THE OFFICIAL®
2006 PRICE GUIDE TO
BASEBALL CARDS

DR. JAMES BECKETT

TWENTY-SIXTH EDITION

House of Collectibles
New York

Important Notice: All of the information, including valuations, in this book has been compiled from reliable sources, and efforts have been made to eliminate errors and questionable data. Nevertheless, the possibility of error, in a work of such immense scope, always exists. The publisher will not be held responsible for losses that may occur in the purchase, sale, or other transaction of items because of information contained herein. Readers who feel they have discovered errors are invited to *write* and inform us, so they may be corrected in subsequent editions. Those seeking further information on the topics covered in this book are advised to refer to the complete line of *Official Price Guides* published by the House of Collectibles.

House of Collectibles and colophon
are trademarks of Random House, Inc.

Published by:
House of Collectibles
Random House Reference
New York, New York

Distributed by Random House Reference,
an imprint of Random House, Inc.,
New York, and simultaneously in Canada by
Random House of Canada Limited, Toronto.

www.houseofcollectibles.com

Manufactured in the United States of America

ISSN: 1062-7138

ISBN-10: 0-375-72101-0
ISBN-13: 978-0-375-72101-4

10 9 8 7 6 5 4 3 2 1

Twenty-sixth Edition: April 2006

Table of Contents

About the Author

Jim Beckett, the leading authority on sports card values in the United States, maintains a wide range of activities in the world of sports. He possesses one of the finest collections of sports cards and autographs in the world, has made numerous appearances on radio and television, and has been frequently cited in many national publications. He was awarded the first "Special Achievement Award" for Contributions to the Hobby by the National Sports Collectors Convention in 1980, the "Jock Jaspersen Award" for Hobby Dedication in 1983, and the "Buck Barker, Spirit of the Hobby" award in 1991.

Dr. Beckett is the author of *Beckett Baseball Card Price Guide, The Official Price Guide to Baseball Cards, Price Guide to Baseball Collectibles, The Sport Americana Baseball Memorabilia and Autograph Price Guide, Beckett Almanac of Baseball Cards and Collectibles, Beckett Football Card Price Guide, The Official Price Guide to Football Cards, Beckett Hockey Card Price Guide, The Official Price Guide to Hockey Cards, Beckett Basketball Card Price Guide, The Official Price Guide to Basketball Cards, The Beckett Baseball Card Alphabetical Checklist, The Beckett Basketball Card Alphabetical Checklist,* and *The Beckett Football Card Alphabetical Checklist.* In addition, he is the founder, publisher, and editor of *Beckett Baseball Card Monthly, Beckett Basketball Monthly, Beckett Football Card Monthly, Beckett Hockey Collector, Beckett Sports Collectibles,* and *Beckett Racing and Motorsports Marketplace.*

Jim Beckett received his Ph.D. in Statistics from Southern Methodist University in 1975. Prior to starting Beckett Publications in 1984, Dr. Beckett served as an Associate Professor of Statistics at Bowling Green State University and as a vice president of a consulting firm in Dallas, Texas.

How to Use This Book

Isn't it great? Every year this book gets better with all the new sets coming out. But even more exciting is that every year there are more options in collecting the cards we love so much. This edition has been enhanced and expanded from the previous edition. The cards you collect — who appears on them, what they look like, where they are from, and (most important to most of you) what their current values are — are enumerated within. Many of the features contained in the other *Beckett Price Guides* have been incorporated into this volume since condition grading, terminology, and many other aspects of collecting are common to the card hobby in general. We hope you find the book both interesting and useful in your collecting pursuits.

The Beckett Guide has been successful where other attempts have failed because it is complete, current, and valid. This price guide contains not just one, but three prices by condition for all the baseball cards listed. The prices were added to the card lists just prior to printing and reflect not the author's opinions or desires but the going retail prices for each card, based on the marketplace (sports memorabilia conventions and shows, sports card shops, hobby papers, current mail-order catalogs, local club meetings, auction results, and other firsthand reportings of actually realized prices).

What is the best price guide available on the market today? Of course, card sellers prefer the price guide with the highest prices, while card buyers naturally prefer the one with the lowest prices. Accuracy, however, is the true test. Use the price guide trusted by more collectors and dealers than all the others combined. Look for the Beckett® name. I won't put my name on anything I won't stake my reputation on. Not the lowest and not the highest — but the most accurate, with integrity.

To facilitate your use of this book, read the complete introductory section on the following pages before going to the pricing pages. Every collectible field has its own terminology; we've tried to capture most of these terms and definitions in our glossary. Please read carefully the section on grading and the condition of your cards, as you cannot determine which price column is appropriate for a given card without first knowing its condition.

Welcome to the world of baseball cards.

How to Collect

Each collection is personal and reflects the individuality of its owner. There are no set rules on how to collect cards. Since card collecting is a hobby or leisure pastime, what you collect, how much you collect, and how much time and money you spend collecting are entirely up to you. The funds you have available for collecting and your own personal taste should determine how you collect. Information and ideas presented here are intended to help you get the most enjoyment from this hobby.

It is impossible to collect every card ever produced. Therefore, beginners as well as intermediate and advanced collectors usually specialize in some way. One of the reasons this hobby is popular is that individual collectors can define and tailor their collecting methods to match their own tastes. To give you some idea of the various approaches to collecting, we will list some of the more popular areas of specialization.

Many collectors select complete sets from particular years. For example, they may concentrate on assembling complete sets from all the years since their birth or since they became avid sports fans. They may try to collect a card for every player during that specified period of time.

Many others wish to acquire only certain players. Usually such players are the superstars of the sport, but occasionally collectors will specialize in all the cards of players who attended a particular college or came from a certain town. Some collectors are interested in only the first cards or Rookie Cards of certain players. A handy guide for collectors interested in pursuing the hobby this way is *The Sport Americana Baseball Card Alphabetical Checklist.*

Another fun way to collect cards is by team. Most fans have a favorite team, and it is natural for that loyalty to be translated into a desire for cards of the players on that favorite team. For most of the recent years, team sets (all the cards from a given team for that year) are readily available at a reasonable price. The Sport *Americana Team Baseball Card Checklist* will open up this field to the collector.

Obtaining Cards

Several avenues are open to card collectors. Cards still can be purchased in the traditional way: by the pack at the local candy, grocery, drug, or major discount store.

But there are also thousands of card shops across the country that specialize in selling cards individually or by the pack, box, or set. Another alternative are the thousands of card shows held each month around the country, which feature anywhere from 8 to 800 tables of sports cards and memorabilia for sale.

For many years, it has been possible to purchase complete sets of baseball cards through mail-order advertisers found in traditional sports media publications, such as the *Sporting News, Baseball Digest*, and, *Street & Smith* yearbooks. These sets also are advertised in the card collecting periodicals. Many collectors will begin by subscribing to at least one of the hobby periodicals, all with good up-to-date information. In fact, subscription offers can be found in the advertising section of this book.

Most serious card collectors obtain old (and new) cards from one or more of several main sources: (1) trading or buying from other collectors or dealers; (2) responding to sale or auction ads in the hobby publications; (3) buying at a local hobby store; (4) attending sports collectibles shows or conventions; and (5) purchasing cards over the Internet.

We advise that you try all five methods since each has its own distinct advantages: (1) trading is a great way to make new friends; (2) hobby periodicals help you keep up with what's going on in the hobby (including when and where the conventions are happening); (3) stores provide the opportunity to enjoy personalized service and consider a great diversity of material in a relaxed sports-oriented atmosphere; (4) shows allow you to choose from multiple dealers and thousands of cards under one roof in a competitive situation; and (5) the Internet allows one to purchase cards in a convenient manner from almost anywhere in the world.

Preserving Your Cards

Cards are fragile. They must be handled properly in order to retain their value. Careless handling can easily result in creased or bent cards. It is, however, not recommended that tweezers or tongs be used to pick up your cards since such utensils might mar or indent card surfaces and thus reduce those cards´ conditions and values.

In general, your cards should be handled directly as little as possible. This is sometimes easier to say than to do.

Although there are still many who use custom boxes, storage trays, or even shoe boxes, plastic sheets are the preferred method of many collectors for storing cards.

A collection stored in plastic pages in a three-ring album allows you to view your collection at any time without the need to touch the card itself. Cards can also be kept in single holders (of various types and thicknesses) designed for the enjoyment of each card individually.

For a large collection, some collectors may use a combination of the above methods. When purchasing plastic sheets for your cards, be sure that you find the pocket size that fits the cards snugly. Don´t put your 1951 Bowman in a sheet designed to fit 1981 Topps.

Most hobby and collectibles shops and virtually all collectors´ conventions will have these plastic pages available in quantity for the various sizes offered, or you can purchase them directly from the advertisers in this book.

Also, remember that pocket size isn´t the only factor to consider when looking for plastic sheets. Other factors such as safety, economy, appearance, availability, or personal preference also may influence which types of sheets a collector may want to buy.

Damp, sunny, and/or hot conditions — no, this is not a weather forecast — are three elements to avoid in extremes if you are interested in preserving your collection. Too much (or too little) humidity can cause the gradual deterioration of a card. Direct, bright sun (or fluorescent light) over time will bleach out the color of a card. Extreme heat accelerates the decomposition of the card. On the other hand, many cards have lasted more than 75 years without much scientific intervention. So be cautious, even if the above factors typically present a problem only when present in the extreme. It never hurts to be prudent.

Collecting vs. Investing

Collecting individual players and collecting complete sets are both popular vehicles for investment and speculation.

Most investors and speculators stock up on complete sets or on quantities of players they think have good investment potential.

There is obviously no guarantee in this book, or anywhere else for that matter, that cards will outperform the stock market or other investment alternatives in the future. After all, baseball cards do not pay quarterly dividends and cards cannot be sold at their "current values" as easily as stocks or bonds.

Nevertheless, investors have noticed a favorable long-term trend in the past performance of baseball and other sports collectibles, and certain cards and sets have outperformed just about any other investment in some years.

Many hobbyists maintain that the best investment is and always will be the building of a collection, which traditionally has held up better than outright speculation.

Some of the obvious questions are: Which cards? When to buy? When to sell? The best investment you can make is in your own education.

The more you know about your collection and the hobby, the more informed the decisions you will be able to make. We´re not selling investment tips. We´re selling information about the current value of baseball cards. It´s up to you to use that information to your best advantage.

Terminology

Each hobby has its own language to describe its area of interest. The nomenclature traditionally used for trading cards is derived from the American Card Catalog, published in 1960 by Nostalgia Press. That catalog, written by Jefferson Burdick (who is called the "Father of Card Collecting" for his pioneering work), uses letter and number designations for each separate set of cards. The letter used in the ACC designation refers to the generic type of card. While both sport and nonsport issues are classified in the ACC, we shall confine ourselves to the sport issues. The following list defines the letters and their meanings as used by the American Card Catalog.

(none) or N - 19th Century U.S. Tobacco.
B - Blankets.
D - Bakery Inserts Including Bread.
E - Early Candy and Gum.
F - Food Inserts.
H - Advertising.
M - Periodicals.
PC - Postcards.
R - Candy and Gum since 1930.
T - Tobacco.

Following the letter prefix and an optional hyphen are one-, two-, or three-digit numbers, R(-)999. These typically represent the company or entity issuing the cards. In several cases, the ACC number is extended by an additional hyphen and another one- or two-digit numerical suffix. For example, the 1957 Topps regular-series baseball card issue carries an ACC designation of R414-11. The "R" indicates a Candy or Gum card produced since 1930. The "414" is the ACC designation for Topps Chewing Gum baseball card issues, and the "11" is the ACC designation for the 1957 regular issue (Topps´ eleventh baseball set). Like other traditional methods of identification, this system provides order to the process of cataloging cards; however, most serious collectors learn the ACC designation of the popular sets by repetition and familiarity, rather than by attempting to "figure out" what they might or should be. From 1948 forward, collectors and dealers commonly refer to all sets by their year, maker, type of issue, and any other distinguishing characteristic. For example, such a characteristic could be an unusual issue or one of several regular issues put out by a specific maker in a single year. Regional issues are usually referred to by year, maker, and sometimes by title or theme of the set.

Glossary/Legend

Our glossary defines terms used in the card collecting hobby and in this book. Many of these terms are also common to other types of sports memorabilia collecting. Some terms may have several meanings depending on use and context.

ACETATE—A transparent plastic.

AS—All-Star card. A card portraying an All-Star Player of the previous year that says "All-Star" on its face.

ATG—All-Time Great card.

ATL—All-Time Leaders card.

AU(TO)—Autographed card.

AW—Award Winner.

BB—Building Blocks.

BC—Bonus Card.

BF—Bright Futures.

BL—Blue Letters.

BNR—Banner Season.

BOX CARD—Card issued on a box (e.g., 1987 Topps Box Bottoms).

BRICK—A group of 50 or more cards having common characteristics that is intended to be bought, sold, or traded as a unit.

CABINETS—Popular and highly valuable photographs on thick card stock produced in the 19th and early 20th century.

CC—Curtain Call.

CG—Cornerstones of the Game.

CHECKLIST—A list of the cards contained in a particular set. The list is always in numerical order if the cards are numbered. Some unnumbered sets are artificially numbered in alphabetical order, by team and alphabetically within the team, or by uniform number for convenience.
CL—Checklist card. A card that lists in order the cards and players in the set or series. Older checklist cards in Mint condition that have not been marked are very desirable and command premiums.
CP—Changing Places.
CO—Coach.
COMM—Commissioner.
COMMON CARD—The typical card of any set; it has no premium value accruing from subject matter, numerical scarcity, popular demand, or anomaly.
CONVENTION—A gathering of dealers and collectors at a single location for the purpose of buying, selling, and trading sports memorabilia items. Conventions are open to the public and sometimes feature autograph guests, door prizes, contests, seminars, etc. They are frequently referred to simply as "shows."
COOP—Cooperstown.
COR—Corrected card.
CT—Cooperstown.
CY—Cy Young Award.
DD—Decade of Dominance.
DEALER—A person who engages in buying, selling, and trading sports collectibles or supplies. A dealer may also be a collector, but as a dealer, his main goal is to earn a profit.
DIE-CUT—A card with part of its stock partially cut, allowing one or more parts to be folded or removed. After removal or appropriate folding, the remaining part of the card can frequently be made to stand up.
DK—Diamond King.
DL—Division Leaders.
DP—Double Print (a card that was printed in double the quantity compared to the other cards in the same series) or a Draft Pick card.
DT—Dream Team.
DUFEX—A method of card manufacturing technology patented by Pinnacle Brands, Inc. It involves a refractive quality to a card with a foil coating.
ERA—Earned Run Average.
ERR—Error card. A card with erroneous information, spelling, or depiction on either side of the card. Most errors are not corrected by the producing card company.
FC—Fan Club.
FDP—First or First-Round Draft Pick.
FF—Future Foundation.
FOIL—Foil embossed stamp on card.
FOLD—Foldout.
FP—Franchise Player.
Fr—Franchise.
FS—Father/son card.
FS—Future Star.
FUN—Fun cards.
FY—First Year.
GL—Green Letters.
GLOSS—A card with luster; a shiny finish as in a card with UV coating.
HG—Heroes of the Game.
HIGH NUMBER—The cards in the last series of numbers in a year in which

such higher-numbered cards were printed or distributed in significantly lesser amounts than the lower-numbered cards. The high-number designation refers to a scarcity of the high-numbered cards. Not all years have high numbers in terms of this definition.

HL—Highlight card.

HOF—Hall of Fame, or a card that portrays a Hall of Famer (HOFer).

HOLOGRAM—A three-dimensional photographic image.

HH—Hometown Heroes.

HOR—Horizontal pose on card as opposed to the standard vertical orientation found on most cards.

IA—In Action card.

IF—Infielder.

INSERT—A card of a different type or any other sports collectible (typically a poster or sticker) contained and sold in the same package along with a card or cards of a major set. An insert card is either unnumbered or not numbered in the same sequence as the major set. Sometimes the inserts are randomly distributed and are not found in every pack.

INTERACTIVE—A concept that involves collector participation.

IRT—International Road Trip.

ISSUE—Synonymous with set, but usually used in conjunction with a manufacturer, e.g., a Topps issue.

JSY—means Jersey.

KM—K-Men.

LHP—Left-handed pitcher.

LL—League Leaders or large letters on card.

LUM—Lumberjack.

MAJOR SET—A set produced by a national manufacturer of cards containing a large number of cards. Usually 100 or more different cards constitute a major set.

MB—Master Blasters.

MEM—Memorial card. For example, the 1990 Donruss and Topps Bart Giamatti cards.

METALLIC—A glossy design method that enhances card features.

MG—Manager.

MI—Maximum Impact.

MINI—A small card; for example, a 1975 Topps card of identical design but smaller dimensions than the regular Topps issue of 1975.

ML—Major League.

MM—Memorable Moments.

MULTI-PLAYER CARD—A single card depicting two or more players (but not a team card).

MVP—Most Valuable Player.

NAU—No autograph on card.

NG—Next Game.

NH—No-Hitter.

NNOF—No name on front.

NOF—Name on front.

NOTCHING—The grooving of the card, usually caused by fingernails, rubber bands, or bumping card edges against other objects.

NT—Now and Then.

NV—Novato.

OF—Outfield or Outfielder.

OLY—Olympics Card.

P—Pitcher or Pitching pose.

P1—First Printing.
P2—Second Printing.
P3—Third Printing.
PACKS—A means by which cards are issued in terms of pack type (wax, cello, foil, rack, etc.) and channel of distribution (hobby, retail, etc.).
PARALLEL— A card that is similar in design to its counterpart from a basic set but offers a distinguishing quality.
PF—Profiles.
PG—Postseason Glory.
PLASTIC SHEET—A clear, plastic page that is punched for insertion into a binder (with standard three-ring spacing) containing pockets for displaying cards. Many different styles of sheets exist with pockets of varying sizes to hold the many differing card formats. Also called a display sheet or storage sheet.
PP—Power Passion.
PLATINUM—A metallic element used in the process of creating a glossy card.
PR—Printed name on back.
PREMIUM—A card, sometimes on photographic stock, that is purchased or obtained in conjunction with, or redemption for, another card or product. The premium is not packaged in the same unit as the primary item.
PRES—President.
PRISMATIC/PRISM—A glossy or bright design that refracts or disperses light.
PS—Pace Setters.
PT—Power Tools.
PUZZLE CARD—A card whose back contains a part of a picture which, when joined correctly with other puzzle cards, forms the completed picture.
PUZZLE PIECE—A die-cut piece designed to interlock with similar pieces (e.g., early 1980s Donruss).
PVC—Polyvinyl chloride, a substance used to make many of the popular card display protective sheets. Non-PVC sheets are considered preferable for long-term storage of cards by many.
RARE—A card or series of cards of very limited availability. Unfortunately, "rare" is a subjective term frequently used indiscriminately to hype value. "Rare" cards are harder to obtain than "scarce" cards.
RB—Record Breaker.
RC—Rookie Card.
REDEMPTION—A program established by multiple card manufacturers that allows collectors to mail in a special card (usually a random insert) in return for special cards, sets, or other prizes not available through conventional channels.
REFRACTORS—A card that features a design element that enhances (distorts) its color/appearance through deflecting light.
REV NEG—Reversed or flopped photo side of the card. This is a major type of error card, but only some are corrected.
RHP—Right-handed pitcher.
RHW—Rookie Home Whites.
RIF—Rifleman.
RPM—Rookie Premiere Materials.
RR—Rated Rookie.
ROO—Rookie.
ROY—Rookie of the Year.
RP—Relief pitcher.
RTC—Rookie True Colors.
SA—Super Action card.
SASE—Self-Addressed, Stamped Envelope.

SB—Scrapbook.

SB—Stolen Bases.

SCARCE—A card or series of cards of limited availability. This subjective term is sometimes used indiscriminately to hype value. "Scarce" cards are not as difficult to obtain as "rare" cards.

SCR—Script name on back.

SD—San Diego Padres.

SEMI-HIGH—A card from the next-to-last series of a sequentially issued set. It has more value than an average card and generally less value than a high number. A card is not called a semi-high unless the next-to-last series in which it exists has an additional premium attached to it.

SERIES—The entire set of cards issued by a particular producer in a particular year; e.g., the 1971 Topps series. Also, within a particular set, series can refer to a group of (consecutively numbered) cards printed at the same time, e.g., the first series of the 1957 Topps issue (#1 through #88).

SET—One each of the entire run of cards of the same type produced by a particular manufacturer during a single year. In other words, if you have a complete set of 1976 Topps then you have every card from #1 up to and including #660; i.e., all the different cards that were produced.

SF—Starflics.

SH—Season Highlight.

SHEEN—Brightness or luster emitted by card.

SKIP-NUMBERED—A set that has many unissued card numbers between the lowest number in the set and the highest number in the set, e.g., the 1948 Leaf baseball set contains 98 cards skip-numbered from #1 to #168. A major set in which a few numbers were not printed is not considered to be skip-numbered.

SP—Single or Short Print (a card that was printed in lesser quantity compared to the other cards in the same series; see also DP and TP).

SPECIAL CARD—A card that portrays something other than a single player or team, for example, a card that portrays the previous year's statistical leaders or the results from the previous year's World Series.

SS—Shortstop.

STANDARD SIZE—Most modern sports cards measure 2-1/2 by 3-1/2 inches. Exceptions are noted in card descriptions throughout this book.

STAR CARD—A card that portrays a player of some repute, usually determined by his ability; but sometimes referring to sheer popularity.

STOCK—The cardboard or paper on which the card is printed.

SUPERIMPOSED—To be affixed on top of something; i.e., a player photo over a solid background.

SUPERSTAR CARD—A card that portrays a superstar, e.g., a Hall of Famer or player with strong Hall of Fame potential.

TC—Team Checklist.

TEAM CARD—A card that depicts an entire team.

THREE-DIMENSIONAL (3D)—A visual image that provides an illusion of depth and perspective.

TOPICAL—A subset or group of cards that have a common theme (e.g., MVP award winners).

TP—Triple Print (a card that was printed in triple the quantity compared to the other cards in the same series).

TR—Trade reference on card.

TRANSPARENT—Clear, see-through.

UDCA—Upper Deck Classic Alumni.

UER—Uncorrected Error.

UMP—Umpire.

USA—Team USA.

UV—Ultraviolet, a glossy coating used in producing cards.

VAR—Variation card. One of two or more cards from the same series with the same number (or player with identical pose if the series is unnumbered) differing from one another by some aspect, the different feature stemming from the printing or stock of the card. This can be caused when the manufacturer of the cards notices an error in one or more of the cards, makes the changes, and then resumes the print run. In this case there will be two versions or variations of the same card. Sometimes one of the variations is relatively scarce.

VERT—Vertical pose on card.

WAS—Washington National League (1974 Topps).

WC—What´s the Call?

WL—White letters on front.

WS—World Series card.

YL—Yellow letters on front.

YT—Yellow team name on front.

*—to denote multi-sport sets.

Understanding Card Values

Determining Value

Why are some cards more valuable than others? Obviously, the economic laws of supply and demand are applicable to card collecting just as they are to any other field where a commodity is bought, sold, or traded in a free, unregulated market.

Supply (the number of cards available on the market) is less than the total number of cards originally produced since attrition diminishes that original quantity. Each year a percentage of cards is typically thrown away, destroyed, or otherwise lost to collectors. This percentage is much, much smaller today than it was in the past because more and more people have become increasingly aware of the value of their cards.

For those who collect only Mint condition cards, the supply of older cards can be quite small indeed. Until recently, collectors were not so conscious of the need to preserve the condition of their cards. For this reason, it is difficult to know exactly how many 1953 Topps are currently available, Mint or otherwise. It is generally accepted that there are fewer 1953 Topps available than 1963, 1973, or 1983 Topps cards. If demand were equal for each of these sets, the law of supply and demand would increase the price for the least available sets. Demand, however, is never equal for all sets, so price correlations can be complicated. The demand for a card is influenced by many factors. These include: (1) the age of the card; (2) the number of cards printed; (3) the player(s) portrayed on the card; (4) the attractiveness and popularity of the set; and (5) the physical condition of the card.

In general, (1) the older the card, (2) the fewer the number of the cards printed, (3) the more famous, popular, and talented the player, (4) the more attractive and popular the set, and (5) the better the condition of the card, the higher the value of the card will be. There are exceptions to all but one of these factors: the condition of the card. Given two cards similar in all respects except condition, the one in the best condition will always be valued higher.

While those guidelines help to establish the value of a card, the countless exceptions and peculiarities make any simple, direct mathematical formula to determine card values impossible.

Regional Variation

Since the market varies from region to region, card prices of local players may be higher. This is known as a regional premium. How significant the premium is — and if there is any premium at all — depends on the local popularity of the team and the player.

The largest regional premiums usually do not apply to superstars, who often are so well known nationwide that the prices of their key cards are too high for local dealers to realize a premium.

Lesser stars often command the strongest premiums. Their popularity is concentrated in their home region, creating local demand that greatly exceeds overall demand.

Regional premiums can apply to popular retired players and sometimes can be found in the areas where the players grew up or starred in college.

A regional discount is the converse of a regional premium. Regional discounts occur when a player has been so popular in his region for so long that local collectors and dealers have accumulated quantities of his key cards. The abundant supply may make the cards available in that area at the lowest prices anywhere.

Set Prices

A somewhat paradoxical situation exists in the price of a complete set versus the combined cost of the individual cards in the set. In nearly every case, the sum of the prices for the individual cards is higher than the cost for the complete set. This is prevalent especially in the cards of the last few years. The reasons for this apparent anomaly stem from the habits of collectors and from the carrying costs to dealers. Today, each card in a set normally is produced in the same quantity as all other cards in its set.

Many collectors pick up only stars, superstars, and particular teams. As a result, the dealer is left with a shortage of certain player cards and an abundance of others. He therefore incurs an expense in simply "carrying" these less desirable cards in stock. On the other hand, if he sells a complete set, he gets rid of large numbers of cards at one time. For this reason, he generally is willing to receive less money for a complete set. By doing this, he recovers all of his costs and also makes a profit.

The disparity between the price of the complete set and the sum of the individual cards also has been influenced by the fact that some of the major manufacturers now are pre-collating card sets. Since "pulling" individual cards from the sets involves a specific type of labor (and cost), the singles or star card market is not affected significantly by pre-collation.

Set prices also do not include rare card varieties, unless specifically stated. Of course, the prices for sets do include one example of each type for the given set, but this is the least expensive variety.

Scarce Series

Scarce series occur because cards issued before 1974 were made available to the public each year in several series of finite numbers of cards, rather than all cards of the set being available for purchase at one time. At some point during the year, usually toward the end of the baseball season, interest in current year baseball cards waned. Consequently, the manufacturers produced smaller numbers of these later-series cards.

Nearly all nationwide issues from post–World War II manufacturers (1948 to 1973) exhibit these series variations. In the past, Topps, for example, may have issued series consisting of many different numbers of cards, including 55, 66, 80, 88, and others. Recently, Topps has settled on what is now its standard sheet size of 132 cards, six of which constitute its 792-card set.

While the number of cards within a given series is usually the same as the number of cards on one printed sheet, this is not always the case. For example, Bowman used 36 cards on its standard printed sheets, but in 1948 substituted 12 cards during later print runs of that year's baseball cards. Twelve of the cards from the initial sheet of 36 cards were removed and replaced by 12 different cards, giving, in effect, a first series of 36 cards and a second series of 12 new cards. This replacement produced a scarcity of 24 cards — the 12 cards removed from the original sheet and the 12 new cards added to the sheet. A full sheet of 1948 Bowman cards (second printing) shows that card numbers 37 through 48 have replaced 12 of the cards on the first printing sheet.

The Topps Company also has created scarcities and/or excesses of certain cards in many of its sets. Topps, however, has most frequently gone the other direction by double printing some of the cards. Double printing causes an abundance of cards of the players who are on the same sheet more than one time. During the years from 1978 to 1981, Topps double printed 66 cards out of their large 726-card set. The Topps practice of double printing cards in earlier years is the most logical explanation for the known scarcities of particular cards in some of these Topps sets.

From 1988 through 1990, Donruss short printed and double printed certain cards in its major sets. Ostensibly this was because of its addition of bonus team MVP cards in its regular-issue wax packs.

We are always looking for information or photographs of printing sheets of cards for research. Each year, we try to update the hobby's knowledge of distribution anomalies. Please let us know at the address in this book if you have firsthand knowledge that would be helpful in this pursuit.

Grading Your Cards

Each hobby has its own grading terminology — stamps, coins, comic books, record collecting, etc. Collectors of sports cards are no exception. The one invariable criterion for determining the value of a card is its condition: The better the condition of the card, the more valuable it is. Condition grading, however, is subjective. Individual card dealers and collectors differ in the strictness of their grading, but the stated condition of a card should be determined without regard to whether it is being bought or sold.

No allowance is made for age. A 1952 card is judged by the same standards as a 1992 card. But there are specific sets and cards that are condition-sensitive (marked with "!" in the Price Guide) because of their border color, consistently poor centering, etc. Such cards and sets sometimes command premiums above the listed percentages in Mint condition.

Centering

Current centering terminology uses numbers representing the percentage of border on either side of the main design. Obviously, centering is diminished in importance for borderless cards such as Stadium Club.

Slightly Off-Center (60/40): A slightly off-center card is one that, upon close inspection, is found to have one border bigger than the opposite border. This degree once was offensive only to purists, but now some hobbyists try to avoid cards that are anything other than perfectly centered.

Off-Center (70/30): An off-center card has one border that is noticeably more than twice as wide as the opposite border.

Badly Off-Center (80/20 or worse): A badly off-center card has virtually no border on one side of the card.

Miscut: A miscut card actually shows part of the adjacent card in its larger border and consequently a corresponding amount of its card is cut off.

Corner Wear

Corner wear is the most scrutinized grading criteria in the hobby. These are the major categories of corner wear:

Corner with a slight touch of wear: The corner still is sharp, but there is a slight touch of wear showing. On a dark-bordered card, this shows as a dot of white.

Fuzzy corner: The corner still comes to a point, but the point has just begun to fray. A slightly "dinged" corner is considered the same as a fuzzy corner.

Slightly rounded corner: The fraying of the corner has increased to where there is only a hint of a point. Mild layering may be evident. A "dinged" corner is considered the same as a slightly rounded corner.

Rounded corner: The point is completely gone. Some layering is noticeable.

Badly rounded corner: The corner is completely round and rough. Severe layering is evident.

Creases

A third common defect is the crease. The degree of creasing in a card is difficult to show in a drawing or picture. On giving the specific condition of an expensive card for sale, the seller should note any creases additionally. Creases can be categorized as to severity according to the following scale:

Light Crease: A light crease is a crease that is barely noticeable upon close inspection. In fact, when cards are in plastic sheets or holders, a light crease may not be seen (until the card is taken out of the holder). A light crease on the front is much more serious than a light crease on the card back only.

Medium Crease: A medium crease is noticeable when held and studied at arm´s length by the naked eye, but does not overly detract from the appearance of the card. It is an obvious crease, but not one that breaks the picture surface of the card.

Heavy Crease: A heavy crease is one that has torn or broken through the card´s picture surface; i.e., puts a tear in the photo surface.

Alterations

Deceptive Trimming: This occurs when someone alters the card in order (1) to shave off edge wear, (2) to improve the sharpness of the corners, or (3) to improve centering — obviously their objective is to falsely increase the perceived value of the card to an unsuspecting buyer. The shrinkage usually is evident only if the trimmed card is compared to an adjacent full-size card or if the trimmed card is itself measured.

Obvious Trimming: Obvious trimming is noticeable and unfortunate. It is usually performed by noncollectors who give no thought to the present or future value of their cards.

Deceptively Retouched Borders: This occurs when the borders (especially on those cards with dark borders) are touched up on the edges and corners with magic marker or crayons of appropriate color in order to make the card appear Mint.

Categorization of Defects—Miscellaneous Flaws

The following are common minor flaws that, depending on severity, lower a card´s condition by one to four grades and often render it no better than Excellent-Mint: bubbles (lumps in surface), gum and wax stains, diamond cutting (slanted borders), notching, off-centered backs, paper wrinkles, scratched-off cartoons or puzzles on back, rubber band marks, scratches, surface impressions, and warping.

The following are common serious flaws that, depending on severity, lower a card´s condition at least four grades and often render it no better than Good: chemical or sun fading, erasure marks, mildew, miscutting (severe off-centering), holes, bleached or retouched borders, tape marks, tears, trimming, water or coffee stains, and writing.

Condition Guide

Grades

Mint (Mt)—A card with no flaws or wear. The card has four perfect corners, 60/40 or better centering from top to bottom and from left to right, original gloss, smooth edges, and original color borders. A Mint card does not have print spots or color or focus imperfections.

Near Mint-Mint (NrMt-Mt)—A card with one minor flaw. Any one of the following would lower a Mint card to Near Mint-Mint: one corner with a slight touch of wear, barely noticeable print spots, or color or focus imperfections. The card must have

60/40 or better centering in both directions, original gloss, smooth edges, and original color borders.

Near Mint (NrMt)—A card with one minor flaw. Any one of the following would lower a Mint card to Near Mint: one fuzzy corner or two to four corners with slight touches of wear, 70/30 to 60/40 centering, slightly rough edges, minor print spots, color or focus imperfections. The card must have original gloss and original color borders.

Excellent-Mint (ExMt)—A card with two or three fuzzy, but not rounded, corners and centering no worse than 80/20. The card may have no more than two of the following: slightly rough edges, very slightly discolored borders, minor print spots, color or focus imperfections. The card must have original gloss.

Excellent (Ex)—A card with four fuzzy but definitely not rounded corners and centering no worse than 80/20. The card may have a small amount of original gloss lost, rough edges, slightly discolored borders, and minor print spots or color or focus imperfections.

Very Good (Vg)—A card that has been handled but not abused: slightly rounded corners with slight layering, slight notching on edges, a significant amount of gloss lost from the surface (but no scuffing) and moderate discoloration of borders. The card may have a few light creases.

Good (G), Fair (F), Poor (P)—A well-worn, mishandled, or abused card: badly rounded and layered corners, scuffing, most or all original gloss missing, seriously discolored borders, moderate or heavy creases, and one or more serious flaws. The grade of Good, Fair, or Poor depends on the severity of wear and flaws. Good, Fair, and Poor cards generally are used only as fillers.

The most widely used grades are defined above. Obviously, many cards will not perfectly fit one of the definitions.

Therefore, categories between the major grades known as in-between grades are used, such as Good to Very Good (G-Vg), Very Good to Excellent (VgEx), and Excellent-Mint to Near Mint (ExMt-NrMt). Such grades indicate a card with all qualities of the lower category but with at least a few qualities of the higher category.

Beckett Baseball Card Price Guide lists each card and set in two grades, with the middle grade valued at about 40%–45% of the top grade.

The value of cards that fall between the listed columns can also be calculated using a percentage of the top grade. For example, a card that falls between the top and middle grades (Ex, ExMt, or NrMt in most cases) will generally be valued at anywhere from 50% to 90% of the top grade.

Similarly, a card that falls between the middle and bottom grades (G-Vg, Vg, or VgEx in most cases) will generally be valued at anywhere from 20%–40% of the top grade.

There are also cases where cards are in better condition than the top grade or worse than the bottom grade. Cards that grade worse than the lowest grade are generally valued at 5%–10% of the top grade.

When a card exceeds the top grade by one — such as NrMt-Mt when the top grade is NrMt, or Mint when the top grade is NrMt-Mt — a premium of up to 50% is possible, with 10%–20% the usual norm.

When a card exceeds the top grade by two — such as Mint when the top grade is NrMt, or NrMt-Mt when the top grade is ExMt — a premium of 25%–50% is the usual norm. But certain condition-sensitive cards or sets, particularly those from the pre-war era, can bring premiums of up to 100% or even more.

Unopened packs, boxes, and factory-collated sets are considered Mint in their unknown (and presumed perfect) state. Once opened, however, each card can be graded (and valued) in its own right by taking into account any defects that may be present in spite of the fact that the card has never been handled.

Selling Your Cards

Just about every collector sells cards or will sell cards eventually. Someday you may be interested in selling your duplicates or maybe even your whole collection. You may sell to other collectors, friends, or dealers. You may even sell cards you purchased from a certain dealer back to that same dealer. In any event, it helps to know some of the mechanics of the typical transaction between buyer and seller.

Dealers will buy cards in order to resell them to other collectors who are interested in the cards. Dealers will always pay a higher percentage for items that (in their opinion) can be resold quickly, and a much lower percentage for those items that are perceived as having low demand and hence are slow moving. In either case, dealers must buy at a price that allows for the expense of doing business and a margin for profit.

If you have cards for sale, the best advice we can give is that you get several offers for your cards — either from card shops or at a card show — and take the best offer, all things considered. Note, the "best" offer may not be the one for the highest amount. And remember, if a dealer really wants your cards, he won't let you get away without making his best competitive offer. Another alternative is to place your cards in an auction as one or several lots.

Many people think nothing of going into a department store and paying $15 for an item of clothing for which the store paid $5. But if you were selling your $15 card to a dealer and he offered you $5 for it, you might consider his markup unreasonable. To complete the analogy: Most department stores (and card dealers) that consistently pay $10 for $15 items eventually go out of business. An exception is when the dealer has lined up a willing buyer for the item(s) you are attempting to sell, or if the cards are so hot that it's likely he'll have to hold the cards for just a short period of time.

In those cases, an offer of up to 75% of book value still will allow the dealer to make a reasonable profit considering the short time he will need to hold the merchandise. In general, however, most cards and collections will bring offers in the range of 25%–50% of retail price. Also consider that most material from the last 5 to 10 years is plentiful. If that's what you're selling, don't be surprised if your best offer is well below that range.

Interesting Notes

The first card numerically of an issue is the single card most likely to obtain excessive wear.

Consequently, you typically will find the price on the #1 card (in NrMt or Mint condition) somewhat higher than might otherwise be the case.

Similarly, but to a lesser extent (because normally the less important, reverse side of the card is the one exposed), the last card numerically in an issue also is prone to abnormal wear. This extra wear and tear occurs because the first and last cards are exposed to the elements (human element included) more than any of the other cards. They are generally end cards in any brick formations and are subject to rubber bandings, stackings on wet surfaces, and like activities.

Sports cards have no intrinsic value. The value of a card, like the value of other collectibles, can be determined only by you and your enjoyment in viewing and possessing these cardboard treasures.

Remember, the buyer ultimately determines the price of each baseball card. You are the determining price factor because you have the ability to say "No" to the price of any card by not exchanging your hard-earned money for a given issue. When the cost of a trading card exceeds the enjoyment you will receive from it, your answer should be "No." We assess and report the prices. You set them!

We are always interested in receiving the price input of collectors and dealers. We happily credit major contributors.

We welcome your opinions, since your contributions assist us in ensuring a better guide each year.

If you would like to join our survey list for the next editions of this book and others authored by Dr. Beckett, please send your name and address to Dr. James Beckett, 15850 Dallas Parkway, Dallas, TX 75248.

History of Baseball Cards

Today's version of the baseball card, with its colorful and oftentimes high-tech front and back, is a far cry from its earliest predecessors. The issue remains cloudy as to which was the very first baseball card ever produced, but the institution of base-

Centering

Well-centered

Slightly Off-centered

Off-centered

Badly Off-centered

Miscut

ball cards dates from the latter half of the 19th century, more than 100 years ago. Early issues, generally printed on heavy cardboard, were of poor quality, with photographs, drawings, and printing far short of today´s standards.

Goodwin & Co., of New York, makers of Gypsy Queen, Old Judge, and other cigarette brands, is considered by many to be the first issuer of baseball and other sports cards. Its issues, predominantly sized 1-1/2 by 2-1/2 inches, generally consisted of photographs of baseball players, boxers, wrestlers, and other subjects mounted on stiff cardboard. More than 2,000 different photos of baseball players alone have been identified. These "Old Judges," a collective name commonly used for the Goodwin & Co. cards, were issued from 1886 to 1890 and are treasured parts of many collections today.

Among the other cigarette companies that issued baseball cards still attracting attention today are Allen & Ginter, D. Buchner & Co. (Gold Coin Chewing Tobacco), and P. H. Mayo & Brother. Cards from the first two companies bear colored line drawings, while the Mayos are sepia photographs on black cardboard. In addition to the small-size cards from this era, several tobacco companies issued cabinet-size baseball cards. These "cabinets" were considerably larger than the small cards, usually about 4-1/4 by 6-1/2 inches, and were printed on heavy stock. Goodwin & Co.´s Old Judge cabinets and the National Tobacco Works´ "Newsboy" baseball photos are two that remain popular today.

By 1895, the American Tobacco Company began to dominate its competition. They discontinued baseball card inserts in their cigarette packages (actually slide boxes in those days). The lack of competition in the cigarette market had made these inserts unnecessary. This marked the end of the first era of baseball cards. At the dawn of the 20th century, few baseball cards were being issued. But once again, it was the cigarette companies, particularly, the American Tobacco Company, followed to a lesser extent by the candy and gum makers that revived the practice of including baseball cards with their products. The bulk of these cards, identified in the American Card Catalog (designated hereafter as ACC) as T or E cards for 20th century "Tobacco" or "Early Candy and Gum" issues, respectively, were released from 1909 to 1915.

This romantic and popular era of baseball card collecting produced many desirable items. The most outstanding is the fabled T-206 Honus Wagner card. Other perennial favorites among collectors are the T-206 Eddie Plank card, and the T-206 Magee error card. The former was once the second most valuable card and only recently relinquished that position to a more distinctive and aesthetically pleasing Napoleon Lajoie card from the 1933–34 Goudey Gum series. The latter misspells the player´s name as "Magie"; the most famous and most valuable blooper card.

The ingenuity and distinctiveness of this era has yet to be surpassed. Highlights include:

- The T-202 Hassan triple-folders, one of the best looking and the most distinctive cards ever issued;
- The durable T-201 Mecca double-folders, one of the first sets with players´ records on the reverse;
- The T-3 Turkey Reds, the hobby´s most popular cabinet card;
- The E-145 Cracker Jacks, the only major set containing Federal League player cards; and
- The T-204 Ramlys, with their distinctive black-and-white oval photos and ornate gold borders.

These are but a few of the varieties issued during this period.

Increasing Popularity

While the American Tobacco Company dominated the field, several other tobacco companies, as well as clothing manufacturers, newspapers and periodicals, game makers, and companies whose identities remain anonymous, also issued cards during this period. In fact, the Collins-McCarthy Candy Company, makers of Zeenuts Pacific Coast League baseball cards, issued cards yearly from 1911 to 1938. Its record for continuous annual card production has been exceeded only by the Topps Chewing Gum Company. The era of the tobacco card issues closed with the onset of World War I, with the exception of the Red Man chewing tobacco sets produced from

Corner Wear

The partial cards here have been photographed at 300%. This was done in order to magnify each card's corner wear to such a degree that differences could be shown on a printed page.

The 1962 Topps Mickey Mantle card definitely has a rounded corner. Some may say that this card is badly rounded, but that is a judgment call.

The 1962 Topps Hank Aaron card has a slightly rounded corner. Note that there is definite corner wear evident by the fraying and that the corner no longer sports a sharp point.

The 1962 Topps Gil Hodges card has corner wear; it is slightly better than the Aaron card above. Nevertheless, some collectors might classify this Hodges corner as slightly rounded.

The 1962 Topps Manager's Dream card showing Mantle and Mays has slight corner wear. This is not a fuzzy corner as very slight wear is noticeable on the card's photo surface.

The 1962 Topps Don Mossi card has very slight corner wear such that it might be called a fuzzy corner. A close look at the original card shows the corner is not perfect, but almost. However, note that corner wear is somewhat academic on this card. As you can plainly see, the heavy crease going across his name breaks through the photo surface.

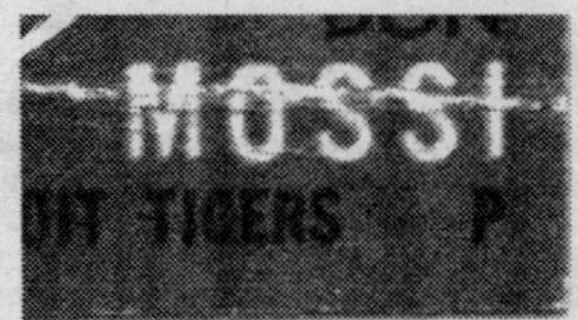

1952 to 1955.

The next flurry of card issues broke out in the roaring and prosperous 1920s, the era of the E card. The caramel companies (National Caramel, American Caramel, York Caramel) were the leading distributors of these E cards. In addition, the strip card, a continuous strip with several cards divided by dotted lines or other sectioning features, flourished during this time. While the E cards and the strip cards generally are considered less imaginative than the T cards or the recent candy and gum issues, they still are pursued by many advanced collectors.

Another significant event of the 1920s was the introduction of the arcade card. Taking its designation from its issuer, the Exhibit Supply Company of Chicago, it is usually known as the "Exhibit" card. Once a trademark of the penny arcades, amusement parks, and county fairs across the country, Exhibit machines dispensed nearly postcard-size photos on thick stock for one penny. These picture cards bore likenesses of a favorite cowboy, actor, actress, or baseball player. Exhibit Supply and its associated companies produced baseball cards during a longer time span, although discontinuous, than any other manufacturer. Its first cards appeared in 1921, while its last issue was in 1966. In 1979, the Exhibit Supply Company was bought and somewhat revived by a collector/dealer who has since reprinted Exhibit photos of the past.

If the T card period, from 1909 to 1915, can be designated the "Golden Age" of baseball card collecting, then perhaps the "Silver Age" commenced with the introduction of the Big League Gum series of 239 cards in 1933 (a 240th card was added in 1934). These are the forerunners of today's baseball gum cards, and the Goudey Gum Company of Boston is responsible for their success. This era spanned the period from the Depression days of 1933 to America's formal involvement in World War II in 1941.

Goudey's attractive designs, with full-color line drawings on thick card stock, greatly influenced other cards being issued at that time. As a result, the most attractive and popular vintage cards in history were produced in this "Silver Age." The 1933 Goudey Big League Gum series also owes its popularity to the more than 40 Hall of Fame players in the set. These include four cards of Babe Ruth and two of Lou Gehrig. Goudey's reign continued in 1934, when it issued a 96-card set in color, together with the single remaining card from the 1933 series, #106, the Napoleon Lajoie card.

In addition to Goudey, several other bubblegum manufacturers issued baseball cards during this era. DeLong Gum Company issued an extremely attractive set in 1933. National Chicle Company's 192-card "Batter-Up" series of 1934-36 became the largest die-cut set in card history. In addition, that company offered the popular "Diamond Stars" series during the same period. Other popular sets included the "Tattoo Orbit" set of 60 color cards issued in 1933 and Gum Products' 75-card "Double Play" set, featuring sepia depictions of two players per card.

In 1939, Gum Inc., which later became Bowman Gum, replaced Goudey Gum as the leading baseball card producer. In 1939 and the following year, it issued two important sets of black-and-white cards. In 1939, its "Play Ball America" set consisted of 162 cards. The larger, 240-card "Play Ball" set of 1940 still is considered by many to be the most attractive black-and-white cards ever produced. That firm introduced its only color set in 1941, consisting of 72 cards titled "Play Ball Sports Hall of Fame." Many of these were colored repeats of poses from the black-and-white 1940 series.

In addition to regular gum cards, many manufacturers distributed premium issues during the 1930s. These premiums were printed on paper or photographic stock, rather than card stock. They were much larger than the regular cards and were sold for a penny across the counter with gum (which was packaged separately from the premium). They often were redeemed at the store or through the mail in exchange for the wrappers of previously purchased gum cards, like proof-of-purchase box-top premiums today. The gum premiums are scarcer than the card issues of the 1930s and in most cases no manufacturer's name is present.

World War II brought an end to this popular era of card collecting when paper and rubber shortages curtailed the production of bubblegum baseball cards. They were resurrected again in 1948 by the Bowman Gum Company (the direct descendent of Gum Inc.). This marked the beginning of the modern era of card collecting.

In 1948, Bowman Gum issued a 48-card set in black and white consisting of one card and one slab of gum in every 1-cent pack. That same year, the Leaf Gum Company also issued a set of cards. Although rather poor in quality, these cards were issued in color. A squabble over the rights to use players´ pictures developed between Bowman and Leaf. Eventually Leaf dropped out of the card market, but not before it had left a lasting heritage to the hobby by issuing some of the rarest cards now in existence. Leaf´s baseball card series of 1948-49 contained 98 cards, skip numbered to #168 (not all numbers were printed). Of these 98 cards, 49 are relatively plentiful; the other 49, however, are rare and quite valuable.

Bowman continued its production of cards in 1949 with a color series of 240 cards. Because there are many scarce "high numbers," this series remains the most difficult Bowman regular issue to complete. Although the set was printed in color and commands great interest due to its scarcity, it is considered aesthetically inferior to the Goudey and National Chicle issues of the 1930s. In addition to the regular issue of 1949, Bowman also produced a set of 36 Pacific Coast League players. Although this was not a regular issue, it still is prized by collectors. In fact, it has become the most valuable Bowman series.

In 1950 (representing Bowman´s one-year monopoly of the baseball card market), the company began a string of top-quality cards that continued until its demise in 1955. The 1950 series was itself something of an oddity because the low numbers, rather than the traditional high numbers, were the more difficult cards to obtain.

The year 1951 marked the beginning of the most competitive and perhaps the highest quality period of baseball card production. In that year, Topps Chewing Gum Company of Brooklyn entered the market. Topps´ 1951 series consisted of two sets of 52 cards each, one set with red backs and the other with blue backs. In addition, Topps also issued 31 insert cards, three of which remain the rarest Topps cards ("Current All-Stars" Konstanty, Roberts, and Stanky). The 1951 Topps cards were unattractive and paled in comparison to the 1951 Bowman issues. They were successful, however, and Topps has continued to produce cards ever since.

Intensified Competition

Topps issued a larger and more attractive card set in 1952. This larger size became standard for the next five years. (Bowman followed with larger-size baseball cards in 1953.) This 1952 Topps set has become, like the 1933 Goudey series and the T-206 white border series, the classic set of its era. The 407-card set is a collector´s dream of scarcities, rarities, errors, and variations. It also contains the first Topps issues of Mickey Mantle and Willie Mays.

As with Bowman and Leaf in the late 1940s, competition over player rights arose. Ensuing court battles occurred between Topps and Bowman. The market split due to stiff competition, and in January 1956, Topps bought out Bowman. (Topps, using the Bowman name, resurrected Bowman as a label in 1989.) Topps remained essentially unchallenged as the primary producer of baseball cards through 1980. So, the story of major baseball card sets from 1956 through 1980 is by and large the story of Topps´ issues. Notable exceptions include the small sets produced by Fleer Gum in 1959, 1960, 1961, and 1963, and the Kellogg´s Cereal and Hostess Cakes baseball cards issued to promote their products.

A court decision in 1980 paved the way for two other large gum companies to enter (or reenter, in Fleer´s case) the baseball card arena. Fleer, which had last made photo cards in 1963, and the Donruss Company (then a division of General Mills) secured rights to produce baseball cards of current players, thus breaking Topps´ monopoly. Each company issued major card sets in 1981 with bubblegum products.

Then a higher court decision in that year overturned the lower court ruling against Topps. It appeared that Topps had regained its sole position as a producer of baseball cards. Undaunted by the revocation ruling, Fleer and Donruss continued to issue cards in 1982 but without bubblegum or any other edible product. Fleer issued its current player baseball cards with "team logo stickers," while Donruss issued its cards with a piece of a baseball jigsaw puzzle.

Sharing the Pie

Since 1981, these three major baseball card producers all have thrived, sharing relatively equal recognition. Each has steadily increased its involvement in terms of numbers of issues per year. To the delight of collectors, their competition has generated novel, and in some cases exceptional, issues of current Major League Baseball players. Collectors also eagerly accepted the debut efforts of Score (1988) and Upper Deck (1989). These five companies were about to embark on a wild ride through the 1990s.

Upper Deck's successful entry into the market turned out to be very important. The company's card stock, photography, packaging, and marketing gave baseball cards a new standard for quality and began the "premium card" trend that continues today. The second premium baseball card set to be issued was the 1990 Leaf set, named for and issued by the parent company of Donruss. To gauge the significance of the premium card trend, one need only note that two of the most valuable post-1986 regular-issue cards in the hobby are the 1989 Upper Deck Ken Griffey Jr. and 1990 Leaf Frank Thomas Rookie Cards.

The impressive debut of Leaf in 1990 was followed by Studio, Ultra, and Stadium Club in 1991. Of those, Stadium Club with its dramatic borderless photo, uncoated card fronts made the biggest impact. In 1992, Bowman and Pinnacle joined the premium fray. In 1992, Donruss and Fleer abandoned the traditional 50-cent pack market and instead produced premium sets comparable to (and presumably designed to compete against) Upper Deck's set. Those moves, combined with the almost instantaneous spread of premium cards to the other major team sports cards, serve as strong indicators that premium cards were here to stay. Bowman had been a lower-level product from 1989 to 1991.

In 1993, Fleer, Topps, and Upper Deck produced the first "super premium" cards with Flair, Finest, and SP, respectively. The success of all three products was an indication the baseball card market was headed toward even higher price levels, and that turned out to be the case in 1994 with the introduction of Bowman's Best (a Topps hybrid of prospect-oriented Bowman and the superpremium Finest) and Leaf Limited. Other 1994 debuts included Upper Deck's entry-level Collector's Choice and Pinnacle's hobby-only Select.

Overall, inserts continued to dominate the hobby scene. Specifically, the parallel chase cards introduced in 1992 with Topps Gold became the latest major hobby trend. Topps Gold was followed by 1993 Finest Refractors (at the time the scarcest insert ever produced and still a landmark set) and the one-per-box Stadium Club First Day Issue.

Of course, the biggest on-field news of 1994 was the owner-provoked players' strike that halted the season prematurely. While the baseball card hobby suffered noticeably from the strike, there was no catastrophic market crash as some had feared. However, the strike drastically slowed down a market that was both strong and growing and contributed to a serious hobby contraction that continues to this day.

By 1995, parallel insert sets were commonplace and had taken on a new complexion: the most popular ones were those that had announced (or at least suspected) print runs of 500 or less, such as Finest Refractors and Select Artist's Proofs.

This trend continued in 1996, with several parallel inserts that were printed in quantities of 250 or less, such as Finest Gold Refractors, Fleer Circa Rave, Studio Silver Press Proofs, and three of the six Select Certified parallels. It could be argued that the high price tags on these extremely limited parallel cards (many exceeded the $1,000 plateau) were driving many single-player collectors to frustration, and even completely out of the hobby. At the same time, average pack prices soared while average number of cards per pack dropped, making the baseball card hobby increasingly expensive.

On the positive side, two trends from 1996 clearly brought in new collectors: Topps' Mickey Mantle retrospective inserts in both series of Topps and Stadium Club and Leaf's Signature Series, which included one certified autograph per pack. Although the Mantle craze following his passing seemed to be a short-term phenomenon, the inclusion of autographs in packs seemed to have more long-term significance.

In 1997 the print runs in selected sets got even lower. Both Fleer/SkyBox and

Pinnacle brands issued cards of which only one exists.

The growth in popularity of autographs also continued. Many products had autographed cards in their packs. A very positive trend was a return to basics. Many collectors bought Rookie Cards, as they understood that concept, and worked on finishing sets.

There was also an increase in international players collecting. Hideo Nomo was incredibly popular in Japan while Chan Ho Park was in demand in Korea. This bodes well for an international growth in the hobby.

Clearly, 1998 was a year of rebirth and growth for the hobby. The big boost came from the home run chase being conducted by Mark McGwire and Sammy Sosa, as well as the continued brilliance of stalwarts like Ken Griffey Jr. and Roger Clemens. The baseball card hobby received a great deal of positive publicity from the renewed interest in the game.

Rookie Cards of the key players of 1998 made significant gains in value as the hobby once again turned to Rookie Cards as the collectible of choice. Also, cards professionally graded by companies such as PSA and SGC were becoming more heavily traded in both older and newer material.

In addition, the Internet and various services such as eBay contributed to the strong growth in collecting interest over the year.

There were downsides in 1998, though. Pinnacle Brands folded, leaving a legacy of innovation and promotions not seen by other companies. In addition, there still was the problem of collectors being frustrated by the extremely short printed cards of their favorite players, making set completion almost impossible.

During 1998, Pacific received a full baseball license and added many innovations to the card market. Their 1998 OnLine set is the most comprehensive set issued in the last five years and many veteran collectors applauded Pacific´s continuing attempts to get as many players as possible into their sets.

In the last couple of years, card companies have been printing specific subsets (usually young players or Rookie Cards) in shorter supply than the regular cards. This is not in every set, but in many sets produced since 1998.

In 1999, many of the trends of the last couple of years continued to gain strength. Buying, selling, and trading cards over the Internet became a dominant factor in the secondary market. Beckett Media LP began its own Marketplace, offering the collectors a chance to search across inventory from many of the finest dealers nationwide in one comprehensive on-line database; eBay continued to flourish, while many other parties began to reap the benefits of the burgeoning online auction market. The Barry Halper collection was auctioned off, bringing many museum quality items to the market and giving the older memorabilia market a significant boost as many treasures were made available to collectors.

Also, the boom in Internet trading created a perfect fit for professionally graded cards, as buyers and sellers traded cards sight unseen with the confidence established by a third-party grader.

From a field of almost a dozen contenders, three companies emerged in 1999 to dominate the field of professional grading, BGS (Beckett Grading Services), PSA (Professional Sports Authenticator), and SGC (Sportscard Guaranty L.L.C.). In 1999 these companies made dramatic expansions in on-site grading and submissions at card shows throughout the nation. In response to the widespread acceptance of graded cards, the line of monthly Beckett Price Guides each added a separate section within the price guide area for professionally graded cards.

Similar to 1998, four licensed manufacturers (Fleer/SkyBox, Pacific, Topps, and Upper Deck) produced slightly more than fifty different products for 1999.

Perhaps the biggest hit of the 1999 card season was created by Topps. Card #220 within the basic issue first series 1999 Topps brand featured Home Run King Mark McGwire in 70 variations, one for each homer he slugged in 1998, and many collectors went after the whole set. Continuing a legacy as strong as the Yankees, the basic Topps issue was one of the most popular sets released in 1999.

Closely trailing the Topps McGwire promotion was Upper Deck´s dynamic A Piece of History bat card promotion. The card that kicked off the frenzy was the Babe Ruth A Piece of History distributed in 1999 Upper Deck series 1 packs. Upper Deck actually purchased a cracked game-used Babe Ruth bat for $24,000 and proceeded to cut it up into approximately 350-400 chips of wood to create the now famous Ruth bat card. The card instantly created polar opposites of opinion among hobbyists. Traditional collectors howled at the sacrilegious act of destroying such a historic piece of memorabilia while more open-minded collectors jumped at the opportunity to chase such an important card. The Ruth card was followed up by the cross-brand "500 Club" bat card promotion, whereby UD produced bat cards from every major league ballplayer who hit 500 or more home runs in their career (except for Mark McGwire, who hit his 500th in the midst of the 1999 season and promptly stated that he did not support Upper Deck's promotion).

More memorabilia cards than ever were offered to collectors in 1999 as Fleer/SkyBox kicked up their efforts to match the standards set by Upper Deck in previous years. Batting gloves, hats, and shoes joined the typical bats and jerseys as pieces of game-used equipment to be featured on trading cards. Sets like E-X Century Authen-Kicks and Fleer Mystique Feel the Game typified the new offerings.

Topps only dabbled with memorabilia cards in 1999, but continued to offer some of the hottest autographed inserts, highlighted by the Topps Stars Rookie Reprint Autographs and the Topps Nolan Ryan Autographs.

Pacific made a clear decision to steer free of memorabilia and autograph inserts, instead focusing on offering collectors a wide selection of beautifully designed insert and parallel cards. Those themes worked beautifully with their established presence for making comprehensive sets, providing collectors with the necessary challenge to pursue regional stars and a favorite team in addition to the typical superstars.

An astounding total of 264 players made their first appearance on a major league licensed trading card in 1999. What may go down as the deepest class of Rookie Cards of all time features a cornucopia of talented youngsters led by Rick Ankiel, Josh Beckett, Pat Burrell, Josh Hamilton, Eric Munson, Corey Patterson, and Alfonso Soriano.

As in years past, Topps continued to provide collectors with a fistful of Rookie Cards within their Bowman, Bowman Chrome, and Bowman's Best brands. In a trend established in 1998 by Fleer when they released their Fleer Update set (fueled largely by a J. D. Drew Rookie Card), hobbyists enjoyed a bevy of late-season sets chock full of RC's. Fleer/SkyBox made an all-out effort by stuffing more than 100 Rookie Cards into their 1999 Fleer Update set. Topps produced their first boxed Traded set since 1994. Each 1999 Topps Traded set contained 1 of 75 different cards autographed by a rookie prospect. Considering how much wider the selection of Rookie Cards became in 1999, it's amazing to see that so few of these RC's were serial numbered. When one looks at the success established with serial numbered Rookie Cards in the basketball and football card markets with brands like SP Authentic and SPx Finite, one can only scratch his head when realizing that Fleer Mystique was the only brand to offer baseball collectors serial numbered RC's. Thus, it's not surprising to see that despite having 25 different Rookie Cards issued in 1999, Pat Burrell's Fleer Mystique RC (#'d of 2,999) had been established as his "best" RC by year's end.

Youngsters weren't the only players in the limelight in 1999 as retired stars and Hall of Famers were featured on more cards than any other year in the 1990s. Upper Deck's Century Legends brand, featuring the top 50 active and top 50 retired players of the decade as chosen by the Sporting News was a runaway hit.

Perhaps the most popular insert set of the year, outpacing all of the dazzling high-dollar memorabilia cards, was Topps Gallery Heritage. Utilizing the design and painting style of artist Gerry Dvorak from the classic 1953 Topps set, these modern masterpieces proved that insert cards can still be a hot commodity in the secondary market, albeit assuming they're well conceived and well made, an unfortunate rarity these days.

The spate of basic issue sets with short-printed subsets continued across many brands in 1999. In reaction to many frustrated dealers and collectors struggling to complete these sets, Fleer/SkyBox created dual versions of each prospect card for the 1999 SkyBox Premium set, an action shot was short-printed and a posed shot was seeded at the same rate as other basic issue cards. The idea was well received by collectors but enjoyed a surprisingly short-lived period of active trading in the secondary market.

The year 2000 was marked by several major developments that would continue shaping the future of our hobby. First off, Pacific decided to forfeit their baseball card license on January 1st, 2000, in an effort to more sharply focus their production expenditures into football and hockey.

In a separate development, Wizards of the Coast (primarily known for their non-sport gaming cards) was granted a license to produce baseball trading cards and debuted their MLB Showdown brand. The cards proved to be quite successful in that they were collected as a set by veteran collectors and played as a game by children (and some adults) both inside and outside of the typical collecting community.

By year´s end, Fleer fazed out their SkyBox and Flair brand names in an effort to take full advantage of the historic significance and brand recognition of their flagship Fleer sets issued sporadically during the late 1950s-1970s and consistently from 1981 to the present.

Almost sixty brands of MLB-licensed cards, issued by five manufacturers, were produced in 2000. In addition, Just Minors and Team Best produced a variety of attractive minor league products. Most shop owners continued to generate their income primarily through the sales of packs and boxes of new product, and, as in years past, they had to make careful decisions as to what to keep in stock for customers and what to pass up in fear of a low sell through.

Vintage (or retro-themed) sets dominated the market highlighted by Fleer Greats of the Game, Upper Deck Yankees Legends, and the run of 3,000 hit club and Joe DiMaggio game-used cards issued by Fleer and Upper Deck. In 2001, Topps Heritage (mimicking the style of the classic ´52 Topps cards), Upper Deck Vintage (in an homage to ´63 Topps baseball), and the return of Topps Archives (after a six-year hiatus) added fuel to the fire.

Using the vintage-theme to tap into a base of wealthy consumers, Upper Deck rolled out their line of Master Collection products (which debuted in basketball a year prior with a Michael Jordan set). Both the Yankees Master Collection and Brooklyn Dodgers Master Collection sets carried initial SRP´s of $4,000 or more, marking the most expensive "factory set" of all-time. Each of these sets was serial numbered (500 Yankees and 250 Dodgers), came in a stylish wood box and contained an assortment of game-used and autograph cards from legends of days gone by.

Game-used memorabilia cards became more abundant in all products to the point where a few early 2001 releases (2001 Pacific Private Stock and 2001 SP Game Bat Edition both carrying SRP´s in the $15-$20 range) included them at a rate of one per pack. Both products enjoyed a dynamic sell through and proved to be very popular in the secondary market. The result, however, on the secondary market values of game-used memorabilia cards has been dramatic. An Alex Rodriguez or Ken Griffey Jr. game bat or game jersey card that sold for $200+ in 1999 could be had for as little as $25-$50 in early 2001.

Patch cards (a swatch of jersey that contains part of a multi-colored patch) really caught on by year´s end as the market formalized premium values on these cards. Upper Deck was the first to create separate "super-premium" jersey Patch inserts within 2000 Upper Deck 1 and 2000 Upper Deck Game Jersey Edition (aka series 2). Pacific followed suit with their Game Gear patch subset within the invincible brand.

By early 2001, Major League Baseball Properties had gotten involved with the trading card autograph and memorabilia programs. From 2001 on, all MLB-licensed trading cards produced by the manufacturers that involved an autograph or game-used memorabilia item had to have the procurement of the item witnessed by a representative of Andersen Consulting, a firm hired by MLB to oversee this historic program. Never before had consumers been provided such an effort by the league and manufacturers to be offered autographed or game-used memorabilia trading cards of such authentic provenance.

Short-printed subset cards, a trend started in 1999, continued to be a common element in most basic sets. The trend, however, evolved to the point where these short prints were now being serial numbered, autographed by the player, or incorporating an element of game-used material onto the card. The result was higher values on the key singles, but lower odds of actually finding a good RC in a pack. By year´s end, a general sentiment of frustration over not being able to pull good Rookie Cards from a box was beginning to be heard more and more often from collectors.

Rookie Cards incorporating game-used material debuted at year's end in 2000 Black Diamond Rookie Edition. Also, Rookie Cards signed by the player, introduced within the basketball and football card markets in 1999 (with Upper Deck's SPx brand), made their baseball debut in 2000 SPx. Serial-numbered Rookie Cards grew in total usage, but shrank in print run numbers as production figures reached an all-time low of 999 copies for a basic issue RC within the 2000 Pacific Omega set.

Year-end boxed sets, a trend brought back from a four-year hiatus by Fleer in 1998 with their Fleer Update set, continued to expand as Topps issued their Bowman Draft Picks and Bowman Chrome Draft Picks sets to cap the now single-series accompanying standard Bowman and Bowman Chrome products.

Fleer broke new ground by blending a 1980s "old-school" concept with some postmodern angles in their 2000 Fleer Glossy boxed set. Harkening back to the run of Glossy parallel factory sets produced from 1987 to 1989, the 2000 Fleer Glossy set included a parallel version of the complete 400-card basic 2000 Fleer set. In addition, 50 new cards (card #'s 401-450, each serial numbered to 1,000 copies) featuring a selection of prospects and rookies were created. Each Glossy factory set contained 5 of the 50 new cards, making it a real challenge to complete the Glossy set.

In a first of its kind for the baseball market, Upper Deck issued a product in December 2000 called Rookie Update that incorporated new cards for three separate popular brands (SP Authentic, SPx, and UD Pros and Prospects) into each pack of cards.

Upper Deck came to terms with Major League Baseball for a license to produce cards featuring members of past and present Team USA squads (bringing back a run of cards last seen in 1993 Topps Traded). That allowed Upper Deck the opportunity to radically expand their production of "true" Rookie Cards in year-end 2000 products, adding a spate of cards featuring heroes from the Olympics in Sydney, Australia, like Ben Sheets. Not surprisingly, the number of prospects making their Rookie Card debut in 2000 sets jumped from about 280 players in 1999 to slightly more than 350 players in 2000.

The influence of sports card dealers and collectors from the Far East (and most noticeably Japan) continued to grow in 2000 as stateside buying approached frenzied levels over scarce Hideo Nomo and Kazuhiro Sasaki cards. A much-traveled starter these days, Nomo's first-ever certified autograph card (issued within the Fleer Mystique Fresh Ink insert set) was the hottest card in the hobby for two months (initially trading for as much as $600-$800).

Not all trends were met with success this year. In particular, low-end products geared towards the youth audience (like 2000 Impact by Fleer) were roundly ignored. The hobby still faces a tough road ahead to keep new waves of collectors involved from generation to generation. Part of the Catch-22 with creating affordable brands catered to youths is that the same customers are most interested in the high-end, expensive material.

Also, Upper Deck's PowerDeck product faced an indifferent audience for a second year in a row, as collectors and even general sports enthusiasts outside the hobby failed to get excited over the CD-ROM cards. More success was met by UD's e-Card insert program, whereby collectors who pulled an e-Card from a pack of UD cards had to go to UD's Website and check the serial number printed on the card to see whether it could evolve into an autograph, game jersey, or game jersey autograph exchange.

The Internet continued to have profound ramifications on shaping the destiny of sports card collecting. By 2000, nearly every dealer (and hard-core collector) was buying or selling cards to some degree in on-line auctions. Auction sales had become so prolific that they were now having a strong effect on the secondary market sales levels of trading cards in arenas entirely outside of cyberspace, like shops, shows, and mail order.

The eBay site continued to dominate the on-line auction action, introducing what appears to be a popular "Buy It Now" option to their already established auction format. The Pit.com opened in mid-year with their concept of buying and selling a portfolio of professionally graded sports cards through their Web site. The concept is based almost exactly upon the methodology used for buying and selling stocks through a brokerage house, with daily ebbs and flows in posted buy and sell prices on your inventory.

Beckett.com made radical improvements to their Marketplace search engines and expanded their inventory of sports cards to the point where they were providing both a wider and a deeper selection of trading cards than any site on the Internet. In addition, a company-wide effort to provide daily news content on their site (coupled with a weekly newsletter sent to over 400,000 collectors) began at year´s end, and the hobby has reaped the benefits ever since.

As the 2001 season approached, hobbyists waited with bated breath for seven-time Japanese batting champ Ichiro Suzuki to make his debut in the Seattle Mariner´s outfield. And what a stunning debut it was. Ichiro led the league in hitting, led the Mariners to their best record ever, and walked off with the A.L. Rookie of the Year and Most Valuable Player awards. Upper Deck obtained the exclusive rights to produce his autograph cards and they hit a grand slam in midsummer by releasing his SPx Rookie Card, featuring a game jersey swatch and a cut signature autograph. In a year studded with notable cards, this one was likely the most memorable.

In the National League, 37-year-old San Francisco Giants superstar Barry Bonds captivated the nation by bashing a jaw-dropping 73 home runs, shattering Mark McGwire´s 1998 single-season home run record.

Cardinals´ rookie Albert Pujols emerged out of the low minor leagues to become an instant hobby superstar and walk away with N.L. Rookie of the Year honors.

The year 2001 was a tumultuous one for sports cards. Topps started the year off with a bang by celebrating their 50th anniversary producing baseball cards. Pacific forfeited its license to make baseball cards after an eight-year run to focus on football and hockey cards. Playoff, a company based out of Grand Prairie, Texas, that had earned its stripes by producing football cards in the late 1990s, purchased the rights to the much-hallowed Donruss corporate name and became a formal MLB licensee in the spring of 2001. Their entrance into the baseball card market heralded the return of benchmark brands like Donruss, Donruss Signature, and Leaf.

Competition was fiercer than ever amongst the four primary licensees (Donruss-Playoff, Fleer, Topps, and Upper Deck) as they cranked out almost 80 different products over the course of 2001.

Of all these, likely the most historically important product, Upper Deck Prospect Premieres, was widely overlooked upon release. In a bold move, Upper Deck created a set of 102 prospects, none of which had played a day in the majors. Each player was pictured, however, in the major league uniforms of their parent ballclubs and signed to individual contracts. Because no active major leaguers were featured, Upper Deck did not have to include licensing rights from the MLB Players Association, though they did get licensing from Major League Properties. The industry had never seen a major release featuring active ballplayers marketed to the mainstream audience that lacked licensing from the MLBPA. Because of its lack of historical predecessors and a mixed reception from collectors, the cards were tagged by Beckett Baseball Card Monthly as XRC´s (or Extended Rookie Cards), a term that had not been used since 1989.

UD´s Prospect Premieres was the first major effort by a manufacturer to level the playing field between Topps and everyone else in that Topps has exclusive rights from the MLBPA to include minor leaguers in their basic brands.

Rookie Cards continued to fascinate collectors, especially in a year with talents like Ichiro and Albert Pujols. The number of players featured on Rookie Cards in 2001 ballooned to an almost absurd figure of 505.

Exchange cards became more prevalent than ever, as manufacturers expanded their use from autograph cards that didn´t get returned in time for pack out to slots within basic sets left open in brands released early in the year to fill in with late-season rookie call-ups.

Certified autograph cards remained a huge player in how brands were structured, but the quality of the players suffered greatly as autograph fees continued to spiral out of control. Signatures from superstars like Barry Bonds and Derek Jeter were now being featured on cards with miniscule print runs of 25 or 50 copies while unknown (and often aging and talentless) prospects signed their serial-numbered Rookies Cards by the hundred count.

More serial-numbered Rookie Cards were produced than ever before, but the quantities produced kept sinking lower and lower as companies tried to create secondary market value by simply limiting supply, a dangerous move to say the least. Donruss-Playoff produced the scarcest Rookie Cards of the year, a handful of Game Base cards (including Ichiro) each serial #'d to a scant 100 copies, within their Leaf Limited set.

After a six-month delay, Topps released their much awaited e-Topps program, a product sold entirely on their Web site whereby trading is conducted in a similar fashion to the buying and selling of stocks, in September.

Several products incorporated non-card memorabilia such as signed caps, bobbing head dolls, and signed baseballs with mixed results.

Memorabilia cards continued their slide into mediocrity as the number of cards featuring various bits and pieces of balls, bases, bats, jerseys, pants, shoes, seats, and whatever else could be dreamt up continued to be offered to consumers, who found the cards less appealing with each passing month. To battle consumer apathy, companies often started to offer combination memorabilia cards featuring notable teammates or several pieces of equipment from a notable star.

Retro-themed cards continued to grow in popularity, and some of the innovations seen in these sets were remarkable. Of particular note was Upper Deck's SP Legendary Cuts Autographs set, featuring 84 deceased players. The set required UD to purchase more than 3,300 autograph cuts, which were then incorporated into a windowpane card design. The result was the first certified autograph cards for legends like Roger Maris, Satchell Paige, and Jackie Robinson. Also, Topps Tribute released at year's end and carrying a hefty $40 per pack suggested retail was widely hailed as one of the most beautiful retro-themed cards ever designed, with their crystal-board fronts encasing full-color, razor-sharp photos.

Pack prices continued to escalate, but surprisingly, the public did not balk as long as they delivered value. The most notable high-end product to hit the market in 2001 was Upper Deck Ultimate Collection with a suggested retail of $100 per pack.

September 11th, 2001, is a day that will go down as one of the most devastating in the history of the United States of America. The game of baseball and the hobby of collecting sports cards were rightfully cast aside as the nation mourned the tragic loss of lives in New York, Pennsylvania, and Washington, D.C. America's economy tumbled as airline traveling ground to a near halt and threats of anthrax crippled the mail system. An economy threatening to slip into recession at the beginning of the year dove headlong into it. The sports card market, along with many other industries, felt the hit for several months. Slowly, Americans looked to move past the grief and the sports card industry, steeped in American nostalgia, provided an ideal retreat for many.

The Arizona Diamondbacks beat the New York Yankees in one of the finest World Series ever played, a much-needed diversion for a grief-stricken nation and a calling card for the dramatic power and glory of our National Pastime.

Last year was a relatively quiet one for baseball cards. Dodger's rookie pitcher Kazuhisa Ishii got off to a blazing first half start and his cards carried many releases through to the All-Star break. Ishii stumbled badly in the second half and no notable rookies were in place to pick up market interest. Cubs hurler Mark Prior created a stir, and his 2001 Rookie Cards were red hot at mid-season. For the second straight season, Barry Bonds was the most dominant star in our sport. His early cards continued to outpace all others in volume trading and professional grading submissions.

The number of players featured on Rookie Cards (or Extended Rookie Cards) reached an all-time high of 524 in 2002 as the manufacturers continued to push the envelope toward more immediate coverage of the current year draft. Though few collectors took notice at the time of release, Upper Deck's incorporation of collegiate Team USA athletes into several year-end brands may take hold and grow into a more prominent position in our industry for collegiate ballplayers. The results of these trends, however, are cards that feature a lot of talented youngsters whom most collectors, unfortunately, have never heard of and won't see in a major league uniform for several years.

To make up for the void in excitement generated by rookies and prospects, the manufacturers made some interesting innovations in product distribution and brand development. In general, base sets got noticeably bigger (including Upper Deck's 1,182 card 40-Man brand and Topps 990-card Topps Total brand). In addition, brands like Topps 206, Leaf Rookies and Stars, and Fleer Fall Classics started to incorporate variations of the base cards directly into the basic issue set (different images, switched out teams, etc.).

One of the bigger surprise hits of the year was the aforementioned Topps 206 brand, which borrowed design elements and set composition from the legendary T-206 tobacco set. Other brands continued to successfully mine from cards and eras long since passed.

Donruss continued to push the creative envelope by incorporating 8½" by 11" framed signature pieces directly into boxes of their Playoff Absolute brand. After a four-year hiatus, Fleer brought back their eponymous "Fleer" name brand with a 540-card set. Donruss introduced their wildly successful Diamond Kings brand, which featured a 150-card painted set. Fleer's Box Score brand was also a popular debut utilizing a unique box-inside-a-box distribution concept. Popular brands like SP Legendary Cuts, Leaf Certified, Topps Heritage, and Topps Tribute all received warm welcomes for their follow-ups to their successes achieved the prior year.

The 2004 season continued to bring us again a growing number of sets with price points ranging from $1.29 to $150. There were also many new heroes during the 2003 season as players such as Josh Beckett, Miguel Cabrera, and Dontrelle Willis of the World Champion Florida Marlins were very strong sellers.

Hideki Matsui, who was the most anticipated rookie for the 2003 season, had a very fine year for the American League Champion Yankees but did not draw the same interest from collectors as Ichiro Suzuki did during the 2001 season.

The 2005 season was most notable for the departure of both Fleer and Donruss/Playoff from the ranks of major manufacturers. One of the issues in recent years has been the staggering amount of sets as well as the complexities of those sets. With some direction from the licensors, the baseball card market was reduced and a maximum of 40 products are expected to be released during the 2006 calendar year.

Despite the struggles the sport of baseball has endured; in recent years, the baseball card market has stepped back to the forefront of the card-collecting hobby, outpacing football, basketball, hockey, golf, and motor sports in volume dollars. As the hobby of collecting baseball cards evolves, we continue to face a market that is blessed with bold creativity and superlative quality; and also challenged with the need to reach new consumers both in mass retail and in cyberspace to continue its growth.

Additional Reading

Each year Beckett Media LP produces comprehensive annual price guides for several sports: *Beckett Baseball Card Price Guide, Beckett Basketball Card Price Guide, Beckett Football Card Price Guide, Beckett Hockey Card Price Guide, Beckett Racing Price Guide,* and a line of *Beckett Alphabetical Checklists Books* have been released as well. The aim of these annual guides is to provide information and accurate pricing on a wide array of sports cards, ranging from main issues by the major card manufacturers to various regional, promotional, and food issues. Alphabetical checklist books are published to assist the collector in identifying all the cards of any particular player. The seasoned collector will find these tools valuable sources of information that will enable him to pursue his hobby interests.

In addition, abridged editions of the *Beckett Price Guides* have been published for each of these major sports as part of the House of Collectibles series: *The Official Price Guide to Baseball Cards, The Official Price Guide to Football Cards,* and *The Official Price Guide to Basketball Cards*. Published in a convenient mass-market paperback format, these price guides provide information and accurate pricing on all the main issues by the major card manufacturers.

Prices in this Guide

Prices found in this guide reflect current retail rates just prior to the printing of this book. They do not reflect the FOR SALE prices of the author, the publisher, the distributors, the advertisers, or any card dealers associated with this guide. No one is obligated in any way to buy, sell, or trade his or her cards based on these prices. The price listings were compiled by the author from actual buy/sell transactions at sports conventions, sports card shops, buy/sell advertisements in the hobby papers, for sale prices from dealer catalogs and price lists, and discussions with leading hobbyists in the United States and Canada. All prices are in U.S. dollars.

Acknowledgments

A great deal of diligence, hard work, and dedicated effort went into this year´s volume. However, the high standards to which we hold ourselves could not have been met without the expert input and generous amount of time contributed by many people. Our sincere thanks are extended to each and every one of you.

A complete list of these invaluable contributors appears after the **Price Guide** section.

2005 Bazooka

	Nm-Mt	Ex-Mt
COMPLETE SET (220)	60.00	18.00
COMMON CARD (1-170)	.40	.12
COMMON CARD (171-190)	.50	.15
COMMON CARD (191-220)	.50	.15

	Nm-Mt	Ex-Mt
❑ 1 Eric Gagne	.40	.12
❑ 2 Aramis Ramirez	.40	.12
❑ 3 Hank Blalock	.40	.12
❑ 4 Jason Kendall	.40	.12
❑ 5 Jeromy Burnitz	.40	.12
❑ 6 Jose Guillen	.40	.12
❑ 7 Tom Glavine	.60	.18
❑ 8 Adrian Beltre	.40	.12
❑ 9 Jason Bay	.40	.12
❑ 10 Mark Teixeira	.60	.18
❑ 11 Moises Alou	.40	.12
❑ 12 Ronnie Belliard	.40	.12
❑ 13 Aaron Guiel	.40	.12
❑ 14 Vladimir Guerrero	1.00	.30
❑ 15 Scott Podsednik	.40	.12
❑ 16 Alfonso Soriano	.40	.12
❑ 17 Craig Wilson	.40	.12
❑ 18 Jose Reyes	.40	.12
❑ 19 Mark Prior	.60	.18
❑ 20 Preston Wilson	.40	.12
❑ 21 Shawn Green	.40	.12
❑ 22 Troy Glaus	.40	.12
❑ 23 Dmitri Young	.40	.12
❑ 24 Garret Anderson	.40	.12
❑ 25 Kazuo Matsui	.40	.12
❑ 26 Kerry Wood	.40	.12
❑ 27 Michael Young	.40	.12
❑ 28 Oliver Perez	.40	.12
❑ 29 Bartolo Colon	.40	.12
❑ 30 Richie Sexson	.40	.12
❑ 31 Brad Penny	.40	.12
❑ 32 Carlos Guillen	.40	.12
❑ 33 Carlos Zambrano	.40	.12
❑ 34 David Wright	1.50	.45
❑ 35 Al Leiter	.40	.12
❑ 36 Jack Wilson	.40	.12
❑ 37 Ryan Drese	.40	.12
❑ 38 Darin Erstad	.40	.12
❑ 39 Derrek Lee	.60	.18
❑ 40 Ivan Rodriguez	.60	.18
❑ 41 Kenny Rogers	.40	.12
❑ 42 Mike Piazza	1.00	.30
❑ 43 Phil Nevin	.40	.12
❑ 44 Geoff Jenkins	.40	.12
❑ 45 Jorge Posada	.60	.18
❑ 46 Khalil Greene	.60	.18
❑ 47 Randy Johnson	1.00	.30
❑ 48 Rondell White	.40	.12
❑ 49 Sammy Sosa	1.00	.30
❑ 50 Vernon Wells	.40	.12
❑ 51 Ben Sheets	.40	.12
❑ 52 Brian Giles	.40	.12
❑ 53 Carlos Delgado	.40	.12
❑ 54 Derek Jeter	2.00	.60
❑ 55 Jeremy Bonderman	.40	.12
❑ 56 Magglio Ordonez	.40	.12
❑ 57 Chad Tracy	.40	.12
❑ 58 Kevin Brown	.40	.12
❑ 59 Luis Castillo	.40	.12
❑ 60 Lyle Overbay	.40	.12
❑ 61 Mark Buehrle	.40	.12
❑ 62 Mark Loretta	.40	.12
❑ 63 Orlando Hudson	.40	.12
❑ 64 Adam Dunn	.40	.12
❑ 65 Frank Thomas	1.00	.30
❑ 66 Jake Peavy	.40	.12
❑ 67 Jason Giambi	.40	.12
❑ 68 Joe Mauer	.40	.12
❑ 69 Marcus Giles	.40	.12
❑ 70 Mike Lowell	.40	.12
❑ 71 Roy Halladay	.40	.12
❑ 72 Aaron Rowand	.40	.12
❑ 73 Alex Rodriguez	1.50	.45
❑ 74 Brian Lawrence	.40	.12
❑ 75 Gabe Gross	.40	.12
❑ 76 Johnny Estrada	.40	.12
❑ 77 Justin Morneau	.40	.12
❑ 78 Miguel Cabrera	.60	.18
❑ 79 Alex Rios	.40	.12
❑ 80 Gary Sheffield	.40	.12
❑ 81 Jason Schmidt	.40	.12
❑ 82 Juan Pierre	.40	.12
❑ 83 Paul Konerko	.40	.12
❑ 84 Jermaine Dye	.40	.12
❑ 85 Rafael Furcal	.40	.12
❑ 86 Torii Hunter	.40	.12
❑ 87 A.J. Pierzynski	.40	.12
❑ 88 Carl Pavano	.40	.12
❑ 89 Carlos Lee	.40	.12
❑ 90 J.D. Drew	.40	.12
❑ 91 Javier Vazquez	.40	.12
❑ 92 Lew Ford	.40	.12
❑ 93 Ted Lilly	.40	.12
❑ 94 Austin Kearns	.40	.12
❑ 95 Chipper Jones	1.00	.30
❑ 96 Erubiel Durazo	.40	.12
❑ 97 Johan Santana	.60	.18
❑ 98 Josh Beckett	.40	.12
❑ 99 Mariano Rivera	.60	.18
❑ 100 Mark Mulder	.40	.12
❑ 101 Andruw Jones	.60	.18
❑ 102 Barry Zito	.40	.12
❑ 103 Bret Boone	.40	.12
❑ 104 Paul LoDuca	.40	.12
❑ 105 Shannon Stewart	.40	.12
❑ 106 Wily Mo Pena	.40	.12
❑ 107 Dontrelle Willis	.40	.12
❑ 108 Eric Chavez	.40	.12
❑ 109 Jamie Moyer	.40	.12
❑ 110 Joe Nathan	.40	.12
❑ 111 Sidney Ponson	.40	.12
❑ 112 John Smoltz	.60	.18
❑ 113 Ichiro Suzuki	2.00	.60
❑ 114 Javy Lopez	.40	.12
❑ 115 Victor Martinez	.40	.12
❑ 116 Ken Griffey Jr.	1.50	.45
❑ 117 Lance Berkman	.40	.12
❑ 118 Scott Hatteberg	.40	.12
❑ 119 Jim Edmonds	.60	.18
❑ 120 Kazuhisa Ishii	.40	.12
❑ 121 Miguel Tejada	.40	.12
❑ 122 Roger Clemens	1.50	.45
❑ 123 Ryan Freel	.40	.12
❑ 124 Albert Pujols	2.00	.60
❑ 125 Hideo Nomo	1.00	.30
❑ 126 Mark Kotsay	.40	.12
❑ 127 Melvin Mora	.40	.12
❑ 128 Roy Oswalt	.40	.12
❑ 129 Sean Casey	.60	.18
❑ 130 Casey Blake	.40	.12
❑ 131 Edgar Renteria	.40	.12
❑ 132 Jeff Kent	.40	.12
❑ 133 Rafael Palmeiro	.60	.18
❑ 134 Tim Hudson	.40	.12
❑ 135 Barry Bonds	2.50	.75
❑ 136 Andy Pettitte	.60	.18
❑ 137 Brian Roberts	.40	.12
❑ 138 Jose Vidro	.40	.12
❑ 139 Omar Vizquel	.60	.18
❑ 140 Rich Harden	.40	.12
❑ 141 Scott Rolen	.60	.18
❑ 142 Carlos Beltran	.40	.12
❑ 143 Chris Carpenter	.40	.12
❑ 144 Manny Ramirez	.60	.18
❑ 145 Nick Johnson	.40	.12
❑ 146 Pat Burrell	.40	.12
❑ 147 C.C. Sabathia	.40	.12
❑ 148 Johnny Damon	.60	.18
❑ 149 Juan Rivera	.40	.12
❑ 150 Ken Harvey	.40	.12
❑ 151 Kevin Millwood	.40	.12
❑ 152 Larry Walker	.60	.18
❑ 153 Aubrey Huff	.40	.12
❑ 154 Curt Schilling	.60	.18
❑ 155 Jake Westbrook	.40	.12
❑ 156 Randy Wolf	.40	.12
❑ 157 Zach Day	.40	.12
❑ 158 Zack Greinke	.40	.12
❑ 159 Brad Wilkerson	.40	.12
❑ 160 Carl Crawford	.40	.12
❑ 161 Jim Thome	.60	.18
❑ 162 Mike Sweeney	.40	.12
❑ 163 Pedro Martinez	.60	.18
❑ 164 Travis Hafner	.40	.12
❑ 165 Bobby Abreu	.40	.12
❑ 166 Cliff Floyd	.40	.12
❑ 167 David DeJesus	.40	.12
❑ 168 David Ortiz	1.00	.30
❑ 169 Rocco Baldelli	.40	.12
❑ 170 Todd Helton	.60	.18
❑ 171 Dallas McPherson PROS	.50	.15
❑ 172 Kevin Youkilis PROS	.50	.15
❑ 173 Val Majewski PROS	.50	.15
❑ 174 Grady Sizemore PROS	.50	.15
❑ 175 Joey Gathright PROS	.50	.15
❑ 176 Rickie Weeks PROS	.50	.15
❑ 177 Jason Kubel PROS	.50	.15
❑ 178 Robinson Cano PROS	.75	.23
❑ 179 Nick Swisher PROS	.50	.15
❑ 180 Ryan Howard PROS	.50	.15
❑ 181 Tim Stauffer PROS	.50	.15
❑ 182 Merkin Valdez PROS	.50	.15
❑ 183 B.J. Upton PROS	.75	.23
❑ 184 Scott Kazmir PROS	1.00	.30
❑ 185 Chris Burke PROS	.50	.15
❑ 186 Felix Hernandez PROS	2.00	.60
❑ 187 Freddy Guzman PROS	.50	.15
❑ 188 Josh Labandeira PROS	.50	.15
❑ 189 Willy Taveras PROS	.50	.15
❑ 190 Casey Kotchman PROS	.50	.15
❑ 191 Steve Doetsch FY RC	.75	.23
❑ 192 Melky Cabrera FY RC	1.00	.30
❑ 193 Luis Ramirez FY RC	.50	.15
❑ 194 Chris Seddon FY RC	.50	.15
❑ 195 Chad Orvella FY RC	.50	.15
❑ 196 Ian Kinsler FY RC	1.00	.30
❑ 197 Brandon Moss FY RC	2.00	.60
❑ 198 Chadd Blasko FY RC	.75	.23
❑ 199 Jeremy West FY RC	.75	.23
❑ 200 Sean Marshall FY RC	.75	.23
❑ 201 Matt DeSalvo FY RC	.75	.23
❑ 202 Ryan Sweeney FY RC	1.00	.30
❑ 203 Matthew Lindstrom FY RC	.50	.15
❑ 204 Ryan Goleski FY RC	.75	.23
❑ 205 Brett Harper FY RC	.75	.23
❑ 206 Chris Roberson FY RC	.50	.15
❑ 207 Andre Ethier FY RC	1.25	.35
❑ 208 Chris Denorfia FY RC	.75	.23
❑ 209 Darren Fenster FY RC	.50	.15
❑ 210 Elvys Quezada FY RC	.50	.15
❑ 211 Kevin West FY RC	.50	.15
❑ 212 Chaz Lytle FY RC	.75	.23
❑ 213 James Jurries FY RC	.75	.23
❑ 214 Matt Rogelstad FY RC	.50	.15
❑ 215 Wade Robinson FY RC	.50	.15
❑ 216 Ian Bladergroen FY RC	.75	.23
❑ 217 Jake Dittler FY	.50	.15
❑ 218 Nate McLouth FY RC	.75	.23
❑ 219 Kole Strayhorn FY RC	.50	.15
❑ 220 Jose Vaquedano FY RC	.50	.15

1948 Bowman

	NM	Ex
COMPLETE SET (48)	3600.00	1800.00
COMMON CARD (1-36)	20.00	10.00
COMMON CARD (37-48)	30.00	15.00
WRAPPER (5-CENT)	700.00	350.00
WRAPPER (1-CENT)	.00	

	NM	Ex
❑ 1 Bob Elliott RC	125.00	19.00
❑ 2 Ewell Blackwell RC	60.00	30.00

❑ 3 Ralph Kiner RC	250.00	125.00
❑ 4 Johnny Mize RC	125.00	60.00
❑ 5 Bob Feller RC	250.00	125.00
❑ 6 Yogi Berra RC	500.00	250.00
❑ 7 Pete Reiser SP	125.00	60.00
❑ 8 Phil Rizzuto SP RC	350.00	180.00
❑ 9 Walker Cooper RC	20.00	10.00
❑ 10 Buddy Rosar	20.00	10.00
❑ 11 Johnny Lindell	25.00	12.50
❑ 12 Johnny Sain RC	80.00	40.00
❑ 13 Willard Marshall SP	40.00	20.00
❑ 14 Allie Reynolds RC	60.00	30.00
❑ 15 Eddie Joost	20.00	10.00
❑ 16 Jack Lohrke SP	40.00	20.00
❑ 17 Enos Slaughter RC	100.00	50.00
❑ 18 Warren Spahn RC	300.00	150.00
❑ 19 Tommy Henrich	60.00	30.00
❑ 20 Buddy Kerr SP	40.00	20.00
❑ 21 Ferris Fain RC	40.00	20.00
❑ 22 Floyd Bevens SP RC	50.00	25.00
❑ 23 Larry Jansen RC	25.00	12.50
❑ 24 Dutch Leonard SP	40.00	20.00
❑ 25 Barney McCosky	20.00	10.00
❑ 26 Frank Shea SP RC	50.00	25.00
❑ 27 Sid Gordon RC	25.00	12.50
❑ 28 Emil Verban SP	40.00	20.00
❑ 29 Joe Page SP RC	80.00	40.00
❑ 30 W.Lockman SP RC	50.00	25.00
❑ 31 Bill McCahan	20.00	10.00
❑ 32 Bill Rigney RC	20.00	10.00
❑ 33 Bill Johnson	25.00	12.50
❑ 34 Sheldon Jones SP	40.00	20.00
❑ 35 Snuffy Stirnweiss RC	40.00	20.00
❑ 36 Stan Musial RC	800.00	400.00
❑ 37 Clint Hartung RC	30.00	15.00
❑ 38 Red Schoendienst RC	200.00	100.00
❑ 39 Augie Galan	30.00	15.00
❑ 40 Marty Marion RC	80.00	40.00
❑ 41 Rex Barney RC	60.00	30.00
❑ 42 Ray Poat	30.00	15.00
❑ 43 Bruce Edwards	40.00	20.00
❑ 44 Johnny Wyrostek	30.00	15.00
❑ 45 Hank Sauer RC	60.00	30.00
❑ 46 Herman Wehmeier	30.00	15.00
❑ 47 Bobby Thomson RC	100.00	50.00
❑ 48 Dave Koslo RC	80.00	19.50

1949 Bowman

	NM	Ex
COMP. MASTER SET (252)	16000.00	8000.00
COMPLETE SET (240)	15000.00	7500.00
COMMON CARD (1-144)	15.00	7.50
COMMON (145-240)	50.00	25.00
WRAPPER (1-CENT,Rd,Wh,Bl)	.00	
WRAPPER (5-CENT, GR.)	250.00	125.00
WRAPPER (5-CENT, BL.)	200.00	100.00
❑ 1 Vern Bickford RC	125.00	25.00
❑ 2 Whitey Lockman	40.00	20.00
❑ 3 Bob Porterfield	15.00	7.50
❑ 4A Jerry Priddy NNOF	15.00	7.50
❑ 4B Jerry Priddy NOF	50.00	25.00
❑ 5 Hank Sauer	40.00	20.00
❑ 6 Phil Cavarretta	40.00	20.00
❑ 7 Joe Dobson	15.00	7.50
❑ 8 Murry Dickson	15.00	7.50
❑ 9 Ferris Fain	40.00	20.00
❑ 10 Ted Gray	15.00	7.50
❑ 11 Lou Boudreau	80.00	40.00
❑ 12 Cass Michaels	15.00	7.50
❑ 13 Bob Chesnes	15.00	7.50
❑ 14 Curt Simmons RC	40.00	20.00
❑ 15 Ned Garver	15.00	7.50
❑ 16 Al Kozar	15.00	7.50
❑ 17 Earl Torgeson	15.00	7.50
❑ 18 Bobby Thomson	40.00	20.00
❑ 19 Bobby Brown RC	60.00	30.00
❑ 20 Gene Hermanski	15.00	7.50
❑ 21 Frank Baumholtz	25.00	12.50
❑ 22 Peanuts Lowrey	15.00	7.50
❑ 23 Bobby Doerr	80.00	40.00
❑ 24 Stan Musial	600.00	300.00
❑ 25 Carl Scheib	15.00	7.50
❑ 26 George Kell RC	80.00	40.00
❑ 27 Bob Feller	300.00	150.00
❑ 28 Don Kolloway	15.00	7.50
❑ 29 Ralph Kiner	125.00	60.00
❑ 30 Andy Seminick	40.00	20.00
❑ 31 Dick Kokos	15.00	7.50
❑ 32 Eddie Yost RC	60.00	30.00
❑ 33 Warren Spahn	200.00	100.00
❑ 34 Dave Koslo	15.00	7.50
❑ 35 Vic Raschi RC	60.00	30.00
❑ 36 Pee Wee Reese	200.00	100.00
❑ 37 Johnny Wyrostek	15.00	7.50
❑ 38 Emil Verban	15.00	7.50
❑ 39 Billy Goodman	25.00	12.50
❑ 40 George Munger	15.00	7.50
❑ 41 Lou Brissie	15.00	7.50
❑ 42 Hoot Evers	15.00	7.50
❑ 43 Dale Mitchell RC	40.00	20.00
❑ 44 Dave Philley	15.00	7.50
❑ 45 Wally Westlake	15.00	7.50
❑ 46 Robin Roberts RC	250.00	125.00
❑ 47 Johnny Sain	60.00	30.00
❑ 48 Willard Marshall	15.00	7.50
❑ 49 Frank Shea	25.00	12.50
❑ 50 Jackie Robinson RC	1200.00	600.00
❑ 51 Herman Wehmeier	15.00	7.50
❑ 52 Johnny Schmitz	15.00	7.50
❑ 53 Jack Kramer	15.00	7.50
❑ 54 Marty Marion	60.00	30.00
❑ 55 Eddie Joost	15.00	7.50
❑ 56 Pat Mullin	15.00	7.50
❑ 57 Gene Bearden	40.00	20.00
❑ 58 Bob Elliott	40.00	20.00
❑ 59 Jack Lohrke	15.00	7.50
❑ 60 Yogi Berra	300.00	150.00
❑ 61 Rex Barney	40.00	20.00
❑ 62 Grady Hatton	15.00	7.50
❑ 63 Andy Pafko	40.00	20.00
❑ 64 Dom DiMaggio	60.00	30.00
❑ 65 Enos Slaughter	80.00	40.00
❑ 66 Elmer Valo	15.00	7.50
❑ 67 Alvin Dark RC	40.00	20.00
❑ 68 Sheldon Jones	15.00	7.50
❑ 69 Tommy Henrich	40.00	20.00
❑ 70 Carl Furillo RC	125.00	60.00
❑ 71 Vern Stephens	15.00	7.50
❑ 72 Tommy Holmes	40.00	20.00
❑ 73 Billy Cox RC	40.00	20.00
❑ 74 Tom McBride	15.00	7.50
❑ 75 Eddie Mayo	15.00	7.50
❑ 76 Bill Nicholson RC	25.00	12.50
❑ 77 Ernie Bonham	15.00	7.50
❑ 78A Sam Zoldak NNOF	15.00	7.50
❑ 78B Sam Zoldak NOF	50.00	25.00
❑ 79 Ron Northey	15.00	7.50
❑ 80 Bill McCahan	15.00	7.50
❑ 81 Virgil Stallcup	15.00	7.50
❑ 82 Joe Page	60.00	30.00
❑ 83A Bob Scheffing NNOF	15.00	7.50
❑ 83B Bob Scheffing NOF	50.00	25.00
❑ 84 Roy Campanella RC	800.00	400.00
❑ 85A Johnny Mize NNOF	100.00	50.00
❑ 85B Johnny Mize NOF	150.00	75.00
❑ 86 Johnny Pesky	60.00	30.00
❑ 87 Randy Gumpert	15.00	7.50
❑ 88A Bill Salkeld NNOF	15.00	7.50
❑ 88B Bill Salkeld NOF	50.00	25.00
❑ 89 Mizell Platt	15.00	7.50
❑ 90 Gil Coan	15.00	7.50
❑ 91 Dick Wakefield	15.00	7.50
❑ 92 Willie Jones	40.00	20.00
❑ 93 Ed Stevens	15.00	7.50
❑ 94 Mickey Vernon RC	40.00	20.00
❑ 95 Howie Pollet RC	15.00	7.50
❑ 96 Taft Wright	15.00	7.50
❑ 97 Danny Litwhiler	15.00	7.50
❑ 98A Phil Rizzuto NNOF	200.00	100.00
❑ 98B Phil Rizzuto NOF	250.00	125.00
❑ 99 Frank Gustine	15.00	7.50
❑ 100 Gil Hodges RC	250.00	125.00
❑ 101 Sid Gordon	15.00	7.50
❑ 102 Stan Spence	15.00	7.50
❑ 103 Joe Tipton	15.00	7.50
❑ 104 Eddie Stanky RC	40.00	20.00
❑ 105 Bill Kennedy	15.00	7.50
❑ 106 Jake Early	15.00	7.50
❑ 107 Eddie Lake	15.00	7.50
❑ 108 Ken Heintzelman	15.00	7.50
❑ 109A Ed Fitzgerald SCR	15.00	7.50
❑ 109B Ed Fitzgerald PR	60.00	30.00
❑ 110 Early Wynn RC	150.00	75.00
❑ 111 Red Schoendienst	100.00	50.00
❑ 112 Sam Chapman	40.00	20.00
❑ 113 Ray LaManno	15.00	7.50
❑ 114 Allie Reynolds	60.00	30.00
❑ 115 Dutch Leonard	15.00	7.50
❑ 116 Joe Hatten	15.00	7.50
❑ 117 Walker Cooper	15.00	7.50
❑ 118 Sam Mele	15.00	7.50
❑ 119 Floyd Baker	15.00	7.50
❑ 120 Cliff Fannin	15.00	7.50
❑ 121 Mark Christman	15.00	7.50
❑ 122 George Vico	15.00	7.50
❑ 123 Johnny Blatnick	15.00	7.50
❑ 124A D.Murtaugh SCR RC	40.00	20.00
❑ 124B D.Murtaugh PR RC	60.00	30.00
❑ 125 Ken Keltner	25.00	12.50
❑ 126A Al Brazle SCR	15.00	7.50
❑ 126B Al Brazle PR	60.00	30.00
❑ 127A Hank Majeski SCR	15.00	7.50
❑ 127B Hank Majeski PR	60.00	30.00
❑ 128 Johnny VanderMeer	60.00	30.00
❑ 129 Bill Johnson	40.00	20.00
❑ 130 Harry Walker	15.00	7.50
❑ 131 Paul Lehner	15.00	7.50
❑ 132A Al Evans SCR	15.00	7.50
❑ 132B Al Evans PR	60.00	30.00
❑ 133 Aaron Robinson	15.00	7.50
❑ 134 Hank Borowy	15.00	7.50
❑ 135 Stan Rojek	15.00	7.50
❑ 136 Hank Edwards	15.00	7.50
❑ 137 Ted Wilks	15.00	7.50
❑ 138 Buddy Rosar	15.00	7.50
❑ 139 Hank Arft	15.00	7.50
❑ 140 Ray Scarborough	15.00	7.50
❑ 141 Tony Lupien	15.00	7.50
❑ 142 Eddie Waitkus RC	40.00	20.00
❑ 143A B.Dillinger RC SCR	25.00	12.50
❑ 143B Bob Dillinger RC PR	60.00	30.00
❑ 144 Mickey Haefner	15.00	7.50
❑ 145 Sylvester Donnelly	50.00	25.00
❑ 146 Mike McCormick	50.00	25.00
❑ 147 Bert Singleton	50.00	25.00
❑ 148 Bob Swift	50.00	25.00
❑ 149 Roy Partee	50.00	25.00
❑ 150 Allie Clark	50.00	25.00
❑ 151 Mickey Harris	50.00	25.00
❑ 152 Clarence Maddern	50.00	25.00
❑ 153 Phil Masi	50.00	25.00

❑ 154 Clint Hartung 60.00 30.00
❑ 155 Mickey Guerra 50.00 25.00
❑ 156 Al Zarilla 50.00 25.00
❑ 157 Walt Masterson 50.00 25.00
❑ 158 Harry Brecheen 60.00 30.00
❑ 159 Glen Moulder 50.00 25.00
❑ 160 Jim Blackburn 50.00 25.00
❑ 161 Jocko Thompson 50.00 25.00
❑ 162 Preacher Roe RC 125.00 60.00
❑ 163 Clyde McCullough 50.00 25.00
❑ 164 Vic Wertz RC 80.00 40.00
❑ 165 Snuffy Stirnweiss 80.00 40.00
❑ 166 Mike Tresh 50.00 25.00
❑ 167 Babe Martin 50.00 25.00
❑ 168 Doyle Lade 50.00 25.00
❑ 169 Jeff Heath 60.00 30.00
❑ 170 Bill Rigney 60.00 30.00
❑ 171 Dick Fowler 50.00 25.00
❑ 172 Eddie Pellagrini 50.00 25.00
❑ 173 Eddie Stewart 50.00 25.00
❑ 174 Terry Moore RC 80.00 40.00
❑ 175 Luke Appling 150.00 75.00
❑ 176 Ken Raffensberger 50.00 25.00
❑ 177 Stan Lopata 60.00 30.00
❑ 178 Tom Brown 60.00 30.00
❑ 179 Hugh Casey 80.00 40.00
❑ 180 Connie Berry 50.00 25.00
❑ 181 Gus Niarhos 50.00 25.00
❑ 182 Hal Peck 50.00 25.00
❑ 183 Lou Stringer 50.00 25.00
❑ 184 Bob Chipman 50.00 25.00
❑ 185 Pete Reiser 80.00 40.00
❑ 186 Buddy Kerr 50.00 25.00
❑ 187 Phil Marchildon 50.00 25.00
❑ 188 Karl Drews 50.00 25.00
❑ 189 Earl Wooten 50.00 25.00
❑ 190 Jim Hearn 50.00 25.00
❑ 191 Joe Haynes 50.00 25.00
❑ 192 Harry Gumbert 50.00 25.00
❑ 193 Ken Trinkle 50.00 25.00
❑ 194 Ralph Branca RC 100.00 50.00
❑ 195 Eddie Bockman 50.00 25.00
❑ 196 Fred Hutchinson 60.00 30.00
❑ 197 Johnny Lindell 60.00 30.00
❑ 198 Steve Gromek 50.00 25.00
❑ 199 Tex Hughson 50.00 25.00
❑ 200 Jess Dobernic 50.00 25.00
❑ 201 Sibby Sisti 50.00 25.00
❑ 202 Larry Jansen 60.00 30.00
❑ 203 Barney McCosky 50.00 25.00
❑ 204 Bob Savage 50.00 25.00
❑ 205 Dick Sisler 60.00 30.00
❑ 206 Bruce Edwards 50.00 25.00
❑ 207 Johnny Hopp 50.00 25.00
❑ 208 Dizzy Trout 60.00 30.00
❑ 209 Charlie Keller 80.00 40.00
❑ 210 Joe Gordon 80.00 40.00
❑ 211 Boo Ferriss 50.00 25.00
❑ 212 Ralph Hamner 50.00 25.00
❑ 213 Red Barrett 50.00 25.00
❑ 214 Richie Ashburn RC 600.00 300.00
❑ 215 Kirby Higbe 50.00 25.00
❑ 216 Schoolboy Rowe 60.00 30.00
❑ 217 Marino Pieretti 50.00 25.00
❑ 218 Dick Kryhoski 50.00 25.00
❑ 219 Virgil Fire Trucks 60.00 30.00
❑ 220 Johnny McCarthy 50.00 25.00
NY Giants Cap but listed as Sioux City MG
❑ 221 Bob Muncrief 50.00 25.00
❑ 222 Alex Kellner 50.00 25.00
❑ 223 Bobby Hofman 50.00 25.00
❑ 224 Satchell Paige RC 1500.00 750.00
❑ 225 Jerry Coleman RC 80.00 40.00
❑ 226 Duke Snider RC 1000.00 500.00
❑ 227 Fritz Ostermueller 50.00 25.00
❑ 228 Jackie Mayo 50.00 25.00
❑ 229 Ed Lopat RC 150.00 75.00
❑ 230 Augie Galan 60.00 30.00
❑ 231 Earl Johnson 50.00 25.00
❑ 232 George McQuinn 60.00 30.00
❑ 233 Larry Doby RC 300.00 150.00
❑ 234 Rip Sewell 50.00 25.00
❑ 235 Jim Russell 50.00 25.00
❑ 236 Fred Sanford 50.00 25.00
❑ 237 Monte Kennedy 50.00 25.00
❑ 238 Bob Lemon RC 200.00 100.00
❑ 239 Frank McCormick 50.00 25.00
❑ 240 Babe Young UER 100.00 25.00
(Photo actually Bobby Young)

1950 Bowman

	NM	Ex
COMPLETE SET (252)	8500.00	4200.00
COMMON CARD (1-72)	50.00	25.00
COMMON CARD (73-252)	15.00	7.50
WRAPPER (1-CENT)	250.00	125.00
WRAPPER (5-CENT)	250.00	125.00

❑ 1 Mel Parnell RC 150.00 30.00
❑ 2 Vern Stephens 60.00 30.00
❑ 3 Dom DiMaggio 80.00 40.00
❑ 4 Gus Zernial RC 60.00 30.00
❑ 5 Bob Kuzava 50.00 25.00
❑ 6 Bob Feller 300.00 150.00
❑ 7 Jim Hegan 60.00 30.00
❑ 8 George Kell 80.00 40.00
❑ 9 Vic Wertz 60.00 30.00
❑ 10 Tommy Henrich 80.00 40.00
❑ 11 Phil Rizzuto 300.00 150.00
❑ 12 Joe Page 80.00 40.00
❑ 13 Ferris Fain 60.00 30.00
❑ 14 Alex Kellner 50.00 25.00
❑ 15 Al Kozar 50.00 25.00
❑ 16 Roy Sievers RC 80.00 40.00
❑ 17 Sid Hudson 50.00 25.00
❑ 18 Eddie Robinson 50.00 25.00
❑ 19 Warren Spahn 300.00 150.00
❑ 20 Bob Elliott 60.00 30.00
❑ 21 Pee Wee Reese 300.00 150.00
❑ 22 Jackie Robinson 1200.00 600.00
❑ 23 Don Newcombe RC 150.00 75.00
❑ 24 Johnny Schmitz 50.00 25.00
❑ 25 Hank Sauer 60.00 30.00
❑ 26 Grady Hatton 50.00 25.00
❑ 27 Herman Wehmeier 50.00 25.00
❑ 28 Bobby Thomson 80.00 40.00
❑ 29 Eddie Stanky 60.00 30.00
❑ 30 Eddie Waitkus 60.00 30.00
❑ 31 Del Ennis 80.00 40.00
❑ 32 Robin Roberts 150.00 75.00
❑ 33 Ralph Kiner 100.00 50.00
❑ 34 Murry Dickson 50.00 25.00
❑ 35 Enos Slaughter 100.00 50.00
❑ 36 Eddie Kazak 60.00 30.00
❑ 37 Luke Appling 80.00 40.00
❑ 38 Bill Wight 50.00 25.00
❑ 39 Larry Doby 100.00 50.00
❑ 40 Bob Lemon 80.00 40.00
❑ 41 Hoot Evers 50.00 25.00
❑ 42 Art Houtteman 50.00 25.00
❑ 43 Bobby Doerr 80.00 40.00
❑ 44 Joe Dobson 50.00 25.00
❑ 45 Al Zarilla 50.00 25.00
❑ 46 Yogi Berra 400.00 200.00
❑ 47 Jerry Coleman 80.00 40.00
❑ 48 Lou Brissie 50.00 25.00
❑ 49 Elmer Valo 50.00 25.00
❑ 50 Dick Kokos 50.00 25.00
❑ 51 Ned Garver 60.00 30.00
❑ 52 Sam Mele 50.00 25.00
❑ 53 Clyde Vollmer 50.00 25.00
❑ 54 Gil Coan 50.00 25.00
❑ 55 Buddy Kerr 50.00 25.00
❑ 56 Del Crandall RC 60.00 30.00
❑ 57 Vern Bickford 50.00 25.00
❑ 58 Carl Furillo 80.00 40.00
❑ 59 Ralph Branca 80.00 40.00
❑ 60 Andy Pafko 60.00 30.00
❑ 61 Bob Rush 50.00 25.00
❑ 62 Ted Kluszewski 125.00 60.00
❑ 63 Ewell Blackwell 60.00 30.00
❑ 64 Alvin Dark 60.00 30.00
❑ 65 Dave Koslo 50.00 25.00
❑ 66 Larry Jansen 60.00 30.00
❑ 67 Willie Jones 60.00 30.00
❑ 68 Curt Simmons 60.00 30.00
❑ 69 Wally Westlake 50.00 25.00
❑ 70 Bob Chesnes 50.00 25.00
❑ 71 Red Schoendienst 80.00 40.00
❑ 72 Howie Pollet 50.00 25.00
❑ 73 Willard Marshall 15.00 7.50
❑ 74 Johnny Antonelli RC 60.00 30.00
❑ 75 Roy Campanella 300.00 150.00
❑ 76 Rex Barney 40.00 20.00
❑ 77 Duke Snider 300.00 150.00
❑ 78 Mickey Owen 25.00 12.50
❑ 79 Johnny VanderMeer 40.00 20.00
❑ 80 Howard Fox 15.00 7.50
❑ 81 Ron Northey 15.00 7.50
❑ 82 Whitey Lockman 25.00 12.50
❑ 83 Sheldon Jones 15.00 7.50
❑ 84 Richie Ashburn 125.00 60.00
❑ 85 Ken Heintzelman 15.00 7.50
❑ 86 Stan Rojek 15.00 7.50
❑ 87 Bill Werle 15.00 7.50
❑ 88 Marty Marion 40.00 20.00
❑ 89 George Munger 15.00 7.50
❑ 90 Harry Brecheen 40.00 20.00
❑ 91 Cass Michaels 15.00 7.50
❑ 92 Hank Majeski 15.00 7.50
❑ 93 Gene Bearden 40.00 20.00
❑ 94 Lou Boudreau 60.00 30.00
❑ 95 Aaron Robinson 15.00 7.50
❑ 96 Virgil Trucks 25.00 12.50
❑ 97 Maurice McDermott RC 15.00 7.50
❑ 98 Ted Williams 1000.00 500.00
❑ 99 Billy Goodman 25.00 12.50
❑ 100 Vic Raschi 60.00 30.00
❑ 101 Bobby Brown 60.00 30.00
❑ 102 Billy Johnson 25.00 12.50
❑ 103 Eddie Joost 15.00 7.50
❑ 104 Sam Chapman 15.00 7.50
❑ 105 Bob Dillinger 15.00 7.50
❑ 106 Cliff Fannin 15.00 7.50
❑ 107 Sam Dente 15.00 7.50
❑ 108 Ray Scarborough 15.00 7.50
❑ 109 Sid Gordon 15.00 7.50
❑ 110 Tommy Holmes 25.00 12.50
❑ 111 Walker Cooper 15.00 7.50
❑ 112 Gil Hodges 125.00 60.00
❑ 113 Gene Hermanski 15.00 7.50
❑ 114 Wayne Terwilliger RC 15.00 7.50
❑ 115 Roy Smalley 15.00 7.50
❑ 116 Virgil Stallcup 15.00 7.50
❑ 117 Bill Rigney 15.00 7.50
❑ 118 Clint Hartung 15.00 7.50
❑ 119 Dick Sisler 25.00 12.50
❑ 120 John Thompson 15.00 7.50
❑ 121 Andy Seminick 25.00 12.50
❑ 122 Johnny Hopp 25.00 12.50
❑ 123 Dino Restelli 15.00 7.50
❑ 124 Clyde McCullough 15.00 7.50
❑ 125 Del Rice 15.00 7.50
❑ 126 Al Brazle 15.00 7.50
❑ 127 Dave Philley 15.00 7.50
❑ 128 Phil Masi 15.00 7.50
❑ 129 Joe Gordon 25.00 12.50
❑ 130 Dale Mitchell 25.00 12.50
❑ 131 Steve Gromek 15.00 7.50
❑ 132 Mickey Vernon 25.00 12.50
❑ 133 Don Kolloway 15.00 7.50
❑ 134 Paul Trout 15.00 7.50
❑ 135 Pat Mullin 15.00 7.50
❑ 136 Buddy Rosar 15.00 7.50
❑ 137 Johnny Pesky 25.00 12.50
❑ 138 Allie Reynolds 60.00 30.00
❑ 139 Johnny Mize 80.00 40.00
❑ 140 Pete Suder 15.00 7.50
❑ 141 Joe Coleman 25.00 12.50
❑ 142 Sherman Lollar RC 40.00 20.00

Card	NM	Ex
❑ 143 Eddie Stewart	15.00	7.50
❑ 144 Al Evans	15.00	7.50
❑ 145 Jack Graham	15.00	7.50
❑ 146 Floyd Baker	15.00	7.50
❑ 147 Mike Garcia RC	40.00	20.00
❑ 148 Early Wynn	80.00	40.00
❑ 149 Bob Swift	15.00	7.50
❑ 150 George Vico	15.00	7.50
❑ 151 Fred Hutchinson	25.00	12.50
❑ 152 Ellis Kinder RC	15.00	7.50
❑ 153 Walt Masterson	15.00	7.50
❑ 154 Gus Niarhos	15.00	7.50
❑ 155 Frank Shea	25.00	12.50
❑ 156 Fred Sanford	25.00	12.50
❑ 157 Mike Guerra	15.00	7.50
❑ 158 Paul Lehner	15.00	7.50
❑ 159 Joe Tipton	15.00	7.50
❑ 160 Mickey Harris	15.00	7.50
❑ 161 Sherry Robertson	15.00	7.50
❑ 162 Eddie Yost	25.00	12.50
❑ 163 Earl Torgeson	15.00	7.50
❑ 164 Sibby Sisti	15.00	7.50
❑ 165 Bruce Edwards	15.00	7.50
❑ 166 Joe Hatton	15.00	7.50
❑ 167 Preacher Roe	60.00	30.00
❑ 168 Bob Scheffing	15.00	7.50
❑ 169 Hank Edwards	15.00	7.50
❑ 170 Dutch Leonard	15.00	7.50
❑ 171 Harry Gumbert	15.00	7.50
❑ 172 Peanuts Lowrey	15.00	7.50
❑ 173 Lloyd Merriman	15.00	7.50
❑ 174 Hank Thompson RC	40.00	20.00
❑ 175 Monte Kennedy	15.00	7.50
❑ 176 Sylvester Donnelly	15.00	7.50
❑ 177 Hank Borowy	15.00	7.50
❑ 178 Ed Fitzgerald	15.00	7.50
❑ 179 Chuck Diering	15.00	7.50
❑ 180 Harry Walker	25.00	12.50
❑ 181 Marino Pieretti	15.00	7.50
❑ 182 Sam Zoldak	15.00	7.50
❑ 183 Mickey Haefner	15.00	7.50
❑ 184 Randy Gumpert	15.00	7.50
❑ 185 Howie Judson	15.00	7.50
❑ 186 Ken Keltner	25.00	12.50
❑ 187 Lou Stringer	15.00	7.50
❑ 188 Earl Johnson	15.00	7.50
❑ 189 Owen Friend	15.00	7.50
❑ 190 Ken Wood	15.00	7.50
❑ 191 Dick Starr	15.00	7.50
❑ 192 Bob Chipman	15.00	7.50
❑ 193 Pete Reiser	40.00	20.00
❑ 194 Billy Cox	60.00	30.00
❑ 195 Phil Cavarretta	40.00	20.00
❑ 196 Doyle Lade	15.00	7.50
❑ 197 Johnny Wyrostek	15.00	7.50
❑ 198 Danny Litwhiler	15.00	7.50
❑ 199 Jack Kramer	15.00	7.50
❑ 200 Kirby Higbe	25.00	12.50
❑ 201 Pete Castiglione	15.00	7.50
❑ 202 Cliff Chambers	15.00	7.50
❑ 203 Danny Murtaugh	25.00	12.50
❑ 204 Granny Hamner RC	40.00	20.00
❑ 205 Mike Goliat	15.00	7.50
❑ 206 Stan Lopata	25.00	12.50
❑ 207 Max Lanier	15.00	7.50
❑ 208 Jim Hearn	15.00	7.50
❑ 209 Johnny Lindell	15.00	7.50
❑ 210 Ted Gray	15.00	7.50
❑ 211 Charlie Keller	40.00	20.00
❑ 212 Jerry Priddy	15.00	7.50
❑ 213 Carl Scheib	15.00	7.50
❑ 214 Dick Fowler	15.00	7.50
❑ 215 Ed Lopat	60.00	30.00
❑ 216 Bob Porterfield	25.00	12.50
❑ 217 Casey Stengel MG	125.00	60.00
❑ 218 Cliff Mapes RC	25.00	12.50
❑ 219 Hank Bauer RC	100.00	50.00
❑ 220 Leo Durocher MG	60.00	30.00
❑ 221 Don Mueller RC	40.00	20.00
❑ 222 Bobby Morgan	15.00	7.50
❑ 223 Jim Russell	15.00	7.50
❑ 224 Jack Banta	15.00	7.50
❑ 225 Eddie Sawyer MG	25.00	12.50
❑ 226 Jim Konstanty RC	60.00	30.00
❑ 227 Bob Miller	25.00	12.50
❑ 228 Bill Nicholson	25.00	12.50
❑ 229 Frank Frisch MG	60.00	30.00
❑ 230 Bill Serena	15.00	7.50
❑ 231 Preston Ward	15.00	7.50
❑ 232 Al Rosen RC	60.00	30.00
❑ 233 Allie Clark	15.00	7.50
❑ 234 Bobby Shantz RC	60.00	30.00
❑ 235 Harold Gilbert	15.00	7.50
❑ 236 Bob Cain	15.00	7.50
❑ 237 Bill Salkeld	15.00	7.50
❑ 238 Nippy Jones	15.00	7.50
❑ 239 Bill Howerton	15.00	7.50
❑ 240 Eddie Lake	15.00	7.50
❑ 241 Neil Berry	15.00	7.50
❑ 242 Dick Kryhoski	15.00	7.50
❑ 243 Johnny Groth	15.00	7.50
❑ 244 Dale Coogan	15.00	7.50
❑ 245 Al Papai	15.00	7.50
❑ 246 Walt Dropo RC	40.00	20.00
❑ 247 Irv Noren RC	25.00	12.50
❑ 248 Sam Jethroe RC	60.00	30.00
❑ 249 Snuffy Stirnweiss	25.00	12.50
❑ 250 Ray Coleman	15.00	7.50
❑ 251 Les Moss	15.00	7.50
❑ 252 Billy DeMars RC	60.00	16.50
❑ 252A Billy DeMars RC NC	.00	

1951 Bowman

	NM	Ex
COMPLETE SET (324)	20000.00	10000.00
COMMON CARD (1-252)	20.00	10.00
COMMON (253-324)	50.00	25.00
WRAPPER (1-CENT)	200.00	100.00
WRAPPER (5-CENT)	250.00	125.00

Card	NM	Ex
❑ 1 Whitey Ford RC	2500.00	600.00
❑ 2 Yogi Berra	400.00	200.00
❑ 3 Robin Roberts	100.00	50.00
❑ 4 Del Ennis	25.00	12.50
❑ 5 Dale Mitchell	25.00	12.50
❑ 6 Don Newcombe	60.00	30.00
❑ 7 Gil Hodges	125.00	60.00
❑ 8 Paul Lehner	20.00	10.00
❑ 9 Sam Chapman	20.00	10.00
❑ 10 Red Schoendienst	60.00	30.00
❑ 11 George Munger	20.00	10.00
❑ 12 Hank Majeski	20.00	10.00
❑ 13 Eddie Stanky	25.00	12.50
❑ 14 Alvin Dark	40.00	20.00
❑ 15 Johnny Pesky	25.00	12.50
❑ 16 Maurice McDermott	20.00	10.00
❑ 17 Pete Castiglione	20.00	10.00
❑ 18 Gil Coan	20.00	10.00
❑ 19 Sid Gordon	20.00	10.00
❑ 20 Del Crandall UER (Misspelled Crandell on card)	25.00	12.50
❑ 21 Snuffy Stirnweiss wearing St.L.Browns hat	25.00	12.50
❑ 22 Hank Sauer	25.00	12.50
❑ 23 Hoot Evers	20.00	10.00
❑ 24 Ewell Blackwell	40.00	20.00
❑ 25 Vic Raschi	60.00	30.00
❑ 26 Phil Rizzuto	150.00	75.00
❑ 27 Jim Konstanty	25.00	12.50
❑ 28 Eddie Waitkus	20.00	10.00
❑ 29 Allie Clark	20.00	10.00
❑ 30 Bob Feller	125.00	60.00
❑ 31 Roy Campanella	300.00	150.00
❑ 32 Duke Snider	250.00	125.00
❑ 33 Bob Hooper	20.00	10.00
❑ 34 Marty Marion	40.00	20.00
❑ 35 Al Zarilla	20.00	10.00
❑ 36 Joe Dobson	20.00	10.00
❑ 37 Whitey Lockman	40.00	20.00
❑ 38 Al Evans	20.00	10.00
❑ 39 Ray Scarborough	20.00	10.00
❑ 40 Gus Bell RC	60.00	30.00
❑ 41 Eddie Yost	25.00	12.50
❑ 42 Vern Bickford	20.00	10.00
❑ 43 Billy DeMars	20.00	10.00
❑ 44 Roy Smalley	20.00	10.00
❑ 45 Art Houtteman	20.00	10.00
❑ 46 George Kell 1941 UER	60.00	30.00
❑ 47 Grady Hatton	20.00	10.00
❑ 48 Ken Raffensberger	20.00	10.00
❑ 49 Jerry Coleman	25.00	12.50
❑ 50 Johnny Mize	80.00	40.00
❑ 51 Andy Seminick	20.00	10.00
❑ 52 Dick Sisler	40.00	20.00
❑ 53 Bob Lemon	60.00	30.00
❑ 54 Ray Boone RC	40.00	20.00
❑ 55 Gene Hermanski	20.00	10.00
❑ 56 Ralph Branca	60.00	30.00
❑ 57 Alex Kellner	20.00	10.00
❑ 58 Enos Slaughter	60.00	30.00
❑ 59 Randy Gumpert	20.00	10.00
❑ 60 Chico Carrasquel RC	60.00	30.00
❑ 61 Jim Hearn	25.00	12.50
❑ 62 Lou Boudreau	60.00	30.00
❑ 63 Bob Dillinger	20.00	10.00
❑ 64 Bill Werle	20.00	10.00
❑ 65 Mickey Vernon	40.00	20.00
❑ 66 Bob Elliott	25.00	12.50
❑ 67 Roy Sievers	25.00	12.50
❑ 68 Dick Kokos	20.00	10.00
❑ 69 Johnny Schmitz	20.00	10.00
❑ 70 Ron Northey	20.00	10.00
❑ 71 Jerry Priddy	20.00	10.00
❑ 72 Lloyd Merriman	20.00	10.00
❑ 73 Tommy Byrne	20.00	10.00
❑ 74 Billy Johnson	25.00	12.50
❑ 75 Russ Meyer RC	25.00	12.50
❑ 76 Stan Lopata	25.00	12.50
❑ 77 Mike Goliat	20.00	10.00
❑ 78 Early Wynn	60.00	30.00
❑ 79 Jim Hegan	25.00	12.50
❑ 80 Pee Wee Reese	200.00	100.00
❑ 81 Carl Furillo	60.00	30.00
❑ 82 Joe Tipton	20.00	10.00
❑ 83 Carl Scheib	20.00	10.00
❑ 84 Barney McCosky	20.00	10.00
❑ 85 Eddie Kazak	20.00	10.00
❑ 86 Harry Brecheen	25.00	12.50
❑ 87 Floyd Baker	20.00	10.00
❑ 88 Eddie Robinson	20.00	10.00
❑ 89 Hank Thompson	25.00	12.50
❑ 90 Dave Koslo	20.00	10.00
❑ 91 Clyde Vollmer	20.00	10.00
❑ 92 Vern Stephens	25.00	12.50
❑ 93 Danny O'Connell	20.00	10.00
❑ 94 Clyde McCullough	20.00	10.00
❑ 95 Sherry Robertson	20.00	10.00
❑ 96 Sandy Consuegra	20.00	10.00
❑ 97 Bob Kuzava	20.00	10.00
❑ 98 Willard Marshall	20.00	10.00
❑ 99 Earl Torgeson	20.00	10.00
❑ 100 Sherm Lollar	25.00	12.50
❑ 101 Owen Friend	20.00	10.00
❑ 102 Dutch Leonard	20.00	10.00
❑ 103 Andy Pafko	40.00	20.00
❑ 104 Virgil Trucks	25.00	12.50
❑ 105 Don Kolloway	20.00	10.00
❑ 106 Pat Mullin	20.00	10.00
❑ 107 Johnny Wyrostek	20.00	10.00
❑ 108 Virgil Stallcup	20.00	10.00
❑ 109 Allie Reynolds	60.00	30.00
❑ 110 Bobby Brown	40.00	20.00
❑ 111 Curt Simmons	25.00	12.50
❑ 112 Willie Jones	20.00	10.00
❑ 113 Bill Nicholson	20.00	10.00
❑ 114 Sam Zoldak Pictured in Indians uniform	20.00	10.00
❑ 115 Steve Gromek	20.00	10.00

❑ 116 Bruce Edwards 20.00 10.00
❑ 117 Eddie Miksis 20.00 10.00
❑ 118 Preacher Roe 60.00 30.00
❑ 119 Eddie Joost 20.00 10.00
❑ 120 Joe Coleman 25.00 12.50
❑ 121 Gerry Staley 20.00 10.00
❑ 122 Joe Garagiola RC 100.00 50.00
❑ 123 Howie Judson 20.00 10.00
❑ 124 Gus Niarhos 20.00 10.00
❑ 125 Bill Rigney 25.00 12.50
❑ 126 Bobby Thomson 60.00 30.00
❑ 127 Sal Maglie RC 60.00 30.00
❑ 128 Ellis Kinder 20.00 10.00
❑ 129 Matt Batts 20.00 10.00
❑ 130 Tom Saffell 20.00 10.00
❑ 131 Cliff Chambers 20.00 10.00
❑ 132 Cass Michaels 20.00 10.00
❑ 133 Sam Dente 20.00 10.00
❑ 134 Warren Spahn 150.00 75.00
❑ 135 Walker Cooper 20.00 10.00
❑ 136 Ray Coleman 20.00 10.00
❑ 137 Dick Starr 20.00 10.00
❑ 138 Phil Cavarretta 25.00 12.50
❑ 139 Doyle Lade 20.00 10.00
❑ 140 Eddie Lake 20.00 10.00
❑ 141 Fred Hutchinson 25.00 12.50
❑ 142 Aaron Robinson 20.00 10.00
❑ 143 Ted Kluszewski 80.00 40.00
❑ 144 Herman Wehmeier 20.00 10.00
❑ 145 Fred Sanford 25.00 12.50
❑ 146 Johnny Hopp 25.00 12.50
❑ 147 Ken Heintzelman 20.00 10.00
❑ 148 Granny Hamner 20.00 10.00
❑ 149 Bubba Church 20.00 10.00
❑ 150 Mike Garcia 25.00 12.50
❑ 151 Larry Doby 60.00 30.00
❑ 152 Cal Abrams 20.00 10.00
❑ 153 Rex Barney 25.00 12.50
❑ 154 Pete Suder 20.00 10.00
❑ 155 Lou Brissie 20.00 10.00
❑ 156 Del Rice 20.00 10.00
❑ 157 Al Brazle 20.00 10.00
❑ 158 Chuck Diering 20.00 10.00
❑ 159 Eddie Stewart 20.00 10.00
❑ 160 Phil Masi 20.00 10.00
❑ 161 Wes Westrum RC 20.00 10.00
❑ 162 Larry Jansen 25.00 12.50
❑ 163 Monte Kennedy 20.00 10.00
❑ 164 Bill Wight 20.00 10.00
❑ 165 Ted Williams UER 800.00 400.00
Wrong birthdate
❑ 166 Stan Rojek 20.00 10.00
Pictured in Pirates uniform
❑ 167 Murry Dickson 20.00 10.00
❑ 168 Sam Mele 20.00 10.00
❑ 169 Sid Hudson 20.00 10.00
❑ 170 Sibby Sisti 20.00 10.00
❑ 171 Buddy Kerr 20.00 10.00
❑ 172 Ned Garver 20.00 10.00
❑ 173 Hank Arft 20.00 10.00
❑ 174 Mickey Owen 25.00 12.50
❑ 175 Wayne Terwilliger 20.00 10.00
❑ 176 Vic Wertz 40.00 20.00
❑ 177 Charlie Keller 25.00 12.50
❑ 178 Ted Gray 20.00 10.00
❑ 179 Danny Litwhiler 20.00 10.00
❑ 180 Howie Fox 20.00 10.00
❑ 181 Casey Stengel MG 80.00 40.00
❑ 182 Tom Ferrick 20.00 10.00
❑ 183 Hank Bauer 60.00 30.00
❑ 184 Eddie Sawyer MG 40.00 20.00
❑ 185 Jimmy Bloodworth 20.00 10.00
❑ 186 Richie Ashburn 100.00 50.00
❑ 187 Al Rosen 40.00 20.00
❑ 188 Bobby Avila RC 25.00 12.50
❑ 189 Erv Palica 20.00 10.00
❑ 190 Joe Hatten 20.00 10.00
❑ 191 Billy Hitchcock 20.00 10.00
❑ 192 Hank Wyse 20.00 10.00
❑ 193 Ted Wilks 20.00 10.00
❑ 194 Peanuts Lowrey 20.00 10.00
❑ 195 Paul Richards MG 25.00 12.50
(Caricature)
❑ 196 Billy Pierce RC 60.00 30.00
❑ 197 Bob Cain 20.00 10.00
❑ 198 Monte Irvin RC 125.00 60.00
❑ 199 Sheldon Jones 20.00 10.00
❑ 200 Jack Kramer 20.00 10.00
Pictured in NY Giants uniform
❑ 201 Steve O'Neill MG 20.00 10.00
❑ 202 Mike Guerra 20.00 10.00
❑ 203 Vernon Law RC 60.00 30.00
❑ 204 Vic Lombardi 20.00 10.00
❑ 205 Mickey Grasso 20.00 10.00
❑ 206 Conrado Marrero 20.00 10.00
❑ 207 Billy Southworth MG 20.00 10.00
❑ 208 Blix Donnelly 20.00 10.00
❑ 209 Ken Wood 20.00 10.00
❑ 210 Les Moss 20.00 10.00
Pictured in St.L.Browns uniform
❑ 211 Hal Jeffcoat 20.00 10.00
❑ 212 Bob Rush 20.00 10.00
❑ 213 Neil Berry 20.00 10.00
❑ 214 Bob Swift 20.00 10.00
❑ 215 Ken Peterson 20.00 10.00
❑ 216 Connie Ryan 20.00 10.00
❑ 217 Joe Page 25.00 12.50
❑ 218 Ed Lopat 60.00 30.00
❑ 219 Gene Woodling RC 60.00 30.00
❑ 220 Bob Miller 20.00 10.00
❑ 221 Dick Whitman 20.00 10.00
❑ 222 Thurman Tucker 20.00 10.00
❑ 223 Johnny VanderMeer 40.00 20.00
❑ 224 Billy Cox 25.00 12.50
❑ 225 Dan Bankhead 40.00 20.00
❑ 226 Jimmy Dykes MG 20.00 10.00
❑ 227 Bobby Shantz UER 25.00 12.50
Sic, Schantz
❑ 228 Cloyd Boyer 25.00 12.50
❑ 229 Bill Howerton 20.00 10.00
Pictured in St.L.Cardinals uniform
❑ 230 Max Lanier 20.00 10.00
❑ 231 Luis Aloma 20.00 10.00
❑ 232 Nelson Fox RC 250.00 125.00
❑ 233 Leo Durocher MG 60.00 30.00
❑ 234 Clint Hartung 25.00 12.50
❑ 235 Jack Lohrke 20.00 10.00
❑ 236 Buddy Rosar 20.00 10.00
❑ 237 Billy Goodman 25.00 12.50
❑ 238 Pete Reiser 40.00 20.00
❑ 239 Bill MacDonald 20.00 10.00
❑ 240 Joe Haynes 20.00 10.00
❑ 241 Irv Noren 25.00 12.50
❑ 242 Sam Jethroe 25.00 12.50
❑ 243 Johnny Antonelli 25.00 12.50
❑ 244 Cliff Fannin 20.00 10.00
❑ 245 John Berardino RC 60.00 30.00
❑ 246 Bill Serena 20.00 10.00
❑ 247 Bob Ramazzotti 20.00 10.00
❑ 248 Johnny Klippstein 20.00 10.00
❑ 249 Johnny Groth 20.00 10.00
❑ 250 Hank Borowy 20.00 10.00
❑ 251 Willard Ramsdell 20.00 10.00
❑ 252 Dixie Howell 20.00 10.00
❑ 253 Mickey Mantle RC 8000.00 4000.00
❑ 254 Jackie Jensen RC 100.00 50.00
❑ 255 Milo Candini 50.00 25.00
❑ 256 Ken Silvestri 50.00 25.00
❑ 257 Birdie Tebbetts RC 60.00 30.00
❑ 258 Luke Easter RC 60.00 30.00
❑ 259 Chuck Dressen MG 60.00 30.00
❑ 260 Carl Erskine RC 100.00 50.00
❑ 261 Wally Moses 60.00 30.00
❑ 262 Gus Zernial 60.00 30.00
❑ 263 Howie Pollet 60.00 30.00
Pictured in Cardinals uniform
❑ 264 Don Richmond 50.00 25.00
❑ 265 Steve Bilko 50.00 25.00
❑ 266 Harry Dorish 50.00 25.00
❑ 267 Ken Holcombe 50.00 25.00
❑ 268 Don Mueller 60.00 30.00
❑ 269 Ray Noble 50.00 25.00
❑ 270 Willard Nixon 50.00 25.00
❑ 271 Tommy Wright 50.00 25.00
❑ 272 Billy Meyer MG 50.00 25.00
❑ 273 Danny Murtaugh 60.00 30.00
❑ 274 George Metkovich 50.00 25.00
❑ 275 Bucky Harris MG 80.00 40.00
❑ 276 Frank Quinn 50.00 25.00
❑ 277 Roy Hartsfield 50.00 25.00
❑ 278 Norman Roy 50.00 25.00
❑ 279 Jim Delsing 50.00 25.00
❑ 280 Frank Overmire 50.00 25.00
Pictured in Browns uniform
❑ 281 Al Widmar 50.00 25.00
❑ 282 Frank Frisch MG 100.00 50.00
❑ 283 Walt Dubiel 50.00 25.00
❑ 284 Gene Bearden 60.00 30.00
❑ 285 Johnny Lipon 50.00 25.00
❑ 286 Bob Usher 50.00 25.00
❑ 287 Jim Blackburn 50.00 25.00
❑ 288 Bobby Adams 50.00 25.00
❑ 289 Cliff Mapes 60.00 30.00
❑ 290 Bill Dickey CO 150.00 75.00
❑ 291 Tommy Henrich CO 80.00 40.00
❑ 292 Eddie Pellagrini 50.00 25.00
❑ 293 Ken Johnson 50.00 25.00
❑ 294 Jocko Thompson 50.00 25.00
❑ 295 Al Lopez MG 125.00 60.00
❑ 296 Bob Kennedy 60.00 30.00
❑ 297 Dave Philley 50.00 25.00
❑ 298 Joe Astroth 50.00 25.00
❑ 299 Clyde King 50.00 25.00
❑ 300 Hal Rice 50.00 25.00
❑ 301 Tommy Glaviano 50.00 25.00
❑ 302 Jim Busby 50.00 25.00
❑ 303 Marv Rotblatt 50.00 25.00
❑ 304 Al Gettell 50.00 25.00
❑ 305 Willie Mays RC 2500.00 1250.00
❑ 306 Jim Piersall RC 125.00 60.00
❑ 307 Walt Masterson 50.00 25.00
❑ 308 Ted Beard 50.00 25.00
❑ 309 Mel Queen 50.00 25.00
❑ 310 Erv Dusak 50.00 25.00
❑ 311 Mickey Harris 50.00 25.00
❑ 312 Gene Mauch RC 60.00 30.00
❑ 313 Ray Mueller 50.00 25.00
❑ 314 Johnny Sain 80.00 40.00
❑ 315 Zack Taylor MG 50.00 25.00
❑ 316 Duane Pillette 50.00 25.00
❑ 317 Smoky Burgess RC 80.00 40.00
❑ 318 Warren Hacker 50.00 25.00
❑ 319 Red Rolfe MG 60.00 30.00
❑ 320 Hal White 50.00 25.00
❑ 321 Earl Johnson 50.00 25.00
❑ 322 Luke Sewell MG 60.00 30.00
❑ 323 Joe Adcock RC 80.00 40.00
❑ 324 Johnny Pramesa RC 125.00 38.00

1952 Bowman

	NM	Ex
COMPLETE SET (252)	8500.00	4200.00
COMMON CARD (1-216)	15.00	6.75
COMMON (217-252)	60.00	30.00
WRAPPER (1-CENT)	200.00	100.00
WRAPPER (5-CENT)	100.00	50.00

❑ 1 Yogi Berra 600.00 190.00
❑ 2 Bobby Thomson 40.00 20.00
❑ 3 Fred Hutchinson 25.00 12.50
❑ 4 Robin Roberts 80.00 40.00
❑ 5 Minnie Minoso RC 125.00 60.00
❑ 6 Virgil Stallcup 15.00 7.50
❑ 7 Mike Garcia 25.00 12.50
❑ 8 Pee Wee Reese 150.00 75.00
❑ 9 Vern Stephens 25.00 12.50
❑ 10 Bob Hooper 15.00 7.50
❑ 11 Ralph Kiner 60.00 30.00
❑ 12 Max Surkont 15.00 7.50

❑ 13 Cliff Mapes 15.00 7.50
❑ 14 Cliff Chambers 15.00 7.50
❑ 15 Sam Mele 15.00 7.50
❑ 16 Turk Lown 15.00 7.50
❑ 17 Ed Lopat 40.00 20.00
❑ 18 Don Mueller 25.00 12.50
❑ 19 Bob Cain 15.00 7.50
❑ 20 Willie Jones 15.00 7.50
❑ 21 Nellie Fox 100.00 50.00
❑ 22 Willard Ramsdell 15.00 7.50
❑ 23 Bob Lemon 60.00 30.00
❑ 24 Carl Furillo 40.00 20.00
❑ 25 Mickey McDermott 15.00 7.50
❑ 26 Eddie Joost 15.00 7.50
❑ 27 Joe Garagiola 40.00 20.00
❑ 28 Roy Hartsfield 15.00 7.50
❑ 29 Ned Garver 15.00 7.50
❑ 30 Red Schoendienst 60.00 30.00
❑ 31 Eddie Yost 25.00 12.50
❑ 32 Eddie Miksis 15.00 7.50
❑ 33 Gil McDougald RC 80.00 40.00
❑ 34 Alvin Dark 25.00 12.50
❑ 35 Granny Hamner 15.00 7.50
❑ 36 Cass Michaels 15.00 7.50
❑ 37 Vic Raschi 25.00 12.50
❑ 38 Whitey Lockman 25.00 12.50
❑ 39 Vic Wertz 25.00 12.50
❑ 40 Bubba Church 15.00 7.50
❑ 41 Chico Carrasquel 25.00 12.50
❑ 42 Johnny Wyrostek 15.00 7.50
❑ 43 Bob Feller 150.00 75.00
❑ 44 Roy Campanella 250.00 125.00
❑ 45 Johnny Pesky 25.00 12.50
❑ 46 Carl Scheib 15.00 7.50
❑ 47 Pete Castiglione 15.00 7.50
❑ 48 Vern Bickford 15.00 7.50
❑ 49 Jim Hearn 15.00 7.50
❑ 50 Gerry Staley 15.00 7.50
❑ 51 Gil Coan 15.00 7.50
❑ 52 Phil Rizzuto 150.00 75.00
❑ 53 Richie Ashburn 125.00 60.00
❑ 54 Billy Pierce 25.00 12.50
❑ 55 Ken Raffensberger 15.00 7.50
❑ 56 Clyde King 25.00 12.50
❑ 57 Clyde Vollmer 15.00 7.50
❑ 58 Hank Majeski 15.00 7.50
❑ 59 Murry Dickson 15.00 7.50
❑ 60 Sid Gordon 15.00 7.50
❑ 61 Tommy Byrne 15.00 7.50
❑ 62 Joe Presko 15.00 7.50
❑ 63 Irv Noren 15.00 7.50
❑ 64 Roy Smalley 15.00 7.50
❑ 65 Hank Bauer 40.00 20.00
❑ 66 Sal Maglie 25.00 12.50
❑ 67 Johnny Groth 15.00 7.50
❑ 68 Jim Busby 15.00 7.50
❑ 69 Joe Adcock 25.00 12.50
❑ 70 Carl Erskine 40.00 20.00
❑ 71 Vernon Law 25.00 12.50
❑ 72 Earl Torgeson 15.00 7.50
❑ 73 Jerry Coleman 25.00 12.50
❑ 74 Wes Westrum 25.00 12.50
❑ 75 George Kell 60.00 30.00
❑ 76 Del Ennis 25.00 12.50
❑ 77 Eddie Robinson 15.00 7.50
❑ 78 Lloyd Merriman 15.00 7.50
❑ 79 Lou Brissie 15.00 7.50
❑ 80 Gil Hodges 100.00 50.00
❑ 81 Billy Goodman 25.00 12.50
❑ 82 Gus Zernial 25.00 12.50
❑ 83 Howie Pollet 15.00 7.50
❑ 84 Sam Jethroe 25.00 12.50
❑ 85 Marty Marion CO 25.00 12.50
❑ 86 Cal Abrams 15.00 7.50
❑ 87 Mickey Vernon 25.00 12.50
❑ 88 Bruce Edwards 15.00 7.50
❑ 89 Billy Hitchcock 15.00 7.50
❑ 90 Larry Jansen 25.00 12.50
❑ 91 Don Kolloway 15.00 7.50
❑ 92 Eddie Waitkus 25.00 12.50
❑ 93 Paul Richards MG 25.00 12.50
❑ 94 Luke Sewell MG 25.00 12.50
❑ 95 Luke Easter 25.00 12.50
❑ 96 Ralph Branca 25.00 12.50
❑ 97 Willard Marshall 15.00 7.50
❑ 98 Jimmy Dykes MG 25.00 12.50
❑ 99 Clyde McCullough 15.00 7.50
❑ 100 Sibby Sisti 15.00 7.50
❑ 101 Mickey Mantle 2500.00 1250.00
❑ 102 Peanuts Lowrey 15.00 7.50
❑ 103 Joe Haynes 15.00 7.50
❑ 104 Hal Jeffcoat 15.00 7.50
❑ 105 Bobby Brown 25.00 12.50
❑ 106 Randy Gumpert 15.00 7.50
❑ 107 Del Rice 15.00 7.50
❑ 108 George Metkovich 15.00 7.50
❑ 109 Tom Morgan 15.00 7.50
❑ 110 Max Lanier 15.00 7.50
❑ 111 Hoot Evers 15.00 7.50
❑ 112 Smoky Burgess 25.00 12.50
❑ 113 Al Zarilla 15.00 7.50
❑ 114 Frank Hiller 15.00 7.50
❑ 115 Larry Doby 60.00 30.00
❑ 116 Duke Snider 200.00 100.00
❑ 117 Bill Wight 15.00 7.50
❑ 118 Ray Murray 15.00 7.50
❑ 119 Bill Howerton 15.00 7.50
❑ 120 Chet Nichols 15.00 7.50
❑ 121 Al Corwin 15.00 7.50
❑ 122 Billy Johnson 15.00 7.50
❑ 123 Sid Hudson 15.00 7.50
❑ 124 Birdie Tebbetts 15.00 7.50
❑ 125 Howie Fox 15.00 7.50
❑ 126 Phil Cavarretta 25.00 12.50
❑ 127 Dick Sisler 15.00 7.50
❑ 128 Don Newcombe 60.00 30.00
❑ 129 Gus Niarhos 15.00 7.50
❑ 130 Allie Clark 15.00 7.50
❑ 131 Bob Swift 15.00 7.50
❑ 132 Dave Cole 15.00 7.50
❑ 133 Dick Kryhoski 15.00 7.50
❑ 134 Al Brazle 15.00 7.50
❑ 135 Mickey Harris 15.00 7.50
❑ 136 Gene Hermanski 15.00 7.50
❑ 137 Stan Rojek 15.00 7.50
❑ 138 Ted Wilks 15.00 7.50
❑ 139 Jerry Priddy 15.00 7.50
❑ 140 Ray Scarborough 15.00 7.50
❑ 141 Hank Edwards 15.00 7.50
❑ 142 Early Wynn 60.00 30.00
❑ 143 Sandy Consuegra 15.00 7.50
❑ 144 Joe Hatton 15.00 7.50
❑ 145 Johnny Mize 60.00 30.00
❑ 146 Leo Durocher MG 60.00 30.00
❑ 147 Marlin Stuart 15.00 7.50
❑ 148 Ken Heintzelman 15.00 7.50
❑ 149 Howie Judson 15.00 7.50
❑ 150 Herman Wehmeier 15.00 7.50
❑ 151 Al Rosen 25.00 12.50
❑ 152 Billy Cox 15.00 7.50
❑ 153 Fred Hatfield 15.00 7.50
❑ 154 Ferris Fain 25.00 12.50
❑ 155 Billy Meyer MG 15.00 7.50
❑ 156 Warren Spahn 125.00 60.00
❑ 157 Jim Delsing 15.00 7.50
❑ 158 Bucky Harris MG 40.00 20.00
❑ 159 Dutch Leonard 15.00 7.50
❑ 160 Eddie Stanky 25.00 12.50
❑ 161 Jackie Jensen 40.00 20.00
❑ 162 Monte Irvin 60.00 30.00
❑ 163 Johnny Lipon 15.00 7.50
❑ 164 Connie Ryan 15.00 7.50
❑ 165 Saul Rogovin 15.00 7.50
❑ 166 Bobby Adams 15.00 7.50
❑ 167 Bobby Avila 25.00 12.50
❑ 168 Preacher Roe 25.00 12.50
❑ 169 Walt Dropo 25.00 12.50
❑ 170 Joe Astroth 15.00 7.50
❑ 171 Mel Queen 15.00 7.50
❑ 172 Ebba St.Claire 15.00 7.50
❑ 173 Gene Bearden 15.00 7.50
❑ 174 Mickey Grasso 15.00 7.50
❑ 175 Randy Jackson 15.00 7.50
❑ 176 Harry Brecheen 25.00 12.50
❑ 177 Gene Woodling 25.00 12.50
❑ 178 Dave Williams RC 25.00 12.50
❑ 179 Pete Suder 15.00 7.50
❑ 180 Ed Fitzgerald 15.00 7.50
❑ 181 Joe Collins RC 25.00 12.50
❑ 182 Dave Koslo 15.00 7.50
❑ 183 Pat Mullin 15.00 7.50
❑ 184 Curt Simmons 25.00 12.50
❑ 185 Eddie Stewart 15.00 7.50
❑ 186 Frank Smith 15.00 7.50
❑ 187 Jim Hegan 25.00 12.50
❑ 188 Chuck Dressen MG 25.00 12.50
❑ 189 Jimmy Piersall 25.00 12.50
❑ 190 Dick Fowler 15.00 7.50
❑ 191 Bob Friend RC 40.00 20.00
❑ 192 John Cusick 15.00 7.50
❑ 193 Bobby Young 15.00 7.50
❑ 194 Bob Porterfield 15.00 7.50
❑ 195 Frank Baumholtz 15.00 7.50
❑ 196 Stan Musial 500.00 250.00
❑ 197 Charlie Silvera RC 15.00 7.50
❑ 198 Chuck Diering 15.00 7.50
❑ 199 Ted Gray 15.00 7.50
❑ 200 Ken Silvestri 15.00 7.50
❑ 201 Ray Coleman 15.00 7.50
❑ 202 Harry Perkowski 15.00 7.50
❑ 203 Steve Gromek 15.00 7.50
❑ 204 Andy Pafko 25.00 12.50
❑ 205 Walt Masterson 15.00 7.50
❑ 206 Elmer Valo 15.00 7.50
❑ 207 George Strickland 15.00 7.50
❑ 208 Walker Cooper 15.00 7.50
❑ 209 Dick Littlefield 15.00 7.50
❑ 210 Archie Wilson 15.00 7.50
❑ 211 Paul Minner 15.00 7.50
❑ 212 Solly Hemus RC 15.00 7.50
❑ 213 Monte Kennedy 15.00 7.50
❑ 214 Ray Boone 15.00 7.50
❑ 215 Sheldon Jones 15.00 7.50
❑ 216 Matt Batts 15.00 7.50
❑ 217 Casey Stengel MG 150.00 75.00
❑ 218 Willie Mays 1500.00 750.00
❑ 219 Neil Berry 60.00 30.00
❑ 220 Russ Meyer 60.00 30.00
❑ 221 Lou Kretlow 60.00 30.00
❑ 222 Dixie Howell 60.00 30.00
❑ 223 Harry Simpson 60.00 30.00
❑ 224 Johnny Schmitz 60.00 30.00
❑ 225 Del Wilber 60.00 30.00
❑ 226 Alex Kellner 60.00 30.00
❑ 227 Clyde Sukeforth CO 60.00 30.00
❑ 228 Bob Chipman 60.00 30.00
❑ 229 Hank Arft 60.00 30.00
❑ 230 Frank Shea 60.00 30.00
❑ 231 Dee Fondy 60.00 30.00
❑ 232 Enos Slaughter 100.00 50.00
❑ 233 Bob Kuzava 60.00 30.00
❑ 234 Fred Fitzsimmons CO 60.00 30.00
❑ 235 Steve Souchock 60.00 30.00
❑ 236 Tommy Brown 60.00 30.00
❑ 237 Sherm Lollar 60.00 30.00
❑ 238 Roy McMillan RC 60.00 30.00
❑ 239 Dale Mitchell 60.00 30.00
❑ 240 Billy Loes RC 60.00 30.00
❑ 241 Mel Parnell 60.00 30.00
❑ 242 Everett Kell 60.00 30.00
❑ 243 George Munger 60.00 30.00
❑ 244 Lew Burdette RC 80.00 40.00
❑ 245 George Schmees 60.00 30.00
❑ 246 Jerry Snyder 60.00 30.00
❑ 247 Johnny Pramesa 60.00 30.00
❑ 248 Bill Werle 60.00 30.00
Full name in signature
❑ 248A Bill Werle 60.00 30.00
Signature on front has no W
❑ 249 Hank Thompson 60.00 30.00
❑ 250 Ike Delock 60.00 30.00
❑ 251 Jack Lohrke 60.00 30.00
❑ 252 Frank Crosetti CO 125.00 31.00

1953 Bowman Color

	NM	Ex
COMPLETE SET (160)	15000.00	7500.00
COMMON CARD (1-112)	40.00	20.00
COMMON (113-128)	80.00	40.00
COMMON (129-160)	75.00	38.00
WRAPPER (1-CENT)	400.00	200.00
WRAPPER (5-CENT)	300.00	150.00

❑ 1 Dave Williams 175.00 35.00
❑ 2 Vic Wertz 50.00 25.00
❑ 3 Sam Jethroe 50.00 25.00
❑ 4 Art Houtteman 40.00 20.00

❑ 5 Sid Gordon 40.00 20.00
❑ 6 Joe Ginsberg 40.00 20.00
❑ 7 Harry Chiti 40.00 20.00
❑ 8 Al Rosen 50.00 25.00
❑ 9 Phil Rizzuto 225.00 110.00
❑ 10 Richie Ashburn 150.00 75.00
❑ 11 Bobby Shantz 50.00 25.00
❑ 12 Carl Erskine 60.00 30.00
❑ 13 Gus Zernial 50.00 25.00
❑ 14 Billy Loes 50.00 25.00
❑ 15 Jim Busby 40.00 20.00
❑ 16 Bob Friend 50.00 25.00
❑ 17 Gerry Staley 40.00 20.00
❑ 18 Nellie Fox 150.00 75.00
❑ 19 Alvin Dark 50.00 25.00
❑ 20 Don Lenhardt 40.00 20.00
❑ 21 Joe Garagiola 60.00 30.00
❑ 22 Bob Porterfield 40.00 20.00
❑ 23 Herman Wehmeier 40.00 20.00
❑ 24 Jackie Jensen 60.00 30.00
❑ 25 Hoot Evers 40.00 20.00
❑ 26 Roy McMillan 50.00 25.00
❑ 27 Vic Raschi 60.00 30.00
❑ 28 Smoky Burgess 50.00 25.00
❑ 29 Bobby Avila 50.00 25.00
❑ 30 Phil Cavarretta 50.00 25.00
❑ 31 Jimmy Dykes MG 50.00 25.00
❑ 32 Stan Musial 600.00 300.00
❑ 33 Pee Wee Reese 1000.00 500.00
❑ 34 Gil Coan 40.00 20.00
❑ 35 Maurice McDermott 40.00 20.00
❑ 36 Minnie Minoso 80.00 40.00
❑ 37 Jim Wilson 40.00 20.00
❑ 38 Harry Byrd 40.00 20.00
❑ 39 Paul Richards MG 50.00 25.00
❑ 40 Larry Doby 100.00 50.00
❑ 41 Sammy White 40.00 20.00
❑ 42 Tommy Brown 40.00 20.00
❑ 43 Mike Garcia 50.00 25.00
❑ 44 Yogi Berra 800.00 400.00
Hank Bauer
Mickey Mantle
❑ 45 Walt Dropo 50.00 25.00
❑ 46 Roy Campanella 350.00 180.00
❑ 47 Ned Garver 40.00 20.00
❑ 48 Hank Sauer 50.00 25.00
❑ 49 Eddie Stanky MG 50.00 25.00
❑ 50 Lou Kretlow 40.00 20.00
❑ 51 Monte Irvin 80.00 40.00
❑ 52 Marty Marion MG 50.00 25.00
❑ 53 Del Rice 40.00 20.00
❑ 54 Chico Carrasquel 40.00 20.00
❑ 55 Leo Durocher MG 80.00 40.00
❑ 56 Bob Cain 40.00 20.00
❑ 57 Lou Boudreau MG 80.00 40.00
❑ 58 Willard Marshall 40.00 20.00
❑ 59 Mickey Mantle 2000.00 1000.00
❑ 60 Granny Hamner 40.00 20.00
❑ 61 George Kell 80.00 40.00
❑ 62 Ted Kluszewski 100.00 50.00
❑ 63 Gil McDougald 80.00 40.00
❑ 64 Curt Simmons 50.00 25.00
❑ 65 Robin Roberts 125.00 60.00
❑ 66 Mel Parnell 50.00 25.00
❑ 67 Mel Clark 40.00 20.00
❑ 68 Allie Reynolds 60.00 30.00
❑ 69 Charlie Grimm MG 50.00 25.00
❑ 70 Clint Courtney 40.00 20.00
❑ 71 Paul Minner 40.00 20.00
❑ 72 Ted Gray 40.00 20.00
❑ 73 Billy Pierce 50.00 25.00
❑ 74 Don Mueller 50.00 25.00
❑ 75 Saul Rogovin 40.00 20.00
❑ 76 Jim Hearn 40.00 20.00
❑ 77 Mickey Grasso 40.00 20.00
❑ 78 Carl Furillo 60.00 30.00
❑ 79 Ray Boone 50.00 25.00
❑ 80 Ralph Kiner 100.00 50.00
❑ 81 Enos Slaughter 100.00 50.00
❑ 82 Joe Astroth 40.00 20.00
❑ 83 Jack Daniels 40.00 20.00
❑ 84 Hank Bauer 60.00 30.00
❑ 85 Solly Hemus 40.00 20.00
❑ 86 Harry Simpson 40.00 20.00
❑ 87 Harry Perkowski 40.00 20.00
❑ 88 Joe Dobson 40.00 20.00
❑ 89 Sandy Consuegra 40.00 20.00
❑ 90 Joe Nuxhall 50.00 25.00
❑ 91 Steve Souchock 40.00 20.00
❑ 92 Gil Hodges 300.00 150.00
❑ 93 Phil Rizzuto and 300.00 150.00
Billy Martin
❑ 94 Bob Addis 40.00 20.00
❑ 95 Wally Moses CO 50.00 25.00
❑ 96 Sal Maglie 50.00 25.00
❑ 97 Eddie Mathews 350.00 180.00
❑ 98 Hector Rodriguez 40.00 20.00
❑ 99 Warren Spahn 350.00 180.00
❑ 100 Bill Wight 40.00 20.00
❑ 101 Red Schoendienst 80.00 40.00
❑ 102 Jim Hegan 50.00 25.00
❑ 103 Del Ennis 50.00 25.00
❑ 104 Luke Easter 50.00 25.00
❑ 105 Eddie Joost 40.00 20.00
❑ 106 Ken Raffensberger 40.00 20.00
❑ 107 Alex Kellner 40.00 20.00
❑ 108 Bobby Adams 40.00 20.00
❑ 109 Ken Wood 40.00 20.00
❑ 110 Bob Rush 40.00 20.00
❑ 111 Jim Dyck 40.00 20.00
❑ 112 Toby Atwell 40.00 20.00
❑ 113 Karl Drews 80.00 40.00
❑ 114 Bob Feller 500.00 250.00
❑ 115 Cloyd Boyer 80.00 40.00
❑ 116 Eddie Yost 100.00 50.00
❑ 117 Duke Snider 600.00 300.00
❑ 118 Billy Martin 400.00 200.00
❑ 119 Dale Mitchell 100.00 50.00
❑ 120 Marlin Stuart 80.00 40.00
❑ 121 Yogi Berra 800.00 400.00
❑ 122 Bill Serena 80.00 40.00
❑ 123 Johnny Lipon 80.00 40.00
❑ 124 Charlie Dressen MG 100.00 50.00
❑ 125 Fred Hatfield 80.00 40.00
❑ 126 Al Corwin 80.00 40.00
❑ 127 Dick Kryhoski 80.00 40.00
❑ 128 Whitey Lockman 100.00 50.00
❑ 129 Russ Meyer 75.00 38.00
❑ 130 Cass Michaels 75.00 38.00
❑ 131 Connie Ryan 75.00 38.00
❑ 132 Fred Hutchinson 90.00 45.00
❑ 133 Willie Jones 75.00 38.00
❑ 134 Johnny Pesky 90.00 45.00
❑ 135 Bobby Morgan 75.00 38.00
❑ 136 Jim Brideweser 75.00 38.00
❑ 137 Sam Dente 75.00 38.00
❑ 138 Bubba Church 75.00 38.00
❑ 139 Pete Runnels 90.00 45.00
❑ 140 Al Brazle 75.00 38.00
❑ 141 Frank Shea 75.00 38.00
❑ 142 Larry Miggins 75.00 38.00
❑ 143 Al Lopez MG 110.00 55.00
❑ 144 Warren Hacker 75.00 38.00
❑ 145 George Shuba 90.00 45.00
❑ 146 Early Wynn 200.00 100.00
❑ 147 Clem Koshorek 75.00 38.00
❑ 148 Billy Goodman 90.00 45.00
❑ 149 Al Corwin 75.00 38.00
❑ 150 Carl Scheib 75.00 38.00
❑ 151 Joe Adcock 110.00 55.00
❑ 152 Clyde Vollmer 75.00 38.00
❑ 153 Whitey Ford 800.00 400.00
❑ 154 Turk Lown 75.00 38.00
❑ 155 Allie Clark 75.00 38.00
❑ 156 Max Surkont 75.00 38.00
❑ 157 Sherm Lollar 90.00 45.00
❑ 158 Howard Fox 75.00 38.00
❑ 159 Mickey Vernon UER 90.00 45.00
(Photo actually
Floyd Baker)
❑ 160 Cal Abrams 500.00 170.00

1954 Bowman

	NM	Ex
COMPLETE SET (224)	4000.00	2000.00
WRAP.(1-CENT, DATED)	150.00	75.00
WRAP.(1-CENT, UNDAT)	200.00	100.00
WRAP.(5-CENT, DATED)	150.00	75.00
WRAP.(5-CENT, UNDAT)	60.00	30.00

❑ 1 Phil Rizzuto 175.00 52.50
❑ 2 Jackie Jensen 30.00 15.00
❑ 3 Marion Fricano 12.00 6.00
❑ 4 Bob Hooper 12.00 6.00
❑ 5 Billy Hunter 12.00 6.00
❑ 6 Nellie Fox 80.00 40.00
❑ 7 Walt Dropo 20.00 10.00
❑ 8 Jim Busby 12.00 6.00
❑ 9 Dave Williams 12.00 6.00
❑ 10 Carl Erskine 20.00 10.00
❑ 11 Sid Gordon 12.00 6.00
❑ 12 Roy McMillan 20.00 10.00
❑ 13 Paul Minner 12.00 6.00
❑ 14 Gerry Staley 12.00 6.00
❑ 15 Richie Ashburn 80.00 40.00
❑ 16 Jim Wilson 12.00 6.00
❑ 17 Tom Gorman 12.00 6.00
❑ 18 Hoot Evers 12.00 6.00
❑ 19 Bobby Shantz 20.00 10.00
❑ 20 Art Houtteman 12.00 6.00
❑ 21 Vic Wertz 20.00 10.00
❑ 22 Sam Mele 12.00 6.00
❑ 23 Harvey Kuenn RC 30.00 15.00
❑ 24 Bob Porterfield 12.00 6.00
❑ 25 Wes Westrum 20.00 10.00
❑ 26 Billy Cox 20.00 10.00
❑ 27 Dick Cole 12.00 6.00
❑ 28 Jim Greengrass 12.00 6.00
❑ 29 Johnny Klippstein 12.00 6.00
❑ 30 Del Rice 12.00 6.00
❑ 31 Smoky Burgess 20.00 10.00
❑ 32 Del Crandall 20.00 10.00
❑ 33A Vic Raschi 20.00 10.00
(No mention of
trade on back)
❑ 33B Vic Raschi 30.00 15.00
(Traded to St.Louis)
❑ 34 Sammy White 12.00 6.00
❑ 35 Eddie Joost 12.00 6.00
❑ 36 George Strickland 12.00 6.00
❑ 37 Dick Kokos 12.00 6.00
❑ 38 Minnie Minoso 30.00 15.00
❑ 39 Ned Garver 12.00 6.00
❑ 40 Gil Coan 12.00 6.00
❑ 41 Alvin Dark 20.00 10.00
❑ 42 Billy Loes 20.00 10.00
❑ 43 Bob Friend 20.00 10.00
❑ 44 Harry Perkowski 12.00 6.00
❑ 45 Ralph Kiner 50.00 25.00
❑ 46 Rip Repulski 12.00 6.00
❑ 47 Granny Hamner 12.00 6.00

Card	NM	Ex
❑ 48 Jack Dittmer	12.00	6.00
❑ 49 Harry Byrd	12.00	6.00
❑ 50 George Kell	50.00	25.00
❑ 51 Alex Kellner	12.00	6.00
❑ 52 Joe Ginsberg	12.00	6.00
❑ 53 Don Lenhardt	12.00	6.00
❑ 54 Chico Carrasquel	12.00	6.00
❑ 55 Jim Delsing	12.00	6.00
❑ 56 Maurice McDermott	12.00	6.00
❑ 57 Hoyt Wilhelm	50.00	25.00
❑ 58 Pee Wee Reese	80.00	40.00
❑ 59 Bob Schultz	12.00	6.00
❑ 60 Fred Baczewski	12.00	6.00
❑ 61 Eddie Miksis	12.00	6.00
❑ 62 Enos Slaughter	50.00	25.00
❑ 63 Earl Torgeson	12.00	6.00
❑ 64 Eddie Mathews	80.00	40.00
❑ 65 Mickey Mantle	1500.00	750.00
❑ 66A Ted Williams	3000.00	1500.00
❑ 66B Jimmy Piersall	80.00	40.00
❑ 67 Carl Scheib	12.00	6.00
❑ 68 Bobby Avila	20.00	10.00
❑ 69 Clint Courtney	12.00	6.00
❑ 70 Willard Marshall	12.00	6.00
❑ 71 Ted Gray	12.00	6.00
❑ 72 Eddie Yost	20.00	10.00
❑ 73 Don Mueller	20.00	10.00
❑ 74 Jim Gilliam	30.00	15.00
❑ 75 Max Surkont	12.00	6.00
❑ 76 Joe Nuxhall	20.00	10.00
❑ 77 Bob Rush	12.00	6.00
❑ 78 Sal Yvars	12.00	6.00
❑ 79 Curt Simmons	20.00	10.00
❑ 80 Johnny Logan	12.00	6.00
❑ 81 Jerry Coleman	20.00	10.00
❑ 82 Billy Goodman	20.00	10.00
❑ 83 Ray Murray	12.00	6.00
❑ 84 Larry Doby	50.00	25.00
❑ 85 Jim Dyck	12.00	6.00
❑ 86 Harry Dorish	12.00	6.00
❑ 87 Don Lund	12.00	6.00
❑ 88 Tom Umphlett	12.00	6.00
❑ 89 Willie Mays	500.00	250.00
❑ 90 Roy Campanella	150.00	75.00
❑ 91 Cal Abrams	12.00	6.00
❑ 92 Ken Raffensberger	12.00	6.00
❑ 93 Bill Serena	12.00	6.00
❑ 94 Solly Hemus	12.00	6.00
❑ 95 Robin Roberts	50.00	25.00
❑ 96 Joe Adcock	20.00	10.00
❑ 97 Gil McDougald	20.00	10.00
❑ 98 Ellis Kinder	12.00	6.00
❑ 99 Pete Suder	12.00	6.00
❑ 100 Mike Garcia	20.00	10.00
❑ 101 Don Larsen RC	80.00	40.00
❑ 102 Billy Pierce	20.00	10.00
❑ 103 Steve Souchock	12.00	6.00
❑ 104 Frank Shea	12.00	6.00
❑ 105 Sal Maglie	20.00	10.00
❑ 106 Clem Labine	20.00	10.00
❑ 107 Paul LaPalme	12.00	6.00
❑ 108 Bobby Adams	12.00	6.00
❑ 109 Roy Smalley	12.00	6.00
❑ 110 Red Schoendienst	50.00	25.00
❑ 111 Murry Dickson	12.00	6.00
❑ 112 Andy Pafko	20.00	10.00
❑ 113 Allie Reynolds	20.00	10.00
❑ 114 Willard Nixon	12.00	6.00
❑ 115 Don Bollweg	12.00	6.00
❑ 116 Luke Easter	20.00	10.00
❑ 117 Dick Kryhoski	12.00	6.00
❑ 118 Bob Boyd	12.00	6.00
❑ 119 Fred Hatfield	12.00	6.00
❑ 120 Mel Hoderlein	12.00	6.00
❑ 121 Ray Katt	12.00	6.00
❑ 122 Carl Furillo	30.00	15.00
❑ 123 Toby Atwell	12.00	6.00
❑ 124 Gus Bell	20.00	10.00
❑ 125 Warren Hacker	12.00	6.00
❑ 126 Cliff Chambers	12.00	6.00
❑ 127 Del Ennis	20.00	10.00
❑ 128 Ebba St.Claire	12.00	6.00
❑ 129 Hank Bauer	30.00	15.00
❑ 130 Milt Bolling	12.00	6.00
❑ 131 Joe Astroth	12.00	6.00
❑ 132 Bob Feller	80.00	40.00
❑ 133 Duane Pillette	12.00	6.00
❑ 134 Luis Aloma	12.00	6.00
❑ 135 Johnny Pesky	20.00	10.00
❑ 136 Clyde Vollmer	12.00	6.00
❑ 137 Al Corwin	12.00	6.00
❑ 138 Gil Hodges	80.00	40.00
❑ 139 Preston Ward	12.00	6.00
❑ 140 Saul Rogovin	12.00	6.00
❑ 141 Joe Garagiola	30.00	15.00
❑ 142 Al Brazle	12.00	6.00
❑ 143 Willie Jones	12.00	6.00
❑ 144 Ernie Johnson RC	30.00	15.00
❑ 145 Billy Martin	80.00	40.00
❑ 146 Dick Gernert	12.00	6.00
❑ 147 Joe DeMaestri	12.00	6.00
❑ 148 Dale Mitchell	20.00	10.00
❑ 149 Bob Young	12.00	6.00
❑ 150 Cass Michaels	12.00	6.00
❑ 151 Pat Mullin	12.00	6.00
❑ 152 Mickey Vernon	20.00	10.00
❑ 153 Whitey Lockman	20.00	10.00
❑ 154 Don Newcombe	30.00	15.00
❑ 155 Frank Thomas RC	20.00	10.00
❑ 156 Rocky Bridges	12.00	6.00
❑ 157 Turk Lown	12.00	6.00
❑ 158 Stu Miller	20.00	10.00
❑ 159 Johnny Lindell	12.00	6.00
❑ 160 Danny O'Connell	12.00	6.00
❑ 161 Yogi Berra	175.00	90.00
❑ 162 Ted Lepcio	12.00	6.00
❑ 163A Dave Philley (No mention of trade on back)	20.00	10.00
❑ 163B Dave Philley (Traded to Cleveland)	30.00	15.00
❑ 164 Early Wynn	50.00	25.00
❑ 165 Johnny Groth	12.00	6.00
❑ 166 Sandy Consuegra	12.00	6.00
❑ 167 Billy Hoeft	12.00	6.00
❑ 168 Ed Fitzgerald	12.00	6.00
❑ 169 Larry Jansen	20.00	10.00
❑ 170 Duke Snider	175.00	90.00
❑ 171 Carlos Bernier	12.00	6.00
❑ 172 Andy Seminick	12.00	6.00
❑ 173 Dee Fondy	12.00	6.00
❑ 174 Pete Castiglione	12.00	6.00
❑ 175 Mel Clark	12.00	6.00
❑ 176 Vern Bickford	12.00	6.00
❑ 177 Whitey Ford	100.00	50.00
❑ 178 Del Wilber	12.00	6.00
❑ 179 Morrie Martin	12.00	6.00
❑ 180 Joe Tipton	12.00	6.00
❑ 181 Les Moss	12.00	6.00
❑ 182 Sherm Lollar	20.00	10.00
❑ 183 Matt Batts	12.00	6.00
❑ 184 Mickey Grasso	12.00	6.00
❑ 185 Daryl Spencer	12.00	6.00
❑ 186 Russ Meyer	12.00	6.00
❑ 187 Vern Law	20.00	10.00
❑ 188 Frank Smith	12.00	6.00
❑ 189 Randy Jackson	12.00	6.00
❑ 190 Joe Presko	12.00	6.00
❑ 191 Karl Drews	12.00	6.00
❑ 192 Lou Burdette	20.00	10.00
❑ 193 Eddie Robinson	12.00	6.00
❑ 194 Sid Hudson	12.00	6.00
❑ 195 Bob Cain	12.00	6.00
❑ 196 Bob Lemon	50.00	25.00
❑ 197 Lou Kretlow	12.00	6.00
❑ 198 Virgil Trucks	12.00	6.00
❑ 199 Steve Gromek	12.00	6.00
❑ 200 Conrado Marrero	12.00	6.00
❑ 201 Bobby Thomson	30.00	15.00
❑ 202 George Shuba	20.00	10.00
❑ 203 Vic Janowicz	20.00	10.00
❑ 204 Jack Collum	12.00	6.00
❑ 205 Hal Jeffcoat	12.00	6.00
❑ 206 Steve Bilko	12.00	6.00
❑ 207 Stan Lopata	12.00	6.00
❑ 208 Johnny Antonelli	20.00	10.00
❑ 209 Gene Woodling	12.00	6.00
❑ 210 Jimmy Piersall	30.00	15.00
❑ 211 Al Robertson	12.00	6.00
❑ 212 Owen Friend	12.00	6.00
❑ 213 Dick Littlefield	12.00	6.00
❑ 214 Ferris Fain	20.00	10.00
❑ 215 Johnny Bucha	12.00	6.00
❑ 216 Jerry Snyder	12.00	6.00
❑ 217 Hank Thompson	20.00	10.00
❑ 218 Preacher Roe	20.00	10.00
❑ 219 Hal Rice	12.00	6.00
❑ 220 Hobie Landrith	12.00	6.00
❑ 221 Frank Baumholtz	12.00	6.00
❑ 222 Memo Luna	12.00	6.00
❑ 223 Steve Ridzik	12.00	6.00
❑ 224 Bill Bruton	50.00	12.50

1955 Bowman

	NM	Ex
COMPLETE SET (320)	5000.00	2500.00
COMMON CARD (1-96)	12.00	6.00
COMMON CARD (97-224)	10.00	5.00
COMMON (225-320)	15.00	7.50
COMMON UMP. 225-320	30.00	15.00
WRAPPER (1-CENT)	60.00	30.00
WRAPPER (5-CENT)	60.00	30.00

Card	NM	Ex
❑ 1 Hoyt Wilhelm	100.00	22.00
❑ 2 Alvin Dark	15.00	7.50
❑ 3 Joe Coleman	15.00	7.50
❑ 4 Eddie Waitkus	15.00	7.50
❑ 5 Jim Robertson	12.00	6.00
❑ 6 Pete Suder	12.00	6.00
❑ 7 Gene Baker	12.00	6.00
❑ 8 Warren Hacker	12.00	6.00
❑ 9 Gil McDougald	20.00	10.00
❑ 10 Phil Rizzuto	125.00	60.00
❑ 11 Bill Bruton	15.00	7.50
❑ 12 Andy Pafko	15.00	7.50
❑ 13 Clyde Vollmer	12.00	6.00
❑ 14 Gus Keriazakos	12.00	6.00
❑ 15 Frank Sullivan	12.00	6.00
❑ 16 Jimmy Piersall	20.00	10.00
❑ 17 Del Ennis	15.00	7.50
❑ 18 Stan Lopata	12.00	6.00
❑ 19 Bobby Avila	15.00	7.50
❑ 20 Al Smith	15.00	7.50
❑ 21 Don Hoak	12.00	6.00
❑ 22 Roy Campanella	125.00	60.00
❑ 23 Al Kaline	150.00	75.00
❑ 24 Al Aber	12.00	6.00
❑ 25 Minnie Minoso	30.00	15.00
❑ 26 Virgil Trucks	15.00	7.50
❑ 27 Preston Ward	12.00	6.00
❑ 28 Dick Cole	12.00	6.00
❑ 29 Red Schoendienst	30.00	15.00
❑ 30 Bill Sarni	12.00	6.00
❑ 31 Johnny Temple RC	15.00	7.50
❑ 32 Wally Post	15.00	7.50
❑ 33 Nellie Fox	50.00	25.00
❑ 34 Clint Courtney	12.00	6.00
❑ 35 Bill Tuttle	12.00	6.00
❑ 36 Wayne Belardi	12.00	6.00
❑ 37 Pee Wee Reese	100.00	50.00
❑ 38 Early Wynn	30.00	15.00
❑ 39 Bob Darnell	15.00	7.50
❑ 40 Vic Wertz	15.00	7.50
❑ 41 Mel Clark	12.00	6.00
❑ 42 Bob Greenwood	12.00	6.00
❑ 43 Bob Buhl	15.00	7.50
❑ 44 Danny O'Connell	12.00	6.00
❑ 45 Tom Umphlett	12.00	6.00

❑ 46 Mickey Vernon 15.00 7.50
❑ 47 Sammy White 12.00 6.00
❑ 48A Milt Bolling ERR 20.00 10.00
(Name on back is
Frank Bolling)
❑ 48B Milt Bolling COR......... 20.00 10.00
❑ 49 Jim Greengrass 12.00 6.00
❑ 50 Hobie Landrith 12.00 6.00
❑ 51 Elvin Tappe 12.00 6.00
❑ 52 Hal Rice............ 12.00 6.00
❑ 53 Alex Kellner............ 12.00 6.00
❑ 54 Don Bollweg 12.00 6.00
❑ 55 Cal Abrams 12.00 6.00
❑ 56 Billy Cox 15.00 7.50
❑ 57 Bob Friend 15.00 7.50
❑ 58 Frank Thomas 15.00 7.50
❑ 59 Whitey Ford............ 100.00 50.00
❑ 60 Enos Slaughter 30.00 15.00
❑ 61 Paul LaPalme 12.00 6.00
❑ 62 Royce Lint 12.00 6.00
❑ 63 Irv Noren............ 15.00 7.50
❑ 64 Curt Simmons............ 15.00 7.50
❑ 65 Don Zimmer RC 20.00 10.00
❑ 66 George Shuba 20.00 10.00
❑ 67 Don Larsen 20.00 10.00
❑ 68 Elston Howard RC 80.00 40.00
❑ 69 Billy Hunter 12.00 6.00
❑ 70 Lou Burdette 20.00 10.00
❑ 71 Dave Jolly 12.00 6.00
❑ 72 Chet Nichols 12.00 6.00
❑ 73 Eddie Yost............ 15.00 7.50
❑ 74 Jerry Snyder 12.00 6.00
❑ 75 Brooks Lawrence RC 12.00 6.00
❑ 76 Tom Poholsky 12.00 6.00
❑ 77 Jim McDonald............ 12.00 6.00
❑ 78 Gil Coan 12.00 6.00
❑ 79 Willie Miranda............ 12.00 6.00
❑ 80 Lou Limmer............ 12.00 6.00
❑ 81 Bobby Morgan 12.00 6.00
❑ 82 Lee Walls 12.00 6.00
❑ 83 Max Surkont 12.00 6.00
❑ 84 George Freese............ 12.00 6.00
❑ 85 Cass Michaels............ 12.00 6.00
❑ 86 Ted Gray 12.00 6.00
❑ 87 Randy Jackson 12.00 6.00
❑ 88 Steve Bilko 12.00 6.00
❑ 89 Lou Boudreau MG......... 30.00 15.00
❑ 90 Art Ditmar 12.00 6.00
❑ 91 Dick Marlowe 12.00 6.00
❑ 92 George Zuverink 12.00 6.00
❑ 93 Andy Seminick 12.00 6.00
❑ 94 Hank Thompson 15.00 7.50
❑ 95 Sal Maglie............ 15.00 7.50
❑ 96 Ray Narleski RC 12.00 6.00
❑ 97 Johnny Podres 30.00 15.00
❑ 98 Jim Gilliam 20.00 10.00
❑ 99 Jerry Coleman............ 15.00 7.50
❑ 100 Tom Morgan 10.00 5.00
❑ 101A Don Johnson ERR...... 20.00 10.00
(Photo actually
Ernie Johnson)
❑ 101B Don Johnson COR 20.00 10.00
❑ 102 Bobby Thomson 15.00 7.50
❑ 103 Eddie Mathews 80.00 40.00
❑ 104 Bob Porterfield 10.00 5.00
❑ 105 Johnny Schmitz......... 10.00 5.00
❑ 106 Del Rice......... 10.00 5.00
❑ 107 Solly Hemus 10.00 5.00
❑ 108 Lou Kretlow......... 10.00 5.00
❑ 109 Vern Stephens......... 15.00 7.50
❑ 110 Bob Miller......... 10.00 5.00
❑ 111 Steve Ridzik......... 10.00 5.00
❑ 112 Granny Hamner 10.00 5.00
❑ 113 Bob Hall 10.00 5.00
❑ 114 Vic Janowicz 15.00 7.50
❑ 115 Roger Bowman 10.00 5.00
❑ 116 Sandy Consuegra 10.00 5.00
❑ 117 Johnny Groth 10.00 5.00
❑ 118 Bobby Adams 10.00 5.00
❑ 119 Joe Astroth 10.00 5.00
❑ 120 Ed Burtschy......... 10.00 5.00
❑ 121 Rufus Crawford 10.00 5.00
❑ 122 Al Corwin 10.00 5.00
❑ 123 Marv Grissom......... 10.00 5.00
❑ 124 Johnny Antonelli......... 15.00 7.50
❑ 125 Paul Giel 15.00 7.50
❑ 126 Billy Goodman 15.00 7.50
❑ 127 Hank Majeski 10.00 5.00
❑ 128 Mike Garcia......... 15.00 7.50
❑ 129 Hal Naragon 10.00 5.00
❑ 130 Richie Ashburn 50.00 25.00
❑ 131 Willard Marshall 10.00 5.00
❑ 132A Harvey Kueen ERR 50.00 25.00
(Sic& Kuenn)
❑ 132B Harvey Kuenn COR 30.00 15.00
❑ 133 Charles King 10.00 5.00
❑ 134 Bob Feller 80.00 40.00
❑ 135 Lloyd Merriman......... 10.00 5.00
❑ 136 Rocky Bridges 10.00 5.00
❑ 137 Bob Talbot......... 10.00 5.00
❑ 138 Davey Williams 15.00 7.50
❑ 139 Shantz Brothers......... 15.00 7.50
Wilmer Shantz
Bobby Shantz
❑ 140 Bobby Shantz 15.00 7.50
❑ 141 Wes Westrum 15.00 7.50
❑ 142 Rudy Regalado 10.00 5.00
❑ 143 Don Newcombe......... 30.00 15.00
❑ 144 Art Houtteman 10.00 5.00
❑ 145 Bob Nieman 10.00 5.00
❑ 146 Don Liddle 10.00 5.00
❑ 147 Sam Mele 10.00 5.00
❑ 148 Bob Chakales 10.00 5.00
❑ 149 Cloyd Boyer 10.00 5.00
❑ 150 Billy Klaus......... 10.00 5.00
❑ 151 Jim Brideweser 10.00 5.00
❑ 152 Johnny Klippstein 10.00 5.00
❑ 153 Eddie Robinson......... 10.00 5.00
❑ 154 Frank Lary RC 15.00 7.50
❑ 155 Gerry Staley......... 10.00 5.00
❑ 156 Jim Hughes......... 15.00 7.50
❑ 157A Ernie Johnson ERR 20.00 10.00
(Photo actually
Don Johnson)
❑ 157B Ernie Johnson COR.... 20.00 10.00
❑ 158 Gil Hodges 50.00 25.00
❑ 159 Harry Byrd......... 10.00 5.00
❑ 160 Bill Skowron 20.00 10.00
❑ 161 Matt Batts 10.00 5.00
❑ 162 Charlie Maxwell 10.00 5.00
❑ 163 Sid Gordon 15.00 7.50
❑ 164 Toby Atwell 10.00 5.00
❑ 165 Maurice McDermott 10.00 5.00
❑ 166 Jim Busby......... 10.00 5.00
❑ 167 Bob Grim RC......... 20.00 10.00
❑ 168 Yogi Berra......... 125.00 60.00
❑ 169 Carl Furillo 30.00 15.00
❑ 170 Carl Erskine......... 20.00 10.00
❑ 171 Robin Roberts 50.00 25.00
❑ 172 Willie Jones 10.00 5.00
❑ 173 Chico Carrasquel 10.00 5.00
❑ 174 Sherm Lollar 15.00 7.50
❑ 175 Wilmer Shantz......... 10.00 5.00
❑ 176 Joe DeMaestri......... 10.00 5.00
❑ 177 Willard Nixon 10.00 5.00
❑ 178 Tom Brewer......... 10.00 5.00
❑ 179 Hank Aaron 250.00 125.00
❑ 180 Johnny Logan 15.00 7.50
❑ 181 Eddie Miksis......... 10.00 5.00
❑ 182 Bob Rush 10.00 5.00
❑ 183 Ray Katt......... 10.00 5.00
❑ 184 Willie Mays......... 250.00 125.00
❑ 185 Vic Raschi......... 10.00 5.00
❑ 186 Alex Grammas......... 10.00 5.00
❑ 187 Fred Hatfield 10.00 5.00
❑ 188 Ned Garver 10.00 5.00
❑ 189 Jack Collum 10.00 5.00
❑ 190 Fred Baczewski 10.00 5.00
❑ 191 Bob Lemon 30.00 15.00
❑ 192 George Strickland 10.00 5.00
❑ 193 Howie Judson 10.00 5.00
❑ 194 Joe Nuxhall......... 15.00 7.50
❑ 195A Erv Palica 15.00 7.50
(Without trade)
❑ 195B Erv Palica 40.00 20.00
(With trade)
❑ 196 Russ Meyer......... 15.00 7.50
❑ 197 Ralph Kiner 30.00 15.00
❑ 198 Dave Pope......... 10.00 5.00
❑ 199 Vern Law......... 15.00 7.50
❑ 200 Dick Littlefield......... 10.00 5.00
❑ 201 Allie Reynolds......... 20.00 10.00
❑ 202 Mickey Mantle UER.... 800.00 400.00
Birthdate listed as 10/30/31
Should be 10/20/31
❑ 203 Steve Gromek 10.00 5.00
❑ 204A Frank Bolling ERR...... 20.00 10.00
(Name on back is
Milt Bolling)
❑ 204B Frank Bolling COR 20.00 10.00
❑ 205 Rip Repulski 10.00 5.00
❑ 206 Ralph Beard......... 10.00 5.00
❑ 207 Frank Shea 10.00 5.00
❑ 208 Ed Fitzgerald 10.00 5.00
❑ 209 Smoky Burgess......... 15.00 7.50
❑ 210 Earl Torgeson 10.00 5.00
❑ 211 Sonny Dixon 10.00 5.00
❑ 212 Jack Dittmer 10.00 5.00
❑ 213 George Kell 30.00 15.00
❑ 214 Billy Pierce 15.00 7.50
❑ 215 Bob Kuzava......... 10.00 5.00
❑ 216 Preacher Roe......... 20.00 10.00
❑ 217 Del Crandall 15.00 7.50
❑ 218 Joe Adcock 15.00 7.50
❑ 219 Whitey Lockman 15.00 7.50
❑ 220 Jim Hearn 10.00 5.00
❑ 221 Hector Brown 10.00 5.00
❑ 222 Russ Kemmerer......... 10.00 5.00
❑ 223 Hal Jeffcoat......... 10.00 5.00
❑ 224 Dee Fondy......... 10.00 5.00
❑ 225 Paul Richards MG 15.00 7.50
❑ 226 Bill McKinley UMP RC 30.00 15.00
❑ 227 Frank Baumholtz 15.00 7.50
❑ 228 John Phillips......... 15.00 7.50
❑ 229 Jim Brosnan RC 20.00 10.00
❑ 230 Al Brazle 15.00 7.50
❑ 231 Jim Konstanty 20.00 10.00
❑ 232 Birdie Tebbetts MG 20.00 10.00
❑ 233 Bill Serena......... 15.00 7.50
❑ 234 Dick Bartell CO 20.00 10.00
❑ 235 Joe Paparella UMP RC 30.00 15.00
❑ 236 Murry Dickson 15.00 7.50
❑ 237 Johnny Wyrostek......... 15.00 7.50
❑ 238 Eddie Stanky MG......... 20.00 10.00
❑ 239 Edwin Rommel UMP 40.00 20.00
❑ 240 Billy Loes 20.00 10.00
❑ 241 Johnny Pesky CO 20.00 10.00
❑ 242 Ernie Banks 350.00 180.00
❑ 243 Gus Bell 20.00 10.00
❑ 244 Duane Pillette 15.00 7.50
❑ 245 Bill Miller 15.00 7.50
❑ 246 Hank Bauer 30.00 15.00
❑ 247 Dutch Leonard CO....... 15.00 7.50
❑ 248 Harry Dorish 15.00 7.50
❑ 249 Billy Gardner RC 20.00 10.00
❑ 250 Larry Napp UMP RC 30.00 15.00
❑ 251 Stan Jok 15.00 7.50
❑ 252 Roy Smalley 15.00 7.50
❑ 253 Jim Wilson 15.00 7.50
❑ 254 Bennett Flowers......... 15.00 7.50
❑ 255 Pete Runnels 20.00 10.00
❑ 256 Owen Friend 15.00 7.50
❑ 257 Tom Alston 15.00 7.50
❑ 258 John Stevens UMP RC 30.00 15.00
❑ 259 Don Mossi RC......... 30.00 15.00
❑ 260 Edwin Hurley UMP RC 30.00 15.00
❑ 261 Walt Moryn 20.00 10.00
❑ 262 Jim Lemon 15.00 7.50
❑ 263 Eddie Joost 15.00 7.50
❑ 264 Bill Henry 15.00 7.50
❑ 265 Albert Barlick UMP RC 80.00 40.00
❑ 266 Mike Fornieles 15.00 7.50
❑ 267 Jim Honochick UMP RC 80.00 40.00
❑ 268 Roy Lee Hawes 15.00 7.50
❑ 269 Joe Amalfitano RC....... 20.00 10.00
❑ 270 Chico Fernandez 20.00 10.00
❑ 271 Bob Hooper......... 15.00 7.50
❑ 272 John Flaherty UMP RC 30.00 15.00
❑ 273 Bubba Church......... 15.00 7.50
❑ 274 Jim Delsing......... 15.00 7.50
❑ 275 William Grieve UMP RC 30.00 15.00
❑ 276 Ike Delock 15.00 7.50
❑ 277 Ed Runge UMP RC 30.00 15.00
❑ 278 Charlie Neal RC......... 40.00 20.00
❑ 279 Hank Soar UMP RC..... 40.00 20.00
❑ 280 Clyde McCullough 15.00 7.50
❑ 281 Charles Berry UMP 40.00 20.00
❑ 282 Phil Cavarretta......... 20.00 10.00

Card	Nm-Mt	Ex-Mt
❑ 283 Nestor Chylak UMP RC	80.00	40.00
❑ 284 Bill Jackowski UMP RC	30.00	15.00
❑ 285 Walt Dropo	20.00	10.00
❑ 286 Frank Secory UMP RC	30.00	15.00
❑ 287 Ron Mrozinski	15.00	7.50
❑ 288 Dick Smith	15.00	7.50
❑ 289 Arthur Gore UMP RC	30.00	15.00
❑ 290 Hershell Freeman	15.00	7.50
❑ 291 Frank Dascoli UMP RC	30.00	15.00
❑ 292 Marv Blaylock	15.00	7.50
❑ 293 Thomas Gorman UMP RC	40.00	20.00
❑ 294 Wally Moses CO	15.00	7.50
❑ 295 Lee Ballanfant UMP RC	30.00	15.00
❑ 296 Bill Virdon RC	30.00	15.00
❑ 297 Dusty Boggess UMP RC	30.00	15.00
❑ 298 Charlie Grimm MG	20.00	10.00
❑ 299 Lon Warneke UMP	40.00	20.00
❑ 300 Tommy Byrne	20.00	10.00
❑ 301 William Engeln UMP RC	30.00	15.00
❑ 302 Frank Malzone RC	30.00	15.00
❑ 303 Jocko Conlan UMP	80.00	40.00
❑ 304 Harry Chiti	15.00	7.50
❑ 305 Frank Umont UMP RC	30.00	15.00
❑ 306 Bob Cerv	20.00	10.00
❑ 307 Babe Pinelli UMP	40.00	20.00
❑ 308 Al Lopez MG	50.00	25.00
❑ 309 Hal Dixon UMP RC	30.00	15.00
❑ 310 Ken Lehman	15.00	7.50
❑ 311 Lawrence Goetz UMP RC	30.00	15.00
❑ 312 Bill Wight	15.00	7.50
❑ 313 Augie Donatelli UMP RC	50.00	25.00
❑ 314 Dale Mitchell	20.00	10.00
❑ 315 Cal Hubbard UMP RC	80.00	40.00
❑ 316 Marion Fricano	15.00	7.50
❑ 317 W. Summers UMP	20.00	10.00
❑ 318 Sid Hudson	15.00	7.50
❑ 319 Al Schroll	15.00	7.50
❑ 320 George Susce RC	50.00	10.00

1989 Bowman

	Nm-Mt	Ex-Mt
COMPLETE SET (484)	25.00	10.00
COMP.FACT.SET (484)	25.00	10.00

Card	Nm-Mt	Ex-Mt
❑ 1 Oswald Peraza	.05	.02
❑ 2 Brian Holton	.05	.02
❑ 3 Jose Bautista RC	.10	.04
❑ 4 Pete Harnisch RC	.25	.10
❑ 5 Dave Schmidt	.05	.02
❑ 6 Gregg Olson RC	.25	.10
❑ 7 Jeff Ballard	.05	.02
❑ 8 Bob Melvin	.05	.02
❑ 9 Cal Ripken	.75	.30
❑ 10 Randy Milligan	.05	.02
❑ 11 Juan Bell RC	.10	.04
❑ 12 Billy Ripken	.05	.02
❑ 13 Jim Traber	.05	.02
❑ 14 Pete Stanicek	.05	.02
❑ 15 Steve Finley RC	.75	.30
❑ 16 Larry Sheets	.05	.02
❑ 17 Phil Bradley	.05	.02
❑ 18 Brady Anderson RC	.40	.16
❑ 19 Lee Smith	.10	.04
❑ 20 Tom Fischer	.05	.02
❑ 21 Mike Boddicker	.05	.02
❑ 22 Rob Murphy	.05	.02
❑ 23 Wes Gardner	.05	.02
❑ 24 John Dopson	.05	.02
❑ 25 Bob Stanley	.05	.02
❑ 26 Roger Clemens	.50	.20
❑ 27 Rich Gedman	.05	.02
❑ 28 Marty Barrett	.05	.02
❑ 29 Luis Rivera	.05	.02
❑ 30 Jody Reed	.05	.02
❑ 31 Nick Esasky	.05	.02
❑ 32 Wade Boggs	.15	.06
❑ 33 Jim Rice	.10	.04
❑ 34 Mike Greenwell	.05	.02
❑ 35 Dwight Evans	.15	.06
❑ 36 Ellis Burks	.10	.04
❑ 37 Chuck Finley	.10	.04
❑ 38 Kirk McCaskill	.05	.02
❑ 39 Jim Abbott RC*	1.00	.40
❑ 40 Bryan Harvey RC *	.25	.10
❑ 41 Bert Blyleven	.10	.04
❑ 42 Mike Witt	.05	.02
❑ 43 Bob McClure	.05	.02
❑ 44 Bill Schroeder	.05	.02
❑ 45 Lance Parrish	.10	.04
❑ 46 Dick Schofield	.05	.02
❑ 47 Wally Joyner	.10	.04
❑ 48 Jack Howell	.05	.02
❑ 49 Johnny Ray	.05	.02
❑ 50 Chili Davis	.10	.04
❑ 51 Tony Armas	.10	.04
❑ 52 Claudell Washington	.05	.02
❑ 53 Brian Downing	.10	.04
❑ 54 Devon White	.10	.04
❑ 55 Bobby Thigpen	.05	.02
❑ 56 Bill Long	.05	.02
❑ 57 Jerry Reuss	.05	.02
❑ 58 Shawn Hillegas	.05	.02
❑ 59 Melido Perez	.05	.02
❑ 60 Jeff Bittiger	.05	.02
❑ 61 Jack McDowell	.10	.04
❑ 62 Carlton Fisk	.15	.06
❑ 63 Steve Lyons	.05	.02
❑ 64 Ozzie Guillen	.10	.04
❑ 65 Robin Ventura RC	.75	.30
❑ 66 Fred Manrique	.05	.02
❑ 67 Dan Pasqua	.05	.02
❑ 68 Ivan Calderon	.05	.02
❑ 69 Ron Kittle	.05	.02
❑ 70 Daryl Boston	.05	.02
❑ 71 Dave Gallagher	.05	.02
❑ 72 Harold Baines	.10	.04
❑ 73 Charles Nagy RC	.25	.10
❑ 74 John Farrell	.05	.02
❑ 75 Kevin Wickander	.05	.02
❑ 76 Greg Swindell	.05	.02
❑ 77 Mike Walker	.05	.02
❑ 78 Doug Jones	.05	.02
❑ 79 Rich Yett	.05	.02
❑ 80 Tom Candiotti	.05	.02
❑ 81 Jesse Orosco	.05	.02
❑ 82 Bud Black	.05	.02
❑ 83 Andy Allanson	.05	.02
❑ 84 Pete O'Brien	.05	.02
❑ 85 Jerry Browne	.05	.02
❑ 86 Brook Jacoby	.05	.02
❑ 87 Mark Lewis RC	.25	.10
❑ 88 Luis Aguayo	.05	.02
❑ 89 Cory Snyder	.05	.02
❑ 90 Oddibe McDowell	.05	.02
❑ 91 Joe Carter	.10	.04
❑ 92 Frank Tanana	.10	.04
❑ 93 Jack Morris	.10	.04
❑ 94 Doyle Alexander	.05	.02
❑ 95 Steve Searcy	.05	.02
❑ 96 Randy Bockus	.05	.02
❑ 97 Jeff M. Robinson	.05	.02
❑ 98 Mike Henneman	.05	.02
❑ 99 Paul Gibson	.05	.02
❑ 100 Frank Williams	.05	.02
❑ 101 Matt Nokes	.05	.02
❑ 102 Rico Brogna RC UER (Misspelled Ricco on card back)	.40	.16
❑ 103 Lou Whitaker	.10	.04
❑ 104 Al Pedrique	.05	.02
❑ 105 Alan Trammell	.10	.04
❑ 106 Chris Brown	.05	.02
❑ 107 Pat Sheridan	.05	.02
❑ 108 Chet Lemon	.10	.04
❑ 109 Keith Moreland	.05	.02
❑ 110 Mel Stottlemyre Jr.	.05	.02
❑ 111 Bret Saberhagen	.10	.04
❑ 112 Floyd Bannister	.05	.02
❑ 113 Jeff Montgomery	.05	.02
❑ 114 Steve Farr	.05	.02
❑ 115 Tom Gordon UER RC (Front shows autograph of Don Gordon)	.40	.16
❑ 116 Charlie Leibrandt	.05	.02
❑ 117 Mark Gubicza	.05	.02
❑ 118 Mike Macfarlane RC	.25	.10
❑ 119 Bob Boone	.10	.04
❑ 120 Kurt Stillwell	.05	.02
❑ 121 George Brett	.60	.24
❑ 122 Frank White	.10	.04
❑ 123 Kevin Seitzer	.05	.02
❑ 124 Willie Wilson	.10	.04
❑ 125 Pat Tabler	.05	.02
❑ 126 Bo Jackson	.25	.10
❑ 127 Hugh Walker RC	.10	.04
❑ 128 Danny Tartabull	.05	.02
❑ 129 Teddy Higuera	.05	.02
❑ 130 Don August	.05	.02
❑ 131 Juan Nieves	.05	.02
❑ 132 Mike Birkbeck	.05	.02
❑ 133 Dan Plesac	.05	.02
❑ 134 Chris Bosio	.05	.02
❑ 135 Bill Wegman	.05	.02
❑ 136 Chuck Crim	.05	.02
❑ 137 B.J. Surhoff	.10	.04
❑ 138 Joey Meyer	.05	.02
❑ 139 Dale Sveum	.05	.02
❑ 140 Paul Molitor	.15	.06
❑ 141 Jim Gantner	.05	.02
❑ 142 Gary Sheffield RC	2.00	.80
❑ 143 Greg Brock	.05	.02
❑ 144 Robin Yount	.40	.16
❑ 145 Glenn Braggs	.05	.02
❑ 146 Rob Deer	.05	.02
❑ 147 Fred Toliver	.05	.02
❑ 148 Jeff Reardon	.10	.04
❑ 149 Allan Anderson	.05	.02
❑ 150 Frank Viola	.10	.04
❑ 151 Shane Rawley	.05	.02
❑ 152 Juan Berenguer	.05	.02
❑ 153 Johnny Ard	.05	.02
❑ 154 Tim Laudner	.05	.02
❑ 155 Brian Harper	.05	.02
❑ 156 Al Newman	.05	.02
❑ 157 Kent Hrbek	.10	.04
❑ 158 Gary Gaetti	.10	.04
❑ 159 Wally Backman	.05	.02
❑ 160 Gene Larkin	.05	.02
❑ 161 Greg Gagne	.05	.02
❑ 162 Kirby Puckett	.25	.10
❑ 163 Dan Gladden	.05	.02
❑ 164 Randy Bush	.05	.02
❑ 165 Dave LaPoint	.05	.02
❑ 166 Andy Hawkins	.05	.02
❑ 167 Dave Righetti	.10	.04
❑ 168 Lance McCullers	.05	.02
❑ 169 Jimmy Jones	.05	.02
❑ 170 Al Leiter	.25	.10
❑ 171 John Candelaria	.05	.02
❑ 172 Don Slaught	.05	.02
❑ 173 Jamie Quirk	.05	.02
❑ 174 Rafael Santana	.05	.02
❑ 175 Mike Pagliarulo	.05	.02
❑ 176 Don Mattingly	.60	.24
❑ 177 Ken Phelps	.05	.02
❑ 178 Steve Sax	.05	.02
❑ 179 Dave Winfield	.10	.04
❑ 180 Stan Jefferson	.05	.02
❑ 181 Rickey Henderson	.25	.10
❑ 182 Bob Brower	.05	.02
❑ 183 Roberto Kelly	.05	.02
❑ 184 Curt Young	.05	.02
❑ 185 Gene Nelson	.05	.02
❑ 186 Bob Welch	.10	.04
❑ 187 Rick Honeycutt	.05	.02
❑ 188 Dave Stewart	.10	.04
❑ 189 Mike Moore	.05	.02
❑ 190 Dennis Eckersley	.15	.06
❑ 191 Eric Plunk	.05	.02

❑ 192	Storm Davis	.05	.02
❑ 193	Terry Steinbach	.10	.04
❑ 194	Ron Hassey	.05	.02
❑ 195	Stan Royer RC	.10	.04
❑ 196	Walt Weiss	.05	.02
❑ 197	Mark McGwire	1.00	.40
❑ 198	Carney Lansford	.10	.04
❑ 199	Glenn Hubbard	.05	.02
❑ 200	Dave Henderson	.05	.02
❑ 201	Jose Canseco	.25	.10
❑ 202	Dave Parker	.10	.04
❑ 203	Scott Bankhead	.05	.02
❑ 204	Tom Niedenfuer	.05	.02
❑ 205	Mark Langston	.05	.02
❑ 206	Erik Hanson RC	.25	.10
❑ 207	Mike Jackson	.05	.02
❑ 208	Dave Valle	.05	.02
❑ 209	Scott Bradley	.05	.02
❑ 210	Harold Reynolds	.10	.04
❑ 211	Tino Martinez RC	2.00	.80
❑ 212	Rich Renteria	.05	.02
❑ 213	Rey Quinones	.05	.02
❑ 214	Jim Presley	.05	.02
❑ 215	Alvin Davis	.05	.02
❑ 216	Edgar Martinez	.25	.10
❑ 217	Darnell Coles	.05	.02
❑ 218	Jeffrey Leonard	.05	.02
❑ 219	Jay Buhner	.10	.04
❑ 220	Ken Griffey Jr. RC	8.00	3.20
❑ 221	Drew Hall	.05	.02
❑ 222	Bobby Witt	.05	.02
❑ 223	Jamie Moyer	.10	.04
❑ 224	Charlie Hough	.10	.04
❑ 225	Nolan Ryan	1.00	.40
❑ 226	Jeff Russell	.05	.02
❑ 227	Jim Sundberg	.10	.04
❑ 228	Julio Franco	.10	.04
❑ 229	Buddy Bell	.10	.04
❑ 230	Scott Fletcher	.05	.02
❑ 231	Jeff Kunkel	.05	.02
❑ 232	Steve Buechele	.05	.02
❑ 233	Monty Fariss	.05	.02
❑ 234	Rick Leach	.05	.02
❑ 235	Ruben Sierra	.05	.02
❑ 236	Cecil Espy	.05	.02
❑ 237	Rafael Palmeiro	.25	.10
❑ 238	Pete Incaviglia	.05	.02
❑ 239	Dave Stieb	.10	.04
❑ 240	Jeff Musselman	.05	.02
❑ 241	Mike Flanagan	.05	.02
❑ 242	Todd Stottlemyre	.05	.02
❑ 243	Jimmy Key	.10	.04
❑ 244	Tony Castillo RC	.10	.04
❑ 245	Alex Sanchez	.05	.02
❑ 246	Tom Henke	.05	.02
❑ 247	John Cerutti	.05	.02
❑ 248	Ernie Whitt	.05	.02
❑ 249	Bob Brenly	.05	.02
❑ 250	Rance Mulliniks	.05	.02
❑ 251	Kelly Gruber	.05	.02
❑ 252	Ed Sprague RC	.25	.10
❑ 253	Fred McGriff	.15	.06
❑ 254	Tony Fernandez	.05	.02
❑ 255	Tom Lawless	.05	.02
❑ 256	George Bell	.10	.04
❑ 257	Jesse Barfield	.10	.04
❑ 258	Roberto Alomar	.15	.06
	Sandy Alomar		
❑ 259	Ken Griffey Jr.	1.00	.40
	Ken Griffey Sr.		
❑ 260	Cal Ripken Jr.	.25	.10
	Cal Ripken Sr.		
❑ 261	Mel Stottlemyre Jr.	.05	.02
	Mel Stottlemyre Sr.		
❑ 262	Zane Smith	.05	.02
❑ 263	Charlie Puleo	.05	.02
❑ 264	Derek Lilliquist RC	.10	.04
❑ 265	Paul Assenmacher	.05	.02
❑ 266	John Smoltz RC	2.00	.80
❑ 267	Tom Glavine	.25	.10
❑ 268	Steve Avery RC	.25	.10
❑ 269	Pete Smith	.05	.02
❑ 270	Jody Davis	.05	.02
❑ 271	Bruce Benedict	.05	.02
❑ 272	Andres Thomas	.05	.02
❑ 273	Gerald Perry	.05	.02
❑ 274	Ron Gant	.10	.04
❑ 275	Darrell Evans	.10	.04
❑ 276	Dale Murphy	.15	.06
❑ 277	Dion James	.05	.02
❑ 278	Lonnie Smith	.05	.02
❑ 279	Geronimo Berroa	.05	.02
❑ 280	Steve Wilson RC	.10	.04
❑ 281	Rick Sutcliffe	.10	.04
❑ 282	Kevin Coffman	.05	.02
❑ 283	Mitch Williams	.05	.02
❑ 284	Greg Maddux	.50	.20
❑ 285	Paul Kilgus	.05	.02
❑ 286	Mike Harkey RC	.10	.04
❑ 287	Lloyd McClendon	.05	.02
❑ 288	Damon Berryhill	.05	.02
❑ 289	Ty Griffin	.05	.02
❑ 290	Ryne Sandberg	.40	.16
❑ 291	Mark Grace	.25	.10
❑ 292	Curt Wilkerson	.05	.02
❑ 293	Vance Law	.05	.02
❑ 294	Shawon Dunston	.05	.02
❑ 295	Jerome Walton RC	.25	.10
❑ 296	Mitch Webster	.05	.02
❑ 297	Dwight Smith RC	.25	.10
❑ 298	Andre Dawson	.10	.04
❑ 299	Jeff Sellers	.05	.02
❑ 300	Jose Rijo	.10	.04
❑ 301	John Franco	.10	.04
❑ 302	Rick Mahler	.05	.02
❑ 303	Ron Robinson	.05	.02
❑ 304	Danny Jackson	.05	.02
❑ 305	Rob Dibble RC	.50	.20
❑ 306	Tom Browning	.05	.02
❑ 307	Bo Diaz	.05	.02
❑ 308	Manny Trillo	.05	.02
❑ 309	Chris Sabo RC *	.40	.16
❑ 310	Ron Oester	.05	.02
❑ 311	Barry Larkin	.15	.06
❑ 312	Todd Benzinger	.05	.02
❑ 313	Paul O'Neill	.15	.06
❑ 314	Kal Daniels	.05	.02
❑ 315	Joel Youngblood	.05	.02
❑ 316	Eric Davis	.10	.04
❑ 317	Dave Smith	.05	.02
❑ 318	Mark Portugal	.05	.02
❑ 319	Brian Meyer	.05	.02
❑ 320	Jim Deshaies	.05	.02
❑ 321	Juan Agosto	.05	.02
❑ 322	Mike Scott	.10	.04
❑ 323	Rick Rhoden	.05	.02
❑ 324	Jim Clancy	.05	.02
❑ 325	Larry Andersen	.05	.02
❑ 326	Alex Trevino	.05	.02
❑ 327	Alan Ashby	.05	.02
❑ 328	Craig Reynolds	.05	.02
❑ 329	Bill Doran	.05	.02
❑ 330	Rafael Ramirez	.05	.02
❑ 331	Glenn Davis	.05	.02
❑ 332	Willie Ansley RC	.10	.04
❑ 333	Gerald Young	.05	.02
❑ 334	Cameron Drew	.05	.02
❑ 335	Jay Howell	.05	.02
❑ 336	Tim Belcher	.05	.02
❑ 337	Fernando Valenzuela	.10	.04
❑ 338	Ricky Horton	.05	.02
❑ 339	Tim Leary	.05	.02
❑ 340	Bill Bene	.05	.02
❑ 341	Orel Hershiser	.10	.04
❑ 342	Mike Scioscia	.10	.04
❑ 343	Rick Dempsey	.05	.02
❑ 344	Willie Randolph	.10	.04
❑ 345	Alfredo Griffin	.05	.02
❑ 346	Eddie Murray	.25	.10
❑ 347	Mickey Hatcher	.05	.02
❑ 348	Mike Sharperson	.05	.02
❑ 349	John Shelby	.05	.02
❑ 350	Mike Marshall	.05	.02
❑ 351	Kirk Gibson	.15	.06
❑ 352	Mike Davis	.05	.02
❑ 353	Bryn Smith	.05	.02
❑ 354	Pascual Perez	.05	.02
❑ 355	Kevin Gross	.05	.02
❑ 356	Andy McGaffigan	.05	.02
❑ 357	Brian Holman RC *	.10	.04
❑ 358	Dave Wainhouse RC	.10	.04
❑ 359	Dennis Martinez	.10	.04
❑ 360	Tim Burke	.05	.02
❑ 361	Nelson Santovenia	.05	.02
❑ 362	Tim Wallach	.05	.02
❑ 363	Spike Owen	.05	.02
❑ 364	Rex Hudler	.05	.02
❑ 365	Andres Galarraga	.10	.04
❑ 366	Otis Nixon	.05	.02
❑ 367	Hubie Brooks	.05	.02
❑ 368	Mike Aldrete	.05	.02
❑ 369	Tim Raines	.10	.04
❑ 370	Dave Martinez	.05	.02
❑ 371	Bob Ojeda	.05	.02
❑ 372	Ron Darling	.10	.04
❑ 373	Wally Whitehurst RC	.10	.04
❑ 374	Randy Myers	.10	.04
❑ 375	David Cone	.10	.04
❑ 376	Dwight Gooden	.10	.04
❑ 377	Sid Fernandez	.05	.02
❑ 378	Dave Proctor	.05	.02
❑ 379	Gary Carter	.10	.04
❑ 380	Keith Miller	.05	.02
❑ 381	Gregg Jefferies	.05	.02
❑ 382	Tim Teufel	.05	.02
❑ 383	Kevin Elster	.05	.02
❑ 384	Dave Magadan	.05	.02
❑ 385	Keith Hernandez	.10	.04
❑ 386	Mookie Wilson	.10	.04
❑ 387	Darryl Strawberry	.10	.04
❑ 388	Kevin McReynolds	.05	.02
❑ 389	Mark Carreon	.05	.02
❑ 390	Jeff Parrett	.05	.02
❑ 391	Mike Maddux	.05	.02
❑ 392	Don Carman	.05	.02
❑ 393	Bruce Ruffin	.05	.02
❑ 394	Ken Howell	.05	.02
❑ 395	Steve Bedrosian	.05	.02
❑ 396	Floyd Youmans	.05	.02
❑ 397	Larry McWilliams	.05	.02
❑ 398	Pat Combs RC *	.10	.04
❑ 399	Steve Lake	.05	.02
❑ 400	Dickie Thon	.05	.02
❑ 401	Ricky Jordan RC *	.25	.10
❑ 402	Mike Schmidt	.50	.20
❑ 403	Tom Herr	.05	.02
❑ 404	Chris James	.05	.02
❑ 405	Juan Samuel	.05	.02
❑ 406	Von Hayes	.05	.02
❑ 407	Ron Jones	.10	.04
❑ 408	Curt Ford	.05	.02
❑ 409	Bob Walk	.05	.02
❑ 410	Jeff D. Robinson	.05	.02
❑ 411	Jim Gott	.05	.02
❑ 412	Scott Medvin	.05	.02
❑ 413	John Smiley	.05	.02
❑ 414	Bob Kipper	.05	.02
❑ 415	Brian Fisher	.05	.02
❑ 416	Doug Drabek	.05	.02
❑ 417	Mike LaValliere	.05	.02
❑ 418	Ken Oberkfell	.05	.02
❑ 419	Sid Bream	.05	.02
❑ 420	Austin Manahan	.05	.02
❑ 421	Jose Lind	.05	.02
❑ 422	Bobby Bonilla	.10	.04
❑ 423	Glenn Wilson	.05	.02
❑ 424	Andy Van Slyke	.15	.06
❑ 425	Gary Redus	.05	.02
❑ 426	Barry Bonds	1.50	.60
❑ 427	Don Heinkel	.05	.02
❑ 428	Ken Dayley	.05	.02
❑ 429	Todd Worrell	.05	.02
❑ 430	Brad DuVall	.05	.02
❑ 431	Jose DeLeon	.05	.02
❑ 432	Joe Magrane	.05	.02
❑ 433	John Ericks	.05	.02
❑ 434	Frank DiPino	.05	.02
❑ 435	Tony Pena	.05	.02
❑ 436	Ozzie Smith	.40	.16
❑ 437	Terry Pendleton	.10	.04
❑ 438	Jose Oquendo	.05	.02
❑ 439	Tim Jones	.05	.02
❑ 440	Pedro Guerrero	.10	.04
❑ 441	Milt Thompson	.05	.02
❑ 442	Willie McGee	.10	.04
❑ 443	Vince Coleman	.05	.02
❑ 444	Tom Brunansky	.05	.02
❑ 445	Walt Terrell	.05	.02

	No.	Player	Nm-Mt	Ex-Mt
❑	446	Eric Show	.05	.02
❑	447	Mark Davis	.05	.02
❑	448	Andy Benes RC	.40	.16
❑	449	Ed Whitson	.05	.02
❑	450	Dennis Rasmussen	.05	.02
❑	451	Bruce Hurst	.05	.02
❑	452	Pat Clements	.05	.02
❑	453	Benito Santiago	.10	.04
❑	454	Sandy Alomar Jr. RC	.40	.16
❑	455	Garry Templeton	.10	.04
❑	456	Jack Clark	.10	.04
❑	457	Tim Flannery	.05	.02
❑	458	Roberto Alomar	.25	.10
❑	459	Carmelo Martinez	.05	.02
❑	460	John Kruk	.10	.04
❑	461	Tony Gwynn	.30	.12
❑	462	Jerald Clark RC	.10	.04
❑	463	Don Robinson	.05	.02
❑	464	Craig Lefferts	.05	.02
❑	465	Kelly Downs	.05	.02
❑	466	Rick Reuschel	.10	.04
❑	467	Scott Garrelts	.05	.02
❑	468	Wil Tejada	.05	.02
❑	469	Kirt Manwaring	.05	.02
❑	470	Terry Kennedy	.05	.02
❑	471	Jose Uribe	.05	.02
❑	472	Royce Clayton RC	.40	.16
❑	473	Robby Thompson	.05	.02
❑	474	Kevin Mitchell	.10	.04
❑	475	Ernie Riles	.05	.02
❑	476	Will Clark	.15	.06
❑	477	Donell Nixon	.05	.02
❑	478	Candy Maldonado	.05	.02
❑	479	Tracy Jones	.05	.02
❑	480	Brett Butler	.10	.04
❑	481	Checklist 1-121	.05	.02
❑	482	Checklist 122-242	.05	.02
❑	483	Checklist 243-363	.05	.02
❑	484	Checklist 364-484	.05	.02

1990 Bowman

	Nm-Mt	Ex-Mt
COMPLETE SET (528)	25.00	7.50
COMP.FACT.SET (528)	25.00	7.50

	No.	Player	Nm-Mt	Ex-Mt
❑	1	Tommy Greene RC	.10	.03
❑	2	Tom Glavine	.15	.04
❑	3	Andy Nezelek	.05	.02
❑	4	Mike Stanton RC	.25	.07
❑	5	Rick Luecken	.05	.02
❑	6	Kent Mercker RC	.25	.07
❑	7	Derek Lilliquist	.05	.02
❑	8	Charlie Leibrandt	.05	.02
❑	9	Steve Avery	.05	.02
❑	10	John Smoltz	.25	.07
❑	11	Mark Lemke	.05	.02
❑	12	Lonnie Smith	.05	.02
❑	13	Oddibe McDowell	.05	.02
❑	14	Tyler Houston RC	.25	.07
❑	15	Jeff Blauser	.05	.02
❑	16	Ernie Whitt	.05	.02
❑	17	Alexis Infante	.05	.02
❑	18	Jim Presley	.05	.02
❑	19	Dale Murphy	.15	.04
❑	20	Nick Esasky	.05	.02
❑	21	Rick Sutcliffe	.10	.03
❑	22	Mike Bielecki	.05	.02
❑	23	Steve Wilson	.05	.02
❑	24	Kevin Blankenship	.05	.02
❑	25	Mitch Williams	.05	.02
❑	26	Dean Wilkins	.05	.02
❑	27	Greg Maddux	.40	.12
❑	28	Mike Harkey	.05	.02
❑	29	Mark Grace	.15	.04
❑	30	Ryne Sandberg	.40	.12
❑	31	Greg Smith	.05	.02
❑	32	Dwight Smith	.05	.02
❑	33	Damon Berryhill	.05	.02
❑	34	E.Cunningham UER RC	.10	.03
		(Errant * by the word "in")		
❑	35	Jerome Walton	.05	.02
❑	36	Lloyd McClendon	.05	.02
❑	37	Ty Griffin	.05	.02
❑	38	Shawon Dunston	.05	.02
❑	39	Andre Dawson	.10	.03
❑	40	Luis Salazar	.05	.02
❑	41	Tim Layana	.05	.02
❑	42	Rob Dibble	.10	.03
❑	43	Tom Browning	.05	.02
❑	44	Danny Jackson	.05	.02
❑	45	Jose Rijo	.05	.02
❑	46	Scott Scudder	.05	.02
❑	47	Randy Myers UER	.10	.03
		(Career ERA .274& should be 2.74)		
❑	48	Brian Lane RC	.10	.03
❑	49	Paul O'Neill	.15	.04
❑	50	Barry Larkin	.15	.04
❑	51	Reggie Jefferson RC	.25	.07
❑	52	Jeff Branson RC**	.10	.03
❑	53	Chris Sabo	.05	.02
❑	54	Joe Oliver	.05	.02
❑	55	Todd Benzinger	.05	.02
❑	56	Rolando Roomes	.05	.02
❑	57	Hal Morris	.05	.02
❑	58	Eric Davis	.10	.03
❑	59	Scott Bryant	.05	.02
❑	60	Ken Griffey Sr.	.10	.03
❑	61	Darryl Kile RC	1.00	.30
❑	62	Dave Smith	.05	.02
❑	63	Mark Portugal	.05	.02
❑	64	Jeff Juden RC	.10	.03
❑	65	Bill Gullickson	.05	.02
❑	66	Danny Darwin	.05	.02
❑	67	Larry Andersen	.05	.02
❑	68	Jose Cano	.05	.02
❑	69	Dan Schatzeder	.05	.02
❑	70	Jim Deshaies	.05	.02
❑	71	Mike Scott	.05	.02
❑	72	Gerald Young	.05	.02
❑	73	Ken Caminiti	.10	.03
❑	74	Ken Oberkfell	.05	.02
❑	75	Dave Rohde	.05	.02
❑	76	Bill Doran	.05	.02
❑	77	Andujar Cedeno RC	.10	.03
❑	78	Craig Biggio	.25	.07
❑	79	Karl Rhodes RC	.25	.07
❑	80	Glenn Davis	.05	.02
❑	81	Eric Anthony RC	.10	.03
❑	82	John Wetteland	.25	.07
❑	83	Jay Howell	.05	.02
❑	84	Orel Hershiser	.10	.03
❑	85	Tim Belcher	.05	.02
❑	86	Kiki Jones	.05	.02
❑	87	Mike Hartley	.05	.02
❑	88	Ramon Martinez	.05	.02
❑	89	Mike Scioscia	.05	.02
❑	90	Willie Randolph	.10	.03
❑	91	Juan Samuel	.05	.02
❑	92	Jose Offerman RC	.25	.07
❑	93	Dave Hansen RC	.25	.07
❑	94	Jeff Hamilton	.05	.02
❑	95	Alfredo Griffin	.05	.02
❑	96	Tom Goodwin RC	.25	.07
❑	97	Kirk Gibson	.15	.04
❑	98	Jose Vizcaino RC	.25	.07
❑	99	Kal Daniels	.05	.02
❑	100	Hubie Brooks	.05	.02
❑	101	Eddie Murray	.25	.07
❑	102	Dennis Boyd	.05	.02
❑	103	Tim Burke	.05	.02
❑	104	Bill Sampen	.05	.02
❑	105	Brett Gideon	.05	.02
❑	106	Mark Gardner RC	.10	.03
❑	107	Howard Farmer	.05	.02
❑	108	Mel Rojas RC	.10	.03
❑	109	Kevin Gross	.05	.02
❑	110	Dave Schmidt	.05	.02
❑	111	Dennis Martinez	.10	.03
❑	112	Jerry Goff	.05	.02
❑	113	Andres Galarraga	.10	.03
❑	114	Tim Wallach	.05	.02
❑	115	Marquis Grissom RC	.50	.15
❑	116	Spike Owen	.05	.02
❑	117	Larry Walker RC	1.00	.30
❑	118	Tim Raines	.10	.03
❑	119	Delino DeShields RC	.25	.07
❑	120	Tom Foley	.05	.02
❑	121	Dave Martinez	.05	.02
❑	122	Frank Viola UER	.05	.02
		(Career ERA .384 should be 3.84)		
❑	123	Julio Valera RC	.05	.02
❑	124	Alejandro Pena	.05	.02
❑	125	David Cone	.10	.03
❑	126	Dwight Gooden	.10	.03
❑	127	Kevin D. Brown	.05	.02
❑	128	John Franco	.10	.03
❑	129	Terry Bross	.05	.02
❑	130	Blaine Beatty	.05	.02
❑	131	Sid Fernandez	.05	.02
❑	132	Mike Marshall	.05	.02
❑	133	Howard Johnson	.05	.02
❑	134	Jaime Roseboro	.05	.02
❑	135	Alan Zinter RC	.10	.03
❑	136	Keith Miller	.05	.02
❑	137	Kevin Elster	.05	.02
❑	138	Kevin McReynolds	.05	.02
❑	139	Barry Lyons	.05	.02
❑	140	Gregg Jefferies	.10	.03
❑	141	Darryl Strawberry	.10	.03
❑	142	Todd Hundley RC	.25	.07
❑	143	Scott Service	.05	.02
❑	144	Chuck Malone	.05	.02
❑	145	Steve Ontiveros	.05	.02
❑	146	Roger McDowell	.05	.02
❑	147	Ken Howell	.05	.02
❑	148	Pat Combs	.05	.02
❑	149	Jeff Parrett	.05	.02
❑	150	Chuck McElroy RC	.10	.03
❑	151	Jason Grimsley RC	.10	.03
❑	152	Len Dykstra	.10	.03
❑	153	M.Morandini RC	.25	.07
❑	154	John Kruk	.10	.03
❑	155	Dickie Thon	.05	.02
❑	156	Ricky Jordan	.05	.02
❑	157	Jeff Jackson RC	.10	.03
❑	158	Darren Daulton	.10	.03
❑	159	Tom Herr	.05	.02
❑	160	Von Hayes	.05	.02
❑	161	Dave Hollins RC	.25	.07
❑	162	Carmelo Martinez	.05	.02
❑	163	Bob Walk	.05	.02
❑	164	Doug Drabek	.05	.02
❑	165	Walt Terrell	.05	.02
❑	166	Bill Landrum	.05	.02
❑	167	Scott Ruskin	.05	.02
❑	168	Bob Patterson	.05	.02
❑	169	Bobby Bonilla	.10	.03
❑	170	Jose Lind	.05	.02
❑	171	Andy Van Slyke	.15	.04
❑	172	Mike LaValliere	.05	.02
❑	173	Willie Greene RC	.10	.03
❑	174	Jay Bell	.10	.03
❑	175	Sid Bream	.05	.02
❑	176	Tom Prince	.05	.02
❑	177	Wally Backman	.05	.02
❑	178	Moises Alou RC	.75	.23
❑	179	Steve Carter	.05	.02
❑	180	Gary Redus	.05	.02
❑	181	Barry Bonds	1.00	.30
❑	182	Don Slaught UER	.05	.02
		(Card back shows headings for a pitcher)		
❑	183	Joe Magrane	.05	.02
❑	184	Bryn Smith	.05	.02
❑	185	Todd Worrell	.05	.02
❑	186	Jose DeLeon	.05	.02

❑ 187 Frank DiPino .05 .02
❑ 188 John Tudor .05 .02
❑ 189 Howard Hilton .05 .02
❑ 190 John Ericks .05 .02
❑ 191 Ken Dayley .05 .02
❑ 192 Ray Lankford RC .50 .15
❑ 193 Todd Zeile .10 .03
❑ 194 Willie McGee .10 .03
❑ 195 Ozzie Smith .40 .12
❑ 196 Milt Thompson .05 .02
❑ 197 Terry Pendleton .10 .03
❑ 198 Vince Coleman .05 .02
❑ 199 Paul Coleman RC .10 .03
❑ 200 Jose Oquendo .05 .02
❑ 201 Pedro Guerrero .05 .02
❑ 202 Tom Brunansky .05 .02
❑ 203 Roger Smithberg .05 .02
❑ 204 Eddie Whitson .05 .02
❑ 205 Dennis Rasmussen .05 .02
❑ 206 Craig Lefferts .05 .02
❑ 207 Andy Benes .10 .03
❑ 208 Bruce Hurst .05 .02
❑ 209 Eric Show .05 .02
❑ 210 Rafael Valdez .05 .02
❑ 211 Joey Cora .10 .03
❑ 212 Thomas Howard .05 .02
❑ 213 Rob Nelson .05 .02
❑ 214 Jack Clark .10 .03
❑ 215 Garry Templeton .05 .02
❑ 216 Fred Lynn .05 .02
❑ 217 Tony Gwynn .30 .09
❑ 218 Benito Santiago .10 .03
❑ 219 Mike Pagliarulo .05 .02
❑ 220 Joe Carter .10 .03
❑ 221 Roberto Alomar .15 .04
❑ 222 Bip Roberts .05 .02
❑ 223 Rick Reuschel .05 .02
❑ 224 Russ Swan .05 .02
❑ 225 Eric Gunderson .05 .02
❑ 226 Steve Bedrosian .05 .02
❑ 227 Mike Remlinger .05 .02
❑ 228 Scott Garrelts .05 .02
❑ 229 Ernie Camacho .05 .02
❑ 230 Andres Santana RC .10 .03
❑ 231 Will Clark .15 .04
❑ 232 Kevin Mitchell .05 .02
❑ 233 Robby Thompson .05 .02
❑ 234 Bill Bathe .05 .02
❑ 235 Tony Perezchica .05 .02
❑ 236 Gary Carter .10 .03
❑ 237 Brett Butler .10 .03
❑ 238 Matt Williams .10 .03
❑ 239 Earnie Riles .05 .02
❑ 240 Kevin Bass .05 .02
❑ 241 Terry Kennedy .05 .02
❑ 242 Steve Hosey RC .10 .03
❑ 243 Ben McDonald RC .25 .07
❑ 244 Jeff Ballard .05 .02
❑ 245 Joe Price .05 .02
❑ 246 Curt Schilling 1.00 .30
❑ 247 Pete Harnisch .05 .02
❑ 248 Mark Williamson .05 .02
❑ 249 Gregg Olson .10 .03
❑ 250 Chris Myers .05 .02
❑ 251 David Segui RC ERR .50 .15
(Missing vital stats at top of card back under name)
❑ 251B David Segui COR RC .50 .15
❑ 252 Joe Orsulak .05 .02
❑ 253 Craig Worthington .05 .02
❑ 254 Mickey Tettleton .05 .02
❑ 255 Cal Ripken .75 .23
❑ 256 Bill Ripken .05 .02
❑ 257 Randy Milligan .05 .02
❑ 258 Brady Anderson .10 .03
❑ 259 Chris Hoiles RC UER .25 .07
Baltimore is spelled Balitmore
❑ 260 Mike Devereaux .05 .02
❑ 261 Phil Bradley .05 .02
❑ 262 Leo Gomez RC .10 .03
❑ 263 Lee Smith .10 .03
❑ 264 Mike Rochford .05 .02
❑ 265 Jeff Reardon .10 .03
❑ 266 Wes Gardner .05 .02
❑ 267 Mike Boddicker .05 .02
❑ 268 Roger Clemens .50 .15
❑ 269 Rob Murphy .05 .02
❑ 270 Mickey Pina .05 .02
❑ 271 Tony Pena .05 .02
❑ 272 Jody Reed .05 .02
❑ 273 Kevin Romine .05 .02
❑ 274 Mike Greenwell .05 .02
❑ 275 Maurice Vaughn RC 1.00 .30
❑ 276 Danny Heep .05 .02
❑ 277 Scott Cooper RC .10 .03
❑ 278 Greg Blosser RC .10 .03
❑ 279 Dwight Evans UER .15 .04
(* by "1990 Team Breakdown")
❑ 280 Ellis Burks .15 .04
❑ 281 Wade Boggs .15 .04
❑ 282 Marty Barrett .05 .02
❑ 283 Kirk McCaskill .05 .02
❑ 284 Mark Langston .05 .02
❑ 285 Bert Blyleven .10 .03
❑ 286 Mike Fetters RC .25 .07
❑ 287 Kyle Abbott .05 .02
❑ 288 Jim Abbott .15 .04
❑ 289 Chuck Finley .10 .03
❑ 290 Gary DiSarcina RC .25 .07
❑ 291 Dick Schofield .05 .02
❑ 292 Devon White .10 .03
❑ 293 Bobby Rose .05 .02
❑ 294 Brian Downing .05 .02
❑ 295 Lance Parrish .05 .02
❑ 296 Jack Howell .05 .02
❑ 297 Claudell Washington .05 .02
❑ 298 John Orton RC .10 .03
❑ 299 Wally Joyner .10 .03
❑ 300 Lee Stevens .10 .03
❑ 301 Chili Davis .10 .03
❑ 302 Johnny Ray .05 .02
❑ 303 Greg Hibbard RC .10 .03
❑ 304 Eric King .05 .02
❑ 305 Jack McDowell .05 .02
❑ 306 Bobby Thigpen .05 .02
❑ 307 Adam Peterson .05 .02
❑ 308 Scott Radinsky RC .25 .07
❑ 309 Wayne Edwards .05 .02
❑ 310 Melido Perez .05 .02
❑ 311 Robin Ventura .25 .07
❑ 312 Sammy Sosa RC 4.00 1.20
❑ 313 Dan Pasqua .05 .02
❑ 314 Carlton Fisk .15 .04
❑ 315 Ozzie Guillen .10 .03
❑ 316 Ivan Calderon .05 .02
❑ 317 Daryl Boston .05 .02
❑ 318 Craig Grebeck RC .25 .07
❑ 319 Scott Fletcher .05 .02
❑ 320 Frank Thomas RC 2.00 .60
❑ 321 Steve Lyons .05 .02
❑ 322 Carlos Martinez .05 .02
❑ 323 Joe Skalski .05 .02
❑ 324 Tom Candiotti .05 .02
❑ 325 Greg Swindell .05 .02
❑ 326 Steve Olin RC .25 .07
❑ 327 Kevin Wickander .05 .02
❑ 328 Doug Jones .05 .02
❑ 329 Jeff Shaw .05 .02
❑ 330 Kevin Bearse .05 .02
❑ 331 Dion James .05 .02
❑ 332 Jerry Browne .05 .02
❑ 333 Joey Belle .25 .07
❑ 334 Felix Fermin .05 .02
❑ 335 Candy Maldonado .05 .02
❑ 336 Cory Snyder .05 .02
❑ 337 Sandy Alomar Jr. .10 .03
❑ 338 Mark Lewis .05 .02
❑ 339 Carlos Baerga RC .25 .07
❑ 340 Chris James .05 .02
❑ 341 Brook Jacoby .05 .02
❑ 342 Keith Hernandez .10 .03
❑ 343 Frank Tanana .05 .02
❑ 344 Scott Aldred .05 .02
❑ 345 Mike Henneman .05 .02
❑ 346 Steve Wapnick .05 .02
❑ 347 Greg Gohr RC .10 .03
❑ 348 Eric Stone .05 .02
❑ 349 Brian DuBois .05 .02
❑ 350 Kevin Ritz .05 .02
❑ 351 Rico Brogna .25 .07
❑ 352 Mike Heath .05 .02
❑ 353 Alan Trammell .10 .03
❑ 354 Chet Lemon .05 .02
❑ 355 Dave Bergman .05 .02
❑ 356 Lou Whitaker .10 .03
❑ 357 Cecil Fielder UER .10 .03
* by 1990 Team Breakdown
❑ 358 Milt Cuyler RC .10 .03
❑ 359 Tony Phillips .05 .02
❑ 360 Travis Fryman RC .50 .15
❑ 361 Ed Romero .05 .02
❑ 362 Lloyd Moseby .05 .02
❑ 363 Mark Gubicza .05 .02
❑ 364 Bret Saberhagen .10 .03
❑ 365 Tom Gordon .10 .03
❑ 366 Steve Farr .05 .02
❑ 367 Kevin Appier .10 .03
❑ 368 Storm Davis .05 .02
❑ 369 Mark Davis .05 .02
❑ 370 Jeff Montgomery .10 .03
❑ 371 Frank White .10 .03
❑ 372 Brent Mayne RC .25 .07
❑ 373 Bob Boone .10 .03
❑ 374 Jim Eisenreich .05 .02
❑ 375 Danny Tartabull .05 .02
❑ 376 Kurt Stillwell .05 .02
❑ 377 Bill Pecota .05 .02
❑ 378 Bo Jackson .25 .07
❑ 379 Bob Hamelin RC .25 .07
❑ 380 Kevin Seitzer .05 .02
❑ 381 Rey Palacios .05 .02
❑ 382 George Brett .60 .18
❑ 383 Gerald Perry .05 .02
❑ 384 Teddy Higuera .05 .02
❑ 385 Tom Filer .05 .02
❑ 386 Dan Plesac .05 .02
❑ 387 Cal Eldred RC .25 .07
❑ 388 Jaime Navarro .05 .02
❑ 389 Chris Bosio .05 .02
❑ 390 Randy Veres .05 .02
❑ 391 Gary Sheffield .25 .07
❑ 392 George Canale .05 .02
❑ 393 B.J. Surhoff .10 .03
❑ 394 Tim McIntosh .05 .02
❑ 395 Greg Brock .05 .02
❑ 396 Greg Vaughn .05 .02
❑ 397 Darryl Hamilton .05 .02
❑ 398 Dave Parker .10 .03
❑ 399 Paul Molitor .15 .04
❑ 400 Jim Gantner .05 .02
❑ 401 Rob Deer .05 .02
❑ 402 Billy Spiers .05 .02
❑ 403 Glenn Braggs .05 .02
❑ 404 Robin Yount .40 .12
❑ 405 Rick Aguilera .10 .03
❑ 406 Johnny Ard .05 .02
❑ 407 Kevin Tapani RC .25 .07
❑ 408 Park Pittman .05 .02
❑ 409 Allan Anderson .05 .02
❑ 410 Juan Berenguer .05 .02
❑ 411 Willie Banks RC .10 .03
❑ 412 Rich Yett .05 .02
❑ 413 Dave West .05 .02
❑ 414 Greg Gagne .05 .02
❑ 415 Chuck Knoblauch RC .50 .15
❑ 416 Randy Bush .05 .02
❑ 417 Gary Gaetti .10 .03
❑ 418 Kent Hrbek .10 .03
❑ 419 Al Newman .05 .02
❑ 420 Danny Gladden .05 .02
❑ 421 Paul Sorrento RC .25 .07
❑ 422 Derek Parks RC .10 .03
❑ 423 Scott Leius RC .10 .03
❑ 424 Kirby Puckett .25 .07
❑ 425 Willie Smith .05 .02
❑ 426 Dave Righetti .05 .02
❑ 427 Jeff D. Robinson .05 .02
❑ 428 Alan Mills RC .10 .03
❑ 429 Tim Leary .05 .02
❑ 430 Pascual Perez .05 .02
❑ 431 Alvaro Espinoza .05 .02
❑ 432 Dave Winfield .10 .03
❑ 433 Jesse Barfield .05 .02
❑ 434 Randy Velarde .05 .02
❑ 435 Rick Cerone .05 .02
❑ 436 Steve Balboni .05 .02

Card	Player	Nm-Mt	Ex-Mt
❑ 437	Mel Hall	.05	.02
❑ 438	Bob Geren	.05	.02
❑ 439	Bernie Williams RC	1.50	.45
❑ 440	Kevin Maas RC	.25	.07
❑ 441	Mike Blowers RC	.10	.03
❑ 442	Steve Sax	.05	.02
❑ 443	Don Mattingly	.60	.18
❑ 444	Roberto Kelly	.05	.02
❑ 445	Mike Moore	.05	.02
❑ 446	Reggie Harris RC	.10	.03
❑ 447	Scott Sanderson	.05	.02
❑ 448	Dave Otto	.05	.02
❑ 449	Dave Stewart	.10	.03
❑ 450	Rick Honeycutt	.05	.02
❑ 451	Dennis Eckersley	.10	.03
❑ 452	Carney Lansford	.10	.03
❑ 453	Scott Hemond RC	.10	.03
❑ 454	Mark McGwire	.60	.18
❑ 455	Felix Jose	.05	.02
❑ 456	Terry Steinbach	.05	.02
❑ 457	Rickey Henderson	.25	.07
❑ 458	Dave Henderson	.05	.02
❑ 459	Mike Gallego	.05	.02
❑ 460	Jose Canseco	.15	.04
❑ 461	Walt Weiss	.05	.02
❑ 462	Ken Phelps	.05	.02
❑ 463	Darren Lewis RC	.10	.03
❑ 464	Ron Hassey	.05	.02
❑ 465	Roger Salkeld RC	.10	.03
❑ 466	Scott Bankhead	.05	.02
❑ 467	Keith Comstock	.05	.02
❑ 468	Randy Johnson	.50	.15
❑ 469	Erik Hanson	.05	.02
❑ 470	Mike Schooler	.05	.02
❑ 471	Gary Eave	.05	.02
❑ 472	Jeffrey Leonard	.05	.02
❑ 473	Dave Valle	.05	.02
❑ 474	Omar Vizquel	.25	.07
❑ 475	Pete O'Brien	.05	.02
❑ 476	Henry Cotto	.05	.02
❑ 477	Jay Buhner	.10	.03
❑ 478	Harold Reynolds	.10	.03
❑ 479	Alvin Davis	.05	.02
❑ 480	Darnell Coles	.05	.02
❑ 481	Ken Griffey Jr.	.75	.23
❑ 482	Greg Briley	.05	.02
❑ 483	Scott Bradley	.05	.02
❑ 484	Tino Martinez	.50	.15
❑ 485	Jeff Russell	.05	.02
❑ 486	Nolan Ryan	1.00	.30
❑ 487	Robb Nen RC	.50	.15
❑ 488	Kevin Brown	.10	.03
❑ 489	Brian Bohanon RC	.10	.03
❑ 490	Ruben Sierra	.05	.02
❑ 491	Pete Incaviglia	.05	.02
❑ 492	Juan Gonzalez RC	1.00	.30
❑ 493	Steve Buechele	.05	.02
❑ 494	Scott Coolbaugh	.05	.02
❑ 495	Geno Petralli	.05	.02
❑ 496	Rafael Palmeiro	.15	.04
❑ 497	Julio Franco	.10	.03
❑ 498	Gary Pettis	.05	.02
❑ 499	Donald Harris	.05	.02
❑ 500	Monty Fariss	.05	.02
❑ 501	Harold Baines	.10	.03
❑ 502	Cecil Espy	.05	.02
❑ 503	Jack Daugherty	.05	.02
❑ 504	Willie Blair RC	.10	.03
❑ 505	Dave Stieb	.10	.03
❑ 506	Tom Henke	.05	.02
❑ 507	John Cerutti	.05	.02
❑ 508	Paul Kilgus	.05	.02
❑ 509	Jimmy Key	.10	.03
❑ 510	John Olerud RC	1.00	.30
❑ 511	Ed Sprague	.10	.03
❑ 512	Manuel Lee	.05	.02
❑ 513	Fred McGriff	.25	.07
❑ 514	Glenallen Hill	.05	.02
❑ 515	George Bell	.05	.02
❑ 516	Mookie Wilson	.10	.03
❑ 517	Luis Sojo RC	.25	.07
❑ 518	Nelson Liriano	.05	.02
❑ 519	Kelly Gruber	.05	.02
❑ 520	Greg Myers	.05	.02
❑ 521	Pat Borders	.05	.02
❑ 522	Junior Felix	.05	.02
❑ 523	Eddie Zosky RC	.10	.03
❑ 524	Tony Fernandez	.05	.02
❑ 525	Checklist 1-132 UER (No copyright mark on the back)	.05	.02
❑ 526	Checklist 133-264	.05	.02
❑ 527	Checklist 265-396	.05	.02
❑ 528	Checklist 397-528	.05	.02

1991 Bowman

	Nm-Mt	Ex-Mt
COMPLETE SET (704)	40.00	12.00
COMP.FACT.SET (704)	40.00	12.00

Card	Player	Nm-Mt	Ex-Mt
❑ 1	Rod Carew I	.15	.04
❑ 2	Rod Carew II	.15	.04
❑ 3	Rod Carew III	.15	.04
❑ 4	Rod Carew IV	.15	.04
❑ 5	Rod Carew V	.15	.04
❑ 6	Willie Fraser	.05	.02
❑ 7	John Olerud	.10	.03
❑ 8	William Suero	.05	.02
❑ 9	Roberto Alomar	.15	.04
❑ 10	Todd Stottlemyre	.05	.02
❑ 11	Joe Carter	.10	.03
❑ 12	Steve Karsay RC	.50	.15
❑ 13	Mark Whiten	.05	.02
❑ 14	Pat Borders	.05	.02
❑ 15	Mike Timlin RC	1.00	.30
❑ 16	Tom Henke	.05	.02
❑ 17	Eddie Zosky	.05	.02
❑ 18	Kelly Gruber	.05	.02
❑ 19	Jimmy Key	.10	.03
❑ 20	Jerry Schunk	.05	.02
❑ 21	Manuel Lee	.05	.02
❑ 22	Dave Stieb	.05	.02
❑ 23	Pat Hentgen RC	.50	.15
❑ 24	Glenallen Hill	.05	.02
❑ 25	Rene Gonzales	.05	.02
❑ 26	Ed Sprague	.05	.02
❑ 27	Ken Dayley	.05	.02
❑ 28	Pat Tabler	.05	.02
❑ 29	Denis Boucher RC	.15	.04
❑ 30	Devon White	.10	.03
❑ 31	Dante Bichette	.10	.03
❑ 32	Paul Molitor	.15	.04
❑ 33	Greg Vaughn	.05	.02
❑ 34	Dan Plesac	.05	.02
❑ 35	Chris George RC	.15	.04
❑ 36	Tim McIntosh	.05	.02
❑ 37	Franklin Stubbs	.05	.02
❑ 38	Bo Dodson RC	.15	.04
❑ 39	Ron Robinson	.05	.02
❑ 40	Ed Nunez	.05	.02
❑ 41	Greg Brock	.05	.02
❑ 42	Jaime Navarro	.05	.02
❑ 43	Chris Bosio	.05	.02
❑ 44	B.J. Surhoff	.10	.03
❑ 45	Chris Johnson	.05	.02
❑ 46	Willie Randolph	.10	.03
❑ 47	Narciso Elvira	.05	.02
❑ 48	Jim Gantner	.05	.02
❑ 49	Kevin Brown	.05	.02
❑ 50	Julio Machado	.05	.02
❑ 51	Chuck Crim	.05	.02
❑ 52	Gary Sheffield	.10	.03
❑ 53	Angel Miranda RC	.15	.04
❑ 54	Ted Higuera	.05	.02
❑ 55	Robin Yount	.40	.12
❑ 56	Cal Eldred	.05	.02
❑ 57	Sandy Alomar Jr.	.05	.02
❑ 58	Greg Swindell	.05	.02
❑ 59	Brook Jacoby	.05	.02
❑ 60	Efrain Valdez	.05	.02
❑ 61	Ever Magallanes	.05	.02
❑ 62	Tom Candiotti	.05	.02
❑ 63	Eric King	.05	.02
❑ 64	Alex Cole	.05	.02
❑ 65	Charles Nagy	.05	.02
❑ 66	Mitch Webster	.05	.02
❑ 67	Chris James	.05	.02
❑ 68	Jim Thome RC	3.00	.90
❑ 69	Carlos Baerga	.05	.02
❑ 70	Mark Lewis	.05	.02
❑ 71	Jerry Browne	.05	.02
❑ 72	Jesse Orosco	.05	.02
❑ 73	Mike Huff	.05	.02
❑ 74	Jose Escobar	.05	.02
❑ 75	Jeff Manto	.05	.02
❑ 76	Turner Ward RC	.15	.04
❑ 77	Doug Jones	.05	.02
❑ 78	Bruce Egloff	.05	.02
❑ 79	Tim Costo RC	.15	.04
❑ 80	Beau Allred	.05	.02
❑ 81	Albert Belle	.10	.03
❑ 82	John Farrell	.05	.02
❑ 83	Glenn Davis	.05	.02
❑ 84	Joe Orsulak	.05	.02
❑ 85	Mark Williamson	.05	.02
❑ 86	Ben McDonald	.05	.02
❑ 87	Billy Ripken	.05	.02
❑ 88	Leo Gomez UER (Baltimore is spelled Balitmore)	.05	.02
❑ 89	Bob Melvin	.05	.02
❑ 90	Jeff M. Robinson	.05	.02
❑ 91	Jose Mesa	.05	.02
❑ 92	Gregg Olson	.05	.02
❑ 93	Mike Devereaux	.05	.02
❑ 94	Luis Mercedes RC	.15	.04
❑ 95	Arthur Rhodes RC	.50	.15
❑ 96	Juan Bell	.05	.02
❑ 97	Mike Mussina RC	3.00	.90
❑ 98	Jeff Ballard	.05	.02
❑ 99	Chris Hoiles	.05	.02
❑ 100	Brady Anderson	.10	.03
❑ 101	Bob Milacki	.05	.02
❑ 102	David Segui	.05	.02
❑ 103	Dwight Evans	.15	.04
❑ 104	Cal Ripken	.75	.23
❑ 105	Mike Linskey	.05	.02
❑ 106	Jeff Tackett RC	.15	.04
❑ 107	Jeff Reardon	.10	.03
❑ 108	Dana Kiecker	.05	.02
❑ 109	Ellis Burks	.10	.03
❑ 110	Dave Owen	.05	.02
❑ 111	Danny Darwin	.05	.02
❑ 112	Mo Vaughn	.10	.03
❑ 113	Jeff McNeely RC	.15	.04
❑ 114	Tom Bolton	.05	.02
❑ 115	Greg Blosser	.05	.02
❑ 116	Mike Greenwell	.05	.02
❑ 117	Phil Plantier RC	.15	.04
❑ 118	Roger Clemens	.50	.15
❑ 119	John Marzano	.05	.02
❑ 120	Jody Reed	.05	.02
❑ 121	Scott Taylor RC	.15	.04
❑ 122	Jack Clark	.10	.03
❑ 123	Derek Livernois	.05	.02
❑ 124	Tony Pena	.05	.02
❑ 125	Tom Brunansky	.05	.02
❑ 126	Carlos Quintana	.05	.02
❑ 127	Tim Naehring	.05	.02
❑ 128	Matt Young	.05	.02
❑ 129	Wade Boggs	.15	.04
❑ 130	Kevin Morton	.05	.02
❑ 131	Pete Incaviglia	.05	.02
❑ 132	Rob Deer	.05	.02
❑ 133	Bill Gullickson	.05	.02
❑ 134	Rico Brogna	.05	.02
❑ 135	Lloyd Moseby	.05	.02
❑ 136	Cecil Fielder	.10	.03
❑ 137	Tony Phillips	.05	.02
❑ 138	Mark Leiter RC	.15	.04

❑ 139 John Cerutti .05 .02
❑ 140 Mickey Tettleton .05 .02
❑ 141 Milt Cuyler .05 .02
❑ 142 Greg Gohr .05 .02
❑ 143 Tony Bernazard .05 .02
❑ 144 Dan Gakeler .05 .02
❑ 145 Travis Fryman .10 .03
❑ 146 Dan Petry .05 .02
❑ 147 Scott Aldred .05 .02
❑ 148 John DeSilva .05 .02
❑ 149 Rusty Meacham RC .15 .04
❑ 150 Lou Whitaker .10 .03
❑ 151 Dave Haas .05 .02
❑ 152 Luis de los Santos .05 .02
❑ 153 Ivan Cruz .05 .02
❑ 154 Alan Trammell .10 .03
❑ 155 Pat Kelly RC .05 .02
❑ 156 Carl Everett RC 1.50 .45
❑ 157 Greg Cadaret .05 .02
❑ 158 Kevin Maas .05 .02
❑ 159 Jeff Johnson .05 .02
❑ 160 Willie Smith .05 .02
❑ 161 Gerald Williams RC .50 .15
❑ 162 Mike Humphreys RC .15 .04
❑ 163 Alvaro Espinoza .05 .02
❑ 164 Matt Nokes .05 .02
❑ 165 Wade Taylor .05 .02
❑ 166 Roberto Kelly .05 .02
❑ 167 John Habyan .05 .02
❑ 168 Steve Farr .05 .02
❑ 169 Jesse Barfield .05 .02
❑ 170 Steve Sax .05 .02
❑ 171 Jim Leyritz .05 .02
❑ 172 Robert Eenhoorn RC .15 .04
❑ 173 Bernie Williams .25 .07
❑ 174 Scott Lusader .05 .02
❑ 175 Torey Lovullo .05 .02
❑ 176 Chuck Cary .05 .02
❑ 177 Scott Sanderson .05 .02
❑ 178 Don Mattingly .60 .18
❑ 179 Mel Hall .05 .02
❑ 180 Juan Gonzalez .25 .07
❑ 181 Hensley Meulens .05 .02
❑ 182 Jose Offerman .05 .02
❑ 183 Jeff Bagwell RC 4.00 1.20
❑ 184 Jeff Conine RC 1.00 .30
❑ 185 Henry Rodriguez RC .50 .15
❑ 186 Jimmie Reese CO .10 .03
❑ 187 Kyle Abbott .05 .02
❑ 188 Lance Parrish .10 .03
❑ 189 Rafael Montalvo .05 .02
❑ 190 Floyd Bannister .05 .02
❑ 191 Dick Schofield .05 .02
❑ 192 Scott Lewis .05 .02
❑ 193 Jeff D. Robinson .05 .02
❑ 194 Kent Anderson .05 .02
❑ 195 Wally Joyner .10 .03
❑ 196 Chuck Finley .10 .03
❑ 197 Luis Sojo .05 .02
❑ 198 Jeff Richardson .05 .02
❑ 199 Dave Parker .10 .03
❑ 200 Jim Abbott .15 .04
❑ 201 Junior Felix .05 .02
❑ 202 Mark Langston .05 .02
❑ 203 Tim Salmon RC 1.50 .45
❑ 204 Cliff Young .05 .02
❑ 205 Scott Bailes .05 .02
❑ 206 Bobby Rose .05 .02
❑ 207 Gary Gaetti .10 .03
❑ 208 Ruben Amaro RC .15 .04
❑ 209 Luis Polonia .05 .02
❑ 210 Dave Winfield .10 .03
❑ 211 Bryan Harvey .05 .02
❑ 212 Mike Moore .05 .02
❑ 213 Rickey Henderson .25 .07
❑ 214 Steve Chitren .05 .02
❑ 215 Bob Welch .05 .02
❑ 216 Terry Steinbach .05 .02
❑ 217 Earnest Riles .05 .02
❑ 218 Todd Van Poppel RC .50 .15
❑ 219 Mike Gallego .05 .02
❑ 220 Curt Young .05 .02
❑ 221 Todd Burns .05 .02
❑ 222 Vance Law .05 .02
❑ 223 Eric Show .05 .02
❑ 224 Don Peters .05 .02
❑ 225 Dave Stewart .10 .03
❑ 226 Dave Henderson .05 .02
❑ 227 Jose Canseco .15 .04
❑ 228 Walt Weiss .05 .02
❑ 229 Dann Howitt .05 .02
❑ 230 Willie Wilson .05 .02
❑ 231 Harold Baines .10 .03
❑ 232 Scott Hemond .05 .02
❑ 233 Joe Slusarski .05 .02
❑ 234 Mark McGwire .60 .18
❑ 235 K.Dressendorfer RC .15 .04
❑ 236 Craig Paquette RC .50 .15
❑ 237 Dennis Eckersley .10 .03
❑ 238 Dana Allison .05 .02
❑ 239 Scott Bradley .05 .02
❑ 240 Brian Holman .05 .02
❑ 241 Mike Schooler .05 .02
❑ 242 Rich DeLucia .05 .02
❑ 243 Edgar Martinez .15 .04
❑ 244 Henry Cotto .05 .02
❑ 245 Omar Vizquel .15 .04
❑ 246 Ken Griffey Jr. .50 .15
(See also 255)
❑ 247 Jay Buhner .10 .03
❑ 248 Bill Krueger .05 .02
❑ 249 Dave Fleming RC .15 .04
❑ 250 Patrick Lennon .05 .02
❑ 251 Dave Valle .05 .02
❑ 252 Harold Reynolds .10 .03
❑ 253 Randy Johnson .30 .09
❑ 254 Scott Bankhead .05 .02
❑ 255 Ken Griffey Sr. UER .05 .02
(Card number is 246)
❑ 256 Greg Briley .05 .02
❑ 257 Tino Martinez .25 .07
❑ 258 Alvin Davis .05 .02
❑ 259 Pete O'Brien .05 .02
❑ 260 Erik Hanson .05 .02
❑ 261 Bret Boone RC 3.00 .90
❑ 262 Roger Salkeld .05 .02
❑ 263 Dave Burba RC .50 .15
❑ 264 Kerry Woodson RC .15 .04
❑ 265 Julio Franco .10 .03
❑ 266 Dan Peltier RC .15 .04
❑ 267 Jeff Russell .05 .02
❑ 268 Steve Buechele .05 .02
❑ 269 Donald Harris .05 .02
❑ 270 Robb Nen .15 .04
❑ 271 Rich Gossage .10 .03
❑ 272 Ivan Rodriguez RC 3.00 .90
❑ 273 Jeff Huson .05 .02
❑ 274 Kevin Brown .10 .03
❑ 275 Dan Smith RC .15 .04
❑ 276 Gary Pettis .05 .02
❑ 277 Jack Daugherty .05 .02
❑ 278 Mike Jeffcoat .05 .02
❑ 279 Brad Arnsberg .05 .02
❑ 280 Nolan Ryan 1.00 .30
❑ 281 Eric McCray .05 .02
❑ 282 Scott Chiamparino .05 .02
❑ 283 Ruben Sierra .05 .02
❑ 284 Geno Petralli .05 .02
❑ 285 Monty Fariss .05 .02
❑ 286 Rafael Palmeiro .15 .04
❑ 287 Bobby Witt .05 .02
❑ 288 Dean Palmer UER .10 .03
Photo is Dan Peltier
❑ 289 Tony Scruggs .05 .02
❑ 290 Kenny Rogers .10 .03
❑ 291 Bret Saberhagen .10 .03
❑ 292 Brian McRae RC .50 .15
❑ 293 Storm Davis .05 .02
❑ 294 Danny Tartabull .05 .02
❑ 295 David Howard .05 .02
❑ 296 Mike Boddicker .05 .02
❑ 297 Joel Johnston RC .15 .04
❑ 298 Tim Spehr .05 .02
❑ 299 Hector Wagner .05 .02
❑ 300 George Brett .60 .18
❑ 301 Mike Macfarlane .05 .02
❑ 302 Kirk Gibson .15 .04
❑ 303 Harvey Pulliam RC .15 .04
❑ 304 Jim Eisenreich .05 .02
❑ 305 Kevin Seitzer .05 .02
❑ 306 Mark Davis .05 .02
❑ 307 Kurt Stillwell .05 .02
❑ 308 Jeff Montgomery .05 .02
❑ 309 Kevin Appier .10 .03
❑ 310 Bob Hamelin .05 .02
❑ 311 Tom Gordon .05 .02
❑ 312 Kerwin Moore RC .15 .04
❑ 313 Hugh Walker .05 .02
❑ 314 Terry Shumpert .05 .02
❑ 315 Warren Cromartie .05 .02
❑ 316 Gary Thurman .05 .02
❑ 317 Steve Bedrosian .05 .02
❑ 318 Danny Gladden .05 .02
❑ 319 Jack Morris .10 .03
❑ 320 Kirby Puckett .25 .07
❑ 321 Kent Hrbek .10 .03
❑ 322 Kevin Tapani .05 .02
❑ 323 Denny Neagle RC .50 .15
❑ 324 Rich Garces RC .15 .04
❑ 325 Larry Casian .05 .02
❑ 326 Shane Mack .05 .02
❑ 327 Allan Anderson .05 .02
❑ 328 Junior Ortiz .05 .02
❑ 329 Paul Abbott RC .50 .15
❑ 330 Chuck Knoblauch .10 .03
❑ 331 Chili Davis .10 .03
❑ 332 Todd Ritchie RC .50 .15
❑ 333 Brian Harper .05 .02
❑ 334 Rick Aguilera .10 .03
❑ 335 Scott Erickson .05 .02
❑ 336 Pedro Munoz RC .15 .04
❑ 337 Scott Leius .05 .02
❑ 338 Greg Gagne .05 .02
❑ 339 Mike Pagliarulo .05 .02
❑ 340 Terry Leach .05 .02
❑ 341 Willie Banks .05 .02
❑ 342 Bobby Thigpen .05 .02
❑ 343 R.Hernandez RC .50 .15
❑ 344 Melido Perez .05 .02
❑ 345 Carlton Fisk .15 .04
❑ 346 Norberto Martin .05 .02
❑ 347 Johnny Ruffin RC .15 .04
❑ 348 Jeff Carter .05 .02
❑ 349 Lance Johnson .05 .02
❑ 350 Sammy Sosa .25 .07
❑ 351 Alex Fernandez .05 .02
❑ 352 Jack McDowell .05 .02
❑ 353 Bob Wickman RC 1.50 .45
❑ 354 Wilson Alvarez .05 .02
❑ 355 Charlie Hough .10 .03
❑ 356 Ozzie Guillen .10 .03
❑ 357 Cory Snyder .05 .02
❑ 358 Robin Ventura .10 .03
❑ 359 Scott Fletcher .05 .02
❑ 360 Cesar Bernhardt .05 .02
❑ 361 Dan Pasqua .05 .02
❑ 362 Tim Raines .10 .03
❑ 363 Brian Drahman .05 .02
❑ 364 Wayne Edwards .05 .02
❑ 365 Scott Radinsky .05 .02
❑ 366 Frank Thomas .25 .07
❑ 367 Cecil Fielder SLUG .05 .02
❑ 368 Julio Franco SLUG .05 .02
❑ 369 Kelly Gruber SLUG .05 .02
❑ 370 Alan Trammell SLUG .10 .03
❑ 371 R.Henderson SLUG .15 .04
❑ 372 Jose Canseco SLUG .10 .03
❑ 373 Ellis Burks SLUG .05 .02
❑ 374 Lance Parrish SLUG .05 .02
❑ 375 Dave Parker SLUG .05 .02
❑ 376 Eddie Murray SLUG .15 .04
❑ 377 Ryne Sandberg SLUG .25 .07
❑ 378 Matt Williams SLUG .05 .02
❑ 379 Barry Larkin SLUG .10 .03
❑ 380 Barry Bonds SLUG .50 .15
❑ 381 Bobby Bonilla SLUG .05 .02
❑ 382 D.Strawberry SLUG .05 .02
❑ 383 Benny Santiago SLUG .05 .02
❑ 384 Don Robinson SLUG .05 .02
❑ 385 Paul Coleman .05 .02
❑ 386 Milt Thompson .05 .02
❑ 387 Lee Smith .10 .03
❑ 388 Ray Lankford .10 .03
❑ 389 Tom Pagnozzi .05 .02
❑ 390 Ken Hill .05 .02
❑ 391 Jamie Moyer .10 .03
❑ 392 Greg Carmona .05 .02
❑ 393 John Ericks .05 .02

❑ 394 Bob Tewksbury .05 .02
❑ 395 Jose Oquendo .05 .02
❑ 396 Rheal Cormier RC .15 .04
❑ 397 Mike Milchin .05 .02
❑ 398 Ozzie Smith .40 .12
❑ 399 Aaron Holbert RC .15 .04
❑ 400 Jose DeLeon .05 .02
❑ 401 Felix Jose .05 .02
❑ 402 Juan Agosto .05 .02
❑ 403 Pedro Guerrero .10 .03
❑ 404 Todd Zeile .05 .02
❑ 405 Gerald Perry .05 .02
❑ 406 D.Osborne UER RC .15 .04
Card number is 410
❑ 407 Bryn Smith .05 .02
❑ 408 Bernard Gilkey .05 .02
❑ 409 Rex Hudler .05 .02
❑ 410 Bobby Thomson .25 .07
Ralph Branca
Shot Heard Round the World
See also 406
❑ 411 Lance Dickson RC .15 .04
❑ 412 Danny Jackson .05 .02
❑ 413 Jerome Walton .05 .02
❑ 414 Sean Cheetham .05 .02
❑ 415 Joe Girardi .05 .02
❑ 416 Ryne Sandberg .40 .12
❑ 417 Mike Harkey .05 .02
❑ 418 George Bell .05 .02
❑ 419 Rick Wilkins RC .15 .04
❑ 420 Earl Cunningham .05 .02
❑ 421 H.Slocumb RC .15 .04
❑ 422 Mike Bielecki .05 .02
❑ 423 Jessie Hollins RC .15 .04
❑ 424 Shawon Dunston .05 .02
❑ 425 Dave Smith .05 .02
❑ 426 Greg Maddux .40 .12
❑ 427 Jose Vizcaino .05 .02
❑ 428 Luis Salazar .05 .02
❑ 429 Andre Dawson .10 .03
❑ 430 Rick Sutcliffe .10 .03
❑ 431 Paul Assenmacher .05 .02
❑ 432 Erik Pappas .05 .02
❑ 433 Mark Grace .15 .04
❑ 434 Dennis Martinez .10 .03
❑ 435 Marquis Grissom .10 .03
❑ 436 Wil Cordero RC .50 .15
❑ 437 Tim Wallach .05 .02
❑ 438 Brian Barnes RC .05 .02
❑ 439 Barry Jones .05 .02
❑ 440 Ivan Calderon .05 .02
❑ 441 Stan Spencer .05 .02
❑ 442 Larry Walker .25 .07
❑ 443 Chris Haney RC .15 .04
❑ 444 Hector Rivera .05 .02
❑ 445 Delino DeShields .10 .03
❑ 446 Andres Galarraga .10 .03
❑ 447 Gilberto Reyes .05 .02
❑ 448 Willie Greene .05 .02
❑ 449 Greg Colbrunn RC .50 .15
❑ 450 Rondell White RC 1.00 .30
❑ 451 Steve Frey .05 .02
❑ 452 Shane Andrews RC .15 .04
❑ 453 Mike Fitzgerald .05 .02
❑ 454 Spike Owen .05 .02
❑ 455 Dave Martinez .05 .02
❑ 456 Dennis Boyd .05 .02
❑ 457 Eric Bullock .05 .02
❑ 458 Reid Cornelius RC .15 .04
❑ 459 Chris Nabholz .05 .02
❑ 460 David Cone .10 .03
❑ 461 Hubie Brooks .05 .02
❑ 462 Sid Fernandez .05 .02
❑ 463 Doug Simons .05 .02
❑ 464 Howard Johnson .05 .02
❑ 465 Chris Donnels .05 .02
❑ 466 Anthony Young RC .15 .04
❑ 467 Todd Hundley .05 .02
❑ 468 Rick Cerone .05 .02
❑ 469 Kevin Elster .05 .02
❑ 470 Wally Whitehurst .05 .02
❑ 471 Vince Coleman .05 .02
❑ 472 Dwight Gooden .10 .03
❑ 473 Charlie O'Brien .05 .02
❑ 474 Jeromy Burnitz RC 1.00 .30
❑ 475 John Franco .10 .03
❑ 476 Daryl Boston .05 .02
❑ 477 Frank Viola .10 .03
❑ 478 D.J. Dozier .05 .02
❑ 479 Kevin McReynolds .05 .02
❑ 480 Tom Herr .05 .02
❑ 481 Gregg Jefferies .05 .02
❑ 482 Pete Schourek RC .15 .04
❑ 483 Ron Darling .05 .02
❑ 484 Dave Magadan .05 .02
❑ 485 Andy Ashby RC .50 .15
❑ 486 Dale Murphy .15 .04
❑ 487 Von Hayes .05 .02
❑ 488 Kim Batiste RC .15 .04
❑ 489 Tony Longmire RC .15 .04
❑ 490 Wally Backman .05 .02
❑ 491 Jeff Jackson .05 .02
❑ 492 Mickey Morandini .05 .02
❑ 493 Darrel Akerfelds .05 .02
❑ 494 Ricky Jordan .05 .02
❑ 495 Randy Ready .05 .02
❑ 496 Darrin Fletcher .05 .02
❑ 497 Chuck Malone .05 .02
❑ 498 Pat Combs .05 .02
❑ 499 Dickie Thon .05 .02
❑ 500 Roger McDowell .05 .02
❑ 501 Len Dykstra .10 .03
❑ 502 Joe Boever .05 .02
❑ 503 John Kruk .10 .03
❑ 504 Terry Mulholland .05 .02
❑ 505 Wes Chamberlain RC .15 .04
❑ 506 Mike Lieberthal RC 1.00 .30
❑ 507 Darren Daulton .10 .03
❑ 508 Charlie Hayes .05 .02
❑ 509 John Smiley .05 .02
❑ 510 Gary Varsho .05 .02
❑ 511 Curt Wilkerson .05 .02
❑ 512 Orlando Merced RC .15 .04
❑ 513 Barry Bonds 1.00 .30
❑ 514 Mike LaValliere .05 .02
❑ 515 Doug Drabek .05 .02
❑ 516 Gary Redus .05 .02
❑ 517 W.Pennyfeather RC .15 .04
❑ 518 Randy Tomlin RC .05 .02
❑ 519 Mike Zimmerman RC .15 .04
❑ 520 Jeff King .05 .02
❑ 521 Kurt Miller RC .15 .04
❑ 522 Jay Bell .10 .03
❑ 523 Bill Landrum .05 .02
❑ 524 Zane Smith .05 .02
❑ 525 Bobby Bonilla .10 .03
❑ 526 Bob Walk .05 .02
❑ 527 Austin Manahan .05 .02
❑ 528 Joe Ausanio .05 .02
❑ 529 Andy Van Slyke .15 .04
❑ 530 Jose Lind .05 .02
❑ 531 Carlos Garcia RC .15 .04
❑ 532 Don Slaught .05 .02
❑ 533 Gen.Colin Powell .50 .15
❑ 534 Frank Bolick RC .15 .04
❑ 535 Gary Scott .05 .02
❑ 536 Nikco Riesgo .05 .02
❑ 537 Reggie Sanders RC 1.50 .45
❑ 538 Tim Howard RC .15 .04
❑ 539 Ryan Bowen RC .15 .04
❑ 540 Eric Anthony .05 .02
❑ 541 Jim Deshaies .05 .02
❑ 542 Tom Nevers RC .15 .04
❑ 543 Ken Caminiti .10 .03
❑ 544 Karl Rhodes .05 .02
❑ 545 Xavier Hernandez .05 .02
❑ 546 Mike Scott .05 .02
❑ 547 Jeff Juden .05 .02
❑ 548 Darryl Kile .10 .03
❑ 549 Willie Ansley .05 .02
❑ 550 Luis Gonzalez RC 1.50 .45
❑ 551 Mike Simms .05 .02
❑ 552 Mark Portugal .05 .02
❑ 553 Jimmy Jones .05 .02
❑ 554 Jim Clancy .05 .02
❑ 555 Pete Harnisch .05 .02
❑ 556 Craig Biggio .15 .04
❑ 557 Eric Yelding .05 .02
❑ 558 Dave Rohde .05 .02
❑ 559 Casey Candaele .05 .02
❑ 560 Curt Schilling .25 .07
❑ 561 Steve Finley .10 .03
❑ 562 Javier Ortiz .05 .02
❑ 563 Andujar Cedeno .05 .02
❑ 564 Rafael Ramirez .05 .02
❑ 565 Kenny Lofton RC 1.50 .45
❑ 566 Steve Avery .05 .02
❑ 567 Lonnie Smith .05 .02
❑ 568 Kent Mercker .05 .02
❑ 569 Chipper Jones RC 5.00 1.50
❑ 570 Terry Pendleton .10 .03
❑ 571 Otis Nixon .05 .02
❑ 572 Juan Berenguer .05 .02
❑ 573 Charlie Leibrandt .05 .02
❑ 574 David Justice .10 .03
❑ 575 Keith Mitchell RC .15 .04
❑ 576 Tom Glavine .15 .04
❑ 577 Greg Olson .05 .02
❑ 578 Rafael Belliard .05 .02
❑ 579 Ben Rivera RC .15 .04
❑ 580 John Smoltz .15 .04
❑ 581 Tyler Houston .05 .02
❑ 582 Mark Wohlers RC .50 .15
❑ 583 Ron Gant .10 .03
❑ 584 Ramon Caraballo RC .15 .04
❑ 585 Sid Bream .05 .02
❑ 586 Jeff Treadway .05 .02
❑ 587 Javy Lopez RC 3.00 .90
❑ 588 Deion Sanders .15 .04
❑ 589 Mike Heath .05 .02
❑ 590 Ryan Klesko RC 1.50 .45
❑ 591 Bob Ojeda .05 .02
❑ 592 Alfredo Griffin .05 .02
❑ 593 Raul Mondesi RC 1.00 .30
❑ 594 Greg Smith .05 .02
❑ 595 Orel Hershiser .10 .03
❑ 596 Juan Samuel .05 .02
❑ 597 Brett Butler .10 .03
❑ 598 Gary Carter .10 .03
❑ 599 Stan Javier .05 .02
❑ 600 Kal Daniels .05 .02
❑ 601 Jamie McAndrew RC .15 .04
❑ 602 Mike Sharperson .05 .02
❑ 603 Jay Howell .05 .02
❑ 604 Eric Karros RC 1.00 .30
❑ 605 Tim Belcher .05 .02
❑ 606 Dan Opperman .05 .02
❑ 607 Lenny Harris .05 .02
❑ 608 Tom Goodwin .05 .02
❑ 609 Darryl Strawberry .10 .03
❑ 610 Ramon Martinez .05 .02
❑ 611 Kevin Gross .05 .02
❑ 612 Zakary Shinall .05 .02
❑ 613 Mike Scioscia .05 .02
❑ 614 Eddie Murray .25 .07
❑ 615 Ronnie Walden RC .15 .04
❑ 616 Will Clark .15 .04
❑ 617 Adam Hyzdu RC .50 .15
❑ 618 Matt Williams .10 .03
❑ 619 Don Robinson .05 .02
❑ 620 Jeff Brantley .05 .02
❑ 621 Greg Litton .05 .02
❑ 622 Steve Decker .05 .02
❑ 623 Robby Thompson .05 .02
❑ 624 Mark Leonard .05 .02
❑ 625 Kevin Bass .05 .02
❑ 626 Scott Garrelts .05 .02
❑ 627 Jose Uribe .05 .02
❑ 628 Eric Gunderson .05 .02
❑ 629 Steve Hosey .05 .02
❑ 630 Trevor Wilson .05 .02
❑ 631 Terry Kennedy .05 .02
❑ 632 Dave Righetti .10 .03
❑ 633 Kelly Downs .05 .02
❑ 634 Johnny Ard .05 .02
❑ 635 E.Christopherson RC .15 .04
❑ 636 Kevin Mitchell .05 .02
❑ 637 John Burkett .05 .02
❑ 638 Kevin Rogers RC .15 .04
❑ 639 Bud Black .05 .02
❑ 640 Willie McGee .10 .03
❑ 641 Royce Clayton .05 .02
❑ 642 Tony Fernandez .05 .02
❑ 643 Ricky Bones RC .15 .04
❑ 644 Thomas Howard .05 .02
❑ 645 Dave Staton RC .15 .04
❑ 646 Jim Presley .05 .02
❑ 647 Tony Gwynn .30 .09

Card	Nm-Mt	Ex-Mt
❑ 648 Marty Barrett	.05	.02
❑ 649 Scott Coolbaugh	.05	.02
❑ 650 Craig Lefferts	.05	.02
❑ 651 Eddie Whitson	.05	.02
❑ 652 Oscar Azocar	.05	.02
❑ 653 Wes Gardner	.05	.02
❑ 654 Bip Roberts	.05	.02
❑ 655 Robbie Beckett RC	.15	.04
❑ 656 Benito Santiago	.10	.03
❑ 657 Greg W.Harris	.05	.02
❑ 658 Jerald Clark	.05	.02
❑ 659 Fred McGriff	.15	.04
❑ 660 Larry Andersen	.05	.02
❑ 661 Bruce Hurst	.05	.02
❑ 662 Steve Martin UER RC	.15	.04
Card said he pitched at Waterloo He's an outfielder		
❑ 663 Rafael Valdez	.05	.02
❑ 664 Paul Faries	.05	.02
❑ 665 Andy Benes	.05	.02
❑ 666 Randy Myers	.05	.02
❑ 667 Rob Dibble	.10	.03
❑ 668 Glenn Sutko	.05	.02
❑ 669 Glenn Braggs	.05	.02
❑ 670 Billy Hatcher	.05	.02
❑ 671 Joe Oliver	.05	.02
❑ 672 Freddie Benavides RC	.15	.04
❑ 673 Barry Larkin	.15	.04
❑ 674 Chris Sabo	.05	.02
❑ 675 Mariano Duncan	.05	.02
❑ 676 Chris Jones RC	.05	.02
❑ 677 Gino Minutelli	.05	.02
❑ 678 Reggie Jefferson	.05	.02
❑ 679 Jack Armstrong	.05	.02
❑ 680 Chris Hammond	.05	.02
❑ 681 Jose Rijo	.05	.02
❑ 682 Bill Doran	.05	.02
❑ 683 Terry Lee	.05	.02
❑ 684 Tom Browning	.05	.02
❑ 685 Paul O'Neill	.15	.04
❑ 686 Eric Davis	.10	.03
❑ 687 Dan Wilson RC	.50	.15
❑ 688 Ted Power	.05	.02
❑ 689 Tim Layana	.05	.02
❑ 690 Norm Charlton	.05	.02
❑ 691 Hal Morris	.05	.02
❑ 692 Rickey Henderson	.15	.04
❑ 693 Sam Militello RC	.15	.04
❑ 694 Matt Mieske RC	.15	.04
❑ 695 Paul Russo RC	.15	.04
❑ 696 Domingo Mota MVP	.05	.02
❑ 697 Todd Guggiana RC	.15	.04
❑ 698 Marc Newfield RC	.15	.04
❑ 699 Checklist 1-122	.05	.02
❑ 700 Checklist 123-244	.05	.02
❑ 701 Checklist 245-366	.05	.02
❑ 702 Checklist 367-471	.05	.02
❑ 703 Checklist 472-593	.05	.02
❑ 704 Checklist 594-704	.05	.02

1992 Bowman

	Nm-Mt	Ex-Mt
COMPLETE SET (705)	150.00	45.00
❑ 1 Ivan Rodriguez	1.25	.35
❑ 2 Kirk McCaskill	.50	.15
❑ 3 Scott Livingstone	.50	.15
❑ 4 Salomon Torres RC	.50	.15
❑ 5 Carlos Hernandez	.50	.15
❑ 6 Dave Hollins	.50	.15
❑ 7 Scott Fletcher	.50	.15
❑ 8 Jorge Fabregas RC	.50	.15
❑ 9 Andujar Cedeno	.50	.15
❑ 10 Howard Johnson	.50	.15
❑ 11 Trevor Hoffman RC	10.00	3.00
❑ 12 Roberto Kelly	.50	.15
❑ 13 Gregg Jefferies	.50	.15
❑ 14 Marquis Grissom	.50	.15
❑ 15 Mike Ignasiak	.50	.15
❑ 16 Jack Morris	.50	.15
❑ 17 William Pennyfeather	.50	.15
❑ 18 Todd Stottlemyre	.50	.15
❑ 19 Chito Martinez	.50	.15
❑ 20 Roberto Alomar	.75	.23
❑ 21 Sam Militello	.50	.15
❑ 22 Hector Fajardo RC	.50	.15
❑ 23 Paul Quantrill RC	.50	.15
❑ 24 Chuck Knoblauch	.50	.15
❑ 25 Reggie Jefferson	.50	.15
❑ 26 Jeremy McGarity RC	.50	.15
❑ 27 Jerome Walton	.50	.15
❑ 28 Chipper Jones	10.00	3.00
❑ 29 Brian Barber RC	.50	.15
❑ 30 Ron Darling	.50	.15
❑ 31 Roberto Petagine RC	.50	.15
❑ 32 Chuck Finley	.50	.15
❑ 33 Edgar Martinez	.75	.23
❑ 34 Napoleon Robinson	.50	.15
❑ 35 Andy Van Slyke	.75	.23
❑ 36 Bobby Thigpen	.50	.15
❑ 37 Travis Fryman	.50	.15
❑ 38 Eric Christopherson	.50	.15
❑ 39 Terry Mulholland	.50	.15
❑ 40 Darryl Strawberry	.50	.15
❑ 41 Manny Alexander RC	.50	.15
❑ 42 Tracy Sanders RC	.50	.15
❑ 43 Pete Incaviglia	.50	.15
❑ 44 Kim Batiste	.50	.15
❑ 45 Frank Rodriguez	.50	.15
❑ 46 Greg Swindell	.50	.15
❑ 47 Delino DeShields	.50	.15
❑ 48 John Ericks	.50	.15
❑ 49 Franklin Stubbs	.50	.15
❑ 50 Tony Gwynn	1.50	.45
❑ 51 Clifton Garrett RC	.50	.15
❑ 52 Mike Gardella	.50	.15
❑ 53 Scott Erickson	.50	.15
❑ 54 Gary Caraballo RC	.50	.15
❑ 55 Jose Oliva RC	.50	.15
❑ 56 Brook Fordyce	.50	.15
❑ 57 Mark Whiten	.50	.15
❑ 58 Joe Slusarski	.50	.15
❑ 59 J.R. Phillips RC	.50	.15
❑ 60 Barry Bonds	4.00	1.20
❑ 61 Bob Milacki	.50	.15
❑ 62 Keith Mitchell	.50	.15
❑ 63 Angel Miranda	.50	.15
❑ 64 Raul Mondesi	.50	.15
❑ 65 Brian Koelling RC	.50	.15
❑ 66 Brian McRae	.50	.15
❑ 67 John Patterson RC	.50	.15
❑ 68 John Wetteland	.50	.15
❑ 69 Wilson Alvarez	.50	.15
❑ 70 Wade Boggs	.75	.23
❑ 71 Darryl Ratliff RC	.50	.15
❑ 72 Jeff Jackson	.50	.15
❑ 73 Jeremy Hernandez RC	.50	.15
❑ 74 Darryl Hamilton	.50	.15
❑ 75 Rafael Belliard	.50	.15
❑ 76 Rick Trlicek RC	.50	.15
❑ 77 Felipe Crespo RC	.50	.15
❑ 78 Carney Lansford	.50	.15
❑ 79 Ryan Long RC	.50	.15
❑ 80 Kirby Puckett	1.25	.35
❑ 81 Earl Cunningham	.50	.15
❑ 82 Pedro Martinez	10.00	3.00
❑ 83 Scott Hatteberg RC	1.00	.30
❑ 84 Juan Gonzalez UER	.75	.23
(65 doubles vs. Tigers)		
❑ 85 Robert Nutting RC	.50	.15
❑ 86 Pokey Reese RC	2.00	.60
❑ 87 Dave Silvestri	.50	.15
❑ 88 Scott Ruffcorn RC	.50	.15
❑ 89 Rick Aguilera	.50	.15
❑ 90 Cecil Fielder	.50	.15
❑ 91 Kirk Dressendorfer	.50	.15
❑ 92 Jerry DiPoto RC	.50	.15
❑ 93 Mike Felder	.50	.15
❑ 94 Craig Paquette	.50	.15
❑ 95 Elvin Paulino RC	.50	.15
❑ 96 Donovan Osborne	.50	.15
❑ 97 Hubie Brooks	.50	.15
❑ 98 Derek Lowe RC	5.00	1.50
❑ 99 David Zancanaro	.50	.15
❑ 100 Ken Griffey Jr.	2.00	.60
❑ 101 Todd Hundley	.50	.15
❑ 102 Mike Trombley RC	.50	.15
❑ 103 Ricky Gutierrez RC	1.00	.30
❑ 104 Braulio Castillo	.50	.15
❑ 105 Craig Lefferts	.50	.15
❑ 106 Rick Sutcliffe	.50	.15
❑ 107 Dean Palmer	.50	.15
❑ 108 Henry Rodriguez	.50	.15
❑ 109 Mark Clark RC	1.00	.30
❑ 110 Kenny Lofton	.75	.23
❑ 111 Mark Carreon	.50	.15
❑ 112 J.T. Bruett	.50	.15
❑ 113 Gerald Williams	.50	.15
❑ 114 Frank Thomas	1.25	.35
❑ 115 Kevin Reimer	.50	.15
❑ 116 Sammy Sosa	1.25	.35
❑ 117 Mickey Tettleton	.50	.15
❑ 118 Reggie Sanders	.50	.15
❑ 119 Trevor Wilson	.50	.15
❑ 120 Cliff Brantley	.50	.15
❑ 121 Spike Owen	.50	.15
❑ 122 Jeff Montgomery	.50	.15
❑ 123 Alex Sutherland	.50	.15
❑ 124 Brien Taylor RC	1.00	.30
❑ 125 Brian Williams RC	.50	.15
❑ 126 Kevin Seitzer	.50	.15
❑ 127 Carlos Delgado RC	12.00	3.60
❑ 128 Gary Scott	.50	.15
❑ 129 Scott Cooper	.50	.15
❑ 130 Domingo Jean RC	.50	.15
❑ 131 Pat Mahomes RC	1.00	.30
❑ 132 Mike Boddicker	.50	.15
❑ 133 Roberto Hernandez	.50	.15
❑ 134 Dave Valle	.50	.15
❑ 135 Kurt Stillwell	.50	.15
❑ 136 Brad Pennington RC	.50	.15
❑ 137 Jermaine Swinton RC	.50	.15
❑ 138 Ryan Hawblitzel RC	.50	.15
❑ 139 Tito Navarro RC	.50	.15
❑ 140 Sandy Alomar Jr.	.50	.15
❑ 141 Todd Benzinger	.50	.15
❑ 142 Danny Jackson	.50	.15
❑ 143 Melvin Nieves RC	.50	.15
❑ 144 Jim Campanis	.50	.15
❑ 145 Luis Gonzalez	.50	.15
❑ 146 D.Dooreneweerd RC	.50	.15
❑ 147 Charlie Hayes	.50	.15
❑ 148 Greg Maddux	2.00	.60
❑ 149 Brian Harper	.50	.15
❑ 150 Brent Miller RC	.50	.15
❑ 151 Shawn Estes RC	1.00	.30
❑ 152 Mike Williams RC	1.00	.30
❑ 153 Charlie Hough	.50	.15
❑ 154 Randy Myers	.50	.15
❑ 155 Kevin Young RC	1.00	.30
❑ 156 Rick Wilkins	.50	.15
❑ 157 Terry Shumpert	.50	.15
❑ 158 Steve Karsay	.50	.15
❑ 159 Gary DiSarcina	.50	.15
❑ 160 Deion Sanders	.75	.23
❑ 161 Tom Browning	.50	.15
❑ 162 Dickie Thon	.50	.15
❑ 163 Luis Mercedes	.50	.15
❑ 164 Riccardo Ingram	.50	.15
❑ 165 Tavo Alvarez RC	.50	.15
❑ 166 Rickey Henderson	1.25	.35
❑ 167 Jaime Navarro	.50	.15
❑ 168 Billy Ashley RC	.50	.15
❑ 169 Phil Dauphin RC	.50	.15
❑ 170 Ivan Cruz	.50	.15
❑ 171 Harold Baines	.50	.15
❑ 172 Bryan Harvey	.50	.15
❑ 173 Alex Cole	.50	.15
❑ 174 Curtis Shaw RC	.50	.15

❑ 175 Matt Williams .50 .15
❑ 176 Felix Jose .50 .15
❑ 177 Sam Horn .50 .15
❑ 178 Randy Johnson 1.25 .35
❑ 179 Ivan Calderon .50 .15
❑ 180 Steve Avery .50 .15
❑ 181 William Suero .50 .15
❑ 182 Bill Swift .50 .15
❑ 183 Howard Battle RC .50 .15
❑ 184 Ruben Amaro .50 .15
❑ 185 Jim Abbott .75 .23
❑ 186 Mike Fitzgerald .50 .15
❑ 187 Bruce Hurst .50 .15
❑ 188 Jeff Juden .50 .15
❑ 189 Jeromy Burnitz .50 .15
❑ 190 Dave Burba .50 .15
❑ 191 Kevin Brown .50 .15
❑ 192 Patrick Lennon .50 .15
❑ 193 Jeff McNeely .50 .15
❑ 194 Wil Cordero .50 .15
❑ 195 Chili Davis .50 .15
❑ 196 Milt Cuyler .50 .15
❑ 197 Von Hayes .50 .15
❑ 198 Todd Revenig RC .50 .15
❑ 199 Joel Johnston .50 .15
❑ 200 Jeff Bagwell 1.25 .35
❑ 201 Alex Fernandez .50 .15
❑ 202 Todd Jones RC 2.00 .60
❑ 203 Charles Nagy .50 .15
❑ 204 Tim Raines .50 .15
❑ 205 Kevin Maas .50 .15
❑ 206 Julio Franco .50 .15
❑ 207 Randy Velarde .50 .15
❑ 208 Lance Johnson .50 .15
❑ 209 Scott Leius .50 .15
❑ 210 Derek Lee .50 .15
❑ 211 Joe Sondrini RC .50 .15
❑ 212 Royce Clayton .50 .15
❑ 213 Chris George .50 .15
❑ 214 Gary Sheffield .50 .15
❑ 215 Mark Gubicza .50 .15
❑ 216 Mike Moore .50 .15
❑ 217 Rick Huisman RC .50 .15
❑ 218 Jeff Russell .50 .15
❑ 219 D.J. Dozier .50 .15
❑ 220 Dave Martinez .50 .15
❑ 221 Alan Newman RC .50 .15
❑ 222 Nolan Ryan 4.00 1.20
❑ 223 Teddy Higuera .50 .15
❑ 224 Damon Buford RC .50 .15
❑ 225 Ruben Sierra .50 .15
❑ 226 Tom Nevers .50 .15
❑ 227 Tommy Greene .50 .15
❑ 228 Nigel Wilson RC .50 .15
❑ 229 John DeSilva .50 .15
❑ 230 Bobby Witt .50 .15
❑ 231 Greg Cadaret .50 .15
❑ 232 John Vander Wal RC 1.00 .30
❑ 233 Jack Clark .50 .15
❑ 234 Bill Doran .50 .15
❑ 235 Bobby Bonilla .50 .15
❑ 236 Steve Olin .50 .15
❑ 237 Derek Bell .50 .15
❑ 238 David Cone .50 .15
❑ 239 Victor Cole .50 .15
❑ 240 Rod Bolton RC .50 .15
❑ 241 Tom Pagnozzi .50 .15
❑ 242 Rob Dibble .50 .15
❑ 243 Michael Carter RC .50 .15
❑ 244 Don Peters .50 .15
❑ 245 Mike LaValliere .50 .15
❑ 246 Joe Perona RC .50 .15
❑ 247 Mitch Williams .50 .15
❑ 248 Jay Buhner .50 .15
❑ 249 Andy Benes .50 .15
❑ 250 Alex Ochoa RC 1.00 .30
❑ 251 Greg Blosser .50 .15
❑ 252 Jack Armstrong .50 .15
❑ 253 Juan Samuel .50 .15
❑ 254 Terry Pendleton .50 .15
❑ 255 Ramon Martinez .50 .15
❑ 256 Rico Brogna .50 .15
❑ 257 John Smiley .50 .15
❑ 258 Carl Everett .75 .23
❑ 259 Tim Salmon .75 .23
❑ 260 Will Clark .75 .23
❑ 261 Ugueth Urbina RC 1.00 .30
❑ 262 Jason Wood RC .50 .15
❑ 263 Dave Magadan .50 .15
❑ 264 Dante Bichette .50 .15
❑ 265 Jose DeLeon .50 .15
❑ 266 Mike Neill RC 1.00 .30
❑ 267 Paul O'Neill .75 .23
❑ 268 Anthony Young .50 .15
❑ 269 Greg W. Harris .50 .15
❑ 270 Todd Van Poppel .50 .15
❑ 271 Pedro Castellano RC .50 .15
❑ 272 Tony Phillips .50 .15
❑ 273 Mike Gallego .50 .15
❑ 274 Steve Cooke RC .50 .15
❑ 275 Robin Ventura .50 .15
❑ 276 Kevin Mitchell .50 .15
❑ 277 Doug Linton RC .50 .15
❑ 278 Robert Eenhoorn .50 .15
❑ 279 Gabe White RC .50 .15
❑ 280 Dave Stewart .50 .15
❑ 281 Mo Sanford .50 .15
❑ 282 Greg Perschke .50 .15
❑ 283 Kevin Flora RC .50 .15
❑ 284 Jeff Williams RC 1.00 .30
❑ 285 Keith Miller .50 .15
❑ 286 Andy Ashby .50 .15
❑ 287 Doug Dascenzo .50 .15
❑ 288 Eric Karros .50 .15
❑ 289 Glenn Murray RC .50 .15
❑ 290 Troy Percival RC 3.00 .90
❑ 291 Orlando Merced .50 .15
❑ 292 Peter Hoy .50 .15
❑ 293 Tony Fernandez .50 .15
❑ 294 Juan Guzman .50 .15
❑ 295 Jesse Barfield .50 .15
❑ 296 Sid Fernandez .50 .15
❑ 297 Scott Cepicky .50 .15
❑ 298 Garret Anderson RC 8.00 2.40
❑ 299 Cal Eldred .50 .15
❑ 300 Ryne Sandberg 2.50 .75
❑ 301 Jim Gantner .50 .15
❑ 302 Mariano Rivera RC 15.00 4.50
❑ 303 Ron Lockett RC .50 .15
❑ 304 Jose Offerman .50 .15
❑ 305 Dennis Martinez .50 .15
❑ 306 Luis Ortiz RC .50 .15
❑ 307 David Howard .50 .15
❑ 308 Russ Springer RC 1.00 .30
❑ 309 Chris Howard .50 .15
❑ 310 Kyle Abbott .50 .15
❑ 311 Aaron Sele RC 2.00 .60
❑ 312 David Justice .50 .15
❑ 313 Pete O'Brien .50 .15
❑ 314 Greg Hansell RC .50 .15
❑ 315 Dave Winfield .50 .15
❑ 316 Lance Dickson .50 .15
❑ 317 Eric King .50 .15
❑ 318 Vaughn Eshelman RC .50 .15
❑ 319 Tim Belcher .50 .15
❑ 320 Andres Galarraga .50 .15
❑ 321 Scott Bullett RC .50 .15
❑ 322 Doug Strange .50 .15
❑ 323 Jerald Clark .50 .15
❑ 324 Dave Righetti .50 .15
❑ 325 Greg Hibbard .50 .15
❑ 326 Eric Hillman RC .50 .15
❑ 327 Shane Reynolds RC 1.00 .30
❑ 328 Chris Hammond .50 .15
❑ 329 Albert Belle .50 .15
❑ 330 Rich Becker RC .50 .15
❑ 331 Eddie Williams RC .50 .15
❑ 332 Donald Harris .50 .15
❑ 333 Dave Smith .50 .15
❑ 334 Steve Fireovid .50 .15
❑ 335 Steve Buechele .50 .15
❑ 336 Mike Schooler .50 .15
❑ 337 Kevin McReynolds .50 .15
❑ 338 Hensley Meulens .50 .15
❑ 339 Benji Gil RC 1.00 .30
❑ 340 Don Mattingly 3.00 .90
❑ 341 Alvin Davis .50 .15
❑ 342 Alan Mills .50 .15
❑ 343 Kelly Downs .50 .15
❑ 344 Leo Gomez .50 .15
❑ 345 Tarrik Brock RC .50 .15
❑ 346 Ryan Turner RC .50 .15
❑ 347 John Smoltz .75 .23
❑ 348 Bill Sampen .50 .15
❑ 349 Paul Byrd RC 3.00 .90
❑ 350 Mike Bordick .50 .15
❑ 351 Jose Lind .50 .15
❑ 352 David Wells .50 .15
❑ 353 Barry Larkin .75 .23
❑ 354 Bruce Ruffin .50 .15
❑ 355 Luis Rivera .50 .15
❑ 356 Sid Bream .50 .15
❑ 357 Julian Vasquez RC .50 .15
❑ 358 Jason Bere RC 1.00 .30
❑ 359 Ben McDonald .50 .15
❑ 360 Scott Stahoviak RC .50 .15
❑ 361 Kirt Manwaring .50 .15
❑ 362 Jeff Johnson .50 .15
❑ 363 Rob Deer .50 .15
❑ 364 Tony Pena .50 .15
❑ 365 Melido Perez .50 .15
❑ 366 Clay Parker .50 .15
❑ 367 Dale Sveum .50 .15
❑ 368 Mike Scioscia .50 .15
❑ 369 Roger Salkeld .50 .15
❑ 370 Mike Stanley .50 .15
❑ 371 Jack McDowell .50 .15
❑ 372 Tim Wallach .50 .15
❑ 373 Billy Ripken .50 .15
❑ 374 Mike Christopher .50 .15
❑ 375 Paul Molitor .75 .23
❑ 376 Dave Stieb .50 .15
❑ 377 Pedro Guerrero .50 .15
❑ 378 Russ Swan .50 .15
❑ 379 Bob Ojeda .50 .15
❑ 380 Donn Pall .50 .15
❑ 381 Eddie Zosky .50 .15
❑ 382 Darnell Coles .50 .15
❑ 383 Tom Smith RC .50 .15
❑ 384 Mark McGwire 3.00 .90
❑ 385 Gary Carter .50 .15
❑ 386 Rich Amaral RC .50 .15
❑ 387 Alan Embree RC 1.00 .30
❑ 388 Jonathan Hurst RC .50 .15
❑ 389 Bobby Jones RC 1.00 .30
❑ 390 Rico Rossy .50 .15
❑ 391 Dan Smith .50 .15
❑ 392 Terry Steinbach .50 .15
❑ 393 Jon Farrell RC .50 .15
❑ 394 Dave Anderson .50 .15
❑ 395 Benny Santiago .50 .15
❑ 396 Mark Wohlers .50 .15
❑ 397 Mo Vaughn .50 .15
❑ 398 Randy Kramer .50 .15
❑ 399 John Jaha RC 1.00 .30
❑ 400 Cal Ripken 4.00 1.20
❑ 401 Ryan Bowen .50 .15
❑ 402 Tim McIntosh .50 .15
❑ 403 Bernard Gilkey .50 .15
❑ 404 Junior Felix .50 .15
❑ 405 Cris Colon RC .50 .15
❑ 406 Marc Newfield .50 .15
❑ 407 Bernie Williams .75 .23
❑ 408 Jay Howell .50 .15
❑ 409 Zane Smith .50 .15
❑ 410 Jeff Shaw .50 .15
❑ 411 Kerry Woodson .50 .15
❑ 412 Wes Chamberlain .50 .15
❑ 413 Dave Mlicki RC 1.00 .30
❑ 414 Benny Distefano .50 .15
❑ 415 Kevin Rogers .50 .15
❑ 416 Tim Naehring .50 .15
❑ 417 Clemente Nunez RC .50 .15
❑ 418 Luis Sojo .50 .15
❑ 419 Kevin Ritz .50 .15
❑ 420 Omar Olivares .50 .15
❑ 421 Manuel Lee .50 .15
❑ 422 Julio Valera .50 .15
❑ 423 Omar Vizquel .75 .23
❑ 424 Darren Burton RC .50 .15
❑ 425 Mel Hall .50 .15
❑ 426 Dennis Powell .50 .15
❑ 427 Lee Stevens .50 .15
❑ 428 Glenn Davis .50 .15
❑ 429 Willie Greene .50 .15
❑ 430 Kevin Wickander .50 .15
❑ 431 Dennis Eckersley .50 .15
❑ 432 Joe Orsulak .50 .15

❑ 433 Eddie Murray 1.25 .35
❑ 434 Matt Stairs RC 1.00 .30
❑ 435 Wally Joyner .50 .15
❑ 436 Rondell White .50 .15
❑ 437 Rob Maurer .50 .15
❑ 438 Joe Redfield .50 .15
❑ 439 Mark Lewis .50 .15
❑ 440 Darren Daulton .50 .15
❑ 441 Mike Henneman .50 .15
❑ 442 John Cangelosi .50 .15
❑ 443 Vince Moore RC .50 .15
❑ 444 John Wehner .50 .15
❑ 445 Kent Hrbek .50 .15
❑ 446 Mark McLemore .50 .15
❑ 447 Bill Wegman .50 .15
❑ 448 Robby Thompson .50 .15
❑ 449 Mark Anthony RC .50 .15
❑ 450 Archi Cianfrocco RC .50 .15
❑ 451 Johnny Ruffin .50 .15
❑ 452 Javy Lopez 2.00 .60
❑ 453 Greg Gohr .50 .15
❑ 454 Tim Scott .50 .15
❑ 455 Stan Belinda .50 .15
❑ 456 Darrin Jackson .50 .15
❑ 457 Chris Gardner .50 .15
❑ 458 Esteban Beltre .50 .15
❑ 459 Phil Plantier .50 .15
❑ 460 Jim Thome 8.00 2.40
❑ 461 Mike Piazza RC 40.00 12.00
❑ 462 Matt Sinatro .50 .15
❑ 463 Scott Servais .50 .15
❑ 464 Brian Jordan RC 2.00 .60
❑ 465 Doug Drabek .50 .15
❑ 466 Carl Willis .50 .15
❑ 467 Bret Barberie .50 .15
❑ 468 Hal Morris .50 .15
❑ 469 Steve Sax .50 .15
❑ 470 Jerry Willard .50 .15
❑ 471 Dan Wilson .50 .15
❑ 472 Chris Hoiles .50 .15
❑ 473 Rheal Cormier .50 .15
❑ 474 John Morris .50 .15
❑ 475 Jeff Reardon .50 .15
❑ 476 Mark Leiter .50 .15
❑ 477 Tom Gordon .50 .15
❑ 478 Kent Bottenfield RC 1.00 .30
❑ 479 Gene Larkin .50 .15
❑ 480 Dwight Gooden .50 .15
❑ 481 B.J. Surhoff .50 .15
❑ 482 Andy Stankiewicz .50 .15
❑ 483 Tino Martinez .75 .23
❑ 484 Craig Biggio .75 .23
❑ 485 Denny Neagle .50 .15
❑ 486 Rusty Meacham .50 .15
❑ 487 Kal Daniels .50 .15
❑ 488 Dave Henderson .50 .15
❑ 489 Tim Costo .50 .15
❑ 490 Doug Davis .50 .15
❑ 491 Frank Viola .50 .15
❑ 492 Cory Snyder .50 .15
❑ 493 Chris Martin .50 .15
❑ 494 Dion James .50 .15
❑ 495 Randy Tomlin .50 .15
❑ 496 Greg Vaughn .50 .15
❑ 497 Dennis Cook .50 .15
❑ 498 Rosario Rodriguez .50 .15
❑ 499 Dave Staton .50 .15
❑ 500 George Brett 3.00 .90
❑ 501 Brian Barnes .50 .15
❑ 502 Butch Henry RC .50 .15
❑ 503 Harold Reynolds .50 .15
❑ 504 David Nied RC .50 .15
❑ 505 Lee Smith .50 .15
❑ 506 Steve Chitren .50 .15
❑ 507 Ken Hill .50 .15
❑ 508 Robbie Beckett .50 .15
❑ 509 Troy Afenir .50 .15
❑ 510 Kelly Gruber .50 .15
❑ 511 Bret Boone 1.25 .35
❑ 512 Jeff Branson .50 .15
❑ 513 Mike Jackson .50 .15
❑ 514 Pete Harnisch .50 .15
❑ 515 Chad Kreuter .50 .15
❑ 516 Joe Vitko RC .50 .15
❑ 517 Orel Hershiser .50 .15
❑ 518 John Doherty RC .50 .15
❑ 519 Jay Bell .50 .15
❑ 520 Mark Langston .50 .15
❑ 521 Dann Howitt .50 .15
❑ 522 Bobby Reed RC .50 .15
❑ 523 Bobby Munoz RC .50 .15
❑ 524 Todd Ritchie .50 .15
❑ 525 Bip Roberts .50 .15
❑ 526 Pat Listach RC 1.00 .30
❑ 527 Scott Brosius RC 2.00 .60
❑ 528 John Roper RC .50 .15
❑ 529 Phil Hiatt RC .50 .15
❑ 530 Denny Walling .50 .15
❑ 531 Carlos Baerga .50 .15
❑ 532 Manny Ramirez RC 25.00 7.50
❑ 533 Pat Clements UER .50 .15
(Mistakenly numbered 553)
❑ 534 Ron Gant .50 .15
❑ 535 Pat Kelly .50 .15
❑ 536 Bill Spiers .50 .15
❑ 537 Darren Reed .50 .15
❑ 538 Ken Caminiti .50 .15
❑ 539 Butch Huskey RC .50 .15
❑ 540 Matt Nokes .50 .15
❑ 541 John Kruk .50 .15
❑ 542 John Jaha FOIL .50 .15
❑ 543 Justin Thompson RC .50 .15
❑ 544 Steve Hosey .50 .15
❑ 545 Joe Kmak .50 .15
❑ 546 John Franco .50 .15
❑ 547 Devon White .50 .15
❑ 548 E.Hansen FOIL RC .50 .15
❑ 549 Ryan Klesko 1.25 .35
❑ 550 Danny Tartabull .50 .15
❑ 551 Frank Thomas FOIL 1.25 .35
❑ 552 Kevin Tapani .50 .15
❑ 553 Willie Banks .50 .15
(See also 533)
❑ 554 B.J. Wallace RC FOIL .50 .15
❑ 555 Orlando Miller RC .50 .15
❑ 556 Mark Smith RC .50 .15
❑ 557 Tim Wallach FOIL .50 .15
❑ 558 Bill Gullickson .50 .15
❑ 559 Derek Bell FOIL .50 .15
❑ 560 Joe Randa FOIL RC 3.00 .90
❑ 561 Frank Seminara RC .50 .15
❑ 562 Mark Gardner .50 .15
❑ 563 Rick Greene RC FOIL .50 .15
❑ 564 Gary Gaetti .50 .15
❑ 565 Ozzie Guillen .50 .15
❑ 566 Charles Nagy FOIL .50 .15
❑ 567 Mike Milchin .50 .15
❑ 568 Ben Shelton RC .50 .15
❑ 569 Chris Roberts FOIL .50 .15
❑ 570 Ellis Burks .50 .15
❑ 571 Scott Scudder .50 .15
❑ 572 Jim Abbott FOIL .75 .23
❑ 573 Joe Carter .50 .15
❑ 574 Steve Finley .50 .15
❑ 575 Jim Olander FOIL .50 .15
❑ 576 Carlos Garcia .50 .15
❑ 577 Gregg Olson .50 .15
❑ 578 Greg Swindell FOIL .50 .15
❑ 579 Matt Williams FOIL .50 .15
❑ 580 Mark Grace .75 .23
❑ 581 Howard House FOIL RC .50 .15
❑ 582 Luis Polonia .50 .15
❑ 583 Erik Hanson .50 .15
❑ 584 Salomon Torres FOIL .50 .15
❑ 585 Carlton Fisk .75 .23
❑ 586 Bret Saberhagen .50 .15
❑ 587 C.McConnell FOIL RC .50 .15
❑ 588 Jimmy Key .50 .15
❑ 589 Mike Macfarlane .50 .15
❑ 590 Barry Bonds FOIL 4.00 1.20
❑ 591 Jamie McAndrew .50 .15
❑ 592 Shane Mack .50 .15
❑ 593 Kerwin Moore .50 .15
❑ 594 Joe Oliver .50 .15
❑ 595 Chris Sabo .50 .15
❑ 596 Alex Gonzalez RC 2.00 .60
❑ 597 Brett Butler .50 .15
❑ 598 Mark Hutton RC .50 .15
❑ 599 Andy Benes FOIL .50 .15
❑ 600 Jose Canseco .75 .23
❑ 601 Darryl Kile .50 .15
❑ 602 Matt Stairs FOIL .50 .15
❑ 603 R.Butler RC FOIL .50 .15
❑ 604 Willie McGee .50 .15
❑ 605 Jack McDowell FOIL .50 .15
❑ 606 Tom Candiotti .50 .15
❑ 607 Ed Martel RC .50 .15
❑ 608 Matt Mieske FOIL .50 .15
❑ 609 Darrin Fletcher .50 .15
❑ 610 Rafael Palmeiro .75 .23
❑ 611 Bill Swift FOIL .50 .15
❑ 612 Mike Mussina 1.25 .35
❑ 613 Vince Coleman .50 .15
❑ 614 Scott Cepicky COR .50 .15
❑ 614A S.Cepicky FOIL UER .50 .15
Bats: LEFLT
❑ 615 Mike Greenwell .50 .15
❑ 616 Kevin McGehee RC .50 .15
❑ 617 J.Hammonds FOIL .50 .15
❑ 618 Scott Taylor .50 .15
❑ 619 Dave Otto .50 .15
❑ 620 Mark McGwire FOIL 3.00 .90
❑ 621 Kevin Tatar RC .50 .15
❑ 622 Steve Farr .50 .15
❑ 623 Ryan Klesko FOIL .50 .15
❑ 624 Dave Fleming .50 .15
❑ 625 Andre Dawson .50 .15
❑ 626 Tino Martinez FOIL .75 .23
❑ 627 Chad Curtis RC 1.00 .30
❑ 628 Mickey Morandini .50 .15
❑ 629 Gregg Olson FOIL .50 .15
❑ 630 Lou Whitaker .50 .15
❑ 631 Arthur Rhodes .50 .15
❑ 632 Brandon Wilson RC .50 .15
❑ 633 Lance Jennings RC .50 .15
❑ 634 Allen Watson RC .50 .15
❑ 635 Len Dykstra .50 .15
❑ 636 Joe Girardi .50 .15
❑ 637 K.Hernandez RC FOIL .50 .15
❑ 638 Mike Hampton RC 2.00 .60
❑ 639 Al Osuna .50 .15
❑ 640 Kevin Appier .50 .15
❑ 641 Rick Helling FOIL .50 .15
❑ 642 Jody Reed .50 .15
❑ 643 Ray Lankford .50 .15
❑ 644 John Olerud .50 .15
❑ 645 Paul Molitor FOIL .75 .23
❑ 646 Pat Borders .50 .15
❑ 647 Mike Morgan .50 .15
❑ 648 Larry Walker .75 .23
❑ 649 P.Castellano FOIL .50 .15
❑ 650 Fred McGriff .75 .23
❑ 651 Walt Weiss .50 .15
❑ 652 C.Murray RC FOIL 1.00 .30
❑ 653 Dave Nilsson .50 .15
❑ 654 Greg Pirkl RC .50 .15
❑ 655 Robin Ventura FOIL .50 .15
❑ 656 Mark Portugal .50 .15
❑ 657 Roger McDowell .50 .15
❑ 658 Rick Hirtensteiner FOIL RC .50 .15
❑ 659 Glenallen Hill .50 .15
❑ 660 Greg Gagne .50 .15
❑ 661 Charles Johnson FOIL .50 .15
❑ 662 Brian Hunter .50 .15
❑ 663 Mark Lemke .50 .15
❑ 664 Tim Belcher FOIL .50 .15
❑ 665 Rich DeLucia .50 .15
❑ 666 Bob Walk .50 .15
❑ 667 Joe Carter FOIL .50 .15
❑ 668 Jose Guzman .50 .15
❑ 669 Otis Nixon .50 .15
❑ 670 Phil Nevin FOIL .75 .23
❑ 671 Eric Davis .50 .15
❑ 672 Damion Easley RC 1.00 .30
❑ 673 Will Clark FOIL .75 .23
❑ 674 Mark Kiefer RC .50 .15
❑ 675 Ozzie Smith 2.00 .60
❑ 676 Manny Ramirez FOIL 5.00 1.50
❑ 677 Gregg Olson .50 .15
❑ 678 Cliff Floyd RC 5.00 1.50
❑ 679 Duane Singleton RC .50 .15
❑ 680 Jose Rijo .50 .15
❑ 681 Willie Randolph .50 .15
❑ 682 M.Tucker FOIL RC 2.00 .60
❑ 683 Darren Lewis .50 .15
❑ 684 Dale Murphy .75 .23
❑ 685 Mike Pagliarulo .50 .15
❑ 686 Paul Miller RC .50 .15

#	Player	Nm-Mt	Ex-Mt
❑ 687	Mike Robertson RC	.50	.15
❑ 688	Mike Devereaux	.50	.15
❑ 689	Pedro Astacio RC	1.00	.30
❑ 690	Alan Trammell	.50	.15
❑ 691	Roger Clemens	2.50	.75
❑ 692	Bud Black	.50	.15
❑ 693	Turk Wendell RC	1.00	.30
❑ 694	Barry Larkin FOIL	.75	.23
❑ 695	Todd Zeile	.50	.15
❑ 696	Pat Hentgen	.50	.15
❑ 697	Eddie Taubensee RC	1.00	.30
❑ 698	G.Velasquez RC	.50	.15
❑ 699	Tom Glavine	.75	.23
❑ 700	Robin Yount	2.00	.60
❑ 701	Checklist 1-141	.50	.15
❑ 702	Checklist 142-282	.50	.15
❑ 703	Checklist 283-423	.50	.15
❑ 704	Checklist 424-564	.50	.15
❑ 705	Checklist 565-705	.50	.15

1993 Bowman

	Nm-Mt	Ex-Mt
COMPLETE SET (708)	50.00	15.00

#	Player	Nm-Mt	Ex-Mt
❑ 1	Glenn Davis	.15	.04
❑ 2	Hector Roa RC	.25	.07
❑ 3	Ken Ryan RC	.25	.07
❑ 4	Derek Wallace RC	.25	.07
❑ 5	Jorge Fabregas	.15	.04
❑ 6	Joe Oliver	.15	.04
❑ 7	Brandon Wilson	.15	.04
❑ 8	Mark Thompson RC	.25	.07
❑ 9	Tracy Sanders	.15	.04
❑ 10	Rich Renteria	.15	.04
❑ 11	Lou Whitaker	.30	.09
❑ 12	Brian L. Hunter RC	.50	.15
❑ 13	Joe Vitiello	.15	.04
❑ 14	Eric Karros	.30	.09
❑ 15	Joe Kmak	.15	.04
❑ 16	Tavo Alvarez	.15	.04
❑ 17	Steve Dunn RC	.25	.07
❑ 18	Tony Fernandez	.15	.04
❑ 19	Melido Perez	.15	.04
❑ 20	Mike Lieberthal	.15	.04
❑ 21	Terry Steinbach	.15	.04
❑ 22	Stan Belinda	.15	.04
❑ 23	Jay Buhner	.30	.09
❑ 24	Allen Watson	.15	.04
❑ 25	Daryl Henderson RC	.25	.07
❑ 26	Ray McDavid RC	.25	.07
❑ 27	Shawn Green	1.00	.30
❑ 28	Bud Black	.15	.04
❑ 29	Sherman Obando RC	.25	.07
❑ 30	Mike Hostetler RC	.25	.07
❑ 31	Nate Minchey RC	.25	.07
❑ 32	Randy Myers	.15	.04
❑ 33	Brian Grebeck	.15	.04
❑ 34	John Roper	.15	.04
❑ 35	Larry Thomas	.15	.04
❑ 36	Alex Cole	.15	.04
❑ 37	Tom Kramer RC	.25	.07
❑ 38	Matt Whisenant RC	.25	.07
❑ 39	Chris Gomez RC	.50	.15
❑ 40	Luis Gonzalez	.30	.09
❑ 41	Kevin Appier	.30	.09
❑ 42	Omar Daal RC	.50	.15
❑ 43	Duane Singleton	.15	.04
❑ 44	Bill Risley	.15	.04
❑ 45	Pat Meares RC	.50	.15
❑ 46	Butch Huskey	.15	.04
❑ 47	Bobby Munoz	.15	.04
❑ 48	Juan Bell	.15	.04
❑ 49	Scott Lydy RC	.25	.07
❑ 50	Dennis Moeller	.15	.04
❑ 51	Marc Newfield	.15	.04
❑ 52	Tripp Cromer RC	.25	.07
❑ 53	Kurt Miller	.15	.04
❑ 54	Jim Pena	.15	.04
❑ 55	Juan Guzman	.15	.04
❑ 56	Matt Williams	.30	.09
❑ 57	Harold Reynolds	.30	.09
❑ 58	Donnie Elliott RC	.25	.07
❑ 59	Jon Shave RC	.25	.07
❑ 60	Kevin Roberson RC	.25	.07
❑ 61	Hilly Hathaway RC	.25	.07
❑ 62	Jose Rijo	.15	.04
❑ 63	Kerry Taylor RC	.15	.04
❑ 64	Ryan Hawblitzel	.15	.04
❑ 65	Glenallen Hill	.15	.04
❑ 66	Ramon Martinez RC	.25	.07
❑ 67	Travis Fryman	.30	.09
❑ 68	Tom Nevers	.15	.04
❑ 69	Phil Hiatt	.15	.04
❑ 70	Tim Wallach	.15	.04
❑ 71	B.J. Surhoff	.30	.09
❑ 72	Rondell White	.30	.09
❑ 73	Denny Hocking RC	.50	.15
❑ 74	Mike Oquist RC	.25	.07
❑ 75	Paul O'Neill	.50	.15
❑ 76	Willie Banks	.15	.04
❑ 77	Bob Welch	.15	.04
❑ 78	Jose Sandoval RC	.25	.07
❑ 79	Bill Haselman	.15	.04
❑ 80	Rheal Cormier	.15	.04
❑ 81	Dean Palmer	.30	.09
❑ 82	Pat Gomez RC	.25	.07
❑ 83	Steve Karsay	.15	.04
❑ 84	Carl Hanselman RC	.25	.07
❑ 85	T.R. Lewis RC	.25	.07
❑ 86	Chipper Jones	.75	.23
❑ 87	Scott Hatteberg	.15	.04
❑ 88	Greg Hibbard	.15	.04
❑ 89	Lance Painter RC	.25	.07
❑ 90	Chad Mottola RC	.50	.15
❑ 91	Jason Bere	.15	.04
❑ 92	Dante Bichette	.30	.09
❑ 93	Sandy Alomar Jr.	.15	.04
❑ 94	Carl Everett	.30	.09
❑ 95	Danny Bautista RC	.50	.15
❑ 96	Steve Finley	.30	.09
❑ 97	David Cone	.30	.09
❑ 98	Todd Hollandsworth	.15	.04
❑ 99	Matt Mieske	.15	.04
❑ 100	Larry Walker	.30	.09
❑ 101	Shane Mack	.15	.04
❑ 102	Aaron Ledesma RC	.25	.07
❑ 103	Andy Pettitte RC	8.00	2.40
❑ 104	Kevin Stocker	.15	.04
❑ 105	Mike Mohler RC	.25	.07
❑ 106	Tony Menendez	.15	.04
❑ 107	Derek Lowe	.30	.09
❑ 108	Basil Shabazz	.15	.04
❑ 109	Dan Smith	.15	.04
❑ 110	Scott Sanders RC	.50	.15
❑ 111	Todd Stottlemyre	.15	.04
❑ 112	Benji Simonton RC	.25	.07
❑ 113	Rick Sutcliffe	.30	.09
❑ 114	Lee Heath RC	.25	.07
❑ 115	Jeff Russell	.15	.04
❑ 116	Dave Stevens RC	.25	.07
❑ 117	Mark Holzemer RC	.25	.07
❑ 118	Tim Belcher	.15	.04
❑ 119	Bobby Thigpen	.15	.04
❑ 120	Roger Bailey RC	.25	.07
❑ 121	Tony Mitchell RC	.25	.07
❑ 122	Junior Felix	.15	.04
❑ 123	Rich Robertson RC	.25	.07
❑ 124	Andy Cook RC	.25	.07
❑ 125	Brian Bevil RC	.25	.07
❑ 126	Darryl Strawberry	.30	.09
❑ 127	Cal Eldred	.15	.04
❑ 128	Cliff Floyd	.30	.09
❑ 129	Alan Newman	.15	.04
❑ 130	Howard Johnson	.15	.04
❑ 131	Jim Abbott	.50	.15
❑ 132	Chad McConnell	.15	.04
❑ 133	Miguel Jimenez RC	.25	.07
❑ 134	Brett Backlund RC	.25	.07
❑ 135	John Cummings RC	.25	.07
❑ 136	Brian Barber	.15	.04
❑ 137	Rafael Palmeiro	.50	.15
❑ 138	Tim Worrell RC	.25	.07
❑ 139	Jose Pett RC	.25	.07
❑ 140	Barry Bonds	2.00	.60
❑ 141	Damon Buford	.15	.04
❑ 142	Jeff Blauser	.15	.04
❑ 143	Frankie Rodriguez	.15	.04
❑ 144	Mike Morgan	.15	.04
❑ 145	Gary DiSarcina	.15	.04
❑ 146	Pokey Reese	.15	.04
❑ 147	Johnny Ruffin	.15	.04
❑ 148	David Nied	.15	.04
❑ 149	Charles Nagy	.15	.04
❑ 150	Mike Myers RC	.25	.07
❑ 151	Kenny Carlyle RC	.25	.07
❑ 152	Eric Anthony	.15	.04
❑ 153	Jose Lind	.15	.04
❑ 154	Pedro Martinez	1.50	.45
❑ 155	Mark Kiefer	.15	.04
❑ 156	Tim Laker RC	.25	.07
❑ 157	Pat Mahomes	.15	.04
❑ 158	Bobby Bonilla	.30	.09
❑ 159	Domingo Jean	.15	.04
❑ 160	Darren Daulton	.30	.09
❑ 161	Mark McGwire	2.00	.60
❑ 162	Jason Kendall RC	1.50	.45
❑ 163	Desi Relaford	.15	.04
❑ 164	Ozzie Canseco	.15	.04
❑ 165	Rick Helling	.15	.04
❑ 166	Steve Pegues RC	.25	.07
❑ 167	Paul Molitor	.50	.15
❑ 168	Larry Carter RC	.15	.04
❑ 169	Arthur Rhodes	.15	.04
❑ 170	Damon Hollins RC	1.00	.30
❑ 171	Frank Viola	.30	.09
❑ 172	Steve Trachsel RC	.50	.15
❑ 173	J.T. Snow RC	1.00	.30
❑ 174	Keith Gordon RC	.25	.07
❑ 175	Carlton Fisk	.50	.15
❑ 176	Jason Bates RC	.25	.07
❑ 177	Mike Crosby RC	.25	.07
❑ 178	Benny Santiago	.30	.09
❑ 179	Mike Moore	.15	.04
❑ 180	Jeff Juden	.15	.04
❑ 181	Darren Burton	.15	.04
❑ 182	Todd Williams RC	.50	.15
❑ 183	John Jaha	.15	.04
❑ 184	Mike Lansing RC	.50	.15
❑ 185	Pedro Grifol RC	.25	.07
❑ 186	Vince Coleman	.15	.04
❑ 187	Pat Kelly	.15	.04
❑ 188	Clemente Alvarez RC	.25	.07
❑ 189	Ron Darling	.15	.04
❑ 190	Orlando Merced	.15	.04
❑ 191	Chris Bosio	.15	.04
❑ 192	Steve Dixon RC	.25	.07
❑ 193	Doug Dascenzo	.15	.04
❑ 194	Ray Holbert RC	.25	.07
❑ 195	Howard Battle	.15	.04
❑ 196	Willie McGee	.30	.09
❑ 197	John O'Donoghue RC	.25	.07
❑ 198	Steve Avery	.15	.04
❑ 199	Greg Blosser	.15	.04
❑ 200	Ryne Sandberg	1.25	.35
❑ 201	Joe Grahe	.15	.04
❑ 202	Dan Wilson	.30	.09
❑ 203	Domingo Martinez RC	.25	.07
❑ 204	Andres Galarraga	.30	.09
❑ 205	Jamie Taylor RC	.25	.07
❑ 206	Darrell Whitmore RC	.25	.07
❑ 207	Ben Blomdahl RC	.25	.07
❑ 208	Doug Drabek	.15	.04
❑ 209	Keith Miller	.15	.04
❑ 210	Billy Ashley	.15	.04
❑ 211	Mike Farrell RC	.25	.07
❑ 212	John Wetteland	.30	.09
❑ 213	Randy Tomlin	.15	.04
❑ 214	Sid Fernandez	.15	.04
❑ 215	Quilvio Veras RC	.50	.15

❑ 216 Dave Hollins .15 .04
❑ 217 Mike Neill .15 .04
❑ 218 Andy Van Slyke .50 .15
❑ 219 Bret Boone .50 .15
❑ 220 Tom Pagnozzi .15 .04
❑ 221 Mike Welch RC .25 .07
❑ 222 Frank Seminara .15 .04
❑ 223 Ron Villone .15 .04
❑ 224 D.J. Thielen RC .25 .07
❑ 225 Cal Ripken 2.50 .75
❑ 226 Pedro Borbon Jr. RC .25 .07
❑ 227 Carlos Quintana .15 .04
❑ 228 Tommy Shields .15 .04
❑ 229 Tim Salmon .50 .15
❑ 230 John Smiley .15 .04
❑ 231 Ellis Burks .30 .09
❑ 232 Pedro Castellano .15 .04
❑ 233 Paul Byrd .30 .09
❑ 234 Bryan Harvey .15 .04
❑ 235 Scott Livingstone .15 .04
❑ 236 James Mouton RC .25 .07
❑ 237 Joe Randa .30 .09
❑ 238 Pedro Astacio .15 .04
❑ 239 Darryl Hamilton .15 .04
❑ 240 Joey Eischen RC .25 .07
❑ 241 Edgar Herrera RC .25 .07
❑ 242 Dwight Gooden .30 .09
❑ 243 Sam Militello .15 .04
❑ 244 Ron Blazier RC .25 .07
❑ 245 Ruben Sierra .15 .04
❑ 246 Al Martin .15 .04
❑ 247 Mike Felder .15 .04
❑ 248 Bob Tewksbury .15 .04
❑ 249 Craig Lefferts .15 .04
❑ 250 Luis Lopez RC .25 .07
❑ 251 Devon White .30 .09
❑ 252 Will Clark .50 .15
❑ 253 Mark Smith .15 .04
❑ 254 Terry Pendleton .30 .09
❑ 255 Aaron Sele .15 .04
❑ 256 Jose Viera RC .25 .07
❑ 257 Damion Easley .15 .04
❑ 258 Rod Lofton RC .25 .07
❑ 259 Chris Snopek RC .25 .07
❑ 260 Q.McCracken RC .50 .15
❑ 261 Mike Matthews RC .25 .07
❑ 262 Hector Carrasco RC .25 .07
❑ 263 Rick Greene .15 .04
❑ 264 Chris Holt RC .50 .15
❑ 265 George Brett 2.00 .60
❑ 266 Rick Gorecki RC .25 .07
❑ 267 Francisco Gamez RC .25 .07
❑ 268 Marquis Grissom .30 .09
❑ 269 Kevin Tapani UER .15 .04
(Misspelled Tapan
on card front)
❑ 270 Ryan Thompson .15 .04
❑ 271 Gerald Williams .15 .04
❑ 272 Paul Fletcher RC .25 .07
❑ 273 Lance Blankenship .15 .04
❑ 274 Marty Neff RC .25 .07
❑ 275 Shawn Estes .15 .04
❑ 276 Rene Arocha RC .50 .15
❑ 277 Scott Eyre RC .25 .07
❑ 278 Phil Plantier .15 .04
❑ 279 Paul Spoljaric RC .25 .07
❑ 280 Chris Gambs .15 .04
❑ 281 Harold Baines .30 .09
❑ 282 Jose Oliva .15 .04
❑ 283 Matt Whiteside RC .25 .07
❑ 284 Brant Brown RC .50 .15
❑ 285 Russ Springer .15 .04
❑ 286 Chris Sabo .15 .04
❑ 287 Ozzie Guillen .30 .09
❑ 288 Marcus Moore RC .25 .07
❑ 289 Chad Ogea .15 .04
❑ 290 Walt Weiss .15 .04
❑ 291 Brian Edmondson .15 .04
❑ 292 Jimmy Gonzalez .15 .04
❑ 293 Danny Miceli RC .50 .15
❑ 294 Jose Offerman .15 .04
❑ 295 Greg Vaughn .15 .04
❑ 296 Frank Bolick .15 .04
❑ 297 Mike Maksudian RC .25 .07
❑ 298 John Franco .30 .09
❑ 299 Danny Tartabull .15 .04
❑ 300 Len Dykstra .30 .09
❑ 301 Bobby Witt .15 .04
❑ 302 Trey Beamon RC .25 .07
❑ 303 Tino Martinez .50 .15
❑ 304 Aaron Holbert .15 .04
❑ 305 Juan Gonzalez .30 .09
❑ 306 Billy Hall RC .25 .07
❑ 307 Duane Ward .15 .04
❑ 308 Rod Beck .15 .04
❑ 309 Jose Mercedes RC .25 .07
❑ 310 Otis Nixon .15 .04
❑ 311 Gettys Glaze RC .25 .07
❑ 312 Candy Maldonado .15 .04
❑ 313 Chad Curtis .15 .04
❑ 314 Tim Costo .15 .04
❑ 315 Mike Robertson .15 .04
❑ 316 Nigel Wilson .15 .04
❑ 317 Greg McMichael RC .50 .15
❑ 318 Scott Pose RC .25 .07
❑ 319 Ivan Cruz .15 .04
❑ 320 Greg Swindell .15 .04
❑ 321 Kevin McReynolds .15 .04
❑ 322 Tom Candiotti .15 .04
❑ 323 Rob Wishnevski RC .25 .07
❑ 324 Ken Hill .15 .04
❑ 325 Kirby Puckett .75 .23
❑ 326 Tim Bogar RC .25 .07
❑ 327 Mariano Rivera 2.00 .60
❑ 328 Mitch Williams .15 .04
❑ 329 Craig Paquette .15 .04
❑ 330 Jay Bell .30 .09
❑ 331 Jose Martinez RC .25 .07
❑ 332 Rob Deer .15 .04
❑ 333 Brook Fordyce .15 .04
❑ 334 Matt Nokes .15 .04
❑ 335 Derek Lee .15 .04
❑ 336 Paul Ellis RC .25 .07
❑ 337 Desi Wilson RC .25 .07
❑ 338 Roberto Alomar .50 .15
❑ 339 Jim Tatum FOIL RC .25 .07
❑ 340 J.T. Snow FOIL 1.00 .30
❑ 341 Tim Salmon FOIL .50 .15
❑ 342 Russ Davis FOIL RC .50 .15
❑ 343 Javy Lopez FOIL .50 .15
❑ 344 Troy O'Leary FOIL RC .50 .15
❑ 345 M.Cordova FOIL RC .50 .15
❑ 346 Bubba Smith RC FOIL .25 .07
❑ 347 Chipper Jones FOIL .75 .23
❑ 348 Jessie Hollins FOIL .15 .04
❑ 349 Willie Greene FOIL .15 .04
❑ 350 Mark Thompson FOIL .15 .04
❑ 351 Nigel Wilson FOIL .15 .04
❑ 352 Todd Jones FOIL .30 .09
❑ 353 Raul Mondesi FOIL .30 .09
❑ 354 Cliff Floyd FOIL .30 .09
❑ 355 Bobby Jones FOIL .30 .09
❑ 356 Kevin Stocker FOIL .15 .04
❑ 357 M.Cummings FOIL .15 .04
❑ 358 Allen Watson FOIL .15 .04
❑ 359 Ray McDavid FOIL .15 .04
❑ 360 Steve Hosey FOIL .15 .04
❑ 361 B.Pennington FOIL .15 .04
❑ 362 F.Rodriguez FOIL .15 .04
❑ 363 Troy Percival FOIL .50 .15
❑ 364 Jason Bere FOIL .15 .04
❑ 365 Manny Ramirez FOIL 1.25 .35
❑ 366 J.Thompson FOIL .15 .04
❑ 367 Joe Vitiello FOIL .15 .04
❑ 368 Tyrone Hill FOIL .15 .04
❑ 369 David McCarty FOIL .15 .04
❑ 370 Brien Taylor FOIL .15 .04
❑ 371 T.Van Poppel FOIL .15 .04
❑ 372 Marc Newfield FOIL .15 .04
❑ 373 T.Lowery RC FOIL .50 .15
❑ 374 Alex Gonzalez FOIL .15 .04
❑ 375 Ken Griffey Jr. 1.25 .35
❑ 376 Donovan Osborne .15 .04
❑ 377 Ritchie Moody RC .25 .07
❑ 378 Shane Andrews .15 .04
❑ 379 Carlos Delgado .75 .23
❑ 380 Bill Swift .15 .04
❑ 381 Leo Gomez .15 .04
❑ 382 Ron Gant .30 .09
❑ 383 Scott Fletcher .15 .04
❑ 384 Matt Walbeck RC .50 .15
❑ 385 Chuck Finley .30 .09
❑ 386 Kevin Mitchell .15 .04
❑ 387 Wilson Alvarez UER .15 .04
(Misspelled Alverez
on card front)
❑ 388 John Burke RC .25 .07
❑ 389 Alan Embree .15 .04
❑ 390 Trevor Hoffman .75 .23
❑ 391 Alan Trammell .30 .09
❑ 392 Todd Jones .30 .09
❑ 393 Felix Jose .15 .04
❑ 394 Orel Hershiser .30 .09
❑ 395 Pat Listach .15 .04
❑ 396 Gabe White .15 .04
❑ 397 Dan Serafini RC .25 .07
❑ 398 Todd Hundley .15 .04
❑ 399 Wade Boggs .50 .15
❑ 400 Tyler Green .15 .04
❑ 401 Mike Bordick .15 .04
❑ 402 Scott Bullett .15 .04
❑ 403 LaGrande Russell RC .25 .07
❑ 404 Ray Lankford .30 .09
❑ 405 Nolan Ryan 3.00 .90
❑ 406 Robbie Beckett .15 .04
❑ 407 Brent Bowers RC .25 .07
❑ 408 Adell Davenport RC .25 .07
❑ 409 Brady Anderson .30 .09
❑ 410 Tom Glavine .50 .15
❑ 411 Doug Hecker RC .25 .07
❑ 412 Jose Guzman .15 .04
❑ 413 Luis Polonia .15 .04
❑ 414 Brian Williams .15 .04
❑ 415 Bo Jackson .75 .23
❑ 416 Eric Young .15 .04
❑ 417 Kenny Lofton .30 .09
❑ 418 Orestes Destrade .15 .04
❑ 419 Tony Phillips .15 .04
❑ 420 Jeff Bagwell .50 .15
❑ 421 Mark Gardner .15 .04
❑ 422 Brett Butler .30 .09
❑ 423 Graeme Lloyd RC .50 .15
❑ 424 Delino DeShields .15 .04
❑ 425 Scott Erickson .15 .04
❑ 426 Jeff Kent .75 .23
❑ 427 Jimmy Key .30 .09
❑ 428 Mickey Morandini .15 .04
❑ 429 Marcos Armas RC .25 .07
❑ 430 Don Slaught .15 .04
❑ 431 Randy Johnson .75 .23
❑ 432 Omar Olivares .15 .04
❑ 433 Charlie Leibrandt .15 .04
❑ 434 Kurt Stillwell .15 .04
❑ 435 Scott Brow RC .25 .07
❑ 436 Robby Thompson .15 .04
❑ 437 Ben McDonald .15 .04
❑ 438 Deion Sanders .50 .15
❑ 439 Tony Pena .15 .04
❑ 440 Mark Grace .50 .15
❑ 441 Eduardo Perez .15 .04
❑ 442 Tim Pugh RC .25 .07
❑ 443 Scott Ruffcorn .15 .04
❑ 444 Jay Gainer RC .25 .07
❑ 445 Albert Belle .30 .09
❑ 446 Bret Barberie .15 .04
❑ 447 Justin Mashore .15 .04
❑ 448 Pete Harnisch .15 .04
❑ 449 Greg Gagne .15 .04
❑ 450 Eric Davis .30 .09
❑ 451 Dave Mlicki .15 .04
❑ 452 Moises Alou .30 .09
❑ 453 Rick Aguilera .15 .04
❑ 454 Eddie Murray .75 .23
❑ 455 Bob Wickman .15 .04
❑ 456 Wes Chamberlain .15 .04
❑ 457 Brent Gates .15 .04
❑ 458 Paul Wagner .15 .04
❑ 459 Mike Hampton .30 .09
❑ 460 Ozzie Smith 1.25 .35
❑ 461 Tom Henke .15 .04
❑ 462 Ricky Gutierrez .15 .04
❑ 463 Jack Morris .30 .09
❑ 464 Joel Chimelis .15 .04
❑ 465 Gregg Olson .15 .04
❑ 466 Javy Lopez .50 .15
❑ 467 Scott Cooper .15 .04
❑ 468 Willie Wilson .15 .04
❑ 469 Mark Langston .15 .04

Card	Nm-Mt	Ex-Mt
❑ 470 Barry Larkin	.50	.15
❑ 471 Rod Bolton	.15	.04
❑ 472 Freddie Benavides	.15	.04
❑ 473 Ken Ramos RC	.25	.07
❑ 474 Chuck Carr	.15	.04
❑ 475 Cecil Fielder	.30	.09
❑ 476 Eddie Taubensee	.15	.04
❑ 477 Chris Eddy RC	.25	.07
❑ 478 Greg Hansell	.15	.04
❑ 479 Kevin Reimer	.15	.04
❑ 480 Dennis Martinez	.30	.09
❑ 481 Chuck Knoblauch	.30	.09
❑ 482 Mike Draper	.15	.04
❑ 483 Spike Owen	.15	.04
❑ 484 Terry Mulholland	.15	.04
❑ 485 Dennis Eckersley	.30	.09
❑ 486 Blas Minor	.15	.04
❑ 487 Dave Fleming	.15	.04
❑ 488 Dan Cholowsky	.15	.04
❑ 489 Ivan Rodriguez	.50	.15
❑ 490 Gary Sheffield	.30	.09
❑ 491 Ed Sprague	.15	.04
❑ 492 Steve Hosey	.15	.04
❑ 493 Jimmy Haynes RC	.50	.15
❑ 494 John Smoltz	.50	.15
❑ 495 Andre Dawson	.30	.09
❑ 496 Rey Sanchez	.15	.04
❑ 497 Ty Van Burkleo	.15	.04
❑ 498 Bobby Ayala RC	.25	.07
❑ 499 Tim Raines	.30	.09
❑ 500 Charlie Hayes	.15	.04
❑ 501 Paul Sorrento	.15	.04
❑ 502 Richie Lewis RC	.25	.07
❑ 503 Jason Pfaff RC	.25	.07
❑ 504 Ken Caminiti	.30	.09
❑ 505 Mike Macfarlane	.15	.04
❑ 506 Jody Reed	.15	.04
❑ 507 Bobby Hughes RC	.25	.07
❑ 508 Wil Cordero	.15	.04
❑ 509 George Tsamis RC	.25	.07
❑ 510 Bret Saberhagen	.30	.09
❑ 511 Derek Jeter RC	20.00	6.00
❑ 512 Gene Schall	.15	.04
❑ 513 Curtis Shaw	.15	.04
❑ 514 Steve Cooke	.15	.04
❑ 515 Edgar Martinez	.50	.15
❑ 516 Mike Milchin	.15	.04
❑ 517 Billy Ripken	.15	.04
❑ 518 Andy Benes	.15	.04
❑ 519 Juan de la Rosa RC	.25	.07
❑ 520 John Burkett	.15	.04
❑ 521 Alex Ochoa	.15	.04
❑ 522 Tony Tarasco RC	.50	.15
❑ 523 Luis Ortiz	.15	.04
❑ 524 Rick Wilkins	.15	.04
❑ 525 Chris Turner RC	.25	.07
❑ 526 Rob Dibble	.30	.09
❑ 527 Jack McDowell	.15	.04
❑ 528 Daryl Boston	.15	.04
❑ 529 Bill Wertz RC	.25	.07
❑ 530 Charlie Hough	.30	.09
❑ 531 Sean Bergman	.15	.04
❑ 532 Doug Jones	.15	.04
❑ 533 Jeff Montgomery	.15	.04
❑ 534 Roger Cedeno RC	.50	.15
❑ 535 Robin Yount	1.25	.35
❑ 536 Mo Vaughn	.30	.09
❑ 537 Brian Harper	.15	.04
❑ 538 Juan Castillo RC	.15	.04
❑ 539 Steve Farr	.15	.04
❑ 540 John Kruk	.30	.09
❑ 541 Troy Neel	.15	.04
❑ 542 Danny Clyburn RC	.25	.07
❑ 543 Jim Converse RC	.25	.07
❑ 544 Gregg Jefferies	.15	.04
❑ 545 Jose Canseco	.50	.15
❑ 546 Julio Bruno RC	.25	.07
❑ 547 Rob Butler	.15	.04
❑ 548 Royce Clayton	.15	.04
❑ 549 Chris Hoiles	.15	.04
❑ 550 Greg Maddux	1.25	.35
❑ 551 Joe Ciccarella RC	.25	.07
❑ 552 Ozzie Timmons	.15	.04
❑ 553 Chili Davis	.30	.09
❑ 554 Brian Koelling	.15	.04
❑ 555 Frank Thomas	.75	.23
❑ 556 Vinny Castilla	.75	.23
❑ 557 Reggie Jefferson	.15	.04
❑ 558 Rob Natal	.15	.04
❑ 559 Mike Henneman	.15	.04
❑ 560 Craig Biggio	.50	.15
❑ 561 Billy Brewer	.15	.04
❑ 562 Dan Melendez	.15	.04
❑ 563 Kenny Felder RC	.25	.07
❑ 564 Miguel Batista RC	1.00	.30
❑ 565 Dave Winfield	.30	.09
❑ 566 Al Shirley	.15	.04
❑ 567 Robert Eenhoorn	.15	.04
❑ 568 Mike Williams	.15	.04
❑ 569 Tanyon Sturtze RC	.50	.15
❑ 570 Tim Wakefield	.75	.23
❑ 571 Greg Pirkl	.15	.04
❑ 572 Sean Lowe RC	.25	.07
❑ 573 Terry Burrows RC	.25	.07
❑ 574 Kevin Higgins	.15	.04
❑ 575 Joe Carter	.30	.09
❑ 576 Kevin Rogers	.15	.04
❑ 577 Manny Alexander	.15	.04
❑ 578 David Justice	.30	.09
❑ 579 Brian Conroy RC	.25	.07
❑ 580 Jessie Hollins	.15	.04
❑ 581 Ron Watson RC	.25	.07
❑ 582 Bip Roberts	.15	.04
❑ 583 Tom Urbani RC	.25	.07
❑ 584 Jason Hutchins RC	.25	.07
❑ 585 Carlos Baerga	.15	.04
❑ 586 Jeff Mutis	.15	.04
❑ 587 Justin Thompson	.15	.04
❑ 588 Orlando Miller	.15	.04
❑ 589 Brian McRae	.15	.04
❑ 590 Ramon Martinez	.15	.04
❑ 591 Dave Nilsson	.15	.04
❑ 592 Jose Vidro RC	1.50	.45
❑ 593 Rich Becker	.15	.04
❑ 594 Preston Wilson RC	1.50	.45
❑ 595 Don Mattingly	2.00	.60
❑ 596 Tony Longmire	.15	.04
❑ 597 Kevin Seitzer	.15	.04
❑ 598 Midre Cummings RC	.25	.07
❑ 599 Omar Vizquel	.50	.15
❑ 600 Lee Smith	.30	.09
❑ 601 David Hulse RC	.25	.07
❑ 602 Darrell Sherman RC	.25	.07
❑ 603 Alex Gonzalez	.15	.04
❑ 604 Geronimo Pena	.15	.04
❑ 605 Mike Devereaux	.15	.04
❑ 606 S.Hitchcock RC	.50	.15
❑ 607 Mike Greenwell	.15	.04
❑ 608 Steve Buechele	.15	.04
❑ 609 Troy Percival	.50	.15
❑ 610 Roberto Kelly	.15	.04
❑ 611 James Baldwin RC	.50	.15
❑ 612 Jerald Clark	.15	.04
❑ 613 Albie Lopez RC	.50	.15
❑ 614 Dave Magadan	.15	.04
❑ 615 Mickey Tettleton	.15	.04
❑ 616 Sean Runyan RC	.25	.07
❑ 617 Bob Hamelin	.15	.04
❑ 618 Raul Mondesi	.30	.09
❑ 619 Tyrone Hill	.15	.04
❑ 620 Darrin Fletcher	.15	.04
❑ 621 Mike Trombley	.15	.04
❑ 622 Jeromy Burnitz	.30	.09
❑ 623 Bernie Williams	.50	.15
❑ 624 Mike Farmer RC	.25	.07
❑ 625 Rickey Henderson	.75	.23
❑ 626 Carlos Garcia	.15	.04
❑ 627 Jeff Darwin RC	.25	.07
❑ 628 Todd Zeile	.15	.04
❑ 629 Benji Gil	.15	.04
❑ 630 Tony Gwynn	1.00	.30
❑ 631 Aaron Small RC	1.00	.30
❑ 632 Joe Rosselli RC	.25	.07
❑ 633 Mike Mussina	.50	.15
❑ 634 Ryan Klesko	.30	.09
❑ 635 Roger Clemens	1.50	.45
❑ 636 Sammy Sosa	.75	.23
❑ 637 Orlando Palmeiro RC	.25	.07
❑ 638 Willie Greene	.15	.04
❑ 639 George Bell	.15	.04
❑ 640 Garvin Alston RC	.25	.07
❑ 641 Pete Janicki RC	.25	.07
❑ 642 Chris Sheff RC	.25	.07
❑ 643 Felipe Lira RC	.25	.07
❑ 644 Roberto Petagine	.15	.04
❑ 645 Wally Joyner	.30	.09
❑ 646 Mike Piazza	3.00	.90
❑ 647 Jaime Navarro	.15	.04
❑ 648 Jeff Hartsock	.15	.04
❑ 649 David McCarty	.15	.04
❑ 650 Bobby Jones	.30	.09
❑ 651 Mark Hutton	.15	.04
❑ 652 Kyle Abbott	.15	.04
❑ 653 Steve Cox RC	.50	.15
❑ 654 Jeff King	.15	.04
❑ 655 Norm Charlton	.15	.04
❑ 656 Mike Gulan RC	.25	.07
❑ 657 Julio Franco	.30	.09
❑ 658 C.Cairncross RC	.25	.07
❑ 659 John Olerud	.30	.09
❑ 660 Salomon Torres	.15	.04
❑ 661 Brad Pennington	.15	.04
❑ 662 Melvin Nieves	.15	.04
❑ 663 Ivan Calderon	.15	.04
❑ 664 Turk Wendell	.15	.04
❑ 665 Chris Pritchett	.15	.04
❑ 666 Reggie Sanders	.30	.09
❑ 667 Robin Ventura	.30	.09
❑ 668 Joe Girardi	.15	.04
❑ 669 Manny Ramirez	1.25	.35
❑ 670 Jeff Conine	.30	.09
❑ 671 Greg Gohr	.15	.04
❑ 672 Andujar Cedeno	.15	.04
❑ 673 Les Norman RC	.25	.07
❑ 674 Mike James RC	.25	.07
❑ 675 Marshall Boze RC	.25	.07
❑ 676 B.J. Wallace	.15	.04
❑ 677 Kent Hrbek	.30	.09
❑ 678 Jack Voigt RC	.25	.07
❑ 679 Brien Taylor	.15	.04
❑ 680 Curt Schilling	.30	.09
❑ 681 Todd Van Poppel	.15	.04
❑ 682 Kevin Young	.30	.09
❑ 683 Tommy Adams	.15	.04
❑ 684 Bernard Gilkey	.15	.04
❑ 685 Kevin Brown	.30	.09
❑ 686 Fred McGriff	.50	.15
❑ 687 Pat Borders	.15	.04
❑ 688 Kirt Manwaring	.15	.04
❑ 689 Sid Bream	.15	.04
❑ 690 John Valentin	.15	.04
❑ 691 Steve Olsen RC	.25	.07
❑ 692 Roberto Mejia RC	.25	.07
❑ 693 Carlos Delgado FOIL	.75	.23
❑ 694 S.Gibralter FOIL RC	.25	.07
❑ 695 Gary Mota FOIL RC	.25	.07
❑ 696 Jose Malave FOIL RC	.25	.07
❑ 697 Larry Sutton FOIL RC	.25	.07
❑ 698 Dan Frye FOIL RC	.25	.07
❑ 699 Tim Clark FOIL RC	.25	.07
❑ 700 Brian Rupp FOIL RC	.25	.07
❑ 701 Felipe Alou FOIL / Moises Alou	.30	.09
❑ 702 Barry Bonds FOIL / Bobby Bonds	1.00	.30
❑ 703 Ken Griffey Sr. FOIL / Ken Griffey Jr.	.75	.23
❑ 704 Brian McRae FOIL / Hal McRae	.15	.04
❑ 705 Checklist 1	.15	.04
❑ 706 Checklist 2	.15	.04
❑ 707 Checklist 3	.15	.04
❑ 708 Checklist 4	.15	.04

1994 Bowman

	Nm-Mt	Ex-Mt
COMPLETE SET (682)	60.00	18.00
❑ 1 Joe Carter	.40	.12
❑ 2 Marcus Moore	.25	.07
❑ 3 Doug Creek RC	.40	.12
❑ 4 Pedro Martinez	1.00	.30
❑ 5 Ken Griffey Jr.	1.50	.45
❑ 6 Greg Swindell	.25	.07
❑ 7 J.J. Johnson	.25	.07
❑ 8 Homer Bush RC	.75	.23
❑ 9 Arquimedez Pozo RC	.40	.12

❑ 10 Bryan Harvey .25 .07
❑ 11 J.T. Snow .40 .12
❑ 12 Alan Benes RC .75 .23
❑ 13 Chad Kreuter .25 .07
❑ 14 Eric Karros .40 .12
❑ 15 Frank Thomas 1.00 .30
❑ 16 Bret Saberhagen .40 .12
❑ 17 Terrell Lowery .25 .07
❑ 18 Rod Bolton .25 .07
❑ 19 Harold Baines .40 .12
❑ 20 Matt Walbeck .25 .07
❑ 21 Tom Glavine .60 .18
❑ 22 Todd Jones .25 .07
❑ 23 Alberto Castillo RC .40 .12
❑ 24 Ruben Sierra .25 .07
❑ 25 Don Mattingly 2.50 .75
❑ 26 Mike Morgan .25 .07
❑ 27 Jim Musselwhite RC .40 .12
❑ 28 Matt Brunson RC .40 .12
❑ 29 A.Meinershagen RC .40 .12
❑ 30 Joe Girardi .25 .07
❑ 31 Shane Halter .25 .07
❑ 32 Jose Paniagua RC .75 .23
❑ 33 Paul Perkins RC .40 .12
❑ 34 John Hudek RC .40 .12
❑ 35 Frank Viola .40 .12
❑ 36 David Lamb RC .40 .12
❑ 37 Marshall Boze .25 .07
❑ 38 Jorge Posada RC 8.00 2.40
❑ 39 Brian Anderson RC .75 .23
❑ 40 Mark Whiten .25 .07
❑ 41 Sean Bergman .25 .07
❑ 42 Jose Parra RC .40 .12
❑ 43 Mike Robertson .25 .07
❑ 44 Pete Walker RC .40 .12
❑ 45 Juan Gonzalez .40 .12
❑ 46 Cleveland Ladell RC .40 .12
❑ 47 Mark Smith .25 .07
❑ 48 Kevin Jarvis UER .40 .12
(team listed as Yankees on back)
❑ 49 Amaury Telemaco RC .40 .12
❑ 50 Andy Van Slyke .60 .18
❑ 51 Rikkert Faneyte RC .40 .12
❑ 52 Curtis Shaw .25 .07
❑ 53 Matt Drews RC .40 .12
❑ 54 Wilson Alvarez .25 .07
❑ 55 Manny Ramirez 1.00 .30
❑ 56 Bobby Munoz .25 .07
❑ 57 Ed Sprague .25 .07
❑ 58 Jamey Wright RC .75 .23
❑ 59 Jeff Montgomery .25 .07
❑ 60 Kirk Rueter .40 .12
❑ 61 Edgar Martinez .60 .18
❑ 62 Luis Gonzalez .40 .12
❑ 63 Tim Vanegmond RC .40 .12
❑ 64 Bip Roberts .25 .07
❑ 65 John Jaha .25 .07
❑ 66 Chuck Carr .25 .07
❑ 67 Chuck Finley .40 .12
❑ 68 Aaron Holbert .25 .07
❑ 69 Cecil Fielder .40 .12
❑ 70 Tom Engle RC .40 .12
❑ 71 Ron Karkovice .25 .07
❑ 72 Joe Orsulak .25 .07
❑ 73 Duff Brumley RC .40 .12
❑ 74 Craig Clayton RC .40 .12
❑ 75 Cal Ripken 3.00 .90
❑ 76 Brad Fulimer RC 1.25 .35
❑ 77 Tony Tarasco .25 .07
❑ 78 Terry Farrar RC .40 .12
❑ 79 Matt Williams .40 .12
❑ 80 Rickey Henderson 1.00 .30
❑ 81 Terry Mulholland .25 .07
❑ 82 Sammy Sosa 1.00 .30
❑ 83 Paul Sorrento .25 .07
❑ 84 Pete Incaviglia .25 .07
❑ 85 Darren Hall RC .40 .12
❑ 86 Scott Klingenbeck .25 .07
❑ 87 Dario Perez RC .40 .12
❑ 88 Ugueth Urbina .25 .07
❑ 89 Dave Vanhof RC .40 .12
❑ 90 Domingo Jean .25 .07
❑ 91 Otis Nixon .25 .07
❑ 92 Andres Berumen .25 .07
❑ 93 Jose Valentin .25 .07
❑ 94 Edgar Renteria RC 4.00 1.20
❑ 95 Chris Turner .25 .07
❑ 96 Ray Lankford .40 .12
❑ 97 Danny Bautista .25 .07
❑ 98 Chan Ho Park RC 1.25 .35
❑ 99 Glenn DiSarcina RC .40 .12
❑ 100 Butch Huskey .25 .07
❑ 101 Ivan Rodriguez .60 .18
❑ 102 Johnny Ruffin .25 .07
❑ 103 Alex Ochoa .25 .07
❑ 104 Torii Hunter RC 5.00 1.50
❑ 105 Ryan Klesko .40 .12
❑ 106 Jay Bell .40 .12
❑ 107 Kurt Peltzer RC .40 .12
❑ 108 Miguel Jimenez .25 .07
❑ 109 Russ Davis .25 .07
❑ 110 Derek Wallace .25 .07
❑ 111 Keith Lockhart RC .75 .23
❑ 112 Mike Lieberthal .25 .07
❑ 113 Dave Stewart .40 .12
❑ 114 Tom Schmidt .25 .07
❑ 115 Brian McRae .25 .07
❑ 116 Moises Alou .40 .12
❑ 117 Dave Fleming .25 .07
❑ 118 Jeff Bagwell .60 .18
❑ 119 Luis Ortiz .25 .07
❑ 120 Tony Gwynn 1.25 .35
❑ 121 Jaime Navarro .25 .07
❑ 122 Benito Santiago .40 .12
❑ 123 Darrell Whitmore .25 .07
❑ 124 John Mabry RC 1.25 .35
❑ 125 Mickey Tettleton .25 .07
❑ 126 Tom Candiotti .25 .07
❑ 127 Tim Raines .40 .12
❑ 128 Bobby Bonilla .40 .12
❑ 129 John Dettmer .25 .07
❑ 130 Hector Carrasco .25 .07
❑ 131 Chris Hoiles .25 .07
❑ 132 Rick Aguilera .25 .07
❑ 133 David Justice .40 .12
❑ 134 Esteban Loaiza RC 1.25 .35
❑ 135 Barry Bonds 2.50 .75
❑ 136 Bob Welch .25 .07
❑ 137 Mike Stanley .25 .07
❑ 138 Roberto Hernandez .25 .07
❑ 139 Sandy Alomar Jr. .25 .07
❑ 140 Darren Daulton .40 .12
❑ 141 Angel Martinez RC .40 .12
❑ 142 Howard Johnson .25 .07
❑ 143 Bob Hamelin UER .25 .07
(name and card number colors don't match)
❑ 144 J.J. Thobe RC .40 .12
❑ 145 Roger Salkeld .25 .07
❑ 146 Orlando Miller .25 .07
❑ 147 Dmitri Young .40 .12
❑ 148 Tim Hyers RC .40 .12
❑ 149 Mark Loretta RC 4.00 1.20
❑ 150 Chris Hammond .25 .07
❑ 151 Joel Moore RC .40 .12
❑ 152 Todd Zeile .25 .07
❑ 153 Wil Cordero .25 .07
❑ 154 Chris Smith .25 .07
❑ 155 James Baldwin .25 .07
❑ 156 Edgardo Alfonzo RC 1.25 .35
❑ 157 Kym Ashworth RC .40 .12
❑ 158 Paul Bako RC .40 .12
❑ 159 Rick Krivda RC .40 .12
❑ 160 Pat Mahomes .25 .07
❑ 161 Damon Hollins .25 .07
❑ 162 Felix Martinez RC .40 .12
❑ 163 Jason Myers RC .40 .12
❑ 164 Izzy Molina RC .40 .12
❑ 165 Brien Taylor .25 .07
❑ 166 Kevin Orie RC .40 .12
❑ 167 Casey Whitten RC .40 .12
❑ 168 Tony Longmire .25 .07
❑ 169 John Olerud .40 .12
❑ 170 Mark Thompson .25 .07
❑ 171 Jorge Fabregas .25 .07
❑ 172 John Wetteland .40 .12
❑ 173 Dan Wilson .25 .07
❑ 174 Doug Drabek .25 .07
❑ 175 Jeff McNeely .25 .07
❑ 176 Melvin Nieves .25 .07
❑ 177 Doug Glanville RC .75 .23
❑ 178 Javier De La Hoya RC .40 .12
❑ 179 Chad Curtis .25 .07
❑ 180 Brian Barber .25 .07
❑ 181 Mike Henneman .25 .07
❑ 182 Jose Offerman .25 .07
❑ 183 Robert Ellis RC .40 .12
❑ 184 John Franco .40 .12
❑ 185 Benji Gil .25 .07
❑ 186 Hal Morris .25 .07
❑ 187 Chris Sabo .25 .07
❑ 188 Blaise Ilsley RC .40 .12
❑ 189 Steve Avery .25 .07
❑ 190 Rick White RC .40 .12
❑ 191 Rod Beck .25 .07
❑ 192 Mark McGwire UER 2.50 .75
(No card number on back)
❑ 193 Jim Abbott .60 .18
❑ 194 Randy Myers .25 .07
❑ 195 Kenny Lofton .40 .12
❑ 196 Mariano Duncan .25 .07
❑ 197 Lee Daniels RC .40 .12
❑ 198 Armando Reynoso .25 .07
❑ 199 Joe Randa .25 .07
❑ 200 Cliff Floyd .40 .12
❑ 201 Tim Harkrider RC .40 .12
❑ 202 Kevin Gallaher RC .40 .12
❑ 203 Scott Cooper .25 .07
❑ 204 Phil Stidham RC .40 .12
❑ 205 Jeff D'Amico RC .75 .23
❑ 206 Matt Whisenant .25 .07
❑ 207 De Shawn Warren .25 .07
❑ 208 Rene Arocha .25 .07
❑ 209 Tony Clark RC 1.25 .35
❑ 210 Jason Jacome RC .40 .12
❑ 211 Scott Christman RC .40 .12
❑ 212 Bill Pulsipher .40 .12
❑ 213 Dean Palmer .40 .12
❑ 214 Chad Mottola .25 .07
❑ 215 Manny Alexander .25 .07
❑ 216 Rich Becker .25 .07
❑ 217 Andre King RC .40 .12
❑ 218 Carlos Garcia .25 .07
❑ 219 Ron Pezzoni RC .40 .12
❑ 220 Steve Karsay .25 .07
❑ 221 Jose Musset RC .40 .12
❑ 222 Karl Rhodes .25 .07
❑ 223 Frank Cimorelli RC .40 .12
❑ 224 Kevin Jordan RC .40 .12
❑ 225 Duane Ward .25 .07
❑ 226 John Burke .25 .07
❑ 227 Mike Macfarlane .25 .07
❑ 228 Mike Lansing .25 .07
❑ 229 Chuck Knoblauch .40 .12
❑ 230 Ken Caminiti .40 .12
❑ 231 Gar Finnvold RC .40 .12
❑ 232 Derrek Lee RC 10.00 3.00
❑ 233 Brady Anderson .40 .12
❑ 234 Vic Darensbourg RC .40 .12
❑ 235 Mark Langston .25 .07
❑ 236 T.J. Mathews RC .40 .12
❑ 237 Lou Whitaker .40 .12
❑ 238 Roger Cedeno .25 .07
❑ 239 Alex Fernandez .25 .07
❑ 240 Ryan Thompson .25 .07
❑ 241 Kerry Lacy RC .40 .12
❑ 242 Reggie Sanders .40 .12
❑ 243 Brad Pennington .25 .07
❑ 244 Bryan Eversgerd RC .40 .12
❑ 245 Greg Maddux 1.50 .45

❑	246	Jason Kendall	.40	.12
❑	247	J.R. Phillips	.25	.07
❑	248	Bobby Witt	.25	.07
❑	249	Paul O'Neill	.60	.18
❑	250	Ryne Sandberg	1.50	.45
❑	251	Charles Nagy	.25	.07
❑	252	Kevin Stocker	.25	.07
❑	253	Shawn Green	1.00	.30
❑	254	Charlie Hayes	.25	.07
❑	255	Donnie Elliott	.25	.07
❑	256	Rob Fitzpatrick RC	.40	.12
❑	257	Tim Davis	.25	.07
❑	258	James Mouton	.25	.07
❑	259	Mike Greenwell	.25	.07
❑	260	Ray McDavid	.25	.07
❑	261	Mike Kelly	.25	.07
❑	262	Andy Larkin RC	.40	.12
❑	263	Marquis Riley UER (No card number on back)	.25	.07
❑	264	Bob Tewksbury	.25	.07
❑	265	Brian Edmondson	.25	.07
❑	266	Eduardo Lantigua RC	.40	.12
❑	267	Brandon Wilson	.25	.07
❑	268	Mike Welch	.25	.07
❑	269	Tom Henke	.25	.07
❑	270	Pokey Reese	.25	.07
❑	271	Greg Zaun RC	.75	.23
❑	272	Todd Ritchie	.25	.07
❑	273	Javier Lopez	.40	.12
❑	274	Kevin Young	.25	.07
❑	275	Kirt Manwaring	.25	.07
❑	276	Bill Taylor RC	.40	.12
❑	277	Robert Eenhoorn	.25	.07
❑	278	Jessie Hollins	.25	.07
❑	279	Julian Tavarez RC	.75	.23
❑	280	Gene Schall	.25	.07
❑	281	Paul Molitor	.60	.18
❑	282	Neifi Perez RC	.75	.23
❑	283	Greg Gagne	.25	.07
❑	284	Marquis Grissom	.40	.12
❑	285	Randy Johnson	1.00	.30
❑	286	Pete Harnisch	.25	.07
❑	287	Joel Bennett RC	.40	.12
❑	288	Derek Bell	.25	.07
❑	289	Darryl Hamilton	.25	.07
❑	290	Gary Sheffield	.40	.12
❑	291	Eduardo Perez	.25	.07
❑	292	Basil Shabazz	.25	.07
❑	293	Eric Davis	.40	.12
❑	294	Pedro Astacio	.25	.07
❑	295	Robin Ventura	.40	.12
❑	296	Jeff Kent	.60	.18
❑	297	Rick Helling	.25	.07
❑	298	Joe Oliver	.25	.07
❑	299	Lee Smith	.40	.12
❑	300	Dave Winfield	.40	.12
❑	301	Deion Sanders	.60	.18
❑	302	R.Manzanillo RC	.40	.12
❑	303	Mark Portugal	.25	.07
❑	304	Brent Gates	.25	.07
❑	305	Wade Boggs	.60	.18
❑	306	Rick Wilkins	.25	.07
❑	307	Carlos Baerga	.25	.07
❑	308	Curt Schilling	.40	.12
❑	309	Shannon Stewart	1.00	.30
❑	310	Darren Holmes	.25	.07
❑	311	Robert Toth RC	.40	.12
❑	312	Gabe White	.25	.07
❑	313	Mac Suzuki RC	.75	.23
❑	314	Alvin Morman RC	.40	.12
❑	315	Mo Vaughn	.40	.12
❑	316	Bryce Florie RC	.40	.12
❑	317	Gabby Martinez RC	.40	.12
❑	318	Carl Everett	.40	.12
❑	319	Kerwin Moore	.25	.07
❑	320	Tom Pagnozzi	.25	.07
❑	321	Chris Gomez	.25	.07
❑	322	Todd Williams	.25	.07
❑	323	Pat Hentgen	.25	.07
❑	324	Kirk Presley RC	.40	.12
❑	325	Kevin Brown	.40	.12
❑	326	J.Isringhausen RC	3.00	.90
❑	327	Rick Forney RC	.40	.12
❑	328	Carlos Pulido RC	.40	.12
❑	329	Terrell Wade RC	.40	.12
❑	330	Al Martin	.25	.07
❑	331	Dan Carlson RC	.40	.12
❑	332	Mark Acre RC	.40	.12
❑	333	Sterling Hitchcock	.25	.07
❑	334	Jon Ratliff RC	.40	.12
❑	335	Alex Ramirez RC	.40	.12
❑	336	Phil Geisler RC	.25	.07
❑	337	E.Zambrano FOIL RC	.40	.12
❑	338	Jim Thome FOIL	.60	.18
❑	339	James Mouton FOIL	.25	.07
❑	340	Cliff Floyd FOIL	.40	.12
❑	341	Carlos Delgado FOIL	.60	.18
❑	342	R.Petagine FOIL	.25	.07
❑	343	Tim Clark FOIL	.25	.07
❑	344	Bubba Smith FOIL	.25	.07
❑	345	Randy Curtis FOIL RC	.40	.12
❑	346	Joe Biasucci FOIL RC	.40	.12
❑	347	D.J. Boston FOIL RC	.40	.12
❑	348	R.Rivera FOIL RC	.40	.12
❑	349	Bryan Link FOIL RC	.40	.12
❑	350	Mike Bell FOIL RC	.40	.12
❑	351	M.Watson FOIL RC	.40	.12
❑	352	Jason Myers FOIL	.25	.07
❑	353	Chipper Jones FOIL	1.00	.30
❑	354	B.Kieschnick FOIL	.25	.07
❑	355	Pokey Reese FOIL	.25	.07
❑	356	John Burke FOIL	.25	.07
❑	357	Kurt Miller FOIL	.25	.07
❑	358	Orlando Miller FOIL	.25	.07
❑	359	T.Hollandsworth FOIL	.25	.07
❑	360	Rondell White FOIL	.40	.12
❑	361	Bill Pulsipher FOIL	.40	.12
❑	362	Tyler Green FOIL	.25	.07
❑	363	M.Cummings FOIL	.25	.07
❑	364	Brian Barber FOIL	.25	.07
❑	365	Melvin Nieves FOIL	.25	.07
❑	366	Salomon Torres FOIL	.25	.07
❑	367	Alex Ochoa FOIL	.25	.07
❑	368	F.Rodriguez FOIL	.25	.07
❑	369	Brian Anderson FOIL	.40	.12
❑	370	James Baldwin FOIL	.25	.07
❑	371	Manny Ramirez FOIL	1.00	.30
❑	372	J.Thompson FOIL	.25	.07
❑	373	Johnny Damon FOIL	.60	.18
❑	374	Jeff D'Amico FOIL	.75	.23
❑	375	Rich Becker FOIL	.25	.07
❑	376	Derek Jeter FOIL	3.00	.90
❑	377	Steve Karsay FOIL	.25	.07
❑	378	Mac Suzuki FOIL	.40	.12
❑	379	Benji Gil FOIL	.25	.07
❑	380	Alex Gonzalez FOIL	.25	.07
❑	381	Jason Bere FOIL	.25	.07
❑	382	Brett Butler FOIL	.40	.12
❑	383	Jeff Conine FOIL	.40	.12
❑	384	Darren Daulton FOIL	.40	.12
❑	385	Jeff Kent FOIL	.60	.18
❑	386	Don Mattingly FOIL	2.50	.75
❑	387	Mike Piazza FOIL	2.00	.60
❑	388	Ryne Sandberg FOIL	1.50	.45
❑	389	Rich Amaral	.25	.07
❑	390	Craig Biggio	.60	.18
❑	391	Jeff Suppan RC	1.25	.35
❑	392	Andy Benes	.25	.07
❑	393	Cal Eldred	.25	.07
❑	394	Jeff Conine	.40	.12
❑	395	Tim Salmon	.60	.18
❑	396	Ray Suplee RC	.40	.12
❑	397	Tony Phillips	.25	.07
❑	398	Ramon Martinez	.25	.07
❑	399	Julio Franco	.40	.12
❑	400	Dwight Gooden	.40	.12
❑	401	Kevin Lomon RC	.40	.12
❑	402	Jose Rijo	.25	.07
❑	403	Mike Devereaux	.25	.07
❑	404	Mike Zolecki RC	.40	.12
❑	405	Fred McGriff	.60	.18
❑	406	Danny Clyburn	.25	.07
❑	407	Robby Thompson	.25	.07
❑	408	Terry Steinbach	.25	.07
❑	409	Luis Polonia	.25	.07
❑	410	Mark Grace	.60	.18
❑	411	Albert Belle	.40	.12
❑	412	John Kruk	.40	.12
❑	413	Scott Spiezio RC	.75	.23
❑	414	Ellis Burks UER (Name spelled Elkis on front)	.40	.12
❑	415	Joe Vitiello	.25	.07
❑	416	Tim Costo	.25	.07
❑	417	Marc Newfield	.25	.07
❑	418	Oscar Henriquez RC	.40	.12
❑	419	Matt Perisho RC	.40	.12
❑	420	Julio Bruno	.25	.07
❑	421	Kenny Felder	.25	.07
❑	422	Tyler Green	.25	.07
❑	423	Jim Edmonds	1.00	.30
❑	424	Ozzie Smith	1.50	.45
❑	425	Rick Greene	.25	.07
❑	426	Todd Hollandsworth	.25	.07
❑	427	Eddie Pearson RC	.40	.12
❑	428	Quilvio Veras	.25	.07
❑	429	Kenny Rogers	.40	.12
❑	430	Willie Greene	.25	.07
❑	431	Vaughn Eshelman	.25	.07
❑	432	Pat Meares	.25	.07
❑	433	Jermaine Dye RC	5.00	1.50
❑	434	Steve Cooke	.25	.07
❑	435	Bill Swift	.25	.07
❑	436	Fausto Cruz RC	.40	.12
❑	437	Mark Hutton	.25	.07
❑	438	B.Kieschnick RC	.75	.23
❑	439	Yorkis Perez	.25	.07
❑	440	Len Dykstra	.40	.12
❑	441	Pat Borders	.25	.07
❑	442	Doug Walls RC	.40	.12
❑	443	Wally Joyner	.40	.12
❑	444	Ken Hill	.25	.07
❑	445	Eric Anthony	.25	.07
❑	446	Mitch Williams	.25	.07
❑	447	Cory Bailey RC	.40	.12
❑	448	Dave Staton	.25	.07
❑	449	Greg Vaughn	.25	.07
❑	450	Dave Magadan	.25	.07
❑	451	Chili Davis	.40	.12
❑	452	Gerald Santos RC	.40	.12
❑	453	Joe Perona	.25	.07
❑	454	Delino DeShields	.25	.07
❑	455	Jack McDowell	.25	.07
❑	456	Todd Hundley	.25	.07
❑	457	Ritchie Moody	.25	.07
❑	458	Bret Boone	.40	.12
❑	459	Ben McDonald	.25	.07
❑	460	Kirby Puckett	1.00	.30
❑	461	Gregg Olson	.25	.07
❑	462	Rich Aude RC	.40	.12
❑	463	John Burkett	.25	.07
❑	464	Troy Neel	.25	.07
❑	465	Jimmy Key	.40	.12
❑	466	Ozzie Timmons	.25	.07
❑	467	Eddie Murray	1.00	.30
❑	468	Mark Tranberg RC	.40	.12
❑	469	Alex Gonzalez	.25	.07
❑	470	David Nied	.25	.07
❑	471	Barry Larkin	.60	.18
❑	472	Brian Looney RC	.40	.12
❑	473	Shawn Estes	.25	.07
❑	474	A.J. Sager RC	.40	.12
❑	475	Roger Clemens	2.00	.60
❑	476	Vince Moore	.25	.07
❑	477	Scott Karl RC	.40	.12
❑	478	Kurt Miller	.25	.07
❑	479	Garret Anderson	1.00	.30
❑	480	Allen Watson	.25	.07
❑	481	Jose Lima RC	1.25	.35
❑	482	Rick Gorecki	.25	.07
❑	483	Jimmy Hurst RC	.40	.12
❑	484	Preston Wilson	.40	.12
❑	485	Will Clark	.60	.18
❑	486	Mike Ferry RC	.40	.12
❑	487	Curtis Goodwin RC	.40	.12
❑	488	Mike Myers	.25	.07
❑	489	Chipper Jones	1.00	.30
❑	490	Jeff King	.25	.07
❑	491	W.VanLandingham RC	.40	.12
❑	492	Carlos Reyes RC	.40	.12
❑	493	Andy Pettitte	1.00	.30
❑	494	Brant Brown	.25	.07
❑	495	Daron Kirkreit	.25	.07
❑	496	Ricky Bottalico RC	.75	.23
❑	497	Devon White	.40	.12
❑	498	Jason Johnson RC	.40	.12
❑	499	Vince Coleman	.25	.07
❑	500	Larry Walker	.40	.12
❑	501	Bobby Ayala	.25	.07

Card	Nm-Mt	Ex-Mt
❑ 502 Steve Finley	.40	.12
❑ 503 Scott Fletcher	.25	.07
❑ 504 Brad Ausmus	.40	.12
❑ 505 Scott Talanoa RC	.40	.12
❑ 506 Orestes Destrade	.25	.07
❑ 507 Gary DiSarcina	.25	.07
❑ 508 Willie Smith RC	.40	.12
❑ 509 Alan Trammell	.40	.12
❑ 510 Mike Piazza	2.00	.60
❑ 511 Ozzie Guillen	.40	.12
❑ 512 Jeromy Burnitz	.40	.12
❑ 513 Darren Oliver RC	.75	.23
❑ 514 Kevin Mitchell	.25	.07
❑ 515 Rafael Palmeiro	.60	.18
❑ 516 David McCarty	.25	.07
❑ 517 Jeff Blauser	.25	.07
❑ 518 Trey Beamon	.25	.07
❑ 519 Royce Clayton	.25	.07
❑ 520 Dennis Eckersley	.40	.12
❑ 521 Bernie Williams	.60	.18
❑ 522 Steve Buechele	.25	.07
❑ 523 Dennis Martinez	.40	.12
❑ 524 Dave Hollins	.25	.07
❑ 525 Joey Hamilton	.25	.07
❑ 526 Andres Galarraga	.40	.12
❑ 527 Jeff Granger	.25	.07
❑ 528 Joey Eischen	.25	.07
❑ 529 Desi Relaford	.25	.07
❑ 530 Roberto Petagine	.25	.07
❑ 531 Andre Dawson	.40	.12
❑ 532 Ray Holbert	.25	.07
❑ 533 Duane Singleton	.25	.07
❑ 534 Kurt Abbott RC	.75	.23
❑ 535 Bo Jackson	1.00	.30
❑ 536 Gregg Jefferies	.25	.07
❑ 537 David Mysel	.25	.07
❑ 538 Raul Mondesi	.40	.12
❑ 539 Chris Snopek	.25	.07
❑ 540 Brook Fordyce	.25	.07
❑ 541 Ron Frazier RC	.40	.12
❑ 542 Brian Koelling	.25	.07
❑ 543 Jimmy Haynes	.25	.07
❑ 544 Marty Cordova	.25	.07
❑ 545 Jason Green RC	.40	.12
❑ 546 Orlando Merced	.25	.07
❑ 547 Lou Pote RC	.40	.12
❑ 548 Todd Van Poppel	.25	.07
❑ 549 Pat Kelly	.25	.07
❑ 550 Turk Wendell	.25	.07
❑ 551 Herbert Perry RC	.75	.23
❑ 552 Ryan Karp RC	.40	.12
❑ 553 Juan Guzman	.25	.07
❑ 554 Bryan Rekar RC	.40	.12
❑ 555 Kevin Appier	.40	.12
❑ 556 Chris Schwab RC	.40	.12
❑ 557 Jay Buhner	.40	.12
❑ 558 Andujar Cedeno	.25	.07
❑ 559 Ryan McGuire RC	.40	.12
❑ 560 Ricky Gutierrez	.25	.07
❑ 561 Keith Kimsey RC	.40	.12
❑ 562 Tim Clark	.25	.07
❑ 563 Damion Easley	.25	.07
❑ 564 Clint Davis RC	.40	.12
❑ 565 Mike Moore	.25	.07
❑ 566 Orel Hershiser	.40	.12
❑ 567 Jason Bere	.25	.07
❑ 568 Kevin McReynolds	.25	.07
❑ 569 Leland Macon RC	.40	.12
❑ 570 John Courtright RC	.40	.12
❑ 571 Sid Fernandez	.25	.07
❑ 572 Chad Roper	.25	.07
❑ 573 Terry Pendleton	.40	.12
❑ 574 Danny Miceli	.25	.07
❑ 575 Joe Rosselli	.25	.07
❑ 576 Mike Bordick	.25	.07
❑ 577 Danny Tartabull	.25	.07
❑ 578 Jose Guzman	.25	.07
❑ 579 Omar Vizquel	.60	.18
❑ 580 Tommy Greene	.25	.07
❑ 581 Paul Spoljaric	.25	.07
❑ 582 Walt Weiss	.25	.07
❑ 583 Oscar Jimenez RC	.40	.12
❑ 584 Rod Henderson	.25	.07
❑ 585 Derek Lowe	.40	.12
❑ 586 Richard Hidalgo RC	1.25	.35
❑ 587 Shayne Bennett RC	.40	.12
❑ 588 Tim Belk RC	.40	.12
❑ 589 Matt Mieske	.25	.07
❑ 590 Nigel Wilson	.25	.07
❑ 591 Jeff Knox RC	.40	.12
❑ 592 Bernard Gilkey	.25	.07
❑ 593 David Cone	.40	.12
❑ 594 Paul LoDuca RC	4.00	1.20
❑ 595 Scott Ruffcorn	.25	.07
❑ 596 Chris Roberts	.25	.07
❑ 597 Oscar Munoz RC	.40	.12
❑ 598 Scott Sullivan RC	.40	.12
❑ 599 Matt Jarvis RC	.40	.12
❑ 600 Jose Canseco	.60	.18
❑ 601 Tony Graffanino RC	1.25	.35
❑ 602 Don Slaught	.25	.07
❑ 603 Brett King RC	.40	.12
❑ 604 Jose Herrera RC	.40	.12
❑ 605 Melido Perez	.25	.07
❑ 606 Mike Hubbard RC	.40	.12
❑ 607 Chad Ogea	.25	.07
❑ 608 Wayne Gomes RC	.75	.23
❑ 609 Roberto Alomar	.60	.18
❑ 610 Angel Echevarria RC	.40	.12
❑ 611 Jose Lind	.25	.07
❑ 612 Darrin Fletcher	.25	.07
❑ 613 Chris Bosio	.25	.07
❑ 614 Darryl Kile	.40	.12
❑ 615 Frankie Rodriguez	.25	.07
❑ 616 Phil Plantier	.25	.07
❑ 617 Pat Listach	.25	.07
❑ 618 Charlie Hough	.40	.12
❑ 619 Ryan Hancock RC	.40	.12
❑ 620 Darrel Deak RC	.40	.12
❑ 621 Travis Fryman	.40	.12
❑ 622 Brett Butler	.40	.12
❑ 623 Lance Johnson	.25	.07
❑ 624 Pete Smith	.25	.07
❑ 625 James Hurst RC	.40	.12
❑ 626 Roberto Kelly	.25	.07
❑ 627 Mike Mussina	.60	.18
❑ 628 Kevin Tapani	.25	.07
❑ 629 John Smoltz	.60	.18
❑ 630 Midre Cummings	.25	.07
❑ 631 Salomon Torres	.25	.07
❑ 632 Willie Adams	.25	.07
❑ 633 Derek Jeter	3.00	.90
❑ 634 Steve Trachsel	.25	.07
❑ 635 Albie Lopez	.25	.07
❑ 636 Jason Moler	.25	.07
❑ 637 Carlos Delgado	.60	.18
❑ 638 Roberto Mejia	.25	.07
❑ 639 Darren Burton	.25	.07
❑ 640 B.J. Wallace	.25	.07
❑ 641 Brad Clontz RC	.40	.12
❑ 642 Billy Wagner RC	4.00	1.20
❑ 643 Aaron Sele	.25	.07
❑ 644 Cameron Cairncross	.25	.07
❑ 645 Brian Harper	.25	.07
❑ 646 Marc Valdes UER (No card number on back)	.25	.07
❑ 647 Mark Ratekin	.25	.07
❑ 648 Terry Bradshaw RC	.40	.12
❑ 649 Justin Thompson	.25	.07
❑ 650 Mike Busch RC	.40	.12
❑ 651 Joe Hall RC	.40	.12
❑ 652 Bobby Jones	.25	.07
❑ 653 Kelly Stinnett RC	.75	.23
❑ 654 Rod Steph RC	.40	.12
❑ 655 Jay Powell RC	.75	.23
❑ 656 K.Garagozzo RC UER No card number on back	.40	.12
❑ 657 Todd Dunn	.25	.07
❑ 658 Charles Peterson RC	.40	.12
❑ 659 Darren Lewis	.25	.07
❑ 660 John Wasdin RC	.40	.12
❑ 661 Tate Seefried RC	.40	.12
❑ 662 Hector Trinidad RC	.40	.12
❑ 663 John Carter RC	.25	.07
❑ 664 Larry Mitchell	.25	.07
❑ 665 David Catlett RC	.40	.12
❑ 666 Dante Bichette	.40	.12
❑ 667 Felix Jose	.25	.07
❑ 668 Rondell White	.40	.12
❑ 669 Tino Martinez	.60	.18
❑ 670 Brian L. Hunter	.25	.07
❑ 671 Jose Malave	.25	.07
❑ 672 Archi Cianfrocco	.25	.07
❑ 673 Mike Matheny RC	2.00	.60
❑ 674 Bret Barberie	.25	.07
❑ 675 Andrew Lorraine RC	.40	.12
❑ 676 Brian Jordan	.40	.12
❑ 677 Tim Belcher	.25	.07
❑ 678 Antonio Osuna RC	.40	.12
❑ 679 Checklist	.25	.07
❑ 680 Checklist	.25	.07
❑ 681 Checklist	.25	.07
❑ 682 Checklist	.25	.07

1995 Bowman

	Nm-Mt	Ex-Mt
COMPLETE SET (439)	150.00	45.00

Card	Nm-Mt	Ex-Mt
❑ 1 Billy Wagner	.75	.23
❑ 2 Chris Widger	.25	.07
❑ 3 Brent Bowers	.25	.07
❑ 4 Bob Abreu RC	10.00	3.00
❑ 5 Lou Collier RC	1.00	.30
❑ 6 Juan Acevedo RC	.50	.15
❑ 7 Jason Kelley RC	.50	.15
❑ 8 Brian Sackinsky	.25	.07
❑ 9 Scott Christman	.25	.07
❑ 10 Damon Hollins	.25	.07
❑ 11 Willis Otanez RC	.50	.15
❑ 12 Jason Ryan RC	.50	.15
❑ 13 Jason Giambi	.75	.23
❑ 14 Andy Taulbee RC	.50	.15
❑ 15 Mark Thompson	.25	.07
❑ 16 Hugo Pivaral RC	.50	.15
❑ 17 Brien Taylor	.25	.07
❑ 18 Antonio Osuna	.25	.07
❑ 19 Edgardo Alfonzo	.25	.07
❑ 20 Carl Everett	.50	.15
❑ 21 Matt Drews	.25	.07
❑ 22 Bartolo Colon RC	5.00	1.50
❑ 23 Andruw Jones RC	30.00	9.00
❑ 24 Robert Person RC	1.00	.30
❑ 25 Derrek Lee	1.25	.35
❑ 26 John Ambrose RC	.50	.15
❑ 27 Eric Knowles RC	.50	.15
❑ 28 Chris Roberts	.25	.07
❑ 29 Don Wengert	.25	.07
❑ 30 Marcus Jensen RC	1.00	.30
❑ 31 Brian Barber	.25	.07
❑ 32 Kevin Brown C	.50	.15
❑ 33 Benji Gil	.25	.07
❑ 34 Mike Hubbard	.25	.07
❑ 35 Bart Evans RC	.50	.15
❑ 36 Enrique Wilson RC	.50	.15
❑ 37 Brian Buchanan RC	1.00	.30
❑ 38 Ken Ray RC	.50	.15
❑ 39 Micah Franklin RC	.50	.15
❑ 40 Ricky Otero RC	.50	.15
❑ 41 Jason Kendall	.50	.15
❑ 42 Jimmy Hurst	.25	.07
❑ 43 Jerry Wolak RC	.50	.15
❑ 44 Jayson Peterson RC	.50	.15
❑ 45 Allen Battle RC	.50	.15
❑ 46 Scott Stahoviak	.25	.07
❑ 47 Steve Schrenk RC	.50	.15
❑ 48 Travis Miller RC	.50	.15
❑ 49 Eddie Rios RC	.50	.15
❑ 50 Mike Hampton	.50	.15
❑ 51 Chad Frontera RC	.50	.15

❑	52	Tom Evans	.25	.07
❑	53	C.J. Nitkowski	.25	.07
❑	54	Clay Caruthers RC	.50	.15
❑	55	Shannon Stewart	.50	.15
❑	56	Jorge Posada	1.25	.35
❑	57	Aaron Holbert	.25	.07
❑	58	Harry Berrios RC	.50	.15
❑	59	Steve Rodriguez	.25	.07
❑	60	Shane Andrews	.25	.07
❑	61	Will Cunnane RC	.50	.15
❑	62	Richard Hidalgo	.25	.07
❑	63	Bill Selby RC	.50	.15
❑	64	Jay Cranford RC	.50	.15
❑	65	Jeff Suppan	.50	.15
❑	66	Curtis Goodwin	.25	.07
❑	67	John Thomson RC	1.00	.30
❑	68	Justin Thompson	.25	.07
❑	69	Troy Percival	.50	.15
❑	70	Matt Wagner RC	.50	.15
❑	71	Terry Bradshaw	.25	.07
❑	72	Greg Hansell	.25	.07
❑	73	John Burke	.25	.07
❑	74	Jeff D'Amico	.25	.07
❑	75	Ernie Young	.25	.07
❑	76	Jason Bates	.25	.07
❑	77	Chris Stynes	.25	.07
❑	78	Cade Gaspar RC	.50	.15
❑	79	Melvin Nieves	.25	.07
❑	80	Rick Gorecki	.25	.07
❑	81	Felix Rodriguez RC	1.00	.30
❑	82	Ryan Hancock	.25	.07
❑	83	Chris Carpenter RC	6.00	1.80
❑	84	Ray McDavid	.25	.07
❑	85	Chris Wimmer	.25	.07
❑	86	Doug Glanville	.25	.07
❑	87	DeShawn Warren	.25	.07
❑	88	Damian Moss RC	1.00	.30
❑	89	Rafael Orellano RC	.50	.15
❑	90	Vladimir Guerrero RC	50.00	15.00
❑	91	Raul Casanova RC	.50	.15
❑	92	Karim Garcia RC	1.00	.30
❑	93	Bryce Florie	.25	.07
❑	94	Kevin Orie	.25	.07
❑	95	Ryan Nye RC	.50	.15
❑	96	Matt Sachse RC	.50	.15
❑	97	Ivan Arteaga RC	.50	.15
❑	98	Glenn Murray	.25	.07
❑	99	Stacy Hollins RC	.50	.15
❑	100	Jim Pittsley	.25	.07
❑	101	Craig Mattson RC	.50	.15
❑	102	Neifi Perez	.25	.07
❑	103	Keith Williams	.25	.07
❑	104	Roger Cedeno	.25	.07
❑	105	Tony Terry RC	.50	.15
❑	106	Jose Malave	.25	.07
❑	107	Joe Rosselli	.25	.07
❑	108	Kevin Jordan	.25	.07
❑	109	Sid Roberson RC	.50	.15
❑	110	Alan Embree	.25	.07
❑	111	Terrell Wade	.25	.07
❑	112	Bob Wolcott	.25	.07
❑	113	Carlos Perez RC	1.00	.30
❑	114	Mike Bovee RC	.50	.15
❑	115	Tommy Davis RC	.50	.15
❑	116	Jeremey Kendall RC	.50	.15
❑	117	Rich Aude	.25	.07
❑	118	Rick Huisman	.25	.07
❑	119	Tim Belk	.25	.07
❑	120	Edgar Renteria	.50	.15
❑	121	Calvin Maduro RC	.50	.15
❑	122	Jerry Martin RC	.50	.15
❑	123	Ramon Fermin RC	.50	.15
❑	124	Kimera Bartee RC	.50	.15
❑	125	Mark Farris	.25	.07
❑	126	Frank Rodriguez	.25	.07
❑	127	Bobby Higginson RC	2.00	.60
❑	128	Bret Wagner	.25	.07
❑	129	Edwin Diaz RC	.50	.15
❑	130	Jimmy Haynes	.25	.07
❑	131	Chris Weinke RC	1.00	.30
❑	132	Damian Jackson RC	1.00	.30
❑	133	Felix Martinez	.25	.07
❑	134	Edwin Hurtado RC	.50	.15
❑	135	Matt Raleigh RC	.50	.15
❑	136	Paul Wilson	.25	.07
❑	137	Ron Villone	.25	.07
❑	138	E.Stuckenschneider RC	.50	.15
❑	139	Tate Seefried	.25	.07
❑	140	Rey Ordonez RC	2.00	.60
❑	141	Eddie Pearson	.25	.07
❑	142	Kevin Gallaher	.25	.07
❑	143	Torii Hunter	.75	.23
❑	144	Daron Kirkreit	.25	.07
❑	145	Craig Wilson	.25	.07
❑	146	Ugueth Urbina	.25	.07
❑	147	Chris Snopek	.25	.07
❑	148	Kym Ashworth	.25	.07
❑	149	Wayne Gomes	.25	.07
❑	150	Mark Loretta	.50	.15
❑	151	Ramon Morel RC	.50	.15
❑	152	Trot Nixon	.75	.23
❑	153	Desi Relaford	.25	.07
❑	154	Scott Sullivan	.25	.07
❑	155	Marc Barcelo	.25	.07
❑	156	Willie Adams	.25	.07
❑	157	Derrick Gibson RC	.50	.15
❑	158	Brian Meadows RC	.50	.15
❑	159	Julian Tavarez	.25	.07
❑	160	Bryan Rekar	.25	.07
❑	161	Steve Gibralter	.25	.07
❑	162	Esteban Loaiza	.25	.07
❑	163	John Wasdin	.25	.07
❑	164	Kirk Presley	.25	.07
❑	165	Mariano Rivera	1.25	.35
❑	166	Andy Larkin	.25	.07
❑	167	Sean Whiteside RC	.50	.15
❑	168	Matt Apana RC	.50	.15
❑	169	Shawn Senior RC	.50	.15
❑	170	Scott Gentile	.25	.07
❑	171	Quilvio Veras	.25	.07
❑	172	Eli Marrero RC	1.50	.45
❑	173	Mendy Lopez RC	.50	.15
❑	174	Homer Bush	.25	.07
❑	175	Brian Stephenson RC	.50	.15
❑	176	Jon Nunnally	.25	.07
❑	177	Jose Herrera	.25	.07
❑	178	Corey Avrard RC	.50	.15
❑	179	David Bell	.25	.07
❑	180	Jason Isringhausen	.50	.15
❑	181	Jamey Wright	.25	.07
❑	182	Lonell Roberts RC	.25	.07
❑	183	Marty Cordova	.25	.07
❑	184	Amaury Telemaco	.25	.07
❑	185	John Mabry	.50	.15
❑	186	Andrew Vessel RC	.50	.15
❑	187	Jim Cole RC	.50	.15
❑	188	Marquis Riley	.25	.07
❑	189	Todd Dunn	.25	.07
❑	190	John Carter	.25	.07
❑	191	Donnie Sadler RC	1.00	.30
❑	192	Mike Bell	.25	.07
❑	193	Chris Cumberland RC	.50	.15
❑	194	Jason Schmidt	1.25	.35
❑	195	Matt Brunson	.25	.07
❑	196	James Baldwin	.25	.07
❑	197	Bill Simas RC	.50	.15
❑	198	Gus Gandarillas	.25	.07
❑	199	Mac Suzuki	.25	.07
❑	200	Rick Holifield RC	.50	.15
❑	201	Fernando Lunar RC	.50	.15
❑	202	Kevin Jarvis	.25	.07
❑	203	Everett Stull	.25	.07
❑	204	Steve Wojciechowski	.25	.07
❑	205	Shawn Estes	.25	.07
❑	206	Jermaine Dye	.50	.15
❑	207	Marc Kroon	.25	.07
❑	208	Peter Munro RC	1.00	.30
❑	209	Pat Watkins	.25	.07
❑	210	Matt Smith	.25	.07
❑	211	Joe Vitiello	.25	.07
❑	212	Gerald Witasick Jr.	.25	.07
❑	213	Freddy A. Garcia RC	.50	.15
❑	214	Glenn Dishman RC	.50	.15
❑	215	Jay Canizaro RC	.50	.15
❑	216	Angel Martinez	.25	.07
❑	217	Yamil Benitez RC	.50	.15
❑	218	Fausto Macey RC	.50	.15
❑	219	Eric Owens	.25	.07
❑	220	Checklist	.25	.07
❑	221	D.Hosey FOIL RC	.50	.15
❑	222	B.Woodall FOIL RC	.50	.15
❑	223	Billy Ashley FOIL	.25	.07
❑	224	M.Grudzielanek FOIL RC	2.00	.60
❑	225	M.Johnson FOIL RC	1.00	.30
❑	226	Tim Unroe FOIL RC	.50	.15
❑	227	Todd Greene FOIL	.25	.07
❑	228	Larry Sutton FOIL	.25	.07
❑	229	Derek Jeter FOIL	4.00	1.20
❑	230	Sal Fasano FOIL RC	.50	.15
❑	231	Ruben Rivera FOIL	.25	.07
❑	232	Chris Truby FOIL RC	.50	.15
❑	233	John Donati FOIL	.25	.07
❑	234	D.Conner FOIL RC	.50	.15
❑	235	Sergio Nunez FOIL RC	.50	.15
❑	236	Ray Brown FOIL RC	.50	.15
❑	237	Juan Melo FOIL RC	.50	.15
❑	238	Hideo Nomo FOIL RC	5.00	1.50
❑	239	Jamie Bluma RC FOIL	.50	.15
❑	240	Jay Payton FOIL RC	2.00	.60
❑	241	Paul Konerko FOIL	4.00	1.20
❑	242	Scott Elarton FOIL RC	1.00	.30
❑	243	Jeff Abbott FOIL RC	1.00	.30
❑	244	Jim Brower FOIL RC	.50	.15
❑	245	Geoff Blum FOIL RC	3.00	.90
❑	246	Aaron Boone FOIL RC	2.00	.60
❑	247	J.R. Phillips FOIL	.25	.07
❑	248	Alex Ochoa FOIL	.25	.07
❑	249	N.Garciaparra FOIL	5.00	1.50
❑	250	Garret Anderson FOIL	.50	.15
❑	251	Ray Durham FOIL	.50	.15
❑	252	Paul Shuey FOIL	.25	.07
❑	253	Tony Clark FOIL	.25	.07
❑	254	Johnny Damon FOIL	.75	.23
❑	255	Duane Singleton FOIL	.25	.07
❑	256	LaTroy Hawkins FOIL	.25	.07
❑	257	Andy Pettitte FOIL	.75	.23
❑	258	Ben Grieve FOIL	.50	.15
❑	259	Marc Newfield FOIL	.25	.07
❑	260	Terrell Lowery FOIL	.25	.07
❑	261	Shawn Green FOIL	.50	.15
❑	262	Chipper Jones FOIL	1.25	.35
❑	263	B.Kieschnick FOIL	.25	.07
❑	264	Pokey Reese FOIL	.25	.07
❑	265	Doug Million FOIL	.25	.07
❑	266	Marc Valdes FOIL	.25	.07
❑	267	Brian L.Hunter FOIL	.25	.07
❑	268	T.Hollandsworth FOIL	.25	.07
❑	269	Rod Henderson FOIL	.25	.07
❑	270	Bill Pulsipher FOIL	.25	.07
❑	271	Scott Rolen FOIL RC	15.00	4.50
❑	272	Trey Beamon FOIL	.25	.07
❑	273	Alan Benes FOIL	.25	.07
❑	274	D.Hermanson FOIL	.25	.07
❑	275	Ricky Bottalico	.25	.07
❑	276	Albert Belle	.50	.15
❑	277	Deion Sanders	.75	.23
❑	278	Matt Williams	.50	.15
❑	279	Jeff Bagwell	.75	.23
❑	280	Kirby Puckett	1.25	.35
❑	281	Dave Hollins	.25	.07
❑	282	Don Mattingly	3.00	.90
❑	283	Joey Hamilton	.25	.07
❑	284	Bobby Bonilla	.50	.15
❑	285	Moises Alou	.50	.15
❑	286	Tom Glavine	.75	.23
❑	287	Brett Butler	.50	.15
❑	288	Chris Hoiles	.25	.07
❑	289	Kenny Rogers	.50	.15
❑	290	Larry Walker	.50	.15
❑	291	Tim Raines	.50	.15
❑	292	Kevin Appier	.50	.15
❑	293	Roger Clemens	2.50	.75
❑	294	Chuck Carr	.25	.07
❑	295	Randy Myers	.25	.07
❑	296	Dave Nilsson	.25	.07
❑	297	Joe Carter	.50	.15
❑	298	Chuck Finley	.50	.15
❑	299	Ray Lankford	.50	.15
❑	300	Roberto Kelly	.25	.07
❑	301	Jon Lieber	.25	.07
❑	302	Travis Fryman	.50	.15
❑	303	Mark McGwire	3.00	.90
❑	304	Tony Gwynn	1.50	.45
❑	305	Kenny Lofton	.50	.15
❑	306	Mark Whiten	.25	.07
❑	307	Doug Drabek	.25	.07
❑	308	Terry Steinbach	.25	.07
❑	309	Ryan Klesko	.50	.15

❑ 310	Mike Piazza	2.00	.60
❑ 311	Ben McDonald	.25	.07
❑ 312	Reggie Sanders	.50	.15
❑ 313	Alex Fernandez	.25	.07
❑ 314	Aaron Sele	.25	.07
❑ 315	Gregg Jefferies	.25	.07
❑ 316	Rickey Henderson	1.25	.35
❑ 317	Brian Anderson	.25	.07
❑ 318	Jose Valentin	.25	.07
❑ 319	Rod Beck	.25	.07
❑ 320	Marquis Grissom	.50	.15
❑ 321	Ken Griffey Jr.	2.00	.60
❑ 322	Bret Saberhagen	.50	.15
❑ 323	Juan Gonzalez	.50	.15
❑ 324	Paul Molitor	.75	.23
❑ 325	Gary Sheffield	.50	.15
❑ 326	Darren Daulton	.50	.15
❑ 327	Bill Swift	.25	.07
❑ 328	Brian McRae	.25	.07
❑ 329	Robin Ventura	.50	.15
❑ 330	Lee Smith	.50	.15
❑ 331	Fred McGriff	.75	.23
❑ 332	Delino DeShields	.25	.07
❑ 333	Edgar Martinez	.75	.23
❑ 334	Mike Mussina	.75	.23
❑ 335	Orlando Merced	.25	.07
❑ 336	Carlos Baerga	.25	.07
❑ 337	Wil Cordero	.25	.07
❑ 338	Tom Pagnozzi	.25	.07
❑ 339	Pat Hentgen	.25	.07
❑ 340	Chad Curtis	.25	.07
❑ 341	Darren Lewis	.25	.07
❑ 342	Jeff Kent	.50	.15
❑ 343	Bip Roberts	.25	.07
❑ 344	Ivan Rodriguez	.75	.23
❑ 345	Jeff Montgomery	.25	.07
❑ 346	Hal Morris	.25	.07
❑ 347	Danny Tartabull	.25	.07
❑ 348	Raul Mondesi	.50	.15
❑ 349	Ken Hill	.25	.07
❑ 350	Pedro Martinez	.75	.23
❑ 351	Frank Thomas	1.25	.35
❑ 352	Manny Ramirez	.75	.23
❑ 353	Tim Salmon	.75	.23
❑ 354	W. VanLandingham	.25	.07
❑ 355	Andres Galarraga	.50	.15
❑ 356	Paul O'Neill	.75	.23
❑ 357	Brady Anderson	.50	.15
❑ 358	Ramon Martinez	.25	.07
❑ 359	John Olerud	.50	.15
❑ 360	Ruben Sierra	.25	.07
❑ 361	Cal Eldred	.25	.07
❑ 362	Jay Buhner	.50	.15
❑ 363	Jay Bell	.50	.15
❑ 364	Wally Joyner	.50	.15
❑ 365	Chuck Knoblauch	.50	.15
❑ 366	Len Dykstra	.50	.15
❑ 367	John Wetteland	.50	.15
❑ 368	Roberto Alomar	.75	.23
❑ 369	Craig Biggio	.75	.23
❑ 370	Ozzie Smith	2.00	.60
❑ 371	Terry Pendleton	.50	.15
❑ 372	Sammy Sosa	1.25	.35
❑ 373	Carlos Garcia	.25	.07
❑ 374	Jose Rijo	.25	.07
❑ 375	Chris Gomez	.25	.07
❑ 376	Barry Bonds	3.00	.90
❑ 377	Steve Avery	.25	.07
❑ 378	Rick Wilkins	.25	.07
❑ 379	Pete Harnisch	.25	.07
❑ 380	Dean Palmer	.50	.15
❑ 381	Bob Hamelin	.25	.07
❑ 382	Jason Bere	.25	.07
❑ 383	Jimmy Key	.50	.15
❑ 384	Dante Bichette	.50	.15
❑ 385	Rafael Palmeiro	.75	.23
❑ 386	David Justice	.50	.15
❑ 387	Chili Davis	.50	.15
❑ 388	Mike Greenwell	.25	.07
❑ 389	Todd Zeile	.25	.07
❑ 390	Jeff Conine	.50	.15
❑ 391	Rick Aguilera	.25	.07
❑ 392	Eddie Murray	1.25	.35
❑ 393	Mike Stanley	.25	.07
❑ 394	Cliff Floyd UER (numbered 294)	.50	.15
❑ 395	Randy Johnson	1.25	.35
❑ 396	David Nied	.25	.07
❑ 397	Devon White	.50	.15
❑ 398	Royce Clayton	.25	.07
❑ 399	Andy Benes	.25	.07
❑ 400	John Hudek	.25	.07
❑ 401	Bobby Jones	.25	.07
❑ 402	Eric Karros	.50	.15
❑ 403	Will Clark	.75	.23
❑ 404	Mark Langston	.25	.07
❑ 405	Kevin Brown	.50	.15
❑ 406	Greg Maddux	2.00	.60
❑ 407	David Cone	.50	.15
❑ 408	Wade Boggs	.75	.23
❑ 409	Steve Trachsel	.25	.07
❑ 410	Greg Vaughn	.25	.07
❑ 411	Mo Vaughn	.50	.15
❑ 412	Wilson Alvarez	.25	.07
❑ 413	Cal Ripken	4.00	1.20
❑ 414	Rico Brogna	.25	.07
❑ 415	Barry Larkin	.75	.23
❑ 416	Cecil Fielder	.50	.15
❑ 417	Jose Canseco	.75	.23
❑ 418	Jack McDowell	.25	.07
❑ 419	Mike Lieberthal	.25	.07
❑ 420	Andrew Lorraine	.25	.07
❑ 421	Rich Becker	.25	.07
❑ 422	Tony Phillips	.25	.07
❑ 423	Scott Ruffcorn	.25	.07
❑ 424	Jeff Granger	.25	.07
❑ 425	Greg Pirkl	.25	.07
❑ 426	Dennis Eckersley	.50	.15
❑ 427	Jose Lima	.25	.07
❑ 428	Russ Davis	.25	.07
❑ 429	Armando Benitez	.50	.15
❑ 430	Alex Gonzalez	.25	.07
❑ 431	Carlos Delgado	.50	.15
❑ 432	Chan Ho Park	.50	.15
❑ 433	Mickey Tettleton	.25	.07
❑ 434	Dave Winfield	.50	.15
❑ 435	John Burkett	.25	.07
❑ 436	Orlando Miller	.25	.07
❑ 437	Rondell White	.50	.15
❑ 438	Jose Oliva	.25	.07
❑ 439	Checklist	.25	.07

1996 Bowman

		Nm-Mt	Ex-Mt
COMPLETE SET (385)		80.00	24.00
❑ 1	Cal Ripken	2.50	.75
❑ 2	Ray Durham	.30	.09
❑ 3	Ivan Rodriguez	.50	.15
❑ 4	Fred McGriff	.50	.15
❑ 5	Hideo Nomo	.75	.23
❑ 6	Troy Percival	.30	.09
❑ 7	Moises Alou	.30	.09
❑ 8	Mike Stanley	.30	.09
❑ 9	Jay Buhner	.30	.09
❑ 10	Shawn Green	.30	.09
❑ 11	Ryan Klesko	.30	.09
❑ 12	Andres Galarraga	.30	.09
❑ 13	Dean Palmer	.30	.09
❑ 14	Jeff Conine	.30	.09
❑ 15	Brian L.Hunter	.30	.09
❑ 16	J.T. Snow	.30	.09
❑ 17	Larry Walker	.30	.09
❑ 18	Barry Larkin	.50	.15
❑ 19	Alex Gonzalez	.30	.09
❑ 20	Edgar Martinez	.50	.15
❑ 21	Mo Vaughn	.30	.09
❑ 22	Mark McGwire	2.00	.60
❑ 23	Jose Canseco	.50	.15
❑ 24	Jack McDowell	.30	.09
❑ 25	Dante Bichette	.30	.09
❑ 26	Wade Boggs	.50	.15
❑ 27	Mike Piazza	1.25	.35
❑ 28	Ray Lankford	.30	.09
❑ 29	Craig Biggio	.50	.15
❑ 30	Rafael Palmeiro	.50	.15
❑ 31	Ron Gant	.30	.09
❑ 32	Javy Lopez	.30	.09
❑ 33	Brian Jordan	.30	.09
❑ 34	Paul O'Neill	.50	.15
❑ 35	Mark Grace	.50	.15
❑ 36	Matt Williams	.30	.09
❑ 37	Pedro Martinez UER Wrong birthdate	.50	.15
❑ 38	Rickey Henderson	.75	.23
❑ 39	Bobby Bonilla	.30	.09
❑ 40	Todd Hollandsworth	.30	.09
❑ 41	Jim Thome	.50	.15
❑ 42	Gary Sheffield	.75	.23
❑ 43	Tim Salmon	.50	.15
❑ 44	Gregg Jefferies	.30	.09
❑ 45	Roberto Alomar	.50	.15
❑ 46	Carlos Baerga	.30	.09
❑ 47	Mark Grudzielanek	.30	.09
❑ 48	Randy Johnson	.75	.23
❑ 49	Tino Martinez	.50	.15
❑ 50	Robin Ventura	.30	.09
❑ 51	Ryne Sandberg	1.25	.35
❑ 52	Jay Bell	.30	.09
❑ 53	Jason Schmidt	.50	.15
❑ 54	Frank Thomas	.75	.23
❑ 55	Kenny Lofton	.30	.09
❑ 56	Ariel Prieto	.30	.09
❑ 57	David Cone	.30	.09
❑ 58	Reggie Sanders	.30	.09
❑ 59	Michael Tucker	.30	.09
❑ 60	Vinny Castilla	.30	.09
❑ 61	Len Dykstra	.30	.09
❑ 62	Todd Hundley	.30	.09
❑ 63	Brian McRae	.30	.09
❑ 64	Dennis Eckersley	.30	.09
❑ 65	Rondell White	.30	.09
❑ 66	Eric Karros	.30	.09
❑ 67	Greg Maddux	1.25	.35
❑ 68	Kevin Appier	.30	.09
❑ 69	Eddie Murray	.75	.23
❑ 70	John Olerud	.30	.09
❑ 71	Tony Gwynn	1.00	.30
❑ 72	David Justice	.30	.09
❑ 73	Ken Caminiti	.30	.09
❑ 74	Terry Steinbach	.30	.09
❑ 75	Alan Benes	.30	.09
❑ 76	Chipper Jones	.75	.23
❑ 77	Jeff Bagwell	.50	.15
❑ 78	Barry Bonds	2.00	.60
❑ 79	Ken Griffey Jr.	1.50	.45
❑ 80	Roger Cedeno	.30	.09
❑ 81	Joe Carter	.30	.09
❑ 82	Henry Rodriguez	.30	.09
❑ 83	Jason Isringhausen	.30	.09
❑ 84	Chuck Knoblauch	.30	.09
❑ 85	Manny Ramirez	.50	.15
❑ 86	Tom Glavine	.50	.15
❑ 87	Jeffrey Hammonds	.30	.09
❑ 88	Paul Molitor	.50	.15
❑ 89	Roger Clemens	1.50	.45
❑ 90	Greg Vaughn	.30	.09
❑ 91	Marty Cordova	.30	.09
❑ 92	Albert Belle	.30	.09
❑ 93	Mike Mussina	.50	.15
❑ 94	Garret Anderson	.30	.09
❑ 95	Juan Gonzalez	.30	.09
❑ 96	John Valentin	.30	.09
❑ 97	Jason Giambi	.30	.09
❑ 98	Kirby Puckett	.75	.23
❑ 99	Jim Edmonds	.30	.09
❑ 100	Cecil Fielder	.30	.09
❑ 101	Mike Aldrete	.30	.09
❑ 102	Marquis Grissom	.30	.09

❑ 103 Derek Bell .30 .09
❑ 104 Raul Mondesi .30 .09
❑ 105 Sammy Sosa .75 .23
❑ 106 Travis Fryman .30 .09
❑ 107 Rico Brogna .30 .09
❑ 108 Will Clark .50 .15
❑ 109 Bernie Williams .50 .15
❑ 110 Brady Anderson .30 .09
❑ 111 Torii Hunter .30 .09
❑ 112 Derek Jeter 2.00 .60
❑ 113 Mike Kusiewicz RC .50 .15
❑ 114 Scott Rolen .75 .23
❑ 115 Ramon Castro .30 .09
❑ 116 Jose Guillen RC 4.00 1.20
❑ 117 Wade Walker RC .50 .15
❑ 118 Shawn Senior .30 .09
❑ 119 Onan Masaoka RC .75 .23
❑ 120 Marlon Anderson RC 1.25 .35
❑ 121 Katsuhiro Maeda RC .75 .23
❑ 122 G.Stephenson RC .75 .23
❑ 123 Butch Huskey .30 .09
❑ 124 D'Angelo Jimenez RC 1.25 .35
❑ 125 Tony Mounce RC .50 .15
❑ 126 Jay Canizaro .30 .09
❑ 127 Juan Melo .30 .09
❑ 128 Steve Gibralter .30 .09
❑ 129 Freddy Garcia .30 .09
❑ 130 Julio Santana UER .30 .09
Card has him born in 1993
❑ 131 Richard Hidalgo .30 .09
❑ 132 Jermaine Dye .30 .09
❑ 133 Willie Adams .30 .09
❑ 134 Everett Stull .30 .09
❑ 135 Ramon Morel .30 .09
❑ 136 Chan Ho Park .30 .09
❑ 137 Jamey Wright .30 .09
❑ 138 Luis R.Garcia RC .50 .15
❑ 139 Dan Serafini .30 .09
❑ 140 Ryan Dempster RC 1.25 .35
❑ 141 Tate Seefried .30 .09
❑ 142 Jimmy Hurst .30 .09
❑ 143 Travis Miller .30 .09
❑ 144 Curtis Goodwin .30 .09
❑ 145 Rocky Coppinger RC .50 .15
❑ 146 Enrique Wilson .30 .09
❑ 147 Jaime Bluma .30 .09
❑ 148 Andrew Vessel .30 .09
❑ 149 Damian Moss .30 .09
❑ 150 Shawn Gallagher RC .50 .15
❑ 151 Pat Watkins .30 .09
❑ 152 Jose Paniagua .30 .09
❑ 153 Danny Graves .30 .09
❑ 154 Bryon Gainey RC .50 .15
❑ 155 Steve Soderstrom .30 .09
❑ 156 Cliff Brumbaugh RC .50 .15
❑ 157 Eugene Kingsale RC .75 .23
❑ 158 Lou Collier .30 .09
❑ 159 Todd Walker .30 .09
❑ 160 Kris Detmers RC .50 .15
❑ 161 Josh Booty RC .75 .23
❑ 162 Greg Whiteman RC .50 .15
❑ 163 Damian Jackson .30 .09
❑ 164 Tony Clark .30 .09
❑ 165 Jeff D'Amico .30 .09
❑ 166 Johnny Damon .50 .15
❑ 167 Rafael Orellano .30 .09
❑ 168 Ruben Rivera .30 .09
❑ 169 Alex Ochoa .30 .09
❑ 170 Jay Powell .30 .09
❑ 171 Tom Evans .30 .09
❑ 172 Ron Villone .30 .09
❑ 173 Shawn Estes .30 .09
❑ 174 John Wasdin .30 .09
❑ 175 Bill Simas .30 .09
❑ 176 Kevin Brown .30 .09
❑ 177 Shannon Stewart .30 .09
❑ 178 Todd Greene .30 .09
❑ 179 Bob Wolcott .30 .09
❑ 180 Chris Snopek .30 .09
❑ 181 Nomar Garciaparra 1.50 .45
❑ 182 Cameron Smith RC .50 .15
❑ 183 Matt Drews .30 .09
❑ 184 Jimmy Haynes .30 .09
❑ 185 Chris Carpenter .50 .15
❑ 186 Desi Relaford .30 .09
❑ 187 Ben Grieve .30 .09
❑ 188 Mike Bell .30 .09
❑ 189 Luis Castillo RC 1.25 .35
❑ 190 Ugueth Urbina .30 .09
❑ 191 Paul Wilson .30 .09
❑ 192 Andruw Jones 1.25 .35
❑ 193 Wayne Gomes .30 .09
❑ 194 Craig Counsell RC 1.25 .35
❑ 195 Jim Cole .30 .09
❑ 196 Brooks Kieschnick .30 .09
❑ 197 Trey Beamon .30 .09
❑ 198 Marino Santana RC .50 .15
❑ 199 Bob Abreu .75 .23
❑ 200 Pokey Reese .30 .09
❑ 201 Dante Powell .30 .09
❑ 202 George Arias .30 .09
❑ 203 Jorge Velandia RC .50 .15
❑ 204 George Lombard RC .50 .15
❑ 205 Byron Browne RC .50 .15
❑ 206 John Frascatore .30 .09
❑ 207 Terry Adams .30 .09
❑ 208 Wilson Delgado RC .50 .15
❑ 209 Billy McMillon .30 .09
❑ 210 Jeff Abbott .30 .09
❑ 211 Trot Nixon .30 .09
❑ 212 Amaury Telemaco .30 .09
❑ 213 Scott Sullivan .30 .09
❑ 214 Justin Thompson .30 .09
❑ 215 Decomba Conner .30 .09
❑ 216 Ryan McGuire .30 .09
❑ 217 Matt Luke .30 .09
❑ 218 Doug Million .30 .09
❑ 219 Jason Dickson RC .50 .15
❑ 220 Ramon Hernandez RC 1.25 .35
❑ 221 Mark Bellhorn RC 4.00 1.20
❑ 222 Eric Ludwick RC .50 .15
❑ 223 Luke Wilcox RC .50 .15
❑ 224 Marty Malloy RC .50 .15
❑ 225 Gary Coffee RC .50 .15
❑ 226 Wendell Magee RC .50 .15
❑ 227 Brett Tomko RC .75 .23
❑ 228 Derek Lowe .30 .09
❑ 229 Jose Rosado RC .50 .15
❑ 230 Steve Bourgeois RC .50 .15
❑ 231 Neil Weber RC .50 .15
❑ 232 Jeff Ware .30 .09
❑ 233 Edwin Diaz .30 .09
❑ 234 Greg Norton .30 .09
❑ 235 Aaron Boone .30 .09
❑ 236 Jeff Suppan .30 .09
❑ 237 Bret Wagner .30 .09
❑ 238 Elieser Marrero .30 .09
❑ 239 Will Cunnane .30 .09
❑ 240 Brian Barkley RC .50 .15
❑ 241 Jay Payton .30 .09
❑ 242 Marcus Jensen .30 .09
❑ 243 Ryan Nye .30 .09
❑ 244 Chad Mottola .30 .09
❑ 245 Scott McClain RC .50 .15
❑ 246 Jessie Ibarra RC .50 .15
❑ 247 Mike Darr RC .75 .23
❑ 248 Bobby Estalella RC .75 .23
❑ 249 Michael Barrett .30 .09
❑ 250 Jamie Lopiccolo RC .50 .15
❑ 251 Shane Spencer RC 1.25 .35
❑ 252 Ben Petrick RC .50 .15
❑ 253 Jason Bell RC .50 .15
❑ 254 Arnold Gooch RC .50 .15
❑ 255 T.J. Mathews .30 .09
❑ 256 Jason Ryan .30 .09
❑ 257 Pat Cline RC .50 .15
❑ 258 Rafael Carmona RC .50 .15
❑ 259 Carl Pavano RC 4.00 1.20
❑ 260 Ben Davis .30 .09
❑ 261 Matt Lawton RC 1.25 .35
❑ 262 Kevin Sefcik RC .50 .15
❑ 263 Chris Fussell RC .50 .15
❑ 264 Mike Cameron RC 1.25 .35
❑ 265 Marty Janzen RC .50 .15
❑ 266 Livan Hernandez RC 4.00 1.20
❑ 267 Raul Ibanez RC 1.25 .35
❑ 268 Juan Encarnacion .30 .09
❑ 269 David Yocum RC .50 .15
❑ 270 Jonathan Johnson RC .50 .15
❑ 271 Reggie Taylor .30 .09
❑ 272 Danny Buxbaum RC .50 .15
❑ 273 Jacob Cruz .30 .09
❑ 274 Bobby Morris RC .50 .15
❑ 275 Andy Fox RC .50 .15
❑ 276 Greg Keagle .30 .09
❑ 277 Charles Peterson .30 .09
❑ 278 Derrek Lee .50 .15
❑ 279 Bryant Nelson RC .50 .15
❑ 280 Antone Williamson .30 .09
❑ 281 Scott Elarton .30 .09
❑ 282 Shad Williams RC .50 .15
❑ 283 Rich Hunter RC .50 .15
❑ 284 Chris Sheff .30 .09
❑ 285 Derrick Gibson .30 .09
❑ 286 Felix Rodriguez .30 .09
❑ 287 Brian Banks RC .50 .15
❑ 288 Jason McDonald .30 .09
❑ 289 Glendon Rusch RC .75 .23
❑ 290 Gary Rath .30 .09
❑ 291 Peter Munro .30 .09
❑ 292 Tom Fordham .30 .09
❑ 293 Jason Kendall .30 .09
❑ 294 Russ Johnson .30 .09
❑ 295 Joe Long .30 .09
❑ 296 Robert Smith RC .75 .23
❑ 297 Jarrod Washburn RC 1.25 .35
❑ 298 Dave Coggin RC .50 .15
❑ 299 Jeff Yoder RC .50 .15
❑ 300 Jed Hansen RC .50 .15
❑ 301 Matt Morris RC 3.00 .90
❑ 302 Josh Bishop RC .50 .15
❑ 303 Dustin Hermanson .30 .09
❑ 304 Mike Gulan .30 .09
❑ 305 Felipe Crespo .30 .09
❑ 306 Quinton McCracken .30 .09
❑ 307 Jim Bonnici RC .50 .15
❑ 308 Sal Fasano .30 .09
❑ 309 Gabe Alvarez RC .50 .15
❑ 310 Heath Murray RC .50 .15
❑ 311 Javier Valentin RC .50 .15
❑ 312 Bartolo Colon .75 .23
❑ 313 Olmedo Saenz .30 .09
❑ 314 Norm Hutchins RC .50 .15
❑ 315 Chris Holt .30 .09
❑ 316 David Doster RC .50 .15
❑ 317 Robert Person .30 .09
❑ 318 Donne Wall RC .50 .15
❑ 319 Adam Riggs RC .50 .15
❑ 320 Homer Bush .30 .09
❑ 321 Brad Rigby RC .50 .15
❑ 322 Lou Merloni RC .75 .23
❑ 323 Neifi Perez .30 .09
❑ 324 Chris Cumberland .30 .09
❑ 325 Alvie Shepherd RC .50 .15
❑ 326 Jarrod Patterson RC .50 .15
❑ 327 Ray Ricken RC .50 .15
❑ 328 Danny Klassen RC .50 .15
❑ 329 David Miller RC .50 .15
❑ 330 Chad Alexander RC .50 .15
❑ 331 Matt Beaumont .30 .09
❑ 332 Damon Hollins .30 .09
❑ 333 Todd Dunn .30 .09
❑ 334 Mike Sweeney RC 3.00 .90
❑ 335 Richie Sexson .50 .15
❑ 336 Billy Wagner .30 .09
❑ 337 Ron Wright RC .50 .15
❑ 338 Paul Konerko .75 .23
❑ 339 Tommy Phelps RC .50 .15
❑ 340 Karim Garcia .30 .09
❑ 341 Mike Grace RC .50 .15
❑ 342 Russell Branyan RC .75 .23
❑ 343 Randy Winn RC 1.25 .35
❑ 344 A.J. Pierzynski RC 4.00 1.20
❑ 345 Mike Busby RC .50 .15
❑ 346 Matt Beech RC .50 .15
❑ 347 Jose Cepeda RC .50 .15
❑ 348 Brian Stephenson .30 .09
❑ 349 Rey Ordonez .30 .09
❑ 350 Rich Aurilla RC 1.25 .35
❑ 351 Edgard Velazquez RC .50 .15
❑ 352 Raul Casanova .30 .09
❑ 353 Carlos Guillen RC 4.00 1.20
❑ 354 Bruce Aven RC .50 .15
❑ 355 Ryan Jones RC .50 .15
❑ 356 Derek Aucoin RC .50 .15
❑ 357 Brian Rose RC .50 .15
❑ 358 Richard Almanzar RC .50 .15
❑ 359 Fletcher Bates RC .50 .15

	Card	Nm-Mt	Ex-Mt
❑	360 Russ Ortiz RC	2.00	.60
❑	361 Wilton Guerrero RC	.75	.23
❑	362 Geoff Jenkins RC	1.25	.35
❑	363 Pete Janicki	.30	.09
❑	364 Yamil Benitez	.30	.09
❑	365 Aaron Holbert	.30	.09
❑	366 Tim Belk	.30	.09
❑	367 Terrell Wade	.30	.09
❑	368 Terrence Long	.30	.09
❑	369 Brad Fullmer	.30	.09
❑	370 Matt Wagner	.30	.09
❑	371 Craig Wilson RC	.50	.15
❑	372 Mark Loretta	.30	.09
❑	373 Eric Owens	.30	.09
❑	374 Vladimir Guerrero	1.50	.45
❑	375 Tommy Davis	.30	.09
❑	376 Donnie Sadler	.30	.09
❑	377 Edgar Renteria	.30	.09
❑	378 Todd Helton	1.50	.45
❑	379 Ralph Milliard RC	.50	.15
❑	380 Darin Blood RC	.50	.15
❑	381 Shayne Bennett	.30	.09
❑	382 Mark Redman	.30	.09
❑	383 Felix Martinez	.30	.09
❑	384 Sean Watkins RC	.50	.15
❑	385 Oscar Henriquez	.30	.09
❑	M20 Mickey Mantle 1952 Bowman Reprint	5.00	1.50
❑	NNO Checklists	.30	.09

1997 Bowman

	Nm-Mt	Ex-Mt
COMPLETE SET (441)	80.00	24.00
COMP. SERIES 1 (221)	40.00	12.00
COMP. SERIES 2 (220)	40.00	12.00

	Card	Nm-Mt	Ex-Mt
❑	1 Derek Jeter	2.00	.60
❑	2 Edgar Renteria	.30	.09
❑	3 Chipper Jones	.75	.23
❑	4 Hideo Nomo	.75	.23
❑	5 Tim Salmon	.50	.15
❑	6 Jason Giambi	.30	.09
❑	7 Robin Ventura	.30	.09
❑	8 Tony Clark	.30	.09
❑	9 Barry Larkin	.50	.15
❑	10 Paul Molitor	.50	.15
❑	11 Bernard Gilkey	.30	.09
❑	12 Jack McDowell	.30	.09
❑	13 Andy Benes	.30	.09
❑	14 Ryan Klesko	.30	.09
❑	15 Mark McGwire	2.00	.60
❑	16 Ken Griffey Jr.	1.25	.35
❑	17 Robb Nen	.30	.09
❑	18 Cal Ripken	2.50	.75
❑	19 John Valentin	.30	.09
❑	20 Ricky Bottalico	.30	.09
❑	21 Mike Lansing	.30	.09
❑	22 Ryne Sandberg	1.25	.35
❑	23 Carlos Delgado	.30	.09
❑	24 Craig Biggio	.50	.15
❑	25 Eric Karros	.30	.09
❑	26 Kevin Appier	.30	.09
❑	27 Mariano Rivera	.50	.15
❑	28 Vinny Castilla	.30	.09
❑	29 Juan Gonzalez	.30	.09
❑	30 Al Martin	.30	.09
❑	31 Jeff Cirillo	.30	.09
❑	32 Eddie Murray	.75	.23
❑	33 Ray Lankford	.30	.09
❑	34 Manny Ramirez	.50	.15
❑	35 Roberto Alomar	.50	.15
❑	36 Will Clark	.50	.15
❑	37 Chuck Knoblauch	.30	.09
❑	38 Harold Baines	.30	.09
❑	39 Trevor Hoffman	.30	.09
❑	40 Edgar Martinez	.50	.15
❑	41 Geronimo Berroa	.30	.09
❑	42 Rey Ordonez	.30	.09
❑	43 Mike Stanley	.30	.09
❑	44 Mike Mussina	.50	.15
❑	45 Kevin Brown	.30	.09
❑	46 Dennis Eckersley	.30	.09
❑	47 Henry Rodriguez	.30	.09
❑	48 Tino Martinez	.50	.15
❑	49 Eric Young	.30	.09
❑	50 Bret Boone	.30	.09
❑	51 Raul Mondesi	.30	.09
❑	52 Sammy Sosa	.75	.23
❑	53 John Smoltz	.50	.15
❑	54 Billy Wagner	.30	.09
❑	55 Jeff D'Amico	.30	.09
❑	56 Ken Caminiti	.30	.09
❑	57 Jason Kendall	.30	.09
❑	58 Wade Boggs	.50	.15
❑	59 Andres Galarraga	.30	.09
❑	60 Jeff Brantley	.30	.09
❑	61 Mel Rojas	.30	.09
❑	62 Brian L. Hunter	.30	.09
❑	63 Bobby Bonilla	.30	.09
❑	64 Roger Clemens	1.50	.45
❑	65 Jeff Kent	.30	.09
❑	66 Matt Williams	.30	.09
❑	67 Albert Belle	.30	.09
❑	68 Jeff King	.30	.09
❑	69 John Wetteland	.30	.09
❑	70 Deion Sanders	.50	.15
❑	71 Bubba Trammell RC	.60	.18
❑	72 Felix Heredia RC	.40	.12
❑	73 Billy Koch RC	1.00	.30
❑	74 Sidney Ponson RC	1.00	.30
❑	75 Ricky Ledee RC	.60	.18
❑	76 Brett Tomko	.30	.09
❑	77 Braden Looper RC	.40	.12
❑	78 Damian Jackson	.30	.09
❑	79 Jason Dickson	.30	.09
❑	80 Chad Green RC	.40	.12
❑	81 R.A. Dickey RC	.40	.12
❑	82 Jeff Liefer	.30	.09
❑	83 Matt Wagner	.30	.09
❑	84 Richard Hidalgo	.30	.09
❑	85 Adam Riggs	.30	.09
❑	86 Robert Smith	.30	.09
❑	87 Chad Hermansen RC	.60	.18
❑	88 Felix Martinez	.30	.09
❑	89 J.J. Johnson	.30	.09
❑	90 Todd Dunwoody	.30	.09
❑	91 Katsuhiro Maeda	.30	.09
❑	92 Darin Erstad	.30	.09
❑	93 Elieser Marrero	.30	.09
❑	94 Bartolo Colon	.30	.09
❑	95 Chris Fussell	.30	.09
❑	96 Ugueth Urbina	.30	.09
❑	97 Josh Paul RC	.40	.12
❑	98 Jaime Bluma	.30	.09
❑	99 Seth Greisinger RC	.40	.12
❑	100 Jose Cruz Jr. RC	1.00	.30
❑	101 Todd Dunn	.30	.09
❑	102 Joe Young RC	.40	.12
❑	103 Jonathan Johnson	.30	.09
❑	104 Justin Towle RC	.40	.12
❑	105 Brian Rose	.30	.09
❑	106 Jose Guillen	.30	.09
❑	107 Andruw Jones	.50	.15
❑	108 Mark Kotsay RC	1.50	.45
❑	109 Wilton Guerrero	.30	.09
❑	110 Jacob Cruz	.30	.09
❑	111 Mike Sweeney	.30	.09
❑	112 Julio Mosquera	.30	.09
❑	113 Matt Morris	.30	.09
❑	114 Wendell Magee	.30	.09
❑	115 John Thomson	.30	.09
❑	116 Javier Valentin	.30	.09
❑	117 Tom Fordham	.30	.09
❑	118 Ruben Rivera	.30	.09
❑	119 Mike Drumright RC	.40	.12
❑	120 Chris Holt	.30	.09
❑	121 Sean Maloney	.30	.09
❑	122 Michael Barrett	.30	.09
❑	123 Tony Saunders RC	.40	.12
❑	124 Kevin Brown C	.30	.09
❑	125 Richard Almanzar	.30	.09
❑	126 Mark Redman	.30	.09
❑	127 Anthony Sanders RC	.40	.12
❑	128 Jeff Abbott	.30	.09
❑	129 Eugene Kingsale	.30	.09
❑	130 Paul Konerko	.50	.15
❑	131 Randall Simon RC	.60	.18
❑	132 Andy Larkin	.30	.09
❑	133 Rafael Medina	.30	.09
❑	134 Mendy Lopez	.30	.09
❑	135 Freddy Adrian Garcia	.30	.09
❑	136 Karim Garcia	.30	.09
❑	137 Larry Rodriguez RC	.40	.12
❑	138 Carlos Guillen	.30	.09
❑	139 Aaron Boone	.30	.09
❑	140 Donnie Sadler	.30	.09
❑	141 Brooks Kieschnick	.30	.09
❑	142 Scott Spiezio	.30	.09
❑	143 Everett Stull	.30	.09
❑	144 Enrique Wilson	.30	.09
❑	145 Milton Bradley RC	2.00	.60
❑	146 Kevin Orie	.30	.09
❑	147 Derek Wallace	.30	.09
❑	148 Russ Johnson	.30	.09
❑	149 Joe Lagarde RC	.40	.12
❑	150 Luis Castillo	.30	.09
❑	151 Jay Payton	.30	.09
❑	152 Joe Long	.30	.09
❑	153 Livan Hernandez	.30	.09
❑	154 Vladimir Nunez RC	.60	.18
❑	155 Pokey Reese UER Card actually numbered 156	.30	.09
❑	156 George Arias	.30	.09
❑	157 Homer Bush	.30	.09
❑	158 Chris Carpenter UER Card numbered 159	.30	.09
❑	159 Eric Milton RC	1.00	.30
❑	160 Richie Sexson	.30	.09
❑	161 Carl Pavano	.30	.09
❑	162 Chris Gissell RC	.40	.12
❑	163 Mac Suzuki	.30	.09
❑	164 Pat Cline	.30	.09
❑	165 Ron Wright	.30	.09
❑	166 Dante Powell	.30	.09
❑	167 Mark Bellhorn	.30	.09
❑	168 George Lombard	.30	.09
❑	169 Pee Wee Lopez RC	.40	.12
❑	170 Paul Wilder RC	.40	.12
❑	171 Brad Fullmer	.30	.09
❑	172 Willie Martinez RC	.40	.12
❑	173 Dario Veras RC	.40	.12
❑	174 Dave Coggin	.30	.09
❑	175 Kris Benson RC	1.00	.30
❑	176 Torii Hunter	.30	.09
❑	177 D.T. Cromer	.30	.09
❑	178 Nelson Figueroa RC	.40	.12
❑	179 Hiram Bocachica RC	.60	.18
❑	180 Shane Monahan	.30	.09
❑	181 Jimmy Anderson RC	.40	.12
❑	182 Juan Melo	.30	.09
❑	183 Pablo Ortega RC	.40	.12
❑	184 Calvin Pickering RC	.60	.18
❑	185 Reggie Taylor	.30	.09
❑	186 Jeff Farnsworth RC	.40	.12
❑	187 Terrence Long	.30	.09
❑	188 Geoff Jenkins	.30	.09
❑	189 Steve Rain RC	.40	.12
❑	190 Nerio Rodriguez RC	.40	.12
❑	191 Derrick Gibson	.30	.09
❑	192 Darin Blood	.30	.09
❑	193 Ben Davis	.30	.09
❑	194 Adrian Beltre RC	5.00	1.50
❑	195 Damian Sapp RC UER	.40	.12
❑	196 Kerry Wood RC	8.00	2.40
❑	197 Nate Rolison RC	.40	.12
❑	198 Fernando Tatis RC	.60	.18
❑	199 Brad Penny RC	1.50	.45
❑	200 Jake Westbrook RC	1.00	.30
❑	201 Edwin Diaz	.30	.09

❑ 202 Joe Fontenot RC .60 .18
❑ 203 Matt Halloran RC .40 .12
❑ 204 Blake Stein RC .40 .12
❑ 205 Onan Masaoka .30 .09
❑ 206 Ben Petrick .30 .09
❑ 207 Matt Clement RC 2.00 .60
❑ 208 Todd Greene .30 .09
❑ 209 Ray Ricken .30 .09
❑ 210 Eric Chavez RC 4.00 1.20
❑ 211 Edgard Velazquez .30 .09
❑ 212 Bruce Chen RC 1.00 .30
❑ 213 Danny Patterson .30 .09
❑ 214 Jeff Yoder .30 .09
❑ 215 Luis Ordaz RC .40 .12
❑ 216 Chris Widger .30 .09
❑ 217 Jason Brester .30 .09
❑ 218 Carlton Loewer .30 .09
❑ 219 Chris Reitsma RC .60 .18
❑ 220 Neifi Perez .30 .09
❑ 221 Hideki Irabu RC .60 .18
❑ 222 Ellis Burks .30 .09
❑ 223 Pedro Martinez UER .50 .15
Wrong birthdate
❑ 224 Kenny Lofton .30 .09
❑ 225 Randy Johnson .75 .23
❑ 226 Terry Steinbach .30 .09
❑ 227 Bernie Williams .50 .15
❑ 228 Dean Palmer .30 .09
❑ 229 Alan Benes .30 .09
❑ 230 Marquis Grissom .30 .09
❑ 231 Gary Sheffield .30 .09
❑ 232 Curt Schilling .30 .09
❑ 233 Reggie Sanders .30 .09
❑ 234 Bobby Higginson .30 .09
❑ 235 Moises Alou .30 .09
❑ 236 Tom Glavine .50 .15
❑ 237 Mark Grace .50 .15
❑ 238 Ramon Martinez .30 .09
❑ 239 Rafael Palmeiro .50 .15
❑ 240 John Olerud .30 .09
❑ 241 Dante Bichette .30 .09
❑ 242 Greg Vaughn .30 .09
❑ 243 Jeff Bagwell .50 .15
❑ 244 Barry Bonds 2.00 .60
❑ 245 Pat Hentgen .30 .09
❑ 246 Jim Thome .50 .15
❑ 247 J.Allensworth .30 .09
❑ 248 Andy Pettitte .50 .15
❑ 249 Jay Bell .30 .09
❑ 250 John Jaha .30 .09
❑ 251 Jim Edmonds .30 .09
❑ 252 Ron Gant .30 .09
❑ 253 David Cone .30 .09
❑ 254 Jose Canseco .50 .15
❑ 255 Jay Buhner .30 .09
❑ 256 Greg Maddux 1.25 .35
❑ 257 Brian McRae .30 .09
❑ 258 Lance Johnson .30 .09
❑ 259 Travis Fryman .30 .09
❑ 260 Paul O'Neill .50 .15
❑ 261 Ivan Rodriguez .50 .15
❑ 262 Gregg Jefferies .30 .09
❑ 263 Fred McGriff .50 .15
❑ 264 Derek Bell .30 .09
❑ 265 Jeff Conine .30 .09
❑ 266 Mike Piazza 1.25 .35
❑ 267 Mark Grudzielanek .30 .09
❑ 268 Brady Anderson .30 .09
❑ 269 Marty Cordova .30 .09
❑ 270 Ray Durham .30 .09
❑ 271 Joe Carter .30 .09
❑ 272 Brian Jordan .30 .09
❑ 273 David Justice .30 .09
❑ 274 Tony Gwynn 1.00 .30
❑ 275 Larry Walker .30 .09
❑ 276 Cecil Fielder .30 .09
❑ 277 Mo Vaughn .30 .09
❑ 278 Alex Fernandez .30 .09
❑ 279 Michael Tucker .30 .09
❑ 280 Jose Valentin .30 .09
❑ 281 Sandy Alomar Jr. .30 .09
❑ 282 Todd Hollandsworth .30 .09
❑ 283 Rico Brogna .30 .09
❑ 284 Rusty Greer .30 .09
❑ 285 Roberto Hernandez .30 .09
❑ 286 Hal Morris .30 .09
❑ 287 Johnny Damon .50 .15
❑ 288 Todd Hundley .30 .09
❑ 289 Rondell White .30 .09
❑ 290 Frank Thomas .75 .23
❑ 291 Don Denbow RC .40 .12
❑ 292 Derrek Lee .50 .15
❑ 293 Todd Walker .30 .09
❑ 294 Scott Rolen .50 .15
❑ 295 Wes Helms .30 .09
❑ 296 Bob Abreu .50 .15
❑ 297 John Patterson RC 2.00 .60
❑ 298 Alex Gonzalez RC 1.00 .30
❑ 299 Grant Roberts RC .60 .18
❑ 300 Jeff Suppan .30 .09
❑ 301 Luke Wilcox .30 .09
❑ 302 Marlon Anderson .30 .09
❑ 303 Ray Brown .30 .09
❑ 304 Mike Caruso RC .40 .12
❑ 305 Sam Marsonek RC .40 .12
❑ 306 Brady Raggio RC .40 .12
❑ 307 Kevin McGlinchy RC .60 .18
❑ 308 Roy Halladay RC 3.00 .90
❑ 309 Jeremi Gonzalez RC .40 .12
❑ 310 Aramis Ramirez RC 4.00 1.20
❑ 311 Dee Brown RC .60 .18
❑ 312 Justin Thompson .30 .09
❑ 313 Jay Tessmer RC .40 .12
❑ 314 Mike Johnson RC .40 .12
❑ 315 Danny Clyburn .30 .09
❑ 316 Bruce Aven .30 .09
❑ 317 Keith Foulke RC 1.50 .45
❑ 318 Jimmy Osting RC .60 .18
❑ 319 Val.De Los Santos RC .40 .12
❑ 320 Shannon Stewart .30 .09
❑ 321 Willie Adams .30 .09
❑ 322 Larry Barnes RC .40 .12
❑ 323 Mark Johnson RC .40 .12
❑ 324 Chris Stowers RC .40 .12
❑ 325 Brandon Reed .30 .09
❑ 326 Randy Winn .30 .09
❑ 327 Steve Chavez RC .40 .12
❑ 328 Nomar Garciaparra 1.25 .35
❑ 329 Jacque Jones RC 1.50 .45
❑ 330 Chris Clemons .30 .09
❑ 331 Todd Helton .75 .23
❑ 332 Ryan Brannan RC .40 .12
❑ 333 Alex Sanchez RC .60 .18
❑ 334 Arnold Gooch .30 .09
❑ 335 Russell Branyan .30 .09
❑ 336 Daryle Ward .60 .18
❑ 337 John LeRoy RC .40 .12
❑ 338 Steve Cox .30 .09
❑ 339 Kevin Witt .30 .09
❑ 340 Norm Hutchins .30 .09
❑ 341 Gabby Martinez .30 .09
❑ 342 Kris Detmers .30 .09
❑ 343 Mike Villano RC .40 .12
❑ 344 Preston Wilson .30 .09
❑ 345 James Manias RC .40 .12
❑ 346 Deivi Cruz RC .60 .18
❑ 347 Donzell McDonald RC .40 .12
❑ 348 Rod Myers RC .40 .12
❑ 349 Shawn Chacon RC 1.00 .30
❑ 350 Elvin Hernandez RC .60 .18
❑ 351 Orlando Cabrera RC 1.50 .45
❑ 352 Brian Banks .30 .09
❑ 353 Robbie Bell .40 .12
❑ 354 Brad Rigby .30 .09
❑ 355 Scott Elarton .30 .09
❑ 356 Kevin Sweeney RC .40 .12
❑ 357 Steve Soderstrom .30 .09
❑ 358 Ryan Nye .30 .09
❑ 359 Marlon Allen RC .40 .12
❑ 360 Donny Leon RC .40 .12
❑ 361 Garrett Neubart RC .60 .18
❑ 362 Abraham Nunez RC .60 .18
❑ 363 Adam Eaton RC 1.50 .45
❑ 364 Octavio Dotel RC .60 .18
❑ 365 Dean Crow RC .40 .12
❑ 366 Jason Baker RC .40 .12
❑ 367 Sean Casey 1.00 .30
❑ 368 Joe Lawrence RC .40 .12
❑ 369 Adam Johnson RC .40 .12
❑ 370 S.Schoeneweis RC .60 .18
❑ 371 Gerald Witasick Jr. .30 .09
❑ 372 Ronnie Belliard RC 1.00 .30
❑ 373 Russ Ortiz .30 .09
❑ 374 Robert Stratton RC .60 .18
❑ 375 Bobby Estalella .30 .09
❑ 376 Corey Lee RC .40 .12
❑ 377 Carlos Beltran 2.00 .60
❑ 378 Mike Cameron .30 .09
❑ 379 Scott Randall RC .40 .12
❑ 380 Corey Erickson RC .40 .12
❑ 381 Jay Canizaro .30 .09
❑ 382 Kerry Robinson RC .40 .12
❑ 383 Todd Noel RC .40 .12
❑ 384 A.J. Zapp RC .40 .12
❑ 385 Jarrod Washburn .30 .09
❑ 386 Ben Grieve .30 .09
❑ 387 Javier Vazquez RC 1.50 .45
❑ 388 Tony Graffanino .30 .09
❑ 389 Travis Lee RC .60 .18
❑ 390 DaRond Stovall .30 .09
❑ 391 Dennis Reyes RC .60 .18
❑ 392 Danny Buxbaum .30 .09
❑ 393 Marc Lewis RC .40 .12
❑ 394 Kelvim Escobar RC 1.00 .30
❑ 395 Danny Klassen .30 .09
❑ 396 Ken Cloude RC .60 .18
❑ 397 Gabe Alvarez .30 .09
❑ 398 Jaret Wright RC 1.00 .30
❑ 399 Raul Casanova .30 .09
❑ 400 Clayton Bruner RC .40 .12
❑ 401 Jason Marquis RC 1.00 .30
❑ 402 Marc Kroon .30 .09
❑ 403 Jamey Wright .30 .09
❑ 404 Matt Snyder RC .40 .12
❑ 405 Josh Garrett RC .40 .12
❑ 406 Juan Encarnacion .30 .09
❑ 407 Heath Murray .30 .09
❑ 408 Brett Herbison RC .60 .18
❑ 409 Brent Butler RC .60 .18
❑ 410 Danny Peoples RC .40 .12
❑ 411 Miguel Tejada RC 10.00 3.00
❑ 412 Damian Moss .30 .09
❑ 413 Jim Pittsley .30 .09
❑ 414 Dmitri Young .30 .09
❑ 415 Glendon Rusch .30 .09
❑ 416 Vladimir Guerrero .75 .23
❑ 417 Cole Liniak RC .60 .18
❑ 418 R.Hernandez UER .30 .09
Card back says 1st Bowman card is 1997, he had a 1996 Bowman
❑ 419 Cliff Politte RC .40 .12
❑ 420 Mel Rosario RC .40 .12
❑ 421 Jorge Carrion RC .40 .12
❑ 422 John Barnes RC .40 .12
❑ 423 Chris Stowe RC .40 .12
❑ 424 Vernon Wells RC 3.00 .90
❑ 425 Brett Caradonna RC .40 .12
❑ 426 Scott Hodges RC .60 .18
❑ 427 Jon Garland RC 3.00 .90
❑ 428 Nathan Haynes RC .60 .18
❑ 429 Geoff Goetz RC .40 .12
❑ 430 Adam Kennedy RC 1.00 .30
❑ 431 T.J. Tucker RC .40 .12
❑ 432 Aaron Akin RC .40 .12
❑ 433 Jayson Werth RC 1.00 .30
❑ 434 Glenn Davis RC .40 .12
❑ 435 Mark Mangum RC .40 .12
❑ 436 Troy Cameron RC .40 .12
❑ 437 J.J. Davis RC .60 .18
❑ 438 Lance Berkman RC 5.00 1.50
❑ 439 Jason Standridge RC .60 .18
❑ 440 Jason Dellaero RC .60 .18
❑ 441 Hideki Irabu .60 .18

1998 Bowman

	Nm-Mt	Ex-Mt
COMPLETE SET (441)	50.00	15.00
COMP. SERIES 1 (221)	25.00	7.50
COMP. SERIES 2 (220)	25.00	7.50

❑ 1 Nomar Garciaparra 1.25 .35
❑ 2 Scott Rolen .50 .15
❑ 3 Andy Pettitte .50 .15
❑ 4 Ivan Rodriguez .50 .15
❑ 5 Mark McGwire 2.00 .60
❑ 6 Jason Dickson .30 .09
❑ 7 Jose Cruz Jr. .30 .09

❑ 8 Jeff Kent .30 .09
❑ 9 Mike Mussina .50 .15
❑ 10 Jason Kendall .30 .09
❑ 11 Brett Tomko .30 .09
❑ 12 Jeff King .30 .09
❑ 13 Brad Radke .30 .09
❑ 14 Robin Ventura .30 .09
❑ 15 Jeff Bagwell .50 .15
❑ 16 Greg Maddux 1.25 .35
❑ 17 John Jaha .30 .09
❑ 18 Mike Piazza 1.25 .35
❑ 19 Edgar Martinez .50 .15
❑ 20 David Justice .30 .09
❑ 21 Todd Hundley .30 .09
❑ 22 Tony Gwynn 1.00 .30
❑ 23 Larry Walker .30 .09
❑ 24 Bernie Williams .50 .15
❑ 25 Edgar Renteria .30 .09
❑ 26 Rafael Palmeiro .50 .15
❑ 27 Tim Salmon .50 .15
❑ 28 Matt Morris .30 .09
❑ 29 Shawn Estes .30 .09
❑ 30 Vladimir Guerrero .75 .23
❑ 31 Fernando Tatis .30 .09
❑ 32 Justin Thompson .30 .09
❑ 33 Ken Griffey Jr. 1.25 .35
❑ 34 Edgardo Alfonzo .30 .09
❑ 35 Mo Vaughn .30 .09
❑ 36 Marty Cordova .30 .09
❑ 37 Craig Biggio .50 .15
❑ 38 Roger Clemens 1.50 .45
❑ 39 Mark Grace .50 .15
❑ 40 Ken Caminiti .30 .09
❑ 41 Tony Womack .30 .09
❑ 42 Albert Belle .30 .09
❑ 43 Tino Martinez .50 .15
❑ 44 Sandy Alomar Jr. .30 .09
❑ 45 Jeff Cirillo .30 .09
❑ 46 Jason Giambi .30 .09
❑ 47 Darin Erstad .30 .09
❑ 48 Livan Hernandez .30 .09
❑ 49 Mark Grudzielanek .30 .09
❑ 50 Sammy Sosa .75 .23
❑ 51 Curt Schilling .30 .09
❑ 52 Brian Hunter .30 .09
❑ 53 Neifi Perez .30 .09
❑ 54 Todd Walker .30 .09
❑ 55 Jose Guillen .30 .09
❑ 56 Jim Thome .50 .15
❑ 57 Tom Glavine .50 .15
❑ 58 Todd Greene .30 .09
❑ 59 Rondell White .30 .09
❑ 60 Roberto Alomar .50 .15
❑ 61 Tony Clark .30 .09
❑ 62 Vinny Castilla .30 .09
❑ 63 Barry Larkin .50 .15
❑ 64 Hideki Irabu .30 .09
❑ 65 Johnny Damon .50 .15
❑ 66 Juan Gonzalez .30 .09
❑ 67 John Olerud .30 .09
❑ 68 Gary Sheffield .30 .09
❑ 69 Raul Mondesi .30 .09
❑ 70 Chipper Jones .75 .23
❑ 71 David Ortiz 2.00 .60
❑ 72 Warren Morris RC .40 .12
❑ 73 Alex Gonzalez .30 .09
❑ 74 Nick Bierbrodt .30 .09
❑ 75 Roy Halladay .30 .09
❑ 76 Danny Buxbaum .30 .09
❑ 77 Adam Kennedy .30 .09
❑ 78 Jared Sandberg .30 .09
❑ 79 Michael Barrett .30 .09
❑ 80 Gil Meche .60 .18
❑ 81 Jayson Werth .30 .09
❑ 82 Abraham Nunez .30 .09
❑ 83 Ben Petrick .30 .09
❑ 84 Brett Caradonna .30 .09
❑ 85 Mike Lowell RC 1.50 .45
❑ 86 Clayton Bruner .30 .09
❑ 87 John Curtice RC .60 .18
❑ 88 Bobby Estalella .30 .09
❑ 89 Juan Melo .30 .09
❑ 90 Arnold Gooch .30 .09
❑ 91 Kevin Millwood RC 1.00 .30
❑ 92 Richie Sexson .30 .09
❑ 93 Orlando Cabrera .30 .09
❑ 94 Pat Cline .30 .09
❑ 95 Anthony Sanders .30 .09
❑ 96 Russ Johnson .30 .09
❑ 97 Ben Grieve .30 .09
❑ 98 Kevin McGlinchy .30 .09
❑ 99 Paul Wilder .30 .09
❑ 100 Russ Ortiz .30 .09
❑ 101 Ryan Jackson RC .40 .12
❑ 102 Heath Murray .30 .09
❑ 103 Brian Rose .30 .09
❑ 104 R.Radmanovich RC .40 .12
❑ 105 Ricky Ledee .30 .09
❑ 106 Jeff Wallace RC .40 .12
❑ 107 Ryan Minor RC .40 .12
❑ 108 Dennis Reyes .30 .09
❑ 109 James Manias .30 .09
❑ 110 Chris Carpenter .30 .09
❑ 111 Daryle Ward .30 .09
❑ 112 Vernon Wells .30 .09
❑ 113 Chad Green .30 .09
❑ 114 Mike Stoner RC .40 .12
❑ 115 Brad Fullmer .30 .09
❑ 116 Adam Eaton .30 .09
❑ 117 Jeff Liefer .30 .09
❑ 118 Corey Koskie RC 1.00 .30
❑ 119 Todd Helton .50 .15
❑ 120 Jaime Jones RC .40 .12
❑ 121 Mel Rosario .30 .09
❑ 122 Geoff Goetz .30 .09
❑ 123 Adrian Beltre .30 .09
❑ 124 Jason Dellaero .30 .09
❑ 125 Gabe Kapler RC 1.00 .30
❑ 126 Scott Schoeneweis .30 .09
❑ 127 Ryan Brannan .30 .09
❑ 128 Aaron Akin .30 .09
❑ 129 Ryan Anderson RC .60 .18
❑ 130 Brad Penny .30 .09
❑ 131 Bruce Chen .30 .09
❑ 132 Eli Marrero .30 .09
❑ 133 Eric Chavez .30 .09
❑ 134 Troy Glaus RC 5.00 1.50
❑ 135 Troy Cameron .30 .09
❑ 136 Brian Sikorski RC .40 .12
❑ 137 Mike Kinkade RC .40 .12
❑ 138 Braden Looper .30 .09
❑ 139 Mark Mangum .30 .09
❑ 140 Danny Peoples .30 .09
❑ 141 J.J. Davis .30 .09
❑ 142 Ben Davis .30 .09
❑ 143 Jacque Jones .30 .09
❑ 144 Derrick Gibson .30 .09
❑ 145 Bronson Arroyo 1.50 .45
❑ 146 L.De Los Santos RC UER .40 .12
has hitting stat line instead of pitching
❑ 147 Jeff Abbott .30 .09
❑ 148 Mike Cuddyer RC 1.00 .30
❑ 149 Jason Romano .30 .09
❑ 150 Shane Monahan .30 .09
❑ 151 Ntema Ndungidi RC .40 .12
❑ 152 Alex Sanchez .30 .09
❑ 153 Jack Cust RC .60 .18
❑ 154 Brent Butler .30 .09
❑ 155 Ramon Hernandez .30 .09
❑ 156 Norm Hutchins .30 .09
❑ 157 Jason Marquis .30 .09
❑ 158 Jacob Cruz .30 .09
❑ 159 Rob Burger RC .40 .12
❑ 160 Dave Coggin .30 .09
❑ 161 Preston Wilson .30 .09
❑ 162 Jason Fitzgerald RC .40 .12
❑ 163 Dan Serafini .30 .09
❑ 164 Peter Munro .30 .09
❑ 165 Trot Nixon .30 .09
❑ 166 Homer Bush .30 .09
❑ 167 Dermal Brown .30 .09
❑ 168 Chad Hermansen .30 .09
❑ 169 Julio Moreno RC .40 .12
❑ 170 John Roskos RC .40 .12
❑ 171 Grant Roberts .30 .09
❑ 172 Ken Cloude .30 .09
❑ 173 Jason Brester .30 .09
❑ 174 Jason Conti .30 .09
❑ 175 Jon Garland .30 .09
❑ 176 Robbie Bell .30 .09
❑ 177 Nathan Haynes .30 .09
❑ 178 Ramon Ortiz RC 1.00 .30
❑ 179 Shannon Stewart .30 .09
❑ 180 Pablo Ortega .30 .09
❑ 181 Jimmy Rollins RC 2.00 .60
❑ 182 Sean Casey .50 .15
❑ 183 Ted Lilly RC 1.00 .30
❑ 184 Chris Enochs RC .40 .12
❑ 185 M.Ordonez RC UER 3.00 .90
Front photo is Mario Valdez
❑ 186 Mike Drumright .30 .09
❑ 187 Aaron Boone .30 .09
❑ 188 Matt Clement .30 .09
❑ 189 Todd Dunwoody .30 .09
❑ 190 Larry Rodriguez .30 .09
❑ 191 Todd Noel .30 .09
❑ 192 Geoff Jenkins .30 .09
❑ 193 George Lombard .30 .09
❑ 194 Lance Berkman .30 .09
❑ 195 Marcus McCain .30 .09
❑ 196 Ryan McGuire .30 .09
❑ 197 Jhensy Sandoval .30 .09
❑ 198 Corey Lee .30 .09
❑ 199 Mario Valdez .30 .09
❑ 200 Robert Fick RC .60 .18
❑ 201 Donnie Sadler .30 .09
❑ 202 Marc Kroon .30 .09
❑ 203 David Miller .30 .09
❑ 204 Jarrod Washburn .30 .09
❑ 205 Miguel Tejada .75 .23
❑ 206 Raul Ibanez .30 .09
❑ 207 John Patterson .30 .09
❑ 208 Calvin Pickering .30 .09
❑ 209 Felix Martinez .30 .09
❑ 210 Mark Redman .30 .09
❑ 211 Scott Elarton .30 .09
❑ 212 Jose Amado RC .40 .12
❑ 213 Kerry Wood .50 .15
❑ 214 Dante Powell .30 .09
❑ 215 Aramis Ramirez .30 .09
❑ 216 A.J. Hinch .30 .09
❑ 217 Dustin Carr RC .40 .12
❑ 218 Mark Kotsay .30 .09
❑ 219 Jason Standridge .30 .09
❑ 220 Luis Ordaz .30 .09
❑ 221 O.Hernandez RC 1.50 .45
❑ 222 Cal Ripken 2.50 .75
❑ 223 Paul Molitor .50 .15
❑ 224 Derek Jeter 2.00 .60
❑ 225 Barry Bonds 2.00 .60
❑ 226 Jim Edmonds .30 .09
❑ 227 John Smoltz .50 .15
❑ 228 Eric Karros .30 .09
❑ 229 Ray Lankford .30 .09
❑ 230 Rey Ordonez .30 .09
❑ 231 Kenny Lofton .30 .09
❑ 232 Alex Rodriguez 1.25 .35
❑ 233 Dante Bichette .30 .09
❑ 234 Pedro Martinez .50 .15
❑ 235 Carlos Delgado .30 .09
❑ 236 Rod Beck .30 .09
❑ 237 Matt Williams .30 .09
❑ 238 Charles Johnson .30 .09
❑ 239 Rico Brogna .30 .09
❑ 240 Frank Thomas .75 .23
❑ 241 Paul O'Neill .50 .15
❑ 242 Jaret Wright .30 .09
❑ 243 Brant Brown .30 .09
❑ 244 Ryan Klesko .30 .09
❑ 245 Chuck Finley .30 .09

❑ 246 Derek Bell	.30	.09
❑ 247 Delino DeShields	.30	.09
❑ 248 Chan Ho Park	.30	.09
❑ 249 Wade Boggs	.50	.15
❑ 250 Jay Buhner	.30	.09
❑ 251 Butch Huskey	.30	.09
❑ 252 Steve Finley	.30	.09
❑ 253 Will Clark	.50	.15
❑ 254 John Valentin	.30	.09
❑ 255 Bobby Higginson	.30	.09
❑ 256 Darryl Strawberry	.30	.09
❑ 257 Randy Johnson	.75	.23
❑ 258 Al Martin	.30	.09
❑ 259 Travis Fryman	.30	.09
❑ 260 Fred McGriff	.50	.15
❑ 261 Jose Valentin	.30	.09
❑ 262 Andruw Jones	.50	.15
❑ 263 Kenny Rogers	.30	.09
❑ 264 Moises Alou	.30	.09
❑ 265 Denny Neagle	.30	.09
❑ 266 Ugueth Urbina	.30	.09
❑ 267 Derrek Lee	.50	.15
❑ 268 Ellis Burks	.30	.09
❑ 269 Mariano Rivera	.50	.15
❑ 270 Dean Palmer	.30	.09
❑ 271 Eddie Taubensee	.30	.09
❑ 272 Brady Anderson	.30	.09
❑ 273 Brian Giles	.30	.09
❑ 274 Quinton McCracken	.30	.09
❑ 275 Henry Rodriguez	.30	.09
❑ 276 Andres Galarraga	.30	.09
❑ 277 Jose Canseco	.50	.15
❑ 278 David Segui	.30	.09
❑ 279 Bret Saberhagen	.30	.09
❑ 280 Kevin Brown	.50	.15
❑ 281 Chuck Knoblauch	.30	.09
❑ 282 Jeromy Burnitz	.30	.09
❑ 283 Jay Bell	.30	.09
❑ 284 Manny Ramirez	.50	.15
❑ 285 Rick Helling	.30	.09
❑ 286 Francisco Cordova	.30	.09
❑ 287 Bob Abreu	.30	.09
❑ 288 J.T. Snow	.30	.09
❑ 289 Hideo Nomo	.75	.23
❑ 290 Brian Jordan	.30	.09
❑ 291 Javy Lopez	.30	.09
❑ 292 Travis Lee	.30	.09
❑ 293 Russell Branyan	.30	.09
❑ 294 Paul Konerko	.30	.09
❑ 295 Masato Yoshii RC	1.00	.30
❑ 296 Kris Benson	.30	.09
❑ 297 Juan Encarnacion	.30	.09
❑ 298 Eric Milton	.30	.09
❑ 299 Mike Caruso	.30	.09
❑ 300 R.Aramboles RC	.60	.18
❑ 301 Bobby Smith	.30	.09
❑ 302 Billy Koch	.30	.09
❑ 303 Richard Hidalgo	.30	.09
❑ 304 Justin Baughman RC	.40	.12
❑ 305 Chris Gissell	.30	.09
❑ 306 Donnie Bridges RC	.40	.12
❑ 307 Nelson Lara RC	.40	.12
❑ 308 Randy Wolf RC	.60	.18
❑ 309 Jason LaRue RC	.60	.18
❑ 310 Jason Gooding RC	.40	.12
❑ 311 Edgard Clemente	.30	.09
❑ 312 Andrew Vessel	.30	.09
❑ 313 Chris Reitsma	.30	.09
❑ 314 Jesus Sanchez RC	.40	.12
❑ 315 Buddy Carlyle RC	.40	.12
❑ 316 Randy Winn	.30	.09
❑ 317 Luis Rivera RC	.40	.12
❑ 318 Marcus Thames RC	.60	.18
❑ 319 A.J. Pierzynski	.30	.09
❑ 320 Scott Randall	.30	.09
❑ 321 Damian Sapp	.30	.09
❑ 322 Ed Yarnall RC	.40	.12
❑ 323 Luke Allen RC	.60	.18
❑ 324 J.D. Smart	.30	.09
❑ 325 Willie Martinez	.30	.09
❑ 326 Alex Ramirez	.30	.09
❑ 327 Eric DuBose RC	.60	.18
❑ 328 Kevin Witt	.30	.09
❑ 329 Dan McKinley RC	.40	.12
❑ 330 Cliff Politte	.30	.09
❑ 331 Vladimir Nunez	.30	.09
❑ 332 John Halama RC	.40	.12
❑ 333 Nerio Rodriguez	.30	.09
❑ 334 Desi Relaford	.30	.09
❑ 335 Robinson Checo	.30	.09
❑ 336 John Nicholson	.50	.15
❑ 337 Tom LaRosa RC	.40	.12
❑ 338 Kevin Nicholson RC	.40	.12
❑ 339 Javier Vazquez	.30	.09
❑ 340 A.J. Zapp	.30	.09
❑ 341 Tom Evans	.30	.09
❑ 342 Kerry Robinson	.30	.09
❑ 343 Gabe Gonzalez RC	.40	.12
❑ 344 Ralph Milliard	.30	.09
❑ 345 Enrique Wilson	.30	.09
❑ 346 Elvin Hernandez	.30	.09
❑ 347 Mike Lincoln RC	.40	.12
❑ 348 Cesar King RC	.40	.12
❑ 349 Cristian Guzman RC	1.00	.30
❑ 350 Donzell McDonald	.30	.09
❑ 351 Jim Parque RC	.40	.12
❑ 352 Mike Saipe RC	.40	.12
❑ 353 Carlos Febles RC	.60	.18
❑ 354 Dernell Stenson RC	.60	.18
❑ 355 Mark Osborne RC	.40	.12
❑ 356 Odalis Perez RC	1.50	.45
❑ 357 Jason Dewey RC	.40	.12
❑ 358 Joe Fontenot	.30	.09
❑ 359 Jason Grilli RC	.40	.12
❑ 360 Kevin Haverbusch RC	.40	.12
❑ 361 Jay Yennaco RC	.40	.12
❑ 362 Brian Buchanan	.30	.09
❑ 363 John Barnes	.30	.09
❑ 364 Chris Fussell	.30	.09
❑ 365 Kevin Gibbs RC	.40	.12
❑ 366 Joe Lawrence	.30	.09
❑ 367 DaRond Stovall	.30	.09
❑ 368 Brian Fuentes RC	.40	.12
❑ 369 Jimmy Anderson	.30	.09
❑ 370 Lariel Gonzalez RC	.40	.12
❑ 371 Scott Williamson RC	.60	.18
❑ 372 Milton Bradley	.30	.09
❑ 373 Jason Halper RC	.40	.12
❑ 374 Brent Billingsley RC	.40	.12
❑ 375 Joe DePastino RC	.40	.12
❑ 376 Jake Westbrook	.30	.09
❑ 377 Octavio Dotel	.30	.09
❑ 378 Jason Williams RC	.40	.12
❑ 379 Julio Ramirez RC	.40	.12
❑ 380 Seth Greisinger	.30	.09
❑ 381 Mike Judd RC	.40	.12
❑ 382 Ben Ford RC	.40	.12
❑ 383 Tom Bennett RC	.40	.12
❑ 384 Adam Butler RC	.40	.12
❑ 385 Wade Miller RC	1.00	.30
❑ 386 Kyle Peterson RC	.40	.12
❑ 387 Tommy Peterman RC	.40	.12
❑ 388 Onan Masaoka	.30	.09
❑ 389 Jason Rakers RC	.40	.12
❑ 390 Rafael Medina	.30	.09
❑ 391 Luis Lopez RC	.40	.12
❑ 392 Jeff Yoder	.30	.09
❑ 393 Vance Wilson RC	.40	.12
❑ 394 F.Seguignol RC	.40	.12
❑ 395 Ron Wright	.30	.09
❑ 396 Ruben Mateo RC	.60	.18
❑ 397 Steve Lomasney RC	.60	.18
❑ 398 Damian Jackson	.30	.09
❑ 399 Mike Jerzembeck RC	.40	.12
❑ 400 Luis Rivas RC	1.00	.30
❑ 401 Kevin Burford RC	.40	.12
❑ 402 Glenn Davis	.30	.09
❑ 403 Robert Luce RC	.40	.12
❑ 404 Cole Liniak	.30	.09
❑ 405 Matt LeCroy RC	.60	.18
❑ 406 Jeremy Giambi RC	.60	.18
❑ 407 Shawn Chacon	.30	.09
❑ 408 Dewayne Wise RC	.40	.12
❑ 409 Steve Woodard	.30	.09
❑ 410 F.Cordero RC	1.00	.30
❑ 411 Damon Minor RC	.40	.12
❑ 412 Lou Collier	.30	.09
❑ 413 Justin Towle	.30	.09
❑ 414 Juan LeBron	.30	.09
❑ 415 Michael Coleman	.30	.09
❑ 416 Felix Rodriguez	.30	.09
❑ 417 Paul Ah Yat RC	.40	.12
❑ 418 Kevin Barker RC	.40	.12
❑ 419 Brian Meadows	.30	.09
❑ 420 Darnell McDonald RC	.40	.12
❑ 421 Matt Kinney RC	.60	.18
❑ 422 Mike Vavrek RC	.40	.12
❑ 423 Courtney Duncan RC	.40	.12
❑ 424 Kevin Millar RC	1.50	.45
❑ 425 Ruben Rivera	.30	.09
❑ 426 Steve Shoemaker RC	.40	.12
❑ 427 Dan Reichert RC	.40	.12
❑ 428 Carlos Lee RC	3.00	.90
❑ 429 Rod Barajas	1.00	.30
❑ 430 Pablo Ozuna RC	.60	.18
❑ 431 Todd Belitz RC	.40	.12
❑ 432 Sidney Ponson	.30	.09
❑ 433 Steve Carver RC	.40	.12
❑ 434 Esteban Yan RC	.60	.18
❑ 435 Cedrick Bowers	.30	.09
❑ 436 Marlon Anderson	.30	.09
❑ 437 Carl Pavano	.30	.09
❑ 438 Jae Weong Seo RC	1.00	.30
❑ 439 Jose Taveras RC	.40	.12
❑ 440 Matt Anderson RC	.60	.18
❑ 441 Darron Ingram RC	.40	.12
❑ NNO S.Hasegawa '91 BBM	10.00	3.00
❑ NNO H.Irabu '91 BBM	10.00	3.00
❑ NNO H.Nomo '91 BBM	25.00	7.50

1999 Bowman

	Nm-Mt	Ex-Mt
COMPLETE SET (440)	80.00	24.00
COMP. SERIES 1 (220)	30.00	9.00
COMP. SERIES 2 (220)	50.00	15.00

❑ 1 Ben Grieve	.30	.09
❑ 2 Kerry Wood	.30	.09
❑ 3 Ruben Rivera	.30	.09
❑ 4 Sandy Alomar Jr.	.30	.09
❑ 5 Cal Ripken	2.50	.75
❑ 6 Mark McGwire	2.00	.60
❑ 7 Vladimir Guerrero	.75	.23
❑ 8 Moises Alou	.30	.09
❑ 9 Jim Edmonds	.30	.09
❑ 10 Greg Maddux	1.25	.35
❑ 11 Gary Sheffield	.30	.09
❑ 12 John Valentin	.30	.09
❑ 13 Chuck Knoblauch	.30	.09
❑ 14 Tony Clark	.30	.09
❑ 15 Rusty Greer	.30	.09
❑ 16 Al Leiter	.30	.09
❑ 17 Travis Lee	.30	.09
❑ 18 Jose Cruz Jr.	.30	.09
❑ 19 Pedro Martinez	.50	.15
❑ 20 Paul O'Neill	.50	.15
❑ 21 Todd Walker	.30	.09
❑ 22 Vinny Castilla	.30	.09
❑ 23 Barry Larkin	.50	.15
❑ 24 Curt Schilling	.30	.09
❑ 25 Jason Kendall	.30	.09
❑ 26 Scott Erickson	.30	.09
❑ 27 Andres Galarraga	.30	.09
❑ 28 Jeff Shaw	.30	.09
❑ 29 John Olerud	.30	.09
❑ 30 Orlando Hernandez	.30	.09
❑ 31 Larry Walker	.30	.09
❑ 32 Andruw Jones	.50	.15
❑ 33 Jeff Cirillo	.30	.09

❑ 34 Barry Bonds 2.00 .60
❑ 35 Manny Ramirez .50 .15
❑ 36 Mark Kotsay .30 .09
❑ 37 Ivan Rodriguez .50 .15
❑ 38 Jeff King .30 .09
❑ 39 Brian Hunter .30 .09
❑ 40 Ray Durham .30 .09
❑ 41 Bernie Williams .50 .15
❑ 42 Darin Erstad .30 .09
❑ 43 Chipper Jones .75 .23
❑ 44 Pat Hentgen .30 .09
❑ 45 Eric Young .30 .09
❑ 46 Jaret Wright .30 .09
❑ 47 Juan Guzman .30 .09
❑ 48 Jorge Posada .50 .15
❑ 49 Bobby Higginson .30 .09
❑ 50 Jose Guillen .30 .09
❑ 51 Trevor Hoffman .30 .09
❑ 52 Ken Griffey Jr. 1.25 .35
❑ 53 David Justice .30 .09
❑ 54 Matt Williams .30 .09
❑ 55 Eric Karros .30 .09
❑ 56 Derek Bell .30 .09
❑ 57 Ray Lankford .30 .09
❑ 58 Mariano Rivera .50 .15
❑ 59 Brett Tomko .30 .09
❑ 60 Mike Mussina .50 .15
❑ 61 Kenny Lofton .30 .09
❑ 62 Chuck Finley .30 .09
❑ 63 Alex Gonzalez .30 .09
❑ 64 Mark Grace .50 .15
❑ 65 Raul Mondesi .30 .09
❑ 66 David Cone .30 .09
❑ 67 Brad Fullmer .30 .09
❑ 68 Andy Benes .30 .09
❑ 69 John Smoltz .50 .15
❑ 70 Shane Reynolds .30 .09
❑ 71 Bruce Chen .30 .09
❑ 72 Adam Kennedy .30 .09
❑ 73 Jack Cust .30 .09
❑ 74 Matt Clement .30 .09
❑ 75 Derrick Gibson .30 .09
❑ 76 Darnell McDonald .30 .09
❑ 77 Adam Everett RC 1.00 .30
❑ 78 Ricardo Aramboles .30 .09
❑ 79 Mark Quinn RC .60 .18
❑ 80 Jason Rakers .30 .09
❑ 81 Seth Etherton RC .40 .12
❑ 82 Jeff Urban RC .60 .18
❑ 83 Manny Aybar .30 .09
❑ 84 Mike Nannini RC .40 .12
❑ 85 Onan Masaoka .30 .09
❑ 86 Rod Barajas .30 .09
❑ 87 Mike Frank .30 .09
❑ 88 Scott Randall .30 .09
❑ 89 Justin Bowles RC .40 .12
❑ 90 Chris Haas .30 .09
❑ 91 Arturo McDowell RC .40 .12
❑ 92 Matt Belisle RC .40 .45
❑ 93 Scott Elarton .30 .09
❑ 94 Vernon Wells .30 .09
❑ 95 Pat Cline .30 .09
❑ 96 Ryan Anderson .30 .09
❑ 97 Kevin Barker .30 .09
❑ 98 Ruben Mateo .30 .09
❑ 99 Robert Fick .30 .09
❑ 100 Corey Koskie .30 .09
❑ 101 Ricky Ledee .30 .09
❑ 102 Rick Elder RC .60 .18
❑ 103 Jack Cressend RC .40 .12
❑ 104 Joe Lawrence .30 .09
❑ 105 Mike Lincoln .30 .09
❑ 106 Kit Pellow RC .40 .12
❑ 107 Matt Burch RC .60 .18
❑ 108 Cole Liniak .30 .09
❑ 109 Jason Dewey .30 .09
❑ 110 Cesar King .30 .09
❑ 111 Julio Ramirez .30 .09
❑ 112 Jake Westbrook .30 .09
❑ 113 Eric Valent RC .60 .18
❑ 114 Roosevelt Brown RC .40 .12
❑ 115 Choo Freeman RC .60 .18
❑ 116 Juan Melo .30 .09
❑ 117 Jason Grilli .30 .09
❑ 118 Jared Sandberg .30 .09
❑ 119 Glenn Davis .30 .09
❑ 120 David Riske RC .40 .12
❑ 121 Jacque Jones .30 .09
❑ 122 Corey Lee .30 .09
❑ 123 Michael Barrett .30 .09
❑ 124 Lariel Gonzalez .30 .09
❑ 125 Mitch Meluskey .30 .09
❑ 126 Freddy Adrian Garcia .30 .09
❑ 127 Tony Torcato RC .60 .18
❑ 128 Jeff Liefer .30 .09
❑ 129 Ntema Ndungidi .30 .09
❑ 130 Andy Brown RC .40 .12
❑ 131 Ryan Mills RC .40 .12
❑ 132 Andy Abad RC .40 .12
❑ 133 Carlos Febles .30 .09
❑ 134 Jason Tyner RC .40 .12
❑ 135 Mark Osborne .30 .09
❑ 136 Phil Norton RC .40 .12
❑ 137 Nathan Haynes .30 .09
❑ 138 Roy Halladay .30 .09
❑ 139 Juan Encarnacion .30 .09
❑ 140 Brad Penny .30 .09
❑ 141 Grant Roberts .30 .09
❑ 142 Aramis Ramirez .30 .09
❑ 143 Cristian Guzman .30 .09
❑ 144 Mamon Tucker RC .40 .12
❑ 145 Ryan Bradley .30 .09
❑ 146 Brian Simmons .30 .09
❑ 147 Dan Reichert .30 .09
❑ 148 Russ Branyan .30 .09
❑ 149 Victor Valencia RC .30 .09
❑ 150 Scott Schoeneweis .30 .09
❑ 151 Sean Spencer RC .40 .12
❑ 152 Odalis Perez .30 .09
❑ 153 Joe Fontenot .30 .09
❑ 154 Milton Bradley .30 1.30
❑ 155 Josh McKinley RC .60 .18
❑ 156 Terrence Long .30 .09
❑ 157 Danny Klassen .30 .09
❑ 158 Paul Hoover RC .60 .18
❑ 159 Ron Belliard .30 .09
❑ 160 Armando Rios .30 .09
❑ 161 Ramon Hernandez .30 .09
❑ 162 Jason Conti .30 .09
❑ 163 Chad Hermansen .30 .09
❑ 164 Jason Standridge .30 .09
❑ 165 Jason Dellaero .30 .09
❑ 166 John Curtice .30 .09
❑ 167 Clayton Andrews RC .40 .12
❑ 168 Jeremy Giambi .30 .09
❑ 169 Alex Ramirez .30 .09
❑ 170 Gabe Molina RC .40 .12
❑ 171 M.Encarnacion RC .40 .12
❑ 172 Mike Zywica RC .40 .12
❑ 173 Chip Ambres RC .40 .12
❑ 174 Trot Nixon .30 .09
❑ 175 Pat Burrell RC 3.00 .90
❑ 176 Jeff Yoder .30 .09
❑ 177 Chris Jones RC .40 .12
❑ 178 Kevin Witt .30 .09
❑ 179 Keith Luuloa RC .40 .12
❑ 180 Billy Koch .30 .09
❑ 181 Damaso Marte RC .40 .12
❑ 182 Ryan Glynn RC .40 .12
❑ 183 Calvin Pickering .30 .09
❑ 184 Michael Cuddyer .30 .09
❑ 185 Nick Johnson RC 2.00 .60
❑ 186 D.Mientkiewicz RC 1.00 .30
❑ 187 Nate Cornejo RC 1.00 .30
❑ 188 Octavio Dotel .30 .09
❑ 189 Wes Helms .30 .09
❑ 190 Nelson Lara .30 .09
❑ 191 Chuck Abbott RC .40 .12
❑ 192 Tony Armas Jr. .30 .09
❑ 193 Gil Meche .30 .09
❑ 194 Ben Petrick .30 .09
❑ 195 Chris George RC .60 .18
❑ 196 Scott Hunter RC .40 .12
❑ 197 Ryan Brannan .30 .09
❑ 198 Amaury Garcia RC .60 .18
❑ 199 Chris Gissell .30 .09
❑ 200 Austin Kearns RC 2.00 .60
❑ 201 Alex Gonzalez .30 .09
❑ 202 Wade Miller .30 .09
❑ 203 Scott Williamson .30 .09
❑ 204 Chris Enochs .30 .09
❑ 205 Fernando Seguignol .30 .09
❑ 206 Marlon Anderson .30 .09
❑ 207 Todd Sears RC .60 .18
❑ 208 Nate Bump RC .40 .12
❑ 209 J.M. Gold RC .40 .12
❑ 210 Matt LeCroy .30 .09
❑ 211 Alex Hernandez .30 .09
❑ 212 Luis Rivera .30 .09
❑ 213 Troy Cameron .30 .09
❑ 214 Alex Escobar RC .60 .18
❑ 215 Jason LaRue .30 .09
❑ 216 Kyle Peterson .30 .09
❑ 217 Brent Butler .30 .09
❑ 218 Dernell Stenson .30 .09
❑ 219 Adrian Beltre .30 .09
❑ 220 Daryle Ward .30 .09
❑ 221 Jim Thome .50 .15
❑ 222 Cliff Floyd .30 .09
❑ 223 Rickey Henderson .75 .23
❑ 224 Garret Anderson .30 .09
❑ 225 Ken Caminiti .30 .09
❑ 226 Bret Boone .30 .09
❑ 227 Jeromy Burnitz .30 .09
❑ 228 Steve Finley .30 .09
❑ 229 Miguel Tejada .30 .09
❑ 230 Greg Vaughn .30 .09
❑ 231 Jose Offerman .30 .09
❑ 232 Andy Ashby .30 .09
❑ 233 Albert Belle .30 .09
❑ 234 Fernando Tatis .30 .09
❑ 235 Todd Helton .50 .15
❑ 236 Sean Casey .50 .15
❑ 237 Brian Giles .30 .09
❑ 238 Andy Pettitte .50 .15
❑ 239 Fred McGriff .50 .15
❑ 240 Roberto Alomar .50 .15
❑ 241 Edgar Martinez .50 .15
❑ 242 Lee Stevens .30 .09
❑ 243 Shawn Green .30 .09
❑ 244 Ryan Klesko .30 .09
❑ 245 Sammy Sosa .75 .23
❑ 246 Todd Hundley .30 .09
❑ 247 Shannon Stewart .30 .09
❑ 248 Randy Johnson .75 .23
❑ 249 Rondell White .30 .09
❑ 250 Mike Piazza 1.25 .35
❑ 251 Craig Biggio .50 .15
❑ 252 David Wells .30 .09
❑ 253 Brian Jordan .30 .09
❑ 254 Edgar Renteria .30 .09
❑ 255 Bartolo Colon .30 .09
❑ 256 Frank Thomas .75 .23
❑ 257 Will Clark .50 .15
❑ 258 Dean Palmer .30 .09
❑ 259 Dmitri Young .30 .09
❑ 260 Scott Rolen .50 .15
❑ 261 Jeff Kent .30 .09
❑ 262 Dante Bichette .30 .09
❑ 263 Nomar Garciaparra 1.25 .35
❑ 264 Tony Gwynn 1.00 .30
❑ 265 Alex Rodriguez 1.25 .35
❑ 266 Jose Canseco .50 .15
❑ 267 Jason Giambi .30 .09
❑ 268 Jeff Bagwell .50 .15
❑ 269 Carlos Delgado .30 .09
❑ 270 Tom Glavine .50 .15
❑ 271 Eric Davis .30 .09
❑ 272 Edgardo Alfonzo .30 .09
❑ 273 Tim Salmon .50 .15
❑ 274 Johnny Damon .50 .15
❑ 275 Rafael Palmeiro .50 .15
❑ 276 Denny Neagle .30 .09
❑ 277 Neifi Perez .30 .09
❑ 278 Roger Clemens 1.50 .45
❑ 279 Brant Brown .30 .09
❑ 280 Kevin Brown .50 .15
❑ 281 Jay Bell .30 .09
❑ 282 Jay Buhner .30 .09
❑ 283 Matt Lawton .30 .09
❑ 284 Robin Ventura .30 .09
❑ 285 Juan Gonzalez .30 .09
❑ 286 Mo Vaughn .30 .09
❑ 287 Kevin Millwood .30 .09
❑ 288 Tino Martinez .50 .15
❑ 289 Justin Thompson .30 .09
❑ 290 Derek Jeter 2.00 .60
❑ 291 Ben Davis .30 .09

Card	Nm-Mt	Ex-Mt
❑ 292 Mike Lowell	.30	.09
❑ 293 Calvin Murray	.30	.09
❑ 294 Micah Bowie RC	.40	.12
❑ 295 Lance Berkman	.30	.09
❑ 296 Jason Marquis	.30	.09
❑ 297 Chad Green	.30	.09
❑ 298 Dee Brown	.30	.09
❑ 299 Jerry Hairston Jr.	.30	.09
❑ 300 Gabe Kapler	.30	.09
❑ 301 Brent Stentz RC	.60	.18
❑ 302 Scott Mullen RC	.40	.12
❑ 303 Brandon Reed	.30	.09
❑ 304 Shea Hillenbrand RC	1.50	.45
❑ 305 J.D. Closser RC	1.00	.30
❑ 306 Gary Matthews Jr.	.30	.09
❑ 307 Toby Hall RC	.60	.18
❑ 308 Jason Phillips RC	.40	.12
❑ 309 Jose Macias RC	.40	.12
❑ 310 Jung Bong RC	.60	.18
❑ 311 Ramon Soler RC	.40	.12
❑ 312 Kelly Dransfeldt RC	.40	.12
❑ 313 Carl. E. Hernandez RC	.60	.18
❑ 314 Kevin Haverbusch	.30	.09
❑ 315 Aaron Myette RC	.40	.12
❑ 316 Chad Harville RC	.40	.12
❑ 317 Kyle Farnsworth RC	1.00	.30
❑ 318 Gookie Dawkins RC	.60	.18
❑ 319 Willie Martinez	.30	.09
❑ 320 Carlos Lee	.30	.09
❑ 321 Carlos Pena RC	.60	.18
❑ 322 Peter Bergeron RC	.60	.18
❑ 323 A.J. Burnett RC	2.00	.60
❑ 324 Bucky Jacobsen RC	1.00	.30
❑ 325 Mo Bruce RC	.40	.12
❑ 326 Reggie Taylor	.30	.09
❑ 327 Jackie Rexrode	.30	.09
❑ 328 Alvin Morrow RC	.40	.12
❑ 329 Carlos Beltran	.50	.15
❑ 330 Eric Chavez	.30	.09
❑ 331 John Patterson	.30	.09
❑ 332 Jayson Werth	.30	.09
❑ 333 Richie Sexson	.30	.09
❑ 334 Randy Wolf	.30	.09
❑ 335 Eli Marrero	.30	.09
❑ 336 Paul LoDuca	.30	.09
❑ 337 J.D Smart	.30	.09
❑ 338 Ryan Minor	.30	.09
❑ 339 Kris Benson	.30	.09
❑ 340 George Lombard	.30	.09
❑ 341 Troy Glaus	.50	.15
❑ 342 Eddie Yarnall	.30	.09
❑ 343 Kip Wells RC	1.00	.30
❑ 344 C.C. Sabathia RC	1.50	.45
❑ 345 Sean Burroughs RC	1.00	.30
❑ 346 Felipe Lopez RC	2.00	.60
❑ 347 Ryan Rupe RC	.40	.12
❑ 348 Orber Moreno RC	.40	.12
❑ 349 Rafael Roque RC	.40	.12
❑ 350 Alfonso Soriano RC	8.00	2.40
❑ 351 Pablo Ozuna	.30	.09
❑ 352 Corey Patterson RC	1.00	.30
❑ 353 Braden Looper	.30	.09
❑ 354 Robbie Bell	.30	.09
❑ 355 Mark Mulder RC	3.00	.90
❑ 356 Angel Pena	.30	.09
❑ 357 Kevin McGlinchy	.30	.09
❑ 358 M.Restovich RC	.60	.18
❑ 359 Eric DuBose	.30	.09
❑ 360 Geoff Jenkins	.30	.09
❑ 361 Mark Harriger RC	.40	.12
❑ 362 Junior Herndon RC	.60	.18
❑ 363 Tim Raines Jr. RC	.60	.18
❑ 364 Rafael Furcal RC	2.00	.60
❑ 365 Marcus Giles RC	1.50	.45
❑ 366 Ted Lilly	.30	.09
❑ 367 Jorge Toca RC	.60	.18
❑ 368 David Kelton RC	.60	.18
❑ 369 Adam Dunn RC	8.00	2.40
❑ 370 Guillermo Mota RC	.40	.12
❑ 371 Brett Laxton RC	.40	.12
❑ 372 Travis Harper RC	.60	.18
❑ 373 Tom Davey RC	.40	.12
❑ 374 Darren Blakely RC	.40	.12
❑ 375 Tim Hudson RC	3.00	.90
❑ 376 Jason Romano	.30	.09
❑ 377 Dan Reichert	.30	.09
❑ 378 Julio Lugo RC	1.00	.30
❑ 379 Jose Garcia RC	.40	.12
❑ 380 Erubiel Durazo RC	1.00	.30
❑ 381 Jose Jimenez	.30	.09
❑ 382 Chris Fussell	.30	.09
❑ 383 Steve Lomasney	.30	.09
❑ 384 Juan Pena RC	.60	.18
❑ 385 Allen Levrault RC	.40	.12
❑ 386 Juan Rivera RC	1.00	.30
❑ 387 Steve Colyer RC	.60	.18
❑ 388 Joe Nathan RC	1.50	.45
❑ 389 Ron Walker RC	.40	.12
❑ 390 Nick Bierbrodt	.30	.09
❑ 391 Luke Prokopec RC	.40	.12
❑ 392 Dave Roberts RC	1.00	.30
❑ 393 Mike Darr	.30	.09
❑ 394 Abraham Nunez RC	.60	.18
❑ 395 G.Chiaramonte RC	.40	.12
❑ 396 J.Van Buren RC	.40	.12
❑ 397 Mike Kusiewicz	.30	.09
❑ 398 Matt Wise RC	.40	.12
❑ 399 Joe McEwing RC	.60	.18
❑ 400 Matt Holliday RC	1.00	.30
❑ 401 Willi Mo Pena RC	3.00	.90
❑ 402 Ruben Quevedo RC	.40	.12
❑ 403 Rob Ryan RC	.40	.12
❑ 404 Freddy Garcia RC	1.50	.45
❑ 405 Kevin Eberwein RC	.40	.12
❑ 406 Jesus Colome RC	.40	.12
❑ 407 Chris Singleton	.30	.09
❑ 408 Bubba Crosby RC	1.00	.30
❑ 409 Jesus Cordero RC	.60	.18
❑ 410 Donny Leon	.30	.09
❑ 411 G.Tomlinson RC	.60	.18
❑ 412 Jeff Winchester RC	.40	.12
❑ 413 Adam Piatt RC	.60	.18
❑ 414 Robert Stratton	.30	.09
❑ 415 T.J. Tucker	.30	.09
❑ 416 Ryan Langerhans RC	2.00	.60
❑ 417 A.Shumaker RC	.40	.12
❑ 418 Matt Miller RC	.40	.12
❑ 419 Doug Clark RC	.40	.12
❑ 420 Kory DeHaan RC	.40	.12
❑ 421 David Eckstein RC	3.00	.90
❑ 422 Brian Cooper RC	.40	.12
❑ 423 Brady Clark RC	1.50	.45
❑ 424 Chris Magruder RC	.60	.18
❑ 425 Bobby Seay RC	.40	.12
❑ 426 Aubrey Huff RC	1.50	.45
❑ 427 Mike Jerzembeck	.30	.09
❑ 428 Matt Blank RC	.60	.18
❑ 429 Benny Agbayani RC	.60	.18
❑ 430 Kevin Beirne RC	.60	.18
❑ 431 Josh Hamilton RC	1.00	.30
❑ 432 Josh Girdley RC	.40	.12
❑ 433 Kyle Snyder RC	.40	.12
❑ 434 Mike Paradis RC	.40	.12
❑ 435 Jason Jennings RC	1.00	.30
❑ 436 David Walling RC	.40	.12
❑ 437 Omar Ortiz RC	.60	.18
❑ 438 Jay Gehrke RC	.60	.18
❑ 439 Casey Burns RC	.60	.18
❑ 440 Carl Crawford RC	3.00	.90

2000 Bowman

	Nm-Mt	Ex-Mt
COMPLETE SET (440)	60.00	18.00

Card	Nm-Mt	Ex-Mt
❑ 1 Vladimir Guerrero	.75	.23
❑ 2 Chipper Jones	.75	.23
❑ 3 Todd Walker	.30	.09
❑ 4 Barry Larkin	.50	.15
❑ 5 Bernie Williams	.50	.15
❑ 6 Todd Helton	.50	.15
❑ 7 Jermaine Dye	.30	.09
❑ 8 Brian Giles	.30	.09
❑ 9 Freddy Garcia	.30	.09
❑ 10 Greg Vaughn	.30	.09
❑ 11 Alex Gonzalez	.30	.09
❑ 12 Luis Gonzalez	.30	.09
❑ 13 Ron Belliard	.30	.09
❑ 14 Ben Grieve	.30	.09
❑ 15 Carlos Delgado	.30	.09
❑ 16 Brian Jordan	.30	.09
❑ 17 Fernando Tatis	.30	.09
❑ 18 Ryan Rupe	.30	.09
❑ 19 Miguel Tejada	.30	.09
❑ 20 Mark Grace	.50	.15
❑ 21 Kenny Lofton	.30	.09
❑ 22 Eric Karros	.30	.09
❑ 23 Cliff Floyd	.30	.09
❑ 24 John Halama	.30	.09
❑ 25 Cristian Guzman	.30	.09
❑ 26 Scott Williamson	.30	.09
❑ 27 Mike Lieberthal	.30	.09
❑ 28 Tim Hudson	.30	.09
❑ 29 Warren Morris	.30	.09
❑ 30 Pedro Martinez	.50	.15
❑ 31 John Smoltz	.50	.15
❑ 32 Ray Durham	.30	.09
❑ 33 Chad Allen	.30	.09
❑ 34 Tony Clark	.30	.09
❑ 35 Tino Martinez	.50	.15
❑ 36 J.T. Snow	.30	.09
❑ 37 Kevin Brown	.30	.09
❑ 38 Bartolo Colon	.30	.09
❑ 39 Rey Ordonez	.30	.09
❑ 40 Jeff Bagwell	.50	.15
❑ 41 Ivan Rodriguez	.50	.15
❑ 42 Eric Chavez	.30	.09
❑ 43 Eric Milton	.30	.09
❑ 44 Jose Canseco	.50	.15
❑ 45 Shawn Green	.30	.09
❑ 46 Rich Aurilia	.30	.09
❑ 47 Roberto Alomar	.50	.15
❑ 48 Brian Daubach	.30	.09
❑ 49 Maggio Ordonez	.30	.09
❑ 50 Derek Jeter	2.00	.60
❑ 51 Kris Benson	.30	.09
❑ 52 Albert Belle	.30	.09
❑ 53 Rondell White	.30	.09
❑ 54 Justin Thompson	.30	.09
❑ 55 Nomar Garciaparra	1.25	.35
❑ 56 Chuck Finley	.30	.09
❑ 57 Omar Vizquel	.50	.15
❑ 58 Luis Castillo	.30	.09
❑ 59 Richard Hidalgo	.30	.09
❑ 60 Barry Bonds	2.00	.60
❑ 61 Craig Biggio	.50	.15
❑ 62 Doug Glanville	.30	.09
❑ 63 Gabe Kapler	.30	.09
❑ 64 Johnny Damon	.50	.15
❑ 65 Pokey Reese	.30	.09
❑ 66 Andy Pettitte	.50	.15
❑ 67 B.J. Surhoff	.30	.09
❑ 68 Richie Sexson	.30	.09
❑ 69 Javy Lopez	.30	.09
❑ 70 Raul Mondesi	.30	.09
❑ 71 Darin Erstad	.30	.09
❑ 72 Kevin Millwood	.30	.09
❑ 73 Ricky Ledee	.30	.09
❑ 74 John Olerud	.30	.09
❑ 75 Sean Casey	.50	.15
❑ 76 Carlos Febles	.30	.09
❑ 77 Paul O'Neill	.50	.15
❑ 78 Bob Abreu	.30	.09
❑ 79 Neifi Perez	.30	.09
❑ 80 Tony Gwynn	1.00	.30
❑ 81 Russ Ortiz	.30	.09
❑ 82 Matt Williams	.30	.09
❑ 83 Chris Carpenter	.30	.09
❑ 84 Roger Cedeno	.30	.09
❑ 85 Tim Salmon	.50	.15
❑ 86 Billy Koch	.30	.09

❑ 87 Jeromy Burnitz	.30	.09
❑ 88 Edgardo Alfonzo	.30	.09
❑ 89 Jay Bell	.30	.09
❑ 90 Manny Ramirez	.50	.15
❑ 91 Frank Thomas	.75	.23
❑ 92 Mike Mussina	.50	.15
❑ 93 J.D. Drew	.30	.09
❑ 94 Adrian Beltre	.30	.09
❑ 95 Alex Rodriguez	1.25	.35
❑ 96 Larry Walker	.30	.09
❑ 97 Juan Encarnacion	.30	.09
❑ 98 Mike Sweeney	.30	.09
❑ 99 Rusty Greer	.30	.09
❑ 100 Randy Johnson	.75	.23
❑ 101 Jose Vidro	.30	.09
❑ 102 Preston Wilson	.30	.09
❑ 103 Greg Maddux	1.25	.35
❑ 104 Jason Giambi	.30	.09
❑ 105 Cal Ripken	2.50	.75
❑ 106 Carlos Beltran	.30	.09
❑ 107 Vinny Castilla	.30	.09
❑ 108 Mariano Rivera	.50	.15
❑ 109 Mo Vaughn	.30	.09
❑ 110 Rafael Palmeiro	.50	.15
❑ 111 Shannon Stewart	.30	.09
❑ 112 Mike Hampton	.30	.09
❑ 113 Joe Nathan	.30	.09
❑ 114 Ben Davis	.30	.09
❑ 115 Andruw Jones	.50	.15
❑ 116 Robin Ventura	.30	.09
❑ 117 Damion Easley	.30	.09
❑ 118 Jeff Cirillo	.30	.09
❑ 119 Kerry Wood	.30	.09
❑ 120 Scott Rolen	.50	.15
❑ 121 Sammy Sosa	.75	.23
❑ 122 Ken Griffey Jr.	1.25	.35
❑ 123 Shane Reynolds	.30	.09
❑ 124 Troy Glaus	.30	.09
❑ 125 Tom Glavine	.50	.15
❑ 126 Michael Barrett	.30	.09
❑ 127 Al Leiter	.30	.09
❑ 128 Jason Kendall	.30	.09
❑ 129 Roger Clemens	1.50	.45
❑ 130 Juan Gonzalez	.30	.09
❑ 131 Corey Koskie	.30	.09
❑ 132 Curt Schilling	.30	.09
❑ 133 Mike Piazza	1.25	.35
❑ 134 Gary Sheffield	.30	.09
❑ 135 Jim Thome	.50	.15
❑ 136 Orlando Hernandez	.30	.09
❑ 137 Ray Lankford	.30	.09
❑ 138 Geoff Jenkins	.30	.09
❑ 139 Jose Lima	.30	.09
❑ 140 Mark McGwire	2.00	.60
❑ 141 Adam Piatt	.30	.09
❑ 142 Pat Manning RC	.30	.09
❑ 143 Marcos Castillo RC	.30	.09
❑ 144 Lesli Brea RC	.30	.09
❑ 145 Humberto Cota RC	.50	.15
❑ 146 Ben Petrick	.30	.09
❑ 147 Kip Wells	.30	.09
❑ 148 Wily Pena	.30	.09
❑ 149 Chris Wakeland RC	.30	.09
❑ 150 Brad Baker RC	.50	.15
❑ 151 Robbie Morrison RC	.30	.09
❑ 152 Reggie Taylor	.30	.09
❑ 153 Matt Ginter RC	.50	.15
❑ 154 Peter Bergeron	.30	.09
❑ 155 Roosevelt Brown	.30	.09
❑ 156 Matt Cepicky RC	.30	.09
❑ 157 Ramon Castro	.30	.09
❑ 158 Brad Baisley RC	.30	.09
❑ 159 Jeff Goldbach RC	.30	.09
❑ 160 Mitch Meluskey	.30	.09
❑ 161 Chad Harville	.30	.09
❑ 162 Brian Cooper	.30	.09
❑ 163 Marcus Giles	.30	.09
❑ 164 Jim Morris	.75	.23
❑ 165 Geoff Goetz	.30	.09
❑ 166 Bobby Bradley RC	.50	.15
❑ 167 Rob Bell	.30	.09
❑ 168 Joe Crede	1.50	.45
❑ 169 Michael Restovich	.30	.09
❑ 170 Quincy Foster RC	.30	.09
❑ 171 Enrique Cruz RC	.30	.09
❑ 172 Mark Quinn	.30	.09
❑ 173 Nick Johnson	.30	.09
❑ 174 Jeff Liefer	.30	.09
❑ 175 Kevin Mench RC	2.00	.60
❑ 176 Steve Lomasney	.30	.09
❑ 177 Jayson Werth	.30	.09
❑ 178 Tim Drew	.30	.09
❑ 179 Chip Ambres	.30	.09
❑ 180 Ryan Anderson	.30	.09
❑ 181 Matt Blank	.30	.09
❑ 182 G.Chiaramonte	.30	.09
❑ 183 Corey Myers RC	.50	.15
❑ 184 Jeff Yoder	.30	.09
❑ 185 Craig Dingman RC	.30	.09
❑ 186 Jon Hamilton RC	.30	.09
❑ 187 Toby Hall	.30	.09
❑ 188 Russell Branyan	.30	.09
❑ 189 Brian Falkenborg RC	.30	.09
❑ 190 Aaron Harang RC	.75	.23
❑ 191 Juan Pena	.30	.09
❑ 192 Travis Thompson RC	.30	.09
❑ 193 Alfonso Soriano	.75	.23
❑ 194 Alejandro Diaz RC	.30	.09
❑ 195 Carlos Pena	.30	.09
❑ 196 Kevin Nicholson	.30	.09
❑ 197 Mo Bruce	.30	.09
❑ 198 C.C. Sabathia	.30	.09
❑ 199 Carl Crawford	.30	.09
❑ 200 Rafael Furcal	.30	.09
❑ 201 Andrew Beinbrink RC	.30	.09
❑ 202 Jimmy Osting	.30	.09
❑ 203 Aaron McNeal RC	.50	.15
❑ 204 Brett Laxton	.30	.09
❑ 205 Chris George	.30	.09
❑ 206 Felipe Lopez	.30	.09
❑ 207 Ben Sheets RC	3.00	.90
❑ 208 Mike Meyers RC	.50	.15
❑ 209 Jason Conti	.30	.09
❑ 210 Milton Bradley	.30	.09
❑ 211 Chris Mears RC	.30	.09
❑ 212 Carlos Hernandez RC	.75	.23
❑ 213 Jason Romano	.30	.09
❑ 214 Geofrey Tomlinson	.30	.09
❑ 215 Jimmy Rollins	.30	.09
❑ 216 Pablo Ozuna	.30	.09
❑ 217 Steve Cox	.30	.09
❑ 218 Terrence Long	.30	.09
❑ 219 Jeff DaVanon RC	.50	.15
❑ 220 Rick Ankiel	.30	.09
❑ 221 Jason Standridge	.30	.09
❑ 222 Tony Armas Jr.	.30	.09
❑ 223 Jason Tyner	.30	.09
❑ 224 Ramon Ortiz	.30	.09
❑ 225 Daryle Ward	.30	.09
❑ 226 Enger Veras RC	.30	.09
❑ 227 Chris Jones	.30	.09
❑ 228 Eric Cammack RC	.30	.09
❑ 229 Ruben Mateo	.30	.09
❑ 230 Ken Harvey RC	.75	.23
❑ 231 Jake Westbrook	.30	.09
❑ 232 Rob Purvis RC	.30	.09
❑ 233 Choo Freeman	.30	.09
❑ 234 Aramis Ramirez	.30	.09
❑ 235 A.J. Burnett	.30	.09
❑ 236 Kevin Barker	.30	.09
❑ 237 Chance Caple RC	.30	.09
❑ 238 Jarrod Washburn	.30	.09
❑ 239 Lance Berkman	.30	.09
❑ 240 Michael Wenner RC	.30	.09
❑ 241 Alex Sanchez	.30	.09
❑ 242 Pat Daneker	.30	.09
❑ 243 Grant Roberts	.30	.09
❑ 244 Mark Ellis RC	.50	.15
❑ 245 Donny Leon	.30	.09
❑ 246 David Eckstein	.30	.09
❑ 247 Dicky Gonzalez RC	.30	.09
❑ 248 John Patterson	.30	.09
❑ 249 Chad Green	.30	.09
❑ 250 Scot Shields RC	.30	.09
❑ 251 Troy Cameron	.30	.09
❑ 252 Jose Molina	.30	.09
❑ 253 Rob Pugmire RC	.30	.09
❑ 254 Rick Elder	.30	.09
❑ 255 Sean Burroughs	.30	.09
❑ 256 Josh Kalinowski RC	.30	.09
❑ 257 Matt LeCroy	.30	.09
❑ 258 Alex Graman RC	.30	.09
❑ 259 Tomo Ohka RC	.50	.15
❑ 260 Brady Clark	.30	.09
❑ 261 Rico Washington RC	.30	.09
❑ 262 Gary Matthews Jr.	.30	.09
❑ 263 Matt Wise	.30	.09
❑ 264 Keith Reed RC	.50	.15
❑ 265 Santiago Ramirez RC	.30	.09
❑ 266 Ben Broussard RC	.75	.23
❑ 267 Ryan Langerhans	.30	.09
❑ 268 Juan Rivera	.30	.09
❑ 269 Shawn Gallagher	.30	.09
❑ 270 Jorge Toca	.30	.09
❑ 271 Brad Lidge	.50	.15
❑ 272 Leoncio Estrella RC	.30	.09
❑ 273 Ruben Quevedo	.30	.09
❑ 274 Jack Cust	.30	.09
❑ 275 T.J. Tucker	.30	.09
❑ 276 Mike Colangelo	.30	.09
❑ 277 Brian Schneider	.30	.09
❑ 278 Calvin Murray	.30	.09
❑ 279 Josh Girdley	.30	.09
❑ 280 Mike Paradis	.30	.09
❑ 281 Chad Hermansen	.30	.09
❑ 282 Ty Howington RC	.50	.15
❑ 283 Aaron Myette	.30	.09
❑ 284 D'Angelo Jimenez	.30	.09
❑ 285 Dernell Stenson	.30	.09
❑ 286 Jerry Hairston Jr.	.30	.09
❑ 287 Gary Majewski RC	.75	.23
❑ 288 Derrin Ebert	.30	.09
❑ 289 Steve Fish RC	.30	.09
❑ 290 Carlos E. Hernandez	.30	.09
❑ 291 Allen Levrault	.30	.09
❑ 292 Sean McNally RC	.30	.09
❑ 293 Randey Dorame RC	.30	.09
❑ 294 Wes Anderson RC	.50	.15
❑ 295 B.J. Ryan	.30	.09
❑ 296 Alan Webb RC	.30	.09
❑ 297 Brandon Inge RC	1.25	.35
❑ 298 David Walling	.30	.09
❑ 299 Sun Woo Kim RC	.50	.15
❑ 300 Pat Burrell	.30	.09
❑ 301 Rick Guttormson RC	.30	.09
❑ 302 Gil Meche	.30	.09
❑ 303 Carlos Zambrano RC	4.00	1.20
❑ 304 Eric Byrnes UER RC Bo Porter pictured	.75	.23
❑ 305 Robb Quinlan RC	.75	.23
❑ 306 Jackie Rexrode	.30	.09
❑ 307 Nate Bump	.30	.09
❑ 308 Sean DePaula RC	.30	.09
❑ 309 Matt Riley	.30	.09
❑ 310 Ryan Minor	.30	.09
❑ 311 J.J. Davis	.30	.09
❑ 312 Randy Wolf	.30	.09
❑ 313 Jason Jennings	.30	.09
❑ 314 Scott Seabol RC	.50	.15
❑ 315 Doug Davis	.30	.09
❑ 316 Todd Moser RC	.30	.09
❑ 317 Rob Ryan	.30	.09
❑ 318 Bubba Crosby	.30	.09
❑ 319 Ryan Knox RC	1.25	.35
❑ 320 Mario Encarnacion	.30	.09
❑ 321 F.Rodriguez RC	2.50	.75
❑ 322 Michael Cuddyer	.30	.09
❑ 323 Ed Yarnall	.30	.09
❑ 324 Cesar Saba RC	.30	.09
❑ 325 Gookie Dawkins	.30	.09
❑ 326 Alex Escobar	.30	.09
❑ 327 Julio Zuleta RC	.30	.09
❑ 328 Josh Hamilton	.30	.09
❑ 329 Nick Neugebauer RC	.30	.09
❑ 330 Matt Belisle	.30	.09
❑ 331 Kurt Ainsworth RC	.50	.15
❑ 332 Tim Raines Jr.	.30	.09
❑ 333 Eric Munson	.30	.09
❑ 334 Donzell McDonald	.30	.09
❑ 335 Larry Bigbie RC	.75	.23
❑ 336 Matt Watson RC	.30	.09
❑ 337 Aubrey Huff	.30	.09
❑ 338 Julio Ramirez	.30	.09
❑ 339 Jason Grabowski RC	.50	.15
❑ 340 Jon Garland	.30	.09
❑ 341 Austin Kearns	.30	.09
❑ 342 Josh Pressley RC	.30	.09
❑ 343 Miguel Olivo RC	.75	.23

No.	Player	Nm-Mt	Ex-Mt
❑ 344	Julio Lugo	.30	.09
❑ 345	Roberto Vaz	.30	.09
❑ 346	Ramon Soler	.30	.09
❑ 347	Brandon Phillips RC	.75	.23
❑ 348	Vince Faison RC	.30	.09
❑ 349	Mike Venafro	.30	.09
❑ 350	Rick Asadoorian RC	.50	.15
❑ 351	B.J. Garbe RC	.30	.09
❑ 352	Dan Reichert	.30	.09
❑ 353	Jason Stumm RC	.30	.09
❑ 354	Ruben Salazar RC	.30	.09
❑ 355	Francisco Cordero	.30	.09
❑ 356	Juan Guzman RC	.30	.09
❑ 357	Mike Bacsik RC	.30	.09
❑ 358	Jared Sandberg	.30	.09
❑ 359	Rod Barajas	.30	.09
❑ 360	Junior Brignac RC	.30	.09
❑ 361	J.M. Gold	.30	.09
❑ 362	Octavio Dotel	.30	.09
❑ 363	David Kelton	.30	.09
❑ 364	Scott Morgan	.30	.09
❑ 365	Wascar Serrano RC	.30	.09
❑ 366	Wilton Veras	.30	.09
❑ 367	Eugene Kingsale	.30	.09
❑ 368	Ted Lilly	.30	.09
❑ 369	George Lombard	.30	.09
❑ 370	Chris Haas	.30	.09
❑ 371	Wilton Pena RC	.30	.09
❑ 372	Vernon Wells	.30	.09
❑ 373	Jason Royer RC	.30	.09
❑ 374	Jeff Heaverlo RC	.30	.09
❑ 375	Calvin Pickering	.30	.09
❑ 376	Mike Lamb RC	.75	.23
❑ 377	Kyle Snyder	.30	.09
❑ 378	Javier Cardona RC	.30	.09
❑ 379	Aaron Rowand RC	2.00	.60
❑ 380	Dee Brown	.30	.09
❑ 381	Brett Myers RC	2.00	.60
❑ 382	Abraham Nunez	.30	.09
❑ 383	Eric Valent	.30	.09
❑ 384	Jody Gerut RC	.75	.23
❑ 385	Adam Dunn	.75	.23
❑ 386	Jay Gehrke	.30	.09
❑ 387	Omar Ortiz	.30	.09
❑ 388	Darnell McDonald	.30	.09
❑ 389	Tony Schrager RC	.30	.09
❑ 390	J.D. Closser	.30	.09
❑ 391	Ben Christensen RC	.30	.09
❑ 392	Adam Kennedy	.30	.09
❑ 393	Nick Green RC	.50	.15
❑ 394	Ramon Hernandez	.30	.09
❑ 395	Roy Oswalt RC	8.00	2.40
❑ 396	Andy Tracy RC	.30	.09
❑ 397	Eric Gagne	.75	.23
❑ 398	Michael Tejera RC	.30	.09
❑ 399	Adam Everett	.30	.09
❑ 400	Corey Patterson	.30	.09
❑ 401	Gary Knotts RC	.30	.09
❑ 402	Ryan Christianson RC	.50	.15
❑ 403	Eric Ireland RC	.30	.09
❑ 404	Andrew Good RC	.30	.09
❑ 405	Brad Penny	.30	.09
❑ 406	Jason LaRue	.30	.09
❑ 407	Kit Pellow	.30	.09
❑ 408	Kevin Beirne	.30	.09
❑ 409	Kelly Dransfeldt	.30	.09
❑ 410	Jason Grilli	.30	.09
❑ 411	Scott Downs RC	.30	.09
❑ 412	Jesus Colome	.30	.09
❑ 413	John Sneed RC	.30	.09
❑ 414	Tony McKnight	.30	.09
❑ 415	Luis Rivera	.30	.09
❑ 416	Adam Eaton	.30	.09
❑ 417	Mike MacDougal RC	.50	.15
❑ 418	Mike Nannini	.30	.09
❑ 419	Barry Zito RC	3.00	.90
❑ 420	DeWayne Wise	.30	.09
❑ 421	Jason Dellaero	.30	.09
❑ 422	Chad Moeller	.30	.09
❑ 423	Jason Marquis	.30	.09
❑ 424	Tim Redding RC	.50	.15
❑ 425	Mark Mulder	.30	.09
❑ 426	Josh Paul	.30	.09
❑ 427	Chris Enochs	.30	.09
❑ 428	W.Rodriguez RC	.30	.09
❑ 429	Kevin Witt	.30	.09
❑ 430	Scott Sobkowiak RC	.30	.09
❑ 431	McKay Christensen	.30	.09
❑ 432	Jung Bong	.30	.09
❑ 433	Keith Evans RC	.30	.09
❑ 434	Garry Maddox Jr. RC	.30	.09
❑ 435	Ramon Santiago RC	.50	.15
❑ 436	Alex Cora	.30	.09
❑ 437	Carlos Lee	.30	.09
❑ 438	Jason Repko RC	.75	.23
❑ 439	Matt Burch	.30	.09
❑ 440	Shawn Sonnier RC	.30	.09

2000 Bowman Draft Picks

	Nm-Mt	Ex-Mt
COMP.FACT.SET (111)	25.00	7.50
COMPLETE SET (110)	15.00	4.50

No.	Player	Nm-Mt	Ex-Mt
❑ 1	Pat Burrell	.30	.09
❑ 2	Rafael Furcal	.30	.09
❑ 3	Grant Roberts	.30	.09
❑ 4	Barry Zito	1.50	.45
❑ 5	Julio Zuleta	.30	.09
❑ 6	Mark Mulder	.30	.09
❑ 7	Rob Bell	.30	.09
❑ 8	Adam Piatt	.30	.09
❑ 9	Mike Lamb	.60	.18
❑ 10	Pablo Ozuna	.30	.09
❑ 11	Jason Tyner	.30	.09
❑ 12	Jason Marquis	.30	.09
❑ 13	Eric Munson	.30	.09
❑ 14	Seth Etherton	.30	.09
❑ 15	Milton Bradley	.30	.09
❑ 16	Nick Green	.30	.09
❑ 17	Chin-Feng Chen RC	.60	.18
❑ 18	Matt Boone RC	.30	.09
❑ 19	Kevin Gregg RC	.40	.12
❑ 20	Eddy Garabito RC	.30	.09
❑ 21	Aaron Capista RC	.30	.09
❑ 22	Esteban German RC	.30	.09
❑ 23	Derek Thompson RC	.30	.09
❑ 24	Phil Merrell RC	.30	.09
❑ 25	Brian O'Connor RC	.30	.09
❑ 26	Yamid Haad	.30	.09
❑ 27	Hector Mercado RC	.30	.09
❑ 28	Jason Woolf RC	.30	.09
❑ 29	Eddy Furniss RC	.30	.09
❑ 30	Cha Sueng Baek RC	.30	.09
❑ 31	Colby Lewis RC	.40	.12
❑ 32	Pasqual Coco RC	.30	.09
❑ 33	Jorge Cantu RC	3.00	.90
❑ 34	Erasmo Ramirez RC	.30	.09
❑ 35	Bobby Kielty RC	.40	.12
❑ 36	Joaquin Benoit RC	.40	.12
❑ 37	Brian Esposito RC	.30	.09
❑ 38	Michael Wenner	.30	.09
❑ 39	Juan Rincon RC	.30	.09
❑ 40	Yorvit Torrealba RC	.30	.09
❑ 41	Chad Durham RC	.30	.09
❑ 42	Jim Mann RC	.30	.09
❑ 43	Shane Loux RC	.30	.09
❑ 44	Luis Rivas	.30	.09
❑ 45	Ken Chenard RC	.30	.09
❑ 46	Mike Lockwood RC	.30	.09
❑ 47	Yovanny Lara RC	.30	.09
❑ 48	Bubba Carpenter RC	.30	.09
❑ 49	Ryan Dittfurth RC	.30	.09
❑ 50	John Stephens RC	.40	.12
❑ 51	Pedro Feliz RC	1.00	.30
❑ 52	Kenny Kelly RC	.40	.12
❑ 53	Neil Jenkins RC	.30	.09
❑ 54	Mike Glendenning RC	.30	.09
❑ 55	Bo Porter	.30	.09
❑ 56	Eric Byrnes	.50	.15
❑ 57	Tony Alvarez RC	.30	.09
❑ 58	Kazuhiro Sasaki RC	.60	.18
❑ 59	Chad Durbin RC	.30	.09
❑ 60	Mike Bynum RC	.30	.09
❑ 61	Travis Wilson RC	.30	.09
❑ 62	Jose Leon RC	.30	.09
❑ 63	Ryan Vogelsong RC	.40	.12
❑ 64	Geraldo Guzman RC	.30	.09
❑ 65	Craig Anderson RC	.30	.09
❑ 66	Carlos Silva RC	.60	.18
❑ 67	Brad Thomas RC	.30	.09
❑ 68	Chin-Hui Tsao RC	2.00	.60
❑ 69	Mark Buehrle RC	3.00	.90
❑ 70	Juan Salas RC	.30	.09
❑ 71	Denny Abreu RC	.30	.09
❑ 72	Keith McDonald RC	.30	.09
❑ 73	Chris Richard RC	.30	.09
❑ 74	Tomas De la Rosa RC	.30	.09
❑ 75	Vicente Padilla RC	.40	.12
❑ 76	Justin Brunette RC	.30	.09
❑ 77	Scott Linebrink RC	.30	.09
❑ 78	Jeff Sparks RC	.30	.09
❑ 79	Tike Redman RC	.60	.18
❑ 80	John Lackey RC	1.00	.30
❑ 81	Joe Strong RC	.30	.09
❑ 82	Brian Tollberg RC	.30	.09
❑ 83	Steve Sisco RC	.30	.09
❑ 84	Chris Clapinski RC	.30	.09
❑ 85	Augie Ojeda RC	.30	.09
❑ 86	Adrian Gonzalez RC	.60	.18
❑ 87	Mike Stodolka RC	.30	.09
❑ 88	Adam Johnson RC	.40	.12
❑ 89	Matt Wheatland RC	.30	.09
❑ 90	Corey Smith RC	.40	.12
❑ 91	Rocco Baldelli RC	2.00	.60
❑ 92	Keith Bucktrot RC	.30	.09
❑ 93	Adam Wainwright RC	.60	.18
❑ 94	Blaine Boyer RC	.30	.09
❑ 95	Aaron Herr RC	.40	.12
❑ 96	Scott Thorman RC	.60	.18
❑ 97	Bryan Digby RC	.40	.12
❑ 98	Josh Shortslef RC	.30	.09
❑ 99	Sean Smith RC	.40	.12
❑ 100	Alex Cruz RC	.30	.09
❑ 101	Marc Love RC	.30	.09
❑ 102	Kevin Lee RC	.30	.09
❑ 103	Victor Ramos RC	.40	.12
❑ 104	Jason Kaanoi RC	.30	.09
❑ 105	Luis Escobar RC	.30	.09
❑ 106	Tripper Johnson RC	.40	.12
❑ 107	Phil Dumatrait RC	.40	.12
❑ 108	Bryan Edwards RC	.30	.09
❑ 109	Grady Sizemore RC	10.00	3.00
❑ 110	Thomas Mitchell RC	.30	.09

2001 Bowman

	Nm-Mt	Ex-Mt
COMPLETE SET (440)	150.00	45.00
COMMON CARD (1-440)	.30	.09
COMMON RC	.40	.12

	Card	Player	Price	Price
❑	1	Jason Giambi	.30	.09
❑	2	Rafael Furcal	.30	.09
❑	3	Rick Ankiel	.30	.09
❑	4	Freddy Garcia	.30	.09
❑	5	Magglio Ordonez	.30	.09
❑	6	Bernie Williams	.50	.15
❑	7	Kenny Lofton	.30	.09
❑	8	Al Leiter	.30	.09
❑	9	Albert Belle	.30	.09
❑	10	Craig Biggio	.50	.15
❑	11	Mark Mulder	.30	.09
❑	12	Carlos Delgado	.30	.09
❑	13	Darin Erstad	.30	.09
❑	14	Richie Sexson	.30	.09
❑	15	Randy Johnson	.75	.23
❑	16	Greg Maddux	1.25	.35
❑	17	Cliff Floyd	.30	.09
❑	18	Mark Buehrle	.50	.15
❑	19	Chris Singleton	.30	.09
❑	20	Orlando Hernandez	.30	.09
❑	21	Javier Vazquez	.30	.09
❑	22	Jeff Kent	.30	.09
❑	23	Jim Thome	.50	.15
❑	24	John Olerud	.30	.09
❑	25	Jason Kendall	.30	.09
❑	26	Scott Rolen	.50	.15
❑	27	Tony Gwynn	1.00	.30
❑	28	Edgardo Alfonzo	.30	.09
❑	29	Pokey Reese	.30	.09
❑	30	Todd Helton	.50	.15
❑	31	Mark Quinn	.30	.09
❑	32	Dan Tosca RC	.60	.18
❑	33	Dean Palmer	.30	.09
❑	34	Jacque Jones	.30	.09
❑	35	Ray Durham	.30	.09
❑	36	Rafael Palmeiro	.50	.15
❑	37	Carl Everett	.30	.09
❑	38	Ryan Dempster	.30	.09
❑	39	Randy Wolf	.30	.09
❑	40	Vladimir Guerrero	.75	.23
❑	41	Livan Hernandez	.30	.09
❑	42	Mo Vaughn	.30	.09
❑	43	Shannon Stewart	.30	.09
❑	44	Preston Wilson	.30	.09
❑	45	Jose Vidro	.30	.09
❑	46	Fred McGriff	.50	.15
❑	47	Kevin Brown	.30	.09
❑	48	Peter Bergeron	.30	.09
❑	49	Miguel Tejada	.30	.09
❑	50	Chipper Jones	.75	.23
❑	51	Edgar Martinez	.50	.15
❑	52	Tony Batista	.30	.09
❑	53	Jorge Posada	.50	.15
❑	54	Ricky Ledee	.30	.09
❑	55	Sammy Sosa	.75	.23
❑	56	Steve Cox	.30	.09
❑	57	Tony Armas Jr.	.30	.09
❑	58	Gary Sheffield	.30	.09
❑	59	Bartolo Colon	.30	.09
❑	60	Pat Burrell	.30	.09
❑	61	Jay Payton	.30	.09
❑	62	Sean Casey	.50	.15
❑	63	Larry Walker	.30	.09
❑	64	Mike Mussina	.50	.15
❑	65	Nomar Garciaparra	1.25	.35
❑	66	Darren Dreifort	.30	.09
❑	67	Richard Hidalgo	.30	.09
❑	68	Troy Glaus	.30	.09
❑	69	Ben Grieve	.30	.09
❑	70	Jim Edmonds	.50	.15
❑	71	Raul Mondesi	.30	.09
❑	72	Andruw Jones	.50	.15
❑	73	Luis Castillo	.30	.09
❑	74	Mike Sweeney	.30	.09
❑	75	Derek Jeter	2.00	.60
❑	76	Ruben Mateo	.30	.09
❑	77	Carlos Lee	.30	.09
❑	78	Cristian Guzman	.30	.09
❑	79	Mike Hampton	.30	.09
❑	80	J.D. Drew	.30	.09
❑	81	Matt Lawton	.30	.09
❑	82	Moises Alou	.30	.09
❑	83	Terrence Long	.30	.09
❑	84	Geoff Jenkins	.30	.09
❑	85	Manny Ramirez Sox	.50	.15
❑	86	Johnny Damon	.50	.15
❑	87	Barry Larkin	.50	.15
❑	88	Pedro Martinez	.50	.15
❑	89	Juan Gonzalez	.30	.09
❑	90	Roger Clemens	1.50	.45
❑	91	Carlos Beltran	.30	.09
❑	92	Brad Radke	.30	.09
❑	93	Orlando Cabrera	.30	.09
❑	94	Roberto Alomar	.50	.15
❑	95	Barry Bonds	2.00	.60
❑	96	Tim Hudson	.30	.09
❑	97	Tom Glavine	.50	.15
❑	98	Jeromy Burnitz	.30	.09
❑	99	Adrian Beltre	.30	.09
❑	100	Mike Piazza	1.25	.35
❑	101	Kerry Wood	.30	.09
❑	102	Steve Finley	.30	.09
❑	103	Alex Cora	.30	.09
❑	104	Bob Abreu	.30	.09
❑	105	Neifi Perez	.30	.09
❑	106	Mark Redman	.30	.09
❑	107	Paul Konerko	.30	.09
❑	108	Jermaine Dye	.30	.09
❑	109	Brian Giles	.30	.09
❑	110	Ivan Rodriguez	.50	.15
❑	111	Vinny Castilla	.30	.09
❑	112	Adam Kennedy	.30	.09
❑	113	Eric Chavez	.30	.09
❑	114	Billy Koch	.30	.09
❑	115	Shawn Green	.30	.09
❑	116	Matt Williams	.30	.09
❑	117	Greg Vaughn	.30	.09
❑	118	Gabe Kapler	.30	.09
❑	119	Jeff Cirillo	.30	.09
❑	120	Frank Thomas	.75	.23
❑	121	David Justice	.30	.09
❑	122	Cal Ripken	2.50	.75
❑	123	Rich Aurilia	.30	.09
❑	124	Curt Schilling	.30	.09
❑	125	Barry Zito	.50	.15
❑	126	Brian Jordan	.30	.09
❑	127	Chan Ho Park	.30	.09
❑	128	J.T. Snow	.30	.09
❑	129	Kazuhiro Sasaki	.30	.09
❑	130	Alex Rodriguez	1.25	.35
❑	131	Mariano Rivera	.50	.15
❑	132	Eric Milton	.30	.09
❑	133	Andy Pettitte	.50	.15
❑	134	Scott Elarton	.30	.09
❑	135	Ken Griffey Jr.	1.25	.35
❑	136	Bengie Molina	.30	.09
❑	137	Jeff Bagwell	.50	.15
❑	138	Kevin Millwood	.30	.09
❑	139	Tino Martinez	.50	.15
❑	140	Mark McGwire	2.00	.60
❑	141	Larry Barnes	.30	.09
❑	142	John Buck RC	1.00	.30
❑	143	Freddie Bynum RC	.60	.18
❑	144	Abraham Nunez	.30	.09
❑	145	Felix Diaz RC	.60	.18
❑	146	Horacio Estrada	.30	.09
❑	147	Ben Diggins	.30	.09
❑	148	Tsuyoshi Shinjo RC	1.00	.30
❑	149	Rocco Baldelli	.30	.09
❑	150	Rod Barajas	.30	.09
❑	151	Luis Terrero	.30	.09
❑	152	Milton Bradley	.30	.09
❑	153	Kurt Ainsworth	.30	.09
❑	154	Russell Branyan	.30	.09
❑	155	Ryan Anderson	.30	.09
❑	156	Mitch Jones RC	.60	.18
❑	157	Chip Ambres	.30	.09
❑	158	Steve Bennett RC	.40	.12
❑	159	Ivanon Coffie	.30	.09
❑	160	Sean Burroughs	.30	.09
❑	161	Keith Bucktrot	.30	.09
❑	162	Tony Alvarez	.30	.09
❑	163	Joaquin Benoit	.30	.09
❑	164	Rick Asadoorian	.30	.09
❑	165	Ben Broussard	.30	.09
❑	166	Ryan Madson RC	.60	.18
❑	167	Dee Brown	.30	.09
❑	168	Sergio Contreras RC	.60	.18
❑	169	John Barnes	.30	.09
❑	170	Ben Washburn RC	.60	.18
❑	171	Erick Almonte RC	.60	.18
❑	172	Shawn Fagan RC	.40	.12
❑	173	Gary Johnson RC	.60	.18
❑	174	Brady Clark	.30	.09
❑	175	Grant Roberts	.30	.09
❑	176	Tony Torcato	.30	.09
❑	177	Ramon Castro	.30	.09
❑	178	Esteban German	.30	.09
❑	179	Joe Hamer RC	.60	.18
❑	180	Nick Neugebauer	.30	.09
❑	181	Dernell Stenson	.30	.09
❑	182	Yhency Brazoban RC	1.00	.30
❑	183	Aaron Myette	.30	.09
❑	184	Juan Sosa	.30	.09
❑	185	Brandon Inge	.30	.09
❑	186	Domingo Guante RC	.60	.18
❑	187	Adrian Brown	.30	.09
❑	188	Deivi Mendez RC	.60	.18
❑	189	Luis Matos	.30	.09
❑	190	Pedro Liriano RC	.60	.18
❑	191	Donnie Bridges	.30	.09
❑	192	Alex Cintron	.30	.09
❑	193	Jace Brewer	.30	.09
❑	194	Ron Davenport RC	.60	.18
❑	195	Jason Belcher RC	.60	.18
❑	196	Adrian Hernandez RC	.30	.09
❑	197	Bobby Kielty	.30	.09
❑	198	Reggie Griggs RC	.60	.18
❑	199	R. Abercrombie RC	.60	.18
❑	200	Troy Farnsworth RC	.60	.18
❑	201	Matt Belisle	.30	.09
❑	202	Miguel Villilo RC	.60	.18
❑	203	Adam Everett	.30	.09
❑	204	John Lackey	.30	.09
❑	205	Pasqual Coco	.30	.09
❑	206	Adam Wainwright	.30	.09
❑	207	Matt White RC	.60	.18
❑	208	Chin-Feng Chen	.30	.09
❑	209	Jeff Andra RC	.60	.18
❑	210	Willie Bloomquist	.30	.09
❑	211	Wes Anderson	.30	.09
❑	212	Enrique Cruz	.30	.09
❑	213	Jerry Hairston Jr.	.30	.09
❑	214	Mike Bynum	.30	.09
❑	215	Brian Hitchcox RC	.60	.18
❑	216	Ryan Christianson	.30	.09
❑	217	J.J. Davis	.30	.09
❑	218	Jovanny Cedeno	.30	.09
❑	219	Elvin Nina	.30	.09
❑	220	Alex Graman	.30	.09
❑	221	Arturo McDowell	.30	.09
❑	222	Deivis Santos RC	.60	.18
❑	223	Jody Gerut	.30	.09
❑	224	Sun Woo Kim	.30	.09
❑	225	Jimmy Rollins	.30	.09
❑	226	Ntema Ndungidi	.30	.09
❑	227	Ruben Salazar	.30	.09
❑	228	Josh Girdley	.30	.09
❑	229	Carl Crawford	.30	.09
❑	230	Luis Montanez RC	.60	.18
❑	231	Ramon Carvajal RC	.60	.18
❑	232	Matt Riley	.30	.09
❑	233	Ben Davis	.30	.09
❑	234	Jason Grabowski	.30	.09
❑	235	Chris George	.30	.09
❑	236	Hank Blalock RC	6.00	1.80
❑	237	Roy Oswalt	.50	.15
❑	238	Eric Reynolds RC	.60	.18
❑	239	Brian Cole	.30	.09
❑	240	Denny Bautista RC	1.00	.30
❑	241	Hector Garcia RC	.60	.18
❑	242	Joe Thurston RC	.60	.18
❑	243	Brad Cresse	.30	.09
❑	244	Corey Patterson	.30	.09
❑	245	Brett Evert RC	.60	.18
❑	246	Elpidio Guzman RC	.60	.18
❑	247	Vernon Wells	.30	.09
❑	248	Roberto Miniel RC	.60	.18
❑	249	Brian Bass RC	.60	.18
❑	250	Mark Burnett RC	.60	.18
❑	251	Juan Silvestre	.30	.09
❑	252	Pablo Ozuna	.30	.09
❑	253	Jayson Werth	.30	.09
❑	254	Russ Jacobson	.30	.09
❑	255	Chad Hermansen	.30	.09
❑	256	Travis Hafner RC	6.00	1.80
❑	257	Brad Baker	.30	.09
❑	258	Gookie Dawkins	.30	.09

❑ 259 Michael Cuddyer .30 .09
❑ 260 Mark Buehrle .50 .15
❑ 261 Ricardo Aramboles .30 .09
❑ 262 Esix Snead RC .60 .18
❑ 263 Wilson Betemit RC 1.00 .30
❑ 264 Albert Pujols RC 70.00 21.00
❑ 265 Joe Lawrence .30 .09
❑ 266 Ramon Ortiz .30 .09
❑ 267 Ben Sheets .50 .15
❑ 268 Luke Lockwood RC .60 .18
❑ 269 Toby Hall .30 .09
❑ 270 Jack Cust .30 .09
❑ 271 Pedro Feliz UER .30 .09
No facsimile signature on card
❑ 272 Noel Devarez RC .60 .18
❑ 273 Josh Beckett .50 .15
❑ 274 Alex Escobar .30 .09
❑ 275 Doug Gredvig RC .60 .18
❑ 276 Marcus Giles .30 .09
❑ 277 Jon Rauch .30 .09
❑ 278 Brian Schmitt RC .60 .18
❑ 279 Seung Song RC .60 .18
❑ 280 Kevin Mench .30 .09
❑ 281 Adam Eaton .30 .09
❑ 282 Shawn Sonnier .30 .09
❑ 283 Andy Van Hekken RC .60 .18
❑ 284 Aaron Rowand .30 .09
❑ 285 Tony Blanco RC .60 .18
❑ 286 Ryan Kohlmeier .30 .09
❑ 287 C.C. Sabathia .30 .09
❑ 288 Bubba Crosby .30 .09
❑ 289 Josh Hamilton .30 .09
❑ 290 Dee Haynes RC .60 .18
❑ 291 Jason Marquis .30 .09
❑ 292 Julio Zuleta .30 .09
❑ 293 Carlos Hernandez .30 .09
❑ 294 Matt Lecroy .30 .09
❑ 295 Andy Beal RC .60 .18
❑ 296 Carlos Pena .30 .09
❑ 297 Reggie Taylor .30 .09
❑ 298 Bob Keppel RC .60 .18
❑ 299 Miguel Cabrera UER 1.50 .45
Photo is Manuel Esquivia
❑ 300 Ryan Franklin .30 .09
❑ 301 Brandon Phillips .30 .09
❑ 302 Victor Hall RC .60 .18
❑ 303 Tony Pena Jr. .30 .09
❑ 304 Jim Journell RC .60 .18
❑ 305 Cristian Guerrero .30 .09
❑ 306 Miguel Olivo .30 .09
❑ 307 Jin Ho Cho .30 .09
❑ 308 Choo Freeman .30 .09
❑ 309 Danny Borrell RC .60 .18
❑ 310 Doug Mientkiewicz .30 .09
❑ 311 Aaron Herr .30 .09
❑ 312 Keith Ginter .30 .09
❑ 313 Felipe Lopez .30 .09
❑ 314 Jeff Goldbach .30 .09
❑ 315 Travis Harper .30 .09
❑ 316 Paul LoDuca .30 .09
❑ 317 Joe Torres .30 .09
❑ 318 Eric Byrnes .30 .09
❑ 319 George Lombard .30 .09
❑ 320 Dave Krynzel .30 .09
❑ 321 Ben Christensen .30 .09
❑ 322 Aubrey Huff .30 .09
❑ 323 Lyle Overbay .30 .09
❑ 324 Sean McGowan .30 .09
❑ 325 Jeff Heaverlo .30 .09
❑ 326 Timo Perez .30 .09
❑ 327 Octavio Martinez RC .60 .18
❑ 328 Vince Faison .30 .09
❑ 329 David Parrish RC .60 .18
❑ 330 Bobby Bradley .30 .09
❑ 331 Jason Miller RC .60 .18
❑ 332 Corey Spencer RC .60 .18
❑ 333 Craig House .30 .09
❑ 334 Maxim St. Pierre RC .60 .18
❑ 335 Adam Johnson .30 .09
❑ 336 Joe Crede .75 .23
❑ 337 Greg Nash RC .60 .18
❑ 338 Chad Durbin .30 .09
❑ 339 Pat Magness RC .60 .18
❑ 340 Matt Wheatland .30 .09
❑ 341 Julio Lugo .30 .09
❑ 342 Grady Sizemore .50 .15
❑ 343 Adrian Gonzalez .30 .09
❑ 344 Tim Raines Jr. .30 .09
❑ 345 Ranier Olmedo RC .60 .18
❑ 346 Phil Dumatrait .30 .09
❑ 347 Brandon Mims RC .60 .18
❑ 348 Jason Jennings .30 .09
❑ 349 Phil Wilson RC .60 .18
❑ 350 Jason Hart .30 .09
❑ 351 Cesar Izturis .30 .09
❑ 352 Matt Butler RC .60 .18
❑ 353 David Kelton .30 .09
❑ 354 Luke Prokopec .30 .09
❑ 355 Corey Smith .30 .09
❑ 356 Joel Pineiro .60 .18
❑ 357 Ken Chenard .30 .09
❑ 358 Keith Reed .30 .09
❑ 359 David Walling .30 .09
❑ 360 Alexis Gomez RC .60 .18
❑ 361 Justin Morneau RC 5.00 1.50
❑ 362 Josh Fogg RC .60 .18
❑ 363 J.R. House .30 .09
❑ 364 Andy Tracy .30 .09
❑ 365 Kenny Kelly .30 .09
❑ 366 Aaron McNeal .30 .09
❑ 367 Nick Johnson .30 .09
❑ 368 Brian Esposito .30 .09
❑ 369 Charles Frazier RC .60 .18
❑ 370 Scott Heard .30 .09
❑ 371 Pat Strange .30 .09
❑ 372 Mike Meyers .30 .09
❑ 373 Ryan Ludwick RC .60 .18
❑ 374 Brad Wilkerson .30 .09
❑ 375 Allen Levrault .30 .09
❑ 376 Seth McClung RC .60 .18
❑ 377 Joe Nathan .30 .09
❑ 378 Rafael Soriano RC .60 .18
❑ 379 Chris Richard .30 .09
❑ 380 Jared Sandberg .30 .09
❑ 381 Tike Redman .30 .09
❑ 382 Adam Dunn UER .50 .15
Card lists him as a pitcher
❑ 383 Jared Abruzzo RC .60 .18
❑ 384 Jason Richardson RC .60 .18
❑ 385 Matt Holliday .30 .09
❑ 386 Darwin Cubillan RC .60 .18
❑ 387 Mike Nannini .30 .09
❑ 388 Blake Williams RC .60 .18
❑ 389 V. Pascucci RC .60 .18
❑ 390 Jon Garland .30 .09
❑ 391 Josh Pressley .30 .09
❑ 392 Jose Ortiz .30 .09
❑ 393 Ryan Hannaman RC .60 .18
❑ 394 Steve Smyth RC .60 .18
❑ 395 John Patterson .30 .09
❑ 396 Chad Petty RC .60 .18
❑ 397 Jake Peavy RC 8.00 2.40
UER last name misspelled Peavey
❑ 398 Onix Mercado RC .60 .18
❑ 399 Jason Romano .30 .09
❑ 400 Luis Torres RC .60 .18
❑ 401 Casey Fossum RC .60 .18
❑ 402 Eduardo Figueroa RC .60 .18
❑ 403 Bryan Barnowski RC .60 .18
❑ 404 Tim Redding .30 .09
❑ 405 Jason Standridge .30 .09
❑ 406 Marvin Seale RC .60 .18
❑ 407 Todd Moser .30 .09
❑ 408 Alex Gordon .30 .09
❑ 409 Steve Smitherman RC .60 .18
❑ 410 Ben Petrick .30 .09
❑ 411 Eric Munson .30 .09
❑ 412 Luis Rivas .30 .09
❑ 413 Matt Ginter .30 .09
❑ 414 Alfonso Soriano .50 .15
❑ 415 Rafael Boitel RC .60 .18
❑ 416 Dany Morban RC .60 .18
❑ 417 Justin Woodrow RC .60 .18
❑ 418 Wilfredo Rodriguez .30 .09
❑ 419 Derrick Van Dusen RC .60 .18
❑ 420 Josh Spoerl RC .60 .18
❑ 421 Juan Pierre .30 .09
❑ 422 J.C. Romero .30 .09
❑ 423 Ed Rogers RC .60 .18
❑ 424 Tomo Ohka .30 .09
❑ 425 Ben Hendrickson RC .60 .18
❑ 426 Carlos Zambrano .50 .15
❑ 427 Brett Myers .30 .09
❑ 428 Scott Seabol .30 .09
❑ 429 Thomas Mitchell .30 .09
❑ 430 Jose Reyes RC 8.00 2.40
❑ 431 Kip Wells .30 .09
❑ 432 Donzell McDonald .30 .09
❑ 433 Adam Pettyjohn RC .60 .18
❑ 434 Austin Kearns .30 .09
❑ 435 Rico Washington .30 .09
❑ 436 Doug Nickle RC .40 .12
❑ 437 Steve Lomasney .30 .09
❑ 438 Jason Jones RC .60 .18
❑ 439 Bobby Seay .30 .09
❑ 440 Justin Wayne RC .60 .18
❑ ROYR Kazuhiro Sasaki 25.00 7.50
Rafael Furcal ROY Jsy
❑ NNO Sean Burroughs Ball/80 15.00 4.50

2001 Bowman Draft Picks

	Nm-Mt	Ex-Mt
COMP.FACT.SET (112)	40.00	12.00
COMPLETE SET (110)	30.00	9.00

❑ BDP1 Alfredo Amezaga RC .40 .12
❑ BDP2 Andrew Good .30 .09
❑ BDP3 Kelly Johnson RC 3.00 .90
❑ BDP4 Larry Bigbie .30 .09
❑ BDP5 Matt Thompson RC .40 .12
❑ BDP6 Wilton Chavez RC .40 .12
❑ BDP7 Joe Borchard RC .40 .12
❑ BDP8 David Espinosa .30 .09
❑ BDP9 Zach Day RC .40 .12
❑ BDP10 Brad Hawpe RC 2.00 .60
❑ BDP11 Nate Cornejo .30 .09
❑ BDP12 Matt Cooper RC .40 .12
❑ BDP13 Brad Lidge .30 .09
❑ BDP14 Angel Berroa RC .60 .18
❑ BDP15 L. Matthews RC .40 .12
❑ BDP16 Jose Garcia .30 .09
❑ BDP17 Grant Balfour RC .30 .09
❑ BDP18 Ron Chiavacci RC .30 .09
❑ BDP19 Jae Seo .30 .09
❑ BDP20 Juan Rivera .30 .09
❑ BDP21 D'Angelo Jimenez .30 .09
❑ BDP22 Juan A.Pena RC .40 .12
❑ BDP23 Marlon Byrd RC .40 .12
❑ BDP24 Sean Burnett .30 .09
❑ BDP25 Josh Pearce RC .40 .12
❑ BDP26 B. Duckworth RC .40 .12
❑ BDP27 Jack Taschner RC .40 .12
❑ BDP28 Marcus Thames .30 .09
❑ BDP29 Brent Abernathy .30 .09
❑ BDP30 David Elder RC .40 .12
❑ BDP31 Scott Cassidy RC .40 .12
❑ BDP32 D. Tankersley RC .40 .12
❑ BDP33 Denny Stark .30 .09
❑ BDP34 Dave Williams RC .40 .12
❑ BDP35 Boof Bonser RC .40 .12
❑ BDP36 Kris Foster RC .30 .09
❑ BDP37 Luis Garcia RC .40 .12
❑ BDP38 Shawn Chacon .30 .09
❑ BDP39 Mike Rivera RC .40 .12
❑ BDP40 Will Smith RC .40 .12
❑ BDP41 M. Ensberg RC 3.00 .90
❑ BDP42 Ken Harvey .30 .09
❑ BDP43 R. Rodriguez RC .40 .12

Card	Nm-Mt	Ex-Mt
❑ BDP44 Jose Mieses RC	.40	.12
❑ BDP45 Luis Maza RC	.40	.12
❑ BDP46 Julio Perez RC	.40	.12
❑ BDP47 Dustan Mohr RC	.40	.12
❑ BDP48 Randy Flores RC	.30	.09
❑ BDP49 Covelli Crisp RC	2.00	.60
❑ BDP50 Kevin Reese RC	.40	.12
❑ BDP51 Brad Thomas UER	.30	.09
Card back is BDP71 Alex Herrera		
❑ BDP52 Xavier Nady	.30	.09
❑ BDP53 Ryan Vogelsong	.30	.09
❑ BDP54 Carlos Silva	.30	.09
❑ BDP55 Dan Wright	.30	.09
❑ BDP56 Brent Butler	.30	.09
❑ BDP57 Brandon Knight RC	.30	.09
❑ BDP58 Brian Reith RC	.40	.12
❑ BDP59 M. Valenzuela RC	.40	.12
❑ BDP60 Bobby Hill RC	.60	.18
❑ BDP61 Rich Rundles RC	.40	.12
❑ BDP62 Rick Elder	.30	.09
❑ BDP63 J.D. Closser	.30	.09
❑ BDP64 Scot Shields	.30	.09
❑ BDP65 Miguel Olivo	.30	.09
❑ BDP66 Stubby Clapp RC	.30	.09
❑ BDP67 J. Williams RC	.60	.18
❑ BDP68 Jason Lane RC	1.50	.45
❑ BDP69 Chase Utley RC	8.00	2.40
❑ BDP70 Erik Bedard RC	1.50	.45
❑ BDP71 A. Herrera UER RC	.30	.09
Card back is BDP51 Brad Thomas		
❑ BDP72 Juan Cruz RC	.40	.12
❑ BDP73 Billy Martin RC	.40	.12
❑ BDP74 Ronnie Merrill RC	.40	.12
❑ BDP75 Jason Kinchen RC	.40	.12
❑ BDP76 Wilkin Ruan RC	.40	.12
❑ BDP77 Cody Ransom RC	.30	.09
❑ BDP78 Bud Smith RC	.40	.12
❑ BDP79 Wily Mo Pena	.30	.09
❑ BDP80 Jeff Nettles RC	.40	.12
❑ BDP81 Jamal Strong RC	.40	.12
❑ BDP82 Bill Ortega RC	.40	.12
❑ BDP83 Mike Bell	.30	.09
❑ BDP84 Ichiro Suzuki RC	8.00	2.40
❑ BDP85 F. Rodney RC	.40	.12
❑ BDP86 Chris Smith RC	.40	.12
❑ BDP87 J.VanBenschoten RC	.40	.12
❑ BDP88 Bobby Crosby RC	5.00	1.50
❑ BDP89 Kenny Baugh RC	.40	.12
❑ BDP90 Jake Gautreau RC	.40	.12
❑ BDP91 Gabe Gross RC	.60	.18
❑ BDP92 Kris Honel RC	.40	.12
❑ BDP93 Dan Denham RC	.40	.12
❑ BDP94 Aaron Heilman RC	.40	.12
❑ BDP95 Irvin Guzman RC	5.00	1.50
❑ BDP96 Mike Jones RC	.60	.18
❑ BDP97 J. Griffin RC	.40	.12
❑ BDP98 Macay McBride RC	1.00	.30
❑ BDP99 J. Rheinecker RC	.40	.12
❑ BDP100 B. Sardinha RC	.40	.12
❑ BDP101 J. Weintraub RC	.40	.12
❑ BDP102 J.D. Martin RC	.40	.12
❑ BDP103 Jayson Nix RC	.40	.12
❑ BDP104 Noah Lowry RC	3.00	.90
❑ BDP105 Richard Lewis RC	.40	.12
❑ BDP106 B. Hennessey RC	.60	.18
❑ BDP107 Jeff Mathis RC	.60	.18
❑ BDP108 Jon Skaggs RC	.40	.12
❑ BDP109 Justin Pope RC	.40	.12
❑ BDP110 Josh Burrus RC	.40	.12

2002 Bowman

	Nm-Mt	Ex-Mt
COMPLETE SET (440)	80.00	24.00
COMMON CARD (1-110)	.30	.09
COMMON CARD (111-440)	.30	.09

Card	Nm-Mt	Ex-Mt
❑ 1 Adam Dunn	.30	.09
❑ 2 Derek Jeter	2.00	.60
❑ 3 Alex Rodriguez	1.25	.35
❑ 4 Miguel Tejada	.30	.09
❑ 5 Nomar Garciaparra	1.25	.35
❑ 6 Toby Hall	.30	.09
❑ 7 Brandon Duckworth	.30	.09
❑ 8 Paul LoDuca	.30	.09
❑ 9 Brian Giles	.30	.09

Card	Nm-Mt	Ex-Mt
❑ 10 C.C. Sabathia	.30	.09
❑ 11 Curt Schilling	.30	.09
❑ 12 Tsuyoshi Shinjo	.30	.09
❑ 13 Ramon Hernandez	.30	.09
❑ 14 Jose Cruz Jr.	.30	.09
❑ 15 Albert Pujols	1.50	.45
❑ 16 Joe Mays	.30	.09
❑ 17 Javy Lopez	.30	.09
❑ 18 J.T. Snow	.30	.09
❑ 19 David Segui	.30	.09
❑ 20 Jorge Posada	.50	.15
❑ 21 Doug Mientkiewicz	.30	.09
❑ 22 Jerry Hairston Jr.	.30	.09
❑ 23 Bernie Williams	.50	.15
❑ 24 Mike Sweeney	.30	.09
❑ 25 Jason Giambi	.30	.09
❑ 26 Ryan Dempster	.30	.09
❑ 27 Ryan Klesko	.30	.09
❑ 28 Mark Quinn	.30	.09
❑ 29 Jeff Kent	.30	.09
❑ 30 Eric Chavez	.30	.09
❑ 31 Adrian Beltre	.30	.09
❑ 32 Andruw Jones	.50	.15
❑ 33 Alfonso Soriano	.30	.09
❑ 34 Aramis Ramirez	.30	.09
❑ 35 Greg Maddux	1.25	.35
❑ 36 Andy Pettitte	.50	.15
❑ 37 Bartolo Colon	.30	.09
❑ 38 Ben Sheets	.30	.09
❑ 39 Bobby Higginson	.30	.09
❑ 40 Ivan Rodriguez	.50	.15
❑ 41 Brad Penny	.30	.09
❑ 42 Carlos Lee	.30	.09
❑ 43 Damion Easley	.30	.09
❑ 44 Preston Wilson	.30	.09
❑ 45 Jeff Bagwell	.50	.15
❑ 46 Eric Milton	.30	.09
❑ 47 Rafael Palmeiro	.50	.15
❑ 48 Gary Sheffield	.30	.09
❑ 49 J.D. Drew	.30	.09
❑ 50 Jim Thome	.50	.15
❑ 51 Ichiro Suzuki	1.50	.45
❑ 52 Bud Smith	.30	.09
❑ 53 Chan Ho Park	.30	.09
❑ 54 D'Angelo Jimenez	.30	.09
❑ 55 Ken Griffey Jr.	1.25	.35
❑ 56 Wade Miller	.30	.09
❑ 57 Vladimir Guerrero	.75	.23
❑ 58 Troy Glaus	.30	.09
❑ 59 Shawn Green	.30	.09
❑ 60 Kerry Wood	.30	.09
❑ 61 Jack Wilson	.30	.09
❑ 62 Kevin Brown	.30	.09
❑ 63 Marcus Giles	.30	.09
❑ 64 Pat Burrell	.30	.09
❑ 65 Larry Walker	.30	.09
❑ 66 Sammy Sosa	.75	.23
❑ 67 Raul Mondesi	.30	.09
❑ 68 Tim Hudson	.30	.09
❑ 69 Lance Berkman	.30	.09
❑ 70 Mike Mussina	.50	.15
❑ 71 Barry Zito	.30	.09
❑ 72 Jimmy Rollins	.30	.09
❑ 73 Barry Bonds	2.00	.60
❑ 74 Craig Biggio	.50	.15
❑ 75 Todd Helton	.50	.15
❑ 76 Roger Clemens	1.50	.45
❑ 77 Frank Catalanotto	.30	.09
❑ 78 Josh Towers	.30	.09
❑ 79 Roy Oswalt	.30	.09
❑ 80 Chipper Jones	.75	.23
❑ 81 Cristian Guzman	.30	.09
❑ 82 Darin Erstad	.30	.09
❑ 83 Freddy Garcia	.30	.09
❑ 84 Jason Tyner	.30	.09
❑ 85 Carlos Delgado	.30	.09
❑ 86 Jon Lieber	.30	.09
❑ 87 Juan Pierre	.30	.09
❑ 88 Matt Morris	.30	.09
❑ 89 Phil Nevin	.30	.09
❑ 90 Jim Edmonds	.50	.15
❑ 91 Magglio Ordonez	.30	.09
❑ 92 Mike Hampton	.30	.09
❑ 93 Rafael Furcal	.30	.09
❑ 94 Richie Sexson	.30	.09
❑ 95 Luis Gonzalez	.30	.09
❑ 96 Scott Rolen	.50	.15
❑ 97 Tim Redding	.30	.09
❑ 98 Moises Alou	.30	.09
❑ 99 Jose Vidro	.30	.09
❑ 100 Mike Piazza	1.25	.35
❑ 101 Pedro Martinez UER	.50	.15
Career strikeout total incorrect		
❑ 102 Geoff Jenkins	.30	.09
❑ 103 Johnny Damon Sox	.50	.15
❑ 104 Mike Cameron	.30	.09
❑ 105 Randy Johnson	.75	.23
❑ 106 David Eckstein	.30	.09
❑ 107 Javier Vazquez	.30	.09
❑ 108 Mark Mulder	.30	.09
❑ 109 Robert Fick	.30	.09
❑ 110 Roberto Alomar	.50	.15
❑ 111 Wilson Betemit	.30	.09
❑ 112 Chris Tritle RC	.30	.09
❑ 113 Ed Rogers	.30	.09
❑ 114 Juan Pena	.30	.09
❑ 115 Josh Beckett	.40	.12
❑ 116 Juan Cruz	.30	.09
❑ 117 Noochie Varner RC	.40	.12
❑ 118 Taylor Buchholz RC	.40	.12
❑ 119 Mike Rivera	.30	.09
❑ 120 Hank Blalock	.60	.18
❑ 121 Hansel Izquierdo RC	.40	.12
❑ 122 Orlando Hudson	.30	.09
❑ 123 Bill Hall	.40	.12
❑ 124 Jose Reyes	.60	.18
❑ 125 Juan Rivera	.30	.09
❑ 126 Eric Valent	.30	.09
❑ 127 Scotty Layfield RC	.40	.12
❑ 128 Austin Kearns	.30	.09
❑ 129 Nic Jackson RC	.40	.12
❑ 130 Chris Baker RC	.40	.12
❑ 131 Chad Qualls RC	.50	.15
❑ 132 Marcus Thames	.30	.09
❑ 133 Nathan Haynes	.30	.09
❑ 134 Brett Evert	.30	.09
❑ 135 Joe Borchard	.30	.09
❑ 136 Ryan Christianson	.30	.09
❑ 137 Josh Hamilton	.30	.09
❑ 138 Corey Patterson	.30	.09
❑ 139 Travis Wilson	.30	.09
❑ 140 Alex Escobar	.30	.09
❑ 141 Alexis Gomez	.30	.09
❑ 142 Nick Johnson	.40	.12
❑ 143 Kenny Kelly	.30	.09
❑ 144 Marlon Byrd	.30	.09
❑ 145 Kory DeHaan	.30	.09
❑ 146 Matt Belisle	.30	.09
❑ 147 Carlos Hernandez	.30	.09
❑ 148 Sean Burroughs	.30	.09
❑ 149 Angel Berroa	.30	.09
❑ 150 Aubrey Huff	.40	.12
❑ 151 Travis Hafner	.40	.12
❑ 152 Brandon Berger	.30	.09
❑ 153 David Krynzel	.30	.09
❑ 154 Ruben Salazar	.30	.09
❑ 155 J.R. House	.30	.09
❑ 156 Juan Silvestre	.30	.09
❑ 157 Dewon Brazelton	.30	.09
❑ 158 Jayson Werth	.30	.09
❑ 159 Larry Barnes	.30	.09
❑ 160 Elvis Pena	.30	.09
❑ 161 Ruben Gotay RC	.50	.15
❑ 162 Tommy Marx RC	.40	.12

❑ 163 John Suomi RC .40 .12
❑ 164 Javier Colina .30 .09
❑ 165 Greg Sain RC .40 .12
❑ 166 Robert Cosby RC .40 .12
❑ 167 Angel Pagan RC .40 .12
❑ 168 Ralph Santana RC .40 .12
❑ 169 Joe Orloski RC .40 .12
❑ 170 Shayne Wright RC .40 .12
❑ 171 Jay Caligiuri RC .40 .12
❑ 172 Greg Montalbano RC .40 .12
❑ 173 Rich Harden RC 5.00 1.50
❑ 174 Rich Thompson RC .40 .12
❑ 175 Fred Bastardo RC .40 .12
❑ 176 Alejandro Giron RC .40 .12
❑ 177 Jesus Medrano RC .40 .12
❑ 178 Kevin Deaton RC .40 .12
❑ 179 Mike Rosamond RC .40 .12
❑ 180 Jon Guzman RC .40 .12
❑ 181 Gerard Oakes RC .40 .12
❑ 182 Francisco Liriano RC 5.00 1.50
❑ 183 Matt Allegra RC .40 .12
❑ 184 Mike Snyder RC .40 .12
❑ 185 James Shanks RC .40 .12
❑ 186 Anderson Hernandez RC .40 .12
❑ 187 Dan Trumble RC .40 .12
❑ 188 Luis DePaula RC .40 .12
❑ 189 Randall Shelley RC .40 .12
❑ 190 Richard Lane RC .40 .12
❑ 191 Antwon Rollins RC .40 .12
❑ 192 Ryan Bukvich RC .40 .12
❑ 193 Derrick Lewis .30 .09
❑ 194 Eric Miller RC .40 .12
❑ 195 Justin Schuda RC .40 .12
❑ 196 Brian West RC .40 .12
❑ 197 Adam Roller RC .40 .12
❑ 198 Neal Frendling RC .40 .12
❑ 199 Jeremy Hill RC .40 .12
❑ 200 James Barrett RC .40 .12
❑ 201 Brett Kay RC .40 .12
❑ 202 Ryan Mottl RC .40 .12
❑ 203 Brad Nelson RC .50 .15
❑ 204 Juan M. Gonzalez RC .40 .12
❑ 205 Curtis Legendre RC .40 .12
❑ 206 Ronald Acuna RC .40 .12
❑ 207 Chris Flinn RC .40 .12
❑ 208 Nick Alvarez RC .40 .12
❑ 209 Jason Ellison RC .75 .23
❑ 210 Blake McGinley RC .40 .12
❑ 211 Dan Phillips RC .40 .12
❑ 212 Demetrius Heath RC .40 .12
❑ 213 Eric Bruntlett RC .40 .12
❑ 214 Joe Jiannetti RC .40 .12
❑ 215 Mike Hill RC .40 .12
❑ 216 Ricardo Cordova RC .40 .12
❑ 217 Mark Hamilton RC .40 .12
❑ 218 David Mattox RC .40 .12
❑ 219 Jose Morban RC .40 .12
❑ 220 Scott Wiggins RC .30 .09
❑ 221 Steve Green .30 .09
❑ 222 Brian Rogers .30 .09
❑ 223 Chin-Hui Tsao .40 .12
❑ 224 Kenny Baugh .30 .09
❑ 225 Nate Teut .30 .09
❑ 226 Josh Wilson RC .40 .12
❑ 227 Christian Parker .30 .09
❑ 228 Tim Raines Jr. .30 .09
❑ 229 Anastacio Martinez RC .40 .12
❑ 230 Richard Lewis .30 .09
❑ 231 Tim Kalita RC .40 .12
❑ 232 Edwin Almonte RC .40 .12
❑ 233 Hee-Seop Choi .40 .12
❑ 234 Ty Howington .30 .09
❑ 235 Victor Alvarez RC .40 .12
❑ 236 Morgan Ensberg .40 .12
❑ 237 Jeff Austin RC .40 .12
❑ 238 Luis Terrero .30 .09
❑ 239 Adam Wainwright .30 .09
❑ 240 Clint Weibl RC .30 .09
❑ 241 Eric Cyr .30 .09
❑ 242 Marlyn Tisdale RC .40 .12
❑ 243 John VanBenschoten .30 .09
❑ 244 Ryan Raburn RC .40 .12
❑ 245 Miguel Cabrera 1.50 .45
❑ 246 Jung Bong .30 .09
❑ 247 Raul Chavez RC .30 .09
❑ 248 Erik Bedard .40 .12
❑ 249 Chris Snelling RC .75 .23
❑ 250 Joe Rogers RC .40 .12
❑ 251 Nate Field RC .40 .12
❑ 252 Matt Herges RC .30 .09
❑ 253 Matt Childers RC .40 .12
❑ 254 Erick Almonte .30 .09
❑ 255 Nick Neugebauer .30 .09
❑ 256 Ron Calloway RC .40 .12
❑ 257 Seung Song .30 .09
❑ 258 Brandon Phillips .30 .09
❑ 259 Cole Barthel RC .40 .12
❑ 260 Jason Lane .40 .12
❑ 261 Jae Seo .30 .09
❑ 262 Randy Flores .30 .09
❑ 263 Scott Chiasson .30 .09
❑ 264 Chase Utley 1.50 .45
❑ 265 Tony Alvarez .30 .09
❑ 266 Ben Howard RC .40 .12
❑ 267 Nelson Castro RC .40 .12
❑ 268 Mark Lukasiewicz RC .30 .09
❑ 269 Eric Glaser RC .40 .12
❑ 270 Rob Henkel RC .40 .12
❑ 271 Jose Valverde RC .40 .12
❑ 272 Ricardo Rodriguez .30 .09
❑ 273 Chris Smith .30 .09
❑ 274 Mark Prior 1.50 .45
❑ 275 Miguel Olivo .30 .09
❑ 276 Ben Broussard .30 .09
❑ 277 Zach Sorensen .30 .09
❑ 278 Brian Mallette RC .30 .09
❑ 279 Brad Wilkerson .30 .09
❑ 280 Carl Crawford .40 .12
❑ 281 Chone Figgins RC .75 .23
❑ 282 Jimmy Alvarez RC .40 .12
❑ 283 Gavin Floyd RC 1.00 .30
❑ 284 Josh Bonifay RC .40 .12
❑ 285 Garrett Guzman RC .40 .12
❑ 286 Blake Williams .30 .09
❑ 287 Matt Holliday .30 .09
❑ 288 Ryan Madson .30 .09
❑ 289 Luis Torres .30 .09
❑ 290 Jeff Verplancke RC .40 .12
❑ 291 Nate Espy RC .40 .12
❑ 292 Jeff Lincoln RC .40 .12
❑ 293 Ryan Snare RC .40 .12
❑ 294 Jose Ortiz .30 .09
❑ 295 Eric Munson .30 .09
❑ 296 Denny Bautista .30 .09
❑ 297 Willy Aybar .30 .09
❑ 298 Kelly Johnson .75 .23
❑ 299 Justin Morneau .40 .12
❑ 300 Derrick Van Dusen .30 .09
❑ 301 Chad Petty .40 .12
❑ 302 Mike Restovich .30 .09
❑ 303 Shawn Fagan .30 .09
❑ 304 Yurendell DeCaster RC .40 .12
❑ 305 Justin Wayne .30 .09
❑ 306 Mike Peeples RC .30 .09
❑ 307 Joel Guzman 1.00 .30
❑ 308 Ryan Vogelsong .30 .09
❑ 309 Jorge Padilla RC .40 .12
❑ 310 Grady Sizemore .40 .12
❑ 311 Joe Jester RC .40 .12
❑ 312 Jim Journell .30 .09
❑ 313 Bobby Seay .30 .09
❑ 314 Ryan Church RC 1.50 .45
❑ 315 Grant Balfour .30 .09
❑ 316 Mitch Jones .30 .09
❑ 317 Travis Foley RC .40 .12
❑ 318 Bobby Crosby 1.00 .30
❑ 319 Adrian Gonzalez .30 .09
❑ 320 Ronnie Merrill .30 .09
❑ 321 Joel Pineiro .30 .09
❑ 322 John-Ford Griffin .30 .09
❑ 323 Brian Forystek RC .40 .12
❑ 324 Sean Douglass .30 .09
❑ 325 Manny Delcarmen RC .50 .15
❑ 326 Donnie Bridges .30 .09
❑ 327 Jim Kavourias RC .40 .12
❑ 328 Gabe Gross .30 .09
❑ 329 Jon Rauch .30 .09
❑ 330 Bill Ortega .30 .09
❑ 331 Joey Hammond RC .40 .12
❑ 332 Ramon Moreta RC .40 .12
❑ 333 Ron Davenport .30 .09
❑ 334 Brett Myers .40 .12
❑ 335 Carlos Pena .30 .09
❑ 336 Ezequiel Astacio RC .40 .12
❑ 337 Edwin Yan RC .40 .12
❑ 338 Josh Girdley .30 .09
❑ 339 Shaun Boyd .30 .09
❑ 340 Juan Rincon .30 .09
❑ 341 Chris Duffy RC 1.00 .30
❑ 342 Jason Kinchen .30 .09
❑ 343 Brad Thomas .30 .09
❑ 344 David Kelton .30 .09
❑ 345 Rafael Soriano .30 .09
❑ 346 Colin Young RC .40 .12
❑ 347 Eric Byrnes .30 .09
❑ 348 Chris Narveson RC .50 .15
❑ 349 John Rheinecker .30 .09
❑ 350 Mike Wilson RC .40 .12
❑ 351 Justin Sherrod RC .40 .12
❑ 352 Deivi Mendez .30 .09
❑ 353 Wily Mo Pena .40 .12
❑ 354 Brett Roneberg RC .40 .12
❑ 355 Trey Lunsford RC .40 .12
❑ 356 Jimmy Gobble RC .40 .12
❑ 357 Brent Butler .30 .09
❑ 358 Aaron Heilman .30 .09
❑ 359 Wilkin Ruan .30 .09
❑ 360 Brian Wolfe RC .40 .12
❑ 361 Cody Ransom .30 .09
❑ 362 Koyie Hill .30 .09
❑ 363 Scott Cassidy .30 .09
❑ 364 Tony Fontana RC .40 .12
❑ 365 Mark Teixeira 1.50 .45
❑ 366 Doug Sessions RC .40 .12
❑ 367 Victor Hall .30 .09
❑ 368 Josh Cisneros RC .40 .12
❑ 369 Kevin Mench .30 .09
❑ 370 Tike Redman .30 .09
❑ 371 Jeff Heaverlo .30 .09
❑ 372 Carlos Brackley RC .40 .12
❑ 373 Brad Hawpe .30 .09
❑ 374 Jesus Colome .30 .09
❑ 375 David Espinosa .30 .09
❑ 376 Jesse Foppert RC .50 .15
❑ 377 Ross Peeples RC .40 .12
❑ 378 Alex Requena RC .40 .12
❑ 379 Joe Mauer RC 4.00 1.20
❑ 380 Carlos Silva .30 .09
❑ 381 David Wright RC 15.00 4.50
❑ 382 Craig Kuzmic RC .40 .12
❑ 383 Pete Zamora RC .40 .12
❑ 384 Matt Parker RC .40 .12
❑ 385 Keith Ginter .30 .09
❑ 386 Gary Cates Jr. .40 .12
❑ 387 Justin Reid RC .40 .12
❑ 388 Jake Mauer RC .40 .12
❑ 389 Dennis Tankersley .30 .09
❑ 390 Josh Barfield RC 1.25 .35
❑ 391 Luis Maza .30 .09
❑ 392 Henry Pichardo RC .40 .12
❑ 393 Michael Floyd RC .40 .12
❑ 394 Clint Nageotte RC .50 .15
❑ 395 Raymond Cabrera RC .40 .12
❑ 396 Mauricio Lara RC .40 .12
❑ 397 Alejandro Cadena RC .40 .12
❑ 398 Jonny Gomes RC 3.00 .90
❑ 399 Jason Bulger RC .40 .12
❑ 400 Bobby Jenks RC 1.50 .45
❑ 401 David Gil RC .40 .12
❑ 402 Joel Crump RC .40 .12
❑ 403 Kazuhisa Ishii RC .50 .15
❑ 404 So Taguchi RC 1.25 .35
❑ 405 Ryan Doumit RC 1.25 .35
❑ 406 Macay McBride .40 .12
❑ 407 Brandon Claussen .30 .09
❑ 408 Chin-Feng Chen .40 .12
❑ 409 Josh Phelps .30 .09
❑ 410 Freddie Money RC .50 .15
❑ 411 Cliff Bartosh RC .40 .12
❑ 412 Josh Pearce .30 .09
❑ 413 Lyle Overbay .30 .09
❑ 414 Ryan Anderson .30 .09
❑ 415 Terrance Hill RC .40 .12
❑ 416 John Rodriguez RC .50 .15
❑ 417 Richard Stahl .30 .09
❑ 418 Brian Specht .30 .09
❑ 419 Chris Latham RC .30 .09
❑ 420 Carlos Cabrera RC .40 .12

❑ 421 Jose Bautista RC .50 .15
❑ 422 Kevin Frederick RC .40 .12
❑ 423 Jerome Williams .30 .09
❑ 424 Napoleon Calzado RC .40 .12
❑ 425 Benito Baez .30 .09
❑ 426 Xavier Nady .30 .09
❑ 427 Jason Botts RC 1.00 .30
❑ 428 Steve Bechler RC .40 .12
❑ 429 Reed Johnson RC .50 .15
❑ 430 Mark Outlaw RC .40 .12
❑ 431 Billy Sylvester .30 .09
❑ 432 Luke Lockwood .30 .09
❑ 433 Jake Peavy .60 .18
❑ 434 Alfredo Amezaga .30 .09
❑ 435 Aaron Cook RC .40 .12
❑ 436 Josh Shaffer RC .40 .12
❑ 437 Dan Wright .30 .09
❑ 438 Ryan Gripp RC .40 .12
❑ 439 Alex Herrera .30 .09
❑ 440 Jason Bay RC 4.00 1.20

2002 Bowman Draft

	Nm-Mt	Ex-Mt
COMPLETE SET (165)	50.00	15.00

❑ BDP1 Clint Everts RC .50 .15
❑ BDP2 Fred Lewis RC .40 .12
❑ BDP3 Jon Broxton RC .75 .23
❑ BDP4 Jason Anderson RC .40 .12
❑ BDP5 Mike Eusebio RC .40 .12
❑ BDP6 Zack Greinke RC 2.50 .75
❑ BDP7 Joe Blanton RC 1.50 .45
❑ BDP8 Sergio Santos RC .50 .15
❑ BDP9 Jason Cooper RC .40 .12
❑ BDP10 Delwyn Young RC 1.00 .30
❑ BDP11 Jeremy Hermida RC 4.00 1.20
❑ BDP12 Dan Ortmeier RC .50 .15
❑ BDP13 Kevin Jepsen RC .50 .15
❑ BDP14 Russ Adams RC .75 .23
❑ BDP15 Mike Nixon RC .40 .12
❑ BDP16 Nick Swisher RC 2.50 .75
❑ BDP17 Cole Hamels RC 2.50 .75
❑ BDP18 Brian Dopirak RC 1.50 .45
❑ BDP19 James Loney RC 1.50 .45
❑ BDP20 Denard Span RC .50 .15
❑ BDP21 Billy Petrick RC .40 .12
❑ BDP22 Jared Doyle RC .40 .12
❑ BDP23 Jeff Francoeur RC 20.00 6.00
❑ BDP24 Nick Bourgeois RC .40 .12
❑ BDP25 Matt Cain RC 5.00 1.50
❑ BDP26 John McCurdy RC .40 .12
❑ BDP27 Mark Kiger RC .40 .12
❑ BDP28 Bill Murphy RC .40 .12
❑ BDP29 Matt Craig RC .50 .15
❑ BDP30 Mike Megrew RC .40 .12
❑ BDP31 Ben Crockett RC .40 .12
❑ BDP32 Luke Hagerty RC .40 .12
❑ BDP33 Matt Whitney RC .40 .12
❑ BDP34 Dan Meyer RC .50 .15
❑ BDP35 Jeremy Brown RC .40 .12
❑ BDP36 Doug Johnson RC .40 .12
❑ BDP37 Steve Obenchain RC .40 .12
❑ BDP38 Matt Clanton RC .40 .12
❑ BDP39 Mark Teahen RC .75 .23
❑ BDP40 Tom Carrow RC .40 .12
❑ BDP41 Micah Schilling RC .40 .12
❑ BDP42 Blair Johnson RC .40 .12
❑ BDP43 Jason Pridie RC .40 .12
❑ BDP44 Joey Votto RC .50 .15
❑ BDP45 Taber Lee RC .40 .12
❑ BDP46 Adam Peterson RC .40 .12
❑ BDP47 Adam Donachie RC .40 .12
❑ BDP48 Josh Murray RC .40 .12
❑ BDP49 Brent Clevlen RC .75 .23
❑ BDP50 Chad Pleiness RC .40 .12
❑ BDP51 Zach Hammes RC .40 .12
❑ BDP52 Chris Snyder RC .50 .15
❑ BDP53 Chris Smith RC .40 .12
❑ BDP54 Justin Maureau RC .40 .12
❑ BDP55 David Bush RC .50 .15
❑ BDP56 Tim Gilhooly RC .40 .12
❑ BDP57 Blair Barbier RC .40 .12
❑ BDP58 Zach Segovia RC .40 .12
❑ BDP59 Jeremy Reed RC 2.00 .60
❑ BDP60 Matt Pender RC .40 .12
❑ BDP61 Eric Thomas RC .40 .12
❑ BDP62 Justin Jones RC .50 .15
❑ BDP63 Brian Slocum RC .40 .12
❑ BDP64 Larry Broadway RC .40 .12
❑ BDP65 Bo Flowers RC .40 .12
❑ BDP66 Scott White RC .40 .12
❑ BDP67 Steve Stanley RC .40 .12
❑ BDP68 Alex Merricks RC .40 .12
❑ BDP69 Josh Womack RC .40 .12
❑ BDP70 Dave Jensen RC .40 .12
❑ BDP71 Curtis Granderson RC 1.50 .45
❑ BDP72 Pat Osborn RC .40 .12
❑ BDP73 Nic Carter RC .40 .12
❑ BDP74 Mitch Talbot RC .40 .12
❑ BDP75 Don Murphy RC .40 .12
❑ BDP76 Val Majewski RC .40 .12
❑ BDP77 Javy Rodriguez RC .40 .12
❑ BDP78 Fernando Pacheco RC .40 .12
❑ BDP79 Steve Russell RC .40 .12
❑ BDP80 Jon Slack RC .40 .12
❑ BDP81 John Baker RC .40 .12
❑ BDP82 Aaron Coonrod RC .40 .12
❑ BDP83 Josh Johnson RC 1.00 .30
❑ BDP84 Jake Blalock RC .75 .23
❑ BDP85 Alex Hart RC .40 .12
❑ BDP86 Wes Bankston RC 1.50 .45
❑ BDP87 Josh Rupe RC .40 .12
❑ BDP88 Dan Cevette RC .40 .12
❑ BDP89 Kiel Fisher RC .50 .15
❑ BDP90 Alan Rick RC .40 .12
❑ BDP91 Charlie Morton RC .40 .12
❑ BDP92 Chad Spann RC .40 .12
❑ BDP93 Kyle Boyer RC .40 .12
❑ BDP94 Bob Malek RC .40 .12
❑ BDP95 Ryan Rodriguez RC .40 .12
❑ BDP96 Jordan Renz RC .40 .12
❑ BDP97 Randy Frye RC .40 .12
❑ BDP98 Rich Hill RC 1.25 .35
❑ BDP99 B.J. Upton RC 6.00 1.80
❑ BDP100 Dan Christensen RC .40 .12
❑ BDP101 Casey Kotchman RC 2.50 .75
❑ BDP102 Eric Good RC .30 .09
❑ BDP103 Mike Fontenot RC .40 .12
❑ BDP104 John Webb RC .40 .12
❑ BDP105 Jason Dubois RC .50 .15
❑ BDP106 Ryan Kibler RC .40 .12
❑ BDP107 Jhonny Peralta RC 3.00 .90
❑ BDP108 Kirk Saarloos RC .40 .12
❑ BDP109 Rhett Parrott RC .40 .12
❑ BDP110 Jason Grove RC .40 .12
❑ BDP111 Colt Griffin RC .40 .12
❑ BDP112 Dallas McPherson RC 2.50 .75
❑ BDP113 Oliver Perez RC 1.50 .45
❑ BDP114 Mar. McDougall RC .40 .12
❑ BDP115 Mike Wood RC .40 .12
❑ BDP116 Scott Hairston RC .50 .15
❑ BDP117 Jason Simontacchi RC .40 .12
❑ BDP118 Taggert Bozied RC .50 .15
❑ BDP119 Shelley Duncan RC .40 .12
❑ BDP120 Dontrelle Willis RC 8.00 2.40
❑ BDP121 Sean Burnett .30 .09
❑ BDP122 Aaron Cook .30 .09
❑ BDP123 Brett Evert .30 .09
❑ BDP124 Jimmy Journell .30 .09
❑ BDP125 Brett Myers .30 .09
❑ BDP126 Brad Baker .30 .09
❑ BDP127 Billy Traber RC .40 .12
❑ BDP128 Adam Wainwright .30 .09
❑ BDP129 Jason Young RC .40 .12
❑ BDP130 John Buck .30 .09
❑ BDP131 Kevin Cash RC .40 .12
❑ BDP132 Jason Stokes RC 1.25 .35
❑ BDP133 Drew Henson .30 .09
❑ BDP134 Chad Tracy RC 1.00 .30
❑ BDP135 Orlando Hudson .30 .09
❑ BDP136 Brandon Phillips .30 .09
❑ BDP137 Joe Borchard .30 .09
❑ BDP138 Marlon Byrd .30 .09
❑ BDP139 Carl Crawford .30 .09
❑ BDP140 Michael Restovich .30 .09
❑ BDP141 Corey Hart RC 1.00 .30
❑ BDP142 Edwin Almonte .30 .09
❑ BDP143 Francis Beltran RC .40 .12
❑ BDP144 Jorge De La Rosa RC .40 .12
❑ BDP145 Gerardo Garcia RC .40 .12
❑ BDP146 Franklyn German RC .40 .12
❑ BDP147 Francisco Liriano 2.00 .60
❑ BDP148 Francisco Rodriguez .30 .09
❑ BDP149 Ricardo Rodriguez .30 .09
❑ BDP150 Seung Song .30 .09
❑ BDP151 John Stephens .30 .09
❑ BDP152 Justin Huber RC .75 .23
❑ BDP153 Victor Martinez .75 .23
❑ BDP154 Hee Seop Choi .30 .09
❑ BDP155 Justin Morneau .30 .09
❑ BDP156 Miguel Cabrera 1.25 .35
❑ BDP157 Victor Diaz RC .75 .23
❑ BDP158 Jose Reyes .50 .15
❑ BDP159 Omar Infante .30 .09
❑ BDP160 Angel Berroa .30 .09
❑ BDP161 Tony Alvarez .30 .09
❑ BDP162 Shin Soo Choo RC .75 .23
❑ BDP163 Wily Mo Pena .30 .09
❑ BDP164 Andres Torres .30 .09
❑ BDP165 Jose Lopez RC 1.25 .35

2003 Bowman

	Nm-Mt	Ex-Mt
COMPLETE SET (330)	60.00	18.00
COMMON CARD (1-155)	.30	.09
COMMON CARD (156-330)	.30	.09

❑ 1 Garret Anderson .30 .09
❑ 2 Derek Jeter 2.00 .60
❑ 3 Gary Sheffield .30 .09
❑ 4 Matt Morris .30 .09
❑ 5 Derek Lowe .30 .09
❑ 6 Andy Van Hekken .30 .09
❑ 7 Sammy Sosa .75 .23
❑ 8 Ken Griffey Jr. 1.25 .35
❑ 9 Omar Vizquel .50 .15
❑ 10 Jorge Posada .50 .15
❑ 11 Lance Berkman .30 .09
❑ 12 Mike Sweeney .30 .09
❑ 13 Adrian Beltre .30 .09
❑ 14 Richie Sexson .30 .09
❑ 15 A.J. Pierzynski .30 .09
❑ 16 Bartolo Colon .30 .09
❑ 17 Mike Mussina .50 .15
❑ 18 Paul Byrd .30 .09
❑ 19 Bobby Abreu .30 .09
❑ 20 Miguel Tejada .30 .09
❑ 21 Aramis Ramirez .30 .09
❑ 22 Edgardo Alfonzo .30 .09
❑ 23 Edgar Martinez .50 .15

❑ 24 Albert Pujols 1.50 .45
❑ 25 Carl Crawford .30 .09
❑ 26 Eric Hinske .30 .09
❑ 27 Tim Salmon .50 .15
❑ 28 Luis Gonzalez .30 .09
❑ 29 Jay Gibbons .30 .09
❑ 30 John Smoltz .50 .15
❑ 31 Tim Wakefield .30 .09
❑ 32 Mark Prior .50 .15
❑ 33 Magglio Ordonez .30 .09
❑ 34 Adam Dunn .30 .09
❑ 35 Larry Walker .30 .09
❑ 36 Luis Castillo .30 .09
❑ 37 Wade Miller .30 .09
❑ 38 Carlos Beltran .30 .09
❑ 39 Odalis Perez .30 .09
❑ 40 Alex Sanchez .30 .09
❑ 41 Torii Hunter .30 .09
❑ 42 Cliff Floyd .30 .09
❑ 43 Andy Pettitte .50 .15
❑ 44 Francisco Rodriguez .30 .09
❑ 45 Eric Chavez .30 .09
❑ 46 Kevin Millwood .30 .09
❑ 47 Dennis Tankersley .30 .09
❑ 48 Hideo Nomo .75 .23
❑ 49 Freddy Garcia .30 .09
❑ 50 Randy Johnson .75 .23
❑ 51 Aubrey Huff .30 .09
❑ 52 Carlos Delgado .30 .09
❑ 53 Troy Glaus .30 .09
❑ 54 Junior Spivey .30 .09
❑ 55 Mike Hampton .30 .09
❑ 56 Sidney Ponson .30 .09
❑ 57 Aaron Boone .30 .09
❑ 58 Kerry Wood .30 .09
❑ 59 Runelvys Hernandez .30 .09
❑ 60 Nomar Garciaparra 1.25 .35
❑ 61 Todd Helton .50 .15
❑ 62 Mike Lowell .30 .09
❑ 63 Roy Oswalt .30 .09
❑ 64 Raul Ibanez .30 .09
❑ 65 Brian Jordan .30 .09
❑ 66 Geoff Jenkins .30 .09
❑ 67 Jermaine Dye .30 .09
❑ 68 Tom Glavine .50 .15
❑ 69 Bernie Williams .50 .15
❑ 70 Vladimir Guerrero .75 .23
❑ 71 Mark Mulder .30 .09
❑ 72 Jimmy Rollins .30 .09
❑ 73 Oliver Perez .30 .09
❑ 74 Rich Aurilia .30 .09
❑ 75 Joel Pineiro .30 .09
❑ 76 J.D. Drew .30 .09
❑ 77 Ivan Rodriguez .50 .15
❑ 78 Josh Phelps .30 .09
❑ 79 Darin Erstad .30 .09
❑ 80 Curt Schilling .30 .09
❑ 81 Paul Lo Duca .30 .09
❑ 82 Marty Cordova .30 .09
❑ 83 Manny Ramirez .50 .15
❑ 84 Bobby Hill .30 .09
❑ 85 Paul Konerko .30 .09
❑ 86 Austin Kearns .30 .09
❑ 87 Jason Jennings .30 .09
❑ 88 Brad Penny .30 .09
❑ 89 Jeff Bagwell .50 .15
❑ 90 Shawn Green .30 .09
❑ 91 Jason Schmidt .30 .09
❑ 92 Doug Mientkiewicz .30 .09
❑ 93 Jose Vidro .30 .09
❑ 94 Bret Boone .30 .09
❑ 95 Jason Giambi .30 .09
❑ 96 Barry Zito .30 .09
❑ 97 Roy Halladay .30 .09
❑ 98 Pat Burrell .30 .09
❑ 99 Sean Burroughs .30 .09
❑ 100 Barry Bonds 2.00 .60
❑ 101 Kazuhiro Sasaki .30 .09
❑ 102 Fernando Vina .30 .09
❑ 103 Chan Ho Park .30 .09
❑ 104 Andruw Jones .50 .15
❑ 105 Adam Kennedy .30 .09
❑ 106 Shea Hillenbrand .30 .09
❑ 107 Greg Maddux 1.25 .35
❑ 108 Jim Edmonds .50 .15
❑ 109 Pedro Martinez .50 .15
❑ 110 Moises Alou .30 .09
❑ 111 Jeff Weaver .30 .09
❑ 112 C.C. Sabathia .30 .09
❑ 113 Robert Fick .30 .09
❑ 114 A.J. Burnett .30 .09
❑ 115 Jeff Kent .30 .09
❑ 116 Kevin Brown .30 .09
❑ 117 Rafael Furcal .30 .09
❑ 118 Cristian Guzman .30 .09
❑ 119 Brad Wilkerson .30 .09
❑ 120 Mike Piazza 1.25 .35
❑ 121 Alfonso Soriano .30 .09
❑ 122 Mark Ellis .30 .09
❑ 123 Vicente Padilla .30 .09
❑ 124 Eric Gagne .30 .09
❑ 125 Ryan Klesko .30 .09
❑ 126 Ichiro Suzuki 1.50 .45
❑ 127 Tony Batista .30 .09
❑ 128 Roberto Alomar .50 .15
❑ 129 Alex Rodriguez 1.25 .35
❑ 130 Jim Thome .50 .15
❑ 131 Jarrod Washburn .30 .09
❑ 132 Orlando Hudson .30 .09
❑ 133 Chipper Jones .75 .23
❑ 134 Rodrigo Lopez .30 .09
❑ 135 Johnny Damon .50 .15
❑ 136 Matt Clement .30 .09
❑ 137 Frank Thomas .75 .23
❑ 138 Ellis Burks .30 .09
❑ 139 Carlos Pena .30 .09
❑ 140 Josh Beckett .30 .09
❑ 141 Joe Randa .30 .09
❑ 142 Brian Giles .30 .09
❑ 143 Kazuhisa Ishii .30 .09
❑ 144 Corey Koskie .30 .09
❑ 145 Orlando Cabrera .30 .09
❑ 146 Mark Buehrle .30 .09
❑ 147 Roger Clemens 1.50 .45
❑ 148 Tim Hudson .30 .09
❑ 149 Randy Wolf UER .30 .09
resume says AL leaders; he pitches in NL
❑ 150 Josh Fogg .30 .09
❑ 151 Phil Nevin .30 .09
❑ 152 John Olerud .30 .09
❑ 153 Scott Rolen .50 .15
❑ 154 Joe Kennedy .30 .09
❑ 155 Rafael Palmeiro .50 .15
❑ 156 Chad Hutchinson .30 .09
❑ 157 Quincy Carter XRC .50 .15
❑ 158 Hee Seop Choi .30 .09
❑ 159 Joe Borchard .30 .09
❑ 160 Brandon Phillips .30 .09
❑ 161 Wily Mo Pena .30 .09
❑ 162 Victor Martinez .50 .15
❑ 163 Jason Stokes .30 .09
❑ 164 Ken Harvey .30 .09
❑ 165 Juan Rivera .30 .09
❑ 166 Jose Contreras RC 1.50 .45
❑ 167 Dan Haren RC .75 .23
❑ 168 Michel Hernandez RC .40 .12
❑ 169 Eider Torres RC .40 .12
❑ 170 Chris De La Cruz RC .40 .12
❑ 171 Ramon Nivar-Martinez RC .40 .12
❑ 172 Mike Adams RC .40 .12
❑ 173 Justin Arneson RC .40 .12
❑ 174 Jamie Athas RC .40 .12
❑ 175 Dwaine Bacon RC .40 .12
❑ 176 Clint Barmes RC 1.50 .45
❑ 177 B.J. Barns RC .40 .12
❑ 178 Tyler Johnson RC .40 .12
❑ 179 Bobby Basham RC .50 .15
❑ 180 T.J. Bohn RC .40 .12
❑ 181 J.D. Durbin RC .40 .12
❑ 182 Brandon Bowe RC .40 .12
❑ 183 Craig Brazell RC .40 .12
❑ 184 Dusty Brown RC .40 .12
❑ 185 Brian Bruney RC .50 .15
❑ 186 Greg Bruso RC .40 .12
❑ 187 Jaime Bubela RC .40 .12
❑ 188 Bryan Bullington RC .40 .12
❑ 189 Brian Burgamy RC .40 .12
❑ 190 Eny Cabreja RC .40 .12
❑ 191 Daniel Cabrera RC .75 .23
❑ 192 Ryan Cameron RC .40 .12
❑ 193 Lance Caraccioli RC .40 .12
❑ 194 David Cash RC .40 .12
❑ 195 Bernie Castro RC .40 .12
❑ 196 Ismael Castro RC .50 .15
❑ 197 Daryl Clark RC .40 .12
❑ 198 Jeff Clark RC .40 .12
❑ 199 Chris Colton RC .40 .12
❑ 200 Dexter Cooper RC .40 .12
❑ 201 Callix Crabbe RC .50 .15
❑ 202 Chien-Ming Wang RC 2.50 .75
❑ 203 Eric Crozier RC .50 .15
❑ 204 Nook Logan RC .50 .15
❑ 205 David DeJesus RC .75 .23
❑ 206 Matt DeMarco RC .40 .12
❑ 207 Chris Duncan RC .40 .12
❑ 208 Eric Eckenstahler .30 .09
❑ 209 Willie Eyre RC .40 .12
❑ 210 Evel Bastida-Martinez RC .40 .12
❑ 211 Chris Fallon RC .40 .12
❑ 212 Mike Flannery RC .40 .12
❑ 213 Mike O'Keefe RC .40 .12
❑ 214 Ben Francisco RC .40 .12
❑ 215 Kason Gabbard RC .40 .12
❑ 216 Mike Gallo RC .40 .12
❑ 217 Jairo Garcia RC .50 .15
❑ 218 Angel Garcia RC .50 .15
❑ 219 Michael Garciaparra RC .30 .09
❑ 220 Joey Gomes RC .40 .12
❑ 221 Dusty Gomon RC .50 .15
❑ 222 Bryan Grace RC .40 .12
❑ 223 Tyson Graham RC .40 .12
❑ 224 Henry Guerrero RC .40 .12
❑ 225 Franklin Gutierrez RC 1.00 .30
❑ 226 Carlos Guzman RC .50 .15
❑ 227 Matthew Hagen RC .40 .12
❑ 228 Josh Hall RC .40 .12
❑ 229 Rob Hammock RC .40 .12
❑ 230 Brendan Harris RC .50 .15
❑ 231 Gary Harris RC .40 .12
❑ 232 Clay Hensley RC .40 .12
❑ 233 Michael Hinckley RC .50 .15
❑ 234 Luis Hodge RC .40 .12
❑ 235 Donnie Hood RC .50 .15
❑ 236 Travis Ishikawa RC .40 .12
❑ 237 Edwin Jackson RC .50 .15
❑ 238 Ardley Jansen RC .50 .15
❑ 239 Ferenc Jongejan RC .40 .12
❑ 240 Matt Kata RC .40 .12
❑ 241 Kazuhiro Takeoka RC .40 .12
❑ 242 Beau Kemp RC .40 .12
❑ 243 Il Kim RC .40 .12
❑ 244 Brennan King RC .40 .12
❑ 245 Chris Kroski RC .40 .12
❑ 246 Jason Kubel RC .75 .23
❑ 247 Pete LaForest RC .40 .12
❑ 248 Wil Ledezma RC .40 .12
❑ 249 Jeremy Bonderman RC 2.50 .75
❑ 250 Gonzalo Lopez RC .40 .12
❑ 251 Brian Luderer RC .40 .12
❑ 252 Ruddy Lugo RC .40 .12
❑ 253 Wayne Lydon RC .40 .12
❑ 254 Mark Malaska RC .40 .12
❑ 255 Andy Marte RC 3.00 .90
❑ 256 Tyler Martin RC .40 .12
❑ 257 Branden Florence RC .40 .12
❑ 258 Aneudis Mateo RC .40 .12
❑ 259 Derell McCall RC .40 .12
❑ 260 Brian McCann RC 3.00 .90
❑ 261 Mike McNutt RC .40 .12
❑ 262 Jacabo Meque RC .40 .12
❑ 263 Derek Michaelis RC .40 .12
❑ 264 Aaron Miles RC .50 .15
❑ 265 Jose Morales RC .40 .12
❑ 266 Dustin Moseley RC .40 .12
❑ 267 Adrian Myers RC .40 .12
❑ 268 Dan Neil RC .40 .12
❑ 269 Jon Nelson RC .50 .15
❑ 270 Mike Neu RC .40 .12
❑ 271 Leigh Neuage RC .40 .12
❑ 272 Wes O'Brien RC .40 .12
❑ 273 Trent Oeltjen RC .50 .15
❑ 274 Tim Olson RC .40 .12
❑ 275 David Pahucki RC .40 .12
❑ 276 Nathan Panther RC .40 .12
❑ 277 Arnie Munoz RC .40 .12
❑ 278 Dave Pember RC .40 .12
❑ 279 Jason Perry RC .50 .15

❑ 280 Matthew Peterson RC ...... .40 .12
❑ 281 Ryan Shealy RC .... .75 .23
❑ 282 Jorge Piedra RC .... .50 .15
❑ 283 Simon Pond RC .... .40 .12
❑ 284 Aaron Rakers RC .... .40 .12
❑ 285 Hanley Ramirez RC .... 2.50 .75
❑ 286 Manuel Ramirez RC .... .50 .15
❑ 287 Kevin Randel RC .... .40 .12
❑ 288 Darrell Rasner RC .... .40 .12
❑ 289 Prentice Redman RC .... .40 .12
❑ 290 Eric Reed RC .... .40 .12
❑ 291 Wilton Reynolds RC .... .50 .15
❑ 292 Eric Riggs RC .... .50 .15
❑ 293 Carlos Rijo RC .... .40 .12
❑ 294 Rajai Davis RC .... .40 .12
❑ 295 Aron Weston RC .... .40 .12
❑ 296 Arturo Rivas RC .... .40 .12
❑ 297 Kyle Roat RC .... .40 .12
❑ 298 Bubba Nelson RC .... .50 .15
❑ 299 Levi Robinson RC .... .40 .12
❑ 300 Ray Sadler RC .... .40 .12
❑ 301 Gary Schneidmiller RC .... .40 .12
❑ 302 Jon Schuerholz RC .... .40 .12
❑ 303 Corey Shafer RC .... .40 .12
❑ 304 Brian Shackelford RC ...... .40 .12
❑ 305 Bill Simon RC .... .40 .12
❑ 306 Haj Turay RC .... .50 .15
❑ 307 Sean Smith RC .... .50 .15
❑ 308 Ryan Spataro RC .... .40 .12
❑ 309 Jemel Spearman RC .... .40 .12
❑ 310 Keith Stamler RC .... .40 .12
❑ 311 Luke Steidlmayer RC .... .40 .12
❑ 312 Adam Stern RC .... .40 .12
❑ 313 Jay Sitzman RC .... .40 .12
❑ 314 Thomari Story-Harden RC .50 .15
❑ 315 Terry Tiffee RC .... .40 .12
❑ 316 Nick Trzesniak RC .... .40 .12
❑ 317 Denny Tussen RC .... .40 .12
❑ 318 Scott Tyler RC .... .50 .15
❑ 319 Shane Victorino RC .... .50 .15
❑ 320 Doug Waechter RC .... .50 .15
❑ 321 Brandon Watson RC .... .40 .12
❑ 322 Todd Wellemeyer RC .... .40 .12
❑ 323 Eli Whiteside RC .... .40 .12
❑ 324 Josh Willingham RC .... .50 .15
❑ 325 Travis Wong RC .... .50 .15
❑ 326 Brian Wright RC .... .40 .12
❑ 327 Kevin Youkilis RC .... .75 .23
❑ 328 Andy Sisco RC .... .50 .15
❑ 329 Dustin Yount RC .... .50 .15
❑ 330 Andrew Dominique RC .... .40 .12
❑ NNO Eric Hinske Bat 15.00 4.50
Jason Jennings Jsy
ROY Relic

2003 Bowman Draft

	MINT	NRMT
COMPLETE SET (165)	40.00	18.00

❑ 1 Dontrelle Willis .... .75 .35
❑ 2 Freddy Sanchez .... .30 .14
❑ 3 Miguel Cabrera .... .75 .35
❑ 4 Ryan Ludwick .... .30 .14
❑ 5 Ty Wigginton .... .30 .14
❑ 6 Mark Teixeira .... .50 .23
❑ 7 Trey Hodges .... .30 .14
❑ 8 Laynce Nix .... .30 .14
❑ 9 Antonio Perez .... .30 .14
❑ 10 Jody Gerut .... .30 .14
❑ 11 Jae Weong Seo .... .30 .14
❑ 12 Erick Almonte .... .30 .14
❑ 13 Lyle Overbay .... .30 .14
❑ 14 Billy Traber .... .30 .14
❑ 15 Andres Torres .... .30 .14
❑ 16 Jose Valverde .... .30 .14
❑ 17 Aaron Heilman .... .30 .14
❑ 18 Brandon Larson .... .30 .14
❑ 19 Jung Bong .... .30 .14
❑ 20 Jesse Foppert .... .30 .14
❑ 21 Angel Berroa .... .30 .14
❑ 22 Jeff DaVanon .... .30 .14
❑ 23 Kurt Ainsworth .... .30 .14
❑ 24 Brandon Claussen .... .30 .14
❑ 25 Xavier Nady .... .30 .14
❑ 26 Travis Hafner .... .30 .14
❑ 27 Jerome Williams .... .30 .14
❑ 28 Jose Reyes .... .30 .14
❑ 29 Sergio Mitre RC .... .50 .23
❑ 30 Bo Hart RC .... .40 .18
❑ 31 Adam Miller RC .... 1.50 .70
❑ 32 Brian Finch RC .... .40 .18
❑ 33 Taylor Mattingly RC .... .50 .23
❑ 34 Daric Barton RC 3.00 1.35
❑ 35 Chris Ray RC .... .75 .35
❑ 36 Jarrod Saltalamacchia RC 3.00 1.35
❑ 37 Dennis Dove RC .... .50 .23
❑ 38 James Houser RC .... .50 .23
❑ 39 Clint King RC .... .50 .23
❑ 40 Lou Palmisano RC .... .50 .23
❑ 41 Dan Moore RC .... .40 .18
❑ 42 Craig Stansberry RC .... .50 .23
❑ 43 Jo Jo Reyes RC .... .50 .23
❑ 44 Jake Stevens RC .... .75 .35
❑ 45 Tom Gorzelanny RC .... .50 .23
❑ 46 Brian Marshall RC .... .40 .18
❑ 47 Scott Beerer RC .... .40 .18
❑ 48 Javi Herrera RC .... .50 .23
❑ 49 Steve LeRud RC .... .50 .23
❑ 50 Josh Banks RC .... .75 .35
❑ 51 Jon Papelbon RC 6.00 2.70
❑ 52 Juan Valdes RC .... .50 .23
❑ 53 Beau Vaughan RC .... .50 .23
❑ 54 Matt Chico RC .... .50 .23
❑ 55 Todd Jennings RC .... .50 .23
❑ 56 Anthony Gwynn RC .... .50 .23
❑ 57 Matt Harrison RC .... .75 .35
❑ 58 Aaron Marsden RC .... .50 .23
❑ 59 Casey Abrams RC .... .40 .18
❑ 60 Cory Stuart RC .... .40 .18
❑ 61 Mike Wagner RC .... .40 .18
❑ 62 Jordan Pratt RC .... .50 .23
❑ 63 Andre Randolph RC .... .50 .23
❑ 64 Blake Balkcom RC .... .50 .23
❑ 65 Josh Muecke RC .... .40 .18
❑ 66 Jamie D'Antona RC .... .75 .35
❑ 67 Cole Seifrig RC .... .40 .18
❑ 68 Josh Anderson RC .... .75 .35
❑ 69 Matt Lorenzo RC .... .50 .23
❑ 70 Nate Spears RC .... .50 .23
❑ 71 Chris Goodman RC .... .40 .18
❑ 72 Brian McFall RC .... .40 .18
❑ 73 Billy Hogan RC .... .50 .23
❑ 74 Jamie Romak RC .... .50 .23
❑ 75 Jeff Cook RC .... .50 .23
❑ 76 Brooks McNiven RC .... .40 .18
❑ 77 Xavier Paul RC .... .50 .23
❑ 78 Bob Zimmerman RC UER .. .40 .18
Name is spelled Zimmermann
❑ 79 Mickey Hall RC .... .50 .23
❑ 80 Shaun Marcum RC .... .75 .35
❑ 81 Matt Nachreiner RC .... .50 .23
❑ 82 Chris Kinsey RC .... .40 .18
❑ 83 Jonathan Fulton RC .... .50 .23
❑ 84 Edgardo Baez RC .... .50 .23
❑ 85 Robert Valido RC .... .50 .23
❑ 86 Kenny Lewis RC .... .50 .23
❑ 87 Trent Peterson RC .... .40 .18
❑ 88 Johnny Woodard RC .... .50 .23
❑ 89 Wes Littleton RC .... .50 .23
❑ 90 Sean Rodriguez RC .... .50 .23
❑ 91 Kyle Pearson RC .... .40 .18
❑ 92 Josh Rainwater RC .... .50 .23
❑ 93 Travis Schlichting RC .... .50 .23
❑ 94 Tim Battle RC .... .50 .23
❑ 95 Aaron Hill RC .... .75 .35
❑ 96 Bob McCrory RC .... .40 .18
❑ 97 Rick Guarno RC .... .50 .23
❑ 98 Brandon Yarbrough RC .... .40 .18
❑ 99 Peter Stonard RC .... .40 .18
❑ 100 Darin Downs RC .... .50 .23
❑ 101 Matt Bruback RC .... .30 .14
❑ 102 Danny Garcia RC .... .40 .18
❑ 103 Cory Stewart RC .... .40 .18
❑ 104 Ferdin Tejeda RC .... .40 .18
❑ 105 Kade Johnson RC .... .40 .18
❑ 106 Andrew Brown RC .... .50 .23
❑ 107 Aquilino Lopez RC .... .40 .18
❑ 108 Stephen Randolph RC .... .40 .18
❑ 109 Dave Matranga RC .... .40 .18
❑ 110 Dustin McGowan RC .... .40 .18
❑ 111 Juan Camacho RC .... .40 .18
❑ 112 Cliff Lee .... .30 .14
❑ 113 Jeff Duncan RC .... .40 .18
❑ 114 C.J. Wilson .... .30 .14
❑ 115 Brandon Roberson RC .... .40 .18
❑ 116 David Corrente RC .... .40 .18
❑ 117 Kevin Beavers RC .... .40 .18
❑ 118 Anthony Webster RC .... .50 .23
❑ 119 Oscar Villarreal RC .... .40 .18
❑ 120 Hong-Chih Kuo RC .... 1.50 .70
❑ 121 Josh Barfield .... .30 .14
❑ 122 Denny Bautista .... .30 .14
❑ 123 Chris Burke RC .... 1.50 .70
❑ 124 Robinson Cano RC 5.00 2.20
❑ 125 Jose Castillo .... .30 .14
❑ 126 Neal Cotts .... .30 .14
❑ 127 Jorge De La Rosa .... .30 .14
❑ 128 J.D. Durbin .... .40 .18
❑ 129 Edwin Encarnacion .... .50 .23
❑ 130 Gavin Floyd .... .30 .14
❑ 131 Alexis Gomez .... .30 .14
❑ 132 Edgar Gonzalez RC .... .40 .18
❑ 133 Khalil Greene .... 1.25 .55
❑ 134 Zack Greinke .... .30 .14
❑ 135 Franklin Gutierrez .... .75 .35
❑ 136 Rich Harden .... .50 .23
❑ 137 J.J. Hardy RC .... 1.25 .55
❑ 138 Ryan Howard RC 5.00 2.20
❑ 139 Justin Huber .... .30 .14
❑ 140 David Kelton .... .30 .14
❑ 141 Dave Krynzel .... .30 .14
❑ 142 Pete LaForest .... .40 .18
❑ 143 Adam LaRoche .... .30 .14
❑ 144 Preston Larrison RC .... .50 .23
❑ 145 John Maine RC .... 1.00 .45
❑ 146 Andy Marte .... 1.50 .70
❑ 147 Jeff Mathis .... .30 .14
❑ 148 Joe Mauer UER .... .50 .23
Card has playing for New Haven
❑ 149 Clint Nageotte .... .30 .14
❑ 150 Chris Narveson .... .30 .14
❑ 151 Ramon Nivar .... .40 .18
❑ 152 Felix Pie RC 4.00 1.80
❑ 153 Guillermo Quiroz RC .... .40 .18
❑ 154 Rene Reyes .... .30 .14
❑ 155 Royce Ring .... .30 .14
❑ 156 Alexis Rios .... .30 .14
❑ 157 Grady Sizemore .... .30 .14
❑ 158 Stephen Smitherman .... .30 .14
❑ 159 Seung Song .... .30 .14
❑ 160 Scott Thorman .... .30 .14
❑ 161 Chad Tracy .... .30 .14
❑ 162 Chin-Hui Tsao .... .30 .14
❑ 163 John VanBenschoten .... .30 .14
❑ 164 Kevin Youkilis .... .75 .35
❑ 165 Chien-Ming Wang .... 1.50 .70

2004 Bowman

	Nm-Mt	Ex-Mt
COMPLETE SET (330)	80.00	24.00
ROY ODDS 1:829 H, 1:284 HTA, 1:1632 R		.00

❑ 1 Garret Anderson .... .30 .09
❑ 2 Larry Walker .... .30 .09
❑ 3 Derek Jeter .... 1.50 .45
❑ 4 Curt Schilling .... .50 .15
❑ 5 Carlos Zambrano .... .30 .09
❑ 6 Shawn Green .... .30 .09
❑ 7 Manny Ramirez .... .50 .15

❑ 8 Randy Johnson .75 .23
❑ 9 Jeremy Bonderman .30 .09
❑ 10 Alfonso Soriano .30 .09
❑ 11 Scott Rolen .50 .15
❑ 12 Kerry Wood .30 .09
❑ 13 Eric Gagne .30 .09
❑ 14 Ryan Klesko .30 .09
❑ 15 Kevin Millar .30 .09
❑ 16 Ty Wigginton .30 .09
❑ 17 David Ortiz .75 .23
❑ 18 Luis Castillo .30 .09
❑ 19 Bernie Williams .50 .15
❑ 20 Edgar Renteria .30 .09
❑ 21 Matt Kata .30 .09
❑ 22 Bartolo Colon .30 .09
❑ 23 Derrek Lee .50 .15
❑ 24 Gary Sheffield .30 .09
❑ 25 Nomar Garciaparra 1.25 .35
❑ 26 Kevin Millwood .30 .09
❑ 27 Corey Patterson .30 .09
❑ 28 Carlos Beltran .30 .09
❑ 29 Mike Lieberthal .30 .09
❑ 30 Troy Glaus .30 .09
❑ 31 Preston Wilson .30 .09
❑ 32 Jorge Posada .50 .15
❑ 33 Bo Hart .30 .09
❑ 34 Mark Prior .50 .15
❑ 35 Hideo Nomo .75 .23
❑ 36 Jason Kendall .30 .09
❑ 37 Roger Clemens 1.50 .45
❑ 38 Dmitri Young .30 .09
❑ 39 Jason Giambi .30 .09
❑ 40 Jim Edmonds .50 .15
❑ 41 Ryan Ludwick .30 .09
❑ 42 Brandon Webb .30 .09
❑ 43 Todd Helton .50 .15
❑ 44 Jacque Jones .30 .09
❑ 45 Jamie Moyer .30 .09
❑ 46 Tim Salmon .50 .15
❑ 47 Kelvim Escobar .30 .09
❑ 48 Tony Batista .30 .09
❑ 49 Nick Johnson .30 .09
❑ 50 Jim Thome .50 .15
❑ 51 Casey Blake .30 .09
❑ 52 Trot Nixon .30 .09
❑ 53 Luis Gonzalez .30 .09
❑ 54 Dontrelle Willis .50 .15
❑ 55 Mike Mussina .50 .15
❑ 56 Carl Crawford .30 .09
❑ 57 Mark Buehrle .30 .09
❑ 58 Scott Podsednik .30 .09
❑ 59 Brian Giles .30 .09
❑ 60 Rafael Furcal .30 .09
❑ 61 Miguel Cabrera .50 .15
❑ 62 Rich Harden .30 .09
❑ 63 Mark Teixeira .50 .15
❑ 64 Frank Thomas .75 .23
❑ 65 Johan Santana .50 .15
❑ 66 Jason Schmidt .30 .09
❑ 67 Aramis Ramirez .30 .09
❑ 68 Jose Reyes .30 .09
❑ 69 Magglio Ordonez .30 .09
❑ 70 Mike Sweeney .30 .09
❑ 71 Eric Chavez .30 .09
❑ 72 Rocco Baldelli .30 .09
❑ 73 Sammy Sosa .75 .23
❑ 74 Javy Lopez .30 .09
❑ 75 Roy Oswalt .30 .09
❑ 76 Raul Ibanez .30 .09
❑ 77 Ivan Rodriguez .50 .15
❑ 78 Jerome Williams .30 .09
❑ 79 Carlos Lee .30 .09
❑ 80 Geoff Jenkins .30 .09
❑ 81 Sean Burroughs .30 .09
❑ 82 Marcus Giles .30 .09
❑ 83 Mike Lowell .30 .09
❑ 84 Barry Zito .30 .09
❑ 85 Aubrey Huff .30 .09
❑ 86 Esteban Loaiza .30 .09
❑ 87 Torii Hunter .30 .09
❑ 88 Phil Nevin .30 .09
❑ 89 Andruw Jones .50 .15
❑ 90 Josh Beckett .30 .09
❑ 91 Mark Mulder .30 .09
❑ 92 Hank Blalock .30 .09
❑ 93 Jason Phillips .30 .09
❑ 94 Russ Ortiz .30 .09
❑ 95 Juan Pierre .30 .09
❑ 96 Tom Glavine .50 .15
❑ 97 Gil Meche .30 .09
❑ 98 Ramon Ortiz .30 .09
❑ 99 Richie Sexson .30 .09
❑ 100 Albert Pujols 1.50 .45
❑ 101 Javier Vazquez .30 .09
❑ 102 Johnny Damon .50 .15
❑ 103 Alex Rodriguez Yanks 1.25 .35
❑ 104 Omar Vizquel .50 .15
❑ 105 Chipper Jones .75 .23
❑ 106 Lance Berkman .30 .09
❑ 107 Tim Hudson .30 .09
❑ 108 Carlos Delgado .30 .09
❑ 109 Austin Kearns .30 .09
❑ 110 Orlando Cabrera .30 .09
❑ 111 Edgar Martinez .50 .15
❑ 112 Melvin Mora .30 .09
❑ 113 Jeff Bagwell .50 .15
❑ 114 Marlon Byrd .30 .09
❑ 115 Vernon Wells .30 .09
❑ 116 C.C. Sabathia .30 .09
❑ 117 Cliff Floyd .30 .09
❑ 118 Ichiro Suzuki 1.50 .45
❑ 119 Miguel Olivo .30 .09
❑ 120 Mike Piazza 1.25 .35
❑ 121 Adam Dunn .30 .09
❑ 122 Paul Lo Duca .30 .09
❑ 123 Brett Myers .30 .09
❑ 124 Michael Young .30 .09
❑ 125 Sidney Ponson .30 .09
❑ 126 Greg Maddux 1.25 .35
❑ 127 Vladimir Guerrero .75 .23
❑ 128 Miguel Tejada .30 .09
❑ 129 Andy Pettitte .50 .15
❑ 130 Rafael Palmeiro .50 .15
❑ 131 Ken Griffey Jr. 1.25 .35
❑ 132 Shannon Stewart .30 .09
❑ 133 Joel Pineiro .30 .09
❑ 134 Luis Matos .30 .09
❑ 135 Jeff Kent .30 .09
❑ 136 Randy Wolf .30 .09
❑ 137 Chris Woodward .30 .09
❑ 138 Jody Gerut .30 .09
❑ 139 Jose Vidro .30 .09
❑ 140 Bret Boone .30 .09
❑ 141 Bill Mueller .30 .09
❑ 142 Angel Berroa .30 .09
❑ 143 Bobby Abreu .30 .09
❑ 144 Roy Halladay .30 .09
❑ 145 Delmon Young .50 .15
❑ 146 Jonny Gomes .30 .09
❑ 147 Rickie Weeks .50 .15
❑ 148 Edwin Jackson .30 .09
❑ 149 Neal Cotts .30 .09
❑ 150 Jason Bay .30 .09
❑ 151 Khalil Greene .75 .23
❑ 152 Joe Mauer .30 .09
❑ 153 Bobby Jenks .30 .09
❑ 154 Chin-Feng Chen .30 .09
❑ 155 Chien-Ming Wang .30 .09
❑ 156 Mickey Hall .30 .09
❑ 157 James Houser .30 .09
❑ 158 Jay Sborz .30 .09
❑ 159 Jonathan Fulton .30 .09
❑ 160 Steven Lerud .30 .09
❑ 161 Grady Sizemore .30 .09
❑ 162 Felix Pie .50 .15
❑ 163 Dustin McGowan .30 .09
❑ 164 Chris Lubanski .30 .09
❑ 165 Tom Gorzelanny .30 .09
❑ 166 Rudy Guillen FY RC .75 .23
❑ 167 Bobby Brownlie FY RC 1.25 .35
❑ 168 Conor Jackson FY RC 3.00 .90
❑ 169 Matt Moses FY RC 1.25 .35
❑ 170 Ervin Santana FY RC 1.50 .45
❑ 171 Merkin Valdez FY RC .50 .15
❑ 172 Erick Aybar FY RC 1.25 .35
❑ 173 Brad Sullivan FY RC .50 .15
❑ 174 David Aardsma FY RC .50 .15
❑ 175 Brad Snyder FY RC 1.25 .35
❑ 176 Alberto Callaspo FY RC .75 .23
❑ 177 Brandon Medders FY RC .40 .12
❑ 178 Zach Miner FY RC .50 .15
❑ 179 Charlie Zink FY RC .30 .09
❑ 180 Adam Greenberg FY RC .75 .23
❑ 181 Kevin Howard FY RC .50 .15
❑ 182 Wanell Severino FY RC .30 .09
❑ 183 Kevin Kouzmanoff FY RC .75 .23
❑ 184 Joel Zumaya FY RC 1.50 .45
❑ 185 Skip Schumaker FY RC .40 .12
❑ 186 Nic Ungs FY RC .40 .12
❑ 187 Todd Self FY RC .50 .15
❑ 188 Brian Steffek FY RC .30 .09
❑ 189 Brock Peterson FY RC .40 .12
❑ 190 Greg Thissen FY RC .40 .12
❑ 191 Frank Brooks FY RC .30 .09
❑ 192 Estee Harris FY RC .50 .15
❑ 193 Chris Mabeus FY RC .40 .12
❑ 194 Dan Giese FY RC .40 .12
❑ 195 Jared Wells FY RC .30 .09
❑ 196 Carlos Sosa FY RC .40 .12
❑ 197 Bobby Madritsch FY .40 .12
❑ 198 Calvin Hayes FY RC .50 .15
❑ 199 Omar Quintanilla FY RC .75 .23
❑ 200 Chris O'Riordan FY RC .40 .12
❑ 201 Tim Hutting FY RC .30 .09
❑ 202 Carlos Quentin FY RC 2.50 .75
❑ 203 Brayan Pena FY RC .40 .12
❑ 204 Jeff Salazar FY RC 1.00 .30
❑ 205 David Murphy FY RC 1.00 .30
❑ 206 Alberto Garcia FY RC .50 .15
❑ 207 Ramon Ramirez FY RC .40 .12
❑ 208 Luis Bolivar FY RC .50 .15
❑ 209 Rodney Choy Foo FY RC .30 .09
❑ 210 Kyle Sleeth FY RC .75 .23
❑ 211 Anthony Acevedo FY RC .40 .12
❑ 212 Chad Santos FY RC .40 .12
❑ 213 Jason Frasor FY RC .40 .12
❑ 214 Jesse Roman FY RC .30 .09
❑ 215 James Tomlin FY RC .40 .12
❑ 216 Josh Labandeira FY RC .40 .12
❑ 217 Joaquin Arias FY RC .75 .23
❑ 218 Don Sutton FY UER RC 1.00 .30
Nick Swisher pictured
❑ 219 Danny Gonzalez FY RC .30 .09
❑ 220 Javier Guzman FY RC .50 .15
❑ 221 Anthony Lerew FY RC .50 .15
❑ 222 Jon Knott FY RC .40 .12
❑ 223 Jesse English FY RC .40 .12
❑ 224 Felix Hernandez FY RC 15.00 4.50
❑ 225 Travis Hanson FY RC .40 .12
❑ 226 Jesse Floyd FY RC .40 .12
❑ 227 Nick Gorneault FY RC .50 .15
❑ 228 Craig Ansman FY RC .40 .12
❑ 229 Wardell Starling FY RC .40 .12
❑ 230 Carl Loadenthal FY RC .50 .15
❑ 231 Dave Crouthers FY RC .30 .09
❑ 232 Harvey Garcia FY RC .30 .09
❑ 233 Casey Kopitzke FY RC .30 .09
❑ 234 Ricky Nolasco FY RC .75 .23
❑ 235 Miguel Perez FY RC .40 .12
❑ 236 Ryan Mulhern FY RC .30 .09
❑ 237 Chris Aguila FY RC .40 .12
❑ 238 Brooks Conrad FY RC .50 .15
❑ 239 Damaso Espino FY RC .30 .09
❑ 240 Jereme Milons FY RC .50 .15
❑ 241 Luke Hughes FY RC .30 .09
❑ 242 Kory Casto FY RC .50 .15
❑ 243 Jose Valdez FY RC .40 .12
❑ 244 J.T. Stotts FY RC .30 .09
❑ 245 Lee Gwaltney FY RC .30 .09
❑ 246 Yoann Torrealba FY RC .30 .09

❑ 247 Omar Falcon FY RC .... .40 .12
❑ 248 Jon Coutlangus FY RC .... .30 .09
❑ 249 George Sherrill FY RC ..... .40 .12
❑ 250 John Santor FY RC .... .30 .09
❑ 251 Tony Richie FY RC .... .40 .12
❑ 252 Kevin Richardson FY RC .. .30 .09
❑ 253 Tim Bittner FY RC .... .40 .12
❑ 254 Dustin Nippert FY RC .... 1.25 .35
❑ 255 Jose Capellan FY RC .... .50 .15
❑ 256 Donald Levinski FY RC .... .30 .09
❑ 257 Jerome Gamble FY RC ..... .30 .09
❑ 258 Jeff Keppinger FY RC ...... .40 .12
❑ 259 Jason Szuminski FY RC .. .30 .09
❑ 260 Akinori Otsuka FY RC ...... .40 .12
❑ 261 Ryan Budde FY RC .... .40 .12
❑ 262 Shingo Takatsu FY RC .... .75 .23
❑ 263 Jeff Allison FY RC .... .40 .12
❑ 264 Hector Gimenez FY RC .... .30 .09
❑ 265 Tim Frend FY RC .... .40 .12
❑ 266 Tom Farmer FY RC .... .40 .12
❑ 267 Shawn Hill FY RC .... .40 .12
❑ 268 Lastings Milledge FY RC 2.00 .60
❑ 269 Scott Proctor FY RC .... .50 .15
❑ 270 Jorge Mejia FY RC .... .40 .12
❑ 271 Terry Jones FY RC .... .50 .15
❑ 272 Zach Duke FY RC 4.00 1.20
❑ 273 Tim Stauffer FY RC .... 1.00 .30
❑ 274 Luke Anderson FY RC ...... .30 .09
❑ 275 Hunter Brown FY RC .... .30 .09
❑ 276 Matt Lemanczyk FY RC .... .40 .12
❑ 277 Fernando Cortez FY RC .... .30 .09
❑ 278 Vince Perkins FY RC .... .50 .15
❑ 279 Tommy Murphy FY RC ..... .40 .12
❑ 280 Mike Gosling FY RC .... .30 .09
❑ 281 Paul Bacot FY RC .... .50 .15
❑ 282 Matt Capps FY RC .... .40 .12
❑ 283 Juan Gutierrez FY RC ...... .40 .12
❑ 284 Teodoro Encarnacion FY RC .50 .15
❑ 285 Juan Cedeno FY RC .... .40 .12
❑ 286 Matt Creighton FY RC ...... .40 .12
❑ 287 Ryan Hankins FY RC .... .30 .09
❑ 288 Leo Nunez FY RC .... .40 .12
❑ 289 Dave Wallace FY RC .... .40 .12
❑ 290 Rob Tejeda FY RC .... .75 .23
❑ 291 Lincoln Holdzkom FY RC .40 .12
❑ 292 Jason Hirsh FY RC .... .75 .23
❑ 293 Tydus Meadows FY RC ..... .40 .12
❑ 294 Khalid Ballouli FY RC ...... .30 .09
❑ 295 Benji DeQuin FY RC .... .30 .09
❑ 296 Tyler Davidson FY RC .... 1.50 .45
❑ 297 Brant Colamarino FY RC .. .75 .23
❑ 298 Marcus McBeth FY RC .... .30 .09
❑ 299 Brad Eldred FY RC .... 2.00 .60
❑ 300 David Pauley FY RC .... .30 .09
❑ 301 Yadier Molina FY RC ...... 1.50 .45
❑ 302 Chris Shelton FY RC ...... 1.50 .45
❑ 303 Travis Blackley FY RC ...... .40 .12
❑ 304 Jon DeVries FY RC .... .40 .12
❑ 305 Sheldon Fulse FY RC .... .30 .09
❑ 306 Vito Chiaravalloti FY RC .. .40 .12
❑ 307 Warner Madrigal FY RC .. .75 .23
❑ 308 Reid Gorecki FY RC .... .40 .12
❑ 309 Sung Jung FY RC .... .30 .09
❑ 310 Pete Shier FY RC .... .30 .09
❑ 311 Michael Mooney FY RC .. .40 .12
❑ 312 Kenny Perez FY RC .... .40 .12
❑ 313 Michael Mallory FY RC ..... .40 .12
❑ 314 Ben Himes FY RC .... .30 .09
❑ 315 Ivan Ochoa FY RC .... .40 .12
❑ 316 Donald Kelly FY RC .... .40 .12
❑ 317 Logan Kensing FY RC ...... .40 .12
❑ 318 Kevin Davidson FY RC .... .30 .09
❑ 319 Brian Pilkington FY RC .... .40 .12
❑ 320 Alex Romero FY RC .... .40 .12
❑ 321 Chad Chop FY RC .... .40 .12
❑ 322 Dioner Navarro FY RC .... 1.50 .45
❑ 323 Casey Myers FY RC .... .30 .09
❑ 324 Mike Rouse FY RC .... .40 .12
❑ 325 Sergio Silva FY RC .... .30 .09
❑ 326 J.J. Furmaniak FY RC ...... .75 .23
❑ 327 Brad Vericker FY RC .... .40 .12
❑ 328 Blake Hawksworth FY RC .50 .15
❑ 329 Brock Jacobsen FY RC .... .30 .09
❑ 330 Alec Zumwalt FY RC .... .30 .09
❑ BW Angel Berroa Bat 15.00 4.50
Dontrelle Willis Jsy ROY

2004 Bowman Draft

	Nm-Mt	Ex-Mt
COMPLETE SET (165)	40.00	12.00
COMMON CARD (1-165)	.30	.09
COMMON RC (1-165)	.30	.09
COMMON RC YR	.30	.09
PLATES ODDS 1:559 HOBBY	.00	
PLATES PRINT RUN 1 SERIAL #'d SET		.00
BLACK-CYAN-MAGENTA-YELLOW EXIST		.00
NO PLATES PRICING DUE TO SCARCITY		.00

❑ 1 Lyle Overbay .... .30 .09
❑ 2 David Newhan .... .30 .09
❑ 3 J.R. House .... .30 .09
❑ 4 Chad Tracy .... .30 .09
❑ 5 Humberto Quintero .... .30 .09
❑ 6 Dave Bush .... .30 .09
❑ 7 Scott Hairston .... .30 .09
❑ 8 Mike Wood .... .30 .09
❑ 9 Alexis Rios .... .30 .09
❑ 10 Sean Burnett .... .30 .09
❑ 11 Wilson Valdez .... .30 .09
❑ 12 Lew Ford .... .30 .09
❑ 13 Freddy Thon RC .... .40 .12
❑ 14 Zack Greinke .... .30 .09
❑ 15 Bucky Jacobsen .... .30 .09
❑ 16 Kevin Youkilis .... .30 .09
❑ 17 Grady Sizemore .... .30 .09
❑ 18 Denny Bautista .... .30 .09
❑ 19 David DeJesus .... .30 .09
❑ 20 Casey Kotchman .... .30 .09
❑ 21 David Kelton .... .30 .09
❑ 22 Charles Thomas RC .... .40 .12
❑ 23 Kazuhito Tadano RC .... .50 .15
❑ 24 Justin Leone RC .... .50 .15
❑ 25 Eduardo Villacis RC .... .40 .12
❑ 26 Brian Dallimore RC .... .30 .09
❑ 27 Nick Green .... .30 .09
❑ 28 Sam McConnell RC .... .40 .12
❑ 29 Brad Halsey RC .... .50 .15
❑ 30 Roman Colon RC .... .30 .09
❑ 31 Josh Fields RC .... 1.25 .35
❑ 32 Cody Bunkelman RC .... .50 .15
❑ 33 Jay Rainville RC .... 1.25 .35
❑ 34 Richie Robnett RC .... 1.00 .30
❑ 35 Jon Poterson RC .... .75 .23
❑ 36 Huston Street RC .... 2.50 .75
❑ 37 Erick San Pedro RC .... .40 .12
❑ 38 Cory Dunlap RC .... 1.25 .35
❑ 39 Kurt Suzuki RC .... 1.25 .35
❑ 40 Anthony Swarzak RC .... .75 .23
❑ 41 Ian Desmond RC .... 1.25 .35
❑ 42 Chris Covington RC .... .50 .15
❑ 43 Christian Garcia RC .... .50 .15
❑ 44 Gaby Hernandez RC .... 1.50 .45
❑ 45 Steven Register RC .... .40 .12
❑ 46 Eduardo Morlan RC .... .75 .23
❑ 47 Collin Balester RC .... .40 .12
❑ 48 Nathan Phillips RC .... .50 .15
❑ 49 Dan Schwartzbauer RC ...... .50 .15
❑ 50 Rafael Gonzalez RC .... .40 .12
❑ 51 K.C. Herren RC .... .75 .23
❑ 52 William Susdorf RC .... .40 .12
❑ 53 Rob Johnson RC .... .50 .15
❑ 54 Louis Marson RC .... .75 .23
❑ 55 Joe Koshansky RC .... 1.00 .30
❑ 56 Jamar Walton RC .... .75 .23
❑ 57 Mark Lowe RC .... .50 .15

❑ 58 Matt Macri RC .... 1.25 .35
❑ 59 Donny Lucy RC .... .40 .12
❑ 60 Mike Ferris RC .... .50 .15
❑ 61 Mike Nickeas RC .... .50 .15
❑ 62 Eric Hurley RC .... .75 .23
❑ 63 Scott Elbert RC .... 1.00 .30
❑ 64 Blake DeWitt RC .... 1.50 .45
❑ 65 Danny Putnam RC .... .75 .23
❑ 66 J.P. Howell RC .... 1.00 .30
❑ 67 John Wiggins RC .... .40 .12
❑ 68 Justin Orenduff RC .... .75 .23
❑ 69 Ray Liotta RC .... 1.25 .35
❑ 70 Billy Buckner RC .... .50 .15
❑ 71 Eric Campbell RC .... 2.00 .60
❑ 72 Olin Wick RC .... .75 .23
❑ 73 Sean Gamble RC .... .50 .15
❑ 74 Seth Smith RC .... 1.00 .30
❑ 75 Wade Davis RC .... .75 .23
❑ 76 Joe Jacobitz RC .... .40 .12
❑ 77 J.A. Happ RC .... .75 .23
❑ 78 Eric Ridener RC .... .40 .12
❑ 79 Matt Tuiasosopo RC .... 3.00 .90
❑ 80 Brad Bergesen RC .... .40 .12
❑ 81 Javy Guerra RC .... .50 .15
❑ 82 Buck Shaw RC .... .50 .15
❑ 83 Paul Janish RC .... .50 .15
❑ 84 Sean Kazmar RC .... .40 .12
❑ 85 Josh Johnson RC .... .50 .15
❑ 86 Angel Salome RC .... 1.25 .35
❑ 87 Jordan Parraz RC .... .75 .23
❑ 88 Kelvin Vazquez RC .... .40 .12
❑ 89 Grant Hansen RC .... .40 .12
❑ 90 Matt Fox RC .... .40 .12
❑ 91 Trevor Plouffe RC .... 1.25 .35
❑ 92 Wes Whisler RC .... .40 .12
❑ 93 Curtis Thigpen RC .... .75 .23
❑ 94 Donnie Smith RC .... .50 .15
❑ 95 Luis Rivera RC .... .50 .15
❑ 96 Jesse Hoover RC .... .50 .15
❑ 97 Jason Vargas RC .... 1.50 .45
❑ 98 Clary Carlsen RC .... .40 .12
❑ 99 Mark Robinson RC .... .40 .12
❑ 100 J.C. Holt RC .... .50 .15
❑ 101 Chad Blackwell RC .... .40 .12
❑ 102 Daryl Jones RC .... 1.00 .30
❑ 103 Jonathan Tierce RC .... .40 .12
❑ 104 Patrick Bryant RC .... .40 .12
❑ 105 Eddie Prasch RC .... .50 .15
❑ 106 Mitch Einertson RC .... 2.50 .75
❑ 107 Kyle Waldrop RC .... 1.00 .30
❑ 108 Jeff Marquez RC .... .50 .15
❑ 109 Zach Jackson RC .... .75 .23
❑ 110 Josh Wahpepah RC .... .40 .12
❑ 111 Adam Lind RC .... 1.25 .35
❑ 112 Kyle Bloom RC .... .50 .15
❑ 113 Ben Harrison RC .... .40 .12
❑ 114 Taylor Tankersley RC .... .75 .23
❑ 115 Steven Jackson RC .... .40 .12
❑ 116 David Purcey RC .... .75 .23
❑ 117 Jacob McGee RC .... .40 .12
❑ 118 Lucas Harrell RC .... .40 .12
❑ 119 Brandon Allen RC .... 1.00 .30
❑ 120 Van Pope RC .... .50 .15
❑ 121 Jeff Francis .... .30 .09
❑ 122 Joe Blanton .... .30 .09
❑ 123 Wil Ledezma .... .30 .09
❑ 124 Bryan Bullington .... .30 .09
❑ 125 Jairo Garcia .... .30 .09
❑ 126 Matt Cain .... 1.00 .30
❑ 127 Arnie Munoz .... .30 .09
❑ 128 Clint Everts .... .30 .09
❑ 129 Jesus Cota .... .30 .09
❑ 130 Gavin Floyd .... .30 .09
❑ 131 Edwin Encarnacion .... .30 .09
❑ 132 Koyie Hill .... .30 .09
❑ 133 Ruben Gotay .... .30 .09
❑ 134 Jeff Mathis .... .30 .09
❑ 135 Andy Marte .... .30 .09
❑ 136 Dallas McPherson .... .30 .09
❑ 137 Justin Morneau .... .30 .09
❑ 138 Rickie Weeks .... .50 .15
❑ 139 Joel Guzman .... .50 .15
❑ 140 Shin Soo Choo .... .30 .09
❑ 141 Yusmeiro Petit RC .... 2.50 .75
❑ 142 Jorge Cortes RC .... .40 .12
❑ 143 Val Majewski .... .30 .09

Card	Nm-Mt	Ex-Mt
❑ 144 Felix Pie	.50	.15
❑ 145 Aaron Hill	.30	.09
❑ 146 Jose Capellan	.30	.09
❑ 147 Dioner Navarro	.75	.23
❑ 148 Fausto Carmona RC	.75	.23
❑ 149 Robinzon Diaz RC	.40	.12
❑ 150 Felix Hernandez	6.00	1.80
❑ 151 Andres Blanco RC	.40	.12
❑ 152 Jason Kubel	.30	.09
❑ 153 Willy Taveras RC	1.25	.35
❑ 154 Merkin Valdez	.50	.15
❑ 155 Robinson Cano	.75	.23
❑ 156 Bill Murphy	.30	.09
❑ 157 Chris Burke	.30	.09
❑ 158 Kyle Sleeth	.50	.15
❑ 159 B.J. Upton	.50	.15
❑ 160 Tim Stauffer	.50	.15
❑ 161 David Wright	1.00	.30
❑ 162 Conor Jackson	1.25	.35
❑ 163 Brad Thompson RC	.75	.23
❑ 164 Delmon Young	.50	.15
❑ 165 Jeremy Reed	.30	.09

2005 Bowman Draft

	Nm-Mt	Ex-Mt
COMPLETE SET (165)	40.00	12.00
COMMON CARD (1-165)	.30	.09
COMMON RC	.30	.09
COMMON RC YR	.30	.09
OVERALL PLATE ODDS 1:826 HOBBY		.00
PLATE PRINT RUN 1 SET PER COLOR		.00
BLACK-CYAN-MAGENTA-YELLOW ISSUED		.00
NO PLATE PRICING DUE TO SCARCITY		.00

Card	Nm-Mt	Ex-Mt
❑ 1 Rickie Weeks	.30	.09
❑ 2 Kyle Davies	.30	.09
❑ 3 Garrett Atkins	.30	.09
❑ 4 Chien-Ming Wang	.75	.23
❑ 5 Dallas McPherson	.30	.09
❑ 6 Dan Johnson	.30	.09
❑ 7 Andy Sisco	.30	.09
❑ 8 Ryan Doumit	.30	.09
❑ 9 J.P. Howell	.30	.09
❑ 10 Tim Stauffer	.30	.09
❑ 11 Willy Taveras	.30	.09
❑ 12 Aaron Hill	.30	.09
❑ 13 Victor Diaz	.30	.09
❑ 14 Wilson Betemit	.30	.09
❑ 15 Ervin Santana	.30	.09
❑ 16 Mike Morse	.50	.15
❑ 17 Yadier Molina	.30	.09
❑ 18 Kelly Johnson	.30	.09
❑ 19 Clint Barmes	.30	.09
❑ 20 Robinson Cano	.50	.15
❑ 21 Brad Thompson	.30	.09
❑ 22 Jorge Cantu	.30	.09
❑ 23 Brad Halsey	.30	.09
❑ 24 Lance Niekro	.30	.09
❑ 25 D.J. Houlton	.30	.09
❑ 26 Ryan Church	.30	.09
❑ 27 Hayden Penn	.30	.09
❑ 28 Chris Young	.30	.09
❑ 29 Chad Orvella RC	.30	.09
❑ 30 Mark Teahen	.30	.09
❑ 31 Mark McCormick FY RC	.50	.15
❑ 32 Jay Bruce FY RC	2.00	.60
❑ 33 Beau Jones FY RC	.75	.23
❑ 34 Tyler Greene FY RC	.75	.23
❑ 35 Zach Ward FY RC	.30	.09
❑ 36 Josh Bell FY RC	.75	.23
❑ 37 Josh Wall FY RC	.50	.15
❑ 38 Nick Webber FY RC	.50	.15
❑ 39 Travis Buck FY RC	.75	.23
❑ 40 Kyle Winters FY RC	.30	.09
❑ 41 Mitch Boggs FY RC	.30	.09
❑ 42 Tommy Mendoza FY RC	.50	.15
❑ 43 Brad Corley FY RC	.50	.15
❑ 44 Drew Butera FY RC	.30	.09
❑ 45 Ryan Mount FY RC	.75	.23
❑ 46 Tyler Herron FY RC	.50	.15
❑ 47 Nick Weglarz FY RC	.75	.23
❑ 48 Brandon Erbe FY RC	1.00	.30
❑ 49 Cody Allen FY RC	.30	.09
❑ 50 Eric Fowler FY RC	.30	.09
❑ 51 James Boone FY RC	.50	.15
❑ 52 Josh Flores FY RC	.75	.23
❑ 53 Brandon Monk FY RC	.50	.15
❑ 54 Kieron Pope FY RC	.75	.23
❑ 55 Kyle Cofield FY RC	.30	.09
❑ 56 Brent Lillibridge FY RC	.30	.09
❑ 57 Daryl Jones FY	.30	.09
❑ 58 Eli Iorg FY RC	.75	.23
❑ 59 Brett Hayes FY RC	.30	.09
❑ 60 Mike Durant FY RC	1.00	.30
❑ 61 Michael Bowden FY RC	.75	.23
❑ 62 Paul Kelly FY RC	.50	.15
❑ 63 Andrew McCutchen FY RC	2.00	.60
❑ 64 Travis Wood FY RC	1.00	.30
❑ 65 Cesar Ramos FY RC	.50	.15
❑ 66 Chaz Roe FY RC	.50	.15
❑ 67 Matt Torra FY RC	.50	.15
❑ 68 Kevin Slowey FY RC	.50	.15
❑ 69 Trayvon Robinson FY RC	.50	.15
❑ 70 Reid Engel FY RC	.30	.09
❑ 71 Kris Harvey FY RC	.50	.15
❑ 72 Craig Italiano FY RC	.75	.23
❑ 73 Matt Maloney FY RC	.50	.15
❑ 74 Sean West FY RC	.75	.23
❑ 75 Henry Sanchez FY RC	.75	.23
❑ 76 Scott Blue FY RC	.30	.09
❑ 77 Jordan Schafer FY RC	.50	.15
❑ 78 Chris Robinson FY RC	.50	.15
❑ 79 Chris Hobdy FY RC	.30	.09
❑ 80 Brandon Durden FY RC	.30	.09
❑ 81 Clay Buchholz FY RC	.50	.15
❑ 82 Josh Geer FY RC	.30	.09
❑ 83 Sam LeCure FY RC	.30	.09
❑ 84 Justin Thomas FY RC	.30	.09
❑ 85 Brett Gardner FY RC	.50	.15
❑ 86 Tommy Manzella FY RC	.30	.09
❑ 87 Matt Green FY RC	.30	.09
❑ 88 Yunel Escobar FY RC	1.00	.30
❑ 89 Mike Costanzo FY RC	.75	.23
❑ 90 Nick Hundley FY RC	.30	.09
❑ 91 Zach Simons FY RC	.30	.09
❑ 92 Jacob Marceaux FY RC	.30	.09
❑ 93 Jed Lowrie FY RC	.75	.23
❑ 94 Brandon Snyder FY RC	1.25	.35
❑ 95 Matt Goyen FY RC	.30	.09
❑ 96 Jon Egan FY RC	.50	.15
❑ 97 Drew Thompson FY RC	.50	.15
❑ 98 Bryan Anderson FY RC	.75	.23
❑ 99 Clayton Richard FY RC	.30	.09
❑ 100 Jimmy Shull FY RC	.50	.15
❑ 101 Mark Pawelek FY RC	2.00	.60
❑ 102 P.J. Phillips FY RC	.75	.23
❑ 103 John Drennen FY RC	.75	.23
❑ 104 Nolan Reimold FY RC	1.25	.35
❑ 105 Troy Tulowitzki FY RC	1.50	.45
❑ 106 Kevin Whelan FY RC	.30	.09
❑ 107 Wade Townsend FY RC	.50	.15
❑ 108 Micah Owings FY RC	.50	.15
❑ 109 Ryan Tucker FY RC	.50	.15
❑ 110 Jeff Clement FY RC	2.50	.75
❑ 111 Josh Sullivan FY RC	.30	.09
❑ 112 Jeff Lyman FY RC	.50	.15
❑ 113 Brian Bogusevic FY RC	.30	.09
❑ 114 Trevor Bell FY RC	.75	.23
❑ 115 Brent Cox FY RC	.50	.15
❑ 116 Michael Billek FY RC	.30	.09
❑ 117 Garrett Olson FY RC	.75	.23
❑ 118 Steven Johnson FY RC	.30	.09
❑ 119 Chase Headley FY RC	.50	.15
❑ 120 Daniel Carte FY RC	.75	.23
❑ 121 Francisco Liriano PROS	.50	.15
❑ 122 Fausto Carmona PROS	.30	.09
❑ 123 Zach Jackson PROS	.30	.09
❑ 124 Adam Loewen PROS	.30	.09
❑ 125 Chris Lambert PROS	.30	.09
❑ 126 Scott Mathieson FY	.30	.09
❑ 127 Paul Maholm PROS	.30	.09
❑ 128 Fernando Nieve PROS	.30	.09
❑ 129 Justin Verlander FY	.50	.15
❑ 130 Yusmeiro Petit PROS	.50	.15
❑ 131 Joel Zumaya PROS	.30	.09
❑ 132 Merkin Valdez PROS	.30	.09
❑ 133 Ryan Garko FY	.30	.09
❑ 134 Edison Volquez FY RC	.75	.23
❑ 135 Russ Martin FY	.30	.09
❑ 136 Conor Jackson PROS	.30	.09
❑ 137 Miguel Montero FY RC	1.00	.30
❑ 138 Josh Barfield PROS	.30	.09
❑ 139 Delmon Young PROS	.50	.15
❑ 140 Andy LaRoche FY	.75	.23
❑ 141 William Bergolla PROS	.30	.09
❑ 142 B.J. Upton PROS	.30	.09
❑ 143 Hernan Iribarren FY	.30	.09
❑ 144 Brandon Wood PROS	.75	.23
❑ 145 Jose Bautista PROS	.30	.09
❑ 146 Edwin Encarnacion PROS	.30	.09
❑ 147 Javier Herrera FY RC	.75	.23
❑ 148 Jeremy Hermida PROS	.50	.15
❑ 149 Frank Diaz PROS RC	.30	.09
❑ 150 Chris B.Young FY	.75	.23
❑ 151 Shin-Soo Choo PROS	.30	.09
❑ 152 Kevin Thompson PROS RC	.30	.09
❑ 153 Hanley Ramirez PROS	.50	.15
❑ 154 Lastings Milledge PROS	.30	.09
❑ 155 Luis Montanez PROS	.30	.09
❑ 156 Justin Huber PROS	.30	.09
❑ 157 Zach Duke PROS	.50	.15
❑ 158 Jeff Francoeur PROS	.75	.23
❑ 159 Melky Cabrera FY	.30	.09
❑ 160 Bobby Jenks PROS	.30	.09
❑ 161 Ian Snell PROS	.30	.09
❑ 162 Fernando Cabrera PROS	.30	.09
❑ 163 Troy Patton PROS	.50	.15
❑ 164 Anthony Lerew PROS	.30	.09
❑ 165 Nelson Cruz FY RC	.50	.15

2005 Bowman

	Nm-Mt	Ex-Mt
COMPLETE SET (330)	80.00	24.00
COMMON CARD (1-140)	.30	.09
COMMON CARD (141-165)	.40	.12
COMMON CARD (166-330)	.40	.12
PLATE ODDS 1:695 HOBBY, 1:177 HTA		.00
PLATE PRINT RUN 1 SET PER COLOR		.00
BLACK-CYAN-MAGENTA-YELLOW ISSUED		.00
NO PLATE PRICING DUE TO SCARCITY		.00
ROY ODDS 1:668 H, 1:248 HTA, 1:1535 R		.00

Card	Nm-Mt	Ex-Mt
❑ 1 Gavin Floyd	.30	.09
❑ 2 Eric Chavez	.30	.09
❑ 3 Miguel Tejada	.30	.09
❑ 4 Dmitri Young	.30	.09
❑ 5 Hank Blalock	.30	.09
❑ 6 Kerry Wood	.30	.09
❑ 7 Andy Pettitte	.50	.15
❑ 8 Pat Burrell	.30	.09
❑ 9 Johnny Estrada	.30	.09
❑ 10 Frank Thomas	.75	.23

❑ 11 Juan Pierre .30 .09
❑ 12 Tom Glavine .50 .15
❑ 13 Lyle Overbay .30 .09
❑ 14 Jim Edmonds .50 .15
❑ 15 Steve Finley .30 .09
❑ 16 Jermaine Dye .30 .09
❑ 17 Omar Vizquel .50 .15
❑ 18 Nick Johnson .30 .09
❑ 19 Brian Giles .30 .09
❑ 20 Justin Morneau .30 .09
❑ 21 Preston Wilson .30 .09
❑ 22 Wily Mo Pena .30 .09
❑ 23 Rafael Palmeiro .50 .15
❑ 24 Scott Kazmir .30 .09
❑ 25 Derek Jeter 1.50 .45
❑ 26 Barry Zito .30 .09
❑ 27 Mike Lowell .30 .09
❑ 28 Jason Bay .30 .09
❑ 29 Ken Harvey .30 .09
❑ 30 Nomar Garciaparra .75 .23
❑ 31 Roy Halladay .30 .09
❑ 32 Todd Helton .50 .15
❑ 33 Mark Kotsay .30 .09
❑ 34 Jake Peavy .30 .09
❑ 35 David Wright 1.25 .35
❑ 36 Dontrelle Willis .30 .09
❑ 37 Marcus Giles .30 .09
❑ 38 Chone Figgins .30 .09
❑ 39 Sidney Ponson .30 .09
❑ 40 Randy Johnson .75 .23
❑ 41 John Smoltz .50 .15
❑ 42 Kevin Millar .30 .09
❑ 43 Mark Teixeira .50 .15
❑ 44 Alex Rios .30 .09
❑ 45 Mike Piazza .75 .23
❑ 46 Victor Martinez .30 .09
❑ 47 Jeff Bagwell .50 .15
❑ 48 Shawn Green .30 .09
❑ 49 Ivan Rodriguez .50 .15
❑ 50 Alex Rodriguez 1.25 .35
❑ 51 Kazuo Matsui .30 .09
❑ 52 Mark Mulder .30 .09
❑ 53 Michael Young .30 .09
❑ 54 Javy Lopez .30 .09
❑ 55 Johnny Damon .50 .15
❑ 56 Jeff Francis .30 .09
❑ 57 Rich Harden .30 .09
❑ 58 Bobby Abreu .30 .09
❑ 59 Mark Loretta .30 .09
❑ 60 Gary Sheffield .30 .09
❑ 61 Jamie Moyer .30 .09
❑ 62 Garret Anderson .30 .09
❑ 63 Vernon Wells .30 .09
❑ 64 Orlando Cabrera .30 .09
❑ 65 Magglio Ordonez .30 .09
❑ 66 Ronnie Belliard .30 .09
❑ 67 Carlos Lee .30 .09
❑ 68 Carl Pavano .30 .09
❑ 69 Jon Lieber .30 .09
❑ 70 Aubrey Huff .30 .09
❑ 71 Rocco Baldelli .30 .09
❑ 72 Jason Schmidt .30 .09
❑ 73 Bernie Williams .50 .15
❑ 74 Hideki Matsui 1.50 .45
❑ 75 Ken Griffey Jr. 1.25 .35
❑ 76 Josh Beckett .30 .09
❑ 77 Mark Buehrle .30 .09
❑ 78 David Ortiz .75 .23
❑ 79 Luis Gonzalez .30 .09
❑ 80 Scott Rolen .50 .15
❑ 81 Joe Mauer .30 .09
❑ 82 Jose Reyes .30 .09
❑ 83 Adam Dunn .30 .09
❑ 84 Greg Maddux 1.25 .35
❑ 85 Bartolo Colon .30 .09
❑ 86 Bret Boone .30 .09
❑ 87 Mike Mussina .50 .15
❑ 88 Ben Sheets .30 .09
❑ 89 Lance Berkman .30 .09
❑ 90 Miguel Cabrera .50 .15
❑ 91 C.C. Sabathia .30 .09
❑ 92 Mike Maroth .30 .09
❑ 93 Andruw Jones .50 .15
❑ 94 Jack Wilson .30 .09
❑ 95 Ichiro Suzuki 1.50 .45
❑ 96 Geoff Jenkins .30 .09
❑ 97 Zack Greinke .30 .09
❑ 98 Jorge Posada .50 .15
❑ 99 Travis Hafner .30 .09
❑ 100 Barry Bonds 2.00 .60
❑ 101 Aaron Rowand .30 .09
❑ 102 Aramis Ramirez .30 .09
❑ 103 Curt Schilling .50 .15
❑ 104 Melvin Mora .30 .09
❑ 105 Albert Pujols 1.50 .45
❑ 106 Austin Kearns .30 .09
❑ 107 Shannon Stewart .30 .09
❑ 108 Carl Crawford .30 .09
❑ 109 Carlos Zambrano .30 .09
❑ 110 Roger Clemens 1.25 .35
❑ 111 Javier Vazquez .30 .09
❑ 112 Randy Wolf .30 .09
❑ 113 Chipper Jones .75 .23
❑ 114 Larry Walker .50 .15
❑ 115 Alfonso Soriano .30 .09
❑ 116 Brad Wilkerson .30 .09
❑ 117 Bobby Crosby .30 .09
❑ 118 Jim Thome .50 .15
❑ 119 Oliver Perez .30 .09
❑ 120 Vladimir Guerrero .75 .23
❑ 121 Roy Oswalt .30 .09
❑ 122 Torii Hunter .30 .09
❑ 123 Rafael Furcal .30 .09
❑ 124 Luis Castillo .30 .09
❑ 125 Carlos Beltran .30 .09
❑ 126 Mike Sweeney .30 .09
❑ 127 Johan Santana .50 .15
❑ 128 Tim Hudson .30 .09
❑ 129 Troy Glaus .30 .09
❑ 130 Manny Ramirez .50 .15
❑ 131 Jeff Kent .30 .09
❑ 132 Jose Vidro .30 .09
❑ 133 Edgar Renteria .30 .09
❑ 134 Russ Ortiz .30 .09
❑ 135 Sammy Sosa .75 .23
❑ 136 Carlos Delgado .30 .09
❑ 137 Richie Sexson .30 .09
❑ 138 Pedro Martinez .50 .15
❑ 139 Adrian Beltre .30 .09
❑ 140 Mark Prior .50 .15
❑ 141 Omar Quintanilla .40 .12
❑ 142 Carlos Quentin .50 .15
❑ 143 Dan Johnson .75 .23
❑ 144 Jake Stevens .40 .12
❑ 145 Nate Schierholtz .50 .15
❑ 146 Neil Walker .40 .12
❑ 147 Bill Bray .40 .12
❑ 148 Taylor Tankersley .40 .12
❑ 149 Trevor Plouffe .50 .15
❑ 150 Felix Hernandez 2.00 .60
❑ 151 Philip Hughes .40 .12
❑ 152 James Houser UER .40 .12
Facsimile Signature is J.R. House
❑ 153 David Murphy .40 .12
❑ 154 Ervin Santana UER .40 .12
Card has Johan Santana's facsimile autograph
❑ 155 Anthony Whittington .40 .12
❑ 156 Chris Lambert .40 .12
❑ 157 Jeremy Sowers .50 .15
❑ 158 Giovanny Gonzalez .40 .12
❑ 159 Blake DeWitt .50 .15
❑ 160 Thomas Diamond .50 .15
❑ 161 Greg Golson .40 .12
❑ 162 David Aardsma .40 .12
❑ 163 Paul Maholm .40 .12
❑ 164 Mark Rogers .50 .15
❑ 165 Homer Bailey .50 .15
❑ 166 Chip Cannon FY RC .75 .23
❑ 167 Tony Giarratano FY RC .50 .15
❑ 168 Darren Fenster FY RC .50 .15
❑ 169 Elvys Quezada FY RC .50 .15
❑ 170 Glen Perkins FY RC 1.00 .30
❑ 171 Ian Kinsler FY RC 1.25 .35
❑ 172 Mike Bourn FY RC 1.00 .30
❑ 173 Jeremy West FY RC .75 .23
❑ 174 Justin Verlander FY RC 2.00 .60
❑ 175 Kevin West FY RC .50 .15
❑ 176 Luis Hernandez FY RC .50 .15
❑ 177 Matt Campbell FY RC .50 .15
❑ 178 Nate McLouth FY RC .75 .23
❑ 179 Ryan Goleski FY RC .75 .23
❑ 180 Matthew Lindstrom FY RC .50 .15
❑ 181 Matt DeSalvo FY RC .75 .23
❑ 182 Kole Strayhorn FY RC .50 .15
❑ 183 Jose Vaquedano FY RC .50 .15
❑ 184 James Jurries FY RC .75 .23
❑ 185 Ian Bladergroen FY RC .75 .23
❑ 186 Eric Nielsen FY RC .50 .15
❑ 187 Chris Vines FY RC .50 .15
❑ 188 Chris Denorfia FY RC .75 .23
❑ 189 Kevin Melillo FY RC 1.00 .30
❑ 190 Melky Cabrera FY RC 1.25 .35
❑ 191 Ryan Sweeney FY RC 1.25 .35
❑ 192 Sean Marshall FY RC .75 .23
❑ 193 Andy LaRoche FY RC 4.00 1.20
❑ 194 Tyler Pelland FY RC .75 .23
❑ 195 Mike Morse FY RC 1.00 .30
❑ 196 Wes Swackhamer FY RC .50 .15
❑ 197 Wade Robinson FY RC .50 .15
❑ 198 Dan Santin FY RC .50 .15
❑ 199 Steve Doetsch FY RC .75 .23
❑ 200 Shane Costa FY RC .50 .15
❑ 201 Scott Mathieson FY RC 1.00 .30
❑ 202 Ben Jones FY RC 1.00 .30
❑ 203 Michael Rogers FY RC .50 .15
❑ 204 Matt Rogelstad FY RC .50 .15
❑ 205 Luis Ramirez FY RC .50 .15
❑ 206 Landon Powell FY RC .75 .23
❑ 207 Erik Cordier FY RC .50 .15
❑ 208 Chris Seddon FY RC .50 .15
❑ 209 Chris Roberson FY RC .50 .15
❑ 210 Thomas Oldham FY RC .50 .15
❑ 211 Dana Eveland FY RC .50 .15
❑ 212 Cody Haerther FY RC .50 .15
❑ 213 Danny Core FY RC .50 .15
❑ 214 Craig Tatum FY RC .50 .15
❑ 215 Elliot Johnson FY RC .50 .15
❑ 216 Ender Chavez FY RC .50 .15
❑ 217 Errol Simonitsch FY RC .75 .23
❑ 218 Matt Van Der Bosch FY RC .50 .15
❑ 219 Eulogio de la Cruz FY RC .50 .15
❑ 220 C.J. Smith FY RC .50 .15
❑ 221 Adam Boeve FY RC .50 .15
❑ 222 Adam Harben FY RC .75 .23
❑ 223 Baltazar Lopez FY RC .50 .15
❑ 224 Russ Martin FY RC 1.00 .30
❑ 225 Brian Bannister FY RC .50 .15
❑ 226 Brian Miller FY RC .50 .15
❑ 227 Casey McGehee FY RC .50 .15
❑ 228 Humberto Sanchez FY RC .50 .15
❑ 229 Javon Moran FY RC .50 .15
❑ 230 Brandon McCarthy FY RC 1.50 .45
❑ 231 Danny Zell FY RC .50 .15
❑ 232 Jake Postlewait FY RC .50 .15
❑ 233 Juan Tejeda FY RC .50 .15
❑ 234 Keith Ramsey FY RC .50 .15
❑ 235 Lorenzo Scott FY RC .50 .15
❑ 236 Wladimir Balentien FY RC 1.25 .35
❑ 237 Martin Prado FY RC .50 .15
❑ 238 Matt Albers FY RC .50 .15
❑ 239 Brian Schweiger FY RC .50 .15
❑ 240 Brian Stavisky FY RC .50 .15
❑ 241 Pat Misch FY RC .50 .15
❑ 242 Pat Osborn FY .40 .12
❑ 243 Ryan Feierabend FY RC .50 .15
❑ 244 Shaun Marcum FY .40 .12
❑ 245 Kevin Collins FY RC .50 .15
❑ 246 Stuart Pomeranz FY RC .50 .15
❑ 247 Tetsu Yofu FY RC .50 .15
❑ 248 Hernan Iribarren FY RC 1.00 .30
❑ 249 Mike Spidale FY RC .50 .15
❑ 250 Tony Arnerich FY RC .50 .15
❑ 251 Manny Parra FY RC .50 .15
❑ 252 Drew Anderson FY RC .50 .15
❑ 253 T.J. Beam FY RC 1.00 .30
❑ 254 Pedro Lopez FY RC .50 .15
❑ 255 Andy Sides FY RC .50 .15
❑ 256 Bear Bay FY RC .75 .23
❑ 257 Bill McCarthy FY RC .50 .15
❑ 258 Daniel Haigwood FY RC 1.25 .35
❑ 259 Brian Sprout FY RC 1.00 .30
❑ 260 Bryan Triplett FY RC .50 .15
❑ 261 Steven Bondurant FY RC .50 .15
❑ 262 Darwinson Salazar FY RC .50 .15
❑ 263 David Shepard FY RC .50 .15
❑ 264 Johan Silva FY RC .50 .15
❑ 265 J.B. Thurmond FY RC .50 .15

- ❑ 266 Brandon Moorhead FY RC .50 .15
- ❑ 267 Kyle Nichols FY RC .75 .23
- ❑ 268 Jonathan Sanchez FY RC .50 .15
- ❑ 269 Mike Esposito FY RC .50 .15
- ❑ 270 Erik Schindewolf FY RC .50 .15
- ❑ 271 Peeter Ramos FY RC .50 .15
- ❑ 272 Juan Senreiso FY RC .50 .15
- ❑ 273 Matthew Kemp FY RC 2.00 .60
- ❑ 274 Vinny Rottino FY RC .50 .15
- ❑ 275 Micah Furtado FY RC .50 .15
- ❑ 276 George Kottaras FY RC 1.00 .30
- ❑ 277 Billy Butler FY RC 3.00 .90
- ❑ 278 Buck Coats FY RC .50 .15
- ❑ 279 Kenny Durost FY RC .50 .15
- ❑ 280 Nick Touchstone FY RC .50 .15
- ❑ 281 Jerry Owens FY RC .75 .23
- ❑ 282 Stefan Bailie FY RC .50 .15
- ❑ 283 Jesse Gutierrez FY RC .50 .15
- ❑ 284 Chuck Tiffany FY RC 1.25 .35
- ❑ 285 Brendan Ryan FY RC .50 .15
- ❑ 286 Hayden Penn FY RC .75 .23
- ❑ 287 Shawn Bowman FY RC .75 .23
- ❑ 288 Alexander Smit FY RC .50 .15
- ❑ 289 Micah Schnurstein FY RC .50 .15
- ❑ 290 Jared Gothreaux FY RC .50 .15
- ❑ 291 Jair Jurrjens FY RC .75 .23
- ❑ 292 Bobby Livingston FY RC .50 .15
- ❑ 293 Ryan Speier FY RC .50 .15
- ❑ 294 Zach Parker FY RC .50 .15
- ❑ 295 Christian Colonel FY RC .50 .15
- ❑ 296 Scott Mitchinson FY RC .50 .15
- ❑ 297 Neil Wilson FY RC .50 .15
- ❑ 298 Chuck James FY RC 2.50 .75
- ❑ 299 Heath Totten FY RC .50 .15
- ❑ 300 Sean Tracey FY RC .50 .15
- ❑ 301 Ismael Ramirez FY RC .50 .15
- ❑ 302 Matt Brown FY RC .50 .15
- ❑ 303 Franklin Morales FY RC .50 .15
- ❑ 304 Brandon Sing FY RC 1.00 .30
- ❑ 305 D.J. Houlton FY RC .50 .15
- ❑ 306 Jayce Tingler FY RC .50 .15
- ❑ 307 Mitchell Arnold FY RC .50 .15
- ❑ 308 Jim Burt FY RC .50 .15
- ❑ 309 Jason Motte FY RC .50 .15
- ❑ 310 David Gassner FY RC .50 .15
- ❑ 311 Andy Santana FY RC UER .50 .15
  Spelled Santan
- ❑ 312 Kelvin Pichardo FY RC .50 .15
- ❑ 313 Carlos Carrasco FY RC .75 .23
- ❑ 314 Willy Mota FY RC .50 .15
- ❑ 315 Frank Mata FY RC .50 .15
- ❑ 316 Carlos Gonzalez FY RC 3.00 .90
- ❑ 317 Jeff Niemann FY RC 1.25 .35
- ❑ 318 Chris B.Young FY RC 2.00 .60
- ❑ 319 Billy Sadler FY RC .50 .15
- ❑ 320 Ricky Barrett FY RC .50 .15
- ❑ 321 Ben Harrison FY .40 .12
- ❑ 322 Steve Nelson FY RC .50 .15
- ❑ 323 Daryl Thompson FY RC .50 .15
- ❑ 324 Philip Humber FY RC 1.25 .35
- ❑ 325 Jeremy Harts FY RC .50 .15
- ❑ 326 Nick Masset FY RC .50 .15
- ❑ 327 Mike Rodriguez FY RC .50 .15
- ❑ 328 Mike Garber FY RC .50 .15
- ❑ 329 Kennard Bibbs FY RC .50 .15
- ❑ 330 Ryan Garko FY RC 1.50 .45
- ❑ BC Jason Bay Bat 15.00 4.50
  Bobby Crosby Bat ROY

1997 Bowman Chrome

	Nm-Mt	Ex-Mt
COMPLETE SET (300)	180.00	55.00

- ❑ 1 Derek Jeter 3.00 .90
- ❑ 2 Chipper Jones 1.25 .35
- ❑ 3 Hideo Nomo 1.25 .35
- ❑ 4 Tim Salmon .75 .23
- ❑ 5 Robin Ventura .50 .15
- ❑ 6 Tony Clark .50 .15
- ❑ 7 Barry Larkin .75 .23
- ❑ 8 Paul Molitor .75 .23
- ❑ 9 Andy Benes .50 .15
- ❑ 10 Ryan Klesko .50 .15
- ❑ 11 Mark McGwire 3.00 .90
- ❑ 12 Ken Griffey Jr. 2.00 .60

- ❑ 13 Robb Nen .50 .15
- ❑ 14 Cal Ripken 4.00 1.20
- ❑ 15 John Valentin .50 .15
- ❑ 16 Ricky Bottalico .50 .15
- ❑ 17 Mike Lansing .50 .15
- ❑ 18 Ryne Sandberg 2.00 .60
- ❑ 19 Carlos Delgado .50 .15
- ❑ 20 Craig Biggio .75 .23
- ❑ 21 Eric Karros .50 .15
- ❑ 22 Kevin Appier .50 .15
- ❑ 23 Mariano Rivera .75 .23
- ❑ 24 Vinny Castilla .50 .15
- ❑ 25 Juan Gonzalez .50 .15
- ❑ 26 Al Martin .50 .15
- ❑ 27 Jeff Cirillo .50 .15
- ❑ 28 Ray Lankford .50 .15
- ❑ 29 Manny Ramirez .75 .23
- ❑ 30 Roberto Alomar .75 .23
- ❑ 31 Will Clark .75 .23
- ❑ 32 Chuck Knoblauch .50 .15
- ❑ 33 Harold Baines .50 .15
- ❑ 34 Edgar Martinez .75 .23
- ❑ 35 Mike Mussina .75 .23
- ❑ 36 Kevin Brown .50 .15
- ❑ 37 Dennis Eckersley .50 .15
- ❑ 38 Tino Martinez .75 .23
- ❑ 39 Raul Mondesi .50 .15
- ❑ 40 Sammy Sosa 1.25 .35
- ❑ 41 John Smoltz .75 .23
- ❑ 42 Billy Wagner .50 .15
- ❑ 43 Ken Caminiti .50 .15
- ❑ 44 Wade Boggs .75 .23
- ❑ 45 Andres Galarraga .50 .15
- ❑ 46 Roger Clemens 2.50 .75
- ❑ 47 Matt Williams .50 .15
- ❑ 48 Albert Belle .50 .15
- ❑ 49 Jeff King .50 .15
- ❑ 50 John Wetteland .50 .15
- ❑ 51 Deion Sanders .75 .23
- ❑ 52 Ellis Burks .50 .15
- ❑ 53 Pedro Martinez .75 .23
- ❑ 54 Kenny Lofton .50 .15
- ❑ 55 Randy Johnson 1.25 .35
- ❑ 56 Bernie Williams .75 .23
- ❑ 57 Marquis Grissom .50 .15
- ❑ 58 Gary Sheffield .50 .15
- ❑ 59 Curt Schilling .50 .15
- ❑ 60 Reggie Sanders .50 .15
- ❑ 61 Bobby Higginson .50 .15
- ❑ 62 Moises Alou .50 .15
- ❑ 63 Tom Glavine .75 .23
- ❑ 64 Mark Grace .75 .23
- ❑ 65 Rafael Palmeiro .75 .23
- ❑ 66 John Olerud .50 .15
- ❑ 67 Dante Bichette .50 .15
- ❑ 68 Jeff Bagwell .75 .23
- ❑ 69 Barry Bonds 3.00 .90
- ❑ 70 Pat Hentgen .50 .15
- ❑ 71 Jim Thome .75 .23
- ❑ 72 Andy Pettitte .75 .23
- ❑ 73 Jay Bell .50 .15
- ❑ 74 Jim Edmonds .50 .15
- ❑ 75 Ron Gant .50 .15
- ❑ 76 David Cone .50 .15
- ❑ 77 Jose Canseco .75 .23
- ❑ 78 Jay Buhner .50 .15
- ❑ 79 Greg Maddux 2.00 .60
- ❑ 80 Lance Johnson .50 .15
- ❑ 81 Travis Fryman .50 .15
- ❑ 82 Paul O'Neill .75 .23
- ❑ 83 Ivan Rodriguez .75 .23
- ❑ 84 Fred McGriff .75 .23
- ❑ 85 Mike Piazza 2.00 .60
- ❑ 86 Brady Anderson .50 .15
- ❑ 87 Marty Cordova .50 .15
- ❑ 88 Joe Carter .50 .15
- ❑ 89 Brian Jordan .50 .15
- ❑ 90 David Justice .50 .15
- ❑ 91 Tony Gwynn 1.50 .45
- ❑ 92 Larry Walker .50 .15
- ❑ 93 Mo Vaughn .50 .15
- ❑ 94 Sandy Alomar Jr. .50 .15
- ❑ 95 Rusty Greer .50 .15
- ❑ 96 Roberto Hernandez .50 .15
- ❑ 97 Hal Morris .50 .15
- ❑ 98 Todd Hundley .50 .15
- ❑ 99 Rondell White .50 .15
- ❑ 100 Frank Thomas 1.25 .35
- ❑ 101 Bubba Trammell RC 1.50 .45
- ❑ 102 Sidney Ponson RC 2.50 .75
- ❑ 103 Ricky Ledee RC 1.50 .45
- ❑ 104 Brett Tomko .50 .15
- ❑ 105 Braden Looper RC 1.00 .30
- ❑ 106 Jason Dickson .50 .15
- ❑ 107 Chad Green RC 1.00 .30
- ❑ 108 R.A. Dickey RC 1.00 .30
- ❑ 109 Jeff Liefer .50 .15
- ❑ 110 Richard Hidalgo .50 .15
- ❑ 111 Chad Hermansen RC 1.50 .45
- ❑ 112 Felix Martinez .50 .15
- ❑ 113 J.J. Johnson .50 .15
- ❑ 114 Todd Dunwoody .50 .15
- ❑ 115 Katsuhiro Maeda .50 .15
- ❑ 116 Darin Erstad .50 .15
- ❑ 117 Elieser Marrero .50 .15
- ❑ 118 Bartolo Colon .50 .15
- ❑ 119 Ugueth Urbina .50 .15
- ❑ 120 Jaime Bluma .50 .15
- ❑ 121 Seth Greisinger RC 1.00 .30
- ❑ 122 Jose Cruz Jr. RC 2.50 .75
- ❑ 123 Todd Dunn .50 .15
- ❑ 124 Justin Towle RC 1.00 .30
- ❑ 125 Brian Rose .50 .15
- ❑ 126 Jose Guillen .50 .15
- ❑ 127 Andruw Jones .75 .23
- ❑ 128 Mark Kotsay RC 4.00 1.20
- ❑ 129 Wilton Guerrero .50 .15
- ❑ 130 Jacob Cruz .50 .15
- ❑ 131 Mike Sweeney .50 .15
- ❑ 132 Matt Morris .50 .15
- ❑ 133 John Thomson .50 .15
- ❑ 134 Javier Valentin .50 .15
- ❑ 135 Mike Drumright RC 1.00 .30
- ❑ 136 Michael Barrett .50 .15
- ❑ 137 Tony Saunders RC 1.00 .30
- ❑ 138 Kevin Brown .50 .15
- ❑ 139 Anthony Sanders RC 1.00 .30
- ❑ 140 Jeff Abbott .50 .15
- ❑ 141 Eugene Kingsale .50 .15
- ❑ 142 Paul Konerko .75 .23
- ❑ 143 Randall Simon RC 1.50 .45
- ❑ 144 Freddy Adrian Garcia .50 .15
- ❑ 145 Karim Garcia .50 .15
- ❑ 146 Carlos Guillen .50 .15
- ❑ 147 Aaron Boone .50 .15
- ❑ 148 Donnie Sadler .50 .15
- ❑ 149 Brooks Kieschnick .50 .15
- ❑ 150 Scott Spiezio .50 .15
- ❑ 151 Kevin Orie .50 .15
- ❑ 152 Russ Johnson .50 .15
- ❑ 153 Livan Hernandez .50 .15
- ❑ 154 Vladimir Nunez RC 1.00 .30
- ❑ 155 Pokey Reese .50 .15
- ❑ 156 Chris Carpenter .50 .15
- ❑ 157 Eric Milton RC 2.50 .75
- ❑ 158 Richie Sexson .50 .15
- ❑ 159 Carl Pavano .50 .15
- ❑ 160 Pat Cline .50 .15
- ❑ 161 Ron Wright .50 .15
- ❑ 162 Dante Powell .50 .15
- ❑ 163 Mark Bellhorn .50 .15
- ❑ 164 George Lombard .50 .15
- ❑ 165 Paul Wilder RC 1.00 .30
- ❑ 166 Brad Fullmer .50 .15

No.	Player	Nm-Mt	Ex-Mt
167	Kris Benson RC	2.50	.75
168	Torii Hunter	.50	.15
169	D.T. Cromer RC	1.00	.30
170	Nelson Figueroa RC	1.00	.30
171	Hiram Bocachica RC	1.50	.45
172	Shane Monahan	.50	.15
173	Juan Melo	.50	.15
174	Calvin Pickering RC	1.50	.45
175	Reggie Taylor	.50	.15
176	Geoff Jenkins	.50	.15
177	Steve Rain RC	1.00	.30
178	Nerio Rodriguez RC	1.00	.30
179	Derrick Gibson	.50	.15
180	Darin Blood	.50	.15
181	Ben Davis	.50	.15
182	Adrian Beltre RC	12.00	3.60
183	Kerry Wood RC	20.00	6.00
184	Nate Rolison RC	1.00	.30
185	Fernando Tatis RC	1.50	.45
186	Jake Westbrook RC	2.50	.75
187	Edwin Diaz	.50	.15
188	Joe Fontenot RC	1.00	.30
189	Matt Halloran RC	1.00	.30
190	Matt Clement RC	5.00	1.50
191	Todd Greene	.50	.15
192	Eric Chavez RC	10.00	3.00
193	Edgard Velazquez	.50	.15
194	Bruce Chen RC	2.50	.75
195	Jason Brester	.50	.15
196	Chris Reitsma RC	1.50	.45
197	Neifi Perez	.50	.15
198	Hideki Irabu RC	1.50	.45
199	Don Denbow RC	1.00	.30
200	Derrek Lee	.75	.23
201	Todd Walker	.50	.15
202	Scott Rolen	.75	.23
203	Wes Helms	.50	.15
204	Bob Abreu	.75	.23
205	John Patterson RC	5.00	1.50
206	Alex Gonzalez RC	2.50	.75
207	Grant Roberts RC	1.50	.45
208	Jeff Suppan	.50	.15
209	Luke Wilcox	.50	.15
210	Marlon Anderson	.50	.15
211	Mike Caruso RC	1.00	.30
212	Roy Halladay RC	8.00	2.40
213	Jeremi Gonzalez RC	1.00	.30
214	Aramis Ramirez RC	10.00	3.00
215	Dee Brown RC	1.50	.45
216	Justin Thompson	.50	.15
217	Danny Clyburn	.50	.15
218	Bruce Aven	.50	.15
219	Keith Foulke RC	4.00	1.20
220	Shannon Stewart	.50	.15
221	Larry Barnes RC	1.00	.30
222	Mark Johnson RC	1.00	.30
223	Randy Winn	.50	.15
224	Nomar Garciaparra	2.00	.60
225	Jacque Jones RC	4.00	1.20
226	Chris Clemons	.50	.15
227	Todd Helton	1.25	.35
228	Ryan Brannan RC	1.00	.30
229	Alex Sanchez RC	1.50	.45
230	Russell Branyan	.50	.15
231	Daryle Ward	1.50	.45
232	Kevin Witt	.50	.15
233	Gabby Martinez	.50	.15
234	Preston Wilson	.50	.15
235	Donzell McDonald RC	1.00	.30
236	Orlando Cabrera RC	4.00	1.20
237	Brian Banks	.50	.15
238	Robbie Bell	1.00	.30
239	Brad Rigby	.50	.15
240	Scott Elarton	.50	.15
241	Donny Leon RC	1.00	.30
242	Abraham Nunez RC	1.00	.30
243	Adam Eaton RC	4.00	1.20
244	Octavio Dotel RC	1.50	.45
245	Sean Casey	2.50	.75
246	Joe Lawrence RC	1.00	.30
247	Adam Johnson RC	1.00	.30
248	Ronnie Belliard RC	2.50	.75
249	Bobby Estalella	.50	.15
250	Corey Lee RC	1.00	.30
251	Mike Cameron	.50	.15
252	Kerry Robinson RC	1.00	.30
253	A.J. Zapp RC	1.00	.30
254	Jarrod Washburn	.50	.15
255	Ben Grieve	.50	.15
256	Javier Vazquez RC	4.00	1.20
257	Travis Lee RC	1.50	.45
258	Dennis Reyes RC	1.00	.30
259	Danny Buxbaum	.50	.15
260	Kelvim Escobar RC	2.50	.75
261	Danny Klassen	.50	.15
262	Ken Cloude RC	1.50	.45
263	Gabe Alvarez	.50	.15
264	Clayton Bruner RC	1.00	.30
265	Jason Marquis RC	2.50	.75
266	Jamey Wright	.50	.15
267	Matt Snyder RC	1.00	.30
268	Josh Garrett RC	1.00	.30
269	Juan Encarnacion	.50	.15
270	Heath Murray	.50	.15
271	Brent Butler RC	1.50	.45
272	Danny Peoples RC	1.00	.30
273	Miguel Tejada RC	30.00	9.00
274	Jim Pittsley	.50	.15
275	Dmitri Young	.50	.15
276	Vladimir Guerrero	1.25	.35
277	Cole Liniak RC	1.00	.30
278	Ramon Hernandez	.50	.15
279	Cliff Politte RC	1.00	.30
280	Mel Rosario RC	1.00	.30
281	Jorge Carrion RC	1.00	.30
282	John Barnes RC	1.00	.30
283	Chris Stowe RC	1.00	.30
284	Vernon Wells RC	8.00	2.40
285	Brett Caradonna RC	1.00	.30
286	Scott Hodges RC	1.00	.30
287	Jon Garland RC	8.00	2.40
288	Nathan Haynes RC	1.50	.45
289	Geoff Goetz RC	1.00	.30
290	Adam Kennedy RC	2.50	.75
291	T.J. Tucker RC	1.00	.30
292	Aaron Akin RC	1.00	.30
293	Jayson Werth RC	2.50	.75
294	Glenn Davis RC	1.00	.30
295	Mark Mangum RC	1.00	.30
296	Troy Cameron RC	1.00	.30
297	J.J. Davis RC	1.50	.45
298	Lance Berkman RC	12.00	3.60
299	Jason Standridge RC	1.50	.45
300	Jason Dellaero RC	1.00	.30

1998 Bowman Chrome

	Nm-Mt	Ex-Mt
COMPLETE SET (441)	160.00	47.50
COMP. SERIES 1 (221)	80.00	24.00
COMP. SERIES 2 (220)	80.00	24.00

No.	Player	Nm-Mt	Ex-Mt
1	Nomar Garciaparra	2.00	.60
2	Scott Rolen	.75	.23
3	Andy Pettitte	.75	.23
4	Ivan Rodriguez	.75	.23
5	Mark McGwire	3.00	.90
6	Jason Dickson	.50	.15
7	Jose Cruz Jr.	.50	.15
8	Jeff Kent	.50	.15
9	Mike Mussina	.75	.23
10	Jason Kendall	.50	.15
11	Brett Tomko	.50	.15
12	Jeff King	.50	.15
13	Brad Radke	.50	.15
14	Robin Ventura	.50	.15
15	Jeff Bagwell	.75	.23
16	Greg Maddux	2.00	.60
17	John Jaha	.50	.15
18	Mike Piazza	2.00	.60
19	Edgar Martinez	.75	.23
20	David Justice	.50	.15
21	Todd Hundley	.50	.15
22	Tony Gwynn	1.50	.45
23	Larry Walker	.50	.15
24	Bernie Williams	.75	.23
25	Edgar Renteria	.50	.15
26	Rafael Palmeiro	.75	.23
27	Tim Salmon	.75	.23
28	Matt Morris	.50	.15
29	Shawn Estes	.50	.15
30	Vladimir Guerrero	1.25	.35
31	Fernando Tatis	.50	.15
32	Justin Thompson	.50	.15
33	Ken Griffey Jr.	2.00	.60
34	Edgardo Alfonzo	.50	.15
35	Mo Vaughn	.50	.15
36	Marty Cordova	.50	.15
37	Craig Biggio	.75	.23
38	Roger Clemens	2.50	.75
39	Mark Grace	.75	.23
40	Ken Caminiti	.50	.15
41	Tony Womack	.50	.15
42	Albert Belle	.50	.15
43	Tino Martinez	.75	.23
44	Sandy Alomar Jr.	.50	.15
45	Jeff Cirillo	.50	.15
46	Jason Giambi	.50	.15
47	Darin Erstad	.50	.15
48	Livan Hernandez	.50	.15
49	Mark Grudzielanek	.50	.15
50	Sammy Sosa	1.25	.35
51	Curt Schilling	.50	.15
52	Brian Hunter	.50	.15
53	Neifi Perez	.50	.15
54	Todd Walker	.50	.15
55	Jose Guillen	.50	.15
56	Jim Thome	.75	.23
57	Tom Glavine	.75	.23
58	Todd Greene	.50	.15
59	Rondell White	.50	.15
60	Roberto Alomar	.75	.23
61	Tony Clark	.50	.15
62	Vinny Castilla	.50	.15
63	Barry Larkin	.75	.23
64	Hideki Irabu	.50	.15
65	Johnny Damon	.75	.23
66	Juan Gonzalez	.50	.15
67	John Olerud	.50	.15
68	Gary Sheffield	.50	.15
69	Raul Mondesi	.50	.15
70	Chipper Jones	1.25	.35
71	David Ortiz	5.00	1.50
72	Warren Morris RC	1.00	.30
73	Alex Gonzalez	.50	.15
74	Nick Bierbrodt	.50	.15
75	Roy Halladay	.50	.15
76	Danny Buxbaum	.50	.15
77	Adam Kennedy	.50	.15
78	Jared Sandberg	.50	.15
79	Michael Barrett	.50	.15
80	Gil Meche	1.50	.45
81	Jayson Werth	.50	.15
82	Abraham Nunez	.50	.15
83	Ben Petrick	.50	.15
84	Brett Caradonna	.50	.15
85	Mike Lowell RC	4.00	1.20
86	Clay Bruner	.50	.15
87	John Curtice RC	1.50	.45
88	Bobby Estalella	.50	.15
89	Juan Melo	.50	.15
90	Arnold Gooch	.50	.15
91	Kevin Millwood RC	2.50	.75
92	Richie Sexson	.50	.15
93	Orlando Cabrera	.50	.15
94	Pat Cline	.50	.15
95	Anthony Sanders	.50	.15
96	Russ Johnson	.50	.15
97	Ben Grieve	.50	.15
98	Kevin McGlinchy	.50	.15
99	Paul Wilder	.50	.15

❑ 100 Russ Ortiz .50 .15
❑ 101 Ryan Jackson RC 1.00 .30
❑ 102 Heath Murray .50 .15
❑ 103 Brian Rose .50 .15
❑ 104 R.Radmanovich RC 1.00 .30
❑ 105 Ricky Ledee .50 .15
❑ 106 Jeff Wallace RC 1.00 .30
❑ 107 Ryan Minor RC 1.00 .30
❑ 108 Dennis Reyes .50 .15
❑ 109 James Manias .50 .15
❑ 110 Chris Carpenter .50 .15
❑ 111 Daryle Ward .50 .15
❑ 112 Vernon Wells .50 .15
❑ 113 Chad Green .50 .15
❑ 114 Mike Stoner RC 1.00 .30
❑ 115 Brad Fullmer .50 .15
❑ 116 Adam Eaton .50 .15
❑ 117 Jeff Liefer .50 .15
❑ 118 Corey Koskie RC 2.50 .75
❑ 119 Todd Helton .75 .23
❑ 120 Jaime Jones RC 1.00 .30
❑ 121 Mel Rosario .50 .15
❑ 122 Geoff Goetz .50 .15
❑ 123 Adrian Beltre .50 .15
❑ 124 Jason Dellaero .50 .15
❑ 125 Gabe Kapler RC 2.50 .75
❑ 126 Scott Schoeneweis .50 .15
❑ 127 Ryan Brannan .50 .15
❑ 128 Aaron Akin .50 .15
❑ 129 Ryan Anderson RC 1.50 .45
❑ 130 Brad Penny .50 .15
❑ 131 Bruce Chen .50 .15
❑ 132 Eli Marrero .50 .15
❑ 133 Eric Chavez .50 .15
❑ 134 Troy Glaus RC 12.00 3.60
❑ 135 Troy Cameron .50 .15
❑ 136 Brian Sikorski RC 1.00 .30
❑ 137 Mike Kinkade RC 1.00 .30
❑ 138 Braden Looper .50 .15
❑ 139 Mark Mangum .50 .15
❑ 140 Danny Peoples .50 .15
❑ 141 J.J. Davis .50 .15
❑ 142 Ben Davis .50 .15
❑ 143 Jacque Jones .50 .15
❑ 144 Derrick Gibson .50 .15
❑ 145 Bronson Arroyo 4.00 1.20
❑ 146 L.De Los Santos RC 1.00 .30
❑ 147 Jeff Abbott .50 .15
❑ 148 Mike Cuddyer RC 2.50 .75
❑ 149 Jason Romano .50 .15
❑ 150 Shane Monahan .50 .15
❑ 151 Ntema Ndungidi RC 1.00 .30
❑ 152 Alex Sanchez .50 .15
❑ 153 Jack Cust RC 1.50 .45
❑ 154 Brent Butler .50 .15
❑ 155 Ramon Hernandez .50 .15
❑ 156 Norm Hutchins .50 .15
❑ 157 Jason Marquis .50 .15
❑ 158 Jacob Cruz .50 .15
❑ 159 Rob Burger RC 1.00 .30
❑ 160 Dave Coggin .50 .15
❑ 161 Preston Wilson .50 .15
❑ 162 Jason Fitzgerald RC 1.00 .30
❑ 163 Dan Serafini .50 .15
❑ 164 Pete Munro .50 .15
❑ 165 Trot Nixon .50 .15
❑ 166 Homer Bush .50 .15
❑ 167 Dermal Brown .50 .15
❑ 168 Chad Hermansen .50 .15
❑ 169 Julio Moreno RC 1.00 .30
❑ 170 John Roskos RC 1.00 .30
❑ 171 Grant Roberts .50 .15
❑ 172 Ken Cloude .50 .15
❑ 173 Jason Brester .50 .15
❑ 174 Jason Conti .50 .15
❑ 175 Jon Garland .50 .15
❑ 176 Robbie Bell .50 .15
❑ 177 Nathan Haynes .50 .15
❑ 178 Ramon Ortiz RC 2.50 .75
❑ 179 Shannon Stewart .50 .15
❑ 180 Pablo Ortega .50 .15
❑ 181 Jimmy Rollins RC 5.00 1.50
❑ 182 Sean Casey .75 .23
❑ 183 Ted Lilly RC 2.50 .75
❑ 184 Chris Enochs RC 1.00 .30
❑ 185 M.Ordonez RC UER 8.00 2.40
Front photo is Mario Valdez
❑ 186 Mike Drumright .50 .15
❑ 187 Aaron Boone .50 .15
❑ 188 Matt Clement .50 .15
❑ 189 Todd Dunwoody .50 .15
❑ 190 Larry Rodriguez .50 .15
❑ 191 Todd Noel .50 .15
❑ 192 Geoff Jenkins .50 .15
❑ 193 George Lombard .50 .15
❑ 194 Lance Berkman .50 .15
❑ 195 Marcus McCain .50 .15
❑ 196 Ryan McGuire .50 .15
❑ 197 Jhensy Sandoval .50 .15
❑ 198 Corey Lee .50 .15
❑ 199 Mario Valdez .50 .15
❑ 200 Robert Fick RC 1.50 .45
❑ 201 Donnie Sadler .50 .15
❑ 202 Marc Kroon .50 .15
❑ 203 David Miller .50 .15
❑ 204 Jarrod Washburn .50 .15
❑ 205 Miguel Tejada 1.25 .35
❑ 206 Raul Ibanez .50 .15
❑ 207 John Patterson .50 .15
❑ 208 Calvin Pickering .50 .15
❑ 209 Felix Martinez .50 .15
❑ 210 Mark Redman .50 .15
❑ 211 Scott Elarton .50 .15
❑ 212 Jose Amado RC 1.00 .30
❑ 213 Kerry Wood .75 .23
❑ 214 Dante Powell .50 .15
❑ 215 Aramis Ramirez .50 .15
❑ 216 A.J. Hinch .50 .15
❑ 217 Dustin Carr RC 1.00 .30
❑ 218 Mark Kotsay .50 .15
❑ 219 Jason Standridge .50 .15
❑ 220 Luis Ordaz .50 .15
❑ 221 O.Hernandez RC 4.00 1.20
❑ 222 Cal Ripken 4.00 1.20
❑ 223 Paul Molitor .75 .23
❑ 224 Derek Jeter 3.00 .90
❑ 225 Barry Bonds 3.00 .90
❑ 226 Jim Edmonds .50 .15
❑ 227 John Smoltz .75 .23
❑ 228 Eric Karros .50 .15
❑ 229 Ray Lankford .50 .15
❑ 230 Rey Ordonez .50 .15
❑ 231 Kenny Lofton .50 .15
❑ 232 Alex Rodriguez 2.00 .60
❑ 233 Dante Bichette .50 .15
❑ 234 Pedro Martinez .75 .23
❑ 235 Carlos Delgado .50 .15
❑ 236 Rod Beck .50 .15
❑ 237 Matt Williams .50 .15
❑ 238 Charles Johnson .50 .15
❑ 239 Rico Brogna .50 .15
❑ 240 Frank Thomas 1.25 .35
❑ 241 Paul O'Neill .75 .23
❑ 242 Jaret Wright .50 .15
❑ 243 Brant Brown .50 .15
❑ 244 Ryan Klesko .50 .15
❑ 245 Chuck Finley .50 .15
❑ 246 Derek Bell .50 .15
❑ 247 Delino DeShields .50 .15
❑ 248 Chan Ho Park .50 .15
❑ 249 Wade Boggs .75 .23
❑ 250 Jay Buhner .50 .15
❑ 251 Butch Huskey .50 .15
❑ 252 Steve Finley .50 .15
❑ 253 Will Clark .75 .23
❑ 254 John Valentin .50 .15
❑ 255 Bobby Higginson .50 .15
❑ 256 Darryl Strawberry .50 .15
❑ 257 Randy Johnson 1.25 .35
❑ 258 Al Martin .50 .15
❑ 259 Travis Fryman .50 .15
❑ 260 Fred McGriff .75 .23
❑ 261 Jose Valentin .50 .15
❑ 262 Andruw Jones .75 .23
❑ 263 Kenny Rogers .50 .15
❑ 264 Moises Alou .50 .15
❑ 265 Denny Neagle .50 .15
❑ 266 Ugueth Urbina .50 .15
❑ 267 Derrek Lee .75 .23
❑ 268 Ellis Burks .50 .15
❑ 269 Mariano Rivera .75 .23
❑ 270 Dean Palmer .50 .15
❑ 271 Eddie Taubensee .50 .15
❑ 272 Brady Anderson .50 .15
❑ 273 Brian Giles .50 .15
❑ 274 Quinton McCracken .50 .15
❑ 275 Henry Rodriguez .50 .15
❑ 276 Andres Galarraga .50 .15
❑ 277 Jose Canseco .75 .23
❑ 278 David Segui .50 .15
❑ 279 Bret Saberhagen .50 .15
❑ 280 Kevin Brown .75 .23
❑ 281 Chuck Knoblauch .50 .15
❑ 282 Jeromy Burnitz .50 .15
❑ 283 Jay Bell .50 .15
❑ 284 Manny Ramirez .75 .23
❑ 285 Rick Helling .50 .15
❑ 286 Francisco Cordova .50 .15
❑ 287 Bob Abreu .50 .15
❑ 288 J.T. Snow .50 .15
❑ 289 Hideo Nomo 1.25 .35
❑ 290 Brian Jordan .50 .15
❑ 291 Javy Lopez .50 .15
❑ 292 Travis Lee .50 .15
❑ 293 Russell Branyan .50 .15
❑ 294 Paul Konerko .50 .15
❑ 295 Masato Yoshii RC 2.50 .75
❑ 296 Kris Benson .50 .15
❑ 297 Juan Encarnacion .50 .15
❑ 298 Eric Milton .50 .15
❑ 299 Mike Caruso .50 .15
❑ 300 R. Aramboles RC 1.50 .45
❑ 301 Bobby Smith .50 .15
❑ 302 Billy Koch .50 .15
❑ 303 Richard Hidalgo .50 .15
❑ 304 Justin Baughman RC 1.00 .30
❑ 305 Chris Gissell .50 .15
❑ 306 Donnie Bridges RC 1.00 .30
❑ 307 Nelson Lara RC 1.00 .30
❑ 308 Randy Wolf RC 1.50 .45
❑ 309 Jason LaRue RC 1.50 .45
❑ 310 Jason Gooding RC 1.00 .30
❑ 311 Edgard Clemente .50 .15
❑ 312 Andrew Vessel .50 .15
❑ 313 Chris Reitsma .50 .15
❑ 314 Jesus Sanchez RC 1.00 .30
❑ 315 Buddy Carlyle RC 1.00 .30
❑ 316 Randy Winn .50 .15
❑ 317 Luis Rivera RC 1.00 .30
❑ 318 Marcus Thames RC 1.50 .45
❑ 319 A.J. Pierzynski .50 .15
❑ 320 Scott Randall .50 .15
❑ 321 Damian Sapp .50 .15
❑ 322 Ed Yarnall RC 1.00 .30
❑ 323 Luke Allen RC 1.50 .45
❑ 324 J.D. Smart .50 .15
❑ 325 Willie Martinez .50 .15
❑ 326 Alex Ramirez .50 .15
❑ 327 Eric DuBose RC 1.50 .45
❑ 328 Kevin Witt .50 .15
❑ 329 Dan McKinley RC 1.00 .30
❑ 330 Cliff Politte .50 .15
❑ 331 Vladimir Nunez .50 .15
❑ 332 John Halama RC 1.00 .30
❑ 333 Nerio Rodriguez .50 .15
❑ 334 Desi Relaford .50 .15
❑ 335 Robinson Checo .50 .15
❑ 336 John Nicholson .75 .23
❑ 337 Tom LaRosa RC 1.00 .30
❑ 338 Kevin Nicholson RC 1.00 .30
❑ 339 Javier Vazquez .50 .15
❑ 340 A.J. Zapp .50 .15
❑ 341 Tom Evans .50 .15
❑ 342 Kerry Robinson .50 .15
❑ 343 Gabe Gonzalez RC 1.00 .30
❑ 344 Ralph Milliard .50 .15
❑ 345 Enrique Wilson .50 .15
❑ 346 Elvin Hernandez .50 .15
❑ 347 Mike Lincoln RC 1.00 .30
❑ 348 Cesar King RC 1.00 .30
❑ 349 Cristian Guzman RC 2.50 .75
❑ 350 Donzell McDonald .50 .15
❑ 351 Jim Parque RC 1.00 .30
❑ 352 Mike Saipe RC 1.00 .30
❑ 353 Carlos Febles RC 1.50 .45
❑ 354 Dernell Stenson RC 1.50 .45
❑ 355 Mark Osborne RC 1.00 .30
❑ 356 Odalis Perez RC 4.00 1.20

Card	Nm-Mt	Ex-Mt
❑ 357 Jason Dewey RC	1.00	.30
❑ 358 Joe Fontenot	.50	.15
❑ 359 Jason Grilli RC	1.00	.30
❑ 360 Kevin Haverbusch RC	1.00	.30
❑ 361 Jay Yennaco RC	1.00	.30
❑ 362 Brian Buchanan	.50	.15
❑ 363 John Barnes	.50	.15
❑ 364 Chris Fussell	.50	.15
❑ 365 Kevin Gibbs RC	1.00	.30
❑ 366 Joe Lawrence	.50	.15
❑ 367 DaRond Stovall	.50	.15
❑ 368 Brian Fuentes RC	1.00	.30
❑ 369 Jimmy Anderson	.50	.15
❑ 370 Lariel Gonzalez RC	1.00	.30
❑ 371 Scott Williamson RC	1.50	.45
❑ 372 Milton Bradley	.50	.15
❑ 373 Jason Halper RC	1.00	.30
❑ 374 Brent Billingsley RC	1.00	.30
❑ 375 Joe DePastino RC	1.00	.30
❑ 376 Jake Westbrook	.50	.15
❑ 377 Octavio Dotel	.50	.15
❑ 378 Jason Williams RC	1.00	.30
❑ 379 Julio Ramirez RC	1.00	.30
❑ 380 Seth Greisinger	.50	.15
❑ 381 Mike Judd RC	1.00	.30
❑ 382 Ben Ford RC	1.00	.30
❑ 383 Tom Bennett RC	1.00	.30
❑ 384 Adam Butler RC	1.00	.30
❑ 385 Wade Miller RC	2.50	.75
❑ 386 Kyle Peterson RC	1.00	.30
❑ 387 Tommy Peterman RC	1.00	.30
❑ 388 Onan Masaoka	.50	.15
❑ 389 Jason Rakers RC	1.00	.30
❑ 390 Rafael Medina	.50	.15
❑ 391 Luis Lopez RC	1.00	.30
❑ 392 Jeff Yoder	.50	.15
❑ 393 Vance Wilson RC	1.00	.30
❑ 394 F. Seguignol RC	1.00	.30
❑ 395 Ron Wright	.50	.15
❑ 396 Ruben Mateo RC	1.50	.45
❑ 397 Steve Lomasney RC	1.50	.45
❑ 398 Damian Jackson	.50	.15
❑ 399 Mike Jerzembeck RC	1.00	.30
❑ 400 Luis Rivas RC	2.50	.75
❑ 401 Kevin Burford RC	1.00	.30
❑ 402 Glenn Davis	.50	.15
❑ 403 Robert Luce RC	1.00	.30
❑ 404 Cole Liniak	.50	.15
❑ 405 Matt LeCroy RC	1.50	.45
❑ 406 Jeremy Giambi RC	1.50	.45
❑ 407 Shawn Chacon	.50	.15
❑ 408 Dewayne Wise RC	1.00	.30
❑ 409 Steve Woodard	.50	.15
❑ 410 F.Cordero RC	2.50	.75
❑ 411 Damon Minor RC	1.00	.30
❑ 412 Lou Collier	.50	.15
❑ 413 Justin Towle	.50	.15
❑ 414 Juan LeBron	.50	.15
❑ 415 Michael Coleman	.50	.15
❑ 416 Felix Rodriguez	.50	.15
❑ 417 Paul Ah Yat RC	1.00	.30
❑ 418 Kevin Barker RC	1.00	.30
❑ 419 Brian Meadows	.50	.15
❑ 420 Darnell McDonald RC	1.00	.30
❑ 421 Matt Kinney RC	1.50	.45
❑ 422 Mike Vavrek RC	1.00	.30
❑ 423 Courtney Duncan RC	1.00	.30
❑ 424 Kevin Millar RC	4.00	1.20
❑ 425 Ruben Rivera	.50	.15
❑ 426 Steve Shoemaker RC	1.00	.30
❑ 427 Dan Reichert RC	1.00	.30
❑ 428 Carlos Lee RC	8.00	2.40
❑ 429 Rod Barajas	2.50	.75
❑ 430 Pablo Ozuna RC	1.50	.45
❑ 431 Todd Belitz RC	1.00	.30
❑ 432 Sidney Ponson	.50	.15
❑ 433 Steve Carver RC	1.00	.30
❑ 434 Esteban Yan RC	1.50	.45
❑ 435 Cedrick Bowers	.50	.15
❑ 436 Marlon Anderson	.50	.15
❑ 437 Carl Pavano	.50	.15
❑ 438 Jae Weong Seo RC	2.50	.75
❑ 439 Jose Taveras RC	1.00	.30
❑ 440 Matt Anderson RC	1.50	.45
❑ 441 Darron Ingram RC	1.00	.30

1999 Bowman Chrome

	Nm-Mt	Ex-Mt
COMPLETE SET (440)	200.00	60.00
COMP. SERIES 1 (220)	80.00	24.00
COMP. SERIES 2 (220)	120.00	36.00

Card	Nm-Mt	Ex-Mt
❑ 1 Ben Grieve	.50	.15
❑ 2 Kerry Wood	.50	.15
❑ 3 Ruben Rivera	.50	.15
❑ 4 Sandy Alomar Jr.	.50	.15
❑ 5 Cal Ripken	4.00	1.20
❑ 6 Mark McGwire	3.00	.90
❑ 7 Vladimir Guerrero	1.25	.35
❑ 8 Moises Alou	.50	.15
❑ 9 Jim Edmonds	.50	.15
❑ 10 Greg Maddux	2.00	.60
❑ 11 Gary Sheffield	.50	.15
❑ 12 John Valentin	.50	.15
❑ 13 Chuck Knoblauch	.50	.15
❑ 14 Tony Clark	.50	.15
❑ 15 Rusty Greer	.50	.15
❑ 16 Al Leiter	.50	.15
❑ 17 Travis Lee	.50	.15
❑ 18 Jose Cruz Jr.	.50	.15
❑ 19 Pedro Martinez	.75	.23
❑ 20 Paul O'Neill	.75	.23
❑ 21 Todd Walker	.50	.15
❑ 22 Vinny Castilla	.50	.15
❑ 23 Barry Larkin	.75	.23
❑ 24 Curt Schilling	.50	.15
❑ 25 Jason Kendall	.50	.15
❑ 26 Scott Erickson	.50	.15
❑ 27 Andres Galarraga	.50	.15
❑ 28 Jeff Shaw	.50	.15
❑ 29 John Olerud	.50	.15
❑ 30 Orlando Hernandez	.50	.15
❑ 31 Larry Walker	.50	.15
❑ 32 Andruw Jones	.75	.23
❑ 33 Jeff Cirillo	.50	.15
❑ 34 Barry Bonds	3.00	.90
❑ 35 Manny Ramirez	.75	.23
❑ 36 Mark Kotsay	.50	.15
❑ 37 Ivan Rodriguez	.75	.23
❑ 38 Jeff King	.50	.15
❑ 39 Brian Hunter	.50	.15
❑ 40 Ray Durham	.50	.15
❑ 41 Bernie Williams	.75	.23
❑ 42 Darin Erstad	.50	.15
❑ 43 Chipper Jones	1.25	.35
❑ 44 Pat Hentgen	.50	.15
❑ 45 Eric Young	.50	.15
❑ 46 Jaret Wright	.50	.15
❑ 47 Juan Guzman	.50	.15
❑ 48 Jorge Posada	.75	.23
❑ 49 Bobby Higginson	.50	.15
❑ 50 Jose Guillen	.50	.15
❑ 51 Trevor Hoffman	.50	.15
❑ 52 Ken Griffey Jr.	2.00	.60
❑ 53 David Justice	.50	.15
❑ 54 Matt Williams	.50	.15
❑ 55 Eric Karros	.50	.15
❑ 56 Derek Bell	.50	.15
❑ 57 Ray Lankford	.50	.15
❑ 58 Mariano Rivera	.75	.23
❑ 59 Brett Tomko	.50	.15
❑ 60 Mike Mussina	.75	.23
❑ 61 Kenny Lofton	.50	.15
❑ 62 Chuck Finley	.50	.15
❑ 63 Alex Gonzalez	.50	.15
❑ 64 Mark Grace	.75	.23
❑ 65 Raul Mondesi	.50	.15
❑ 66 David Cone	.50	.15
❑ 67 Brad Fullmer	.50	.15
❑ 68 Andy Benes	.50	.15
❑ 69 John Smoltz	.75	.23
❑ 70 Shane Reynolds	.50	.15
❑ 71 Bruce Chen	.50	.15
❑ 72 Adam Kennedy	.50	.15
❑ 73 Jack Cust	.50	.15
❑ 74 Matt Clement	.50	.15
❑ 75 Derrick Gibson	.50	.15
❑ 76 Darnell McDonald	.50	.15
❑ 77 Adam Everett RC	2.50	.75
❑ 78 Ricardo Aramboles	.50	.15
❑ 79 Mark Quinn RC	1.50	.45
❑ 80 Jason Rakers	.50	.15
❑ 81 Seth Etherton RC	1.00	.30
❑ 82 Jeff Urban RC	1.00	.30
❑ 83 Manny Aybar	.50	.15
❑ 84 Mike Nannini RC	1.00	.30
❑ 85 Onan Masaoka	.50	.15
❑ 86 Rod Barajas	.50	.15
❑ 87 Mike Frank	.50	.15
❑ 88 Scott Randall	.50	.15
❑ 89 Justin Bowles RC	1.00	.30
❑ 90 Chris Haas	.50	.15
❑ 91 Arturo McDowell RC	1.00	.30
❑ 92 Matt Belisle RC	1.00	.30
❑ 93 Scott Elarton	.50	.15
❑ 94 Vernon Wells	.50	.15
❑ 95 Pat Cline	.50	.15
❑ 96 Ryan Anderson	.50	.15
❑ 97 Kevin Barker	.50	.15
❑ 98 Ruben Mateo	.50	.15
❑ 99 Robert Fick	.50	.15
❑ 100 Corey Koskie	.50	.15
❑ 101 Ricky Ledee	.50	.15
❑ 102 Rick Elder RC	1.50	.45
❑ 103 Jack Cressend RC	1.00	.30
❑ 104 Joe Lawrence	.50	.15
❑ 105 Mike Lincoln	.50	.15
❑ 106 Kit Pellow RC	1.00	.30
❑ 107 Matt Burch RC	1.00	.30
❑ 108 Cole Liniak	.50	.15
❑ 109 Jason Dewey	.50	.15
❑ 110 Cesar King	.50	.15
❑ 111 Julio Ramirez	.50	.15
❑ 112 Jake Westbrook	.50	.15
❑ 113 Eric Valent RC	1.50	.45
❑ 114 Roosevelt Brown RC	1.00	.30
❑ 115 Choo Freeman RC	1.50	.45
❑ 116 Juan Melo	.50	.15
❑ 117 Jason Grilli	.50	.15
❑ 118 Jared Sandberg	.50	.15
❑ 119 Glenn Davis	.50	.15
❑ 120 David Riske RC	1.00	.30
❑ 121 Jacque Jones	.50	.15
❑ 122 Corey Lee	.50	.15
❑ 123 Michael Barrett	.50	.15
❑ 124 Lariel Gonzalez	.50	.15
❑ 125 Mitch Meluskey	.50	.15
❑ 126 Freddy Adrian Garcia	.50	.15
❑ 127 Tony Torcato RC	1.50	.45
❑ 128 Jeff Liefer	.50	.15
❑ 129 Ntema Ndungidi	.50	.15
❑ 130 Andy Brown RC	1.00	.30
❑ 131 Ryan Mills RC	1.00	.30
❑ 132 Andy Abad RC	1.00	.30
❑ 133 Carlos Febles	.50	.15
❑ 134 Jason Tyner RC	1.00	.30
❑ 135 Mark Osborne	.50	.15
❑ 136 Phil Norton RC	1.00	.30
❑ 137 Nathan Haynes	.50	.15
❑ 138 Roy Halladay	.50	.15
❑ 139 Juan Encarnacion	.50	.15
❑ 140 Brad Penny	.50	.15
❑ 141 Grant Roberts	.50	.15
❑ 142 Aramis Ramirez	.50	.15
❑ 143 Cristian Guzman	.50	.15
❑ 144 Mamon Tucker RC	1.00	.30
❑ 145 Ryan Bradley	.50	.15
❑ 146 Brian Simmons	.50	.15
❑ 147 Dan Reichert	.50	.15

❑ 148 Russell Branyan .50 .15
❑ 149 Victor Valencia RC 1.00 .30
❑ 150 Scott Schoeneweis .50 .15
❑ 151 Sean Spencer RC 1.00 .30
❑ 152 Odalis Perez .50 .15
❑ 153 Joe Fontenot .50 .15
❑ 154 Milton Bradley .50 .15
❑ 155 Josh McKinley RC 1.50 .45
❑ 156 Terrence Long .50 .15
❑ 157 Danny Klassen .50 .15
❑ 158 Paul Hoover RC 1.00 .30
❑ 159 Ron Belliard .50 .15
❑ 160 Armando Rios .50 .15
❑ 161 Ramon Hernandez .50 .15
❑ 162 Jason Conti .50 .15
❑ 163 Chad Hermansen .50 .15
❑ 164 Jason Standridge .50 .15
❑ 165 Jason Dellaero .50 .15
❑ 166 John Curtice .50 .15
❑ 167 Clayton Andrews RC 1.00 .30
❑ 168 Jeremy Giambi .50 .15
❑ 169 Alex Ramirez .50 .15
❑ 170 Gabe Molina RC 1.00 .30
❑ 171 M.Encarnacion RC 1.00 .30
❑ 172 Mike Zywica RC 1.00 .30
❑ 173 Chip Ambres RC 1.00 .30
❑ 174 Trot Nixon .50 .15
❑ 175 Pat Burrell RC 8.00 2.40
❑ 176 Jeff Yoder .50 .15
❑ 177 Chris Jones RC 1.00 .30
❑ 178 Kevin Witt .50 .15
❑ 179 Keith Luuloa RC 1.00 .30
❑ 180 Billy Koch .50 .15
❑ 181 Damaso Marte RC 1.00 .30
❑ 182 Ryan Glynn RC 1.00 .30
❑ 183 Calvin Pickering .50 .15
❑ 184 Michael Cuddyer .50 .15
❑ 185 Nick Johnson RC 5.00 1.50
❑ 186 D.Mientkiewicz RC 2.50 .75
❑ 187 Nate Cornejo RC 1.50 .45
❑ 188 Octavio Dotel .50 .15
❑ 189 Wes Helms .50 .15
❑ 190 Nelson Lara .50 .15
❑ 191 Chuck Abbott RC 1.00 .30
❑ 192 Tony Armas Jr. .50 .15
❑ 193 Gil Meche .50 .15
❑ 194 Ben Petrick .50 .15
❑ 195 Chris George RC 1.50 .45
❑ 196 Scott Hunter RC 1.00 .30
❑ 197 Ryan Brannan .50 .15
❑ 198 Amaury Garcia RC 1.00 .30
❑ 199 Chris Gissell .50 .15
❑ 200 Austin Kearns RC 5.00 1.50
❑ 201 Alex Gonzalez .50 .15
❑ 202 Wade Miller .50 .15
❑ 203 Scott Williamson .50 .15
❑ 204 Chris Enochs .50 .15
❑ 205 Fernando Seguignol .50 .15
❑ 206 Marlon Anderson .50 .15
❑ 207 Todd Sears RC 1.50 .45
❑ 208 Nate Bump RC 1.00 .30
❑ 209 J.M. Gold RC 1.00 .30
❑ 210 Matt LeCroy .50 .15
❑ 211 Alex Hernandez .50 .15
❑ 212 Luis Rivera .50 .15
❑ 213 Troy Cameron .50 .15
❑ 214 Alex Escobar RC 1.50 .45
❑ 215 Jason LaRue .50 .15
❑ 216 Kyle Peterson .50 .15
❑ 217 Brent Butler .50 .15
❑ 218 Dernell Stenson .50 .15
❑ 219 Adrian Beltre .50 .15
❑ 220 Daryle Ward .50 .15
❑ 221 Jim Thome .75 .23
❑ 222 Cliff Floyd .50 .15
❑ 223 Rickey Henderson 1.25 .35
❑ 224 Garret Anderson .50 .15
❑ 225 Ken Caminiti .50 .15
❑ 226 Bret Boone .50 .15
❑ 227 Jeromy Burnitz .50 .15
❑ 228 Steve Finley .50 .15
❑ 229 Miguel Tejada .50 .15
❑ 230 Greg Vaughn .50 .15
❑ 231 Jose Offerman .50 .15
❑ 232 Andy Ashby .50 .15
❑ 233 Albert Belle .50 .15
❑ 234 Fernando Tatis .50 .15
❑ 235 Todd Helton .75 .23
❑ 236 Sean Casey .75 .23
❑ 237 Brian Giles .50 .15
❑ 238 Andy Pettitte .75 .23
❑ 239 Fred McGriff .75 .23
❑ 240 Roberto Alomar .75 .23
❑ 241 Edgar Martinez .75 .23
❑ 242 Lee Stevens .50 .15
❑ 243 Shawn Green .50 .15
❑ 244 Ryan Klesko .50 .15
❑ 245 Sammy Sosa 1.25 .35
❑ 246 Todd Hundley .50 .15
❑ 247 Shannon Stewart .50 .15
❑ 248 Randy Johnson 1.25 .35
❑ 249 Rondell White .50 .15
❑ 250 Mike Piazza 2.00 .60
❑ 251 Craig Biggio .75 .23
❑ 252 David Wells .50 .15
❑ 253 Brian Jordan .50 .15
❑ 254 Edgar Renteria .50 .15
❑ 255 Bartolo Colon .50 .15
❑ 256 Frank Thomas 1.25 .35
❑ 257 Will Clark .75 .23
❑ 258 Dean Palmer .50 .15
❑ 259 Dmitri Young .50 .15
❑ 260 Scott Rolen .75 .23
❑ 261 Jeff Kent .50 .15
❑ 262 Dante Bichette .50 .15
❑ 263 Nomar Garciaparra 2.00 .60
❑ 264 Tony Gwynn 1.50 .45
❑ 265 Alex Rodriguez 2.00 .60
❑ 266 Jose Canseco .75 .23
❑ 267 Jason Giambi .50 .15
❑ 268 Jeff Bagwell .75 .23
❑ 269 Carlos Delgado .50 .15
❑ 270 Tom Glavine .75 .23
❑ 271 Eric Davis .50 .15
❑ 272 Edgardo Alfonzo .50 .15
❑ 273 Tim Salmon .75 .23
❑ 274 Johnny Damon .75 .23
❑ 275 Rafael Palmeiro .75 .23
❑ 276 Denny Neagle .50 .15
❑ 277 Neifi Perez .50 .15
❑ 278 Roger Clemens 2.50 .75
❑ 279 Brant Brown .50 .15
❑ 280 Kevin Brown .75 .23
❑ 281 Jay Bell .50 .15
❑ 282 Jay Buhner .50 .15
❑ 283 Matt Lawton .50 .15
❑ 284 Robin Ventura .50 .15
❑ 285 Juan Gonzalez .50 .15
❑ 286 Mo Vaughn .50 .15
❑ 287 Kevin Millwood .50 .15
❑ 288 Tino Martinez .75 .23
❑ 289 Justin Thompson .50 .15
❑ 290 Derek Jeter 3.00 .90
❑ 291 Ben Davis .50 .15
❑ 292 Mike Lowell .50 .15
❑ 293 Calvin Murray .50 .15
❑ 294 Micah Bowie RC 1.00 .30
❑ 295 Lance Berkman .50 .15
❑ 296 Jason Marquis .50 .15
❑ 297 Chad Green .50 .15
❑ 298 Dee Brown .50 .15
❑ 299 Jerry Hairston Jr. .50 .15
❑ 300 Gabe Kapler .50 .15
❑ 301 Brent Stentz RC 1.00 .30
❑ 302 Scott Mullen RC 1.00 .30
❑ 303 Brandon Reed .50 .15
❑ 304 Shea Hillenbrand RC 4.00 1.20
❑ 305 J.D. Closser RC 2.50 .75
❑ 306 Gary Matthews Jr. .50 .15
❑ 307 Toby Hall RC 1.50 .45
❑ 308 Jason Phillips RC 1.00 .30
❑ 309 Jose Macias RC 1.00 .30
❑ 310 Jung Bong RC 1.50 .45
❑ 311 Ramon Soler RC 1.00 .30
❑ 312 Kelly Dransfeldt RC 1.00 .30
❑ 313 Carlos E. Hernandez RC 1.50 .45
❑ 314 Kevin Haverbusch .50 .15
❑ 315 Aaron Myette RC 1.00 .30
❑ 316 Chad Harville RC 1.00 .30
❑ 317 Kyle Farnsworth RC 2.50 .75
❑ 318 Gookie Dawkins RC 1.50 .45
❑ 319 Willie Martinez .50 .15
❑ 320 Carlos Lee .50 .15
❑ 321 Carlos Pena RC 1.50 .45
❑ 322 Peter Bergeron RC 1.50 .45
❑ 323 A.J. Burnett RC 5.00 1.50
❑ 324 Bucky Jacobsen RC 2.50 .75
❑ 325 Mo Bruce RC 1.00 .30
❑ 326 Reggie Taylor .50 .15
❑ 327 Jackie Rexrode .50 .15
❑ 328 Alvin Morrow RC 1.00 .30
❑ 329 Carlos Beltran .75 .23
❑ 330 Eric Chavez .50 .15
❑ 331 John Patterson .50 .15
❑ 332 Jayson Werth .50 .15
❑ 333 Richie Sexson .50 .15
❑ 334 Randy Wolf .50 .15
❑ 335 Eli Marrero .50 .15
❑ 336 Paul LoDuca .50 .15
❑ 337 J.D Smart .50 .15
❑ 338 Ryan Minor .50 .15
❑ 339 Kris Benson .50 .15
❑ 340 George Lombard .50 .15
❑ 341 Troy Glaus .75 .23
❑ 342 Eddie Yarnall .50 .15
❑ 343 Kip Wells RC 2.50 .75
❑ 344 C.C. Sabathia RC 4.00 1.20
❑ 345 Sean Burroughs RC 2.50 .75
❑ 346 Felipe Lopez RC 5.00 1.50
❑ 347 Ryan Rupe RC 1.00 .30
❑ 348 Orber Moreno RC 1.00 .30
❑ 349 Rafael Roque RC 1.00 .30
❑ 350 Alfonso Soriano RC 25.00 7.50
❑ 351 Pablo Ozuna .50 .15
❑ 352 Corey Patterson RC 2.50 .75
❑ 353 Braden Looper .50 .15
❑ 354 Robbie Bell .50 .15
❑ 355 Mark Mulder RC 8.00 2.40
❑ 356 Angel Pena .50 .15
❑ 357 Kevin McGlinchy .50 .15
❑ 358 M.Restovich RC 1.50 .45
❑ 359 Eric DuBose .50 .15
❑ 360 Geoff Jenkins .50 .15
❑ 361 Mark Harriger RC 1.00 .30
❑ 362 Junior Herndon RC 1.50 .45
❑ 363 Tim Raines Jr. RC 1.50 .45
❑ 364 Rafael Furcal RC 5.00 1.50
❑ 365 Marcus Giles RC 4.00 1.20
❑ 366 Ted Lilly .50 .15
❑ 367 Jorge Toca RC 1.50 .45
❑ 368 David Kelton RC 1.50 .45
❑ 369 Adam Dunn RC 25.00 7.50
❑ 370 Guillermo Mota RC 1.00 .30
❑ 371 Brett Laxton RC 1.00 .30
❑ 372 Travis Harper RC 1.00 .30
❑ 373 Tom Davey RC 1.00 .30
❑ 374 Darren Blakely RC 1.00 .30
❑ 375 Tim Hudson RC 8.00 2.40
❑ 376 Jason Romano .50 .15
❑ 377 Dan Reichert .50 .15
❑ 378 Julio Lugo RC 2.50 .75
❑ 379 Jose Garcia RC 1.00 .30
❑ 380 Erubiel Durazo RC 2.50 .75
❑ 381 Jose Jimenez .50 .15
❑ 382 Chris Fussell .50 .15
❑ 383 Steve Lomasney .50 .15
❑ 384 Juan Pena RC 1.00 .30
❑ 385 Allen Levrault RC 1.00 .30
❑ 386 Juan Rivera RC 2.50 .75
❑ 387 Steve Colyer RC 1.50 .45
❑ 388 Joe Nathan RC 4.00 1.20
❑ 389 Ron Walker RC 1.00 .30
❑ 390 Nick Bierbrodt .50 .15
❑ 391 Luke Prokopec RC 1.00 .30
❑ 392 Dave Roberts RC 2.50 .75
❑ 393 Mike Darr .50 .15
❑ 394 Abraham Nunez RC 1.50 .45
❑ 395 G.Chiaramonte RC 1.00 .30
❑ 396 J.Van Buren RC 1.00 .30
❑ 397 Mike Kusiewicz .50 .15
❑ 398 Matt Wise RC 1.00 .30
❑ 399 Joe McEwing RC 1.50 .45
❑ 400 Matt Holliday RC 2.50 .75
❑ 401 Willi Mo Pena RC 8.00 2.40
❑ 402 Ruben Quevedo RC 1.00 .30
❑ 403 Rob Ryan RC 1.00 .30
❑ 404 Freddy Garcia RC 4.00 1.20
❑ 405 Kevin Eberwein RC 1.00 .30

Card	Nm-Mt	Ex-Mt
❑ 406 Jesus Colome RC	1.00	.30
❑ 407 Chris Singleton	.50	.15
❑ 408 Bubba Crosby RC	2.50	.75
❑ 409 Jesus Cordero RC	1.50	.45
❑ 410 Donny Leon	.50	.15
❑ 411 G.Tomlinson RC	1.00	.30
❑ 412 Jeff Winchester RC	1.00	.30
❑ 413 Adam Piatt RC	1.50	.45
❑ 414 Robert Stratton	.50	.15
❑ 415 T.J. Tucker	.50	.15
❑ 416 Ryan Langerhans RC	5.00	1.50
❑ 417 A.Shumaker RC	1.00	.30
❑ 418 Matt Miller RC	1.00	.30
❑ 419 Doug Clark RC	1.00	.30
❑ 420 Kory DeHaan RC	1.00	.30
❑ 421 David Eckstein RC	8.00	2.40
❑ 422 Brian Cooper RC	1.00	.30
❑ 423 Brady Clark RC	4.00	1.20
❑ 424 Chris Magruder RC	1.00	.30
❑ 425 Bobby Seay RC	1.00	.30
❑ 426 Aubrey Huff RC	4.00	1.20
❑ 427 Mike Jerzembeck	.50	.15
❑ 428 Matt Blank RC	1.00	.30
❑ 429 Benny Agbayani RC	1.50	.45
❑ 430 Kevin Beirne RC	1.50	.45
❑ 431 Josh Hamilton RC	2.50	.75
❑ 432 Josh Girdley RC	1.00	.30
❑ 433 Kyle Snyder RC	1.00	.30
❑ 434 Mike Paradis RC	1.00	.30
❑ 435 Jason Jennings RC	2.50	.75
❑ 436 David Walling RC	1.00	.30
❑ 437 Omar Ortiz RC	1.00	.30
❑ 438 Jay Gehrke RC	1.50	.45
❑ 439 Casey Burns RC	1.00	.30
❑ 440 Carl Crawford RC	8.00	2.40

2000 Bowman Chrome

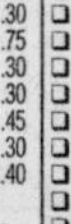
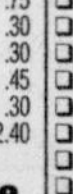
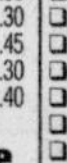

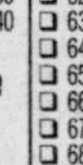

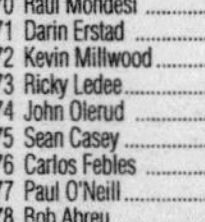
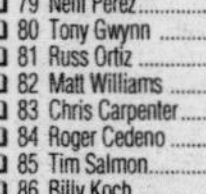

	Nm-Mt	Ex-Mt
COMPLETE SET (440)	120.00	36.00
❑ 1 Vladimir Guerrero	1.25	.35
❑ 2 Chipper Jones	1.25	.35
❑ 3 Todd Walker	.50	.15
❑ 4 Barry Larkin	.75	.23
❑ 5 Bernie Williams	.75	.23
❑ 6 Todd Helton	.75	.23
❑ 7 Jermaine Dye	.50	.15
❑ 8 Brian Giles	.50	.15
❑ 9 Freddy Garcia	.50	.15
❑ 10 Greg Vaughn	.50	.15
❑ 11 Alex Gonzalez	.50	.15
❑ 12 Luis Gonzalez	.50	.15
❑ 13 Ron Belliard	.50	.15
❑ 14 Ben Grieve	.50	.15
❑ 15 Carlos Delgado	.50	.15
❑ 16 Brian Jordan	.50	.15
❑ 17 Fernando Tatis	.50	.15
❑ 18 Ryan Rupe	.50	.15
❑ 19 Miguel Tejada	.50	.15
❑ 20 Mark Grace	.75	.23
❑ 21 Kenny Lofton	.50	.15
❑ 22 Eric Karros	.50	.15
❑ 23 Cliff Floyd	.50	.15
❑ 24 John Halama	.50	.15
❑ 25 Cristian Guzman	.50	.15
❑ 26 Scott Williamson	.50	.15
❑ 27 Mike Lieberthal	.50	.15
❑ 28 Tim Hudson	.50	.15
❑ 29 Warren Morris	.50	.15
❑ 30 Pedro Martinez	.75	.23
❑ 31 John Smoltz	.75	.23
❑ 32 Ray Durham	.50	.15
❑ 33 Chad Allen	.50	.15
❑ 34 Tony Clark	.50	.15
❑ 35 Tino Martinez	.75	.23
❑ 36 J.T. Snow	.50	.15
❑ 37 Kevin Brown	.75	.23
❑ 38 Bartolo Colon	.50	.15
❑ 39 Rey Ordonez	.50	.15
❑ 40 Jeff Bagwell	.75	.23
❑ 41 Ivan Rodriguez	.75	.23
❑ 42 Eric Chavez	.50	.15
❑ 43 Eric Milton	.50	.15
❑ 44 Jose Canseco	.75	.23
❑ 45 Shawn Green	.50	.15
❑ 46 Rich Aurilia	.50	.15
❑ 47 Roberto Alomar	.75	.23
❑ 48 Brian Daubach	.50	.15
❑ 49 Magglio Ordonez	.50	.15
❑ 50 Derek Jeter	3.00	.90
❑ 51 Kris Benson	.50	.15
❑ 52 Albert Belle	.50	.15
❑ 53 Rondell White	.50	.15
❑ 54 Justin Thompson	.50	.15
❑ 55 Nomar Garciaparra	2.00	.60
❑ 56 Chuck Finley	.50	.15
❑ 57 Omar Vizquel	.75	.23
❑ 58 Luis Castillo	.50	.15
❑ 59 Richard Hidalgo	.50	.15
❑ 60 Barry Bonds	3.00	.90
❑ 61 Craig Biggio	.75	.23
❑ 62 Doug Glanville	.50	.15
❑ 63 Gabe Kapler	.50	.15
❑ 64 Johnny Damon	.75	.23
❑ 65 Pokey Reese	.50	.15
❑ 66 Andy Pettitte	.75	.23
❑ 67 B.J. Surhoff	.50	.15
❑ 68 Richie Sexson	.50	.15
❑ 69 Javy Lopez	.50	.15
❑ 70 Raul Mondesi	.50	.15
❑ 71 Darin Erstad	.50	.15
❑ 72 Kevin Millwood	.50	.15
❑ 73 Ricky Ledee	.50	.15
❑ 74 John Olerud	.50	.15
❑ 75 Sean Casey	.75	.23
❑ 76 Carlos Febles	.50	.15
❑ 77 Paul O'Neill	.75	.23
❑ 78 Bob Abreu	.50	.15
❑ 79 Neifi Perez	.50	.15
❑ 80 Tony Gwynn	1.50	.45
❑ 81 Russ Ortiz	.50	.15
❑ 82 Matt Williams	.50	.15
❑ 83 Chris Carpenter	.50	.15
❑ 84 Roger Cedeno	.50	.15
❑ 85 Tim Salmon	.75	.23
❑ 86 Billy Koch	.50	.15
❑ 87 Jeromy Burnitz	.50	.15
❑ 88 Edgardo Alfonzo	.50	.15
❑ 89 Jay Bell	.50	.15
❑ 90 Manny Ramirez	.75	.23
❑ 91 Frank Thomas	1.25	.35
❑ 92 Mike Mussina	.75	.23
❑ 93 J.D. Drew	.50	.15
❑ 94 Adrian Beltre	.50	.15
❑ 95 Alex Rodriguez	2.00	.60
❑ 96 Larry Walker	.50	.15
❑ 97 Juan Encarnacion	.50	.15
❑ 98 Mike Sweeney	.50	.15
❑ 99 Rusty Greer	.50	.15
❑ 100 Randy Johnson	1.25	.35
❑ 101 Jose Vidro	.50	.15
❑ 102 Preston Wilson	.50	.15
❑ 103 Greg Maddux	2.00	.60
❑ 104 Jason Giambi	.50	.15
❑ 105 Cal Ripken	4.00	1.20
❑ 106 Carlos Beltran	.50	.15
❑ 107 Vinny Castilla	.50	.15
❑ 108 Mariano Rivera	.75	.23
❑ 109 Mo Vaughn	.50	.15
❑ 110 Rafael Palmeiro	.75	.23
❑ 111 Shannon Stewart	.50	.15
❑ 112 Mike Hampton	.50	.15
❑ 113 Joe Nathan	.50	.15
❑ 114 Ben Davis	.50	.15
❑ 115 Andruw Jones	.75	.23
❑ 116 Robin Ventura	.50	.15
❑ 117 Damion Easley	.50	.15
❑ 118 Jeff Cirillo	.50	.15
❑ 119 Kerry Wood	.50	.15
❑ 120 Scott Rolen	.75	.23
❑ 121 Sammy Sosa	1.25	.35
❑ 122 Ken Griffey Jr.	2.00	.60
❑ 123 Shane Reynolds	.50	.15
❑ 124 Troy Glaus	.50	.15
❑ 125 Tom Glavine	.75	.23
❑ 126 Michael Barrett	.50	.15
❑ 127 Al Leiter	.50	.15
❑ 128 Jason Kendall	.50	.15
❑ 129 Roger Clemens	2.50	.75
❑ 130 Juan Gonzalez	.50	.15
❑ 131 Corey Koskie	.50	.15
❑ 132 Curt Schilling	.50	.15
❑ 133 Mike Piazza	2.00	.60
❑ 134 Gary Sheffield	.50	.15
❑ 135 Jim Thome	.75	.23
❑ 136 Orlando Hernandez	.50	.15
❑ 137 Ray Lankford	.50	.15
❑ 138 Geoff Jenkins	.50	.15
❑ 139 Jose Lima	.50	.15
❑ 140 Mark McGwire	3.00	.90
❑ 141 Adam Piatt	.50	.15
❑ 142 Pat Manning RC	.75	.23
❑ 143 Marcos Castillo RC	.75	.23
❑ 144 Lesli Brea RC	.75	.23
❑ 145 Humberto Cota RC	1.25	.35
❑ 146 Ben Petrick	.50	.15
❑ 147 Kip Wells	.50	.15
❑ 148 Wily Pena	.50	.15
❑ 149 Chris Wakeland RC	.75	.23
❑ 150 Brad Baker RC	1.25	.35
❑ 151 Robbie Morrison RC	.75	.23
❑ 152 Reggie Taylor	.50	.15
❑ 153 Matt Ginter RC	1.25	.35
❑ 154 Peter Bergeron	.50	.15
❑ 155 Roosevelt Brown	.50	.15
❑ 156 Matt Cepicky RC	.75	.23
❑ 157 Ramon Castro	.50	.15
❑ 158 Brad Baisley RC	.75	.23
❑ 159 Jason Hart RC	.75	.23
❑ 160 Mitch Meluskey	.50	.15
❑ 161 Chad Harville	.50	.15
❑ 162 Brian Cooper	.50	.15
❑ 163 Marcus Giles	.50	.15
❑ 164 Jim Morris	1.25	.35
❑ 165 Geoff Goetz	.50	.15
❑ 166 Bobby Bradley RC	1.25	.35
❑ 167 Rob Bell	.50	.15
❑ 168 Joe Crede	2.50	.75
❑ 169 Michael Restovich	.50	.15
❑ 170 Quincy Foster RC	.75	.23
❑ 171 Enrique Cruz RC	.75	.23
❑ 172 Mark Quinn	.50	.15
❑ 173 Nick Johnson	.50	.15
❑ 174 Jeff Liefer	.50	.15
❑ 175 Kevin Mench RC	5.00	1.50
❑ 176 Steve Lomasney	.50	.15
❑ 177 Jayson Werth	.50	.15
❑ 178 Tim Drew	.50	.15
❑ 179 Chip Ambres	.50	.15
❑ 180 Ryan Anderson	.50	.15
❑ 181 Matt Blank	.50	.15
❑ 182 G. Chiaramonte	.50	.15
❑ 183 Corey Myers RC	1.25	.35
❑ 184 Jeff Yoder	.50	.15
❑ 185 Craig Dingman RC	.75	.23
❑ 186 Jon Hamilton RC	.75	.23
❑ 187 Toby Hall	.50	.15
❑ 188 Russell Branyan	.50	.15
❑ 189 Brian Falkenborg RC	.75	.23
❑ 190 Aaron Harang RC	2.00	.60
❑ 191 Juan Pena	.50	.15
❑ 192 Chin-Hui Tsao RC	5.00	1.50
❑ 193 Alfonso Soriano	1.25	.35
❑ 194 Alejandro Diaz RC	.75	.23
❑ 195 Carlos Pena	.50	.15
❑ 196 Kevin Nicholson	.50	.15
❑ 197 Mo Bruce	.50	.15
❑ 198 C.C. Sabathia	.50	.15
❑ 199 Carl Crawford	.50	.15
❑ 200 Rafael Furcal	.50	.15

❑ 201 Andrew Beinbrink RC .75 .23
❑ 202 Jimmy Osting .50 .15
❑ 203 Aaron McNeal RC 1.25 .35
❑ 204 Brett Laxton .50 .15
❑ 205 Chris George .50 .15
❑ 206 Felipe Lopez .50 .15
❑ 207 Ben Sheets RC 8.00 2.40
❑ 208 Mike Meyers RC 1.25 .35
❑ 209 Jason Conti .50 .15
❑ 210 Milton Bradley .50 .15
❑ 211 Chris Mears RC .75 .23
❑ 212 Carlos Hernandez RC 1.25 .35
❑ 213 Jason Romano .50 .15
❑ 214 Geofrey Tomlinson .50 .15
❑ 215 Jimmy Rollins .50 .15
❑ 216 Pablo Ozuna .50 .15
❑ 217 Steve Cox .50 .15
❑ 218 Terrence Long .50 .15
❑ 219 Jeff DaVanon RC 1.25 .35
❑ 220 Rick Ankiel .50 .15
❑ 221 Jason Standridge .50 .15
❑ 222 Tony Armas Jr. .50 .15
❑ 223 Jason Tyner .50 .15
❑ 224 Ramon Ortiz .50 .15
❑ 225 Daryle Ward .50 .15
❑ 226 Enger Veras RC .75 .23
❑ 227 Chris Jones .50 .15
❑ 228 Eric Cammack RC .75 .23
❑ 229 Ruben Mateo .50 .15
❑ 230 Ken Harvey RC 2.00 .60
❑ 231 Jake Westbrook .50 .15
❑ 232 Rob Purvis RC .75 .23
❑ 233 Choo Freeman .50 .15
❑ 234 Aramis Ramirez .50 .15
❑ 235 A.J. Burnett .50 .15
❑ 236 Kevin Barker .50 .15
❑ 237 Chance Caple RC .75 .23
❑ 238 Jarrod Washburn .50 .15
❑ 239 Lance Berkman .50 .15
❑ 240 Michael Wenner RC .75 .23
❑ 241 Alex Sanchez .50 .15
❑ 242 Pat Daneker .50 .15
❑ 243 Grant Roberts .50 .15
❑ 244 Mark Ellis RC 1.25 .35
❑ 245 Donny Leon .50 .15
❑ 246 David Eckstein .50 .15
❑ 247 Dicky Gonzalez RC .75 .23
❑ 248 John Patterson .50 .15
❑ 249 Chad Green .50 .15
❑ 250 Scot Shields RC .75 .23
❑ 251 Troy Cameron .50 .15
❑ 252 Jose Molina .50 .15
❑ 253 Rob Pugmire RC .75 .23
❑ 254 Rick Elder .50 .15
❑ 255 Sean Burroughs .50 .15
❑ 256 Josh Kalinowski RC .75 .23
❑ 257 Matt LeCroy .50 .15
❑ 258 Alex Graman RC .75 .23
❑ 259 Juan Silvestre RC .75 .23
❑ 260 Brady Clark .50 .15
❑ 261 Rico Washington RC .75 .23
❑ 262 Gary Matthews Jr. .50 .15
❑ 263 Matt Wise .50 .15
❑ 264 Keith Reed RC 1.25 .35
❑ 265 Santiago Ramirez RC .75 .23
❑ 266 Ben Broussard RC 2.00 .60
❑ 267 Ryan Langerhans .50 .15
❑ 268 Juan Rivera .50 .15
❑ 269 Shawn Gallagher .50 .15
❑ 270 Jorge Toca .50 .15
❑ 271 Brad Lidge .75 .23
❑ 272 Leoncio Estrella RC .75 .23
❑ 273 Ruben Quevedo .50 .15
❑ 274 Jack Cust .50 .15
❑ 275 T.J. Tucker .50 .15
❑ 276 Mike Colangelo .50 .15
❑ 277 Brian Schneider .50 .15
❑ 278 Calvin Murray .50 .15
❑ 279 Josh Girdley .50 .15
❑ 280 Mike Paradis .50 .15
❑ 281 Chad Hermansen .50 .15
❑ 282 Ty Howington RC 1.25 .35
❑ 283 Aaron Myette .50 .15
❑ 284 D'Angelo Jimenez .50 .15
❑ 285 Dernell Stenson .50 .15
❑ 286 Jerry Hairston Jr. .50 .15
❑ 287 Gary Majewski RC 2.00 .60
❑ 288 Derrin Ebert .50 .15
❑ 289 Steve Fish RC .75 .23
❑ 290 Carlos E. Hernandez .50 .15
❑ 291 Allen Levrault .50 .15
❑ 292 Sean McNally RC .75 .23
❑ 293 Randey Dorame RC .75 .23
❑ 294 Wes Anderson RC 1.25 .35
❑ 295 B.J. Ryan .50 .15
❑ 296 Alan Webb RC .75 .23
❑ 297 Brandon Inge RC 3.00 .90
❑ 298 David Walling .50 .15
❑ 299 Sun Woo Kim RC 1.25 .35
❑ 300 Pat Burrell .50 .15
❑ 301 Rick Guttormson RC .75 .23
❑ 302 Gil Meche .50 .15
❑ 303 Carlos Zambrano RC 10.00 3.00
❑ 304 Eric Byrnes UER RC 2.00 .60
Bo Porter pictured
❑ 305 Robb Quinlan RC 2.00 .60
❑ 306 Jackie Rexrode .50 .15
❑ 307 Nate Bump .50 .15
❑ 308 Sean DePaula RC .75 .23
❑ 309 Matt Riley .50 .15
❑ 310 Ryan Minor .50 .15
❑ 311 J.J. Davis .50 .15
❑ 312 Randy Wolf .50 .15
❑ 313 Jason Jennings .50 .15
❑ 314 Scott Seabol RC 1.25 .35
❑ 315 Doug Davis .50 .15
❑ 316 Todd Moser RC .75 .23
❑ 317 Rob Ryan .50 .15
❑ 318 Bubba Crosby .50 .15
❑ 319 Lyle Overbay RC 3.00 .90
❑ 320 Mario Encarnacion .50 .15
❑ 321 F.Rodriguez RC 6.00 1.80
❑ 322 Michael Cuddyer .50 .15
❑ 323 Ed Yarnall .50 .15
❑ 324 Cesar Saba RC .75 .23
❑ 325 Gookie Dawkins .50 .15
❑ 326 Alex Escobar .50 .15
❑ 327 Julio Zuleta RC .75 .23
❑ 328 Josh Hamilton .50 .15
❑ 329 Carlos Urquiola RC .75 .23
❑ 330 Matt Belisle .50 .15
❑ 331 Kurt Ainsworth RC 1.25 .35
❑ 332 Tim Raines Jr. .50 .15
❑ 333 Eric Munson .50 .15
❑ 334 Donzell McDonald .50 .15
❑ 335 Larry Bigbie RC 2.00 .60
❑ 336 Matt Watson RC .75 .23
❑ 337 Aubrey Huff .50 .15
❑ 338 Julio Ramirez .50 .15
❑ 339 Jason Grabowski RC 1.25 .35
❑ 340 Jon Garland .50 .15
❑ 341 Austin Kearns .50 .15
❑ 342 Josh Pressley RC .75 .23
❑ 343 Miguel Olivo RC 2.00 .60
❑ 344 Julio Lugo .50 .15
❑ 345 Roberto Vaz .50 .15
❑ 346 Ramon Soler .50 .15
❑ 347 Brandon Phillips RC 2.00 .60
❑ 348 Vince Faison RC .75 .23
❑ 349 Mike Venafro .50 .15
❑ 350 Rick Asadoorian RC 1.25 .35
❑ 351 B.J. Garbe RC .75 .23
❑ 352 Dan Reichert .50 .15
❑ 353 Jason Stumm RC .75 .23
❑ 354 Ruben Salazar RC .75 .23
❑ 355 Francisco Cordero .50 .15
❑ 356 Juan Guzman RC .75 .23
❑ 357 Mike Bacsik RC .75 .23
❑ 358 Jared Sandberg .50 .15
❑ 359 Rod Barajas .50 .15
❑ 360 Junior Brignac RC .75 .23
❑ 361 J.M. Gold .50 .15
❑ 362 Octavio Dotel .50 .15
❑ 363 David Kelton .50 .15
❑ 364 Scott Morgan .50 .15
❑ 365 Wascar Serrano RC .75 .23
❑ 366 Wilton Veras .50 .15
❑ 367 Eugene Kingsale .50 .15
❑ 368 Ted Lilly .50 .15
❑ 369 George Lombard .50 .15
❑ 370 Chris Haas .50 .15
❑ 371 Wilton Pena RC .75 .23
❑ 372 Vernon Wells .50 .15
❑ 373 Keith Ginter RC .75 .23
❑ 374 Jeff Heaverlo RC .75 .23
❑ 375 Calvin Pickering .50 .15
❑ 376 Mike Lamb RC 2.00 .60
❑ 377 Kyle Snyder .50 .15
❑ 378 Javier Cardona RC .75 .23
❑ 379 Aaron Rowand RC 5.00 1.50
❑ 380 Dee Brown .50 .15
❑ 381 Brett Myers RC 5.00 1.50
❑ 382 Abraham Nunez .50 .15
❑ 383 Eric Valent .50 .15
❑ 384 Jody Gerut RC 2.00 .60
❑ 385 Adam Dunn 1.25 .35
❑ 386 Jay Gehrke .50 .15
❑ 387 Omar Ortiz .50 .15
❑ 388 Darnell McDonald .50 .15
❑ 389 Tony Schrager RC .75 .23
❑ 390 J.D. Closser .50 .15
❑ 391 Ben Christensen RC .75 .23
❑ 392 Adam Kennedy .50 .15
❑ 393 Nick Green RC 1.25 .35
❑ 394 Ramon Hernandez .50 .15
❑ 395 Roy Oswalt RC 15.00 4.50
❑ 396 Andy Tracy RC .75 .23
❑ 397 Eric Gagne 1.25 .35
❑ 398 Michael Tejera RC .75 .23
❑ 399 Adam Everett .50 .15
❑ 400 Corey Patterson .50 .15
❑ 401 Gary Knotts RC .75 .23
❑ 402 Ryan Christianson RC 1.25 .35
❑ 403 Eric Ireland RC .75 .23
❑ 404 Andrew Good RC .75 .23
❑ 405 Brad Penny .50 .15
❑ 406 Jason LaRue .50 .15
❑ 407 Kit Pellow .50 .15
❑ 408 Kevin Beirne .50 .15
❑ 409 Kelly Dransfeldt .50 .15
❑ 410 Jason Grilli .50 .15
❑ 411 Scott Downs RC .75 .23
❑ 412 Jesus Colome .50 .15
❑ 413 John Sneed RC .75 .23
❑ 414 Tony McKnight .50 .15
❑ 415 Luis Rivera .50 .15
❑ 416 Adam Eaton .50 .15
❑ 417 Mike MacDougal RC 1.25 .35
❑ 418 Mike Nannini .50 .15
❑ 419 Barry Zito RC 8.00 2.40
❑ 420 DeWayne Wise .50 .15
❑ 421 Jason Dellaero .50 .15
❑ 422 Chad Moeller .50 .15
❑ 423 Jason Marquis .50 .15
❑ 424 Tim Redding RC 1.25 .35
❑ 425 Mark Mulder .50 .15
❑ 426 Josh Paul .50 .15
❑ 427 Chris Enochs .50 .15
❑ 428 W.Rodriguez RC .75 .23
❑ 429 Kevin Witt .50 .15
❑ 430 Scott Sobkowiak RC .75 .23
❑ 431 McKay Christensen .50 .15
❑ 432 Jung Bong .50 .15
❑ 433 Keith Evans RC .75 .23
❑ 434 Garry Maddox Jr. RC .75 .23
❑ 435 Ramon Santiago RC 1.25 .35
❑ 436 Alex Cora .50 .15
❑ 437 Carlos Lee .50 .15
❑ 438 Jason Repko RC 2.00 .60
❑ 439 Matt Burch .50 .15
❑ 440 Shawn Sonnier RC .75 .23

2000 Bowman Chrome Draft Picks

	Nm-Mt	Ex-Mt
COMP.FACT.SET (110)	50.00	15.00

❑ 1 Pat Burrell .50 .15
❑ 2 Rafael Furcal .50 .15
❑ 3 Grant Roberts .50 .15
❑ 4 Barry Zito 4.00 1.20
❑ 5 Julio Zuleta .50 .15
❑ 6 Mark Mulder .50 .15
❑ 7 Rob Bell .50 .15
❑ 8 Adam Piatt .50 .15
❑ 9 Mike Lamb .75 .23
❑ 10 Pablo Ozuna .50 .15

	Card	Nm-Mt	Ex-Mt
❑	11 Jason Tyner	.50	.15
❑	12 Jason Marquis	.50	.15
❑	13 Eric Munson	.50	.15
❑	14 Seth Etherton	.50	.15
❑	15 Milton Bradley	.50	.15
❑	16 Nick Green	.50	.15
❑	17 Chin-Feng Chen RC	1.50	.45
❑	18 Matt Boone RC	.50	.15
❑	19 Kevin Gregg RC	1.00	.30
❑	20 Eddy Garabito RC	.50	.15
❑	21 Aaron Capista RC	.50	.15
❑	22 Esteban German RC	.50	.15
❑	23 Derek Thompson RC	.50	.15
❑	24 Phil Merrell RC	.50	.15
❑	25 Brian O'Connor RC	.50	.15
❑	26 Yamid Haad	.50	.15
❑	27 Hector Mercado RC	.50	.15
❑	28 Jason Woolf RC	.50	.15
❑	29 Eddy Furniss RC	.50	.15
❑	30 Cha Sueng Baek RC	.50	.15
❑	31 Colby Lewis RC	1.00	.30
❑	32 Pasqual Coco RC	.50	.15
❑	33 Jorge Cantu RC	8.00	2.40
❑	34 Erasmo Ramirez RC	.50	.15
❑	35 Bobby Kielty RC	1.00	.30
❑	36 Joaquin Benoit RC	1.00	.30
❑	37 Brian Esposito RC	.50	.15
❑	38 Michael Wenner	.50	.15
❑	39 Juan Rincon RC	.50	.15
❑	40 Yorvit Torrealba RC	.50	.15
❑	41 Chad Durham RC	.50	.15
❑	42 Jim Mann RC	.50	.15
❑	43 Shane Loux RC	.50	.15
❑	44 Luis Rivas	.50	.15
❑	45 Ken Chenard RC	.50	.15
❑	46 Mike Lockwood RC	.50	.15
❑	47 Yovanny Lara RC	.50	.15
❑	48 Bubba Carpenter RC	.50	.15
❑	49 Ryan Dittfurth RC	.50	.15
❑	50 John Stephens RC	1.00	.30
❑	51 Pedro Feliz RC	2.50	.75
❑	52 Kenny Kelly RC	1.00	.30
❑	53 Neil Jenkins RC	.50	.15
❑	54 Mike Glendenning RC	.50	.15
❑	55 Bo Porter	.50	.15
❑	56 Eric Byrnes	.75	.23
❑	57 Tony Alvarez RC	.50	.15
❑	58 Kazuhiro Sasaki RC	1.50	.45
❑	59 Chad Durbin RC	.50	.15
❑	60 Mike Bynum RC	.50	.15
❑	61 Travis Wilson RC	.50	.15
❑	62 Jose Leon RC	.50	.15
❑	63 Ryan Vogelsong RC	1.00	.30
❑	64 Geraldo Guzman RC	.50	.15
❑	65 Craig Anderson RC	.50	.15
❑	66 Carlos Silva RC	1.50	.45
❑	67 Brad Thomas RC	.50	.15
❑	68 Chin-Hui Tsao	1.50	.45
❑	69 Mark Buehrle RC	8.00	2.40
❑	70 Juan Salas RC	.50	.15
❑	71 Denny Abreu RC	.50	.15
❑	72 Keith McDonald RC	.50	.15
❑	73 Chris Richard RC	.50	.15
❑	74 Tomas De la Rosa RC	.50	.15
❑	75 Vicente Padilla RC	1.00	.30
❑	76 Justin Brunette RC	.50	.15
❑	77 Scott Linebrink RC	.50	.15
❑	78 Jeff Sparks RC	.50	.15
❑	79 Tike Redman RC	1.50	.45
❑	80 John Lackey RC	2.50	.75
❑	81 Joe Strong RC	.50	.15
❑	82 Brian Tollberg RC	.50	.15
❑	83 Steve Sisco RC	.50	.15
❑	84 Chris Clapinski RC	.50	.15
❑	85 Augie Ojeda RC	.50	.15
❑	86 Adrian Gonzalez RC	1.50	.45
❑	87 Mike Stodolka RC	.50	.15
❑	88 Adam Johnson RC	1.00	.30
❑	89 Matt Wheatland RC	.50	.15
❑	90 Corey Smith RC	1.00	.30
❑	91 Rocco Baldelli RC	5.00	1.50
❑	92 Keith Bucktrot RC	.50	.15
❑	93 Adam Wainwright RC	1.50	.45
❑	94 Blaine Boyer RC	.50	.15
❑	95 Aaron Herr RC	1.00	.30
❑	96 Scott Thorman RC	1.00	.30
❑	97 Bryan Digby RC	1.00	.30
❑	98 Josh Shortslef RC	.50	.15
❑	99 Sean Smith RC	1.00	.30
❑	100 Alex Cruz RC	.50	.15
❑	101 Marc Love RC	.50	.15
❑	102 Kevin Lee RC	.50	.15
❑	103 Timo Perez RC	1.00	.30
❑	104 Alex Cabrera RC	1.00	.30
❑	105 Shane Heams RC	.50	.15
❑	106 Tripper Johnson RC	1.00	.30
❑	107 Brent Abernathy RC	.50	.15
❑	108 John Cotton RC	.50	.15
❑	109 Brad Wilkerson RC	2.50	.75
❑	110 Jon Rauch RC	1.00	.30

2001 Bowman Chrome

	Nm-Mt	Ex-Mt
COMP.SET w/o SP's (220)	50.00	15.00
COMMON (1-110/201-310)	.50	.15
COMMON (111-200/311-330)	5.00	1.50
COMMON (331-350)	50.00	15.00

	Card	Nm-Mt	Ex-Mt
❑	1 Jason Giambi	.50	.15
❑	2 Rafael Furcal	.50	.15
❑	3 Bernie Williams	.75	.23
❑	4 Kenny Lofton	.50	.15
❑	5 Al Leiter	.50	.15
❑	6 Albert Belle	.50	.15
❑	7 Craig Biggio	.75	.23
❑	8 Mark Mulder	.50	.15
❑	9 Carlos Delgado	.50	.15
❑	10 Darin Erstad	.50	.15
❑	11 Richie Sexson	.50	.15
❑	12 Randy Johnson	1.25	.35
❑	13 Greg Maddux	2.00	.60
❑	14 Orlando Hernandez	.50	.15
❑	15 Javier Vazquez	.50	.15
❑	16 Jeff Kent	.50	.15
❑	17 Jim Thome	.75	.23
❑	18 John Olerud	.50	.15
❑	19 Jason Kendall	.50	.15
❑	20 Scott Rolen	.75	.23
❑	21 Tony Gwynn	1.50	.45
❑	22 Edgardo Alfonzo	.50	.15
❑	23 Pokey Reese	.50	.15
❑	24 Todd Helton	.75	.23
❑	25 Mark Quinn	.50	.15
❑	26 Dean Palmer	.50	.15
❑	27 Ray Durham	.50	.15
❑	28 Rafael Palmeiro	.75	.23
❑	29 Carl Everett	.50	.15
❑	30 Vladimir Guerrero	1.25	.35
❑	31 Livan Hernandez	.50	.15
❑	32 Preston Wilson	.50	.15
❑	33 Jose Vidro	.50	.15
❑	34 Fred McGriff	.75	.23
❑	35 Kevin Brown	.50	.15
❑	36 Miguel Tejada	.50	.15
❑	37 Chipper Jones	1.25	.35
❑	38 Edgar Martinez	.75	.23
❑	39 Tony Batista	.50	.15
❑	40 Jorge Posada	.75	.23
❑	41 Sammy Sosa	1.25	.35
❑	42 Gary Sheffield	.50	.15
❑	43 Bartolo Colon	.50	.15
❑	44 Pat Burrell	.50	.15
❑	45 Jay Payton	.50	.15
❑	46 Mike Mussina	.75	.23
❑	47 Nomar Garciaparra	2.00	.60
❑	48 Darren Dreifort	.50	.15
❑	49 Richard Hidalgo	.50	.15
❑	50 Troy Glaus	.50	.15
❑	51 Ben Grieve	.50	.15
❑	52 Jim Edmonds	.75	.23
❑	53 Raul Mondesi	.50	.15
❑	54 Andruw Jones	.75	.23
❑	55 Mike Sweeney	.50	.15
❑	56 Derek Jeter	3.00	.90
❑	57 Ruben Mateo	.50	.15
❑	58 Cristian Guzman	.50	.15
❑	59 Mike Hampton	.50	.15
❑	60 J.D. Drew	.50	.15
❑	61 Matt Lawton	.50	.15
❑	62 Moises Alou	.50	.15
❑	63 Terrence Long	.50	.15
❑	64 Geoff Jenkins	.50	.15
❑	65 Manny Ramirez Sox	.75	.23
❑	66 Johnny Damon	.75	.23
❑	67 Pedro Martinez	.75	.23
❑	68 Juan Gonzalez	.50	.15
❑	69 Roger Clemens	2.50	.75
❑	70 Carlos Beltran	.50	.15
❑	71 Roberto Alomar	.75	.23
❑	72 Barry Bonds	3.00	.90
❑	73 Tim Hudson	.50	.15
❑	74 Tom Glavine	.75	.23
❑	75 Jeromy Burnitz	.50	.15
❑	76 Adrian Beltre	.50	.15
❑	77 Mike Piazza	2.00	.60
❑	78 Kerry Wood	.50	.15
❑	79 Steve Finley	.50	.15
❑	80 Bob Abreu	.50	.15
❑	81 Neifi Perez	.50	.15
❑	82 Mark Redman	.50	.15
❑	83 Paul Konerko	.50	.15
❑	84 Jermaine Dye	.50	.15
❑	85 Brian Giles	.50	.15
❑	86 Ivan Rodriguez	.75	.23
❑	87 Adam Kennedy	.50	.15
❑	88 Eric Chavez	.50	.15
❑	89 Billy Koch	.50	.15
❑	90 Shawn Green	.50	.15
❑	91 Matt Williams	.50	.15
❑	92 Greg Vaughn	.50	.15
❑	93 Jeff Cirillo	.50	.15
❑	94 Frank Thomas	1.25	.35
❑	95 David Justice	.50	.15
❑	96 Cal Ripken	4.00	1.20
❑	97 Curt Schilling	.50	.15
❑	98 Barry Zito	.75	.23
❑	99 Brian Jordan	.50	.15
❑	100 Chan Ho Park	.50	.15
❑	101 J.T. Snow	.50	.15
❑	102 Kazuhiro Sasaki	.50	.15
❑	103 Alex Rodriguez	2.00	.60
❑	104 Mariano Rivera	.75	.23
❑	105 Eric Milton	.50	.15
❑	106 Andy Pettitte	.75	.23
❑	107 Ken Griffey Jr.	2.00	.60
❑	108 Bengie Molina	.50	.15
❑	109 Jeff Bagwell	.75	.23
❑	110 Mark McGwire	3.00	.90
❑	111 Dan Tosca RC	8.00	2.40
❑	112 Sergio Contreras RC	8.00	2.40
❑	113 Mitch Jones RC	8.00	2.40
❑	114 Ramon Carvajal RC	8.00	2.40

- ❑ 115 Ryan Madson RC 8.00 2.40
- ❑ 116 Hank Blalock RC 40.00 12.00
- ❑ 117 Ben Washburn RC 8.00 2.40
- ❑ 118 Erick Almonte RC 8.00 2.40
- ❑ 119 Shawn Fagan RC 8.00 2.40
- ❑ 120 Gary Johnson RC 8.00 2.40
- ❑ 121 Brett Evert RC 8.00 2.40
- ❑ 122 Joe Hamer RC 8.00 2.40
- ❑ 123 Yhency Brazoban RC 10.00 3.00
- ❑ 124 Domingo Guante RC 8.00 2.40
- ❑ 125 Deivi Mendez RC 8.00 2.40
- ❑ 126 Adrian Hernandez RC 8.00 2.40
- ❑ 127 R. Abercrombie RC 8.00 2.40
- ❑ 128 Steve Bennett RC 5.00 1.50
- ❑ 129 Matt White RC 8.00 2.40
- ❑ 130 Brian Hitchcox RC 5.00 1.50
- ❑ 131 Deivis Santos RC 8.00 2.40
- ❑ 132 Luis Montanez RC 8.00 2.40
- ❑ 133 Eric Reynolds RC 5.00 1.50
- ❑ 134 Denny Bautista RC 10.00 3.00
- ❑ 135 Hector Garcia RC 8.00 2.40
- ❑ 136 Joe Thurston RC 8.00 2.40
- ❑ 137 Tsuyoshi Shinjo RC 10.00 3.00
- ❑ 138 Elpidio Guzman RC 8.00 2.40
- ❑ 139 Brian Bass RC 8.00 2.40
- ❑ 140 Mark Burnett RC 8.00 2.40
- ❑ 141 Russ Jacobson UER 5.00 1.50
  Last name misspelled Jacobsen on front
- ❑ 142 Travis Hafner RC 40.00 12.00
- ❑ 143 Wilson Betemit RC 10.00 3.00
- ❑ 144 Luke Lockwood RC 8.00 2.40
- ❑ 145 Noel Devarez RC 8.00 2.40
- ❑ 146 Doug Gredvig RC 8.00 2.40
- ❑ 147 Seung Song RC 8.00 2.40
- ❑ 148 Andy Van Hekken RC 8.00 2.40
- ❑ 149 Ryan Kohlmeier 5.00 1.50
- ❑ 150 Dee Haynes RC 8.00 2.40
- ❑ 151 Jim Journell RC 8.00 2.40
- ❑ 152 Chad Petty RC 8.00 2.40
- ❑ 153 Danny Borrell RC 8.00 2.40
- ❑ 154 Dave Krynzel 5.00 1.50
- ❑ 155 Octavio Martinez RC 8.00 2.40
- ❑ 156 David Parrish RC 8.00 2.40
- ❑ 157 Jason Miller RC 8.00 2.40
- ❑ 158 Corey Spencer RC 5.00 1.50
- ❑ 159 Maxim St. Pierre RC 8.00 2.40
- ❑ 160 Pat Magness RC 8.00 2.40
- ❑ 161 Ranier Olmedo RC 8.00 2.40
- ❑ 162 Brandon Mims RC 8.00 2.40
- ❑ 163 Phil Wilson RC 8.00 2.40
- ❑ 164 Jose Reyes RC 50.00 15.00
- ❑ 165 Matt Butler RC 8.00 2.40
- ❑ 166 Joel Pineiro 8.00 2.40
- ❑ 167 Ken Chenard 5.00 1.50
- ❑ 168 Alexis Gomez RC 8.00 2.40
- ❑ 169 Justin Morneau RC 30.00 9.00
- ❑ 170 Josh Fogg RC 8.00 2.40
- ❑ 171 Charles Frazier RC 8.00 2.40
- ❑ 172 Ryan Ludwick RC 8.00 2.40
- ❑ 173 Seth McClung RC 8.00 2.40
- ❑ 174 Justin Wayne RC 8.00 2.40
- ❑ 175 Rafael Soriano RC 8.00 2.40
- ❑ 176 Jared Abruzzo RC 8.00 2.40
- ❑ 177 Jason Richardson RC 8.00 2.40
- ❑ 178 Darwin Cubillan RC 5.00 1.50
- ❑ 179 Blake Williams RC 8.00 2.40
- ❑ 180 V. Pascucci RC 8.00 2.40
- ❑ 181 Ryan Hannaman RC 8.00 2.40
- ❑ 182 Steve Smyth RC 8.00 2.40
- ❑ 183 Jake Peavy RC 50.00 15.00
- ❑ 184 Onix Mercado RC 8.00 2.40
- ❑ 185 Luis Torres RC 8.00 2.40
- ❑ 186 Casey Fossum RC 8.00 2.40
- ❑ 187 Eduardo Figueroa RC 8.00 2.40
- ❑ 188 Bryan Barnowski RC 8.00 2.40
- ❑ 189 Jason Standridge 5.00 1.50
- ❑ 190 Marvin Seale RC 8.00 2.40
- ❑ 191 Steve Smitherman RC 8.00 2.40
- ❑ 192 Rafael Boitel RC 8.00 2.40
- ❑ 193 Dany Morban RC 8.00 2.40
- ❑ 194 Justin Woodrow RC 8.00 2.40
- ❑ 195 Ed Rogers RC 8.00 2.40
- ❑ 196 Ben Hendrickson RC 8.00 2.40
- ❑ 197 Thomas Mitchell 5.00 1.50
- ❑ 198 Adam Pettyjohn RC 8.00 2.40
- ❑ 199 Doug Nickle RC 5.00 1.50
- ❑ 200 Jason Jones RC 8.00 2.40
- ❑ 201 Larry Barnes .50 .15
- ❑ 202 Ben Diggins .50 .15
- ❑ 203 Dee Brown .50 .15
- ❑ 204 Rocco Baldelli .50 .15
- ❑ 205 Luis Terrero .50 .15
- ❑ 206 Milton Bradley .50 .15
- ❑ 207 Kurt Ainsworth .50 .15
- ❑ 208 Sean Burroughs .50 .15
- ❑ 209 Rick Asadoorian .50 .15
- ❑ 210 Ramon Castro .50 .15
- ❑ 211 Nick Neugebauer .50 .15
- ❑ 212 Aaron Myette .50 .15
- ❑ 213 Luis Matos .50 .15
- ❑ 214 Donnie Bridges .50 .15
- ❑ 215 Alex Cintron .50 .15
- ❑ 216 Bobby Kielty .50 .15
- ❑ 217 Matt Belisle .50 .15
- ❑ 218 Adam Everett .50 .15
- ❑ 219 John Lackey .50 .15
- ❑ 220 Adam Wainwright .50 .15
- ❑ 221 Jerry Hairston Jr. .50 .15
- ❑ 222 Mike Bynum .50 .15
- ❑ 223 Ryan Christianson .50 .15
- ❑ 224 J.J. Davis .50 .15
- ❑ 225 Alex Graman .50 .15
- ❑ 226 Abraham Nunez .50 .15
- ❑ 227 Sun Woo Kim .50 .15
- ❑ 228 Jimmy Rollins .50 .15
- ❑ 229 Ruben Salazar .50 .15
- ❑ 230 Josh Girdley .50 .15
- ❑ 231 Carl Crawford .50 .15
- ❑ 232 Ben Davis .50 .15
- ❑ 233 Jason Grabowski .50 .15
- ❑ 234 Chris George .50 .15
- ❑ 235 Roy Oswalt .75 .23
- ❑ 236 Brian Cole .50 .15
- ❑ 237 Corey Patterson .50 .15
- ❑ 238 Vernon Wells .50 .15
- ❑ 239 Brad Baker .50 .15
- ❑ 240 Gookie Dawkins .50 .15
- ❑ 241 Michael Cuddyer .50 .15
- ❑ 242 Ricardo Aramboles .50 .15
- ❑ 243 Ben Sheets .75 .23
- ❑ 244 Toby Hall .50 .15
- ❑ 245 Jack Cust .50 .15
- ❑ 246 Pedro Feliz .50 .15
- ❑ 247 Josh Beckett .75 .23
- ❑ 248 Alex Escobar .50 .15
- ❑ 249 Marcus Giles .50 .15
- ❑ 250 Jon Rauch .50 .15
- ❑ 251 Kevin Mench .50 .15
- ❑ 252 Shawn Sonnier .50 .15
- ❑ 253 Aaron Rowand .50 .15
- ❑ 254 C.C. Sabathia .50 .15
- ❑ 255 Bubba Crosby .50 .15
- ❑ 256 Josh Hamilton .50 .15
- ❑ 257 Carlos Hernandez .50 .15
- ❑ 258 Carlos Pena .50 .15
- ❑ 259 Miguel Cabrera 4.00 1.20
- ❑ 260 Brandon Phillips .50 .15
- ❑ 261 Tony Pena Jr. .50 .15
- ❑ 262 Cristian Guerrero .50 .15
- ❑ 263 Jin Ho Cho .50 .15
- ❑ 264 Aaron Herr .50 .15
- ❑ 265 Keith Ginter .50 .15
- ❑ 266 Felipe Lopez .50 .15
- ❑ 267 Travis Harper .50 .15
- ❑ 268 Joe Torres .50 .15
- ❑ 269 Eric Byrnes .50 .15
- ❑ 270 Ben Christensen .50 .15
- ❑ 271 Aubrey Huff .50 .15
- ❑ 272 Lyle Overbay .50 .15
- ❑ 273 Vince Faison .50 .15
- ❑ 274 Bobby Bradley .50 .15
- ❑ 275 Joe Crede 1.25 .35
- ❑ 276 Matt Wheatland .50 .15
- ❑ 277 Grady Sizemore .75 .23
- ❑ 278 Adrian Gonzalez .50 .15
- ❑ 279 Tim Raines Jr. .50 .15
- ❑ 280 Phil Dumatrait .50 .15
- ❑ 281 Jason Hart .50 .15
- ❑ 282 David Kelton .50 .15
- ❑ 283 David Walling .50 .15
- ❑ 284 J.R. House .50 .15
- ❑ 285 Kenny Kelly .50 .15
- ❑ 286 Aaron McNeal .50 .15
- ❑ 287 Nick Johnson .50 .15
- ❑ 288 Scott Heard .50 .15
- ❑ 289 Brad Wilkerson .50 .15
- ❑ 290 Allen Levrault .50 .15
- ❑ 291 Chris Richard .50 .15
- ❑ 292 Jared Sandberg .50 .15
- ❑ 293 Tike Redman .50 .15
- ❑ 294 Adam Dunn .75 .23
- ❑ 295 Josh Pressley .50 .15
- ❑ 296 Jose Ortiz .50 .15
- ❑ 297 Jason Romano .50 .15
- ❑ 298 Tim Redding .50 .15
- ❑ 299 Alex Gordon .50 .15
- ❑ 300 Ben Petrick .50 .15
- ❑ 301 Eric Munson .50 .15
- ❑ 302 Luis Rivas .50 .15
- ❑ 303 Matt Ginter .50 .15
- ❑ 304 Alfonso Soriano .75 .23
- ❑ 305 Wilfredo Rodriguez .50 .15
- ❑ 306 Brett Myers .50 .15
- ❑ 307 Scott Seabol .50 .15
- ❑ 308 Tony Alvarez .50 .15
- ❑ 309 Donzell McDonald .50 .15
- ❑ 310 Austin Kearns .50 .15
- ❑ 311 Will Ohman RC 8.00 2.40
- ❑ 312 Ryan Soules RC 5.00 1.50
- ❑ 313 Cody Ross RC 8.00 2.40
- ❑ 314 Bill Whitecotton RC 8.00 2.40
- ❑ 315 Mike Burns RC 8.00 2.40
- ❑ 316 Manuel Acosta RC 8.00 2.40
- ❑ 317 Lance Niekro RC 15.00 4.50
- ❑ 318 Travis Thompson RC 8.00 2.40
- ❑ 319 Zach Sorensen RC 8.00 2.40
- ❑ 320 Austin Evans RC 5.00 1.50
- ❑ 321 Brad Stiles RC 8.00 2.40
- ❑ 322 Joe Kennedy RC 10.00 3.00
- ❑ 323 Luke Martin RC 8.00 2.40
- ❑ 324 Juan Diaz RC 8.00 2.40
- ❑ 325 Pat Hallmark RC 5.00 1.50
- ❑ 326 Christian Parker RC 5.00 1.50
- ❑ 327 Ronny Corona RC 8.00 2.40
- ❑ 328 Jermaine Clark RC 5.00 1.50
- ❑ 329 Scott Dunn RC 8.00 2.40
- ❑ 330 Scott Chiasson RC 8.00 2.40
- ❑ 331 Greg Nash AU RC 50.00 15.00
- ❑ 332 Brad Cresse AU 50.00 15.00
- ❑ 333 John Buck AU RC 80.00 24.00
- ❑ 334 Freddie Bynum AU RC 50.00 15.00
- ❑ 335 Felix Diaz AU RC 50.00 15.00
- ❑ 336 Jason Belcher AU RC 50.00 15.00
- ❑ 337 T.Farnsworth AU RC 50.00 15.00
- ❑ 338 Roberto Miniel AU RC 50.00 15.00
- ❑ 339 Esix Snead AU RC 50.00 15.00
- ❑ 340 Albert Pujols AU RC 2500.00 750.00
- ❑ 341 Jeff Andra AU RC 50.00 15.00
- ❑ 342 Victor Hall AU RC 50.00 15.00
- ❑ 343 Pedro Liriano AU RC 50.00 15.00
- ❑ 344 Andy Beal AU RC 50.00 15.00
- ❑ 345 Bob Keppel AU RC 50.00 15.00
- ❑ 346 Brian Schmitt AU RC 50.00 15.00
- ❑ 347 Ron Davenport AU RC 200.00 60.00
- ❑ 348 Tony Blanco AU RC 50.00 15.00
- ❑ 349 Reggie Griggs AU RC 50.00 15.00
- ❑ 350 D. Van Dusen AU RC 50.00 15.00
- ❑ 351A I. Suzuki English RC 100.00 30.00
- ❑ 351B I. Suzuki Japan RC 100.00 30.00

2002 Bowman Chrome

	Nm-Mt	Ex-Mt
COMP.RED SET (110)	40.00	12.00
COMP.BLUE w/o SP's (110)	40.00	12.00
COMMON RED (1-110)	.50	.15
COMMON BLUE (111-383)	.75	.23
COMMON AU (324B/384-405)	10.00	3.00
324B/384-405 GROUP A AUTO ODDS 1:28		.00
403-404 GROUP B AUTO ODDS 1:1290		.00
324B/384-405 OVERALL AUTO ODDS 1:27		.00

- ❑ 1 Adam Dunn .50 .15
- ❑ 2 Derek Jeter 3.00 .90
- ❑ 3 Alex Rodriguez 2.00 .60
- ❑ 4 Miguel Tejada .50 .15
- ❑ 5 Nomar Garciaparra 2.00 .60

❑ 6 Toby Hall .50 .15
❑ 7 Brandon Duckworth .50 .15
❑ 8 Paul LoDuca .50 .15
❑ 9 Brian Giles .50 .15
❑ 10 C.C. Sabathia .50 .15
❑ 11 Curt Schilling .50 .15
❑ 12 Tsuyoshi Shinjo .50 .15
❑ 13 Ramon Hernandez .50 .15
❑ 14 Jose Cruz Jr. .50 .15
❑ 15 Albert Pujols 2.50 .75
❑ 16 Joe Mays .50 .15
❑ 17 Javy Lopez .50 .15
❑ 18 J.T. Snow .50 .15
❑ 19 David Segui .50 .15
❑ 20 Jorge Posada .75 .23
❑ 21 Doug Mientkiewicz .50 .15
❑ 22 Jerry Hairston Jr. .50 .15
❑ 23 Bernie Williams .75 .23
❑ 24 Mike Sweeney .50 .15
❑ 25 Jason Giambi .50 .15
❑ 26 Ryan Dempster .50 .15
❑ 27 Ryan Klesko .50 .15
❑ 28 Mark Quinn .50 .15
❑ 29 Jeff Kent .50 .15
❑ 30 Eric Chavez .50 .15
❑ 31 Adrian Beltre .50 .15
❑ 32 Andruw Jones .75 .23
❑ 33 Alfonso Soriano .50 .15
❑ 34 Aramis Ramirez .50 .15
❑ 35 Greg Maddux 2.00 .60
❑ 36 Andy Pettitte .75 .23
❑ 37 Bartolo Colon .50 .15
❑ 38 Ben Sheets .50 .15
❑ 39 Bobby Higginson .50 .15
❑ 40 Ivan Rodriguez .75 .23
❑ 41 Brad Penny .50 .15
❑ 42 Carlos Lee .50 .15
❑ 43 Damion Easley .50 .15
❑ 44 Preston Wilson .50 .15
❑ 45 Jeff Bagwell .75 .23
❑ 46 Eric Milton .50 .15
❑ 47 Rafael Palmeiro .75 .23
❑ 48 Gary Sheffield .50 .15
❑ 49 J.D. Drew .50 .15
❑ 50 Jim Thome .75 .23
❑ 51 Ichiro Suzuki 2.50 .75
❑ 52 Bud Smith .50 .15
❑ 53 Chan Ho Park .50 .15
❑ 54 D'Angelo Jimenez .50 .15
❑ 55 Ken Griffey Jr. 2.00 .60
❑ 56 Wade Miller .50 .15
❑ 57 Vladimir Guerrero 1.25 .35
❑ 58 Troy Glaus .50 .15
❑ 59 Shawn Green .50 .15
❑ 60 Kerry Wood .50 .15
❑ 61 Jack Wilson .50 .15
❑ 62 Kevin Brown .50 .15
❑ 63 Marcus Giles .50 .15
❑ 64 Pat Burrell .50 .15
❑ 65 Larry Walker .50 .15
❑ 66 Sammy Sosa 1.25 .35
❑ 67 Raul Mondesi .50 .15
❑ 68 Tim Hudson .50 .15
❑ 69 Lance Berkman .50 .15
❑ 70 Mike Mussina .75 .23
❑ 71 Barry Zito .50 .15
❑ 72 Jimmy Rollins .50 .15
❑ 73 Barry Bonds 3.00 .90
❑ 74 Craig Biggio .75 .23
❑ 75 Todd Helton .75 .23
❑ 76 Roger Clemens 2.50 .75
❑ 77 Frank Catalanotto .50 .15
❑ 78 Josh Towers .50 .15
❑ 79 Roy Oswalt .50 .15
❑ 80 Chipper Jones 1.25 .35
❑ 81 Cristian Guzman .50 .15
❑ 82 Darin Erstad .50 .15
❑ 83 Freddy Garcia .50 .15
❑ 84 Jason Tyner .50 .15
❑ 85 Carlos Delgado .50 .15
❑ 86 Jon Lieber .50 .15
❑ 87 Juan Pierre .50 .15
❑ 88 Matt Morris .50 .15
❑ 89 Phil Nevin .50 .15
❑ 90 Jim Edmonds .75 .23
❑ 91 Magglio Ordonez .50 .15
❑ 92 Mike Hampton .50 .15
❑ 93 Rafael Furcal .50 .15
❑ 94 Richie Sexson .50 .15
❑ 95 Luis Gonzalez .50 .15
❑ 96 Scott Rolen .75 .23
❑ 97 Tim Redding .50 .15
❑ 98 Moises Alou .50 .15
❑ 99 Jose Vidro .50 .15
❑ 100 Mike Piazza 2.00 .60
❑ 101 Pedro Martinez .75 .23
❑ 102 Geoff Jenkins .50 .15
❑ 103 Johnny Damon Sox .75 .23
❑ 104 Mike Cameron UER .50 .15
Card has fascimile autograph of Troy Cameron
❑ 105 Randy Johnson 1.25 .35
❑ 106 David Eckstein .50 .15
❑ 107 Javier Vazquez .50 .15
❑ 108 Mark Mulder .50 .15
❑ 109 Robert Fick .50 .15
❑ 110 Roberto Alomar .75 .23
❑ 111 Wilson Betemit .75 .23
❑ 112 Chris Tritle SP RC 5.00 1.50
❑ 113 Ed Rogers .75 .23
❑ 114 Juan Pena .75 .23
❑ 115 Josh Beckett 1.25 .35
❑ 116 Juan Cruz .75 .23
❑ 117 Noochie Varner SP RC 5.00 1.50
❑ 118 Blake Williams .75 .23
❑ 119 Mike Rivera .75 .23
❑ 120 Hank Blalock 2.00 .60
❑ 121 Hansel Izquierdo SP RC 5.00 1.50
❑ 122 Orlando Hudson .75 .23
❑ 123 Bill Hall SP 5.00 1.50
❑ 124 Jose Reyes 2.00 .60
❑ 125 Juan Rivera .75 .23
❑ 126 Eric Valent .75 .23
❑ 127 Scotty Layfield SP RC 5.00 1.50
❑ 128 Austin Kearns .75 .23
❑ 129 Nic Jackson SP RC 5.00 1.50
❑ 130 Scott Chiasson .75 .23
❑ 131 Chad Qualls SP RC 8.00 2.40
❑ 132 Marcus Thames .75 .23
❑ 133 Nathan Haynes .75 .23
❑ 134 Joe Borchard .75 .23
❑ 135 Josh Hamilton .75 .23
❑ 136 Corey Patterson .75 .23
❑ 137 Travis Wilson .75 .23
❑ 138 Alex Escobar .75 .23
❑ 139 Alexis Gomez .75 .23
❑ 140 Nick Johnson 1.25 .35
❑ 141 Marlon Byrd .75 .23
❑ 142 Kory DeHaan .75 .23
❑ 143 Carlos Hernandez .75 .23
❑ 144 Sean Burroughs .75 .23
❑ 145 Angel Berroa .75 .23
❑ 146 Aubrey Huff 1.25 .35
❑ 147 Travis Hafner 1.25 .35
❑ 148 Brandon Berger .75 .23
❑ 149 J.R. House .75 .23
❑ 150 Dewon Brazelton .75 .23
❑ 151 Jayson Werth .75 .23
❑ 152 Larry Barnes .75 .23
❑ 153 Ruben Gotay SP RC 8.00 2.40
❑ 154 Tommy Marx SP RC 5.00 1.50
❑ 155 John Suomi SP RC 5.00 1.50
❑ 156 Javier Colina SP 5.00 1.50
❑ 157 Greg Sain SP RC 5.00 1.50
❑ 158 Robert Cosby SP RC 5.00 1.50
❑ 159 Angel Pagan SP RC 5.00 1.50
❑ 160 Ralph Santana RC 1.25 .35
❑ 161 Joe Orloski RC 1.25 .35
❑ 162 Shayne Wright SP RC 5.00 1.50
❑ 163 Jay Caligiuri SP RC 5.00 1.50
❑ 164 Greg Montalbano SP RC 5.00 1.50
❑ 165 Rich Harden SP RC 30.00 9.00
❑ 166 Rich Thompson SP RC 5.00 1.50
❑ 167 Fred Bastardo SP RC 5.00 1.50
❑ 168 Alejandro Giron SP RC 5.00 1.50
❑ 169 Jesus Medrano SP RC 5.00 1.50
❑ 170 Kevin Deaton SP RC 5.00 1.50
❑ 171 Mike Rosamond RC 1.25 .35
❑ 172 Jon Guzman SP RC 5.00 1.50
❑ 173 Gerard Oakes SP RC 5.00 1.50
❑ 174 Francisco Liriano SP RC 30.00 9.00
❑ 175 Matt Allegra SP RC 5.00 1.50
❑ 176 Mike Snyder SP RC 5.00 1.50
❑ 177 James Shanks SP RC 5.00 1.50
❑ 178 And. Hernandez SP RC 5.00 1.50
❑ 179 Dan Trumble SP RC 5.00 1.50
❑ 180 Luis DePaula SP RC 5.00 1.50
❑ 181 Randall Shelley SP RC 5.00 1.50
❑ 182 Richard Lane SP RC 5.00 1.50
❑ 183 Antwon Rollins SP RC 5.00 1.50
❑ 184 Ryan Bukvich SP RC 5.00 1.50
❑ 185 Derrick Lewis SP 5.00 1.50
❑ 186 Eric Miller SP RC 5.00 1.50
❑ 187 Justin Schuda SP RC 5.00 1.50
❑ 188 Brian West SP RC 5.00 1.50
❑ 189 Brad Wilkerson .75 .23
❑ 190 Neal Frendling SP RC 5.00 1.50
❑ 191 Jeremy Hill SP RC 5.00 1.50
❑ 192 James Barrett SP RC 5.00 1.50
❑ 193 Brett Kay SP RC 5.00 1.50
❑ 194 Ryan Mottl SP RC 5.00 1.50
❑ 195 Brad Nelson SP RC 8.00 2.40
❑ 196 Juan M. Gonzalez SP RC 5.00 1.50
❑ 197 Curtis Legendre SP RC 5.00 1.50
❑ 198 Ronald Acuna SP RC 5.00 1.50
❑ 199 Chris Flinn SP RC 5.00 1.50
❑ 200 Nick Alvarez SP RC 5.00 1.50
❑ 201 Jason Ellison SP RC 10.00 3.00
❑ 202 Blake McGinley SP RC 5.00 1.50
❑ 203 Dan Phillips SP RC 5.00 1.50
❑ 204 Demetrius Heath SP RC 5.00 1.50
❑ 205 Eric Bruntlett SP RC 5.00 1.50
❑ 206 Joe Jiannetti SP RC 5.00 1.50
❑ 207 Mike Hill SP RC 5.00 1.50
❑ 208 Ricardo Cordova SP RC 5.00 1.50
❑ 209 Mark Hamilton SP RC 5.00 1.50
❑ 210 David Mattox SP RC 5.00 1.50
❑ 211 Jose Morban SP RC 5.00 1.50
❑ 212 Scott Wiggins SP RC 5.00 1.50
❑ 213 Steve Green .75 .23
❑ 214 Brian Rogers SP 5.00 1.50
❑ 215 Kenny Baugh .75 .23
❑ 216 Anastacio Martinez SP RC 5.00 1.50
❑ 217 Richard Lewis .75 .23
❑ 218 Tim Kalita SP RC 5.00 1.50
❑ 219 Edwin Almonte SP RC 5.00 1.50
❑ 220 Hee Seop Choi 1.25 .35
❑ 221 Ty Howington .75 .23
❑ 222 Victor Alvarez SP RC 5.00 1.50
❑ 223 Morgan Ensberg 1.25 .35
❑ 224 Jeff Austin SP RC 5.00 1.50
❑ 225 Clint Weibl SP RC 5.00 1.50
❑ 226 Eric Cyr .75 .23
❑ 227 Marlyn Tisdale SP RC 5.00 1.50
❑ 228 John VanBenschoten .75 .23
❑ 229 David Krynzel .75 .23
❑ 230 Raul Chavez SP RC 5.00 1.50
❑ 231 Brett Evert .75 .23
❑ 232 Joe Rogers SP RC 5.00 1.50
❑ 233 Adam Wainwright .75 .23
❑ 234 Matt Herges RC .75 .23
❑ 235 Matt Childers SP RC 5.00 1.50
❑ 236 Nick Neugebauer .75 .23
❑ 237 Carl Crawford 1.25 .35
❑ 238 Seung Song .75 .23
❑ 239 Randy Flores .75 .23
❑ 240 Jason Lane 1.25 .35
❑ 241 Chase Utley 5.00 1.50
❑ 242 Ben Howard SP RC 5.00 1.50
❑ 243 Eric Glaser SP RC 5.00 1.50

❑ 244 Josh Wilson RC .... 1.25 .35
❑ 245 Jose Valverde SP RC...... 5.00 1.50
❑ 246 Chris Smith..................... .75 .23
❑ 247 Mark Prior....................... 5.00 1.50
❑ 248 Brian Mallette SP RC...... 5.00 1.50
❑ 249 Chone Figgins SP RC .. 10.00 3.00
❑ 250 Jimmy Alvarez SP RC 5.00 1.50
❑ 251 Luis Terrero..................... .75 .23
❑ 252 Josh Bonifay SP RC 5.00 1.50
❑ 253 Garrett Guzman SP RC .. 5.00 1.50
❑ 254 Jeff Verplancke SP RC.... 5.00 1.50
❑ 255 Nate Espy SP RC........... 5.00 1.50
❑ 256 Jeff Lincoln SP RC 5.00 1.50
❑ 257 Ryan Snare SP RC.......... 5.00 1.50
❑ 258 Jose Ortiz .... .75 .23
❑ 259 Denny Bautista .... .75 .23
❑ 260 Willy Aybar .... .75 .23
❑ 261 Kelly Johnson 4.00 1.20
❑ 262 Shawn Fagan.................... .75 .23
❑ 263 Yurendell DeCaster SP RC 5.00 1.50
❑ 264 Mike Peeples SP RC 5.00 1.50
❑ 265 Joel Guzman .... 3.00 .90
❑ 266 Ryan Vogelsong .... .75 .23
❑ 267 Jorge Padilla SP RC 5.00 1.50
❑ 268 Joe Jester SP RC............ 5.00 1.50
❑ 269 Ryan Church SP RC 15.00 4.50
❑ 270 Mitch Jones .... .75 .23
❑ 271 Travis Foley SP RC 5.00 1.50
❑ 272 Bobby Crosby 5.00 1.50
❑ 273 Adrian Gonzalez .... .75 .23
❑ 274 Ronnie Merrill .... .75 .23
❑ 275 Joel Pineiro..................... .75 .23
❑ 276 John-Ford Griffin .... .75 .23
❑ 277 Brian Forystek SP RC 5.00 1.50
❑ 278 Sean Douglass .... .75 .23
❑ 279 Manny Delcarmen SP RC 8.00 2.40
❑ 280 Jim Kavourias SP RC 5.00 1.50
❑ 281 Gabe Gross .... .75 .23
❑ 282 Bill Ortega........................ .75 .23
❑ 283 Joey Hammond SP RC .. 5.00 1.50
❑ 284 Brett Myers .... 1.25 .35
❑ 285 Carlos Pena...................... .75 .23
❑ 286 Ezequiel Astacio SP RC.. 5.00 1.50
❑ 287 Edwin Yan SP RC 5.00 1.50
❑ 288 Chris Duffy SP RC........ 10.00 3.00
❑ 289 Jason Kinchen.................. .75 .23
❑ 290 Rafael Soriano.................. .75 .23
❑ 291 Colin Young RC 5.00 1.50
❑ 292 Eric Byrnes .... .75 .23
❑ 293 Chris Narveson SP RC .. 8.00 2.40
❑ 294 John Rheinecker .... .75 .23
❑ 295 Mike Wilson SP RC......... 5.00 1.50
❑ 296 Justin Sherrod SP RC 5.00 1.50
❑ 297 Deivi Mendez .... .75 .23
❑ 298 Wily Mo Pena .... 1.25 .35
❑ 299 Brett Roneberg SP RC.... 5.00 1.50
❑ 300 Trey Lunsford SP RC...... 5.00 1.50
❑ 301 Christian Parker .... .75 .23
❑ 302 Brent Butler...................... .75 .23
❑ 303 Aaron Heilman .... .75 .23
❑ 304 Wilkin Ruan...................... .75 .23
❑ 305 Kenny Kelly...................... .75 .23
❑ 306 Cody Ransom .... .75 .23
❑ 307 Koyie Hill SP.................. 5.00 1.50
❑ 308 Tony Fontana SP RC...... 5.00 1.50
❑ 309 Mark Teixeira 5.00 1.50
❑ 310 Doug Sessions SP RC.... 5.00 1.50
❑ 311 Josh Cisneros SP RC 5.00 1.50
❑ 312 Carlos Brackley SP RC .. 5.00 1.50
❑ 313 Tim Raines Jr. .... .75 .23
❑ 314 Ross Peeples SP RC 5.00 1.50
❑ 315 Alex Requena SP RC...... 5.00 1.50
❑ 316 Chin-Hui Tsao................ 1.25 .35
❑ 317 Tony Alvarez .... .75 .23
❑ 318 Craig Kuzmic SP RC 5.00 1.50
❑ 319 Pete Zamora SP RC........ 5.00 1.50
❑ 320 Matt Parker SP RC 5.00 1.50
❑ 321 Keith Ginter .... .75 .23
❑ 322 Gary Cates Jr. SP RC 5.00 1.50
❑ 323 Matt Belisle...................... .75 .23
❑ 324A Ben Broussard .... .75 .23
❑ 324B Ja.Mauer AU A RC EXCH UER 10.00 3.00
Card was mistakenly numbered as 324
❑ 325 Dennis Tankersley............ .75 .23
❑ 326 Juan Silvestre .... .75 .23
❑ 327 Henry Pichardo SP RC .. 5.00 1.50
❑ 328 Michael Floyd SP RC 5.00 1.50
❑ 329 Clint Nageotte SP RC 8.00 2.40
❑ 330 Raymond Cabrera SP RC 5.00 1.50
❑ 331 Mauricio Lara SP RC...... 5.00 1.50
❑ 332 Alejandro Cadena SP RC 5.00 1.50
❑ 333 Jonny Gomes SP RC.... 15.00 4.50
❑ 334 Jason Bulger SP RC 5.00 1.50
❑ 335 Nate Teut........................... .75 .23
❑ 336 David Gil SP RC 5.00 1.50
❑ 337 Joel Crump SP RC 5.00 1.50
❑ 338 Brandon Phillips .... .75 .23
❑ 339 Macay McBride.............. 1.25 .35
❑ 340 Brandon Claussen............ .75 .23
❑ 341 Josh Phelps .... .75 .23
❑ 342 Freddie Money SP RC.... 5.00 1.50
❑ 343 Cliff Bartosh SP RC........ 5.00 1.50
❑ 344 Terrance Hill SP RC 5.00 1.50
❑ 345 John Rodriguez SP RC .. 8.00 2.40
❑ 346 Chris Latham SP RC 5.00 1.50
❑ 347 Carlos Cabrera SP RC.... 5.00 1.50
❑ 348 Jose Bautista SP RC 8.00 2.40
❑ 349 Kevin Frederick SP RC .. 5.00 1.50
❑ 350 Jerome Williams .... .75 .23
❑ 351 Napoleon Calzado SP RC 5.00 1.50
❑ 352 Benito Baez SP 5.00 1.50
❑ 353 Xavier Nady....................... .75 .23
❑ 354 Jason Botts SP RC 10.00 3.00
❑ 355 Steve Bechler SP RC...... 5.00 1.50
❑ 356 Reed Johnson SP RC 8.00 2.40
❑ 357 Mark Outlaw SP RC........ 5.00 1.50
❑ 358 Jake Peavy .... 2.00 .60
❑ 359 Josh Shafler SP RC........ 5.00 1.50
❑ 360 Dan Wright SP 5.00 1.50
❑ 361 Ryan Gripp SP RC.......... 5.00 1.50
❑ 362 Nelson Castro SP RC 5.00 1.50
❑ 363 Jason Bay SP RC 25.00 7.50
❑ 364 Franklyn German SP RC 5.00 1.50
❑ 365 Corwin Malone SP RC .. 5.00 1.50
❑ 366 Kelly Ramos SP RC........ 5.00 1.50
❑ 367 John Ennis SP RC.......... 5.00 1.50
❑ 368 George Perez SP 5.00 1.50
❑ 369 Rene Reyes SP RC 5.00 1.50
❑ 370 Rolando Viera SP RC 5.00 1.50
❑ 371 Earl Snyder SP RC 5.00 1.50
❑ 372 Kyle Kane SP RC............ 5.00 1.50
❑ 373 Mario Ramos SP RC 5.00 1.50
❑ 374 Tyler Yates SP RC.......... 5.00 1.50
❑ 375 Jason Young SP RC 5.00 1.50
❑ 376 Chris Bootcheck SP RC.. 5.00 1.50
❑ 377 Jesus Cota SP RC 5.00 1.50
❑ 378 Corky Miller SP............... 5.00 1.50
❑ 379 Matt Erickson SP RC...... 5.00 1.50
❑ 380 Justin Huber SP RC 10.00 3.00
❑ 381 Felix Escalona SP RC 5.00 1.50
❑ 382 Kevin Cash SP RC.......... 5.00 1.50
❑ 383 J.J. Putz SP RC.............. 5.00 1.50
❑ 384 Chris Snelling AU A RC 25.00 7.50
❑ 385 David Wright AU A RC 160.00 47.50
❑ 386 Brian Wolfe AU A RC.... 10.00 3.00
❑ 387 Justin Reid AU A RC.... 10.00 3.00
❑ 389 Ryan Raburn AU A RC.. 10.00 3.00
❑ 390 Josh Barfield AU A RC 25.00 7.50
❑ 391 Joe Mauer AU A RC 80.00 24.00
❑ 392 Bobby Jenks AU A RC.. 25.00 7.50
❑ 393 Rob Henkel AU A RC.... 10.00 3.00
❑ 394 Jimmy Gobble AU A RC 10.00 3.00
❑ 395 Jesse Foppert AU A RC 15.00 4.50
❑ 396 Gavin Floyd AU A RC .. 25.00 7.50
❑ 397 Nate Field AU A RC...... 10.00 3.00
❑ 398 Ryan Doumit AU A RC.. 25.00 7.50
❑ 399 Ron Calloway AU A RC 10.00 3.00
❑ 400 Taylor Buchholz AU A RC 10.00 3.00
❑ 401 Adam Roller AU A RC .. 10.00 3.00
❑ 402 Cole Barthel AU A RC .. 10.00 3.00
❑ 403 Kazuhisa Ishii SP RC...... 8.00 2.40
❑ 403A Kazuhisa Ishii AU B.... 60.00 18.00
❑ 404 So Taguchi SP RC.......... 8.00 2.40
❑ 404A So Taguchi AU B....... 50.00 15.00
❑ 405 Chris Baker AU A RC.... 10.00 3.00

2002 Bowman Chrome Draft

	Nm-Mt	Ex-Mt
COMPLETE SET (175)	300.00	90.00
COMP.SET w/o AU's (165)	175.00	52.50
COMMON CARD (1-165)	.40	.12
COMMON CARD (166-175)	10.00	3.00

❑ 1 Clint Everts RC .... 1.50 .45
❑ 2 Fred Lewis RC.................. 1.00 .30
❑ 3 Jon Broxton RC................ 2.50 .75
❑ 4 Jason Anderson RC.......... 1.00 .30
❑ 5 Mike Eusebio RC.............. 1.00 .30
❑ 6 Zack Greinke RC 8.00 2.40
❑ 7 Joe Blanton RC 5.00 1.50
❑ 8 Sergio Santos RC .... 1.50 .45
❑ 9 Jason Cooper RC .... 1.00 .30
❑ 10 Delwyn Young RC.......... 3.00 .90
❑ 11 Jeremy Hermida RC 12.00 3.60
❑ 12 Dan Ortmeier RC........... 1.50 .45
❑ 13 Kevin Jepsen RC........... 1.50 .45
❑ 14 Russ Adams RC .... 2.50 .75
❑ 15 Mike Nixon RC .... 1.00 .30
❑ 16 Nick Swisher RC 8.00 2.40
❑ 17 Cole Hamels RC 8.00 2.40
❑ 18 Brian Dopirak RC 5.00 1.50
❑ 19 James Loney RC 5.00 1.50
❑ 20 Denard Span RC .... 1.50 .45
❑ 21 Billy Petrick RC............. 1.00 .30
❑ 22 Jared Doyle RC .... 1.00 .30
❑ 23 Jeff Francoeur RC 60.00 18.00
❑ 24 Nick Bourgeois RC .... 1.00 .30
❑ 25 Matt Cain RC................ 15.00 4.50
❑ 26 John McCurdy RC........... 1.00 .30
❑ 27 Mark Kiger RC................ 1.00 .30
❑ 28 Bill Murphy RC .... 1.00 .30
❑ 29 Matt Craig RC .... 1.50 .45
❑ 30 Mike Megrew RC............ 1.00 .30
❑ 31 Ben Crockett RC .... 1.00 .30
❑ 32 Luke Hagerty RC .... 1.00 .30
❑ 33 Matt Whitney RC............ 1.00 .30
❑ 34 Dan Meyer RC................. 1.50 .45
❑ 35 Jeremy Brown RC .... 1.00 .30
❑ 36 Doug Johnson RC........... 1.00 .30
❑ 37 Steve Obenchain RC .... 1.00 .30
❑ 38 Matt Clanton RC .... 1.00 .30
❑ 39 Mark Teahen RC .... 2.50 .75
❑ 40 Tom Carrow RC.............. 1.00 .30
❑ 41 Micah Schilling RC .... 1.00 .30
❑ 42 Blair Johnson RC .... 1.00 .30
❑ 43 Jason Pridie RC .... 1.00 .30
❑ 44 Joey Votto RC .... 1.50 .45
❑ 45 Taber Lee RC.................. 1.00 .30
❑ 46 Adam Peterson RC .... 1.00 .30
❑ 47 Adam Donachie RC......... 1.00 .30
❑ 48 Josh Murray RC .... 1.00 .30
❑ 49 Brent Clevlen RC............ 2.50 .75
❑ 50 Chad Pleiness RC........... 1.00 .30
❑ 51 Zach Hammes RC .... 1.00 .30
❑ 52 Chris Snyder RC............. 1.50 .45
❑ 53 Chris Smith RC .... 1.00 .30
❑ 54 Justin Maureau RC .... 1.00 .30
❑ 55 David Bush RC .... 1.50 .45
❑ 56 Tim Gilhooly RC .... 1.00 .30
❑ 57 Blair Barbier RC .... 1.00 .30
❑ 58 Zach Segovia RC............ 1.00 .30
❑ 59 Jeremy Reed RC 6.00 1.80
❑ 60 Matt Pender RC.............. 1.00 .30
❑ 61 Eric Thomas RC .... 1.00 .30
❑ 62 Justin Jones RC .... 1.50 .45
❑ 63 Brian Slocum RC............. 1.00 .30
❑ 64 Larry Broadway RC .... 1.00 .30
❑ 65 Bo Flowers RC .... 1.00 .30

❑ 66 Scott White RC 1.00 .30
❑ 67 Steve Stanley RC 1.00 .30
❑ 68 Alex Merricks RC 1.00 .30
❑ 69 Josh Womack RC 1.00 .30
❑ 70 Dave Jensen RC 1.00 .30
❑ 71 Curtis Granderson RC 5.00 1.50
❑ 72 Pat Osborn RC 1.00 .30
❑ 73 Nic Carter RC 1.00 .30
❑ 74 Mitch Talbot RC 1.00 .30
❑ 75 Don Murphy RC 1.00 .30
❑ 76 Val Majewski RC 1.00 .30
❑ 77 Javy Rodriguez RC 1.00 .30
❑ 78 Fernando Pacheco RC 1.00 .30
❑ 79 Steve Russell RC 1.00 .30
❑ 80 Jon Slack RC 1.00 .30
❑ 81 John Baker RC 1.00 .30
❑ 82 Aaron Coonrod RC 1.00 .30
❑ 83 Josh Johnson RC 3.00 .90
❑ 84 Jake Blalock RC 2.50 .75
❑ 85 Alex Hart RC 1.00 .30
❑ 86 Wes Bankston RC 5.00 1.50
❑ 87 Josh Rupe RC 1.00 .30
❑ 88 Dan Cevette RC 1.00 .30
❑ 89 Kiel Fisher RC 1.50 .45
❑ 90 Alan Rick RC 1.00 .30
❑ 91 Charlie Morton RC 1.00 .30
❑ 92 Chad Spann RC 1.00 .30
❑ 93 Kyle Boyer RC 1.00 .30
❑ 94 Bob Malek RC 1.00 .30
❑ 95 Ryan Rodriguez RC 1.00 .30
❑ 96 Jordan Renz RC 1.00 .30
❑ 97 Randy Frye RC 1.00 .30
❑ 98 Rich Hill RC 3.00 .90
❑ 99 B.J. Upton RC 20.00 6.00
❑ 100 Dan Christensen RC 1.00 .30
❑ 101 Casey Kotchman RC 8.00 2.40
❑ 102 Eric Good RC 1.00 .30
❑ 103 Mike Fontenot RC 1.00 .30
❑ 104 John Webb RC 1.00 .30
❑ 105 Jason Dubois RC 1.50 .45
❑ 106 Ryan Kibler RC 1.00 .30
❑ 107 Jhonny Peralta RC 10.00 3.00
❑ 108 Kirk Saarloos RC 1.00 .30
❑ 109 Rhett Parrott RC 1.00 .30
❑ 110 Jason Grove RC 1.00 .30
❑ 111 Colt Griffin RC 1.00 .30
❑ 112 Dallas McPherson RC UER 8.00 2.40
Reversed Negative
❑ 113 Oliver Perez RC 5.00 1.50
❑ 114 Marshall McDougall RC 1.00 .30
❑ 115 Mike Wood RC 1.00 .30
❑ 116 Scott Hairston RC 1.50 .45
❑ 117 Jason Simontacchi RC 1.00 .30
❑ 118 Taggert Bozied RC 1.50 .45
❑ 119 Shelley Duncan RC 1.00 .30
❑ 120 Dontrelle Willis RC 25.00 7.50
❑ 121 Sean Burnett .40 .12
❑ 122 Aaron Cook .60 .18
❑ 123 Brett Evert .40 .12
❑ 124 Jimmy Journell .40 .12
❑ 125 Brett Myers .60 .18
❑ 126 Brad Baker .40 .12
❑ 127 Billy Traber RC 1.00 .30
❑ 128 Adam Wainwright .40 .12
❑ 129 Jason Young 1.00 .30
❑ 130 John Buck .40 .12
❑ 131 Kevin Cash 1.00 .30
❑ 132 Jason Stokes RC 4.00 1.20
❑ 133 Drew Henson .60 .18
❑ 134 Chad Tracy RC 3.00 .90
❑ 135 Orlando Hudson .40 .12
❑ 136 Brandon Phillips .40 .12
❑ 137 Joe Borchard .40 .12
❑ 138 Marlon Byrd .40 .12
❑ 139 Carl Crawford .60 .18
❑ 140 Michael Restovich .40 .12
❑ 141 Corey Hart RC 3.00 .90
❑ 142 Edwin Almonte .60 .18
❑ 143 Francis Beltran RC 1.00 .30
❑ 144 Jorge De La Rosa RC 1.00 .30
❑ 145 Gerardo Garcia RC 1.00 .30
❑ 146 Franklyn German RC 1.00 .30
❑ 147 Francisco Liriano 8.00 2.40
❑ 148 Francisco Rodriguez .60 .18
❑ 149 Ricardo Rodriguez .40 .12
❑ 150 Seung Song .40 .12
❑ 151 John Stephens .40 .12
❑ 152 Justin Huber RC 2.50 .75
❑ 153 Victor Martinez 1.50 .45
❑ 154 Hee Seop Choi .60 .18
❑ 155 Justin Morneau .60 .18
❑ 156 Miguel Cabrera 2.50 .75
❑ 157 Victor Diaz RC 2.50 .75
❑ 158 Jose Reyes 1.00 .30
❑ 159 Omar Infante .40 .12
❑ 160 Angel Berroa .40 .12
❑ 161 Tony Alvarez .40 .12
❑ 162 Shin Soo Choo RC 2.50 .75
❑ 163 Wily Mo Pena .60 .18
❑ 164 Andres Torres .40 .12
❑ 165 Jose Lopez RC 4.00 1.20
❑ 166 Scott Moore AU RC 15.00 4.50
❑ 167 Chris Gruler AU RC 10.00 3.00
❑ 168 Joe Saunders AU RC 15.00 4.50
❑ 169 Jeff Francis AU RC 25.00 7.50
❑ 170 Royce Ring AU RC 10.00 3.00
❑ 171 Greg Miller AU RC 25.00 7.50
❑ 172 Brandon Weeden AU RC 10.00 3.00
❑ 173 Drew Meyer AU RC 10.00 3.00
❑ 174 Khalil Greene AU RC 60.00 18.00
❑ 175 Mark Schramek AU RC 10.00 3.00

2003 Bowman Chrome

	MINT	NRMT
COMPLETE SET (351)	500.00	220.00
COMP.SET w/o AU's (331)	150.00	70.00
COMMON CARD (1-165)	.50	.23
COMMON CARD (166-330)	.50	.23
COMMON RC (156-330)	1.00	.45
COMP.SET w/o AU'S INCLUDES 351 MAYS		.00
MAYS AU IS NOT PART OF 351-CARD SET		.00

❑ 1 Garret Anderson .50 .23
❑ 2 Derek Jeter 3.00 1.35
❑ 3 Gary Sheffield .50 .23
❑ 4 Matt Morris .50 .23
❑ 5 Derek Lowe .50 .23
❑ 6 Andy Van Hekken .50 .23
❑ 7 Sammy Sosa 1.25 .55
❑ 8 Ken Griffey Jr. 2.00 .90
❑ 9 Omar Vizquel .75 .35
❑ 10 Jorge Posada .75 .35
❑ 11 Lance Berkman .50 .23
❑ 12 Mike Sweeney .50 .23
❑ 13 Adrian Beltre .50 .23
❑ 14 Richie Sexson .50 .23
❑ 15 A.J. Pierzynski .50 .23
❑ 16 Bartolo Colon .50 .23
❑ 17 Mike Mussina .75 .35
❑ 18 Paul Byrd .50 .23
❑ 19 Bobby Abreu .50 .23
❑ 20 Miguel Tejada .50 .23
❑ 21 Aramis Ramirez .50 .23
❑ 22 Edgardo Alfonzo .50 .23
❑ 23 Edgar Martinez .75 .35
❑ 24 Albert Pujols 2.50 1.10
❑ 25 Carl Crawford .50 .23
❑ 26 Eric Hinske .50 .23
❑ 27 Tim Salmon .75 .35
❑ 28 Luis Gonzalez .50 .23
❑ 29 Jay Gibbons .50 .23
❑ 30 John Smoltz .50 .23
❑ 31 Tim Wakefield .50 .23
❑ 32 Mark Prior .75 .35
❑ 33 Magglio Ordonez .50 .23
❑ 34 Adam Dunn .50 .23
❑ 35 Larry Walker .50 .23
❑ 36 Luis Castillo .50 .23
❑ 37 Wade Miller .50 .23
❑ 38 Carlos Beltran .50 .23
❑ 39 Odalis Perez .50 .23
❑ 40 Alex Sanchez .50 .23
❑ 41 Torii Hunter .50 .23
❑ 42 Cliff Floyd .50 .23
❑ 43 Andy Pettitte .75 .35
❑ 44 Francisco Rodriguez .50 .23
❑ 45 Eric Chavez .50 .23
❑ 46 Kevin Millwood .50 .23
❑ 47 Dennis Tankersley .50 .23
❑ 48 Hideo Nomo 1.25 .55
❑ 49 Freddy Garcia .50 .23
❑ 50 Randy Johnson 1.25 .55
❑ 51 Aubrey Huff .50 .23
❑ 52 Carlos Delgado .50 .23
❑ 53 Troy Glaus .50 .23
❑ 54 Junior Spivey .50 .23
❑ 55 Mike Hampton .50 .23
❑ 56 Sidney Ponson .50 .23
❑ 57 Aaron Boone .50 .23
❑ 58 Kerry Wood .50 .23
❑ 59 Willie Harris .50 .23
❑ 60 Nomar Garciaparra 2.00 .90
❑ 61 Todd Helton .75 .35
❑ 62 Mike Lowell .50 .23
❑ 63 Roy Oswalt .50 .23
❑ 64 Raul Ibanez .50 .23
❑ 65 Brian Jordan .50 .23
❑ 66 Geoff Jenkins .50 .23
❑ 67 Jermaine Dye .50 .23
❑ 68 Tom Glavine .75 .35
❑ 69 Bernie Williams .75 .35
❑ 70 Vladimir Guerrero 1.25 .55
❑ 71 Mark Mulder .50 .23
❑ 72 Jimmy Rollins .50 .23
❑ 73 Oliver Perez .50 .23
❑ 74 Rich Aurilia .50 .23
❑ 75 Joel Pineiro .50 .23
❑ 76 J.D. Drew .50 .23
❑ 77 Ivan Rodriguez .75 .35
❑ 78 Josh Phelps .50 .23
❑ 79 Darin Erstad .50 .23
❑ 80 Curt Schilling .50 .23
❑ 81 Paul Lo Duca .50 .23
❑ 82 Marty Cordova .50 .23
❑ 83 Manny Ramirez .75 .35
❑ 84 Bobby Hill .50 .23
❑ 85 Paul Konerko .50 .23
❑ 86 Austin Kearns .50 .23
❑ 87 Jason Jennings .50 .23
❑ 88 Brad Penny .50 .23
❑ 89 Jeff Bagwell .75 .35
❑ 90 Shawn Green .50 .23
❑ 91 Jason Schmidt .50 .23
❑ 92 Doug Mientkiewicz .50 .23
❑ 93 Jose Vidro .50 .23
❑ 94 Bret Boone .50 .23
❑ 95 Jason Giambi .50 .23
❑ 96 Barry Zito .50 .23
❑ 97 Roy Halladay .50 .23
❑ 98 Pat Burrell .50 .23
❑ 99 Sean Burroughs .50 .23
❑ 100 Barry Bonds 3.00 1.35
❑ 101 Kazuhiro Sasaki .50 .23
❑ 102 Fernando Vina .50 .23
❑ 103 Chan Ho Park .50 .23
❑ 104 Andruw Jones .75 .35
❑ 105 Adam Kennedy .50 .23
❑ 106 Shea Hillenbrand .50 .23
❑ 107 Greg Maddux 2.00 .90
❑ 108 Jim Edmonds .75 .35
❑ 109 Pedro Martinez .75 .35
❑ 110 Moises Alou .50 .23
❑ 111 Jeff Weaver .50 .23
❑ 112 C.C. Sabathia .50 .23
❑ 113 Robert Fick .50 .23
❑ 114 A.J. Burnett .50 .23
❑ 115 Jeff Kent .50 .23
❑ 116 Kevin Brown .50 .23
❑ 117 Rafael Furcal .50 .23
❑ 118 Cristian Guzman .50 .23

❑ 119 Brad Wilkerson .50 .23
❑ 120 Mike Piazza 2.00 .90
❑ 121 Alfonso Soriano .50 .23
❑ 122 Mark Ellis .50 .23
❑ 123 Vicente Padilla .50 .23
❑ 124 Eric Gagne .50 .23
❑ 125 Ryan Klesko .50 .23
❑ 126 Ichiro Suzuki 2.50 1.10
❑ 127 Tony Batista .50 .23
❑ 128 Roberto Alomar .75 .35
❑ 129 Alex Rodriguez 2.00 .90
❑ 130 Jim Thome .75 .35
❑ 131 Jarrod Washburn .50 .23
❑ 132 Orlando Hudson .50 .23
❑ 133 Chipper Jones 1.25 .55
❑ 134 Rodrigo Lopez .50 .23
❑ 135 Johnny Damon .75 .35
❑ 136 Matt Clement .50 .23
❑ 137 Frank Thomas 1.25 .55
❑ 138 Ellis Burks .50 .23
❑ 139 Carlos Pena .50 .23
❑ 140 Josh Beckett .50 .23
❑ 141 Joe Randa .50 .23
❑ 142 Brian Giles .50 .23
❑ 143 Kazuhisa Ishii .50 .23
❑ 144 Corey Koskie .50 .23
❑ 145 Orlando Cabrera .50 .23
❑ 146 Mark Buehrle .50 .23
❑ 147 Roger Clemens 2.50 1.10
❑ 148 Tim Hudson .50 .23
❑ 149 Randy Wolf .50 .23
❑ 150 Josh Fogg .50 .23
❑ 151 Phil Nevin .50 .23
❑ 152 John Olerud .50 .23
❑ 153 Scott Rolen .75 .35
❑ 154 Joe Kennedy .50 .23
❑ 155 Rafael Palmeiro .75 .35
❑ 156 Chad Hutchinson .50 .23
❑ 157 Quincy Carter XRC 2.00 .90
❑ 158 Hee Seop Choi .50 .23
❑ 159 Joe Borchard .50 .23
❑ 160 Brandon Phillips .50 .23
❑ 161 Wily Mo Pena .50 .23
❑ 162 Victor Martinez .75 .35
❑ 163 Jason Stokes .50 .23
❑ 164 Ken Harvey .50 .23
❑ 165 Juan Rivera .50 .23
❑ 166 Joe Valentine RC 1.50 .70
❑ 167 Dan Haren RC 3.00 1.35
❑ 168 Michel Hernandez RC 1.50 .70
❑ 169 Eider Torres RC 1.50 .70
❑ 170 Chris De La Cruz RC 1.50 .70
❑ 171 Ramon Nivar-Martinez RC 1.50 .70
❑ 172 Mike Adams RC 1.50 .70
❑ 173 Justin Arneson RC 1.50 .70
❑ 174 Jamie Athas RC 1.50 .70
❑ 175 Dwaine Bacon RC 1.50 .70
❑ 176 Clint Barmes RC 6.00 2.70
❑ 177 B.J. Barns RC 1.50 .70
❑ 178 Tyler Johnson RC 1.50 .70
❑ 179 Brandon Webb RC 4.00 1.80
❑ 180 T.J. Bohn RC 1.50 .70
❑ 181 Ozzie Chavez RC 1.50 .70
❑ 182 Brandon Bowe RC 1.50 .70
❑ 183 Craig Brazell RC 1.50 .70
❑ 184 Dusty Brown RC 1.50 .70
❑ 185 Brian Bruney RC 2.00 .90
❑ 186 Greg Bruso RC 1.50 .70
❑ 187 Jaime Bubela RC 1.50 .70
❑ 188 Matt Diaz RC 2.00 .90
❑ 189 Brian Burgamy RC 1.50 .70
❑ 190 Eny Cabreja RC 1.50 .70
❑ 191 Daniel Cabrera RC 3.00 1.35
❑ 192 Ryan Cameron RC 1.50 .70
❑ 193 Lance Caraccioli RC 1.50 .70
❑ 194 David Cash RC 1.50 .70
❑ 195 Bernie Castro RC 1.50 .70
❑ 196 Ismael Castro RC 2.00 .90
❑ 197 Cory Doyne RC 1.50 .70
❑ 198 Jeff Clark RC 1.50 .70
❑ 199 Chris Colton RC 1.50 .70
❑ 200 Dexter Cooper RC 1.50 .70
❑ 201 Calfix Crabbe RC 2.00 .90
❑ 202 Chien-Ming Wang RC 10.00 4.50
❑ 203 Eric Crozier RC 2.00 .90
❑ 204 Nook Logan RC 2.00 .90
❑ 205 David DeJesus RC 3.00 1.35
❑ 206 Matt DeMarco RC 1.50 .70
❑ 207 Chris Duncan RC 1.50 .70
❑ 208 Eric Eckenstahler .50 .23
❑ 209 Willie Eyre RC 1.50 .70
❑ 210 Evel Bastida-Martinez RC 1.50 .70
❑ 211 Chris Fallon RC 1.50 .70
❑ 212 Mike Flannery RC 1.50 .70
❑ 213 Mike O'Keefe RC 1.50 .70
❑ 214 Lew Ford RC 2.00 .90
❑ 215 Kason Gabbard RC 1.50 .70
❑ 216 Mike Gallo RC 1.50 .70
❑ 217 Jairo Garcia RC 2.00 .90
❑ 218 Angel Garcia RC 2.00 .90
❑ 219 Michael Garciaparra RC 1.50 .70
❑ 220 Jeremy Griffiths RC 1.50 .70
❑ 221 Dusty Gomon RC 2.00 .90
❑ 222 Bryan Grace RC 1.50 .70
❑ 223 Tyson Graham RC 1.50 .70
❑ 224 Henry Guerrero RC 1.50 .70
❑ 225 Franklin Gutierrez RC 4.00 1.80
❑ 226 Carlos Guzman RC 2.00 .90
❑ 227 Matthew Hagen RC 1.50 .70
❑ 228 Josh Hall RC 1.50 .70
❑ 229 Rob Hammock RC 1.50 .70
❑ 230 Brendan Harris RC 2.00 .90
❑ 231 Gary Harris RC 1.50 .70
❑ 232 Clay Hensley RC 1.50 .70
❑ 233 Michael Hinckley RC 2.00 .90
❑ 234 Luis Hodge RC 1.50 .70
❑ 235 Donnie Hood RC 2.00 .90
❑ 236 Matt Hensley RC 1.50 .70
❑ 237 Edwin Jackson RC 2.00 .90
❑ 238 Ardley Jansen RC 2.00 .90
❑ 239 Ferenc Jongejan RC 1.50 .70
❑ 240 Matt Kata RC 1.50 .70
❑ 241 Kazuhiro Takeoka RC 1.50 .70
❑ 242 Charlie Manning RC 1.50 .70
❑ 243 Il Kim RC 1.50 .70
❑ 244 Brennan King RC 1.50 .70
❑ 245 Chris Kroski RC 1.50 .70
❑ 246 David Martinez RC 1.50 .70
❑ 247 Pete LaForest RC 1.50 .70
❑ 248 Wil Ledezma RC 1.50 .70
❑ 249 Jeremy Bonderman RC 10.00 4.50
❑ 250 Gonzalo Lopez RC 1.50 .70
❑ 251 Brian Luderer RC 1.50 .70
❑ 252 Ruddy Lugo RC 1.50 .70
❑ 253 Wayne Lydon RC 1.50 .70
❑ 254 Mark Malaska RC 1.50 .70
❑ 255 Andy Marte RC 12.00 5.50
❑ 256 Tyler Martin RC 1.50 .70
❑ 257 Branden Florence RC 1.50 .70
❑ 258 Aneudis Mateo RC 1.50 .70
❑ 259 Derell McCall RC 1.50 .70
❑ 260 Elizardo Ramirez RC 2.00 .90
❑ 261 Mike McNutt RC 1.50 .70
❑ 262 Jacobo Meque RC 1.50 .70
❑ 263 Derek Michaelis RC 1.50 .70
❑ 264 Aaron Miles RC 2.00 .90
❑ 265 Jose Morales RC 1.50 .70
❑ 266 Dustin Moseley RC 1.50 .70
❑ 267 Adrian Myers RC 1.50 .70
❑ 268 Dan Neil RC 1.50 .70
❑ 269 Jon Nelson RC 2.00 .90
❑ 270 Mike Neu RC 1.50 .70
❑ 271 Leigh Neuage RC 1.50 .70
❑ 272 Wes O'Brien RC 1.50 .70
❑ 273 Trent Oeltjen RC 2.00 .90
❑ 274 Tim Olson RC 1.50 .70
❑ 275 David Pahucki RC 1.50 .70
❑ 276 Nathan Panther RC 1.50 .70
❑ 277 Arnie Munoz RC 1.50 .70
❑ 278 Dave Pember RC 1.50 .70
❑ 279 Jason Perry RC 2.00 .90
❑ 280 Matthew Peterson RC 1.50 .70
❑ 281 Greg Aquino RC 1.50 .70
❑ 282 Jorge Piedra RC 2.00 .90
❑ 283 Simon Pond RC 1.50 .70
❑ 284 Aaron Rakers RC 1.50 .70
❑ 285 Felix Sanchez RC 1.50 .70
❑ 286 Manuel Ramirez RC 2.00 .90
❑ 287 Kevin Randel RC 1.50 .70
❑ 288 Kelly Shoppach RC 3.00 1.35
❑ 289 Prentice Redman RC 1.50 .70
❑ 290 Eric Reed RC 1.50 .70
❑ 291 Wilton Reynolds RC 2.00 .90
❑ 292 Eric Riggs RC 2.00 .90
❑ 293 Carlos Rijo RC 1.50 .70
❑ 294 Tyler Adamczyk RC 1.50 .70
❑ 295 Jon-Mark Sprowl RC 1.50 .70
❑ 296 Arturo Rivas RC 1.50 .70
❑ 297 Kyle Roat RC 1.50 .70
❑ 298 Bubba Nelson RC .75 .35
❑ 299 Levi Robinson RC 1.50 .70
❑ 300 Ray Sadler RC 1.50 .70
❑ 301 Rylan Reed RC 1.50 .70
❑ 302 Jon Schuerholz RC 1.50 .70
❑ 303 Nobuaki Yoshida RC 1.50 .70
❑ 304 Brian Shackelford RC 1.50 .70
❑ 305 Bill Simon RC 1.50 .70
❑ 306 Haj Turay RC 2.00 .90
❑ 307 Sean Smith RC 2.00 .90
❑ 308 Ryan Spataro RC 1.50 .70
❑ 309 Jemel Spearman RC 1.50 .70
❑ 310 Keith Stamler RC 1.50 .70
❑ 311 Luke Steidlmayer RC 1.50 .70
❑ 312 Adam Stern RC 1.50 .70
❑ 313 Jay Sitzman RC 1.50 .70
❑ 314 Mike Wodnicki RC 1.50 .70
❑ 315 Terry Tiffee RC 1.50 .70
❑ 316 Nick Trzesniak RC 1.50 .70
❑ 317 Denny Tussen RC 1.50 .70
❑ 318 Scott Tyler RC 2.00 .90
❑ 319 Shane Victorino RC 2.00 .90
❑ 320 Doug Waechter RC 2.00 .90
❑ 321 Brandon Watson RC 1.50 .70
❑ 322 Todd Wellemeyer RC 1.50 .70
❑ 323 Eli Whiteside RC 1.50 .70
❑ 324 Josh Willingham RC 2.00 .90
❑ 325 Travis Wong RC 2.00 .90
❑ 326 Brian Wright RC 1.50 .70
❑ 327 Felix Pie RC 15.00 6.75
❑ 328 Andy Sisco RC .75 .35
❑ 329 Dustin Yount RC 2.00 .90
❑ 330 Andrew Dominique RC 1.50 .70
❑ 331 Brian McCann AU A RC 35.00 16.00
❑ 332 Jose Contreras AU B RC 150.00 70.00
❑ 333 Corey Shafer AU A RC 10.00 4.50
❑ 334 Hanley Ramirez AU A RC 40.00 18.00
❑ 335 Ryan Shealy AU A RC 15.00 6.75
❑ 336 Kevin Youkilis AU A RC 15.00 6.75
❑ 337 Jason Kubel AU A RC 15.00 6.75
❑ 338 Aron Weston AU A RC 10.00 4.50
❑ 338B Rajai Davis AU A ERR .00
❑ 339 J.D. Durbin AU A RC 10.00 4.50
❑ 340 G. Schneidmiller AU A RC 10.00 4.50
❑ 341 Travis Ishikawa AU A RC 10.00 4.50
❑ 342 Ben Francisco AU A RC 10.00 4.50
❑ 343 Bobby Basham AU A RC 15.00 6.75
❑ 344 Joey Gomes AU A RC 10.00 4.50
❑ 345 Beau Kemp AU A RC 10.00 4.50
❑ 346 T.Story-Harden AU A RC 10.00 4.50
❑ 347 Daryl Clark AU A RC 10.00 4.50
❑ 348 Bryan Bullington AU A RC 10.00 4.50
❑ 349 Rajai Davis AU A RC 10.00 4.50
❑ 350 Darrell Rasner AU A RC 10.00 4.50
❑ 351 Willie Mays 2.00 .90
❑ 351AU Willie Mays AU 300.00 135.00

2003 Bowman Chrome Draft

	MINT	NRMT
COMPLETE SET (176)	300.00	135.00
COMP.SET w/o AU's (165)	100.00	45.00
COMMON CARD (1-165)	.40	.18
1-165 TWO PER BOWMAN DRAFT PACK		.00
COMMON CARD (166-176)	10.00	4.50
166-176 STATED ODDS 1:41 H/R	.00	
LUBANSKI IS AN SP BY 1000 COPIES		.00
❑ 1 Dontrelle Willis	1.50	.70
❑ 2 Freddy Sanchez	.40	.18
❑ 3 Miguel Cabrera	1.50	.70
❑ 4 Ryan Ludwick	.40	.18
❑ 5 Ty Wigginton	.40	.18
❑ 6 Mark Teixeira	1.00	.45
❑ 7 Trey Hodges	.40	.18
❑ 8 Laynce Nix	.60	.25
❑ 9 Antonio Perez	.40	.18
❑ 10 Jody Gerut	.40	.18
❑ 11 Jae Weong Seo	.40	.18
❑ 12 Erick Almonte	.40	.18
❑ 13 Lyle Overbay	.40	.18
❑ 14 Billy Traber	.40	.18
❑ 15 Andres Torres	.40	.18
❑ 16 Jose Valverde	.40	.18
❑ 17 Aaron Heilman	.40	.18
❑ 18 Brandon Larson	.40	.18
❑ 19 Jung Bong	.40	.18
❑ 20 Jesse Foppert	.40	.18
❑ 21 Angel Berroa	.40	.18
❑ 22 Jeff DaVanon	.40	.18
❑ 23 Kurt Ainsworth	.40	.18
❑ 24 Brandon Claussen	.40	.18
❑ 25 Xavier Nady	.40	.18
❑ 26 Travis Hafner	.60	.25
❑ 27 Jerome Williams	.40	.18
❑ 28 Jose Reyes	.60	.25
❑ 29 Sergio Mitre RC	1.50	.70
❑ 30 Bo Hart RC	1.00	.45
❑ 31 Adam Miller RC	5.00	2.20
❑ 32 Brian Finch RC	1.00	.45
❑ 33 Taylor Mattingly RC	1.50	.70
❑ 34 Daric Barton RC	10.00	4.50
❑ 35 Chris Ray RC	2.50	1.10
❑ 36 Jarrod Saltalamacchia RC	10.00	4.50
❑ 37 Dennis Dove RC	1.50	.70
❑ 38 James Houser RC	1.50	.70
❑ 39 Clint King RC	1.50	.70
❑ 40 Lou Palmisano RC	1.50	.70
❑ 41 Dan Moore RC	1.00	.45
❑ 42 Craig Stansberry RC	1.50	.70
❑ 43 Jo Jo Reyes RC	1.50	.70
❑ 44 Jake Stevens RC	2.50	1.10
❑ 45 Tom Gorzelanny RC	1.50	.70
❑ 46 Brian Marshall RC	1.00	.45
❑ 47 Scott Beerer RC	1.00	.45
❑ 48 Javi Herrera RC	1.50	.70
❑ 49 Steve LeRud RC	1.50	.70
❑ 50 Josh Banks RC	2.50	1.10
❑ 51 Jon Papelbon RC	20.00	9.00
❑ 52 Juan Valdes RC	1.50	.70
❑ 53 Beau Vaughan RC	1.50	.70
❑ 54 Matt Chico RC	1.50	.70
❑ 55 Todd Jennings RC	1.50	.70
❑ 56 Anthony Gwynn RC	1.50	.70
❑ 57 Matt Harrison RC	2.50	1.10
❑ 58 Aaron Marsden RC	1.50	.70
❑ 59 Casey Abrams RC	1.00	.45
❑ 60 Cory Stuart RC	1.00	.45
❑ 61 Mike Wagner RC	1.00	.45
❑ 62 Jordan Pratt RC	1.50	.70
❑ 63 Andre Randolph RC	1.50	.70
❑ 64 Blake Balkcom RC	1.50	.70
❑ 65 Josh Muecke RC	1.00	.45
❑ 66 Jamie D'Antona RC	2.50	1.10
❑ 67 Cole Seifrig RC	1.00	.45
❑ 68 Josh Anderson RC	2.50	1.10
❑ 69 Matt Lorenzo RC	1.50	.70
❑ 70 Nate Spears RC	1.50	.70
❑ 71 Chris Goodman RC	1.00	.45
❑ 72 Brian McFall RC	1.00	.45
❑ 73 Billy Hogan RC	1.50	.70
❑ 74 Jamie Romak RC	1.50	.70
❑ 75 Jeff Cook RC	1.50	.70
❑ 76 Brooks McNiven RC	1.00	.45
❑ 77 Xavier Paul RC	1.50	.70
❑ 78 Bob Zimmerman RC UER Name is really Zimmermann	1.00	.45
❑ 79 Mickey Hall RC	1.50	.70
❑ 80 Shaun Marcum RC	2.50	1.10
❑ 81 Matt Nachreiner RC	1.50	.70
❑ 82 Chris Kinsey RC	1.00	.45
❑ 83 Jonathan Fulton RC	1.50	.70
❑ 84 Edgardo Baez RC	1.50	.70
❑ 85 Robert Valido RC	1.50	.70
❑ 86 Kenny Lewis RC	1.50	.70
❑ 87 Trent Peterson RC	1.00	.45
❑ 88 Johnny Woodard RC	1.50	.70
❑ 89 Wes Littleton RC	1.50	.70
❑ 90 Sean Rodriguez RC	1.50	.70
❑ 91 Kyle Pearson RC	1.00	.45
❑ 92 Josh Rainwater RC	1.50	.70
❑ 93 Travis Schlichting RC	1.50	.70
❑ 94 Tim Battle RC	1.50	.70
❑ 95 Aaron Hill RC	2.50	1.10
❑ 96 Bob McCrory RC	1.00	.45
❑ 97 Rick Guarno RC	1.50	.70
❑ 98 Brandon Yarbrough RC	1.00	.45
❑ 99 Peter Stonard RC	1.00	.45
❑ 100 Darin Downs RC	1.50	.70
❑ 101 Matt Bruback RC	1.00	.45
❑ 102 Danny Garcia RC	1.00	.45
❑ 103 Cory Stewart RC	1.00	.45
❑ 104 Ferdin Tejeda RC	1.00	.45
❑ 105 Kade Johnson RC	1.00	.45
❑ 106 Andrew Brown RC	1.50	.70
❑ 107 Aquilino Lopez RC	1.00	.45
❑ 108 Stephen Randolph RC	1.00	.45
❑ 109 Dave Matranga RC	1.00	.45
❑ 110 Dustin McGowan RC	1.00	.45
❑ 111 Juan Camacho RC	1.00	.45
❑ 112 Cliff Lee	.40	.18
❑ 113 Jeff Duncan RC	1.00	.45
❑ 114 C.J. Wilson	.40	.18
❑ 115 Brandon Roberson RC	1.00	.45
❑ 116 David Corrente RC	1.00	.45
❑ 117 Kevin Beavers RC	1.00	.45
❑ 118 Anthony Webster RC	1.50	.70
❑ 119 Oscar Villarreal RC	1.00	.45
❑ 120 Hong-Chih Kuo RC	5.00	2.20
❑ 121 Josh Barfield	.60	.25
❑ 122 Denny Bautista	.40	.18
❑ 123 Chris Burke RC	5.00	2.20
❑ 124 Robinson Cano RC	15.00	6.75
❑ 125 Jose Castillo	.40	.18
❑ 126 Neal Cotts	.40	.18
❑ 127 Jorge De La Rosa	.40	.18
❑ 128 J.D. Durbin	.50	.23
❑ 129 Edwin Encarnacion	1.00	.45
❑ 130 Gavin Floyd	.40	.18
❑ 131 Alexis Gomez	.40	.18
❑ 132 Edgar Gonzalez RC	1.00	.45
❑ 133 Khalil Greene	2.50	1.10
❑ 134 Zack Greinke	.60	.25
❑ 135 Franklin Gutierrez	1.50	.70
❑ 136 Rich Harden	1.00	.45
❑ 137 J.J. Hardy RC	4.00	1.80
❑ 138 Ryan Howard RC	15.00	6.75
❑ 139 Justin Huber	.40	.18
❑ 140 David Kelton	.40	.18
❑ 141 Dave Krynzel	.40	.18
❑ 142 Pete LaForest	.50	.23
❑ 143 Adam LaRoche	.40	.18
❑ 144 Preston Larrison RC	1.00	.45
❑ 145 John Maine RC	3.00	1.35
❑ 146 Andy Marte	5.00	2.20
❑ 147 Jeff Mathis	.40	.18
❑ 148 Joe Mauer	1.00	.45
❑ 149 Clint Nageotte	.40	.18
❑ 150 Chris Narveson	.40	.18
❑ 151 Ramon Nivar	.50	.23
❑ 152 Felix Pie	6.00	2.70
❑ 153 Guillermo Quiroz RC	1.00	.45
❑ 154 Rene Reyes	.40	.18
❑ 155 Royce Ring	.40	.18
❑ 156 Alexis Rios	1.50	.70
❑ 157 Grady Sizemore	.60	.25
❑ 158 Stephen Smitherman	.40	.18
❑ 159 Seung Song	.40	.18
❑ 160 Scott Thorman	.40	.18
❑ 161 Chad Tracy	.40	.18
❑ 162 Chin-Hui Tsao	.60	.25
❑ 163 John VanBenschoten	.40	.18
❑ 164 Kevin Youkilis	1.50	.70
❑ 165 Chien-Ming Wang	4.00	1.80
❑ 166 Chris Lubanski AU SP RC	30.00	13.50
❑ 167 Ryan Harvey AU RC	30.00	13.50
❑ 168 Matt Murton AU RC	30.00	13.50
❑ 169 Jay Sborz AU RC	10.00	4.50
❑ 170 Brandon Wood AU RC	85.00	38.00
❑ 171 Nick Markakis AU RC	30.00	13.50
❑ 172 Rickie Weeks AU RC	60.00	27.00
❑ 173 Eric Duncan AU RC	40.00	18.00
❑ 174 Chad Billingsley AU RC	40.00	18.00
❑ 175 Ryan Wagner AU RC	10.00	4.50
❑ 176 Delmon Young AU RC	110.00	50.00

2004 Bowman Chrome

	Nm-Mt	Ex-Mt
COMPLETE SET (350)	400.00	120.00
COMP.SET w/o AU's (330)	120.00	36.00
COMMON CARD (1-150)	.50	.15
COMMON CARD (151-165)	.50	.15
COMMON AUTO (331-350)	15.00	4.50
331-350 AU'S ARE NOT SERIAL-NUMBERED		.00
331-350 PRINT RUN PROVIDED BY TOPPS		.00
❑ 1 Garret Anderson	.50	.15
❑ 2 Larry Walker	.50	.15
❑ 3 Derek Jeter	2.50	.75
❑ 4 Curt Schilling	.75	.23
❑ 5 Carlos Zambrano	.50	.15
❑ 6 Shawn Green	.50	.15
❑ 7 Manny Ramirez	.75	.23
❑ 8 Randy Johnson	1.25	.35
❑ 9 Jeremy Bonderman	.50	.15
❑ 10 Alfonso Soriano	.50	.15
❑ 11 Scott Rolen	.75	.23
❑ 12 Kerry Wood	.50	.15
❑ 13 Eric Gagne	.50	.15
❑ 14 Ryan Klesko	.50	.15
❑ 15 Kevin Millar	.50	.15
❑ 16 Ty Wigginton	.50	.15
❑ 17 David Ortiz	1.25	.35
❑ 18 Luis Castillo	.50	.15
❑ 19 Bernie Williams	.75	.23
❑ 20 Edgar Renteria	.50	.15
❑ 21 Matt Kata	.50	.15
❑ 22 Bartolo Colon	.50	.15
❑ 23 Derrek Lee	.75	.23
❑ 24 Gary Sheffield	.50	.15
❑ 25 Nomar Garciaparra	2.00	.60
❑ 26 Kevin Millwood	.50	.15
❑ 27 Corey Patterson	.50	.15
❑ 28 Carlos Beltran	.50	.15
❑ 29 Mike Lieberthal	.50	.15
❑ 30 Troy Glaus	.50	.15
❑ 31 Preston Wilson	.50	.15
❑ 32 Jorge Posada	.75	.23
❑ 33 Bo Hart	.50	.15
❑ 34 Mark Prior	.75	.23
❑ 35 Hideo Nomo	1.25	.35
❑ 36 Jason Kendall	.50	.15
❑ 37 Roger Clemens	2.50	.75
❑ 38 Dmitri Young	.50	.15
❑ 39 Jason Giambi	.50	.15
❑ 40 Jim Edmonds	.75	.23
❑ 41 Ryan Ludwick	.50	.15
❑ 42 Brandon Webb	.50	.15
❑ 43 Todd Helton	.75	.23

❑	44	Jacque Jones	.50	.15
❑	45	Jamie Moyer	.50	.15
❑	46	Tim Salmon	.75	.23
❑	47	Kelvim Escobar	.50	.15
❑	48	Tony Batista	.50	.15
❑	49	Nick Johnson	.50	.15
❑	50	Jim Thome	.75	.23
❑	51	Casey Blake	.50	.15
❑	52	Trot Nixon	.50	.15
❑	53	Luis Gonzalez	.50	.15
❑	54	Dontrelle Willis	.75	.23
❑	55	Mike Mussina	.75	.23
❑	56	Carl Crawford	.50	.15
❑	57	Mark Buehrle	.50	.15
❑	58	Scott Podsednik	.50	.15
❑	59	Brian Giles	.50	.15
❑	60	Rafael Furcal	.50	.15
❑	61	Miguel Cabrera	.75	.23
❑	62	Rich Harden	.50	.15
❑	63	Mark Teixeira	.75	.23
❑	64	Frank Thomas	1.25	.35
❑	65	Johan Santana	.75	.23
❑	66	Jason Schmidt	.50	.15
❑	67	Aramis Ramirez	.50	.15
❑	68	Jose Reyes	.50	.15
❑	69	Maggio Ordonez	.50	.15
❑	70	Mike Sweeney	.50	.15
❑	71	Eric Chavez	.50	.15
❑	72	Rocco Baldelli	.50	.15
❑	73	Sammy Sosa	1.25	.35
❑	74	Javy Lopez	.50	.15
❑	75	Roy Oswalt	.50	.15
❑	76	Raul Ibanez	.50	.15
❑	77	Ivan Rodriguez	.75	.23
❑	78	Jerome Williams	.50	.15
❑	79	Carlos Lee	.50	.15
❑	80	Geoff Jenkins	.50	.15
❑	81	Sean Burroughs	.50	.15
❑	82	Marcus Giles	.50	.15
❑	83	Mike Lowell	.50	.15
❑	84	Barry Zito	.50	.15
❑	85	Aubrey Huff	.50	.15
❑	86	Esteban Loaiza	.50	.15
❑	87	Torii Hunter	.50	.15
❑	88	Phil Nevin	.50	.15
❑	89	Andruw Jones	.75	.23
❑	90	Josh Beckett	.50	.15
❑	91	Mark Mulder	.50	.15
❑	92	Hank Blalock	.50	.15
❑	93	Jason Phillips	.50	.15
❑	94	Russ Ortiz	.50	.15
❑	95	Juan Pierre	.50	.15
❑	96	Tom Glavine	.75	.23
❑	97	Gil Meche	.50	.15
❑	98	Ramon Ortiz	.50	.15
❑	99	Richie Sexson	.50	.15
❑	100	Albert Pujols	2.50	.75
❑	101	Javier Vazquez	.50	.15
❑	102	Johnny Damon	.75	.23
❑	103	Alex Rodriguez	2.00	.60
❑	104	Omar Vizquel	.75	.23
❑	105	Chipper Jones	1.25	.35
❑	106	Lance Berkman	.50	.15
❑	107	Tim Hudson	.50	.15
❑	108	Carlos Delgado	.50	.15
❑	109	Austin Kearns	.50	.15
❑	110	Orlando Cabrera	.50	.15
❑	111	Edgar Martinez	.75	.23
❑	112	Melvin Mora	.50	.15
❑	113	Jeff Bagwell	.75	.23
❑	114	Marlon Byrd	.50	.15
❑	115	Vernon Wells	.50	.15
❑	116	C.C. Sabathia	.50	.15
❑	117	Cliff Floyd	.50	.15
❑	118	Ichiro Suzuki	2.50	.75
❑	119	Miguel Olivo	.50	.15
❑	120	Mike Piazza	2.00	.60
❑	121	Adam Dunn	.50	.15
❑	122	Paul Lo Duca	.50	.15
❑	123	Brett Myers	.50	.15
❑	124	Michael Young	.50	.15
❑	125	Sidney Ponson	.50	.15
❑	126	Greg Maddux	2.00	.60
❑	127	Vladimir Guerrero	1.25	.35
❑	128	Miguel Tejada	.50	.15
❑	129	Andy Pettitte	.75	.23
❑	130	Rafael Palmeiro	.75	.23
❑	131	Ken Griffey Jr.	2.00	.60
❑	132	Shannon Stewart	.50	.15
❑	133	Joel Pineiro	.50	.15
❑	134	Luis Matos	.50	.15
❑	135	Jeff Kent	.50	.15
❑	136	Randy Wolf	.50	.15
❑	137	Chris Woodward	.50	.15
❑	138	Jody Gerut	.50	.15
❑	139	Jose Vidro	.50	.15
❑	140	Bret Boone	.50	.15
❑	141	Bill Mueller	.50	.15
❑	142	Angel Berroa	.50	.15
❑	143	Bobby Abreu	.50	.15
❑	144	Roy Halladay	.50	.15
❑	145	Delmon Young	.75	.23
❑	146	Jonny Gomes	.50	.15
❑	147	Rickie Weeks	.75	.23
❑	148	Edwin Jackson	.50	.15
❑	149	Neal Cotts	.50	.15
❑	150	Jason Bay	.50	.15
❑	151	Khalil Greene	1.50	.45
❑	152	Joe Mauer	.75	.23
❑	153	Bobby Jenks	.75	.23
❑	154	Chin-Feng Chen	.50	.15
❑	155	Chien-Ming Wang	.75	.23
❑	156	Mickey Hall	.50	.15
❑	157	James Houser	.50	.15
❑	158	Jay Sborz	.50	.15
❑	159	Jonathan Fulton	.50	.15
❑	160	Steven Lerud	.50	.15
❑	161	Grady Sizemore	.75	.23
❑	162	Felix Pie	2.00	.60
❑	163	Dustin McGowan	.50	.15
❑	164	Chris Lubanski	.75	.23
❑	165	Tom Gorzelanny	.50	.15
❑	166	Rudy Guillen RC	3.00	.90
❑	167	Aarom Baldiris RC	2.00	.60
❑	168	Conor Jackson RC	12.00	3.60
❑	169	Matt Moses RC	5.00	1.50
❑	170	Ervin Santana RC	6.00	1.80
❑	171	Merkin Valdez RC	2.00	.60
❑	172	Erick Aybar RC	5.00	1.50
❑	173	Brad Sullivan RC	2.00	.60
❑	174	Joey Gathright RC	4.00	1.20
❑	175	Brad Snyder RC	5.00	1.50
❑	176	Alberto Callaspo RC	3.00	.90
❑	177	Brandon Medders RC	1.50	.45
❑	178	Zach Miner RC	2.00	.60
❑	179	Charlie Zink RC	1.00	.30
❑	180	Adam Greenberg RC	3.00	.90
❑	181	Kevin Howard RC	2.00	.60
❑	182	Wanell Severino RC	1.00	.30
❑	183	Chin-Lung Hu RC	4.00	1.20
❑	184	Joel Zumaya RC	6.00	1.80
❑	185	Skip Schumaker RC	1.50	.45
❑	186	Nic Ungs RC	1.50	.45
❑	187	Todd Self RC	2.00	.60
❑	188	Brian Steffek RC	1.00	.30
❑	189	Brock Peterson RC	1.50	.45
❑	190	Greg Thissen RC	1.50	.45
❑	191	Frank Brooks RC	1.00	.30
❑	192	Scott Olsen RC	4.00	1.20
❑	193	Chris Mabeus RC	1.50	.45
❑	194	Dan Giese RC	1.50	.45
❑	195	Jared Wells RC	1.00	.30
❑	196	Carlos Sosa RC	1.50	.45
❑	197	Bobby Madritsch	1.50	.45
❑	198	Calvin Hayes RC	2.00	.60
❑	199	Omar Quintanilla RC	3.00	.90
❑	200	Chris O'Riordan RC	1.50	.45
❑	201	Tim Hutting RC	1.00	.30
❑	202	Carlos Quentin RC	10.00	3.00
❑	203	Brayan Pena RC	1.50	.45
❑	204	Jeff Salazar RC	4.00	1.20
❑	205	David Murphy RC	4.00	1.20
❑	206	Alberto Garcia RC	2.00	.60
❑	207	Ramon Ramirez RC	1.50	.45
❑	208	Luis Bolivar RC	1.50	.45
❑	209	Rodney Choy Foo RC	1.00	.30
❑	210	Fausto Carmona RC	3.00	.90
❑	211	Anthony Acevedo RC	1.50	.45
❑	212	Chad Santos RC	1.50	.45
❑	213	Jason Frasor RC	1.50	.45
❑	214	Jesse Roman RC	1.00	.30
❑	215	James Tomlin RC	1.50	.45
❑	216	Josh Labandeira RC	1.50	.45
❑	217	Ryan Meaux RC	1.50	.45
❑	218	Don Sutton RC	4.00	1.20
❑	219	Danny Gonzalez RC	1.00	.30
❑	220	Javier Guzman RC	2.00	.60
❑	221	Anthony Lerew RC	2.00	.60
❑	222	Jon Connolly RC	4.00	1.20
❑	223	Jesse English RC	1.50	.45
❑	224	Hector Made RC	3.00	.90
❑	225	Travis Hanson RC	1.50	.45
❑	226	Jesse Floyd RC	1.50	.45
❑	227	Nick Gorneault RC	2.00	.60
❑	228	Craig Ansman RC	1.50	.45
❑	229	Paul McAnulty RC	3.00	.90
❑	230	Carl Loadenthal RC	2.00	.60
❑	231	Dave Crouthers RC	1.00	.30
❑	232	Harvey Garcia RC	1.00	.30
❑	233	Casey Kopitzke RC	1.00	.30
❑	234	Ricky Nolasco RC	3.00	.90
❑	235	Miguel Perez RC	1.50	.45
❑	236	Ryan Mulhern RC	1.00	.30
❑	237	Chris Aguila RC	1.50	.45
❑	238	Brooks Conrad RC	2.00	.60
❑	239	Damaso Espino RC	1.00	.30
❑	240	Jereme Milons RC	2.00	.60
❑	241	Luke Hughes RC	1.00	.30
❑	242	Kory Casto RC	2.00	.60
❑	243	Jose Valdez RC	1.50	.45
❑	244	J.T. Stotts RC	1.00	.30
❑	245	Lee Gwaltney RC	1.00	.30
❑	246	Yoann Torrealba RC	1.00	.30
❑	247	Omar Falcon RC	1.50	.45
❑	248	Jon Coutlangus RC	1.00	.30
❑	249	George Sherrill RC	1.50	.45
❑	250	John Santor RC	1.00	.30
❑	251	Tony Richie RC	1.50	.45
❑	252	Kevin Richardson RC	1.00	.30
❑	253	Tim Bittner RC	1.50	.45
❑	254	Chris Saenz RC	1.50	.45
❑	255	Jose Capellan RC	2.00	.60
❑	256	Donald Levinski RC	1.00	.30
❑	257	Jerome Gamble RC	1.00	.30
❑	258	Jeff Keppinger RC	1.50	.45
❑	259	Jason Szuminski RC	1.00	.30
❑	260	Akinori Otsuka RC	1.50	.45
❑	261	Ryan Budde RC	1.50	.45
❑	262	Marland Williams RC	2.00	.60
❑	263	Jeff Allison RC	1.50	.45
❑	264	Hector Gimenez RC	1.00	.30
❑	265	Tim Frend RC	1.50	.45
❑	266	Tom Farmer RC	1.50	.45
❑	267	Shawn Hill RC	1.50	.45
❑	268	Mike Huggins RC	1.50	.45
❑	269	Scott Proctor RC	2.00	.60
❑	270	Jorge Mejia RC	1.50	.45
❑	271	Terry Jones RC	2.00	.60
❑	272	Zach Duke RC	15.00	4.50
❑	273	Jesse Crain RC	3.00	.90
❑	274	Luke Anderson RC	1.00	.30
❑	275	Hunter Brown RC	1.00	.30
❑	276	Matt Lemanczyk RC	1.50	.45
❑	277	Fernando Cortez RC	1.00	.30
❑	278	Vince Perkins RC	2.00	.60
❑	279	Tommy Murphy RC	1.50	.45
❑	280	Mike Gosling RC	1.00	.30
❑	281	Paul Bacot RC	2.00	.60
❑	282	Matt Capps RC	1.50	.45
❑	283	Juan Gutierrez RC	1.50	.45
❑	284	Teodoro Encarnacion RC	2.00	.60
❑	285	Chad Bentz RC	1.50	.45
❑	286	Kazuo Matsui RC	3.00	.90
❑	287	Ryan Hankins RC	1.00	.30
❑	288	Leo Nunez RC	1.50	.45
❑	289	Dave Wallace RC	1.50	.45
❑	290	Rob Tejeda RC	3.00	.90
❑	291	Paul Maholm RC	4.00	1.20
❑	292	Casey Daigle RC	1.50	.45
❑	293	Tydus Meadows RC	1.00	.30
❑	294	Khalid Ballouli RC	1.00	.30
❑	295	Benji DeQuin RC	1.00	.30
❑	296	Tyler Davidson RC	2.00	.60
❑	297	Brant Colamarino RC	3.00	.90
❑	298	Marcus McBeth RC	1.00	.30
❑	299	Brad Eldred RC	8.00	2.40
❑	300	David Pauley RC	1.00	.30
❑	301	Yadier Molina RC	6.00	1.80

Card	Nm-Mt	Ex-Mt
❑ 302 Chris Shelton RC	5.00	1.50
❑ 303 Nyjer Morgan RC	1.00	.30
❑ 304 Jon DeVries RC	1.50	.45
❑ 305 Sheldon Fulse RC	1.00	.30
❑ 306 Vito Chiaravalloti RC	1.50	.45
❑ 307 Warner Madrigal RC	3.00	.90
❑ 308 Reid Gorecki RC	1.50	.45
❑ 309 Sung Jung RC	1.00	.30
❑ 310 Pete Shier RC	1.00	.30
❑ 311 Michael Mooney RC	1.50	.45
❑ 312 Kenny Perez RC	1.50	.45
❑ 313 Michael Mallory RC	1.50	.45
❑ 314 Ben Himes RC	1.00	.30
❑ 315 Ivan Ochoa RC	1.50	.45
❑ 316 Donald Kelly RC	1.50	.45
❑ 317 Tom Mastny RC	1.50	.45
❑ 318 Kevin Davidson RC	1.00	.30
❑ 319 Brian Pilkington RC	1.50	.45
❑ 320 Alex Romero RC	1.50	.45
❑ 321 Chad Chop RC	1.50	.45
❑ 322 Kody Kirkland RC	2.00	.60
❑ 323 Casey Myers RC	1.00	.30
❑ 324 Mike Rouse RC	1.50	.45
❑ 325 Sergio Silva RC	1.00	.30
❑ 326 J.J. Furmaniak RC	3.00	.90
❑ 327 Brad Vericker RC	1.50	.45
❑ 328 Blake Hawksworth RC	2.00	.60
❑ 329 Brock Jacobsen RC	1.00	.30
❑ 330 Alec Zumwalt RC	1.00	.30
❑ 331 Wardell Starling AU RC	15.00	4.50
❑ 332 Estee Harris AU RC	20.00	6.00
❑ 333 Kyle Sleeth AU RC	20.00	6.00
❑ 334 Dioner Navarro AU RC	30.00	9.00
❑ 335 Logan Kensing AU RC	15.00	4.50
❑ 336 Travis Blackley AU RC	15.00	4.50
❑ 337 Lincoln Holdzkom AU RC	15.00	4.50
❑ 338 Jason Hirsh AU RC	20.00	6.00
❑ 339 Juan Cedeno AU RC	15.00	4.50
❑ 340 Matt Creighton AU RC	15.00	4.50
❑ 341 Tim Stauffer AU RC	20.00	6.00
❑ 342 Shingo Takatsu AU RC	20.00	6.00
❑ 343 Lastings Milledge AU RC	60.00	18.00
❑ 344 Dustin Nippert AU RC	20.00	6.00
❑ 345 Felix Hernandez AU RC	160.00	47.50
❑ 346 Joaquin Arias AU RC	20.00	6.00
❑ 347 Kevin Kouzmanoff AU RC	20.00	6.00
❑ 348 B.Brownlie AU RC EXCH	25.00	7.50
❑ 349 David Aardsma AU RC	20.00	6.00
❑ 350 Jon Knott AU RC	15.00	4.50

2004 Bowman Chrome Draft

	Nm-Mt	Ex-Mt
COMPLETE SET (175)	300.00	90.00
COMP.SET w/o SP's (165)	100.00	30.00
COMMON CARD (1-165)	.40	.12
COMMON RC YR	.40	.12
1-165 TWO PER BOWMAN DRAFT PACK		.00

166-175 ODDS 1:60 BOWMAN DRAFT HOBBY
166-175 ODDS 1:60 BOWMAN DRAFT RETAIL
166-175 STATED PRINT RUN 1695 SETS
166-175 ARE NOT SERIAL-NUMBERED
166-175 PRINT RUN PROVIDED BY TOPPS
PLATES 1-165 ODDS 1:559 HOBBY
PLATES 166-175 ODDS 1:18,354 HOBBY
PLATES PRINT RUN 1 SERIAL #'d SET
BLACK-CYAN-MAGENTA-YELLOW EXIST
NO PLATES PRICING DUE TO SCARCITY

Card	Nm-Mt	Ex-Mt
❑ 1 Lyle Overbay	.40	.12
❑ 2 David Newhan	.40	.12
❑ 3 J.R. House	.40	.12
❑ 4 Chad Tracy	.40	.12
❑ 5 Humberto Quintero	.40	.12
❑ 6 Dave Bush	.40	.12
❑ 7 Scott Hairston	.40	.12
❑ 8 Mike Wood	.40	.12
❑ 9 Alexis Rios	.60	.18
❑ 10 Sean Burnett	.40	.12
❑ 11 Wilson Valdez	.40	.12
❑ 12 Lew Ford	.40	.12
❑ 13 Freddy Thon RC	1.00	.30
❑ 14 Zack Greinke	.60	.18
❑ 15 Bucky Jacobsen	.40	.12
❑ 16 Kevin Youkilis	.40	.12
❑ 17 Grady Sizemore	.60	.18
❑ 18 Denny Bautista	.40	.12
❑ 19 David DeJesus	.40	.12
❑ 20 Casey Kotchman	.60	.18
❑ 21 David Kelton	.40	.12
❑ 22 Charles Thomas RC	1.00	.30
❑ 23 Kazuhito Tadano RC	1.50	.45
❑ 24 Justin Leone RC	1.50	.45
❑ 25 Eduardo Villacis RC	1.00	.30
❑ 26 Brian Dallimore RC	1.00	.30
❑ 27 Nick Green	.40	.12
❑ 28 Sam McConnell RC	1.00	.30
❑ 29 Brad Halsey RC	1.50	.45
❑ 30 Roman Colon RC	1.00	.30
❑ 31 Josh Fields RC	4.00	1.20
❑ 32 Cody Bunkelman RC	1.50	.45
❑ 33 Jay Rainville RC	4.00	1.20
❑ 34 Richie Robnett RC	3.00	.90
❑ 35 Jon Poterson RC	2.50	.75
❑ 36 Huston Street RC	6.00	1.80
❑ 37 Erick San Pedro RC	1.00	.30
❑ 38 Cory Dunlap RC	3.00	.90
❑ 39 Kurt Suzuki RC	4.00	1.20
❑ 40 Anthony Swarzak RC	2.50	.75
❑ 41 Ian Desmond RC	4.00	1.20
❑ 42 Chris Covington RC	1.50	.45
❑ 43 Christian Garcia RC	1.50	.45
❑ 44 Gaby Hernandez RC	5.00	1.50
❑ 45 Steven Register RC	1.00	.30
❑ 46 Eduardo Morlan RC	2.50	.75
❑ 47 Collin Balester RC	1.00	.30
❑ 48 Nathan Phillips RC	1.50	.45
❑ 49 Dan Schwartzbauer RC	1.50	.45
❑ 50 Rafael Gonzalez RC	1.00	.30
❑ 51 K.C. Herren RC	2.50	.75
❑ 52 William Susdorf RC	1.00	.30
❑ 53 Rob Johnson RC	1.50	.45
❑ 54 Louis Marson RC	2.50	.75
❑ 55 Joe Koshansky RC	3.00	.90
❑ 56 Jamar Walton RC	2.50	.75
❑ 57 Mark Lowe RC	1.50	.45
❑ 58 Matt Macri RC	4.00	1.20
❑ 59 Donny Lucy RC	1.00	.30
❑ 60 Mike Ferris RC	1.50	.45
❑ 61 Mike Nickeas RC	1.50	.45
❑ 62 Eric Hurley RC	2.50	.75
❑ 63 Scott Elbert RC	3.00	.90
❑ 64 Blake DeWitt RC	5.00	1.50
❑ 65 Danny Putnam RC	2.50	.75
❑ 66 J.P. Howell RC	3.00	.90
❑ 67 John Wiggins RC	1.00	.30
❑ 68 Justin Orenduff RC	2.50	.75
❑ 69 Ray Liotta RC	3.00	.90
❑ 70 Billy Buckner RC	1.50	.45
❑ 71 Eric Campbell RC	6.00	1.80
❑ 72 Olin Wick RC	2.50	.75
❑ 73 Sean Gamble RC	1.50	.45
❑ 74 Seth Smith RC	3.00	.90
❑ 75 Wade Davis RC	2.50	.75
❑ 76 Joe Jacobitz RC	1.00	.30
❑ 77 J.A. Happ RC	2.50	.75
❑ 78 Eric Ridener RC	1.00	.30
❑ 79 Matt Tuiasosopo RC	8.00	2.40
❑ 80 Brad Bergesen RC	1.00	.30
❑ 81 Javy Guerra RC	1.50	.45
❑ 82 Buck Shaw RC	1.50	.45
❑ 83 Paul Janish RC	1.50	.45
❑ 84 Sean Kazmar RC	1.00	.30
❑ 85 Josh Johnson RC	1.50	.45
❑ 86 Angel Salome RC	4.00	1.20
❑ 87 Jordan Parraz RC	2.50	.75
❑ 88 Kelvin Vazquez RC	1.00	.30
❑ 89 Grant Hansen RC	1.00	.30
❑ 90 Matt Fox RC	1.00	.30
❑ 91 Trevor Plouffe RC	4.00	1.20
❑ 92 Wes Whisler RC	1.00	.30
❑ 93 Curtis Thigpen RC	2.50	.75
❑ 94 Donnie Smith RC	1.50	.45
❑ 95 Luis Rivera RC	1.50	.45
❑ 96 Jesse Hoover RC	1.50	.45
❑ 97 Jason Vargas RC	4.00	1.20
❑ 98 Clary Carlsen RC	1.00	.30
❑ 99 Mark Robinson RC	1.00	.30
❑ 100 J.C. Holt RC	1.50	.45
❑ 101 Chad Blackwell RC	1.00	.30
❑ 102 Daryl Jones RC	3.00	.90
❑ 103 Jonathan Tierce RC	1.00	.30
❑ 104 Patrick Bryant RC	1.00	.30
❑ 105 Eddie Prasch RC	1.50	.45
❑ 106 Mitch Einertson RC	6.00	1.80
❑ 107 Kyle Waldrop RC	3.00	.90
❑ 108 Jeff Marquez RC	1.50	.45
❑ 109 Zach Jackson RC	2.50	.75
❑ 110 Josh Wahpepah RC	1.00	.30
❑ 111 Adam Lind RC	4.00	1.20
❑ 112 Kyle Bloom RC	1.50	.45
❑ 113 Ben Harrison RC	1.00	.30
❑ 114 Taylor Tankersley RC	2.50	.75
❑ 115 Steven Jackson RC	1.00	.30
❑ 116 David Purcey RC	2.50	.75
❑ 117 Jacob McGee RC	1.00	.30
❑ 118 Lucas Harrell RC	1.00	.30
❑ 119 Brandon Allen RC	3.00	.90
❑ 120 Van Pope RC	1.50	.45
❑ 121 Jeff Francis	.60	.18
❑ 122 Joe Blanton	.60	.18
❑ 123 Wil Ledezma	.40	.12
❑ 124 Bryan Bullington	.40	.12
❑ 125 Jairo Garcia	.40	.12
❑ 126 Matt Cain	2.00	.60
❑ 127 Arnie Munoz	.40	.12
❑ 128 Clint Everts	.40	.12
❑ 129 Jesus Cota	.40	.12
❑ 130 Gavin Floyd	.40	.12
❑ 131 Edwin Encarnacion	.60	.18
❑ 132 Koyie Hill	.40	.12
❑ 133 Ruben Gotay	.40	.12
❑ 134 Jeff Mathis	.40	.12
❑ 135 Andy Marte	.60	.18
❑ 136 Dallas McPherson	.60	.18
❑ 137 Justin Morneau	.60	.18
❑ 138 Rickie Weeks	1.00	.30
❑ 139 Joel Guzman	1.00	.30
❑ 140 Shin Soo Choo	.40	.12
❑ 141 Yusmeiro Petit RC	6.00	1.80
❑ 142 Jorge Cortes RC	1.00	.30
❑ 143 Val Majewski	.40	.12
❑ 144 Felix Pie	1.00	.30
❑ 145 Aaron Hill	.40	.12
❑ 146 Jose Capellan	.60	.18
❑ 147 Dioner Navarro	1.50	.45
❑ 148 Fausto Carmona	1.00	.30
❑ 149 Robinzon Diaz RC	1.00	.30
❑ 150 Felix Hernandez	15.00	4.50
❑ 151 Andres Blanco RC	1.00	.30
❑ 152 Jason Kubel	.40	.12
❑ 153 Willy Taveras RC	4.00	1.20
❑ 154 Merkin Valdez	1.00	.30
❑ 155 Robinson Cano	1.50	.45
❑ 156 Bill Murphy	.40	.12
❑ 157 Chris Burke	.60	.18
❑ 158 Kyle Sleeth	.60	.18
❑ 159 B.J. Upton	1.00	.30
❑ 160 Tim Stauffer	1.00	.30
❑ 161 David Wright	2.00	.60
❑ 162 Conor Jackson	4.00	1.20
❑ 163 Brad Thompson RC	2.50	.75
❑ 164 Delmon Young	1.00	.30
❑ 165 Jeremy Reed	.60	.18
❑ 166 Matt Bush AU RC	30.00	9.00
❑ 167 Mark Rogers AU RC	20.00	6.00
❑ 168 Thomas Diamond AU RC UER Many errors in informational blurb	25.00	7.50
❑ 169 Greg Golson AU RC	25.00	7.50

❑ 170 Homer Bailey AU RC 25.00 7.50
❑ 171 Chris Lambert AU RC .. 15.00 4.50
❑ 172 Neil Walker AU RC 30.00 9.00
❑ 173 Bill Bray AU RC 10.00 3.00
❑ 174 Phillip Hughes AU RC .. 40.00 12.00
❑ 175 Gio Gonzalez AU RC 20.00 6.00

2005 Bowman Chrome

	Nm-Mt	Ex-Mt
COMP.SET w/o AU's (330)	120.00	36.00
COMMON CARD (1-140)	.50	.15
COMMON CARD (141-165)	.50	.15
COMMON CARD (166-330)	1.00	.30
COMMON AUTO (331-353)	12.00	3.60

1-330 PLATE ODDS 1:779 HOBBY..
331-353 AU PLATE ODDS 1:10,996 HOBBY
PLATE PRINT RUN 1 SET PER COLOR
BLACK-CYAN-MAGENTA-YELLOW ISSUED
NO PLATE PRICING DUE TO SCARCITY

❑ 1 Gavin Floyd .... .50 .15
❑ 2 Eric Chavez .... .50 .15
❑ 3 Miguel Tejada .... .50 .15
❑ 4 Dmitri Young .... .50 .15
❑ 5 Hank Blalock .... .50 .15
❑ 6 Kerry Wood .... .50 .15
❑ 7 Andy Pettitte .... .75 .23
❑ 8 Pat Burrell .... .50 .15
❑ 9 Johnny Estrada .... .50 .15
❑ 10 Frank Thomas .... 1.25 .35
❑ 11 Juan Pierre .... .50 .15
❑ 12 Tom Glavine .... .75 .23
❑ 13 Lyle Overbay .... .50 .15
❑ 14 Jim Edmonds .... .75 .23
❑ 15 Steve Finley .... .50 .15
❑ 16 Jermaine Dye .... .50 .15
❑ 17 Omar Vizquel .... .75 .23
❑ 18 Nick Johnson .... .50 .15
❑ 19 Brian Giles .... .50 .15
❑ 20 Justin Morneau .... .50 .15
❑ 21 Preston Wilson .... .50 .15
❑ 22 Wily Mo Pena .... .50 .15
❑ 23 Rafael Palmeiro .... .75 .23
❑ 24 Scott Kazmir .... .50 .15
❑ 25 Derek Jeter .... 2.50 .75
❑ 26 Barry Zito .... .50 .15
❑ 27 Mike Lowell .... .50 .15
❑ 28 Jason Bay .... .50 .15
❑ 29 Ken Harvey .... .50 .15
❑ 30 Nomar Garciaparra .... 1.25 .35
❑ 31 Roy Halladay .... .50 .15
❑ 32 Todd Helton .... .75 .23
❑ 33 Mark Kotsay .... .50 .15
❑ 34 Jake Peavy .... .50 .15
❑ 35 David Wright .... 2.00 .60
❑ 36 Dontrelle Willis .... .50 .15
❑ 37 Marcus Giles .... .50 .15
❑ 38 Chone Figgins .... .50 .15
❑ 39 Sidney Ponson .... .50 .15
❑ 40 Randy Johnson .... 1.25 .35
❑ 41 John Smoltz .... .75 .23
❑ 42 Kevin Millar .... .50 .15
❑ 43 Mark Teixeira .... .75 .23
❑ 44 Alex Rios .... .50 .15
❑ 45 Mike Piazza .... 1.25 .35
❑ 46 Victor Martinez .... .50 .15
❑ 47 Jeff Bagwell .... .75 .23
❑ 48 Shawn Green .... .50 .15
❑ 49 Ivan Rodriguez .... .75 .23
❑ 50 Alex Rodriguez .... 2.00 .60
❑ 51 Kazuo Matsui .... .50 .15
❑ 52 Mark Mulder .... .50 .15
❑ 53 Michael Young .... .50 .15
❑ 54 Javy Lopez .... .50 .15
❑ 55 Johnny Damon .... .75 .23
❑ 56 Jeff Francis .... .50 .15
❑ 57 Rich Harden .... .50 .15
❑ 58 Bobby Abreu .... .50 .15
❑ 59 Mark Loretta .... .50 .15
❑ 60 Gary Sheffield .... .50 .15
❑ 61 Jamie Moyer .... .50 .15
❑ 62 Garret Anderson .... .50 .15
❑ 63 Vernon Wells .... .50 .15
❑ 64 Orlando Cabrera .... .50 .15
❑ 65 Magglio Ordonez .... .50 .15
❑ 66 Ronnie Belliard .... .50 .15
❑ 67 Carlos Lee .... .50 .15
❑ 68 Carl Pavano .... .50 .15
❑ 69 Jon Lieber .... .50 .15
❑ 70 Aubrey Huff .... .50 .15
❑ 71 Rocco Baldelli .... .50 .15
❑ 72 Jason Schmidt .... .50 .15
❑ 73 Bernie Williams .... .75 .23
❑ 74 Hideki Matsui .... 2.50 .75
❑ 75 Ken Griffey Jr. .... 2.00 .60
❑ 76 Josh Beckett .... .50 .15
❑ 77 Mark Buehrle .... .50 .15
❑ 78 David Ortiz .... 1.25 .35
❑ 79 Luis Gonzalez .... .50 .15
❑ 80 Scott Rolen .... .75 .23
❑ 81 Joe Mauer .... .50 .15
❑ 82 Jose Reyes .... .50 .15
❑ 83 Adam Dunn .... .50 .15
❑ 84 Greg Maddux .... 2.00 .60
❑ 85 Bartolo Colon .... .50 .15
❑ 86 Bret Boone .... .50 .15
❑ 87 Mike Mussina .... .75 .23
❑ 88 Ben Sheets .... .50 .15
❑ 89 Lance Berkman .... .50 .15
❑ 90 Miguel Cabrera .... .75 .23
❑ 91 C.C. Sabathia .... .50 .15
❑ 92 Mike Maroth .... .50 .15
❑ 93 Andruw Jones .... .75 .23
❑ 94 Jack Wilson .... .50 .15
❑ 95 Ichiro Suzuki .... 2.50 .75
❑ 96 Geoff Jenkins .... .50 .15
❑ 97 Zack Greinke .... .50 .15
❑ 98 Jorge Posada .... .75 .23
❑ 99 Travis Hafner .... .50 .15
❑ 100 Barry Bonds .... 3.00 .90
❑ 101 Aaron Rowand .... .50 .15
❑ 102 Aramis Ramirez .... .50 .15
❑ 103 Curt Schilling .... .75 .23
❑ 104 Melvin Mora .... .50 .15
❑ 105 Albert Pujols .... 2.50 .75
❑ 106 Austin Kearns .... .50 .15
❑ 107 Shannon Stewart .... .50 .15
❑ 108 Carl Crawford .... .50 .15
❑ 109 Carlos Zambrano .... .50 .15
❑ 110 Roger Clemens .... 2.00 .60
❑ 111 Javier Vazquez .... .50 .15
❑ 112 Randy Wolf .... .50 .15
❑ 113 Chipper Jones .... 1.25 .35
❑ 114 Larry Walker .... .75 .23
❑ 115 Alfonso Soriano .... .50 .15
❑ 116 Brad Wilkerson .... .50 .15
❑ 117 Bobby Crosby .... .50 .15
❑ 118 Jim Thome .... .75 .23
❑ 119 Oliver Perez .... .50 .15
❑ 120 Vladimir Guerrero .... 1.25 .35
❑ 121 Roy Oswalt .... .50 .15
❑ 122 Torii Hunter .... .50 .15
❑ 123 Rafael Furcal .... .50 .15
❑ 124 Luis Castillo .... .50 .15
❑ 125 Carlos Beltran .... .50 .15
❑ 126 Mike Sweeney .... .50 .15
❑ 127 Johan Santana .... .75 .23
❑ 128 Tim Hudson .... .50 .15
❑ 129 Troy Glaus .... .50 .15
❑ 130 Manny Ramirez .... .75 .23
❑ 131 Jeff Kent .... .50 .15
❑ 132 Jose Vidro .... .50 .15
❑ 133 Edgar Renteria .... .50 .15
❑ 134 Russ Ortiz .... .50 .15
❑ 135 Sammy Sosa .... 1.25 .35
❑ 136 Carlos Delgado .... .50 .15
❑ 137 Richie Sexson .... .50 .15
❑ 138 Pedro Martinez .... .75 .23
❑ 139 Adrian Beltre .... .50 .15
❑ 140 Mark Prior .... .75 .23
❑ 141 Omar Quintanilla .... .50 .15
❑ 142 Carlos Quentin .... .75 .23
❑ 143 Dan Johnson .... .75 .23
❑ 144 Jake Stevens .... .50 .15
❑ 145 Nate Schierholtz .... .75 .23
❑ 146 Neil Walker .... .50 .15
❑ 147 Bill Bray .... .50 .15
❑ 148 Taylor Tankersley .... .50 .15
❑ 149 Trevor Plouffe .... .75 .23
❑ 150 Felix Hernandez 6.00 1.80
❑ 151 Philip Hughes .... .50 .15
❑ 152 James Houser .... .50 .15
❑ 153 David Murphy .... .50 .15
❑ 154 Ervin Santana .... .75 .23
❑ 155 Anthony Whittington .... .50 .15
❑ 156 Chris Lambert .... .50 .15
❑ 157 Jeremy Sowers .... .75 .23
❑ 158 Giovanny Gonzalez .... .75 .23
❑ 159 Blake DeWitt .... .75 .23
❑ 160 Thomas Diamond .... .75 .23
❑ 161 Greg Golson .... .75 .23
❑ 162 David Aardsma .... .50 .15
❑ 163 Paul Maholm .... .50 .15
❑ 164 Mark Rogers .... .75 .23
❑ 165 Homer Bailey .... .75 .23
❑ 166 Elvin Puello RC .... 1.50 .45
❑ 167 Tony Giarratano RC .... 1.50 .45
❑ 168 Darren Fenster RC .... 1.50 .45
❑ 169 Elvys Quezada RC .... 1.50 .45
❑ 170 Glen Perkins RC .... 3.00 .90
❑ 171 Ian Kinsler RC .... 3.00 .90
❑ 172 Adam Bostick RC .... 1.50 .45
❑ 173 Jeremy West RC .... 2.00 .60
❑ 174 Brett Harper RC .... 2.00 .60
❑ 175 Kevin West RC .... 1.50 .45
❑ 176 Luis Hernandez RC .... 1.50 .45
❑ 177 Matt Campbell RC .... 1.50 .45
❑ 178 Nate McLouth RC .... 2.00 .60
❑ 179 Ryan Goleski RC .... 2.00 .60
❑ 180 Matthew Lindstrom RC .. 1.50 .45
❑ 181 Matt DeSalvo RC .... 2.00 .60
❑ 182 Kole Strayhorn RC .... 1.50 .45
❑ 183 Jose Vaquedano RC .... 1.50 .45
❑ 184 James Jurries RC .... 2.00 .60
❑ 185 Ian Bladergroen RC .... 2.00 .60
❑ 186 Kila Kaaihue RC 4.00 1.20
❑ 187 Luke Scott RC .... 2.00 .60
❑ 188 Chris Denorfia RC .... 2.00 .60
❑ 189 Jai Miller RC .... 2.00 .60
❑ 190 Melky Cabrera RC 4.00 1.20
❑ 191 Ryan Sweeney RC 4.00 1.20
❑ 192 Sean Marshall RC .... 2.00 .60
❑ 193 Erick Abreu RC .... 3.00 .90
❑ 194 Tyler Pelland RC .... 2.00 .60
❑ 195 Cole Armstrong RC .... 1.50 .45
❑ 196 John Hudgins RC .... 1.50 .45
❑ 197 Wade Robinson RC .... 1.50 .45
❑ 198 Dan Santin RC .... 1.50 .45
❑ 199 Steve Doetsch RC .... 1.50 .45
❑ 200 Shane Costa RC .... 1.50 .45
❑ 201 Scott Mathieson RC .... 3.00 .90
❑ 202 Ben Jones RC .... 2.00 .60
❑ 203 Michael Rogers RC .... 1.50 .45
❑ 204 Matt Rogelstad RC .... 1.50 .45
❑ 205 Luis Ramirez RC .... 1.50 .45
❑ 206 Landon Powell RC .... 2.00 .60
❑ 207 Erik Cordier RC .... 1.50 .45
❑ 208 Chris Seddon RC .... 1.50 .45
❑ 209 Chris Roberson RC .... 1.50 .45
❑ 210 Thomas Oldham RC .... 1.50 .45
❑ 211 Dana Eveland RC .... 1.50 .45
❑ 212 Cody Haerther RC .... 1.50 .45
❑ 213 Danny Core RC .... 1.50 .45
❑ 214 Craig Tatum RC .... 1.50 .45
❑ 215 Elliot Johnson RC .... 1.50 .45
❑ 216 Ender Chavez RC .... 1.50 .45
❑ 217 Errol Simonitsch RC .... 2.00 .60
❑ 218 Matt Van Der Bosch RC .. 1.50 .45
❑ 219 Eulogio de la Cruz RC .... 1.50 .45

❑ 220 Drew Toussaint RC 1.50 .45
❑ 221 Adam Boeve RC 1.50 .45
❑ 222 Adam Harben RC 2.00 .60
❑ 223 Baltazar Lopez RC 1.50 .45
❑ 224 Russ Martin RC 3.00 .90
❑ 225 Brian Bannister RC 1.50 .45
❑ 226 Chris Walker RC 1.50 .45
❑ 227 Casey McGehee RC 1.50 .45
❑ 228 Humberto Sanchez RC 1.50 .45
❑ 229 Javon Moran RC 1.50 .45
❑ 230 Brandon McCarthy RC 5.00 1.50
❑ 231 Danny Zell RC 1.50 .45
❑ 232 Kevin Barry RC 1.50 .45
❑ 233 Juan Tejeda RC 1.50 .45
❑ 234 Keith Ramsey RC 1.50 .45
❑ 235 Lorenzo Scott RC 1.50 .45
❑ 236 Jon Barratt RC 1.50 .45
❑ 237 Martin Prado RC 1.50 .45
❑ 238 Matt Albers RC 1.50 .45
❑ 239 Brian Schweiger RC 1.50 .45
❑ 240 Raul Tablado RC 1.50 .45
❑ 241 Pat Misch RC 1.50 .45
❑ 242 Pat Osborn 1.50 .45
❑ 243 Ryan Feierabend RC 1.50 .45
❑ 244 Shaun Marcum 1.00 .30
❑ 245 Kevin Collins RC 1.50 .45
❑ 246 Stuart Pomeranz RC 1.50 .45
❑ 247 Tetsu Yofu RC 1.50 .45
❑ 248 Hernan Iribarren RC 3.00 .90
❑ 249 Mike Spidale RC 1.50 .45
❑ 250 Tony Arnerich RC 1.50 .45
❑ 251 Manny Parra RC 1.50 .45
❑ 252 Drew Anderson RC 1.50 .45
❑ 253 T.J. Beam RC 3.00 .90
❑ 254 Claudio Arias RC 2.00 .60
❑ 255 Andy Sides RC 1.50 .45
❑ 256 Bear Bay RC 2.00 .60
❑ 257 Bill McCarthy RC 1.50 .45
❑ 258 Daniel Haigwood RC 4.00 1.20
❑ 259 Brian Sprout RC 2.00 .60
❑ 260 Bryan Triplett RC 1.50 .45
❑ 261 Steven Bondurant RC 1.50 .45
❑ 262 Darwinson Salazar RC 1.50 .45
❑ 263 David Shepard RC 1.50 .45
❑ 264 Johan Silva RC 1.50 .45
❑ 265 J.B. Thurmond RC 1.50 .45
❑ 266 Brandon Moorhead RC 1.50 .45
❑ 267 Kyle Nichols RC 2.00 .60
❑ 268 Jonathan Sanchez RC 1.50 .45
❑ 269 Mike Esposito RC 1.50 .45
❑ 270 Erik Schindewolf RC 1.50 .45
❑ 271 Peeter Ramos RC 1.50 .45
❑ 272 Juan Senreiso RC 1.50 .45
❑ 273 Travis Chick RC 2.00 .60
❑ 274 Vinny Rottino RC 1.50 .45
❑ 275 Micah Furtado RC 1.50 .45
❑ 276 George Kottaras RC 3.00 .90
❑ 277 Abel Gomez RC 2.00 .60
❑ 278 Buck Coats RC 1.50 .45
❑ 279 Kenny Durost RC 1.50 .45
❑ 280 Nick Touchstone RC 1.50 .45
❑ 281 Jerry Owens RC 2.00 .60
❑ 282 Stefan Bailie RC 1.50 .45
❑ 283 Jesse Gutierrez RC 1.50 .45
❑ 284 Chuck Tiffany RC 4.00 1.20
❑ 285 Brendan Ryan RC 1.50 .45
❑ 286 Julio Pimentel RC 2.00 .60
❑ 287 Shawn Bowman RC 2.00 .60
❑ 288 Alexander Smit RC 1.50 .45
❑ 289 Micah Schnurstein RC 1.50 .45
❑ 290 Jared Gothreaux RC 1.50 .45
❑ 291 Jair Jurrjens RC 2.00 .60
❑ 292 Bobby Livingston RC 1.50 .45
❑ 293 Ryan Speier RC 1.50 .45
❑ 294 Zach Parker RC 1.50 .45
❑ 295 Christian Colonel RC 1.50 .45
❑ 296 Scott Mitchinson RC 1.50 .45
❑ 297 Neil Wilson RC 1.50 .45
❑ 298 Chuck James RC 8.00 2.40
❑ 299 Heath Totten RC 1.50 .45
❑ 300 Sean Tracey RC 1.50 .45
❑ 301 Tadahito Iguchi RC 5.00 1.50
❑ 302 Matt Brown RC 1.50 .45
❑ 303 Franklin Morales RC 1.50 .45
❑ 304 Brandon Sing RC 3.00 .90
❑ 305 D.J. Houlton RC 1.50 .45
❑ 306 Jayce Tingler RC 1.50 .45
❑ 307 Mitchell Arnold RC 1.50 .45
❑ 308 Jim Burt RC 1.50 .45
❑ 309 Jason Motte RC 1.50 .45
❑ 310 David Gassner RC 1.50 .45
❑ 311 Andy Santana RC 1.50 .45
❑ 312 Kelvin Pichardo RC 1.50 .45
❑ 313 Carlos Carrasco RC 2.00 .60
❑ 314 Willy Mota RC 1.50 .45
❑ 315 Frank Mata RC 1.50 .45
❑ 316 Carlos Gonzalez RC 10.00 3.00
❑ 317 Jesse Floyd 1.00 .30
❑ 318 Chris B.Young RC 6.00 1.80
❑ 319 Billy Sadler RC 1.50 .45
❑ 320 Ricky Barrett RC 1.50 .45
❑ 321 Ben Harrison 1.50 .45
❑ 322 Steve Nelson RC 1.50 .45
❑ 323 Daryl Thompson RC 1.50 .45
❑ 324 Davis Romero RC 1.50 .45
❑ 325 Jeremy Harts RC 1.50 .45
❑ 326 Nick Masset RC 1.50 .45
❑ 327 Thomas Pauly RC 1.50 .45
❑ 328 Mike Garber RC 1.50 .45
❑ 329 Kennard Bibbs RC 1.50 .45
❑ 330 Colter Bean RC 1.50 .45
❑ 331 Justin Verlander AU RC 40.00 12.00
❑ 332 Chip Cannon AU RC 15.00 4.50
❑ 333 Kevin Melillo AU RC 20.00 6.00
❑ 334 Jake Postlewait AU RC 12.00 3.60
❑ 335 Wes Swackhamer AU RC 15.00 4.50
❑ 336 Mike Rodriguez AU RC 15.00 4.50
❑ 337 Philip Humber AU RC 25.00 7.50
❑ 338 Jeff Niemann AU RC 25.00 7.50
❑ 339 Brian Miller AU RC 15.00 4.50
❑ 340 Chris Vines AU RC 15.00 4.50
❑ 341 Andy LaRoche AU RC 50.00 15.00
❑ 342 Mike Bourn AU RC 20.00 6.00
❑ 343 Eric Nielsen AU RC 12.00 3.60
❑ 344 Wladimir Balentien AU RC 25.00 7.50
❑ 345 Ismael Ramirez AU RC 15.00 4.50
❑ 346 Pedro Lopez AU RC 12.00 3.60
❑ 347 Shawn Bowman AU 20.00 6.00
❑ 348 Hayden Penn AU RC 25.00 7.50
❑ 349 Matthew Kemp AU RC 40.00 12.00
❑ 350 Brian Stavisky AU RC 15.00 4.50
❑ 351 C.J. Smith AU RC 15.00 4.50
❑ 352 Mike Morse AU RC 25.00 7.50
❑ 353 Billy Butler AU RC 60.00 18.00

2005 Bowman Chrome Draft

	Nm-Mt	Ex-Mt
COMP.SET w/o SP's (165)	100.00	30.00
COMMON CARD (1-165)	.40	.12
COMMON RC	1.00	.30
COMMON RC YR	.40	.12

1-165 TWO PER BOWMAN DRAFT PACK
166-180 GROUP A ODDS 1:671 H, 1:643 R
166-180 GROUP B ODDS 1:69 H, 1:69 R
1-165 PLATE ODDS 1:826 HOBBY
166-180 AU PLATE ODDS 1:18,411 HOBBY
PLATE PRINT RUN 1 SET PER COLOR
BLACK-CYAN-MAGENTA-YELLOW ISSUED
NO PLATE PRICING DUE TO SCARCITY

❑ 1 Rickie Weeks .60 .18
❑ 2 Kyle Davies .40 .12
❑ 3 Garrett Atkins .40 .12
❑ 4 Chien-Ming Wang 1.50 .45
❑ 5 Dallas McPherson .40 .12
❑ 6 Dan Johnson .60 .18
❑ 7 Andy Sisco .40 .12
❑ 8 Ryan Doumit .40 .12
❑ 9 J.P. Howell .40 .12
❑ 10 Tim Stauffer .40 .12
❑ 11 Willy Taveras .60 .18
❑ 12 Aaron Hill .40 .12
❑ 13 Victor Diaz .40 .12
❑ 14 Wilson Betemit .40 .12
❑ 15 Ervin Santana .60 .18
❑ 16 Mike Morse 1.00 .30
❑ 17 Yadier Molina .60 .18
❑ 18 Kelly Johnson .40 .12
❑ 19 Clint Barmes .60 .18
❑ 20 Robinson Cano 1.00 .30
❑ 21 Brad Thompson .40 .12
❑ 22 Jorge Cantu .60 .18
❑ 23 Brad Halsey .40 .12
❑ 24 Lance Niekro .60 .18
❑ 25 D.J. Houlton .40 .12
❑ 26 Ryan Church .40 .12
❑ 27 Hayden Penn .60 .18
❑ 28 Chris Young .40 .12
❑ 29 Chad Orvella RC 1.00 .30
❑ 30 Mark Teahen .40 .12
❑ 31 Mark McCormick FY RC 1.50 .45
❑ 32 Jay Bruce FY RC 8.00 2.40
❑ 33 Beau Jones FY RC 3.00 .90
❑ 34 Tyler Greene FY RC 2.50 .75
❑ 35 Zach Ward FY RC 1.00 .30
❑ 36 Josh Bell FY RC 2.50 .75
❑ 37 Josh Wall FY RC 1.50 .45
❑ 38 Nick Webber FY RC 1.50 .45
❑ 39 Travis Buck FY RC 2.50 .75
❑ 40 Kyle Winters FY RC 1.00 .30
❑ 41 Mitch Boggs FY RC 1.00 .30
❑ 42 Tommy Mendoza FY RC 1.50 .45
❑ 43 Brad Corley FY RC 1.50 .45
❑ 44 Drew Butera FY RC 1.00 .30
❑ 45 Ryan Mount FY RC 2.50 .75
❑ 46 Tyler Herron FY RC 1.50 .45
❑ 47 Nick Weglarz FY RC 3.00 .90
❑ 48 Brandon Erbe FY RC 4.00 1.20
❑ 49 Cody Allen FY RC 1.00 .30
❑ 50 Eric Fowler FY RC 1.00 .30
❑ 51 James Boone FY RC 1.50 .45
❑ 52 Josh Flores FY RC 2.50 .75
❑ 53 Brandon Monk FY RC 1.50 .45
❑ 54 Kieron Pope FY RC 2.50 .75
❑ 55 Kyle Cofield FY RC 1.00 .30
❑ 56 Brent Lillibridge FY RC 1.00 .30
❑ 57 Daryl Jones FY 1.00 .30
❑ 58 Eli Iorg FY RC 3.00 .90
❑ 59 Brett Hayes FY RC 1.00 .30
❑ 60 Mike Durant FY RC 4.00 1.20
❑ 61 Michael Bowden FY RC 2.50 .75
❑ 62 Paul Kelly FY RC 1.50 .45
❑ 63 Andrew McCutchen FY RC 8.00 2.40
❑ 64 Travis Wood FY RC 4.00 1.20
❑ 65 Cesar Ramos FY RC 1.50 .45
❑ 66 Chaz Roe FY RC 1.50 .45
❑ 67 Matt Torra FY RC 1.50 .45
❑ 68 Kevin Slowey FY RC 1.50 .45
❑ 69 Trayvon Robinson FY RC 1.50 .45
❑ 70 Reid Engel FY RC 1.00 .30
❑ 71 Kris Harvey FY RC 1.50 .45
❑ 72 Craig Italiano FY RC 2.50 .75
❑ 73 Matt Maloney FY RC 1.50 .45
❑ 74 Sean West FY RC 2.50 .75
❑ 75 Henry Sanchez FY RC 3.00 .90
❑ 76 Scott Blue FY RC 1.00 .30
❑ 77 Jordan Schafer FY RC 1.50 .45
❑ 78 Chris Robinson FY RC 1.50 .45
❑ 79 Chris Hobdy FY RC 1.00 .30
❑ 80 Brandon Durden FY RC 1.00 .30
❑ 81 Clay Buchholz FY RC 1.50 .45
❑ 82 Josh Geer FY RC 1.00 .30
❑ 83 Sam LeCure FY RC 1.00 .30
❑ 84 Justin Thomas FY RC 1.00 .30
❑ 85 Brett Gardner FY RC 1.50 .45
❑ 86 Tommy Manzella FY RC 1.00 .30
❑ 87 Matt Green FY RC 1.00 .30
❑ 88 Yunel Escobar FY RC 4.00 1.20

No.	Player	Nm-Mt	Ex-Mt
❑ 89	Mike Costanzo FY RC	3.00	.90
❑ 90	Nick Hundley FY RC	1.00	.30
❑ 91	Zach Simons FY RC	1.00	.30
❑ 92	Jacob Marceaux FY RC	1.00	.30
❑ 93	Jed Lowrie FY RC	2.50	.75
❑ 94	Brandon Snyder FY RC	5.00	1.50
❑ 95	Matt Goyen FY RC	1.00	.30
❑ 96	Jon Egan FY RC	1.50	.45
❑ 97	Drew Thompson FY RC	1.50	.45
❑ 98	Bryan Anderson FY RC	3.00	.90
❑ 99	Clayton Richard FY RC	1.00	.30
❑ 100	Jimmy Shull FY RC	1.50	.45
❑ 101	Mark Pawelek FY RC	8.00	2.40
❑ 102	P.J. Phillips FY RC	2.50	.75
❑ 103	John Drennen FY RC	2.50	.75
❑ 104	Nolan Reimold FY RC	5.00	1.50
❑ 105	Troy Tulowitzki FY RC	6.00	1.80
❑ 106	Kevin Whelan FY RC	1.00	.30
❑ 107	Wade Townsend FY RC	1.50	.45
❑ 108	Micah Owings FY RC	1.50	.45
❑ 109	Ryan Tucker FY RC	1.50	.45
❑ 110	Jeff Clement FY RC	10.00	3.00
❑ 111	Josh Sullivan FY RC	1.00	.30
❑ 112	Jeff Lyman FY RC	1.50	.45
❑ 113	Brian Bogusevic FY RC	1.00	.30
❑ 114	Trevor Bell FY RC	2.50	.75
❑ 115	Brent Cox FY RC	1.50	.45
❑ 116	Michael Billek FY RC	1.00	.30
❑ 117	Garrett Olson FY RC	2.50	.75
❑ 118	Steven Johnson FY RC	1.00	.30
❑ 119	Chase Headley FY RC	1.50	.45
❑ 120	Daniel Carte FY RC	2.50	.75
❑ 121	Francisco Liriano PROS	1.00	.30
❑ 122	Fausto Carmona PROS	.40	.12
❑ 123	Zach Jackson PROS	.40	.12
❑ 124	Adam Loewen PROS	.40	.12
❑ 125	Chris Lambert PROS	.40	.12
❑ 126	Scott Mathieson FY	.60	.18
❑ 127	Paul Maholm PROS	.60	.18
❑ 128	Fernando Nieve PROS	.40	.12
❑ 129	Justin Verlander FY	1.00	.30
❑ 130	Yusmeiro Petit PROS	1.00	.30
❑ 131	Joel Zumaya PROS	.60	.18
❑ 132	Merkin Valdez PROS	.40	.12
❑ 133	Ryan Garko FY RC	3.00	.90
❑ 134	Edison Volquez FY RC	2.50	.75
❑ 135	Russ Martin FY	.60	.18
❑ 136	Conor Jackson PROS	.60	.18
❑ 137	Miguel Montero FY RC	4.00	1.20
❑ 138	Josh Barfield PROS	.40	.12
❑ 139	Delmon Young PROS	1.00	.30
❑ 140	Andy LaRoche FY	1.50	.45
❑ 141	William Bergolla PROS	.40	.12
❑ 142	B.J. Upton PROS	.60	.18
❑ 143	Hernan Iribarren FY	.60	.18
❑ 144	Brandon Wood PROS	2.00	.60
❑ 145	Jose Bautista PROS	.40	.12
❑ 146	Edwin Encarnacion PROS	.40	.12
❑ 147	Javier Herrera FY RC	2.50	.75
❑ 148	Jeremy Hermida PROS	1.00	.30
❑ 149	Frank Diaz PROS RC	1.00	.30
❑ 150	Chris B.Young FY	1.50	.45
❑ 151	Shin-Soo Choo PROS	.40	.12
❑ 152	Kevin Thompson PROS RC	1.00	.30
❑ 153	Hanley Ramirez PROS	1.00	.30
❑ 154	Lastings Milledge PROS	.60	.18
❑ 155	Luis Montanez PROS	.40	.12
❑ 156	Justin Huber PROS	.40	.12
❑ 157	Zach Duke PROS	1.00	.30
❑ 158	Jeff Francoeur PROS	1.50	.45
❑ 159	Melky Cabrera FY	.60	.18
❑ 160	Bobby Jenks PROS	.60	.18
❑ 161	Ian Snell PROS	.40	.12
❑ 162	Fernando Cabrera PROS	.40	.12
❑ 163	Troy Patton PROS	1.00	.30
❑ 164	Anthony Lerew PROS	.60	.18
❑ 165	Nelson Cruz FY RC	1.50	.45
❑ 166	Stephen Drew AU A RC	80.00	24.00
❑ 167	Jered Weaver AU A RC	50.00	15.00
❑ 168	Ryan Braun AU B RC	40.00	12.00
❑ 169	John Mayberry Jr. AU B RC	20.00	6.00
❑ 170	Aaron Thompson AU B RC	15.00	4.50
❑ 171	Cesar Carrillo AU B RC	20.00	6.00
❑ 172	Jacoby Ellsbury AU B RC	20.00	6.00
❑ 173	Matt Garza AU B RC	15.00	4.50
❑ 174	Cliff Pennington AU B RC	15.00	4.50
❑ 175	Colby Rasmus AU B RC	40.00	12.00
❑ 176	Chris Volstad AU B RC	20.00	6.00
❑ 177	Ricky Romero AU B RC	15.00	4.50
❑ 178	Ryan Zimmerman AU B RC	80.00	24.00
❑ 179	C.J. Henry AU B RC	30.00	9.00
❑ 180	Eddy Martinez AU B RC	20.00	6.00

2001 Bowman Heritage

	Nm-Mt	Ex-Mt
COMPLETE SET (440)	200.00	60.00
COMP.SET w/o SP's (330)	50.00	15.00
COMMON CARD (1-330)	.40	.12
COMMON RC (1-330)	.40	.12
COMMON (331-440)	2.00	.60

No.	Player	Nm-Mt	Ex-Mt
❑ 1	Chipper Jones	1.00	.30
❑ 2	Pete Harnisch	.40	.12
❑ 3	Brian Giles	.40	.12
❑ 4	J.T. Snow	.40	.12
❑ 5	Bartolo Colon	.40	.12
❑ 6	Jorge Posada	.60	.18
❑ 7	Shawn Green	.40	.12
❑ 8	Derek Jeter	2.50	.75
❑ 9	Benito Santiago	.40	.12
❑ 10	Ramon Hernandez	.40	.12
❑ 11	Bernie Williams	.60	.18
❑ 12	Greg Maddux	1.50	.45
❑ 13	Barry Bonds	2.50	.75
❑ 14	Roger Clemens	2.00	.60
❑ 15	Miguel Tejada	.40	.12
❑ 16	Pedro Feliz	.40	.12
❑ 17	Jim Edmonds	.60	.18
❑ 18	Tom Glavine	.60	.18
❑ 19	David Justice	.40	.12
❑ 20	Rich Aurilia	.40	.12
❑ 21	Jason Giambi	.40	.12
❑ 22	Orlando Hernandez	.40	.12
❑ 23	Shawn Estes	.40	.12
❑ 24	Nelson Figueroa	.40	.12
❑ 25	Terrence Long	.40	.12
❑ 26	Mike Mussina	.60	.18
❑ 27	Eric Davis	.40	.12
❑ 28	Jimmy Rollins	.40	.12
❑ 29	Andy Pettitte	.60	.18
❑ 30	Shawon Dunston	.40	.12
❑ 31	Tim Hudson	.40	.12
❑ 32	Jeff Kent	.40	.12
❑ 33	Scott Brosius	.40	.12
❑ 34	Livan Hernandez	.40	.12
❑ 35	Alfonso Soriano	.60	.18
❑ 36	Mark McGwire	2.50	.75
❑ 37	Russ Ortiz	.40	.12
❑ 38	Fernando Vina	.40	.12
❑ 39	Ken Griffey Jr.	1.50	.45
❑ 40	Edgar Renteria	.40	.12
❑ 41	Kevin Brown	.40	.12
❑ 42	Robb Nen	.40	.12
❑ 43	Paul LoDuca	.40	.12
❑ 44	Bobby Abreu	.40	.12
❑ 45	Adam Dunn	.60	.18
❑ 46	Osvaldo Fernandez	.40	.12
❑ 47	Marvin Benard	.40	.12
❑ 48	Mark Gardner	.40	.12
❑ 49	Alex Rodriguez	1.50	.45
❑ 50	Preston Wilson	.40	.12
❑ 51	Roberto Alomar	.60	.18
❑ 52	Ben Davis	.40	.12
❑ 53	Derek Bell	.40	.12
❑ 54	Ken Caminiti	.40	.12
❑ 55	Barry Zito	.60	.18
❑ 56	Scott Rolen	.60	.18
❑ 57	Geoff Jenkins	.40	.12
❑ 58	Mike Cameron	.40	.12
❑ 59	Ben Grieve	.40	.12
❑ 60	Chuck Knoblauch	.40	.12
❑ 61	Matt Lawton	.40	.12
❑ 62	Chan Ho Park	.40	.12
❑ 63	Lance Berkman	.40	.12
❑ 64	Carlos Beltran	.40	.12
❑ 65	Dean Palmer	.40	.12
❑ 66	Alex Gonzalez	.40	.12
❑ 67	Larry Walker	.40	.12
❑ 68	Magglio Ordonez	.40	.12
❑ 69	Ellis Burks	.40	.12
❑ 70	Mark Mulder	.40	.12
❑ 71	Randy Johnson	1.00	.30
❑ 72	John Smoltz	.60	.18
❑ 73	Jerry Hairston Jr.	.40	.12
❑ 74	Pedro Martinez	.60	.18
❑ 75	Fred McGriff	.60	.18
❑ 76	Sean Casey	.60	.18
❑ 77	C.C. Sabathia	.40	.12
❑ 78	Todd Helton	.60	.18
❑ 79	Brad Penny	.40	.12
❑ 80	Mike Sweeney	.40	.12
❑ 81	Billy Wagner	.40	.12
❑ 82	Mark Buehrle	.60	.18
❑ 83	Cristian Guzman	.40	.12
❑ 84	Jose Vidro	.40	.12
❑ 85	Pat Burrell	.40	.12
❑ 86	Jermaine Dye	.40	.12
❑ 87	Brandon Inge	.40	.12
❑ 88	David Wells	.40	.12
❑ 89	Mike Piazza	1.50	.45
❑ 90	Jose Cabrera	.40	.12
❑ 91	Cliff Floyd	.40	.12
❑ 92	Matt Morris	.40	.12
❑ 93	Raul Mondesi	.40	.12
❑ 94	Joe Kennedy RC	.60	.18
❑ 95	Jack Wilson RC	.60	.18
❑ 96	Andruw Jones	.60	.18
❑ 97	Mariano Rivera	.60	.18
❑ 98	Mike Hampton	.40	.12
❑ 99	Roger Cedeno	.40	.12
❑ 100	Jose Cruz	.40	.12
❑ 101	Mike Lowell	.40	.12
❑ 102	Pedro Astacio	.40	.12
❑ 103	Joe Mays	.40	.12
❑ 104	John Franco	.40	.12
❑ 105	Tim Redding	.40	.12
❑ 106	Sandy Alomar Jr.	.40	.12
❑ 107	Bret Boone	.40	.12
❑ 108	Josh Towers RC	.60	.18
❑ 109	Matt Stairs	.40	.12
❑ 110	Chris Truby	.40	.12
❑ 111	Jeff Suppan	.40	.12
❑ 112	J.C. Romero	.40	.12
❑ 113	Felipe Lopez	.40	.12
❑ 114	Ben Sheets	.60	.18
❑ 115	Frank Thomas	1.00	.30
❑ 116	A.J. Burnett	.40	.12
❑ 117	Tony Clark	.40	.12
❑ 118	Mac Suzuki	.40	.12
❑ 119	Brad Radke	.40	.12
❑ 120	Jeff Shaw	.40	.12
❑ 121	Nick Neugebauer	.40	.12
❑ 122	Kenny Lofton	.40	.12
❑ 123	Jacque Jones	.40	.12
❑ 124	Brent Mayne	.40	.12
❑ 125	Carlos Hernandez	.40	.12
❑ 126	Shane Spencer	.40	.12
❑ 127	John Lackey	.40	.12
❑ 128	Sterling Hitchcock	.40	.12
❑ 129	Darren Dreifort	.40	.12
❑ 130	Rusty Greer	.40	.12
❑ 131	Michael Cuddyer	.40	.12
❑ 132	Tyler Houston	.40	.12
❑ 133	Chin-Feng Chen	.40	.12
❑ 134	Ken Harvey	.40	.12
❑ 135	Marquis Grissom	.40	.12
❑ 136	Russell Branyan	.40	.12
❑ 137	Eric Karros	.40	.12
❑ 138	Josh Beckett	.60	.18

❑ 139	Todd Zeile	.40	.12
❑ 140	Corey Koskie	.40	.12
❑ 141	Steve Sparks	.40	.12
❑ 142	Bobby Seay	.40	.12
❑ 143	Tim Raines Jr.	.40	.12
❑ 144	Julio Zuleta	.40	.12
❑ 145	Jose Lima	.40	.12
❑ 146	Dante Bichette	.40	.12
❑ 147	Randy Keisler	.40	.12
❑ 148	Brent Butler	.40	.12
❑ 149	Antonio Alfonseca	.40	.12
❑ 150	Bryan Rekar	.40	.12
❑ 151	Jeffrey Hammonds	.40	.12
❑ 152	Larry Bigbie	.40	.12
❑ 153	Blake Stein	.40	.12
❑ 154	Robin Ventura	.40	.12
❑ 155	Rondell White	.40	.12
❑ 156	Juan Silvestre	.40	.12
❑ 157	Marcus Thames	.40	.12
❑ 158	Sidney Ponson	.40	.12
❑ 159	Juan A. Pena RC	.40	.12
❑ 160	C.J. Nitkowski	.40	.12
❑ 161	Adam Everett	.40	.12
❑ 162	Eric Munson	.40	.12
❑ 163	Jason Isringhausen	.40	.12
❑ 164	Brad Fullmer	.40	.12
❑ 165	Miguel Olivo	.40	.12
❑ 166	Fernando Tatis	.40	.12
❑ 167	Freddy Garcia	.40	.12
❑ 168	Tom Goodwin	.40	.12
❑ 169	Armando Benitez	.40	.12
❑ 170	Paul Konerko	.40	.12
❑ 171	Jeff Cirillo	.40	.12
❑ 172	Shane Reynolds	.40	.12
❑ 173	Kevin Tapani	.40	.12
❑ 174	Joe Crede	1.00	.30
❑ 175	Omar Infante RC	.60	.18
❑ 176	Jake Peavy RC	5.00	1.50
❑ 177	Corey Patterson	.40	.12
❑ 178	Mike Penney RC	.40	.12
❑ 179	Jeromy Burnitz	.40	.12
❑ 180	David Segui	.40	.12
❑ 181	Marcus Giles	.40	.12
❑ 182	Paul O'Neill	.60	.18
❑ 183	John Olerud	.40	.12
❑ 184	Andy Benes	.40	.12
❑ 185	Brad Cresse	.40	.12
❑ 186	Ricky Ledee	.40	.12
❑ 187	Allen Levrault UER	.40	.12
	Last name misspelled Leverault		
❑ 188	Royce Clayton	.40	.12
❑ 189	Kelly Johnson RC	3.00	.90
❑ 190	Quilvio Veras	.40	.12
❑ 191	Mike Williams	.40	.12
❑ 192	Jason Lane RC	1.50	.45
❑ 193	Rick Helling	.40	.12
❑ 194	Tim Wakefield	.40	.12
❑ 195	James Baldwin	.40	.12
❑ 196	Cody Ransom RC	.40	.12
❑ 197	Bobby Kielty	.40	.12
❑ 198	Bobby Jones	.40	.12
❑ 199	Steve Cox	.40	.12
❑ 200	Jamal Strong RC	.40	.12
❑ 201	Steve Lomasney	.40	.12
❑ 202	Brian Cardwell RC	.40	.12
❑ 203	Mike Matheny	.40	.12
❑ 204	Jeff Randazzo RC	.40	.12
❑ 205	Aubrey Huff	.40	.12
❑ 206	Chuck Finley	.40	.12
❑ 207	Denny Bautista RC	.60	.18
❑ 208	Terry Mulholland	.40	.12
❑ 209	Rey Ordonez	.40	.12
❑ 210	Keith Surkont RC	.40	.12
❑ 211	Orlando Cabrera	.40	.12
❑ 212	Juan Encarnacion	.40	.12
❑ 213	Dustin Hermanson	.40	.12
❑ 214	Luis Rivas	.40	.12
❑ 215	Mark Quinn	.40	.12
❑ 216	Randy Velarde	.40	.12
❑ 217	Billy Koch	.40	.12
❑ 218	Ryan Rupe	.40	.12
❑ 219	Keith Ginter	.40	.12
❑ 220	Woody Williams	.40	.12
❑ 221	Ryan Franklin	.40	.12
❑ 222	Aaron Myette	.40	.12
❑ 223	Joe Borchard RC	.40	.12
❑ 224	Nate Cornejo	.40	.12
❑ 225	Julian Tavarez	.40	.12
❑ 226	Kevin Millwood	.40	.12
❑ 227	Travis Hafner RC	4.00	1.20
❑ 228	Charles Nagy	.40	.12
❑ 229	Mike Lieberthal	.40	.12
❑ 230	Jeff Nelson	.40	.12
❑ 231	Ryan Dempster	.40	.12
❑ 232	Andres Galarraga	.40	.12
❑ 233	Chad Durbin	.40	.12
❑ 234	Timo Perez	.40	.12
❑ 235	Troy O'Leary	.40	.12
❑ 236	Kevin Young	.40	.12
❑ 237	Gabe Kapler	.40	.12
❑ 238	Juan Cruz RC	.40	.12
❑ 239	Masato Yoshii	.40	.12
❑ 240	Aramis Ramirez	.40	.12
❑ 241	Matt Cooper RC	.40	.12
❑ 242	Randy Flores RC	.40	.12
❑ 243	Rafael Furcal	.40	.12
❑ 244	David Eckstein	.40	.12
❑ 245	Matt Clement	.40	.12
❑ 246	Craig Biggio	.60	.18
❑ 247	Rick Reed	.40	.12
❑ 248	Jose Macias	.40	.12
❑ 249	Alex Escobar	.40	.12
❑ 250	Roberto Hernandez	.40	.12
❑ 251	Andy Ashby	.40	.12
❑ 252	Tony Armas Jr.	.40	.12
❑ 253	Jamie Moyer	.40	.12
❑ 254	Jason Tyner	.40	.12
❑ 255	Charles Kegley RC	.40	.12
❑ 256	Jeff Conine	.40	.12
❑ 257	Francisco Cordova	.40	.12
❑ 258	Ted Lilly	.40	.12
❑ 259	Joe Randa	.40	.12
❑ 260	Jeff D'Amico	.40	.12
❑ 261	Albie Lopez	.40	.12
❑ 262	Kevin Appier	.40	.12
❑ 263	Richard Hidalgo	.40	.12
❑ 264	Omar Daal	.40	.12
❑ 265	Ricky Gutierrez	.40	.12
❑ 266	John Rocker	.40	.12
❑ 267	Ray Lankford	.40	.12
❑ 268	Beau Hale RC	.40	.12
❑ 269	Tony Blanco RC	.40	.12
❑ 270	Derrek Lee UER	.60	.18
	First name misspelled Derrick		
❑ 271	Jamey Wright	.40	.12
❑ 272	Alex Gordon	.40	.12
❑ 273	Jeff Weaver	.40	.12
❑ 274	Jaret Wright	.40	.12
❑ 275	Jose Hernandez	.40	.12
❑ 276	Bruce Chen	.40	.12
❑ 277	Todd Hollandsworth	.40	.12
❑ 278	Wade Miller	.40	.12
❑ 279	Luke Prokopec	.40	.12
❑ 280	Rafael Soriano RC	.40	.12
❑ 281	Damion Easley	.40	.12
❑ 282	Darren Oliver	.40	.12
❑ 283	B. Duckworth RC	.40	.12
❑ 284	Aaron Herr	.40	.12
❑ 285	Ray Durham	.40	.12
❑ 286	Wilmy Caceras RC	.40	.12
❑ 287	Ugueth Urbina	.40	.12
❑ 288	Scott Seabol	.40	.12
❑ 289	Lance Niekro RC	2.00	.60
❑ 290	Trot Nixon	.40	.12
❑ 291	Adam Kennedy	.40	.12
❑ 292	Brian Schmitt RC	.40	.12
❑ 293	Grant Roberts	.40	.12
❑ 294	Benny Agbayani	.40	.12
❑ 295	Travis Lee	.40	.12
❑ 296	Erick Almonte RC	.40	.12
❑ 297	Jim Thome	.60	.18
❑ 298	Eric Young	.40	.12
❑ 299	Dan Denham RC	.40	.12
❑ 300	Boof Bonser RC	.40	.12
❑ 301	Denny Neagle	.40	.12
❑ 302	Kenny Rogers	.40	.12
❑ 303	J.D. Closser	.40	.12
❑ 304	Chase Utley RC	8.00	2.40
❑ 305	Rey Sanchez	.40	.12
❑ 306	Sean McGowan	.40	.12
❑ 307	Justin Pope RC	.40	.12
❑ 308	Torii Hunter	.40	.12
❑ 309	B.J. Surhoff	.40	.12
❑ 310	Aaron Heilman RC	.40	.12
❑ 311	Gabe Gross RC	.60	.18
❑ 312	Lee Stevens	.40	.12
❑ 313	Todd Hundley	.40	.12
❑ 314	Macay McBride RC	1.00	.30
❑ 315	Edgar Martinez	.60	.18
❑ 316	Omar Vizquel	.60	.18
❑ 317	Reggie Sanders	.40	.12
❑ 318	John-Ford Griffin RC	.40	.12
❑ 319	Tim Salmon UER	.40	.12
	Photo is Troy Glaus		
❑ 320	Pokey Reese	.40	.12
❑ 321	Jay Payton	.40	.12
❑ 322	Doug Glanville	.40	.12
❑ 323	Greg Vaughn	.40	.12
❑ 324	Ruben Sierra	.40	.12
❑ 325	Kip Wells	.40	.12
❑ 326	Carl Everett	.40	.12
❑ 327	Garret Anderson	.40	.12
❑ 328	Jay Bell	.40	.12
❑ 329	Barry Larkin	.60	.18
❑ 330	Jeff Mathis RC	.60	.18
❑ 331	Adrian Gonzalez SP	2.00	.60
❑ 332	Juan Rivera SP	2.00	.60
❑ 333	Tony Alvarez SP	2.00	.60
❑ 334	Xavier Nady SP	2.00	.60
❑ 335	Josh Hamilton SP	2.00	.60
❑ 336	Will Smith SP RC	2.00	.60
❑ 337	Israel Alcantara SP	2.00	.60
❑ 338	Chris George SP	2.00	.60
❑ 339	Sean Burroughs SP	2.00	.60
❑ 340	Jack Cust SP	2.00	.60
❑ 341	Henry Mateo SP RC	2.00	.60
❑ 342	Carlos Pena SP	2.00	.60
❑ 343	J.R. House SP	2.00	.60
❑ 344	Carlos Silva SP	2.00	.60
❑ 345	Mike Rivera SP RC	2.00	.60
❑ 346	Adam Johnson SP	2.00	.60
❑ 347	Scott Heard SP	2.00	.60
❑ 348	Alex Cintron SP	2.00	.60
❑ 349	Miguel Cabrera SP	8.00	2.40
❑ 350	Nick Johnson SP	2.00	.60
❑ 351	Albert Pujols SP RC	60.00	18.00
❑ 352	Ichiro Suzuki SP RC	40.00	12.00
❑ 353	Carlos Delgado SP	2.00	.60
❑ 354	Troy Glaus SP	2.00	.60
❑ 355	Sammy Sosa SP	3.00	.90
❑ 356	Ivan Rodriguez SP	3.00	.90
❑ 357	Vladimir Guerrero SP	3.00	.90
❑ 358	Manny Ramirez Sox SP	3.00	.90
❑ 359	Luis Gonzalez SP	2.00	.60
❑ 360	Roy Oswalt SP	3.00	.90
❑ 361	Moises Alou SP	2.00	.60
❑ 362	Juan Gonzalez SP	2.00	.60
❑ 363	Tony Gwynn SP	4.00	1.20
❑ 364	Hideo Nomo SP	3.00	.90
❑ 365	T. Shinjo SP RC	3.00	.90
❑ 366	Kazuhiro Sasaki SP	2.00	.60
❑ 367	Cal Ripken SP	10.00	3.00
❑ 368	Rafael Palmeiro SP	3.00	.90
❑ 369	J.D. Drew SP	2.00	.60
❑ 370	Doug Mientkiewicz SP	2.00	.60
❑ 371	Jeff Bagwell SP	3.00	.90
❑ 372	Darin Erstad SP	2.00	.60
❑ 373	Tom Gordon SP	2.00	.60
❑ 374	Ben Petrick SP	2.00	.60
❑ 375	Eric Milton SP	2.00	.60
❑ 376	N. Garciaparra SP	5.00	1.50
❑ 377	Julio Lugo SP	2.00	.60
❑ 378	Tino Martinez SP	3.00	.90
❑ 379	Javier Vazquez SP	2.00	.60
❑ 380	Jeremy Giambi SP	2.00	.60
❑ 381	Marty Cordova SP	2.00	.60
❑ 382	Adrian Beltre SP	2.00	.60
❑ 383	John Burkett SP	2.00	.60
❑ 384	Aaron Boone SP	2.00	.60
❑ 385	Eric Chavez SP	2.00	.60
❑ 386	Curt Schilling SP	2.00	.60
❑ 387	Cory Lidle UER	2.00	.60
	First name misspelled Corey		
❑ 388	Jason Schmidt SP	2.00	.60
❑ 389	Johnny Damon SP	3.00	.90
❑ 390	Steve Finley SP	2.00	.60
❑ 391	Edgardo Alfonzo SP	2.00	.60
❑ 392	Jose Valentin SP	2.00	.60

❑ 393 Jose Canseco SP 3.00 .90
❑ 394 Ryan Klesko SP 2.00 .60
❑ 395 David Cone SP 2.00 .60
❑ 396 Jason Kendall UER 2.00 .60
Last name misspelled Kendell
❑ 397 Placido Polanco SP 2.00 .60
❑ 398 Glendon Rusch SP 2.00 .60
❑ 399 Aaron Sele SP 2.00 .60
❑ 400 D'Angelo Jimenez SP 2.00 .60
❑ 401 Mark Grace SP 3.00 .90
❑ 402 Al Leiter SP 2.00 .60
❑ 403 Brian Jordan SP 2.00 .60
❑ 404 Phil Nevin SP 2.00 .60
❑ 405 Brent Abernathy SP 2.00 .60
❑ 406 Kerry Wood SP 2.00 .60
❑ 407 Alex Gonzalez SP 2.00 .60
❑ 408 Robert Fick SP 2.00 .60
❑ 409 Dmitri Young UER 2.00 .60
First name misspelled Dimitri
❑ 410 Wes Helms SP 2.00 .60
❑ 411 Trevor Hoffman SP 2.00 .60
❑ 412 Rickey Henderson SP 3.00 .90
❑ 413 Bobby Higginson SP 2.00 .60
❑ 414 Gary Sheffield SP 2.00 .60
❑ 415 Darryl Kile SP 2.00 .60
❑ 416 Richie Sexson SP 2.00 .60
❑ 417 F. Menechino SP RC 2.00 .60
❑ 418 Javy Lopez SP 2.00 .60
❑ 419 Carlos Lee SP 2.00 .60
❑ 420 Jon Lieber SP 2.00 .60
❑ 421 Hank Blalock SP RC 8.00 2.40
❑ 422 Marlon Byrd SP RC .40 .12
❑ 423 Jason Kinchen SP RC 2.00 .60
❑ 424 M. Ensberg SP RC UER 6.00 1.80
Front photo is Adam Everett
❑ 425 Greg Nash SP RC 2.00 .60
❑ 426 D. Tankersley SP RC 2.00 .60
❑ 427 Nate Murphy SP RC 2.00 .60
❑ 428 Chris Smith SP RC 2.00 .60
❑ 429 Jake Gautreau SP RC 2.00 .60
❑ 430 J. VanBenschoten SP RC 2.00 .60
❑ 431 T.Thompson SP RC 2.00 .60
❑ 432 O.Hudson SP RC 3.00 .90
❑ 433 J.Williams SP RC 3.00 .90
❑ 434 Kevin Reese SP RC 2.00 .60
❑ 435 Ed Rogers SP RC 2.00 .60
❑ 436 Ryan Jamison SP RC 2.00 .60
❑ 437 A. Pettyjohn SP RC 2.00 .60
❑ 438 Hee Seop Choi SP RC 3.00 .90
❑ 439 J. Morneau SP RC 6.00 1.80
❑ 440 Mitch Jones SP RC 2.00 .60

2002 Bowman Heritage

	Nm-Mt	Ex-Mt
COMP.SET w/o SP's (324)	50.00	15.00
COMMON CARD (1-439)	.40	.12
COMMON SP	2.00	.60

❑ 1 Brent Abernathy .40 .12
❑ 2 Jermaine Dye .40 .12
❑ 3 James Shanks RC .40 .12
❑ 4 Chris Flinn RC .40 .12
❑ 5 Mike Peeples SP RC 2.00 .60
❑ 6 Gary Sheffield .40 .12
❑ 7 Livan Hernandez SP 2.00 .60
❑ 8 Jeff Austin RC .40 .12
❑ 9 Jeremy Giambi .40 .12
❑ 10 Adam Roller RC .40 .12
❑ 11 Sandy Alomar Jr. SP 2.00 .60
❑ 12 Matt Williams SP 2.00 .60
❑ 13 Hee Seop Choi .40 .12
❑ 14 Jose Offerman .40 .12
❑ 15 Robin Ventura .40 .12
❑ 16 Craig Biggio .60 .18
❑ 17 David Wells .40 .12
❑ 18 Rob Henkel RC .40 .12
❑ 19 Edgar Martinez .60 .18
❑ 20 Matt Morris SP 2.00 .60
❑ 21 Jose Valentin .40 .12
❑ 22 Barry Bonds 2.50 .75
❑ 23 Justin Schuda RC .40 .12
❑ 24 Josh Phelps .40 .12
❑ 25 John Rodriguez RC .50 .15
❑ 26 Angel Pagan RC .40 .12
❑ 27 Aramis Ramirez .40 .12
❑ 28 Jack Wilson .40 .12
❑ 29 Roger Clemens 2.00 .60
❑ 30 Kazuhisa Ishii RC .50 .15
❑ 31 Carlos Beltran .40 .12
❑ 32 Drew Henson SP 2.00 .60
❑ 33 Kevin Young SP 2.00 .60
❑ 34 Juan Cruz SP 2.00 .60
❑ 35 Curtis Legendre RC .40 .12
❑ 36 Jose Morban RC .40 .12
❑ 37 Ricardo Cordova SP RC 2.00 .60
❑ 38 Adam Everett .40 .12
❑ 39 Mark Prior 1.00 .30
❑ 40 Jose Bautista RC .50 .15
❑ 41 Travis Foley RC .40 .12
❑ 42 Kerry Wood .40 .12
❑ 43 B.J. Surhoff .40 .12
❑ 44 Moises Alou .40 .12
❑ 45 Joey Hammond .40 .12
❑ 46 Eric Bruntlett RC .40 .12
❑ 47 Carlos Guillen .40 .12
❑ 48 Joe Crede .40 .12
❑ 49 Dan Phillips RC .40 .12
❑ 50 Jason LaRue .40 .12
❑ 51 Javy Lopez .40 .12
❑ 52 Larry Bigbie SP 2.00 .60
❑ 53 Chris Baker RC .40 .12
❑ 54 Marty Cordova .40 .12
❑ 55 C.C. Sabathia .40 .12
❑ 56 Mike Piazza 1.50 .45
❑ 57 Brian Giles .40 .12
❑ 58 Mike Bordick SP 2.00 .60
❑ 59 Tyler Houston SP 2.00 .60
❑ 60 Gabe Kapler .40 .12
❑ 61 Ben Broussard .40 .12
❑ 62 Steve Finley SP 2.00 .60
❑ 63 Koyie Hill .40 .12
❑ 64 Jeff D'Amico .40 .12
❑ 65 Edwin Almonte RC .40 .12
❑ 66 Pedro Martinez .60 .18
❑ 66B Nomar Garciaparra 66 1.50 .45
❑ 67 Travis Fryman SP 2.00 .60
❑ 68 Brady Clark SP 2.00 .60
❑ 69 Reed Johnson SP RC 3.00 .90
❑ 70 Mark Grace SP 3.00 .90
❑ 71 Tony Batista SP 2.00 .60
❑ 72 Roy Oswalt .40 .12
❑ 73 Pat Burrell SP 2.00 .60
❑ 74 Dennis Tankersley .40 .12
❑ 75 Ramon Ortiz .40 .12
❑ 76 Neal Frendling SP RC 2.00 .60
❑ 77 Omar Vizquel SP 3.00 .90
❑ 78 Hideo Nomo 1.00 .30
❑ 79 Orlando Hernandez SP 2.00 .60
❑ 80 Andy Pettitte .60 .18
❑ 81 Cole Barthel RC .40 .12
❑ 82 Bret Boone .40 .12
❑ 83 Alfonso Soriano .40 .12
❑ 84 Brandon Duckworth .40 .12
❑ 85 Ben Grieve .40 .12
❑ 86 Mike Rosamond SP RC 2.00 .60
❑ 87 Luke Prokopec .40 .12
❑ 88 Chone Figgins RC .75 .23
❑ 89 Rick Ankiel SP 2.00 .60
❑ 90 David Eckstein .40 .12
❑ 91 Corey Koskie .40 .12
❑ 92 David Justice .40 .12
❑ 93 Jimmy Alvarez RC .40 .12
❑ 94 Jason Schmidt .40 .12
❑ 95 Reggie Sanders .40 .12
❑ 96 Victor Alvarez RC .40 .12
❑ 97 Brett Roneberg RC .40 .12
❑ 98 D'Angelo Jimenez .40 .12
❑ 99 Hank Blalock .60 .18
❑ 100 Juan Rivera .40 .12
❑ 101 Mark Buehrle SP 2.00 .60
❑ 102 Juan Uribe .40 .12
❑ 103 Royce Clayton SP 2.00 .60
❑ 104 Brett Kay RC .40 .12
❑ 105 John Olerud .40 .12
❑ 106 Richie Sexson .40 .12
❑ 107 Chipper Jones 1.00 .30
❑ 108 Adam Dunn .40 .12
❑ 109 Tim Salmon SP 3.00 .90
❑ 110 Eric Karros .40 .12
❑ 111 Jose Vidro .40 .12
❑ 112 Jerry Hairston Jr. .40 .12
❑ 113 Anastacio Martinez RC .40 .12
❑ 114 Robert Fick SP 2.00 .60
❑ 115 Randy Johnson 1.00 .30
❑ 116 Trot Nixon SP 2.00 .60
❑ 117 Nick Bierbrodt SP 2.00 .60
❑ 118 Jim Edmonds .60 .18
❑ 119 Rafael Palmeiro .60 .18
❑ 120 Jose Macias .40 .12
❑ 121 Josh Beckett .40 .12
❑ 122 Sean Douglass .40 .12
❑ 123 Jeff Kent .40 .12
❑ 124 Tim Redding .40 .12
❑ 125 Xavier Nady .40 .12
❑ 126 Carl Everett .40 .12
❑ 127 Joe Randa .40 .12
❑ 128 Luke Hudson SP 2.00 .60
❑ 129 Eric Miller RC .40 .12
❑ 130 Melvin Mora .40 .12
❑ 131 Adrian Gonzalez .40 .12
❑ 132 Larry Walker SP 2.00 .60
❑ 133 Nic Jackson SP RC 2.00 .60
❑ 134 Mike Lowell SP 2.00 .60
❑ 135 Jim Thome .60 .18
❑ 136 Eric Milton .40 .12
❑ 137 Rich Thompson SP RC 2.00 .60
❑ 138 Placido Polanco SP 2.00 .60
❑ 139 Juan Pierre .40 .12
❑ 140 David Segui .40 .12
❑ 141 Chuck Finley .40 .12
❑ 142 Felipe Lopez .40 .12
❑ 143 Toby Hall .40 .12
❑ 144 Fred Bastardo RC .40 .12
❑ 145 Troy Glaus .40 .12
❑ 146 Todd Helton .60 .18
❑ 147 Ruben Gotay SP RC 3.00 .90
❑ 148 Darin Erstad .40 .12
❑ 149 Ryan Gripp SP RC 2.00 .60
❑ 150 Orlando Cabrera .40 .12
❑ 151 Jason Young RC .40 .12
❑ 152 Sterling Hitchcock SP 2.00 .60
❑ 153 Miguel Tejada .40 .12
❑ 154 Al Leiter .40 .12
❑ 155 Taylor Buchholz RC .40 .12
❑ 156 Juan M. Gonzalez RC .40 .12
❑ 157 Damion Easley .40 .12
❑ 158 Jimmy Gobble RC .40 .12
❑ 159 Dennis Ulacia SP RC 2.00 .60
❑ 160 Shane Reynolds SP 2.00 .60
❑ 161 Javier Colina .40 .12
❑ 162 Frank Thomas 1.00 .30
❑ 163 Chuck Knoblauch .40 .12
❑ 164 Sean Burroughs .40 .12
❑ 165 Greg Maddux 1.50 .45
❑ 166 Jason Ellison RC .75 .23
❑ 167 Tony Womack .40 .12
❑ 168 Randall Shelley SP RC 2.00 .60
❑ 169 Jason Marquis .40 .12
❑ 170 Brian Jordan .40 .12
❑ 171 Vicente Padilla .40 .12
❑ 172 Barry Zito .40 .12
❑ 173 Matt Allegra SP RC 2.00 .60
❑ 174 Ralph Santana SP RC 2.00 .60
❑ 175 Carlos Lee .40 .12
❑ 176 Richard Hidalgo SP 2.00 .60
❑ 177 Kevin Deaton RC .40 .12
❑ 178 Juan Encarnacion .40 .12
❑ 179 Mark Quinn .40 .12
❑ 180 Rafael Furcal .40 .12
❑ 181 Garret Anderson UER .40 .12
Photo is Chone Figgins

❑ 182 David Wright RC 12.00 3.60
❑ 183 Jose Reyes .60 .18
❑ 184 Mario Ramos SP RC 2.00 .60
❑ 185 J.D. Drew .40 .12
❑ 186 Juan Gonzalez .40 .12
❑ 187 Nick Neugebauer .40 .12
❑ 188 Alejandro Giron RC .40 .12
❑ 189 John Burkett .40 .12
❑ 190 Ben Sheets .40 .12
❑ 191 Vinny Castilla SP 2.00 .60
❑ 192 Cory Lidle .40 .12
❑ 193 Fernando Vina .40 .12
❑ 194 Russell Branyan SP 2.00 .60
❑ 195 Ben Davis .40 .12
❑ 196 Angel Berroa .40 .12
❑ 197 Alex Gonzalez .40 .12
❑ 198 Jared Sandberg .40 .12
❑ 199 Travis Lee SP 2.00 .60
❑ 200 Luis DePaula SP 2.00 .60
❑ 201 Ramon Hernandez SP 2.00 .60
❑ 202 Brandon Inge .40 .12
❑ 203 Aubrey Huff .40 .12
❑ 204 Mike Rivera .40 .12
❑ 205 Brad Nelson RC .50 .15
❑ 206 Colt Griffin SP RC 2.00 .60
❑ 207 Joel Pineiro .40 .12
❑ 208 Adam Pettyjohn .40 .12
❑ 209 Mark Redman .40 .12
❑ 210 Roberto Alomar SP 3.00 .90
❑ 211 Denny Neagle .40 .12
❑ 212 Adam Kennedy .40 .12
❑ 213 Jason Arnold SP RC 2.00 .60
❑ 214 Jamie Moyer .40 .12
❑ 215 Aaron Boone .40 .12
❑ 216 Doug Glanville .40 .12
❑ 217 Nick Johnson SP 2.00 .60
❑ 218 Mike Cameron SP 2.00 .60
❑ 219 Tim Wakefield SP 2.00 .60
❑ 220 Todd Stottlemyre SP 2.00 .60
❑ 221 Mo Vaughn SP 2.00 .60
❑ 222 Vladimir Guerrero 1.00 .30
❑ 223 Bill Ortega .40 .12
❑ 224 Kevin Brown .40 .12
❑ 225 Peter Bergeron SP 2.00 .60
❑ 226 Shannon Stewart SP 2.00 .60
❑ 227 Eric Chavez .40 .12
❑ 228 Clint Weibl RC .40 .12
❑ 229 Todd Hollandsworth SP 2.00 .60
❑ 230 Jeff Bagwell .60 .18
❑ 231 Chad Qualls RC .50 .15
❑ 232 Ben Howard RC .40 .12
❑ 233 Rondell White SP 2.00 .60
❑ 234 Fred McGriff .60 .18
❑ 235 Steve Cox SP 2.00 .60
❑ 236 Chris Tritle RC .40 .12
❑ 237 Eric Valent .40 .12
❑ 238 Joe Mauer RC 4.00 1.20
❑ 239 Shawn Green .40 .12
❑ 240 Jimmy Rollins .40 .12
❑ 241 Edgar Renteria .40 .12
❑ 242 Edwin Yan RC .40 .12
❑ 243 Noochie Varner RC .40 .12
❑ 244 Kris Benson SP 2.00 .60
❑ 245 Mike Hampton .40 .12
❑ 246 So Taguchi RC .50 .15
❑ 247 Sammy Sosa 1.00 .30
❑ 248 Terrence Long .40 .12
❑ 249 Jason Bay RC 4.00 1.20
❑ 250 Kevin Millar SP 2.00 .60
❑ 251 Albert Pujols 2.00 .60
❑ 252 Chris Latham RC .40 .12
❑ 253 Eric Byrnes .40 .12
❑ 254 Napoleon Calzado SP RC 2.00 .60
❑ 255 Bobby Higginson .40 .12
❑ 256 Ben Molina .40 .12
❑ 257 Torii Hunter SP 2.00 .60
❑ 258 Jason Giambi .40 .12
❑ 259 Bartolo Colon .40 .12
❑ 260 Benito Baez .40 .12
❑ 261 Ichiro Suzuki 2.00 .60
❑ 262 Mike Sweeney .40 .12
❑ 263 Brian West RC .40 .12
❑ 264 Brad Penny .40 .12
❑ 265 Kevin Millwood SP 2.00 .60
❑ 266 Orlando Hudson .40 .12
❑ 267 Doug Mientkiewicz .40 .12
❑ 268 Luis Gonzalez SP 2.00 .60
❑ 269 Jay Caligiuri RC .40 .12
❑ 270 Nate Cornejo SP 2.00 .60
❑ 271 Lee Stevens .40 .12
❑ 272 Eric Hinske .40 .12
❑ 273 Antwon Rollins RC .40 .12
❑ 274 Bobby Jenks RC 1.50 .45
❑ 275 Joe Mays .40 .12
❑ 276 Josh Shaffer RC .40 .12
❑ 277 Jonny Gomes RC 3.00 .90
❑ 278 Bernie Williams .60 .18
❑ 279 Ed Rogers .40 .12
❑ 280 Carlos Delgado .40 .12
❑ 281 Raul Mondesi SP 2.00 .60
❑ 282 Jose Ortiz .40 .12
❑ 283 Cesar Izturis .40 .12
❑ 284 Ryan Dempster SP 2.00 .60
❑ 285 Brian Daubach .40 .12
❑ 286 Hansel Izquierdo RC .40 .12
❑ 287 Mike Lieberthal SP 2.00 .60
❑ 288 Marcus Thames .40 .12
❑ 289 Nomar Garciaparra 1.50 .45
❑ 290 Brad Fullmer .40 .12
❑ 291 Tino Martinez .60 .18
❑ 292 James Barrett RC .40 .12
❑ 293 Jacque Jones .40 .12
❑ 294 Nick Alvarez SP RC 2.00 .60
❑ 295 Jason Grove SP RC 2.00 .60
❑ 296 Mike Wilson SP RC 2.00 .60
❑ 297 J.T. Snow .40 .12
❑ 298 Cliff Floyd .40 .12
❑ 299 Todd Hundley SP 2.00 .60
❑ 300 Tony Clark SP 2.00 .60
❑ 301 Demetrius Heath RC .40 .12
❑ 302 Morgan Ensberg .40 .12
❑ 303 Cristian Guzman .40 .12
❑ 304 Frank Catalanotto .40 .12
❑ 305 Jeff Weaver .40 .12
❑ 306 Tim Hudson .40 .12
❑ 307 Scott Wiggins SP RC 2.00 .60
❑ 308 Shea Hillenbrand SP 2.00 .60
❑ 309 Todd Walker SP 2.00 .60
❑ 310 Tsuyoshi Shinjo .40 .12
❑ 311 Adrian Beltre .40 .12
❑ 312 Craig Kuzmic RC .40 .12
❑ 313 Paul Konerko .40 .12
❑ 314 Scott Hairston RC .50 .15
❑ 315 Chan Ho Park .40 .12
❑ 316 Jorge Posada .60 .18
❑ 317 Chris Snelling RC .75 .23
❑ 318 Keith Foulke .40 .12
❑ 319 John Smoltz .60 .18
❑ 320 Ryan Church SP RC 8.00 2.40
❑ 321 Mike Mussina .60 .18
❑ 322 Tony Armas Jr. SP 2.00 .60
❑ 323 Craig Counsell .40 .12
❑ 324 Marcus Giles .40 .12
❑ 325 Greg Vaughn .40 .12
❑ 326 Curt Schilling .40 .12
❑ 327 Jeromy Burnitz .40 .12
❑ 328 Eric Byrnes .40 .12
❑ 329 Johnny Damon Sox .60 .18
❑ 330 Michael Floyd SP RC 2.00 .60
❑ 331 Edgardo Alfonzo .40 .12
❑ 332 Jeremy Hill RC .40 .12
❑ 333 Josh Bonifay RC .40 .12
❑ 334 Byung-Hyun Kim .40 .12
❑ 335 Keith Ginter .40 .12
❑ 336 Ronald Acuna SP RC 2.00 .60
❑ 337 Mike Hill SP RC 2.00 .60
❑ 338 Sean Casey .60 .18
❑ 339 Matt Anderson SP 2.00 .60
❑ 340 Dan Wright .40 .12
❑ 341 Ben Petrick .40 .12
❑ 342 Mike Sirotka SP 2.00 .60
❑ 343 Alex Rodriguez 1.50 .45
❑ 344 Einar Diaz .40 .12
❑ 345 Derek Jeter 2.50 .75
❑ 346 Jeff Conine .40 .12
❑ 347 Ray Durham SP 2.00 .60
❑ 348 Wilson Betemit SP 2.00 .60
❑ 349 Jeffrey Hammonds .40 .12
❑ 350 Dan Trumble RC .40 .12
❑ 351 Phil Nevin SP 2.00 .60
❑ 352 A.J. Burnett .40 .12
❑ 353 Bill Mueller .40 .12
❑ 354 Charles Nagy .40 .12
❑ 355 Rusty Greer SP 2.00 .60
❑ 356 Jason Botts RC .75 .23
❑ 357 Magglio Ordonez .40 .12
❑ 358 Kevin Appier .40 .12
❑ 359 Brad Radke .40 .12
❑ 360 Chris George .40 .12
❑ 361 Chris Piersoll RC .40 .12
❑ 362 Ivan Rodriguez .60 .18
❑ 363 Jim Kavourias RC .40 .12
❑ 364 Rick Helling SP 2.00 .60
❑ 365 Dean Palmer .40 .12
❑ 366 Rich Aurilia SP 2.00 .60
❑ 367 Ryan Vogelsong .40 .12
❑ 368 Matt Lawton .40 .12
❑ 369 Wade Miller .40 .12
❑ 370 Dustin Hermanson .40 .12
❑ 371 Craig Wilson .40 .12
❑ 372 Todd Zeile SP 2.00 .60
❑ 373 Jon Guzman RC .40 .12
❑ 374 Ellis Burks .40 .12
❑ 375 Robert Cosby SP RC 2.00 .60
❑ 376 Jason Kendall .40 .12
❑ 377 Scott Rolen SP 3.00 .90
❑ 378 Andruw Jones .60 .18
❑ 379 Greg Sain RC .40 .12
❑ 380 Paul LoDuca .40 .12
❑ 381 Scotty Layfield RC .40 .12
❑ 382 Tomo Ohka .40 .12
❑ 383 Garrett Guzman RC .40 .12
❑ 384 Jack Cust SP 2.00 .60
❑ 385 Shayne Wright RC .40 .12
❑ 386 Derrek Lee .60 .18
❑ 387 Jesus Medrano RC .40 .12
❑ 388 Javier Vazquez .40 .12
❑ 389 Preston Wilson SP 2.00 .60
❑ 390 Gavin Floyd RC 1.00 .30
❑ 391 Sidney Ponson SP 2.00 .60
❑ 392 Jose Hernandez .40 .12
❑ 393 Scott Erickson SP 2.00 .60
❑ 394 Jose Valverde RC .40 .12
❑ 395 Mark Hamilton SP RC 2.00 .60
❑ 396 Brad Cresse .40 .12
❑ 397 Danny Bautista .40 .12
❑ 398 Ray Lankford SP 2.00 .60
❑ 399 Miguel Batista SP 2.00 .60
❑ 400 Brent Butler .40 .12
❑ 401 Manny Delcarmen SP RC 3.00 .90
❑ 402 Kyle Farnsworth SP 2.00 .60
❑ 403 Freddy Garcia .40 .12
❑ 404 Joe Jiannetti RC .40 .12
❑ 405 Josh Barfield RC 1.25 .35
❑ 406 Corey Patterson .40 .12
❑ 407 Josh Towers .40 .12
❑ 408 Carlos Pena .40 .12
❑ 409 Jeff Cirillo .40 .12
❑ 410 Jon Lieber .40 .12
❑ 411 Woody Williams SP 2.00 .60
❑ 412 Richard Lane SP RC 2.00 .60
❑ 413 Alex Gonzalez .40 .12
❑ 414 Wilkin Ruan .40 .12
❑ 415 Geoff Jenkins .40 .12
❑ 416 Carlos Hernandez .40 .12
❑ 417 Matt Clement SP 2.00 .60
❑ 418 Jose Cruz Jr. .40 .12
❑ 419 Jake Mauer RC .40 .12
❑ 420 Matt Childers RC .40 .12
❑ 421 Tom Glavine SP 3.00 .90
❑ 422 Ken Griffey Jr. 1.50 .45
❑ 423 Anderson Hernandez RC .40 .12
❑ 424 John Suomi RC .40 .12
❑ 425 Doug Sessions RC .40 .12
❑ 426 Jaret Wright .40 .12
❑ 427 Rolando Viera SP RC 2.00 .60
❑ 428 Aaron Sele .40 .12
❑ 429 Dmitri Young .40 .12
❑ 430 Ryan Klesko .40 .12
❑ 431 Kevin Tapani SP 2.00 .60
❑ 432 Joe Kennedy .40 .12
❑ 433 Austin Kearns .40 .12
❑ 434 Roger Cedeno SP 2.00 .60
❑ 435 Lance Berkman .40 .12
❑ 436 Frank Menechino .40 .12
❑ 437 Brett Myers .40 .12
❑ 438 Bob Abreu .40 .12
❑ 439 Shawn Estes SP 2.00 .60

2003 Bowman Heritage

		MINT	NRMT
COMPLETE SET (300)		100.00	45.00
❑ 1	Jorge Posada	.60	.25
❑ 2	Todd Helton	.60	.25
❑ 3	Marcus Giles	.40	.18
❑ 4	Eric Chavez	.40	.18
❑ 5	Edgar Martinez	.60	.25
❑ 6	Luis Gonzalez	.40	.18
❑ 7	Corey Patterson	.40	.18
❑ 8	Preston Wilson	.40	.18
❑ 9	Ryan Klesko	.40	.18
❑ 10	Randy Johnson	1.00	.45
❑ 11	Jose Guillen	.40	.18
❑ 12	Carlos Lee	.40	.18
❑ 13	Steve Finley	.40	.18
❑ 14	A.J. Pierzynski	.40	.18
❑ 15	Troy Glaus	.40	.18
❑ 16	Darin Erstad	.40	.18
❑ 17	Moises Alou	.40	.18
❑ 18	Torii Hunter	.40	.18
❑ 19	Marlon Byrd	.40	.18
❑ 20	Mark Prior	.60	.25
❑ 21	Shannon Stewart	.40	.18
❑ 22	Craig Biggio	.60	.25
❑ 23	Johnny Damon	.60	.25
❑ 24	Robert Fick	.40	.18
❑ 25	Jason Giambi	.40	.18
❑ 26	Fernando Vina	.40	.18
❑ 27	Aubrey Huff	.40	.18
❑ 28	Benito Santiago	.40	.18
❑ 29	Jay Gibbons	.40	.18
❑ 30	Ken Griffey Jr.	1.50	.70
❑ 31	Rocco Baldelli	.40	.18
❑ 32	Pat Burrell	.40	.18
❑ 33	A.J. Burnett	.40	.18
❑ 34	Omar Vizquel	.60	.25
❑ 35	Greg Maddux	1.50	.70
❑ 36	Cliff Floyd	.40	.18
❑ 37	C.C. Sabathia	.40	.18
❑ 38	Geoff Jenkins	.40	.18
❑ 39	Ty Wigginton	.40	.18
❑ 40	Jeff Kent	.40	.18
❑ 41	Orlando Hudson	.40	.18
❑ 42	Edgardo Alfonzo	.40	.18
❑ 43	Greg Myers	.40	.18
❑ 44	Melvin Mora	.40	.18
❑ 45	Sammy Sosa	1.00	.45
❑ 46	Russ Ortiz	.40	.18
❑ 47	Josh Beckett	.40	.18
❑ 48	David Wells	.40	.18
❑ 49	Woody Williams	.40	.18
❑ 50	Alex Rodriguez	1.50	.70
❑ 51	Randy Wolf	.40	.18
❑ 52	Carlos Beltran	.40	.18
❑ 53	Austin Kearns	.40	.18
❑ 54	Trot Nixon	.40	.18
❑ 55	Ivan Rodriguez	.60	.25
❑ 56	Shea Hillenbrand	.40	.18
❑ 57	Roberto Alomar	.60	.25
❑ 58	John Olerud	.40	.18
❑ 59	Michael Young	.60	.25
❑ 60	Garret Anderson	.40	.18
❑ 61	Mike Lieberthal	.40	.18
❑ 62	Adam Dunn	.40	.18
❑ 63	Raul Ibanez	.40	.18
❑ 64	Kenny Lofton	.40	.18
❑ 65	Ichiro Suzuki	2.00	.90
❑ 66	Jarrod Washburn	.40	.18
❑ 67	Shawn Chacon	.40	.18
❑ 68	Alex Gonzalez	.40	.18
❑ 69	Roy Halladay	.40	.18
❑ 70	Vladimir Guerrero	1.00	.45
❑ 71	Hee Seop Choi	.40	.18
❑ 72	Jody Gerut	.40	.18
❑ 73	Ray Durham	.40	.18
❑ 74	Mark Teixeira	.60	.25
❑ 75	Hank Blalock	.40	.18
❑ 76	Jerry Hairston Jr.	.40	.18
❑ 77	Erubiel Durazo	.40	.18
❑ 78	Frank Catalanotto	.40	.18
❑ 79	Jacque Jones	.40	.18
❑ 80	Bobby Abreu	.40	.18
❑ 81	Mike Hampton	.40	.18
❑ 82	Zach Day	.40	.18
❑ 83	Jimmy Rollins	.40	.18
❑ 84	Joel Pineiro	.40	.18
❑ 85	Brett Myers	.40	.18
❑ 86	Frank Thomas	1.00	.45
❑ 87	Aramis Ramirez	.40	.18
❑ 88	Paul Lo Duca	.40	.18
❑ 89	Dmitri Young	.40	.18
❑ 90	Brian Giles	.40	.18
❑ 91	Jose Cruz Jr.	.40	.18
❑ 92	Derek Lowe	.40	.18
❑ 93	Mark Buehrle	.40	.18
❑ 94	Wade Miller	.40	.18
❑ 95	Derek Jeter	2.50	1.10
❑ 96	Bret Boone	.40	.18
❑ 97	Tony Batista	.40	.18
❑ 98	Sean Casey	.60	.25
❑ 99	Eric Hinske	.40	.18
❑ 100	Albert Pujols	2.00	.90
❑ 101	Runelvys Hernandez	.40	.18
❑ 102	Vernon Wells	.40	.18
❑ 103	Kerry Wood	.40	.18
❑ 104	Lance Berkman	.40	.18
❑ 105	Alfonso Soriano	.40	.18
❑ 106	Bill Mueller	.40	.18
❑ 107	Bartolo Colon	.40	.18
❑ 108	Andy Pettitte	.60	.25
❑ 109	Rafael Furcal	.40	.18
❑ 110	Dontrelle Willis	1.00	.45
❑ 111	Carl Crawford	.40	.18
❑ 112	Scott Rolen	.60	.25
❑ 113	Chipper Jones	1.00	.45
❑ 114	Magglio Ordonez	.40	.18
❑ 115	Bernie Williams	.60	.25
❑ 116	Roy Oswalt	.40	.18
❑ 117	Kevin Brown	.40	.18
❑ 118	Cristian Guzman	.40	.18
❑ 119	Kazuhisa Ishii	.40	.18
❑ 120	Larry Walker	.40	.18
❑ 121	Miguel Tejada	.40	.18
❑ 122	Manny Ramirez	.60	.25
❑ 123	Mike Mussina	.60	.25
❑ 124	Mike Lowell	.40	.18
❑ 125	Scott Podsednik	.40	.18
❑ 126	Aaron Boone	.40	.18
❑ 127	Carlos Delgado	.40	.18
❑ 128	Jose Vidro	.40	.18
❑ 129	Brad Radke	.40	.18
❑ 130	Rafael Palmeiro	.60	.25
❑ 131	Mark Mulder	.40	.18
❑ 132	Jason Schmidt	.40	.18
❑ 133	Gary Sheffield	.40	.18
❑ 134	Richie Sexson	.40	.18
❑ 135	Barry Zito	.40	.18
❑ 136	Tom Glavine	.60	.25
❑ 137	Jim Edmonds	.60	.25
❑ 138	Andruw Jones	.60	.25
❑ 139	Pedro Martinez	.60	.25
❑ 140	Curt Schilling	.40	.18
❑ 141	Phil Nevin	.40	.18
❑ 142	Nomar Garciaparra	1.50	.70
❑ 143	Vicente Padilla	.40	.18
❑ 144	Kevin Millwood	.40	.18
❑ 145	Shawn Green	.40	.18
❑ 146	Jeff Bagwell	.60	.25
❑ 147	Hideo Nomo	1.00	.45
❑ 148	Fred McGriff	.60	.25
❑ 149	Matt Morris	.40	.18
❑ 150	Roger Clemens	2.00	.90
❑ 151	Jerome Williams	.40	.18
❑ 152	Orlando Cabrera	.40	.18
❑ 153	Tim Hudson	.40	.18
❑ 154	Mike Sweeney	.40	.18
❑ 155	Jim Thome	.60	.25
❑ 156	Rich Aurilia	.40	.18
❑ 157	Mike Piazza	1.50	.70
❑ 158	Edgar Renteria	.40	.18
❑ 159	Javy Lopez	.40	.18
❑ 160	Jamie Moyer	.40	.18
❑ 161	Miguel Cabrera DI	1.00	.45
❑ 162	Adam Loewen DI RC	.60	.25
❑ 163	Jose Reyes DI	.40	.18
❑ 164	Zack Greinke DI	.40	.18
❑ 165	Gavin Floyd DI	.40	.18
❑ 166	Jeremy Guthrie DI	.40	.18
❑ 167	Victor Martinez DI	.60	.25
❑ 168	Rich Harden DI	.60	.25
❑ 169	Joe Mauer DI	.60	.25
❑ 170	Khalil Greene DI	1.50	.70
❑ 171A	Willie Mays	2.00	.90
❑ 171B	Willie Mays DI	2.00	.90
❑ 171C	Willie Mays KN	2.00	.90
❑ 172A	Phil Rizzuto	.60	.25
❑ 172B	Phil Rizzuto DI	.60	.25
❑ 172C	Phil Rizzuto KN	.60	.25
❑ 173A	Al Kaline	1.00	.45
❑ 173B	Al Kaline DI	1.00	.45
❑ 173C	Al Kaline KN	1.00	.45
❑ 174A	Warren Spahn	.60	.25
❑ 174B	Warren Spahn DI	.60	.25
❑ 174C	Warren Spahn KN	.60	.25
❑ 175A	Jimmy Piersall	.40	.18
❑ 175B	Jimmy Piersall DI	.40	.18
❑ 175C	Jimmy Piersall KN	.40	.18
❑ 176A	Luis Aparicio	.40	.18
❑ 176B	Luis Aparicio DI	.40	.18
❑ 176C	Luis Aparicio KN	.40	.18
❑ 177A	Whitey Ford	.60	.25
❑ 177B	Whitey Ford DI	.60	.25
❑ 177C	Whitey Ford KN	.60	.25
❑ 178A	Harmon Killebrew	1.00	.45
❑ 178B	Harmon Killebrew DI	1.00	.45
❑ 178C	Harmon Killebrew KN	1.00	.45
❑ 179A	Duke Snider	.60	.25
❑ 179B	Duke Snider DI	.60	.25
❑ 179C	Duke Snider KN	.60	.25
❑ 180A	Roberto Clemente	2.50	1.10
❑ 180B	Roberto Clemente DI	2.50	1.10
❑ 180C	Roberto Clemente KN	2.50	1.10
❑ 181	David Martinez KN RC	.40	.18
❑ 182	Felix Pie KN RC	4.00	1.80
❑ 183	Kevin Correia KN RC	.40	.18
❑ 184	Brandon Webb KN RC	.75	.35
❑ 185	Matt Diaz KN RC	.50	.23
❑ 186	Lew Ford KN RC	.50	.23
❑ 187	Jeremy Griffiths KN RC	.40	.18
❑ 188	Matt Hensley KN RC	.40	.18
❑ 189	Danny Garcia KN RC	.40	.18
❑ 190	Elizardo Ramirez KN RC	.50	.23
❑ 191	Greg Aquino KN RC	.40	.18
❑ 192	Felix Sanchez KN RC	.40	.18
❑ 193	Kelly Shoppach KN RC	.75	.35
❑ 194	Bubba Nelson KN RC	.50	.23
❑ 195	Mike O'Keefe KN RC	.40	.18
❑ 196	Hanley Ramirez KN RC	2.50	1.10
❑ 197	Todd Wellemeyer KN RC	.40	.18
❑ 198	Dustin Moseley KN RC	.40	.18
❑ 199	Eric Crozier KN RC	.50	.23
❑ 200	Ryan Shealy KN RC	.75	.35
❑ 201	Jeremy Bonderman KN RC	2.50	1.10
❑ 202	Bo Hart KN RC	.40	.18
❑ 203	Dusty Brown KN RC	.40	.18
❑ 204	Rob Hammock KN RC	.40	.18
❑ 205	Jorge Piedra KN RC	.50	.23
❑ 206	Jason Kubel KN RC	.75	.35
❑ 207	Stephen Randolph KN RC	.40	.18
❑ 208	Andy Sisco KN RC	.50	.23
❑ 209	Matt Kata KN RC	.40	.18
❑ 210	Robinson Cano KN RC	5.00	2.20
❑ 211	Ben Francisco KN RC	.40	.18
❑ 212	Arnie Munoz KN RC	.40	.18
❑ 213	Ozzie Chavez KN RC	.40	.18
❑ 214	Beau Kemp KN RC	.40	.18
❑ 215	Travis Wong KN RC	.50	.23
❑ 216	Brian McCann KN RC	3.00	1.35

	Card	Nm-Mt	Ex-Mt
❑ 217	Aquilino Lopez KN RC	.40	.18
❑ 218	Bobby Basham KN RC	.50	.23
❑ 219	Tim Olson KN RC	.40	.18
❑ 220	Nathan Panther KN RC	.40	.18
❑ 221	Wil Ledezma KN RC	.40	.18
❑ 222	Josh Willingham KN RC	.50	.23
❑ 223	David Cash KN RC	.40	.18
❑ 224	Oscar Villarreal KN RC	.40	.18
❑ 225	Jeff Duncan KN RC	.40	.18
❑ 226	Dan Haren KN RC	.75	.35
❑ 227	Michel Hernandez KN RC	.40	.18
❑ 228	Matt Murton KN RC	2.00	.90
❑ 229	Clay Hensley KN RC	.40	.18
❑ 230	Tyler Johnson KN RC	.40	.18
❑ 231	Tyler Martin KN RC	.40	.18
❑ 232	J.D. Durbin KN RC	.40	.18
❑ 233	Shane Victorino KN RC	.50	.23
❑ 234	Rajai Davis KN RC	.40	.18
❑ 235	Chien-Ming Wang KN RC	2.50	1.10
❑ 236	Travis Ishikawa KN RC	.40	.18
❑ 237	Eric Eckenstahler KN	.40	.18
❑ 238	Dustin McGowan KN RC	.40	.18
❑ 239	Prentice Redman KN RC	.40	.18
❑ 240	Haj Turay KN RC	.50	.23
❑ 241	Matt DeMarco KN RC	.40	.18
❑ 242	Lou Palmisano KN RC	.50	.23
❑ 243	Eric Reed KN RC	.40	.18
❑ 244	Willie Eyre KN RC	.40	.18
❑ 245	Ferdin Tejeda KN RC	.40	.18
❑ 246	Michael Garciaparra KN RC	.40	.18
❑ 247	Michael Hinckley KN RC	.50	.23
❑ 248	Branden Florence KN RC	.40	.18
❑ 249	Trent Oeltjen KN RC	.50	.23
❑ 250	Mike Neu KN RC	.40	.18
❑ 251	Chris Lubanski KN RC	1.00	.45
❑ 252	Brandon Wood KN RC	10.00	4.50
❑ 253	Delmon Young KN RC	5.00	2.20
❑ 254	Matt Harrison KN RC	.75	.35
❑ 255	Chad Billingsley KN RC	2.50	1.10
❑ 256	Josh Anderson KN RC	.75	.35
❑ 257	Brian McFall KN RC	.40	.18
❑ 258	Ryan Wagner KN RC	.40	.18
❑ 259	Billy Hogan KN RC	.50	.23
❑ 260	Nate Spears KN RC	.50	.23
❑ 261	Ryan Harvey KN RC	2.00	.90
❑ 262	Wes Littleton KN RC	.50	.23
❑ 263	Xavier Paul KN RC	.50	.23
❑ 264	Sean Rodriguez KN RC	.50	.23
❑ 265	Brian Finch KN RC	.40	.18
❑ 266	Josh Rainwater KN RC	.50	.23
❑ 267	Brian Snyder KN RC	.50	.23
❑ 268	Eric Duncan KN RC	2.50	1.10
❑ 269	Rickie Weeks KN RC	4.00	1.80
❑ 270	Tim Battle KN RC	.50	.23
❑ 271	Scott Beerer KN RC	.40	.18
❑ 272	Aaron Hill KN RC	.75	.35
❑ 273	Casey Abrams KN RC	.40	.18
❑ 274	Jonathan Fulton KN RC	.50	.23
❑ 275	Todd Jennings KN RC	.50	.23
❑ 276	Jordan Pratt KN RC	.50	.23
❑ 277	Tom Gorzelanny KN RC	.50	.23
❑ 278	Matt Lorenzo KN RC	.50	.23
❑ 279	Jarrod Saltalamacchia KN RC	3.00	1.35
❑ 280	Mike Wagner KN RC	.40	.18

2004 Bowman Heritage

	Nm-Mt	Ex-Mt
COMPLETE SET (351)	300.00	90.00
COMP.SET w/o SP's (300)	50.00	15.00

SP STATED ODDS 1:3 HOBBY, 1:3 RETAIL
SP's: 2/9/13/21/25/40B/46/48B/50/55/61
SP's: 77/80/87/89/95/100/104/109/127/130
SP's: 132/141/183A/189/204/206/208/210
SP's: 213/216/220/224/228/234/240/243
SP's: 246/249/259/268/270-271/282/291
SP's: 304/318/327/334/342/348 ....
PLATES STATED ODDS 1:240 HOBBY
PLATES PRINT RUN 1 #'d SET PER COLOR
PLATES: BLACK, CYAN, MAGENTA & YELLOW
NO PLATES PRICING DUE TO SCARCITY
ROOP BINDER ODDS 1:240 HOBBY.00
ROOP BINDER EXCH.DEADLINE 12/31/05

	Card	Nm-Mt	Ex-Mt
❑ 1	Tom Glavine	.60	.18
❑ 2	Mike Piazza SP	8.00	2.40
❑ 3	Sidney Ponson	.40	.12
❑ 4	Jerry Hairston Jr.	.40	.12
❑ 5	Jermaine Dye	.40	.12
❑ 6	Bobby Crosby	.40	.12
❑ 7	Carlos Zambrano	.40	.12
❑ 8	Moises Alou	.40	.12
❑ 9	Alex Rodriguez SP	8.00	2.40
❑ 10	Derek Jeter	2.00	.60
❑ 11	Rafael Furcal	.40	.12
❑ 12	J.D. Drew	.40	.12
❑ 13	Joe Mauer SP	5.00	1.50
❑ 14	Brad Radke	.40	.12
❑ 15	Johnny Damon	.60	.18
❑ 16	Derek Lowe	.40	.12
❑ 17	Pat Burrell	.40	.12
❑ 18	Mike Lieberthal	.40	.12
❑ 19	Cliff Lee	.40	.12
❑ 20	Ronnie Belliard	.40	.12
❑ 21	Eric Gagne SP	5.00	1.50
❑ 22	Brad Penny	.40	.12
❑ 23	Al Kaline RET	1.50	.45
❑ 24	Mike Maroth	.40	.12
❑ 25	Magglio Ordonez SP	5.00	1.50
❑ 26	Mark Buehrle	.40	.12
❑ 27	Jack Wilson	.40	.12
❑ 28	Oliver Perez	.40	.12
❑ 29	Red Schoendienst RET	.60	.18
❑ 30	Yadier Molina FY RC	2.00	.60
❑ 31	Ryan Freel	.40	.12
❑ 32	Adam Dunn	.40	.12
❑ 33	Paul Konerko	.40	.12
❑ 34	Esteban Loaiza	.40	.12
❑ 35	Ivan Rodriguez	.60	.18
❑ 36	Carlos Guillen	.40	.12
❑ 37	Adrian Beltre	.40	.12
❑ 38	C.C. Sabathia	.40	.12
❑ 39	Hideo Nomo	1.00	.30
❑ 40A	Victor Martinez	.40	.12
❑ 40B	V.Martinez Pedro Stats SP	5.00	1.50
❑ 41	Bobby Abreu	.40	.12
❑ 42	Randy Wolf	.40	.12
❑ 43	Johnny Estrada	.40	.12
❑ 44	Russ Ortiz	.40	.12
❑ 45	Kenny Rogers	.40	.12
❑ 46	Hank Blalock SP	5.00	1.50
❑ 47	David Ortiz	1.00	.30
❑ 48A	Pedro Martinez	.60	.18
❑ 48B	P.Martinez Victor Stats SP	8.00	2.40
❑ 49	Austin Kearns	.40	.12
❑ 50	Ken Griffey Jr. SP	8.00	2.40
❑ 51	Mark Prior	.60	.18
❑ 52	Kerry Wood	.40	.12
❑ 53	Eric Chavez	.40	.12
❑ 54	Tim Hudson	.40	.12
❑ 55	Rafael Palmeiro SP	8.00	2.40
❑ 56	Javy Lopez	.40	.12
❑ 57	Jason Bay	.40	.12
❑ 58	Craig Wilson	.40	.12
❑ 59	Whitey Ford RET	1.00	.30
❑ 60	Jason Giambi	.40	.12
❑ 61	Scott Rolen SP	8.00	2.40
❑ 62	Matt Morris	.40	.12
❑ 63	Javier Vazquez	.40	.12
❑ 64	Jim Thome	.60	.18
❑ 65	Don Zimmer RET	.60	.18
❑ 66	Shawn Green	.40	.12
❑ 67	Don Larsen RET	1.00	.30
❑ 68	Gary Sheffield	.40	.12
❑ 69	Jorge Posada	.60	.18
❑ 70	Bernie Williams	.60	.18
❑ 71	Chipper Jones	1.00	.30
❑ 72	Andruw Jones	.60	.18
❑ 73	John Thomson	.40	.12
❑ 74	Jim Edmonds	.60	.18
❑ 75	Albert Pujols	2.00	.60
❑ 76	Chris Carpenter	.40	.12
❑ 77	Aubrey Huff SP	5.00	1.50
❑ 78	Carl Crawford	.40	.12
❑ 79	Victor Zambrano	.40	.12
❑ 80	Alfonso Soriano SP	5.00	1.50
❑ 81	Lance Berkman	.40	.12
❑ 82	Mike Sweeney	.40	.12
❑ 83	Ken Harvey	.40	.12
❑ 84	Angel Berroa	.40	.12
❑ 85	A.J. Burnett	.40	.12
❑ 86	Mike Lowell	.40	.12
❑ 87	Miguel Cabrera SP	8.00	2.40
❑ 88	Preston Wilson	.40	.12
❑ 89	Todd Helton SP	8.00	2.40
❑ 90	Larry Walker Cards	.60	.18
❑ 91	Vladimir Guerrero	1.00	.30
❑ 92	Garret Anderson	.40	.12
❑ 93	Bartolo Colon	.40	.12
❑ 94	Scott Hairston	.40	.12
❑ 95	Richie Sexson SP	5.00	1.50
❑ 96	Sean Casey	.60	.18
❑ 97	John Podres RET	.60	.18
❑ 98	Andy Pettitte	.60	.18
❑ 99	Roy Oswalt	.40	.12
❑ 100	Roger Clemens SP	8.00	2.40
❑ 101	Scott Podsednik	.40	.12
❑ 102	Ben Sheets	.40	.12
❑ 103	Lyle Overbay	.40	.12
❑ 104	Nick Johnson SP	5.00	1.50
❑ 105	Zach Day	.40	.12
❑ 106	Jose Reyes	.40	.12
❑ 107	Khalil Greene	1.00	.30
❑ 108	Sean Burroughs	.40	.12
❑ 109	David Wells SP	5.00	1.50
❑ 110	Jason Schmidt	.40	.12
❑ 111	Neifi Perez	.40	.12
❑ 112	Edgar Renteria	.40	.12
❑ 113	Rich Aurilia	.40	.12
❑ 114	Edgar Martinez	.60	.18
❑ 115	Joel Pineiro	.40	.12
❑ 116	Mark Teixeira	.60	.18
❑ 117	Michael Young	.40	.12
❑ 118	Ricardo Rodriguez	.40	.12
❑ 119	Carlos Delgado	.40	.12
❑ 120	Roy Halladay	.40	.12
❑ 121	Jose Guillen	.40	.12
❑ 122	Troy Glaus	.40	.12
❑ 123	Shea Hillenbrand	.40	.12
❑ 124	Luis Gonzalez	.40	.12
❑ 125	Horacio Ramirez	.40	.12
❑ 126	Melvin Mora	.40	.12
❑ 127	Miguel Tejada SP	5.00	1.50
❑ 128	Manny Ramirez	.60	.18
❑ 129	Tim Wakefield	.40	.12
❑ 130	Curt Schilling SP	8.00	2.40
❑ 131	Aramis Ramirez	.40	.12
❑ 132	Sammy Sosa SP	8.00	2.40
❑ 133	Matt Clement	.40	.12
❑ 134	Juan Uribe	.40	.12
❑ 135	Dontrelle Willis	.60	.18
❑ 136	Paul Lo Duca	.40	.12
❑ 137	Juan Pierre	.40	.12
❑ 138	Kevin Brown	.40	.12
❑ 139	Brian Giles Marcus Giles	.40	.12
❑ 140	Brian Giles	.40	.12
❑ 141	Nomar Garciaparra SP	8.00	2.40
❑ 142	Cesar Izturis	.40	.12
❑ 143	Don Newcombe RET	.60	.18
❑ 144	Craig Biggio	.60	.18
❑ 145	Carlos Beltran	.40	.12
❑ 146	Torii Hunter	.40	.12
❑ 147	Livan Hernandez	.40	.12
❑ 148	Cliff Floyd	.40	.12
❑ 149	Barry Zito	.40	.12
❑ 150	Mark Mulder	.40	.12
❑ 151	Rocco Baldelli	.40	.12
❑ 152	Bret Boone	.40	.12

❑ 153 Jamie Moyer .40 .12
❑ 154 Ichiro Suzuki 2.00 .60
❑ 155 Brett Myers .40 .12
❑ 156 Carl Pavano .40 .12
❑ 157 Josh Beckett .40 .12
❑ 158 Randy Johnson 1.00 .30
❑ 159 Trot Nixon .40 .12
❑ 160 Dmitri Young .40 .12
❑ 161 Jacque Jones .40 .12
❑ 162 Lew Ford .40 .12
❑ 163 Jose Vidro .40 .12
❑ 164 Mark Kotsay .40 .12
❑ 165 A.J. Pierzynski .40 .12
❑ 166 Dewon Brazelton .40 .12
❑ 167 Jeromy Burnitz .40 .12
❑ 168 Johan Santana .60 .18
❑ 169 Greg Maddux 1.50 .45
❑ 170 Carl Erskine RET .60 .18
❑ 171 Robin Roberts RET .60 .18
❑ 172 Freddy Garcia .40 .12
❑ 173 Carlos Lee .40 .12
❑ 174 Jeff Bagwell .60 .18
❑ 175 Jeff Kent .40 .12
❑ 176 Kazuhisa Ishii .40 .12
❑ 177 Orlando Cabrera .40 .12
❑ 178 Shannon Stewart .40 .12
❑ 179 Mike Cameron .40 .12
❑ 180 Mike Mussina .60 .18
❑ 181 Frank Thomas 1.00 .30
❑ 182 Jaret Wright .40 .12
❑ 183A Alex Gonzalez Marlins SP 5.00 1.50
❑ 183B Alex Gonzalez Padres .40 .12
❑ 184 Matt Lawton .40 .12
❑ 185 Derrek Lee .60 .18
❑ 186 Omar Vizquel .60 .18
❑ 187 Jeremy Bonderman .40 .12
❑ 188 Jake Westbrook .40 .12
❑ 189 Zack Greinke SP 5.00 1.50
❑ 190 Chad Tracy .40 .12
❑ 191 Rondell White .40 .12
❑ 192 Alex Gonzalez .40 .12
❑ 193 Geoff Jenkins .40 .12
❑ 194 Ralph Kiner RET 1.00 .30
❑ 195 Al Leiter .40 .12
❑ 196 Kevin Millwood .40 .12
❑ 197 Jason Kendall .40 .12
❑ 198 Kris Benson .40 .12
❑ 199 Ryan Klesko .40 .12
❑ 200 Mark Loretta .40 .12
❑ 201 Richard Hidalgo .40 .12
❑ 202 Reed Johnson .40 .12
❑ 203 Luis Castillo .40 .12
❑ 204 Jon Zeringue DP SP RC 8.00 2.40
❑ 205 Matt Bush DP RC 3.00 .90
❑ 206 Kurt Suzuki DP SP RC 10.00 3.00
❑ 207 Mark Rogers DP RC 2.00 .60
❑ 208 Jason Vargas DP SP RC 8.00 2.40
❑ 209 Homer Bailey DP RC 2.50 .75
❑ 210 Ray Liotta DP SP RC 8.00 2.40
❑ 211 Eric Campbell DP RC 3.00 .90
❑ 212 Thomas Diamond DP RC 2.50 .75
❑ 213 Gaby Hernandez DP SP RC 10.00 3.00
❑ 214 Neil Walker DP RC 2.50 .75
❑ 215 Bill Bray DP RC .75 .23
❑ 216 Wade Davis DP SP RC 8.00 2.40
❑ 217 David Purcey DP RC 1.50 .45
❑ 218 Scott Elbert DP RC 2.00 .60
❑ 219 Josh Fields DP RC 2.50 .75
❑ 220 Josh Johnson DP SP RC 8.00 2.40
❑ 221 Chris Lambert DP RC 1.00 .30
❑ 222 Trevor Plouffe DP RC 2.50 .75
❑ 223 Bruce Froemming UMP .50 .15
❑ 224 Matt Macri DP SP RC 8.00 2.40
❑ 225 Greg Golson DP RC 2.50 .75
❑ 226 Philip Hughes DP RC 3.00 .90
❑ 227 Kyle Waldrop DP RC 2.00 .60
❑ 228 Matt Tuiasosopo DP SP RC 12.00 3.60
❑ 229 Richie Robnett DP RC 2.00 .60
❑ 230 Taylor Tankersley DP RC 1.50 .45
❑ 231 Blake DeWitt DP RC 3.00 .90
❑ 232 Charlie Reliford UMP .50 .15
❑ 233 Eric Hurley DP RC 1.50 .45
❑ 234 Jordan Parraz DP SP RC 8.00 2.40
❑ 235 J.P. Howell DP RC 2.00 .60
❑ 236 Dana DeMuth UMP .50 .15
❑ 237 Zach Jackson DP RC 1.50 .45
❑ 238 Justin Orenduff DP RC 1.50 .45
❑ 239 Brad Thompson FY RC .75 .23
❑ 240 J.C. Holt DP SP RC 8.00 2.40
❑ 241 Matt Fox DP RC .75 .23
❑ 242 Danny Putnam DP RC 1.50 .45
❑ 243 Daryl Jones DP SP RC 8.00 2.40
❑ 244 Jon Poterson DP RC .75 .23
❑ 245 Gio Gonzalez DP RC 2.00 .60
❑ 246 Lucas Harrell DP SP RC 5.00 1.50
❑ 247 Jerry Crawford UMP .50 .15
❑ 248 Jay Rainville DP RC 2.50 .75
❑ 249 Donnie Smith DP SP RC 8.00 2.40
❑ 250 Huston Street DP RC 4.00 1.20
❑ 251 Jeff Marquez DP RC 1.00 .30
❑ 252 Reid Brignac DP RC 3.00 .90
❑ 253 Yusmeiro Petit FY RC 2.50 .75
❑ 254 K.C. Herren DP RC 1.50 .45
❑ 255 Dale Scott UMP .50 .15
❑ 256 Erick San Pedro DP RC .75 .23
❑ 257 Ed Montague UMP .50 .15
❑ 258 Billy Buckner DP RC 1.00 .30
❑ 259 Mitch Einertson DP SP RC 8.00 2.40
❑ 260 Aarom Baldiris FY RC .50 .15
❑ 261 Conor Jackson FY RC 3.00 .90
❑ 262 Rick Reed UMP .50 .15
❑ 263 Ervin Santana FY RC UER 2.00 .60
Facsimile Signature is Johan Santana
❑ 264 Gerry Davis UMP .50 .15
❑ 265 Merkin Valdez FY RC .50 .15
❑ 266 Joey Gathright FY RC 1.00 .30
❑ 267 Alberto Callaspo FY RC .75 .23
❑ 268 Carlos Quentin FY SP RC 10.00 3.00
❑ 269 Gary Darling UMP .50 .15
❑ 270 Jeff Salazar FY SP RC 8.00 2.40
❑ 271 Akinori Otsuka FY SP RC 5.00 1.50
❑ 272 Joe Brinkman UMP .50 .15
❑ 273 Omar Quintanilla FY RC 1.00 .30
❑ 274 Brian Runge UMP .50 .15
❑ 275 Tom Mastny FY RC .40 .12
❑ 276 John Hirschbeck UMP .50 .15
❑ 277 Warner Madrigal FY RC .75 .23
❑ 278 Joe West UMP .50 .15
❑ 279 Paul Maholm FY RC 1.00 .30
❑ 280 Larry Young UMP .50 .15
❑ 281 Mike Reilly UMP .50 .15
❑ 282 Kazuo Matsui FY SP RC 8.00 2.40
❑ 283 Randy Marsh UMP .50 .15
❑ 284 Frank Francisco FY RC .40 .12
❑ 285 Zach Duke FY RC 4.00 1.20
❑ 286 Tim McClelland UMP .50 .15
❑ 287 Jesse Crain FY RC .75 .23
❑ 288 Hector Gimenez FY RC .40 .12
❑ 289 Marland Williams FY RC .50 .15
❑ 290 Brian Gorman UMP .50 .15
❑ 291 Jose Capellan FY SP RC 8.00 2.40
❑ 292 Tim Welke UMP .50 .15
❑ 293 Javier Guzman FY RC .50 .15
❑ 294 Paul McAnulty FY RC .75 .23
❑ 295 Hector Made FY RC .75 .23
❑ 296 Jon Connolly FY RC 1.00 .30
❑ 297 Don Sutton FY RC 1.00 .30
❑ 298 Fausto Carmona FY RC .75 .23
❑ 299 Ramon Ramirez FY RC .40 .12
❑ 300 Brad Snyder FY RC 1.25 .35
❑ 301 Chin-Lung Hu FY RC 1.00 .30
❑ 302 Rudy Guillen FY RC .75 .23
❑ 303 Matt Moses FY RC 1.25 .35
❑ 304 Brad Halsey FY SP RC 8.00 2.40
❑ 305 Erick Aybar FY RC 1.25 .35
❑ 306 Brad Sullivan FY RC .50 .15
❑ 307 Nick Gorneault FY RC .50 .15
❑ 308 Craig Ansman FY RC .40 .12
❑ 309 Ricky Nolasco FY RC .75 .23
❑ 310 Luke Hughes FY RC .40 .12
❑ 311 Danny Gonzalez FY RC .40 .12
❑ 312 Josh Labandeira FY RC .40 .12
❑ 313 Donald Levinski FY RC .40 .12
❑ 314 Vince Perkins FY RC .50 .15
❑ 315 Tommy Murphy FY RC .40 .12
❑ 316 Chad Bentz FY RC .40 .12
❑ 317 Chris Shelton FY RC 1.50 .45
❑ 318 Nyjer Morgan FY SP RC 5.00 1.50
❑ 319 Kody Kirkland FY RC .50 .15
❑ 320 Blake Hawksworth FY RC .50 .15
❑ 321 Alex Romero FY RC .40 .12
❑ 322 Mike Gosling FY RC .40 .12
❑ 323 Ryan Budde FY RC .40 .12
❑ 324 Kevin Howard FY RC .50 .15
❑ 325 Wanell Macia FY RC .40 .12
❑ 326 Travis Blackley FY RC .40 .12
❑ 327 Kazuhito Tadano FY SP RC 8.00 2.40
❑ 328 Shingo Takatsu FY RC .75 .23
❑ 329 Joaquin Arias FY RC .75 .23
❑ 330 Juan Cedeno FY RC .40 .12
❑ 331 Bobby Brownlie FY RC 1.25 .35
❑ 332 Lastings Milledge FY RC 2.00 .60
❑ 333 Estee Harris FY RC .50 .15
❑ 334 Tim Stauffer FY SP RC 8.00 2.40
❑ 335 Jon Knott FY RC .40 .12
❑ 336 David Aardsma FY RC .50 .15
❑ 337 Wardell Starling FY RC .40 .12
❑ 338 Dioner Navarro FY RC 1.50 .45
❑ 339 Logan Kensing FY RC .40 .12
❑ 340 Jason Hirsh FY RC 1.00 .30
❑ 341 Matt Creighton FY RC .40 .12
❑ 342 Felix Hernandez FY SP RC 25.00 7.50
❑ 343 Kyle Sleeth FY RC .75 .23
❑ 344 Dustin Nippert FY RC .50 .15
❑ 345 Anthony Lerew FY RC .50 .15
❑ 346 Chris Saenz FY RC .40 .12
❑ 347 Steve Palermo SUP 1.00 .30
❑ 348 Barry Bonds SP 20.00 6.00
❑ MJ Roop Binder EXCH 15.00 4.50

2004 Bowman Sterling

Nm-Mt Ex-Mt

FY ODDS APPX.TWO PER HOBBY PACK .00
FY AU ODDS APPX.ONE PER HOBBY PACK .00
AU-GU ODDS APPX.ONE PER HOBBY PACK .00
AU-GU 1:2 WRAPPER ODDS IS AN ERROR .00
GU ODDS APPX. 1.5 PER HOBBY PACK .00
GU 1:2 WRAPPER ODDS IS AN ERROR .00

❑ AB Angel Berroa Bat 8.00 2.40
❑ ABA Aarom Baldiris FY RC 5.00 1.50
❑ AC Alberto Callaspo FY AU RC 10.00 3.00
❑ AD Adam Dunn Bat 8.00 2.40
❑ AER Alex Rodriguez Bat 15.00 4.50
❑ AJ Andruw Jones Jsy 10.00 3.00
❑ AK Austin Kearns Jsy 8.00 2.40
❑ ANR Aramis Ramirez Bat 8.00 2.40
❑ AP Albert Pujols Jsy 20.00 6.00
❑ AR Alex Romero FY AU RC 8.00 2.40
❑ AW Adam Wainwright AU Jsy 15.00 4.50
❑ AWH A.Whittington FY RC 5.00 1.50
❑ AZ Alec Zumwalt FY AU RC 8.00 2.40
❑ BB Brian Bixler AU Jsy RC 15.00 4.50
❑ BBR Bill Bray FY RC 4.00 1.20
❑ BBU Billy Buckner FY RC 5.00 1.50
❑ BC2 Bobby Crosby Jsy 8.00 2.40
❑ BD Blake DeWitt AU Jsy RC 25.00 7.50
❑ BE Brad Eldred FY RC 15.00 4.50
❑ BH B.Hawksworth FY AU RC 10.00 3.00
❑ BT Brad Thompson FY RC 8.00 2.40
❑ BU B.J. Upton AU Bat 30.00 9.00
❑ BW Bernie Williams Jsy 10.00 3.00
❑ CA Chris Aguila FY AU RC 8.00 2.40
❑ CB Craig Biggio Jsy 10.00 3.00
❑ CC Chad Cordero AU Jsy 15.00 4.50
❑ CG Christian Garcia AU Jsy RC 15.00 4.50
❑ CH Chin-Lung Hu FY RC 8.00 2.40
❑ CIB Carlos Beltran Bat 8.00 2.40
❑ CJ Conor Jackson FY RC 20.00 6.00
❑ CL Chris Lubanski AU Bat 15.00 4.50

❑ CLA Chris Lambert FY RC 5.00 1.50
❑ CN Chris Nelson FY RC 12.00 3.60
❑ CQ Carlos Quentin FY AU RC 30.00 9.00
❑ CT Curtis Thigpen FY RC 8.00 2.40
❑ DD David DeJesus AU Jsy 15.00 4.50
❑ DP Danny Putnam AU Jsy RC 20.00 6.00
❑ DPU David Purcey FY RC 8.00 2.40
❑ DW David Wright AU Jsy 50.00 15.00
❑ DWW Dontrelle Willis Jsy 10.00 3.00
❑ DY Delmon Young AU Bat 30.00 9.00
❑ EG Eric Gagne Jsy 8.00 2.40
❑ EH Eric Hurley FY RC 8.00 2.40
❑ ESP Erick San Pedro FY RC 4.00 1.20
❑ FC Fausto Carmona FY RC 8.00 2.40
❑ FG Freddy Guzman FY RC 4.00 1.20
❑ FH Felix Hernandez FY RC 40.00 12.00
❑ FP Felix Pie AU Jsy 30.00 9.00
❑ FT Frank Thomas Bat 10.00 3.00
❑ GG Greg Golson FY RC 8.00 2.40
❑ GH Gaby Hernandez FY RC 10.00 3.00
❑ GIG Gio Gonzalez FY RC 8.00 2.40
❑ GS Gary Sheffield Bat 8.00 2.40
❑ HB Homer Bailey AU Jsy RC 25.00 7.50
❑ HC Hee Seop Choi Bat 8.00 2.40
❑ HG Hector Gimenez FY AU RC 8.00 2.40
❑ HJB Hank Blalock Bat 8.00 2.40
❑ HM Hector Made FY RC 8.00 2.40
❑ HS Huston Street AU Jsy RC 40.00 12.00
❑ IR Ivan Rodriguez Bat 10.00 3.00
❑ JB Jeff Bagwell Jsy 10.00 3.00
❑ JC Jose Capellan FY RC 5.00 1.50
❑ JCR Jesse Crain FY RC 8.00 2.40
❑ JD Johnny Damon Bat 10.00 3.00
❑ JE Johnny Estrada Bat 8.00 2.40
❑ JFI Josh Fields FY RC 8.00 2.40
❑ JG Joey Gathright FY RC 8.00 2.40
❑ JH Jesse Hoover FY RC 5.00 1.50
❑ JK Jason Kendall Bat 8.00 2.40
❑ JM Jeff Marquez AU Jsy RC 15.00 4.50
❑ JO Justin Orenduff FY RC 8.00 2.40
❑ JP Juan Pierre Bat 8.00 2.40
❑ JPH J.P. Howell FY RC 6.00 1.80
❑ JR Jay Rainville FY AU RC 20.00 6.00
❑ JS Jeremy Sowers FY AU RC 20.00 6.00
❑ JZ Jon Zeringue FY RC 8.00 2.40
❑ KCH K.C. Herren FY RC 8.00 2.40
❑ KS Kurt Suzuki FY RC 8.00 2.40
❑ KT Kazuhito Tadano FY RC 5.00 1.50
❑ KW Kerry Wood Jsy 8.00 2.40
❑ KWA Kyle Waldrop AU Jsy RC 20.00 6.00
❑ LB Lance Berkman Jsy 8.00 2.40
❑ LC Luis Castillo Jsy 8.00 2.40
❑ LH Linc Holdzkom FY AU RC 8.00 2.40
❑ LN Laynce Nix Bat 8.00 2.40
❑ MA Moises Alou Bat 8.00 2.40
❑ MAM Mark Mulder Jsy 8.00 2.40
❑ MAR Manny Ramirez Bat 10.00 3.00
❑ MB Matt Bush AU Jsy RC 25.00 7.50
❑ MC Miguel Cabrera Bat 10.00 3.00
❑ MCT Mark Teixeira Bat 10.00 3.00
❑ ME Mitch Einertson FY RC 15.00 4.50
❑ MF Mike Ferris FY RC 5.00 1.50
❑ MFO Matt Fox FY RC 4.00 1.20
❑ MJP Mike Piazza Bat 10.00 3.00
❑ MM Matt Moses FY AU RC 20.00 6.00
❑ MMC Matt Macri FY RC 8.00 2.40
❑ MP Mark Prior Jsy 10.00 3.00
❑ MR Mike Rouse FY AU RC 8.00 2.40
❑ MRO Mark Rogers FY RC 8.00 2.40
❑ MT M.Tuiasosopo AU Bat RC 30.00 9.00
❑ MT1 Miguel Tejada Bat 8.00 2.40
❑ MT2 Miguel Tejada Jsy 8.00 2.40
❑ MW Marland Williams FY RC 5.00 1.50
❑ MY Michael Young Bat 8.00 2.40
❑ NJ Nick Johnson Bat 8.00 2.40
❑ NM Nyjer Morgan FY RC 4.00 1.20
❑ NS Nate Schierholtz FY RC 25.00 7.50
❑ NW Neil Walker FY RC 10.00 3.00
❑ OQ Omar Quintanilla FY RC 8.00 2.40
❑ PGM Paul Maholm FY RC 8.00 2.40
❑ PH Philip Hughes FY RC 10.00 3.00
❑ PL Paul LoDuca Bat 8.00 2.40
❑ PR Pokey Reese Bat 8.00 2.40
❑ RB Rocco Baldelli Bat 8.00 2.40
❑ RBR Reid Brignac FY RC 8.00 2.40
❑ RC Robinson Cano AU Jsy 60.00 18.00
❑ RH Ryan Harvey AU Bat 25.00 7.50
❑ RJH Richard Hidalgo Bat 8.00 2.40
❑ RM Ryan Meaux FY AU RC 8.00 2.40
❑ RO Russ Ortiz Jsy 8.00 2.40
❑ RP Rafael Palmeiro Bat 10.00 3.00
❑ SK Scott Kazmir AU Jsy RC 30.00 9.00
❑ SO Scott Olsen AU Jsy RC 20.00 6.00
❑ SS Sammy Sosa Jsy 10.00 3.00
❑ SSM Seth Smith FY RC 8.00 2.40
❑ TD Thomas Diamond FY RC 8.00 2.40
❑ TG Troy Glaus Bat 8.00 2.40
❑ TLH Todd Helton Bat 10.00 3.00
❑ TM Tino Martinez Bat 10.00 3.00
❑ TMG Tom Glavine Jsy 10.00 3.00
❑ TP Trevor Plouffe AU Jsy RC 20.00 6.00
❑ TT T.Tankersley AU Jsy RC 20.00 6.00
❑ VG Vladimir Guerrero Bat 10.00 3.00
❑ VP Vince Perkins FY AU RC 10.00 3.00
❑ YP Yusmeiro Petit FY RC 15.00 4.50
❑ ZD Zach Duke FY RC 25.00 7.50
❑ ZJ Zach Jackson FY RC 8.00 2.40

1994 Bowman's Best

	Nm-Mt	Ex-Mt
COMPLETE SET (200)	40.00	12.00

❑ B1 Chipper Jones 1.25 .35
❑ B2 Derek Jeter 4.00 1.20
❑ B3 Bill Pulsipher .50 .15
❑ B4 James Baldwin .25 .07
❑ B5 Brooks Kieschnick RC 1.00 .30
❑ B6 Justin Thompson .25 .07
❑ B7 Midre Cummings .25 .07
❑ B8 Joey Hamilton .25 .07
❑ B9 Pokey Reese .25 .07
❑ B10 Brian Barber .25 .07
❑ B11 John Burke .25 .07
❑ B12 DeShawn Warren .25 .07
❑ B13 Edgardo Alfonzo RC 1.50 .45
❑ B14 Eddie Pearson RC .50 .15
❑ B15 Jimmy Haynes .25 .07
❑ B16 Danny Bautista .25 .07
❑ B17 Roger Cedeno .25 .07
❑ B18 Jon Lieber .50 .15
❑ B19 Billy Wagner RC 5.00 1.50
❑ B20 Tate Seefried RC .50 .15
❑ B21 Chad Mottola .25 .07
❑ B22 Jose Malave .25 .07
❑ B23 Terrell Wade RC .50 .15
❑ B24 Shane Andrews .25 .07
❑ B25 Chan Ho Park RC 1.50 .45
❑ B26 Kirk Presley RC .50 .15
❑ B27 Robbie Beckett .25 .07
❑ B28 Orlando Miller .25 .07
❑ B29 Jorge Posada RC 10.00 3.00
❑ B30 Frankie Rodriguez .25 .07
❑ B31 Brian L. Hunter .25 .07
❑ B32 Billy Ashley .25 .07
❑ B33 Rondell White .50 .15
❑ B34 John Roper .25 .07
❑ B35 Marc Valdes .25 .07
❑ B36 Scott Ruffcorn .25 .07
❑ B37 Rod Henderson .25 .07
❑ B38 Curtis Goodwin RC .50 .15
❑ B39 Russ Davis .25 .07
❑ B40 Rick Gorecki .25 .07
❑ B41 Johnny Damon 1.25 .35
❑ B42 Roberto Petagine .25 .07
❑ B43 Chris Snopek .25 .07
❑ B44 Mark Acre RC .50 .15
❑ B45 Todd Hollandsworth .25 .07
❑ B46 Shawn Green 1.25 .35
❑ B47 John Carter RC .50 .15
❑ B48 Jim Pittsley RC .50 .15
❑ B49 John Wasdin RC .50 .15
❑ B50 D.J. Boston RC .50 .15
❑ B51 Tim Clark .25 .07
❑ B52 Alex Ochoa .25 .07
❑ B53 Chad Roper .25 .07
❑ B54 Mike Kelly .25 .07
❑ B55 Brad Fullmer RC 1.50 .45
❑ B56 Carl Everett .50 .15
❑ B57 Tim Belk RC .50 .15
❑ B58 Jimmy Hurst RC .50 .15
❑ B59 Mac Suzuki RC 1.00 .30
❑ B60 Mike Moore .25 .07
❑ B61 Alan Benes RC .50 .15
❑ B62 Tony Clark RC 1.50 .45
❑ B63 Edgar Renteria RC 5.00 1.50
❑ B64 Trey Beamon .25 .07
❑ B65 LaTroy Hawkins RC 1.50 .45
❑ B66 Wayne Gomes RC 1.00 .30
❑ B67 Ray McDavid .25 .07
❑ B68 John Dettmer .25 .07
❑ B69 Willie Greene .25 .07
❑ B70 Dave Stevens .25 .07
❑ B71 Kevin Orie RC .25 .07
❑ B72 Chad Ogea .25 .07
❑ B73 Ben Van Ryn RC .50 .15
❑ B74 Kym Ashworth RC .50 .15
❑ B75 Dmitri Young .50 .15
❑ B76 Herbert Perry RC 1.00 .30
❑ B77 Joey Eischen .25 .07
❑ B78 Arquimedez Pozo RC .50 .15
❑ B79 Ugueth Urbina .25 .07
❑ B80 Keith Williams RC .50 .15
❑ B81 John Frascatore RC .50 .15
❑ B82 Garey Ingram RC .50 .15
❑ B83 Aaron Small .50 .15
❑ B84 Olmedo Saenz RC .50 .15
❑ B85 Jesus Tavarez RC .50 .15
❑ B86 Jose Silva RC 1.00 .30
❑ B87 Jay Witasick RC .50 .15
❑ B88 Jay Maldonado RC .50 .15
❑ B89 Keith Heberling RC .50 .15
❑ B90 Rusty Greer RC 1.50 .45
❑ R1 Paul Molitor .75 .23
❑ R2 Eddie Murray 1.25 .35
❑ R3 Ozzie Smith 2.00 .60
❑ R4 Rickey Henderson 1.25 .35
❑ R5 Lee Smith .50 .15
❑ R6 Dave Winfield .50 .15
❑ R7 Roberto Alomar .75 .23
❑ R8 Matt Williams .50 .15
❑ R9 Mark Grace .75 .23
❑ R10 Lance Johnson .25 .07
❑ R11 Darren Daulton .50 .15
❑ R12 Tom Glavine .75 .23
❑ R13 Gary Sheffield .50 .15
❑ R14 Rod Beck .25 .07
❑ R15 Fred McGriff .75 .23
❑ R16 Joe Carter .50 .15
❑ R17 Dante Bichette .50 .15
❑ R18 Danny Tartabull .25 .07
❑ R19 Juan Gonzalez .50 .15
❑ R20 Steve Avery .25 .07
❑ R21 John Wetteland .50 .15
❑ R22 Ben McDonald .25 .07
❑ R23 Jack McDowell .25 .07
❑ R24 Jose Canseco .75 .23
❑ R25 Tim Salmon .75 .23
❑ R26 Wilson Alvarez .25 .07
❑ R27 Gregg Jefferies .25 .07
❑ R28 John Burkett .25 .07
❑ R29 Greg Vaughn .25 .07
❑ R30 Robin Ventura .50 .15
❑ R31 Paul O'Neill .75 .23
❑ R32 Cecil Fielder .50 .15
❑ R33 Kevin Mitchell .25 .07
❑ R34 Jeff Conine .50 .15
❑ R35 Carlos Baerga .25 .07
❑ R36 Greg Maddux 2.00 .60
❑ R37 Roger Clemens 2.50 .75
❑ R38 Deion Sanders .75 .23

❑ R39 Delino DeShields .25 .07
❑ R40 Ken Griffey Jr. 2.00 .60
❑ R41 Albert Belle .50 .15
❑ R42 Wade Boggs .75 .23
❑ R43 Andres Galarraga .50 .15
❑ R44 Aaron Sele .25 .07
❑ R45 Don Mattingly 3.00 .90
❑ R46 David Cone .50 .15
❑ R47 Len Dykstra .50 .15
❑ R48 Brett Butler .50 .15
❑ R49 Bill Swift .25 .07
❑ R50 Bobby Bonilla .50 .15
❑ R51 Rafael Palmeiro .75 .23
❑ R52 Moises Alou .50 .15
❑ R53 Jeff Bagwell .75 .23
❑ R54 Mike Mussina .75 .23
❑ R55 Frank Thomas 1.25 .35
❑ R56 Jose Rijo .25 .07
❑ R57 Ruben Sierra .25 .07
❑ R58 Randy Myers .25 .07
❑ R59 Barry Bonds 3.00 .90
❑ R60 Jimmy Key .50 .15
❑ R61 Travis Fryman .50 .15
❑ R62 John Olerud .50 .15
❑ R63 David Justice .50 .15
❑ R64 Ray Lankford .50 .15
❑ R65 Bob Tewksbury .25 .07
❑ R66 Chuck Carr .25 .07
❑ R67 Jay Buhner .50 .15
❑ R68 Kenny Lofton .50 .15
❑ R69 Marquis Grissom .50 .15
❑ R70 Sammy Sosa 1.25 .35
❑ R71 Cal Ripken 4.00 1.20
❑ R72 Ellis Burks .50 .15
❑ R73 Jeff Montgomery .25 .07
❑ R74 Julio Franco .50 .15
❑ R75 Kirby Puckett 1.25 .35
❑ R76 Larry Walker .50 .15
❑ R77 Andy Van Slyke .75 .23
❑ R78 Tony Gwynn 1.50 .45
❑ R79 Will Clark .75 .23
❑ R80 Mo Vaughn .50 .15
❑ R81 Mike Piazza 2.50 .75
❑ R82 James Mouton .25 .07
❑ R83 Carlos Delgado .75 .23
❑ R84 Ryan Klesko .50 .15
❑ R85 Javier Lopez .50 .15
❑ R86 Raul Mondesi .50 .15
❑ R87 Cliff Floyd .50 .15
❑ R88 Manny Ramirez 1.25 .35
❑ R89 Hector Carrasco .25 .07
❑ R90 Jeff Granger .25 .07
❑ X91 Frank Thomas / Dmitri Young .75 .23
❑ X92 Fred McGriff / Brooks Kieschnick .50 .15
❑ X93 Matt Williams / Shane Andrews .25 .07
❑ X94 Cal Ripken / Kevin Orie 2.00 .60
❑ X95 Barry Larkin / Derek Jeter 2.00 .60
❑ X96 Ken Griffey Jr. / Johnny Damon 1.00 .30
❑ X97 Barry Bonds / Rondell White 1.50 .45
❑ X98 Albert Belle / Jimmy Hurst .50 .15
❑ X99 Raul Mondesi / Ruben Rivera RC .50 .15
❑ X100 Roger Clemens / Scott Ruffcorn 1.25 .35
❑ X101 Greg Maddux / John Wasdin 1.25 .35
❑ X102 Tim Salmon / Chad Mottola .75 .23
❑ X103 Carlos Baerga / Arquimedez Pozo .25 .07
❑ X104 Mike Piazza / Bobby Hughes 1.25 .35
❑ X105 Carlos Delgado / Melvin Nieves .75 .23
❑ X106 Javier Lopez / Jorge Posada 2.50 .75
❑ X107 Manny Ramirez / Jose Malave 1.25 .35
❑ X108 Travis Fryman / Chipper Jones .75 .23
❑ X109 Steve Avery / Bill Pulsipher .25 .07
❑ X110 John Olerud / Shawn Green 1.25 .35

1995 Bowman's Best

	Nm-Mt	Ex-Mt
COMPLETE SET (195)	250.00	75.00
COMMON CARD (B1-R90)	.50	.15
COMMON CARD (X1-X15)	.50	.15

❑ B1 Derek Jeter 3.00 .90
❑ B2 Vladimir Guerrero RC 80.00 24.00
❑ B3 Bob Abreu RC 15.00 4.50
❑ B4 Chan Ho Park .50 .15
❑ B5 Paul Wilson .50 .15
❑ B6 Chad Ogea .50 .15
❑ B7 Andruw Jones RC 50.00 15.00
❑ B8 Brian Barber .50 .15
❑ B9 Andy Larkin .50 .15
❑ B10 Richie Sexson RC 12.00 3.60
❑ B11 Everett Stull .50 .15
❑ B12 Brooks Kieschnick .50 .15
❑ B13 Matt Murray .50 .15
❑ B14 John Wasdin .50 .15
❑ B15 Shannon Stewart .50 .15
❑ B16 Luis Ortiz .50 .15
❑ B17 Marc Kroon .50 .15
❑ B18 Todd Greene .50 .15
❑ B19 Juan Acevedo RC 1.00 .30
❑ B20 Tony Clark .50 .15
❑ B21 Jermaine Dye .50 .15
❑ B22 Derrek Lee 1.25 .35
❑ B23 Pat Watkins .50 .15
❑ B24 Pokey Reese .50 .15
❑ B25 Ben Grieve .50 .15
❑ B26 Julio Santana RC .50 .15
❑ B27 Felix Rodriguez RC 2.00 .60
❑ B28 Paul Konerko 8.00 2.40
❑ B29 Nomar Garciaparra 5.00 1.50
❑ B30 Pat Ahearne .50 .15
❑ B31 Jason Schmidt 1.25 .35
❑ B32 Billy Wagner .75 .23
❑ B33 Rey Ordonez RC 3.00 .90
❑ B34 Curtis Goodwin .50 .15
❑ B35 Sergio Nunez RC 1.00 .30
❑ B36 Tim Belk .50 .15
❑ B37 Scott Elarton RC 2.00 .60
❑ B38 Jason Isringhausen .50 .15
❑ B39 Trot Nixon .75 .23
❑ B40 Sid Roberson RC 1.00 .30
❑ B41 Ron Villone .50 .15
❑ B42 Ruben Rivera .50 .15
❑ B43 Rick Huisman .50 .15
❑ B44 Todd Hollandsworth .50 .15
❑ B45 Johnny Damon .75 .23
❑ B46 Garret Anderson .50 .15
❑ B47 Jeff D'Amico .50 .15
❑ B48 Dustin Hermanson .50 .15
❑ B49 Juan Encarnacion RC 3.00 .90
❑ B50 Andy Pettitte .75 .23
❑ B51 Chris Stynes .50 .15
❑ B52 Troy Percival .50 .15
❑ B53 LaTroy Hawkins .50 .15
❑ B54 Roger Cedeno .50 .15
❑ B55 Alan Benes .50 .15
❑ B56 Karim Garcia RC 2.00 .60
❑ B57 Andrew Lorraine .50 .15
❑ B58 Gary Rath RC 1.00 .30
❑ B59 Bret Wagner .50 .15
❑ B60 Jeff Suppan .50 .15
❑ B61 Bill Pulsipher .50 .15
❑ B62 Jay Payton RC 3.00 .90
❑ B63 Alex Ochoa .50 .15
❑ B64 Ugueth Urbina .50 .15
❑ B65 Armando Benitez .50 .15
❑ B66 George Arias .50 .15
❑ B67 Raul Casanova RC 1.00 .30
❑ B68 Matt Drews .50 .15
❑ B69 Jimmy Haynes .50 .15
❑ B70 Jimmy Hurst .50 .15
❑ B71 C.J. Nitkowski .50 .15
❑ B72 Tommy Davis RC 1.00 .30
❑ B73 Bartolo Colon RC 8.00 2.40
❑ B74 Chris Carpenter RC 10.00 3.00
❑ B75 Trey Beamon .50 .15
❑ B76 Bryan Rekar .50 .15
❑ B77 James Baldwin .50 .15
❑ B78 Marc Valdes .50 .15
❑ B79 Tom Fordham RC 1.00 .30
❑ B80 Marc Newfield .50 .15
❑ B81 Angel Martinez .50 .15
❑ B82 Brian L. Hunter .50 .15
❑ B83 Jose Herrera .50 .15
❑ B84 Glenn Dishman RC 1.00 .30
❑ B85 Jacob Cruz RC 2.00 .60
❑ B86 Paul Shuey .50 .15
❑ B87 Scott Rolen RC 25.00 7.50
❑ B88 Doug Million .50 .15
❑ B89 Desi Relaford .50 .15
❑ B90 Michael Tucker .50 .15
❑ R1 Randy Johnson 1.25 .35
❑ R2 Joe Carter .50 .15
❑ R3 Chili Davis .50 .15
❑ R4 Moises Alou .50 .15
❑ R5 Gary Sheffield .50 .15
❑ R6 Kevin Appier .50 .15
❑ R7 Denny Neagle .50 .15
❑ R8 Ruben Sierra .50 .15
❑ R9 Darren Daulton .50 .15
❑ R10 Cal Ripken 4.00 1.20
❑ R11 Bobby Bonilla .50 .15
❑ R12 Manny Ramirez .75 .23
❑ R13 Barry Bonds 3.00 .90
❑ R14 Eric Karros .50 .15
❑ R15 Greg Maddux 2.00 .60
❑ R16 Jeff Bagwell .75 .23
❑ R17 Paul Molitor .75 .23
❑ R18 Ray Lankford .50 .15
❑ R19 Mark Grace .75 .23
❑ R20 Kenny Lofton .50 .15
❑ R21 Tony Gwynn 1.50 .45
❑ R22 Will Clark .75 .23
❑ R23 Roger Clemens 2.50 .75
❑ R24 Dante Bichette .50 .15
❑ R25 Barry Larkin .75 .23
❑ R26 Wade Boggs .75 .23
❑ R27 Kirby Puckett 1.25 .35
❑ R28 Cecil Fielder .50 .15
❑ R29 Jose Canseco .75 .23
❑ R30 Juan Gonzalez .50 .15
❑ R31 David Cone .50 .15
❑ R32 Craig Biggio .75 .23
❑ R33 Tim Salmon .75 .23
❑ R34 David Justice .50 .15
❑ R35 Sammy Sosa 1.25 .35
❑ R36 Mike Piazza 2.00 .60
❑ R37 Carlos Baerga .50 .15
❑ R38 Jeff Conine .50 .15
❑ R39 Rafael Palmeiro .75 .23
❑ R40 Bret Saberhagen .50 .15
❑ R41 Len Dykstra .50 .15
❑ R42 Mo Vaughn .50 .15
❑ R43 Wally Joyner .50 .15
❑ R44 Chuck Knoblauch .50 .15
❑ R45 Robin Ventura .50 .15
❑ R46 Don Mattingly 3.00 .90
❑ R47 Dave Hollins .50 .15
❑ R48 Andy Benes .50 .15
❑ R49 Ken Griffey Jr. 2.00 .60
❑ R50 Albert Belle .50 .15

❑ R51 Matt Williams .50 .15
❑ R52 Rondell White .50 .15
❑ R53 Raul Mondesi .50 .15
❑ R54 Brian Jordan .50 .15
❑ R55 Greg Vaughn .50 .15
❑ R56 Fred McGriff .75 .23
❑ R57 Roberto Alomar .75 .23
❑ R58 Dennis Eckersley .50 .15
❑ R59 Lee Smith .50 .15
❑ R60 Eddie Murray 1.25 .35
❑ R61 Kenny Rogers .50 .15
❑ R62 Ron Gant .50 .15
❑ R63 Larry Walker .50 .15
❑ R64 Chad Curtis .50 .15
❑ R65 Frank Thomas 1.25 .35
❑ R66 Paul O'Neill .75 .23
❑ R67 Kevin Seitzer .50 .15
❑ R68 Marquis Grissom .50 .15
❑ R69 Mark McGwire 4.00 1.20
❑ R70 Travis Fryman .50 .15
❑ R71 Andres Galarraga .50 .15
❑ R72 Carlos Perez RC 2.00 .60
❑ R73 Tyler Green .50 .15
❑ R74 Marty Cordova .50 .15
❑ R75 Shawn Green .50 .15
❑ R76 Vaughn Eshelman .50 .15
❑ R77 John Mabry .50 .15
❑ R78 Jason Bates .50 .15
❑ R79 Jon Nunnally .50 .15
❑ R80 Ray Durham .50 .15
❑ R81 Edgardo Alfonzo .50 .15
❑ R82 Esteban Loaiza .50 .15
❑ R83 Hideo Nomo RC 8.00 2.40
❑ R84 Orlando Miller .50 .15
❑ R85 Alex Gonzalez .50 .15
❑ R86 M.Grudzielanek RC 3.00 .90
❑ R87 Julian Tavarez .50 .15
❑ R88 Benji Gil .50 .15
❑ R89 Quilvio Veras .50 .15
❑ R90 Ricky Bottalico .50 .15
❑ X1 Ben Davis RC 1.50 .45
Ivan Rodriguez
❑ X2 Mark Redman RC 1.50 .45
Manny Ramirez
❑ X3 Reggie Taylor RC 1.50 .45
Deion Sanders
❑ X4 Ryan Jaroncyk RC .50 .15
Shawn Green
❑ X5 Juan LeBron RC 8.00 2.40
Juan Gonzalez UER
Card pictures Carlos Beltran instead of Juan LeBron.
❑ X6 Tony McKnight RC .50 .15
Craig Biggio
❑ X7 Michael Barrett RC 1.50 .45
Travis Fryman
❑ X8 Corey Jenkins RC .50 .15
Mo Vaughn
❑ X9 Ruben Rivera 1.25 .35
Frank Thomas
❑ X10 Curtis Goodwin .50 .15
Kenny Lofton
❑ X11 Brian L. Hunter .75 .23
Tony Gwynn
❑ X12 Todd Greene 1.25 .35
Ken Griffey Jr.
❑ X13 Karim Garcia .50 .15
Matt Williams
❑ X14 Billy Wagner .75 .23
Randy Johnson
❑ X15 Pat Watkins .75 .23
Jeff Bagwell

1996 Bowman's Best

	Nm-Mt	Ex-Mt
COMPLETE SET (180)	40.00	12.00

❑ 1 Hideo Nomo 1.00 .30
❑ 2 Edgar Martinez .60 .18
❑ 3 Cal Ripken 3.00 .90
❑ 4 Wade Boggs .60 .18
❑ 5 Cecil Fielder .40 .12
❑ 6 Albert Belle .40 .12
❑ 7 Chipper Jones 1.00 .30
❑ 8 Ryne Sandberg 1.50 .45

❑ 9 Tim Salmon .60 .18
❑ 10 Barry Bonds 2.50 .75
❑ 11 Ken Caminiti .40 .12
❑ 12 Ron Gant .40 .12
❑ 13 Frank Thomas 1.00 .30
❑ 14 Dante Bichette .40 .12
❑ 15 Jason Kendall .40 .12
❑ 16 Mo Vaughn .40 .12
❑ 17 Rey Ordonez .40 .12
❑ 18 Henry Rodriguez .40 .12
❑ 19 Ryan Klesko .40 .12
❑ 20 Jeff Bagwell .60 .18
❑ 21 Randy Johnson 1.00 .30
❑ 22 Jim Edmonds .40 .12
❑ 23 Kenny Lofton .40 .12
❑ 24 Andy Pettitte .60 .18
❑ 25 Brady Anderson .40 .12
❑ 26 Mike Piazza 1.50 .45
❑ 27 Greg Vaughn .40 .12
❑ 28 Joe Carter .40 .12
❑ 29 Jason Giambi .40 .12
❑ 30 Ivan Rodriguez .60 .18
❑ 31 Jeff Conine .40 .12
❑ 32 Rafael Palmeiro .60 .18
❑ 33 Roger Clemens UER 2.00 .60
Actually card #32
❑ 34 Chuck Knoblauch .40 .12
❑ 35 Reggie Sanders .40 .12
❑ 36 Andres Galarraga .40 .12
❑ 37 Paul O'Neill .60 .18
❑ 38 Tony Gwynn 1.25 .35
❑ 39 Paul Wilson .40 .12
❑ 40 Garret Anderson .40 .12
❑ 41 David Justice .40 .12
❑ 42 Eddie Murray 1.00 .30
❑ 43 Mike Grace RC .50 .15
❑ 44 Marty Cordova .40 .12
❑ 45 Kevin Appier .40 .12
❑ 46 Raul Mondesi .40 .12
❑ 47 Jim Thome .60 .18
❑ 48 Sammy Sosa 1.00 .30
❑ 49 Craig Biggio .60 .18
❑ 50 Marquis Grissom .40 .12
❑ 51 Alan Benes .40 .12
❑ 52 Manny Ramirez .60 .18
❑ 53 Gary Sheffield .40 .12
❑ 54 Mike Mussina .60 .18
❑ 55 Robin Ventura .40 .12
❑ 56 Johnny Damon .60 .18
❑ 57 Jose Canseco .60 .18
❑ 58 Juan Gonzalez .40 .12
❑ 59 Tino Martinez .60 .18
❑ 60 Brian Hunter .40 .12
❑ 61 Fred McGriff .60 .18
❑ 62 Jay Buhner .40 .12
❑ 63 Carlos Delgado .40 .12
❑ 64 Moises Alou .40 .12
❑ 65 Roberto Alomar .60 .18
❑ 66 Barry Larkin .60 .18
❑ 67 Vinny Castilla .40 .12
❑ 68 Ray Durham .40 .12
❑ 69 Travis Fryman .40 .12
❑ 70 Jason Isringhausen .40 .12
❑ 71 Ken Griffey Jr. 1.50 .45
❑ 72 John Smoltz .60 .18
❑ 73 Matt Williams .40 .12
❑ 74 Chan Ho Park .40 .12
❑ 75 Mark McGwire 3.00 .90
❑ 76 Jeffrey Hammonds .40 .12
❑ 77 Will Clark .60 .18
❑ 78 Kirby Puckett 1.00 .30
❑ 79 Derek Jeter 2.50 .75
❑ 80 Derek Bell .40 .12
❑ 81 Eric Karros .40 .12
❑ 82 Len Dykstra .40 .12
❑ 83 Larry Walker .40 .12
❑ 84 Mark Grudzielanek .40 .12
❑ 85 Greg Maddux 1.50 .45
❑ 86 Carlos Baerga .40 .12
❑ 87 Paul Molitor .60 .18
❑ 88 John Valentin .40 .12
❑ 89 Mark Grace .60 .18
❑ 90 Ray Lankford .40 .12
❑ 91 Andruw Jones 1.50 .45
❑ 92 Nomar Garciaparra 2.00 .60
❑ 93 Alex Ochoa .40 .12
❑ 94 Derrick Gibson .40 .12
❑ 95 Jeff D'Amico .40 .12
❑ 96 Ruben Rivera .40 .12
❑ 97 Vladimir Guerrero 2.00 .60
❑ 98 Pokey Reese .40 .12
❑ 99 Richard Hidalgo .40 .12
❑ 100 Bartolo Colon 1.00 .30
❑ 101 Karim Garcia .40 .12
❑ 102 Ben Davis .40 .12
❑ 103 Jay Powell .40 .12
❑ 104 Chris Snopek .40 .12
❑ 105 Glendon Rusch RC 1.00 .30
❑ 106 Enrique Wilson .40 .12
❑ 107 A.Alfonseca RC 1.00 .30
❑ 108 Wilton Guerrero RC 1.00 .30
❑ 109 Jose Guillen RC 5.00 1.50
❑ 110 Miguel Mejia RC .50 .15
❑ 111 Jay Payton .40 .12
❑ 112 Scott Elarton .40 .12
❑ 113 Brooks Kieschnick .40 .12
❑ 114 Dustin Hermanson .40 .12
❑ 115 Roger Cedeno .40 .12
❑ 116 Matt Wagner .40 .12
❑ 117 Lee Daniels .40 .12
❑ 118 Ben Grieve .40 .12
❑ 119 Ugueth Urbina .40 .12
❑ 120 Danny Graves .40 .12
❑ 121 Dan Donato RC .50 .15
❑ 122 Matt Ruebel RC .50 .15
❑ 123 Mark Sievert RC .50 .15
❑ 124 Chris Stynes .40 .12
❑ 125 Jeff Abbott .40 .12
❑ 126 Rocky Coppinger RC .50 .15
❑ 127 Jermaine Dye .40 .12
❑ 128 Todd Greene .40 .12
❑ 129 Chris Carpenter .60 .18
❑ 130 Edgar Renteria .40 .12
❑ 131 Matt Drews .40 .12
❑ 132 Edgard Velazquez RC .50 .15
❑ 133 Casey Whitten .40 .12
❑ 134 Ryan Jones RC .50 .15
❑ 135 Todd Walker .40 .12
❑ 136 Geoff Jenkins RC 1.50 .45
❑ 137 Matt Morris RC 4.00 1.20
❑ 138 Richie Sexson .60 .18
❑ 139 Todd Dunwoody RC .50 .15
❑ 140 Gabe Alvarez RC .50 .15
❑ 141 J.J. Johnson .40 .12
❑ 142 Shannon Stewart .40 .12
❑ 143 Brad Fullmer .40 .12
❑ 144 Julio Santana .40 .12
❑ 145 Scott Rolen 1.00 .30
❑ 146 Amaury Telemaco .40 .12
❑ 147 Trey Beamon .40 .12
❑ 148 Billy Wagner .40 .12
❑ 149 Todd Hollandsworth .40 .12
❑ 150 Doug Million .40 .12
❑ 151 Javier Valentin RC .50 .15
❑ 152 Wes Helms RC 1.50 .45
❑ 153 Jeff Suppan .40 .12
❑ 154 Luis Castillo RC 1.50 .45
❑ 155 Bob Abreu 1.00 .30
❑ 156 Paul Konerko 1.00 .30
❑ 157 Jamey Wright .40 .12
❑ 158 Eddie Pearson .40 .12
❑ 159 Jimmy Haynes .40 .12
❑ 160 Derrek Lee .60 .18
❑ 161 Damian Moss .40 .12

#	Player	Nm-Mt	Ex-Mt
❑ 162	Carlos Guillen RC	5.00	1.50
❑ 163	Chris Fussell RC	.50	.15
❑ 164	Mike Sweeney RC	4.00	1.20
❑ 165	Donnie Sadler	.40	.12
❑ 166	Desi Relaford	.40	.12
❑ 167	Steve Gibralter	.40	.12
❑ 168	Neifi Perez	.40	.12
❑ 169	Antone Williamson	.40	.12
❑ 170	Marty Janzen RC	.50	.15
❑ 171	Todd Helton	2.00	.60
❑ 172	Raul Ibanez RC	1.50	.45
❑ 173	Bill Selby	.40	.12
❑ 174	Shane Monahan RC	.50	.15
❑ 175	Robin Jennings	.40	.12
❑ 176	Bobby Chouinard	.40	.12
❑ 177	Einar Diaz	.40	.12
❑ 178	Jason Thompson RC	.40	.12
❑ 179	Rafael Medina RC	.50	.15
❑ 180	Kevin Orie	.40	.12
❑ NNO	Mickey Mantle 1952 Bowman Atomic Ref.	10.00	3.00
❑ NNO	Mickey Mantle 1952 Bowman Refractor	5.00	1.50
❑ NNO	Mickey Mantle 1952 Bowman Chrome	2.50	.75

1997 Bowman's Best

	Nm-Mt	Ex-Mt
COMPLETE SET (200)	40.00	12.00

#	Player	Nm-Mt	Ex-Mt
❑ 1	Ken Griffey Jr.	1.50	.45
❑ 2	Cecil Fielder	.40	.12
❑ 3	Albert Belle	.40	.12
❑ 4	Todd Hundley	.40	.12
❑ 5	Mike Piazza	1.50	.45
❑ 6	Matt Williams	.40	.12
❑ 7	Mo Vaughn	.40	.12
❑ 8	Ryne Sandberg	1.50	.45
❑ 9	Chipper Jones	1.00	.30
❑ 10	Edgar Martinez	.60	.18
❑ 11	Kenny Lofton	.40	.12
❑ 12	Ron Gant	.40	.12
❑ 13	Moises Alou	.40	.12
❑ 14	Pat Hentgen	.40	.12
❑ 15	Steve Finley	.40	.12
❑ 16	Mark Grace	.60	.18
❑ 17	Jay Buhner	.40	.12
❑ 18	Jeff Conine	.40	.12
❑ 19	Jim Edmonds	.40	.12
❑ 20	Todd Hollandsworth	.40	.12
❑ 21	Andy Pettitte	.60	.18
❑ 22	Jim Thome	.60	.18
❑ 23	Eric Young	.40	.12
❑ 24	Ray Lankford	.40	.12
❑ 25	Marquis Grissom	.40	.12
❑ 26	Tony Clark	.40	.12
❑ 27	Jermaine Allensworth	.40	.12
❑ 28	Ellis Burks	.40	.12
❑ 29	Tony Gwynn	1.25	.35
❑ 30	Barry Larkin	.60	.18
❑ 31	John Olerud	.40	.12
❑ 32	Mariano Rivera	.60	.18
❑ 33	Paul Molitor	.60	.18
❑ 34	Ken Caminiti	.40	.12
❑ 35	Gary Sheffield	.40	.12
❑ 36	Al Martin	.40	.12
❑ 37	John Valentin	.40	.12
❑ 38	Frank Thomas	1.00	.30
❑ 39	John Jaha	.40	.12
❑ 40	Greg Maddux	1.50	.45
❑ 41	Alex Fernandez	.40	.12
❑ 42	Dean Palmer	.40	.12
❑ 43	Bernie Williams	.60	.18
❑ 44	Deion Sanders	.60	.18
❑ 45	Mark McGwire	3.00	.90
❑ 46	Brian Jordan	.40	.12
❑ 47	Bernard Gilkey	.40	.12
❑ 48	Will Clark	.60	.18
❑ 49	Kevin Appier	.40	.12
❑ 50	Tom Glavine	.60	.18
❑ 51	Chuck Knoblauch	.40	.12
❑ 52	Rondell White	.40	.12
❑ 53	Greg Vaughn	.40	.12
❑ 54	Mike Mussina	.60	.18
❑ 55	Brian McRae	.40	.12
❑ 56	Chili Davis	.40	.12
❑ 57	Wade Boggs	.60	.18
❑ 58	Jeff Bagwell	.60	.18
❑ 59	Roberto Alomar	.60	.18
❑ 60	Dennis Eckersley	.40	.12
❑ 61	Ryan Klesko	.40	.12
❑ 62	Manny Ramirez	.60	.18
❑ 63	John Wetteland	.40	.12
❑ 64	Cal Ripken	3.00	.90
❑ 65	Edgar Renteria	.40	.12
❑ 66	Tino Martinez	.60	.18
❑ 67	Larry Walker	.40	.12
❑ 68	Gregg Jefferies	.40	.12
❑ 69	Lance Johnson	.40	.12
❑ 70	Carlos Delgado	.40	.12
❑ 71	Craig Biggio	.60	.18
❑ 72	Jose Canseco	.60	.18
❑ 73	Barry Bonds	2.50	.75
❑ 74	Juan Gonzalez	.40	.12
❑ 75	Eric Karros	.40	.12
❑ 76	Reggie Sanders	.40	.12
❑ 77	Robin Ventura	.40	.12
❑ 78	Hideo Nomo	1.00	.30
❑ 79	David Justice	.40	.12
❑ 80	Vinny Castilla	.40	.12
❑ 81	Travis Fryman	.40	.12
❑ 82	Derek Jeter	2.50	.75
❑ 83	Sammy Sosa	1.00	.30
❑ 84	Ivan Rodriguez	.60	.18
❑ 85	Rafael Palmeiro	.60	.18
❑ 86	Roger Clemens	2.00	.60
❑ 87	Jason Giambi	.40	.12
❑ 88	Andres Galarraga	.40	.12
❑ 89	Jermaine Dye	.40	.12
❑ 90	Joe Carter	.40	.12
❑ 91	Brady Anderson	.40	.12
❑ 92	Derek Bell	.40	.12
❑ 93	Randy Johnson	1.00	.30
❑ 94	Fred McGriff	.60	.18
❑ 95	John Smoltz	.60	.18
❑ 96	Harold Baines	.40	.12
❑ 97	Raul Mondesi	.40	.12
❑ 98	Tim Salmon	.60	.18
❑ 99	Carlos Baerga	.40	.12
❑ 100	Dante Bichette	.40	.12
❑ 101	Vladimir Guerrero	1.00	.30
❑ 102	Richard Hidalgo	.40	.12
❑ 103	Paul Konerko	.60	.18
❑ 104	Alex Gonzalez RC	1.00	.30
❑ 105	Jason Dickson	.40	.12
❑ 106	Jose Rosado	.40	.12
❑ 107	Todd Walker	.40	.12
❑ 108	Seth Greisinger RC	.40	.12
❑ 109	Todd Helton	1.00	.30
❑ 110	Ben Davis	.40	.12
❑ 111	Bartolo Colon	.40	.12
❑ 112	Elieser Marrero	.40	.12
❑ 113	Jeff D'Amico	.40	.12
❑ 114	Miguel Tejada RC	10.00	3.00
❑ 115	Darin Erstad	.40	.12
❑ 116	Kris Benson RC	1.00	.30
❑ 117	Adrian Beltre RC	5.00	1.50
❑ 118	Neifi Perez	.40	.12
❑ 119	Pokey Reese	.40	.12
❑ 120	Carl Pavano	.40	.12
❑ 121	Juan Melo	.40	.12
❑ 122	Kevin McGlinchy RC	.40	.12
❑ 123	Pat Cline	.40	.12
❑ 124	Felix Heredia RC	.40	.12
❑ 125	Aaron Boone	.40	.12
❑ 126	Glendon Rusch	.40	.12
❑ 127	Mike Cameron	.40	.12
❑ 128	Justin Thompson	.40	.12
❑ 129	Chad Hermansen RC	.60	.18
❑ 130	Sidney Ponson RC	1.00	.30
❑ 131	Willie Martinez RC	.40	.12
❑ 132	Paul Wilder RC	.40	.12
❑ 133	Geoff Jenkins	.40	.12
❑ 134	Roy Halladay RC	3.00	.90
❑ 135	Carlos Guillen	.40	.12
❑ 136	Tony Batista	.40	.12
❑ 137	Todd Greene	.40	.12
❑ 138	Luis Castillo	.40	.12
❑ 139	Jimmy Anderson RC	.40	.12
❑ 140	Edgard Velazquez	.40	.12
❑ 141	Chris Snopek	.40	.12
❑ 142	Ruben Rivera	.40	.12
❑ 143	Javier Valentin	.40	.12
❑ 144	Brian Rose	.40	.12
❑ 145	Fernando Tatis RC	.60	.18
❑ 146	Dean Crow RC	.40	.12
❑ 147	Karim Garcia	.40	.12
❑ 148	Dante Powell	.40	.12
❑ 149	Hideki Irabu RC	.60	.18
❑ 150	Matt Morris	.40	.12
❑ 151	Wes Helms	.40	.12
❑ 152	Russ Johnson	.40	.12
❑ 153	Jarrod Washburn	.40	.12
❑ 154	Kerry Wood RC	8.00	2.40
❑ 155	Joe Fontenot RC	.40	.12
❑ 156	Eugene Kingsale	.40	.12
❑ 157	Terrence Long	.40	.12
❑ 158	Calvin Maduro	.40	.12
❑ 159	Jeff Suppan	.40	.12
❑ 160	DaRond Stovall	.40	.12
❑ 161	Mark Redman	.40	.12
❑ 162	Ken Cloude RC	.60	.18
❑ 163	Bobby Estalella	.40	.12
❑ 164	Abraham Nunez RC	.40	.12
❑ 165	Derrick Gibson	.40	.12
❑ 166	Mike Drumright RC	.40	.12
❑ 167	Katsuhiro Maeda	.40	.12
❑ 168	Jeff Liefer	.40	.12
❑ 169	Ben Grieve	.40	.12
❑ 170	Bob Abreu	.60	.18
❑ 171	Shannon Stewart	.40	.12
❑ 172	Braden Looper RC	.40	.12
❑ 173	Brant Brown	.40	.12
❑ 174	Marlon Anderson	.40	.12
❑ 175	Brad Fullmer	.40	.12
❑ 176	Carlos Beltran	2.00	.60
❑ 177	Nomar Garciaparra	1.50	.45
❑ 178	Derrek Lee	.60	.18
❑ 179	Val.De Los Santos RC	.40	.12
❑ 180	Dmitri Young	.40	.12
❑ 181	Jamey Wright	.40	.12
❑ 182	Hiram Bocachica RC	.60	.18
❑ 183	Wilton Guerrero	.40	.12
❑ 184	Chris Carpenter	.40	.12
❑ 185	Scott Spiezio	.40	.12
❑ 186	Andruw Jones	.60	.18
❑ 187	Travis Lee RC	.60	.18
❑ 188	Jose Cruz Jr. RC	1.00	.30
❑ 189	Jose Guillen	.40	.12
❑ 190	Jeff Abbott	.40	.12
❑ 191	Ricky Ledee RC	.60	.18
❑ 192	Mike Sweeney	.40	.12
❑ 193	Donnie Sadler	.40	.12
❑ 194	Scott Rolen	.60	.18
❑ 195	Kevin Orie	.40	.12
❑ 196	Jason Conti RC	.40	.12
❑ 197	Mark Kotsay RC	1.50	.45
❑ 198	Eric Milton RC	1.00	.30
❑ 199	Russell Branyan	.40	.12
❑ 200	Alex Sanchez RC	.60	.18

1998 Bowman's Best

	Nm-Mt	Ex-Mt
COMPLETE SET (200)	40.00	12.00

#	Player	Nm-Mt	Ex-Mt
❑ 1	Mark McGwire	2.50	.75
❑ 2	Jeromy Burnitz	.40	.12
❑ 3	Barry Bonds	2.50	.75
❑ 4	Dante Bichette	.40	.12

❑ 5 Chipper Jones 1.00 .30
❑ 6 Frank Thomas 1.00 .30
❑ 7 Kevin Brown .60 .18
❑ 8 Juan Gonzalez .40 .12
❑ 9 Jay Buhner .40 .12
❑ 10 Chuck Knoblauch .40 .12
❑ 11 Cal Ripken 3.00 .90
❑ 12 Matt Williams .40 .12
❑ 13 Jim Edmonds .40 .12
❑ 14 Manny Ramirez .60 .18
❑ 15 Tony Clark .40 .12
❑ 16 Mo Vaughn .40 .12
❑ 17 Bernie Williams .60 .18
❑ 18 Scott Rolen .60 .18
❑ 19 Gary Sheffield .40 .12
❑ 20 Albert Belle .40 .12
❑ 21 Mike Piazza 1.50 .45
❑ 22 John Olerud .40 .12
❑ 23 Tony Gwynn 1.25 .35
❑ 24 Jay Bell .40 .12
❑ 25 Jose Cruz Jr. .40 .12
❑ 26 Justin Thompson .40 .12
❑ 27 Ken Griffey Jr. 1.50 .45
❑ 28 Sandy Alomar Jr. .40 .12
❑ 29 Mark Grudzielanek .40 .12
❑ 30 Mark Grace .60 .18
❑ 31 Ron Gant .40 .12
❑ 32 Javy Lopez .40 .12
❑ 33 Jeff Bagwell .60 .18
❑ 34 Fred McGriff .60 .18
❑ 35 Rafael Palmeiro .60 .18
❑ 36 Vinny Castilla .40 .12
❑ 37 Andy Benes .40 .12
❑ 38 Pedro Martinez .60 .18
❑ 39 Andy Pettitte .60 .18
❑ 40 Marty Cordova .40 .12
❑ 41 Rusty Greer .40 .12
❑ 42 Kevin Orie .40 .12
❑ 43 Chan Ho Park .40 .12
❑ 44 Ryan Klesko .40 .12
❑ 45 Alex Rodriguez 1.50 .45
❑ 46 Travis Fryman .40 .12
❑ 47 Jeff King .40 .12
❑ 48 Roger Clemens 2.00 .60
❑ 49 Darin Erstad .40 .12
❑ 50 Brady Anderson .40 .12
❑ 51 Jason Kendall .40 .12
❑ 52 John Valentin .40 .12
❑ 53 Ellis Burks .40 .12
❑ 54 Brian Hunter .40 .12
❑ 55 Paul O'Neill .60 .18
❑ 56 Ken Caminiti .40 .12
❑ 57 David Justice .40 .12
❑ 58 Eric Karros .40 .12
❑ 59 Pat Hentgen .40 .12
❑ 60 Greg Maddux 1.50 .45
❑ 61 Craig Biggio .60 .18
❑ 62 Edgar Martinez .60 .18
❑ 63 Mike Mussina .60 .18
❑ 64 Larry Walker .40 .12
❑ 65 Tino Martinez .60 .18
❑ 66 Jim Thome .60 .18
❑ 67 Tom Glavine .60 .18
❑ 68 Raul Mondesi .40 .12
❑ 69 Marquis Grissom .40 .12
❑ 70 Randy Johnson 1.00 .30
❑ 71 Steve Finley .40 .12
❑ 72 Jose Guillen .40 .12
❑ 73 Nomar Garciaparra 1.50 .45
❑ 74 Wade Boggs .60 .18
❑ 75 Bobby Higginson .40 .12
❑ 76 Robin Ventura .40 .12
❑ 77 Derek Jeter 2.50 .75
❑ 78 Andruw Jones .60 .18
❑ 79 Ray Lankford .40 .12
❑ 80 Vladimir Guerrero 1.00 .30
❑ 81 Kenny Lofton .40 .12
❑ 82 Ivan Rodriguez .60 .18
❑ 83 Neifi Perez .40 .12
❑ 84 John Smoltz .60 .18
❑ 85 Tim Salmon .60 .18
❑ 86 Carlos Delgado .40 .12
❑ 87 Sammy Sosa 1.00 .30
❑ 88 Jaret Wright .40 .12
❑ 89 Roberto Alomar .60 .18
❑ 90 Paul Molitor .60 .18
❑ 91 Dean Palmer .40 .12
❑ 92 Barry Larkin .60 .18
❑ 93 Jason Giambi .40 .12
❑ 94 Curt Schilling .40 .12
❑ 95 Eric Young .40 .12
❑ 96 Denny Neagle .40 .12
❑ 97 Moises Alou .40 .12
❑ 98 Livan Hernandez .40 .12
❑ 99 Todd Hundley .40 .12
❑ 100 Andres Galarraga .40 .12
❑ 101 Travis Lee .40 .12
❑ 102 Lance Berkman .40 .12
❑ 103 Orlando Cabrera .40 .12
❑ 104 Mike Lowell RC 1.50 .45
❑ 105 Ben Grieve .40 .12
❑ 106 Jae Weong Seo RC 1.00 .30
❑ 107 Richie Sexson .40 .12
❑ 108 Eli Marrero .40 .12
❑ 109 Aramis Ramirez .40 .12
❑ 110 Paul Konerko .40 .12
❑ 111 Carl Pavano .40 .12
❑ 112 Brad Fullmer .40 .12
❑ 113 Matt Clement .40 .12
❑ 114 Donzell McDonald .40 .12
❑ 115 Todd Helton .60 .18
❑ 116 Mike Caruso .40 .12
❑ 117 Donnie Sadler .40 .12
❑ 118 Bruce Chen .40 .12
❑ 119 Jarrod Washburn .40 .12
❑ 120 Adrian Beltre .40 .12
❑ 121 Ryan Jackson RC .40 .12
❑ 122 Kevin Millar RC 1.50 .45
❑ 123 Corey Koskie RC 1.00 .30
❑ 124 Dermal Brown .40 .12
❑ 125 Kerry Wood .60 .18
❑ 126 Juan Melo .40 .12
❑ 127 Ramon Hernandez .40 .12
❑ 128 Roy Halladay .40 .12
❑ 129 Ron Wright .40 .12
❑ 130 Darnell McDonald RC .60 .18
❑ 131 Odalis Perez RC 1.50 .45
❑ 132 Alex Cora RC .60 .18
❑ 133 Justin Towle .40 .12
❑ 134 Juan Encarnacion .40 .12
❑ 135 Brian Rose .40 .12
❑ 136 Russell Branyan .40 .12
❑ 137 Cesar King RC .40 .12
❑ 138 Ruben Rivera .40 .12
❑ 139 Ricky Ledee .40 .12
❑ 140 Vernon Wells .40 .12
❑ 141 Luis Rivas RC 1.00 .30
❑ 142 Brent Butler .40 .12
❑ 143 Karim Garcia .40 .12
❑ 144 George Lombard .40 .12
❑ 145 Masato Yoshii RC 1.00 .30
❑ 146 Braden Looper .40 .12
❑ 147 Alex Sanchez .40 .12
❑ 148 Kris Benson .40 .12
❑ 149 Mark Kotsay .40 .12
❑ 150 Richard Hidalgo .40 .12
❑ 151 Scott Elarton .40 .12
❑ 152 Ryan Minor RC .40 .12
❑ 153 Troy Glaus RC 5.00 1.50
❑ 154 Carlos Lee RC 3.00 .90
❑ 155 Michael Coleman .40 .12
❑ 156 Jason Grilli RC .40 .12
❑ 157 Julio Ramirez RC .40 .12
❑ 158 Randy Wolf RC .60 .18
❑ 159 Ryan Brannan .40 .12
❑ 160 Edgard Clemente .40 .12
❑ 161 Miguel Tejada 1.00 .30
❑ 162 Chad Hermansen .40 .12
❑ 163 Ryan Anderson RC .60 .18
❑ 164 Ben Petrick .40 .12
❑ 165 Alex Gonzalez .40 .12
❑ 166 Ben Davis .40 .12
❑ 167 John Patterson .40 .12
❑ 168 Cliff Politte .40 .12
❑ 169 Randall Simon .40 .12
❑ 170 Javier Vazquez .40 .12
❑ 171 Kevin Witt .40 .12
❑ 172 Geoff Jenkins .40 .12
❑ 173 David Ortiz 3.00 .90
❑ 174 Derrick Gibson .40 .12
❑ 175 Abraham Nunez .40 .12
❑ 176 A.J. Hinch .40 .12
❑ 177 Ruben Mateo RC .60 .18
❑ 178 Magglio Ordonez RC 3.00 .90
❑ 179 Todd Dunwoody .40 .12
❑ 180 Daryle Ward .40 .12
❑ 181 Mike Kinkade RC .40 .12
❑ 182 Willie Martinez .40 .12
❑ 183 O.Hernandez RC 1.50 .45
❑ 184 Eric Milton .40 .12
❑ 185 Eric Chavez .40 .12
❑ 186 Damian Jackson .40 .12
❑ 187 Jim Parque RC .60 .18
❑ 188 Dan Reichert RC .60 .18
❑ 189 Mike Drumright .40 .12
❑ 190 Todd Walker .40 .12
❑ 191 Shane Monahan .40 .12
❑ 192 Derrek Lee .60 .18
❑ 193 Jeremy Giambi RC .60 .18
❑ 194 Dan McKinley RC .40 .12
❑ 195 Tony Armas Jr. RC .60 .18
❑ 196 Matt Anderson RC .60 .18
❑ 197 Jim Chamblee RC .40 .12
❑ 198 F.Cordero RC 1.00 .30
❑ 199 Calvin Pickering .40 .12
❑ 200 Reggie Taylor .40 .12

1999 Bowman's Best

	Nm-Mt	Ex-Mt
COMPLETE SET (200)	40.00	12.00
COMP.SET w/o SP's (150)	25.00	7.50
COMMON CARD (1-150)	.40	.12
COMMON (151-200)	.50	.15

❑ 1 Chipper Jones 1.00 .30
❑ 2 Brian Jordan .40 .12
❑ 3 David Justice .40 .12
❑ 4 Jason Kendall .40 .12
❑ 5 Mo Vaughn .40 .12
❑ 6 Jim Edmonds .40 .12
❑ 7 Wade Boggs .60 .18
❑ 8 Jeromy Burnitz .40 .12
❑ 9 Todd Hundley .40 .12
❑ 10 Rondell White .40 .12
❑ 11 Cliff Floyd .40 .12
❑ 12 Sean Casey .60 .18
❑ 13 Bernie Williams .60 .18
❑ 14 Dante Bichette .40 .12
❑ 15 Greg Vaughn .40 .12
❑ 16 Andres Galarraga .40 .12
❑ 17 Ray Durham .40 .12
❑ 18 Jim Thome .60 .18

Card	Nm-Mt	Ex-Mt
❑ 19 Gary Sheffield	.40	.12
❑ 20 Frank Thomas	1.00	.30
❑ 21 Orlando Hernandez	.40	.12
❑ 22 Ivan Rodriguez	.60	.18
❑ 23 Jose Cruz Jr.	.40	.12
❑ 24 Jason Giambi	.40	.12
❑ 25 Craig Biggio	.60	.18
❑ 26 Kerry Wood	.40	.12
❑ 27 Manny Ramirez	.60	.18
❑ 28 Curt Schilling	.40	.12
❑ 29 Mike Mussina	.60	.18
❑ 30 Tim Salmon	.60	.18
❑ 31 Mike Piazza	1.50	.45
❑ 32 Roberto Alomar	.60	.18
❑ 33 Larry Walker	.40	.12
❑ 34 Barry Larkin	.60	.18
❑ 35 Nomar Garciaparra	1.50	.45
❑ 36 Paul O'Neill	.60	.18
❑ 37 Todd Walker	.40	.12
❑ 38 Eric Karros	.40	.12
❑ 39 Brad Fullmer	.40	.12
❑ 40 John Olerud	.40	.12
❑ 41 Todd Helton	.60	.18
❑ 42 Raul Mondesi	.40	.12
❑ 43 Jose Canseco	.60	.18
❑ 44 Matt Williams	.40	.12
❑ 45 Ray Lankford	.40	.12
❑ 46 Carlos Delgado	.40	.12
❑ 47 Darin Erstad	.40	.12
❑ 48 Vladimir Guerrero	1.00	.30
❑ 49 Robin Ventura	.40	.12
❑ 50 Alex Rodriguez	1.50	.45
❑ 51 Vinny Castilla	.40	.12
❑ 52 Tony Clark	.40	.12
❑ 53 Pedro Martinez	.60	.18
❑ 54 Rafael Palmeiro	.60	.18
❑ 55 Scott Rolen	.60	.18
❑ 56 Tino Martinez	.60	.18
❑ 57 Tony Gwynn	1.25	.35
❑ 58 Barry Bonds	2.50	.75
❑ 59 Kenny Lofton	.40	.12
❑ 60 Javy Lopez	.40	.12
❑ 61 Mark Grace	.60	.18
❑ 62 Travis Lee	.40	.12
❑ 63 Kevin Brown	.60	.18
❑ 64 Al Leiter	.40	.12
❑ 65 Albert Belle	.40	.12
❑ 66 Sammy Sosa	1.00	.30
❑ 67 Greg Maddux	1.50	.45
❑ 68 Mark Kotsay	.40	.12
❑ 69 Dmitri Young	.40	.12
❑ 70 Mark McGwire	2.50	.75
❑ 71 Juan Gonzalez	.40	.12
❑ 72 Andruw Jones	.60	.18
❑ 73 Derek Jeter	2.50	.75
❑ 74 Randy Johnson	1.00	.30
❑ 75 Cal Ripken	3.00	.90
❑ 76 Shawn Green	.40	.12
❑ 77 Moises Alou	.40	.12
❑ 78 Tom Glavine	.60	.18
❑ 79 Sandy Alomar Jr.	.40	.12
❑ 80 Ken Griffey Jr.	1.50	.45
❑ 81 Ryan Klesko	.40	.12
❑ 82 Jeff Bagwell	.60	.18
❑ 83 Ben Grieve	.40	.12
❑ 84 John Smoltz	.60	.18
❑ 85 Roger Clemens	2.00	.60
❑ 86 Ken Griffey Jr. BP	1.00	.30
❑ 87 Roger Clemens BP	1.00	.30
❑ 88 Derek Jeter BP	1.25	.35
❑ 89 Nomar Garciaparra BP	.75	.23
❑ 90 Mark McGwire BP	1.25	.35
❑ 91 Sammy Sosa BP	.60	.18
❑ 92 Alex Rodriguez BP	.75	.23
❑ 93 Greg Maddux BP	.75	.23
❑ 94 Vladimir Guerrero BP	.60	.18
❑ 95 Chipper Jones BP	.60	.18
❑ 96 Kerry Wood BP	.40	.12
❑ 97 Ben Grieve BP	.40	.12
❑ 98 Tony Gwynn BP	.60	.18
❑ 99 Juan Gonzalez BP	.40	.12
❑ 100 Mike Piazza BP	.75	.23
❑ 101 Eric Chavez	.40	.12
❑ 102 Billy Koch	.40	.12
❑ 103 Dernell Stenson	.40	.12
❑ 104 Marlon Anderson	.40	.12
❑ 105 Ron Belliard	.40	.12
❑ 106 Bruce Chen	.40	.12
❑ 107 Carlos Beltran	.60	.18
❑ 108 Chad Hermansen	.40	.12
❑ 109 Ryan Anderson	.40	.12
❑ 110 Michael Barrett	.40	.12
❑ 111 Matt Clement	.40	.12
❑ 112 Ben Davis	.40	.12
❑ 113 Calvin Pickering	.40	.12
❑ 114 Brad Penny	.40	.12
❑ 115 Paul Konerko	.40	.12
❑ 116 Alex Gonzalez	.40	.12
❑ 117 George Lombard	.40	.12
❑ 118 John Patterson	.40	.12
❑ 119 Rob Bell	.40	.12
❑ 120 Ruben Mateo	.40	.12
❑ 121 Troy Glaus	.60	.18
❑ 122 Ryan Bradley	.40	.12
❑ 123 Carlos Lee	.40	.12
❑ 124 Gabe Kapler	.40	.12
❑ 125 Ramon Hernandez	.40	.12
❑ 126 Carlos Febles	.40	.12
❑ 127 Mitch Meluskey	.40	.12
❑ 128 Michael Cuddyer	.40	.12
❑ 129 Pablo Ozuna	.40	.12
❑ 130 Jayson Werth	.40	.12
❑ 131 Ricky Ledee	.40	.12
❑ 132 Jeremy Giambi	.40	.12
❑ 133 Danny Klassen	.40	.12
❑ 134 Mark DeRosa	.40	.12
❑ 135 Randy Wolf	.40	.12
❑ 136 Roy Halladay	.40	.12
❑ 137 Derrick Gibson	.40	.12
❑ 138 Ben Petrick	.40	.12
❑ 139 Warren Morris	.40	.12
❑ 140 Lance Berkman	.40	.12
❑ 141 Russell Branyan	.40	.12
❑ 142 Adrian Beltre	.40	.12
❑ 143 Juan Encarnacion	.40	.12
❑ 144 Fernando Seguignol	.40	.12
❑ 145 Corey Koskie	.40	.12
❑ 146 Preston Wilson	.40	.12
❑ 147 Homer Bush	.40	.12
❑ 148 Daryle Ward	.40	.12
❑ 149 Joe McEwing RC	.60	.18
❑ 150 Peter Bergeron RC	.60	.18
❑ 151 Pat Burrell RC	3.00	.90
❑ 152 Choo Freeman RC	.60	.18
❑ 153 Matt Belisle RC	.50	.15
❑ 154 Carlos Pena RC	.60	.18
❑ 155 A.J. Burnett RC	2.00	.60
❑ 156 D.Mientkiewicz RC	1.00	.30
❑ 157 Sean Burroughs RC	1.00	.30
❑ 158 Mike Zywica RC	.50	.15
❑ 159 Corey Patterson RC	1.00	.30
❑ 160 Austin Kearns RC	2.00	.60
❑ 161 Chip Ambres RC	.50	.15
❑ 162 Kelly Dransfeldt RC	.50	.15
❑ 163 Mike Nannini RC	.50	.15
❑ 164 Mark Mulder RC	3.00	.90
❑ 165 Jason Tyner RC	.50	.15
❑ 166 Bobby Seay RC	.50	.15
❑ 167 Alex Escobar RC	.60	.18
❑ 168 Nick Johnson RC	1.50	.45
❑ 169 Alfonso Soriano RC	8.00	2.40
❑ 170 Clayton Andrews RC	.50	.15
❑ 171 C.C. Sabathia RC	1.50	.45
❑ 172 Matt Holliday RC	1.00	.30
❑ 173 Brad Lidge RC	5.00	1.50
❑ 174 Kit Pellow RC	.50	.15
❑ 175 J.M. Gold RC	.50	.15
❑ 176 Roosevelt Brown RC	.50	.15
❑ 177 Eric Valent RC	.60	.18
❑ 178 Adam Everett RC	1.00	.30
❑ 179 Jorge Toca RC	.60	.18
❑ 180 Matt Roney RC	.50	.15
❑ 181 Andy Brown RC	.50	.15
❑ 182 Phil Norton RC	.50	.15
❑ 183 Mickey Lopez RC	.50	.15
❑ 184 Chris George RC	.60	.18
❑ 185 Arturo McDowell RC	.50	.15
❑ 186 Jose Fernandez RC	.50	.15
❑ 187 Seth Etherton RC	.50	.15
❑ 188 Josh McKinley RC	.60	.18
❑ 189 Nate Cornejo RC	.60	.18
❑ 190 G.Chiaramonte RC	.50	.15
❑ 191 Mamon Tucker RC	.50	.15
❑ 192 Ryan Mills RC	.50	.15
❑ 193 Chad Moeller RC	.50	.15
❑ 194 Tony Torcato RC	.60	.18
❑ 195 Jeff Winchester RC	.50	.15
❑ 196 Rick Elder RC	.60	.18
❑ 197 Matt Burch RC	.60	.18
❑ 198 Jeff Urban RC	.60	.18
❑ 199 Chris Jones RC	.50	.15
❑ 200 Masao Kida RC	.60	.18

2000 Bowman's Best

	Nm-Mt	Ex-Mt
COMP.SET w/o RC's (150)	40.00	12.00
COMMON CARD (1-150)	.40	.12
COMMON (151-200)	5.00	1.50

Card	Nm-Mt	Ex-Mt
❑ 1 Nomar Garciaparra	1.50	.45
❑ 2 Chipper Jones	1.00	.30
❑ 3 Tony Clark	.40	.12
❑ 4 Bernie Williams	.60	.18
❑ 5 Barry Bonds	2.50	.75
❑ 6 Jermaine Dye	.40	.12
❑ 7 John Olerud	.40	.12
❑ 8 Mike Hampton	.40	.12
❑ 9 Cal Ripken	3.00	.90
❑ 10 Jeff Bagwell	.60	.18
❑ 11 Troy Glaus	.40	.12
❑ 12 J.D. Drew	.40	.12
❑ 13 Jeromy Burnitz	.40	.12
❑ 14 Carlos Delgado	.40	.12
❑ 15 Shawn Green	.40	.12
❑ 16 Kevin Millwood	.40	.12
❑ 17 Rondell White	.40	.12
❑ 18 Scott Rolen	.60	.18
❑ 19 Jeff Cirillo	.40	.12
❑ 20 Barry Larkin	.60	.18
❑ 21 Brian Giles	.40	.12
❑ 22 Roger Clemens	2.00	.60
❑ 23 Manny Ramirez	.60	.18
❑ 24 Alex Gonzalez	.40	.12
❑ 25 Mark Grace	.60	.18
❑ 26 Fernando Tatis	.40	.12
❑ 27 Randy Johnson	1.00	.30
❑ 28 Roger Cedeno	.40	.12
❑ 29 Brian Jordan	.40	.12
❑ 30 Kevin Brown	.40	.12
❑ 31 Greg Vaughn	.40	.12
❑ 32 Roberto Alomar	.60	.18
❑ 33 Larry Walker	.40	.12
❑ 34 Rafael Palmeiro	.60	.18
❑ 35 Curt Schilling	.40	.12
❑ 36 Orlando Hernandez	.40	.12
❑ 37 Todd Walker	.40	.12
❑ 38 Juan Gonzalez	.40	.12
❑ 39 Sean Casey	.60	.18
❑ 40 Tony Gwynn	1.25	.35
❑ 41 Albert Belle	.40	.12
❑ 42 Gary Sheffield	.40	.12
❑ 43 Michael Barrett	.40	.12
❑ 44 Preston Wilson	.40	.12
❑ 45 Jim Thome	.60	.18
❑ 46 Shannon Stewart	.40	.12
❑ 47 Mo Vaughn	.40	.12
❑ 48 Ben Grieve	.40	.12
❑ 49 Adrian Beltre	.40	.12
❑ 50 Sammy Sosa	1.00	.30
❑ 51 Bob Abreu	.40	.12

Card	Nm-Mt	Ex-Mt
❑ 52 Edgardo Alfonzo	.40	.12
❑ 53 Carlos Febles	.40	.12
❑ 54 Frank Thomas	1.00	.30
❑ 55 Alex Rodriguez	1.50	.45
❑ 56 Cliff Floyd	.40	.12
❑ 57 Jose Canseco	.60	.18
❑ 58 Erubiel Durazo	.40	.12
❑ 59 Tim Hudson	.40	.12
❑ 60 Craig Biggio	.60	.18
❑ 61 Eric Karros	.40	.12
❑ 62 Mike Mussina	.60	.18
❑ 63 Robin Ventura	.40	.12
❑ 64 Carlos Beltran	.40	.12
❑ 65 Pedro Martinez	.60	.18
❑ 66 Gabe Kapler	.40	.12
❑ 67 Jason Kendall	.40	.12
❑ 68 Derek Jeter	2.50	.75
❑ 69 Magglio Ordonez	.40	.12
❑ 70 Mike Piazza	1.50	.45
❑ 71 Mike Lieberthal	.40	.12
❑ 72 Andres Galarraga	.40	.12
❑ 73 Raul Mondesi	.40	.12
❑ 74 Eric Chavez	.40	.12
❑ 75 Greg Maddux	1.50	.45
❑ 76 Matt Williams	.40	.12
❑ 77 Kris Benson	.40	.12
❑ 78 Ivan Rodriguez	.60	.18
❑ 79 Pokey Reese	.40	.12
❑ 80 Vladimir Guerrero	1.00	.30
❑ 81 Mark McGwire	2.50	.75
❑ 82 Vinny Castilla	.40	.12
❑ 83 Todd Helton	.60	.18
❑ 84 Andruw Jones	.60	.18
❑ 85 Ken Griffey Jr.	1.50	.45
❑ 86 Mark McGwire BP	1.25	.35
❑ 87 Derek Jeter BP	1.25	.35
❑ 88 Chipper Jones BP	.60	.18
❑ 89 Nomar Garciaparra BP	1.00	.30
❑ 90 Sammy Sosa BP	.60	.18
❑ 91 Cal Ripken BP	1.50	.45
❑ 92 Juan Gonzalez BP	.40	.12
❑ 93 Alex Rodriguez BP	1.00	.30
❑ 94 Barry Bonds BP	1.25	.35
❑ 95 Sean Casey BP	.40	.12
❑ 96 Vladimir Guerrero BP	.60	.18
❑ 97 Mike Piazza BP	1.00	.30
❑ 98 Shawn Green BP	.40	.12
❑ 99 Jeff Bagwell BP	.40	.12
❑ 100 Ken Griffey Jr. BP	1.00	.30
❑ 101 Rick Ankiel	.40	.12
❑ 102 John Patterson	.40	.12
❑ 103 David Walling	.40	.12
❑ 104 Michael Restovich	.40	.12
❑ 105 A.J. Burnett	.40	.12
❑ 106 Pablo Ozuna	.40	.12
❑ 107 Chad Hermansen	.40	.12
❑ 108 Choo Freeman	.40	.12
❑ 109 Mark Quinn	.40	.12
❑ 110 Corey Patterson	.40	.12
❑ 111 Ramon Ortiz	.40	.12
❑ 112 Vernon Wells	.40	.12
❑ 113 Milton Bradley	.40	.12
❑ 114 Gookie Dawkins	.40	.12
❑ 115 Sean Burroughs	.40	.12
❑ 116 Wily Mo Pena	.40	.12
❑ 117 Dee Brown	.40	.12
❑ 118 C.C. Sabathia	.40	.12
❑ 119 Adam Kennedy	.40	.12
❑ 120 Octavio Dotel	.40	.12
❑ 121 Kip Wells	.40	.12
❑ 122 Ben Petrick	.40	.12
❑ 123 Mark Mulder	.40	.12
❑ 124 Jason Standridge	.40	.12
❑ 125 Adam Piatt	.40	.12
❑ 126 Steve Lomasney	.40	.12
❑ 127 Jayson Werth	.40	.12
❑ 128 Alex Escobar	.40	.12
❑ 129 Ryan Anderson	.40	.12
❑ 130 Adam Dunn	1.00	.30
❑ 131 Ted Lilly	.40	.12
❑ 132 Brad Penny	.40	.12
❑ 133 Daryle Ward	.40	.12
❑ 134 Eric Munson	.40	.12
❑ 135 Nick Johnson	.40	.12
❑ 136 Jason Jennings	.40	.12
❑ 137 Tim Raines Jr.	.40	.12
❑ 138 Ruben Mateo	.40	.12
❑ 139 Jack Cust	.40	.12
❑ 140 Rafael Furcal	.40	.12
❑ 141 Eric Gagne	1.00	.30
❑ 142 Tony Armas Jr.	.40	.12
❑ 143 Mike Paradis	.40	.12
❑ 144 Peter Bergeron	.40	.12
❑ 145 Alfonso Soriano	1.00	.30
❑ 146 Josh Hamilton	.40	.12
❑ 147 Michael Cuddyer	.40	.12
❑ 148 Jay Gehrke	.40	.12
❑ 149 Josh Girdley	.40	.12
❑ 150 Pat Burrell	.40	.12
❑ 151 Brett Myers RC	15.00	4.50
❑ 152 Scott Seabol RC	5.00	1.50
❑ 153 Keith Reed RC	5.00	1.50
❑ 154 F.Rodriguez RC	20.00	6.00
❑ 155 Barry Zito RC	25.00	7.50
❑ 156 Pat Manning RC	5.00	1.50
❑ 157 Ben Christensen RC	5.00	1.50
❑ 158 Corey Myers RC	5.00	1.50
❑ 159 Wascar Serrano RC	5.00	1.50
❑ 160 Wes Anderson RC	5.00	1.50
❑ 161 Andy Tracy RC	5.00	1.50
❑ 162 Cesar Saba RC	5.00	1.50
❑ 163 Mike Lamb RC	8.00	2.40
❑ 164 Bobby Bradley RC	5.00	1.50
❑ 165 Vince Faison RC	5.00	1.50
❑ 166 Ty Howington RC	5.00	1.50
❑ 167 Ken Harvey RC UER	8.00	2.40
Card has pitching stats on the back		
❑ 168 Josh Kalinowski RC	5.00	1.50
❑ 169 Ruben Salazar RC	5.00	1.50
❑ 170 Aaron Rowand RC	10.00	3.00
❑ 171 Ramon Santiago RC	5.00	1.50
❑ 172 Scott Sobkowiak RC	5.00	1.50
❑ 173 Lyle Overbay RC	8.00	2.40
❑ 174 Rico Washington RC	5.00	1.50
❑ 175 Rick Asadoorian RC	5.00	1.50
❑ 176 Matt Ginter RC	5.00	1.50
❑ 177 Jason Stumm RC	5.00	1.50
❑ 178 B.J. Garbe RC	5.00	1.50
❑ 179 Mike MacDougal RC	5.00	1.50
❑ 180 Ryan Christianson RC	5.00	1.50
❑ 181 Kurt Ainsworth RC	5.00	1.50
❑ 182 Brad Baisley RC	5.00	1.50
❑ 183 Ben Broussard RC	8.00	2.40
❑ 184 Aaron McNeal RC	5.00	1.50
❑ 185 John Sneed RC	5.00	1.50
❑ 186 Junior Brignac RC	5.00	1.50
❑ 187 Chance Caple RC	5.00	1.50
❑ 188 Scott Downs RC	5.00	1.50
❑ 189 Matt Cepicky RC	5.00	1.50
❑ 190 Chin-Feng Chen RC	30.00	9.00
❑ 191 Johan Santana RC	60.00	18.00
❑ 192 Brad Baker RC	5.00	1.50
❑ 193 Jason Repko RC	8.00	2.40
❑ 194 Craig Dingman RC	5.00	1.50
❑ 195 Chris Wakeland RC	5.00	1.50
❑ 196 Rogelio Arias RC	5.00	1.50
❑ 197 Luis Matos RC	5.00	1.50
❑ 198 Rob Ramsay	5.00	1.50
❑ 199 Willie Bloomquist RC	25.00	7.50
❑ 200 Tony Pena Jr. RC	5.00	1.50

2001 Bowman's Best

	Nm-Mt	Ex-Mt
COMP.SET w/o SP's (150)	50.00	15.00
COMMON CARD (1-150)	.40	.12
COMMON (151-200)	5.00	1.50
❑ 1 Vladimir Guerrero	1.00	.30
❑ 2 Miguel Tejada	.40	.12
❑ 3 Geoff Jenkins	.40	.12
❑ 4 Jeff Bagwell	.60	.18
❑ 5 Todd Helton	.60	.18
❑ 6 Ken Griffey Jr.	1.50	.45
❑ 7 Nomar Garciaparra	1.50	.45
❑ 8 Chipper Jones	1.00	.30
❑ 9 Darin Erstad	.40	.12
❑ 10 Frank Thomas	1.00	.30
❑ 11 Jim Thome	.60	.18
❑ 12 Preston Wilson	.40	.12
❑ 13 Kevin Brown	.40	.12
❑ 14 Derek Jeter	2.50	.75
❑ 15 Scott Rolen	.60	.18
❑ 16 Ryan Klesko	.40	.12
❑ 17 Jeff Kent	.40	.12
❑ 18 Raul Mondesi	.40	.12
❑ 19 Greg Vaughn	.40	.12
❑ 20 Bernie Williams	.60	.18
❑ 21 Mike Piazza	1.50	.45
❑ 22 Richard Hidalgo	.40	.12
❑ 23 Dean Palmer	.40	.12
❑ 24 Roberto Alomar	.60	.18
❑ 25 Sammy Sosa	1.00	.30
❑ 26 Randy Johnson	1.00	.30
❑ 27 Manny Ramirez Sox	.60	.18
❑ 28 Roger Clemens	2.00	.60
❑ 29 Terrence Long	.40	.12
❑ 30 Jason Kendall	.40	.12
❑ 31 Richie Sexson	.40	.12
❑ 32 David Wells	.40	.12
❑ 33 Andruw Jones	.60	.18
❑ 34 Pokey Reese	.40	.12
❑ 35 Juan Gonzalez	.40	.12
❑ 36 Carlos Beltran	.40	.12
❑ 37 Shawn Green	.40	.12
❑ 38 Mariano Rivera	.60	.18
❑ 39 John Olerud	.40	.12
❑ 40 Jim Edmonds	.60	.18
❑ 41 Andres Galarraga	.40	.12
❑ 42 Carlos Delgado	.40	.12
❑ 43 Kris Benson	.40	.12
❑ 44 Andy Pettitte	.60	.18
❑ 45 Jeff Cirillo	.40	.12
❑ 46 Maggio Ordonez	.40	.12
❑ 47 Tom Glavine	.60	.18
❑ 48 Garret Anderson	.40	.12
❑ 49 Cal Ripken	3.00	.90
❑ 50 Pedro Martinez	.60	.18
❑ 51 Barry Bonds	2.50	.75
❑ 52 Alex Rodriguez	1.50	.45
❑ 53 Ben Grieve	.40	.12
❑ 54 Edgar Martinez	.60	.18
❑ 55 Jason Giambi	.40	.12
❑ 56 Jeromy Burnitz	.40	.12
❑ 57 Mike Mussina	.60	.18
❑ 58 Moises Alou	.40	.12
❑ 59 Sean Casey	.60	.18
❑ 60 Greg Maddux	1.50	.45
❑ 61 Tim Hudson	.40	.12
❑ 62 Mark McGwire	2.50	.75
❑ 63 Rafael Palmeiro	.60	.18
❑ 64 Tony Batista	.40	.12
❑ 65 Kazuhiro Sasaki	.40	.12
❑ 66 Jorge Posada	.60	.18
❑ 67 Johnny Damon	.60	.18
❑ 68 Brian Giles	.40	.12
❑ 69 Jose Vidro	.40	.12
❑ 70 Jermaine Dye	.40	.12
❑ 71 Craig Biggio	.60	.18
❑ 72 Larry Walker	.40	.12
❑ 73 Eric Chavez	.40	.12
❑ 74 David Segui	.40	.12
❑ 75 Tim Salmon	.60	.18
❑ 76 Javy Lopez	.40	.12
❑ 77 Paul Konerko	.40	.12
❑ 78 Barry Larkin	.60	.18
❑ 79 Mike Hampton	.40	.12
❑ 80 Bobby Higginson	.40	.12
❑ 81 Mark Mulder	.40	.12

	Nm-Mt	Ex-Mt
❑ 82 Pat Burrell	.40	.12
❑ 83 Kerry Wood	.40	.12
❑ 84 J.T. Snow	.40	.12
❑ 85 Ivan Rodriguez	.60	.18
❑ 86 Edgardo Alfonzo	.40	.12
❑ 87 Orlando Hernandez	.40	.12
❑ 88 Gary Sheffield	.40	.12
❑ 89 Mike Sweeney	.40	.12
❑ 90 Carlos Lee	.40	.12
❑ 91 Rafael Furcal	.40	.12
❑ 92 Troy Glaus	.40	.12
❑ 93 Bartolo Colon	.40	.12
❑ 94 Cliff Floyd	.40	.12
❑ 95 Barry Zito	.60	.18
❑ 96 J.D. Drew	.40	.12
❑ 97 Eric Karros	.40	.12
❑ 98 Jose Valentin	.40	.12
❑ 99 Ellis Burks	.40	.12
❑ 100 David Justice	.40	.12
❑ 101 Larry Barnes	.40	.12
❑ 102 Rod Barajas	.40	.12
❑ 103 Tony Pena Jr.	.40	.12
❑ 104 Jerry Hairston Jr.	.40	.12
❑ 105 Keith Ginter	.40	.12
❑ 106 Corey Patterson	.40	.12
❑ 107 Aaron Rowand	.40	.12
❑ 108 Miguel Olivo	.40	.12
❑ 109 Gookie Dawkins	.40	.12
❑ 110 C.C. Sabathia	.40	.12
❑ 111 Ben Petrick	.40	.12
❑ 112 Eric Munson	.40	.12
❑ 113 Ramon Castro	.40	.12
❑ 114 Alex Escobar	.40	.12
❑ 115 Josh Hamilton	.40	.12
❑ 116 Jason Marquis	.40	.12
❑ 117 Ben Davis	.40	.12
❑ 118 Alex Cintron	.40	.12
❑ 119 Julio Zuleta	.40	.12
❑ 120 Ben Broussard	.40	.12
❑ 121 Adam Everett	.40	.12
❑ 122 Ramon Carvajal RC	.40	.12
❑ 123 Felipe Lopez	.40	.12
❑ 124 Alfonso Soriano	.60	.18
❑ 125 Jayson Werth	.40	.12
❑ 126 Donzell McDonald	.40	.12
❑ 127 Jason Hart	.40	.12
❑ 128 Joe Crede	1.00	.30
❑ 129 Sean Burroughs	.40	.12
❑ 130 Jack Cust	.40	.12
❑ 131 Corey Smith	.40	.12
❑ 132 Adrian Gonzalez	.40	.12
❑ 133 J.R. House	.40	.12
❑ 134 Steve Lomasney	.40	.12
❑ 135 Tim Raines Jr.	.40	.12
❑ 136 Tony Alvarez	.40	.12
❑ 137 Doug Mientkiewicz	.40	.12
❑ 138 Rocco Baldelli	.40	.12
❑ 139 Jason Romano	.40	.12
❑ 140 Vernon Wells	.40	.12
❑ 141 Mike Bynum	.40	.12
❑ 142 Xavier Nady	.40	.12
❑ 143 Brad Wilkerson	.40	.12
❑ 144 Ben Diggins	.40	.12
❑ 145 Aubrey Huff	.40	.12
❑ 146 Eric Byrnes	.40	.12
❑ 147 Alex Gordon	.40	.12
❑ 148 Roy Oswalt	.60	.18
❑ 149 Brian Esposito	.40	.12
❑ 150 Scott Seabol	.40	.12
❑ 151 Erick Almonte RC	5.00	1.50
❑ 152 Gary Johnson RC	5.00	1.50
❑ 153 Pedro Liriano RC	5.00	1.50
❑ 154 Matt White RC	5.00	1.50
❑ 155 Luis Montanez RC	5.00	1.50
❑ 156 Brad Cresse	5.00	1.50
❑ 157 Wilson Betemit RC	8.00	2.40
❑ 158 Octavio Martinez RC	5.00	1.50
❑ 159 Adam Pettyjohn RC	5.00	1.50
❑ 160 Corey Spencer RC	5.00	1.50
❑ 161 Mark Burnett RC	5.00	1.50
❑ 162 Ichiro Suzuki RC	60.00	18.00
❑ 163 Alexis Gomez RC	5.00	1.50
❑ 164 Greg Nash RC	5.00	1.50
❑ 165 Roberto Miniel RC	5.00	1.50
❑ 166 Justin Morneau RC	20.00	6.00
❑ 167 Ben Washburn RC	5.00	1.50
❑ 168 Bob Keppel RC	5.00	1.50
❑ 169 Deivi Mendez RC	5.00	1.50
❑ 170 Tsuyoshi Shinjo RC	8.00	2.40
❑ 171 Jared Abruzzo RC	5.00	1.50
❑ 172 Derrick Van Dusen RC	5.00	1.50
❑ 173 Hee Seop Choi RC	10.00	3.00
❑ 174 Albert Pujols RC	250.00	75.00
❑ 175 Travis Hafner RC	25.00	7.50
❑ 176 Ron Davenport RC	5.00	1.50
❑ 177 Luis Torres RC	5.00	1.50
❑ 178 Jake Peavy RC	40.00	12.00
❑ 179 Elvis Corporan RC	5.00	1.50
❑ 180 Dave Krynzel	5.00	1.50
❑ 181 Tony Blanco RC	5.00	1.50
❑ 182 Elpidio Guzman RC	5.00	1.50
❑ 183 Matt Butler RC	5.00	1.50
❑ 184 Joe Thurston RC	5.00	1.50
❑ 185 Andy Beal RC	5.00	1.50
❑ 186 Kevin Nulton RC	5.00	1.50
❑ 187 Sneideer Santos RC	5.00	1.50
❑ 188 Joe Dillon RC	5.00	1.50
❑ 189 Jeremy Blevins RC	5.00	1.50
❑ 190 Chris Amador RC	5.00	1.50
❑ 191 Mark Hendrickson RC	5.00	1.50
❑ 192 Willy Aybar RC	8.00	2.40
❑ 193 Antoine Cameron RC	5.00	1.50
❑ 194 J.J. Johnson RC	5.00	1.50
❑ 195 Ryan Ketchner RC	8.00	2.40
❑ 196 Bjorn Ivy RC	5.00	1.50
❑ 197 Josh Kroeger RC	8.00	2.40
❑ 198 Ty Wigginton RC	5.00	1.50
❑ 199 Stubby Clapp RC	5.00	1.50
❑ 200 Jerrod Riggan RC	5.00	1.50

2002 Bowman's Best

	Nm-Mt	Ex-Mt
COMP.SET w/o SP's (90)	100.00	30.00
COMMON CARD (1-90)	.75	.23
COMMON AUTO A (91-180)	8.00	2.40
AUTO GROUP A ODDS 1:3	.00	
COMMON AUTO B (91-180)	10.00	3.00
AUTO GROUP B ODDS 1:19	.00	
COMMON BAT (91-180)	5.00	1.50
91-180 BAT STATED ODDS 1:5	.00	
181 ISHII BAT EXCHANGE ODDS 1:131		.00

	Nm-Mt	Ex-Mt
❑ 1 Josh Beckett	.75	.23
❑ 2 Derek Jeter	5.00	1.50
❑ 3 Alex Rodriguez	3.00	.90
❑ 4 Miguel Tejada	.75	.23
❑ 5 Nomar Garciaparra	3.00	.90
❑ 6 Aramis Ramirez	.75	.23
❑ 7 Jeremy Giambi	.75	.23
❑ 8 Bernie Williams	1.25	.35
❑ 9 Juan Pierre	.75	.23
❑ 10 Chipper Jones	2.00	.60
❑ 11 Jimmy Rollins	.75	.23
❑ 12 Alfonso Soriano	.75	.23
❑ 13 Mark Prior	2.00	.60
❑ 14 Paul Konerko	.75	.23
❑ 15 Tim Hudson	.75	.23
❑ 16 Doug Mientkiewicz	.75	.23
❑ 17 Todd Helton	1.25	.35
❑ 18 Moises Alou	.75	.23
❑ 19 Juan Gonzalez	.75	.23
❑ 20 Jorge Posada	1.25	.35
❑ 21 Jeff Kent	.75	.23
❑ 22 Roger Clemens	4.00	1.20
❑ 23 Phil Nevin	.75	.23
❑ 24 Brian Giles	.75	.23
❑ 25 Carlos Delgado	.75	.23
❑ 26 Jason Giambi	.75	.23
❑ 27 Vladimir Guerrero	2.00	.60
❑ 28 Cliff Floyd	.75	.23
❑ 29 Shea Hillenbrand	.75	.23
❑ 30 Ken Griffey Jr.	3.00	.90
❑ 31 Mike Piazza	3.00	.90
❑ 32 Carlos Pena	.75	.23
❑ 33 Larry Walker	.75	.23
❑ 34 Magglio Ordonez	.75	.23
❑ 35 Mike Mussina	1.25	.35
❑ 36 Andruw Jones	1.25	.35
❑ 37 Nick Johnson	.75	.23
❑ 38 Curt Schilling	.75	.23
❑ 39 Eric Chavez	.75	.23
❑ 40 Bartolo Colon	.75	.23
❑ 41 Eric Hinske	.75	.23
❑ 42 Sean Burroughs	.75	.23
❑ 43 Randy Johnson	2.00	.60
❑ 44 Adam Dunn	.75	.23
❑ 45 Pedro Martinez	1.25	.35
❑ 46 Garret Anderson	.75	.23
❑ 47 Jim Thome	1.25	.35
❑ 48 Gary Sheffield	.75	.23
❑ 49 Tsuyoshi Shinjo	.75	.23
❑ 50 Albert Pujols	4.00	1.20
❑ 51 Ichiro Suzuki	4.00	1.20
❑ 52 C.C. Sabathia	.75	.23
❑ 53 Bobby Abreu	.75	.23
❑ 54 Ivan Rodriguez	1.25	.35
❑ 55 J.D. Drew	.75	.23
❑ 56 Jacque Jones	.75	.23
❑ 57 Jason Kendall	.75	.23
❑ 58 Javier Vazquez	.75	.23
❑ 59 Jeff Bagwell	1.25	.35
❑ 60 Greg Maddux	3.00	.90
❑ 61 Jim Edmonds	1.25	.35
❑ 62 Hank Blalock	1.25	.35
❑ 63 Jose Vidro	.75	.23
❑ 64 Kevin Brown	.75	.23
❑ 65 Mark Teixeira	2.00	.60
❑ 66 Sammy Sosa	2.00	.60
❑ 67 Lance Berkman	.75	.23
❑ 68 Mark Mulder	.75	.23
❑ 69 Marty Cordova	.75	.23
❑ 70 Frank Thomas	2.00	.60
❑ 71 Mike Cameron	.75	.23
❑ 72 Mike Sweeney	.75	.23
❑ 73 Barry Bonds	5.00	1.50
❑ 74 Troy Glaus	.75	.23
❑ 75 Barry Zito	.75	.23
❑ 76 Pat Burrell	.75	.23
❑ 77 Paul LoDuca	.75	.23
❑ 78 Rafael Palmeiro	1.25	.35
❑ 79 Austin Kearns	.75	.23
❑ 80 Darin Erstad	.75	.23
❑ 81 Richie Sexson	.75	.23
❑ 82 Roberto Alomar	1.25	.35
❑ 83 Roy Oswalt	.75	.23
❑ 84 Ryan Klesko	.75	.23
❑ 85 Luis Gonzalez	.75	.23
❑ 86 Scott Rolen	1.25	.35
❑ 87 Shannon Stewart	.75	.23
❑ 88 Shawn Green	.75	.23
❑ 89 Toby Hall	.75	.23
❑ 90 Bret Boone	.75	.23
❑ 91 Casey Kotchman Bat RC	10.00	3.00
❑ 92 Jose Valverde AU A RC	8.00	2.40
❑ 93 Cole Barthel Bat RC	5.00	1.50
❑ 94 Brad Nelson AU A RC	10.00	3.00
❑ 95 Mauricio Lara AU A RC	8.00	2.40
❑ 96 Ryan Gripp Bat RC	5.00	1.50
❑ 97 Brian West AU A RC	8.00	2.40
❑ 98 Chris Piersoll AU B RC	10.00	3.00
❑ 99 Ryan Church AU B RC	25.00	7.50
❑ 100 Javier Colina AU A	8.00	2.40
❑ 101 Juan M. Gonzalez AU A RC	8.00	2.40
❑ 102 Benito Baez AU A	8.00	2.40
❑ 103 Mike Hill Bat RC	5.00	1.50
❑ 104 Jason Grove AU B RC	10.00	3.00
❑ 105 Koyie Hill AU B	10.00	3.00
❑ 106 Mark Outlaw AU A RC	8.00	2.40
❑ 107 Jason Bay Bat RC	15.00	4.50
❑ 108 Jorge Padilla AU A RC	8.00	2.40

❑ 109 Pete Zamora AU A RC 8.00 2.40
❑ 110 Joe Mauer AU A RC 50.00 15.00
❑ 111 Franklyn German AU A RC 8.00 2.40
❑ 112 Chris Flinn AU A RC 8.00 2.40
❑ 113 David Wright Bat RC 50.00 15.00
❑ 114 An. Martinez AU A RC 8.00 2.40
❑ 115 Nic Jackson Bat RC 5.00 1.50
❑ 116 Rene Reyes AU A RC 8.00 2.40
❑ 117 Colin Young AU A RC 8.00 2.40
❑ 118 Joe Orloski AU A RC 8.00 2.40
❑ 119 Mike Wilson AU A RC 8.00 2.40
❑ 120 Rich Thompson AU A RC 8.00 2.40
❑ 121 Jake Mauer AU B RC 10.00 3.00
❑ 122 Mario Ramos AU A RC .. 8.00 2.40
❑ 123 Doug Sessions AU B RC 10.00 3.00
❑ 124 Doug Devore Bat RC 5.00 1.50
❑ 125 Travis Foley AU A RC 8.00 2.40
❑ 126 Chris Baker AU A RC 8.00 2.40
❑ 127 Michael Floyd AU A RC .. 8.00 2.40
❑ 128 Josh Barfield Bat RC 8.00 2.40
❑ 129 Jose Bautista Bat RC 8.00 2.40
❑ 130 Gavin Floyd AU A RC .. 15.00 4.50
❑ 131 Jason Botts Bat RC 8.00 2.40
❑ 132 Clint Nageotte AU A RC 10.00 3.00
❑ 133 Jesus Cota AU B RC 10.00 3.00
❑ 134 Ron Calloway Bat RC 5.00 1.50
❑ 135 Kevin Cash Bat RC 5.00 1.50
❑ 136 Jonny Gomes AU B RC 30.00 9.00
❑ 137 Dennis Ulacia AU A RC .. 8.00 2.40
❑ 138 Ryan Snare AU A RC 8.00 2.40
❑ 139 Kevin Deaton AU A RC .. 8.00 2.40
❑ 140 Bobby Jenks AU B RC .. 20.00 6.00
❑ 141 Casey Kotchman AU A RC 30.00 9.00
❑ 142 Adam Walker AU A RC .. 8.00 2.40
❑ 143 Mike Gonzalez AU A RC 8.00 2.40
❑ 144 Ruben Gotay Bat RC 8.00 2.40
❑ 145 Jason Grove Bat RC 5.00 1.50
❑ 146 Freddy Sanchez AU B RC 10.00 3.00
❑ 147 Jason Arnold AU B RC 10.00 3.00
❑ 148 Scott Hairston AU A RC 10.00 3.00
❑ 149 Jason St. Clair AU B RC 10.00 3.00
❑ 150 Chris Tritle Bat RC 5.00 1.50
❑ 151 Edwin Yan Bat RC 5.00 1.50
❑ 152 Freddy Sanchez Bat RC .. 5.00 1.50
❑ 153 Greg Sain Bat RC 5.00 1.50
❑ 154 Yurendell De Caster Bat RC 5.00 1.50
❑ 155 Noochie Varner Bat RC .. 5.00 1.50
❑ 156 Nelson Castro AU B RC 10.00 3.00
❑ 157 Randall Shelley Bat RC .. 5.00 1.50
❑ 158 Reed Johnson Bat RC 8.00 2.40
❑ 159 Ryan Raburn AU A RC 8.00 2.40
❑ 160 Jose Morban Bat RC 5.00 1.50
❑ 161 Justin Schuda AU A RC .. 8.00 2.40
❑ 162 Henry Pichardo AU A RC 8.00 2.40
❑ 163 Josh Bard AU A RC 8.00 2.40
❑ 164 Josh Bonifay AU A RC 8.00 2.40
❑ 165 Brandon League AU B RC 10.00 3.00
❑ 166 Jorge-Julio DePaula AU A RC 8.00 2.40
❑ 167 Todd Linden AU B RC .. 15.00 4.50
❑ 168 Francisco Liriano AU A RC 50.00 15.00
❑ 169 Chris Snelling AU A RC 15.00 4.50
❑ 170 Blake McGinley AU A RC 8.00 2.40
❑ 171 Cody McKay AU A RC 8.00 2.40
❑ 172 Jason Stanford AU A RC 8.00 2.40
❑ 173 Lenny Dinardo AU A RC 8.00 2.40
❑ 174 Greg Montalbano AU A RC 8.00 2.40
❑ 175 Earl Snyder AU A RC 8.00 2.40
❑ 176 Justin Huber AU A RC .. 10.00 3.00
❑ 177 Chris Narveson AU A RC 8.00 2.40
❑ 178 Jon Switzer AU A RC 8.00 2.40
❑ 179 Ronald Acuna AU A RC .. 8.00 2.40
❑ 180 Chris Duffy Bat RC 10.00 3.00
❑ 181 Kazuhisa Ishii Bat RC 8.00 2.40

2003 Bowman's Best

	MINT	NRMT
COMP.SET w/o SP's (50)	40.00	18.00
COMMON CARD	1.00	.45
COMMON AUTO	8.00	3.60
COMMON BAT	4.00	1.80

❑ AB Andrew Brown FY AU RC 10.00 4.50
❑ AK Austin Kearns .... 1.00 .45
❑ AM Aneudis Mateo FY AU RC 8.00 3.60
❑ AP Albert Pujols 3.00 1.35

❑ AR Alex Rodriguez 2.50 1.10
❑ AS Alfonso Soriano .... 1.00 .45
❑ AW Aron Weston FY AU RC .. 8.00 3.60
❑ BB Bryan Bullington FY AU RC 8.00 3.60
❑ BC Bernie Castro FY RC .... 1.00 .45
❑ BFL Br. Florence FY AU RC .. 8.00 3.60
❑ BFR Ben Francisco FY AU RC 8.00 3.60
❑ BH Brendan Harris FY AU RC 10.00 4.50
❑ BJH Bo Hart FY RC .... 1.00 .45
❑ BK Beau Kemp FY AU RC 8.00 3.60
❑ BLB Barry Bonds 4.00 1.80
❑ BM Brian McCann FY AU RC 30.00 13.50
❑ BSG Brian Giles .... 1.00 .45
❑ BWB Bobby Basham FY AU RC 10.00 4.50
❑ BZ Barry Zito .... 1.00 .45
❑ CAD Carlos Duran FY AU RC 8.00 3.60
❑ CDC C. De La Cruz FY AU RC 8.00 3.60
❑ CJ Chipper Jones .... 1.50 .70
❑ CJW C.J. Wilson FY AU 8.00 3.60
❑ CM Charlie Manning FY AU RC 8.00 3.60
❑ CMS Curt Schilling .... 1.00 .45
❑ CS Cory Stewart FY AU RC .. 8.00 3.60
❑ CSS Corey Shafer FY AU RC 8.00 3.60
❑ CW Chien-Ming Wang FY RC 3.00 1.35
❑ CWA Chien-Ming Wang FY AU 60.00 27.00
❑ DAM D. Moseley FY AU RC .. 8.00 3.60
❑ DC David Cash FY AU RC 8.00 3.60
❑ DH Dan Haren FY AU RC 15.00 6.75
❑ DJ Derek Jeter 4.00 1.80
❑ DM David Martinez FY AU RC 8.00 3.60
❑ DMM D. McGowan FY AU RC 8.00 3.60
❑ DR Darrell Rasner FY AU RC 8.00 3.60
❑ DW Doug Waechter FY AU RC 10.00 4.50
❑ DY Dustin Yount FY RC .... 1.50 .70
❑ ERA El. Ramirez FY AU RC .. 10.00 4.50
❑ ERI Eric Riggs FY AU RC 10.00 4.50
❑ ET Eider Torres FY AU RC 8.00 3.60
❑ FP Felix Pie FY AU RC 50.00 22.00
❑ FS Felix Sanchez FY AU RC .. 8.00 3.60
❑ FT Ferdin Tejeda FY AU RC .. 8.00 3.60
❑ GA Greg Aquino FY AU RC .. 8.00 3.60
❑ GB Gregor Blanco FY AU RC 8.00 3.60
❑ GJA Garret Anderson .... 1.00 .45
❑ GM Greg Maddux 2.50 1.10
❑ GS G. Schneidmiller FY AU RC 8.00 3.60
❑ HR Hanley Ramirez FY AU RC 35.00 16.00
❑ HRB Hanley Ramirez FY Bat 10.00 4.50
❑ HT Haj Turay FY RC .... 1.50 .70
❑ IS Ichiro Suzuki 3.00 1.35
❑ JB Jeremy Bonderman FY RC 3.00 1.35
❑ JC Jose Contreras FY RC ...... 1.50 .70
❑ JDD J.D. Durbin FY AU RC .. 8.00 3.60
❑ JFK Jeff Kent .... 1.00 .45
❑ JG Joey Gomes FY AU RC 8.00 3.60
❑ JGB Joey Gomes FY Bat 4.00 1.80
❑ JGG Jason Giambi .... 1.00 .45
❑ JK Jason Kubel FY AU RC .. 10.00 4.50
❑ JKB Jason Kubel FY Bat 5.00 2.20
❑ JLB Jaime Bubela FY AU RC 8.00 3.60
❑ JM Jose Morales FY AU RC .. 8.00 3.60
❑ JMS Jon-Mark Sprowl FY RC 1.00 .45
❑ JRG Jeremy Griffiths FY AU RC 8.00 3.60
❑ JT Jim Thome .... 1.00 .45
❑ JV Joe Valentine FY AU RC .. 8.00 3.60
❑ JW Josh Willingham FY AU RC 10.00 4.50
❑ KBS Kelly Shoppach FY Bat .. 5.00 2.20
❑ KG Ken Griffey Jr. 2.50 1.10
❑ KJ Kade Johnson FY AU RC .. 8.00 3.60
❑ KS Kelly Shoppach FY AU RC 10.00 4.50
❑ KY Kevin Youkilis FY AU RC 10.00 4.50
❑ KYE Kevin Youkilis FY Bat 5.00 2.20
❑ LB Lance Berkman .... 1.00 .45
❑ LF Lew Ford FY AU RC 10.00 4.50
❑ LFJ Lew Ford FY Bat 5.00 2.20
❑ LW Larry Walker .... 1.00 .45
❑ MB Matt Bruback FY RC ...... 1.00 .45
❑ MD Matt Diaz FY RC .... 1.50 .70
❑ MDA Matt Diaz FY AU 10.00 4.50
❑ MDH Matt Hensley FY AU RC 8.00 3.60
❑ MDM Mark Malaska FY AU RC 8.00 3.60
❑ MH Mi. Hernandez FY AU RC 8.00 3.60
❑ MHI Mi. Hinckley FY AU RC 10.00 4.50
❑ MJP Mike Piazza 2.50 1.10
❑ MK Matt Kata FY AU RC 8.00 3.60
❑ MNH Matt Hagen FY AU RC .. 8.00 3.60
❑ MO Mike O'Keefe FY RC ...... 1.00 .45
❑ MOR Magglio Ordonez .... 1.00 .45
❑ MP Mark Prior .... 1.00 .45
❑ MR Manny Ramirez .... 1.00 .45
❑ MS Mike Sweeney .... 1.00 .45
❑ MT Miguel Tejada .... 1.00 .45
❑ NG Nomar Garciaparra 2.50 1.10
❑ NL Nook Logan FY AU RC .. 10.00 4.50
❑ OC Ozzie Chavez FY AU RC .. 8.00 3.60
❑ PB Pat Burrell .... 1.00 .45
❑ PL Pete LaForest FY AU RC .. 8.00 3.60
❑ PM Pedro Martinez .... 1.00 .45
❑ PR Prentice Redman FY AU RC 8.00 3.60
❑ RC Ryan Cameron FY AU RC 8.00 3.60
❑ RD Rajai Davis FY AU RC 8.00 3.60
❑ RH Ryan Howard FY AU RC 80.00 36.00
❑ RHJ Ryan Howard FY Bat 15.00 6.75
❑ RJ Randy Johnson .... 1.50 .70
❑ RLD Rajai Davis FY Bat 4.00 1.80
❑ RM R. Nivar-Martinez FY RC 1.00 .45
❑ RS Ryan Shealy FY AU RC .. 10.00 4.50
❑ RSB Ryan Shealy FY Bat 5.00 2.20
❑ RWH Rob. Hammock FY AU RC 8.00 3.60
❑ SG Shawn Green .... 1.00 .45
❑ SS Sammy Sosa .... 1.50 .70
❑ ST Scott Tyler FY AU RC 10.00 4.50
❑ SV Shane Victorino FY RC .... 1.50 .70
❑ TA Tyler Adamczyk FY AU RC 8.00 3.60
❑ TH Todd Helton .... 1.00 .45
❑ TI Travis Ishikawa FY AU RC 8.00 3.60
❑ TJ Tyler Johnson FY AU RC .. 8.00 3.60
❑ TJB T.J. Bohn FY RC .... 1.00 .45
❑ TKH Torii Hunter .... 1.00 .45
❑ TO Tim Olson FY AU RC 8.00 3.60
❑ TS T.Story-Harden FY AU RC 8.00 3.60
❑ TSB T.Story-Harden FY Bat .. 4.00 1.80
❑ TT Terry Tiffee FY RC .... 1.00 .45
❑ VG Vladimir Guerrero .... 1.50 .70
❑ WE Willie Eyre FY AU RC 8.00 3.60
❑ WL Wil Ledezma FY AU RC .. 8.00 3.60
❑ WRC Roger Clemens 3.00 1.35
❑ NNO Bryan Bullington 25.00 11.00
Opened Box AU
❑ NNO Bryan Bullington .... .00
Sealed Box AU

2004 Bowman's Best

	Nm-Mt	Ex-Mt
COMP.SET w/o SP'S (50)	25.00	7.50
COMMON CARD	1.00	.30
COMMON RC	1.00	.30

ONE AUTO PER HOBBY PACK
ONE RELIC PER BOX-LOADER PACK
ONE BOX-LOADER PACK PER HOBBY BOX
STAUFFER BOX RANDOM IN HOBBY CASES
OVERALL AU PLATE ODDS 1:391 HOBBY
AU PLATE PRINT RUN 1 SET PER COLOR
BLACK-CYAN-MAGENTA-YELLOW ISSUED
NO AU PLATE PRICING DUE TO SCARCITY

❑ AER Alex Rodriguez .... 2.50 .75
❑ AG Adam Greenberg FY AU RC 15.00 4.50
❑ AL Anthony Lerew FY RC ...... 1.50 .45
❑ AO Akinori Otsuka FY RC...... 1.00 .30
❑ AP Albert Pujols.................. 3.00 .90
❑ AS Alfonso Soriano .... 1.00 .30
❑ BB Bobby Brownlie FY AU RC 15.00 4.50
❑ BEM Brandon Medders FY AU RC 8.00 2.40
❑ BG Brian Giles .... 1.00 .30
❑ BMS Brad Snyder FY AU RC 15.00 4.50
❑ BP Brayan Pena FY AU RC.... 8.00 2.40
❑ BS Brad Sullivan FY AU RC 10.00 3.00
❑ CB Carlos Beltran.................. 1.00 .30
❑ CD Carlos Delgado .... 1.00 .30
❑ CJ Conor Jackson FY AU RC 40.00 12.00
❑ CLH Chin-Lung Hu FY RC .... 2.00 .60
❑ CMA Craig Ansman FY AU RC 8.00 2.40
❑ CMS Curt Schilling .... 1.00 .30
❑ CZ Charlie Zink FY AU RC 8.00 2.40
❑ DA David Aardsma FY AU RC 10.00 3.00
❑ DC Dave Crouthers FY AU RC 8.00 2.40
❑ DDN Dustin Nippert FY AU RC 10.00 3.00
❑ DG Danny Gonzalez FY RC.... 1.00 .30
❑ DK Donald Kelly FY AU RC .. 8.00 2.40
❑ DL Donald Levinski FY AU RC 8.00 2.40
❑ DM David Murphy FY AU RC 12.00 3.60
❑ DN Dioner Navarro FY AU RC 20.00 6.00
❑ DS Don Sutton FY RC .... 2.50 .75
❑ EA Erick Aybar FY AU RC.... 15.00 4.50
❑ EC Eric Chavez.................... 1.00 .30
❑ EH Estee Harris FY AU RC .. 10.00 3.00
❑ ES Ervin Santana FY AU RC 25.00 7.50
❑ FH Felix Hernandez FY AU RC 100.00 30.00
❑ GA Garret Anderson .... 1.00 .30
❑ HB Hank Blalock .... 1.00 .30
❑ HM Hector Made FY RC........ 1.50 .45
❑ IR Ivan Rodriguez.............. 1.00 .30
❑ IS Ichiro Suzuki .... 3.00 .90
❑ JA Joaquin Arias FY AU RC 12.00 3.60
❑ JAV Jose Vidro.................... 1.00 .30
❑ JC Juan Cedeno FY AU RC .. 8.00 2.40
❑ JDS Jason Schmidt .... 1.00 .30
❑ JE Jesse English FY AU RC .. 8.00 2.40
❑ JGG Jason Giambi .... 1.00 .30
❑ JH Jason Hirsh FY AU RC .. 10.00 3.00
❑ JJC Jon Connolly FY RC ...... 2.00 .60
❑ JK Jon Knott FY AU RC 8.00 2.40
❑ JL Josh Labandeira FY AU RC 8.00 2.40
❑ JLO Javy Lopez .... 1.00 .30
❑ JP Jorge Posada .... 1.00 .30
❑ JRG Joey Gathright FY RC .... 2.00 .60
❑ JS Jeff Salazar FY AU RC.... 12.00 3.60
❑ JSZ Jason Szuminski FY AU RC 8.00 2.40
❑ JT Jim Thome .... 1.00 .30
❑ KC Kory Casto FY AU RC.... 10.00 3.00
❑ KK Kevin Kouzmanoff FY AU RC 10.00 3.00
❑ KM Kazuo Matsui FY Uni RC 8.00 2.40
❑ KRK Kody Kirkland FY Bat RC 8.00 2.40
❑ KS Kyle Sleeth FY RC............ 1.50 .45
❑ KT Kazuhito Tadano FY Jsy RC 8.00 2.40
❑ LK Logan Kensing FY AU RC 8.00 2.40
❑ LM Lastings Milledge FY AU RC 30.00 9.00
❑ LO Lyle Overbay.................. 1.00 .30
❑ LTH Luke Hughes FY AU RC 8.00 2.40
❑ LWJ Chipper Jones .... 1.50 .45
❑ MAR Manny Ramirez .... 1.00 .30
❑ MDC Matt Creighton FY AU RC 8.00 2.40
❑ MG Mike Gosling FY RC ...... 1.00 .30
❑ MJP Mike Piazza .... 2.50 .75
❑ MO Magglio Ordonez.......... 1.00 .30
❑ MT Miguel Tejada .... 1.00 .30
❑ MTC Miguel Cabrera .... 1.00 .30
❑ MV Merkin Valdez FY AU RC 10.00 3.00
❑ MWP Mark Prior .... 1.00 .30
❑ MY Michael Young .... 1.00 .30
❑ NAG Nomar Garciaparra........ 2.50 .75
❑ NG Nick Gorneault FY RC .... 1.50 .45
❑ NU Nic Ungs FY AU RC 8.00 2.40
❑ OQ Omar Quintanilla FY AU RC 10.00 3.00
❑ PM Paul Maholm FY AU RC 25.00 7.50
❑ PMM Paul McAnulty FY RC.. 1.50 .45
❑ RB Ryan Budde FY AU RC 8.00 2.40
❑ RC Roger Clemens................ 3.00 .90
❑ RG Rudy Guillen FY AU RC 10.00 3.00
❑ RJ Randy Johnson .... 1.50 .45
❑ RN Ricky Nolasco FY AU RC 20.00 6.00
❑ RR Ramon Ramirez FY AU RC 8.00 2.40
❑ RS Richie Sexson................ 1.00 .30
❑ RT Rob Tejeda FY AU RC 15.00 4.50
❑ SH Shawn Hill FY AU RC...... 8.00 2.40
❑ SR Scott Rolen.................... 1.00 .30
❑ SS Sammy Sosa.................... 1.50 .45
❑ ST Shingo Takatsu FY Jsy RC 10.00 3.00
❑ TB Travis Blackley FY Jsy RC 5.00 1.50
❑ TD Tyler Davidson FY AU RC 10.00 3.00
❑ TJ Terry Jones FY RC.......... 1.50 .45
❑ TJS Tim Stauffer FY AU RC 12.00 3.60
❑ TLH Todd Helton .... 1.00 .30
❑ TOH Travis Hanson FY AU RC 8.00 2.40
❑ TRM Tom Mastny FY AU RC 8.00 2.40
❑ TS Todd Self FY RC .... 1.50 .45
❑ VC Vito Chiaravalloti FY AU RC 8.00 2.40
❑ VG Vladimir Guerrero.......... 1.50 .45
❑ WM Warner Madrigal FY RC 1.50 .45
❑ WS Wardell Starling FY AU RC 8.00 2.40
❑ YM Yadier Molina FY AU RC 25.00 7.50
❑ ZD Zach Duke FY AU RC 60.00 18.00
❑ NNO Tim Stauffer AU Box/100 30.00 9.00

2005 Bowman's Best

	Nm-Mt	Ex-Mt
COMP.SET w/o SP's (100)........	50.00	15.00
COMMON CARD (1-30)................	.50	.15
COMMON CARD (31-100)..............	1.00	.30
COMMON AU (101-143)	8.00	2.40
OVERALL 1-100 PLATE ODDS 1:345 H		
OVERALL 101-143 AU PLATE ODDS 1:805 H		.00
PLATE PRINT RUN 1 SET PER COLOR		
BLACK-CYAN-MAGENTA-YELLOW ISSUED		
NO PLATE PRICING DUE TO SCARCITY		

❑ 1 Jose Vidro.......................... .50 .15
❑ 2 Adam Dunn.......................... .50 .15
❑ 3 Manny Ramirez.................. .75 .23
❑ 4 Miguel Tejada .... .50 .15
❑ 5 Ken Griffey Jr.................. 2.00 .60
❑ 6 Pedro Martinez .... .75 .23
❑ 7 Alex Rodriguez .... 2.00 .60
❑ 8 Ichiro Suzuki...................... 2.50 .75
❑ 9 Alfonso Soriano .... .50 .15
❑ 10 Brian Giles .... .50 .15
❑ 11 Roger Clemens .... 2.00 .60
❑ 12 Todd Helton .... .75 .23
❑ 13 Ivan Rodriguez .... .75 .23
❑ 14 David Ortiz .... 1.25 .35
❑ 15 Sammy Sosa...................... 1.25 .35
❑ 16 Chipper Jones.................. 1.25 .35
❑ 17 Mark Buehrle...................... .50 .15
❑ 18 Miguel Cabrera .... .75 .23
❑ 19 Johan Santana.................. .75 .23
❑ 20 Randy Johnson .... 1.25 .35
❑ 21 Jim Thome .... .75 .23
❑ 22 Vladimir Guerrero .... 1.25 .35
❑ 23 Dontrelle Willis .... .50 .15
❑ 24 Nomar Garciaparra .... 1.25 .35
❑ 25 Barry Bonds .... 3.00 .90
❑ 26 Curt Schilling .... .75 .23
❑ 27 Carlos Beltran .... .50 .15
❑ 28 Albert Pujols .... 2.50 .75
❑ 29 Mark Prior.......................... .75 .23
❑ 30 Derek Jeter .... 2.50 .75
❑ 31 Ryan Garko FY RC............ 2.50 .75
❑ 32 Eulogio De La Cruz FY RC 1.00 .30
❑ 33 Luke Scott FY RC .... 1.50 .45
❑ 34 Shane Costa FY RC.......... 1.00 .30
❑ 35 Casey McGehee FY RC .... 1.00 .30
❑ 36 Jered Weaver FY RC 8.00 2.40
❑ 37 Kevin Melillo FY RC .... 2.00 .60
❑ 38 D.J. Houlton FY RC.......... 1.00 .30
❑ 39 Brandon Moorhead FY RC 1.00 .30
❑ 40 Jerry Owens FY RC .... 1.50 .45
❑ 41 Elliot Johnson FY RC ...... 1.00 .30
❑ 42 Kevin West FY RC............ 1.00 .30
❑ 43 Hernan Iribarren FY RC .... 2.00 .60
❑ 44 Miguel Montero FY RC 5.00 1.50
❑ 45 Craig Tatum FY RC .... 1.00 .30
❑ 46 Ryan Sweeney FY RC ...... 2.50 .75
❑ 47 Micah Furtado FY RC ...... 1.00 .30
❑ 48 Cody Haerther FY RC ...... 1.00 .30
❑ 49 Erick Abreu FY RC............ 2.00 .60
❑ 50 Chuck Tiffany FY RC........ 2.50 .75
❑ 51 Tadahito Iguchi FY RC 4.00 1.20
❑ 52 Frank Diaz FY RC .... 1.00 .30
❑ 53 Errol Simonitsch FY RC .. 1.50 .45
❑ 54 Wade Robinson FY RC .... 1.00 .30
❑ 55 Adam Boeve FY RC.......... 1.00 .30
❑ 56 Steven Bondurant FY RC.. 1.00 .30
❑ 57 Jason Motte FY RC .... 1.00 .30
❑ 58 Juan Senreiso FY RC ...... 1.00 .30
❑ 59 Vinny Rottino FY RC .... 1.00 .30
❑ 60 Jai Miller FY RC .... 1.50 .45
❑ 61 Thomas Pauly FY RC ...... 1.00 .30
❑ 62 Tony Giarratano FY RC .... 1.00 .30
❑ 63 Alexander Smit FY RC...... 1.00 .30
❑ 64 Keiichi Yabu FY RC.......... 1.00 .30
❑ 65 Brian Bannister FY RC...... 1.00 .30
❑ 66 Kennard Bibbs FY RC ...... 1.00 .30
❑ 67 Anthony Reyes FY RC 5.00 1.50
❑ 68 Thomas Oldham FY RC .... 1.00 .30
❑ 69 Ben Harrison FY .... 1.00 .30
❑ 70 Daryl Thompson FY RC...... 1.00 .30
❑ 71 Kevin Collins FY RC .... 1.00 .30
❑ 72 Wes Swackhamer FY RC.. 1.00 .30
❑ 73 Landon Powell FY RC ...... 1.50 .45
❑ 74 Matt Brown FY RC............ 1.00 .30
❑ 75 Russ Martin FY RC .... 2.00 .60
❑ 76 Nick Touchstone FY RC .. 1.00 .30
❑ 77 Steven White FY RC .... 2.00 .60
❑ 78 Ian Bladergroen FY RC .... 1.50 .45
❑ 79 Sean Marshall FY RC ...... 1.50 .45
❑ 80 Nick Masset FY RC .... 1.00 .30
❑ 81 Ryan Goleski FY RC .... 1.00 .30
❑ 82 Matt Campbell FY RC ...... 1.00 .30
❑ 83 Manny Parra FY RC.......... 1.00 .30
❑ 84 Melky Cabrera FY RC ...... 2.50 .75
❑ 85 Ryan Feierabend FY RC.... 1.00 .30
❑ 86 Nate McLouth FY RC........ 1.50 .45
❑ 87 Glen Perkins FY RC.......... 2.00 .60
❑ 88 Kila Kaaihue FY RC .... 2.50 .75
❑ 89 Dana Eveland FY RC .... 1.00 .30
❑ 90 Tyler Pelland FY RC .... 1.50 .45
❑ 91 Matt Van Der Bosch FY RC 1.00 .30
❑ 92 Andy Santana FY RC........ 1.00 .30
❑ 93 Eric Nielsen FY RC .... 1.00 .30
❑ 94 Brendan Ryan FY RC........ 1.00 .30
❑ 95 Ian Kinsler FY RC .... 2.50 .75
❑ 96 Matthew Kemp FY RC 4.00 1.20
❑ 97 Stephen Drew FY RC...... 10.00 3.00
❑ 98 Peeter Ramos FY RC........ 1.00 .30
❑ 99 Chris Seddon FY RC........ 1.00 .30
❑ 100 Chuck James FY RC 5.00 1.50
❑ 101 Travis Chick FY AU RC 10.00 3.00
❑ 102 Justin Verlander FY AU RC 20.00 6.00
❑ 103 Billy Butler FY AU RC .. 40.00 12.00
❑ 104 Chris B.Young FY AU RC 25.00 7.50
❑ 105 Jake Postlewait FY AU RC 8.00 2.40
❑ 106 C.J. Smith FY AU RC 8.00 2.40
❑ 107 Mike Rodriguez FY AU RC 8.00 2.40
❑ 108 Philip Humber FY AU RC 12.00 3.60
❑ 109 Jeff Niemann FY AU RC 12.00 3.60
❑ 110 Brian Miller FY AU RC .. 8.00 2.40

❑ 111 Chris Vines FY AU RC	8.00	2.40
❑ 112 Andy LaRoche FY AU RC	35.00	10.50
❑ 113 Mike Bourn FY AU RC	10.00	3.00
❑ 114 Wlad Balentein FY AU RC	12.00	3.60
❑ 115 Ismael Ramirez FY AU RC	8.00	2.40
❑ 116 Hayden Penn FY AU RC	10.00	3.00
❑ 117 Pedro Lopez FY AU RC	8.00	2.40
❑ 118 Shawn Bowman FY AU RC	10.00	3.00
❑ 119 Chad Orvella FY AU RC	8.00	2.40
❑ 120 Sean Tracey FY AU RC	8.00	2.40
❑ 121 Bobby Livingston FY AU RC	8.00	2.40
❑ 122 Michael Rogers FY AU RC	8.00	2.40
❑ 123 Willy Mota FY AU RC	8.00	2.40
❑ 124 Bran McCarthy FY AU RC	25.00	7.50
❑ 125 Mike Morse FY AU RC	15.00	4.50
❑ 126 Matt Lindstrom FY AU RC	8.00	2.40
❑ 127 Brian Stavisky FY AU RC	8.00	2.40
❑ 128 Richie Gardner FY AU RC	8.00	2.40
❑ 129 Scott Mitchinson FY AU RC	8.00	2.40
❑ 130 Billy McCarthy FY AU RC	8.00	2.40
❑ 131 Brandon Sing FY AU RC	12.00	3.60
❑ 132 Matt Albers FY AU RC	8.00	2.40
❑ 133 George Kottaras FY AU RC	10.00	3.00
❑ 134 Luis Hernandez FY AU RC	8.00	2.40
❑ 135 Hum Sanchez FY AU RC	8.00	2.40
❑ 136 Buck Coats FY AU RC	8.00	2.40
❑ 137 Jon Barratt FY AU RC	8.00	2.40
❑ 138 Raul Tablado FY AU RC	8.00	2.40
❑ 139 Jake Mullinax FY AU RC	8.00	2.40
❑ 140 Edgar Varela FY AU RC	8.00	2.40
❑ 141 Ryan Garko FY AU	15.00	4.50
❑ 142 Nate McLouth FY AU	10.00	3.00
❑ 143 Shane Costa FY AU	8.00	2.40

1914 Cracker Jack

	Ex-Mt	VG
COMPLETE SET (144)	45000.00	22500.00
❑ 1 Otto Knabe	250.00	125.00
❑ 2 Frank Baker	400.00	200.00
❑ 3 Joe Tinker	400.00	200.00
❑ 4 Larry Doyle	175.00	90.00
❑ 5 Ward Miller	150.00	75.00
❑ 6 Eddie Plank	600.00	300.00
Phila. AL		
❑ 7 Eddie Collins	450.00	220.00
Phila. AL		
❑ 8 Rube Oldring	150.00	75.00
❑ 9 Artie Hoffman	150.00	75.00
❑ 10 John McInnis	150.00	75.00
❑ 11 George Stovall	150.00	75.00
❑ 12 Connie Mack MG	500.00	250.00
❑ 13 Art Wilson	150.00	75.00
❑ 14 Sam Crawford	300.00	150.00
❑ 15 Reb Russell	150.00	75.00
❑ 16 Howie Camnitz	150.00	75.00
❑ 17 Roger Bresnahan	350.00	180.00
Catcher		
❑ 18 Johnny Evers	350.00	180.00
❑ 19 Chief Bender	450.00	220.00
Phila. AL		
❑ 20 Cy Falkenberg	150.00	75.00
❑ 21 Heinie Zimmerman	150.00	75.00
❑ 22 Joe Wood	300.00	150.00
❑ 23 Chas.Comiskey OWN	350.00	180.00
❑ 24 George Mullen	150.00	75.00
❑ 25 Michael Simon	150.00	75.00
❑ 26 James Scott	150.00	75.00
❑ 27 Bill Carrigan	150.00	75.00
❑ 28 Jack Barry	150.00	75.00
❑ 29 Vean Gregg	200.00	100.00
Cleveland		
❑ 30 Ty Cobb	6000.00	3000.00
❑ 31 Heinie Wagner	150.00	75.00
❑ 32 Mordecai Brown	350.00	180.00
❑ 33 Amos Strunk	150.00	75.00
❑ 34 Ira Thomas	150.00	75.00
❑ 35 Harry Hooper	300.00	150.00
❑ 36 Ed Walsh	300.00	150.00
❑ 37 Grover C. Alexander	800.00	400.00
❑ 38 Red Dooin	200.00	100.00
Phila. NL		
❑ 39 Chick Gandil	350.00	180.00
❑ 40 Jimmy Austin	200.00	100.00
St.L. AL		
❑ 41 Tommy Leach	150.00	75.00
❑ 42 Al Bridwell	150.00	75.00
❑ 43 Rube Marquard	350.00	180.00
NY NL		
❑ 44 Charles Tesreau	150.00	75.00
❑ 45 Fred Luderus	150.00	75.00
❑ 46 Bob Groom	150.00	75.00
❑ 47 Josh Devore	200.00	100.00
Phila. NL		
❑ 48 Harry Lord	250.00	125.00
❑ 49 John Miller	150.00	75.00
❑ 50 John Hummell	150.00	75.00
❑ 51 Nap Rucker	175.00	90.00
❑ 52 Zach Wheat	350.00	180.00
❑ 53 Otto Miller	150.00	75.00
❑ 54 Marty O'Toole	150.00	75.00
❑ 55 Dick Hoblitzel	200.00	100.00
Cinc.		
❑ 56 Clyde Milan	175.00	90.00
❑ 57 Walter Johnson	2000.00	1000.00
❑ 58 Wally Schang	175.00	90.00
❑ 59 Harry Gessler	150.00	75.00
❑ 60 Rollie Zeider	250.00	125.00
❑ 61 Ray Schalk	300.00	150.00
❑ 62 Jay Cashion	300.00	150.00
❑ 63 Babe Adams	175.00	90.00
❑ 64 Jimmy Archer	150.00	75.00
❑ 65 Tris Speaker	700.00	350.00
❑ 66 Napoleon Lajoie	800.00	400.00
Cleve.		
❑ 67 Otis Crandall	150.00	75.00
❑ 68 Honus Wagner	2500.00	1250.00
❑ 69 John McGraw	450.00	220.00
❑ 70 Fred Clarke	300.00	150.00
❑ 71 Chief Meyers	175.00	90.00
❑ 72 John Boehling	150.00	75.00
❑ 73 Max Carey	300.00	150.00
❑ 74 Frank Owens	150.00	75.00
❑ 75 Miller Huggins	300.00	150.00
❑ 76 Claude Hendrix	150.00	75.00
❑ 77 Hughie Jennings MG	300.00	150.00
❑ 78 Fred Merkle	200.00	100.00
❑ 79 Ping Bodie	175.00	90.00
❑ 80 Ed Ruelbach	175.00	90.00
❑ 81 Jim C. Delehanty	175.00	90.00
❑ 82 Gavvy Cravath	200.00	100.00
❑ 83 Russ Ford	150.00	75.00
❑ 84 Elmer E. Knetzer	150.00	75.00
❑ 85 Buck Herzog	150.00	75.00
❑ 86 Burt Shotton	150.00	75.00
❑ 87 Forrest Cady	150.00	75.00
❑ 88 Christy Mathewson	3000.00	1500.00
Pitching		
❑ 89 Lawrence Cheney	150.00	75.00
❑ 90 Frank Smith	150.00	75.00
❑ 91 Roger Peckinpaugh	175.00	90.00
❑ 92 Al Demaree N.Y. NL	200.00	100.00
❑ 93 Del Pratt	250.00	125.00
Throwing		
❑ 94 Eddie Cicotte	325.00	160.00
❑ 95 Ray Keating	150.00	75.00
❑ 96 Beals Becker	150.00	75.00
❑ 97 John(Rube) Benton	150.00	75.00
❑ 98 Frank LaPorte	150.00	75.00
❑ 99 Frank Chance	1500.00	750.00
❑ 100 Thomas Seaton	150.00	75.00
❑ 101 Frank Schulte	150.00	75.00
❑ 102 Ray Fisher	150.00	75.00
❑ 103 Joe Jackson	8000.00	4000.00
❑ 104 Vic Saier	150.00	75.00
❑ 105 James Lavender	150.00	75.00
❑ 106 Joe Birmingham	150.00	75.00
❑ 107 Tom Downey	150.00	75.00
❑ 108 Sherry Magee	200.00	100.00
Phila. NL		
❑ 109 Fred Blanding	150.00	75.00
❑ 110 Bob Bescher	150.00	75.00
❑ 111 Jim Callahan	300.00	150.00
❑ 112 Ed Sweeney	150.00	75.00
❑ 113 George Suggs	150.00	75.00
❑ 114 Geo.J. Moriarty	175.00	90.00
❑ 115 Addison Brennan	150.00	75.00
❑ 116 Rollie Zeider	150.00	75.00
❑ 117 Ted Easterly	150.00	75.00
❑ 118 Ed Konetchy	200.00	100.00
Pittsburgh		
❑ 119 George Perring	150.00	75.00
❑ 120 Mike Doolan	150.00	75.00
❑ 121 Hub Perdue	200.00	100.00
Boston NL		
❑ 122 Owen Bush	150.00	75.00
❑ 123 Slim Sallee	150.00	75.00
❑ 124 Earl Moore	150.00	75.00
❑ 125 Bert Niehoff	200.00	100.00
❑ 126 Walter Blair	150.00	75.00
❑ 127 Butch Schmidt	150.00	75.00
❑ 128 Steve Evans	150.00	75.00
❑ 129 Ray Caldwell	150.00	75.00
❑ 130 Ivy Wingo	150.00	75.00
❑ 131 George Baumgardner	150.00	75.00
❑ 132 Les Nunamaker	150.00	75.00
❑ 133 Branch Rickey MG	450.00	220.00
❑ 134 Armando Marsans	200.00	100.00
Cincinnati		
❑ 135 Bill Killefer	150.00	75.00
❑ 136 Rabbit Maranville	350.00	180.00
❑ 137 William Rariden	150.00	75.00
❑ 138 Hank Gowdy	150.00	75.00
❑ 139 Rebel Oakes	150.00	75.00
❑ 140 Danny Murphy	150.00	75.00
❑ 141 Cy Barger	150.00	75.00
❑ 142 Eugene Packard	150.00	75.00
❑ 143 Jake Daubert	175.00	90.00
❑ 144 James C. Walsh	200.00	100.00

1915 Cracker Jack

	Ex-Mt	VG
COMPLETE SET (176)	35000.00	17500.00
COMMON CARD (1-144)	100.00	50.00
COMM. CARD (145-176)	125.00	60.00
❑ 1 Otto Knabe	175.00	90.00
❑ 2 Frank Baker	350.00	180.00
❑ 3 Joe Tinker	350.00	180.00
❑ 4 Larry Doyle	100.00	50.00
❑ 5 Ward Miller	100.00	50.00
❑ 6 Eddie Plank	500.00	250.00
St.L. FED		
❑ 7 Eddie Collins	350.00	180.00
Chicago AL		
❑ 8 Rube Oldring	100.00	50.00
❑ 9 Artie Hoffman	100.00	50.00
❑ 10 John McInnis	100.00	50.00
❑ 11 George Stovall	100.00	50.00
❑ 12 Connie Mack MG	400.00	200.00
❑ 13 Art Wilson	100.00	50.00
❑ 14 Sam Crawford	300.00	150.00

Card	Price 1	Price 2
❑ 15 Reb Russell	100.00	50.00
❑ 16 Howie Camnitz	100.00	50.00
❑ 17 Roger Bresnahan	300.00	150.00
❑ 18 Johnny Evers	300.00	150.00
❑ 19 Chief Bender	350.00	180.00
Baltimore FED		
❑ 20 Cy Falkenberg	100.00	50.00
❑ 21 Heinie Zimmerman	100.00	50.00
❑ 22 Joe Wood	250.00	125.00
❑ 23 C. Comiskey OWN	300.00	150.00
❑ 24 George Mullen	100.00	50.00
❑ 25 Michael Simon	100.00	50.00
❑ 26 James Scott	100.00	50.00
❑ 27 Bill Carrigan	100.00	50.00
❑ 28 Jack Barry	100.00	50.00
❑ 29 Vean Gregg	125.00	60.00
Boston AL		
❑ 30 Ty Cobb	4000.00	2000.00
❑ 31 Heinie Wagner	100.00	50.00
❑ 32 Mordecai Brown	300.00	150.00
❑ 33 Amos Strunk	100.00	50.00
❑ 34 Ira Thomas	100.00	50.00
❑ 35 Harry Hooper	250.00	125.00
❑ 36 Ed Walsh	300.00	150.00
❑ 37 Grover C. Alexander	600.00	300.00
❑ 38 Red Dooin	125.00	60.00
Cincinnati		
❑ 39 Chick Gandil	300.00	150.00
❑ 40 Jimmy Austin	125.00	60.00
Pitts. FED UER		
Biographical Information is wrong		
❑ 41 Tommy Leach	100.00	50.00
❑ 42 Al Bridwell	100.00	50.00
❑ 43 Rube Marquard	350.00	180.00
Brooklyn FED		
❑ 44 Charles(Jeff) Tesreau	100.00	50.00
❑ 45 Fred Luderus	100.00	50.00
❑ 46 Bob Groom	100.00	50.00
❑ 47 Josh Devore	125.00	60.00
Boston NL		
❑ 48 Steve O'Neill	125.00	60.00
❑ 49 John Miller	100.00	50.00
❑ 50 John Hummell	100.00	50.00
❑ 51 Nap Rucker	125.00	60.00
❑ 52 Zach Wheat	300.00	150.00
❑ 53 Otto Miller	100.00	50.00
❑ 54 Marty O'Toole	100.00	50.00
❑ 55 Dick Hoblitzel	125.00	60.00
Boston AL		
❑ 56 Clyde Milan	125.00	60.00
❑ 57 Walter Johnson	1500.00	750.00
❑ 58 Wally Schang	125.00	60.00
❑ 59 Harry Gessler	100.00	50.00
❑ 60 Oscar Dugey	125.00	60.00
❑ 61 Ray Schalk	250.00	125.00
❑ 62 Willie Mitchell	125.00	60.00
❑ 63 Babe Adams	125.00	60.00
❑ 64 Jimmy Archer	100.00	50.00
❑ 65 Tris Speaker	600.00	300.00
❑ 66 Napoleon Lajoie	600.00	300.00
Phila. AL		
❑ 67 Otis Crandall	100.00	50.00
❑ 68 Honus Wagner	1500.00	750.00
❑ 69 John McGraw MG	300.00	150.00
❑ 70 Fred Clarke	250.00	125.00
❑ 71 Chief Meyers	100.00	50.00
❑ 72 John Boehling	100.00	50.00
❑ 73 Max Carey	250.00	125.00
❑ 74 Frank Owens	100.00	50.00
❑ 75 Miller Huggins	300.00	150.00
❑ 76 Claude Hendrix	100.00	50.00
❑ 77 Hughie Jennings MG	300.00	150.00
❑ 78 Fred Merkle	125.00	60.00
❑ 79 Ping Bodie	125.00	60.00
❑ 80 Ed Ruelbach	125.00	60.00
❑ 81 Jim C. Delehanty	125.00	60.00
❑ 82 Gavvy Cravath	125.00	60.00
❑ 83 Russ Ford	100.00	50.00
❑ 84 Elmer E. Knetzer	100.00	50.00
❑ 85 Buck Herzog	100.00	50.00
❑ 86 Burt Shotton	100.00	50.00
❑ 87 Forrest Cady	100.00	50.00
❑ 88 Christy Mathewson	1500.00	750.00
Portrait		
❑ 89 Lawrence Cheney	100.00	50.00
❑ 90 Frank Smith	100.00	50.00
❑ 91 Roger Peckinpaugh	125.00	60.00
❑ 92 Al Demaree	125.00	60.00
Phila. NL		
❑ 93 Del Pratt	175.00	90.00
Portrait		
❑ 94 Eddie Cicotte	300.00	150.00
❑ 95 Ray Keating	100.00	50.00
❑ 96 Beals Becker	100.00	50.00
❑ 97 John(Rube) Benton	100.00	50.00
❑ 98 Frank LaPorte	100.00	50.00
❑ 99 Hal Chase	300.00	150.00
❑ 100 Thomas Seaton	100.00	50.00
❑ 101 Frank Schulte	100.00	50.00
❑ 102 Ray Fisher	100.00	50.00
❑ 103 Joe Jackson	8000.00	4000.00
❑ 104 Vic Saier	100.00	50.00
❑ 105 James Lavender	100.00	50.00
❑ 106 Joe Birmingham MG	100.00	50.00
❑ 107 Thomas Downey	100.00	50.00
❑ 108 Sherry Magee	125.00	60.00
Boston NL		
❑ 109 Fred Blanding	100.00	50.00
❑ 110 Bob Bescher	100.00	50.00
❑ 111 Herbie Moran	125.00	60.00
❑ 112 Ed Sweeney	100.00	50.00
❑ 113 George Suggs	100.00	50.00
❑ 114 Geo.J. Moriarty	125.00	60.00
❑ 115 Addison Brennan	100.00	50.00
❑ 116 Rollie Zeider	100.00	50.00
❑ 117 Ted Easterly	100.00	50.00
❑ 118 Ed Konetchy	125.00	60.00
Pitts. FED		
❑ 119 George Perring	100.00	50.00
❑ 120 Mike Doolan	100.00	50.00
❑ 121 Hub Perdue	125.00	60.00
St. Louis NL		
❑ 122 Owen Bush	100.00	50.00
❑ 123 Slim Sallee	100.00	50.00
❑ 124 Earl Moore	100.00	50.00
❑ 125 Bert Niehoff	125.00	60.00
Phila. NL		
❑ 126 Walter Blair	100.00	50.00
❑ 127 Butch Schmidt	100.00	50.00
❑ 128 Steve Evans	100.00	50.00
❑ 129 Ray Caldwell	100.00	50.00
❑ 130 Ivy Wingo	100.00	50.00
❑ 131 Geo. Baumgardner	100.00	50.00
❑ 132 Les Nunamaker	100.00	50.00
❑ 133 Branch Rickey MG	300.00	150.00
❑ 134 Armando Marsans	125.00	60.00
St.L. FED		
❑ 135 William Killefer	100.00	50.00
❑ 136 Rabbit Maranville	250.00	125.00
❑ 137 William Rariden	100.00	50.00
❑ 138 Hank Gowdy	100.00	50.00
❑ 139 Rebel Oakes	100.00	50.00
❑ 140 Danny Murphy	100.00	50.00
❑ 141 Cy Barger	100.00	50.00
❑ 142 Eugene Packard	100.00	50.00
❑ 143 Jake Daubert	100.00	50.00
❑ 144 James C. Walsh	100.00	50.00
❑ 145 Ted Cather	125.00	60.00
❑ 146 George Tyler	125.00	60.00
❑ 147 Lee Magee	125.00	60.00
❑ 148 Owen Wilson	125.00	60.00
❑ 149 Hal Janvrin	125.00	60.00
❑ 150 Doc Johnston	125.00	60.00
❑ 151 George Whitted	125.00	60.00
❑ 152 George McQuillen	125.00	60.00
❑ 153 Bill James	125.00	60.00
❑ 154 Dick Rudolph	125.00	60.00
❑ 155 Joe Connolly	125.00	60.00
❑ 156 Jean Dubuc	125.00	60.00
❑ 157 George Kaiserling	125.00	60.00
❑ 158 Fritz Maisel	125.00	60.00
❑ 159 Heinie Groh	125.00	60.00
❑ 160 Benny Kauff	125.00	60.00
❑ 161 Edd Roush	300.00	150.00
❑ 162 George Stallings MG	125.00	60.00
❑ 163 Bert Whaling	125.00	60.00
❑ 164 Bob Shawkey	125.00	60.00
❑ 165 Eddie Murphy	125.00	60.00
❑ 166 Joe Bush	125.00	60.00
❑ 167 Clark Griffith	300.00	150.00
❑ 168 Vin Campbell	125.00	60.00
❑ 169 Raymond Collins	125.00	60.00
❑ 170 Hans Lobert	125.00	60.00
❑ 171 Earl Hamilton	125.00	60.00
❑ 172 Erskine Mayer	125.00	60.00
❑ 173 Tilly Walker	125.00	60.00
❑ 174 Robert Veach	125.00	60.00
❑ 175 Joseph Benz	125.00	60.00
❑ 176 Hippo Vaughn	175.00	90.00

2002 Diamond Kings

	Nm-Mt	Ex-Mt
COMP.LOW SET (150)	200.00	60.00
COMP.LOW w/o SP's (100)	50.00	15.00
COMP.UPDATE SET (10)	40.00	12.00
COMMON CARD (1-100)	.50	.15
COMMON PROSPECT (101-150)	4.00	1.20
COMMON RETIRED (101-150)	4.00	1.20
COMMON CARD (151-160)	4.00	1.20

Card	Nm-Mt	Ex-Mt
❑ 1 Vladimir Guerrero	1.25	.35
❑ 2 Adam Dunn	.50	.15
❑ 3 Tsuyoshi Shinjo	.50	.15
❑ 4 Adrian Beltre	.50	.15
❑ 5 Troy Glaus	.50	.15
❑ 6 Albert Pujols	2.50	.75
❑ 7 Trot Nixon	.50	.15
❑ 8 Alex Rodriguez	2.00	.60
❑ 9 Tom Glavine	.75	.23
❑ 10 Alfonso Soriano	.50	.15
❑ 11 Todd Helton	.75	.23
❑ 12 Joe Torre	.75	.23
❑ 13 Tim Hudson	.50	.15
❑ 14 Andruw Jones	.75	.23
❑ 15 Shawn Green	.50	.15
❑ 16 Aramis Ramirez	.50	.15
❑ 17 Shannon Stewart	.50	.15
❑ 18 Barry Bonds	3.00	.90
❑ 19 Sean Casey	.75	.23
❑ 20 Barry Larkin	.75	.23
❑ 21 Scott Rolen	.75	.23
❑ 22 Barry Zito	.50	.15
❑ 23 Sammy Sosa	1.25	.35
❑ 24 Bartolo Colon	.50	.15
❑ 25 Ryan Klesko	.50	.15
❑ 26 Ben Grieve	.50	.15
❑ 27 Roy Oswalt	.50	.15
❑ 28 Kazuhiro Sasaki	.50	.15
❑ 29 Roger Clemens	2.50	.75
❑ 30 Bernie Williams	.75	.23
❑ 31 Roberto Alomar	.75	.23
❑ 32 Bobby Abreu	.50	.15
❑ 33 Robert Fick	.50	.15
❑ 34 Bret Boone	.50	.15
❑ 35 Rickey Henderson	1.25	.35
❑ 36 Brian Giles	.50	.15
❑ 37 Richie Sexson	.50	.15
❑ 38 Bud Smith	.50	.15
❑ 39 Richard Hidalgo	.50	.15
❑ 40 C. C. Sabathia	.50	.15
❑ 41 Rich Aurilia	.50	.15
❑ 42 Carlos Beltran	.50	.15
❑ 43 Raul Mondesi	.50	.15
❑ 44 Carlos Delgado	.50	.15
❑ 45 Randy Johnson	1.25	.35
❑ 46 Chan Ho Park	.50	.15
❑ 47 Rafael Palmeiro	.75	.23
❑ 48 Chipper Jones	1.25	.35
❑ 49 Phil Nevin	.50	.15
❑ 50 Cliff Floyd	.50	.15

	Nm-Mt	Ex-Mt
❑ 51 Pedro Martinez	.75	.23
❑ 52 Craig Biggio	.75	.23
❑ 53 Paul LoDuca	.50	.15
❑ 54 Cristian Guzman	.50	.15
❑ 55 Pat Burrell	.50	.15
❑ 56 Curt Schilling	.50	.15
❑ 57 Orlando Cabrera	.50	.15
❑ 58 Darin Erstad	.50	.15
❑ 59 Omar Vizquel	.75	.23
❑ 60 Derek Jeter	3.00	.90
❑ 61 Nomar Garciaparra	2.00	.60
❑ 62 Edgar Martinez	.75	.23
❑ 63 Moises Alou	.50	.15
❑ 64 Eric Chavez	.50	.15
❑ 65 Mike Sweeney	.50	.15
❑ 66 Frank Thomas	1.25	.35
❑ 67 Mike Piazza	2.00	.60
❑ 68 Gary Sheffield	.50	.15
❑ 69 Mike Mussina	.75	.23
❑ 70 Greg Maddux	2.00	.60
❑ 71 Juan Gonzalez	.50	.15
❑ 72 Hideo Nomo	1.25	.35
❑ 73 Miguel Tejada	.50	.15
❑ 74 Ichiro Suzuki	2.50	.75
❑ 75 Matt Morris	.50	.15
❑ 76 Ivan Rodriguez	.75	.23
❑ 77 Mark Mulder	.50	.15
❑ 78 J.D. Drew	.50	.15
❑ 79 Mark Grace	.75	.23
❑ 80 Jason Giambi	.50	.15
❑ 81 Mark Buehrle	.50	.15
❑ 82 Jose Vidro	.50	.15
❑ 83 Manny Ramirez	.75	.23
❑ 84 Jeff Bagwell	.75	.23
❑ 85 Magglio Ordonez	.50	.15
❑ 86 Ken Griffey Jr.	2.00	.60
❑ 87 Luis Gonzalez	.50	.15
❑ 88 Jim Edmonds	.75	.23
❑ 89 Larry Walker	.50	.15
❑ 90 Jim Thome	.75	.23
❑ 91 Lance Berkman	.50	.15
❑ 92 Jorge Posada	.75	.23
❑ 93 Kevin Brown	.50	.15
❑ 94 Joe Mays	.50	.15
❑ 95 Kerry Wood	.50	.15
❑ 96 Mark Ellis	.50	.15
❑ 97 Austin Kearns	.50	.15
❑ 98 Jorge De La Rosa RC	.50	.15
❑ 99 Brandon Berger	.50	.15
❑ 100 Ryan Ludwick	.50	.15
❑ 101 Marlon Byrd SP	4.00	1.20
❑ 102 Brandon Backe SP RC	4.00	1.20
❑ 103 Juan Cruz SP	4.00	1.20
❑ 104 Anderson Machado SP RC	4.00	1.20
❑ 105 So Taguchi SP RC	4.00	1.20
❑ 106 Dewon Brazelton SP	4.00	1.20
❑ 107 Josh Beckett SP	4.00	1.20
❑ 108 John Buck SP	4.00	1.20
❑ 109 Jorge Padilla SP RC	4.00	1.20
❑ 110 Hee Seop Choi SP	4.00	1.20
❑ 111 Angel Berroa SP	4.00	1.20
❑ 112 Mark Teixeira SP	5.00	1.50
❑ 113 Victor Martinez SP	5.00	1.50
❑ 114 Kazuhisa Ishii SP RC	4.00	1.20
❑ 115 Dennis Tankersley SP	4.00	1.20
❑ 116 Wilson Valdez SP RC	4.00	1.20
❑ 117 Antonio Perez SP	4.00	1.20
❑ 118 Ed Rogers SP	4.00	1.20
❑ 119 Wilson Betemit SP	4.00	1.20
❑ 120 Mike Rivera SP	4.00	1.20
❑ 121 Mark Prior SP	5.00	1.50
❑ 122 Roberto Clemente SP	8.00	2.40
❑ 123 Roberto Clemente SP	8.00	2.40
❑ 124 Roberto Clemente SP	8.00	2.40
❑ 125 Roberto Clemente SP	8.00	2.40
❑ 126 Roberto Clemente SP	8.00	2.40
❑ 127 Babe Ruth SP	10.00	3.00
❑ 128 Ted Williams SP	8.00	2.40
❑ 129 Andre Dawson SP	4.00	1.20
❑ 130 Eddie Murray SP	5.00	1.50
❑ 131 Juan Marichal SP	4.00	1.20
❑ 132 Kirby Puckett SP	5.00	1.50
❑ 133 Alan Trammell SP	4.00	1.20
❑ 134 Bobby Doerr SP	4.00	1.20
❑ 135 Carlton Fisk SP	4.00	1.20
❑ 136 Eddie Mathews SP	5.00	1.50
❑ 137 Mike Schmidt SP	10.00	3.00
❑ 138 Catfish Hunter SP	4.00	1.20
❑ 139 Nolan Ryan SP	12.00	3.60
❑ 140 George Brett SP	10.00	3.00
❑ 141 Gary Carter SP	4.00	1.20
❑ 142 Paul Molitor SP	4.00	1.20
❑ 143 Lou Gehrig SP	6.00	1.80
❑ 144 Ryne Sandberg SP	10.00	3.00
❑ 145 Tony Gwynn SP	6.00	1.80
❑ 146 Ron Santo SP	4.00	1.20
❑ 147 Cal Ripken SP	15.00	4.50
❑ 148 Al Kaline SP	5.00	1.50
❑ 149 Bo Jackson SP	5.00	1.50
❑ 150 Don Mattingly SP	10.00	3.00
❑ 151 Chris Snelling RC	5.00	1.50
❑ 152 Satoru Komiyama RC	4.00	1.20
❑ 153 Oliver Perez RC	6.00	1.80
❑ 154 Kirk Saarloos RC	4.00	1.20
❑ 155 Rene Reyes RC	4.00	1.20
❑ 156 Runelvys Hernandez RC	4.00	1.20
❑ 157 Rodrigo Rosario RC	4.00	1.20
❑ 158 Jason Simontacchi RC	4.00	1.20
❑ 159 Miguel Asencio RC	4.00	1.20
❑ 160 Aaron Cook RC	4.00	1.20

2003 Diamond Kings

	Nm-Mt	Ex-Mt
COMP.LO SET (176)	150.00	45.00
COMP.LO SET w/o SP's (150)	50.00	15.00
COMMON CARD (1-150)	.50	.15
COMMON CARD (151-158)	2.00	.60
COMMON CARD (159-175)	4.00	1.20
COMMON CARD (177-201)	4.00	1.20
❑ 1 Darin Erstad	.50	.15
❑ 2 Garret Anderson	.50	.15
❑ 3 Troy Glaus	.50	.15
❑ 4 David Eckstein	.50	.15
❑ 5 Jarrod Washburn	.50	.15
❑ 6 Adam Kennedy	.50	.15
❑ 7 Jay Gibbons	.50	.15
❑ 8 Tony Batista	.50	.15
❑ 9 Melvin Mora	.50	.15
❑ 10 Rodrigo Lopez	.50	.15
❑ 11 Manny Ramirez	.75	.23
❑ 12 Pedro Martinez	.75	.23
❑ 13 Nomar Garciaparra	2.00	.60
❑ 14 Rickey Henderson	1.25	.35
❑ 15 Johnny Damon	.75	.23
❑ 16 Derek Lowe	.50	.15
❑ 17 Cliff Floyd	.50	.15
❑ 18 Frank Thomas	1.25	.35
❑ 19 Magglio Ordonez	.50	.15
❑ 20 Paul Konerko	.50	.15
❑ 21 Mark Buehrle	.50	.15
❑ 22 C.C. Sabathia	.50	.15
❑ 23 Omar Vizquel	.75	.23
❑ 24 Jim Thome	.75	.23
❑ 25 Ellis Burks	.50	.15
❑ 26 Robert Fick	.50	.15
❑ 27 Bobby Higginson	.50	.15
❑ 28 Randall Simon	.50	.15
❑ 29 Carlos Pena	.50	.15
❑ 30 Carlos Beltran	.50	.15
❑ 31 Paul Byrd	.50	.15
❑ 32 Raul Ibanez	.50	.15
❑ 33 Mike Sweeney	.50	.15
❑ 34 Torii Hunter	.50	.15
❑ 35 Corey Koskie	.50	.15
❑ 36 A.J. Pierzynski	.50	.15
❑ 37 Cristian Guzman	.50	.15
❑ 38 Jacque Jones	.50	.15
❑ 39 Derek Jeter	3.00	.90
❑ 40 Bernie Williams	.75	.23
❑ 41 Roger Clemens	2.50	.75
❑ 42 Mike Mussina	.75	.23
❑ 43 Jorge Posada	.75	.23
❑ 44 Alfonso Soriano	.50	.15
❑ 45 Jason Giambi	.50	.15
❑ 46 Robin Ventura	.50	.15
❑ 47 David Wells	.50	.15
❑ 48 Tim Hudson	.50	.15
❑ 49 Barry Zito	.50	.15
❑ 50 Mark Mulder	.50	.15
❑ 51 Miguel Tejada	.50	.15
❑ 52 Eric Chavez	.50	.15
❑ 53 Jermaine Dye	.50	.15
❑ 54 Ichiro Suzuki	2.50	.75
❑ 55 Edgar Martinez	.75	.23
❑ 56 John Olerud	.50	.15
❑ 57 Dan Wilson	.50	.15
❑ 58 Joel Pineiro	.50	.15
❑ 59 Kazuhiro Sasaki	.50	.15
❑ 60 Freddy Garcia	.50	.15
❑ 61 Aubrey Huff	.50	.15
❑ 62 Steve Cox	.50	.15
❑ 63 Randy Winn	.50	.15
❑ 64 Alex Rodriguez	2.00	.60
❑ 65 Juan Gonzalez	.50	.15
❑ 66 Rafael Palmeiro	.75	.23
❑ 67 Ivan Rodriguez	.75	.23
❑ 68 Kenny Rogers	.50	.15
❑ 69 Carlos Delgado	.50	.15
❑ 70 Eric Hinske	.50	.15
❑ 71 Roy Halladay	.50	.15
❑ 72 Vernon Wells	.50	.15
❑ 73 Shannon Stewart	.50	.15
❑ 74 Curt Schilling	.50	.15
❑ 75 Randy Johnson	1.25	.35
❑ 76 Luis Gonzalez	.50	.15
❑ 77 Mark Grace	.75	.23
❑ 78 Junior Spivey	.50	.15
❑ 79 Greg Maddux	2.00	.60
❑ 80 Tom Glavine	.75	.23
❑ 81 John Smoltz	.75	.23
❑ 82 Chipper Jones	1.25	.35
❑ 83 Gary Sheffield	.50	.15
❑ 84 Andruw Jones	.75	.23
❑ 85 Kerry Wood	.50	.15
❑ 86 Fred McGriff	.75	.23
❑ 87 Sammy Sosa	1.25	.35
❑ 88 Mark Prior	.75	.23
❑ 89 Ken Griffey Jr.	2.00	.60
❑ 90 Barry Larkin	.75	.23
❑ 91 Adam Dunn	.50	.15
❑ 92 Sean Casey	.75	.23
❑ 93 Austin Kearns	.50	.15
❑ 94 Aaron Boone	.50	.15
❑ 95 Larry Walker	.50	.15
❑ 96 Todd Helton	.75	.23
❑ 97 Jason Jennings	.50	.15
❑ 98 Jay Payton	.50	.15
❑ 99 Josh Beckett	.50	.15
❑ 100 Mike Lowell	.50	.15
❑ 101 A.J. Burnett	.50	.15
❑ 102 Jeff Bagwell	.75	.23
❑ 103 Craig Biggio	.75	.23
❑ 104 Lance Berkman	.50	.15
❑ 105 Roy Oswalt	.50	.15
❑ 106 Wade Miller	.50	.15
❑ 107 Shawn Green	.50	.15
❑ 108 Adrian Beltre	.50	.15
❑ 109 Hideo Nomo	1.25	.35
❑ 110 Kazuhisa Ishii	.50	.15
❑ 111 Odalis Perez	.50	.15
❑ 112 Paul Lo Duca	.50	.15
❑ 113 Ben Sheets	.50	.15
❑ 114 Richie Sexson	.50	.15
❑ 115 Jose Hernandez	.50	.15
❑ 116 Vladimir Guerrero	1.25	.35
❑ 117 Jose Vidro	.50	.15
❑ 118 Tomo Ohka	.50	.15
❑ 119 Andres Galarraga	.50	.15
❑ 120 Bartolo Colon	.50	.15

❑ 121 Mike Piazza 2.00 .60
❑ 122 Roberto Alomar .75 .23
❑ 123 Mo Vaughn .50 .15
❑ 124 Al Leiter .50 .15
❑ 125 Edgardo Alfonzo .50 .15
❑ 126 Pat Burrell .50 .15
❑ 127 Bobby Abreu .50 .15
❑ 128 Mike Lieberthal .50 .15
❑ 129 Vicente Padilla .50 .15
❑ 130 Marlon Byrd .50 .15
❑ 131 Jason Kendall .50 .15
❑ 132 Brian Giles .50 .15
❑ 133 Aramis Ramirez .50 .15
❑ 134 Kip Wells .50 .15
❑ 135 Ryan Klesko .50 .15
❑ 136 Phil Nevin .50 .15
❑ 137 Brian Lawrence .50 .15
❑ 138 Sean Burroughs .50 .15
❑ 139 Mark Kotsay .50 .15
❑ 140 Barry Bonds 3.00 .90
❑ 141 Jeff Kent .50 .15
❑ 142 Benito Santiago .50 .15
❑ 143 Kirk Rueter .50 .15
❑ 144 Jason Schmidt .50 .15
❑ 145 Jim Edmonds .75 .23
❑ 146 J.D. Drew .50 .15
❑ 147 Albert Pujols 2.50 .75
❑ 148 Tino Martinez .75 .23
❑ 149 Matt Morris .50 .15
❑ 150 Scott Rolen .75 .23
❑ 151 Joe Borchard ROO 2.00 .60
❑ 152 Cliff Lee ROO 2.00 .60
❑ 153 Brian Tallet ROO 2.00 .60
❑ 154 Freddy Sanchez ROO 2.00 .60
❑ 155 Chone Figgins ROO 2.00 .60
❑ 156 Kevin Cash ROO 2.00 .60
❑ 157 Justin Wayne ROO 2.00 .60
❑ 158 Ben Kozlowski ROO 2.00 .60
❑ 159 Babe Ruth RET 10.00 3.00
❑ 160 Jackie Robinson RET 5.00 1.50
❑ 161 Ozzie Smith RET 8.00 2.40
❑ 162 Lou Gehrig RET 6.00 1.80
❑ 163 Stan Musial RET 6.00 1.80
❑ 164 Mike Schmidt RET 10.00 3.00
❑ 165 Carlton Fisk RET 5.00 1.50
❑ 166 George Brett RET 10.00 3.00
❑ 167 Dale Murphy RET 8.00 2.40
❑ 168 Cal Ripken RET 12.00 3.60
❑ 169 Tony Gwynn RET 5.00 1.50
❑ 170 Don Mattingly RET 10.00 3.00
❑ 171 Jack Morris RET 4.00 1.20
❑ 172 Ty Cobb RET 5.00 1.50
❑ 173 Nolan Ryan RET 10.00 3.00
❑ 174 Ryne Sandberg RET 8.00 2.40
❑ 175 Thurman Munson RET 5.00 1.50
❑ 176 Jose Contreras ROO RC 5.00 1.50
❑ 177 Hideki Matsui ROO RC 10.00 3.00
❑ 178 Jeremy Bonderman ROO RC 8.00 2.40
❑ 179 Brandon Webb ROO RC 5.00 1.50
❑ 180 Adam Loewen ROO RC 5.00 1.50
❑ 181 Chien-Ming Wang ROO RC 8.00 2.40
❑ 182 Hong-Chih Kuo ROO RC 5.00 1.50
❑ 183 Clint Barmes ROO RC 5.00 1.50
❑ 184 Guillermo Quiroz ROO RC 4.00 1.20
❑ 185 Edgar Gonzalez ROO RC 4.00 1.20
❑ 186 Todd Wellemeyer ROO RC 4.00 1.20
❑ 187 Dan Haren ROO RC 5.00 1.50
❑ 188 Dustin McGowan ROO RC 4.00 1.20
❑ 189 Preston Larrison ROO RC 5.00 1.50
❑ 190 Does Not Exist .00
❑ 191 Kevin Youkilis ROO RC 5.00 1.50
❑ 192 Bubba Nelson ROO RC 5.00 1.50
❑ 193 Chris Burke ROO RC 5.00 1.50
❑ 194 J.D. Durbin ROO RC 4.00 1.20
❑ 195 Ryan Howard ROO RC 10.00 3.00
❑ 196 Jason Kubel ROO RC 5.00 1.50
❑ 197 Brendan Harris ROO RC 5.00 1.50
❑ 198 Brian Bruney ROO RC 5.00 1.50
❑ 199 Ramon Nivar ROO RC 4.00 1.20
❑ 200 Rickie Weeks ROO RC 10.00 3.00
❑ 201 Delmon Young ROO RC 10.00 3.00

2004 Diamond Kings

	Nm-Mt	Ex-Mt
COMPLETE SET w/Sepia (200)	200.00	60.00

COMPLETE SET (175)	100.00	30.00
COMP.SET w/o SP's (150)	40.00	12.00
COMMON CARD (1-150)	.50	.15
COMMON CARD (151-175)	3.00	.90
151-175 RANDOM INSERTS IN PACKS		.00

❑ 1 Alex Rodriguez 2.00 .60
❑ 2 Andruw Jones .75 .23
❑ 3 Nomar Garciaparra 2.00 .60
❑ 4 Kerry Wood .50 .15
❑ 5 Magglio Ordonez .50 .15
❑ 6 Victor Martinez .50 .15
❑ 7 Jeremy Bonderman .50 .15
❑ 8 Josh Beckett .50 .15
❑ 9 Jeff Kent .50 .15
❑ 10 Carlos Beltran .50 .15
❑ 11 Hideo Nomo 1.25 .35
❑ 12 Richie Sexson .50 .15
❑ 13 Jose Vidro .50 .15
❑ 14 Jae Weong Seo .50 .15
❑ 15 Alfonso Soriano .50 .15
❑ 16 Barry Zito .50 .15
❑ 17 Brett Myers .50 .15
❑ 18 Brian Giles .50 .15
❑ 19 Edgar Martinez .75 .23
❑ 20 Jim Edmonds .75 .23
❑ 21 Rocco Baldelli .50 .15
❑ 22 Mark Teixeira .75 .23
❑ 23 Carlos Delgado .50 .15
❑ 24 Julius Matos .50 .15
❑ 25 Jose Reyes .50 .15
❑ 26 Marlon Byrd .50 .15
❑ 27 Albert Pujols 2.50 .75
❑ 28 Vernon Wells .50 .15
❑ 29 Garret Anderson .50 .15
❑ 30 Jerome Williams .50 .15
❑ 31 Chipper Jones 1.25 .35
❑ 32 Rich Harden .50 .15
❑ 33 Manny Ramirez .75 .23
❑ 34 Derek Jeter 2.50 .75
❑ 35 Brandon Webb .50 .15
❑ 36 Mark Prior .75 .23
❑ 37 Roy Halladay .50 .15
❑ 38 Frank Thomas 1.25 .35
❑ 39 Rafael Palmeiro .75 .23
❑ 40 Adam Dunn .50 .15
❑ 41 Aubrey Huff .50 .15
❑ 42 Todd Helton .75 .23
❑ 43 Matt Morris .50 .15
❑ 44 Dontrelle Willis .75 .23
❑ 45 Lance Berkman .50 .15
❑ 46 Mike Sweeney .50 .15
❑ 47 Kazuhisa Ishii .50 .15
❑ 48 Torii Hunter .50 .15
❑ 49 Vladimir Guerrero 1.25 .35
❑ 50 Mike Piazza 2.00 .60
❑ 51 Alexis Rios .50 .15
❑ 52 Shannon Stewart .50 .15
❑ 53 Eric Hinske .50 .15
❑ 54 Jason Jennings .50 .15
❑ 55 Jason Giambi .50 .15
❑ 56 Brandon Claussen .50 .15
❑ 57 Joe Thurston .50 .15
❑ 58 Ramon Nivar .50 .15
❑ 59 Jay Gibbons .50 .15
❑ 60 Eric Chavez .50 .15
❑ 61 Jimmy Gobble .50 .15
❑ 62 Walter Young .50 .15
❑ 63 Mark Grace .75 .23
❑ 64 Austin Kearns .50 .15
❑ 65 Bob Abreu .50 .15
❑ 66 Hee Seop Choi .50 .15
❑ 67 Brandon Phillips .50 .15
❑ 68 Rickie Weeks .75 .23
❑ 69 Luis Gonzalez .50 .15
❑ 70 Mariano Rivera .75 .23
❑ 71 Jason Lane .50 .15
❑ 72 Xavier Nady .50 .15
❑ 73 Runelvys Hernandez .50 .15
❑ 74 Aramis Ramirez .50 .15
❑ 75 Ichiro Suzuki 2.50 .75
❑ 76 Cliff Lee .50 .15
❑ 77 Chris Snelling .50 .15
❑ 78 Ryan Wagner .50 .15
❑ 79 Miguel Tejada .50 .15
❑ 80 Juan Gonzalez .50 .15
❑ 81 Joe Borchard .50 .15
❑ 82 Gary Sheffield .50 .15
❑ 83 Wade Miller .50 .15
❑ 84 Jeff Bagwell .75 .23
❑ 85 Ryan Church .50 .15
❑ 86 Adrian Beltre .50 .15
❑ 87 Jeff Baker .50 .15
❑ 88 Adam Loewen .50 .15
❑ 89 Bernie Williams .75 .23
❑ 90 Pedro Martinez .75 .23
❑ 91 Carlos Rivera .50 .15
❑ 92 Junior Spivey .50 .15
❑ 93 Tim Hudson .50 .15
❑ 94 Troy Glaus .50 .15
❑ 95 Ken Griffey Jr. 2.00 .60
❑ 96 Alexis Gomez .50 .15
❑ 97 Antonio Perez .50 .15
❑ 98 Dan Haren .50 .15
❑ 99 Ivan Rodriguez .75 .23
❑ 100 Randy Johnson 1.25 .35
❑ 101 Lyle Overbay .50 .15
❑ 102 Oliver Perez .50 .15
❑ 103 Miguel Cabrera .75 .23
❑ 104 Scott Rolen .75 .23
❑ 105 Roger Clemens 2.50 .75
❑ 106 Brian Tallet .50 .15
❑ 107 Nic Jackson .50 .15
❑ 108 Angel Berroa .50 .15
❑ 109 Hank Blalock .50 .15
❑ 110 Ryan Klesko .50 .15
❑ 111 Jose Castillo .50 .15
❑ 112 Paul Konerko .50 .15
❑ 113 Greg Maddux 2.00 .60
❑ 114 Mark Mulder .50 .15
❑ 115 Pat Burrell .50 .15
❑ 116 Garrett Atkins .50 .15
❑ 117 Jeremy Guthrie .50 .15
❑ 118 Orlando Cabrera .50 .15
❑ 119 Nick Johnson .50 .15
❑ 120 Tom Glavine .75 .23
❑ 121 Morgan Ensberg .50 .15
❑ 122 Sean Casey .75 .23
❑ 123 Orlando Hudson .50 .15
❑ 124 Hideki Matsui 2.50 .75
❑ 125 Craig Biggio .75 .23
❑ 126 Adam LaRoche .50 .15
❑ 127 Hong-Chih Kuo .50 .15
❑ 128 Paul Lo Duca .50 .15
❑ 129 Shawn Green .50 .15
❑ 130 Luis Castillo .50 .15
❑ 131 Joe Crede .50 .15
❑ 132 Ken Harvey .50 .15
❑ 133 Freddy Sanchez .50 .15
❑ 134 Roy Oswalt .50 .15
❑ 135 Curt Schilling .75 .23
❑ 136 Alfredo Amezaga .50 .15
❑ 137 Chien-Ming Wang .50 .15
❑ 138 Barry Larkin .75 .23
❑ 139 Trot Nixon .50 .15
❑ 140 Jim Thome .75 .23
❑ 141 Bret Boone .50 .15
❑ 142 Jacque Jones .50 .15
❑ 143 Travis Hafner .50 .15
❑ 144 Sammy Sosa 1.25 .35
❑ 145 Mike Mussina .75 .23
❑ 146 Vinny Chulk .50 .15
❑ 147 Chad Gaudin .50 .15
❑ 148 Delmon Young .75 .23
❑ 149 Mike Lowell .50 .15

❑ 150 Rickey Henderson 1.25 .35
❑ 151 Roger Clemens FB 6.00 1.80
❑ 152 Mark Grace FB 4.00 1.20
❑ 153 Rickey Henderson FB 4.00 1.20
❑ 154 Alex Rodriguez FB 5.00 1.50
❑ 155 Rafael Palmeiro FB 4.00 1.20
❑ 156 Greg Maddux FB 5.00 1.50
❑ 157 Mike Piazza FB 5.00 1.50
❑ 158 Mike Mussina FB 4.00 1.20
❑ 159 Dale Murphy LGD 4.00 1.20
❑ 160 Cal Ripken LGD 10.00 3.00
❑ 161 Carl Yastrzemski LGD 5.00 1.50
❑ 162 Marty Marion LGD 3.00 .90
❑ 163 Don Mattingly LGD 6.00 1.80
❑ 164 Robin Yount LGD 4.00 1.20
❑ 165 Andre Dawson LGD 3.00 .90
❑ 166 Jim Palmer LGD 3.00 .90
❑ 167 George Brett LGD 6.00 1.80
❑ 168 Whitey Ford LGD 4.00 1.20
❑ 169 Roy Campanella LGD 4.00 1.20
❑ 170 Roger Maris LGD 4.00 1.20
❑ 171 Duke Snider LGD 4.00 1.20
❑ 172 Steve Carlton LGD 3.00 .90
❑ 173 Stan Musial LGD 5.00 1.50
❑ 174 Nolan Ryan LGD 8.00 2.40
❑ 175 Deion Sanders LGD 4.00 1.20

2005 Diamond Kings

	Nm-Mt	Ex-Mt
COMPLETE SET (450)	180.00	55.00
COMP.SERIES 1 SET (300)	120.00	36.00
COMP.SERIES 2 SET (150)	60.00	18.00
COMMON CARD	.50	.15
COMMON RC	.50	.15
COMMON RETIRED	.50	.15
COMP.SET DOES NOT CONTAIN ANY SP's		.00

❑ 1 Garret Anderson .50 .15
❑ 2 Vladimir Guerrero 1.25 .35
❑ 3 Jose Guillen .50 .15
❑ 4 Troy Glaus UER .50 .15
Previous Diamond King appearences in wrong years
❑ 5 Tim Salmon .75 .23
❑ 6 Casey Kotchman .50 .15
❑ 7 Chone Figgins .50 .15
❑ 8 Robb Quinlan .50 .15
❑ 9 Francisco Rodriguez .50 .15
❑ 10 Troy Percival .50 .15
❑ 11 Randy Johnson 1.25 .35
❑ 12 Brandon Webb .50 .15
❑ 13 Richie Sexson .50 .15
❑ 14 Shea Hillenbrand .50 .15
❑ 15 Chad Tracy .50 .15
❑ 16 Alex Cintron .50 .15
❑ 17 Luis Gonzalez .50 .15
❑ 18 Rafael Furcal .50 .15
❑ 19 Andruw Jones .75 .23
❑ 20 Marcus Giles .50 .15
❑ 21 John Smoltz .75 .23
❑ 22 Adam LaRoche .50 .15
❑ 23 Russ Ortiz .50 .15
❑ 24 J.D. Drew .50 .15
❑ 25 Chipper Jones 1.25 .35
❑ 26 Nick Green .50 .15
❑ 27 Rafael Palmeiro O's .75 .23
❑ 28 Miguel Tejada .50 .15
❑ 29 Javy Lopez .50 .15
❑ 30 Luis Matos .50 .15
❑ 31 Larry Bigbie .50 .15
❑ 32 Rodrigo Lopez .50 .15
❑ 33 Brian Roberts .50 .15
❑ 34 Melvin Mora .50 .15
❑ 35 Adam Loewen .50 .15
❑ 36 Manny Ramirez .75 .23
❑ 37 Jason Varitek 1.25 .35
❑ 38 Trot Nixon .50 .15
❑ 39 Curt Schilling .75 .23
❑ 40 Keith Foulke .50 .15
❑ 41 Pedro Martinez .75 .23
❑ 42 Johnny Damon .75 .23
❑ 43 Kevin Youkilis .50 .15
❑ 44 Orlando Cabrera Sox .50 .15
❑ 45 Abe Alvarez .50 .15
❑ 46 David Ortiz 1.25 .35
❑ 47 Kerry Wood .50 .15
❑ 48 Mark Prior .75 .23
❑ 49 Aramis Ramirez .50 .15
❑ 50 Greg Maddux Cubs 2.00 .60
❑ 51 Carlos Zambrano .50 .15
❑ 52 Derrek Lee .75 .23
❑ 53 Corey Patterson .50 .15
❑ 54 Moises Alou .50 .15
❑ 55 Matt Clement .50 .15
❑ 56 Sammy Sosa 1.25 .35
❑ 57 Nomar Garciaparra Cubs 1.25 .35
❑ 58 Todd Walker .50 .15
❑ 59 Angel Guzman .50 .15
❑ 60 Magglio Ordonez .50 .15
❑ 61 Carlos Lee .50 .15
❑ 62 Joe Crede .50 .15
❑ 63 Paul Konerko .50 .15
❑ 64 Shingo Takatsu .50 .15
❑ 65 Frank Thomas 1.25 .35
❑ 66 Freddy Garcia .50 .15
❑ 67 Aaron Rowand .50 .15
❑ 68 Jose Contreras .50 .15
❑ 69 Adam Dunn .50 .15
❑ 70 Austin Kearns .50 .15
❑ 71 Barry Larkin .75 .23
❑ 72 Ken Griffey Jr. 2.00 .60
❑ 73 Ryan Wagner .50 .15
❑ 74 Sean Casey .75 .23
❑ 75 Danny Graves .50 .15
❑ 76 C.C. Sabathia .50 .15
❑ 77 Jody Gerut .50 .15
❑ 78 Omar Vizquel .75 .23
❑ 79 Victor Martinez .50 .15
❑ 80 Matt Lawton .50 .15
❑ 81 Jake Westbrook .50 .15
❑ 82 Kazuhito Tadano .50 .15
❑ 83 Travis Hafner .50 .15
❑ 84 Todd Helton .75 .23
❑ 85 Preston Wilson .50 .15
❑ 86 Matt Holliday .50 .15
❑ 87 Jeromy Burnitz .50 .15
❑ 88 Vinny Castilla .50 .15
❑ 89 Jeremy Bonderman .50 .15
❑ 90 Ivan Rodriguez Tigers .75 .23
❑ 91 Carlos Guillen .50 .15
❑ 92 Brandon Inge .50 .15
❑ 93 Rondell White .50 .15
❑ 94 Dontrelle Willis .50 .15
❑ 95 Miguel Cabrera .75 .23
❑ 96 Josh Beckett .50 .15
❑ 97 Mike Lowell .50 .15
❑ 98 Luis Castillo .50 .15
❑ 99 Juan Pierre .50 .15
❑ 100 Paul LoDuca Marlins .50 .15
❑ 101 Guillermo Mota .50 .15
❑ 102 Craig Biggio .75 .23
❑ 103 Lance Berkman .50 .15
❑ 104 Roy Oswalt .50 .15
❑ 105 Roger Clemens Astros 2.00 .60
❑ 106 Jeff Kent .50 .15
❑ 107 Morgan Ensberg .50 .15
❑ 108 Jeff Bagwell .75 .23
❑ 109 Carlos Beltran Astros .50 .15
❑ 110 Angel Berroa .50 .15
❑ 111 Mike Sweeney .50 .15
❑ 112 Jeremy Affeldt .50 .15
❑ 113 Zack Greinke .50 .15
❑ 114 Juan Gonzalez .50 .15
❑ 115 Andres Blanco .50 .15
❑ 116 Shawn Green .50 .15
❑ 117 Milton Bradley .50 .15
❑ 118 Adrian Beltre .50 .15
❑ 119 Hideo Nomo 1.25 .35
❑ 120 Steve Finley .50 .15
❑ 121 Eric Gagne .50 .15
❑ 122 Brad Penny Dgr .50 .15
❑ 123 Scott Podsednik .50 .15
❑ 124 Ben Sheets .50 .15
❑ 125 Lyle Overbay .50 .15
❑ 126 Junior Spivey .50 .15
❑ 127 Bill Hall .50 .15
❑ 128 Rickie Weeks .50 .15
❑ 129 Jacque Jones .50 .15
❑ 130 Torii Hunter .50 .15
❑ 131 Johan Santana .75 .23
❑ 132 Lew Ford .50 .15
❑ 133 Joe Mauer .50 .15
❑ 134 Justin Morneau .50 .15
❑ 135 Jason Kubel .50 .15
❑ 136 Jose Vidro .50 .15
❑ 137 Chad Cordero .50 .15
❑ 138 Brad Wilkerson .50 .15
❑ 139 Nick Johnson .50 .15
❑ 140 Livan Hernandez .50 .15
❑ 141 Tom Glavine .75 .23
❑ 142 Jae Weong Seo .50 .15
❑ 143 Jose Reyes .50 .15
❑ 144 Al Leiter .50 .15
❑ 145 Mike Piazza 1.25 .35
❑ 146 Kazuo Matsui .50 .15
❑ 147 Richard Hidalgo Mets .50 .15
❑ 148 David Wright 2.00 .60
❑ 149 Mariano Rivera .75 .23
❑ 150 Mike Mussina .75 .23
❑ 151 Alex Rodriguez 2.00 .60
❑ 152 Derek Jeter 2.50 .75
❑ 153 Jorge Posada .75 .23
❑ 154 Jason Giambi .50 .15
❑ 155 Gary Sheffield .50 .15
❑ 156 Bubba Crosby .50 .15
❑ 157 Javier Vazquez .50 .15
❑ 158 Kevin Brown .50 .15
❑ 159 Tom Gordon .50 .15
❑ 160 Esteban Loaiza Yanks .50 .15
❑ 161 Hideki Matsui 2.50 .75
❑ 162 Eric Chavez .50 .15
❑ 163 Mark Mulder .50 .15
❑ 164 Barry Zito .50 .15
❑ 165 Tim Hudson .50 .15
❑ 166 Jermaine Dye .50 .15
❑ 167 Octavio Dotel .50 .15
❑ 168 Bobby Crosby .50 .15
❑ 169 Mark Kotsay .50 .15
❑ 170 Scott Hatteberg .50 .15
❑ 171 Jim Thome Phils .75 .23
❑ 172 Bobby Abreu .50 .15
❑ 173 Kevin Millwood .50 .15
❑ 174 Mike Lieberthal .50 .15
❑ 175 Jimmy Rollins .50 .15
❑ 176 Chase Utley .50 .15
❑ 177 Randy Wolf .50 .15
❑ 178 Craig Wilson .50 .15
❑ 179 Jason Kendall .50 .15
❑ 180 Jack Wilson .50 .15
❑ 181 Jose Castillo .50 .15
❑ 182 Rob Mackowiak .50 .15
❑ 183 Oliver Perez .50 .15
❑ 184 Jason Bay .50 .15
❑ 185 Sean Burroughs .50 .15
❑ 186 Jay Payton .50 .15
❑ 187 Brian Giles .50 .15
❑ 188 Akinori Otsuka .50 .15
❑ 189 Jake Peavy .50 .15
❑ 190 Phil Nevin .50 .15
❑ 191 Mark Loretta .50 .15
❑ 192 Khalil Greene .75 .23
❑ 193 Trevor Hoffman .50 .15
❑ 194 Freddy Guzman .50 .15
❑ 195 Jerome Williams .50 .15
❑ 196 Jason Schmidt .50 .15
❑ 197 Todd Linden .50 .15
❑ 198 Merkin Valdez .50 .15
❑ 199 J.T. Snow .50 .15
❑ 200 A.J. Pierzynski .50 .15
❑ 201 Edgar Martinez .75 .23

❑ 202 Ichiro Suzuki 2.50 .75
❑ 203 Raul Ibanez .50 .15
❑ 204 Bret Boone .50 .15
❑ 205 Shigetoshi Hasegawa .50 .15
❑ 206 Miguel Olivo .50 .15
❑ 207 Bucky Jacobsen .50 .15
❑ 208 Jamie Moyer .50 .15
❑ 209 Jim Edmonds .75 .23
❑ 210 Scott Rolen .75 .23
❑ 211 Edgar Renteria .50 .15
❑ 212 Dan Haren .50 .15
❑ 213 Matt Morris .50 .15
❑ 214 Albert Pujols 2.50 .75
❑ 215 Larry Walker Cards .75 .23
❑ 216 Jason Isringhausen .50 .15
❑ 217 Chris Carpenter .50 .15
❑ 218 Jason Marquis .50 .15
❑ 219 Jeff Suppan .50 .15
❑ 220 Aubrey Huff .50 .15
❑ 221 Carl Crawford .50 .15
❑ 222 Rocco Baldelli .50 .15
❑ 223 Fred McGriff .75 .23
❑ 224 Dewon Brazelton .50 .15
❑ 225 B.J. Upton .75 .23
❑ 226 Joey Gathright .50 .15
❑ 227 Scott Kazmir .50 .15
❑ 228 Hank Blalock .50 .15
❑ 229 Mark Teixeira .75 .23
❑ 230 Michael Young .50 .15
❑ 231 Adrian Gonzalez .50 .15
❑ 232 Laynce Nix .50 .15
❑ 233 Alfonso Soriano Rgr .50 .15
❑ 234 Rafael Palmeiro Rgr .75 .23
❑ 235 Kevin Mench .50 .15
❑ 236 David Dellucci .50 .15
❑ 237 Francisco Cordero .50 .15
❑ 238 Kenny Rogers .50 .15
❑ 239 Roy Halladay .50 .15
❑ 240 Carlos Delgado .50 .15
❑ 241 Alexis Rios .50 .15
❑ 242 Vernon Wells .50 .15
❑ 243 Yadier Molina .50 .15
❑ 244 Rene Rivera .50 .15
❑ 245 Logan Kensing .50 .15
❑ 246 Gavin Floyd .50 .15
❑ 247 Russ Adams .50 .15
❑ 248 Dioner Navarro .50 .15
❑ 249 Ryan Howard .50 .15
❑ 250 Ryan Church .50 .15
❑ 251 Jeff Francis .50 .15
❑ 252 John VanBenschoten .50 .15
❑ 253 Yhency Brazoban .50 .15
❑ 254 Dave Krynzel .50 .15
❑ 255 Victor Diaz .50 .15
❑ 256 Jairo Garcia .50 .15
❑ 257 Scott Proctor .50 .15
❑ 258 Shawn Hill .50 .15
❑ 259 Jeff Baker .50 .15
❑ 260 Matt Peterson .50 .15
❑ 261 Josh Kroeger .50 .15
❑ 262 Grady Sizemore .50 .15
❑ 263 Clint Nageotte .50 .15
❑ 264 Andy Green .50 .15
❑ 265 Justin Verlander RC 2.00 .60
❑ 266 Jim Thome Indians .75 .23
❑ 267 Larry Walker Rockies .50 .15
❑ 268 Ivan Rodriguez Rgr .75 .23
❑ 269 Brad Penny Marlins .50 .15
❑ 270 Carlos Beltran Royals .50 .15
❑ 271 Paul LoDuca Dgr .50 .15
❑ 272 Orlando Cabrera Expos .50 .15
❑ 273 Nomar Garciaparra Sox 1.25 .35
❑ 274 Esteban Loaiza Sox .50 .15
❑ 275 Richard Hidalgo Astros .50 .15
❑ 276 John Olerud .50 .15
❑ 277 Greg Maddux Braves 2.00 .60
❑ 278 Roger Clemens Yanks 2.00 .60
❑ 279 Alfonso Soriano Yanks .50 .15
❑ 280 Dale Murphy .75 .23
❑ 281 Cal Ripken 5.00 1.50
❑ 282 Dwight Evans .75 .23
❑ 283 Ron Santo .75 .23
❑ 284 Andre Dawson .50 .15
❑ 285 Harold Baines .50 .15
❑ 286 Jack Morris .50 .15
❑ 287 Kirk Gibson .75 .23
❑ 288 Bo Jackson 1.25 .35
❑ 289 Orel Hershiser .50 .15
❑ 290 Maury Wills .50 .15
❑ 291 Tony Oliva .50 .15
❑ 292 Darryl Strawberry .50 .15
❑ 293 Roger Maris 1.25 .35
❑ 294 Don Mattingly 2.50 .75
❑ 295 Rickey Henderson 1.25 .35
❑ 296 Dave Stewart .50 .15
❑ 297 Dave Parker .50 .15
❑ 298 Steve Garvey .50 .15
❑ 299 Matt Williams .50 .15
❑ 300 Keith Hernandez .50 .15
❑ 301 John Lackey .50 .15
❑ 302 Vladimir Guerrero Angels 1.25 .35
❑ 303 Garret Anderson .50 .15
❑ 304 Dallas McPherson .50 .15
❑ 305 Orlando Cabrera .50 .15
❑ 306 Steve Finley Angels .50 .15
❑ 307 Luis Gonzalez .50 .15
❑ 308 Randy Johnson D'backs 1.25 .35
❑ 309 Scott Hairston .50 .15
❑ 310 Shawn Green .50 .15
❑ 311 Troy Glaus .50 .15
❑ 312 Javier Vazquez .50 .15
❑ 313 Russ Ortiz .50 .15
❑ 314 Chipper Jones 1.25 .35
❑ 315 Johnny Estrada .50 .15
❑ 316 Andruw Jones .75 .23
❑ 317 Tim Hudson .50 .15
❑ 318 Danny Kolb .50 .15
❑ 319 Jay Gibbons .50 .15
❑ 320 Melvin Mora .50 .15
❑ 321 Rafael Palmeiro O's .75 .23
❑ 322 Val Majewski .50 .15
❑ 323 David Ortiz 1.25 .35
❑ 324 Manny Ramirez .75 .23
❑ 325 Edgar Renteria .50 .15
❑ 326 Matt Clement .50 .15
❑ 327 Curt Schilling Sox .75 .23
❑ 328 Sammy Sosa Cubs 1.25 .35
❑ 329 Mark Prior .75 .23
❑ 330 Greg Maddux 2.00 .60
❑ 331 Nomar Garciaparra 1.25 .35
❑ 332 Frank Thomas 1.25 .35
❑ 333 Mark Buehrle .50 .15
❑ 334 Jermaine Dye .50 .15
❑ 335 Scott Podsednik .50 .15
❑ 336 Sean Casey .50 .15
❑ 337 Adam Dunn .50 .15
❑ 338 Ken Griffey Jr. 2.00 .60
❑ 339 Travis Hafner .50 .15
❑ 340 Victor Martinez .50 .15
❑ 341 Cliff Lee .50 .15
❑ 342 Todd Helton .75 .23
❑ 343 Preston Wilson .50 .15
❑ 344 Ivan Rodriguez Tigers .75 .23
❑ 345 Dmitri Young .50 .15
❑ 346 Nate Robertson .50 .15
❑ 347 Miguel Cabrera .75 .23
❑ 348 Jeff Bagwell .75 .23
❑ 349 Andy Pettitte .75 .23
❑ 350 Roger Clemens Astros 2.00 .60
❑ 351 Ken Harvey .50 .15
❑ 352 Denny Bautista .50 .15
❑ 353 Hideo Nomo 1.25 .35
❑ 354 Kazuhisa Ishii .50 .15
❑ 355 Edwin Jackson .50 .15
❑ 356 J.D. Drew .50 .15
❑ 357 Jeff Kent .50 .15
❑ 358 Geoff Jenkins .50 .15
❑ 359 Carlos Lee .50 .15
❑ 360 Shannon Stewart .50 .15
❑ 361 Joe Nathan .50 .15
❑ 362 Johan Santana .75 .23
❑ 363 Mike Piazza Mets 1.25 .35
❑ 364 Kazuo Matsui .50 .15
❑ 365 Carlos Beltran .50 .15
❑ 366 Pedro Martinez .75 .23
❑ 367 Ambiorix Concepcion RC .75 .23
❑ 368 Hideki Matsui 2.50 .75
❑ 369 Bernie Williams .75 .23
❑ 370 Gary Sheffield Yanks .50 .15
❑ 371 Randy Johnson Yanks 1.25 .35
❑ 372 Jaret Wright .50 .15
❑ 373 Carl Pavano .50 .15
❑ 374 Derek Jeter 2.50 .75
❑ 375 Alex Rodriguez 2.00 .60
❑ 376 Eric Byrnes .50 .15
❑ 377 Rich Harden .50 .15
❑ 378 Mark Mulder A's .50 .15
❑ 379 Nick Swisher .50 .15
❑ 380 Eric Chavez .50 .15
❑ 381 Jason Kendall .50 .15
❑ 382 Marlon Byrd .50 .15
❑ 383 Pat Burrell .50 .15
❑ 384 Brett Myers .50 .15
❑ 385 Jim Thome .75 .23
❑ 386 Jason Bay .50 .15
❑ 387 Jake Peavy .50 .15
❑ 388 Moises Alou .50 .15
❑ 389 Omar Vizquel .75 .23
❑ 390 Travis Blackley .50 .15
❑ 391 Jose Lopez .50 .15
❑ 392 Jeremy Reed .50 .15
❑ 393 Adrian Beltre .50 .15
❑ 394 Richie Sexson .50 .15
❑ 395 Wladimir Balentien RC 1.25 .35
❑ 396 Ichiro Suzuki 2.50 .75
❑ 397 Albert Pujols 2.50 .75
❑ 398 Scott Rolen Cards .75 .23
❑ 399 Mark Mulder Cards .50 .15
❑ 400 David Eckstein .50 .15
❑ 401 Delmon Young .50 .15
❑ 402 Aubrey Huff .50 .15
❑ 403 Alfonso Soriano .50 .15
❑ 404 Hank Blalock .50 .15
❑ 405 Richard Hidalgo .50 .15
❑ 406 Vernon Wells .50 .15
❑ 407 Orlando Hudson .50 .15
❑ 408 Alexis Rios .50 .15
❑ 409 Shea Hillenbrand .50 .15
❑ 410 Jose Guillen .50 .15
❑ 411 Vinny Castilla .50 .15
❑ 412 Jose Vidro .50 .15
❑ 413 Nick Johnson .50 .15
❑ 414 Livan Hernandez .50 .15
❑ 415 Miguel Tejada .50 .15
❑ 416 Gary Sheffield Braves .50 .15
❑ 417 Curt Schilling D'backs .50 .15
❑ 418 Rafael Palmeiro Rgr .75 .23
❑ 419 Scott Rolen Phils .75 .23
❑ 420 Aramis Ramirez .50 .15
❑ 421 Vladimir Guerrero Expos 1.25 .35
❑ 422 Steve Finley D'backs .50 .15
❑ 423 Roger Clemens Sox 2.00 .60
❑ 424 Mike Piazza Dgr 1.25 .35
❑ 425 Ivan Rodriguez M's .75 .23
❑ 426 David Justice 1.50 .45
❑ 427 Mark Grace .75 .23
❑ 428 Alan Trammell .50 .15
❑ 429 Bert Blyleven .50 .15
❑ 430 Dwight Gooden .50 .15
❑ 431 Deion Sanders .75 .23
❑ 432 Joe Torre MG .75 .23
❑ 433 Jose Canseco 1.25 .35
❑ 434 Tony Gwynn 1.50 .45
❑ 435 Will Clark .75 .23
❑ 436 Marty Marion .50 .15
❑ 437 Nolan Ryan 3.00 .90
❑ 438 Billy Martin .75 .23
❑ 439 Carlos Delgado .50 .15
❑ 440 Magglio Ordonez .50 .15
❑ 441 Sammy Sosa O's 1.25 .35
❑ 442 Keiichi Yabu RC .50 .15
❑ 443 Yuniesky Betancourt RC 2.00 .60
❑ 444 Jeff Niemann RC 1.25 .35
❑ 445 Brandon McCarthy RC 1.50 .45
❑ 446 Phil Humber RC 1.25 .35
❑ 447 Tadahito Iguchi RC 2.00 .60
❑ 448 Cal Ripken 5.00 1.50
❑ 449 Ryne Sandberg 2.50 .75
❑ 450 Willie Mays 2.50 .75

1981 Donruss

	Nm-Mt	Ex-Mt
COMPLETE SET (605)	40.00	16.00
❑ 1 Ozzie Smith	3.00	1.20
❑ 2 Rollie Fingers	.25	.10
❑ 3 Rick Wise	.10	.04

❑ 4 Gene Richards .10 .04
❑ 5 Alan Trammell .50 .20
❑ 6 Tom Brookens .10 .04
❑ 7A Duffy Dyer P1 .25 .10
1980 batting average
has decimal point
❑ 7B Duffy Dyer P2 .10 .04
1980 batting average
has no decimal point
❑ 8 Mark Fidrych .25 .10
❑ 9 Dave Rozema .10 .04
❑ 10 Ricky Peters .10 .04
❑ 11 Mike Schmidt 2.50 1.00
❑ 12 Willie Stargell .50 .20
❑ 13 Tim Foli .10 .04
❑ 14 Manny Sanguillen .25 .10
❑ 15 Grant Jackson .10 .04
❑ 16 Eddie Solomon .10 .04
❑ 17 Omar Moreno .10 .04
❑ 18 Joe Morgan .50 .20
❑ 19 Rafael Landestoy .10 .04
❑ 20 Bruce Bochy .10 .04
❑ 21 Joe Sambito .10 .04
❑ 22 Manny Trillo .10 .04
❑ 23A Dave Smith RC P1 .50 .20
Line box around stats
is not complete
❑ 23B Dave Smith RC P2 .50 .20
Box totally encloses
stats at top
❑ 24 Terry Puhl .10 .04
❑ 25 Bump Wills .10 .04
❑ 26A John Ellis P1 ERR .50 .20
Danny Walton photo on front
❑ 26B John Ellis P2 COR .25 .10
❑ 27 Jim Kern .10 .04
❑ 28 Richie Zisk .10 .04
❑ 29 John Mayberry .10 .04
❑ 30 Bob Davis .10 .04
❑ 31 Jackson Todd .10 .04
❑ 32 Alvis Woods .10 .04
❑ 33 Steve Carlton .50 .20
❑ 34 Lee Mazzilli .25 .10
❑ 35 John Stearns .10 .04
❑ 36 Roy Lee Jackson .10 .04
❑ 37 Mike Scott .25 .10
❑ 38 Lamar Johnson .10 .04
❑ 39 Kevin Bell .10 .04
❑ 40 Ed Farmer .10 .04
❑ 41 Ross Baumgarten .10 .04
❑ 42 Leo Sutherland .10 .04
❑ 43 Dan Meyer .10 .04
❑ 44 Ron Reed .10 .04
❑ 45 Mario Mendoza .10 .04
❑ 46 Rick Honeycutt .10 .04
❑ 47 Glenn Abbott .10 .04
❑ 48 Leon Roberts .10 .04
❑ 49 Rod Carew .50 .20
❑ 50 Bert Campaneris .25 .10
❑ 51A T.Donahue P1 ERR .25 .10
Name on front
misspelled Donahue
❑ 51B Tom Donohue .10 .04
P2 COR
❑ 52 Dave Frost .10 .04
❑ 53 Ed Halicki .10 .04
❑ 54 Dan Ford .10 .04
❑ 55 Garry Maddox .10 .04
❑ 56A Steve Garvey P1 .25 .10
Surpassed 25 HR
❑ 56B Steve Garvey P2 .25 .10
Surpassed 21 HR
❑ 57 Bill Russell .25 .10
❑ 58 Don Sutton .25 .10
❑ 59 Reggie Smith .25 .10
❑ 60 Rick Monday .25 .10
❑ 61 Ray Knight .25 .10
❑ 62 Johnny Bench 1.00 .40
❑ 63 Mario Soto .25 .10
❑ 64 Doug Bair .10 .04
❑ 65 George Foster .25 .10
❑ 66 Jeff Burroughs .25 .10
❑ 67 Keith Hernandez .25 .10
❑ 68 Tom Herr .10 .04
❑ 69 Bob Forsch .10 .04
❑ 70 John Fulgham .10 .04
❑ 71A Bobby Bonds P1 ERR 1.00 .40
986 lifetime HR
❑ 71B Bobby Bonds P2 COR .50 .20
326 lifetime HR
❑ 72A Rennie Stennett P1 .25 .10
Breaking broke leg
❑ 72B Rennie Stennett P2 .10 .04
Word "broke" deleted
❑ 73 Joe Strain .10 .04
❑ 74 Ed Whitson .10 .04
❑ 75 Tom Griffin .10 .04
❑ 76 Billy North .10 .04
❑ 77 Gene Garber .10 .04
❑ 78 Mike Hargrove .10 .04
❑ 79 Dave Rosello .10 .04
❑ 80 Ron Hassey .10 .04
❑ 81 Sid Monge .10 .04
❑ 82A J.Charboneau P1 RC 1.00 .40
'78 highlights
For some reason
❑ 82B J.Charboneau P2 RC 1.00 .40
Phrase "For some reason" deleted
❑ 83 Cecil Cooper .25 .10
❑ 84 Sal Bando .25 .10
❑ 85 Moose Haas .10 .04
❑ 86 Mike Caldwell .10 .04
❑ 87A Larry Hisle P1 .25 .10
'77 highlights
line ends with "28 RBI"
❑ 87B Larry Hisle P2 .10 .04
Correct line "28 HR"
❑ 88 Luis Gomez .10 .04
❑ 89 Larry Parrish .10 .04
❑ 90 Gary Carter .50 .20
❑ 91 Bill Gullickson RC .50 .20
❑ 92 Fred Norman .10 .04
❑ 93 Tommy Hutton .10 .04
❑ 94 Carl Yastrzemski 1.50 .60
❑ 95 Glenn Hoffman .10 .04
❑ 96 Dennis Eckersley .50 .20
❑ 97A Tom Burgmeier P1 .25 .10
ERR Throws: Right
❑ 97B Tom Burgmeier P2 .10 .04
COR Throws: Left
❑ 98 Win Remmerswaal .10 .04
❑ 99 Bob Horner .25 .10
❑ 100 George Brett 2.50 1.00
❑ 101 Dave Chalk .10 .04
❑ 102 Dennis Leonard .10 .04
❑ 103 Renie Martin .10 .04
❑ 104 Amos Otis .25 .10
❑ 105 Graig Nettles .25 .10
❑ 106 Eric Soderholm .10 .04
❑ 107 Tommy John .25 .10
❑ 108 Tom Underwood .10 .04
❑ 109 Lou Piniella .25 .10
❑ 110 Mickey Klutts .10 .04
❑ 111 Bobby Murcer .25 .10
❑ 112 Eddie Murray 1.50 .60
❑ 113 Rick Dempsey .10 .04
❑ 114 Scott McGregor .10 .04
❑ 115 Ken Singleton .25 .10
❑ 116 Gary Roenicke .10 .04
❑ 117 Dave Revering .10 .04
❑ 118 Mike Norris .10 .04
❑ 119 Rickey Henderson 6.00 2.40
❑ 120 Mike Heath .10 .04
❑ 121 Dave Cash .10 .04
❑ 122 Randy Jones .25 .10
❑ 123 Eric Rasmussen .10 .04
❑ 124 Jerry Mumphrey .10 .04
❑ 125 Richie Hebner .10 .04
❑ 126 Mark Wagner .10 .04
❑ 127 Jack Morris .50 .20
❑ 128 Dan Petry .10 .04
❑ 129 Bruce Robbins .10 .04
❑ 130 Champ Summers .10 .04
❑ 131 Pete Rose P1 3.00 1.20
Last line ends with
see card 251
❑ 131B Pete Rose P2 2.00 .80
Last line corrected
see card 371
❑ 132 Willie Stargell .50 .20
❑ 133 Ed Ott .10 .04
❑ 134 Jim Bibby .10 .04
❑ 135 Bert Blyleven .25 .10
❑ 136 Dave Parker .25 .10
❑ 137 Bill Robinson .10 .04
❑ 138 Enos Cabell .10 .04
❑ 139 Dave Bergman .10 .04
❑ 140 J.R. Richard .25 .10
❑ 141 Ken Forsch .10 .04
❑ 142 Larry Bowa UER .25 .10
Shortshop on front
❑ 143 Frank LaCorte UER .10 .04
Photo actually Randy Niemann
❑ 144 Denny Walling .10 .04
❑ 145 Buddy Bell .25 .10
❑ 146 Ferguson Jenkins .25 .10
❑ 147 Danny Darwin .25 .10
❑ 148 John Grubb .10 .04
❑ 149 Alfredo Griffin .10 .04
❑ 150 Jerry Garvin .10 .04
❑ 151 Paul Mirabella .10 .04
❑ 152 Rick Bosetti .10 .04
❑ 153 Dick Ruthven .10 .04
❑ 154 Frank Taveras .10 .04
❑ 155 Craig Swan .10 .04
❑ 156 Jeff Reardon RC 1.00 .40
❑ 157 Steve Henderson .10 .04
❑ 158 Jim Morrison .10 .04
❑ 159 Glenn Borgmann .10 .04
❑ 160 LaMarr Hoyt RC .50 .20
❑ 161 Rich Wortham .10 .04
❑ 162 Thad Bosley .10 .04
❑ 163 Julio Cruz .10 .04
❑ 164A Del Unser P1 .25 .10
No "3B" heading
❑ 164B Del Unser P2 .10 .04
Batting record on back
corrected "3B"
❑ 165 Jim Anderson .10 .04
❑ 166 Jim Beattie .10 .04
❑ 167 Shane Rawley .10 .04
❑ 168 Joe Simpson .10 .04
❑ 169 Rod Carew .50 .20
❑ 170 Fred Patek .10 .04
❑ 171 Frank Tanana .25 .10
❑ 172 Alfredo Martinez .10 .04
❑ 173 Chris Knapp .10 .04
❑ 174 Joe Rudi .25 .10
❑ 175 Greg Luzinski .25 .10
❑ 176 Steve Garvey .50 .20
❑ 177 Joe Ferguson .10 .04
❑ 178 Bob Welch .25 .10
❑ 179 Dusty Baker .25 .10
❑ 180 Rudy Law .10 .04
❑ 181 Dave Concepcion .25 .10
❑ 182 Johnny Bench 1.00 .40
❑ 183 Mike LaCoss .10 .04
❑ 184 Ken Griffey .25 .10
❑ 185 Dave Collins .10 .04
❑ 186 Brian Asselstine .10 .04
❑ 187 Garry Templeton .25 .10
❑ 188 Mike Phillips .10 .04
❑ 189 Pete Vuckovich .10 .04
❑ 190 John Urrea .10 .04
❑ 191 Tony Scott .10 .04
❑ 192 Darrell Evans .25 .10
❑ 193 Milt May .10 .04
❑ 194 Bob Knepper .10 .04
❑ 195 Randy Moffitt .10 .04
❑ 196 Larry Herndon .10 .04

❑	197	Rick Camp	.10	.04
❑	198	Andre Thornton	.25	.10
❑	199	Tom Veryzer	.10	.04
❑	200	Gary Alexander	.10	.04
❑	201	Rick Waits	.10	.04
❑	202	Rick Manning	.10	.04
❑	203	Paul Molitor	1.00	.40
❑	204	Jim Gantner	.10	.04
❑	205	Paul Mitchell	.10	.04
❑	206	Reggie Cleveland	.10	.04
❑	207	Sixto Lezcano	.10	.04
❑	208	Bruce Benedict	.10	.04
❑	209	Rodney Scott	.10	.04
❑	210	John Tamargo	.10	.04
❑	211	Bill Lee	.25	.10
❑	212	Andre Dawson UER	.50	.20
		Middle name Fernando should be Nolan		
❑	213	Rowland Office	.10	.04
❑	214	Carl Yastrzemski	1.50	.60
❑	215	Jerry Remy	.10	.04
❑	216	Mike Torrez	.10	.04
❑	217	Skip Lockwood	.10	.04
❑	218	Fred Lynn	.25	.10
❑	219	Chris Chambliss	.25	.10
❑	220	Willie Aikens	.10	.04
❑	221	John Wathan	.10	.04
❑	222	Dan Quisenberry	.10	.04
❑	223	Willie Wilson	.25	.10
❑	224	Clint Hurdle	.10	.04
❑	225	Bob Watson	.10	.04
❑	226	Jim Spencer	.10	.04
❑	227	Ron Guidry	.25	.10
❑	228	Reggie Jackson	1.00	.40
❑	229	Oscar Gamble	.10	.04
❑	230	Jeff Cox	.10	.04
❑	231	Luis Tiant	.25	.10
❑	232	Rich Dauer	.10	.04
❑	233	Dan Graham	.10	.04
❑	234	Mike Flanagan	.10	.04
❑	235	John Lowenstein	.10	.04
❑	236	Benny Ayala	.10	.04
❑	237	Wayne Gross	.10	.04
❑	238	Rick Langford	.10	.04
❑	239	Tony Armas	.25	.10
❑	240A	Bob Lacey P1 ERR	.50	.20
		Name misspelled Lacy		
❑	240B	Bob Lacey P2 COR	.10	.04
❑	241	Gene Tenace	.25	.10
❑	242	Bob Shirley	.10	.04
❑	243	Gary Lucas	.10	.04
❑	244	Jerry Turner	.10	.04
❑	245	John Wockenfuss	.10	.04
❑	246	Stan Papi	.10	.04
❑	247	Milt Wilcox	.10	.04
❑	248	Dan Schatzeder	.10	.04
❑	249	Steve Kemp	.10	.04
❑	250	Jim Lentine	.10	.04
❑	251	Pete Rose	3.00	1.20
❑	252	Bill Madlock	.25	.10
❑	253	Dale Berra	.10	.04
❑	254	Kent Tekulve	.10	.04
❑	255	Enrique Romo	.10	.04
❑	256	Mike Easler	.10	.04
❑	257	Chuck Tanner MG	.10	.04
❑	258	Art Howe	.10	.04
❑	259	Alan Ashby	.10	.04
❑	260	Nolan Ryan	5.00	2.00
❑	261A	Vern Ruhle P1 ERR	.50	.20
		Ken Forsch photo on front		
❑	261B	Vern Ruhle P2 COR	.25	.10
❑	262	Bob Boone	.25	.10
❑	263	Cesar Cedeno	.25	.10
❑	264	Jeff Leonard	.25	.10
❑	265	Pat Putnam	.10	.04
❑	266	Jon Matlack	.10	.04
❑	267	Dave Rajsich	.10	.04
❑	268	Billy Sample	.10	.04
❑	269	Damaso Garcia	.10	.04
❑	270	Tom Buskey	.10	.04
❑	271	Joey McLaughlin	.10	.04
❑	272	Barry Bonnell	.10	.04
❑	273	Tug McGraw	.25	.10
❑	274	Mike Jorgensen	.10	.04
❑	275	Pat Zachry	.10	.04
❑	276	Neil Allen	.10	.04
❑	277	Joel Youngblood	.10	.04
❑	278	Greg Pryor	.10	.04
❑	279	Britt Burns	.10	.04
❑	280	Rich Dotson	.10	.04
❑	281	Chet Lemon	.25	.10
❑	282	Rusty Kuntz	.10	.04
❑	283	Ted Cox	.10	.04
❑	284	Sparky Lyle	.25	.10
❑	285	Larry Cox	.10	.04
❑	286	Floyd Bannister	.10	.04
❑	287	Byron McLaughlin	.10	.04
❑	288	Rodney Craig	.10	.04
❑	289	Bobby Grich	.25	.10
❑	290	Dickie Thon	.10	.04
❑	291	Mark Clear	.10	.04
❑	292	Dave Lemanczyk	.10	.04
❑	293	Jason Thompson	.10	.04
❑	294	Rick Miller	.10	.04
❑	295	Lonnie Smith	.25	.10
❑	296	Ron Cey	.25	.10
❑	297	Steve Yeager	.25	.10
❑	298	Bobby Castillo	.10	.04
❑	299	Manny Mota	.25	.10
❑	300	Jay Johnstone	.10	.04
❑	301	Dan Driessen	.10	.04
❑	302	Joe Nolan	.10	.04
❑	303	Paul Householder	.10	.04
❑	304	Harry Spilman	.10	.04
❑	305	Cesar Geronimo	.10	.04
❑	306A	G.Mathews P1 ERR	.50	.20
		Name misspelled		
❑	306B	G.Matthews P2 COR	.25	.10
❑	307	Ken Reitz	.10	.04
❑	308	Ted Simmons	.25	.10
❑	309	John Littlefield	.10	.04
❑	310	George Frazier	.10	.04
❑	311	Dane Iorg	.10	.04
❑	312	Mike Ivie	.10	.04
❑	313	Dennis Littlejohn	.10	.04
❑	314	Gary Lavelle	.10	.04
❑	315	Jack Clark	.25	.10
❑	316	Jim Wohlford	.10	.04
❑	317	Rick Matula	.10	.04
❑	318	Toby Harrah	.25	.10
❑	319A	D.Kuiper P1 ERR	.25	.10
		Name misspelled		
❑	319B	D.Kuiper P2 COR	.10	.04
❑	320	Len Barker	.25	.10
❑	321	Victor Cruz	.10	.04
❑	322	Dell Alston	.10	.04
❑	323	Robin Yount	1.50	.60
❑	324	Charlie Moore	.10	.04
❑	325	Lary Sorensen	.10	.04
❑	326A	Gorman Thomas P1	.50	.20
		2nd line on back: "30 HR mark 4th"		
❑	326B	Gorman Thomas P2	.25	.10
		30 HR mark 3rd		
❑	327	Bob Rodgers MG	.10	.04
❑	328	Phil Niekro	.25	.10
❑	329	Chris Speier	.10	.04
❑	330A	Steve Rodgers P1	.25	.10
		ERR Name misspelled		
❑	330B	S.Rogers P2 COR	.25	.10
❑	331	Woodie Fryman	.10	.04
❑	332	Warren Cromartie	.10	.04
❑	333	Jerry White	.10	.04
❑	334	Tony Perez	.50	.20
❑	335	Carlton Fisk	.50	.20
❑	336	Dick Drago	.10	.04
❑	337	Steve Renko	.10	.04
❑	338	Jim Rice	.25	.10
❑	339	Jerry Royster	.10	.04
❑	340	Frank White	.25	.10
❑	341	Jamie Quirk	.10	.04
❑	342A	P.Spittorff P1 ERR	.25	.10
		Name misspelled		
❑	342B	Paul Splittorff P2 COR	.10	.04
❑	343	Marty Pattin	.10	.04
❑	344	Pete LaCock	.10	.04
❑	345	Willie Randolph	.25	.10
❑	346	Rick Cerone	.10	.04
❑	347	Rich Gossage	.25	.10
❑	348	Reggie Jackson	1.00	.40
❑	349	Ruppert Jones	.10	.04
❑	350	Dave McKay	.10	.04
❑	351	Yogi Berra CO	1.00	.40
❑	352	Doug DeCinces	.10	.04
❑	353	Jim Palmer	.50	.20
❑	354	Tippy Martinez	.10	.04
❑	355	Al Bumbry	.10	.04
❑	356	Earl Weaver MG	.25	.10
❑	357A	Bob Picciolo P1 ERR	.25	.10
		Name misspelled		
❑	357B	R.Picciolo P2 COR	.10	.04
❑	358	Matt Keough	.10	.04
❑	359	Dwayne Murphy	.10	.04
❑	360	Brian Kingman	.10	.04
❑	361	Bill Fahey	.10	.04
❑	362	Steve Mura	.10	.04
❑	363	Dennis Kinney	.10	.04
❑	364	Dave Winfield	.50	.20
❑	365	Lou Whitaker	.50	.20
❑	366	Lance Parrish	.25	.10
❑	367	Tim Corcoran	.10	.04
❑	368	Pat Underwood	.10	.04
❑	369	Al Cowens	.10	.04
❑	370	Sparky Anderson MG	.25	.10
❑	371	Pete Rose	3.00	1.20
❑	372	Phil Garner	.25	.10
❑	373	Steve Nicosia	.10	.04
❑	374	John Candelaria	.25	.10
❑	375	Don Robinson	.10	.04
❑	376	Lee Lacy	.10	.04
❑	377	John Milner	.10	.04
❑	378	Craig Reynolds	.10	.04
❑	379A	Luis Pujols P1 ERR	.25	.10
		Name misspelled Pujois		
❑	379B	Luis Pujols P2 COR	.10	.04
❑	380	Joe Niekro	.10	.04
❑	381	Joaquin Andujar	.25	.10
❑	382	Keith Moreland	.10	.04
❑	383	Jose Cruz	.25	.10
❑	384	Bill Virdon MG	.10	.04
❑	385	Jim Sundberg	.25	.10
❑	386	Doc Medich	.10	.04
❑	387	Al Oliver	.25	.10
❑	388	Jim Norris	.10	.04
❑	389	Bob Bailor	.10	.04
❑	390	Ernie Whitt	.10	.04
❑	391	Otto Velez	.10	.04
❑	392	Roy Howell	.10	.04
❑	393	Bob Walk RC	.50	.20
❑	394	Doug Flynn	.10	.04
❑	395	Pete Falcone	.10	.04
❑	396	Tom Hausman	.10	.04
❑	397	Elliott Maddox	.10	.04
❑	398	Mike Squires	.10	.04
❑	399	Marvis Foley	.10	.04
❑	400	Steve Trout	.10	.04
❑	401	Wayne Nordhagen	.10	.04
❑	402	Tony LaRussa MG	.25	.10
❑	403	Bruce Bochte	.10	.04
❑	404	Bake McBride	.25	.10
❑	405	Jerry Narron	.10	.04
❑	406	Rob Dressler	.10	.04
❑	407	Dave Heaverlo	.10	.04
❑	408	Tom Paciorek	.10	.04
❑	409	Carney Lansford	.25	.10
❑	410	Brian Downing	.25	.10
❑	411	Don Aase	.10	.04
❑	412	Jim Barr	.10	.04
❑	413	Don Baylor	.25	.10
❑	414	Jim Fregosi MG	.10	.04
❑	415	Dallas Green MG	.10	.04
❑	416	Dave Lopes	.25	.10
❑	417	Jerry Reuss	.10	.04
❑	418	Rick Sutcliffe	.25	.10
❑	419	Derrel Thomas	.10	.04
❑	420	Tom Lasorda MG	.50	.20
❑	421	Charlie Leibrandt RC	.50	.20
❑	422	Tom Seaver	1.00	.40
❑	423	Ron Oester	.10	.04
❑	424	Junior Kennedy	.10	.04
❑	425	Tom Seaver	1.00	.40
❑	426	Bobby Cox MG	.25	.10
❑	427	Leon Durham RC	.50	.20
❑	428	Terry Kennedy	.10	.04
❑	429	Silvio Martinez	.10	.04
❑	430	George Hendrick	.25	.10

❑ 431 Red Schoendienst MG .50 .20
❑ 432 Johnnie LeMaster .10 .04
❑ 433 Vida Blue .25 .10
❑ 434 John Montefusco .10 .04
❑ 435 Terry Whitfield .10 .04
❑ 436 Dave Bristol MG .10 .04
❑ 437 Dale Murphy .50 .20
❑ 438 Jerry Dybzinski .10 .04
❑ 439 Jorge Orta .10 .04
❑ 440 Wayne Garland .10 .04
❑ 441 Miguel Dilone .10 .04
❑ 442 Dave Garcia MG .10 .04
❑ 443 Don Money .10 .04
❑ 444A B.Martinez P1 ERR .25 .10
Reverse negative
❑ 444B Buck Martinez .10 .04
P2 COR
❑ 445 Jerry Augustine .10 .04
❑ 446 Ben Oglivie .25 .10
❑ 447 Jim Slaton .10 .04
❑ 448 Doyle Alexander .10 .04
❑ 449 Tony Bernazard .10 .04
❑ 450 Scott Sanderson .10 .04
❑ 451 David Palmer .10 .04
❑ 452 Stan Bahnsen .10 .04
❑ 453 Dick Williams MG .10 .04
❑ 454 Rick Burleson .10 .04
❑ 455 Gary Allenson .10 .04
❑ 456 Bob Stanley .10 .04
❑ 457A J. Tudor P1 ERR RC 1.00 .40
Lifetime W-L 9.7
❑ 457B J.Tudor P2 COR RC 1.00 .40
Lifetime W-L 9-7
❑ 458 Dwight Evans .50 .20
❑ 459 Glenn Hubbard .10 .04
❑ 460 U.L. Washington .10 .04
❑ 461 Larry Gura .10 .04
❑ 462 Rich Gale .10 .04
❑ 463 Hal McRae .25 .10
❑ 464 Jim Frey MG .10 .04
❑ 465 Bucky Dent .25 .10
❑ 466 Dennis Werth .10 .04
❑ 467 Ron Davis .10 .04
❑ 468 Reggie Jackson UER 1.00 .40
32 HR in 1970
should be 23
❑ 469 Bobby Brown .10 .04
❑ 470 Mike Davis RC .50 .20
❑ 471 Gaylord Perry .25 .10
❑ 472 Mark Belanger .10 .04
❑ 473 Jim Palmer .50 .20
❑ 474 Sammy Stewart .10 .04
❑ 475 Tim Stoddard .10 .04
❑ 476 Steve Stone .10 .04
❑ 477 Jeff Newman .10 .04
❑ 478 Steve McCatty .10 .04
❑ 479 Billy Martin MG .50 .20
❑ 480 Mitchell Page .10 .04
❑ 481 Steve Carlton CY .25 .10
❑ 482 Bill Buckner .25 .10
❑ 483A I.DeJesus P1 ERR .25 .10
Lifetime hits 702
❑ 483B I.DeJesus P2 COR .10 .04
Lifetime hits 642
❑ 484 Cliff Johnson .10 .04
❑ 485 Lenny Randle .10 .04
❑ 486 Larry Milbourne .10 .04
❑ 487 Roy Smalley .10 .04
❑ 488 John Castino .10 .04
❑ 489 Ron Jackson .10 .04
❑ 490A Dave Roberts P1 .25 .10
Career Highlights
Showed pop in
❑ 490B Dave Roberts P2 .10 .04
Declared himself
❑ 491 George Brett MVP 1.50 .60
❑ 492 Mike Cubbage .10 .04
❑ 493 Rob Wilfong .10 .04
❑ 494 Danny Goodwin .10 .04
❑ 495 Jose Morales .10 .04
❑ 496 Mickey Rivers .10 .04
❑ 497 Mike Edwards .10 .04
❑ 498 Mike Sadek .10 .04
❑ 499 Lenn Sakata .10 .04
❑ 500 Gene Michael MG .10 .04
❑ 501 Dave Roberts .10 .04
❑ 502 Steve Dillard .10 .04
❑ 503 Jim Essian .10 .04
❑ 504 Rance Mulliniks .10 .04
❑ 505 Darrell Porter .10 .04
❑ 506 Joe Torre MG .25 .10
❑ 507 Terry Crowley .10 .04
❑ 508 Bill Travers .10 .04
❑ 509 Nelson Norman .10 .04
❑ 510 Bob McClure .10 .04
❑ 511 Steve Howe RC .50 .20
❑ 512 Dave Rader .10 .04
❑ 513 Mick Kelleher .10 .04
❑ 514 Kiko Garcia .10 .04
❑ 515 Larry Biittner .10 .04
❑ 516A Willie Norwood P1 .25 .10
Career Highlights
Spent most of
❑ 516B Willie Norwood P2 .10 .04
Traded to Seattle
❑ 517 Bo Diaz .10 .04
❑ 518 Juan Beniquez .10 .04
❑ 519 Scot Thompson .10 .04
❑ 520 Jim Tracy RC 1.00 .40
❑ 521 Carlos Lezcano .10 .04
❑ 522 Joe Amalfitano MG .10 .04
❑ 523 Preston Hanna .10 .04
❑ 524A Ray Burris P1 .25 .10
Career Highlights
Went on ...
❑ 524B Ray Burris P2 .10 .04
Drafted by ...
❑ 525 Broderick Perkins .10 .04
❑ 526 Mickey Hatcher .10 .04
❑ 527 John Goryl MG .10 .04
❑ 528 Dick Davis .10 .04
❑ 529 Butch Wynegar .10 .04
❑ 530 Sal Butera .10 .04
❑ 531 Jerry Koosman .25 .10
❑ 532A Geoff Zahn P1 .25 .10
(Career Highlights
Was 2nd in
❑ 532B Geoff Zahn P2 .10 .04
Signed a 3 year
❑ 533 Dennis Martinez .25 .10
❑ 534 Gary Thomasson .10 .04
❑ 535 Steve Macko .10 .04
❑ 536 Jim Kaat .25 .10
❑ 537 George Brett 1.50 .60
Rod Carew
❑ 538 Tim Raines RC 2.50 1.00
❑ 539 Keith Smith .10 .04
❑ 540 Ken Macha .10 .04
❑ 541 Burt Hooton .10 .04
❑ 542 Butch Hobson .10 .04
❑ 543 Bill Stein .10 .04
❑ 544 Dave Stapleton .10 .04
❑ 545 Bob Pate .10 .04
❑ 546 Doug Corbett .10 .04
❑ 547 Darrell Jackson .10 .04
❑ 548 Pete Redfern .10 .04
❑ 549 Roger Erickson .10 .04
❑ 550 Al Hrabosky .25 .10
❑ 551 Dick Tidrow .10 .04
❑ 552 Dave Ford .10 .04
❑ 553 Dave Kingman .25 .10
❑ 554A Mike Vail P1 .25 .10
Career Highlights
After two
❑ 554B Mike Vail P2 .10 .04
Traded to
❑ 555A Jerry Martin P1 .25 .10
Career Highlights
Overcame a
❑ 555B Jerry Martin P2 .10 .04
Traded to
❑ 556A Jesus Figueroa P1 .25 .10
Career Highlights
Had an
❑ 556B Jesus Figueroa P2 .10 .04
Traded to
❑ 557 Don Stanhouse .10 .04
❑ 558 Barry Foote .10 .04
❑ 559 Tim Blackwell .10 .04
❑ 560 Bruce Sutter .25 .10
❑ 561 Rick Reuschel .25 .10
❑ 562 Lynn McGlothen .10 .04
❑ 563A Bob Owchinko P1 .25 .10
Career Highlights
Traded to
❑ 563B Bob Owchinko P2 .10 .04
Involved in a
❑ 564 John Verhoeven .10 .04
❑ 565 Ken Landreaux .10 .04
❑ 566A Glen Adams P1 ERR .25 .10
Name misspelled
❑ 566B G. Adams P2 COR .10 .04
❑ 567 Hosken Powell .10 .04
❑ 568 Dick Noles .10 .04
❑ 569 Danny Ainge RC 3.00 1.20
❑ 570 Bobby Mattick MG .10 .04
❑ 571 Joe Lefebvre .10 .04
❑ 572 Bobby Clark .10 .04
❑ 573 Dennis Lamp .10 .04
❑ 574 Randy Lerch .10 .04
❑ 575 Mookie Wilson RC 3.00 1.20
❑ 576 Ron LeFlore .25 .10
❑ 577 Jim Dwyer .10 .04
❑ 578 Bill Castro .10 .04
❑ 579 Greg Minton .10 .04
❑ 580 Mark Littell .10 .04
❑ 581 Andy Hassler .10 .04
❑ 582 Dave Stieb .25 .10
❑ 583 Ken Oberkfell .10 .04
❑ 584 Larry Bradford .10 .04
❑ 585 Fred Stanley .10 .04
❑ 586 Bill Caudill .10 .04
❑ 587 Doug Capilla .10 .04
❑ 588 George Riley .10 .04
❑ 589 Willie Hernandez .10 .04
❑ 590 Mike Schmidt MVP 2.50 1.00
❑ 591 Steve Stone CY .10 .04
❑ 592 Rick Sofield .10 .04
❑ 593 Bombo Rivera .10 .04
❑ 594 Gary Ward .10 .04
❑ 595A Dave Edwards P1 .25 .10
Career Highlights
Sidelined the
❑ 595B Dave Edwards P2 .10 .04
Traded to
❑ 596 Mike Proly .10 .04
❑ 597 Tommy Boggs .10 .04
❑ 598 Greg Gross .10 .04
❑ 599 Elias Sosa .10 .04
❑ 600 Pat Kelly .10 .04
❑ 601A Checklist 1-120 P1 .25 .10
ERR Unnumbered
51 Donahue
❑ 601B Checklist 1-120 P2 .50 .20
COR Unnumbered
51 Donohue
❑ 602 Checklist 121-240 .25 .10
Unnumbered
❑ 603A CL 241-360 P1 .25 .10
ERR Unnumbered
306 Mathews
❑ 603B CL 241-360 P2 .25 .10
COR Unnumbered
306 Matthews
❑ 604A CL 361-480 P1 .25 .10
ERR Unnumbered
379 Pujois
❑ 604B CL 361-480 P2 .25 .10
COR Unnumbered
379 Pujols
❑ 605A CL 481-600 P1 .25 .10
ERR Unnumbered
566 Glen Adams
❑ 605B CL 481-600 P2 .25 .10
COR Unnumbered
566 Glenn Adams

1982 Donruss

	Nm-Mt	Ex-Mt
COMPLETE SET (660)	60.00	24.00
COMP.FACT.SET (660)	60.00	24.00
COMP.RUTH PUZZLE	10.00	4.00

❑ 1 Pete Rose DK 2.50 1.00
❑ 2 Gary Carter DK .20 .08
❑ 3 Steve Garvey DK .20 .08
❑ 4 Vida Blue DK .20 .08

❑ 5 Alan Trammell DK COR .20 .08
❑ 5A Alan Trammel DK ERR .20 .08
(Name misspelled)
❑ 6 Len Barker DK .10 .04
❑ 7 Dwight Evans DK .40 .16
❑ 8 Rod Carew DK .40 .16
❑ 9 George Hendrick DK .20 .08
❑ 10 Phil Niekro DK .20 .08
❑ 11 Richie Zisk DK .10 .04
❑ 12 Dave Parker DK .20 .08
❑ 13 Nolan Ryan DK 4.00 1.60
❑ 14 Ivan DeJesus DK .10 .04
❑ 15 George Brett DK 2.00 .80
❑ 16 Tom Seaver DK .40 .16
❑ 17 Dave Kingman DK .20 .08
❑ 18 Dave Winfield DK .20 .08
❑ 19 Mike Norris DK .10 .04
❑ 20 Carlton Fisk DK .40 .16
❑ 21 Ozzie Smith DK 1.50 .60
❑ 22 Roy Smalley DK .10 .04
❑ 23 Buddy Bell DK .20 .08
❑ 24 Ken Singleton DK .20 .08
❑ 25 John Mayberry DK .10 .04
❑ 26 Gorman Thomas DK .20 .08
❑ 27 Earl Weaver MG .20 .08
❑ 28 Rollie Fingers .20 .08
❑ 29 Sparky Anderson MG .20 .08
❑ 30 Dennis Eckersley .40 .16
❑ 31 Dave Winfield .20 .08
❑ 32 Burt Hooton .10 .04
❑ 33 Rick Waits .10 .04
❑ 34 George Brett 2.00 .80
❑ 35 Steve McCatty .10 .04
❑ 36 Steve Rogers .20 .08
❑ 37 Bill Stein .10 .04
❑ 38 Steve Renko .10 .04
❑ 39 Mike Squires .10 .04
❑ 40 George Hendrick .20 .08
❑ 41 Bob Knepper .10 .04
❑ 42 Steve Carlton .40 .16
❑ 43 Larry Biittner .10 .04
❑ 44 Chris Welsh .10 .04
❑ 45 Steve Nicosia .10 .04
❑ 46 Jack Clark .20 .08
❑ 47 Chris Chambliss .20 .08
❑ 48 Ivan DeJesus .10 .04
❑ 49 Lee Mazzilli .20 .08
❑ 50 Julio Cruz .10 .04
❑ 51 Pete Redfern .10 .04
❑ 52 Dave Stieb .20 .08
❑ 53 Doug Corbett .10 .04
❑ 54 Jorge Bell RC 1.00 .40
❑ 55 Joe Simpson .10 .04
❑ 56 Rusty Staub .20 .08
❑ 57 Hector Cruz .10 .04
❑ 58 Claudell Washington .10 .04
❑ 59 Enrique Romo .10 .04
❑ 60 Gary Lavelle .10 .04
❑ 61 Tim Flannery .10 .04
❑ 62 Joe Nolan .10 .04
❑ 63 Larry Bowa .20 .08
❑ 64 Sixto Lezcano .10 .04
❑ 65 Joe Sambito .10 .04
❑ 66 Bruce Kison .10 .04
❑ 67 Wayne Nordhagen .10 .04
❑ 68 Woodie Fryman .10 .04
❑ 69 Billy Sample .10 .04
❑ 70 Amos Otis .20 .08
❑ 71 Matt Keough .10 .04
❑ 72 Toby Harrah .20 .08
❑ 73 Dave Righetti RC 1.50 .60
❑ 74 Carl Yastrzemski 1.25 .50
❑ 75 Bob Welch .20 .08
❑ 76 Alan Trammell COR .20 .08
❑ 76A Alan Trammel ERR .20 .08
(Name misspelled)
❑ 77 Rick Dempsey .10 .04
❑ 78 Paul Molitor .40 .16
❑ 79 Dennis Martinez .20 .08
❑ 80 Jim Slaton .10 .04
❑ 81 Champ Summers .10 .04
❑ 82 Carney Lansford .20 .08
❑ 83 Barry Foote .10 .04
❑ 84 Steve Garvey .20 .08
❑ 85 Rick Manning .10 .04
❑ 86 John Wathan .10 .04
❑ 87 Brian Kingman .10 .04
❑ 88 Andre Dawson UER .20 .08
(Middle name Fernando should be Nolan)
❑ 89 Jim Kern .10 .04
❑ 90 Bobby Grich .20 .08
❑ 91 Bob Forsch .10 .04
❑ 92 Art Howe .10 .04
❑ 93 Marty Bystrom .10 .04
❑ 94 Ozzie Smith 1.50 .60
❑ 95 Dave Parker .20 .08
❑ 96 Doyle Alexander .10 .04
❑ 97 Al Hrabosky .10 .04
❑ 98 Frank Taveras .10 .04
❑ 99 Tim Blackwell .10 .04
❑ 100 Floyd Bannister .10 .04
❑ 101 Alfredo Griffin .10 .04
❑ 102 Dave Engle .10 .04
❑ 103 Mario Soto .20 .08
❑ 104 Ross Baumgarten .10 .04
❑ 105 Ken Singleton .20 .08
❑ 106 Ted Simmons .20 .08
❑ 107 Jack Morris .20 .08
❑ 108 Bob Watson .10 .04
❑ 109 Dwight Evans .40 .16
❑ 110 Tom Lasorda MG .40 .16
❑ 111 Bert Blyleven .20 .08
❑ 112 Dan Quisenberry .10 .04
❑ 113 Rickey Henderson 2.50 1.00
❑ 114 Gary Carter .20 .08
❑ 115 Brian Downing .20 .08
❑ 116 Al Oliver .20 .08
❑ 117 LaMarr Hoyt .10 .04
❑ 118 Cesar Cedeno .20 .08
❑ 119 Keith Moreland .10 .04
❑ 120 Bob Shirley .10 .04
❑ 121 Terry Kennedy .10 .04
❑ 122 Frank Pastore .10 .04
❑ 123 Gene Garber .10 .04
❑ 124 Tony Pena .20 .08
❑ 125 Allen Ripley .10 .04
❑ 126 Randy Martz .10 .04
❑ 127 Richie Zisk .10 .04
❑ 128 Mike Scott .20 .08
❑ 129 Lloyd Moseby .10 .04
❑ 130 Rob Wilfong .10 .04
❑ 131 Tim Stoddard .10 .04
❑ 132 Gorman Thomas .20 .08
❑ 133 Dan Petry .10 .04
❑ 134 Bob Stanley .10 .04
❑ 135 Lou Piniella .20 .08
❑ 136 Pedro Guerrero .20 .08
❑ 137 Len Barker .10 .04
❑ 138 Rich Gale .10 .04
❑ 139 Wayne Gross .10 .04
❑ 140 Tim Wallach RC 1.00 .40
❑ 141 Gene Mauch MG .10 .04
❑ 142 Doc Medich .10 .04
❑ 143 Tony Bernazard .10 .04
❑ 144 Bill Virdon MG .10 .04
❑ 145 John Littlefield .10 .04
❑ 146 Dave Bergman .10 .04
❑ 147 Dick Davis .10 .04
❑ 148 Tom Seaver .75 .30
❑ 149 Matt Sinatro .10 .04
❑ 150 Chuck Tanner MG .10 .04
❑ 151 Leon Durham .10 .04
❑ 152 Gene Tenace .20 .08
❑ 153 Al Bumbry .10 .04
❑ 154 Mark Brouhard .10 .04
❑ 155 Rick Peters .10 .04
❑ 156 Jerry Remy .10 .04
❑ 157 Rick Reuschel .20 .08
❑ 158 Steve Howe .10 .04
❑ 159 Alan Bannister .10 .04
❑ 160 U.L. Washington .10 .04
❑ 161 Rick Langford .10 .04
❑ 162 Bill Gullickson .10 .04
❑ 163 Mark Wagner .10 .04
❑ 164 Geoff Zahn .10 .04
❑ 165 Ron LeFlore .20 .08
❑ 166 Dane Iorg .10 .04
❑ 167 Joe Niekro .10 .04
❑ 168 Pete Rose 2.50 1.00
❑ 169 Dave Collins .10 .04
❑ 170 Rick Wise .10 .04
❑ 171 Jim Bibby .10 .04
❑ 172 Larry Herndon .10 .04
❑ 173 Bob Horner .20 .08
❑ 174 Steve Dillard .10 .04
❑ 175 Mookie Wilson .20 .08
❑ 176 Dan Meyer .10 .04
❑ 177 Fernando Arroyo .10 .04
❑ 178 Jackson Todd .10 .04
❑ 179 Darrell Jackson .10 .04
❑ 180 Alvis Woods .10 .04
❑ 181 Jim Anderson .10 .04
❑ 182 Dave Kingman .20 .08
❑ 183 Steve Henderson .10 .04
❑ 184 Brian Asselstine .10 .04
❑ 185 Rod Scurry .10 .04
❑ 186 Fred Breining .10 .04
❑ 187 Danny Boone .10 .04
❑ 188 Junior Kennedy .10 .04
❑ 189 Sparky Lyle .20 .08
❑ 190 Whitey Herzog MG .20 .08
❑ 191 Dave Smith .10 .04
❑ 192 Ed Ott .10 .04
❑ 193 Greg Luzinski .20 .08
❑ 194 Bill Lee .20 .08
❑ 195 Don Zimmer MG .20 .08
❑ 196 Hal McRae .20 .08
❑ 197 Mike Norris .10 .04
❑ 198 Duane Kuiper .10 .04
❑ 199 Rick Cerone .10 .04
❑ 200 Jim Rice .20 .08
❑ 201 Steve Yeager .20 .08
❑ 202 Tom Brookens .10 .04
❑ 203 Jose Morales .10 .04
❑ 204 Roy Howell .10 .04
❑ 205 Tippy Martinez .10 .04
❑ 206 Moose Haas .10 .04
❑ 207 Al Cowens .10 .04
❑ 208 Dave Stapleton .10 .04
❑ 209 Bucky Dent .20 .08
❑ 210 Ron Cey .20 .08
❑ 211 Jorge Orta .10 .04
❑ 212 Jamie Quirk .10 .04
❑ 213 Jeff Jones .10 .04
❑ 214 Tim Raines .40 .16
❑ 215 Jon Matlack .10 .04
❑ 216 Rod Carew .40 .16
❑ 217 Jim Kaat .20 .08
❑ 218 Joe Pittman .10 .04
❑ 219 Larry Christenson .10 .04
❑ 220 Juan Bonilla RC .15 .06
❑ 221 Mike Easler .10 .04
❑ 222 Vida Blue .20 .08
❑ 223 Rick Camp .10 .04
❑ 224 Mike Jorgensen .10 .04
❑ 225 Jody Davis .10 .04
❑ 226 Mike Parrott .10 .04
❑ 227 Jim Clancy .10 .04
❑ 228 Hosken Powell .10 .04
❑ 229 Tom Hume .10 .04
❑ 230 Britt Burns .10 .04
❑ 231 Jim Palmer .20 .08
❑ 232 Bob Rodgers MG .10 .04
❑ 233 Milt Wilcox .10 .04
❑ 234 Dave Revering .10 .04
❑ 235 Mike Torrez .10 .04
❑ 236 Robert Castillo .10 .04
❑ 237 Von Hayes RC .50 .20

❑	238	Renie Martin	.10	.04
❑	239	Dwayne Murphy	.10	.04
❑	240	Rodney Scott	.10	.04
❑	241	Fred Patek	.10	.04
❑	242	Mickey Rivers	.10	.04
❑	243	Steve Trout	.10	.04
❑	244	Jose Cruz	.20	.08
❑	245	Manny Trillo	.10	.04
❑	246	Lary Sorensen	.10	.04
❑	247	Dave Edwards	.10	.04
❑	248	Dan Driessen	.10	.04
❑	249	Tommy Boggs	.10	.04
❑	250	Dale Berra	.10	.04
❑	251	Ed Whitson	.10	.04
❑	252	Lee Smith RC	2.00	.80
❑	253	Tom Paciorek	.10	.04
❑	254	Pat Zachry	.10	.04
❑	255	Luis Leal	.10	.04
❑	256	John Castino	.10	.04
❑	257	Rich Dauer	.10	.04
❑	258	Cecil Cooper	.20	.08
❑	259	Dave Rozema	.10	.04
❑	260	John Tudor	.20	.08
❑	261	Jerry Mumphrey	.10	.04
❑	262	Jay Johnstone	.10	.04
❑	263	Bo Diaz	.10	.04
❑	264	Dennis Leonard	.10	.04
❑	265	Jim Spencer	.10	.04
❑	266	John Milner	.10	.04
❑	267	Don Aase	.10	.04
❑	268	Jim Sundberg	.20	.08
❑	269	Lamar Johnson	.10	.04
❑	270	Frank LaCorte	.10	.04
❑	271	Barry Evans	.10	.04
❑	272	Enos Cabell	.10	.04
❑	273	Del Unser	.10	.04
❑	274	George Foster	.20	.08
❑	275	Brett Butler RC	1.00	.40
❑	276	Lee Lacy	.10	.04
❑	277	Ken Reitz	.10	.04
❑	278	Keith Hernandez	.20	.08
❑	279	Doug DeCinces	.10	.04
❑	280	Charlie Moore	.10	.04
❑	281	Lance Parrish	.20	.08
❑	282	Ralph Houk MG	.10	.04
❑	283	Rich Gossage	.20	.08
❑	284	Jerry Reuss	.10	.04
❑	285	Mike Stanton	.10	.04
❑	286	Frank White	.20	.08
❑	287	Bob Owchinko	.10	.04
❑	288	Scott Sanderson	.10	.04
❑	289	Bump Wills	.10	.04
❑	290	Dave Frost	.10	.04
❑	291	Chet Lemon	.20	.08
❑	292	Tito Landrum	.10	.04
❑	293	Vern Ruhle	.10	.04
❑	294	Mike Schmidt	2.00	.80
❑	295	Sam Mejias	.10	.04
❑	296	Gary Lucas	.10	.04
❑	297	John Candelaria	.10	.04
❑	298	Jerry Martin	.10	.04
❑	299	Dale Murphy	.40	.16
❑	300	Mike Lum	.10	.04
❑	301	Tom Hausman	.10	.04
❑	302	Glenn Abbott	.10	.04
❑	303	Roger Erickson	.10	.04
❑	304	Otto Velez	.10	.04
❑	305	Danny Goodwin	.10	.04
❑	306	John Mayberry	.10	.04
❑	307	Lenny Randle	.10	.04
❑	308	Bob Bailor	.10	.04
❑	309	Jerry Morales	.10	.04
❑	310	Rufino Linares	.10	.04
❑	311	Kent Tekulve	.10	.04
❑	312	Joe Morgan	.20	.08
❑	313	John Urrea	.10	.04
❑	314	Paul Householder	.10	.04
❑	315	Garry Maddox	.10	.04
❑	316	Mike Ramsey	.10	.04
❑	317	Alan Ashby	.10	.04
❑	318	Bob Clark	.10	.04
❑	319	Tony LaRussa MG	.20	.08
❑	320	Charlie Lea	.10	.04
❑	321	Danny Darwin	.10	.04
❑	322	Cesar Geronimo	.10	.04
❑	323	Tom Underwood	.10	.04
❑	324	Andre Thornton	.10	.04
❑	325	Rudy May	.10	.04
❑	326	Frank Tanana	.20	.08
❑	327	Dave Lopes	.20	.08
❑	328	Richie Hebner	.10	.04
❑	329	Mike Flanagan	.10	.04
❑	330	Mike Caldwell	.10	.04
❑	331	Scott McGregor	.10	.04
❑	332	Jerry Augustine	.10	.04
❑	333	Stan Papi	.10	.04
❑	334	Rick Miller	.10	.04
❑	335	Graig Nettles	.20	.08
❑	336	Dusty Baker	.20	.08
❑	337	Dave Garcia MG	.10	.04
❑	338	Larry Gura	.10	.04
❑	339	Cliff Johnson	.10	.04
❑	340	Warren Cromartie	.10	.04
❑	341	Steve Comer	.10	.04
❑	342	Rick Burleson	.10	.04
❑	343	John Martin RC	.15	.06
❑	344	Craig Reynolds	.10	.04
❑	345	Mike Proly	.10	.04
❑	346	Ruppert Jones	.10	.04
❑	347	Omar Moreno	.10	.04
❑	348	Greg Minton	.10	.04
❑	349	Rick Mahler	.10	.04
❑	350	Alex Trevino	.10	.04
❑	351	Mike Krukow	.10	.04
❑	352A	Shane Rawley ERR (Photo actually Jim Anderson)	.40	.16
❑	352B	Shane Rawley COR	.10	.04
❑	353	Garth Iorg	.10	.04
❑	354	Pete Mackanin	.10	.04
❑	355	Paul Moskau	.10	.04
❑	356	Richard Dotson	.10	.04
❑	357	Steve Stone	.10	.04
❑	358	Larry Hisle	.10	.04
❑	359	Aurelio Lopez	.10	.04
❑	360	Oscar Gamble	.10	.04
❑	361	Tom Burgmeier	.10	.04
❑	362	Terry Forster	.20	.08
❑	363	Joe Charboneau	.20	.08
❑	364	Ken Brett	.10	.04
❑	365	Tony Armas	.20	.08
❑	366	Chris Speier	.10	.04
❑	367	Fred Lynn	.20	.08
❑	368	Buddy Bell	.20	.08
❑	369	Jim Essian	.10	.04
❑	370	Terry Puhl	.10	.04
❑	371	Greg Gross	.10	.04
❑	372	Bruce Sutter	.20	.08
❑	373	Joe Lefebvre	.10	.04
❑	374	Ray Knight	.20	.08
❑	375	Bruce Benedict	.10	.04
❑	376	Tim Foli	.10	.04
❑	377	Al Holland	.10	.04
❑	378	Ken Kravec	.10	.04
❑	379	Jeff Burroughs	.10	.04
❑	380	Pete Falcone	.10	.04
❑	381	Ernie Whitt	.10	.04
❑	382	Brad Havens	.10	.04
❑	383	Terry Crowley	.10	.04
❑	384	Don Money	.10	.04
❑	385	Dan Schatzeder	.10	.04
❑	386	Gary Allenson	.10	.04
❑	387	Yogi Berra CO	.75	.30
❑	388	Ken Landreaux	.10	.04
❑	389	Mike Hargrove	.10	.04
❑	390	Darryl Motley	.10	.04
❑	391	Dave McKay	.10	.04
❑	392	Stan Bahnsen	.10	.04
❑	393	Ken Forsch	.10	.04
❑	394	Mario Mendoza	.10	.04
❑	395	Jim Morrison	.10	.04
❑	396	Mike Ivie	.10	.04
❑	397	Broderick Perkins	.10	.04
❑	398	Darrell Evans	.20	.08
❑	399	Ron Reed	.10	.04
❑	400	Johnny Bench	.75	.30
❑	401	Steve Bedrosian RC	.50	.20
❑	402	Bill Robinson	.10	.04
❑	403	Bill Buckner	.20	.08
❑	404	Ken Oberkfell	.10	.04
❑	405	Cal Ripken RC	40.00	16.00
❑	406	Jim Gantner	.10	.04
❑	407	Kirk Gibson	.75	.30
❑	408	Tony Perez	.40	.16
❑	409	Tommy John UER (Text says 52-56 as Yankee, should be 52-26)	.20	.08
❑	410	Dave Stewart RC	1.50	.60
❑	411	Dan Spillner	.10	.04
❑	412	Willie Aikens	.10	.04
❑	413	Mike Heath	.10	.04
❑	414	Ray Burris	.10	.04
❑	415	Leon Roberts	.10	.04
❑	416	Mike Witt	.50	.20
❑	417	Bob Molinaro	.10	.04
❑	418	Steve Braun	.10	.04
❑	419	Nolan Ryan UER (Nisnumbering of Nolan's no-hitters on card back)	4.00	1.60
❑	420	Tug McGraw	.20	.08
❑	421	Dave Concepcion	.20	.08
❑	422A	Juan Eichelberger ERR (Photo actually Gary Lucas)	.40	.16
❑	422B	Juan Eichelberger COR	.10	.04
❑	423	Rick Rhoden	.10	.04
❑	424	Frank Robinson MG	.40	.16
❑	425	Eddie Miller	.10	.04
❑	426	Bill Caudill	.10	.04
❑	427	Doug Flynn	.10	.04
❑	428	Larry Andersen UER (Misspelled Anderson on card front)	.10	.04
❑	429	Al Williams	.10	.04
❑	430	Jerry Garvin	.10	.04
❑	431	Glenn Adams	.10	.04
❑	432	Barry Bonnell	.10	.04
❑	433	Jerry Narron	.10	.04
❑	434	John Stearns	.10	.04
❑	435	Mike Tyson	.10	.04
❑	436	Glenn Hubbard	.10	.04
❑	437	Eddie Solomon	.10	.04
❑	438	Jeff Leonard	.10	.04
❑	439	Randy Bass RC	.50	.20
❑	440	Mike LaCoss	.10	.04
❑	441	Gary Matthews	.20	.08
❑	442	Mark Littell	.10	.04
❑	443	Don Sutton	.20	.08
❑	444	John Harris	.10	.04
❑	445	Vada Pinson CO	.20	.08
❑	446	Elias Sosa	.10	.04
❑	447	Charlie Hough	.20	.08
❑	448	Willie Wilson	.20	.08
❑	449	Fred Stanley	.10	.04
❑	450	Tom Veryzer	.10	.04
❑	451	Ron Davis	.10	.04
❑	452	Mark Clear	.10	.04
❑	453	Bill Russell	.20	.08
❑	454	Lou Whitaker	.20	.08
❑	455	Dan Graham	.10	.04
❑	456	Reggie Cleveland	.10	.04
❑	457	Sammy Stewart	.10	.04
❑	458	Pete Vuckovich	.10	.04
❑	459	John Wockenfuss	.10	.04
❑	460	Glenn Hoffman	.10	.04
❑	461	Willie Randolph	.20	.08
❑	462	Fernando Valenzuela	.75	.30
❑	463	Ron Hassey	.10	.04
❑	464	Paul Splittorff	.10	.04
❑	465	Rob Picciolo	.10	.04
❑	466	Larry Parrish	.10	.04
❑	467	Johnny Grubb	.10	.04
❑	468	Dan Ford	.10	.04
❑	469	Silvio Martinez	.10	.04
❑	470	Kiko Garcia	.10	.04
❑	471	Bob Boone	.20	.08
❑	472	Luis Salazar	.10	.04
❑	473	Randy Niemann UER (Card says Pirate, but in an Astro uniform)	.10	.04
❑	474	Tom Griffin	.10	.04
❑	475	Phil Niekro	.20	.08
❑	476	Hubie Brooks	.10	.04
❑	477	Dick Tidrow	.10	.04
❑	478	Jim Beattie	.10	.04

- ❑ 479 Damaso Garcia .10 .04
- ❑ 480 Mickey Hatcher .10 .04
- ❑ 481 Joe Price .10 .04
- ❑ 482 Ed Farmer .10 .04
- ❑ 483 Eddie Murray .75 .30
- ❑ 484 Ben Oglivie .20 .08
- ❑ 485 Kevin Saucier .10 .04
- ❑ 486 Bobby Murcer .20 .08
- ❑ 487 Bill Campbell .10 .04
- ❑ 488 Reggie Smith .20 .08
- ❑ 489 Wayne Garland .10 .04
- ❑ 490 Jim Wright .10 .04
- ❑ 491 Billy Martin MG .40 .16
- ❑ 492 Jim Fanning MG .10 .04
- ❑ 493 Don Baylor .20 .08
- ❑ 494 Rick Honeycutt .10 .04
- ❑ 495 Carlton Fisk .40 .16
- ❑ 496 Denny Walling .10 .04
- ❑ 497 Bake McBride .20 .08
- ❑ 498 Darrell Porter .10 .04
- ❑ 499 Gene Richards .10 .04
- ❑ 500 Ron Oester .10 .04
- ❑ 501 Ken Dayley .10 .04
- ❑ 502 Jason Thompson .10 .04
- ❑ 503 Milt May .10 .04
- ❑ 504 Doug Bird .10 .04
- ❑ 505 Bruce Bochte .10 .04
- ❑ 506 Neil Allen .10 .04
- ❑ 507 Joey McLaughlin .10 .04
- ❑ 508 Butch Wynegar .10 .04
- ❑ 509 Gary Roenicke .10 .04
- ❑ 510 Robin Yount 1.25 .50
- ❑ 511 Dave Tobik .10 .04
- ❑ 512 Rich Gedman .50 .20
- ❑ 513 Gene Nelson .10 .04
- ❑ 514 Rick Monday .20 .08
- ❑ 515 Miguel Dilone .10 .04
- ❑ 516 Clint Hurdle .10 .04
- ❑ 517 Jeff Newman .10 .04
- ❑ 518 Grant Jackson .10 .04
- ❑ 519 Andy Hassler .10 .04
- ❑ 520 Pat Putnam .10 .04
- ❑ 521 Greg Pryor .10 .04
- ❑ 522 Tony Scott .10 .04
- ❑ 523 Steve Mura .10 .04
- ❑ 524 Johnnie LeMaster .10 .04
- ❑ 525 Dick Ruthven .10 .04
- ❑ 526 John McNamara MG .10 .04
- ❑ 527 Larry McWilliams .10 .04
- ❑ 528 Johnny Ray RC .50 .20
- ❑ 529 Pat Tabler .10 .04
- ❑ 530 Tom Herr .10 .04
- ❑ 531A SD Chicken 1.00 .40
  ERR (Without TM)
- ❑ 531B San Diego Chicken 1.00 .40
  COR (With TM)
- ❑ 532 Sal Butera .10 .04
- ❑ 533 Mike Griffin .10 .04
- ❑ 534 Kelvin Moore .10 .04
- ❑ 535 Reggie Jackson .40 .16
- ❑ 536 Ed Romero .10 .04
- ❑ 537 Derrel Thomas .10 .04
- ❑ 538 Mike O'Berry .10 .04
- ❑ 539 Jack O'Connor .10 .04
- ❑ 540 Bob Ojeda RC .50 .20
- ❑ 541 Roy Lee Jackson .10 .04
- ❑ 542 Lynn Jones .10 .04
- ❑ 543 Gaylord Perry .20 .08
- ❑ 544A Phil Garner ERR .20 .08
  (Reverse negative)
- ❑ 544B Phil Garner COR .20 .08
- ❑ 545 Garry Templeton .20 .08
- ❑ 546 Rafael Ramirez .10 .04
- ❑ 547 Jeff Reardon .20 .08
- ❑ 548 Ron Guidry .20 .08
- ❑ 549 Tim Laudner .10 .04
- ❑ 550 John Henry Johnson .10 .04
- ❑ 551 Chris Bando .10 .04
- ❑ 552 Bobby Brown .10 .04
- ❑ 553 Larry Bradford .10 .04
- ❑ 554 Scott Fletcher RC .50 .20
- ❑ 555 Jerry Royster .10 .04
- ❑ 556 Shooty Babitt UER .10 .04
  (Spelled Babbitt
  on front)
- ❑ 557 Kent Hrbek RC 1.00 .40
- ❑ 558 Ron Guidry .20 .08
  Tommy John
- ❑ 559 Mark Bomback .10 .04
- ❑ 560 Julio Valdez .10 .04
- ❑ 561 Buck Martinez .10 .04
- ❑ 562 Mike A. Marshall RC .50 .20
- ❑ 563 Rennie Stennett .10 .04
- ❑ 564 Steve Crawford .10 .04
- ❑ 565 Bob Babcock .10 .04
- ❑ 566 Johnny Podres CO .20 .08
- ❑ 567 Paul Serna .10 .04
- ❑ 568 Harold Baines .20 .08
- ❑ 569 Dave LaRoche .10 .04
- ❑ 570 Lee May .10 .04
- ❑ 571 Gary Ward .10 .04
- ❑ 572 John Denny .10 .04
- ❑ 573 Roy Smalley .10 .04
- ❑ 574 Bob Brenly RC 1.00 .40
- ❑ 575 Reggie Jackson .20 .08
  Dave Winfield
- ❑ 576 Luis Pujols .10 .04
- ❑ 577 Butch Hobson .10 .04
- ❑ 578 Harvey Kuenn MG .10 .04
- ❑ 579 Cal Ripken Sr. CO .20 .08
- ❑ 580 Juan Berenguer .10 .04
- ❑ 581 Benny Ayala .10 .04
- ❑ 582 Vance Law .10 .04
- ❑ 583 Rick Leach .10 .04
- ❑ 584 George Frazier .10 .04
- ❑ 585 Phillies Finest 1.50 .60
  Pete Rose
  Mike Schmidt
- ❑ 586 Joe Rudi .20 .08
- ❑ 587 Juan Beniquez .10 .04
- ❑ 588 Luis DeLeon .10 .04
- ❑ 589 Craig Swan .10 .04
- ❑ 590 Dave Chalk .10 .04
- ❑ 591 Billy Gardner MG .10 .04
- ❑ 592 Sal Bando .20 .08
- ❑ 593 Bert Campaneris .20 .08
- ❑ 594 Steve Kemp .10 .04
- ❑ 595A Randy Lerch ERR .40 .16
  (Braves)
- ❑ 595B Randy Lerch COR .10 .04
  (Brewers)
- ❑ 596 Bryan Clark RC .15 .06
- ❑ 597 Dave Ford .10 .04
- ❑ 598 Mike Scioscia .20 .08
- ❑ 599 John Lowenstein .10 .04
- ❑ 600 Rene Lachemann MG .10 .04
- ❑ 601 Mick Kelleher .10 .04
- ❑ 602 Ron Jackson .10 .04
- ❑ 603 Jerry Koosman .20 .08
- ❑ 604 Dave Goltz .10 .04
- ❑ 605 Ellis Valentine .10 .04
- ❑ 606 Lonnie Smith .10 .04
- ❑ 607 Joaquin Andujar .20 .08
- ❑ 608 Garry Hancock .10 .04
- ❑ 609 Jerry Turner .10 .04
- ❑ 610 Bob Bonner .10 .04
- ❑ 611 Jim Dwyer .10 .04
- ❑ 612 Terry Bulling .10 .04
- ❑ 613 Joel Youngblood .10 .04
- ❑ 614 Larry Milbourne .10 .04
- ❑ 615 Gene Roof UER .10 .04
  (Name on front
  is Phil Roof)
- ❑ 616 Keith Drumwright .10 .04
- ❑ 617 Dave Rosello .10 .04
- ❑ 618 Rickey Keeton .10 .04
- ❑ 619 Dennis Lamp .10 .04
- ❑ 620 Sid Monge .10 .04
- ❑ 621 Jerry White .10 .04
- ❑ 622 Luis Aguayo .10 .04
- ❑ 623 Jamie Easterly .10 .04
- ❑ 624 Steve Sax RC 1.00 .40
- ❑ 625 Dave Roberts .10 .04
- ❑ 626 Rick Bosetti .10 .04
- ❑ 627 Terry Francona RC 3.00 1.20
- ❑ 628 Tom Seaver .75 .30
  Johnny Bench
- ❑ 629 Paul Mirabella .10 .04
- ❑ 630 Rance Mulliniks .10 .04
- ❑ 631 Kevin Hickey RC .15 .06
- ❑ 632 Reid Nichols .10 .04
- ❑ 633 Dave Geisel .10 .04
- ❑ 634 Ken Griffey .20 .08
- ❑ 635 Bob Lemon MG .40 .16
- ❑ 636 Orlando Sanchez .10 .04
- ❑ 637 Bill Almon .10 .04
- ❑ 638 Danny Ainge .20 .08
- ❑ 639 Willie Stargell .40 .16
- ❑ 640 Bob Sykes .10 .04
- ❑ 641 Ed Lynch .10 .04
- ❑ 642 John Ellis .10 .04
- ❑ 643 Ferguson Jenkins .20 .08
- ❑ 644 Lenn Sakata .10 .04
- ❑ 645 Julio Gonzalez .10 .04
- ❑ 646 Jesse Orosco .10 .04
- ❑ 647 Jerry Dybzinski .10 .04
- ❑ 648 Tommy Davis CO .20 .08
- ❑ 649 Ron Gardenhire RC .50 .20
- ❑ 650 Felipe Alou CO .20 .08
- ❑ 651 Harvey Haddix CO .20 .08
- ❑ 652 Willie Upshaw .50 .20
- ❑ 653 Bill Madlock .20 .08
- ❑ 654A DK Checklist 1-26 .40 .16
  ERR (Unnumbered)
  (With Trammel)
- ❑ 654B DK Checklist 1-26 .20 .08
  COR (Unnumbered)
  (With Trammell)
- ❑ 655 Checklist 27-130 .20 .08
  (Unnumbered)
- ❑ 656 Checklist 131-234 .20 .08
  (Unnumbered)
- ❑ 657 Checklist 235-338 .20 .08
  (Unnumbered)
- ❑ 658 Checklist 339-442 .20 .08
  (Unnumbered)
- ❑ 659 Checklist 443-544 .20 .08
  (Unnumbered)
- ❑ 660 Checklist 545-653 .20 .08
  (Unnumbered)

1983 Donruss

	Nm-Mt	Ex-Mt
COMPLETE SET (660)	60.00	24.00
COMP.FACT.SET (660)	80.00	32.00
COMP.COBB PUZZLE	5.00	2.00

- ❑ 1 Fernando Valenzuela DK .20 .08
- ❑ 2 Rollie Fingers DK .20 .08
- ❑ 3 Reggie Jackson DK .40 .16
- ❑ 4 Jim Palmer DK .20 .08
- ❑ 5 Jack Morris DK .20 .08
- ❑ 6 George Foster DK .20 .08
- ❑ 7 Jim Sundberg DK .20 .08
- ❑ 8 Willie Stargell DK .40 .16
- ❑ 9 Dave Stieb DK .20 .08
- ❑ 10 Joe Niekro DK .10 .04
- ❑ 11 Rickey Henderson DK 1.50 .60
- ❑ 12 Dale Murphy DK .40 .16
- ❑ 13 Toby Harrah DK .20 .08
- ❑ 14 Bill Buckner DK .20 .08
- ❑ 15 Willie Wilson DK .20 .08
- ❑ 16 Steve Carlton DK .40 .16
- ❑ 17 Ron Guidry DK .20 .08
- ❑ 18 Steve Rogers DK .20 .08
- ❑ 19 Kent Hrbek DK .20 .08
- ❑ 20 Keith Hernandez DK .20 .08
- ❑ 21 Floyd Bannister DK .10 .04
- ❑ 22 Johnny Bench DK .75 .30
- ❑ 23 Britt Burns DK .10 .04

❑ 24 Joe Morgan DK .20 .08
❑ 25 Carl Yastrzemski DK .75 .30
❑ 26 Terry Kennedy DK .10 .04
❑ 27 Gary Roenicke .10 .04
❑ 28 Dwight Bernard .10 .04
❑ 29 Pat Underwood .10 .04
❑ 30 Gary Allenson .10 .04
❑ 31 Ron Guidry .20 .08
❑ 32 Burt Hooton .10 .04
❑ 33 Chris Bando .10 .04
❑ 34 Vida Blue .20 .08
❑ 35 Rickey Henderson 1.50 .60
❑ 36 Ray Burris .10 .04
❑ 37 John Butcher .10 .04
❑ 38 Don Aase .10 .04
❑ 39 Jerry Koosman .20 .08
❑ 40 Bruce Sutter .20 .08
❑ 41 Jose Cruz .20 .08
❑ 42 Pete Rose 2.50 1.00
❑ 43 Cesar Cedeno .20 .08
❑ 44 Floyd Chiffer .10 .04
❑ 45 Larry McWilliams .10 .04
❑ 46 Alan Fowlkes .10 .04
❑ 47 Dale Murphy .40 .16
❑ 48 Doug Bird .10 .04
❑ 49 Hubie Brooks .10 .04
❑ 50 Floyd Bannister .10 .04
❑ 51 Jack O'Connor .10 .04
❑ 52 Steve Senteney .10 .04
❑ 53 Gary Gaetti RC 1.00 .40
❑ 54 Damaso Garcia .10 .04
❑ 55 Gene Nelson .10 .04
❑ 56 Mookie Wilson .20 .08
❑ 57 Allen Ripley .10 .04
❑ 58 Bob Horner .20 .08
❑ 59 Tony Pena .10 .04
❑ 60 Gary Lavelle .10 .04
❑ 61 Tim Lollar .10 .04
❑ 62 Frank Pastore .10 .04
❑ 63 Garry Maddox .10 .04
❑ 64 Bob Forsch .10 .04
❑ 65 Harry Spilman .10 .04
❑ 66 Geoff Zahn .10 .04
❑ 67 Salome Barojas .10 .04
❑ 68 David Palmer .10 .04
❑ 69 Charlie Hough .20 .08
❑ 70 Dan Quisenberry .10 .04
❑ 71 Tony Armas .20 .08
❑ 72 Rick Sutcliffe .20 .08
❑ 73 Steve Balboni .10 .04
❑ 74 Jerry Remy .10 .04
❑ 75 Mike Scioscia .20 .08
❑ 76 John Wockenfuss .10 .04
❑ 77 Jim Palmer .20 .08
❑ 78 Rollie Fingers .20 .08
❑ 79 Joe Nolan .10 .04
❑ 80 Pete Vuckovich .10 .04
❑ 81 Rick Leach .10 .04
❑ 82 Rick Miller .10 .04
❑ 83 Graig Nettles .20 .08
❑ 84 Ron Cey .20 .08
❑ 85 Miguel Dilone .10 .04
❑ 86 John Wathan .10 .04
❑ 87 Kelvin Moore .10 .04
❑ 88A Byrn Smith ERR .20 .08
(Sic, Bryn)
❑ 88B Bryn Smith COR .40 .16
❑ 89 Dave Hostetler .10 .04
❑ 90 Rod Carew .40 .16
❑ 91 Lonnie Smith .10 .04
❑ 92 Bob Knepper .10 .04
❑ 93 Marty Bystrom .10 .04
❑ 94 Chris Welsh .10 .04
❑ 95 Jason Thompson .10 .04
❑ 96 Tom O'Malley .10 .04
❑ 97 Phil Niekro .20 .08
❑ 98 Neil Allen .10 .04
❑ 99 Bill Buckner .20 .08
❑ 100 Ed VandeBerg .10 .04
❑ 101 Jim Clancy .10 .04
❑ 102 Robert Castillo .10 .04
❑ 103 Bruce Berenyi .10 .04
❑ 104 Carlton Fisk .40 .16
❑ 105 Mike Flanagan .10 .04
❑ 106 Cecil Cooper .20 .08
❑ 107 Jack Morris .20 .08
❑ 108 Mike Morgan .10 .04
❑ 109 Luis Aponte .10 .04
❑ 110 Pedro Guerrero .20 .08
❑ 111 Len Barker .10 .04
❑ 112 Willie Wilson .20 .08
❑ 113 Dave Beard .10 .04
❑ 114 Mike Gates .10 .04
❑ 115 Reggie Jackson .40 .16
❑ 116 George Wright RC .50 .20
❑ 117 Vance Law .10 .04
❑ 118 Nolan Ryan 4.00 1.60
❑ 119 Mike Krukow .10 .04
❑ 120 Ozzie Smith 1.25 .50
❑ 121 Broderick Perkins .10 .04
❑ 122 Tom Seaver .75 .30
❑ 123 Chris Chambliss .20 .08
❑ 124 Chuck Tanner MG .10 .04
❑ 125 Johnnie LeMaster .10 .04
❑ 126 Mel Hall RC .50 .20
❑ 127 Bruce Bochte .10 .04
❑ 128 Charlie Puleo .10 .04
❑ 129 Luis Leal .10 .04
❑ 130 John Pacella .10 .04
❑ 131 Glenn Gulliver .10 .04
❑ 132 Don Money .10 .04
❑ 133 Dave Rozema .10 .04
❑ 134 Bruce Hurst .10 .04
❑ 135 Rudy May .10 .04
❑ 136 Tom Lasorda MG .40 .16
❑ 137 Dan Spillner UER .10 .04
(Photo actually
Ed Whitson)
❑ 138 Jerry Martin .10 .04
❑ 139 Mike Norris .10 .04
❑ 140 Al Oliver .20 .08
❑ 141 Daryl Sconiers .10 .04
❑ 142 Lamar Johnson .10 .04
❑ 143 Harold Baines .20 .08
❑ 144 Alan Ashby .10 .04
❑ 145 Garry Templeton .20 .08
❑ 146 Al Holland .10 .04
❑ 147 Bo Diaz .10 .04
❑ 148 Dave Concepcion .20 .08
❑ 149 Rick Camp .10 .04
❑ 150 Jim Morrison .10 .04
❑ 151 Randy Martz .10 .04
❑ 152 Keith Hernandez .20 .08
❑ 153 John Lowenstein .10 .04
❑ 154 Mike Caldwell .10 .04
❑ 155 Milt Wilcox .10 .04
❑ 156 Rich Gedman .10 .04
❑ 157 Rich Gossage .20 .08
❑ 158 Jerry Reuss .10 .04
❑ 159 Ron Hassey .10 .04
❑ 160 Larry Gura .10 .04
❑ 161 Dwayne Murphy .10 .04
❑ 162 Woodie Fryman .10 .04
❑ 163 Steve Comer .10 .04
❑ 164 Ken Forsch .10 .04
❑ 165 Dennis Lamp .10 .04
❑ 166 David Green RC .50 .20
❑ 167 Terry Puhl .10 .04
❑ 168 Mike Schmidt 2.00 .80
(Wearing 37
rather than 20)
❑ 169 Eddie Milner .10 .04
❑ 170 John Curtis .10 .04
❑ 171 Don Robinson .10 .04
❑ 172 Rich Gale .10 .04
❑ 173 Steve Bedrosian .10 .04
❑ 174 Willie Hernandez .10 .04
❑ 175 Ron Gardenhire .10 .04
❑ 176 Jim Beattie .10 .04
❑ 177 Tim Laudner .10 .04
❑ 178 Buck Martinez .10 .04
❑ 179 Kent Hrbek .20 .08
❑ 180 Alfredo Griffin .10 .04
❑ 181 Larry Andersen .10 .04
❑ 182 Pete Falcone .10 .04
❑ 183 Jody Davis .10 .04
❑ 184 Glenn Hubbard .10 .04
❑ 185 Dale Berra .10 .04
❑ 186 Greg Minton .10 .04
❑ 187 Gary Lucas .10 .04
❑ 188 Dave Van Gorder .10 .04
❑ 189 Bob Dernier .10 .04
❑ 190 Willie McGee RC 1.50 .60
❑ 191 Dickie Thon .10 .04
❑ 192 Bob Boone .20 .08
❑ 193 Britt Burns .10 .04
❑ 194 Jeff Reardon .20 .08
❑ 195 Jon Matlack .10 .04
❑ 196 Don Slaught RC .50 .20
❑ 197 Fred Stanley .10 .04
❑ 198 Rick Manning .10 .04
❑ 199 Dave Righetti .20 .08
❑ 200 Dave Stapleton .10 .04
❑ 201 Steve Yeager .20 .08
❑ 202 Enos Cabell .10 .04
❑ 203 Sammy Stewart .10 .04
❑ 204 Moose Haas .10 .04
❑ 205 Lenn Sakata .10 .04
❑ 206 Charlie Moore .10 .04
❑ 207 Alan Trammell .20 .08
❑ 208 Jim Rice .20 .08
❑ 209 Roy Smalley .10 .04
❑ 210 Bill Russell .20 .08
❑ 211 Andre Thornton .10 .04
❑ 212 Willie Aikens .10 .04
❑ 213 Dave McKay .10 .04
❑ 214 Tim Blackwell .10 .04
❑ 215 Buddy Bell .20 .08
❑ 216 Doug DeCinces .10 .04
❑ 217 Tom Herr .10 .04
❑ 218 Frank LaCorte .10 .04
❑ 219 Steve Carlton .40 .16
❑ 220 Terry Kennedy .10 .04
❑ 221 Mike Easler .10 .04
❑ 222 Jack Clark .20 .08
❑ 223 Gene Garber .10 .04
❑ 224 Scott Holman .10 .04
❑ 225 Mike Proly .10 .04
❑ 226 Terry Bulling .10 .04
❑ 227 Jerry Garvin .10 .04
❑ 228 Ron Davis .10 .04
❑ 229 Tom Hume .10 .04
❑ 230 Marc Hill .10 .04
❑ 231 Dennis Martinez .20 .08
❑ 232 Jim Gantner .10 .04
❑ 233 Larry Pashnick .10 .04
❑ 234 Dave Collins .10 .04
❑ 235 Tom Burgmeier .10 .04
❑ 236 Ken Landreaux .10 .04
❑ 237 John Denny .10 .04
❑ 238 Hal McRae .20 .08
❑ 239 Matt Keough .10 .04
❑ 240 Doug Flynn .10 .04
❑ 241 Fred Lynn .20 .08
❑ 242 Billy Sample .10 .04
❑ 243 Tom Paciorek .10 .04
❑ 244 Joe Sambito .10 .04
❑ 245 Sid Monge .10 .04
❑ 246 Ken Oberkfell .10 .04
❑ 247 Joe Pittman UER .10 .04
(Photo actually
Juan Eichelberger)
❑ 248 Mario Soto .20 .08
❑ 249 Claudell Washington .10 .04
❑ 250 Rick Rhoden .10 .04
❑ 251 Darrell Evans .20 .08
❑ 252 Steve Henderson .10 .04
❑ 253 Manny Castillo .10 .04
❑ 254 Craig Swan .10 .04
❑ 255 Joey McLaughlin .10 .04
❑ 256 Pete Redfern .10 .04
❑ 257 Ken Singleton .20 .08
❑ 258 Robin Yount 1.25 .50
❑ 259 Elias Sosa .10 .04
❑ 260 Bob Ojeda .10 .04
❑ 261 Bobby Murcer .20 .08
❑ 262 Candy Maldonado RC .50 .20
❑ 263 Rick Waits .10 .04
❑ 264 Greg Pryor .10 .04
❑ 265 Bob Owchinko .10 .04
❑ 266 Chris Speier .10 .04
❑ 267 Bruce Kison .10 .04
❑ 268 Mark Wagner .10 .04
❑ 269 Steve Kemp .10 .04
❑ 270 Phil Garner .20 .08
❑ 271 Gene Richards .10 .04
❑ 272 Renie Martin .10 .04
❑ 273 Dave Roberts .10 .04

❑ 274	Dan Driessen	.10	.04
❑ 275	Rufino Linares	.10	.04
❑ 276	Lee Lacy	.10	.04
❑ 277	Ryne Sandberg RC	10.00	4.00
❑ 278	Darrell Porter	.10	.04
❑ 279	Cal Ripken	6.00	2.40
❑ 280	Jamie Easterly	.10	.04
❑ 281	Bill Fahey	.10	.04
❑ 282	Glenn Hoffman	.10	.04
❑ 283	Willie Randolph	.20	.08
❑ 284	Fernando Valenzuela	.20	.08
❑ 285	Alan Bannister	.10	.04
❑ 286	Paul Splittorff	.10	.04
❑ 287	Joe Rudi	.20	.08
❑ 288	Bill Gullickson	.10	.04
❑ 289	Danny Darwin	.10	.04
❑ 290	Andy Hassler	.10	.04
❑ 291	Ernesto Escarrega	.10	.04
❑ 292	Steve Mura	.10	.04
❑ 293	Tony Scott	.10	.04
❑ 294	Manny Trillo	.10	.04
❑ 295	Greg Harris	.10	.04
❑ 296	Luis DeLeon	.10	.04
❑ 297	Kent Tekulve	.10	.04
❑ 298	Atlee Hammaker	.10	.04
❑ 299	Bruce Benedict	.10	.04
❑ 300	Fergie Jenkins	.20	.08
❑ 301	Dave Kingman	.20	.08
❑ 302	Bill Caudill	.10	.04
❑ 303	John Castino	.10	.04
❑ 304	Ernie Whitt	.10	.04
❑ 305	Randy Johnson	.10	.04
❑ 306	Garth Iorg	.10	.04
❑ 307	Gaylord Perry	.20	.08
❑ 308	Ed Lynch	.10	.04
❑ 309	Keith Moreland	.10	.04
❑ 310	Rafael Ramirez	.10	.04
❑ 311	Bill Madlock	.20	.08
❑ 312	Milt May	.10	.04
❑ 313	John Montefusco	.10	.04
❑ 314	Wayne Krenchicki	.10	.04
❑ 315	George Vukovich	.10	.04
❑ 316	Joaquin Andujar	.20	.08
❑ 317	Craig Reynolds	.10	.04
❑ 318	Rick Burleson	.10	.04
❑ 319	Richard Dotson	.10	.04
❑ 320	Steve Rogers	.20	.08
❑ 321	Dave Schmidt	.10	.04
❑ 322	Bud Black RC	.50	.20
❑ 323	Jeff Burroughs	.10	.04
❑ 324	Von Hayes	.10	.04
❑ 325	Butch Wynegar	.10	.04
❑ 326	Carl Yastrzemski	1.25	.50
❑ 327	Ron Roenicke	.10	.04
❑ 328	Howard Johnson RC	1.00	.40
❑ 329	Rick Dempsey UER (Posing as a left-handed batter)	.10	.04
❑ 330A	Jim Slaton (Bio printed black on white)	.10	.04
❑ 330B	Jim Slaton (Bio printed black on yellow)	.20	.08
❑ 331	Benny Ayala	.10	.04
❑ 332	Ted Simmons	.20	.08
❑ 333	Lou Whitaker	.20	.08
❑ 334	Chuck Rainey	.10	.04
❑ 335	Lou Piniella	.20	.08
❑ 336	Steve Sax	.20	.08
❑ 337	Toby Harrah	.20	.08
❑ 338	George Brett	2.00	.80
❑ 339	Dave Lopes	.20	.08
❑ 340	Gary Carter	.20	.08
❑ 341	John Grubb	.10	.04
❑ 342	Tim Foli	.10	.04
❑ 343	Jim Kaat	.20	.08
❑ 344	Mike LaCoss	.10	.04
❑ 345	Larry Christenson	.10	.04
❑ 346	Juan Bonilla	.10	.04
❑ 347	Omar Moreno	.10	.04
❑ 348	Chili Davis	.20	.08
❑ 349	Tommy Boggs	.10	.04
❑ 350	Rusty Staub	.20	.08
❑ 351	Bump Wills	.10	.04
❑ 352	Rick Sweet	.10	.04
❑ 353	Jim Gott RC	.50	.20
❑ 354	Terry Felton	.10	.04
❑ 355	Jim Kern	.10	.04
❑ 356	Bill Almon UER (Expos/Mets in 1983, not Padres/Mets)	.10	.04
❑ 357	Tippy Martinez	.10	.04
❑ 358	Roy Howell	.10	.04
❑ 359	Dan Petry	.10	.04
❑ 360	Jerry Mumphrey	.10	.04
❑ 361	Mark Clear	.10	.04
❑ 362	Mike Marshall	.10	.04
❑ 363	Lary Sorensen	.10	.04
❑ 364	Amos Otis	.20	.08
❑ 365	Rick Langford	.10	.04
❑ 366	Brad Mills	.10	.04
❑ 367	Brian Downing	.20	.08
❑ 368	Mike Richardt	.10	.04
❑ 369	Aurelio Rodriguez	.10	.04
❑ 370	Dave Smith	.10	.04
❑ 371	Tug McGraw	.20	.08
❑ 372	Doug Bair	.10	.04
❑ 373	Ruppert Jones	.10	.04
❑ 374	Alex Trevino	.10	.04
❑ 375	Ken Dayley	.10	.04
❑ 376	Rod Scurry	.10	.04
❑ 377	Bob Brenly	.10	.04
❑ 378	Scot Thompson	.10	.04
❑ 379	Julio Cruz	.10	.04
❑ 380	John Stearns	.10	.04
❑ 381	Dale Murray	.10	.04
❑ 382	Frank Viola RC	1.50	.60
❑ 383	Al Bumbry	.10	.04
❑ 384	Ben Oglivie	.20	.08
❑ 385	Dave Tobik	.10	.04
❑ 386	Bob Stanley	.10	.04
❑ 387	Andre Robertson	.10	.04
❑ 388	Jorge Orta	.10	.04
❑ 389	Ed Whitson	.10	.04
❑ 390	Don Hood	.10	.04
❑ 391	Tom Underwood	.10	.04
❑ 392	Tim Wallach	.20	.08
❑ 393	Steve Renko	.10	.04
❑ 394	Mickey Rivers	.10	.04
❑ 395	Greg Luzinski	.20	.08
❑ 396	Art Howe	.10	.04
❑ 397	Alan Wiggins	.10	.04
❑ 398	Jim Barr	.10	.04
❑ 399	Ivan DeJesus	.10	.04
❑ 400	Tom Lawless	.10	.04
❑ 401	Bob Walk	.10	.04
❑ 402	Jimmy Smith	.10	.04
❑ 403	Lee Smith	.40	.16
❑ 404	George Hendrick	.20	.08
❑ 405	Eddie Murray	.75	.30
❑ 406	Marshall Edwards	.10	.04
❑ 407	Lance Parrish	.20	.08
❑ 408	Carney Lansford	.20	.08
❑ 409	Dave Winfield	.20	.08
❑ 410	Bob Welch	.20	.08
❑ 411	Larry Milbourne	.10	.04
❑ 412	Dennis Leonard	.10	.04
❑ 413	Dan Meyer	.10	.04
❑ 414	Charlie Lea	.10	.04
❑ 415	Rick Honeycutt	.10	.04
❑ 416	Mike Witt	.10	.04
❑ 417	Steve Trout	.10	.04
❑ 418	Glenn Brummer	.10	.04
❑ 419	Denny Walling	.10	.04
❑ 420	Gary Matthews	.20	.08
❑ 421	Charlie Leibrandt UER (Liebrandt on front of card)	.10	.04
❑ 422	J.Eichelberger UER Photo actually Joe Pittman	.10	.04
❑ 423	Cecilio Guante UER (Listed as Matt on card)	.10	.04
❑ 424	Bill Laskey	.10	.04
❑ 425	Jerry Royster	.10	.04
❑ 426	Dickie Noles	.10	.04
❑ 427	George Foster	.20	.08
❑ 428	Mike Moore RC	.50	.20
❑ 429	Gary Ward	.10	.04
❑ 430	Barry Bonnell	.10	.04
❑ 431	Ron Washington	.10	.04
❑ 432	Rance Mulliniks	.10	.04
❑ 433	Mike Stanton	.10	.04
❑ 434	Jesse Orosco	.10	.04
❑ 435	Larry Bowa	.20	.08
❑ 436	Biff Pocoroba	.10	.04
❑ 437	Johnny Ray	.10	.04
❑ 438	Joe Morgan	.20	.08
❑ 439	Eric Show RC	.50	.20
❑ 440	Larry Biittner	.10	.04
❑ 441	Greg Gross	.10	.04
❑ 442	Gene Tenace	.20	.08
❑ 443	Danny Heep	.10	.04
❑ 444	Bobby Clark	.10	.04
❑ 445	Kevin Hickey	.10	.04
❑ 446	Scott Sanderson	.10	.04
❑ 447	Frank Tanana	.20	.08
❑ 448	Cesar Geronimo	.10	.04
❑ 449	Jimmy Sexton	.10	.04
❑ 450	Mike Hargrove	.10	.04
❑ 451	Doyle Alexander	.10	.04
❑ 452	Dwight Evans	.40	.16
❑ 453	Terry Forster	.20	.08
❑ 454	Tom Brookens	.10	.04
❑ 455	Rich Dauer	.10	.04
❑ 456	Rob Picciolo	.10	.04
❑ 457	Terry Crowley	.10	.04
❑ 458	Ned Yost	.10	.04
❑ 459	Kirk Gibson	.40	.16
❑ 460	Reid Nichols	.10	.04
❑ 461	Oscar Gamble	.10	.04
❑ 462	Dusty Baker	.20	.08
❑ 463	Jack Perconte	.10	.04
❑ 464	Frank White	.20	.08
❑ 465	Mickey Klutts	.10	.04
❑ 466	Warren Cromartie	.10	.04
❑ 467	Larry Parrish	.10	.04
❑ 468	Bobby Grich	.20	.08
❑ 469	Dane Iorg	.10	.04
❑ 470	Joe Niekro	.10	.04
❑ 471	Ed Farmer	.10	.04
❑ 472	Tim Flannery	.10	.04
❑ 473	Dave Parker	.20	.08
❑ 474	Jeff Leonard	.10	.04
❑ 475	Al Hrabosky	.10	.04
❑ 476	Ron Hodges	.10	.04
❑ 477	Leon Durham	.10	.04
❑ 478	Jim Essian	.10	.04
❑ 479	Roy Lee Jackson	.10	.04
❑ 480	Brad Havens	.10	.04
❑ 481	Joe Price	.10	.04
❑ 482	Tony Bernazard	.10	.04
❑ 483	Scott McGregor	.10	.04
❑ 484	Paul Molitor	.40	.16
❑ 485	Mike Ivie	.10	.04
❑ 486	Ken Griffey	.20	.08
❑ 487	Dennis Eckersley	.40	.16
❑ 488	Steve Garvey	.20	.08
❑ 489	Mike Fischlin	.10	.04
❑ 490	U.L. Washington	.10	.04
❑ 491	Steve McCatty	.10	.04
❑ 492	Roy Johnson	.10	.04
❑ 493	Don Baylor	.20	.08
❑ 494	Bobby Johnson	.10	.04
❑ 495	Mike Squires	.10	.04
❑ 496	Bert Roberge	.10	.04
❑ 497	Dick Ruthven	.10	.04
❑ 498	Tito Landrum	.10	.04
❑ 499	Sixto Lezcano	.10	.04
❑ 500	Johnny Bench	.75	.30
❑ 501	Larry Whisenton	.10	.04
❑ 502	Manny Sarmiento	.10	.04
❑ 503	Fred Breining	.10	.04
❑ 504	Bill Campbell	.10	.04
❑ 505	Todd Cruz	.10	.04
❑ 506	Bob Bailor	.10	.04
❑ 507	Dave Stieb	.20	.08
❑ 508	Al Williams	.10	.04
❑ 509	Dan Ford	.10	.04
❑ 510	Gorman Thomas	.20	.08
❑ 511	Chet Lemon	.20	.08
❑ 512	Mike Torrez	.10	.04
❑ 513	Shane Rawley	.10	.04
❑ 514	Mark Belanger	.10	.04
❑ 515	Rodney Craig	.10	.04
❑ 516	Onix Concepcion	.10	.04

❑ 517 Mike Heath .10 .04
❑ 518 Andre Dawson UER .20 .08
(Middle name Fernando,
should be Nolan)
❑ 519 Luis Sanchez .10 .04
❑ 520 Terry Bogener .10 .04
❑ 521 Rudy Law .10 .04
❑ 522 Ray Knight .20 .08
❑ 523 Joe Lefebvre .10 .04
❑ 524 Jim Wohlford .10 .04
❑ 525 Julio Franco RC 5.00 2.00
❑ 526 Ron Oester .10 .04
❑ 527 Rick Mahler .10 .04
❑ 528 Steve Nicosia .10 .04
❑ 529 Junior Kennedy .10 .04
❑ 530A Whitey Herzog MG .20 .08
(Bio printed
black on white)
❑ 530B Whitey Herzog MG .20 .08
(Bio printed
black on yellow)
❑ 531A Don Sutton .20 .08
(Blue border
on photo)
❑ 531B Don Sutton .20 .08
(Green border
on photo)
❑ 532 Mark Brouhard .10 .04
❑ 533A S.Anderson MG .20 .08
(Bio printed
black on white)
❑ 533B S.Anderson MG .20 .08
(Bio printed
black on yellow)
❑ 534 Roger LaFrancois .10 .04
❑ 535 George Frazier .10 .04
❑ 536 Tom Niedenfuer .10 .04
❑ 537 Ed Glynn .10 .04
❑ 538 Lee May .10 .04
❑ 539 Bob Kearney .10 .04
❑ 540 Tim Raines .20 .08
❑ 541 Paul Mirabella .10 .04
❑ 542 Luis Tiant .20 .08
❑ 543 Ron LeFlore .20 .08
❑ 544 Dave LaPoint .10 .04
❑ 545 Randy Moffitt .10 .04
❑ 546 Luis Aguayo .10 .04
❑ 547 Brad Lesley .15 .06
❑ 548 Luis Salazar .10 .04
❑ 549 John Candelaria .10 .04
❑ 550 Dave Bergman .10 .04
❑ 551 Bob Watson .10 .04
❑ 552 Pat Tabler .10 .04
❑ 553 Brent Gaff .10 .04
❑ 554 Al Cowens .10 .04
❑ 555 Tom Brunansky .20 .08
❑ 556 Lloyd Moseby .10 .04
❑ 557A Pascual Perez ERR 2.00 .80
(Twins in glove)
❑ 557B Pascual Perez COR .20 .08
(Braves in glove)
❑ 558 Willie Upshaw .10 .04
❑ 559 Richie Zisk .10 .04
❑ 560 Pat Zachry .10 .04
❑ 561 Jay Johnstone .10 .04
❑ 562 Carlos Diaz RC .15 .06
❑ 563 John Tudor .20 .08
❑ 564 Frank Robinson MG .40 .16
❑ 565 Dave Edwards .10 .04
❑ 566 Paul Householder .10 .04
❑ 567 Ron Reed .10 .04
❑ 568 Mike Ramsey .10 .04
❑ 569 Kiko Garcia .10 .04
❑ 570 Tommy John .20 .08
❑ 571 Tony LaRussa MG .20 .08
❑ 572 Joel Youngblood .10 .04
❑ 573 Wayne Tolleson .10 .04
❑ 574 Keith Creel .10 .04
❑ 575 Billy Martin MG .40 .16
❑ 576 Jerry Dybzinski .10 .04
❑ 577 Rick Cerone .10 .04
❑ 578 Tony Perez .40 .16
❑ 579 Greg Brock .10 .04
❑ 580 Glenn Wilson .50 .20
❑ 581 Tim Stoddard .10 .04
❑ 582 Bob McClure .10 .04
❑ 583 Jim Dwyer .10 .04
❑ 584 Ed Romero .10 .04
❑ 585 Larry Herndon .10 .04
❑ 586 Wade Boggs RC 10.00 4.00
❑ 587 Jay Howell .10 .04
❑ 588 Dave Stewart .20 .08
❑ 589 Bert Blyleven .20 .08
❑ 590 Dick Howser MG .10 .04
❑ 591 Wayne Gross .10 .04
❑ 592 Terry Francona .20 .08
❑ 593 Don Werner .10 .04
❑ 594 Bill Stein .10 .04
❑ 595 Jesse Barfield .20 .08
❑ 596 Bob Molinaro .10 .04
❑ 597 Mike Vail .10 .04
❑ 598 Tony Gwynn RC 15.00 6.00
❑ 599 Gary Rajsich .10 .04
❑ 600 Jerry Ujdur .10 .04
❑ 601 Cliff Johnson .10 .04
❑ 602 Jerry White .10 .04
❑ 603 Bryan Clark .10 .04
❑ 604 Joe Ferguson .10 .04
❑ 605 Guy Sularz .10 .04
❑ 606A Ozzie Virgil .20 .08
(Green border
on photo)
❑ 606B Ozzie Virgil .20 .08
(Orange border
on photo)
❑ 607 Terry Harper .10 .04
❑ 608 Harvey Kuenn MG .10 .04
❑ 609 Jim Sundberg .20 .08
❑ 610 Willie Stargell .40 .16
❑ 611 Reggie Smith .20 .08
❑ 612 Rob Wilfong .10 .04
❑ 613 Joe Niekro .20 .08
Phil Niekro
❑ 614 Lee Elia MG .10 .04
❑ 615 Mickey Hatcher .10 .04
❑ 616 Jerry Hairston .10 .04
❑ 617 John Martin .10 .04
❑ 618 Wally Backman .10 .04
❑ 619 Storm Davis RC .50 .20
❑ 620 Alan Knicely .10 .04
❑ 621 John Stuper .10 .04
❑ 622 Matt Sinatro .10 .04
❑ 623 Geno Petralli .50 .20
❑ 624 Duane Walker .10 .04
❑ 625 Dick Williams MG .10 .04
❑ 626 Pat Corrales MG .10 .04
❑ 627 Vern Ruhle .10 .04
❑ 628 Joe Torre MG .20 .08
❑ 629 Anthony Johnson .10 .04
❑ 630 Steve Howe .10 .04
❑ 631 Gary Woods .10 .04
❑ 632 LaMarr Hoyt .10 .04
❑ 633 Steve Swisher .10 .04
❑ 634 Terry Leach .10 .04
❑ 635 Jeff Newman .10 .04
❑ 636 Brett Butler .20 .08
❑ 637 Gary Gray .10 .04
❑ 638 Lee Mazzilli .20 .08
❑ 639A Ron Jackson ERR 20.00 8.00
(A's in glove)
❑ 639B Ron Jackson COR .10 .04
(Angels in glove,
red border
on photo)
❑ 639C Ron Jackson COR .40 .16
(Angels in glove,
green border
on photo)
❑ 640 Juan Beniquez .10 .04
❑ 641 Dave Rucker .10 .04
❑ 642 Luis Pujols .10 .04
❑ 643 Rick Monday .20 .08
❑ 644 Hosken Powell .10 .04
❑ 645 The Chicken .40 .16
❑ 646 Dave Engle .10 .04
❑ 647 Dick Davis .10 .04
❑ 648 Frank Robinson .40 .16
Vida Blue
Joe Morgan
❑ 649 Al Chambers .10 .04
❑ 650 Jesus Vega .10 .04
❑ 651 Jeff Jones .10 .04
❑ 652 Marvis Foley .10 .04
❑ 653 Ty Cobb Puzzle Card .75 .30
❑ 654A Dick Perez/Diamond .40 .16
King Checklist 1-26
(Unnumbered) ERR
(Word "checklist"
omitted from back)
❑ 654B Dick Perez/Diamond .40 .16
King Checklist 1-26
(Unnumbered) COR
(Word "checklist"
is on back)
❑ 655 Checklist 27-130 .10 .04
(Unnumbered)
❑ 656 Checklist 131-234 .10 .04
(Unnumbered)
❑ 657 Checklist 235-338 .10 .04
(Unnumbered)
❑ 658 Checklist 339-442 .10 .04
(Unnumbered)
❑ 659 Checklist 443-544 .10 .04
(Unnumbered)
❑ 660 Checklist 545-653 .10 .04
(Unnumbered)

1984 Donruss

	Nm-Mt	Ex-Mt
COMPLETE SET (660)	100.00	40.00
COMP.FACT.SET (658)	150.00	60.00
COMP.SNIDER PUZZLE	5.00	2.00

❑ 1 Robin Yount DK COR 2.50 1.00
❑ 1A Robin Yount DK ERR 5.00 2.00
❑ 2 Dave Concepcion DK .75 .30
COR
❑ 2A Dave Concepcion DK .75 .30
ERR (Perez Steel)
❑ 3 Dwayne Murphy DK .25 .10
COR
❑ 3A Dwayne Murphy DK .25 .10
ERR (Perez Steel)
❑ 4 John Castino DK COR .25 .10
❑ 4A John Castino DK ERR .25 .10
(Perez Steel)
❑ 5 Leon Durham DK COR .75 .30
❑ 5A Leon Durham DK ERR .25 .10
(Perez Steel)
❑ 6 Rusty Staub DK COR .75 .30
❑ 6A Rusty Staub DK ERR .75 .30
(Perez Steel)
❑ 7 Jack Clark DK COR .75 .30
❑ 7A Jack Clark DK ERR .75 .30
(Perez Steel)
❑ 8 Dave Dravecky DK .25 .10
COR
❑ 8A Dave Dravecky DK .25 .10
ERR (Perez Steel)
❑ 9 Al Oliver DK COR .75 .30
❑ 9A Al Oliver DK ERR .75 .30
(Perez Steel)
❑ 10 Dave Righetti DK .75 .30
COR
❑ 10A Dave Righetti DK .75 .30
ERR (Perez Steel)
❑ 11 Hal McRae DK COR .75 .30
❑ 11A Hal McRae DK ERR .75 .30
(Perez Steel)
❑ 12 Ray Knight DK COR .75 .30

❑ 12A Ray Knight DK ERR (Perez Steel) .75 .30
❑ 13 Bruce Sutter DK COR .75 .30
❑ 13A Bruce Sutter DK ERR (Perez Steel) .75 .30
❑ 14 Bob Horner DK COR .75 .30
❑ 14A Bob Horner DK ERR (Perez Steel) .75 .30
❑ 15 Lance Parrish DK COR .75 .30
❑ 15A Lance Parrish DK ERR (Perez Steel) .75 .30
❑ 16 Matt Young DK COR .75 .30
❑ 16A Matt Young DK ERR (Perez Steel) .75 .30
❑ 17 Fred Lynn DK COR .75 .30
❑ 17A Fred Lynn DK ERR (Perez Steel) (A's logo on back) .75 .30
❑ 18 Ron Kittle DK COR .25 .10
❑ 18A Ron Kittle DK ERR (Perez Steel) .25 .10
❑ 19 Jim Clancy DK COR .25 .10
❑ 19A Jim Clancy DK ERR (Perez Steel) .25 .10
❑ 20 Bill Madlock DK COR .75 .30
❑ 20A Bill Madlock DK ERR (Perez Steel) .75 .30
❑ 21 Larry Parrish DK COR .25 .10
❑ 21A Larry Parrish DK ERR (Perez Steel) .25 .10
❑ 22 Eddie Murray DK COR 3.00 1.20
❑ 22A Eddie Murray DK ERR 3.00 1.20
❑ 23 Mike Schmidt DK COR 5.00 2.00
❑ 23A M.Schmidt DK ERR 5.00 2.00
❑ 24 Pedro Guerrero DK COR .75 .30
❑ 24A Pedro Guerrero DK ERR (Perez Steel) .75 .30
❑ 25 Andre Thornton DK COR .25 .10
❑ 25A Andre Thornton DK ERR (Perez Steel) .25 .10
❑ 26 Wade Boggs DK COR 3.00 1.20
❑ 26A Wade Boggs DK ERR 3.00 1.20
❑ 27 Joel Skinner RR RC .25 .10
❑ 28 Tommy Dunbar RR RC .25 .10
❑ 29A M.Stenhouse RC RR ERR (No number on back) .25 .10
❑ 29B Mike Stenhouse RR (COR Numbered on back) 3.00 1.20
❑ 30A R.Darling RC RR ERR (No number on back) 2.00 .80
❑ 30B Ron Darling RR COR (Numbered on back) 3.00 1.20
❑ 31 Dion James RR RC .25 .10
❑ 32 Tony Fernandez RR RC 2.00 .80
❑ 33 Angel Salazar RR RC .25 .10
❑ 34 K. McReynolds RR RC 2.00 .80
❑ 35 Dick Schofield RR RC 1.00 .40
❑ 36 Brad Komminsk RR RC .25 .10
❑ 37 Tim Teufel RR RC 1.00 .40
❑ 38 Doug Frobel RR RC .25 .10
❑ 39 Greg Gagne RR RC 1.00 .40
❑ 40 Mike Fuentes RR RC .25 .10
❑ 41 Joe Carter RR RC 8.00 3.20
❑ 42 Mike Brown RC RR (Angels OF) .25 .10
❑ 43 Mike Jeffcoat RR RC .25 .10
❑ 44 Sid Fernandez RR RC 2.00 .80
❑ 45 Brian Dayett RR RC .25 .10
❑ 46 Chris Smith RR RC .25 .10
❑ 47 Eddie Murray 3.00 1.20
❑ 48 Robin Yount 5.00 2.00
❑ 49 Lance Parrish 1.50 .60
❑ 50 Jim Rice .75 .30
❑ 51 Dave Winfield .75 .30
❑ 52 Fernando Valenzuela .75 .30
❑ 53 George Brett 8.00 3.20
❑ 54 Rickey Henderson 5.00 2.00
❑ 55 Gary Carter .75 .30
❑ 56 Buddy Bell .75 .30
❑ 57 Reggie Jackson 1.50 .60
❑ 58 Harold Baines .75 .30
❑ 59 Ozzie Smith 5.00 2.00
❑ 60 Nolan Ryan UER (Text on back refers to 1972 as the year he struck out 383; the year was 1973) 15.00 6.00
❑ 61 Pete Rose 10.00 4.00
❑ 62 Ron Oester .25 .10
❑ 63 Steve Garvey .75 .30
❑ 64 Jason Thompson .25 .10
❑ 65 Jack Clark .75 .30
❑ 66 Dale Murphy 1.50 .60
❑ 67 Leon Durham .25 .10
❑ 68 Darryl Strawberry RC 8.00 3.20
❑ 69 Richie Zisk .25 .10
❑ 70 Kent Hrbek .75 .30
❑ 71 Dave Stieb .75 .30
❑ 72 Ken Schrom .25 .10
❑ 73 George Bell .75 .30
❑ 74 John Moses .25 .10
❑ 75 Ed Lynch .25 .10
❑ 76 Chuck Rainey .25 .10
❑ 77 Biff Pocoroba .25 .10
❑ 78 Cecilio Guante .25 .10
❑ 79 Jim Barr .25 .10
❑ 80 Kurt Bevacqua .25 .10
❑ 81 Tom Foley .25 .10
❑ 82 Joe Lefebvre .25 .10
❑ 83 Andy Van Slyke RC 4.00 1.60
❑ 84 Bob Lillis MG .25 .10
❑ 85 Ricky Adams .25 .10
❑ 86 Jerry Hairston .25 .10
❑ 87 Bob James .25 .10
❑ 88 Joe Altobelli MG .25 .10
❑ 89 Ed Romero .25 .10
❑ 90 John Grubb .25 .10
❑ 91 John Henry Johnson .25 .10
❑ 92 Juan Espino .25 .10
❑ 93 Candy Maldonado .25 .10
❑ 94 Andre Thornton .25 .10
❑ 95 Onix Concepcion .25 .10
❑ 96 Donnie Hill UER (Listed as P, should be 2B) .25 .10
❑ 97 Andre Dawson UER (Wrong middle name, should be Nolan) .75 .30
❑ 98 Frank Tanana .75 .30
❑ 99 Curtis Wilkerson .25 .10
❑ 100 Larry Gura .25 .10
❑ 101 Dwayne Murphy .25 .10
❑ 102 Tom Brennan .25 .10
❑ 103 Dave Righetti .75 .30
❑ 104 Steve Sax .25 .10
❑ 105 Dan Petry .75 .30
❑ 106 Cal Ripken 20.00 8.00
❑ 107 Paul Molitor UER ('83 stats should say .270 BA, 608 AB, and 164 hits) 1.50 .60
❑ 108 Fred Lynn .75 .30
❑ 109 Neil Allen .25 .10
❑ 110 Joe Niekro .25 .10
❑ 111 Steve Carlton 1.50 .60
❑ 112 Terry Kennedy .25 .10
❑ 113 Bill Madlock .75 .30
❑ 114 Chili Davis .75 .30
❑ 115 Jim Gantner .25 .10
❑ 116 Tom Seaver 3.00 1.20
❑ 117 Bill Buckner .75 .30
❑ 118 Bill Caudill .25 .10
❑ 119 Jim Clancy .25 .10
❑ 120 John Castino .25 .10
❑ 121 Dave Concepcion .75 .30
❑ 122 Greg Luzinski .75 .30
❑ 123 Mike Boddicker .25 .10
❑ 124 Pete Ladd .25 .10
❑ 125 Juan Berenguer .25 .10
❑ 126 John Montefusco .25 .10
❑ 127 Ed Jurak .25 .10
❑ 128 Tom Niedenfuer .25 .10
❑ 129 Bert Blyleven .75 .30
❑ 130 Bud Black .25 .10
❑ 131 Gorman Heimueller .25 .10
❑ 132 Dan Schatzeder .25 .10
❑ 133 Ron Jackson .25 .10
❑ 134 Tom Henke RC 2.00 .80
❑ 135 Kevin Hickey .25 .10
❑ 136 Mike Scott .75 .30
❑ 137 Bo Diaz .25 .10
❑ 138 Glenn Brummer .25 .10
❑ 139 Sid Monge .25 .10
❑ 140 Rich Gale .25 .10
❑ 141 Brett Butler .75 .30
❑ 142 Brian Harper RC 1.00 .40
❑ 143 John Rabb .25 .10
❑ 144 Gary Woods .25 .10
❑ 145 Pat Putnam .25 .10
❑ 146 Jim Acker .25 .10
❑ 147 Mickey Hatcher .25 .10
❑ 148 Todd Cruz .25 .10
❑ 149 Tom Tellmann .25 .10
❑ 150 John Wockenfuss .25 .10
❑ 151 Wade Boggs UER (1983 runs 10; should be 100) 8.00 3.20
❑ 152 Don Baylor .75 .30
❑ 153 Bob Welch .75 .30
❑ 154 Alan Bannister .25 .10
❑ 155 Willie Aikens .25 .10
❑ 156 Jeff Burroughs .25 .10
❑ 157 Bryan Little .25 .10
❑ 158 Bob Boone .75 .30
❑ 159 Dave Hostetler .25 .10
❑ 160 Jerry Dybzinski .25 .10
❑ 161 Mike Madden .25 .10
❑ 162 Luis DeLeon .25 .10
❑ 163 Willie Hernandez .25 .10
❑ 164 Frank Pastore .25 .10
❑ 165 Rick Camp .25 .10
❑ 166 Lee Mazzilli .75 .30
❑ 167 Scot Thompson .25 .10
❑ 168 Bob Forsch .25 .10
❑ 169 Mike Flanagan .25 .10
❑ 170 Rick Manning .25 .10
❑ 171 Chet Lemon .75 .30
❑ 172 Jerry Remy .25 .10
❑ 173 Ron Guidry .75 .30
❑ 174 Pedro Guerrero .75 .30
❑ 175 Willie Wilson .75 .30
❑ 176 Carney Lansford .75 .30
❑ 177 Al Oliver .75 .30
❑ 178 Jim Sundberg .75 .30
❑ 179 Bobby Grich .75 .30
❑ 180 Rich Dotson .25 .10
❑ 181 Joaquin Andujar .75 .30
❑ 182 Jose Cruz .75 .30
❑ 183 Mike Schmidt 8.00 3.20
❑ 184 Gary Redus RC 1.00 .40
❑ 185 Garry Templeton .75 .30
❑ 186 Tony Pena .25 .10
❑ 187 Greg Minton .25 .10
❑ 188 Phil Niekro .75 .30
❑ 189 Ferguson Jenkins .75 .30
❑ 190 Mookie Wilson .75 .30
❑ 191 Jim Beattie .25 .10
❑ 192 Gary Ward .25 .10
❑ 193 Jesse Barfield .75 .30
❑ 194 Pete Filson .25 .10
❑ 195 Roy Lee Jackson .25 .10
❑ 196 Rick Sweet .25 .10
❑ 197 Jesse Orosco .25 .10
❑ 198 Steve Lake .25 .10
❑ 199 Ken Dayley .25 .10
❑ 200 Manny Sarmiento .25 .10
❑ 201 Mark Davis .25 .10
❑ 202 Tim Flannery .25 .10
❑ 203 Bill Scherrer .25 .10
❑ 204 Al Holland .25 .10
❑ 205 Dave Von Ohlen .25 .10
❑ 206 Mike LaCoss .25 .10
❑ 207 Juan Beniquez .25 .10
❑ 208 Juan Agosto .25 .10
❑ 209 Bobby Ramos .25 .10
❑ 210 Al Bumbry .25 .10
❑ 211 Mark Brouhard .25 .10
❑ 212 Howard Bailey .25 .10
❑ 213 Bruce Hurst .25 .10
❑ 214 Bob Shirley .25 .10
❑ 215 Pat Zachry .25 .10
❑ 216 Julio Franco 3.00 1.20
❑ 217 Mike Armstrong .25 .10
❑ 218 Dave Beard .25 .10
❑ 219 Steve Rogers .75 .30
❑ 220 John Butcher .25 .10

- ❑ 221 Mike Smithson .25 .10
- ❑ 222 Frank White .75 .30
- ❑ 223 Mike Heath .25 .10
- ❑ 224 Chris Bando .25 .10
- ❑ 225 Roy Smalley .25 .10
- ❑ 226 Dusty Baker .75 .30
- ❑ 227 Lou Whitaker .75 .30
- ❑ 228 John Lowenstein .25 .10
- ❑ 229 Ben Oglivie .75 .30
- ❑ 230 Doug DeCinces .25 .10
- ❑ 231 Lonnie Smith .25 .10
- ❑ 232 Ray Knight .75 .30
- ❑ 233 Gary Matthews .75 .30
- ❑ 234 Juan Bonilla .25 .10
- ❑ 235 Rod Scurry .25 .10
- ❑ 236 Atlee Hammaker .25 .10
- ❑ 237 Mike Caldwell .25 .10
- ❑ 238 Keith Hernandez .75 .30
- ❑ 239 Larry Bowa .75 .30
- ❑ 240 Tony Bernazard .25 .10
- ❑ 241 Damaso Garcia .25 .10
- ❑ 242 Tom Brunansky .25 .10
- ❑ 243 Dan Driessen .25 .10
- ❑ 244 Ron Kittle .25 .10
- ❑ 245 Tim Stoddard .25 .10
- ❑ 246 Bob L. Gibson RC .25 .10
  (Brewers Pitcher)
- ❑ 247 Marty Castillo .25 .10
- ❑ 248 D.Mattingly RC UER 40.00 16.00
  traiing on back
- ❑ 249 Jeff Newman .25 .10
- ❑ 250 Alejandro Pena RC 2.00 .80
- ❑ 251 Toby Harrah .75 .30
- ❑ 252 Cesar Geronimo .25 .10
- ❑ 253 Tom Underwood .25 .10
- ❑ 254 Doug Flynn .25 .10
- ❑ 255 Andy Hassler .25 .10
- ❑ 256 Odell Jones .25 .10
- ❑ 257 Rudy Law .25 .10
- ❑ 258 Harry Spilman .25 .10
- ❑ 259 Marty Bystrom .25 .10
- ❑ 260 Dave Rucker .25 .10
- ❑ 261 Ruppert Jones .25 .10
- ❑ 262 Jeff R. Jones .25 .10
  (Reds OF)
- ❑ 263 Gerald Perry 1.00 .40
- ❑ 264 Gene Tenace .75 .30
- ❑ 265 Brad Wellman .25 .10
- ❑ 266 Dickie Noles .25 .10
- ❑ 267 Jamie Allen .25 .10
- ❑ 268 Jim Gott .25 .10
- ❑ 269 Ron Davis .25 .10
- ❑ 270 Benny Ayala .25 .10
- ❑ 271 Ned Yost .25 .10
- ❑ 272 Dave Rozema .25 .10
- ❑ 273 Dave Stapleton .25 .10
- ❑ 274 Lou Piniella .75 .30
- ❑ 275 Jose Morales .25 .10
- ❑ 276 Broderick Perkins .25 .10
- ❑ 277 Butch Davis RC .25 .10
- ❑ 278 Tony Phillips RC 2.00 .80
- ❑ 279 Jeff Reardon .75 .30
- ❑ 280 Ken Forsch .25 .10
- ❑ 281 Pete O'Brien RC 1.00 .40
- ❑ 282 Tom Paciorek .25 .10
- ❑ 283 Frank LaCorte .25 .10
- ❑ 284 Tim Lollar .25 .10
- ❑ 285 Greg Gross .25 .10
- ❑ 286 Alex Trevino .25 .10
- ❑ 287 Gene Garber .25 .10
- ❑ 288 Dave Parker .75 .30
- ❑ 289 Lee Smith .75 .30
- ❑ 290 Dave LaPoint .25 .10
- ❑ 291 John Shelby .25 .10
- ❑ 292 Charlie Moore .25 .10
- ❑ 293 Alan Trammell .75 .30
- ❑ 294 Tony Armas .75 .30
- ❑ 295 Shane Rawley .25 .10
- ❑ 296 Greg Brock .25 .10
- ❑ 297 Hal McRae .75 .30
- ❑ 298 Mike Davis .25 .10
- ❑ 299 Tim Raines .75 .30
- ❑ 300 Bucky Dent .75 .30
- ❑ 301 Tommy John .75 .30
- ❑ 302 Carlton Fisk 1.50 .60
- ❑ 303 Darrell Porter .25 .10
- ❑ 304 Dickie Thon .25 .10
- ❑ 305 Garry Maddox .25 .10
- ❑ 306 Cesar Cedeno .75 .30
- ❑ 307 Gary Lucas .25 .10
- ❑ 308 Johnny Ray .25 .10
- ❑ 309 Andy McGaffigan .25 .10
- ❑ 310 Claudell Washington .25 .10
- ❑ 311 Ryne Sandberg 12.00 4.80
- ❑ 312 George Foster .75 .30
- ❑ 313 Spike Owen RC 1.00 .40
- ❑ 314 Gary Gaetti 1.50 .60
- ❑ 315 Willie Upshaw .25 .10
- ❑ 316 Al Williams .25 .10
- ❑ 317 Jorge Orta .25 .10
- ❑ 318 Orlando Mercado .25 .10
- ❑ 319 Junior Ortiz .25 .10
- ❑ 320 Mike Proly .25 .10
- ❑ 321 Randy Johnson UER .25 .10
  ('72-'82 stats are from Twins' Randy Johnson, '83 stats are from Braves' Randy Johnson)
- ❑ 322 Jim Morrison .25 .10
- ❑ 323 Max Venable .25 .10
- ❑ 324 Tony Gwynn 12.00 4.80
- ❑ 325 Duane Walker .25 .10
- ❑ 326 Ozzie Virgil .25 .10
- ❑ 327 Jeff Lahti .25 .10
- ❑ 328 Bill Dawley .25 .10
- ❑ 329 Rob Wilfong .25 .10
- ❑ 330 Marc Hill .25 .10
- ❑ 331 Ray Burris .25 .10
- ❑ 332 Allan Ramirez .25 .10
- ❑ 333 Chuck Porter .25 .10
- ❑ 334 Wayne Krenchicki .25 .10
- ❑ 335 Gary Allenson .25 .10
- ❑ 336 Bobby Meacham .25 .10
- ❑ 337 Joe Beckwith .25 .10
- ❑ 338 Rick Sutcliffe .75 .30
- ❑ 339 Mark Huismann .25 .10
- ❑ 340 Tim Conroy .25 .10
- ❑ 341 Scott Sanderson .25 .10
- ❑ 342 Larry Biittner .25 .10
- ❑ 343 Dave Stewart .75 .30
- ❑ 344 Darryl Motley .25 .10
- ❑ 345 Chris Codiroli .25 .10
- ❑ 346 Rich Behenna .25 .10
- ❑ 347 Andre Robertson .25 .10
- ❑ 348 Mike Marshall .25 .10
- ❑ 349 Larry Herndon .75 .30
- ❑ 350 Rich Dauer .25 .10
- ❑ 351 Cecil Cooper .75 .30
- ❑ 352 Rod Carew 1.50 .60
- ❑ 353 Willie McGee .75 .30
- ❑ 354 Phil Garner .75 .30
- ❑ 355 Joe Morgan .75 .30
- ❑ 356 Luis Salazar .25 .10
- ❑ 357 John Candelaria .25 .10
- ❑ 358 Bill Laskey .25 .10
- ❑ 359 Bob McClure .25 .10
- ❑ 360 Dave Kingman .75 .30
- ❑ 361 Ron Cey .75 .30
- ❑ 362 Matt Young RC 1.00 .40
- ❑ 363 Lloyd Moseby .25 .10
- ❑ 364 Frank Viola 1.50 .60
- ❑ 365 Eddie Milner .25 .10
- ❑ 366 Floyd Bannister .25 .10
- ❑ 367 Dan Ford .25 .10
- ❑ 368 Moose Haas .25 .10
- ❑ 369 Doug Bair .25 .10
- ❑ 370 Ray Fontenot .25 .10
- ❑ 371 Luis Aponte .25 .10
- ❑ 372 Jack Fimple .25 .10
- ❑ 373 Neal Heaton .25 .10
- ❑ 374 Greg Pryor .25 .10
- ❑ 375 Wayne Gross .25 .10
- ❑ 376 Charlie Lea .25 .10
- ❑ 377 Steve Lubratich .25 .10
- ❑ 378 Jon Matlack .25 .10
- ❑ 379 Julio Cruz .25 .10
- ❑ 380 John Mizerock .25 .10
- ❑ 381 Kevin Gross RC 1.00 .40
- ❑ 382 Mike Ramsey .25 .10
- ❑ 383 Doug Gwosdz .25 .10
- ❑ 384 Kelly Paris .25 .10
- ❑ 385 Pete Falcone .25 .10
- ❑ 386 Milt May .25 .10
- ❑ 387 Fred Breining .25 .10
- ❑ 388 Craig Lefferts RC .25 .10
- ❑ 389 Steve Henderson .25 .10
- ❑ 390 Randy Moffitt .25 .10
- ❑ 391 Ron Washington .25 .10
- ❑ 392 Gary Roenicke .25 .10
- ❑ 393 Tom Candiotti RC 2.00 .80
- ❑ 394 Larry Pashnick .25 .10
- ❑ 395 Dwight Evans 1.50 .60
- ❑ 396 Rich Gossage .75 .30
- ❑ 397 Derrel Thomas .25 .10
- ❑ 398 Juan Eichelberger .25 .10
- ❑ 399 Leon Roberts .25 .10
- ❑ 400 Dave Lopes .75 .30
- ❑ 401 Bill Gullickson .25 .10
- ❑ 402 Geoff Zahn .25 .10
- ❑ 403 Billy Sample .25 .10
- ❑ 404 Mike Squires .25 .10
- ❑ 405 Craig Reynolds .25 .10
- ❑ 406 Eric Show .25 .10
- ❑ 407 John Denny .25 .10
- ❑ 408 Dann Bilardello .25 .10
- ❑ 409 Bruce Benedict .25 .10
- ❑ 410 Kent Tekulve .25 .10
- ❑ 411 Mel Hall .75 .30
- ❑ 412 John Stuper .25 .10
- ❑ 413 Rick Dempsey .25 .10
- ❑ 414 Don Sutton .75 .30
- ❑ 415 Jack Morris .75 .30
- ❑ 416 John Tudor .75 .30
- ❑ 417 Willie Randolph .75 .30
- ❑ 418 Jerry Reuss .25 .10
- ❑ 419 Don Slaught .75 .30
- ❑ 420 Steve McCatty .25 .10
- ❑ 421 Tim Wallach .25 .10
- ❑ 422 Larry Parrish .25 .10
- ❑ 423 Brian Downing .75 .30
- ❑ 424 Britt Burns .25 .10
- ❑ 425 David Green .25 .10
- ❑ 426 Jerry Mumphrey .25 .10
- ❑ 427 Ivan DeJesus .25 .10
- ❑ 428 Mario Soto .75 .30
- ❑ 429 Gene Richards .25 .10
- ❑ 430 Dale Berra .25 .10
- ❑ 431 Darrell Evans .75 .30
- ❑ 432 Glenn Hubbard .25 .10
- ❑ 433 Jody Davis .25 .10
- ❑ 434 Danny Heep .25 .10
- ❑ 435 Ed Nunez RC .25 .10
- ❑ 436 Bobby Castillo .25 .10
- ❑ 437 Ernie Whitt .25 .10
- ❑ 438 Scott Ullger .25 .10
- ❑ 439 Doyle Alexander .25 .10
- ❑ 440 Domingo Ramos .25 .10
- ❑ 441 Craig Swan .25 .10
- ❑ 442 Warren Brusstar .25 .10
- ❑ 443 Len Barker .25 .10
- ❑ 444 Mike Easler .25 .10
- ❑ 445 Renie Martin .25 .10
- ❑ 446 D.Rasmussen RC 1.00 .40
- ❑ 447 Ted Power .25 .10
- ❑ 448 Charles Hudson .25 .10
- ❑ 449 Danny Cox RC .25 .10
- ❑ 450 Kevin Bass .25 .10
- ❑ 451 Daryl Sconiers .25 .10
- ❑ 452 Scott Fletcher .25 .10
- ❑ 453 Bryn Smith .25 .10
- ❑ 454 Jim Dwyer .25 .10
- ❑ 455 Rob Picciolo .25 .10
- ❑ 456 Enos Cabell .25 .10
- ❑ 457 Dennis Boyd .75 .30
- ❑ 458 Butch Wynegar .25 .10
- ❑ 459 Burt Hooton .25 .10
- ❑ 460 Ron Hassey .25 .10
- ❑ 461 Danny Jackson RC 1.00 .40
- ❑ 462 Bob Kearney .25 .10
- ❑ 463 Terry Francona .75 .30
- ❑ 464 Wayne Tolleson .25 .10
- ❑ 465 Mickey Rivers .25 .10
- ❑ 466 John Wathan .25 .10
- ❑ 467 Bill Almon .25 .10
- ❑ 468 George Vukovich .25 .10
- ❑ 469 Steve Kemp .25 .10
- ❑ 470 Ken Landreaux .25 .10
- ❑ 471 Milt Wilcox .25 .10

❑ 472 Tippy Martinez .25 .10
❑ 473 Ted Simmons .75 .30
❑ 474 Tim Foli .25 .10
❑ 475 George Hendrick .75 .30
❑ 476 Terry Puhl .25 .10
❑ 477 Von Hayes .25 .10
❑ 478 Bobby Brown .25 .10
❑ 479 Lee Lacy .25 .10
❑ 480 Joel Youngblood .25 .10
❑ 481 Jim Slaton .25 .10
❑ 482 Mike Fitzgerald .25 .10
❑ 483 Keith Moreland .25 .10
❑ 484 Ron Roenicke .25 .10
❑ 485 Luis Leal .25 .10
❑ 486 Bryan Oelkers .25 .10
❑ 487 Bruce Berenyi .25 .10
❑ 488 LaMarr Hoyt .25 .10
❑ 489 Joe Nolan .25 .10
❑ 490 Marshall Edwards .25 .10
❑ 491 Mike Laga .75 .30
❑ 492 Rick Cerone .25 .10
❑ 493 Rick Miller UER .25 .10
(Listed as Mike on card front)
❑ 494 Rick Honeycutt .25 .10
❑ 495 Mike Hargrove .25 .10
❑ 496 Joe Simpson .25 .10
❑ 497 Keith Atherton .25 .10
❑ 498 Chris Welsh .25 .10
❑ 499 Bruce Kison .25 .10
❑ 500 Bobby Johnson .25 .10
❑ 501 Jerry Koosman .75 .30
❑ 502 Frank DiPino .25 .10
❑ 503 Tony Perez 1.50 .60
❑ 504 Ken Oberkfell .25 .10
❑ 505 Mark Thurmond .25 .10
❑ 506 Joe Price .25 .10
❑ 507 Pascual Perez .25 .10
❑ 508 Marvell Wynne 1.00 .40
❑ 509 Mike Krukow .25 .10
❑ 510 Dick Ruthven .25 .10
❑ 511 Al Cowens .25 .10
❑ 512 Cliff Johnson .25 .10
❑ 513 Randy Bush .25 .10
❑ 514 Sammy Stewart .25 .10
❑ 515 Bill Schroeder .25 .10
❑ 516 Aurelio Lopez .75 .30
❑ 517 Mike C. Brown .25 .10
❑ 518 Graig Nettles .75 .30
❑ 519 Dave Sax .25 .10
❑ 520 Jerry Willard .25 .10
❑ 521 Paul Splittorff .25 .10
❑ 522 Tom Burgmeier .25 .10
❑ 523 Chris Speier .25 .10
❑ 524 Bobby Clark .25 .10
❑ 525 George Wright .25 .10
❑ 526 Dennis Lamp .25 .10
❑ 527 Tony Scott .25 .10
❑ 528 Ed Whitson .25 .10
❑ 529 Ron Reed .25 .10
❑ 530 Charlie Puleo .25 .10
❑ 531 Jerry Royster .25 .10
❑ 532 Don Robinson .25 .10
❑ 533 Steve Trout .25 .10
❑ 534 Bruce Sutter .75 .30
❑ 535 Bob Horner .75 .30
❑ 536 Pat Tabler .25 .10
❑ 537 Chris Chambliss .75 .30
❑ 538 Bob Ojeda .25 .10
❑ 539 Alan Ashby .25 .10
❑ 540 Jay Johnstone .25 .10
❑ 541 Bob Dernier .25 .10
❑ 542 Brook Jacoby 1.00 .40
❑ 543 U.L. Washington .25 .10
❑ 544 Danny Darwin .25 .10
❑ 545 Kiko Garcia .25 .10
❑ 546 Vance Law UER .25 .10
(Listed as P on card front)
❑ 547 Tug McGraw .75 .30
❑ 548 Dave Smith .25 .10
❑ 549 Len Matuszek .25 .10
❑ 550 Tom Hume .25 .10
❑ 551 Dave Dravecky .25 .10
❑ 552 Rick Rhoden .25 .10
❑ 553 Duane Kuiper .25 .10
❑ 554 Rusty Staub .75 .30
❑ 555 Bill Campbell .25 .10
❑ 556 Mike Torrez .25 .10
❑ 557 Dave Henderson .75 .30
❑ 558 Len Whitehouse .25 .10
❑ 559 Barry Bonnell .25 .10
❑ 560 Rick Lysander .25 .10
❑ 561 Garth Iorg .25 .10
❑ 562 Bryan Clark .25 .10
❑ 563 Brian Giles .25 .10
❑ 564 Vern Ruhle .25 .10
❑ 565 Steve Bedrosian .25 .10
❑ 566 Larry McWilliams .25 .10
❑ 567 Jeff Leonard UER .25 .10
(Listed as P on card front)
❑ 568 Alan Wiggins .25 .10
❑ 569 Jeff Russell RC 1.00 .40
❑ 570 Salome Barojas .25 .10
❑ 571 Dane Iorg .25 .10
❑ 572 Bob Knepper .25 .10
❑ 573 Gary Lavelle .25 .10
❑ 574 Gorman Thomas .75 .30
❑ 575 Manny Trillo .25 .10
❑ 576 Jim Palmer .75 .30
❑ 577 Dale Murray .25 .10
❑ 578 Tom Brookens .75 .30
❑ 579 Rich Gedman .25 .10
❑ 580 Bill Doran RC 1.00 .40
❑ 581 Steve Yeager .75 .30
❑ 582 Dan Spillner .25 .10
❑ 583 Dan Quisenberry .25 .10
❑ 584 Rance Mulliniks .25 .10
❑ 585 Storm Davis .25 .10
❑ 586 Dave Schmidt .25 .10
❑ 587 Bill Russell .75 .30
❑ 588 Pat Sheridan .25 .10
❑ 589 Rafael Ramirez .25 .10
UER (A's on front)
❑ 590 Bud Anderson .25 .10
❑ 591 George Frazier .25 .10
❑ 592 Lee Tunnell .25 .10
❑ 593 Kirk Gibson 3.00 1.20
❑ 594 Scott McGregor .25 .10
❑ 595 Bob Bailor .25 .10
❑ 596 Tom Herr .25 .10
❑ 597 Luis Sanchez .25 .10
❑ 598 Dave Engle .25 .10
❑ 599 Craig McMurtry .25 .10
❑ 600 Carlos Diaz .25 .10
❑ 601 Tom O'Malley .25 .10
❑ 602 Nick Esasky .25 .10
❑ 603 Ron Hodges .25 .10
❑ 604 Ed VandeBerg .25 .10
❑ 605 Alfredo Griffin .25 .10
❑ 606 Glenn Hoffman .25 .10
❑ 607 Hubie Brooks .25 .10
❑ 608 Richard Barnes UER .25 .10
(Photo actually Neal Heaton)
❑ 609 Greg Walker 1.00 .40
❑ 610 Ken Singleton .75 .30
❑ 611 Mark Clear .25 .10
❑ 612 Buck Martinez .25 .10
❑ 613 Ken Griffey .75 .30
❑ 614 Reid Nichols .25 .10
❑ 615 Doug Sisk .25 .10
❑ 616 Bob Brenly .25 .10
❑ 617 Joey McLaughlin .25 .10
❑ 618 Glenn Wilson .75 .30
❑ 619 Bob Stoddard .25 .10
❑ 620 Lenn Sakata UER .25 .10
(Listed as Len on card front)
❑ 621 Mike Young RC .25 .10
❑ 622 John Stefero .25 .10
❑ 623 Carmelo Martinez .25 .10
❑ 624 Dave Bergman .25 .10
❑ 625 Runnin' Reds UER 3.00 1.20
(Sic, Redbirds)
David Green
Willie McGee
Lonnie Smith
Ozzie Smith
❑ 626 Rudy May .25 .10
❑ 627 Matt Keough .25 .10
❑ 628 Jose DeLeon RC 1.00 .40
❑ 629 Jim Essian .25 .10
❑ 630 Darnell Coles RC 1.00 .40
❑ 631 Mike Warren .25 .10
❑ 632 Del Crandall MG .25 .10
❑ 633 Dennis Martinez .75 .30
❑ 634 Mike Moore .25 .10
❑ 635 Lary Sorensen .25 .10
❑ 636 Ricky Nelson .25 .10
❑ 637 Omar Moreno .25 .10
❑ 638 Charlie Hough .75 .30
❑ 639 Dennis Eckersley 1.50 .60
❑ 640 Walt Terrell .25 .10
❑ 641 Denny Walling .25 .10
❑ 642 Dave Anderson RC .25 .10
❑ 643 Jose Oquendo RC 1.00 .40
❑ 644 Bob Stanley .25 .10
❑ 645 Dave Geisel .25 .10
❑ 646 Scott Garrelts .25 .10
❑ 647 Gary Pettis .25 .10
❑ 648 Duke Snider 1.50 .60
Puzzle Card
❑ 649 Johnnie LeMaster .25 .10
❑ 650 Dave Collins .25 .10
❑ 651 The Chicken 1.50 .60
❑ 652 DK Checklist 1-26 .75 .30
(Unnumbered)
❑ 653 Checklist 27-130 .25 .10
(Unnumbered)
❑ 654 Checklist 131-234 .25 .10
(Unnumbered)
❑ 655 Checklist 235-338 .25 .10
(Unnumbered)
❑ 656 Checklist 339-442 .25 .10
(Unnumbered)
❑ 657 Checklist 443-546 .25 .10
(Unnumbered)
❑ 658 Checklist 547-651 .25 .10
(Unnumbered)
❑ A Living Legends A 2.50 1.00
Gaylord Perry
Rollie Fingers
❑ B Living Legends B 5.00 2.00
Carl Yastrzemski
Johnny Bench

1985 Donruss

	Nm-Mt	Ex-Mt
COMPLETE SET (660)	60.00	24.00
COMP.FACT.SET (660)	100.00	40.00
COMP.GEHRIG PUZZLE	4.00	1.60

❑ 1 Ryne Sandberg DK 1.25 .50
❑ 2 Doug DeCinces DK .15 .06
❑ 3 Richard Dotson DK .15 .06
❑ 4 Bert Blyleven DK .40 .16
❑ 5 Lou Whitaker DK .40 .16
❑ 6 Dan Quisenberry DK .15 .06
❑ 7 Don Mattingly DK 2.50 1.00
❑ 8 Carney Lansford DK .40 .16
❑ 9 Frank Tanana DK .40 .16
❑ 10 Willie Upshaw DK .15 .06
❑ 11 C.Washington DK .15 .06
❑ 12 Mike Marshall DK .15 .06
❑ 13 Joaquin Andujar DK .40 .16
❑ 14 Cal Ripken DK 2.50 1.00
❑ 15 Jim Rice DK .40 .16
❑ 16 Don Sutton DK .40 .16

❑ 17 Frank Viola DK .40 .16
❑ 18 Alvin Davis DK .40 .16
❑ 19 Mario Soto DK .40 .16
❑ 20 Jose Cruz DK .40 .16
❑ 21 Charlie Lea DK .15 .06
❑ 22 Jesse Orosco DK .15 .06
❑ 23 Juan Samuel DK .15 .06
❑ 24 Tony Pena DK .15 .06
❑ 25 Tony Gwynn DK 1.25 .50
❑ 26 Bob Brenly DK .15 .06
❑ 27 Danny Tartabull RR RC 1.00 .40
❑ 28 Mike Bielecki RC .25 .10
❑ 29 Steve Lyons RR RC .50 .20
❑ 30 Jeff Reed RC .25 .10
❑ 31 Tony Brewer RC .25 .10
❑ 32 John Morris RC .25 .10
❑ 33 Daryl Boston RR RC .25 .10
❑ 34 Al Pulido RR .25 .10
❑ 35 Steve Kiefer RC .25 .10
❑ 36 Larry Sheets RC .25 .10
❑ 37 Scott Bradley RC .25 .10
❑ 38 Calvin Schiraldi RC .50 .20
❑ 39 S.Dunston RR RC 1.00 .40
❑ 40 Charlie Mitchell RC .25 .10
❑ 41 Billy Hatcher RR RC .50 .20
❑ 42 Russ Stephans RC .25 .10
❑ 43 Alejandro Sanchez RC .25 .10
❑ 44 Steve Jeltz RC .25 .10
❑ 45 Jim Traber RC .25 .10
❑ 46 Doug Loman RC .25 .10
❑ 47 Eddie Murray 1.25 .50
❑ 48 Robin Yount 2.00 .80
❑ 49 Lance Parrish .40 .16
❑ 50 Jim Rice .40 .16
❑ 51 Dave Winfield .40 .16
❑ 52 Fernando Valenzuela .40 .16
❑ 53 George Brett 3.00 1.20
❑ 54 Dave Kingman .40 .16
❑ 55 Gary Carter .40 .16
❑ 56 Buddy Bell .40 .16
❑ 57 Reggie Jackson .75 .30
❑ 58 Harold Baines .40 .16
❑ 59 Ozzie Smith 2.00 .80
❑ 60 Nolan Ryan UER 6.00 2.40
(Set strikeout record in 1973, not 1972)
❑ 61 Mike Schmidt 3.00 1.20
❑ 62 Dave Parker .40 .16
❑ 63 Tony Gwynn 2.50 1.00
❑ 64 Tony Pena .15 .06
❑ 65 Jack Clark .40 .16
❑ 66 Dale Murphy .75 .30
❑ 67 Ryne Sandberg 2.50 1.00
❑ 68 Keith Hernandez .40 .16
❑ 69 Alvin Davis RC* .50 .20
❑ 70 Kent Hrbek .40 .16
❑ 71 Willie Upshaw .15 .06
❑ 72 Dave Engle .15 .06
❑ 73 Alfredo Griffin .15 .06
❑ 74A Jack Perconte .15 .06
(Career Highlights takes four lines)
❑ 74B Jack Perconte .15 .06
(Career Highlights takes three lines)
❑ 75 Jesse Orosco .15 .06
❑ 76 Jody Davis .15 .06
❑ 77 Bob Horner .40 .16
❑ 78 Larry McWilliams .15 .06
❑ 79 Joel Youngblood .15 .06
❑ 80 Alan Wiggins .15 .06
❑ 81 Ron Oester .15 .06
❑ 82 Ozzie Virgil .15 .06
❑ 83 Ricky Horton .15 .06
❑ 84 Bill Doran .15 .06
❑ 85 Rod Carew .75 .30
❑ 86 LaMarr Hoyt .15 .06
❑ 87 Tim Wallach .15 .06
❑ 88 Mike Flanagan .15 .06
❑ 89 Jim Sundberg .40 .16
❑ 90 Chet Lemon .40 .16
❑ 91 Bob Stanley .15 .06
❑ 92 Willie Randolph .40 .16
❑ 93 Bill Russell .40 .16
❑ 94 Julio Franco .40 .16
❑ 95 Dan Quisenberry .15 .06
❑ 96 Bill Caudill .15 .06
❑ 97 Bill Gullickson .15 .06
❑ 98 Danny Darwin .15 .06
❑ 99 Curtis Wilkerson .15 .06
❑ 100 Bud Black .15 .06
❑ 101 Tony Phillips .15 .06
❑ 102 Tony Bernazard .15 .06
❑ 103 Jay Howell .15 .06
❑ 104 Burt Hooton .15 .06
❑ 105 Milt Wilcox .15 .06
❑ 106 Rich Dauer .15 .06
❑ 107 Don Sutton .40 .16
❑ 108 Mike Witt .15 .06
❑ 109 Bruce Sutter .40 .16
❑ 110 Enos Cabell .15 .06
❑ 111 John Denny .15 .06
❑ 112 Dave Dravecky .15 .06
❑ 113 Marvell Wynne .15 .06
❑ 114 Johnnie LeMaster .15 .06
❑ 115 Chuck Porter .15 .06
❑ 116 John Gibbons .15 .06
❑ 117 Keith Moreland .15 .06
❑ 118 Darnell Coles .15 .06
❑ 119 Dennis Lamp .15 .06
❑ 120 Ron Davis .15 .06
❑ 121 Nick Esasky .15 .06
❑ 122 Vance Law .15 .06
❑ 123 Gary Roenicke .15 .06
❑ 124 Bill Schroeder .15 .06
❑ 125 Dave Rozema .15 .06
❑ 126 Bobby Meacham .15 .06
❑ 127 Marty Barrett .15 .06
❑ 128 R.J. Reynolds .15 .06
❑ 129 Ernie Camacho UER .15 .06
(Photo actually Rich Thompson)
❑ 130 Jorge Orta .15 .06
❑ 131 Lary Sorensen .15 .06
❑ 132 Terry Francona .40 .16
❑ 133 Fred Lynn .40 .16
❑ 134 Bob Jones .15 .06
❑ 135 Jerry Hairston .15 .06
❑ 136 Kevin Bass .15 .06
❑ 137 Garry Maddox .15 .06
❑ 138 Dave LaPoint .15 .06
❑ 139 Kevin McReynolds .40 .16
❑ 140 Wayne Krenchicki .15 .06
❑ 141 Rafael Ramirez .15 .06
❑ 142 Rod Scurry .15 .06
❑ 143 Greg Minton .15 .06
❑ 144 Tim Stoddard .15 .06
❑ 145 Steve Henderson .15 .06
❑ 146 George Bell .40 .16
❑ 147 Dave Meier .15 .06
❑ 148 Sammy Stewart .15 .06
❑ 149 Mark Brouhard .15 .06
❑ 150 Larry Herndon .15 .06
❑ 151 Oil Can Boyd .15 .06
❑ 152 Brian Dayett .15 .06
❑ 153 Tom Niedenfuer .15 .06
❑ 154 Brook Jacoby .15 .06
❑ 155 Onix Concepcion .15 .06
❑ 156 Tim Conroy .15 .06
❑ 157 Joe Hesketh .15 .06
❑ 158 Brian Downing .40 .16
❑ 159 Tommy Dunbar .15 .06
❑ 160 Marc Hill .15 .06
❑ 161 Phil Garner .40 .16
❑ 162 Jerry Davis .15 .06
❑ 163 Bill Campbell .15 .06
❑ 164 John Franco RC 1.00 .40
❑ 165 Len Barker .15 .06
❑ 166 Benny Distefano .15 .06
❑ 167 George Frazier .15 .06
❑ 168 Tito Landrum .15 .06
❑ 169 Cal Ripken 5.00 2.00
❑ 170 Cecil Cooper .40 .16
❑ 171 Alan Trammell .40 .16
❑ 172 Wade Boggs 1.25 .50
❑ 173 Don Baylor .40 .16
❑ 174 Pedro Guerrero .40 .16
❑ 175 Frank White .40 .16
❑ 176 Rickey Henderson 1.50 .60
❑ 177 Charlie Lea .15 .06
❑ 178 Pete O'Brien .15 .06
❑ 179 Doug DeCinces .15 .06
❑ 180 Ron Kittle .15 .06
❑ 181 George Hendrick .40 .16
❑ 182 Joe Niekro .15 .06
❑ 183 Juan Samuel .15 .06
❑ 184 Mario Soto .40 .16
❑ 185 Rich Gossage .40 .16
❑ 186 Johnny Ray .15 .06
❑ 187 Bob Brenly .15 .06
❑ 188 Craig McMurtry .15 .06
❑ 189 Leon Durham .15 .06
❑ 190 Dwight Gooden RC 3.00 1.20
❑ 191 Barry Bonnell .15 .06
❑ 192 Tim Teufel .15 .06
❑ 193 Dave Stieb .40 .16
❑ 194 Mickey Hatcher .15 .06
❑ 195 Jesse Barfield .40 .16
❑ 196 Al Cowens .15 .06
❑ 197 Hubie Brooks .15 .06
❑ 198 Steve Trout .15 .06
❑ 199 Glenn Hubbard .15 .06
❑ 200 Bill Madlock .40 .16
❑ 201 Jeff D. Robinson .15 .06
❑ 202 Eric Show .15 .06
❑ 203 Dave Concepcion .40 .16
❑ 204 Ivan DeJesus .15 .06
❑ 205 Neil Allen .15 .06
❑ 206 Jerry Mumphrey .15 .06
❑ 207 Mike C. Brown .15 .06
❑ 208 Carlton Fisk .75 .30
❑ 209 Bryn Smith .15 .06
❑ 210 Tippy Martinez .15 .06
❑ 211 Dion James .15 .06
❑ 212 Willie Hernandez .15 .06
❑ 213 Mike Easler .15 .06
❑ 214 Ron Guidry .40 .16
❑ 215 Rick Honeycutt .15 .06
❑ 216 Brett Butler .40 .16
❑ 217 Larry Gura .15 .06
❑ 218 Ray Burris .15 .06
❑ 219 Steve Rogers .40 .16
❑ 220 Frank Tanana UER .40 .16
(Bats Left listed twice on card back)
❑ 221 Ned Yost .15 .06
❑ 222 B.Saberhagen RC UER 1.50 .60
18 career IP on back
❑ 223 Mike Davis .15 .06
❑ 224 Bert Blyleven .40 .16
❑ 225 Steve Kemp .15 .06
❑ 226 Jerry Reuss .15 .06
❑ 227 Darrell Evans UER .40 .16
(80 homers in 1980)
❑ 228 Wayne Gross .15 .06
❑ 229 Jim Gantner .15 .06
❑ 230 Bob Boone .40 .16
❑ 231 Lonnie Smith .15 .06
❑ 232 Frank DiPino .15 .06
❑ 233 Jerry Koosman .40 .16
❑ 234 Graig Nettles .40 .16
❑ 235 John Tudor .40 .16
❑ 236 John Rabb .15 .06
❑ 237 Rick Manning .15 .06
❑ 238 Mike Fitzgerald .15 .06
❑ 239 Gary Matthews .40 .16
❑ 240 Jim Presley .50 .20
❑ 241 Dave Collins .15 .06
❑ 242 Gary Gaetti .40 .16
❑ 243 Dann Bilardello .15 .06
❑ 244 Rudy Law .15 .06
❑ 245 John Lowenstein .15 .06
❑ 246 Tom Tellmann .15 .06
❑ 247 Howard Johnson .40 .16
❑ 248 Ray Fontenot .15 .06
❑ 249 Tony Armas .40 .16
❑ 250 Candy Maldonado .15 .06
❑ 251 Mike Jeffcoat .15 .06
❑ 252 Dane Iorg .15 .06
❑ 253 Bruce Bochte .15 .06
❑ 254 Pete Rose Expos 4.00 1.60
❑ 255 Don Aase .15 .06
❑ 256 George Wright .15 .06
❑ 257 Britt Burns .15 .06
❑ 258 Mike Scott .40 .16
❑ 259 Len Matuszek .15 .06
❑ 260 Dave Rucker .15 .06
❑ 261 Craig Lefferts .15 .06

❑ 262	Jay Tibbs	.15	.06
❑ 263	Bruce Benedict	.15	.06
❑ 264	Don Robinson	.15	.06
❑ 265	Gary Lavelle	.15	.06
❑ 266	Scott Sanderson	.15	.06
❑ 267	Matt Young	.15	.06
❑ 268	Ernie Whitt	.15	.06
❑ 269	Houston Jimenez	.15	.06
❑ 270	Ken Dixon	.15	.06
❑ 271	Pete Ladd	.15	.06
❑ 272	Juan Berenguer	.15	.06
❑ 273	Roger Clemens RC	40.00	16.00
❑ 274	Rick Cerone	.15	.06
❑ 275	Dave Anderson	.15	.06
❑ 276	George Vukovich	.15	.06
❑ 277	Greg Pryor	.15	.06
❑ 278	Mike Warren	.15	.06
❑ 279	Bob James	.15	.06
❑ 280	Bobby Grich	.40	.16
❑ 281	Mike Mason RC	.25	.10
❑ 282	Ron Reed	.15	.06
❑ 283	Alan Ashby	.15	.06
❑ 284	Mark Thurmond	.15	.06
❑ 285	Joe Lefebvre	.15	.06
❑ 286	Ted Power	.15	.06
❑ 287	Chris Chambliss	.40	.16
❑ 288	Lee Tunnell	.15	.06
❑ 289	Rich Bordi	.15	.06
❑ 290	Glenn Brummer	.15	.06
❑ 291	Mike Boddicker	.15	.06
❑ 292	Rollie Fingers	.40	.16
❑ 293	Lou Whitaker	.40	.16
❑ 294	Dwight Evans	.75	.30
❑ 295	Don Mattingly	5.00	2.00
❑ 296	Mike Marshall	.15	.06
❑ 297	Willie Wilson	.40	.16
❑ 298	Mike Heath	.15	.06
❑ 299	Tim Raines	.40	.16
❑ 300	Larry Parrish	.15	.06
❑ 301	Geoff Zahn	.15	.06
❑ 302	Rich Dotson	.15	.06
❑ 303	David Green	.15	.06
❑ 304	Jose Cruz	.40	.16
❑ 305	Steve Carlton	.40	.16
❑ 306	Gary Redus	.15	.06
❑ 307	Steve Garvey	.40	.16
❑ 308	Jose DeLeon	.15	.06
❑ 309	Randy Lerch	.15	.06
❑ 310	Claudell Washington	.15	.06
❑ 311	Lee Smith	.40	.16
❑ 312	Darryl Strawberry	1.25	.50
❑ 313	Jim Beattie	.15	.06
❑ 314	John Butcher	.15	.06
❑ 315	Damaso Garcia	.15	.06
❑ 316	Mike Smithson	.15	.06
❑ 317	Luis Leal	.15	.06
❑ 318	Ken Phelps	.15	.06
❑ 319	Wally Backman	.15	.06
❑ 320	Ron Cey	.40	.16
❑ 321	Brad Komminsk	.15	.06
❑ 322	Jason Thompson	.15	.06
❑ 323	Frank Williams	.15	.06
❑ 324	Tim Lollar	.15	.06
❑ 325	Eric Davis RC	3.00	1.20
❑ 326	Von Hayes	.15	.06
❑ 327	Andy Van Slyke	.75	.30
❑ 328	Craig Reynolds	.15	.06
❑ 329	Dick Schofield	.15	.06
❑ 330	Scott Fletcher	.15	.06
❑ 331	Jeff Reardon	.40	.16
❑ 332	Rick Dempsey	.15	.06
❑ 333	Ben Oglivie	.40	.16
❑ 334	Dan Petry	.15	.06
❑ 335	Jackie Gutierrez	.15	.06
❑ 336	Dave Righetti	.40	.16
❑ 337	Alejandro Pena	.15	.06
❑ 338	Mel Hall	.15	.06
❑ 339	Pat Sheridan	.15	.06
❑ 340	Keith Atherton	.15	.06
❑ 341	David Palmer	.15	.06
❑ 342	Gary Ward	.15	.06
❑ 343	Dave Stewart	.40	.16
❑ 344	Mark Gubicza RC*	.50	.20
❑ 345	Carney Lansford	.40	.16
❑ 346	Jerry Willard	.15	.06
❑ 347	Ken Griffey	.40	.16
❑ 348	Franklin Stubbs	.15	.06
❑ 349	Aurelio Lopez	.15	.06
❑ 350	Al Bumbry	.15	.06
❑ 351	Charlie Moore	.15	.06
❑ 352	Luis Sanchez	.15	.06
❑ 353	Darrell Porter	.15	.06
❑ 354	Bill Dawley	.15	.06
❑ 355	Charles Hudson	.15	.06
❑ 356	Garry Templeton	.40	.16
❑ 357	Cecilio Guante	.15	.06
❑ 358	Jeff Leonard	.15	.06
❑ 359	Paul Molitor	.75	.30
❑ 360	Ron Gardenhire	.15	.06
❑ 361	Larry Bowa	.40	.16
❑ 362	Bob Kearney	.15	.06
❑ 363	Garth Iorg	.15	.06
❑ 364	Tom Brunansky	.15	.06
❑ 365	Brad Gulden	.15	.06
❑ 366	Greg Walker	.15	.06
❑ 367	Mike Young	.15	.06
❑ 368	Rick Waits	.15	.06
❑ 369	Doug Bair	.15	.06
❑ 370	Bob Shirley	.15	.06
❑ 371	Bob Ojeda	.15	.06
❑ 372	Bob Welch	.40	.16
❑ 373	Neal Heaton	.15	.06
❑ 374	Danny Jackson UER (Photo actually Frank Wills)	.15	.06
❑ 375	Donnie Hill	.15	.06
❑ 376	Mike Stenhouse	.15	.06
❑ 377	Bruce Kison	.15	.06
❑ 378	Wayne Tolleson	.15	.06
❑ 379	Floyd Bannister	.15	.06
❑ 380	Vern Ruhle	.15	.06
❑ 381	Tim Corcoran	.15	.06
❑ 382	Kurt Kepshire	.15	.06
❑ 383	Bobby Brown	.15	.06
❑ 384	Dave Van Gorder	.15	.06
❑ 385	Rick Mahler	.15	.06
❑ 386	Lee Mazzilli	.40	.16
❑ 387	Bill Laskey	.15	.06
❑ 388	Thad Bosley	.15	.06
❑ 389	Al Chambers	.15	.06
❑ 390	Tony Fernandez	.40	.16
❑ 391	Ron Washington	.15	.06
❑ 392	Bill Swaggerty	.15	.06
❑ 393	Bob L. Gibson	.15	.06
❑ 394	Marty Castillo	.15	.06
❑ 395	Steve Crawford	.15	.06
❑ 396	Clay Christiansen	.15	.06
❑ 397	Bob Bailor	.15	.06
❑ 398	Mike Hargrove	.15	.06
❑ 399	Charlie Leibrandt	.15	.06
❑ 400	Tom Burgmeier	.15	.06
❑ 401	Razor Shines	.15	.06
❑ 402	Rob Wilfong	.15	.06
❑ 403	Tom Henke	.40	.16
❑ 404	Al Jones	.15	.06
❑ 405	Mike LaCoss	.15	.06
❑ 406	Luis DeLeon	.15	.06
❑ 407	Greg Gross	.15	.06
❑ 408	Tom Hume	.15	.06
❑ 409	Rick Camp	.15	.06
❑ 410	Milt May	.15	.06
❑ 411	Henry Cotto RC	.25	.10
❑ 412	David Von Ohlen	.15	.06
❑ 413	Scott McGregor	.15	.06
❑ 414	Ted Simmons	.40	.16
❑ 415	Jack Morris	.40	.16
❑ 416	Bill Buckner	.40	.16
❑ 417	Butch Wynegar	.15	.06
❑ 418	Steve Sax	.15	.06
❑ 419	Steve Balboni	.15	.06
❑ 420	Dwayne Murphy	.15	.06
❑ 421	Andre Dawson	.40	.16
❑ 422	Charlie Hough	.40	.16
❑ 423	Tommy John	.40	.16
❑ 424A	Tom Seaver ERR (Photo actually Floyd Bannister)	.75	.30
❑ 424B	Tom Seaver COR	10.00	4.00
❑ 425	Tom Herr	.15	.06
❑ 426	Terry Puhl	.15	.06
❑ 427	Al Holland	.15	.06
❑ 428	Eddie Milner	.15	.06
❑ 429	Terry Kennedy	.15	.06
❑ 430	John Candelaria	.15	.06
❑ 431	Manny Trillo	.15	.06
❑ 432	Ken Oberkfell	.15	.06
❑ 433	Rick Sutcliffe	.40	.16
❑ 434	Ron Darling	.40	.16
❑ 435	Spike Owen	.15	.06
❑ 436	Frank Viola	.40	.16
❑ 437	Lloyd Moseby	.15	.06
❑ 438	Kirby Puckett RC	10.00	4.00
❑ 439	Jim Clancy	.15	.06
❑ 440	Mike Moore	.15	.06
❑ 441	Doug Sisk	.15	.06
❑ 442	Dennis Eckersley	.75	.30
❑ 443	Gerald Perry	.15	.06
❑ 444	Dale Berra	.15	.06
❑ 445	Dusty Baker	.40	.16
❑ 446	Ed Whitson	.15	.06
❑ 447	Cesar Cedeno	.40	.16
❑ 448	Rick Schu	.15	.06
❑ 449	Joaquin Andujar	.40	.16
❑ 450	Mark Bailey	.15	.06
❑ 451	Ron Romanick	.15	.06
❑ 452	Julio Cruz	.15	.06
❑ 453	Miguel Dilone	.15	.06
❑ 454	Storm Davis	.15	.06
❑ 455	Jaime Cocanower	.15	.06
❑ 456	Barbaro Garbey	.15	.06
❑ 457	Rich Gedman	.15	.06
❑ 458	Phil Niekro	.40	.16
❑ 459	Mike Scioscia	.40	.16
❑ 460	Pat Tabler	.15	.06
❑ 461	Darryl Motley	.15	.06
❑ 462	Chris Codiroli	.15	.06
❑ 463	Doug Flynn	.15	.06
❑ 464	Billy Sample	.15	.06
❑ 465	Mickey Rivers	.15	.06
❑ 466	John Wathan	.15	.06
❑ 467	Bill Krueger	.15	.06
❑ 468	Andre Thornton	.15	.06
❑ 469	Rex Hudler	.15	.06
❑ 470	Sid Bream RC	.50	.20
❑ 471	Kirk Gibson	.75	.30
❑ 472	John Shelby	.15	.06
❑ 473	Moose Haas	.15	.06
❑ 474	Doug Corbett	.15	.06
❑ 475	Willie McGee	.40	.16
❑ 476	Bob Knepper	.15	.06
❑ 477	Kevin Gross	.15	.06
❑ 478	Carmelo Martinez	.15	.06
❑ 479	Kent Tekulve	.15	.06
❑ 480	Chili Davis	.40	.16
❑ 481	Bobby Clark	.15	.06
❑ 482	Mookie Wilson	.40	.16
❑ 483	Dave Owen	.15	.06
❑ 484	Ed Nunez	.15	.06
❑ 485	Rance Mulliniks	.15	.06
❑ 486	Ken Schrom	.15	.06
❑ 487	Jeff Russell	.15	.06
❑ 488	Tom Paciorek	.15	.06
❑ 489	Dan Ford	.15	.06
❑ 490	Mike Caldwell	.15	.06
❑ 491	Scottie Earl	.15	.06
❑ 492	Jose Rijo RC	1.00	.40
❑ 493	Bruce Hurst	.15	.06
❑ 494	Ken Landreaux	.15	.06
❑ 495	Mike Fischlin	.15	.06
❑ 496	Don Slaught	.15	.06
❑ 497	Steve McCatty	.15	.06
❑ 498	Gary Lucas	.15	.06
❑ 499	Gary Pettis	.15	.06
❑ 500	Marvis Foley	.15	.06
❑ 501	Mike Squires	.15	.06
❑ 502	Jim Pankovits	.15	.06
❑ 503	Luis Aguayo	.15	.06
❑ 504	Ralph Citarella	.15	.06
❑ 505	Bruce Bochy	.15	.06
❑ 506	Bob Owchinko	.15	.06
❑ 507	Pascual Perez	.15	.06
❑ 508	Lee Lacy	.15	.06
❑ 509	Atlee Hammaker	.15	.06
❑ 510	Bob Dernier	.15	.06
❑ 511	Ed VandeBerg	.15	.06
❑ 512	Cliff Johnson	.15	.06
❑ 513	Len Whitehouse	.15	.06
❑ 514	Dennis Martinez	.40	.16

❑ 515 Ed Romero .15 .06
❑ 516 Rusty Kuntz .15 .06
❑ 517 Rick Miller .15 .06
❑ 518 Dennis Rasmussen .15 .06
❑ 519 Steve Yeager .40 .16
❑ 520 Chris Bando .15 .06
❑ 521 U.L. Washington .15 .06
❑ 522 Curt Young .15 .06
❑ 523 Angel Salazar .15 .06
❑ 524 Curt Kaufman .15 .06
❑ 525 Odell Jones .15 .06
❑ 526 Juan Agosto .15 .06
❑ 527 Denny Walling .15 .06
❑ 528 Andy Hawkins .15 .06
❑ 529 Sixto Lezcano .15 .06
❑ 530 Skeeter Barnes RC .25 .10
❑ 531 Randy Johnson .15 .06
❑ 532 Jim Morrison .15 .06
❑ 533 Warren Brusstar .15 .06
❑ 534A J.Pendleton ERR RC 1.00 .40
Wrong first name
❑ 534B T.Pendleton COR RC 1.00 .40
❑ 535 Vic Rodriguez .15 .06
❑ 536 Bob McClure .15 .06
❑ 537 Dave Bergman .15 .06
❑ 538 Mark Clear .15 .06
❑ 539 Mike Pagliarulo .15 .06
❑ 540 Terry Whitfield .15 .06
❑ 541 Joe Beckwith .15 .06
❑ 542 Jeff Burroughs .15 .06
❑ 543 Dan Schatzeder .15 .06
❑ 544 Donnie Scott .15 .06
❑ 545 Jim Slaton .15 .06
❑ 546 Greg Luzinski .40 .16
❑ 547 Mark Salas .15 .06
❑ 548 Dave Smith .15 .06
❑ 549 John Wockenfuss .15 .06
❑ 550 Frank Pastore .15 .06
❑ 551 Tim Flannery .15 .06
❑ 552 Rick Rhoden .15 .06
❑ 553 Mark Davis .15 .06
❑ 554 Jeff Dedmon .15 .06
❑ 555 Gary Woods .15 .06
❑ 556 Danny Heep .15 .06
❑ 557 Mark Langston RC 1.00 .40
❑ 558 Darrell Brown .15 .06
❑ 559 Jimmy Key RC 1.00 .40
❑ 560 Rick Lysander .15 .06
❑ 561 Doyle Alexander .15 .06
❑ 562 Mike Stanton .15 .06
❑ 563 Sid Fernandez .40 .16
❑ 564 Richie Hebner .15 .06
❑ 565 Alex Trevino .15 .06
❑ 566 Brian Harper .15 .06
❑ 567 Dan Gladden RC .50 .20
❑ 568 Luis Salazar .15 .06
❑ 569 Tom Foley .15 .06
❑ 570 Larry Andersen .15 .06
❑ 571 Danny Cox .15 .06
❑ 572 Joe Sambito .15 .06
❑ 573 Juan Beniquez .15 .06
❑ 574 Joel Skinner .15 .06
❑ 575 Randy St.Claire .15 .06
❑ 576 Floyd Rayford .15 .06
❑ 577 Roy Howell .15 .06
❑ 578 John Grubb .15 .06
❑ 579 Ed Jurak .15 .06
❑ 580 John Montefusco .15 .06
❑ 581 Orel Hershiser RC 3.00 1.20
❑ 582 Tom Waddell .15 .06
❑ 583 Mark Huismann .15 .06
❑ 584 Joe Morgan .40 .16
❑ 585 Jim Wohlford .15 .06
❑ 586 Dave Schmidt .15 .06
❑ 587 Jeff Kunkel .15 .06
❑ 588 Hal McRae .40 .16
❑ 589 Bill Almon .15 .06
❑ 590 Carmelo Castillo .15 .06
❑ 591 Omar Moreno .15 .06
❑ 592 Ken Howell .15 .06
❑ 593 Tom Brookens .15 .06
❑ 594 Joe Nolan .15 .06
❑ 595 Willie Lozado .15 .06
❑ 596 Tom Nieto .15 .06
❑ 597 Walt Terrell .15 .06
❑ 598 Al Oliver .40 .16

❑ 599 Shane Rawley .15 .06
❑ 600 Denny Gonzalez .15 .06
❑ 601 Mark Grant .15 .06
❑ 602 Mike Armstrong .15 .06
❑ 603 George Foster .40 .16
❑ 604 Dave Lopes .40 .16
❑ 605 Salome Barojas .15 .06
❑ 606 Roy Lee Jackson .15 .06
❑ 607 Pete Filson .15 .06
❑ 608 Duane Walker .15 .06
❑ 609 Glenn Wilson .15 .06
❑ 610 Rafael Santana .15 .06
❑ 611 Roy Smith .15 .06
❑ 612 Ruppert Jones .15 .06
❑ 613 Joe Cowley .15 .06
❑ 614 Al Nipper UER .15 .06
(Photo actually
Mike Brown)
❑ 615 Gene Nelson .15 .06
❑ 616 Joe Carter 1.25 .50
❑ 617 Ray Knight .40 .16
❑ 618 Chuck Rainey .15 .06
❑ 619 Dan Driessen .15 .06
❑ 620 Daryl Sconiers .15 .06
❑ 621 Bill Stein .15 .06
❑ 622 Roy Smalley .15 .06
❑ 623 Ed Lynch .15 .06
❑ 624 Jeff Stone .15 .06
❑ 625 Bruce Berenyi .15 .06
❑ 626 Kelvin Chapman .15 .06
❑ 627 Joe Price .15 .06
❑ 628 Steve Bedrosian .15 .06
❑ 629 Vic Mata .15 .06
❑ 630 Mike Krukow .15 .06
❑ 631 Phil Bradley .50 .20
❑ 632 Jim Gott .15 .06
❑ 633 Randy Bush .15 .06
❑ 634 Tom Browning RC .50 .20
❑ 635 Lou Gehrig 1.25 .50
Puzzle Card
❑ 636 Reid Nichols .15 .06
❑ 637 Dan Pasqua RC .50 .20
❑ 638 German Rivera .15 .06
❑ 639 Don Schulze .15 .06
❑ 640A Mike Jones .15 .06
(Career Highlights,
takes five lines)
❑ 640B Mike Jones .15 .06
(Career Highlights,
takes four lines)
❑ 641 Pete Rose 4.00 1.60
❑ 642 Wade Rowdon .15 .06
❑ 643 Jerry Narron .15 .06
❑ 644 Darrell Miller .15 .06
❑ 645 Tim Hulett RC .25 .10
❑ 646 Andy McGaffigan .15 .06
❑ 647 Kurt Bevacqua .15 .06
❑ 648 John Russell .15 .06
❑ 649 Ron Robinson .15 .06
❑ 650 Donnie Moore .15 .06
❑ 651A Two for the Title 2.00 .80
Dave Winfield
Don Mattingly
(Yellow letters)
❑ 651B Two for the Title 5.00 2.00
Dave Winfield
Don Mattingly
(White letters)
❑ 652 Tim Laudner .15 .06
❑ 653 Steve Farr RC .50 .20
❑ 654 DK Checklist 1-26 .15 .06
(Unnumbered)
❑ 655 Checklist 27-130 .15 .06
(Unnumbered)
❑ 656 Checklist 131-234 .15 .06
(Unnumbered)
❑ 657 Checklist 235-338 .15 .06
(Unnumbered)
❑ 658 Checklist 339-442 .15 .06
(Unnumbered)
❑ 659 Checklist 443-546 .15 .06
(Unnumbered)
❑ 660 Checklist 547-653 .15 .06
(Unnumbered)

1986 Donruss

	Nm-Mt	Ex-Mt
COMPLETE SET (660)	40.00	16.00
COMP.FACT.SET (660)	40.00	16.00
COMP.AARON PUZZLE	2.00	.80

❑ 1 Kirk Gibson DK .50 .20
❑ 2 Rich Gossage DK .25 .10
❑ 3 Willie McGee DK .25 .10
❑ 4 George Bell DK .25 .10
❑ 5 Tony Armas DK .25 .10
❑ 6 Chili Davis DK .25 .10
❑ 7 Cecil Cooper DK .25 .10
❑ 8 Mike Boddicker DK .15 .06
❑ 9 Dave Lopes DK .25 .10
❑ 10 Bill Doran DK .15 .06
❑ 11 Bret Saberhagen DK .25 .10
❑ 12 Brett Butler DK .25 .10
❑ 13 Harold Baines DK .25 .10
❑ 14 Mike Davis DK .15 .06
❑ 15 Tony Perez DK .50 .20
❑ 16 Willie Randolph DK .25 .10
❑ 17 Bob Boone DK .25 .10
❑ 18 Orel Hershiser DK .50 .20
❑ 19 Johnny Ray DK .15 .06
❑ 20 Gary Ward DK .15 .06
❑ 21 Rick Mahler DK .15 .06
❑ 22 Phil Bradley DK .15 .06
❑ 23 Jerry Koosman DK .25 .10
❑ 24 Tom Brunansky DK .15 .06
❑ 25 Andre Dawson DK .15 .06
❑ 26 Dwight Gooden DK .75 .30
❑ 27 Kal Daniels RR .50 .20
❑ 28 Fred McGriff RR RC 8.00 3.20
❑ 29 Cory Snyder RR .15 .06
❑ 30 Jose Guzman RR RC .15 .06
❑ 31 Ty Gainey RC .15 .06
❑ 32 Johnny Abrego RC .15 .06
❑ 33A A.Galarraga RC RR 1.50 .60
No accent
❑ 33B A.Galarraga RC RR 1.50 .60
Accent over e
❑ 34 Dave Shipanoff RC .15 .06
❑ 35 M.McLemore RR RC 1.00 .40
❑ 36 Marty Clary RC .15 .06
❑ 37 Paul O'Neill RR RC 4.00 1.60
❑ 38 Danny Tartabull RR .25 .10
❑ 39 Jose Canseco RR RC 10.00 4.00
❑ 40 Juan Nieves RC .15 .06
❑ 41 Lance McCullers RC .15 .06
❑ 42 Rick Surhoff RC .15 .06
❑ 43 Todd Worrell RR RC .50 .20
❑ 44 Bob Kipper RC .15 .06
❑ 45 John Habyan RR RC .15 .06
❑ 46 Mike Woodard RC .15 .06
❑ 47 Mike Boddicker .15 .06
❑ 48 Robin Yount 1.25 .50
❑ 49 Lou Whitaker .25 .10
❑ 50 Oil Can Boyd .15 .06
❑ 51 Rickey Henderson .75 .30
❑ 52 Mike Marshall .15 .06
❑ 53 George Brett 2.00 .80
❑ 54 Dave Kingman .25 .10
❑ 55 Hubie Brooks .15 .06
❑ 56 Oddibe McDowell .15 .06
❑ 57 Doug DeCinces .15 .06
❑ 58 Britt Burns .15 .06
❑ 59 Ozzie Smith 1.25 .50

❑ 60 Jose Cruz .25 .10
❑ 61 Mike Schmidt 2.00 .80
❑ 62 Pete Rose 2.50 1.00
❑ 63 Steve Garvey .25 .10
❑ 64 Tony Pena .15 .06
❑ 65 Chili Davis .25 .10
❑ 66 Dale Murphy .50 .20
❑ 67 Ryne Sandberg 1.50 .60
❑ 68 Gary Carter .25 .10
❑ 69 Alvin Davis .15 .06
❑ 70 Kent Hrbek .25 .10
❑ 71 George Bell .25 .10
❑ 72 Kirby Puckett 2.00 .80
❑ 73 Lloyd Moseby .15 .06
❑ 74 Bob Kearney .15 .06
❑ 75 Dwight Gooden .75 .30
❑ 76 Gary Matthews .25 .10
❑ 77 Rick Mahler .15 .06
❑ 78 Benny Distefano .15 .06
❑ 79 Jeff Leonard .15 .06
❑ 80 Kevin McReynolds .25 .10
❑ 81 Ron Oester .15 .06
❑ 82 John Russell .15 .06
❑ 83 Tommy Herr .15 .06
❑ 84 Jerry Mumphrey .15 .06
❑ 85 Ron Romanick .15 .06
❑ 86 Daryl Boston .15 .06
❑ 87 Andre Dawson .25 .10
❑ 88 Eddie Murray .75 .30
❑ 89 Dion James .15 .06
❑ 90 Chet Lemon .25 .10
❑ 91 Bob Stanley .15 .06
❑ 92 Willie Randolph .25 .10
❑ 93 Mike Scioscia .25 .10
❑ 94 Tom Waddell .15 .06
❑ 95 Danny Jackson .15 .06
❑ 96 Mike Davis .15 .06
❑ 97 Mike Fitzgerald .15 .06
❑ 98 Gary Ward .15 .06
❑ 99 Pete O'Brien .15 .06
❑ 100 Bret Saberhagen .25 .10
❑ 101 Alfredo Griffin .15 .06
❑ 102 Brett Butler .25 .10
❑ 103 Ron Guidry .25 .10
❑ 104 Jerry Reuss .15 .06
❑ 105 Jack Morris .25 .10
❑ 106 Rick Dempsey .15 .06
❑ 107 Ray Burris .15 .06
❑ 108 Brian Downing .25 .10
❑ 109 Willie McGee .25 .10
❑ 110 Bill Doran .15 .06
❑ 111 Kent Tekulve .15 .06
❑ 112 Tony Gwynn 1.25 .50
❑ 113 Marvell Wynne .15 .06
❑ 114 David Green .15 .06
❑ 115 Jim Gantner .15 .06
❑ 116 George Foster .25 .10
❑ 117 Steve Trout .15 .06
❑ 118 Mark Langston .25 .10
❑ 119 Tony Fernandez .15 .06
❑ 120 John Butcher .15 .06
❑ 121 Ron Robinson .15 .06
❑ 122 Dan Spillner .15 .06
❑ 123 Mike Young .15 .06
❑ 124 Paul Molitor .50 .20
❑ 125 Kirk Gibson .50 .20
❑ 126 Ken Griffey .25 .10
❑ 127 Tony Armas .25 .10
❑ 128 Mariano Duncan RC* .50 .20
❑ 129 Pat Tabler .15 .06
❑ 130 Frank White .25 .10
❑ 131 Carney Lansford .25 .10
❑ 132 Vance Law .15 .06
❑ 133 Dick Schofield .15 .06
❑ 134 Wayne Tolleson .15 .06
❑ 135 Greg Walker .15 .06
❑ 136 Denny Walling .15 .06
❑ 137 Ozzie Virgil .15 .06
❑ 138 Ricky Horton .15 .06
❑ 139 LaMarr Hoyt .15 .06
❑ 140 Wayne Krenchicki .15 .06
❑ 141 Glenn Hubbard .15 .06
❑ 142 Cecilio Guante .15 .06
❑ 143 Mike Krukow .15 .06
❑ 144 Lee Smith .25 .10
❑ 145 Edwin Nunez .15 .06
❑ 146 Dave Stieb .25 .10
❑ 147 Mike Smithson .15 .06
❑ 148 Ken Dixon .15 .06
❑ 149 Danny Darwin .15 .06
❑ 150 Chris Pittaro .15 .06
❑ 151 Bill Buckner .25 .10
❑ 152 Mike Pagliarulo .15 .06
❑ 153 Bill Russell .25 .10
❑ 154 Brook Jacoby .15 .06
❑ 155 Pat Sheridan .15 .06
❑ 156 Mike Gallego RC .15 .06
❑ 157 Jim Wohlford .15 .06
❑ 158 Gary Pettis .15 .06
❑ 159 Toby Harrah .25 .10
❑ 160 Richard Dotson .15 .06
❑ 161 Bob Knepper .15 .06
❑ 162 Dave Dravecky .15 .06
❑ 163 Greg Gross .15 .06
❑ 164 Eric Davis .75 .30
❑ 165 Gerald Perry .15 .06
❑ 166 Rick Rhoden .15 .06
❑ 167 Keith Moreland .15 .06
❑ 168 Jack Clark .25 .10
❑ 169 Storm Davis .15 .06
❑ 170 Cecil Cooper .25 .10
❑ 171 Alan Trammell .25 .10
❑ 172 Roger Clemens 5.00 2.00
❑ 173 Don Mattingly 2.50 1.00
❑ 174 Pedro Guerrero .25 .10
❑ 175 Willie Wilson .25 .10
❑ 176 Dwayne Murphy .15 .06
❑ 177 Tim Raines .25 .10
❑ 178 Larry Parrish .15 .06
❑ 179 Mike Witt .15 .06
❑ 180 Harold Baines .25 .10
❑ 181 V.Coleman RC* UER 1.00 .40
BA 2.67 on back
❑ 182 Jeff Heathcock .15 .06
❑ 183 Steve Carlton .25 .10
❑ 184 Mario Soto .25 .10
❑ 185 Rich Gossage .25 .10
❑ 186 Johnny Ray .15 .06
❑ 187 Dan Gladden .15 .06
❑ 188 Bob Horner .25 .10
❑ 189 Rick Sutcliffe .25 .10
❑ 190 Keith Hernandez .25 .10
❑ 191 Phil Bradley .15 .06
❑ 192 Tom Brunansky .15 .06
❑ 193 Jesse Barfield .25 .10
❑ 194 Frank Viola .25 .10
❑ 195 Willie Upshaw .15 .06
❑ 196 Jim Beattie .15 .06
❑ 197 Darryl Strawberry .50 .20
❑ 198 Ron Cey .25 .10
❑ 199 Steve Bedrosian .15 .06
❑ 200 Steve Kemp .15 .06
❑ 201 Manny Trillo .15 .06
❑ 202 Garry Templeton .25 .10
❑ 203 Dave Parker .25 .10
❑ 204 John Denny .15 .06
❑ 205 Terry Pendleton .25 .10
❑ 206 Terry Puhl .15 .06
❑ 207 Bobby Grich .25 .10
❑ 208 Ozzie Guillen RC 2.00 .80
❑ 209 Jeff Reardon .25 .10
❑ 210 Cal Ripken 3.00 1.20
❑ 211 Bill Schroeder .15 .06
❑ 212 Dan Petry .15 .06
❑ 213 Jim Rice .25 .10
❑ 214 Dave Righetti .25 .10
❑ 215 Fernando Valenzuela .25 .10
❑ 216 Julio Franco .25 .10
❑ 217 Darryl Motley .15 .06
❑ 218 Dave Collins .15 .06
❑ 219 Tim Wallach .15 .06
❑ 220 George Wright .15 .06
❑ 221 Tommy Dunbar .15 .06
❑ 222 Steve Balboni .15 .06
❑ 223 Jay Howell .15 .06
❑ 224 Joe Carter .25 .10
❑ 225 Ed Whitson .15 .06
❑ 226 Orel Hershiser .75 .30
❑ 227 Willie Hernandez .15 .06
❑ 228 Lee Lacy .15 .06
❑ 229 Rollie Fingers .25 .10
❑ 230 Bob Boone .25 .10
❑ 231 Joaquin Andujar .25 .10
❑ 232 Craig Reynolds .15 .06
❑ 233 Shane Rawley .15 .06
❑ 234 Eric Show .15 .06
❑ 235 Jose DeLeon .15 .06
❑ 236 Jose Uribe .15 .06
❑ 237 Moose Haas .15 .06
❑ 238 Wally Backman .15 .06
❑ 239 Dennis Eckersley .50 .20
❑ 240 Mike Moore .15 .06
❑ 241 Damaso Garcia .15 .06
❑ 242 Tim Teufel .15 .06
❑ 243 Dave Concepcion .25 .10
❑ 244 Floyd Bannister .15 .06
❑ 245 Fred Lynn .25 .10
❑ 246 Charlie Moore .15 .06
❑ 247 Walt Terrell .15 .06
❑ 248 Dave Winfield .25 .10
❑ 249 Dwight Evans .50 .20
❑ 250 Dennis Powell .15 .06
❑ 251 Andre Thornton .15 .06
❑ 252 Onix Concepcion .15 .06
❑ 253 Mike Heath .15 .06
❑ 254A David Palmer ERR .15 .06
(Position 2B)
❑ 254B David Palmer COR .50 .20
(Position P)
❑ 255 Donnie Moore .15 .06
❑ 256 Curtis Wilkerson .15 .06
❑ 257 Julio Cruz .15 .06
❑ 258 Nolan Ryan 4.00 1.60
❑ 259 Jeff Stone .15 .06
❑ 260 John Tudor .25 .10
❑ 261 Mark Thurmond .15 .06
❑ 262 Jay Tibbs .15 .06
❑ 263 Rafael Ramirez .15 .06
❑ 264 Larry McWilliams .15 .06
❑ 265 Mark Davis .15 .06
❑ 266 Bob Dernier .15 .06
❑ 267 Matt Young .15 .06
❑ 268 Jim Clancy .15 .06
❑ 269 Mickey Hatcher .15 .06
❑ 270 Sammy Stewart .15 .06
❑ 271 Bob L. Gibson .15 .06
❑ 272 Nelson Simmons .15 .06
❑ 273 Rich Gedman .15 .06
❑ 274 Butch Wynegar .15 .06
❑ 275 Ken Howell .15 .06
❑ 276 Mel Hall .15 .06
❑ 277 Jim Sundberg .25 .10
❑ 278 Chris Codiroli .15 .06
❑ 279 Herm Winningham .15 .06
❑ 280 Rod Carew .50 .20
❑ 281 Don Slaught .15 .06
❑ 282 Scott Fletcher .15 .06
❑ 283 Bill Dawley .15 .06
❑ 284 Andy Hawkins .15 .06
❑ 285 Glenn Wilson .15 .06
❑ 286 Nick Esasky .15 .06
❑ 287 Claudell Washington .15 .06
❑ 288 Lee Mazzilli .25 .10
❑ 289 Jody Davis .15 .06
❑ 290 Darrell Porter .15 .06
❑ 291 Scott McGregor .15 .06
❑ 292 Ted Simmons .25 .10
❑ 293 Aurelio Lopez .15 .06
❑ 294 Marty Barrett .15 .06
❑ 295 Dale Berra .15 .06
❑ 296 Greg Brock .15 .06
❑ 297 Charlie Leibrandt .15 .06
❑ 298 Bill Krueger .15 .06
❑ 299 Bryn Smith .15 .06
❑ 300 Burt Hooton .15 .06
❑ 301 Stu Cliburn .15 .06
❑ 302 Luis Salazar .15 .06
❑ 303 Ken Dayley .15 .06
❑ 304 Frank DiPino .15 .06
❑ 305 Von Hayes .15 .06
❑ 306 Gary Redus .15 .06
❑ 307 Craig Lefferts .15 .06
❑ 308 Sammy Khalifa .15 .06
❑ 309 Scott Garrelts .15 .06
❑ 310 Rick Cerone .15 .06
❑ 311 Shawon Dunston .25 .10
❑ 312 Howard Johnson .25 .10
❑ 313 Jim Presley .15 .06

314	Gary Gaetti	.25	.10
315	Luis Leal	.15	.06
316	Mark Salas	.15	.06
317	Bill Caudill	.15	.06
318	Dave Henderson	.15	.06
319	Rafael Santana	.15	.06
320	Leon Durham	.15	.06
321	Bruce Sutter	.25	.10
322	Jason Thompson	.15	.06
323	Bob Brenly	.15	.06
324	Carmelo Martinez	.15	.06
325	Eddie Milner	.15	.06
326	Juan Samuel	.15	.06
327	Tom Nieto	.15	.06
328	Dave Smith	.15	.06
329	Urbano Lugo	.15	.06
330	Joel Skinner	.15	.06
331	Bill Gullickson	.15	.06
332	Floyd Rayford	.15	.06
333	Ben Oglivie	.25	.10
334	Lance Parrish	.25	.10
335	Jackie Gutierrez	.15	.06
336	Dennis Rasmussen	.15	.06
337	Terry Whitfield	.15	.06
338	Neal Heaton	.15	.06
339	Jorge Orta	.15	.06
340	Donnie Hill	.15	.06
341	Joe Hesketh	.15	.06
342	Charlie Hough	.25	.10
343	Dave Rozema	.15	.06
344	Greg Pryor	.15	.06
345	Mickey Tettleton RC	.50	.20
346	George Vukovich	.15	.06
347	Don Baylor	.25	.10
348	Carlos Diaz	.15	.06
349	Barbaro Garbey	.15	.06
350	Larry Sheets	.15	.06
351	Ted Higuera RC*	.50	.20
352	Juan Beniquez	.15	.06
353	Bob Forsch	.15	.06
354	Mark Bailey	.15	.06
355	Larry Andersen	.15	.06
356	Terry Kennedy	.15	.06
357	Don Robinson	.15	.06
358	Jim Gott	.15	.06
359	Earnie Riles	.15	.06
360	John Christensen	.15	.06
361	Ray Fontenot	.15	.06
362	Spike Owen	.15	.06
363	Jim Acker	.15	.06
364	Ron Davis	.15	.06
365	Tom Hume	.15	.06
366	Carlton Fisk	.50	.20
367	Nate Snell	.15	.06
368	Rick Manning	.15	.06
369	Darrell Evans	.25	.10
370	Ron Hassey	.15	.06
371	Wade Boggs	.50	.20
372	Rick Honeycutt	.15	.06
373	Chris Bando	.15	.06
374	Bud Black	.15	.06
375	Steve Henderson	.15	.06
376	Charlie Lea	.15	.06
377	Reggie Jackson	.50	.20
378	Dave Schmidt	.15	.06
379	Bob James	.15	.06
380	Glenn Davis	.15	.06
381	Tim Corcoran	.15	.06
382	Danny Cox	.15	.06
383	Tim Flannery	.15	.06
384	Tom Browning	.15	.06
385	Rick Camp	.15	.06
386	Jim Morrison	.15	.06
387	Dave LaPoint	.15	.06
388	Dave Lopes	.25	.10
389	Al Cowens	.15	.06
390	Doyle Alexander	.15	.06
391	Tim Laudner	.15	.06
392	Don Aase	.15	.06
393	Jaime Cocanower	.15	.06
394	Randy O'Neal	.15	.06
395	Mike Easler	.15	.06
396	Scott Bradley	.15	.06
397	Tom Niedenfuer	.15	.06
398	Jerry Willard	.15	.06
399	Lonnie Smith	.15	.06
400	Bruce Bochte	.15	.06
401	Terry Francona	.25	.10
402	Jim Slaton	.15	.06
403	Bill Stein	.15	.06
404	Tim Hulett	.15	.06
405	Alan Ashby	.15	.06
406	Tim Stoddard	.15	.06
407	Garry Maddox	.15	.06
408	Ted Power	.15	.06
409	Len Barker	.15	.06
410	Denny Gonzalez	.15	.06
411	George Frazier	.15	.06
412	Andy Van Slyke	.50	.20
413	Jim Dwyer	.15	.06
414	Paul Householder	.15	.06
415	Alejandro Sanchez	.15	.06
416	Steve Crawford	.15	.06
417	Dan Pasqua	.15	.06
418	Enos Cabell	.15	.06
419	Mike Jones	.15	.06
420	Steve Kiefer	.15	.06
421	Tim Burke	.15	.06
422	Mike Mason	.15	.06
423	Ruppert Jones	.15	.06
424	Jerry Hairston	.15	.06
425	Tito Landrum	.15	.06
426	Jeff Calhoun	.15	.06
427	Don Carman	.15	.06
428	Tony Perez	.50	.20
429	Jerry Davis	.15	.06
430	Bob Walk	.15	.06
431	Brad Wellman	.15	.06
432	Terry Forster	.25	.10
433	Billy Hatcher	.15	.06
434	Clint Hurdle	.15	.06
435	Ivan Calderon RC*	.50	.20
436	Pete Filson	.15	.06
437	Tom Henke	.25	.10
438	Dave Engle	.15	.06
439	Tom Filer	.15	.06
440	Gorman Thomas	.25	.10
441	Rick Aguilera RC	.50	.20
442	Scott Sanderson	.15	.06
443	Jeff Dedmon	.15	.06
444	Joe Orsulak RC*	.50	.20
445	Atlee Hammaker	.15	.06
446	Jerry Royster	.15	.06
447	Buddy Bell	.25	.10
448	Dave Rucker	.15	.06
449	Ivan DeJesus	.15	.06
450	Jim Pankovits	.15	.06
451	Jerry Narron	.15	.06
452	Bryan Little	.15	.06
453	Gary Lucas	.15	.06
454	Dennis Martinez	.25	.10
455	Ed Romero	.15	.06
456	Bob Melvin	.15	.06
457	Glenn Hoffman	.15	.06
458	Bob Shirley	.15	.06
459	Bob Welch	.25	.10
460	Carmen Castillo	.15	.06
461	Dave Leeper	.15	.06
462	Tim Birtsas	.15	.06
463	Randy St.Claire	.15	.06
464	Chris Welsh	.15	.06
465	Greg Harris	.15	.06
466	Lynn Jones	.15	.06
467	Dusty Baker	.25	.10
468	Roy Smith	.15	.06
469	Andre Robertson	.15	.06
470	Ken Landreaux	.15	.06
471	Dave Bergman	.15	.06
472	Gary Roenicke	.15	.06
473	Pete Vuckovich	.15	.06
474	Kirk McCaskill RC	.50	.20
475	Jeff Lahti	.15	.06
476	Mike Scott	.25	.10
477	Darren Daulton RC	1.00	.40
478	Graig Nettles	.25	.10
479	Bill Almon	.15	.06
480	Greg Minton	.15	.06
481	Randy Ready	.15	.06
482	Len Dykstra RC	1.50	.60
483	Thad Bosley	.15	.06
484	Harold Reynolds RC	1.50	.60
485	Al Oliver	.25	.10
486	Roy Smalley	.15	.06
487	John Franco	.25	.10
488	Juan Agosto	.15	.06
489	Al Pardo	.15	.06
490	Bill Wegman RC	.15	.06
491	Frank Tanana	.25	.10
492	Brian Fisher RC	.15	.06
493	Mark Clear	.15	.06
494	Len Matuszek	.15	.06
495	Ramon Romero	.15	.06
496	John Wathan	.15	.06
497	Rob Picciolo	.15	.06
498	U.L. Washington	.15	.06
499	John Candelaria	.15	.06
500	Duane Walker	.15	.06
501	Gene Nelson	.15	.06
502	John Mizerock	.15	.06
503	Luis Aguayo	.15	.06
504	Kurt Kepshire	.15	.06
505	Ed Wojna	.15	.06
506	Joe Price	.15	.06
507	Milt Thompson RC	.50	.20
508	Junior Ortiz	.15	.06
509	Vida Blue	.25	.10
510	Steve Engel	.15	.06
511	Karl Best	.15	.06
512	Cecil Fielder RC	2.00	.80
513	Frank Eufemia	.15	.06
514	Tippy Martinez	.15	.06
515	Billy Joe Robidoux	.15	.06
516	Bill Scherrer	.15	.06
517	Bruce Hurst	.15	.06
518	Rich Bordi	.15	.06
519	Steve Yeager	.25	.10
520	Tony Bernazard	.15	.06
521	Hal McRae	.25	.10
522	Jose Rijo	.25	.10
523	Mitch Webster	.15	.06
524	Jack Howell	.15	.06
525	Alan Bannister	.15	.06
526	Ron Kittle	.15	.06
527	Phil Garner	.25	.10
528	Kurt Bevacqua	.15	.06
529	Kevin Gross	.15	.06
530	Bo Diaz	.15	.06
531	Ken Oberkfell	.15	.06
532	Rick Reuschel	.25	.10
533	Ron Meridith	.15	.06
534	Steve Braun	.15	.06
535	Wayne Gross	.15	.06
536	Ray Searage	.15	.06
537	Tom Brookens	.15	.06
538	Al Nipper	.15	.06
539	Billy Sample	.15	.06
540	Steve Sax	.15	.06
541	Dan Quisenberry	.15	.06
542	Tony Phillips	.15	.06
543	Floyd Youmans	.15	.06
544	Steve Buechele RC	.50	.20
545	Craig Gerber	.15	.06
546	Joe DeSa	.15	.06
547	Brian Harper	.15	.06
548	Kevin Bass	.15	.06
549	Tom Foley	.15	.06
550	Dave Van Gorder	.15	.06
551	Bruce Bochy	.15	.06
552	R.J. Reynolds	.15	.06
553	Chris Brown	.15	.06
554	Bruce Benedict	.15	.06
555	Warren Brusstar	.15	.06
556	Danny Heep	.15	.06
557	Darnell Coles	.15	.06
558	Greg Gagne	.15	.06
559	Ernie Whitt	.15	.06
560	Ron Washington	.15	.06
561	Jimmy Key	.25	.10
562	Billy Swift	.15	.06
563	Ron Darling	.25	.10
564	Dick Ruthven	.15	.06
565	Zane Smith	.15	.06
566	Sid Bream	.15	.06
567A	J.Youngblood ERR Position P	.15	.06
567B	J.Youngblood COR Position IF	.50	.20
568	Mario Ramirez	.15	.06

❑ 569 Tom Runnells .15 .06
❑ 570 Rick Schu .15 .06
❑ 571 Bill Campbell .15 .06
❑ 572 Dickie Thon .15 .06
❑ 573 Al Holland .15 .06
❑ 574 Reid Nichols .15 .06
❑ 575 Bert Roberge .15 .06
❑ 576 Mike Flanagan .15 .06
❑ 577 Tim Leary .15 .06
❑ 578 Mike Laga .15 .06
❑ 579 Steve Lyons .15 .06
❑ 580 Phil Niekro .25 .10
❑ 581 Gilberto Reyes .15 .06
❑ 582 Jamie Easterly .15 .06
❑ 583 Mark Gubicza .15 .06
❑ 584 Stan Javier RC .50 .20
❑ 585 Bill Laskey .15 .06
❑ 586 Jeff Russell .15 .06
❑ 587 Dickie Noles .15 .06
❑ 588 Steve Farr .15 .06
❑ 589 Steve Ontiveros RC .15 .06
❑ 590 Mike Hargrove .15 .06
❑ 591 Marty Bystrom .15 .06
❑ 592 Franklin Stubbs .15 .06
❑ 593 Larry Herndon .15 .06
❑ 594 Bill Swaggerty .15 .06
❑ 595 Carlos Ponce .15 .06
❑ 596 Pat Perry .15 .06
❑ 597 Ray Knight .25 .10
❑ 598 Steve Lombardozzi .15 .06
❑ 599 Brad Havens .15 .06
❑ 600 Pat Clements .15 .06
❑ 601 Joe Niekro .15 .06
❑ 602 Hank Aaron .75 .30
Puzzle Card
❑ 603 Dwayne Henry .15 .06
❑ 604 Mookie Wilson .25 .10
❑ 605 Buddy Biancalana .15 .06
❑ 606 Rance Mulliniks .15 .06
❑ 607 Alan Wiggins .15 .06
❑ 608 Joe Cowley .15 .06
❑ 609 Tom Seaver .50 .20
(Green borders on name)
❑ 609B Tom Seaver 2.00 .80
(Yellow borders on name)
❑ 610 Neil Allen .15 .06
❑ 611 Don Sutton .25 .10
❑ 612 Fred Toliver .15 .06
❑ 613 Jay Baller .15 .06
❑ 614 Marc Sullivan .15 .06
❑ 615 John Grubb .15 .06
❑ 616 Bruce Kison .15 .06
❑ 617 Bill Madlock .25 .10
❑ 618 Chris Chambliss .25 .10
❑ 619 Dave Stewart .25 .10
❑ 620 Tim Lollar .15 .06
❑ 621 Gary Lavelle .15 .06
❑ 622 Charles Hudson .15 .06
❑ 623 Joel Davis .15 .06
❑ 624 Joe Johnson .15 .06
❑ 625 Sid Fernandez .15 .06
❑ 626 Dennis Lamp .15 .06
❑ 627 Terry Harper .15 .06
❑ 628 Jack Lazorko .15 .06
❑ 629 Roger McDowell RC* .50 .20
❑ 630 Mark Funderburk .15 .06
❑ 631 Ed Lynch .15 .06
❑ 632 Rudy Law .15 .06
❑ 633 Roger Mason RC .15 .06
❑ 634 Mike Felder RC .15 .06
❑ 635 Ken Schrom .15 .06
❑ 636 Bob Ojeda .15 .06
❑ 637 Ed VandeBerg .15 .06
❑ 638 Bobby Meacham .15 .06
❑ 639 Cliff Johnson .15 .06
❑ 640 Garth Iorg .15 .06
❑ 641 Dan Driessen .15 .06
❑ 642 Mike Brown OF .15 .06
❑ 643 John Shelby .15 .06
❑ 644 Pete Rose RB .75 .30
❑ 645 Phil Niekro .25 .10
Joe Niekro
❑ 646 Jesse Orosco .15 .06
❑ 647 Billy Beane RC 1.00 .40
❑ 648 Cesar Cedeno .25 .10
❑ 649 Bert Blyleven .25 .10
❑ 650 Max Venable .15 .06
❑ 651 Vince Coleman .15 .06
Willie McGee
❑ 652 Calvin Schiraldi .15 .06
❑ 653 Pete Rose KING .75 .30
❑ 654 Dia. Kings CL 1-26 .15 .06
(Unnumbered)
❑ 655A CL 1: 27-130 .15 .06
(Unnumbered)
(45 Beane ERR)
❑ 655B CL 1: 27-130 .15 .06
(Unnumbered)
(45 Habyan COR)
❑ 656 CL 2: 131-234 .15 .06
(Unnumbered)
❑ 657 CL 3: 235-338 .15 .06
(Unnumbered)
❑ 658 CL 4: 339-442 .15 .06
(Unnumbered)
❑ 659 CL 5: 443-546 .15 .06
(Unnumbered)
❑ 660 CL 6: 547-653 .15 .06
(Unnumbered)

1986 Donruss Rookies

	Nm-Mt	Ex-Mt
COMP.FACT.SET (56)	40.00	16.00

❑ 1 Wally Joyner XRC 1.00 .40
❑ 2 Tracy Jones .15 .06
❑ 3 Allan Anderson .15 .06
❑ 4 Ed Correa .15 .06
❑ 5 Reggie Williams .15 .06
❑ 6 Charlie Kerfeld .15 .06
❑ 7 Andres Galarraga 1.25 .50
❑ 8 Bob Tewksbury XRC .50 .20
❑ 9 Al Newman .25 .10
❑ 10 Andres Thomas .15 .06
❑ 11 Barry Bonds XRC 30.00 12.00
❑ 12 Juan Nieves .15 .06
❑ 13 Mark Eichhorn .15 .06
❑ 14 Dan Plesac XRC .50 .20
❑ 15 Cory Snyder .15 .06
❑ 16 Kelly Gruber .15 .06
❑ 17 Kevin Mitchell XRC 1.00 .40
❑ 18 Steve Lombardozzi .15 .06
❑ 19 Mitch Williams XRC .50 .20
❑ 20 John Cerutti .15 .06
❑ 21 Todd Worrell .50 .20
❑ 22 Jose Canseco 4.00 1.60
❑ 23 Pete Incaviglia XRC .50 .20
❑ 24 Jose Guzman .15 .06
❑ 25 Scott Bailes .15 .06
❑ 26 Greg Mathews .15 .06
❑ 27 Eric King .15 .06
❑ 28 Paul Assenmacher .50 .20
❑ 29 Jeff Sellers .15 .06
❑ 30 Bobby Bonilla XRC 1.00 .40
❑ 31 Doug Drabek XRC 1.00 .40
❑ 32 Will Clark UER 2.00 .80
(Listed as throwing right, should be left) XRC
❑ 33 Bip Roberts XRC .50 .20
❑ 34 Jim Deshaies XRC .15 .06
❑ 35 Mike LaValliere XRC .50 .20
❑ 36 Scott Bankhead .15 .06
❑ 37 Dale Sveum .15 .06
❑ 38 Bo Jackson XRC 5.00 2.00
❑ 39 Robby Thompson XRC .50 .20
❑ 40 Eric Plunk .15 .06
❑ 41 Bill Bathe .15 .06
❑ 42 John Kruk XRC 1.50 .60
❑ 43 Andy Allanson .15 .06
❑ 44 Mark Portugal XRC .50 .20
❑ 45 Danny Tartabull .25 .10
❑ 46 Bob Kipper .15 .06
❑ 47 Gene Walter .15 .06
❑ 48 Rey Quinones UER .15 .06
(Misspelled Quinonez)
❑ 49 Bobby Witt XRC .50 .20
❑ 50 Bill Mooneyham .15 .06
❑ 51 John Cangelosi .15 .06
❑ 52 Ruben Sierra XRC 1.25 .50
❑ 53 Rob Woodward .15 .06
❑ 54 Ed Hearn .15 .06
❑ 55 Joel McKeon .15 .06
❑ 56 Checklist 1-56 .15 .06

1987 Donruss

	Nm-Mt	Ex-Mt
COMPLETE SET (660)	40.00	16.00
COMP.FACT.SET (660)	50.00	20.00
COMP.CLEMENTE PUZZLE	1.50	.60

❑ 1 Wally Joyner DK .40 .16
❑ 2 Roger Clemens DK 1.00 .40
❑ 3 Dale Murphy DK .25 .10
❑ 4 Darryl Strawberry DK .15 .06
❑ 5 Ozzie Smith DK .60 .24
❑ 6 Jose Canseco DK 1.00 .40
❑ 7 Charlie Hough DK .15 .06
❑ 8 Brook Jacoby DK .10 .04
❑ 9 Fred Lynn DK .15 .06
❑ 10 Rick Rhoden DK .10 .04
❑ 11 Chris Brown DK .10 .04
❑ 12 Von Hayes DK .10 .04
❑ 13 Jack Morris DK .15 .06
❑ 14A Kevin McReynolds DK .40 .16
ERR (Yellow strip missing on back)
❑ 14B Kevin McReynolds DK .10 .04
COR
❑ 15 George Brett DK 1.00 .40
❑ 16 Ted Higuera DK .10 .04
❑ 17 Hubie Brooks DK .10 .04
❑ 18 Mike Scott DK .15 .06
❑ 19 Kirby Puckett DK .40 .16
❑ 20 Dave Winfield DK .15 .06
❑ 21 Lloyd Moseby DK .10 .04
❑ 22A Eric Davis DK ERR .40 .16
(Yellow strip missing on back)
❑ 22B Eric Davis DK COR .25 .10
❑ 23 Jim Presley DK .10 .04
❑ 24 Keith Moreland DK .10 .04
❑ 25A Greg Walker DK ERR .40 .16
(Yellow strip missing on back)
❑ 25B Greg Walker DK COR .10 .04
❑ 26 Steve Sax DK .10 .04
❑ 27 DK Checklist 1-26 .10 .04
❑ 28 B.J. Surhoff RR RC .60 .24
❑ 29 Randy Myers RR RC .60 .24
❑ 30 Ken Gerhart RC .15 .06

❑ 31 Benito Santiago .15 .06
❑ 32 Greg Swindell RR RC .40 .16
❑ 33 Mike Birkbeck RC .15 .06
❑ 34 Terry Steinbach RR RC .60 .24
❑ 35 Bo Jackson RR RC 5.00 2.00
❑ 36 Greg Maddux UER RC 10.00 4.00
middle name misspelled "Allen"
❑ 37 Jim Lindeman RC .15 .06
❑ 38 Devon White RR RC .60 .24
❑ 39 Eric Bell RC .15 .06
❑ 40 Willie Fraser RC .15 .06
❑ 41 Jerry Browne RR RC .15 .06
❑ 42 Chris James RR RC* .15 .06
❑ 43 Rafael Palmeiro RR RC 5.00 2.00
❑ 44 Pat Dodson RC .15 .06
❑ 45 Duane Ward RR RC* .40 .16
❑ 46 Mark McGwire RR 8.00 3.20
❑ 47 Bruce Fields UER RC .15 .06
(Photo actually
Darnell Coles)
❑ 48 Eddie Murray .40 .16
❑ 49 Ted Higuera .10 .04
❑ 50 Kirk Gibson .25 .10
❑ 51 Oil Can Boyd .10 .04
❑ 52 Don Mattingly 1.25 .50
❑ 53 Pedro Guerrero .15 .06
❑ 54 George Brett 1.00 .40
❑ 55 Jose Rijo .15 .06
❑ 56 Tim Raines .15 .06
❑ 57 Ed Correa .10 .04
❑ 58 Mike Witt .10 .04
❑ 59 Greg Walker .10 .04
❑ 60 Ozzie Smith .60 .24
❑ 61 Glenn Davis .10 .04
❑ 62 Glenn Wilson .10 .04
❑ 63 Tom Browning .10 .04
❑ 64 Tony Gwynn .60 .24
❑ 65 R.J. Reynolds .10 .04
❑ 66 Will Clark RC 1.50 .60
❑ 67 Ozzie Virgil .10 .04
❑ 68 Rick Sutcliffe .15 .06
❑ 69 Gary Carter .15 .06
❑ 70 Mike Moore .10 .04
❑ 71 Bert Blyleven .15 .06
❑ 72 Tony Fernandez .10 .04
❑ 73 Kent Hrbek .15 .06
❑ 74 Lloyd Moseby .10 .04
❑ 75 Alvin Davis .10 .04
❑ 76 Keith Hernandez .15 .06
❑ 77 Ryne Sandberg .75 .30
❑ 78 Dale Murphy .25 .10
❑ 79 Sid Bream .10 .04
❑ 80 Chris Brown .10 .04
❑ 81 Steve Garvey .15 .06
❑ 82 Mario Soto .15 .06
❑ 83 Shane Rawley .10 .04
❑ 84 Willie McGee .15 .06
❑ 85 Jose Cruz .15 .06
❑ 86 Brian Downing .15 .06
❑ 87 Ozzie Guillen .25 .10
❑ 88 Hubie Brooks .10 .04
❑ 89 Cal Ripken 1.50 .60
❑ 90 Juan Nieves .10 .04
❑ 91 Lance Parrish .15 .06
❑ 92 Jim Rice .15 .06
❑ 93 Ron Guidry .15 .06
❑ 94 Fernando Valenzuela .15 .06
❑ 95 Andy Allanson .10 .04
❑ 96 Willie Wilson .15 .06
❑ 97 Jose Canseco 1.00 .40
❑ 98 Jeff Reardon .15 .06
❑ 99 Bobby Witt RC .40 .16
❑ 100 Checklist 28-133 .10 .04
❑ 101 Jose Guzman .10 .04
❑ 102 Steve Balboni .10 .04
❑ 103 Tony Phillips .10 .04
❑ 104 Brook Jacoby .10 .04
❑ 105 Dave Winfield .15 .06
❑ 106 Orel Hershiser .25 .10
❑ 107 Lou Whitaker .15 .06
❑ 108 Fred Lynn .15 .06
❑ 109 Bill Wegman .10 .04
❑ 110 Donnie Moore .10 .04
❑ 111 Jack Clark .15 .06
❑ 112 Bob Knepper .10 .04
❑ 113 Von Hayes .10 .04
❑ 114 Bip Roberts RC* .40 .16
❑ 115 Tony Pena .10 .04
❑ 116 Scott Garrelts .10 .04
❑ 117 Paul Molitor .25 .10
❑ 118 Darryl Strawberry .15 .06
❑ 119 Shawon Dunston .10 .04
❑ 120 Jim Presley .10 .04
❑ 121 Jesse Barfield .15 .06
❑ 122 Gary Gaetti .15 .06
❑ 123 Kurt Stillwell .10 .04
❑ 124 Joel Davis .10 .04
❑ 125 Mike Boddicker .10 .04
❑ 126 Robin Yount .60 .24
❑ 127 Alan Trammell .15 .06
❑ 128 Dave Righetti .15 .06
❑ 129 Dwight Evans .25 .10
❑ 130 Mike Scioscia .15 .06
❑ 131 Julio Franco .15 .06
❑ 132 Bret Saberhagen .15 .06
❑ 133 Mike Davis .10 .04
❑ 134 Joe Hesketh .10 .04
❑ 135 Wally Joyner RC .60 .24
❑ 136 Don Slaught .10 .04
❑ 137 Daryl Boston .10 .04
❑ 138 Nolan Ryan 2.00 .80
❑ 139 Mike Schmidt 1.00 .40
❑ 140 Tommy Herr .10 .04
❑ 141 Garry Templeton .15 .06
❑ 142 Kal Daniels .10 .04
❑ 143 Billy Sample .10 .04
❑ 144 Johnny Ray .10 .04
❑ 145 Rob Thompson RC* .40 .16
❑ 146 Bob Dernier .10 .04
❑ 147 Danny Tartabull .10 .04
❑ 148 Ernie Whitt .10 .04
❑ 149 Kirby Puckett .40 .16
❑ 150 Mike Young .10 .04
❑ 151 Ernest Riles .10 .04
❑ 152 Frank Tanana .15 .06
❑ 153 Rich Gedman .10 .04
❑ 154 Willie Randolph .15 .06
❑ 155 Bill Madlock .15 .06
❑ 156 Joe Carter .15 .06
❑ 157 Danny Jackson .10 .04
❑ 158 Carney Lansford .15 .06
❑ 159 Bryn Smith .10 .04
❑ 160 Gary Pettis .10 .04
❑ 161 Oddibe McDowell .10 .04
❑ 162 John Cangelosi .10 .04
❑ 163 Mike Scott .15 .06
❑ 164 Eric Show .10 .04
❑ 165 Juan Samuel .10 .04
❑ 166 Nick Esasky .10 .04
❑ 167 Zane Smith .10 .04
❑ 168 Mike C. Brown OF .10 .04
❑ 169 Keith Moreland .10 .04
❑ 170 John Tudor .15 .06
❑ 171 Ken Dixon .10 .04
❑ 172 Jim Gantner .10 .04
❑ 173 Jack Morris .15 .06
❑ 174 Bruce Hurst .10 .04
❑ 175 Dennis Rasmussen .10 .04
❑ 176 Mike Marshall .10 .04
❑ 177 Dan Quisenberry .10 .04
❑ 178 Eric Plunk .10 .04
❑ 179 Tim Wallach .10 .04
❑ 180 Steve Buechele .10 .04
❑ 181 Don Sutton .15 .06
❑ 182 Dave Schmidt .10 .04
❑ 183 Terry Pendleton .15 .06
❑ 184 Jim Deshaies RC * .15 .06
❑ 185 Steve Bedrosian .10 .04
❑ 186 Pete Rose 1.25 .50
❑ 187 Dave Dravecky .10 .04
❑ 188 Rick Reuschel .15 .06
❑ 189 Dan Gladden .10 .04
❑ 190 Rick Mahler .10 .04
❑ 191 Thad Bosley .10 .04
❑ 192 Ron Darling .15 .06
❑ 193 Matt Young .10 .04
❑ 194 Tom Brunansky .10 .04
❑ 195 Dave Stieb .15 .06
❑ 196 Frank Viola .15 .06
❑ 197 Tom Henke .10 .04
❑ 198 Karl Best .10 .04
❑ 199 Dwight Gooden .25 .10
❑ 200 Checklist 134-239 .10 .04
❑ 201 Steve Trout .10 .04
❑ 202 Rafael Ramirez .10 .04
❑ 203 Bob Walk .10 .04
❑ 204 Roger Mason .10 .04
❑ 205 Terry Kennedy .10 .04
❑ 206 Ron Oester .10 .04
❑ 207 John Russell .10 .04
❑ 208 Greg Mathews .10 .04
❑ 209 Charlie Kerfeld .10 .04
❑ 210 Reggie Jackson .25 .10
❑ 211 Floyd Bannister .10 .04
❑ 212 Vance Law .10 .04
❑ 213 Rich Bordi .10 .04
❑ 214 Dan Plesac .10 .04
❑ 215 Dave Collins .10 .04
❑ 216 Bob Stanley .10 .04
❑ 217 Joe Niekro .10 .04
❑ 218 Tom Niedenfuer .10 .04
❑ 219 Brett Butler .15 .06
❑ 220 Charlie Leibrandt .10 .04
❑ 221 Steve Ontiveros .10 .04
❑ 222 Tim Burke .10 .04
❑ 223 Curtis Wilkerson .10 .04
❑ 224 Pete Incaviglia RC * .40 .16
❑ 225 Lonnie Smith .10 .04
❑ 226 Chris Codiroli .10 .04
❑ 227 Scott Bailes .10 .04
❑ 228 Rickey Henderson .40 .16
❑ 229 Ken Howell .10 .04
❑ 230 Darnell Coles .10 .04
❑ 231 Don Aase .10 .04
❑ 232 Tim Leary .10 .04
❑ 233 Bob Boone .15 .06
❑ 234 Ricky Horton .10 .04
❑ 235 Mark Bailey .10 .04
❑ 236 Kevin Gross .10 .04
❑ 237 Lance McCullers .10 .04
❑ 238 Cecilio Guante .10 .04
❑ 239 Bob Melvin .10 .04
❑ 240 Billy Joe Robidoux .10 .04
❑ 241 Roger McDowell .10 .04
❑ 242 Leon Durham .10 .04
❑ 243 Ed Nunez .10 .04
❑ 244 Jimmy Key .15 .06
❑ 245 Mike Smithson .10 .04
❑ 246 Bo Diaz .10 .04
❑ 247 Carlton Fisk .25 .10
❑ 248 Larry Sheets .10 .04
❑ 249 Juan Castillo RC .15 .06
❑ 250 Eric King .10 .04
❑ 251 Doug Drabek RC .60 .24
❑ 252 Wade Boggs .25 .10
❑ 253 Mariano Duncan .10 .04
❑ 254 Pat Tabler .10 .04
❑ 255 Frank White .15 .06
❑ 256 Alfredo Griffin .10 .04
❑ 257 Floyd Youmans .10 .04
❑ 258 Rob Wilfong .10 .04
❑ 259 Pete O'Brien .10 .04
❑ 260 Tim Hulett .10 .04
❑ 261 Dickie Thon .10 .04
❑ 262 Darren Daulton .15 .06
❑ 263 Vince Coleman .10 .04
❑ 264 Andy Hawkins .10 .04
❑ 265 Eric Davis .25 .10
❑ 266 Andres Thomas .10 .04
❑ 267 Mike Diaz .10 .04
❑ 268 Chili Davis .15 .06
❑ 269 Jody Davis .10 .04
❑ 270 Phil Bradley .10 .04
❑ 271 George Bell .15 .06
❑ 272 Keith Atherton .10 .04
❑ 273 Storm Davis .10 .04
❑ 274 Rob Deer .10 .04
❑ 275 Walt Terrell .10 .04
❑ 276 Roger Clemens 1.00 .40
❑ 277 Mike Easler .10 .04
❑ 278 Steve Sax .10 .04
❑ 279 Andre Thornton .10 .04
❑ 280 Jim Sundberg .15 .06
❑ 281 Bill Bathe .10 .04
❑ 282 Jay Tibbs .10 .04
❑ 283 Dick Schofield .10 .04
❑ 284 Mike Mason .10 .04
❑ 285 Jerry Hairston .10 .04

	No.	Player	Mint	Ex
❑	286	Bill Doran	.10	.04
❑	287	Tim Flannery	.10	.04
❑	288	Gary Redus	.10	.04
❑	289	John Franco	.15	.06
❑	290	Paul Assenmacher	.40	.16
❑	291	Joe Orsulak	.10	.04
❑	292	Lee Smith	.15	.06
❑	293	Mike Laga	.10	.04
❑	294	Rick Dempsey	.10	.04
❑	295	Mike Felder	.10	.04
❑	296	Tom Brookens	.10	.04
❑	297	Al Nipper	.10	.04
❑	298	Mike Pagliarulo	.10	.04
❑	299	Franklin Stubbs	.10	.04
❑	300	Checklist 240-345	.10	.04
❑	301	Steve Farr	.10	.04
❑	302	Bill Mooneyham	.10	.04
❑	303	Andres Galarraga	.15	.06
❑	304	Scott Fletcher	.10	.04
❑	305	Jack Howell	.10	.04
❑	306	Russ Morman	.10	.04
❑	307	Todd Worrell	.10	.04
❑	308	Dave Smith	.10	.04
❑	309	Jeff Stone	.10	.04
❑	310	Ron Robinson	.10	.04
❑	311	Bruce Bochy	.10	.04
❑	312	Jim Winn	.10	.04
❑	313	Mark Davis	.10	.04
❑	314	Jeff Dedmon	.10	.04
❑	315	Jamie Moyer RC	1.00	.40
❑	316	Wally Backman	.10	.04
❑	317	Ken Phelps	.10	.04
❑	318	Steve Lombardozzi	.10	.04
❑	319	Rance Mulliniks	.10	.04
❑	320	Tim Laudner	.10	.04
❑	321	Mark Eichhorn	.10	.04
❑	322	Lee Guetterman	.10	.04
❑	323	Sid Fernandez	.10	.04
❑	324	Jerry Mumphrey	.10	.04
❑	325	David Palmer	.10	.04
❑	326	Bill Almon	.10	.04
❑	327	Candy Maldonado	.10	.04
❑	328	John Kruk RC	1.25	.50
❑	329	John Denny	.10	.04
❑	330	Milt Thompson	.10	.04
❑	331	Mike LaValliere RC *	.40	.16
❑	332	Alan Ashby	.10	.04
❑	333	Doug Corbett	.10	.04
❑	334	Ron Karkovice RC	.40	.16
❑	335	Mitch Webster	.10	.04
❑	336	Lee Lacy	.10	.04
❑	337	Glenn Braggs RC	.15	.06
❑	338	Dwight Lowry	.10	.04
❑	339	Don Baylor	.15	.06
❑	340	Brian Fisher	.10	.04
❑	341	Reggie Williams	.10	.04
❑	342	Tom Candiotti	.10	.04
❑	343	Rudy Law	.10	.04
❑	344	Curt Young	.10	.04
❑	345	Mike Fitzgerald	.10	.04
❑	346	Ruben Sierra RC	1.00	.40
❑	347	Mitch Williams RC *	.40	.16
❑	348	Jorge Orta	.10	.04
❑	349	Mickey Tettleton	.10	.04
❑	350	Ernie Camacho	.10	.04
❑	351	Ron Kittle	.10	.04
❑	352	Ken Landreaux	.10	.04
❑	353	Chet Lemon	.15	.06
❑	354	John Shelby	.10	.04
❑	355	Mark Clear	.10	.04
❑	356	Doug DeCinces	.10	.04
❑	357	Ken Dayley	.10	.04
❑	358	Phil Garner	.15	.06
❑	359	Steve Jeltz	.10	.04
❑	360	Ed Whitson	.10	.04
❑	361	Barry Bonds RC	15.00	6.00
❑	362	Vida Blue	.15	.06
❑	363	Cecil Cooper	.15	.06
❑	364	Bob Ojeda	.10	.04
❑	365	Dennis Eckersley	.25	.10
❑	366	Mike Morgan	.10	.04
❑	367	Willie Upshaw	.10	.04
❑	368	Allan Anderson	.10	.04
❑	369	Bill Gullickson	.10	.04
❑	370	Bobby Thigpen RC	.40	.16
❑	371	Juan Beniquez	.10	.04
❑	372	Charlie Moore	.10	.04
❑	373	Dan Petry	.10	.04
❑	374	Rod Scurry	.10	.04
❑	375	Tom Seaver	.25	.10
❑	376	Ed VandeBerg	.10	.04
❑	377	Tony Bernazard	.10	.04
❑	378	Greg Pryor	.10	.04
❑	379	Dwayne Murphy	.10	.04
❑	380	Andy McGaffigan	.10	.04
❑	381	Kirk McCaskill	.10	.04
❑	382	Greg Harris	.10	.04
❑	383	Rich Dotson	.10	.04
❑	384	Craig Reynolds	.10	.04
❑	385	Greg Gross	.10	.04
❑	386	Tito Landrum	.10	.04
❑	387	Craig Lefferts	.10	.04
❑	388	Dave Parker	.15	.06
❑	389	Bob Horner	.15	.06
❑	390	Pat Clements	.10	.04
❑	391	Jeff Leonard	.10	.04
❑	392	Chris Speier	.10	.04
❑	393	John Moses	.10	.04
❑	394	Garth Iorg	.10	.04
❑	395	Greg Gagne	.10	.04
❑	396	Nate Snell	.10	.04
❑	397	Bryan Clutterbuck	.10	.04
❑	398	Darrell Evans	.15	.06
❑	399	Steve Crawford	.10	.04
❑	400	Checklist 346-451	.10	.04
❑	401	Phil Lombardi	.10	.04
❑	402	Rick Honeycutt	.10	.04
❑	403	Ken Schrom	.10	.04
❑	404	Bud Black	.10	.04
❑	405	Donnie Hill	.10	.04
❑	406	Wayne Krenchicki	.10	.04
❑	407	Chuck Finley RC	.60	.24
❑	408	Toby Harrah	.15	.06
❑	409	Steve Lyons	.10	.04
❑	410	Kevin Bass	.10	.04
❑	411	Marvell Wynne	.10	.04
❑	412	Ron Roenicke	.10	.04
❑	413	Tracy Jones	.10	.04
❑	414	Gene Garber	.10	.04
❑	415	Mike Bielecki	.10	.04
❑	416	Frank DiPino	.10	.04
❑	417	Andy Van Slyke	.25	.10
❑	418	Jim Dwyer	.10	.04
❑	419	Ben Oglivie	.15	.06
❑	420	Dave Bergman	.10	.04
❑	421	Joe Sambito	.10	.04
❑	422	Bob Tewksbury RC *	.40	.16
❑	423	Len Matuszek	.10	.04
❑	424	Mike Kingery RC	.15	.06
❑	425	Dave Kingman	.15	.06
❑	426	Al Newman	.10	.04
❑	427	Gary Ward	.10	.04
❑	428	Ruppert Jones	.10	.04
❑	429	Harold Baines	.15	.06
❑	430	Pat Perry	.10	.04
❑	431	Terry Puhl	.10	.04
❑	432	Don Carman	.10	.04
❑	433	Eddie Milner	.10	.04
❑	434	LaMarr Hoyt	.10	.04
❑	435	Rick Rhoden	.10	.04
❑	436	Jose Uribe	.10	.04
❑	437	Ken Oberkfell	.10	.04
❑	438	Ron Davis	.10	.04
❑	439	Jesse Orosco	.10	.04
❑	440	Scott Bradley	.10	.04
❑	441	Randy Bush	.10	.04
❑	442	John Cerutti	.10	.04
❑	443	Roy Smalley	.10	.04
❑	444	Kelly Gruber	.10	.04
❑	445	Bob Kearney	.10	.04
❑	446	Ed Hearn	.10	.04
❑	447	Scott Sanderson	.10	.04
❑	448	Bruce Benedict	.10	.04
❑	449	Junior Ortiz	.10	.04
❑	450	Mike Aldrete	.10	.04
❑	451	Kevin McReynolds	.10	.04
❑	452	Rob Murphy	.10	.04
❑	453	Kent Tekulve	.10	.04
❑	454	Curt Ford	.10	.04
❑	455	Dave Lopes	.15	.06
❑	456	Bob Grich	.15	.06
❑	457	Jose DeLeon	.10	.04
❑	458	Andre Dawson	.15	.06
❑	459	Mike Flanagan	.10	.04
❑	460	Joey Meyer	.15	.06
❑	461	Chuck Cary	.10	.04
❑	462	Bill Buckner	.15	.06
❑	463	Bob Shirley	.10	.04
❑	464	Jeff Hamilton	.10	.04
❑	465	Phil Niekro	.15	.06
❑	466	Mark Gubicza	.10	.04
❑	467	Jerry Willard	.10	.04
❑	468	Bob Sebra	.10	.04
❑	469	Larry Parrish	.10	.04
❑	470	Charlie Hough	.15	.06
❑	471	Hal McRae	.15	.06
❑	472	Dave Leiper	.10	.04
❑	473	Mel Hall	.10	.04
❑	474	Dan Pasqua	.10	.04
❑	475	Bob Welch	.15	.06
❑	476	Johnny Grubb	.10	.04
❑	477	Jim Traber	.10	.04
❑	478	Chris Bosio RC	.40	.16
❑	479	Mark McLemore	.15	.06
❑	480	John Morris	.10	.04
❑	481	Billy Hatcher	.10	.04
❑	482	Dan Schatzeder	.10	.04
❑	483	Rich Gossage	.15	.06
❑	484	Jim Morrison	.10	.04
❑	485	Bob Brenly	.10	.04
❑	486	Bill Schroeder	.10	.04
❑	487	Mookie Wilson	.15	.06
❑	488	Dave Martinez RC	.40	.16
❑	489	Harold Reynolds	.15	.06
❑	490	Jeff Hearron	.10	.04
❑	491	Mickey Hatcher	.10	.04
❑	492	Barry Larkin RC	1.50	.60
❑	493	Bob James	.10	.04
❑	494	John Habyan	.10	.04
❑	495	Jim Adduci	.10	.04
❑	496	Mike Heath	.10	.04
❑	497	Tim Stoddard	.10	.04
❑	498	Tony Armas	.15	.06
❑	499	Dennis Powell	.10	.04
❑	500	Checklist 452-557	.10	.04
❑	501	Chris Bando	.10	.04
❑	502	David Cone RC	1.00	.40
❑	503	Jay Howell	.10	.04
❑	504	Tom Foley	.10	.04
❑	505	Ray Chadwick	.10	.04
❑	506	Mike Loynd RC	.15	.06
❑	507	Neil Allen	.10	.04
❑	508	Danny Darwin	.10	.04
❑	509	Rick Schu	.10	.04
❑	510	Jose Oquendo	.10	.04
❑	511	Gene Walter	.10	.04
❑	512	Terry McGriff	.10	.04
❑	513	Ken Griffey	.15	.06
❑	514	Benny Distefano	.10	.04
❑	515	Terry Mulholland RC	.40	.16
❑	516	Ed Lynch	.10	.04
❑	517	Bill Swift	.10	.04
❑	518	Manny Lee	.10	.04
❑	519	Andre David	.10	.04
❑	520	Scott McGregor	.10	.04
❑	521	Rick Manning	.10	.04
❑	522	Willie Hernandez	.10	.04
❑	523	Marty Barrett	.10	.04
❑	524	Wayne Tolleson	.10	.04
❑	525	Jose Gonzalez RC	.15	.06
❑	526	Cory Snyder	.10	.04
❑	527	Buddy Biancalana	.10	.04
❑	528	Moose Haas	.10	.04
❑	529	Wilfredo Tejada	.10	.04
❑	530	Stu Cliburn	.10	.04
❑	531	Dale Mohorcic	.10	.04
❑	532	Ron Hassey	.10	.04
❑	533	Ty Gainey	.10	.04
❑	534	Jerry Royster	.10	.04
❑	535	Mike Maddux	.10	.04
❑	536	Ted Power	.10	.04
❑	537	Ted Simmons	.15	.06
❑	538	Rafael Belliard RC	.40	.16
❑	539	Chico Walker	.10	.04
❑	540	Bob Forsch	.10	.04
❑	541	John Stefero	.10	.04
❑	542	Dale Sveum	.10	.04
❑	543	Mark Thurmond	.10	.04

		Nm-Mt	Ex-Mt
❑ 544	Jeff Sellers	.10	.04
❑ 545	Joel Skinner	.10	.04
❑ 546	Alex Trevino	.10	.04
❑ 547	Randy Kutcher	.10	.04
❑ 548	Joaquin Andujar	.15	.06
❑ 549	Casey Candaele	.10	.04
❑ 550	Jeff Russell	.10	.04
❑ 551	John Candelaria	.10	.04
❑ 552	Joe Cowley	.10	.04
❑ 553	Danny Cox	.10	.04
❑ 554	Denny Walling	.10	.04
❑ 555	Bruce Ruffin RC	.15	.06
❑ 556	Buddy Bell	.15	.06
❑ 557	Jimmy Jones RC	.15	.06
❑ 558	Bobby Bonilla RC	.60	.24
❑ 559	Jeff D. Robinson	.10	.04
❑ 560	Ed Olwine	.10	.04
❑ 561	Glenallen Hill RC	.40	.16
❑ 562	Lee Mazzilli	.15	.06
❑ 563	Mike G. Brown P	.10	.04
❑ 564	George Frazier	.10	.04
❑ 565	Mike Sharperson RC	.15	.06
❑ 566	Mark Portugal RC *	.40	.16
❑ 567	Rick Leach	.10	.04
❑ 568	Mark Langston	.10	.04
❑ 569	Rafael Santana	.10	.04
❑ 570	Manny Trillo	.10	.04
❑ 571	Cliff Speck	.10	.04
❑ 572	Bob Kipper	.10	.04
❑ 573	Kelly Downs RC	.15	.06
❑ 574	Randy Asadoor	.10	.04
❑ 575	Dave Magadan RC	.40	.16
❑ 576	Marvin Freeman RC	.15	.06
❑ 577	Jeff Lahti	.10	.04
❑ 578	Jeff Calhoun	.10	.04
❑ 579	Gus Polidor	.10	.04
❑ 580	Gene Nelson	.10	.04
❑ 581	Tim Teufel	.10	.04
❑ 582	Odell Jones	.10	.04
❑ 583	Mark Ryal	.10	.04
❑ 584	Randy O'Neal	.10	.04
❑ 585	Mike Greenwell RC	.40	.16
❑ 586	Ray Knight	.15	.06
❑ 587	Ralph Bryant	.10	.04
❑ 588	Carmen Castillo	.10	.04
❑ 589	Ed Wojna	.10	.04
❑ 590	Stan Javier	.10	.04
❑ 591	Jeff Musselman	.10	.04
❑ 592	Mike Stanley RC	.40	.16
❑ 593	Darrell Porter	.10	.04
❑ 594	Drew Hall	.10	.04
❑ 595	Rob Nelson	.10	.04
❑ 596	Bryan Oelkers	.10	.04
❑ 597	Scott Nielsen	.10	.04
❑ 598	Brian Holton	.10	.04
❑ 599	Kevin Mitchell RC *	.60	.24
❑ 600	Checklist 558-660	.10	.04
❑ 601	Jackie Gutierrez	.10	.04
❑ 602	Barry Jones	.10	.04
❑ 603	Jerry Narron	.10	.04
❑ 604	Steve Lake	.10	.04
❑ 605	Jim Pankovits	.10	.04
❑ 606	Ed Romero	.10	.04
❑ 607	Dave LaPoint	.10	.04
❑ 608	Don Robinson	.10	.04
❑ 609	Mike Krukow	.10	.04
❑ 610	Dave Valle RC **	.15	.06
❑ 611	Len Dykstra	.15	.06
❑ 612	R.Clemente PUZ	.50	.20
❑ 613	Mike Trujillo	.10	.04
❑ 614	Damaso Garcia	.10	.04
❑ 615	Neal Heaton	.10	.04
❑ 616	Juan Berenguer	.10	.04
❑ 617	Steve Carlton	.15	.06
❑ 618	Gary Lucas	.10	.04
❑ 619	Geno Petralli	.10	.04
❑ 620	Rick Aguilera	.10	.04
❑ 621	Fred McGriff	.75	.30
❑ 622	Dave Henderson	.10	.04
❑ 623	Dave Clark RC	.15	.06
❑ 624	Angel Salazar	.10	.04
❑ 625	Randy Hunt	.10	.04
❑ 626	John Gibbons	.10	.04
❑ 627	Kevin Brown RC	1.50	.60
❑ 628	Bill Dawley	.10	.04
❑ 629	Aurelio Lopez	.10	.04
❑ 630	Charles Hudson	.10	.04
❑ 631	Ray Soff	.10	.04
❑ 632	Ray Hayward	.10	.04
❑ 633	Spike Owen	.10	.04
❑ 634	Glenn Hubbard	.10	.04
❑ 635	Kevin Elster RC	.40	.16
❑ 636	Mike LaCoss	.10	.04
❑ 637	Dwayne Henry	.10	.04
❑ 638	Rey Quinones	.10	.04
❑ 639	Jim Clancy	.10	.04
❑ 640	Larry Andersen	.10	.04
❑ 641	Calvin Schiraldi	.10	.04
❑ 642	Stan Jefferson	.10	.04
❑ 643	Marc Sullivan	.10	.04
❑ 644	Mark Grant	.10	.04
❑ 645	Cliff Johnson	.10	.04
❑ 646	Howard Johnson	.15	.06
❑ 647	Dave Sax	.10	.04
❑ 648	Dave Stewart	.15	.06
❑ 649	Danny Heep	.10	.04
❑ 650	Joe Johnson	.10	.04
❑ 651	Bob Brower	.10	.04
❑ 652	Rob Woodward	.10	.04
❑ 653	John Mizerock	.10	.04
❑ 654	Tim Pyznarski	.10	.04
❑ 655	Luis Aquino	.10	.04
❑ 656	Mickey Brantley	.10	.04
❑ 657	Doyle Alexander	.10	.04
❑ 658	Sammy Stewart	.10	.04
❑ 659	Jim Acker	.10	.04
❑ 660	Pete Ladd	.10	.04

1987 Donruss Rookies

		Nm-Mt	Ex-Mt
COMP.FACT.SET (56)		25.00	10.00
❑ 1	Mark McGwire	10.00	4.00
❑ 2	Eric Bell	.15	.06
❑ 3	Mark Williamson	.10	.04
❑ 4	Mike Greenwell	.40	.16
❑ 5	Ellis Burks XRC	.60	.24
❑ 6	DeWayne Buice	.10	.04
❑ 7	Mark McLemore	.25	.10
❑ 8	Devon White	.60	.24
❑ 9	Willie Fraser	.15	.06
❑ 10	Les Lancaster	.10	.04
❑ 11	Ken Williams XRC	.10	.04
❑ 12	Matt Nokes XRC	.40	.16
❑ 13	Jeff M. Robinson	.10	.04
❑ 14	Bo Jackson	5.00	2.00
❑ 15	Kevin Seitzer XRC	.40	.16
❑ 16	Billy Ripken XRC	.40	.16
❑ 17	B.J. Surhoff	.60	.24
❑ 18	Chuck Crim	.10	.04
❑ 19	Mike Birkbeck	.15	.06
❑ 20	Chris Bosio	.40	.16
❑ 21	Les Straker	.10	.04
❑ 22	Mark Davidson	.10	.04
❑ 23	Gene Larkin XRC	.40	.16
❑ 24	Ken Gerhart	.10	.04
❑ 25	Luis Polonia XRC	.40	.16
❑ 26	Terry Steinbach	.60	.24
❑ 27	Mickey Brantley	.10	.04
❑ 28	Mike Stanley	.40	.16
❑ 29	Jerry Browne	.15	.06
❑ 30	Todd Benzinger XRC	.40	.16
❑ 31	Fred McGriff	1.50	.60
❑ 32	Mike Henneman XRC	.40	.16
❑ 33	Casey Candaele	.10	.04
❑ 34	Dave Magadan	.40	.16
❑ 35	David Cone	1.00	.40
❑ 36	Mike Jackson XRC	.40	.16
❑ 37	John Mitchell XRC	.15	.06
❑ 38	Mike Dunne	.10	.04
❑ 39	John Smiley XRC	.40	.16
❑ 40	Joe Magrane XRC	.15	.06
❑ 41	Jim Lindeman	.15	.06
❑ 42	Shane Mack	.10	.04
❑ 43	Stan Jefferson	.10	.04
❑ 44	Benito Santiago	.25	.10
❑ 45	Matt Williams XRC	2.50	1.00
❑ 46	Dave Meads	.10	.04
❑ 47	Rafael Palmeiro	5.00	2.00
❑ 48	Bill Long	.10	.04
❑ 49	Bob Brower	.10	.04
❑ 50	James Steels	.10	.04
❑ 51	Paul Noce	.10	.04
❑ 52	Greg Maddux	8.00	3.20
❑ 53	Jeff Musselman	.10	.04
❑ 54	Brian Holton	.10	.04
❑ 55	Chuck Jackson	.10	.04
❑ 56	Checklist 1-56	.10	.04

1987 Donruss Opening Day

		Nm-Mt	Ex-Mt
COMP.FACT. SET (272)		50.00	20.00
163A LISTED IN NEAR MINT CONDITION			.00
❑ 1	Doug DeCinces	.10	.04
❑ 2	Mike Witt	.10	.04
❑ 3	George Hendrick	.15	.06
❑ 4	Dick Schofield	.10	.04
❑ 5	Devon White	.60	.24
❑ 6	Butch Wynegar	.10	.04
❑ 7	Wally Joyner	.25	.10
❑ 8	Mark McLemore	.15	.06
❑ 9	Brian Downing	.15	.06
❑ 10	Gary Pettis	.10	.04
❑ 11	Bill Doran	.10	.04
❑ 12	Phil Garner	.15	.06
❑ 13	Jose Cruz	.15	.06
❑ 14	Kevin Bass	.10	.04
❑ 15	Mike Scott	.15	.06
❑ 16	Glenn Davis	.10	.04
❑ 17	Alan Ashby	.10	.04
❑ 18	Billy Hatcher	.10	.04
❑ 19	Craig Reynolds	.10	.04
❑ 20	Carney Lansford	.15	.06
❑ 21	Mike Davis	.10	.04
❑ 22	Reggie Jackson	.25	.10
❑ 23	Mickey Tettleton	.10	.04
❑ 24	Jose Canseco	1.50	.60
❑ 25	Rob Nelson	.10	.04
❑ 26	Tony Phillips	.10	.04
❑ 27	Dwayne Murphy	.10	.04
❑ 28	Alfredo Griffin	.10	.04
❑ 29	Curt Young	.10	.04
❑ 30	Willie Upshaw	.10	.04
❑ 31	Mike Sharperson	.10	.04
❑ 32	Rance Mulliniks	.10	.04
❑ 33	Ernie Whitt	.10	.04
❑ 34	Jesse Barfield	.15	.06
❑ 35	Tony Fernandez	.10	.04
❑ 36	Lloyd Moseby	.10	.04

No.	Player	Nm-Mt	Ex-Mt
37	Jimmy Key	.15	.06
38	Fred McGriff	.75	.30
39	George Bell	.15	.06
40	Dale Murphy	.25	.10
41	Rick Mahler	.10	.04
42	Ken Griffey	.15	.06
43	Andres Thomas	.10	.04
44	Dion James	.10	.04
45	Ozzie Virgil	.10	.04
46	Ken Oberkfell	.10	.04
47	Gary Roenicke	.10	.04
48	Glenn Hubbard	.10	.04
49	Bill Schroeder	.10	.04
50	Greg Brock	.10	.04
51	Billy Joe Robidoux	.10	.04
52	Glenn Braggs	.15	.06
53	Jim Gantner	.10	.04
54	Paul Molitor	.25	.10
55	Dale Sveum	.10	.04
56	Ted Higuera	.10	.04
57	Rob Deer	.10	.04
58	Robin Yount	.60	.24
59	Jim Lindeman	.15	.06
60	Vince Coleman	.10	.04
61	Tommy Herr	.10	.04
62	Terry Pendleton	.15	.06
63	John Tudor	.15	.06
64	Tony Pena	.10	.04
65	Ozzie Smith	.60	.24
66	Tito Landrum	.10	.04
67	Jack Clark	.15	.06
68	Bob Dernier	.10	.04
69	Rick Sutcliffe	.15	.06
70	Andre Dawson	.15	.06
71	Keith Moreland	.10	.04
72	Jody Davis	.10	.04
73	Brian Dayett	.10	.04
74	Leon Durham	.10	.04
75	Ryne Sandberg	.75	.30
76	Shawon Dunston	.10	.04
77	Mike Marshall	.10	.04
78	Bill Madlock	.15	.06
79	Orel Hershiser	.25	.10
80	Mike Ramsey	.10	.04
81	Ken Landreaux	.10	.04
82	Mike Scioscia	.15	.06
83	Franklin Stubbs	.10	.04
84	Mariano Duncan	.10	.04
85	Steve Sax	.10	.04
86	Mitch Webster	.10	.04
87	Reid Nichols	.10	.04
88	Tim Wallach	.10	.04
89	Floyd Youmans	.10	.04
90	Andres Galarraga	.15	.06
91	Hubie Brooks	.10	.04
92	Jeff Reed	.10	.04
93	Alonzo Powell	.10	.04
94	Vance Law	.10	.04
95	Bob Brenly	.10	.04
96	Will Clark	2.00	.80
97	Chili Davis	.15	.06
98	Mike Krukow	.10	.04
99	Jose Uribe	.10	.04
100	Chris Brown	.10	.04
101	Robby Thompson	.40	.16
102	Candy Maldonado	.10	.04
103	Jeff Leonard	.10	.04
104	Tom Candiotti	.10	.04
105	Chris Bando	.10	.04
106	Cory Snyder	.10	.04
107	Pat Tabler	.10	.04
108	Andre Thornton	.10	.04
109	Joe Carter	.15	.06
110	Tony Bernazard	.10	.04
111	Julio Franco	.15	.06
112	Brook Jacoby	.10	.04
113	Brett Butler	.15	.06
114	Donell Nixon	.10	.04
115	Alvin Davis	.10	.04
116	Mark Langston	.10	.04
117	Harold Reynolds	.15	.06
118	Ken Phelps	.10	.04
119	Mike Kingery	.15	.06
120	Dave Valle	.15	.06
121	Rey Quinones	.10	.04
122	Phil Bradley	.10	.04
123	Jim Presley	.10	.04
124	Keith Hernandez	.15	.06
125	Kevin McReynolds	.10	.04
126	Rafael Santana	.10	.04
127	Bob Ojeda	.10	.04
128	Darryl Strawberry	.15	.06
129	Mookie Wilson	.15	.06
130	Gary Carter	.15	.06
131	Tim Teufel	.10	.04
132	Howard Johnson	.15	.06
133	Cal Ripken	1.50	.60
134	Rick Burleson	.10	.04
135	Fred Lynn	.15	.06
136	Eddie Murray	.40	.16
137	Ray Knight	.15	.06
138	Alan Wiggins	.10	.04
139	John Shelby	.10	.04
140	Mike Boddicker	.10	.04
141	Ken Gerhart	.10	.04
142	Terry Kennedy	.10	.04
143	Steve Garvey	.15	.06
144	Marvell Wynne	.10	.04
145	Kevin Mitchell	.25	.10
146	Tony Gwynn	.60	.24
147	Joey Cora	.40	.16
148	Benito Santiago	.15	.06
149	Eric Show	.10	.04
150	Garry Templeton	.15	.06
151	Carmelo Martinez	.10	.04
152	Von Hayes	.10	.04
153	Lance Parrish	.15	.06
154	Milt Thompson	.10	.04
155	Mike Easler	.10	.04
156	Juan Samuel	.10	.04
157	Steve Jeltz	.10	.04
158	Glenn Wilson	.10	.04
159	Shane Rawley	.10	.04
160	Mike Schmidt	1.00	.40
161	Andy Van Slyke	.25	.10
162	Johnny Ray	.10	.04
163A	Barry Bonds ERR (Photo actually Johnny Ray wearing a black shirt)	300.00	120.00
163B	Barry Bonds COR	15.00	6.00
164	Junior Ortiz	.10	.04
165	Rafael Belliard	.40	.16
166	Bob Patterson	.10	.04
167	Bobby Bonilla	.60	.24
168	Sid Bream	.10	.04
169	Jim Morrison	.10	.04
170	Jerry Browne	.15	.06
171	Scott Fletcher	.10	.04
172	Ruben Sierra	1.00	.40
173	Larry Parrish	.10	.04
174	Pete O'Brien	.10	.04
175	Pete Incaviglia	.40	.16
176	Don Slaught	.10	.04
177	Oddibe McDowell	.10	.04
178	Charlie Hough	.15	.06
179	Steve Buechele	.10	.04
180	Bob Stanley	.10	.04
181	Wade Boggs	.25	.10
182	Jim Rice	.15	.06
183	Bill Buckner	.15	.06
184	Dwight Evans	.25	.10
185	Spike Owen	.10	.04
186	Don Baylor	.15	.06
187	Marc Sullivan	.10	.04
188	Marty Barrett	.10	.04
189	Dave Henderson	.10	.04
190	Bo Diaz	.10	.04
191	Barry Larkin	2.00	.80
192	Kal Daniels	.10	.04
193	Terry Francona	.15	.06
194	Tom Browning	.10	.04
195	Ron Oester	.10	.04
196	Buddy Bell	.15	.06
197	Eric Davis	.25	.10
198	Dave Parker	.15	.06
199	Steve Balboni	.10	.04
200	Danny Tartabull	.10	.04
201	Ed Hearn	.10	.04
202	Buddy Biancalana	.10	.04
203	Danny Jackson	.10	.04
204	Frank White	.15	.06
205	Bo Jackson	5.00	2.00
206	George Brett	1.00	.40
207	Kevin Seitzer	.15	.06
208	Willie Wilson	.15	.06
209	Orlando Mercado	.10	.04
210	Darrell Evans	.15	.06
211	Larry Herndon	.10	.04
212	Jack Morris	.15	.06
213	Chet Lemon	.15	.06
214	Mike Heath	.10	.04
215	Darnell Coles	.10	.04
216	Alan Trammell	.15	.06
217	Terry Harper	.10	.04
218	Lou Whitaker	.15	.06
219	Gary Gaetti	.15	.06
220	Tom Nieto	.10	.04
221	Kirby Puckett	.40	.16
222	Tom Brunansky	.10	.04
223	Greg Gagne	.10	.04
224	Dan Gladden	.10	.04
225	Mark Davidson	.10	.04
226	Bert Blyleven	.15	.06
227	Steve Lombardozzi	.10	.04
228	Kent Hrbek	.15	.06
229	Gary Redus	.10	.04
230	Ivan Calderon	.10	.04
231	Tim Hulett	.10	.04
232	Carlton Fisk	.25	.10
233	Greg Walker	.10	.04
234	Ron Karkovice	.40	.16
235	Ozzie Guillen	.25	.10
236	Harold Baines	.15	.06
237	Donnie Hill	.10	.04
238	Rich Dotson	.10	.04
239	Mike Pagliarulo	.10	.04
240	Joel Skinner	.10	.04
241	Don Mattingly	1.25	.50
242	Gary Ward	.10	.04
243	Dave Winfield	.15	.06
244	Dan Pasqua	.10	.04
245	Wayne Tolleson	.10	.04
246	Willie Randolph	.15	.06
247	Dennis Rasmussen	.10	.04
248	Rickey Henderson	.40	.16
249	Angels Logo	.00	.00
250	Astros Logo	.00	.00
251	A's Logo	.00	.00
252	Blue Jays Logo	.00	.00
253	Braves Logo	.00	.00
254	Brewers Logo	.00	.00
255	Cardinals Logo	.00	.00
256	Dodgers Logo	.00	.00
257	Expos Logo	.00	.00
258	Giants Logo	.00	.00
259	Indians Logo	.00	.00
260	Mariners Logo	.00	.00
261	Orioles Logo	.00	.00
262	Padres Logo	.00	.00
263	Phillies Logo	.00	.00
264	Pirates Logo	.00	.00
265	Rangers Logo	.00	.00
266	Red Sox Logo	.00	.00
267	Reds Logo	.00	.00
268	Royals Logo	.00	.00
269	Tigers Logo	.00	.00
270	Twins Logo	.00	.00
271	Chicago Logos	.00	.00
272	New York Logos	.00	.00

1988 Donruss

	Nm-Mt	Ex-Mt
COMPLETE SET (660)	10.00	4.00
COMP.FACT.SET (660)	15.00	6.00
COMMON CARD (1-660)	.05	.02
COMMON SP (648-660)	.10	.04

No.	Player	Nm-Mt	Ex-Mt
1	Mark McGwire DK	.75	.30
2	Tim Raines DK	.10	.04
3	Benito Santiago DK	.10	.04
4	Alan Trammell DK	.10	.04
5	Danny Tartabull DK	.05	.02
6	Ron Darling DK	.10	.04
7	Paul Molitor DK	.15	.06
8	Devon White DK	.10	.04
9	Andre Dawson DK	.05	.02

❑ 10	Julio Franco DK	.10	.04
❑ 11	Scott Fletcher DK	.05	.02
❑ 12	Tony Fernandez DK	.05	.02
❑ 13	Shane Rawley DK	.05	.02
❑ 14	Kal Daniels DK	.05	.02
❑ 15	Jack Clark DK	.10	.04
❑ 16	Dwight Evans DK	.15	.06
❑ 17	Tommy John DK	.10	.04
❑ 18	Andy Van Slyke DK	.15	.06
❑ 19	Gary Gaetti DK	.10	.04
❑ 20	Mark Langston DK	.05	.02
❑ 21	Will Clark DK	.20	.08
❑ 22	Glenn Hubbard DK	.05	.02
❑ 23	Billy Hatcher DK	.05	.02
❑ 24	Bob Welch DK	.10	.04
❑ 25	Ivan Calderon DK	.05	.02
❑ 26	Cal Ripken DK	.40	.16
❑ 27	DK Checklist 1-26	.05	.02
❑ 28	Mackey Sasser RR RC	.25	.10
❑ 29	Jeff Treadway RR RC	.25	.10
❑ 30	Mike Campbell RR	.05	.02
❑ 31	Lance Johnson RR RC	.25	.10
❑ 32	Nelson Liriano RR	.05	.02
❑ 33	Shawn Abner RR	.05	.02
❑ 34	Roberto Alomar RR RC	2.00	.80
❑ 35	Shawn Hillegas RR	.05	.02
❑ 36	Joey Meyer RR	.05	.02
❑ 37	Kevin Elster RR	.05	.02
❑ 38	Jose Lind RR RC	.25	.10
❑ 39	Kirt Manwaring RR RC	.25	.10
❑ 40	Mark Grace RR RC	2.00	.80
❑ 41	Jody Reed RR RC	.25	.10
❑ 42	John Farrell RR RC	.10	.04
❑ 43	Al Leiter RR RC	.75	.30
❑ 44	Gary Thurman RR	.05	.02
❑ 45	Vicente Palacios RR	.05	.02
❑ 46	Eddie Williams RR RC	.10	.04
❑ 47	Jack McDowell RR RC	.40	.16
❑ 48	Ken Dixon	.05	.02
❑ 49	Mike Birkbeck	.05	.02
❑ 50	Eric King	.05	.02
❑ 51	Roger Clemens	.50	.20
❑ 52	Pat Clements	.05	.02
❑ 53	Fernando Valenzuela	.10	.04
❑ 54	Mark Gubicza	.05	.02
❑ 55	Jay Howell	.05	.02
❑ 56	Floyd Youmans	.05	.02
❑ 57	Ed Correa	.05	.02
❑ 58	DeWayne Buice	.05	.02
❑ 59	Jose DeLeon	.05	.02
❑ 60	Danny Cox	.05	.02
❑ 61	Nolan Ryan	1.00	.40
❑ 62	Steve Bedrosian	.05	.02
❑ 63	Tom Browning	.05	.02
❑ 64	Mark Davis	.05	.02
❑ 65	R.J. Reynolds	.05	.02
❑ 66	Kevin Mitchell	.10	.04
❑ 67	Ken Oberkfell	.05	.02
❑ 68	Rick Sutcliffe	.10	.04
❑ 69	Dwight Gooden	.10	.04
❑ 70	Scott Bankhead	.05	.02
❑ 71	Bert Blyleven	.10	.04
❑ 72	Jimmy Key	.10	.04
❑ 73	Les Straker	.05	.02
❑ 74	Jim Clancy	.05	.02
❑ 75	Mike Moore	.05	.02
❑ 76	Ron Darling	.10	.04
❑ 77	Ed Lynch	.05	.02
❑ 78	Dale Murphy	.15	.06
❑ 79	Doug Drabek	.05	.02
❑ 80	Scott Garrelts	.05	.02
❑ 81	Ed Whitson	.05	.02
❑ 82	Rob Murphy	.05	.02
❑ 83	Shane Rawley	.05	.02
❑ 84	Greg Mathews	.05	.02
❑ 85	Jim Deshaies	.05	.02
❑ 86	Mike Witt	.05	.02
❑ 87	Donnie Hill	.05	.02
❑ 88	Jeff Reed	.05	.02
❑ 89	Mike Boddicker	.05	.02
❑ 90	Ted Higuera	.05	.02
❑ 91	Walt Terrell	.05	.02
❑ 92	Bob Stanley	.05	.02
❑ 93	Dave Righetti	.10	.04
❑ 94	Orel Hershiser	.10	.04
❑ 95	Chris Bando	.05	.02
❑ 96	Bret Saberhagen	.10	.04
❑ 97	Curt Young	.05	.02
❑ 98	Tim Burke	.05	.02
❑ 99	Charlie Hough	.10	.04
❑ 100A	Checklist 28-137	.05	.02
❑ 100B	Checklist 28-133	.05	.02
❑ 101	Bobby Witt	.05	.02
❑ 102	George Brett	.50	.20
❑ 103	Mickey Tettleton	.05	.02
❑ 104	Scott Bailes	.05	.02
❑ 105	Mike Pagliarulo	.05	.02
❑ 106	Mike Scioscia	.10	.04
❑ 107	Tom Brookens	.05	.02
❑ 108	Ray Knight	.10	.04
❑ 109	Dan Plesac	.05	.02
❑ 110	Wally Joyner	.10	.04
❑ 111	Bob Forsch	.05	.02
❑ 112	Mike Scott	.10	.04
❑ 113	Kevin Gross	.05	.02
❑ 114	Benito Santiago	.10	.04
❑ 115	Bob Kipper	.05	.02
❑ 116	Mike Krukow	.05	.02
❑ 117	Chris Bosio	.05	.02
❑ 118	Sid Fernandez	.05	.02
❑ 119	Jody Davis	.05	.02
❑ 120	Mike Morgan	.05	.02
❑ 121	Mark Eichhorn	.05	.02
❑ 122	Jeff Reardon	.10	.04
❑ 123	John Franco	.10	.04
❑ 124	Richard Dotson	.05	.02
❑ 125	Eric Bell	.05	.02
❑ 126	Juan Nieves	.05	.02
❑ 127	Jack Morris	.10	.04
❑ 128	Rick Rhoden	.05	.02
❑ 129	Rich Gedman	.05	.02
❑ 130	Ken Howell	.05	.02
❑ 131	Brook Jacoby	.05	.02
❑ 132	Danny Jackson	.05	.02
❑ 133	Gene Nelson	.05	.02
❑ 134	Neal Heaton	.05	.02
❑ 135	Willie Fraser	.05	.02
❑ 136	Jose Guzman	.05	.02
❑ 137	Ozzie Guillen	.10	.04
❑ 138	Bob Knepper	.05	.02
❑ 139	Mike Jackson RC*	.25	.10
❑ 140	Joe Magrane RC*	.25	.10
❑ 141	Jimmy Jones	.05	.02
❑ 142	Ted Power	.05	.02
❑ 143	Ozzie Virgil	.05	.02
❑ 144	Felix Fermin	.05	.02
❑ 145	Kelly Downs	.05	.02
❑ 146	Shawon Dunston	.05	.02
❑ 147	Scott Bradley	.05	.02
❑ 148	Dave Stieb	.10	.04
❑ 149	Frank Viola	.10	.04
❑ 150	Terry Kennedy	.05	.02
❑ 151	Bill Wegman	.05	.02
❑ 152	Matt Nokes RC*	.25	.10
❑ 153	Wade Boggs	.15	.06
❑ 154	Wayne Tolleson	.05	.02
❑ 155	Mariano Duncan	.05	.02
❑ 156	Julio Franco	.10	.04
❑ 157	Charlie Leibrandt	.05	.02
❑ 158	Terry Steinbach	.10	.04
❑ 159	Mike Fitzgerald	.05	.02
❑ 160	Jack Lazorko	.05	.02
❑ 161	Mitch Williams	.05	.02
❑ 162	Greg Walker	.05	.02
❑ 163	Alan Ashby	.05	.02
❑ 164	Tony Gwynn	.30	.12
❑ 165	Bruce Ruffin	.05	.02
❑ 166	Ron Robinson	.05	.02
❑ 167	Zane Smith	.05	.02
❑ 168	Junior Ortiz	.05	.02
❑ 169	Jamie Moyer	.10	.04
❑ 170	Tony Pena	.05	.02
❑ 171	Cal Ripken	.75	.30
❑ 172	B.J. Surhoff	.10	.04
❑ 173	Lou Whitaker	.10	.04
❑ 174	Ellis Burks RC	.40	.16
❑ 175	Ron Guidry	.10	.04
❑ 176	Steve Sax	.05	.02
❑ 177	Danny Tartabull	.05	.02
❑ 178	Carney Lansford	.10	.04
❑ 179	Casey Candaele	.05	.02
❑ 180	Scott Fletcher	.05	.02
❑ 181	Mark McLemore	.05	.02
❑ 182	Ivan Calderon	.05	.02
❑ 183	Jack Clark	.10	.04
❑ 184	Glenn Davis	.05	.02
❑ 185	Luis Aguayo	.05	.02
❑ 186	Bo Diaz	.05	.02
❑ 187	Stan Jefferson	.05	.02
❑ 188	Sid Bream	.05	.02
❑ 189	Bob Brenly	.05	.02
❑ 190	Dion James	.05	.02
❑ 191	Leon Durham	.05	.02
❑ 192	Jesse Orosco	.05	.02
❑ 193	Alvin Davis	.05	.02
❑ 194	Gary Gaetti	.10	.04
❑ 195	Fred McGriff	.20	.08
❑ 196	Steve Lombardozzi	.05	.02
❑ 197	Rance Mulliniks	.05	.02
❑ 198	Rey Quinones	.05	.02
❑ 199	Gary Carter	.10	.04
❑ 200A	Checklist 138-247	.05	.02
❑ 200B	Checklist 134-239	.05	.02
❑ 201	Keith Moreland	.05	.02
❑ 202	Ken Griffey	.10	.04
❑ 203	Tommy Gregg	.05	.02
❑ 204	Will Clark	.20	.08
❑ 205	John Kruk	.10	.04
❑ 206	Buddy Bell	.10	.04
❑ 207	Von Hayes	.05	.02
❑ 208	Tommy Herr	.05	.02
❑ 209	Craig Reynolds	.05	.02
❑ 210	Gary Pettis	.05	.02
❑ 211	Harold Baines	.10	.04
❑ 212	Vance Law	.05	.02
❑ 213	Ken Gerhart	.05	.02
❑ 214	Jim Gantner	.05	.02
❑ 215	Chet Lemon	.10	.04
❑ 216	Dwight Evans	.15	.06
❑ 217	Don Mattingly	.60	.24
❑ 218	Franklin Stubbs	.05	.02
❑ 219	Pat Tabler	.05	.02
❑ 220	Bo Jackson	.20	.08
❑ 221	Tony Phillips	.05	.02
❑ 222	Tim Wallach	.05	.02
❑ 223	Ruben Sierra	.10	.04
❑ 224	Steve Buechele	.05	.02
❑ 225	Frank White	.10	.04
❑ 226	Alfredo Griffin	.05	.02
❑ 227	Greg Swindell	.05	.02
❑ 228	Willie Randolph	.10	.04
❑ 229	Mike Marshall	.05	.02
❑ 230	Alan Trammell	.10	.04
❑ 231	Eddie Murray	.20	.08
❑ 232	Dale Sveum	.05	.02
❑ 233	Dick Schofield	.05	.02
❑ 234	Jose Oquendo	.05	.02
❑ 235	Bill Doran	.05	.02
❑ 236	Milt Thompson	.05	.02
❑ 237	Marvell Wynne	.05	.02
❑ 238	Bobby Bonilla	.10	.04
❑ 239	Chris Speier	.05	.02
❑ 240	Glenn Braggs	.05	.02
❑ 241	Wally Backman	.05	.02
❑ 242	Ryne Sandberg	.40	.16
❑ 243	Phil Bradley	.05	.02
❑ 244	Kelly Gruber	.05	.02
❑ 245	Tom Brunansky	.05	.02
❑ 246	Ron Oester	.05	.02
❑ 247	Bobby Thigpen	.05	.02

❑ 248	Fred Lynn	.10	.04
❑ 249	Paul Molitor	.15	.06
❑ 250	Darrell Evans	.10	.04
❑ 251	Gary Ward	.05	.02
❑ 252	Bruce Hurst	.05	.02
❑ 253	Bob Welch	.10	.04
❑ 254	Joe Carter	.10	.04
❑ 255	Willie Wilson	.10	.04
❑ 256	Mark McGwire	1.50	.60
❑ 257	Mitch Webster	.05	.02
❑ 258	Brian Downing	.10	.04
❑ 259	Mike Stanley	.05	.02
❑ 260	Carlton Fisk	.15	.06
❑ 261	Billy Hatcher	.05	.02
❑ 262	Glenn Wilson	.05	.02
❑ 263	Ozzie Smith	.30	.12
❑ 264	Randy Ready	.05	.02
❑ 265	Kurt Stillwell	.05	.02
❑ 266	David Palmer	.05	.02
❑ 267	Mike Diaz	.05	.02
❑ 268	Robby Thompson	.05	.02
❑ 269	Andre Dawson	.10	.04
❑ 270	Lee Guetterman	.05	.02
❑ 271	Willie Upshaw	.05	.02
❑ 272	Randy Bush	.05	.02
❑ 273	Larry Sheets	.05	.02
❑ 274	Rob Deer	.05	.02
❑ 275	Kirk Gibson	.20	.08
❑ 276	Marty Barrett	.05	.02
❑ 277	Rickey Henderson	.20	.08
❑ 278	Pedro Guerrero	.10	.04
❑ 279	Brett Butler	.10	.04
❑ 280	Kevin Seitzer	.05	.02
❑ 281	Mike Davis	.05	.02
❑ 282	Andres Galarraga	.10	.04
❑ 283	Devon White	.10	.04
❑ 284	Pete O'Brien	.05	.02
❑ 285	Jerry Hairston	.05	.02
❑ 286	Kevin Bass	.05	.02
❑ 287	Carmelo Martinez	.05	.02
❑ 288	Juan Samuel	.05	.02
❑ 289	Kal Daniels	.05	.02
❑ 290	Albert Hall	.05	.02
❑ 291	Andy Van Slyke	.15	.06
❑ 292	Lee Smith	.10	.04
❑ 293	Vince Coleman	.05	.02
❑ 294	Tom Niedenfuer	.05	.02
❑ 295	Robin Yount	.30	.12
❑ 296	Jeff M. Robinson	.05	.02
❑ 297	Todd Benzinger RC*	.25	.10
❑ 298	Dave Winfield	.10	.04
❑ 299	Mickey Hatcher	.05	.02
❑ 300A	Checklist 248-357	.05	.02
❑ 300B	Checklist 240-345	.05	.02
❑ 301	Bud Black	.05	.02
❑ 302	Jose Canseco	.50	.20
❑ 303	Tom Foley	.05	.02
❑ 304	Pete Incaviglia	.05	.02
❑ 305	Bob Boone	.10	.04
❑ 306	Bill Long	.05	.02
❑ 307	Willie McGee	.10	.04
❑ 308	Ken Caminiti RC	2.00	.80
❑ 309	Darren Daulton	.10	.04
❑ 310	Tracy Jones	.05	.02
❑ 311	Greg Booker	.05	.02
❑ 312	Mike LaValliere	.05	.02
❑ 313	Chili Davis	.10	.04
❑ 314	Glenn Hubbard	.05	.02
❑ 315	Paul Noce	.05	.02
❑ 316	Keith Hernandez	.10	.04
❑ 317	Mark Langston	.05	.02
❑ 318	Keith Atherton	.05	.02
❑ 319	Tony Fernandez	.05	.02
❑ 320	Kent Hrbek	.10	.04
❑ 321	John Cerutti	.05	.02
❑ 322	Mike Kingery	.05	.02
❑ 323	Dave Magadan	.05	.02
❑ 324	Rafael Palmeiro	.40	.16
❑ 325	Jeff Dedmon	.05	.02
❑ 326	Barry Bonds	2.00	.80
❑ 327	Jeffrey Leonard	.05	.02
❑ 328	Tim Flannery	.05	.02
❑ 329	Dave Concepcion	.10	.04
❑ 330	Mike Schmidt	.50	.20
❑ 331	Bill Dawley	.05	.02
❑ 332	Larry Andersen	.05	.02
❑ 333	Jack Howell	.05	.02
❑ 334	Ken Williams RC	.05	.02
❑ 335	Bryn Smith	.05	.02
❑ 336	Bill Ripken RC*	.25	.10
❑ 337	Greg Brock	.05	.02
❑ 338	Mike Heath	.05	.02
❑ 339	Mike Greenwell	.05	.02
❑ 340	Claudell Washington	.05	.02
❑ 341	Jose Gonzalez	.05	.02
❑ 342	Mel Hall	.05	.02
❑ 343	Jim Eisenreich	.05	.02
❑ 344	Tony Bernazard	.05	.02
❑ 345	Tim Raines	.10	.04
❑ 346	Bob Brower	.05	.02
❑ 347	Larry Parrish	.05	.02
❑ 348	Thad Bosley	.05	.02
❑ 349	Dennis Eckersley	.15	.06
❑ 350	Cory Snyder	.05	.02
❑ 351	Rick Cerone	.05	.02
❑ 352	John Shelby	.05	.02
❑ 353	Larry Herndon	.05	.02
❑ 354	John Habyan	.05	.02
❑ 355	Chuck Crim	.05	.02
❑ 356	Gus Polidor	.05	.02
❑ 357	Ken Dayley	.05	.02
❑ 358	Danny Darwin	.05	.02
❑ 359	Lance Parrish	.10	.04
❑ 360	James Steels	.05	.02
❑ 361	Al Pedrique	.05	.02
❑ 362	Mike Aldrete	.05	.02
❑ 363	Juan Castillo	.05	.02
❑ 364	Len Dykstra	.10	.04
❑ 365	Luis Quinones	.05	.02
❑ 366	Jim Presley	.05	.02
❑ 367	Lloyd Moseby	.05	.02
❑ 368	Kirby Puckett	.20	.08
❑ 369	Eric Davis	.10	.04
❑ 370	Gary Redus	.05	.02
❑ 371	Dave Schmidt	.05	.02
❑ 372	Mark Clear	.05	.02
❑ 373	Dave Bergman	.05	.02
❑ 374	Charles Hudson	.05	.02
❑ 375	Calvin Schiraldi	.05	.02
❑ 376	Alex Trevino	.05	.02
❑ 377	Tom Candiotti	.05	.02
❑ 378	Steve Farr	.05	.02
❑ 379	Mike Gallego	.05	.02
❑ 380	Andy McGaffigan	.05	.02
❑ 381	Kirk McCaskill	.05	.02
❑ 382	Oddibe McDowell	.05	.02
❑ 383	Floyd Bannister	.05	.02
❑ 384	Denny Walling	.05	.02
❑ 385	Don Carman	.05	.02
❑ 386	Todd Worrell	.05	.02
❑ 387	Eric Show	.05	.02
❑ 388	Dave Parker	.10	.04
❑ 389	Rick Mahler	.05	.02
❑ 390	Mike Dunne	.05	.02
❑ 391	Candy Maldonado	.05	.02
❑ 392	Bob Dernier	.05	.02
❑ 393	Dave Valle	.05	.02
❑ 394	Ernie Whitt	.05	.02
❑ 395	Juan Berenguer	.05	.02
❑ 396	Mike Young	.05	.02
❑ 397	Mike Felder	.05	.02
❑ 398	Willie Hernandez	.05	.02
❑ 399	Jim Rice	.10	.04
❑ 400A	Checklist 358-467	.05	.02
❑ 400B	Checklist 346-451	.05	.02
❑ 401	Tommy John	.10	.04
❑ 402	Brian Holton	.05	.02
❑ 403	Carmen Castillo	.05	.02
❑ 404	Jamie Quirk	.05	.02
❑ 405	Dwayne Murphy	.05	.02
❑ 406	Jeff Parrett	.05	.02
❑ 407	Don Sutton	.10	.04
❑ 408	Jerry Browne	.05	.02
❑ 409	Jim Winn	.05	.02
❑ 410	Dave Smith	.05	.02
❑ 411	Shane Mack	.05	.02
❑ 412	Greg Gross	.05	.02
❑ 413	Nick Esasky	.05	.02
❑ 414	Damaso Garcia	.05	.02
❑ 415	Brian Fisher	.05	.02
❑ 416	Brian Dayett	.05	.02
❑ 417	Curt Ford	.05	.02
❑ 418	Mark Williamson	.05	.02
❑ 419	Bill Schroeder	.05	.02
❑ 420	Mike Henneman RC*	.25	.10
❑ 421	John Marzano	.05	.02
❑ 422	Ron Kittle	.05	.02
❑ 423	Matt Young	.05	.02
❑ 424	Steve Balboni	.05	.02
❑ 425	Luis Polonia RC*	.25	.10
❑ 426	Randy St.Claire	.05	.02
❑ 427	Greg Harris	.05	.02
❑ 428	Johnny Ray	.05	.02
❑ 429	Ray Searage	.05	.02
❑ 430	Ricky Horton	.05	.02
❑ 431	Gerald Young	.05	.02
❑ 432	Rick Schu	.05	.02
❑ 433	Paul O'Neill	.15	.06
❑ 434	Rich Gossage	.10	.04
❑ 435	John Cangelosi	.05	.02
❑ 436	Mike LaCoss	.05	.02
❑ 437	Gerald Perry	.05	.02
❑ 438	Dave Martinez	.05	.02
❑ 439	Darryl Strawberry	.10	.04
❑ 440	John Moses	.05	.02
❑ 441	Greg Gagne	.05	.02
❑ 442	Jesse Barfield	.10	.04
❑ 443	George Frazier	.05	.02
❑ 444	Garth Iorg	.05	.02
❑ 445	Ed Nunez	.05	.02
❑ 446	Rick Aguilera	.05	.02
❑ 447	Jerry Mumphrey	.05	.02
❑ 448	Rafael Ramirez	.05	.02
❑ 449	John Smiley RC*	.25	.10
❑ 450	Atlee Hammaker	.05	.02
❑ 451	Lance McCullers	.05	.02
❑ 452	Guy Hoffman	.05	.02
❑ 453	Chris James	.05	.02
❑ 454	Terry Pendleton	.10	.04
❑ 455	Dave Meads	.05	.02
❑ 456	Bill Buckner	.10	.04
❑ 457	John Pawlowski	.05	.02
❑ 458	Bob Sebra	.05	.02
❑ 459	Jim Dwyer	.05	.02
❑ 460	Jay Aldrich	.05	.02
❑ 461	Frank Tanana	.10	.04
❑ 462	Oil Can Boyd	.05	.02
❑ 463	Dan Pasqua	.05	.02
❑ 464	Tim Crews RC	.25	.10
❑ 465	Andy Allanson	.05	.02
❑ 466	Bill Pecota RC*	.10	.04
❑ 467	Steve Ontiveros	.05	.02
❑ 468	Hubie Brooks	.05	.02
❑ 469	Paul Kilgus	.05	.02
❑ 470	Dale Mohorcic	.05	.02
❑ 471	Dan Quisenberry	.05	.02
❑ 472	Dave Stewart	.10	.04
❑ 473	Dave Clark	.05	.02
❑ 474	Joel Skinner	.05	.02
❑ 475	Dave Anderson	.05	.02
❑ 476	Dan Petry	.05	.02
❑ 477	Carl Nichols	.05	.02
❑ 478	Ernest Riles	.05	.02
❑ 479	George Hendrick	.10	.04
❑ 480	John Morris	.05	.02
❑ 481	Manny Hernandez	.05	.02
❑ 482	Jeff Stone	.05	.02
❑ 483	Chris Brown	.05	.02
❑ 484	Mike Bielecki	.05	.02
❑ 485	Dave Dravecky	.05	.02
❑ 486	Rick Manning	.05	.02
❑ 487	Bill Almon	.05	.02
❑ 488	Jim Sundberg	.10	.04
❑ 489	Ken Phelps	.05	.02
❑ 490	Tom Henke	.05	.02
❑ 491	Dan Gladden	.05	.02
❑ 492	Barry Larkin	.15	.06
❑ 493	Fred Manrique	.05	.02
❑ 494	Mike Griffin	.05	.02
❑ 495	Mark Knudson	.05	.02
❑ 496	Bill Madlock	.10	.04
❑ 497	Tim Stoddard	.05	.02
❑ 498	Sam Horn RC	.10	.04
❑ 499	Tracy Woodson RC	.10	.04
❑ 500A	Checklist 468-577	.05	.02
❑ 500B	Checklist 452-557	.05	.02
❑ 501	Ken Schrom	.05	.02
❑ 502	Angel Salazar	.05	.02

❑ 503 Eric Plunk .05 .02
❑ 504 Joe Hesketh .05 .02
❑ 505 Greg Minton .05 .02
❑ 506 Geno Petralli .05 .02
❑ 507 Bob James .05 .02
❑ 508 Robbie Wine .05 .02
❑ 509 Jeff Calhoun .05 .02
❑ 510 Steve Lake .05 .02
❑ 511 Mark Grant .05 .02
❑ 512 Frank Williams .05 .02
❑ 513 Jeff Blauser RC .25 .10
❑ 514 Bob Walk .05 .02
❑ 515 Craig Lefferts .05 .02
❑ 516 Manny Trillo .05 .02
❑ 517 Jerry Reed .05 .02
❑ 518 Rick Leach .05 .02
❑ 519 Mark Davidson .05 .02
❑ 520 Jeff Ballard .05 .02
❑ 521 Dave Stapleton .05 .02
❑ 522 Pat Sheridan .05 .02
❑ 523 Al Nipper .05 .02
❑ 524 Steve Trout .05 .02
❑ 525 Jeff Hamilton .05 .02
❑ 526 Tommy Hinzo .05 .02
❑ 527 Lonnie Smith .05 .02
❑ 528 Greg Cadaret .05 .02
❑ 529 Bob McClure UER .05 .02
(Rob on front)
❑ 530 Chuck Finley .10 .04
❑ 531 Jeff Russell .05 .02
❑ 532 Steve Lyons .05 .02
❑ 533 Terry Puhl .05 .02
❑ 534 Eric Nolte .05 .02
❑ 535 Kent Tekulve .05 .02
❑ 536 Pat Pacillo .05 .02
❑ 537 Charlie Puleo .05 .02
❑ 538 Tom Prince .05 .02
❑ 539 Greg Maddux 1.00 .40
❑ 540 Jim Lindeman .05 .02
❑ 541 Pete Stanicek .05 .02
❑ 542 Steve Kiefer .05 .02
❑ 543A Jim Morrison ERR .15 .06
(No decimal before lifetime average)
❑ 543B Jim Morrison COR .05 .02
❑ 544 Spike Owen .05 .02
❑ 545 Jay Buhner RC .50 .20
❑ 546 Mike Devereaux RC .25 .10
❑ 547 Jerry Don Gleaton .05 .02
❑ 548 Jose Rijo .10 .04
❑ 549 Dennis Martinez .10 .04
❑ 550 Mike Loynd .05 .02
❑ 551 Darrell Miller .05 .02
❑ 552 Dave LaPoint .05 .02
❑ 553 John Tudor .10 .04
❑ 554 Rocky Childress .05 .02
❑ 555 Wally Ritchie .05 .02
❑ 556 Terry McGriff .05 .02
❑ 557 Dave Leiper .05 .02
❑ 558 Jeff D. Robinson .05 .02
❑ 559 Jose Uribe .05 .02
❑ 560 Ted Simmons .10 .04
❑ 561 Les Lancaster .05 .02
❑ 562 Keith A. Miller RC .25 .10
❑ 563 Harold Reynolds .10 .04
❑ 564 Gene Larkin RC* .25 .10
❑ 565 Cecil Fielder .10 .04
❑ 566 Roy Smalley .05 .02
❑ 567 Duane Ward .05 .02
❑ 568 Bill Wilkinson .05 .02
❑ 569 Howard Johnson .10 .04
❑ 570 Frank DiPino .05 .02
❑ 571 Pete Smith RC .10 .04
❑ 572 Darnell Coles .05 .02
❑ 573 Don Robinson .05 .02
❑ 574 Rob Nelson UER .05 .02
(Career 0 RBI, but 1 RBI in '87)
❑ 575 Dennis Rasmussen .05 .02
❑ 576 Steve Jeltz UER .05 .02
(Photo actually Juan Samuel; Samuel noted for one batting glove and black bat)
❑ 577 Tom Pagnozzi RC .10 .04
❑ 578 Ty Gainey .05 .02
❑ 579 Gary Lucas .05 .02
❑ 580 Ron Hassey .05 .02
❑ 581 Herm Winningham .05 .02
❑ 582 Rene Gonzales RC .10 .04
❑ 583 Brad Komminsk .05 .02
❑ 584 Doyle Alexander .05 .02
❑ 585 Jeff Sellers .05 .02
❑ 586 Bill Gullickson .05 .02
❑ 587 Tim Belcher .05 .02
❑ 588 Doug Jones RC .25 .10
❑ 589 Melido Perez RC .25 .10
❑ 590 Rick Honeycutt .05 .02
❑ 591 Pascual Perez .05 .02
❑ 592 Curt Wilkerson .05 .02
❑ 593 Steve Howe .05 .02
❑ 594 John Davis .05 .02
❑ 595 Storm Davis .05 .02
❑ 596 Sammy Stewart .05 .02
❑ 597 Neil Allen .05 .02
❑ 598 Alejandro Pena .05 .02
❑ 599 Mark Thurmond .05 .02
❑ 600A Checklist 578-660 .05 .02
BC1-BC26
❑ 600B Checklist 558-660 .05 .02
❑ 601 Jose Mesa RC .25 .10
❑ 602 Don August .05 .02
❑ 603 Terry Leach SP .10 .04
❑ 604 Tom Newell .05 .02
❑ 605 Randall Byers SP .10 .04
❑ 606 Jim Gott .05 .02
❑ 607 Harry Spilman .05 .02
❑ 608 John Candelaria .05 .02
❑ 609 Mike Brumley .05 .02
❑ 610 Mickey Brantley .05 .02
❑ 611 Jose Nunez SP .10 .04
❑ 612 Tom Nieto .05 .02
❑ 613 Rick Reuschel .10 .04
❑ 614 Lee Mazzilli SP .10 .04
❑ 615 Scott Lusader .05 .02
❑ 616 Bobby Meacham .05 .02
❑ 617 Kevin McReynolds SP .10 .04
❑ 618 Gene Garber .05 .02
❑ 619 Barry Lyons SP .10 .04
❑ 620 Randy Myers .10 .04
❑ 621 Donnie Moore .05 .02
❑ 622 Domingo Ramos .05 .02
❑ 623 Ed Romero .05 .02
❑ 624 Greg Myers RC .25 .10
❑ 625 Ripken Family .40 .16
Cal Ripken Sr.
Cal Ripken Jr.
Billy Ripken
❑ 626 Pat Perry .05 .02
❑ 627 Andres Thomas SP .10 .04
❑ 628 Matt Williams SP RC .75 .30
❑ 629 Dave Hengel .05 .02
❑ 630 Jeff Musselman SP .10 .04
❑ 631 Tim Laudner .05 .02
❑ 632 Bob Ojeda SP .10 .04
❑ 633 Rafael Santana .05 .02
❑ 634 Wes Gardner .05 .02
❑ 635 Roberto Kelly SP RC .25 .10
❑ 636 Mike Flanagan SP .10 .04
❑ 637 Jay Bell RC .40 .16
❑ 638 Bob Melvin .05 .02
❑ 639 D.Berryhill RC UER .25 .10
Bats: Swithch
❑ 640 David Wells SP RC 1.00 .40
❑ 641 Stan Musial PUZ .20 .08
❑ 642 Doug Sisk .05 .02
❑ 643 Keith Hughes .05 .02
❑ 644 Tom Glavine RC 2.00 .80
❑ 645 Al Newman .05 .02
❑ 646 Scott Sanderson .05 .02
❑ 647 Scott Terry .05 .02
❑ 648 Tim Teufel SP .10 .04
❑ 649 Garry Templeton SP .10 .04
❑ 650 Manny Lee SP .10 .04
❑ 651 Roger McDowell SP .10 .04
❑ 652 Mookie Wilson SP .10 .04
❑ 653 David Cone SP .10 .04
❑ 654 Ron Gant SP RC .40 .16
❑ 655 Joe Price SP .10 .04
❑ 656 George Bell SP .10 .04
❑ 657 Gregg Jefferies SP RC .25 .10
❑ 658 T.Stottlemyre SP RC .25 .10
❑ 659 G.Berroa SP RC .25 .10
❑ 660 Jerry Royster SP .10 .04
❑ XX Kirby Puckett 1.25 .50
Blister Pack

1988 Donruss Rookies

	Nm-Mt	Ex-Mt
COMP.FACT.SET (56)	10.00	4.00

❑ 1 Mark Grace 2.00 .80
❑ 2 Mike Campbell .15 .06
❑ 3 Todd Frohwirth .15 .06
❑ 4 Dave Stapleton .15 .06
❑ 5 Shawn Abner .15 .06
❑ 6 Jose Cecena .15 .06
❑ 7 Dave Gallagher .15 .06
❑ 8 Mark Parent .15 .06
❑ 9 Cecil Espy .15 .06
❑ 10 Pete Smith .15 .06
❑ 11 Jay Buhner 1.00 .40
❑ 12 Pat Borders XRC .50 .20
❑ 13 Doug Jennings .15 .06
❑ 14 Brady Anderson XRC .75 .30
❑ 15 Pete Stanicek .15 .06
❑ 16 Roberto Kelly .50 .20
❑ 17 Jeff Treadway .15 .06
❑ 18 Walt Weiss XRC* .75 .30
❑ 19 Paul Gibson .15 .06
❑ 20 Tim Crews .15 .06
❑ 21 Melido Perez .15 .06
❑ 22 Steve Peters .15 .06
❑ 23 Craig Worthington .15 .06
❑ 24 John Trautwein .15 .06
❑ 25 DeWayne Vaughn .15 .06
❑ 26 David Wells 1.50 .60
❑ 27 Al Leiter 1.00 .40
❑ 28 Tim Belcher .15 .06
❑ 29 Johnny Paredes .15 .06
❑ 30 Chris Sabo XRC .40 .16
❑ 31 Damon Berryhill .15 .06
❑ 32 Randy Milligan XRC* .25 .10
❑ 33 Gary Thurman .15 .06
❑ 34 Kevin Elster .15 .06
❑ 35 Roberto Alomar 4.00 1.60
❑ 36 E.Martinez UER XRC 5.00 2.00
Photo actually Edwin Nunez
❑ 37 Todd Stottlemyre .15 .06
❑ 38 Joey Meyer .15 .06
❑ 39 Carl Nichols .15 .06
❑ 40 Jack McDowell .75 .30
❑ 41 Jose Bautista XRC .25 .10
❑ 42 Sil Campusano .15 .06
❑ 43 John Dopson .15 .06
❑ 44 Jody Reed .50 .20
❑ 45 Darrin Jackson XRC* .25 .10
❑ 46 Mike Capel .15 .06
❑ 47 Ron Gant .75 .30
❑ 48 John Davis .15 .06
❑ 49 Kevin Coffman .15 .06
❑ 50 Cris Carpenter XRC .25 .10
❑ 51 Mackey Sasser .15 .06
❑ 52 Luis Alicea XRC .50 .20
❑ 53 Bryan Harvey XRC .30 .12
❑ 54 Steve Ellsworth .15 .06
❑ 55 Mike Macfarlane XRC .50 .20
❑ 56 Checklist 1-56 .15 .06

1989 Donruss

	Nm-Mt	Ex-Mt
COMPLETE SET (660)	25.00	10.00
COMP.FACT.SET (672)	25.00	10.00
❑ 1 Mike Greenwell DK	.05	.02
❑ 2 Bobby Bonilla DK DP	.10	.04
❑ 3 Pete Incaviglia DK	.05	.02
❑ 4 Chris Sabo DK DP	.10	.04
❑ 5 Robin Yount DK	.40	.16
❑ 6 Tony Gwynn DK DP	.15	.06
❑ 7 Carlton Fisk DK UER (OF on back)	.15	.06
❑ 8 Cory Snyder DK	.05	.02
❑ 9 David Cone DK UER ("hurdlers")	.10	.04
❑ 10 Kevin Seitzer DK	.05	.02
❑ 11 Rick Reuschel DK	.10	.04
❑ 12 Johnny Ray DK	.05	.02
❑ 13 Dave Schmidt DK	.05	.02
❑ 14 Andres Galarraga DK	.10	.04
❑ 15 Kirk Gibson DK	.15	.06
❑ 16 Fred McGriff DK	.15	.06
❑ 17 Mark Grace DK	.25	.10
❑ 18 Jeff M. Robinson DK	.05	.02
❑ 19 Vince Coleman DK DP	.05	.02
❑ 20 Dave Henderson DK	.05	.02
❑ 21 Harold Reynolds DK	.10	.04
❑ 22 Gerald Perry DK	.05	.02
❑ 23 Frank Viola DK	.10	.04
❑ 24 Steve Bedrosian DK	.05	.02
❑ 25 Glenn Davis DK	.05	.02
❑ 26 Don Mattingly DK UER (Doesn't mention Don's previous DK in 1985)	.30	.12
❑ 27 DK Checklist 1-26 DP	.05	.02
❑ 28 S.Alomar Jr. RR RC	.40	.16
❑ 29 Steve Searcy RR	.05	.02
❑ 30 Cameron Drew RR	.05	.02
❑ 31 Gary Sheffield RR RC	2.00	.80
❑ 32 Erik Hanson RR RC	.25	.10
❑ 33 Ken Griffey Jr. RR RC	8.00	3.20
❑ 34 Greg W. Harris RR RC	.10	.04
❑ 35 Gregg Jefferies RR	.05	.02
❑ 36 Luis Medina RR	.05	.02
❑ 37 Carlos Quintana RR RC	.10	.04
❑ 38 Felix Jose RR RC	.10	.04
❑ 39 Cris Carpenter RR RC*	.10	.04
❑ 40 Ron Jones RR	.10	.04
❑ 41 Dave West RR RC	.10	.04
❑ 42 R.Johnson RC RR UER (Card says born in 1964 he was born in 1963)	5.00	2.00
❑ 43 Mike Harkey RR RC	.10	.04
❑ 44 P.Harnisch RR DP RC	.25	.10
❑ 45 Tom Gordon RR DP RC	.40	.16
❑ 46 Gregg Olson RC RR DP	.25	.10
❑ 47 Alex Sanchez RR DP	.05	.02
❑ 48 Ruben Sierra	.05	.02
❑ 49 Rafael Palmeiro	.25	.10
❑ 50 Ron Gant	.10	.04
❑ 51 Cal Ripken	.75	.30
❑ 52 Wally Joyner	.10	.04
❑ 53 Gary Carter	.10	.04
❑ 54 Andy Van Slyke	.15	.06
❑ 55 Robin Yount	.40	.16
❑ 56 Pete Incaviglia	.05	.02
❑ 57 Greg Brock	.05	.02
❑ 58 Melido Perez	.05	.02
❑ 59 Craig Lefferts	.05	.02
❑ 60 Gary Pettis	.05	.02
❑ 61 Danny Tartabull	.05	.02
❑ 62 Guillermo Hernandez	.05	.02
❑ 63 Ozzie Smith	.40	.16
❑ 64 Gary Gaetti	.10	.04
❑ 65 Mark Davis	.05	.02
❑ 66 Lee Smith	.10	.04
❑ 67 Dennis Eckersley	.15	.06
❑ 68 Wade Boggs	.15	.06
❑ 69 Mike Scott	.10	.04
❑ 70 Fred McGriff	.15	.06
❑ 71 Tom Browning	.05	.02
❑ 72 Claudell Washington	.05	.02
❑ 73 Mel Hall	.05	.02
❑ 74 Don Mattingly	.60	.24
❑ 75 Steve Bedrosian	.05	.02
❑ 76 Juan Samuel	.05	.02
❑ 77 Mike Scioscia	.10	.04
❑ 78 Dave Righetti	.10	.04
❑ 79 Alfredo Griffin	.05	.02
❑ 80 Eric Davis UER (165 games in 1988, should be 135)	.10	.04
❑ 81 Juan Berenguer	.05	.02
❑ 82 Todd Worrell	.05	.02
❑ 83 Joe Carter	.10	.04
❑ 84 Steve Sax	.05	.02
❑ 85 Frank White	.10	.04
❑ 86 John Kruk	.10	.04
❑ 87 Rance Mulliniks	.05	.02
❑ 88 Alan Ashby	.05	.02
❑ 89 Charlie Leibrandt	.05	.02
❑ 90 Frank Tanana	.10	.04
❑ 91 Jose Canseco	.25	.10
❑ 92 Barry Bonds	1.50	.60
❑ 93 Harold Reynolds	.10	.04
❑ 94 Mark McLemore	.05	.02
❑ 95 Mark McGwire	1.00	.40
❑ 96 Eddie Murray	.25	.10
❑ 97 Tim Raines	.10	.04
❑ 98 Robby Thompson	.05	.02
❑ 99 Kevin McReynolds	.05	.02
❑ 100 Checklist 28-137	.05	.02
❑ 101 Carlton Fisk	.15	.06
❑ 102 Dave Martinez	.05	.02
❑ 103 Glenn Braggs	.05	.02
❑ 104 Dale Murphy	.15	.06
❑ 105 Ryne Sandberg	.40	.16
❑ 106 Dennis Martinez	.10	.04
❑ 107 Pete O'Brien	.05	.02
❑ 108 Dick Schofield	.05	.02
❑ 109 Henry Cotto	.05	.02
❑ 110 Mike Marshall	.05	.02
❑ 111 Keith Moreland	.05	.02
❑ 112 Tom Brunansky	.05	.02
❑ 113 Kelly Gruber UER (Wrong birthdate)	.05	.02
❑ 114 Brook Jacoby	.05	.02
❑ 115 Keith Brown	.05	.02
❑ 116 Matt Nokes	.05	.02
❑ 117 Keith Hernandez	.10	.04
❑ 118 Bob Forsch	.05	.02
❑ 119 Bert Blyleven UER (... 3000 strikeouts in 1987, should be 1986)	.10	.04
❑ 120 Willie Wilson	.10	.04
❑ 121 Tommy Gregg	.05	.02
❑ 122 Jim Rice	.10	.04
❑ 123 Bob Knepper	.05	.02
❑ 124 Danny Jackson	.05	.02
❑ 125 Eric Plunk	.05	.02
❑ 126 Brian Fisher	.05	.02
❑ 127 Mike Pagliarulo	.05	.02
❑ 128 Tony Gwynn	.30	.12
❑ 129 Lance McCullers	.05	.02
❑ 130 Andres Galarraga	.10	.04
❑ 131 Jose Uribe	.05	.02
❑ 132 Kirk Gibson UER (Wrong birthdate)	.15	.06
❑ 133 David Palmer	.05	.02
❑ 134 R.J. Reynolds	.05	.02
❑ 135 Greg Walker	.05	.02
❑ 136 Kirk McCaskill UER (Wrong birthdate)	.05	.02
❑ 137 Shawon Dunston	.05	.02
❑ 138 Andy Allanson	.05	.02
❑ 139 Rob Murphy	.05	.02
❑ 140 Mike Aldrete	.05	.02
❑ 141 Terry Kennedy	.05	.02
❑ 142 Scott Fletcher	.05	.02
❑ 143 Steve Balboni	.05	.02
❑ 144 Bret Saberhagen	.10	.04
❑ 145 Ozzie Virgil	.05	.02
❑ 146 Dale Sveum	.05	.02
❑ 147 Darryl Strawberry	.10	.04
❑ 148 Harold Baines	.10	.04
❑ 149 George Bell	.10	.04
❑ 150 Dave Parker	.10	.04
❑ 151 Bobby Bonilla	.10	.04
❑ 152 Mookie Wilson	.10	.04
❑ 153 Ted Power	.05	.02
❑ 154 Nolan Ryan	1.00	.40
❑ 155 Jeff Reardon	.10	.04
❑ 156 Tim Wallach	.05	.02
❑ 157 Jamie Moyer	.10	.04
❑ 158 Rich Gossage	.10	.04
❑ 159 Dave Winfield	.10	.04
❑ 160 Von Hayes	.05	.02
❑ 161 Willie McGee	.10	.04
❑ 162 Rich Gedman	.05	.02
❑ 163 Tony Pena	.05	.02
❑ 164 Mike Morgan	.05	.02
❑ 165 Charlie Hough	.10	.04
❑ 166 Mike Stanley	.05	.02
❑ 167 Andre Dawson	.10	.04
❑ 168 Joe Boever	.05	.02
❑ 169 Pete Stanicek	.05	.02
❑ 170 Bob Boone	.10	.04
❑ 171 Ron Darling	.10	.04
❑ 172 Bob Walk	.05	.02
❑ 173 Rob Deer	.05	.02
❑ 174 Steve Buechele	.05	.02
❑ 175 Ted Higuera	.05	.02
❑ 176 Ozzie Guillen	.10	.04
❑ 177 Candy Maldonado	.05	.02
❑ 178 Doyle Alexander	.05	.02
❑ 179 Mark Gubicza	.05	.02
❑ 180 Alan Trammell	.10	.04
❑ 181 Vince Coleman	.05	.02
❑ 182 Kirby Puckett	.25	.10
❑ 183 Chris Brown	.05	.02
❑ 184 Marty Barrett	.05	.02
❑ 185 Stan Javier	.05	.02
❑ 186 Mike Greenwell	.05	.02
❑ 187 Billy Hatcher	.05	.02
❑ 188 Jimmy Key	.10	.04
❑ 189 Nick Esasky	.05	.02
❑ 190 Don Slaught	.05	.02
❑ 191 Cory Snyder	.05	.02
❑ 192 John Candelaria	.05	.02
❑ 193 Mike Schmidt	.50	.20
❑ 194 Kevin Gross	.05	.02
❑ 195 John Tudor	.10	.04
❑ 196 Neil Allen	.05	.02
❑ 197 Orel Hershiser	.10	.04
❑ 198 Kal Daniels	.05	.02
❑ 199 Kent Hrbek	.10	.04
❑ 200 Checklist 138-247	.05	.02
❑ 201 Joe Magrane	.05	.02
❑ 202 Scott Bailes	.05	.02
❑ 203 Tim Belcher	.05	.02
❑ 204 George Brett	.60	.24
❑ 205 Benito Santiago	.10	.04
❑ 206 Tony Fernandez	.05	.02
❑ 207 Gerald Young	.05	.02
❑ 208 Bo Jackson	.25	.10
❑ 209 Chet Lemon	.10	.04
❑ 210 Storm Davis	.05	.02
❑ 211 Doug Drabek	.05	.02
❑ 212 Mickey Brantley UER (Photo actually Nelson Simmons)	.05	.02
❑ 213 Devon White	.10	.04
❑ 214 Dave Stewart	.10	.04
❑ 215 Dave Schmidt	.05	.02
❑ 216 Bryn Smith	.05	.02
❑ 217 Brett Butler	.10	.04
❑ 218 Bob Ojeda	.05	.02
❑ 219 Steve Rosenberg	.05	.02
❑ 220 Hubie Brooks	.05	.02

❑	221	B.J. Surhoff	.10	.04
❑	222	Rick Mahler	.05	.02
❑	223	Rick Sutcliffe	.10	.04
❑	224	Neal Heaton	.05	.02
❑	225	Mitch Williams	.05	.02
❑	226	Chuck Finley	.10	.04
❑	227	Mark Langston	.05	.02
❑	228	Jesse Orosco	.05	.02
❑	229	Ed Whitson	.05	.02
❑	230	Terry Pendleton	.10	.04
❑	231	Lloyd Moseby	.05	.02
❑	232	Greg Swindell	.05	.02
❑	233	John Franco	.10	.04
❑	234	Jack Morris	.10	.04
❑	235	Howard Johnson	.10	.04
❑	236	Glenn Davis	.05	.02
❑	237	Frank Viola	.10	.04
❑	238	Kevin Seitzer	.05	.02
❑	239	Gerald Perry	.05	.02
❑	240	Dwight Evans	.15	.06
❑	241	Jim Deshaies	.05	.02
❑	242	Bo Diaz	.05	.02
❑	243	Carney Lansford	.10	.04
❑	244	Mike LaValliere	.05	.02
❑	245	Rickey Henderson	.25	.10
❑	246	Roberto Alomar	.25	.10
❑	247	Jimmy Jones	.05	.02
❑	248	Pascual Perez	.05	.02
❑	249	Will Clark	.15	.06
❑	250	Fernando Valenzuela	.10	.04
❑	251	Shane Rawley	.05	.02
❑	252	Sid Bream	.05	.02
❑	253	Steve Lyons	.05	.02
❑	254	Brian Downing	.10	.04
❑	255	Mark Grace	.25	.10
❑	256	Tom Candiotti	.05	.02
❑	257	Barry Larkin	.15	.06
❑	258	Mike Krukow	.05	.02
❑	259	Billy Ripken	.05	.02
❑	260	Cecilio Guante	.05	.02
❑	261	Scott Bradley	.05	.02
❑	262	Floyd Bannister	.05	.02
❑	263	Pete Smith	.05	.02
❑	264	Jim Gantner UER (Wrong birthdate)	.05	.02
❑	265	Roger McDowell	.05	.02
❑	266	Bobby Thigpen	.05	.02
❑	267	Jim Clancy	.05	.02
❑	268	Terry Steinbach	.10	.04
❑	269	Mike Dunne	.05	.02
❑	270	Dwight Gooden	.10	.04
❑	271	Mike Heath	.05	.02
❑	272	Dave Smith	.05	.02
❑	273	Keith Atherton	.05	.02
❑	274	Tim Burke	.05	.02
❑	275	Damon Berryhill	.05	.02
❑	276	Vance Law	.05	.02
❑	277	Rich Dotson	.05	.02
❑	278	Lance Parrish	.10	.04
❑	279	Denny Walling	.05	.02
❑	280	Roger Clemens	.50	.20
❑	281	Greg Mathews	.05	.02
❑	282	Tom Niedenfuer	.05	.02
❑	283	Paul Kilgus	.05	.02
❑	284	Jose Guzman	.05	.02
❑	285	Calvin Schiraldi	.05	.02
❑	286	Charlie Puleo UER (Career ERA 4.24, should be 4.23)	.05	.02
❑	287	Joe Orsulak	.05	.02
❑	288	Jack Howell	.05	.02
❑	289	Kevin Elster	.05	.02
❑	290	Jose Lind	.05	.02
❑	291	Paul Molitor	.15	.06
❑	292	Cecil Espy	.05	.02
❑	293	Bill Wegman	.05	.02
❑	294	Dan Pasqua	.05	.02
❑	295	Scott Garrelts UER (Wrong birthdate)	.05	.02
❑	296	Walt Terrell	.05	.02
❑	297	Ed Hearn	.05	.02
❑	298	Lou Whitaker	.10	.04
❑	299	Ken Dayley	.05	.02
❑	300	Checklist 248-357	.05	.02
❑	301	Tommy Herr	.05	.02
❑	302	Mike Brumley	.05	.02
❑	303	Ellis Burks	.10	.04
❑	304	Curt Young UER (Wrong birthdate)	.05	.02
❑	305	Jody Reed	.05	.02
❑	306	Bill Doran	.05	.02
❑	307	David Wells	.10	.04
❑	308	Ron Robinson	.05	.02
❑	309	Rafael Santana	.05	.02
❑	310	Julio Franco	.10	.04
❑	311	Jack Clark	.10	.04
❑	312	Chris James	.05	.02
❑	313	Milt Thompson	.05	.02
❑	314	John Shelby	.05	.02
❑	315	Al Leiter	.25	.10
❑	316	Mike Davis	.05	.02
❑	317	Chris Sabo RC *	.40	.16
❑	318	Greg Gagne	.05	.02
❑	319	Jose Oquendo	.05	.02
❑	320	John Farrell	.05	.02
❑	321	Franklin Stubbs	.05	.02
❑	322	Kurt Stillwell	.05	.02
❑	323	Shawn Abner	.05	.02
❑	324	Mike Flanagan	.05	.02
❑	325	Kevin Bass	.05	.02
❑	326	Pat Tabler	.05	.02
❑	327	Mike Henneman	.05	.02
❑	328	Rick Honeycutt	.05	.02
❑	329	John Smiley	.05	.02
❑	330	Rey Quinones	.05	.02
❑	331	Johnny Ray	.05	.02
❑	332	Bob Welch	.10	.04
❑	333	Larry Sheets	.05	.02
❑	334	Jeff Parrett	.05	.02
❑	335	Rick Reuschel UER (For Don Robinson& should be Jeff)	.10	.04
❑	336	Randy Myers	.10	.04
❑	337	Ken Williams	.05	.02
❑	338	Andy McGaffigan	.05	.02
❑	339	Joey Meyer	.05	.02
❑	340	Dion James	.05	.02
❑	341	Les Lancaster	.05	.02
❑	342	Tom Foley	.05	.02
❑	343	Geno Petralli	.05	.02
❑	344	Dan Petry	.05	.02
❑	345	Alvin Davis	.05	.02
❑	346	Mickey Hatcher	.05	.02
❑	347	Marvell Wynne	.05	.02
❑	348	Danny Cox	.05	.02
❑	349	Dave Stieb	.10	.04
❑	350	Jay Bell	.10	.04
❑	351	Jeff Treadway	.05	.02
❑	352	Luis Salazar	.05	.02
❑	353	Len Dykstra	.10	.04
❑	354	Juan Agosto	.05	.02
❑	355	Gene Larkin	.05	.02
❑	356	Steve Farr	.05	.02
❑	357	Paul Assenmacher	.05	.02
❑	358	Todd Benzinger	.05	.02
❑	359	Larry Andersen	.05	.02
❑	360	Paul O'Neill	.15	.06
❑	361	Ron Hassey	.05	.02
❑	362	Jim Gott	.05	.02
❑	363	Ken Phelps	.05	.02
❑	364	Tim Flannery	.05	.02
❑	365	Randy Ready	.05	.02
❑	366	Nelson Santovenia	.05	.02
❑	367	Kelly Downs	.05	.02
❑	368	Danny Heep	.05	.02
❑	369	Phil Bradley	.05	.02
❑	370	Jeff D. Robinson	.05	.02
❑	371	Ivan Calderon	.05	.02
❑	372	Mike Witt	.05	.02
❑	373	Greg Maddux	.50	.20
❑	374	Carmen Castillo	.05	.02
❑	375	Jose Rijo	.10	.04
❑	376	Joe Price	.05	.02
❑	377	Rene Gonzales	.05	.02
❑	378	Oddibe McDowell	.05	.02
❑	379	Jim Presley	.05	.02
❑	380	Brad Wellman	.05	.02
❑	381	Tom Glavine	.25	.10
❑	382	Dan Plesac	.05	.02
❑	383	Wally Backman	.05	.02
❑	384	Dave Gallagher	.05	.02
❑	385	Tom Henke	.05	.02
❑	386	Luis Polonia	.05	.02
❑	387	Junior Ortiz	.05	.02
❑	388	David Cone	.10	.04
❑	389	Dave Bergman	.05	.02
❑	390	Danny Darwin	.05	.02
❑	391	Dan Gladden	.05	.02
❑	392	John Dopson	.05	.02
❑	393	Frank DiPino	.05	.02
❑	394	Al Nipper	.05	.02
❑	395	Willie Randolph	.10	.04
❑	396	Don Carman	.05	.02
❑	397	Scott Terry	.05	.02
❑	398	Rick Cerone	.05	.02
❑	399	Tom Pagnozzi	.05	.02
❑	400	Checklist 358-467	.05	.02
❑	401	Mickey Tettleton	.05	.02
❑	402	Curtis Wilkerson	.05	.02
❑	403	Jeff Russell	.05	.02
❑	404	Pat Perry	.05	.02
❑	405	Jose Alvarez RC	.10	.04
❑	406	Rick Schu	.05	.02
❑	407	Sherman Corbett	.05	.02
❑	408	Dave Magadan	.05	.02
❑	409	Bob Kipper	.05	.02
❑	410	Don August	.05	.02
❑	411	Bob Brower	.05	.02
❑	412	Chris Bosio	.05	.02
❑	413	Jerry Reuss	.05	.02
❑	414	Atlee Hammaker	.05	.02
❑	415	Jim Walewander	.05	.02
❑	416	Mike Macfarlane RC *	.25	.10
❑	417	Pat Sheridan	.05	.02
❑	418	Pedro Guerrero	.10	.04
❑	419	Allan Anderson	.05	.02
❑	420	Mark Parent	.05	.02
❑	421	Bob Stanley	.05	.02
❑	422	Mike Gallego	.05	.02
❑	423	Bruce Hurst	.05	.02
❑	424	Dave Meads	.05	.02
❑	425	Jesse Barfield	.10	.04
❑	426	Rob Dibble RC	.50	.20
❑	427	Joel Skinner	.05	.02
❑	428	Ron Kittle	.05	.02
❑	429	Rick Rhoden	.05	.02
❑	430	Bob Dernier	.05	.02
❑	431	Steve Jeltz	.05	.02
❑	432	Rick Dempsey	.05	.02
❑	433	Roberto Kelly	.05	.02
❑	434	Dave Anderson	.05	.02
❑	435	Herm Winningham	.05	.02
❑	436	Al Newman	.05	.02
❑	437	Jose DeLeon	.05	.02
❑	438	Doug Jones	.05	.02
❑	439	Brian Holton	.05	.02
❑	440	Jeff Montgomery	.05	.02
❑	441	Dickie Thon	.05	.02
❑	442	Cecil Fielder	.10	.04
❑	443	John Fishel	.05	.02
❑	444	Jerry Don Gleaton	.05	.02
❑	445	Paul Gibson	.05	.02
❑	446	Walt Weiss	.05	.02
❑	447	Glenn Wilson	.05	.02
❑	448	Mike Moore	.05	.02
❑	449	Chili Davis	.10	.04
❑	450	Dave Henderson	.05	.02
❑	451	Jose Bautista RC	.10	.04
❑	452	Rex Hudler	.05	.02
❑	453	Bob Brenly	.05	.02
❑	454	Mackey Sasser	.05	.02
❑	455	Daryl Boston	.05	.02
❑	456	Mike R. Fitzgerald	.05	.02
❑	457	Jeffrey Leonard	.05	.02
❑	458	Bruce Sutter	.10	.04
❑	459	Mitch Webster	.05	.02
❑	460	Joe Hesketh	.05	.02
❑	461	Bobby Witt	.05	.02
❑	462	Stu Cliburn	.05	.02
❑	463	Scott Bankhead	.05	.02
❑	464	Ramon Martinez RC	.25	.10
❑	465	Dave Leiper	.05	.02
❑	466	Luis Alicea RC *	.25	.10
❑	467	John Cerutti	.05	.02
❑	468	Ron Washington	.05	.02
❑	469	Jeff Reed	.05	.02
❑	470	Jeff M. Robinson	.05	.02
❑	471	Sid Fernandez	.05	.02

❑ 472 Terry Puhl .05 .02
❑ 473 Charlie Lea .05 .02
❑ 474 Israel Sanchez .05 .02
❑ 475 Bruce Benedict .05 .02
❑ 476 Oil Can Boyd .05 .02
❑ 477 Craig Reynolds .05 .02
❑ 478 Frank Williams .05 .02
❑ 479 Greg Cadaret .05 .02
❑ 480 Randy Kramer .05 .02
❑ 481 Dave Eiland .05 .02
❑ 482 Eric Show .05 .02
❑ 483 Garry Templeton .10 .04
❑ 484 Wallace Johnson .05 .02
❑ 485 Kevin Mitchell .10 .04
❑ 486 Tim Crews .05 .02
❑ 487 Mike Maddux .05 .02
❑ 488 Dave LaPoint .05 .02
❑ 489 Fred Manrique .05 .02
❑ 490 Greg Minton .05 .02
❑ 491 Doug Dascenzo UER .05 .02
(Photo actually
Damon Berryhill)
❑ 492 Willie Upshaw .05 .02
❑ 493 Jack Armstrong RC * .25 .10
❑ 494 Kirt Manwaring .05 .02
❑ 495 Jeff Ballard .05 .02
❑ 496 Jeff Kunkel .05 .02
❑ 497 Mike Campbell .05 .02
❑ 498 Gary Thurman .05 .02
❑ 499 Zane Smith .05 .02
❑ 500 Checklist 468-577 DP .05 .02
❑ 501 Mike Birkbeck .05 .02
❑ 502 Terry Leach .05 .02
❑ 503 Shawn Hillegas .05 .02
❑ 504 Manny Lee .05 .02
❑ 505 Doug Jennings .05 .02
❑ 506 Ken Oberkfell .05 .02
❑ 507 Tim Teufel .05 .02
❑ 508 Tom Brookens .05 .02
❑ 509 Rafael Ramirez .05 .02
❑ 510 Fred Toliver .05 .02
❑ 511 Brian Holman RC * .10 .04
❑ 512 Mike Bielecki .05 .02
❑ 513 Jeff Pico .05 .02
❑ 514 Charles Hudson .05 .02
❑ 515 Bruce Ruffin .05 .02
❑ 516 L.McWilliams UER .05 .02
(New Richland, should
be North Richland)
❑ 517 Jeff Sellers .05 .02
❑ 518 John Costello .05 .02
❑ 519 Brady Anderson RC .40 .16
❑ 520 Craig McMurtry .05 .02
❑ 521 Ray Hayward DP .05 .02
❑ 522 Drew Hall DP .05 .02
❑ 523 Mark Lemke DP RC .40 .16
❑ 524 Oswald Peraza DP .05 .02
❑ 525 Bryan Harvey DP RC * .25 .10
❑ 526 Rick Aguilera DP .05 .02
❑ 527 Tom Prince DP .05 .02
❑ 528 Mark Clear DP .05 .02
❑ 529 Jerry Browne DP .05 .02
❑ 530 Juan Castillo DP .05 .02
❑ 531 Jack McDowell DP .10 .04
❑ 532 Chris Speier DP .05 .02
❑ 533 Darrell Evans DP .10 .04
❑ 534 Luis Aquino DP .05 .02
❑ 535 Eric King DP .05 .02
❑ 536 Ken Hill DP RC .25 .10
❑ 537 Randy Bush DP .05 .02
❑ 538 Shane Mack DP .05 .02
❑ 539 Tom Bolton DP .05 .02
❑ 540 Gene Nelson DP .05 .02
❑ 541 Wes Gardner DP .05 .02
❑ 542 Ken Caminiti DP .15 .06
❑ 543 Duane Ward DP .05 .02
❑ 544 Norm Charlton DP RC .25 .10
❑ 545 Hal Morris DP RC .25 .10
❑ 546 Rich Yett DP .05 .02
❑ 547 H.Meulens DP RC .10 .04
❑ 548 Greg A. Harris DP .05 .02
❑ 549 Darren Daulton DP .10 .04
(Posing as right-
handed hitter)
❑ 550 Jeff Hamilton DP .05 .02
❑ 551 Luis Aguayo DP .05 .02
❑ 552 Tim Leary DP .05 .02
(Resembles M.Marshall)
❑ 553 Ron Oester DP .05 .02
❑ 554 S.Lombardozzi DP .05 .02
❑ 555 Tim Jones DP .05 .02
❑ 556 Bud Black DP .05 .02
❑ 557 Alejandro Pena DP .05 .02
❑ 558 Jose DeJesus DP .05 .02
❑ 559 D.Rasmussen DP .05 .02
❑ 560 Pat Borders DP RC* .25 .10
❑ 561 Craig Biggio DP RC 1.50 .60
❑ 562 Luis DeLosSantos DP .05 .02
❑ 563 Fred Lynn DP .10 .04
❑ 564 Todd Burns DP .05 .02
❑ 565 Felix Fermin DP .05 .02
❑ 566 Darnell Coles DP .05 .02
❑ 567 Willie Fraser DP .05 .02
❑ 568 Glenn Hubbard DP .05 .02
❑ 569 Craig Worthington DP .05 .02
❑ 570 Johnny Paredes DP .05 .02
❑ 571 Don Robinson DP .05 .02
❑ 572 Barry Lyons DP .05 .02
❑ 573 Bill Long DP .05 .02
❑ 574 Tracy Jones DP .05 .02
❑ 575 Juan Nieves DP .05 .02
❑ 576 Andres Thomas DP .05 .02
❑ 577 Rolando Roomes DP .05 .02
❑ 578 Luis Rivera UER DP .05 .02
(Wrong birthdate)
❑ 579 Chad Kreuter DP RC .25 .10
❑ 580 Tony Armas DP .10 .04
❑ 581 Jay Buhner .10 .04
❑ 582 Ricky Horton DP .05 .02
❑ 583 Andy Hawkins DP .05 .02
❑ 584 Sil Campusano .05 .02
❑ 585 Dave Clark .05 .02
❑ 586 Van Snider DP .05 .02
❑ 587 Todd Frohwirth DP .05 .02
❑ 588 W.Spahn DP PUZ .15 .06
❑ 589 William Brennan .05 .02
❑ 590 German Gonzalez .05 .02
❑ 591 Ernie Whitt DP .05 .02
❑ 592 Jeff Blauser .05 .02
❑ 593 Spike Owen DP .05 .02
❑ 594 Matt Williams .25 .10
❑ 595 Lloyd McClendon DP .05 .02
❑ 596 Steve Ontiveros .05 .02
❑ 597 Scott Medvin .05 .02
❑ 598 Hipolito Pena DP .05 .02
❑ 599 Jerald Clark DP RC .10 .04
❑ 600A CL 578-660 DP .05 .02
635 Kurt Schilling
❑ 600B CL 578-660 DP .05 .02
635 Curt Schilling;
MVP's not listed
on checklist card
❑ 600C CL 578-660 DP .05 .02
635 Curt Schilling;
MVP's listed
following 660
❑ 601 Carmelo Martinez DP .05 .02
❑ 602 Mike LaCoss .05 .02
❑ 603 Mike Devereaux .05 .02
❑ 604 Alex Madrid DP .05 .02
❑ 605 Gary Redus DP .05 .02
❑ 606 Lance Johnson .05 .02
❑ 607 Terry Clark DP .05 .02
❑ 608 Manny Trillo DP .05 .02
❑ 609 Scott Jordan RC .25 .10
❑ 610 Jay Howell DP .05 .02
❑ 611 Francisco Melendez .05 .02
❑ 612 Mike Boddicker .05 .02
❑ 613 Kevin Brown DP .25 .10
❑ 614 Dave Valle .05 .02
❑ 615 Tim Laudner DP .05 .02
❑ 616 Andy Nezelek UER .05 .02
(Wrong birthdate)
❑ 617 Chuck Crim .05 .02
❑ 618 Jack Savage DP .05 .02
❑ 619 Adam Peterson .05 .02
❑ 620 Todd Stottlemyre .05 .02
❑ 621 Lance Blankenship RC .10 .04
❑ 622 Miguel Garcia DP .05 .02
❑ 623 Keith A. Miller DP .05 .02
❑ 624 Ricky Jordan DP RC* .25 .10
❑ 625 Ernest Riles DP .05 .02
❑ 626 John Moses DP .05 .02
❑ 627 Nelson Liriano DP .05 .02
❑ 628 Mike Smithson DP .05 .02
❑ 629 Scott Sanderson .05 .02
❑ 630 Dale Mohorcic .05 .02
❑ 631 Marvin Freeman DP .05 .02
❑ 632 Mike Young DP .05 .02
❑ 633 Dennis Lamp .05 .02
❑ 634 Dante Bichette DP RC .40 .16
❑ 635 Curt Schilling DP RC 4.00 1.60
❑ 636 Scott May DP .05 .02
❑ 637 Mike Schooler .05 .02
❑ 638 Rick Leach .05 .02
❑ 639 Tom Lampkin UER .05 .02
(Throws Left, should
be Throws Right)
❑ 640 Brian Meyer .05 .02
❑ 641 Brian Harper .05 .02
❑ 642 John Smoltz RC 2.00 .80
❑ 643 Jose Canseco .25 .10
(40/40 Club)
❑ 644 Bill Schroeder .05 .02
❑ 645 Edgar Martinez .25 .10
❑ 646 Dennis Cook RC .25 .10
❑ 647 Barry Jones .05 .02
❑ 648 Orel Hershiser .10 .04
(59 and Counting)
❑ 649 Rod Nichols .05 .02
❑ 650 Jody Davis .05 .02
❑ 651 Bob Milacki .05 .02
❑ 652 Mike Jackson .05 .02
❑ 653 Derek Lilliquist RC .10 .04
❑ 654 Paul Mirabella .05 .02
❑ 655 Mike Diaz .05 .02
❑ 656 Jeff Musselman .05 .02
❑ 657 Jerry Reed .05 .02
❑ 658 Kevin Blankenship .05 .02
❑ 659 Wayne Tolleson .05 .02
❑ 660 Eric Hetzel .05 .02
❑ BC Jose Canseco 2.00 .80
Blister Pack

1989 Donruss Rookies

	Nm-Mt	Ex-Mt
COMP.FACT.SET (56)	15.00	6.00

❑ 1 Gary Sheffield 2.00 .80
❑ 2 Gregg Jefferies .10 .04
❑ 3 Ken Griffey Jr. 8.00 3.20
❑ 4 Tom Gordon .15 .06
❑ 5 Billy Spiers RC .25 .10
❑ 6 Deion Sanders RC 1.50 .60
❑ 7 Donn Pall .05 .02
❑ 8 Steve Carter .05 .02
❑ 9 Francisco Oliveras .05 .02
❑ 10 Steve Wilson RC .10 .04
❑ 11 Bob Geren RC .05 .02
❑ 12 Tony Castillo RC .10 .04
❑ 13 Kenny Rogers RC 1.00 .40
❑ 14 Carlos Martinez RC .10 .04
❑ 15 Edgar Martinez .25 .10
❑ 16 Jim Abbott RC 1.00 .40
❑ 17 Torey Lovullo RC .10 .04
❑ 18 Mark Carreon .05 .02
❑ 19 Geronimo Berroa .05 .02
❑ 20 Luis Medina .05 .02
❑ 21 Sandy Alomar Jr. .15 .06
❑ 22 Bob Milacki .05 .02

❑ 23 Joe Girardi RC .40 .16
❑ 24 German Gonzalez .05 .02
❑ 25 Craig Worthington .05 .02
❑ 26 Jerome Walton RC .25 .10
❑ 27 Gary Wayne .05 .02
❑ 28 Tim Jones .05 .02
❑ 29 Dante Bichette .15 .06
❑ 30 Alexis Infante .05 .02
❑ 31 Ken Hill .25 .10
❑ 32 Dwight Smith RC .25 .10
❑ 33 Luis de los Santos .05 .02
❑ 34 Eric Yelding .05 .02
❑ 35 Gregg Olson .25 .10
❑ 36 Phil Stephenson .05 .02
❑ 37 Ken Patterson .05 .02
❑ 38 Rick Wrona .05 .02
❑ 39 Mike Brumley .05 .02
❑ 40 Cris Carpenter .05 .02
❑ 41 Jeff Brantley RC .25 .10
❑ 42 Ron Jones .05 .02
❑ 43 Randy Johnson 3.00 1.20
❑ 44 Kevin Brown .25 .10
❑ 45 Ramon Martinez .10 .04
❑ 46 Greg W.Harris .05 .02
❑ 47 Steve Finley RC .75 .30
❑ 48 Randy Kramer .05 .02
❑ 49 Erik Hanson .10 .04
❑ 50 Matt Merullo .05 .02
❑ 51 Mike Devereaux .05 .02
❑ 52 Clay Parker .05 .02
❑ 53 Omar Vizquel RC 1.00 .40
❑ 54 Derek Lilliquist .05 .02
❑ 55 Junior Felix RC .10 .04
❑ 56 Checklist 1-56 .05 .02

1989 Donruss Baseball's Best

	Nm-Mt	Ex-Mt
COMP.FACT.SET (336)	80.00	32.00

❑ 1 Don Mattingly 1.50 .60
❑ 2 Tom Glavine .60 .24
❑ 3 Bert Blyleven .25 .10
❑ 4 Andre Dawson .25 .10
❑ 5 Pete O'Brien .15 .06
❑ 6 Eric Davis .25 .10
❑ 7 George Brett 1.50 .60
❑ 8 Glenn Davis .15 .06
❑ 9 Ellis Burks .25 .10
❑ 10 Kirk Gibson .40 .16
❑ 11 Carlton Fisk .40 .16
❑ 12 Andres Galarraga .25 .10
❑ 13 Alan Trammell .25 .10
❑ 14 Dwight Gooden .25 .10
❑ 15 Paul Molitor .40 .16
❑ 16 Roger McDowell .15 .06
❑ 17 Doug Drabek .15 .06
❑ 18 Kent Hrbek .25 .10
❑ 19 Vince Coleman .15 .06
❑ 20 Steve Sax .15 .06
❑ 21 Roberto Alomar .60 .24
❑ 22 Carney Lansford .25 .10
❑ 23 Will Clark .40 .16
❑ 24 Alvin Davis .15 .06
❑ 25 Bobby Thigpen .15 .06
❑ 26 Ryne Sandberg 1.00 .40
❑ 27 Devon White .25 .10
❑ 28 Mike Greenwell .15 .06
❑ 29 Dale Murphy .40 .16
❑ 30 Jeff Ballard .15 .06
❑ 31 Kelly Gruber .15 .06
❑ 32 Julio Franco .25 .10
❑ 33 Bobby Bonilla .25 .10
❑ 34 Tim Wallach .15 .06
❑ 35 Lou Whitaker .25 .10
❑ 36 Jay Howell .15 .06
❑ 37 Greg Maddux 1.25 .50
❑ 38 Bill Doran .15 .06
❑ 39 Danny Tartabull .15 .06
❑ 40 Darryl Strawberry .25 .10
❑ 41 Ron Darling .25 .10
❑ 42 Tony Gwynn .75 .30
❑ 43 Mark McGwire 2.50 1.00
❑ 44 Ozzie Smith 1.00 .40
❑ 45 Andy Van Slyke .40 .16
❑ 46 Juan Berenguer .15 .06
❑ 47 Von Hayes .15 .06
❑ 48 Tony Fernandez .15 .06
❑ 49 Eric Plunk .15 .06
❑ 50 Ernest Riles .15 .06
❑ 51 Harold Reynolds .25 .10
❑ 52 Andy Hawkins .15 .06
❑ 53 Robin Yount 1.00 .40
❑ 54 Danny Jackson .15 .06
❑ 55 Nolan Ryan 2.50 1.00
❑ 56 Joe Carter .25 .10
❑ 57 Jose Canseco .60 .24
❑ 58 Jody Davis .15 .06
❑ 59 Lance Parrish .25 .10
❑ 60 Mitch Williams .15 .06
❑ 61 Brook Jacoby .15 .06
❑ 62 Tom Browning .15 .06
❑ 63 Kurt Stillwell .15 .06
❑ 64 Rafael Ramirez .15 .06
❑ 65 Roger Clemens 1.25 .50
❑ 66 Mike Scioscia .25 .10
❑ 67 Dave Gallagher .15 .06
❑ 68 Mark Langston .15 .06
❑ 69 Chet Lemon .25 .10
❑ 70 Kevin McReynolds .15 .06
❑ 71 Rob Deer .15 .06
❑ 72 Tommy Herr .15 .06
❑ 73 Barry Bonds 3.00 1.20
❑ 74 Frank Viola .25 .10
❑ 75 Pedro Guerrero .25 .10
❑ 76 Dave Righetti UER .15 .06
(ML total of 7
wins incorrect)
❑ 77 Bruce Hurst .15 .06
❑ 78 Rickey Henderson .60 .24
❑ 79 Robby Thompson .15 .06
❑ 80 Randy Johnson 10.00 4.00
❑ 81 Harold Baines .25 .10
❑ 82 Calvin Schiraldi .15 .06
❑ 83 Kirk McCaskill .15 .06
❑ 84 Lee Smith .25 .10
❑ 85 John Smoltz 4.00 1.60
❑ 86 Mickey Tettleton .15 .06
❑ 87 Jimmy Key .25 .10
❑ 88 Rafael Palmeiro .60 .24
❑ 89 Sid Bream .15 .06
❑ 90 Dennis Martinez .25 .10
❑ 91 Frank Tanana .25 .10
❑ 92 Eddie Murray .60 .24
❑ 93 Shawon Dunston .15 .06
❑ 94 Mike Scott .25 .10
❑ 95 Bret Saberhagen .25 .10
❑ 96 David Cone .25 .10
❑ 97 Kevin Elster .15 .06
❑ 98 Jack Clark .25 .10
❑ 99 Dave Stewart .25 .10
❑ 100 Jose Oquendo .15 .06
❑ 101 Jose Lind .15 .06
❑ 102 Gary Gaetti .25 .10
❑ 103 Ricky Jordan .50 .20
❑ 104 Fred McGriff .40 .16
❑ 105 Don Slaught .15 .06
❑ 106 Jose Uribe .15 .06
❑ 107 Jeffrey Leonard .15 .06
❑ 108 Lee Guetterman .15 .06
❑ 109 Chris Bosio .15 .06
❑ 110 Barry Larkin .40 .16
❑ 111 Ruben Sierra .15 .06
❑ 112 Greg Swindell .15 .06
❑ 113 Gary Sheffield 4.00 1.60
❑ 114 Lonnie Smith .15 .06
❑ 115 Chili Davis .25 .10
❑ 116 Damon Berryhill .15 .06
❑ 117 Tom Candiotti .15 .06
❑ 118 Kal Daniels .15 .06
❑ 119 Mark Gubicza .15 .06
❑ 120 Jim Deshaies .15 .06
❑ 121 Dwight Evans .40 .16
❑ 122 Mike Morgan .15 .06
❑ 123 Dan Pasqua .15 .06
❑ 124 Bryn Smith .15 .06
❑ 125 Doyle Alexander .15 .06
❑ 126 Howard Johnson .25 .10
❑ 127 Chuck Crim .15 .06
❑ 128 Darren Daulton .25 .10
❑ 129 Jeff Robinson .15 .06
❑ 130 Kirby Puckett .60 .24
❑ 131 Joe Magrane .15 .06
❑ 132 Jesse Barfield .25 .10
❑ 133 Mark Davis UER .15 .06
(Photo actually
Dave Leiper)
❑ 134 Dennis Eckersley .40 .16
❑ 135 Mike Krukow .15 .06
❑ 136 Jay Buhner .25 .10
❑ 137 Ozzie Guillen .25 .10
❑ 138 Rick Sutcliffe .25 .10
❑ 139 Wally Joyner .25 .10
❑ 140 Wade Boggs .40 .16
❑ 141 Jeff Treadway .15 .06
❑ 142 Cal Ripken 2.00 .80
❑ 143 Dave Stieb .25 .10
❑ 144 Pete Incaviglia .15 .06
❑ 145 Bob Walk .15 .06
❑ 146 Nelson Santovenia .15 .06
❑ 147 Mike Heath .15 .06
❑ 148 Willie Randolph .25 .10
❑ 149 Paul Kilgus .15 .06
❑ 150 Billy Hatcher .15 .06
❑ 151 Steve Farr .15 .06
❑ 152 Gregg Jefferies .15 .06
❑ 153 Randy Myers .25 .10
❑ 154 Garry Templeton .25 .10
❑ 155 Walt Weiss .15 .06
❑ 156 Terry Pendleton .25 .10
❑ 157 John Smiley .15 .06
❑ 158 Greg Gagne .15 .06
❑ 159 Len Dykstra .25 .10
❑ 160 Nelson Liriano .15 .06
❑ 161 Alvaro Espinoza .15 .06
❑ 162 Rick Reuschel .25 .10
❑ 163 Omar Vizquel UER 2.00 .80
(Photo actually
Darnell Coles)
❑ 164 Clay Parker .15 .06
❑ 165 Dan Plesac .15 .06
❑ 166 John Franco .25 .10
❑ 167 Scott Fletcher .15 .06
❑ 168 Cory Snyder .15 .06
❑ 169 Bo Jackson .60 .24
❑ 170 Tommy Gregg .15 .06
❑ 171 Jim Abbott 2.00 .80
❑ 172 Jerome Walton .50 .20
❑ 173 Doug Jones .15 .06
❑ 174 Todd Benzinger .15 .06
❑ 175 Frank White .25 .10
❑ 176 Craig Biggio 3.00 1.20
❑ 177 John Dopson .15 .06
❑ 178 Alfredo Griffin .15 .06
❑ 179 Melido Perez .15 .06
❑ 180 Tim Burke .15 .06
❑ 181 Matt Nokes .15 .06
❑ 182 Gary Carter .25 .10
❑ 183 Ted Higuera .15 .06
❑ 184 Ken Howell .15 .06
❑ 185 Rey Quinones .15 .06
❑ 186 Wally Backman .15 .06
❑ 187 Tom Brunansky .15 .06
❑ 188 Steve Balboni .15 .06
❑ 189 Marvell Wynne .15 .06
❑ 190 Dave Henderson .15 .06
❑ 191 Don Robinson .15 .06
❑ 192 Ken Griffey Jr. 15.00 6.00
❑ 193 Ivan Calderon .15 .06

❑ 194	Mike Bielecki	.15	.06
❑ 195	Johnny Ray	.15	.06
❑ 196	Rob Murphy	.15	.06
❑ 197	Andres Thomas	.15	.06
❑ 198	Phil Bradley	.15	.06
❑ 199	Junior Felix	.25	.10
❑ 200	Jeff Russell	.15	.06
❑ 201	Mike LaValliere	.15	.06
❑ 202	Kevin Gross	.15	.06
❑ 203	Keith Moreland	.15	.06
❑ 204	Mike Marshall	.15	.06
❑ 205	Dwight Smith	.50	.20
❑ 206	Jim Clancy	.15	.06
❑ 207	Kevin Seitzer	.15	.06
❑ 208	Keith Hernandez	.25	.10
❑ 209	Bob Ojeda	.15	.06
❑ 210	Ed Whitson	.15	.06
❑ 211	Tony Phillips	.15	.06
❑ 212	Milt Thompson	.15	.06
❑ 213	Randy Kramer	.15	.06
❑ 214	Randy Bush	.15	.06
❑ 215	Randy Ready	.15	.06
❑ 216	Duane Ward	.15	.06
❑ 217	Jimmy Jones	.15	.06
❑ 218	Scott Garrelts	.15	.06
❑ 219	Scott Bankhead	.15	.06
❑ 220	Lance McCullers	.15	.06
❑ 221	B.J. Surhoff	.25	.10
❑ 222	Chris Sabo	.75	.30
❑ 223	Steve Buechele	.15	.06
❑ 224	Joel Skinner	.15	.06
❑ 225	Orel Hershiser	.25	.10
❑ 226	Derek Lilliquist	.25	.10
❑ 227	Claudell Washington	.15	.06
❑ 228	Lloyd McClendon	.15	.06
❑ 229	Felix Fermin	.15	.06
❑ 230	Paul O'Neill	.40	.16
❑ 231	Charlie Leibrandt	.15	.06
❑ 232	Dave Smith	.15	.06
❑ 233	Bob Stanley	.15	.06
❑ 234	Tim Belcher	.15	.06
❑ 235	Eric King	.15	.06
❑ 236	Spike Owen	.15	.06
❑ 237	Mike Henneman	.15	.06
❑ 238	Juan Samuel	.15	.06
❑ 239	Greg Brock	.15	.06
❑ 240	John Kruk	.25	.10
❑ 241	Glenn Wilson	.15	.06
❑ 242	Jeff Reardon	.25	.10
❑ 243	Todd Worrell	.15	.06
❑ 244	Dave LaPoint	.15	.06
❑ 245	Walt Terrell	.15	.06
❑ 246	Mike Moore	.15	.06
❑ 247	Kelly Downs	.15	.06
❑ 248	Dave Valle	.15	.06
❑ 249	Ron Kittle	.15	.06
❑ 250	Steve Wilson	.25	.10
❑ 251	Dick Schofield	.15	.06
❑ 252	Marty Barrett	.15	.06
❑ 253	Dion James	.15	.06
❑ 254	Bob Milacki	.15	.06
❑ 255	Ernie Whitt	.15	.06
❑ 256	Kevin Brown	.60	.24
❑ 257	R.J. Reynolds	.15	.06
❑ 258	Tim Raines	.25	.10
❑ 259	Frank Williams	.15	.06
❑ 260	Jose Gonzalez	.15	.06
❑ 261	Mitch Webster	.15	.06
❑ 262	Ken Caminiti	.40	.16
❑ 263	Bob Boone	.25	.10
❑ 264	Dave Magadan	.15	.06
❑ 265	Rick Aguilera	.15	.06
❑ 266	Chris James	.15	.06
❑ 267	Bob Welch	.25	.10
❑ 268	Ken Dayley	.15	.06
❑ 269	Junior Ortiz	.15	.06
❑ 270	Allan Anderson	.15	.06
❑ 271	Steve Jeltz	.15	.06
❑ 272	George Bell	.25	.10
❑ 273	Roberto Kelly	.15	.06
❑ 274	Brett Butler	.25	.10
❑ 275	Mike Schooler	.25	.10
❑ 276	Ken Phelps	.15	.06
❑ 277	Glenn Braggs	.15	.06
❑ 278	Jose Rijo	.25	.10
❑ 279	Bobby Witt	.15	.06
❑ 280	Jerry Browne	.15	.06
❑ 281	Kevin Mitchell	.25	.10
❑ 282	Craig Worthington	.15	.06
❑ 283	Greg Minton	.15	.06
❑ 284	Nick Esasky	.15	.06
❑ 285	John Farrell	.15	.06
❑ 286	Rick Mahler	.15	.06
❑ 287	Tom Gordon	.75	.30
❑ 288	Gerald Young	.15	.06
❑ 289	Jody Reed	.15	.06
❑ 290	Jeff Hamilton	.15	.06
❑ 291	Gerald Perry	.15	.06
❑ 292	Hubie Brooks	.15	.06
❑ 293	Bo Diaz	.15	.06
❑ 294	Terry Puhl	.15	.06
❑ 295	Jim Gantner	.15	.06
❑ 296	Jeff Parrett	.15	.06
❑ 297	Mike Boddicker	.15	.06
❑ 298	Dan Gladden	.15	.06
❑ 299	Tony Pena	.15	.06
❑ 300	Checklist Card	.15	.06
❑ 301	Tom Henke	.15	.06
❑ 302	Pascual Perez	.15	.06
❑ 303	Steve Bedrosian	.15	.06
❑ 304	Ken Hill	.50	.20
❑ 305	Jerry Reuss	.15	.06
❑ 306	Jim Eisenreich	.15	.06
❑ 307	Jack Howell	.15	.06
❑ 308	Rick Cerone	.15	.06
❑ 309	Tim Leary	.15	.06
❑ 310	Joe Orsulak	.15	.06
❑ 311	Jim Dwyer	.15	.06
❑ 312	Geno Petralli	.15	.06
❑ 313	Rick Honeycutt	.15	.06
❑ 314	Tom Foley	.15	.06
❑ 315	Kenny Rogers	2.00	.80
❑ 316	Mike Flanagan	.15	.06
❑ 317	Bryan Harvey	.15	.06
❑ 318	Billy Ripken	.15	.06
❑ 319	Jeff Montgomery	.15	.06
❑ 320	Erik Hanson	.50	.20
❑ 321	Brian Downing	.25	.10
❑ 322	Gregg Olson	.50	.20
❑ 323	Terry Steinbach	.25	.10
❑ 324	Sammy Sosa	15.00	6.00
❑ 325	Gene Harris	.15	.06
❑ 326	Mike Devereaux	.15	.06
❑ 327	Dennis Cook	.50	.20
❑ 328	David Wells	.25	.10
❑ 329	Checklist Card	.15	.06
❑ 330	Kirt Manwaring	.15	.06
❑ 331	Jim Presley	.15	.06
❑ 332	Checklist Card	.15	.06
❑ 333	Chuck Finley	.25	.10
❑ 334	Rob Dibble	1.00	.40
❑ 335	Cecil Espy	.15	.06
❑ 336	Dave Parker	.25	.10

1990 Donruss

	Nm-Mt	Ex-Mt
COMPLETE SET (716)	15.00	4.50
COMP.FACT.SET (728)	15.00	4.50
COMP.YAZ PUZZLE	1.00	.30

❑ 1	Bo Jackson DK	.15	.04
❑ 2	Steve Sax DK	.05	.02
❑ 3A	Ruben Sierra DK ERR (No small line on top border on card back)	.05	.02
❑ 3B	Ruben Sierra DK COR	.05	.02
❑ 4	Ken Griffey Jr. DK	.40	.12
❑ 5	Mickey Tettleton DK	.05	.02
❑ 6	Dave Stewart DK	.05	.02
❑ 7	Jim Deshaies DK DP	.05	.02
❑ 8	John Smoltz DK	.25	.07
❑ 9	Mike Bielecki DK	.05	.02
❑ 10A	Brian Downing DK ERR (Reverse negative on card front)	.15	.04
❑ 10B	Brian Downing DK COR	.05	.02
❑ 11	Kevin Mitchell DK	.05	.02
❑ 12	Kelly Gruber DK	.05	.02
❑ 13	Joe Magrane DK	.05	.02
❑ 14	John Franco DK	.10	.03
❑ 15	Ozzie Guillen DK	.10	.03
❑ 16	Lou Whitaker DK	.05	.02
❑ 17	John Smiley DK	.05	.02
❑ 18	Howard Johnson DK	.05	.02
❑ 19	Willie Randolph DK	.10	.03
❑ 20	Chris Bosio DK	.05	.02
❑ 21	Tommy Herr DK DP	.05	.02
❑ 22	Dan Gladden DK	.05	.02
❑ 23	Ellis Burks DK	.10	.03
❑ 24	Pete O'Brien DK	.05	.02
❑ 25	Bryn Smith DK	.05	.02
❑ 26	Ed Whitson DK DP	.05	.02
❑ 27	DK Checklist 1-27 DP (Comments on Perez-Steele on back)	.05	.02
❑ 28	Robin Ventura RR	.25	.07
❑ 29	Todd Zeile RR	.10	.03
❑ 30	Sandy Alomar Jr.	.10	.03
❑ 31	Kent Mercker RR RC	.25	.07
❑ 32	B.McDonald RC UER Middle name Benard not Benjamin	.25	.07
❑ 33A	J.Gonzalez RC ERR Reverse negative	2.00	.60
❑ 33B	J.Gonzalez COR RC	1.00	.30
❑ 34	Eric Anthony RR RC	.10	.03
❑ 35	Mike Fetters RR RC	.25	.07
❑ 36	Marquis Grissom RC	.40	.12
❑ 37	Greg Vaughn RR	.05	.02
❑ 38	Brian DuBois RC	.10	.03
❑ 39	Steve Avery RR UER (Born in MI, not NJ)	.05	.02
❑ 40	Mark Gardner RR RC	.10	.03
❑ 41	Andy Benes	.10	.03
❑ 42	D.DeShields RR RC	.25	.07
❑ 43	Scott Coolbaugh RC	.10	.03
❑ 44	Pat Combs DP	.05	.02
❑ 45	Alex Sanchez DP	.05	.02
❑ 46	Kelly Mann DP RC	.10	.03
❑ 47	Julio Machado DP RC	.10	.03
❑ 48	Pete Incaviglia	.05	.02
❑ 49	Shawon Dunston	.05	.02
❑ 50	Jeff Treadway	.05	.02
❑ 51	Jeff Ballard	.05	.02
❑ 52	Claudell Washington	.05	.02
❑ 53	Juan Samuel	.05	.02
❑ 54	John Smiley	.05	.02
❑ 55	Rob Deer	.05	.02
❑ 56	Geno Petralli	.05	.02
❑ 57	Chris Bosio	.05	.02
❑ 58	Carlton Fisk	.15	.04
❑ 59	Kirt Manwaring	.05	.02
❑ 60	Chet Lemon	.05	.02
❑ 61	Bo Jackson	.25	.07
❑ 62	Doyle Alexander	.05	.02
❑ 63	Pedro Guerrero	.05	.02
❑ 64	Allan Anderson	.05	.02
❑ 65	Greg W. Harris	.05	.02
❑ 66	Mike Greenwell	.05	.02
❑ 67	Walt Weiss	.05	.02
❑ 68	Wade Boggs	.15	.04
❑ 69	Jim Clancy	.05	.02
❑ 70	Junior Felix	.05	.02
❑ 71	Barry Larkin	.15	.04
❑ 72	Dave LaPoint	.05	.02
❑ 73	Joel Skinner	.05	.02
❑ 74	Jesse Barfield	.05	.02
❑ 75	Tommy Herr	.05	.02

☐ 76 Ricky Jordan .05 .02
☐ 77 Eddie Murray .25 .07
☐ 78 Steve Sax .05 .02
☐ 79 Tim Belcher .05 .02
☐ 80 Danny Jackson .05 .02
☐ 81 Kent Hrbek .10 .03
☐ 82 Milt Thompson .05 .02
☐ 83 Brook Jacoby .05 .02
☐ 84 Mike Marshall .05 .02
☐ 85 Kevin Seitzer .05 .02
☐ 86 Tony Gwynn .30 .09
☐ 87 Dave Stieb .10 .03
☐ 88 Dave Smith .05 .02
☐ 89 Bret Saberhagen .10 .03
☐ 90 Alan Trammell .10 .03
☐ 91 Tony Phillips .05 .02
☐ 92 Doug Drabek .05 .02
☐ 93 Jeffrey Leonard .05 .02
☐ 94 Wally Joyner .10 .03
☐ 95 Carney Lansford .10 .03
☐ 96 Cal Ripken .75 .23
☐ 97 Andres Galarraga .10 .03
☐ 98 Kevin Mitchell .05 .02
☐ 99 Howard Johnson .05 .02
☐ 100A Checklist 28-129 .05 .02
☐ 100B Checklist 28-125 .05 .02
☐ 101 Melido Perez .05 .02
☐ 102 Spike Owen .05 .02
☐ 103 Paul Molitor .15 .04
☐ 104 Geronimo Berroa .05 .02
☐ 105 Ryne Sandberg .40 .12
☐ 106 Bryn Smith .05 .02
☐ 107 Steve Buechele .05 .02
☐ 108 Jim Abbott .15 .04
☐ 109 Alvin Davis .05 .02
☐ 110 Lee Smith .10 .03
☐ 111 Roberto Alomar .15 .04
☐ 112 Rick Reuschel .05 .02
☐ 113A Kelly Gruber ERR .05 .02
(Born 2/22)
☐ 113B Kelly Gruber COR .05 .02
(Born 2/26; corrected
in factory sets)
☐ 114 Joe Carter .10 .03
☐ 115 Jose Rijo .05 .02
☐ 116 Greg Minton .05 .02
☐ 117 Bob Ojeda .05 .02
☐ 118 Glenn Davis .05 .02
☐ 119 Jeff Reardon .10 .03
☐ 120 Kurt Stillwell .05 .02
☐ 121 John Smoltz .25 .07
☐ 122 Dwight Evans .15 .04
☐ 123 Eric Yelding .05 .02
☐ 124 John Franco .10 .03
☐ 125 Jose Canseco .15 .04
☐ 126 Barry Bonds 1.00 .30
☐ 127 Lee Guetterman .05 .02
☐ 128 Jack Clark .10 .03
☐ 129 Dave Valle .05 .02
☐ 130 Hubie Brooks .05 .02
☐ 131 Ernest Riles .05 .02
☐ 132 Mike Morgan .05 .02
☐ 133 Steve Jeltz .05 .02
☐ 134 Jeff D. Robinson .05 .02
☐ 135 Ozzie Guillen .10 .03
☐ 136 Chili Davis .10 .03
☐ 137 Mitch Webster .05 .02
☐ 138 Jerry Browne .05 .02
☐ 139 Bo Diaz .05 .02
☐ 140 Robby Thompson .05 .02
☐ 141 Craig Worthington .05 .02
☐ 142 Julio Franco .10 .03
☐ 143 Brian Holman .05 .02
☐ 144 George Brett .60 .18
☐ 145 Tom Glavine .15 .04
☐ 146 Robin Yount .40 .12
☐ 147 Gary Carter .10 .03
☐ 148 Ron Kittle .05 .02
☐ 149 Tony Fernandez .05 .02
☐ 150 Dave Stewart .10 .03
☐ 151 Gary Gaetti .10 .03
☐ 152 Kevin Elster .05 .02
☐ 153 Gerald Perry .05 .02
☐ 154 Jesse Orosco .05 .02
☐ 155 Wally Backman .05 .02
☐ 156 Dennis Martinez .10 .03
☐ 157 Rick Sutcliffe .10 .03
☐ 158 Greg Maddux .40 .12
☐ 159 Andy Hawkins .05 .02
☐ 160 John Kruk .10 .03
☐ 161 Jose Oquendo .05 .02
☐ 162 John Dopson .05 .02
☐ 163 Joe Magrane .05 .02
☐ 164 Bill Ripken .05 .02
☐ 165 Fred Manrique .05 .02
☐ 166 Nolan Ryan UER 1.00 .30
(Did not lead NL in
K's in '89 as he was
in AL in '89)
☐ 167 Damon Berryhill .05 .02
☐ 168 Dale Murphy .15 .04
☐ 169 Mickey Tettleton .05 .02
☐ 170A Kirk McCaskill ERR .05 .02
(Born 4/19)
☐ 170B Kirk McCaskill COR .05 .02
(Born 4/9; corrected
in factory sets)
☐ 171 Dwight Gooden .10 .03
☐ 172 Jose Lind .05 .02
☐ 173 B.J. Surhoff .10 .03
☐ 174 Ruben Sierra .05 .02
☐ 175 Dan Plesac .05 .02
☐ 176 Dan Pasqua .05 .02
☐ 177 Kelly Downs .05 .02
☐ 178 Matt Nokes .05 .02
☐ 179 Luis Aquino .05 .02
☐ 180 Frank Tanana .05 .02
☐ 181 Tony Pena .05 .02
☐ 182 Dan Gladden .05 .02
☐ 183 Bruce Hurst .05 .02
☐ 184 Roger Clemens .50 .15
☐ 185 Mark McGwire .60 .18
☐ 186 Rob Murphy .05 .02
☐ 187 Jim Deshaies .05 .02
☐ 188 Fred McGriff .25 .07
☐ 189 Rob Dibble .10 .03
☐ 190 Don Mattingly .60 .18
☐ 191 Felix Fermin .05 .02
☐ 192 Roberto Kelly .05 .02
☐ 193 Dennis Cook .05 .02
☐ 194 Darren Daulton .10 .03
☐ 195 Alfredo Griffin .05 .02
☐ 196 Eric Plunk .05 .02
☐ 197 Orel Hershiser .10 .03
☐ 198 Paul O'Neill .15 .04
☐ 199 Randy Bush .05 .02
☐ 200A Checklist 130-231 .05 .02
☐ 200B Checklist 126-223 .05 .02
☐ 201 Ozzie Smith .40 .12
☐ 202 Pete O'Brien .05 .02
☐ 203 Jay Howell .05 .02
☐ 204 Mark Gubicza .05 .02
☐ 205 Ed Whitson .05 .02
☐ 206 George Bell .05 .02
☐ 207 Mike Scott .05 .02
☐ 208 Charlie Leibrandt .05 .02
☐ 209 Mike Heath .05 .02
☐ 210 Dennis Eckersley .10 .03
☐ 211 Mike LaValliere .05 .02
☐ 212 Darnell Coles .05 .02
☐ 213 Lance Parrish .05 .02
☐ 214 Mike Moore .05 .02
☐ 215 Steve Finley .10 .03
☐ 216 Tim Raines .10 .03
☐ 217A Scott Garrelts ERR .05 .02
(Born 10/20)
☐ 217B Scott Garrelts COR .05 .02
(Born 10/30; corrected
in factory sets)
☐ 218 Kevin McReynolds .05 .02
☐ 219 Dave Gallagher .05 .02
☐ 220 Tim Wallach .05 .02
☐ 221 Chuck Crim .05 .02
☐ 222 Lonnie Smith .05 .02
☐ 223 Andre Dawson .10 .03
☐ 224 Nelson Santovenia .05 .02
☐ 225 Rafael Palmeiro .15 .04
☐ 226 Devon White .10 .03
☐ 227 Harold Reynolds .10 .03
☐ 228 Ellis Burks .15 .04
☐ 229 Mark Parent .05 .02
☐ 230 Will Clark .15 .04
☐ 231 Jimmy Key .10 .03
☐ 232 John Farrell .05 .02
☐ 233 Eric Davis .10 .03
☐ 234 Johnny Ray .05 .02
☐ 235 Darryl Strawberry .10 .03
☐ 236 Bill Doran .05 .02
☐ 237 Greg Gagne .05 .02
☐ 238 Jim Eisenreich .05 .02
☐ 239 Tommy Gregg .05 .02
☐ 240 Marty Barrett .05 .02
☐ 241 Rafael Ramirez .05 .02
☐ 242 Chris Sabo .05 .02
☐ 243 Dave Henderson .05 .02
☐ 244 Andy Van Slyke .15 .04
☐ 245 Alvaro Espinoza .05 .02
☐ 246 Garry Templeton .05 .02
☐ 247 Gene Harris .05 .02
☐ 248 Kevin Gross .05 .02
☐ 249 Brett Butler .10 .03
☐ 250 Willie Randolph .10 .03
☐ 251 Roger McDowell .05 .02
☐ 252 Rafael Belliard .05 .02
☐ 253 Steve Rosenberg .05 .02
☐ 254 Jack Howell .05 .02
☐ 255 Marvell Wynne .05 .02
☐ 256 Tom Candiotti .05 .02
☐ 257 Todd Benzinger .05 .02
☐ 258 Don Robinson .05 .02
☐ 259 Phil Bradley .05 .02
☐ 260 Cecil Espy .05 .02
☐ 261 Scott Bankhead .05 .02
☐ 262 Frank White .10 .03
☐ 263 Andres Thomas .05 .02
☐ 264 Glenn Braggs .05 .02
☐ 265 David Cone .10 .03
☐ 266 Bobby Thigpen .05 .02
☐ 267 Nelson Liriano .05 .02
☐ 268 Terry Steinbach .05 .02
☐ 269 Kirby Puckett UER .25 .07
(Back doesn't consider
Joe Torre's .363 in '71)
☐ 270 Gregg Jefferies .10 .03
☐ 271 Jeff Blauser .05 .02
☐ 272 Cory Snyder .05 .02
☐ 273 Roy Smith .05 .02
☐ 274 Tom Foley .05 .02
☐ 275 Mitch Williams .05 .02
☐ 276 Paul Kilgus .05 .02
☐ 277 Don Slaught .05 .02
☐ 278 Von Hayes .05 .02
☐ 279 Vince Coleman .05 .02
☐ 280 Mike Boddicker .05 .02
☐ 281 Ken Dayley .05 .02
☐ 282 Mike Devereaux .05 .02
☐ 283 Kenny Rogers .10 .03
☐ 284 Jeff Russell .05 .02
☐ 285 Jerome Walton .05 .02
☐ 286 Derek Lilliquist .05 .02
☐ 287 Joe Orsulak .05 .02
☐ 288 Dick Schofield .05 .02
☐ 289 Ron Darling .05 .02
☐ 290 Bobby Bonilla .10 .03
☐ 291 Jim Gantner .05 .02
☐ 292 Bobby Witt .05 .02
☐ 293 Greg Brock .05 .02
☐ 294 Ivan Calderon .05 .02
☐ 295 Steve Bedrosian .05 .02
☐ 296 Mike Henneman .05 .02
☐ 297 Tom Gordon .10 .03
☐ 298 Lou Whitaker .10 .03
☐ 299 Terry Pendleton .10 .03
☐ 300A Checklist 232-333 .05 .02
☐ 300B Checklist 224-321 .05 .02
☐ 301 Juan Berenguer .05 .02
☐ 302 Mark Davis .05 .02
☐ 303 Nick Esasky .05 .02
☐ 304 Rickey Henderson .25 .07
☐ 305 Rick Cerone .05 .02
☐ 306 Craig Biggio .25 .07
☐ 307 Duane Ward .05 .02
☐ 308 Tom Browning .05 .02
☐ 309 Walt Terrell .05 .02
☐ 310 Greg Swindell .05 .02
☐ 311 Dave Righetti .05 .02
☐ 312 Mike Maddux .05 .02
☐ 313 Len Dykstra .10 .03

❑	314	Jose Gonzalez	.05	.02
❑	315	Steve Balboni	.05	.02
❑	316	Mike Scioscia	.05	.02
❑	317	Ron Oester	.05	.02
❑	318	Gary Wayne	.05	.02
❑	319	Todd Worrell	.05	.02
❑	320	Doug Jones	.05	.02
❑	321	Jeff Hamilton	.05	.02
❑	322	Danny Tartabull	.05	.02
❑	323	Chris James	.05	.02
❑	324	Mike Flanagan	.05	.02
❑	325	Gerald Young	.05	.02
❑	326	Bob Boone	.10	.03
❑	327	Frank Williams	.05	.02
❑	328	Dave Parker	.10	.03
❑	329	Sid Bream	.05	.02
❑	330	Mike Schooler	.05	.02
❑	331	Bert Blyleven	.10	.03
❑	332	Bob Welch	.05	.02
❑	333	Bob Milacki	.05	.02
❑	334	Tim Burke	.05	.02
❑	335	Jose Uribe	.05	.02
❑	336	Randy Myers	.10	.03
❑	337	Eric King	.05	.02
❑	338	Mark Langston	.05	.02
❑	339	Teddy Higuera	.05	.02
❑	340	Oddibe McDowell	.05	.02
❑	341	Lloyd McClendon	.05	.02
❑	342	Pascual Perez	.05	.02
❑	343	Kevin Brown UER	.10	.03
		(Signed is misspelled as signeed on back)		
❑	344	Chuck Finley	.10	.03
❑	345	Erik Hanson	.05	.02
❑	346	Rich Gedman	.05	.02
❑	347	Bip Roberts	.05	.02
❑	348	Matt Williams	.10	.03
❑	349	Tom Henke	.05	.02
❑	350	Brad Komminsk	.05	.02
❑	351	Jeff Reed	.05	.02
❑	352	Brian Downing	.05	.02
❑	353	Frank Viola	.05	.02
❑	354	Terry Puhl	.05	.02
❑	355	Brian Harper	.05	.02
❑	356	Steve Farr	.05	.02
❑	357	Joe Boever	.05	.02
❑	358	Danny Heep	.05	.02
❑	359	Larry Andersen	.05	.02
❑	360	Rolando Roomes	.05	.02
❑	361	Mike Gallego	.05	.02
❑	362	Bob Kipper	.05	.02
❑	363	Clay Parker	.05	.02
❑	364	Mike Pagliarulo	.05	.02
❑	365	Ken Griffey Jr. UER	.75	.23
		(Signed through 1990, should be 1991)		
❑	366	Rex Hudler	.05	.02
❑	367	Pat Sheridan	.05	.02
❑	368	Kirk Gibson	.15	.04
❑	369	Jeff Parrett	.05	.02
❑	370	Bob Walk	.05	.02
❑	371	Ken Patterson	.05	.02
❑	372	Bryan Harvey	.05	.02
❑	373	Mike Bielecki	.05	.02
❑	374	Tom Magrann	.05	.02
❑	375	Rick Mahler	.05	.02
❑	376	Craig Lefferts	.05	.02
❑	377	Gregg Olson	.10	.03
❑	378	Jamie Moyer	.10	.03
❑	379	Randy Johnson	.50	.15
❑	380	Jeff Montgomery	.10	.03
❑	381	Marty Clary	.05	.02
❑	382	Bill Spiers	.05	.02
❑	383	Dave Magadan	.05	.02
❑	384	Greg Hibbard RC	.10	.03
❑	385	Ernie Whitt	.05	.02
❑	386	Rick Honeycutt	.05	.02
❑	387	Dave West	.05	.02
❑	388	Keith Hernandez	.10	.03
❑	389	Jose Alvarez	.05	.02
❑	390	Joey Belle	.25	.07
❑	391	Rick Aguilera	.10	.03
❑	392	Mike Fitzgerald	.05	.02
❑	393	Dwight Smith	.05	.02
❑	394	Steve Wilson	.05	.02
❑	395	Bob Geren	.05	.02
❑	396	Randy Ready	.05	.02
❑	397	Ken Hill	.10	.03
❑	398	Jody Reed	.05	.02
❑	399	Tom Brunansky	.05	.02
❑	400A	Checklist 334-435	.05	.02
❑	400B	Checklist 322-419	.05	.02
❑	401	Rene Gonzales	.05	.02
❑	402	Harold Baines	.10	.03
❑	403	Cecilio Guante	.05	.02
❑	404	Joe Girardi	.15	.04
❑	405A	Sergio Valdez ERR	.05	.02
		(Card front shows black line crossing S in Sergio)		
❑	405B	Sergio Valdez COR	.05	.02
❑	406	Mark Williamson	.05	.02
❑	407	Glenn Hoffman	.05	.02
❑	408	Jeff Innis	.05	.02
❑	409	Randy Kramer	.05	.02
❑	410	Charlie O'Brien	.05	.02
❑	411	Charlie Hough	.10	.03
❑	412	Gus Polidor	.05	.02
❑	413	Ron Karkovice	.05	.02
❑	414	Trevor Wilson	.05	.02
❑	415	Kevin Ritz	.05	.02
❑	416	Gary Thurman	.05	.02
❑	417	Jeff M. Robinson	.05	.02
❑	418	Scott Terry	.05	.02
❑	419	Tim Laudner	.05	.02
❑	420	Dennis Rasmussen	.05	.02
❑	421	Luis Rivera	.05	.02
❑	422	Jim Corsi	.05	.02
❑	423	Dennis Lamp	.05	.02
❑	424	Ken Caminiti	.10	.03
❑	425	David Wells	.10	.03
❑	426	Norm Charlton	.05	.02
❑	427	Deion Sanders	.25	.07
❑	428	Dion James	.05	.02
❑	429	Chuck Cary	.05	.02
❑	430	Ken Howell	.05	.02
❑	431	Steve Lake	.05	.02
❑	432	Kal Daniels	.05	.02
❑	433	Lance McCullers	.05	.02
❑	434	Lenny Harris	.05	.02
❑	435	Scott Scudder	.05	.02
❑	436	Gene Larkin	.05	.02
❑	437	Dan Quisenberry	.05	.02
❑	438	Steve Olin RC	.25	.07
❑	439	Mickey Hatcher	.05	.02
❑	440	Willie Wilson	.05	.02
❑	441	Mark Grant	.05	.02
❑	442	Mookie Wilson	.10	.03
❑	443	Alex Trevino	.05	.02
❑	444	Pat Tabler	.05	.02
❑	445	Dave Bergman	.05	.02
❑	446	Todd Burns	.05	.02
❑	447	R.J. Reynolds	.05	.02
❑	448	Jay Buhner	.10	.03
❑	449	Lee Stevens	.10	.03
❑	450	Ron Hassey	.05	.02
❑	451	Bob Melvin	.05	.02
❑	452	Dave Martinez	.05	.02
❑	453	Greg Litton	.05	.02
❑	454	Mark Carreon	.05	.02
❑	455	Scott Fletcher	.05	.02
❑	456	Otis Nixon	.05	.02
❑	457	Tony Fossas	.05	.02
❑	458	John Russell	.05	.02
❑	459	Paul Assenmacher	.05	.02
❑	460	Zane Smith	.05	.02
❑	461	Jack Daugherty	.05	.02
❑	462	Rich Monteleone	.05	.02
❑	463	Greg Briley	.05	.02
❑	464	Mike Smithson	.05	.02
❑	465	Benito Santiago	.10	.03
❑	466	Jeff Brantley	.05	.02
❑	467	Jose Nunez	.05	.02
❑	468	Scott Bailes	.05	.02
❑	469	Ken Griffey Sr.	.10	.03
❑	470	Bob McClure	.05	.02
❑	471	Mackey Sasser	.05	.02
❑	472	Glenn Wilson	.05	.02
❑	473	Kevin Tapani RC	.25	.07
❑	474	Bill Buckner	.05	.02
❑	475	Ron Gant	.10	.03
❑	476	Kevin Romine	.05	.02
❑	477	Juan Agosto	.05	.02
❑	478	Herm Winningham	.05	.02
❑	479	Storm Davis	.05	.02
❑	480	Jeff King	.05	.02
❑	481	Kevin Mmahat	.05	.02
❑	482	Carmelo Martinez	.05	.02
❑	483	Omar Vizquel	.25	.07
❑	484	Jim Dwyer	.05	.02
❑	485	Bob Knepper	.05	.02
❑	486	Dave Anderson	.05	.02
❑	487	Ron Jones	.05	.02
❑	488	Jay Bell	.10	.03
❑	489	Sammy Sosa RC	3.00	.90
❑	490	Kent Anderson	.05	.02
❑	491	Domingo Ramos	.05	.02
❑	492	Dave Clark	.05	.02
❑	493	Tim Birtsas	.05	.02
❑	494	Ken Oberkfell	.05	.02
❑	495	Larry Sheets	.05	.02
❑	496	Jeff Kunkel	.05	.02
❑	497	Jim Presley	.05	.02
❑	498	Mike Macfarlane	.05	.02
❑	499	Pete Smith	.05	.02
❑	500A	Checklist 436-537 DP	.05	.02
❑	500B	Checklist 420-517	.05	.02
❑	501	Gary Sheffield	.25	.07
❑	502	Terry Bross	.05	.02
❑	503	Jerry Kutzler	.05	.02
❑	504	Lloyd Moseby	.05	.02
❑	505	Curt Young	.05	.02
❑	506	Al Newman	.05	.02
❑	507	Keith Miller	.05	.02
❑	508	Mike Stanton RC	.25	.07
❑	509	Rich Yett	.05	.02
❑	510	Tim Drummond	.05	.02
❑	511	Joe Hesketh	.05	.02
❑	512	Rick Wrona	.05	.02
❑	513	Luis Salazar	.05	.02
❑	514	Hal Morris	.05	.02
❑	515	Terry Mulholland	.05	.02
❑	516	John Morris	.05	.02
❑	517	Carlos Quintana	.05	.02
❑	518	Frank DiPino	.05	.02
❑	519	Randy Milligan	.05	.02
❑	520	Chad Kreuter	.05	.02
❑	521	Mike Jeffcoat	.05	.02
❑	522	Mike Harkey	.05	.02
❑	523A	Andy Nezelek ERR	.05	.02
		(Wrong birth year)		
❑	523B	Andy Nezelek COR	.15	.04
		(Finally corrected in factory sets)		
❑	524	Dave Schmidt	.05	.02
❑	525	Tony Armas	.05	.02
❑	526	Barry Lyons	.05	.02
❑	527	Rick Reed RC	.25	.07
❑	528	Jerry Reuss	.05	.02
❑	529	Dean Palmer RC	.25	.07
❑	530	Jeff Peterek	.05	.02
❑	531	Carlos Martinez	.05	.02
❑	532	Atlee Hammaker	.05	.02
❑	533	Mike Brumley	.05	.02
❑	534	Terry Leach	.05	.02
❑	535	Doug Strange	.05	.02
❑	536	Jose DeLeon	.05	.02
❑	537	Shane Rawley	.05	.02
❑	538	Joey Cora	.10	.03
❑	539	Eric Hetzel	.05	.02
❑	540	Gene Nelson	.05	.02
❑	541	Wes Gardner	.05	.02
❑	542	Mark Portugal	.05	.02
❑	543	Al Leiter	.25	.07
❑	544	Jack Armstrong	.05	.02
❑	545	Greg Cadaret	.05	.02
❑	546	Rod Nichols	.05	.02
❑	547	Luis Polonia	.05	.02
❑	548	Charlie Hayes	.05	.02
❑	549	Dickie Thon	.05	.02
❑	550	Tim Crews	.05	.02
❑	551	Dave Winfield	.10	.03
❑	552	Mike Davis	.05	.02
❑	553	Ron Robinson	.05	.02
❑	554	Carmen Castillo	.05	.02
❑	555	John Costello	.05	.02
❑	556	Bud Black	.05	.02
❑	557	Rick Dempsey	.05	.02

❑	558	Jim Acker	.05	.02
❑	559	Eric Show	.05	.02
❑	560	Pat Borders	.05	.02
❑	561	Danny Darwin	.05	.02
❑	562	Rick Luecken	.05	.02
❑	563	Edwin Nunez	.05	.02
❑	564	Felix Jose	.05	.02
❑	565	John Cangelosi	.05	.02
❑	566	Bill Swift	.05	.02
❑	567	Bill Schroeder	.05	.02
❑	568	Stan Javier	.05	.02
❑	569	Jim Traber	.05	.02
❑	570	Wallace Johnson	.05	.02
❑	571	Donell Nixon	.05	.02
❑	572	Sid Fernandez	.05	.02
❑	573	Lance Johnson	.05	.02
❑	574	Andy McGaffigan	.05	.02
❑	575	Mark Knudson	.05	.02
❑	576	Tommy Greene RC	.10	.03
❑	577	Mark Grace	.15	.04
❑	578	Larry Walker RC	1.00	.30
❑	579	Mike Stanley	.05	.02
❑	580	Mike Witt DP	.05	.02
❑	581	Scott Bradley	.05	.02
❑	582	Greg A. Harris	.05	.02
❑	583A	Kevin Hickey ERR	.25	.07
❑	583B	Kevin Hickey COR	.05	.02
❑	584	Lee Mazzilli	.05	.02
❑	585	Jeff Pico	.05	.02
❑	586	Joe Oliver	.05	.02
❑	587	Willie Fraser DP	.05	.02
❑	588	Carl Yastrzemski Puzzle Card DP	.25	.07
❑	589	Kevin Bass DP	.05	.02
❑	590	John Moses DP	.05	.02
❑	591	Tom Pagnozzi DP	.05	.02
❑	592	Tony Castillo DP	.05	.02
❑	593	Jerald Clark DP	.05	.02
❑	594	Dan Schatzeder	.05	.02
❑	595	Luis Quinones DP	.05	.02
❑	596	Pete Harnisch DP	.05	.02
❑	597	Gary Redus	.05	.02
❑	598	Mel Hall	.05	.02
❑	599	Rick Schu	.05	.02
❑	600A	Checklist 538-639	.05	.02
❑	600B	Checklist 518-617	.05	.02
❑	601	Mike Kingery DP	.05	.02
❑	602	Terry Kennedy DP	.05	.02
❑	603	Mike Sharperson DP	.05	.02
❑	604	Don Carman DP	.05	.02
❑	605	Jim Gott	.05	.02
❑	606	Donn Pall DP	.05	.02
❑	607	Rance Mulliniks	.05	.02
❑	608	Curt Wilkerson DP	.05	.02
❑	609	Mike Felder DP	.05	.02
❑	610	G.Hernandez DP	.05	.02
❑	611	Candy Maldonado DP	.05	.02
❑	612	Mark Thurmond DP	.05	.02
❑	613	Rick Leach DP	.05	.02
❑	614	Jerry Reed DP	.05	.02
❑	615	Franklin Stubbs	.05	.02
❑	616	Billy Hatcher DP	.05	.02
❑	617	Don August DP	.05	.02
❑	618	Tim Teufel	.05	.02
❑	619	Shawn Hillegas DP	.05	.02
❑	620	Manny Lee	.05	.02
❑	621	Gary Ward DP	.05	.02
❑	622	Mark Guthrie DP	.05	.02
❑	623	Jeff Musselman DP	.05	.02
❑	624	Mark Lemke DP	.05	.02
❑	625	Fernando Valenzuela	.10	.03
❑	626	Paul Sorrento DP RC	.25	.07
❑	627	Glenallen Hill DP	.05	.02
❑	628	Les Lancaster DP	.05	.02
❑	629	Vance Law DP	.05	.02
❑	630	Randy Velarde DP	.05	.02
❑	631	Todd Frohwirth DP	.05	.02
❑	632	Willie McGee	.10	.03
❑	633	Dennis Boyd DP	.05	.02
❑	634	Cris Carpenter DP	.05	.02
❑	635	Brian Holton	.05	.02
❑	636	Tracy Jones DP	.05	.02
❑	637A	Terry Steinbach AS (Recent Major League Performance)	.05	.02
❑	637B	Terry Steinbach AS (All-Star Game Performance)	.05	.02
❑	638	Brady Anderson	.10	.03
❑	639A	Jack Morris ERR (Card front shows black line crossing J in Jack)	.10	.03
❑	639B	Jack Morris COR	.10	.03
❑	640	Jaime Navarro	.05	.02
❑	641	Darrin Jackson	.05	.02
❑	642	Mike Dyer RC	.05	.02
❑	643	Mike Schmidt	.50	.15
❑	644	Henry Cotto	.05	.02
❑	645	John Cerutti	.05	.02
❑	646	Francisco Cabrera	.05	.02
❑	647	Scott Sanderson	.05	.02
❑	648	Brian Meyer	.05	.02
❑	649	Ray Searage	.05	.02
❑	650A	Bo Jackson AS (Recent Major League Performance)	.25	.07
❑	650B	Bo Jackson AS (All-Star Game Performance)	.25	.07
❑	651	Steve Lyons	.05	.02
❑	652	Mike LaCoss	.05	.02
❑	653	Ted Power	.05	.02
❑	654A	Howard Johnson AS (Recent Major League Performance)	.05	.02
❑	654B	Howard Johnson AS (All-Star Game Performance)	.05	.02
❑	655	Mauro Gozzo	.05	.02
❑	656	Mike Blowers RC	.10	.03
❑	657	Paul Gibson	.05	.02
❑	658	Neal Heaton	.05	.02
❑	659	Nolan Ryan 5000K COR (Still an error as Ryan did not lead AL in K's in '75)	.50	.15
❑	659A	Nolan Ryan 5000K ERR (665 King of Kings back)	1.50	.45
❑	660A	Harold Baines AS (Black line through star on front; Recent Major League Performance)	.75	.23
❑	660B	Harold Baines AS (Black line through star on front; All-Star Game Performance)	1.00	.30
❑	660C	Harold Baines AS (Black line behind star on front; Recent Major League Performance)	.25	.07
❑	660D	Harold Baines AS (Black line behind star on front; All-Star Game Performance)	.05	.02
❑	661	Gary Pettis	.05	.02
❑	662	Clint Zavaras	.05	.02
❑	663A	Rick Reuschel AS (Recent Major League Performance)	.05	.02
❑	663B	Rick Reuschel AS (All-Star Game Performance)	.05	.02
❑	664	Alejandro Pena	.05	.02
❑	665	N.Ryan KING COR	.50	.15
❑	665A	Nolan Ryan KING (659 5000 K back) ERR	1.50	.45
❑	665C	N.Ryan KING ERR No number on back in factory sets	.75	.23
❑	666	Ricky Horton	.05	.02
❑	667	Curt Schilling	1.00	.30
❑	668	Bill Landrum	.05	.02
❑	669	Todd Stottlemyre	.10	.03
❑	670	Tim Leary	.05	.02
❑	671	John Wetteland	.25	.07
❑	672	Calvin Schiraldi	.05	.02
❑	673A	Ruben Sierra AS (Recent Major League Performance)	.05	.02
❑	673B	Ruben Sierra AS (All-Star Game Performance)	.05	.02
❑	674A	Pedro Guerrero AS (Recent Major League Performance)	.05	.02
❑	674B	Pedro Guerrero AS (All-Star Game Performance)	.05	.02
❑	675	Ken Phelps	.05	.02
❑	676A	Cal Ripken AS (All-Star Game Performance)	.40	.12
❑	676B	Cal Ripken AS (Recent Major League Performance)	.75	.23
❑	677	Denny Walling	.05	.02
❑	678	Goose Gossage	.10	.03
❑	679	Gary Mielke	.05	.02
❑	680	Bill Bathe	.05	.02
❑	681	Tom Lawless	.05	.02
❑	682	Xavier Hernandez RC	.05	.02
❑	683A	Kirby Puckett AS (Recent Major League Performance)	.15	.04
❑	683B	Kirby Puckett AS (All-Star Game Performance)	.15	.04
❑	684	Mariano Duncan	.05	.02
❑	685	Ramon Martinez	.05	.02
❑	686	Tim Jones	.05	.02
❑	687	Tom Filer	.05	.02
❑	688	Steve Lombardozzi	.05	.02
❑	689	Bernie Williams RC	1.50	.45
❑	690	Chip Hale	.05	.02
❑	691	Beau Allred RC	.05	.02
❑	692A	Ryne Sandberg AS (Recent Major League Performance)	.25	.07
❑	692B	Ryne Sandberg AS (All-Star Game Performance)	.25	.07
❑	693	Jeff Huson RC	.10	.03
❑	694	Curt Ford	.05	.02
❑	695A	Eric Davis AS (Recent Major League Performance)	.05	.02
❑	695B	Eric Davis AS (All-Star Game Performance)	.05	.02
❑	696	Scott Lusader	.05	.02
❑	697A	Mark McGwire AS (Recent Major League Performance)	.30	.09
❑	697B	Mark McGwire AS (All-Star Game Performance)	.30	.09
❑	698	Steve Cummings RC	.05	.02
❑	699	George Canale	.05	.02
❑	700A	Checklist 640-715 and BC1-BC26	.25	.07
❑	700B	Checklist 640-716 and BC1-BC26	.10	.03
❑	700C	Checklist 618-716	.05	.02
❑	701A	Julio Franco AS (Recent Major League Performance)	.05	.02
❑	701B	Julio Franco AS (All-Star Game Performance)	.05	.02
❑	702	Dave Johnson (P)	.05	.02
❑	703A	Dave Stewart AS (Recent Major League Performance)	.05	.02
❑	703B	Dave Stewart AS (All-Star Game Performance)	.05	.02
❑	704	Dave Justice RC	.50	.15
❑	705	Tony Gwynn AS (All-Star Game Performance)	.15	.04
❑	705A	Tony Gwynn AS	.15	.04

(Recent Major League Performance)
❑ 706 Greg Myers .05 .02
❑ 707A Will Clark AS .15 .04
(Recent Major League Performance)
❑ 707B Will Clark AS .15 .04
(All-Star Game Performance)
❑ 708A Benito Santiago AS .05 .02
(Recent Major League Performance)
❑ 708B Benito Santiago AS .05 .02
(All-Star Game Performance)
❑ 709 Larry McWilliams .05 .02
❑ 710A Ozzie Smith AS .25 .07
(Recent Major League Performance)
❑ 710B Ozzie Smith AS Perf .25 .07
❑ 711 John Olerud RC .50 .15
❑ 712A Wade Boggs AS .10 .03
(Recent Major League Performance)
❑ 712B Wade Boggs AS .10 .03
(All-Star Game Performance)
❑ 713 Gary Eave .05 .02
❑ 714 Bob Tewksbury .05 .02
❑ 715A Kevin Mitchell AS .05 .02
(Recent Major League Performance)
❑ 715B Kevin Mitchell AS .05 .02
(All-Star Game Performance)
❑ 716 B.Giamatti COMM .25 .07
In Memoriam

1990 Donruss Best AL

	Nm-Mt	Ex-Mt
COMP.FACT.SET (144)	40.00	12.00

❑ 1 Ken Griffey Jr. 1.25 .35
❑ 2 Bob Milacki .15 .04
❑ 3 Mike Boddicker .15 .04
❑ 4 Bert Blyleven .20 .06
❑ 5 Carlton Fisk .30 .09
❑ 6 Greg Swindell .15 .04
❑ 7 Alan Trammell .20 .06
❑ 8 Mark Davis .15 .04
❑ 9 Chris Bosio .15 .04
❑ 10 Gary Gaetti .20 .06
❑ 11 Matt Nokes .15 .04
❑ 12 Dennis Eckersley .20 .06
❑ 13 Kevin Brown .20 .06
❑ 14 Tom Henke .15 .04
❑ 15 Mickey Tettleton .15 .04
❑ 16 Jody Reed .15 .04
❑ 17 Mark Langston .15 .04
❑ 18 Melido Perez UER .15 .04
(Listed as an Expo rather than White Sox)
❑ 19 John Farrell .15 .04
❑ 20 Tony Phillips .15 .04
❑ 21 Bret Saberhagen .20 .06
❑ 22 Robin Yount .75 .23
❑ 23 Kirby Puckett .50 .15
❑ 24 Steve Sax .15 .04
❑ 25 Dave Stewart .20 .06
❑ 26 Alvin Davis .15 .04
❑ 27 Geno Petralli .15 .04
❑ 28 Mookie Wilson .20 .06
❑ 29 Jeff Ballard .15 .04
❑ 30 Ellis Burks .20 .06
❑ 31 Wally Joyner .20 .06
❑ 32 Bobby Thigpen .15 .04
❑ 33 Keith Hernandez .20 .06
❑ 34 Jack Morris .20 .06
❑ 35 George Brett 1.25 .35
❑ 36 Dan Plesac .15 .04
❑ 37 Brian Harper .15 .04
❑ 38 Don Mattingly 1.25 .35
❑ 39 Dave Henderson .15 .04
❑ 40 Scott Bankhead UER .15 .04
(Asheboro misspelled as Ashboro on card)
❑ 41 Rafael Palmeiro .30 .09
❑ 42 Jimmy Key .20 .06
❑ 43 Gregg Olson .15 .04
❑ 44 Tony Pena .15 .04
❑ 45 Jack Howell .15 .04
❑ 46 Eric King .15 .04
❑ 47 Cory Snyder .15 .04
❑ 48 Frank Tanana .20 .06
❑ 49 Nolan Ryan 1.50 .45
❑ 50 Bob Boone .20 .06
❑ 51 Dave Parker .20 .06
❑ 52 Allan Anderson .15 .04
❑ 53 Tim Leary .15 .04
❑ 54 Mark McGwire 1.50 .45
❑ 55 Dave Valle .15 .04
❑ 56 Fred McGriff .30 .09
❑ 57 Cal Ripken 1.50 .45
❑ 58 Roger Clemens 1.00 .30
❑ 59 Lance Parrish .20 .06
❑ 60 Robin Ventura .50 .15
❑ 61 Doug Jones .15 .04
❑ 62 Lloyd Moseby .15 .04
❑ 63 Bo Jackson .50 .15
❑ 64 Paul Molitor .30 .09
❑ 65 Kent Hrbek .20 .06
❑ 66 Mel Hall .15 .04
❑ 67 Bob Welch .20 .06
❑ 68 Erik Hanson .15 .04
❑ 69 Harold Baines .20 .06
❑ 70 Junior Felix .15 .04
❑ 71 Craig Worthington .15 .04
❑ 72 Jeff Reardon .20 .06
❑ 73 Johnny Ray .15 .04
❑ 74 Ozzie Guillen .20 .06
❑ 75 Brook Jacoby .15 .04
❑ 76 Chet Lemon .15 .04
❑ 77 Mark Gubicza .15 .04
❑ 78 B.J. Surhoff .20 .06
❑ 79 Rick Aguilera .20 .06
❑ 80 Pascual Perez .15 .04
❑ 81 Jose Canseco .30 .09
❑ 82 Mike Schooler .15 .04
❑ 83 Jeff Huson .15 .04
❑ 84 Kelly Gruber .15 .04
❑ 85 Randy Milligan .15 .04
❑ 86 Wade Boggs .30 .09
❑ 87 Dave Winfield .20 .06
❑ 88 Scott Fletcher .15 .04
❑ 89 Tom Candiotti .15 .04
❑ 90 Mike Heath .15 .04
❑ 91 Kevin Seitzer .15 .04
❑ 92 Ted Higuera .15 .04
❑ 93 Kevin Tapani .50 .15
❑ 94 Roberto Kelly .15 .04
❑ 95 Walt Weiss .15 .04
❑ 96 Checklist Card .15 .04
❑ 97 Sandy Alomar Jr. .20 .06
❑ 98 Pete O'Brien .15 .04
❑ 99 Jeff Russell .15 .04
❑ 100 John Olerud 1.50 .45
❑ 101 Pete Harnisch .15 .04
❑ 102 Dwight Evans .30 .09
❑ 103 Chuck Finley .20 .06
❑ 104 Sammy Sosa 8.00 2.40
❑ 105 Mike Henneman .15 .04
❑ 106 Kurt Stillwell .15 .04
❑ 107 Greg Vaughn .15 .04
❑ 108 Dan Gladden .15 .04
❑ 109 Jesse Barfield .15 .04
❑ 110 Willie Randolph .20 .06
❑ 111 Randy Johnson .75 .23
❑ 112 Julio Franco .20 .06
❑ 113 Tony Fernandez .15 .04
❑ 114 Ben McDonald .15 .04
❑ 115 Mike Greenwell .15 .04
❑ 116 Luis Polonia .15 .04
❑ 117 Carney Lansford .20 .06
❑ 118 Bud Black .15 .04
❑ 119 Lou Whitaker .20 .06
❑ 120 Jim Eisenreich .15 .04
❑ 121 Gary Sheffield .50 .15
❑ 122 Shane Mack .15 .04
❑ 123 Alvaro Espinoza .15 .04
❑ 124 Rickey Henderson .50 .15
❑ 125 Jeffrey Leonard .15 .04
❑ 126 Gary Pettis .15 .04
❑ 127 Dave Stieb .20 .06
❑ 128 Danny Tartabull .15 .04
❑ 129 Joe Orsulak .15 .04
❑ 130 Tom Brunansky .15 .04
❑ 131 Dick Schofield .15 .04
❑ 132 Candy Maldonado .15 .04
❑ 133 Cecil Fielder .20 .06
❑ 134 Terry Shumpert .15 .04
❑ 135 Greg Gagne .15 .04
❑ 136 Dave Righetti .20 .06
❑ 137 Terry Steinbach .15 .04
❑ 138 Harold Reynolds .20 .06
❑ 139 George Bell .15 .04
❑ 140 Carlos Quintana .15 .04
❑ 141 Ivan Calderon .15 .04
❑ 142 Greg Brock .15 .04
❑ 143 Ruben Sierra .15 .04
❑ 144 Checklist Card .15 .04

1992 Donruss Rookies

	Nm-Mt	Ex-Mt
COMPLETE SET (132)	10.00	3.00

❑ 1 Kyle Abbott .05 .02
❑ 2 Troy Afenir .05 .02
❑ 3 Rich Amaral RC .10 .03
❑ 4 Ruben Amaro .05 .02
❑ 5 Billy Ashley RC .10 .03
❑ 6 Pedro Astacio RC .25 .07
❑ 7 Jim Austin .05 .02
❑ 8 Robert Ayrault .05 .02
❑ 9 Kevin Baez .05 .02
❑ 10 Esteban Beltre .05 .02
❑ 11 Brian Bohanon .05 .02
❑ 12 Kent Bottenfield RC .25 .07
❑ 13 Jeff Branson .05 .02
❑ 14 Brad Brink .05 .02
❑ 15 John Briscoe .05 .02
❑ 16 Doug Brocail RC .10 .03
❑ 17 Rico Brogna .05 .02
❑ 18 J.T. Bruett .05 .02
❑ 19 Jacob Brumfield .05 .02
❑ 20 Jim Bullinger .05 .02
❑ 21 Kevin Campbell .05 .02
❑ 22 Pedro Castellano RC .10 .03
❑ 23 Mike Christopher .05 .02
❑ 24 Archi Cianfrocco RC .10 .03
❑ 25 Mark Clark RC .10 .03
❑ 26 Craig Colbert .05 .02
❑ 27 Victor Cole .05 .02

	Card	Nm-Mt	Ex-Mt
❑	28 Steve Cooke RC	.10	.03
❑	29 Tim Costo	.05	.02
❑	30 Chad Curtis RC	.25	.07
❑	31 Doug Davis	.05	.02
❑	32 Gary DiSarcina	.05	.02
❑	33 John Doherty RC	.10	.03
❑	34 Mike Draper	.05	.02
❑	35 Monty Fariss	.05	.02
❑	36 Bien Figueroa	.05	.02
❑	37 John Flaherty	.05	.02
❑	38 Tim Fortugno	.05	.02
❑	39 Eric Fox RC	.10	.03
❑	40 Jeff Frye RC	.10	.03
❑	41 Ramon Garcia	.05	.02
❑	42 Brent Gates RC	.10	.03
❑	43 Tom Goodwin	.05	.02
❑	44 Buddy Groom RC	.10	.03
❑	45 Jeff Grotewold	.05	.02
❑	46 Juan Guerrero	.05	.02
❑	47 Johnny Guzman RC	.10	.03
❑	48 Shawn Hare RC	.10	.03
❑	49 Ryan Hawblitzel RC	.10	.03
❑	50 Bert Hefferman	.05	.02
❑	51 Butch Henry	.05	.02
❑	52 Cesar Hernandez RC	.10	.03
❑	53 Vince Horsman	.05	.02
❑	54 Steve Hosey	.05	.02
❑	55 Pat Howell	.05	.02
❑	56 Peter Hoy	.05	.02
❑	57 Jonathan Hurst RC	.10	.03
❑	58 Mark Hutton RC	.10	.03
❑	59 Shawn Jeter RC	.10	.03
❑	60 Joel Johnston	.05	.02
❑	61 Jeff Kent RC	3.00	.90
❑	62 Kurt Knudsen RC	.10	.03
❑	63 Kevin Koslofski	.05	.02
❑	64 Danny Leon	.05	.02
❑	65 Jesse Levis	.05	.02
❑	66 Tom Marsh	.05	.02
❑	67 Ed Martel	.05	.02
❑	68 Al Martin RC	.25	.07
❑	69 Pedro Martinez	2.00	.60
❑	70 Derrick May	.05	.02
❑	71 Matt Maysey	.05	.02
❑	72 Russ McGinnis	.05	.02
❑	73 Tim McIntosh	.05	.02
❑	74 Jim McNamara	.05	.02
❑	75 Jeff McNeely	.05	.02
❑	76 Rusty Meacham	.05	.02
❑	77 Tony Menendez	.05	.02
❑	78 Henry Mercedes	.05	.02
❑	79 Paul Miller	.05	.02
❑	80 Joe Millette	.05	.02
❑	81 Blas Minor	.05	.02
❑	82 Dennis Moeller	.05	.02
❑	83 Raul Mondesi	.10	.03
❑	84 Rob Natal	.05	.02
❑	85 Troy Neel RC	.10	.03
❑	86 David Nied RC	.10	.03
❑	87 Jerry Nielson	.05	.02
❑	88 Donovan Osborne	.05	.02
❑	89 John Patterson RC	.10	.03
❑	90 Roger Pavlik RC	.10	.03
❑	91 Dan Peltier	.05	.02
❑	92 Jim Pena	.05	.02
❑	93 William Pennyfeather	.05	.02
❑	94 Mike Perez	.05	.02
❑	95 Hipolito Pichardo RC	.10	.03
❑	96 Greg Pirkl RC	.10	.03
❑	97 Harvey Pulliam	.05	.02
❑	98 Manny Ramirez RC	4.00	1.20
❑	99 Pat Rapp RC	.10	.03
❑	100 Jeff Reboulet	.05	.02
❑	101 Darren Reed	.05	.02
❑	102 Shane Reynolds RC	.25	.07
❑	103 Bill Risley	.05	.02
❑	104 Ben Rivera	.05	.02
❑	105 Henry Rodriguez	.05	.02
❑	106 Rico Rossy	.05	.02
❑	107 Johnny Ruffin	.05	.02
❑	108 Steve Scarsone	.05	.02
❑	109 Tim Scott	.05	.02
❑	110 Steve Shifflett	.05	.02
❑	111 Dave Silvestri	.05	.02
❑	112 Matt Stairs RC	.25	.07
❑	113 William Suero	.05	.02
❑	114 Jeff Tackett	.05	.02
❑	115 Eddie Taubensee	.10	.03
❑	116 Rick Trlicek RC	.10	.03
❑	117 Scooter Tucker	.05	.02
❑	118 Shane Turner	.05	.02
❑	119 Julio Valera	.05	.02
❑	120 Paul Wagner RC	.10	.03
❑	121 Tim Wakefield RC	3.00	.90
❑	122 Mike Walker	.05	.02
❑	123 Bruce Walton	.05	.02
❑	124 Lenny Webster	.05	.02
❑	125 Bob Wickman	.25	.07
❑	126 Mike Williams RC	.25	.07
❑	127 Kerry Woodson	.05	.02
❑	128 Eric Young RC	.25	.07
❑	129 Kevin Young RC	.25	.07
❑	130 Pete Young	.05	.02
❑	131 Checklist 1-66	.05	.02
❑	132 Checklist 67-132	.05	.02

2001 Donruss

	Nm-Mt	Ex-Mt
COMP.SET w/o SP's (150)	25.00	7.50
COMMON CARD (1-150)	.30	.09
COMMON (151-200)	8.00	2.40
COMMON (201-220)	2.50	.75

	Card	Nm-Mt	Ex-Mt
❑	1 Alex Rodriguez	1.25	.35
❑	2 Barry Bonds	2.00	.60
❑	3 Cal Ripken	2.50	.75
❑	4 Chipper Jones	.75	.23
❑	5 Derek Jeter	2.00	.60
❑	6 Troy Glaus	.30	.09
❑	7 Frank Thomas	.75	.23
❑	8 Greg Maddux	1.25	.35
❑	9 Ivan Rodriguez	.50	.15
❑	10 Jeff Bagwell	.50	.15
❑	11 Jose Canseco	.50	.15
❑	12 Todd Helton	.50	.15
❑	13 Ken Griffey Jr.	1.25	.35
❑	14 Manny Ramirez Sox	.50	.15
❑	15 Mark McGwire	2.00	.60
❑	16 Mike Piazza	1.25	.35
❑	17 Nomar Garciaparra	1.25	.35
❑	18 Pedro Martinez	.50	.15
❑	19 Randy Johnson	.75	.23
❑	20 Rick Ankiel	.30	.09
❑	21 Rickey Henderson	.75	.23
❑	22 Roger Clemens	1.50	.45
❑	23 Sammy Sosa	.75	.23
❑	24 Tony Gwynn	1.00	.30
❑	25 Vladimir Guerrero	.75	.23
❑	26 Eric Davis	.30	.09
❑	27 Roberto Alomar	.30	.09
❑	28 Mark Mulder	.30	.09
❑	29 Pat Burrell	.30	.09
❑	30 Harold Baines	.30	.09
❑	31 Carlos Delgado	.30	.09
❑	32 J.D. Drew	.30	.09
❑	33 Jim Edmonds	.50	.15
❑	34 Darin Erstad	.30	.09
❑	35 Jason Giambi	.30	.09
❑	36 Tom Glavine	.50	.15
❑	37 Juan Gonzalez	.30	.09
❑	38 Mark Grace	.50	.15
❑	39 Shawn Green	.30	.09
❑	40 Tim Hudson	.30	.09
❑	41 Andruw Jones	.50	.15
❑	42 David Justice	.30	.09
❑	43 Jeff Kent	.30	.09
❑	44 Barry Larkin	.50	.15
❑	45 Pokey Reese	.30	.09
❑	46 Mike Mussina	.50	.15
❑	47 Hideo Nomo	.75	.23
❑	48 Rafael Palmeiro	.50	.15
❑	49 Adam Piatt	.30	.09
❑	50 Scott Rolen	.50	.15
❑	51 Gary Sheffield	.30	.09
❑	52 Bernie Williams	.50	.15
❑	53 Bob Abreu	.30	.09
❑	54 Edgardo Alfonzo	.30	.09
❑	55 Jermaine Clark RC	.50	.15
❑	56 Albert Belle	.30	.09
❑	57 Craig Biggio	.50	.15
❑	58 Andres Galarraga	.30	.09
❑	59 Edgar Martinez	.50	.15
❑	60 Fred McGriff	.50	.15
❑	61 Magglio Ordonez	.30	.09
❑	62 Jim Thome	.50	.15
❑	63 Matt Williams	.30	.09
❑	64 Kerry Wood	.30	.09
❑	65 Moises Alou	.30	.09
❑	66 Brady Anderson	.30	.09
❑	67 Garret Anderson	.30	.09
❑	68 Tony Armas Jr.	.30	.09
❑	69 Tony Batista	.30	.09
❑	70 Jose Cruz Jr.	.30	.09
❑	71 Carlos Beltran	.30	.09
❑	72 Adrian Beltre	.30	.09
❑	73 Kris Benson	.30	.09
❑	74 Lance Berkman	.30	.09
❑	75 Kevin Brown	.30	.09
❑	76 Jay Buhner	.30	.09
❑	77 Jeromy Burnitz	.30	.09
❑	78 Ken Caminiti	.30	.09
❑	79 Sean Casey	.50	.15
❑	80 Luis Castillo	.30	.09
❑	81 Eric Chavez	.30	.09
❑	82 Jeff Cirillo	.30	.09
❑	83 Bartolo Colon	.30	.09
❑	84 David Cone	.30	.09
❑	85 Freddy Garcia	.30	.09
❑	86 Johnny Damon	.50	.15
❑	87 Ray Durham	.30	.09
❑	88 Jermaine Dye	.30	.09
❑	89 Juan Encarnacion	.30	.09
❑	90 Terrence Long	.30	.09
❑	91 Carl Everett	.30	.09
❑	92 Steve Finley	.30	.09
❑	93 Cliff Floyd	.30	.09
❑	94 Brad Fullmer	.30	.09
❑	95 Brian Giles	.30	.09
❑	96 Luis Gonzalez	.30	.09
❑	97 Rusty Greer	.30	.09
❑	98 Jeffrey Hammonds	.30	.09
❑	99 Mike Hampton	.30	.09
❑	100 Orlando Hernandez	.30	.09
❑	101 Richard Hidalgo	.30	.09
❑	102 Geoff Jenkins	.30	.09
❑	103 Jacque Jones	.30	.09
❑	104 Brian Jordan	.30	.09
❑	105 Gabe Kapler	.30	.09
❑	106 Eric Karros	.30	.09
❑	107 Jason Kendall	.30	.09
❑	108 Adam Kennedy	.30	.09
❑	109 Byung-Hyun Kim	.30	.09
❑	110 Ryan Klesko	.30	.09
❑	111 Chuck Knoblauch	.30	.09
❑	112 Paul Konerko	.30	.09
❑	113 Carlos Lee	.30	.09
❑	114 Kenny Lofton	.30	.09
❑	115 Javy Lopez	.30	.09
❑	116 Tino Martinez	.50	.15
❑	117 Ruben Mateo	.30	.09
❑	118 Kevin Millwood	.30	.09
❑	119 Ben Molina	.30	.09
❑	120 Raul Mondesi	.30	.09
❑	121 Trot Nixon	.30	.09
❑	122 John Olerud	.30	.09
❑	123 Paul O'Neill	.50	.15
❑	124 Chan Ho Park	.30	.09
❑	125 Andy Pettitte	.50	.15
❑	126 Jorge Posada	.50	.15
❑	127 Mark Quinn	.30	.09

❑ 128 Aramis Ramirez .30 .09
❑ 129 Mariano Rivera .50 .15
❑ 130 Tim Salmon .50 .15
❑ 131 Curt Schilling .30 .09
❑ 132 Richie Sexson .30 .09
❑ 133 John Smoltz .50 .15
❑ 134 J.T. Snow .30 .09
❑ 135 Jay Payton .30 .09
❑ 136 Shannon Stewart .30 .09
❑ 137 B.J. Surhoff .30 .09
❑ 138 Mike Sweeney .30 .09
❑ 139 Fernando Tatis .30 .09
❑ 140 Miguel Tejada .30 .09
❑ 141 Jason Varitek .75 .23
❑ 142 Greg Vaughn .30 .09
❑ 143 Mo Vaughn .30 .09
❑ 144 Robin Ventura UER .30 .09
Listed as playing for Yankees last 2 years
Also Bat and Throw information is wrong
❑ 145 Jose Vidro .30 .09
❑ 146 Omar Vizquel .50 .15
❑ 147 Larry Walker .30 .09
❑ 148 David Wells .30 .09
❑ 149 Rondell White .30 .09
❑ 150 Preston Wilson .30 .09
❑ 151 Brent Abernathy RR 8.00 2.40
❑ 152 Cory Aldridge RR RC 8.00 2.40
❑ 153 Gene Altman RR RC 8.00 2.40
❑ 154 Josh Beckett RR 10.00 3.00
❑ 155 W. Betemit RR RC 10.00 3.00
❑ 156 A.Pujols RR/500 RC .. 250.00 75.00
❑ 157 Joe Crede RR 10.00 3.00
❑ 158 Jack Cust RR 8.00 2.40
❑ 159 Ben Sheets RR/500 40.00 12.00
❑ 160 Alex Escobar RR 8.00 2.40
❑ 161 A. Hernandez RR RC 8.00 2.40
❑ 162 Pedro Feliz RR 8.00 2.40
❑ 163 Nate Frese RR RC 8.00 2.40
❑ 164 Carlos Garcia RR RC 8.00 2.40
❑ 165 Marcus Giles RR 8.00 2.40
❑ 166 Alexis Gomez RR RC 8.00 2.40
❑ 167 Jason Hart RR 8.00 2.40
❑ 168 Eric Hinske RR RC 10.00 3.00
❑ 169 Cesar Izturis RR 8.00 2.40
❑ 170 Nick Johnson RR 8.00 2.40
❑ 171 Mike Young RR 10.00 3.00
❑ 172 B. Lawrence RR RC 8.00 2.40
❑ 173 Steve Lomasney RR 8.00 2.40
❑ 174 Nick Maness RR 8.00 2.40
❑ 175 Jose Mieses RR RC 8.00 2.40
❑ 176 Greg Miller RR RC 8.00 2.40
❑ 177 Eric Munson RR 8.00 2.40
❑ 178 Xavier Nady RR 8.00 2.40
❑ 179 Blaine Neal RR RC 8.00 2.40
❑ 180 Abraham Nunez RR 8.00 2.40
❑ 181 Jose Ortiz RR 8.00 2.40
❑ 182 Jeremy Owens RR RC 8.00 2.40
❑ 183 Pablo Ozuna RR 8.00 2.40
❑ 184 Corey Patterson RR 8.00 2.40
❑ 185 Carlos Pena RR 8.00 2.40
❑ 186 Wily Mo Pena RR 8.00 2.40
❑ 187 Timo Perez RR 8.00 2.40
❑ 188 A. Pettyjohn RR RC 8.00 2.40
❑ 189 Luis Rivas RR 8.00 2.40
❑ 190 J. Melian RR RC 8.00 2.40
❑ 191 Wilken Ruan RR RC 8.00 2.40
❑ 192 D. Sanchez RR RC 8.00 2.40
❑ 193 Alfonso Soriano RR 10.00 3.00
❑ 194 Rafael Soriano RR RC 8.00 2.40
❑ 195 Ichiro Suzuki RR RC 60.00 18.00
❑ 196 Billy Sylvester RR RC 8.00 2.40
❑ 197 Juan Uribe RR RC 10.00 3.00
❑ 198 Eric Valent RR 8.00 2.40
❑ 199 C.Valderrama RR RC 8.00 2.40
❑ 200 Matt White RR RC 8.00 2.40
❑ 201 Alex Rodriguez FC 6.00 1.80
❑ 202 Barry Bonds FC 10.00 3.00
❑ 203 Cal Ripken FC 12.00 3.60
❑ 204 Chipper Jones FC 4.00 1.20
❑ 205 Derek Jeter FC 10.00 3.00
❑ 206 Troy Glaus FC 2.50 .75
❑ 207 Frank Thomas FC 4.00 1.20
❑ 208 Greg Maddux FC 6.00 1.80
❑ 209 Ivan Rodriguez FC 2.50 .75
❑ 210 Jeff Bagwell FC 2.50 .75
❑ 211 Todd Helton FC 2.50 .75
❑ 212 Ken Griffey Jr. FC 6.00 1.80
❑ 213 Manny Ramirez Sox FC .. 2.50 .75
❑ 214 Mark McGwire FC 10.00 3.00
❑ 215 Mike Piazza FC 6.00 1.80
❑ 216 Pedro Martinez FC 2.50 .75
❑ 217 Sammy Sosa FC 4.00 1.20
❑ 218 Tony Gwynn FC 5.00 1.50
❑ 219 Vladimir Guerrero FC 4.00 1.20
❑ 220 Nomar Garciaparra FC 6.00 1.80
❑ NNO BB Best Coupon 2.00 .60
❑ NNO The Rookies Coupon .50 .15

2001 Donruss Rookies

	Nm-Mt	Ex-Mt
COMP.FACT.SET (106)	80.00	24.00
COMP.SET w/o SP's (105)	60.00	18.00

❑ R1 Adam Dunn .75 .23
❑ R2 Ryan Drese RC .75 .23
❑ R3 Bud Smith RC .50 .15
❑ R4 Tsuyoshi Shinjo RC .75 .23
❑ R5 Roy Oswalt .75 .23
❑ R6 Wilmy Caceres RC .50 .15
❑ R7 Willie Harris RC .50 .15
❑ R8 Andres Torres RC .50 .15
❑ R9 Brandon Knight RC .50 .15
❑ R10 Horacio Ramirez RC .75 .23
❑ R11 Benito Baez RC .50 .15
❑ R12 Jeremy Affeldt RC .50 .15
❑ R13 Ryan Jensen RC .50 .15
❑ R14 Casey Fossum RC .50 .15
❑ R15 Ramon Vazquez RC .50 .15
❑ R16 Dustan Mohr RC .50 .15
❑ R17 Saul Rivera RC .50 .15
❑ R18 Zach Day RC .50 .15
❑ R19 Erik Hiljus RC .50 .15
❑ R20 Cesar Crespo RC .50 .15
❑ R21 Wilson Guzman RC .50 .15
❑ R22 Travis Hafner RC 4.00 1.20
❑ R23 Grant Balfour RC .50 .15
❑ R24 Johnny Estrada RC .75 .23
❑ R25 Morgan Ensberg RC 3.00 .90
❑ R26 Jack Wilson RC .75 .23
❑ R27 Aubrey Huff .50 .15
❑ R28 Endy Chavez RC .50 .15
❑ R29 Delvin James RC .50 .15
❑ R30 Michael Cuddyer .40 .12
❑ R31 Jason Michaels RC .50 .15
❑ R32 Martin Vargas RC .50 .15
❑ R33 Donaldo Mendez RC .50 .15
❑ R34 Jorge Julio RC .50 .15
❑ R35 T.Spooneybarger RC .50 .15
❑ R36 Kurt Ainsworth .40 .12
❑ R37 Josh Fogg RC .50 .15
❑ R38 Brian Reith RC .50 .15
❑ R39 Rick Bauer RC .50 .15
❑ R40 Tim Redding .40 .12
❑ R41 Erick Almonte RC .50 .15
❑ R42 Juan A.Pena RC .40 .12
❑ R43 Ken Harvey .40 .12
❑ R44 David Brous RC .50 .15
❑ R45 Kevin Olsen RC .50 .15
❑ R46 Henry Mateo RC .50 .15
❑ R47 Nick Neugebauer .40 .12
❑ R48 Mike Penney RC .50 .15
❑ R49 Jay Gibbons RC .75 .23
❑ R50 Tim Christman RC .40 .12
❑ R51 B.Duckworth RC .50 .15
❑ R52 Brett Jodie RC .50 .15
❑ R53 Christian Parker RC .50 .15
❑ R54 Carlos Hernandez .40 .12
❑ R55 Brandon Larson RC .50 .15
❑ R56 Nick Punto RC .50 .15
❑ R57 Elpidio Guzman RC .50 .15
❑ R58 Joe Beimel RC .40 .12
❑ R59 Junior Spivey RC .75 .23
❑ R60 Will Ohman RC .50 .15
❑ R61 Brandon Lyon RC .50 .15
❑ R62 Stubby Clapp RC .40 .12
❑ R63 J.Duchscherer RC .50 .15
❑ R64 Jimmy Rollins .50 .15
❑ R65 David Williams RC .50 .15
❑ R66 Craig Monroe RC .75 .23
❑ R67 Jose Acevedo RC .50 .15
❑ R68 Jason Jennings .40 .12
❑ R69 Josh Phelps .40 .12
❑ R70 Brian Roberts RC 3.00 .90
❑ R71 Claudio Vargas RC .50 .15
❑ R72 Adam Johnson .40 .12
❑ R73 Bart Miadich RC .40 .12
❑ R74 Juan Rivera .40 .12
❑ R75 Brad Voyles RC .40 .12
❑ R76 Nate Cornejo .40 .12
❑ R77 Juan Moreno RC .50 .15
❑ R78 Brian Rogers RC .50 .15
❑ R79 R.Rodriguez RC .50 .15
❑ R80 Geronimo Gil RC .40 .12
❑ R81 Joe Kennedy RC .75 .23
❑ R82 Kevin Joseph RC .50 .15
❑ R83 Josue Perez RC .50 .15
❑ R84 Victor Zambrano RC .75 .23
❑ R85 Josh Towers RC .75 .23
❑ R86 Mike Rivera RC .50 .15
❑ R87 Mark Prior RC 8.00 2.40
❑ R88 Juan Cruz RC .50 .15
❑ R89 Dewon Brazelton RC .50 .15
❑ R90 Angel Berroa RC .75 .23
❑ R91 Mark Teixeira RC 10.00 3.00
❑ R92 Cody Ransom RC .50 .15
❑ R93 Angel Santos RC .50 .15
❑ R94 Corky Miller RC .50 .15
❑ R95 Brandon Berger RC .50 .15
❑ R96 Corey Patterson UPD .40 .12
❑ R97 A. Pujols UPD UER 40.00 12.00
Homers and RBI Stats wrong
❑ R98 Josh Beckett UPD .75 .23
❑ R99 C.C. Sabathia UPD .50 .15
❑ R100 A. Soriano UPD .75 .23
❑ R101 Ben Sheets UPD .75 .23
❑ R102 Rafael Soriano UPD .50 .15
❑ R103 Wilson Betemit UPD .75 .23
❑ R104 Ichiro Suzuki UPD 15.00 4.50
❑ R105 Jose Ortiz UPD .40 .12

2003 Donruss Rookies

	MINT	NRMT
COMPLETE SET (65)	20.00	9.00
COMMON CARD (1-65)	.20	.09
COMMON RC	.25	.11

❑ 1 Jeremy Bonderman RC 1.50 .70
❑ 2 Adam Loewen RC .40 .18
❑ 3 Dan Haren RC .50 .23
❑ 4 Jose Contreras RC .50 .23

❑ 5 Hideki Matsui RC	2.00	.90
❑ 6 Arnie Munoz RC	.25	.11
❑ 7 Miguel Cabrera	.50	.23
❑ 8 Andrew Brown RC	.40	.18
❑ 9 Josh Hall RC	.25	.11
❑ 10 Josh Stewart RC	.25	.11
❑ 11 Clint Barmes RC	1.00	.45
❑ 12 Luis Ayala RC	.25	.11
❑ 13 Brandon Webb RC	.50	.23
❑ 14 Greg Aquino RC	.25	.11
❑ 15 Chien-Ming Wang RC	1.50	.70
❑ 16 Rickie Weeks RC	2.00	.90
❑ 17 Edgar Gonzalez RC	.25	.11
❑ 18 Dontrelle Willis	.50	.23
❑ 19 Bo Hart RC	.25	.11
❑ 20 Rosman Garcia RC	.25	.11
❑ 21 Jeremy Griffiths RC	.25	.11
❑ 22 Craig Brazell RC	.25	.11
❑ 23 Daniel Cabrera RC	.50	.23
❑ 24 Fernando Cabrera RC	.25	.11
❑ 25 Terrmel Sledge RC	.25	.11
❑ 26 Ramon Nivar RC	.25	.11
❑ 27 Rob Hammock RC	.25	.11
❑ 28 Francisco Rosario RC	.25	.11
❑ 29 Cory Stewart RC	.25	.11
❑ 30 Felix Sanchez RC	.25	.11
❑ 31 Jorge Cordova RC	.25	.11
❑ 32 Rocco Baldelli	.20	.09
❑ 33 Beau Kemp RC	.25	.11
❑ 34 Mike Nakamura RC	.25	.11
❑ 35 Rett Johnson RC	.25	.11
❑ 36 Guillermo Quiroz RC	.25	.11
❑ 37 Hong-Chih Kuo RC	1.00	.45
❑ 38 Ian Ferguson RC	.25	.11
❑ 39 Franklin Perez RC	.25	.11
❑ 40 Tim Olson RC	.25	.11
❑ 41 Jerome Williams	.20	.09
❑ 42 Rich Fischer RC	.25	.11
❑ 43 Phil Seibel RC	.25	.11
❑ 44 Aaron Looper RC	.25	.11
❑ 45 Jae Weong Seo	.20	.09
❑ 46 Chad Gaudin RC	.25	.11
❑ 47 Matt Kata RC	.25	.11
❑ 48 Ryan Wagner RC	.25	.11
❑ 49 Michel Hernandez RC	.25	.11
❑ 50 Diegomar Markwell RC	.25	.11
❑ 51 Doug Waechter RC	.40	.18
❑ 52 Mike Nicolas RC	.25	.11
❑ 53 Prentice Redman RC	.25	.11
❑ 54 Shane Bazzell RC	.25	.11
❑ 55 Delmon Young RC	2.50	1.10
❑ 56 Brian Stokes RC	.25	.11
❑ 57 Matt Bruback RC	.25	.11
❑ 58 Nook Logan RC	.40	.18
❑ 59 Oscar Villarreal RC	.25	.11
❑ 60 Pete LaForest RC	.25	.11
❑ 61 Shea Hillenbrand	.20	.09
❑ 62 Aramis Ramirez	.20	.09
❑ 63 Aaron Boone	.20	.09
❑ 64 Roberto Alomar	.30	.14
❑ 65 Rickey Henderson	.50	.23

2004 Donruss

	MINT	NRMT
COMPLETE SET (400)	150.00	70.00
COMP.SET w/o SP's (300)	25.00	11.00
COMMON CARD (71-370)	.30	.14
COMMON CARD (1-25/371-400)	2.00	.90
COMMON CARD (26-70)	2.00	.90

1-70/370-400 RANDOM INSERTS IN PACKS

❑ 1 Derek Jeter DK	4.00	1.80
❑ 2 Greg Maddux DK	3.00	1.35
❑ 3 Albert Pujols DK	4.00	1.80
❑ 4 Ichiro Suzuki DK	4.00	1.80
❑ 5 Alex Rodriguez DK	3.00	1.35
❑ 6 Roger Clemens DK	4.00	1.80
❑ 7 Andruw Jones DK	2.00	.90
❑ 8 Barry Bonds DK	5.00	2.20
❑ 9 Jeff Bagwell DK	2.00	.90
❑ 10 Randy Johnson DK	2.00	.90
❑ 11 Scott Rolen DK	2.00	.90
❑ 12 Lance Berkman DK	2.00	.90
❑ 13 Barry Zito DK	2.00	.90
❑ 14 Manny Ramirez DK	2.00	.90
❑ 15 Carlos Delgado DK	2.00	.90
❑ 16 Alfonso Soriano DK	2.00	.90
❑ 17 Todd Helton DK	2.00	.90
❑ 18 Mike Mussina DK	2.00	.90
❑ 19 Austin Kearns DK	2.00	.90
❑ 20 Nomar Garciaparra DK	3.00	1.35
❑ 21 Chipper Jones DK	2.00	.90
❑ 22 Mark Prior DK	2.00	.90
❑ 23 Jim Thome DK	2.00	.90
❑ 24 Vladimir Guerrero DK	2.00	.90
❑ 25 Pedro Martinez DK	2.00	.90
❑ 26 Sergio Mitre RR	2.00	.90
❑ 27 Adam Loewen RR	2.00	.90
❑ 28 Alfredo Gonzalez RR	2.00	.90
❑ 29 Miguel Ojeda RR	2.00	.90
❑ 30 Rosman Garcia RR	2.00	.90
❑ 31 Arnie Munoz RR	2.00	.90
❑ 32 Andrew Brown RR	2.00	.90
❑ 33 Josh Hall RR	2.00	.90
❑ 34 Josh Stewart RR	2.00	.90
❑ 35 Clint Barmes RR	3.00	1.35
❑ 36 Brandon Webb RR	2.00	.90
❑ 37 Chien-Ming Wang RR	3.00	1.35
❑ 38 Edgar Gonzalez RR	2.00	.90
❑ 39 Alejandro Machado RR	2.00	.90
❑ 40 Jeremy Griffiths RR	2.00	.90
❑ 41 Craig Brazell RR	2.00	.90
❑ 42 Daniel Cabrera RR	2.00	.90
❑ 43 Fernando Cabrera RR	2.00	.90
❑ 44 Terrmel Sledge RR	2.00	.90
❑ 45 Rob Hammock RR	2.00	.90
❑ 46 Francisco Rosario RR	2.00	.90
❑ 47 Francisco Cruceta RR	2.00	.90
❑ 48 Rett Johnson RR	2.00	.90
❑ 49 Guillermo Quiroz RR	2.00	.90
❑ 50 Hong-Chih Kuo RR	3.00	1.35
❑ 51 Ian Ferguson RR	2.00	.90
❑ 52 Tim Olson RR	2.00	.90
❑ 53 Todd Wellemeyer RR	2.00	.90
❑ 54 Rich Fischer RR	2.00	.90
❑ 55 Phil Seibel RR	2.00	.90
❑ 56 Joe Valentine RR	2.00	.90
❑ 57 Matt Kata RR	2.00	.90
❑ 58 Michael Hessman RR	2.00	.90
❑ 59 Michel Hernandez RR	2.00	.90
❑ 60 Doug Waechter RR	2.00	.90
❑ 61 Prentice Redman RR	2.00	.90
❑ 62 Nook Logan RR	2.00	.90
❑ 63 Oscar Villarreal RR	2.00	.90
❑ 64 Pete LaForest RR	2.00	.90
❑ 65 Matt Bruback RR	2.00	.90
❑ 66 Dan Haren RR	2.00	.90
❑ 67 Greg Aquino RR	2.00	.90
❑ 68 Lew Ford RR	2.00	.90
❑ 69 Jeff Duncan RR	2.00	.90
❑ 70 Ryan Wagner RR	2.00	.90
❑ 71 Bengie Molina	.30	.14
❑ 72 Brad Fullmer	.30	.14
❑ 73 Darin Erstad	.30	.14
❑ 74 David Eckstein	.30	.14
❑ 75 Garret Anderson	.30	.14
❑ 76 Jarrod Washburn	.30	.14
❑ 77 Kevin Appier	.30	.14
❑ 78 Scott Spiezio	.30	.14
❑ 79 Tim Salmon	.50	.23
❑ 80 Troy Glaus	.30	.14
❑ 81 Troy Percival	.30	.14
❑ 82 Jason Johnson	.30	.14
❑ 83 Jay Gibbons	.30	.14
❑ 84 Melvin Mora	.30	.14
❑ 85 Sidney Ponson	.30	.14
❑ 86 Tony Batista	.30	.14
❑ 87 Bill Mueller	.30	.14
❑ 88 Byung-Hyun Kim	.30	.14
❑ 89 David Ortiz	.75	.35
❑ 90 Derek Lowe	.30	.14
❑ 91 Johnny Damon	.50	.23
❑ 92 Casey Fossum	.30	.14
❑ 93 Manny Ramirez	.50	.23
❑ 94 Nomar Garciaparra	1.25	.55
❑ 95 Pedro Martinez	.50	.23
❑ 96 Todd Walker	.30	.14
❑ 97 Trot Nixon	.30	.14
❑ 98 Bartolo Colon	.30	.14
❑ 99 Carlos Lee	.30	.14
❑ 100 D'Angelo Jimenez	.30	.14
❑ 101 Esteban Loaiza	.30	.14
❑ 102 Frank Thomas	.75	.35
❑ 103 Joe Crede	.30	.14
❑ 104 Jose Valentin	.30	.14
❑ 105 Magglio Ordonez	.30	.14
❑ 106 Mark Buehrle	.30	.14
❑ 107 Paul Konerko	.30	.14
❑ 108 Brandon Phillips	.30	.14
❑ 109 C.C Sabathia	.30	.14
❑ 110 Ellis Burks	.30	.14
❑ 111 Jeremy Guthrie	.30	.14
❑ 112 Josh Bard	.30	.14
❑ 113 Matt Lawton	.30	.14
❑ 114 Milton Bradley	.30	.14
❑ 115 Omar Vizquel	.50	.23
❑ 116 Travis Hafner	.30	.14
❑ 117 Bobby Higginson	.30	.14
❑ 118 Carlos Pena	.30	.14
❑ 119 Dmitri Young	.30	.14
❑ 120 Eric Munson	.30	.14
❑ 121 Jeremy Bonderman	.30	.14
❑ 122 Nate Cornejo	.30	.14
❑ 123 Omar Infante	.30	.14
❑ 124 Ramon Santiago	.30	.14
❑ 125 Angel Berroa	.30	.14
❑ 126 Carlos Beltran	.30	.14
❑ 127 Desi Relaford	.30	.14
❑ 128 Jeremy Affeldt	.30	.14
❑ 129 Joe Randa	.30	.14
❑ 130 Ken Harvey	.30	.14
❑ 131 Mike MacDougal	.30	.14
❑ 132 Michael Tucker	.30	.14
❑ 133 Mike Sweeney	.30	.14
❑ 134 Raul Ibanez	.30	.14
❑ 135 Runelvys Hernandez	.30	.14
❑ 136 A.J. Pierzynski	.30	.14
❑ 137 Brad Radke	.30	.14
❑ 138 Corey Koskie	.30	.14
❑ 139 Cristian Guzman	.30	.14
❑ 140 Doug Mientkiewicz	.30	.14
❑ 141 Dustan Mohr	.30	.14
❑ 142 Jacque Jones	.30	.14
❑ 143 Kenny Rogers	.30	.14
❑ 144 Bobby Kielty	.30	.14
❑ 145 Kyle Lohse	.30	.14
❑ 146 Luis Rivas	.30	.14
❑ 147 Torii Hunter	.30	.14
❑ 148 Alfonso Soriano	.30	.14
❑ 149 Andy Pettitte	.50	.23
❑ 150 Bernie Williams	.50	.23
❑ 151 David Wells	.30	.14
❑ 152 Derek Jeter	1.50	.70
❑ 153 Hideki Matsui	1.50	.70
❑ 154 Jason Giambi	.30	.14
❑ 155 Jorge Posada	.50	.23
❑ 156 Jose Contreras	.30	.14
❑ 157 Mike Mussina	.50	.23
❑ 158 Nick Johnson	.30	.14
❑ 159 Robin Ventura	.30	.14
❑ 160 Roger Clemens	1.50	.70
❑ 161 Barry Zito	.30	.14
❑ 162 Chris Singleton	.30	.14
❑ 163 Eric Byrnes	.30	.14
❑ 164 Eric Chavez	.30	.14
❑ 165 Erubiel Durazo	.30	.14
❑ 166 Keith Foulke	.30	.14
❑ 167 Mark Ellis	.30	.14
❑ 168 Miguel Tejada	.30	.14
❑ 169 Mark Mulder	.30	.14

❑ 170 Ramon Hernandez .30 .14
❑ 171 Ted Lilly .30 .14
❑ 172 Terrence Long .30 .14
❑ 173 Tim Hudson .30 .14
❑ 174 Bret Boone .30 .14
❑ 175 Carlos Guillen .30 .14
❑ 176 Dan Wilson .30 .14
❑ 177 Edgar Martinez .50 .23
❑ 178 Freddy Garcia .30 .14
❑ 179 Gil Meche .30 .14
❑ 180 Ichiro Suzuki 1.50 .70
❑ 181 Jamie Moyer .30 .14
❑ 182 Joel Pineiro .30 .14
❑ 183 John Olerud .30 .14
❑ 184 Mike Cameron .30 .14
❑ 185 Randy Winn .30 .14
❑ 186 Ryan Franklin .30 .14
❑ 187 Kazuhiro Sasaki .30 .14
❑ 188 Aubrey Huff .30 .14
❑ 189 Carl Crawford .30 .14
❑ 190 Joe Kennedy .30 .14
❑ 191 Marlon Anderson .30 .14
❑ 192 Rey Ordonez .30 .14
❑ 193 Rocco Baldelli .30 .14
❑ 194 Toby Hall .30 .14
❑ 195 Travis Lee .30 .14
❑ 196 Alex Rodriguez 1.25 .55
❑ 197 Carl Everett .30 .14
❑ 198 Chan Ho Park .30 .14
❑ 199 Einar Diaz .30 .14
❑ 200 Hank Blalock .30 .14
❑ 201 Ismael Valdes .30 .14
❑ 202 Juan Gonzalez .30 .14
❑ 203 Mark Teixeira .50 .23
❑ 204 Mike Young .30 .14
❑ 205 Rafael Palmeiro .50 .23
❑ 206 Carlos Delgado .30 .14
❑ 207 Kelvim Escobar .30 .14
❑ 208 Eric Hinske .30 .14
❑ 209 Frank Catalanotto .30 .14
❑ 210 Josh Phelps .30 .14
❑ 211 Orlando Hudson .30 .14
❑ 212 Roy Halladay .30 .14
❑ 213 Shannon Stewart .30 .14
❑ 214 Vernon Wells .30 .14
❑ 215 Carlos Baerga .30 .14
❑ 216 Curt Schilling .30 .14
❑ 217 Junior Spivey .30 .14
❑ 218 Luis Gonzalez .30 .14
❑ 219 Lyle Overbay .30 .14
❑ 220 Mark Grace .50 .23
❑ 221 Matt Williams .30 .14
❑ 222 Randy Johnson .75 .35
❑ 223 Shea Hillenbrand .30 .14
❑ 224 Steve Finley .30 .14
❑ 225 Andruw Jones .50 .23
❑ 226 Chipper Jones .75 .35
❑ 227 Gary Sheffield .30 .14
❑ 228 Greg Maddux 1.25 .55
❑ 229 Javy Lopez .30 .14
❑ 230 John Smoltz .50 .23
❑ 231 Marcus Giles .30 .14
❑ 232 Mike Hampton .30 .14
❑ 233 Rafael Furcal .30 .14
❑ 234 Robert Fick .30 .14
❑ 235 Russ Ortiz .30 .14
❑ 236 Alex Gonzalez .30 .14
❑ 237 Carlos Zambrano .30 .14
❑ 238 Corey Patterson .30 .14
❑ 239 Hee Seop Choi .30 .14
❑ 240 Kerry Wood .30 .14
❑ 241 Mark Bellhorn .30 .14
❑ 242 Mark Prior .50 .23
❑ 243 Moises Alou .30 .14
❑ 244 Sammy Sosa .75 .35
❑ 245 Aaron Boone .30 .14
❑ 246 Adam Dunn .30 .14
❑ 247 Austin Kearns .30 .14
❑ 248 Barry Larkin .50 .23
❑ 249 Felipe Lopez .30 .14
❑ 250 Jose Guillen .30 .14
❑ 251 Ken Griffey Jr. 1.25 .55
❑ 252 Jason LaRue .30 .14
❑ 253 Scott Williamson .30 .14
❑ 254 Sean Casey .50 .23
❑ 255 Shawn Chacon .30 .14
❑ 256 Chris Stynes .30 .14
❑ 257 Jason Jennings .30 .14
❑ 258 Jay Payton .30 .14
❑ 259 Jose Hernandez .30 .14
❑ 260 Larry Walker .30 .14
❑ 261 Preston Wilson .30 .14
❑ 262 Ronnie Belliard .30 .14
❑ 263 Todd Helton .50 .23
❑ 264 A.J. Burnett .30 .14
❑ 265 Alex Gonzalez .30 .14
❑ 266 Brad Penny .30 .14
❑ 267 Derrek Lee .50 .23
❑ 268 Ivan Rodriguez .50 .23
❑ 269 Josh Beckett .30 .14
❑ 270 Juan Encarnacion .30 .14
❑ 271 Juan Pierre .30 .14
❑ 272 Luis Castillo .30 .14
❑ 273 Mike Lowell .30 .14
❑ 274 Todd Hollandsworth .30 .14
❑ 275 Billy Wagner .30 .14
❑ 276 Brad Ausmus .30 .14
❑ 277 Craig Biggio .50 .23
❑ 278 Jeff Bagwell .50 .23
❑ 279 Jeff Kent .30 .14
❑ 280 Lance Berkman .30 .14
❑ 281 Richard Hidalgo .30 .14
❑ 282 Roy Oswalt .30 .14
❑ 283 Wade Miller .30 .14
❑ 284 Adrian Beltre .30 .14
❑ 285 Brian Jordan .30 .14
❑ 286 Cesar Izturis .30 .14
❑ 287 Dave Roberts .30 .14
❑ 288 Eric Gagne .30 .14
❑ 289 Fred McGriff .50 .23
❑ 290 Hideo Nomo .75 .35
❑ 291 Kazuhisa Ishii .30 .14
❑ 292 Kevin Brown .30 .14
❑ 293 Paul Lo Duca .30 .14
❑ 294 Shawn Green .30 .14
❑ 295 Ben Sheets .30 .14
❑ 296 Geoff Jenkins .30 .14
❑ 297 Rey Sanchez .30 .14
❑ 298 Richie Sexson .30 .14
❑ 299 Wes Helms .30 .14
❑ 300 Brad Wilkerson .30 .14
❑ 301 Claudio Vargas .30 .14
❑ 302 Endy Chavez .30 .14
❑ 303 Fernando Tatis .30 .14
❑ 304 Javier Vazquez .30 .14
❑ 305 Jose Vidro .30 .14
❑ 306 Michael Barrett .30 .14
❑ 307 Orlando Cabrera .30 .14
❑ 308 Tony Armas Jr. .30 .14
❑ 309 Vladimir Guerrero .75 .35
❑ 310 Zach Day .30 .14
❑ 311 Al Leiter .30 .14
❑ 312 Cliff Floyd .30 .14
❑ 313 Jae Weong Seo .30 .14
❑ 314 Jeromy Burnitz .30 .14
❑ 315 Mike Piazza 1.25 .55
❑ 316 Mo Vaughn .30 .14
❑ 317 Roberto Alomar .50 .23
❑ 318 Roger Cedeno .30 .14
❑ 319 Tom Glavine .50 .23
❑ 320 Jose Reyes .30 .14
❑ 321 Bobby Abreu .30 .14
❑ 322 Brett Myers .30 .14
❑ 323 David Bell .30 .14
❑ 324 Jim Thome .50 .23
❑ 325 Jimmy Rollins .30 .14
❑ 326 Kevin Millwood .30 .14
❑ 327 Marlon Byrd .30 .14
❑ 328 Mike Lieberthal .30 .14
❑ 329 Pat Burrell .30 .14
❑ 330 Randy Wolf .30 .14
❑ 331 Aramis Ramirez .30 .14
❑ 332 Brian Giles .30 .14
❑ 333 Jason Kendall .30 .14
❑ 334 Kenny Lofton .30 .14
❑ 335 Kip Wells .30 .14
❑ 336 Kris Benson .30 .14
❑ 337 Randall Simon .30 .14
❑ 338 Reggie Sanders .30 .14
❑ 339 Albert Pujols 1.50 .70
❑ 340 Edgar Renteria .30 .14
❑ 341 Fernando Vina .30 .14
❑ 342 J.D. Drew .30 .14
❑ 343 Jim Edmonds .50 .23
❑ 344 Matt Morris .30 .14
❑ 345 Mike Matheny .30 .14
❑ 346 Scott Rolen .50 .23
❑ 347 Tino Martinez .50 .23
❑ 348 Woody Williams .30 .14
❑ 349 Brian Lawrence .30 .14
❑ 350 Mark Kotsay .30 .14
❑ 351 Mark Loretta .30 .14
❑ 352 Ramon Vazquez .30 .14
❑ 353 Rondell White .30 .14
❑ 354 Ryan Klesko .30 .14
❑ 355 Sean Burroughs .30 .14
❑ 356 Trevor Hoffman .30 .14
❑ 357 Xavier Nady .30 .14
❑ 358 Andres Galarraga .30 .14
❑ 359 Barry Bonds 2.00 .90
❑ 360 Benito Santiago .30 .14
❑ 361 Deivi Cruz .30 .14
❑ 362 Edgardo Alfonzo .30 .14
❑ 363 J.T. Snow .30 .14
❑ 364 Jason Schmidt .30 .14
❑ 365 Kirk Rueter .30 .14
❑ 366 Kurt Ainsworth .30 .14
❑ 367 Marquis Grissom .30 .14
❑ 368 Ray Durham .30 .14
❑ 369 Rich Aurilia .30 .14
❑ 370 Tim Worrell .30 .14
❑ 371 Troy Glaus TC 2.00 .90
❑ 372 Melvin Mora TC 2.00 .90
❑ 373 Nomar Garciaparra TC 3.00 1.35
❑ 374 Magglio Ordonez TC 2.00 .90
❑ 375 Omar Vizquel TC 2.00 .90
❑ 376 Dmitri Young TC 2.00 .90
❑ 377 Mike Sweeney TC 2.00 .90
❑ 378 Torii Hunter TC 2.00 .90
❑ 379 Derek Jeter TC 4.00 1.80
❑ 380 Barry Zito TC 2.00 .90
❑ 381 Ichiro Suzuki TC 4.00 1.80
❑ 382 Rocco Baldelli TC 2.00 .90
❑ 383 Alex Rodriguez TC 3.00 1.35
❑ 384 Carlos Delgado TC 2.00 .90
❑ 385 Randy Johnson TC 2.00 .90
❑ 386 Greg Maddux TC 3.00 1.35
❑ 387 Sammy Sosa TC 2.00 .90
❑ 388 Ken Griffey Jr. TC 3.00 1.35
❑ 389 Todd Helton TC 2.00 .90
❑ 390 Ivan Rodriguez TC 2.00 .90
❑ 391 Jeff Bagwell TC 2.00 .90
❑ 392 Hideo Nomo TC 2.00 .90
❑ 393 Richie Sexson TC 2.00 .90
❑ 394 Vladimir Guerrero TC 2.00 .90
❑ 395 Mike Piazza TC 3.00 1.35
❑ 396 Jim Thome TC 2.00 .90
❑ 397 Jason Kendall TC 2.00 .90
❑ 398 Albert Pujols TC 4.00 1.80
❑ 399 Ryan Klesko TC 2.00 .90
❑ 400 Barry Bonds TC 5.00 2.20

2005 Donruss

	Nm-Mt	Ex-Mt
COMPLETE SET (400)	150.00	45.00
COMP.SET w/o SP's (300)	25.00	7.50
COMMON CARD (71-370)	.30	.09
COMMON (1-25/371-400)	2.00	.60
COMMON CARD (26-70)	2.00	.60
1-25 STATED ODDS 1:6	.00	

26-70 STATED ODDS 1:6 .00
371-400 STATED ODDS 1:6 .00

❑ 1 Garret Anderson DK 2.00 .60
❑ 2 Vladimir Guerrero DK 2.00 .60
❑ 3 Manny Ramirez DK 2.00 .60
❑ 4 Kerry Wood DK 2.00 .60
❑ 5 Sammy Sosa DK 2.00 .60
❑ 6 Magglio Ordonez DK 2.00 .60
❑ 7 Adam Dunn DK 2.00 .60
❑ 8 Todd Helton DK 2.00 .60
❑ 9 Josh Beckett DK 2.00 .60
❑ 10 Miguel Cabrera DK 2.00 .60
❑ 11 Lance Berkman DK 2.00 .60
❑ 12 Carlos Beltran DK 2.00 .60
❑ 13 Shawn Green DK 2.00 .60
❑ 14 Roger Clemens DK 3.00 .90
❑ 15 Mike Piazza DK 2.00 .60
❑ 16 Alex Rodriguez DK 3.00 .90
❑ 17 Derek Jeter DK 4.00 1.20
❑ 18 Mark Mulder DK 2.00 .60
❑ 19 Jim Thome DK 2.00 .60
❑ 20 Albert Pujols DK 4.00 1.20
❑ 21 Scott Rolen DK 2.00 .60
❑ 22 Aubrey Huff DK 2.00 .60
❑ 23 Alfonso Soriano DK 2.00 .60
❑ 24 Hank Blalock DK 2.00 .60
❑ 25 Vernon Wells DK 2.00 .60
❑ 26 Kazuo Matsui RR 3.00 .90
❑ 27 B.J. Upton RR 5.00 1.50
❑ 28 Charles Thomas RR 2.00 .60
❑ 29 Akinori Otsuka RR 3.00 .90
❑ 30 David Aardsma RR 2.00 .60
❑ 31 Travis Blackley RR 2.00 .60
❑ 32 Brad Halsey RR 2.00 .60
❑ 33 David Wright RR 8.00 2.40
❑ 34 Kazuhito Tadano RR 3.00 .90
❑ 35 Casey Kotchman RR 3.00 .90
❑ 36 Khalil Greene RR 5.00 1.50
❑ 37 Adrian Gonzalez RR 2.00 .60
❑ 38 Zack Greinke RR 3.00 .90
❑ 39 Chad Cordero RR 2.00 .60
❑ 40 Scott Kazmir RR 5.00 1.50
❑ 41 Jeremy Guthrie RR 2.00 .60
❑ 42 Noah Lowry RR 3.00 .90
❑ 43 Chase Utley RR 3.00 .90
❑ 44 Billy Traber RR 2.00 .60
❑ 45 Aarom Baldiris RR 2.00 .60
❑ 46 Abe Alvarez RR 2.00 .60
❑ 47 Angel Chavez RR 2.00 .60
❑ 48 Joe Mauer RR 3.00 .90
❑ 49 Joey Gathright RR 3.00 .90
❑ 50 John Gall RR 2.00 .60
❑ 51 Ronald Belisario RR 2.00 .60
❑ 52 Ryan Wing RR 2.00 .60
❑ 53 Scott Proctor RR 2.00 .60
❑ 54 Yadier Molina RR 3.00 .90
❑ 55 Carlos Hines RR 2.00 .60
❑ 56 Frankie Francisco RR 2.00 .60
❑ 57 Graham Koonce RR 2.00 .60
❑ 58 Jake Woods RR 2.00 .60
❑ 59 Jason Bartlett RR 3.00 .90
❑ 60 Mike Rouse RR 2.00 .60
❑ 61 Phil Stockman RR 2.00 .60
❑ 62 Renyel Pinto RR 2.00 .60
❑ 63 Roberto Novoa RR 2.00 .60
❑ 64 Ryan Meaux RR 2.00 .60
❑ 65 Dave Crouthers RR 2.00 .60
❑ 66 Justin Knoedler RR 2.00 .60
❑ 67 Justin Leone RR 2.00 .60
❑ 68 Nick Regilio RR 2.00 .60
❑ 69 Mike Gosling RR 2.00 .60
❑ 70 Onil Joseph RR 2.00 .60
❑ 71 Bartolo Colon .30 .09
❑ 72 Brad Fullmer .30 .09
❑ 73 Chone Figgins .30 .09
❑ 74 Darin Erstad .30 .09
❑ 75 Francisco Rodriguez .30 .09
❑ 76 Garret Anderson .30 .09
❑ 77 Jarrod Washburn .30 .09
❑ 78 John Lackey .30 .09
❑ 79 Jose Guillen .30 .09
❑ 80 Robb Quinlan .30 .09
❑ 81 Tim Salmon .50 .15
❑ 82 Troy Glaus .30 .09
❑ 83 Troy Percival .30 .09
❑ 84 Vladimir Guerrero .75 .23
❑ 85 Brandon Webb .30 .09
❑ 86 Casey Fossum .30 .09
❑ 87 Luis Gonzalez .30 .09
❑ 88 Randy Johnson .75 .23
❑ 89 Richie Sexson .30 .09
❑ 90 Robby Hammock .30 .09
❑ 91 Roberto Alomar .50 .15
❑ 92 Adam LaRoche .30 .09
❑ 93 Andruw Jones .50 .15
❑ 94 Bubba Nelson .30 .09
❑ 95 Chipper Jones .75 .23
❑ 96 J.D. Drew .30 .09
❑ 97 John Smoltz .50 .15
❑ 98 Johnny Estrada .30 .09
❑ 99 Marcus Giles .30 .09
❑ 100 Mike Hampton .30 .09
❑ 101 Nick Green .30 .09
❑ 102 Rafael Furcal .30 .09
❑ 103 Russ Ortiz .30 .09
❑ 104 Adam Loewen .30 .09
❑ 105 Brian Roberts .30 .09
❑ 106 Javy Lopez .30 .09
❑ 107 Jay Gibbons .30 .09
❑ 108 Larry Bigbie UER .30 .09
Player pictured is Brian Roberts
❑ 109 Luis Matos .30 .09
❑ 110 Melvin Mora .30 .09
❑ 111 Miguel Tejada .30 .09
❑ 112 Rafael Palmeiro .50 .15
❑ 113 Rodrigo Lopez .30 .09
❑ 114 Sidney Ponson .30 .09
❑ 115 Bill Mueller .30 .09
❑ 116 Byung-Hyun Kim .30 .09
❑ 117 Curt Schilling .50 .15
❑ 118 David Ortiz .75 .23
❑ 119 Derek Lowe .30 .09
❑ 120 Doug Mientkiewicz .30 .09
❑ 121 Jason Varitek .75 .23
❑ 122 Johnny Damon .50 .15
❑ 123 Keith Foulke .30 .09
❑ 124 Kevin Youkilis .30 .09
❑ 125 Manny Ramirez .50 .15
❑ 126 Orlando Cabrera .30 .09
❑ 127 Pedro Martinez .50 .15
❑ 128 Trot Nixon .30 .09
❑ 129 Aramis Ramirez .30 .09
❑ 130 Carlos Zambrano .30 .09
❑ 131 Corey Patterson .30 .09
❑ 132 Derrek Lee .50 .15
❑ 133 Greg Maddux 1.25 .35
❑ 134 Kerry Wood .30 .09
❑ 135 Mark Prior .50 .15
❑ 136 Matt Clement .30 .09
❑ 137 Moises Alou .30 .09
❑ 138 Nomar Garciaparra .75 .23
❑ 139 Sammy Sosa .75 .23
❑ 140 Todd Walker .30 .09
❑ 141 Angel Guzman .30 .09
❑ 142 Billy Koch .30 .09
❑ 143 Carlos Lee .30 .09
❑ 144 Frank Thomas .75 .23
❑ 145 Magglio Ordonez .30 .09
❑ 146 Mark Buehrle .30 .09
❑ 147 Paul Konerko .30 .09
❑ 148 Wilson Valdez .30 .09
❑ 149 Adam Dunn .30 .09
❑ 150 Austin Kearns .30 .09
❑ 151 Barry Larkin .50 .15
❑ 152 Benito Santiago .30 .09
❑ 153 Jason LaRue .30 .09
❑ 154 Ken Griffey Jr. 1.25 .35
❑ 155 Ryan Wagner .30 .09
❑ 156 Sean Casey .50 .15
❑ 157 Brandon Phillips .30 .09
❑ 158 Brian Tallet .30 .09
❑ 159 C.C. Sabathia .30 .09
❑ 160 Cliff Lee .30 .09
❑ 161 Jeremy Guthrie .30 .09
❑ 162 Jody Gerut .30 .09
❑ 163 Matt Lawton .30 .09
❑ 164 Omar Vizquel .50 .15
❑ 165 Travis Hafner .30 .09
❑ 166 Victor Martinez .30 .09
❑ 167 Charles Johnson .30 .09
❑ 168 Garrett Atkins .30 .09
❑ 169 Jason Jennings .30 .09
❑ 170 Jay Payton .30 .09
❑ 171 Jeromy Burnitz .30 .09
❑ 172 Joe Kennedy .30 .09
❑ 173 Larry Walker .50 .15
❑ 174 Preston Wilson .30 .09
❑ 175 Todd Helton .50 .15
❑ 176 Vinny Castilla .30 .09
❑ 177 Bobby Higginson .30 .09
❑ 178 Brandon Inge .30 .09
❑ 179 Carlos Guillen .30 .09
❑ 180 Carlos Pena .30 .09
❑ 181 Craig Monroe .30 .09
❑ 182 Dmitri Young .30 .09
❑ 183 Eric Munson .30 .09
❑ 184 Fernando Vina .30 .09
❑ 185 Ivan Rodriguez .50 .15
❑ 186 Jeremy Bonderman .30 .09
❑ 187 Rondell White .30 .09
❑ 188 A.J. Burnett .30 .09
❑ 189 Dontrelle Willis .30 .09
❑ 190 Guillermo Mota .30 .09
❑ 191 Hee Seop Choi .30 .09
❑ 192 Jeff Conine .30 .09
❑ 193 Josh Beckett .30 .09
❑ 194 Juan Encarnacion .30 .09
❑ 195 Juan Pierre .30 .09
❑ 196 Luis Castillo .30 .09
❑ 197 Miguel Cabrera .50 .15
❑ 198 Mike Lowell .30 .09
❑ 199 Paul Lo Duca .30 .09
❑ 200 Andy Pettitte .50 .15
❑ 201 Brad Ausmus .30 .09
❑ 202 Carlos Beltran .30 .09
❑ 203 Chris Burke .30 .09
❑ 204 Craig Biggio .50 .15
❑ 205 Jeff Bagwell .50 .15
❑ 206 Jeff Kent .30 .09
❑ 207 Lance Berkman .30 .09
❑ 208 Morgan Ensberg .30 .09
❑ 209 Octavio Dotel .30 .09
❑ 210 Roger Clemens 1.25 .35
❑ 211 Roy Oswalt .30 .09
❑ 212 Tim Redding .30 .09
❑ 213 Angel Berroa .30 .09
❑ 214 Juan Gonzalez .30 .09
❑ 215 Ken Harvey .30 .09
❑ 216 Mike Sweeney .30 .09
❑ 217 Adrian Beltre .30 .09
❑ 218 Brad Penny .30 .09
❑ 219 Eric Gagne .30 .09
❑ 220 Hideo Nomo .75 .23
❑ 221 Hong-Chih Kuo .30 .09
❑ 222 Jeff Weaver .30 .09
❑ 223 Kazuhisa Ishii .30 .09
❑ 224 Milton Bradley .30 .09
❑ 225 Shawn Green .30 .09
❑ 226 Steve Finley .30 .09
❑ 227 Danny Kolb .30 .09
❑ 228 Geoff Jenkins .30 .09
❑ 229 Junior Spivey .30 .09
❑ 230 Lyle Overbay .30 .09
❑ 231 Rickie Weeks .30 .09
❑ 232 Scott Podsednik .30 .09
❑ 233 Brad Radke .30 .09
❑ 234 Corey Koskie .30 .09
❑ 235 Cristian Guzman .30 .09
❑ 236 Dustan Mohr .30 .09
❑ 237 Eddie Guardado .30 .09
❑ 238 J.D. Durbin .30 .09
❑ 239 Jacque Jones .30 .09
❑ 240 Joe Nathan .30 .09
❑ 241 Johan Santana .50 .15
❑ 242 Lew Ford .30 .09
❑ 243 Michael Cuddyer .30 .09
❑ 244 Shannon Stewart .30 .09
❑ 245 Torii Hunter .30 .09
❑ 246 Brad Wilkerson .30 .09
❑ 247 Carl Everett .30 .09
❑ 248 Jeff Fassero .30 .09
❑ 249 Jose Vidro .30 .09
❑ 250 Livan Hernandez .30 .09
❑ 251 Michael Barrett .30 .09
❑ 252 Tony Batista .30 .09
❑ 253 Zach Day .30 .09
❑ 254 Al Leiter .30 .09

	Nm-Mt	Ex-Mt
❑ 255 Cliff Floyd	.30	.09
❑ 256 Jae Weong Seo	.30	.09
❑ 257 John Olerud	.30	.09
❑ 258 Jose Reyes	.30	.09
❑ 259 Mike Cameron	.30	.09
❑ 260 Mike Piazza	.75	.23
❑ 261 Richard Hidalgo	.30	.09
❑ 262 Tom Glavine	.50	.15
❑ 263 Vance Wilson	.30	.09
❑ 264 Alex Rodriguez	1.25	.35
❑ 265 Armando Benitez	.30	.09
❑ 266 Bernie Williams	.50	.15
❑ 267 Bubba Crosby	.30	.09
❑ 268 Chien-Ming Wang	.30	.09
❑ 269 Derek Jeter	1.50	.45
❑ 270 Esteban Loaiza	.30	.09
❑ 271 Gary Sheffield	.30	.09
❑ 272 Hideki Matsui	1.50	.45
❑ 273 Jason Giambi	.30	.09
❑ 274 Javier Vazquez	.30	.09
❑ 275 Jorge Posada	.50	.15
❑ 276 Jose Contreras	.30	.09
❑ 277 Kenny Lofton	.30	.09
❑ 278 Kevin Brown	.30	.09
❑ 279 Mariano Rivera	.50	.15
❑ 280 Mike Mussina	.50	.15
❑ 281 Barry Zito	.30	.09
❑ 282 Bobby Crosby	.30	.09
❑ 283 Eric Byrnes	.30	.09
❑ 284 Eric Chavez	.30	.09
❑ 285 Erubiel Durazo	.30	.09
❑ 286 Jermaine Dye	.30	.09
❑ 287 Mark Kotsay	.30	.09
❑ 288 Mark Mulder	.30	.09
❑ 289 Rich Harden	.30	.09
❑ 290 Tim Hudson	.30	.09
❑ 291 Billy Wagner	.30	.09
❑ 292 Bobby Abreu	.30	.09
❑ 293 Brett Myers	.30	.09
❑ 294 Eric Milton	.30	.09
❑ 295 Jim Thome	.50	.15
❑ 296 Jimmy Rollins	.30	.09
❑ 297 Kevin Millwood	.30	.09
❑ 298 Marlon Byrd	.30	.09
❑ 299 Mike Lieberthal	.30	.09
❑ 300 Pat Burrell	.30	.09
❑ 301 Randy Wolf	.30	.09
❑ 302 Craig Wilson	.30	.09
❑ 303 Jack Wilson	.30	.09
❑ 304 Jacob Cruz	.30	.09
❑ 305 Jason Bay	.30	.09
❑ 306 Jason Kendall	.30	.09
❑ 307 Jose Castillo	.30	.09
❑ 308 Kip Wells	.30	.09
❑ 309 Brian Giles	.30	.09
❑ 310 Brian Lawrence	.30	.09
❑ 311 Chris Oxspring	.30	.09
❑ 312 David Wells	.30	.09
❑ 313 Freddy Guzman	.30	.09
❑ 314 Jake Peavy	.30	.09
❑ 315 Mark Loretta	.30	.09
❑ 316 Ryan Klesko	.30	.09
❑ 317 Sean Burroughs	.30	.09
❑ 318 Trevor Hoffman	.30	.09
❑ 319 Xavier Nady	.30	.09
❑ 320 A.J. Pierzynski	.30	.09
❑ 321 Edgardo Alfonzo	.30	.09
❑ 322 J.T. Snow	.30	.09
❑ 323 Jason Schmidt	.30	.09
❑ 324 Jerome Williams	.30	.09
❑ 325 Kirk Rueter	.30	.09
❑ 326 Bret Boone	.30	.09
❑ 327 Bucky Jacobsen	.30	.09
❑ 328 Edgar Martinez	.50	.15
❑ 329 Freddy Garcia	.30	.09
❑ 330 Ichiro Suzuki	1.50	.45
❑ 331 Jamie Moyer	.30	.09
❑ 332 Joel Pineiro	.30	.09
❑ 333 Scott Spiezio	.30	.09
❑ 334 Shigetoshi Hasegawa	.30	.09
❑ 335 Albert Pujols	1.50	.45
❑ 336 Edgar Renteria	.30	.09
❑ 337 Jason Isringhausen	.30	.09
❑ 338 Jim Edmonds	.50	.15
❑ 339 Matt Morris	.30	.09
❑ 340 Mike Matheny	.30	.09
❑ 341 Reggie Sanders	.30	.09
❑ 342 Scott Rolen	.50	.15
❑ 343 Woody Williams	.30	.09
❑ 344 Jeff Suppan	.30	.09
❑ 345 Aubrey Huff	.30	.09
❑ 346 Carl Crawford	.30	.09
❑ 347 Chad Gaudin	.30	.09
❑ 348 Delmon Young	.30	.09
❑ 349 Dewon Brazelton	.30	.09
❑ 350 Jose Cruz Jr.	.30	.09
❑ 351 Rocco Baldelli	.30	.09
❑ 352 Tino Martinez	.50	.15
❑ 353 Toby Hall	.30	.09
❑ 354 Alfonso Soriano	.30	.09
❑ 355 Brian Jordan	.30	.09
❑ 356 Francisco Cordero	.30	.09
❑ 357 Hank Blalock	.30	.09
❑ 358 Kenny Rogers	.30	.09
❑ 359 Kevin Mench	.30	.09
❑ 360 Laynce Nix	.30	.09
❑ 361 Mark Teixeira	.50	.15
❑ 362 Michael Young	.30	.09
❑ 363 Alex S. Gonzalez	.30	.09
❑ 364 Alexis Rios	.30	.09
❑ 365 Carlos Delgado	.30	.09
❑ 366 Eric Hinske	.30	.09
❑ 367 Frank Catalanotto	.30	.09
❑ 368 Josh Phelps	.30	.09
❑ 369 Roy Halladay	.30	.09
❑ 370 Vernon Wells	.30	.09
❑ 371 Vladimir Guerrero TC	2.00	.60
❑ 372 Randy Johnson TC	2.00	.60
❑ 373 Chipper Jones TC	2.00	.60
❑ 374 Miguel Tejada TC	2.00	.60
❑ 375 Pedro Martinez TC	2.00	.60
❑ 376 Sammy Sosa TC	2.00	.60
❑ 377 Frank Thomas TC	2.00	.60
❑ 378 Ken Griffey Jr. TC	3.00	.90
❑ 379 Victor Martinez TC	2.00	.60
❑ 380 Todd Helton TC	2.00	.60
❑ 381 Ivan Rodriguez TC	2.00	.60
❑ 382 Miguel Cabrera TC	2.00	.60
❑ 383 Roger Clemens TC	3.00	.90
❑ 384 Ken Harvey TC	2.00	.60
❑ 385 Eric Gagne TC	2.00	.60
❑ 386 Lyle Overbay TC	2.00	.60
❑ 387 Shannon Stewart TC	2.00	.60
❑ 388 Brad Wilkerson TC	2.00	.60
❑ 389 Mike Piazza TC	2.00	.60
❑ 390 Alex Rodriguez TC	3.00	.90
❑ 391 Mark Mulder TC	2.00	.60
❑ 392 Jim Thome TC	2.00	.60
❑ 393 Jack Wilson TC	2.00	.60
❑ 394 Khalil Greene TC	2.00	.60
❑ 395 Jason Schmidt TC	2.00	.60
❑ 396 Ichiro Suzuki TC	4.00	1.20
❑ 397 Albert Pujols TC	4.00	1.20
❑ 398 Rocco Baldelli TC	2.00	.60
❑ 399 Alfonso Soriano TC	2.00	.60
❑ 400 Vernon Wells TC	2.00	.60

2001 eTopps

	Nm-Mt	Ex-Mt
❑ 1 Nomar Garciaparra/1315	20.00	6.00
❑ 2 Chipper Jones/674	125.00	38.00
❑ 3 Jeff Bagwell/485	50.00	15.00
❑ 4 Randy Johnson/1499	30.00	9.00
❑ 7 Adam Dunn/4197	8.00	2.40
❑ 8 J.D. Drew/767	15.00	4.50
❑ 9 Larry Walker/420	40.00	12.00
❑ 10 Edgardo Alfonzo/338	100.00	30.00
❑ 11 Lance Berkman/595	50.00	15.00
❑ 12 Tony Gwynn/828	40.00	12.00
❑ 13 Andruw Jones/908	25.00	7.50
❑ 15 Troy Glaus/862	15.00	4.50
❑ 17 Sammy Sosa/2487	10.00	3.00
❑ 21 Darin Erstad/664	20.00	6.00
❑ 22 Barry Bonds/1567	125.00	38.00
❑ 27 Derek Jeter/1041	60.00	18.00
❑ 29 Curt Schilling/2125	8.00	2.40
❑ 30 Roberto Alomar/448	40.00	12.00
❑ 31 Luis Gonzalez/1104	10.00	3.00
❑ 32 Jimmy Rollins/1307	10.00	3.00
❑ 34 Joe Crede/1050	12.00	3.60
❑ 39 Sean Casey/537	30.00	9.00
❑ 46 Alex Rodriguez/2212	50.00	15.00
❑ 47 Tom Glavine/437	50.00	15.00
❑ 50 Jose Ortiz/738	15.00	4.50
❑ 51 Cal Ripken/2201	40.00	12.00
❑ 52 Bob Abreu/677	30.00	9.00
❑ 55 Alex Escobar/931	10.00	3.00
❑ 56 Ivan Rodriguez/698	20.00	6.00
❑ 59 Jeff Kent/452	40.00	12.00
❑ 62 Rick Ankiel/752	10.00	3.00
❑ 65 Craig Biggio/410	50.00	15.00
❑ 66 Carlos Delgado/398	60.00	18.00
❑ 68 Greg Maddux/1031	25.00	7.50
❑ 69 Kerry Wood/1056	20.00	6.00
❑ 71 Todd Helton/978	30.00	9.00
❑ 72 Mariano Rivera/824	25.00	7.50
❑ 73 Jason Kendall/672	20.00	6.00
❑ 75 Scott Rolen/498	60.00	18.00
❑ 76 Kazuhiro Sasaki/5000	5.00	1.50
❑ 77 Roy Oswalt/915	25.00	7.50
❑ 78 C.C. Sabathia/1974	10.00	3.00
❑ 83 Brian Giles/400	40.00	12.00
❑ 87 Rafael Furcal/646	20.00	6.00
❑ 88 Mike Mussina/793	25.00	7.50
❑ 89 Gary Sheffield/359	80.00	24.00
❑ 92 Mark McGwire/2908	15.00	4.50
❑ 94 Tsuyoshi Shinjo/3000	5.00	1.50
❑ 99 Jose Vidro/443	40.00	12.00
❑ 100 Ichiro Suzuki/10000	20.00	6.00
❑ 105 Manny Ramirez Sox/1074	20.00	6.00
❑ 109 Juan Gonzalez/558	20.00	6.00
❑ 112 Ken Griffey Jr./2398	15.00	4.50
❑ 114 Tim Hudson/663	30.00	9.00
❑ 115 Nick Johnson/1217	10.00	3.00
❑ 118 Jason Giambi/897	15.00	4.50
❑ 122 Rafael Palmeiro/464	50.00	15.00
❑ 124 V. Guerrero/854	40.00	12.00
❑ 125 Vernon Wells/349	150.00	45.00
❑ 127 Roger Clemens/1462	40.00	12.00
❑ 128 Frank Thomas/834	25.00	7.50
❑ 129 Carlos Beltran/489	80.00	24.00
❑ 130 Pat Burrell/1253	25.00	7.50
❑ 131 Pedro Martinez/1038	25.00	7.50
❑ 132 Mike Piazza/1379	15.00	4.50
❑ 135 Luis Montanez/5000	4.00	1.20
❑ 140 Sean Burroughs/5000	4.00	1.20
❑ 141 Barry Zito/843	30.00	9.00
❑ 142 Bobby Bradley/5000	4.00	1.20
❑ 143 Albert Pujols/5000	80.00	24.00
❑ 144 Ben Sheets/1713	12.00	3.60
❑ 145 Alfonso Soriano/1699	25.00	7.50
❑ 146 Josh Hamilton/5000	4.00	1.20
❑ 147 Eric Munson/5000	4.00	1.20
❑ 150 Mark Mulder/4335	5.00	1.50

1996 Finest

	Nm-Mt	Ex-Mt
COMP.BRONZE SER.1 (110)	25.00	7.50
COMP.BRONZE SER.2 (110)	25.00	7.50
COMMON BRONZE	.50	.15
COMMON GOLD	5.00	1.50
COMMON SILVER	2.50	.75
❑ B5 Roberto Hernandez B	.50	.15
❑ B8 Terry Pendleton B	.50	.15
❑ B12 Ken Caminiti B	.50	.15
❑ B15 Dan Miceli B	.50	.15
❑ B16 Chipper Jones B	1.25	.35
❑ B17 John Wetteland B	.50	.15

❑	B19 Tim Naehring B	.50	.15
❑	B21 Eddie Murray B	1.25	.35
❑	B23 Kevin Appier B	.50	.15
❑	B24 Ken Griffey Jr. B	2.00	.60
❑	B26 Brian McRae B	.50	.15
❑	B27 Pedro Martinez B	.75	.23
❑	B28 Brian Jordan B	.50	.15
❑	B29 Mike Fetters B	.50	.15
❑	B30 Carlos Delgado B	.50	.15
❑	B31 Shane Reynolds B	.50	.15
❑	B32 Terry Steinbach B	.50	.15
❑	B34 Mark Leiter B	.50	.15
❑	B36 David Segui B	.50	.15
❑	B40 Fred McGriff B	.75	.23
❑	B44 Glenallen Hill B	.50	.15
❑	B45 Brady Anderson B	.50	.15
❑	B47 Jim Thome B	.75	.23
❑	B48 Frank Thomas B	1.25	.35
❑	B49 Chuck Knoblauch B	.50	.15
❑	B50 Len Dykstra B	.50	.15
❑	B53 Tom Pagnozzi B	.50	.15
❑	B55 Ricky Bones B	.50	.15
❑	B56 David Justice B	.50	.15
❑	B57 Steve Avery B	.50	.15
❑	B58 Robby Thompson B	.50	.15
❑	B61 Tony Gwynn B	1.50	.45
❑	B63 Denny Neagle B	.50	.15
❑	B67 Robin Ventura B	.50	.15
❑	B70 Kevin Seitzer B	.50	.15
❑	B71 Ramon Martinez B	.50	.15
❑	B75 Brian L.Hunter B	.50	.15
❑	B76 Alan Benes B	.50	.15
❑	B80 Ozzie Guillen B	.50	.15
❑	B82 Benji Gil B	.50	.15
❑	B85 Todd Hundley B	.50	.15
❑	B87 Pat Hentgen B	.50	.15
❑	B89 Chuck Finley B	.50	.15
❑	B92 Derek Jeter B	3.00	.90
❑	B93 Paul O'Neill B	.75	.23
❑	B94 Darrin Fletcher B	.50	.15
❑	B96 Delino DeShields B	.50	.15
❑	B97 Tim Salmon B	.75	.23
❑	B98 John Olerud B	.50	.15
❑	B101 Tim Wakefield B	.50	.15
❑	B103 Dave Stevens B	.50	.15
❑	B104 Orlando Merced B	.50	.15
❑	B106 Jay Bell B	.50	.15
❑	B107 John Burkett B	.50	.15
❑	B108 Chris Hoiles B	.50	.15
❑	B110 Dave Nilsson B	.50	.15
❑	B111 Rod Beck B	.50	.15
❑	B113 Mike Piazza B	2.00	.60
❑	B114 Mark Langston B	.50	.15
❑	B116 Rico Brogna B	.50	.15
❑	B118 Tom Goodwin B	.50	.15
❑	B119 Bryan Rekar B	.50	.15
❑	B120 David Cone B	.50	.15
❑	B122 Andy Pettitte B	.75	.23
❑	B123 Chili Davis B	.50	.15
❑	B124 John Smoltz B	.75	.23
❑	B125 H.Slocumb B	.50	.15
❑	B126 Dante Bichette B	.50	.15
❑	B128 Alex Gonzalez B	.50	.15
❑	B129 Jeff Montgomery B	.50	.15
❑	B131 Denny Martinez B	.50	.15
❑	B132 Mel Rojas B	.50	.15
❑	B133 Derek Bell B	.50	.15
❑	B134 Trevor Hoffman B	.50	.15
❑	B136 Darren Daulton B	.50	.15
❑	B137 Pete Schourek B	.50	.15
❑	B138 Phil Nevin B	.50	.15
❑	B139 Andres Galarraga B	.50	.15
❑	B140 Chad Fonville B	.50	.15
❑	B144 J.T. Snow B	.50	.15
❑	B146 Barry Bonds B	3.00	.90
❑	B147 Orel Hershiser B	.50	.15
❑	B148 Quilvio Veras B	.50	.15
❑	B149 Will Clark B	.75	.23
❑	B150 Jose Rijo B	.50	.15
❑	B152 Travis Fryman B	.50	.15
❑	B154 Alex Fernandez B	.50	.15
❑	B155 Wade Boggs B	.75	.23
❑	B156 Troy Percival B	.50	.15
❑	B157 Moises Alou B	.50	.15
❑	B158 Javy Lopez B	.50	.15
❑	B159 Jason Giambi B	.50	.15
❑	B162 Mark McGwire B	3.00	.90
❑	B163 Eric Karros B	.50	.15
❑	B166 Mickey Tettleton B	.50	.15
❑	B167 Barry Larkin B	.75	.23
❑	B169 Ruben Sierra B	.50	.15
❑	B170 Bill Swift B	.50	.15
❑	B172 Chad Curtis B	.50	.15
❑	B173 Dean Palmer B	.50	.15
❑	B175 Bobby Bonilla B	.50	.15
❑	B176 Greg Colbrunn B	.50	.15
❑	B177 Jose Mesa B	.50	.15
❑	B178 Mike Greenwell B	.50	.15
❑	B181 Doug Drabek B	.50	.15
❑	B183 Wilson Alvarez B	.50	.15
❑	B184 Marty Cordova B	.50	.15
❑	B185 Hal Morris B	.50	.15
❑	B187 Carlos Garcia B	.50	.15
❑	B190 Marquis Grissom B	.50	.15
❑	B193 Will Clark B	.75	.23
❑	B194 Paul Molitor B	.75	.23
❑	B195 Kenny Rogers B	.50	.15
❑	B196 Reggie Sanders B	.50	.15
❑	B199 Raul Mondesi B	.50	.15
❑	B200 Lance Johnson B	.50	.15
❑	B201 Alvin Morman B	.50	.15
❑	B203 Jack McDowell B	.50	.15
❑	B204 Randy Myers B	.50	.15
❑	B205 Harold Baines B	.50	.15
❑	B206 Marty Cordova B	.50	.15
❑	B207 Rich Hunter B RC	.50	.15
❑	B208 Al Leiter B	.50	.15
❑	B209 Greg Gagne B	.50	.15
❑	B210 Ben McDonald B	.50	.15
❑	B212 Terry Adams B	.50	.15
❑	B213 Paul Sorrento B	.50	.15
❑	B214 Albert Belle B	.50	.15
❑	B215 Mike Blowers B	.50	.15
❑	B216 Jim Edmonds B	.50	.15
❑	B217 Felipe Crespo B	.50	.15
❑	B219 Shawon Dunston B	.50	.15
❑	B220 Jimmy Haynes B	.50	.15
❑	B221 Jose Canseco B	.75	.23
❑	B222 Eric Davis B	.50	.15
❑	B224 Tim Raines B	.50	.15
❑	B225 Tony Phillips B	.50	.15
❑	B226 Charlie Hayes B	.50	.15
❑	B227 Eric Owens B	.50	.15
❑	B228 Roberto Alomar B	.75	.23
❑	B233 Kenny Lofton B	.50	.15
❑	B236 Mark McGwire B	3.00	.90
❑	B237 Jay Buhner B	.50	.15
❑	B238 Craig Biggio B	.75	.23
❑	B240 Barry Bonds B	3.00	.90
❑	B244 Ron Gant B	.50	.15
❑	B245 Paul Wilson B	.50	.15
❑	B246 T.Hollandsworth B	.50	.15
❑	B247 Todd Zeile B	.50	.15
❑	B248 David Justice B	.50	.15
❑	B250 Moises Alou B	.50	.15
❑	B251 Bob Wolcott B	.50	.15
❑	B252 David Wells B	.50	.15
❑	B253 Juan Gonzalez B	.50	.15
❑	B254 Andres Galarraga B	.50	.15
❑	B255 Dave Hollins B	.50	.15
❑	B257 Sammy Sosa B	1.25	.35
❑	B258 Ivan Rodriguez B	.75	.23
❑	B259 Bip Roberts B	.50	.15
❑	B260 Tino Martinez B	.75	.23
❑	B262 Mike Stanley B	.50	.15
❑	B264 Butch Huskey B	.50	.15
❑	B265 Jeff Conine B	.50	.15
❑	B267 Mark Grace B	.75	.23
❑	B268 Jason Schmidt B	.75	.23
❑	B269 Otis Nixon B	.50	.15
❑	B271 Kirby Puckett B	1.25	.35
❑	B273 Andy Benes B	.50	.15
❑	B275 Mike Piazza B	2.00	.60
❑	B276 Rey Ordonez B	.50	.15
❑	B278 Gary Gaetti B	.50	.15
❑	B280 Robin Ventura B	.50	.15
❑	B281 Cal Ripken B	4.00	1.20
❑	B282 Carlos Baerga B	.50	.15
❑	B283 Roger Cedeno B	.50	.15
❑	B285 Terrell Wade B	.50	.15
❑	B286 Kevin Brown B	.50	.15
❑	B287 Rafael Palmeiro B	.75	.23
❑	B288 Mo Vaughn B	.50	.15
❑	B292 Bob Tewksbury B	.50	.15
❑	B297 T.J. Mathews B	.50	.15
❑	B298 Manny Ramirez B	.75	.23
❑	B299 Jeff Bagwell B	.75	.23
❑	B301 Wade Boggs B	.75	.23
❑	B303 Steve Gibralter B	.50	.15
❑	B304 B.J. Surhoff B	.50	.15
❑	B306 Royce Clayton B	.50	.15
❑	B307 Sal Fasano B	.50	.15
❑	B309 Gary Sheffield B	.50	.15
❑	B310 Ken Hill B	.50	.15
❑	B311 Joe Girardi B	.50	.15
❑	B312 Matt Lawton B RC	1.00	.30
❑	B314 Julio Franco B	.50	.15
❑	B315 Joe Carter B	.50	.15
❑	B316 Brooks Kieschnick B	.50	.15
❑	B318 H.Slocumb B	.50	.15
❑	B319 Barry Larkin B	.75	.23
❑	B320 Tony Gwynn B	1.50	.45
❑	B322 Frank Thomas B	1.25	.35
❑	B323 Edgar Martinez B	.75	.23
❑	B325 Henry Rodriguez B	.50	.15
❑	B326 Marvin Benard B RC	.50	.15
❑	B329 Ugueth Urbina B	.50	.15
❑	B331 Roger Salkeld B	.50	.15
❑	B332 Edgar Renteria B	.50	.15
❑	B333 Ryan Klesko B	.50	.15
❑	B334 Ray Lankford B	.50	.15
❑	B336 Justin Thompson B	.50	.15
❑	B339 Mark Clark B	.50	.15
❑	B340 Ruben Rivera B	.50	.15
❑	B342 Matt Williams B	.50	.15
❑	B343 F.Cordova B RC	.50	.15
❑	B344 Cecil Fielder B	.50	.15
❑	B348 Mark Grudzielanek B	.50	.15
❑	B349 Ron Coomer B	.50	.15
❑	B351 Rich Aurilia B RC	1.00	.30
❑	B352 Jose Herrera B	.50	.15
❑	B356 Tony Clark B	.50	.15
❑	B358 Dan Naulty B	.50	.15
❑	B359 Checklist B	.50	.15
❑	G4 Marty Cordova G	5.00	1.50
❑	G6 Tony Gwynn G	15.00	4.50
❑	G9 Albert Belle G	5.00	1.50
❑	G18 Kirby Puckett G	12.00	3.60
❑	G20 Karim Garcia G	5.00	1.50
❑	G25 Cal Ripken G	40.00	12.00
❑	G33 Hideo Nomo G	12.00	3.60
❑	G39 Ryne Sandberg G	20.00	6.00
❑	G42 Jeff Bagwell G	4.00	1.20
❑	G51 Jason Isringhausen G	5.00	1.50
❑	G64 Mo Vaughn G	5.00	1.50
❑	G66 Dante Bichette G	5.00	1.50
❑	G74 Mark McGwire G	30.00	9.00
❑	G81 Kenny Lofton G	5.00	1.50
❑	G83 Jim Edmonds G	5.00	1.50
❑	G90 Mike Mussina G	8.00	2.40
❑	G100 Jeff Conine G	5.00	1.50
❑	G102 Johnny Damon G	8.00	2.40
❑	G105 Barry Bonds G	30.00	9.00
❑	G117 Jose Canseco G	8.00	2.40
❑	G135 Ken Griffey Jr. G	20.00	6.00
❑	G141 Chipper Jones G	12.00	3.60
❑	G145 Greg Maddux G	20.00	6.00
❑	G164 Jay Buhner G	5.00	1.50
❑	G186 Frank Thomas G	12.00	3.60
❑	G191 Checklist G	5.00	1.50

❑ G192 Chipper Jones G	12.00	3.60
❑ G197 Roberto Alomar G	8.00	2.40
❑ G198 Dennis Eckersley G	5.00	1.50
❑ G202 George Arias G	5.00	1.50
❑ G232 Hideo Nomo G	12.00	3.60
❑ G243 Chris Snopek G	5.00	1.50
❑ G249 Tim Salmon G	8.00	2.40
❑ G266 Matt Williams G	5.00	1.50
❑ G270 Randy Johnson G	12.00	3.60
❑ G279 Paul Molitor G	8.00	2.40
❑ G290 Cecil Fielder G	5.00	1.50
❑ G294 L.Hernandez G RC	15.00	4.50
❑ G300 Marty Janzen G RC	5.00	1.50
❑ G308 Ron Gant G	5.00	1.50
❑ G321 Ryan Klesko G	5.00	1.50
❑ G324 Jermaine Dye G	5.00	1.50
❑ G330 Jason Giambi G	5.00	1.50
❑ G335 Edgar Martinez G	8.00	2.40
❑ G338 Rey Ordonez G	5.00	1.50
❑ G347 Sammy Sosa G	12.00	3.60
❑ G354 Juan Gonzalez G	5.00	1.50
❑ G355 Craig Biggio G	8.00	2.40
❑ S1 Greg Maddux S UER 95 stats listed as Mariners	10.00	3.00
❑ S2 Bernie Williams S	4.00	1.20
❑ S3 Ivan Rodriguez S	4.00	1.20
❑ S7 Barry Larkin S	4.00	1.20
❑ S10 Ray Lankford S	2.50	.75
❑ S11 Mike Piazza S	10.00	3.00
❑ S13 Larry Walker S	2.50	.75
❑ S14 Matt Williams S	2.50	.75
❑ S22 Tim Salmon S	4.00	1.20
❑ S35 Edgar Martinez S	4.00	1.20
❑ S37 Gregg Jefferies S	2.50	.75
❑ S38 Bill Pulsipher S	2.50	.75
❑ S41 Shawn Green S	2.50	.75
❑ S43 Jim Abbott S	4.00	1.20
❑ S46 Roger Clemens S	12.00	3.60
❑ S52 Rondell White S	2.50	.75
❑ S54 Dennis Eckersley S	2.50	.75
❑ S59 Hideo Nomo S	6.00	1.80
❑ S60 Gary Sheffield S	2.50	.75
❑ S62 Will Clark S	4.00	1.20
❑ S65 Bret Boone S	2.50	.75
❑ S68 Rafael Palmeiro S	4.00	1.20
❑ S69 Carlos Baerga S	2.50	.75
❑ S72 Tom Glavine S	4.00	1.20
❑ S73 Garret Anderson S	2.50	.75
❑ S77 Randy Johnson S	6.00	1.80
❑ S78 Jeff King S	2.50	.75
❑ S79 Kirby Puckett S	6.00	1.80
❑ S84 Cecil Fielder S	2.50	.75
❑ S86 Reggie Sanders S	2.50	.75
❑ S88 Ryan Klesko S	2.50	.75
❑ S91 John Valentin S	2.50	.75
❑ S95 Manny Ramirez S	4.00	1.20
❑ S99 Vinny Castilla S	2.50	.75
❑ S109 Carlos Perez S	2.50	.75
❑ S112 Craig Biggio S	4.00	1.20
❑ S115 Juan Gonzalez S	2.50	.75
❑ S121 Ray Durham S	2.50	.75
❑ S127 C.J. Nitkowski S	2.50	.75
❑ S130 Raul Mondesi S	2.50	.75
❑ S142 Lee Smith S	2.50	.75
❑ S143 Joe Carter S	2.50	.75
❑ S151 Mo Vaughn S	2.50	.75
❑ S153 Frank Rodriguez S	2.50	.75
❑ S160 Steve Finley S	2.50	.75
❑ S161 Jeff Bagwell S	4.00	1.20
❑ S165 Cal Ripken S	20.00	6.00
❑ S168 Lyle Mouton S	2.50	.75
❑ S171 Sammy Sosa S	1.50	.45
❑ S174 John Franco S	2.50	.75
❑ S179 Greg Vaughn S	2.50	.75
❑ S180 Mark Wohlers S	2.50	.75
❑ S182 Paul O'Neill S	4.00	1.20
❑ S188 Albert Belle S	2.50	.75
❑ S189 Mark Grace S	4.00	1.20
❑ S211 Ernie Young S	2.50	.75
❑ S218 Fred McGriff S	4.00	1.20
❑ S223 Kimera Bartee S	2.50	.75
❑ S229 Rickey Henderson S	6.00	1.80
❑ S230 Sterling Hitchcock S	2.50	.75
❑ S231 Bernard Gilkey S	2.50	.75
❑ S234 Ryne Sandberg S	10.00	3.00
❑ S235 Greg Maddux S	10.00	3.00
❑ S239 Todd Stottlemyre S	2.50	.75
❑ S241 Jason Kendall S	2.50	.75
❑ S242 Paul O'Neill S	4.00	1.20
❑ S256 Devon White S	2.50	.75
❑ S261 Chuck Knoblauch S	2.50	.75
❑ S263 Wally Joyner S	2.50	.75
❑ S272 Andy Fox S	2.50	.75
❑ S274 Sean Berry S	2.50	.75
❑ S277 Benito Santiago S	2.50	.75
❑ S284 Chad Mottola S	2.50	.75
❑ S289 Dante Bichette S	2.50	.75
❑ S291 Dwight Gooden S	2.50	.75
❑ S293 Kevin Mitchell S	2.50	.75
❑ S295 Russ Davis S	2.50	.75
❑ S296 Chan Ho Park S	2.50	.75
❑ S302 Larry Walker S	2.50	.75
❑ S305 Ken Griffey Jr. S	10.00	3.00
❑ S313 Billy Wagner S	2.50	.75
❑ S317 Mike Grace S RC	2.50	.75
❑ S327 Kenny Lofton S	2.50	.75
❑ S328 Derek Bell S	2.50	.75
❑ S337 Gary Sheffield S	2.50	.75
❑ S341 Mark Grace S	4.00	1.20
❑ S345 Andres Galarraga S	2.50	.75
❑ S346 Brady Anderson S	2.50	.75
❑ S350 Derek Jeter S	12.00	3.60
❑ S353 Jay Buhner S	2.50	.75
❑ S357 Tino Martinez S	4.00	1.20

1999 Finest

	Nm-Mt	Ex-Mt
COMPLETE SET (300)	80.00	24.00
COMP.SERIES 1 (150)	40.00	12.00
COMP.SERIES 2 (150)	40.00	12.00
COMP.SER.1 w/o SP's (100)	15.00	4.50
COMP.SER.2 w/o SP's (100)	15.00	4.50
COMMON (1-100/151-250)	.40	.12
COMMON (101-150/251-300)	.50	.15

❑ 1 Darin Erstad	.40	.12
❑ 2 Javy Lopez	.40	.12
❑ 3 Vinny Castilla	.40	.12
❑ 4 Jim Thome	.60	.18
❑ 5 Tino Martinez	.60	.18
❑ 6 Mark Grace	.60	.18
❑ 7 Shawn Green	.40	.12
❑ 8 Dustin Hermanson	.40	.12
❑ 9 Kevin Young	.40	.12
❑ 10 Tony Clark	.40	.12
❑ 11 Scott Brosius	.40	.12
❑ 12 Craig Biggio	.60	.18
❑ 13 Brian McRae	.40	.12
❑ 14 Chan Ho Park	.40	.12
❑ 15 Manny Ramirez	.60	.18
❑ 16 Chipper Jones	1.00	.30
❑ 17 Rico Brogna	.40	.12
❑ 18 Quinton McCracken	.40	.12
❑ 19 J.T. Snow	.40	.12
❑ 20 Tony Gwynn	1.25	.35
❑ 21 Juan Guzman	.40	.12
❑ 22 John Valentin	.40	.12
❑ 23 Rick Helling	.40	.12
❑ 24 Sandy Alomar Jr.	.40	.12
❑ 25 Frank Thomas	1.00	.30
❑ 26 Jorge Posada	.60	.18
❑ 27 Dmitri Young	.40	.12
❑ 28 Rick Reed	.40	.12
❑ 29 Kevin Tapani	.40	.12
❑ 30 Troy Glaus	.60	.18
❑ 31 Kenny Rogers	.40	.12
❑ 32 Jeromy Burnitz	.40	.12
❑ 33 Mark Grudzielanek	.40	.12
❑ 34 Mike Mussina	.60	.18
❑ 35 Scott Rolen	.60	.18
❑ 36 Neifi Perez	.40	.12
❑ 37 Brad Radke	.40	.12
❑ 38 Darryl Strawberry	.40	.12
❑ 39 Robb Nen	.40	.12
❑ 40 Moises Alou	.40	.12
❑ 41 Eric Young	.40	.12
❑ 42 Livan Hernandez	.40	.12
❑ 43 John Wetteland	.40	.12
❑ 44 Matt Lawton	.40	.12
❑ 45 Ben Grieve	.40	.12
❑ 46 Fernando Tatis	.40	.12
❑ 47 Travis Fryman	.40	.12
❑ 48 David Segui	.40	.12
❑ 49 Bob Abreu	.40	.12
❑ 50 Nomar Garciaparra	1.50	.45
❑ 51 Paul O'Neill	.60	.18
❑ 52 Jeff King	.40	.12
❑ 53 Francisco Cordova	.40	.12
❑ 54 John Olerud	.40	.12
❑ 55 Vladimir Guerrero	1.00	.30
❑ 56 Fernando Vina	.40	.12
❑ 57 Shane Reynolds	.40	.12
❑ 58 Chuck Finley	.40	.12
❑ 59 Rondell White	.40	.12
❑ 60 Greg Vaughn	.40	.12
❑ 61 Ryan Minor	.40	.12
❑ 62 Tom Gordon	.40	.12
❑ 63 Damion Easley	.40	.12
❑ 64 Ray Durham	.40	.12
❑ 65 Orlando Hernandez	.40	.12
❑ 66 Bartolo Colon	.40	.12
❑ 67 Jaret Wright	.40	.12
❑ 68 Royce Clayton	.40	.12
❑ 69 Tim Salmon	.60	.18
❑ 70 Mark McGwire	2.50	.75
❑ 71 Alex Gonzalez	.40	.12
❑ 72 Tom Glavine	.60	.18
❑ 73 David Justice	.40	.12
❑ 74 Omar Vizquel	.60	.18
❑ 75 Juan Gonzalez	.40	.12
❑ 76 Bobby Higginson	.40	.12
❑ 77 Todd Walker	.40	.12
❑ 78 Dante Bichette	.40	.12
❑ 79 Kevin Millwood	.40	.12
❑ 80 Roger Clemens	2.00	.60
❑ 81 Kerry Wood	.40	.12
❑ 82 Cal Ripken	3.00	.90
❑ 83 Jay Bell	.40	.12
❑ 84 Barry Bonds	2.50	.75
❑ 85 Alex Rodriguez	1.50	.45
❑ 86 Doug Glanville	.40	.12
❑ 87 Jason Kendall	.40	.12
❑ 88 Sean Casey	.60	.18
❑ 89 Aaron Sele	.40	.12
❑ 90 Derek Jeter	2.50	.75
❑ 91 Andy Ashby	.40	.12
❑ 92 Rusty Greer	.40	.12
❑ 93 Rod Beck	.40	.12
❑ 94 Matt Williams	.40	.12
❑ 95 Mike Piazza	1.50	.45
❑ 96 Wally Joyner	.40	.12
❑ 97 Barry Larkin	.60	.18
❑ 98 Eric Milton	.40	.12
❑ 99 Gary Sheffield	.40	.12
❑ 100 Greg Maddux	1.50	.45
❑ 101 Ken Griffey Jr. GEM	2.50	.75
❑ 102 Frank Thomas GEM	1.50	.45
❑ 103 N.Garciaparra GEM	2.50	.75
❑ 104 Mark McGwire GEM	4.00	1.20
❑ 105 Alex Rodriguez GEM	2.50	.75
❑ 106 Tony Gwynn GEM	2.00	.60
❑ 107 Juan Gonzalez GEM	.60	.18
❑ 108 Jeff Bagwell GEM	1.00	.30
❑ 109 Sammy Sosa GEM	1.50	.45
❑ 110 V.Guerrero GEM	1.50	.45
❑ 111 Roger Clemens GEM	3.00	.90
❑ 112 Barry Bonds GEM	4.00	1.20
❑ 113 Darin Erstad GEM	.60	.18
❑ 114 Mike Piazza GEM	2.50	.75
❑ 115 Derek Jeter GEM	4.00	1.20

#	Player	Nm-Mt	Ex-Mt
❑ 116	Chipper Jones GEM	1.50	.45
❑ 117	Larry Walker GEM	.60	.18
❑ 118	Scott Rolen GEM	1.00	.30
❑ 119	Cal Ripken GEM	5.00	1.50
❑ 120	Greg Maddux GEM	2.50	.75
❑ 121	Troy Glaus SENS	1.00	.30
❑ 122	Ben Grieve SENS	.50	.15
❑ 123	Ryan Minor SENS	.50	.15
❑ 124	Kerry Wood SENS	.60	.18
❑ 125	Travis Lee SENS	.50	.15
❑ 126	Adrian Beltre SENS	.60	.18
❑ 127	Brad Fullmer SENS	.50	.15
❑ 128	Aramis Ramirez SENS	.60	.18
❑ 129	Eric Chavez SENS	.60	.18
❑ 130	Todd Helton SENS	1.00	.30
❑ 131	Pat Burrell RC	3.00	.90
❑ 132	Ryan Mills RC	.50	.15
❑ 133	Austin Kearns RC	2.00	.60
❑ 134	Josh McKinley RC	.60	.18
❑ 135	Adam Everett RC	1.00	.30
❑ 136	Marlon Anderson	.50	.15
❑ 137	Bruce Chen	.50	.15
❑ 138	Matt Clement	.60	.18
❑ 139	Alex Gonzalez	.50	.15
❑ 140	Roy Halladay	.60	.18
❑ 141	Calvin Pickering	.50	.15
❑ 142	Randy Wolf	.50	.15
❑ 143	Ryan Anderson	.50	.15
❑ 144	Ruben Mateo	.50	.15
❑ 145	Alex Escobar RC	.60	.18
❑ 146	Jeremy Giambi	.50	.15
❑ 147	Lance Berkman	.60	.18
❑ 148	Michael Barrett	.50	.15
❑ 149	Preston Wilson	.60	.18
❑ 150	Gabe Kapler	.60	.18
❑ 151	Roger Clemens	2.00	.60
❑ 152	Jay Buhner	.40	.12
❑ 153	Brad Fullmer	.40	.12
❑ 154	Ray Lankford	.40	.12
❑ 155	Jim Edmonds	.40	.12
❑ 156	Jason Giambi	.40	.12
❑ 157	Bret Boone	.40	.12
❑ 158	Jeff Cirillo	.40	.12
❑ 159	Rickey Henderson	1.00	.30
❑ 160	Edgar Martinez	.60	.18
❑ 161	Ron Gant	.40	.12
❑ 162	Mark Kotsay	.40	.12
❑ 163	Trevor Hoffman	.40	.12
❑ 164	Jason Schmidt	.40	.12
❑ 165	Brett Tomko	.40	.12
❑ 166	David Ortiz	.60	.18
❑ 167	Dean Palmer	.40	.12
❑ 168	Hideki Irabu	.40	.12
❑ 169	Mike Cameron	.40	.12
❑ 170	Pedro Martinez	.60	.18
❑ 171	Tom Goodwin	.40	.12
❑ 172	Brian Hunter	.40	.12
❑ 173	Al Leiter	.40	.12
❑ 174	Charles Johnson	.40	.12
❑ 175	Curt Schilling	.40	.12
❑ 176	Robin Ventura	.40	.12
❑ 177	Travis Lee	.40	.12
❑ 178	Jeff Shaw	.40	.12
❑ 179	Ugueth Urbina	.40	.12
❑ 180	Roberto Alomar	.60	.18
❑ 181	Cliff Floyd	.40	.12
❑ 182	Adrian Beltre	.40	.12
❑ 183	Tony Womack	.40	.12
❑ 184	Brian Jordan	.40	.12
❑ 185	Randy Johnson	1.00	.30
❑ 186	Mickey Morandini	.40	.12
❑ 187	Todd Hundley	.40	.12
❑ 188	Jose Valentin	.40	.12
❑ 189	Eric Davis	.40	.12
❑ 190	Ken Caminiti	.40	.12
❑ 191	David Wells	.40	.12
❑ 192	Ryan Klesko	.40	.12
❑ 193	Garret Anderson	.40	.12
❑ 194	Eric Karros	.40	.12
❑ 195	Ivan Rodriguez	.60	.18
❑ 196	Aramis Ramirez	.40	.12
❑ 197	Mike Lieberthal	.40	.12
❑ 198	Will Clark	.60	.18
❑ 199	Rey Ordonez	.40	.12
❑ 200	Ken Griffey Jr.	1.50	.45
❑ 201	Jose Guillen	.40	.12
❑ 202	Scott Erickson	.40	.12
❑ 203	Paul Konerko	.40	.12
❑ 204	Johnny Damon	.60	.18
❑ 205	Larry Walker	.40	.12
❑ 206	Denny Neagle	.40	.12
❑ 207	Jose Offerman	.40	.12
❑ 208	Andy Pettitte	.60	.18
❑ 209	Bobby Jones	.40	.12
❑ 210	Kevin Brown	.60	.18
❑ 211	John Smoltz	.60	.18
❑ 212	Henry Rodriguez	.40	.12
❑ 213	Tim Belcher	.40	.12
❑ 214	Carlos Delgado	.40	.12
❑ 215	Andruw Jones	.60	.18
❑ 216	Andy Benes	.40	.12
❑ 217	Fred McGriff	.60	.18
❑ 218	Edgar Renteria	.40	.12
❑ 219	Miguel Tejada	.40	.12
❑ 220	Bernie Williams	.60	.18
❑ 221	Justin Thompson	.40	.12
❑ 222	Marty Cordova	.40	.12
❑ 223	Delino DeShields	.40	.12
❑ 224	Ellis Burks	.40	.12
❑ 225	Kenny Lofton	.40	.12
❑ 226	Steve Finley	.40	.12
❑ 227	Eric Chavez	.40	.12
❑ 228	Jose Cruz Jr.	.40	.12
❑ 229	Marquis Grissom	.40	.12
❑ 230	Jeff Bagwell	.60	.18
❑ 231	Jose Canseco	.60	.18
❑ 232	Edgardo Alfonzo	.40	.12
❑ 233	Richie Sexson	.40	.12
❑ 234	Jeff Kent	.40	.12
❑ 235	Rafael Palmeiro	.60	.18
❑ 236	David Cone	.40	.12
❑ 237	Gregg Jefferies	.40	.12
❑ 238	Mike Lansing	.40	.12
❑ 239	Mariano Rivera	.60	.18
❑ 240	Albert Belle	.40	.12
❑ 241	Chuck Knoblauch	.40	.12
❑ 242	Derek Bell	.40	.12
❑ 243	Pat Hentgen	.40	.12
❑ 244	Andres Galarraga	.40	.12
❑ 245	Mo Vaughn	.40	.12
❑ 246	Wade Boggs	.60	.18
❑ 247	Devon White	.40	.12
❑ 248	Todd Helton	.60	.18
❑ 249	Raul Mondesi	.40	.12
❑ 250	Sammy Sosa	1.00	.30
❑ 251	Nomar Garciaparra ST	2.50	.75
❑ 252	Mark McGwire ST	4.00	1.20
❑ 253	Alex Rodriguez ST	2.50	.75
❑ 254	Juan Gonzalez ST	.60	.18
❑ 255	Vladimir Guerrero ST	1.50	.45
❑ 256	Ken Griffey Jr. ST	2.50	.75
❑ 257	Mike Piazza ST	2.50	.75
❑ 258	Derek Jeter ST	4.00	1.20
❑ 259	Albert Belle ST	.60	.18
❑ 260	Greg Vaughn ST	.50	.15
❑ 261	Sammy Sosa ST	1.50	.45
❑ 262	Greg Maddux ST	2.50	.75
❑ 263	Frank Thomas ST	1.50	.45
❑ 264	Mark Grace ST	1.00	.30
❑ 265	Ivan Rodriguez ST	1.00	.30
❑ 266	Roger Clemens GM	3.00	.90
❑ 267	Mo Vaughn GM	.60	.18
❑ 268	Jim Thome GM	1.00	.30
❑ 269	Darin Erstad GM	.60	.18
❑ 270	Chipper Jones GM	1.50	.45
❑ 271	Larry Walker GM	.60	.18
❑ 272	Cal Ripken GM	5.00	1.50
❑ 273	Scott Rolen GM	1.00	.30
❑ 274	Randy Johnson GM	1.50	.45
❑ 275	Tony Gwynn GM	2.00	.60
❑ 276	Barry Bonds GM	4.00	1.20
❑ 277	Sean Burroughs RC	1.00	.30
❑ 278	J.M. Gold RC	.50	.15
❑ 279	Carlos Lee	.60	.18
❑ 280	George Lombard	.50	.15
❑ 281	Carlos Beltran	1.00	.30
❑ 282	Fernando Seguignol	.50	.15
❑ 283	Eric Chavez	.60	.18
❑ 284	Carlos Pena RC	.60	.18
❑ 285	Corey Patterson RC	1.00	.30
❑ 286	Alfonso Soriano RC	8.00	2.40
❑ 287	Nick Johnson RC	1.50	.45
❑ 288	Jorge Toca RC	.60	.18
❑ 289	A.J. Burnett RC	2.00	.60
❑ 290	Andy Brown RC	.50	.15
❑ 291	D.Mientkiewicz RC	1.00	.30
❑ 292	Bobby Seay RC	.50	.15
❑ 293	Chip Ambres RC	.50	.15
❑ 294	C.C. Sabathia RC	1.50	.45
❑ 295	Choo Freeman RC	.60	.18
❑ 296	Eric Valent RC	.60	.18
❑ 297	Matt Belisle RC	.50	.15
❑ 298	Jason Tyner RC	.50	.15
❑ 299	Masao Kida RC	.60	.18
❑ 300	Hank Aaron Mark McGwire	3.00	.90

2000 Finest

	Nm-Mt	Ex-Mt
COMP.SERIES 1 w/o SP's (100)	25.00	7.50
COMP.SERIES 2 w/o SP's (100)	25.00	7.50
COMMON (1-100/147-246)	.40	.12
COMMON (101-120)	5.00	1.50
COMMON (121-135)	1.50	.45
COMMON (136-145/277-286)	2.00	.60
COMMON (247-266)	5.00	1.50
COMMON (267-276)	1.00	.30

#	Player	Nm-Mt	Ex-Mt
❑ 1	Nomar Garciaparra	1.50	.45
❑ 2	Chipper Jones	1.00	.30
❑ 3	Erubiel Durazo	.40	.12
❑ 4	Robin Ventura	.60	.18
❑ 5	Garret Anderson	.40	.12
❑ 6	Dean Palmer	.40	.12
❑ 7	Mariano Rivera	.60	.18
❑ 8	Rusty Greer	.40	.12
❑ 9	Jim Thome	.60	.18
❑ 10	Jeff Bagwell	.60	.18
❑ 11	Jason Giambi	.40	.12
❑ 12	Jeromy Burnitz	.40	.12
❑ 13	Mark Grace	.60	.18
❑ 14	Russ Ortiz	.40	.12
❑ 15	Kevin Brown	.60	.18
❑ 16	Kevin Millwood	.40	.12
❑ 17	Scott Williamson	.40	.12
❑ 18	Orlando Hernandez	.40	.12
❑ 19	Todd Walker	.40	.12
❑ 20	Carlos Beltran	.40	.12
❑ 21	Ruben Rivera	.40	.12
❑ 22	Curt Schilling	.40	.12
❑ 23	Brian Giles	.40	.12
❑ 24	Eric Karros	.40	.12
❑ 25	Preston Wilson	.40	.12
❑ 26	Al Leiter	.40	.12
❑ 27	Juan Encarnacion	.40	.12
❑ 28	Tim Salmon	.60	.18
❑ 29	B.J. Surhoff	.40	.12
❑ 30	Bernie Williams	.60	.18
❑ 31	Lee Stevens	.40	.12
❑ 32	Pokey Reese	.40	.12
❑ 33	Mike Sweeney	.40	.12
❑ 34	Corey Koskie	.40	.12
❑ 35	Roberto Alomar	.60	.18
❑ 36	Tim Hudson	.40	.12
❑ 37	Tom Glavine	.60	.18
❑ 38	Jeff Kent	.40	.12
❑ 39	Mike Lieberthal	.40	.12
❑ 40	Barry Larkin	.60	.18
❑ 41	Paul O'Neill	.60	.18
❑ 42	Rico Brogna	.40	.12

❑ 43 Brian Daubach .40 .12
❑ 44 Rich Aurilia .40 .12
❑ 45 Vladimir Guerrero 1.00 .30
❑ 46 Luis Castillo .40 .12
❑ 47 Bartolo Colon .40 .12
❑ 48 Kevin Appier .40 .12
❑ 49 Mo Vaughn .40 .12
❑ 50 Alex Rodriguez 1.50 .45
❑ 51 Randy Johnson 1.00 .30
❑ 52 Kris Benson .40 .12
❑ 53 Tony Clark .40 .12
❑ 54 Chad Allen .40 .12
❑ 55 Larry Walker .40 .12
❑ 56 Freddy Garcia .40 .12
❑ 57 Paul Konerko .40 .12
❑ 58 Edgardo Alfonzo .40 .12
❑ 59 Brady Anderson .40 .12
❑ 60 Derek Jeter 2.50 .75
❑ 61 John Smoltz .60 .18
❑ 62 Doug Glanville .40 .12
❑ 63 Shannon Stewart .40 .12
❑ 64 Greg Maddux 1.50 .45
❑ 65 Mark McGwire 2.50 .75
❑ 66 Gary Sheffield .40 .12
❑ 67 Kevin Young .40 .12
❑ 68 Tony Gwynn 1.25 .35
❑ 69 Rey Ordonez .40 .12
❑ 70 Cal Ripken 3.00 .90
❑ 71 Todd Helton .60 .18
❑ 72 Brian Jordan .40 .12
❑ 73 Jose Canseco .60 .18
❑ 74 Luis Gonzalez .40 .12
❑ 75 Barry Bonds 2.50 .75
❑ 76 Jermaine Dye .40 .12
❑ 77 Jose Offerman .40 .12
❑ 78 Magglio Ordonez .40 .12
❑ 79 Fred McGriff .60 .18
❑ 80 Ivan Rodriguez .60 .18
❑ 81 Josh Hamilton .40 .12
❑ 82 Vernon Wells .40 .12
❑ 83 Mark Mulder .40 .12
❑ 84 John Patterson .40 .12
❑ 85 Nick Johnson .40 .12
❑ 86 Pablo Ozuna .40 .12
❑ 87 A.J. Burnett .40 .12
❑ 88 Jack Cust .40 .12
❑ 89 Adam Piatt .40 .12
❑ 90 Rob Ryan .40 .12
❑ 91 Sean Burroughs .40 .12
❑ 92 D'Angelo Jimenez .40 .12
❑ 93 Chad Hermansen .40 .12
❑ 94 Robert Fick .40 .12
❑ 95 Ruben Mateo .40 .12
❑ 96 Alex Escobar .40 .12
❑ 97 Wily Pena .40 .12
❑ 98 Corey Patterson .40 .12
❑ 99 Eric Munson .40 .12
❑ 100 Pat Burrell .40 .12
❑ 101 Michael Tejera RC 5.00 1.50
❑ 102 Bobby Bradley RC 5.00 1.50
❑ 103 Larry Bigbie RC 8.00 2.40
❑ 104 B.J. Garbe RC 5.00 1.50
❑ 105 Josh Kalinowski RC 5.00 1.50
❑ 106 Brett Myers RC 10.00 3.00
❑ 107 Chris Mears RC 5.00 1.50
❑ 108 Aaron Rowand RC 10.00 3.00
❑ 109 Corey Myers RC 5.00 1.50
❑ 110 John Sneed RC 5.00 1.50
❑ 111 Ryan Christianson RC 5.00 1.50
❑ 112 Kyle Snyder 5.00 1.50
❑ 113 Mike Paradis 5.00 1.50
❑ 114 Chance Caple RC 5.00 1.50
❑ 115 Ben Christensen RC 5.00 1.50
❑ 116 Brad Baker RC 5.00 1.50
❑ 117 Rob Purvis RC 5.00 1.50
❑ 118 Rick Asadoorian RC 5.00 1.50
❑ 119 Ruben Salazar RC 5.00 1.50
❑ 120 Julio Zuleta RC 5.00 1.50
❑ 121 Alex Rodriguez 2.50 .75
Ken Griffey Jr.
❑ 122 Nomar Garciaparra 3.00 .90
Derek Jeter
❑ 123 Mark Mcgwire 4.00 1.20
Sammy Sosa
❑ 124 Randy Johnson 2.50 .75
Pedro Martinez
❑ 125 Ivan Rodriguez 2.50 .75
Mike Piazza
❑ 126 Manny Ramirez 1.50 .45
Roberto Alomar
❑ 127 Chipper Jones 2.50 .75
Andruw Jones
❑ 128 Cal Ripken 5.00 1.50
Tony Gwynn
❑ 129 Jeff Bagwell 1.50 .45
Craig Biggio
❑ 130 Barry Bonds 4.00 1.20
Vladimir Guerrero
❑ 131 Nick Johnson 2.50 .75
Alfonso Soriano
❑ 132 Josh Hamilton 5.00 1.50
Pat Burrell
❑ 133 Corey Patterson 1.50 .45
Ruben Mateo
❑ 134 Larry Walker 1.50 .45
Todd Helton
❑ 135 Rey Ordonez 1.50 .45
Edgardo Alfonzo
❑ 136 Derek Jeter GEM 8.00 2.40
❑ 137 Alex Rodriguez GEM 5.00 1.50
❑ 138 Chipper Jones GEM 5.00 1.50
❑ 139 Mike Piazza GEM 5.00 1.50
❑ 140 Mark McGwire GEM 8.00 2.40
❑ 141 Ivan Rodriguez GEM 3.00 .90
❑ 142 Cal Ripken GEM 10.00 3.00
❑ 143 V.Guerrero GEM 5.00 1.50
❑ 144 Randy Johnson GEM 5.00 1.50
❑ 145 Jeff Bagwell GEM 3.00 .90
❑ 146 K.Griffey Jr. ACTION 1.50 .45
❑ 146A Ken Griffey Jr. PORT 1.50 .45
❑ 147 Andruw Jones .60 .18
❑ 148 Kerry Wood .40 .12
❑ 149 Jim Edmonds .40 .12
❑ 150 Pedro Martinez .60 .18
❑ 151 Warren Morris .40 .12
❑ 152 Trevor Hoffman .40 .12
❑ 153 Ryan Klesko .40 .12
❑ 154 Andy Pettitte .60 .18
❑ 155 Frank Thomas 1.00 .30
❑ 156 Damion Easley .40 .12
❑ 157 Cliff Floyd .40 .12
❑ 158 Ben Davis .40 .12
❑ 159 John Valentin .40 .12
❑ 160 Rafael Palmeiro .60 .18
❑ 161 Andy Ashby .40 .12
❑ 162 J.D. Drew .40 .12
❑ 163 Jay Bell .40 .12
❑ 164 Adam Kennedy .40 .12
❑ 165 Manny Ramirez .60 .18
❑ 166 John Halama .40 .12
❑ 167 Octavio Dotel .40 .12
❑ 168 Darin Erstad .40 .12
❑ 169 Jose Lima .40 .12
❑ 170 Andres Galarraga .40 .12
❑ 171 Scott Rolen .60 .18
❑ 172 Delino DeShields .40 .12
❑ 173 J.T. Snow .40 .12
❑ 174 Tony Womack .40 .12
❑ 175 John Olerud .40 .12
❑ 176 Jason Kendall .40 .12
❑ 177 Carlos Lee .40 .12
❑ 178 Eric Milton .40 .12
❑ 179 Jeff Cirillo .40 .12
❑ 180 Gabe Kapler .40 .12
❑ 181 Greg Vaughn .40 .12
❑ 182 Denny Neagle .40 .12
❑ 183 Tino Martinez .60 .18
❑ 184 Doug Mientkiewicz .40 .12
❑ 185 Juan Gonzalez .40 .12
❑ 186 Ellis Burks .40 .12
❑ 187 Mike Hampton .40 .12
❑ 188 Royce Clayton .40 .12
❑ 189 Mike Mussina .60 .18
❑ 190 Carlos Delgado .40 .12
❑ 191 Ben Grieve .40 .12
❑ 192 Fernando Tatis .40 .12
❑ 193 Matt Williams .40 .12
❑ 194 Rondell White .40 .12
❑ 195 Shawn Green .40 .12
❑ 196 Hideki Irabu .40 .12
❑ 197 Troy Glaus .40 .12
❑ 198 Roger Cedeno .40 .12
❑ 199 Ray Lankford .40 .12
❑ 200 Sammy Sosa 1.00 .30
❑ 201 Kenny Lofton .40 .12
❑ 202 Edgar Martinez .60 .18
❑ 203 Mark Kotsay .40 .12
❑ 204 David Wells .40 .12
❑ 205 Craig Biggio .60 .18
❑ 206 Ray Durham .40 .12
❑ 207 Troy O'Leary .40 .12
❑ 208 Rickey Henderson 1.00 .30
❑ 209 Bob Abreu .40 .12
❑ 210 Neifi Perez .40 .12
❑ 211 Carlos Febles .40 .12
❑ 212 Chuck Knoblauch .40 .12
❑ 213 Moises Alou .40 .12
❑ 214 Omar Vizquel .60 .18
❑ 215 Vinny Castilla .40 .12
❑ 216 Javy Lopez .40 .12
❑ 217 Johnny Damon .60 .18
❑ 218 Roger Clemens 2.00 .60
❑ 219 Miguel Tejada .40 .12
❑ 220 Carl Everett .40 .12
❑ 221 Matt Lawton .40 .12
❑ 222 Albert Belle .40 .12
❑ 223 Adrian Beltre .40 .12
❑ 224 Dante Bichette .40 .12
❑ 225 Raul Mondesi .40 .12
❑ 226 Mike Piazza 1.50 .45
❑ 227 Brad Penny .40 .12
❑ 228 Kip Wells .40 .12
❑ 229 Adam Everett .40 .12
❑ 230 Eddie Yarnall .40 .12
❑ 231 Matt LeCroy .40 .12
❑ 232 Jason Tyner .40 .12
❑ 233 Rick Ankiel .40 .12
❑ 234 Lance Berkman .40 .12
❑ 235 Rafael Furcal .40 .12
❑ 236 Dee Brown .40 .12
❑ 237 Gookie Dawkins .40 .12
❑ 238 Eric Valent .40 .12
❑ 239 Peter Bergeron .40 .12
❑ 240 Alfonso Soriano 1.00 .30
❑ 241 Adam Dunn 1.00 .30
❑ 242 Jorge Toca .40 .12
❑ 243 Ryan Anderson .40 .12
❑ 244 Jason Dellaero .40 .12
❑ 245 Jason Grilli .40 .12
❑ 246 Milton Bradley .40 .12
❑ 247 Scott Downs RC 5.00 1.50
❑ 248 Keith Reed RC 5.00 1.50
❑ 249 Edgar Cruz RC 5.00 1.50
❑ 250 Wes Anderson RC 5.00 1.50
❑ 251 Lyle Overbay RC 8.00 2.40
❑ 252 Mike Lamb RC 8.00 2.40
❑ 253 Vince Faison RC 5.00 1.50
❑ 254 Chad Alexander 5.00 1.50
❑ 255 Chris Wakeland RC 5.00 1.50
❑ 256 Aaron McNeal RC 5.00 1.50
❑ 257 Tomo Ohka RC 5.00 1.50
❑ 258 Ty Howington RC 5.00 1.50
❑ 259 Javier Colina RC 5.00 1.50
❑ 260 Jason Jennings 5.00 1.50
❑ 261 Ramon Santiago RC 5.00 1.50
❑ 262 Johan Santana RC 60.00 18.00
❑ 263 Quincy Foster RC 5.00 1.50
❑ 264 Junior Brignac RC 5.00 1.50
❑ 265 Rico Washington RC 5.00 1.50
❑ 266 Scott Sobkowiak RC 5.00 1.50
❑ 267 Pedro Martinez 1.50 .45
Rick Ankiel
❑ 268 Manny Ramirez 2.50 .75
Vladimir Guerrero
❑ 269 A.J.Burnett 1.00 .30
Mark Mulder
❑ 270 Mike Piazza 2.50 .75
Eric Munson
❑ 271 Josh Hamilton 1.00 .30
Corey Patterson
❑ 272 Ken Griffey Jr. 2.00 .60
Sammy Sosa
❑ 273 Derek Jeter 4.00 1.20
Alfonso Soriano
❑ 274 Mark McGwire 4.00 1.20
Pat Burrell
❑ 275 Chipper Jones 4.00 1.20
Cal Ripken

❑ 276 Nomar Garciaparra .... 2.50 .75
Alex Rodriguez
❑ 277 Pedro Martinez GEM ...... 3.00 .90
❑ 278 Tony Gwynn GEM 4.00 1.20
❑ 279 Barry Bonds GEM 8.00 2.40
❑ 280 Juan Gonzalez GEM .... 2.00 .60
❑ 281 Larry Walker GEM .... 2.00 .60
❑ 282 N.Garciaparra GEM 5.00 1.50
❑ 283 Ken Griffey Jr. GEM........ 5.00 1.50
❑ 284 Manny Ramirez GEM...... 3.00 .90
❑ 285 Shawn Green GEM .... 2.00 .60
❑ 286 Sammy Sosa GEM 5.00 1.50
❑ NNO Graded Gems Ser.1 EXCH/10
❑ NNO Graded Gems Ser.2 EXCH/10

2001 Finest

	Nm-Mt	Ex-Mt
COMP.SET w/o SP's	25.00	7.50
COMMON CARD (1-110)	.40	.12
COMMON SP	10.00	3.00
COMMON (111-140)	10.00	3.00

❑ 1 Mike Piazza SP 20.00 6.00
❑ 2 Andruw Jones .... .60 .18
❑ 3 Jason Giambi .... .40 .12
❑ 4 Fred McGriff .... .60 .18
❑ 5 Vladimir Guerrero SP .... 1.00 .30
❑ 6 Adrian Gonzalez .... .40 .12
❑ 7 Pedro Martinez .... .60 .18
❑ 8 Mike Lieberthal .... .40 .12
❑ 9 Warren Morris....................... .40 .12
❑ 10 Juan Gonzalez..................... .40 .12
❑ 11 Jose Canseco .... .60 .18
❑ 12 Jose Valentin....................... .40 .12
❑ 13 Jeff Cirillo .... .40 .12
❑ 14 Pokey Reese .... .40 .12
❑ 15 Scott Rolen .... .60 .18
❑ 16 Greg Maddux .... 1.50 .45
❑ 17 Carlos Delgado .... .40 .12
❑ 18 Rick Ankiel .... .40 .12
❑ 19 Steve Finley......................... .40 .12
❑ 20 Shawn Green....................... .40 .12
❑ 21 Orlando Cabrera .... .40 .12
❑ 22 Roberto Alomar.................. .60 .18
❑ 23 John Olerud .... .40 .12
❑ 24 Albert Belle .... .40 .12
❑ 25 Edgardo Alfonzo .... .40 .12
❑ 26 Rafael Palmeiro.................. .60 .18
❑ 27 Mike Sweeney..................... .40 .12
❑ 28 Bernie Williams.................. .60 .18
❑ 29 Larry Walker .... .40 .12
❑ 30 Barry Bonds SP............. 25.00 7.50
❑ 31 Orlando Hernandez .... .40 .12
❑ 32 Randy Johnson .... 1.00 .30
❑ 33 Shannon Stewart................ .40 .12
❑ 34 Mark Grace .... .60 .18
❑ 35 Alex Rodriguez SP......... 25.00 7.50
❑ 36 Tino Martinez .... .60 .18
❑ 37 Carlos Febles .... .40 .12
❑ 38 Al Leiter................................ .40 .12
❑ 39 Omar Vizquel....................... .60 .18
❑ 40 Chuck Knoblauch .... .40 .12
❑ 41 Tim Salmon.......................... .60 .18
❑ 42 Brian Jordan .... .40 .12
❑ 43 Edgar Renteria.................... .40 .12
❑ 44 Preston Wilson .... .40 .12
❑ 45 Mariano Rivera .... .60 .18
❑ 46 Gabe Kapler......................... .40 .12
❑ 47 Jason Kendall .... .40 .12
❑ 48 Rickey Henderson .... 1.00 .30
❑ 49 Luis Gonzalez .... .40 .12
❑ 50 Tom Glavine .... .60 .18
❑ 51 Jeromy Burnitz .... .40 .12
❑ 52 Garret Anderson .... .40 .12
❑ 53 Craig Biggio .... .60 .18
❑ 54 Vinny Castilla .... .40 .12
❑ 55 Jeff Kent .... .40 .12
❑ 56 Gary Sheffield .... .40 .12
❑ 57 Jorge Posada .... .60 .18
❑ 58 Sean Casey .... .60 .18
❑ 59 Johnny Damon .... .60 .18
❑ 60 Dean Palmer .... .40 .12
❑ 61 Todd Helton .... .60 .18
❑ 62 Barry Larkin........................... .60 .18
❑ 63 Robin Ventura .... .40 .12
❑ 64 Kenny Lofton......................... .40 .12
❑ 65 Sammy Sosa SP 10.00 3.00
❑ 66 Rafael Furcal .... .40 .12
❑ 67 Jay Bell .... .40 .12
❑ 68 J.T. Snow .... .40 .12
❑ 69 Jose Vidro .... .40 .12
❑ 70 Ivan Rodriguez .... .60 .18
❑ 71 Jermaine Dye .... .40 .12
❑ 72 Chipper Jones SP 10.00 3.00
❑ 73 Fernando Vina........................ .40 .12
❑ 74 Ben Grieve.............................. .40 .12
❑ 75 Mark McGwire SP 25.00 7.50
❑ 76 Matt Williams .... .40 .12
❑ 77 Mark Grudzielanek .... .40 .12
❑ 78 Mike Hampton........................ .40 .12
❑ 79 Brian Giles .... .40 .12
❑ 80 Tony Gwynn .... 1.25 .35
❑ 81 Carlos Beltran .... .40 .12
❑ 82 Ray Durham .... .40 .12
❑ 83 Brad Radke .... .40 .12
❑ 84 David Justice.......................... .40 .12
❑ 85 Frank Thomas .... 1.00 .30
❑ 86 Todd Zeile............................... .40 .12
❑ 87 Pat Burrell............................... .40 .12
❑ 88 Jim Thome .... .60 .18
❑ 89 Greg Vaughn........................... .40 .12
❑ 90 Ken Griffey Jr. SP 15.00 4.50
❑ 91 Mike Mussina .... .60 .18
❑ 92 Magglio Ordonez.................... .40 .12
❑ 93 Bob Abreu................................ .40 .12
❑ 94 Alex Gonzalez .... .40 .12
❑ 95 Kevin Brown .... .40 .12
❑ 96 Jay Buhner .... .40 .12
❑ 97 Roger Clemens .... 2.00 .60
❑ 98 Nomar Garciaparra SP.... 15.00 4.50
❑ 99 Derrek Lee................................ .60 .18
❑ 100 Derek Jeter SP............. 25.00 7.50
❑ 101 Adrian Beltre .... .40 .12
❑ 102 Geoff Jenkins .... .40 .12
❑ 103 Javy Lopez .... .40 .12
❑ 104 Raul Mondesi .... .40 .12
❑ 105 Troy Glaus............................. .40 .12
❑ 106 Jeff Bagwell.......................... .60 .18
❑ 107 Eric Karros .... .40 .12
❑ 108 Mo Vaughn .... .40 .12
❑ 109 Cal Ripken........................ 3.00 .90
❑ 110 Manny Ramirez Sox .... .60 .18
❑ 111 Scott Heard PROS 10.00 3.00
❑ 112 L. Montanez PROS RC 10.00 3.00
❑ 113 Ben Diggins PROS 10.00 3.00
❑ 114 Shaun Boyd PROS RC.. 10.00 3.00
❑ 115 Sean Burnett PROS 10.00 3.00
❑ 116 Carmen Cali PROS RC 10.00 3.00
❑ 117 D.Thompson PROS...... 10.00 3.00
❑ 118 D.Parrish PROS RC...... 10.00 3.00
❑ 119 D.Rich PROS RC 10.00 3.00
❑ 120 Chad Petty PROS RC.... 10.00 3.00
❑ 121 S.Smyth PROS RC 10.00 3.00
❑ 122 John Lackey PROS 10.00 3.00
❑ 123 M.Galante PROS RC 10.00 3.00
❑ 124 D.Borrell PROS RC 10.00 3.00
❑ 125 Bob Keppel PROS RC .. 10.00 3.00
❑ 126 J.Wayne PROS RC 10.00 3.00
❑ 127 J.R. House PROS 10.00 3.00
❑ 128 Brian Sellier PROS RC 10.00 3.00
❑ 129 Dan Moylan PROS RC.. 10.00 3.00
❑ 130 Scott Pratt PROS RC 10.00 3.00
❑ 131 Victor Hall PROS RC 10.00 3.00
❑ 132 Joel Pineiro PROS........ 10.00 3.00
❑ 133 J.Axelson PROS RC 10.00 3.00
❑ 134 Jose Reyes PROS RC .. 50.00 15.00
❑ 135 G. Runser PROS RC 10.00 3.00
❑ 136 B. Hebson PROS RC 10.00 3.00
❑ 137 S.Serrano PROS RC 10.00 3.00
❑ 138 K. Joseph PROS RC 10.00 3.00
❑ 139 J. Richardson PROS RC 10.00 3.00
❑ 140 M. Fischer PROS RC.... 10.00 3.00

2002 Finest

	Nm-Mt	Ex-Mt
COMP.SET w/o SP's (100)	25.00	7.50
COMMON CARD (1-100)	.50	.15
COMMON CARD (101-110)	10.00	3.00

❑ 1 Mike Mussina .... .75 .23
❑ 2 Steve Sparks .... .50 .15
❑ 3 Randy Johnson .... 1.25 .35
❑ 4 Orlando Cabrera .... .50 .15
❑ 5 Jeff Kent .... .50 .15
❑ 6 Carlos Delgado .... .50 .15
❑ 7 Ivan Rodriguez .... .75 .23
❑ 8 Jose Cruz .... .50 .15
❑ 9 Jason Giambi .... .50 .15
❑ 10 Brad Penny .... .50 .15
❑ 11 Moises Alou .... .50 .15
❑ 12 Mike Piazza .... 2.00 .60
❑ 13 Ben Grieve........................... .50 .15
❑ 14 Derek Jeter .... 3.00 .90
❑ 15 Roy Oswalt .... .50 .15
❑ 16 Pat Burrell............................ .50 .15
❑ 17 Preston Wilson .... .50 .15
❑ 18 Kevin Brown .... .50 .15
❑ 19 Barry Bonds .... 3.00 .90
❑ 20 Phil Nevin .... .50 .15
❑ 21 Aramis Ramirez.................. .50 .15
❑ 22 Carlos Beltran .... .50 .15
❑ 23 Chipper Jones................ 1.25 .35
❑ 24 Curt Schilling....................... .50 .15
❑ 25 Jorge Posada .... .75 .23
❑ 26 Alfonso Soriano .... .50 .15
❑ 27 Cliff Floyd .... .50 .15
❑ 28 Rafael Palmeiro.................. .75 .23
❑ 29 Terrence Long..................... .50 .15
❑ 30 Ken Griffey Jr. .... 2.00 .60
❑ 31 Jason Kendall .... .50 .15
❑ 32 Jose Vidro .... .50 .15
❑ 33 Jermaine Dye .... .50 .15
❑ 34 Bobby Higginson .... .50 .15
❑ 35 Albert Pujols .... 2.50 .75
❑ 36 Miguel Tejada .... .50 .15
❑ 37 Jim Edmonds .... .75 .23
❑ 38 Barry Zito .... .50 .15
❑ 39 Jimmy Rollins...................... .50 .15
❑ 40 Rafael Furcal .... .50 .15
❑ 41 Omar Vizquel....................... .75 .23
❑ 42 Kazuhiro Sasaki.................. .50 .15
❑ 43 Brian Giles .... .50 .15
❑ 44 Darin Erstad .... .50 .15
❑ 45 Mariano Rivera .... .75 .23
❑ 46 Troy Percival .... .50 .15
❑ 47 Mike Sweeney..................... .50 .15
❑ 48 Vladimir Guerrero .... 1.25 .35
❑ 49 Troy Glaus........................... .50 .15
❑ 50 So Taguchi RC .... 3.00 .90
❑ 51 Edgardo Alfonzo .... .50 .15
❑ 52 Roger Clemens .... 2.50 .75
❑ 53 Eric Chavez .... .50 .15

❑ 54 Alex Rodriguez 2.00 .60
❑ 55 Cristian Guzman .50 .15
❑ 56 Jeff Bagwell .75 .23
❑ 57 Bernie Williams .75 .23
❑ 58 Kerry Wood .50 .15
❑ 59 Ryan Klesko .50 .15
❑ 60 Ichiro Suzuki 2.50 .75
❑ 61 Larry Walker .50 .15
❑ 62 Nomar Garciaparra 2.00 .60
❑ 63 Craig Biggio .75 .23
❑ 64 J.D. Drew .50 .15
❑ 65 Juan Pierre .50 .15
❑ 66 Roberto Alomar .75 .23
❑ 67 Luis Gonzalez .50 .15
❑ 68 Bud Smith .50 .15
❑ 69 Magglio Ordonez .50 .15
❑ 70 Scott Rolen .75 .23
❑ 71 Tsuyoshi Shinjo .50 .15
❑ 72 Paul Konerko .50 .15
❑ 73 Garret Anderson .50 .15
❑ 74 Tim Hudson .50 .15
❑ 75 Adam Dunn .50 .15
❑ 76 Gary Sheffield .50 .15
❑ 77 Johnny Damon Sox .75 .23
❑ 78 Todd Helton .75 .23
❑ 79 Geoff Jenkins .50 .15
❑ 80 Shawn Green .50 .15
❑ 81 C.C. Sabathia .50 .15
❑ 82 Kazuhisa Ishii RC UER 2.50 .75
2001 ERA is incorrect
❑ 83 Rich Aurilia .50 .15
❑ 84 Mike Hampton .50 .15
❑ 85 Ben Sheets .50 .15
❑ 86 Andruw Jones .75 .23
❑ 87 Richie Sexson .50 .15
❑ 88 Jim Thome .75 .23
❑ 89 Sammy Sosa 1.25 .35
❑ 90 Greg Maddux 2.00 .60
❑ 91 Pedro Martinez .75 .23
❑ 92 Jeromy Burnitz .50 .15
❑ 93 Raul Mondesi .50 .15
❑ 94 Bret Boone .50 .15
❑ 95 Jerry Hairston .50 .15
❑ 96 Mike Rivera .50 .15
❑ 97 Juan Cruz .50 .15
❑ 98 Morgan Ensberg .50 .15
❑ 99 Nathan Haynes .50 .15
❑ 100 Xavier Nady .50 .15
❑ 101 Nic Jackson FY AU RC 10.00 3.00
❑ 102 Mauricio Lara FY AU RC 10.00 3.00
❑ 103 Freddy Sanchez FY AU RC 10.00 3.00
❑ 104 Clint Nageotte FY AU RC 15.00 4.50
❑ 105 Beltran Perez FY AU RC 10.00 3.00
❑ 106 Garrett Gentry FY AU RC 10.00 3.00
❑ 107 Chad Qualls FY AU RC 15.00 4.50
❑ 108 Jason Bay FY AU RC 40.00 12.00
❑ 109 Michael Hill FY AU RC 10.00 3.00
❑ 110 Brian Tallet FY AU RC 10.00 3.00

2003 Finest

	Nm-Mt	Ex-Mt
COMP.SET w/o SP's (100)	25.00	7.50
COMMON CARD (1-100)	.50	.15
COMMON CARD (101-110)	15.00	4.50

❑ 1 Sammy Sosa 1.25 .35
❑ 2 Paul Konerko .50 .15
❑ 3 Todd Helton .75 .23
❑ 4 Mike Lowell .50 .15
❑ 5 Lance Berkman .50 .15
❑ 6 Kazuhisa Ishii .50 .15
❑ 7 A.J. Pierzynski .50 .15
❑ 8 Jose Vidro .50 .15
❑ 9 Roberto Alomar .75 .23
❑ 10 Derek Jeter 3.00 .90
❑ 11 Barry Zito .50 .15
❑ 12 Jimmy Rollins .50 .15
❑ 13 Brian Giles .50 .15
❑ 14 Ryan Klesko .50 .15
❑ 15 Rich Aurilia .50 .15
❑ 16 Jim Edmonds .75 .23
❑ 17 Aubrey Huff .50 .15
❑ 18 Ivan Rodriguez .75 .23
❑ 19 Eric Hinske .50 .15
❑ 20 Barry Bonds 3.00 .90
❑ 21 Darin Erstad .50 .15
❑ 22 Curt Schilling .50 .15
❑ 23 Andruw Jones .75 .23
❑ 24 Jay Gibbons .50 .15
❑ 25 Nomar Garciaparra 2.00 .60
❑ 26 Kerry Wood .50 .15
❑ 27 Magglio Ordonez .50 .15
❑ 28 Austin Kearns .50 .15
❑ 29 Jason Jennings .50 .15
❑ 30 Jason Giambi .50 .15
❑ 31 Tim Hudson .50 .15
❑ 32 Edgar Martinez .75 .23
❑ 33 Carl Crawford .50 .15
❑ 34 Hee Seop Choi .50 .15
❑ 35 Vladimir Guerrero 1.25 .35
❑ 36 Jeff Kent .50 .15
❑ 37 John Smoltz .75 .23
❑ 38 Frank Thomas 1.25 .35
❑ 39 Cliff Floyd .50 .15
❑ 40 Mike Piazza 2.00 .60
❑ 41 Mark Prior .75 .23
❑ 42 Tim Salmon .75 .23
❑ 43 Shawn Green .50 .15
❑ 44 Bernie Williams .75 .23
❑ 45 Jim Thome .75 .23
❑ 46 John Olerud .50 .15
❑ 47 Orlando Hudson .50 .15
❑ 48 Mark Teixeira .75 .23
❑ 49 Gary Sheffield .50 .15
❑ 50 Ichiro Suzuki 2.50 .75
❑ 51 Tom Glavine .75 .23
❑ 52 Torii Hunter .50 .15
❑ 53 Craig Biggio .75 .23
❑ 54 Carlos Beltran .50 .15
❑ 55 Bartolo Colon .50 .15
❑ 56 Jorge Posada .75 .23
❑ 57 Pat Burrell .50 .15
❑ 58 Edgar Renteria .50 .15
❑ 59 Rafael Palmeiro .75 .23
❑ 60 Alfonso Soriano .50 .15
❑ 61 Brandon Phillips .50 .15
❑ 62 Luis Gonzalez .50 .15
❑ 63 Manny Ramirez .75 .23
❑ 64 Garret Anderson .50 .15
❑ 65 Ken Griffey Jr. 2.00 .60
❑ 66 A.J. Burnett .50 .15
❑ 67 Mike Sweeney .50 .15
❑ 68 Doug Mientkiewicz .50 .15
❑ 69 Eric Chavez .50 .15
❑ 70 Adam Dunn .50 .15
❑ 71 Shea Hillenbrand .50 .15
❑ 72 Troy Glaus .50 .15
❑ 73 Rodrigo Lopez .50 .15
❑ 74 Moises Alou .50 .15
❑ 75 Chipper Jones 1.25 .35
❑ 76 Bobby Abreu .50 .15
❑ 77 Mark Mulder .50 .15
❑ 78 Kevin Brown .50 .15
❑ 79 Josh Beckett .50 .15
❑ 80 Larry Walker .50 .15
❑ 81 Randy Johnson 1.25 .35
❑ 82 Greg Maddux 2.00 .60
❑ 83 Johnny Damon .75 .23
❑ 84 Omar Vizquel .75 .23
❑ 85 Jeff Bagwell .75 .23
❑ 86 Carlos Pena .50 .15
❑ 87 Roy Oswalt .50 .15
❑ 88 Richie Sexson .50 .15
❑ 89 Roger Clemens 2.50 .75
❑ 90 Miguel Tejada .50 .15
❑ 91 Vicente Padilla .50 .15
❑ 92 Phil Nevin .50 .15
❑ 93 Edgardo Alfonzo .50 .15
❑ 94 Bret Boone .50 .15
❑ 95 Albert Pujols 2.50 .75
❑ 96 Carlos Delgado .50 .15
❑ 97 Jose Contreras RC 2.00 .60
❑ 98 Scott Rolen .75 .23
❑ 99 Pedro Martinez .75 .23
❑ 100 Alex Rodriguez 2.00 .60
❑ 101 Adam LaRoche AU 15.00 4.50
❑ 102 Andy Marte AU RC 50.00 15.00
❑ 103 Daryl Clark AU RC 10.00 3.00
❑ 104 J.D. Durbin AU RC 10.00 3.00
❑ 105 Craig Brazell AU RC 10.00 3.00
❑ 106 Brian Burgamy AU RC 10.00 3.00
❑ 107 Tyler Johnson AU RC 10.00 3.00
❑ 108 Joey Gomes AU RC 10.00 3.00
❑ 109 Bryan Bullington AU RC 15.00 4.50
❑ 110 Byron Gettis AU RC 10.00 3.00

2004 Finest

	Nm-Mt	Ex-Mt
COMP.SET w/o SP's (100)	25.00	7.50
COMMON CARD (1-100)	.50	.15
COMMON CARD (101-110)	8.00	2.40
101-110 STATED ODDS 1:7 MINI-BOXES		.00
COMMON CARD (111-122)	10.00	3.00
111-122 STATED ODDS 1:3 MINI-BOXES		.00
EXCHANGE DEADLINE 04/30/06	.00	
CARD 112 EXCH UNABLE TO BE FULFILLED		.00
04 WS HL B.THOMSON AU SENT INSTEAD		.00

❑ 1 Juan Pierre .50 .15
❑ 2 Derek Jeter 2.50 .75
❑ 3 Garret Anderson .50 .15
❑ 4 Javy Lopez .50 .15
❑ 5 Corey Patterson .50 .15
❑ 6 Todd Helton .75 .23
❑ 7 Roy Oswalt .50 .15
❑ 8 Shawn Green .50 .15
❑ 9 Vladimir Guerrero 1.25 .35
❑ 10 Jorge Posada .75 .23
❑ 11 Jason Kendall .50 .15
❑ 12 Scott Rolen .75 .23
❑ 13 Randy Johnson 1.25 .35
❑ 14 Bill Mueller .50 .15
❑ 15 Magglio Ordonez .50 .15
❑ 16 Larry Walker .50 .15
❑ 17 Lance Berkman .50 .15
❑ 18 Richie Sexson .50 .15
❑ 19 Orlando Cabrera .50 .15
❑ 20 Alfonso Soriano .50 .15
❑ 21 Kevin Millwood .50 .15
❑ 22 Edgar Martinez .75 .23
❑ 23 Aubrey Huff .50 .15
❑ 24 Carlos Delgado .50 .15
❑ 25 Vernon Wells .50 .15
❑ 26 Mark Teixeira .75 .23
❑ 27 Troy Glaus .50 .15
❑ 28 Jeff Kent .50 .15
❑ 29 Hideo Nomo 1.25 .35
❑ 30 Torii Hunter .50 .15
❑ 31 Hank Blalock .50 .15
❑ 32 Brandon Webb .50 .15
❑ 33 Tony Batista .50 .15
❑ 34 Bret Boone .50 .15

❑ 35 Ryan Klesko .50 .15
❑ 36 Barry Zito .50 .15
❑ 37 Edgar Renteria .50 .15
❑ 38 Geoff Jenkins .50 .15
❑ 39 Jeff Bagwell .75 .23
❑ 40 Dontrelle Willis .75 .23
❑ 41 Adam Dunn .50 .15
❑ 42 Mark Buehrle .50 .15
❑ 43 Esteban Loaiza .50 .15
❑ 44 Angel Berroa .50 .15
❑ 45 Ivan Rodriguez .75 .23
❑ 46 Jose Vidro .50 .15
❑ 47 Mark Mulder .50 .15
❑ 48 Roger Clemens 2.50 .75
❑ 49 Jim Edmonds .75 .23
❑ 50 Eric Gagne .50 .15
❑ 51 Marcus Giles .50 .15
❑ 52 Curt Schilling .75 .23
❑ 53 Ken Griffey Jr. 2.00 .60
❑ 54 Jason Schmidt .50 .15
❑ 55 Miguel Tejada .50 .15
❑ 56 Dmitri Young .50 .15
❑ 57 Mike Lowell .50 .15
❑ 58 Mike Sweeney .50 .15
❑ 59 Scott Podsednik .50 .15
❑ 60 Miguel Cabrera .75 .23
❑ 61 Johan Santana .75 .23
❑ 62 Bernie Williams .75 .23
❑ 63 Eric Chavez .50 .15
❑ 64 Bobby Abreu .50 .15
❑ 65 Brian Giles .50 .15
❑ 66 Michael Young .50 .15
❑ 67 Paul Lo Duca .50 .15
❑ 68 Austin Kearns .50 .15
❑ 69 Jody Gerut .50 .15
❑ 70 Kerry Wood .50 .15
❑ 71 Luis Matos .50 .15
❑ 72 Greg Maddux 2.00 .60
❑ 73 Alex Rodriguez Yanks 2.00 .60
❑ 74 Mike Lieberthal .50 .15
❑ 75 Jim Thome .75 .23
❑ 76 Javier Vazquez .50 .15
❑ 77 Bartolo Colon .50 .15
❑ 78 Manny Ramirez .75 .23
❑ 79 Jacque Jones .50 .15
❑ 80 Johnny Damon .75 .23
❑ 81 Carlos Beltran .50 .15
❑ 82 C.C. Sabathia .50 .15
❑ 83 Preston Wilson .50 .15
❑ 84 Luis Castillo .50 .15
❑ 85 Kevin Brown .50 .15
❑ 86 Shannon Stewart .50 .15
❑ 87 Cliff Floyd .50 .15
❑ 88 Mike Mussina .75 .23
❑ 89 Rafael Furcal .50 .15
❑ 90 Roy Halladay .50 .15
❑ 91 Frank Thomas 1.25 .35
❑ 92 Melvin Mora .50 .15
❑ 93 Andruw Jones .75 .23
❑ 94 Luis Gonzalez .50 .15
❑ 95 David Ortiz 1.25 .35
❑ 96 Gary Sheffield .50 .15
❑ 97 Tim Hudson .50 .15
❑ 98 Phil Nevin .50 .15
❑ 99 Ichiro Suzuki 2.50 .75
❑ 100 Albert Pujols 2.50 .75
❑ 101 Nomar Garciaparra SR Jsy 15.00 4.50
❑ 102 Sammy Sosa SR Jsy 10.00 3.00
❑ 103 Josh Beckett SR Jsy 8.00 2.40
❑ 104 Jason Giambi SR Jsy 8.00 2.40
❑ 105 Rocco Baldelli SR Jsy 8.00 2.40
❑ 106 Jose Reyes SR Jsy 8.00 2.40
❑ 107 Chipper Jones SR Jsy 10.00 3.00
❑ 108 Pedro Martinez SR Jsy 10.00 3.00
❑ 109 Mike Piazza SR Jsy 15.00 4.50
❑ 110 Mark Prior SR Jsy 10.00 3.00
❑ 111 Craig Ansman AU RC 10.00 3.00
❑ 112 J.Allison AU RC EXCH UER
❑ 113 David Murphy AU RC EXCH 20.00 6.00
❑ 114 Jason Hirsh AU RC 20.00 6.00
❑ 115 Matt Moses AU RC 25.00 7.50
❑ 116 Estee Harris AU RC 15.00 4.50
❑ 117 Logan Kensing AU RC 10.00 3.00
❑ 118 L.Milledge AU RC EXCH 30.00 9.00
❑ 119 Merkin Valdez AU RC 15.00 4.50
❑ 120 Travis Blackley AU RC 10.00 3.00
❑ 121 Vito Chiaravalloti AU RC 10.00 3.00
❑ 122 Dioner Navarro AU RC 25.00 7.50

2005 Finest

	Nm-Mt	Ex-Mt
COMP.SET w/o SP's (150)	80.00	24.00
COMMON CARD (1-140)	.50	.15
COMMON CARD (157-166)	1.00	.30
AU p/r 970 ODDS 1:3 MINI BOXES	.00	
AU p/r 970 PRINT RUN 970 #'d SETS		.00
AU p/r 375 ODDS 1:41 MINI BOXES		.00
AU p/r 375 PRINT RUN 375 #'d SETS		.00
OVERALL PLATE ODDS 1:51 MINI BOX		.00
OVERALL AU PLATE ODDS 1:478 MINI BOX		.00
PLATE PRINT RUN 1 SET PER COLOR		.00
BLACK-CYAN-MAGENTA-YELLOW ISSUED		.00
NO PLATE PRICING DUE TO SCARCITY		.00

❑ 1 Alexis Rios .50 .15
❑ 2 Hank Blalock .50 .15
❑ 3 Bobby Abreu .50 .15
❑ 4 Curt Schilling .75 .23
❑ 5 Albert Pujols 2.50 .75
❑ 6 Aaron Rowand .50 .15
❑ 7 B.J. Upton .50 .15
❑ 8 Andruw Jones .75 .23
❑ 9 Jeff Francis .50 .15
❑ 10 Sammy Sosa 1.25 .35
❑ 11 Aramis Ramirez .50 .15
❑ 12 Carl Pavano .50 .15
❑ 13 Bartolo Colon .50 .15
❑ 14 Greg Maddux 2.00 .60
❑ 15 Scott Kazmir .50 .15
❑ 16 Melvin Mora .50 .15
❑ 17 Brandon Backe .50 .15
❑ 18 Bobby Crosby .50 .15
❑ 19 Carlos Lee .50 .15
❑ 20 Carl Crawford .50 .15
❑ 21 Brian Giles .50 .15
❑ 22 Jeff Bagwell .75 .23
❑ 23 J.D. Drew .50 .15
❑ 24 C.C. Sabathia .50 .15
❑ 25 Alfonso Soriano .50 .15
❑ 26 Chipper Jones 1.25 .35
❑ 27 Austin Kearns .50 .15
❑ 28 Carlos Delgado .50 .15
❑ 29 Jack Wilson .50 .15
❑ 30 Dmitri Young .50 .15
❑ 31 Carlos Guillen .50 .15
❑ 32 Jim Thome .75 .23
❑ 33 Eric Chavez .50 .15
❑ 34 Jason Schmidt .50 .15
❑ 35 Brad Radke .50 .15
❑ 36 Frank Thomas 1.25 .35
❑ 37 Darin Erstad .50 .15
❑ 38 Javier Vazquez .50 .15
❑ 39 Garret Anderson .50 .15
❑ 40 David Ortiz 1.25 .35
❑ 41 Javy Lopez .50 .15
❑ 42 Geoff Jenkins .50 .15
❑ 43 Jose Vidro .50 .15
❑ 44 Aubrey Huff .50 .15
❑ 45 Bernie Williams .75 .23
❑ 46 Dontrelle Willis .50 .15
❑ 47 Jim Edmonds .75 .23
❑ 48 Ivan Rodriguez .75 .23
❑ 49 Gary Sheffield .50 .15
❑ 50 Alex Rodriguez 2.00 .60
❑ 51 John Buck .50 .15
❑ 52 Andy Pettitte .75 .23
❑ 53 Ichiro Suzuki 2.50 .75
❑ 54 Johnny Estrada .50 .15
❑ 55 Jake Peavy .50 .15
❑ 56 Carlos Zambrano .50 .15
❑ 57 Jose Reyes .50 .15
❑ 58 Bret Boone .50 .15
❑ 59 Jason Bay .50 .15
❑ 60 David Wright 2.00 .60
❑ 61 Jeromy Burnitz .50 .15
❑ 62 Corey Patterson .50 .15
❑ 63 Juan Pierre .50 .15
❑ 64 Zack Greinke .50 .15
❑ 65 Mike Lowell .50 .15
❑ 66 Ken Griffey Jr. 2.00 .60
❑ 67 Marcus Giles .50 .15
❑ 68 Edgar Renteria .50 .15
❑ 69 Ken Harvey .50 .15
❑ 70 Pedro Martinez .75 .23
❑ 71 Johnny Damon .75 .23
❑ 72 Lyle Overbay .50 .15
❑ 73 Mike Maroth .50 .15
❑ 74 Jorge Posada .75 .23
❑ 75 Carlos Beltran .50 .15
❑ 76 Mark Buehrle .50 .15
❑ 77 Khalil Greene .75 .23
❑ 78 Josh Beckett .50 .15
❑ 79 Mark Loretta .50 .15
❑ 80 Rafael Palmeiro .75 .23
❑ 81 Justin Morneau .50 .15
❑ 82 Rocco Baldelli .50 .15
❑ 83 Ben Sheets .50 .15
❑ 84 Kerry Wood .50 .15
❑ 85 Miguel Tejada .50 .15
❑ 86 Magglio Ordonez .50 .15
❑ 87 Livan Hernandez .50 .15
❑ 88 Kazuo Matsui .50 .15
❑ 89 Manny Ramirez .75 .23
❑ 90 Hideki Matsui 2.50 .75
❑ 91 Jeff Kent .50 .15
❑ 92 Matt Lawton .50 .15
❑ 93 Richie Sexson .50 .15
❑ 94 Mike Mussina .75 .23
❑ 95 Adam Dunn .50 .15
❑ 96 Johan Santana .75 .23
❑ 97 Nomar Garciaparra 1.25 .35
❑ 98 Michael Young .50 .15
❑ 99 Victor Martinez .50 .15
❑ 100 Barry Bonds 3.00 .90
❑ 101 Oliver Perez .50 .15
❑ 102 Randy Johnson 1.25 .35
❑ 103 Mark Mulder .50 .15
❑ 104 Pat Burrell .50 .15
❑ 105 Mike Sweeney .50 .15
❑ 106 Mark Teixeira .75 .23
❑ 107 Paul Lo Duca .50 .15
❑ 108 Jon Lieber .50 .15
❑ 109 Mike Piazza 1.25 .35
❑ 110 Roger Clemens 2.00 .60
❑ 111 Rafael Furcal .50 .15
❑ 112 Troy Glaus .50 .15
❑ 113 Miguel Cabrera .75 .23
❑ 114 Randy Wolf .50 .15
❑ 115 Lance Berkman .50 .15
❑ 116 Mark Prior .75 .23
❑ 117 Rich Harden .50 .15
❑ 118 Preston Wilson .50 .15
❑ 119 Roy Oswalt .50 .15
❑ 120 Luis Gonzalez .50 .15
❑ 121 Ronnie Belliard .50 .15
❑ 122 Sean Casey .50 .15
❑ 123 Barry Zito .50 .15
❑ 124 Larry Walker .75 .23
❑ 125 Derek Jeter 2.50 .75
❑ 126 Tim Hudson .50 .15
❑ 127 Tom Glavine .75 .23
❑ 128 Scott Rolen .75 .23
❑ 129 Torii Hunter .50 .15
❑ 130 Paul Konerko .50 .15
❑ 131 Shawn Green .50 .15
❑ 132 Travis Hafner .50 .15
❑ 133 Vernon Wells .50 .15
❑ 134 Sidney Ponson .50 .15
❑ 135 Vladimir Guerrero 1.25 .35
❑ 136 Mark Kotsay .50 .15

❑ 137 Todd Helton	.75	.23
❑ 138 Adrian Beltre	.50	.15
❑ 139 Wily Mo Pena	.50	.15
❑ 140 Joe Mauer	.50	.15
❑ 141 Brian Stavisky AU/970 RC	10.00	3.00
❑ 142 Nate McLouth AU/970 RC	15.00	4.50
❑ 143 Glen Perkins AU/375 RC	25.00	7.50
❑ 144 Chip Cannon AU/970 RC	15.00	4.50
❑ 145 Shane Costa AU/970 RC	10.00	3.00
❑ 146 W.Swackhamer AU/970 RC	10.00	3.00
❑ 147 Kevin Melillo AU/970 RC	15.00	4.50
❑ 148 Billy Butler AU/970 RC	40.00	12.00
❑ 149 Landon Powell AU/970 RC	15.00	4.50
❑ 150 Scott Mathieson AU/970 RC	15.00	4.50
❑ 151 Chris Roberson AU/970	10.00	3.00
❑ 152 Chad Orvella AU/375 RC	30.00	9.00
❑ 153 Eric Nielsen AU/970 RC	10.00	3.00
❑ 154 Matt Campbell AU/970 RC	10.00	3.00
❑ 155 Mike Rogers AU/970 RC	10.00	3.00
❑ 156 Melky Cabrera AU/970 RC	15.00	4.50
❑ 157 Nolan Ryan RET	5.00	1.50
❑ 158 Bo Jackson RET	2.00	.60
❑ 159 Wade Boggs RET	1.50	.45
❑ 160 Andre Dawson RET	1.00	.30
❑ 161 Dave Winfield RET	1.00	.30
❑ 162 Reggie Jackson RET	1.50	.45
❑ 163 David Justice RET	2.00	.60
❑ 164 Dale Murphy RET	1.50	.45
❑ 165 Paul O'Neill RET	1.50	.45
❑ 166 Tom Seaver RET	1.50	.45

1963 Fleer

	NM	Ex
COMPLETE SET (67)	1500.00	600.00
WRAPPER (5-CENT)	100.00	40.00
❑ 1 Steve Barber	25.00	7.50
❑ 2 Ron Hansen	15.00	6.00
❑ 3 Milt Pappas	20.00	8.00
❑ 4 Brooks Robinson	100.00	40.00
❑ 5 Willie Mays	175.00	70.00
❑ 6 Lou Clinton	15.00	6.00
❑ 7 Bill Monbouquette	15.00	6.00
❑ 8 Carl Yastrzemski	100.00	40.00
❑ 9 Ray Herbert	15.00	6.00
❑ 10 Jim Landis	15.00	6.00
❑ 11 Dick Donovan	15.00	6.00
❑ 12 Tito Francona	15.00	6.00
❑ 13 Jerry Kindall	15.00	6.00
❑ 14 Frank Lary	20.00	8.00
❑ 15 Dick Howser	20.00	8.00
❑ 16 Jerry Lumpe	15.00	6.00
❑ 17 Norm Siebern	15.00	6.00
❑ 18 Don Lee	15.00	6.00
❑ 19 Albie Pearson	20.00	8.00
❑ 20 Bob Rodgers	20.00	8.00
❑ 21 Leon Wagner	15.00	6.00
❑ 22 Jim Kaat	25.00	10.00
❑ 23 Vic Power	20.00	8.00
❑ 24 Rich Rollins	20.00	8.00
❑ 25 Bobby Richardson	25.00	10.00
❑ 26 Ralph Terry	20.00	8.00
❑ 27 Tom Cheney	15.00	6.00
❑ 28 Chuck Cottier	15.00	6.00
❑ 29 Jimmy Piersall	20.00	8.00
❑ 30 Dave Stenhouse	15.00	6.00
❑ 31 Glen Hobbie	15.00	6.00
❑ 32 Ron Santo	25.00	10.00
❑ 33 Gene Freese	15.00	6.00
❑ 34 Vada Pinson	25.00	10.00
❑ 35 Bob Purkey	15.00	6.00
❑ 36 Joe Amalfitano	15.00	6.00
❑ 37 Bob Aspromonte	15.00	6.00
❑ 38 Dick Farrell	15.00	6.00
❑ 39 Al Spangler	15.00	6.00
❑ 40 Tommy Davis	20.00	8.00
❑ 41 Don Drysdale	80.00	32.00
❑ 42 Sandy Koufax	200.00	80.00
❑ 43 Maury Wills RC	100.00	40.00
❑ 44 Frank Bolling	15.00	6.00
❑ 45 Warren Spahn	80.00	32.00
❑ 46 Joe Adcock SP	150.00	60.00
❑ 47 Roger Craig	20.00	8.00
❑ 48 Al Jackson	20.00	8.00
❑ 49 Rod Kanehl	20.00	8.00
❑ 50 Ruben Amaro	15.00	6.00
❑ 51 Johnny Callison	20.00	8.00
❑ 52 Clay Dalrymple	15.00	6.00
❑ 53 Don Demeter	15.00	6.00
❑ 54 Art Mahaffey	15.00	6.00
❑ 55 Smoky Burgess	20.00	8.00
❑ 56 Roberto Clemente	175.00	70.00
❑ 57 Roy Face	20.00	8.00
❑ 58 Vern Law	20.00	8.00
❑ 59 Bill Mazeroski	30.00	12.00
❑ 60 Ken Boyer	25.00	10.00
❑ 61 Bob Gibson	80.00	32.00
❑ 62 Gene Oliver	15.00	6.00
❑ 63 Bill White	20.00	8.00
❑ 64 Orlando Cepeda	30.00	12.00
❑ 65 Jim Davenport	15.00	6.00
❑ 66 Billy O'Dell	25.00	7.50
❑ NNO Checklist card	500.00	160.00

1981 Fleer

	Nm-Mt	Ex-Mt
COMPLETE SET (660)	40.00	16.00
❑ 1 Pete Rose UER 270 hits in 63 should be 170	3.00	1.20
❑ 2 Larry Bowa	.25	.10
❑ 3 Manny Trillo	.10	.04
❑ 4 Bob Boone	.25	.10
❑ 5 Mike Schmidt See also 640A	2.50	1.00
❑ 6 Steve Carlton P1 Golden Arm Back 1066 Cardinals Number on back 6	.50	.20
❑ 6B Steve Carlton P2 Pitcher of Year Back 1066 Cardinals	1.50	.60
❑ 6C Steve Carlton P3 1966 Cardinals	2.00	.80
❑ 7 Tug McGraw See 657A	.25	.10
❑ 8 Larry Christenson	.10	.04
❑ 9 Bake McBride	.25	.10
❑ 10 Greg Luzinski	.25	.10
❑ 11 Ron Reed	.10	.04
❑ 12 Dickie Noles	.10	.04
❑ 13 Keith Moreland	.10	.04
❑ 14 Bob Walk RC	.50	.20
❑ 15 Lonnie Smith	.25	.10
❑ 16 Dick Ruthven	.10	.04
❑ 17 Sparky Lyle	.25	.10
❑ 18 Greg Gross	.10	.04
❑ 19 Garry Maddox	.10	.04
❑ 20 Nino Espinosa	.10	.04
❑ 21 George Vukovich	.10	.04
❑ 22 John Vukovich	.10	.04
❑ 23 Ramon Aviles	.10	.04
❑ 24A Kevin Saucier P1 (Name on back Ken)	.10	.04
❑ 24B Kevin Saucier P2 (Name on back Ken)	.10	.04
❑ 24C Kevin Saucier P3 (Name on back Kevin)	.50	.20
❑ 25 Randy Lerch	.10	.04
❑ 26 Del Unser	.10	.04
❑ 27 Tim McCarver	.25	.10
❑ 28 George Brett See also 655A	2.50	1.00
❑ 29 Willie Wilson See also 653A	.25	.10
❑ 30 Paul Splittorff	.10	.04
❑ 31 Dan Quisenberry	.10	.04
❑ 32A Amos Otis P1 (Batting Pose Outfield 32 on back)	.25	.10
❑ 32B Amos Otis P2 (Series Starter 483 on back)	.25	.10
❑ 33 Steve Busby	.10	.04
❑ 34 U.L. Washington	.10	.04
❑ 35 Dave Chalk	.10	.04
❑ 36 Darrell Porter	.10	.04
❑ 37 Marty Pattin	.10	.04
❑ 38 Larry Gura	.10	.04
❑ 39 Renie Martin	.10	.04
❑ 40 Rich Gale	.10	.04
❑ 41A Hal McRae P1 (Royals on front in black letters)	.50	.20
❑ 41B Hal McRae P2 (Royals on front in blue letters)	.25	.10
❑ 42 Dennis Leonard	.10	.04
❑ 43 Willie Aikens	.10	.04
❑ 44 Frank White	.25	.10
❑ 45 Clint Hurdle	.10	.04
❑ 46 John Wathan	.10	.04
❑ 47 Pete LaCock	.10	.04
❑ 48 Rance Mulliniks	.10	.04
❑ 49 Jeff Twitty	.10	.04
❑ 50 Jamie Quirk	.10	.04
❑ 51 Art Howe	.10	.04
❑ 52 Ken Forsch	.10	.04
❑ 53 Vern Ruhle	.10	.04
❑ 54 Joe Niekro	.10	.04
❑ 55 Frank LaCorte	.10	.04
❑ 56 J.R. Richard	.25	.10
❑ 57 Nolan Ryan	5.00	2.00
❑ 58 Enos Cabell	.10	.04
❑ 59 Cesar Cedeno	.25	.10
❑ 60 Jose Cruz	.25	.10
❑ 61 Bill Virdon MG	.10	.04
❑ 62 Terry Puhl	.10	.04
❑ 63 Joaquin Andujar	.25	.10
❑ 64 Alan Ashby	.10	.04
❑ 65 Joe Sambito	.10	.04
❑ 66 Denny Walling	.10	.04
❑ 67 Jeff Leonard	.25	.10
❑ 68 Luis Pujols	.10	.04
❑ 69 Bruce Bochy	.10	.04
❑ 70 Rafael Landestoy	.10	.04
❑ 71 Dave Smith RC	.50	.20
❑ 72 Danny Heep	.10	.04
❑ 73 Julio Gonzalez	.10	.04
❑ 74 Craig Reynolds	.10	.04
❑ 75 Gary Woods	.10	.04
❑ 76 Dave Bergman	.10	.04
❑ 77 Randy Niemann	.10	.04
❑ 78 Joe Morgan	.50	.20
❑ 79 Reggie Jackson See also 650A	1.00	.40
❑ 80 Bucky Dent	.25	.10
❑ 81 Tommy John	.25	.10
❑ 82 Luis Tiant	.25	.10
❑ 83 Rick Cerone	.10	.04

❑ 84 Dick Howser MG .10 .04
❑ 85 Lou Piniella .25 .10
❑ 86 Ron Davis .10 .04
❑ 87A Graig Nettles ERR 5.00 2.00
Name on back spelled Craig
❑ 87B Graig Nettles COR .25 .10
Graig
❑ 88 Ron Guidry .25 .10
❑ 89 Rich Gossage .25 .10
❑ 90 Rudy May .10 .04
❑ 91 Gaylord Perry .25 .10
❑ 92 Eric Soderholm .10 .04
❑ 93 Bob Watson .10 .04
❑ 94 Bobby Murcer .25 .10
❑ 95 Bobby Brown .10 .04
❑ 96 Jim Spencer .10 .04
❑ 97 Tom Underwood .10 .04
❑ 98 Oscar Gamble .10 .04
❑ 99 Johnny Oates .25 .10
❑ 100 Fred Stanley .10 .04
❑ 101 Ruppert Jones .10 .04
❑ 102 Dennis Werth .10 .04
❑ 103 Joe Lefebvre .10 .04
❑ 104 Brian Doyle .10 .04
❑ 105 Aurelio Rodriguez .10 .04
❑ 106 Doug Bird .10 .04
❑ 107 Mike Griffin RC .15 .06
❑ 108 Tim Lollar .10 .04
❑ 109 Willie Randolph .25 .10
❑ 110 Steve Garvey .50 .20
❑ 111 Reggie Smith .25 .10
❑ 112 Don Sutton .25 .10
❑ 113 Burt Hooton .10 .04
❑ 114A Dave Lopes P1 .50 .20
Small hand on back
❑ 114B Dave Lopes P2 .25 .10
No hand
❑ 115 Dusty Baker .25 .10
❑ 116 Tom Lasorda MG .50 .20
❑ 117 Bill Russell .25 .10
❑ 118 Jerry Reuss UER .10 .04
Home omitted
❑ 119 Terry Forster .25 .10
❑ 120A Bob Welch P1 .25 .10
(Name on back is Bob)
❑ 120B Bob Welch P2 .25 .10
(Name on back is Robert)
❑ 121 Don Stanhouse .10 .04
❑ 122 Rick Monday .25 .10
❑ 123 Derrel Thomas .10 .04
❑ 124 Joe Ferguson .10 .04
❑ 125 Rick Sutcliffe .25 .10
❑ 126A Ron Cey P1 .25 .10
Small hand on back
❑ 126B Ron Cey P2 .25 .10
No hand
❑ 127 Dave Goltz .10 .04
❑ 128 Jay Johnstone .10 .04
❑ 129 Steve Yeager .25 .10
❑ 130 Gary Weiss .10 .04
❑ 131 Mike Scioscia RC 1.50 .60
❑ 132 Vic Davalillo .10 .04
❑ 133 Doug Rau .10 .04
❑ 134 Pepe Frias .10 .04
❑ 135 Mickey Hatcher .10 .04
❑ 136 Steve Howe RC .50 .20
❑ 137 Robert Castillo .10 .04
❑ 138 Gary Thomasson .10 .04
❑ 139 Rudy Law .10 .04
❑ 140 F.Valenzuela RC UER 5.00 2.00
Misspelled Fernand on card
❑ 141 Manny Mota .25 .10
❑ 142 Gary Carter .50 .20
❑ 143 Steve Rogers .25 .10
❑ 144 Warren Cromartie .10 .04
❑ 145 Andre Dawson .50 .20
❑ 146 Larry Parrish .10 .04
❑ 147 Rowland Office .10 .04
❑ 148 Ellis Valentine .10 .04
❑ 149 Dick Williams MG .10 .04
❑ 150 Bill Gullickson RC .50 .20
❑ 151 Elias Sosa .10 .04
❑ 152 John Tamargo .10 .04
❑ 153 Chris Speier .10 .04
❑ 154 Ron LeFlore .25 .10
❑ 155 Rodney Scott .10 .04
❑ 156 Stan Bahnsen .10 .04
❑ 157 Bill Lee .25 .10
❑ 158 Fred Norman .10 .04
❑ 159 Woodie Fryman .10 .04
❑ 160 David Palmer .10 .04
❑ 161 Jerry White .10 .04
❑ 162 Roberto Ramos .10 .04
❑ 163 John D'Acquisto .10 .04
❑ 164 Tommy Hutton .10 .04
❑ 165 Charlie Lea .10 .04
❑ 166 Scott Sanderson .10 .04
❑ 167 Ken Macha .10 .04
❑ 168 Tony Bernazard .10 .04
❑ 169 Jim Palmer .50 .20
❑ 170 Steve Stone .10 .04
❑ 171 Mike Flanagan .10 .04
❑ 172 Al Bumbry .10 .04
❑ 173 Doug DeCinces .10 .04
❑ 174 Scott McGregor .10 .04
❑ 175 Mark Belanger .10 .04
❑ 176 Tim Stoddard .10 .04
❑ 177A Rick Dempsey P1 .25 .10
Small hand on front
❑ 177B Rick Dempsey P2 .10 .04
No hand
❑ 178 Earl Weaver MG .25 .10
❑ 179 Tippy Martinez .10 .04
❑ 180 Dennis Martinez .25 .10
❑ 181 Sammy Stewart .10 .04
❑ 182 Rich Dauer .10 .04
❑ 183 Lee May .10 .04
❑ 184 Eddie Murray 1.50 .60
❑ 185 Benny Ayala .10 .04
❑ 186 John Lowenstein .10 .04
❑ 187 Gary Roenicke .10 .04
❑ 188 Ken Singleton .25 .10
❑ 189 Dan Graham .10 .04
❑ 190 Terry Crowley .10 .04
❑ 191 Kiko Garcia .10 .04
❑ 192 Dave Ford .10 .04
❑ 193 Mark Corey .10 .04
❑ 194 Lenn Sakata .10 .04
❑ 195 Doug DeCinces .10 .04
❑ 196 Johnny Bench 1.00 .40
❑ 197 Dave Concepcion .25 .10
❑ 198 Ray Knight .25 .10
❑ 199 Ken Griffey .25 .10
❑ 200 Tom Seaver 1.00 .40
❑ 201 Dave Collins .10 .04
❑ 202A George Foster P1 .50 .20
Slugger
Number on back 216
❑ 202B George Foster P2 .50 .20
Slugger
Number on back 202
❑ 203 Junior Kennedy .10 .04
❑ 204 Frank Pastore .10 .04
❑ 205 Dan Driessen .10 .04
❑ 206 Hector Cruz .10 .04
❑ 207 Paul Moskau .10 .04
❑ 208 Charlie Leibrandt RC .50 .20
❑ 209 Harry Spilman .10 .04
❑ 210 Joe Price .10 .04
❑ 211 Tom Hume .10 .04
❑ 212 Joe Nolan .10 .04
❑ 213 Doug Bair .10 .04
❑ 214 Mario Soto .25 .10
❑ 215A Bill Bonham P1 .50 .20
(Small hand on back)
❑ 215B Bill Bonham P2 .10 .04
(No hand)
❑ 216 George Foster .25 .10
(See 202)
❑ 217 Paul Householder .10 .04
❑ 218 Ron Oester .10 .04
❑ 219 Sam Mejias .10 .04
❑ 220 Sheldon Burnside .10 .04
❑ 221 Carl Yastrzemski 1.50 .60
❑ 222 Jim Rice .25 .10
❑ 223 Fred Lynn .25 .10
❑ 224 Carlton Fisk .50 .20
❑ 225 Rick Burleson .10 .04
❑ 226 Dennis Eckersley .50 .20
❑ 227 Butch Hobson .10 .04
❑ 228 Tom Burgmeier .10 .04
❑ 229 Garry Hancock .10 .04
❑ 230 Don Zimmer MG .25 .10
❑ 231 Steve Renko .10 .04
❑ 232 Dwight Evans .50 .20
❑ 233 Mike Torrez .10 .04
❑ 234 Bob Stanley .10 .04
❑ 235 Jim Dwyer .10 .04
❑ 236 Dave Stapleton .10 .04
❑ 237 Glenn Hoffman .10 .04
❑ 238 Jerry Remy .10 .04
❑ 239 Dick Drago .10 .04
❑ 240 Bill Campbell .10 .04
❑ 241 Tony Perez .50 .20
❑ 242 Phil Niekro .25 .10
❑ 243 Dale Murphy .50 .20
❑ 244 Bob Horner .25 .10
❑ 245 Jeff Burroughs .25 .10
❑ 246 Rick Camp .10 .04
❑ 247 Bobby Cox MG .25 .10
❑ 248 Bruce Benedict .10 .04
❑ 249 Gene Garber .10 .04
❑ 250 Jerry Royster .10 .04
❑ 251A Gary Matthews P1 .50 .20
Small hand on back
❑ 251B Gary Matthews P2 .25 .10
No hand
❑ 252 Chris Chambliss .25 .10
❑ 253 Luis Gomez .10 .04
❑ 254 Bill Nahorodny .10 .04
❑ 255 Doyle Alexander .10 .04
❑ 256 Brian Asselstine .10 .04
❑ 257 Biff Pocoroba .10 .04
❑ 258 Mike Lum .10 .04
❑ 259 Charlie Spikes .10 .04
❑ 260 Glenn Hubbard .10 .04
❑ 261 Tommy Boggs .10 .04
❑ 262 Al Hrabosky UER .25 .10
Card lists him as 5' 1"
❑ 263 Rick Matula .10 .04
❑ 264 Preston Hanna .10 .04
❑ 265 Larry Bradford .10 .04
❑ 266 Rafael Ramirez .10 .04
❑ 267 Larry McWilliams .10 .04
❑ 268 Rod Carew .50 .20
❑ 269 Bobby Grich .25 .10
❑ 270 Carney Lansford .25 .10
❑ 271 Don Baylor .25 .10
❑ 272 Joe Rudi .25 .10
❑ 273 Dan Ford .10 .04
❑ 274 Jim Fregosi MG .10 .04
❑ 275 Dave Frost .10 .04
❑ 276 Frank Tanana .25 .10
❑ 277 Dickie Thon .10 .04
❑ 278 Jason Thompson .10 .04
❑ 279 Rick Miller .10 .04
❑ 280 Bert Campaneris .25 .10
❑ 281 Tom Donohue .10 .04
❑ 282 Brian Downing .25 .10
❑ 283 Fred Patek .10 .04
❑ 284 Bruce Kison .10 .04
❑ 285 Dave LaRoche .10 .04
❑ 286 Don Aase .10 .04
❑ 287 Jim Barr .10 .04
❑ 288 Alfredo Martinez .10 .04
❑ 289 Larry Harlow .10 .04
❑ 290 Andy Hassler .10 .04
❑ 291 Dave Kingman .25 .10
❑ 292 Bill Buckner .25 .10
❑ 293 Rick Reuschel .25 .10
❑ 294 Bruce Sutter .25 .10
❑ 295 Jerry Martin .10 .04
❑ 296 Scot Thompson .10 .04
❑ 297 Ivan DeJesus .10 .04
❑ 298 Steve Dillard .10 .04
❑ 299 Dick Tidrow .10 .04
❑ 300 Randy Martz .10 .04
❑ 301 Lenny Randle .10 .04
❑ 302 Lynn McGlothen .10 .04
❑ 303 Cliff Johnson .10 .04
❑ 304 Tim Blackwell .10 .04
❑ 305 Dennis Lamp .10 .04
❑ 306 Bill Caudill .10 .04
❑ 307 Carlos Lezcano .10 .04
❑ 308 Jim Tracy RC 1.00 .40
❑ 309 Doug Capilla UER .10 .04
Cubs on front but
Braves on back

	Card		
❑	310 Willie Hernandez	.10	.04
❑	311 Mike Vail	.10	.04
❑	312 Mike Krukow	.10	.04
❑	313 Barry Foote	.10	.04
❑	314 Larry Biittner	.10	.04
❑	315 Mike Tyson	.10	.04
❑	316 Lee Mazzilli	.25	.10
❑	317 John Stearns	.10	.04
❑	318 Alex Trevino	.10	.04
❑	319 Craig Swan	.10	.04
❑	320 Frank Taveras	.10	.04
❑	321 Steve Henderson	.10	.04
❑	322 Neil Allen	.10	.04
❑	323 Mark Bomback	.10	.04
❑	324 Mike Jorgensen	.10	.04
❑	325 Joe Torre MG	.25	.10
❑	326 Elliott Maddox	.10	.04
❑	327 Pete Falcone	.10	.04
❑	328 Ray Burris	.10	.04
❑	329 Claudell Washington	.10	.04
❑	330 Doug Flynn	.10	.04
❑	331 Joel Youngblood	.10	.04
❑	332 Bill Almon	.10	.04
❑	333 Tom Hausman	.10	.04
❑	334 Pat Zachry	.10	.04
❑	335 Jeff Reardon RC	1.00	.40
❑	336 Wally Backman RC	.50	.20
❑	337 Dan Norman	.10	.04
❑	338 Jerry Morales	.10	.04
❑	339 Ed Farmer	.10	.04
❑	340 Bob Molinaro	.10	.04
❑	341 Todd Cruz	.10	.04
❑	342A Britt Burns P1 Small hand on front	.50	.20
❑	342B Britt Burns P2 No hand	.25	.10
❑	343 Kevin Bell	.10	.04
❑	344 Tony LaRussa MG	.25	.10
❑	345 Steve Trout	.10	.04
❑	346 Harold Baines RC	2.00	.80
❑	347 Richard Wortham	.10	.04
❑	348 Wayne Nordhagen	.10	.04
❑	349 Mike Squires	.10	.04
❑	350 Lamar Johnson	.10	.04
❑	351 Rickey Henderson Most Stolen Bases AL	3.00	1.20
❑	352 Francisco Barrios	.10	.04
❑	353 Thad Bosley	.10	.04
❑	354 Chet Lemon	.25	.10
❑	355 Bruce Kimm	.10	.04
❑	356 Richard Dotson	.10	.04
❑	357 Jim Morrison	.10	.04
❑	358 Mike Proly	.10	.04
❑	359 Greg Pryor	.10	.04
❑	360 Dave Parker	.25	.10
❑	361 Omar Moreno	.10	.04
❑	362A Kent Tekulve P1 Back 1071 Waterbury and 1078 Pirates	.10	.04
❑	362B Kent Tekulve P2 1971 Waterbury and 1978 Pirates	.10	.04
❑	363 Willie Stargell	.50	.20
❑	364 Phil Garner	.25	.10
❑	365 Ed Ott	.10	.04
❑	366 Don Robinson	.10	.04
❑	367 Chuck Tanner MG	.10	.04
❑	368 Jim Rooker	.10	.04
❑	369 Dale Berra	.10	.04
❑	370 Jim Bibby	.10	.04
❑	371 Steve Nicosia	.10	.04
❑	372 Mike Easler	.10	.04
❑	373 Bill Robinson	.10	.04
❑	374 Lee Lacy	.10	.04
❑	375 John Candelaria	.25	.10
❑	376 Manny Sanguillen	.25	.10
❑	377 Rick Rhoden	.10	.04
❑	378 Grant Jackson	.10	.04
❑	379 Tim Foli	.10	.04
❑	380 Rod Scurry	.10	.04
❑	381 Bill Madlock	.25	.10
❑	382A Kurt Bevacqua P1 ERR P on cap backwards	.25	.10
❑	382B Kurt Bevacqua P2 COR	.10	.04
❑	383 Bert Blyleven	.25	.10
❑	384 Eddie Solomon	.10	.04
❑	385 Enrique Romo	.10	.04
❑	386 John Milner	.10	.04
❑	387 Mike Hargrove	.10	.04
❑	388 Jorge Orta	.10	.04
❑	389 Toby Harrah	.25	.10
❑	390 Tom Veryzer	.10	.04
❑	391 Miguel Dilone	.10	.04
❑	392 Dan Spillner	.10	.04
❑	393 Jack Brohamer	.10	.04
❑	394 Wayne Garland	.10	.04
❑	395 Sid Monge	.10	.04
❑	396 Rick Waits	.10	.04
❑	397 Joe Charboneau RC	1.00	.40
❑	398 Gary Alexander	.10	.04
❑	399 Jerry Dybzinski	.10	.04
❑	400 Mike Stanton	.10	.04
❑	401 Mike Paxton	.10	.04
❑	402 Gary Gray	.10	.04
❑	403 Rick Manning	.10	.04
❑	404 Bo Diaz	.10	.04
❑	405 Ron Hassey	.10	.04
❑	406 Ross Grimsley	.10	.04
❑	407 Victor Cruz	.10	.04
❑	408 Len Barker	.25	.10
❑	409 Bob Bailor	.10	.04
❑	410 Otto Velez	.10	.04
❑	411 Ernie Whitt	.10	.04
❑	412 Jim Clancy	.10	.04
❑	413 Barry Bonnell	.10	.04
❑	414 Dave Stieb	.25	.10
❑	415 Damaso Garcia	.10	.04
❑	416 John Mayberry	.10	.04
❑	417 Roy Howell	.10	.04
❑	418 Danny Ainge RC	3.00	1.20
❑	419A Jesse Jefferson P1 Back says Pirates	.10	.04
❑	419B Jesse Jefferson P2 Back says Pirates	.10	.04
❑	419C Jesse Jefferson P3 Back says Blue Jays	.50	.20
❑	420 Joey McLaughlin	.10	.04
❑	421 Lloyd Moseby RC	.50	.20
❑	422 Alvis Woods	.10	.04
❑	423 Garth Iorg	.10	.04
❑	424 Doug Ault	.10	.04
❑	425 Ken Schrom	.10	.04
❑	426 Mike Willis	.10	.04
❑	427 Steve Braun	.10	.04
❑	428 Bob Davis	.10	.04
❑	429 Jerry Garvin	.10	.04
❑	430 Alfredo Griffin	.10	.04
❑	431 Bob Mattick MG	.10	.04
❑	432 Vida Blue	.25	.10
❑	433 Jack Clark	.25	.10
❑	434 Willie McCovey	.50	.20
❑	435 Mike Ivie	.10	.04
❑	436A Darrel Evans P1 ERR Name on front Darrel	.50	.20
❑	436B Darrell Evans P2 COR Name on front Darrell	.50	.20
❑	437 Terry Whitfield	.10	.04
❑	438 Rennie Stennett	.10	.04
❑	439 John Montefusco	.10	.04
❑	440 Jim Wohlford	.10	.04
❑	441 Bill North	.10	.04
❑	442 Milt May	.10	.04
❑	443 Max Venable	.10	.04
❑	444 Ed Whitson	.10	.04
❑	445 Al Holland	.10	.04
❑	446 Randy Moffitt	.10	.04
❑	447 Bob Knepper	.10	.04
❑	448 Gary Lavelle	.10	.04
❑	449 Greg Minton	.10	.04
❑	450 Johnnie LeMaster	.10	.04
❑	451 Larry Herndon	.10	.04
❑	452 Rich Murray	.10	.04
❑	453 Joe Pettini	.10	.04
❑	454 Allen Ripley	.10	.04
❑	455 Dennis Littlejohn	.10	.04
❑	456 Tom Griffin	.10	.04
❑	457 Alan Hargesheimer	.10	.04
❑	458 Joe Strain	.10	.04
❑	459 Steve Kemp	.10	.04
❑	460 Sparky Anderson MG	.25	.10
❑	461 Alan Trammell	.50	.20
❑	462 Mark Fidrych	.25	.10
❑	463 Lou Whitaker	.50	.20
❑	464 Dave Rozema	.10	.04
❑	465 Milt Wilcox	.10	.04
❑	466 Champ Summers	.10	.04
❑	467 Lance Parrish	.25	.10
❑	468 Dan Petry	.10	.04
❑	469 Pat Underwood	.10	.04
❑	470 Rick Peters	.10	.04
❑	471 Al Cowens	.10	.04
❑	472 John Wockenfuss	.10	.04
❑	473 Tom Brookens	.10	.04
❑	474 Richie Hebner	.10	.04
❑	475 Jack Morris	.50	.20
❑	476 Jim Lentine	.10	.04
❑	477 Bruce Robbins	.10	.04
❑	478 Mark Wagner	.10	.04
❑	479 Tim Corcoran	.10	.04
❑	480A Stan Papi P1 Front as Pitcher	.25	.10
❑	480B Stan Papi P2 Front as Shortstop	.10	.04
❑	481 Kirk Gibson RC	5.00	2.00
❑	482 Dan Schatzeder	.10	.04
❑	483A Amos Otis P1 See card 32	.25	.10
❑	483B Amos Otis P2 See card 32	.25	.10
❑	484 Dave Winfield	.50	.20
❑	485 Rollie Fingers	.25	.10
❑	486 Gene Richards	.10	.04
❑	487 Randy Jones	.10	.04
❑	488 Ozzie Smith	3.00	1.20
❑	489 Gene Tenace	.25	.10
❑	490 Bill Fahey	.10	.04
❑	491 John Curtis	.10	.04
❑	492 Dave Cash	.10	.04
❑	493A Tim Flannery P1 Batting right	.25	.10
❑	493B Tim Flannery P2 Batting left	.10	.04
❑	494 Jerry Mumphrey	.10	.04
❑	495 Bob Shirley	.10	.04
❑	496 Steve Mura	.10	.04
❑	497 Eric Rasmussen	.10	.04
❑	498 Broderick Perkins	.10	.04
❑	499 Barry Evans	.10	.04
❑	500 Chuck Baker	.10	.04
❑	501 Luis Salazar RC	.50	.20
❑	502 Gary Lucas	.10	.04
❑	503 Mike Armstrong	.10	.04
❑	504 Jerry Turner	.10	.04
❑	505 Dennis Kinney	.10	.04
❑	506 Willie Montanez UER Spelled Willy on card front	.10	.04
❑	507 Gorman Thomas	.25	.10
❑	508 Ben Oglivie	.25	.10
❑	509 Larry Hisle	.10	.04
❑	510 Sal Bando	.25	.10
❑	511 Robin Yount	1.50	.60
❑	512 Mike Caldwell	.10	.04
❑	513 Sixto Lezcano	.10	.04
❑	514A Bill Travers P1 ERR Jerry Augustine with Augustine back	.25	.10
❑	514B Bill Travers P2 COR	.10	.04
❑	515 Paul Molitor	1.00	.40
❑	516 Moose Haas	.10	.04
❑	517 Bill Castro	.10	.04
❑	518 Jim Slaton	.10	.04
❑	519 Lary Sorensen	.10	.04
❑	520 Bob McClure	.10	.04
❑	521 Charlie Moore	.10	.04
❑	522 Jim Gantner	.10	.04
❑	523 Reggie Cleveland	.10	.04
❑	524 Don Money	.10	.04
❑	525 Bill Travers	.10	.04
❑	526 Buck Martinez	.10	.04
❑	527 Dick Davis	.10	.04
❑	528 Ted Simmons	.25	.10
❑	529 Garry Templeton	.25	.10
❑	530 Ken Reitz	.10	.04
❑	531 Tony Scott	.10	.04
❑	532 Ken Oberkfell	.10	.04
❑	533 Bob Sykes	.10	.04

❑ 534 Keith Smith .10 .04
❑ 535 John Littlefield .10 .04
❑ 536 Jim Kaat .25 .10
❑ 537 Bob Forsch .10 .04
❑ 538 Mike Phillips .10 .04
❑ 539 Terry Landrum .10 .04
❑ 540 Leon Durham RC .50 .20
❑ 541 Terry Kennedy .10 .04
❑ 542 George Hendrick .25 .10
❑ 543 Dane Iorg .10 .04
❑ 544 Mark Littell .10 .04
❑ 545 Keith Hernandez .25 .10
❑ 546 Silvio Martinez .10 .04
❑ 547A Don Hood P1 ERR .25 .10
Pete Vuckovich
with Vuckovich back
❑ 547B Don Hood P2 COR .10 .04
❑ 548 Bobby Bonds .25 .10
❑ 549 Mike Ramsey RC .15 .06
❑ 550 Tom Herr .10 .04
❑ 551 Roy Smalley .10 .04
❑ 552 Jerry Koosman .25 .10
❑ 553 Ken Landreaux .10 .04
❑ 554 John Castino .10 .04
❑ 555 Doug Corbett .10 .04
❑ 556 Bombo Rivera .10 .04
❑ 557 Ron Jackson .10 .04
❑ 558 Butch Wynegar .10 .04
❑ 559 Hosken Powell .10 .04
❑ 560 Pete Redfern .10 .04
❑ 561 Roger Erickson .10 .04
❑ 562 Glenn Adams .10 .04
❑ 563 Rick Sofield .10 .04
❑ 564 Geoff Zahn .10 .04
❑ 565 Pete Mackanin .10 .04
❑ 566 Mike Cubbage .10 .04
❑ 567 Darrell Jackson .10 .04
❑ 568 Dave Edwards .10 .04
❑ 569 Rob Wilfong .10 .04
❑ 570 Sal Butera .10 .04
❑ 571 Jose Morales .10 .04
❑ 572 Rick Langford .10 .04
❑ 573 Mike Norris .10 .04
❑ 574 Rickey Henderson 6.00 2.40
❑ 575 Tony Armas .25 .10
❑ 576 Dave Revering .10 .04
❑ 577 Jeff Newman .10 .04
❑ 578 Bob Lacey .10 .04
❑ 579 Brian Kingman .10 .04
❑ 580 Mitchell Page .10 .04
❑ 581 Billy Martin MG .50 .20
❑ 582 Rob Picciolo .10 .04
❑ 583 Mike Heath .10 .04
❑ 584 Mickey Klutts .10 .04
❑ 585 Orlando Gonzalez .10 .04
❑ 586 Mike Davis RC .50 .20
❑ 587 Wayne Gross .10 .04
❑ 588 Matt Keough .10 .04
❑ 589 Steve McCatty .10 .04
❑ 590 Dwayne Murphy .10 .04
❑ 591 Mario Guerrero .10 .04
❑ 592 Dave McKay .10 .04
❑ 593 Jim Essian .10 .04
❑ 594 Dave Heaverlo .10 .04
❑ 595 Maury Wills MG .25 .10
❑ 596 Juan Beniquez .10 .04
❑ 597 Rodney Craig .10 .04
❑ 598 Jim Anderson .10 .04
❑ 599 Floyd Bannister .10 .04
❑ 600 Bruce Bochte .10 .04
❑ 601 Julio Cruz .10 .04
❑ 602 Ted Cox .10 .04
❑ 603 Dan Meyer .10 .04
❑ 604 Larry Cox .10 .04
❑ 605 Bill Stein .10 .04
❑ 606 Steve Garvey .50 .20
Most Hits NL
❑ 607 Dave Roberts .10 .04
❑ 608 Leon Roberts .10 .04
❑ 609 Reggie Walton .10 .04
❑ 610 Dave Edler .10 .04
❑ 611 Larry Milbourne .10 .04
❑ 612 Kim Allen .10 .04
❑ 613 Mario Mendoza .10 .04
❑ 614 Tom Paciorek .10 .04
❑ 615 Glenn Abbott .10 .04
❑ 616 Joe Simpson .10 .04
❑ 617 Mickey Rivers .10 .04
❑ 618 Jim Kern .10 .04
❑ 619 Jim Sundberg .25 .10
❑ 620 Richie Zisk .10 .04
❑ 621 Jon Matlack .10 .04
❑ 622 Ferguson Jenkins .25 .10
❑ 623 Pat Corrales MG .10 .04
❑ 624 Ed Figueroa .10 .04
❑ 625 Buddy Bell .25 .10
❑ 626 Al Oliver .25 .10
❑ 627 Doc Medich .10 .04
❑ 628 Bump Wills .10 .04
❑ 629 Rusty Staub .25 .10
❑ 630 Pat Putnam .10 .04
❑ 631 John Grubb .10 .04
❑ 632 Danny Darwin .10 .04
❑ 633 Ken Clay .10 .04
❑ 634 Jim Norris .10 .04
❑ 635 John Butcher .10 .04
❑ 636 Dave Roberts .10 .04
❑ 637 Billy Sample .10 .04
❑ 638 Carl Yastrzemski 1.50 .60
❑ 639 Cecil Cooper .25 .10
❑ 640 Mike Schmidt P1 2.50 1.00
Portrait
Third Base
number on back 5
❑ 640B Mike Schmidt P2 2.50 1.00
1980 Home Run King
640 on back
❑ 641A CL: Phils/Royals P1 .25 .10
41 is Hal McRae
❑ 641B CL: Phils/Royals P2 .25 .10
41 is Hal McRae
Double Threat
❑ 642 CL: Astros/Yankees .10 .04
❑ 643 CL: Expos/Dodgers .10 .04
❑ 644A CL: Reds/Orioles P1 .25 .10
202 is George Foster
Joe Nolan pitcher
should be catcher
❑ 644B CL: Reds/Orioles P2 .25 .10
202 is Foster Slugger
Joe Nolan pitcher
should be catcher
❑ 645 Pete Rose 1.50 .60
Larry Bowa
Mike Schmidt
Triple Threat P1
No number on back
❑ 645B Pete Rose 2.50 1.00
Larry Bowa
Mike Schmidt
Triple Threat P2
Back numbered 645
❑ 646 CL: Braves/Red Sox .10 .04
❑ 647 CL: Cubs/Angels .10 .04
❑ 648 CL: Mets/White Sox .10 .04
❑ 649 CL: Indians/Pirates .10 .04
❑ 650 Reggie Jackson 1.00 .40
Mr. Baseball P1
Number on back 79
❑ 650B Reggie Jackson .50 .20
Mr. Baseball P2
Number on back 650
❑ 651 CL: Giants/Blue Jays .10 .04
❑ 652A CL:Tigers/Padres P1 .25 .10
483 is listed
❑ 652B CL:Tigers/Padres P2 .25 .10
483 is deleted
❑ 653A Willie Wilson P1 .25 .10
Most Hits Most Runs
Number on back 29
❑ 653B Willie Wilson P2 .25 .10
Most Hits Most Runs
Number on back 653
❑ 654A Checklist Brewers .25 .10
Cards P1
514 Jerry Augustine
547 Pete Vuckovich
❑ 654B Checklist Brewers .25 .10
Cards P2
514 Billy Travers
547 Don Hood
❑ 655 George Brett P1 2.50 1.00
.390 Average
Number on back 28
❑ 655B George Brett P2 2.50 1.00
.390 Average
Number on back 655
❑ 656 CL:Twins/Oakland A's .25 .10
❑ 657A Tug McGraw P1 .25 .10
Game Saver
Number on back 7
❑ 657B Tug McGraw P2 .25 .10
Game Saver
Number on back 657
❑ 658 CL: Rangers/Mariners .10 .04
❑ 659A Checklist P1 .10 .04
of Special Cards
Last lines on front
Wilson Most Hits
❑ 659B Checklist P2 .10 .04
of Special Cards
Last lines on front
Otis Series Starter
❑ 660 Steve Carlton P1 .50 .20
Golden Arm
(Number on back 660
Back 1066 Cardinals
❑ 660B Steve Carlton P2 2.00 .80
Golden Arm
1966 Cardinals

1982 Fleer

	Nm-Mt	Ex-Mt
COMPLETE SET (660)	50.00	20.00

❑ 1 Dusty Baker .20 .08
❑ 2 Robert Castillo .10 .04
❑ 3 Ron Cey .20 .08
❑ 4 Terry Forster .20 .08
❑ 5 Steve Garvey .20 .08
❑ 6 Dave Goltz .10 .04
❑ 7 Pedro Guerrero .20 .08
❑ 8 Burt Hooton .10 .04
❑ 9 Steve Howe .10 .04
❑ 10 Jay Johnstone .10 .04
❑ 11 Ken Landreaux .10 .04
❑ 12 Dave Lopes .20 .08
❑ 13 Mike A. Marshall RC .50 .20
❑ 14 Bobby Mitchell .10 .04
❑ 15 Rick Monday .20 .08
❑ 16 Tom Niedenfuer RC .50 .20
❑ 17 Ted Power RC .15 .06
❑ 18 Jerry Reuss UER .10 .04
("Home:" omitted)
❑ 19 Ron Roenicke .10 .04
❑ 20 Bill Russell .20 .08
❑ 21 Steve Sax RC 1.00 .40
❑ 22 Mike Scioscia .20 .08
❑ 23 Reggie Smith .20 .08
❑ 24 Dave Stewart RC 1.50 .60
❑ 25 Rick Sutcliffe .20 .08
❑ 26 Derrel Thomas .10 .04
❑ 27 Fernando Valenzuela .75 .30
❑ 28 Bob Welch .20 .08
❑ 29 Steve Yeager .20 .08
❑ 30 Bobby Brown .10 .04
❑ 31 Rick Cerone .10 .04
❑ 32 Ron Davis .10 .04
❑ 33 Bucky Dent .20 .08
❑ 34 Barry Foote .10 .04

❑ 35 George Frazier .10 .04
❑ 36 Oscar Gamble .10 .04
❑ 37 Rich Gossage .20 .08
❑ 38 Ron Guidry .20 .08
❑ 39 Reggie Jackson .40 .16
❑ 40 Tommy John .20 .08
❑ 41 Rudy May .10 .04
❑ 42 Larry Milbourne .10 .04
❑ 43 Jerry Mumphrey .10 .04
❑ 44 Bobby Murcer .20 .08
❑ 45 Gene Nelson .10 .04
❑ 46 Graig Nettles .20 .08
❑ 47 Johnny Oates .20 .08
❑ 48 Lou Piniella .20 .08
❑ 49 Willie Randolph .20 .08
❑ 50 Rick Reuschel .20 .08
❑ 51 Dave Revering .10 .04
❑ 52 Dave Righetti RC 1.50 .60
❑ 53 Aurelio Rodriguez .10 .04
❑ 54 Bob Watson .10 .04
❑ 55 Dennis Werth .10 .04
❑ 56 Dave Winfield .20 .08
❑ 57 Johnny Bench .75 .30
❑ 58 Bruce Berenyi .10 .04
❑ 59 Larry Biittner .10 .04
❑ 60 Scott Brown .10 .04
❑ 61 Dave Collins .10 .04
❑ 62 Geoff Combe .10 .04
❑ 63 Dave Concepcion .20 .08
❑ 64 Dan Driessen .10 .04
❑ 65 Joe Edelen .10 .04
❑ 66 George Foster .20 .08
❑ 67 Ken Griffey .20 .08
❑ 68 Paul Householder .10 .04
❑ 69 Tom Hume .10 .04
❑ 70 Junior Kennedy .10 .04
❑ 71 Ray Knight .20 .08
❑ 72 Mike LaCoss .10 .04
❑ 73 Rafael Landestoy .10 .04
❑ 74 Charlie Leibrandt .10 .04
❑ 75 Sam Mejias .10 .04
❑ 76 Paul Moskau .10 .04
❑ 77 Joe Nolan .10 .04
❑ 78 Mike O'Berry .10 .04
❑ 79 Ron Oester .10 .04
❑ 80 Frank Pastore .10 .04
❑ 81 Joe Price .10 .04
❑ 82 Tom Seaver .75 .30
❑ 83 Mario Soto .20 .08
❑ 84 Mike Vail .10 .04
❑ 85 Tony Armas .20 .08
❑ 86 Shooty Babitt .10 .04
❑ 87 Dave Beard .10 .04
❑ 88 Rick Bosetti .10 .04
❑ 89 Keith Drumwright .10 .04
❑ 90 Wayne Gross .10 .04
❑ 91 Mike Heath .10 .04
❑ 92 Rickey Henderson 2.50 1.00
❑ 93 Cliff Johnson .10 .04
❑ 94 Jeff Jones .10 .04
❑ 95 Matt Keough .10 .04
❑ 96 Brian Kingman .10 .04
❑ 97 Mickey Klutts .10 .04
❑ 98 Rick Langford .10 .04
❑ 99 Steve McCatty .10 .04
❑ 100 Dave McKay .10 .04
❑ 101 Dwayne Murphy .10 .04
❑ 102 Jeff Newman .10 .04
❑ 103 Mike Norris .10 .04
❑ 104 Bob Owchinko .10 .04
❑ 105 Mitchell Page .10 .04
❑ 106 Rob Picciolo .10 .04
❑ 107 Jim Spencer .10 .04
❑ 108 Fred Stanley .10 .04
❑ 109 Tom Underwood .10 .04
❑ 110 Joaquin Andujar .20 .08
❑ 111 Steve Braun .10 .04
❑ 112 Bob Forsch .10 .04
❑ 113 George Hendrick .20 .08
❑ 114 Keith Hernandez .20 .08
❑ 115 Tom Herr .10 .04
❑ 116 Dane Iorg .10 .04
❑ 117 Jim Kaat .20 .08
❑ 118 Tito Landrum .10 .04
❑ 119 Sixto Lezcano .10 .04
❑ 120 Mark Littell .10 .04
❑ 121 John Martin RC .15 .06
❑ 122 Silvio Martinez .10 .04
❑ 123 Ken Oberkfell .10 .04
❑ 124 Darrell Porter .10 .04
❑ 125 Mike Ramsey .10 .04
❑ 126 Orlando Sanchez .10 .04
❑ 127 Bob Shirley .10 .04
❑ 128 Lary Sorensen .10 .04
❑ 129 Bruce Sutter .20 .08
❑ 130 Bob Sykes .10 .04
❑ 131 Garry Templeton .20 .08
❑ 132 Gene Tenace .20 .08
❑ 133 Jerry Augustine .10 .04
❑ 134 Sal Bando .20 .08
❑ 135 Mark Brouhard .10 .04
❑ 136 Mike Caldwell .10 .04
❑ 137 Reggie Cleveland .10 .04
❑ 138 Cecil Cooper .20 .08
❑ 139 Jamie Easterly .10 .04
❑ 140 Marshall Edwards .10 .04
❑ 141 Rollie Fingers .20 .08
❑ 142 Jim Gantner .10 .04
❑ 143 Moose Haas .10 .04
❑ 144 Larry Hisle .10 .04
❑ 145 Roy Howell .10 .04
❑ 146 Rickey Keeton .10 .04
❑ 147 Randy Lerch .10 .04
❑ 148 Paul Molitor .40 .16
❑ 149 Don Money .10 .04
❑ 150 Charlie Moore .10 .04
❑ 151 Ben Oglivie .20 .08
❑ 152 Ted Simmons .20 .08
❑ 153 Jim Slaton .10 .04
❑ 154 Gorman Thomas .20 .08
❑ 155 Robin Yount 1.25 .50
❑ 156 Pete Vuckovich .10 .04
(Should precede Yount
in the team order)
❑ 157 Benny Ayala .10 .04
❑ 158 Mark Belanger .10 .04
❑ 159 Al Bumbry .10 .04
❑ 160 Terry Crowley .10 .04
❑ 161 Rich Dauer .10 .04
❑ 162 Doug DeCinces .10 .04
❑ 163 Rick Dempsey .10 .04
❑ 164 Jim Dwyer .10 .04
❑ 165 Mike Flanagan .10 .04
❑ 166 Dave Ford .10 .04
❑ 167 Dan Graham .10 .04
❑ 168 Wayne Krenchicki .10 .04
❑ 169 John Lowenstein .10 .04
❑ 170 Dennis Martinez .20 .08
❑ 171 Tippy Martinez .10 .04
❑ 172 Scott McGregor .10 .04
❑ 173 Jose Morales .10 .04
❑ 174 Eddie Murray .75 .30
❑ 175 Jim Palmer .20 .08
❑ 176 Cal Ripken RC 40.00 16.00
Fleer Ripken cards from 1982
through 1993 erroneously have 22
games played in 1981;not 23.
❑ 177 Gary Roenicke .10 .04
❑ 178 Lenn Sakata .10 .04
❑ 179 Ken Singleton .20 .08
❑ 180 Sammy Stewart .10 .04
❑ 181 Tim Stoddard .10 .04
❑ 182 Steve Stone .10 .04
❑ 183 Stan Bahnsen .10 .04
❑ 184 Ray Burris .10 .04
❑ 185 Gary Carter .20 .08
❑ 186 Warren Cromartie .10 .04
❑ 187 Andre Dawson .20 .08
❑ 188 Terry Francona RC 3.00 1.20
❑ 189 Woodie Fryman .10 .04
❑ 190 Bill Gullickson .10 .04
❑ 191 Grant Jackson .10 .04
❑ 192 Wallace Johnson .10 .04
❑ 193 Charlie Lea .10 .04
❑ 194 Bill Lee .20 .08
❑ 195 Jerry Manuel .10 .04
❑ 196 Brad Mills .10 .04
❑ 197 John Milner .10 .04
❑ 198 Rowland Office .10 .04
❑ 199 David Palmer .10 .04
❑ 200 Larry Parrish .10 .04
❑ 201 Mike Phillips .10 .04
❑ 202 Tim Raines .40 .16
❑ 203 Bobby Ramos .10 .04
❑ 204 Jeff Reardon .20 .08
❑ 205 Steve Rogers .20 .08
❑ 206 Scott Sanderson .10 .04
❑ 207 Rodney Scott UER .40 .16
(Photo actually
Tim Raines)
❑ 208 Elias Sosa .10 .04
❑ 209 Chris Speier .10 .04
❑ 210 Tim Wallach RC 1.00 .40
❑ 211 Jerry White .10 .04
❑ 212 Alan Ashby .10 .04
❑ 213 Cesar Cedeno .20 .08
❑ 214 Jose Cruz .20 .08
❑ 215 Kiko Garcia .10 .04
❑ 216 Phil Garner .20 .08
❑ 217 Danny Heep .10 .04
❑ 218 Art Howe .10 .04
❑ 219 Bob Knepper .10 .04
❑ 220 Frank LaCorte .10 .04
❑ 221 Joe Niekro .10 .04
❑ 222 Joe Pittman .10 .04
❑ 223 Terry Puhl .10 .04
❑ 224 Luis Pujols .10 .04
❑ 225 Craig Reynolds .10 .04
❑ 226 J.R. Richard .20 .08
❑ 227 Dave Roberts .10 .04
❑ 228 Vern Ruhle .10 .04
❑ 229 Nolan Ryan 4.00 1.60
❑ 230 Joe Sambito .10 .04
❑ 231 Tony Scott .10 .04
❑ 232 Dave Smith .10 .04
❑ 233 Harry Spilman .10 .04
❑ 234 Don Sutton .20 .08
❑ 235 Dickie Thon .10 .04
❑ 236 Denny Walling .10 .04
❑ 237 Gary Woods .10 .04
❑ 238 Luis Aguayo .10 .04
❑ 239 Ramon Aviles .10 .04
❑ 240 Bob Boone .20 .08
❑ 241 Larry Bowa .20 .08
❑ 242 Warren Brusstar .10 .04
❑ 243 Steve Carlton .40 .16
❑ 244 Larry Christenson .10 .04
❑ 245 Dick Davis .10 .04
❑ 246 Greg Gross .10 .04
❑ 247 Sparky Lyle .20 .08
❑ 248 Garry Maddox .10 .04
❑ 249 Gary Matthews .20 .08
❑ 250 Bake McBride .20 .08
❑ 251 Tug McGraw .20 .08
❑ 252 Keith Moreland .10 .04
❑ 253 Dickie Noles .10 .04
❑ 254 Mike Proly .10 .04
❑ 255 Ron Reed .10 .04
❑ 256 Pete Rose 2.50 1.00
❑ 257 Dick Ruthven .10 .04
❑ 258 Mike Schmidt 2.00 .80
❑ 259 Lonnie Smith .10 .04
❑ 260 Manny Trillo .10 .04
❑ 261 Del Unser .10 .04
❑ 262 George Vukovich .10 .04
❑ 263 Tom Brookens .10 .04
❑ 264 George Cappuzzello .10 .04
❑ 265 Marty Castillo .10 .04
❑ 266 Al Cowens .10 .04
❑ 267 Kirk Gibson .75 .30
❑ 268 Richie Hebner .10 .04
❑ 269 Ron Jackson .10 .04
❑ 270 Lynn Jones .10 .04
❑ 271 Steve Kemp .10 .04
❑ 272 Rick Leach .10 .04
❑ 273 Aurelio Lopez .10 .04
❑ 274 Jack Morris .20 .08
❑ 275 Kevin Saucier .10 .04
❑ 276 Lance Parrish .20 .08
❑ 277 Rick Peters .10 .04
❑ 278 Dan Petry .10 .04
❑ 279 Dave Rozema .10 .04
❑ 280 Stan Papi .10 .04
❑ 281 Dan Schatzeder .10 .04
❑ 282 Champ Summers .10 .04
❑ 283 Alan Trammell .20 .08
❑ 284 Lou Whitaker .20 .08
❑ 285 Milt Wilcox .10 .04

❑ 286 John Wockenfuss .10 .04
❑ 287 Gary Allenson .10 .04
❑ 288 Tom Burgmeier .10 .04
❑ 289 Bill Campbell .10 .04
❑ 290 Mark Clear .10 .04
❑ 291 Steve Crawford .10 .04
❑ 292 Dennis Eckersley .40 .16
❑ 293 Dwight Evans .40 .16
❑ 294 Rich Gedman .50 .20
❑ 295 Garry Hancock .10 .04
❑ 296 Glenn Hoffman .10 .04
❑ 297 Bruce Hurst .10 .04
❑ 298 Carney Lansford .20 .08
❑ 299 Rick Miller .10 .04
❑ 300 Reid Nichols .10 .04
❑ 301 Bob Ojeda RC .50 .20
❑ 302 Tony Perez .40 .16
❑ 303 Chuck Rainey .10 .04
❑ 304 Jerry Remy .10 .04
❑ 305 Jim Rice .20 .08
❑ 306 Joe Rudi .20 .08
❑ 307 Bob Stanley .10 .04
❑ 308 Dave Stapleton .10 .04
❑ 309 Frank Tanana .20 .08
❑ 310 Mike Torrez .10 .04
❑ 311 John Tudor .20 .08
❑ 312 Carl Yastrzemski 1.25 .50
❑ 313 Buddy Bell .20 .08
❑ 314 Steve Comer .10 .04
❑ 315 Danny Darwin .10 .04
❑ 316 John Ellis .10 .04
❑ 317 John Grubb .10 .04
❑ 318 Rick Honeycutt .10 .04
❑ 319 Charlie Hough .20 .08
❑ 320 Ferguson Jenkins .20 .08
❑ 321 John Henry Johnson .10 .04
❑ 322 Jim Kern .10 .04
❑ 323 Jon Matlack .10 .04
❑ 324 Doc Medich .10 .04
❑ 325 Mario Mendoza .10 .04
❑ 326 Al Oliver .20 .08
❑ 327 Pat Putnam .10 .04
❑ 328 Mickey Rivers .10 .04
❑ 329 Leon Roberts .10 .04
❑ 330 Billy Sample .10 .04
❑ 331 Bill Stein .10 .04
❑ 332 Jim Sundberg .20 .08
❑ 333 Mark Wagner .10 .04
❑ 334 Bump Wills .10 .04
❑ 335 Bill Almon .10 .04
❑ 336 Harold Baines .20 .08
❑ 337 Ross Baumgarten .10 .04
❑ 338 Tony Bernazard .10 .04
❑ 339 Britt Burns .10 .04
❑ 340 Richard Dotson .10 .04
❑ 341 Jim Essian .10 .04
❑ 342 Ed Farmer .10 .04
❑ 343 Carlton Fisk .40 .16
❑ 344 Kevin Hickey RC .15 .06
❑ 345 LaMarr Hoyt .10 .04
❑ 346 Lamar Johnson .10 .04
❑ 347 Jerry Koosman .20 .08
❑ 348 Rusty Kuntz .10 .04
❑ 349 Dennis Lamp .10 .04
❑ 350 Ron LeFlore .20 .08
❑ 351 Chet Lemon .20 .08
❑ 352 Greg Luzinski .20 .08
❑ 353 Bob Molinaro .10 .04
❑ 354 Jim Morrison .10 .04
❑ 355 Wayne Nordhagen .10 .04
❑ 356 Greg Pryor .10 .04
❑ 357 Mike Squires .10 .04
❑ 358 Steve Trout .10 .04
❑ 359 Alan Bannister .10 .04
❑ 360 Len Barker .10 .04
❑ 361 Bert Blyleven .20 .08
❑ 362 Joe Charboneau .20 .08
❑ 363 John Denny .10 .04
❑ 364 Bo Diaz .10 .04
❑ 365 Miguel Dilone .10 .04
❑ 366 Jerry Dybzinski .10 .04
❑ 367 Wayne Garland .10 .04
❑ 368 Mike Hargrove .10 .04
❑ 369 Toby Harrah .20 .08
❑ 370 Ron Hassey .10 .04
❑ 371 Von Hayes RC .50 .20
❑ 372 Pat Kelly .10 .04
❑ 373 Duane Kuiper .10 .04
❑ 374 Rick Manning .10 .04
❑ 375 Sid Monge .10 .04
❑ 376 Jorge Orta .10 .04
❑ 377 Dave Rosello .10 .04
❑ 378 Dan Spillner .10 .04
❑ 379 Mike Stanton .10 .04
❑ 380 Andre Thornton .10 .04
❑ 381 Tom Veryzer .10 .04
❑ 382 Rick Waits .10 .04
❑ 383 Doyle Alexander .10 .04
❑ 384 Vida Blue .20 .08
❑ 385 Fred Breining .10 .04
❑ 386 Enos Cabell .10 .04
❑ 387 Jack Clark .20 .08
❑ 388 Darrell Evans .20 .08
❑ 389 Tom Griffin .10 .04
❑ 390 Larry Herndon .10 .04
❑ 391 Al Holland .10 .04
❑ 392 Gary Lavelle .10 .04
❑ 393 Johnnie LeMaster .10 .04
❑ 394 Jerry Martin .10 .04
❑ 395 Milt May .10 .04
❑ 396 Greg Minton .10 .04
❑ 397 Joe Morgan .20 .08
❑ 398 Joe Pettini .10 .04
❑ 399 Allen Ripley .10 .04
❑ 400 Billy Smith .10 .04
❑ 401 Rennie Stennett .10 .04
❑ 402 Ed Whitson .10 .04
❑ 403 Jim Wohlford .10 .04
❑ 404 Willie Aikens .10 .04
❑ 405 George Brett 2.00 .80
❑ 406 Ken Brett .10 .04
❑ 407 Dave Chalk .10 .04
❑ 408 Rich Gale .10 .04
❑ 409 Cesar Geronimo .10 .04
❑ 410 Larry Gura .10 .04
❑ 411 Clint Hurdle .10 .04
❑ 412 Mike Jones .10 .04
❑ 413 Dennis Leonard .10 .04
❑ 414 Renie Martin .10 .04
❑ 415 Lee May .10 .04
❑ 416 Hal McRae .20 .08
❑ 417 Darryl Motley .10 .04
❑ 418 Rance Mulliniks .10 .04
❑ 419 Amos Otis .20 .08
❑ 420 Ken Phelps .10 .04
❑ 421 Jamie Quirk .10 .04
❑ 422 Dan Quisenberry .10 .04
❑ 423 Paul Splittorff .10 .04
❑ 424 U.L. Washington .10 .04
❑ 425 John Wathan .10 .04
❑ 426 Frank White .20 .08
❑ 427 Willie Wilson .20 .08
❑ 428 Brian Asselstine .10 .04
❑ 429 Bruce Benedict .10 .04
❑ 430 Tommy Boggs .10 .04
❑ 431 Larry Bradford .10 .04
❑ 432 Rick Camp .10 .04
❑ 433 Chris Chambliss .20 .08
❑ 434 Gene Garber .10 .04
❑ 435 Preston Hanna .10 .04
❑ 436 Bob Horner .20 .08
❑ 437 Glenn Hubbard .10 .04
❑ 438A All Hrabosky ERR 8.00 3.20
(Height 5'1" All on reverse)
❑ 438B Al Hrabosky ERR .40 .16
(Height 5'1")
❑ 438C Al Hrabosky .20 .08
(Height 5'10")
❑ 439 Rufino Linares .10 .04
❑ 440 Rick Mahler .10 .04
❑ 441 Ed Miller .10 .04
❑ 442 John Montefusco .10 .04
❑ 443 Dale Murphy .40 .16
❑ 444 Phil Niekro .20 .08
❑ 445 Gaylord Perry .20 .08
❑ 446 Biff Pocoroba .10 .04
❑ 447 Rafael Ramirez .10 .04
❑ 448 Jerry Royster .10 .04
❑ 449 Claudell Washington .10 .04
❑ 450 Don Aase .10 .04
❑ 451 Don Baylor .20 .08
❑ 452 Juan Beniquez .10 .04
❑ 453 Rick Burleson .10 .04
❑ 454 Bert Campaneris .20 .08
❑ 455 Rod Carew .40 .16
❑ 456 Bob Clark .10 .04
❑ 457 Brian Downing .20 .08
❑ 458 Dan Ford .10 .04
❑ 459 Ken Forsch .10 .04
❑ 460A Dave Frost (5 mm space before ERA) .10 .04
❑ 460B Dave Frost .10 .04
(1 mm space)
❑ 461 Bobby Grich .20 .08
❑ 462 Larry Harlow .10 .04
❑ 463 John Harris .10 .04
❑ 464 Andy Hassler .10 .04
❑ 465 Butch Hobson .10 .04
❑ 466 Jesse Jefferson .10 .04
❑ 467 Bruce Kison .10 .04
❑ 468 Fred Lynn .20 .08
❑ 469 Angel Moreno .10 .04
❑ 470 Ed Ott .10 .04
❑ 471 Fred Patek .10 .04
❑ 472 Steve Renko .10 .04
❑ 473 Mike Witt .50 .20
❑ 474 Geoff Zahn .10 .04
❑ 475 Gary Alexander .10 .04
❑ 476 Dale Berra .10 .04
❑ 477 Kurt Bevacqua .10 .04
❑ 478 Jim Bibby .10 .04
❑ 479 John Candelaria .10 .04
❑ 480 Victor Cruz .10 .04
❑ 481 Mike Easler .10 .04
❑ 482 Tim Foli .10 .04
❑ 483 Lee Lacy .10 .04
❑ 484 Vance Law .10 .04
❑ 485 Bill Madlock .20 .08
❑ 486 Willie Montanez .10 .04
❑ 487 Omar Moreno .10 .04
❑ 488 Steve Nicosia .10 .04
❑ 489 Dave Parker .20 .08
❑ 490 Tony Pena .20 .08
❑ 491 Pascual Perez .10 .04
❑ 492 Johnny Ray RC .50 .20
❑ 493 Rick Rhoden .10 .04
❑ 494 Bill Robinson .10 .04
❑ 495 Don Robinson .10 .04
❑ 496 Enrique Romo .10 .04
❑ 497 Rod Scurry .10 .04
❑ 498 Eddie Solomon .10 .04
❑ 499 Willie Stargell .40 .16
❑ 500 Kent Tekulve .10 .04
❑ 501 Jason Thompson .10 .04
❑ 502 Glenn Abbott .10 .04
❑ 503 Jim Anderson .10 .04
❑ 504 Floyd Bannister .10 .04
❑ 505 Bruce Bochte .10 .04
❑ 506 Jeff Burroughs .10 .04
❑ 507 Bryan Clark RC .15 .06
❑ 508 Ken Clay .10 .04
❑ 509 Julio Cruz .10 .04
❑ 510 Dick Drago .10 .04
❑ 511 Gary Gray .10 .04
❑ 512 Dan Meyer .10 .04
❑ 513 Jerry Narron .10 .04
❑ 514 Tom Paciorek .10 .04
❑ 515 Casey Parsons .10 .04
❑ 516 Lenny Randle .10 .04
❑ 517 Shane Rawley .10 .04
❑ 518 Joe Simpson .10 .04
❑ 519 Richie Zisk .10 .04
❑ 520 Neil Allen .10 .04
❑ 521 Bob Bailor .10 .04
❑ 522 Hubie Brooks .10 .04
❑ 523 Mike Cubbage .10 .04
❑ 524 Pete Falcone .10 .04
❑ 525 Doug Flynn .10 .04
❑ 526 Tom Hausman .10 .04
❑ 527 Ron Hodges .10 .04
❑ 528 Randy Jones .10 .04
❑ 529 Mike Jorgensen .10 .04
❑ 530 Dave Kingman .20 .08
❑ 531 Ed Lynch .10 .04
❑ 532 Mike G. Marshall .10 .04
❑ 533 Lee Mazzilli .20 .08
❑ 534 Dyar Miller .10 .04

❑ 535 Mike Scott .20 .08
❑ 536 Rusty Staub .20 .08
❑ 537 John Stearns .10 .04
❑ 538 Craig Swan .10 .04
❑ 539 Frank Taveras .10 .04
❑ 540 Alex Trevino .10 .04
❑ 541 Ellis Valentine .10 .04
❑ 542 Mookie Wilson .20 .08
❑ 543 Joel Youngblood .10 .04
❑ 544 Pat Zachry .10 .04
❑ 545 Glenn Adams .10 .04
❑ 546 Fernando Arroyo .10 .04
❑ 547 John Verhoeven .10 .04
❑ 548 Sal Butera .10 .04
❑ 549 John Castino .10 .04
❑ 550 Don Cooper .10 .04
❑ 551 Doug Corbett .10 .04
❑ 552 Dave Engle .10 .04
❑ 553 Roger Erickson .10 .04
❑ 554 Danny Goodwin .10 .04
❑ 555A Darrell Jackson .40 .16
(Black cap)
❑ 555B Darrell Jackson .20 .08
(Red cap with T)
❑ 555C Darrell Jackson 3.00 1.20
(Red cap, no emblem)
❑ 556 Pete Mackanin .10 .04
❑ 557 Jack O'Connor .10 .04
❑ 558 Hosken Powell .10 .04
❑ 559 Pete Redfern .10 .04
❑ 560 Roy Smalley .10 .04
❑ 561 Chuck Baker UER .10 .04
(Shortshop on front)
❑ 562 Gary Ward .10 .04
❑ 563 Rob Wilfong .10 .04
❑ 564 Al Williams .10 .04
❑ 565 Butch Wynegar .10 .04
❑ 566 Randy Bass RC .50 .20
❑ 567 Juan Bonilla RC .15 .06
❑ 568 Danny Boone .10 .04
❑ 569 John Curtis .10 .04
❑ 570 Juan Eichelberger .10 .04
❑ 571 Barry Evans .10 .04
❑ 572 Tim Flannery .10 .04
❑ 573 Ruppert Jones .10 .04
❑ 574 Terry Kennedy .10 .04
❑ 575 Joe Lefebvre .10 .04
❑ 576A John Littlefield ERR 150.00 60.00
(Left handed;
reverse negative)
❑ 576B John Littlefield COR .20 .08
(Right handed)
❑ 577 Gary Lucas .10 .04
❑ 578 Steve Mura .10 .04
❑ 579 Broderick Perkins .10 .04
❑ 580 Gene Richards .10 .04
❑ 581 Luis Salazar .10 .04
❑ 582 Ozzie Smith 1.50 .60
❑ 583 John Urrea .10 .04
❑ 584 Chris Welsh .10 .04
❑ 585 Rick Wise .10 .04
❑ 586 Doug Bird .10 .04
❑ 587 Tim Blackwell .10 .04
❑ 588 Bobby Bonds .20 .08
❑ 589 Bill Buckner .20 .08
❑ 590 Bill Caudill .10 .04
❑ 591 Hector Cruz .10 .04
❑ 592 Jody Davis .10 .04
❑ 593 Ivan DeJesus .10 .04
❑ 594 Steve Dillard .10 .04
❑ 595 Leon Durham .10 .04
❑ 596 Rawly Eastwick .20 .08
❑ 597 Steve Henderson .10 .04
❑ 598 Mike Krukow .10 .04
❑ 599 Mike Lum .10 .04
❑ 600 Randy Martz .10 .04
❑ 601 Jerry Morales .10 .04
❑ 602 Ken Reitz .10 .04
❑ 603 Lee Smith RC ERR 2.00 .80
(Cubs logo reversed)
❑ 603B Lee Smith RC COR 6.00 2.40
❑ 604 Dick Tidrow .10 .04
❑ 605 Jim Tracy .20 .08
❑ 606 Mike Tyson .10 .04
❑ 607 Ty Waller .10 .04
❑ 608 Danny Ainge .20 .08
❑ 609 Jorge Bell RC 1.00 .40
❑ 610 Mark Bomback .10 .04
❑ 611 Barry Bonnell .10 .04
❑ 612 Jim Clancy .10 .04
❑ 613 Damaso Garcia .10 .04
❑ 614 Jerry Garvin .10 .04
❑ 615 Alfredo Griffin .10 .04
❑ 616 Garth Iorg .10 .04
❑ 617 Luis Leal .10 .04
❑ 618 Ken Macha .10 .04
❑ 619 John Mayberry .10 .04
❑ 620 Joey McLaughlin .10 .04
❑ 621 Lloyd Moseby .10 .04
❑ 622 Dave Stieb .20 .08
❑ 623 Jackson Todd .10 .04
❑ 624 Willie Upshaw .50 .20
❑ 625 Otto Velez .10 .04
❑ 626 Ernie Whitt .10 .04
❑ 627 Alvis Woods .10 .04
❑ 628 All Star Game .20 .08
Cleveland, Ohio
❑ 629 Frank White .20 .08
Bucky Dent
❑ 630 Dan Driessen .20 .08
Dave Concepcion
George Foster
❑ 631 Bruce Sutter .10 .04
Top NL Relief Pitcher
❑ 632 Steve Carlton .20 .08
Carlton Fisk
❑ 633 Carl Yastrzemski .75 .30
3000th Game
❑ 634 Johnny Bench .75 .30
Tom Seaver
❑ 635 Fernando Valenzuela .10 .04
Gary Carter
❑ 636A Fernando Valenzuela: .40 .16
NL SO King "he" NL
❑ 636B Fernando Valenzuela: .40 .16
NL SO King "the" NL
❑ 637 Mike Schmidt .75 .30
Home Run King
❑ 638 Gary Carter .10 .04
Dave Parker
❑ 639 Perfect Game UER .20 .08
Len Barker
Bo Diaz
(Catcher actually
Ron Hassey)
❑ 640 Pete Rose .75 .30
Pete Rose Jr.
❑ 641 Lonnie Smith .75 .30
Mike Schmidt
Steve Carlton
❑ 642 Fred Lynn .40 .16
Dwight Evans
❑ 643 Rickey Henderson 1.25 .50
Most Hits and Runs
❑ 644 Rollie Fingers .20 .08
Most Saves AL
❑ 645 Tom Seaver .20 .08
Most 1981 Wins
❑ 646 Yankee Powerhouse .20 .08
Reggie Jackson
Dave Winfield
(Comma on back
after outfielder)
❑ 646B Yankee Powerhouse .20 .08
Reggie Jackson
Dave Winfield
(No comma)
❑ 647 CL: Yankees/Dodgers .10 .04
❑ 648 CL: A's/Reds .10 .04
❑ 649 CL: Cards/Brewers .10 .04
❑ 650 CL: Expos/Orioles .10 .04
❑ 651 CL: Astros/Phillies .10 .04
❑ 652 CL: Tigers/Red Sox .10 .04
❑ 653 CL: Rangers/White Sox .10 .04
❑ 654 CL: Giants/Indians .10 .04
❑ 655 CL: Royals/Braves .10 .04
❑ 656 CL: Angels/Pirates .10 .04
❑ 657 CL: Mariners/Mets .10 .04
❑ 658 CL: Padres/Twins .10 .04
❑ 659 CL: Blue Jays/Cubs .10 .04
❑ 660 Specials Checklist .10 .04

1983 Fleer

	Nm-Mt	Ex-Mt
COMPLETE SET (660)	60.00	24.00

❑ 1 Joaquin Andujar .20 .08
❑ 2 Doug Bair .10 .04
❑ 3 Steve Braun .10 .04
❑ 4 Glenn Brummer .10 .04
❑ 5 Bob Forsch .10 .04
❑ 6 David Green RC .50 .20
❑ 7 George Hendrick .20 .08
❑ 8 Keith Hernandez .20 .08
❑ 9 Tom Herr .10 .04
❑ 10 Dane Iorg .10 .04
❑ 11 Jim Kaat .20 .08
❑ 12 Jeff Lahti .10 .04
❑ 13 Tito Landrum .10 .04
❑ 14 Dave LaPoint .10 .04
❑ 15 Willie McGee RC 1.50 .60
❑ 16 Steve Mura .10 .04
❑ 17 Ken Oberkfell .10 .04
❑ 18 Darrell Porter .10 .04
❑ 19 Mike Ramsey .10 .04
❑ 20 Gene Roof .10 .04
❑ 21 Lonnie Smith .10 .04
❑ 22 Ozzie Smith 1.25 .50
❑ 23 John Stuper .10 .04
❑ 24 Bruce Sutter .20 .08
❑ 25 Gene Tenace .20 .08
❑ 26 Jerry Augustine .10 .04
❑ 27 Dwight Bernard .10 .04
❑ 28 Mark Brouhard .10 .04
❑ 29 Mike Caldwell .10 .04
❑ 30 Cecil Cooper .20 .08
❑ 31 Jamie Easterly .10 .04
❑ 32 Marshall Edwards .10 .04
❑ 33 Rollie Fingers .20 .08
❑ 34 Jim Gantner .10 .04
❑ 35 Moose Haas .10 .04
❑ 36 Roy Howell .10 .04
❑ 37 Pete Ladd .10 .04
❑ 38 Bob McClure .10 .04
❑ 39 Doc Medich .10 .04
❑ 40 Paul Molitor .40 .16
❑ 41 Don Money .10 .04
❑ 42 Charlie Moore .10 .04
❑ 43 Ben Oglivie .20 .08
❑ 44 Ed Romero .10 .04
❑ 45 Ted Simmons .20 .08
❑ 46 Jim Slaton .10 .04
❑ 47 Don Sutton .20 .08
❑ 48 Gorman Thomas .20 .08
❑ 49 Pete Vuckovich .10 .04
❑ 50 Ned Yost .10 .04
❑ 51 Robin Yount 1.25 .50
❑ 52 Benny Ayala .10 .04
❑ 53 Bob Bonner .10 .04
❑ 54 Al Bumbry .10 .04
❑ 55 Terry Crowley .10 .04
❑ 56 Storm Davis RC .50 .20
❑ 57 Rich Dauer .10 .04
❑ 58 Rick Dempsey UER .10 .04
(Posing batting lefty)
❑ 59 Jim Dwyer .10 .04
❑ 60 Mike Flanagan .10 .04
❑ 61 Dan Ford .10 .04
❑ 62 Glenn Gulliver .10 .04
❑ 63 John Lowenstein .10 .04

❑ 64 Dennis Martinez .20 .08
❑ 65 Tippy Martinez .10 .04
❑ 66 Scott McGregor .10 .04
❑ 67 Eddie Murray .75 .30
❑ 68 Joe Nolan .10 .04
❑ 69 Jim Palmer .20 .08
❑ 70 Cal Ripken 6.00 2.40
❑ 71 Gary Roenicke .10 .04
❑ 72 Lenn Sakata .10 .04
❑ 73 Ken Singleton .20 .08
❑ 74 Sammy Stewart .10 .04
❑ 75 Tim Stoddard .10 .04
❑ 76 Don Aase .10 .04
❑ 77 Don Baylor .20 .08
❑ 78 Juan Beniquez .10 .04
❑ 79 Bob Boone .20 .08
❑ 80 Rick Burleson .10 .04
❑ 81 Rod Carew .40 .16
❑ 82 Bobby Clark .10 .04
❑ 83 Doug Corbett .10 .04
❑ 84 John Curtis .10 .04
❑ 85 Doug DeCinces .10 .04
❑ 86 Brian Downing .20 .08
❑ 87 Joe Ferguson .10 .04
❑ 88 Tim Foli .10 .04
❑ 89 Ken Forsch .10 .04
❑ 90 Dave Goltz .10 .04
❑ 91 Bobby Grich .20 .08
❑ 92 Andy Hassler .10 .04
❑ 93 Reggie Jackson .40 .16
❑ 94 Ron Jackson .10 .04
❑ 95 Tommy John .20 .08
❑ 96 Bruce Kison .10 .04
❑ 97 Fred Lynn .20 .08
❑ 98 Ed Ott .10 .04
❑ 99 Steve Renko .10 .04
❑ 100 Luis Sanchez .10 .04
❑ 101 Rob Wilfong .10 .04
❑ 102 Mike Witt .10 .04
❑ 103 Geoff Zahn .10 .04
❑ 104 Willie Aikens .10 .04
❑ 105 Mike Armstrong .10 .04
❑ 106 Vida Blue .20 .08
❑ 107 Bud Black RC .50 .20
❑ 108 George Brett 2.00 .80
❑ 109 Bill Castro .10 .04
❑ 110 Onix Concepcion .10 .04
❑ 111 Dave Frost .10 .04
❑ 112 Cesar Geronimo .10 .04
❑ 113 Larry Gura .10 .04
❑ 114 Steve Hammond .10 .04
❑ 115 Don Hood .10 .04
❑ 116 Dennis Leonard .10 .04
❑ 117 Jerry Martin .10 .04
❑ 118 Lee May .10 .04
❑ 119 Hal McRae .20 .08
❑ 120 Amos Otis .20 .08
❑ 121 Greg Pryor .10 .04
❑ 122 Dan Quisenberry .10 .04
❑ 123 Don Slaught RC .50 .20
❑ 124 Paul Splittorff .10 .04
❑ 125 U.L. Washington .10 .04
❑ 126 John Wathan .10 .04
❑ 127 Frank White .20 .08
❑ 128 Willie Wilson .20 .08
❑ 129 Steve Bedrosian UER .10 .04
(Height 6'33")
❑ 130 Bruce Benedict .10 .04
❑ 131 Tommy Boggs .10 .04
❑ 132 Brett Butler .20 .08
❑ 133 Rick Camp .10 .04
❑ 134 Chris Chambliss .20 .08
❑ 135 Ken Dayley .10 .04
❑ 136 Gene Garber .10 .04
❑ 137 Terry Harper .10 .04
❑ 138 Bob Horner .20 .08
❑ 139 Glenn Hubbard .10 .04
❑ 140 Rufino Linares .10 .04
❑ 141 Rick Mahler .10 .04
❑ 142 Dale Murphy .40 .16
❑ 143 Phil Niekro .20 .08
❑ 144 Pascual Perez .10 .04
❑ 145 Biff Pocoroba .10 .04
❑ 146 Rafael Ramirez .10 .04
❑ 147 Jerry Royster .10 .04
❑ 148 Ken Smith .10 .04
❑ 149 Bob Walk .10 .04
❑ 150 Claudell Washington .10 .04
❑ 151 Bob Watson .10 .04
❑ 152 Larry Whisenton .10 .04
❑ 153 Porfirio Altamirano .10 .04
❑ 154 Marty Bystrom .10 .04
❑ 155 Steve Carlton .40 .16
❑ 156 Larry Christenson .10 .04
❑ 157 Ivan DeJesus .10 .04
❑ 158 John Denny .10 .04
❑ 159 Bob Dernier .10 .04
❑ 160 Bo Diaz .10 .04
❑ 161 Ed Farmer .10 .04
❑ 162 Greg Gross .10 .04
❑ 163 Mike Krukow .10 .04
❑ 164 Garry Maddox .10 .04
❑ 165 Gary Matthews .20 .08
❑ 166 Tug McGraw .20 .08
❑ 167 Bob Molinaro .10 .04
❑ 168 Sid Monge .10 .04
❑ 169 Ron Reed .10 .04
❑ 170 Bill Robinson .10 .04
❑ 171 Pete Rose 2.50 1.00
❑ 172 Dick Ruthven .10 .04
❑ 173 Mike Schmidt 2.00 .80
❑ 174 Manny Trillo .10 .04
❑ 175 Ozzie Virgil .10 .04
❑ 176 George Vukovich .10 .04
❑ 177 Gary Allenson .10 .04
❑ 178 Luis Aponte .10 .04
❑ 179 Wade Boggs RC 10.00 4.00
❑ 180 Tom Burgmeier .10 .04
❑ 181 Mark Clear .10 .04
❑ 182 Dennis Eckersley .40 .16
❑ 183 Dwight Evans .40 .16
❑ 184 Rich Gedman .10 .04
❑ 185 Glenn Hoffman .10 .04
❑ 186 Bruce Hurst .10 .04
❑ 187 Carney Lansford .20 .08
❑ 188 Rick Miller .10 .04
❑ 189 Reid Nichols .10 .04
❑ 190 Bob Ojeda .10 .04
❑ 191 Tony Perez .40 .16
❑ 192 Chuck Rainey .10 .04
❑ 193 Jerry Remy .10 .04
❑ 194 Jim Rice .20 .08
❑ 195 Bob Stanley .10 .04
❑ 196 Dave Stapleton .10 .04
❑ 197 Mike Torrez .10 .04
❑ 198 John Tudor .20 .08
❑ 199 Julio Valdez .10 .04
❑ 200 Carl Yastrzemski 1.25 .50
❑ 201 Dusty Baker .20 .08
❑ 202 Joe Beckwith .10 .04
❑ 203 Greg Brock .10 .04
❑ 204 Ron Cey .20 .08
❑ 205 Terry Forster .20 .08
❑ 206 Steve Garvey .20 .08
❑ 207 Pedro Guerrero .20 .08
❑ 208 Burt Hooton .10 .04
❑ 209 Steve Howe .10 .04
❑ 210 Ken Landreaux .10 .04
❑ 211 Mike Marshall .10 .04
❑ 212 Candy Maldonado RC .50 .20
❑ 213 Rick Monday .20 .08
❑ 214 Tom Niedenfuer .10 .04
❑ 215 Jorge Orta .10 .04
❑ 216 Jerry Reuss UER .10 .04
("Home:" omitted)
❑ 217 Ron Roenicke .10 .04
❑ 218 Vicente Romo .10 .04
❑ 219 Bill Russell .20 .08
❑ 220 Steve Sax .20 .08
❑ 221 Mike Scioscia .20 .08
❑ 222 Dave Stewart .20 .08
❑ 223 Derrel Thomas .10 .04
❑ 224 Fernando Valenzuela .20 .08
❑ 225 Bob Welch .20 .08
❑ 226 Ricky Wright .10 .04
❑ 227 Steve Yeager .20 .08
❑ 228 Bill Almon .10 .04
❑ 229 Harold Baines .20 .08
❑ 230 Salome Barojas .10 .04
❑ 231 Tony Bernazard .10 .04
❑ 232 Britt Burns .10 .04
❑ 233 Richard Dotson .10 .04
❑ 234 Ernesto Escarrega .10 .04
❑ 235 Carlton Fisk .40 .16
❑ 236 Jerry Hairston .10 .04
❑ 237 Kevin Hickey .10 .04
❑ 238 LaMarr Hoyt .10 .04
❑ 239 Steve Kemp .10 .04
❑ 240 Jim Kern .10 .04
❑ 241 Ron Kittle RC 1.00 .40
❑ 242 Jerry Koosman .20 .08
❑ 243 Dennis Lamp .10 .04
❑ 244 Rudy Law .10 .04
❑ 245 Vance Law .10 .04
❑ 246 Ron LeFlore .20 .08
❑ 247 Greg Luzinski .20 .08
❑ 248 Tom Paciorek .10 .04
❑ 249 Aurelio Rodriguez .10 .04
❑ 250 Mike Squires .10 .04
❑ 251 Steve Trout .10 .04
❑ 252 Jim Barr .10 .04
❑ 253 Dave Bergman .10 .04
❑ 254 Fred Breining .10 .04
❑ 255 Bob Brenly .10 .04
❑ 256 Jack Clark .20 .08
❑ 257 Chili Davis .20 .08
❑ 258 Darrell Evans .20 .08
❑ 259 Alan Fowlkes .10 .04
❑ 260 Rich Gale .10 .04
❑ 261 Atlee Hammaker .10 .04
❑ 262 Al Holland .10 .04
❑ 263 Duane Kuiper .10 .04
❑ 264 Bill Laskey .10 .04
❑ 265 Gary Lavelle .10 .04
❑ 266 Johnnie LeMaster .10 .04
❑ 267 Renie Martin .10 .04
❑ 268 Milt May .10 .04
❑ 269 Greg Minton .10 .04
❑ 270 Joe Morgan .20 .08
❑ 271 Tom O'Malley .10 .04
❑ 272 Reggie Smith .20 .08
❑ 273 Guy Sularz .10 .04
❑ 274 Champ Summers .10 .04
❑ 275 Max Venable .10 .04
❑ 276 Jim Wohlford .10 .04
❑ 277 Ray Burris .10 .04
❑ 278 Gary Carter .20 .08
❑ 279 Warren Cromartie .10 .04
❑ 280 Andre Dawson .20 .08
❑ 281 Terry Francona .20 .08
❑ 282 Doug Flynn .10 .04
❑ 283 Woodie Fryman .10 .04
❑ 284 Bill Gullickson .10 .04
❑ 285 Wallace Johnson .10 .04
❑ 286 Charlie Lea .10 .04
❑ 287 Randy Lerch .10 .04
❑ 288 Brad Mills .10 .04
❑ 289 Dan Norman .10 .04
❑ 290 Al Oliver .20 .08
❑ 291 David Palmer .10 .04
❑ 292 Tim Raines .20 .08
❑ 293 Jeff Reardon .20 .08
❑ 294 Steve Rogers .20 .08
❑ 295 Scott Sanderson .10 .04
❑ 296 Dan Schatzeder .10 .04
❑ 297 Bryn Smith .10 .04
❑ 298 Chris Speier .10 .04
❑ 299 Tim Wallach .20 .08
❑ 300 Jerry White .10 .04
❑ 301 Joel Youngblood .10 .04
❑ 302 Ross Baumgarten .10 .04
❑ 303 Dale Berra .10 .04
❑ 304 John Candelaria .10 .04
❑ 305 Dick Davis .10 .04
❑ 306 Mike Easler .10 .04
❑ 307 Richie Hebner .10 .04
❑ 308 Lee Lacy .10 .04
❑ 309 Bill Madlock .20 .08
❑ 310 Larry McWilliams .10 .04
❑ 311 John Milner .10 .04
❑ 312 Omar Moreno .10 .04
❑ 313 Jim Morrison .10 .04
❑ 314 Steve Nicosia .10 .04
❑ 315 Dave Parker .20 .08
❑ 316 Tony Pena .10 .04
❑ 317 Johnny Ray .10 .04
❑ 318 Rick Rhoden .10 .04
❑ 319 Don Robinson .10 .04

❑ 320 Enrique Romo .10 .04
❑ 321 Manny Sarmiento .10 .04
❑ 322 Rod Scurry .10 .04
❑ 323 Jimmy Smith .10 .04
❑ 324 Willie Stargell .40 .16
❑ 325 Jason Thompson .10 .04
❑ 326 Kent Tekulve .10 .04
❑ 327A Tom Brookens .10 .04
(Short .375" brown box shaded in on card back)
❑ 327B Tom Brookens .10 .04
(Longer 1.25" brown box shaded in on card back)
❑ 328 Enos Cabell .10 .04
❑ 329 Kirk Gibson .40 .16
❑ 330 Larry Herndon .10 .04
❑ 331 Mike Ivie .10 .04
❑ 332 Howard Johnson RC 1.00 .40
❑ 333 Lynn Jones .10 .04
❑ 334 Rick Leach .10 .04
❑ 335 Chet Lemon .20 .08
❑ 336 Jack Morris .20 .08
❑ 337 Lance Parrish .20 .08
❑ 338 Larry Pashnick .10 .04
❑ 339 Dan Petry .10 .04
❑ 340 Dave Rozema .10 .04
❑ 341 Dave Rucker .10 .04
❑ 342 Elias Sosa .10 .04
❑ 343 Dave Tobik .10 .04
❑ 344 Alan Trammell .20 .08
❑ 345 Jerry Turner .10 .04
❑ 346 Jerry Ujdur .10 .04
❑ 347 Pat Underwood .10 .04
❑ 348 Lou Whitaker .20 .08
❑ 349 Milt Wilcox .10 .04
❑ 350 Glenn Wilson .50 .20
❑ 351 John Wockenfuss .10 .04
❑ 352 Kurt Bevacqua .10 .04
❑ 353 Juan Bonilla .10 .04
❑ 354 Floyd Chiffer .10 .04
❑ 355 Luis DeLeon .10 .04
❑ 356 Dave Dravecky RC 1.00 .40
❑ 357 Dave Edwards .10 .04
❑ 358 Juan Eichelberger .10 .04
❑ 359 Tim Flannery .10 .04
❑ 360 Tony Gwynn RC 15.00 6.00
❑ 361 Ruppert Jones .10 .04
❑ 362 Terry Kennedy .10 .04
❑ 363 Joe Lefebvre .10 .04
❑ 364 Sixto Lezcano .10 .04
❑ 365 Tim Lollar .10 .04
❑ 366 Gary Lucas .10 .04
❑ 367 John Montefusco .10 .04
❑ 368 Broderick Perkins .10 .04
❑ 369 Joe Pittman .10 .04
❑ 370 Gene Richards .10 .04
❑ 371 Luis Salazar .10 .04
❑ 372 Eric Show RC .50 .20
❑ 373 Garry Templeton .20 .08
❑ 374 Chris Welsh .10 .04
❑ 375 Alan Wiggins .10 .04
❑ 376 Rick Cerone .10 .04
❑ 377 Dave Collins .10 .04
❑ 378 Roger Erickson .10 .04
❑ 379 George Frazier .10 .04
❑ 380 Oscar Gamble .10 .04
❑ 381 Rich Gossage .20 .08
❑ 382 Ken Griffey .20 .08
❑ 383 Ron Guidry .20 .08
❑ 384 Dave LaRoche .10 .04
❑ 385 Rudy May .10 .04
❑ 386 John Mayberry .10 .04
❑ 387 Lee Mazzilli .20 .08
❑ 388 Mike Morgan .10 .04
❑ 389 Jerry Mumphrey .10 .04
❑ 390 Bobby Murcer .20 .08
❑ 391 Graig Nettles .20 .08
❑ 392 Lou Piniella .20 .08
❑ 393 Willie Randolph .20 .08
❑ 394 Shane Rawley .10 .04
❑ 395 Dave Righetti .20 .08
❑ 396 Andre Robertson .10 .04
❑ 397 Roy Smalley .10 .04
❑ 398 Dave Winfield .20 .08
❑ 399 Butch Wynegar .10 .04
❑ 400 Chris Bando .10 .04
❑ 401 Alan Bannister .10 .04
❑ 402 Len Barker .10 .04
❑ 403 Tom Brennan .10 .04
❑ 404 Carmelo Castillo .10 .04
❑ 405 Miguel Dilone .10 .04
❑ 406 Jerry Dybzinski .10 .04
❑ 407 Mike Fischlin .10 .04
❑ 408 Ed Glynn UER .10 .04
(Photo actually Bud Anderson)
❑ 409 Mike Hargrove .10 .04
❑ 410 Toby Harrah .20 .08
❑ 411 Ron Hassey .10 .04
❑ 412 Von Hayes .10 .04
❑ 413 Rick Manning .10 .04
❑ 414 Bake McBride .20 .08
❑ 415 Larry Milbourne .10 .04
❑ 416 Bill Nahorodny .10 .04
❑ 417 Jack Perconte .10 .04
❑ 418 Lary Sorensen .10 .04
❑ 419 Dan Spillner .10 .04
❑ 420 Rick Sutcliffe .20 .08
❑ 421 Andre Thornton .10 .04
❑ 422 Rick Waits .10 .04
❑ 423 Eddie Whitson .10 .04
❑ 424 Jesse Barfield .20 .08
❑ 425 Barry Bonnell .10 .04
❑ 426 Jim Clancy .10 .04
❑ 427 Damaso Garcia .10 .04
❑ 428 Jerry Garvin .10 .04
❑ 429 Alfredo Griffin .10 .04
❑ 430 Garth Iorg .10 .04
❑ 431 Roy Lee Jackson .10 .04
❑ 432 Luis Leal .10 .04
❑ 433 Buck Martinez .10 .04
❑ 434 Joey McLaughlin .10 .04
❑ 435 Lloyd Moseby .10 .04
❑ 436 Rance Mulliniks .10 .04
❑ 437 Dale Murray .10 .04
❑ 438 Wayne Nordhagen .10 .04
❑ 439 Geno Petralli .50 .20
❑ 440 Hosken Powell .10 .04
❑ 441 Dave Stieb .20 .08
❑ 442 Willie Upshaw .10 .04
❑ 443 Ernie Whitt .10 .04
❑ 444 Alvis Woods .10 .04
❑ 445 Alan Ashby .10 .04
❑ 446 Jose Cruz .20 .08
❑ 447 Kiko Garcia .10 .04
❑ 448 Phil Garner .20 .08
❑ 449 Danny Heep .10 .04
❑ 450 Art Howe .10 .04
❑ 451 Bob Knepper .10 .04
❑ 452 Alan Knicely .10 .04
❑ 453 Ray Knight .20 .08
❑ 454 Frank LaCorte .10 .04
❑ 455 Mike LaCoss .10 .04
❑ 456 Randy Moffitt .10 .04
❑ 457 Joe Niekro .10 .04
❑ 458 Terry Puhl .10 .04
❑ 459 Luis Pujols .10 .04
❑ 460 Craig Reynolds .10 .04
❑ 461 Bert Roberge .10 .04
❑ 462 Vern Ruhle .10 .04
❑ 463 Nolan Ryan 4.00 1.60
❑ 464 Joe Sambito .10 .04
❑ 465 Tony Scott .10 .04
❑ 466 Dave Smith .10 .04
❑ 467 Harry Spilman .10 .04
❑ 468 Dickie Thon .10 .04
❑ 469 Denny Walling .10 .04
❑ 470 Larry Andersen .10 .04
❑ 471 Floyd Bannister .10 .04
❑ 472 Jim Beattie .10 .04
❑ 473 Bruce Bochte .10 .04
❑ 474 Manny Castillo .10 .04
❑ 475 Bill Caudill .10 .04
❑ 476 Bryan Clark .10 .04
❑ 477 Al Cowens .10 .04
❑ 478 Julio Cruz .10 .04
❑ 479 Todd Cruz .10 .04
❑ 480 Gary Gray .10 .04
❑ 481 Dave Henderson .10 .04
❑ 482 Mike Moore RC .50 .20
❑ 483 Gaylord Perry .20 .08
❑ 484 Dave Revering .10 .04
❑ 485 Joe Simpson .10 .04
❑ 486 Mike Stanton .10 .04
❑ 487 Rick Sweet .10 .04
❑ 488 Ed VandeBerg .10 .04
❑ 489 Richie Zisk .10 .04
❑ 490 Doug Bird .10 .04
❑ 491 Larry Bowa .20 .08
❑ 492 Bill Buckner .20 .08
❑ 493 Bill Campbell .10 .04
❑ 494 Jody Davis .10 .04
❑ 495 Leon Durham .10 .04
❑ 496 Steve Henderson .10 .04
❑ 497 Willie Hernandez .10 .04
❑ 498 Ferguson Jenkins .20 .08
❑ 499 Jay Johnstone .10 .04
❑ 500 Junior Kennedy .10 .04
❑ 501 Randy Martz .10 .04
❑ 502 Jerry Morales .10 .04
❑ 503 Keith Moreland .10 .04
❑ 504 Dickie Noles .10 .04
❑ 505 Mike Proly .10 .04
❑ 506 Allen Ripley .10 .04
❑ 507 R.Sandberg RC UER 10.00 4.00
Should say High School in Spokane, Washington
❑ 508 Lee Smith .40 .16
❑ 509 Pat Tabler .10 .04
❑ 510 Dick Tidrow .10 .04
❑ 511 Bump Wills .10 .04
❑ 512 Gary Woods .10 .04
❑ 513 Tony Armas .20 .08
❑ 514 Dave Beard .10 .04
❑ 515 Jeff Burroughs .10 .04
❑ 516 John D'Acquisto .10 .04
❑ 517 Wayne Gross .10 .04
❑ 518 Mike Heath .10 .04
❑ 519 R.Henderson UER 1.50 .60
Brock record listed as 120 steals
❑ 520 Cliff Johnson .10 .04
❑ 521 Matt Keough .10 .04
❑ 522 Brian Kingman .10 .04
❑ 523 Rick Langford .10 .04
❑ 524 Dave Lopes .20 .08
❑ 525 Steve McCatty .10 .04
❑ 526 Dave McKay .10 .04
❑ 527 Dan Meyer .10 .04
❑ 528 Dwayne Murphy .10 .04
❑ 529 Jeff Newman .10 .04
❑ 530 Mike Norris .10 .04
❑ 531 Bob Owchinko .10 .04
❑ 532 Joe Rudi .20 .08
❑ 533 Jimmy Sexton .10 .04
❑ 534 Fred Stanley .10 .04
❑ 535 Tom Underwood .10 .04
❑ 536 Neil Allen .10 .04
❑ 537 Wally Backman .10 .04
❑ 538 Bob Bailor .10 .04
❑ 539 Hubie Brooks .10 .04
❑ 540 Carlos Diaz RC .25 .10
❑ 541 Pete Falcone .10 .04
❑ 542 George Foster .20 .08
❑ 543 Ron Gardenhire .10 .04
❑ 544 Brian Giles .10 .04
❑ 545 Ron Hodges .10 .04
❑ 546 Randy Jones .10 .04
❑ 547 Mike Jorgensen .10 .04
❑ 548 Dave Kingman .20 .08
❑ 549 Ed Lynch .10 .04
❑ 550 Jesse Orosco .10 .04
❑ 551 Rick Ownbey .10 .04
❑ 552 Charlie Puleo .10 .04
❑ 553 Gary Rajsich .10 .04
❑ 554 Mike Scott .20 .08
❑ 555 Rusty Staub .20 .08
❑ 556 John Stearns .10 .04
❑ 557 Craig Swan .10 .04
❑ 558 Ellis Valentine .10 .04
❑ 559 Tom Veryzer .10 .04
❑ 560 Mookie Wilson .20 .08
❑ 561 Pat Zachry .10 .04
❑ 562 Buddy Bell .20 .08
❑ 563 John Butcher .10 .04
❑ 564 Steve Comer .10 .04
❑ 565 Danny Darwin .10 .04
❑ 566 Bucky Dent .20 .08

- ❑ 567 John Grubb .10 .04
- ❑ 568 Rick Honeycutt .10 .04
- ❑ 569 Dave Hostetler .10 .04
- ❑ 570 Charlie Hough .20 .08
- ❑ 571 Lamar Johnson .10 .04
- ❑ 572 Jon Matlack .10 .04
- ❑ 573 Paul Mirabella .10 .04
- ❑ 574 Larry Parrish .10 .04
- ❑ 575 Mike Richardt .10 .04
- ❑ 576 Mickey Rivers .10 .04
- ❑ 577 Billy Sample .10 .04
- ❑ 578 Dave Schmidt .10 .04
- ❑ 579 Bill Stein .10 .04
- ❑ 580 Jim Sundberg .20 .08
- ❑ 581 Frank Tanana .20 .08
- ❑ 582 Mark Wagner .10 .04
- ❑ 583 George Wright RC .50 .20
- ❑ 584 Johnny Bench .75 .30
- ❑ 585 Bruce Berenyi .10 .04
- ❑ 586 Larry Biittner .10 .04
- ❑ 587 Cesar Cedeno .20 .08
- ❑ 588 Dave Concepcion .20 .08
- ❑ 589 Dan Driessen .10 .04
- ❑ 590 Greg Harris .10 .04
- ❑ 591 Ben Hayes .10 .04
- ❑ 592 Paul Householder .10 .04
- ❑ 593 Tom Hume .10 .04
- ❑ 594 Wayne Krenchicki .10 .04
- ❑ 595 Rafael Landestoy .10 .04
- ❑ 596 Charlie Leibrandt .10 .04
- ❑ 597 Eddie Milner .10 .04
- ❑ 598 Ron Oester .10 .04
- ❑ 599 Frank Pastore .10 .04
- ❑ 600 Joe Price .10 .04
- ❑ 601 Tom Seaver .75 .30
- ❑ 602 Bob Shirley .10 .04
- ❑ 603 Mario Soto .20 .08
- ❑ 604 Alex Trevino .10 .04
- ❑ 605 Mike Vail .10 .04
- ❑ 606 Duane Walker .10 .04
- ❑ 607 Tom Brunansky .20 .08
- ❑ 608 Bobby Castillo .10 .04
- ❑ 609 John Castino .10 .04
- ❑ 610 Ron Davis .10 .04
- ❑ 611 Lenny Faedo .10 .04
- ❑ 612 Terry Felton .10 .04
- ❑ 613 Gary Gaetti RC 1.00 .40
- ❑ 614 Mickey Hatcher .10 .04
- ❑ 615 Brad Havens .10 .04
- ❑ 616 Kent Hrbek .20 .08
- ❑ 617 Randy Johnson .10 .04
- ❑ 618 Tim Laudner .10 .04
- ❑ 619 Jeff Little .10 .04
- ❑ 620 Bobby Mitchell .10 .04
- ❑ 621 Jack O'Connor .10 .04
- ❑ 622 John Pacella .10 .04
- ❑ 623 Pete Redfern .10 .04
- ❑ 624 Jesus Vega .10 .04
- ❑ 625 Frank Viola RC 1.50 .60
- ❑ 626 Ron Washington .10 .04
- ❑ 627 Gary Ward .10 .04
- ❑ 628 Al Williams .10 .04
- ❑ 629 Carl Yastrzemski .75 .30
  Dennis Eckersley
  Mark Clear
- ❑ 630 Gaylord Perry .10 .04
  Terry Bulling 5/6/82
- ❑ 631 Dave Concepcion .20 .08
  Manny Trillo
- ❑ 632 Robin Yount .75 .30
  Buddy Bell
- ❑ 633 Dave Winfield .10 .04
  Kent Hrbek
- ❑ 634 Willie Stargell .75 .30
  Pete Rose
- ❑ 635 Toby Harrah .20 .08
  Andre Thornton
- ❑ 636 Ozzie Smith .75 .30
  Lonnie Smith
- ❑ 637 Bo Diaz .10 .04
  Gary Carter
- ❑ 638 Carlton Fisk .20 .08
  Gary Carter
- ❑ 639 Rickey Henderson IA .75 .30
- ❑ 640 Ben Oglivie .40 .16
  Reggie Jackson
- ❑ 641 Joel Youngblood .10 .04
  August 4, 1982
- ❑ 642 Ron Hassey .20 .08
  Len Barker
- ❑ 643 Black and Blue .20 .08
  Vida Blue
- ❑ 644 Black and Blue .10 .04
  Bud Black
- ❑ 645 Reggie Jackson Power .20 .08
- ❑ 646 Rickey Henderson Speed .75 .30
- ❑ 647 CL: Cards/Brewers .10 .04
- ❑ 648 CL: Orioles/Angels .10 .04
- ❑ 649 CL: Royals/Braves .10 .04
- ❑ 650 CL: Phillies/Red Sox .10 .04
- ❑ 651 CL: Dodgers/White Sox .10 .04
- ❑ 652 CL: Giants/Expos .10 .04
- ❑ 653 CL: Pirates/Tigers .10 .04
- ❑ 654 CL: Padres/Yankees .10 .04
- ❑ 655 CL: Indians/Blue Jays .10 .04
- ❑ 656 CL: Astros/Mariners .10 .04
- ❑ 657 CL: Cubs/A's .10 .04
- ❑ 658 CL: Mets/Rangers .10 .04
- ❑ 659 CL: Reds/Twins .10 .04
- ❑ 660 CL: Specials/Teams .10 .04

1984 Fleer

	Nm-Mt	Ex-Mt
COMPLETE SET (660)	50.00	20.00

- ❑ 1 Mike Boddicker .15 .06
- ❑ 2 Al Bumbry .15 .06
- ❑ 3 Todd Cruz .15 .06
- ❑ 4 Rich Dauer .15 .06
- ❑ 5 Storm Davis .15 .06
- ❑ 6 Rick Dempsey .15 .06
- ❑ 7 Jim Dwyer .15 .06
- ❑ 8 Mike Flanagan .15 .06
- ❑ 9 Dan Ford .15 .06
- ❑ 10 John Lowenstein .15 .06
- ❑ 11 Dennis Martinez .40 .16
- ❑ 12 Tippy Martinez .15 .06
- ❑ 13 Scott McGregor .15 .06
- ❑ 14 Eddie Murray 1.50 .60
- ❑ 15 Joe Nolan .15 .06
- ❑ 16 Jim Palmer .40 .16
- ❑ 17 Cal Ripken 10.00 4.00
- ❑ 18 Gary Roenicke .15 .06
- ❑ 19 Lenn Sakata .15 .06
- ❑ 20 John Shelby .15 .06
- ❑ 21 Ken Singleton .40 .16
- ❑ 22 Sammy Stewart .15 .06
- ❑ 23 Tim Stoddard .15 .06
- ❑ 24 Marty Bystrom .15 .06
- ❑ 25 Steve Carlton .75 .30
- ❑ 26 Ivan DeJesus .15 .06
- ❑ 27 John Denny .15 .06
- ❑ 28 Bob Dernier .15 .06
- ❑ 29 Bo Diaz .15 .06
- ❑ 30 Kiko Garcia .15 .06
- ❑ 31 Greg Gross .15 .06
- ❑ 32 Kevin Gross RC .50 .20
- ❑ 33 Von Hayes .15 .06
- ❑ 34 Willie Hernandez .15 .06
- ❑ 35 Al Holland .15 .06
- ❑ 36 Charles Hudson .15 .06
- ❑ 37 Joe Lefebvre .15 .06
- ❑ 38 Sixto Lezcano .15 .06
- ❑ 39 Garry Maddox .15 .06
- ❑ 40 Gary Matthews .40 .16
- ❑ 41 Len Matuszek .15 .06
- ❑ 42 Tug McGraw .40 .16
- ❑ 43 Joe Morgan .40 .16
- ❑ 44 Tony Perez .75 .30
- ❑ 45 Ron Reed .15 .06
- ❑ 46 Pete Rose 5.00 2.00
- ❑ 47 Juan Samuel RC 1.00 .40
- ❑ 48 Mike Schmidt 4.00 1.60
- ❑ 49 Ozzie Virgil .15 .06
- ❑ 50 Juan Agosto .15 .06
- ❑ 51 Harold Baines .40 .16
- ❑ 52 Floyd Bannister .15 .06
- ❑ 53 Salome Barojas .15 .06
- ❑ 54 Britt Burns .15 .06
- ❑ 55 Julio Cruz .15 .06
- ❑ 56 Richard Dotson .15 .06
- ❑ 57 Jerry Dybzinski .15 .06
- ❑ 58 Carlton Fisk .75 .30
- ❑ 59 Scott Fletcher .15 .06
- ❑ 60 Jerry Hairston .15 .06
- ❑ 61 Kevin Hickey .15 .06
- ❑ 62 Marc Hill .15 .06
- ❑ 63 LaMarr Hoyt .15 .06
- ❑ 64 Ron Kittle .15 .06
- ❑ 65 Jerry Koosman .40 .16
- ❑ 66 Dennis Lamp .15 .06
- ❑ 67 Rudy Law .15 .06
- ❑ 68 Vance Law .15 .06
- ❑ 69 Greg Luzinski .40 .16
- ❑ 70 Tom Paciorek .15 .06
- ❑ 71 Mike Squires .15 .06
- ❑ 72 Dick Tidrow .15 .06
- ❑ 73 Greg Walker .50 .20
- ❑ 74 Glenn Abbott .15 .06
- ❑ 75 Howard Bailey .15 .06
- ❑ 76 Doug Bair .15 .06
- ❑ 77 Juan Berenguer .15 .06
- ❑ 78 Tom Brookens .40 .16
- ❑ 79 Enos Cabell .15 .06
- ❑ 80 Kirk Gibson 1.50 .60
- ❑ 81 John Grubb .15 .06
- ❑ 82 Larry Herndon .40 .16
- ❑ 83 Wayne Krenchicki .15 .06
- ❑ 84 Rick Leach .15 .06
- ❑ 85 Chet Lemon .40 .16
- ❑ 86 Aurelio Lopez .40 .16
- ❑ 87 Jack Morris .40 .16
- ❑ 88 Lance Parrish .75 .30
- ❑ 89 Dan Petry .40 .16
- ❑ 90 Dave Rozema .15 .06
- ❑ 91 Alan Trammell .40 .16
- ❑ 92 Lou Whitaker .40 .16
- ❑ 93 Milt Wilcox .15 .06
- ❑ 94 Glenn Wilson .40 .16
- ❑ 95 John Wockenfuss .15 .06
- ❑ 96 Dusty Baker .40 .16
- ❑ 97 Joe Beckwith .15 .06
- ❑ 98 Greg Brock .15 .06
- ❑ 99 Jack Fimple .15 .06
- ❑ 100 Pedro Guerrero .40 .16
- ❑ 101 Rick Honeycutt .15 .06
- ❑ 102 Burt Hooton .15 .06
- ❑ 103 Steve Howe .15 .06
- ❑ 104 Ken Landreaux .15 .06
- ❑ 105 Mike Marshall .15 .06
- ❑ 106 Rick Monday .40 .16
- ❑ 107 Jose Morales .15 .06
- ❑ 108 Tom Niedenfuer .15 .06
- ❑ 109 Alejandro Pena RC* 1.00 .40
- ❑ 110 Jerry Reuss UER .15 .06
  ("Home:" omitted)
- ❑ 111 Bill Russell .40 .16
- ❑ 112 Steve Sax .15 .06
- ❑ 113 Mike Scioscia .40 .16
- ❑ 114 Derrel Thomas .15 .06
- ❑ 115 Fernando Valenzuela .40 .16
- ❑ 116 Bob Welch .40 .16
- ❑ 117 Steve Yeager .40 .16
- ❑ 118 Pat Zachry .15 .06
- ❑ 119 Don Baylor .40 .16
- ❑ 120 Bert Campaneris .40 .16
- ❑ 121 Rick Cerone .15 .06
- ❑ 122 Ray Fontenot .15 .06
- ❑ 123 George Frazier .15 .06
- ❑ 124 Oscar Gamble .15 .06

❑ 125 Rich Gossage .40 .16
❑ 126 Ken Griffey .40 .16
❑ 127 Ron Guidry .40 .16
❑ 128 Jay Howell .15 .06
❑ 129 Steve Kemp .15 .06
❑ 130 Matt Keough .15 .06
❑ 131 Don Mattingly RC 25.00 10.00
❑ 132 John Montefusco .15 .06
❑ 133 Omar Moreno .15 .06
❑ 134 Dale Murray .15 .06
❑ 135 Graig Nettles .40 .16
❑ 136 Lou Piniella .40 .16
❑ 137 Willie Randolph .40 .16
❑ 138 Shane Rawley .15 .06
❑ 139 Dave Righetti .40 .16
❑ 140 Andre Robertson .15 .06
❑ 141 Bob Shirley .15 .06
❑ 142 Roy Smalley .15 .06
❑ 143 Dave Winfield .40 .16
❑ 144 Butch Wynegar .15 .06
❑ 145 Jim Acker .15 .06
❑ 146 Doyle Alexander .15 .06
❑ 147 Jesse Barfield .40 .16
❑ 148 Jorge Bell .40 .16
❑ 149 Barry Bonnell .15 .06
❑ 150 Jim Clancy .15 .06
❑ 151 Dave Collins .15 .06
❑ 152 Tony Fernandez RC 1.00 .40
❑ 153 Damaso Garcia .15 .06
❑ 154 Dave Geisel .15 .06
❑ 155 Jim Gott .15 .06
❑ 156 Alfredo Griffin .15 .06
❑ 157 Garth Iorg .15 .06
❑ 158 Roy Lee Jackson .15 .06
❑ 159 Cliff Johnson .15 .06
❑ 160 Luis Leal .15 .06
❑ 161 Buck Martinez .15 .06
❑ 162 Joey McLaughlin .15 .06
❑ 163 Randy Moffitt .15 .06
❑ 164 Lloyd Moseby .15 .06
❑ 165 Rance Mulliniks .15 .06
❑ 166 Jorge Orta .15 .06
❑ 167 Dave Stieb .40 .16
❑ 168 Willie Upshaw .15 .06
❑ 169 Ernie Whitt .15 .06
❑ 170 Len Barker .15 .06
❑ 171 Steve Bedrosian .15 .06
❑ 172 Bruce Benedict .15 .06
❑ 173 Brett Butler .40 .16
❑ 174 Rick Camp .15 .06
❑ 175 Chris Chambliss .40 .16
❑ 176 Ken Dayley .15 .06
❑ 177 Pete Falcone .15 .06
❑ 178 Terry Forster .40 .16
❑ 179 Gene Garber .15 .06
❑ 180 Terry Harper .15 .06
❑ 181 Bob Horner .40 .16
❑ 182 Glenn Hubbard .15 .06
❑ 183 Randy Johnson .15 .06
❑ 184 Craig McMurtry .15 .06
❑ 185 Donnie Moore .15 .06
❑ 186 Dale Murphy .75 .30
❑ 187 Phil Niekro .40 .16
❑ 188 Pascual Perez .15 .06
❑ 189 Biff Pocoroba .15 .06
❑ 190 Rafael Ramirez .15 .06
❑ 191 Jerry Royster .15 .06
❑ 192 Claudell Washington .15 .06
❑ 193 Bob Watson .15 .06
❑ 194 Jerry Augustine .15 .06
❑ 195 Mark Brouhard .15 .06
❑ 196 Mike Caldwell .15 .06
❑ 197 Tom Candiotti RC 1.00 .40
❑ 198 Cecil Cooper .40 .16
❑ 199 Rollie Fingers .40 .16
❑ 200 Jim Gantner .15 .06
❑ 201 Bob L. Gibson RC .25 .10
❑ 202 Moose Haas .15 .06
❑ 203 Roy Howell .15 .06
❑ 204 Pete Ladd .15 .06
❑ 205 Rick Manning .15 .06
❑ 206 Bob McClure .15 .06
❑ 207 Paul Molitor UER .75 .30
('83 stats should say .270 BA and 608 AB)
❑ 208 Don Money .15 .06
❑ 209 Charlie Moore .15 .06
❑ 210 Ben Oglivie .40 .16
❑ 211 Chuck Porter .15 .06
❑ 212 Ed Romero .15 .06
❑ 213 Ted Simmons .40 .16
❑ 214 Jim Slaton .15 .06
❑ 215 Don Sutton .40 .16
❑ 216 Tom Tellmann .15 .06
❑ 217 Pete Vuckovich .15 .06
❑ 218 Ned Yost .15 .06
❑ 219 Robin Yount 2.50 1.00
❑ 220 Alan Ashby .15 .06
❑ 221 Kevin Bass .15 .06
❑ 222 Jose Cruz .40 .16
❑ 223 Bill Dawley .15 .06
❑ 224 Frank DiPino .15 .06
❑ 225 Bill Doran RC* .50 .20
❑ 226 Phil Garner .40 .16
❑ 227 Art Howe .15 .06
❑ 228 Bob Knepper .15 .06
❑ 229 Ray Knight .40 .16
❑ 230 Frank LaCorte .15 .06
❑ 231 Mike LaCoss .15 .06
❑ 232 Mike Madden .15 .06
❑ 233 Jerry Mumphrey .15 .06
❑ 234 Joe Niekro .15 .06
❑ 235 Terry Puhl .15 .06
❑ 236 Luis Pujols .15 .06
❑ 237 Craig Reynolds .15 .06
❑ 238 Vern Ruhle .15 .06
❑ 239 Nolan Ryan 8.00 3.20
❑ 240 Mike Scott .40 .16
❑ 241 Tony Scott .15 .06
❑ 242 Dave Smith .15 .06
❑ 243 Dickie Thon .15 .06
❑ 244 Denny Walling .15 .06
❑ 245 Dale Berra .15 .06
❑ 246 Jim Bibby .15 .06
❑ 247 John Candelaria .15 .06
❑ 248 Jose DeLeon RC .50 .20
❑ 249 Mike Easler .15 .06
❑ 250 Cecilio Guante .15 .06
❑ 251 Richie Hebner .15 .06
❑ 252 Lee Lacy .15 .06
❑ 253 Bill Madlock .40 .16
❑ 254 Milt May .15 .06
❑ 255 Lee Mazzilli .40 .16
❑ 256 Larry McWilliams .15 .06
❑ 257 Jim Morrison .15 .06
❑ 258 Dave Parker .40 .16
❑ 259 Tony Pena .15 .06
❑ 260 Johnny Ray .15 .06
❑ 261 Rick Rhoden .15 .06
❑ 262 Don Robinson .15 .06
❑ 263 Manny Sarmiento .15 .06
❑ 264 Rod Scurry .15 .06
❑ 265 Kent Tekulve .15 .06
❑ 266 Gene Tenace .40 .16
❑ 267 Jason Thompson .15 .06
❑ 268 Lee Tunnell .15 .06
❑ 269 Marvell Wynne .50 .20
❑ 270 Ray Burris .15 .06
❑ 271 Gary Carter .40 .16
❑ 272 Warren Cromartie .15 .06
❑ 273 Andre Dawson .40 .16
❑ 274 Doug Flynn .15 .06
❑ 275 Terry Francona .40 .16
❑ 276 Bill Gullickson .15 .06
❑ 277 Bob James .15 .06
❑ 278 Charlie Lea .15 .06
❑ 279 Bryan Little .15 .06
❑ 280 Al Oliver .40 .16
❑ 281 Tim Raines .40 .16
❑ 282 Bobby Ramos .15 .06
❑ 283 Jeff Reardon .40 .16
❑ 284 Steve Rogers .40 .16
❑ 285 Scott Sanderson .15 .06
❑ 286 Dan Schatzeder .15 .06
❑ 287 Bryn Smith .15 .06
❑ 288 Chris Speier .15 .06
❑ 289 Manny Trillo .15 .06
❑ 290 Mike Vail .15 .06
❑ 291 Tim Wallach .15 .06
❑ 292 Chris Welsh .15 .06
❑ 293 Jim Wohlford .15 .06
❑ 294 Kurt Bevacqua .15 .06
❑ 295 Juan Bonilla .15 .06
❑ 296 Bobby Brown .15 .06
❑ 297 Luis DeLeon .15 .06
❑ 298 Dave Dravecky .15 .06
❑ 299 Tim Flannery .15 .06
❑ 300 Steve Garvey .40 .16
❑ 301 Tony Gwynn 6.00 2.40
❑ 302 Andy Hawkins .15 .06
❑ 303 Ruppert Jones .15 .06
❑ 304 Terry Kennedy .15 .06
❑ 305 Tim Lollar .15 .06
❑ 306 Gary Lucas .15 .06
❑ 307 Kevin McReynolds RC 1.00 .40
❑ 308 Sid Monge .15 .06
❑ 309 Mario Ramirez .15 .06
❑ 310 Gene Richards .15 .06
❑ 311 Luis Salazar .15 .06
❑ 312 Eric Show .15 .06
❑ 313 Elias Sosa .15 .06
❑ 314 Garry Templeton .40 .16
❑ 315 Mark Thurmond .15 .06
❑ 316 Ed Whitson .15 .06
❑ 317 Alan Wiggins .15 .06
❑ 318 Neil Allen .15 .06
❑ 319 Joaquin Andujar .40 .16
❑ 320 Steve Braun .15 .06
❑ 321 Glenn Brummer .15 .06
❑ 322 Bob Forsch .15 .06
❑ 323 David Green .15 .06
❑ 324 George Hendrick .40 .16
❑ 325 Tom Herr .15 .06
❑ 326 Dane Iorg .15 .06
❑ 327 Jeff Lahti .15 .06
❑ 328 Dave LaPoint .15 .06
❑ 329 Willie McGee .40 .16
❑ 330 Ken Oberkfell .15 .06
❑ 331 Darrell Porter .15 .06
❑ 332 Jamie Quirk .15 .06
❑ 333 Mike Ramsey .15 .06
❑ 334 Floyd Rayford .15 .06
❑ 335 Lonnie Smith .15 .06
❑ 336 Ozzie Smith 2.50 1.00
❑ 337 John Stuper .15 .06
❑ 338 Bruce Sutter .40 .16
❑ 339 A.Van Slyke RC UER 2.50 1.00
Batting and throwing both wrong on card back
❑ 340 Dave Von Ohlen .15 .06
❑ 341 Willie Aikens .15 .06
❑ 342 Mike Armstrong .15 .06
❑ 343 Bud Black .15 .06
❑ 344 George Brett 4.00 1.60
❑ 345 Onix Concepcion .15 .06
❑ 346 Keith Creel .15 .06
❑ 347 Larry Gura .15 .06
❑ 348 Don Hood .15 .06
❑ 349 Dennis Leonard .15 .06
❑ 350 Hal McRae .40 .16
❑ 351 Amos Otis .40 .16
❑ 352 Gaylord Perry .40 .16
❑ 353 Greg Pryor .15 .06
❑ 354 Dan Quisenberry .15 .06
❑ 355 Steve Renko .15 .06
❑ 356 Leon Roberts .15 .06
❑ 357 Pat Sheridan .15 .06
❑ 358 Joe Simpson .15 .06
❑ 359 Don Slaught .40 .16
❑ 360 Paul Splittorff .15 .06
❑ 361 U.L. Washington .15 .06
❑ 362 John Wathan .15 .06
❑ 363 Frank White .40 .16
❑ 364 Willie Wilson .40 .16
❑ 365 Jim Barr .15 .06
❑ 366 Dave Bergman .15 .06
❑ 367 Fred Breining .15 .06
❑ 368 Bob Brenly .15 .06
❑ 369 Jack Clark .40 .16
❑ 370 Chili Davis .40 .16
❑ 371 Mark Davis .15 .06
❑ 372 Darrell Evans .40 .16
❑ 373 Atlee Hammaker .15 .06
❑ 374 Mike Krukow .15 .06
❑ 375 Duane Kuiper .15 .06
❑ 376 Bill Laskey .15 .06
❑ 377 Gary Lavelle .15 .06
❑ 378 Johnnie LeMaster .15 .06

❑ 379 Jeff Leonard	.15	.06
❑ 380 Randy Lerch	.15	.06
❑ 381 Renie Martin	.15	.06
❑ 382 Andy McGaffigan	.15	.06
❑ 383 Greg Minton	.15	.06
❑ 384 Tom O'Malley	.15	.06
❑ 385 Max Venable	.15	.06
❑ 386 Brad Wellman	.15	.06
❑ 387 Joel Youngblood	.15	.06
❑ 388 Gary Allenson	.15	.06
❑ 389 Luis Aponte	.15	.06
❑ 390 Tony Armas	.40	.16
❑ 391 Doug Bird	.15	.06
❑ 392 Wade Boggs	4.00	1.60
❑ 393 Dennis Boyd	.40	.16
❑ 394 Mike Brown UER (shown with record of 31-104)	.25	.10
❑ 395 Mark Clear	.15	.06
❑ 396 Dennis Eckersley	.75	.30
❑ 397 Dwight Evans	.75	.30
❑ 398 Rich Gedman	.15	.06
❑ 399 Glenn Hoffman	.15	.06
❑ 400 Bruce Hurst	.15	.06
❑ 401 John Henry Johnson	.15	.06
❑ 402 Ed Jurak	.15	.06
❑ 403 Rick Miller	.15	.06
❑ 404 Jeff Newman	.15	.06
❑ 405 Reid Nichols	.15	.06
❑ 406 Bob Ojeda	.15	.06
❑ 407 Jerry Remy	.15	.06
❑ 408 Jim Rice	.40	.16
❑ 409 Bob Stanley	.15	.06
❑ 410 Dave Stapleton	.15	.06
❑ 411 John Tudor	.40	.16
❑ 412 Carl Yastrzemski	1.50	.60
❑ 413 Buddy Bell	.40	.16
❑ 414 Larry Biittner	.15	.06
❑ 415 John Butcher	.15	.06
❑ 416 Danny Darwin	.15	.06
❑ 417 Bucky Dent	.40	.16
❑ 418 Dave Hostetler	.15	.06
❑ 419 Charlie Hough	.40	.16
❑ 420 Bobby Johnson	.15	.06
❑ 421 Odell Jones	.15	.06
❑ 422 Jon Matlack	.15	.06
❑ 423 Pete O'Brien RC*	.50	.20
❑ 424 Larry Parrish	.15	.06
❑ 425 Mickey Rivers	.15	.06
❑ 426 Billy Sample	.15	.06
❑ 427 Dave Schmidt	.15	.06
❑ 428 Mike Smithson	.15	.06
❑ 429 Bill Stein	.15	.06
❑ 430 Dave Stewart	.40	.16
❑ 431 Jim Sundberg	.40	.16
❑ 432 Frank Tanana	.40	.16
❑ 433 Dave Tobik	.15	.06
❑ 434 Wayne Tolleson	.15	.06
❑ 435 George Wright	.15	.06
❑ 436 Bill Almon	.15	.06
❑ 437 Keith Atherton	.15	.06
❑ 438 Dave Beard	.15	.06
❑ 439 Tom Burgmeier	.15	.06
❑ 440 Jeff Burroughs	.15	.06
❑ 441 Chris Codiroli	.15	.06
❑ 442 Tim Conroy	.15	.06
❑ 443 Mike Davis	.15	.06
❑ 444 Wayne Gross	.15	.06
❑ 445 Garry Hancock	.15	.06
❑ 446 Mike Heath	.15	.06
❑ 447 Rickey Henderson	2.50	1.00
❑ 448 Donnie Hill	.15	.06
❑ 449 Bob Kearney	.15	.06
❑ 450 Bill Krueger RC	.25	.10
❑ 451 Rick Langford	.15	.06
❑ 452 Carney Lansford	.40	.16
❑ 453 Dave Lopes	.40	.16
❑ 454 Steve McCatty	.15	.06
❑ 455 Dan Meyer	.15	.06
❑ 456 Dwayne Murphy	.15	.06
❑ 457 Mike Norris	.15	.06
❑ 458 Ricky Peters	.15	.06
❑ 459 Tony Phillips RC	1.00	.40
❑ 460 Tom Underwood	.15	.06
❑ 461 Mike Warren	.15	.06
❑ 462 Johnny Bench	1.50	.60
❑ 463 Bruce Berenyi	.15	.06
❑ 464 Dann Bilardello	.15	.06
❑ 465 Cesar Cedeno	.40	.16
❑ 466 Dave Concepcion	.40	.16
❑ 467 Dan Driessen	.15	.06
❑ 468 Nick Esasky	.15	.06
❑ 469 Rich Gale	.15	.06
❑ 470 Ben Hayes	.15	.06
❑ 471 Paul Householder	.15	.06
❑ 472 Tom Hume	.15	.06
❑ 473 Alan Knicely	.15	.06
❑ 474 Eddie Milner	.15	.06
❑ 475 Ron Oester	.15	.06
❑ 476 Kelly Paris	.15	.06
❑ 477 Frank Pastore	.15	.06
❑ 478 Ted Power	.15	.06
❑ 479 Joe Price	.15	.06
❑ 480 Charlie Puleo	.15	.06
❑ 481 Gary Redus RC*	.50	.20
❑ 482 Bill Scherrer	.15	.06
❑ 483 Mario Soto	.40	.16
❑ 484 Alex Trevino	.15	.06
❑ 485 Duane Walker	.15	.06
❑ 486 Larry Bowa	.40	.16
❑ 487 Warren Brusstar	.15	.06
❑ 488 Bill Buckner	.40	.16
❑ 489 Bill Campbell	.15	.06
❑ 490 Ron Cey	.40	.16
❑ 491 Jody Davis	.15	.06
❑ 492 Leon Durham	.15	.06
❑ 493 Mel Hall	.40	.16
❑ 494 Ferguson Jenkins	.40	.16
❑ 495 Jay Johnstone	.15	.06
❑ 496 Craig Lefferts RC	.25	.10
❑ 497 Carmelo Martinez	.15	.06
❑ 498 Jerry Morales	.15	.06
❑ 499 Keith Moreland	.15	.06
❑ 500 Dickie Noles	.15	.06
❑ 501 Mike Proly	.15	.06
❑ 502 Chuck Rainey	.15	.06
❑ 503 Dick Ruthven	.15	.06
❑ 504 Ryne Sandberg	6.00	2.40
❑ 505 Lee Smith	.40	.16
❑ 506 Steve Trout	.15	.06
❑ 507 Gary Woods	.15	.06
❑ 508 Juan Beniquez	.15	.06
❑ 509 Bob Boone	.40	.16
❑ 510 Rick Burleson	.15	.06
❑ 511 Rod Carew	.75	.30
❑ 512 Bobby Clark	.15	.06
❑ 513 John Curtis	.15	.06
❑ 514 Doug DeCinces	.15	.06
❑ 515 Brian Downing	.40	.16
❑ 516 Tim Foli	.15	.06
❑ 517 Ken Forsch	.15	.06
❑ 518 Bobby Grich	.40	.16
❑ 519 Andy Hassler	.15	.06
❑ 520 Reggie Jackson	.75	.30
❑ 521 Ron Jackson	.15	.06
❑ 522 Tommy John	.40	.16
❑ 523 Bruce Kison	.15	.06
❑ 524 Steve Lubratich	.15	.06
❑ 525 Fred Lynn	.40	.16
❑ 526 Gary Pettis	.15	.06
❑ 527 Luis Sanchez	.15	.06
❑ 528 Daryl Sconiers	.15	.06
❑ 529 Ellis Valentine	.15	.06
❑ 530 Rob Wilfong	.15	.06
❑ 531 Mike Witt	.15	.06
❑ 532 Geoff Zahn	.15	.06
❑ 533 Bud Anderson	.15	.06
❑ 534 Chris Bando	.15	.06
❑ 535 Alan Bannister	.15	.06
❑ 536 Bert Blyleven	.40	.16
❑ 537 Tom Brennan	.15	.06
❑ 538 Jamie Easterly	.15	.06
❑ 539 Juan Eichelberger	.15	.06
❑ 540 Jim Essian	.15	.06
❑ 541 Mike Fischlin	.15	.06
❑ 542 Julio Franco	.40	.16
❑ 543 Mike Hargrove	.15	.06
❑ 544 Toby Harrah	.40	.16
❑ 545 Ron Hassey	.15	.06
❑ 546 Neal Heaton	.15	.06
❑ 547 Bake McBride	.40	.16
❑ 548 Broderick Perkins	.15	.06
❑ 549 Lary Sorensen	.15	.06
❑ 550 Dan Spillner	.15	.06
❑ 551 Rick Sutcliffe	.40	.16
❑ 552 Pat Tabler	.15	.06
❑ 553 Gorman Thomas	.40	.16
❑ 554 Andre Thornton	.15	.06
❑ 555 George Vukovich	.15	.06
❑ 556 Darrell Brown	.15	.06
❑ 557 Tom Brunansky	.15	.06
❑ 558 Randy Bush	.15	.06
❑ 559 Bobby Castillo	.15	.06
❑ 560 John Castino	.15	.06
❑ 561 Ron Davis	.15	.06
❑ 562 Dave Engle	.15	.06
❑ 563 Lenny Faedo	.15	.06
❑ 564 Pete Filson	.15	.06
❑ 565 Gary Gaetti	.75	.30
❑ 566 Mickey Hatcher	.15	.06
❑ 567 Kent Hrbek	.40	.16
❑ 568 Rusty Kuntz	.15	.06
❑ 569 Tim Laudner	.15	.06
❑ 570 Rick Lysander	.15	.06
❑ 571 Bobby Mitchell	.15	.06
❑ 572 Ken Schrom	.15	.06
❑ 573 Ray Smith	.15	.06
❑ 574 Tim Teufel RC	.50	.20
❑ 575 Frank Viola	.75	.30
❑ 576 Gary Ward	.15	.06
❑ 577 Ron Washington	.15	.06
❑ 578 Len Whitehouse	.15	.06
❑ 579 Al Williams	.15	.06
❑ 580 Bob Bailor	.15	.06
❑ 581 Mark Bradley	.15	.06
❑ 582 Hubie Brooks	.15	.06
❑ 583 Carlos Diaz	.15	.06
❑ 584 George Foster	.40	.16
❑ 585 Brian Giles	.15	.06
❑ 586 Danny Heep	.15	.06
❑ 587 Keith Hernandez	.40	.16
❑ 588 Ron Hodges	.15	.06
❑ 589 Scott Holman	.15	.06
❑ 590 Dave Kingman	.40	.16
❑ 591 Ed Lynch	.15	.06
❑ 592 Jose Oquendo RC	.50	.20
❑ 593 Jesse Orosco	.15	.06
❑ 594 Junior Ortiz	.15	.06
❑ 595 Tom Seaver	1.50	.60
❑ 596 Doug Sisk	.15	.06
❑ 597 Rusty Staub	.40	.16
❑ 598 John Stearns	.15	.06
❑ 599 Darryl Strawberry RC	5.00	2.00
❑ 600 Craig Swan	.15	.06
❑ 601 Walt Terrell	.15	.06
❑ 602 Mike Torrez	.15	.06
❑ 603 Mookie Wilson	.40	.16
❑ 604 Jamie Allen	.15	.06
❑ 605 Jim Beattie	.15	.06
❑ 606 Tony Bernazard	.15	.06
❑ 607 Manny Castillo	.15	.06
❑ 608 Bill Caudill	.15	.06
❑ 609 Bryan Clark	.15	.06
❑ 610 Al Cowens	.15	.06
❑ 611 Dave Henderson	.40	.16
❑ 612 Steve Henderson	.15	.06
❑ 613 Orlando Mercado	.15	.06
❑ 614 Mike Moore	.15	.06
❑ 615 Ricky Nelson UER (Jamie Nelson's stats on back)	.15	.06
❑ 616 Spike Owen RC	.50	.20
❑ 617 Pat Putnam	.15	.06
❑ 618 Ron Roenicke	.15	.06
❑ 619 Mike Stanton	.15	.06
❑ 620 Bob Stoddard	.15	.06
❑ 621 Rick Sweet	.15	.06
❑ 622 Roy Thomas	.15	.06
❑ 623 Ed VandeBerg	.15	.06
❑ 624 Matt Young RC	.50	.20
❑ 625 Richie Zisk	.15	.06
❑ 626 Fred Lynn IA	.40	.16
❑ 627 Manny Trillo IA	.15	.06
❑ 628 Steve Garvey IA	.15	.06
❑ 629 Rod Carew IA	.40	.16
❑ 630 Wade Boggs IA	1.50	.60
❑ 631 Tim Raines IA	.15	.06
❑ 632 Al Oliver IA	.40	.16

❑ 633 Steve Sax IA .15 .06
❑ 634 Dickie Thon IA .15 .06
❑ 635 Dan Quisenberry .15 .06
Tippy Martinez
❑ 636 Joe Morgan 1.50 .60
Pete Rose
Tony Perez
❑ 637 Lance Parrish .75 .30
Bob Boone
❑ 638 George Brett 2.00 .80
Gaylord Perry
❑ 639 Dave Righetti .75 .30
Mike Warren
Bob Forsch
❑ 640 Johnny Bench 1.50 .60
Carl Yastrzemski
❑ 641 Gaylord Perry IA .15 .06
❑ 642 Steve Carlton IA .40 .16
❑ 643 Joe Altobelli MG .15 .06
Paul Owens MG
❑ 644 Rick Dempsey WS .15 .06
❑ 645 Mike Boddicker WS .15 .06
❑ 646 Scott McGregor WS .15 .06
❑ 647 CL: Orioles/Royals .15 .06
Joe Altobelli MG
❑ 648 CL: Phillies/Giants .15 .06
Paul Owens MG
❑ 649 CL: White Sox/Red Sox .75 .30
Tony LaRussa MG
❑ 650 CL: Tigers/Rangers .75 .30
Sparky Anderson MG
❑ 651 CL: Dodgers/A's .75 .30
Tommy Lasorda MG
❑ 652 CL: Yankees/Reds .75 .30
Billy Martin MG
❑ 653 CL: Blue Jays/Cubs .40 .16
Bobby Cox MG
❑ 654 CL: Braves/Angels .75 .30
Joe Torre MG
❑ 655 CL: Brewers/Indians .15 .06
Rene Lachemann MG
❑ 656 CL: Astros/Twins .15 .06
Bob Lillis MG
❑ 657 CL: Pirates/Mets .15 .06
Chuck Tanner MG
❑ 658 CL: Expos/Mariners .15 .06
Bill Virdon MG
❑ 659 CL: Padres/Specials .40 .16
Dick Williams MG
❑ 660 CL: Cardinals/Teams .75 .30
Whitey Herzog MG

1984 Fleer Update

	Nm-Mt	Ex-Mt
COMP.FACT.SET (132)	400.00	160.00

❑ 1 Willie Aikens 1.00 .40
❑ 2 Luis Aponte 1.00 .40
❑ 3 Mark Bailey 1.00 .40
❑ 4 Bob Bailor 1.00 .40
❑ 5 Dusty Baker 1.50 .60
❑ 6 Steve Balboni 1.00 .40
❑ 7 Alan Bannister 1.00 .40
❑ 8 Marty Barrett XRC 2.00 .80
❑ 9 Dave Beard 1.00 .40
❑ 10 Joe Beckwith 1.00 .40
❑ 11 Dave Bergman 1.00 .40
❑ 12 Tony Bernazard 1.00 .40
❑ 13 Bruce Bochte 1.00 .40
❑ 14 Barry Bonnell 1.00 .40
❑ 15 Phil Bradley 2.00 .80
❑ 16 Fred Breining 1.00 .40
❑ 17 Mike C. Brown 1.00 .40
❑ 18 Bill Buckner 1.50 .60
❑ 19 Ray Burris 1.00 .40
❑ 20 John Butcher 1.00 .40
❑ 21 Brett Butler 1.50 .60
❑ 22 Enos Cabell 1.00 .40
❑ 23 Bill Campbell 1.00 .40
❑ 24 Bill Caudill 1.00 .40
❑ 25 Bobby Clark 1.00 .40
❑ 26 Bryan Clark 1.00 .40
❑ 27 Roger Clemens XRC 300.00 120.00
❑ 28 Jaime Cocanower 1.00 .40
❑ 29 Ron Darling XRC* 5.00 2.00
❑ 30 Alvin Davis XRC 2.00 .80
❑ 31 Bob Dernier 1.00 .40
❑ 32 Carlos Diaz 1.00 .40
❑ 33 Mike Easler 1.00 .40
❑ 34 Dennis Eckersley 2.50 1.00
❑ 35 Jim Essian 1.00 .40
❑ 36 Darrell Evans 1.50 .60
❑ 37 Mike Fitzgerald 1.00 .40
❑ 38 Tim Foli 1.00 .40
❑ 39 John Franco XRC 5.00 2.00
❑ 40 George Frazier 1.00 .40
❑ 41 Rich Gale 1.00 .40
❑ 42 Barbaro Garbey 1.00 .40
❑ 43 Dwight Gooden XRC 25.00 10.00
❑ 44 Rich Gossage 1.50 .60
❑ 45 Wayne Gross 1.00 .40
❑ 46 Mark Gubicza XRC 2.00 .80
❑ 47 Jackie Gutierrez 1.00 .40
❑ 48 Toby Harrah 1.50 .60
❑ 49 Ron Hassey 1.00 .40
❑ 50 Richie Hebner 1.00 .40
❑ 51 Willie Hernandez 1.00 .40
❑ 52 Ed Hodge 1.00 .40
❑ 53 Ricky Horton 1.00 .40
❑ 54 Art Howe 1.00 .40
❑ 55 Dane Iorg 1.00 .40
❑ 56 Brook Jacoby 2.00 .80
❑ 57 Dion James XRC* 1.00 .40
❑ 58 Mike Jeffcoat XRC 1.00 .40
❑ 59 Ruppert Jones 1.00 .40
❑ 60 Bob Kearney 1.00 .40
❑ 61 Jimmy Key XRC 5.00 2.00
❑ 62 Dave Kingman 1.50 .60
❑ 63 Brad Komminsk XRC 1.00 .40
❑ 64 Jerry Koosman 1.50 .60
❑ 65 Wayne Krenchicki 1.00 .40
❑ 66 Rusty Kuntz 1.00 .40
❑ 67 Frank LaCorte 1.00 .40
❑ 68 Dennis Lamp 1.00 .40
❑ 69 Tito Landrum 1.00 .40
❑ 70 Mark Langston XRC 5.00 2.00
❑ 71 Rick Leach 1.00 .40
❑ 72 Craig Lefferts 1.00 .40
❑ 73 Gary Lucas 1.00 .40
❑ 74 Jerry Martin 1.00 .40
❑ 75 Carmelo Martinez 1.00 .40
❑ 76 Mike Mason XRC 1.00 .40
❑ 77 Gary Matthews 1.50 .60
❑ 78 Andy McGaffigan 1.00 .40
❑ 79 Joey McLaughlin 1.00 .40
❑ 80 Joe Morgan 1.50 .60
❑ 81 Darryl Motley 1.00 .40
❑ 82 Graig Nettles 1.50 .60
❑ 83 Phil Niekro 1.50 .60
❑ 84 Ken Oberkfell 1.00 .40
❑ 85 Al Oliver 1.50 .60
❑ 86 Jorge Orta 1.00 .40
❑ 87 Amos Otis 1.50 .60
❑ 88 Bob Owchinko 1.00 .40
❑ 89 Dave Parker 1.50 .60
❑ 90 Jack Perconte 1.00 .40
❑ 91 Tony Perez 2.50 1.00
❑ 92 Gerald Perry 2.00 .80
❑ 93 Kirby Puckett XRC 60.00 24.00
❑ 94 Shane Rawley 1.00 .40
❑ 95 Floyd Rayford 1.00 .40
❑ 96 Ron Reed 1.00 .40
❑ 97 R.J. Reynolds 1.00 .40
❑ 98 Gene Richards 1.00 .40
❑ 99 Jose Rijo XRC 5.00 2.00
❑ 100 Jeff D. Robinson 1.00 .40
❑ 101 Ron Romanick 1.00 .40
❑ 102 Pete Rose 12.00 4.80
❑ 103 Bret Saberhagen XRC 10.00 4.00
❑ 104 Scott Sanderson 1.00 .40
❑ 105 Dick Schofield XRC* 2.00 .80
❑ 106 Tom Seaver 4.00 1.60
❑ 107 Jim Slaton 1.00 .40
❑ 108 Mike Smithson 1.00 .40
❑ 109 Lary Sorensen 1.00 .40
❑ 110 Tim Stoddard 1.00 .40
❑ 111 Jeff Stone 1.00 .40
❑ 112 Champ Summers 1.00 .40
❑ 113 Jim Sundberg 1.50 .60
❑ 114 Rick Sutcliffe 1.50 .60
❑ 115 Craig Swan 1.00 .40
❑ 116 Derrel Thomas 1.00 .40
❑ 117 Gorman Thomas 1.50 .60
❑ 118 Alex Trevino 1.00 .40
❑ 119 Manny Trillo 1.00 .40
❑ 120 John Tudor 1.50 .60
❑ 121 Tom Underwood 1.00 .40
❑ 122 Mike Vail 1.00 .40
❑ 123 Tom Waddell 1.00 .40
❑ 124 Gary Ward 1.00 .40
❑ 125 Terry Whitfield 1.00 .40
❑ 126 Curtis Wilkerson 1.00 .40
❑ 127 Frank Williams 1.00 .40
❑ 128 Glenn Wilson 1.50 .60
❑ 129 John Wockenfuss 1.00 .40
❑ 130 Ned Yost 1.00 .40
❑ 131 Mike Young RC 1.00 .40
❑ 132 Checklist 1-132 1.00 .40

1985 Fleer

	Nm-Mt	Ex-Mt
COMPLETE SET (660)	60.00	24.00
COMP.FACT.SET (660)	100.00	40.00

❑ 1 Doug Bair .15 .06
❑ 2 Juan Berenguer .15 .06
❑ 3 Dave Bergman .15 .06
❑ 4 Tom Brookens .15 .06
❑ 5 Marty Castillo .15 .06
❑ 6 Darrell Evans .40 .16
❑ 7 Barbaro Garbey .15 .06
❑ 8 Kirk Gibson .75 .30
❑ 9 John Grubb .15 .06
❑ 10 Willie Hernandez .15 .06
❑ 11 Larry Herndon .15 .06
❑ 12 Howard Johnson .40 .16
❑ 13 Ruppert Jones .15 .06
❑ 14 Rusty Kuntz .15 .06
❑ 15 Chet Lemon .40 .16
❑ 16 Aurelio Lopez .15 .06
❑ 17 Sid Monge .15 .06
❑ 18 Jack Morris .40 .16
❑ 19 Lance Parrish .40 .16
❑ 20 Dan Petry .15 .06
❑ 21 Dave Rozema .15 .06
❑ 22 Bill Scherrer .15 .06
❑ 23 Alan Trammell .40 .16
❑ 24 Lou Whitaker .40 .16
❑ 25 Milt Wilcox .15 .06
❑ 26 Kurt Bevacqua .15 .06
❑ 27 Greg Booker .15 .06
❑ 28 Bobby Brown .15 .06

❑ 29 Luis DeLeon .15 .06
❑ 30 Dave Dravecky .15 .06
❑ 31 Tim Flannery .15 .06
❑ 32 Steve Garvey .40 .16
❑ 33 Rich Gossage .40 .16
❑ 34 Tony Gwynn 2.50 1.00
❑ 35 Greg Harris .15 .06
❑ 36 Andy Hawkins .15 .06
❑ 37 Terry Kennedy .15 .06
❑ 38 Craig Lefferts .15 .06
❑ 39 Tim Lollar .15 .06
❑ 40 Carmelo Martinez .15 .06
❑ 41 Kevin McReynolds .40 .16
❑ 42 Graig Nettles .40 .16
❑ 43 Luis Salazar .15 .06
❑ 44 Eric Show .15 .06
❑ 45 Garry Templeton .40 .16
❑ 46 Mark Thurmond .15 .06
❑ 47 Ed Whitson .15 .06
❑ 48 Alan Wiggins .15 .06
❑ 49 Rich Bordi .15 .06
❑ 50 Larry Bowa .40 .16
❑ 51 Warren Brusstar .15 .06
❑ 52 Ron Cey .40 .16
❑ 53 Henry Cotto RC .25 .10
❑ 54 Jody Davis .15 .06
❑ 55 Bob Dernier .15 .06
❑ 56 Leon Durham .15 .06
❑ 57 Dennis Eckersley .75 .30
❑ 58 George Frazier .15 .06
❑ 59 Richie Hebner .15 .06
❑ 60 Dave Lopes .40 .16
❑ 61 Gary Matthews .40 .16
❑ 62 Keith Moreland .15 .06
❑ 63 Rick Reuschel .40 .16
❑ 64 Dick Ruthven .15 .06
❑ 65 Ryne Sandberg 2.50 1.00
❑ 66 Scott Sanderson .15 .06
❑ 67 Lee Smith .40 .16
❑ 68 Tim Stoddard .15 .06
❑ 69 Rick Sutcliffe .40 .16
❑ 70 Steve Trout .15 .06
❑ 71 Gary Woods .15 .06
❑ 72 Wally Backman .15 .06
❑ 73 Bruce Berenyi .15 .06
❑ 74 Hubie Brooks UER .15 .06
(Kelvin Chapman's stats on card back)
❑ 75 Kelvin Chapman .15 .06
❑ 76 Ron Darling .40 .16
❑ 77 Sid Fernandez .40 .16
❑ 78 Mike Fitzgerald .15 .06
❑ 79 George Foster .40 .16
❑ 80 Brent Gaff .15 .06
❑ 81 Ron Gardenhire .15 .06
❑ 82 Dwight Gooden RC 3.00 1.20
❑ 83 Tom Gorman .15 .06
❑ 84 Danny Heep .15 .06
❑ 85 Keith Hernandez .40 .16
❑ 86 Ray Knight .40 .16
❑ 87 Ed Lynch .15 .06
❑ 88 Jose Oquendo .15 .06
❑ 89 Jesse Orosco .15 .06
❑ 90 Rafael Santana .15 .06
❑ 91 Doug Sisk .15 .06
❑ 92 Rusty Staub .40 .16
❑ 93 Darryl Strawberry 1.25 .50
❑ 94 Walt Terrell .15 .06
❑ 95 Mookie Wilson .40 .16
❑ 96 Jim Acker .15 .06
❑ 97 Willie Aikens .15 .06
❑ 98 Doyle Alexander .15 .06
❑ 99 Jesse Barfield .40 .16
❑ 100 George Bell .40 .16
❑ 101 Jim Clancy .15 .06
❑ 102 Dave Collins .15 .06
❑ 103 Tony Fernandez .40 .16
❑ 104 Damaso Garcia .15 .06
❑ 105 Jim Gott .15 .06
❑ 106 Alfredo Griffin .15 .06
❑ 107 Garth Iorg .15 .06
❑ 108 Roy Lee Jackson .15 .06
❑ 109 Cliff Johnson .15 .06
❑ 110 Jimmy Key RC 1.00 .40
❑ 111 Dennis Lamp .15 .06
❑ 112 Rick Leach .15 .06
❑ 113 Luis Leal .15 .06
❑ 114 Buck Martinez .15 .06
❑ 115 Lloyd Moseby .15 .06
❑ 116 Rance Mulliniks .15 .06
❑ 117 Dave Stieb .40 .16
❑ 118 Willie Upshaw .15 .06
❑ 119 Ernie Whitt .15 .06
❑ 120 Mike Armstrong .15 .06
❑ 121 Don Baylor .40 .16
❑ 122 Marty Bystrom .15 .06
❑ 123 Rick Cerone .15 .06
❑ 124 Joe Cowley .15 .06
❑ 125 Brian Dayett .15 .06
❑ 126 Tim Foli .15 .06
❑ 127 Ray Fontenot .15 .06
❑ 128 Ken Griffey .40 .16
❑ 129 Ron Guidry .40 .16
❑ 130 Toby Harrah .40 .16
❑ 131 Jay Howell .15 .06
❑ 132 Steve Kemp .15 .06
❑ 133 Don Mattingly 5.00 2.00
❑ 134 Bobby Meacham .15 .06
❑ 135 John Montefusco .15 .06
❑ 136 Omar Moreno .15 .06
❑ 137 Dale Murray .15 .06
❑ 138 Phil Niekro .40 .16
❑ 139 Mike Pagliarulo .15 .06
❑ 140 Willie Randolph .40 .16
❑ 141 Dennis Rasmussen .15 .06
❑ 142 Dave Righetti .40 .16
❑ 143 Jose Rijo RC 1.00 .40
❑ 144 Andre Robertson .15 .06
❑ 145 Bob Shirley .15 .06
❑ 146 Dave Winfield .40 .16
❑ 147 Butch Wynegar .15 .06
❑ 148 Gary Allenson .15 .06
❑ 149 Tony Armas .40 .16
❑ 150 Marty Barrett .15 .06
❑ 151 Wade Boggs 1.25 .50
❑ 152 Dennis Boyd .15 .06
❑ 153 Bill Buckner .40 .16
❑ 154 Mark Clear .15 .06
❑ 155 Roger Clemens RC 40.00 16.00
❑ 156 Steve Crawford .15 .06
❑ 157 Mike Easler .15 .06
❑ 158 Dwight Evans .75 .30
❑ 159 Rich Gedman .15 .06
❑ 160 Jackie Gutierrez .40 .16
(Wade Boggs shown on deck)
❑ 161 Bruce Hurst .15 .06
❑ 162 John Henry Johnson .15 .06
❑ 163 Rick Miller .15 .06
❑ 164 Reid Nichols .15 .06
❑ 165 Al Nipper .15 .06
❑ 166 Bob Ojeda .15 .06
❑ 167 Jerry Remy .15 .06
❑ 168 Jim Rice .40 .16
❑ 169 Bob Stanley .15 .06
❑ 170 Mike Boddicker .15 .06
❑ 171 Al Bumbry .15 .06
❑ 172 Todd Cruz .15 .06
❑ 173 Rich Dauer .15 .06
❑ 174 Storm Davis .15 .06
❑ 175 Rick Dempsey .15 .06
❑ 176 Jim Dwyer .15 .06
❑ 177 Mike Flanagan .15 .06
❑ 178 Dan Ford .15 .06
❑ 179 Wayne Gross .15 .06
❑ 180 John Lowenstein .15 .06
❑ 181 Dennis Martinez .40 .16
❑ 182 Tippy Martinez .15 .06
❑ 183 Scott McGregor .15 .06
❑ 184 Eddie Murray 1.25 .50
❑ 185 Joe Nolan .15 .06
❑ 186 Floyd Rayford .15 .06
❑ 187 Cal Ripken 5.00 2.00
❑ 188 Gary Roenicke .15 .06
❑ 189 Lenn Sakata .15 .06
❑ 190 John Shelby .15 .06
❑ 191 Ken Singleton .40 .16
❑ 192 Sammy Stewart .15 .06
❑ 193 Bill Swaggerty .15 .06
❑ 194 Tom Underwood .15 .06
❑ 195 Mike Young .15 .06
❑ 196 Steve Balboni .15 .06
❑ 197 Joe Beckwith .15 .06
❑ 198 Bud Black .15 .06
❑ 199 George Brett 3.00 1.20
❑ 200 Onix Concepcion .15 .06
❑ 201 Mark Gubicza RC* .50 .20
❑ 202 Larry Gura .15 .06
❑ 203 Mark Huismann .15 .06
❑ 204 Dane Iorg .15 .06
❑ 205 Danny Jackson .15 .06
❑ 206 Charlie Leibrandt .15 .06
❑ 207 Hal McRae .40 .16
❑ 208 Darryl Motley .15 .06
❑ 209 Jorge Orta .15 .06
❑ 210 Greg Pryor .15 .06
❑ 211 Dan Quisenberry .15 .06
❑ 212 Bret Saberhagen RC 1.50 .60
❑ 213 Pat Sheridan .15 .06
❑ 214 Don Slaught .15 .06
❑ 215 U.L. Washington .15 .06
❑ 216 John Wathan .15 .06
❑ 217 Frank White .40 .16
❑ 218 Willie Wilson .40 .16
❑ 219 Neil Allen .15 .06
❑ 220 Joaquin Andujar .40 .16
❑ 221 Steve Braun .15 .06
❑ 222 Danny Cox .15 .06
❑ 223 Bob Forsch .15 .06
❑ 224 David Green .15 .06
❑ 225 George Hendrick .40 .16
❑ 226 Tom Herr .15 .06
❑ 227 Ricky Horton .15 .06
❑ 228 Art Howe .15 .06
❑ 229 Mike Jorgensen .15 .06
❑ 230 Kurt Kepshire .15 .06
❑ 231 Jeff Lahti .15 .06
❑ 232 Tito Landrum .15 .06
❑ 233 Dave LaPoint .15 .06
❑ 234 Willie McGee .40 .16
❑ 235 Tom Nieto .15 .06
❑ 236 Terry Pendleton RC 1.00 .40
❑ 237 Darrell Porter .15 .06
❑ 238 Dave Rucker .15 .06
❑ 239 Lonnie Smith .15 .06
❑ 240 Ozzie Smith 2.00 .80
❑ 241 Bruce Sutter .40 .16
❑ 242 Andy Van Slyke UER .75 .30
(Bats Right, Throws Left)
❑ 243 Dave Von Ohlen .15 .06
❑ 244 Larry Andersen .15 .06
❑ 245 Bill Campbell .15 .06
❑ 246 Steve Carlton .40 .16
❑ 247 Tim Corcoran .15 .06
❑ 248 Ivan DeJesus .15 .06
❑ 249 John Denny .15 .06
❑ 250 Bo Diaz .15 .06
❑ 251 Greg Gross .15 .06
❑ 252 Kevin Gross .15 .06
❑ 253 Von Hayes .15 .06
❑ 254 Al Holland .15 .06
❑ 255 Charles Hudson .15 .06
❑ 256 Jerry Koosman .40 .16
❑ 257 Joe Lefebvre .15 .06
❑ 258 Sixto Lezcano .15 .06
❑ 259 Garry Maddox .15 .06
❑ 260 Len Matuszek .15 .06
❑ 261 Tug McGraw .40 .16
❑ 262 Al Oliver .40 .16
❑ 263 Shane Rawley .15 .06
❑ 264 Juan Samuel .15 .06
❑ 265 Mike Schmidt 3.00 1.20
❑ 266 Jeff Stone .15 .06
❑ 267 Ozzie Virgil .15 .06
❑ 268 Glenn Wilson .15 .06
❑ 269 John Wockenfuss .15 .06
❑ 270 Darrell Brown .15 .06
❑ 271 Tom Brunansky .15 .06
❑ 272 Randy Bush .15 .06
❑ 273 John Butcher .15 .06
❑ 274 Bobby Castillo .15 .06
❑ 275 Ron Davis .15 .06
❑ 276 Dave Engle .15 .06
❑ 277 Pete Filson .15 .06
❑ 278 Gary Gaetti .40 .16
❑ 279 Mickey Hatcher .15 .06
❑ 280 Ed Hodge .15 .06

Card		
❑ 281 Kent Hrbek	.40	.16
❑ 282 Houston Jimenez	.15	.06
❑ 283 Tim Laudner	.15	.06
❑ 284 Rick Lysander	.15	.06
❑ 285 Dave Meier	.15	.06
❑ 286 Kirby Puckett RC	10.00	4.00
❑ 287 Pat Putnam	.15	.06
❑ 288 Ken Schrom	.15	.06
❑ 289 Mike Smithson	.15	.06
❑ 290 Tim Teufel	.15	.06
❑ 291 Frank Viola	.40	.16
❑ 292 Ron Washington	.15	.06
❑ 293 Don Aase	.15	.06
❑ 294 Juan Beniquez	.15	.06
❑ 295 Bob Boone	.40	.16
❑ 296 Mike C. Brown	.15	.06
❑ 297 Rod Carew	.75	.30
❑ 298 Doug Corbett	.15	.06
❑ 299 Doug DeCinces	.15	.06
❑ 300 Brian Downing	.40	.16
❑ 301 Ken Forsch	.15	.06
❑ 302 Bobby Grich	.40	.16
❑ 303 Reggie Jackson	.75	.30
❑ 304 Tommy John	.40	.16
❑ 305 Curt Kaufman	.15	.06
❑ 306 Bruce Kison	.15	.06
❑ 307 Fred Lynn	.40	.16
❑ 308 Gary Pettis	.15	.06
❑ 309 Ron Romanick	.15	.06
❑ 310 Luis Sanchez	.15	.06
❑ 311 Dick Schofield	.15	.06
❑ 312 Daryl Sconiers	.15	.06
❑ 313 Jim Slaton	.15	.06
❑ 314 Derrel Thomas	.15	.06
❑ 315 Rob Wilfong	.15	.06
❑ 316 Mike Witt	.15	.06
❑ 317 Geoff Zahn	.15	.06
❑ 318 Len Barker	.15	.06
❑ 319 Steve Bedrosian	.15	.06
❑ 320 Bruce Benedict	.15	.06
❑ 321 Rick Camp	.15	.06
❑ 322 Chris Chambliss	.40	.16
❑ 323 Jeff Dedmon	.15	.06
❑ 324 Terry Forster	.40	.16
❑ 325 Gene Garber	.15	.06
❑ 326 Albert Hall	.15	.06
❑ 327 Terry Harper	.15	.06
❑ 328 Bob Horner	.40	.16
❑ 329 Glenn Hubbard	.15	.06
❑ 330 Randy Johnson	.15	.06
❑ 331 Brad Komminsk	.15	.06
❑ 332 Rick Mahler	.15	.06
❑ 333 Craig McMurtry	.15	.06
❑ 334 Donnie Moore	.15	.06
❑ 335 Dale Murphy	.75	.30
❑ 336 Ken Oberkfell	.15	.06
❑ 337 Pascual Perez	.15	.06
❑ 338 Gerald Perry	.15	.06
❑ 339 Rafael Ramirez	.15	.06
❑ 340 Jerry Royster	.15	.06
❑ 341 Alex Trevino	.15	.06
❑ 342 Claudell Washington	.15	.06
❑ 343 Alan Ashby	.15	.06
❑ 344 Mark Bailey	.15	.06
❑ 345 Kevin Bass	.15	.06
❑ 346 Enos Cabell	.15	.06
❑ 347 Jose Cruz	.40	.16
❑ 348 Bill Dawley	.15	.06
❑ 349 Frank DiPino	.15	.06
❑ 350 Bill Doran	.15	.06
❑ 351 Phil Garner	.40	.16
❑ 352 Bob Knepper	.15	.06
❑ 353 Mike LaCoss	.15	.06
❑ 354 Jerry Mumphrey	.15	.06
❑ 355 Joe Niekro	.15	.06
❑ 356 Terry Puhl	.15	.06
❑ 357 Craig Reynolds	.15	.06
❑ 358 Vern Ruhle	.15	.06
❑ 359 Nolan Ryan	6.00	2.40
❑ 360 Joe Sambito	.15	.06
❑ 361 Mike Scott	.40	.16
❑ 362 Dave Smith	.15	.06
❑ 363 Julio Solano	.15	.06
❑ 364 Dickie Thon	.15	.06
❑ 365 Denny Walling	.15	.06
❑ 366 Dave Anderson	.15	.06
❑ 367 Bob Bailor	.15	.06
❑ 368 Greg Brock	.15	.06
❑ 369 Carlos Diaz	.15	.06
❑ 370 Pedro Guerrero	.40	.16
❑ 371 Orel Hershiser RC	3.00	1.20
❑ 372 Rick Honeycutt	.15	.06
❑ 373 Burt Hooton	.15	.06
❑ 374 Ken Howell	.15	.06
❑ 375 Ken Landreaux	.15	.06
❑ 376 Candy Maldonado	.15	.06
❑ 377 Mike Marshall	.15	.06
❑ 378 Tom Niedenfuer	.15	.06
❑ 379 Alejandro Pena	.15	.06
❑ 380 Jerry Reuss UER	.15	.06
("Home:" omitted)		
❑ 381 R.J. Reynolds	.15	.06
❑ 382 German Rivera	.15	.06
❑ 383 Bill Russell	.40	.16
❑ 384 Steve Sax	.15	.06
❑ 385 Mike Scioscia	.40	.16
❑ 386 Franklin Stubbs	.15	.06
❑ 387 Fernando Valenzuela	.40	.16
❑ 388 Bob Welch	.40	.16
❑ 389 Terry Whitfield	.15	.06
❑ 390 Steve Yeager	.40	.16
❑ 391 Pat Zachry	.15	.06
❑ 392 Fred Breining	.15	.06
❑ 393 Gary Carter	.40	.16
❑ 394 Andre Dawson	.40	.16
❑ 395 Miguel Dilone	.15	.06
❑ 396 Dan Driessen	.15	.06
❑ 397 Doug Flynn	.15	.06
❑ 398 Terry Francona	.40	.16
❑ 399 Bill Gullickson	.15	.06
❑ 400 Bob James	.15	.06
❑ 401 Charlie Lea	.15	.06
❑ 402 Bryan Little	.15	.06
❑ 403 Gary Lucas	.15	.06
❑ 404 David Palmer	.15	.06
❑ 405 Tim Raines	.40	.16
❑ 406 Mike Ramsey	.15	.06
❑ 407 Jeff Reardon	.40	.16
❑ 408 Steve Rogers	.40	.16
❑ 409 Dan Schatzeder	.15	.06
❑ 410 Bryn Smith	.15	.06
❑ 411 Mike Stenhouse	.15	.06
❑ 412 Tim Wallach	.15	.06
❑ 413 Jim Wohlford	.15	.06
❑ 414 Bill Almon	.15	.06
❑ 415 Keith Atherton	.15	.06
❑ 416 Bruce Bochte	.15	.06
❑ 417 Tom Burgmeier	.15	.06
❑ 418 Ray Burris	.15	.06
❑ 419 Bill Caudill	.15	.06
❑ 420 Chris Codiroli	.15	.06
❑ 421 Tim Conroy	.15	.06
❑ 422 Mike Davis	.15	.06
❑ 423 Jim Essian	.15	.06
❑ 424 Mike Heath	.15	.06
❑ 425 Rickey Henderson	1.50	.60
❑ 426 Donnie Hill	.15	.06
❑ 427 Dave Kingman	.40	.16
❑ 428 Bill Krueger	.15	.06
❑ 429 Carney Lansford	.40	.16
❑ 430 Steve McCatty	.15	.06
❑ 431 Joe Morgan	.40	.16
❑ 432 Dwayne Murphy	.15	.06
❑ 433 Tony Phillips	.15	.06
❑ 434 Lary Sorensen	.15	.06
❑ 435 Mike Warren	.15	.06
❑ 436 Curt Young	.15	.06
❑ 437 Luis Aponte	.15	.06
❑ 438 Chris Bando	.15	.06
❑ 439 Tony Bernazard	.15	.06
❑ 440 Bert Blyleven	.40	.16
❑ 441 Brett Butler	.40	.16
❑ 442 Ernie Camacho	.15	.06
❑ 443 Joe Carter	1.25	.50
❑ 444 Carmelo Castillo	.15	.06
❑ 445 Jamie Easterly	.15	.06
❑ 446 Steve Farr RC	.50	.20
❑ 447 Mike Fischlin	.15	.06
❑ 448 Julio Franco	.40	.16
❑ 449 Mel Hall	.15	.06
❑ 450 Mike Hargrove	.15	.06
❑ 451 Neal Heaton	.15	.06
❑ 452 Brook Jacoby	.15	.06
❑ 453 Mike Jeffcoat	.15	.06
❑ 454 Don Schulze	.15	.06
❑ 455 Roy Smith	.15	.06
❑ 456 Pat Tabler	.15	.06
❑ 457 Andre Thornton	.15	.06
❑ 458 George Vukovich	.15	.06
❑ 459 Tom Waddell	.15	.06
❑ 460 Jerry Willard	.15	.06
❑ 461 Dale Berra	.15	.06
❑ 462 John Candelaria	.15	.06
❑ 463 Jose DeLeon	.15	.06
❑ 464 Doug Frobel	.15	.06
❑ 465 Cecilio Guante	.15	.06
❑ 466 Brian Harper	.15	.06
❑ 467 Lee Lacy	.15	.06
❑ 468 Bill Madlock	.40	.16
❑ 469 Lee Mazzilli	.40	.16
❑ 470 Larry McWilliams	.15	.06
❑ 471 Jim Morrison	.15	.06
❑ 472 Tony Pena	.15	.06
❑ 473 Johnny Ray	.15	.06
❑ 474 Rick Rhoden	.15	.06
❑ 475 Don Robinson	.15	.06
❑ 476 Rod Scurry	.15	.06
❑ 477 Kent Tekulve	.15	.06
❑ 478 Jason Thompson	.15	.06
❑ 479 John Tudor	.40	.16
❑ 480 Lee Tunnell	.15	.06
❑ 481 Marvell Wynne	.15	.06
❑ 482 Salome Barojas	.15	.06
❑ 483 Dave Beard	.15	.06
❑ 484 Jim Beattie	.15	.06
❑ 485 Barry Bonnell	.15	.06
❑ 486 Phil Bradley	.50	.20
❑ 487 Al Cowens	.15	.06
❑ 488 Alvin Davis RC*	.50	.20
❑ 489 Dave Henderson	.15	.06
❑ 490 Steve Henderson	.15	.06
❑ 491 Bob Kearney	.15	.06
❑ 492 Mark Langston RC	1.00	.40
❑ 493 Larry Milbourne	.15	.06
❑ 494 Paul Mirabella	.15	.06
❑ 495 Mike Moore	.15	.06
❑ 496 Edwin Nunez	.15	.06
❑ 497 Spike Owen	.15	.06
❑ 498 Jack Perconte	.15	.06
❑ 499 Ken Phelps	.15	.06
❑ 500 Jim Presley	.50	.20
❑ 501 Mike Stanton	.15	.06
❑ 502 Bob Stoddard	.15	.06
❑ 503 Gorman Thomas	.40	.16
❑ 504 Ed VandeBerg	.15	.06
❑ 505 Matt Young	.15	.06
❑ 506 Juan Agosto	.15	.06
❑ 507 Harold Baines	.40	.16
❑ 508 Floyd Bannister	.15	.06
❑ 509 Britt Burns	.15	.06
❑ 510 Julio Cruz	.15	.06
❑ 511 Richard Dotson	.15	.06
❑ 512 Jerry Dybzinski	.15	.06
❑ 513 Carlton Fisk	.75	.30
❑ 514 Scott Fletcher	.15	.06
❑ 515 Jerry Hairston	.15	.06
❑ 516 Marc Hill	.15	.06
❑ 517 LaMarr Hoyt	.15	.06
❑ 518 Ron Kittle	.15	.06
❑ 519 Rudy Law	.15	.06
❑ 520 Vance Law	.15	.06
❑ 521 Greg Luzinski	.40	.16
❑ 522 Gene Nelson	.15	.06
❑ 523 Tom Paciorek	.15	.06
❑ 524 Ron Reed	.15	.06
❑ 525 Bert Roberge	.15	.06
❑ 526 Tom Seaver	.75	.30
❑ 527 Roy Smalley	.15	.06
❑ 528 Dan Spillner	.15	.06
❑ 529 Mike Squires	.15	.06
❑ 530 Greg Walker	.15	.06
❑ 531 Cesar Cedeno	.40	.16
❑ 532 Dave Concepcion	.40	.16
❑ 533 Eric Davis RC	3.00	1.20
❑ 534 Nick Esasky	.15	.06
❑ 535 Tom Foley	.15	.06
❑ 536 John Franco UER RC	1.00	.40
(Koufax misspelled		

as Kofax on back)
❏ 537 Brad Gulden .15 .06
❏ 538 Tom Hume .15 .06
❏ 539 Wayne Krenchicki .15 .06
❏ 540 Andy McGaffigan .15 .06
❏ 541 Eddie Milner .15 .06
❏ 542 Ron Oester .15 .06
❏ 543 Bob Owchinko .15 .06
❏ 544 Dave Parker .40 .16
❏ 545 Frank Pastore .15 .06
❏ 546 Tony Perez .75 .30
❏ 547 Ted Power .15 .06
❏ 548 Joe Price .15 .06
❏ 549 Gary Redus .15 .06
❏ 550 Pete Rose 4.00 1.60
❏ 551 Jeff Russell .15 .06
❏ 552 Mario Soto .40 .16
❏ 553 Jay Tibbs .15 .06
❏ 554 Duane Walker .15 .06
❏ 555 Alan Bannister .15 .06
❏ 556 Buddy Bell .40 .16
❏ 557 Danny Darwin .15 .06
❏ 558 Charlie Hough .40 .16
❏ 559 Bobby Jones .15 .06
❏ 560 Odell Jones .15 .06
❏ 561 Jeff Kunkel .15 .06
❏ 562 Mike Mason RC .25 .10
❏ 563 Pete O'Brien .15 .06
❏ 564 Larry Parrish .15 .06
❏ 565 Mickey Rivers .15 .06
❏ 566 Billy Sample .15 .06
❏ 567 Dave Schmidt .15 .06
❏ 568 Donnie Scott .15 .06
❏ 569 Dave Stewart .40 .16
❏ 570 Frank Tanana .40 .16
❏ 571 Wayne Tolleson .15 .06
❏ 572 Gary Ward .15 .06
❏ 573 Curtis Wilkerson .15 .06
❏ 574 George Wright .15 .06
❏ 575 Ned Yost .15 .06
❏ 576 Mark Brouhard .15 .06
❏ 577 Mike Caldwell .15 .06
❏ 578 Bobby Clark .15 .06
❏ 579 Jaime Cocanower .15 .06
❏ 580 Cecil Cooper .40 .16
❏ 581 Rollie Fingers .40 .16
❏ 582 Jim Gantner .15 .06
❏ 583 Moose Haas .15 .06
❏ 584 Dion James .15 .06
❏ 585 Pete Ladd .15 .06
❏ 586 Rick Manning .15 .06
❏ 587 Bob McClure .15 .06
❏ 588 Paul Molitor .75 .30
❏ 589 Charlie Moore .15 .06
❏ 590 Ben Oglivie .40 .16
❏ 591 Chuck Porter .15 .06
❏ 592 Randy Ready RC* .25 .10
❏ 593 Ed Romero .15 .06
❏ 594 Bill Schroeder .15 .06
❏ 595 Ray Searage .15 .06
❏ 596 Ted Simmons .40 .16
❏ 597 Jim Sundberg .40 .16
❏ 598 Don Sutton .40 .16
❏ 599 Tom Tellmann .15 .06
❏ 600 Rick Waits .15 .06
❏ 601 Robin Yount 2.00 .80
❏ 602 Dusty Baker .40 .16
❏ 603 Bob Brenly .15 .06
❏ 604 Jack Clark .40 .16
❏ 605 Chili Davis .40 .16
❏ 606 Mark Davis .15 .06
❏ 607 Dan Gladden RC .50 .20
❏ 608 Atlee Hammaker .15 .06
❏ 609 Mike Krukow .15 .06
❏ 610 Duane Kuiper .15 .06
❏ 611 Bob Lacey .15 .06
❏ 612 Bill Laskey .15 .06
❏ 613 Gary Lavelle .15 .06
❏ 614 Johnnie LeMaster .15 .06
❏ 615 Jeff Leonard .15 .06
❏ 616 Randy Lerch .15 .06
❏ 617 Greg Minton .15 .06
❏ 618 Steve Nicosia .15 .06
❏ 619 Gene Richards .15 .06
❏ 620 Jeff D. Robinson .15 .06
❏ 621 Scot Thompson .15 .06
❏ 622 Manny Trillo .15 .06
❏ 623 Brad Wellman .15 .06
❏ 624 Frank Williams .15 .06
❏ 625 Joel Youngblood .15 .06
❏ 626 Cal Ripken IA 3.00 1.20
❏ 627 Mike Schmidt IA 1.25 .50
❏ 628 Sparky Anderson IA .40 .16
❏ 629 Dave Winfield .40 .16
Rickey Henderson
❏ 630 Mike Schmidt 2.00 .80
Ryne Sandberg
❏ 631 Darryl Strawberry 1.25 .50
Gary Carter
Steve Garvey
Ozzie Smith
❏ 632 Gary Carter .15 .06
Charlie Lea
❏ 633 Steve Garvey .40 .16
Rich Gossage
❏ 634 Dwight Gooden 1.25 .50
Juan Samuel
❏ 635 Willie Upshaw IA .15 .06
❏ 636 Lloyd Moseby IA .15 .06
❏ 637 HOLLAND: Al Holland .15 .06
❏ 638 TUNNELL .15 .06
Lee Tunnell
❏ 639 Reggie Jackson IA .40 .16
❏ 640 4000th Hit IA 1.25 .50
❏ 641 Cal Ripken Jr. 3.00 1.20
Cal Ripken Sr.
❏ 642 Cubs Division Champs .40 .16
❏ 643 Two Perfect Games .40 .16
and One No-Hitter:
Mike Witt
David Palmer
Jack Morris
❏ 644 Willie Lozado and .15 .06
Vic Mata
❏ 645 Kelly Gruber RC and .50 .20
Randy O'Neal
❏ 646 Jose Roman .15 .06
Joel Skinner
❏ 647 Steve Kiefer RC and 1.00 .40
Danny Tartabull
❏ 648 Rob Dee RC and .50 .20
Alejandro Sanchez
❏ 649 Billy Hatcher RC and 1.00 .40
Shawon Dunston
❏ 650 Ron Robinson and .15 .06
Mike Bielecki
❏ 651 Zane Smith RC and .50 .20
Paul Zuvella
❏ 652 Joe Hesketh RC and .50 .20
Glenn Davis
❏ 653 John Russell and .15 .06
Steve Jeltz
❏ 654 CL: Tigers/Padres .15 .06
and Cubs/Mets
❏ 655 CL: Blue Jays/Yankees .15 .06
and Red Sox/Orioles
❏ 656 CL: Royals/Cardinals .15 .06
and Phillies/Twins
❏ 657 CL: Angels/Braves .15 .06
and Astros/Dodgers
❏ 658 CL: Expos/A's .15 .06
and Indians/Pirates
❏ 659 CL: Mariners/White Sox .15 .06
and Reds/Rangers
❏ 660 CL: Brewers/Giants .15 .06
and Special Cards

1985 Fleer Update

	Nm-Mt	Ex-Mt
COMP.FACT.SET (132)	8.00	3.20

❏ 1 Don Aase .15 .06
❏ 2 Bill Almon .15 .06
❏ 3 Dusty Baker .40 .16
❏ 4 Dale Berra .15 .06
❏ 5 Karl Best .15 .06
❏ 6 Tim Birtsas .15 .06
❏ 7 Vida Blue .40 .16
❏ 8 Rich Bordi .15 .06
❏ 9 Daryl Boston XRC* .25 .10
❏ 10 Hubie Brooks .15 .06

❏ 11 Chris Brown .25 .10
❏ 12 Tom Browning XRC* .50 .20
❏ 13 Al Bumbry .15 .06
❏ 14 Tim Burke .15 .06
❏ 15 Ray Burris .15 .06
❏ 16 Jeff Burroughs .15 .06
❏ 17 Ivan Calderon XRC .50 .20
❏ 18 Jeff Calhoun .15 .06
❏ 19 Bill Campbell .15 .06
❏ 20 Don Carman .15 .06
❏ 21 Gary Carter .40 .16
❏ 22 Bobby Castillo .15 .06
❏ 23 Bill Caudill .15 .06
❏ 24 Rick Cerone .15 .06
❏ 25 Jack Clark .40 .16
❏ 26 Pat Clements .15 .06
❏ 27 Stu Cliburn .15 .06
❏ 28 Vince Coleman XRC 1.00 .40
❏ 29 Dave Collins .15 .06
❏ 30 Fritz Connally .15 .06
❏ 31 Henry Cotto .25 .10
❏ 32 Danny Darwin .15 .06
❏ 33 Darren Daulton XRC 1.00 .40
❏ 34 Jerry Davis .15 .06
❏ 35 Brian Dayett .15 .06
❏ 36 Ken Dixon .15 .06
❏ 37 Tommy Dunbar .15 .06
❏ 38 Mariano Duncan XRC .50 .20
❏ 39 Bob Fallon .15 .06
❏ 40 Brian Fisher XRC .25 .10
❏ 41 Mike Fitzgerald .15 .06
❏ 42 Ray Fontenot .15 .06
❏ 43 Greg Gagne XRC* .50 .20
❏ 44 Oscar Gamble .15 .06
❏ 45 Jim Gott .15 .06
❏ 46 David Green .15 .06
❏ 47 Alfredo Griffin .15 .06
❏ 48 Ozzie Guillen XRC 4.00 1.60
❏ 49 Toby Harrah .40 .16
❏ 50 Ron Hassey .15 .06
❏ 51 Rickey Henderson 2.50 1.00
❏ 52 Steve Henderson .15 .06
❏ 53 George Hendrick .40 .16
❏ 54 Teddy Higuera XRC .50 .20
❏ 55 Al Holland .15 .06
❏ 56 Burt Hooton .15 .06
❏ 57 Jay Howell .15 .06
❏ 58 LaMarr Hoyt .15 .06
❏ 59 Tim Hulett XRC* .25 .10
❏ 60 Bob James .15 .06
❏ 61 Cliff Johnson .15 .06
❏ 62 Howard Johnson .40 .16
❏ 63 Ruppert Jones .15 .06
❏ 64 Steve Kemp .15 .06
❏ 65 Bruce Kison .15 .06
❏ 66 Mike LaCoss .15 .06
❏ 67 Lee Lacy .15 .06
❏ 68 Dave LaPoint .15 .06
❏ 69 Gary Lavelle .15 .06
❏ 70 Vance Law .15 .06
❏ 71 Manny Lee XRC .25 .10
❏ 72 Sixto Lezcano .15 .06
❏ 73 Tim Lollar .15 .06
❏ 74 Urbano Lugo .15 .06
❏ 75 Fred Lynn .40 .16
❏ 76 Steve Lyons XRC .50 .20
❏ 77 Mickey Mahler .15 .06
❏ 78 Ron Mathis .15 .06

❑ 79 Len Matuszek .15 .06
❑ 80 O.McDowell XRC UER .50 .20
Part of bio
actually Roger's
❑ 81 R.McDowell XRC UER .50 .20
Part of bio
actually Oddibe's
❑ 82 Donnie Moore .15 .06
❑ 83 Ron Musselman .15 .06
❑ 84 Al Oliver .40 .16
❑ 85 Joe Orsulak XRC .50 .20
❑ 86 Dan Pasqua XRC* .50 .20
❑ 87 Chris Pittaro .15 .06
❑ 88 Rick Reuschel .40 .16
❑ 89 Earnie Riles .15 .06
❑ 90 Jerry Royster .15 .06
❑ 91 Dave Rozema .15 .06
❑ 92 Dave Rucker .15 .06
❑ 93 Vern Ruhle .15 .06
❑ 94 Mark Salas .15 .06
❑ 95 Luis Salazar .15 .06
❑ 96 Joe Sambito .15 .06
❑ 97 Billy Sample .15 .06
❑ 98 Alejandro Sanchez XRC .25 .10
❑ 99 Calvin Schiraldi XRC .50 .20
❑ 100 Rick Schu .15 .06
❑ 101 Larry Sheets XRC .25 .10
❑ 102 Ron Shephard .15 .06
❑ 103 Nelson Simmons .15 .06
❑ 104 Don Slaught .15 .06
❑ 105 Roy Smalley .15 .06
❑ 106 Lonnie Smith .15 .06
❑ 107 Nate Snell .15 .06
❑ 108 Lary Sorensen .15 .06
❑ 109 Chris Speier .15 .06
❑ 110 Mike Stenhouse .15 .06
❑ 111 Tim Stoddard .15 .06
❑ 112 John Stuper .15 .06
❑ 113 Jim Sundberg .40 .16
❑ 114 Bruce Sutter .40 .16
❑ 115 Don Sutton .40 .16
❑ 116 Bruce Tanner .15 .06
❑ 117 Kent Tekulve .15 .06
❑ 118 Walt Terrell .15 .06
❑ 119 Mickey Tettleton XRC .50 .20
❑ 120 Rich Thompson .15 .06
❑ 121 Louis Thornton .15 .06
❑ 122 Alex Trevino .15 .06
❑ 123 John Tudor .40 .16
❑ 124 Jose Uribe .15 .06
❑ 125 Dave Valle XRC .50 .20
❑ 126 Dave Von Ohlen .15 .06
❑ 127 Curt Wardle .15 .06
❑ 128 U.L. Washington .15 .06
❑ 129 Ed Whitson .15 .06
❑ 130 Herm Winningham .15 .06
❑ 131 Rich Yett .15 .06
❑ 132 Checklist U1-U132 .15 .06

1986 Fleer

	Nm-Mt	Ex-Mt
COMPLETE SET (660)	40.00	16.00
COMP.FACT.SET (660)	40.00	16.00

❑ 1 Steve Balboni .15 .06
❑ 2 Joe Beckwith .15 .06
❑ 3 Buddy Biancalana .15 .06
❑ 4 Bud Black .15 .06
❑ 5 George Brett 2.00 .80
❑ 6 Onix Concepcion .15 .06
❑ 7 Steve Farr .15 .06
❑ 8 Mark Gubicza .15 .06
❑ 9 Dane Iorg .15 .06
❑ 10 Danny Jackson .15 .06
❑ 11 Lynn Jones .15 .06
❑ 12 Mike Jones .15 .06
❑ 13 Charlie Leibrandt .15 .06
❑ 14 Hal McRae .25 .10
❑ 15 Omar Moreno .15 .06
❑ 16 Darryl Motley .15 .06
❑ 17 Jorge Orta .15 .06
❑ 18 Dan Quisenberry .15 .06
❑ 19 Bret Saberhagen .25 .10
❑ 20 Pat Sheridan .15 .06
❑ 21 Lonnie Smith .15 .06
❑ 22 Jim Sundberg .25 .10
❑ 23 John Wathan .15 .06
❑ 24 Frank White .25 .10
❑ 25 Willie Wilson .25 .10
❑ 26 Joaquin Andujar .25 .10
❑ 27 Steve Braun .15 .06
❑ 28 Bill Campbell .15 .06
❑ 29 Cesar Cedeno .25 .10
❑ 30 Jack Clark .25 .10
❑ 31 Vince Coleman RC* 1.00 .40
❑ 32 Danny Cox .15 .06
❑ 33 Ken Dayley .15 .06
❑ 34 Ivan DeJesus .15 .06
❑ 35 Bob Forsch .15 .06
❑ 36 Brian Harper .15 .06
❑ 37 Tom Herr .15 .06
❑ 38 Ricky Horton .15 .06
❑ 39 Kurt Kepshire .15 .06
❑ 40 Jeff Lahti .15 .06
❑ 41 Tito Landrum .15 .06
❑ 42 Willie McGee .25 .10
❑ 43 Tom Nieto .15 .06
❑ 44 Terry Pendleton .25 .10
❑ 45 Darrell Porter .15 .06
❑ 46 Ozzie Smith 1.25 .50
❑ 47 John Tudor .25 .10
❑ 48 Andy Van Slyke .50 .20
❑ 49 Todd Worrell RC .50 .20
❑ 50 Jim Acker .15 .06
❑ 51 Doyle Alexander .15 .06
❑ 52 Jesse Barfield .25 .10
❑ 53 George Bell .25 .10
❑ 54 Jeff Burroughs .15 .06
❑ 55 Bill Caudill .15 .06
❑ 56 Jim Clancy .15 .06
❑ 57 Tony Fernandez .15 .06
❑ 58 Tom Filer .15 .06
❑ 59 Damaso Garcia .15 .06
❑ 60 Tom Henke .25 .10
❑ 61 Garth Iorg .15 .06
❑ 62 Cliff Johnson .15 .06
❑ 63 Jimmy Key .25 .10
❑ 64 Dennis Lamp .15 .06
❑ 65 Gary Lavelle .15 .06
❑ 66 Buck Martinez .15 .06
❑ 67 Lloyd Moseby .15 .06
❑ 68 Rance Mulliniks .15 .06
❑ 69 Al Oliver .25 .10
❑ 70 Dave Stieb .25 .10
❑ 71 Louis Thornton .15 .06
❑ 72 Willie Upshaw .15 .06
❑ 73 Ernie Whitt .15 .06
❑ 74 Rick Aguilera RC .50 .20
❑ 75 Wally Backman .15 .06
❑ 76 Gary Carter .25 .10
❑ 77 Ron Darling .25 .10
❑ 78 Len Dykstra RC 1.50 .60
❑ 79 Sid Fernandez .15 .06
❑ 80 George Foster .25 .10
❑ 81 Dwight Gooden .75 .30
❑ 82 Tom Gorman .15 .06
❑ 83 Danny Heep .15 .06
❑ 84 Keith Hernandez .25 .10
❑ 85 Howard Johnson .25 .10
❑ 86 Ray Knight .25 .10
❑ 87 Terry Leach .15 .06
❑ 88 Ed Lynch .15 .06
❑ 89 Roger McDowell RC* .50 .20
❑ 90 Jesse Orosco .15 .06
❑ 91 Tom Paciorek .15 .06
❑ 92 Ronn Reynolds .15 .06
❑ 93 Rafael Santana .15 .06
❑ 94 Doug Sisk .15 .06
❑ 95 Rusty Staub .25 .10
❑ 96 Darryl Strawberry .50 .20
❑ 97 Mookie Wilson .25 .10
❑ 98 Neil Allen .15 .06
❑ 99 Don Baylor .25 .10
❑ 100 Dale Berra .15 .06
❑ 101 Rich Bordi .15 .06
❑ 102 Marty Bystrom .15 .06
❑ 103 Joe Cowley .15 .06
❑ 104 Brian Fisher RC .15 .06
❑ 105 Ken Griffey .25 .10
❑ 106 Ron Guidry .25 .10
❑ 107 Ron Hassey .15 .06
❑ 108 R.Henderson UER .75 .30
SB Record of 120, sic
❑ 109 Don Mattingly 2.50 1.00
❑ 110 Bobby Meacham .15 .06
❑ 111 John Montefusco .15 .06
❑ 112 Phil Niekro .25 .10
❑ 113 Mike Pagliarulo .15 .06
❑ 114 Dan Pasqua .15 .06
❑ 115 Willie Randolph .25 .10
❑ 116 Dave Righetti .25 .10
❑ 117 Andre Robertson .15 .06
❑ 118 Billy Sample .15 .06
❑ 119 Bob Shirley .15 .06
❑ 120 Ed Whitson .15 .06
❑ 121 Dave Winfield .25 .10
❑ 122 Butch Wynegar .15 .06
❑ 123 Dave Anderson .15 .06
❑ 124 Bob Bailor .15 .06
❑ 125 Greg Brock .15 .06
❑ 126 Enos Cabell .15 .06
❑ 127 Bobby Castillo .15 .06
❑ 128 Carlos Diaz .15 .06
❑ 129 Mariano Duncan RC* .50 .20
❑ 130 Pedro Guerrero .25 .10
❑ 131 Orel Hershiser .75 .30
❑ 132 Rick Honeycutt .15 .06
❑ 133 Ken Howell .15 .06
❑ 134 Ken Landreaux .15 .06
❑ 135 Bill Madlock .25 .10
❑ 136 Candy Maldonado .15 .06
❑ 137 Mike Marshall .15 .06
❑ 138 Len Matuszek .15 .06
❑ 139 Tom Niedenfuer .15 .06
❑ 140 Alejandro Pena .15 .06
❑ 141 Jerry Reuss .15 .06
❑ 142 Bill Russell .25 .10
❑ 143 Steve Sax .15 .06
❑ 144 Mike Scioscia .25 .10
❑ 145 Fernando Valenzuela .25 .10
❑ 146 Bob Welch .25 .10
❑ 147 Terry Whitfield .15 .06
❑ 148 Juan Beniquez .15 .06
❑ 149 Bob Boone .25 .10
❑ 150 John Candelaria .15 .06
❑ 151 Rod Carew .50 .20
❑ 152 Stu Cliburn .15 .06
❑ 153 Doug DeCinces .15 .06
❑ 154 Brian Downing .25 .10
❑ 155 Ken Forsch .15 .06
❑ 156 Craig Gerber .15 .06
❑ 157 Bobby Grich .25 .10
❑ 158 George Hendrick .25 .10
❑ 159 Al Holland .15 .06
❑ 160 Reggie Jackson .50 .20
❑ 161 Ruppert Jones .15 .06
❑ 162 Urbano Lugo .15 .06
❑ 163 Kirk McCaskill RC .50 .20
❑ 164 Donnie Moore .15 .06
❑ 165 Gary Pettis .15 .06
❑ 166 Ron Romanick .15 .06
❑ 167 Dick Schofield .15 .06
❑ 168 Daryl Sconiers .15 .06
❑ 169 Jim Slaton .15 .06
❑ 170 Don Sutton .25 .10
❑ 171 Mike Witt .15 .06
❑ 172 Buddy Bell .25 .10
❑ 173 Tom Browning .15 .06
❑ 174 Dave Concepcion .25 .10
❑ 175 Eric Davis .75 .30

No.	Player	Price	Price
❑ 176	Bo Diaz	.15	.06
❑ 177	Nick Esasky	.15	.06
❑ 178	John Franco	.25	.10
❑ 179	Tom Hume	.15	.06
❑ 180	Wayne Krenchicki	.15	.06
❑ 181	Andy McGaffigan	.15	.06
❑ 182	Eddie Milner	.15	.06
❑ 183	Ron Oester	.15	.06
❑ 184	Dave Parker	.25	.10
❑ 185	Frank Pastore	.15	.06
❑ 186	Tony Perez	.50	.20
❑ 187	Ted Power	.15	.06
❑ 188	Joe Price	.15	.06
❑ 189	Gary Redus	.15	.06
❑ 190	Ron Robinson	.15	.06
❑ 191	Pete Rose	2.50	1.00
❑ 192	Mario Soto	.25	.10
❑ 193	John Stuper	.15	.06
❑ 194	Jay Tibbs	.15	.06
❑ 195	Dave Van Gorder	.15	.06
❑ 196	Max Venable	.15	.06
❑ 197	Juan Agosto	.15	.06
❑ 198	Harold Baines	.25	.10
❑ 199	Floyd Bannister	.15	.06
❑ 200	Britt Burns	.15	.06
❑ 201	Julio Cruz	.15	.06
❑ 202	Joel Davis	.15	.06
❑ 203	Richard Dotson	.15	.06
❑ 204	Carlton Fisk	.50	.20
❑ 205	Scott Fletcher	.15	.06
❑ 206	Ozzie Guillen RC	2.00	.80
❑ 207	Jerry Hairston	.15	.06
❑ 208	Tim Hulett	.15	.06
❑ 209	Bob James	.15	.06
❑ 210	Ron Kittle	.15	.06
❑ 211	Rudy Law	.15	.06
❑ 212	Bryan Little	.15	.06
❑ 213	Gene Nelson	.15	.06
❑ 214	Reid Nichols	.15	.06
❑ 215	Luis Salazar	.15	.06
❑ 216	Tom Seaver	.50	.20
❑ 217	Dan Spillner	.15	.06
❑ 218	Bruce Tanner	.15	.06
❑ 219	Greg Walker	.15	.06
❑ 220	Dave Wehrmeister	.15	.06
❑ 221	Juan Berenguer	.15	.06
❑ 222	Dave Bergman	.15	.06
❑ 223	Tom Brookens	.15	.06
❑ 224	Darrell Evans	.25	.10
❑ 225	Barbaro Garbey	.15	.06
❑ 226	Kirk Gibson	.50	.20
❑ 227	John Grubb	.15	.06
❑ 228	Willie Hernandez	.15	.06
❑ 229	Larry Herndon	.15	.06
❑ 230	Chet Lemon	.25	.10
❑ 231	Aurelio Lopez	.15	.06
❑ 232	Jack Morris	.25	.10
❑ 233	Randy O'Neal	.15	.06
❑ 234	Lance Parrish	.25	.10
❑ 235	Dan Petry	.15	.06
❑ 236	Alejandro Sanchez	.15	.06
❑ 237	Bill Scherrer	.15	.06
❑ 238	Nelson Simmons	.15	.06
❑ 239	Frank Tanana	.25	.10
❑ 240	Walt Terrell	.15	.06
❑ 241	Alan Trammell	.25	.10
❑ 242	Lou Whitaker	.25	.10
❑ 243	Milt Wilcox	.15	.06
❑ 244	Hubie Brooks	.15	.06
❑ 245	Tim Burke	.15	.06
❑ 246	Andre Dawson	.25	.10
❑ 247	Mike Fitzgerald	.15	.06
❑ 248	Terry Francona	.25	.10
❑ 249	Bill Gullickson	.15	.06
❑ 250	Joe Hesketh	.15	.06
❑ 251	Bill Laskey	.15	.06
❑ 252	Vance Law	.15	.06
❑ 253	Charlie Lea	.15	.06
❑ 254	Gary Lucas	.15	.06
❑ 255	David Palmer	.15	.06
❑ 256	Tim Raines	.25	.10
❑ 257	Jeff Reardon	.25	.10
❑ 258	Bert Roberge	.15	.06
❑ 259	Dan Schatzeder	.15	.06
❑ 260	Bryn Smith	.15	.06
❑ 261	Randy St.Claire	.15	.06
❑ 262	Scot Thompson	.15	.06
❑ 263	Tim Wallach	.15	.06
❑ 264	U.L. Washington	.15	.06
❑ 265	Mitch Webster	.15	.06
❑ 266	Herm Winningham	.15	.06
❑ 267	Floyd Youmans	.15	.06
❑ 268	Don Aase	.15	.06
❑ 269	Mike Boddicker	.15	.06
❑ 270	Rich Dauer	.15	.06
❑ 271	Storm Davis	.15	.06
❑ 272	Rick Dempsey	.15	.06
❑ 273	Ken Dixon	.15	.06
❑ 274	Jim Dwyer	.15	.06
❑ 275	Mike Flanagan	.15	.06
❑ 276	Wayne Gross	.15	.06
❑ 277	Lee Lacy	.15	.06
❑ 278	Fred Lynn	.25	.10
❑ 279	Tippy Martinez	.15	.06
❑ 280	Dennis Martinez	.25	.10
❑ 281	Scott McGregor	.15	.06
❑ 282	Eddie Murray	.75	.30
❑ 283	Floyd Rayford	.15	.06
❑ 284	Cal Ripken	3.00	1.20
❑ 285	Gary Roenicke	.15	.06
❑ 286	Larry Sheets	.15	.06
❑ 287	John Shelby	.15	.06
❑ 288	Nate Snell	.15	.06
❑ 289	Sammy Stewart	.15	.06
❑ 290	Alan Wiggins	.15	.06
❑ 291	Mike Young	.15	.06
❑ 292	Alan Ashby	.15	.06
❑ 293	Mark Bailey	.15	.06
❑ 294	Kevin Bass	.15	.06
❑ 295	Jeff Calhoun	.15	.06
❑ 296	Jose Cruz	.25	.10
❑ 297	Glenn Davis	.15	.06
❑ 298	Bill Dawley	.15	.06
❑ 299	Frank DiPino	.15	.06
❑ 300	Bill Doran	.15	.06
❑ 301	Phil Garner	.25	.10
❑ 302	Jeff Heathcock	.15	.06
❑ 303	Charlie Kerfeld	.15	.06
❑ 304	Bob Knepper	.15	.06
❑ 305	Ron Mathis	.15	.06
❑ 306	Jerry Mumphrey	.15	.06
❑ 307	Jim Pankovits	.15	.06
❑ 308	Terry Puhl	.15	.06
❑ 309	Craig Reynolds	.15	.06
❑ 310	Nolan Ryan	4.00	1.60
❑ 311	Mike Scott	.25	.10
❑ 312	Dave Smith	.15	.06
❑ 313	Dickie Thon	.15	.06
❑ 314	Denny Walling	.15	.06
❑ 315	Kurt Bevacqua	.15	.06
❑ 316	Al Bumbry	.15	.06
❑ 317	Jerry Davis	.15	.06
❑ 318	Luis DeLeon	.15	.06
❑ 319	Dave Dravecky	.15	.06
❑ 320	Tim Flannery	.15	.06
❑ 321	Steve Garvey	.25	.10
❑ 322	Rich Gossage	.25	.10
❑ 323	Tony Gwynn	1.25	.50
❑ 324	Andy Hawkins	.15	.06
❑ 325	LaMarr Hoyt	.15	.06
❑ 326	Roy Lee Jackson	.15	.06
❑ 327	Terry Kennedy	.15	.06
❑ 328	Craig Lefferts	.15	.06
❑ 329	Carmelo Martinez	.15	.06
❑ 330	Lance McCullers	.15	.06
❑ 331	Kevin McReynolds	.15	.06
❑ 332	Graig Nettles	.25	.10
❑ 333	Jerry Royster	.15	.06
❑ 334	Eric Show	.15	.06
❑ 335	Tim Stoddard	.15	.06
❑ 336	Garry Templeton	.25	.10
❑ 337	Mark Thurmond	.15	.06
❑ 338	Ed Wojna	.15	.06
❑ 339	Tony Armas	.25	.10
❑ 340	Marty Barrett	.15	.06
❑ 341	Wade Boggs	.50	.20
❑ 342	Dennis Boyd	.15	.06
❑ 343	Bill Buckner	.25	.10
❑ 344	Mark Clear	.15	.06
❑ 345	Roger Clemens	5.00	2.00
❑ 346	Steve Crawford	.15	.06
❑ 347	Mike Easler	.15	.06
❑ 348	Dwight Evans	.50	.20
❑ 349	Rich Gedman	.15	.06
❑ 350	Jackie Gutierrez	.15	.06
❑ 351	Glenn Hoffman	.15	.06
❑ 352	Bruce Hurst	.15	.06
❑ 353	Bruce Kison	.15	.06
❑ 354	Tim Lollar	.15	.06
❑ 355	Steve Lyons	.15	.06
❑ 356	Al Nipper	.15	.06
❑ 357	Bob Ojeda	.15	.06
❑ 358	Jim Rice	.25	.10
❑ 359	Bob Stanley	.15	.06
❑ 360	Mike Trujillo	.15	.06
❑ 361	Thad Bosley	.15	.06
❑ 362	Warren Brusstar	.15	.06
❑ 363	Ron Cey	.25	.10
❑ 364	Jody Davis	.15	.06
❑ 365	Bob Dernier	.15	.06
❑ 366	Shawon Dunston	.25	.10
❑ 367	Leon Durham	.15	.06
❑ 368	Dennis Eckersley	.50	.20
❑ 369	Ray Fontenot	.15	.06
❑ 370	George Frazier	.15	.06
❑ 371	Billy Hatcher	.15	.06
❑ 372	Dave Lopes	.25	.10
❑ 373	Gary Matthews	.25	.10
❑ 374	Ron Meridith	.15	.06
❑ 375	Keith Moreland	.15	.06
❑ 376	Reggie Patterson	.15	.06
❑ 377	Dick Ruthven	.15	.06
❑ 378	Ryne Sandberg	1.50	.60
❑ 379	Scott Sanderson	.15	.06
❑ 380	Lee Smith	.25	.10
❑ 381	Lary Sorensen	.15	.06
❑ 382	Chris Speier	.15	.06
❑ 383	Rick Sutcliffe	.25	.10
❑ 384	Steve Trout	.15	.06
❑ 385	Gary Woods	.15	.06
❑ 386	Bert Blyleven	.25	.10
❑ 387	Tom Brunansky	.15	.06
❑ 388	Randy Bush	.15	.06
❑ 389	John Butcher	.15	.06
❑ 390	Ron Davis	.15	.06
❑ 391	Dave Engle	.15	.06
❑ 392	Frank Eufemia	.15	.06
❑ 393	Pete Filson	.15	.06
❑ 394	Gary Gaetti	.25	.10
❑ 395	Greg Gagne	.15	.06
❑ 396	Mickey Hatcher	.15	.06
❑ 397	Kent Hrbek	.25	.10
❑ 398	Tim Laudner	.15	.06
❑ 399	Rick Lysander	.15	.06
❑ 400	Dave Meier	.15	.06
❑ 401	Kirby Puckett UER Card has him in NL, should be AL	2.00	.80
❑ 402	Mark Salas	.15	.06
❑ 403	Ken Schrom	.15	.06
❑ 404	Roy Smalley	.15	.06
❑ 405	Mike Smithson	.15	.06
❑ 406	Mike Stenhouse	.15	.06
❑ 407	Tim Teufel	.15	.06
❑ 408	Frank Viola	.25	.10
❑ 409	Ron Washington	.15	.06
❑ 410	Keith Atherton	.15	.06
❑ 411	Dusty Baker	.25	.10
❑ 412	Tim Birtsas	.15	.06
❑ 413	Bruce Bochte	.15	.06
❑ 414	Chris Codiroli	.15	.06
❑ 415	Dave Collins	.15	.06
❑ 416	Mike Davis	.15	.06
❑ 417	Alfredo Griffin	.15	.06
❑ 418	Mike Heath	.15	.06
❑ 419	Steve Henderson	.15	.06
❑ 420	Donnie Hill	.15	.06
❑ 421	Jay Howell	.15	.06
❑ 422	Tommy John	.25	.10
❑ 423	Dave Kingman	.25	.10
❑ 424	Bill Krueger	.15	.06
❑ 425	Rick Langford	.15	.06
❑ 426	Carney Lansford	.25	.10
❑ 427	Steve McCatty	.15	.06
❑ 428	Dwayne Murphy	.15	.06
❑ 429	Steve Ontiveros RC	.15	.06
❑ 430	Tony Phillips	.15	.06
❑ 431	Jose Rijo	.25	.10

❑ 432 Mickey Tettleton RC .50 .20
❑ 433 Luis Aguayo .15 .06
❑ 434 Larry Andersen .15 .06
❑ 435 Steve Carlton .25 .10
❑ 436 Don Carman .15 .06
❑ 437 Tim Corcoran .15 .06
❑ 438 Darren Daulton RC 1.00 .40
❑ 439 John Denny .15 .06
❑ 440 Tom Foley .15 .06
❑ 441 Greg Gross .15 .06
❑ 442 Kevin Gross .15 .06
❑ 443 Von Hayes .15 .06
❑ 444 Charles Hudson .15 .06
❑ 445 Garry Maddox .15 .06
❑ 446 Shane Rawley .15 .06
❑ 447 Dave Rucker .15 .06
❑ 448 John Russell .15 .06
❑ 449 Juan Samuel .15 .06
❑ 450 Mike Schmidt 2.00 .80
❑ 451 Rick Schu .15 .06
❑ 452 Dave Shipanoff .15 .06
❑ 453 Dave Stewart .25 .10
❑ 454 Jeff Stone .15 .06
❑ 455 Kent Tekulve .15 .06
❑ 456 Ozzie Virgil .15 .06
❑ 457 Glenn Wilson .15 .06
❑ 458 Jim Beattie .15 .06
❑ 459 Karl Best .15 .06
❑ 460 Barry Bonnell .15 .06
❑ 461 Phil Bradley .15 .06
❑ 462 Ivan Calderon RC* .50 .20
❑ 463 Al Cowens .15 .06
❑ 464 Alvin Davis .15 .06
❑ 465 Dave Henderson .15 .06
❑ 466 Bob Kearney .15 .06
❑ 467 Mark Langston .25 .10
❑ 468 Bob Long .15 .06
❑ 469 Mike Moore .15 .06
❑ 470 Edwin Nunez .15 .06
❑ 471 Spike Owen .15 .06
❑ 472 Jack Perconte .15 .06
❑ 473 Jim Presley .15 .06
❑ 474 Donnie Scott .15 .06
❑ 475 Bill Swift .15 .06
❑ 476 Danny Tartabull .25 .10
❑ 477 Gorman Thomas .25 .10
❑ 478 Roy Thomas .15 .06
❑ 479 Ed VandeBerg .15 .06
❑ 480 Frank Wills .15 .06
❑ 481 Matt Young .15 .06
❑ 482 Ray Burris .15 .06
❑ 483 Jaime Cocanower .15 .06
❑ 484 Cecil Cooper .25 .10
❑ 485 Danny Darwin .15 .06
❑ 486 Rollie Fingers .25 .10
❑ 487 Jim Gantner .15 .06
❑ 488 Bob L. Gibson .15 .06
❑ 489 Moose Haas .15 .06
❑ 490 Teddy Higuera RC* .50 .20
❑ 491 Paul Householder .15 .06
❑ 492 Pete Ladd .15 .06
❑ 493 Rick Manning .15 .06
❑ 494 Bob McClure .15 .06
❑ 495 Paul Molitor .50 .20
❑ 496 Charlie Moore .15 .06
❑ 497 Ben Oglivie .25 .10
❑ 498 Randy Ready .15 .06
❑ 499 Earnie Riles .15 .06
❑ 500 Ed Romero .15 .06
❑ 501 Bill Schroeder .15 .06
❑ 502 Ray Searage .15 .06
❑ 503 Ted Simmons .25 .10
❑ 504 Pete Vuckovich .15 .06
❑ 505 Rick Waits .15 .06
❑ 506 Robin Yount 1.25 .50
❑ 507 Len Barker .15 .06
❑ 508 Steve Bedrosian .15 .06
❑ 509 Bruce Benedict .15 .06
❑ 510 Rick Camp .15 .06
❑ 511 Rick Cerone .15 .06
❑ 512 Chris Chambliss .25 .10
❑ 513 Jeff Dedmon .15 .06
❑ 514 Terry Forster .25 .10
❑ 515 Gene Garber .15 .06
❑ 516 Terry Harper .15 .06
❑ 517 Bob Horner .25 .10
❑ 518 Glenn Hubbard .15 .06
❑ 519 Joe Johnson .15 .06
❑ 520 Brad Komminsk .15 .06
❑ 521 Rick Mahler .15 .06
❑ 522 Dale Murphy .50 .20
❑ 523 Ken Oberkfell .15 .06
❑ 524 Pascual Perez .15 .06
❑ 525 Gerald Perry .15 .06
❑ 526 Rafael Ramirez .15 .06
❑ 527 Steve Shields .15 .06
❑ 528 Zane Smith .15 .06
❑ 529 Bruce Sutter .25 .10
❑ 530 Milt Thompson RC .50 .20
❑ 531 Claudell Washington .15 .06
❑ 532 Paul Zuvella .15 .06
❑ 533 Vida Blue .25 .10
❑ 534 Bob Brenly .15 .06
❑ 535 Chris Brown .15 .06
❑ 536 Chili Davis .25 .10
❑ 537 Mark Davis .15 .06
❑ 538 Rob Deer .15 .06
❑ 539 Dan Driessen .15 .06
❑ 540 Scott Garrelts .15 .06
❑ 541 Dan Gladden .15 .06
❑ 542 Jim Gott .15 .06
❑ 543 David Green .15 .06
❑ 544 Atlee Hammaker .15 .06
❑ 545 Mike Jeffcoat .15 .06
❑ 546 Mike Krukow .15 .06
❑ 547 Dave LaPoint .15 .06
❑ 548 Jeff Leonard .15 .06
❑ 549 Greg Minton .15 .06
❑ 550 Alex Trevino .15 .06
❑ 551 Manny Trillo .15 .06
❑ 552 Jose Uribe .15 .06
❑ 553 Brad Wellman .15 .06
❑ 554 Frank Williams .15 .06
❑ 555 Joel Youngblood .15 .06
❑ 556 Alan Bannister .15 .06
❑ 557 Glenn Brummer .15 .06
❑ 558 Steve Buechele RC .50 .20
❑ 559 Jose Guzman RC .15 .06
❑ 560 Toby Harrah .25 .10
❑ 561 Greg Harris .15 .06
❑ 562 Dwayne Henry .15 .06
❑ 563 Burt Hooton .15 .06
❑ 564 Charlie Hough .25 .10
❑ 565 Mike Mason .15 .06
❑ 566 Oddibe McDowell .15 .06
❑ 567 Dickie Noles .15 .06
❑ 568 Pete O'Brien .15 .06
❑ 569 Larry Parrish .15 .06
❑ 570 Dave Rozema .15 .06
❑ 571 Dave Schmidt .15 .06
❑ 572 Don Slaught .15 .06
❑ 573 Wayne Tolleson .15 .06
❑ 574 Duane Walker .15 .06
❑ 575 Gary Ward .15 .06
❑ 576 Chris Welsh .15 .06
❑ 577 Curtis Wilkerson .15 .06
❑ 578 George Wright .15 .06
❑ 579 Chris Bando .15 .06
❑ 580 Tony Bernazard .15 .06
❑ 581 Brett Butler .25 .10
❑ 582 Ernie Camacho .15 .06
❑ 583 Joe Carter .25 .10
❑ 584 Carmen Castillo .15 .06
❑ 585 Jamie Easterly .15 .06
❑ 586 Julio Franco .25 .10
❑ 587 Mel Hall .15 .06
❑ 588 Mike Hargrove .15 .06
❑ 589 Neal Heaton .15 .06
❑ 590 Brook Jacoby .15 .06
❑ 591 Otis Nixon RC 1.00 .40
❑ 592 Jerry Reed .15 .06
❑ 593 Vern Ruhle .15 .06
❑ 594 Pat Tabler .15 .06
❑ 595 Rich Thompson .15 .06
❑ 596 Andre Thornton .15 .06
❑ 597 Dave Von Ohlen .15 .06
❑ 598 George Vukovich .15 .06
❑ 599 Tom Waddell .15 .06
❑ 600 Curt Wardle .15 .06
❑ 601 Jerry Willard .15 .06
❑ 602 Bill Almon .15 .06
❑ 603 Mike Bielecki .15 .06
❑ 604 Sid Bream .15 .06
❑ 605 Mike C. Brown .15 .06
❑ 606 Pat Clements .15 .06
❑ 607 Jose DeLeon .15 .06
❑ 608 Denny Gonzalez .15 .06
❑ 609 Cecilio Guante .15 .06
❑ 610 Steve Kemp .15 .06
❑ 611 Sammy Khalifa .15 .06
❑ 612 Lee Mazzilli .25 .10
❑ 613 Larry McWilliams .15 .06
❑ 614 Jim Morrison .15 .06
❑ 615 Joe Orsulak RC* .50 .20
❑ 616 Tony Pena .15 .06
❑ 617 Johnny Ray .15 .06
❑ 618 Rick Reuschel .25 .10
❑ 619 R.J. Reynolds .15 .06
❑ 620 Rick Rhoden .15 .06
❑ 621 Don Robinson .15 .06
❑ 622 Jason Thompson .15 .06
❑ 623 Lee Tunnell .15 .06
❑ 624 Jim Winn .15 .06
❑ 625 Marvell Wynne .15 .06
❑ 626 Dwight Gooden IA .50 .20
❑ 627 Don Mattingly IA 1.25 .50
❑ 628 Pete Rose 4192 .50 .20
❑ 629 Rod Carew 3000 Hits .25 .10
❑ 630 Tom Seaver .25 .10
Phil Niekro
❑ 631 Don Baylor Ouch .25 .10
❑ 632 Darryl Strawberry .25 .10
Tim Raines
❑ 633 Cal Ripken 1.50 .60
Alan Trammell
❑ 634 Wade Boggs 1.00 .40
George Brett
❑ 635 Bob Horner .50 .20
Dale Murphy
❑ 636 Willie McGee .25 .10
Vince Coleman
❑ 637 Vince Coleman IA .25 .10
❑ 638 Pete Rose .75 .30
Dwight Gooden
❑ 639 Wade Boggs 1.25 .50
Don Mattingly
❑ 640 Dale Murphy .50 .20
Steve Garvey
Dave Parker
❑ 641 Fernando Valenzuela .50 .20
Dwight Gooden
❑ 642 Jimmy Key .25 .10
Dave Stieb
❑ 643 Carlton Fisk .25 .10
Rich Gedman
❑ 644 Gene Walter RC and 2.00 .80
Benito Santiago
❑ 645 Mike Woodard and .15 .06
Colin Ward
❑ 646 Kal Daniels RC and 4.00 1.60
Paul O'Neill
❑ 647 Andres Galarraga RC 1.50 .60
Fred Toliver
❑ 648 Bob Kipper and .15 .06
Curt Ford
❑ 649 Jose Canseco RC and 8.00 3.20
Eric Plunk
❑ 650 Mark McLemore RC 1.00 .40
Gus Polidor
❑ 651 Rob Woodward and .15 .06
Mickey Brantley
❑ 652 Billy Joe Robidoux .15 .06
Mark Funderburk
❑ 653 Cecil Fielder RC and 2.00 .80
Cory Snyder
❑ 654 CL: Royals/Cardinals .15 .06
Blue Jays/Mets
❑ 655 CL: Yankees/Dodgers .15 .06
Angels/Reds UER
(168 Darly Sconiers)
❑ 656 CL: White Sox/Tigers .15 .06
Expos/Orioles
(279 Dennis&
280 Tippy)
❑ 657 CL: Astros/Padres .15 .06
Red Sox/Cubs
❑ 658 CL: Twins/A's .15 .06
Phillies/Mariners

Card	Nm-Mt	Ex-Mt
❑ 659 CL: Brewers/Braves Giants/Rangers	.15	.06
❑ 660 CL: Indians/Pirates Special Cards	.15	.06

1986 Fleer Update

	Nm-Mt	Ex-Mt
COMP.FACT.SET (132)	50.00	20.00
❑ 1 Mike Aldrete	.15	.06
❑ 2 Andy Allanson	.15	.06
❑ 3 Neil Allen	.15	.06
❑ 4 Joaquin Andujar	.25	.10
❑ 5 Paul Assenmacher	.50	.20
❑ 6 Scott Bailes	.15	.06
❑ 7 Jay Baller	.15	.06
❑ 8 Scott Bankhead	.15	.06
❑ 9 Bill Bathe	.15	.06
❑ 10 Don Baylor	.25	.10
❑ 11 Billy Beane XRC	1.00	.40
❑ 12 Steve Bedrosian	.15	.06
❑ 13 Juan Beniquez	.15	.06
❑ 14 Barry Bonds XRC	40.00	16.00
❑ 15 Bobby Bonilla UER (Wrong birthday) XRC	1.00	.40
❑ 16 Rich Bordi	.15	.06
❑ 17 Bill Campbell	.15	.06
❑ 18 Tom Candiotti	.15	.06
❑ 19 John Cangelosi	.15	.06
❑ 20 Jose Canseco UER (Headings on back for a pitcher)	4.00	1.60
❑ 21 Chuck Cary	.15	.06
❑ 22 Juan Castillo XRC	.15	.06
❑ 23 Rick Cerone	.15	.06
❑ 24 John Cerutti	.15	.06
❑ 25 Will Clark XRC	2.00	.80
❑ 26 Mark Clear	.15	.06
❑ 27 Darnell Coles	.15	.06
❑ 28 Dave Collins	.15	.06
❑ 29 Tim Conroy	.15	.06
❑ 30 Ed Correa	.15	.06
❑ 31 Joe Cowley	.15	.06
❑ 32 Bill Dawley	.15	.06
❑ 33 Rob Deer	.15	.06
❑ 34 John Denny	.15	.06
❑ 35 Jim Deshaies XRC	.15	.06
❑ 36 Doug Drabek XRC	1.00	.40
❑ 37 Mike Easler	.15	.06
❑ 38 Mark Eichhorn	.15	.06
❑ 39 Dave Engle	.15	.06
❑ 40 Mike Fischlin	.15	.06
❑ 41 Scott Fletcher	.15	.06
❑ 42 Terry Forster	.25	.10
❑ 43 Terry Francona	.25	.10
❑ 44 Andres Galarraga	1.25	.50
❑ 45 Lee Guetterman	.15	.06
❑ 46 Bill Gullickson	.15	.06
❑ 47 Jackie Gutierrez	.15	.06
❑ 48 Moose Haas	.15	.06
❑ 49 Billy Hatcher	.15	.06
❑ 50 Mike Heath	.15	.06
❑ 51 Guy Hoffman	.15	.06
❑ 52 Tom Hume	.15	.06
❑ 53 Pete Incaviglia XRC	.50	.20
❑ 54 Dane Iorg	.15	.06
❑ 55 Chris James XRC	.15	.06
❑ 56 Stan Javier XRC*	.50	.20
❑ 57 Tommy John	.25	.10
❑ 58 Tracy Jones	.15	.06
❑ 59 Wally Joyner XRC	1.00	.40
❑ 60 Wayne Krenchicki	.15	.06
❑ 61 John Kruk XRC	1.50	.60
❑ 62 Mike LaCoss	.15	.06
❑ 63 Pete Ladd	.15	.06
❑ 64 Dave LaPoint	.15	.06
❑ 65 Mike LaValliere XRC	.50	.20
❑ 66 Rudy Law	.15	.06
❑ 67 Dennis Leonard	.15	.06
❑ 68 Steve Lombardozzi	.15	.06
❑ 69 Aurelio Lopez	.15	.06
❑ 70 Mickey Mahler	.15	.06
❑ 71 Candy Maldonado	.15	.06
❑ 72 Roger Mason XRC*	.15	.06
❑ 73 Greg Mathews	.15	.06
❑ 74 Andy McGaffigan	.15	.06
❑ 75 Joel McKeon	.15	.06
❑ 76 Kevin Mitchell XRC	1.00	.40
❑ 77 Bill Mooneyham	.15	.06
❑ 78 Omar Moreno	.15	.06
❑ 79 Jerry Mumphrey	.15	.06
❑ 80 Al Newman	.25	.10
❑ 81 Phil Niekro	.25	.10
❑ 82 Randy Niemann	.15	.06
❑ 83 Juan Nieves	.15	.06
❑ 84 Bob Ojeda	.15	.06
❑ 85 Rick Ownbey	.15	.06
❑ 86 Tom Paciorek	.15	.06
❑ 87 David Palmer	.15	.06
❑ 88 Jeff Parrett XRC	.15	.06
❑ 89 Pat Perry	.15	.06
❑ 90 Dan Plesac	.15	.06
❑ 91 Darrell Porter	.15	.06
❑ 92 Luis Quinones	.15	.06
❑ 93 Rey Quinones UER (Misspelled Quinonez)	.15	.06
❑ 94 Gary Redus	.15	.06
❑ 95 Jeff Reed	.15	.06
❑ 96 Bip Roberts XRC	.50	.20
❑ 97 Billy Joe Robidoux	.15	.06
❑ 98 Gary Roenicke	.15	.06
❑ 99 Ron Roenicke	.15	.06
❑ 100 Angel Salazar	.15	.06
❑ 101 Joe Sambito	.15	.06
❑ 102 Billy Sample	.15	.06
❑ 103 Dave Schmidt	.15	.06
❑ 104 Ken Schrom	.15	.06
❑ 105 Ruben Sierra XRC	1.25	.50
❑ 106 Ted Simmons	.25	.10
❑ 107 Sammy Stewart	.15	.06
❑ 108 Kurt Stillwell	.15	.06
❑ 109 Dale Sveum	.15	.06
❑ 110 Tim Teufel	.15	.06
❑ 111 Bob Tewksbury XRC	.50	.20
❑ 112 Andres Thomas	.15	.06
❑ 113 Jason Thompson	.15	.06
❑ 114 Milt Thompson	.50	.20
❑ 115 R. Thompson XRC	.50	.20
❑ 116 Jay Tibbs	.15	.06
❑ 117 Fred Toliver	.15	.06
❑ 118 Wayne Tolleson	.15	.06
❑ 119 Alex Trevino	.15	.06
❑ 120 Manny Trillo	.15	.06
❑ 121 Ed VandeBerg	.15	.06
❑ 122 Ozzie Virgil	.15	.06
❑ 123 Tony Walker	.15	.06
❑ 124 Gene Walter	.15	.06
❑ 125 Duane Ward XRC	.50	.20
❑ 126 Jerry Willard	.15	.06
❑ 127 Mitch Williams XRC	.50	.20
❑ 128 Reggie Williams	.15	.06
❑ 129 Bobby Witt XRC	.50	.20
❑ 130 Marvell Wynne	.15	.06
❑ 131 Steve Yeager	.25	.10
❑ 132 Checklist 1-132	.15	.06

1987 Fleer

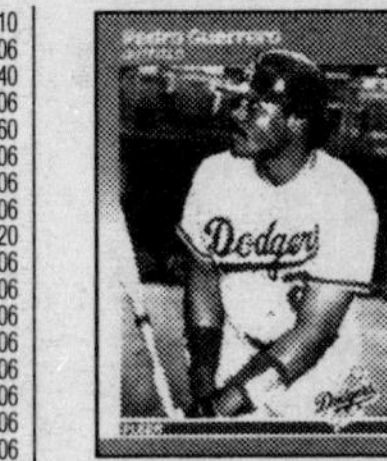

	Nm-Mt	Ex-Mt
COMPLETE SET (660)	80.00	32.00
COMP.FACT.SET (672)	80.00	32.00
❑ 1 Rick Aguilera	.15	.06
❑ 2 Richard Anderson	.15	.06
❑ 3 Wally Backman	.15	.06
❑ 4 Gary Carter	.25	.10
❑ 5 Ron Darling	.25	.10
❑ 6 Len Dykstra	.25	.10
❑ 7 Kevin Elster RC	.50	.20
❑ 8 Sid Fernandez	.15	.06
❑ 9 Dwight Gooden	.40	.16
❑ 10 Ed Hearn	.15	.06
❑ 11 Danny Heep	.15	.06
❑ 12 Keith Hernandez	.25	.10
❑ 13 Howard Johnson	.25	.10
❑ 14 Ray Knight	.25	.10
❑ 15 Lee Mazzilli	.25	.10
❑ 16 Roger McDowell	.15	.06
❑ 17 Kevin Mitchell RC *	1.25	.50
❑ 18 Randy Niemann	.15	.06
❑ 19 Bob Ojeda	.15	.06
❑ 20 Jesse Orosco	.15	.06
❑ 21 Rafael Santana	.15	.06
❑ 22 Doug Sisk	.15	.06
❑ 23 Darryl Strawberry	.25	.10
❑ 24 Tim Teufel	.15	.06
❑ 25 Mookie Wilson	.25	.10
❑ 26 Tony Armas	.25	.10
❑ 27 Marty Barrett	.15	.06
❑ 28 Don Baylor	.25	.10
❑ 29 Wade Boggs	.40	.16
❑ 30 Oil Can Boyd	.15	.06
❑ 31 Bill Buckner	.25	.10
❑ 32 Roger Clemens	1.50	.60
❑ 33 Steve Crawford	.15	.06
❑ 34 Dwight Evans	.40	.16
❑ 35 Rich Gedman	.15	.06
❑ 36 Dave Henderson	.15	.06
❑ 37 Bruce Hurst	.15	.06
❑ 38 Tim Lollar	.15	.06
❑ 39 Al Nipper	.15	.06
❑ 40 Spike Owen	.15	.06
❑ 41 Jim Rice	.25	.10
❑ 42 Ed Romero	.15	.06
❑ 43 Joe Sambito	.15	.06
❑ 44 Calvin Schiraldi	.15	.06
❑ 45 Tom Seaver UER (Lifetime saves total 0, should be 1)	.40	.16
❑ 46 Jeff Sellers	.15	.06
❑ 47 Bob Stanley	.15	.06
❑ 48 Sammy Stewart	.15	.06
❑ 49 Larry Andersen	.15	.06
❑ 50 Alan Ashby	.15	.06
❑ 51 Kevin Bass	.15	.06
❑ 52 Jeff Calhoun	.15	.06
❑ 53 Jose Cruz	.25	.10
❑ 54 Danny Darwin	.15	.06
❑ 55 Glenn Davis	.15	.06
❑ 56 Jim Deshaies RC *	.25	.10
❑ 57 Bill Doran	.15	.06
❑ 58 Phil Garner	.25	.10
❑ 59 Billy Hatcher	.15	.06
❑ 60 Charlie Kerfeld	.15	.06
❑ 61 Bob Knepper	.15	.06
❑ 62 Dave Lopes	.25	.10
❑ 63 Aurelio Lopez	.15	.06
❑ 64 Jim Pankovits	.15	.06
❑ 65 Terry Puhl	.15	.06
❑ 66 Craig Reynolds	.15	.06
❑ 67 Nolan Ryan	3.00	1.20
❑ 68 Mike Scott	.25	.10
❑ 69 Dave Smith	.15	.06

❑ 70 Dickie Thon .15 .06
❑ 71 Tony Walker .15 .06
❑ 72 Denny Walling .15 .06
❑ 73 Bob Boone .25 .10
❑ 74 Rick Burleson .15 .06
❑ 75 John Candelaria .15 .06
❑ 76 Doug Corbett .15 .06
❑ 77 Doug DeCinces .15 .06
❑ 78 Brian Downing .25 .10
❑ 79 Chuck Finley RC 1.25 .50
❑ 80 Terry Forster .25 .10
❑ 81 Bob Grich .25 .10
❑ 82 George Hendrick .25 .10
❑ 83 Jack Howell .15 .06
❑ 84 Reggie Jackson .40 .16
❑ 85 Ruppert Jones .15 .06
❑ 86 Wally Joyner RC 1.25 .50
❑ 87 Gary Lucas .15 .06
❑ 88 Kirk McCaskill .15 .06
❑ 89 Donnie Moore .15 .06
❑ 90 Gary Pettis .15 .06
❑ 91 Vern Ruhle .15 .06
❑ 92 Dick Schofield .15 .06
❑ 93 Don Sutton .25 .10
❑ 94 Rob Wilfong .15 .06
❑ 95 Mike Witt .15 .06
❑ 96 Doug Drabek RC 1.25 .50
❑ 97 Mike Easler .15 .06
❑ 98 Mike Fischlin .15 .06
❑ 99 Brian Fisher .15 .06
❑ 100 Ron Guidry .25 .10
❑ 101 Rickey Henderson .60 .24
❑ 102 Tommy John .25 .10
❑ 103 Ron Kittle .15 .06
❑ 104 Don Mattingly 2.00 .80
❑ 105 Bobby Meacham .15 .06
❑ 106 Joe Niekro .15 .06
❑ 107 Mike Pagliarulo .15 .06
❑ 108 Dan Pasqua .15 .06
❑ 109 Willie Randolph .25 .10
❑ 110 Dennis Rasmussen .15 .06
❑ 111 Dave Righetti .25 .10
❑ 112 Gary Roenicke .15 .06
❑ 113 Rod Scurry .15 .06
❑ 114 Bob Shirley .15 .06
❑ 115 Joel Skinner .15 .06
❑ 116 Tim Stoddard .15 .06
❑ 117 Bob Tewksbury RC * .50 .20
❑ 118 Wayne Tolleson .15 .06
❑ 119 Claudell Washington .15 .06
❑ 120 Dave Winfield .25 .10
❑ 121 Steve Buechele .15 .06
❑ 122 Ed Correa .15 .06
❑ 123 Scott Fletcher .15 .06
❑ 124 Jose Guzman .15 .06
❑ 125 Toby Harrah .25 .10
❑ 126 Greg Harris .15 .06
❑ 127 Charlie Hough .25 .10
❑ 128 Pete Incaviglia RC * .50 .20
❑ 129 Mike Mason .15 .06
❑ 130 Oddibe McDowell .15 .06
❑ 131 Dale Mohorcic .15 .06
❑ 132 Pete O'Brien .15 .06
❑ 133 Tom Paciorek .15 .06
❑ 134 Larry Parrish .15 .06
❑ 135 Geno Petralli .15 .06
❑ 136 Darrell Porter .15 .06
❑ 137 Jeff Russell .15 .06
❑ 138 Ruben Sierra RC 2.00 .80
❑ 139 Don Slaught .15 .06
❑ 140 Gary Ward .15 .06
❑ 141 Curtis Wilkerson .15 .06
❑ 142 Mitch Williams RC * .50 .20
❑ 143 Bobby Witt RC UER .50 .20
(Tulsa misspelled as Tusla; ERA should be 6.43, not .643)
❑ 144 Dave Bergman .15 .06
❑ 145 Tom Brookens .15 .06
❑ 146 Bill Campbell .15 .06
❑ 147 Chuck Cary .15 .06
❑ 148 Darnell Coles .15 .06
❑ 149 Dave Collins .15 .06
❑ 150 Darrell Evans .25 .10
❑ 151 Kirk Gibson .40 .16
❑ 152 John Grubb .15 .06
❑ 153 Willie Hernandez .15 .06
❑ 154 Larry Herndon .15 .06
❑ 155 Eric King .15 .06
❑ 156 Chet Lemon .25 .10
❑ 157 Dwight Lowry .15 .06
❑ 158 Jack Morris .25 .10
❑ 159 Randy O'Neal .15 .06
❑ 160 Lance Parrish .25 .10
❑ 161 Dan Petry .15 .06
❑ 162 Pat Sheridan .15 .06
❑ 163 Jim Slaton .15 .06
❑ 164 Frank Tanana .25 .10
❑ 165 Walt Terrell .15 .06
❑ 166 Mark Thurmond .15 .06
❑ 167 Alan Trammell .25 .10
❑ 168 Lou Whitaker .25 .10
❑ 169 Luis Aguayo .15 .06
❑ 170 Steve Bedrosian .15 .06
❑ 171 Don Carman .15 .06
❑ 172 Darren Daulton .25 .10
❑ 173 Greg Gross .15 .06
❑ 174 Kevin Gross .15 .06
❑ 175 Von Hayes .15 .06
❑ 176 Charles Hudson .15 .06
❑ 177 Tom Hume .15 .06
❑ 178 Steve Jeltz .15 .06
❑ 179 Mike Maddux .15 .06
❑ 180 Shane Rawley .15 .06
❑ 181 Gary Redus .15 .06
❑ 182 Ron Roenicke .15 .06
❑ 183 Bruce Ruffin RC .25 .10
❑ 184 John Russell .15 .06
❑ 185 Juan Samuel .15 .06
❑ 186 Dan Schatzeder .15 .06
❑ 187 Mike Schmidt 1.50 .60
❑ 188 Rick Schu .15 .06
❑ 189 Jeff Stone .15 .06
❑ 190 Kent Tekulve .15 .06
❑ 191 Milt Thompson .15 .06
❑ 192 Glenn Wilson .15 .06
❑ 193 Buddy Bell .25 .10
❑ 194 Tom Browning .15 .06
❑ 195 Sal Butera .15 .06
❑ 196 Dave Concepcion .25 .10
❑ 197 Kal Daniels .15 .06
❑ 198 Eric Davis .40 .16
❑ 199 John Denny .15 .06
❑ 200 Bo Diaz .15 .06
❑ 201 Nick Esasky .15 .06
❑ 202 John Franco .25 .10
❑ 203 Bill Gullickson .15 .06
❑ 204 Barry Larkin RC 3.00 1.20
❑ 205 Eddie Milner .15 .06
❑ 206 Rob Murphy .15 .06
❑ 207 Ron Oester .15 .06
❑ 208 Dave Parker .25 .10
❑ 209 Tony Perez .40 .16
❑ 210 Ted Power .15 .06
❑ 211 Joe Price .15 .06
❑ 212 Ron Robinson .15 .06
❑ 213 Pete Rose 2.00 .80
❑ 214 Mario Soto .25 .10
❑ 215 Kurt Stillwell .15 .06
❑ 216 Max Venable .15 .06
❑ 217 Chris Welsh .15 .06
❑ 218 Carl Willis RC .25 .10
❑ 219 Jesse Barfield .25 .10
❑ 220 George Bell .25 .10
❑ 221 Bill Caudill .15 .06
❑ 222 John Cerutti .15 .06
❑ 223 Jim Clancy .15 .06
❑ 224 Mark Eichhorn .15 .06
❑ 225 Tony Fernandez .15 .06
❑ 226 Damaso Garcia .15 .06
❑ 227 Kelly Gruber ERR .15 .06
(Wrong birth year)
❑ 228 Tom Henke .15 .06
❑ 229 Garth Iorg .15 .06
❑ 230 Joe Johnson .15 .06
❑ 231 Cliff Johnson .15 .06
❑ 232 Jimmy Key .25 .10
❑ 233 Dennis Lamp .15 .06
❑ 234 Rick Leach .15 .06
❑ 235 Buck Martinez .15 .06
❑ 236 Lloyd Moseby .15 .06
❑ 237 Rance Mulliniks .15 .06
❑ 238 Dave Stieb .25 .10
❑ 239 Willie Upshaw .15 .06
❑ 240 Ernie Whitt .15 .06
❑ 241 Andy Allanson .15 .06
❑ 242 Scott Bailes .15 .06
❑ 243 Chris Bando .15 .06
❑ 244 Tony Bernazard .15 .06
❑ 245 John Butcher .15 .06
❑ 246 Brett Butler .25 .10
❑ 247 Ernie Camacho .15 .06
❑ 248 Tom Candiotti .15 .06
❑ 249 Joe Carter .25 .10
❑ 250 Carmen Castillo .15 .06
❑ 251 Julio Franco .25 .10
❑ 252 Mel Hall .15 .06
❑ 253 Brook Jacoby .15 .06
❑ 254 Phil Niekro .25 .10
❑ 255 Otis Nixon .15 .06
❑ 256 Dickie Noles .15 .06
❑ 257 Bryan Oelkers .15 .06
❑ 258 Ken Schrom .15 .06
❑ 259 Don Schulze .15 .06
❑ 260 Cory Snyder .15 .06
❑ 261 Pat Tabler .15 .06
❑ 262 Andre Thornton .15 .06
❑ 263 Rich Yett .15 .06
❑ 264 Mike Aldrete .15 .06
❑ 265 Juan Berenguer .15 .06
❑ 266 Vida Blue .25 .10
❑ 267 Bob Brenly .15 .06
❑ 268 Chris Brown .15 .06
❑ 269 Will Clark RC 3.00 1.20
❑ 270 Chili Davis .25 .10
❑ 271 Mark Davis .15 .06
❑ 272 Kelly Downs RC .25 .10
❑ 273 Scott Garrelts .15 .06
❑ 274 Dan Gladden .15 .06
❑ 275 Mike Krukow .15 .06
❑ 276 Randy Kutcher .15 .06
❑ 277 Mike LaCoss .15 .06
❑ 278 Jeff Leonard .15 .06
❑ 279 Candy Maldonado .15 .06
❑ 280 Roger Mason .15 .06
❑ 281 Bob Melvin .15 .06
❑ 282 Greg Minton .15 .06
❑ 283 Jeff D. Robinson .15 .06
❑ 284 Harry Spilman .15 .06
❑ 285 R.Thompson RC* .50 .20
❑ 286 Jose Uribe .15 .06
❑ 287 Frank Williams .15 .06
❑ 288 Joel Youngblood .15 .06
❑ 289 Jack Clark .25 .10
❑ 290 Vince Coleman .15 .06
❑ 291 Tim Conroy .15 .06
❑ 292 Danny Cox .15 .06
❑ 293 Ken Dayley .15 .06
❑ 294 Curt Ford .15 .06
❑ 295 Bob Forsch .15 .06
❑ 296 Tom Herr .15 .06
❑ 297 Ricky Horton .15 .06
❑ 298 Clint Hurdle .15 .06
❑ 299 Jeff Lahti .15 .06
❑ 300 Steve Lake .15 .06
❑ 301 Tito Landrum .15 .06
❑ 302 Mike LaValliere RC * .50 .20
❑ 303 Greg Mathews .15 .06
❑ 304 Willie McGee .25 .10
❑ 305 Jose Oquendo .15 .06
❑ 306 Terry Pendleton .25 .10
❑ 307 Pat Perry .15 .06
❑ 308 Ozzie Smith 1.00 .40
❑ 309 Ray Soff .15 .06
❑ 310 John Tudor .25 .10
❑ 311 Andy Van Slyke UER .40 .16
(Bats R, Throws L)
❑ 312 Todd Worrell .15 .06
❑ 313 Dann Bilardello .15 .06
❑ 314 Hubie Brooks .15 .06
❑ 315 Tim Burke .15 .06
❑ 316 Andre Dawson .25 .10
❑ 317 Mike Fitzgerald .15 .06
❑ 318 Tom Foley .15 .06
❑ 319 Andres Galarraga .25 .10
❑ 320 Joe Hesketh .15 .06
❑ 321 Wallace Johnson .15 .06
❑ 322 Wayne Krenchicki .15 .06

❑	323	Vance Law	.15	.06
❑	324	Dennis Martinez	.25	.10
❑	325	Bob McClure	.15	.06
❑	326	Andy McGaffigan	.15	.06
❑	327	Al Newman	.15	.06
❑	328	Tim Raines	.25	.10
❑	329	Jeff Reardon	.25	.10
❑	330	Luis Rivera RC	.25	.10
❑	331	Bob Sebra	.15	.06
❑	332	Bryn Smith	.15	.06
❑	333	Jay Tibbs	.15	.06
❑	334	Tim Wallach	.15	.06
❑	335	Mitch Webster	.15	.06
❑	336	Jim Wohlford	.15	.06
❑	337	Floyd Youmans	.15	.06
❑	338	Chris Bosio RC	.50	.20
❑	339	Glenn Braggs RC	.25	.10
❑	340	Rick Cerone	.15	.06
❑	341	Mark Clear	.15	.06
❑	342	Bryan Clutterbuck	.15	.06
❑	343	Cecil Cooper	.25	.10
❑	344	Rob Deer	.15	.06
❑	345	Jim Gantner	.15	.06
❑	346	Ted Higuera	.15	.06
❑	347	John Henry Johnson	.15	.06
❑	348	Tim Leary	.15	.06
❑	349	Rick Manning	.15	.06
❑	350	Paul Molitor	.40	.16
❑	351	Charlie Moore	.15	.06
❑	352	Juan Nieves	.15	.06
❑	353	Ben Oglivie	.25	.10
❑	354	Dan Plesac	.15	.06
❑	355	Ernest Riles	.15	.06
❑	356	Billy Joe Robidoux	.15	.06
❑	357	Bill Schroeder	.15	.06
❑	358	Dale Sveum	.15	.06
❑	359	Gorman Thomas	.25	.10
❑	360	Bill Wegman	.15	.06
❑	361	Robin Yount	1.00	.40
❑	362	Steve Balboni	.15	.06
❑	363	Scott Bankhead	.15	.06
❑	364	Buddy Biancalana	.15	.06
❑	365	Bud Black	.15	.06
❑	366	George Brett	1.50	.60
❑	367	Steve Farr	.15	.06
❑	368	Mark Gubicza	.15	.06
❑	369	Bo Jackson RC	8.00	3.20
❑	370	Danny Jackson	.15	.06
❑	371	Mike Kingery RC	.25	.10
❑	372	Rudy Law	.15	.06
❑	373	Charlie Leibrandt	.15	.06
❑	374	Dennis Leonard	.15	.06
❑	375	Hal McRae	.25	.10
❑	376	Jorge Orta	.15	.06
❑	377	Jamie Quirk	.15	.06
❑	378	Dan Quisenberry	.15	.06
❑	379	Bret Saberhagen	.25	.10
❑	380	Angel Salazar	.15	.06
❑	381	Lonnie Smith	.15	.06
❑	382	Jim Sundberg	.25	.10
❑	383	Frank White	.25	.10
❑	384	Willie Wilson	.25	.10
❑	385	Joaquin Andujar	.25	.10
❑	386	Doug Bair	.15	.06
❑	387	Dusty Baker	.25	.10
❑	388	Bruce Bochte	.15	.06
❑	389	Jose Canseco	1.50	.60
❑	390	Chris Codiroli	.15	.06
❑	391	Mike Davis	.15	.06
❑	392	Alfredo Griffin	.15	.06
❑	393	Moose Haas	.15	.06
❑	394	Donnie Hill	.15	.06
❑	395	Jay Howell	.15	.06
❑	396	Dave Kingman	.25	.10
❑	397	Carney Lansford	.25	.10
❑	398	Dave Leiper	.15	.06
❑	399	Bill Mooneyham	.15	.06
❑	400	Dwayne Murphy	.15	.06
❑	401	Steve Ontiveros	.15	.06
❑	402	Tony Phillips	.15	.06
❑	403	Eric Plunk	.15	.06
❑	404	Jose Rijo	.25	.10
❑	405	Terry Steinbach RC	1.25	.50
❑	406	Dave Stewart	.25	.10
❑	407	Mickey Tettleton	.15	.06
❑	408	Dave Von Ohlen	.15	.06
❑	409	Jerry Willard	.15	.06
❑	410	Curt Young	.15	.06
❑	411	Bruce Bochy	.15	.06
❑	412	Dave Dravecky	.15	.06
❑	413	Tim Flannery	.15	.06
❑	414	Steve Garvey	.25	.10
❑	415	Rich Gossage	.25	.10
❑	416	Tony Gwynn	1.00	.40
❑	417	Andy Hawkins	.15	.06
❑	418	LaMarr Hoyt	.15	.06
❑	419	Terry Kennedy	.15	.06
❑	420	John Kruk RC	2.50	1.00
❑	421	Dave LaPoint	.15	.06
❑	422	Craig Lefferts	.15	.06
❑	423	Carmelo Martinez	.15	.06
❑	424	Lance McCullers	.15	.06
❑	425	Kevin McReynolds	.15	.06
❑	426	Graig Nettles	.25	.10
❑	427	Bip Roberts RC	.50	.20
❑	428	Jerry Royster	.15	.06
❑	429	Benito Santiago	.25	.10
❑	430	Eric Show	.15	.06
❑	431	Bob Stoddard	.15	.06
❑	432	Garry Templeton	.25	.10
❑	433	Gene Walter	.15	.06
❑	434	Ed Whitson	.15	.06
❑	435	Marvell Wynne	.15	.06
❑	436	Dave Anderson	.15	.06
❑	437	Greg Brock	.15	.06
❑	438	Enos Cabell	.15	.06
❑	439	Mariano Duncan	.15	.06
❑	440	Pedro Guerrero	.25	.10
❑	441	Orel Hershiser	.40	.16
❑	442	Rick Honeycutt	.15	.06
❑	443	Ken Howell	.15	.06
❑	444	Ken Landreaux	.15	.06
❑	445	Bill Madlock	.25	.10
❑	446	Mike Marshall	.15	.06
❑	447	Len Matuszek	.15	.06
❑	448	Tom Niedenfuer	.15	.06
❑	449	Alejandro Pena	.15	.06
❑	450	Dennis Powell	.15	.06
❑	451	Jerry Reuss	.15	.06
❑	452	Bill Russell	.25	.10
❑	453	Steve Sax	.15	.06
❑	454	Mike Scioscia	.25	.10
❑	455	Franklin Stubbs	.15	.06
❑	456	Alex Trevino	.15	.06
❑	457	Fernando Valenzuela	.25	.10
❑	458	Ed VandeBerg	.15	.06
❑	459	Bob Welch	.25	.10
❑	460	Reggie Williams	.15	.06
❑	461	Don Aase	.15	.06
❑	462	Juan Beniquez	.15	.06
❑	463	Mike Boddicker	.15	.06
❑	464	Juan Bonilla	.15	.06
❑	465	Rich Bordi	.15	.06
❑	466	Storm Davis	.15	.06
❑	467	Rick Dempsey	.15	.06
❑	468	Ken Dixon	.15	.06
❑	469	Jim Dwyer	.15	.06
❑	470	Mike Flanagan	.15	.06
❑	471	Jackie Gutierrez	.15	.06
❑	472	Brad Havens	.15	.06
❑	473	Lee Lacy	.15	.06
❑	474	Fred Lynn	.25	.10
❑	475	Scott McGregor	.15	.06
❑	476	Eddie Murray	.60	.24
❑	477	Tom O'Malley	.15	.06
❑	478	Cal Ripken Jr.	2.50	1.00
❑	479	Larry Sheets	.15	.06
❑	480	John Shelby	.15	.06
❑	481	Nate Snell	.15	.06
❑	482	Jim Traber	.15	.06
❑	483	Mike Young	.15	.06
❑	484	Neil Allen	.15	.06
❑	485	Harold Baines	.25	.10
❑	486	Floyd Bannister	.15	.06
❑	487	Daryl Boston	.15	.06
❑	488	Ivan Calderon	.15	.06
❑	489	John Cangelosi	.15	.06
❑	490	Steve Carlton	.25	.10
❑	491	Joe Cowley	.15	.06
❑	492	Julio Cruz	.15	.06
❑	493	Bill Dawley	.15	.06
❑	494	Jose DeLeon	.15	.06
❑	495	Richard Dotson	.15	.06
❑	496	Carlton Fisk	.40	.16
❑	497	Ozzie Guillen	.40	.16
❑	498	Jerry Hairston	.15	.06
❑	499	Ron Hassey	.15	.06
❑	500	Tim Hulett	.15	.06
❑	501	Bob James	.15	.06
❑	502	Steve Lyons	.15	.06
❑	503	Joel McKeon	.15	.06
❑	504	Gene Nelson	.15	.06
❑	505	Dave Schmidt	.15	.06
❑	506	Ray Searage	.15	.06
❑	507	Bobby Thigpen RC	.50	.20
❑	508	Greg Walker	.15	.06
❑	509	Jim Acker	.15	.06
❑	510	Doyle Alexander	.15	.06
❑	511	Paul Assenmacher	.50	.20
❑	512	Bruce Benedict	.15	.06
❑	513	Chris Chambliss	.25	.10
❑	514	Jeff Dedmon	.15	.06
❑	515	Gene Garber	.15	.06
❑	516	Ken Griffey	.25	.10
❑	517	Terry Harper	.15	.06
❑	518	Bob Horner	.25	.10
❑	519	Glenn Hubbard	.15	.06
❑	520	Rick Mahler	.15	.06
❑	521	Omar Moreno	.15	.06
❑	522	Dale Murphy	.40	.16
❑	523	Ken Oberkfell	.15	.06
❑	524	Ed Olwine	.15	.06
❑	525	David Palmer	.15	.06
❑	526	Rafael Ramirez	.15	.06
❑	527	Billy Sample	.15	.06
❑	528	Ted Simmons	.25	.10
❑	529	Zane Smith	.15	.06
❑	530	Bruce Sutter	.25	.10
❑	531	Andres Thomas	.15	.06
❑	532	Ozzie Virgil	.15	.06
❑	533	Allan Anderson	.15	.06
❑	534	Keith Atherton	.15	.06
❑	535	Billy Beane	.25	.10
❑	536	Bert Blyleven	.25	.10
❑	537	Tom Brunansky	.15	.06
❑	538	Randy Bush	.15	.06
❑	539	George Frazier	.15	.06
❑	540	Gary Gaetti	.25	.10
❑	541	Greg Gagne	.15	.06
❑	542	Mickey Hatcher	.15	.06
❑	543	Neal Heaton	.15	.06
❑	544	Kent Hrbek	.25	.10
❑	545	Roy Lee Jackson	.15	.06
❑	546	Tim Laudner	.15	.06
❑	547	Steve Lombardozzi	.15	.06
❑	548	Mark Portugal RC *	.50	.20
❑	549	Kirby Puckett	.60	.24
❑	550	Jeff Reed	.15	.06
❑	551	Mark Salas	.15	.06
❑	552	Roy Smalley	.15	.06
❑	553	Mike Smithson	.15	.06
❑	554	Frank Viola	.25	.10
❑	555	Thad Bosley	.15	.06
❑	556	Ron Cey	.25	.10
❑	557	Jody Davis	.15	.06
❑	558	Ron Davis	.15	.06
❑	559	Bob Dernier	.15	.06
❑	560	Frank DiPino	.15	.06
❑	561	Shawon Dunston UER (Wrong birth year listed on card back)	.15	.06
❑	562	Leon Durham	.15	.06
❑	563	Dennis Eckersley	.40	.16
❑	564	Terry Francona	.25	.10
❑	565	Dave Gumpert	.15	.06
❑	566	Guy Hoffman	.15	.06
❑	567	Ed Lynch	.15	.06
❑	568	Gary Matthews	.25	.10
❑	569	Keith Moreland	.15	.06
❑	570	Jamie Moyer RC	2.00	.80
❑	571	Jerry Mumphrey	.15	.06
❑	572	Ryne Sandberg	1.25	.50
❑	573	Scott Sanderson	.15	.06
❑	574	Lee Smith	.25	.10
❑	575	Chris Speier	.15	.06
❑	576	Rick Sutcliffe	.25	.10
❑	577	Manny Trillo	.15	.06
❑	578	Steve Trout	.15	.06

❑ 579 Karl Best .15 .06
❑ 580 Scott Bradley .15 .06
❑ 581 Phil Bradley .15 .06
❑ 582 Mickey Brantley .15 .06
❑ 583 Mike G. Brown P .15 .06
❑ 584 Alvin Davis .15 .06
❑ 585 Lee Guetterman .15 .06
❑ 586 Mark Huismann .15 .06
❑ 587 Bob Kearney .15 .06
❑ 588 Pete Ladd .15 .06
❑ 589 Mark Langston .15 .06
❑ 590 Mike Moore .15 .06
❑ 591 Mike Morgan .15 .06
❑ 592 John Moses .15 .06
❑ 593 Ken Phelps .15 .06
❑ 594 Jim Presley .15 .06
❑ 595 Rey Quinones UER .15 .06
(Quinonez on front)
❑ 596 Harold Reynolds .25 .10
❑ 597 Billy Swift .15 .06
❑ 598 Danny Tartabull .15 .06
❑ 599 Steve Yeager .25 .10
❑ 600 Matt Young .15 .06
❑ 601 Bill Almon .15 .06
❑ 602 Rafael Belliard RC .50 .20
❑ 603 Mike Bielecki .15 .06
❑ 604 Barry Bonds RC 50.00 20.00
❑ 605 Bobby Bonilla RC 1.25 .50
❑ 606 Sid Bream .15 .06
❑ 607 Mike C. Brown .15 .06
❑ 608 Pat Clements .15 .06
❑ 609 Mike Diaz .15 .06
❑ 610 Cecilio Guante .15 .06
❑ 611 Barry Jones .15 .06
❑ 612 Bob Kipper .15 .06
❑ 613 Larry McWilliams .15 .06
❑ 614 Jim Morrison .15 .06
❑ 615 Joe Orsulak .15 .06
❑ 616 Junior Ortiz .15 .06
❑ 617 Tony Pena .15 .06
❑ 618 Johnny Ray .15 .06
❑ 619 Rick Reuschel .25 .10
❑ 620 R.J. Reynolds .15 .06
❑ 621 Rick Rhoden .15 .06
❑ 622 Don Robinson .15 .06
❑ 623 Bob Walk .15 .06
❑ 624 Jim Winn .15 .06
❑ 625 Pete Incaviglia .75 .30
Jose Canseco
❑ 626 Don Sutton .25 .10
Phil Niekro
❑ 627 Dave Righetti .15 .06
Don Aase
❑ 628 Wally Joyner .75 .30
Jose Canseco
❑ 629 Gary Carter .40 .16
Sid Fernandez
Dwight Gooden
Keith Hernandez
Darryl Strawberry
❑ 630 Mike Scott .15 .06
Mike Krukow
❑ 631 Fernando Valenzuela .15 .06
John Franco
❑ 632 Bob Horner 4 Homers .15 .06
❑ 633 Jose Canseco .75 .30
Jim Rice
Kirby Puckett
❑ 634 Gary Carter .60 .24
Roger Clemens
❑ 635 Steve Carlton 4000K's .25 .10
❑ 636 Glenn Davis .60 .24
Eddie Murray
❑ 637 Wade Boggs .25 .10
Keith Hernandez
❑ 638 Don Mattingly 1.00 .40
Darryl Strawberry
❑ 639 Dave Parker .60 .24
Ryne Sandberg
❑ 640 Dwight Gooden .60 .24
Roger Clemens
❑ 641 Mike Witt .15 .06
Charlie Hough
❑ 642 Juan Samuel .25 .10
Tim Raines
❑ 643 Harold Baines .25 .10
Jesse Barfield
❑ 644 Dave Clark RC and .50 .20
Greg Swindell
❑ 645 Ron Karkovice RC .50 .20
Russ Morman
❑ 646 Devon White RC and 1.25 .50
Willie Fraser
❑ 647 Mike Stanley RC and .50 .20
Jerry Browne
❑ 648 Dave Magadan RC .50 .20
Phil Lombardi
❑ 649 Jose Gonzalez RC .25 .10
Ralph Bryant
❑ 650 Jimmy Jones RC and .25 .10
Randy Asadoor
❑ 651 Tracy Jones RC and .25 .10
Marvin Freeman
❑ 652 John Stefero and .50 .20
Kevin Seitzer RC
❑ 653 Rob Nelson and .25 .10
Steve Fireovid
❑ 654 CL: Mets/Red Sox .15 .06
Astros/Angels
❑ 655 CL: Yankees/Rangers .15 .06
Tigers/Phillies
❑ 656 CL: Reds/Blue Jays .15 .06
Indians/Giants
ERR (230/231 wrong)
❑ 657 CL: Cardinals/Expos .15 .06
Brewers/Royals
❑ 658 CL: A's/Padres .15 .06
Dodgers/Orioles
❑ 659 CL: White Sox/Braves .15 .06
Twins/Cubs
❑ 660 CL: Mariners/Pirates .15 .06
Special Cards
ER (580/581 wrong)

1987 Fleer Update

	Nm-Mt	Ex-Mt
COMP.FACT.SET (132)	15.00	6.00

❑ 1 Scott Bankhead .10 .04
❑ 2 Eric Bell .15 .06
❑ 3 Juan Beniquez .10 .04
❑ 4 Juan Berenguer .10 .04
❑ 5 Mike Birkbeck .15 .06
❑ 6 Randy Bockus .10 .04
❑ 7 Rod Booker .10 .04
❑ 8 Thad Bosley .10 .04
❑ 9 Greg Brock .10 .04
❑ 10 Bob Brower .10 .04
❑ 11 Chris Brown .10 .04
❑ 12 Jerry Browne .15 .06
❑ 13 Ralph Bryant .10 .04
❑ 14 DeWayne Buice .10 .04
❑ 15 Ellis Burks XRC .75 .30
❑ 16 Casey Candaele .10 .04
❑ 17 Steve Carlton .15 .06
❑ 18 Juan Castillo .15 .06
❑ 19 Chuck Crim .10 .04
❑ 20 Mark Davidson .10 .04
❑ 21 Mark Davis .10 .04
❑ 22 Storm Davis .10 .04
❑ 23 Bill Dawley .10 .04
❑ 24 Andre Dawson .15 .06
❑ 25 Brian Dayett .10 .04
❑ 26 Rick Dempsey .10 .04
❑ 27 Ken Dowell .10 .04
❑ 28 Dave Dravecky .10 .04
❑ 29 Mike Dunne .10 .04
❑ 30 Dennis Eckersley .25 .10
❑ 31 Cecil Fielder .15 .06
❑ 32 Brian Fisher .10 .04
❑ 33 Willie Fraser .15 .06
❑ 34 Ken Gerhart .10 .04
❑ 35 Jim Gott .10 .04
❑ 36 Dan Gladden .10 .04
❑ 37 Mike Greenwell XRC* .30 .12
❑ 38 Cecilio Guante .10 .04
❑ 39 Albert Hall .10 .04
❑ 40 Atlee Hammaker .10 .04
❑ 41 Mickey Hatcher .10 .04
❑ 42 Mike Heath .10 .04
❑ 43 Neal Heaton .10 .04
❑ 44 Mike Henneman XRC .30 .12
❑ 45 Guy Hoffman .10 .04
❑ 46 Charles Hudson .10 .04
❑ 47 Chuck Jackson .10 .04
❑ 48 Mike Jackson XRC .30 .12
❑ 49 Reggie Jackson .25 .10
❑ 50 Chris James .10 .04
❑ 51 Dion James .10 .04
❑ 52 Stan Javier .10 .04
❑ 53 Stan Jefferson .10 .04
❑ 54 Jimmy Jones .15 .06
❑ 55 Tracy Jones .10 .04
❑ 56 Terry Kennedy .10 .04
❑ 57 Mike Kingery .15 .06
❑ 58 Ray Knight .15 .06
❑ 59 Gene Larkin XRC .30 .12
❑ 60 Mike LaValliere .30 .12
❑ 61 Jack Lazorko .10 .04
❑ 62 Terry Leach .10 .04
❑ 63 Rick Leach .10 .04
❑ 64 Craig Lefferts .10 .04
❑ 65 Jim Lindeman .15 .06
❑ 66 Bill Long .10 .04
❑ 67 Mike Loynd XRC .15 .06
❑ 68 Greg Maddux XRC 8.00 3.20
❑ 69 Bill Madlock .15 .06
❑ 70 Dave Magadan .30 .12
❑ 71 Joe Magrane XRC .15 .06
❑ 72 Fred Manrique .10 .04
❑ 73 Mike Mason .10 .04
❑ 74 Lloyd McClendon XRC .30 .12
❑ 75 Fred McGriff 1.00 .40
❑ 76 Mark McGwire 5.00 2.00
❑ 77 Mark McLemore .15 .06
❑ 78 Kevin McReynolds .10 .04
❑ 79 Dave Meads .10 .04
❑ 80 Greg Minton .10 .04
❑ 81 John Mitchell XRC .15 .06
❑ 82 Kevin Mitchell .25 .10
❑ 83 John Morris .10 .04
❑ 84 Jeff Musselman .10 .04
❑ 85 Randy Myers XRC .75 .30
❑ 86 Gene Nelson .10 .04
❑ 87 Joe Niekro .10 .04
❑ 88 Tom Nieto .10 .04
❑ 89 Reid Nichols .10 .04
❑ 90 Matt Nokes XRC .30 .12
❑ 91 Dickie Noles .10 .04
❑ 92 Edwin Nunez .10 .04
❑ 93 Jose Nunez .10 .04
❑ 94 Paul O'Neill .40 .16
❑ 95 Jim Paciorek .10 .04
❑ 96 Lance Parrish .15 .06
❑ 97 Bill Pecota XRC .15 .06
❑ 98 Tony Pena .10 .04
❑ 99 Luis Polonia XRC .30 .12
❑ 100 Randy Ready .10 .04
❑ 101 Jeff Reardon .15 .06
❑ 102 Gary Redus .10 .04
❑ 103 Rick Rhoden .10 .04
❑ 104 Wally Ritchie .10 .04
❑ 105 Jeff M. Robinson UER .10 .04
(Wrong Jeff's
stats on back)
❑ 106 Mark Salas .10 .04
❑ 107 Dave Schmidt .10 .04
❑ 108 Kevin Seitzer UER .30 .12
(Wrong birth year)
❑ 109 John Shelby .10 .04

❑ 110 John Smiley XRC .30 .12
❑ 111 Lary Sorensen .10 .04
❑ 112 Chris Speier .10 .04
❑ 113 Randy St.Claire .10 .04
❑ 114 Jim Sundberg .15 .06
❑ 115 B.J. Surhoff XRC .75 .30
❑ 116 Greg Swindell .30 .12
❑ 117 Danny Tartabull .10 .04
❑ 118 Dorn Taylor .10 .04
❑ 119 Lee Tunnell .10 .04
❑ 120 Ed VandeBerg .10 .04
❑ 121 Andy Van Slyke .25 .10
❑ 122 Gary Ward .10 .04
❑ 123 Devon White .75 .30
❑ 124 Alan Wiggins .10 .04
❑ 125 Bill Wilkinson .10 .04
❑ 126 Jim Winn .10 .04
❑ 127 Frank Williams .10 .04
❑ 128 Ken Williams XRC .10 .04
❑ 129 Matt Williams XRC 1.50 .60
❑ 130 Herm Winningham .10 .04
❑ 131 Matt Young .10 .04
❑ 132 Checklist 1-132 .10 .04

1988 Fleer

	Nm-Mt	Ex-Mt
COMPLETE SET (660)	15.00	6.00
COMP.RETAIL SET (660)	15.00	6.00
COMP.HOBBY SET (672)	15.00	6.00

❑ 1 Keith Atherton .10 .04
❑ 2 Don Baylor .15 .06
❑ 3 Juan Berenguer .10 .04
❑ 4 Bert Blyleven .15 .06
❑ 5 Tom Brunansky .10 .04
❑ 6 Randy Bush .10 .04
❑ 7 Steve Carlton .15 .06
❑ 8 Mark Davidson .10 .04
❑ 9 George Frazier .10 .04
❑ 10 Gary Gaetti .15 .06
❑ 11 Greg Gagne .10 .04
❑ 12 Dan Gladden .10 .04
❑ 13 Kent Hrbek .15 .06
❑ 14 Gene Larkin RC* .40 .16
❑ 15 Tim Laudner .10 .04
❑ 16 Steve Lombardozzi .10 .04
❑ 17 Al Newman .10 .04
❑ 18 Joe Niekro .10 .04
❑ 19 Kirby Puckett .30 .12
❑ 20 Jeff Reardon .15 .06
❑ 21A Dan Schatzeder ERR .15 .06
(Misspelled Schatzader on both sides of the card)
❑ 21B Dan Schatzeder COR .10 .04
❑ 22 Roy Smalley .10 .04
❑ 23 Mike Smithson .10 .04
❑ 24 Les Straker .10 .04
❑ 25 Frank Viola .15 .06
❑ 26 Jack Clark .15 .06
❑ 27 Vince Coleman .10 .04
❑ 28 Danny Cox .10 .04
❑ 29 Bill Dawley .10 .04
❑ 30 Ken Dayley .10 .04
❑ 31 Doug DeCinces .10 .04
❑ 32 Curt Ford .10 .04
❑ 33 Bob Forsch .10 .04
❑ 34 David Green .10 .04
❑ 35 Tom Herr .10 .04
❑ 36 Ricky Horton .10 .04
❑ 37 Lance Johnson RC .40 .16
❑ 38 Steve Lake .10 .04
❑ 39 Jim Lindeman .10 .04
❑ 40 Joe Magrane RC* .40 .16
❑ 41 Greg Mathews .10 .04
❑ 42 Willie McGee .15 .06
❑ 43 John Morris .10 .04
❑ 44 Jose Oquendo .10 .04
❑ 45 Tony Pena .10 .04
❑ 46 Terry Pendleton .15 .06
❑ 47 Ozzie Smith .50 .20
❑ 48 John Tudor .15 .06
❑ 49 Lee Tunnell .10 .04
❑ 50 Todd Worrell .10 .04
❑ 51 Doyle Alexander .10 .04
❑ 52 Dave Bergman .10 .04
❑ 53 Tom Brookens .10 .04
❑ 54 Darrell Evans .15 .06
❑ 55 Kirk Gibson .30 .12
❑ 56 Mike Heath .10 .04
❑ 57 Mike Henneman RC* .40 .16
❑ 58 Willie Hernandez .10 .04
❑ 59 Larry Herndon .10 .04
❑ 60 Eric King .10 .04
❑ 61 Chet Lemon .15 .06
❑ 62 Scott Lusader .10 .04
❑ 63 Bill Madlock .15 .06
❑ 64 Jack Morris .15 .06
❑ 65 Jim Morrison .10 .04
❑ 66 Matt Nokes RC* .40 .16
❑ 67 Dan Petry .10 .04
❑ 68A Jeff M. Robinson .20 .08
ERR (Stats for Jeff D. Robinson on card back)
Born 12-13-60
❑ 68B Jeff M. Robinson .10 .04
COR, Born 12-14-61
❑ 69 Pat Sheridan .10 .04
❑ 70 Nate Snell .10 .04
❑ 71 Frank Tanana .15 .06
❑ 72 Walt Terrell .10 .04
❑ 73 Mark Thurmond .10 .04
❑ 74 Alan Trammell .15 .06
❑ 75 Lou Whitaker .15 .06
❑ 76 Mike Aldrete .10 .04
❑ 77 Bob Brenly .10 .04
❑ 78 Will Clark .30 .12
❑ 79 Chili Davis .15 .06
❑ 80 Kelly Downs .10 .04
❑ 81 Dave Dravecky .10 .04
❑ 82 Scott Garrelts .10 .04
❑ 83 Atlee Hammaker .10 .04
❑ 84 Dave Henderson .10 .04
❑ 85 Mike Krukow .10 .04
❑ 86 Mike LaCoss .10 .04
❑ 87 Craig Lefferts .10 .04
❑ 88 Jeff Leonard .10 .04
❑ 89 Candy Maldonado .10 .04
❑ 90 Eddie Milner .10 .04
❑ 91 Bob Melvin .10 .04
❑ 92 Kevin Mitchell .15 .06
❑ 93 Jon Perlman .10 .04
❑ 94 Rick Reuschel .15 .06
❑ 95 Don Robinson .10 .04
❑ 96 Chris Speier .10 .04
❑ 97 Harry Spilman .10 .04
❑ 98 Robby Thompson .10 .04
❑ 99 Jose Uribe .10 .04
❑ 100 Mark Wasinger .10 .04
❑ 101 Matt Williams RC 1.50 .60
❑ 102 Jesse Barfield .15 .06
❑ 103 George Bell .15 .06
❑ 104 Juan Beniquez .10 .04
❑ 105 John Cerutti .10 .04
❑ 106 Jim Clancy .10 .04
❑ 107 Rob Ducey .10 .04
❑ 108 Mark Eichhorn .10 .04
❑ 109 Tony Fernandez .10 .04
❑ 110 Cecil Fielder .15 .06
❑ 111 Kelly Gruber .10 .04
❑ 112 Tom Henke .10 .04
❑ 113A Garth Iorg ERR .20 .08
(Misspelled Iorq on card front)
❑ 113B Garth Iorg COR .10 .04
❑ 114 Jimmy Key .15 .06
❑ 115 Rick Leach .10 .04
❑ 116 Manny Lee .10 .04
❑ 117 Nelson Liriano .10 .04
❑ 118 Fred McGriff .30 .12
❑ 119 Lloyd Moseby .10 .04
❑ 120 Rance Mulliniks .10 .04
❑ 121 Jeff Musselman .10 .04
❑ 122 Jose Nunez .10 .04
❑ 123 Dave Stieb .15 .06
❑ 124 Willie Upshaw .10 .04
❑ 125 Duane Ward .10 .04
❑ 126 Ernie Whitt .10 .04
❑ 127 Rick Aguilera .10 .04
❑ 128 Wally Backman .10 .04
❑ 129 Mark Carreon RC .15 .06
❑ 130 Gary Carter .15 .06
❑ 131 David Cone .15 .06
❑ 132 Ron Darling .15 .06
❑ 133 Len Dykstra .15 .06
❑ 134 Sid Fernandez .10 .04
❑ 135 Dwight Gooden .15 .06
❑ 136 Keith Hernandez .15 .06
❑ 137 Gregg Jefferies RC .40 .16
❑ 138 Howard Johnson .15 .06
❑ 139 Terry Leach .10 .04
❑ 140 Barry Lyons .10 .04
❑ 141 Dave Magadan .10 .04
❑ 142 Roger McDowell .10 .04
❑ 143 Kevin McReynolds .10 .04
❑ 144 Keith A. Miller RC .40 .16
❑ 145 John Mitchell RC .15 .06
❑ 146 Randy Myers .15 .06
❑ 147 Bob Ojeda .10 .04
❑ 148 Jesse Orosco .10 .04
❑ 149 Rafael Santana .10 .04
❑ 150 Doug Sisk .10 .04
❑ 151 Darryl Strawberry .15 .06
❑ 152 Tim Teufel .10 .04
❑ 153 Gene Walter .10 .04
❑ 154 Mookie Wilson .15 .06
❑ 155 Jay Aldrich .10 .04
❑ 156 Chris Bosio .10 .04
❑ 157 Glenn Braggs .10 .04
❑ 158 Greg Brock .10 .04
❑ 159 Juan Castillo .10 .04
❑ 160 Mark Clear .10 .04
❑ 161 Cecil Cooper .15 .06
❑ 162 Chuck Crim .10 .04
❑ 163 Rob Deer .10 .04
❑ 164 Mike Felder .10 .04
❑ 165 Jim Gantner .10 .04
❑ 166 Ted Higuera .10 .04
❑ 167 Steve Kiefer .10 .04
❑ 168 Rick Manning .10 .04
❑ 169 Paul Molitor .20 .08
❑ 170 Juan Nieves .10 .04
❑ 171 Dan Plesac .10 .04
❑ 172 Earnest Riles .10 .04
❑ 173 Bill Schroeder .10 .04
❑ 174 Steve Stanicek .10 .04
❑ 175 B.J. Surhoff .15 .06
❑ 176 Dale Sveum .10 .04
❑ 177 Bill Wegman .10 .04
❑ 178 Robin Yount .50 .20
❑ 179 Hubie Brooks .10 .04
❑ 180 Tim Burke .10 .04
❑ 181 Casey Candaele .10 .04
❑ 182 Mike Fitzgerald .10 .04
❑ 183 Tom Foley .10 .04
❑ 184 Andres Galarraga .15 .06
❑ 185 Neal Heaton .10 .04
❑ 186 Wallace Johnson .10 .04
❑ 187 Vance Law .10 .04
❑ 188 Dennis Martinez .15 .06
❑ 189 Bob McClure .10 .04
❑ 190 Andy McGaffigan .10 .04
❑ 191 Reid Nichols .10 .04
❑ 192 Pascual Perez .10 .04
❑ 193 Tim Raines .15 .06
❑ 194 Jeff Reed .10 .04
❑ 195 Bob Sebra .10 .04
❑ 196 Bryn Smith .10 .04
❑ 197 Randy St.Claire .10 .04
❑ 198 Tim Wallach .10 .04
❑ 199 Mitch Webster .10 .04

❑ 200 Herm Winningham .10 .04
❑ 201 Floyd Youmans .10 .04
❑ 202 Brad Arnsberg .10 .04
❑ 203 Rick Cerone .10 .04
❑ 204 Pat Clements .10 .04
❑ 205 Henry Cotto .10 .04
❑ 206 Mike Easler .10 .04
❑ 207 Ron Guidry .15 .06
❑ 208 Bill Gullickson .10 .04
❑ 209 Rickey Henderson .30 .12
❑ 210 Charles Hudson .10 .04
❑ 211 Tommy John .15 .06
❑ 212 Roberto Kelly RC .40 .16
❑ 213 Ron Kittle .10 .04
❑ 214 Don Mattingly 1.00 .40
❑ 215 Bobby Meacham .10 .04
❑ 216 Mike Pagliarulo .10 .04
❑ 217 Dan Pasqua .10 .04
❑ 218 Willie Randolph .15 .06
❑ 219 Rick Rhoden .10 .04
❑ 220 Dave Righetti .15 .06
❑ 221 Jerry Royster .10 .04
❑ 222 Tim Stoddard .10 .04
❑ 223 Wayne Tolleson .10 .04
❑ 224 Gary Ward .10 .04
❑ 225 Claudell Washington .10 .04
❑ 226 Dave Winfield .15 .06
❑ 227 Buddy Bell .15 .06
❑ 228 Tom Browning .10 .04
❑ 229 Dave Concepcion .15 .06
❑ 230 Kal Daniels .10 .04
❑ 231 Eric Davis .15 .06
❑ 232 Bo Diaz .10 .04
❑ 233 Nick Esasky .10 .04
(Has a dollar sign before '87 SB totals)
❑ 234 John Franco .15 .06
❑ 235 Guy Hoffman .10 .04
❑ 236 Tom Hume .10 .04
❑ 237 Tracy Jones .10 .04
❑ 238 Bill Landrum .10 .04
❑ 239 Barry Larkin .20 .08
❑ 240 Terry McGriff .10 .04
❑ 241 Rob Murphy .10 .04
❑ 242 Ron Oester .10 .04
❑ 243 Dave Parker .15 .06
❑ 244 Pat Perry .10 .04
❑ 245 Ted Power .10 .04
❑ 246 Dennis Rasmussen .10 .04
❑ 247 Ron Robinson .10 .04
❑ 248 Kurt Stillwell .10 .04
❑ 249 Jeff Treadway RC .40 .16
❑ 250 Frank Williams .10 .04
❑ 251 Steve Balboni .10 .04
❑ 252 Bud Black .10 .04
❑ 253 Thad Bosley .10 .04
❑ 254 George Brett .75 .30
❑ 255 John Davis .10 .04
❑ 256 Steve Farr .10 .04
❑ 257 Gene Garber .10 .04
❑ 258 Jerry Don Gleaton .10 .04
❑ 259 Mark Gubicza .10 .04
❑ 260 Bo Jackson .30 .12
❑ 261 Danny Jackson .10 .04
❑ 262 Ross Jones .10 .04
❑ 263 Charlie Leibrandt .10 .04
❑ 264 Bill Pecota RC* .15 .06
❑ 265 Melido Perez RC .40 .16
❑ 266 Jamie Quirk .10 .04
❑ 267 Dan Quisenberry .10 .04
❑ 268 Bret Saberhagen .15 .06
❑ 269 Angel Salazar .10 .04
❑ 270 Kevin Seitzer UER .15 .06
(Wrong birth year)
❑ 271 Danny Tartabull .10 .04
❑ 272 Gary Thurman .10 .04
❑ 273 Frank White .15 .06
❑ 274 Willie Wilson .15 .06
❑ 275 Tony Bernazard .10 .04
❑ 276 Jose Canseco .75 .30
❑ 277 Mike Davis .10 .04
❑ 278 Storm Davis .10 .04
❑ 279 Dennis Eckersley .20 .08
❑ 280 Alfredo Griffin .10 .04
❑ 281 Rick Honeycutt .10 .04
❑ 282 Jay Howell .10 .04
❑ 283 Reggie Jackson .20 .08
❑ 284 Dennis Lamp .10 .04
❑ 285 Carney Lansford .15 .06
❑ 286 Mark McGwire 2.50 1.00
❑ 287 Dwayne Murphy .10 .04
❑ 288 Gene Nelson .10 .04
❑ 289 Steve Ontiveros .10 .04
❑ 290 Tony Phillips .10 .04
❑ 291 Eric Plunk .10 .04
❑ 292 Luis Polonia RC* .40 .16
❑ 293 Rick Rodriguez .10 .04
❑ 294 Terry Steinbach .15 .06
❑ 295 Dave Stewart .15 .06
❑ 296 Curt Young .10 .04
❑ 297 Luis Aguayo .10 .04
❑ 298 Steve Bedrosian .10 .04
❑ 299 Jeff Calhoun .10 .04
❑ 300 Don Carman .10 .04
❑ 301 Todd Frohwirth .10 .04
❑ 302 Greg Gross .10 .04
❑ 303 Kevin Gross .10 .04
❑ 304 Von Hayes .10 .04
❑ 305 Keith Hughes .10 .04
❑ 306 Mike Jackson RC* .40 .16
❑ 307 Chris James .10 .04
❑ 308 Steve Jeltz .10 .04
❑ 309 Mike Maddux .10 .04
❑ 310 Lance Parrish .15 .06
❑ 311 Shane Rawley .10 .04
❑ 312 Wally Ritchie .10 .04
❑ 313 Bruce Ruffin .10 .04
❑ 314 Juan Samuel .10 .04
❑ 315 Mike Schmidt .75 .30
❑ 316 Rick Schu .10 .04
❑ 317 Jeff Stone .10 .04
❑ 318 Kent Tekulve .10 .04
❑ 319 Milt Thompson .10 .04
❑ 320 Glenn Wilson .10 .04
❑ 321 Rafael Belliard .10 .04
❑ 322 Barry Bonds 3.00 1.20
❑ 323 Bobby Bonilla UER .15 .06
(Wrong birth year)
❑ 324 Sid Bream .10 .04
❑ 325 John Cangelosi .10 .04
❑ 326 Mike Diaz .10 .04
❑ 327 Doug Drabek .10 .04
❑ 328 Mike Dunne .10 .04
❑ 329 Brian Fisher .10 .04
❑ 330 Brett Gideon .10 .04
❑ 331 Terry Harper .10 .04
❑ 332 Bob Kipper .10 .04
❑ 333 Mike LaValliere .10 .04
❑ 334 Jose Lind RC .40 .16
❑ 335 Junior Ortiz .10 .04
❑ 336 Vicente Palacios .10 .04
❑ 337 Bob Patterson .10 .04
❑ 338 Al Pedrique .10 .04
❑ 339 R.J. Reynolds .10 .04
❑ 340 John Smiley RC* .40 .16
❑ 341 Andy Van Slyke UER .20 .08
(Wrong batting and throwing listed)
❑ 342 Bob Walk .10 .04
❑ 343 Marty Barrett .10 .04
❑ 344 Todd Benzinger RC* .40 .16
❑ 345 Wade Boggs .20 .08
❑ 346 Tom Bolton .10 .04
❑ 347 Oil Can Boyd .10 .04
❑ 348 Ellis Burks RC .50 .20
❑ 349 Roger Clemens .75 .30
❑ 350 Steve Crawford .10 .04
❑ 351 Dwight Evans .20 .08
❑ 352 Wes Gardner .10 .04
❑ 353 Rich Gedman .10 .04
❑ 354 Mike Greenwell .10 .04
❑ 355 Sam Horn RC .15 .06
❑ 356 Bruce Hurst .10 .04
❑ 357 John Marzano .10 .04
❑ 358 Al Nipper .10 .04
❑ 359 Spike Owen .10 .04
❑ 360 Jody Reed RC .40 .16
❑ 361 Jim Rice .15 .06
❑ 362 Ed Romero .10 .04
❑ 363 Kevin Romine .10 .04
❑ 364 Joe Sambito .10 .04
❑ 365 Calvin Schiraldi .10 .04
❑ 366 Jeff Sellers .10 .04
❑ 367 Bob Stanley .10 .04
❑ 368 Scott Bankhead .10 .04
❑ 369 Phil Bradley .10 .04
❑ 370 Scott Bradley .10 .04
❑ 371 Mickey Brantley .10 .04
❑ 372 Mike Campbell .10 .04
❑ 373 Alvin Davis .10 .04
❑ 374 Lee Guetterman .10 .04
❑ 375 Dave Hengel .10 .04
❑ 376 Mike Kingery .10 .04
❑ 377 Mark Langston .10 .04
❑ 378 Edgar Martinez RC 5.00 2.00
❑ 379 Mike Moore .10 .04
❑ 380 Mike Morgan .10 .04
❑ 381 John Moses .10 .04
❑ 382 Donell Nixon .10 .04
❑ 383 Edwin Nunez .10 .04
❑ 384 Ken Phelps .10 .04
❑ 385 Jim Presley .10 .04
❑ 386 Rey Quinones .10 .04
❑ 387 Jerry Reed .10 .04
❑ 388 Harold Reynolds .15 .06
❑ 389 Dave Valle .10 .04
❑ 390 Bill Wilkinson .10 .04
❑ 391 Harold Baines .15 .06
❑ 392 Floyd Bannister .10 .04
❑ 393 Daryl Boston .10 .04
❑ 394 Ivan Calderon .10 .04
❑ 395 Jose DeLeon .10 .04
❑ 396 Richard Dotson .10 .04
❑ 397 Carlton Fisk .20 .08
❑ 398 Ozzie Guillen .15 .06
❑ 399 Ron Hassey .10 .04
❑ 400 Donnie Hill .10 .04
❑ 401 Bob James .10 .04
❑ 402 Dave LaPoint .10 .04
❑ 403 Bill Lindsey .10 .04
❑ 404 Bill Long .10 .04
❑ 405 Steve Lyons .10 .04
❑ 406 Fred Manrique .10 .04
❑ 407 Jack McDowell RC .50 .20
❑ 408 Gary Redus .10 .04
❑ 409 Ray Searage .10 .04
❑ 410 Bobby Thigpen .10 .04
❑ 411 Greg Walker .10 .04
❑ 412 Ken Williams RC .10 .04
❑ 413 Jim Winn .10 .04
❑ 414 Jody Davis .10 .04
❑ 415 Andre Dawson .15 .06
❑ 416 Brian Dayett .10 .04
❑ 417 Bob Dernier .10 .04
❑ 418 Frank DiPino .10 .04
❑ 419 Shawon Dunston .10 .04
❑ 420 Leon Durham .10 .04
❑ 421 Les Lancaster .10 .04
❑ 422 Ed Lynch .10 .04
❑ 423 Greg Maddux 1.50 .60
❑ 424 Dave Martinez .10 .04
❑ 425A Keith Moreland ERR 1.50 .60
(Photo actually Jody Davis)
❑ 425B Keith Moreland COR .15 .06
(Bat on shoulder)
❑ 426 Jamie Moyer .15 .06
❑ 427 Jerry Mumphrey .10 .04
❑ 428 Paul Noce .10 .04
❑ 429 Rafael Palmeiro .60 .24
❑ 430 Wade Rowdon .10 .04
❑ 431 Ryne Sandberg .60 .24
❑ 432 Scott Sanderson .10 .04
❑ 433 Lee Smith .15 .06
❑ 434 Jim Sundberg .15 .06
❑ 435 Rick Sutcliffe .15 .06
❑ 436 Manny Trillo .10 .04
❑ 437 Juan Agosto .10 .04
❑ 438 Larry Andersen .10 .04
❑ 439 Alan Ashby .10 .04
❑ 440 Kevin Bass .10 .04
❑ 441 Ken Caminiti RC 3.00 1.20
❑ 442 Rocky Childress .10 .04
❑ 443 Jose Cruz .15 .06
❑ 444 Danny Darwin .10 .04
❑ 445 Glenn Davis .10 .04
❑ 446 Jim Deshaies .10 .04
❑ 447 Bill Doran .10 .04

❑ 448 Ty Gainey	.10	.04
❑ 449 Billy Hatcher	.10	.04
❑ 450 Jeff Heathcock	.10	.04
❑ 451 Bob Knepper	.10	.04
❑ 452 Rob Mallicoat	.10	.04
❑ 453 Dave Meads	.10	.04
❑ 454 Craig Reynolds	.10	.04
❑ 455 Nolan Ryan	1.50	.60
❑ 456 Mike Scott	.15	.06
❑ 457 Dave Smith	.10	.04
❑ 458 Denny Walling	.10	.04
❑ 459 Robbie Wine	.10	.04
❑ 460 Gerald Young	.10	.04
❑ 461 Bob Brower	.10	.04
❑ 462A Jerry Browne ERR	1.50	.60
(Photo actually		
Bob Brower,		
white player)		
❑ 462B Jerry Browne COR	.15	.06
(Black player)		
❑ 463 Steve Buechele	.10	.04
❑ 464 Edwin Correa	.10	.04
❑ 465 Cecil Espy	.10	.04
❑ 466 Scott Fletcher	.10	.04
❑ 467 Jose Guzman	.10	.04
❑ 468 Greg Harris	.10	.04
❑ 469 Charlie Hough	.15	.06
❑ 470 Pete Incaviglia	.10	.04
❑ 471 Paul Kilgus	.10	.04
❑ 472 Mike Loynd	.10	.04
❑ 473 Oddibe McDowell	.10	.04
❑ 474 Dale Mohorcic	.10	.04
❑ 475 Pete O'Brien	.10	.04
❑ 476 Larry Parrish	.10	.04
❑ 477 Geno Petralli	.10	.04
❑ 478 Jeff Russell	.10	.04
❑ 479 Ruben Sierra	.15	.06
❑ 480 Mike Stanley	.10	.04
❑ 481 Curtis Wilkerson	.10	.04
❑ 482 Mitch Williams	.10	.04
❑ 483 Bobby Witt	.10	.04
❑ 484 Tony Armas	.15	.06
❑ 485 Bob Boone	.15	.06
❑ 486 Bill Buckner	.15	.06
❑ 487 DeWayne Buice	.10	.04
❑ 488 Brian Downing	.15	.06
❑ 489 Chuck Finley	.15	.06
❑ 490 Willie Fraser UER	.10	.04
(Wrong bio stats,		
for George Hendrick)		
❑ 491 Jack Howell	.10	.04
❑ 492 Ruppert Jones	.10	.04
❑ 493 Wally Joyner	.15	.06
❑ 494 Jack Lazorko	.10	.04
❑ 495 Gary Lucas	.10	.04
❑ 496 Kirk McCaskill	.10	.04
❑ 497 Mark McLemore	.10	.04
❑ 498 Darrell Miller	.10	.04
❑ 499 Greg Minton	.10	.04
❑ 500 Donnie Moore	.10	.04
❑ 501 Gus Polidor	.10	.04
❑ 502 Johnny Ray	.10	.04
❑ 503 Mark Ryal	.10	.04
❑ 504 Dick Schofield	.10	.04
❑ 505 Don Sutton	.15	.06
❑ 506 Devon White	.15	.06
❑ 507 Mike Witt	.10	.04
❑ 508 Dave Anderson	.10	.04
❑ 509 Tim Belcher	.10	.04
❑ 510 Ralph Bryant	.10	.04
❑ 511 Tim Crews RC	.40	.16
❑ 512 Mike Devereaux RC	.40	.16
❑ 513 Mariano Duncan	.10	.04
❑ 514 Pedro Guerrero	.15	.06
❑ 515 Jeff Hamilton	.10	.04
❑ 516 Mickey Hatcher	.10	.04
❑ 517 Brad Havens	.10	.04
❑ 518 Orel Hershiser	.15	.06
❑ 519 Shawn Hillegas	.10	.04
❑ 520 Ken Howell	.10	.04
❑ 521 Tim Leary	.10	.04
❑ 522 Mike Marshall	.10	.04
❑ 523 Steve Sax	.10	.04
❑ 524 Mike Scioscia	.15	.06
❑ 525 Mike Sharperson	.10	.04
❑ 526 John Shelby	.10	.04
❑ 527 Franklin Stubbs	.10	.04
❑ 528 Fernando Valenzuela	.15	.06
❑ 529 Bob Welch	.15	.06
❑ 530 Matt Young	.10	.04
❑ 531 Jim Acker	.10	.04
❑ 532 Paul Assenmacher	.10	.04
❑ 533 Jeff Blauser RC	.40	.16
❑ 534 Joe Boever	.10	.04
❑ 535 Martin Clary	.10	.04
❑ 536 Kevin Coffman	.10	.04
❑ 537 Jeff Dedmon	.10	.04
❑ 538 Ron Gant RC	.50	.20
❑ 539 Tom Glavine RC	3.00	1.20
❑ 540 Ken Griffey	.15	.06
❑ 541 Albert Hall	.10	.04
❑ 542 Glenn Hubbard	.10	.04
❑ 543 Dion James	.10	.04
❑ 544 Dale Murphy	.20	.08
❑ 545 Ken Oberkfell	.10	.04
❑ 546 David Palmer	.10	.04
❑ 547 Gerald Perry	.10	.04
❑ 548 Charlie Puleo	.10	.04
❑ 549 Ted Simmons	.15	.06
❑ 550 Zane Smith	.10	.04
❑ 551 Andres Thomas	.10	.04
❑ 552 Ozzie Virgil	.10	.04
❑ 553 Don Aase	.10	.04
❑ 554 Jeff Ballard	.10	.04
❑ 555 Eric Bell	.10	.04
❑ 556 Mike Boddicker	.10	.04
❑ 557 Ken Dixon	.10	.04
❑ 558 Jim Dwyer	.10	.04
❑ 559 Ken Gerhart	.10	.04
❑ 560 Rene Gonzales RC	.15	.06
❑ 561 Mike Griffin	.10	.04
❑ 562 John Habyan UER	.10	.04
(Misspelled Hayban on		
both sides of card)		
❑ 563 Terry Kennedy	.10	.04
❑ 564 Ray Knight	.15	.06
❑ 565 Lee Lacy	.10	.04
❑ 566 Fred Lynn	.15	.06
❑ 567 Eddie Murray	.30	.12
❑ 568 Tom Niedenfuer	.10	.04
❑ 569 Bill Ripken RC*	.40	.16
❑ 570 Cal Ripken	1.25	.50
❑ 571 Dave Schmidt	.10	.04
❑ 572 Larry Sheets	.10	.04
❑ 573 Pete Stanicek	.10	.04
❑ 574 Mark Williamson	.10	.04
❑ 575 Mike Young	.10	.04
❑ 576 Shawn Abner	.10	.04
❑ 577 Greg Booker	.10	.04
❑ 578 Chris Brown	.10	.04
❑ 579 Keith Comstock	.10	.04
❑ 580 Joey Cora RC	.40	.16
❑ 581 Mark Davis	.10	.04
❑ 582 Tim Flannery	.20	.08
(With surfboard)		
❑ 583 Goose Gossage	.15	.06
❑ 584 Mark Grant	.10	.04
❑ 585 Tony Gwynn	.50	.20
❑ 586 Andy Hawkins	.10	.04
❑ 587 Stan Jefferson	.10	.04
❑ 588 Jimmy Jones	.10	.04
❑ 589 John Kruk	.15	.06
❑ 590 Shane Mack	.10	.04
❑ 591 Carmelo Martinez	.10	.04
❑ 592 Lance McCullers UER	.10	.04
(6'11" tall)		
❑ 593 Eric Nolte	.10	.04
❑ 594 Randy Ready	.10	.04
❑ 595 Luis Salazar	.10	.04
❑ 596 Benito Santiago	.15	.06
❑ 597 Eric Show	.10	.04
❑ 598 Garry Templeton	.15	.06
❑ 599 Ed Whitson	.10	.04
❑ 600 Scott Bailes	.10	.04
❑ 601 Chris Bando	.10	.04
❑ 602 Jay Bell RC	.50	.20
❑ 603 Brett Butler	.15	.06
❑ 604 Tom Candiotti	.10	.04
❑ 605 Joe Carter	.15	.06
❑ 606 Carmen Castillo	.10	.04
❑ 607 Brian Dorsett	.10	.04
❑ 608 John Farrell RC	.15	.06
❑ 609 Julio Franco	.15	.06
❑ 610 Mel Hall	.10	.04
❑ 611 Tommy Hinzo	.10	.04
❑ 612 Brook Jacoby	.10	.04
❑ 613 Doug Jones RC	.40	.16
❑ 614 Ken Schrom	.10	.04
❑ 615 Cory Snyder	.10	.04
❑ 616 Sammy Stewart	.10	.04
❑ 617 Greg Swindell	.10	.04
❑ 618 Pat Tabler	.10	.04
❑ 619 Ed VandeBerg	.10	.04
❑ 620 Eddie Williams RC	.15	.06
❑ 621 Rich Yett	.10	.04
❑ 622 Wally Joyner	.15	.06
Cory Snyder		
❑ 623 George Bell	.10	.04
Pedro Guerrero		
❑ 624 Mark McGwire	1.50	.60
Jose Canseco		
❑ 625 Dave Righetti	.10	.04
Dan Plesac		
❑ 626 Bret Saberhagen	.15	.06
Mike Witt		
Jack Morris		
❑ 627 John Franco	.10	.04
Steve Bedrosian		
❑ 628 Ozzie Smith	.30	.12
Ryne Sandberg		
❑ 629 Mark McGwire HL	1.25	.50
❑ 630 Mike Greenwell	.30	.12
Ellis Burks		
Todd Benzinger		
❑ 631 Tony Gwynn	.20	.08
Tim Raines		
❑ 632 Mike Scott	.15	.06
Orel Hershiser		
❑ 633 Pat Tabler	1.25	.50
Mark McGwire		
❑ 634 Tony Gwynn	.20	.08
Vince Coleman		
❑ 635 Tony Fernandez	.50	.20
Cal Ripken		
Alan Trammell		
❑ 636 Mike Schmidt	.30	.12
Gary Carter		
❑ 637 Darryl Strawberry	.15	.06
Eric Davis		
❑ 638 Matt Nokes	.20	.08
Kirby Puckett		
❑ 639 Keith Hernandez	.15	.06
Dale Murphy		
❑ 640 Billy Ripken	.75	.30
Cal Ripken		
❑ 641 Mark Grace RC and	3.00	1.20
Darrin Jackson		
❑ 642 Damon Berryhill RC	.40	.16
Jeff Montgomery RC		
❑ 643 Felix Fermin	.15	.06
Jesse Reid RC		
❑ 644 Greg Myers	.40	.16
Greg Tabor RC		
❑ 645 Joey Meyer	.15	.06
Jim Eppard RC		
❑ 646 Adam Peterson	.40	.16
Randy Velarde RC		
❑ 647 Pete Smith	.40	.16
Chris Gwynn RC		
❑ 648 Tom Newell and	.15	.06
Greg Jelks RC		
❑ 649 Mario Diaz	.15	.06
Clay Parker RC		
❑ 650 Jack Savage and	.15	.06
Todd Simmons RC		
❑ 651 John Burkett	.40	.16
Kirt Manwaring RC		
❑ 652 Dave Otto	.50	.20
Walt Weiss RC		
❑ 653 Jeff King	.40	.16
Randell Byers RC		
❑ 654 CL: Twins/Cards	.10	.04
Tigers/Giants UER		
(90 Bob Melvin,		
91 Eddie Milner)		
❑ 655 CL: Blue Jays/Mets	.10	.04
Brewers/Expos UER		
(Mets listed before		

Card	Nm-Mt	Ex-Mt
Blue Jays on card)		
❑ 656 CL: Yankees/Reds Royals/A's	.10	.04
❑ 657 CL: Phillies/Pirates Red Sox/Mariners	.10	.04
❑ 658 CL: White Sox/Cubs Astros/Rangers	.10	.04
❑ 659 CL: Angels/Dodgers Braves/Orioles	.10	.04
❑ 660 CL: Padres/Indians Rookies/Specials	.10	.04

1988 Fleer Update

Card	Nm-Mt	Ex-Mt
COMP.FACT.SET (132)	10.00	4.00
❑ 1 Jose Bautista XRC	.25	.10
❑ 2 Joe Orsulak	.10	.04
❑ 3 Doug Sisk	.10	.04
❑ 4 Craig Worthington	.10	.04
❑ 5 Mike Boddicker	.10	.04
❑ 6 Rick Cerone	.10	.04
❑ 7 Larry Parrish	.10	.04
❑ 8 Lee Smith	.20	.08
❑ 9 Mike Smithson	.10	.04
❑ 10 John Trautwein	.10	.04
❑ 11 Sherman Corbett	.10	.04
❑ 12 Chili Davis	.20	.08
❑ 13 Jim Eppard	.10	.04
❑ 14 Bryan Harvey XRC	.50	.20
❑ 15 John Davis	.10	.04
❑ 16 Dave Gallagher	.10	.04
❑ 17 Ricky Horton	.10	.04
❑ 18 Dan Pasqua	.10	.04
❑ 19 Melido Perez	.10	.04
❑ 20 Jose Segura	.10	.04
❑ 21 Andy Allanson	.10	.04
❑ 22 Jon Perlman	.10	.04
❑ 23 Domingo Ramos	.10	.04
❑ 24 Rick Rodriguez	.10	.04
❑ 25 Willie Upshaw	.10	.04
❑ 26 Paul Gibson	.10	.04
❑ 27 Don Heinkel	.10	.04
❑ 28 Ray Knight	.20	.08
❑ 29 Gary Pettis	.10	.04
❑ 30 Luis Salazar	.10	.04
❑ 31 Mike Macfarlane XRC	.50	.20
❑ 32 Jeff Montgomery	.50	.20
❑ 33 Ted Power	.10	.04
❑ 34 Israel Sanchez	.10	.04
❑ 35 Kurt Stillwell	.10	.04
❑ 36 Pat Tabler	.10	.04
❑ 37 Don August	.10	.04
❑ 38 Darryl Hamilton XRC	.50	.20
❑ 39 Jeff Leonard	.10	.04
❑ 40 Joey Meyer	.10	.04
❑ 41 Allan Anderson	.10	.04
❑ 42 Brian Harper	.10	.04
❑ 43 Tom Herr	.10	.04
❑ 44 Charlie Lea	.10	.04
❑ 45 John Moses (Listed as Hohn on checklist card)	.10	.04
❑ 46 John Candelaria	.10	.04
❑ 47 Jack Clark	.20	.08
❑ 48 Richard Dotson	.10	.04
❑ 49 Al Leiter XRC*	1.00	.40
❑ 50 Rafael Santana	.10	.04
❑ 51 Don Slaught	.10	.04
❑ 52 Todd Burns	.10	.04
❑ 53 Dave Henderson	.10	.04
❑ 54 Doug Jennings	.10	.04
❑ 55 Dave Parker	.20	.08
❑ 56 Walt Weiss	.75	.30
❑ 57 Bob Welch	.20	.08
❑ 58 Henry Cotto	.10	.04
❑ 59 Mario Diaz UER (Listed as Marion on card front)	.10	.04
❑ 60 Mike Jackson	.20	.08
❑ 61 Bill Swift	.10	.04
❑ 62 Jose Cecena	.10	.04
❑ 63 Ray Hayward	.10	.04
❑ 64 Jim Steels UER (Listed as Jim Steele on card back)	.10	.04
❑ 65 Pat Borders XRC	.50	.20
❑ 66 Sil Campusano	.10	.04
❑ 67 Mike Flanagan	.10	.04
❑ 68 Todd Stottlemyre XRC	.50	.20
❑ 69 David Wells XRC	1.50	.60
❑ 70 Jose Alvarez XRC	.25	.10
❑ 71 Paul Runge	.10	.04
❑ 72 Cesar Jimenez (Card was intended for German Jiminez& it's his photo)	.10	.04
❑ 73 Pete Smith	.10	.04
❑ 74 John Smoltz XRC	5.00	2.00
❑ 75 Damon Berryhill	.25	.10
❑ 76 Goose Gossage	.20	.08
❑ 77 Mark Grace	2.00	.80
❑ 78 Darrin Jackson	.25	.10
❑ 79 Vance Law	.10	.04
❑ 80 Jeff Pico	.10	.04
❑ 81 Gary Varsho	.10	.04
❑ 82 Tim Birtsas	.10	.04
❑ 83 Rob Dibble XRC	1.00	.40
❑ 84 Danny Jackson	.10	.04
❑ 85 Paul O'Neill	.30	.12
❑ 86 Jose Rijo	.20	.08
❑ 87 Chris Sabo XRC	.75	.30
❑ 88 John Fishel	.10	.04
❑ 89 Craig Biggio XRC	4.00	1.60
❑ 90 Terry Puhl	.10	.04
❑ 91 Rafael Ramirez	.10	.04
❑ 92 Louie Meadows	.10	.04
❑ 93 Kirk Gibson	.50	.20
❑ 94 Alfredo Griffin	.10	.04
❑ 95 Jay Howell	.10	.04
❑ 96 Jesse Orosco	.10	.04
❑ 97 Alejandro Pena	.10	.04
❑ 98 Tracy Woodson XRC*	.25	.10
❑ 99 John Dopson	.10	.04
❑ 100 Brian Holman XRC	.25	.10
❑ 101 Rex Hudler	.10	.04
❑ 102 Jeff Parrett	.10	.04
❑ 103 Nelson Santovenia	.10	.04
❑ 104 Kevin Elster	.10	.04
❑ 105 Jeff Innis	.10	.04
❑ 106 Mackey Sasser XRC*	.50	.20
❑ 107 Phil Bradley	.10	.04
❑ 108 Danny Clay	.10	.04
❑ 109 Greg A.Harris	.10	.04
❑ 110 Ricky Jordan XRC	.50	.20
❑ 111 David Palmer	.10	.04
❑ 112 Jim Gott	.10	.04
❑ 113 Tommy Gregg UER (Photo actually Randy Milligan)	.10	.04
❑ 114 Barry Jones	.10	.04
❑ 115 Randy Milligan XRC*	.25	.10
❑ 116 Luis Alicea XRC	.50	.20
❑ 117 Tom Brunansky	.10	.04
❑ 118 John Costello	.10	.04
❑ 119 Jose DeLeon	.10	.04
❑ 120 Bob Horner	.20	.08
❑ 121 Scott Terry	.10	.04
❑ 122 Roberto Alomar XRC	2.00	.80
❑ 123 Dave Leiper	.10	.04
❑ 124 Keith Moreland	.10	.04
❑ 125 Mark Parent	.10	.04
❑ 126 Dennis Rasmussen	.10	.04
❑ 127 Randy Bockus	.10	.04
❑ 128 Brett Butler	.20	.08
❑ 129 Donell Nixon	.10	.04
❑ 130 Earnest Riles	.10	.04
❑ 131 Roger Samuels	.10	.04
❑ 132 Checklist U1-U132	.10	.04

1989 Fleer

Card	Nm-Mt	Ex-Mt
COMPLETE SET (660)	15.00	6.00
COMP.FACT.SET (672)	15.00	6.00
❑ 1 Don Baylor	.10	.04
❑ 2 Lance Blankenship RC	.10	.04
❑ 3 Todd Burns UER (Wrong birthdate; before/after All-Star stats missing)	.05	.02
❑ 4 Greg Cadaret UER (All-Star Break stats show 3 losses, should be 2	.05	.02
❑ 5 Jose Canseco	.25	.10
❑ 6 Storm Davis	.05	.02
❑ 7 Dennis Eckersley	.15	.06
❑ 8 Mike Gallego	.05	.02
❑ 9 Ron Hassey	.05	.02
❑ 10 Dave Henderson	.05	.02
❑ 11 Rick Honeycutt	.05	.02
❑ 12 Glenn Hubbard	.05	.02
❑ 13 Stan Javier	.05	.02
❑ 14 Doug Jennings	.05	.02
❑ 15 Felix Jose RC	.10	.04
❑ 16 Carney Lansford	.10	.04
❑ 17 Mark McGwire	1.00	.40
❑ 18 Gene Nelson	.05	.02
❑ 19 Dave Parker	.10	.04
❑ 20 Eric Plunk	.05	.02
❑ 21 Luis Polonia	.05	.02
❑ 22 Terry Steinbach	.10	.04
❑ 23 Dave Stewart	.10	.04
❑ 24 Walt Weiss	.05	.02
❑ 25 Bob Welch	.10	.04
❑ 26 Curt Young	.05	.02
❑ 27 Rick Aguilera	.05	.02
❑ 28 Wally Backman	.05	.02
❑ 29 Mark Carreon UER (After All-Star Break batting 7.14)	.05	.02
❑ 30 Gary Carter	.10	.04
❑ 31 David Cone	.10	.04
❑ 32 Ron Darling	.10	.04
❑ 33 Len Dykstra	.10	.04
❑ 34 Kevin Elster	.05	.02
❑ 35 Sid Fernandez	.05	.02
❑ 36 Dwight Gooden	.10	.04
❑ 37 Keith Hernandez	.10	.04
❑ 38 Gregg Jefferies	.05	.02
❑ 39 Howard Johnson	.10	.04
❑ 40 Terry Leach	.05	.02
❑ 41 Dave Magadan UER (Bio says 15 doubles, should be 13)	.05	.02
❑ 42 Bob McClure	.05	.02
❑ 43 Roger McDowell UER (Led Mets with 58, should be 62)	.05	.02
❑ 44 Kevin McReynolds	.05	.02
❑ 45 Keith A. Miller	.05	.02
❑ 46 Randy Myers	.10	.04

❑ 47 Bob Ojeda .05 .02
❑ 48 Mackey Sasser .05 .02
❑ 49 Darryl Strawberry .10 .04
❑ 50 Tim Teufel .05 .02
❑ 51 Dave West RC .10 .04
❑ 52 Mookie Wilson .10 .04
❑ 53 Dave Anderson .05 .02
❑ 54 Tim Belcher .05 .02
❑ 55 Mike Davis .05 .02
❑ 56 Mike Devereaux .05 .02
❑ 57 Kirk Gibson .15 .06
❑ 58 Alfredo Griffin .05 .02
❑ 59 Chris Gwynn .05 .02
❑ 60 Jeff Hamilton .05 .02
❑ 61A Danny Heep ERR .25 .10
Lake Hills
❑ 61B Danny Heep COR .05 .02
San Antonio
❑ 62 Orel Hershiser .10 .04
❑ 63 Brian Holton .05 .02
❑ 64 Jay Howell .05 .02
❑ 65 Tim Leary .05 .02
❑ 66 Mike Marshall .05 .02
❑ 67 Ramon Martinez RC .25 .10
❑ 68 Jesse Orosco .05 .02
❑ 69 Alejandro Pena .05 .02
❑ 70 Steve Sax .05 .02
❑ 71 Mike Scioscia .10 .04
❑ 72 Mike Sharperson .05 .02
❑ 73 John Shelby .05 .02
❑ 74 Franklin Stubbs .05 .02
❑ 75 John Tudor .10 .04
❑ 76 Fernando Valenzuela .10 .04
❑ 77 Tracy Woodson .05 .02
❑ 78 Marty Barrett .05 .02
❑ 79 Todd Benzinger .05 .02
❑ 80 Mike Boddicker UER .05 .02
(Rochester in '76,
should be '78)
❑ 81 Wade Boggs .15 .06
❑ 82 Oil Can Boyd .05 .02
❑ 83 Ellis Burks .10 .04
❑ 84 Rick Cerone .05 .02
❑ 85 Roger Clemens .50 .20
❑ 86 Steve Curry .05 .02
❑ 87 Dwight Evans .15 .06
❑ 88 Wes Gardner .05 .02
❑ 89 Rich Gedman .05 .02
❑ 90 Mike Greenwell .05 .02
❑ 91 Bruce Hurst .05 .02
❑ 92 Dennis Lamp .05 .02
❑ 93 Spike Owen .05 .02
❑ 94 Larry Parrish UER .05 .02
(Before All-Star Break
batting 1.90)
❑ 95 Carlos Quintana RC .10 .04
❑ 96 Jody Reed .05 .02
❑ 97 Jim Rice .10 .04
❑ 98A Kevin Romine ERR .25 .10
(Photo actually
Randy Kutcher batting)
❑ 98B Kevin Romine COR .05 .02
(Arms folded)
❑ 99 Lee Smith .10 .04
❑ 100 Mike Smithson .05 .02
❑ 101 Bob Stanley .05 .02
❑ 102 Allan Anderson .05 .02
❑ 103 Keith Atherton .05 .02
❑ 104 Juan Berenguer .05 .02
❑ 105 Bert Blyleven .10 .04
❑ 106 Eric Bullock UER .05 .02
Bats/Throws Right,
should be Left
❑ 107 Randy Bush .05 .02
❑ 108 John Christensen .05 .02
❑ 109 Mark Davidson .05 .02
❑ 110 Gary Gaetti .10 .04
❑ 111 Greg Gagne .05 .02
❑ 112 Dan Gladden .05 .02
❑ 113 German Gonzalez .05 .02
❑ 114 Brian Harper .05 .02
❑ 115 Tom Herr .05 .02
❑ 116 Kent Hrbek .10 .04
❑ 117 Gene Larkin .05 .02
❑ 118 Tim Laudner .05 .02
❑ 119 Charlie Lea .05 .02
❑ 120 Steve Lombardozzi .05 .02
❑ 121A John Moses ERR .25 .10
Tempe
❑ 121B John Moses COR .05 .02
Phoenix
❑ 122 Al Newman .05 .02
❑ 123 Mark Portugal .05 .02
❑ 124 Kirby Puckett .25 .10
❑ 125 Jeff Reardon .10 .04
❑ 126 Fred Toliver .05 .02
❑ 127 Frank Viola .10 .04
❑ 128 Doyle Alexander .05 .02
❑ 129 Dave Bergman .05 .02
❑ 130A Tom Brookens ERR .75 .30
(Mike Heath back)
❑ 130B Tom Brookens COR .05 .02
❑ 131 Paul Gibson .05 .02
❑ 132A Mike Heath ERR .75 .30
(Tom Brookens back)
❑ 132B Mike Heath COR .05 .02
❑ 133 Don Heinkel .05 .02
❑ 134 Mike Henneman .05 .02
❑ 135 Guillermo Hernandez .05 .02
❑ 136 Eric King .05 .02
❑ 137 Chet Lemon .10 .04
❑ 138 Fred Lynn UER .10 .04
'74 and '75 stats missing
❑ 139 Jack Morris .10 .04
❑ 140 Matt Nokes .05 .02
❑ 141 Gary Pettis .05 .02
❑ 142 Ted Power .05 .02
❑ 143 Jeff M. Robinson .05 .02
❑ 144 Luis Salazar .05 .02
❑ 145 Steve Searcy .05 .02
❑ 146 Pat Sheridan .05 .02
❑ 147 Frank Tanana .10 .04
❑ 148 Alan Trammell .10 .04
❑ 149 Walt Terrell .05 .02
❑ 150 Jim Walewander .05 .02
❑ 151 Lou Whitaker .10 .04
❑ 152 Tim Birtsas .05 .02
❑ 153 Tom Browning .05 .02
❑ 154 Keith Brown .05 .02
❑ 155 Norm Charlton RC .25 .10
❑ 156 Dave Concepcion .10 .04
❑ 157 Kal Daniels .05 .02
❑ 158 Eric Davis .10 .04
❑ 159 Bo Diaz .05 .02
❑ 160 Rob Dibble RC .50 .20
❑ 161 Nick Esasky .05 .02
❑ 162 John Franco .10 .04
❑ 163 Danny Jackson .05 .02
❑ 164 Barry Larkin .15 .06
❑ 165 Rob Murphy .05 .02
❑ 166 Paul O'Neill .15 .06
❑ 167 Jeff Reed .05 .02
❑ 168 Jose Rijo .10 .04
❑ 169 Ron Robinson .05 .02
❑ 170 Chris Sabo RC .40 .16
❑ 171 Candy Sierra .05 .02
❑ 172 Van Snider .05 .02
❑ 173A Jeff Treadway 25.00 10.00
(Target registration
mark above head
on front in
light blue)
❑ 173B Jeff Treadway .05 .02
(No target on front)
❑ 174 Frank Williams UER .05 .02
(After All-Star Break
stats are jumbled)
❑ 175 Herm Winningham .05 .02
❑ 176 Jim Adduci .05 .02
❑ 177 Don August .05 .02
❑ 178 Mike Birkbeck .05 .02
❑ 179 Chris Bosio .05 .02
❑ 180 Glenn Braggs .05 .02
❑ 181 Greg Brock .05 .02
❑ 182 Mark Clear .05 .02
❑ 183 Chuck Crim .05 .02
❑ 184 Rob Deer .05 .02
❑ 185 Tom Filer .05 .02
❑ 186 Jim Gantner .05 .02
❑ 187 Darryl Hamilton RC .25 .10
❑ 188 Ted Higuera .05 .02
❑ 189 Odell Jones .05 .02
❑ 190 Jeffrey Leonard .05 .02
❑ 191 Joey Meyer .05 .02
❑ 192 Paul Mirabella .05 .02
❑ 193 Paul Molitor .15 .06
❑ 194 Charlie O'Brien .05 .02
❑ 195 Dan Plesac .05 .02
❑ 196 Gary Sheffield RC 2.00 .80
❑ 197 B.J. Surhoff .10 .04
❑ 198 Dale Sveum .05 .02
❑ 199 Bill Wegman .05 .02
❑ 200 Robin Yount .40 .16
❑ 201 Rafael Belliard .05 .02
❑ 202 Barry Bonds 1.50 .60
❑ 203 Bobby Bonilla .10 .04
❑ 204 Sid Bream .05 .02
❑ 205 Benny Distefano .05 .02
❑ 206 Doug Drabek .05 .02
❑ 207 Mike Dunne .05 .02
❑ 208 Felix Fermin .05 .02
❑ 209 Brian Fisher .05 .02
❑ 210 Jim Gott .05 .02
❑ 211 Bob Kipper .05 .02
❑ 212 Dave LaPoint .05 .02
❑ 213 Mike LaValliere .05 .02
❑ 214 Jose Lind .05 .02
❑ 215 Junior Ortiz .05 .02
❑ 216 Vicente Palacios .05 .02
❑ 217 Tom Prince .05 .02
❑ 218 Gary Redus .05 .02
❑ 219 R.J. Reynolds .05 .02
❑ 220 Jeff D. Robinson .05 .02
❑ 221 John Smiley .05 .02
❑ 222 Andy Van Slyke .15 .06
❑ 223 Bob Walk .05 .02
❑ 224 Glenn Wilson .05 .02
❑ 225 Jesse Barfield .10 .04
❑ 226 George Bell .10 .04
❑ 227 Pat Borders RC .25 .10
❑ 228 John Cerutti .05 .02
❑ 229 Jim Clancy .05 .02
❑ 230 Mark Eichhorn .05 .02
❑ 231 Tony Fernandez .05 .02
❑ 232 Cecil Fielder .10 .04
❑ 233 Mike Flanagan .05 .02
❑ 234 Kelly Gruber .05 .02
❑ 235 Tom Henke .05 .02
❑ 236 Jimmy Key .10 .04
❑ 237 Rick Leach .05 .02
❑ 238 Manny Lee UER .05 .02
(Bio says regular
shortstop, sic,
Tony Fernandez)
❑ 239 Nelson Liriano .05 .02
❑ 240 Fred McGriff .15 .06
❑ 241 Lloyd Moseby .05 .02
❑ 242 Rance Mulliniks .05 .02
❑ 243 Jeff Musselman .05 .02
❑ 244 Dave Stieb .10 .04
❑ 245 Todd Stottlemyre .05 .02
❑ 246 Duane Ward .05 .02
❑ 247 David Wells .10 .04
❑ 248 Ernie Whitt UER .05 .02
(HR total 21,
should be 121)
❑ 249 Luis Aguayo .05 .02
❑ 250A Neil Allen ERR .75 .30
Sarasota, FL
❑ 250B Neil Allen COR .05 .02
Syosset, NY
❑ 251 John Candelaria .05 .02
❑ 252 Jack Clark .10 .04
❑ 253 Richard Dotson .05 .02
❑ 254 Rickey Henderson .25 .10
❑ 255 Tommy John .10 .04
❑ 256 Roberto Kelly .05 .02
❑ 257 Al Leiter .25 .10
❑ 258 Don Mattingly .60 .24
❑ 259 Dale Mohorcic .05 .02
❑ 260 Hal Morris RC .25 .10
❑ 261 Scott Nielsen .05 .02
❑ 262 Mike Pagliarulo UER .05 .02
(Wrong birthdate)
❑ 263 Hipolito Pena .05 .02
❑ 264 Ken Phelps .05 .02
❑ 265 Willie Randolph .10 .04
❑ 266 Rick Rhoden .05 .02

❑ 267	Dave Righetti	.10	.04
❑ 268	Rafael Santana	.05	.02
❑ 269	Steve Shields	.05	.02
❑ 270	Joel Skinner	.05	.02
❑ 271	Don Slaught	.05	.02
❑ 272	Claudell Washington	.05	.02
❑ 273	Gary Ward	.05	.02
❑ 274	Dave Winfield	.10	.04
❑ 275	Luis Aquino	.05	.02
❑ 276	Floyd Bannister	.05	.02
❑ 277	George Brett	.60	.24
❑ 278	Bill Buckner	.10	.04
❑ 279	Nick Capra	.05	.02
❑ 280	Jose DeJesus	.05	.02
❑ 281	Steve Farr	.05	.02
❑ 282	Jerry Don Gleaton	.05	.02
❑ 283	Mark Gubicza	.05	.02
❑ 284	Tom Gordon RC UER (16.2 innings in '88, should be 15.2)	.40	.16
❑ 285	Bo Jackson	.25	.10
❑ 286	Charlie Leibrandt	.05	.02
❑ 287	Mike Macfarlane RC	.25	.10
❑ 288	Jeff Montgomery	.05	.02
❑ 289	Bill Pecota UER (Photo actually Brad Wellman)	.05	.02
❑ 290	Jamie Quirk	.05	.02
❑ 291	Bret Saberhagen	.10	.04
❑ 292	Kevin Seitzer	.05	.02
❑ 293	Kurt Stillwell	.05	.02
❑ 294	Pat Tabler	.05	.02
❑ 295	Danny Tartabull	.05	.02
❑ 296	Gary Thurman	.05	.02
❑ 297	Frank White	.10	.04
❑ 298	Willie Wilson	.10	.04
❑ 299	Roberto Alomar	.25	.10
❑ 300	S.Alomar Jr. RC UER Wrong birthdate, says 6/16/66, should say 6/18/66	.40	.16
❑ 301	Chris Brown	.05	.02
❑ 302	Mike Brumley UER (133 hits in '88, should be 134)	.05	.02
❑ 303	Mark Davis	.05	.02
❑ 304	Mark Grant	.05	.02
❑ 305	Tony Gwynn	.30	.12
❑ 306	Greg W. Harris RC	.10	.04
❑ 307	Andy Hawkins	.05	.02
❑ 308	Jimmy Jones	.05	.02
❑ 309	John Kruk	.10	.04
❑ 310	Dave Leiper	.05	.02
❑ 311	Carmelo Martinez	.05	.02
❑ 312	Lance McCullers	.05	.02
❑ 313	Keith Moreland	.05	.02
❑ 314	Dennis Rasmussen	.05	.02
❑ 315	Randy Ready UER (1214 games in '88, should be 114)	.05	.02
❑ 316	Benito Santiago	.10	.04
❑ 317	Eric Show	.05	.02
❑ 318	Todd Simmons	.05	.02
❑ 319	Garry Templeton	.10	.04
❑ 320	Dickie Thon	.05	.02
❑ 321	Ed Whitson	.05	.02
❑ 322	Marvell Wynne	.05	.02
❑ 323	Mike Aldrete	.05	.02
❑ 324	Brett Butler	.10	.04
❑ 325	Will Clark UER (Three consecutive 100 RBI seasons)	.15	.06
❑ 326	Kelly Downs UER ('88 stats missing)	.05	.02
❑ 327	Dave Dravecky	.05	.02
❑ 328	Scott Garrelts	.05	.02
❑ 329	Atlee Hammaker	.05	.02
❑ 330	Charlie Hayes RC	.25	.10
❑ 331	Mike Krukow	.05	.02
❑ 332	Craig Lefferts	.05	.02
❑ 333	Candy Maldonado	.05	.02
❑ 334	Kirt Manwaring UER (Bats Rights)	.05	.02
❑ 335	Bob Melvin	.05	.02
❑ 336	Kevin Mitchell	.10	.04
❑ 337	Donell Nixon	.05	.02
❑ 338	Tony Perezchica	.05	.02
❑ 339	Joe Price	.05	.02
❑ 340	Rick Reuschel	.10	.04
❑ 341	Earnest Riles	.05	.02
❑ 342	Don Robinson	.05	.02
❑ 343	Chris Speier	.05	.02
❑ 344	Robby Thompson UER (West Plam Beach)	.05	.02
❑ 345	Jose Uribe	.05	.02
❑ 346	Matt Williams	.25	.10
❑ 347	Trevor Wilson RC	.10	.04
❑ 348	Juan Agosto	.05	.02
❑ 349	Larry Andersen	.05	.02
❑ 350A	Alan Ashby ERR (Throws Rig)	2.00	.80
❑ 350B	Alan Ashby COR	.05	.02
❑ 351	Kevin Bass	.05	.02
❑ 352	Buddy Bell	.10	.04
❑ 353	Craig Biggio RC	1.50	.60
❑ 354	Danny Darwin	.05	.02
❑ 355	Glenn Davis	.05	.02
❑ 356	Jim Deshaies	.05	.02
❑ 357	Bill Doran	.05	.02
❑ 358	John Fishel	.05	.02
❑ 359	Billy Hatcher	.05	.02
❑ 360	Bob Knepper	.05	.02
❑ 361	L.Meadows UER Bio says 10 EBH's and 6 SB's in '88, should be 3 and 4	.05	.02
❑ 362	Dave Meads	.05	.02
❑ 363	Jim Pankovits	.05	.02
❑ 364	Terry Puhl	.05	.02
❑ 365	Rafael Ramirez	.05	.02
❑ 366	Craig Reynolds	.05	.02
❑ 367	Mike Scott (Card number listed as 368 on Astros CL)	.10	.04
❑ 368	Nolan Ryan (Card number listed as 367 on Astros CL)	1.00	.40
❑ 369	Dave Smith	.05	.02
❑ 370	Gerald Young	.05	.02
❑ 371	Hubie Brooks	.05	.02
❑ 372	Tim Burke	.05	.02
❑ 373	John Dopson	.05	.02
❑ 374	Mike R. Fitzgerald	.05	.02
❑ 375	Tom Foley	.05	.02
❑ 376	Andres Galarraga UER (Home: Caracus)	.10	.04
❑ 377	Neal Heaton	.05	.02
❑ 378	Joe Hesketh	.05	.02
❑ 379	Brian Holman RC	.10	.04
❑ 380	Rex Hudler	.05	.02
❑ 381	R.Johnson RC UER Innings for '85 and '86 shown as 27 and 120, should be 27.1 and 119.2	5.00	2.00
❑ 381B	R.Johnson Marlboro ERR	40.00	16.00
❑ 382	Wallace Johnson	.05	.02
❑ 383	Tracy Jones	.05	.02
❑ 384	Dave Martinez	.05	.02
❑ 385	Dennis Martinez	.10	.04
❑ 386	Andy McGaffigan	.05	.02
❑ 387	Otis Nixon	.05	.02
❑ 388	Johnny Paredes	.05	.02
❑ 389	Jeff Parrett	.05	.02
❑ 390	Pascual Perez	.05	.02
❑ 391	Tim Raines	.10	.04
❑ 392	Luis Rivera	.05	.02
❑ 393	Nelson Santovenia	.05	.02
❑ 394	Bryn Smith	.05	.02
❑ 395	Tim Wallach	.05	.02
❑ 396	Andy Allanson UER 1214 hits in '88, should be 114	.05	.02
❑ 397	Rod Allen	.05	.02
❑ 398	Scott Bailes	.05	.02
❑ 399	Tom Candiotti	.05	.02
❑ 400	Joe Carter	.10	.04
❑ 401	Carmen Castillo UER (After All-Star Break batting 2.50)	.05	.02
❑ 402	Dave Clark UER (Card front shows position as Rookie; after All-Star Break batting 3.14)	.05	.02
❑ 403	John Farrell UER (Typo in runs allowed in '88)	.05	.02
❑ 404	Julio Franco	.10	.04
❑ 405	Don Gordon	.05	.02
❑ 406	Mel Hall	.05	.02
❑ 407	Brad Havens	.05	.02
❑ 408	Brook Jacoby	.05	.02
❑ 409	Doug Jones	.05	.02
❑ 410	Jeff Kaiser	.05	.02
❑ 411	Luis Medina	.05	.02
❑ 412	Cory Snyder	.05	.02
❑ 413	Greg Swindell	.05	.02
❑ 414	Ron Tingley UER (Hit HR in first ML at-bat, should be first AL at-bat)	.05	.02
❑ 415	Willie Upshaw	.05	.02
❑ 416	Ron Washington	.05	.02
❑ 417	Rich Yett	.05	.02
❑ 418	Damon Berryhill	.05	.02
❑ 419	Mike Bielecki	.05	.02
❑ 420	Doug Dascenzo	.05	.02
❑ 421	Jody Davis UER (Braves stats for '88 missing)	.05	.02
❑ 422	Andre Dawson	.10	.04
❑ 423	Frank DiPino	.05	.02
❑ 424	Shawon Dunston	.05	.02
❑ 425	Rich Gossage	.10	.04
❑ 426	Mark Grace UER (Minor League stats for '88 missing)	.25	.10
❑ 427	Mike Harkey RC	.10	.04
❑ 428	Darrin Jackson	.10	.04
❑ 429	Les Lancaster	.05	.02
❑ 430	Vance Law	.05	.02
❑ 431	Greg Maddux	.50	.20
❑ 432	Jamie Moyer	.10	.04
❑ 433	Al Nipper	.05	.02
❑ 434	Rafael Palmeiro UER 170 hits in '88, should be 178	.25	.10
❑ 435	Pat Perry	.05	.02
❑ 436	Jeff Pico	.05	.02
❑ 437	Ryne Sandberg	.40	.16
❑ 438	Calvin Schiraldi	.05	.02
❑ 439	Rick Sutcliffe	.10	.04
❑ 440A	Manny Trillo ERR (Throws Rig)	2.00	.80
❑ 440B	Manny Trillo COR	.05	.02
❑ 441	Gary Varsho UER (Wrong birthdate; .303 should be .302; 11/28 should be 9/19)	.05	.02
❑ 442	Mitch Webster	.05	.02
❑ 443	Luis Alicea RC	.25	.10
❑ 444	Tom Brunansky	.05	.02
❑ 445	Vince Coleman UER Third straight with 83 should be fourth straight with 81	.05	.02
❑ 446	John Costello UER (Home California, should be New York)	.05	.02
❑ 447	Danny Cox	.05	.02
❑ 448	Ken Dayley	.05	.02
❑ 449	Jose DeLeon	.05	.02
❑ 450	Curt Ford	.05	.02
❑ 451	Pedro Guerrero	.10	.04
❑ 452	Bob Horner	.10	.04
❑ 453	Tim Jones	.05	.02
❑ 454	Steve Lake	.05	.02
❑ 455	Joe Magrane UER (Des Moines& IO)	.05	.02
❑ 456	Greg Mathews	.05	.02
❑ 457	Willie McGee	.10	.04
❑ 458	Larry McWilliams	.05	.02
❑ 459	Jose Oquendo	.05	.02
❑ 460	Tony Pena	.05	.02
❑ 461	Terry Pendleton	.10	.04
❑ 462	Steve Peters UER (Lives in Harrah, not Harah)	.05	.02

❑ 463 Ozzie Smith .40 .16
❑ 464 Scott Terry .05 .02
❑ 465 Denny Walling .05 .02
❑ 466 Todd Worrell .05 .02
❑ 467 Tony Armas UER .10 .04
(Before All-Star Break
batting 2.39)
❑ 468 Dante Bichette RC .40 .16
❑ 469 Bob Boone .10 .04
❑ 470 Terry Clark .05 .02
❑ 471 Stu Cliburn .05 .02
❑ 472 Mike Cook UER .05 .02
(TM near Angels logo
missing from front)
❑ 473 Sherman Corbett .05 .02
❑ 474 Chili Davis .10 .04
❑ 475 Brian Downing .10 .04
❑ 476 Jim Eppard .05 .02
❑ 477 Chuck Finley .10 .04
❑ 478 Willie Fraser .05 .02
❑ 479 Bryan Harvey UER RC .25 .10
ML record shows 0-0,
should be 7-5
❑ 480 Jack Howell .05 .02
❑ 481 Wally Joyner UER .10 .04
(Yorba Linda, GA)
❑ 482 Jack Lazorko .05 .02
❑ 483 Kirk McCaskill .05 .02
❑ 484 Mark McLemore .05 .02
❑ 485 Greg Minton .05 .02
❑ 486 Dan Petry .05 .02
❑ 487 Johnny Ray .05 .02
❑ 488 Dick Schofield .05 .02
❑ 489 Devon White .10 .04
❑ 490 Mike Witt .05 .02
❑ 491 Harold Baines .10 .04
❑ 492 Daryl Boston .05 .02
❑ 493 Ivan Calderon UER .05 .02
('80 stats shifted)
❑ 494 Mike Diaz .05 .02
❑ 495 Carlton Fisk .15 .06
❑ 496 Dave Gallagher .05 .02
❑ 497 Ozzie Guillen .10 .04
❑ 498 Shawn Hillegas .05 .02
❑ 499 Lance Johnson .05 .02
❑ 500 Barry Jones .05 .02
❑ 501 Bill Long .05 .02
❑ 502 Steve Lyons .05 .02
❑ 503 Fred Manrique .05 .02
❑ 504 Jack McDowell .10 .04
❑ 505 Donn Pall .05 .02
❑ 506 Kelly Paris .05 .02
❑ 507 Dan Pasqua .05 .02
❑ 508 Ken Patterson .05 .02
❑ 509 Melido Perez .05 .02
❑ 510 Jerry Reuss .05 .02
❑ 511 Mark Salas .05 .02
❑ 512 Bobby Thigpen UER .05 .02
('86 ERA 4.69,
should be 4.68)
❑ 513 Mike Woodard .05 .02
❑ 514 Bob Brower .05 .02
❑ 515 Steve Buechele .05 .02
❑ 516 Jose Cecena .05 .02
❑ 517 Cecil Espy .05 .02
❑ 518 Scott Fletcher .05 .02
❑ 519 Cecilio Guante .05 .02
('87 Yankee stats
are off-centered)
❑ 520 Jose Guzman .05 .02
❑ 521 Ray Hayward .05 .02
❑ 522 Charlie Hough .10 .04
❑ 523 Pete Incaviglia .05 .02
❑ 524 Mike Jeffcoat .05 .02
❑ 525 Paul Kilgus .05 .02
❑ 526 Chad Kreuter RC .25 .10
❑ 527 Jeff Kunkel .05 .02
❑ 528 Oddibe McDowell .05 .02
❑ 529 Pete O'Brien .05 .02
❑ 530 Geno Petralli .05 .02
❑ 531 Jeff Russell .05 .02
❑ 532 Ruben Sierra .05 .02
❑ 533 Mike Stanley .05 .02
❑ 534A Ed VandeBerg ERR 2.00 .80
(Throws Lef)
❑ 534B Ed VandeBerg COR .05 .02
❑ 535 Curtis Wilkerson ERR .05 .02
(Pitcher headings
at bottom)
❑ 536 Mitch Williams .05 .02
❑ 537 Bobby Witt UER .05 .02
('85 ERA .643,
should be 6.43)
❑ 538 Steve Balboni .05 .02
❑ 539 Scott Bankhead .05 .02
❑ 540 Scott Bradley .05 .02
❑ 541 Mickey Brantley .05 .02
❑ 542 Jay Buhner .10 .04
❑ 543 Mike Campbell .05 .02
❑ 544 Darnell Coles .05 .02
❑ 545 Henry Cotto .05 .02
❑ 546 Alvin Davis .05 .02
❑ 547 Mario Diaz .05 .02
❑ 548 Ken Griffey Jr. RC 8.00 3.20
❑ 549 Erik Hanson RC .25 .10
❑ 550 Mike Jackson UER .05 .02
(Lifetime ERA 3.345,
should be 3.45)
❑ 551 Mark Langston .05 .02
❑ 552 Edgar Martinez .25 .10
❑ 553 Bill McGuire .05 .02
❑ 554 Mike Moore .05 .02
❑ 555 Jim Presley .05 .02
❑ 556 Rey Quinones .05 .02
❑ 557 Jerry Reed .05 .02
❑ 558 Harold Reynolds .10 .04
❑ 559 Mike Schooler .05 .02
❑ 560 Bill Swift .05 .02
❑ 561 Dave Valle .05 .02
❑ 562 Steve Bedrosian .05 .02
❑ 563 Phil Bradley .05 .02
❑ 564 Don Carman .05 .02
❑ 565 Bob Dernier .05 .02
❑ 566 Marvin Freeman .05 .02
❑ 567 Todd Frohwirth .05 .02
❑ 568 Greg Gross .05 .02
❑ 569 Kevin Gross .05 .02
❑ 570 Greg A. Harris .05 .02
❑ 571 Von Hayes .05 .02
❑ 572 Chris James .05 .02
❑ 573 Steve Jeltz .05 .02
❑ 574 Ron Jones UER .10 .04
(Led IL in '88 with
85, should be 75)
❑ 575 Ricky Jordan RC .25 .10
❑ 576 Mike Maddux .05 .02
❑ 577 David Palmer .05 .02
❑ 578 Lance Parrish .10 .04
❑ 579 Shane Rawley .05 .02
❑ 580 Bruce Ruffin .05 .02
❑ 581 Juan Samuel .05 .02
❑ 582 Mike Schmidt .50 .20
❑ 583 Kent Tekulve .05 .02
❑ 584 Milt Thompson UER .05 .02
(19 hits in '88,
should be 109)
❑ 585 Jose Alvarez RC .10 .04
❑ 586 Paul Assenmacher .05 .02
❑ 587 Bruce Benedict .05 .02
❑ 588 Jeff Blauser .05 .02
❑ 589 Terry Blocker .05 .02
❑ 590 Ron Gant .10 .04
❑ 591 Tom Glavine .25 .10
❑ 592 Tommy Gregg .05 .02
❑ 593 Albert Hall .05 .02
❑ 594 Dion James .05 .02
❑ 595 Rick Mahler .05 .02
❑ 596 Dale Murphy .15 .06
❑ 597 Gerald Perry .05 .02
❑ 598 Charlie Puleo .05 .02
❑ 599 Ted Simmons .10 .04
❑ 600 Pete Smith .05 .02
❑ 601 Zane Smith .05 .02
❑ 602 John Smoltz RC 2.00 .80
❑ 603 Bruce Sutter .10 .04
❑ 604 Andres Thomas .05 .02
❑ 605 Ozzie Virgil .05 .02
❑ 606 Brady Anderson RC .40 .16
❑ 607 Jeff Ballard .05 .02
❑ 608 Jose Bautista RC .10 .04
❑ 609 Ken Gerhart .05 .02
❑ 610 Terry Kennedy .05 .02
❑ 611 Eddie Murray .25 .10
❑ 612 Carl Nichols UER .05 .02
(Before All-Star Break
batting 1.88)
❑ 613 Tom Niedenfuer .05 .02
❑ 614 Joe Orsulak .05 .02
❑ 615 Oswald Peraza UER .05 .02
(Shown as Oswaldo)
❑ 616A Bill Ripken ERR 15.00 6.00
(Rick Face written
on knob of bat)
❑ 616B Bill Ripken 120.00 47.50
(Bat knob
whited out)
❑ 616C Bill Ripken 25.00 10.00
(Words on bat knob
scribbled out in White)
❑ 616D Bill Ripken 15.00 6.00
Words on Bat
covered by black scribble
❑ 616E Bill Ripken DP 5.00 2.00
(Black box covering
bat knob)
❑ 617 Cal Ripken .75 .30
❑ 618 Dave Schmidt .05 .02
❑ 619 Rick Schu .05 .02
❑ 620 Larry Sheets .05 .02
❑ 621 Doug Sisk .05 .02
❑ 622 Pete Stanicek .05 .02
❑ 623 Mickey Tettleton .05 .02
❑ 624 Jay Tibbs .05 .02
❑ 625 Jim Traber .05 .02
❑ 626 Mark Williamson .05 .02
❑ 627 Craig Worthington .05 .02
❑ 628 Jose Canseco 40/40 .25 .10
❑ 629 Tom Browning Perfect .05 .02
❑ 630 Roberto Alomar .25 .10
Sandy Alomar Jr. UER
(Names on card listed
in wrong order)
❑ 631 Will Clark .15 .06
Rafael Palmeiro UER
(Gallaraga, sic;
Clark 3 consecutive
100 RBI seasons;
third with 102 RBI's)
❑ 632 Darryl Strawberry .10 .04
Will Clark UER (Homeruns
should be two words)
❑ 633 Wade Boggs .10 .04
Carney Lansford UER
(Boggs hit .366 in
'86, should be '88)
❑ 634 Jose Canseco .75 .30
Terry Steinbach
Mark McGwire
❑ 635 Mark Davis .05 .02
Dwight Gooden
❑ 636 Danny Jackson .05 .02
David Cone UER
Hersheiser, sic
❑ 637 Chris Sabo .10 .04
Bobby Bonilla UER
Bobby Bonds, sic
❑ 638 Andres Galarraga UER .05 .02
(Misspelled Gallaraga
on card back)
Gerald Perry
❑ 639 Kirby Puckett .15 .06
Eric Davis
❑ 640 Steve Wilson and .05 .02
Cameron Drew
❑ 641 Kevin Brown and .25 .10
Kevin Reimer
❑ 642 Brad Pounders RC .10 .04
Jerald Clark
❑ 643 Mike Capel and .05 .02
Drew Hall
❑ 644 Joe Girardi RC and .40 .16
Rolando Roomes
❑ 645 Lenny Harris RC and .25 .10
Marty Brown
❑ 646 Luis DeLosSantos .05 .02
and Jim Campbell
❑ 647 Randy Kramer and .05 .02
Miguel Garcia

❑ 648 Torey Lovullo RC and ...... .10 .04
Robert Palacios
❑ 649 Jim Corsi and .... .05 .02
Bob Milacki
❑ 650 Grady Hall and .... .05 .02
Mike Rochford
❑ 651 Terry Taylor RC .... .10 .04
Vance Lovelace
❑ 652 Ken Hill RC and .... .25 .10
Dennis Cook
❑ 653 Scott Service and .... .05 .02
Shane Turner
❑ 654 CL: Oakland/Mets .... .05 .02
Dodgers/Red Sox
(10 Henderson;
68 Jess Orosco)
❑ 655A CL: Twins/Tigers ERR .... .05 .02
Reds/Brewers
(179 Boslo and
Twins/Tigers positions
listed)
❑ 655B CL: Twins/Tigers COR .. .05 .02
Reds/Brewers
(179 Boslo but
Twins/Tigers positions
not listed)
❑ 656 CL: Pirates/Blue Jays ...... .05 .02
Yankees/Royals
(225 Jess Barfield)
❑ 657 CL: Padres/Giants .... .05 .02
Astros/Expos
(367/368 wrong)
❑ 658 CL: Indians/Cubs .... .05 .02
Cardinals/Angels
(449 Deleon)
❑ 659 CL: White Sox/Rangers .... .05 .02
Mariners/Phillies
❑ 660 CL: Braves/Orioles .... .05 .02
Specials/Checklists
(632 hyphenated diff-
erently and 650 Hali;
595 Rich Mahler;
619 Rich Schu)

1989 Fleer Update

	Nm-Mt	Ex-Mt
COMP.FACT.SET (132)	5.00	2.00

❑ 1 Phil Bradley .05 .02
❑ 2 Mike Devereaux .05 .02
❑ 3 Steve Finley RC .75 .30
❑ 4 Kevin Hickey .05 .02
❑ 5 Brian Holton .05 .02
❑ 6 Bob Milacki .05 .02
❑ 7 Randy Milligan .05 .02
❑ 8 John Dopson .05 .02
❑ 9 Nick Esasky .05 .02
❑ 10 Rob Murphy .05 .02
❑ 11 Jim Abbott RC* 1.00 .40
❑ 12 Bert Blyleven .10 .04
❑ 13 Jeff Manto RC .10 .04
❑ 14 Bob McClure .05 .02
❑ 15 Lance Parrish .10 .04
❑ 16 Lee Stevens RC .25 .10
❑ 17 Claudell Washington .05 .02
❑ 18 Mark Davis RC .25 .10
❑ 19 Eric King .05 .02
❑ 20 Ron Kittle .05 .02
❑ 21 Matt Merullo .05 .02
❑ 22 Steve Rosenberg .05 .02
❑ 23 Robin Ventura RC .75 .30
❑ 24 Keith Atherton .05 .02
❑ 25 Joey Belle RC 1.00 .40
❑ 26 Jerry Browne .05 .02
❑ 27 Felix Fermin .05 .02
❑ 28 Brad Komminsk .05 .02
❑ 29 Pete O'Brien .05 .02
❑ 30 Mike Brumley .05 .02
❑ 31 Tracy Jones .05 .02
❑ 32 Mike Schwabe .05 .02
❑ 33 Gary Ward .05 .02
❑ 34 Frank Williams .05 .02
❑ 35 Kevin Appier RC .50 .20
❑ 36 Bob Boone .10 .04
❑ 37 Luis DeLosSantos .05 .02
❑ 38 Jim Eisenreich .05 .02
❑ 39 Jaime Navarro RC .10 .04
❑ 40 Bill Spiers RC .25 .10
❑ 41 Greg Vaughn RC .40 .16
❑ 42 Randy Veres .05 .02
❑ 43 Wally Backman .05 .02
❑ 44 Shane Rawley .05 .02
❑ 45 Steve Balboni .05 .02
❑ 46 Jesse Barfield .10 .04
❑ 47 Alvaro Espinoza .05 .02
❑ 48 Bob Geren RC .05 .02
❑ 49 Mel Hall .05 .02
❑ 50 Andy Hawkins .05 .02
❑ 51 Hensley Meulens RC .10 .04
❑ 52 Steve Sax .05 .02
❑ 53 Deion Sanders RC 1.50 .60
❑ 54 Rickey Henderson .25 .10
❑ 55 Mike Moore .05 .02
❑ 56 Tony Phillips .05 .02
❑ 57 Greg Briley .10 .04
❑ 58 Gene Harris RC .10 .04
❑ 59 Randy Johnson 3.00 1.20
❑ 60 Jeffrey Leonard .05 .02
❑ 61 Dennis Powell .05 .02
❑ 62 Omar Vizquel RC 1.00 .40
❑ 63 Kevin Brown .25 .10
❑ 64 Julio Franco .10 .04
❑ 65 Jamie Moyer .10 .04
❑ 66 Rafael Palmeiro .25 .10
❑ 67 Nolan Ryan 1.50 .60
❑ 68 Francisco Cabrera RC .10 .04
❑ 69 Junior Felix RC .10 .04
❑ 70 Al Leiter .25 .10
❑ 71 Alex Sanchez .05 .02
❑ 72 Geronimo Berroa .05 .02
❑ 73 Derek Lilliquist RC .10 .04
❑ 74 Lonnie Smith .05 .02
❑ 75 Jeff Treadway .05 .02
❑ 76 Paul Kilgus .05 .02
❑ 77 Lloyd McClendon .05 .02
❑ 78 Scott Sanderson .05 .02
❑ 79 Dwight Smith RC .25 .10
❑ 80 Jerome Walton RC .25 .10
❑ 81 Mitch Williams .05 .02
❑ 82 Steve Wilson .10 .04
❑ 83 Todd Benzinger .05 .02
❑ 84 Ken Griffey Sr. .10 .04
❑ 85 Rick Mahler .05 .02
❑ 86 Rolando Roomes .05 .02
❑ 87 Scott Scudder RC .10 .04
❑ 88 Jim Clancy .05 .02
❑ 89 Rick Rhoden .05 .02
❑ 90 Dan Schatzeder .05 .02
❑ 91 Mike Morgan .05 .02
❑ 92 Eddie Murray .25 .10
❑ 93 Willie Randolph .10 .04
❑ 94 Ray Searage .05 .02
❑ 95 Mike Aldrete .05 .02
❑ 96 Kevin Gross .05 .02
❑ 97 Mark Langston .05 .02
❑ 98 Spike Owen .05 .02
❑ 99 Zane Smith .05 .02
❑ 100 Don Aase .05 .02
❑ 101 Barry Lyons .05 .02
❑ 102 Juan Samuel .05 .02
❑ 103 Wally Whitehurst RC .10 .04
❑ 104 Dennis Cook .05 .02
❑ 105 Len Dykstra .10 .04
❑ 106 Charlie Hayes .25 .10
❑ 107 Tommy Herr .05 .02
❑ 108 Ken Howell .05 .02
❑ 109 John Kruk .10 .04
❑ 110 Roger McDowell .05 .02
❑ 111 Terry Mulholland .05 .02
❑ 112 Jeff Parrett .05 .02
❑ 113 Neal Heaton .05 .02
❑ 114 Jeff King .05 .02
❑ 115 Randy Kramer .05 .02
❑ 116 Bill Landrum .05 .02
❑ 117 Cris Carpenter RC * .10 .04
❑ 118 Frank DiPino .05 .02
❑ 119 Ken Hill .25 .10
❑ 120 Dan Quisenberry .05 .02
❑ 121 Milt Thompson .05 .02
❑ 122 Todd Zeile RC .40 .16
❑ 123 Jack Clark .10 .04
❑ 124 Bruce Hurst .05 .02
❑ 125 Mark Parent .05 .02
❑ 126 Bip Roberts .05 .02
❑ 127 Jeff Brantley RC UER .25 .10
(Photo actually
Joe Kmak)
❑ 128 Terry Kennedy .05 .02
❑ 129 Mike LaCoss .05 .02
❑ 130 Greg Litton .05 .02
❑ 131 Mike Schmidt .75 .30
❑ 132 Checklist 1-132 .05 .02

1990 Fleer

	Nm-Mt	Ex-Mt
COMPLETE SET (660)	15.00	4.50
COMP.RETAIL SET (660)	15.00	4.50
COMP.HOBBY SET (672)	15.00	4.50

❑ 1 Lance Blankenship .05 .02
❑ 2 Todd Burns .05 .02
❑ 3 Jose Canseco .15 .04
❑ 4 Jim Corsi .05 .02
❑ 5 Storm Davis .05 .02
❑ 6 Dennis Eckersley .10 .03
❑ 7 Mike Gallego .05 .02
❑ 8 Ron Hassey .05 .02
❑ 9 Dave Henderson .05 .02
❑ 10 Rickey Henderson .25 .07
❑ 11 Rick Honeycutt .05 .02
❑ 12 Stan Javier .05 .02
❑ 13 Felix Jose .05 .02
❑ 14 Carney Lansford .10 .03
❑ 15 Mark McGwire UER .60 .18
(1989 runs listed as
4, should be 74)
❑ 16 Mike Moore .05 .02
❑ 17 Gene Nelson .05 .02
❑ 18 Dave Parker .10 .03
❑ 19 Tony Phillips .05 .02
❑ 20 Terry Steinbach .05 .02
❑ 21 Dave Stewart .10 .03
❑ 22 Walt Weiss .05 .02
❑ 23 Bob Welch .05 .02
❑ 24 Curt Young .05 .02
❑ 25 Paul Assenmacher .05 .02
❑ 26 Damon Berryhill .05 .02
❑ 27 Mike Bielecki .05 .02
❑ 28 Kevin Blankenship .05 .02
❑ 29 Andre Dawson .10 .03
❑ 30 Shawon Dunston .05 .02
❑ 31 Joe Girardi .15 .04

❑ 32 Mark Grace .15 .04
❑ 33 Mike Harkey .05 .02
❑ 34 Paul Kilgus .05 .02
❑ 35 Les Lancaster .05 .02
❑ 36 Vance Law .05 .02
❑ 37 Greg Maddux .40 .12
❑ 38 Lloyd McClendon .05 .02
❑ 39 Jeff Pico .05 .02
❑ 40 Ryne Sandberg .40 .12
❑ 41 Scott Sanderson .05 .02
❑ 42 Dwight Smith .05 .02
❑ 43 Rick Sutcliffe .10 .03
❑ 44 Jerome Walton .05 .02
❑ 45 Mitch Webster .05 .02
❑ 46 Curt Wilkerson .05 .02
❑ 47 Dean Wilkins .05 .02
❑ 48 Mitch Williams .05 .02
❑ 49 Steve Wilson .05 .02
❑ 50 Steve Bedrosian .05 .02
❑ 51 Mike Benjamin RC .10 .03
❑ 52 Jeff Brantley .05 .02
❑ 53 Brett Butler .10 .03
❑ 54 Will Clark UER .10 .03
(Did You Know says first in runs, should say tied for first)
❑ 55 Kelly Downs .05 .02
❑ 56 Scott Garrelts .05 .02
❑ 57 Atlee Hammaker .05 .02
❑ 58 Terry Kennedy .05 .02
❑ 59 Mike LaCoss .05 .02
❑ 60 Craig Lefferts .05 .02
❑ 61 Greg Litton .05 .02
❑ 62 Candy Maldonado .05 .02
❑ 63 Kirt Manwaring UER .05 .02
(No '88 Phoenix stats as noted in box)
❑ 64 Randy McCament .05 .02
❑ 65 Kevin Mitchell .05 .02
❑ 66 Donell Nixon .05 .02
❑ 67 Ken Oberkfell .05 .02
❑ 68 Rick Reuschel .05 .02
❑ 69 Ernest Riles .05 .02
❑ 70 Don Robinson .05 .02
❑ 71 Pat Sheridan .05 .02
❑ 72 Chris Speier .05 .02
❑ 73 Robby Thompson .05 .02
❑ 74 Jose Uribe .05 .02
❑ 75 Matt Williams .10 .03
❑ 76 George Bell .05 .02
❑ 77 Pat Borders .05 .02
❑ 78 John Cerutti .05 .02
❑ 79 Junior Felix .05 .02
❑ 80 Tony Fernandez .05 .02
❑ 81 Mike Flanagan .05 .02
❑ 82 Mauro Gozzo .05 .02
❑ 83 Kelly Gruber .05 .02
❑ 84 Tom Henke .05 .02
❑ 85 Jimmy Key .10 .03
❑ 86 Manny Lee .05 .02
❑ 87 Nelson Liriano UER .05 .02
(Should say "led the IL" instead of "led the TL")
❑ 88 Lee Mazzilli .05 .02
❑ 89 Fred McGriff .25 .07
❑ 90 Lloyd Moseby .05 .02
❑ 91 Rance Mulliniks .05 .02
❑ 92 Alex Sanchez .05 .02
❑ 93 Dave Stieb .10 .03
❑ 94 Todd Stottlemyre .10 .03
❑ 95 Duane Ward UER .05 .02
(Double line of '87 Syracuse stats)
❑ 96 David Wells .10 .03
❑ 97 Ernie Whitt .05 .02
❑ 98 Frank Wills .05 .02
❑ 99 Mookie Wilson .10 .03
❑ 100 Kevin Appier .10 .03
❑ 101 Luis Aquino .05 .02
❑ 102 Bob Boone .10 .03
❑ 103 George Brett .60 .18
❑ 104 Jose DeJesus .05 .02
❑ 105 Luis De Los Santos .05 .02
❑ 106 Jim Eisenreich .05 .02
❑ 107 Steve Farr .05 .02
❑ 108 Tom Gordon .10 .03
❑ 109 Mark Gubicza .05 .02
❑ 110 Bo Jackson .25 .07
❑ 111 Terry Leach .05 .02
❑ 112 Charlie Leibrandt .05 .02
❑ 113 Rick Luecken .05 .02
❑ 114 Mike Macfarlane .05 .02
❑ 115 Jeff Montgomery .10 .03
❑ 116 Bret Saberhagen .10 .03
❑ 117 Kevin Seitzer .05 .02
❑ 118 Kurt Stillwell .05 .02
❑ 119 Pat Tabler .05 .02
❑ 120 Danny Tartabull .05 .02
❑ 121 Gary Thurman .05 .02
❑ 122 Frank White .10 .03
❑ 123 Willie Wilson .05 .02
❑ 124 Matt Winters .05 .02
❑ 125 Jim Abbott .15 .04
❑ 126 Tony Armas .05 .02
❑ 127 Dante Bichette .10 .03
❑ 128 Bert Blyleven .10 .03
❑ 129 Chili Davis .10 .03
❑ 130 Brian Downing .05 .02
❑ 131 Mike Fetters RC .25 .07
❑ 132 Chuck Finley .10 .03
❑ 133 Willie Fraser .05 .02
❑ 134 Bryan Harvey .05 .02
❑ 135 Jack Howell .05 .02
❑ 136 Wally Joyner .10 .03
❑ 137 Jeff Manto .05 .02
❑ 138 Kirk McCaskill .05 .02
❑ 139 Bob McClure .05 .02
❑ 140 Greg Minton .05 .02
❑ 141 Lance Parrish .05 .02
❑ 142 Dan Petry .05 .02
❑ 143 Johnny Ray .05 .02
❑ 144 Dick Schofield .05 .02
❑ 145 Lee Stevens .10 .03
❑ 146 Claudell Washington .05 .02
❑ 147 Devon White .10 .03
❑ 148 Mike Witt .05 .02
❑ 149 Roberto Alomar .15 .04
❑ 150 Sandy Alomar Jr. .10 .03
❑ 151 Andy Benes .10 .03
❑ 152 Jack Clark .10 .03
❑ 153 Pat Clements .05 .02
❑ 154 Joey Cora .10 .03
❑ 155 Mark Davis .05 .02
❑ 156 Mark Grant .05 .02
❑ 157 Tony Gwynn .30 .09
❑ 158 Greg W. Harris .05 .02
❑ 159 Bruce Hurst .05 .02
❑ 160 Darrin Jackson .05 .02
❑ 161 Chris James .05 .02
❑ 162 Carmelo Martinez .05 .02
❑ 163 Mike Pagliarulo .05 .02
❑ 164 Mark Parent .05 .02
❑ 165 Dennis Rasmussen .05 .02
❑ 166 Bip Roberts .05 .02
❑ 167 Benito Santiago .10 .03
❑ 168 Calvin Schiraldi .05 .02
❑ 169 Eric Show .05 .02
❑ 170 Garry Templeton .05 .02
❑ 171 Ed Whitson .05 .02
❑ 172 Brady Anderson .10 .03
❑ 173 Jeff Ballard .05 .02
❑ 174 Phil Bradley .05 .02
❑ 175 Mike Devereaux .05 .02
❑ 176 Steve Finley .10 .03
❑ 177 Pete Harnisch .05 .02
❑ 178 Kevin Hickey .05 .02
❑ 179 Brian Holton .05 .02
❑ 180 Ben McDonald RC .25 .07
❑ 181 Bob Melvin .05 .02
❑ 182 Bob Milacki .05 .02
❑ 183 Randy Milligan UER .05 .02
(Double line of '87 stats)
❑ 184 Gregg Olson .10 .03
❑ 185 Joe Orsulak .05 .02
❑ 186 Bill Ripken .05 .02
❑ 187 Cal Ripken .75 .23
❑ 188 Dave Schmidt .05 .02
❑ 189 Larry Sheets .05 .02
❑ 190 Mickey Tettleton .05 .02
❑ 191 Mark Thurmond .05 .02
❑ 192 Jay Tibbs .05 .02
❑ 193 Jim Traber .05 .02
❑ 194 Mark Williamson .05 .02
❑ 195 Craig Worthington .05 .02
❑ 196 Don Aase .05 .02
❑ 197 Blaine Beatty .05 .02
❑ 198 Mark Carreon .05 .02
❑ 199 Gary Carter .10 .03
❑ 200 David Cone .10 .03
❑ 201 Ron Darling .05 .02
❑ 202 Kevin Elster .05 .02
❑ 203 Sid Fernandez .05 .02
❑ 204 Dwight Gooden .10 .03
❑ 205 Keith Hernandez .10 .03
❑ 206 Jeff Innis .05 .02
❑ 207 Gregg Jefferies .10 .03
❑ 208 Howard Johnson .05 .02
❑ 209 Barry Lyons UER .05 .02
(Double line of '87 stats)
❑ 210 Dave Magadan .05 .02
❑ 211 Kevin McReynolds .05 .02
❑ 212 Jeff Musselman .05 .02
❑ 213 Randy Myers .10 .03
❑ 214 Bob Ojeda .05 .02
❑ 215 Juan Samuel .05 .02
❑ 216 Mackey Sasser .05 .02
❑ 217 Darryl Strawberry .10 .03
❑ 218 Tim Teufel .05 .02
❑ 219 Frank Viola .05 .02
❑ 220 Juan Agosto .05 .02
❑ 221 Larry Andersen .05 .02
❑ 222 Eric Anthony RC .10 .03
❑ 223 Kevin Bass .05 .02
❑ 224 Craig Biggio .25 .07
❑ 225 Ken Caminiti .10 .03
❑ 226 Jim Clancy .05 .02
❑ 227 Danny Darwin .05 .02
❑ 228 Glenn Davis .05 .02
❑ 229 Jim Deshaies .05 .02
❑ 230 Bill Doran .05 .02
❑ 231 Bob Forsch .05 .02
❑ 232 Brian Meyer .05 .02
❑ 233 Terry Puhl .05 .02
❑ 234 Rafael Ramirez .05 .02
❑ 235 Rick Rhoden .05 .02
❑ 236 Dan Schatzeder .05 .02
❑ 237 Mike Scott .05 .02
❑ 238 Dave Smith .05 .02
❑ 239 Alex Trevino .05 .02
❑ 240 Glenn Wilson .05 .02
❑ 241 Gerald Young .05 .02
❑ 242 Tom Brunansky .05 .02
❑ 243 Cris Carpenter .05 .02
❑ 244 Alex Cole RC .10 .03
❑ 245 Vince Coleman .05 .02
❑ 246 John Costello .05 .02
❑ 247 Ken Dayley .05 .02
❑ 248 Jose DeLeon .05 .02
❑ 249 Frank DiPino .05 .02
❑ 250 Pedro Guerrero .05 .02
❑ 251 Ken Hill .10 .03
❑ 252 Joe Magrane .05 .02
❑ 253 Willie McGee UER .10 .03
(No decimal point before 353)
❑ 254 John Morris .05 .02
❑ 255 Jose Oquendo .05 .02
❑ 256 Tony Pena .05 .02
❑ 257 Terry Pendleton .10 .03
❑ 258 Ted Power .05 .02
❑ 259 Dan Quisenberry .05 .02
❑ 260 Ozzie Smith .40 .12
❑ 261 Scott Terry .05 .02
❑ 262 Milt Thompson .05 .02
❑ 263 Denny Walling .05 .02
❑ 264 Todd Worrell .05 .02
❑ 265 Todd Zeile .10 .03
❑ 266 Marty Barrett .05 .02
❑ 267 Mike Boddicker .05 .02
❑ 268 Wade Boggs .15 .04
❑ 269 Ellis Burks .15 .04
❑ 270 Rick Cerone .05 .02
❑ 271 Roger Clemens .50 .15
❑ 272 John Dopson .05 .02
❑ 273 Nick Esasky .05 .02

No.	Player		
❑ 274	Dwight Evans	.15	.04
❑ 275	Wes Gardner	.05	.02
❑ 276	Rich Gedman	.05	.02
❑ 277	Mike Greenwell	.05	.02
❑ 278	Danny Heep	.05	.02
❑ 279	Eric Hetzel	.05	.02
❑ 280	Dennis Lamp	.05	.02
❑ 281	Rob Murphy UER ('89 stats say Reds, should say Red Sox)	.05	.02
❑ 282	Joe Price	.05	.02
❑ 283	Carlos Quintana	.05	.02
❑ 284	Jody Reed	.05	.02
❑ 285	Luis Rivera	.05	.02
❑ 286	Kevin Romine	.05	.02
❑ 287	Lee Smith	.10	.03
❑ 288	Mike Smithson	.05	.02
❑ 289	Bob Stanley	.05	.02
❑ 290	Harold Baines	.10	.03
❑ 291	Kevin Brown	.10	.03
❑ 292	Steve Buechele	.05	.02
❑ 293	Scott Coolbaugh	.05	.02
❑ 294	Jack Daugherty	.05	.02
❑ 295	Cecil Espy	.05	.02
❑ 296	Julio Franco	.10	.03
❑ 297	Juan Gonzalez RC	1.00	.30
❑ 298	Cecilio Guante	.05	.02
❑ 299	Drew Hall	.05	.02
❑ 300	Charlie Hough	.10	.03
❑ 301	Pete Incaviglia	.05	.02
❑ 302	Mike Jeffcoat	.05	.02
❑ 303	Chad Kreuter	.05	.02
❑ 304	Jeff Kunkel	.05	.02
❑ 305	Rick Leach	.05	.02
❑ 306	Fred Manrique	.05	.02
❑ 307	Jamie Moyer	.10	.03
❑ 308	Rafael Palmeiro	.15	.04
❑ 309	Geno Petralli	.05	.02
❑ 310	Kevin Reimer	.05	.02
❑ 311	Kenny Rogers	.10	.03
❑ 312	Jeff Russell	.05	.02
❑ 313	Nolan Ryan	1.00	.30
❑ 314	Ruben Sierra	.05	.02
❑ 315	Bobby Witt	.05	.02
❑ 316	Chris Bosio	.05	.02
❑ 317	Glenn Braggs UER (Stats say 111 K's, but bio says 117 K's)	.05	.02
❑ 318	Greg Brock	.05	.02
❑ 319	Chuck Crim	.05	.02
❑ 320	Rob Deer	.05	.02
❑ 321	Mike Felder	.05	.02
❑ 322	Tom Filer	.05	.02
❑ 323	Tony Fossas	.05	.02
❑ 324	Jim Gantner	.05	.02
❑ 325	Darryl Hamilton	.05	.02
❑ 326	Teddy Higuera	.05	.02
❑ 327	Mark Knudson	.05	.02
❑ 328	Bill Krueger UER ('86 stats missing)	.05	.02
❑ 329	Tim McIntosh RC	.10	.03
❑ 330	Paul Molitor	.15	.04
❑ 331	Jaime Navarro	.05	.02
❑ 332	Charlie O'Brien	.05	.02
❑ 333	Jeff Peterek	.05	.02
❑ 334	Dan Plesac	.05	.02
❑ 335	Jerry Reuss	.05	.02
❑ 336	Gary Sheffield UER (Bio says played for 3 teams in '87, but stats say in '88)	.25	.07
❑ 337	Bill Spiers	.05	.02
❑ 338	B.J. Surhoff	.10	.03
❑ 339	Greg Vaughn	.05	.02
❑ 340	Robin Yount	.40	.12
❑ 341	Hubie Brooks	.05	.02
❑ 342	Tim Burke	.05	.02
❑ 343	Mike Fitzgerald	.05	.02
❑ 344	Tom Foley	.05	.02
❑ 345	Andres Galarraga	.10	.03
❑ 346	Damaso Garcia	.05	.02
❑ 347	Marquis Grissom RC	.40	.12
❑ 348	Kevin Gross	.05	.02
❑ 349	Joe Hesketh	.05	.02
❑ 350	Jeff Huson RC	.05	.02
❑ 351	Wallace Johnson	.05	.02
❑ 352	Mark Langston	.05	.02
❑ 353A	Dave Martinez (Yellow on front)	2.00	.60
❑ 353B	Dave Martinez (Red on front)	.05	.02
❑ 354	Dennis Martinez UER ('87 ERA is 616, should be 6.16)	.10	.03
❑ 355	Andy McGaffigan	.05	.02
❑ 356	Otis Nixon	.05	.02
❑ 357	Spike Owen	.05	.02
❑ 358	Pascual Perez	.05	.02
❑ 359	Tim Raines	.10	.03
❑ 360	Nelson Santovenia	.05	.02
❑ 361	Bryn Smith	.05	.02
❑ 362	Zane Smith	.05	.02
❑ 363	Larry Walker RC	1.00	.30
❑ 364	Tim Wallach	.05	.02
❑ 365	Rick Aguilera	.10	.03
❑ 366	Allan Anderson	.05	.02
❑ 367	Wally Backman	.05	.02
❑ 368	Doug Baker	.05	.02
❑ 369	Juan Berenguer	.05	.02
❑ 370	Randy Bush	.05	.02
❑ 371	Carmelo Castillo	.05	.02
❑ 372	Mike Dyer RC	.05	.02
❑ 373	Gary Gaetti	.10	.03
❑ 374	Greg Gagne	.05	.02
❑ 375	Dan Gladden	.05	.02
❑ 376	G.Gonzalez UER Bio says 31 saves in '88, but stats say 30	.05	.02
❑ 377	Brian Harper	.05	.02
❑ 378	Kent Hrbek	.10	.03
❑ 379	Gene Larkin	.05	.02
❑ 380	Tim Laudner UER (No decimal point before '85 BA of 238)	.05	.02
❑ 381	John Moses	.05	.02
❑ 382	Al Newman	.05	.02
❑ 383	Kirby Puckett	.25	.07
❑ 384	Shane Rawley	.05	.02
❑ 385	Jeff Reardon	.10	.03
❑ 386	Roy Smith	.05	.02
❑ 387	Gary Wayne	.05	.02
❑ 388	Dave West	.05	.02
❑ 389	Tim Belcher	.05	.02
❑ 390	Tim Crews UER (Stats say 163 IP for '83, but bio says 136)	.05	.02
❑ 391	Mike Davis	.05	.02
❑ 392	Rick Dempsey	.05	.02
❑ 393	Kirk Gibson	.15	.04
❑ 394	Jose Gonzalez	.05	.02
❑ 395	Alfredo Griffin	.05	.02
❑ 396	Jeff Hamilton	.05	.02
❑ 397	Lenny Harris	.05	.02
❑ 398	Mickey Hatcher	.05	.02
❑ 399	Orel Hershiser	.10	.03
❑ 400	Jay Howell	.05	.02
❑ 401	Mike Marshall	.05	.02
❑ 402	Ramon Martinez	.05	.02
❑ 403	Mike Morgan	.05	.02
❑ 404	Eddie Murray	.25	.07
❑ 405	Alejandro Pena	.05	.02
❑ 406	Willie Randolph	.10	.03
❑ 407	Mike Scioscia	.05	.02
❑ 408	Ray Searage	.05	.02
❑ 409	Fernando Valenzuela	.10	.03
❑ 410	Jose Vizcaino RC	.25	.07
❑ 411	John Wetteland	.25	.07
❑ 412	Jack Armstrong	.05	.02
❑ 413	Todd Benzinger UER (Bio says .323 at Pawtucket, but stats say .321)	.05	.02
❑ 414	Tim Birtsas	.05	.02
❑ 415	Tom Browning	.05	.02
❑ 416	Norm Charlton	.05	.02
❑ 417	Eric Davis	.10	.03
❑ 418	Rob Dibble	.10	.03
❑ 419	John Franco	.10	.03
❑ 420	Ken Griffey Sr.	.10	.03
❑ 421	Chris Hammond RC (No 1989 used for "Did Not Play" stat, actually did play for Nashville in 1989)	.10	.03
❑ 422	Danny Jackson	.05	.02
❑ 423	Barry Larkin	.15	.04
❑ 424	Tim Leary	.05	.02
❑ 425	Rick Mahler	.05	.02
❑ 426	Joe Oliver	.05	.02
❑ 427	Paul O'Neill	.15	.04
❑ 428	Luis Quinones UER ('86-'88 stats are omitted from card but included in totals)	.05	.02
❑ 429	Jeff Reed	.05	.02
❑ 430	Jose Rijo	.05	.02
❑ 431	Ron Robinson	.05	.02
❑ 432	Rolando Roomes	.05	.02
❑ 433	Chris Sabo	.05	.02
❑ 434	Scott Scudder	.05	.02
❑ 435	Herm Winningham	.05	.02
❑ 436	Steve Balboni	.05	.02
❑ 437	Jesse Barfield	.05	.02
❑ 438	Mike Blowers RC	.10	.03
❑ 439	Tom Brookens	.05	.02
❑ 440	Greg Cadaret	.05	.02
❑ 441	Alvaro Espinoza UER (Career games say 218, should be 219)	.05	.02
❑ 442	Bob Geren	.05	.02
❑ 443	Lee Guetterman	.05	.02
❑ 444	Mel Hall	.05	.02
❑ 445	Andy Hawkins	.05	.02
❑ 446	Roberto Kelly	.05	.02
❑ 447	Don Mattingly	.60	.18
❑ 448	Lance McCullers	.05	.02
❑ 449	Hensley Meulens	.05	.02
❑ 450	Dale Mohorcic	.05	.02
❑ 451	Clay Parker	.05	.02
❑ 452	Eric Plunk	.05	.02
❑ 453	Dave Righetti	.05	.02
❑ 454	Deion Sanders	.25	.07
❑ 455	Steve Sax	.05	.02
❑ 456	Don Slaught	.05	.02
❑ 457	Walt Terrell	.05	.02
❑ 458	Dave Winfield	.10	.03
❑ 459	Jay Bell	.10	.03
❑ 460	Rafael Belliard	.05	.02
❑ 461	Barry Bonds	1.00	.30
❑ 462	Bobby Bonilla	.10	.03
❑ 463	Sid Bream	.05	.02
❑ 464	Benny Distefano	.05	.02
❑ 465	Doug Drabek	.05	.02
❑ 466	Jim Gott	.05	.02
❑ 467	Billy Hatcher UER (.1 hits for Cubs in 1984)	.05	.02
❑ 468	Neal Heaton	.05	.02
❑ 469	Jeff King	.05	.02
❑ 470	Bob Kipper	.05	.02
❑ 471	Randy Kramer	.05	.02
❑ 472	Bill Landrum	.05	.02
❑ 473	Mike LaValliere	.05	.02
❑ 474	Jose Lind	.05	.02
❑ 475	Junior Ortiz	.05	.02
❑ 476	Gary Redus	.05	.02
❑ 477	Rick Reed RC	.25	.07
❑ 478	R.J. Reynolds	.05	.02
❑ 479	Jeff D. Robinson	.05	.02
❑ 480	John Smiley	.05	.02
❑ 481	Andy Van Slyke	.15	.04
❑ 482	Bob Walk	.05	.02
❑ 483	Andy Allanson	.05	.02
❑ 484	Scott Bailes	.05	.02
❑ 485	Joey Belle UER (Has Jay Bell "Did You Know") Later changed his name to Albert	.25	.07
❑ 486	Bud Black	.05	.02
❑ 487	Jerry Browne	.05	.02
❑ 488	Tom Candiotti	.05	.02
❑ 489	Joe Carter	.10	.03
❑ 490	Dave Clark (No '84 stats)	.05	.02
❑ 491	John Farrell	.05	.02
❑ 492	Felix Fermin	.05	.02
❑ 493	Brook Jacoby	.05	.02
❑ 494	Dion James	.05	.02

❑ 495 Doug Jones .05 .02
❑ 496 Brad Komminsk .05 .02
❑ 497 Rod Nichols .05 .02
❑ 498 Pete O'Brien .05 .02
❑ 499 Steve Olin RC .10 .03
❑ 500 Jesse Orosco .05 .02
❑ 501 Joel Skinner .05 .02
❑ 502 Cory Snyder .05 .02
❑ 503 Greg Swindell .05 .02
❑ 504 Rich Yett .05 .02
❑ 505 Scott Bankhead .05 .02
❑ 506 Scott Bradley .05 .02
❑ 507 Greg Briley UER .05 .02
(28 SB's in bio, but 27 in stats)
❑ 508 Jay Buhner .10 .03
❑ 509 Darnell Coles .05 .02
❑ 510 Keith Comstock .05 .02
❑ 511 Henry Cotto .05 .02
❑ 512 Alvin Davis .05 .02
❑ 513 Ken Griffey Jr. .75 .23
❑ 514 Erik Hanson .05 .02
❑ 515 Gene Harris .05 .02
❑ 516 Brian Holman .05 .02
❑ 517 Mike Jackson .05 .02
❑ 518 Randy Johnson .50 .15
❑ 519 Jeffrey Leonard .05 .02
❑ 520 Edgar Martinez .15 .04
❑ 521 Dennis Powell .05 .02
❑ 522 Jim Presley .05 .02
❑ 523 Jerry Reed .05 .02
❑ 524 Harold Reynolds .10 .03
❑ 525 Mike Schooler .05 .02
❑ 526 Bill Swift .05 .02
❑ 527 Dave Valle .05 .02
❑ 528 Omar Vizquel .25 .07
❑ 529 Ivan Calderon .05 .02
❑ 530 Carlton Fisk UER .15 .04
(Bellow Falls, should be Bellows Falls)
❑ 531 Scott Fletcher .05 .02
❑ 532 Dave Gallagher .05 .02
❑ 533 Ozzie Guillen .10 .03
❑ 534 Greg Hibbard RC .10 .03
❑ 535 Shawn Hillegas .05 .02
❑ 536 Lance Johnson .05 .02
❑ 537 Eric King .05 .02
❑ 538 Ron Kittle .05 .02
❑ 539 Steve Lyons .05 .02
❑ 540 Carlos Martinez .05 .02
❑ 541 Tom McCarthy .05 .02
❑ 542 Matt Merullo .05 .02
(Had 5 ML runs scored entering '90, not 6)
❑ 543 Donn Pall UER .05 .02
(Stats say pro career began in '85, bio says '88)
❑ 544 Dan Pasqua .05 .02
❑ 545 Ken Patterson .05 .02
❑ 546 Melido Perez .05 .02
❑ 547 Steve Rosenberg .05 .02
❑ 548 Sammy Sosa RC 3.00 .90
❑ 549 Bobby Thigpen .05 .02
❑ 550 Robin Ventura .25 .07
❑ 551 Greg Walker .05 .02
❑ 552 Don Carman .05 .02
❑ 553 Pat Combs .05 .02
(6 walks for Phillies in '89 in stats, brief bio says 4)
❑ 554 Dennis Cook .05 .02
❑ 555 Darren Daulton .10 .03
❑ 556 Len Dykstra .10 .03
❑ 557 Curt Ford .05 .02
❑ 558 Charlie Hayes .05 .02
❑ 559 Von Hayes .05 .02
❑ 560 Tommy Herr .05 .02
❑ 561 Ken Howell .05 .02
❑ 562 Steve Jeltz .05 .02
❑ 563 Ron Jones .05 .02
❑ 564 Ricky Jordan UER .05 .02
(Duplicate line of statistics on back)
❑ 565 John Kruk .10 .03
❑ 566 Steve Lake .05 .02
❑ 567 Roger McDowell .05 .02
❑ 568 Terry Mulholland UER .05 .02
(Did You Know refers to Dave Magadan)
❑ 569 Dwayne Murphy .05 .02
❑ 570 Jeff Parrett .05 .02
❑ 571 Randy Ready .05 .02
❑ 572 Bruce Ruffin .05 .02
❑ 573 Dickie Thon .05 .02
❑ 574 Jose Alvarez UER .05 .02
('78 and '79 stats are reversed)
❑ 575 Geronimo Berroa .05 .02
❑ 576 Jeff Blauser .05 .02
❑ 577 Joe Boever .05 .02
❑ 578 Marty Clary UER .05 .02
(No comma between city and state)
❑ 579 Jody Davis .05 .02
❑ 580 Mark Eichhorn .05 .02
❑ 581 Darrell Evans .10 .03
❑ 582 Ron Gant .10 .03
❑ 583 Tom Glavine .15 .04
❑ 584 Tommy Greene RC .10 .03
❑ 585 Tommy Gregg .05 .02
❑ 586 Dave Justice RC UER .50 .15
(Actually had 16 2B in Sumter in '86)
❑ 587 Mark Lemke .05 .02
❑ 588 Derek Lilliquist .05 .02
❑ 589 Oddibe McDowell .05 .02
❑ 590 Kent Mercker RC ERA .05 .02
(Bio says 2.75 ERA, stats say 2.68 ERA)
❑ 591 Dale Murphy .15 .04
❑ 592 Gerald Perry .05 .02
❑ 593 Lonnie Smith .05 .02
❑ 594 Pete Smith .05 .02
❑ 595 John Smoltz .25 .07
❑ 596 Mike Stanton RC UER .25 .07
(No comma between city and state)
❑ 597 Andres Thomas .05 .02
❑ 598 Jeff Treadway .05 .02
❑ 599 Doyle Alexander .05 .02
❑ 600 Dave Bergman .05 .02
❑ 601 Brian DuBois .05 .02
❑ 602 Paul Gibson .05 .02
❑ 603 Mike Heath .05 .02
❑ 604 Mike Henneman .05 .02
❑ 605 Guillermo Hernandez .05 .02
❑ 606 Shawn Holman .05 .02
❑ 607 Tracy Jones .05 .02
❑ 608 Chet Lemon .05 .02
❑ 609 Fred Lynn .05 .02
❑ 610 Jack Morris .10 .03
❑ 611 Matt Nokes .05 .02
❑ 612 Gary Pettis .05 .02
❑ 613 Kevin Ritz .05 .02
❑ 614 Jeff M. Robinson .05 .02
('88 stats are not in line)
❑ 615 Steve Searcy .05 .02
❑ 616 Frank Tanana .05 .02
❑ 617 Alan Trammell .10 .03
❑ 618 Gary Ward .05 .02
❑ 619 Lou Whitaker .10 .03
❑ 620 Frank Williams .05 .02
❑ 621A George Brett '80 2.00 .60
ERR (Had 10 .390 hitting seasons)
❑ 621B George Brett '80 .30 .09
COR
❑ 622 Fern.Valenzuela '81 .05 .02
❑ 623 Dale Murphy '82 .15 .04
❑ 624A Cal Ripken '83 ERR 5.00 1.50
(Misspelled Ripkin on card back)
❑ 624B Cal Ripken '83 COR .40 .12
❑ 625 Ryne Sandberg '84 .25 .07
❑ 626 Don Mattingly '85 .20 .06
❑ 627 Roger Clemens '86 .25 .07
❑ 628 George Bell '87 .05 .02
❑ 629 J.Canseco '88 UER .10 .03
Reggie won MVP in '83, should say '73
❑ 630A Will Clark '89 ERR 1.00 .30
(32 total bases on card back)
❑ 630B Will Clark '89 COR .15 .04
(321 total bases; technically still an error, listing only 24 runs)
❑ 631 Mark Davis .05 .02
Mitch Williams
❑ 632 Wade Boggs .10 .03
Mike Greenwell
❑ 633 Mark Gubicza .05 .02
Jeff Russell
❑ 634 Tony Fernandez .25 .07
Cal Ripken
❑ 635 Kirby Puckett .15 .04
Bo Jackson
❑ 636 Nolan Ryan .40 .12
Mike Scott
❑ 637 Will Clark .10 .03
Kevin Mitchell
❑ 638 Don Mattingly .30 .09
Mark McGwire
❑ 639 Howard Johnson .25 .07
Ryne Sandberg
❑ 640 Rudy Seanez RC .10 .03
Colin Charland
❑ 641 George Canale RC .25 .07
Kevin Maas UER
(Canale listed as INF on front, 1B on back)
❑ 642 Kelly Mann .25 .07
and Dave Hansen RC
❑ 643 Greg Smith .10 .03
and Stu Tate
❑ 644 Tom Drees RC .10 .03
Dann Howitt RC
❑ 645 Mike Roesler RC .10 .03
and Derrick May
❑ 646 Scott Hemond .10 .03
and Mark Gardner RC
❑ 647 John Orton .10 .03
and Scott Leius RC
❑ 648 Rich Monteleone .10 .03
and Dana Williams
❑ 649 Mike Huff .10 .03
and Steve Frey
❑ 650 Chuck McElroy .75 .23
and Moises Alou RC
❑ 651 Bobby Rose .25 .07
and Mike Hartley
❑ 652 Matt Kinzer .10 .03
and Wayne Edwards
❑ 653 Delino DeShields RC .25 .07
and Jason Grimsley
❑ 654 CL: A's/Cubs .05 .02
Giants/Blue Jays
❑ 655 CL: Royals/Angels .05 .02
Padres/Orioles
❑ 656 CL: Mets/Astros .05 .02
Cards/Red Sox
❑ 657 CL: Rangers/Brewers .05 .02
Expos/Twins
❑ 658 CL: Dodgers/Reds .05 .02
Yankees/Pirates
❑ 659 CL: Indians/Mariners .05 .02
White Sox/Phillies
❑ 660A CL: Braves/Tigers .05 .02
Specials/Checklists
(Checklist-660 in smaller print on card front)
❑ 660B CL: Braves/Tigers .05 .02
Specials/Checklists
(Checklist-660 in normal print on card front)

1992 Fleer Update

	Nrm-Mt	Ex-Mt
COMP.FACT.SET (136)	100.00	30.00
COMPLETE SET (132)	80.00	24.00

❑ 1 Todd Frohwirth .50 .15
❑ 2 Alan Mills .50 .15
❑ 3 Rick Sutcliffe 1.00 .30

❑ 4 John Valentin RC 1.50 .45
❑ 5 Frank Viola 1.00 .30
❑ 6 Bob Zupcic RC .50 .15
❑ 7 Mike Butcher .50 .15
❑ 8 Chad Curtis RC 1.50 .45
❑ 9 Damion Easley RC 1.50 .45
❑ 10 Tim Salmon 1.50 .45
❑ 11 Julio Valera .50 .15
❑ 12 George Bell .50 .15
❑ 13 Roberto Hernandez .50 .15
❑ 14 Shawn Jeter RC .50 .15
❑ 15 Thomas Howard .50 .15
❑ 16 Jesse Levis .50 .15
❑ 17 Kenny Lofton 1.50 .45
❑ 18 Paul Sorrento .50 .15
❑ 19 Rico Brogna .50 .15
❑ 20 John Doherty RC .50 .15
❑ 21 Dan Gladden .50 .15
❑ 22 Buddy Groom RC .50 .15
❑ 23 Shawn Hare RC .50 .15
❑ 24 John Kiely .50 .15
❑ 25 Kurt Knudsen .50 .15
❑ 26 Gregg Jefferies .50 .15
❑ 27 Wally Joyner 1.00 .30
❑ 28 Kevin Koslofski .50 .15
❑ 29 Kevin McReynolds .50 .15
❑ 30 Rusty Meacham .50 .15
❑ 31 Keith Miller .50 .15
❑ 32 Hipolito Pichardo RC .50 .15
❑ 33 Jim Austin .50 .15
❑ 34 Scott Fletcher .50 .15
❑ 35 John Jaha RC 1.50 .45
❑ 36 Pat Listach RC 1.50 .45
❑ 37 Dave Nilsson .50 .15
❑ 38 Kevin Seitzer .50 .15
❑ 39 Tom Edens .50 .15
❑ 40 Pat Mahomes RC 1.50 .45
❑ 41 John Smiley .50 .15
❑ 42 Charlie Hayes .50 .15
❑ 43 Sam Militello .50 .15
❑ 44 Andy Stankiewicz .50 .15
❑ 45 Danny Tartabull .50 .15
❑ 46 Bob Wickman 2.50 .75
❑ 47 Jerry Browne .50 .15
❑ 48 Kevin Campbell .50 .15
❑ 49 Vince Horsman .50 .15
❑ 50 Troy Neel RC .50 .15
❑ 51 Ruben Sierra .50 .15
❑ 52 Bruce Walton .50 .15
❑ 53 Willie Wilson .50 .15
❑ 54 Bret Boone 2.50 .75
❑ 55 Dave Fleming .50 .15
❑ 56 Kevin Mitchell .50 .15
❑ 57 Jeff Nelson RC 2.50 .75
❑ 58 Shane Turner .50 .15
❑ 59 Jose Canseco 1.50 .45
❑ 60 Jeff Frye RC .50 .15
❑ 61 Danny Leon .50 .15
❑ 62 Roger Pavlik RC .50 .15
❑ 63 David Cone 1.00 .30
❑ 64 Pat Hentgen .50 .15
❑ 65 Randy Knorr .50 .15
❑ 66 Jack Morris 1.00 .30
❑ 67 Dave Winfield 1.00 .30
❑ 68 David Nied RC .50 .15
❑ 69 Otis Nixon .50 .15
❑ 70 Alejandro Pena .50 .15
❑ 71 Jeff Reardon 1.00 .30
❑ 72 Alex Arias RC .50 .15
❑ 73 Jim Bullinger .50 .15
❑ 74 Mike Morgan .50 .15
❑ 75 Rey Sanchez RC 1.50 .45
❑ 76 Bob Scanlan .50 .15
❑ 77 Sammy Sosa 4.00 1.20
❑ 78 Scott Bankhead .50 .15
❑ 79 Tim Belcher .50 .15
❑ 80 Steve Foster .50 .15
❑ 81 Willie Greene .50 .15
❑ 82 Bip Roberts .50 .15
❑ 83 Scott Ruskin .50 .15
❑ 84 Greg Swindell .50 .15
❑ 85 Juan Guerrero .50 .15
❑ 86 Butch Henry .50 .15
❑ 87 Doug Jones .50 .15
❑ 88 Brian Williams RC .50 .15
❑ 89 Tom Candiotti .50 .15
❑ 90 Eric Davis 1.00 .30
❑ 91 Carlos Hernandez .50 .15
❑ 92 Mike Piazza RC 60.00 18.00
❑ 93 Mike Sharperson .50 .15
❑ 94 Eric Young RC 1.50 .45
❑ 95 Moises Alou 1.00 .30
❑ 96 Greg Colbrunn .50 .15
❑ 97 Wil Cordero .50 .15
❑ 98 Ken Hill .50 .15
❑ 99 John Vander Wal RC 1.50 .45
❑ 100 John Wetteland 1.00 .30
❑ 101 Bobby Bonilla 1.00 .30
❑ 102 Eric Hillman RC .50 .15
❑ 103 Pat Howell .50 .15
❑ 104 Jeff Kent RC 25.00 7.50
❑ 105 Dick Schofield .50 .15
❑ 106 Ryan Thompson RC .50 .15
❑ 107 Chico Walker .50 .15
❑ 108 Juan Bell .50 .15
❑ 109 Mariano Duncan .50 .15
❑ 110 Jeff Grotewold .50 .15
❑ 111 Ben Rivera .50 .15
❑ 112 Curt Schilling 1.50 .45
❑ 113 Victor Cole .50 .15
❑ 114 Al Martin RC 1.50 .45
❑ 115 Roger Mason .50 .15
❑ 116 Blas Minor .50 .15
❑ 117 Tim Wakefield RC 10.00 3.00
❑ 118 Mark Clark RC .50 .15
❑ 119 Rheal Cormier .50 .15
❑ 120 Donovan Osborne .50 .15
❑ 121 Todd Worrell .50 .15
❑ 122 Jeremy Hernandez RC .50 .15
❑ 123 Randy Myers .50 .15
❑ 124 Frank Seminara RC .50 .15
❑ 125 Gary Sheffield 1.00 .30
❑ 126 Dan Walters .50 .15
❑ 127 Steve Hosey .50 .15
❑ 128 Mike Jackson .50 .15
❑ 129 Jim Pena .50 .15
❑ 130 Cory Snyder .50 .15
❑ 131 Bill Swift .50 .15
❑ 132 Checklist U1-U132 .50 .15

1993 Fleer Final Edition

	Nm-Mt	Ex-Mt
COMP.FACT.SET (310)	10.00	3.00
COMPLETE SET (300)	8.00	2.40

❑ 1 Steve Bedrosian .10 .03
❑ 2 Jay Howell .10 .03
❑ 3 Greg Maddux .75 .23
❑ 4 Greg McMichael RC .15 .04
❑ 5 Tony Tarasco RC .15 .04
❑ 6 Jose Bautista .10 .03
❑ 7 Jose Guzman .10 .03
❑ 8 Greg Hibbard .10 .03
❑ 9 Candy Maldonado .10 .03
❑ 10 Randy Myers .10 .03
❑ 11 Matt Walbeck RC .40 .12
❑ 12 Turk Wendell .10 .03
❑ 13 Willie Wilson .10 .03
❑ 14 Greg Cadaret .10 .03
❑ 15 Roberto Kelly .10 .03
❑ 16 Randy Milligan .10 .03
❑ 17 Kevin Mitchell .10 .03
❑ 18 Jeff Reardon .20 .06
❑ 19 John Roper .10 .03
❑ 20 John Smiley .10 .03
❑ 21 Andy Ashby .10 .03
❑ 22 Dante Bichette .20 .06
❑ 23 Willie Blair .10 .03
❑ 24 Pedro Castellano .10 .03
❑ 25 Vinny Castilla .50 .15
❑ 26 Jerald Clark .10 .03
❑ 27 Alex Cole .10 .03
❑ 28 Scott Fredrickson RC .15 .04
❑ 29 Jay Gainer RC .15 .04
❑ 30 Andres Galarraga .20 .06
❑ 31 Joe Girardi .10 .03
❑ 32 Ryan Hawblitzel .10 .03
❑ 33 Charlie Hayes .10 .03
❑ 34 Darren Holmes .10 .03
❑ 35 Chris Jones .10 .03
❑ 36 David Nied .10 .03
❑ 37 J.Owens RC .15 .04
❑ 38 Lance Painter RC .40 .12
❑ 39 Jeff Parrett .10 .03
❑ 40 Steve Reed .10 .03
❑ 41 Armando Reynoso .10 .03
❑ 42 Bruce Ruffin .10 .03
❑ 43 Danny Sheaffer RC .15 .04
❑ 44 Keith Shepherd .10 .03
❑ 45 Jim Tatum .10 .03
❑ 46 Gary Wayne .10 .03
❑ 47 Eric Young .10 .03
❑ 48 Luis Aquino .10 .03
❑ 49 Alex Arias .10 .03
❑ 50 Jack Armstrong .10 .03
❑ 51 Bret Barberie .10 .03
❑ 52 Geronimo Berroa .10 .03
❑ 53 Ryan Bowen .10 .03
❑ 54 Greg Briley .10 .03
❑ 55 Cris Carpenter .10 .03
❑ 56 Chuck Carr .10 .03
❑ 57 Jeff Conine .20 .06
❑ 58 Jim Corsi .10 .03
❑ 59 Orestes Destrade .10 .03
❑ 60 Junior Felix .10 .03
❑ 61 Chris Hammond .10 .03
❑ 62 Bryan Harvey .10 .03
❑ 63 Charlie Hough .20 .06
❑ 64 Joe Klink .10 .03
❑ 65 Richie Lewis RC UER .15 .04
(Refers to place of birth and residence as Illinois instead of Indiana)
❑ 66 Mitch Lyden RC .15 .04
❑ 67 Bob Natal .10 .03
❑ 68 Scott Pose RC .15 .04
❑ 69 Rich Renteria .10 .03
❑ 70 Benito Santiago .20 .06
❑ 71 Gary Sheffield .20 .06
❑ 72 Matt Turner RC .15 .04
❑ 73 Walt Weiss .10 .03
❑ 74 Darrell Whitmore RC .15 .04
❑ 75 Nigel Wilson .10 .03
❑ 76 Kevin Bass .10 .03
❑ 77 Doug Drabek .10 .03
❑ 78 Tom Edens .10 .03
❑ 79 Chris James .10 .03
❑ 80 Greg Swindell .10 .03
❑ 81 Omar Daal RC .40 .12
❑ 82 Raul Mondesi .20 .06
❑ 83 Jody Reed .10 .03
❑ 84 Cory Snyder .10 .03
❑ 85 Rick Trlicek .10 .03

❑ 86 Tim Wallach .10 .03
❑ 87 Todd Worrell .10 .03
❑ 88 Tavo Alvarez .10 .03
❑ 89 Frank Bolick .10 .03
❑ 90 Kent Bottenfield .10 .03
❑ 91 Greg Colbrunn .10 .03
❑ 92 Cliff Floyd .20 .06
❑ 93 Lou Frazier RC .15 .04
❑ 94 Mike Gardiner .10 .03
❑ 95 Mike Lansing RC .40 .12
❑ 96 Bill Risley .10 .03
❑ 97 Jeff Shaw .10 .03
❑ 98 Kevin Baez .10 .03
❑ 99 Tim Bogar RC .15 .04
❑ 100 Jeromy Burnitz .20 .06
❑ 101 Mike Draper .10 .03
❑ 102 Darrin Jackson .10 .03
❑ 103 Mike Maddux .10 .03
❑ 104 Joe Orsulak .10 .03
❑ 105 Doug Saunders RC .15 .04
❑ 106 Frank Tanana .10 .03
❑ 107 Dave Telgheder RC .15 .04
❑ 108 Larry Andersen .10 .03
❑ 109 Jim Eisenreich .10 .03
❑ 110 Pete Incaviglia .10 .03
❑ 111 Danny Jackson .10 .03
❑ 112 David West .10 .03
❑ 113 Al Martin .10 .03
❑ 114 Blas Minor .10 .03
❑ 115 Dennis Moeller .10 .03
❑ 116 William Pennyfeather .10 .03
❑ 117 Rich Robertson RC .15 .04
❑ 118 Ben Shelton .10 .03
❑ 119 Lonnie Smith .10 .03
❑ 120 Freddie Toliver .10 .03
❑ 121 Paul Wagner .10 .03
❑ 122 Kevin Young .20 .06
❑ 123 Rene Arocha RC .40 .12
❑ 124 Gregg Jefferies .10 .03
❑ 125 Paul Kilgus .10 .03
❑ 126 Les Lancaster .10 .03
❑ 127 Joe Magrane .10 .03
❑ 128 Rob Murphy .10 .03
❑ 129 Erik Pappas .10 .03
❑ 130 Stan Royer .10 .03
❑ 131 Ozzie Smith .75 .23
❑ 132 Tom Urbani RC .15 .04
❑ 133 Mark Whiten .10 .03
❑ 134 Derek Bell .10 .03
❑ 135 Doug Brocail .10 .03
❑ 136 Phil Clark .10 .03
❑ 137 Mark Ettles RC .15 .04
❑ 138 Jeff Gardner .10 .03
❑ 139 Pat Gomez RC .15 .04
❑ 140 Ricky Gutierrez .10 .03
❑ 141 Gene Harris .10 .03
❑ 142 Kevin Higgins .10 .03
❑ 143 Trevor Hoffman .50 .15
❑ 144 Phil Plantier .10 .03
❑ 145 Kerry Taylor RC .15 .04
❑ 146 Guillermo Velasquez .10 .03
❑ 147 Wally Whitehurst .10 .03
❑ 148 Tim Worrell RC .40 .12
❑ 149 Todd Benzinger .10 .03
❑ 150 Barry Bonds 1.50 .45
❑ 151 Greg Brummett RC .15 .04
❑ 152 Mark Carreon .10 .03
❑ 153 Dave Martinez .10 .03
❑ 154 Jeff Reed .10 .03
❑ 155 Kevin Rogers .10 .03
❑ 156 Harold Baines .20 .06
❑ 157 Damon Buford .10 .03
❑ 158 Paul Carey RC .15 .04
❑ 159 Jeffrey Hammonds .10 .03
❑ 160 Jamie Moyer .20 .06
❑ 161 Sherman Obando RC .15 .04
❑ 162 John O'Donoghue RC .15 .04
❑ 163 Brad Pennington .10 .03
❑ 164 Jim Poole .10 .03
❑ 165 Harold Reynolds .20 .06
❑ 166 Fernando Valenzuela .20 .06
❑ 167 Jack Voigt RC .15 .04
❑ 168 Mark Williamson .10 .03
❑ 169 Scott Bankhead .10 .03
❑ 170 Greg Blosser .10 .03
❑ 171 Jim Byrd RC .15 .04
❑ 172 Ivan Calderon .10 .03
❑ 173 Andre Dawson .20 .06
❑ 174 Scott Fletcher .10 .03
❑ 175 Jose Melendez .10 .03
❑ 176 Carlos Quintana .10 .03
❑ 177 Jeff Russell .10 .03
❑ 178 Aaron Sele .10 .03
❑ 179 Rod Correia RC .15 .04
❑ 180 Chili Davis .20 .06
❑ 181 Jim Edmonds RC 3.00 .90
❑ 182 Rene Gonzales .10 .03
❑ 183 Hilly Hathaway RC .15 .04
❑ 184 Torey Lovullo .10 .03
❑ 185 Greg Myers .10 .03
❑ 186 Gene Nelson .10 .03
❑ 187 Troy Percival .30 .09
❑ 188 Scott Sanderson .10 .03
❑ 189 Darryl Scott RC .15 .04
❑ 190 J.T. Snow RC .60 .18
❑ 191 Russ Springer .10 .03
❑ 192 Jason Bere .10 .03
❑ 193 Rodney Bolton .10 .03
❑ 194 Ellis Burks .20 .06
❑ 195 Bo Jackson .50 .15
❑ 196 Mike LaValliere .10 .03
❑ 197 Scott Ruffcorn .10 .03
❑ 198 Jeff Schwarz .10 .03
❑ 199 Jerry DiPoto .10 .03
❑ 200 Alvaro Espinoza .10 .03
❑ 201 Wayne Kirby .10 .03
❑ 202 Tom Kramer RC .15 .04
❑ 203 Jesse Levis .10 .03
❑ 204 Manny Ramirez .75 .23
❑ 205 Jeff Treadway .10 .03
❑ 206 Bill Wertz RC .15 .04
❑ 207 Cliff Young .10 .03
❑ 208 Matt Young .10 .03
❑ 209 Kirk Gibson .30 .09
❑ 210 Greg Gohr .10 .03
❑ 211 Bill Krueger .10 .03
❑ 212 Bob MacDonald .10 .03
❑ 213 Mike Moore .10 .03
❑ 214 David Wells .20 .06
❑ 215 Billy Brewer .10 .03
❑ 216 David Cone .20 .06
❑ 217 Greg Gagne .10 .03
❑ 218 Mark Gardner .10 .03
❑ 219 Chris Haney .10 .03
❑ 220 Phil Hiatt .10 .03
❑ 221 Jose Lind .10 .03
❑ 222 Juan Bell .10 .03
❑ 223 Tom Brunansky .10 .03
❑ 224 Mike Ignasiak .10 .03
❑ 225 Joe Kmak .10 .03
❑ 226 Tom Lampkin .10 .03
❑ 227 Graeme Lloyd RC .40 .12
❑ 228 Carlos Maldonado .10 .03
❑ 229 Matt Mieske .10 .03
❑ 230 Angel Miranda .10 .03
❑ 231 Troy O'Leary RC .40 .12
❑ 232 Kevin Reimer .10 .03
❑ 233 Larry Casian .10 .03
❑ 234 Jim Deshaies .10 .03
❑ 235 Eddie Guardado RC .60 .18
❑ 236 Chip Hale .10 .03
❑ 237 Mike Maksudian RC .15 .04
❑ 238 David McCarty .10 .03
❑ 239 Pat Meares RC .40 .12
❑ 240 George Tsamis RC .15 .04
❑ 241 Dave Winfield .20 .06
❑ 242 Jim Abbott .30 .09
❑ 243 Wade Boggs .30 .09
❑ 244 Andy Cook RC .15 .04
❑ 245 Russ Davis RC .15 .04
❑ 246 Mike Humphreys .10 .03
❑ 247 Jimmy Key .20 .06
❑ 248 Jim Leyritz .10 .03
❑ 249 Bobby Munoz .10 .03
❑ 250 Paul O'Neill .30 .09
❑ 251 Spike Owen .10 .03
❑ 252 Dave Silvestri .10 .03
❑ 253 Marcos Armas RC .15 .04
❑ 254 Brent Gates .10 .03
❑ 255 Rich Gossage .20 .06
❑ 256 Scott Lydy RC .15 .04
❑ 257 Henry Mercedes .10 .03
❑ 258 Mike Mohler RC .40 .12
❑ 259 Troy Neel .10 .03
❑ 260 Edwin Nunez .10 .03
❑ 261 Craig Paquette .10 .03
❑ 262 Kevin Seitzer .10 .03
❑ 263 Rich Amaral .10 .03
❑ 264 Mike Blowers .10 .03
❑ 265 Chris Bosio .10 .03
❑ 266 Norm Charlton .10 .03
❑ 267 Jim Converse RC .15 .04
❑ 268 John Cummings RC .15 .04
❑ 269 Mike Felder .10 .03
❑ 270 Mike Hampton .20 .06
❑ 271 Bill Haselman .10 .03
❑ 272 Dwayne Henry .10 .03
❑ 273 Greg Litton .10 .03
❑ 274 Mackey Sasser .10 .03
❑ 275 Lee Tinsley .10 .03
❑ 276 David Wainhouse .10 .03
❑ 277 Jeff Bronkey .10 .03
❑ 278 Benji Gil .10 .03
❑ 279 Tom Henke .10 .03
❑ 280 Charlie Leibrandt .10 .03
❑ 281 Robb Nen .20 .06
❑ 282 Bill Ripken .10 .03
❑ 283 Jon Shave RC .15 .04
❑ 284 Doug Strange .10 .03
❑ 285 Matt Whiteside RC .15 .04
❑ 286 Scott Brow RC .15 .04
❑ 287 Willie Canate RC .15 .04
❑ 288 Tony Castillo .10 .03
❑ 289 Domingo Cedeno RC .15 .04
❑ 290 Darnell Coles .10 .03
❑ 291 Danny Cox .10 .03
❑ 292 Mark Eichhorn .10 .03
❑ 293 Tony Fernandez .10 .03
❑ 294 Al Leiter .20 .06
❑ 295 Paul Molitor .30 .09
❑ 296 Dave Stewart .20 .06
❑ 297 Woody Williams RC .60 .18
❑ 298 Checklist F1-F100 .10 .03
❑ 299 Checklist F101-F200 .10 .03
❑ 300 Checklist F201-F300 .10 .03

1994 Fleer Update

	Nm-Mt	Ex-Mt
COMP.FACT.SET (210)	50.00	15.00

❑ 1 Mark Eichhorn .25 .07
❑ 2 Sid Fernandez .25 .07
❑ 3 Leo Gomez .25 .07
❑ 4 Mike Oquist .25 .07
❑ 5 Rafael Palmeiro .75 .23
❑ 6 Chris Sabo .25 .07
❑ 7 Dwight Smith .25 .07
❑ 8 Lee Smith .50 .15
❑ 9 Damon Berryhill .25 .07
❑ 10 Wes Chamberlain .25 .07
❑ 11 Gar Finnvold .25 .07
❑ 12 Chris Howard .25 .07
❑ 13 Tim Naehring .25 .07
❑ 14 Otis Nixon .25 .07
❑ 15 Brian Anderson RC .50 .15
❑ 16 Jorge Fabregas .25 .07
❑ 17 Rex Hudler .25 .07
❑ 18 Bo Jackson 1.25 .35
❑ 19 Mark Leiter .25 .07
❑ 20 Spike Owen .25 .07

❑ 21 Harold Reynolds .50 .15
❑ 22 Chris Turner .25 .07
❑ 23 Dennis Cook .25 .07
❑ 24 Jose DeLeon .25 .07
❑ 25 Julio Franco .50 .15
❑ 26 Joe Hall .25 .07
❑ 27 Darrin Jackson .25 .07
❑ 28 Dane Johnson .25 .07
❑ 29 Norberto Martin .25 .07
❑ 30 Scott Sanderson .25 .07
❑ 31 Jason Grimsley .25 .07
❑ 32 Dennis Martinez .50 .15
❑ 33 Jack Morris .50 .15
❑ 34 Eddie Murray 1.25 .35
❑ 35 Chad Ogea .25 .07
❑ 36 Tony Pena .25 .07
❑ 37 Paul Shuey .25 .07
❑ 38 Omar Vizquel .75 .23
❑ 39 Danny Bautista .25 .07
❑ 40 Tim Belcher .25 .07
❑ 41 Joe Boever .25 .07
❑ 42 Storm Davis .25 .07
❑ 43 Junior Felix .25 .07
❑ 44 Mike Gardiner .25 .07
❑ 45 Buddy Groom .25 .07
❑ 46 Juan Samuel .25 .07
❑ 47 Vince Coleman .25 .07
❑ 48 Bob Hamelin .25 .07
❑ 49 Dave Henderson .25 .07
❑ 50 Rusty Meacham .25 .07
❑ 51 Terry Shumpert .25 .07
❑ 52 Jeff Bronkey .25 .07
❑ 53 Alex Diaz .25 .07
❑ 54 Brian Harper .25 .07
❑ 55 Jose Mercedes .25 .07
❑ 56 Jody Reed .25 .07
❑ 57 Bob Scanlan .25 .07
❑ 58 Turner Ward .25 .07
❑ 59 Rich Becker .25 .07
❑ 60 Alex Cole .25 .07
❑ 61 Denny Hocking .25 .07
❑ 62 Scott Leius .25 .07
❑ 63 Pat Mahomes .25 .07
❑ 64 Carlos Pulido .25 .07
❑ 65 Dave Stevens .25 .07
❑ 66 Matt Walbeck .25 .07
❑ 67 Xavier Hernandez .25 .07
❑ 68 Sterling Hitchcock .25 .07
❑ 69 Terry Mulholland .25 .07
❑ 70 Luis Polonia .25 .07
❑ 71 Gerald Williams .25 .07
❑ 72 Mark Acre RC .25 .07
❑ 73 Geronimo Berroa .25 .07
❑ 74 Rickey Henderson 1.25 .35
❑ 75 Stan Javier .25 .07
❑ 76 Steve Karsay .25 .07
❑ 77 Carlos Reyes .25 .07
❑ 78 Bill Taylor RC .50 .15
❑ 79 Eric Anthony .25 .07
❑ 80 Bobby Ayala .25 .07
❑ 81 Tim Davis .25 .07
❑ 82 Felix Fermin .25 .07
❑ 83 Reggie Jefferson .25 .07
❑ 84 Keith Mitchell .25 .07
❑ 85 Bill Risley .25 .07
❑ 86 Alex Rodriguez RC 40.00 12.00
❑ 87 Roger Salkeld .25 .07
❑ 88 Dan Wilson .25 .07
❑ 89 Cris Carpenter .25 .07
❑ 90 Will Clark .75 .23
❑ 91 Jeff Frye .25 .07
❑ 92 Rick Helling .25 .07
❑ 93 Chris James .25 .07
❑ 94 Oddibe McDowell .25 .07
❑ 95 Billy Ripken .25 .07
❑ 96 Carlos Delgado .75 .23
❑ 97 Alex Gonzalez .25 .07
❑ 98 Shawn Green 1.25 .35
❑ 99 Darren Hall .25 .07
❑ 100 Mike Huff .25 .07
❑ 101 Mike Kelly .25 .07
❑ 102 Roberto Kelly .25 .07
❑ 103 Charlie O'Brien .25 .07
❑ 104 Jose Oliva .25 .07
❑ 105 Gregg Olson .25 .07
❑ 106 Willie Banks .25 .07
❑ 107 Jim Bullinger .25 .07
❑ 108 Chuck Crim .25 .07
❑ 109 Shawon Dunston .25 .07
❑ 110 Karl Rhodes .25 .07
❑ 111 Steve Trachsel .25 .07
❑ 112 Anthony Young .25 .07
❑ 113 Eddie Zambrano .25 .07
❑ 114 Bret Boone .50 .15
❑ 115 Jeff Brantley .25 .07
❑ 116 Hector Carrasco .25 .07
❑ 117 Tony Fernandez .25 .07
❑ 118 Tim Fortugno .25 .07
❑ 119 Erik Hanson .25 .07
❑ 120 Chuck McElroy .25 .07
❑ 121 Deion Sanders .75 .23
❑ 122 Ellis Burks .50 .15
❑ 123 Marvin Freeman .25 .07
❑ 124 Mike Harkey .25 .07
❑ 125 Howard Johnson .25 .07
❑ 126 Mike Kingery .25 .07
❑ 127 Nelson Liriano .25 .07
❑ 128 Marcus Moore .25 .07
❑ 129 Mike Munoz .25 .07
❑ 130 Kevin Ritz .25 .07
❑ 131 Walt Weiss .25 .07
❑ 132 Kurt Abbott RC .50 .15
❑ 133 Jerry Browne .25 .07
❑ 134 Greg Colbrunn .25 .07
❑ 135 Jeremy Hernandez .25 .07
❑ 136 Dave Magadan .25 .07
❑ 137 Kurt Miller .25 .07
❑ 138 Robb Nen .50 .15
❑ 139 Jesus Tavarez RC .25 .07
❑ 140 Sid Bream .25 .07
❑ 141 Tom Edens .25 .07
❑ 142 Tony Eusebio .25 .07
❑ 143 John Hudek RC .25 .07
❑ 144 Brian L. Hunter .25 .07
❑ 145 Orlando Miller .25 .07
❑ 146 James Mouton .25 .07
❑ 147 Shane Reynolds .25 .07
❑ 148 Rafael Bournigal .25 .07
❑ 149 Delino DeShields .25 .07
❑ 150 Garey Ingram RC .25 .07
❑ 151 Chan Ho Park RC .75 .23
❑ 152 Wil Cordero .25 .07
❑ 153 Pedro Martinez 1.25 .35
❑ 154 Randy Milligan .25 .07
❑ 155 Lenny Webster .25 .07
❑ 156 Rico Brogna .25 .07
❑ 157 Josias Manzanillo .25 .07
❑ 158 Kevin McReynolds .25 .07
❑ 159 Mike Remlinger .25 .07
❑ 160 David Segui .25 .07
❑ 161 Pete Smith .25 .07
❑ 162 Kelly Stinnett RC .50 .15
❑ 163 Jose Vizcaino .25 .07
❑ 164 Billy Hatcher .25 .07
❑ 165 Doug Jones .25 .07
❑ 166 Mike Lieberthal .25 .07
❑ 167 Tony Longmire .25 .07
❑ 168 Bobby Munoz .25 .07
❑ 169 Paul Quantrill .25 .07
❑ 170 Heathcliff Slocumb .25 .07
❑ 171 Fernando Valenzuela .50 .15
❑ 172 Mark Dewey .25 .07
❑ 173 Brian R. Hunter .25 .07
❑ 174 Jon Lieber .50 .15
❑ 175 Ravelo Manzanillo .25 .07
❑ 176 Dan Miceli .25 .07
❑ 177 Rick White .25 .07
❑ 178 Bryan Eversgerd .25 .07
❑ 179 John Habyan .25 .07
❑ 180 Terry McGriff .25 .07
❑ 181 Vicente Palacios .25 .07
❑ 182 Rich Rodriguez .25 .07
❑ 183 Rick Sutcliffe .50 .15
❑ 184 Donnie Elliott .25 .07
❑ 185 Joey Hamilton .25 .07
❑ 186 Tim Hyers RC .25 .07
❑ 187 Luis Lopez .25 .07
❑ 188 Ray McDavid .25 .07
❑ 189 Bip Roberts .25 .07
❑ 190 Scott Sanders .25 .07
❑ 191 Eddie Williams .25 .07
❑ 192 Steve Frey .25 .07
❑ 193 Pat Gomez .25 .07
❑ 194 Rich Monteleone .25 .07
❑ 195 Mark Portugal .25 .07
❑ 196 Darryl Strawberry .50 .15
❑ 197 Salomon Torres .25 .07
❑ 198 W.VanLandingham RC .25 .07
❑ 199 Checklist .25 .07
❑ 200 Checklist .25 .07

1997 Fleer

	Nm-Mt	Ex-Mt
COMPLETE SET (761)	110.00	33.00
COMP. SERIES 1 (500)	60.00	18.00
COMP. SERIES 2 (261)	50.00	15.00
COMMON CARD (1-750)	.30	.09
COMMON CARD (751-761)	.50	.15

❑ 1 Roberto Alomar .50 .15
❑ 2 Brady Anderson .30 .09
❑ 3 Bobby Bonilla .30 .09
❑ 4 Rocky Coppinger .30 .09
❑ 5 Cesar Devarez .30 .09
❑ 6 Scott Erickson .30 .09
❑ 7 Jeffrey Hammonds .30 .09
❑ 8 Chris Hoiles .30 .09
❑ 9 Eddie Murray .75 .23
❑ 10 Mike Mussina .50 .15
❑ 11 Randy Myers .30 .09
❑ 12 Rafael Palmeiro .50 .15
❑ 13 Cal Ripken 2.50 .75
❑ 14 B.J. Surhoff .30 .09
❑ 15 David Wells .30 .09
❑ 16 Todd Zeile .30 .09
❑ 17 Darren Bragg .30 .09
❑ 18 Jose Canseco .50 .15
❑ 19 Roger Clemens 1.50 .45
❑ 20 Wil Cordero .30 .09
❑ 21 Jeff Frye .30 .09
❑ 22 Nomar Garciaparra 1.25 .35
❑ 23 Tom Gordon .30 .09
❑ 24 Mike Greenwell .30 .09
❑ 25 Reggie Jefferson .30 .09
❑ 26 Jose Malave .30 .09
❑ 27 Tim Naehring .30 .09
❑ 28 Troy O'Leary .30 .09
❑ 29 Heathcliff Slocumb .30 .09
❑ 30 Mike Stanley .30 .09
❑ 31 John Valentin .30 .09
❑ 32 Mo Vaughn .30 .09
❑ 33 Tim Wakefield .30 .09
❑ 34 Garret Anderson .30 .09
❑ 35 George Arias .30 .09
❑ 36 Shawn Boskie .30 .09
❑ 37 Chili Davis .30 .09
❑ 38 Jason Dickson .30 .09
❑ 39 Gary DiSarcina .30 .09
❑ 40 Jim Edmonds .30 .09
❑ 41 Darin Erstad .30 .09
❑ 42 Jorge Fabregas .30 .09
❑ 43 Chuck Finley .30 .09
❑ 44 Todd Greene .30 .09
❑ 45 Mike Holtz .30 .09
❑ 46 Rex Hudler .30 .09
❑ 47 Mike James .30 .09
❑ 48 Mark Langston .30 .09
❑ 49 Troy Percival .30 .09
❑ 50 Tim Salmon .50 .15

❑ 51 Jeff Schmidt .30 .09
❑ 52 J.T. Snow .30 .09
❑ 53 Randy Velarde .30 .09
❑ 54 Wilson Alvarez .30 .09
❑ 55 Harold Baines .30 .09
❑ 56 James Baldwin .30 .09
❑ 57 Jason Bere .30 .09
❑ 58 Mike Cameron .30 .09
❑ 59 Ray Durham .30 .09
❑ 60 Alex Fernandez .30 .09
❑ 61 Ozzie Guillen .30 .09
❑ 62 Roberto Hernandez .30 .09
❑ 63 Ron Karkovice .30 .09
❑ 64 Darren Lewis .30 .09
❑ 65 Dave Martinez .30 .09
❑ 66 Lyle Mouton .30 .09
❑ 67 Greg Norton .30 .09
❑ 68 Tony Phillips .30 .09
❑ 69 Chris Snopek .30 .09
❑ 70 Kevin Tapani .30 .09
❑ 71 Danny Tartabull .30 .09
❑ 72 Frank Thomas .75 .23
❑ 73 Robin Ventura .30 .09
❑ 74 Sandy Alomar Jr. .30 .09
❑ 75 Albert Belle .30 .09
❑ 76 Mark Carreon .30 .09
❑ 77 Julio Franco .30 .09
❑ 78 Brian Giles RC 1.50 .45
❑ 79 Orel Hershiser .30 .09
❑ 80 Kenny Lofton .30 .09
❑ 81 Dennis Martinez .30 .09
❑ 82 Jack McDowell .30 .09
❑ 83 Jose Mesa .30 .09
❑ 84 Charles Nagy .30 .09
❑ 85 Chad Ogea .30 .09
❑ 86 Eric Plunk .30 .09
❑ 87 Manny Ramirez .50 .15
❑ 88 Kevin Seitzer .30 .09
❑ 89 Julian Tavarez .30 .09
❑ 90 Jim Thome .50 .15
❑ 91 Jose Vizcaino .30 .09
❑ 92 Omar Vizquel .50 .15
❑ 93 Brad Ausmus .30 .09
❑ 94 Kimera Bartee .30 .09
❑ 95 Raul Casanova .30 .09
❑ 96 Tony Clark .30 .09
❑ 97 John Cummings .30 .09
❑ 98 Travis Fryman .30 .09
❑ 99 Bob Higginson .30 .09
❑ 100 Mark Lewis .30 .09
❑ 101 Felipe Lira .30 .09
❑ 102 Phil Nevin .30 .09
❑ 103 Melvin Nieves .30 .09
❑ 104 Curtis Pride .30 .09
❑ 105 A.J. Sager .30 .09
❑ 106 Ruben Sierra .30 .09
❑ 107 Justin Thompson .30 .09
❑ 108 Alan Trammell .30 .09
❑ 109 Kevin Appier .30 .09
❑ 110 Tim Belcher .30 .09
❑ 111 Jaime Bluma .30 .09
❑ 112 Johnny Damon .50 .15
❑ 113 Tom Goodwin .30 .09
❑ 114 Chris Haney .30 .09
❑ 115 Keith Lockhart .30 .09
❑ 116 Mike Macfarlane .30 .09
❑ 117 Jeff Montgomery .30 .09
❑ 118 Jose Offerman .30 .09
❑ 119 Craig Paquette .30 .09
❑ 120 Joe Randa .30 .09
❑ 121 Bip Roberts .30 .09
❑ 122 Jose Rosado .30 .09
❑ 123 Mike Sweeney .30 .09
❑ 124 Michael Tucker .30 .09
❑ 125 Jeromy Burnitz .30 .09
❑ 126 Jeff Cirillo .30 .09
❑ 127 Jeff D'Amico .30 .09
❑ 128 Mike Fetters .30 .09
❑ 129 John Jaha .30 .09
❑ 130 Scott Karl .30 .09
❑ 131 Jesse Levis .30 .09
❑ 132 Mark Loretta .30 .09
❑ 133 Mike Matheny .30 .09
❑ 134 Ben McDonald .30 .09
❑ 135 Matt Mieske .30 .09
❑ 136 Marc Newfield .30 .09
❑ 137 Dave Nilsson .30 .09
❑ 138 Jose Valentin .30 .09
❑ 139 Fernando Vina .30 .09
❑ 140 Bob Wickman .30 .09
❑ 141 Gerald Williams .30 .09
❑ 142 Rick Aguilera .30 .09
❑ 143 Rich Becker .30 .09
❑ 144 Ron Coomer .30 .09
❑ 145 Marty Cordova .30 .09
❑ 146 Roberto Kelly .30 .09
❑ 147 Chuck Knoblauch .30 .09
❑ 148 Matt Lawton .30 .09
❑ 149 Pat Meares .30 .09
❑ 150 Travis Miller .30 .09
❑ 151 Paul Molitor .50 .15
❑ 152 Greg Myers .30 .09
❑ 153 Dan Naulty .30 .09
❑ 154 Kirby Puckett .75 .23
❑ 155 Brad Radke .30 .09
❑ 156 Frank Rodriguez .30 .09
❑ 157 Scott Stahoviak .30 .09
❑ 158 Dave Stevens .30 .09
❑ 159 Matt Walbeck .30 .09
❑ 160 Todd Walker .30 .09
❑ 161 Wade Boggs .50 .15
❑ 162 David Cone .30 .09
❑ 163 Mariano Duncan .30 .09
❑ 164 Cecil Fielder .30 .09
❑ 165 Joe Girardi .30 .09
❑ 166 Dwight Gooden .30 .09
❑ 167 Charlie Hayes .30 .09
❑ 168 Derek Jeter 2.00 .60
❑ 169 Jimmy Key .30 .09
❑ 170 Jim Leyritz .30 .09
❑ 171 Tino Martinez .50 .15
❑ 172 Ramiro Mendoza RC .30 .09
❑ 173 Jeff Nelson .30 .09
❑ 174 Paul O'Neill .50 .15
❑ 175 Andy Pettitte .50 .15
❑ 176 Mariano Rivera .50 .15
❑ 177 Ruben Rivera .30 .09
❑ 178 Kenny Rogers .30 .09
❑ 179 Darryl Strawberry .30 .09
❑ 180 John Wetteland .30 .09
❑ 181 Bernie Williams .50 .15
❑ 182 Willie Adams .30 .09
❑ 183 Tony Batista .30 .09
❑ 184 Geronimo Berroa .30 .09
❑ 185 Mike Bordick .30 .09
❑ 186 Scott Brosius .30 .09
❑ 187 Bobby Chouinard .30 .09
❑ 188 Jim Corsi .30 .09
❑ 189 Brent Gates .30 .09
❑ 190 Jason Giambi .30 .09
❑ 191 Jose Herrera .30 .09
❑ 192 Damon Mashore .30 .09
❑ 193 Mark McGwire 2.00 .60
❑ 194 Mike Mohler .30 .09
❑ 195 Scott Spiezio .30 .09
❑ 196 Terry Steinbach .30 .09
❑ 197 Bill Taylor .30 .09
❑ 198 John Wasdin .30 .09
❑ 199 Steve Wojciechowski .30 .09
❑ 200 Ernie Young .30 .09
❑ 201 Rich Amaral .30 .09
❑ 202 Jay Buhner .30 .09
❑ 203 Norm Charlton .30 .09
❑ 204 Joey Cora .30 .09
❑ 205 Russ Davis .30 .09
❑ 206 Ken Griffey Jr. 1.25 .35
❑ 207 Sterling Hitchcock .30 .09
❑ 208 Brian Hunter .30 .09
❑ 209 Raul Ibanez .30 .09
❑ 210 Randy Johnson .75 .23
❑ 211 Edgar Martinez .50 .15
❑ 212 Jamie Moyer .30 .09
❑ 213 Alex Rodriguez 1.25 .35
❑ 214 Paul Sorrento .30 .09
❑ 215 Matt Wagner .30 .09
❑ 216 Bob Wells .30 .09
❑ 217 Dan Wilson .30 .09
❑ 218 Damon Buford .30 .09
❑ 219 Will Clark .50 .15
❑ 220 Kevin Elster .30 .09
❑ 221 Juan Gonzalez .30 .09
❑ 222 Rusty Greer .30 .09
❑ 223 Kevin Gross .30 .09
❑ 224 Darryl Hamilton .30 .09
❑ 225 Mike Henneman .30 .09
❑ 226 Ken Hill .30 .09
❑ 227 Mark McLemore .30 .09
❑ 228 Darren Oliver .30 .09
❑ 229 Dean Palmer .30 .09
❑ 230 Roger Pavlik .30 .09
❑ 231 Ivan Rodriguez .50 .15
❑ 232 Mickey Tettleton .30 .09
❑ 233 Bobby Witt .30 .09
❑ 234 Jacob Brumfield .30 .09
❑ 235 Joe Carter .30 .09
❑ 236 Tim Crabtree .30 .09
❑ 237 Carlos Delgado .30 .09
❑ 238 Huck Flener .30 .09
❑ 239 Alex Gonzalez .30 .09
❑ 240 Shawn Green .30 .09
❑ 241 Juan Guzman .30 .09
❑ 242 Pat Hentgen .30 .09
❑ 243 Marty Janzen .30 .09
❑ 244 Sandy Martinez .30 .09
❑ 245 Otis Nixon .30 .09
❑ 246 Charlie O'Brien .30 .09
❑ 247 John Olerud .30 .09
❑ 248 Robert Perez .30 .09
❑ 249 Ed Sprague .30 .09
❑ 250 Mike Timlin .30 .09
❑ 251 Steve Avery .30 .09
❑ 252 Jeff Blauser .30 .09
❑ 253 Brad Clontz .30 .09
❑ 254 Jermaine Dye .30 .09
❑ 255 Tom Glavine .50 .15
❑ 256 Marquis Grissom .30 .09
❑ 257 Andruw Jones .50 .15
❑ 258 Chipper Jones .75 .23
❑ 259 David Justice .30 .09
❑ 260 Ryan Klesko .30 .09
❑ 261 Mark Lemke .30 .09
❑ 262 Javier Lopez .30 .09
❑ 263 Greg Maddux 1.25 .35
❑ 264 Fred McGriff .50 .15
❑ 265 Greg McMichael .30 .09
❑ 266 Denny Neagle .30 .09
❑ 267 Terry Pendleton .30 .09
❑ 268 Eddie Perez .30 .09
❑ 269 John Smoltz .50 .15
❑ 270 Terrell Wade .30 .09
❑ 271 Mark Wohlers .30 .09
❑ 272 Terry Adams .30 .09
❑ 273 Brant Brown .30 .09
❑ 274 Leo Gomez .30 .09
❑ 275 Luis Gonzalez .30 .09
❑ 276 Mark Grace .50 .15
❑ 277 Tyler Houston .30 .09
❑ 278 Robin Jennings .30 .09
❑ 279 Brooks Kieschnick .30 .09
❑ 280 Brian McRae .30 .09
❑ 281 Jaime Navarro .30 .09
❑ 282 Ryne Sandberg 1.25 .35
❑ 283 Scott Servais .30 .09
❑ 284 Sammy Sosa .75 .23
❑ 285 Dave Swartzbaugh .30 .09
❑ 286 Amaury Telemaco .30 .09
❑ 287 Steve Trachsel .30 .09
❑ 288 Pedro Valdes .30 .09
❑ 289 Turk Wendell .30 .09
❑ 290 Bret Boone .30 .09
❑ 291 Jeff Branson .30 .09
❑ 292 Jeff Brantley .30 .09
❑ 293 Eric Davis .30 .09
❑ 294 Willie Greene .30 .09
❑ 295 Thomas Howard .30 .09
❑ 296 Barry Larkin .50 .15
❑ 297 Kevin Mitchell .30 .09
❑ 298 Hal Morris .30 .09
❑ 299 Chad Mottola .30 .09
❑ 300 Joe Oliver .30 .09
❑ 301 Mark Portugal .30 .09
❑ 302 Roger Salkeld .30 .09
❑ 303 Reggie Sanders .30 .09
❑ 304 Pete Schourek .30 .09
❑ 305 John Smiley .30 .09
❑ 306 Eddie Taubensee .30 .09
❑ 307 Dante Bichette .30 .09
❑ 308 Ellis Burks .30 .09

	No.	Player		
❑	309	Vinny Castilla	.30	.09
❑	310	Andres Galarraga	.30	.09
❑	311	Curt Leskanic	.30	.09
❑	312	Quinton McCracken	.30	.09
❑	313	Neifi Perez	.30	.09
❑	314	Jeff Reed	.30	.09
❑	315	Steve Reed	.30	.09
❑	316	Armando Reynoso	.30	.09
❑	317	Kevin Ritz	.30	.09
❑	318	Bruce Ruffin	.30	.09
❑	319	Larry Walker	.30	.09
❑	320	Walt Weiss	.30	.09
❑	321	Jamey Wright	.30	.09
❑	322	Eric Young	.30	.09
❑	323	Kurt Abbott	.30	.09
❑	324	Alex Arias	.30	.09
❑	325	Kevin Brown	.30	.09
❑	326	Luis Castillo	.30	.09
❑	327	Greg Colbrunn	.30	.09
❑	328	Jeff Conine	.30	.09
❑	329	Andre Dawson	.30	.09
❑	330	Charles Johnson	.30	.09
❑	331	Al Leiter	.30	.09
❑	332	Ralph Milliard	.30	.09
❑	333	Robb Nen	.30	.09
❑	334	Pat Rapp	.30	.09
❑	335	Edgar Renteria	.30	.09
❑	336	Gary Sheffield	.30	.09
❑	337	Devon White	.30	.09
❑	338	Bob Abreu	.50	.15
❑	339	Jeff Bagwell	.50	.15
❑	340	Derek Bell	.30	.09
❑	341	Sean Berry	.30	.09
❑	342	Craig Biggio	.50	.15
❑	343	Doug Drabek	.30	.09
❑	344	Tony Eusebio	.30	.09
❑	345	Ricky Gutierrez	.30	.09
❑	346	Mike Hampton	.30	.09
❑	347	Brian Hunter	.30	.09
❑	348	Todd Jones	.30	.09
❑	349	Darryl Kile	.30	.09
❑	350	Derrick May	.30	.09
❑	351	Orlando Miller	.30	.09
❑	352	James Mouton	.30	.09
❑	353	Shane Reynolds	.30	.09
❑	354	Billy Wagner	.30	.09
❑	355	Donne Wall	.30	.09
❑	356	Mike Blowers	.30	.09
❑	357	Brett Butler	.30	.09
❑	358	Roger Cedeno	.30	.09
❑	359	Chad Curtis	.30	.09
❑	360	Delino DeShields	.30	.09
❑	361	Greg Gagne	.30	.09
❑	362	Karim Garcia	.30	.09
❑	363	Wilton Guerrero	.30	.09
❑	364	Todd Hollandsworth	.30	.09
❑	365	Eric Karros	.30	.09
❑	366	Ramon Martinez	.30	.09
❑	367	Raul Mondesi	.30	.09
❑	368	Hideo Nomo	.75	.23
❑	369	Antonio Osuna	.30	.09
❑	370	Chan Ho Park	.30	.09
❑	371	Mike Piazza	1.25	.35
❑	372	Ismael Valdes	.30	.09
❑	373	Todd Worrell	.30	.09
❑	374	Moises Alou	.30	.09
❑	375	Shane Andrews	.30	.09
❑	376	Yamil Benitez	.30	.09
❑	377	Jeff Fassero	.30	.09
❑	378	Darrin Fletcher	.30	.09
❑	379	Cliff Floyd	.30	.09
❑	380	Mark Grudzielanek	.30	.09
❑	381	Mike Lansing	.30	.09
❑	382	Barry Manuel	.30	.09
❑	383	Pedro Martinez	.50	.15
❑	384	Henry Rodriguez	.30	.09
❑	385	Mel Rojas	.30	.09
❑	386	F.P. Santangelo	.30	.09
❑	387	David Segui	.30	.09
❑	388	Ugueth Urbina	.30	.09
❑	389	Rondell White	.30	.09
❑	390	Edgardo Alfonzo	.30	.09
❑	391	Carlos Baerga	.30	.09
❑	392	Mark Clark	.30	.09
❑	393	Alvaro Espinoza	.30	.09
❑	394	John Franco	.30	.09
❑	395	Bernard Gilkey	.30	.09
❑	396	Pete Harnisch	.30	.09
❑	397	Todd Hundley	.30	.09
❑	398	Butch Huskey	.30	.09
❑	399	Jason Isringhausen	.30	.09
❑	400	Lance Johnson	.30	.09
❑	401	Bobby Jones	.30	.09
❑	402	Alex Ochoa	.30	.09
❑	403	Rey Ordonez	.30	.09
❑	404	Robert Person	.30	.09
❑	405	Paul Wilson	.30	.09
❑	406	Matt Beech	.30	.09
❑	407	Ron Blazier	.30	.09
❑	408	Ricky Bottalico	.30	.09
❑	409	Lenny Dykstra	.30	.09
❑	410	Jim Eisenreich	.30	.09
❑	411	Bobby Estalella	.30	.09
❑	412	Mike Grace	.30	.09
❑	413	Gregg Jefferies	.30	.09
❑	414	Mike Lieberthal	.30	.09
❑	415	Wendell Magee	.30	.09
❑	416	Mickey Morandini	.30	.09
❑	417	Ricky Otero	.30	.09
❑	418	Scott Rolen	.50	.15
❑	419	Ken Ryan	.30	.09
❑	420	Benito Santiago	.30	.09
❑	421	Curt Schilling	.30	.09
❑	422	Kevin Sefcik	.30	.09
❑	423	Jermaine Allensworth	.30	.09
❑	424	Trey Beamon	.30	.09
❑	425	Jay Bell	.30	.09
❑	426	Francisco Cordova	.30	.09
❑	427	Carlos Garcia	.30	.09
❑	428	Mark Johnson	.30	.09
❑	429	Jason Kendall	.30	.09
❑	430	Jeff King	.30	.09
❑	431	Jon Lieber	.30	.09
❑	432	Al Martin	.30	.09
❑	433	Orlando Merced	.30	.09
❑	434	Ramon Morel	.30	.09
❑	435	Matt Ruebel	.30	.09
❑	436	Jason Schmidt	.30	.09
❑	437	Marc Wilkins	.30	.09
❑	438	Alan Benes	.30	.09
❑	439	Andy Benes	.30	.09
❑	440	Royce Clayton	.30	.09
❑	441	Dennis Eckersley	.30	.09
❑	442	Gary Gaetti	.30	.09
❑	443	Ron Gant	.30	.09
❑	444	Aaron Holbert	.30	.09
❑	445	Brian Jordan	.30	.09
❑	446	Ray Lankford	.30	.09
❑	447	John Mabry	.30	.09
❑	448	T.J. Mathews	.30	.09
❑	449	Willie McGee	.30	.09
❑	450	Donovan Osborne	.30	.09
❑	451	Tom Pagnozzi	.30	.09
❑	452	Ozzie Smith	1.25	.35
❑	453	Todd Stottlemyre	.30	.09
❑	454	Mark Sweeney	.30	.09
❑	455	Dmitri Young	.30	.09
❑	456	Andy Ashby	.30	.09
❑	457	Ken Caminiti	.30	.09
❑	458	Archi Cianfrocco	.30	.09
❑	459	Steve Finley	.30	.09
❑	460	John Flaherty	.30	.09
❑	461	Chris Gomez	.30	.09
❑	462	Tony Gwynn	1.00	.30
❑	463	Joey Hamilton	.30	.09
❑	464	Rickey Henderson	.75	.23
❑	465	Trevor Hoffman	.30	.09
❑	466	Brian Johnson	.30	.09
❑	467	Wally Joyner	.30	.09
❑	468	Jody Reed	.30	.09
❑	469	Scott Sanders	.30	.09
❑	470	Bob Tewksbury	.30	.09
❑	471	Fernando Valenzuela	.30	.09
❑	472	Greg Vaughn	.30	.09
❑	473	Tim Worrell	.30	.09
❑	474	Rich Aurilia	.30	.09
❑	475	Rod Beck	.30	.09
❑	476	Marvin Benard	.30	.09
❑	477	Barry Bonds	2.00	.60
❑	478	Jay Canizaro	.30	.09
❑	479	Shawon Dunston	.30	.09
❑	480	Shawn Estes	.30	.09
❑	481	Mark Gardner	.30	.09
❑	482	Glenallen Hill	.30	.09
❑	483	Stan Javier	.30	.09
❑	484	Marcus Jensen	.30	.09
❑	485	Bill Mueller RC	1.50	.45
❑	486	Wm. VanLandingham	.30	.09
❑	487	Allen Watson	.30	.09
❑	488	Rick Wilkins	.30	.09
❑	489	Matt Williams	.30	.09
❑	490	Desi Wilson	.30	.09
❑	491	Albert Belle CL	.30	.09
❑	492	Ken Griffey Jr. CL	.75	.23
❑	493	Andruw Jones CL	.30	.09
❑	494	Chipper Jones CL	.50	.15
❑	495	Mark McGwire CL	1.00	.30
❑	496	Paul Molitor CL	.30	.09
❑	497	Mike Piazza CL	.75	.23
❑	498	Cal Ripken CL	1.25	.35
❑	499	Alex Rodriguez CL	.75	.23
❑	500	Frank Thomas CL	.50	.15
❑	501	Kenny Lofton	.30	.09
❑	502	Carlos Perez	.30	.09
❑	503	Tim Raines	.30	.09
❑	504	Danny Patterson	.30	.09
❑	505	Derrick May	.30	.09
❑	506	Dave Hollins	.30	.09
❑	507	Felipe Crespo	.30	.09
❑	508	Brian Banks	.30	.09
❑	509	Jeff Kent	.30	.09
❑	510	Bubba Trammell RC	.40	.12
❑	511	Robert Person	.30	.09
❑	512	David Arias-Ortiz RC	30.00	9.00
❑	513	Ryan Jones	.30	.09
❑	514	David Justice	.30	.09
❑	515	Will Cunnane	.30	.09
❑	516	Russ Johnson	.30	.09
❑	517	John Burkett	.30	.09
❑	518	Robinson Checo RC	.30	.09
❑	519	Ricardo Rincon RC	.30	.09
❑	520	Woody Williams	.30	.09
❑	521	Rick Helling	.30	.09
❑	522	Jorge Posada	.50	.15
❑	523	Kevin Orie	.30	.09
❑	524	Fernando Tatis RC	.40	.12
❑	525	Jermaine Dye	.30	.09
❑	526	Brian Hunter	.30	.09
❑	527	Greg McMichael	.30	.09
❑	528	Matt Wagner	.30	.09
❑	529	Richie Sexson	.30	.09
❑	530	Scott Ruffcorn	.30	.09
❑	531	Luis Gonzalez	.30	.09
❑	532	Mike Johnson RC	.30	.09
❑	533	Mark Petkovsek	.30	.09
❑	534	Doug Drabek	.30	.09
❑	535	Jose Canseco	.50	.15
❑	536	Bobby Bonilla	.30	.09
❑	537	J.T. Snow	.30	.09
❑	538	Shawon Dunston	.30	.09
❑	539	John Ericks	.30	.09
❑	540	Terry Steinbach	.30	.09
❑	541	Jay Bell	.30	.09
❑	542	Joe Borowski RC	.30	.09
❑	543	David Wells	.30	.09
❑	544	Justin Towle RC	.30	.09
❑	545	Mike Blowers	.30	.09
❑	546	Shannon Stewart	.30	.09
❑	547	Rudy Pemberton	.30	.09
❑	548	Bill Swift	.30	.09
❑	549	Osvaldo Fernandez	.30	.09
❑	550	Eddie Murray	.75	.23
❑	551	Don Wengert	.30	.09
❑	552	Brad Ausmus	.30	.09
❑	553	Carlos Garcia	.30	.09
❑	554	Jose Guillen	.30	.09
❑	555	Rheal Cormier	.30	.09
❑	556	Doug Brocail	.30	.09
❑	557	Rex Hudler	.30	.09
❑	558	Armando Benitez	.30	.09
❑	559	Eli Marrero	.30	.09
❑	560	Ricky Ledee RC	.40	.12
❑	561	Bartolo Colon	.30	.09
❑	562	Quilvio Veras	.30	.09
❑	563	Alex Fernandez	.30	.09
❑	564	Darren Dreifort	.30	.09
❑	565	Benji Gil	.30	.09
❑	566	Kent Mercker	.30	.09

Card	Nm-Mt	Ex-Mt
567 Glendon Rusch	.30	.09
568 Ramon Tatis RC	.30	.09
569 Roger Clemens	1.50	.45
570 Mark Lewis	.30	.09
571 Emil Brown RC	.30	.09
572 Jaime Navarro	.30	.09
573 Sherman Obando	.30	.09
574 John Wasdin	.30	.09
575 Calvin Maduro	.30	.09
576 Todd Jones	.30	.09
577 Orlando Merced	.30	.09
578 Cal Eldred	.30	.09
579 Mark Gubicza	.30	.09
580 Michael Tucker	.30	.09
581 Tony Saunders RC	.30	.09
582 Garvin Alston	.30	.09
583 Joe Roa	.30	.09
584 Brady Raggio RC	.30	.09
585 Jimmy Key	.30	.09
586 Marc Sagmoen RC	.30	.09
587 Jim Bullinger	.30	.09
588 Yorkis Perez	.30	.09
589 Jose Cruz Jr. RC	.50	.15
590 Mike Stanton	.30	.09
591 Deivi Cruz RC	.40	.12
592 Steve Karsay	.30	.09
593 Mike Trombley	.30	.09
594 Doug Glanville	.30	.09
595 Scott Sanders	.30	.09
596 Thomas Howard	.30	.09
597 T.J. Staton RC	.30	.09
598 Garrett Stephenson	.30	.09
599 Rico Brogna	.30	.09
600 Albert Belle	.30	.09
601 Jose Vizcaino	.30	.09
602 Chili Davis	.30	.09
603 Shane Mack	.30	.09
604 Jim Eisenreich	.30	.09
605 Todd Zeile	.30	.09
606 Brian Boehringer RC	.30	.09
607 Paul Shuey	.30	.09
608 Kevin Tapani	.30	.09
609 John Wetteland	.30	.09
610 Jim Leyritz	.30	.09
611 Ray Montgomery RC	.30	.09
612 Doug Bochtler	.30	.09
613 Wady Almonte RC	.30	.09
614 Danny Tartabull	.30	.09
615 Orlando Miller	.30	.09
616 Bobby Ayala	.30	.09
617 Tony Graffanino	.30	.09
618 Marc Valdes	.30	.09
619 Ron Villone	.30	.09
620 Derrek Lee	.50	.15
621 Greg Colbrunn	.30	.09
622 Felix Heredia RC	.40	.12
623 Carl Everett	.30	.09
624 Mark Thompson	.30	.09
625 Jeff Granger	.30	.09
626 Damian Jackson	.30	.09
627 Mark Leiter	.30	.09
628 Chris Holt	.30	.09
629 Dario Veras RC	.30	.09
630 Dave Burba	.30	.09
631 Darryl Hamilton	.30	.09
632 Mark Acre	.30	.09
633 F.Hernandez RC	.30	.09
634 Terry Mulholland	.30	.09
635 Dustin Hermanson	.30	.09
636 Delino DeShields	.30	.09
637 Steve Avery	.30	.09
638 Tony Womack RC	.50	.15
639 Mark Whiten	.30	.09
640 Marquis Grissom	.30	.09
641 Xavier Hernandez	.30	.09
642 Eric Davis	.30	.09
643 Bob Tewksbury	.30	.09
644 Dante Powell	.30	.09
645 Carlos Castillo RC	.30	.09
646 Chris Widger	.30	.09
647 Moises Alou	.30	.09
648 Pat Listach	.30	.09
649 Edgar Ramos RC	.30	.09
650 Deion Sanders	.50	.15
651 John Olerud	.30	.09
652 Todd Dunwoody	.30	.09
653 Randall Simon RC	.40	.12
654 Dan Carlson	.30	.09
655 Matt Williams	.30	.09
656 Jeff King	.30	.09
657 Luis Alicea	.30	.09
658 Brian Moehler RC	.30	.09
659 Ariel Prieto	.30	.09
660 Kevin Elster	.30	.09
661 Mark Hutton	.30	.09
662 Aaron Sele	.30	.09
663 Graeme Lloyd	.30	.09
664 John Burke	.30	.09
665 Mel Rojas	.30	.09
666 Sid Fernandez	.30	.09
667 Pedro Astacio	.30	.09
668 Jeff Abbott	.30	.09
669 Darren Daulton	.30	.09
670 Mike Bordick	.30	.09
671 Sterling Hitchcock	.30	.09
672 Damion Easley	.30	.09
673 Armando Reynoso	.30	.09
674 Pat Cline	.30	.09
675 Orlando Cabrera RC	.75	.23
676 Alan Embree	.30	.09
677 Brian Bevil	.30	.09
678 David Weathers	.30	.09
679 Cliff Floyd	.30	.09
680 Joe Randa	.30	.09
681 Bill Haselman	.30	.09
682 Jeff Fassero	.30	.09
683 Matt Morris	.30	.09
684 Mark Portugal	.30	.09
685 Lee Smith	.30	.09
686 Pokey Reese	.30	.09
687 Benito Santiago	.30	.09
688 Brian Johnson	.30	.09
689 Brent Brede RC	.30	.09
690 S.Hasegawa RC	.50	.15
691 Julio Santana	.30	.09
692 Steve Kline	.30	.09
693 Julian Tavarez	.30	.09
694 John Hudek	.30	.09
695 Manny Alexander	.30	.09
696 Roberto Alomar ENC	.30	.09
697 Jeff Bagwell ENC	.30	.09
698 Barry Bonds ENC	1.00	.30
699 Ken Caminiti ENC	.30	.09
700 Juan Gonzalez ENC	.30	.09
701 Ken Griffey Jr. ENC	.75	.23
702 Tony Gwynn ENC	.50	.15
703 Derek Jeter ENC	1.00	.30
704 Andruw Jones ENC	.50	.15
705 Chipper Jones ENC	.50	.15
706 Barry Larkin ENC	.30	.09
707 Greg Maddux ENC	.75	.23
708 Mark McGwire ENC	1.00	.30
709 Paul Molitor ENC	.30	.09
710 Hideo Nomo ENC	.30	.09
711 Andy Pettitte ENC	.30	.09
712 Mike Piazza ENC	.75	.23
713 Manny Ramirez ENC	.50	.15
714 Cal Ripken ENC	1.25	.35
715 Alex Rodriguez ENC	.75	.23
716 Ryne Sandberg ENC	.75	.23
717 John Smoltz ENC	.30	.09
718 Frank Thomas ENC	.50	.15
719 Mo Vaughn ENC	.30	.09
720 Bernie Williams ENC	.30	.09
721 Tim Salmon CL	.30	.09
722 Greg Maddux CL	.75	.23
723 Cal Ripken CL	1.25	.35
724 Mo Vaughn CL	.30	.09
725 Ryne Sandberg CL	.75	.23
726 Frank Thomas CL	.50	.15
727 Barry Larkin CL	.30	.09
728 Manny Ramirez CL	.30	.09
729 Andres Galarraga CL	.30	.09
730 Tony Clark CL	.30	.09
731 Gary Sheffield CL	.30	.09
732 Jeff Bagwell CL	.30	.09
733 Kevin Appier CL	.30	.09
734 Mike Piazza CL	.75	.23
735 Jeff Cirillo CL	.30	.09
736 Paul Molitor CL	.30	.09
737 Henry Rodriguez CL	.30	.09
738 Todd Hundley CL	.30	.09
739 Derek Jeter CL	1.00	.30
740 Mark McGwire CL	1.00	.30
741 Curt Schilling CL	.30	.09
742 Jason Kendall CL	.30	.09
743 Tony Gwynn CL	.50	.15
744 Barry Bonds CL	1.00	.30
745 Ken Griffey Jr. CL	.75	.23
746 Brian Jordan CL	.30	.09
747 Juan Gonzalez CL	.30	.09
748 Joe Carter CL	.30	.09
749 Ariz. Diamondbacks CL Inserts	.30	.09
750 Tampa Bay Devil Rays CL Inserts	.30	.09
751 Hideki Irabu RC	.75	.23
752 Jeremi Gonzalez RC	.50	.15
753 Mario Valdez RC	.50	.15
754 Aaron Boone	.75	.23
755 Brett Tomko	.50	.15
756 Jaret Wright RC	1.25	.35
757 Ryan McGuire	.50	.15
758 Jason McDonald	.50	.15
759 Adrian Brown RC	.50	.15
760 Keith Foulke RC	2.00	.60
761 Bonus Checklist	.50	.15
P489 M.Williams Promo	1.00	.30
NNO Andruw Jones Circa AU/200	25.00	7.50

1998 Fleer Tradition Update

	Nm-Mt	Ex-Mt
COMP.FACT.SET (100)	15.00	4.50
U1 Mark McGwire HL	1.25	.35
U2 Sammy Sosa HL	.30	.09
U3 Roger Clemens HL	1.00	.30
U4 Barry Bonds HL	1.50	.45
U5 Kerry Wood HL	.30	.09
U6 Paul Molitor HL	.30	.09
U7 Ken Griffey Jr. HL	.75	.23
U8 Cal Ripken HL	1.50	.45
U9 David Wells HL	.20	.06
U10 Alex Rodriguez HL	.75	.23
U11 Angel Pena RC	.40	.12
U12 Bruce Chen	.20	.06
U13 Craig Wilson	.20	.06
U14 O.Hernandez RC	1.50	.45
U15 Aramis Ramirez	.20	.06
U16 Aaron Boone	.20	.06
U17 Bob Henley	.20	.06
U18 Juan Guzman	.20	.06
U19 Darryl Hamilton	.20	.06
U20 Jay Payton	.20	.06
U21 Jeremy Powell	.20	.06
U22 Ben Davis	.20	.06
U23 Preston Wilson	.20	.06
U24 Jim Parque RC	.60	.18
U25 Odalis Perez RC	1.50	.45
U26 Ronnie Belliard	.20	.06
U27 Royce Clayton	.20	.06
U28 George Lombard	.20	.06
U29 Tony Phillips	.20	.06
U30 F.Seguignol RC	.40	.12
U31 Armando Rios RC	.60	.18
U32 Jerry Hairston Jr. RC	1.00	.30
U33 Justin Baughman RC	.40	.12

- ❑ U34 Seth Greisinger .20 .06
- ❑ U35 Alex Gonzalez .20 .06
- ❑ U36 Michael Barrett .20 .06
- ❑ U37 Carlos Beltran 1.00 .30
- ❑ U38 Ellis Burks .20 .06
- ❑ U39 Jose Jimenez RC 1.00 .30
- ❑ U40 Carlos Guillen .20 .06
- ❑ U41 Marlon Anderson .20 .06
- ❑ U42 Scott Elarton .20 .06
- ❑ U43 Glenallen Hill .20 .06
- ❑ U44 Shane Monahan .20 .06
- ❑ U45 Dennis Martinez .20 .06
- ❑ U46 Carlos Febles RC .60 .18
- ❑ U47 Carlos Perez .20 .06
- ❑ U48 Wilton Guerrero .20 .06
- ❑ U49 Randy Johnson .50 .15
- ❑ U50 Brian Simmons RC .40 .12
- ❑ U51 Carlton Loewer .20 .06
- ❑ U52 Mark DeRosa RC .60 .18
- ❑ U53 Tim Young RC .40 .12
- ❑ U54 Gary Gaetti .20 .06
- ❑ U55 Eric Chavez .20 .06
- ❑ U56 Carl Pavano .20 .06
- ❑ U57 Mike Stanley .20 .06
- ❑ U58 Todd Stottlemyre .20 .06
- ❑ U59 Gabe Kapler RC 1.00 .30
- ❑ U60 Mike Jerzembeck RC .40 .12
- ❑ U61 Mitch Meluskey RC .60 .18
- ❑ U62 Bill Pulsipher .20 .06
- ❑ U63 Derrick Gibson .20 .06
- ❑ U64 John Rocker RC 1.00 .30
- ❑ U65 Calvin Pickering .20 .06
- ❑ U66 Blake Stein .20 .06
- ❑ U67 Fernando Tatis .20 .06
- ❑ U68 Gabe Alvarez .20 .06
- ❑ U69 Jeffrey Hammonds .20 .06
- ❑ U70 Adrian Beltre .20 .06
- ❑ U71 Ryan Bradley RC .40 .12
- ❑ U72 Edgard Clemente .20 .06
- ❑ U73 Rick Croushore RC .40 .12
- ❑ U74 Matt Clement .20 .06
- ❑ U75 Dermal Brown .20 .06
- ❑ U76 Paul Bako .20 .06
- ❑ U77 Placido Polanco RC .60 .18
- ❑ U78 Jay Tessmer .20 .06
- ❑ U79 Jarrod Washburn .20 .06
- ❑ U80 Kevin Witt .20 .06
- ❑ U81 Mike Metcalfe .20 .06
- ❑ U82 Daryle Ward .20 .06
- ❑ U83 Benj Sampson RC .40 .12
- ❑ U84 Mike Kinkade RC .40 .12
- ❑ U85 Randy Winn .20 .06
- ❑ U86 Jeff Shaw .20 .06
- ❑ U87 Troy Glaus RC 4.00 1.20
- ❑ U88 Hideo Nomo .50 .15
- ❑ U89 Mark Grudzielanek .20 .06
- ❑ U90 Mike Frank RC .40 .12
- ❑ U91 Bobby Howry RC .60 .18
- ❑ U92 Ryan Minor RC .40 .12
- ❑ U93 Corey Koskie RC 1.00 .30
- ❑ U94 Matt Anderson RC .60 .18
- ❑ U95 Joe Carter .20 .06
- ❑ U96 Paul Konerko .20 .06
- ❑ U97 Sidney Ponson .20 .06
- ❑ U98 Jeremy Giambi RC .60 .18
- ❑ U99 Jeff Kubenka RC .40 .12
- ❑ U100 J.D. Drew RC 2.00 .60

1999 Fleer Tradition Update

	Nm-Mt	Ex-Mt
COMP.FACT.SET (150)	25.00	7.50

- ❑ U1 Rick Ankiel RC .75 .23
- ❑ U2 Peter Bergeron RC .40 .12
- ❑ U3 Pat Burrell RC 2.00 .60
- ❑ U4 Eric Munson RC .75 .23
- ❑ U5 Alfonso Soriano RC 5.00 1.50
- ❑ U6 Tim Hudson RC 2.00 .60
- ❑ U7 Erubiel Durazo RC .75 .23
- ❑ U8 Chad Hermansen .20 .06
- ❑ U9 Jeff Zimmerman RC .25 .07
- ❑ U10 Jesus Pena RC .25 .07
- ❑ U11 Ramon Hernandez .25 .07
- ❑ U12 Trent Durrington RC .25 .07

- ❑ U13 Tony Armas Jr. .20 .06
- ❑ U14 Mike Fyhrie RC .25 .07
- ❑ U15 Danny Kolb RC .75 .23
- ❑ U16 Mike Porzio RC .25 .07
- ❑ U17 Will Brunson RC .25 .07
- ❑ U18 Mike Duvall RC .25 .07
- ❑ U19 D.Mientkiewicz RC .75 .23
- ❑ U20 Gabe Molina RC .25 .07
- ❑ U21 Luis Vizcaino RC .25 .07
- ❑ U22 Robinson Cancel RC .25 .07
- ❑ U23 Brett Laxton RC .25 .07
- ❑ U24 Joe McEwing RC .25 .07
- ❑ U25 Justin Speier RC .25 .07
- ❑ U26 Kip Wells RC .75 .23
- ❑ U27 Armando Almanza RC .25 .07
- ❑ U28 Joe Davenport RC .25 .07
- ❑ U29 Yamid Haad RC .25 .07
- ❑ U30 John Halama .20 .06
- ❑ U31 Adam Kennedy .20 .06
- ❑ U32 Micah Bowie RC .25 .07
- ❑ U33 Gookie Dawkins RC .40 .12
- ❑ U34 Ryan Rupe RC .25 .07
- ❑ U35 B.J. Ryan RC 1.00 .30
- ❑ U36 Chance Sanford RC .25 .07
- ❑ U37 A.Shumaker RC .25 .07
- ❑ U38 Ryan Glynn RC .25 .07
- ❑ U39 Roosevelt Brown RC .25 .07
- ❑ U40 Ben Molina RC .75 .23
- ❑ U41 Scott Williamson .20 .06
- ❑ U42 Eric Gagne RC 5.00 1.50
- ❑ U43 John McDonald RC .40 .12
- ❑ U44 Scott Sauerbeck RC .25 .07
- ❑ U45 Mike Venafro RC .25 .07
- ❑ U46 Edwards Guzman RC .25 .07
- ❑ U47 Richard Barker RC .25 .07
- ❑ U48 Braden Looper .20 .06
- ❑ U49 Chad Meyers RC .25 .07
- ❑ U50 Scott Strickland RC .25 .07
- ❑ U51 Billy Koch .20 .06
- ❑ U52 David Newhan RC .40 .12
- ❑ U53 David Riske RC .25 .07
- ❑ U54 Jose Santiago RC .25 .07
- ❑ U55 Miguel Del Toro RC .25 .07
- ❑ U56 Orber Moreno RC .25 .07
- ❑ U57 Dave Roberts RC .75 .23
- ❑ U58 Tim Byrdak RC .25 .07
- ❑ U59 David Lee RC .25 .07
- ❑ U60 Guillermo Mota RC .25 .07
- ❑ U61 Wilton Veras RC .25 .07
- ❑ U62 Joe Mays RC .40 .12
- ❑ U63 Jose Fernandez RC .25 .07
- ❑ U64 Ray King RC .25 .07
- ❑ U65 Chris Petersen RC .25 .07
- ❑ U66 Vernon Wells .20 .06
- ❑ U67 Ruben Mateo .20 .06
- ❑ U68 Ben Petrick .20 .06
- ❑ U69 Chris Tremie RC .25 .07
- ❑ U70 Lance Berkman .20 .06
- ❑ U71 Dan Smith RC .25 .07
- ❑ U72 Carlos E. Hernandez RC .40 .12
- ❑ U73 Chad Harville RC .25 .07
- ❑ U74 Damaso Marte RC .25 .07
- ❑ U75 Aaron Myette RC .25 .07
- ❑ U76 Willis Roberts RC .25 .07
- ❑ U77 Erik Sabel RC .25 .07
- ❑ U78 Hector Almonte RC .25 .07
- ❑ U79 Kris Benson .20 .06
- ❑ U80 Pat Daneker RC .25 .07
- ❑ U81 Freddy Garcia RC 1.00 .30
- ❑ U82 Byung-Hyun Kim RC 1.00 .30
- ❑ U83 Wily Pena RC 2.00 .60
- ❑ U84 Dan Wheeler RC .40 .12
- ❑ U85 Tim Harikkala RC .25 .07
- ❑ U86 Derrin Ebert RC .25 .07
- ❑ U87 Horacio Estrada RC .25 .07
- ❑ U88 Liu Rodriguez RC .25 .07
- ❑ U89 J.Zimmerman RC .25 .07
- ❑ U90 A.J. Burnett RC 1.25 .35
- ❑ U91 Doug Davis RC 1.00 .30
- ❑ U92 Rob Ramsay RC .25 .07
- ❑ U93 Clay Bellinger RC .25 .07
- ❑ U94 Charlie Greene RC .25 .07
- ❑ U95 Bo Porter RC .25 .07
- ❑ U96 Jorge Toca RC .40 .12
- ❑ U97 Casey Blake RC .75 .23
- ❑ U98 Amaury Garcia RC .25 .07
- ❑ U99 Jose Molina RC .25 .07
- ❑ U100 Melvin Mora RC 3.00 .90
- ❑ U101 Joe Nathan RC 1.00 .30
- ❑ U102 Juan Pena RC .25 .07
- ❑ U103 Dave Borkowski RC .25 .07
- ❑ U104 Eddie Gaillard RC .25 .07
- ❑ U105 Glen Barker RC .25 .07
- ❑ U106 Brett Hinchliffe RC .25 .07
- ❑ U107 Carlos Lee .20 .06
- ❑ U108 Rob Ryan RC .25 .07
- ❑ U109 Jeff Weaver RC .75 .23
- ❑ U110 Ed Yarnall .20 .06
- ❑ U111 Nelson Cruz RC .25 .07
- ❑ U112 C.Davidson RC .25 .07
- ❑ U113 Tim Kubinski RC .25 .07
- ❑ U114 Sean Spencer RC .25 .07
- ❑ U115 Joe Winkelsas RC .25 .07
- ❑ U116 Mike Colangelo RC .25 .07
- ❑ U117 Tom Davey RC .25 .07
- ❑ U118 Warren Morris .20 .06
- ❑ U119 Dan Murray RC .25 .07
- ❑ U120 Jose Nieves RC .25 .07
- ❑ U121 Mark Quinn RC .40 .12
- ❑ U122 Josh Beckett RC 10.00 3.00
- ❑ U123 Chad Allen RC .25 .07
- ❑ U124 Mike Figga .25 .07
- ❑ U125 Beiker Graterol RC .25 .07
- ❑ U126 Aaron Scheffer RC .25 .07
- ❑ U127 Wiki Gonzalez RC .40 .12
- ❑ U128 Ramon E.Martinez RC .25 .07
- ❑ U129 Matt Riley RC .40 .12
- ❑ U130 Chris Woodward RC .25 .07
- ❑ U131 Albert Belle .20 .06
- ❑ U132 Roger Cedeno .20 .06
- ❑ U133 Roger Clemens 1.00 .30
- ❑ U134 Brian Giles .20 .06
- ❑ U135 Rickey Henderson .50 .15
- ❑ U136 Randy Johnson .50 .15
- ❑ U137 Brian Jordan .20 .06
- ❑ U138 Paul Konerko .20 .06
- ❑ U139 Hideo Nomo .50 .15
- ❑ U140 Kenny Rogers .20 .06
- ❑ U141 Wade Boggs HL .30 .09
- ❑ U142 Jose Canseco HL .20 .06
- ❑ U143 Roger Clemens HL 1.00 .30
- ❑ U144 David Cone HL .20 .06
- ❑ U145 Tony Gwynn HL .60 .18
- ❑ U146 Mark McGwire HL 1.25 .35
- ❑ U147 Cal Ripken HL 1.50 .45
- ❑ U148 Alex Rodriguez HL .75 .23
- ❑ U149 Fernando Tatis HL .20 .06
- ❑ U150 Robin Ventura HL .20 .06

2000 Fleer Tradition Update

	Nm-Mt	Ex-Mt
COMP.FACT.SET (149)	25.00	7.50

- ❑ 1 Ken Griffey Jr. SH .75 .23
- ❑ 2 Cal Ripken SH 1.00 .30
- ❑ 3 Randy Velarde SH .30 .09
- ❑ 4 Fred McGriff SH .30 .09
- ❑ 5 Derek Jeter SH .75 .23
- ❑ 6 Tom Glavine SH .30 .09
- ❑ 7 Brent Mayne SH .30 .09
- ❑ 8 Alex Ochoa SH .30 .09
- ❑ 9 Scott Sheldon SH .30 .09

❑ 10 Randy Johnson SH .50 .15
❑ 11 Daniel Garibay RC .30 .09
❑ 12 Brad Fullmer .30 .09
❑ 13 Kazuhiro Sasaki RC .60 .18
❑ 14 Andy Tracy RC .30 .09
❑ 15 Bret Boone .30 .09
❑ 16 Chad Durbin RC .40 .12
❑ 17 Mark Buehrle RC 2.00 .60
❑ 18 Julio Zuleta RC .30 .09
❑ 19 Jeremy Giambi .30 .09
❑ 20 Gene Stechschulte RC .30 .09
❑ 21 Lou Pote .30 .09
Bengie Molina
❑ 22 Darrell Einertson RC .30 .09
❑ 23 Ken Griffey Jr. 1.25 .35
❑ 24 Jeff Sparks RC .30 .09
Dan Wheeler
❑ 25 Aaron Fultz RC .30 .09
❑ 26 Derek Bell .30 .09
❑ 27 Rob Bell .30 .09
D.T. Cromer
❑ 28 Robert Fick .30 .09
❑ 29 Darryl Kile .30 .09
❑ 30 Clayton Andrews .30 .09
John Bale RC
❑ 31 Dave Veres .30 .09
❑ 32 Hector Mercado RC .30 .09
❑ 33 Willie Morales RC .30 .09
❑ 34 Kelly Wunsch .30 .09
Kip Wells
❑ 35 Hideki Irabu .30 .09
❑ 36 Sean DePaula RC .30 .09
❑ 37 DeWayne Wise .30 .09
Chris Woodward
❑ 38 Curt Schilling .30 .09
❑ 39 Mark Johnson .30 .09
❑ 40 Mike Cameron .30 .09
❑ 41 Scott Sheldon .30 .09
Tom Evans
❑ 42 Brett Tomko .30 .09
❑ 43 Johan Santana RC 10.00 3.00
❑ 44 Andy Benes .30 .09
❑ 45 Matt LeCroy .30 .09
Mark Redman
❑ 46 Ryan Klesko .30 .09
❑ 47 Andy Ashby .30 .09
❑ 48 Octavio Dotel .30 .09
❑ 49 Eric Byrnes RC .60 .18
❑ 50 Does Not Exist .00
❑ 51 Kenny Rogers .30 .09
❑ 52 Ben Weber RC .40 .12
❑ 53 Matt Blank .30 .09
Scott Strickland
❑ 54 Tom Goodwin .30 .09
❑ 55 Jim Edmonds Cards .50 .15
❑ 56 Derrick Turnbow RC .60 .18
❑ 57 Mark Mulder .30 .09
❑ 58 Tarrick Brock .30 .09
Ruben Quevedo
❑ 59 Danny Young RC .30 .09
❑ 60 Fernando Vina .30 .09
❑ 61 Justin Brunette RC .30 .09
❑ 62 Jimmy Anderson .30 .09
❑ 63 Reggie Sanders .30 .09
❑ 64 Adam Kennedy .30 .09
❑ 65 Jesse Garcia .30 .09
B.J. Ryan
❑ 66 Al Martin .30 .09
❑ 67 Kevin Walker RC .30 .09
❑ 68 Brad Penny .30 .09
❑ 69 B.J. Surhoff .30 .09
❑ 70 Geoff Blum .30 .09
Trace Coquillette RC
❑ 71 Jose Jimenez .30 .09
❑ 72 Chuck Finley .30 .09
❑ 73 Valerio De Los Santos .30 .09
Everett Stull
❑ 74 Terry Adams .30 .09
❑ 75 Rafael Furcal .30 .09
❑ 76 John Roskos .30 .09
Mike Darr
❑ 77 Quilvio Veras .30 .09
❑ 78 Armando Almanza .30 .09
Nate Rolison
❑ 79 Greg Vaughn .30 .09
❑ 80 Keith McDonald RC .30 .09
❑ 81 Eric Cammack RC .30 .09
❑ 82 Horacio Estrada .30 .09
Ray King
❑ 83 Kory DeHaan .30 .09
❑ 84 Kevin Hodges RC .30 .09
❑ 85 Mike Lamb RC .60 .18
❑ 86 Shawn Green .30 .09
❑ 87 Dan Reichert .30 .09
Jason Rakers
❑ 88 Adam Piatt .30 .09
❑ 89 Mike Garcia .30 .09
❑ 90 Rodrigo Lopez RC .60 .18
❑ 91 John Olerud .30 .09
❑ 92 Barry Zito RC 2.50 .75
Terrence Long
❑ 93 Jimmy Rollins .30 .09
❑ 94 Denny Neagle .30 .09
❑ 95 Rickey Henderson .75 .23
❑ 96 Adam Eaton .30 .09
Buddy Carlyle
❑ 97 Brian O'Connor RC .30 .09
❑ 98 Andy Thompson RC .30 .09
❑ 99 Jason Boyd RC .30 .09
❑ 100 Joel Pineiro RC 1.00 .30
Carlos Guillen
❑ 101 Raul Gonzalez RC .30 .09
❑ 102 Brandon Kolb RC .30 .09
❑ 103 Jason Maxwell .30 .09
Mike Lincoln
❑ 104 Luis Matos RC .40 .12
❑ 105 Morgan Burkhart RC .30 .09
❑ 106 Ismael Villegas RC .30 .09
Steve Sisco RC
❑ 107 David Justice Yankees .30 .09
❑ 108 Pablo Ozuna .30 .09
❑ 109 Jose Canseco .50 .15
❑ 110 Alex Cora .30 .09
Shawn Gilbert
❑ 111 Will Clark Cardinals .50 .15
❑ 112 Keith Luuloa .30 .09
Eric Weaver
❑ 113 Bruce Chen .30 .09
❑ 114 Adam Hyzdu .30 .09
❑ 115 Scott Forster RC .30 .09
Yovanny Lara RC
❑ 116 Allen McDill RC .30 .09
Jose Macias
❑ 117 Kevin Nicholson .30 .09
❑ 118 Israel Alcantara .30 .09
Tim Young
❑ 119 Juan Alvarez RC .30 .09
❑ 120 Julio Lugo .30 .09
Mitch Meluskey
❑ 121 B.J. Waszgis RC .30 .09
❑ 122 Jeff M. D'Amico RC .30 .09
Brett Laxton
❑ 123 Ricky Ledee .30 .09
❑ 124 Mark DeRosa .30 .09
Jason Marquis
❑ 125 Alex Cabrera RC .40 .12
❑ 126 Augie Ojeda RC .30 .09
Gary Matthews Jr.
❑ 127 Richie Sexson .30 .09
❑ 128 Santiago Perez RC .30 .09
Hector Ramirez RC
❑ 129 Rondell White .30 .09
❑ 130 Craig House RC .30 .09
❑ 131 Kevin Beirne .30 .09
Jon Garland
❑ 132 Wayne Franklin RC .30 .09
❑ 133 Henry Rodriguez .30 .09
❑ 134 Jay Payton .30 .09
Jim Mann
❑ 135 Ron Gant .30 .09
❑ 136 Paxton Crawford RC .30 .09
Sang-Hoon Lee RC
❑ 137 Kent Bottenfield .30 .09
❑ 138 Rocky Biddle RC .30 .09
❑ 139 Travis Lee .30 .09
❑ 140 Ryan Vogelsong RC .40 .12
❑ 141 Jason Conti .30 .09
Geraldo Guzman RC
❑ 142 Tim Drew .30 .09
Mark Watson RC
❑ 143 John Parrish RC .30 .09
Chris Richard RC
❑ 144 Javier Cardona RC .30 .09
Brandon Villafuerte RC
❑ 145 Tike Redman RC .60 .18
Steve Sparks RC
❑ 146 Brian Schneider .40 .12
Matt Skrmetta RC
❑ 147 Pasqual Coco RC .30 .09
❑ 148 Lorenzo Barcelo RC 1.00 .30
Joe Crede
❑ 149 Jace Brewer RC .30 .09
❑ 150 Milton Bradley .40 .12
Tomas De La Rosa RC
❑ MP1 Mickey Mantle Pants 200.00 60.00

2001 Fleer Tradition

	Nm-Mt	Ex-Mt
COMP.FACT.SET (485)	100.00	30.00
COMPLETE SET (450)	50.00	15.00
COMMON CARD (1-450)	.30	.09
COMMON (451-485)	.50	.15

❑ 1 Andres Galarraga .30 .09
❑ 2 Armando Rios .30 .09
❑ 3 Julio Lugo .30 .09
❑ 4 Darryl Hamilton .30 .09
❑ 5 Dave Veres .30 .09
❑ 6 Edgardo Alfonzo .30 .09
❑ 7 Brook Fordyce .30 .09
❑ 8 Eric Karros .30 .09
❑ 9 Neifi Perez .30 .09
❑ 10 Jim Edmonds .50 .15
❑ 11 Barry Larkin .50 .15
❑ 12 Trot Nixon .30 .09
❑ 13 Andy Pettitte .50 .15
❑ 14 Jose Guillen .30 .09
❑ 15 David Wells .30 .09
❑ 16 Magglio Ordonez .30 .09
❑ 17 David Segui .30 .09
❑ 17A David Segui ERR .30 .09
Card has no number on the back
❑ 18 Juan Encarnacion .30 .09
❑ 19 Robert Person .30 .09
❑ 20 Quilvio Veras .30 .09
❑ 21 Mo Vaughn .30 .09
❑ 22 B.J. Surhoff .30 .09
❑ 23 Ken Caminiti .30 .09
❑ 24 Frank Catalanotto .30 .09
❑ 25 Luis Gonzalez .30 .09
❑ 26 Pete Harnisch .30 .09
❑ 27 Alex Gonzalez .30 .09

No.	Player		
❑ 28	Mark Quinn	.30	.09
❑ 29	Luis Castillo	.30	.09
❑ 30	Rick Helling	.30	.09
❑ 31	Barry Bonds	2.00	.60
❑ 32	Warren Morris	.30	.09
❑ 33	Aaron Boone	.30	.09
❑ 34	Ricky Gutierrez	.30	.09
❑ 35	Preston Wilson	.30	.09
❑ 36	Erubiel Durazo	.30	.09
❑ 37	Jermaine Dye	.30	.09
❑ 38	John Rocker	.30	.09
❑ 39	Mark Grudzielanek	.30	.09
❑ 40	Pedro Martinez	.50	.15
❑ 41	Phil Nevin	.30	.09
❑ 42	Luis Matos	.30	.09
❑ 43	Orlando Hernandez	.30	.09
❑ 44	Steve Cox	.30	.09
❑ 45	James Baldwin	.30	.09
❑ 46	Rafael Furcal	.30	.09
❑ 47	Todd Zeile	.30	.09
❑ 48	Elmer Dessens	.30	.09
❑ 49	Russell Branyan	.30	.09
❑ 50	Juan Gonzalez	.30	.09
❑ 51	Mac Suzuki	.30	.09
❑ 52	Adam Kennedy	.30	.09
❑ 53	Randy Velarde	.30	.09
❑ 54	David Bell	.30	.09
❑ 55	Royce Clayton	.30	.09
❑ 56	Greg Colbrunn	.30	.09
❑ 57	Rey Ordonez	.30	.09
❑ 58	Kevin Millwood	.30	.09
❑ 59	Fernando Vina	.30	.09
❑ 60	Eddie Taubensee	.30	.09
❑ 61	Enrique Wilson	.30	.09
❑ 62	Jay Bell	.30	.09
❑ 63	Brian Moehler	.30	.09
❑ 64	Brad Fullmer	.30	.09
❑ 65	Ben Petrick	.30	.09
❑ 66	Orlando Cabrera	.30	.09
❑ 67	Shane Reynolds	.30	.09
❑ 68	Mitch Meluskey	.30	.09
❑ 69	Jeff Shaw	.30	.09
❑ 70	Chipper Jones	.75	.23
❑ 71	Tomo Ohka	.30	.09
❑ 72	Ruben Rivera	.30	.09
❑ 73	Mike Sirotka	.30	.09
❑ 74	Scott Rolen	.50	.15
❑ 75	Glendon Rusch	.30	.09
❑ 76	Miguel Tejada	.30	.09
❑ 77	Brady Anderson	.30	.09
❑ 78	Bartolo Colon	.30	.09
❑ 79	Ron Coomer	.30	.09
❑ 80	Gary DiSarcina	.30	.09
❑ 81	Geoff Jenkins	.30	.09
❑ 82	Billy Koch	.30	.09
❑ 83	Mike Lamb	.30	.09
❑ 84	Alex Rodriguez	1.25	.35
❑ 85	Denny Neagle	.30	.09
❑ 86	Michael Tucker	.30	.09
❑ 87	Edgar Renteria	.30	.09
❑ 88	Brian Anderson	.30	.09
❑ 89	Glenallen Hill	.30	.09
❑ 90	Aramis Ramirez	.30	.09
❑ 91	Rondell White	.30	.09
❑ 92	Tony Womack	.30	.09
❑ 93	Jeffrey Hammonds	.30	.09
❑ 94	Freddy Garcia	.30	.09
❑ 95	Bill Mueller	.30	.09
❑ 96	Mike Lieberthal	.30	.09
❑ 97	Michael Barrett	.30	.09
❑ 98	Derrek Lee	.50	.15
❑ 99	Bill Spiers	.30	.09
❑ 100	Derek Lowe	.30	.09
❑ 101	Javy Lopez	.30	.09
❑ 102	Adrian Beltre	.30	.09
❑ 103	Jim Parque	.30	.09
❑ 104	Marquis Grissom	.30	.09
❑ 105	Eric Chavez	.30	.09
❑ 106	Todd Jones	.30	.09
❑ 107	Eric Owens	.30	.09
❑ 108	Roger Clemens	1.50	.45
❑ 109	Denny Hocking	.30	.09
❑ 110	Roberto Hernandez	.30	.09
❑ 111	Albert Belle	.30	.09
❑ 112	Troy Glaus	.30	.09
❑ 113	Ivan Rodriguez	.50	.15
❑ 114	Carlos Guillen	.30	.09
❑ 115	Chuck Finley	.30	.09
❑ 116	Dmitri Young	.30	.09
❑ 117	Paul Konerko	.30	.09
❑ 118	Damon Buford	.30	.09
❑ 119	Fernando Tatis	.30	.09
❑ 120	Larry Walker	.30	.09
❑ 121	Jason Kendall	.30	.09
❑ 122	Matt Williams	.30	.09
❑ 123	Henry Rodriguez	.30	.09
❑ 124	Placido Polanco	.30	.09
❑ 125	Bobby Estalella	.30	.09
❑ 126	Pat Burrell	.30	.09
❑ 127	Mark Loretta	.30	.09
❑ 128	Moises Alou	.30	.09
❑ 129	Tino Martinez	.50	.15
❑ 130	Milton Bradley	.30	.09
❑ 131	Todd Hundley	.30	.09
❑ 132	Keith Foulke	.30	.09
❑ 133	Robert Fick	.30	.09
❑ 134	Cristian Guzman	.30	.09
❑ 135	Rusty Greer	.30	.09
❑ 136	John Olerud	.30	.09
❑ 137	Mariano Rivera	.50	.15
❑ 138	Jeromy Burnitz	.30	.09
❑ 139	Dave Burba	.30	.09
❑ 140	Ken Griffey Jr.	1.25	.35
❑ 141	Tony Gwynn	1.00	.30
❑ 142	Carlos Delgado	.30	.09
❑ 143	Edgar Martinez	.50	.15
❑ 144	Ramon Hernandez	.30	.09
❑ 145	Pedro Astacio	.30	.09
❑ 146	Ray Lankford	.30	.09
❑ 147	Mike Mussina	.50	.15
❑ 148	Ray Durham	.30	.09
❑ 149	Lee Stevens	.30	.09
❑ 150	Jay Canizaro	.30	.09
❑ 151	Adrian Brown	.30	.09
❑ 152	Mike Piazza	1.25	.35
❑ 153	Cliff Floyd	.30	.09
❑ 154	Jose Vidro	.30	.09
❑ 155	Jason Giambi	.30	.09
❑ 156	Andruw Jones	.50	.15
❑ 157	Robin Ventura	.30	.09
❑ 158	Gary Sheffield	.30	.09
❑ 159	Jeff D'Amico	.30	.09
❑ 160	Chuck Knoblauch	.30	.09
❑ 161	Roger Cedeno	.30	.09
❑ 162	Jim Thome	.50	.15
❑ 163	Peter Bergeron	.30	.09
❑ 164	Kerry Wood	.30	.09
❑ 165	Gabe Kapler	.30	.09
❑ 166	Corey Koskie	.30	.09
❑ 167	Doug Glanville	.30	.09
❑ 168	Brent Mayne	.30	.09
❑ 169	Scott Spiezio	.30	.09
❑ 170	Steve Karsay	.30	.09
❑ 171	Al Martin	.30	.09
❑ 172	Fred McGriff	.50	.15
❑ 173	Gabe White	.30	.09
❑ 174	Alex Gonzalez	.30	.09
❑ 175	Mike Darr	.30	.09
❑ 176	Bengie Molina	.30	.09
❑ 177	Ben Grieve	.30	.09
❑ 178	Marlon Anderson	.30	.09
❑ 179	Brian Giles	.30	.09
❑ 180	Jose Valentin	.30	.09
❑ 181	Brian Jordan	.30	.09
❑ 182	Randy Johnson	.75	.23
❑ 183	Ricky Ledee	.30	.09
❑ 184	Russ Ortiz	.30	.09
❑ 185	Mike Lowell	.30	.09
❑ 186	Curtis Leskanic	.30	.09
❑ 187	Bob Abreu	.30	.09
❑ 188	Derek Jeter	2.00	.60
❑ 189	Lance Berkman	.30	.09
❑ 190	Roberto Alomar	.50	.15
❑ 191	Darin Erstad	.30	.09
❑ 192	Richie Sexson	.30	.09
❑ 193	Alex Ochoa	.30	.09
❑ 194	Carlos Febles	.30	.09
❑ 195	David Ortiz	.50	.15
❑ 196	Shawn Green	.30	.09
❑ 197	Mike Sweeney	.30	.09
❑ 198	Vladimir Guerrero	.75	.23
❑ 199	Jose Jimenez	.30	.09
❑ 200	Travis Lee	.30	.09
❑ 201	Rickey Henderson	.75	.23
❑ 202	Bob Wickman	.30	.09
❑ 203	Miguel Cairo	.30	.09
❑ 204	Steve Finley	.30	.09
❑ 205	Tony Batista	.30	.09
❑ 206	Jamey Wright	.30	.09
❑ 207	Terrence Long	.30	.09
❑ 208	Trevor Hoffman	.30	.09
❑ 209	John VanderWal	.30	.09
❑ 210	Greg Maddux	1.25	.35
❑ 211	Tim Salmon	.50	.15
❑ 212	Herbert Perry	.30	.09
❑ 213	Marvin Benard	.30	.09
❑ 214	Jose Offerman	.30	.09
❑ 215	Jay Payton	.30	.09
❑ 216	Jon Lieber	.30	.09
❑ 217	Mark Kotsay	.30	.09
❑ 218	Scott Brosius	.30	.09
❑ 219	Scott Williamson	.30	.09
❑ 220	Omar Vizquel	.50	.15
❑ 221	Mike Hampton	.30	.09
❑ 222	Richard Hidalgo	.30	.09
❑ 223	Rey Sanchez	.30	.09
❑ 224	Matt Lawton	.30	.09
❑ 225	Bruce Chen	.30	.09
❑ 226	Ryan Klesko	.30	.09
❑ 227	Garret Anderson	.30	.09
❑ 228	Kevin Brown	.30	.09
❑ 229	Mike Cameron	.30	.09
❑ 230	Tony Clark	.30	.09
❑ 231	Curt Schilling	.30	.09
❑ 232	Vinny Castilla	.30	.09
❑ 233	Carl Pavano	.30	.09
❑ 234	Eric Davis	.30	.09
❑ 235	Darrin Fletcher	.30	.09
❑ 236	Matt Stairs	.30	.09
❑ 237	Octavio Dotel	.30	.09
❑ 238	Mark Grace	.50	.15
❑ 239	John Smoltz	.50	.15
❑ 240	Matt Clement	.30	.09
❑ 241	Ellis Burks	.30	.09
❑ 242	Charles Johnson	.30	.09
❑ 243	Jeff Bagwell	.50	.15
❑ 244	Derek Bell	.30	.09
❑ 245	Nomar Garciaparra	1.25	.35
❑ 246	Jorge Posada	.50	.15
❑ 247	Ryan Dempster	.30	.09
❑ 248	J.T. Snow	.30	.09
❑ 249	Eric Young	.30	.09
❑ 250	Daryle Ward	.30	.09
❑ 251	Joe Randa	.30	.09
❑ 252	Travis Fryman	.30	.09
❑ 253	Mike Williams	.30	.09
❑ 254	Jacque Jones	.30	.09
❑ 255	Scott Elarton	.30	.09
❑ 256	Mark McGwire	2.00	.60
❑ 257	Jay Buhner	.30	.09
❑ 258	Randy Wolf	.30	.09
❑ 259	Sammy Sosa	.75	.23
❑ 260	Chan Ho Park	.30	.09
❑ 261	Damion Easley	.30	.09
❑ 262	Rick Ankiel	.30	.09
❑ 263	Frank Thomas	.75	.23
❑ 264	Kris Benson	.30	.09
❑ 265	Luis Alicea	.30	.09
❑ 266	Jeromy Burnitz	.30	.09
❑ 267	Geoff Blum	.30	.09
❑ 268	Joe Girardi	.30	.09
❑ 269	Livan Hernandez	.30	.09
❑ 270	Jeff Conine	.30	.09
❑ 271	Danny Graves	.30	.09
❑ 272	Craig Biggio	.50	.15
❑ 273	Jose Canseco	.50	.15
❑ 274	Tom Glavine	.50	.15
❑ 275	Ruben Mateo	.30	.09
❑ 276	Jeff Kent	.30	.09
❑ 277	Kevin Young	.30	.09
❑ 278	A.J. Burnett	.30	.09
❑ 279	Dante Bichette	.30	.09
❑ 280	Sandy Alomar Jr.	.30	.09
❑ 281	John Wetteland	.30	.09
❑ 282	Torii Hunter	.30	.09
❑ 283	Jarrod Washburn	.30	.09
❑ 284	Rich Aurilia	.30	.09
❑ 285	Jeff Cirillo	.30	.09

☐ 286	Fernando Seguignol	.30	.09
☐ 287	Darren Dreifort	.30	.09
☐ 288	Deivi Cruz	.30	.09
☐ 289	Pokey Reese	.30	.09
☐ 290	Garrett Stephenson	.30	.09
☐ 291	Bret Boone	.30	.09
☐ 292	Tim Hudson	.30	.09
☐ 293	John Flaherty	.30	.09
☐ 294	Shannon Stewart	.30	.09
☐ 295	Shawn Estes	.30	.09
☐ 296	Wilton Guerrero	.30	.09
☐ 297	Delino DeShields	.30	.09
☐ 298	David Justice	.30	.09
☐ 299	Harold Baines	.30	.09
☐ 300	Al Leiter	.30	.09
☐ 301	Wil Cordero	.30	.09
☐ 302	Antonio Alfonseca	.30	.09
☐ 303	Sean Casey	.50	.15
☐ 304	Carlos Beltran	.30	.09
☐ 305	Brad Radke	.30	.09
☐ 306	Jason Varitek	.75	.23
☐ 307	Shigetoshi Hasegawa	.30	.09
☐ 308	Todd Stottlemyre	.30	.09
☐ 309	Raul Mondesi	.30	.09
☐ 310	Mike Bordick	.30	.09
☐ 311	Darryl Kile	.30	.09
☐ 312	Dean Palmer	.30	.09
☐ 313	Johnny Damon	.50	.15
☐ 314	Todd Helton	.50	.15
☐ 315	Chad Hermansen	.30	.09
☐ 316	Kevin Appier	.30	.09
☐ 317	Greg Vaughn	.30	.09
☐ 318	Robb Nen	.30	.09
☐ 319	Jose Cruz Jr.	.30	.09
☐ 320	Ron Belliard	.30	.09
☐ 321	Bernie Williams	.50	.15
☐ 322	Melvin Mora	.30	.09
☐ 323	Kenny Lofton	.30	.09
☐ 324	Armando Benitez	.30	.09
☐ 325	Carlos Lee	.30	.09
☐ 326	Damian Jackson	.30	.09
☐ 327	Eric Milton	.30	.09
☐ 328	J.D. Drew	.30	.09
☐ 329	Byung-Hyun Kim	.30	.09
☐ 330	Chris Stynes	.30	.09
☐ 331	Kazuhiro Sasaki	.30	.09
☐ 332	Troy O'Leary	.30	.09
☐ 333	Pat Hentgen	.30	.09
☐ 334	Brad Ausmus	.30	.09
☐ 335	Todd Walker	.30	.09
☐ 336	Jason Isringhausen	.30	.09
☐ 337	Gerald Williams	.30	.09
☐ 338	Aaron Sele	.30	.09
☐ 339	Paul O'Neill	.50	.15
☐ 340	Cal Ripken	2.50	.75
☐ 341	Manny Ramirez	.50	.15
☐ 342	Will Clark	.50	.15
☐ 343	Mark Redman	.30	.09
☐ 344	Bubba Trammell	.30	.09
☐ 345	Troy Percival	.30	.09
☐ 346	Chris Singleton	.30	.09
☐ 347	Rafael Palmeiro	.50	.15
☐ 348	Carl Everett	.30	.09
☐ 349	Andy Benes	.30	.09
☐ 350	Bobby Higginson	.30	.09
☐ 351	Alex Cabrera	.30	.09
☐ 352	Barry Zito	.50	.15
☐ 353	Jace Brewer	.30	.09
☐ 354	Paxton Crawford	.30	.09
☐ 355	Oswaldo Mairena	.30	.09
☐ 356	Joe Crede	.75	.23
☐ 357	A.J. Pierzynski	.30	.09
☐ 358	Daniel Garibay	.30	.09
☐ 359	Jason Tyner	.30	.09
☐ 360	Nate Rolison	.30	.09
☐ 361	Scott Downs	.30	.09
☐ 362	Keith Ginter	.30	.09
☐ 363	Juan Pierre	.30	.09
☐ 364	Adam Bernero	.30	.09
☐ 365	Chris Richard	.30	.09
☐ 366	Joey Nation	.30	.09
☐ 367	Aubrey Huff	.30	.09
☐ 368	Adam Eaton	.30	.09
☐ 369	Jose Ortiz	.30	.09
☐ 370	Eric Munson	.30	.09
☐ 371	Matt Kinney	.30	.09
☐ 372	Eric Byrnes	.30	.09
☐ 373	Keith McDonald	.30	.09
☐ 374	Matt Wise	.30	.09
☐ 375	Timo Perez	.30	.09
☐ 376	Julio Zuleta	.30	.09
☐ 377	Jimmy Rollins	.30	.09
☐ 378	Xavier Nady	.30	.09
☐ 379	Ryan Kohlmeier	.30	.09
☐ 380	Corey Patterson	.30	.09
☐ 381	Todd Helton LL	.30	.09
☐ 382	Moises Alou LL	.30	.09
☐ 383	Vladimir Guerrero LL	.50	.15
☐ 384	Luis Castillo LL	.30	.09
☐ 385	Jeffrey Hammonds LL	.30	.09
☐ 386	Nomar Garciaparra LL	.75	.23
☐ 387	Carlos Delgado LL	.30	.09
☐ 388	Darin Erstad LL	.30	.09
☐ 389	Manny Ramirez LL	.30	.09
☐ 390	Mike Sweeney LL	.30	.09
☐ 391	Sammy Sosa LL	.50	.15
☐ 392	Barry Bonds LL	1.00	.30
☐ 393	Jeff Bagwell LL	.30	.09
☐ 394	Richard Hidalgo LL	.30	.09
☐ 395	Vladimir Guerrero LL	.50	.15
☐ 396	Troy Glaus LL	.30	.09
☐ 397	Frank Thomas LL	.50	.15
☐ 398	Carlos Delgado LL	.30	.09
☐ 399	David Justice LL	.30	.09
☐ 400	Jason Giambi LL	.30	.09
☐ 401	Randy Johnson LL	.50	.15
☐ 402	Kevin Brown LL	.30	.09
☐ 403	Greg Maddux LL	.75	.23
☐ 404	Al Leiter LL	.30	.09
☐ 405	Mike Hampton LL	.30	.09
☐ 406	Pedro Martinez LL	.50	.15
☐ 407	Roger Clemens LL	.75	.23
☐ 408	Mike Sirotka LL	.30	.09
☐ 409	Mike Mussina LL	.30	.09
☐ 410	Bartolo Colon LL	.30	.09
☐ 411	Subway Series WS	.50	.15
☐ 412	Jose Vizcaino WS	.50	.15
☐ 413	Jose Vizcaino WS	.50	.15
☐ 414	Roger Clemens WS	.75	.23
☐ 415	Armando Benitez	.30	.09
	Edgardo Alfonzo		
	Timo Perez WS		
☐ 416	Al Leiter WS	.50	.15
☐ 417	Luis Sojo WS	.50	.15
☐ 418	Yankees 3-Peat WS	.75	.23
☐ 419	Derek Jeter WS	1.00	.30
☐ 420	Toast of the Town WS	.50	.15
☐ 421	Rafael Furcal	.30	.09
	Chipper Jones		
	Greg Maddux		
	John Rocker		
	Tom Glavine CL		
☐ 422	Armando Benitez	.75	.23
	Mike Piazza		
	Mike Hampton		
	Al Leiter CL		
☐ 423	Ryan Dempster	.30	.09
	Luis Castillo		
	Antonio Alfonseca		
	Preston Wilson CL		
☐ 424	Robert Person	.30	.09
	Scott Rolen		
	Randy Wolf		
	Bob Abreu		
	Doug Glanville CL		
☐ 425	Vladimir Guerrero	.50	.15
	Peter Bergeron CL		
☐ 426	Fernando Vina	.30	.09
	Dave Veres		
	Jim Edmonds		
	Rick Ankiel		
	Edgar Renteria		
	Darryl Kile CL		
☐ 427	Danny Graves	.30	.09
	Ken Griffey Jr.		
	Sean Casey		
	Pokey Reese CL		
☐ 428	Jon Lieber	.50	.15
	Sammy Sosa		
	Eric Young CL		
☐ 429	Curtis Leskanic	.30	.09
	Geoff Jenkins		
	Jeff D'Amico		
	Jeromy Burnitz		
	Marquis Grissom CL		
☐ 430	Scott Elarton	.30	.09
	Jeff Bagwell		
	Octavio Dotel		
	Moises Alou		
	Roger Cedeno CL		
☐ 431	Mike Williams	.50	.15
	Jason Kendall		
	Kris Benson		
	Brian Giles CL		
☐ 432	Livan Hernandez	.30	.09
	Jeff Kent		
	Robb Nen		
	Barry Bonds		
	Marvin Benard CL		
☐ 433	Luis Gonzalez	.30	.09
	Steve Finley		
	Tony Womack		
	Randy Johnson CL		
☐ 434	Jeff Shaw	.30	.09
	Gary Sheffield		
	Kevin Brown		
	Shawn Green		
	Chan Ho Park CL UER		
	B.Shaw should be J.Shaw		
☐ 435	Jose Jimenez	.30	.09
	Todd Helton		
	Brian Bohanon		
	Tom Goodwin CL UER		
	C.Goodwin should be T.Goodwin		
☐ 436	Trevor Hoffman	.30	.09
	Phil Nevin		
	Matt Clement		
	Eric Owens CL		
☐ 437	Mariano Rivera	.75	.23
	Derek Jeter		
	Roger Clemens		
	Bernie Williams		
	Andy Pettitte CL		
☐ 438	Pedro Martinez	.50	.15
	Nomar Garciaparra		
	Derek Lowe		
	Carl Everett CL		
☐ 439	Ryan Kohlmeier	.30	.09
	Delino DeShields		
	Mike Mussina		
	Albert Belle CL		
☐ 440	David Wells	.30	.09
	Carlos Delgado		
	Billy Koch		
	Raul Mondesi CL		
☐ 441	Ramon Hernandez	.30	.09
	Fred McGriff		
	Miguel Cairo		
	Greg Vaughn CL		
☐ 442	Mike Sirotka	.50	.15
	Frank Thomas		
	Keith Foulke		
	Ray Durham CL		
☐ 443	Steve Karsay	.30	.09
	Manny Ramirez		
	Bartolo Colon		
	Roberto Alomar CL		
☐ 444	Brian Moehler	.30	.09
	Deivi Cruz		
	Juan Encarnacion		
	Todd Jones		
	Bobby Higginson CL		
☐ 445	Mac Suzuki	.30	.09
	Mike Sweeney		
	Johnny Damon		
	Jermaine Dye CL		
☐ 446	Brad Radke	.30	.09
	Matt Lawton		
	Eric Milton		
	Jacque Jones		
	Cristian Guzman CL		
☐ 447	Kazuhiro Sasaki	.30	.09
	Edgar Martinez		
	Aaron Sele		
	Rickey Henderson CL		
☐ 448	Jason Isringhausen	.30	.09
	Jason Giambi		
	Tim Hudson		

Card	Mint	NrMt
Randy Velarde CL		
❑ 449 Shigetoshi Hasegawa	.30	.09
Darin Erstad		
Troy Percival		
Troy Glaus CL		
❑ 450 Rick Helling	.30	.09
Rafael Palmeiro		
John Wetteland		
Luis Alicea CL		
❑ 451 Albert Pujols RC	50.00	15.00
❑ 452 Ichiro Suzuki RC	15.00	4.50
❑ 453 Tsuyoshi Shinjo RC	.75	.23
❑ 454 Johnny Estrada RC	.75	.23
❑ 455 Elpidio Guzman RC	.50	.15
❑ 456 Adrian Hernandez RC	.50	.15
❑ 457 Rafael Soriano RC	.50	.15
❑ 458 Drew Henson RC	1.25	.35
❑ 459 Juan Uribe RC	.75	.23
❑ 460 Matt White RC	.50	.15
❑ 461 Endy Chavez RC	.50	.15
❑ 462 Bud Smith RC	.50	.15
❑ 463 Morgan Ensberg RC	4.00	1.20
❑ 464 Jay Gibbons RC	.75	.23
❑ 465 Jackson Melian RC	.50	.15
❑ 466 Junior Spivey RC	.75	.23
❑ 467 Juan Cruz RC	.50	.15
❑ 468 Wilson Betemit RC	.75	.23
❑ 469 Alexis Gomez RC	.50	.15
❑ 470 Mark Teixeira RC	15.00	4.50
❑ 471 Erick Almonte RC	.50	.15
❑ 472 Travis Hafner RC	5.00	1.50
❑ 473 Carlos Valderrama RC	.50	.15
❑ 474 Brandon Duckworth RC	.50	.15
❑ 475 Ryan Freel RC	.75	.23
❑ 476 Wilkin Ruan RC	.50	.15
❑ 477 Andres Torres RC	.50	.15
❑ 478 Josh Towers RC	.75	.23
❑ 479 Kyle Lohse RC	.75	.23
❑ 480 Jason Michaels RC	.50	.15
❑ 481 Alfonso Soriano	.75	.23
❑ 482 C.C. Sabathia	.50	.15
❑ 483 Roy Oswalt	.75	.23
❑ 484 Ben Sheets UER	.75	.23
Wrong team logo on the front		
❑ 485 Adam Dunn	.75	.23
❑ NNO Uncut Sheet EXCH/100	2.00	.60

2003 Fleer Tradition Update

	MINT	NRMT
COMP.SET w/o SP's (285)	40.00	18.00
COMMON CARD (1-285)	.30	.14
COMMON CARD (286-299)	1.00	.45
COMMON RC (286-299)	1.00	.45
286-299 STATED ODDS 1:4 HOB/RET		.00
COMMON CARD (300-398)	1.00	.45
COMMON RC (300-398)	1.00	.45
300-398 ISSUED IN MINI-BOXES	.00	
ONE MINI-BOX PER UPDATE BOX	.00	
25 CARDS PER MINI-BOX	.00	

Card	Mint	NrMt
❑ 1 Aaron Boone	.30	.14
❑ 2 Carl Everett	.30	.14
❑ 3 Eduardo Perez	.30	.14
❑ 4 Jason Michaels	.30	.14
❑ 5 Karim Garcia	.30	.14
❑ 6 Rainer Olmedo	.30	.14
❑ 7 Scott Williamson	.30	.14
❑ 8 Adam Kennedy	.30	.14
❑ 9 Carl Pavano	.30	.14
❑ 10 Eli Marrero	.30	.14
❑ 11 Jason Simontacchi	.30	.14
❑ 12 Keith Foulke	.30	.14
❑ 13 Preston Wilson	.30	.14
❑ 14 Scott Hatteberg	.30	.14
❑ 15 Adam Dunn	.30	.14
❑ 16 Carlos Baerga	.30	.14
❑ 17 Elmer Dessens	.30	.14
❑ 18 Javier Vazquez	.30	.14
❑ 19 Kenny Rogers	.30	.14
❑ 20 Quinton McCracken	.30	.14
❑ 21 Shane Reynolds	.30	.14
❑ 22 Adam Eaton	.30	.14
❑ 23 Carlos Zambrano	.30	.14
❑ 24 Enrique Wilson	.30	.14
❑ 25 Jeff DaVanon	.30	.14
❑ 26 Kenny Lofton	.30	.14
❑ 27 Ramon Castro	.30	.14
❑ 28 Shannon Stewart	.30	.14
❑ 29 Al Martin	.30	.14
❑ 30 Carlos Guillen	.30	.14
❑ 31 Eric Karros	.30	.14
❑ 32 Tim Worrell	.30	.14
❑ 33 Kevin Millwood	.30	.14
❑ 34 Randall Simon	.30	.14
❑ 35 Shawn Chacon	.30	.14
❑ 36 Alex Rodriguez	1.25	.55
❑ 37 Casey Blake	.30	.14
❑ 38 Eric Munson	.30	.14
❑ 39 Jeff Kent	.30	.14
❑ 40 Kris Benson	.30	.14
❑ 41 Randy Winn	.30	.14
❑ 42 Shea Hillenbrand	.30	.14
❑ 43 Alfonso Soriano	.30	.14
❑ 44 Chris George	.30	.14
❑ 45 Eric Bruntlett	.30	.14
❑ 46 Jeromy Burnitz	.30	.14
❑ 47 Kyle Farnsworth	.30	.14
❑ 48 Torii Hunter	.30	.14
❑ 49 Sidney Ponson	.30	.14
❑ 50 Andres Galarraga	.30	.14
❑ 51 Chris Singleton	.30	.14
❑ 52 Eric Gagne	.30	.14
❑ 53 Jesse Foppert	.30	.14
❑ 54 Lance Carter	.30	.14
❑ 55 Ray Durham	.30	.14
❑ 56 Tanyon Sturtze	.30	.14
❑ 57 Andy Ashby	.30	.14
❑ 58 Cliff Floyd	.30	.14
❑ 59 Eric Young	.30	.14
❑ 60 Jhonny Peralta	.75	.35
❑ 61 Livan Hernandez	.30	.14
❑ 62 Reggie Sanders	.30	.14
❑ 63 Tim Spooneybarger	.30	.14
❑ 64 Angel Berroa	.30	.14
❑ 65 Coco Crisp	.30	.14
❑ 66 Eric Hinske	.30	.14
❑ 67 Jim Edmonds	.50	.23
❑ 68 Luis Matos	.30	.14
❑ 69 Rickey Henderson	.75	.35
❑ 70 Todd Walker	.30	.14
❑ 71 Antonio Alfonseca	.30	.14
❑ 72 Corey Koskie	.30	.14
❑ 73 Erubiel Durazo	.30	.14
❑ 74 Jim Thome	.50	.23
❑ 75 Lyle Overbay	.30	.14
❑ 76 Robert Fick	.30	.14
❑ 77 Todd Hollandsworth	.30	.14
❑ 78 Aramis Ramirez	.30	.14
❑ 79 Cristian Guzman	.30	.14
❑ 80 Esteban Loaiza	.30	.14
❑ 81 Jody Gerut	.30	.14
❑ 82 Mark Grudzielanek	.30	.14
❑ 83 Roberto Alomar	.50	.23
❑ 84 Todd Hundley	.30	.14
❑ 85 Mike Hampton	.30	.14
❑ 86 Curt Schilling	.30	.14
❑ 87 Francisco Rodriguez	.30	.14
❑ 88 John Lackey	.30	.14
❑ 89 Mark Redman	.30	.14
❑ 90 Robin Ventura	.30	.14
❑ 91 Todd Zeile	.30	.14
❑ 92 B.J. Surhoff	.30	.14
❑ 93 Raul Mondesi	.30	.14
❑ 94 Frank Catalanotto	.30	.14
❑ 95 John Smoltz	.50	.23
❑ 96 Mark Ellis	.30	.14
❑ 97 Rocco Baldelli	.30	.14
❑ 98 Todd Pratt	.30	.14
❑ 99 Barry Bonds	2.00	.90
❑ 100 Danny Graves	.30	.14
❑ 101 Fred McGriff	.50	.23
❑ 102 John Burkett	.30	.14
❑ 103 Marquis Grissom	.30	.14
❑ 104 Rocky Biddle	.30	.14
❑ 105 Tom Glavine	.50	.23
❑ 106 Bartolo Colon	.30	.14
❑ 107 Darren Bragg	.30	.14
❑ 108 Gabe Kapler	.30	.14
❑ 109 John Franco	.30	.14
❑ 110 Matt Mantei	.30	.14
❑ 111 Rod Beck	.30	.14
❑ 112 Tomo Ohka	.30	.14
❑ 113 Ben Petrick	.30	.14
❑ 114 Darren Dreifort	.30	.14
❑ 115 Garret Anderson	.30	.14
❑ 116 John Vander Wal	.30	.14
❑ 117 Melvin Mora	.30	.14
❑ 118 Rodrigo Lopez	.30	.14
❑ 119 Raul Ibanez	.30	.14
❑ 120 Benito Santiago	.30	.14
❑ 121 David Ortiz Sox	.75	.35
❑ 122 Gary Bennett	.30	.14
❑ 123 Jon Garland	.30	.14
❑ 124 Michael Young	.50	.23
❑ 125 Rodrigo Rosario	.30	.14
❑ 126 Travis Lee	.30	.14
❑ 127 Bill Mueller	.30	.14
❑ 128 Derek Lowe	.30	.14
❑ 129 Gil Meche	.30	.14
❑ 130 Jose Guillen	.30	.14
❑ 131 Miguel Cabrera	.75	.35
❑ 132 Ron Calloway	.30	.14
❑ 133 Troy Percival	.30	.14
❑ 134 Billy Koch	.30	.14
❑ 135 Dmitri Young	.30	.14
❑ 136 Glendon Rusch	.30	.14
❑ 137 Jose Jimenez	.30	.14
❑ 138 Miguel Tejada	.30	.14
❑ 139 John Thomson	.30	.14
❑ 140 Troy O'Leary	.30	.14
❑ 141 Bobby Kielty	.30	.14
❑ 142 Dontrelle Willis	.75	.35
❑ 143 Greg Myers	.30	.14
❑ 144 Jose Vizcaino	.30	.14
❑ 145 Mike MacDougal	.30	.14
❑ 146 Ronnie Belliard	.30	.14
❑ 147 Tyler Houston	.30	.14
❑ 148 Brady Clark	.30	.14
❑ 149 Edgardo Alfonzo	.30	.14
❑ 150 Guillermo Mota	.30	.14
❑ 151 Jose Lima	.30	.14
❑ 152 Mike Williams	.30	.14
❑ 153 Roy Oswalt	.30	.14
❑ 154 Scott Podsednik	5.00	2.20
❑ 155 Brandon Lyon	.30	.14
❑ 156 Henry Mateo	.30	.14
❑ 157 Jose Macias	.30	.14
❑ 158 Mike Bordick	.30	.14
❑ 159 Royce Clayton	.30	.14
❑ 160 Vance Wilson	.30	.14
❑ 161 Brent Abernathy	.30	.14
❑ 162 Horacio Ramirez	.30	.14
❑ 163 Jose Reyes	.30	.14
❑ 164 Nick Punto	.30	.14
❑ 165 Ruben Sierra	.30	.14
❑ 166 Victor Zambrano	.30	.14
❑ 167 Brett Tomko	.30	.14
❑ 168 Ivan Rodriguez	.50	.23
❑ 169 Jose Mesa	.30	.14
❑ 170 Octavio Dotel	.30	.14
❑ 171 Russ Ortiz	.30	.14
❑ 172 Vladimir Guerrero	.75	.35
❑ 173 Brian Lawrence	.30	.14
❑ 174 Jae Weong Seo	.30	.14
❑ 175 Jose Cruz Jr.	.30	.14
❑ 176 Pat Burrell	.30	.14
❑ 177 Russell Branyan	.30	.14
❑ 178 Warren Morris	.30	.14

❑ 179 Brian Boehringer .30 .14
❑ 180 Jason Johnson .30 .14
❑ 181 Josh Phelps .30 .14
❑ 182 Paul Konerko .30 .14
❑ 183 Ryan Franklin .30 .14
❑ 184 Wes Helms .30 .14
❑ 185 Brooks Kieschnick .30 .14
❑ 186 Jason Davis .30 .14
❑ 187 Juan Pierre .30 .14
❑ 188 Paul Wilson .30 .14
❑ 189 Sammy Sosa .75 .35
❑ 190 Wil Cordero .30 .14
❑ 191 Byung-Hyun Kim .30 .14
❑ 192 Juan Encarnacion .30 .14
❑ 193 Placido Polanco .30 .14
❑ 194 Sandy Alomar Jr. .30 .14
❑ 195 Julio Lugo .30 .14
❑ 196 Junior Spivey .30 .14
❑ 197 Woody Williams .30 .14
❑ 198 Xavier Nady .30 .14
❑ 199 Mark Loretta .30 .14
❑ 200 Deivi Cruz .30 .14
❑ 201 Jorge Posada AS .30 .14
❑ 202 Carlos Delgado AS .30 .14
❑ 203 Alfonso Soriano AS .30 .14
❑ 204 Alex Rodriguez AS .75 .35
❑ 205 Troy Glaus AS .30 .14
❑ 206 Garret Anderson AS .30 .14
❑ 207 Hideki Matsui AS 2.00 .90
❑ 208 Ichiro Suzuki AS .75 .35
❑ 209 Esteban Loaiza AS .30 .14
❑ 210 Manny Ramirez AS .50 .23
❑ 211 Roger Clemens AS .75 .35
❑ 212 Roy Halladay AS .30 .14
❑ 213 Jason Giambi AS .30 .14
❑ 214 Edgar Martinez AS .30 .14
❑ 215 Bret Boone AS .30 .14
❑ 216 Hank Blalock AS .30 .14
❑ 217 Nomar Garciaparra AS .75 .35
❑ 218 Vernon Wells AS .30 .14
❑ 219 Melvin Mora AS .30 .14
❑ 220 Magglio Ordonez AS .30 .14
❑ 221 Mike Sweeney AS .30 .14
❑ 222 Barry Zito AS .30 .14
❑ 223 Carl Everett AS .30 .14
❑ 224 Shigetoshi Hasegawa AS .30 .14
❑ 225 Jamie Moyer AS .30 .14
❑ 226 Mark Mulder AS .30 .14
❑ 227 Eddie Guardado AS .30 .14
❑ 228 Ramon Hernandez AS .30 .14
❑ 229 Keith Foulke AS .30 .14
❑ 230 Javy Lopez AS .30 .14
❑ 231 Todd Helton AS .30 .14
❑ 232 Marcus Giles AS .30 .14
❑ 233 Edgar Renteria AS .30 .14
❑ 234 Scott Rolen AS .30 .14
❑ 235 Barry Bonds AS 1.00 .45
❑ 236 Albert Pujols AS .75 .35
❑ 237 Gary Sheffield AS .30 .14
❑ 238 Jim Edmonds AS .30 .14
❑ 239 Jason Schmidt AS .30 .14
❑ 240 Mark Prior AS .30 .14
❑ 241 Dontrelle Willis AS .50 .23
❑ 242 Kerry Wood AS .30 .14
❑ 243 Kevin Brown AS .30 .14
❑ 244 Woody Williams AS .30 .14
❑ 245 Paul Lo Duca AS .30 .14
❑ 246 Richie Sexson AS .30 .14
❑ 247 Jose Vidro AS .30 .14
❑ 248 Luis Castillo AS .30 .14
❑ 249 Aaron Boone AS .30 .14
❑ 250 Mike Lowell AS .30 .14
❑ 251 Rafael Furcal AS .30 .14
❑ 252 Andruw Jones AS .30 .14
❑ 253 Preston Wilson AS .30 .14
❑ 254 John Smoltz AS .30 .14
❑ 255 Eric Gagne AS .30 .14
❑ 256 Randy Wolf AS .30 .14
❑ 257 Billy Wagner AS .30 .14
❑ 258 Luis Gonzalez AS .30 .14
❑ 259 Russ Ortiz AS .30 .14
❑ 260 Jim Thome .50 .23
Pedro Martinez IL
❑ 261 Alfonso Soriano .50 .23
Jeff Bagwell IL
❑ 262 Dontrelle Willis .50 .23
Rocco Baldelli IL
❑ 263 Carlos Delgado .50 .23
Vladimir Guerrero IL
❑ 264 Sammy Sosa .75 .35
Magglio Ordonez IL
❑ 265 Jason Giambi .30 .14
Adam Dunn IL
❑ 266 Mike Sweeney .75 .35
Albert Pujols IL
❑ 267 Barry Bonds 1.00 .45
Torii Hunter IL
❑ 268 Ichiro Suzuki .75 .35
Andruw Jones IL
❑ 269 Chipper Jones .50 .23
Hank Blalock IL
❑ 270 Mark Prior .30 .14
Vernon Wells IL
❑ 271 Nomar Garciaparra .75 .35
Scott Rolen IL
❑ 272 Alex Rodriguez .75 .35
Lance Berkman IL
❑ 273 Roger Clemens .75 .35
Kerry Wood IL
❑ 274 Derek Jeter 1.00 .45
Jose Reyes IL
❑ 275 Greg Maddux .75 .35
Barry Zito IL
❑ 276 Carlos Delgado TT .30 .14
❑ 277 J.D. Drew TT .30 .14
❑ 278 Barry Bonds TT 1.00 .45
❑ 279 Albert Pujols TT .75 .35
❑ 280 Jim Thome TT .30 .14
❑ 281 Sammy Sosa TT .50 .23
❑ 282 Alfonso Soriano TT .30 .14
❑ 283 Hideki Matsui TT 2.00 .90
❑ 284 Mike Piazza TT .75 .35
❑ 285 Vladimir Guerrero TT .50 .23
❑ 286 Rich Harden ROO 1.50 .70
❑ 287 Chin-Hui Tsao ROO 1.00 .45
❑ 288 Edwin Jackson ROO RC 1.50 .70
❑ 289 Chien-Ming Wang ROO RC 5.00 2.20
❑ 290 Josh Willingham ROO RC 1.50 .70
❑ 291 Matt Kata ROO RC 1.00 .45
❑ 292 Jose Contreras ROO RC 2.00 .90
❑ 293 Chris Bootcheck ROO 1.00 .45
❑ 294 Javier A. Lopez ROO RC 1.00 .45
❑ 295 Delmon Young ROO RC 8.00 3.60
❑ 296 Pedro Liriano ROO 1.00 .45
❑ 297 Noah Lowry ROO 1.50 .70
❑ 298 Khalil Greene ROO UER 4.00 1.80
First Name misspelled
❑ 299 Rob Bowen ROO 1.00 .45
❑ 300 Bo Hart ROO RC 1.00 .45
❑ 301 Beau Kemp ROO RC 1.00 .45
❑ 302 Gerald Laird ROO 1.00 .45
❑ 303 Miguel Ojeda ROO RC 1.00 .45
❑ 304 Todd Wellemeyer ROO RC 1.00 .45
❑ 305 Ryan Wagner ROO RC 1.00 .45
❑ 306 Jeff Duncan ROO RC 1.00 .45
❑ 307 Wilfredo Ledezma ROO RC 1.00 .45
❑ 308 Wes Obermueller ROO 1.00 .45
❑ 309 Bernie Castro ROO RC 1.00 .45
❑ 310 Tim Olson ROO RC 1.00 .45
❑ 311 Colin Porter ROO RC 1.00 .45
❑ 312 Francisco Cruceta ROO RC 1.00 .45
❑ 313 Guillermo Quiroz ROO RC 1.00 .45
❑ 314 Brian Stokes ROO RC 1.00 .45
❑ 315 Robby Hammock ROO RC 1.00 .45
❑ 316 Lew Ford ROO RC 1.50 .70
❑ 317 Todd Linden ROO 1.00 .45
❑ 318 Mike Gallo ROO RC 1.00 .45
❑ 319 Francisco Rosario ROO RC 1.00 .45
❑ 320 Rosman Garcia ROO RC 1.00 .45
❑ 321 Felix Sanchez ROO RC 1.00 .45
❑ 322 Chad Gaudin ROO RC 1.00 .45
❑ 323 Phil Seibel ROO RC 1.00 .45
❑ 324 Jason Gilfillan ROO RC 1.00 .45
❑ 325 Termel Sledge ROO RC 1.00 .45
❑ 326 Alfredo Gonzalez ROO RC 1.00 .45
❑ 327 Josh Stewart ROO RC 1.00 .45
❑ 328 Jeremy Griffiths ROO RC 1.00 .45
❑ 329 Cory Stewart ROO RC 1.00 .45
❑ 330 Josh Hall ROO RC 1.00 .45
❑ 331 Arnie Munoz ROO RC 1.00 .45
❑ 332 Garrett Atkins ROO 1.00 .45
❑ 333 Neal Cotts ROO 1.00 .45
❑ 334 Dan Haren ROO RC 2.00 .90
❑ 335 Shane Victorino ROO RC 1.50 .70
❑ 336 David Sanders ROO RC 1.00 .45
❑ 337 Oscar Villarreal ROO RC 1.00 .45
❑ 338 Michael Hessman ROO RC 1.00 .45
❑ 339 Andrew Brown ROO RC 1.50 .70
❑ 340 Kevin Hooper ROO 1.00 .45
❑ 341 Prentice Redman ROO RC 1.00 .45
❑ 342 Brandon Webb ROO RC 2.00 .90
❑ 343 Jimmy Gobble ROO 1.00 .45
❑ 344 Pete LaForest ROO RC 1.00 .45
❑ 345 Chris Waters ROO RC 1.00 .45
❑ 346 Hideki Matsui ROO RC 8.00 3.60
❑ 347 Chris Capuano ROO RC 1.00 .45
❑ 348 Jon Leicester ROO RC 1.00 .45
❑ 349 Mike Nicolas ROO RC 1.00 .45
❑ 350 Nook Logan ROO RC 1.50 .70
❑ 351 Craig Brazell ROO RC 1.00 .45
❑ 352 Aaron Looper ROO RC 1.00 .45
❑ 353 D.J. Carrasco ROO RC 1.00 .45
❑ 354 Clint Barmes ROO RC 3.00 1.35
❑ 355 Doug Waechter ROO RC 1.50 .70
❑ 356 Julio Manon ROO RC 1.00 .45
❑ 357 Jer. Bonderman ROO RC 5.00 2.20
❑ 358 D. Markwell ROO RC 1.00 .45
❑ 359 Dave Matranga ROO RC 1.00 .45
❑ 360 Luis Ayala ROO RC 1.00 .45
❑ 361 Jason Stanford ROO 1.00 .45
❑ 362 Roger Deago ROO RC 1.00 .45
❑ 363 Geoff Geary ROO RC 1.00 .45
❑ 364 Edgar Gonzalez ROO RC 1.00 .45
❑ 365 Michel Hernandez ROO RC 1.00 .45
❑ 366 Aquilino Lopez ROO RC 1.00 .45
❑ 367 David Manning ROO 1.00 .45
❑ 368 Carlos Mendez ROO RC 1.00 .45
❑ 369 Matt Miller ROO RC 1.00 .45
❑ 370 Mi. Nakamura ROO RC 1.00 .45
❑ 371 Mike Neu ROO RC 1.00 .45
❑ 372 Ramon Nivar ROO RC 1.00 .45
❑ 373 Kevin Ohme ROO RC 1.00 .45
❑ 374 Alex Prieto ROO RC 1.00 .45
❑ 375 Stephen Randolph ROO RC 1.00 .45
❑ 376 Brian Sweeney ROO RC 1.00 .45
❑ 377 Matt Diaz ROO RC 1.50 .70
❑ 378 Mike Gonzalez ROO 1.00 .45
❑ 379 Daniel Cabrera ROO RC 2.00 .90
❑ 380 Fernando Cabrera ROO RC 1.00 .45
❑ 381 David DeJesus ROO RC 2.00 .90
❑ 382 Mike Ryan ROO RC 1.00 .45
❑ 383 Rick Roberts ROO RC 1.00 .45
❑ 384 Seung Song ROO 1.00 .45
❑ 385 Rickie Weeks ROO RC 6.00 2.70
❑ 386 Hum. Quintero ROO RC 1.00 .45
❑ 387 Alexis Rios ROO 1.00 .45
❑ 388 Aaron Miles ROO RC 1.50 .70
❑ 389 Tom Gregorio ROO RC 1.00 .45
❑ 390 Anthony Ferrari ROO RC 1.00 .45
❑ 391 Kevin Correia ROO RC 1.00 .45
❑ 392 Rafael Betancourt ROO RC 1.50 .70
❑ 393 Rett Johnson ROO RC 1.00 .45
❑ 394 Richard Fischer ROO RC 1.00 .45
❑ 395 Greg Aquino ROO RC 1.00 .45
❑ 396 Daniel Garcia ROO RC 1.00 .45
❑ 397 Sergio Mitre ROO RC 1.50 .70
❑ 398 Edwin Almonte ROO 1.00 .45

2004 Fleer Tradition

	Nm-Mt	Ex-Mt
COMPLETE SET (500)	150.00	45.00
COMP.SET w/o SP's (400)	40.00	12.00
COMMON CARD (1-400)	.30	.09
COMMON CARD (401-470)	1.00	.30
COMMON CARD (471-500)	1.00	.30
401-445 STATED ODDS 1:2	.00	
446-461 STATED ODDS 1:6	.00	
462-470 STATED ODDS 1:9	.00	
471-500 STATED ODDS 1:3	.00	
❑ 1 Juan Pierre WS	.30	.09
❑ 2 Josh Beckett WS	.30	.09
❑ 3 Ivan Rodriguez WS	.50	.15
❑ 4 Miguel Cabrera WS	.50	.15
❑ 5 Dontrelle Willis WS	.50	.15
❑ 6 Derek Jeter WS	1.50	.45
❑ 7 Jason Giambi WS	.30	.09
❑ 8 Bernie Williams WS	.50	.15
❑ 9 Alfonso Soriano WS	.30	.09
❑ 10 Hideki Matsui WS	1.50	.45
❑ 11 Garret Anderson Garret Anderson Ramon Ortiz John Lackey TL	.30	.09
❑ 12 Luis Gonzalez Luis Gonzalez Brandon Webb Curt Schilling TL	.30	.09
❑ 13 Javy Lopez Gary Sheffield Russ Ortiz Russ Ortiz TL	.30	.09
❑ 14 Tony Batista Jay Gibbons Sidney Ponson Jason Johnson TL	.30	.09
❑ 15 Manny Ramirez Nomar Garciaparra Derek Lowe Pedro Martinez TL	.50	.15
❑ 16 Sammy Sosa Sammy Sosa Mark Prior Kerry Wood TL	.50	.15
❑ 17 Frank Thomas Carlos Lee Esteban Loaiza Esteban Loaiza TL	.50	.15
❑ 18 Adam Dunn Sean Casey Chris Reitsma Paul Wilson TL	.30	.09
❑ 19 Jody Gerut Jody Gerut C.C. Sabathia C.C. Sabathia TL	.30	.09
❑ 20 Preston Wilson Preston Wilson Darren Oliver Jason Jennings TL	.30	.09
❑ 21 Dmitri Young Dmitri Young Mike Maroth Jeremy Bonderman TL	.30	.09
❑ 22 Mike Lowell Mike Lowell Dontrelle Willis Josh Beckett TL	.50	.15
❑ 23 Jeff Bagwell Jeff Bagwell Jeriome Robertson Wade Miller TL	.30	.09
❑ 24 Carlos Beltran Carlos Beltran Darrell May Darrell May TL	.30	.09
❑ 25 Adrian Beltre Shawn Green Hideo Nomo Kevin Brown TL	.30	.09
❑ 26 Richie Sexson Richie Sexson Ben Sheets Ben Sheets TL	.30	.09
❑ 27 Torii Hunter Torii Hunter Brad Radke Johan Santana TL	.30	.09
❑ 28 Vladimir Guerrero Orlando Cabrera Livan Hernandez Javier Vazquez TL	.50	.15
❑ 29 Cliff Floyd Ty Wigginton Steve Trachsel Al Leiter TL	.30	.09
❑ 30 Jason Giambi Jason Giambi Andy Pettitte Mike Mussina TL	.50	.15
❑ 31 Eric Chavez Miguel Tejada Tim Hudson Tim Hudson TL	.30	.09
❑ 32 Jim Thome Jim Thome Randy Wolf Randy Wolf TL	.30	.09
❑ 33 Reggie Sanders Reggie Sanders Josh Fogg Kip Wells TL	.30	.09
❑ 34 Ryan Klesko Mark Loretta Jake Peavy Jake Peavy TL	.30	.09
❑ 35 Jose Cruz Jr. Edgardo Alfonzo Jason Schmidt Jason Schmidt TL	.30	.09
❑ 36 Bret Boone Bret Boone Jamie Moyer Joel Pineiro TL	.30	.09
❑ 37 Albert Pujols Albert Pujols Woody Williams Woody Williams TL	.75	.23
❑ 38 Aubrey Huff Aubrey Huff Victor Zambrano Victor Zambrano TL	.30	.09
❑ 39 Alex Rodriguez Alex Rodriguez John Thomson John Thomson TL	.75	.23
❑ 40 Carlos Delgado Carlos Delgado Roy Halladay Roy Halladay TL	.30	.09
❑ 41 Greg Maddux	1.25	.35
❑ 42 Ben Grieve	.30	.09
❑ 43 Darin Erstad	.30	.09
❑ 44 Ruben Sierra	.30	.09
❑ 45 Byung-Hyung Kim	.30	.09
❑ 46 Freddy Garcia	.30	.09
❑ 47 Richard Hidalgo	.30	.09
❑ 48 Tike Redman	.30	.09
❑ 49 Kevin Millwood	.30	.09
❑ 50 Marquis Grissom	.30	.09
❑ 51 Jae Weong Seo	.30	.09
❑ 52 Wil Cordero	.30	.09
❑ 53 LaTroy Hawkins	.30	.09
❑ 54 Jolbert Cabrera	.30	.09
❑ 55 Kevin Appier	.30	.09
❑ 56 John Lackey	.30	.09
❑ 57 Garret Anderson	.30	.09
❑ 58 R.A. Dickey	.30	.09
❑ 59 David Segui	.30	.09
❑ 60 Erubiel Durazo	.30	.09
❑ 61 Bobby Abreu	.30	.09
❑ 62 Travis Hafner	.30	.09
❑ 63 Victor Zambrano	.30	.09
❑ 64 Randy Johnson	.75	.23
❑ 65 Bernie Williams	.50	.15
❑ 66 J.T. Snow	.30	.09
❑ 67 Sammy Sosa	.75	.23
❑ 68 Al Leiter	.30	.09
❑ 69 Jason Jennings	.30	.09
❑ 70 Matt Morris	.30	.09
❑ 71 Mike Hampton	.30	.09
❑ 72 Juan Encarnacion	.30	.09
❑ 73 Alex Gonzalez	.30	.09
❑ 74 Bartolo Colon	.30	.09
❑ 75 Brett Myers	.30	.09
❑ 76 Michael Young	.30	.09
❑ 77 Ichiro Suzuki	1.50	.45
❑ 78 Jason Johnson	.30	.09
❑ 79 Brad Ausmus	.30	.09
❑ 80 Ted Lilly	.30	.09
❑ 81 Ken Griffey Jr.	1.25	.35
❑ 82 Chone Figgins	.30	.09
❑ 83 Edgar Martinez	.50	.15
❑ 84 Adam Eaton	.30	.09
❑ 85 Ken Harvey	.30	.09
❑ 86 Francisco Rodriguez	.30	.09
❑ 87 Bill Mueller	.30	.09
❑ 88 Mike Maroth	.30	.09
❑ 89 Charles Johnson	.30	.09
❑ 90 Jhonny Peralta	.30	.09
❑ 91 Kip Wells	.30	.09
❑ 92 Cesar Izturis	.30	.09
❑ 93 Matt Clement	.30	.09
❑ 94 Lyle Overbay	.30	.09
❑ 95 Kirk Rueter	.30	.09
❑ 96 Cristian Guzman	.30	.09
❑ 97 Garrett Stephenson	.30	.09
❑ 98 Lance Berkman	.30	.09
❑ 99 Brett Tomko	.30	.09
❑ 100 Chris Stynes	.30	.09
❑ 101 Nate Cornejo	.30	.09
❑ 102 Aaron Rowand	.30	.09
❑ 103 Javier Vazquez	.30	.09
❑ 104 Jason Kendall	.30	.09
❑ 105 Mark Redman	.30	.09
❑ 106 Benito Santiago	.30	.09
❑ 107 C.C. Sabathia	.30	.09
❑ 108 David Wells	.30	.09
❑ 109 Mark Ellis	.30	.09
❑ 110 Casey Blake	.30	.09
❑ 111 Sean Burroughs	.30	.09
❑ 112 Carlos Beltran	.30	.09
❑ 113 Ramon Hernandez	.30	.09
❑ 114 Eric Hinske	.30	.09
❑ 115 Luis Gonzalez	.30	.09
❑ 116 Jarrod Washburn	.30	.09
❑ 117 Ronnie Belliard	.30	.09
❑ 118 Troy Percival	.30	.09
❑ 119 Jose Valentin	.30	.09
❑ 120 Chase Utley	.50	.15
❑ 121 Odalis Perez	.30	.09
❑ 122 Steve Finley	.30	.09
❑ 123 Bret Boone	.30	.09
❑ 124 Jeff Conine	.30	.09
❑ 125 Josh Fogg	.30	.09
❑ 126 Neifi Perez	.30	.09
❑ 127 Ben Sheets	.30	.09
❑ 128 Randy Winn	.30	.09
❑ 129 Matt Stairs	.30	.09
❑ 130 Carlos Delgado	.30	.09
❑ 131 Morgan Ensberg	.30	.09
❑ 132 Vinny Castilla	.30	.09
❑ 133 Matt Mantei	.30	.09
❑ 134 Alex Rodriguez	1.25	.35
❑ 135 Matthew LeCroy	.30	.09
❑ 136 Woody Williams	.30	.09
❑ 137 Frank Catalanotto	.30	.09
❑ 138 Rondell White	.30	.09
❑ 139 Scott Rolen	.50	.15
❑ 140 Cliff Floyd	.30	.09
❑ 141 Chipper Jones	.75	.23
❑ 142 Robin Ventura	.30	.09
❑ 143 Mariano Rivera	.50	.15
❑ 144 Brady Clark	.30	.09
❑ 145 Ramon Ortiz	.30	.09
❑ 146 Omar Infante	.30	.09
❑ 147 Mike Matheny	.30	.09
❑ 148 Pedro Martinez	.50	.15
❑ 149 Carlos Baerga	.30	.09
❑ 150 Shannon Stewart	.30	.09
❑ 151 Travis Lee	.30	.09
❑ 152 Eric Byrnes	.30	.09
❑ 153 Rafael Furcal	.30	.09
❑ 154 B.J. Surhoff	.30	.09
❑ 155 Zach Day	.30	.09
❑ 156 Marlon Anderson	.30	.09
❑ 157 Mark Hendrickson	.30	.09

❑ 158 Mike Mussina .50 .15
❑ 159 Randall Simon .30 .09
❑ 160 Jeff DaVanon .30 .09
❑ 161 Joel Pineiro .30 .09
❑ 162 Vernon Wells .30 .09
❑ 163 Adam Kennedy .30 .09
❑ 164 Trot Nixon .30 .09
❑ 165 Rodrigo Lopez .30 .09
❑ 166 Curt Schilling .30 .09
❑ 167 Horacio Ramirez .30 .09
❑ 168 Jason Marquis .30 .09
❑ 169 Magglio Ordonez .30 .09
❑ 170 Scott Schoeneweis .30 .09
❑ 171 Andruw Jones .50 .15
❑ 172 Tino Martinez .50 .15
❑ 173 Moises Alou .30 .09
❑ 174 Kelvim Escobar .30 .09
❑ 175 Xavier Nady .30 .09
❑ 176 Ramon Martinez .30 .09
❑ 177 Pat Hentgen .30 .09
❑ 178 Austin Kearns .30 .09
❑ 179 D'Angelo Jimenez .30 .09
❑ 180 Deivi Cruz .30 .09
❑ 181 John Smoltz .50 .15
❑ 182 Toby Hall .30 .09
❑ 183 Mark Buehrle .30 .09
❑ 184 Howie Clark .30 .09
❑ 185 David Ortiz .75 .23
❑ 186 Raul Mondesi .30 .09
❑ 187 Milton Bradley .30 .09
❑ 188 Jorge Julio .30 .09
❑ 189 Victor Martinez .30 .09
❑ 190 Gabe Kapler .30 .09
❑ 191 Julio Franco .30 .09
❑ 192 Ryan Freel .30 .09
❑ 193 Brad Fullmer .30 .09
❑ 194 Joe Borowski .30 .09
❑ 195 Darren Oliver .30 .09
❑ 196 Jason Varitek .75 .23
❑ 197 Greg Myers .30 .09
❑ 198 Eric Munson .30 .09
❑ 199 Tim Wakefield .30 .09
❑ 200 Kyle Farnsworth .30 .09
❑ 201 Johnny Vander Wal .30 .09
❑ 202 Alex Escobar .30 .09
❑ 203 Sean Casey .50 .15
❑ 204 John Thomson .30 .09
❑ 205 Carlos Zambrano .30 .09
❑ 206 Kenny Lofton .30 .09
❑ 207 Marcus Giles .30 .09
❑ 208 Wade Miller .30 .09
❑ 209 Geoff Blum .30 .09
❑ 210 Jason LaRue .30 .09
❑ 211 Omar Vizquel .50 .15
❑ 212 Carlos Pena .30 .09
❑ 213 Adam Dunn .30 .09
❑ 214 Oscar Villarreal .30 .09
❑ 215 Paul Konerko .30 .09
❑ 216 Hideo Nomo .75 .23
❑ 217 Mike Sweeney .30 .09
❑ 218 Coco Crisp .30 .09
❑ 219 Shawn Chacon .30 .09
❑ 220 Brook Fordyce .30 .09
❑ 221 Josh Beckett .30 .09
❑ 222 Paul Wilson .30 .09
❑ 223 Josh Towers .30 .09
❑ 224 Geoff Jenkins .30 .09
❑ 225 Shawn Green .30 .09
❑ 226 Derrek Lee .50 .15
❑ 227 Karim Garcia .30 .09
❑ 228 Preston Wilson .30 .09
❑ 229 Dane Sardinha .30 .09
❑ 230 Aramis Ramirez .30 .09
❑ 231 Doug Mientkiewicz .30 .09
❑ 232 Jay Gibbons .30 .09
❑ 233 Adam Everett .30 .09
❑ 234 Brooks Kieschnick .30 .09
❑ 235 Dmitri Young .30 .09
❑ 236 Brad Penny .30 .09
❑ 237 Todd Zeile .30 .09
❑ 238 Eric Gagne .30 .09
❑ 239 Esteban Loaiza .30 .09
❑ 240 Billy Wagner .30 .09
❑ 241 Nomar Garciaparra 1.25 .35
❑ 242 Desi Relaford .30 .09
❑ 243 Luis Rivas .30 .09
❑ 244 Andy Pettitte .50 .15
❑ 245 Ty Wigginton .30 .09
❑ 246 Edgar Gonzalez .30 .09
❑ 247 Brian Anderson .30 .09
❑ 248 Richie Sexson .30 .09
❑ 249 Russell Branyan .30 .09
❑ 250 Jose Guillen .30 .09
❑ 251 Chin-Hui Tsao .30 .09
❑ 252 Jose Hernandez .30 .09
❑ 253 Kevin Brown .30 .09
❑ 254 Pete LaForest .30 .09
❑ 255 Adrian Beltre .30 .09
❑ 256 Jacque Jones .30 .09
❑ 257 Jimmy Rollins .30 .09
❑ 258 Brandon Phillips .30 .09
❑ 259 Derek Jeter 1.50 .45
❑ 260 Carl Everett .30 .09
❑ 261 Wes Helms .30 .09
❑ 262 Kyle Lohse .30 .09
❑ 263 Jason Phillips .30 .09
❑ 264 Jake Peavy .30 .09
❑ 265 Orlando Hernandez .30 .09
❑ 266 Keith Foulke .30 .09
❑ 267 Brad Wilkerson .30 .09
❑ 268 Corey Koskie .30 .09
❑ 269 Josh Hall .30 .09
❑ 270 Bobby Higginson .30 .09
❑ 271 Andres Galarraga .30 .09
❑ 272 Alfonso Soriano .30 .09
❑ 273 Carlos Rivera .30 .09
❑ 274 Steve Trachsel .30 .09
❑ 275 David Bell .30 .09
❑ 276 Endy Chavez .30 .09
❑ 277 Jay Payton .30 .09
❑ 278 Mark Mulder .30 .09
❑ 279 Terrence Long .30 .09
❑ 280 A.J. Burnett .30 .09
❑ 281 Pokey Reese .30 .09
❑ 282 Phil Nevin .30 .09
❑ 283 Jose Contreras .30 .09
❑ 284 Jim Thome .50 .15
❑ 285 Pat Burrell .30 .09
❑ 286 Luis Castillo .30 .09
❑ 287 Juan Uribe .30 .09
❑ 288 Raul Ibanez .30 .09
❑ 289 Sidney Ponson .30 .09
❑ 290 Scott Hatteberg .30 .09
❑ 291 Jack Wilson .30 .09
❑ 292 Reggie Sanders .30 .09
❑ 293 Brian Giles .30 .09
❑ 294 Craig Biggio .50 .15
❑ 295 Kazuhisa Ishii .30 .09
❑ 296 Jim Edmonds .50 .15
❑ 297 Trevor Hoffman .30 .09
❑ 298 Ray Durham .30 .09
❑ 299 Mike Lieberthal .30 .09
❑ 300 Tim Worrell .30 .09
❑ 301 Chris George .30 .09
❑ 302 Jamie Moyer .30 .09
❑ 303 Mike Cameron .30 .09
❑ 304 Matt Kinney .30 .09
❑ 305 Aubrey Huff .30 .09
❑ 306 Brian Lawrence .30 .09
❑ 307 Carlos Guillen .30 .09
❑ 308 J.D. Drew .30 .09
❑ 309 Paul Lo Duca .30 .09
❑ 310 Tim Salmon .50 .15
❑ 311 Jason Schmidt .30 .09
❑ 312 A.J. Pierzynski .30 .09
❑ 313 Lance Carter .30 .09
❑ 314 Julio Lugo .30 .09
❑ 315 Johan Santana .50 .15
❑ 316 Laynce Nix .30 .09
❑ 317 John Olerud .30 .09
❑ 318 Robb Quinlan .30 .09
❑ 319 Scott Spiezio .30 .09
❑ 320 Tony Clark .30 .09
❑ 321 Jose Vidro .30 .09
❑ 322 Shea Hillenbrand .30 .09
❑ 323 Doug Glanville .30 .09
❑ 324 Orlando Palmeiro .30 .09
❑ 325 Juan Gonzalez .30 .09
❑ 326 Jason Giambi .30 .09
❑ 327 Junior Spivey .30 .09
❑ 328 Tom Glavine .50 .15
❑ 329 Reed Johnson .30 .09
❑ 330 David Eckstein .30 .09
❑ 331 Damian Jackson .30 .09
❑ 332 Orlando Hudson .30 .09
❑ 333 Barry Zito .30 .09
❑ 334 Robert Fick .30 .09
❑ 335 Aaron Boone .30 .09
❑ 336 Rafael Palmeiro .50 .15
❑ 337 Bobby Kielty .30 .09
❑ 338 Tony Batista .30 .09
❑ 339 Ryan Dempster .30 .09
❑ 340 Derek Lowe .30 .09
❑ 341 Alex Cintron .30 .09
❑ 342 Jermaine Dye .30 .09
❑ 343 John Burkett .30 .09
❑ 344 Javy Lopez .30 .09
❑ 345 Eric Karros .30 .09
❑ 346 Corey Patterson .30 .09
❑ 347 Josh Phelps .30 .09
❑ 348 Ryan Klesko .30 .09
❑ 349 Craig Wilson .30 .09
❑ 350 Brian Roberts .30 .09
❑ 351 Roberto Alomar .50 .15
❑ 352 Frank Thomas .75 .23
❑ 353 Gary Sheffield .30 .09
❑ 354 Alex Gonzalez .30 .09
❑ 355 Jose Cruz Jr. .30 .09
❑ 356 Jerome Williams .30 .09
❑ 357 Mark Kotsay .30 .09
❑ 358 Chris Reitsma .30 .09
❑ 359 Carlos Lee .30 .09
❑ 360 Todd Helton .50 .15
❑ 361 Gil Meche .30 .09
❑ 362 Ryan Franklin .30 .09
❑ 363 Josh Bard .30 .09
❑ 364 Juan Pierre .30 .09
❑ 365 Barry Larkin .50 .15
❑ 366 Edgar Renteria .30 .09
❑ 367 Alex Sanchez .30 .09
❑ 368 Jeff Bagwell .50 .15
❑ 369 Ben Broussard .30 .09
❑ 370 Chan-Ho Park .30 .09
❑ 371 Darrell May .30 .09
❑ 372 Roy Oswalt .30 .09
❑ 373 Craig Monroe .30 .09
❑ 374 Fred McGriff .50 .15
❑ 375 Bengie Molina .30 .09
❑ 376 Aaron Guiel .30 .09
❑ 377 Jeriome Robertson .30 .09
❑ 378 Kenny Rogers .30 .09
❑ 379 Colby Lewis .30 .09
❑ 380 Jeromy Burnitz .30 .09
❑ 381 Orlando Cabrera .30 .09
❑ 382 Joe Randa .30 .09
❑ 383 Miguel Batista .30 .09
❑ 384 Brad Radke .30 .09
❑ 385 Jeremy Giambi .30 .09
❑ 386 Vladimir Guerrero .75 .23
❑ 387 Melvin Mora .30 .09
❑ 388 Royce Clayton .30 .09
❑ 389 Danny Garcia .30 .09
❑ 390 Manny Ramirez .50 .15
❑ 391 Dave McCarty .30 .09
❑ 392 Mark Grudzielanek .30 .09
❑ 393 Mike Piazza 1.25 .35
❑ 394 Jorge Posada .50 .15
❑ 395 Tim Hudson .30 .09
❑ 396 Placido Polanco .30 .09
❑ 397 Mark Loretta .30 .09
❑ 398 Jesse Foppert .30 .09
❑ 399 Albert Pujols 1.50 .45
❑ 400 Jeremi Gonzalez .30 .09
❑ 401 Paul Bako SP 1.00 .30
❑ 402 Luis Matos SP 1.00 .30
❑ 403 Johnny Damon SP 1.50 .45
❑ 404 Kerry Wood SP 1.00 .30
❑ 405 Joe Crede SP 1.00 .30
❑ 406 Jason Davis SP 1.00 .30
❑ 407 Larry Walker SP 1.00 .30
❑ 408 Ivan Rodriguez SP 1.50 .45
❑ 409 Nick Johnson SP 1.00 .30
❑ 410 Jose Lima SP 1.00 .30
❑ 411 Brian Jordan SP 1.00 .30
❑ 412 Eddie Guardado SP 1.00 .30
❑ 413 Ron Calloway SP 1.00 .30
❑ 414 Aaron Heilman SP 1.00 .30
❑ 415 Eric Chavez SP 1.00 .30

❑ 416 Randy Wolf SP .... 1.00 .30
❑ 417 Jason Bay SP .... 1.00 .30
❑ 418 Edgardo Alfonzo SP ...... 1.00 .30
❑ 419 Kazuhiro Sasaki SP .... 1.00 .30
❑ 420 Eduardo Perez SP .... 1.00 .30
❑ 421 Carl Crawford SP .... 1.00 .30
❑ 422 Troy Glaus SP .... 1.00 .30
❑ 423 Joaquin Benoit SP .... 1.00 .30
❑ 424 Russ Ortiz SP .... 1.00 .30
❑ 425 Larry Bigbie SP .... 1.00 .30
❑ 426 Todd Walker SP .... 1.00 .30
❑ 427 Kris Benson SP .... 1.00 .30
❑ 428 Sandy Alomar Jr. SP ...... 1.00 .30
❑ 429 Jody Gerut SP .... 1.00 .30
❑ 430 Rene Reyes SP .... 1.00 .30
❑ 431 Mike Lowell SP .... 1.00 .30
❑ 432 Jeff Kent SP .... 1.00 .30
❑ 433 Mike MacDougal SP ...... 1.00 .30
❑ 434 Dave Roberts SP .... 1.00 .30
❑ 435 Torii Hunter SP .... 1.00 .30
❑ 436 Tomo Ohka SP .... 1.00 .30
❑ 437 Jeremy Griffiths SP .... 1.00 .30
❑ 438 Miguel Tejada SP .... 1.00 .30
❑ 439 Vicente Padilla SP .... 1.00 .30
❑ 440 Bobby Hill SP .... 1.00 .30
❑ 441 Rich Aurilia SP .... 1.00 .30
❑ 442 Shigetoshi Hasegawa SP 1.00 .30
❑ 443 So Taguchi SP .... 1.00 .30
❑ 444 Damian Rolls SP .... 1.00 .30
❑ 445 Roy Halladay SP .... 1.00 .30
❑ 446 Rocco Baldelli SO SP .... 1.00 .30
❑ 447 Dontrelle Willis SO SP .. 1.50 .45
❑ 448 Mark Prior SO SP .... 1.50 .45
❑ 449 Jason Lane SO SP .... 1.00 .30
❑ 450 Angel Berroa SO SP ...... 1.00 .30
❑ 451 Jose Reyes SO SP .... 1.00 .30
❑ 452 Ryan Wagner SO SP ...... 1.00 .30
❑ 453 Marlon Byrd SO SP .... 1.00 .30
❑ 454 Hee Seop Choi SO SP .... 1.00 .30
❑ 455 Brandon Webb SO SP .... 1.00 .30
❑ 456 Bo Hart SO SP .... 1.00 .30
❑ 457 Hank Blalock SO SP ...... 1.00 .30
❑ 458 Mark Teixeira SO SP ...... 1.50 .45
❑ 459 Hideki Matsui SO SP 5.00 1.50
❑ 460 Scott Podsednik SO SP .. 1.00 .30
❑ 461 Miguel Cabrera SO SP .. 1.50 .45
❑ 462 Josh Beckett AW SP ...... 1.00 .30
❑ 463 Mariano Rivera AW SP .. 1.50 .45
❑ 464 Ivan Rodriguez AW SP .. 1.50 .45
❑ 465 Alex Rodriguez AW SP .. 4.00 1.20
❑ 466 Albert Pujols AW SP 5.00 1.50
❑ 467 Roy Halladay AW SP ...... 1.00 .30
❑ 468 Eric Gagne AW SP .... 1.00 .30
❑ 469 Angel Berroa AW SP ...... 1.00 .30
❑ 470 Dontrelle Willis AW SP .. 1.50 .45
❑ 471 Chris Bootcheck .... 1.00 .30
Tom Gregorio
Richard Fischer SP
❑ 472 Matt Kata .... 1.00 .30
Tim Olson
Robby Hammock SP
❑ 473 Michael Hessman .... 1.00 .30
Chris Waters
Greg Aquino SP
❑ 474 Carlos Mendez .... 1.00 .30
Daniel Cabrera
Jeremy Guthrie SP
❑ 475 Edwin Almonte .... 1.00 .30
Phil Seibel
Felix Sanchez SP
❑ 476 Todd Wellemeyer .... 1.00 .30
Jon Leicester
Sergio Mitre SP
❑ 477 Josh Stewart .... 1.00 .30
Neal Cotts
Aaron Miles SP
❑ 478 Terrmel Sledge .... 1.00 .30
Josh Hall
Brandon Claussen SP
❑ 479 Francisco Cruceta .... 1.00 .30
Jason Stanford
Rafael Betancourt SP
❑ 480 Javier A.Lopez .... 1.50 .45
Garrett Atkins
Clint Barmes SP
❑ 481 Wilfredo Ledezma .... 1.50 .45
Nook Logan
Jeremy Bonderman SP
❑ 482 Josh Willingham .... 1.00 .30
Kevin Hooper
Rick Roberts SP
❑ 483 Colin Porter .... 1.00 .30
Mike Gallo
Dave Matranga SP
❑ 484 David DeJesus .... 1.00 .30
Jason Gilfillan
Jimmy Gobble SP
❑ 485 Koyie Hill .... 1.00 .30
Alfredo Gonzalez
Andrew Brown SP
❑ 486 Rickie Weeks .... 1.50 .45
Pedro Liriano
Wes Obermueller SP
❑ 487 Alex Prieto .... 1.00 .30
Mike Ryan
Lew Ford SP
❑ 488 Julio Manon .... 1.00 .30
Luis Ayala
Seung Song SP
❑ 489 Jeff Duncan .... 1.50 .45
Prentice Redman
Craig Brazell SP
❑ 490 Chien-Ming Wang .... 1.50 .45
Michel Hernandez
Mike Gonzalez SP
❑ 491 Rich Harden .... 1.50 .45
Mike Neu
Geoff Geary SP
❑ 492 Diegomar Markwell .... 1.00 .30
Chad Gaudin
David Sanders SP
❑ 493 Beau Kemp .... 1.00 .30
Micheal Nakamura
D.J. Carrasco SP
❑ 494 Khalil Greene 4.00 1.20
Miguel Ojeda
Bernie Castro SP
❑ 495 Noah Lowry .... 1.50 .45
Todd Linden
Kevin Correia SP
❑ 496 Aaron Looper .... 1.00 .30
Brian Sweeney
Rett Johnson SP
❑ 497 John Gall RC .... 2.50 .75
Dan Haren
Kevin Ohme SP
❑ 498 Delmon Young .... 2.50 .75
Doug Waechter
Matt Diaz SP
❑ 499 Gerald Laird .... 1.00 .30
Rosman Garcia
Ramon Nivar SP
❑ 500 Alexis Rios .... 1.50 .45
Guillermo Quiroz
Francisco Rosario SP

2005 Fleer Tradition

	Nm-Mt	Ex-Mt
COMPLETE SET (350)	150.00	45.00
COMP.SET w/o SP's (300)	40.00	12.00
COMMON CARD (1-300)	.30	.09
COMMON CARD (301-330)	5.00	1.50
COMMON CARD (331-350)	1.00	.30

301-350 STATED ODDS 1:2 H, 1:4 R

❑ 1 Johan Santana .... .50 .15
Curt Schilling
Jake Westbrook SL
❑ 2 Ben Sheets .... .50 .15
Jake Peavy
Randy Johnson SL
❑ 3 Johan Santana .... .30 .09
Bartolo Colon
Curt Schilling SL
❑ 4 Carl Pavano .... .75 .23
Roy Oswalt
Roger Clemens SL
❑ 5 Johan Santana .... .30 .09
Pedro Martinez
Curt Schilling SL
❑ 6 Jason Schmidt .... .50 .15
Randy Johnson
Ben Sheets SL
❑ 7 Melvin Mora .... .75 .23
Vladimir Guerrero
Ichiro Suzuki SL
❑ 8 Adrian Beltre .... .30 .09
Todd Helton
Mark Loretta SL
❑ 9 Manny Ramirez .... .50 .15
Paul Konerko
David Ortiz SL
❑ 10 Albert Pujols .... .75 .23
Adrian Beltre
Adam Dunn SL
❑ 11 David Ortiz .... .50 .15
Manny Ramirez
Miguel Tejada SL
❑ 12 Albert Pujols .... .50 .15
Vinny Castilla
Scott Rolen SL
❑ 13 Jason Bay .... .30 .09
❑ 14 Greg Maddux .... 1.25 .35
❑ 15 Melvin Mora .... .30 .09
❑ 16 Matt Stairs .... .30 .09
❑ 17 Scott Podsednik .... .30 .09
❑ 18 Bartolo Colon .... .30 .09
❑ 19 Roger Clemens .... 1.25 .35
❑ 20 Eric Hinske .... .30 .09
❑ 21 Johnny Estrada .... .30 .09
❑ 22 Brett Tomko .... .30 .09
❑ 23 John Buck .... .30 .09
❑ 24 Nomar Garciaparra .... .75 .23
❑ 25 Milton Bradley .... .30 .09
❑ 26 Craig Biggio .... .50 .15
❑ 27 Kyle Denney .... .30 .09
❑ 28 Brad Penny .... .30 .09
❑ 29 Todd Helton .... .50 .15
❑ 30 Luis Gonzalez .... .30 .09
❑ 31 Bill Hall .... .30 .09
❑ 32 Ruben Sierra .... .30 .09
❑ 33 Zach Greinke .... .30 .09
❑ 34 Sandy Alomar Jr. .... .30 .09
❑ 35 Jason Giambi .... .30 .09
❑ 36 Ben Sheets .... .30 .09
❑ 37 Edgardo Alfonzo .... .30 .09
❑ 38 Kenny Rogers .... .30 .09
❑ 39 Coco Crisp .... .30 .09
❑ 40 Randy Choate .... .30 .09
❑ 41 Braden Looper .... .30 .09
❑ 42 Adam Dunn .... .30 .09
❑ 43 Adam Eaton .... .30 .09
❑ 44 Luis Castillo .... .30 .09
❑ 45 Casey Fossum .... .30 .09
❑ 46 Mike Piazza .... .75 .23
❑ 47 Juan Pierre .... .30 .09
❑ 48 Doug Davis .... .30 .09
❑ 49 Manny Ramirez .... .50 .15
❑ 50 Travis Hafner .... .30 .09
❑ 51 Jack Wilson .... .30 .09
❑ 52 Mike Maroth .... .30 .09
❑ 53 Ken Harvey .... .30 .09
❑ 54 Brooks Kieschnick .... .30 .09
❑ 55 Brad Fullmer .... .30 .09
❑ 56 Octavio Dotel .... .30 .09
❑ 57 Mike Matheny .... .30 .09
❑ 58 Andruw Jones .... .50 .15
❑ 59 Alfonso Soriano .... .30 .09
❑ 60 Royce Clayton .... .30 .09
❑ 61 Jon Garland .... .30 .09
❑ 62 John Mabry .... .30 .09

❑ 63 Rafael Palmeiro .50 .15
❑ 64 Garett Atkins .30 .09
❑ 65 Brian Meadows .30 .09
❑ 66 Tony Armas Jr. .30 .09
❑ 67 Toby Hall .30 .09
❑ 68 Carlos Baerga .30 .09
❑ 69 Barry Larkin .50 .15
❑ 70 Jody Gerut .30 .09
❑ 71 Brent Mayne .30 .09
❑ 72 Shigetoshi Hasegawa .30 .09
❑ 73 Jose Cruz Jr. .30 .09
❑ 74 Dan Wilson .30 .09
❑ 75 Sidney Ponson .30 .09
❑ 76 Jason Jennings .30 .09
❑ 77 A.J. Burnett .30 .09
❑ 78 Tony Batista .30 .09
❑ 79 Kris Benson .30 .09
❑ 80 Sean Burroughs .30 .09
❑ 81 Eric Young .30 .09
❑ 82 Casey Kotchman .30 .09
❑ 83 Derrek Lee .50 .15
❑ 84 Mariano Rivera .50 .15
❑ 85 Julio Franco .30 .09
❑ 86 Corey Patterson .30 .09
❑ 87 Carlos Beltran .30 .09
❑ 88 Trevor Hoffman .30 .09
❑ 89 Danny Garcia .30 .09
❑ 90 Marcos Scutaro .30 .09
❑ 91 Marquis Grissom .30 .09
❑ 92 Aubrey Huff .30 .09
❑ 93 Tony Womack .30 .09
❑ 94 Placido Polanco .30 .09
❑ 95 Bengie Molina .30 .09
❑ 96 Roger Cedeno .30 .09
❑ 97 Geoff Jenkins .30 .09
❑ 98 Kip Wells .30 .09
❑ 99 Derek Jeter 1.50 .45
❑ 100 Omar Infante .30 .09
❑ 101 Phil Nevin .30 .09
❑ 102 Edgar Renteria .30 .09
❑ 103 B.J. Surhoff .30 .09
❑ 104 David DeJesus .30 .09
❑ 105 Raul Ibanez .30 .09
❑ 106 Hank Blalock .30 .09
❑ 107 Shawn Estes .30 .09
❑ 108 Wily Mo Pena .30 .09
❑ 109 Shawn Green .30 .09
❑ 110 David Wright 2.00 .60
❑ 111 Kenny Lofton .30 .09
❑ 112 Matt Clement .30 .09
❑ 113 Cesar Izturis .30 .09
❑ 114 John Lackey .30 .09
❑ 115 Torii Hunter .30 .09
❑ 116 Charles Johnson .30 .09
❑ 117 Ray Durham .30 .09
❑ 118 Luke Hudson .30 .09
❑ 119 Jeremy Bonderman .30 .09
❑ 120 Sean Casey .50 .15
❑ 121 Johnny Damon .50 .15
❑ 122 Eric Milton .30 .09
❑ 123 Shea Hillenbrand .30 .09
❑ 124 Johan Santana .50 .15
❑ 125 Jim Edmonds .50 .15
❑ 126 Javier Vazquez .30 .09
❑ 127 Jon Adkins .30 .09
❑ 128 Mike Lowell .30 .09
❑ 129 Khalil Greene .50 .15
❑ 130 Quinton McCracken .30 .09
❑ 131 Edgar Martinez .50 .15
❑ 132 Matt Lawton .30 .09
❑ 133 Jeff Weaver .30 .09
❑ 134 Marlon Byrd .30 .09
❑ 135 John Smoltz .50 .15
❑ 136 Grady Sizemore .30 .09
❑ 137 Brian Roberts .30 .09
❑ 138 Dee Brown .30 .09
❑ 139 Joel Pineiro .30 .09
❑ 140 David Dellucci .30 .09
❑ 141 Bobby Higginson .30 .09
❑ 142 Ryan Madson .30 .09
❑ 143 Scott Hatteberg .30 .09
❑ 144 Greg Zaun .30 .09
❑ 145 Brian Jordan .30 .09
❑ 146 Jason Isringhausen .30 .09
❑ 147 Vinnie Chulk .30 .09
❑ 148 Al Leiter .30 .09
❑ 149 Pedro Martinez .50 .15
❑ 150 Carlos Guillen .30 .09
❑ 151 Randy Wolf .30 .09
❑ 152 Vernon Wells .30 .09
❑ 153 Barry Zito .30 .09
❑ 154 Pedro Feliz .30 .09
❑ 155 Omar Vizquel .50 .15
❑ 156 Chone Figgins .30 .09
❑ 157 David Ortiz .75 .23
❑ 158 Sunny Kim .30 .09
❑ 159 Adam Kennedy .30 .09
❑ 160 Carlos Lee .30 .09
❑ 161 Rick Ankiel .30 .09
❑ 162 Roy Oswalt .30 .09
❑ 163 Armando Benitez .30 .09
❑ 164 Erubiel Durazo .30 .09
❑ 165 Adam Hyzdu .30 .09
❑ 166 Esteban Yan .30 .09
❑ 167 Victor Santos .30 .09
❑ 168 Kevin Millwood .30 .09
❑ 169 Andy Pettitte .50 .15
❑ 170 Mike Cameron .30 .09
❑ 171 Scott Rolen .50 .15
❑ 172 Trot Nixon .30 .09
❑ 173 Eric Munson .30 .09
❑ 174 Roy Halladay .30 .09
❑ 175 Juan Encarnacion .30 .09
❑ 176 Eric Chavez .30 .09
❑ 177 Terrmel Sledge .30 .09
❑ 178 Jason Schmidt .30 .09
❑ 179 Endy Chavez .30 .09
❑ 180 Carlos Zambrano .30 .09
❑ 181 Carlos Delgado .30 .09
❑ 182 Dewon Brazelton .30 .09
❑ 183 J.D. Drew .30 .09
❑ 184 Orlando Cabrera .30 .09
❑ 185 Craig Wilson .30 .09
❑ 186 Chin-Hui Tsao .30 .09
❑ 187 Jolbert Cabrera .30 .09
❑ 188 Rod Barajas .30 .09
❑ 189 Craig Monroe .30 .09
❑ 190 Dave Berg .30 .09
❑ 191 Carlos Silva .30 .09
❑ 192 Eric Gagne .30 .09
❑ 193 Marcus Giles .30 .09
❑ 194 Nick Johnson .30 .09
❑ 195 Kelvim Escobar .30 .09
❑ 196 Wade Miller .30 .09
❑ 197 David Bell .30 .09
❑ 198 Rondell White .30 .09
❑ 199 Brian Giles .30 .09
❑ 200 Jeromy Burnitz .30 .09
❑ 201 Carl Pavano .30 .09
❑ 202 Alex Rios .30 .09
❑ 203 Ryan Freel .30 .09
❑ 204 R.A. Dickey .30 .09
❑ 205 Miguel Cairo .30 .09
❑ 206 Kerry Wood .30 .09
❑ 207 C.C. Sabathia .30 .09
❑ 208 Jaime Cerda .30 .09
❑ 209 Jerome Williams .30 .09
❑ 210 Ryan Wagner .30 .09
❑ 211 Javy Lopez .30 .09
❑ 212 Tike Redman .30 .09
❑ 213 Richie Sexson .30 .09
❑ 214 Shannon Stewart .30 .09
❑ 215 Ben Davis .30 .09
❑ 216 Jeff Bagwell .50 .15
❑ 217 David Wells .30 .09
❑ 218 Justin Leone .30 .09
❑ 219 Brad Radke .30 .09
❑ 220 Ramon Santiago .30 .09
❑ 221 Richard Hidalgo .30 .09
❑ 222 Aaron Miles .30 .09
❑ 223 Mark Loretta .30 .09
❑ 224 Aaron Boone .30 .09
❑ 225 Steve Trachsel .30 .09
❑ 226 Geoff Blum .30 .09
❑ 227 Shingo Takatsu .30 .09
❑ 228 Kevin Youkilis .30 .09
❑ 229 Laynce Nix .30 .09
❑ 230 Daniel Cabrera .30 .09
❑ 231 Kyle Lohse .30 .09
❑ 232 Todd Pratt .30 .09
❑ 233 Reed Johnson .30 .09
❑ 234 Lance Berkman .30 .09
❑ 235 Hideki Matsui 1.50 .45
❑ 236 Randy Winn .30 .09
❑ 237 Joe Randa .30 .09
❑ 238 Bob Howry .30 .09
❑ 239 Jason LaRue .30 .09
❑ 240 Jose Valentin .30 .09
❑ 241 Livan Hernandez .30 .09
❑ 242 Jamie Moyer .30 .09
❑ 243 Garret Anderson .30 .09
❑ 244 Brad Ausmus .30 .09
❑ 245 Russell Branyan .30 .09
❑ 246 Paul Wilson .30 .09
❑ 247 Tim Wakefield .30 .09
❑ 248 Roberto Alomar .50 .15
❑ 249 Kazuhisa Ishii .30 .09
❑ 250 Tino Martinez .50 .15
❑ 251 Tomo Ohka .30 .09
❑ 252 Mark Redman .30 .09
❑ 253 Paul Byrd .30 .09
❑ 254 Greg Aquino .30 .09
❑ 255 Adrian Beltre .30 .09
❑ 256 Ricky Ledee .30 .09
❑ 257 Josh Fogg .30 .09
❑ 258 Derek Lowe .30 .09
❑ 259 Lew Ford .30 .09
❑ 260 Bobby Crosby .30 .09
❑ 261 Jim Thome .50 .15
❑ 262 Jaret Wright .30 .09
❑ 263 Chin-Feng Chen .30 .09
❑ 264 Troy Glaus .30 .09
❑ 265 Jorge Sosa .30 .09
❑ 266 Mike Lamb .30 .09
❑ 267 Russ Ortiz .30 .09
❑ 268 Reggie Sanders .30 .09
❑ 269 Orlando Hudson .30 .09
❑ 270 Rodrigo Lopez .30 .09
❑ 271 Jose Vidro .30 .09
❑ 272 Akinori Otsuka .30 .09
❑ 273 Victor Martinez .30 .09
❑ 274 Carl Crawford .30 .09
❑ 275 Roberto Novoa .30 .09
❑ 276 Brian Lawrence .30 .09
❑ 277 Angel Berroa .30 .09
❑ 278 Josh Beckett .30 .09
❑ 279 Lyle Overbay .30 .09
❑ 280 Dustin Hermanson .30 .09
❑ 281 Jeff Conine .30 .09
❑ 282 Mark Prior .50 .15
❑ 283 Kevin Brown .30 .09
❑ 284 Magglio Ordonez .30 .09
❑ 285 Dontrelle Willis .30 .09
❑ 286 Dallas McPherson .30 .09
❑ 287 Rafael Furcal .30 .09
❑ 288 Ty Wigginton .30 .09
❑ 289 Moises Alou .30 .09
❑ 290 A.J. Pierzynski .30 .09
❑ 291 Todd Walker .30 .09
❑ 292 Hideo Nomo .75 .23
❑ 293 Larry Walker .50 .15
❑ 294 Choo Freeman .30 .09
❑ 295 Eduardo Perez .30 .09
❑ 296 Miguel Tejada .30 .09
❑ 297 Corey Koskie .30 .09
❑ 298 Jermaine Dye .30 .09
❑ 299 John Riedling .30 .09
❑ 300 John Olerud .30 .09
❑ 301 Tim Bittner 5.00 1.50
Jake Woods
Bobby Jenks TP
❑ 302 Josh Kroeger 5.00 1.50
Casey Daigle
Brandon Medders TP
❑ 303 Kelly Johnson 5.00 1.50
Charles Thomas
Dan Meyer TP
❑ 304 Eddy Rodriguez 5.00 1.50
Ryan Hannaman
John Maine TP
❑ 305 Anastacio Martinez 5.00 1.50
Jerome Gamble
Lenny Dinardo TP
❑ 306 Ronny Cedeno 5.00 1.50
Carlos Vasquez
Renyel Pinto TP
❑ 307 Arnie Munoz 5.00 1.50
Ryan Wing

Felix Diaz TP
❑ 308 William Bergolla 5.00 1.50
Ray Olmedo
Edwin Encarnacion TP
❑ 309 Mariano Gomez 5.00 1.50
Ivan Ochoa
Kazuhito Tadano TP
❑ 310 Tony Miller 5.00 1.50
Jeff Baker
Matt Holliday TP
❑ 311 Preston Larrison 5.00 1.50
Curtis Granderson
Ryan Raburn TP
❑ 312 Josh Wilson 5.00 1.50
Logan Kensing
Kevin Cave TP
❑ 313 Hector Gimenez 5.00 1.50
Willy Taveras
Taylor Buchholz TP
❑ 314 Ruben Gotay 5.00 1.50
Brian Bass
Andres Blanco TP
❑ 315 Joel Hanrahan 5.00 1.50
Willy Aybar
Yhency Brazoban TP
❑ 316 Dave Krynzel 5.00 1.50
Ben Hendrickson
Corey Hart TP
❑ 317 Colby Miller 5.00 1.50
Jason Kubel
J.D. Durbin TP
❑ 318 Maicer Izturis 5.00 1.50
Chad Cordero
Brandon Watson TP
❑ 319 Victor Diaz 5.00 1.50
Aarom Baldiris
Wayne Lydon TP
❑ 320 Edwardo Sierra 5.00 1.50
Dioner Navarro
Sean Henn TP
❑ 321 Nick Swisher 5.00 1.50
Joe Blanton
Dan Johnson TP
❑ 322 Ryan Howard 5.00 1.50
Gavin Floyd
Keith Bucktrot TP
❑ 323 Ryan Doumit 5.00 1.50
Sean Burnett
Bobby Bradley TP
❑ 324 Justin Germano 5.00 1.50
Rusty Tucker
Freddy Guzman TP
❑ 325 David Aardsma 5.00 1.50
Justin Knoedler
Alfredo Simon TP
❑ 326 Jose Lopez 5.00 1.50
Rene Rivera
Cha Seung Baek TP
❑ 327 Yadier Molina 5.00 1.50
Evan Rust
Adam Wainwright TP
❑ 328 Jorge Cantu 5.00 1.50
Scott Kazmir
B.J. Upton TP
❑ 329 Adrian Gonzalez 5.00 1.50
Ramon Nivar
Jason Bourgeois TP
❑ 330 Russ Adams 5.00 1.50
Dustin McGowan
Gustavo Chacin TP
❑ 331 Alfonso Soriano AW .... 1.00 .30
❑ 332 Albert Pujols AW .... 3.00 .90
❑ 333 David Ortiz AW .... 1.50 .45
❑ 334 Manny Ramirez AW .... 1.50 .45
❑ 335 Jason Bay AW .... 1.00 .30
❑ 336 Bobby Crosby AW .... 1.00 .30
❑ 337 Roger Clemens AW .... 2.50 .75
❑ 338 Johan Santana AW .... 1.50 .45
❑ 339 Jim Thome AW .... 1.50 .45
❑ 340 Vladimir Guerrero AW .... 1.50 .45
❑ 341 David Ortiz PS .... 1.50 .45
❑ 342 Alex Rodriguez PS .... 2.50 .75
❑ 343 Albert Pujols PS .... 3.00 .90
❑ 344 Carlos Beltran PS .... 1.00 .30
❑ 345 Johnny Damon PS .... 1.50 .45
❑ 346 Scott Rolen PS .... 1.50 .45
❑ 347 Larry Walker PS .... 1.50 .45
❑ 348 Curt Schilling PS .... 1.50 .45
❑ 349 Pedro Martinez PS .... 1.50 .45
❑ 350 David Ortiz PS .... 1.50 .45

1933 Goudey

	Ex-Mt	VG
COMPLETE SET (239)	40000.00	20000.00
COMMON CARD (1-52)	75.00	38.00
COMMON (41/43/53-240)	60.00	30.00
WRAPPER (1-CENT, BAT.)	100.00	50.00
WRAPPER (1-CENT, AD)	175.00	90.00

❑ 1 Benny Bengough 1500.00 450.00
❑ 2 Dazzy Vance 200.00 100.00
❑ 3 Hugh Critz 75.00 38.00
❑ 4 Heinie Schuble 75.00 38.00
❑ 5 Babe Herman 75.00 38.00
❑ 6 Jimmy Dykes 75.00 38.00
❑ 7 Ted Lyons 150.00 75.00
❑ 8 Roy Johnson 75.00 38.00
❑ 9 Dave Harris 75.00 38.00
❑ 10 Glenn Myatt 75.00 38.00
❑ 11 Billy Rogell 75.00 38.00
❑ 12 George Pipgras 75.00 38.00
❑ 13 Fresco Thompson 75.00 38.00
❑ 14 Henry Johnson 75.00 38.00
❑ 15 Victor Sorrell 75.00 38.00
❑ 16 George Blaeholder 75.00 38.00
❑ 17 Watson Clark 75.00 38.00
❑ 18 Muddy Ruel 75.00 38.00
❑ 19 Bill Dickey 350.00 180.00
❑ 20 Bill Terry THROW 250.00 125.00
❑ 21 Phil Collins 75.00 38.00
❑ 22 Pie Traynor 250.00 125.00
❑ 23 Kiki Cuyler 200.00 100.00
❑ 24 Horace Ford 75.00 38.00
❑ 25 Paul Waner 200.00 100.00
❑ 26 Bill Cissell 75.00 38.00
❑ 27 George Connally 75.00 38.00
❑ 28 Dick Bartell 75.00 38.00
❑ 29 Jimmie Foxx 600.00 300.00
❑ 30 Frank Hogan 75.00 38.00
❑ 31 Tony Lazzeri 400.00 200.00
❑ 32 Bud Clancy 75.00 38.00
❑ 33 Ralph Kress 75.00 38.00
❑ 34 Bob O'Farrell 75.00 38.00
❑ 35 Al Simmons 350.00 180.00
❑ 36 Tommy Thevenow 75.00 38.00
❑ 37 Jimmy Wilson 75.00 38.00
❑ 38 Fred Brickell 75.00 38.00
❑ 39 Mark Koenig 75.00 38.00
❑ 40 Taylor Douthit 75.00 38.00
❑ 41 Gus Mancuso 60.00 30.00
❑ 42 Eddie Collins 150.00 75.00
❑ 43 Lew Fonseca 60.00 30.00
❑ 44 Jim Bottomley 150.00 75.00
❑ 45 Larry Benton 75.00 38.00
❑ 46 Ethan Allen 75.00 38.00
❑ 47 Heinie Manush BAT 175.00 90.00
❑ 48 Marty McManus 75.00 38.00
❑ 49 Frankie Frisch 300.00 150.00
❑ 50 Ed Brandt 75.00 38.00
❑ 51 Charlie Grimm 75.00 38.00
❑ 52 Andy Cohen 75.00 38.00
❑ 53 Babe Ruth 6000.00 3000.00
❑ 54 Ray Kremer 60.00 30.00
❑ 55 Pat Malone 60.00 30.00
❑ 56 Red Ruffing 175.00 90.00
❑ 57 Earl Clark 60.00 30.00
❑ 58 Lefty O'Doul 125.00 60.00
❑ 59 Bing Miller 60.00 30.00
❑ 60 Waite Hoyt 125.00 60.00
❑ 61 Max Bishop 60.00 30.00
❑ 62 Pepper Martin 125.00 60.00
❑ 63 Joe Cronin BAT 150.00 75.00
❑ 64 Burleigh Grimes 250.00 125.00
❑ 65 Milt Gaston 60.00 30.00
❑ 66 George Grantham 60.00 30.00
❑ 67 Guy Bush 60.00 30.00
❑ 68 Horace Lisenbee 60.00 30.00
❑ 69 Randy Moore 60.00 30.00
❑ 70 Floyd (Pete) Scott 60.00 30.00
❑ 71 Robert J. Burke 60.00 30.00
❑ 72 Owen Carroll 60.00 30.00
❑ 73 Jesse Haines 125.00 60.00
❑ 74 Eppa Rixey 150.00 75.00
❑ 75 Willie Kamm 60.00 30.00
❑ 76 Mickey Cochrane 250.00 125.00
❑ 77 Adam Comorosky 60.00 30.00
❑ 78 Jack Quinn 60.00 30.00
❑ 79 Red Faber 125.00 60.00
❑ 80 Clyde Manion 60.00 30.00
❑ 81 Sam Jones 60.00 30.00
❑ 82 Dib Williams 60.00 30.00
❑ 83 Pete Jablonowski 60.00 30.00
❑ 84 Glenn Spencer 60.00 30.00
❑ 85 Heinie Sand 60.00 30.00
❑ 86 Phil Todt 60.00 30.00
❑ 87 Frank O'Rourke 60.00 30.00
❑ 88 Russell Rollings 60.00 30.00
❑ 89 Tris Speaker RET 300.00 150.00
❑ 90 Jess Petty 60.00 30.00
❑ 91 Tom Zachary 60.00 30.00
❑ 92 Lou Gehrig 2500.00 1250.00
❑ 93 John Welch 60.00 30.00
❑ 94 Bill Walker 60.00 30.00
❑ 95 Alvin Crowder 60.00 30.00
❑ 96 Willis Hudlin 60.00 30.00
❑ 97 Joe Morrissey 60.00 30.00
❑ 98 Wally Berger 75.00 38.00
❑ 99 Tony Cuccinello 75.00 38.00
❑ 100 George Uhle 60.00 30.00
❑ 101 Richard Coffman 60.00 30.00
❑ 102 Travis Jackson 150.00 75.00
❑ 103 Earle Combs 125.00 60.00
❑ 104 Fred Marberry 60.00 30.00
❑ 105 Bernie Friberg 60.00 30.00
❑ 106 Napoleon Lajoie SP 25000.00 12500.00
(Not issued
until 1934)
❑ 107 Heinie Manush 125.00 60.00
❑ 108 Joe Kuhel 60.00 30.00
❑ 109 Joe Cronin 300.00 150.00
❑ 110 Goose Goslin 250.00 125.00
❑ 111 Monte Weaver 60.00 30.00
❑ 112 Fred Schulte 60.00 30.00
❑ 113 Oswald Bluege POR 60.00 30.00
❑ 114 Luke Sewell FIELD 75.00 38.00
❑ 115 Cliff Heathcote 60.00 30.00
❑ 116 Eddie Morgan 60.00 30.00
❑ 117 Rabbit Maranville 125.00 60.00
❑ 118 Val Picinich 60.00 30.00
❑ 119 R. Hornsby FIELD 600.00 300.00
❑ 120 Carl Reynolds 60.00 30.00
❑ 121 Walter Stewart 60.00 30.00
❑ 122 Alvin Crowder 60.00 30.00
❑ 123 Jack Russell 60.00 30.00
❑ 124 Earl Whitehill 60.00 30.00
❑ 125 Bill Terry 250.00 125.00
❑ 126 Joe Moore 60.00 30.00
❑ 127 Mel Ott 400.00 200.00
❑ 128 Chuck Klein 175.00 90.00
❑ 129 Hal Schumacher PIT 60.00 30.00
❑ 130 Fred Fitzsimmons POR 60.00 30.00
❑ 131 Fred Frankhouse 60.00 30.00
❑ 132 Jim Elliott 60.00 30.00
❑ 133 Fred Lindstrom 125.00 60.00
❑ 134 Sam Rice 200.00 100.00
❑ 135 Woody English 60.00 30.00
❑ 136 Flint Rhem 60.00 30.00
❑ 137 Red Lucas 60.00 30.00
❑ 138 Herb Pennock 175.00 90.00
❑ 139 Ben Cantwell 60.00 30.00
❑ 140 Bump Hadley 60.00 30.00

❑ 141 Ray Benge 60.00 30.00
❑ 142 Paul Richards 75.00 38.00
❑ 143 Glenn Wright 60.00 30.00
❑ 144 Babe Ruth Bat DP 4000.00 2000.00
❑ 145 Rube Walberg 60.00 30.00
❑ 146 Walter Stewart PIT 60.00 30.00
❑ 147 Leo Durocher 200.00 100.00
❑ 148 Eddie Farrell 60.00 30.00
❑ 149 Babe Ruth 5000.00 2500.00
❑ 150 Ray Kolp 60.00 30.00
❑ 151 Jake Flowers 60.00 30.00
❑ 152 Zack Taylor 60.00 30.00
❑ 153 Buddy Myer 60.00 30.00
❑ 154 Jimmie Foxx 600.00 300.00
❑ 155 Joe Judge 60.00 30.00
❑ 156 Danny MacFayden 60.00 30.00
❑ 157 Sam Byrd 60.00 30.00
❑ 158 Moe Berg 400.00 200.00
❑ 159 Oswald Bluege FIELD 60.00 30.00
❑ 160 Lou Gehrig 3000.00 1500.00
❑ 161 Al Spohrer 60.00 30.00
❑ 162 Leo Mangum 60.00 30.00
❑ 163 Luke Sewell POR 75.00 38.00
❑ 164 Lloyd Waner 250.00 125.00
❑ 165 Joe Sewell 125.00 60.00
❑ 166 Sam West 60.00 30.00
❑ 167 Jack Russell 60.00 30.00
❑ 168 Goose Goslin 200.00 100.00
❑ 169 Al Thomas 60.00 30.00
❑ 170 Harry McCurdy 60.00 30.00
❑ 171 Charlie Jamieson 60.00 30.00
❑ 172 Billy Hargrave 60.00 30.00
❑ 173 Roscoe Holm 60.00 30.00
❑ 174 Warren(Curly) Ogden 60.00 30.00
❑ 175 Dan Howley MG 60.00 30.00
❑ 176 John Ogden 60.00 30.00
❑ 177 Walter French 60.00 30.00
❑ 178 Jackie Warner 60.00 30.00
❑ 179 Fred Leach 60.00 30.00
❑ 180 Eddie Moore 60.00 30.00
❑ 181 Babe Ruth 4000.00 2000.00
❑ 182 Andy High 60.00 30.00
❑ 183 Rube Walberg 60.00 30.00
❑ 184 Charley Berry 60.00 30.00
❑ 185 Bob Smith 60.00 30.00
❑ 186 John Schulte 60.00 30.00
❑ 187 Heinie Manush 150.00 75.00
❑ 188 Rogers Hornsby 600.00 300.00
❑ 189 Joe Cronin 200.00 100.00
❑ 190 Fred Schulte 60.00 30.00
❑ 191 Ben Chapman 75.00 38.00
❑ 192 Walter Brown 60.00 30.00
❑ 193 Lynford Lary 60.00 30.00
❑ 194 Earl Averill 200.00 100.00
❑ 195 Evar Swanson 60.00 30.00
❑ 196 Leroy Mahaffey 60.00 30.00
❑ 197 Rick Ferrell 125.00 60.00
❑ 198 Jack Burns 60.00 30.00
❑ 199 Tom Bridges 60.00 30.00
❑ 200 Bill Hallahan 60.00 30.00
❑ 201 Ernie Orsatti 60.00 30.00
❑ 202 Gabby Hartnett 250.00 125.00
❑ 203 Lon Warneke 60.00 30.00
❑ 204 Riggs Stephenson 60.00 30.00
❑ 205 Heinie Meine 60.00 30.00
❑ 206 Gus Suhr 60.00 30.00
❑ 207 Mel Ott Bat 400.00 200.00
❑ 208 Bernie James 60.00 30.00
❑ 209 Adolfo Luque 75.00 38.00
❑ 210 Spud Davis 60.00 30.00
❑ 211 Hack Wilson 400.00 200.00
❑ 212 Billy Urbanski 60.00 30.00
❑ 213 Earl Adams 60.00 30.00
❑ 214 John Kerr 60.00 30.00
❑ 215 Russ Van Atta 60.00 30.00
❑ 216 Lefty Gomez 300.00 150.00
❑ 217 Frank Crosetti 150.00 75.00
❑ 218 Wes Ferrell 75.00 38.00
❑ 219 Mule Haas UER 60.00 30.00
Name spelled Hass on front
❑ 220 Lefty Grove 500.00 250.00
❑ 221 Dale Alexander 60.00 30.00
❑ 222 Charley Gehringer 400.00 200.00
❑ 223 Dizzy Dean 800.00 400.00
❑ 224 Frank Demaree 60.00 30.00
❑ 225 Bill Jurges 60.00 30.00
❑ 226 Charley Root 60.00 30.00
❑ 227 Billy Herman 150.00 75.00
❑ 228 Tony Piet 60.00 30.00
❑ 229 Arky Vaughan 150.00 75.00
❑ 230 Carl Hubbell PIT 400.00 200.00
❑ 231 Joe Moore FIELD 60.00 30.00
❑ 232 Lefty O'Doul 125.00 60.00
❑ 233 Johnny Vergez 60.00 30.00
❑ 234 Carl Hubbell 400.00 200.00
❑ 235 Fred Fitzsimmons PIT 60.00 30.00
❑ 236 George Davis 60.00 30.00
❑ 237 Gus Mancuso 60.00 30.00
❑ 238 Hugh Critz 60.00 30.00
❑ 239 Leroy Parmelee 60.00 30.00
❑ 240 Hal Schumacher 125.00 60.00

1934 Goudey

	Ex-Mt	VG
COMPLETE SET (96)	16000.00	8000.00
COMMON CARD (1-48)	50.00	25.00
COMMON CARD (49-72)	75.00	38.00
COMMON CARD (73-96)	175.00	90.00
WRAPPER (1-CENT, WHT.)	100.00	50.00
WRAPPER (1-CENT, CLR.)	100.00	50.00

❑ 1 Jimmie Foxx 750.00 220.00
❑ 2 Mickey Cochrane 175.00 90.00
❑ 3 Charlie Grimm 60.00 30.00
❑ 4 Woody English 50.00 25.00
❑ 5 Ed Brandt 50.00 25.00
❑ 6 Dizzy Dean 700.00 350.00
❑ 7 Leo Durocher 175.00 90.00
❑ 8 Tony Piet 50.00 25.00
❑ 9 Ben Chapman 60.00 30.00
❑ 10 Chuck Klein 150.00 75.00
❑ 11 Paul Waner 150.00 75.00
❑ 12 Carl Hubbell 175.00 90.00
❑ 13 Frankie Frisch 175.00 90.00
❑ 14 Willie Kamm 50.00 25.00
❑ 15 Alvin Crowder 50.00 25.00
❑ 16 Joe Kuhel 50.00 25.00
❑ 17 Hugh Critz 50.00 25.00
❑ 18 Heinie Manush 125.00 60.00
❑ 19 Lefty Grove 300.00 150.00
❑ 20 Frank Hogan 50.00 25.00
❑ 21 Bill Terry 200.00 100.00
❑ 22 Arky Vaughan 125.00 60.00
❑ 23 Charley Gehringer 200.00 100.00
❑ 24 Ray Benge 50.00 25.00
❑ 25 Roger Cramer 60.00 30.00
❑ 26 Gerald Walker 50.00 25.00
❑ 27 Luke Appling 150.00 75.00
❑ 28 Ed Coleman 50.00 25.00
❑ 29 Larry French 50.00 25.00
❑ 30 Julius Solters 50.00 25.00
❑ 31 Buck Jordan 50.00 25.00
❑ 32 Blondy Ryan 50.00 25.00
❑ 33 Don Hurst 50.00 25.00
❑ 34 Chick Hafey 125.00 60.00
❑ 35 Ernie Lombardi 150.00 75.00
❑ 36 Walter Betts 50.00 25.00
❑ 37 Lou Gehrig 3000.00 1500.00
❑ 38 Oral Hildebrand 50.00 25.00
❑ 39 Fred Walker 50.00 25.00
❑ 40 John Stone 50.00 25.00
❑ 41 George Earnshaw 50.00 25.00
❑ 42 John Allen 50.00 25.00
❑ 43 Dick Porter 50.00 25.00
❑ 44 Tom Bridges 60.00 30.00
❑ 45 Oscar Melillo 50.00 25.00
❑ 46 Joe Stripp 50.00 25.00
❑ 47 John Frederick 50.00 25.00
❑ 48 Tex Carleton 50.00 25.00
❑ 49 Sam Leslie 75.00 38.00
❑ 50 Walter Beck 75.00 38.00
❑ 51 Rip Collins 75.00 38.00
❑ 52 Herman Bell 75.00 38.00
❑ 53 George Watkins 75.00 38.00
❑ 54 Wesley Schulmerich 75.00 38.00
❑ 55 Ed Holley 75.00 38.00
❑ 56 Mark Koenig 100.00 50.00
❑ 57 Bill Swift 75.00 38.00
❑ 58 Earl Grace 75.00 38.00
❑ 59 Joe Mowry 75.00 38.00
❑ 60 Lynn Nelson 75.00 38.00
❑ 61 Lou Gehrig 3000.00 1500.00
❑ 62 Hank Greenberg 700.00 350.00
❑ 63 Minter Hayes 75.00 38.00
❑ 64 Frank Grube 75.00 38.00
❑ 65 Cliff Bolton 75.00 38.00
❑ 66 Mel Harder 100.00 50.00
❑ 67 Bob Weiland 75.00 38.00
❑ 68 Bob Johnson 100.00 50.00
❑ 69 John Marcum 75.00 38.00
❑ 70 Pete Fox 75.00 38.00
❑ 71 Lyle Tinning 75.00 38.00
❑ 72 Arndt Jorgens 75.00 38.00
❑ 73 Ed Wells 175.00 90.00
❑ 74 Bob Boken 175.00 90.00
❑ 75 Bill Werber 175.00 90.00
❑ 76 Hal Trosky 200.00 100.00
❑ 77 Joe Vosmik 175.00 90.00
❑ 78 Pinky Higgins 200.00 100.00
❑ 79 Eddie Durham 175.00 90.00
❑ 80 Marty McManus CK 175.00 90.00
❑ 81 Bob Brown CK 175.00 90.00
❑ 82 Bill Hallahan CK 175.00 90.00
❑ 83 Jim Mooney CK 175.00 90.00
❑ 84 Paul Derringer CK 225.00 110.00
❑ 85 Adam Comorosky CK 175.00 90.00
❑ 86 Lloyd Johnson CK 175.00 90.00
❑ 87 George Darrow CK 175.00 90.00
❑ 88 Homer Peel CK 175.00 90.00
❑ 89 Linus Frey CK 175.00 90.00
❑ 90 KiKi Cuyler CK 350.00 180.00
❑ 91 Dolph Camilli CK 200.00 100.00
❑ 92 Steve Larkin 175.00 90.00
❑ 93 Fred Ostermueller 175.00 90.00
❑ 94 Red Rolfe 200.00 100.00
❑ 95 Myril Hoag 175.00 90.00
❑ 96 James DeShong 500.00 250.00

1949 Leaf

	NM	Ex
COMPLETE SET (98)	30000.00	15000.00
COMMON CARD (1-168)	25.00	12.50
COMMON SP's	300.00	150.00
WRAPPER (1-CENT)	160.00	80.00

❑ 1 Joe DiMaggio 3000.00 1200.00
❑ 3 Babe Ruth 2500.00 1250.00
❑ 4 Stan Musial 1000.00 500.00
❑ 5 Virgil Trucks SP RC 400.00 200.00
❑ 8 S.Paige SP RC 12000.00 6000.00
❑ 10 Dizzy Trout 40.00 20.00
❑ 11 Phil Rizzuto 350.00 180.00
❑ 13 Cass Michaels SP 300.00 150.00
❑ 14 Billy Johnson 40.00 20.00
❑ 17 Frank Overmire 25.00 12.50
❑ 19 Johnny Wyrostek SP 300.00 150.00

❑ 20 Hank Sauer SP 400.00 200.00
❑ 22 Al Evans 25.00 12.50
❑ 26 Sam Chapman 40.00 20.00
❑ 27 Mickey Harris 25.00 12.50
❑ 28 Jim Hegan RC 40.00 20.00
❑ 29 Elmer Valo RC 40.00 20.00
❑ 30 Billy Goodman SP RC .. 400.00 200.00
❑ 31 Lou Brissie 25.00 12.50
❑ 32 Warren Spahn 350.00 180.00
❑ 33 Peanuts Lowrey SP 300.00 150.00
❑ 36 Al Zarilla SP 300.00 150.00
❑ 38 Ted Kluszewski RC 200.00 100.00
❑ 39 Ewell Blackwell 60.00 30.00
❑ 42 Kent Peterson 25.00 12.50
❑ 43 Ed Stevens SP 300.00 150.00
❑ 45 Ken Keltner SP 300.00 150.00
❑ 46 Johnny Mize 100.00 50.00
❑ 47 George Vico 25.00 12.50
❑ 48 Johnny Schmitz SP 300.00 150.00
❑ 49 Del Ennis RC 60.00 30.00
❑ 50 Dick Wakefield 25.00 12.50
❑ 51 Al Dark SP RC 500.00 250.00
❑ 53 Johnny VanderMeer 100.00 50.00
❑ 54 Bobby Adams SP 300.00 150.00
❑ 55 Tommy Henrich SP 500.00 250.00
❑ 56 Larry Jansen RC UER 40.00 20.00
(Misspelled Jensen)
❑ 57 Bob McCall 25.00 12.50
❑ 59 Luke Appling 100.00 50.00
❑ 61 Jake Early 25.00 12.50
❑ 62 Eddie Joost SP 300.00 150.00
❑ 63 Barney McCosky SP 300.00 150.00
❑ 65 Robert Elliott RC UER .. 100.00 50.00
(Misspelled Elliot
on card front)
❑ 66 Orval Grove SP 300.00 150.00
❑ 68 Eddie Miller SP 300.00 150.00
❑ 70 Honus Wagner CO 350.00 180.00
❑ 72 Hank Edwards 25.00 12.50
❑ 73 Pat Seerey 25.00 12.50
❑ 75 Dom DiMaggio SP 600.00 300.00
❑ 76 Ted Williams 1200.00 600.00
❑ 77 Roy Smalley RC 25.00 12.50
❑ 78 Hoot Evers SP 300.00 150.00
❑ 79 Jackie Robinson RC .. 1500.00 750.00
❑ 81 Whitey Kurowski SP 300.00 150.00
❑ 82 Johnny Lindell 40.00 20.00
❑ 83 Bobby Doerr 100.00 50.00
❑ 84 Sid Hudson 25.00 12.50
❑ 85 Dave Philley SP RC 400.00 200.00
❑ 86 Ralph Weigel 25.00 12.50
❑ 88 Frank Gustine SP 300.00 150.00
❑ 91 Ralph Kiner 200.00 100.00
❑ 93 Bob Feller SP 2000.00 1000.00
❑ 95 George Stirnweiss RC 40.00 20.00
❑ 97 Marty Marion 60.00 30.00
❑ 98 Hal Newhouser SP RC .. 600.00 300.00
❑ 102A Gene Hermansk ERR 250.00 125.00
❑ 102B G.Hermanski COR 40.00 20.00
❑ 104 Eddie Stewart SP 300.00 150.00
❑ 106 Lou Boudreau 100.00 50.00
❑ 108 Matt Batts SP 300.00 150.00
❑ 111 Jerry Priddy 25.00 12.50
❑ 113 Dutch Leonard SP 300.00 150.00
❑ 117 Joe Gordon 40.00 20.00
❑ 120 George Kell SP RC 600.00 300.00
❑ 121 Johnny Pesky SP RC .. 400.00 200.00
❑ 123 Cliff Fannin SP 300.00 150.00
❑ 125 Andy Pafko RC 25.00 12.50
❑ 127 Enos Slaughter SP 800.00 400.00
❑ 128 Buddy Rosar 25.00 12.50
❑ 129 Kirby Higbe SP 300.00 150.00
❑ 131 Sid Gordon SP 300.00 150.00
❑ 133 Tommy Holmes SP 500.00 250.00
❑ 136A Cliff Aberson 25.00 12.50
(Full sleeve)
❑ 136B Cliff Aberson 250.00 125.00
(Short sleeve)
❑ 137 Harry Walker SP 400.00 200.00
❑ 138 Larry Doby SP RC 700.00 350.00
❑ 139 Johnny Hopp RC 25.00 12.50
❑ 142 D.Murtaugh SP RC 400.00 200.00
❑ 143 Dick Sisler SP 300.00 150.00
❑ 144 Bob Dillinger SP 300.00 150.00
❑ 146 Pete Reiser SP 500.00 250.00
❑ 149 Hank Majeski SP 300.00 150.00
❑ 153 Floyd Baker SP 300.00 150.00
❑ 158 H. Brecheen SP RC 400.00 200.00
❑ 159 Mizell Platt 25.00 12.50
❑ 160 Bob Scheffing SP 300.00 150.00
❑ 161 Vern Stephens SP RC 400.00 200.00
❑ 163 F.Hutchinson SP RC .. 400.00 200.00
❑ 165 Dale Mitchell SP RC .. 400.00 200.00
❑ 168 P.Cavarretta SP UER .. 500.00 200.00
Name spelled Cavaretta
❑ NNO Album ....

1990 Leaf

	Nm-Mt	Ex-Mt
COMPLETE SET (528)	100.00	30.00
COMPLETE SERIES 1 (264)	60.00	18.00
COMPLETE SERIES 2 (264)	40.00	12.00
COMP. BERRA PUZZLE	1.00	.30

❑ 1 Introductory Card .... .40 .12
❑ 2 Mike Henneman .... .40 .12
❑ 3 Steve Bedrosian .... .40 .12
❑ 4 Mike Scott .... .40 .12
❑ 5 Allan Anderson .... .40 .12
❑ 6 Rick Sutcliffe .... .60 .18
❑ 7 Gregg Olson .... .60 .18
❑ 8 Kevin Elster .... .40 .12
❑ 9 Pete O'Brien .... .40 .12
❑ 10 Carlton Fisk .... 1.00 .30
❑ 11 Joe Magrane .... .40 .12
❑ 12 Roger Clemens .... 3.00 .90
❑ 13 Tom Glavine .... 1.00 .30
❑ 14 Tom Gordon .... .60 .18
❑ 15 Todd Benzinger .... .40 .12
❑ 16 Hubie Brooks .... .40 .12
❑ 17 Roberto Kelly .... .40 .12
❑ 18 Barry Larkin .... 1.00 .30
❑ 19 Mike Boddicker .... .40 .12
❑ 20 Roger McDowell .... .40 .12
❑ 21 Nolan Ryan 5.00 1.50
❑ 22 John Farrell .... .40 .12
❑ 23 Bruce Hurst .... .40 .12
❑ 24 Wally Joyner .... .60 .18
❑ 25 Greg Maddux 5.00 1.50
❑ 26 Chris Bosio .... .40 .12
❑ 27 John Cerutti .... .40 .12
❑ 28 Tim Burke .... .40 .12
❑ 29 Dennis Eckersley .... .60 .18
❑ 30 Glenn Davis .... .40 .12
❑ 31 Jim Abbott .... 1.00 .30
❑ 32 Mike LaValliere .... .40 .12
❑ 33 Andres Thomas .... .40 .12
❑ 34 Lou Whitaker .... .60 .18
❑ 35 Alvin Davis .... .40 .12
❑ 36 Melido Perez .... .40 .12
❑ 37 Craig Biggio .... 1.50 .45
❑ 38 Rick Aguilera .... .60 .18
❑ 39 Pete Harnisch .... .40 .12
❑ 40 David Cone .... .60 .18
❑ 41 Scott Garrelts .... .40 .12
❑ 42 Jay Howell .... .40 .12
❑ 43 Eric King .... .40 .12
❑ 44 Pedro Guerrero .... .40 .12
❑ 45 Mike Bielecki .... .40 .12
❑ 46 Bob Boone .... .60 .18
❑ 47 Kevin Brown .... .60 .18
❑ 48 Jerry Browne .... .40 .12
❑ 49 Mike Scioscia .... .40 .12
❑ 50 Chuck Cary .... .40 .12
❑ 51 Wade Boggs .... 1.00 .30
❑ 52 Von Hayes .... .40 .12
❑ 53 Tony Fernandez .... .40 .12
❑ 54 Dennis Martinez .... .60 .18
❑ 55 Tom Candiotti .... .40 .12
❑ 56 Andy Benes .... .60 .18
❑ 57 Rob Dibble .... .60 .18
❑ 58 Chuck Crim .... .40 .12
❑ 59 John Smoltz .... 1.50 .45
❑ 60 Mike Heath .... .40 .12
❑ 61 Kevin Gross .... .40 .12
❑ 62 Mark McGwire 4.00 1.20
❑ 63 Bert Blyleven .... .60 .18
❑ 64 Bob Walk .... .40 .12
❑ 65 Mickey Tettleton .... .40 .12
❑ 66 Sid Fernandez .... .40 .12
❑ 67 Terry Kennedy .... .40 .12
❑ 68 Fernando Valenzuela .... .60 .18
❑ 69 Don Mattingly 4.00 1.20
❑ 70 Paul O'Neill .... 1.00 .30
❑ 71 Robin Yount .... 2.50 .75
❑ 72 Bret Saberhagen .... .60 .18
❑ 73 Geno Petralli .... .40 .12
❑ 74 Brook Jacoby .... .40 .12
❑ 75 Roberto Alomar .... 1.00 .30
❑ 76 Devon White .... .60 .18
❑ 77 Jose Lind .... .40 .12
❑ 78 Pat Combs .... .40 .12
❑ 79 Dave Stieb .... .60 .18
❑ 80 Tim Wallach .... .40 .12
❑ 81 Dave Stewart .... .60 .18
❑ 82 Eric Anthony RC .... .40 .12
❑ 83 Randy Bush .... .40 .12
❑ 84 Rickey Henderson CL .... .60 .18
❑ 85 Jaime Navarro .... .40 .12
❑ 86 Tommy Gregg .... .40 .12
❑ 87 Frank Tanana .... .40 .12
❑ 88 Omar Vizquel .... 1.50 .45
❑ 89 Ivan Calderon .... .40 .12
❑ 90 Vince Coleman .... .40 .12
❑ 91 Barry Bonds 5.00 1.50
❑ 92 Randy Milligan .... .40 .12
❑ 93 Frank Viola .... .40 .12
❑ 94 Matt Williams .... .60 .18
❑ 95 Alfredo Griffin .... .40 .12
❑ 96 Steve Sax .... .40 .12
❑ 97 Gary Gaetti .... .60 .18
❑ 98 Ryne Sandberg .... 3.00 .90
❑ 99 Danny Tartabull .... .40 .12
❑ 100 Rafael Palmeiro .... 1.00 .30
❑ 101 Jesse Orosco .... .40 .12
❑ 102 Garry Templeton .... .40 .12
❑ 103 Frank DiPino .... .40 .12
❑ 104 Tony Pena .... .40 .12
❑ 105 Dickie Thon .... .40 .12
❑ 106 Kelly Gruber .... .40 .12
❑ 107 Marquis Grissom RC .... 2.00 .60
❑ 108 Jose Canseco .... 1.00 .30
❑ 109 Mike Blowers RC .... .40 .12
❑ 110 Tom Browning .... .40 .12
❑ 111 Greg Vaughn .... .40 .12
❑ 112 Oddibe McDowell .... .40 .12
❑ 113 Gary Ward .... .40 .12
❑ 114 Jay Buhner .... .60 .18
❑ 115 Eric Show .... .40 .12
❑ 116 Bryan Harvey .... .40 .12
❑ 117 Andy Van Slyke .... 1.00 .30
❑ 118 Jeff Ballard .... .40 .12
❑ 119 Barry Lyons .... .40 .12
❑ 120 Kevin Mitchell .... .40 .12
❑ 121 Mike Gallego .... .40 .12
❑ 122 Dave Smith .... .40 .12
❑ 123 Kirby Puckett .... 1.50 .45
❑ 124 Jerome Walton .... .40 .12
❑ 125 Bo Jackson .... 1.50 .45
❑ 126 Harold Baines .... .60 .18
❑ 127 Scott Bankhead .... .40 .12
❑ 128 Ozzie Guillen .... .60 .18
❑ 129 Jose Oquendo UER .... .40 .12
(League misspelled
as Legue)
❑ 130 John Dopson .... .40 .12
❑ 131 Charlie Hayes .... .40 .12
❑ 132 Fred McGriff .... 1.50 .45
❑ 133 Chet Lemon .... .40 .12
❑ 134 Gary Carter .... .60 .18

- ❑ 135 Rafael Ramirez .40 .12
- ❑ 136 Shane Mack .40 .12
- ❑ 137 Mark Grace UER 1.00 .30
  (Card back has OB:L, should be B:L)
- ❑ 138 Phil Bradley .40 .12
- ❑ 139 Dwight Gooden .60 .18
- ❑ 140 Harold Reynolds .60 .18
- ❑ 141 Scott Fletcher .40 .12
- ❑ 142 Ozzie Smith 2.50 .75
- ❑ 143 Mike Greenwell .40 .12
- ❑ 144 Pete Smith .40 .12
- ❑ 145 Mark Gubicza .40 .12
- ❑ 146 Chris Sabo .40 .12
- ❑ 147 Ramon Martinez .40 .12
- ❑ 148 Tim Leary .40 .12
- ❑ 149 Randy Myers .60 .18
- ❑ 150 Jody Reed .40 .12
- ❑ 151 Bruce Ruffin .40 .12
- ❑ 152 Jeff Russell .40 .12
- ❑ 153 Doug Jones .40 .12
- ❑ 154 Tony Gwynn 2.00 .60
- ❑ 155 Mark Langston .40 .12
- ❑ 156 Mitch Williams .40 .12
- ❑ 157 Gary Sheffield 1.50 .45
- ❑ 158 Tom Henke .40 .12
- ❑ 159 Oil Can Boyd .40 .12
- ❑ 160 Rickey Henderson 1.50 .45
- ❑ 161 Bill Doran .40 .12
- ❑ 162 Chuck Finley .60 .18
- ❑ 163 Jeff King .40 .12
- ❑ 164 Nick Esasky .40 .12
- ❑ 165 Cecil Fielder .60 .18
- ❑ 166 Dave Valle .40 .12
- ❑ 167 Robin Ventura 1.50 .45
- ❑ 168 Jim Deshaies .40 .12
- ❑ 169 Juan Berenguer .40 .12
- ❑ 170 Craig Worthington .40 .12
- ❑ 171 Gregg Jefferies .60 .18
- ❑ 172 Will Clark 1.00 .30
- ❑ 173 Kirk Gibson 1.00 .30
- ❑ 174 Carlton Fisk CL .60 .18
- ❑ 175 Bobby Thigpen .40 .12
- ❑ 176 John Tudor .40 .12
- ❑ 177 Andre Dawson .60 .18
- ❑ 178 George Brett 4.00 1.20
- ❑ 179 Steve Buechele .40 .12
- ❑ 180 Joey Belle 1.50 .45
- ❑ 181 Eddie Murray 1.50 .45
- ❑ 182 Bob Geren .40 .12
- ❑ 183 Rob Murphy .40 .12
- ❑ 184 Tom Herr .40 .12
- ❑ 185 George Bell .40 .12
- ❑ 186 Spike Owen .40 .12
- ❑ 187 Cory Snyder .40 .12
- ❑ 188 Fred Lynn .40 .12
- ❑ 189 Eric Davis .60 .18
- ❑ 190 Dave Parker .60 .18
- ❑ 191 Jeff Blauser .40 .12
- ❑ 192 Matt Nokes .40 .12
- ❑ 193 Delino DeShields RC 1.00 .30
- ❑ 194 Scott Sanderson .40 .12
- ❑ 195 Lance Parrish .40 .12
- ❑ 196 Bobby Bonilla .60 .18
- ❑ 197 Cal Ripken UER 5.00 1.50
  (Reistertown, should be Reisterstown)
- ❑ 198 Kevin McReynolds .40 .12
- ❑ 199 Robby Thompson .40 .12
- ❑ 200 Tim Belcher .40 .12
- ❑ 201 Jesse Barfield .40 .12
- ❑ 202 Mariano Duncan .40 .12
- ❑ 203 Bill Spiers .40 .12
- ❑ 204 Frank White .60 .18
- ❑ 205 Julio Franco .60 .18
- ❑ 206 Greg Swindell .40 .12
- ❑ 207 Benito Santiago .60 .18
- ❑ 208 Johnny Ray .40 .12
- ❑ 209 Gary Redus .40 .12
- ❑ 210 Jeff Parrett .40 .12
- ❑ 211 Jimmy Key .60 .18
- ❑ 212 Tim Raines .60 .18
- ❑ 213 Carney Lansford .60 .18
- ❑ 214 Gerald Young .40 .12
- ❑ 215 Gene Larkin .40 .12
- ❑ 216 Dan Plesac .40 .12
- ❑ 217 Lonnie Smith .40 .12
- ❑ 218 Alan Trammell .60 .18
- ❑ 219 Jeffrey Leonard .40 .12
- ❑ 220 Sammy Sosa RC 25.00 7.50
- ❑ 221 Todd Zeile .60 .18
- ❑ 222 Bill Landrum .40 .12
- ❑ 223 Mike Devereaux .40 .12
- ❑ 224 Mike Marshall .40 .12
- ❑ 225 Jose Uribe .40 .12
- ❑ 226 Juan Samuel .40 .12
- ❑ 227 Mel Hall .40 .12
- ❑ 228 Kent Hrbek .60 .18
- ❑ 229 Shawon Dunston .40 .12
- ❑ 230 Kevin Seitzer .40 .12
- ❑ 231 Pete Incaviglia .40 .12
- ❑ 232 Sandy Alomar Jr. .60 .18
- ❑ 233 Bip Roberts .40 .12
- ❑ 234 Scott Terry .40 .12
- ❑ 235 Dwight Evans 1.00 .30
- ❑ 236 Ricky Jordan .40 .12
- ❑ 237 John Olerud RC 3.00 .90
- ❑ 238 Zane Smith .40 .12
- ❑ 239 Walt Weiss .40 .12
- ❑ 240 Alvaro Espinoza .40 .12
- ❑ 241 Billy Hatcher .40 .12
- ❑ 242 Paul Molitor 1.00 .30
- ❑ 243 Dale Murphy 1.00 .30
- ❑ 244 Dave Bergman .40 .12
- ❑ 245 Ken Griffey Jr. 5.00 1.50
- ❑ 246 Ed Whitson .40 .12
- ❑ 247 Kirk McCaskill .40 .12
- ❑ 248 Jay Bell .60 .18
- ❑ 249 Ben McDonald RC 1.00 .30
- ❑ 250 Darryl Strawberry .60 .18
- ❑ 251 Brett Butler .60 .18
- ❑ 252 Terry Steinbach .40 .12
- ❑ 253 Ken Caminiti .60 .18
- ❑ 254 Dan Gladden .40 .12
- ❑ 255 Dwight Smith .40 .12
- ❑ 256 Kurt Stillwell .40 .12
- ❑ 257 Ruben Sierra .40 .12
- ❑ 258 Mike Schooler .40 .12
- ❑ 259 Lance Johnson .40 .12
- ❑ 260 Terry Pendleton .60 .18
- ❑ 261 Ellis Burks 1.00 .30
- ❑ 262 Len Dykstra .60 .18
- ❑ 263 Mookie Wilson .60 .18
- ❑ 264 Nolan Ryan CL UER 1.50 .45
  No TM after Ranger logo
- ❑ 265 Nolan Ryan 2.50 .75
  No Hit King
- ❑ 266 Brian DuBois .40 .12
- ❑ 267 Don Robinson .40 .12
- ❑ 268 Glenn Wilson .40 .12
- ❑ 269 Kevin Tapani RC 1.00 .30
- ❑ 270 Marvell Wynne .40 .12
- ❑ 271 Bill Ripken .40 .12
- ❑ 272 Howard Johnson .40 .12
- ❑ 273 Brian Holman .40 .12
- ❑ 274 Dan Pasqua .40 .12
- ❑ 275 Ken Dayley .40 .12
- ❑ 276 Jeff Reardon .60 .18
- ❑ 277 Jim Presley .40 .12
- ❑ 278 Jim Eisenreich .40 .12
- ❑ 279 Danny Jackson .40 .12
- ❑ 280 Orel Hershiser .60 .18
- ❑ 281 Andy Hawkins .40 .12
- ❑ 282 Jose Rijo .40 .12
- ❑ 283 Luis Rivera .40 .12
- ❑ 284 John Kruk .60 .18
- ❑ 285 Jeff Huson RC .40 .12
- ❑ 286 Joel Skinner .40 .12
- ❑ 287 Jack Clark .60 .18
- ❑ 288 Chili Davis .60 .18
- ❑ 289 Joe Girardi 1.00 .30
- ❑ 290 B.J. Surhoff .60 .18
- ❑ 291 Luis Sojo .40 .12
- ❑ 292 Tom Foley .40 .12
- ❑ 293 Mike Moore .40 .12
- ❑ 294 Ken Oberkfell .40 .12
- ❑ 295 Luis Polonia .60 .18
- ❑ 296 Doug Drabek .40 .12
- ❑ 297 Dave Justice RC 3.00 .90
- ❑ 298 Paul Gibson .40 .12
- ❑ 299 Edgar Martinez 1.00 .30
- ❑ 300 F.Thomas RC UER 20.00 6.00
  No B in front of birthdate
- ❑ 301 Eric Yelding .40 .12
- ❑ 302 Greg Gagne .40 .12
- ❑ 303 Brad Komminsk .40 .12
- ❑ 304 Ron Darling .40 .12
- ❑ 305 Kevin Bass .40 .12
- ❑ 306 Jeff Hamilton .40 .12
- ❑ 307 Ron Karkovice .40 .12
- ❑ 308 Milt Thompson UER 1.00 .30
  (Ray Lankford pictured on card back)
- ❑ 309 Mike Harkey .40 .12
- ❑ 310 Mel Stottlemyre Jr. .40 .12
- ❑ 311 Kenny Rogers .60 .18
- ❑ 312 Mitch Webster .40 .12
- ❑ 313 Kal Daniels .40 .12
- ❑ 314 Matt Nokes .40 .12
- ❑ 315 Dennis Lamp .40 .12
- ❑ 316 Ken Howell .40 .12
- ❑ 317 Glenallen Hill .40 .12
- ❑ 318 Dave Martinez .40 .12
- ❑ 319 Chris James .40 .12
- ❑ 320 Mike Pagliarulo .40 .12
- ❑ 321 Hal Morris .40 .12
- ❑ 322 Rob Deer .40 .12
- ❑ 323 Greg Olson .40 .12
- ❑ 324 Tony Phillips .40 .12
- ❑ 325 Larry Walker RC 8.00 2.40
- ❑ 326 Ron Hassey .40 .12
- ❑ 327 Jack Howell .40 .12
- ❑ 328 John Smiley .40 .12
- ❑ 329 Steve Finley .60 .18
- ❑ 330 Dave Magadan .40 .12
- ❑ 331 Greg Litton .40 .12
- ❑ 332 Mickey Hatcher .40 .12
- ❑ 333 Lee Guetterman .40 .12
- ❑ 334 Norm Charlton .40 .12
- ❑ 335 Edgar Diaz .40 .12
- ❑ 336 Willie Wilson .40 .12
- ❑ 337 Bobby Witt .40 .12
- ❑ 338 Candy Maldonado .40 .12
- ❑ 339 Craig Lefferts .40 .12
- ❑ 340 Dante Bichette .60 .18
- ❑ 341 Wally Backman .40 .12
- ❑ 342 Dennis Cook .40 .12
- ❑ 343 Pat Borders .40 .12
- ❑ 344 Wallace Johnson .40 .12
- ❑ 345 Willie Randolph .60 .18
- ❑ 346 Danny Darwin .40 .12
- ❑ 347 Al Newman .40 .12
- ❑ 348 Mark Knudson .40 .12
- ❑ 349 Joe Boever .40 .12
- ❑ 350 Larry Sheets .40 .12
- ❑ 351 Mike Jackson .40 .12
- ❑ 352 Wayne Edwards .40 .12
- ❑ 353 Bernard Gilkey RC 1.00 .30
- ❑ 354 Don Slaught .40 .12
- ❑ 355 Joe Orsulak .40 .12
- ❑ 356 John Franco .60 .18
- ❑ 357 Jeff Brantley .40 .12
- ❑ 358 Mike Morgan .40 .12
- ❑ 359 Deion Sanders 1.50 .45
- ❑ 360 Terry Leach .40 .12
- ❑ 361 Les Lancaster .40 .12
- ❑ 362 Storm Davis .40 .12
- ❑ 363 Scott Coolbaugh .40 .12
- ❑ 364 Ozzie Smith CL 1.00 .30
- ❑ 365 Cecilio Guante .40 .12
- ❑ 366 Joey Cora .60 .18
- ❑ 367 Willie McGee .60 .18
- ❑ 368 Jerry Reed .40 .12
- ❑ 369 Darren Daulton .60 .18
- ❑ 370 Manny Lee .40 .12
- ❑ 371 Mark Gardner .40 .12
- ❑ 372 Rick Honeycutt .40 .12
- ❑ 373 Steve Balboni .40 .12
- ❑ 374 Jack Armstrong .40 .12
- ❑ 375 Charlie O'Brien .40 .12
- ❑ 376 Ron Gant .60 .18
- ❑ 377 Lloyd Moseby .40 .12
- ❑ 378 Gene Harris .40 .12
- ❑ 379 Joe Carter .60 .18
- ❑ 380 Scott Bailes .40 .12
- ❑ 381 R.J. Reynolds .40 .12
- ❑ 382 Bob Melvin .40 .12

❑ 383 Tim Teufel .40 .12
❑ 384 John Burkett .40 .12
❑ 385 Felix Jose .40 .12
❑ 386 Larry Andersen .40 .12
❑ 387 David West .40 .12
❑ 388 Luis Salazar .40 .12
❑ 389 Mike Macfarlane .40 .12
❑ 390 Charlie Hough .60 .18
❑ 391 Greg Briley .40 .12
❑ 392 Donn Pall .40 .12
❑ 393 Bryn Smith .40 .12
❑ 394 Carlos Quintana .40 .12
❑ 395 Steve Lake .40 .12
❑ 396 Mark Whiten RC 1.00 .30
❑ 397 Edwin Nunez .40 .12
❑ 398 Rick Parker .40 .12
❑ 399 Mark Portugal .40 .12
❑ 400 Roy Smith .40 .12
❑ 401 Hector Villanueva .40 .12
❑ 402 Bob Milacki .40 .12
❑ 403 Alejandro Pena .40 .12
❑ 404 Scott Bradley .40 .12
❑ 405 Ron Kittle .40 .12
❑ 406 Bob Tewksbury .40 .12
❑ 407 Wes Gardner .40 .12
❑ 408 Ernie Whitt .40 .12
❑ 409 Terry Shumpert .40 .12
❑ 410 Tim Layana .40 .12
❑ 411 Chris Gwynn .40 .12
❑ 412 Jeff D. Robinson .40 .12
❑ 413 Scott Scudder .40 .12
❑ 414 Kevin Romine .40 .12
❑ 415 Jose DeJesus .40 .12
❑ 416 Mike Jeffcoat .40 .12
❑ 417 Rudy Seanez .40 .12
❑ 418 Mike Dunne .40 .12
❑ 419 Dick Schofield .40 .12
❑ 420 Steve Wilson .40 .12
❑ 421 Bill Krueger .40 .12
❑ 422 Junior Felix .40 .12
❑ 423 Drew Hall .40 .12
❑ 424 Curt Young .40 .12
❑ 425 Franklin Stubbs .40 .12
❑ 426 Dave Winfield .60 .18
❑ 427 Rick Reed RC 1.00 .30
❑ 428 Charlie Leibrandt .40 .12
❑ 429 Jeff M. Robinson .40 .12
❑ 430 Erik Hanson .40 .12
❑ 431 Barry Jones .40 .12
❑ 432 Alex Trevino .40 .12
❑ 433 John Moses .40 .12
❑ 434 Dave Johnson .40 .12
❑ 435 Mackey Sasser .40 .12
❑ 436 Rick Leach .40 .12
❑ 437 Lenny Harris .40 .12
❑ 438 Carlos Martinez .40 .12
❑ 439 Rex Hudler .40 .12
❑ 440 Domingo Ramos .40 .12
❑ 441 Gerald Perry .40 .12
❑ 442 Jeff Russell .40 .12
❑ 443 Carlos Baerga RC 1.00 .30
❑ 444 Will Clark CL .60 .18
❑ 445 Stan Javier .40 .12
❑ 446 Kevin Maas RC 1.00 .30
❑ 447 Tom Brunansky .40 .12
❑ 448 Carmelo Martinez .40 .12
❑ 449 Willie Blair RC .40 .12
❑ 450 Andres Galarraga .60 .18
❑ 451 Bud Black .40 .12
❑ 452 Greg W. Harris .40 .12
❑ 453 Joe Oliver .40 .12
❑ 454 Greg Brock .40 .12
❑ 455 Jeff Treadway .40 .12
❑ 456 Lance McCullers .40 .12
❑ 457 Dave Schmidt .40 .12
❑ 458 Todd Burns .40 .12
❑ 459 Max Venable .40 .12
❑ 460 Neal Heaton .40 .12
❑ 461 Mark Williamson .40 .12
❑ 462 Keith Miller .40 .12
❑ 463 Mike LaCoss .40 .12
❑ 464 Jose Offerman RC 1.00 .30
❑ 465 Jim Leyritz RC 1.00 .30
❑ 466 Glenn Braggs .40 .12
❑ 467 Ron Robinson .40 .12
❑ 468 Mark Davis .40 .12
❑ 469 Gary Pettis .40 .12
❑ 470 Keith Hernandez .60 .18
❑ 471 Dennis Rasmussen .40 .12
❑ 472 Mark Eichhorn .40 .12
❑ 473 Ted Power .40 .12
❑ 474 Terry Mulholland .40 .12
❑ 475 Todd Stottlemyre .60 .18
❑ 476 Jerry Goff .40 .12
❑ 477 Gene Nelson .40 .12
❑ 478 Rich Gedman .40 .12
❑ 479 Brian Harper .40 .12
❑ 480 Mike Felder .40 .12
❑ 481 Steve Avery .40 .12
❑ 482 Jack Morris .60 .18
❑ 483 Randy Johnson 3.00 .90
❑ 484 Scott Radinsky RC .40 .12
❑ 485 Jose DeLeon .40 .12
❑ 486 Stan Belinda RC .40 .12
❑ 487 Brian Holton .40 .12
❑ 488 Mark Carreon .40 .12
❑ 489 Trevor Wilson .40 .12
❑ 490 Mike Sharperson .40 .12
❑ 491 Alan Mills RC .40 .12
❑ 492 John Candelaria .40 .12
❑ 493 Paul Assenmacher .40 .12
❑ 494 Steve Crawford .40 .12
❑ 495 Brad Arnsberg .40 .12
❑ 496 Sergio Valdez .40 .12
❑ 497 Mark Parent .40 .12
❑ 498 Tom Pagnozzi .40 .12
❑ 499 Greg A. Harris .40 .12
❑ 500 Randy Ready .40 .12
❑ 501 Duane Ward .40 .12
❑ 502 Nelson Santovenia .40 .12
❑ 503 Joe Klink .40 .12
❑ 504 Eric Plunk .40 .12
❑ 505 Jeff Reed .40 .12
❑ 506 Ted Higuera .40 .12
❑ 507 Joe Hesketh .40 .12
❑ 508 Dan Petry .40 .12
❑ 509 Matt Young .40 .12
❑ 510 Jerald Clark .40 .12
❑ 511 John Orton .40 .12
❑ 512 Scott Ruskin .40 .12
❑ 513 Chris Hoiles RC 1.00 .30
❑ 514 Daryl Boston .40 .12
❑ 515 Francisco Oliveras .40 .12
❑ 516 Ozzie Canseco .40 .12
❑ 517 Xavier Hernandez RC .40 .12
❑ 518 Fred Manrique .40 .12
❑ 519 Shawn Boskie RC .40 .12
❑ 520 Jeff Montgomery .60 .18
❑ 521 Jack Daugherty .40 .12
❑ 522 Keith Comstock .40 .12
❑ 523 Greg Hibbard RC .40 .12
❑ 524 Lee Smith .60 .18
❑ 525 Dana Kiecker .40 .12
❑ 526 Darrel Akerfelds .40 .12
❑ 527 Greg Myers .40 .12
❑ 528 Ryne Sandberg CL 1.50 .45

1993 Leaf

	Nm-Mt	Ex-Mt
COMPLETE SET (550)	35.00	10.50
COMP. SERIES 1 (220)	15.00	4.50
COMP. SERIES 2 (220)	15.00	4.50
COMPLETE UPDATE (110)	5.00	1.50
COMMON RC	.15	.04

❑ 1 Ben McDonald .15 .04
❑ 2 Sid Fernandez .15 .04
❑ 3 Juan Guzman .15 .04
❑ 4 Curt Schilling .30 .09
❑ 5 Ivan Rodriguez .50 .15
❑ 6 Don Slaught .15 .04
❑ 7 Terry Steinbach .15 .04
❑ 8 Todd Zeile .15 .04
❑ 9 Andy Stankiewicz .15 .04
❑ 10 Tim Teufel .15 .04
❑ 11 Marvin Freeman .15 .04
❑ 12 Jim Austin .15 .04
❑ 13 Bob Scanlan .15 .04
❑ 14 Rusty Meacham .15 .04
❑ 15 Casey Candaele .15 .04
❑ 16 Travis Fryman .30 .09
❑ 17 Jose Offerman .15 .04
❑ 18 Albert Belle .30 .09
❑ 19 John Vander Wal .15 .04
❑ 20 Dan Pasqua .15 .04
❑ 21 Frank Viola .30 .09
❑ 22 Terry Mulholland .15 .04
❑ 23 Gregg Olson .15 .04
❑ 24 Randy Tomlin .15 .04
❑ 25 Todd Stottlemyre .15 .04
❑ 26 Jose Oquendo .15 .04
❑ 27 Julio Franco .30 .09
❑ 28 Tony Gwynn 1.00 .30
❑ 29 Ruben Sierra .15 .04
❑ 30 Robby Thompson .15 .04
❑ 31 Jim Bullinger .15 .04
❑ 32 Rick Aguilera .15 .04
❑ 33 Scott Servais .15 .04
❑ 34 Cal Eldred .15 .04
❑ 35 Mike Piazza 3.00 .90
❑ 36 Brent Mayne .15 .04
❑ 37 Wil Cordero .15 .04
❑ 38 Milt Cuyler .15 .04
❑ 39 Howard Johnson .15 .04
❑ 40 Kenny Lofton .30 .09
❑ 41 Alex Fernandez .15 .04
❑ 42 Denny Neagle .30 .09
❑ 43 Tony Pena .15 .04
❑ 44 Bob Tewksbury .15 .04
❑ 45 Glenn Davis .15 .04
❑ 46 Fred McGriff .50 .15
❑ 47 John Olerud .30 .09
❑ 48 Steve Hosey .15 .04
❑ 49 Rafael Palmeiro .50 .15
❑ 50 David Justice .30 .09
❑ 51 Pete Harnisch .15 .04
❑ 52 Sam Militello .15 .04
❑ 53 Orel Hershiser .30 .09
❑ 54 Pat Mahomes .15 .04
❑ 55 Greg Colbrunn .15 .04
❑ 56 Greg Vaughn .15 .04
❑ 57 Vince Coleman .15 .04
❑ 58 Brian McRae .15 .04
❑ 59 Len Dykstra .30 .09
❑ 60 Dan Gladden .15 .04
❑ 61 Ted Power .15 .04
❑ 62 Donovan Osborne .15 .04
❑ 63 Ron Karkovice .15 .04
❑ 64 Frank Seminara .15 .04
❑ 65 Bob Zupcic .15 .04
❑ 66 Kirt Manwaring .15 .04
❑ 67 Mike Devereaux .15 .04
❑ 68 Mark Lemke .15 .04
❑ 69 Devon White .30 .09
❑ 70 Sammy Sosa .75 .23
❑ 71 Pedro Astacio .15 .04
❑ 72 Dennis Eckersley .30 .09
❑ 73 Chris Nabholz .15 .04
❑ 74 Melido Perez .15 .04
❑ 75 Todd Hundley .15 .04
❑ 76 Kent Hrbek .30 .09
❑ 77 Mickey Morandini .15 .04
❑ 78 Tim McIntosh .15 .04
❑ 79 Andy Van Slyke .50 .15
❑ 80 Kevin McReynolds .15 .04
❑ 81 Mike Henneman .15 .04
❑ 82 Greg W. Harris .15 .04
❑ 83 Sandy Alomar Jr. .15 .04
❑ 84 Mike Jackson .15 .04

❑ 85 Ozzie Guillen .30 .09
❑ 86 Jeff Blauser .15 .04
❑ 87 John Valentin .15 .04
❑ 88 Rey Sanchez .15 .04
❑ 89 Rick Sutcliffe .30 .09
❑ 90 Luis Gonzalez .30 .09
❑ 91 Jeff Fassero .15 .04
❑ 92 Kenny Rogers .30 .09
❑ 93 Bret Saberhagen .30 .09
❑ 94 Bob Welch .15 .04
❑ 95 Darren Daulton .30 .09
❑ 96 Mike Gallego .15 .04
❑ 97 Orlando Merced .15 .04
❑ 98 Chuck Knoblauch .30 .09
❑ 99 Bernard Gilkey .15 .04
❑ 100 Billy Ashley .15 .04
❑ 101 Kevin Appier .30 .09
❑ 102 Jeff Brantley .15 .04
❑ 103 Bill Gullickson .15 .04
❑ 104 John Smoltz .50 .15
❑ 105 Paul Sorrento .15 .04
❑ 106 Steve Buechele .15 .04
❑ 107 Steve Sax .15 .04
❑ 108 Andujar Cedeno .15 .04
❑ 109 Billy Hatcher .15 .04
❑ 110 Checklist .15 .04
❑ 111 Alan Mills .15 .04
❑ 112 John Franco .30 .09
❑ 113 Jack Morris .30 .09
❑ 114 Mitch Williams .15 .04
❑ 115 Nolan Ryan 3.00 .90
❑ 116 Jay Bell .30 .09
❑ 117 Mike Bordick .15 .04
❑ 118 Geronimo Pena .15 .04
❑ 119 Danny Tartabull .15 .04
❑ 120 Checklist .15 .04
❑ 121 Steve Avery .15 .04
❑ 122 Ricky Bones .15 .04
❑ 123 Mike Morgan .15 .04
❑ 124 Jeff Montgomery .15 .04
❑ 125 Jeff Bagwell .50 .15
❑ 126 Tony Phillips .15 .04
❑ 127 Lenny Harris .15 .04
❑ 128 Glenallen Hill .15 .04
❑ 129 Marquis Grissom .30 .09
❑ 130 Gerald Williams UER .15 .04
(Bernie Williams picture and stats)
❑ 131 Greg A. Harris .15 .04
❑ 132 Tommy Greene .15 .04
❑ 133 Chris Hoiles .15 .04
❑ 134 Bob Walk .15 .04
❑ 135 Duane Ward .15 .04
❑ 136 Tom Pagnozzi .15 .04
❑ 137 Jeff Huson .15 .04
❑ 138 Kurt Stillwell .15 .04
❑ 139 Dave Henderson .15 .04
❑ 140 Darrin Jackson .15 .04
❑ 141 Frank Castillo .15 .04
❑ 142 Scott Erickson .15 .04
❑ 143 Darryl Kile .30 .09
❑ 144 Bill Wegman .15 .04
❑ 145 Steve Wilson .15 .04
❑ 146 George Brett 2.00 .60
❑ 147 Moises Alou .30 .09
❑ 148 Lou Whitaker .30 .09
❑ 149 Chico Walker .15 .04
❑ 150 Jerry Browne .15 .04
❑ 151 Kirk McCaskill .15 .04
❑ 152 Zane Smith .15 .04
❑ 153 Matt Young .15 .04
❑ 154 Lee Smith .30 .09
❑ 155 Leo Gomez .15 .04
❑ 156 Dan Walters .15 .04
❑ 157 Pat Borders .15 .04
❑ 158 Matt Williams .30 .09
❑ 159 Dean Palmer .30 .09
❑ 160 John Patterson .15 .04
❑ 161 Doug Jones .15 .04
❑ 162 John Habyan .15 .04
❑ 163 Pedro Martinez 1.50 .45
❑ 164 Carl Willis .15 .04
❑ 165 Darrin Fletcher .15 .04
❑ 166 B.J. Surhoff .30 .09
❑ 167 Eddie Murray .75 .23
❑ 168 Keith Miller .15 .04
❑ 169 Ricky Jordan .15 .04
❑ 170 Juan Gonzalez .30 .09
❑ 171 Charles Nagy .15 .04
❑ 172 Mark Clark .15 .04
❑ 173 Bobby Thigpen .15 .04
❑ 174 Tim Scott .15 .04
❑ 175 Scott Cooper .15 .04
❑ 176 Royce Clayton .15 .04
❑ 177 Brady Anderson .30 .09
❑ 178 Sid Bream .15 .04
❑ 179 Derek Bell .15 .04
❑ 180 Otis Nixon .15 .04
❑ 181 Kevin Gross .15 .04
❑ 182 Ron Darling .15 .04
❑ 183 John Wetteland .30 .09
❑ 184 Mike Stanley .15 .04
❑ 185 Jeff Kent .75 .23
❑ 186 Brian Harper .15 .04
❑ 187 Mariano Duncan .15 .04
❑ 188 Robin Yount 1.25 .35
❑ 189 Al Martin .15 .04
❑ 190 Eddie Zosky .15 .04
❑ 191 Mike Munoz .15 .04
❑ 192 Andy Benes .15 .04
❑ 193 Dennis Cook .15 .04
❑ 194 Bill Swift .15 .04
❑ 195 Frank Thomas .75 .23
❑ 195A Frank Thomas 1.25 .35
Franklin visible on batting glove
❑ 196 Damon Berryhill .15 .04
❑ 197 Mike Greenwell .15 .04
❑ 198 Mark Grace .50 .15
❑ 199 Darryl Hamilton .15 .04
❑ 200 Derrick May .15 .04
❑ 201 Ken Hill .15 .04
❑ 202 Kevin Brown .30 .09
❑ 203 Dwight Gooden .30 .09
❑ 204 Bobby Witt .15 .04
❑ 205 Juan Bell .15 .04
❑ 206 Kevin Maas .15 .04
❑ 207 Jeff King .15 .04
❑ 208 Scott Leius .15 .04
❑ 209 Rheal Cormier .15 .04
❑ 210 Darryl Strawberry .30 .09
❑ 211 Tom Gordon .15 .04
❑ 212 Bud Black .15 .04
❑ 213 Mickey Tettleton .15 .04
❑ 214 Pete Smith .15 .04
❑ 215 Felix Fermin .15 .04
❑ 216 Rick Wilkins .15 .04
❑ 217 George Bell .15 .04
❑ 218 Eric Anthony .15 .04
❑ 219 Pedro Munoz .15 .04
❑ 220 Checklist .15 .04
❑ 221 Lance Blankenship .15 .04
❑ 222 Deion Sanders .50 .15
❑ 223 Craig Biggio .50 .15
❑ 224 Ryne Sandberg 1.25 .35
❑ 225 Ron Gant .30 .09
❑ 226 Tom Brunansky .15 .04
❑ 227 Chad Curtis .15 .04
❑ 228 Joe Carter .30 .09
❑ 229 Brian Jordan .30 .09
❑ 230 Brett Butler .30 .09
❑ 231 Frank Bolick .15 .04
❑ 232 Rod Beck .15 .04
❑ 233 Carlos Baerga .15 .04
❑ 234 Eric Karros .30 .09
❑ 235 Jack Armstrong .15 .04
❑ 236 Bobby Bonilla .30 .09
❑ 237 Don Mattingly 2.00 .60
❑ 238 Jeff Gardner .15 .04
❑ 239 Dave Hollins .15 .04
❑ 240 Steve Cooke .15 .04
❑ 241 Jose Canseco .50 .15
❑ 242 Ivan Calderon .15 .04
❑ 243 Tim Belcher .15 .04
❑ 244 Freddie Benavides .15 .04
❑ 245 Roberto Alomar .50 .15
❑ 246 Rob Deer .15 .04
❑ 247 Will Clark .50 .15
❑ 248 Mike Felder .15 .04
❑ 249 Harold Baines .30 .09
❑ 250 David Cone .30 .09
❑ 251 Mark Guthrie .15 .04
❑ 252 Ellis Burks .30 .09
❑ 253 Jim Abbott .50 .15
❑ 254 Chili Davis .30 .09
❑ 255 Chris Bosio .15 .04
❑ 256 Bret Barberie .15 .04
❑ 257 Hal Morris .15 .04
❑ 258 Dante Bichette .30 .09
❑ 259 Storm Davis .15 .04
❑ 260 Gary DiSarcina .15 .04
❑ 261 Ken Caminiti .30 .09
❑ 262 Paul Molitor .50 .15
❑ 263 Joe Oliver .15 .04
❑ 264 Pat Listach .15 .04
❑ 265 Gregg Jefferies .15 .04
❑ 266 Jose Guzman .15 .04
❑ 267 Eric Davis .30 .09
❑ 268 Delino DeShields .15 .04
❑ 269 Barry Bonds 2.00 .60
❑ 270 Mike Bielecki .15 .04
❑ 271 Jay Buhner .30 .09
❑ 272 Scott Pose RC .15 .04
❑ 273 Tony Fernandez .15 .04
❑ 274 Chito Martinez .15 .04
❑ 275 Phil Plantier .15 .04
❑ 276 Pete Incaviglia .15 .04
❑ 277 Carlos Garcia .15 .04
❑ 278 Tom Henke .15 .04
❑ 279 Roger Clemens 1.50 .45
❑ 280 Rob Dibble .30 .09
❑ 281 Daryl Boston .15 .04
❑ 282 Greg Gagne .15 .04
❑ 283 Cecil Fielder .30 .09
❑ 284 Carlton Fisk .50 .15
❑ 285 Wade Boggs .50 .15
❑ 286 Damion Easley .15 .04
❑ 287 Norm Charlton .15 .04
❑ 288 Jeff Conine .30 .09
❑ 289 Roberto Kelly .15 .04
❑ 290 Jerald Clark .15 .04
❑ 291 Rickey Henderson .75 .23
❑ 292 Chuck Finley .30 .09
❑ 293 Doug Drabek .15 .04
❑ 294 Dave Stewart .30 .09
❑ 295 Tom Glavine .50 .15
❑ 296 Jaime Navarro .15 .04
❑ 297 Ray Lankford .30 .09
❑ 298 Greg Hibbard .15 .04
❑ 299 Jody Reed .15 .04
❑ 300 Dennis Martinez .30 .09
❑ 301 Dave Martinez .15 .04
❑ 302 Reggie Jefferson .15 .04
❑ 303 John Cummings RC .15 .04
❑ 304 Orestes Destrade .15 .04
❑ 305 Mike Maddux .15 .04
❑ 306 David Segui .15 .04
❑ 307 Gary Sheffield .30 .09
❑ 308 Danny Jackson .15 .04
❑ 309 Craig Lefferts .15 .04
❑ 310 Andre Dawson .30 .09
❑ 311 Barry Larkin .50 .15
❑ 312 Alex Cole .15 .04
❑ 313 Mark Gardner .15 .04
❑ 314 Kirk Gibson .50 .15
❑ 315 Shane Mack .15 .04
❑ 316 Bo Jackson .75 .23
❑ 317 Jimmy Key .30 .09
❑ 318 Greg Myers .15 .04
❑ 319 Ken Griffey Jr. 1.25 .35
❑ 320 Monty Fariss .15 .04
❑ 321 Kevin Mitchell .15 .04
❑ 322 Andres Galarraga .30 .09
❑ 323 Mark McGwire 2.00 .60
❑ 324 Mark Langston .15 .04
❑ 325 Steve Finley .30 .09
❑ 326 Greg Maddux 1.25 .35
❑ 327 Dave Nilsson .15 .04
❑ 328 Ozzie Smith 1.25 .35
❑ 329 Candy Maldonado .15 .04
❑ 330 Checklist .15 .04
❑ 331 Tim Pugh RC .15 .04
❑ 332 Joe Girardi .15 .04
❑ 333 Junior Felix .15 .04
❑ 334 Greg Swindell .15 .04
❑ 335 Ramon Martinez .15 .04
❑ 336 Sean Berry .15 .04
❑ 337 Joe Orsulak .15 .04
❑ 338 Wes Chamberlain .15 .04

❑ 339 Stan Belinda .15 .04
❑ 340 Checklist UER .15 .04
(306 Luis Mercedes)
❑ 341 Bruce Hurst .15 .04
❑ 342 John Burkett .15 .04
❑ 343 Mike Mussina .50 .15
❑ 344 Scott Fletcher .15 .04
❑ 345 Rene Gonzales .15 .04
❑ 346 Roberto Hernandez .15 .04
❑ 347 Carlos Martinez .15 .04
❑ 348 Bill Krueger .15 .04
❑ 349 Felix Jose .15 .04
❑ 350 John Jaha .15 .04
❑ 351 Willie Banks .15 .04
❑ 352 Matt Nokes .15 .04
❑ 353 Kevin Seitzer .15 .04
❑ 354 Erik Hanson .15 .04
❑ 355 David Hulse RC .15 .04
❑ 356 Domingo Martinez RC .15 .04
❑ 357 Greg Olson .15 .04
❑ 358 Randy Myers .15 .04
❑ 359 Tom Browning .15 .04
❑ 360 Charlie Hayes .15 .04
❑ 361 Bryan Harvey .15 .04
❑ 362 Eddie Taubensee .15 .04
❑ 363 Tim Wallach .15 .04
❑ 364 Mel Rojas .15 .04
❑ 365 Frank Tanana .15 .04
❑ 366 John Kruk .30 .09
❑ 367 Tim Laker RC .15 .04
❑ 368 Rich Rodriguez .15 .04
❑ 369 Darren Lewis .15 .04
❑ 370 Harold Reynolds .30 .09
❑ 371 Jose Melendez .15 .04
❑ 372 Joe Grahe .15 .04
❑ 373 Lance Johnson .15 .04
❑ 374 Jose Mesa .15 .04
❑ 375 Scott Livingstone .15 .04
❑ 376 Wally Joyner .30 .09
❑ 377 Kevin Reimer .15 .04
❑ 378 Kirby Puckett .75 .23
❑ 379 Paul O'Neill .50 .15
❑ 380 Randy Johnson .75 .23
❑ 381 Manuel Lee .15 .04
❑ 382 Dick Schofield .15 .04
❑ 383 Darren Holmes .15 .04
❑ 384 Charlie Hough .30 .09
❑ 385 John Orton .15 .04
❑ 386 Edgar Martinez .50 .15
❑ 387 Terry Pendleton .30 .09
❑ 388 Dan Plesac .15 .04
❑ 389 Jeff Reardon .30 .09
❑ 390 David Nied .15 .04
❑ 391 Dave Magadan .15 .04
❑ 392 Larry Walker .30 .09
❑ 393 Ben Rivera .15 .04
❑ 394 Lonnie Smith .15 .04
❑ 395 Craig Shipley .15 .04
❑ 396 Willie McGee .30 .09
❑ 397 Arthur Rhodes .15 .04
❑ 398 Mike Stanton .15 .04
❑ 399 Luis Polonia .15 .04
❑ 400 Jack McDowell .15 .04
❑ 401 Mike Moore .15 .04
❑ 402 Jose Lind .15 .04
❑ 403 Bill Spiers .15 .04
❑ 404 Kevin Tapani .15 .04
❑ 405 Spike Owen .15 .04
❑ 406 Tino Martinez .50 .15
❑ 407 Charlie Leibrandt .15 .04
❑ 408 Ed Sprague .15 .04
❑ 409 Bryn Smith .15 .04
❑ 410 Benito Santiago .30 .09
❑ 411 Jose Rijo .15 .04
❑ 412 Pete O'Brien .15 .04
❑ 413 Willie Wilson .15 .04
❑ 414 Bip Roberts .15 .04
❑ 415 Eric Young .15 .04
❑ 416 Walt Weiss .15 .04
❑ 417 Milt Thompson .15 .04
❑ 418 Chris Sabo .15 .04
❑ 419 Scott Sanderson .15 .04
❑ 420 Tim Raines .30 .09
❑ 421 Alan Trammell .30 .09
❑ 422 Mike Macfarlane .15 .04
❑ 423 Dave Winfield .30 .09
❑ 424 Bob Wickman .15 .04
❑ 425 David Valle .15 .04
❑ 426 Gary Redus .15 .04
❑ 427 Turner Ward .15 .04
❑ 428 Reggie Sanders .30 .09
❑ 429 Todd Worrell .15 .04
❑ 430 Julio Valera .15 .04
❑ 431 Cal Ripken Jr. 2.50 .75
❑ 432 Mo Vaughn .30 .09
❑ 433 John Smiley .15 .04
❑ 434 Omar Vizquel .50 .15
❑ 435 Billy Ripken .15 .04
❑ 436 Cory Snyder .15 .04
❑ 437 Carlos Quintana .15 .04
❑ 438 Omar Olivares .15 .04
❑ 439 Robin Ventura .30 .09
❑ 440 Checklist .15 .04
❑ 441 Kevin Higgins .15 .04
❑ 442 Carlos Hernandez .15 .04
❑ 443 Dan Peltier .15 .04
❑ 444 Derek Lilliquist .15 .04
❑ 445 Tim Salmon .50 .15
❑ 446 Sherman Obando RC .15 .04
❑ 447 Pat Kelly .15 .04
❑ 448 Todd Van Poppel .15 .04
❑ 449 Mark Whiten .15 .04
❑ 450 Checklist .15 .04
❑ 451 Pat Meares RC .40 .12
❑ 452 Tony Tarasco RC .15 .04
❑ 453 Chris Gwynn .15 .04
❑ 454 Armando Reynoso .15 .04
❑ 455 Danny Darwin .15 .04
❑ 456 Willie Greene .15 .04
❑ 457 Mike Blowers .15 .04
❑ 458 Kevin Roberson RC .15 .04
❑ 459 Graeme Lloyd RC .40 .12
❑ 460 David West .15 .04
❑ 461 Joey Cora .15 .04
❑ 462 Alex Arias .15 .04
❑ 463 Chad Kreuter .15 .04
❑ 464 Mike Lansing RC .40 .12
❑ 465 Mike Timlin .15 .04
❑ 466 Paul Wagner .15 .04
❑ 467 Mark Portugal .15 .04
❑ 468 Jim Leyritz .15 .04
❑ 469 Ryan Klesko .30 .09
❑ 470 Mario Diaz .15 .04
❑ 471 Guillermo Velasquez .15 .04
❑ 472 Fernando Valenzuela .30 .09
❑ 473 Raul Mondesi .30 .09
❑ 474 Mike Pagliarulo .15 .04
❑ 475 Chris Hammond .15 .04
❑ 476 Torey Lovullo .15 .04
❑ 477 Trevor Wilson .15 .04
❑ 478 Marcos Armas RC .15 .04
❑ 479 Dave Gallagher .15 .04
❑ 480 Jeff Treadway .15 .04
❑ 481 Jeff Branson .15 .04
❑ 482 Dickie Thon .15 .04
❑ 483 Eduardo Perez .15 .04
❑ 484 David Wells .30 .09
❑ 485 Brian Williams .15 .04
❑ 486 Domingo Cedeno RC .15 .04
❑ 487 Tom Candiotti .15 .04
❑ 488 Steve Frey .15 .04
❑ 489 Greg McMichael RC .15 .04
❑ 490 Marc Newfield .15 .04
❑ 491 Larry Andersen .15 .04
❑ 492 Damon Buford .15 .04
❑ 493 Ricky Gutierrez .15 .04
❑ 494 Jeff Russell .15 .04
❑ 495 Vinny Castilla .75 .23
❑ 496 Wilson Alvarez .15 .04
❑ 497 Scott Bullett .15 .04
❑ 498 Larry Casian .15 .04
❑ 499 Jose Vizcaino .15 .04
❑ 500 J.T. Snow RC .60 .18
❑ 501 Bryan Hickerson .15 .04
❑ 502 Jeremy Hernandez .15 .04
❑ 503 Jeromy Burnitz .30 .09
❑ 504 Steve Farr .15 .04
❑ 505 J. Owens RC .15 .04
❑ 506 Craig Paquette .15 .04
❑ 507 Jim Eisenreich .15 .04
❑ 508 Matt Whiteside RC .15 .04
❑ 509 Luis Aquino .15 .04
❑ 510 Mike LaValliere .15 .04
❑ 511 Jim Gott .15 .04
❑ 512 Mark McLemore .15 .04
❑ 513 Randy Milligan .15 .04
❑ 514 Gary Gaetti .30 .09
❑ 515 Lou Frazier RC .15 .04
❑ 516 Rich Amaral .15 .04
❑ 517 Gene Harris .15 .04
❑ 518 Aaron Sele .15 .04
❑ 519 Mark Wohlers .15 .04
❑ 520 Scott Kamieniecki .15 .04
❑ 521 Kent Mercker .15 .04
❑ 522 Jim Deshaies .15 .04
❑ 523 Kevin Stocker .15 .04
❑ 524 Jason Bere .15 .04
❑ 525 Tim Bogar RC .15 .04
❑ 526 Brad Pennington .15 .04
❑ 527 Curt Leskanic RC .60 .18
❑ 528 Wayne Kirby .15 .04
❑ 529 Tim Costo .15 .04
❑ 530 Doug Henry .15 .04
❑ 531 Trevor Hoffman .75 .23
❑ 532 Kelly Gruber .15 .04
❑ 533 Mike Harkey .15 .04
❑ 534 John Doherty .15 .04
❑ 535 Erik Pappas .15 .04
❑ 536 Brent Gates .15 .04
❑ 537 Roger McDowell .15 .04
❑ 538 Chris Haney .15 .04
❑ 539 Blas Minor .15 .04
❑ 540 Pat Hentgen .15 .04
❑ 541 Chuck Carr .15 .04
❑ 542 Doug Strange .15 .04
❑ 543 Xavier Hernandez .15 .04
❑ 544 Paul Quantrill .15 .04
❑ 545 Anthony Young .15 .04
❑ 546 Bret Boone .50 .15
❑ 547 Dwight Smith .15 .04
❑ 548 Bobby Munoz .15 .04
❑ 549 Russ Springer .15 .04
❑ 550 Roger Pavlik .15 .04
❑ DW Dave Winfield 1.00 .30
3000 Hits
❑ FT Frank Thomas AU/3500 50.00 15.00
(Certified autograph)

2005 Leaf

	Nm-Mt	Ex-Mt
COMPLETE SET (300)	150.00	45.00
COMP.SETw/o SP's (200)	25.00	7.50
COMMON CARD (1-200)	.30	.09
COMMON CARD (201-250)	2.00	.60
201-250 STATED ODDS 1:3	.00	
COMMON CARD (251-300)	1.50	.45
251-270 STATED ODDS 1:6	.00	
271-300 STATED ODDS 1:4	.00	

❑ 1 Bartolo Colon .30 .09
❑ 2 Casey Kotchman .30 .09
❑ 3 Chone Figgins .30 .09
❑ 4 Darin Erstad .30 .09
❑ 5 Francisco Rodriguez .30 .09
❑ 6 Garret Anderson .30 .09
❑ 7 Jarrod Washburn .30 .09
❑ 8 Troy Glaus .30 .09
❑ 9 Vladimir Guerrero .75 .23
❑ 10 Brandon Webb .30 .09
❑ 11 Casey Fossum .30 .09

❑ 12 Luis Gonzalez .30 .09
❑ 13 Randy Johnson .75 .23
❑ 14 Richie Sexson .30 .09
❑ 15 Andruw Jones .50 .15
❑ 16 Chipper Jones .75 .23
❑ 17 J.D. Drew .30 .09
❑ 18 John Smoltz .50 .15
❑ 19 Johnny Estrada .30 .09
❑ 20 Marcus Giles .30 .09
❑ 21 Rafael Furcal .30 .09
❑ 22 Russ Ortiz .30 .09
❑ 23 Javy Lopez .30 .09
❑ 24 Jay Gibbons .30 .09
❑ 25 Melvin Mora .30 .09
❑ 26 Miguel Tejada .30 .09
❑ 27 Rafael Palmeiro .50 .15
❑ 28 Sidney Ponson .30 .09
❑ 29 Bill Mueller .30 .09
❑ 30 Curt Schilling .50 .15
❑ 31 David Ortiz .75 .23
❑ 32 Doug Mientkiewicz .30 .09
❑ 33 Jason Varitek .75 .23
❑ 34 Johnny Damon .50 .15
❑ 35 Manny Ramirez .50 .15
❑ 36 Pedro Martinez .50 .15
❑ 37 Trot Nixon .30 .09
❑ 38 Aramis Ramirez .30 .09
❑ 39 Corey Patterson .30 .09
❑ 40 Derrek Lee .50 .15
❑ 41 Greg Maddux 1.25 .35
❑ 42 Kerry Wood .30 .09
❑ 43 Mark Prior .50 .15
❑ 44 Moises Alou .30 .09
❑ 45 Nomar Garciaparra .75 .23
❑ 46 Sammy Sosa .75 .23
❑ 47 Carlos Lee .30 .09
❑ 48 Kip Wells .30 .09
❑ 49 Magglio Ordonez .30 .09
❑ 50 Mark Buehrle .30 .09
❑ 51 Paul Konerko .30 .09
❑ 52 Roberto Alomar .50 .15
❑ 53 Adam Dunn .30 .09
❑ 54 Austin Kearns .30 .09
❑ 55 Barry Larkin .50 .15
❑ 56 Danny Graves .30 .09
❑ 57 Ken Griffey Jr. 1.25 .35
❑ 58 Sean Casey .50 .15
❑ 59 C.C. Sabathia .30 .09
❑ 60 Cliff Lee .30 .09
❑ 61 Jody Gerut .30 .09
❑ 62 Omar Vizquel .30 .09
❑ 63 Travis Hafner .30 .09
❑ 64 Victor Martinez .30 .09
❑ 65 Charles Johnson .30 .09
❑ 66 Jason Jennings .30 .09
❑ 67 Jeromy Burnitz .30 .09
❑ 68 Preston Wilson .30 .09
❑ 69 Todd Helton .50 .15
❑ 70 Bobby Higginson .30 .09
❑ 71 Dmitri Young .30 .09
❑ 72 Eric Munson .30 .09
❑ 73 Ivan Rodriguez .50 .15
❑ 74 Jeremy Bonderman .30 .09
❑ 75 Rondell White .30 .09
❑ 76 A.J. Burnett .30 .09
❑ 77 Carl Pavano .30 .09
❑ 78 Dontrelle Willis .30 .09
❑ 79 Hee Seop Choi .30 .09
❑ 80 Josh Beckett .30 .09
❑ 81 Juan Pierre .30 .09
❑ 82 Miguel Cabrera .50 .15
❑ 83 Mike Lowell .30 .09
❑ 84 Paul Lo Duca .30 .09
❑ 85 Andy Pettitte .50 .15
❑ 86 Carlos Beltran .30 .09
❑ 87 Craig Biggio .50 .15
❑ 88 Jeff Bagwell .50 .15
❑ 89 Jeff Kent .30 .09
❑ 90 Lance Berkman .30 .09
❑ 91 Roger Clemens 1.25 .35
❑ 92 Roy Oswalt .30 .09
❑ 93 Andres Blanco .30 .09
❑ 94 Jeremy Affeldt .30 .09
❑ 95 Juan Gonzalez .30 .09
❑ 96 Ken Harvey .30 .09
❑ 97 Mike Sweeney .30 .09
❑ 98 Zack Greinke .30 .09
❑ 99 Adrian Beltre .30 .09
❑ 100 Brad Penny .30 .09
❑ 101 Eric Gagne .30 .09
❑ 102 Kazuhisa Ishii .30 .09
❑ 103 Milton Bradley .30 .09
❑ 104 Shawn Green .30 .09
❑ 105 Steve Finley .30 .09
❑ 106 Ben Sheets .30 .09
❑ 107 Bill Hall .30 .09
❑ 108 Danny Kolb .30 .09
❑ 109 Geoff Jenkins .30 .09
❑ 110 Junior Spivey .30 .09
❑ 111 Lyle Overbay .30 .09
❑ 112 Scott Podsednik .30 .09
❑ 113 A.J. Pierzynski .30 .09
❑ 114 Brad Radke .30 .09
❑ 115 Corey Koskie .30 .09
❑ 116 Jacque Jones .30 .09
❑ 117 Joe Mauer .30 .09
❑ 118 Joe Nathan .30 .09
❑ 119 Shannon Stewart .30 .09
❑ 120 Torii Hunter .30 .09
❑ 121 Brad Wilkerson .30 .09
❑ 122 Jeff Fassero .30 .09
❑ 123 Jose Vidro .30 .09
❑ 124 Livan Hernandez .30 .09
❑ 125 Nick Johnson .30 .09
❑ 126 Al Leiter .30 .09
❑ 127 Jose Reyes .30 .09
❑ 128 Kazuo Matsui .30 .09
❑ 129 Mike Cameron .30 .09
❑ 130 Mike Piazza .75 .23
❑ 131 Richard Hidalgo .30 .09
❑ 132 Tom Glavine .50 .15
❑ 133 Alex Rodriguez 1.25 .35
❑ 134 Bernie Williams .50 .15
❑ 135 Derek Jeter 1.50 .45
❑ 136 Gary Sheffield .30 .09
❑ 137 Jason Giambi .30 .09
❑ 138 Javier Vazquez .30 .09
❑ 139 Jorge Posada .50 .15
❑ 140 Kevin Brown .30 .09
❑ 141 Mariano Rivera .50 .15
❑ 142 Mike Mussina .50 .15
❑ 143 Barry Zito .30 .09
❑ 144 Bobby Crosby .30 .09
❑ 145 Eric Chavez .30 .09
❑ 146 Erubiel Durazo .30 .09
❑ 147 Jermaine Dye .30 .09
❑ 148 Mark Mulder .30 .09
❑ 149 Tim Hudson .30 .09
❑ 150 Bobby Abreu .30 .09
❑ 151 Eric Milton .30 .09
❑ 152 Jim Thome .50 .15
❑ 153 Kevin Millwood .30 .09
❑ 154 Mike Lieberthal .30 .09
❑ 155 Pat Burrell .30 .09
❑ 156 Randy Wolf .30 .09
❑ 157 Craig Wilson .30 .09
❑ 158 Jack Wilson .30 .09
❑ 159 Jason Bay .30 .09
❑ 160 Jason Kendall .30 .09
❑ 161 Kris Benson .30 .09
❑ 162 Brian Giles .30 .09
❑ 163 Jake Peavy .30 .09
❑ 164 Jay Payton .30 .09
❑ 165 Khalil Greene .50 .15
❑ 166 Mark Loretta .30 .09
❑ 167 Ryan Klesko .30 .09
❑ 168 Sean Burroughs .30 .09
❑ 169 David Aardsma .30 .09
❑ 170 Edgardo Alfonzo .30 .09
❑ 171 Jason Schmidt .30 .09
❑ 172 Merkin Valdez .30 .09
❑ 173 Ray Durham .30 .09
❑ 174 Bret Boone .30 .09
❑ 175 Dan Wilson .30 .09
❑ 176 Ichiro Suzuki 1.50 .45
❑ 177 Jamie Moyer .30 .09
❑ 178 Rich Aurilia .30 .09
❑ 179 Albert Pujols 1.50 .45
❑ 180 Edgar Renteria .30 .09
❑ 181 Jason Isringhausen .30 .09
❑ 182 Jeff Suppan .30 .09
❑ 183 Jim Edmonds .50 .15
❑ 184 Scott Rolen .50 .15
❑ 185 Woody Williams .30 .09
❑ 186 Aubrey Huff .30 .09
❑ 187 Carl Crawford .30 .09
❑ 188 Dewon Brazelton .30 .09
❑ 189 Jose Cruz Jr. .30 .09
❑ 190 Rocco Baldelli .30 .09
❑ 191 Alfonso Soriano .30 .09
❑ 192 Hank Blalock .30 .09
❑ 193 Kenny Rogers .30 .09
❑ 194 Laynce Nix .30 .09
❑ 195 Mark Teixeira .50 .15
❑ 196 Michael Young .30 .09
❑ 197 Alexis Rios .30 .09
❑ 198 Carlos Delgado .30 .09
❑ 199 Roy Halladay .30 .09
❑ 200 Vernon Wells .30 .09
❑ 201 Josh Kroeger PROS 2.00 .60
❑ 202 Angel Guzman PROS 2.00 .60
❑ 203 Brad Halsey PROS 2.00 .60
❑ 204 Bucky Jacobsen PROS 2.00 .60
❑ 205 Carlos Hines PROS 2.00 .60
❑ 206 Carlos Vasquez PROS 2.00 .60
❑ 207 Billy Traber PROS 2.00 .60
❑ 208 Bubba Crosby PROS 2.00 .60
❑ 209 Chris Oxspring PROS 2.00 .60
❑ 210 Chris Shelton PROS 2.00 .60
❑ 211 Colby Miller PROS 2.00 .60
❑ 212 Dave Crouthers PROS 2.00 .60
❑ 213 Dennis Sarfate PROS 2.00 .60
❑ 214 Don Kelly PROS 2.00 .60
❑ 215 Edwardo Sierra PROS 2.00 .60
❑ 216 Edwin Moreno PROS 2.00 .60
❑ 217 Fernando Nieve PROS 2.00 .60
❑ 218 Freddy Guzman PROS 2.00 .60
❑ 219 Greg Dobbs PROS 2.00 .60
❑ 220 Hector Gimenez PROS 2.00 .60
❑ 221 Andy Green PROS 2.00 .60
❑ 222 Jason Bartlett PROS 3.00 .90
❑ 223 Jerry Gil PROS 2.00 .60
❑ 224 Jesse Crain PROS 3.00 .90
❑ 225 Joey Gathright PROS 2.00 .60
❑ 226 John Gall PROS 2.00 .60
❑ 227 Jorge Sequea PROS 2.00 .60
❑ 228 Jorge Vasquez PROS 2.00 .60
❑ 229 Josh Labandeira PROS 2.00 .60
❑ 230 Justin Leone PROS 2.00 .60
❑ 231 Lance Cormier PROS 2.00 .60
❑ 232 Lincoln Holdzkom PROS 2.00 .60
❑ 233 Miguel Olivo PROS 2.00 .60
❑ 234 Mike Rouse PROS 2.00 .60
❑ 235 Onil Joseph PROS 2.00 .60
❑ 236 Phil Stockman PROS 2.00 .60
❑ 237 Ramon Ramirez PROS 2.00 .60
❑ 238 Robb Quinlan PROS 2.00 .60
❑ 239 Roberto Novoa PROS 2.00 .60
❑ 240 Ronald Belisario PROS 2.00 .60
❑ 241 Ronny Cedeno PROS 2.00 .60
❑ 242 Ruddy Yan PROS 2.00 .60
❑ 243 Ryan Meaux PROS 2.00 .60
❑ 244 Ryan Wing PROS 2.00 .60
❑ 245 Scott Proctor PROS 2.00 .60
❑ 246 Sean Henn PROS 2.00 .60
❑ 247 Tim Bausher PROS 2.00 .60
❑ 248 Tim Bittner PROS 2.00 .60
❑ 249 William Bergolla PROS 2.00 .60
❑ 250 Yadier Molina PROS 3.00 .90
❑ 251 Bernie Williams PTT 2.00 .60
❑ 252 Craig Biggio PTT 2.00 .60
❑ 253 Chipper Jones PTT 2.00 .60
❑ 254 Greg Maddux PTT 3.00 .90
❑ 255 Sammy Sosa PTT 2.00 .60
❑ 256 Mike Mussina PTT 2.00 .60
❑ 257 Tim Salmon PTT 2.00 .60
❑ 258 Barry Larkin PTT 2.00 .60
❑ 259 Randy Johnson PTT 2.00 .60
❑ 260 Jeff Bagwell PTT 2.00 .60
❑ 261 Roberto Alomar PTT 2.00 .60
❑ 262 Tom Glavine PTT 2.00 .60
❑ 263 Roger Clemens PTT 3.00 .90
❑ 264 Alex Rodriguez PTT 3.00 .90
❑ 265 Ivan Rodriguez PTT 2.00 .60
❑ 266 Pedro Martinez PTT 2.00 .60
❑ 267 Ken Griffey Jr. PTT 3.00 .90
❑ 268 Jim Thome PTT 2.00 .60
❑ 269 Frank Thomas PTT 2.00 .60

❑ 270 Mike Piazza PTT 2.00 .60
❑ 271 Garret Anderson TC 1.50 .45
❑ 272 Luis Gonzalez TC 1.50 .45
❑ 273 John Smoltz TC 2.00 .60
❑ 274 Rafael Palmeiro TC 2.00 .60
❑ 275 Curt Schilling TC 2.00 .60
❑ 276 Mark Prior TC 2.00 .60
❑ 277 Magglio Ordonez TC 1.50 .45
❑ 278 Adam Dunn TC 1.50 .45
❑ 279 Travis Hafner TC 1.50 .45
❑ 280 Jeromy Burnitz TC 1.50 .45
❑ 281 Carlos Guillen TC 1.50 .45
❑ 282 Dontrelle Willis TC 1.50 .45
❑ 283 Carlos Beltran TC 1.50 .45
❑ 284 Zack Greinke TC 1.50 .45
❑ 285 Adrian Beltre TC 1.50 .45
❑ 286 Ben Sheets TC 1.50 .45
❑ 287 Johan Santana TC 2.00 .60
❑ 288 Livan Hernandez TC 1.50 .45
❑ 289 Kazuo Matsui TC 1.50 .45
❑ 290 Derek Jeter TC 4.00 1.20
❑ 291 Tim Hudson TC 1.50 .45
❑ 292 Eric Milton TC 1.50 .45
❑ 293 Jason Kendall TC 1.50 .45
❑ 294 Jake Peavy TC 1.50 .45
❑ 295 Ray Durham TC 1.50 .45
❑ 296 Ichiro Suzuki TC 4.00 1.20
❑ 297 Scott Rolen TC 2.00 .60
❑ 298 Carl Crawford TC 1.50 .45
❑ 299 Hank Blalock TC 1.50 .45
❑ 300 Roy Halladay TC 1.50 .45

2005 MLB Artifacts

	Nm-Mt	Ex-Mt
COMP.SET w/o SP's (100)	40.00	12.00
COMMON CARD (1-100)	.50	.15
COMMON CARD (101-150)	3.00	.90
COMMON CARD (151-200)	3.00	.90

❑ 1 Adam Dunn .50 .15
❑ 2 Adrian Beltre .50 .15
❑ 3 Albert Pujols 2.50 .75
❑ 4 Alex Rodriguez 2.00 .60
❑ 5 Alfonso Soriano .50 .15
❑ 6 Andruw Jones .75 .23
❑ 7 Andy Pettitte .75 .23
❑ 8 Aramis Ramirez .50 .15
❑ 9 Aubrey Huff .50 .15
❑ 10 Barry Larkin .75 .23
❑ 11 Ben Sheets .50 .15
❑ 12 Bernie Williams .75 .23
❑ 13 Bobby Abreu .50 .15
❑ 14 Brad Penny .50 .15
❑ 15 Bret Boone .50 .15
❑ 16 Brian Giles .50 .15
❑ 17 Carl Crawford .50 .15
❑ 18 Carl Pavano .50 .15
❑ 19 Carlos Beltran .50 .15
❑ 20 Carlos Delgado .50 .15
❑ 21 Carlos Guillen .50 .15
❑ 22 Carlos Lee .50 .15
❑ 23 Carlos Zambrano .50 .15
❑ 24 Chipper Jones 1.25 .35
❑ 25 Craig Biggio .75 .23
❑ 26 Craig Wilson .50 .15
❑ 27 Curt Schilling .75 .23
❑ 28 David Ortiz 1.25 .35
❑ 29 Derek Jeter 2.50 .75
❑ 30 Eric Chavez .50 .15
❑ 31 Eric Gagne .50 .15
❑ 32 Frank Thomas 1.25 .35
❑ 33 Garret Anderson .50 .15
❑ 34 Gary Sheffield .50 .15
❑ 35 Greg Maddux 2.00 .60
❑ 36 Hank Blalock .50 .15
❑ 37 Hideki Matsui 2.50 .75
❑ 38 Ichiro Suzuki 2.50 .75
❑ 39 Ivan Rodriguez .75 .23
❑ 40 J.D. Drew .50 .15
❑ 41 Jake Peavy .50 .15
❑ 42 Jason Kendall .50 .15
❑ 43 Jason Schmidt .50 .15
❑ 44 Jeff Bagwell .75 .23
❑ 45 Jeff Kent .50 .15
❑ 46 Jim Edmonds .75 .23
❑ 47 Jim Thome .75 .23
❑ 48 Joe Mauer .50 .15
❑ 49 Johan Santana .75 .23
❑ 50 John Smoltz .75 .23
❑ 51 Jose Reyes .50 .15
❑ 52 Jose Vidro .50 .15
❑ 53 Josh Beckett .50 .15
❑ 54 Ken Griffey Jr. 2.00 .60
❑ 55 Kerry Wood .50 .15
❑ 56 Kevin Brown .50 .15
❑ 57 Lance Berkman .50 .15
❑ 58 Larry Walker .75 .23
❑ 59 Livan Hernandez .50 .15
❑ 60 Luis Gonzalez .50 .15
❑ 61 Lyle Overbay .50 .15
❑ 62 Magglio Ordonez .50 .15
❑ 63 Manny Ramirez .75 .23
❑ 64 Mark Mulder .50 .15
❑ 65 Mark Prior .75 .23
❑ 66 Mark Teixeira .75 .23
❑ 67 Melvin Mora .50 .15
❑ 68 Michael Young .50 .15
❑ 69 Miguel Cabrera .75 .23
❑ 70 Miguel Tejada .50 .15
❑ 71 Mike Lowell .50 .15
❑ 72 Mike Mussina .75 .23
❑ 73 Mike Piazza 1.25 .35
❑ 74 Mike Sweeney .50 .15
❑ 75 Nomar Garciaparra 1.25 .35
❑ 76 Oliver Perez .50 .15
❑ 77 Paul Konerko .50 .15
❑ 78 Pedro Martinez .75 .23
❑ 79 Preston Wilson .50 .15
❑ 80 Rafael Furcal .50 .15
❑ 81 Rafael Palmeiro .75 .23
❑ 82 Randy Johnson 1.25 .35
❑ 83 Richie Sexson .50 .15
❑ 84 Roger Clemens 2.00 .60
❑ 85 Roy Halladay .50 .15
❑ 86 Roy Oswalt .50 .15
❑ 87 Sammy Sosa 1.25 .35
❑ 88 Scott Podsednik .50 .15
❑ 89 Scott Rolen .75 .23
❑ 90 Shawn Green .50 .15
❑ 91 Steve Finley .50 .15
❑ 92 Tim Hudson .50 .15
❑ 93 Todd Helton .75 .23
❑ 94 Tom Glavine .75 .23
❑ 95 Torii Hunter .50 .15
❑ 96 Travis Hafner .50 .15
❑ 97 Troy Glaus .50 .15
❑ 98 Vernon Wells .50 .15
❑ 99 Victor Martinez .50 .15
❑ 100 Vladimir Guerrero 1.25 .35
❑ 101 Aaron Rowand FS 3.00 .90
❑ 102 Adam LaRoche FS 3.00 .90
❑ 103 Adrian Gonzalez FS 3.00 .90
❑ 104 Alexis Rios FS 3.00 .90
❑ 105 Angel Guzman FS 3.00 .90
❑ 106 B.J. Upton FS 3.00 .90
❑ 107 Bobby Crosby FS 3.00 .90
❑ 108 Bobby Madritsch FS 3.00 .90
❑ 109 Brandon Claussen FS 3.00 .90
❑ 110 Bucky Jacobsen FS 3.00 .90
❑ 111 Casey Kotchman FS 3.00 .90
❑ 112 Chad Cordero FS 3.00 .90
❑ 113 Chase Utley FS 3.00 .90
❑ 114 Chris Burke FS 3.00 .90
❑ 115 Dallas McPherson FS 3.00 .90
❑ 116 Daniel Cabrera FS 3.00 .90
❑ 117 David DeJesus FS 3.00 .90
❑ 118 David Wright FS 8.00 2.40
❑ 119 Eddy Rodriguez FS 3.00 .90
❑ 120 Edwin Jackson FS 3.00 .90
❑ 121 Gabe Gross FS 3.00 .90
❑ 122 Garrett Atkins FS 3.00 .90
❑ 123 Gavin Floyd FS 3.00 .90
❑ 124 Gerald Laird FS 3.00 .90
❑ 125 Guillermo Quiroz FS 3.00 .90
❑ 126 J.D. Closser FS 3.00 .90
❑ 127 Jason Bay FS 3.00 .90
❑ 128 Jason DuBois FS 3.00 .90
❑ 129 Jason Lane FS 3.00 .90
❑ 130 Jayson Werth FS 3.00 .90
❑ 131 Jeff Francis FS 3.00 .90
❑ 132 Jesse Crain FS 3.00 .90
❑ 133 Joe Blanton FS 3.00 .90
❑ 134 Joe Mauer FS 3.00 .90
❑ 135 Jose Capellan FS 3.00 .90
❑ 136 Kevin Youkilis FS 3.00 .90
❑ 137 Khalil Greene FS 3.00 .90
❑ 138 Laynce Nix FS 3.00 .90
❑ 139 Nick Swisher FS 3.00 .90
❑ 140 Oliver Perez FS 3.00 .90
❑ 141 Rickie Weeks FS 3.00 .90
❑ 142 Robb Quinlan FS 3.00 .90
❑ 143 Roman Colon FS 3.00 .90
❑ 144 Ryan Howard FS 3.00 .90
❑ 145 Ryan Wagner FS 3.00 .90
❑ 146 Scott Kazmir FS 3.00 .90
❑ 147 Scott Proctor FS 3.00 .90
❑ 148 Wily Mo Pena FS 3.00 .90
❑ 149 Yhency Brazoban FS 3.00 .90
❑ 150 Zack Greinke FS 3.00 .90
❑ 151 Al Kaline LGD 4.00 1.20
❑ 152 Babe Ruth LGD 10.00 3.00
❑ 153 Billy Williams LGD 3.00 .90
❑ 154 Bob Feller LGD 3.00 .90
❑ 155 Bob Gibson LGD 3.00 .90
❑ 156 Bob Lemon LGD 3.00 .90
❑ 157 Bobby Doerr LGD 3.00 .90
❑ 158 Brooks Robinson LGD 3.00 .90
❑ 159 Cal Ripken LGD 10.00 3.00
❑ 160 Christy Mathewson LGD 4.00 1.20
❑ 161 Cy Young LGD 4.00 1.20
❑ 162 Dizzy Dean LGD 3.00 .90
❑ 163 Don Drysdale LGD 3.00 .90
❑ 164 Eddie Mathews LGD 4.00 1.20
❑ 165 Enos Slaughter LGD 3.00 .90
❑ 166 Ernie Banks LGD 4.00 1.20
❑ 167 Fergie Jenkins LGD 3.00 .90
❑ 168 George Sisler LGD 3.00 .90
❑ 169 Harmon Killebrew LGD 4.00 1.20
❑ 170 Honus Wagner LGD 4.00 1.20
❑ 171 Jackie Robinson LGD 4.00 1.20
❑ 172 Jimmie Foxx LGD 4.00 1.20
❑ 173 Joe DiMaggio LGD 5.00 1.50
❑ 174 Joe Morgan LGD 3.00 .90
❑ 175 Juan Marichal LGD 3.00 .90
❑ 176 Lou Brock LGD 3.00 .90
❑ 177 Lou Gehrig LGD 5.00 1.50
❑ 178 Luis Aparicio LGD 3.00 .90
❑ 179 Mel Ott LGD 3.00 .90
❑ 180 Mickey Cochrane LGD 3.00 .90
❑ 181 Mickey Mantle LGD 15.00 4.50
❑ 182 Mike Schmidt LGD 5.00 1.50
❑ 183 Nolan Ryan LGD 8.00 2.40
❑ 184 Pee Wee Reese LGD 3.00 .90
❑ 185 Phil Rizzuto LGD 3.00 .90
❑ 186 Ralph Kiner LGD 3.00 .90
❑ 187 Rogers Hornsby LGD 3.00 .90
❑ 188 Roy Campanella LGD 4.00 1.20
❑ 189 Satchel Paige LGD 4.00 1.20
❑ 190 Stan Musial LGD 4.00 1.20
❑ 191 Rick Ferrell LGD 3.00 .90
❑ 192 Thurman Munson LGD 4.00 1.20
❑ 193 Tom Seaver LGD 3.00 .90
❑ 194 Ty Cobb LGD 4.00 1.20
❑ 195 Walter Johnson LGD 4.00 1.20
❑ 196 Warren Spahn LGD 3.00 .90
❑ 197 Whitey Ford LGD 3.00 .90
❑ 198 Willie McCovey LGD 3.00 .90
❑ 199 Willie Stargell LGD 3.00 .90
❑ 200 Yogi Berra LGD 4.00 1.20

2005 MLB Showdown

	Nm-Mt	Ex-Mt
COMP.SET w/o FOIL (298)	80.00	24.00
FOIL STATED ODDS 1:3		

#	Player	Nm-Mt	Ex-Mt
❑ 1	Garret Anderson	1.00	.30
❑ 2	David Eckstein	1.00	.30
❑ 3	Darin Erstad	1.00	.30
❑ 4	Chone Figgins	.50	.15
❑ 5	Troy Glaus	1.00	.30
❑ 6	Kevin Gregg	.50	.15
❑ 7	Vladimir Guerrero FOIL	10.00	3.00
❑ 8	Jose Guillen	1.00	.30
❑ 9	Adam Kennedy	.50	.15
❑ 10	Troy Percival	1.00	.30
❑ 11	Francisco Rodriguez FOIL	5.00	1.50
❑ 12	Tim Salmon	1.50	.45
❑ 13	Danny Bautista	.50	.15
❑ 14	Alex Cintron	.50	.15
❑ 15	Luis Gonzalez	1.00	.30
❑ 16	Scott Hairston	.50	.15
❑ 17	Shea Hillenbrand	1.00	.30
❑ 18	Randy Johnson FOIL	15.00	4.50
❑ 19	Mike Koplove	.50	.15
❑ 20	Chad Tracy	.50	.15
❑ 21	Brandon Webb	.50	.15
❑ 22	Antonio Alfonseca	.50	.15
❑ 23	J.D. Drew FOIL	8.00	2.40
❑ 24	Johnny Estrada FOIL	3.00	.90
❑ 25	Julio Franco	1.00	.30
❑ 26	Rafael Furcal	1.00	.30
❑ 27	Marcus Giles	1.00	.30
❑ 28	Andruw Jones	1.50	.45
❑ 29	Chipper Jones	2.50	.75
❑ 30	Eli Marrero	.50	.15
❑ 31	John Smoltz	1.50	.45
❑ 32	John Thomson	.50	.15
❑ 33	Jaret Wright	.50	.15
❑ 34	Buddy Groom	.50	.15
❑ 35	Jerry Hairston	.50	.15
❑ 36	Jorge Julio	.50	.15
❑ 37	Rodrigo Lopez	.50	.15
❑ 38	Melvin Mora FOIL	8.00	2.40
❑ 39	Rafael Palmeiro	1.50	.45
❑ 40	Brian Roberts	1.00	.30
❑ 41	B.J. Ryan	.50	.15
❑ 42	B.J. Surhoff	1.00	.30
❑ 43	Miguel Tejada FOIL	8.00	2.40
❑ 44	Mark Bellhorn	1.00	.30
❑ 45	Johnny Damon	1.50	.45
❑ 46	Alan Embree	.50	.15
❑ 47	Keith Foulke	1.00	.30
❑ 48	Gabe Kapler	1.00	.30
❑ 49	Pedro Martinez	1.50	.45
❑ 50	Bill Mueller	1.00	.30
❑ 51	David Ortiz FOIL	10.00	3.00
❑ 52	Manny Ramirez FOIL	12.00	3.60
❑ 53	Pokey Reese	1.00	.30
❑ 54	Curt Schilling FOIL	8.00	2.40
❑ 55	Mike Timlin	1.00	.30
❑ 56	Jason Varitek	2.50	.75
❑ 57	Moises Alou	1.00	.30
❑ 58	Michael Barrett	.50	.15
❑ 59	Matt Clement	1.00	.30
❑ 60	Kyle Farnsworth	.50	.15
❑ 61	Nomar Garciaparra	2.50	.75
❑ 62	LaTroy Hawkins	.50	.15
❑ 63	Todd Hollandsworth	.50	.15
❑ 64	Derrek Lee	1.50	.45
❑ 65	Greg Maddux	4.00	1.20
❑ 66	Kent Mercker	.50	.15
❑ 67	Corey Patterson	.50	.15
❑ 68	Aramis Ramirez	1.00	.30
❑ 69	Kerry Wood	1.00	.30
❑ 70	Mark Buehrle	1.00	.30
❑ 71	Joe Crede	1.00	.30
❑ 72	Freddy Garcia	1.00	.30
❑ 73	Paul Konerko FOIL	5.00	1.50
❑ 74	Carlos Lee	1.00	.30
❑ 75	Damaso Marte	.50	.15
❑ 76	Aaron Rowand	1.00	.30
❑ 77	Shingo Takatsu	.50	.15
❑ 78	Juan Uribe	.50	.15
❑ 79	Jose Valentin	.50	.15
❑ 80	Sean Casey	1.50	.45
❑ 81	Juan Castro	.50	.15
❑ 82	Adam Dunn FOIL	5.00	1.50
❑ 83	Ryan Freel	.50	.15
❑ 84	Aaron Harang	.50	.15
❑ 85	D'Angelo Jimenez	.50	.15
❑ 86	Barry Larkin	1.50	.45
❑ 87	Jason LaRue	.50	.15
❑ 88	Wily Mo Pena	1.00	.30
❑ 89	Phil Norton	.50	.15
❑ 90	John Riedling	.50	.15
❑ 91	Paul Wilson	.50	.15
❑ 92	Ronnie Belliard	.50	.15
❑ 93	Casey Blake	.50	.15
❑ 94	Ben Broussard	.50	.15
❑ 95	Coco Crisp	.50	.15
❑ 96	Travis Hafner FOIL	5.00	1.50
❑ 97	Matt Lawton	.50	.15
❑ 98	Cliff Lee	.50	.15
❑ 99	Victor Martinez	1.00	.30
❑ 100	David Riske	.50	.15
❑ 101	C.C. Sabathia	1.00	.30
❑ 102	Omar Vizquel	1.50	.45
❑ 103	Jake Westbrook	.50	.15
❑ 104	Jeromy Burnitz	1.00	.30
❑ 105	Vinny Castilla	1.00	.30
❑ 106	Shawn Chacon	.50	.15
❑ 107	Royce Clayton	.50	.15
❑ 108	Todd Helton FOIL	8.00	2.40
❑ 109	Jason Jennings	.50	.15
❑ 110	Charles Johnson	.50	.15
❑ 111	Aaron Miles	.50	.15
❑ 112	Steve Reed	.50	.15
❑ 113	Mark Sweeney	.50	.15
❑ 114	Carlos Guillen	1.00	.30
❑ 115	Omar Infante	.50	.15
❑ 116	Mike Maroth	.50	.15
❑ 117	Craig Monroe	.50	.15
❑ 118	Carlos Pena	.50	.15
❑ 119	Nate Robertson	.50	.15
❑ 120	Ivan Rodriguez FOIL	8.00	2.40
❑ 121	Alex Sanchez	.50	.15
❑ 122	Ugueth Urbina	.50	.15
❑ 123	Rondell White	1.00	.30
❑ 124	Esteban Yan	.50	.15
❑ 125	Dmitri Young	1.00	.30
❑ 126	Josh Beckett	1.00	.30
❑ 127	Armando Benitez FOIL	5.00	1.50
❑ 128	Miguel Cabrera FOIL	8.00	2.40
❑ 129	Luis Castillo	.50	.15
❑ 130	Jeff Conine	1.00	.30
❑ 131	Alex Gonzalez	.50	.15
❑ 132	Mike Lowell	1.00	.30
❑ 133	Carl Pavano FOIL	5.00	1.50
❑ 134	Matt Perisho	.50	.15
❑ 135	Juan Pierre	1.00	.30
❑ 136	Tim Spooneybarger	.50	.15
❑ 137	Dontrelle Willis	1.00	.30
❑ 138	Brad Ausmus	1.00	.30
❑ 139	Jeff Bagwell	1.50	.45
❑ 140	Carlos Beltran FOIL	5.00	1.50
❑ 141	Lance Berkman FOIL	8.00	2.40
❑ 142	Craig Biggio	1.50	.45
❑ 143	Roger Clemens FOIL	10.00	3.00
❑ 144	Morgan Ensberg	1.00	.30
❑ 145	Adam Everett	.50	.15
❑ 146	Mike Gallo	.50	.15
❑ 147	Jeff Kent	1.00	.30
❑ 148	Mike Lamb	.50	.15
❑ 149	Brad Lidge	1.00	.30
❑ 150	Dan Miceli	.50	.15
❑ 151	Wade Miller	.50	.15
❑ 152	Roy Oswalt FOIL	8.00	2.40
❑ 153	Angel Berroa	.50	.15
❑ 154	Shawn Camp	.50	.15
❑ 155	Tony Graffanino	.50	.15
❑ 156	Ken Harvey	.50	.15
❑ 157	Darrell May	.50	.15
❑ 158	Joe Randa	.50	.15
❑ 159	Desi Relaford	.50	.15
❑ 160	Matt Stairs	.50	.15
❑ 161	Scott Sullivan	.50	.15
❑ 162	Mike Sweeney	1.00	.30
❑ 163	Wilson Alvarez	.50	.15
❑ 164	Adrian Beltre FOIL	5.00	1.50
❑ 165	Milton Bradley	1.00	.30
❑ 166	Hee Seop Choi	1.00	.30
❑ 167	Eric Gagne FOIL	5.00	1.50
❑ 168	Shawn Green	1.00	.30
❑ 169	Kazuhisa Ishii	1.00	.30
❑ 170	Cesar Izturis	.50	.15
❑ 171	Jose Lima	.50	.15
❑ 172	Jeff Weaver	.50	.15
❑ 173	Jeff Bennett	.50	.15
❑ 174	Javy Lopez	1.00	.30
❑ 175	Brady Clark	.50	.15
❑ 176	Craig Counsell	.50	.15
❑ 177	Doug Davis	.50	.15
❑ 178	Bill Hall	.50	.15
❑ 179	Geoff Jenkins	.50	.15
❑ 180	Brooks Kieschnick	.50	.15
❑ 181	Dan Kolb FOIL	5.00	1.50
❑ 182	Chad Moeller	.50	.15
❑ 183	Lyle Overbay	.50	.15
❑ 184	Scott Podsednik	1.00	.30
❑ 185	Victor Santos	.50	.15
❑ 186	Henry Blanco	.50	.15
❑ 187	Michael Cuddyer	.50	.15
❑ 188	Lew Ford	.50	.15
❑ 189	Christian Guzman	.50	.15
❑ 190	Torii Hunter	1.00	.30
❑ 191	Jacque Jones	1.00	.30
❑ 192	Corey Koskie	.50	.15
❑ 193	Scott Linebrink	.50	.15
❑ 194	Brad Radke	1.00	.30
❑ 195	Johan Santana FOIL	25.00	7.50
❑ 196	Ben Sheets	1.00	.30
❑ 197	Wes Helms	.50	.15
❑ 198	Ken Griffey Jr.	4.00	1.20
❑ 199	Danny Graves	.50	.15
❑ 200	Runelvys Hernandez	.50	.15
❑ 201	Chris Woodward	.50	.15
❑ 202	Paul Lo Duca	1.00	.30
❑ 203	Scot Shields	.50	.15
❑ 204	Todd Walker	.50	.15
❑ 205	Gregg Zaun	.50	.15
❑ 206	Ricky Bottalico	.50	.15
❑ 207	Mike Cameron	.50	.15
❑ 208	Cliff Floyd	1.00	.30
❑ 209	Tom Glavine	1.50	.45
❑ 210	Richard Hidalgo	.50	.15
❑ 211	Al Leiter	1.00	.30
❑ 212	Braden Looper	.50	.15
❑ 213	Kazuo Matsui	1.00	.30
❑ 214	Jason Phillips	.50	.15
❑ 215	Mike Piazza FOIL	10.00	3.00
❑ 216	Jose Reyes	1.00	.30
❑ 217	David Wright	4.00	1.20
❑ 218	Kevin Brown	1.00	.30
❑ 219	Miguel Cairo	.50	.15
❑ 220	Tom Gordon	.50	.15
❑ 221	Derek Jeter	5.00	1.50
❑ 222	Kenny Lofton	1.00	.30
❑ 223	Jorge Posada FOIL	8.00	2.40
❑ 224	Paul Quantrill	.50	.15
❑ 225	Mariano Rivera	1.50	.45
❑ 226	Alex Rodriguez FOIL	15.00	4.50
❑ 227	Gary Sheffield FOIL	5.00	1.50
❑ 228	Javier Vazquez FOIL	5.00	1.50
❑ 229	Enrique Wilson	.50	.15
❑ 230	Eric Byrnes	.50	.15
❑ 231	Eric Chavez FOIL	8.00	2.40
❑ 232	Bobby Crosby	1.00	.30
❑ 233	Erubiel Durazo FOIL	5.00	1.50
❑ 234	Jermaine Dye	1.00	.30
❑ 235	Scott Hatteberg	.50	.15
❑ 236	Bobby Kielty	.50	.15

Card	Nm-Mt	Ex-Mt
❑ 237 Mark Kotsay	1.00	.30
❑ 238 Mark Mulder FOIL	5.00	1.50
❑ 239 Ricardo Rincon	.50	.15
❑ 240 Marco Scutaro	.50	.15
❑ 241 Barry Zito	1.00	.30
❑ 242 Bobby Abreu FOIL	5.00	1.50
❑ 243 David Bell	.50	.15
❑ 244 Pat Burrell	1.00	.30
❑ 245 Rheal Cormier	.50	.15
❑ 246 Mike Lieberthal	.50	.15
❑ 247 Jason Michaels	.50	.15
❑ 248 Eric Milton FOIL	5.00	1.50
❑ 249 Vicente Padilla	.50	.15
❑ 250 Placido Polanco	.50	.15
❑ 251 Lance Carter	.50	.15
❑ 252 Jimmy Rollins	1.00	.30
❑ 253 Jim Thome FOIL	8.00	2.40
❑ 254 Chase Utley	1.00	.30
❑ 255 Billy Wagner	1.00	.30
❑ 256 Randy Wolf	.50	.15
❑ 257 Jason Bay	1.00	.30
❑ 258 Jose Castillo	.50	.15
❑ 259 Jason Kendall FOIL	5.00	1.50
❑ 260 Rob Mackowiak	.50	.15
❑ 261 Jose Mesa	.50	.15
❑ 262 Oliver Perez	.50	.15
❑ 263 Tike Redman	.50	.15
❑ 264 Salomon Torres	.50	.15
❑ 265 Daryle Ward	.50	.15
❑ 266 Kip Wells	.50	.15
❑ 267 Eric Munson	.50	.15
❑ 268 Craig Wilson	1.00	.30
❑ 269 Jack Wilson	.50	.15
❑ 270 Sean Burroughs	.50	.15
❑ 271 Brian Giles	1.00	.30
❑ 272 Khalil Greene	1.50	.45
❑ 273 Ramon Hernandez	.50	.15
❑ 274 Trevor Hoffman	1.00	.30
❑ 275 Ryan Klesko	1.00	.30
❑ 276 Mark Loretta FOIL	5.00	1.50
❑ 277 Phil Nevin	1.00	.30
❑ 278 Akinori Otsuka	1.00	.30
❑ 279 Jay Payton	.50	.15
❑ 280 Jake Peavy FOIL	5.00	1.50
❑ 281 David Wells	1.00	.30
❑ 282 Edgardo Alfonzo	.50	.15
❑ 283 Jim Brower	.50	.15
❑ 284 Deivi Cruz	.50	.15
❑ 285 Ray Durham	1.00	.30
❑ 286 Scott Eyre	.50	.15
❑ 287 Marquis Grissom	1.00	.30
❑ 288 Dustan Mohr	.50	.15
❑ 289 A.J. Pierzynski	1.00	.30
❑ 290 Jason Schmidt FOIL	5.00	1.50
❑ 291 J.T. Snow FOIL	5.00	1.50
❑ 292 Brett Tomko	.50	.15
❑ 293 Michael Tucker	.50	.15
❑ 294 Bret Boone	1.00	.30
❑ 295 Ryan Franklin	.50	.15
❑ 296 Eddie Guardado	1.00	.30
❑ 297 Shigetoshi Hasegawa	1.00	.30
❑ 298 Raul Ibanez	.50	.15
❑ 299 Edgar Martinez	1.50	.45
❑ 300 Joel Pineiro	.50	.15
❑ 301 Scott Spiezio	.50	.15
❑ 302 Ichiro Suzuki FOIL	15.00	4.50
❑ 303 Dan Wilson	.50	.15
❑ 304 Randy Winn	.50	.15
❑ 305 Chris Carpenter FOIL	5.00	1.50
❑ 306 Jim Edmonds FOIL	8.00	2.40
❑ 307 Jason Isringhausen	1.00	.30
❑ 308 Ray King	.50	.15
❑ 309 Mike Matheny	.50	.15
❑ 310 Matt Morris	1.00	.30
❑ 311 Albert Pujols FOIL	15.00	4.50
❑ 312 Edgar Renteria	1.00	.30
❑ 313 Scott Rolen FOIL	8.00	2.40
❑ 314 Reggie Sanders	1.00	.30
❑ 315 Julian Tavarez	.50	.15
❑ 316 Larry Walker	1.50	.45
❑ 317 Woody Williams	.50	.15
❑ 318 Tony Womack	.50	.15
❑ 319 Danys Baez	.50	.15
❑ 320 Rocco Baldelli	1.00	.30
❑ 321 Dewon Brazelton	.50	.15
❑ 322 Carl Crawford	1.00	.30
❑ 323 Jose Cruz Jr.	.50	.15
❑ 324 Toby Hall	.50	.15
❑ 325 Travis Harper	.50	.15
❑ 326 Aubrey Huff	1.00	.30
❑ 327 Julio Lugo	.50	.15
❑ 328 Tino Martinez	1.50	.45
❑ 329 Rod Barajas	.50	.15
❑ 330 Hank Blalock FOIL	5.00	1.50
❑ 331 Francisco Cordero FOIL	3.00	.90
❑ 332 Chan Ho Park	1.00	.30
❑ 333 Kevin Mench	.50	.15
❑ 334 Laynce Nix	.50	.15
❑ 335 Kenny Rogers	1.00	.30
❑ 336 Brian Shouse	.50	.15
❑ 337 Alfonso Soriano FOIL	5.00	1.50
❑ 338 Mark Teixeira	1.50	.45
❑ 339 Michael Young	1.00	.30
❑ 340 Miguel Batista	.50	.15
❑ 341 Frank Catalanotto	.50	.15
❑ 342 Carlos Delgado	1.00	.30
❑ 343 Roy Halladay	1.00	.30
❑ 344 Eric Hinske	.50	.15
❑ 345 Orlando Hudson	.50	.15
❑ 346 Reed Johnson	.50	.15
❑ 347 Justin Speier	.50	.15
❑ 348 Vernon Wells	1.00	.30

2001 MLB Showdown Pennant Run

	Nm-Mt	Ex-Mt
COMPLETE SET (175)	200.00	60.00
COMP.SET w/o FOIL (150)	40.00	12.00
COMMON CARD (1-175)	.25	.07
COMMON FOIL	5.00	1.50

Card	Nm-Mt	Ex-Mt
❑ 1 Randy Velarde	.25	.07
❑ 2 Dustin Hermanson	.25	.07
❑ 3 Jamie Moyer	.75	.23
❑ 4 Aaron Fultz	.25	.07
❑ 5 Barry Zito FOIL	8.00	2.40
❑ 6 Adam Piatt	.25	.07
❑ 7 Ben Grieve	.25	.07
❑ 8 C.C. Sabathia FOIL	5.00	1.50
❑ 9 Eddie Guardado	.25	.07
❑ 10 Matt Kinney	.25	.07
❑ 11 Blake Stein	.25	.07
❑ 12 Billy Wagner FOIL	5.00	1.50
❑ 13 Chris Holt	.25	.07
❑ 14 Homer Bush	.25	.07
❑ 15 Vladimir Nunez	.25	.07
❑ 16 C.J. Nitkowski	.25	.07
❑ 17 Juan Pierre	.75	.23
❑ 18 Jose Valentin	.25	.07
❑ 19 Juan Gonzalez	.75	.23
❑ 20 Derek Bell	.25	.07
❑ 21 Wade Miller	.25	.07
❑ 22 Shawn Estes	.25	.07
❑ 23 Enrique Wilson	.25	.07
❑ 24 Dave Magadan	.25	.07
❑ 25 Jason Christiansen	.25	.07
❑ 26 Paul Shuey	.25	.07
❑ 27 Mark Wohlers	.25	.07
❑ 28 John Riedling	.25	.07
❑ 29 Francisco Cordova	.25	.07
❑ 30 Craig House	.25	.07
❑ 31 Scott Strickland	.25	.07
❑ 32 Octavio Dotel	.25	.07
❑ 33 Jimmy Rollins FOIL	5.00	1.50
❑ 34 Carl Pavano	.75	.23
❑ 35 Sandy Alomar Jr.	.25	.07
❑ 36 Hideki Irabu	.25	.07
❑ 37 Tom Gordon	.25	.07
❑ 38 Roosevelt Brown	.25	.07
❑ 39 Alex Rodriguez FOIL	15.00	4.50
❑ 40 Andres Galarraga	.75	.23
❑ 41 Rob Bell	.25	.07
❑ 42 Jason Schmidt	.75	.23
❑ 43 Rod Beck	.25	.07
❑ 44 Paul Rigdon	.25	.07
❑ 45 Dan Miceli	.25	.07
❑ 46 Ricky Bones	.25	.07
❑ 47 Mike Hampton FOIL	8.00	2.40
❑ 48 Cliff Politte	.25	.07
❑ 49 Chris Stynes	.25	.07
❑ 50 Ramiro Mendoza	.25	.07
❑ 51 Todd Walker	.25	.07
❑ 52 Fernando Seguignol	.25	.07
❑ 53 Mark Guthrie	.25	.07
❑ 54 Tony Armas Jr.	.25	.07
❑ 55 Billy McMillon	.25	.07
❑ 56 Gary Bennett	.25	.07
❑ 57 Corey Patterson FOIL	5.00	1.50
❑ 58 Juan Guzman	.25	.07
❑ 59 Joe Crede	2.50	.75
❑ 60 A.J. Pierzynski	.75	.23
❑ 61 Ben Davis	.25	.07
❑ 62 Alan Embree	.25	.07
❑ 63 Jon Garland FOIL	5.00	1.50
❑ 64 Ryan Kohlmeier	.25	.07
❑ 65 Andy Benes	.25	.07
❑ 66 Ron Gant	.75	.23
❑ 67 Jerry Hairston Jr.	.25	.07
❑ 68 Odalis Perez	.25	.07
❑ 69 Lance Painter	.25	.07
❑ 70 David Segui	.25	.07
❑ 71 Russ Davis	.25	.07
❑ 72 Jeff Zimmerman	.25	.07
❑ 73 Dennys Reyes	.25	.07
❑ 74 Jamey Wright	.25	.07
❑ 75 Rico Brogna	.25	.07
❑ 76 Geraldo Guzman	.25	.07
❑ 77 Eric Gagne	.75	.23
❑ 78 Bruce Chen	.25	.07
❑ 79 Justin Speier	.25	.07
❑ 80 Randy Keisler	.25	.07
❑ 81 Ellis Burks FOIL	8.00	2.40
❑ 82 Alfonso Soriano	1.50	.45
❑ 83 Jeff Nelson	.25	.07
❑ 84 Wes Helms	.25	.07
❑ 85 Freddy Garcia FOIL	5.00	1.50
❑ 86 Erubiel Durazo	.25	.07
❑ 87 Ben Sheets FOIL	8.00	2.40
❑ 88 Jose Ortiz FOIL	5.00	1.50
❑ 89 Paul Wilson	.25	.07
❑ 90 Onan Masaoka	.25	.07
❑ 91 Jose Rosado	.25	.07
❑ 92 A.J. Burnett	.75	.23
❑ 93 Bubba Trammell	.25	.07
❑ 94 Mike Fetters	.25	.07
❑ 95 Jacob Cruz	.25	.07
❑ 96 John Franco	.75	.23
❑ 97 Armando Reynoso	.75	.23
❑ 98 Lou Pote	.25	.07
❑ 99 D'Angelo Jimenez FOIL	5.00	1.50
❑ 100 Julio Zuleta	.25	.07
❑ 101 Charles Johnson FOIL	8.00	2.40
❑ 102 Tsuyoshi Shinjo RC	1.50	.45
❑ 103 Brett Tomko	.25	.07
❑ 104 Marcus Giles	.75	.23
❑ 105 Craig Counsell	.25	.07
❑ 106 Ruben Mateo	.25	.07
❑ 107 Andy Ashby	.25	.07
❑ 108 Marlon Anderson	.25	.07
❑ 109 Mark Grace	1.50	.45
❑ 110 Russ Branyan	.25	.07
❑ 111 Julian Tavarez	.25	.07
❑ 112 Joey Hamilton	.25	.07
❑ 113 Jason LaRue	.25	.07
❑ 114 Benji Gil	.25	.07
❑ 115 Bill Mueller	.75	.23
❑ 116 Mike Stanton	.25	.07
❑ 117 Ray King	.25	.07
❑ 118 Timo Perez	.25	.07
❑ 119 Johnny Damon FOIL	8.00	2.40

❑ 120 Matt Morris .75 .23
❑ 121 Kevin Appier .75 .23
❑ 122 Frank Castillo .25 .07
❑ 123 Mike Darr .25 .07
❑ 124 Felipe Crespo .25 .07
❑ 125 John Smoltz FOIL 8.00 2.40
❑ 126 Ben Weber .25 .07
❑ 127 Luis Rivas .25 .07
❑ 128 Travis Harper .25 .07
❑ 129 Aubrey Huff .75 .23
❑ 130 Paul LoDuca .75 .23
❑ 131 Eric Davis .75 .23
❑ 132 Fernando Tatis .25 .07
❑ 133 Ugueth Urbina .25 .07
❑ 134 Steve Kline .25 .07
❑ 135 Tanyon Sturtze .25 .07
❑ 136 Scott Hatteberg .25 .07
❑ 137 Tomokazu Ohka FOIL 5.00 1.50
❑ 138 Melvin Mora .75 .23
❑ 139 Kip Wells .25 .07
❑ 140 Ken Caminiti .75 .23
❑ 141 Dave Martinez .25 .07
❑ 142 Robert Fick .25 .07
❑ 143 Mike Bordick .75 .23
❑ 144 Doug Mientkiewicz .75 .23
❑ 145 Darryl Hamilton .25 .07
❑ 146 Shane Reynolds .25 .07
❑ 147 Vernon Wells FOIL 5.00 1.50
❑ 148 Rey Ordonez .25 .07
❑ 149 Brad Ausmus .75 .23
❑ 150 Jay Powell .25 .07
❑ 151 Todd Hundley .25 .07
❑ 152 Travis Miller .25 .07
❑ 153 Tyler Houston .25 .07
❑ 154 Nelson Cruz .25 .07
❑ 155 Manny Ramirez Sox FOIL 8.00 2.40
❑ 156 Luis Lopez .25 .07
❑ 157 Luis Sojo .25 .07
❑ 158 Tony Gwynn FOIL 8.00 2.40
❑ 159 Roger Cedeno .25 .07
❑ 160 Royce Clayton .25 .07
❑ 161 Olmedo Saenz .25 .07
❑ 162 Brook Fordyce .25 .07
❑ 163 Dee Brown .25 .07
❑ 164 David Wells FOIL 5.00 1.50
❑ 165 Jack Wilson RC 1.50 .45
❑ 166 Pedro Feliz .25 .07
❑ 167 Hideo Nomo 2.50 .75
❑ 168 Albert Pujols FOIL RC 50.00 15.00
❑ 169 Ichiro Suzuki FOIL RC 20.00 6.00
❑ 170 Ramon Ortiz .75 .23
❑ 171 Mike Holtz .25 .07
❑ 172 Chris Woodward .25 .07
❑ 173 Mike Mussina FOIL 8.00 2.40
❑ 174 Carlos Guillen .75 .23
❑ 175 Ben Petrick FOIL 5.00 1.50

2005 MLB Showdown Trading Deadline

	Nm-Mt	Ex-Mt
COMP.SET w/o FOIL (150)	50.00	15.00
COMMON CARD (1-165)	.50	.15
COMMON FOIL 1-165	3.00	.90
COMMON CARD (166-175)	.50	.15
FOIL STATED ODDS 1:3		

❑ 1 Steve Finley 1.00 .30
❑ 2 Josh Phelps .50 .15
❑ 3 Magglio Ordonez 1.00 .30
❑ 4 Nick Johnson 1.00 .30
❑ 5 Carlos Lee FOIL 5.00 1.50
❑ 6 Quinton McCracken .50 .15
❑ 7 Shawn Estes .50 .15
❑ 8 J.J. Putz .50 .15
❑ 9 Mike DeJean .50 .15
❑ 10 Juan Gonzalez 1.00 .30
❑ 11 Eric Young .50 .15
❑ 12 Matt Mantei .50 .15
❑ 13 Neal Cotts .50 .15
❑ 14 Mark Sweeney .50 .15
❑ 15 Glendon Rusch .50 .15
❑ 16 Terrmel Sledge .50 .15
❑ 17 Ron Villone .50 .15
❑ 18 Troy Glaus 1.00 .30
❑ 19 Wilson Valdez .50 .15
❑ 20 B.J. Surhoff 1.00 .30
❑ 21 Kazuhisa Ishii 1.00 .30
❑ 22 Dustin Hermanson .50 .15
❑ 23 Al Leiter 1.00 .30
❑ 24 Octavio Dotel .50 .15
❑ 25 Henry Blanco .50 .15
❑ 26 J.D. Drew FOIL 5.00 1.50
❑ 27 Kevin Millwood .50 .15
❑ 28 Sandy Alomar Jr. .50 .15
❑ 29 John Riedling .50 .15
❑ 30 Rich Harden FOIL 5.00 1.50
❑ 31 Aaron Sele .50 .15
❑ 32 Carlos Beltran FOIL 5.00 1.50
❑ 33 Jose Lima .50 .15
❑ 34 Richard Hidalgo .50 .15
❑ 35 Placido Polanco .50 .15
❑ 36 Neifi Perez .50 .15
❑ 37 Wilson Alvarez .50 .15
❑ 38 So Taguchi 1.00 .30
❑ 39 Matt Perisho .50 .15
❑ 40 Roberto Hernandez .50 .15
❑ 41 Todd Walker .50 .15
❑ 42 Jason Kendall 1.00 .30
❑ 43 Brett Myers 1.00 .30
❑ 44 Carlos Silva .50 .15
❑ 45 Randy Johnson FOIL 12.00 3.60
❑ 46 Jeremy Bonderman 1.00 .30
❑ 47 Orlando Cabrera 1.00 .30
❑ 48 Carlos Delgado FOIL 5.00 1.50
❑ 49 A.J. Pierzynski 1.00 .30
❑ 50 Omar Vizquel 1.50 .45
❑ 51 Lenny Harris .50 .15
❑ 52 Chris Carpenter 1.00 .30
❑ 53 Miguel Cairo .50 .15
❑ 54 Sammy Sosa FOIL 10.00 3.00
❑ 55 Royce Clayton .50 .15
❑ 56 Cal Eldred .50 .15
❑ 57 Rich Aurilia .50 .15
❑ 58 Orlando Palmeiro .50 .15
❑ 59 Bengie Molina .50 .15
❑ 60 Ismael Valdez .50 .15
❑ 61 Nate Bump .50 .15
❑ 62 David Wells 1.00 .30
❑ 63 Jermaine Dye 1.00 .30
❑ 64 Carlos Zambrano 1.00 .30
❑ 65 David Newhan .50 .15
❑ 66 Russ Springer .50 .15
❑ 67 Elmer Dessens .50 .15
❑ 68 Kris Benson .50 .15
❑ 69 Al Reyes .50 .15
❑ 70 Tino Martinez 1.50 .45
❑ 71 Ruben Sierra 1.00 .30
❑ 72 Antonio Osuna .50 .15
❑ 73 Moises Alou 1.00 .30
❑ 74 Brad Wilkerson FOIL 3.00 .90
❑ 75 Jason Christiansen .50 .15
❑ 76 Geoff Blum .50 .15
❑ 77 Dennys Reyes .50 .15
❑ 78 Craig Counsell .50 .15
❑ 79 Rey Sanchez .50 .15
❑ 80 Mark Hendrickson .50 .15
❑ 81 Doug Mirabelli .50 .15
❑ 82 Jeromy Burnitz 1.00 .30
❑ 83 Carl Pavano 1.00 .30
❑ 84 Richie Sexson 1.00 .30
❑ 85 Eric Milton .50 .15
❑ 86 Mark DeRosa .50 .15
❑ 87 Bob Wickman .50 .15
❑ 88 Hideo Nomo 2.50 .75
❑ 89 Tony Armas Jr. .50 .15
❑ 90 Desi Relaford .50 .15
❑ 91 Russ Ortiz 1.00 .30
❑ 92 Jose Vidro 1.00 .30
❑ 93 Jeff Kent FOIL 5.00 1.50
❑ 94 Esteban Yan .50 .15
❑ 95 Tim Hudson FOIL 5.00 1.50
❑ 96 Jay Payton .50 .15
❑ 97 Tony Womack .50 .15
❑ 98 Gregg Zaun .50 .15
❑ 99 David Weathers .50 .15
❑ 100 Scott Podsednik FOIL 5.00 1.50
❑ 101 Mark Mulder FOIL 5.00 1.50
❑ 102 Jose Guillen 1.00 .30
❑ 103 Grady Sizemore 1.00 .30
❑ 104 Paul Bako .50 .15
❑ 105 Jeff DaVanon .50 .15
❑ 106 Jeff Nelson .50 .15
❑ 107 Troy Percival 1.00 .30
❑ 108 Brian Lawrence .50 .15
❑ 109 Mike Redmond .50 .15
❑ 110 Odalis Perez .50 .15
❑ 111 John Franco 1.00 .30
❑ 112 Doug Brocail .50 .15
❑ 113 Einar Diaz .50 .15
❑ 114 Mark Grudzielanek .50 .15
❑ 115 Jason Marquis .50 .15
❑ 116 Jayson Werth .50 .15
❑ 117 John Mabry .50 .15
❑ 118 Alexis Rios 1.00 .30
❑ 119 Livan Hernandez 1.00 .30
❑ 120 Zack Greinke 1.00 .30
❑ 121 Chris Hammond .50 .15
❑ 122 Kent Mercker .50 .15
❑ 123 Ryan Drese .50 .15
❑ 124 Pedro Martinez FOIL 12.00 3.60
❑ 125 Alex Cora .50 .15
❑ 126 Kenny Lofton 1.00 .30
❑ 127 Adrian Beltre FOIL 5.00 1.50
❑ 128 David Eckstein 1.00 .30
❑ 129 Derek Lowe 1.00 .30
❑ 130 Joe Randa .50 .15
❑ 131 Jose Valentin .50 .15
❑ 132 David Bush .50 .15
❑ 133 Brian Schneider .50 .15
❑ 134 Matt Clement 1.00 .30
❑ 135 Paul Byrd .50 .15
❑ 136 Jose Vizcaino .50 .15
❑ 137 Todd Pratt .50 .15
❑ 138 Jose Offerman .50 .15
❑ 139 Dan Wilson .50 .15
❑ 140 Frank Francisco .50 .15
❑ 141 Woody Williams .50 .15
❑ 142 Juan Castro .50 .15
❑ 143 Jerry Hairston Jr. .50 .15
❑ 144 Jeff Suppan .50 .15
❑ 145 Steve Reed .50 .15
❑ 146 Jon Lieber .50 .15
❑ 147 Cristian Guzman .50 .15
❑ 148 Shawn Green FOIL 5.00 1.50
❑ 149 Damion Easley .50 .15
❑ 150 Bronson Arroyo .50 .15
❑ 151 Raul Mondesi .50 .15
❑ 152 Roger Cedeno .50 .15
❑ 153 Carlos Baerga .50 .15
❑ 154 Jose Hernandez .50 .15
❑ 155 Antonio Alfonseca .50 .15
❑ 156 Ricky Ledee .50 .15
❑ 157 Armando Benitez .50 .15
❑ 158 Esteban Loaiza .50 .15
❑ 159 Steve Kline .50 .15
❑ 160 Corey Koskie .50 .15
❑ 161 Vinny Castilla FOIL 5.00 1.50
❑ 162 Tony Clark .50 .15
❑ 163 Edgar Renteria FOIL 5.00 1.50
❑ 164 Brian Jordan 1.00 .30
❑ 165 David Dellucci 1.00 .30
❑ 166 Hoyt Wilhelm FOIL 15.00 4.50
❑ 167 Pee Wee Reese 1.50 .45
❑ 168 Larry Doby 1.00 .30
❑ 169 Yogi Berra FOIL 20.00 6.00
❑ 170 Robin Yount FOIL 20.00 6.00
❑ 171 Brooks Robinson FOIL 10.00 3.00
❑ 172 Reggie Jackson FOIL 30.00 9.00
❑ 173 Rod Carew FOIL 15.00 4.50
❑ 174 Harmon Killebrew FOIL 25.00 7.50
❑ 175 Nolan Ryan FOIL 30.00 9.00

2005 Origins

	Nm-Mt	Ex-Mt
COMMON CARD (1-100)	1.50	.45
COMMON CARD (101-150)	1.50	.45
COMMON CARD (151-200)	1.50	.45
APPX EIGHT BASIC CARDS PER TIN		.00
*OLD JUDGE 1-200: .4X TO 1X BASIC 1-200		.00
APPX EIGHT OLD JUDGE CARDS PER TIN		.00

Card	Nm-Mt	Ex-Mt
❑ 1 Jim Edmonds	2.00	.60
❑ 2 Jason Schmidt	1.50	.45
❑ 3 J.D. Drew	1.50	.45
❑ 4 Luis Gonzalez	1.50	.45
❑ 5 Nomar Garciaparra	3.00	.90
❑ 6 Jake Peavy	1.50	.45
❑ 7 Rafael Furcal	1.50	.45
❑ 8 Craig Biggio	2.00	.60
❑ 9 Ken Griffey Jr.	5.00	1.50
❑ 10 Mike Piazza	3.00	.90
❑ 11 Jose Vidro	1.50	.45
❑ 12 Ivan Rodriguez	2.00	.60
❑ 13 Carl Crawford	1.50	.45
❑ 14 Roger Clemens	5.00	1.50
❑ 15 Kerry Wood	1.50	.45
❑ 16 Vernon Wells	1.50	.45
❑ 17 Carlos Guillen	1.50	.45
❑ 18 Tim Hudson	1.50	.45
❑ 19 Carl Pavano	1.50	.45
❑ 20 Carlos Beltran	1.50	.45
❑ 21 Pedro Martinez	2.00	.60
❑ 22 Hideki Matsui	6.00	1.80
❑ 23 Frank Thomas	3.00	.90
❑ 24 Curt Schilling	2.00	.60
❑ 25 Manny Ramirez	2.00	.60
❑ 26 Alex Rodriguez	5.00	1.50
❑ 27 Aubrey Huff	1.50	.45
❑ 28 David Ortiz	3.00	.90
❑ 29 Mark Prior	2.00	.60
❑ 30 Albert Pujols	6.00	1.80
❑ 31 Miguel Cabrera	2.00	.60
❑ 32 Brad Penny	1.50	.45
❑ 33 Carlos Delgado	1.50	.45
❑ 34 Aramis Ramirez	1.50	.45
❑ 35 Josh Beckett	1.50	.45
❑ 36 Rafael Palmeiro	2.00	.60
❑ 37 Bret Boone	1.50	.45
❑ 38 Lance Berkman	1.50	.45
❑ 39 Carlos Zambrano	1.50	.45
❑ 40 Adam Dunn	1.50	.45
❑ 41 Livan Hernandez	1.50	.45
❑ 42 Mike Mussina	2.00	.60
❑ 43 Ben Sheets	1.50	.45
❑ 44 Derek Jeter	8.00	2.40
❑ 45 Kazuo Matsui	1.50	.45
❑ 46 Bobby Abreu	1.50	.45
❑ 47 Jeff Bagwell	2.00	.60
❑ 48 Travis Hafner	1.50	.45
❑ 49 Torii Hunter	1.50	.45
❑ 50 Kevin Brown	1.50	.45
❑ 51 Alfonso Soriano	1.50	.45
❑ 52 Jim Thome	2.00	.60
❑ 53 John Smoltz	2.00	.60
❑ 54 Mike Sweeney	1.50	.45
❑ 55 Andy Pettitte	2.00	.60
❑ 56 Chipper Jones	3.00	.90
❑ 57 Randy Johnson	3.00	.90
❑ 58 Steve Finley	1.50	.45
❑ 59 Larry Walker	2.00	.60
❑ 60 Troy Glaus	1.50	.45
❑ 61 Greg Maddux	5.00	1.50
❑ 62 Shawn Green	1.50	.45
❑ 63 Roy Halladay	1.50	.45
❑ 64 Jeff Kent	1.50	.45
❑ 65 Scott Podsednik	1.50	.45
❑ 66 Miguel Tejada	1.50	.45
❑ 67 Lyle Overbay	1.50	.45
❑ 68 Bernie Williams	2.00	.60
❑ 69 Todd Helton	1.50	.45
❑ 70 Melvin Mora	1.50	.45
❑ 71 Magglio Ordonez	1.50	.45
❑ 72 Carlos Lee	1.50	.45
❑ 73 Roy Oswalt	1.50	.45
❑ 74 Victor Martinez	1.50	.45
❑ 75 Scott Rolen	2.00	.60
❑ 76 Eric Chavez	1.50	.45
❑ 77 Paul Konerko	1.50	.45
❑ 78 Jose Reyes	1.50	.45
❑ 79 Barry Larkin	2.00	.60
❑ 80 Johnny Damon	2.00	.60
❑ 81 Eric Gagne	1.50	.45
❑ 82 Andruw Jones	2.00	.60
❑ 83 Gary Sheffield	1.50	.45
❑ 84 Richie Sexson	1.50	.45
❑ 85 Sammy Sosa	3.00	.90
❑ 86 Mark Teixeira	2.00	.60
❑ 87 Vladimir Guerrero	3.00	.90
❑ 88 Michael Young	1.50	.45
❑ 89 Johan Santana	2.00	.60
❑ 90 Adrian Beltre	1.50	.45
❑ 91 Tom Glavine	2.00	.60
❑ 92 Hank Blalock	1.50	.45
❑ 93 Preston Wilson	1.50	.45
❑ 94 Jason Kendall	1.50	.45
❑ 95 Mike Lowell	1.50	.45
❑ 96 Craig Wilson	1.50	.45
❑ 97 Ichiro Suzuki	8.00	2.40
❑ 98 Mark Mulder	1.50	.45
❑ 99 Garret Anderson	1.50	.45
❑ 100 Brian Giles	1.50	.45
❑ 101 Robin Yount RET	4.00	1.20
❑ 102 Ernie Banks RET	4.00	1.20
❑ 103 Mike Schmidt RET	8.00	2.40
❑ 104 Enos Slaughter RET	1.50	.45
❑ 105 Red Schoendienst RET	1.50	.45
❑ 106 Hoyt Wilhelm RET	1.50	.45
❑ 107 Lou Brock RET	2.50	.75
❑ 108 Rollie Fingers RET	1.50	.45
❑ 109 Gaylord Perry RET	1.50	.45
❑ 110 Bobby Doerr RET	1.50	.45
❑ 111 Larry Doby RET	1.50	.45
❑ 112 Al Lopez RET	1.50	.45
❑ 113 Joe Morgan RET	1.50	.45
❑ 114 Luis Aparicio RET	1.50	.45
❑ 115 Willie McCovey RET	2.50	.75
❑ 116 Bob Lemon RET	1.50	.45
❑ 117 Early Wynn RET	1.50	.45
❑ 118 Bob Feller RET	2.50	.75
❑ 119 Cal Ripken RET	12.00	3.60
❑ 120 George Kell RET	1.50	.45
❑ 121 Juan Marichal RET	1.50	.45
❑ 122 Monte Irvin RET	1.50	.45
❑ 123 Harmon Killebrew RET	4.00	1.20
❑ 124 Lou Boudreau RET	2.50	.75
❑ 125 Mickey Mantle RET	15.00	4.50
❑ 126 Richie Ashburn RET	2.50	.75
❑ 127 Pee Wee Reese RET	2.50	.75
❑ 128 Whitey Ford RET	2.50	.75
❑ 129 Tom Seaver RET	2.50	.75
❑ 130 Phil Rizzuto RET	2.50	.75
❑ 131 Yogi Berra RET	4.00	1.20
❑ 132 Warren Spahn RET	2.50	.75
❑ 133 Billy Williams RET	1.50	.45
❑ 134 Jim Bunning RET	1.50	.45
❑ 135 Ralph Kiner RET	1.50	.45
❑ 136 Ted Williams RET	6.00	1.80
❑ 137 Rick Ferrell RET	1.50	.45
❑ 138 Robin Roberts RET	1.50	.45
❑ 139 Brooks Robinson RET	2.50	.75
❑ 140 Hal Newhouser RET	1.50	.45
❑ 141 Catfish Hunter RET	1.50	.45
❑ 142 Phil Niekro RET	1.50	.45
❑ 143 Fergie Jenkins RET	1.50	.45
❑ 144 Al Kaline RET	4.00	1.20
❑ 145 Stan Musial RET	5.00	1.50
❑ 146 Joe DiMaggio RET	6.00	1.80
❑ 147 Willie Stargell RET	2.50	.75
❑ 148 Nolan Ryan RET	10.00	3.00
❑ 149 Babe Ruth RET	8.00	2.40
❑ 150 Bob Gibson RET	2.50	.75
❑ 151 David DeJesus YS	1.50	.45
❑ 152 Chris Burke YS	1.50	.45
❑ 153 Chad Cordero YS	1.50	.45
❑ 154 Kevin Youkilis YS	1.50	.45
❑ 155 Bucky Jacobsen YS	1.50	.45
❑ 156 B.J. Upton YS	1.50	.45
❑ 157 Aaron Rowand YS	1.50	.45
❑ 158 Jose Capellan YS	1.50	.45
❑ 159 David Wright YS	5.00	1.50
❑ 160 Jason Bay YS	1.50	.45
❑ 161 Edwin Jackson YS	1.50	.45
❑ 162 Scott Kazmir YS	1.50	.45
❑ 163 J.D. Closser YS	1.50	.45
❑ 164 Chase Utley YS	2.50	.75
❑ 165 Nick Swisher YS	1.50	.45
❑ 166 Casey Kotchman YS	1.50	.45
❑ 167 Bobby Crosby YS	1.50	.45
❑ 168 Zack Greinke YS	1.50	.45
❑ 169 Gavin Floyd YS	1.50	.45
❑ 170 Jeff Francis YS	1.50	.45
❑ 171 Dallas McPherson YS	1.50	.45
❑ 172 Gabe Gross YS	1.50	.45
❑ 173 Brandon Claussen YS	1.50	.45
❑ 174 Wily Mo Pena YS	1.50	.45
❑ 175 Robb Quinlan YS	1.50	.45
❑ 176 Oliver Perez YS	1.50	.45
❑ 177 Guillermo Quiroz YS	1.50	.45
❑ 178 Ryan Howard YS	1.50	.45
❑ 179 Gerald Laird YS	1.50	.45
❑ 180 Jayson Werth YS	1.50	.45
❑ 181 Bobby Madritsch YS	1.50	.45
❑ 182 Laynce Nix YS	1.50	.45
❑ 183 Eddy Rodriguez YS	1.50	.45
❑ 184 Rickie Weeks YS	1.50	.45
❑ 185 Scott Proctor YS	1.50	.45
❑ 186 Adam LaRoche YS	1.50	.45
❑ 187 Yhency Brazoban YS	1.50	.45
❑ 188 Adrian Gonzalez YS	1.50	.45
❑ 189 Jason Lane YS	1.50	.45
❑ 190 Ryan Wagner YS	1.50	.45
❑ 191 Roman Colon YS	1.50	.45
❑ 192 Alexis Rios YS	1.50	.45
❑ 193 Joe Mauer YS	1.50	.45
❑ 194 Garrett Atkins YS	1.50	.45
❑ 195 Daniel Cabrera YS	1.50	.45
❑ 196 Khalil Greene YS	2.50	.75
❑ 197 Joe Blanton YS	1.50	.45
❑ 198 Jason DuBois YS	1.50	.45
❑ 199 Angel Guzman YS	1.50	.45
❑ 200 Jesse Crain YS	1.50	.45

1992 Pinnacle

	Nm-Mt	Ex-Mt
COMPLETE SET (620)	40.00	12.00
COMP. SERIES 1 (310)	25.00	7.50
COMP. SERIES 2 (310)	15.00	4.50

Card	Nm-Mt	Ex-Mt
❑ 1 Frank Thomas	.50	.15
❑ 2 Benito Santiago	.20	.06
❑ 3 Carlos Baerga	.10	.03
❑ 4 Cecil Fielder	.20	.06
❑ 5 Barry Larkin	.30	.09
❑ 6 Ozzie Smith	.75	.23

❑ 7 Willie McGee .20 .06
❑ 8 Paul Molitor .30 .09
❑ 9 Andy Van Slyke .30 .09
❑ 10 Ryne Sandberg .75 .23
❑ 11 Kevin Seitzer .10 .03
❑ 12 Len Dykstra .20 .06
❑ 13 Edgar Martinez .30 .09
❑ 14 Ruben Sierra .10 .03
❑ 15 Howard Johnson .10 .03
❑ 16 Dave Henderson .10 .03
❑ 17 Devon White .20 .06
❑ 18 Terry Pendleton .20 .06
❑ 19 Steve Finley .20 .06
❑ 20 Kirby Puckett .50 .15
❑ 21 Orel Hershiser .20 .06
❑ 22 Hal Morris .10 .03
❑ 23 Don Mattingly 1.25 .35
❑ 24 Delino DeShields .10 .03
❑ 25 Dennis Eckersley .20 .06
❑ 26 Ellis Burks .20 .06
❑ 27 Jay Buhner .20 .06
❑ 28 Matt Williams .20 .06
❑ 29 Lou Whitaker .20 .06
❑ 30 Alex Fernandez .10 .03
❑ 31 Albert Belle .20 .06
❑ 32 Todd Zeile .10 .03
❑ 33 Tony Pena .10 .03
❑ 34 Jay Bell .20 .06
❑ 35 Rafael Palmeiro .30 .09
❑ 36 Wes Chamberlain .10 .03
❑ 37 George Bell .10 .03
❑ 38 Robin Yount .75 .23
❑ 39 Vince Coleman .10 .03
❑ 40 Bruce Hurst .10 .03
❑ 41 Harold Baines .20 .06
❑ 42 Chuck Finley .20 .06
❑ 43 Ken Caminiti .20 .06
❑ 44 Ben McDonald .10 .03
❑ 45 Roberto Alomar .30 .09
❑ 46 Chili Davis .20 .06
❑ 47 Bill Doran .10 .03
❑ 48 Jerald Clark .10 .03
❑ 49 Jose Lind .10 .03
❑ 50 Nolan Ryan 2.00 .60
❑ 51 Phil Plantier .10 .03
❑ 52 Gary DiSarcina .10 .03
❑ 53 Kevin Bass .10 .03
❑ 54 Pat Kelly .10 .03
❑ 55 Mark Wohlers .10 .03
❑ 56 Walt Weiss .10 .03
❑ 57 Lenny Harris .10 .03
❑ 58 Ivan Calderon .10 .03
❑ 59 Harold Reynolds .20 .06
❑ 60 George Brett 1.25 .35
❑ 61 Gregg Olson .10 .03
❑ 62 Orlando Merced .10 .03
❑ 63 Steve Decker .10 .03
❑ 64 John Franco .20 .06
❑ 65 Greg Maddux .75 .23
❑ 66 Alex Cole .10 .03
❑ 67 Dave Hollins .10 .03
❑ 68 Kent Hrbek .20 .06
❑ 69 Tom Pagnozzi .10 .03
❑ 70 Jeff Bagwell .50 .15
❑ 71 Jim Gantner .10 .03
❑ 72 Matt Nokes .10 .03
❑ 73 Brian Harper .10 .03
❑ 74 Andy Benes .10 .03
❑ 75 Tom Glavine .30 .09
❑ 76 Terry Steinbach .10 .03
❑ 77 Dennis Martinez .20 .06
❑ 78 John Olerud .20 .06
❑ 79 Ozzie Guillen .20 .06
❑ 80 Darryl Strawberry .20 .06
❑ 81 Gary Gaetti .20 .06
❑ 82 Dave Righetti .20 .06
❑ 83 Chris Hoiles .10 .03
❑ 84 Andujar Cedeno .10 .03
❑ 85 Jack Clark .20 .06
❑ 86 David Howard .10 .03
❑ 87 Bill Gullickson .10 .03
❑ 88 Bernard Gilkey .10 .03
❑ 89 Kevin Elster .10 .03
❑ 90 Kevin Maas .10 .03
❑ 91 Mark Lewis .10 .03
❑ 92 Greg Vaughn .10 .03
❑ 93 Bret Barberie .10 .03
❑ 94 Dave Smith .10 .03
❑ 95 Roger Clemens 1.00 .30
❑ 96 Doug Drabek .10 .03
❑ 97 Omar Vizquel .30 .09
❑ 98 Jose Guzman .10 .03
❑ 99 Juan Samuel .10 .03
❑ 100 Dave Justice .20 .06
❑ 101 Tom Browning .10 .03
❑ 102 Mark Gubicza .10 .03
❑ 103 Mickey Morandini .10 .03
❑ 104 Ed Whitson .10 .03
❑ 105 Lance Parrish .20 .06
❑ 106 Scott Erickson .10 .03
❑ 107 Jack McDowell .10 .03
❑ 108 Dave Stieb .10 .03
❑ 109 Mike Moore .10 .03
❑ 110 Travis Fryman .20 .06
❑ 111 Dwight Gooden .20 .06
❑ 112 Fred McGriff .30 .09
❑ 113 Alan Trammell .20 .06
❑ 114 Roberto Kelly .10 .03
❑ 115 Andre Dawson .20 .06
❑ 116 Bill Landrum .10 .03
❑ 117 Brian McRae .10 .03
❑ 118 B.J. Surhoff .20 .06
❑ 119 Chuck Knoblauch .20 .06
❑ 120 Steve Olin .10 .03
❑ 121 Robin Ventura .20 .06
❑ 122 Will Clark .30 .09
❑ 123 Tino Martinez .30 .09
❑ 124 Dale Murphy .30 .09
❑ 125 Pete O'Brien .10 .03
❑ 126 Ray Lankford .20 .06
❑ 127 Juan Gonzalez .30 .09
❑ 128 Ron Gant .20 .06
❑ 129 Marquis Grissom .20 .06
❑ 130 Jose Canseco .30 .09
❑ 131 Mike Greenwell .10 .03
❑ 132 Mark Langston .10 .03
❑ 133 Brett Butler .20 .06
❑ 134 Kelly Gruber .10 .03
❑ 135 Chris Sabo .10 .03
❑ 136 Mark Grace .30 .09
❑ 137 Tony Fernandez .10 .03
❑ 138 Glenn Davis .10 .03
❑ 139 Pedro Munoz .10 .03
❑ 140 Craig Biggio .30 .09
❑ 141 Pete Schourek .10 .03
❑ 142 Mike Boddicker .10 .03
❑ 143 Robby Thompson .10 .03
❑ 144 Mel Hall .10 .03
❑ 145 Bryan Harvey .10 .03
❑ 146 Mike LaValliere .10 .03
❑ 147 John Kruk .20 .06
❑ 148 Joe Carter .20 .06
❑ 149 Greg Olson .10 .03
❑ 150 Julio Franco .20 .06
❑ 151 Darryl Hamilton .10 .03
❑ 152 Felix Fermin .10 .03
❑ 153 Jose Offerman .10 .03
❑ 154 Paul O'Neill .30 .09
❑ 155 Tommy Greene .10 .03
❑ 156 Ivan Rodriguez .50 .15
❑ 157 Dave Stewart .20 .06
❑ 158 Jeff Reardon .20 .06
❑ 159 Felix Jose .10 .03
❑ 160 Doug Dascenzo .10 .03
❑ 161 Tim Wallach .10 .03
❑ 162 Dan Plesac .10 .03
❑ 163 Luis Gonzalez .20 .06
❑ 164 Mike Henneman .10 .03
❑ 165 Mike Devereaux .10 .03
❑ 166 Luis Polonia .10 .03
❑ 167 Mike Sharperson .10 .03
❑ 168 Chris Donnels .10 .03
❑ 169 Greg W. Harris .10 .03
❑ 170 Deion Sanders .30 .09
❑ 171 Mike Schooler .10 .03
❑ 172 Jose DeJesus .10 .03
❑ 173 Jeff Montgomery .10 .03
❑ 174 Milt Cuyler .10 .03
❑ 175 Wade Boggs .30 .09
❑ 176 Kevin Tapani .10 .03
❑ 177 Bill Spiers .10 .03
❑ 178 Tim Raines .20 .06
❑ 179 Randy Milligan .10 .03
❑ 180 Rob Dibble .20 .06
❑ 181 Kirt Manwaring .10 .03
❑ 182 Pascual Perez .10 .03
❑ 183 Juan Guzman .10 .03
❑ 184 John Smiley .10 .03
❑ 185 David Segui .10 .03
❑ 186 Omar Olivares .10 .03
❑ 187 Joe Slusarski .10 .03
❑ 188 Erik Hanson .10 .03
❑ 189 Mark Portugal .10 .03
❑ 190 Walt Terrell .10 .03
❑ 191 John Smoltz .30 .09
❑ 192 Wilson Alvarez .10 .03
❑ 193 Jimmy Key .20 .06
❑ 194 Larry Walker .30 .09
❑ 195 Lee Smith .20 .06
❑ 196 Pete Harnisch .10 .03
❑ 197 Mike Harkey .10 .03
❑ 198 Frank Tanana .10 .03
❑ 199 Terry Mulholland .10 .03
❑ 200 Cal Ripken 1.50 .45
❑ 201 Dave Magadan .10 .03
❑ 202 Bud Black .10 .03
❑ 203 Terry Shumpert .10 .03
❑ 204 Mike Mussina .50 .15
❑ 205 Mo Vaughn .20 .06
❑ 206 Steve Farr .10 .03
❑ 207 Darrin Jackson .10 .03
❑ 208 Jerry Browne .10 .03
❑ 209 Jeff Russell .10 .03
❑ 210 Mike Scioscia .10 .03
❑ 211 Rick Aguilera .20 .06
❑ 212 Jaime Navarro .10 .03
❑ 213 Randy Tomlin .10 .03
❑ 214 Bobby Thigpen .10 .03
❑ 215 Mark Gardner .10 .03
❑ 216 Norm Charlton .10 .03
❑ 217 Mark McGwire 1.25 .35
❑ 218 Skeeter Barnes .10 .03
❑ 219 Bob Tewksbury .10 .03
❑ 220 Junior Felix .10 .03
❑ 221 Sam Horn .10 .03
❑ 222 Jody Reed .10 .03
❑ 223 Luis Sojo .10 .03
❑ 224 Jerome Walton .10 .03
❑ 225 Darryl Kile .20 .06
❑ 226 Mickey Tettleton .10 .03
❑ 227 Dan Pasqua .10 .03
❑ 228 Jim Gott .10 .03
❑ 229 Bernie Williams .30 .09
❑ 230 Shane Mack .10 .03
❑ 231 Steve Avery .10 .03
❑ 232 Dave Valle .10 .03
❑ 233 Mark Leonard .10 .03
❑ 234 Spike Owen .10 .03
❑ 235 Gary Sheffield .20 .06
❑ 236 Steve Chitren .10 .03
❑ 237 Zane Smith .10 .03
❑ 238 Tom Gordon .10 .03
❑ 239 Jose Oquendo .10 .03
❑ 240 Todd Stottlemyre .10 .03
❑ 241 Darren Daulton .20 .06
❑ 242 Tim Naehring .10 .03
❑ 243 Tony Phillips .10 .03
❑ 244 Shawon Dunston .10 .03
❑ 245 Manuel Lee .10 .03
❑ 246 Mike Pagliarulo .10 .03
❑ 247 Jim Thome .50 .15
❑ 248 Luis Mercedes .10 .03
❑ 249 Cal Eldred .10 .03
❑ 250 Derek Bell .20 .06
❑ 251 Arthur Rhodes .10 .03
❑ 252 Scott Cooper .10 .03
❑ 253 Roberto Hernandez .10 .03
❑ 254 Mo Sanford .10 .03
❑ 255 Scott Servais .10 .03
❑ 256 Eric Karros .20 .06
❑ 257 Andy Mota .10 .03
❑ 258 Keith Mitchell .10 .03
❑ 259 Joel Johnston .10 .03
❑ 260 John Wehner .10 .03
❑ 261 Gino Minutelli .10 .03
❑ 262 Greg Gagne .10 .03
❑ 263 Stan Royer .10 .03
❑ 264 Carlos Garcia .10 .03

	No.	Player	Price 1	Price 2
❑	265	Andy Ashby	.10	.03
❑	266	Kim Batiste	.10	.03
❑	267	Julio Valera	.10	.03
❑	268	Royce Clayton	.10	.03
❑	269	Gary Scott	.10	.03
❑	270	Kirk Dressendorfer	.10	.03
❑	271	Sean Berry	.10	.03
❑	272	Lance Dickson	.10	.03
❑	273	Rob Maurer	.10	.03
❑	274	Scott Brosius RC	.50	.15
❑	275	Dave Fleming	.10	.03
❑	276	Lenny Webster	.10	.03
❑	277	Mike Humphreys	.10	.03
❑	278	Freddie Benavides	.10	.03
❑	279	Harvey Pulliam	.10	.03
❑	280	Jeff Carter	.10	.03
❑	281	Jim Abbott I Nolan Ryan	.50	.15
❑	282	Wade Boggs I George Brett	.50	.15
❑	283	Ken Griffey Jr. I Rickey Henderson	.50	.15
❑	284	Wally Joyner Dale Murphy	.30	.09
❑	285	Chuck Knoblauch I Ozzie Smith	.30	.09
❑	286	Robin Ventura I Lou Gehrig	.50	.15
❑	287	Robin Yount SIDE	.50	.15
❑	288	Bob Tewksbury SIDE	.10	.03
❑	289	Kirby Puckett SIDE	.30	.09
❑	290	Kenny Lofton SIDE	.20	.06
❑	291	Jack McDowell SIDE	.10	.03
❑	292	John Burkett SIDE	.10	.03
❑	293	Dwight Smith SIDE	.10	.03
❑	294	Nolan Ryan SIDE	1.00	.30
❑	295	M.Ramirez DP RC	4.00	1.20
❑	296	Cliff Floyd RC DP UER (Throws right, not left as indicated on back)	1.50	.45
❑	297	Al Shirley DP RC	.15	.04
❑	298	Brian Barber DP RC	.15	.04
❑	299	Jon Farrell DP RC	.15	.04
❑	300	Scott Ruffcorn DP RC	.15	.04
❑	301	Tyrone Hill DP RC	.15	.04
❑	302	Benji Gil DP RC	.25	.07
❑	303	Tyler Green DP RC	.15	.04
❑	304	Allen Watson DP RC	.15	.04
❑	305	Jay Buhner SH	.10	.03
❑	306	Roberto Alomar SH	.20	.06
❑	307	Chuck Knoblauch SH	.10	.03
❑	308	Darryl Strawberry SH	.10	.03
❑	309	Danny Tartabull SH	.10	.03
❑	310	Bobby Bonilla SH	.10	.03
❑	311	Mike Felder	.10	.03
❑	312	Storm Davis	.10	.03
❑	313	Tim Teufel	.10	.03
❑	314	Tom Brunansky	.10	.03
❑	315	Rex Hudler	.10	.03
❑	316	Dave Otto	.10	.03
❑	317	Jeff King	.10	.03
❑	318	Dan Gladden	.10	.03
❑	319	Bill Pecota	.10	.03
❑	320	Franklin Stubbs	.10	.03
❑	321	Gary Carter	.20	.06
❑	322	Melido Perez	.10	.03
❑	323	Eric Davis	.20	.06
❑	324	Greg Myers	.10	.03
❑	325	Pete Incaviglia	.10	.03
❑	326	Von Hayes	.10	.03
❑	327	Greg Swindell	.10	.03
❑	328	Steve Sax	.10	.03
❑	329	Chuck McElroy	.10	.03
❑	330	Gregg Jefferies	.10	.03
❑	331	Joe Oliver	.10	.03
❑	332	Paul Faries	.10	.03
❑	333	David West	.10	.03
❑	334	Craig Grebeck	.10	.03
❑	335	Chris Hammond	.10	.03
❑	336	Billy Ripken	.10	.03
❑	337	Scott Sanderson	.10	.03
❑	338	Dick Schofield	.10	.03
❑	339	Bob Milacki	.10	.03
❑	340	Kevin Reimer	.10	.03
❑	341	Jose DeLeon	.10	.03
❑	342	Henry Cotto	.10	.03
❑	343	Daryl Boston	.10	.03
❑	344	Kevin Gross	.10	.03
❑	345	Milt Thompson	.10	.03
❑	346	Luis Rivera	.10	.03
❑	347	Al Osuna	.10	.03
❑	348	Rob Deer	.10	.03
❑	349	Tim Leary	.10	.03
❑	350	Mike Stanton	.10	.03
❑	351	Dean Palmer	.20	.06
❑	352	Trevor Wilson	.10	.03
❑	353	Mark Eichhorn	.10	.03
❑	354	Scott Aldred	.10	.03
❑	355	Mark Whiten	.10	.03
❑	356	Leo Gomez	.10	.03
❑	357	Rafael Belliard	.10	.03
❑	358	Carlos Quintana	.10	.03
❑	359	Mark Davis	.10	.03
❑	360	Chris Nabholz	.10	.03
❑	361	Carlton Fisk	.30	.09
❑	362	Joe Orsulak	.10	.03
❑	363	Eric Anthony	.10	.03
❑	364	Greg Hibbard	.10	.03
❑	365	Scott Leius	.10	.03
❑	366	Hensley Meulens	.10	.03
❑	367	Chris Bosio	.10	.03
❑	368	Brian Downing	.10	.03
❑	369	Sammy Sosa	.50	.15
❑	370	Stan Belinda	.10	.03
❑	371	Joe Grahe	.10	.03
❑	372	Luis Salazar	.10	.03
❑	373	Lance Johnson	.10	.03
❑	374	Kal Daniels	.10	.03
❑	375	Dave Winfield	.20	.06
❑	376	Brook Jacoby	.10	.03
❑	377	Mariano Duncan	.10	.03
❑	378	Ron Darling	.10	.03
❑	379	Randy Johnson	.50	.15
❑	380	Chito Martinez	.10	.03
❑	381	Andres Galarraga	.20	.06
❑	382	Willie Randolph	.20	.06
❑	383	Charles Nagy	.10	.03
❑	384	Tim Belcher	.10	.03
❑	385	Duane Ward	.10	.03
❑	386	Vicente Palacios	.10	.03
❑	387	Mike Gallego	.10	.03
❑	388	Rich DeLucia	.10	.03
❑	389	Scott Radinsky	.10	.03
❑	390	Damon Berryhill	.10	.03
❑	391	Kirk McCaskill	.10	.03
❑	392	Pedro Guerrero	.20	.06
❑	393	Kevin Mitchell	.10	.03
❑	394	Dickie Thon	.10	.03
❑	395	Bobby Bonilla	.20	.06
❑	396	Bill Wegman	.10	.03
❑	397	Dave Martinez	.10	.03
❑	398	Rick Sutcliffe	.20	.06
❑	399	Larry Andersen	.10	.03
❑	400	Tony Gwynn	.60	.18
❑	401	Rickey Henderson	.50	.15
❑	402	Greg Cadaret	.10	.03
❑	403	Keith Miller	.10	.03
❑	404	Bip Roberts	.10	.03
❑	405	Kevin Brown	.20	.06
❑	406	Mitch Williams	.10	.03
❑	407	Frank Viola	.20	.06
❑	408	Darren Lewis	.10	.03
❑	409	Bob Welch	.10	.03
❑	410	Bob Walk	.10	.03
❑	411	Todd Frohwirth	.10	.03
❑	412	Brian Hunter	.10	.03
❑	413	Ron Karkovice	.10	.03
❑	414	Mike Morgan	.10	.03
❑	415	Joe Hesketh	.10	.03
❑	416	Don Slaught	.10	.03
❑	417	Tom Henke	.10	.03
❑	418	Kurt Stillwell	.10	.03
❑	419	Hector Villaneuva	.10	.03
❑	420	Glenallen Hill	.10	.03
❑	421	Pat Borders	.10	.03
❑	422	Charlie Hough	.20	.06
❑	423	Charlie Leibrandt	.10	.03
❑	424	Eddie Murray	.50	.15
❑	425	Jesse Barfield	.10	.03
❑	426	Mark Lemke	.10	.03
❑	427	Kevin McReynolds	.10	.03
❑	428	Gilberto Reyes	.10	.03
❑	429	Ramon Martinez	.10	.03
❑	430	Steve Buechele	.10	.03
❑	431	David Wells	.20	.06
❑	432	Kyle Abbott	.10	.03
❑	433	John Habyan	.10	.03
❑	434	Kevin Appier	.20	.06
❑	435	Gene Larkin	.10	.03
❑	436	Sandy Alomar Jr.	.10	.03
❑	437	Mike Jackson	.10	.03
❑	438	Todd Benzinger	.10	.03
❑	439	Teddy Higuera	.10	.03
❑	440	Reggie Sanders	.20	.06
❑	441	Mark Carreon	.10	.03
❑	442	Bret Saberhagen	.20	.06
❑	443	Gene Nelson	.10	.03
❑	444	Jay Howell	.10	.03
❑	445	Roger McDowell	.10	.03
❑	446	Sid Bream	.10	.03
❑	447	Mackey Sasser	.10	.03
❑	448	Bill Swift	.10	.03
❑	449	Hubie Brooks	.10	.03
❑	450	David Cone	.20	.06
❑	451	Bobby Witt	.10	.03
❑	452	Brady Anderson	.20	.06
❑	453	Lee Stevens	.10	.03
❑	454	Luis Aquino	.10	.03
❑	455	Carney Lansford	.20	.06
❑	456	Carlos Hernandez	.10	.03
❑	457	Danny Jackson	.10	.03
❑	458	Gerald Young	.10	.03
❑	459	Tom Candiotti	.10	.03
❑	460	Billy Hatcher	.10	.03
❑	461	John Wetteland	.20	.06
❑	462	Mike Bordick	.10	.03
❑	463	Don Robinson	.10	.03
❑	464	Jeff Johnson	.10	.03
❑	465	Lonnie Smith	.10	.03
❑	466	Paul Assenmacher	.10	.03
❑	467	Alvin Davis	.10	.03
❑	468	Jim Eisenreich	.10	.03
❑	469	Brent Mayne	.10	.03
❑	470	Jeff Brantley	.10	.03
❑	471	Tim Burke	.10	.03
❑	472	Pat Mahomes RC	.25	.07
❑	473	Ryan Bowen	.10	.03
❑	474	Bryn Smith	.10	.03
❑	475	Mike Flanagan	.10	.03
❑	476	Reggie Jefferson	.10	.03
❑	477	Jeff Blauser	.10	.03
❑	478	Craig Lefferts	.10	.03
❑	479	Todd Worrell	.10	.03
❑	480	Scott Scudder	.10	.03
❑	481	Kirk Gibson	.30	.09
❑	482	Kenny Rogers	.20	.06
❑	483	Jack Morris	.20	.06
❑	484	Russ Swan	.10	.03
❑	485	Mike Huff	.10	.03
❑	486	Ken Hill	.10	.03
❑	487	Geronimo Pena	.10	.03
❑	488	Charlie O'Brien	.10	.03
❑	489	Mike Maddux	.10	.03
❑	490	Scott Livingstone	.10	.03
❑	491	Carl Willis	.10	.03
❑	492	Kelly Downs	.10	.03
❑	493	Dennis Cook	.10	.03
❑	494	Joe Magrane	.10	.03
❑	495	Bob Kipper	.10	.03
❑	496	Jose Mesa	.10	.03
❑	497	Charlie Hayes	.10	.03
❑	498	Joe Girardi	.10	.03
❑	499	Doug Jones	.10	.03
❑	500	Barry Bonds	1.50	.45
❑	501	Bill Krueger	.10	.03
❑	502	Glenn Braggs	.10	.03
❑	503	Eric King	.10	.03
❑	504	Frank Castillo	.10	.03
❑	505	Mike Gardiner	.10	.03
❑	506	Cory Snyder	.10	.03
❑	507	Steve Howe	.10	.03
❑	508	Jose Rijo	.10	.03
❑	509	Sid Fernandez	.10	.03
❑	510	Archi Cianfrocco RC	.15	.04
❑	511	Mark Guthrie	.10	.03
❑	512	Bob Ojeda	.10	.03
❑	513	John Doherty RC	.15	.04
❑	514	Dante Bichette	.20	.06

No.	Player	Nm-Mt	Ex-Mt
❑ 515	Juan Berenguer	.10	.03
❑ 516	Jeff M. Robinson	.10	.03
❑ 517	Mike Macfarlane	.10	.03
❑ 518	Matt Young	.10	.03
❑ 519	Otis Nixon	.10	.03
❑ 520	Brian Holman	.10	.03
❑ 521	Chris Haney	.10	.03
❑ 522	Jeff Kent RC	3.00	.90
❑ 523	Chad Curtis RC	.25	.07
❑ 524	Vince Horsman	.10	.03
❑ 525	Rod Nichols	.10	.03
❑ 526	Peter Hoy	.10	.03
❑ 527	Shawn Boskie	.10	.03
❑ 528	Alejandro Pena	.10	.03
❑ 529	Dave Burba	.10	.03
❑ 530	Ricky Jordan	.10	.03
❑ 531	Dave Silvestri	.10	.03
❑ 532	John Patterson UER RC	.10	.03
	(Listed as being born in 1960; should be 1967)		
❑ 533	Jeff Branson	.10	.03
❑ 534	Derrick May	.10	.03
❑ 535	Esteban Beltre	.10	.03
❑ 536	Jose Melendez	.10	.03
❑ 537	Wally Joyner	.20	.06
❑ 538	Eddie Taubensee RC	.25	.07
❑ 539	Jim Abbott	.30	.09
❑ 540	Brian Williams RC	.15	.04
❑ 541	Donovan Osborne	.10	.03
❑ 542	Patrick Lennon	.10	.03
❑ 543	Mike Groppuso RC	.15	.04
❑ 544	Jarvis Brown	.10	.03
❑ 545	Shawn Livsey RC	.15	.04
❑ 546	Jeff Ware	.10	.03
❑ 547	Danny Tartabull	.10	.03
❑ 548	Bobby Jones RC	.25	.07
❑ 549	Ken Griffey Jr.	.75	.23
❑ 550	Rey Sanchez RC	.25	.07
❑ 551	Pedro Astacio RC	.25	.07
❑ 552	Juan Guerrero	.10	.03
❑ 553	Jacob Brumfield	.10	.03
❑ 554	Ben Rivera	.10	.03
❑ 555	Brian Jordan RC	.50	.15
❑ 556	Denny Neagle	.20	.06
❑ 557	Cliff Brantley	.10	.03
❑ 558	Anthony Young	.10	.03
❑ 559	John Vander Wal	.10	.03
❑ 560	Monty Fariss	.10	.03
❑ 561	Russ Springer RC	.15	.04
❑ 562	Pat Listach RC	.25	.07
❑ 563	Pat Hentgen	.10	.03
❑ 564	Andy Stankiewicz	.10	.03
❑ 565	Mike Perez	.10	.03
❑ 566	Mike Bielecki	.10	.03
❑ 567	Butch Henry RC	.15	.04
❑ 568	Dave Nilsson	.10	.03
❑ 569	Scott Hatteberg RC	.25	.07
❑ 570	Ruben Amaro	.10	.03
❑ 571	Todd Hundley	.10	.03
❑ 572	Moises Alou	.20	.06
❑ 573	Hector Fajardo RC	.15	.04
❑ 574	Todd Van Poppel	.10	.03
❑ 575	Willie Banks	.10	.03
❑ 576	Bob Zupcic RC	.15	.04
❑ 577	J.J. Johnson RC	.15	.04
❑ 578	John Burkett	.10	.03
❑ 579	Trever Miller RC	.15	.04
❑ 580	Scott Bankhead	.10	.03
❑ 581	Rich Amaral	.10	.03
❑ 582	Kenny Lofton	.30	.09
❑ 583	Matt Stairs RC	.25	.07
❑ 584	Don Mattingly	.50	.15
	Rod Carew IDOLS		
❑ 585	Steve Avery	.10	.03
	Jack Morris IDOLS		
❑ 586	Roberto Alomar	.20	.06
	Sandy Alomar SR. IDOLS		
❑ 587	Scott Sanderson	.20	.06
	Catfish Hunter IDOLS		
❑ 588	Dave Justice	.20	.06
	Willie Stargell IDOLS		
❑ 589	Rex Hudler	.50	.15
	Roger Staubach IDOLS		
❑ 590	David Cone	.20	.06
	Jackie Gleason IDOLS		
❑ 591	Tony Gwynn	.30	.09
	Willie Davis IDOLS		
❑ 592	Orel Hershiser SIDE	.10	.03
❑ 593	John Wetteland SIDE	.10	.03
❑ 594	Tom Glavine SIDE	.20	.06
❑ 595	Randy Johnson SIDE	.30	.09
❑ 596	Jim Gott SIDE	.10	.03
❑ 597	Donald Harris	.10	.03
❑ 598	Shawn Hare RC	.15	.04
❑ 599	Chris Gardner	.10	.03
❑ 600	Rusty Meacham	.10	.03
❑ 601	Benito Santiago	.20	.06
❑ 602	Eric Davis SHADE	.10	.03
❑ 603	Jose Lind SHADE	.10	.03
❑ 604	Dave Justice SHADE	.10	.03
❑ 605	Tim Raines SHADE	.10	.03
❑ 606	Randy Tomlin GRIP	.10	.03
❑ 607	Jack McDowell GRIP	.10	.03
❑ 608	Greg Maddux GRIP	.50	.15
❑ 609	Charles Nagy GRIP	.10	.03
❑ 610	Tom Candiotti GRIP	.10	.03
❑ 611	David Cone GRIP	.10	.03
❑ 612	Steve Avery GRIP	.10	.03
❑ 613	Rod Beck GRIP RC	.25	.07
❑ 614	R. Henderson TECH	.30	.09
❑ 615	Benito Santiago TECH	.10	.03
❑ 616	Ruben Sierra TECH	.10	.03
❑ 617	Ryne Sandberg TECH	.50	.15
❑ 618	Nolan Ryan TECH	1.00	.30
❑ 619	Brett Butler TECH	.10	.03
❑ 620	Dave Justice TECH	.10	.03

1993 Pinnacle

	Nm-Mt	Ex-Mt
COMPLETE SET (620)	40.00	12.00
COMP. SERIES 1 (310)	15.00	4.50
COMP. SERIES 2 (310)	25.00	7.50

No.	Player	Nm-Mt	Ex-Mt
❑ 1	Gary Sheffield	.30	.09
❑ 2	Cal Eldred	.15	.04
❑ 3	Larry Walker	.30	.09
❑ 4	Deion Sanders	.50	.15
❑ 5	Dave Fleming	.15	.04
❑ 6	Carlos Baerga	.15	.04
❑ 7	Bernie Williams	.50	.15
❑ 8	John Kruk	.30	.09
❑ 9	Jimmy Key	.30	.09
❑ 10	Jeff Bagwell	.50	.15
❑ 11	Jim Abbott	.50	.15
❑ 12	Terry Steinbach	.15	.04
❑ 13	Bob Tewksbury	.15	.04
❑ 14	Eric Karros	.30	.09
❑ 15	Ryne Sandberg	1.25	.35
❑ 16	Will Clark	.50	.15
❑ 17	Edgar Martinez	.50	.15
❑ 18	Eddie Murray	.75	.23
❑ 19	Andy Van Slyke	.50	.15
❑ 20	Cal Ripken Jr.	2.50	.75
❑ 21	Ivan Rodriguez	.50	.15
❑ 22	Barry Larkin	.50	.15
❑ 23	Don Mattingly	2.00	.60
❑ 24	Gregg Jefferies	.15	.04
❑ 25	Roger Clemens	1.50	.45
❑ 26	Cecil Fielder	.30	.09
❑ 27	Kent Hrbek	.30	.09
❑ 28	Robin Ventura	.30	.09
❑ 29	Rickey Henderson	.75	.23
❑ 30	Roberto Alomar	.50	.15
❑ 31	Luis Polonia	.15	.04
❑ 32	Andujar Cedeno	.15	.04
❑ 33	Pat Listach	.15	.04
❑ 34	Mark Grace	.50	.15
❑ 35	Otis Nixon	.15	.04
❑ 36	Felix Jose	.15	.04
❑ 37	Mike Sharperson	.15	.04
❑ 38	Dennis Martinez	.30	.09
❑ 39	Willie McGee	.30	.09
❑ 40	Kenny Lofton	.30	.09
❑ 41	Randy Johnson	.75	.23
❑ 42	Andy Benes	.15	.04
❑ 43	Bobby Bonilla	.30	.09
❑ 44	Mike Mussina	.50	.15
❑ 45	Len Dykstra	.30	.09
❑ 46	Ellis Burks	.30	.09
❑ 47	Chris Sabo	.15	.04
❑ 48	Jay Bell	.30	.09
❑ 49	Jose Canseco	.50	.15
❑ 50	Craig Biggio	.50	.15
❑ 51	Wally Joyner	.30	.09
❑ 52	Mickey Tettleton	.15	.04
❑ 53	Tim Raines	.30	.09
❑ 54	Brian Harper	.15	.04
❑ 55	Rene Gonzales	.15	.04
❑ 56	Mark Langston	.15	.04
❑ 57	Jack Morris	.30	.09
❑ 58	Mark McGwire	2.00	.60
❑ 59	Ken Caminiti	.30	.09
❑ 60	Terry Pendleton	.30	.09
❑ 61	Dave Nilsson	.15	.04
❑ 62	Tom Pagnozzi	.15	.04
❑ 63	Mike Morgan	.15	.04
❑ 64	Darryl Strawberry	.30	.09
❑ 65	Charles Nagy	.15	.04
❑ 66	Ken Hill	.15	.04
❑ 67	Matt Williams	.30	.09
❑ 68	Jay Buhner	.30	.09
❑ 69	Vince Coleman	.15	.04
❑ 70	Brady Anderson	.30	.09
❑ 71	Fred McGriff	.50	.15
❑ 72	Ben McDonald	.15	.04
❑ 73	Terry Mulholland	.15	.04
❑ 74	Randy Tomlin	.15	.04
❑ 75	Nolan Ryan	3.00	.90
❑ 76	Frank Viola UER	.30	.09
	(Card incorrectly states he has a surgically repaired elbow)		
❑ 77	Jose Rijo	.15	.04
❑ 78	Shane Mack	.15	.04
❑ 79	Travis Fryman	.30	.09
❑ 80	Jack McDowell	.15	.04
❑ 81	Mark Gubicza	.15	.04
❑ 82	Matt Nokes	.15	.04
❑ 83	Bert Blyleven	.30	.09
❑ 84	Eric Anthony	.15	.04
❑ 85	Mike Bordick	.15	.04
❑ 86	John Olerud	.30	.09
❑ 87	B.J. Surhoff	.30	.09
❑ 88	Bernard Gilkey	.15	.04
❑ 89	Shawon Dunston	.15	.04
❑ 90	Tom Glavine	.50	.15
❑ 91	Brett Butler	.30	.09
❑ 92	Moises Alou	.30	.09
❑ 93	Albert Belle	.30	.09
❑ 94	Darren Lewis	.15	.04
❑ 95	Omar Vizquel	.50	.15
❑ 96	Dwight Gooden	.30	.09
❑ 97	Gregg Olson	.15	.04
❑ 98	Tony Gwynn	1.00	.30
❑ 99	Darren Daulton	.30	.09
❑ 100	Dennis Eckersley	.30	.09
❑ 101	Rob Dibble	.30	.09
❑ 102	Mike Greenwell	.15	.04
❑ 103	Jose Lind	.15	.04
❑ 104	Julio Franco	.30	.09
❑ 105	Tom Gordon	.15	.04
❑ 106	Scott Livingstone	.15	.04
❑ 107	Chuck Knoblauch	.30	.09
❑ 108	Frank Thomas	.75	.23
❑ 109	Melido Perez	.15	.04
❑ 110	Ken Griffey Jr.	1.25	.35
❑ 111	Harold Baines	.30	.09
❑ 112	Gary Gaetti	.30	.09
❑ 113	Pete Harnisch	.15	.04
❑ 114	David Wells	.30	.09

❑	115	Charlie Leibrandt	.15	.04
❑	116	Ray Lankford	.30	.09
❑	117	Kevin Seitzer	.15	.04
❑	118	Robin Yount	1.25	.35
❑	119	Lenny Harris	.15	.04
❑	120	Chris James	.15	.04
❑	121	Delino DeShields	.15	.04
❑	122	Kirt Manwaring	.15	.04
❑	123	Glenallen Hill	.15	.04
❑	124	Hensley Meulens	.15	.04
❑	125	Darrin Jackson	.15	.04
❑	126	Todd Hundley	.15	.04
❑	127	Dave Hollins	.15	.04
❑	128	Sam Horn	.15	.04
❑	129	Roberto Hernandez	.15	.04
❑	130	Vicente Palacios	.15	.04
❑	131	George Brett	2.00	.60
❑	132	Dave Martinez	.15	.04
❑	133	Kevin Appier	.30	.09
❑	134	Pat Kelly	.15	.04
❑	135	Pedro Munoz	.15	.04
❑	136	Mark Carreon	.15	.04
❑	137	Lance Johnson	.15	.04
❑	138	Devon White	.30	.09
❑	139	Julio Valera	.15	.04
❑	140	Eddie Taubensee	.15	.04
❑	141	Willie Wilson	.15	.04
❑	142	Stan Belinda	.15	.04
❑	143	John Smoltz	.50	.15
❑	144	Darryl Hamilton	.15	.04
❑	145	Sammy Sosa	.75	.23
❑	146	Carlos Hernandez	.15	.04
❑	147	Tom Candiotti	.15	.04
❑	148	Mike Felder	.15	.04
❑	149	Rusty Meacham	.15	.04
❑	150	Ivan Calderon	.15	.04
❑	151	Pete O'Brien	.15	.04
❑	152	Erik Hanson	.15	.04
❑	153	Billy Ripken	.15	.04
❑	154	Kurt Stillwell	.15	.04
❑	155	Jeff Kent	.75	.23
❑	156	Mickey Morandini	.15	.04
❑	157	Randy Milligan	.15	.04
❑	158	Reggie Sanders	.30	.09
❑	159	Luis Rivera	.15	.04
❑	160	Orlando Merced	.15	.04
❑	161	Dean Palmer	.30	.09
❑	162	Mike Perez	.15	.04
❑	163	Scott Erickson	.15	.04
❑	164	Kevin McReynolds	.15	.04
❑	165	Kevin Maas	.15	.04
❑	166	Ozzie Guillen	.30	.09
❑	167	Rob Deer	.15	.04
❑	168	Danny Tartabull	.15	.04
❑	169	Lee Stevens	.15	.04
❑	170	Dave Henderson	.15	.04
❑	171	Derek Bell	.15	.04
❑	172	Steve Finley	.30	.09
❑	173	Greg Olson	.15	.04
❑	174	Geronimo Pena	.15	.04
❑	175	Paul Quantrill	.15	.04
❑	176	Steve Buechele	.15	.04
❑	177	Kevin Gross	.15	.04
❑	178	Tim Wallach	.15	.04
❑	179	Dave Valle	.15	.04
❑	180	Dave Silvestri	.15	.04
❑	181	Bud Black	.15	.04
❑	182	Henry Rodriguez	.15	.04
❑	183	Tim Teufel	.15	.04
❑	184	Mark McLemore	.15	.04
❑	185	Bret Saberhagen	.30	.09
❑	186	Chris Hoiles	.15	.04
❑	187	Ricky Jordan	.15	.04
❑	188	Don Slaught	.15	.04
❑	189	Mo Vaughn	.30	.09
❑	190	Joe Oliver	.15	.04
❑	191	Juan Gonzalez	.30	.09
❑	192	Scott Leius	.15	.04
❑	193	Milt Cuyler	.15	.04
❑	194	Chris Haney	.15	.04
❑	195	Ron Karkovice	.15	.04
❑	196	Steve Farr	.15	.04
❑	197	John Orton	.15	.04
❑	198	Kelly Gruber	.15	.04
❑	199	Ron Darling	.15	.04
❑	200	Ruben Sierra	.15	.04
❑	201	Chuck Finley	.30	.09
❑	202	Mike Moore	.15	.04
❑	203	Pat Borders	.15	.04
❑	204	Sid Bream	.15	.04
❑	205	Todd Zeile	.15	.04
❑	206	Rick Wilkins	.15	.04
❑	207	Jim Gantner	.15	.04
❑	208	Frank Castillo	.15	.04
❑	209	Dave Hansen	.15	.04
❑	210	Trevor Wilson	.15	.04
❑	211	Sandy Alomar Jr.	.15	.04
❑	212	Sean Berry	.15	.04
❑	213	Tino Martinez	.50	.15
❑	214	Chito Martinez	.15	.04
❑	215	Dan Walters	.15	.04
❑	216	John Franco	.30	.09
❑	217	Glenn Davis	.15	.04
❑	218	Mariano Duncan	.15	.04
❑	219	Mike LaValliere	.15	.04
❑	220	Rafael Palmeiro	.50	.15
❑	221	Jack Clark	.30	.09
❑	222	Hal Morris	.15	.04
❑	223	Ed Sprague	.15	.04
❑	224	John Valentin	.15	.04
❑	225	Sam Militello	.15	.04
❑	226	Bob Wickman	.15	.04
❑	227	Damion Easley	.15	.04
❑	228	John Jaha	.15	.04
❑	229	Bob Ayrault	.15	.04
❑	230	Mo Sanford	.15	.04
❑	231	Walt Weiss	.15	.04
❑	232	Dante Bichette	.30	.09
❑	233	Steve Decker	.15	.04
❑	234	Jerald Clark	.15	.04
❑	235	Bryan Harvey	.15	.04
❑	236	Joe Girardi	.15	.04
❑	237	Dave Magadan	.15	.04
❑	238	David Nied	.15	.04
❑	239	Eric Wedge RC	.40	.12
❑	240	Rico Brogna	.15	.04
❑	241	J.T. Bruett	.15	.04
❑	242	Jonathan Hurst	.15	.04
❑	243	Bret Boone	.50	.15
❑	244	Manny Alexander	.15	.04
❑	245	Scooter Tucker	.15	.04
❑	246	Troy Neel	.15	.04
❑	247	Eddie Zosky	.15	.04
❑	248	Melvin Nieves	.15	.04
❑	249	Ryan Thompson	.15	.04
❑	250	Shawn Barton RC	.15	.04
❑	251	Ryan Klesko	.30	.09
❑	252	Mike Piazza	3.00	.90
❑	253	Steve Hosey	.15	.04
❑	254	Shane Reynolds	.15	.04
❑	255	Dan Wilson	.30	.09
❑	256	Tom Marsh	.15	.04
❑	257	Barry Manuel	.15	.04
❑	258	Paul Miller	.15	.04
❑	259	Pedro Martinez	1.50	.45
❑	260	Steve Cooke	.15	.04
❑	261	Johnny Guzman	.15	.04
❑	262	Mike Butcher	.15	.04
❑	263	Bien Figueroa	.15	.04
❑	264	Rich Rowland	.15	.04
❑	265	Shawn Jeter	.15	.04
❑	266	Gerald Williams	.15	.04
❑	267	Derek Parks	.15	.04
❑	268	Henry Mercedes	.15	.04
❑	269	David Hulse RC	.15	.04
❑	270	Tim Pugh RC	.15	.04
❑	271	William Suero	.15	.04
❑	272	Ozzie Canseco	.15	.04
❑	273	Fernando Ramsey RC	.15	.04
❑	274	Bernardo Brito	.15	.04
❑	275	Dave Mlicki	.15	.04
❑	276	Tim Salmon	.50	.15
❑	277	Mike Raczka	.15	.04
❑	278	Ken Ryan RC	.40	.12
❑	279	Rafael Bournigal	.15	.04
❑	280	Wil Cordero	.15	.04
❑	281	Billy Ashley	.15	.04
❑	282	Paul Wagner	.15	.04
❑	283	Blas Minor	.15	.04
❑	284	Rick Trlicek	.15	.04
❑	285	Willie Greene	.15	.04
❑	286	Ted Wood	.15	.04
❑	287	Phil Clark	.15	.04
❑	288	Jesse Levis	.15	.04
❑	289	Tony Gwynn NT	.50	.15
❑	290	Nolan Ryan NT	1.50	.45
❑	291	Dennis Martinez NT	.15	.04
❑	292	Eddie Murray NT	.50	.15
❑	293	Robin Yount NT	.75	.23
❑	294	George Brett NT	1.00	.30
❑	295	Dave Winfield NT	.15	.04
❑	296	Bert Blyleven NT	.15	.04
❑	297	Jeff Bagwell Carl Yastrzemski	.75	.23
❑	298	John Smoltz Jack Morris	.30	.09
❑	299	Larry Walker Mike Bossy	.30	.09
❑	300	Gary Sheffield Barry Larkin	.30	.09
❑	301	Ivan Rodriguez Carlton Fisk	.30	.09
❑	302	Delino DeShields Malcolm X	.75	.23
❑	303	Tim Salmon Dwight Evans	.50	.15
❑	304	Bernard Gilkey HH	.15	.04
❑	305	Cal Ripken Jr. HH	1.25	.35
❑	306	Barry Larkin HH	.30	.09
❑	307	Kent Hrbek HH	.15	.04
❑	308	Rickey Henderson HH	.50	.15
❑	309	Darryl Strawberry HH	.15	.04
❑	310	John Franco HH	.15	.04
❑	311	Todd Stottlemyre	.15	.04
❑	312	Luis Gonzalez	.30	.09
❑	313	Tommy Greene	.15	.04
❑	314	Randy Velarde	.15	.04
❑	315	Steve Avery	.15	.04
❑	316	Jose Oquendo	.15	.04
❑	317	Rey Sanchez	.15	.04
❑	318	Greg Vaughn	.15	.04
❑	319	Orel Hershiser	.30	.09
❑	320	Paul Sorrento	.15	.04
❑	321	Royce Clayton	.15	.04
❑	322	John Vander Wal	.15	.04
❑	323	Henry Cotto	.15	.04
❑	324	Pete Schourek	.15	.04
❑	325	David Segui	.15	.04
❑	326	Arthur Rhodes	.15	.04
❑	327	Bruce Hurst	.15	.04
❑	328	Wes Chamberlain	.15	.04
❑	329	Ozzie Smith	1.25	.35
❑	330	Scott Cooper	.15	.04
❑	331	Felix Fermin	.15	.04
❑	332	Mike Macfarlane	.15	.04
❑	333	Dan Gladden	.15	.04
❑	334	Kevin Tapani	.15	.04
❑	335	Steve Sax	.15	.04
❑	336	Jeff Montgomery	.15	.04
❑	337	Gary DiSarcina	.15	.04
❑	338	Lance Blankenship	.15	.04
❑	339	Brian Williams	.15	.04
❑	340	Duane Ward	.15	.04
❑	341	Chuck McElroy	.15	.04
❑	342	Joe Magrane	.15	.04
❑	343	Jaime Navarro	.15	.04
❑	344	Dave Justice	.30	.09
❑	345	Jose Offerman	.15	.04
❑	346	Marquis Grissom	.30	.09
❑	347	Bill Swift	.15	.04
❑	348	Jim Thome	.50	.15
❑	349	Archi Cianfrocco	.15	.04
❑	350	Anthony Young	.15	.04
❑	351	Leo Gomez	.15	.04
❑	352	Bill Gullickson	.15	.04
❑	353	Alan Trammell	.30	.09
❑	354	Dan Pasqua	.15	.04
❑	355	Jeff King	.15	.04
❑	356	Kevin Brown	.30	.09
❑	357	Tim Belcher	.15	.04
❑	358	Bip Roberts	.15	.04
❑	359	Brent Mayne	.15	.04
❑	360	Rheal Cormier	.15	.04
❑	361	Mark Guthrie	.15	.04
❑	362	Craig Grebeck	.15	.04
❑	363	Andy Stankiewicz	.15	.04
❑	364	Juan Guzman	.15	.04
❑	365	Bobby Witt	.15	.04

❏	366	Mark Portugal	.15	.04
❏	367	Brian McRae	.15	.04
❏	368	Mark Lemke	.15	.04
❏	369	Bill Wegman	.15	.04
❏	370	Donovan Osborne	.15	.04
❏	371	Derrick May	.15	.04
❏	372	Carl Willis	.15	.04
❏	373	Chris Nabholz	.15	.04
❏	374	Mark Lewis	.15	.04
❏	375	John Burkett	.15	.04
❏	376	Luis Mercedes	.15	.04
❏	377	Ramon Martinez	.15	.04
❏	378	Kyle Abbott	.15	.04
❏	379	Mark Wohlers	.15	.04
❏	380	Bob Walk	.15	.04
❏	381	Kenny Rogers	.30	.09
❏	382	Tim Naehring	.15	.04
❏	383	Alex Fernandez	.15	.04
❏	384	Keith Miller	.15	.04
❏	385	Mike Henneman	.15	.04
❏	386	Rick Aguilera	.15	.04
❏	387	George Bell	.15	.04
❏	388	Mike Gallego	.15	.04
❏	389	Howard Johnson	.15	.04
❏	390	Kim Batiste	.15	.04
❏	391	Jerry Browne	.15	.04
❏	392	Damon Berryhill	.15	.04
❏	393	Ricky Bones	.15	.04
❏	394	Omar Olivares	.15	.04
❏	395	Mike Harkey	.15	.04
❏	396	Pedro Astacio	.15	.04
❏	397	John Wetteland	.30	.09
❏	398	Rod Beck	.15	.04
❏	399	Thomas Howard	.15	.04
❏	400	Mike Devereaux	.15	.04
❏	401	Tim Wakefield	.75	.23
❏	402	Curt Schilling	.30	.09
❏	403	Zane Smith	.15	.04
❏	404	Bob Zupcic	.15	.04
❏	405	Tom Browning	.15	.04
❏	406	Tony Phillips	.15	.04
❏	407	John Doherty	.15	.04
❏	408	Pat Mahomes	.15	.04
❏	409	John Habyan	.15	.04
❏	410	Steve Olin	.15	.04
❏	411	Chad Curtis	.15	.04
❏	412	Joe Grahe	.15	.04
❏	413	John Patterson	.15	.04
❏	414	Brian Hunter	.15	.04
❏	415	Doug Henry	.15	.04
❏	416	Lee Smith	.30	.09
❏	417	Bob Scanlan	.15	.04
❏	418	Kent Mercker	.15	.04
❏	419	Mel Rojas	.15	.04
❏	420	Mark Whiten	.15	.04
❏	421	Carlton Fisk	.50	.15
❏	422	Candy Maldonado	.15	.04
❏	423	Doug Drabek	.15	.04
❏	424	Wade Boggs	.50	.15
❏	425	Mark Davis	.15	.04
❏	426	Kirby Puckett	.75	.23
❏	427	Joe Carter	.30	.09
❏	428	Paul Molitor	.50	.15
❏	429	Eric Davis	.30	.09
❏	430	Darryl Kile	.30	.09
❏	431	Jeff Parrett	.15	.04
❏	432	Jeff Blauser	.15	.04
❏	433	Dan Plesac	.15	.04
❏	434	Andres Galarraga	.30	.09
❏	435	Jim Gott	.15	.04
❏	436	Jose Mesa	.15	.04
❏	437	Ben Rivera	.15	.04
❏	438	Dave Winfield	.30	.09
❏	439	Norm Charlton	.15	.04
❏	440	Chris Bosio	.15	.04
❏	441	Wilson Alvarez	.15	.04
❏	442	Dave Stewart	.30	.09
❏	443	Doug Jones	.15	.04
❏	444	Jeff Russell	.15	.04
❏	445	Ron Gant	.30	.09
❏	446	Paul O'Neill	.50	.15
❏	447	Charlie Hayes	.15	.04
❏	448	Joe Hesketh	.15	.04
❏	449	Chris Hammond	.15	.04
❏	450	Hipolito Pichardo	.15	.04
❏	451	Scott Radinsky	.15	.04
❏	452	Bobby Thigpen	.15	.04
❏	453	Xavier Hernandez	.15	.04
❏	454	Lonnie Smith	.15	.04
❏	455	Jamie Arnold DP RC	.15	.04
❏	456	B.J. Wallace DP	.15	.04
❏	457	Derek Jeter DP RC	15.00	4.50
❏	458	Jason Kendall DP RC	1.00	.30
❏	459	Rick Helling DP	.15	.04
❏	460	Derek Wallace DP RC	.15	.04
❏	461	Sean Lowe DP RC	.15	.04
❏	462	S. Stewart DP RC	1.00	.30
❏	463	Benji Grigsby DP RC	.15	.04
❏	464	T. Steverson DP RC	.15	.04
❏	465	Dan Serafini DP RC	.15	.04
❏	466	Michael Tucker DP	.30	.09
❏	467	Chris Roberts DP	.15	.04
❏	468	Pete Janicki DP RC	.15	.04
❏	469	Jeff Schmidt DP RC	.15	.04
❏	470	Don Mattingly NT	1.00	.30
❏	471	Cal Ripken Jr. NT	1.25	.35
❏	472	Jack Morris NT	.15	.04
❏	473	Terry Pendleton NT	.15	.04
❏	474	Dennis Eckersley NT	.30	.09
❏	475	Carlton Fisk NT	.30	.09
❏	476	Wade Boggs NT	.30	.09
❏	477	Len Dykstra	.30	.09
		Ken Stabler		
❏	478	Danny Tartabull	.15	.04
		Jose Tartabull		
❏	479	Jeff Conine	.50	.15
		Dale Murphy		
❏	480	Gregg Jefferies	.15	.04
		Ron Cey		
❏	481	Paul Molitor	.30	.09
		Harmon Killebrew		
❏	482	John Valentin	.15	.04
		Dave Concepcion		
❏	483	Alex Arias	.15	.04
		Dave Winfield		
❏	484	Barry Bonds HH	1.00	.30
❏	485	Doug Drabek HH	.15	.04
❏	486	Dave Winfield HH	.15	.04
❏	487	Brett Butler HH	.15	.04
❏	488	Harold Baines HH	.15	.04
❏	489	David Cone HH	.15	.04
❏	490	Willie McGee HH	.15	.04
❏	491	Robby Thompson	.15	.04
❏	492	Pete Incaviglia	.15	.04
❏	493	Manuel Lee	.15	.04
❏	494	Rafael Belliard	.15	.04
❏	495	Scott Fletcher	.15	.04
❏	496	Jeff Frye	.15	.04
❏	497	Andre Dawson	.30	.09
❏	498	Mike Scioscia	.15	.04
❏	499	Spike Owen	.15	.04
❏	500	Sid Fernandez	.15	.04
❏	501	Joe Orsulak	.15	.04
❏	502	Benito Santiago	.30	.09
❏	503	Dale Murphy	.50	.15
❏	504	Barry Bonds	2.00	.60
❏	505	Jose Guzman	.15	.04
❏	506	Tony Pena	.15	.04
❏	507	Greg Swindell	.15	.04
❏	508	Mike Pagliarulo	.15	.04
❏	509	Lou Whitaker	.30	.09
❏	510	Greg Gagne	.15	.04
❏	511	Butch Henry	.15	.04
❏	512	Jeff Brantley	.15	.04
❏	513	Jack Armstrong	.15	.04
❏	514	Danny Jackson	.15	.04
❏	515	Junior Felix	.15	.04
❏	516	Milt Thompson	.15	.04
❏	517	Greg Maddux	1.25	.35
❏	518	Eric Young	.15	.04
❏	519	Jody Reed	.15	.04
❏	520	Roberto Kelly	.15	.04
❏	521	Darren Holmes	.15	.04
❏	522	Craig Lefferts	.15	.04
❏	523	Charlie Hough	.30	.09
❏	524	Bo Jackson	.75	.23
❏	525	Bill Spiers	.15	.04
❏	526	Orestes Destrade	.15	.04
❏	527	Greg Hibbard	.15	.04
❏	528	Roger McDowell	.15	.04
❏	529	Cory Snyder	.15	.04
❏	530	Harold Reynolds	.30	.09
❏	531	Kevin Reimer	.15	.04
❏	532	Rick Sutcliffe	.30	.09
❏	533	Tony Fernandez	.15	.04
❏	534	Tom Brunansky	.15	.04
❏	535	Jeff Reardon	.30	.09
❏	536	Chili Davis	.30	.09
❏	537	Bob Ojeda	.15	.04
❏	538	Greg Colbrunn	.15	.04
❏	539	Phil Plantier	.15	.04
❏	540	Brian Jordan	.30	.09
❏	541	Pete Smith	.15	.04
❏	542	Frank Tanana	.15	.04
❏	543	John Smiley	.15	.04
❏	544	David Cone	.30	.09
❏	545	Daryl Boston	.15	.04
❏	546	Tom Henke	.15	.04
❏	547	Bill Krueger	.15	.04
❏	548	Freddie Benavides	.15	.04
❏	549	Randy Myers	.15	.04
❏	550	Reggie Jefferson	.15	.04
❏	551	Kevin Mitchell	.15	.04
❏	552	Dave Stieb	.15	.04
❏	553	Bret Barberie	.15	.04
❏	554	Tim Crews	.15	.04
❏	555	Doug Dascenzo	.15	.04
❏	556	Alex Cole	.15	.04
❏	557	Jeff Innis	.15	.04
❏	558	Carlos Garcia	.15	.04
❏	559	Steve Howe	.15	.04
❏	560	Kirk McCaskill	.15	.04
❏	561	Frank Seminara	.15	.04
❏	562	Cris Carpenter	.15	.04
❏	563	Mike Stanley	.15	.04
❏	564	Carlos Quintana	.15	.04
❏	565	Mitch Williams	.15	.04
❏	566	Juan Bell	.15	.04
❏	567	Eric Fox	.15	.04
❏	568	Al Leiter	.30	.09
❏	569	Mike Stanton	.15	.04
❏	570	Scott Kamieniecki	.15	.04
❏	571	Ryan Bowen	.15	.04
❏	572	Andy Ashby	.15	.04
❏	573	Bob Welch	.15	.04
❏	574	Scott Sanderson	.15	.04
❏	575	Joe Kmak	.15	.04
❏	576	Scott Pose RC	.15	.04
❏	577	Ricky Gutierrez	.15	.04
❏	578	Mike Trombley	.15	.04
❏	579	Sterling Hitchcock RC	.40	.12
❏	580	Rodney Bolton	.15	.04
❏	581	Tyler Green	.15	.04
❏	582	Tim Costo	.15	.04
❏	583	Tim Laker RC	.15	.04
❏	584	Steve Reed RC	.15	.04
❏	585	Tom Kramer RC	.15	.04
❏	586	Robb Nen	.30	.09
❏	587	Jim Tatum RC	.15	.04
❏	588	Frank Bolick	.15	.04
❏	589	Kevin Young	.30	.09
❏	590	Matt Whiteside RC	.15	.04
❏	591	Cesar Hernandez	.15	.04
❏	592	Mike Mohler RC	.40	.12
❏	593	Alan Embree	.15	.04
❏	594	Terry Jorgensen	.15	.04
❏	595	John Cummings RC	.15	.04
❏	596	Domingo Martinez RC	.15	.04
❏	597	Benji Gil	.15	.04
❏	598	Todd Pratt RC	.40	.12
❏	599	Rene Arocha RC	.40	.12
❏	600	Dennis Moeller	.15	.04
❏	601	Jeff Conine	.30	.09
❏	602	Trevor Hoffman	.75	.23
❏	603	Daniel Smith	.15	.04
❏	604	Lee Tinsley	.15	.04
❏	605	Dan Peltier	.15	.04
❏	606	Billy Brewer	.15	.04
❏	607	Matt Walbeck RC	.40	.12
❏	608	Richie Lewis RC	.15	.04
❏	609	J.T. Snow RC	.60	.18
❏	610	Pat Gomez RC	.15	.04
❏	611	Phil Hiatt	.15	.04
❏	612	Alex Arias	.15	.04
❏	613	Kevin Rogers	.15	.04
❏	614	Al Martin	.15	.04
❏	615	Greg Gohr	.15	.04
❏	616	Graeme Lloyd RC	.40	.12

Card	Nm-Mt	Ex-Mt
❑ 617 Kent Bottenfield	.15	.04
❑ 618 Chuck Carr	.15	.04
❑ 619 Darrell Sherman RC	.15	.04
❑ 620 Mike Lansing RC	.40	.12

1994 Pinnacle

	Nm-Mt	Ex-Mt
COMPLETE SET (540)	20.00	6.00
COMP. SERIES 1 (270)	10.00	3.00
COMP. SERIES 2 (270)	10.00	3.00

Card	Nm-Mt	Ex-Mt
❑ 1 Frank Thomas	.50	.15
❑ 2 Carlos Baerga	.10	.03
❑ 3 Sammy Sosa	.50	.15
❑ 4 Tony Gwynn	.60	.18
❑ 5 John Olerud	.20	.06
❑ 6 Ryne Sandberg	.75	.23
❑ 7 Moises Alou	.20	.06
❑ 8 Steve Avery	.10	.03
❑ 9 Tim Salmon	.30	.09
❑ 10 Cecil Fielder	.20	.06
❑ 11 Greg Maddux	.75	.23
❑ 12 Barry Larkin	.30	.09
❑ 13 Mike Devereaux	.10	.03
❑ 14 Charlie Hayes	.10	.03
❑ 15 Albert Belle	.20	.06
❑ 16 Andy Van Slyke	.30	.09
❑ 17 Mo Vaughn	.20	.06
❑ 18 Brian McRae	.10	.03
❑ 19 Cal Eldred	.10	.03
❑ 20 Craig Biggio	.30	.09
❑ 21 Kirby Puckett	.50	.15
❑ 22 Derek Bell	.10	.03
❑ 23 Don Mattingly	1.25	.35
❑ 24 John Burkett	.10	.03
❑ 25 Roger Clemens	1.00	.30
❑ 26 Barry Bonds	1.50	.45
❑ 27 Paul Molitor	.30	.09
❑ 28 Mike Piazza	1.00	.30
❑ 29 Robin Ventura	.20	.06
❑ 30 Jeff Conine	.20	.06
❑ 31 Wade Boggs	.30	.09
❑ 32 Dennis Eckersley	.20	.06
❑ 33 Bobby Bonilla	.20	.06
❑ 34 Lenny Dykstra	.20	.06
❑ 35 Manny Alexander	.10	.03
❑ 36 Ray Lankford	.20	.06
❑ 37 Greg Vaughn	.10	.03
❑ 38 Chuck Finley	.20	.06
❑ 39 Todd Benzinger	.10	.03
❑ 40 Dave Justice	.20	.06
❑ 41 Rob Dibble	.20	.06
❑ 42 Tom Henke	.10	.03
❑ 43 David Nied	.10	.03
❑ 44 Sandy Alomar Jr.	.10	.03
❑ 45 Pete Harnisch	.10	.03
❑ 46 Jeff Russell	.10	.03
❑ 47 Terry Mulholland	.10	.03
❑ 48 Kevin Appier	.20	.06
❑ 49 Randy Tomlin	.10	.03
❑ 50 Cal Ripken Jr.	1.50	.45
❑ 51 Andy Benes	.10	.03
❑ 52 Jimmy Key	.20	.06
❑ 53 Kirt Manwaring	.10	.03
❑ 54 Kevin Tapani	.10	.03
❑ 55 Jose Guzman	.10	.03
❑ 56 Todd Stottlemyre	.10	.03
❑ 57 Jack McDowell	.10	.03
❑ 58 Orel Hershiser	.20	.06
❑ 59 Chris Hammond	.10	.03
❑ 60 Chris Nabholz	.10	.03
❑ 61 Ruben Sierra	.10	.03
❑ 62 Dwight Gooden	.20	.06
❑ 63 John Kruk	.20	.06
❑ 64 Omar Vizquel	.30	.09
❑ 65 Tim Naehring	.10	.03
❑ 66 Dwight Smith	.10	.03
❑ 67 Mickey Tettleton	.10	.03
❑ 68 J.T. Snow	.20	.06
❑ 69 Greg McMichael	.10	.03
❑ 70 Kevin Mitchell	.10	.03
❑ 71 Kevin Brown	.20	.06
❑ 72 Scott Cooper	.10	.03
❑ 73 Jim Thome	.30	.09
❑ 74 Joe Girardi	.10	.03
❑ 75 Eric Anthony	.10	.03
❑ 76 Orlando Merced	.10	.03
❑ 77 Felix Jose	.10	.03
❑ 78 Tommy Greene	.10	.03
❑ 79 Bernard Gilkey	.10	.03
❑ 80 Phil Plantier	.10	.03
❑ 81 Danny Tartabull	.10	.03
❑ 82 Trevor Wilson	.10	.03
❑ 83 Chuck Knoblauch	.20	.06
❑ 84 Rick Wilkins	.10	.03
❑ 85 Devon White	.20	.06
❑ 86 Lance Johnson	.10	.03
❑ 87 Eric Karros	.20	.06
❑ 88 Gary Sheffield	.20	.06
❑ 89 Wil Cordero	.10	.03
❑ 90 Ron Darling	.10	.03
❑ 91 Darren Daulton	.20	.06
❑ 92 Joe Orsulak	.10	.03
❑ 93 Steve Cooke	.10	.03
❑ 94 Darryl Hamilton	.10	.03
❑ 95 Aaron Sele	.10	.03
❑ 96 John Doherty	.10	.03
❑ 97 Gary DiSarcina	.10	.03
❑ 98 Jeff Blauser	.10	.03
❑ 99 John Smiley	.10	.03
❑ 100 Ken Griffey Jr.	.75	.23
❑ 101 Dean Palmer	.20	.06
❑ 102 Felix Fermin	.10	.03
❑ 103 Jerald Clark	.10	.03
❑ 104 Doug Drabek	.10	.03
❑ 105 Curt Schilling	.20	.06
❑ 106 Jeff Montgomery	.10	.03
❑ 107 Rene Arocha	.10	.03
❑ 108 Carlos Garcia	.10	.03
❑ 109 Wally Whitehurst	.10	.03
❑ 110 Jim Abbott	.30	.09
❑ 111 Royce Clayton	.10	.03
❑ 112 Chris Hoiles	.10	.03
❑ 113 Mike Morgan	.10	.03
❑ 114 Joe Magrane	.10	.03
❑ 115 Tom Candiotti	.10	.03
❑ 116 Ron Karkovice	.10	.03
❑ 117 Ryan Bowen	.10	.03
❑ 118 Rod Beck	.10	.03
❑ 119 John Wetteland	.20	.06
❑ 120 Terry Steinbach	.10	.03
❑ 121 Dave Hollins	.10	.03
❑ 122 Jeff Kent	.30	.09
❑ 123 Ricky Bones	.10	.03
❑ 124 Brian Jordan	.20	.06
❑ 125 Chad Kreuter	.10	.03
❑ 126 John Valentin	.10	.03
❑ 127 Hilly Hathaway	.10	.03
❑ 128 Wilson Alvarez	.10	.03
❑ 129 Tino Martinez	.30	.09
❑ 130 Rodney Bolton	.10	.03
❑ 131 David Segui	.10	.03
❑ 132 Wayne Kirby	.10	.03
❑ 133 Eric Young	.10	.03
❑ 134 Scott Servais	.10	.03
❑ 135 Scott Radinsky	.10	.03
❑ 136 Bret Barberie	.10	.03
❑ 137 John Roper	.10	.03
❑ 138 Ricky Gutierrez	.10	.03
❑ 139 Bernie Williams	.30	.09
❑ 140 Bud Black	.10	.03
❑ 141 Jose Vizcaino	.10	.03
❑ 142 Gerald Williams	.10	.03
❑ 143 Duane Ward	.10	.03
❑ 144 Danny Jackson	.10	.03
❑ 145 Allen Watson	.10	.03
❑ 146 Scott Fletcher	.10	.03
❑ 147 Delino DeShields	.10	.03
❑ 148 Shane Mack	.10	.03
❑ 149 Jim Eisenreich	.10	.03
❑ 150 Troy Neel	.10	.03
❑ 151 Jay Bell	.20	.06
❑ 152 B.J. Surhoff	.20	.06
❑ 153 Mark Whiten	.10	.03
❑ 154 Mike Henneman	.10	.03
❑ 155 Todd Hundley	.10	.03
❑ 156 Greg Myers	.10	.03
❑ 157 Ryan Klesko	.20	.06
❑ 158 Dave Fleming	.10	.03
❑ 159 Mickey Morandini	.10	.03
❑ 160 Blas Minor	.10	.03
❑ 161 Reggie Jefferson	.10	.03
❑ 162 David Hulse	.10	.03
❑ 163 Greg Swindell	.10	.03
❑ 164 Roberto Hernandez	.10	.03
❑ 165 Brady Anderson	.20	.06
❑ 166 Jack Armstrong	.10	.03
❑ 167 Phil Clark	.10	.03
❑ 168 Melido Perez	.10	.03
❑ 169 Darren Lewis	.10	.03
❑ 170 Sam Horn	.10	.03
❑ 171 Mike Harkey	.10	.03
❑ 172 Juan Guzman	.10	.03
❑ 173 Bob Natal	.10	.03
❑ 174 Deion Sanders	.30	.09
❑ 175 Carlos Quintana	.10	.03
❑ 176 Mel Rojas	.10	.03
❑ 177 Willie Banks	.10	.03
❑ 178 Ben Rivera	.10	.03
❑ 179 Kenny Lofton	.20	.06
❑ 180 Leo Gomez	.10	.03
❑ 181 Roberto Mejia	.10	.03
❑ 182 Mike Perez	.10	.03
❑ 183 Travis Fryman	.20	.06
❑ 184 Ben McDonald	.10	.03
❑ 185 Steve Frey	.10	.03
❑ 186 Kevin Young	.10	.03
❑ 187 Dave Magadan	.10	.03
❑ 188 Bobby Munoz	.10	.03
❑ 189 Pat Rapp	.10	.03
❑ 190 Jose Offerman	.10	.03
❑ 191 Vinny Castilla	.20	.06
❑ 192 Ivan Calderon	.10	.03
❑ 193 Ken Caminiti	.20	.06
❑ 194 Benji Gil	.10	.03
❑ 195 Chuck Carr	.10	.03
❑ 196 Derrick May	.10	.03
❑ 197 Pat Kelly	.10	.03
❑ 198 Jeff Brantley	.10	.03
❑ 199 Jose Lind	.10	.03
❑ 200 Steve Buechele	.10	.03
❑ 201 Wes Chamberlain	.10	.03
❑ 202 Eduardo Perez	.10	.03
❑ 203 Bret Saberhagen	.20	.06
❑ 204 Gregg Jefferies	.10	.03
❑ 205 Darrin Fletcher	.10	.03
❑ 206 Kent Hrbek	.20	.06
❑ 207 Kim Batiste	.10	.03
❑ 208 Jeff King	.10	.03
❑ 209 Donovan Osborne	.10	.03
❑ 210 Dave Nilsson	.10	.03
❑ 211 Al Martin	.10	.03
❑ 212 Mike Moore	.10	.03
❑ 213 Sterling Hitchcock	.10	.03
❑ 214 Geronimo Pena	.10	.03
❑ 215 Kevin Higgins	.10	.03
❑ 216 Norm Charlton	.10	.03
❑ 217 Don Slaught	.10	.03
❑ 218 Mitch Williams	.10	.03
❑ 219 Derek Lilliquist	.10	.03
❑ 220 Armando Reynoso	.10	.03
❑ 221 Kenny Rogers	.20	.06
❑ 222 Doug Jones	.10	.03
❑ 223 Luis Aquino	.10	.03
❑ 224 Mike Oquist	.10	.03
❑ 225 Darryl Scott	.10	.03
❑ 226 Kurt Abbott RC	.40	.12
❑ 227 Andy Tomberlin	.10	.03
❑ 228 Norberto Martin	.10	.03
❑ 229 Pedro Castellano	.10	.03

- ❑ 230 Curtis Pride RC .40 .12
- ❑ 231 Jeff McNeely .10 .03
- ❑ 232 Scott Lydy .10 .03
- ❑ 233 Darren Oliver RC .40 .12
- ❑ 234 Danny Bautista .10 .03
- ❑ 235 Butch Huskey .10 .03
- ❑ 236 Chipper Jones .50 .15
- ❑ 237 Eddie Zambrano RC .10 .03
- ❑ 238 Domingo Jean .10 .03
- ❑ 239 Javier Lopez .20 .06
- ❑ 240 Nigel Wilson .10 .03
- ❑ 241 Drew Denson .10 .03
- ❑ 242 Raul Mondesi .20 .06
- ❑ 243 Luis Ortiz .10 .03
- ❑ 244 Manny Ramirez .50 .15
- ❑ 245 Greg Blosser .10 .03
- ❑ 246 Rondell White .20 .06
- ❑ 247 Steve Karsay .10 .03
- ❑ 248 Scott Stahoviak .10 .03
- ❑ 249 Jose Valentin .10 .03
- ❑ 250 Marc Newfield .10 .03
- ❑ 251 Keith Kessinger .10 .03
- ❑ 252 Carl Everett .20 .06
- ❑ 253 John O'Donoghue .10 .03
- ❑ 254 Turk Wendell .10 .03
- ❑ 255 Scott Ruffcorn .10 .03
- ❑ 256 Tony Tarasco .10 .03
- ❑ 257 Andy Cook .10 .03
- ❑ 258 Matt Mieske .10 .03
- ❑ 259 Luis Lopez .10 .03
- ❑ 260 Ramon Caraballo .10 .03
- ❑ 261 Salomon Torres .10 .03
- ❑ 262 Brooks Kieschnick RC .40 .12
- ❑ 263 Daron Kirkreit .10 .03
- ❑ 264 Bill Wagner RC 1.50 .45
- ❑ 265 Matt Drews RC .10 .03
- ❑ 266 Scott Christman RC .10 .03
- ❑ 267 Torii Hunter RC 1.50 .45
- ❑ 268 Jamey Wright RC .10 .03
- ❑ 269 Jeff Granger .10 .03
- ❑ 270 Trot Nixon RC 1.50 .45
- ❑ 271 Randy Myers .10 .03
- ❑ 272 Trevor Hoffman .30 .09
- ❑ 273 Bob Wickman .10 .03
- ❑ 274 Willie McGee .20 .06
- ❑ 275 Hipolito Pichardo .10 .03
- ❑ 276 Bobby Witt .10 .03
- ❑ 277 Gregg Olson .10 .03
- ❑ 278 Randy Johnson .50 .15
- ❑ 279 Robb Nen .20 .06
- ❑ 280 Paul O'Neill .30 .09
- ❑ 281 Lou Whitaker .20 .06
- ❑ 282 Chad Curtis .10 .03
- ❑ 283 Doug Henry .10 .03
- ❑ 284 Tom Glavine .30 .09
- ❑ 285 Mike Greenwell .10 .03
- ❑ 286 Roberto Kelly .10 .03
- ❑ 287 Roberto Alomar .30 .09
- ❑ 288 Charlie Hough .20 .06
- ❑ 289 Alex Fernandez .10 .03
- ❑ 290 Jeff Bagwell .30 .09
- ❑ 291 Wally Joyner .20 .06
- ❑ 292 Andujar Cedeno .10 .03
- ❑ 293 Rick Aguilera .10 .03
- ❑ 294 Darryl Strawberry .20 .06
- ❑ 295 Mike Mussina .30 .09
- ❑ 296 Jeff Gardner .10 .03
- ❑ 297 Chris Gwynn .10 .03
- ❑ 298 Matt Williams .20 .06
- ❑ 299 Brent Gates .10 .03
- ❑ 300 Mark McGwire 1.25 .35
- ❑ 301 Jim Deshaies .10 .03
- ❑ 302 Edgar Martinez .30 .09
- ❑ 303 Danny Darwin .10 .03
- ❑ 304 Pat Meares .10 .03
- ❑ 305 Benito Santiago .20 .06
- ❑ 306 Jose Canseco .30 .09
- ❑ 307 Jim Gott .10 .03
- ❑ 308 Paul Sorrento .10 .03
- ❑ 309 Scott Kamieniecki .10 .03
- ❑ 310 Larry Walker .20 .06
- ❑ 311 Mark Langston .10 .03
- ❑ 312 John Jaha .10 .03
- ❑ 313 Stan Javier .10 .03
- ❑ 314 Hal Morris .10 .03
- ❑ 315 Robby Thompson .10 .03
- ❑ 316 Pat Hentgen .10 .03
- ❑ 317 Tom Gordon .10 .03
- ❑ 318 Joey Cora .10 .03
- ❑ 319 Luis Alicea .10 .03
- ❑ 320 Andre Dawson .20 .06
- ❑ 321 Darryl Kile .20 .06
- ❑ 322 Jose Rijo .10 .03
- ❑ 323 Luis Gonzalez .20 .06
- ❑ 324 Billy Ashley .10 .03
- ❑ 325 David Cone .20 .06
- ❑ 326 Bill Swift .10 .03
- ❑ 327 Phil Hiatt .10 .03
- ❑ 328 Craig Paquette .10 .03
- ❑ 329 Bob Welch .10 .03
- ❑ 330 Tony Phillips .10 .03
- ❑ 331 Archi Cianfrocco .10 .03
- ❑ 332 Dave Winfield .20 .06
- ❑ 333 David McCarty .10 .03
- ❑ 334 Al Leiter .20 .06
- ❑ 335 Tom Browning .10 .03
- ❑ 336 Mark Grace .30 .09
- ❑ 337 Jose Mesa .10 .03
- ❑ 338 Mike Stanley .10 .03
- ❑ 339 Roger McDowell .10 .03
- ❑ 340 Damion Easley .10 .03
- ❑ 341 Angel Miranda .10 .03
- ❑ 342 John Smoltz .30 .09
- ❑ 343 Jay Buhner .20 .06
- ❑ 344 Bryan Harvey .10 .03
- ❑ 345 Joe Carter .20 .06
- ❑ 346 Dante Bichette .20 .06
- ❑ 347 Jason Bere .10 .03
- ❑ 348 Frank Viola .20 .06
- ❑ 349 Ivan Rodriguez .30 .09
- ❑ 350 Juan Gonzalez .20 .06
- ❑ 351 Steve Finley .20 .06
- ❑ 352 Mike Felder .10 .03
- ❑ 353 Ramon Martinez .10 .03
- ❑ 354 Greg Gagne .10 .03
- ❑ 355 Ken Hill .10 .03
- ❑ 356 Pedro Munoz .10 .03
- ❑ 357 Todd Van Poppel .10 .03
- ❑ 358 Marquis Grissom .20 .06
- ❑ 359 Milt Cuyler .10 .03
- ❑ 360 Reggie Sanders .20 .06
- ❑ 361 Scott Erickson .10 .03
- ❑ 362 Billy Hatcher .10 .03
- ❑ 363 Gene Harris .10 .03
- ❑ 364 Rene Gonzales .10 .03
- ❑ 365 Kevin Rogers .10 .03
- ❑ 366 Eric Plunk .10 .03
- ❑ 367 Todd Zeile .10 .03
- ❑ 368 John Franco .20 .06
- ❑ 369 Brett Butler .20 .06
- ❑ 370 Bill Spiers .10 .03
- ❑ 371 Terry Pendleton .20 .06
- ❑ 372 Chris Bosio .10 .03
- ❑ 373 Orestes Destrade .10 .03
- ❑ 374 Dave Stewart .20 .06
- ❑ 375 Darren Holmes .10 .03
- ❑ 376 Doug Strange .10 .03
- ❑ 377 Brian Turang .10 .03
- ❑ 378 Carl Wills .10 .03
- ❑ 379 Mark McLemore .10 .03
- ❑ 380 Bobby Jones .10 .03
- ❑ 381 Scott Sanders .10 .03
- ❑ 382 Kirk Rueter .20 .06
- ❑ 383 Randy Velarde .10 .03
- ❑ 384 Fred McGriff .30 .09
- ❑ 385 Charles Nagy .10 .03
- ❑ 386 Rich Amaral .10 .03
- ❑ 387 Geronimo Berroa .10 .03
- ❑ 388 Eric Davis .20 .06
- ❑ 389 Ozzie Smith .75 .23
- ❑ 390 Alex Arias .10 .03
- ❑ 391 Brad Ausmus .20 .06
- ❑ 392 Cliff Floyd .20 .06
- ❑ 393 Roger Salkeld .10 .03
- ❑ 394 Jim Edmonds .50 .15
- ❑ 395 Jeromy Burnitz .20 .06
- ❑ 396 Dave Staton .10 .03
- ❑ 397 Rob Butler .10 .03
- ❑ 398 Marcos Armas .10 .03
- ❑ 399 Darrell Whitmore .10 .03
- ❑ 400 Ryan Thompson .10 .03
- ❑ 401 Ross Powell RC .10 .03
- ❑ 402 Joe Oliver .10 .03
- ❑ 403 Paul Carey .10 .03
- ❑ 404 Bob Hamelin .10 .03
- ❑ 405 Chris Turner .10 .03
- ❑ 406 Nate Minchey .10 .03
- ❑ 407 Lonnie Maclin RC .10 .03
- ❑ 408 Harold Baines .20 .06
- ❑ 409 Brian Williams .10 .03
- ❑ 410 Johnny Ruffin .10 .03
- ❑ 411 Julian Tavarez RC .10 .03
- ❑ 412 Mark Hutton .10 .03
- ❑ 413 Carlos Delgado .30 .09
- ❑ 414 Chris Gomez .10 .03
- ❑ 415 Mike Hampton .20 .06
- ❑ 416 Alex Diaz RC .10 .03
- ❑ 417 Jeffrey Hammonds .10 .03
- ❑ 418 Jayhawk Owens .10 .03
- ❑ 419 J.R. Phillips .10 .03
- ❑ 420 Cory Bailey RC .10 .03
- ❑ 421 Denny Hocking .10 .03
- ❑ 422 Jon Shave .10 .03
- ❑ 423 Damon Buford .10 .03
- ❑ 424 Troy O'Leary .10 .03
- ❑ 425 Tripp Cromer .10 .03
- ❑ 426 Albie Lopez .10 .03
- ❑ 427 Tony Fernandez .10 .03
- ❑ 428 Ozzie Guillen .20 .06
- ❑ 429 Alan Trammell .20 .06
- ❑ 430 John Wasdin RC .10 .03
- ❑ 431 Marc Valdes .10 .03
- ❑ 432 Brian Anderson RC .40 .12
- ❑ 433 Matt Brunson RC .10 .03
- ❑ 434 Wayne Gomes RC .10 .03
- ❑ 435 Jay Powell RC .10 .03
- ❑ 436 Kirk Presley RC .10 .03
- ❑ 437 Jon Ratliff RC .10 .03
- ❑ 438 Derrek Lee RC 4.00 1.20
- ❑ 439 Tom Pagnozzi .10 .03
- ❑ 440 Kent Mercker .10 .03
- ❑ 441 Phil Leftwich RC .10 .03
- ❑ 442 Jamie Moyer .20 .06
- ❑ 443 John Flaherty .10 .03
- ❑ 444 Mark Wohlers .10 .03
- ❑ 445 Jose Bautista .10 .03
- ❑ 446 Andres Galarraga .20 .06
- ❑ 447 Mark Lemke .10 .03
- ❑ 448 Tim Wakefield .30 .09
- ❑ 449 Pat Listach .10 .03
- ❑ 450 Rickey Henderson .50 .15
- ❑ 451 Mike Gallego .10 .03
- ❑ 452 Bob Tewksbury .10 .03
- ❑ 453 Kirk Gibson .30 .09
- ❑ 454 Pedro Astacio .10 .03
- ❑ 455 Mike Lansing .10 .03
- ❑ 456 Sean Berry .10 .03
- ❑ 457 Bob Walk .10 .03
- ❑ 458 Chili Davis .20 .06
- ❑ 459 Ed Sprague .10 .03
- ❑ 460 Kevin Stocker .10 .03
- ❑ 461 Mike Stanton .10 .03
- ❑ 462 Tim Raines .20 .06
- ❑ 463 Mike Bordick .10 .03
- ❑ 464 David Wells .20 .06
- ❑ 465 Tim Laker .10 .03
- ❑ 466 Cory Snyder .10 .03
- ❑ 467 Alex Cole .10 .03
- ❑ 468 Pete Incaviglia .10 .03
- ❑ 469 Roger Pavlik .10 .03
- ❑ 470 Greg W. Harris .10 .03
- ❑ 471 Xavier Hernandez .10 .03
- ❑ 472 Erik Hanson .10 .03
- ❑ 473 Jesse Orosco .10 .03
- ❑ 474 Greg Colbrunn .10 .03
- ❑ 475 Harold Reynolds .20 .06
- ❑ 476 Greg A. Harris .10 .03
- ❑ 477 Pat Borders .10 .03
- ❑ 478 Melvin Nieves .10 .03
- ❑ 479 Mariano Duncan .10 .03
- ❑ 480 Greg Hibbard .10 .03
- ❑ 481 Tim Pugh .10 .03
- ❑ 482 Bobby Ayala .10 .03
- ❑ 483 Sid Fernandez .10 .03
- ❑ 484 Tim Wallach .10 .03
- ❑ 485 Randy Milligan .10 .03
- ❑ 486 Walt Weiss .10 .03
- ❑ 487 Matt Walbeck .10 .03

❑ 488 Mike Macfarlane .10 .03
❑ 489 Jerry Browne .10 .03
❑ 490 Chris Sabo .10 .03
❑ 491 Tim Belcher .10 .03
❑ 492 Spike Owen .10 .03
❑ 493 Rafael Palmeiro .30 .09
❑ 494 Brian Harper .10 .03
❑ 495 Eddie Murray .50 .15
❑ 496 Ellis Burks .20 .06
❑ 497 Karl Rhodes .10 .03
❑ 498 Otis Nixon .10 .03
❑ 499 Lee Smith .20 .06
❑ 500 Bip Roberts .10 .03
❑ 501 Pedro Martinez .50 .15
❑ 502 Brian Hunter .10 .03
❑ 503 Tyler Green .10 .03
❑ 504 Bruce Hurst .10 .03
❑ 505 Alex Gonzalez .10 .03
❑ 506 Mark Portugal .10 .03
❑ 507 Bob Ojeda .10 .03
❑ 508 Dave Henderson .10 .03
❑ 509 Bo Jackson .50 .15
❑ 510 Bret Boone .20 .06
❑ 511 Mark Eichhorn .10 .03
❑ 512 Luis Polonia .10 .03
❑ 513 Will Clark .30 .09
❑ 514 Dave Valle .10 .03
❑ 515 Dan Wilson .10 .03
❑ 516 Dennis Martinez .20 .06
❑ 517 Jim Leyritz .10 .03
❑ 518 Howard Johnson .10 .03
❑ 519 Jody Reed .10 .03
❑ 520 Julio Franco .20 .06
❑ 521 Jeff Reardon .20 .06
❑ 522 Willie Greene .10 .03
❑ 523 Shawon Dunston .10 .03
❑ 524 Keith Mitchell .10 .03
❑ 525 Rick Helling .10 .03
❑ 526 Mark Kiefer .10 .03
❑ 527 Chan Ho Park RC .50 .15
❑ 528 Tony Longmire .10 .03
❑ 529 Rich Becker .10 .03
❑ 530 Tim Hyers RC .10 .03
❑ 531 Darrin Jackson .10 .03
❑ 532 Jack Morris .20 .06
❑ 533 Rick White .10 .03
❑ 534 Mike Kelly .10 .03
❑ 535 James Mouton .10 .03
❑ 536 Steve Trachsel .10 .03
❑ 537 Tony Eusebio .10 .03
❑ 538 Kelly Stinnett RC .40 .12
❑ 539 Paul Spoljaric .10 .03
❑ 540 Darren Dreifort .10 .03
❑ SR1 Carlos Delgado 5.00 1.50
Super Rookie

1939 Play Ball

	Ex-Mt	VG
COMPLETE SET (161)	10000.00	5000.00
COMMON CARD (1-115)	20.00	10.00
COMMON (116-162)	75.00	38.00
WRAPPER (1-CENT)	200.00	100.00

❑ 1 Jake Powell 60.00 18.00
❑ 2 Lee Grissom 20.00 10.00
❑ 3 Red Ruffing 75.00 38.00
❑ 4 Eldon Auker 20.00 10.00
❑ 5 Luke Sewell 25.00 12.50
❑ 6 Leo Durocher 100.00 50.00
❑ 7 Bobby Doerr 75.00 38.00
❑ 8 Henry Pippen 20.00 10.00
❑ 9 James Tobin 20.00 10.00
❑ 10 James DeShong 20.00 10.00
❑ 11 Johnny Rizzo 20.00 10.00
❑ 12 Hershel Martin 20.00 10.00
❑ 13 Luke Hamlin 20.00 10.00
❑ 14 Jim Tabor 20.00 10.00
❑ 15 Paul Derringer 30.00 15.00
❑ 16 John Peacock 20.00 10.00
❑ 17 Emerson Dickman 20.00 10.00
❑ 18 Harry Danning 20.00 10.00
❑ 19 Paul Dean 40.00 20.00
❑ 20 Joe Heving 20.00 10.00
❑ 21 Dutch Leonard 30.00 15.00
❑ 22 Bucky Walters 30.00 15.00
❑ 23 Burgess Whitehead 20.00 10.00
❑ 24 Richard Coffman 20.00 10.00
❑ 25 George Selkirk 40.00 20.00
❑ 26 Joe DiMaggio 1400.00 700.00
❑ 27 Fred Ostermueller 20.00 10.00
❑ 28 Sylvester Johnson 20.00 10.00
❑ 29 John(Jack) Wilson 20.00 10.00
❑ 30 Bill Dickey 125.00 60.00
❑ 31 Sam West 20.00 10.00
❑ 32 Bob Seeds 20.00 10.00
❑ 33 Del Young 20.00 10.00
❑ 34 Frank Demaree 20.00 10.00
❑ 35 Bill Jurges 20.00 10.00
❑ 36 Frank McCormick 20.00 10.00
❑ 37 Virgil Davis 20.00 10.00
❑ 38 Billy Myers 20.00 10.00
❑ 39 Rick Ferrell 75.00 38.00
❑ 40 James Bagby Jr. 20.00 10.00
❑ 41 Lon Warneke 25.00 12.50
❑ 42 Arndt Jorgens 20.00 10.00
❑ 43 Melo Almada 25.00 12.50
❑ 44 Don Heffner 20.00 10.00
❑ 45 Merrill May 20.00 10.00
❑ 46 Morris Arnovich 20.00 10.00
❑ 47 Buddy Lewis 20.00 10.00
❑ 48 Lefty Gomez 125.00 60.00
❑ 49 Eddie Miller 20.00 10.00
❑ 50 Charley Gehringer 125.00 60.00
❑ 51 Mel Ott 125.00 60.00
❑ 52 Tommy Henrich 40.00 20.00
❑ 53 Carl Hubbell 125.00 60.00
❑ 54 Harry Gumpert 20.00 10.00
❑ 55 Arky Vaughan 75.00 38.00
❑ 56 Hank Greenberg 200.00 100.00
❑ 57 Buddy Hassett 20.00 10.00
❑ 58 Lou Chiozza 20.00 10.00
❑ 59 Ken Chase 20.00 10.00
❑ 60 Schoolboy Rowe 40.00 20.00
❑ 61 Tony Cuccinello 25.00 12.50
❑ 62 Tom Carey 20.00 10.00
❑ 63 Emmett Mueller 20.00 10.00
❑ 64 Wally Moses 25.00 12.50
❑ 65 Harry Craft 25.00 12.50
❑ 66 Jimmy Ripple 20.00 10.00
❑ 67 Ed Joost 25.00 12.50
❑ 68 Fred Sington 20.00 10.00
❑ 69 Elbie Fletcher 20.00 10.00
❑ 70 Fred Frankhouse 20.00 10.00
❑ 71 Monte Pearson 30.00 15.00
❑ 72 Debs Garms 20.00 10.00
❑ 73 Hal Schumacher 25.00 12.50
❑ 74 Cookie Lavagetto 25.00 12.50
❑ 75 Stan Bordagaray 20.00 10.00
❑ 76 Goody Rosen 20.00 10.00
❑ 77 Lew Riggs 20.00 10.00
❑ 78 Julius Solters 20.00 10.00
❑ 79 Jo Jo Moore 20.00 10.00
❑ 80 Pete Fox 20.00 10.00
❑ 81 Babe Dahlgren 30.00 15.00
❑ 82 Chuck Klein 100.00 50.00
❑ 83 Gus Suhr 20.00 10.00
❑ 84 Skeeter Newsom 20.00 10.00
❑ 85 Johnny Cooney 20.00 10.00
❑ 86 Dolph Camilli 25.00 12.50
❑ 87 Milburn Shoffner 20.00 10.00
❑ 88 Charlie Keller 40.00 20.00
❑ 89 Lloyd Waner 75.00 38.00
❑ 90 Robert Klinger 20.00 10.00
❑ 91 John Knott 20.00 10.00
❑ 92 Ted Williams 1500.00 750.00
❑ 93 Charles Gelbert 20.00 10.00
❑ 94 Heinie Manush 75.00 38.00
❑ 95 Whit Wyatt 25.00 12.50
❑ 96 Babe Phelps 20.00 10.00
❑ 97 Bob Johnson 30.00 15.00
❑ 98 Pinky Whitney 20.00 10.00
❑ 99 Wally Berger 30.00 15.00
❑ 100 Buddy Myer 25.00 12.50
❑ 101 Roger Cramer 25.00 12.50
❑ 102 Lem Young 20.00 10.00
❑ 103 Moe Berg 125.00 60.00
❑ 104 Tom Bridges 25.00 12.50
❑ 105 Rabbit McNair 20.00 10.00
❑ 106 Dolly Stark UMP 30.00 15.00
❑ 107 Joe Vosmik 20.00 10.00
❑ 108 Frank Hayes 20.00 10.00
❑ 109 Myril Hoag 20.00 10.00
❑ 110 Fred Fitzsimmons 25.00 12.50
❑ 111 Van Lingle Mungo 30.00 15.00
❑ 112 Paul Waner 100.00 50.00
❑ 113 Al Schacht 30.00 15.00
❑ 114 Cecil Travis 25.00 12.50
❑ 115 Ralph Kress 20.00 10.00
❑ 116 Gene Desautels 75.00 38.00
❑ 117 Wayne Ambler 75.00 38.00
❑ 118 Lynn Nelson 75.00 38.00
❑ 119 Will Hershberger 100.00 50.00
❑ 120 Rabbit Warstler 75.00 38.00
❑ 121 Bill Posedel 75.00 38.00
❑ 122 George McQuinn 75.00 38.00
❑ 123 Ray T. Davis 75.00 38.00
❑ 124 Walter Brown 75.00 38.00
❑ 125 Cliff Melton 75.00 38.00
❑ 126 Not issued .00
❑ 127 Gil Brack 75.00 38.00
❑ 128 Joe Bowman 75.00 38.00
❑ 129 Bill Swift 75.00 38.00
❑ 130 Bill Brubaker 75.00 38.00
❑ 131 Mort Cooper 100.00 50.00
❑ 132 Jim Brown 75.00 38.00
❑ 133 Lynn Myers 75.00 38.00
❑ 134 Tot Presnell 75.00 38.00
❑ 135 Mickey Owen 100.00 50.00
❑ 136 Roy Bell 75.00 38.00
❑ 137 Pete Appleton 75.00 38.00
❑ 138 George Case 100.00 50.00
❑ 139 Vito Tamulis 75.00 38.00
❑ 140 Ray Hayworth 75.00 38.00
❑ 141 Pete Coscarart 75.00 38.00
❑ 142 Ira Hutchinson 75.00 38.00
❑ 143 Earl Averill 175.00 90.00
❑ 144 Zeke Bonura 100.00 50.00
❑ 145 Hugh Mulcahy 75.00 38.00
❑ 146 Tom Sunkel 75.00 38.00
❑ 147 George Coffman 75.00 38.00
❑ 148 Bill Trotter 75.00 38.00
❑ 149 Max West 75.00 38.00
❑ 150 James Walkup 75.00 38.00
❑ 151 Hugh Casey 100.00 50.00
❑ 152 Roy Weatherly 75.00 38.00
❑ 153 Dizzy Trout 100.00 50.00
❑ 154 Johnny Hudson 75.00 38.00
❑ 155 Jimmy Outlaw 75.00 38.00
❑ 156 Ray Berres 75.00 38.00
❑ 157 Don Padgett 75.00 38.00
❑ 158 Bud Thomas 75.00 38.00
❑ 159 Red Evans 75.00 38.00
❑ 160 Gene Moore 75.00 38.00
❑ 161 Lonnie Frey 75.00 38.00
❑ 162 Whitey Moore 100.00 50.00

1940 Play Ball

	Ex-Mt	VG
COMPLETE SET (240)	15000.00	7500.00
COMMON CARD (1-120)	20.00	10.00
COMMON (121-180)	20.00	10.00
COMMON (181-240)	70.00	35.00
WRAP.(1-CENT, DIFF. COL.)	800.00	400.00

❑ 1 Joe DiMaggio 2500.00 1000.00
❑ 2 Art Jorgens 25.00 12.50
❑ 3 Babe Dahlgren 25.00 12.50
❑ 4 Tommy Henrich .00 .00
❑ 5 Monte Pearson 25.00 12.50
❑ 6 Lefty Gomez 150.00 75.00
❑ 7 Bill Dickey 175.00 90.00

	No.	Player	Ex-Mt	VG
❑	8	George Selkirk	25.00	12.50
❑	9	Charlie Keller	.00	.00
❑	10	Red Ruffing	90.00	45.00
❑	11	Jake Powell	25.00	12.50
❑	12	Johnny Schulte	20.00	10.00
❑	13	Jack Knott	20.00	10.00
❑	14	Rabbit McNair	20.00	10.00
❑	15	George Case	25.00	12.50
❑	16	Cecil Travis	25.00	12.50
❑	17	Buddy Myer	25.00	12.50
❑	18	Charlie Gelbert	20.00	10.00
❑	19	Ken Chase	20.00	10.00
❑	20	Buddy Lewis	20.00	10.00
❑	21	Rick Ferrell	80.00	40.00
❑	22	Sammy West	20.00	10.00
❑	23	Dutch Leonard	25.00	12.50
❑	24	Frank Hayes	20.00	10.00
❑	25	Bob Johnson	25.00	12.50
❑	26	Wally Moses	25.00	12.50
❑	27	Ted Williams	1200.00	600.00
❑	28	Gene Desautels	20.00	10.00
❑	29	Doc Cramer	25.00	12.50
❑	30	Moe Berg	150.00	75.00
❑	31	Jack Wilson	20.00	10.00
❑	32	Jim Bagby	20.00	10.00
❑	33	Fritz Ostermueller	20.00	10.00
❑	34	John Peacock	20.00	10.00
❑	35	Joe Heving	20.00	10.00
❑	36	Jim Tabor	20.00	10.00
❑	37	Emerson Dickman	20.00	10.00
❑	38	Bobby Doerr	90.00	45.00
❑	39	Tom Carey	20.00	10.00
❑	40	Hank Greenberg	200.00	100.00
❑	41	Charley Gehringer	150.00	75.00
❑	42	Bud Thomas	20.00	10.00
❑	43	Pete Fox	20.00	10.00
❑	44	Dizzy Trout	25.00	12.50
❑	45	Red Kress	20.00	10.00
❑	46	Earl Averill	90.00	45.00
❑	47	Oscar Vitt	20.00	10.00
❑	48	Luke Sewell	25.00	12.50
❑	49	Stormy Weatherly	20.00	10.00
❑	50	Hal Trosky	25.00	12.50
❑	51	Don Heffner	20.00	10.00
❑	52	Myril Hoag	20.00	10.00
❑	53	George McQuinn	25.00	12.50
❑	54	Bill Trotter	20.00	10.00
❑	55	Slick Coffman	20.00	10.00
❑	56	Eddie Miller	25.00	12.50
❑	57	Max West	20.00	10.00
❑	58	Bill Posedel	20.00	10.00
❑	59	Rabbit Warstler	20.00	10.00
❑	60	John Cooney	20.00	10.00
❑	61	Tony Cuccinello	25.00	12.50
❑	62	Buddy Hassett	20.00	10.00
❑	63	Pete Coscarart	20.00	10.00
❑	64	Van Lingle Mungo	25.00	12.50
❑	65	Fred Fitzsimmons	25.00	12.50
❑	66	Babe Phelps	20.00	10.00
❑	67	Whit Wyatt	25.00	12.50
❑	68	Dolph Camilli	25.00	12.50
❑	69	Cookie Lavagetto	25.00	12.50
❑	70	Luke Hamlin (Hot Potato)	20.00	10.00
❑	71	Mel Almada	20.00	10.00
❑	72	Chuck Dressen	25.00	12.50
❑	73	Bucky Walters	25.00	12.50
❑	74	Paul(Duke) Derringer	25.00	12.50
❑	75	Frank(Buck)McCormick	25.00	12.50
❑	76	Lonny Frey	20.00	10.00
❑	77	Willard Hershberger	25.00	12.50
❑	78	Lew Riggs	20.00	10.00
❑	79	Harry Craft	25.00	12.50
❑	80	Billy Myers	20.00	10.00
❑	81	Wally Berger	25.00	12.50
❑	82	Hank Gowdy CO	25.00	12.50
❑	83	Cliff Melton	20.00	10.00
❑	84	Jo Jo Moore	20.00	10.00
❑	85	Hal Schumacher	25.00	12.50
❑	86	Harry Gumbert	20.00	10.00
❑	87	Carl Hubbell	125.00	60.00
❑	88	Mel Ott	175.00	90.00
❑	89	Bill Jurges	20.00	10.00
❑	90	Frank Demaree	20.00	10.00
❑	91	Bob Seeds	20.00	10.00
❑	92	Whitey Whitehead	20.00	10.00
❑	93	Harry Danning	20.00	10.00
❑	94	Gus Suhr	20.00	10.00
❑	95	Hugh Mulcahy	20.00	10.00
❑	96	Heinie Mueller	20.00	10.00
❑	97	Morry Arnovich	20.00	10.00
❑	98	Pinky May	20.00	10.00
❑	99	Syl Johnson	20.00	10.00
❑	100	Hersh Martin	20.00	10.00
❑	101	Del Young	20.00	10.00
❑	102	Chuck Klein	100.00	50.00
❑	103	Elbie Fletcher	20.00	10.00
❑	104	Paul Waner	90.00	45.00
❑	105	Lloyd Waner	80.00	40.00
❑	106	Pep Young	20.00	10.00
❑	107	Arky Vaughan	80.00	40.00
❑	108	Johnny Rizzo	20.00	10.00
❑	109	Don Padgett	20.00	10.00
❑	110	Tom Sunkel	20.00	10.00
❑	111	Mickey Owen	25.00	12.50
❑	112	Jimmy Brown	20.00	10.00
❑	113	Mort Cooper	25.00	12.50
❑	114	Lon Warneke	25.00	12.50
❑	115	Mike Gonzalez CO	25.00	12.50
❑	116	Al Schacht	25.00	12.50
❑	117	Dolly Stark UMP	25.00	12.50
❑	118	Waite Hoyt	90.00	45.00
❑	119	Grover C. Alexander	175.00	90.00
❑	120	Walter Johnson	200.00	100.00
❑	121	Atley Donald	25.00	12.50
❑	122	Sandy Sundra	25.00	12.50
❑	123	Hildy Hildebrand	25.00	12.50
❑	124	Earle Combs	100.00	50.00
❑	125	Art Fletcher	25.00	12.50
❑	126	Jake Solters	20.00	10.00
❑	127	Muddy Ruel	20.00	10.00
❑	128	Pete Appleton	20.00	10.00
❑	129	Bucky Harris	80.00	40.00
❑	130	Clyde Milan	25.00	12.50
❑	131	Zeke Bonura	25.00	12.50
❑	132	Connie Mack MG	150.00	75.00
❑	133	Jimmie Foxx	200.00	100.00
❑	134	Joe Cronin	100.00	50.00
❑	135	Line Drive Nelson	20.00	10.00
❑	136	Cotton Pippen	20.00	10.00
❑	137	Bing Miller	20.00	10.00
❑	138	Beau Bell	20.00	10.00
❑	139	Elden Auker	20.00	10.00
❑	140	Dick Coffman	20.00	10.00
❑	141	Casey Stengel MG	175.00	90.00
❑	142	George Kelly	90.00	45.00
❑	143	Gene Moore	20.00	10.00
❑	144	Joe Vosmik	20.00	10.00
❑	145	Vito Tamulis	20.00	10.00
❑	146	Tot Pressnell	20.00	10.00
❑	147	Johnny Hudson	20.00	10.00
❑	148	Hugh Casey	25.00	12.50
❑	149	Pinky Shoffner	20.00	10.00
❑	150	Whitey Moore	20.00	10.00
❑	151	Edwin Joost	25.00	12.50
❑	152	Jimmy Wilson	20.00	10.00
❑	153	Bill McKechnie MG	80.00	40.00
❑	154	Jumbo Brown	20.00	10.00
❑	155	Ray Hayworth	20.00	10.00
❑	156	Daffy Dean	.00	.00
❑	157	Lou Chiozza	20.00	10.00
❑	158	Travis Jackson	90.00	45.00
❑	159	Pancho Snyder	20.00	10.00
❑	160	Hans Lobert CO	20.00	10.00
❑	161	Debs Garms	20.00	10.00
❑	162	Joe Bowman	20.00	10.00
❑	163	Spud Davis	20.00	10.00
❑	164	Ray Berres	20.00	10.00
❑	165	Bob Klinger	20.00	10.00
❑	166	Bill Brubaker	20.00	10.00
❑	167	Frankie Frisch MG	90.00	45.00
❑	168	Honus Wagner CO	200.00	100.00
❑	169	Gabby Street	20.00	10.00
❑	170	Tris Speaker	175.00	90.00
❑	171	Harry Heilmann	80.00	40.00
❑	172	Chief Bender	80.00	40.00
❑	173	Napoleon Lajoie	175.00	90.00
❑	174	Johnny Evers	90.00	45.00
❑	175	Christy Mathewson	250.00	125.00
❑	176	Heinie Manush	90.00	45.00
❑	177	Frank Baker	100.00	50.00
❑	178	Max Carey	90.00	45.00
❑	179	George Sisler	125.00	60.00
❑	180	Mickey Cochrane	150.00	75.00
❑	181	Spud Chandler	80.00	40.00
❑	182	Knick Knickerbocker	70.00	35.00
❑	183	Marvin Breuer	70.00	35.00
❑	184	Mule Haas	70.00	35.00
❑	185	Joe Kuhel	70.00	35.00
❑	186	Taft Wright	70.00	35.00
❑	187	Jimmy Dykes MG	80.00	40.00
❑	188	Joe Krakauskas	70.00	35.00
❑	189	Jim Bloodworth	70.00	35.00
❑	190	Charley Berry	70.00	35.00
❑	191	John Babich	70.00	35.00
❑	192	Dick Siebert	70.00	35.00
❑	193	Chubby Dean	70.00	35.00
❑	194	Sam Chapman	70.00	35.00
❑	195	Dee Miles	70.00	35.00
❑	196	Red(Nonny)Nonnenkamp	70.00	35.00
❑	197	Lou Finney	70.00	35.00
❑	198	Denny Galehouse	70.00	35.00
❑	199	Pinky Higgins	70.00	35.00
❑	200	Soup Campbell	70.00	35.00
❑	201	Barney McCosky	70.00	35.00
❑	202	Al Milnar	70.00	35.00
❑	203	Bad News Hale	70.00	35.00
❑	204	Harry Eisenstat	70.00	35.00
❑	205	Rollie Hemsley	70.00	35.00
❑	206	Chet Laabs	70.00	35.00
❑	207	Gus Mancuso	70.00	35.00
❑	208	Lee Gamble	70.00	35.00
❑	209	Hy Vandenberg	70.00	35.00
❑	210	Bill Lohrman	70.00	35.00
❑	211	Pop Joiner	70.00	35.00
❑	212	Babe Young	70.00	35.00
❑	213	John Rucker	70.00	35.00
❑	214	Ken O'Dea	70.00	35.00
❑	215	Johnnie McCarthy	70.00	35.00
❑	216	Joe Marty	70.00	35.00
❑	217	Walter Beck	70.00	35.00
❑	218	Wally Millies	70.00	35.00
❑	219	Russ Bauers	70.00	35.00
❑	220	Mace Brown	70.00	35.00
❑	221	Lee Handley	70.00	35.00
❑	222	Max Butcher	70.00	35.00
❑	223	Hughie Jennings	150.00	75.00
❑	224	Pie Traynor	175.00	90.00
❑	225	Joe Jackson	2500.00	1250.00
❑	226	Harry Hooper	150.00	75.00
❑	227	Jesse Haines	150.00	75.00
❑	228	Charlie Grimm	80.00	40.00
❑	229	Buck Herzog	70.00	35.00
❑	230	Red Faber	175.00	90.00
❑	231	Dolf Luque	100.00	50.00
❑	232	Goose Goslin	150.00	75.00
❑	233	George Earnshaw	80.00	40.00
❑	234	Frank Chance	150.00	75.00
❑	235	John McGraw	175.00	90.00
❑	236	Jim Bottomley	150.00	75.00
❑	237	Willie Keeler	175.00	90.00
❑	238	Tony Lazzeri	175.00	90.00
❑	239	George Uhle	70.00	35.00
❑	240	Bill Atwood	100.00	50.00

1941 Play Ball

	Ex-Mt	VG
COMPLETE SET (72)	10000.00	5000.00
COMMON CARD (1-48)	40.00	20.00
COMMON CARD (49-72)	60.00	30.00
WRAPPER (1-CENT)	800.00	400.00

	Card	Nm-Mt	Ex-Mt
❑	1 Eddie Miller	125.00	60.00
❑	2 Max West	40.00	20.00
❑	3 Bucky Walters	45.00	22.00
❑	4 Paul Derringer	50.00	25.00
❑	5 Frank(Buck) McCormick	45.00	22.00
❑	6 Carl Hubbell	175.00	90.00
❑	7 Harry Danning	40.00	20.00
❑	8 Mel Ott	225.00	110.00
❑	9 Pinky May	40.00	20.00
❑	10 Arky Vaughan	100.00	50.00
❑	11 Debs Garms	40.00	20.00
❑	12 Jimmy Brown	40.00	20.00
❑	13 Jimmie Foxx	300.00	150.00
❑	14 Ted Williams	1500.00	750.00
❑	15 Joe Cronin	125.00	60.00
❑	16 Hal Trosky	45.00	22.00
❑	17 Roy Weatherly	40.00	20.00
❑	18 Hank Greenberg	300.00	150.00
❑	19 Charley Gehringer	200.00	100.00
❑	20 Red Ruffing	125.00	60.00
❑	21 Charlie Keller	60.00	30.00
❑	22 Bob Johnson	50.00	25.00
❑	23 George McQuinn	40.00	20.00
❑	24 Dutch Leonard	45.00	22.00
❑	25 Gene Moore	40.00	20.00
❑	26 Harry Gumpert	40.00	20.00
❑	27 Babe Young	40.00	20.00
❑	28 Joe Marty	40.00	20.00
❑	29 Jack Wilson	40.00	20.00
❑	30 Lou Finney	40.00	20.00
❑	31 Joe Kuhel	40.00	20.00
❑	32 Taft Wright	40.00	20.00
❑	33 Al Milnar	40.00	20.00
❑	34 Rollie Hemsley	40.00	20.00
❑	35 Pinky Higgins	45.00	22.00
❑	36 Barney McCosky	40.00	20.00
❑	37 Bruce Campbell	40.00	20.00
❑	38 Atley Donald	50.00	25.00
❑	39 Tommy Henrich	60.00	30.00
❑	40 John Babich	40.00	20.00
❑	41 Frank(Blimp) Hayes	40.00	20.00
❑	42 Wally Moses	45.00	22.00
❑	43 Al Brancato	40.00	20.00
❑	44 Sam Chapman	40.00	20.00
❑	45 Eldon Auker	40.00	20.00
❑	46 Sid Hudson	40.00	20.00
❑	47 Buddy Lewis	40.00	20.00
❑	48 Cecil Travis	45.00	22.00
❑	49 Babe Dahlgren	65.00	32.00
❑	50 Johnny Cooney	60.00	30.00
❑	51 Dolph Camilli	65.00	32.00
❑	52 Kirby Higbe	60.00	30.00
❑	53 Luke Hamlin	60.00	30.00
❑	54 Pee Wee Reese	600.00	300.00
❑	55 Whit Wyatt	65.00	32.00
❑	56 Johnny VanderMeer	100.00	50.00
❑	57 Moe Arnovich	60.00	30.00
❑	58 Frank Demaree	60.00	30.00
❑	59 Bill Jurges	60.00	30.00
❑	60 Chuck Klein	150.00	75.00
❑	61 Vince DiMaggio	225.00	110.00
❑	62 Elbie Fletcher	60.00	30.00
❑	63 Dom DiMaggio	250.00	125.00
❑	64 Bobby Doerr	175.00	90.00
❑	65 Tommy Bridges	65.00	32.00
❑	66 Harland Clift	60.00	30.00
❑	67 Walt Judnich	60.00	30.00
❑	68 John Knott	60.00	30.00
❑	69 George Case	65.00	32.00
❑	70 Bill Dickey	400.00	200.00
❑	71 Joe DiMaggio	2500.00	1250.00
❑	72 Lefty Gomez	475.00	240.00

2004 Reflections

	Nm-Mt	Ex-Mt
COMP.SET w/o SP's (100)	40.00	12.00
COMP.UPDATE SET (50)	30.00	9.00
COMMON CARD (1-100)	.75	.23
COMMON CARD (101-130)	4.00	1.20
COMMON CARD (131-214)	6.00	1.80
SP CL: 132/142/144/146/153/156/159		.00
SP CL: 161-162/164/178/184/186/188		.00
SP CL: 190-191/197-198/201/207/214		.00
SP INFO PROVIDED BY UPPER DECK		.00
COMMON CARD (215-298)	8.00	2.40
COMMON CARD (299-340)	25.00	7.50
COMMON CARD (341-390)	.60	.18

	Card	Nm-Mt	Ex-Mt
❑	1 Adam Dunn	.75	.23
❑	2 Albert Pujols	4.00	1.20
❑	3 Alex Rodriguez Yanks	3.00	.90
❑	4 Alfonso Soriano	.75	.23
❑	5 Andruw Jones	1.25	.35
❑	6 Austin Kearns	.75	.23
❑	7 Rafael Furcal	.75	.23
❑	8 Barry Zito	.75	.23
❑	9 Bartolo Colon	.75	.23
❑	10 Ben Sheets	.75	.23
❑	11 Bernie Williams	1.25	.35
❑	12 Bobby Abreu	.75	.23
❑	13 Brandon Webb	.75	.23
❑	14 Bret Boone	.75	.23
❑	15 Brian Giles	.75	.23
❑	16 Carlos Beltran	.75	.23
❑	17 Carlos Delgado	.75	.23
❑	18 Carlos Lee	.75	.23
❑	19 Chipper Jones	2.00	.60
❑	20 Corey Patterson	.75	.23
❑	21 Curt Schilling	1.25	.35
❑	22 Delmon Young	1.25	.35
❑	23 Derek Jeter	4.00	1.20
❑	24 Dmitri Young	.75	.23
❑	25 Dontrelle Willis	1.25	.35
❑	26 Edgar Martinez	1.25	.35
❑	27 Edgar Renteria	.75	.23
❑	28 Eric Chavez	.75	.23
❑	29 Eric Gagne	.75	.23
❑	30 Frank Thomas	2.00	.60
❑	31 Garrett Anderson	.75	.23
❑	32 Gary Sheffield	.75	.23
❑	33 Geoff Jenkins	.75	.23
❑	34 Greg Maddux	3.00	.90
❑	35 Hank Blalock	.75	.23
❑	36 Hideki Matsui	4.00	1.20
❑	37 Hideo Nomo	2.00	.60
❑	38 Ichiro Suzuki	4.00	1.20
❑	39 Ivan Rodriguez	1.25	.35
❑	40 Jacque Jones	.75	.23
❑	41 Jason Giambi	.75	.23
❑	42 Jason Schmidt	.75	.23
❑	43 Javy Lopez	.75	.23
❑	44 Jay Gibbons	.75	.23
❑	45 Jeff Bagwell	1.25	.35
❑	46 Jeff Kent	.75	.23
❑	47 Jeremy Bonderman	.75	.23
❑	48 Jim Edmonds	1.25	.35
❑	49 Jim Thome	1.25	.35
❑	50 Johnny Damon	1.25	.35
❑	51 Jorge Posada	1.25	.35
❑	52 Jose Contreras	.75	.23
❑	53 Jose Reyes	.75	.23
❑	54 Jose Vidro	.75	.23
❑	55 Josh Beckett	.75	.23
❑	56 Juan Gonzalez	.75	.23
❑	57 Ken Griffey Jr.	3.00	.90
❑	58 Kerry Wood	.75	.23
❑	59 Kevin Brown	.75	.23
❑	60 Kevin Millwood	.75	.23
❑	61 Lance Berkman	.75	.23
❑	62 Larry Walker	.75	.23
❑	63 Luis Gonzalez	.75	.23
❑	64 Magglio Ordonez	.75	.23
❑	65 Manny Ramirez	1.25	.35
❑	66 Mark Mulder	.75	.23
❑	67 Mark Prior	1.25	.35
❑	68 Mark Teixeira	1.25	.35
❑	69 Miguel Cabrera	1.25	.35
❑	70 Miguel Tejada	.75	.23
❑	71 Mike Lowell	.75	.23
❑	72 Mike Mussina	1.25	.35
❑	73 Mike Piazza	3.00	.90
❑	74 Mike Sweeney	.75	.23
❑	75 Milton Bradley	.75	.23
❑	76 Nomar Garciaparra	3.00	.90
❑	77 Orlando Cabrera	.75	.23
❑	78 Pedro Martinez	1.25	.35
❑	79 Phil Nevin	.75	.23
❑	80 Preston Wilson	.75	.23
❑	81 Rafael Palmeiro	1.25	.35
❑	82 Randy Johnson	2.00	.60
❑	83 Rich Harden	.75	.23
❑	84 Richie Sexson	.75	.23
❑	85 Rickie Weeks	1.25	.35
❑	86 Rocco Baldelli	.75	.23
❑	87 Roy Halladay	.75	.23
❑	88 Roy Oswalt	.75	.23
❑	89 Ryan Klesko	.75	.23
❑	90 Sammy Sosa	2.00	.60
❑	91 Scott Rolen	1.25	.35
❑	92 Shannon Stewart	.75	.23
❑	93 Shawn Green	.75	.23
❑	94 Tim Hudson	.75	.23
❑	95 Todd Helton	1.25	.35
❑	96 Torii Hunter	.75	.23
❑	97 Trot Nixon	.75	.23
❑	98 Troy Glaus	.75	.23
❑	99 Vernon Wells	.75	.23
❑	100 Vladimir Guerrero	2.00	.60
❑	101 Brandon Medders RC	4.00	1.20
❑	102 Colby Miller RC	4.00	1.20
❑	103 Dave Crouthers RC	4.00	1.20
❑	104 Dennis Sarfate RC	4.00	1.20
❑	105 Donnie Kelly RC	4.00	1.20
❑	106 Alec Zumwalt RC	4.00	1.20
❑	107 Chris Aguila RC	4.00	1.20
❑	108 Greg Dobbs RC	4.00	1.20
❑	109 Ian Snell RC	5.00	1.50
❑	110 Jake Woods RC	4.00	1.20
❑	111 Jamie Brown RC	4.00	1.20
❑	112 Jason Frasor RC	4.00	1.20
❑	113 Jerome Gamble RC	4.00	1.20
❑	114 Jesse Harper RC	4.00	1.20
❑	115 Josh Labandeira RC	4.00	1.20
❑	116 Justin Hampson RC	4.00	1.20
❑	117 Justin Huisman RC	4.00	1.20
❑	118 Justin Leone RC	5.00	1.50
❑	119 Kazuo Matsui RC	5.00	1.50
❑	120 Lincoln Holdzkom RC	4.00	1.20
❑	121 Mike Bumatay RC	4.00	1.20
❑	122 Mike Gosling RC	4.00	1.20
❑	123 Mike Johnston RC	4.00	1.20
❑	124 Mike Rouse RC	4.00	1.20
❑	125 Nick Regilio RC	4.00	1.20
❑	126 Ryan Meaux RC	4.00	1.20
❑	127 Scott Dohmann RC	4.00	1.20
❑	128 Sean Henn RC	4.00	1.20
❑	129 Tim Bausher RC	4.00	1.20
❑	130 Tim Bittner RC	4.00	1.20
❑	131 Adam Dunn Jsy L1	6.00	1.80
❑	132 Andruw Jones Jsy L1 SP	12.00	3.60
❑	133 Austin Kearns Jsy L1	6.00	1.80
❑	134 Bartolo Colon Jsy L1	6.00	1.80
❑	135 Ben Sheets Jsy L1	6.00	1.80

❑	136	Bernie Williams Jsy L1	10.00	3.00
❑	137	Bobby Abreu Jsy L1	6.00	1.80
❑	138	Brian Giles Jsy L1	6.00	1.80
❑	139	Carlos Lee Jsy L1	6.00	1.80
❑	140	Chipper Jones Jsy L1	10.00	3.00
❑	141	Corey Patterson Jsy L1	6.00	1.80
❑	142	Darin Erstad Jsy L1 SP	8.00	2.40
❑	143	Edgar Martinez Jsy L1	10.00	3.00
❑	144	Vladimir Guerrero Jsy L1 SP	12.00	3.60
❑	145	Eric Gagne Jsy L1	6.00	1.80
❑	146	Frank Thomas Jsy L1 SP	12.00	3.60
❑	147	Garret Anderson Jsy L1	6.00	1.80
❑	148	Roger Clemens Jsy L1	15.00	4.50
❑	149	Greg Maddux Jsy L1	10.00	3.00
❑	150	Jacque Jones Jsy L1	6.00	1.80
❑	151	Randy Johnson Jsy L1	10.00	3.00
❑	152	Javy Lopez Jsy L1	6.00	1.80
❑	153	Mike Piazza Jsy L1 SP	15.00	4.50
❑	154	Albert Pujols Jsy L1	15.00	4.50
❑	155	Jim Edmonds Jsy L1	10.00	3.00
❑	156	Eric Milton Jsy L1 SP	8.00	2.40
❑	157	Jorge Posada Jsy L1	10.00	3.00
❑	158	J.D. Drew Jsy L1	6.00	1.80
❑	159	Jose Vidro Jsy L1 SP	8.00	2.40
❑	160	Kevin Millwood Jsy L1	6.00	1.80
❑	161	Larry Walker Jsy L1 SP	8.00	2.40
❑	162	Luis Gonzalez Jsy L1 SP	8.00	2.40
❑	163	Mike Sweeney Jsy L1	6.00	1.80
❑	164	Kerry Wood Jsy L1 SP	8.00	2.40
❑	165	Mike Cameron Jsy L1	6.00	1.80
❑	166	Phil Nevin Jsy L1	6.00	1.80
❑	167	Rocco Baldelli Jsy L1	6.00	1.80
❑	168	Ryan Klesko Jsy L1	6.00	1.80
❑	169	Shannon Stewart Jsy L1	6.00	1.80
❑	170	Torii Hunter Jsy L1	6.00	1.80
❑	171	Trot Nixon Jsy L1	6.00	1.80
❑	172	Vernon Wells Jsy L1	6.00	1.80
❑	173	Alfonso Soriano Jsy L2	6.00	1.80
❑	174	Andruw Jones Jsy L2	10.00	3.00
❑	175	Barry Zito Jsy L2	6.00	1.80
❑	176	Brandon Webb Jsy L2	6.00	1.80
❑	177	Bret Boone Jsy L2	6.00	1.80
❑	178	Scott Rolen Jsy L2 SP	12.00	3.60
❑	179	Carlos Delgado Jsy L2	6.00	1.80
❑	180	Curt Schilling Jsy L2	10.00	3.00
❑	181	Dontrelle Willis Jsy L2	10.00	3.00
❑	182	Eric Chavez Jsy L2	6.00	1.80
❑	183	Frank Thomas Jsy L2	10.00	3.00
❑	184	Gary Sheffield Jsy L2 SP	8.00	2.40
❑	185	Greg Maddux Jsy L2	10.00	3.00
❑	186	Hank Blalock Jsy L2 SP	8.00	2.40
❑	187	Hideki Matsui Jsy L2	25.00	7.50
❑	188	Hideo Nomo Jsy L2 SP	12.00	3.60
❑	189	Ichiro Suzuki Jsy L2	15.00	4.50
❑	190	Ivan Rodriguez Jsy L2 SP	12.00	3.60
❑	191	Jason Giambi Jsy L2 SP	8.00	2.40
❑	192	Rafael Furcal Jsy L2	6.00	1.80
❑	193	Jeff Bagwell Jsy L2	10.00	3.00
❑	194	Jeff Kent Jsy L2	6.00	1.80
❑	195	Jim Thome Jsy L2	10.00	3.00
❑	196	Jose Reyes Jsy L2	6.00	1.80
❑	197	Josh Beckett Jsy L2 SP	8.00	2.40
❑	198	Juan Gonzalez Jsy L2 SP	8.00	2.40
❑	199	Ken Griffey Jr. Jsy L2	15.00	4.50
❑	200	Kevin Brown Jsy L2	6.00	1.80
❑	201	Lance Berkman Jsy L2 SP	8.00	2.40
❑	202	Magglio Ordonez Jsy L2	6.00	1.80
❑	203	Mark Mulder Jsy L2	6.00	1.80
❑	204	Mark Teixeira Jsy L2	10.00	3.00
❑	205	Miguel Tejada Jsy L2	6.00	1.80
❑	206	Mike Mussina Jsy L2	10.00	3.00
❑	207	Preston Wilson Jsy L2 SP	8.00	2.40
❑	208	Rafael Palmeiro Jsy L2	10.00	3.00
❑	209	Alex Rodriguez Jsy L2	15.00	4.50
❑	210	Richie Sexson Jsy L2	6.00	1.80
❑	211	Roy Halladay Jsy L2	6.00	1.80
❑	212	Roy Oswalt Jsy L2	6.00	1.80
❑	213	Tim Hudson Jsy L2	6.00	1.80
❑	214	Troy Glaus Jsy L2 SP	8.00	2.40
❑	215	Adam Dunn Jsy L3	8.00	2.40
❑	216	Austin Kearns Jsy L3	8.00	2.40
❑	217	Bartolo Colon Jsy L3	8.00	2.40
❑	218	Ben Sheets Jsy L3	8.00	2.40
❑	219	Bernie Williams Jsy L3	12.00	3.60
❑	220	Bobby Abreu Jsy L3	8.00	2.40
❑	221	Bret Boone Jsy L3	8.00	2.40
❑	222	Todd Helton Jsy L3	12.00	3.60
❑	223	Chipper Jones Jsy L3	12.00	3.60
❑	224	Corey Patterson Jsy L3	8.00	2.40
❑	225	Darin Erstad Jsy L3	8.00	2.40
❑	226	Dontrelle Willis Jsy L3	12.00	3.60
❑	227	Edgar Martinez Jsy L3	12.00	3.60
❑	228	Eric Gagne Jsy L3	8.00	2.40
❑	229	Garret Anderson Jsy L3	8.00	2.40
❑	230	Roger Clemens Jsy L3	20.00	6.00
❑	231	Hank Blalock Jsy L3	8.00	2.40
❑	232	Jacque Jones Jsy L3	8.00	2.40
❑	233	Jeff Bagwell Jsy L3	12.00	3.60
❑	234	Jeff Kent Jsy L3	8.00	2.40
❑	235	Jeremy Bonderman Jsy L3	8.00	2.40
❑	236	Jim Edmonds Jsy L3	12.00	3.60
❑	237	Jorge Posada Jsy L3	12.00	3.60
❑	238	J.D. Drew Jsy L3	8.00	2.40
❑	239	Jose Reyes Jsy L3	8.00	2.40
❑	240	Jose Vidro Jsy L3	8.00	2.40
❑	241	Kevin Millwood Jsy L3	8.00	2.40
❑	242	Luis Gonzalez Jsy L3	8.00	2.40
❑	243	Mike Sweeney Jsy L3	8.00	2.40
❑	244	Jason Giambi Jsy L3	8.00	2.40
❑	245	Manny Ramirez Jsy L3	12.00	3.60
❑	246	Phil Nevin Jsy L3	8.00	2.40
❑	247	Preston Wilson Jsy L3	8.00	2.40
❑	248	Alex Rodriguez Jsy L3	20.00	6.00
❑	249	Richie Sexson Jsy L3	8.00	2.40
❑	250	Rocco Baldelli Jsy L3	8.00	2.40
❑	251	Ryan Klesko Jsy L3	8.00	2.40
❑	252	Sammy Sosa Jsy L3	12.00	3.60
❑	253	Torii Hunter Jsy L3	8.00	2.40
❑	254	Mike Lowell Jsy L3	8.00	2.40
❑	255	Troy Glaus Jsy L3	8.00	2.40
❑	256	Vernon Wells Jsy L3	8.00	2.40
❑	257	Albert Pujols Jsy L4	25.00	7.50
❑	258	Alex Rodriguez Jsy L4	20.00	6.00
❑	259	Alfonso Soriano Jsy L4	8.00	2.40
❑	260	Roger Clemens Jsy L4	20.00	6.00
❑	261	Barry Zito Jsy L4	8.00	2.40
❑	262	Brandon Webb Jsy L4	8.00	2.40
❑	263	Carlos Delgado Jsy L4	8.00	2.40
❑	264	Curt Schilling Jsy L4	12.00	3.60
❑	265	Derek Jeter Jsy L4	30.00	9.00
❑	266	Eric Chavez Jsy L4	8.00	2.40
❑	267	Gary Sheffield Jsy L4	8.00	2.40
❑	268	Hideki Matsui Jsy L4	30.00	9.00
❑	269	Hideo Nomo Jsy L4	12.00	3.60
❑	270	Ichiro Suzuki Jsy L4	25.00	7.50
❑	271	Ivan Rodriguez Jsy L4	12.00	3.60
❑	272	Jason Giambi Jsy L4	8.00	2.40
❑	273	Jim Thome Jsy L4	12.00	3.60
❑	274	Josh Beckett Jsy L4	8.00	2.40
❑	275	Juan Gonzalez Jsy L4	8.00	2.40
❑	276	Ken Griffey Jr. Jsy L4	20.00	6.00
❑	277	Kerry Wood Jsy L4	8.00	2.40
❑	278	Kevin Brown Jsy L4	8.00	2.40
❑	279	Lance Berkman Jsy L4	8.00	2.40
❑	280	Magglio Ordonez Jsy L4	8.00	2.40
❑	281	Manny Ramirez Jsy L4	12.00	3.60
❑	282	Mark Mulder Jsy L4	8.00	2.40
❑	283	Mark Prior Jsy L4	12.00	3.60
❑	284	Mark Teixeira Jsy L4	12.00	3.60
❑	285	Miguel Tejada Jsy L4	8.00	2.40
❑	286	Mike Mussina Jsy L4	12.00	3.60
❑	287	Mike Piazza Jsy L4	20.00	6.00
❑	288	Pedro Martinez Jsy L4	12.00	3.60
❑	289	Rafael Palmeiro Jsy L4	12.00	3.60
❑	290	Randy Johnson Jsy L4	12.00	3.60
❑	291	Roy Halladay Jsy L4	8.00	2.40
❑	292	Roy Oswalt Jsy L4	8.00	2.40
❑	293	Sammy Sosa Jsy L4	12.00	3.60
❑	294	Scott Rolen Jsy L4	12.00	3.60
❑	295	Shawn Green Jsy L4	8.00	2.40
❑	296	Tim Hudson Jsy L4	8.00	2.40
❑	297	Todd Helton Jsy L4	12.00	3.60
❑	298	Vladimir Guerrero Jsy L4	12.00	3.60
❑	299	Bret Boone AU	40.00	12.00
❑	300	Alex Rodriguez AU	200.00	60.00
❑	301	Dontrelle Willis AU	50.00	15.00
❑	302	Barry Larkin AU	50.00	15.00
❑	303	Barry Zito AU	50.00	15.00
❑	304	Eric Chavez AU	40.00	12.00
❑	305	Bernie Williams AU	120.00	36.00
❑	306	Brandon Webb AU	25.00	7.50
❑	307	Cal Ripken AU	200.00	60.00
❑	308	Carl Yastrzemski AU	80.00	24.00
❑	309	Carlos Delgado AU	40.00	12.00
❑	310	Shawn Green AU	50.00	15.00
❑	311	Eric Gagne AU	12.00	3.60
❑	312	Frank Thomas AU	60.00	18.00
❑	313	Carlos Lee AU	25.00	7.50
❑	314	Garret Anderson AU	40.00	12.00
❑	315	Hideki Matsui AU	350.00	105.00
❑	316	Jim Edmonds AU	50.00	15.00
❑	317	Jeff Bagwell AU	50.00	15.00
❑	318	Luis Gonzalez AU	40.00	12.00
❑	319	Mike Mussina AU	50.00	15.00
❑	320	John Smoltz AU	100.00	30.00
❑	321	Jose Reyes AU	40.00	12.00
❑	322	Josh Beckett AU	50.00	15.00
❑	323	Juan Gonzalez AU	40.00	12.00
❑	324	Ken Griffey Jr. AU	150.00	45.00
❑	325	Rich Harden AU	25.00	7.50
❑	326	Pat Burrell AU	40.00	12.00
❑	327	Mark Teixeira AU	50.00	15.00
❑	328	Roy Oswalt AU	50.00	15.00
❑	329	Miguel Tejada AU	50.00	15.00
❑	330	Mike Hampton AU	40.00	12.00
❑	331	Mike Piazza AU	200.00	60.00
❑	332	Nolan Ryan AU	150.00	45.00
❑	333	Orlando Hernandez AU	40.00	12.00
❑	334	Paul Lo Duca AU	40.00	12.00
❑	335	Roberto Alomar AU	50.00	15.00
❑	336	Rocco Baldelli AU	40.00	12.00
❑	337	Trevor Hoffman AU	50.00	15.00
❑	338	Tom Glavine AU	50.00	15.00
❑	339	Tom Seaver AU	60.00	18.00
❑	340	Mark Prior AU	60.00	18.00
❑	341	Shingo Takatsu RC	2.50	.75
❑	342	Franklyn Gracesqui RC	.60	.18
❑	343	Angel Chavez RC	1.00	.30
❑	344	Jorge Sequea RC	1.00	.30
❑	345	David Aardsma RC	1.50	.45
❑	346	Ramon Ramirez RC	1.00	.30
❑	347	Lino Urdaneta RC	1.00	.30
❑	348	Orlando Rodriguez RC	1.00	.30
❑	349	Jason Szuminski RC	.60	.18
❑	350	Luis A. Gonzalez RC	1.50	.45
❑	351	John Gall RC	1.50	.45
❑	352	Kevin Cave RC	1.00	.30
❑	353	Chris Oxspring RC	1.00	.30
❑	354	Freddy Guzman RC	1.00	.30
❑	355	Jeff Bennett RC	1.00	.30
❑	356	Jorge Vasquez RC	1.00	.30
❑	357	Merkin Valdez RC	1.50	.45
❑	358	Tim Hamulack RC	.60	.18
❑	359	Hector Gimenez RC	.60	.18
❑	360	Jerry Gil RC	1.00	.30
❑	361	Ryan Wing RC	1.00	.30
❑	362	Shawn Hill RC	1.00	.30
❑	363	Jason Bartlett RC	2.50	.75
❑	364	Renyel Pinto RC	1.50	.45
❑	365	Carlos Vasquez RC	1.50	.45
❑	366	Mike Vento RC	1.50	.45
❑	367	Casey Daigle RC	1.00	.30
❑	368	Chad Bentz RC	1.00	.30
❑	369	Chris Saenz RC	1.00	.30
❑	370	Shawn Camp RC	.60	.18
❑	371	Carlos Hines RC	1.00	.30
❑	372	Edwin Moreno RC	1.00	.30
❑	373	Michael Wuertz RC	1.50	.45
❑	374	Aarom Baldiris RC	1.50	.45
❑	375	Ronny Cedeno RC	2.50	.75
❑	376	Akinori Otsuka RC	4.00	1.20
❑	377	Jose Capellan RC	1.50	.45
❑	378	Justin Germano RC	1.00	.30
❑	379	Justin Knoedler RC	1.00	.30
❑	380	Mariano Gomez RC	1.00	.30
❑	381	Fernando Nieve RC	2.50	.75
❑	382	Scott Proctor RC	5.00	1.50
❑	383	Roman Colon RC	.60	.18
❑	384	Onil Joseph RC	1.00	.30
❑	385	Eddy Rodriguez RC	1.50	.45
❑	386	Enemencio Pacheco RC	1.00	.30
❑	387	William Bergolla RC	1.00	.30
❑	388	Ivan Ochoa RC	1.00	.30
❑	389	Rusty Tucker RC	1.50	.45
❑	390	Roberto Novoa RC	1.50	.45
❑	S38	Ichiro Suzuki Promo	.00	

2005 Reflections

	Nm-Mt	Ex-Mt
COMP.SET w/o SP's (100)	40.00	12.00
COMMON CARD (1-100)	.75	.23
COMMON CARD (101-150)	3.00	.90
COMMON CARD (151-200)	3.00	.90

Card	Nm-Mt	Ex-Mt
1 Corey Patterson	.75	.23
2 Curt Schilling	1.25	.35
3 Todd Helton	1.25	.35
4 Johnny Damon	1.25	.35
5 Alex Rodriguez	3.00	.90
6 Vladimir Guerrero	2.00	.60
7 John Smoltz	1.25	.35
8 Ivan Rodriguez	1.25	.35
9 Roy Halladay	.75	.23
10 Carlos Beltran	.75	.23
11 Ichiro Suzuki	4.00	1.20
12 Jim Edmonds	1.25	.35
13 Andruw Jones	1.25	.35
14 Scott Podsednik	.75	.23
15 Troy Glaus	.75	.23
16 Miguel Cabrera	1.25	.35
17 Adrian Beltre	.75	.23
18 Ben Sheets	.75	.23
19 Alfonso Soriano	.75	.23
20 Brian Giles	.75	.23
21 Carl Crawford	.75	.23
22 Frank Thomas	2.00	.60
23 Jeff Kent	.75	.23
24 Eric Gagne	.75	.23
25 Shawn Green	.75	.23
26 Sammy Sosa	2.00	.60
27 Carlos Lee	.75	.23
28 Ken Griffey Jr.	3.00	.90
29 Mike Lowell	.75	.23
30 Magglio Ordonez	.75	.23
31 Aubrey Huff	.75	.23
32 Travis Hafner	.75	.23
33 Albert Pujols	4.00	1.20
34 Vernon Wells	.75	.23
35 Roy Oswalt	.75	.23
36 Jose Guillen	.75	.23
37 Jim Thome	1.25	.35
38 Bobby Abreu	.75	.23
39 Bret Boone	.75	.23
40 Mark Teixeira	1.25	.35
41 Garret Anderson	.75	.23
42 Jose Reyes	.75	.23
43 Bernie Williams	1.25	.35
44 Greg Maddux	3.00	.90
45 Gary Sheffield	.75	.23
46 Josh Beckett	.75	.23
47 Chipper Jones	2.00	.60
48 Hank Blalock	.75	.23
49 C.C. Sabathia	.75	.23
50 Manny Ramirez	1.25	.35
51 Pedro Martinez	1.25	.35
52 Michael Young	.75	.23
53 Jacque Jones	.75	.23
54 Marcus Giles	.75	.23
55 Steve Finley	.75	.23
56 Miguel Tejada	.75	.23
57 Mike Sweeney	.75	.23
58 Lance Berkman	.75	.23
59 J.D. Drew	.75	.23
60 Jeromy Burnitz	.75	.23
61 Johan Santana	1.25	.35
62 Victor Martinez	.75	.23
63 Carl Pavano	.75	.23
64 Roger Clemens	3.00	.90
65 Richie Sexson	.75	.23
66 Tim Hudson	.75	.23
67 Melvin Mora	.75	.23
68 Angel Berroa	.75	.23
69 Rafael Palmeiro	1.25	.35
70 Randy Johnson	2.00	.60
71 Torii Hunter	.75	.23
72 Luis Gonzalez	.75	.23
73 Kazuo Matsui	.75	.23
74 Hideki Matsui	4.00	1.20
75 Mark Prior	1.25	.35
76 Jeff Bagwell	1.25	.35
77 Eric Chavez	.75	.23
78 Mark Loretta	.75	.23
79 Adam Dunn	.75	.23
80 Kerry Wood	.75	.23
81 Jose Vidro	.75	.23
82 Jason Schmidt	.75	.23
83 Carlos Delgado	.75	.23
84 Scott Rolen	1.25	.35
85 David Ortiz	2.00	.60
86 Edgar Renteria	.75	.23
87 Nomar Garciaparra	2.00	.60
88 Mike Piazza	2.00	.60
89 Mark Mulder	.75	.23
90 Tom Glavine	1.25	.35
91 Paul Konerko	.75	.23
92 Larry Walker	1.25	.35
93 Derek Jeter	4.00	1.20
94 Jake Peavy	.75	.23
95 Carlos Zambrano	.75	.23
96 Russ Ortiz	.75	.23
97 Barry Zito	.75	.23
98 Austin Kearns	.75	.23
99 Pedro Feliz	.75	.23
100 Rich Harden	.75	.23
101 Adam LaRoche FUT	3.00	.90
102 Brandon Claussen FUT	3.00	.90
103 Gavin Floyd FUT	3.00	.90
104 Daniel Cabrera FUT	3.00	.90
105 Joe Mauer FUT	3.00	.90
106 Khalil Greene FUT	4.00	1.20
107 David Wright FUT	5.00	1.50
108 Rickie Weeks FUT	3.00	.90
109 Robb Quinlan FUT	3.00	.90
110 Bucky Jacobsen FUT	3.00	.90
111 Ryan Howard FUT	3.00	.90
112 Jeff Francis FUT	3.00	.90
113 Jason Lane FUT	3.00	.90
114 Alexis Rios FUT	3.00	.90
115 Bobby Madritsch FUT	3.00	.90
116 Jesse Crain FUT	3.00	.90
117 Oliver Perez FUT	3.00	.90
118 Garrett Atkins FUT	3.00	.90
119 Casey Kotchman FUT	3.00	.90
120 B.J. Upton FUT	3.00	.90
121 Laynce Nix FUT	3.00	.90
122 Adrian Gonzalez FUT	3.00	.90
123 Joe Blanton FUT	3.00	.90
124 Gabe Gross FUT	3.00	.90
125 Scott Kazmir FUT	3.00	.90
126 Zack Greinke FUT	3.00	.90
127 Edwin Jackson FUT	3.00	.90
128 Jason Bay FUT	3.00	.90
129 J.D. Closser FUT	3.00	.90
130 Jason DuBois FUT	3.00	.90
131 Dallas McPherson FUT	3.00	.90
132 Chad Cordero FUT	3.00	.90
133 Angel Guzman FUT	3.00	.90
134 Jayson Werth FUT	3.00	.90
135 Ryan Wagner FUT	3.00	.90
136 Guillermo Quiroz FUT	3.00	.90
137 Scott Proctor FUT	3.00	.90
138 Chris Burke FUT	3.00	.90
139 Nick Swisher FUT	3.00	.90
140 David DeJesus FUT	3.00	.90
141 Yhency Brazoban FUT	3.00	.90
142 Bobby Crosby FUT	3.00	.90
143 Chase Utley FUT	3.00	.90
144 Wily Mo Pena FUT	3.00	.90
145 Roman Colon FUT	3.00	.90
146 Eddy Rodriguez FUT	3.00	.90
147 Gerald Laird FUT	3.00	.90
148 Jose Capellan FUT	3.00	.90
149 Aaron Rowand FUT	3.00	.90
150 Kevin Youkilis FUT	3.00	.90
151 Bob Feller LGD	4.00	1.20
152 Robin Yount LGD	4.00	1.20
153 Willie Stargell LGD	4.00	1.20
154 Cal Ripken LGD	10.00	3.00
155 Monte Irvin LGD	3.00	.90
156 Nolan Ryan LGD	8.00	2.40
157 Bob Lemon LGD	3.00	.90
158 Richie Ashburn LGD	4.00	1.20
159 Billy Williams LGD	3.00	.90
160 Luis Aparicio LGD	3.00	.90
161 Phil Niekro LGD	3.00	.90
162 Bobby Doerr LGD	3.00	.90
163 Mike Schmidt LGD	6.00	1.80
164 Stan Musial LGD	5.00	1.50
165 George Kell LGD	3.00	.90
166 Joe Morgan LGD	3.00	.90
167 Whitey Ford LGD	4.00	1.20
168 Rick Ferrell LGD	3.00	.90
169 Catfish Hunter LGD	4.00	1.20
170 Red Schoendienst LGD	3.00	.90
171 Tom Seaver LGD	4.00	1.20
172 Pee Wee Reese LGD	4.00	1.20
173 Lou Boudreau LGD	3.00	.90
174 Hal Newhouser LGD	3.00	.90
175 Harmon Killebrew LGD	4.00	1.20
176 Jim Bunning LGD	3.00	.90
177 Willie McCovey LGD	4.00	1.20
178 Bob Gibson LGD	4.00	1.20
179 Juan Marichal LGD	3.00	.90
180 Robin Roberts LGD	3.00	.90
181 Gaylord Perry LGD	3.00	.90
182 Brooks Robinson LGD	4.00	1.20
183 Al Lopez LGD	3.00	.90
184 Joe DiMaggio LGD	6.00	1.80
185 Al Kaline LGD	4.00	1.20
186 Rollie Fingers LGD	3.00	.90
187 Mickey Mantle LGD	20.00	6.00
188 Enos Slaughter LGD	3.00	.90
189 Ernie Banks LGD	4.00	1.20
190 Eddie Mathews LGD	4.00	1.20
191 Tommy Lasorda LGD	3.00	.90
192 Fergie Jenkins LGD	3.00	.90
193 Lou Brock LGD	4.00	1.20
194 Larry Doby LGD	3.00	.90
195 Phil Rizzuto LGD	4.00	1.20
196 Warren Spahn LGD	4.00	1.20
197 Ralph Kiner LGD	4.00	1.20
198 Hoyt Wilhelm LGD	3.00	.90
199 Early Wynn LGD	3.00	.90
200 Yogi Berra LGD	4.00	1.20

1988 Score

	Nm-Mt	Ex-Mt
COMPLETE SET (660)	10.00	4.00
COMP.FACT.SET (660)	12.00	4.80

Card	Nm-Mt	Ex-Mt
1 Don Mattingly	.60	.24
2 Wade Boggs	.15	.06
3 Tim Raines	.10	.04
4 Andre Dawson	.10	.04
5 Mark McGwire	1.50	.60
6 Kevin Seitzer	.05	.02
7 Wally Joyner	.10	.04
8 Jesse Barfield	.10	.04
9 Pedro Guerrero	.10	.04

❑ 10 Eric Davis .10 .04
❑ 11 George Brett .50 .20
❑ 12 Ozzie Smith .30 .12
❑ 13 Rickey Henderson .20 .08
❑ 14 Jim Rice .10 .04
❑ 15 Matt Nokes RC* .25 .10
❑ 16 Mike Schmidt .50 .20
❑ 17 Dave Parker .10 .04
❑ 18 Eddie Murray .20 .08
❑ 19 Andres Galarraga .10 .04
❑ 20 Tony Fernandez .05 .02
❑ 21 Kevin McReynolds .05 .02
❑ 22 B.J. Surhoff .10 .04
❑ 23 Pat Tabler .05 .02
❑ 24 Kirby Puckett .20 .08
❑ 25 Benny Santiago .10 .04
❑ 26 Ryne Sandberg .40 .16
❑ 27 Kelly Downs .05 .02
(Will Clark in background, out of focus)
❑ 28 Jose Cruz .10 .04
❑ 29 Pete O'Brien .05 .02
❑ 30 Mark Langston .05 .02
❑ 31 Lee Smith .10 .04
❑ 32 Juan Samuel .05 .02
❑ 33 Kevin Bass .05 .02
❑ 34 R.J. Reynolds .05 .02
❑ 35 Steve Sax .05 .02
❑ 36 John Kruk .10 .04
❑ 37 Alan Trammell .10 .04
❑ 38 Chris Bosio .05 .02
❑ 39 Brook Jacoby .05 .02
❑ 40 Willie McGee UER .10 .04
(Excited misspelled as excitd)
❑ 41 Dave Magadan .05 .02
❑ 42 Fred Lynn .10 .04
❑ 43 Kent Hrbek .10 .04
❑ 44 Brian Downing .10 .04
❑ 45 Jose Canseco .50 .20
❑ 46 Jim Presley .05 .02
❑ 47 Mike Stanley .05 .02
❑ 48 Tony Pena .05 .02
❑ 49 David Cone .10 .04
❑ 50 Rick Sutcliffe .10 .04
❑ 51 Doug Drabek .05 .02
❑ 52 Bill Doran .05 .02
❑ 53 Mike Scioscia .10 .04
❑ 54 Candy Maldonado .05 .02
❑ 55 Dave Winfield .10 .04
❑ 56 Lou Whitaker .10 .04
❑ 57 Tom Henke .05 .02
❑ 58 Ken Gerhart .05 .02
❑ 59 Glenn Braggs .05 .02
❑ 60 Julio Franco .10 .04
❑ 61 Charlie Leibrandt .05 .02
❑ 62 Gary Gaetti .10 .04
❑ 63 Bob Boone .10 .04
❑ 64 Luis Polonia RC* .25 .10
❑ 65 Dwight Evans .15 .06
❑ 66 Phil Bradley .05 .02
❑ 67 Mike Boddicker .05 .02
❑ 68 Vince Coleman .05 .02
❑ 69 Howard Johnson .10 .04
❑ 70 Tim Wallach .05 .02
❑ 71 Keith Moreland .05 .02
❑ 72 Barry Larkin .15 .06
❑ 73 Alan Ashby .05 .02
❑ 74 Rick Rhoden .05 .02
❑ 75 Darrell Evans .10 .04
❑ 76 Dave Stieb .10 .04
❑ 77 Dan Plesac .05 .02
❑ 78 Will Clark UER .20 .08
(Born 3/17/64, should be 3/13/64)
❑ 79 Frank White .10 .04
❑ 80 Joe Carter .10 .04
❑ 81 Mike Witt .05 .02
❑ 82 Terry Steinbach .10 .04
❑ 83 Alvin Davis .05 .02
❑ 84 Tommy Herr .10 .04
(Will Clark shown sliding into second)
❑ 85 Vance Law .05 .02
❑ 86 Kal Daniels .05 .02
❑ 87 Rick Honeycutt UER .05 .02
(Wrong years for stats on back)
❑ 88 Alfredo Griffin .05 .02
❑ 89 Bret Saberhagen .10 .04
❑ 90 Bert Blyleven .10 .04
❑ 91 Jeff Reardon .10 .04
❑ 92 Cory Snyder .05 .02
❑ 93A Greg Walker ERR 2.00 .80
(93 of 66)
❑ 93B Greg Walker COR .05 .02
(93 of 660)
❑ 94 Joe Magrane RC* .25 .10
❑ 95 Rob Deer .05 .02
❑ 96 Ray Knight .10 .04
❑ 97 Casey Candaele .05 .02
❑ 98 John Cerutti .05 .02
❑ 99 Buddy Bell .10 .04
❑ 100 Jack Clark .10 .04
❑ 101 Eric Bell .05 .02
❑ 102 Willie Wilson .10 .04
❑ 103 Dave Schmidt .05 .02
❑ 104 Dennis Eckersley UER .15 .06
(Complete games stats are wrong)
❑ 105 Don Sutton .10 .04
❑ 106 Danny Tartabull .05 .02
❑ 107 Fred McGriff .20 .08
❑ 108 Les Straker .05 .02
❑ 109 Lloyd Moseby .05 .02
❑ 110 Roger Clemens .50 .20
❑ 111 Glenn Hubbard .05 .02
❑ 112 Ken Williams RC .05 .02
❑ 113 Ruben Sierra .10 .04
❑ 114 Stan Jefferson .05 .02
❑ 115 Milt Thompson .05 .02
❑ 116 Bobby Bonilla .10 .04
❑ 117 Wayne Tolleson .05 .02
❑ 118 Matt Williams RC .75 .30
❑ 119 Chet Lemon .10 .04
❑ 120 Dale Sveum .05 .02
❑ 121 Dennis Boyd .05 .02
❑ 122 Brett Butler .10 .04
❑ 123 Terry Kennedy .05 .02
❑ 124 Jack Howell .05 .02
❑ 125 Curt Young .05 .02
❑ 126A Dave Valle ERR .10 .04
(Misspelled Dale on card front)
❑ 126B Dave Valle COR .05 .02
❑ 127 Curt Wilkerson .05 .02
❑ 128 Tim Teufel .05 .02
❑ 129 Ozzie Virgil .05 .02
❑ 130 Brian Fisher .05 .02
❑ 131 Lance Parrish .10 .04
❑ 132 Tom Browning .05 .02
❑ 133A Larry Andersen ERR .10 .04
(Misspelled Anderson on card front)
❑ 133B Larry Andersen COR .05 .02
❑ 134A Bob Brenly ERR .10 .04
(Misspelled Brenley on card front)
❑ 134B Bob Brenly COR .05 .02
❑ 135 Mike Marshall .05 .02
❑ 136 Gerald Perry .05 .02
❑ 137 Bobby Meacham .05 .02
❑ 138 Larry Herndon .05 .02
❑ 139 Fred Manrique .05 .02
❑ 140 Charlie Hough .10 .04
❑ 141 Ron Darling .10 .04
❑ 142 Herm Winningham .05 .02
❑ 143 Mike Diaz .05 .02
❑ 144 Mike Jackson RC* .25 .10
❑ 145 Denny Walling .05 .02
❑ 146 Robby Thompson .05 .02
❑ 147 Franklin Stubbs .05 .02
❑ 148 Albert Hall .05 .02
❑ 149 Bobby Witt .05 .02
❑ 150 Lance McCullers .05 .02
❑ 151 Scott Bradley .05 .02
❑ 152 Mark McLemore .05 .02
❑ 153 Tim Laudner .05 .02
❑ 154 Greg Swindell .05 .02
❑ 155 Marty Barrett .05 .02
❑ 156 Mike Heath .05 .02
❑ 157 Gary Ward .05 .02
❑ 158A Lee Mazzilli ERR .10 .04
(Misspelled Mazilli on card front)
❑ 158B Lee Mazzilli COR .10 .04
❑ 159 Tom Foley .05 .02
❑ 160 Robin Yount .30 .12
❑ 161 Steve Bedrosian .05 .02
❑ 162 Bob Walk .05 .02
❑ 163 Nick Esasky .05 .02
❑ 164 Ken Caminiti RC 2.00 .80
❑ 165 Jose Uribe .05 .02
❑ 166 Dave Anderson .05 .02
❑ 167 Ed Whitson .05 .02
❑ 168 Ernie Whitt .05 .02
❑ 169 Cecil Cooper .10 .04
❑ 170 Mike Pagliarulo .05 .02
❑ 171 Pat Sheridan .05 .02
❑ 172 Chris Bando .05 .02
❑ 173 Lee Lacy .05 .02
❑ 174 Steve Lombardozzi .05 .02
❑ 175 Mike Greenwell .05 .02
❑ 176 Greg Minton .05 .02
❑ 177 Moose Haas .05 .02
❑ 178 Mike Kingery .05 .02
❑ 179 Greg A. Harris .05 .02
❑ 180 Bo Jackson .20 .08
❑ 181 Carmelo Martinez .05 .02
❑ 182 Alex Trevino .05 .02
❑ 183 Ron Oester .05 .02
❑ 184 Danny Darwin .05 .02
❑ 185 Mike Krukow .05 .02
❑ 186 Rafael Palmeiro .40 .16
❑ 187 Tim Burke .05 .02
❑ 188 Roger McDowell .05 .02
❑ 189 Garry Templeton .10 .04
❑ 190 Terry Pendleton .10 .04
❑ 191 Larry Parrish .05 .02
❑ 192 Rey Quinones .05 .02
❑ 193 Joaquin Andujar .10 .04
❑ 194 Tom Brunansky .05 .02
❑ 195 Donnie Moore .05 .02
❑ 196 Dan Pasqua .05 .02
❑ 197 Jim Gantner .05 .02
❑ 198 Mark Eichhorn .05 .02
❑ 199 John Grubb .05 .02
❑ 200 Bill Ripken RC* .25 .10
❑ 201 Sam Horn RC .10 .04
❑ 202 Todd Worrell .05 .02
❑ 203 Terry Leach .05 .02
❑ 204 Garth Iorg .05 .02
❑ 205 Brian Dayett .05 .02
❑ 206 Bo Diaz .05 .02
❑ 207 Craig Reynolds .05 .02
❑ 208 Brian Holton .05 .02
❑ 209 Marvell Wynne UER .05 .02
(Misspelled Marvelle on card front)
❑ 210 Dave Concepcion .10 .04
❑ 211 Mike Davis .05 .02
❑ 212 Devon White .10 .04
❑ 213 Mickey Brantley .05 .02
❑ 214 Greg Gagne .05 .02
❑ 215 Oddibe McDowell .05 .02
❑ 216 Jimmy Key .10 .04
❑ 217 Dave Bergman .05 .02
❑ 218 Calvin Schiraldi .05 .02
❑ 219 Larry Sheets .05 .02
❑ 220 Mike Easler .05 .02
❑ 221 Kurt Stillwell .05 .02
❑ 222 Chuck Jackson .05 .02
❑ 223 Dave Martinez .05 .02
❑ 224 Tim Leary .05 .02
❑ 225 Steve Garvey .10 .04
❑ 226 Greg Mathews .05 .02
❑ 227 Doug Sisk .05 .02
❑ 228 Dave Henderson .05 .02
(Wearing Red Sox uniform; Red Sox logo on back)
❑ 229 Jimmy Dwyer .05 .02
❑ 230 Larry Owen .05 .02
❑ 231 Andre Thornton .05 .02
❑ 232 Mark Salas .05 .02
❑ 233 Tom Brookens .05 .02
❑ 234 Greg Brock .05 .02
❑ 235 Rance Mulliniks .05 .02
❑ 236 Bob Brower .05 .02

❑ 237 Joe Niekro .05 .02
❑ 238 Scott Bankhead .05 .02
❑ 239 Doug DeCinces .05 .02
❑ 240 Tommy John .10 .04
❑ 241 Rich Gedman .05 .02
❑ 242 Ted Power .05 .02
❑ 243 Dave Meads .05 .02
❑ 244 Jim Sundberg .10 .04
❑ 245 Ken Oberkfell .05 .02
❑ 246 Jimmy Jones .05 .02
❑ 247 Ken Landreaux .05 .02
❑ 248 Jose Oquendo .05 .02
❑ 249 John Mitchell RC .10 .04
❑ 250 Don Baylor .10 .04
❑ 251 Scott Fletcher .05 .02
❑ 252 Al Newman .05 .02
❑ 253 Carney Lansford .10 .04
❑ 254 Johnny Ray .05 .02
❑ 255 Gary Pettis .05 .02
❑ 256 Ken Phelps .05 .02
❑ 257 Rick Leach .05 .02
❑ 258 Tim Stoddard .05 .02
❑ 259 Ed Romero .05 .02
❑ 260 Sid Bream .05 .02
❑ 261A T.Niedenfuer ERR .10 .04
(Misspelled Neidenfuer on card front)
❑ 261B T.Niedenfuer COR .05 .02
❑ 262 Rick Dempsey .05 .02
❑ 263 Lonnie Smith .05 .02
❑ 264 Bob Forsch .05 .02
❑ 265 Barry Bonds 2.00 .80
❑ 266 Willie Randolph .10 .04
❑ 267 Mike Ramsey .05 .02
❑ 268 Don Slaught .05 .02
❑ 269 Mickey Tettleton .05 .02
❑ 270 Jerry Reuss .05 .02
❑ 271 Marc Sullivan .05 .02
❑ 272 Jim Morrison .05 .02
❑ 273 Steve Balboni .05 .02
❑ 274 Dick Schofield .05 .02
❑ 275 John Tudor .10 .04
❑ 276 Gene Larkin RC* .25 .10
❑ 277 Harold Reynolds .10 .04
❑ 278 Jerry Browne .05 .02
❑ 279 Willie Upshaw .05 .02
❑ 280 Ted Higuera .05 .02
❑ 281 Terry McGriff .05 .02
❑ 282 Terry Puhl .05 .02
❑ 283 Mark Wasinger .05 .02
❑ 284 Luis Salazar .05 .02
❑ 285 Ted Simmons .10 .04
❑ 286 John Shelby .05 .02
❑ 287 John Smiley RC* .25 .10
❑ 288 Curt Ford .05 .02
❑ 289 Steve Crawford .05 .02
❑ 290 Dan Quisenberry .05 .02
❑ 291 Alan Wiggins .05 .02
❑ 292 Randy Bush .05 .02
❑ 293 John Candelaria .05 .02
❑ 294 Tony Phillips .05 .02
❑ 295 Mike Morgan .05 .02
❑ 296 Bill Wegman .05 .02
❑ 297A Terry Francona ERR .10 .04
(Misspelled Franconia on card front)
❑ 297B Terry Francona COR .10 .04
❑ 298 Mickey Hatcher .05 .02
❑ 299 Andres Thomas .05 .02
❑ 300 Bob Stanley .05 .02
❑ 301 Al Pedrique .05 .02
❑ 302 Jim Lindeman .05 .02
❑ 303 Wally Backman .05 .02
❑ 304 Paul O'Neill .15 .06
❑ 305 Hubie Brooks .05 .02
❑ 306 Steve Buechele .05 .02
❑ 307 Bobby Thigpen .05 .02
❑ 308 George Hendrick .10 .04
❑ 309 John Moses .05 .02
❑ 310 Ron Guidry .10 .04
❑ 311 Bill Schroeder .05 .02
❑ 312 Jose Nunez .05 .02
❑ 313 Bud Black .05 .02
❑ 314 Joe Sambito .05 .02
❑ 315 Scott McGregor .05 .02
❑ 316 Rafael Santana .05 .02
❑ 317 Frank Williams .05 .02
❑ 318 Mike Fitzgerald .05 .02
❑ 319 Rick Mahler .05 .02
❑ 320 Jim Gott .05 .02
❑ 321 Mariano Duncan .05 .02
❑ 322 Jose Guzman .05 .02
❑ 323 Lee Guetterman .05 .02
❑ 324 Dan Gladden .05 .02
❑ 325 Gary Carter .10 .04
❑ 326 Tracy Jones .05 .02
❑ 327 Floyd Youmans .05 .02
❑ 328 Bill Dawley .05 .02
❑ 329 Paul Noce .05 .02
❑ 330 Angel Salazar .05 .02
❑ 331 Goose Gossage .10 .04
❑ 332 George Frazier .05 .02
❑ 333 Ruppert Jones .05 .02
❑ 334 Billy Joe Robidoux .05 .02
❑ 335 Mike Scott .10 .04
❑ 336 Randy Myers .10 .04
❑ 337 Bob Sebra .05 .02
❑ 338 Eric Show .05 .02
❑ 339 Mitch Williams .05 .02
❑ 340 Paul Molitor .15 .06
❑ 341 Gus Polidor .05 .02
❑ 342 Steve Trout .05 .02
❑ 343 Jerry Don Gleaton .05 .02
❑ 344 Bob Knepper .05 .02
❑ 345 Mitch Webster .05 .02
❑ 346 John Morris .05 .02
❑ 347 Andy Hawkins .05 .02
❑ 348 Dave Leiper .05 .02
❑ 349 Ernest Riles .05 .02
❑ 350 Dwight Gooden .10 .04
❑ 351 Dave Righetti .10 .04
❑ 352 Pat Dodson .05 .02
❑ 353 John Habyan .05 .02
❑ 354 Jim Deshaies .05 .02
❑ 355 Butch Wynegar .05 .02
❑ 356 Bryn Smith .05 .02
❑ 357 Matt Young .05 .02
❑ 358 Tom Pagnozzi RC .10 .04
❑ 359 Floyd Rayford .05 .02
❑ 360 Darryl Strawberry .10 .04
❑ 361 Sal Butera .05 .02
❑ 362 Domingo Ramos .05 .02
❑ 363 Chris Brown .05 .02
❑ 364 Jose Gonzalez .05 .02
❑ 365 Dave Smith .05 .02
❑ 366 Andy McGaffigan .05 .02
❑ 367 Stan Javier .05 .02
❑ 368 Henry Cotto .05 .02
❑ 369 Mike Birkbeck .05 .02
❑ 370 Len Dykstra .10 .04
❑ 371 Dave Collins .05 .02
❑ 372 Spike Owen .05 .02
❑ 373 Geno Petralli .05 .02
❑ 374 Ron Karkovice .05 .02
❑ 375 Shane Rawley .05 .02
❑ 376 DeWayne Buice .05 .02
❑ 377 Bill Pecota RC* .10 .04
❑ 378 Leon Durham .05 .02
❑ 379 Ed Olwine .05 .02
❑ 380 Bruce Hurst .05 .02
❑ 381 Bob McClure .05 .02
❑ 382 Mark Thurmond .05 .02
❑ 383 Buddy Biancalana .05 .02
❑ 384 Tim Conroy .05 .02
❑ 385 Tony Gwynn .30 .12
❑ 386 Greg Gross .05 .02
❑ 387 Barry Lyons .05 .02
❑ 388 Mike Felder .05 .02
❑ 389 Pat Clements .05 .02
❑ 390 Ken Griffey .10 .04
❑ 391 Mark Davis .05 .02
❑ 392 Jose Rijo .10 .04
❑ 393 Mike Young .05 .02
❑ 394 Willie Fraser .05 .02
❑ 395 Dion James .05 .02
❑ 396 Steve Shields .05 .02
❑ 397 Randy St.Claire .05 .02
❑ 398 Danny Jackson .05 .02
❑ 399 Cecil Fielder .10 .04
❑ 400 Keith Hernandez .10 .04
❑ 401 Don Carman .05 .02
❑ 402 Chuck Crim .05 .02
❑ 403 Rob Woodward .05 .02
❑ 404 Junior Ortiz .05 .02
❑ 405 Glenn Wilson .05 .02
❑ 406 Ken Howell .05 .02
❑ 407 Jeff Kunkel .05 .02
❑ 408 Jeff Reed .05 .02
❑ 409 Chris James .05 .02
❑ 410 Zane Smith .05 .02
❑ 411 Ken Dixon .05 .02
❑ 412 Ricky Horton .05 .02
❑ 413 Frank DiPino .05 .02
❑ 414 Shane Mack .05 .02
❑ 415 Danny Cox .05 .02
❑ 416 Andy Van Slyke .15 .06
❑ 417 Danny Heep .05 .02
❑ 418 John Cangelosi .05 .02
❑ 419A J.Christensen ERR .10 .04
(Christiansen on card front)
❑ 419B J.Christensen COR .05 .02
❑ 420 Joey Cora RC .25 .10
❑ 421 Mike LaValliere .05 .02
❑ 422 Kelly Gruber .05 .02
❑ 423 Bruce Benedict .05 .02
❑ 424 Len Matuszek .05 .02
❑ 425 Kent Tekulve .05 .02
❑ 426 Rafael Ramirez .05 .02
❑ 427 Mike Flanagan .05 .02
❑ 428 Mike Gallego .05 .02
❑ 429 Juan Castillo .05 .02
❑ 430 Neal Heaton .05 .02
❑ 431 Phil Garner .10 .04
❑ 432 Mike Dunne .05 .02
❑ 433 Wallace Johnson .05 .02
❑ 434 Jack O'Connor .05 .02
❑ 435 Steve Jeltz .05 .02
❑ 436 Donell Nixon .05 .02
❑ 437 Jack Lazorko .05 .02
❑ 438 Keith Comstock .05 .02
❑ 439 Jeff D. Robinson .05 .02
❑ 440 Graig Nettles .10 .04
❑ 441 Mel Hall .05 .02
❑ 442 Gerald Young .05 .02
❑ 443 Gary Redus .05 .02
❑ 444 Charlie Moore .05 .02
❑ 445 Bill Madlock .10 .04
❑ 446 Mark Clear .05 .02
❑ 447 Greg Booker .05 .02
❑ 448 Rick Schu .05 .02
❑ 449 Ron Kittle .05 .02
❑ 450 Dale Murphy .15 .06
❑ 451 Bob Dernier .05 .02
❑ 452 Dale Mohorcic .05 .02
❑ 453 Rafael Belliard .05 .02
❑ 454 Charlie Puleo .05 .02
❑ 455 Dwayne Murphy .05 .02
❑ 456 Jim Eisenreich .05 .02
❑ 457 David Palmer .05 .02
❑ 458 Dave Stewart .10 .04
❑ 459 Pascual Perez .05 .02
❑ 460 Glenn Davis .05 .02
❑ 461 Dan Petry .05 .02
❑ 462 Jim Winn .05 .02
❑ 463 Darrell Miller .05 .02
❑ 464 Mike Moore .05 .02
❑ 465 Mike LaCoss .05 .02
❑ 466 Steve Farr .05 .02
❑ 467 Jerry Mumphrey .05 .02
❑ 468 Kevin Gross .05 .02
❑ 469 Bruce Bochy .05 .02
❑ 470 Orel Hershiser .10 .04
❑ 471 Eric King .05 .02
❑ 472 Ellis Burks RC .40 .16
❑ 473 Darren Daulton .10 .04
❑ 474 Mookie Wilson .10 .04
❑ 475 Frank Viola .10 .04
❑ 476 Ron Robinson .05 .02
❑ 477 Bob Melvin .05 .02
❑ 478 Jeff Musselman .05 .02
❑ 479 Charlie Kerfeld .05 .02
❑ 480 Richard Dotson .05 .02
❑ 481 Kevin Mitchell .10 .04
❑ 482 Gary Roenicke .05 .02
❑ 483 Tim Flannery .05 .02
❑ 484 Rich Yett .05 .02
❑ 485 Pete Incaviglia .05 .02

- ❑ 486 Rick Cerone .05 .02
- ❑ 487 Tony Armas .10 .04
- ❑ 488 Jerry Reed .05 .02
- ❑ 489 Dave Lopes .10 .04
- ❑ 490 Frank Tanana .10 .04
- ❑ 491 Mike Loynd .05 .02
- ❑ 492 Bruce Ruffin .05 .02
- ❑ 493 Chris Speier .05 .02
- ❑ 494 Tom Hume .05 .02
- ❑ 495 Jesse Orosco .05 .02
- ❑ 496 Robbie Wine UER .05 .02 (Misspelled Robby on card front)
- ❑ 497 Jeff Montgomery RC .25 .10
- ❑ 498 Jeff Dedmon .05 .02
- ❑ 499 Luis Aguayo .05 .02
- ❑ 500 Reggie Jackson A's .15 .06
- ❑ 501 Reggie Jackson O's .15 .06
- ❑ 502 Reggie Jackson Yanks .15 .06
- ❑ 503 Reggie Jackson Angels .15 .06
- ❑ 504 Reggie Jackson A's .15 .06
- ❑ 505 Billy Hatcher .05 .02
- ❑ 506 Ed Lynch .05 .02
- ❑ 507 Willie Hernandez .05 .02
- ❑ 508 Jose DeLeon .05 .02
- ❑ 509 Joel Youngblood .05 .02
- ❑ 510 Bob Welch .10 .04
- ❑ 511 Steve Ontiveros .05 .02
- ❑ 512 Randy Ready .05 .02
- ❑ 513 Juan Nieves .05 .02
- ❑ 514 Jeff Russell .05 .02
- ❑ 515 Von Hayes .05 .02
- ❑ 516 Mark Gubicza .05 .02
- ❑ 517 Ken Dayley .05 .02
- ❑ 518 Don Aase .05 .02
- ❑ 519 Rick Reuschel .10 .04
- ❑ 520 Mike Henneman RC* .25 .10
- ❑ 521 Rick Aguilera .05 .02
- ❑ 522 Jay Howell .05 .02
- ❑ 523 Ed Correa .05 .02
- ❑ 524 Manny Trillo .05 .02
- ❑ 525 Kirk Gibson .20 .08
- ❑ 526 Wally Ritchie .05 .02
- ❑ 527 Al Nipper .05 .02
- ❑ 528 Atlee Hammaker .05 .02
- ❑ 529 Shawon Dunston .05 .02
- ❑ 530 Jim Clancy .05 .02
- ❑ 531 Tom Paciorek .05 .02
- ❑ 532 Joel Skinner .05 .02
- ❑ 533 Scott Garrelts .05 .02
- ❑ 534 Tom O'Malley .05 .02
- ❑ 535 John Franco .10 .04
- ❑ 536 Paul Kilgus .05 .02
- ❑ 537 Darrell Porter .05 .02
- ❑ 538 Walt Terrell .05 .02
- ❑ 539 Bill Long .05 .02
- ❑ 540 George Bell .10 .04
- ❑ 541 Jeff Sellers .05 .02
- ❑ 542 Joe Boever .05 .02
- ❑ 543 Steve Howe .05 .02
- ❑ 544 Scott Sanderson .05 .02
- ❑ 545 Jack Morris .10 .04
- ❑ 546 Todd Benzinger RC* .25 .10
- ❑ 547 Steve Henderson .05 .02
- ❑ 548 Eddie Milner .05 .02
- ❑ 549 Jeff M. Robinson .05 .02
- ❑ 550 Cal Ripken .75 .30
- ❑ 551 Jody Davis .05 .02
- ❑ 552 Kirk McCaskill .05 .02
- ❑ 553 Craig Lefferts .05 .02
- ❑ 554 Darnell Coles .05 .02
- ❑ 555 Phil Niekro .10 .04
- ❑ 556 Mike Aldrete .05 .02
- ❑ 557 Pat Perry .05 .02
- ❑ 558 Juan Agosto .05 .02
- ❑ 559 Rob Murphy .05 .02
- ❑ 560 Dennis Rasmussen .05 .02
- ❑ 561 Manny Lee .05 .02
- ❑ 562 Jeff Blauser RC .25 .10
- ❑ 563 Bob Ojeda .05 .02
- ❑ 564 Dave Dravecky .05 .02
- ❑ 565 Gene Garber .05 .02
- ❑ 566 Ron Roenicke .05 .02
- ❑ 567 Tommy Hinzo .05 .02
- ❑ 568 Eric Nolte .05 .02
- ❑ 569 Ed Hearn .05 .02
- ❑ 570 Mark Davidson .05 .02
- ❑ 571 Jim Walewander .05 .02
- ❑ 572 Donnie Hill UER .05 .02 (84 Stolen Base total listed as 7)
- ❑ 573 Jamie Moyer .10 .04
- ❑ 574 Ken Schrom .05 .02
- ❑ 575 Nolan Ryan 1.00 .40
- ❑ 576 Jim Acker .05 .02
- ❑ 577 Jamie Quirk .05 .02
- ❑ 578 Jay Aldrich .05 .02
- ❑ 579 Claudell Washington .05 .02
- ❑ 580 Jeff Leonard .05 .02
- ❑ 581 Carmen Castillo .05 .02
- ❑ 582 Daryl Boston .05 .02
- ❑ 583 Jeff DeWillis .05 .02
- ❑ 584 John Marzano .05 .02
- ❑ 585 Bill Gullickson .05 .02
- ❑ 586 Andy Allanson .05 .02
- ❑ 587 Lee Tunnell UER .05 .02 (1987 stat line reads .4.84 ERA)
- ❑ 588 Gene Nelson .05 .02
- ❑ 589 Dave LaPoint .05 .02
- ❑ 590 Harold Baines .10 .04
- ❑ 591 Bill Buckner .10 .04
- ❑ 592 Carlton Fisk .15 .06
- ❑ 593 Rick Manning .05 .02
- ❑ 594 Doug Jones RC .25 .10
- ❑ 595 Tom Candiotti .05 .02
- ❑ 596 Steve Lake .05 .02
- ❑ 597 Jose Lind RC .25 .10
- ❑ 598 Ross Jones .05 .02
- ❑ 599 Gary Matthews .10 .04
- ❑ 600 Fernando Valenzuela .10 .04
- ❑ 601 Dennis Martinez .10 .04
- ❑ 602 Les Lancaster .05 .02
- ❑ 603 Ozzie Guillen .10 .04
- ❑ 604 Tony Bernazard .05 .02
- ❑ 605 Chili Davis .10 .04
- ❑ 606 Roy Smalley .05 .02
- ❑ 607 Ivan Calderon .05 .02
- ❑ 608 Jay Tibbs .05 .02
- ❑ 609 Guy Hoffman .05 .02
- ❑ 610 Doyle Alexander .05 .02
- ❑ 611 Mike Bielecki .05 .02
- ❑ 612 Shawn Hillegas .05 .02
- ❑ 613 Keith Atherton .05 .02
- ❑ 614 Eric Plunk .05 .02
- ❑ 615 Sid Fernandez .05 .02
- ❑ 616 Dennis Lamp .05 .02
- ❑ 617 Dave Engle .05 .02
- ❑ 618 Harry Spilman .05 .02
- ❑ 619 Don Robinson .05 .02
- ❑ 620 John Farrell RC .10 .04
- ❑ 621 Nelson Liriano .05 .02
- ❑ 622 Floyd Bannister .05 .02
- ❑ 623 Randy Milligan RC .10 .04
- ❑ 624 Kevin Elster .05 .02
- ❑ 625 Jody Reed RC .25 .10
- ❑ 626 Shawn Abner .05 .02
- ❑ 627 Kirt Manwaring RC .25 .10
- ❑ 628 Pete Stanicek .05 .02
- ❑ 629 Rob Ducey .05 .02
- ❑ 630 Steve Kiefer .05 .02
- ❑ 631 Gary Thurman .05 .02
- ❑ 632 Darrel Akerfelds .05 .02
- ❑ 633 Dave Clark .05 .02
- ❑ 634 Roberto Kelly RC .25 .10
- ❑ 635 Keith Hughes .05 .02
- ❑ 636 John Davis .05 .02
- ❑ 637 Mike Devereaux RC .25 .10
- ❑ 638 Tom Glavine RC 2.00 .80
- ❑ 639 Keith A. Miller RC .25 .10
- ❑ 640 Chris Gwynn UER RC .25 .10 (Wrong batting and throwing on back)
- ❑ 641 Tim Crews RC .25 .10
- ❑ 642 Mackey Sasser RC .25 .10
- ❑ 643 Vicente Palacios .05 .02
- ❑ 644 Kevin Romine .05 .02
- ❑ 645 Gregg Jefferies RC .25 .10
- ❑ 646 Jeff Treadway RC .25 .10
- ❑ 647 Ron Gant RC .40 .16
- ❑ 648 Mark McGwire .75 .30 Matt Nokes
- ❑ 649 Eric Davis .10 .04 Tim Raines
- ❑ 650 Don Mattingly .30 .12 Jack Clark
- ❑ 651 Tony Fernandez .25 .10 Alan Trammell Cal Ripken
- ❑ 652 Vince Coleman HL .05 .02
- ❑ 653 Kirby Puckett HL .15 .06
- ❑ 654 Benito Santiago HL .05 .02
- ❑ 655 Juan Nieves HL .05 .02
- ❑ 656 Steve Bedrosian HL .05 .02
- ❑ 657 Mike Schmidt HL .20 .08
- ❑ 658 Don Mattingly HL .30 .12
- ❑ 659 Mark McGwire HL .75 .30
- ❑ 660 Paul Molitor HL .10 .04

1988 Score Rookie/Traded

	Nm-Mt	Ex-Mt
COMP.FACT.SET (110)	40.00	16.00
❑ 1T Jack Clark	.75	.30
❑ 2T Danny Jackson	.25	.10
❑ 3T Brett Butler	.75	.30
❑ 4T Kurt Stillwell	.25	.10
❑ 5T Tom Brunansky	.25	.10
❑ 6T Dennis Lamp	.25	.10
❑ 7T Jose DeLeon	.25	.10
❑ 8T Tom Herr	.25	.10
❑ 9T Keith Moreland	.25	.10
❑ 10T Kirk Gibson	2.00	.80
❑ 11T Bud Black	.25	.10
❑ 12T Rafael Ramirez	.25	.10
❑ 13T Luis Salazar	.25	.10
❑ 14T Goose Gossage	.75	.30
❑ 15T Bob Welch	.75	.30
❑ 16T Vance Law	.25	.10
❑ 17T Ray Knight	.75	.30
❑ 18T Dan Quisenberry	.25	.10
❑ 19T Don Slaught	.25	.10
❑ 20T Lee Smith	.75	.30
❑ 21T Rick Cerone	.25	.10
❑ 22T Pat Tabler	.25	.10
❑ 23T Larry McWilliams	.25	.10
❑ 24T Ricky Horton	.25	.10
❑ 25T Graig Nettles	.75	.30
❑ 26T Dan Petry	.25	.10
❑ 27T Jose Rijo	.75	.30
❑ 28T Chili Davis	.75	.30
❑ 29T Dickie Thon	.25	.10
❑ 30T Mackey Sasser	.25	.10
❑ 31T Mickey Tettleton	.25	.10
❑ 32T Rick Dempsey	.25	.10
❑ 33T Ron Hassey	.25	.10
❑ 34T Phil Bradley	.25	.10
❑ 35T Jay Howell	.25	.10
❑ 36T Bill Buckner	.75	.30
❑ 37T Alfredo Griffin	.25	.10
❑ 38T Gary Pettis	.25	.10
❑ 39T Calvin Schiraldi	.25	.10
❑ 40T John Candelaria	.25	.10
❑ 41T Joe Orsulak	.25	.10
❑ 42T Willie Upshaw	.25	.10
❑ 43T Herm Winningham	.25	.10
❑ 44T Ron Kittle	.25	.10
❑ 45T Bob Dernier	.25	.10
❑ 46T Steve Balboni	.25	.10

❑ 47T Steve Shields	.25	.10
❑ 48T Henry Cotto	.25	.10
❑ 49T Dave Henderson	.25	.10
❑ 50T Dave Parker	.75	.30
❑ 51T Mike Young	.25	.10
❑ 52T Mark Salas	.25	.10
❑ 53T Mike Davis	.25	.10
❑ 54T Rafael Santana	.25	.10
❑ 55T Don Baylor	.75	.30
❑ 56T Dan Pasqua	.25	.10
❑ 57T Ernest Riles	.25	.10
❑ 58T Glenn Hubbard	.25	.10
❑ 59T Mike Smithson	.25	.10
❑ 60T Richard Dotson	.25	.10
❑ 61T Jerry Reuss	.25	.10
❑ 62T Mike Jackson	.75	.30
❑ 63T Floyd Bannister	.25	.10
❑ 64T Jesse Orosco	.25	.10
❑ 65T Larry Parrish	.25	.10
❑ 66T Jeff Bittiger	.25	.10
❑ 67T Ray Hayward	.25	.10
❑ 68T Ricky Jordan XRC	.75	.30
❑ 69T Tommy Gregg	.25	.10
❑ 70T Brady Anderson XRC	1.25	.50
❑ 71T Jeff Montgomery	.75	.30
❑ 72T Darryl Hamilton XRC	.75	.30
❑ 73T Cecil Espy	.25	.10
❑ 74T Greg Briley XRC	.25	.10
❑ 75T Joey Meyer	.25	.10
❑ 76T Mike Macfarlane XRC	.75	.30
❑ 77T Oswald Peraza	.25	.10
❑ 78T Jack Armstrong XRC	.25	.10
❑ 79T Don Heinkel	.25	.10
❑ 80T Mark Grace XRC	8.00	3.20
❑ 81T Steve Curry	.25	.10
❑ 82T Damon Berryhill XRC	.75	.30
❑ 83T Steve Ellsworth	.25	.10
❑ 84T Pete Smith XRC*	.25	.10
❑ 85T Jack McDowell XRC	1.25	.50
❑ 86T Rob Dibble XRC	2.00	.80
❑ 87T Bryan Harvey UER (Games Pitched 47, Innings 5) XRC	.75	.30
❑ 88T John Dopson	.25	.10
❑ 89T Dave Gallagher	.25	.10
❑ 90T Todd Stottlemyre XRC	.75	.30
❑ 91T Mike Schooler	.25	.10
❑ 92T Don Gordon	.25	.10
❑ 93T Sil Campusano	.25	.10
❑ 94T Jeff Pico	.25	.10
❑ 95T Jay Buhner XRC	2.00	.80
❑ 96T Nelson Santovenia	.25	.10
❑ 97T Al Leiter XRC*	3.00	1.20
❑ 98T Luis Alicea XRC	.75	.30
❑ 99T Pat Borders XRC	.75	.30
❑ 100T Chris Sabo XRC	1.25	.50
❑ 101T Tim Belcher	.25	.10
❑ 102T Walt Weiss XRC*	1.25	.50
❑ 103T Craig Biggio XRC	10.00	4.00
❑ 104T Don August	.25	.10
❑ 105T Roberto Alomar XRC	10.00	4.00
❑ 106T Todd Burns	.25	.10
❑ 107T John Costello	.25	.10
❑ 108T Melido Perez XRC*	.75	.30
❑ 109T Darrin Jackson XRC	.25	.10
❑ 110T O.Destrade XRC	.25	.10

1989 Score Rookie/Traded

	Nm-Mt	Ex-Mt
COMP.FACT.SET (110)	15.00	6.00
❑ 1T Rafael Palmeiro	.25	.10
❑ 2T Nolan Ryan	1.50	.60
❑ 3T Jack Clark	.10	.04
❑ 4T Dave LaPoint	.05	.02
❑ 5T Mike Moore	.05	.02
❑ 6T Pete O'Brien	.05	.02
❑ 7T Jeffrey Leonard	.05	.02
❑ 8T Rob Murphy	.05	.02
❑ 9T Tom Herr	.05	.02
❑ 10T Claudell Washington	.05	.02
❑ 11T Mike Pagliarulo	.05	.02
❑ 12T Steve Lake	.05	.02
❑ 13T Spike Owen	.05	.02

❑ 14T Andy Hawkins	.05	.02
❑ 15T Todd Benzinger	.05	.02
❑ 16T Mookie Wilson	.10	.04
❑ 17T Bert Blyleven	.10	.04
❑ 18T Jeff Treadway	.05	.02
❑ 19T Bruce Hurst	.05	.02
❑ 20T Steve Sax	.05	.02
❑ 21T Juan Samuel	.05	.02
❑ 22T Jesse Barfield	.10	.04
❑ 23T Carmen Castillo	.05	.02
❑ 24T Terry Leach	.05	.02
❑ 25T Mark Langston	.05	.02
❑ 26T Eric King	.05	.02
❑ 27T Steve Balboni	.05	.02
❑ 28T Len Dykstra	.10	.04
❑ 29T Keith Moreland	.05	.02
❑ 30T Terry Kennedy	.05	.02
❑ 31T Eddie Murray	.25	.10
❑ 32T Mitch Williams	.05	.02
❑ 33T Jeff Parrett	.05	.02
❑ 34T Wally Backman	.05	.02
❑ 35T Julio Franco	.10	.04
❑ 36T Lance Parrish	.10	.04
❑ 37T Nick Esasky	.05	.02
❑ 38T Luis Polonia	.05	.02
❑ 39T Kevin Gross	.05	.02
❑ 40T John Dopson	.05	.02
❑ 41T Willie Randolph	.10	.04
❑ 42T Jim Clancy	.05	.02
❑ 43T Tracy Jones	.05	.02
❑ 44T Phil Bradley	.05	.02
❑ 45T Milt Thompson	.05	.02
❑ 46T Chris James	.05	.02
❑ 47T Scott Fletcher	.05	.02
❑ 48T Kal Daniels	.05	.02
❑ 49T Steve Bedrosian	.05	.02
❑ 50T Rickey Henderson	.25	.10
❑ 51T Dion James	.05	.02
❑ 52T Tim Leary	.05	.02
❑ 53T Roger McDowell	.05	.02
❑ 54T Mel Hall	.05	.02
❑ 55T Dickie Thon	.05	.02
❑ 56T Zane Smith	.05	.02
❑ 57T Danny Heep	.05	.02
❑ 58T Bob McClure	.05	.02
❑ 59T Brian Holton	.05	.02
❑ 60T Randy Ready	.05	.02
❑ 61T Bob Melvin	.05	.02
❑ 62T Harold Baines	.10	.04
❑ 63T Lance McCullers	.05	.02
❑ 64T Jody Davis	.05	.02
❑ 65T Darrell Evans	.10	.04
❑ 66T Joel Youngblood	.05	.02
❑ 67T Frank Viola	.10	.04
❑ 68T Mike Aldrete	.05	.02
❑ 69T Greg Cadaret	.05	.02
❑ 70T John Kruk	.10	.04
❑ 71T Pat Sheridan	.05	.02
❑ 72T Oddibe McDowell	.05	.02
❑ 73T Tom Brookens	.05	.02
❑ 74T Bob Boone	.10	.04
❑ 75T Walt Terrell	.05	.02
❑ 76T Joel Skinner	.05	.02
❑ 77T Randy Johnson	3.00	1.20
❑ 78T Felix Fermin	.05	.02
❑ 79T Rick Mahler	.05	.02
❑ 80T Richard Dotson	.05	.02
❑ 81T Cris Carpenter RC *	.10	.04
❑ 82T Bill Spiers RC	.25	.10
❑ 83T Junior Felix RC	.10	.04
❑ 84T Joe Girardi RC	.40	.16
❑ 85T Jerome Walton RC	.25	.10
❑ 86T Greg Litton	.05	.02
❑ 87T Greg W.Harris RC	.10	.04
❑ 88T Jim Abbott RC*	1.00	.40
❑ 89T Kevin Brown	.25	.10
❑ 90T John Wetteland RC	.40	.16
❑ 91T Gary Wayne	.05	.02
❑ 92T Rich Monteleone	.05	.02
❑ 93T Bob Geren RC	.05	.02
❑ 94T Clay Parker	.05	.02
❑ 95T Steve Finley RC	.75	.30
❑ 96T Gregg Olson RC	.25	.10
❑ 97T Ken Patterson	.05	.02
❑ 98T Ken Hill RC	.25	.10
❑ 99T Scott Scudder RC	.10	.04
❑ 100T Ken Griffey Jr. RC	8.00	3.20
❑ 101T Jeff Brantley RC	.25	.10
❑ 102T Donn Pall	.05	.02
❑ 103T Carlos Martinez RC	.10	.04
❑ 104T Joe Oliver RC	.25	.10
❑ 105T Omar Vizquel RC	1.00	.40
❑ 106T Joey Belle RC	1.00	.40
❑ 107T Kenny Rogers RC	1.00	.40
❑ 108T Mark Carreon	.05	.02
❑ 109T Rolando Roomes	.05	.02
❑ 110T Pete Harnisch RC	.25	.10

1990 Score

	Nm-Mt	Ex-Mt
COMPLETE SET (704)	15.00	4.50
COMP.RETAIL SET (704)	15.00	4.50
COMP.HOBBY SET (714)	15.00	4.50
❑ 1 Don Mattingly	.60	.18
❑ 2 Cal Ripken	.75	.23
❑ 3 Dwight Evans	.15	.04
❑ 4 Barry Bonds	1.00	.30
❑ 5 Kevin McReynolds	.05	.02
❑ 6 Ozzie Guillen	.10	.03
❑ 7 Terry Kennedy	.05	.02
❑ 8 Bryan Harvey	.05	.02
❑ 9 Alan Trammell	.10	.03
❑ 10 Cory Snyder	.05	.02
❑ 11 Jody Reed	.05	.02
❑ 12 Roberto Alomar	.15	.04
❑ 13 Pedro Guerrero	.05	.02
❑ 14 Gary Redus	.05	.02
❑ 15 Marty Barrett	.05	.02
❑ 16 Ricky Jordan	.05	.02
❑ 17 Joe Magrane	.05	.02
❑ 18 Sid Fernandez	.05	.02
❑ 19 Richard Dotson	.05	.02
❑ 20 Jack Clark	.10	.03
❑ 21 Bob Walk	.05	.02
❑ 22 Ron Karkovice	.05	.02
❑ 23 Lenny Harris	.05	.02
❑ 24 Phil Bradley	.05	.02
❑ 25 Andres Galarraga	.10	.03
❑ 26 Brian Downing	.05	.02
❑ 27 Dave Martinez	.05	.02
❑ 28 Eric King	.05	.02
❑ 29 Barry Lyons	.05	.02
❑ 30 Dave Schmidt	.05	.02
❑ 31 Mike Boddicker	.05	.02
❑ 32 Tom Foley	.05	.02

❑ 33 Brady Anderson .10 .03
❑ 34 Jim Presley .05 .02
❑ 35 Lance Parrish .05 .02
❑ 36 Von Hayes .05 .02
❑ 37 Lee Smith .10 .03
❑ 38 Herm Winningham .05 .02
❑ 39 Alejandro Pena .05 .02
❑ 40 Mike Scott .05 .02
❑ 41 Joe Orsulak .05 .02
❑ 42 Rafael Ramirez .05 .02
❑ 43 Gerald Young .05 .02
❑ 44 Dick Schofield .05 .02
❑ 45 Dave Smith .05 .02
❑ 46 Dave Magadan .05 .02
❑ 47 Dennis Martinez .10 .03
❑ 48 Greg Minton .05 .02
❑ 49 Milt Thompson .05 .02
❑ 50 Orel Hershiser .10 .03
❑ 51 Bip Roberts .05 .02
❑ 52 Jerry Browne .05 .02
❑ 53 Bob Ojeda .05 .02
❑ 54 Fernando Valenzuela .10 .03
❑ 55 Matt Nokes .05 .02
❑ 56 Brook Jacoby .05 .02
❑ 57 Frank Tanana .05 .02
❑ 58 Scott Fletcher .05 .02
❑ 59 Ron Oester .05 .02
❑ 60 Bob Boone .10 .03
❑ 61 Dan Gladden .05 .02
❑ 62 Darnell Coles .05 .02
❑ 63 Gregg Olson .10 .03
❑ 64 Todd Burns .05 .02
❑ 65 Todd Benzinger .05 .02
❑ 66 Dale Murphy .15 .04
❑ 67 Mike Flanagan .05 .02
❑ 68 Jose Oquendo .05 .02
❑ 69 Cecil Espy .05 .02
❑ 70 Chris Sabo .05 .02
❑ 71 Shane Rawley .05 .02
❑ 72 Tom Brunansky .05 .02
❑ 73 Vance Law .05 .02
❑ 74 B.J. Surhoff .10 .03
❑ 75 Lou Whitaker .10 .03
❑ 76 Ken Caminiti UER .10 .03
Euclid and Ohio should be Hanford and California
❑ 77 Nelson Liriano .05 .02
❑ 78 Tommy Gregg .05 .02
❑ 79 Don Slaught .05 .02
❑ 80 Eddie Murray .25 .07
❑ 81 Joe Boever .05 .02
❑ 82 Charlie Leibrandt .05 .02
❑ 83 Jose Lind .05 .02
❑ 84 Tony Phillips .05 .02
❑ 85 Mitch Webster .05 .02
❑ 86 Dan Plesac .05 .02
❑ 87 Rick Mahler .05 .02
❑ 88 Steve Lyons .05 .02
❑ 89 Tony Fernandez .05 .02
❑ 90 Ryne Sandberg .40 .12
❑ 91 Nick Esasky .05 .02
❑ 92 Luis Salazar .05 .02
❑ 93 Pete Incaviglia .05 .02
❑ 94 Ivan Calderon .05 .02
❑ 95 Jeff Treadway .05 .02
❑ 96 Kurt Stillwell .05 .02
❑ 97 Gary Sheffield .25 .07
❑ 98 Jeffrey Leonard .05 .02
❑ 99 Andres Thomas .05 .02
❑ 100 Roberto Kelly .05 .02
❑ 101 Alvaro Espinoza .05 .02
❑ 102 Greg Gagne .05 .02
❑ 103 John Farrell .05 .02
❑ 104 Willie Wilson .05 .02
❑ 105 Glenn Braggs .05 .02
❑ 106 Chet Lemon .05 .02
❑ 107A Jamie Moyer ERR .10 .03
(Scintilating)
❑ 107B Jamie Moyer COR .50 .15
(Scintillating)
❑ 108 Chuck Crim .05 .02
❑ 109 Dave Valle .05 .02
❑ 110 Walt Weiss .05 .02
❑ 111 Larry Sheets .05 .02
❑ 112 Don Robinson .05 .02
❑ 113 Danny Heep .05 .02
❑ 114 Carmelo Martinez .05 .02
❑ 115 Dave Gallagher .05 .02
❑ 116 Mike LaValliere .05 .02
❑ 117 Bob McClure .05 .02
❑ 118 Rene Gonzales .05 .02
❑ 119 Mark Parent .05 .02
❑ 120 Wally Joyner .10 .03
❑ 121 Mark Gubicza .05 .02
❑ 122 Tony Pena .05 .02
❑ 123 Carmelo Castillo .05 .02
❑ 124 Howard Johnson .05 .02
❑ 125 Steve Sax .05 .02
❑ 126 Tim Belcher .05 .02
❑ 127 Tim Burke .05 .02
❑ 128 Al Newman .05 .02
❑ 129 Dennis Rasmussen .05 .02
❑ 130 Doug Jones .05 .02
❑ 131 Fred Lynn .05 .02
❑ 132 Jeff Hamilton .05 .02
❑ 133 German Gonzalez .05 .02
❑ 134 John Morris .05 .02
❑ 135 Dave Parker .10 .03
❑ 136 Gary Pettis .05 .02
❑ 137 Dennis Boyd .05 .02
❑ 138 Candy Maldonado .05 .02
❑ 139 Rick Cerone .05 .02
❑ 140 George Brett .60 .18
❑ 141 Dave Clark .05 .02
❑ 142 Dickie Thon .05 .02
❑ 143 Junior Ortiz .05 .02
❑ 144 Don August .05 .02
❑ 145 Gary Gaetti .10 .03
❑ 146 Kirt Manwaring .05 .02
❑ 147 Jeff Reed .05 .02
❑ 148 Jose Alvarez .05 .02
❑ 149 Mike Schooler .05 .02
❑ 150 Mark Grace .15 .04
❑ 151 Geronimo Berroa .05 .02
❑ 152 Barry Jones .05 .02
❑ 153 Geno Petralli .05 .02
❑ 154 Jim Deshaies .05 .02
❑ 155 Barry Larkin .15 .04
❑ 156 Alfredo Griffin .05 .02
❑ 157 Tom Henke .05 .02
❑ 158 Mike Jeffcoat .05 .02
❑ 159 Bob Welch .05 .02
❑ 160 Julio Franco .10 .03
❑ 161 Henry Cotto .05 .02
❑ 162 Terry Steinbach .05 .02
❑ 163 Damon Berryhill .05 .02
❑ 164 Tim Crews .05 .02
❑ 165 Tom Browning .05 .02
❑ 166 Fred Manrique .05 .02
❑ 167 Harold Reynolds .10 .03
❑ 168A Ron Hassey ERR .05 .02
(27 on back)
❑ 168B Ron Hassey COR .50 .15
(24 on back)
❑ 169 Shawon Dunston .05 .02
❑ 170 Bobby Bonilla .10 .03
❑ 171 Tommy Herr .05 .02
❑ 172 Mike Heath .05 .02
❑ 173 Rich Gedman .05 .02
❑ 174 Bill Ripken .05 .02
❑ 175 Pete O'Brien .05 .02
❑ 176A L.McClendon ERR .05 .02
Uniform number on back listed as 1
❑ 176B L.McClendon COR .50 .15
Uniform number on back listed as 10
❑ 177 Brian Holton .05 .02
❑ 178 Jeff Blauser .05 .02
❑ 179 Jim Eisenreich .05 .02
❑ 180 Bert Blyleven .10 .03
❑ 181 Rob Murphy .05 .02
❑ 182 Bill Doran .05 .02
❑ 183 Curt Ford .05 .02
❑ 184 Mike Henneman .05 .02
❑ 185 Eric Davis .10 .03
❑ 186 Lance McCullers .05 .02
❑ 187 Steve Davis .05 .02
❑ 188 Bill Wegman .05 .02
❑ 189 Brian Harper .05 .02
❑ 190 Mike Moore .05 .02
❑ 191 Dale Mohorcic .05 .02
❑ 192 Tim Wallach .05 .02
❑ 193 Keith Hernandez .10 .03
❑ 194 Dave Righetti .05 .02
❑ 195A B.Saberhagen ERR .10 .03
Joke
❑ 195B B.Saberhagen COR .50 .15
Joker
❑ 196 Paul Kilgus .05 .02
❑ 197 Bud Black .05 .02
❑ 198 Juan Samuel .05 .02
❑ 199 Kevin Seitzer .05 .02
❑ 200 Darryl Strawberry .10 .03
❑ 201 Dave Stieb .10 .03
❑ 202 Charlie Hough .10 .03
❑ 203 Jack Morris .10 .03
❑ 204 Rance Mulliniks .05 .02
❑ 205 Alvin Davis .05 .02
❑ 206 Jack Howell .05 .02
❑ 207 Ken Patterson .05 .02
❑ 208 Terry Pendleton .10 .03
❑ 209 Craig Lefferts .05 .02
❑ 210 Kevin Brown UER .10 .03
(First mention of '89 Rangers should be '88)
❑ 211 Dan Petry .05 .02
❑ 212 Dave Leiper .05 .02
❑ 213 Daryl Boston .05 .02
❑ 214 Kevin Hickey .05 .02
❑ 215 Mike Krukow .05 .02
❑ 216 Terry Francona .10 .03
❑ 217 Kirk McCaskill .05 .02
❑ 218 Scott Bailes .05 .02
❑ 219 Bob Forsch .05 .02
❑ 220A Mike Aldrete ERR .05 .02
(25 on back)
❑ 220B Mike Aldrete COR .50 .15
(24 on back)
❑ 221 Steve Buechele .05 .02
❑ 222 Jesse Barfield .05 .02
❑ 223 Juan Berenguer .05 .02
❑ 224 Andy McGaffigan .05 .02
❑ 225 Pete Smith .05 .02
❑ 226 Mike Witt .05 .02
❑ 227 Jay Howell .05 .02
❑ 228 Scott Bradley .05 .02
❑ 229 Jerome Walton .05 .02
❑ 230 Greg Swindell .05 .02
❑ 231 Atlee Hammaker .05 .02
❑ 232A Mike Devereaux ERR .05 .02
(RF on front)
❑ 232B M.Devereaux COR .50 .15
CF on front
❑ 233 Ken Hill .10 .03
❑ 234 Craig Worthington .05 .02
❑ 235 Scott Terry .05 .02
❑ 236 Brett Butler .10 .03
❑ 237 Doyle Alexander .05 .02
❑ 238 Dave Anderson .05 .02
❑ 239 Bob Milacki .05 .02
❑ 240 Dwight Smith .05 .02
❑ 241 Otis Nixon .05 .02
❑ 242 Pat Tabler .05 .02
❑ 243 Derek Lilliquist .05 .02
❑ 244 Danny Tartabull .05 .02
❑ 245 Wade Boggs .15 .04
❑ 246 Scott Garrelts .05 .02
(Should say Relief Pitcher on front)
❑ 247 Spike Owen .05 .02
❑ 248 Norm Charlton .05 .02
❑ 249 Gerald Perry .05 .02
❑ 250 Nolan Ryan 1.00 .30
❑ 251 Kevin Gross .05 .02
❑ 252 Randy Milligan .05 .02
❑ 253 Mike LaCoss .05 .02
❑ 254 Dave Bergman .05 .02
❑ 255 Tony Gwynn .30 .09
❑ 256 Felix Fermin .05 .02
❑ 257 Greg W. Harris .05 .02
❑ 258 Junior Felix .05 .02
❑ 259 Mark Davis .05 .02
❑ 260 Vince Coleman .05 .02
❑ 261 Paul Gibson .05 .02
❑ 262 Mitch Williams .05 .02
❑ 263 Jeff Russell .05 .02
❑ 264 Omar Vizquel .25 .07

❑ 265 Andre Dawson .10 .03
❑ 266 Storm Davis .05 .02
❑ 267 Guillermo Hernandez .05 .02
❑ 268 Mike Felder .05 .02
❑ 269 Tom Candiotti .05 .02
❑ 270 Bruce Hurst .05 .02
❑ 271 Fred McGriff .25 .07
❑ 272 Glenn Davis .05 .02
❑ 273 John Franco .10 .03
❑ 274 Rich Yett .05 .02
❑ 275 Craig Biggio .25 .07
❑ 276 Gene Larkin .05 .02
❑ 277 Rob Dibble .10 .03
❑ 278 Randy Bush .05 .02
❑ 279 Kevin Bass .05 .02
❑ 280A Bo Jackson ERR .25 .07
(Watham)
❑ 280B Bo Jackson COR .75 .23
(Wathan)
❑ 281 Wally Backman .05 .02
❑ 282 Larry Andersen .05 .02
❑ 283 Chris Bosio .05 .02
❑ 284 Juan Agosto .05 .02
❑ 285 Ozzie Smith .40 .12
❑ 286 George Bell .05 .02
❑ 287 Rex Hudler .05 .02
❑ 288 Pat Borders .05 .02
❑ 289 Danny Jackson .05 .02
❑ 290 Carlton Fisk .15 .04
❑ 291 Tracy Jones .05 .02
❑ 292 Allan Anderson .05 .02
❑ 293 Johnny Ray .05 .02
❑ 294 Lee Guetterman .05 .02
❑ 295 Paul O'Neill .15 .04
❑ 296 Carney Lansford .10 .03
❑ 297 Tom Brookens .05 .02
❑ 298 Claudell Washington .05 .02
❑ 299 Hubie Brooks .05 .02
❑ 300 Will Clark .15 .04
❑ 301 Kenny Rogers .10 .03
❑ 302 Darrell Evans .10 .03
❑ 303 Greg Briley .05 .02
❑ 304 Donn Pall .05 .02
❑ 305 Teddy Higuera .05 .02
❑ 306 Dan Pasqua .05 .02
❑ 307 Dave Winfield .10 .03
❑ 308 Dennis Powell .05 .02
❑ 309 Jose DeLeon .05 .02
❑ 310 Roger Clemens UER .50 .15
(Dominate, should say dominant)
❑ 311 Melido Perez .05 .02
❑ 312 Devon White .10 .03
❑ 313 Dwight Gooden .10 .03
❑ 314 Carlos Martinez .05 .02
❑ 315 Dennis Eckersley .10 .03
❑ 316 Clay Parker UER .05 .02
(Height 6'11")
❑ 317 Rick Honeycutt .05 .02
❑ 318 Tim Laudner .05 .02
❑ 319 Joe Carter .10 .03
❑ 320 Robin Yount .40 .12
❑ 321 Felix Jose .05 .02
❑ 322 Mickey Tettleton .05 .02
❑ 323 Mike Gallego .05 .02
❑ 324 Edgar Martinez .15 .04
❑ 325 Dave Henderson .05 .02
❑ 326 Chili Davis .10 .03
❑ 327 Steve Balboni .05 .02
❑ 328 Jody Davis .05 .02
❑ 329 Shawn Hillegas .05 .02
❑ 330 Jim Abbott .15 .04
❑ 331 John Dopson .05 .02
❑ 332 Mark Williamson .05 .02
❑ 333 Jeff D. Robinson .05 .02
❑ 334 John Smiley .05 .02
❑ 335 Bobby Thigpen .05 .02
❑ 336 Garry Templeton .05 .02
❑ 337 Marvell Wynne .05 .02
❑ 338A Ken Griffey Sr. ERR .10 .03
(Uniform number on back listed as 25)
❑ 338B Ken Griffey Sr. COR .50 .15
(Uniform number on back listed as 30)
❑ 339 Steve Finley .10 .03
❑ 340 Ellis Burks .15 .04
❑ 341 Frank Williams .05 .02
❑ 342 Mike Morgan .05 .02
❑ 343 Kevin Mitchell .05 .02
❑ 344 Joel Youngblood .05 .02
❑ 345 Mike Greenwell .05 .02
❑ 346 Glenn Wilson .05 .02
❑ 347 John Costello .05 .02
❑ 348 Wes Gardner .05 .02
❑ 349 Jeff Ballard .05 .02
❑ 350 Mark Thurmond UER .05 .02
(ERA is 192, should be 1.92)
❑ 351 Randy Myers .10 .03
❑ 352 Shawn Abner .05 .02
❑ 353 Jesse Orosco .05 .02
❑ 354 Greg Walker .05 .02
❑ 355 Pete Harnisch .05 .02
❑ 356 Steve Farr .05 .02
❑ 357 Dave LaPoint .05 .02
❑ 358 Willie Fraser .05 .02
❑ 359 Mickey Hatcher .05 .02
❑ 360 Rickey Henderson .25 .07
❑ 361 Mike Fitzgerald .05 .02
❑ 362 Bill Schroeder .05 .02
❑ 363 Mark Carreon .05 .02
❑ 364 Ron Jones .05 .02
❑ 365 Jeff Montgomery .10 .03
❑ 366 Bill Krueger .05 .02
❑ 367 John Cangelosi .05 .02
❑ 368 Jose Gonzalez .05 .02
❑ 369 Greg Hibbard RC .10 .03
❑ 370 John Smoltz .25 .07
❑ 371 Jeff Brantley .05 .02
❑ 372 Frank White .10 .03
❑ 373 Ed Whitson .05 .02
❑ 374 Willie McGee .10 .03
❑ 375 Jose Canseco .15 .04
❑ 376 Randy Ready .05 .02
❑ 377 Don Aase .05 .02
❑ 378 Tony Armas .05 .02
❑ 379 Steve Bedrosian .05 .02
❑ 380 Chuck Finley .10 .03
❑ 381 Kent Hrbek .10 .03
❑ 382 Jim Gantner .05 .02
❑ 383 Mel Hall .05 .02
❑ 384 Mike Marshall .05 .02
❑ 385 Mark McGwire .60 .18
❑ 386 Wayne Tolleson .05 .02
❑ 387 Brian Holman .05 .02
❑ 388 John Wetteland .25 .07
❑ 389 Darren Daulton .10 .03
❑ 390 Rob Deer .05 .02
❑ 391 John Moses .05 .02
❑ 392 Todd Worrell .05 .02
❑ 393 Chuck Cary .05 .02
❑ 394 Stan Javier .05 .02
❑ 395 Willie Randolph .10 .03
❑ 396 Bill Buckner .05 .02
❑ 397 Robby Thompson .05 .02
❑ 398 Mike Scioscia .05 .02
❑ 399 Lonnie Smith .05 .02
❑ 400 Kirby Puckett .25 .07
❑ 401 Mark Langston .05 .02
❑ 402 Danny Darwin .05 .02
❑ 403 Greg Maddux .40 .12
❑ 404 Lloyd Moseby .05 .02
❑ 405 Rafael Palmeiro .15 .04
❑ 406 Chad Kreuter .05 .02
❑ 407 Jimmy Key .10 .03
❑ 408 Tim Birtsas .05 .02
❑ 409 Tim Raines .10 .03
❑ 410 Dave Stewart .10 .03
❑ 411 Eric Yelding .05 .02
❑ 412 Kent Anderson .05 .02
❑ 413 Les Lancaster .05 .02
❑ 414 Rick Dempsey .05 .02
❑ 415 Randy Johnson .50 .15
❑ 416 Gary Carter .10 .03
❑ 417 Rolando Roomes .05 .02
❑ 418 Dan Schatzeder .05 .02
❑ 419 Bryn Smith .05 .02
❑ 420 Ruben Sierra .05 .02
❑ 421 Steve Jeltz .05 .02
❑ 422 Ken Oberkfell .05 .02
❑ 423 Sid Bream .05 .02
❑ 424 Jim Clancy .05 .02
❑ 425 Kelly Gruber .05 .02
❑ 426 Rick Leach .05 .02
❑ 427 Len Dykstra .10 .03
❑ 428 Jeff Pico .05 .02
❑ 429 John Cerutti .05 .02
❑ 430 David Cone .10 .03
❑ 431 Jeff Kunkel .05 .02
❑ 432 Luis Aquino .05 .02
❑ 433 Ernie Whitt .05 .02
❑ 434 Bo Diaz .05 .02
❑ 435 Steve Lake .05 .02
❑ 436 Pat Perry .05 .02
❑ 437 Mike Davis .05 .02
❑ 438 Cecilio Guante .05 .02
❑ 439 Duane Ward .05 .02
❑ 440 Andy Van Slyke .15 .04
❑ 441 Gene Nelson .05 .02
❑ 442 Luis Polonia .05 .02
❑ 443 Kevin Elster .05 .02
❑ 444 Keith Moreland .05 .02
❑ 445 Roger McDowell .05 .02
❑ 446 Ron Darling .05 .02
❑ 447 Ernest Riles .05 .02
❑ 448 Mookie Wilson .10 .03
❑ 449A Billy Spiers ERR .05 .02
(No birth year)
❑ 449B Billy Spiers COR .50 .15
(Born in 1966)
❑ 450 Rick Sutcliffe .10 .03
❑ 451 Nelson Santovenia .05 .02
❑ 452 Andy Allanson .05 .02
❑ 453 Bob Melvin .05 .02
❑ 454 Benito Santiago .10 .03
❑ 455 Jose Uribe .05 .02
❑ 456 Bill Landrum .05 .02
❑ 457 Bobby Witt .05 .02
❑ 458 Kevin Romine .05 .02
❑ 459 Lee Mazzilli .05 .02
❑ 460 Paul Molitor .15 .04
❑ 461 Ramon Martinez .05 .02
❑ 462 Frank DiPino .05 .02
❑ 463 Walt Terrell .05 .02
❑ 464 Bob Geren .05 .02
❑ 465 Rick Reuschel .05 .02
❑ 466 Mark Grant .05 .02
❑ 467 John Kruk .10 .03
❑ 468 Gregg Jefferies .10 .03
❑ 469 R.J. Reynolds .05 .02
❑ 470 Harold Baines .10 .03
❑ 471 Dennis Lamp .05 .02
❑ 472 Tom Gordon .10 .03
❑ 473 Terry Puhl .05 .02
❑ 474 Curt Wilkerson .05 .02
❑ 475 Dan Quisenberry .05 .02
❑ 476 Oddibe McDowell .05 .02
❑ 477A Zane Smith ERR .05 .02
(Career ERA .393)
❑ 477B Zane Smith COR .50 .15
(career ERA 3.93)
❑ 478 Franklin Stubbs .05 .02
❑ 479 Wallace Johnson .05 .02
❑ 480 Jay Tibbs .05 .02
❑ 481 Tom Glavine .15 .04
❑ 482 Manny Lee .05 .02
❑ 483 Joe Hesketh UER .05 .02
Says Rookiess on back, should say Rookies
❑ 484 Mike Bielecki .05 .02
❑ 485 Greg Brock .05 .02
❑ 486 Pascual Perez .05 .02
❑ 487 Kirk Gibson .15 .04
❑ 488 Scott Sanderson .05 .02
❑ 489 Domingo Ramos .05 .02
❑ 490 Kal Daniels .05 .02
❑ 491A David Wells ERR .10 .03
(Reverse negative photo on card back)
❑ 491B David Wells COR .50 .15
❑ 492 Jerry Reed .05 .02
❑ 493 Eric Show .05 .02
❑ 494 Mike Pagliarulo .05 .02
❑ 495 Ron Robinson .05 .02
❑ 496 Brad Komminsk .05 .02
❑ 497 Greg Litton .05 .02
❑ 498 Chris James .05 .02

❑ 499 Luis Quinones .05 .02
❑ 500 Frank Viola .05 .02
❑ 501 Tim Teufel UER .05 .02
(Twins '85, the s is lower case, should be upper case)
❑ 502 Terry Leach .05 .02
❑ 503 Matt Williams UER .10 .03
(Wearing 10 on front, listed as 9 on back)
❑ 504 Tim Leary .05 .02
❑ 505 Doug Drabek .05 .02
❑ 506 Mariano Duncan .05 .02
❑ 507 Charlie Hayes .05 .02
❑ 508 Joey Belle .25 .07
❑ 509 Pat Sheridan .05 .02
❑ 510 Mackey Sasser .05 .02
❑ 511 Jose Rijo .05 .02
❑ 512 Mike Smithson .05 .02
❑ 513 Gary Ward .05 .02
❑ 514 Dion James .05 .02
❑ 515 Jim Gott .05 .02
❑ 516 Drew Hall .05 .02
❑ 517 Doug Bair .05 .02
❑ 518 Scott Scudder .05 .02
❑ 519 Rick Aguilera .10 .03
❑ 520 Rafael Belliard .05 .02
❑ 521 Jay Buhner .10 .03
❑ 522 Jeff Reardon .10 .03
❑ 523 Steve Rosenberg .05 .02
❑ 524 Randy Velarde .05 .02
❑ 525 Jeff Musselman .05 .02
❑ 526 Bill Long .05 .02
❑ 527 Gary Wayne .05 .02
❑ 528 Dave Johnson (P) .05 .02
❑ 529 Ron Kittle .05 .02
❑ 530 Erik Hanson UER .05 .02
(5th line on back says seson, should say season)
❑ 531 Steve Wilson .05 .02
❑ 532 Joey Meyer .05 .02
❑ 533 Curt Young .05 .02
❑ 534 Kelly Downs .05 .02
❑ 535 Joe Girardi .15 .04
❑ 536 Lance Blankenship .05 .02
❑ 537 Greg Mathews .05 .02
❑ 538 Donell Nixon .05 .02
❑ 539 Mark Knudson .05 .02
❑ 540 Jeff Wetherby .05 .02
❑ 541 Darrin Jackson .05 .02
❑ 542 Terry Mulholland .05 .02
❑ 543 Eric Hetzel .05 .02
❑ 544 Rick Reed RC .25 .07
❑ 545 Dennis Cook .05 .02
❑ 546 Mike Jackson .05 .02
❑ 547 Brian Fisher .05 .02
❑ 548 Gene Harris .05 .02
❑ 549 Jeff King .05 .02
❑ 550 Dave Dravecky .25 .07
❑ 551 Randy Kutcher .05 .02
❑ 552 Mark Portugal .05 .02
❑ 553 Jim Corsi .05 .02
❑ 554 Todd Stottlemyre .10 .03
❑ 555 Scott Bankhead .05 .02
❑ 556 Ken Dayley .05 .02
❑ 557 Rick Wrona .05 .02
❑ 558 Sammy Sosa RC 3.00 .90
❑ 559 Keith Miller .05 .02
❑ 560 Ken Griffey Jr. .75 .23
❑ 561A R.Sandberg HL ERR 8.00 2.40
Position on front listed as 3B
❑ 561B R.Sandberg HL COR .25 .07
❑ 562 Billy Hatcher .05 .02
❑ 563 Jay Bell .10 .03
❑ 564 Jack Daugherty .05 .02
❑ 565 Rich Monteleone .05 .02
❑ 566 Bo Jackson AS-MVP .10 .03
❑ 567 Tony Fossas .05 .02
❑ 568 Roy Smith .05 .02
❑ 569 Jaime Navarro .05 .02
❑ 570 Lance Johnson .05 .02
❑ 571 Mike Dyer RC .05 .02
❑ 572 Kevin Ritz .05 .02
❑ 573 Dave West .05 .02
❑ 574 Gary Mielke .05 .02
❑ 575 Scott Lusader .05 .02
❑ 576 Joe Oliver .05 .02
❑ 577 Sandy Alomar Jr. .10 .03
❑ 578 Andy Benes UER .10 .03
(Extra comma between day and year)
❑ 579 Tim Jones .05 .02
❑ 580 Randy McCament .05 .02
❑ 581 Curt Schilling 1.00 .30
❑ 582 John Orton RC .10 .03
❑ 583A Milt Cuyler ERR RC .10 .03
(998 games)
❑ 583B Milt Cuyler RC COR .50 .15
(98 games; the extra 9 was ghosted out and may still be visible)
❑ 584 Eric Anthony RC .10 .03
❑ 585 Greg Vaughn .05 .02
❑ 586 Deion Sanders .25 .07
❑ 587 Jose DeJesus .05 .02
❑ 588 Chip Hale .05 .02
❑ 589 John Olerud RC .50 .15
❑ 590 Steve Olin RC .25 .07
❑ 591 Marquis Grissom RC .40 .12
❑ 592 Moises Alou RC .75 .23
❑ 593 Mark Lemke .05 .02
❑ 594 Dean Palmer RC .25 .07
❑ 595 Robin Ventura .25 .07
❑ 596 Tino Martinez .50 .15
❑ 597 Mike Huff .05 .02
❑ 598 Scott Hemond RC .10 .03
❑ 599 Wally Whitehurst .05 .02
❑ 600 Todd Zeile .10 .03
❑ 601 Glenallen Hill .05 .02
❑ 602 Hal Morris .05 .02
❑ 603 Juan Bell .05 .02
❑ 604 Bobby Rose .05 .02
❑ 605 Matt Merullo .05 .02
❑ 606 Kevin Maas RC .25 .07
❑ 607 Randy Nosek .05 .02
❑ 608A Billy Bates .05 .02
(Text mentions 12 triples in tenth line)
❑ 608B Billy Bates .05 .02
(Text has no mention of triples)
❑ 609 Mike Stanton RC .25 .07
❑ 610 Mauro Gozzo .05 .02
❑ 611 Charles Nagy .05 .02
❑ 612 Scott Coolbaugh .05 .02
❑ 613 Jose Vizcaino RC .25 .07
❑ 614 Greg Smith .05 .02
❑ 615 Jeff Huson RC .10 .03
❑ 616 Mickey Weston .05 .02
❑ 617 John Pawlowski .05 .02
❑ 618A Joe Skalski ERR .05 .02
(27 on back)
❑ 618B Joe Skalski COR .50 .15
(67 on back)
❑ 619 Bernie Williams RC 1.50 .45
❑ 620 Shawn Holman .05 .02
❑ 621 Gary Eave .05 .02
❑ 622 Darrin Fletcher UER .10 .03
Elmherst, should be Elmhurst
❑ 623 Pat Combs .05 .02
❑ 624 Mike Blowers RC .10 .03
❑ 625 Kevin Appier .10 .03
❑ 626 Pat Austin .05 .02
❑ 627 Kelly Mann .05 .02
❑ 628 Matt Kinzer .05 .02
❑ 629 Chris Hammond RC .10 .03
❑ 630 Dean Wilkins .05 .02
❑ 631 Larry Walker RC UER 1.00 .30
Uniform number 55 on front and 33 on back; Home is Maple Ridge, not Maple River
❑ 632 Blaine Beatty .05 .02
❑ 633A Tommy Barrett ERR .05 .02
(29 on back)
❑ 633B Tommy Barrett COR .50 .15
(14 on back)
❑ 634 Stan Belinda RC .10 .03
❑ 635 Mike (Tex) Smith .05 .02
❑ 636 Hensley Meulens .05 .02
❑ 637 J.Gonzalez RC UER 1.00 .30
Sarasots on back, should be Sarasota
❑ 638 Lenny Webster RC .10 .03
❑ 639 Mark Gardner RC .10 .03
❑ 640 Tommy Greene RC .10 .03
❑ 641 Mike Hartley .05 .02
❑ 642 Phil Stephenson .05 .02
❑ 643 Kevin Mmahat .05 .02
❑ 644 Ed Whited .05 .02
❑ 645 Delino DeShields RC .25 .07
❑ 646 Kevin Blankenship .05 .02
❑ 647 Paul Sorrento RC .25 .07
❑ 648 Mike Roesler .05 .02
❑ 649 Jason Grimsley RC .10 .03
❑ 650 Dave Justice RC .50 .15
❑ 651 Scott Cooper RC .10 .03
❑ 652 Dave Eiland .05 .02
❑ 653 Mike Munoz .05 .02
❑ 654 Jeff Fischer .05 .02
❑ 655 Terry Jorgensen .05 .02
❑ 656 George Canale .05 .02
❑ 657 Brian DuBois UER .05 .02
(Misspelled Dubois on card)
❑ 658 Carlos Quintana .05 .02
❑ 659 Luis de los Santos .05 .02
❑ 660 Jerald Clark .05 .02
❑ 661 Donald Harris DC .05 .02
❑ 662 Paul Coleman DC RC .10 .03
❑ 663 Frank Thomas DC RC 2.00 .60
❑ 664 Brent Mayne DC RC .25 .07
❑ 665 Eddie Zosky DC RC .10 .03
❑ 666 Steve Hosey DC RC .10 .03
❑ 667 Scott Bryant DC .10 .03
❑ 668 Tom Goodwin DC RC .25 .07
❑ 669 Cal Eldred DC RC .25 .07
❑ 670 E.Cunningham DC RC .10 .03
❑ 671 Alan Zinter DC RC .10 .03
❑ 672 C.Knoblauch DC RC .40 .12
❑ 673 Kyle Abbott DC .05 .02
❑ 674 Roger Salkeld DC RC .05 .02
❑ 675 M.Vaughn DC RC .50 .15
❑ 676 Keith (Kiki) Jones DC .05 .02
❑ 677 Tyler Houston DC RC .25 .07
❑ 678 Jeff Jackson DC RC .10 .03
❑ 679 Greg Gohr DC RC .10 .03
❑ 680 Ben McDonald DC RC .25 .07
❑ 681 Greg Blosser DC RC .10 .03
❑ 682 W.Greene RC DC UER .25 .07
Name spelled as Green
❑ 683A W.Boggs DT ERR .10 .03
Text says 215 hits in '89, should be 205
❑ 683B W.Boggs DT COR .50 .15
Text says 205 hits in '89
❑ 684 Will Clark DT .10 .03
❑ 685 Tony Gwynn DT UER .15 .04
(Text reads battling instead of batting)
❑ 686 Rickey Henderson DT .15 .04
❑ 687 Bo Jackson DT .10 .03
❑ 688 Mark Langston DT .05 .02
❑ 689 Barry Larkin DT .10 .03
❑ 690 Kirby Puckett DT .15 .04
❑ 691 Ryne Sandberg DT .25 .07
❑ 692 Mike Scott DT .05 .02
❑ 693A Terry Steinbach DT .05 .02
ERR (cathers)
❑ 693B Terry Steinbach DT .05 .02
COR (catchers)
❑ 694 Bobby Thigpen DT .05 .02
❑ 695 Mitch Williams DT .05 .02
❑ 696 Nolan Ryan HL .40 .12
❑ 697 Bo Jackson FB/BB .50 .15
❑ 698 Rickey Henderson .15 .04
ALCS-MVP
❑ 699 Will Clark .10 .03
NLCS-MVP
❑ 700 Dave Stewart .10 .03
Mike Moore WS
❑ 701 Lights Out .25 .07
❑ 702 Carney Lansford .15 .04
Rickey Henderson
Jose Canseco
Dave Henderson WS

❑ 703 WS Game 4/Wrap-up .05 .02
❑ 704 Wade Boggs HL .10 .03

1991 Score

	Nm-Mt	Ex-Mt
COMPLETE SET (893)	20.00	6.00
COMP.FACT.SET (900)	25.00	7.50

❑ 1 Jose Canseco .15 .04
❑ 2 Ken Griffey Jr. .50 .15
❑ 3 Ryne Sandberg .40 .12
❑ 4 Nolan Ryan 1.00 .30
❑ 5 Bo Jackson .25 .07
❑ 6 Bret Saberhagen UER .05 .02
(In bio, missed misspelled as mised)
❑ 7 Will Clark .15 .04
❑ 8 Ellis Burks .10 .03
❑ 9 Joe Carter .10 .03
❑ 10 Rickey Henderson .25 .07
❑ 11 Ozzie Guillen .10 .03
❑ 12 Wade Boggs .15 .04
❑ 13 Jerome Walton .05 .02
❑ 14 John Franco .10 .03
❑ 15 Ricky Jordan UER .05 .02
(League misspelled as legue)
❑ 16 Wally Backman .05 .02
❑ 17 Rob Dibble .10 .03
❑ 18 Glenn Braggs .05 .02
❑ 19 Cory Snyder .05 .02
❑ 20 Kal Daniels .05 .02
❑ 21 Mark Langston .05 .02
❑ 22 Kevin Gross .05 .02
❑ 23 Don Mattingly UER .60 .18
First line is missing from Yankee
❑ 24 Dave Righetti .10 .03
❑ 25 Roberto Alomar .15 .04
❑ 26 Robby Thompson .05 .02
❑ 27 Jack McDowell .05 .02
❑ 28 Bip Roberts UER .05 .02
(Bio reads playd)
❑ 29 Jay Howell .05 .02
❑ 30 Dave Stieb UER .05 .02
(17 wins in bio, 18 in stats)
❑ 31 Johnny Ray .05 .02
❑ 32 Steve Sax .05 .02
❑ 33 Terry Mulholland .05 .02
❑ 34 Lee Guetterman .05 .02
❑ 35 Tim Raines .10 .03
❑ 36 Scott Fletcher .05 .02
❑ 37 Lance Parrish .10 .03
❑ 38 Tony Phillips UER .05 .02
(Born 4/15 should be 4/25)
❑ 39 Todd Stottlemyre .05 .02
❑ 40 Alan Trammell .10 .03
❑ 41 Todd Burns .05 .02
❑ 42 Mookie Wilson .10 .03
❑ 43 Chris Bosio .05 .02
❑ 44 Jeffrey Leonard .05 .02
❑ 45 Doug Jones .05 .02
❑ 46 Mike Scott UER .05 .02
(In first line, dominate should read dominating)
❑ 47 Andy Hawkins .05 .02
❑ 48 Harold Reynolds .10 .03
❑ 49 Paul Molitor .15 .04
❑ 50 John Farrell .05 .02
❑ 51 Danny Darwin .05 .02
❑ 52 Jeff Blauser .05 .02
❑ 53 John Tudor UER .05 .02
(41 wins in '81)
❑ 54 Milt Thompson .05 .02
❑ 55 Dave Justice .10 .03
❑ 56 Greg Olson .05 .02
❑ 57 Willie Blair .05 .02
❑ 58 Rick Parker .05 .02
❑ 59 Shawn Boskie .05 .02
❑ 60 Kevin Tapani .05 .02
❑ 61 Dave Hollins .05 .02
❑ 62 Scott Radinsky .05 .02
❑ 63 Francisco Cabrera .05 .02
❑ 64 Tim Layana .05 .02
❑ 65 Jim Leyritz .05 .02
❑ 66 Wayne Edwards .05 .02
❑ 67 Lee Stevens .05 .02
❑ 68 Bill Sampen UER .05 .02
Fourth line, long is spelled along
❑ 69 Craig Grebeck UER .05 .02
Born in Cerritos, not Johnstown
❑ 70 John Burkett .05 .02
❑ 71 Hector Villanueva .05 .02
❑ 72 Oscar Azocar .05 .02
❑ 73 Alan Mills .05 .02
❑ 74 Carlos Baerga .05 .02
❑ 75 Charles Nagy .05 .02
❑ 76 Tim Drummond .05 .02
❑ 77 Dana Kiecker .05 .02
❑ 78 Tom Edens .05 .02
❑ 79 Kent Mercker .05 .02
❑ 80 Steve Avery .05 .02
❑ 81 Lee Smith .10 .03
❑ 82 Dave Martinez .05 .02
❑ 83 Dave Winfield .10 .03
❑ 84 Bill Spiers .05 .02
❑ 85 Dan Pasqua .05 .02
❑ 86 Randy Milligan .05 .02
❑ 87 Tracy Jones .05 .02
❑ 88 Greg Myers .05 .02
❑ 89 Keith Hernandez .10 .03
❑ 90 Todd Benzinger .05 .02
❑ 91 Mike Jackson .05 .02
❑ 92 Mike Stanley .05 .02
❑ 93 Candy Maldonado .05 .02
❑ 94 John Kruk UER .10 .03
(No decimal point before 1990 BA)
❑ 95 Cal Ripken UER .75 .23
(Genius spelled genuis)
❑ 96 Willie Fraser .05 .02
❑ 97 Mike Felder .05 .02
❑ 98 Bill Landrum .05 .02
❑ 99 Chuck Crim .05 .02
❑ 100 Chuck Finley .10 .03
❑ 101 Kirt Manwaring .05 .02
❑ 102 Jaime Navarro .05 .02
❑ 103 Dickie Thon .05 .02
❑ 104 Brian Downing .05 .02
❑ 105 Jim Abbott .15 .04
❑ 106 Tom Brookens .05 .02
❑ 107 Darryl Hamilton UER .05 .02
(Bio info is for Jeff Hamilton)
❑ 108 Bryan Harvey .05 .02
❑ 109 Greg A. Harris UER .05 .02
Shown pitching lefty, bio says righty
❑ 110 Greg Swindell .05 .02
❑ 111 Juan Berenguer .05 .02
❑ 112 Mike Heath .05 .02
❑ 113 Scott Bradley .05 .02
❑ 114 Jack Morris .10 .03
❑ 115 Barry Jones .05 .02
❑ 116 Kevin Romine .05 .02
❑ 117 Garry Templeton .05 .02
❑ 118 Scott Sanderson .05 .02
❑ 119 Roberto Kelly .05 .02
❑ 120 George Brett .60 .18
❑ 121 Oddibe McDowell .05 .02
❑ 122 Jim Acker .05 .02
❑ 123 Bill Swift UER .05 .02
(Born 12/27/61, should be 10/27)
❑ 124 Eric King .05 .02
❑ 125 Jay Buhner .10 .03
❑ 126 Matt Young .05 .02
❑ 127 Alvaro Espinoza .05 .02
❑ 128 Greg Hibbard .05 .02
❑ 129 Jeff M. Robinson .05 .02
❑ 130 Mike Greenwell .05 .02
❑ 131 Dion James .05 .02
❑ 132 Donn Pall UER .05 .02
(1988 ERA in stats 0.00)
❑ 133 Lloyd Moseby .05 .02
❑ 134 Randy Velarde .05 .02
❑ 135 Allan Anderson .05 .02
❑ 136 Mark Davis .05 .02
❑ 137 Eric Davis .10 .03
❑ 138 Phil Stephenson .05 .02
❑ 139 Felix Fermin .05 .02
❑ 140 Pedro Guerrero .10 .03
❑ 141 Charlie Hough .10 .03
❑ 142 Mike Henneman .05 .02
❑ 143 Jeff Montgomery .05 .02
❑ 144 Lenny Harris .05 .02
❑ 145 Bruce Hurst .05 .02
❑ 146 Eric Anthony .05 .02
❑ 147 Paul Assenmacher .05 .02
❑ 148 Jesse Barfield .05 .02
❑ 149 Carlos Quintana .05 .02
❑ 150 Dave Stewart .10 .03
❑ 151 Roy Smith .05 .02
❑ 152 Paul Gibson .05 .02
❑ 153 Mickey Hatcher .05 .02
❑ 154 Jim Eisenreich .05 .02
❑ 155 Kenny Rogers .10 .03
❑ 156 Dave Schmidt .05 .02
❑ 157 Lance Johnson .05 .02
❑ 158 Dave West .05 .02
❑ 159 Steve Balboni .05 .02
❑ 160 Jeff Brantley .05 .02
❑ 161 Craig Biggio .15 .04
❑ 162 Brook Jacoby .05 .02
❑ 163 Dan Gladden .05 .02
❑ 164 Jeff Reardon UER .10 .03
(Total IP shown as 943.2, should be 943.1)
❑ 165 Mark Carreon .05 .02
❑ 166 Mel Hall .05 .02
❑ 167 Gary Mielke .05 .02
❑ 168 Cecil Fielder .10 .03
❑ 169 Darrin Jackson .05 .02
❑ 170 Rick Aguilera .10 .03
❑ 171 Walt Weiss .05 .02
❑ 172 Steve Farr .05 .02
❑ 173 Jody Reed .05 .02
❑ 174 Mike Jeffcoat .05 .02
❑ 175 Mark Grace .15 .04
❑ 176 Larry Sheets .05 .02
❑ 177 Bill Gullickson .05 .02
❑ 178 Chris Gwynn .05 .02
❑ 179 Melido Perez .05 .02
❑ 180 Sid Fernandez UER .05 .02
(779 runs in 1990)
❑ 181 Tim Burke .05 .02
❑ 182 Gary Pettis .05 .02
❑ 183 Rob Murphy .05 .02
❑ 184 Craig Lefferts .05 .02
❑ 185 Howard Johnson .05 .02
❑ 186 Ken Caminiti .10 .03
❑ 187 Tim Belcher .05 .02
❑ 188 Greg Cadaret .05 .02
❑ 189 Matt Williams .10 .03
❑ 190 Dave Magadan .05 .02
❑ 191 Geno Petralli .05 .02
❑ 192 Jeff D. Robinson .05 .02
❑ 193 Jim Deshaies .05 .02
❑ 194 Willie Randolph .10 .03
❑ 195 George Bell .05 .02
❑ 196 Hubie Brooks .05 .02
❑ 197 Tom Gordon .05 .02
❑ 198 Mike Fitzgerald .05 .02
❑ 199 Mike Pagliarulo .05 .02
❑ 200 Kirby Puckett .25 .07
❑ 201 Shawon Dunston .05 .02
❑ 202 Dennis Boyd .05 .02
❑ 203 Junior Felix UER .05 .02
(Text has him in NL)

❑	204	Alejandro Pena	.05	.02
❑	205	Pete Smith	.05	.02
❑	206	Tom Glavine UER (Lefty spelled leftie)	.15	.04
❑	207	Luis Salazar	.05	.02
❑	208	John Smoltz	.15	.04
❑	209	Doug Dascenzo	.05	.02
❑	210	Tim Wallach	.05	.02
❑	211	Greg Gagne	.05	.02
❑	212	Mark Gubicza	.05	.02
❑	213	Mark Parent	.05	.02
❑	214	Ken Oberkfell	.05	.02
❑	215	Gary Carter	.10	.03
❑	216	Rafael Palmeiro	.15	.04
❑	217	Tom Niedenfuer	.05	.02
❑	218	Dave LaPoint	.05	.02
❑	219	Jeff Treadway	.05	.02
❑	220	Mitch Williams UER ('89 ERA shown as 2.76, should be 2.64)	.05	.02
❑	221	Jose DeLeon	.05	.02
❑	222	Mike LaValliere	.05	.02
❑	223	Darrel Akerfelds	.05	.02
❑	224A	Kent Anderson ERR (First line& flachy should read flashy)	.10	.03
❑	224B	Kent Anderson COR (Corrected in factory sets)	.10	.03
❑	225	Dwight Evans	.15	.04
❑	226	Gary Redus	.05	.02
❑	227	Paul O'Neill	.15	.04
❑	228	Marty Barrett	.05	.02
❑	229	Tom Browning	.05	.02
❑	230	Terry Pendleton	.10	.03
❑	231	Jack Armstrong	.05	.02
❑	232	Mike Boddicker	.05	.02
❑	233	Neal Heaton	.05	.02
❑	234	Marquis Grissom	.10	.03
❑	235	Bert Blyleven	.10	.03
❑	236	Curt Young	.05	.02
❑	237	Don Carman	.05	.02
❑	238	Charlie Hayes	.05	.02
❑	239	Mark Knudson	.05	.02
❑	240	Todd Zeile	.05	.02
❑	241	Larry Walker UER (Maple River, should be Maple Ridge)	.25	.07
❑	242	Jerald Clark	.05	.02
❑	243	Jeff Ballard	.05	.02
❑	244	Jeff King	.05	.02
❑	245	Tom Brunansky	.05	.02
❑	246	Darren Daulton	.10	.03
❑	247	Scott Terry	.05	.02
❑	248	Rob Deer	.05	.02
❑	249	Brady Anderson UER (1990 Hagerstown 1 hit, should say 13 hits)	.10	.03
❑	250	Len Dykstra	.10	.03
❑	251	Greg W. Harris	.05	.02
❑	252	Mike Hartley	.05	.02
❑	253	Joey Cora	.05	.02
❑	254	Ivan Calderon	.05	.02
❑	255	Ted Power	.05	.02
❑	256	Sammy Sosa	.25	.07
❑	257	Steve Buechele	.05	.02
❑	258	Mike Devereaux UER (No comma between city and state)	.05	.02
❑	259	Brad Komminsk UER (Last text line, Ba should be BA)	.05	.02
❑	260	Ted Higuera	.05	.02
❑	261	Shawn Abner	.05	.02
❑	262	Dave Valle	.05	.02
❑	263	Jeff Huson	.05	.02
❑	264	Edgar Martinez	.15	.04
❑	265	Carlton Fisk	.15	.04
❑	266	Steve Finley	.10	.03
❑	267	John Wetteland	.10	.03
❑	268	Kevin Appier	.10	.03
❑	269	Steve Lyons	.05	.02
❑	270	Mickey Tettleton	.05	.02
❑	271	Luis Rivera	.05	.02
❑	272	Steve Jeltz	.05	.02
❑	273	R.J. Reynolds	.05	.02
❑	274	Carlos Martinez	.05	.02
❑	275	Dan Plesac	.05	.02
❑	276	Mike Morgan UER (Total IP shown as 1149.1, should be 1149)	.05	.02
❑	277	Jeff Russell	.05	.02
❑	278	Pete Incaviglia	.05	.02
❑	279	Kevin Seitzer UER (Bio has 200 hits twice and .300 four times, should be once and three times)	.05	.02
❑	280	Bobby Thigpen	.05	.02
❑	281	Stan Javier UER (Born 1/9, should say 9/1)	.05	.02
❑	282	Henry Cotto	.05	.02
❑	283	Gary Wayne	.05	.02
❑	284	Shane Mack	.05	.02
❑	285	Brian Holman	.05	.02
❑	286	Gerald Perry	.05	.02
❑	287	Steve Crawford	.05	.02
❑	288	Nelson Liriano	.05	.02
❑	289	Don Aase	.05	.02
❑	290	Randy Johnson	.30	.09
❑	291	Harold Baines	.10	.03
❑	292	Kent Hrbek	.10	.03
❑	293A	Les Lancaster ERR (No comma between Dallas and Texas)	.05	.02
❑	293B	Les Lancaster COR (Corrected in factory sets)	.05	.02
❑	294	Jeff Musselman	.05	.02
❑	295	Kurt Stillwell	.05	.02
❑	296	Stan Belinda	.05	.02
❑	297	Lou Whitaker	.10	.03
❑	298	Glenn Wilson	.05	.02
❑	299	Omar Vizquel UER (Born 5/15, should be 4/24, there is a decimal before GP total for '90)	.15	.04
❑	300	Ramon Martinez	.05	.02
❑	301	Dwight Smith	.05	.02
❑	302	Tim Crews	.05	.02
❑	303	Lance Blankenship	.05	.02
❑	304	Sid Bream	.05	.02
❑	305	Rafael Ramirez	.05	.02
❑	306	Steve Wilson	.05	.02
❑	307	Mackey Sasser	.05	.02
❑	308	Franklin Stubbs	.05	.02
❑	309	Jack Daugherty UER (Born 6/3/60, should say July)	.05	.02
❑	310	Eddie Murray	.25	.07
❑	311	Bob Welch	.05	.02
❑	312	Brian Harper	.05	.02
❑	313	Lance McCullers	.05	.02
❑	314	Dave Smith	.05	.02
❑	315	Bobby Bonilla	.10	.03
❑	316	Jerry Don Gleaton	.05	.02
❑	317	Greg Maddux	.40	.12
❑	318	Keith Miller	.05	.02
❑	319	Mark Portugal	.05	.02
❑	320	Robin Ventura	.10	.03
❑	321	Bob Ojeda	.05	.02
❑	322	Mike Harkey	.05	.02
❑	323	Jay Bell	.10	.03
❑	324	Mark McGwire	.60	.18
❑	325	Gary Gaetti	.10	.03
❑	326	Jeff Pico	.05	.02
❑	327	Kevin McReynolds	.05	.02
❑	328	Frank Tanana	.05	.02
❑	329	Eric Yelding UER (Listed as 6'3" should be 5'11")	.05	.02
❑	330	Barry Bonds	1.00	.30
❑	331	Brian McRae RC UER (No comma between city and state)	.25	.07
❑	332	Pedro Munoz RC	.10	.03
❑	333	Daryl Irvine	.05	.02
❑	334	Chris Hoiles	.05	.02
❑	335	Thomas Howard	.05	.02
❑	336	Jeff Schulz	.05	.02
❑	337	Jeff Manto	.05	.02
❑	338	Beau Allred	.05	.02
❑	339	Mike Bordick RC	.40	.12
❑	340	Todd Hundley	.05	.02
❑	341	Jim Vatcher UER (Height 6'9", should be 5'9")	.05	.02
❑	342	Luis Sojo	.05	.02
❑	343	Jose Offerman UER (Born 1969, should say 1968)	.05	.02
❑	344	Pete Coachman	.05	.02
❑	345	Mike Benjamin	.05	.02
❑	346	Ozzie Canseco	.05	.02
❑	347	Tim McIntosh	.05	.02
❑	348	Phil Plantier RC	.10	.03
❑	349	Terry Shumpert	.05	.02
❑	350	Darren Lewis	.05	.02
❑	351	David Walsh RC	.05	.02
❑	352A	Scott Chiamparino ERR Bats left, should be right	.10	.03
❑	352B	Scott Chiamparino COR corrected in factory sets	.10	.03
❑	353	Julio Valera UER (Progressed misspelled as progessed)	.05	.02
❑	354	Anthony Telford	.05	.02
❑	355	Kevin Wickander	.05	.02
❑	356	Tim Naehring	.05	.02
❑	357	Jim Poole	.05	.02
❑	358	Mark Whiten UER Shown hitting lefty, bio says righty	.05	.02
❑	359	Terry Wells	.05	.02
❑	360	Rafael Valdez	.05	.02
❑	361	Mel Stottlemyre Jr.	.05	.02
❑	362	David Segui	.05	.02
❑	363	Paul Abbott RC	.10	.03
❑	364	Steve Howard	.05	.02
❑	365	Karl Rhodes	.05	.02
❑	366	Rafael Novoa	.05	.02
❑	367	Joe Grahe RC	.05	.02
❑	368	Darren Reed	.05	.02
❑	369	Jeff McKnight	.05	.02
❑	370	Scott Leius	.05	.02
❑	371	Mark Dewey	.05	.02
❑	372	Mark Lee UER RC (Shown hitting left, bio says righty, born in Dakota, should say North Dakota)	.10	.03
❑	373	Rosario Rodriguez UER Shown hitting lefty, bio says righty	.05	.02
❑	374	Chuck McElroy	.05	.02
❑	375	Mike Bell	.05	.02
❑	376	Mickey Morandini	.05	.02
❑	377	Bill Haselman	.05	.02
❑	378	Dave Pavlas	.05	.02
❑	379	Derrick May	.05	.02
❑	380	J.Burnitz FDP RC	.40	.12
❑	381	Donald Peters FDP	.05	.02
❑	382	Alex Fernandez FDP	.05	.02
❑	383	Mike Mussina FDP RC	1.50	.45
❑	384	Dan Smith FDP RC	.10	.03
❑	385	L.Dickson FDP RC	.10	.03
❑	386	Carl Everett FDP RC	.50	.15
❑	387	Tom Nevers FDP RC	.10	.03
❑	388	Adam Hyzdu FDP RC	.25	.07
❑	389	T.Van Poppel FDP RC	.25	.07
❑	390	R.White FDP RC	.40	.12
❑	391	M.Newfield FDP RC	.10	.03
❑	392	Julio Franco AS	.05	.02
❑	393	Wade Boggs AS	.10	.03
❑	394	Ozzie Guillen AS	.05	.02
❑	395	Cecil Fielder AS	.05	.02
❑	396	Ken Griffey Jr. AS	.25	.07
❑	397	Rickey Henderson AS	.15	.04
❑	398	Jose Canseco AS	.10	.03
❑	399	Roger Clemens AS	.25	.07
❑	400	Sandy Alomar Jr. AS	.05	.02
❑	401	Bobby Thigpen AS	.05	.02
❑	402	Bobby Bonilla MB	.05	.02
❑	403	Eric Davis MB	.05	.02
❑	404	Fred McGriff MB	.10	.03
❑	405	Glenn Davis MB	.05	.02
❑	406	Kevin Mitchell MB	.05	.02

❑	407	Rob Dibble KM	.05	.02
❑	408	Ramon Martinez KM	.05	.02
❑	409	David Cone KM	.05	.02
❑	410	Bobby Witt KM	.05	.02
❑	411	Mark Langston KM	.05	.02
❑	412	Bo Jackson RIF	.10	.03
❑	413	Shawon Dunston RIF UER	.05	.02
		In the baseball, should say in baseball		
❑	414	Jesse Barfield RIF	.05	.02
❑	415	Ken Caminiti RIF	.05	.02
❑	416	Benito Santiago RIF	.05	.02
❑	417	Nolan Ryan HL	.50	.15
❑	418	B.Thigpen HL UER	.05	.02
		Back refers to Hal McRae Jr., should say Brian McRae		
❑	419	Ramon Martinez HL	.05	.02
❑	420	Bo Jackson HL	.10	.03
❑	421	Carlton Fisk HL	.10	.03
❑	422	Jimmy Key	.10	.03
❑	423	Junior Noboa	.05	.02
❑	424	Al Newman	.05	.02
❑	425	Pat Borders	.05	.02
❑	426	Von Hayes	.05	.02
❑	427	Tim Teufel	.05	.02
❑	428	Eric Plunk UER	.05	.02
		Text says Eric's had, no apostrophe needed		
❑	429	John Moses	.05	.02
❑	430	Mike Witt	.05	.02
❑	431	Otis Nixon	.05	.02
❑	432	Tony Fernandez	.05	.02
❑	433	Rance Mulliniks	.05	.02
❑	434	Dan Petry	.05	.02
❑	435	Bob Geren	.05	.02
❑	436	Steve Frey	.05	.02
❑	437	Jamie Moyer	.10	.03
❑	438	Junior Ortiz	.05	.02
❑	439	Tom O'Malley	.05	.02
❑	440	Pat Combs	.05	.02
❑	441	Jose Canseco DT	.15	.04
❑	442	Alfredo Griffin	.05	.02
❑	443	Andres Galarraga	.10	.03
❑	444	Bryn Smith	.05	.02
❑	445	Andre Dawson	.10	.03
❑	446	Juan Samuel	.05	.02
❑	447	Mike Aldrete	.05	.02
❑	448	Ron Gant	.10	.03
❑	449	Fernando Valenzuela	.10	.03
❑	450	Vince Coleman UER	.05	.02
		Should say topped majors in steals four times, not three times		
❑	451	Kevin Mitchell	.05	.02
❑	452	Spike Owen	.05	.02
❑	453	Mike Bielecki	.05	.02
❑	454	Dennis Martinez	.10	.03
❑	455	Brett Butler	.10	.03
❑	456	Ron Darling	.05	.02
❑	457	Dennis Rasmussen	.05	.02
❑	458	Ken Howell	.05	.02
❑	459	Steve Bedrosian	.05	.02
❑	460	Frank Viola	.10	.03
❑	461	Jose Lind	.05	.02
❑	462	Chris Sabo	.05	.02
❑	463	Dante Bichette	.10	.03
❑	464	Rick Mahler	.05	.02
❑	465	John Smiley	.05	.02
❑	466	Devon White	.10	.03
❑	467	John Orton	.05	.02
❑	468	Mike Stanton	.05	.02
❑	469	Billy Hatcher	.05	.02
❑	470	Wally Joyner	.10	.03
❑	471	Gene Larkin	.05	.02
❑	472	Doug Drabek	.05	.02
❑	473	Gary Sheffield	.10	.03
❑	474	David Wells	.10	.03
❑	475	Andy Van Slyke	.15	.04
❑	476	Mike Gallego	.05	.02
❑	477	B.J. Surhoff	.10	.03
❑	478	Gene Nelson	.05	.02
❑	479	Mariano Duncan	.05	.02
❑	480	Fred McGriff	.15	.04
❑	481	Jerry Browne	.05	.02
❑	482	Alvin Davis	.05	.02
❑	483	Bill Wegman	.05	.02
❑	484	Dave Parker	.10	.03
❑	485	Dennis Eckersley	.10	.03
❑	486	Erik Hanson UER	.05	.02
		(Basketball misspelled as baseketball)		
❑	487	Bill Ripken	.05	.02
❑	488	Tom Candiotti	.05	.02
❑	489	Mike Schooler	.05	.02
❑	490	Gregg Olson	.05	.02
❑	491	Chris James	.05	.02
❑	492	Pete Harnisch	.05	.02
❑	493	Julio Franco	.10	.03
❑	494	Greg Briley	.05	.02
❑	495	Ruben Sierra	.05	.02
❑	496	Steve Olin	.05	.02
❑	497	Mike Fetters	.05	.02
❑	498	Mark Williamson	.05	.02
❑	499	Bob Tewksbury	.05	.02
❑	500	Tony Gwynn	.30	.09
❑	501	Randy Myers	.05	.02
❑	502	Keith Comstock	.05	.02
❑	503	C.Worthington UER	.05	.02
		DeCinces misspelled DiCinces on back		
❑	504	Mark Eichhorn UER	.05	.02
		Stats incomplete, doesn't have '89 Braves stint		
❑	505	Barry Larkin	.15	.04
❑	506	Dave Johnson	.05	.02
❑	507	Bobby Witt	.05	.02
❑	508	Joe Orsulak	.05	.02
❑	509	Pete O'Brien	.05	.02
❑	510	Brad Arnsberg	.05	.02
❑	511	Storm Davis	.05	.02
❑	512	Bob Milacki	.05	.02
❑	513	Bill Pecota	.05	.02
❑	514	Glenallen Hill	.05	.02
❑	515	Danny Tartabull	.05	.02
❑	516	Mike Moore	.05	.02
❑	517	Ron Robinson UER	.05	.02
		(577 K's in 1990)		
❑	518	Mark Gardner	.05	.02
❑	519	Rick Wrona	.05	.02
❑	520	Mike Scioscia	.05	.02
❑	521	Frank Wills	.05	.02
❑	522	Greg Brock	.05	.02
❑	523	Jack Clark	.10	.03
❑	524	Bruce Ruffin	.05	.02
❑	525	Robin Yount	.40	.12
❑	526	Tom Foley	.05	.02
❑	527	Pat Perry	.05	.02
❑	528	Greg Vaughn	.05	.02
❑	529	Wally Whitehurst	.05	.02
❑	530	Norm Charlton	.05	.02
❑	531	Marvell Wynne	.05	.02
❑	532	Jim Gantner	.05	.02
❑	533	Greg Litton	.05	.02
❑	534	Manny Lee	.05	.02
❑	535	Scott Bailes	.05	.02
❑	536	Charlie Leibrandt	.05	.02
❑	537	Roger McDowell	.05	.02
❑	538	Andy Benes	.05	.02
❑	539	Rick Honeycutt	.05	.02
❑	540	Dwight Gooden	.10	.03
❑	541	Scott Garrelts	.05	.02
❑	542	Dave Clark	.05	.02
❑	543	Lonnie Smith	.05	.02
❑	544	Rick Reuschel	.05	.02
❑	545	Delino DeShields UER	.10	.03
		(Rockford misspelled as Rock Ford in '88)		
❑	546	Mike Sharperson	.05	.02
❑	547	Mike Kingery	.05	.02
❑	548	Terry Kennedy	.05	.02
❑	549	David Cone	.10	.03
❑	550	Orel Hershiser	.10	.03
❑	551	Matt Nokes	.05	.02
❑	552	Eddie Williams	.05	.02
❑	553	Frank DiPino	.05	.02
❑	554	Fred Lynn	.05	.02
❑	555	Alex Cole	.05	.02
❑	556	Terry Leach	.05	.02
❑	557	Chet Lemon	.05	.02
❑	558	Paul Mirabella	.05	.02
❑	559	Bill Long	.05	.02
❑	560	Phil Bradley	.05	.02
❑	561	Duane Ward	.05	.02
❑	562	Dave Bergman	.05	.02
❑	563	Eric Show	.05	.02
❑	564	Xavier Hernandez	.05	.02
❑	565	Jeff Parrett	.05	.02
❑	566	Chuck Cary	.05	.02
❑	567	Ken Hill	.05	.02
❑	568	Bob Welch Hand	.05	.02
		(Complement should be compliment) UER		
❑	569	John Mitchell	.05	.02
❑	570	Travis Fryman	.10	.03
❑	571	Derek Lilliquist	.05	.02
❑	572	Steve Lake	.05	.02
❑	573	John Barfield	.05	.02
❑	574	Randy Bush	.05	.02
❑	575	Joe Magrane	.05	.02
❑	576	Eddie Diaz	.05	.02
❑	577	Casey Candaele	.05	.02
❑	578	Jesse Orosco	.05	.02
❑	579	Tom Henke	.05	.02
❑	580	Rick Cerone UER	.05	.02
		(Actually his third go-round with Yankees)		
❑	581	Drew Hall	.05	.02
❑	582	Tony Castillo	.05	.02
❑	583	Jimmy Jones	.05	.02
❑	584	Rick Reed	.05	.02
❑	585	Joe Girardi	.05	.02
❑	586	Jeff Gray	.05	.02
❑	587	Luis Polonia	.05	.02
❑	588	Joe Klink	.05	.02
❑	589	Rex Hudler	.05	.02
❑	590	Kirk McCaskill	.05	.02
❑	591	Juan Agosto	.05	.02
❑	592	Wes Gardner	.05	.02
❑	593	Rich Rodriguez	.05	.02
❑	594	Mitch Webster	.05	.02
❑	595	Kelly Gruber	.05	.02
❑	596	Dale Mohorcic	.05	.02
❑	597	Willie McGee	.10	.03
❑	598	Bill Krueger	.05	.02
❑	599	Bob Walk UER	.05	.02
		Cards says he's 33, but actually he's 34		
❑	600	Kevin Maas	.05	.02
❑	601	Danny Jackson	.05	.02
❑	602	Craig McMurtry UER	.05	.02
		(Anonymously misspelled anonimously)		
❑	603	Curtis Wilkerson	.05	.02
❑	604	Adam Peterson	.05	.02
❑	605	Sam Horn	.05	.02
❑	606	Tommy Gregg	.05	.02
❑	607	Ken Dayley	.05	.02
❑	608	Carmelo Castillo	.05	.02
❑	609	John Shelby	.05	.02
❑	610	Don Slaught	.05	.02
❑	611	Calvin Schiraldi	.05	.02
❑	612	Dennis Lamp	.05	.02
❑	613	Andres Thomas	.05	.02
❑	614	Jose Gonzalez	.05	.02
❑	615	Randy Ready	.05	.02
❑	616	Kevin Bass	.05	.02
❑	617	Mike Marshall	.05	.02
❑	618	Daryl Boston	.05	.02
❑	619	Andy McGaffigan	.05	.02
❑	620	Joe Oliver	.05	.02
❑	621	Jim Gott	.05	.02
❑	622	Jose Oquendo	.05	.02
❑	623	Jose DeJesus	.05	.02
❑	624	Mike Brumley	.05	.02
❑	625	John Olerud	.10	.03
❑	626	Ernest Riles	.05	.02
❑	627	Gene Harris	.05	.02
❑	628	Jose Uribe	.05	.02
❑	629	Darnell Coles	.05	.02
❑	630	Carney Lansford	.10	.03
❑	631	Tim Leary	.05	.02
❑	632	Tim Hulett	.05	.02
❑	633	Kevin Elster	.05	.02
❑	634	Tony Fossas	.05	.02
❑	635	Francisco Oliveras	.05	.02
❑	636	Bob Patterson	.05	.02
❑	637	Gary Ward	.05	.02

❑ 638 Rene Gonzales .05 .02
❑ 639 Don Robinson .05 .02
❑ 640 Darryl Strawberry .10 .03
❑ 641 Dave Anderson .05 .02
❑ 642 Scott Scudder .05 .02
❑ 643 Reggie Harris UER .05 .02
(Hepatitis misspelled as hepititis)
❑ 644 Dave Henderson .05 .02
❑ 645 Ben McDonald .05 .02
❑ 646 Bob Kipper .05 .02
❑ 647 Hal Morris UER .05 .02
(It's should be its)
❑ 648 Tim Birtsas .05 .02
❑ 649 Steve Searcy .05 .02
❑ 650 Dale Murphy .15 .04
❑ 651 Ron Oester .05 .02
❑ 652 Mike LaCoss .05 .02
❑ 653 Ron Jones .05 .02
❑ 654 Kelly Downs .05 .02
❑ 655 Roger Clemens .50 .15
❑ 656 Herm Winningham .05 .02
❑ 657 Trevor Wilson .05 .02
❑ 658 Jose Rijo .05 .02
❑ 659 Dann Bilardello UER .05 .02
Bio has 13 games, 1 hit, and 32 AB, stats show 19, 2, and 37
❑ 660 Gregg Jefferies .05 .02
❑ 661 Doug Drabek AS UER .05 .02
(Through is misspelled though)
❑ 662 Randy Myers AS .05 .02
❑ 663 Benny Santiago AS .05 .02
❑ 664 Will Clark AS .10 .03
❑ 665 Ryne Sandberg AS .25 .07
❑ 666 Barry Larkin AS UER .10 .03
Line 13, coolly misspelled cooly
❑ 667 Matt Williams AS .05 .02
❑ 668 Barry Bonds AS .50 .15
❑ 669 Eric Davis AS .05 .02
❑ 670 Bobby Bonilla AS .05 .02
❑ 671 C.Jones FDP RC 4.00 1.20
❑ 672 E.Christopherson RC .10 .03
FDP
❑ 673 R.Beckett FDP RC .10 .03
❑ 674 S.Andrews FDP RC .25 .07
❑ 675 Steve Karsay FDP RC .25 .07
❑ 676 Aaron Holbert FDP RC .10 .03
❑ 677 D.Osborne FDP RC .10 .03
❑ 678 Todd Ritchie FDP RC .25 .07
❑ 679 Ron Walden FDP RC .10 .03
❑ 680 Tim Costo FDP RC .10 .03
❑ 681 Dan Wilson FDP RC .25 .07
❑ 682 Kurt Miller FDP RC .10 .03
❑ 683 M.Lieberthal FDP RC .40 .12
❑ 684 Roger Clemens KM .25 .07
❑ 685 Dwight Gooden KM .05 .02
❑ 686 Nolan Ryan KM .50 .15
❑ 687 Frank Viola KM .05 .02
❑ 688 Erik Hanson KM .05 .02
❑ 689 Matt Williams MB .05 .02
❑ 690 J.Canseco MB UER .10 .03
Mammoth misspelled as monmouth
❑ 691 Darryl Strawberry MB .05 .02
❑ 692 Bo Jackson MB .10 .03
❑ 693 Cecil Fielder MB .05 .02
❑ 694 Sandy Alomar Jr. RF .05 .02
❑ 695 Cory Snyder RF .05 .02
❑ 696 Eric Davis RF .05 .02
❑ 697 Ken Griffey Jr. RF .25 .07
❑ 698 A.Van Slyke RF UER .10 .03
Line 2, outfielders does not need
❑ 699 Mark Langston NH .05 .02
Mike Witt
❑ 700 Randy Johnson NH .15 .04
❑ 701 Nolan Ryan NH .50 .15
❑ 702 Dave Stewart NH .05 .02
❑ 703 F.Valenzuela NH .05 .02
❑ 704 Andy Hawkins NH .05 .02
❑ 705 Melido Perez NH .05 .02
❑ 706 Terry Mulholland NH .05 .02
❑ 707 Dave Stieb NH .05 .02
❑ 708 Brian Barnes RC .05 .02
❑ 709 Bernard Gilkey .05 .02
❑ 710 Steve Decker .05 .02
❑ 711 Paul Faries .05 .02
❑ 712 Paul Marak .05 .02
❑ 713 Wes Chamberlain RC .10 .03
❑ 714 Kevin Belcher .05 .02
❑ 715 Dan Boone UER .05 .02
(IP adds up to 101, but card has 101.2)
❑ 716 Steve Adkins .05 .02
❑ 717 Geronimo Pena .05 .02
❑ 718 Howard Farmer .05 .02
❑ 719 Mark Leonard .05 .02
❑ 720 Tom Lampkin .05 .02
❑ 721 Mike Gardiner .05 .02
❑ 722 Jeff Conine RC .40 .12
❑ 723 Efrain Valdez .05 .02
❑ 724 Chuck Malone .05 .02
❑ 725 Leo Gomez .05 .02
❑ 726 Paul McClellan .05 .02
❑ 727 Mark Leiter RC .10 .03
❑ 728 Rich DeLucia UER .05 .02
(Line 2, all told is written alltold)
❑ 729 Mel Rojas .05 .02
❑ 730 Hector Wagner .05 .02
❑ 731 Ray Lankford .10 .03
❑ 732 Turner Ward RC .10 .03
❑ 733 Gerald Alexander .05 .02
❑ 734 Scott Anderson .05 .02
❑ 735 Tony Perezchica .05 .02
❑ 736 Jimmy Kremers .05 .02
❑ 737 American Flag .25 .07
(Pray for Peace)
❑ 738 Mike York .05 .02
❑ 739 Mike Rochford .05 .02
❑ 740 Scott Aldred .05 .02
❑ 741 Rico Brogna .05 .02
❑ 742 Dave Burba RC .25 .07
❑ 743 Ray Stephens .05 .02
❑ 744 Eric Gunderson .05 .02
❑ 745 Troy Afenir .05 .02
❑ 746 Jeff Shaw .05 .02
❑ 747 Orlando Merced RC .10 .03
❑ 748 O.Olivares UER RC .10 .03
Line 9, league is misspelled legaue
❑ 749 Jerry Kutzler .05 .02
❑ 750 Mo Vaughn UER .10 .03
(44 SB's in 1990)
❑ 751 Matt Stark .05 .02
❑ 752 Randy Hennis .05 .02
❑ 753 Andujar Cedeno .05 .02
❑ 754 Kelvin Torve .05 .02
❑ 755 Joe Kraemer .05 .02
❑ 756 Phil Clark RC .10 .03
❑ 757 Ed Vosberg .05 .02
❑ 758 Mike Perez RC .10 .03
❑ 759 Scott Lewis .05 .02
❑ 760 Steve Chitren .05 .02
❑ 761 Ray Young .05 .02
❑ 762 Andres Santana .05 .02
❑ 763 Rodney McCray .05 .02
❑ 764 Sean Berry UER RC .10 .03
(Name misspelled Barry on card front)
❑ 765 Brent Mayne .05 .02
❑ 766 Mike Simms .05 .02
❑ 767 Glenn Sutko .05 .02
❑ 768 Gary DiSarcina .05 .02
❑ 769 George Brett HL .25 .07
❑ 770 Cecil Fielder HL .05 .02
❑ 771 Jim Presley .05 .02
❑ 772 John Dopson .05 .02
❑ 773 Bo Jackson Breaker .10 .03
❑ 774 Brent Knackert UER .05 .02
Born in 1954, shown throwing righty, but bio says lefty
❑ 775 Bill Doran UER .05 .02
(Reds in NL East)
❑ 776 Dick Schofield .05 .02
❑ 777 Nelson Santovenia .05 .02
❑ 778 Mark Guthrie .05 .02
❑ 779 Mark Lemke .05 .02
❑ 780 Terry Steinbach .05 .02
❑ 781 Tom Bolton .05 .02
❑ 782 Randy Tomlin RC .10 .03
❑ 783 Jeff Kunkel .05 .02
❑ 784 Felix Jose .05 .02
❑ 785 Rick Sutcliffe .10 .03
❑ 786 John Cerutti .05 .02
❑ 787 Jose Vizcaino UER .05 .02
(Offerman, not Opperman)
❑ 788 Curt Schilling .25 .07
❑ 789 Ed Whitson .05 .02
❑ 790 Tony Pena .05 .02
❑ 791 John Candelaria .05 .02
❑ 792 Carmelo Martinez .05 .02
❑ 793 Sandy Alomar Jr. UER .05 .02
(Indian's should say Indians')
❑ 794 Jim Neidlinger .05 .02
❑ 795 Barry Larkin WS .10 .03
and Chris Sabo
❑ 796 Paul Sorrento .05 .02
❑ 797 Tom Pagnozzi .05 .02
❑ 798 Tino Martinez .25 .07
❑ 799 Scott Ruskin UER .05 .02
(Text says first three seasons but lists averages for four)
❑ 800 Kirk Gibson .15 .04
❑ 801 Walt Terrell .05 .02
❑ 802 John Russell .05 .02
❑ 803 Chili Davis .10 .03
❑ 804 Chris Nabholz .05 .02
❑ 805 Juan Gonzalez .25 .07
❑ 806 Ron Hassey .05 .02
❑ 807 Todd Worrell .05 .02
❑ 808 Tommy Greene .05 .02
❑ 809 Joel Skinner UER .05 .02
Joel, not Bob, was drafted in 1979
❑ 810 Benito Santiago .10 .03
❑ 811 Pat Tabler UER .05 .02
Line 3, always misspelled always
❑ 812 Scott Erickson UER .05 .02
(Record spelled rcord)
❑ 813 Moises Alou .10 .03
❑ 814 Dale Sveum .05 .02
❑ 815 R.Sandberg MANYR .25 .07
❑ 816 Rick Dempsey .05 .02
❑ 817 Scott Bankhead .05 .02
❑ 818 Jason Grimsley .05 .02
❑ 819 Doug Jennings .05 .02
❑ 820 Tom Herr .05 .02
❑ 821 Rob Ducey .05 .02
❑ 822 Luis Quinones .05 .02
❑ 823 Greg Minton .05 .02
❑ 824 Mark Grant .05 .02
❑ 825 Ozzie Smith UER .40 .12
(Shortstop misspelled shortsop)
❑ 826 Dave Eiland .05 .02
❑ 827 Danny Heep .05 .02
❑ 828 Hensley Meulens .05 .02
❑ 829 Charlie O'Brien .05 .02
❑ 830 Glenn Davis .05 .02
❑ 831 John Marzano UER .05 .02
(International misspelled Internaional)
❑ 832 Steve Ontiveros .05 .02
❑ 833 Ron Karkovice .05 .02
❑ 834 Jerry Goff .05 .02
❑ 835 Ken Griffey Sr. .10 .03
❑ 836 Kevin Reimer .05 .02
❑ 837 Randy Kutcher UER .05 .02
(Infectious misspelled infectous)
❑ 838 Mike Blowers .05 .02
❑ 839 Mike Macfarlane .05 .02
❑ 840 Frank Thomas UER .25 .07
1989 Sarasota stats, 15 games but 188 AB
❑ 841 Ken Griffey Jr. .40 .12
Ken Griffey Sr.
❑ 842 Jack Howell .05 .02
❑ 843 Goose Gozzo .05 .02
❑ 844 Gerald Young .05 .02
❑ 845 Zane Smith .05 .02
❑ 846 Kevin Brown .10 .03
❑ 847 Sil Campusano .05 .02
❑ 848 Larry Andersen .05 .02

❑	849 Cal Ripken FRAN	.40	.12
❑	850 Roger Clemens FRAN	.25	.07
❑	851 S.Alomar Jr. FRAN	.05	.02
❑	852 Alan Trammell FRAN	.10	.03
❑	853 George Brett FRAN	.25	.07
❑	854 Robin Yount FRAN	.25	.07
❑	855 Kirby Puckett FRAN	.15	.04
❑	856 Don Mattingly FRAN	.30	.09
❑	857 R.Henderson FRAN	.15	.04
❑	858 Ken Griffey Jr. FRAN	.25	.07
❑	859 Ruben Sierra FRAN	.05	.02
❑	860 John Olerud FRAN	.05	.02
❑	861 Dave Justice FRAN	.05	.02
❑	862 Ryne Sandberg FRAN	.25	.07
❑	863 Eric Davis FRAN	.05	.02
❑	864 D.Strawberry FRAN	.05	.02
❑	865 Tim Wallach FRAN	.05	.02
❑	866 Dwight Gooden FRAN	.05	.02
❑	867 Len Dykstra FRAN	.05	.02
❑	868 Barry Bonds FRAN	.50	.15
❑	869 Todd Zeile FRAN UER (Powerful misspelled as poweful)	.05	.02
❑	870 Benito Santiago FRAN	.05	.02
❑	871 Will Clark FRAN	.10	.03
❑	872 Craig Biggio FRAN	.10	.03
❑	873 Wally Joyner FRAN	.05	.02
❑	874 Frank Thomas FRAN	.15	.04
❑	875 R.Henderson MVP	.15	.04
❑	876 Barry Bonds MVP	.50	.15
❑	877 Bob Welch CY	.05	.02
❑	878 Doug Drabek CY	.05	.02
❑	879 S.Alomar Jr. ROY	.05	.02
❑	880 Dave Justice ROY	.05	.02
❑	881 Damon Berryhill	.05	.02
❑	882 Frank Viola DT	.05	.02
❑	883 Dave Stewart DT	.05	.02
❑	884 Doug Jones DT	.05	.02
❑	885 Randy Myers DT	.05	.02
❑	886 Will Clark DT	.10	.03
❑	887 Roberto Alomar DT	.10	.03
❑	888 Barry Larkin DT	.10	.03
❑	889 Wade Boggs DT	.15	.04
❑	890 Rickey Henderson DT	.25	.07
❑	891 Kirby Puckett DT	.15	.04
❑	892 Ken Griffey Jr DT	.50	.15
❑	893 Benny Santiago DT	.10	.03

1992 Score

	Nm-Mt	Ex-Mt
COMPLETE SET (893)	15.00	4.50
COMP.FACT.SET (910)	20.00	6.00
COMP. SERIES 1 (442)	8.00	2.40
COMP. SERIES 2 (451)	8.00	2.40

❑	1 Ken Griffey Jr.	.40	.12
❑	2 Nolan Ryan	1.00	.30
❑	3 Will Clark	.15	.04
❑	4 Dave Justice	.10	.03
❑	5 Dave Henderson	.05	.02
❑	6 Bret Saberhagen	.10	.03
❑	7 Fred McGriff	.15	.04
❑	8 Erik Hanson	.05	.02
❑	9 Darryl Strawberry	.10	.03
❑	10 Dwight Gooden	.10	.03
❑	11 Juan Gonzalez	.15	.04
❑	12 Mark Langston	.05	.02
❑	13 Lonnie Smith	.05	.02
❑	14 Jeff Montgomery	.05	.02
❑	15 Roberto Alomar	.15	.04
❑	16 Delino DeShields	.05	.02
❑	17 Steve Bedrosian	.05	.02
❑	18 Terry Pendleton	.10	.03
❑	19 Mark Carreon	.05	.02
❑	20 Mark McGwire	.60	.18
❑	21 Roger Clemens	.50	.15
❑	22 Chuck Crim	.05	.02
❑	23 Don Mattingly	.60	.18
❑	24 Dickie Thon	.05	.02
❑	25 Ron Gant	.10	.03
❑	26 Milt Cuyler	.05	.02
❑	27 Mike Macfarlane	.05	.02
❑	28 Dan Gladden	.05	.02
❑	29 Melido Perez	.05	.02
❑	30 Willie Randolph	.10	.03
❑	31 Albert Belle	.10	.03
❑	32 Dave Winfield	.10	.03
❑	33 Jimmy Jones	.05	.02
❑	34 Kevin Gross	.05	.02
❑	35 Andres Galarraga	.10	.03
❑	36 Mike Devereaux	.05	.02
❑	37 Chris Bosio	.05	.02
❑	38 Mike LaValliere	.05	.02
❑	39 Gary Gaetti	.10	.03
❑	40 Felix Jose	.05	.02
❑	41 Alvaro Espinoza	.05	.02
❑	42 Rick Aguilera	.10	.03
❑	43 Mike Gallego	.05	.02
❑	44 Eric Davis	.10	.03
❑	45 George Bell	.05	.02
❑	46 Tom Brunansky	.05	.02
❑	47 Steve Farr	.05	.02
❑	48 Duane Ward	.05	.02
❑	49 David Wells	.10	.03
❑	50 Cecil Fielder	.10	.03
❑	51 Walt Weiss	.05	.02
❑	52 Todd Zeile	.05	.02
❑	53 Doug Jones	.05	.02
❑	54 Bob Walk	.05	.02
❑	55 Rafael Palmeiro	.15	.04
❑	56 Rob Deer	.05	.02
❑	57 Paul O'Neill	.15	.04
❑	58 Jeff Reardon	.10	.03
❑	59 Randy Ready	.05	.02
❑	60 Scott Erickson	.05	.02
❑	61 Paul Molitor	.15	.04
❑	62 Jack McDowell	.05	.02
❑	63 Jim Acker	.05	.02
❑	64 Jay Buhner	.10	.03
❑	65 Travis Fryman	.10	.03
❑	66 Marquis Grissom	.10	.03
❑	67 Mike Harkey	.05	.02
❑	68 Luis Polonia	.05	.02
❑	69 Ken Caminiti	.10	.03
❑	70 Chris Sabo	.05	.02
❑	71 Gregg Olson	.05	.02
❑	72 Carlton Fisk	.15	.04
❑	73 Juan Samuel	.05	.02
❑	74 Todd Stottlemyre	.05	.02
❑	75 Andre Dawson	.10	.03
❑	76 Alvin Davis	.05	.02
❑	77 Bill Doran	.05	.02
❑	78 B.J. Surhoff	.10	.03
❑	79 Kirk McCaskill	.05	.02
❑	80 Dale Murphy	.15	.04
❑	81 Jose DeLeon	.05	.02
❑	82 Alex Fernandez	.05	.02
❑	83 Ivan Calderon	.05	.02
❑	84 Brent Mayne	.05	.02
❑	85 Jody Reed	.05	.02
❑	86 Randy Tomlin	.05	.02
❑	87 Randy Milligan	.05	.02
❑	88 Pascual Perez	.05	.02
❑	89 Hensley Meulens	.05	.02
❑	90 Joe Carter	.10	.03
❑	91 Mike Moore	.05	.02
❑	92 Ozzie Guillen	.10	.03
❑	93 Shawn Hillegas	.05	.02
❑	94 Chili Davis	.10	.03
❑	95 Vince Coleman	.05	.02
❑	96 Jimmy Key	.10	.03
❑	97 Billy Ripken	.05	.02
❑	98 Dave Smith	.05	.02
❑	99 Tom Bolton	.05	.02
❑	100 Barry Larkin	.15	.04
❑	101 Kenny Rogers	.10	.03
❑	102 Mike Boddicker	.05	.02
❑	103 Kevin Elster	.05	.02
❑	104 Ken Hill	.05	.02
❑	105 Charlie Leibrandt	.05	.02
❑	106 Pat Combs	.05	.02
❑	107 Hubie Brooks	.05	.02
❑	108 Julio Franco	.10	.03
❑	109 Vicente Palacios	.05	.02
❑	110 Kal Daniels	.05	.02
❑	111 Bruce Hurst	.05	.02
❑	112 Willie McGee	.10	.03
❑	113 Ted Power	.05	.02
❑	114 Milt Thompson	.05	.02
❑	115 Doug Drabek	.05	.02
❑	116 Rafael Belliard	.05	.02
❑	117 Scott Garrelts	.05	.02
❑	118 Terry Mulholland	.05	.02
❑	119 Jay Howell	.05	.02
❑	120 Danny Jackson	.05	.02
❑	121 Scott Ruskin	.05	.02
❑	122 Robin Ventura	.10	.03
❑	123 Bip Roberts	.05	.02
❑	124 Jeff Russell	.05	.02
❑	125 Hal Morris	.05	.02
❑	126 Teddy Higuera	.05	.02
❑	127 Luis Sojo	.05	.02
❑	128 Carlos Baerga	.05	.02
❑	129 Jeff Ballard	.05	.02
❑	130 Tom Gordon	.05	.02
❑	131 Sid Bream	.05	.02
❑	132 Rance Mulliniks	.05	.02
❑	133 Andy Benes	.05	.02
❑	134 Mickey Tettleton	.05	.02
❑	135 Rich DeLucia	.05	.02
❑	136 Tom Pagnozzi	.05	.02
❑	137 Harold Baines	.10	.03
❑	138 Danny Darwin	.05	.02
❑	139 Kevin Bass	.05	.02
❑	140 Chris Nabholz	.05	.02
❑	141 Pete O'Brien	.05	.02
❑	142 Jeff Treadway	.05	.02
❑	143 Mickey Morandini	.05	.02
❑	144 Eric King	.05	.02
❑	145 Danny Tartabull	.05	.02
❑	146 Lance Johnson	.05	.02
❑	147 Casey Candaele	.05	.02
❑	148 Felix Fermin	.05	.02
❑	149 Rich Rodriguez	.05	.02
❑	150 Dwight Evans	.15	.04
❑	151 Joe Klink	.05	.02
❑	152 Kevin Reimer	.05	.02
❑	153 Orlando Merced	.05	.02
❑	154 Mel Hall	.05	.02
❑	155 Randy Myers	.05	.02
❑	156 Greg A. Harris	.05	.02
❑	157 Jeff Brantley	.05	.02
❑	158 Jim Eisenreich	.05	.02
❑	159 Luis Rivera	.05	.02
❑	160 Cris Carpenter	.05	.02
❑	161 Bruce Ruffin	.05	.02
❑	162 Omar Vizquel	.15	.04
❑	163 Gerald Alexander	.05	.02
❑	164 Mark Guthrie	.05	.02
❑	165 Scott Lewis	.05	.02
❑	166 Bill Sampen	.05	.02
❑	167 Dave Anderson	.05	.02
❑	168 Kevin McReynolds	.05	.02
❑	169 Jose Vizcaino	.05	.02
❑	170 Bob Geren	.05	.02
❑	171 Mike Morgan	.05	.02
❑	172 Jim Gott	.05	.02
❑	173 Mike Pagliarulo	.05	.02
❑	174 Mike Jeffcoat	.05	.02
❑	175 Craig Lefferts	.05	.02
❑	176 Steve Finley	.10	.03
❑	177 Wally Backman	.05	.02
❑	178 Kent Mercker	.05	.02
❑	179 John Cerutti	.05	.02
❑	180 Jay Bell	.10	.03
❑	181 Dale Sveum	.05	.02
❑	182 Greg Gagne	.05	.02
❑	183 Donnie Hill	.05	.02
❑	184 Rex Hudler	.05	.02
❑	185 Pat Kelly	.05	.02

❑	186	Jeff D. Robinson	.05	.02
❑	187	Jeff Gray	.05	.02
❑	188	Jerry Willard	.05	.02
❑	189	Carlos Quintana	.05	.02
❑	190	Dennis Eckersley	.10	.03
❑	191	Kelly Downs	.05	.02
❑	192	Gregg Jefferies	.05	.02
❑	193	Darrin Fletcher	.05	.02
❑	194	Mike Jackson	.05	.02
❑	195	Eddie Murray	.25	.07
❑	196	Bill Landrum	.05	.02
❑	197	Eric Yelding	.05	.02
❑	198	Devon White	.10	.03
❑	199	Larry Walker	.15	.04
❑	200	Ryne Sandberg	.40	.12
❑	201	Dave Magadan	.05	.02
❑	202	Steve Chitren	.05	.02
❑	203	Scott Fletcher	.05	.02
❑	204	Dwayne Henry	.05	.02
❑	205	Scott Coolbaugh	.05	.02
❑	206	Tracy Jones	.05	.02
❑	207	Von Hayes	.05	.02
❑	208	Bob Melvin	.05	.02
❑	209	Scott Scudder	.05	.02
❑	210	Luis Gonzalez	.10	.03
❑	211	Scott Sanderson	.05	.02
❑	212	Chris Donnels	.05	.02
❑	213	Heathcliff Slocumb	.05	.02
❑	214	Mike Timlin	.05	.02
❑	215	Brian Harper	.05	.02
❑	216	Juan Berenguer UER (Decimal point missing in IP total)	.05	.02
❑	217	Mike Henneman	.05	.02
❑	218	Bill Spiers	.05	.02
❑	219	Scott Terry	.05	.02
❑	220	Frank Viola	.10	.03
❑	221	Mark Eichhorn	.05	.02
❑	222	Ernest Riles	.05	.02
❑	223	Ray Lankford	.10	.03
❑	224	Pete Harnisch	.05	.02
❑	225	Bobby Bonilla	.10	.03
❑	226	Mike Scioscia	.05	.02
❑	227	Joel Skinner	.05	.02
❑	228	Brian Holman	.05	.02
❑	229	Gilberto Reyes	.05	.02
❑	230	Matt Williams	.10	.03
❑	231	Jaime Navarro	.05	.02
❑	232	Jose Rijo	.05	.02
❑	233	Atlee Hammaker	.05	.02
❑	234	Tim Teufel	.05	.02
❑	235	John Kruk	.10	.03
❑	236	Kurt Stillwell	.05	.02
❑	237	Dan Pasqua	.05	.02
❑	238	Tim Crews	.05	.02
❑	239	Dave Gallagher	.05	.02
❑	240	Leo Gomez	.05	.02
❑	241	Steve Avery	.05	.02
❑	242	Bill Gullickson	.05	.02
❑	243	Mark Portugal	.05	.02
❑	244	Lee Guetterman	.05	.02
❑	245	Benito Santiago	.10	.03
❑	246	Jim Gantner	.05	.02
❑	247	Robby Thompson	.05	.02
❑	248	Terry Shumpert	.05	.02
❑	249	Mike Bell	.05	.02
❑	250	Harold Reynolds	.10	.03
❑	251	Mike Felder	.05	.02
❑	252	Bill Pecota	.05	.02
❑	253	Bill Krueger	.05	.02
❑	254	Alfredo Griffin	.05	.02
❑	255	Lou Whitaker	.10	.03
❑	256	Roy Smith	.05	.02
❑	257	Jerald Clark	.05	.02
❑	258	Sammy Sosa	.25	.07
❑	259	Tim Naehring	.05	.02
❑	260	Dave Righetti	.10	.03
❑	261	Paul Gibson	.05	.02
❑	262	Chris James	.05	.02
❑	263	Larry Andersen	.05	.02
❑	264	Storm Davis	.05	.02
❑	265	Jose Lind	.05	.02
❑	266	Greg Hibbard	.05	.02
❑	267	Norm Charlton	.05	.02
❑	268	Paul Kilgus	.05	.02
❑	269	Greg Maddux	.40	.12
❑	270	Ellis Burks	.10	.03
❑	271	Frank Tanana	.05	.02
❑	272	Gene Larkin	.05	.02
❑	273	Ron Hassey	.05	.02
❑	274	Jeff M. Robinson	.05	.02
❑	275	Steve Howe	.05	.02
❑	276	Daryl Boston	.05	.02
❑	277	Mark Lee	.05	.02
❑	278	Jose Segura	.05	.02
❑	279	Lance Blankenship	.05	.02
❑	280	Don Slaught	.05	.02
❑	281	Russ Swan	.05	.02
❑	282	Bob Tewksbury	.05	.02
❑	283	Geno Petralli	.05	.02
❑	284	Shane Mack	.05	.02
❑	285	Bob Scanlan	.05	.02
❑	286	Tim Leary	.05	.02
❑	287	John Smoltz	.15	.04
❑	288	Pat Borders	.05	.02
❑	289	Mark Davidson	.05	.02
❑	290	Sam Horn	.05	.02
❑	291	Lenny Harris	.05	.02
❑	292	Franklin Stubbs	.05	.02
❑	293	Thomas Howard	.05	.02
❑	294	Steve Lyons	.05	.02
❑	295	Francisco Oliveras	.05	.02
❑	296	Terry Leach	.05	.02
❑	297	Barry Jones	.05	.02
❑	298	Lance Parrish	.10	.03
❑	299	Wally Whitehurst	.05	.02
❑	300	Bob Welch	.05	.02
❑	301	Charlie Hayes	.05	.02
❑	302	Charlie Hough	.10	.03
❑	303	Gary Redus	.05	.02
❑	304	Scott Bradley	.05	.02
❑	305	Jose Oquendo	.05	.02
❑	306	Pete Incaviglia	.05	.02
❑	307	Marvin Freeman	.05	.02
❑	308	Gary Pettis	.05	.02
❑	309	Joe Slusarski	.05	.02
❑	310	Kevin Seitzer	.05	.02
❑	311	Jeff Reed	.05	.02
❑	312	Pat Tabler	.05	.02
❑	313	Mike Maddux	.05	.02
❑	314	Bob Milacki	.05	.02
❑	315	Eric Anthony	.05	.02
❑	316	Dante Bichette	.10	.03
❑	317	Steve Decker	.05	.02
❑	318	Jack Clark	.10	.03
❑	319	Doug Dascenzo	.05	.02
❑	320	Scott Leius	.05	.02
❑	321	Jim Lindeman	.05	.02
❑	322	Bryan Harvey	.05	.02
❑	323	Spike Owen	.05	.02
❑	324	Roberto Kelly	.05	.02
❑	325	Stan Belinda	.05	.02
❑	326	Joey Cora	.05	.02
❑	327	Jeff Innis	.05	.02
❑	328	Willie Wilson	.05	.02
❑	329	Juan Agosto	.05	.02
❑	330	Charles Nagy	.05	.02
❑	331	Scott Bailes	.05	.02
❑	332	Pete Schourek	.05	.02
❑	333	Mike Flanagan	.05	.02
❑	334	Omar Olivares	.05	.02
❑	335	Dennis Lamp	.05	.02
❑	336	Tommy Greene	.05	.02
❑	337	Randy Velarde	.05	.02
❑	338	Tom Lampkin	.05	.02
❑	339	John Russell	.05	.02
❑	340	Bob Kipper	.05	.02
❑	341	Todd Burns	.05	.02
❑	342	Ron Jones	.05	.02
❑	343	Dave Valle	.05	.02
❑	344	Mike Heath	.05	.02
❑	345	John Olerud	.10	.03
❑	346	Gerald Young	.05	.02
❑	347	Ken Patterson	.05	.02
❑	348	Les Lancaster	.05	.02
❑	349	Steve Crawford	.05	.02
❑	350	John Candelaria	.05	.02
❑	351	Mike Aldrete	.05	.02
❑	352	Mariano Duncan	.05	.02
❑	353	Julio Machado	.05	.02
❑	354	Ken Williams	.05	.02
❑	355	Walt Terrell	.05	.02
❑	356	Mitch Williams	.05	.02
❑	357	Al Newman	.05	.02
❑	358	Bud Black	.05	.02
❑	359	Joe Hesketh	.05	.02
❑	360	Paul Assenmacher	.05	.02
❑	361	Bo Jackson	.25	.07
❑	362	Jeff Blauser	.05	.02
❑	363	Mike Brumley	.05	.02
❑	364	Jim Deshaies	.05	.02
❑	365	Brady Anderson	.10	.03
❑	366	Chuck McElroy	.05	.02
❑	367	Matt Merullo	.05	.02
❑	368	Tim Belcher	.05	.02
❑	369	Luis Aquino	.05	.02
❑	370	Joe Oliver	.05	.02
❑	371	Greg Swindell	.05	.02
❑	372	Lee Stevens	.05	.02
❑	373	Mark Knudson	.05	.02
❑	374	Bill Wegman	.05	.02
❑	375	Jerry Don Gleaton	.05	.02
❑	376	Pedro Guerrero	.10	.03
❑	377	Randy Bush	.05	.02
❑	378	Greg W. Harris	.05	.02
❑	379	Eric Plunk	.05	.02
❑	380	Jose DeJesus	.05	.02
❑	381	Bobby Witt	.05	.02
❑	382	Curtis Wilkerson	.05	.02
❑	383	Gene Nelson	.05	.02
❑	384	Wes Chamberlain	.05	.02
❑	385	Tom Henke	.05	.02
❑	386	Mark Lemke	.05	.02
❑	387	Greg Briley	.05	.02
❑	388	Rafael Ramirez	.05	.02
❑	389	Tony Fossas	.05	.02
❑	390	Henry Cotto	.05	.02
❑	391	Tim Hulett	.05	.02
❑	392	Dean Palmer	.10	.03
❑	393	Glenn Braggs	.05	.02
❑	394	Mark Salas	.05	.02
❑	395	Rusty Meacham	.05	.02
❑	396	Andy Ashby	.05	.02
❑	397	Jose Melendez	.05	.02
❑	398	Warren Newson	.05	.02
❑	399	Frank Castillo	.05	.02
❑	400	Chito Martinez	.05	.02
❑	401	Bernie Williams	.15	.04
❑	402	Derek Bell	.10	.03
❑	403	Javier Ortiz	.05	.02
❑	404	Tim Sherrill	.05	.02
❑	405	Rob MacDonald	.05	.02
❑	406	Phil Plantier	.05	.02
❑	407	Troy Afenir	.05	.02
❑	408	Gino Minutelli	.05	.02
❑	409	Reggie Jefferson	.05	.02
❑	410	Mike Remlinger	.05	.02
❑	411	Carlos Rodriguez	.05	.02
❑	412	Joe Redfield	.05	.02
❑	413	Alonzo Powell	.05	.02
❑	414	S.Livingstone UER (Travis Fryman, not Woodie, should be referenced on back	.05	.02
❑	415	Scott Kamieniecki	.05	.02
❑	416	Tim Spehr	.05	.02
❑	417	Brian Hunter	.05	.02
❑	418	Ced Landrum	.05	.02
❑	419	Bret Barberie	.05	.02
❑	420	Kevin Morton	.05	.02
❑	421	Doug Henry RC	.10	.03
❑	422	Doug Piatt	.05	.02
❑	423	Pat Rice	.05	.02
❑	424	Juan Guzman	.05	.02
❑	425	Nolan Ryan NH	.50	.15
❑	426	Tommy Greene NH	.05	.02
❑	427	Bob Milacki and Mike Flanagan NH (Mark Williamson and Gregg Olson)	.05	.02
❑	428	Wilson Alvarez NH	.05	.02
❑	429	Otis Nixon HL	.05	.02
❑	430	Rickey Henderson HL	.15	.04
❑	431	Cecil Fielder AS	.05	.02
❑	432	Julio Franco AS	.05	.02
❑	433	Cal Ripken AS	.40	.12
❑	434	Wade Boggs AS	.10	.03
❑	435	Joe Carter AS	.05	.02

❑ 436 Ken Griffey Jr. AS .25 .07
❑ 437 Ruben Sierra AS .05 .02
❑ 438 Scott Erickson AS .05 .02
❑ 439 Tom Henke AS .05 .02
❑ 440 Terry Steinbach AS .05 .02
❑ 441 Rickey Henderson DT .25 .07
❑ 442 Ryne Sandberg DT .40 .12
❑ 443 Otis Nixon .05 .02
❑ 444 Scott Radinsky UER .05 .02
  Photo on front is Tom Drees
❑ 445 Mark Grace .15 .04
❑ 446 Tony Pena .05 .02
❑ 447 Billy Hatcher .05 .02
❑ 448 Glenallen Hill .05 .02
❑ 449 Chris Gwynn .05 .02
❑ 450 Tom Glavine .15 .04
❑ 451 John Habyan .05 .02
❑ 452 Al Osuna .05 .02
❑ 453 Tony Phillips .05 .02
❑ 454 Greg Cadaret .05 .02
❑ 455 Rob Dibble .10 .03
❑ 456 Rick Honeycutt .05 .02
❑ 457 Jerome Walton .05 .02
❑ 458 Mookie Wilson .10 .03
❑ 459 Mark Gubicza .05 .02
❑ 460 Craig Biggio .15 .04
❑ 461 Dave Cochrane .05 .02
❑ 462 Keith Miller .05 .02
❑ 463 Alex Cole .05 .02
❑ 464 Pete Smith .05 .02
❑ 465 Brett Butler .10 .03
❑ 466 Jeff Huson .05 .02
❑ 467 Steve Lake .05 .02
❑ 468 Lloyd Moseby .05 .02
❑ 469 Tim McIntosh .05 .02
❑ 470 Dennis Martinez .10 .03
❑ 471 Greg Myers .05 .02
❑ 472 Mackey Sasser .05 .02
❑ 473 Junior Ortiz .05 .02
❑ 474 Greg Olson .05 .02
❑ 475 Steve Sax .05 .02
❑ 476 Ricky Jordan .05 .02
❑ 477 Max Venable .05 .02
❑ 478 Brian McRae .05 .02
❑ 479 Doug Simons .05 .02
❑ 480 Rickey Henderson .25 .07
❑ 481 Gary Varsho .05 .02
❑ 482 Carl Willis .05 .02
❑ 483 Rick Wilkins .05 .02
❑ 484 Donn Pall .05 .02
❑ 485 Edgar Martinez .15 .04
❑ 486 Tom Foley .05 .02
❑ 487 Mark Williamson .05 .02
❑ 488 Jack Armstrong .05 .02
❑ 489 Gary Carter .10 .03
❑ 490 Ruben Sierra .05 .02
❑ 491 Gerald Perry .05 .02
❑ 492 Rob Murphy .05 .02
❑ 493 Zane Smith .05 .02
❑ 494 Darryl Kile .10 .03
❑ 495 Kelly Gruber .05 .02
❑ 496 Jerry Browne .05 .02
❑ 497 Darryl Hamilton .05 .02
❑ 498 Mike Stanton .05 .02
❑ 499 Mark Leonard .05 .02
❑ 500 Jose Canseco .15 .04
❑ 501 Dave Martinez .05 .02
❑ 502 Jose Guzman .05 .02
❑ 503 Terry Kennedy .05 .02
❑ 504 Ed Sprague .05 .02
❑ 505 Frank Thomas UER .25 .07
  (His Gulf Coast League
  stats are wrong)
❑ 506 Darren Daulton .10 .03
❑ 507 Kevin Tapani .05 .02
❑ 508 Luis Salazar .05 .02
❑ 509 Paul Faries .05 .02
❑ 510 Sandy Alomar Jr. .05 .02
❑ 511 Jeff King .05 .02
❑ 512 Gary Thurman .05 .02
❑ 513 Chris Hammond .05 .02
❑ 514 Pedro Munoz .05 .02
❑ 515 Alan Trammell .10 .03
❑ 516 Geronimo Pena .05 .02
❑ 517 Rodney McCray UER .05 .02
  Stole 6 bases in 1990, not 5;
  career totals are correct at 7
❑ 518 Manny Lee .05 .02
❑ 519 Junior Felix .05 .02
❑ 520 Kirk Gibson .15 .04
❑ 521 Darrin Jackson .05 .02
❑ 522 John Burkett .05 .02
❑ 523 Jeff Johnson .05 .02
❑ 524 Jim Corsi .05 .02
❑ 525 Robin Yount .40 .12
❑ 526 Jamie Quirk .05 .02
❑ 527 Bob Ojeda .05 .02
❑ 528 Mark Lewis .05 .02
❑ 529 Bryn Smith .05 .02
❑ 530 Kent Hrbek .10 .03
❑ 531 Dennis Boyd .05 .02
❑ 532 Ron Karkovice .05 .02
❑ 533 Don August .05 .02
❑ 534 Todd Frohwirth .05 .02
❑ 535 Wally Joyner .10 .03
❑ 536 Dennis Rasmussen .05 .02
❑ 537 Andy Allanson .05 .02
❑ 538 Rich Gossage .10 .03
❑ 539 John Marzano .05 .02
❑ 540 Cal Ripken .75 .23
❑ 541 Bill Swift UER .05 .02
  (Brewers logo on front)
❑ 542 Kevin Appier .10 .03
❑ 543 Dave Bergman .05 .02
❑ 544 Bernard Gilkey .05 .02
❑ 545 Mike Greenwell .05 .02
❑ 546 Jose Uribe .05 .02
❑ 547 Jesse Orosco .05 .02
❑ 548 Bob Patterson .05 .02
❑ 549 Mike Stanley .05 .02
❑ 550 Howard Johnson .05 .02
❑ 551 Joe Orsulak .05 .02
❑ 552 Dick Schofield .05 .02
❑ 553 Dave Hollins .05 .02
❑ 554 David Segui .05 .02
❑ 555 Barry Bonds 1.00 .30
❑ 556 Mo Vaughn .10 .03
❑ 557 Craig Wilson .05 .02
❑ 558 Bobby Rose .05 .02
❑ 559 Rod Nichols .05 .02
❑ 560 Len Dykstra .10 .03
❑ 561 Craig Grebeck .05 .02
❑ 562 Darren Lewis .05 .02
❑ 563 Todd Benzinger .05 .02
❑ 564 Ed Whitson .05 .02
❑ 565 Jesse Barfield .05 .02
❑ 566 Lloyd McClendon .05 .02
❑ 567 Dan Plesac .05 .02
❑ 568 Danny Cox .05 .02
❑ 569 Skeeter Barnes .05 .02
❑ 570 Bobby Thigpen .05 .02
❑ 571 Deion Sanders .15 .04
❑ 572 Chuck Knoblauch .10 .03
❑ 573 Matt Nokes .05 .02
❑ 574 Herm Winningham .05 .02
❑ 575 Tom Candiotti .05 .02
❑ 576 Jeff Bagwell .25 .07
❑ 577 Brook Jacoby .05 .02
❑ 578 Chico Walker .05 .02
❑ 579 Brian Downing .05 .02
❑ 580 Dave Stewart .10 .03
❑ 581 Francisco Cabrera .05 .02
❑ 582 Rene Gonzales .05 .02
❑ 583 Stan Javier .05 .02
❑ 584 Randy Johnson .25 .07
❑ 585 Chuck Finley .10 .03
❑ 586 Mark Gardner .05 .02
❑ 587 Mark Whiten .05 .02
❑ 588 Garry Templeton .05 .02
❑ 589 Gary Sheffield .10 .03
❑ 590 Ozzie Smith .40 .12
❑ 591 Candy Maldonado .05 .02
❑ 592 Mike Sharperson .05 .02
❑ 593 Carlos Martinez .05 .02
❑ 594 Scott Bankhead .05 .02
❑ 595 Tim Wallach .05 .02
❑ 596 Tino Martinez .15 .04
❑ 597 Roger McDowell .05 .02
❑ 598 Cory Snyder .05 .02
❑ 599 Andujar Cedeno .05 .02
❑ 600 Kirby Puckett .25 .07
❑ 601 Rick Parker .05 .02
❑ 602 Todd Hundley .05 .02
❑ 603 Greg Litton .05 .02
❑ 604 Dave Johnson .05 .02
❑ 605 John Franco .10 .03
❑ 606 Mike Fetters .05 .02
❑ 607 Luis Alicea .05 .02
❑ 608 Trevor Wilson .05 .02
❑ 609 Rob Ducey .05 .02
❑ 610 Ramon Martinez .05 .02
❑ 611 Dave Burba .05 .02
❑ 612 Dwight Smith .05 .02
❑ 613 Kevin Maas .05 .02
❑ 614 John Costello .05 .02
❑ 615 Glenn Davis .05 .02
❑ 616 Shawn Abner .05 .02
❑ 617 Scott Hemond .05 .02
❑ 618 Tom Prince .05 .02
❑ 619 Wally Ritchie .05 .02
❑ 620 Jim Abbott .15 .04
❑ 621 Charlie O'Brien .05 .02
❑ 622 Jack Daugherty .05 .02
❑ 623 Tommy Gregg .05 .02
❑ 624 Jeff Shaw .05 .02
❑ 625 Tony Gwynn .30 .09
❑ 626 Mark Leiter .05 .02
❑ 627 Jim Clancy .05 .02
❑ 628 Tim Layana .05 .02
❑ 629 Jeff Schaefer .05 .02
❑ 630 Lee Smith .10 .03
❑ 631 Wade Taylor .05 .02
❑ 632 Mike Simms .05 .02
❑ 633 Terry Steinbach .05 .02
❑ 634 Shawon Dunston .05 .02
❑ 635 Tim Raines .10 .03
❑ 636 Kirt Manwaring .05 .02
❑ 637 Warren Cromartie .05 .02
❑ 638 Luis Quinones .05 .02
❑ 639 Greg Vaughn .05 .02
❑ 640 Kevin Mitchell .05 .02
❑ 641 Chris Hoiles .05 .02
❑ 642 Tom Browning .05 .02
❑ 643 Mitch Webster .05 .02
❑ 644 Steve Olin .05 .02
❑ 645 Tony Fernandez .05 .02
❑ 646 Juan Bell .05 .02
❑ 647 Joe Boever .05 .02
❑ 648 Carney Lansford .10 .03
❑ 649 Mike Benjamin .05 .02
❑ 650 George Brett .60 .18
❑ 651 Tim Burke .05 .02
❑ 652 Jack Morris .10 .03
❑ 653 Orel Hershiser .10 .03
❑ 654 Mike Schooler .05 .02
❑ 655 Andy Van Slyke .15 .04
❑ 656 Dave Stieb .05 .02
❑ 657 Dave Clark .05 .02
❑ 658 Ben McDonald .05 .02
❑ 659 John Smiley .05 .02
❑ 660 Wade Boggs .15 .04
❑ 661 Eric Bullock .05 .02
❑ 662 Eric Show .05 .02
❑ 663 Lenny Webster .05 .02
❑ 664 Mike Huff .05 .02
❑ 665 Rick Sutcliffe .10 .03
❑ 666 Jeff Manto .05 .02
❑ 667 Mike Fitzgerald .05 .02
❑ 668 Matt Young .05 .02
❑ 669 Dave West .05 .02
❑ 670 Mike Hartley .05 .02
❑ 671 Curt Schilling .15 .04
❑ 672 Brian Bohanon .05 .02
❑ 673 Cecil Espy .05 .02
❑ 674 Joe Grahe .05 .02
❑ 675 Sid Fernandez .05 .02
❑ 676 Edwin Nunez .05 .02
❑ 677 Hector Villanueva .05 .02
❑ 678 Sean Berry .05 .02
❑ 679 Dave Eiland .05 .02
❑ 680 David Cone .10 .03
❑ 681 Mike Bordick .05 .02
❑ 682 Tony Castillo .05 .02
❑ 683 John Barfield .05 .02
❑ 684 Jeff Hamilton .05 .02
❑ 685 Ken Dayley .05 .02
❑ 686 Carmelo Martinez .05 .02
❑ 687 Mike Capel .05 .02

❑ 688 Scott Chiamparino .05 .02
❑ 689 Rich Gedman .05 .02
❑ 690 Rich Monteleone .05 .02
❑ 691 Alejandro Pena .05 .02
❑ 692 Oscar Azocar .05 .02
❑ 693 Jim Poole .05 .02
❑ 694 Mike Gardiner .05 .02
❑ 695 Steve Buechele .05 .02
❑ 696 Rudy Seanez .05 .02
❑ 697 Paul Abbott .05 .02
❑ 698 Steve Searcy .05 .02
❑ 699 Jose Offerman .05 .02
❑ 700 Ivan Rodriguez .25 .07
❑ 701 Joe Girardi .05 .02
❑ 702 Tony Perezchica .05 .02
❑ 703 Paul McClellan .05 .02
❑ 704 David Howard .05 .02
❑ 705 Dan Petry .05 .02
❑ 706 Jack Howell .05 .02
❑ 707 Jose Mesa .05 .02
❑ 708 Randy St. Claire .05 .02
❑ 709 Kevin Brown .10 .03
❑ 710 Ron Darling .05 .02
❑ 711 Jason Grimsley .05 .02
❑ 712 John Orton .05 .02
❑ 713 Shawn Boskie .05 .02
❑ 714 Pat Clements .05 .02
❑ 715 Brian Barnes .05 .02
❑ 716 Luis Lopez .05 .02
❑ 717 Bob McClure .05 .02
❑ 718 Mark Davis .05 .02
❑ 719 Dann Bilardello .05 .02
❑ 720 Tom Edens .05 .02
❑ 721 Willie Fraser .05 .02
❑ 722 Curt Young .05 .02
❑ 723 Neal Heaton .05 .02
❑ 724 Craig Worthington .05 .02
❑ 725 Mel Rojas .05 .02
❑ 726 Daryl Irvine .05 .02
❑ 727 Roger Mason .05 .02
❑ 728 Kirk Dressendorfer .05 .02
❑ 729 Scott Aldred .05 .02
❑ 730 Willie Blair .05 .02
❑ 731 Allan Anderson .05 .02
❑ 732 Dana Kiecker .05 .02
❑ 733 Jose Gonzalez .05 .02
❑ 734 Brian Drahman .05 .02
❑ 735 Brad Komminsk .05 .02
❑ 736 Arthur Rhodes .05 .02
❑ 737 Terry Mathews .05 .02
❑ 738 Jeff Fassero .05 .02
❑ 739 Mike Magnante RC .10 .03
❑ 740 Kip Gross .05 .02
❑ 741 Jim Hunter .05 .02
❑ 742 Jose Mota .05 .02
❑ 743 Joe Bitker .05 .02
❑ 744 Tim Mauser .05 .02
❑ 745 Ramon Garcia .05 .02
❑ 746 Rod Beck RC .25 .07
❑ 747 Jim Austin RC .05 .02
❑ 748 Keith Mitchell .05 .02
❑ 749 Wayne Rosenthal .05 .02
❑ 750 Bryan Hickerson RC .10 .03
❑ 751 Bruce Egloff .05 .02
❑ 752 John Wehner .05 .02
❑ 753 Darren Holmes .05 .02
❑ 754 Dave Hansen .05 .02
❑ 755 Mike Mussina .25 .07
❑ 756 Anthony Young .05 .02
❑ 757 Ron Tingley .05 .02
❑ 758 Ricky Bones .05 .02
❑ 759 Mark Wohlers .05 .02
❑ 760 Wilson Alvarez .05 .02
❑ 761 Harvey Pulliam .05 .02
❑ 762 Ryan Bowen .05 .02
❑ 763 Terry Bross .05 .02
❑ 764 Joel Johnston .05 .02
❑ 765 Terry McDaniel .05 .02
❑ 766 Esteban Beltre .05 .02
❑ 767 Rob Maurer .05 .02
❑ 768 Ted Wood .05 .02
❑ 769 Mo Sanford .05 .02
❑ 770 Jeff Carter .05 .02
❑ 771 Gil Heredia RC .25 .07
❑ 772 Monty Fariss .05 .02
❑ 773 Will Clark AS .10 .03
❑ 774 Ryne Sandberg AS .25 .07
❑ 775 Barry Larkin AS .10 .03
❑ 776 Howard Johnson AS .05 .02
❑ 777 Barry Bonds AS .50 .15
❑ 778 Brett Butler AS .05 .02
❑ 779 Tony Gwynn AS .15 .04
❑ 780 Ramon Martinez AS .05 .02
❑ 781 Lee Smith AS .05 .02
❑ 782 Mike Scioscia AS .05 .02
❑ 783 D.Martinez HL UER .05 .02
Card has both 13th
and 15th perfect game
in Major League history
❑ 784 Dennis Martinez NH .05 .02
❑ 785 Mark Gardner NH .05 .02
❑ 786 Bret Saberhagen NH .05 .02
❑ 787 Kent Mercker NH .05 .02
Mark Wohlers
Alejandro Pena
❑ 788 Cal Ripken MVP .40 .12
❑ 789 Terry Pendleton MVP .05 .02
❑ 790 Roger Clemens CY .25 .07
❑ 791 Tom Glavine CY .10 .03
❑ 792 C.Knoblauch ROY .05 .02
❑ 793 Jeff Bagwell ROY .15 .04
❑ 794 Cal Ripken MANYR .40 .12
❑ 795 David Cone HL .05 .02
❑ 796 Kirby Puckett HL .15 .04
❑ 797 Steve Avery HL .05 .02
❑ 798 Jack Morris HL .05 .02
❑ 799 Allen Watson DC RC .10 .03
❑ 800 M.Ramirez DC RC 4.00 1.20
❑ 801 Cliff Floyd DC RC 1.00 .30
❑ 802 Al Shirley DC RC .10 .03
❑ 803 Brian Barber DC RC .10 .03
❑ 804 Jon Farrell DC RC .10 .03
❑ 805 Brent Gates DC RC .10 .03
❑ 806 Scott Ruffcorn DC RC .10 .03
❑ 807 Tyrone Hill DC RC .10 .03
❑ 808 Benji Gil DC RC .25 .07
❑ 809 Aaron Sele DC RC .40 .12
❑ 810 Tyler Green DC RC .10 .03
❑ 811 Chris Jones .05 .02
❑ 812 Steve Wilson .05 .02
❑ 813 Freddie Benavides .05 .02
❑ 814 Don Wakamatsu .05 .02
❑ 815 Mike Humphreys .05 .02
❑ 816 Scott Servais .05 .02
❑ 817 Rico Rossy .05 .02
❑ 818 John Ramos .05 .02
❑ 819 Rob Mallicoat .05 .02
❑ 820 Milt Hill .05 .02
❑ 821 Carlos Garcia .05 .02
❑ 822 Stan Royer .05 .02
❑ 823 Jeff Plympton .05 .02
❑ 824 Braulio Castillo .05 .02
❑ 825 David Haas .05 .02
❑ 826 Luis Mercedes .05 .02
❑ 827 Eric Karros .10 .03
❑ 828 Shawn Hare RC .10 .03
❑ 829 Reggie Sanders .10 .03
❑ 830 Tom Goodwin .05 .02
❑ 831 Dan Gakeler .05 .02
❑ 832 Stacy Jones .05 .02
❑ 833 Kim Batiste .05 .02
❑ 834 Cal Eldred .05 .02
❑ 835 Chris George .05 .02
❑ 836 Wayne Housie .05 .02
❑ 837 Mike Ignasiak .05 .02
❑ 838 Josias Manzanillo RC .10 .03
❑ 839 Jim Olander .05 .02
❑ 840 Gary Cooper .05 .02
❑ 841 Royce Clayton .05 .02
❑ 842 Hector Fajardo RC .10 .03
❑ 843 Blaine Beatty .05 .02
❑ 844 Jorge Pedre .05 .02
❑ 845 Kenny Lofton .15 .04
❑ 846 Scott Brosius RC .40 .12
❑ 847 Chris Cron .05 .02
❑ 848 Denis Boucher .05 .02
❑ 849 Kyle Abbott .05 .02
❑ 850 Bob Zupcic RC .10 .03
❑ 851 Rheal Cormier .05 .02
❑ 852 Jimmy Lewis RC .05 .02
❑ 853 Anthony Telford .05 .02
❑ 854 Cliff Brantley .05 .02
❑ 855 Kevin Campbell .05 .02
❑ 856 Craig Shipley .05 .02
❑ 857 Chuck Carr .05 .02
❑ 858 Tony Eusebio .10 .03
❑ 859 Jim Thome .25 .07
❑ 860 Vinny Castilla RC 1.00 .30
❑ 861 Dann Howitt .05 .02
❑ 862 Kevin Ward .05 .02
❑ 863 Steve Wapnick .05 .02
❑ 864 Rod Brewer RC .10 .03
❑ 865 Todd Van Poppel .05 .02
❑ 866 Jose Hernandez RC .40 .12
❑ 867 Amalio Carreno .05 .02
❑ 868 Calvin Jones .05 .02
❑ 869 Jeff Gardner .05 .02
❑ 870 Jarvis Brown .05 .02
❑ 871 Eddie Taubensee RC .25 .07
❑ 872 Andy Mota .05 .02
❑ 873 Chris Haney .05 .02
❑ 874 Roberto Hernandez .05 .02
❑ 875 Laddie Renfroe .05 .02
❑ 876 Scott Cooper .05 .02
❑ 877 Armando Reynoso RC .25 .07
❑ 878 Ty Cobb MEMO .25 .07
❑ 879 Babe Ruth MEMO .50 .15
❑ 880 Honus Wagner MEMO .25 .07
❑ 881 Lou Gehrig MEMO .40 .12
❑ 882 Satchel Paige MEMO .25 .07
❑ 883 Will Clark DT .10 .03
❑ 884 Cal Ripken DT 2.00 .60
❑ 885 Wade Boggs DT .10 .03
❑ 886 Kirby Puckett DT .15 .04
❑ 887 Tony Gwynn DT .15 .04
❑ 888 Craig Biggio DT .10 .03
❑ 889 Scott Erickson DT .05 .02
❑ 890 Tom Glavine DT .10 .03
❑ 891 Rob Dibble DT .10 .03
❑ 892 Mitch Williams DT .05 .02
❑ 893 Frank Thomas DT .15 .04
❑ X672 Chuck Knoblauch AU 25.00 7.50
1990 Score card,
3000 copies signed

1992 Score Rookie/Traded

	Nm-Mt	Ex-Mt
COMP.FACT.SET (110)	8.00	2.40

❑ 1T Gary Sheffield .30 .09
❑ 2T Kevin Seitzer .20 .06
❑ 3T Danny Tartabull .20 .06
❑ 4T Steve Sax .20 .06
❑ 5T Bobby Bonilla .30 .09
❑ 6T Frank Viola .30 .09
❑ 7T Dave Winfield .30 .09
❑ 8T Rick Sutcliffe .30 .09
❑ 9T Jose Canseco .50 .15
❑ 10T Greg Swindell .20 .06
❑ 11T Eddie Murray .75 .23
❑ 12T Randy Myers .20 .06
❑ 13T Wally Joyner .30 .09
❑ 14T Kenny Lofton .50 .15
❑ 15T Jack Morris .30 .09
❑ 16T Charlie Hayes .20 .06
❑ 17T Pete Incaviglia .20 .06
❑ 18T Kevin Mitchell .20 .06
❑ 19T Kurt Stillwell .20 .06

Card	Player	Nm-Mt	Ex-Mt
❑ 20T	Bret Saberhagen	.30	.09
❑ 21T	Steve Buechele	.20	.06
❑ 22T	John Smiley	.20	.06
❑ 23T	Sammy Sosa	.75	.23
❑ 24T	George Bell	.20	.06
❑ 25T	Curt Schilling	.50	.15
❑ 26T	Dick Schofield	.20	.06
❑ 27T	David Cone	.30	.09
❑ 28T	Dan Gladden	.20	.06
❑ 29T	Kirk McCaskill	.20	.06
❑ 30T	Mike Gallego	.20	.06
❑ 31T	Kevin McReynolds	.20	.06
❑ 32T	Bill Swift	.20	.06
❑ 33T	Dave Martinez	.20	.06
❑ 34T	Storm Davis	.20	.06
❑ 35T	Willie Randolph	.30	.09
❑ 36T	Melido Perez	.20	.06
❑ 37T	Mark Carreon	.20	.06
❑ 38T	Doug Jones	.20	.06
❑ 39T	Gregg Jefferies	.20	.06
❑ 40T	Mike Jackson	.20	.06
❑ 41T	Dickie Thon	.20	.06
❑ 42T	Eric King	.20	.06
❑ 43T	Herm Winningham	.20	.06
❑ 44T	Derek Lilliquist	.20	.06
❑ 45T	Dave Anderson	.20	.06
❑ 46T	Jeff Reardon	.30	.09
❑ 47T	Scott Bankhead	.20	.06
❑ 48T	Cory Snyder	.20	.06
❑ 49T	Al Newman	.20	.06
❑ 50T	Keith Miller	.20	.06
❑ 51T	Dave Burba	.20	.06
❑ 52T	Bill Pecota	.20	.06
❑ 53T	Chuck Crim	.20	.06
❑ 54T	Mariano Duncan	.20	.06
❑ 55T	Dave Gallagher	.20	.06
❑ 56T	Chris Gwynn	.20	.06
❑ 57T	Scott Ruskin	.20	.06
❑ 58T	Jack Armstrong	.20	.06
❑ 59T	Gary Carter	.30	.09
❑ 60T	Andres Galarraga	.30	.09
❑ 61T	Ken Hill	.20	.06
❑ 62T	Eric Davis	.30	.09
❑ 63T	Ruben Sierra	.20	.06
❑ 64T	Darrin Fletcher	.20	.06
❑ 65T	Tim Belcher	.20	.06
❑ 66T	Mike Morgan	.20	.06
❑ 67T	Scott Scudder	.20	.06
❑ 68T	Tom Candiotti	.20	.06
❑ 69T	Hubie Brooks	.20	.06
❑ 70T	Kal Daniels	.20	.06
❑ 71T	Bruce Ruffin	.20	.06
❑ 72T	Billy Hatcher	.20	.06
❑ 73T	Bob Melvin	.20	.06
❑ 74T	Lee Guetterman	.20	.06
❑ 75T	Rene Gonzales	.20	.06
❑ 76T	Kevin Bass	.20	.06
❑ 77T	Tom Bolton	.20	.06
❑ 78T	John Wetteland	.30	.09
❑ 79T	Bip Roberts	.20	.06
❑ 80T	Pat Listach RC	.40	.12
❑ 81T	John Doherty RC	.20	.06
❑ 82T	Sam Militello	.20	.06
❑ 83T	Brian Jordan RC	.60	.18
❑ 84T	Jeff Kent RC	4.00	1.20
❑ 85T	Dave Fleming	.20	.06
❑ 86T	Jeff Tackett	.20	.06
❑ 87T	Chad Curtis RC	.40	.12
❑ 88T	Eric Fox RC	.20	.06
❑ 89T	Denny Neagle	.30	.09
❑ 90T	Donovan Osborne	.20	.06
❑ 91T	Carlos Hernandez	.20	.06
❑ 92T	Tim Wakefield RC	4.00	1.20
❑ 93T	Tim Salmon	.50	.15
❑ 94T	Dave Nilsson	.20	.06
❑ 95T	Mike Perez	.20	.06
❑ 96T	Pat Hentgen	.20	.06
❑ 97T	Frank Seminara RC	.20	.06
❑ 98T	Ruben Amaro	.20	.06
❑ 99T	Archi Cianfrocco RC	.20	.06
❑ 100T	Andy Stankiewicz	.20	.06
❑ 101T	Jim Bullinger	.20	.06
❑ 102T	Pat Mahomes RC	.40	.12
❑ 103T	Hipolito Pichardo RC	.20	.06
❑ 104T	Bret Boone	.75	.23
❑ 105T	John Vander Wal	.20	.06
❑ 106T	Vince Horsman	.20	.06
❑ 107T	Jim Austin	.20	.06
❑ 108T	Brian Williams RC	.20	.06
❑ 109T	Dan Walters	.20	.06
❑ 110T	Wil Cordero	.20	.06

1993 Score

Card	Player	Nm-Mt	Ex-Mt
	COMPLETE SET (660)	40.00	12.00
❑ 1	Ken Griffey Jr.	.75	.23
❑ 2	Gary Sheffield	.20	.06
❑ 3	Frank Thomas	.50	.15
❑ 4	Ryne Sandberg	.75	.23
❑ 5	Larry Walker	.20	.06
❑ 6	Cal Ripken Jr.	1.50	.45
❑ 7	Roger Clemens	1.00	.30
❑ 8	Bobby Bonilla	.20	.06
❑ 9	Carlos Baerga	.10	.03
❑ 10	Darren Daulton	.20	.06
❑ 11	Travis Fryman	.20	.06
❑ 12	Andy Van Slyke	.30	.09
❑ 13	Jose Canseco	.30	.09
❑ 14	Roberto Alomar	.30	.09
❑ 15	Tom Glavine	.30	.09
❑ 16	Barry Larkin	.30	.09
❑ 17	Gregg Jefferies	.10	.03
❑ 18	Craig Biggio	.30	.09
❑ 19	Shane Mack	.10	.03
❑ 20	Brett Butler	.20	.06
❑ 21	Dennis Eckersley	.20	.06
❑ 22	Will Clark	.30	.09
❑ 23	Don Mattingly	1.25	.35
❑ 24	Tony Gwynn	.60	.18
❑ 25	Ivan Rodriguez	.30	.09
❑ 26	Shawon Dunston	.10	.03
❑ 27	Mike Mussina	.30	.09
❑ 28	Marquis Grissom	.20	.06
❑ 29	Charles Nagy	.10	.03
❑ 30	Len Dykstra	.20	.06
❑ 31	Cecil Fielder	.20	.06
❑ 32	Jay Bell	.20	.06
❑ 33	B.J. Surhoff	.20	.06
❑ 34	Bob Tewksbury	.10	.03
❑ 35	Danny Tartabull	.10	.03
❑ 36	Terry Pendleton	.20	.06
❑ 37	Jack Morris	.20	.06
❑ 38	Hal Morris	.10	.03
❑ 39	Luis Polonia	.10	.03
❑ 40	Ken Caminiti	.20	.06
❑ 41	Robin Ventura	.20	.06
❑ 42	Darryl Strawberry	.20	.06
❑ 43	Wally Joyner	.20	.06
❑ 44	Fred McGriff	.30	.09
❑ 45	Kevin Tapani	.10	.03
❑ 46	Matt Williams	.20	.06
❑ 47	Robin Yount	.75	.23
❑ 48	Ken Hill	.10	.03
❑ 49	Edgar Martinez	.30	.09
❑ 50	Mark Grace	.30	.09
❑ 51	Juan Gonzalez	.20	.06
❑ 52	Curt Schilling	.20	.06
❑ 53	Dwight Gooden	.20	.06
❑ 54	Chris Hoiles	.10	.03
❑ 55	Frank Viola	.20	.06
❑ 56	Ray Lankford	.20	.06
❑ 57	George Brett	1.25	.35
❑ 58	Kenny Lofton	.20	.06
❑ 59	Nolan Ryan	2.00	.60
❑ 60	Mickey Tettleton	.10	.03
❑ 61	John Smoltz	.30	.09
❑ 62	Howard Johnson	.10	.03
❑ 63	Eric Karros	.20	.06
❑ 64	Rick Aguilera	.10	.03
❑ 65	Steve Finley	.20	.06
❑ 66	Mark Langston	.10	.03
❑ 67	Bill Swift	.10	.03
❑ 68	John Olerud	.20	.06
❑ 69	Kevin McReynolds	.10	.03
❑ 70	Jack McDowell	.10	.03
❑ 71	Rickey Henderson	.50	.15
❑ 72	Brian Harper	.10	.03
❑ 73	Mike Morgan	.10	.03
❑ 74	Rafael Palmeiro	.30	.09
❑ 75	Dennis Martinez	.20	.06
❑ 76	Tino Martinez	.30	.09
❑ 77	Eddie Murray	.50	.15
❑ 78	Ellis Burks	.20	.06
❑ 79	John Kruk	.20	.06
❑ 80	Gregg Olson	.10	.03
❑ 81	Bernard Gilkey	.10	.03
❑ 82	Milt Cuyler	.10	.03
❑ 83	Mike LaValliere	.10	.03
❑ 84	Albert Belle	.20	.06
❑ 85	Bip Roberts	.10	.03
❑ 86	Melido Perez	.10	.03
❑ 87	Otis Nixon	.10	.03
❑ 88	Bill Spiers	.10	.03
❑ 89	Jeff Bagwell	.30	.09
❑ 90	Orel Hershiser	.20	.06
❑ 91	Andy Benes	.10	.03
❑ 92	Devon White	.20	.06
❑ 93	Willie McGee	.20	.06
❑ 94	Ozzie Guillen	.20	.06
❑ 95	Ivan Calderon	.10	.03
❑ 96	Keith Miller	.10	.03
❑ 97	Steve Buechele	.10	.03
❑ 98	Kent Hrbek	.20	.06
❑ 99	Dave Hollins	.10	.03
❑ 100	Mike Bordick	.10	.03
❑ 101	Randy Tomlin	.10	.03
❑ 102	Omar Vizquel	.30	.09
❑ 103	Lee Smith	.20	.06
❑ 104	Leo Gomez	.10	.03
❑ 105	Jose Rijo	.10	.03
❑ 106	Mark Whiten	.10	.03
❑ 107	Dave Justice	.20	.06
❑ 108	Eddie Taubensee	.10	.03
❑ 109	Lance Johnson	.10	.03
❑ 110	Felix Jose	.10	.03
❑ 111	Mike Harkey	.10	.03
❑ 112	Randy Milligan	.10	.03
❑ 113	Anthony Young	.10	.03
❑ 114	Rico Brogna	.10	.03
❑ 115	Bret Saberhagen	.20	.06
❑ 116	Sandy Alomar Jr.	.10	.03
❑ 117	Terry Mulholland	.10	.03
❑ 118	Darryl Hamilton	.10	.03
❑ 119	Todd Zeile	.10	.03
❑ 120	Bernie Williams	.30	.09
❑ 121	Zane Smith	.10	.03
❑ 122	Derek Bell	.10	.03
❑ 123	Deion Sanders	.30	.09
❑ 124	Luis Sojo	.10	.03
❑ 125	Joe Oliver	.10	.03
❑ 126	Craig Grebeck	.10	.03
❑ 127	Andujar Cedeno	.10	.03
❑ 128	Brian McRae	.10	.03
❑ 129	Jose Offerman	.10	.03
❑ 130	Pedro Munoz	.10	.03
❑ 131	Bud Black	.10	.03
❑ 132	Mo Vaughn	.20	.06
❑ 133	Bruce Hurst	.10	.03
❑ 134	Dave Henderson	.10	.03
❑ 135	Tom Pagnozzi	.10	.03
❑ 136	Erik Hanson	.10	.03
❑ 137	Orlando Merced	.10	.03
❑ 138	Dean Palmer	.20	.06
❑ 139	John Franco	.20	.06
❑ 140	Brady Anderson	.20	.06
❑ 141	Ricky Jordan	.10	.03
❑ 142	Jeff Blauser	.10	.03
❑ 143	Sammy Sosa	.50	.15
❑ 144	Bob Walk	.10	.03

❑	145	Delino DeShields	.10	.03
❑	146	Kevin Brown	.20	.06
❑	147	Mark Lemke	.10	.03
❑	148	Chuck Knoblauch	.20	.06
❑	149	Chris Sabo	.10	.03
❑	150	Bobby Witt	.10	.03
❑	151	Luis Gonzalez	.20	.06
❑	152	Ron Karkovice	.10	.03
❑	153	Jeff Brantley	.10	.03
❑	154	Kevin Appier	.20	.06
❑	155	Darrin Jackson	.10	.03
❑	156	Kelly Gruber	.10	.03
❑	157	Royce Clayton	.10	.03
❑	158	Chuck Finley	.20	.06
❑	159	Jeff King	.10	.03
❑	160	Greg Vaughn	.10	.03
❑	161	Geronimo Pena	.10	.03
❑	162	Steve Farr	.10	.03
❑	163	Jose Oquendo	.10	.03
❑	164	Mark Lewis	.10	.03
❑	165	John Wetteland	.20	.06
❑	166	Mike Henneman	.10	.03
❑	167	Todd Hundley	.10	.03
❑	168	Wes Chamberlain	.10	.03
❑	169	Steve Avery	.10	.03
❑	170	Mike Devereaux	.10	.03
❑	171	Reggie Sanders	.20	.06
❑	172	Jay Buhner	.20	.06
❑	173	Eric Anthony	.10	.03
❑	174	John Burkett	.10	.03
❑	175	Tom Candiotti	.10	.03
❑	176	Phil Plantier	.10	.03
❑	177	Doug Henry	.10	.03
❑	178	Scott Leius	.10	.03
❑	179	Kirt Manwaring	.10	.03
❑	180	Jeff Parrett	.10	.03
❑	181	Don Slaught	.10	.03
❑	182	Scott Radinsky	.10	.03
❑	183	Luis Alicea	.10	.03
❑	184	Tom Gordon	.10	.03
❑	185	Rick Wilkins	.10	.03
❑	186	Todd Stottlemyre	.10	.03
❑	187	Moises Alou	.20	.06
❑	188	Joe Grahe	.10	.03
❑	189	Jeff Kent	.50	.15
❑	190	Bill Wegman	.10	.03
❑	191	Kim Batiste	.10	.03
❑	192	Matt Nokes	.10	.03
❑	193	Mark Wohlers	.10	.03
❑	194	Paul Sorrento	.10	.03
❑	195	Chris Hammond	.10	.03
❑	196	Scott Livingstone	.10	.03
❑	197	Doug Jones	.10	.03
❑	198	Scott Cooper	.10	.03
❑	199	Ramon Martinez	.10	.03
❑	200	Dave Valle	.10	.03
❑	201	Mariano Duncan	.10	.03
❑	202	Ben McDonald	.10	.03
❑	203	Darren Lewis	.10	.03
❑	204	Kenny Rogers	.20	.06
❑	205	Manuel Lee	.10	.03
❑	206	Scott Erickson	.10	.03
❑	207	Dan Gladden	.10	.03
❑	208	Bob Welch	.10	.03
❑	209	Greg Olson	.10	.03
❑	210	Dan Pasqua	.10	.03
❑	211	Tim Wallach	.10	.03
❑	212	Jeff Montgomery	.10	.03
❑	213	Derrick May	.10	.03
❑	214	Ed Sprague	.10	.03
❑	215	David Haas	.10	.03
❑	216	Darrin Fletcher	.10	.03
❑	217	Brian Jordan	.20	.06
❑	218	Jaime Navarro	.10	.03
❑	219	Randy Velarde	.10	.03
❑	220	Ron Gant	.20	.06
❑	221	Paul Quantrill	.10	.03
❑	222	Damion Easley	.10	.03
❑	223	Charlie Hough	.20	.06
❑	224	Brad Brink	.10	.03
❑	225	Barry Manuel	.10	.03
❑	226	Kevin Koslofski	.10	.03
❑	227	Ryan Thompson	.10	.03
❑	228	Mike Munoz	.10	.03
❑	229	Dan Wilson	.20	.06
❑	230	Peter Hoy	.10	.03
❑	231	Pedro Astacio	.10	.03
❑	232	Matt Stairs	.10	.03
❑	233	Jeff Reboulet	.10	.03
❑	234	Manny Alexander	.10	.03
❑	235	Willie Banks	.10	.03
❑	236	John Jaha	.10	.03
❑	237	Scooter Tucker	.10	.03
❑	238	Russ Springer	.10	.03
❑	239	Paul Miller	.10	.03
❑	240	Dan Peltier	.10	.03
❑	241	Ozzie Canseco	.10	.03
❑	242	Ben Rivera	.10	.03
❑	243	John Valentin	.10	.03
❑	244	Henry Rodriguez	.10	.03
❑	245	Derek Parks	.10	.03
❑	246	Carlos Garcia	.10	.03
❑	247	Tim Pugh RC	.10	.03
❑	248	Melvin Nieves	.10	.03
❑	249	Rich Amaral	.10	.03
❑	250	Willie Greene	.10	.03
❑	251	Tim Scott	.10	.03
❑	252	Dave Silvestri	.10	.03
❑	253	Rob Mallicoat	.10	.03
❑	254	Donald Harris	.10	.03
❑	255	Craig Colbert	.10	.03
❑	256	Jose Guzman	.10	.03
❑	257	Domingo Martinez RC	.10	.03
❑	258	William Suero	.10	.03
❑	259	Juan Guerrero	.10	.03
❑	260	J.T. Snow RC	.50	.15
❑	261	Tony Pena	.10	.03
❑	262	Tim Fortugno	.10	.03
❑	263	Tom Marsh	.10	.03
❑	264	Kurt Knudsen	.10	.03
❑	265	Tim Costo	.10	.03
❑	266	Steve Shifflett	.10	.03
❑	267	Billy Ashley	.10	.03
❑	268	Jerry Nielsen	.10	.03
❑	269	Pete Young	.10	.03
❑	270	Johnny Guzman	.10	.03
❑	271	Greg Colbrunn	.10	.03
❑	272	Jeff Nelson	.10	.03
❑	273	Kevin Young	.20	.06
❑	274	Jeff Frye	.10	.03
❑	275	J.T. Bruett	.10	.03
❑	276	Todd Pratt RC	.25	.07
❑	277	Mike Butcher	.10	.03
❑	278	John Flaherty	.10	.03
❑	279	John Patterson	.10	.03
❑	280	Eric Hillman	.10	.03
❑	281	Bien Figueroa	.10	.03
❑	282	Shane Reynolds	.10	.03
❑	283	Rich Rowland	.10	.03
❑	284	Steve Foster	.10	.03
❑	285	Dave Mlicki	.10	.03
❑	286	Mike Piazza	3.00	.90
❑	287	Mike Trombley	.10	.03
❑	288	Jim Pena	.10	.03
❑	289	Bob Ayrault	.10	.03
❑	290	Henry Mercedes	.10	.03
❑	291	Bob Wickman	.10	.03
❑	292	Jacob Brumfield	.10	.03
❑	293	David Hulse RC	.10	.03
❑	294	Ryan Klesko	.20	.06
❑	295	Doug Linton	.10	.03
❑	296	Steve Cooke	.10	.03
❑	297	Eddie Zosky	.10	.03
❑	298	Gerald Williams	.10	.03
❑	299	Jonathan Hurst	.10	.03
❑	300	Larry Carter RC	.10	.03
❑	301	William Pennyfeather	.10	.03
❑	302	Cesar Hernandez	.10	.03
❑	303	Steve Hosey	.10	.03
❑	304	Blas Minor	.10	.03
❑	305	Jeff Grotewald	.10	.03
❑	306	Bernardo Brito	.10	.03
❑	307	Rafael Bournigal	.10	.03
❑	308	Jeff Branson	.10	.03
❑	309	Tom Quinlan RC	.10	.03
❑	310	Pat Gomez RC	.10	.03
❑	311	Sterling Hitchcock RC	.25	.07
❑	312	Kent Bottenfield	.10	.03
❑	313	Alan Trammell	.20	.06
❑	314	Cris Colon	.10	.03
❑	315	Paul Wagner	.10	.03
❑	316	Matt Maysey	.10	.03
❑	317	Mike Stanton	.10	.03
❑	318	Rick Trlicek	.10	.03
❑	319	Kevin Rogers	.10	.03
❑	320	Mark Clark	.10	.03
❑	321	Pedro Martinez	1.00	.30
❑	322	Al Martin	.10	.03
❑	323	Mike Macfarlane	.10	.03
❑	324	Rey Sanchez	.10	.03
❑	325	Roger Pavlik	.10	.03
❑	326	Troy Neel	.10	.03
❑	327	Kerry Woodson	.10	.03
❑	328	Wayne Kirby	.10	.03
❑	329	Ken Ryan RC	.25	.07
❑	330	Jesse Levis	.10	.03
❑	331	Jim Austin	.10	.03
❑	332	Dan Walters	.10	.03
❑	333	Brian Williams	.10	.03
❑	334	Wil Cordero	.10	.03
❑	335	Bret Boone	.30	.09
❑	336	Hipolito Pichardo	.10	.03
❑	337	Pat Mahomes	.10	.03
❑	338	Andy Stankiewicz	.10	.03
❑	339	Jim Bullinger	.10	.03
❑	340	Archi Cianfrocco	.10	.03
❑	341	Ruben Amaro	.10	.03
❑	342	Frank Seminara	.10	.03
❑	343	Pat Hentgen	.10	.03
❑	344	Dave Nilsson	.10	.03
❑	345	Mike Perez	.10	.03
❑	346	Tim Salmon	.30	.09
❑	347	Tim Wakefield	.50	.15
❑	348	Carlos Hernandez	.10	.03
❑	349	Donovan Osborne	.10	.03
❑	350	Denny Neagle	.20	.06
❑	351	Sam Militello	.10	.03
❑	352	Eric Fox	.10	.03
❑	353	John Doherty	.10	.03
❑	354	Chad Curtis	.10	.03
❑	355	Jeff Tackett	.10	.03
❑	356	Dave Fleming	.10	.03
❑	357	Pat Listach	.10	.03
❑	358	Kevin Wickander	.10	.03
❑	359	John Vander Wal	.10	.03
❑	360	Arthur Rhodes	.10	.03
❑	361	Bob Scanlan	.10	.03
❑	362	Bob Zupcic	.10	.03
❑	363	Mel Rojas	.10	.03
❑	364	Jim Thome	.30	.09
❑	365	Bill Pecota	.10	.03
❑	366	Mark Carreon	.10	.03
❑	367	Mitch Williams	.10	.03
❑	368	Cal Eldred	.10	.03
❑	369	Stan Belinda	.10	.03
❑	370	Pat Kelly	.10	.03
❑	371	Rheal Cormier	.10	.03
❑	372	Juan Guzman	.10	.03
❑	373	Damon Berryhill	.10	.03
❑	374	Gary DiSarcina	.10	.03
❑	375	Norm Charlton	.10	.03
❑	376	Roberto Hernandez	.10	.03
❑	377	Scott Kamieniecki	.10	.03
❑	378	Rusty Meacham	.10	.03
❑	379	Kurt Stillwell	.10	.03
❑	380	Lloyd McClendon	.10	.03
❑	381	Mark Leonard	.10	.03
❑	382	Jerry Browne	.10	.03
❑	383	Glenn Davis	.10	.03
❑	384	Randy Johnson	.50	.15
❑	385	Mike Greenwell	.10	.03
❑	386	Scott Chiamparino	.10	.03
❑	387	George Bell	.10	.03
❑	388	Steve Olin	.10	.03
❑	389	Chuck McElroy	.10	.03
❑	390	Mark Gardner	.10	.03
❑	391	Rod Beck	.10	.03
❑	392	Dennis Rasmussen	.10	.03
❑	393	Charlie Leibrandt	.10	.03
❑	394	Julio Franco	.20	.06
❑	395	Pete Harnisch	.10	.03
❑	396	Sid Bream	.10	.03
❑	397	Milt Thompson	.10	.03
❑	398	Glenallen Hill	.10	.03
❑	399	Chico Walker	.10	.03
❑	400	Alex Cole	.10	.03
❑	401	Trevor Wilson	.10	.03
❑	402	Jeff Conine	.20	.06

403	Kyle Abbott	.10	.03
404	Tom Browning	.10	.03
405	Jerald Clark	.10	.03
406	Vince Horsman	.10	.03
407	Kevin Mitchell	.10	.03
408	Pete Smith	.10	.03
409	Jeff Innis	.10	.03
410	Mike Timlin	.10	.03
411	Charlie Hayes	.10	.03
412	Alex Fernandez	.10	.03
413	Jeff Russell	.10	.03
414	Jody Reed	.10	.03
415	Mickey Morandini	.10	.03
416	Darnell Coles	.10	.03
417	Xavier Hernandez	.10	.03
418	Steve Sax	.10	.03
419	Joe Girardi	.10	.03
420	Mike Fetters	.10	.03
421	Danny Jackson	.10	.03
422	Jim Gott	.10	.03
423	Tim Belcher	.10	.03
424	Jose Mesa	.10	.03
425	Junior Felix	.10	.03
426	Thomas Howard	.10	.03
427	Julio Valera	.10	.03
428	Dante Bichette	.20	.06
429	Mike Sharperson	.10	.03
430	Darryl Kile	.20	.06
431	Lonnie Smith	.10	.03
432	Monty Fariss	.10	.03
433	Reggie Jefferson	.10	.03
434	Bob McClure	.10	.03
435	Craig Lefferts	.10	.03
436	Duane Ward	.10	.03
437	Shawn Abner	.10	.03
438	Roberto Kelly	.10	.03
439	Paul O'Neill	.30	.09
440	Alan Mills	.10	.03
441	Roger Mason	.10	.03
442	Gary Pettis	.10	.03
443	Steve Lake	.10	.03
444	Gene Larkin	.10	.03
445	Larry Andersen	.10	.03
446	Doug Dascenzo	.10	.03
447	Daryl Boston	.10	.03
448	John Candelaria	.10	.03
449	Storm Davis	.10	.03
450	Tom Edens	.10	.03
451	Mike Maddux	.10	.03
452	Tim Naehring	.10	.03
453	John Orton	.10	.03
454	Joey Cora	.10	.03
455	Chuck Crim	.10	.03
456	Dan Plesac	.10	.03
457	Mike Bielecki	.10	.03
458	Terry Jorgensen	.10	.03
459	John Habyan	.10	.03
460	Pete O'Brien	.10	.03
461	Jeff Treadway	.10	.03
462	Frank Castillo	.10	.03
463	Jimmy Jones	.10	.03
464	Tommy Greene	.10	.03
465	Tracy Woodson	.10	.03
466	Rich Rodriguez	.10	.03
467	Joe Hesketh	.10	.03
468	Greg Myers	.10	.03
469	Kirk McCaskill	.10	.03
470	Ricky Bones	.10	.03
471	Lenny Webster	.10	.03
472	Francisco Cabrera	.10	.03
473	Turner Ward	.10	.03
474	Dwayne Henry	.10	.03
475	Al Osuna	.10	.03
476	Craig Wilson	.10	.03
477	Chris Nabholz	.10	.03
478	Rafael Belliard	.10	.03
479	Terry Leach	.10	.03
480	Tim Teufel	.10	.03
481	Dennis Eckersley AW	.20	.06
482	Barry Bonds AW	.75	.23
483	Dennis Eckersley AW	.20	.06
484	Greg Maddux AW	.50	.15
485	Pat Listach AW	.10	.03
486	Eric Karros AW	.10	.03
487	Jamie Arnold DP RC	.10	.03
488	B.J. Wallace DP	.10	.03
489	Derek Jeter DP RC	10.00	3.00
490	Jason Kendall DP RC	.75	.23
491	Rick Helling DP	.10	.03
492	Derek Wallace DP RC	.10	.03
493	Sean Lowe DP RC	.10	.03
494	S.Stewart DP RC	.75	.23
495	Benji Grigsby DP RC	.10	.03
496	T.Steverson DP RC	.10	.03
497	Dan Serafini DP RC	.10	.03
498	Michael Tucker DP	.20	.06
499	Chris Roberts DP	.10	.03
500	Pete Janicki DP RC	.10	.03
501	Jeff Schmidt DP RC	.10	.03
502	Edgar Martinez AS	.20	.06
503	Omar Vizquel AS	.20	.06
504	Ken Griffey Jr. AS	.50	.15
505	Kirby Puckett AS	.30	.09
506	Joe Carter AS	.10	.03
507	Ivan Rodriguez AS	.20	.06
508	Jack Morris AS	.10	.03
509	Dennis Eckersley AS	.20	.06
510	Frank Thomas AS	.30	.09
511	Roberto Alomar AS	.20	.06
512	Mickey Morandini AS	.10	.03
513	Dennis Eckersley HL	.20	.06
514	Jeff Reardon HL	.10	.03
515	Danny Tartabull HL	.10	.03
516	Bip Roberts HL	.10	.03
517	George Brett HL	.60	.18
518	Robin Yount HL	.50	.15
519	Kevin Gross HL	.10	.03
520	Ed Sprague WS	.10	.03
521	Dave Winfield WS	.10	.03
522	Ozzie Smith AS	.50	.15
523	Barry Bonds AS	.75	.23
524	Andy Van Slyke AS	.20	.06
525	Tony Gwynn AS	.30	.09
526	Darren Daulton AS	.10	.03
527	Greg Maddux AS	.50	.15
528	Fred McGriff AS	.30	.09
529	Lee Smith AS	.10	.03
530	Ryne Sandberg AS	.50	.15
531	Gary Sheffield AS	.10	.03
532	Ozzie Smith DT	.50	.15
533	Kirby Puckett DT	.30	.09
534	Gary Sheffield DT	.10	.03
535	Andy Van Slyke DT	.20	.06
536	Ken Griffey Jr. DT	.50	.15
537	Ivan Rodriguez DT	.20	.06
538	Charles Nagy DT	.10	.03
539	Tom Glavine DT	.20	.06
540	Dennis Eckersley DT	.20	.06
541	Frank Thomas DT	.30	.09
542	Roberto Alomar DT	.20	.06
543	Sean Berry	.10	.03
544	Mike Schooler	.10	.03
545	Chuck Carr	.10	.03
546	Lenny Harris	.10	.03
547	Gary Scott	.10	.03
548	Derek Lilliquist	.10	.03
549	Brian Hunter	.10	.03
550	Kirby Puckett MOY	.30	.09
551	Jim Eisenreich	.10	.03
552	Andre Dawson	.20	.06
553	David Nied	.10	.03
554	Spike Owen	.10	.03
555	Greg Gagne	.10	.03
556	Sid Fernandez	.10	.03
557	Mark McGwire	1.25	.35
558	Bryan Harvey	.10	.03
559	Harold Reynolds	.20	.06
560	Barry Bonds	1.50	.45
561	Eric Wedge RC	.25	.07
562	Ozzie Smith	.75	.23
563	Rick Sutcliffe	.20	.06
564	Jeff Reardon	.20	.06
565	Alex Arias	.10	.03
566	Greg Swindell	.10	.03
567	Brook Jacoby	.10	.03
568	Pete Incaviglia	.10	.03
569	Butch Henry	.10	.03
570	Eric Davis	.20	.06
571	Kevin Seitzer	.10	.03
572	Tony Fernandez	.10	.03
573	Steve Reed RC	.10	.03
574	Cory Snyder	.10	.03
575	Joe Carter	.20	.06
576	Greg Maddux	.75	.23
577	Bert Blyleven UER (Should say 3701 career strikeouts)	.20	.06
578	Kevin Bass	.10	.03
579	Carlton Fisk	.30	.09
580	Doug Drabek	.10	.03
581	Mark Gubicza	.10	.03
582	Bobby Thigpen	.10	.03
583	Chili Davis	.20	.06
584	Scott Bankhead	.10	.03
585	Harold Baines	.20	.06
586	Eric Young	.10	.03
587	Lance Parrish	.20	.06
588	Juan Bell	.10	.03
589	Bob Ojeda	.10	.03
590	Joe Orsulak	.10	.03
591	Benito Santiago	.20	.06
592	Wade Boggs	.30	.09
593	Robby Thompson	.10	.03
594	Eric Plunk	.10	.03
595	Hensley Meulens	.10	.03
596	Lou Whitaker	.20	.06
597	Dale Murphy	.30	.09
598	Paul Molitor	.30	.09
599	Greg W. Harris	.10	.03
600	Darren Holmes	.10	.03
601	Dave Martinez	.10	.03
602	Tom Henke	.10	.03
603	Mike Benjamin	.10	.03
604	Rene Gonzales	.10	.03
605	Roger McDowell	.10	.03
606	Kirby Puckett	.50	.15
607	Randy Myers	.10	.03
608	Ruben Sierra	.10	.03
609	Wilson Alvarez	.10	.03
610	David Segui	.10	.03
611	Juan Samuel	.10	.03
612	Tom Brunansky	.10	.03
613	Willie Randolph	.20	.06
614	Tony Phillips	.10	.03
615	Candy Maldonado	.10	.03
616	Chris Bosio	.10	.03
617	Bret Barberie	.10	.03
618	Scott Sanderson	.10	.03
619	Ron Darling	.10	.03
620	Dave Winfield	.20	.06
621	Mike Felder	.10	.03
622	Greg Hibbard	.10	.03
623	Mike Scioscia	.10	.03
624	John Smiley	.10	.03
625	Alejandro Pena	.10	.03
626	Terry Steinbach	.10	.03
627	Freddie Benavides	.10	.03
628	Kevin Reimer	.10	.03
629	Braulio Castillo	.10	.03
630	Dave Stieb	.10	.03
631	Dave Magadan	.10	.03
632	Scott Fletcher	.10	.03
633	Cris Carpenter	.10	.03
634	Kevin Maas	.10	.03
635	Todd Worrell	.10	.03
636	Rob Deer	.10	.03
637	Dwight Smith	.10	.03
638	Chito Martinez	.10	.03
639	Jimmy Key	.20	.06
640	Greg A. Harris	.10	.03
641	Mike Moore	.10	.03
642	Pat Borders	.10	.03
643	Bill Gullickson	.10	.03
644	Gary Gaetti	.20	.06
645	David Howard	.10	.03
646	Jim Abbott	.30	.09
647	Willie Wilson	.10	.03
648	David Wells	.20	.06
649	Andres Galarraga	.20	.06
650	Vince Coleman	.10	.03
651	Rob Dibble	.20	.06
652	Frank Tanana	.10	.03
653	Steve Decker	.10	.03
654	David Cone	.20	.06
655	Jack Armstrong	.10	.03
656	Dave Stewart	.20	.06
657	Billy Hatcher	.10	.03
658	Tim Raines	.20	.06

❑ 659 Walt Weiss .10 .03
❑ 660 Jose Lind .10 .03

1994 Score

	Nm-Mt	Ex-Mt
COMPLETE SET (660)	24.00	7.25
COMP.SERIES 1 (330)	12.00	3.60
COMP.SERIES 2 (330)	12.00	3.60

❑ 1 Barry Bonds 1.50 .45
❑ 2 John Olerud .20 .06
❑ 3 Ken Griffey Jr. .75 .23
❑ 4 Jeff Bagwell .30 .09
❑ 5 John Burkett .10 .03
❑ 6 Jack McDowell .10 .03
❑ 7 Albert Belle .20 .06
❑ 8 Andres Galarraga .20 .06
❑ 9 Mike Mussina .30 .09
❑ 10 Will Clark .30 .09
❑ 11 Travis Fryman .20 .06
❑ 12 Tony Gwynn .60 .18
❑ 13 Robin Yount .75 .23
❑ 14 Dave Magadan .10 .03
❑ 15 Paul O'Neill .30 .09
❑ 16 Ray Lankford .20 .06
❑ 17 Damion Easley .10 .03
❑ 18 Andy Van Slyke .30 .09
❑ 19 Brian McRae .10 .03
❑ 20 Ryne Sandberg .75 .23
❑ 21 Kirby Puckett .50 .15
❑ 22 Dwight Gooden .20 .06
❑ 23 Don Mattingly 1.25 .35
❑ 24 Kevin Mitchell .10 .03
❑ 25 Roger Clemens 1.00 .30
❑ 26 Eric Karros .20 .06
❑ 27 Juan Gonzalez .20 .06
❑ 28 John Kruk .20 .06
❑ 29 Gregg Jefferies .10 .03
❑ 30 Tom Glavine .30 .09
❑ 31 Ivan Rodriguez .30 .09
❑ 32 Jay Bell .20 .06
❑ 33 Randy Johnson .50 .15
❑ 34 Darren Daulton .20 .06
❑ 35 Rickey Henderson .50 .15
❑ 36 Eddie Murray .50 .15
❑ 37 Brian Harper .10 .03
❑ 38 Delino DeShields .10 .03
❑ 39 Jose Lind .10 .03
❑ 40 Benito Santiago .20 .06
❑ 41 Frank Thomas .50 .15
❑ 42 Mark Grace .30 .09
❑ 43 Roberto Alomar .30 .09
❑ 44 Andy Benes .10 .03
❑ 45 Luis Polonia .10 .03
❑ 46 Brett Butler .20 .06
❑ 47 Terry Steinbach .10 .03
❑ 48 Craig Biggio .30 .09
❑ 49 Greg Vaughn .10 .03
❑ 50 Charlie Hayes .10 .03
❑ 51 Mickey Tettleton .10 .03
❑ 52 Jose Rijo .10 .03
❑ 53 Carlos Baerga .10 .03
❑ 54 Jeff Blauser .10 .03
❑ 55 Leo Gomez .10 .03
❑ 56 Bob Tewksbury .10 .03
❑ 57 Mo Vaughn .20 .06
❑ 58 Orlando Merced .10 .03
❑ 59 Tino Martinez .30 .09
❑ 60 Lenny Dykstra .20 .06
❑ 61 Jose Canseco .30 .09
❑ 62 Tony Fernandez .10 .03
❑ 63 Donovan Osborne .10 .03
❑ 64 Ken Hill .10 .03
❑ 65 Kent Hrbek .20 .06
❑ 66 Bryan Harvey .10 .03
❑ 67 Wally Joyner .20 .06
❑ 68 Derrick May .10 .03
❑ 69 Lance Johnson .10 .03
❑ 70 Willie McGee .20 .06
❑ 71 Mark Langston .10 .03
❑ 72 Terry Pendleton .20 .06
❑ 73 Joe Carter .20 .06
❑ 74 Barry Larkin .30 .09
❑ 75 Jimmy Key .20 .06
❑ 76 Joe Girardi .10 .03
❑ 77 B.J. Surhoff .20 .06
❑ 78 Pete Harnisch .10 .03
❑ 79 Lou Whitaker UER .20 .06
(Milt Cuyler
pictured on front)
❑ 80 Cory Snyder .10 .03
❑ 81 Kenny Lofton .20 .06
❑ 82 Fred McGriff .30 .09
❑ 83 Mike Greenwell .10 .03
❑ 84 Mike Perez .10 .03
❑ 85 Cal Ripken 1.50 .45
❑ 86 Don Slaught .10 .03
❑ 87 Omar Vizquel .30 .09
❑ 88 Curt Schilling .20 .06
❑ 89 Chuck Knoblauch .20 .06
❑ 90 Moises Alou .20 .06
❑ 91 Greg Gagne .10 .03
❑ 92 Bret Saberhagen .20 .06
❑ 93 Ozzie Guillen .20 .06
❑ 94 Matt Williams .20 .06
❑ 95 Chad Curtis .10 .03
❑ 96 Mike Harkey .10 .03
❑ 97 Devon White .20 .06
❑ 98 Walt Weiss .10 .03
❑ 99 Kevin Brown .20 .06
❑ 100 Gary Sheffield .20 .06
❑ 101 Wade Boggs .30 .09
❑ 102 Orel Hershiser .20 .06
❑ 103 Tony Phillips .10 .03
❑ 104 Andujar Cedeno .10 .03
❑ 105 Bill Spiers .10 .03
❑ 106 Otis Nixon .10 .03
❑ 107 Felix Fermin .10 .03
❑ 108 Bip Roberts .10 .03
❑ 109 Dennis Eckersley .20 .06
❑ 110 Dante Bichette .20 .06
❑ 111 Ben McDonald .10 .03
❑ 112 Jim Poole .10 .03
❑ 113 John Dopson .10 .03
❑ 114 Rob Dibble .20 .06
❑ 115 Jeff Treadway .10 .03
❑ 116 Ricky Jordan .10 .03
❑ 117 Mike Henneman .10 .03
❑ 118 Willie Blair .10 .03
❑ 119 Doug Henry .10 .03
❑ 120 Gerald Perry .10 .03
❑ 121 Greg Myers .10 .03
❑ 122 John Franco .20 .06
❑ 123 Roger Mason .10 .03
❑ 124 Chris Hammond .10 .03
❑ 125 Hubie Brooks .10 .03
❑ 126 Kent Mercker .10 .03
❑ 127 Jim Abbott .30 .09
❑ 128 Kevin Bass .10 .03
❑ 129 Rick Aguilera .10 .03
❑ 130 Mitch Webster .10 .03
❑ 131 Eric Plunk .10 .03
❑ 132 Mark Carreon .10 .03
❑ 133 Dave Stewart .20 .06
❑ 134 Willie Wilson .10 .03
❑ 135 Dave Fleming .10 .03
❑ 136 Jeff Tackett .10 .03
❑ 137 Geno Petralli .10 .03
❑ 138 Gene Harris .10 .03
❑ 139 Scott Bankhead .10 .03
❑ 140 Trevor Wilson .10 .03
❑ 141 Alvaro Espinoza .10 .03
❑ 142 Ryan Bowen .10 .03
❑ 143 Mike Moore .10 .03
❑ 144 Bill Pecota .10 .03
❑ 145 Jaime Navarro .10 .03
❑ 146 Jack Daugherty .10 .03
❑ 147 Bob Wickman .10 .03
❑ 148 Chris Jones .10 .03
❑ 149 Todd Stottlemyre .10 .03
❑ 150 Brian Williams .10 .03
❑ 151 Chuck Finley .20 .06
❑ 152 Lenny Harris .10 .03
❑ 153 Alex Fernandez .10 .03
❑ 154 Candy Maldonado .10 .03
❑ 155 Jeff Montgomery .10 .03
❑ 156 David West .10 .03
❑ 157 Mark Williamson .10 .03
❑ 158 Milt Thompson .10 .03
❑ 159 Ron Darling .10 .03
❑ 160 Stan Belinda .10 .03
❑ 161 Henry Cotto .10 .03
❑ 162 Mel Rojas .10 .03
❑ 163 Doug Strange .10 .03
❑ 164 Rene Arocha .10 .03
❑ 165 Tim Hulett .10 .03
❑ 166 Steve Avery .10 .03
❑ 167 Jim Thome .30 .09
❑ 168 Tom Browning .10 .03
❑ 169 Mario Diaz .10 .03
❑ 170 Steve Reed .10 .03
❑ 171 Scott Livingstone .10 .03
❑ 172 Chris Donnels .10 .03
❑ 173 John Jaha .10 .03
❑ 174 Carlos Hernandez .10 .03
❑ 175 Dion James .10 .03
❑ 176 Bud Black .10 .03
❑ 177 Tony Castillo .10 .03
❑ 178 Jose Guzman .10 .03
❑ 179 Torey Lovullo .10 .03
❑ 180 John Vander Wal .10 .03
❑ 181 Mike LaValliere .10 .03
❑ 182 Sid Fernandez .10 .03
❑ 183 Brent Mayne .10 .03
❑ 184 Terry Mulholland .10 .03
❑ 185 Willie Banks .10 .03
❑ 186 Steve Cooke .10 .03
❑ 187 Brent Gates .10 .03
❑ 188 Erik Pappas .10 .03
❑ 189 Bill Haselman .10 .03
❑ 190 Fernando Valenzuela .20 .06
❑ 191 Gary Redus .10 .03
❑ 192 Danny Darwin .10 .03
❑ 193 Mark Portugal .10 .03
❑ 194 Derek Lilliquist .10 .03
❑ 195 Charlie O'Brien .10 .03
❑ 196 Matt Nokes .10 .03
❑ 197 Danny Sheaffer .10 .03
❑ 198 Bill Gullickson .10 .03
❑ 199 Alex Arias .10 .03
❑ 200 Mike Fetters .10 .03
❑ 201 Brian Jordan .20 .06
❑ 202 Joe Grahe .10 .03
❑ 203 Tom Candiotti .10 .03
❑ 204 Jeremy Hernandez .10 .03
❑ 205 Mike Stanton .10 .03
❑ 206 David Howard .10 .03
❑ 207 Darren Holmes .10 .03
❑ 208 Rick Honeycutt .10 .03
❑ 209 Danny Jackson .10 .03
❑ 210 Rich Amaral .10 .03
❑ 211 Blas Minor .10 .03
❑ 212 Kenny Rogers .20 .06
❑ 213 Jim Leyritz .10 .03
❑ 214 Mike Morgan .10 .03
❑ 215 Dan Gladden .10 .03
❑ 216 Randy Velarde .10 .03
❑ 217 Mitch Williams .10 .03
❑ 218 Hipolito Pichardo .10 .03
❑ 219 Dave Burba .10 .03
❑ 220 Wilson Alvarez .10 .03
❑ 221 Bob Zupcic .10 .03
❑ 222 Francisco Cabrera .10 .03
❑ 223 Julio Valera .10 .03
❑ 224 Paul Assenmacher .10 .03
❑ 225 Jeff Branson .10 .03
❑ 226 Todd Frohwirth .10 .03
❑ 227 Armando Reynoso .10 .03
❑ 228 Rich Rowland .10 .03
❑ 229 Freddie Benavides .10 .03

❑ 230 Wayne Kirby .10 .03
❑ 231 Darryl Kile .20 .06
❑ 232 Skeeter Barnes .10 .03
❑ 233 Ramon Martinez .10 .03
❑ 234 Tom Gordon .10 .03
❑ 235 Dave Gallagher .10 .03
❑ 236 Ricky Bones .10 .03
❑ 237 Larry Andersen .10 .03
❑ 238 Pat Meares .10 .03
❑ 239 Zane Smith .10 .03
❑ 240 Tim Leary .10 .03
❑ 241 Phil Clark .10 .03
❑ 242 Danny Cox .10 .03
❑ 243 Mike Jackson .10 .03
❑ 244 Mike Gallego .10 .03
❑ 245 Lee Smith .20 .06
❑ 246 Todd Jones .10 .03
❑ 247 Steve Bedrosian .10 .03
❑ 248 Troy Neel .10 .03
❑ 249 Jose Bautista .10 .03
❑ 250 Steve Frey .10 .03
❑ 251 Jeff Reardon .20 .06
❑ 252 Stan Javier .10 .03
❑ 253 Mo Sanford .10 .03
❑ 254 Steve Sax .10 .03
❑ 255 Luis Aquino .10 .03
❑ 256 Domingo Jean .10 .03
❑ 257 Scott Servais .10 .03
❑ 258 Brad Pennington .10 .03
❑ 259 Dave Hansen .10 .03
❑ 260 Rich Gossage .20 .06
❑ 261 Jeff Fassero .10 .03
❑ 262 Junior Ortiz .10 .03
❑ 263 Anthony Young .10 .03
❑ 264 Chris Bosio .10 .03
❑ 265 Ruben Amaro .10 .03
❑ 266 Mark Eichhorn .10 .03
❑ 267 Dave Clark .10 .03
❑ 268 Gary Thurman .10 .03
❑ 269 Les Lancaster .10 .03
❑ 270 Jamie Moyer .20 .06
❑ 271 Ricky Gutierrez .10 .03
❑ 272 Greg A. Harris .10 .03
❑ 273 Mike Benjamin .10 .03
❑ 274 Gene Nelson .10 .03
❑ 275 Damon Berryhill .10 .03
❑ 276 Scott Radinsky .10 .03
❑ 277 Mike Aldrete .10 .03
❑ 278 Jerry DiPoto .10 .03
❑ 279 Chris Haney .10 .03
❑ 280 Richie Lewis .10 .03
❑ 281 Jarvis Brown .10 .03
❑ 282 Juan Bell .10 .03
❑ 283 Joe Klink .10 .03
❑ 284 Graeme Lloyd .10 .03
❑ 285 Casey Candaele .10 .03
❑ 286 Bob MacDonald .10 .03
❑ 287 Mike Sharperson .10 .03
❑ 288 Gene Larkin .10 .03
❑ 289 Brian Barnes .10 .03
❑ 290 David McCarty .10 .03
❑ 291 Jeff Innis .10 .03
❑ 292 Bob Patterson .10 .03
❑ 293 Ben Rivera .10 .03
❑ 294 John Habyan .10 .03
❑ 295 Rich Rodriguez .10 .03
❑ 296 Edwin Nunez .10 .03
❑ 297 Rod Brewer .10 .03
❑ 298 Mike Timlin .10 .03
❑ 299 Jesse Orosco .10 .03
❑ 300 Gary Gaetti .20 .06
❑ 301 Todd Benzinger .10 .03
❑ 302 Jeff Nelson .10 .03
❑ 303 Rafael Belliard .10 .03
❑ 304 Matt Whiteside .10 .03
❑ 305 Vinny Castilla .20 .06
❑ 306 Matt Turner .10 .03
❑ 307 Eduardo Perez .10 .03
❑ 308 Joel Johnston .10 .03
❑ 309 Chris Gomez .10 .03
❑ 310 Pat Rapp .10 .03
❑ 311 Jim Tatum .10 .03
❑ 312 Kirk Rueter .20 .06
❑ 313 John Flaherty .10 .03
❑ 314 Tom Kramer .10 .03
❑ 315 Mark Whiten .10 .03
❑ 316 Chris Bosio .10 .03
❑ 317 Baltimore Orioles CL .10 .03
❑ 318 Bos.Red Sox CL UER .10 .03
Viola listed as 316; should be 331
❑ 319 California Angels CL .10 .03
❑ 320 Chicago White Sox CL .10 .03
❑ 321 Cleveland Indians CL .10 .03
❑ 322 Detroit Tigers CL .10 .03
❑ 323 KC Royals CL .10 .03
❑ 324 Milw. Brewers CL .10 .03
❑ 325 Minnesota Twins CL .10 .03
❑ 326 New York Yankees CL .10 .03
❑ 327 Oakland Athletics CL .10 .03
❑ 328 Seattle Mariners CL .10 .03
❑ 329 Texas Rangers CL .10 .03
❑ 330 Toronto Blue Jays CL .10 .03
❑ 331 Frank Viola .20 .06
❑ 332 Ron Gant .20 .06
❑ 333 Charles Nagy .10 .03
❑ 334 Roberto Kelly .10 .03
❑ 335 Brady Anderson .20 .06
❑ 336 Alex Cole .10 .03
❑ 337 Alan Trammell .20 .06
❑ 338 Derek Bell .10 .03
❑ 339 Bernie Williams .30 .09
❑ 340 Jose Offerman .10 .03
❑ 341 Bill Wegman .10 .03
❑ 342 Ken Caminiti .20 .06
❑ 343 Pat Borders .10 .03
❑ 344 Kirt Manwaring .10 .03
❑ 345 Chili Davis .20 .06
❑ 346 Steve Buechele .10 .03
❑ 347 Robin Ventura .20 .06
❑ 348 Teddy Higuera .10 .03
❑ 349 Jerry Browne .10 .03
❑ 350 Scott Kamieniecki .10 .03
❑ 351 Kevin Tapani .10 .03
❑ 352 Marquis Grissom .20 .06
❑ 353 Jay Buhner .20 .06
❑ 354 Dave Hollins .10 .03
❑ 355 Dan Wilson .10 .03
❑ 356 Bob Walk .10 .03
❑ 357 Chris Hoiles .10 .03
❑ 358 Todd Zeile .10 .03
❑ 359 Kevin Appier .20 .06
❑ 360 Chris Sabo .10 .03
❑ 361 David Segui .10 .03
❑ 362 Jerald Clark .10 .03
❑ 363 Tony Pena .10 .03
❑ 364 Steve Finley .20 .06
❑ 365 Roger Pavlik .10 .03
❑ 366 John Smoltz .30 .09
❑ 367 Scott Fletcher .10 .03
❑ 368 Jody Reed .10 .03
❑ 369 David Wells .20 .06
❑ 370 Jose Vizcaino .10 .03
❑ 371 Pat Listach .10 .03
❑ 372 Orestes Destrade .10 .03
❑ 373 Danny Tartabull .10 .03
❑ 374 Greg W. Harris .10 .03
❑ 375 Juan Guzman .10 .03
❑ 376 Larry Walker .20 .06
❑ 377 Gary DiSarcina .10 .03
❑ 378 Bobby Bonilla .20 .06
❑ 379 Tim Raines .20 .06
❑ 380 Tommy Greene .10 .03
❑ 381 Chris Gwynn .10 .03
❑ 382 Jeff King .10 .03
❑ 383 Shane Mack .10 .03
❑ 384 Ozzie Smith .75 .23
❑ 385 Eddie Zambrano RC .10 .03
❑ 386 Mike Devereaux .10 .03
❑ 387 Erik Hanson .10 .03
❑ 388 Scott Cooper .10 .03
❑ 389 Dean Palmer .20 .06
❑ 390 John Wetteland .20 .06
❑ 391 Reggie Jefferson .10 .03
❑ 392 Mark Lemke .10 .03
❑ 393 Cecil Fielder .20 .06
❑ 394 Reggie Sanders .20 .06
❑ 395 Darryl Hamilton .10 .03
❑ 396 Daryl Boston .10 .03
❑ 397 Pat Kelly .10 .03
❑ 398 Joe Orsulak .10 .03
❑ 399 Ed Sprague .10 .03
❑ 400 Eric Anthony .10 .03
❑ 401 Scott Sanderson .10 .03
❑ 402 Jim Gott .10 .03
❑ 403 Ron Karkovice .10 .03
❑ 404 Phil Plantier .10 .03
❑ 405 David Cone .20 .06
❑ 406 Robby Thompson .10 .03
❑ 407 Dave Winfield .20 .06
❑ 408 Dwight Smith .10 .03
❑ 409 Ruben Sierra .10 .03
❑ 410 Jack Armstrong .10 .03
❑ 411 Mike Felder .10 .03
❑ 412 Wil Cordero .10 .03
❑ 413 Julio Franco .20 .06
❑ 414 Howard Johnson .10 .03
❑ 415 Mark McLemore .10 .03
❑ 416 Pete Incaviglia .10 .03
❑ 417 John Valentin .10 .03
❑ 418 Tim Wakefield .30 .09
❑ 419 Jose Mesa .10 .03
❑ 420 Bernard Gilkey .10 .03
❑ 421 Kirk Gibson .30 .09
❑ 422 Dave Justice .20 .06
❑ 423 Tom Brunansky .10 .03
❑ 424 John Smiley .10 .03
❑ 425 Kevin Maas .10 .03
❑ 426 Doug Drabek .10 .03
❑ 427 Paul Molitor .30 .09
❑ 428 Darryl Strawberry .20 .06
❑ 429 Tim Naehring .10 .03
❑ 430 Bill Swift .10 .03
❑ 431 Ellis Burks .20 .06
❑ 432 Greg Hibbard .10 .03
❑ 433 Felix Jose .10 .03
❑ 434 Bret Barberie .10 .03
❑ 435 Pedro Munoz .10 .03
❑ 436 Darrin Fletcher .10 .03
❑ 437 Bobby Witt .10 .03
❑ 438 Wes Chamberlain .10 .03
❑ 439 Mackey Sasser .10 .03
❑ 440 Mark Whiten .10 .03
❑ 441 Harold Reynolds .20 .06
❑ 442 Greg Olson .10 .03
❑ 443 Billy Hatcher .10 .03
❑ 444 Joe Oliver .10 .03
❑ 445 Sandy Alomar Jr. .10 .03
❑ 446 Tim Wallach .10 .03
❑ 447 Karl Rhodes .10 .03
❑ 448 Royce Clayton .10 .03
❑ 449 Cal Eldred .10 .03
❑ 450 Rick Wilkins .10 .03
❑ 451 Mike Stanley .10 .03
❑ 452 Charlie Hough .20 .06
❑ 453 Jack Morris .20 .06
❑ 454 Jon Ratliff RC .10 .03
❑ 455 Rene Gonzales .10 .03
❑ 456 Eddie Taubensee .10 .03
❑ 457 Roberto Hernandez .10 .03
❑ 458 Todd Hundley .10 .03
❑ 459 Mike Macfarlane .10 .03
❑ 460 Mickey Morandini .10 .03
❑ 461 Scott Erickson .10 .03
❑ 462 Lonnie Smith .10 .03
❑ 463 Dave Henderson .10 .03
❑ 464 Ryan Klesko .20 .06
❑ 465 Edgar Martinez .30 .09
❑ 466 Tom Pagnozzi .10 .03
❑ 467 Charlie Leibrandt .10 .03
❑ 468 Brian Anderson RC .25 .07
❑ 469 Harold Baines .20 .06
❑ 470 Tim Belcher .10 .03
❑ 471 Andre Dawson .20 .06
❑ 472 Eric Young .10 .03
❑ 473 Paul Sorrento .10 .03
❑ 474 Luis Gonzalez .20 .06
❑ 475 Rob Deer .10 .03
❑ 476 Mike Piazza 1.00 .30
❑ 477 Kevin Reimer .10 .03
❑ 478 Jeff Gardner .10 .03
❑ 479 Melido Perez .10 .03
❑ 480 Darren Lewis .10 .03
❑ 481 Duane Ward .10 .03
❑ 482 Rey Sanchez .10 .03
❑ 483 Mark Lewis .10 .03
❑ 484 Jeff Conine .20 .06
❑ 485 Joey Cora .10 .03

- ❑ 486 Trot Nixon RC 1.00 .30
- ❑ 487 Kevin McReynolds .10 .03
- ❑ 488 Mike Lansing .10 .03
- ❑ 489 Mike Pagliarulo .10 .03
- ❑ 490 Mariano Duncan .10 .03
- ❑ 491 Mike Bordick .10 .03
- ❑ 492 Kevin Young .10 .03
- ❑ 493 Dave Valle .10 .03
- ❑ 494 Wayne Gomes RC .10 .03
- ❑ 495 Rafael Palmeiro .30 .09
- ❑ 496 Deion Sanders .30 .09
- ❑ 497 Rick Sutcliffe .20 .06
- ❑ 498 Randy Milligan .10 .03
- ❑ 499 Carlos Quintana .10 .03
- ❑ 500 Chris Turner .10 .03
- ❑ 501 Thomas Howard .10 .03
- ❑ 502 Greg Swindell .10 .03
- ❑ 503 Chad Kreuter .10 .03
- ❑ 504 Eric Davis .20 .06
- ❑ 505 Dickie Thon .10 .03
- ❑ 506 Matt Drews RC .10 .03
- ❑ 507 Spike Owen .10 .03
- ❑ 508 Rod Beck .10 .03
- ❑ 509 Pat Hentgen .10 .03
- ❑ 510 Sammy Sosa .50 .15
- ❑ 511 J.T. Snow .20 .06
- ❑ 512 Chuck Carr .10 .03
- ❑ 513 Bo Jackson .50 .15
- ❑ 514 Dennis Martinez .20 .06
- ❑ 515 Phil Hiatt .10 .03
- ❑ 516 Jeff Kent .30 .09
- ❑ 517 Brooks Kieschnick RC .25 .07
- ❑ 518 Kirk Presley RC .10 .03
- ❑ 519 Kevin Seitzer .10 .03
- ❑ 520 Carlos Garcia .10 .03
- ❑ 521 Mike Blowers .10 .03
- ❑ 522 Luis Alicea .10 .03
- ❑ 523 David Hulse .10 .03
- ❑ 524 Greg Maddux UER .75 .23
  (Career strikeout totals listed as 113; should be 1134)
- ❑ 525 Gregg Olson .10 .03
- ❑ 526 Hal Morris .10 .03
- ❑ 527 Daron Kirkreit .10 .03
- ❑ 528 David Nied .10 .03
- ❑ 529 Jeff Russell .10 .03
- ❑ 530 Kevin Gross .10 .03
- ❑ 531 John Doherty .10 .03
- ❑ 532 Matt Brunson RC .10 .03
- ❑ 533 Dave Nilsson .10 .03
- ❑ 534 Randy Myers .10 .03
- ❑ 535 Steve Farr .10 .03
- ❑ 536 Billy Wagner RC 1.00 .30
- ❑ 537 Darnell Coles .10 .03
- ❑ 538 Frank Tanana .10 .03
- ❑ 539 Tim Salmon .30 .09
- ❑ 540 Kim Batiste .10 .03
- ❑ 541 George Bell .10 .03
- ❑ 542 Tom Henke .10 .03
- ❑ 543 Sam Horn .10 .03
- ❑ 544 Doug Jones .10 .03
- ❑ 545 Scott Leius .10 .03
- ❑ 546 Al Martin .10 .03
- ❑ 547 Bob Welch .10 .03
- ❑ 548 Scott Christman RC .10 .03
- ❑ 549 Norm Charlton .10 .03
- ❑ 550 Mark McGwire 1.25 .35
- ❑ 551 Greg McMichael .10 .03
- ❑ 552 Tim Costo .10 .03
- ❑ 553 Rodney Bolton .10 .03
- ❑ 554 Pedro Martinez .50 .15
- ❑ 555 Marc Valdes .10 .03
- ❑ 556 Darrell Whitmore .10 .03
- ❑ 557 Tim Bogar .10 .03
- ❑ 558 Steve Karsay .10 .03
- ❑ 559 Danny Bautista .10 .03
- ❑ 560 Jeffrey Hammonds .10 .03
- ❑ 561 Aaron Sele .10 .03
- ❑ 562 Russ Springer .10 .03
- ❑ 563 Jason Bere .10 .03
- ❑ 564 Billy Brewer .10 .03
- ❑ 565 Sterling Hitchcock .10 .03
- ❑ 566 Bobby Munoz .10 .03
- ❑ 567 Craig Paquette .10 .03
- ❑ 568 Bret Boone .20 .06
- ❑ 569 Dan Peltier .10 .03
- ❑ 570 Jeromy Burnitz .20 .06
- ❑ 571 John Wasdin RC .10 .03
- ❑ 572 Chipper Jones .50 .15
- ❑ 573 Jamey Wright RC .10 .03
- ❑ 574 Jeff Granger .10 .03
- ❑ 575 Jay Powell RC .10 .03
- ❑ 576 Ryan Thompson .10 .03
- ❑ 577 Lou Frazier .10 .03
- ❑ 578 Paul Wagner .10 .03
- ❑ 579 Brad Ausmus .20 .06
- ❑ 580 Jack Voigt .10 .03
- ❑ 581 Kevin Rogers .10 .03
- ❑ 582 Damon Buford .10 .03
- ❑ 583 Paul Quantrill .10 .03
- ❑ 584 Marc Newfield .10 .03
- ❑ 585 Derrek Lee RC 2.00 .60
- ❑ 586 Shane Reynolds .10 .03
- ❑ 587 Cliff Floyd .20 .06
- ❑ 588 Jeff Schwarz .10 .03
- ❑ 589 Ross Powell RC .10 .03
- ❑ 590 Gerald Williams .10 .03
- ❑ 591 Mike Trombley .10 .03
- ❑ 592 Ken Ryan .10 .03
- ❑ 593 John O'Donoghue .10 .03
- ❑ 594 Rod Correia .10 .03
- ❑ 595 Darrell Sherman .10 .03
- ❑ 596 Steve Scarsone .10 .03
- ❑ 597 Sherman Obando .10 .03
- ❑ 598 Kurt Abbott RC .25 .07
- ❑ 599 Dave Telgheder .10 .03
- ❑ 600 Rick Trlicek .10 .03
- ❑ 601 Carl Everett .20 .06
- ❑ 602 Luis Ortiz .10 .03
- ❑ 603 Larry Luebbers .10 .03
- ❑ 604 Kevin Roberson .10 .03
- ❑ 605 Butch Huskey .10 .03
- ❑ 606 Benji Gil .10 .03
- ❑ 607 Todd Van Poppel .10 .03
- ❑ 608 Mark Hutton .10 .03
- ❑ 609 Chip Hale .10 .03
- ❑ 610 Matt Maysey .10 .03
- ❑ 611 Scott Ruffcorn .10 .03
- ❑ 612 Hilly Hathaway .10 .03
- ❑ 613 Allen Watson .10 .03
- ❑ 614 Carlos Delgado .30 .09
- ❑ 615 Roberto Mejia .10 .03
- ❑ 616 Turk Wendell .10 .03
- ❑ 617 Tony Tarasco .10 .03
- ❑ 618 Raul Mondesi .20 .06
- ❑ 619 Kevin Stocker .10 .03
- ❑ 620 Javier Lopez .20 .06
- ❑ 621 Keith Kessinger .10 .03
- ❑ 622 Bob Hamelin .10 .03
- ❑ 623 John Roper .10 .03
- ❑ 624 Lenny Dykstra WS .10 .03
- ❑ 625 Joe Carter WS .10 .03
- ❑ 626 Jim Abbott HL .20 .06
- ❑ 627 Lee Smith HL .10 .03
- ❑ 628 Ken Griffey Jr. HL .50 .15
- ❑ 629 Dave Winfield HL .10 .03
- ❑ 630 Darryl Kile HL .10 .03
- ❑ 631 F.Thomas AL MVP .30 .09
- ❑ 632 Barry Bonds NL MVP .75 .23
- ❑ 633 Jack McDowell AL CY .10 .03
- ❑ 634 Greg Maddux NL CY .50 .15
- ❑ 635 Tim Salmon AL ROY .20 .06
- ❑ 636 Mike Piazza NL ROY .50 .15
- ❑ 637 Brian Turang RC .10 .03
- ❑ 638 Rondell White .20 .06
- ❑ 639 Nigel Wilson .10 .03
- ❑ 640 Torii Hunter RC 1.00 .30
- ❑ 641 Salomon Torres .10 .03
- ❑ 642 Kevin Higgins .10 .03
- ❑ 643 Eric Wedge .10 .03
- ❑ 644 Roger Salkeld .10 .03
- ❑ 645 Manny Ramirez .50 .15
- ❑ 646 Jeff McNeely .10 .03
- ❑ 647 Atlanta Braves CL .10 .03
- ❑ 648 Chicago Cubs CL .10 .03
- ❑ 649 Cincinnati Reds CL .10 .03
- ❑ 650 Colorado Rockies CL .10 .03
- ❑ 651 Florida Marlins CL .10 .03
- ❑ 652 Houston Astros CL .10 .03
- ❑ 653 L.A. Dodgers CL .10 .03
- ❑ 654 Montreal Expos CL .10 .03
- ❑ 655 New York Mets CL .10 .03
- ❑ 656 Phi. Phillies CL .10 .03
- ❑ 657 Pittsburgh Pirates CL .10 .03
- ❑ 658 St. Louis Cardinals CL .10 .03
- ❑ 659 San Diego Padres CL .10 .03
- ❑ 660 S.F. Giants CL .10 .03

1994 Score Rookie/Traded

	Nm-Mt	Ex-Mt
COMPLETE SET (165)	15.00	4.50
ACTUAL CARD REDEEMED IN 1995		.00

- ❑ RT1 Will Clark .50 .15
- ❑ RT2 Lee Smith .30 .09
- ❑ RT3 Bo Jackson .75 .23
- ❑ RT4 Ellis Burks .30 .09
- ❑ RT5 Eddie Murray .75 .23
- ❑ RT6 Delino DeShields .15 .04
- ❑ RT7 Erik Hanson .15 .04
- ❑ RT8 Rafael Palmeiro .50 .15
- ❑ RT9 Luis Polonia .15 .04
- ❑ RT10 Omar Vizquel .50 .15
- ❑ RT11 Kurt Abbott .30 .09
- ❑ RT12 Vince Coleman .15 .04
- ❑ RT13 Rickey Henderson .75 .23
- ❑ RT14 Terry Mulholland .15 .04
- ❑ RT15 Greg Hibbard .15 .04
- ❑ RT16 Walt Weiss .15 .04
- ❑ RT17 Chris Sabo .15 .04
- ❑ RT18 Dave Henderson .15 .04
- ❑ RT19 Rick Sutcliffe .30 .09
- ❑ RT20 Harold Reynolds .30 .09
- ❑ RT21 Jack Morris .30 .09
- ❑ RT22 Dan Wilson .15 .04
- ❑ RT23 Dave Magadan .15 .04
- ❑ RT24 Dennis Martinez .30 .09
- ❑ RT25 Wes Chamberlain .15 .04
- ❑ RT26 Otis Nixon .15 .04
- ❑ RT27 Eric Anthony .15 .04
- ❑ RT28 Randy Milligan .15 .04
- ❑ RT29 Julio Franco .30 .09
- ❑ RT30 Kevin McReynolds .15 .04
- ❑ RT31 Anthony Young .15 .04
- ❑ RT32 Brian Harper .15 .04
- ❑ RT33 Gene Harris .15 .04
- ❑ RT34 Eddie Taubensee .15 .04
- ❑ RT35 David Segui .15 .04
- ❑ RT36 Stan Javier .15 .04
- ❑ RT37 Felix Fermin .15 .04
- ❑ RT38 Darrin Jackson .15 .04
- ❑ RT39 Tony Fernandez .15 .04
- ❑ RT40 Jose Vizcaino .15 .04
- ❑ RT41 Willie Banks .15 .04
- ❑ RT42 Brian Hunter .15 .04
- ❑ RT43 Reggie Jefferson .15 .04
- ❑ RT44 Junior Felix .15 .04
- ❑ RT45 Jack Armstrong .15 .04
- ❑ RT46 Bip Roberts .15 .04
- ❑ RT47 Jerry Browne .15 .04
- ❑ RT48 Marvin Freeman .15 .04
- ❑ RT49 Jody Reed .15 .04
- ❑ RT50 Alex Cole .15 .04
- ❑ RT51 Sid Fernandez .15 .04
- ❑ RT52 Pete Smith .15 .04
- ❑ RT53 Xavier Hernandez .15 .04
- ❑ RT54 Scott Sanderson .15 .04
- ❑ RT55 Turner Ward .15 .04

Card	Player	Nm-Mt	Ex-Mt
❑ RT56	Rex Hudler	.15	.04
❑ RT57	Deion Sanders	.50	.15
❑ RT58	Sid Bream	.15	.04
❑ RT59	Tony Pena	.15	.04
❑ RT60	Bret Boone	.30	.09
❑ RT61	Bobby Ayala	.15	.04
❑ RT62	Pedro Martinez	.75	.23
❑ RT63	Howard Johnson	.15	.04
❑ RT64	Mark Portugal	.15	.04
❑ RT65	Roberto Kelly	.15	.04
❑ RT66	Spike Owen	.15	.04
❑ RT67	Jeff Treadway	.15	.04
❑ RT68	Mike Harkey	.15	.04
❑ RT69	Doug Jones	.15	.04
❑ RT70	Steve Farr	.15	.04
❑ RT71	Billy Taylor RC	.15	.04
❑ RT72	Manny Ramirez	.75	.23
❑ RT73	Bob Hamelin	.15	.04
❑ RT74	Steve Karsay	.15	.04
❑ RT75	Ryan Klesko	.30	.09
❑ RT76	Cliff Floyd	.30	.09
❑ RT77	Jeffrey Hammonds	.15	.04
❑ RT78	Javier Lopez	.30	.09
❑ RT79	Roger Salkeld	.15	.04
❑ RT80	Hector Carrasco	.15	.04
❑ RT81	Gerald Williams	.15	.04
❑ RT82	Raul Mondesi	.30	.09
❑ RT83	Sterling Hitchcock	.15	.04
❑ RT84	Danny Bautista	.15	.04
❑ RT85	Chris Turner	.15	.04
❑ RT86	Shane Reynolds	.15	.04
❑ RT87	Rondell White	.30	.09
❑ RT88	Salomon Torres	.15	.04
❑ RT89	Turk Wendell	.15	.04
❑ RT90	Tony Tarasco	.15	.04
❑ RT91	Shawn Green	.75	.23
❑ RT92	Greg Colbrunn	.15	.04
❑ RT93	Eddie Zambrano	.15	.04
❑ RT94	Rich Becker	.15	.04
❑ RT95	Chris Gomez	.15	.04
❑ RT96	John Patterson	.15	.04
❑ RT97	Derek Parks	.15	.04
❑ RT98	Rich Rowland	.15	.04
❑ RT99	James Mouton	.15	.04
❑ RT100	Tim Hyers RC	.15	.04
❑ RT101	Jose Valentin	.15	.04
❑ RT102	Carlos Delgado	.50	.15
❑ RT103	Robert Eenhoorn	.15	.04
❑ RT104	John Hudek RC	.15	.04
❑ RT105	Domingo Cedeno	.15	.04
❑ RT106	Denny Hocking	.15	.04
❑ RT107	Greg Pirkl	.15	.04
❑ RT108	Mark Smith	.15	.04
❑ RT109	Paul Shuey	.15	.04
❑ RT110	Jorge Fabregas	.15	.04
❑ RT111	Rikkert Faneyte RC	.15	.04
❑ RT112	Rob Butler	.15	.04
❑ RT113	Darren Oliver RC	.30	.09
❑ RT114	Troy O'Leary	.15	.04
❑ RT115	Scott Brow	.15	.04
❑ RT116	Tony Eusebio	.15	.04
❑ RT117	Carlos Reyes	.15	.04
❑ RT118	J.R. Phillips	.15	.04
❑ RT119	Alex Diaz	.15	.04
❑ RT120	Charles Johnson	.30	.09
❑ RT121	Nate Minchey	.15	.04
❑ RT122	Scott Sanders	.15	.04
❑ RT123	Daryl Boston	.15	.04
❑ RT124	Joey Hamilton	.15	.04
❑ RT125	Brian Anderson	.30	.09
❑ RT126	Dan Miceli	.15	.04
❑ RT127	Tom Brunansky	.15	.04
❑ RT128	Dave Staton	.15	.04
❑ RT129	Mike Oquist	.15	.04
❑ RT130	John Mabry RC	.50	.15
❑ RT131	Norberto Martin	.15	.04
❑ RT132	Hector Fajardo	.15	.04
❑ RT133	Mark Hutton	.15	.04
❑ RT134	Fernando Vina	.15	.04
❑ RT135	Lee Tinsley	.15	.04
❑ RT136	Chan Ho Park RC	.50	.15
❑ RT137	Paul Spoljaric	.15	.04
❑ RT138	Matias Carrillo	.15	.04
❑ RT139	Mark Kiefer	.15	.04
❑ RT140	Stan Royer	.15	.04
❑ RT141	Bryan Eversgerd	.15	.04
❑ RT142	Brian L. Hunter	.15	.04
❑ RT143	Joe Hall	.15	.04
❑ RT144	Johnny Ruffin	.15	.04
❑ RT145	Alex Gonzalez	.15	.04
❑ RT146	Keith Lockhart RC	.30	.09
❑ RT147	Tom Marsh	.15	.04
❑ RT148	Tony Longmire	.15	.04
❑ RT149	Keith Mitchell	.15	.04
❑ RT150	Melvin Nieves	.15	.04
❑ RT151	Kelly Stinnett RC	.15	.04
❑ RT152	Miguel Jimenez	.15	.04
❑ RT153	Jeff Juden	.15	.04
❑ RT154	Matt Walbeck	.15	.04
❑ RT155	Marc Newfield	.15	.04
❑ RT156	Matt Mieske	.15	.04
❑ RT157	Marcus Moore	.15	.04
❑ RT158	Jose Lima RC SP	5.00	1.50
❑ RT159	Mike Kelly	.15	.04
❑ RT160	Jim Edmonds	.75	.23
❑ RT161	Steve Trachsel	.15	.04
❑ RT162	Greg Blosser	.15	.04
❑ RT163	Marc Acre RC	.15	.04
❑ RT164	AL Checklist	.15	.04
❑ RT165	NL Checklist	.15	.04
❑ HC1	Alex Rodriguez Call-Up Redemption	400.00	120.00
❑ NNO	Sept. Call-Up Trade EXP	2.00	.60

1993 Select

Card	Player	Nm-Mt	Ex-Mt
	COMPLETE SET (405)	25.00	7.50
❑ 1	Barry Bonds	1.50	.45
❑ 2	Ken Griffey Jr.	.75	.23
❑ 3	Will Clark	.30	.09
❑ 4	Kirby Puckett	.50	.15
❑ 5	Tony Gwynn	.60	.18
❑ 6	Frank Thomas	.50	.15
❑ 7	Tom Glavine	.30	.09
❑ 8	Roberto Alomar	.30	.09
❑ 9	Andre Dawson	.20	.06
❑ 10	Ron Darling	.15	.04
❑ 11	Bobby Bonilla	.20	.06
❑ 12	Danny Tartabull	.15	.04
❑ 13	Darren Daulton	.20	.06
❑ 14	Roger Clemens	1.00	.30
❑ 15	Ozzie Smith	.75	.23
❑ 16	Mark McGwire	1.25	.35
❑ 17	Terry Pendleton	.20	.06
❑ 18	Cal Ripken	1.50	.45
❑ 19	Fred McGriff	.30	.09
❑ 20	Cecil Fielder	.20	.06
❑ 21	Darryl Strawberry	.20	.06
❑ 22	Robin Yount	.75	.23
❑ 23	Barry Larkin	.30	.09
❑ 24	Don Mattingly	1.25	.35
❑ 25	Craig Biggio	.30	.09
❑ 26	Sandy Alomar Jr.	.15	.04
❑ 27	Larry Walker	.20	.06
❑ 28	Junior Felix	.15	.04
❑ 29	Eddie Murray	.50	.15
❑ 30	Robin Ventura	.20	.06
❑ 31	Greg Maddux	.75	.23
❑ 32	Dave Winfield	.20	.06
❑ 33	John Kruk	.20	.06
❑ 34	Wally Joyner	.20	.06
❑ 35	Andy Van Slyke	.30	.09
❑ 36	Chuck Knoblauch	.20	.06
❑ 37	Tom Pagnozzi	.15	.04
❑ 38	Dennis Eckersley	.20	.06
❑ 39	Dave Justice	.20	.06
❑ 40	Juan Gonzalez	.20	.06
❑ 41	Gary Sheffield	.20	.06
❑ 42	Paul Molitor	.30	.09
❑ 43	Delino DeShields	.15	.04
❑ 44	Travis Fryman	.20	.06
❑ 45	Hal Morris	.15	.04
❑ 46	Greg Olson	.15	.04
❑ 47	Ken Caminiti	.20	.06
❑ 48	Wade Boggs	.30	.09
❑ 49	Orel Hershiser	.20	.06
❑ 50	Albert Belle	.20	.06
❑ 51	Bill Swift	.15	.04
❑ 52	Mark Langston	.15	.04
❑ 53	Joe Girardi	.15	.04
❑ 54	Keith Miller	.15	.04
❑ 55	Gary Carter	.20	.06
❑ 56	Brady Anderson	.20	.06
❑ 57	Dwight Gooden	.20	.06
❑ 58	Julio Franco	.20	.06
❑ 59	Lenny Dykstra	.20	.06
❑ 60	Mickey Tettleton	.15	.04
❑ 61	Randy Tomlin	.15	.04
❑ 62	B.J. Surhoff	.20	.06
❑ 63	Todd Zeile	.15	.04
❑ 64	Roberto Kelly	.15	.04
❑ 65	Rob Dibble	.20	.06
❑ 66	Leo Gomez	.15	.04
❑ 67	Doug Jones	.15	.04
❑ 68	Ellis Burks	.20	.06
❑ 69	Mike Scioscia	.15	.04
❑ 70	Charles Nagy	.15	.04
❑ 71	Cory Snyder	.15	.04
❑ 72	Devon White	.20	.06
❑ 73	Mark Grace	.30	.09
❑ 74	Luis Polonia	.15	.04
❑ 75	John Smiley 2X	.15	.04
❑ 76	Carlton Fisk	.30	.09
❑ 77	Luis Sojo	.15	.04
❑ 78	George Brett	1.25	.35
❑ 79	Mitch Williams	.15	.04
❑ 80	Kent Hrbek	.20	.06
❑ 81	Jay Bell	.20	.06
❑ 82	Edgar Martinez	.30	.09
❑ 83	Lee Smith	.20	.06
❑ 84	Deion Sanders	.30	.09
❑ 85	Bill Gullickson	.15	.04
❑ 86	Paul O'Neill	.30	.09
❑ 87	Kevin Seitzer	.15	.04
❑ 88	Steve Finley	.20	.06
❑ 89	Mel Hall	.15	.04
❑ 90	Nolan Ryan	2.00	.60
❑ 91	Eric Davis	.20	.06
❑ 92	Mike Mussina	.30	.09
❑ 93	Tony Fernandez	.15	.04
❑ 94	Frank Viola	.20	.06
❑ 95	Matt Williams	.20	.06
❑ 96	Joe Carter	.20	.06
❑ 97	Ryne Sandberg	.75	.23
❑ 98	Jim Abbott	.30	.09
❑ 99	Marquis Grissom	.20	.06
❑ 100	George Bell	.15	.04
❑ 101	Howard Johnson	.15	.04
❑ 102	Kevin Appier	.20	.06
❑ 103	Dale Murphy	.30	.09
❑ 104	Shane Mack	.15	.04
❑ 105	Jose Lind	.15	.04
❑ 106	Rickey Henderson	.50	.15
❑ 107	Bob Tewksbury	.15	.04
❑ 108	Kevin Mitchell	.15	.04
❑ 109	Steve Avery	.15	.04
❑ 110	Candy Maldonado	.15	.04
❑ 111	Bip Roberts	.15	.04
❑ 112	Lou Whitaker	.20	.06
❑ 113	Jeff Bagwell	.30	.09
❑ 114	Dante Bichette	.20	.06
❑ 115	Brett Butler	.20	.06
❑ 116	Melido Perez	.15	.04
❑ 117	Andy Benes	.15	.04
❑ 118	Randy Johnson	.50	.15
❑ 119	Willie McGee	.20	.06
❑ 120	Jody Reed	.15	.04
❑ 121	Shawon Dunston	.15	.04
❑ 122	Carlos Baerga	.15	.04

❑ 123 Bret Saberhagen .20 .06
❑ 124 John Olerud .20 .06
❑ 125 Ivan Calderon .15 .04
❑ 126 Bryan Harvey .15 .04
❑ 127 Terry Mulholland .15 .04
❑ 128 Ozzie Guillen .20 .06
❑ 129 Steve Buechele .15 .04
❑ 130 Kevin Tapani .15 .04
❑ 131 Felix Jose .15 .04
❑ 132 Terry Steinbach .15 .04
❑ 133 Ron Gant .20 .06
❑ 134 Harold Reynolds .20 .06
❑ 135 Chris Sabo .15 .04
❑ 136 Ivan Rodriguez .30 .09
❑ 137 Eric Anthony .15 .04
❑ 138 Mike Henneman .15 .04
❑ 139 Robby Thompson .15 .04
❑ 140 Scott Fletcher .15 .04
❑ 141 Bruce Hurst .15 .04
❑ 142 Kevin Maas .15 .04
❑ 143 Tom Candiotti .15 .04
❑ 144 Chris Hoiles .15 .04
❑ 145 Mike Morgan .15 .04
❑ 146 Mark Whiten .15 .04
❑ 147 Dennis Martinez .20 .06
❑ 148 Tony Pena .15 .04
❑ 149 Dave Magadan .15 .04
❑ 150 Mark Lewis .15 .04
❑ 151 Mariano Duncan .15 .04
❑ 152 Gregg Jefferies .15 .04
❑ 153 Doug Drabek .15 .04
❑ 154 Brian Harper .15 .04
❑ 155 Ray Lankford .20 .06
❑ 156 Carney Lansford .20 .06
❑ 157 Mike Sharperson .15 .04
❑ 158 Jack Morris .20 .06
❑ 159 Otis Nixon .15 .04
❑ 160 Steve Sax .15 .04
❑ 161 Mark Lemke .15 .04
❑ 162 Rafael Palmeiro .30 .09
❑ 163 Jose Rijo .15 .04
❑ 164 Omar Vizquel .30 .09
❑ 165 Sammy Sosa .50 .15
❑ 166 Milt Cuyler .15 .04
❑ 167 John Franco .20 .06
❑ 168 Darryl Hamilton .15 .04
❑ 169 Ken Hill .15 .04
❑ 170 Mike Devereaux .15 .04
❑ 171 Don Slaught .15 .04
❑ 172 Steve Farr .15 .04
❑ 173 Bernard Gilkey .15 .04
❑ 174 Mike Fetters .15 .04
❑ 175 Vince Coleman .15 .04
❑ 176 Kevin McReynolds .15 .04
❑ 177 John Smoltz .30 .09
❑ 178 Greg Gagne .15 .04
❑ 179 Greg Swindell .15 .04
❑ 180 Juan Guzman .15 .04
❑ 181 Kal Daniels .15 .04
❑ 182 Rick Sutcliffe .20 .06
❑ 183 Orlando Merced .15 .04
❑ 184 Bill Wegman .15 .04
❑ 185 Mark Gardner .15 .04
❑ 186 Rob Deer .15 .04
❑ 187 Dave Hollins .15 .04
❑ 188 Jack Clark .20 .06
❑ 189 Brian Hunter .15 .04
❑ 190 Tim Wallach .15 .04
❑ 191 Tim Belcher .15 .04
❑ 192 Walt Weiss .15 .04
❑ 193 Kurt Stillwell .15 .04
❑ 194 Charlie Hayes .15 .04
❑ 195 Willie Randolph .20 .06
❑ 196 Jack McDowell .15 .04
❑ 197 Jose Offerman .15 .04
❑ 198 Chuck Finley .20 .06
❑ 199 Darrin Jackson .15 .04
❑ 200 Kelly Gruber .15 .04
❑ 201 John Wetteland .20 .06
❑ 202 Jay Buhner .20 .06
❑ 203 Mike LaValliere .15 .04
❑ 204 Kevin Brown .20 .06
❑ 205 Luis Gonzalez .20 .06
❑ 206 Rick Aguilera .15 .04
❑ 207 Norm Charlton .15 .04
❑ 208 Mike Bordick .15 .04
❑ 209 Charlie Leibrandt .15 .04
❑ 210 Tom Brunansky .15 .04
❑ 211 Tom Henke .15 .04
❑ 212 Randy Milligan .15 .04
❑ 213 Ramon Martinez .15 .04
❑ 214 Mo Vaughn .20 .06
❑ 215 Randy Myers .15 .04
❑ 216 Greg Hibbard .15 .04
❑ 217 Wes Chamberlain .15 .04
❑ 218 Tony Phillips .15 .04
❑ 219 Pete Harnisch .15 .04
❑ 220 Mike Gallego .15 .04
❑ 221 Bud Black .15 .04
❑ 222 Greg Vaughn .15 .04
❑ 223 Milt Thompson .15 .04
❑ 224 Ben McDonald .15 .04
❑ 225 Billy Hatcher .15 .04
❑ 226 Paul Sorrento .15 .04
❑ 227 Mark Gubicza .15 .04
❑ 228 Mike Greenwell .15 .04
❑ 229 Curt Schilling .20 .06
❑ 230 Alan Trammell .20 .06
❑ 231 Zane Smith .15 .04
❑ 232 Bobby Thigpen .15 .04
❑ 233 Greg Olson .15 .04
❑ 234 Joe Orsulak .15 .04
❑ 235 Joe Oliver .15 .04
❑ 236 Tim Raines .20 .06
❑ 237 Juan Samuel .15 .04
❑ 238 Chili Davis .20 .06
❑ 239 Spike Owen .15 .04
❑ 240 Dave Stewart .20 .06
❑ 241 Jim Eisenreich .15 .04
❑ 242 Phil Plantier .15 .04
❑ 243 Sid Fernandez .15 .04
❑ 244 Dan Gladden .15 .04
❑ 245 Mickey Morandini .15 .04
❑ 246 Tino Martinez .30 .09
❑ 247 Kirt Manwaring .15 .04
❑ 248 Dean Palmer .20 .06
❑ 249 Tom Browning .15 .04
❑ 250 Brian McRae .15 .04
❑ 251 Scott Leius .15 .04
❑ 252 Bert Blyleven .20 .06
❑ 253 Scott Erickson .15 .04
❑ 254 Bob Welch .15 .04
❑ 255 Pat Kelly .15 .04
❑ 256 Felix Fermin .15 .04
❑ 257 Harold Baines .20 .06
❑ 258 Duane Ward .15 .04
❑ 259 Bill Spiers .15 .04
❑ 260 Jaime Navarro .15 .04
❑ 261 Scott Sanderson .15 .04
❑ 262 Gary Gaetti .20 .06
❑ 263 Bob Ojeda .15 .04
❑ 264 Jeff Montgomery .15 .04
❑ 265 Scott Bankhead .15 .04
❑ 266 Lance Johnson .15 .04
❑ 267 Rafael Belliard .15 .04
❑ 268 Kevin Reimer .15 .04
❑ 269 Benito Santiago .20 .06
❑ 270 Mike Moore .15 .04
❑ 271 Dave Fleming .15 .04
❑ 272 Moises Alou .20 .06
❑ 273 Pat Listach .15 .04
❑ 274 Reggie Sanders .20 .06
❑ 275 Kenny Lofton .20 .06
❑ 276 Donovan Osborne .15 .04
❑ 277 Rusty Meacham .15 .04
❑ 278 Eric Karros .20 .06
❑ 279 Andy Stankiewicz .15 .04
❑ 280 Brian Jordan .20 .06
❑ 281 Gary DiSarcina .15 .04
❑ 282 Mark Wohlers .15 .04
❑ 283 Dave Nilsson .15 .04
❑ 284 Anthony Young .15 .04
❑ 285 Jim Bullinger .15 .04
❑ 286 Derek Bell .15 .04
❑ 287 Brian Williams .15 .04
❑ 288 Julio Valera .15 .04
❑ 289 Dan Walters .15 .04
❑ 290 Chad Curtis .15 .04
❑ 291 Michael Tucker DP .20 .06
❑ 292 Bob Zupcic .15 .04
❑ 293 Todd Hundley .15 .04
❑ 294 Jeff Tackett .15 .04
❑ 295 Greg Colbrunn .15 .04
❑ 296 Cal Eldred .15 .04
❑ 297 Chris Roberts DP .15 .04
❑ 298 John Doherty .15 .04
❑ 299 Denny Neagle .20 .06
❑ 300 Arthur Rhodes .15 .04
❑ 301 Mark Clark .15 .04
❑ 302 Scott Cooper .15 .04
❑ 303 Jamie Arnold DP RC .15 .04
❑ 304 Jim Thome .30 .09
❑ 305 Frank Seminara .15 .04
❑ 306 Kurt Knudsen .15 .04
❑ 307 Tim Wakefield .50 .15
❑ 308 John Jaha .15 .04
❑ 309 Pat Hentgen .15 .04
❑ 310 B.J. Wallace DP .15 .04
❑ 311 Roberto Hernandez .15 .04
❑ 312 Hipolito Pichardo .15 .04
❑ 313 Eric Fox .15 .04
❑ 314 Willie Banks .15 .04
❑ 315 Sam Militello .15 .04
❑ 316 Vince Horsman .15 .04
❑ 317 Carlos Hernandez .15 .04
❑ 318 Jeff Kent .50 .15
❑ 319 Mike Perez .15 .04
❑ 320 Scott Livingstone .15 .04
❑ 321 Jeff Conine .20 .06
❑ 322 Jim Austin .15 .04
❑ 323 John Vander Wal .15 .04
❑ 324 Pat Mahomes .15 .04
❑ 325 Pedro Astacio .15 .04
❑ 326 Bret Boone UER .30 .09
(Misspelled Brett)
❑ 327 Matt Stairs .15 .04
❑ 328 Damion Easley .15 .04
❑ 329 Ben Rivera .15 .04
❑ 330 Reggie Jefferson .15 .04
❑ 331 Luis Mercedes .15 .04
❑ 332 Kyle Abbott .15 .04
❑ 333 Eddie Taubensee .15 .04
❑ 334 Tim McIntosh .15 .04
❑ 335 Phil Clark .15 .04
❑ 336 Wil Cordero .15 .04
❑ 337 Russ Springer .15 .04
❑ 338 Craig Colbert .15 .04
❑ 339 Tim Salmon .30 .09
❑ 340 Braulio Castillo .15 .04
❑ 341 Donald Harris .15 .04
❑ 342 Eric Young .15 .04
❑ 343 Bob Wickman .15 .04
❑ 344 John Valentin .15 .04
❑ 345 Dan Wilson .20 .06
❑ 346 Steve Hosey .15 .04
❑ 347 Mike Piazza 3.00 .90
❑ 348 Willie Greene .15 .04
❑ 349 Tom Goodwin .15 .04
❑ 350 Eric Hillman .15 .04
❑ 351 Steve Reed RC .15 .04
❑ 352 Dan Serafini DP RC .15 .04
❑ 353 T.Steverson DP RC .15 .04
❑ 354 Benji Grigsby DP RC .15 .04
❑ 355 S.Stewart DP RC .75 .23
❑ 356 Sean Lowe DP RC .15 .04
❑ 357 Derek Wallace DP RC .15 .04
❑ 358 Rick Helling DP .15 .04
❑ 359 Jason Kendall DP RC .75 .23
❑ 360 Derek Jeter DP RC 10.00 3.00
❑ 361 David Cone .20 .06
❑ 362 Jeff Reardon .20 .06
❑ 363 Bobby Witt .15 .04
❑ 364 Jose Canseco .30 .09
❑ 365 Jeff Russell .15 .04
❑ 366 Ruben Sierra .15 .04
❑ 367 Alan Mills .15 .04
❑ 368 Matt Nokes .15 .04
❑ 369 Pat Borders .15 .04
❑ 370 Pedro Munoz .15 .04
❑ 371 Danny Jackson .15 .04
❑ 372 Geronimo Pena .15 .04
❑ 373 Craig Lefferts .15 .04
❑ 374 Joe Grahe .15 .04
❑ 375 Roger McDowell .15 .04
❑ 376 Jimmy Key .20 .06
❑ 377 Steve Olin .15 .04
❑ 378 Glenn Davis .15 .04
❑ 379 Rene Gonzales .15 .04

❑ 380 Manuel Lee	.15	.04
❑ 381 Ron Karkovice	.15	.04
❑ 382 Sid Bream	.15	.04
❑ 383 Gerald Williams	.15	.04
❑ 384 Lenny Harris	.15	.04
❑ 385 J.T. Snow RC	.50	.15
❑ 386 Dave Stieb	.15	.04
❑ 387 Kirk McCaskill	.15	.04
❑ 388 Lance Parrish	.20	.06
❑ 389 Craig Grebeck	.15	.04
❑ 390 Rick Wilkins	.15	.04
❑ 391 Manny Alexander	.15	.04
❑ 392 Mike Schooler	.15	.04
❑ 393 Bernie Williams	.30	.09
❑ 394 Kevin Koslofski	.15	.04
❑ 395 Willie Wilson	.15	.04
❑ 396 Jeff Parrett	.15	.04
❑ 397 Mike Harkey	.15	.04
❑ 398 Frank Tanana	.15	.04
❑ 399 Doug Henry	.15	.04
❑ 400 Royce Clayton	.15	.04
❑ 401 Eric Wedge RC	.25	.07
❑ 402 Derrick May	.15	.04
❑ 403 Carlos Garcia	.15	.04
❑ 404 Henry Rodriguez	.15	.04
❑ 405 Ryan Klesko	.20	.06

1993 SP

	Nm-Mt	Ex-Mt
COMPLETE SET (290)	80.00	24.00
COMMON CARD (1-270)	.50	.15
COMMON FOIL (271-290)	1.00	.30
❑ 1 Roberto Alomar AS	1.25	.35
❑ 2 Wade Boggs AS	1.25	.35
❑ 3 Joe Carter AS	.50	.15
❑ 4 Ken Griffey Jr. AS	3.00	.90
❑ 5 Mark Langston AS	.50	.15
❑ 6 John Olerud AS	.75	.23
❑ 7 Kirby Puckett AS	2.00	.60
❑ 8 Cal Ripken Jr. AS	6.00	1.80
❑ 9 Ivan Rodriguez AS	1.25	.35
❑ 10 Barry Bonds AS	5.00	1.50
❑ 11 Darren Daulton AS	.75	.23
❑ 12 Marquis Grissom AS	.75	.23
❑ 13 David Justice AS	.75	.23
❑ 14 John Kruk AS	.75	.23
❑ 15 Barry Larkin AS	1.25	.35
❑ 16 Terry Mulholland AS	.50	.15
❑ 17 Ryne Sandberg AS	3.00	.90
❑ 18 Gary Sheffield AS	.75	.23
❑ 19 Chad Curtis	.50	.15
❑ 20 Chili Davis	.75	.23
❑ 21 Gary DiSarcina	.50	.15
❑ 22 Damion Easley	.50	.15
❑ 23 Chuck Finley	.75	.23
❑ 24 Luis Polonia	.50	.15
❑ 25 Tim Salmon	1.25	.35
❑ 26 J.T. Snow RC	1.25	.35
❑ 27 Russ Springer	.50	.15
❑ 28 Jeff Bagwell	1.25	.35
❑ 29 Craig Biggio	1.25	.35
❑ 30 Ken Caminiti	.75	.23
❑ 31 Andujar Cedeno	.50	.15
❑ 32 Doug Drabek	.50	.15
❑ 33 Steve Finley	.75	.23
❑ 34 Luis Gonzalez	.75	.23
❑ 35 Pete Harnisch	.50	.15
❑ 36 Darryl Kile	.75	.23
❑ 37 Mike Bordick	.50	.15
❑ 38 Dennis Eckersley	.75	.23
❑ 39 Brent Gates	.50	.15
❑ 40 Rickey Henderson	2.00	.60
❑ 41 Mark McGwire	5.00	1.50
❑ 42 Craig Paquette	.50	.15
❑ 43 Ruben Sierra	.50	.15
❑ 44 Terry Steinbach	.50	.15
❑ 45 Todd Van Poppel	.50	.15
❑ 46 Pat Borders	.50	.15
❑ 47 Tony Fernandez	.50	.15
❑ 48 Juan Guzman	.50	.15
❑ 49 Pat Hentgen	.50	.15
❑ 50 Paul Molitor	1.25	.35
❑ 51 Jack Morris	.75	.23
❑ 52 Ed Sprague	.50	.15
❑ 53 Duane Ward	.50	.15
❑ 54 Devon White	.75	.23
❑ 55 Steve Avery	.50	.15
❑ 56 Jeff Blauser	.50	.15
❑ 57 Ron Gant	.75	.23
❑ 58 Tom Glavine	1.25	.35
❑ 59 Greg Maddux	3.00	.90
❑ 60 Fred McGriff	1.25	.35
❑ 61 Terry Pendleton	.75	.23
❑ 62 Deion Sanders	1.25	.35
❑ 63 John Smoltz	1.25	.35
❑ 64 Cal Eldred	.50	.15
❑ 65 Darryl Hamilton	.50	.15
❑ 66 John Jaha	.50	.15
❑ 67 Pat Listach	.50	.15
❑ 68 Jaime Navarro	.50	.15
❑ 69 Kevin Reimer	.50	.15
❑ 70 B.J. Surhoff	.75	.23
❑ 71 Greg Vaughn	.50	.15
❑ 72 Robin Yount	3.00	.90
❑ 73 Rene Arocha RC	.75	.23
❑ 74 Bernard Gilkey	.50	.15
❑ 75 Gregg Jefferies	.50	.15
❑ 76 Ray Lankford	.75	.23
❑ 77 Tom Pagnozzi	.50	.15
❑ 78 Lee Smith	.75	.23
❑ 79 Ozzie Smith	3.00	.90
❑ 80 Bob Tewksbury	.50	.15
❑ 81 Mark Whiten	.50	.15
❑ 82 Steve Buechele	.50	.15
❑ 83 Mark Grace	1.25	.35
❑ 84 Jose Guzman	.50	.15
❑ 85 Derrick May	.50	.15
❑ 86 Mike Morgan	.50	.15
❑ 87 Randy Myers	.50	.15
❑ 88 Kevin Roberson RC	.50	.15
❑ 89 Sammy Sosa	2.00	.60
❑ 90 Rick Wilkins	.50	.15
❑ 91 Brett Butler	.75	.23
❑ 92 Eric Davis	.75	.23
❑ 93 Orel Hershiser	.75	.23
❑ 94 Eric Karros	.75	.23
❑ 95 Ramon Martinez	.50	.15
❑ 96 Raul Mondesi	.75	.23
❑ 97 Jose Offerman	.50	.15
❑ 98 Mike Piazza	5.00	1.50
❑ 99 Darryl Strawberry	.75	.23
❑ 100 Moises Alou	.75	.23
❑ 101 Wil Cordero	.50	.15
❑ 102 Delino DeShields	.50	.15
❑ 103 Darrin Fletcher	.50	.15
❑ 104 Ken Hill	.50	.15
❑ 105 Mike Lansing RC	.75	.23
❑ 106 Dennis Martinez	.75	.23
❑ 107 Larry Walker	.75	.23
❑ 108 John Wetteland	.75	.23
❑ 109 Rod Beck	.50	.15
❑ 110 John Burkett	.50	.15
❑ 111 Will Clark	1.25	.35
❑ 112 Royce Clayton	.50	.15
❑ 113 Darren Lewis	.50	.15
❑ 114 Willie McGee	.75	.23
❑ 115 Bill Swift	.50	.15
❑ 116 Robby Thompson	.50	.15
❑ 117 Matt Williams	.75	.23
❑ 118 Sandy Alomar Jr.	.50	.15
❑ 119 Carlos Baerga	.50	.15
❑ 120 Albert Belle	.75	.23
❑ 121 Reggie Jefferson	.50	.15
❑ 122 Wayne Kirby	.50	.15
❑ 123 Kenny Lofton	.75	.23
❑ 124 Carlos Martinez	.50	.15
❑ 125 Charles Nagy	.50	.15
❑ 126 Paul Sorrento	.50	.15
❑ 127 Rich Amaral	.50	.15
❑ 128 Jay Buhner	.75	.23
❑ 129 Norm Charlton	.50	.15
❑ 130 Dave Fleming	.50	.15
❑ 131 Erik Hanson	.50	.15
❑ 132 Randy Johnson	2.00	.60
❑ 133 Edgar Martinez	1.25	.35
❑ 134 Tino Martinez	1.25	.35
❑ 135 Omar Vizquel	1.25	.35
❑ 136 Bret Barberie	.50	.15
❑ 137 Chuck Carr	.50	.15
❑ 138 Jeff Conine	.75	.23
❑ 139 Orestes Destrade	.50	.15
❑ 140 Chris Hammond	.50	.15
❑ 141 Bryan Harvey	.50	.15
❑ 142 Benito Santiago	.75	.23
❑ 143 Walt Weiss	.50	.15
❑ 144 Darrell Whitmore RC	.50	.15
❑ 145 Tim Bogar RC	.50	.15
❑ 146 Bobby Bonilla	.75	.23
❑ 147 Jeromy Burnitz	.75	.23
❑ 148 Vince Coleman	.50	.15
❑ 149 Dwight Gooden	.75	.23
❑ 150 Todd Hundley	.50	.15
❑ 151 Howard Johnson	.50	.15
❑ 152 Eddie Murray	2.00	.60
❑ 153 Bret Saberhagen	.75	.23
❑ 154 Brady Anderson	.75	.23
❑ 155 Mike Devereaux	.50	.15
❑ 156 Jeffrey Hammonds	.50	.15
❑ 157 Chris Hoiles	.50	.15
❑ 158 Ben McDonald	.50	.15
❑ 159 Mark McLemore	.50	.15
❑ 160 Mike Mussina	1.25	.35
❑ 161 Gregg Olson	.50	.15
❑ 162 David Segui	.50	.15
❑ 163 Derek Bell	.50	.15
❑ 164 Andy Benes	.50	.15
❑ 165 Archi Cianfrocco	.50	.15
❑ 166 Ricky Gutierrez	.50	.15
❑ 167 Tony Gwynn	2.50	.75
❑ 168 Gene Harris	.50	.15
❑ 169 Trevor Hoffman	2.00	.60
❑ 170 Ray McDavid RC	.50	.15
❑ 171 Phil Plantier	.50	.15
❑ 172 Mariano Duncan	.50	.15
❑ 173 Len Dykstra	.75	.23
❑ 174 Tommy Greene	.50	.15
❑ 175 Dave Hollins	.50	.15
❑ 176 Pete Incaviglia	.50	.15
❑ 177 Mickey Morandini	.50	.15
❑ 178 Curt Schilling	.75	.23
❑ 179 Kevin Stocker	.50	.15
❑ 180 Mitch Williams	.50	.15
❑ 181 Stan Belinda	.50	.15
❑ 182 Jay Bell	.75	.23
❑ 183 Steve Cooke	.50	.15
❑ 184 Carlos Garcia	.50	.15
❑ 185 Jeff King	.50	.15
❑ 186 Orlando Merced	.50	.15
❑ 187 Don Slaught	.50	.15
❑ 188 Andy Van Slyke	1.25	.35
❑ 189 Kevin Young	.75	.23
❑ 190 Kevin Brown	.75	.23
❑ 191 Jose Canseco	1.25	.35
❑ 192 Julio Franco	.75	.23
❑ 193 Benji Gil	.50	.15
❑ 194 Juan Gonzalez	.75	.23
❑ 195 Tom Henke	.50	.15
❑ 196 Rafael Palmeiro	1.25	.35
❑ 197 Dean Palmer	.75	.23
❑ 198 Nolan Ryan	8.00	2.40
❑ 199 Roger Clemens	4.00	1.20
❑ 200 Scott Cooper	.50	.15
❑ 201 Andre Dawson	.75	.23
❑ 202 Mike Greenwell	.50	.15
❑ 203 Carlos Quintana	.50	.15
❑ 204 Jeff Russell	.50	.15
❑ 205 Aaron Sele	.50	.15
❑ 206 Mo Vaughn	.75	.23
❑ 207 Frank Viola	.75	.23

No.	Player	Nm-Mt	Ex-Mt
❑ 208	Rob Dibble	.75	.23
❑ 209	Roberto Kelly	.50	.15
❑ 210	Kevin Mitchell	.50	.15
❑ 211	Hal Morris	.50	.15
❑ 212	Joe Oliver	.50	.15
❑ 213	Jose Rijo	.50	.15
❑ 214	Bip Roberts	.50	.15
❑ 215	Chris Sabo	.50	.15
❑ 216	Reggie Sanders	.75	.23
❑ 217	Dante Bichette	.75	.23
❑ 218	Jerald Clark	.50	.15
❑ 219	Alex Cole	.50	.15
❑ 220	Andres Galarraga	.75	.23
❑ 221	Joe Girardi	.50	.15
❑ 222	Charlie Hayes	.50	.15
❑ 223	Roberto Mejia RC	.50	.15
❑ 224	Armando Reynoso	.50	.15
❑ 225	Eric Young	.50	.15
❑ 226	Kevin Appier	.75	.23
❑ 227	George Brett	5.00	1.50
❑ 228	David Cone	.75	.23
❑ 229	Phil Hiatt	.50	.15
❑ 230	Felix Jose	.50	.15
❑ 231	Wally Joyner	.75	.23
❑ 232	Mike Macfarlane	.50	.15
❑ 233	Brian McRae	.50	.15
❑ 234	Jeff Montgomery	.50	.15
❑ 235	Rob Deer	.50	.15
❑ 236	Cecil Fielder	.75	.23
❑ 237	Travis Fryman	.75	.23
❑ 238	Mike Henneman	.50	.15
❑ 239	Tony Phillips	.50	.15
❑ 240	Mickey Tettleton	.50	.15
❑ 241	Alan Trammell	.75	.23
❑ 242	David Wells	.75	.23
❑ 243	Lou Whitaker	.75	.23
❑ 244	Rick Aguilera	.50	.15
❑ 245	Scott Erickson	.50	.15
❑ 246	Brian Harper	.50	.15
❑ 247	Kent Hrbek	.75	.23
❑ 248	Chuck Knoblauch	.75	.23
❑ 249	Shane Mack	.50	.15
❑ 250	David McCarty	.50	.15
❑ 251	Pedro Munoz	.50	.15
❑ 252	Dave Winfield	.75	.23
❑ 253	Alex Fernandez	.50	.15
❑ 254	Ozzie Guillen	.75	.23
❑ 255	Bo Jackson	2.00	.60
❑ 256	Lance Johnson	.50	.15
❑ 257	Ron Karkovice	.50	.15
❑ 258	Jack McDowell	.50	.15
❑ 259	Tim Raines	.75	.23
❑ 260	Frank Thomas	2.00	.60
❑ 261	Robin Ventura	.75	.23
❑ 262	Jim Abbott	1.25	.35
❑ 263	Steve Farr	.50	.15
❑ 264	Jimmy Key	.75	.23
❑ 265	Don Mattingly	5.00	1.50
❑ 266	Paul O'Neill	1.25	.35
❑ 267	Mike Stanley	.50	.15
❑ 268	Danny Tartabull	.50	.15
❑ 269	Bob Wickman	.50	.15
❑ 270	Bernie Williams	1.25	.35
❑ 271	Jason Bere FOIL	1.00	.30
❑ 272	R.Cedeno FOIL RC	1.50	.45
❑ 273	J.Damon FOIL RC	10.00	3.00
❑ 274	Russ Davis FOIL RC	1.50	.45
❑ 275	Carlos Delgado FOIL	4.00	1.20
❑ 276	Carl Everett FOIL	1.50	.45
❑ 277	Cliff Floyd FOIL	.75	.23
❑ 278	Alex Gonzalez FOIL	1.00	.30
❑ 279	Derek Jeter FOIL RC	60.00	18.00
❑ 280	Chipper Jones FOIL	4.00	1.20
❑ 281	Javier Lopez FOIL	1.25	.35
❑ 282	Chad Mottola FOIL RC	1.00	.30
❑ 283	Marc Newfield FOIL	1.00	.30
❑ 284	Eduardo Perez FOIL	1.00	.30
❑ 285	Manny Ramirez FOIL	5.00	1.50
❑ 286	T.Steverson FOIL RC	1.00	.30
❑ 287	Michael Tucker FOIL	1.50	.45
❑ 288	Allen Watson FOIL	1.00	.30
❑ 289	Rondell White FOIL	1.50	.45
❑ 290	Dmitri Young FOIL	2.50	.75

1994 SP

	Nm-Mt	Ex-Mt
COMPLETE SET (200)	120.00	36.00
COMMON CARD (21-200)	.20	.06
COMMON FOIL (1-20)	.50	.15

No.	Player	Nm-Mt	Ex-Mt
❑ 1	Mike Bell FOIL RC	.50	.15
❑ 2	D.J. Boston FOIL RC	.50	.15
❑ 3	Johnny Damon FOIL	1.50	.45
❑ 4	Brad Fullmer FOIL RC	1.50	.45
❑ 5	Joey Hamilton FOIL	.50	.15
❑ 6	T.Hollandsworth FOIL	.50	.15
❑ 7	Brian L. Hunter FOIL	.50	.15
❑ 8	L.Hawkins FOIL RC	1.50	.45
❑ 9	B.Kieschnick FOIL RC	1.00	.30
❑ 10	Derrek Lee FOIL RC	15.00	4.50
❑ 11	Trot Nixon FOIL RC	3.00	.90
❑ 12	Alex Ochoa FOIL	.50	.15
❑ 13	Chan Ho Park FOIL RC	1.50	.45
❑ 14	Kirk Presley FOIL RC	.50	.15
❑ 15	A.Rodriguez FOIL RC	100.00	30.00
❑ 16	Jose Silva FOIL RC	.50	.15
❑ 17	Terrell Wade FOIL RC	.50	.15
❑ 18	Billy Wagner FOIL RC	3.00	.90
❑ 19	G.Williams FOIL RC	.50	.15
❑ 20	Preston Wilson FOIL	1.00	.30
❑ 21	Brian Anderson RC	.40	.12
❑ 22	Chad Curtis	.20	.06
❑ 23	Chili Davis	.40	.12
❑ 24	Bo Jackson	1.00	.30
❑ 25	Mark Langston	.20	.06
❑ 26	Tim Salmon	.60	.18
❑ 27	Jeff Bagwell	.60	.18
❑ 28	Craig Biggio	.60	.18
❑ 29	Ken Caminiti	.40	.12
❑ 30	Doug Drabek	.20	.06
❑ 31	John Hudek RC	.20	.06
❑ 32	Greg Swindell	.20	.06
❑ 33	Brent Gates	.20	.06
❑ 34	Rickey Henderson	1.00	.30
❑ 35	Steve Karsay	.20	.06
❑ 36	Mark McGwire	2.50	.75
❑ 37	Ruben Sierra	.20	.06
❑ 38	Terry Steinbach	.20	.06
❑ 39	Roberto Alomar	.60	.18
❑ 40	Joe Carter	.40	.12
❑ 41	Carlos Delgado	.60	.18
❑ 42	Alex Gonzalez	.20	.06
❑ 43	Juan Guzman	.20	.06
❑ 44	Paul Molitor	.60	.18
❑ 45	John Olerud	.40	.12
❑ 46	Devon White	.40	.12
❑ 47	Steve Avery	.20	.06
❑ 48	Jeff Blauser	.20	.06
❑ 49	Tom Glavine	.60	.18
❑ 50	David Justice	.40	.12
❑ 51	Roberto Kelly	.20	.06
❑ 52	Ryan Klesko	.40	.12
❑ 53	Javier Lopez	.40	.12
❑ 54	Greg Maddux	1.50	.45
❑ 55	Fred McGriff	.60	.18
❑ 56	Ricky Bones	.20	.06
❑ 57	Cal Eldred	.20	.06
❑ 58	Brian Harper	.20	.06
❑ 59	Pat Listach	.20	.06
❑ 60	B.J. Surhoff	.40	.12
❑ 61	Greg Vaughn	.20	.06
❑ 62	Bernard Gilkey	.20	.06
❑ 63	Gregg Jefferies	.20	.06
❑ 64	Ray Lankford	.40	.12
❑ 65	Ozzie Smith	1.50	.45
❑ 66	Bob Tewksbury	.20	.06
❑ 67	Mark Whiten	.20	.06
❑ 68	Todd Zeile	.20	.06
❑ 69	Mark Grace	.60	.18
❑ 70	Randy Myers	.20	.06
❑ 71	Ryne Sandberg	1.50	.45
❑ 72	Sammy Sosa	1.00	.30
❑ 73	Steve Trachsel	.20	.06
❑ 74	Rick Wilkins	.20	.06
❑ 75	Brett Butler	.40	.12
❑ 76	Delino DeShields	.20	.06
❑ 77	Orel Hershiser	.40	.12
❑ 78	Eric Karros	.40	.12
❑ 79	Raul Mondesi	.40	.12
❑ 80	Mike Piazza	2.00	.60
❑ 81	Tim Wallach	.20	.06
❑ 82	Moises Alou	.40	.12
❑ 83	Cliff Floyd	.40	.12
❑ 84	Marquis Grissom	.40	.12
❑ 85	Pedro Martinez	1.00	.30
❑ 86	Larry Walker	.40	.12
❑ 87	John Wetteland	.40	.12
❑ 88	Rondell White	.40	.12
❑ 89	Rod Beck	.20	.06
❑ 90	Barry Bonds	2.50	.75
❑ 91	John Burkett	.20	.06
❑ 92	Royce Clayton	.20	.06
❑ 93	Billy Swift	.20	.06
❑ 94	Robby Thompson	.20	.06
❑ 95	Matt Williams	.40	.12
❑ 96	Carlos Baerga	.20	.06
❑ 97	Albert Belle	.40	.12
❑ 98	Kenny Lofton	.40	.12
❑ 99	Dennis Martinez	.40	.12
❑ 100	Eddie Murray	1.00	.30
❑ 101	Manny Ramirez	1.00	.30
❑ 102	Eric Anthony	.20	.06
❑ 103	Chris Bosio	.20	.06
❑ 104	Jay Buhner	.40	.12
❑ 105	Ken Griffey Jr.	1.50	.45
❑ 106	Randy Johnson	1.00	.30
❑ 107	Edgar Martinez	.60	.18
❑ 108	Chuck Carr	.20	.06
❑ 109	Jeff Conine	.40	.12
❑ 110	Carl Everett	.40	.12
❑ 111	Chris Hammond	.20	.06
❑ 112	Bryan Harvey	.20	.06
❑ 113	Charles Johnson	.40	.12
❑ 114	Gary Sheffield	.40	.12
❑ 115	Bobby Bonilla	.40	.12
❑ 116	Dwight Gooden	.40	.12
❑ 117	Todd Hundley	.20	.06
❑ 118	Bobby Jones	.20	.06
❑ 119	Jeff Kent	.60	.18
❑ 120	Bret Saberhagen	.40	.12
❑ 121	Jeffrey Hammonds	.20	.06
❑ 122	Chris Hoiles	.20	.06
❑ 123	Ben McDonald	.20	.06
❑ 124	Mike Mussina	.60	.18
❑ 125	Rafael Palmeiro	.60	.18
❑ 126	Cal Ripken Jr.	3.00	.90
❑ 127	Lee Smith	.40	.12
❑ 128	Derek Bell	.20	.06
❑ 129	Andy Benes	.20	.06
❑ 130	Tony Gwynn	1.25	.35
❑ 131	Trevor Hoffman	.60	.18
❑ 132	Phil Plantier	.20	.06
❑ 133	Bip Roberts	.20	.06
❑ 134	Darren Daulton	.40	.12
❑ 135	Lenny Dykstra	.40	.12
❑ 136	Dave Hollins	.20	.06
❑ 137	Danny Jackson	.20	.06
❑ 138	John Kruk	.40	.12
❑ 139	Kevin Stocker	.20	.06
❑ 140	Jay Bell	.40	.12
❑ 141	Carlos Garcia	.20	.06
❑ 142	Jeff King	.20	.06
❑ 143	Orlando Merced	.20	.06
❑ 144	Andy Van Slyke	.60	.18
❑ 145	Rick White	.20	.06
❑ 146	Jose Canseco	.60	.18
❑ 147	Will Clark	.60	.18
❑ 148	Juan Gonzalez	.40	.12

❑ 149 Rick Helling	.20	.06
❑ 150 Dean Palmer	.40	.12
❑ 151 Ivan Rodriguez	.60	.18
❑ 152 Roger Clemens	2.00	.60
❑ 153 Scott Cooper	.20	.06
❑ 154 Andre Dawson	.40	.12
❑ 155 Mike Greenwell	.20	.06
❑ 156 Aaron Sele	.20	.06
❑ 157 Mo Vaughn	.40	.12
❑ 158 Bret Boone	.40	.12
❑ 159 Barry Larkin	.60	.18
❑ 160 Kevin Mitchell	.20	.06
❑ 161 Jose Rijo	.20	.06
❑ 162 Deion Sanders	.60	.18
❑ 163 Reggie Sanders	.40	.12
❑ 164 Dante Bichette	.40	.12
❑ 165 Ellis Burks	.40	.12
❑ 166 Andres Galarraga	.40	.12
❑ 167 Charlie Hayes	.20	.06
❑ 168 David Nied	.20	.06
❑ 169 Walt Weiss	.20	.06
❑ 170 Kevin Appier	.40	.12
❑ 171 David Cone	.40	.12
❑ 172 Jeff Granger	.20	.06
❑ 173 Felix Jose	.20	.06
❑ 174 Wally Joyner	.40	.12
❑ 175 Brian McRae	.20	.06
❑ 176 Cecil Fielder	.40	.12
❑ 177 Travis Fryman	.40	.12
❑ 178 Mike Henneman	.20	.06
❑ 179 Tony Phillips	.20	.06
❑ 180 Mickey Tettleton	.20	.06
❑ 181 Alan Trammell	.40	.12
❑ 182 Rick Aguilera	.20	.06
❑ 183 Rich Becker	.20	.06
❑ 184 Scott Erickson	.20	.06
❑ 185 Chuck Knoblauch	.40	.12
❑ 186 Kirby Puckett	1.00	.30
❑ 187 Dave Winfield	.40	.12
❑ 188 Wilson Alvarez	.20	.06
❑ 189 Jason Bere	.20	.06
❑ 190 Alex Fernandez	.20	.06
❑ 191 Julio Franco	.40	.12
❑ 192 Jack McDowell	.20	.06
❑ 193 Frank Thomas	1.00	.30
❑ 194 Robin Ventura	.40	.12
❑ 195 Jim Abbott	.60	.18
❑ 196 Wade Boggs	.60	.18
❑ 197 Jimmy Key	.40	.12
❑ 198 Don Mattingly	2.50	.75
❑ 199 Paul O'Neill	.60	.18
❑ 200 Danny Tartabull	.20	.06
❑ P24 Ken Griffey Jr. Promo	2.00	.60

2000 SP Authentic

	Nm-Mt	Ex-Mt
COMP.BASIC w/o SP's (90)	25.00	7.50
COMP.UPDATE w/o SP'S (30)	10.00	3.00
COMMON CARD (1-90)	.40	.12
COMMON SUP (91-105)	3.00	.90
COMMON FW (106-135)	5.00	1.50
COMMON FW (136-164)	5.00	1.50
COMMON (166-195)	.60	.18

Card	Nm-Mt	Ex-Mt
❑ 1 Mo Vaughn	.40	.12
❑ 2 Troy Glaus	.40	.12
❑ 3 Jason Giambi	.40	.12
❑ 4 Tim Hudson	.40	.12
❑ 5 Eric Chavez	.40	.12
❑ 6 Shannon Stewart	.40	.12
❑ 7 Raul Mondesi	.40	.12
❑ 8 Carlos Delgado	.40	.12
❑ 9 Jose Canseco	.60	.18
❑ 10 Vinny Castilla	.40	.12
❑ 11 Greg Vaughn	.40	.12
❑ 12 Manny Ramirez	.60	.18
❑ 13 Roberto Alomar	.60	.18
❑ 14 Jim Thome	.60	.18
❑ 15 Richie Sexson	.40	.12
❑ 16 Alex Rodriguez	1.50	.45
❑ 17 Freddy Garcia	.40	.12
❑ 18 John Olerud	.40	.12
❑ 19 Albert Belle	.40	.12
❑ 20 Cal Ripken	3.00	.90
❑ 21 Mike Mussina	.60	.18
❑ 22 Ivan Rodriguez	.60	.18
❑ 23 Gabe Kapler	.40	.12
❑ 24 Rafael Palmeiro	.60	.18
❑ 25 Nomar Garciaparra	1.50	.45
❑ 26 Pedro Martinez	.60	.18
❑ 27 Carl Everett	.40	.12
❑ 28 Carlos Beltran	.40	.12
❑ 29 Jermaine Dye	.40	.12
❑ 30 Juan Gonzalez	.40	.12
❑ 31 Dean Palmer	.40	.12
❑ 32 Corey Koskie	.40	.12
❑ 33 Jacque Jones	.40	.12
❑ 34 Frank Thomas	1.00	.30
❑ 35 Paul Konerko	.40	.12
❑ 36 Magglio Ordonez	.40	.12
❑ 37 Bernie Williams	.60	.18
❑ 38 Derek Jeter	2.50	.75
❑ 39 Roger Clemens	2.00	.60
❑ 40 Mariano Rivera	.60	.18
❑ 41 Jeff Bagwell	.60	.18
❑ 42 Craig Biggio	.60	.18
❑ 43 Jose Lima	.40	.12
❑ 44 Moises Alou	.40	.12
❑ 45 Chipper Jones	1.00	.30
❑ 46 Greg Maddux	1.50	.45
❑ 47 Andruw Jones	.60	.18
❑ 48 Andres Galarraga	.40	.12
❑ 49 Jeromy Burnitz	.40	.12
❑ 50 Geoff Jenkins	.40	.12
❑ 51 Mark McGwire	2.50	.75
❑ 52 Fernando Tatis	.40	.12
❑ 53 J.D. Drew	.40	.12
❑ 54 Sammy Sosa	1.00	.30
❑ 55 Kerry Wood	.40	.12
❑ 56 Mark Grace	.60	.18
❑ 57 Matt Williams	.40	.12
❑ 58 Randy Johnson	1.00	.30
❑ 59 Erubiel Durazo	.40	.12
❑ 60 Gary Sheffield	.40	.12
❑ 61 Kevin Brown	.60	.18
❑ 62 Shawn Green	.40	.12
❑ 63 Vladimir Guerrero	1.00	.30
❑ 64 Michael Barrett	.40	.12
❑ 65 Barry Bonds	2.50	.75
❑ 66 Jeff Kent	.40	.12
❑ 67 Russ Ortiz	.40	.12
❑ 68 Preston Wilson	.40	.12
❑ 69 Mike Lowell	.40	.12
❑ 70 Mike Piazza	1.50	.45
❑ 71 Mike Hampton	.40	.12
❑ 72 Robin Ventura	.40	.12
❑ 73 Edgardo Alfonzo	.40	.12
❑ 74 Tony Gwynn	1.25	.35
❑ 75 Ryan Klesko	.40	.12
❑ 76 Trevor Hoffman	.40	.12
❑ 77 Scott Rolen	.60	.18
❑ 78 Bob Abreu	.40	.12
❑ 79 Mike Lieberthal	.40	.12
❑ 80 Curt Schilling	.40	.12
❑ 81 Jason Kendall	.40	.12
❑ 82 Brian Giles	.40	.12
❑ 83 Kris Benson	.40	.12
❑ 84 Ken Griffey Jr.	1.50	.45
❑ 85 Sean Casey	.60	.18
❑ 86 Pokey Reese	.40	.12
❑ 87 Barry Larkin	.60	.18
❑ 88 Larry Walker	.40	.12
❑ 89 Todd Helton	.60	.18
❑ 90 Jeff Cirillo	.40	.12
❑ 91 Ken Griffey Jr. SUP	8.00	2.40
❑ 92 Mark McGwire SUP	12.00	3.60
❑ 93 Chipper Jones SUP	5.00	1.50
❑ 94 Derek Jeter SUP	12.00	3.60
❑ 95 Shawn Green SUP	3.00	.90
❑ 96 Pedro Martinez SUP	3.00	.90
❑ 97 Mike Piazza SUP	8.00	2.40
❑ 98 Alex Rodriguez SUP	8.00	2.40
❑ 99 Jeff Bagwell SUP	3.00	.90
❑ 100 Cal Ripken SUP	15.00	4.50
❑ 101 Sammy Sosa SUP	5.00	1.50
❑ 102 Barry Bonds SUP	12.00	3.60
❑ 103 Jose Canseco SUP	3.00	.90
❑ 104 N.Garciaparra SUP	8.00	2.40
❑ 105 Ivan Rodriguez SUP	3.00	.90
❑ 106 Rick Ankiel FW	5.00	1.50
❑ 107 Pat Burrell FW	3.00	.90
❑ 108 Vernon Wells FW	5.00	1.50
❑ 109 Nick Johnson FW	5.00	1.50
❑ 110 Kip Wells FW	5.00	1.50
❑ 111 Matt Riley FW	5.00	1.50
❑ 112 Alfonso Soriano FW	8.00	2.40
❑ 113 Josh Beckett FW	8.00	2.40
❑ 114 Danys Baez FW RC	5.00	1.50
❑ 115 Travis Dawkins FW	5.00	1.50
❑ 116 Eric Gagne FW	8.00	2.40
❑ 117 Mike Lamb FW RC	8.00	2.40
❑ 118 Eric Munson FW	5.00	1.50
❑ 119 W.Rodriguez FW RC	5.00	1.50
❑ 120 K.Sasaki FW RC	8.00	2.40
❑ 121 Chad Hutchinson FW	5.00	1.50
❑ 122 Peter Bergeron FW	5.00	1.50
❑ 123 W.Serrano FW RC	5.00	1.50
❑ 124 Tony Armas Jr. FW	5.00	1.50
❑ 125 Ramon Ortiz FW	5.00	1.50
❑ 126 Adam Kennedy FW	5.00	1.50
❑ 127 Joe Crede FW	10.00	3.00
❑ 128 Roosevelt Brown FW	5.00	1.50
❑ 129 Mark Mulder FW	5.00	1.50
❑ 130 Brad Penny FW	5.00	1.50
❑ 131 Terrence Long FW	5.00	1.50
❑ 132 Ruben Mateo FW	5.00	1.50
❑ 133 Wily Mo Pena FW	5.00	1.50
❑ 134 Rafael Furcal FW	5.00	1.50
❑ 135 M.Encarnacion FW	5.00	1.50
❑ 136 Barry Zito FW RC	15.00	4.50
❑ 137 Aaron McNeal FW RC	5.00	1.50
❑ 138 Timo Perez FW RC	5.00	1.50
❑ 139 Sun Woo Kim FW RC	5.00	1.50
❑ 140 Xavier Nady FW RC	8.00	2.40
❑ 141 M.Wheatland FW RC	5.00	1.50
❑ 142 B.Abernathy FW RC	5.00	1.50
❑ 143 Cory Vance FW RC	5.00	1.50
❑ 144 Scott Heard FW RC	5.00	1.50
❑ 145 Mike Meyers FW RC	5.00	1.50
❑ 146 Ben Diggins FW RC	5.00	1.50
❑ 147 Luis Matos FW RC	5.00	1.50
❑ 148 Ben Sheets FW RC	15.00	4.50
❑ 149 K.Ainsworth FW RC	5.00	1.50
❑ 150 Dave Krynzel FW RC	8.00	2.40
❑ 151 Alex Cabrera FW RC	5.00	1.50
❑ 152 Mike Tonis FW RC	5.00	1.50
❑ 153 Dane Sardinha FW RC	5.00	1.50
❑ 154 Keith Ginter FW RC	5.00	1.50
❑ 155 D.Espinosa FW RC	5.00	1.50
❑ 156 Joe Torres FW RC	5.00	1.50
❑ 157 Daylan Holt FW RC	5.00	1.50
❑ 158 Koyie Hill FW RC	5.00	1.50
❑ 159 B.Wilkerson FW RC	8.00	2.40
❑ 160 Juan Pierre FW RC	8.00	2.40
❑ 161 Matt Ginter FW RC	5.00	1.50
❑ 162 Dane Artman FW RC	5.00	1.50
❑ 163 Jon Rauch FW RC	5.00	1.50
❑ 164 Sean Burnett FW RC	8.00	2.40
❑ 165 Does Not Exist	.00	
❑ 166 Darin Erstad	.60	.18
❑ 167 Ben Grieve	.60	.18
❑ 168 David Wells	.60	.18
❑ 169 Fred McGriff	1.00	.30
❑ 170 Bob Wickman	.60	.18
❑ 171 Al Martin	.60	.18
❑ 172 Melvin Mora	.60	.18
❑ 173 Ricky Ledee	.60	.18
❑ 174 Dante Bichette	.60	.18
❑ 175 Mike Sweeney	.60	.18
❑ 176 Bobby Higginson	.60	.18

Card	Nm-Mt	Ex-Mt
❑ 177 Matt Lawton	.60	.18
❑ 178 Charles Johnson	.60	.18
❑ 179 David Justice	.60	.18
❑ 180 Richard Hidalgo	.60	.18
❑ 181 B.J. Surhoff	.60	.18
❑ 182 Richie Sexson	.60	.18
❑ 183 Jim Edmonds	.60	.18
❑ 184 Rondell White	.60	.18
❑ 185 Curt Schilling	.60	.18
❑ 186 Tom Goodwin	.60	.18
❑ 187 Jose Vidro	.60	.18
❑ 188 Ellis Burks	.60	.18
❑ 189 Henry Rodriguez	.60	.18
❑ 190 Mike Bordick	.60	.18
❑ 191 Eric Owens	.60	.18
❑ 192 Travis Lee	.60	.18
❑ 193 Kevin Young	.60	.18
❑ 194 Aaron Boone	.60	.18
❑ 195 Todd Hollandsworth	.60	.18
❑ SPA K.Griffey Jr. Sample	2.00	.60

2001 SP Authentic

	Nm-Mt	Ex-Mt
COMP.BASIC w/o SP's (90)	25.00	7.50
COMP.UPDATE w/o SP's (30)	10.00	3.00
COMMON CARD (1-90)	.40	.12
COMMON FW (91-135)	8.00	2.40
COMMON SS (136-180)	5.00	1.50
COMMON (181-210)	.60	.18
COMMON (211-240)	6.00	1.80

Card	Nm-Mt	Ex-Mt
❑ 1 Troy Glaus	.40	.12
❑ 2 Darin Erstad	.40	.12
❑ 3 Jason Giambi	.40	.12
❑ 4 Tim Hudson	.40	.12
❑ 5 Eric Chavez	.40	.12
❑ 6 Miguel Tejada	.40	.12
❑ 7 Jose Ortiz	.40	.12
❑ 8 Carlos Delgado	.40	.12
❑ 9 Tony Batista	.40	.12
❑ 10 Raul Mondesi	.40	.12
❑ 11 Aubrey Huff	.40	.12
❑ 12 Greg Vaughn	.40	.12
❑ 13 Roberto Alomar	.60	.18
❑ 14 Juan Gonzalez	.40	.12
❑ 15 Jim Thome	.60	.18
❑ 16 Omar Vizquel	.60	.18
❑ 17 Edgar Martinez	.60	.18
❑ 18 Freddy Garcia	.40	.12
❑ 19 Cal Ripken	3.00	.90
❑ 20 Ivan Rodriguez	.60	.18
❑ 21 Rafael Palmeiro	.60	.18
❑ 22 Alex Rodriguez	1.50	.45
❑ 23 Manny Ramirez Sox	.60	.18
❑ 24 Pedro Martinez	.60	.18
❑ 25 Nomar Garciaparra	1.50	.45
❑ 26 Mike Sweeney	.40	.12
❑ 27 Jermaine Dye	.40	.12
❑ 28 Bobby Higginson	.40	.12
❑ 29 Dean Palmer	.40	.12
❑ 30 Matt Lawton	.40	.12
❑ 31 Eric Milton	.40	.12
❑ 32 Frank Thomas	1.00	.30
❑ 33 Magglio Ordonez	.40	.12
❑ 34 David Wells	.40	.12
❑ 35 Paul Konerko	.40	.12
❑ 36 Derek Jeter	2.50	.75
❑ 37 Bernie Williams	.60	.18
❑ 38 Roger Clemens	2.00	.60
❑ 39 Mike Mussina	.60	.18
❑ 40 Jorge Posada	.60	.18
❑ 41 Jeff Bagwell	.60	.18
❑ 42 Richard Hidalgo	.40	.12
❑ 43 Craig Biggio	.60	.18
❑ 44 Greg Maddux	1.50	.45
❑ 45 Chipper Jones	1.00	.30
❑ 46 Andruw Jones	.60	.18
❑ 47 Rafael Furcal	.40	.12
❑ 48 Tom Glavine	.60	.18
❑ 49 Jeromy Burnitz	.40	.12
❑ 50 Jeffrey Hammonds	.40	.12
❑ 51 Mark McGwire	2.50	.75
❑ 52 Jim Edmonds	.60	.18
❑ 53 Rick Ankiel	.40	.12
❑ 54 J.D. Drew	.40	.12
❑ 55 Sammy Sosa	1.00	.30
❑ 56 Corey Patterson	.40	.12
❑ 57 Kerry Wood	.40	.12
❑ 58 Randy Johnson	1.00	.30
❑ 59 Luis Gonzalez	.40	.12
❑ 60 Curt Schilling	.40	.12
❑ 61 Gary Sheffield	.40	.12
❑ 62 Shawn Green	.40	.12
❑ 63 Kevin Brown	.40	.12
❑ 64 Vladimir Guerrero	1.00	.30
❑ 65 Jose Vidro	.40	.12
❑ 66 Barry Bonds	2.50	.75
❑ 67 Jeff Kent	.40	.12
❑ 68 Livan Hernandez	.40	.12
❑ 69 Preston Wilson	.40	.12
❑ 70 Charles Johnson	.40	.12
❑ 71 Ryan Dempster	.40	.12
❑ 72 Mike Piazza	1.50	.45
❑ 73 Al Leiter	.40	.12
❑ 74 Edgardo Alfonzo	.40	.12
❑ 75 Robin Ventura	.40	.12
❑ 76 Tony Gwynn	1.25	.35
❑ 77 Phil Nevin	.40	.12
❑ 78 Trevor Hoffman	.40	.12
❑ 79 Scott Rolen	.60	.18
❑ 80 Pat Burrell	.40	.12
❑ 81 Bob Abreu	.40	.12
❑ 82 Jason Kendall	.40	.12
❑ 83 Brian Giles	.40	.12
❑ 84 Kris Benson	.40	.12
❑ 85 Ken Griffey Jr.	1.50	.45
❑ 86 Barry Larkin	.60	.18
❑ 87 Sean Casey	.60	.18
❑ 88 Todd Helton	.60	.18
❑ 89 Mike Hampton	.40	.12
❑ 90 Larry Walker	.40	.12
❑ 91 Ichiro Suzuki FW RC	150.00	45.00
❑ 92 Wilson Betemit FW RC	10.00	3.00
❑ 93 A. Hernandez FW RC	8.00	2.40
❑ 94 Juan Uribe FW RC	10.00	3.00
❑ 95 Travis Hafner FW RC	40.00	12.00
❑ 96 M. Ensberg FW RC	30.00	9.00
❑ 97 Sean Douglass FW RC	8.00	2.40
❑ 98 Juan Diaz FW RC	8.00	2.40
❑ 99 Erick Almonte FW RC	8.00	2.40
❑ 100 Ryan Freel FW RC	10.00	3.00
❑ 101 E. Guzman FW RC	8.00	2.40
❑ 102 C. Parker FW RC	8.00	2.40
❑ 103 Josh Fogg FW RC	8.00	2.40
❑ 104 Bert Snow FW RC	8.00	2.40
❑ 105 H. Ramirez FW RC	10.00	3.00
❑ 106 R. Rodriguez FW RC	8.00	2.40
❑ 107 Tyler Walker FW RC	8.00	2.40
❑ 108 Jose Mieses FW RC	8.00	2.40
❑ 109 Billy Sylvester FW RC	8.00	2.40
❑ 110 Martin Vargas FW RC	8.00	2.40
❑ 111 Andres Torres FW RC	8.00	2.40
❑ 112 Greg Miller FW RC	8.00	2.40
❑ 113 Alexis Gomez FW RC	8.00	2.40
❑ 114 Grant Balfour FW RC	8.00	2.40
❑ 115 Henry Mateo FW RC	8.00	2.40
❑ 116 Esix Snead FW RC	8.00	2.40
❑ 117 J. Melian FW RC	8.00	2.40
❑ 118 Nate Teut FW RC	8.00	2.40
❑ 119 T. Shinjo FW RC	10.00	3.00
❑ 120 C. Valderrama FW RC	8.00	2.40
❑ 121 J. Estrada FW RC	10.00	3.00
❑ 122 J. Michaels FW RC	8.00	2.40
❑ 123 William Ortega FW RC	8.00	2.40
❑ 124 Jason Smith FW RC	8.00	2.40
❑ 125 B. Lawrence FW RC	8.00	2.40
❑ 126 Albert Pujols FW RC	400.00	120.00
❑ 127 Wilkin Ruan FW RC	8.00	2.40
❑ 128 Josh Towers FW RC	10.00	3.00
❑ 129 Kris Keller FW RC	8.00	2.40
❑ 130 Nick Maness FW RC	8.00	2.40
❑ 131 Jack Wilson FW RC	10.00	3.00
❑ 132 B. Duckworth FW RC	8.00	2.40
❑ 133 Mike Penney FW RC	8.00	2.40
❑ 134 Jay Gibbons FW RC	10.00	3.00
❑ 135 Cesar Crespo FW RC	8.00	2.40
❑ 136 Ken Griffey Jr. SS	10.00	3.00
❑ 137 Mark McGwire SS	15.00	4.50
❑ 138 Derek Jeter SS	15.00	4.50
❑ 139 Alex Rodriguez SS	10.00	3.00
❑ 140 Sammy Sosa SS	6.00	1.80
❑ 141 Carlos Delgado SS	5.00	1.50
❑ 142 Cal Ripken SS	20.00	6.00
❑ 143 Pedro Martinez SS	5.00	1.50
❑ 144 Frank Thomas SS	6.00	1.80
❑ 145 Juan Gonzalez SS	5.00	1.50
❑ 146 Troy Glaus SS	5.00	1.50
❑ 147 Jason Giambi SS	5.00	1.50
❑ 148 Ivan Rodriguez SS	5.00	1.50
❑ 149 Chipper Jones SS	6.00	1.80
❑ 150 Vladimir Guerrero SS	6.00	1.80
❑ 151 Mike Piazza SS	10.00	3.00
❑ 152 Jeff Bagwell SS	5.00	1.50
❑ 153 Randy Johnson SS	6.00	1.80
❑ 154 Todd Helton SS	5.00	1.50
❑ 155 Gary Sheffield SS	5.00	1.50
❑ 156 Tony Gwynn SS	8.00	2.40
❑ 157 Barry Bonds SS	15.00	4.50
❑ 158 N. Garciaparra SS	10.00	3.00
❑ 159 Bernie Williams SS	5.00	1.50
❑ 160 Greg Vaughn SS	5.00	1.50
❑ 161 David Wells SS	5.00	1.50
❑ 162 Roberto Alomar SS	5.00	1.50
❑ 163 Jermaine Dye SS	5.00	1.50
❑ 164 Rafael Palmeiro SS	5.00	1.50
❑ 165 Andruw Jones SS	5.00	1.50
❑ 166 Preston Wilson SS	5.00	1.50
❑ 167 Edgardo Alfonzo SS	5.00	1.50
❑ 168 Pat Burrell SS	5.00	1.50
❑ 169 Jim Edmonds SS	5.00	1.50
❑ 170 Mike Hampton SS	5.00	1.50
❑ 171 Jeff Kent SS	5.00	1.50
❑ 172 Kevin Brown SS	5.00	1.50
❑ 173 Manny Ramirez Sox SS	5.00	1.50
❑ 174 Magglio Ordonez SS	5.00	1.50
❑ 175 Roger Clemens SS	12.00	3.60
❑ 176 Jim Thome SS	5.00	1.50
❑ 177 Barry Zito SS	5.00	1.50
❑ 178 Brian Giles SS	5.00	1.50
❑ 179 Rick Ankiel SS	5.00	1.50
❑ 180 Corey Patterson SS	5.00	1.50
❑ 181 Garret Anderson	.60	.18
❑ 182 Jermaine Dye	.60	.18
❑ 183 Shannon Stewart	.60	.18
❑ 184 Ben Grieve	.60	.18
❑ 185 Ellis Burks	.60	.18
❑ 186 John Olerud	.60	.18
❑ 187 Tony Batista	.60	.18
❑ 188 Ruben Sierra	.60	.18
❑ 189 Carl Everett	.60	.18
❑ 190 Neifi Perez	.60	.18
❑ 191 Tony Clark	.60	.18
❑ 192 Doug Mientkiewicz	.60	.18
❑ 193 Carlos Lee	.60	.18
❑ 194 Jorge Posada	1.00	.30
❑ 195 Lance Berkman	5.00	1.50
❑ 196 Ken Caminiti	.60	.18
❑ 197 Ben Sheets	1.00	.30
❑ 198 Matt Morris	.60	.18
❑ 199 Fred McGriff	1.00	.30
❑ 200 Mark Grace	1.00	.30
❑ 201 Paul LoDuca	.60	.18
❑ 202 Tony Armas Jr.	.60	.18
❑ 203 Andres Galarraga	.60	.18
❑ 204 Cliff Floyd	.60	.18
❑ 205 Matt Lawton	.60	.18
❑ 206 Ryan Klesko	.60	.18
❑ 207 Jimmy Rollins	.60	.18
❑ 208 Aramis Ramirez	.60	.18
❑ 209 Aaron Boone	.60	.18

❑ 210 Jose Ortiz .60 .18
❑ 211 Mark Prior FW RC 80.00 24.00
❑ 212 Mark Teixeira FW RC 100.00 30.00
❑ 213 Bud Smith FW RC 6.00 1.80
❑ 214 W.Caceres FW RC 6.00 1.80
❑ 215 Dave Williams FW RC 6.00 1.80
❑ 216 Delvin James FW RC 6.00 1.80
❑ 217 Endy Chavez FW RC 6.00 1.80
❑ 218 Doug Nickle FW RC 6.00 1.80
❑ 219 Bret Prinz FW RC 6.00 1.80
❑ 220 Troy Mattes FW RC 6.00 1.80
❑ 221 D.Sanchez FW RC 6.00 1.80
❑ 222 D.Brazelton FW RC 6.00 1.80
❑ 223 Brian Bowles FW RC 6.00 1.80
❑ 224 D.Mendez FW RC 6.00 1.80
❑ 225 Jorge Julio FW RC 6.00 1.80
❑ 226 Matt White FW RC 6.00 1.80
❑ 227 Casey Fossum FW RC 6.00 1.80
❑ 228 Mike Rivera FW RC 6.00 1.80
❑ 229 Joe Kennedy FW RC 8.00 2.40
❑ 230 Kyle Lohse FW RC 8.00 2.40
❑ 231 Juan Cruz FW RC 6.00 1.80
❑ 232 Jeremy Affeldt FW RC 6.00 1.80
❑ 233 Brandon Lyon FW RC 6.00 1.80
❑ 234 Brian Roberts FW RC 30.00 9.00
❑ 235 Willie Harris FW RC 6.00 1.80
❑ 236 Pedro Santana FW RC 6.00 1.80
❑ 237 Rafael Soriano FW RC 6.00 1.80
❑ 238 Steve Green FW RC 6.00 1.80
❑ 239 Junior Spivey FW RC 8.00 2.40
❑ 240 R.Mackowiak FW RC 8.00 2.40
❑ NNO K.Griffey Jr. Promo 2.00 .60

2002 SP Authentic

	Nm-Mt	Ex-Mt
COMP.LOW w/o SP's (90)	15.00	4.50
COMP.UPDATE w/o SP's (30)	10.00	3.00
COMMON CARD (1-90)	.40	.12
COMMON (91-135/201-230)	5.00	1.50
COMMON CARD (136-170)	15.00	4.50
COMMON CARD (171-200)	.60	.18

❑ 1 Troy Glaus .40 .12
❑ 2 Darin Erstad .40 .12
❑ 3 Barry Zito .40 .12
❑ 4 Eric Chavez .40 .12
❑ 5 Tim Hudson .40 .12
❑ 6 Miguel Tejada .40 .12
❑ 7 Carlos Delgado .40 .12
❑ 8 Shannon Stewart .40 .12
❑ 9 Ben Grieve .40 .12
❑ 10 Jim Thome .60 .18
❑ 11 C.C. Sabathia .40 .12
❑ 12 Ichiro Suzuki 2.00 .60
❑ 13 Freddy Garcia .40 .12
❑ 14 Edgar Martinez .60 .18
❑ 15 Bret Boone .40 .12
❑ 16 Jeff Conine .40 .12
❑ 17 Alex Rodriguez 1.50 .45
❑ 18 Juan Gonzalez .40 .12
❑ 19 Ivan Rodriguez .60 .18
❑ 20 Rafael Palmeiro .60 .18
❑ 21 Hank Blalock .60 .18
❑ 22 Pedro Martinez .60 .18
❑ 23 Manny Ramirez .60 .18
❑ 24 Nomar Garciaparra 1.50 .45
❑ 25 Carlos Beltran .40 .12
❑ 26 Mike Sweeney .40 .12
❑ 27 Randall Simon .40 .12
❑ 28 Dmitri Young .40 .12
❑ 29 Bobby Higginson .40 .12
❑ 30 Corey Koskie .40 .12
❑ 31 Eric Milton .40 .12
❑ 32 Torii Hunter .40 .12
❑ 33 Joe Mays .40 .12
❑ 34 Frank Thomas 1.00 .30
❑ 35 Mark Buehrle .40 .12
❑ 36 Magglio Ordonez .40 .12
❑ 37 Kenny Lofton .40 .12
❑ 38 Roger Clemens 2.00 .60
❑ 39 Derek Jeter 2.50 .75
❑ 40 Jason Giambi .40 .12
❑ 41 Bernie Williams .60 .18
❑ 42 Alfonso Soriano .40 .12
❑ 43 Lance Berkman .40 .12
❑ 44 Roy Oswalt .40 .12
❑ 45 Jeff Bagwell .60 .18
❑ 46 Craig Biggio .60 .18
❑ 47 Chipper Jones 1.00 .30
❑ 48 Greg Maddux 1.50 .45
❑ 49 Gary Sheffield .40 .12
❑ 50 Andruw Jones .60 .18
❑ 51 Ben Sheets .40 .12
❑ 52 Richie Sexson .40 .12
❑ 53 Albert Pujols 2.00 .60
❑ 54 Matt Morris .40 .12
❑ 55 J.D. Drew .40 .12
❑ 56 Sammy Sosa 1.00 .30
❑ 57 Kerry Wood .40 .12
❑ 58 Corey Patterson .40 .12
❑ 59 Mark Prior 1.00 .30
❑ 60 Randy Johnson 1.00 .30
❑ 61 Luis Gonzalez .40 .12
❑ 62 Curt Schilling .40 .12
❑ 63 Shawn Green .40 .12
❑ 64 Kevin Brown .40 .12
❑ 65 Hideo Nomo 1.00 .30
❑ 66 Vladimir Guerrero 1.00 .30
❑ 67 Jose Vidro .40 .12
❑ 68 Barry Bonds 2.50 .75
❑ 69 Jeff Kent .40 .12
❑ 70 Rich Aurilia .40 .12
❑ 71 Preston Wilson .40 .12
❑ 72 Josh Beckett .40 .12
❑ 73 Mike Lowell .40 .12
❑ 74 Roberto Alomar .60 .18
❑ 75 Mo Vaughn .40 .12
❑ 76 Jeromy Burnitz .40 .12
❑ 77 Mike Piazza 1.50 .45
❑ 78 Sean Burroughs .40 .12
❑ 79 Phil Nevin .40 .12
❑ 80 Bobby Abreu .40 .12
❑ 81 Pat Burrell .40 .12
❑ 82 Scott Rolen .60 .18
❑ 83 Jason Kendall .40 .12
❑ 84 Brian Giles .40 .12
❑ 85 Ken Griffey Jr. 1.50 .45
❑ 86 Adam Dunn .40 .12
❑ 87 Sean Casey .60 .18
❑ 88 Todd Helton .60 .18
❑ 89 Larry Walker .40 .12
❑ 90 Mike Hampton .40 .12
❑ 91 Brandon Puffer FW 5.00 1.50
❑ 92 Tom Shearn FW RC 5.00 1.50
❑ 93 Chris Baker FW RC 5.00 1.50
❑ 94 Gustavo Chacin FW RC 8.00 2.40
❑ 95 Joe Orloski FW RC 5.00 1.50
❑ 96 Mike Smith FW RC 5.00 1.50
❑ 97 John Ennis FW RC 5.00 1.50
❑ 98 John Foster FW RC 5.00 1.50
❑ 99 Kevin Gryboski FW RC 5.00 1.50
❑ 100 Brian Mallette FW RC 5.00 1.50
❑ 101 Takahito Nomura FW RC 5.00 1.50
❑ 102 So Taguchi FW RC 8.00 2.40
❑ 103 Jeremy Lambert FW RC 5.00 1.50
❑ 104 J.Simontacchi FW RC 5.00 1.50
❑ 105 Jorge Sosa FW RC 8.00 2.40
❑ 106 Brandon Backe FW RC 8.00 2.40
❑ 107 P.J. Bevis FW RC 5.00 1.50
❑ 108 Jeremy Ward FW RC 5.00 1.50
❑ 109 Doug Devore FW RC 5.00 1.50
❑ 110 Ron Chiavacci FW 5.00 1.50
❑ 111 Ron Calloway FW RC 5.00 1.50
❑ 112 Nelson Castro FW RC 5.00 1.50
❑ 113 Deivis Santos FW 5.00 1.50
❑ 114 Earl Snyder FW RC 5.00 1.50
❑ 115 Julio Mateo FW RC 5.00 1.50
❑ 116 J.J. Putz FW RC 5.00 1.50
❑ 117 Allan Simpson FW RC 5.00 1.50
❑ 118 Satoru Komiyama FW RC 5.00 1.50
❑ 119 Adam Walker FW RC 5.00 1.50
❑ 120 Oliver Perez FW RC 10.00 3.00
❑ 121 Cliff Bartosh FW RC 5.00 1.50
❑ 122 Todd Donovan FW RC 5.00 1.50
❑ 123 Elio Serrano FW RC 5.00 1.50
❑ 124 Pete Zamora FW RC 5.00 1.50
❑ 125 Mike Gonzalez FW RC 5.00 1.50
❑ 126 Travis Hughes FW RC 5.00 1.50
❑ 127 J.De La Rosa FW RC 5.00 1.50
❑ 128 An.Martinez FW RC 5.00 1.50
❑ 129 Colin Young FW RC 5.00 1.50
❑ 130 Nate Field FW RC 5.00 1.50
❑ 131 Tim Kalita FW RC 5.00 1.50
❑ 132 Julius Matos FW RC 5.00 1.50
❑ 133 Terry Pearson FW RC 5.00 1.50
❑ 134 Kyle Kane FW RC 5.00 1.50
❑ 135 Mitch Wylie FW RC 5.00 1.50
❑ 136 Rodrigo Rosario AU RC 15.00 4.50
❑ 137 Franklyn German AU RC 15.00 4.50
❑ 138 Reed Johnson AU RC 20.00 6.00
❑ 139 Luis Martinez AU RC 15.00 4.50
❑ 140 Michael Crudale AU RC 15.00 4.50
❑ 141 Francis Beltran AU RC 15.00 4.50
❑ 142 Steve Kent AU RC 15.00 4.50
❑ 143 Felix Escalona AU RC 15.00 4.50
❑ 144 Jose Valverde AU RC 15.00 4.50
❑ 145 Victor Alvarez AU RC 15.00 4.50
❑ 146 Kazuhisa Ishii AU/249 RC 40.00 12.00
❑ 147 Jorge Nunez AU RC 15.00 4.50
❑ 148 Eric Good AU RC 15.00 4.50
❑ 149 Luis Ugueto AU RC 15.00 4.50
❑ 150 Matt Thornton AU RC 15.00 4.50
❑ 151 Wilson Valdez AU RC 15.00 4.50
❑ 152 Han Izquierdo AU/249 RC 40.00 12.00
❑ 153 Jaime Cerda AU RC 15.00 4.50
❑ 154 Mark Corey AU RC 15.00 4.50
❑ 155 Tyler Yates AU RC 15.00 4.50
❑ 156 Steve Bechler AU RC 15.00 4.50
❑ 157 Ben Howard AU/249 RC 40.00 12.00
❑ 158 And. Machado AU RC 15.00 4.50
❑ 159 Jorge Padilla AU RC 15.00 4.50
❑ 160 Eric Junge AU RC 15.00 4.50
❑ 161 Adrian Burnside AU RC 15.00 4.50
❑ 162 Josh Hancock AU RC 15.00 4.50
❑ 163 Chris Booker AU RC 15.00 4.50
❑ 164 Cam Esslinger AU RC 15.00 4.50
❑ 165 Rene Reyes AU RC 15.00 4.50
❑ 166 Aaron Cook AU RC 15.00 4.50
❑ 167 Juan Brito AU RC 15.00 4.50
❑ 168 Miguel Ascencio AU RC 15.00 4.50
❑ 169 Kevin Frederick AU RC 15.00 4.50
❑ 170 Edwin Almonte AU RC 15.00 4.50
❑ 171 Erubiel Durazo .60 .18
❑ 172 Junior Spivey .60 .18
❑ 173 Geronimo Gil .60 .18
❑ 174 Cliff Floyd .60 .18
❑ 175 Brandon Larson .60 .18
❑ 176 Aaron Boone .60 .18
❑ 177 Shawn Estes .60 .18
❑ 178 Austin Kearns .60 .18
❑ 179 Joe Borchard .60 .18
❑ 180 Russell Branyan .60 .18
❑ 181 Jay Payton .60 .18
❑ 182 Andres Torres .60 .18
❑ 183 Andy Van Hekken .60 .18
❑ 184 Alex Sanchez .60 .18
❑ 185 Endy Chavez .60 .18
❑ 186 Bartolo Colon .60 .18
❑ 187 Raul Mondesi .60 .18
❑ 188 Robin Ventura .60 .18
❑ 189 Mike Mussina 1.00 .30
❑ 190 Jorge Posada 1.00 .30
❑ 191 Ted Lilly .60 .18
❑ 192 Ray Durham .60 .18
❑ 193 Brett Myers .60 .18
❑ 194 Marlon Byrd .60 .18
❑ 195 Vicente Padilla .60 .18
❑ 196 Josh Fogg .60 .18
❑ 197 Kenny Lofton .60 .18
❑ 198 Scott Rolen 1.00 .30

Card	Nm-Mt	Ex-Mt
199 Jason Lane	.60	.18
200 Josh Phelps	.60	.18
201 Travis Driskill FW RC	5.00	1.50
202 Howie Clark FW RC	5.00	1.50
203 Mike Mahoney FW	5.00	1.50
204 Brian Tallet FW RC	5.00	1.50
205 Kirk Saarloos FW RC	5.00	1.50
206 Barry Wesson FW RC	5.00	1.50
207 Aaron Guiel FW RC	5.00	1.50
208 Shawn Sedlacek FW RC	5.00	1.50
209 Jose Diaz FW RC	5.00	1.50
210 Jorge Nunez FW	5.00	1.50
211 Danny Mota FW RC	5.00	1.50
212 David Ross FW RC	5.00	1.50
213 Jayson Durocher FW RC	5.00	1.50
214 Shane Nance FW RC	5.00	1.50
215 Wil Nieves FW RC	5.00	1.50
216 Freddy Sanchez FW RC	5.00	1.50
217 Alex Pelaez FW RC	5.00	1.50
218 Jamey Carroll FW RC	5.00	1.50
219 J.J. Trujillo FW RC	5.00	1.50
220 Kevin Pickford FW RC	5.00	1.50
221 Clay Condrey FW RC	5.00	1.50
222 Chris Snelling FW RC	8.00	2.40
223 Cliff Lee FW RC	8.00	2.40
224 Jeremy Hill FW RC	5.00	1.50
225 Jose Rodriguez FW RC	5.00	1.50
226 Lance Carter FW RC	5.00	1.50
227 Ken Huckaby FW RC	5.00	1.50
228 Scott Wiggins FW RC	5.00	1.50
229 Corey Thurman FW RC	5.00	1.50
230 Kevin Cash FW RC	5.00	1.50
RJ-D Joe DiMaggio AU Poster	200.00	60.00

2003 SP Authentic

	Nm-Mt	Ex-Mt
COMP.LO SET w/o SP's (90)	15.00	4.50
COMMON CARD (1-90)	.40	.12
COMMON CARD (91-123)	3.00	.90
COMMON CARD (124-150)	3.00	.90
COMMON CARD (151-180)	5.00	1.50
COMMON CARD (181-189)	15.00	4.50
91-189 RANDOM INSERTS IN PACKS		.00
COMMON CARD (190-239)	5.00	1.50
190-239 RANDOM IN 03 UD FINITE PACKS		.00
190-239 PRINT RUN 699 SERIAL #'d SETS		.00

Card	Nm-Mt	Ex-Mt
1 Darin Erstad	.40	.12
2 Garret Anderson	.40	.12
3 Troy Glaus	.40	.12
4 Eric Chavez	.40	.12
5 Barry Zito	.40	.12
6 Miguel Tejada	.40	.12
7 Eric Hinske	.40	.12
8 Carlos Delgado	.40	.12
9 Josh Phelps	.40	.12
10 Ben Grieve	.40	.12
11 Carl Crawford	.40	.12
12 Omar Vizquel	.60	.18
13 Matt Lawton	.40	.12
14 C.C. Sabathia	.40	.12
15 Ichiro Suzuki	2.00	.60
16 John Olerud	.40	.12
17 Freddy Garcia	.40	.12
18 Jay Gibbons	.40	.12
19 Tony Batista	.40	.12
20 Melvin Mora	.40	.12
21 Alex Rodriguez	1.50	.45
22 Rafael Palmeiro	.60	.18
23 Hank Blalock	.40	.12
24 Nomar Garciaparra	1.50	.45
25 Pedro Martinez	.60	.18
26 Johnny Damon	.60	.18
27 Mike Sweeney	.40	.12
28 Carlos Febles	.40	.12
29 Carlos Beltran	.40	.12
30 Carlos Pena	.40	.12
31 Eric Munson	.40	.12
32 Bobby Higginson	.40	.12
33 Torii Hunter	.40	.12
34 Doug Mientkiewicz	.40	.12
35 Jacque Jones	.40	.12
36 Paul Konerko	.40	.12
37 Bartolo Colon	.40	.12
38 Magglio Ordonez	.40	.12
39 Derek Jeter	2.50	.75
40 Bernie Williams	.60	.18
41 Jason Giambi	.40	.12
42 Alfonso Soriano	.40	.12
43 Roger Clemens	2.00	.60
44 Jeff Bagwell	.60	.18
45 Jeff Kent	.40	.12
46 Lance Berkman	.40	.12
47 Chipper Jones	1.00	.30
48 Andruw Jones	.60	.18
49 Gary Sheffield	.40	.12
50 Ben Sheets	.40	.12
51 Richie Sexson	.40	.12
52 Geoff Jenkins	.40	.12
53 Jim Edmonds	.60	.18
54 Albert Pujols	2.00	.60
55 Scott Rolen	.60	.18
56 Sammy Sosa	1.00	.30
57 Kerry Wood	.40	.12
58 Eric Karros	.40	.12
59 Luis Gonzalez	.40	.12
60 Randy Johnson	1.00	.30
61 Curt Schilling	.40	.12
62 Fred McGriff	.60	.18
63 Shawn Green	.40	.12
64 Paul Lo Duca	.40	.12
65 Vladimir Guerrero	1.00	.30
66 Jose Vidro	.40	.12
67 Barry Bonds	2.50	.75
68 Rich Aurilia	.40	.12
69 Edgardo Alfonzo	.40	.12
70 Ivan Rodriguez	.60	.18
71 Mike Lowell	.40	.12
72 Derrek Lee	.60	.18
73 Tom Glavine	.60	.18
74 Mike Piazza	1.50	.45
75 Roberto Alomar	.60	.18
76 Ryan Klesko	.40	.12
77 Phil Nevin	.40	.12
78 Mark Kotsay	.40	.12
79 Jim Thome	.60	.18
80 Pat Burrell	.40	.12
81 Bobby Abreu	.40	.12
82 Jason Kendall	.40	.12
83 Brian Giles	.40	.12
84 Aramis Ramirez	.40	.12
85 Austin Kearns	.40	.12
86 Ken Griffey Jr.	1.50	.45
87 Adam Dunn	.40	.12
88 Larry Walker	.40	.12
89 Todd Helton	.60	.18
90 Preston Wilson	.40	.12
91 Derek Jeter RA	8.00	2.40
92 Johnny Damon RA	3.00	.90
93 Chipper Jones RA	3.00	.90
94 Manny Ramirez RA	3.00	.90
95 Trot Nixon RA	3.00	.90
96 Alex Rodriguez RA	5.00	1.50
97 Chan Ho Park RA	3.00	.90
98 Brad Fullmer RA	3.00	.90
99 Billy Wagner RA	3.00	.90
100 Hideo Nomo RA	3.00	.90
101 Freddy Garcia RA	3.00	.90
102 Darin Erstad RA	3.00	.90
103 Jose Cruz Jr. RA	3.00	.90
104 Nomar Garciaparra RA	5.00	1.50
105 Magglio Ordonez RA	3.00	.90
106 Kerry Wood RA	3.00	.90
107 Troy Glaus RA	3.00	.90
108 J.D. Drew RA	3.00	.90
109 Alfonso Soriano RA	3.00	.90
110 Danys Baez RA	3.00	.90
111 Kazuhiro Sasaki RA	3.00	.90
112 Barry Zito RA	3.00	.90
113 Brent Abernathy RA	3.00	.90
114 Ben Diggins RA	3.00	.90
115 Ben Sheets RA	3.00	.90
116 Brad Wilkerson RA	3.00	.90
117 Juan Pierre RA	3.00	.90
118 Jon Rauch RA	3.00	.90
119 Ichiro Suzuki RA	6.00	1.80
120 Albert Pujols RA	6.00	1.80
121 Mark Prior RA	3.00	.90
122 Mark Teixeira RA	3.00	.90
123 Kazuhisa Ishii RA	3.00	.90
124 Troy Glaus B93	3.00	.90
125 Randy Johnson B93	3.00	.90
126 Curt Schilling B93	3.00	.90
127 Chipper Jones B93	3.00	.90
128 Greg Maddux B93	5.00	1.50
129 Nomar Garciaparra B93	5.00	1.50
130 Pedro Martinez B93	3.00	.90
131 Sammy Sosa B93	3.00	.90
132 Mark Prior B93	3.00	.90
133 Ken Griffey Jr. B93	5.00	1.50
134 Adam Dunn B93	3.00	.90
135 Jeff Bagwell B93	3.00	.90
136 Vladimir Guerrero B93	3.00	.90
137 Mike Piazza B93	5.00	1.50
138 Tom Glavine B93	3.00	.90
139 Derek Jeter B93	8.00	2.40
140 Roger Clemens B93	6.00	1.80
141 Jason Giambi B93	3.00	.90
142 Alfonso Soriano B93	3.00	.90
143 Miguel Tejada B93	3.00	.90
144 Barry Zito B93	3.00	.90
145 Jim Thome B93	3.00	.90
146 Barry Bonds B93	8.00	2.40
147 Ichiro Suzuki B93	6.00	1.80
148 Albert Pujols B93	6.00	1.80
149 Alex Rodriguez B93	5.00	1.50
150 Carlos Delgado B93	3.00	.90
151 Rich Fischer FW RC	5.00	1.50
152 Brandon Webb FW RC	8.00	2.40
153 Rob Hammock FW RC	5.00	1.50
154 Matt Kata FW RC	5.00	1.50
155 Tim Olson FW RC	5.00	1.50
156 Oscar Villarreal FW RC	5.00	1.50
157 Michael Hessman FW RC	5.00	1.50
158 Daniel Cabrera FW RC	8.00	2.40
159 Jon Leicester FW RC	5.00	1.50
160 Todd Wellemeyer FW RC	5.00	1.50
161 Felix Sanchez FW RC	5.00	1.50
162 David Sanders FW RC	5.00	1.50
163 Josh Stewart FW RC	5.00	1.50
164 Arnie Munoz FW RC	5.00	1.50
165 Ryan Cameron FW RC	5.00	1.50
166 Clint Barmes FW RC	8.00	2.40
167 Josh Willingham FW RC	8.00	2.40
169 Willie Eyre FW RC	5.00	1.50
170 Brent Hoard FW RC	5.00	1.50
171 Terrmel Sledge FW RC	5.00	1.50
172 Phil Seibel FW RC	5.00	1.50
173 Craig Brazell FW RC	5.00	1.50
174 Jeff Duncan FW RC	5.00	1.50
176 Bernie Castro FW RC	5.00	1.50
177 Mike Nicolas FW RC	5.00	1.50
178 Rett Johnson FW RC	5.00	1.50
179 Bobby Madritsch FW RC	8.00	2.40
180 Chris Capuano FW RC	5.00	1.50
181 Hid Matsui FW AU RC	300.00	90.00
182 J.Contreras FW AU RC	25.00	7.50
183 Lew Ford FW AU RC	25.00	7.50
184 Jer. Griffiths FW AU RC	15.00	4.50
185 G.Quiroz FW AU RC	15.00	4.50
186 Alej Machado FW AU RC	15.00	4.50
187 Fran Cruceta FW AU RC	15.00	4.50
188 Pr. Redman FW AU RC	15.00	4.50
189 S.Bazzell FW AU RC	15.00	4.50
190 Aaron Looper FW RC	5.00	1.50
191 Alex Prieto FW RC	5.00	1.50
192 Alfredo Gonzalez FW RC	5.00	1.50
193 Andrew Brown FW RC	8.00	2.40
194 Anthony Ferrari FW RC	5.00	1.50
195 Aquilino Lopez FW RC	5.00	1.50

❑ 196 Beau Kemp FW RC	5.00	1.50
❑ 197 Bo Hart FW RC	5.00	1.50
❑ 198 Chad Gaudin FW RC	5.00	1.50
❑ 199 Colin Porter FW RC	5.00	1.50
❑ 200 D.J. Carrasco FW RC	5.00	1.50
❑ 201 Dan Haren FW RC	8.00	2.40
❑ 202 Danny Garcia FW RC	5.00	1.50
❑ 203 Jon Switzer FW	5.00	1.50
❑ 204 Edwin Jackson FW RC	8.00	2.40
❑ 205 Fernando Cabrera FW RC	5.00	1.50
❑ 206 Garrett Atkins FW	5.00	1.50
❑ 207 Gerald Laird FW	5.00	1.50
❑ 208 Greg Jones FW RC	5.00	1.50
❑ 209 Ian Ferguson FW RC	5.00	1.50
❑ 210 Jason Roach FW RC	5.00	1.50
❑ 211 Jason Shiell FW RC	5.00	1.50
❑ 212 Jeremy Bonderman FW RC	20.00	6.00
❑ 213 Jeremy Wedel FW RC	5.00	1.50
❑ 214 Jhonny Peralta FW	8.00	2.40
❑ 215 Delmon Young FW RC	40.00	12.00
❑ 216 Jorge DePaula FW	5.00	1.50
❑ 217 Josh Hall FW RC	5.00	1.50
❑ 218 Julio Manon FW RC	5.00	1.50
❑ 219 Kevin Correia FW RC	5.00	1.50
❑ 220 Kevin Ohme FW RC	5.00	1.50
❑ 221 Kevin Tolar FW RC	5.00	1.50
❑ 222 Luis Ayala FW RC	5.00	1.50
❑ 223 Luis De Los Santos FW	5.00	1.50
❑ 224 Chad Cordero FW RC	10.00	3.00
❑ 225 Mark Malaska FW RC	5.00	1.50
❑ 226 Khalil Greene FW	10.00	3.00
❑ 227 Michael Nakamura FW RC	5.00	1.50
❑ 228 Michel Hernandez FW RC	5.00	1.50
❑ 229 Miguel Ojeda FW RC	5.00	1.50
❑ 230 Mike Neu FW RC	5.00	1.50
❑ 231 Nate Bland FW RC	5.00	1.50
❑ 232 Pete LaForest FW RC	5.00	1.50
❑ 233 Rickie Weeks FW RC	25.00	7.50
❑ 234 Rosman Garcia FW RC	5.00	1.50
❑ 235 Ryan Wagner FW RC	5.00	1.50
❑ 236 Lance Niekro FW	5.00	1.50
❑ 237 Tom Gregorio FW RC	5.00	1.50
❑ 238 Tommy Phelps FW	5.00	1.50
❑ 239 Wilfredo Ledezma FW RC	5.00	1.50

2004 SP Authentic

	Nm-Mt	Ex-Mt
COMP.SET w/o SP's (90)	15.00	4.50
COMMON CARD (1-90)	.40	.12
COMMON (91-132/178-191)	5.00	1.50
91-132/178-191 OVERALL FW ODDS 1:24		.00
91-132/178-179/181-191 PRINT 704 #'d SETS		
91-132/178-179/181-191 #'d FROM 296-999		.00
CARD 180 PRINT RUN 999 #'d COPIES		.00
CARD 180 #'d FROM 1-999	.00	
COMMON CARD (133-177)	3.00	.90
133-177 STATED ODDS 1:24	.00	
133-177 PRINT RUN 999 SERIAL #'d SETS		.00

❑ 1 Bret Boone	.40	.12
❑ 2 Gary Sheffield	.40	.12
❑ 3 Rafael Palmeiro	.60	.18
❑ 4 Jorge Posada	.60	.18
❑ 5 Derek Jeter	2.00	.60
❑ 6 Garret Anderson	.40	.12
❑ 7 Bartolo Colon	.40	.12
❑ 8 Kevin Brown	.40	.12
❑ 9 Shea Hillenbrand	.40	.12
❑ 10 Ryan Klesko	.40	.12
❑ 11 Bobby Abreu	.40	.12
❑ 12 Scott Rolen	.60	.18
❑ 13 Alfonso Soriano	.40	.12
❑ 14 Jason Giambi	.40	.12
❑ 15 Tom Glavine	.60	.18
❑ 16 Hideo Nomo	1.00	.30
❑ 17 Johan Santana	.60	.18
❑ 18 Sammy Sosa	1.00	.30
❑ 19 Rickie Weeks	.60	.18
❑ 20 Barry Zito	.40	.12
❑ 21 Kerry Wood	.40	.12
❑ 22 Austin Kearns	.40	.12
❑ 23 Shawn Green	.40	.12
❑ 24 Miguel Cabrera	.60	.18
❑ 25 Richard Hidalgo	.40	.12
❑ 26 Andruw Jones	.60	.18
❑ 27 Randy Wolf	.40	.12
❑ 28 David Ortiz	1.00	.30
❑ 29 Roy Oswalt	.40	.12
❑ 30 Vernon Wells	.40	.12
❑ 31 Ben Sheets	.40	.12
❑ 32 Mike Lowell	.40	.12
❑ 33 Todd Helton	.60	.18
❑ 34 Jacque Jones	.40	.12
❑ 35 Mike Sweeney	.40	.12
❑ 36 Hank Blalock	.40	.12
❑ 37 Jason Schmidt	.40	.12
❑ 38 Jeff Kent	.40	.12
❑ 39 Josh Beckett	.40	.12
❑ 40 Manny Ramirez	.60	.18
❑ 41 Torii Hunter	.40	.12
❑ 42 Brian Giles	.40	.12
❑ 43 Javier Vazquez	.40	.12
❑ 44 Jim Edmonds	.60	.18
❑ 45 Dmitri Young	.40	.12
❑ 46 Preston Wilson	.40	.12
❑ 47 Jeff Bagwell	.60	.18
❑ 48 Pedro Martinez	.60	.18
❑ 49 Eric Chavez	.40	.12
❑ 50 Ken Griffey Jr.	1.50	.45
❑ 51 Shannon Stewart	.40	.12
❑ 52 Rafael Furcal	.40	.12
❑ 53 Brandon Webb	.40	.12
❑ 54 Juan Pierre	.40	.12
❑ 55 Roger Clemens	2.00	.60
❑ 56 Geoff Jenkins	.40	.12
❑ 57 Lance Berkman	.40	.12
❑ 58 Albert Pujols	2.00	.60
❑ 59 Frank Thomas	1.00	.30
❑ 60 Edgar Martinez	.60	.18
❑ 61 Tim Hudson	.40	.12
❑ 62 Eric Gagne	.40	.12
❑ 63 Richie Sexson	.40	.12
❑ 64 Corey Patterson	.40	.12
❑ 65 Nomar Garciaparra	1.50	.45
❑ 66 Hideki Matsui	2.00	.60
❑ 67 Mark Teixeira	.60	.18
❑ 68 Troy Glaus	.40	.12
❑ 69 Carlos Lee	.40	.12
❑ 70 Mike Mussina	.60	.18
❑ 71 Magglio Ordonez	.40	.12
❑ 72 Roy Halladay	.40	.12
❑ 73 Ichiro Suzuki	2.00	.60
❑ 74 Randy Johnson	1.00	.30
❑ 75 Luis Gonzalez	.40	.12
❑ 76 Mark Prior	.60	.18
❑ 77 Carlos Beltran	.40	.12
❑ 78 Ivan Rodriguez	.60	.18
❑ 79 Alex Rodriguez	1.50	.45
❑ 80 Dontrelle Willis	.60	.18
❑ 81 Mike Piazza	1.50	.45
❑ 82 Curt Schilling	.60	.18
❑ 83 Vladimir Guerrero	1.00	.30
❑ 84 Greg Maddux	1.50	.45
❑ 85 Jim Thome	.60	.18
❑ 86 Miguel Tejada	.40	.12
❑ 87 Carlos Delgado	.40	.12
❑ 88 Jose Reyes	.40	.12
❑ 89 Matt Morris	.40	.12
❑ 90 Mark Mulder	.40	.12
❑ 91 Angel Chavez FW RC	5.00	1.50
❑ 92 Brandon Medders FW RC	5.00	1.50
❑ 93 Carlos Vasquez FW RC	5.00	1.50
❑ 94 Chris Aguila FW RC	5.00	1.50
❑ 95 Colby Miller FW RC	5.00	1.50
❑ 96 Dave Crouthers FW RC	5.00	1.50
❑ 97 Dennis Sarfate FW RC	5.00	1.50
❑ 98 Donnie Kelly FW RC	5.00	1.50
❑ 99 Merkin Valdez FW RC	5.00	1.50
❑ 100 Eddy Rodriguez FW RC	5.00	1.50
❑ 101 Edwin Moreno FW RC	5.00	1.50
❑ 102 Enemencio Pacheco FW RC	5.00	1.50
❑ 103 Roberto Novoa FW RC	5.00	1.50
❑ 104 Greg Dobbs FW RC	5.00	1.50
❑ 105 Hector Gimenez FW RC	5.00	1.50
❑ 106 Ian Snell FW RC	8.00	2.40
❑ 107 Jake Woods FW RC	5.00	1.50
❑ 108 Jamie Brown FW RC	5.00	1.50
❑ 109 Jason Frasor FW RC	5.00	1.50
❑ 110 Jerome Gamble FW RC	5.00	1.50
❑ 111 Jerry Gil FW RC	5.00	1.50
❑ 112 Jesse Harper FW RC	5.00	1.50
❑ 113 Jorge Vasquez FW RC	5.00	1.50
❑ 114 Jose Capellan FW RC	5.00	1.50
❑ 115 Josh Labandeira FW RC	5.00	1.50
❑ 116 Justin Hampson FW RC	5.00	1.50
❑ 117 Justin Huisman FW RC	5.00	1.50
❑ 118 Justin Leone FW RC	5.00	1.50
❑ 119 Lincoln Holdzkom FW RC	5.00	1.50
❑ 120 Lino Urdaneta FW RC	5.00	1.50
❑ 121 Mike Gosling FW RC	5.00	1.50
❑ 122 Mike Johnston FW RC	5.00	1.50
❑ 123 Mike Rouse FW RC	5.00	1.50
❑ 124 Scott Proctor FW RC	5.00	1.50
❑ 125 Roman Colon FW RC	5.00	1.50
❑ 126 Ronny Cedeno FW RC	8.00	2.40
❑ 127 Ryan Meaux FW RC	5.00	1.50
❑ 128 Scott Dohmann FW RC	5.00	1.50
❑ 129 Sean Henn FW RC	5.00	1.50
❑ 130 Tim Bausher FW RC	5.00	1.50
❑ 131 Tim Bittner FW RC	5.00	1.50
❑ 132 William Bergolla FW RC	5.00	1.50
❑ 133 Rick Ferrell ASM	3.00	.90
❑ 134 Joe DiMaggio ASM	5.00	1.50
❑ 135 Bob Feller ASM	3.00	.90
❑ 136 Ted Williams ASM	8.00	2.40
❑ 137 Stan Musial ASM	5.00	1.50
❑ 138 Larry Doby ASM	3.00	.90
❑ 139 Red Schoendienst ASM	3.00	.90
❑ 140 Enos Slaughter ASM	3.00	.90
❑ 141 Stan Musial ASM	5.00	1.50
❑ 142 Mickey Mantle ASM	10.00	3.00
❑ 143 Ted Williams ASM	8.00	2.40
❑ 144 Mickey Mantle ASM	10.00	3.00
❑ 145 Stan Musial ASM	5.00	1.50
❑ 146 Tom Seaver ASM	4.00	1.20
❑ 147 Willie McCovey ASM	4.00	1.20
❑ 148 Bob Gibson ASM	4.00	1.20
❑ 149 Frank Robinson ASM	3.00	.90
❑ 150 Joe Morgan ASM	3.00	.90
❑ 151 Billy Williams ASM	3.00	.90
❑ 152 Catfish Hunter ASM	4.00	1.20
❑ 153 Joe Morgan ASM	3.00	.90
❑ 154 Joe Morgan ASM	3.00	.90
❑ 155 Mike Schmidt ASM	8.00	2.40
❑ 156 Tommy Lasorda ASM	3.00	.90
❑ 157 Robin Yount ASM	4.00	1.20
❑ 158 Nolan Ryan ASM	10.00	3.00
❑ 159 John Franco ASM	3.00	.90
❑ 160 Nolan Ryan ASM	10.00	3.00
❑ 161 Ken Griffey Jr. ASM	5.00	1.50
❑ 162 Cal Ripken ASM	10.00	3.00
❑ 163 Ken Griffey Jr. ASM	5.00	1.50
❑ 164 Gary Sheffield ASM	3.00	.90
❑ 165 Fred McGriff ASM	4.00	1.20
❑ 166 Hideo Nomo ASM	4.00	1.20
❑ 167 Mike Piazza ASM	5.00	1.50
❑ 168 Sandy Alomar Jr. ASM	3.00	.90
❑ 169 Roberto Alomar ASM	4.00	1.20
❑ 170 Ted Williams ASM	8.00	2.40
❑ 171 Pedro Martinez ASM	4.00	1.20
❑ 172 Derek Jeter ASM	6.00	1.80
❑ 173 Cal Ripken ASM	10.00	3.00
❑ 174 Torii Hunter ASM	3.00	.90
❑ 175 Alfonso Soriano ASM	3.00	.90
❑ 176 Hank Blalock ASM	3.00	.90
❑ 177 Ichiro Suzuki ASM	6.00	1.80
❑ 178 Orlando Rodriguez FW RC	5.00	1.50
❑ 179 Ramon Ramirez FW RC	5.00	1.50
❑ 180 Kazuo Matsui FW RC	8.00	2.40
❑ 181 Kevin Cave FW RC	5.00	1.50

Card	Nm-Mt	Ex-Mt
❑ 182 John Gall FW RC	5.00	1.50
❑ 183 Freddy Guzman FW RC	5.00	1.50
❑ 184 Chris Oxspring FW RC	5.00	1.50
❑ 185 Rusty Tucker FW RC	5.00	1.50
❑ 186 Jorge Sequea FW RC	5.00	1.50
❑ 187 Carlos Hines FW RC	5.00	1.50
❑ 188 Michael Vento FW RC	5.00	1.50
❑ 189 Ryan Wing FW RC	5.00	1.50
❑ 190 Jeff Bennett FW RC	5.00	1.50
❑ 191 Luis A. Gonzalez FW RC	5.00	1.50

2005 SP Authentic

	Nm-Mt	Ex-Mt
COMPLETE SET (100)	25.00	7.50
COMMON CARD (1-100)	.40	.12
COMMON RETIRED	.40	.12
ISSUED IN 05 SP COLLECTION PACKS		.00
❑ 1 A.J. Burnett	.40	.12
❑ 2 Aaron Rowand	.40	.12
❑ 3 Adam Dunn	.40	.12
❑ 4 Adrian Beltre	.40	.12
❑ 5 Adrian Gonzalez	.40	.12
❑ 6 Akinori Otsuka	.40	.12
❑ 7 Albert Pujols	2.00	.60
❑ 8 Andre Dawson	.40	.12
❑ 9 Andruw Jones	.60	.18
❑ 10 Aramis Ramirez	.40	.12
❑ 11 Barry Larkin	.60	.18
❑ 12 Ben Sheets	.40	.12
❑ 13 Bo Jackson	1.00	.30
❑ 14 Bobby Abreu	.40	.12
❑ 15 Bobby Crosby	.40	.12
❑ 16 Bronson Arroyo	.40	.12
❑ 17 Cal Ripken	3.00	.90
❑ 18 Carl Crawford	.40	.12
❑ 19 Carlos Zambrano	.40	.12
❑ 20 Casey Kotchman	.40	.12
❑ 21 Cesar Izturis	.40	.12
❑ 22 Chone Figgins	.40	.12
❑ 23 Corey Patterson	.40	.12
❑ 24 Craig Biggio	.60	.18
❑ 25 Dale Murphy	.60	.18
❑ 26 Dallas McPherson	.40	.12
❑ 27 Danny Haren	.40	.12
❑ 28 Darryl Strawberry	.40	.12
❑ 29 David Ortiz	1.00	.30
❑ 30 David Wright	1.50	.45
❑ 31 Derek Jeter	2.00	.60
❑ 32 Derrek Lee	.60	.18
❑ 33 Don Mattingly	2.00	.60
❑ 34 Dwight Gooden	.40	.12
❑ 35 Edgar Renteria	.40	.12
❑ 36 Eric Chavez	.40	.12
❑ 37 Eric Gagne	.40	.12
❑ 38 Gary Sheffield	.40	.12
❑ 39 Gavin Floyd	.40	.12
❑ 40 Pedro Martinez	.60	.18
❑ 41 Greg Maddux	1.50	.45
❑ 42 Hank Blalock	.40	.12
❑ 43 Huston Street	.60	.18
❑ 44 J.D. Drew	.40	.12
❑ 45 Jake Peavy	.40	.12
❑ 46 Jake Westbrook	.40	.12
❑ 47 Jason Bay	.40	.12
❑ 48 Austin Kearns	.40	.12
❑ 49 Jeremy Reed	.40	.12
❑ 50 Jim Rice	.40	.12
❑ 51 Jimmy Rollins	.40	.12
❑ 52 Joe Blanton	.40	.12
❑ 53 Joe Mauer	.40	.12
❑ 54 Johan Santana	.60	.18
❑ 55 John Smoltz	.60	.18
❑ 56 Johnny Estrada	.40	.12
❑ 57 Jose Reyes	.40	.12
❑ 58 Ken Griffey Jr.	1.50	.45
❑ 59 Kerry Wood	.40	.12
❑ 60 Khalil Greene	.60	.18
❑ 61 Marcus Giles	.40	.12
❑ 62 Melvin Mora	.40	.12
❑ 63 Mark Grace	.60	.18
❑ 64 Mark Mulder	.40	.12
❑ 65 Mark Prior	.60	.18
❑ 66 Mark Teixeria	.60	.18
❑ 67 Matt Clement	.40	.12
❑ 68 Michael Young	.40	.12
❑ 69 Miguel Cabrera	.60	.18
❑ 70 Miguel Tejada	.40	.12
❑ 71 Mike Piazza	1.00	.30
❑ 72 Mike Schmidt	2.00	.60
❑ 73 Nolan Ryan	2.50	.75
❑ 74 Oliver Perez	.40	.12
❑ 75 Nick Johnson	.40	.12
❑ 76 Paul Molitor	.60	.18
❑ 77 Rafael Palmeiro	.60	.18
❑ 78 Randy Johnson	1.00	.30
❑ 79 Reggie Jackson	.60	.18
❑ 80 Rich Harden	.40	.12
❑ 81 Rickie Weeks	.40	.12
❑ 82 Robin Yount	1.00	.30
❑ 83 Roger Clemens	1.50	.45
❑ 84 Roy Oswalt	.40	.12
❑ 85 Ryan Howard	.40	.12
❑ 86 Ryne Sandberg	2.00	.60
❑ 87 Scott Kazmir	.40	.12
❑ 88 Scott Rolen	.60	.18
❑ 89 Sean Burroughs	.40	.12
❑ 90 Sean Casey	.40	.12
❑ 91 Shingo Takatsu	.40	.12
❑ 92 Tim Hudson	.40	.12
❑ 93 Tony Gwynn	1.25	.35
❑ 94 Torii Hunter	.40	.12
❑ 95 Travis Hafner	.40	.12
❑ 96 Victor Martinez	.40	.12
❑ 97 Vladimir Guerrero	1.00	.30
❑ 98 Wade Boggs	.60	.18
❑ 99 Will Clark	.60	.18
❑ 100 Yadier Molina	.40	.12

2001 SP Game Bat Milestone

	Nm-Mt	Ex-Mt
COMP.SET w/o SP's (90)	80.00	24.00
COMMON CARD (1-90)	1.00	.30
COMMON BAT (91-96)	10.00	3.00
❑ 1 Troy Glaus	1.00	.30
❑ 2 Darin Erstad	1.00	.30
❑ 3 Jason Giambi	1.00	.30
❑ 4 Jermaine Dye	1.00	.30
❑ 5 Eric Chavez	1.00	.30
❑ 6 Carlos Delgado	1.00	.30
❑ 7 Raul Mondesi	1.00	.30
❑ 8 Shannon Stewart	1.00	.30
❑ 9 Greg Vaughn	1.00	.30
❑ 10 Aubrey Huff	1.00	.30
❑ 11 Juan Gonzalez	1.00	.30
❑ 12 Roberto Alomar	1.50	.45
❑ 13 Jim Thome	1.50	.45
❑ 14 Omar Vizquel	1.50	.45
❑ 15 Mike Cameron	1.00	.30
❑ 16 Edgar Martinez	1.50	.45
❑ 17 John Olerud	1.00	.30
❑ 18 Bret Boone	1.00	.30
❑ 19 Cal Ripken	8.00	2.40
❑ 20 Tony Batista	1.00	.30
❑ 21 Alex Rodriguez	4.00	1.20
❑ 22 Ivan Rodriguez	1.50	.45
❑ 23 Rafael Palmeiro	1.50	.45
❑ 24 Manny Ramirez Sox	1.50	.45
❑ 25 Pedro Martinez	1.50	.45
❑ 26 Nomar Garciaparra	4.00	1.20
❑ 27 Carl Everett	1.00	.30
❑ 28 Mike Sweeney	1.00	.30
❑ 29 Neifi Perez	1.00	.30
❑ 30 Mark Quinn	1.00	.30
❑ 31 Bobby Higginson	1.00	.30
❑ 32 Tony Clark	1.00	.30
❑ 33 Doug Mientkiewicz	1.00	.30
❑ 34 Cristian Guzman	1.00	.30
❑ 35 Joe Mays	1.00	.30
❑ 36 David Ortiz	1.50	.45
❑ 37 Frank Thomas	2.50	.75
❑ 38 Magglio Ordonez	1.00	.30
❑ 39 Carlos Lee	1.00	.30
❑ 40 Alfonso Soriano	1.50	.45
❑ 41 Bernie Williams	1.50	.45
❑ 42 Derek Jeter	6.00	1.80
❑ 43 Roger Clemens	5.00	1.50
❑ 44 Jeff Bagwell	1.50	.45
❑ 45 Richard Hidalgo	1.00	.30
❑ 46 Moises Alou	1.00	.30
❑ 47 Chipper Jones	2.50	.75
❑ 48 Greg Maddux	4.00	1.20
❑ 49 Rafael Furcal	1.00	.30
❑ 50 Andruw Jones	1.50	.45
❑ 51 Jeromy Burnitz	1.00	.30
❑ 52 Geoff Jenkins	1.00	.30
❑ 53 Richie Sexson	1.00	.30
❑ 54 Edgar Renteria	1.00	.30
❑ 55 Mark McGwire	6.00	1.80
❑ 56 Jim Edmonds	1.50	.45
❑ 57 J.D. Drew	1.00	.30
❑ 58 Sammy Sosa	2.50	.75
❑ 59 Fred McGriff	1.50	.45
❑ 60 Luis Gonzalez	1.00	.30
❑ 61 Randy Johnson	2.50	.75
❑ 62 Gary Sheffield	1.00	.30
❑ 63 Shawn Green	1.00	.30
❑ 64 Kevin Brown	1.00	.30
❑ 65 Vladimir Guerrero	2.50	.75
❑ 66 Jose Vidro	1.00	.30
❑ 67 Fernando Tatis	1.00	.30
❑ 68 Barry Bonds	6.00	1.80
❑ 69 Jeff Kent	1.00	.30
❑ 70 Rich Aurilia	1.00	.30
❑ 71 Preston Wilson	1.00	.30
❑ 72 Charles Johnson	1.00	.30
❑ 73 Cliff Floyd	1.00	.30
❑ 74 Mike Piazza	4.00	1.20
❑ 75 Matt Lawton	1.00	.30
❑ 76 Edgardo Alfonzo	1.00	.30
❑ 77 Tony Gwynn	3.00	.90
❑ 78 Phil Nevin	1.00	.30
❑ 79 Scott Rolen	1.50	.45
❑ 80 Pat Burrell	1.00	.30
❑ 81 Bobby Abreu	1.00	.30
❑ 82 Brian Giles	1.00	.30
❑ 83 Jason Kendall	1.00	.30
❑ 84 Aramis Ramirez	1.00	.30
❑ 85 Sean Casey	1.50	.45
❑ 86 Ken Griffey Jr.	4.00	1.20
❑ 87 Barry Larkin	1.50	.45
❑ 88 Todd Helton	1.50	.45
❑ 89 Mike Hampton	1.00	.30
❑ 90 Larry Walker	1.00	.30
❑ 91 Ichiro Suzuki BAT RC	100.00	30.00
❑ 92 Albert Pujols BAT RC	200.00	60.00
❑ 93 T. Shinjo BAT RC	15.00	4.50
❑ 94 Jack Wilson BAT RC	15.00	4.50
❑ 95 D. Mendez BAT RC	10.00	3.00
❑ 96 Junior Spivey BAT RC	15.00	4.50

2001 SP Game Used Edition

	Nm-Mt	Ex-Mt
COMP.SET w/o SP's (60)	80.00	24.00
COMMON CARD (1-60)	1.25	.35
COMMON CARD (61-90)	8.00	2.40

#	Player	Nm-Mt	Ex-Mt
❑ 1	Garret Anderson	1.25	.35
❑ 2	Troy Glaus	1.25	.35
❑ 3	Darin Erstad	1.25	.35
❑ 4	Jason Giambi	1.25	.35
❑ 5	Tim Hudson	1.25	.35
❑ 6	Johnny Damon	2.00	.60
❑ 7	Carlos Delgado	1.25	.35
❑ 8	Greg Vaughn	1.25	.35
❑ 9	Juan Gonzalez	1.25	.35
❑ 10	Roberto Alomar	2.00	.60
❑ 11	Jim Thome	2.00	.60
❑ 12	Edgar Martinez	2.00	.60
❑ 13	Cal Ripken	10.00	3.00
❑ 14	Andres Galarraga	1.25	.35
❑ 15	Alex Rodriguez	5.00	1.50
❑ 16	Rafael Palmeiro	2.00	.60
❑ 17	Ivan Rodriguez	2.00	.60
❑ 18	Manny Ramirez Sox	2.00	.60
❑ 19	Nomar Garciaparra	5.00	1.50
❑ 20	Pedro Martinez	2.00	.60
❑ 21	Jermaine Dye	1.25	.35
❑ 22	Dean Palmer	1.25	.35
❑ 23	Matt Lawton	1.25	.35
❑ 24	Frank Thomas	3.00	.90
❑ 25	David Wells	1.25	.35
❑ 26	Magglio Ordonez	1.25	.35
❑ 27	Derek Jeter	8.00	2.40
❑ 28	Bernie Williams	2.00	.60
❑ 29	Roger Clemens	6.00	1.80
❑ 30	Jeff Bagwell	2.00	.60
❑ 31	Richard Hidalgo	1.25	.35
❑ 32	Chipper Jones	3.00	.90
❑ 33	Andruw Jones	2.00	.60
❑ 34	Greg Maddux	5.00	1.50
❑ 35	Jeffrey Hammonds	1.25	.35
❑ 36	Mark McGwire	8.00	2.40
❑ 37	Jim Edmonds	2.00	.60
❑ 38	Sammy Sosa	3.00	.90
❑ 39	Corey Patterson	1.25	.35
❑ 40	Randy Johnson	3.00	.90
❑ 41	Luis Gonzalez	1.25	.35
❑ 42	Gary Sheffield	1.25	.35
❑ 43	Shawn Green	1.25	.35
❑ 44	Kevin Brown	1.25	.35
❑ 45	Vladimir Guerrero	3.00	.90
❑ 46	Barry Bonds	8.00	2.40
❑ 47	Jeff Kent	1.25	.35
❑ 48	Preston Wilson	1.25	.35
❑ 49	Charles Johnson	1.25	.35
❑ 50	Mike Piazza	5.00	1.50
❑ 51	Edgardo Alfonzo	1.25	.35
❑ 52	Tony Gwynn	4.00	1.20
❑ 53	Scott Rolen	2.00	.60
❑ 54	Pat Burrell	1.25	.35
❑ 55	Brian Giles	1.25	.35
❑ 56	Jason Kendall	1.25	.35
❑ 57	Ken Griffey Jr.	5.00	1.50
❑ 58	Mike Hampton	1.25	.35
❑ 59	Todd Helton	2.00	.60
❑ 60	Larry Walker	1.25	.35
❑ 61	Wilson Betemit RC	10.00	3.00
❑ 62	Travis Hafner RC	25.00	7.50
❑ 63	Ichiro Suzuki RC	80.00	24.00
❑ 64	Juan Diaz RC	8.00	2.40
❑ 65	Morgan Ensberg RC	20.00	6.00
❑ 66	Horacio Ramirez RC	10.00	3.00
❑ 67	Ricardo Rodriguez RC	8.00	2.40
❑ 68	Sean Douglass RC	8.00	2.40
❑ 69	Brandon Duckworth RC	8.00	2.40
❑ 70	Jackson Melian RC	8.00	2.40
❑ 71	Adrian Hernandez RC	8.00	2.40
❑ 72	Kyle Kessel RC	8.00	2.40
❑ 73	Jason Michaels RC	8.00	2.40
❑ 74	Esix Snead RC	8.00	2.40
❑ 75	Jason Smith RC	8.00	2.40
❑ 76	Tyler Walker RC	8.00	2.40
❑ 77	Juan Uribe RC	10.00	3.00
❑ 78	Adam Pettyjohn RC	8.00	2.40
❑ 79	Tsuyoshi Shinjo RC	10.00	3.00
❑ 80	Mike Penney RC	8.00	2.40
❑ 81	Josh Towers RC	10.00	3.00
❑ 82	Erick Almonte RC	8.00	2.40
❑ 83	Ryan Freel RC	10.00	3.00
❑ 84	Juan Pena	8.00	2.40
❑ 85	Albert Pujols RC	250.00	75.00
❑ 86	Henry Mateo RC	8.00	2.40
❑ 87	Greg Miller RC	8.00	2.40
❑ 88	Jose Mieses RC	8.00	2.40
❑ 89	Jack Wilson RC	10.00	3.00
❑ 90	Carlos Valderrama RC	8.00	2.40

2004 SP Game Used Patch

	Nm-Mt	Ex-Mt
COMP.UPDATE SET (50)	100.00	30.00
COMMON CARD 1-60	4.00	1.20
61-90 PRINT RUN B/WN 86-684 COPIES PER		.00
COMMON CARD (91-119)	8.00	2.40
COMMON CARD (121-135)	2.50	.75
COMMON CARD (136-170)	2.50	.75
ONE UPDATE SET PER 48 UD2 HOB.BOXES		.00

#	Player	Nm-Mt	Ex-Mt
❑ 1	Miguel Cabrera	4.00	1.20
❑ 2	Alex Rodriguez Yanks	8.00	2.40
❑ 3	Edgar Renteria	4.00	1.20
❑ 4	Juan Gonzalez	4.00	1.20
❑ 5	Mike Lowell	4.00	1.20
❑ 6	Andruw Jones	4.00	1.20
❑ 7	Eric Chavez	4.00	1.20
❑ 8	Jim Edmonds	4.00	1.20
❑ 9	Mike Piazza	8.00	2.40
❑ 10	Angel Berroa	4.00	1.20
❑ 11	Eric Gagne	4.00	1.20
❑ 12	Jody Gerut	4.00	1.20
❑ 13	Orlando Cabrera	4.00	1.20
❑ 14	Austin Kearns	4.00	1.20
❑ 15	Frank Thomas	5.00	1.50
❑ 16	Johan Santana	4.00	1.20
❑ 17	Randy Johnson	5.00	1.50
❑ 18	Preston Wilson	4.00	1.20
❑ 19	Garret Anderson	4.00	1.20
❑ 20	Jorge Posada	4.00	1.20
❑ 21	Rich Harden	4.00	1.20
❑ 22	Barry Zito	4.00	1.20
❑ 23	Gary Sheffield	4.00	1.20
❑ 24	Jose Reyes	4.00	1.20
❑ 25	Roy Halladay	4.00	1.20
❑ 26	Ben Sheets	4.00	1.20
❑ 27	Geoff Jenkins	4.00	1.20
❑ 28	Josh Beckett	4.00	1.20
❑ 29	Roy Oswalt	4.00	1.20
❑ 30	Bobby Abreu	4.00	1.20
❑ 31	Hank Blalock	4.00	1.20
❑ 32	Kerry Wood	4.00	1.20
❑ 33	Ryan Klesko	4.00	1.20
❑ 34	Rafael Furcal	4.00	1.20
❑ 35	Tom Glavine	4.00	1.20
❑ 36	Kevin Brown	4.00	1.20
❑ 37	Scott Rolen	4.00	1.20
❑ 38	Bret Boone	4.00	1.20
❑ 39	Ichiro Suzuki	10.00	3.00
❑ 40	Lance Berkman	4.00	1.20
❑ 41	Tim Hudson	4.00	1.20
❑ 42	Carlos Delgado	4.00	1.20
❑ 43	Ivan Rodriguez	4.00	1.20
❑ 44	Luis Gonzalez	4.00	1.20
❑ 45	Torii Hunter	4.00	1.20
❑ 46	Carlos Lee	4.00	1.20
❑ 47	Jacque Jones	4.00	1.20
❑ 48	Manny Ramirez	4.00	1.20
❑ 49	Troy Glaus	4.00	1.20
❑ 50	Corey Patterson	4.00	1.20
❑ 51	Jason Schmidt	4.00	1.20
❑ 52	Mark Mulder	4.00	1.20
❑ 53	Vernon Wells	4.00	1.20
❑ 54	Curt Schilling	4.00	1.20
❑ 55	Javy Lopez	4.00	1.20
❑ 56	Mark Prior	4.00	1.20
❑ 57	Dontrelle Willis	4.00	1.20
❑ 58	Derek Jeter	10.00	3.00
❑ 59	Jeff Bagwell	4.00	1.20
❑ 60	Marlon Byrd	4.00	1.20
❑ 61	Rafael Palmeiro SN/500	5.00	1.50
❑ 62	Kevin Millwood SN/165	5.00	1.50
❑ 63	Greg Maddux SN/273	10.00	3.00
❑ 64	Adam Dunn SN/400	5.00	1.50
❑ 65	Richie Sexson SN/469	5.00	1.50
❑ 66	Magglio Ordonez SN/567	5.00	1.50
❑ 67	Hideo Nomo SN/236	6.00	1.80
❑ 68	Albert Pujols SN/194	12.00	3.60
❑ 69	Rocco Baldelli SN/368	5.00	1.50
❑ 70	Mark Teixeira SN/86	6.00	1.80
❑ 71	Jason Giambi SN/660	5.00	1.50
❑ 72	Alfonso Soriano SN/230	5.00	1.50
❑ 73	Roger Clemens SN/300	12.00	3.60
❑ 74	Miguel Tejada SN/359	5.00	1.50
❑ 75	Jeff Kent SN/684	5.00	1.50
❑ 76	Bernie Williams SN/342	5.00	1.50
❑ 77	Sammy Sosa SN/470	6.00	1.80
❑ 78	Mike Mussina SN/641	5.00	1.50
❑ 79	Jim Thome SN/334	5.00	1.50
❑ 80	Brian Giles SN/506	5.00	1.50
❑ 81	Shawn Green SN/234	5.00	1.50
❑ 82	Mike Sweeney SN/340	5.00	1.50
❑ 83	John Smoltz SN/262	5.00	1.50
❑ 84	Carlos Beltran SN/319	5.00	1.50
❑ 85	Todd Helton SN/384	5.00	1.50
❑ 86	Nomar Garciaparra SN/372	10.00	3.00
❑ 87	Ken Griffey Jr. SN/481	10.00	3.00
❑ 88	Chipper Jones SN/633	6.00	1.80
❑ 89	Vladimir Guerrero SN/226	6.00	1.80
❑ 90	Pedro Martinez SN/313	5.00	1.50
❑ 91	Brandon Medders RD RC	8.00	2.40
❑ 92	Colby Miller RD RC	8.00	2.40
❑ 93	Dave Crouthers RD RC	8.00	2.40
❑ 94	Dennis Sarfate RD RC	8.00	2.40
❑ 95	Donald Kelly RD RC	8.00	2.40
❑ 96	Alec Zumwalt RD RC	8.00	2.40
❑ 97	Chris Aguila RD RC	8.00	2.40
❑ 98	Greg Dobbs RD RC	8.00	2.40
❑ 99	Ian Snell RD RC	10.00	3.00
❑ 100	Jake Woods RD RC	8.00	2.40
❑ 101	Jamie Brown RD RC	8.00	2.40
❑ 102	Jason Frasor RD RC	8.00	2.40
❑ 103	Jerome Gamble RD RC	8.00	2.40
❑ 104	Jesse Harper RD RC	8.00	2.40
❑ 105	Josh Labandeira RD RC	8.00	2.40
❑ 106	Justin Hampson RD RC	8.00	2.40
❑ 107	Justin Huisman RD RC	8.00	2.40
❑ 108	Justin Leone RD RC	10.00	3.00
❑ 109	Lincoln Holdzkom RD RC	8.00	2.40
❑ 110	Mike Bumatay RD RC	8.00	2.40
❑ 111	Mike Gosling RD RC	8.00	2.40
❑ 112	Mike Johnston RD RC	8.00	2.40

Card	Nm-Mt	Ex-Mt
❑ 113 Mike Rouse RD RC	8.00	2.40
❑ 114 Nick Regilio RD RC	8.00	2.40
❑ 115 Ryan Meaux RD RC	8.00	2.40
❑ 116 Scott Dohmann RD RC	8.00	2.40
❑ 117 Sean Henn RD RC	8.00	2.40
❑ 118 Tim Bausher RD RC	8.00	2.40
❑ 119 Tim Bittner RD RC	8.00	2.40
❑ 121 Richie Sexson	2.50	.75
❑ 122 Javier Vazquez	2.50	.75
❑ 123 Alex Rodriguez Yanks	8.00	2.40
❑ 124 Javy Lopez	2.50	.75
❑ 125 Miguel Tejada	2.50	.75
❑ 126 Bartolo Colon	2.50	.75
❑ 127 Ivan Rodriguez	4.00	1.20
❑ 128 Rafael Palmeiro	4.00	1.20
❑ 129 Kevin Brown	2.50	.75
❑ 130 Gary Sheffield	2.50	.75
❑ 131 Greg Maddux	8.00	2.40
❑ 132 Curt Schilling	4.00	1.20
❑ 133 Roger Clemens	10.00	3.00
❑ 134 Alfonso Soriano	2.50	.75
❑ 135 Vladimir Guerrero	5.00	1.50
❑ 136 Carlos Vasquez RC	2.50	.75
❑ 137 Roman Colon RC	2.50	.75
❑ 138 William Bergolla RC	2.50	.75
❑ 139 Jason Bartlett RC	5.00	1.50
❑ 140 Casey Daigle RC	2.50	.75
❑ 141 Ryan Wing RC	2.50	.75
❑ 142 Chris Saenz RC	2.50	.75
❑ 143 Edwin Moreno RC	2.50	.75
❑ 144 Shawn Hill RC	2.50	.75
❑ 145 Eddy Rodriguez RC	3.00	.90
❑ 146 Justin Knoedler RC	2.50	.75
❑ 147 Renyel Pinto RC	3.00	.90
❑ 148 Kevin Cave RC	2.50	.75
❑ 149 Carlos Hines RC	2.50	.75
❑ 150 Merkin Valdez RC	3.00	.90
❑ 151 Tim Hamulack RC	2.50	.75
❑ 152 Hector Gimenez RC	2.50	.75
❑ 153 Mike Vento RC	3.00	.90
❑ 154 Scott Proctor RC	3.00	.90
❑ 155 Rusty Tucker RC	3.00	.90
❑ 156 Akinori Otsuka RC	2.50	.75
❑ 157 Ronny Cedeno RC	5.00	1.50
❑ 158 Jose Capellan RC	3.00	.90
❑ 159 Justin Germano RC	2.50	.75
❑ 160 Shingo Takatsu RC	5.00	1.50
❑ 161 Fernando Nieve RC	5.00	1.50
❑ 162 Michael Wuertz RC	3.00	.90
❑ 163 Jerry Gil RC	2.50	.75
❑ 164 Jorge Vasquez RC	2.50	.75
❑ 165 Chad Bentz RC	2.50	.75
❑ 166 Luis A. Gonzalez RC	3.00	.90
❑ 167 Ivan Ochoa RC	2.50	.75
❑ 168 Onil Joseph RC	2.50	.75
❑ 169 Enemencio Pacheco RC	2.50	.75
❑ 170 Kazuo Matsui RC	5.00	1.50

2004 SP Legendary Cuts

	Nm-Mt	Ex-Mt
COMPLETE SET (126)	40.00	12.00
❑ 1 Al Kaline	1.50	.45
❑ 2 Al Lopez	.60	.18
❑ 3 Alan Trammell	.60	.18
❑ 4 Andre Dawson	.60	.18
❑ 5 Babe Ruth	5.00	1.50
❑ 6 Bert Campaneris	.40	.12
❑ 7 Bill Mazeroski	1.00	.30
❑ 8 Bill Russell	.40	.12
❑ 9 Billy Williams	.60	.18
❑ 10 Bob Feller	1.00	.30
❑ 11 Bob Gibson	1.00	.30
❑ 12 Bob Lemon	.60	.18
❑ 13 Bobby Doerr	.60	.18
❑ 14 Brooks Robinson	1.00	.30
❑ 15 Cal Ripken	5.00	1.50
❑ 16 Carl Yastrzemski	2.50	.75
❑ 17 Carlton Fisk	1.00	.30
❑ 18 Catfish Hunter	.60	.18
❑ 19 Dale Murphy	1.00	.30
❑ 20 Darryl Strawberry	.60	.18
❑ 21 Dave Concepcion	.60	.18
❑ 22 Dave Winfield	.60	.18
❑ 23 Dennis Eckersley	.60	.18
❑ 24 Denny McLain	.60	.18
❑ 25 Don Drysdale	1.00	.30
❑ 26 Don Larsen	.60	.18
❑ 27 Don Mattingly	3.00	.90
❑ 28 Don Sutton	.60	.18
❑ 29 Duke Snider UER Tris Speaker's stats are on the back	1.00	.30
❑ 30 Dusty Baker	.60	.18
❑ 31 Dwight Gooden	.60	.18
❑ 32 Earl Weaver	.40	.12
❑ 33 Early Wynn	.60	.18
❑ 34 Eddie Mathews	1.50	.45
❑ 35 Eddie Murray	1.50	.45
❑ 36 Enos Slaughter	.60	.18
❑ 37 Ernie Banks	1.50	.45
❑ 38 Fergie Jenkins	.60	.18
❑ 39 Frank Robinson	.60	.18
❑ 40 Fred Lynn	.40	.12
❑ 41 Gary Carter	.60	.18
❑ 42 Gaylord Perry	.60	.18
❑ 43 George Brett	3.00	.90
❑ 44 George Foster	.40	.12
❑ 45 George Kell	.60	.18
❑ 46 Greg Luzinski	.60	.18
❑ 47 Hal Newhouser	.60	.18
❑ 48 Hank Greenberg	1.50	.45
❑ 49 Harmon Killebrew	1.50	.45
❑ 50 Honus Wagner	1.50	.45
❑ 51 Hoyt Wilhelm	.60	.18
❑ 52 Jackie Robinson	1.50	.45
❑ 53 Jim Bunning	1.00	.30
❑ 54 Jim Palmer	.60	.18
❑ 55 Jimmie Foxx	1.50	.45
❑ 56 Joe Carter	.60	.18
❑ 57 Joe DiMaggio	2.50	.75
❑ 58 Joe Morgan	.60	.18
❑ 59 Joe Torre	1.00	.30
❑ 60 Johnny Bench	1.50	.45
❑ 61 Johnny Podres	.60	.18
❑ 62 Johnny Roseboro	.40	.12
❑ 63 Johnny Sain	.60	.18
❑ 64 Juan Marichal	.60	.18
❑ 65 Keith Hernandez	.60	.18
❑ 66 Kirby Puckett	1.50	.45
❑ 67 Kirk Gibson	.60	.18
❑ 68 Will Clark	1.00	.30
❑ 69 Jim Rice	.60	.18
❑ 70 Larry Doby	.60	.18
❑ 71 Lou Boudreau	.60	.18
❑ 72 Lou Brock	1.00	.30
❑ 73 Lou Gehrig	2.50	.75
❑ 74 Lou Piniella	.60	.18
❑ 75 Luis Aparicio	.60	.18
❑ 76 Mark Grace	1.00	.30
❑ 77 Mel Ott	1.50	.45
❑ 78 Mickey Lolich	.60	.18
❑ 79 Mickey Mantle	8.00	2.40
❑ 80 Mike Greenwell	.40	.12
❑ 81 Mike Schmidt	3.00	.90
❑ 82 Monte Irvin	.60	.18
❑ 83 Nellie Fox	1.00	.30
❑ 84 Nolan Ryan	4.00	1.20
❑ 85 Orlando Cepeda	.60	.18
❑ 86 Ozzie Smith	2.50	.75
❑ 87 Paul Molitor	1.00	.30
❑ 88 Pee Wee Reese	1.00	.30
❑ 89 Phil Niekro	.60	.18
❑ 90 Phil Rizzuto	1.00	.30
❑ 91 Ralph Kiner	1.00	.30
❑ 92 Red Rolfe	.40	.12
❑ 93 Red Schoendienst	.60	.18
❑ 94 Reggie Smith	.40	.12
❑ 95 Rich Gossage	.60	.18
❑ 96 Richie Ashburn	1.00	.30
❑ 97 Rick Ferrell	.60	.18
❑ 98 Elston Howard	.60	.18
❑ 99 Roberto Clemente	4.00	1.20
❑ 100 Robin Roberts	.60	.18
❑ 101 Robin Yount	1.50	.45
❑ 102 Roger Maris	1.50	.45
❑ 103 Rollie Fingers	.60	.18
❑ 104 Ron Santo	1.00	.30
❑ 105 Roy Campanella	1.50	.45
❑ 106 Ryne Sandberg	3.00	.90
❑ 107 Sparky Anderson	.60	.18
❑ 108 Sparky Lyle	.40	.12
❑ 109 Stan Musial	2.50	.75
❑ 110 Steve Carlton	.60	.18
❑ 111 Steve Garvey	.60	.18
❑ 112 Ted Williams	3.00	.90
❑ 113 Thurman Munson	1.50	.45
❑ 114 Tom Seaver	1.00	.30
❑ 115 Tommy Henrich	.60	.18
❑ 116 Tommy Lasorda	.60	.18
❑ 117 Tony Gwynn	2.00	.60
❑ 118 Tony Perez	.60	.18
❑ 119 Ty Cobb	2.00	.60
❑ 120 Wade Boggs	1.00	.30
❑ 121 Warren Spahn	1.00	.30
❑ 122 Whitey Ford	1.00	.30
❑ 123 Willie McCovey	1.00	.30
❑ 124 Willie Randolph	.60	.18
❑ 125 Willie Stargell	1.00	.30
❑ 126 Yogi Berra	1.50	.45

2005 SP Legendary Cuts

	Nm-Mt	Ex-Mt
COMPLETE SET (90)	25.00	7.50
COMMON CARD (1-90)	.40	.12
❑ 1 Al Kaline	1.50	.45
❑ 2 Babe Ruth	5.00	1.50
❑ 3 Bill Mazeroski	1.00	.30
❑ 4 Billy Williams	.60	.18
❑ 5 Bob Feller	1.00	.30
❑ 6 Bob Gibson	1.00	.30
❑ 7 Bob Lemon	.60	.18
❑ 8 Bobby Doerr	.60	.18
❑ 9 Brooks Robinson	1.00	.30
❑ 10 Carl Yastrzemski	2.50	.75
❑ 11 Carlton Fisk	1.00	.30
❑ 12 Casey Stengel	1.00	.30
❑ 13 Catfish Hunter	.60	.18
❑ 14 Christy Mathewson	1.50	.45
❑ 15 Cy Young	1.50	.45
❑ 16 Dennis Eckersley	.60	.18
❑ 17 Dizzy Dean	1.00	.30
❑ 18 Don Drysdale	1.00	.30
❑ 19 Don Sutton	.60	.18
❑ 20 Duke Snider	1.00	.30
❑ 21 Early Wynn	.60	.18
❑ 22 Eddie Mathews	1.50	.45
❑ 23 Eddie Murray	1.50	.45
❑ 24 Enos Slaughter	.60	.18
❑ 25 Ernie Banks	1.50	.45
❑ 26 Fergie Jenkins	.60	.18
❑ 27 Frank Robinson	.60	.18

❑ 28 Gary Carter .60 .18
❑ 29 Gaylord Perry .60 .18
❑ 30 Reggie Jackson 1.00 .30
❑ 31 George Kell .60 .18
❑ 32 George Sisler .60 .18
❑ 33 Hal Newhouser .60 .18
❑ 34 Harmon Killebrew 1.50 .45
❑ 35 Honus Wagner 1.50 .45
❑ 36 Jackie Robinson 1.50 .45
❑ 37 Jim Bunning 1.00 .30
❑ 38 Jim Palmer .60 .18
❑ 39 Jimmie Foxx 1.50 .45
❑ 40 Joe DiMaggio 2.50 .75
❑ 41 Joe Morgan .60 .18
❑ 42 Johnny Bench 1.50 .45
❑ 43 Johnny Mize .60 .18
❑ 44 Juan Marichal .60 .18
❑ 45 Kirby Puckett 1.50 .45
❑ 46 Larry Doby .60 .18
❑ 47 Lefty Grove 1.00 .30
❑ 48 Lou Boudreau .60 .18
❑ 49 Lou Brock 1.00 .30
❑ 50 Lou Gehrig 2.50 .75
❑ 51 Luis Aparicio .60 .18
❑ 52 Mel Ott 1.50 .45
❑ 53 Mickey Cochrane .60 .18
❑ 54 Mickey Mantle 8.00 2.40
❑ 55 Mike Schmidt 3.00 .90
❑ 56 Monte Irvin .60 .18
❑ 57 Nolan Ryan 4.00 1.20
❑ 58 Orlando Cepeda .60 .18
❑ 59 Ozzie Smith 2.50 .75
❑ 60 Paul Molitor 1.00 .30
❑ 61 Pee Wee Reese 1.00 .30
❑ 62 Phil Niekro .60 .18
❑ 63 Phil Rizzuto 1.00 .30
❑ 64 Ralph Kiner 1.00 .30
❑ 65 Red Schoendienst .60 .18
❑ 66 Richie Ashburn 1.00 .30
❑ 67 Rick Ferrell .60 .18
❑ 68 Robin Roberts .60 .18
❑ 69 Robin Yount 1.50 .45
❑ 70 Rod Carew 1.00 .30
❑ 71 Rogers Hornsby 1.00 .30
❑ 72 Rollie Fingers .60 .18
❑ 73 Roy Campanella 1.50 .45
❑ 74 Ryne Sandberg 3.00 .90
❑ 75 Satchel Paige 1.50 .45
❑ 76 Stan Musial 2.50 .75
❑ 77 Steve Carlton .60 .18
❑ 78 Ted Williams 3.00 .90
❑ 79 Thurman Munson 1.50 .45
❑ 80 Tom Seaver 1.00 .30
❑ 81 Tony Gwynn 2.00 .60
❑ 82 Tony Perez .60 .18
❑ 83 Ty Cobb 2.00 .60
❑ 84 Wade Boggs 1.00 .30
❑ 85 Walter Johnson 1.50 .45
❑ 86 Warren Spahn 1.00 .30
❑ 87 Whitey Ford 1.00 .30
❑ 88 Willie McCovey 1.00 .30
❑ 89 Willie Stargell 1.00 .30
❑ 90 Yogi Berra 1.50 .45

2004 SP Prospects

Nm-Mt Ex-Mt
COMP.ROOKIES SET (198) 50.00 15.00
COMMON CARD (1-90) 1.00 .30
1-90 APPX. 2X TOUGHER THAN 91-290 .00
COMMON CARD (91-190 1.00 .30
91-190 ODDS TWO PER PACK .00
COMMON CARD (191-290) 1.00 .30
191-290 APPX.TWO PER PACK .00
OVERALL AU ODDS 1:5 .00
AU PRINT RUNS B/WN 400-600 PER .00
233/237/345/438-443/445 DO NOT EXIST .00

❑ 1 Roger Clemens 5.00 1.50
❑ 2 Melvin Mora 1.00 .30
❑ 3 Dontrelle Willis 1.50 .45
❑ 4 Jose Vidro 1.00 .30
❑ 5 Oliver Perez 1.00 .30
❑ 6 Carlos Zambrano 1.00 .30
❑ 7 Chipper Jones 2.50 .75
❑ 8 Greg Maddux 4.00 1.20
❑ 9 Curt Schilling 1.50 .45
❑ 10 Jose Reyes 1.00 .30
❑ 11 David Ortiz 2.50 .75
❑ 12 Mike Piazza 4.00 1.20
❑ 13 Jason Schmidt 1.00 .30
❑ 14 Randy Johnson 2.50 .75
❑ 15 Magglio Ordonez 1.00 .30
❑ 16 Mike Mussina 1.50 .45
❑ 17 Jake Peavy 1.00 .30
❑ 18 Jim Edmonds 1.50 .45
❑ 19 Ken Griffey Jr. 4.00 1.20
❑ 20 Jason Giambi 1.00 .30
❑ 21 Mike Sweeney 1.00 .30
❑ 22 Carlos Lee 1.00 .30
❑ 23 Craig Wilson 1.00 .30
❑ 24 Pedro Martinez 1.50 .45
❑ 25 Bobby Abreu 1.00 .30
❑ 26 Mike Lowell 1.00 .30
❑ 27 Miguel Cabrera 1.50 .45
❑ 28 Hank Blalock 1.00 .30
❑ 29 Frank Thomas 2.50 .75
❑ 30 Manny Ramirez 1.50 .45
❑ 31 Mark Mulder 1.00 .30
❑ 32 Scott Podsednik 1.00 .30
❑ 33 Albert Pujols 5.00 1.50
❑ 34 Preston Wilson 1.00 .30
❑ 35 Todd Helton 1.50 .45
❑ 36 Victor Martinez 1.00 .30
❑ 37 Kerry Wood 1.00 .30
❑ 38 Carlos Beltran 1.00 .30
❑ 39 Vernon Wells 1.00 .30
❑ 40 Sammy Sosa 2.50 .75
❑ 41 Pat Burrell 1.00 .30
❑ 42 Tim Hudson 1.00 .30
❑ 43 Eric Gagne 1.00 .30
❑ 44 Jim Thome 1.50 .45
❑ 45 Vladimir Guerrero 2.50 .75
❑ 46 Travis Hafner 1.00 .30
❑ 47 Rickie Weeks 1.50 .45
❑ 48 Miguel Tejada 1.00 .30
❑ 49 Ivan Rodriguez 1.50 .45
❑ 50 J.D. Drew 1.00 .30
❑ 51 Ben Sheets 1.00 .30
❑ 52 Garret Anderson 1.00 .30
❑ 53 Aubrey Huff 1.00 .30
❑ 54 Nomar Garciaparra 4.00 1.20
❑ 55 Luis Gonzalez 1.00 .30
❑ 56 Lance Berkman 1.00 .30
❑ 57 Ichiro Suzuki 5.00 1.50
❑ 58 Torii Hunter 1.00 .30
❑ 59 Adam Dunn 1.00 .30
❑ 60 Mark Teixeira 1.50 .45
❑ 61 Bret Boone 1.00 .30
❑ 62 Roy Oswalt 1.00 .30
❑ 63 Joe Mauer 1.00 .30
❑ 64 Scott Rolen 1.50 .45
❑ 65 Hideki Matsui 5.00 1.50
❑ 66 Richie Sexson 1.00 .30
❑ 67 Jeff Kent 1.00 .30
❑ 68 Barry Zito 1.00 .30
❑ 69 C.C. Sabathia 1.00 .30
❑ 70 Carlos Delgado 1.00 .30
❑ 71 Gary Sheffield 1.00 .30
❑ 72 Shawn Green 1.00 .30
❑ 73 Jason Bay 1.00 .30
❑ 74 Andruw Jones 1.50 .45
❑ 75 Jeff Bagwell 1.50 .45
❑ 76 Rafael Palmeiro 1.50 .45
❑ 77 Alex Rodriguez 4.00 1.20
❑ 78 Adrian Beltre 1.00 .30
❑ 79 Troy Glaus 1.00 .30
❑ 80 Tom Glavine 1.50 .45
❑ 81 Paul Konerko 1.00 .30
❑ 82 Alfonso Soriano 1.00 .30
❑ 83 Roy Halladay 1.00 .30
❑ 84 Derek Jeter 5.00 1.50
❑ 85 Josh Beckett 1.00 .30
❑ 86 Delmon Young 1.50 .45
❑ 87 Brian Giles 1.00 .30
❑ 88 Eric Chavez 1.00 .30
❑ 89 Lyle Overbay 1.00 .30
❑ 90 Mark Prior 1.50 .45
❑ 91 Shawn Camp RC 1.00 .30
❑ 92 Travis Smith 1.00 .30
❑ 93 Juan Padilla RC 1.00 .30
❑ 94 Brad Halsey RC 1.50 .45
❑ 95 Scott Kazmir RC 4.00 1.20
❑ 96 Sam Narron RC 1.00 .30
❑ 97 Frank Francisco RC 1.00 .30
❑ 98 Mike Johnston RC 1.00 .30
❑ 99 Sam McConnell RC 1.00 .30
❑ 100 Josh Labandeira RC 1.00 .30
❑ 101 Kazuhito Tadano RC 1.50 .45
❑ 102 Hector Gimenez RC 1.00 .30
❑ 103 David Aardsma RC 1.50 .45
❑ 104 Charles Thomas RC 1.00 .30
❑ 105 Ian Snell RC 2.00 .60
❑ 106 Jeff Keppinger RC 1.00 .30
❑ 107 Michael Vento RC 1.50 .45
❑ 108 Jerry Gil RC 1.00 .30
❑ 109 Marty McLeary RC 1.00 .30
❑ 110 Donnie Kelly RC 1.00 .30
❑ 111 Roman Colon RC 1.00 .30
❑ 112 Travis Blackley RC 1.00 .30
❑ 113 Edwardo Sierra RC 1.50 .45
❑ 114 Chris Shelton RC 2.50 .75
❑ 115 Bartolome Fortunato RC 1.00 .30
❑ 116 Brandon Medders RC 1.00 .30
❑ 117 Merkin Valdez RC 1.50 .45
❑ 118 Carlos Vasquez RC 1.50 .45
❑ 119 Shingo Takatsu RC 1.50 .45
❑ 120 Aarom Baldiris RC 1.50 .45
❑ 121 Chris Aguila RC 1.00 .30
❑ 122 Jimmy Serrano RC 1.00 .30
❑ 123 Mike Gosling RC 1.00 .30
❑ 124 Brian Dallimore RC 1.00 .30
❑ 125 Ronald Belisario RC 1.00 .30
❑ 126 George Sherrill RC 1.00 .30
❑ 127 Fernando Nieve RC 1.50 .45
❑ 128 Abe Alvarez RC 1.50 .45
❑ 129 Jeff Bennett RC 1.00 .30
❑ 130 Ryan Meaux RC 1.00 .30
❑ 131 Edwin Moreno RC 1.50 .45
❑ 132 Jesse Crain RC 1.50 .45
❑ 133 Scott Dohmann RC 1.00 .30
❑ 134 Ronny Cedeno RC 1.50 .45
❑ 135 Orlando Rodriguez RC 1.00 .30
❑ 136 Michael Wuertz RC 1.50 .45
❑ 137 Justin Hampson RC 1.00 .30
❑ 138 Matt Treanor RC 1.00 .30
❑ 139 Andy Green RC 1.00 .30
❑ 140 Yadier Molina RC 2.50 .75
❑ 141 Joe Nelson RC 1.00 .30
❑ 142 Justin Lehr RC 1.00 .30
❑ 143 Ryan Wing RC 1.00 .30
❑ 144 Kevin Cave RC 1.00 .30
❑ 145 Evan Rust RC 1.00 .30
❑ 146 Mike Rouse RC 1.00 .30
❑ 147 Lance Cormier RC 1.00 .30
❑ 148 Eduardo Villacis RC 1.00 .30
❑ 149 Justin Knoedler RC 1.00 .30
❑ 150 Freddy Guzman RC 1.00 .30
❑ 151 Casey Daigle RC 1.00 .30
❑ 152 Joey Gathright RC 2.00 .60
❑ 153 Tim Bittner RC 1.00 .30
❑ 154 Scott Atchison RC 1.00 .30
❑ 155 Ivan Ochoa RC 1.00 .30
❑ 156 Lincoln Holdzkom RC 1.00 .30
❑ 157 Onil Joseph RC 1.00 .30
❑ 158 Jason Bartlett RC 1.50 .45
❑ 159 Jon Knott RC 1.00 .30
❑ 160 Jake Woods RC 1.00 .30
❑ 161 Jerome Gamble RC 1.00 .30
❑ 162 Sean Henn RC 1.00 .30
❑ 163 Kazuo Matsui RC 1.50 .45

❑ 164 Roberto Novoa RC 1.50 .45
❑ 165 Eddy Rodriguez RC 1.50 .45
❑ 166 Ramon Ramirez RC 1.00 .30
❑ 167 Enemencio Pacheco RC 1.00 .30
❑ 168 Chad Bentz RC 1.00 .30
❑ 169 Chris Oxspring RC 1.00 .30
❑ 170 Justin Leone RC 1.50 .45
❑ 171 Joe Horgan RC 1.00 .30
❑ 172 Jose Capellan RC 1.50 .45
❑ 173 Greg Dobbs RC 1.00 .30
❑ 174 Jason Frasor RC 1.00 .30
❑ 175 Shawn Hill RC 1.00 .30
❑ 176 Carlos Hines RC 1.00 .30
❑ 177 John Gall RC 1.50 .45
❑ 178 Steve Andrade RC 1.00 .30
❑ 179 Scott Proctor RC 1.50 .45
❑ 180 Rusty Tucker RC 1.50 .45
❑ 181 Dave Crouthers RC 1.00 .30
❑ 182 Franklyn Gracesqui RC 1.00 .30
❑ 183 Justin Germano RC 1.00 .30
❑ 184 Alfredo Simon RC 1.00 .30
❑ 185 Jorge Sequea RC 1.00 .30
❑ 186 Nick Regilio RC 1.00 .30
❑ 187 Justin Huisman RC 1.00 .30
❑ 188 Akinori Otsuka RC 1.00 .30
❑ 189 Luis Gonzalez RC 1.00 .30
❑ 190 Renyel Pinto RC 1.50 .45
❑ 191 Joshua Leblanc RC 1.50 .45
❑ 192 Devin Ivany RC 2.00 .60
❑ 193 Chad Blackwell RC 1.50 .45
❑ 194 Brandon Burgess RC 1.50 .45
❑ 195 Cory Patton RC 1.50 .45
❑ 196 Daniel Batz RC 1.50 .45
❑ 197 Adam Russell RC 1.50 .45
❑ 198 Jarrett Hoffpauir RC 2.00 .60
❑ 199 Patrick Bryant RC 1.50 .45
❑ 200 Sean Gamble RC 2.00 .60
❑ 201 Jermaine Brock RC 2.00 .60
❑ 202 Ben Zobrist RC 2.00 .60
❑ 203 Clay Meredith RC 2.00 .60
❑ 204 Derek Tharpe RC 1.50 .45
❑ 205 Bradley McCann RC 3.00 .90
❑ 206 Justin Hedrick RC 1.50 .45
❑ 207 Clint Sammons RC 2.00 .60
❑ 208 Richard Steik RC 1.50 .45
❑ 209 Fernando Perez RC 2.00 .60
❑ 210 Mark Jecmen RC 1.50 .45
❑ 211 Benjamin Harrison RC 1.50 .45
❑ 212 Jason Quarles RC 1.50 .45
❑ 213 William Layman RC 1.50 .45
❑ 214 Koley Kolberg RC 1.50 .45
❑ 215 Randy Dicken RC 1.00 .30
❑ 216 Barry Richmond RC 1.50 .45
❑ 217 Timothy Murphey RC 1.50 .45
❑ 218 John Hardy RC 1.50 .45
❑ 219 Sebastien Boucher RC 2.00 .60
❑ 220 Andrew Alvarado RC 1.50 .45
❑ 221 Patrick Perry RC 2.00 .60
❑ 222 Jarod McAuliff RC 1.50 .45
❑ 223 Jared Gaston RC 1.50 .45
❑ 224 William Thompson RC 1.50 .45
❑ 225 Lucas French RC 1.50 .45
❑ 226 Brandon Parillo RC 2.00 .60
❑ 227 Gregory Goetz RC 1.50 .45
❑ 228 David Haehnel RC 2.00 .60
❑ 229 James Miller RC 1.50 .45
❑ 230 Mark Roberts RC 1.50 .45
❑ 231 Eric Ridener RC 1.50 .45
❑ 232 Freddy Sandoval RC 1.50 .45
❑ 234 Carlos Medero-Stullz RC 1.50 .45
❑ 235 Matthew Shepherd RC 1.50 .45
❑ 236 Thomas Hubbard RC 1.50 .45
❑ 238 Kyle Bono RC 2.00 .60
❑ 239 Craig Moldrem RC 1.00 .30
❑ 240 Brandon Timm RC UER 2.00 .60
Photo is Cory Middleton
❑ 241 Mike Carp RC 3.00 .90
❑ 242 Joseph Muro RC 1.50 .45
❑ 243 Derek Decarlo RC 1.50 .45
❑ 244 Christopher Niesel RC 2.00 .60
❑ 245 Trevor Lawhorn RC 2.00 .60
❑ 246 Joey Howell RC 2.00 .60
❑ 247 Dustin Hahn RC 1.50 .45
❑ 248 James Fasano RC 2.00 .60
❑ 249 Hainley Statia RC 2.00 .60
❑ 250 Brandon Conway RC 1.50 .45
❑ 251 Christopher McConnell RC 2.50 .75
❑ 252 Austin Shappi RC 2.00 .60
❑ 253 Joseph Metropoulos RC 2.00 .60
❑ 254 David Nicholson RC 2.00 .60
❑ 255 Ryan McCarthy RC 2.00 .60
❑ 256 Michael Parisi RC 1.50 .45
❑ 257 Andrew Macfarlane RC 1.50 .45
❑ 258 Jeffrey Dominguez RC 2.00 .60
❑ 259 Troy Patton RC 4.00 1.20
❑ 260 Ryan Norwood RC 2.50 .75
❑ 261 Chad Boyd RC 1.50 .45
❑ 262 Grant Plumley RC 1.50 .45
❑ 263 Jeffrey Katz RC 2.00 .60
❑ 264 Cory Middleton RC 1.50 .45
❑ 265 Andrew Moffitt RC 1.00 .30
❑ 266 Jarrett Grube RC 1.50 .45
❑ 267 Derek Hankins RC 1.50 .45
❑ 268 Douglas Reinhardt RC 1.50 .45
❑ 269 Duron Legrande RC 1.50 .45
❑ 270 Steven Jackson RC 1.50 .45
❑ 271 Brian Hall RC 2.00 .60
❑ 272 Cory Wade RC 2.00 .60
❑ 273 John Grogan RC 1.50 .45
❑ 274 Robert Asanovich RC 2.00 .60
❑ 275 Kevin Hart RC 2.00 .60
❑ 276 Matthew Guillory RC 1.50 .45
❑ 277 Clifton Remole RC 1.50 .45
❑ 278 David Trahan RC 1.50 .45
❑ 279 Kristian Bell RC 1.00 .30
❑ 280 Christopher Westervelt RC 1.50 .45
❑ 281 Garry Bakker RC 1.50 .45
❑ 282 Jonathan Ash RC 2.00 .60
❑ 283 Ryan Phillips RC 1.50 .45
❑ 284 Wesley Letson RC UER 1.50 .45
Name spelled Lesly on the back
❑ 285 Jeffrey Landing RC 1.50 .45
❑ 286 Mark Worrell RC 1.50 .45
❑ 287 Sean Gallagher RC 5.00 1.50
❑ 288 Nicholas Blasi RC 1.50 .45
❑ 289 Kevin Frandsen RC 2.00 .60
❑ 290 Richard Mercado RC 1.50 .45
❑ 291 Matt Bush AU 400/RC 50.00 15.00
❑ 292 Mark Rogers AU 400/RC 25.00 7.50
❑ 293 Homer Bailey AU 400/RC 30.00 9.00
❑ 294 Chris Nelson AU 400/RC 60.00 18.00
❑ 295 T.Diamond AU 400/RC 40.00 12.00
❑ 296 Neil Walker AU 400/RC 50.00 15.00
❑ 297 Bill Bray AU 400/RC 10.00 3.00
❑ 298 David Purcey AU 400/RC 20.00 6.00
❑ 299 Scott Elbert AU 400/RC 25.00 7.50
❑ 300 Josh Fields AU 400/RC 30.00 9.00
❑ 301 Chris Lambert AU 400/RC 25.00 7.50
❑ 302 Trevor Plouffe AU 400/RC 30.00 9.00
❑ 303 Greg Golson AU 400/RC 30.00 9.00
❑ 304 Philip Hughes AU 400/RC 40.00 12.00
❑ 305 Kyle Waldrop AU 400/RC 25.00 7.50
❑ 306 Richie Robnett AU 350/RC 25.00 7.50
❑ 307 T.Tankersley AU 400/RC 20.00 6.00
❑ 308 Blake Dewitt AU 400/RC 40.00 12.00
❑ 309 Eric Hurley AU 400/RC 25.00 7.50
❑ 310 J.Howell AU 400/RC EX * 30.00 9.00
❑ 311 Zachary Jackson AU 400/RC 20.00 6.00
❑ 312 Justin Orenduff AU 400/RC 20.00 6.00
❑ 313 Tyler Lumsden AU 400/RC 15.00 4.50
❑ 314 Matthew Fox AU 600/RC 8.00 2.40
❑ 315 Danny Putnam AU 450/RC 20.00 6.00
❑ 316 Jon Poterson AU 400/RC 20.00 6.00
❑ 317 Gio Gonzalez AU 400/RC 25.00 7.50
❑ 318 Jay Rainville AU 475/RC 30.00 9.00
❑ 319 Huston Street AU 400/RC 50.00 15.00
❑ 320 Jeff Marquez AU 400/RC 15.00 4.50
❑ 321 Eric Beattie AU 500/RC 12.00 3.60
❑ 322 Reid Brignac AU 325/RC 50.00 15.00
❑ 323 Y.Gallardo AU 400/RC 20.00 6.00
❑ 324 Justin Hoyman AU 400/RC 20.00 6.00
❑ 325 B.J. Szymanski AU 400/RC 25.00 7.50
❑ 326 Seth Smith AU 600/RC 20.00 6.00
❑ 327 Karl Herren AU 600/RC 15.00 4.50
❑ 328 Brian Bixler AU 600/RC 8.00 2.40
❑ 329 Wesley Whisler AU 600/RC 8.00 2.40
❑ 330 E.San Pedro AU 400/RC 15.00 4.50
❑ 331 Billy Buckner AU 400/RC 15.00 4.50
❑ 332 Jon Zeringue AU 400/RC 30.00 9.00
❑ 333 Curtis Thigpen AU 400/RC 20.00 6.00
❑ 334 Blake Johnson AU 400/RC 25.00 7.50
❑ 335 Donald Lucy AU 400/RC 10.00 3.00
❑ 336 Michael Ferris AU 600/RC 12.00 3.60
❑ 337 A.Swarzak AU 600/RC 20.00 6.00
❑ 338 Jason Jaramillo AU 400/RC 15.00 4.50
❑ 339 Hunter Pence AU 600/RC 40.00 12.00
❑ 340 Dustin Pedroia AU 400/RC 50.00 15.00
❑ 341 Grant Johnson AU 400/RC 20.00 6.00
❑ 342 Kurt Suzuki AU 400/RC 30.00 9.00
❑ 343 Jason Vargas AU 600/RC 30.00 9.00
❑ 344 Raymond Liotta AU 400/RC 30.00 9.00
❑ 346 Eric Campbell AU 400/RC 60.00 18.00
❑ 347 Jeffrey Frazier AU 400/RC 15.00 4.50
❑ 348 G.Hernandez AU 400/RC 40.00 12.00
❑ 349 Wade Davis AU 600/RC 15.00 4.50
❑ 350 J.Wahpepah AU 400/RC 10.00 3.00
❑ 351 Scott Lewis AU 400/RC 15.00 4.50
❑ 352 Jeff Fiorentino AU 400/RC 25.00 7.50
❑ 353 S.Register AU 600/RC 8.00 2.40
❑ 354 Michael Schlact AU 400/RC 10.00 3.00
❑ 355 Eddie Prasch AU 400/RC 15.00 4.50
❑ 356 Adam Lind AU 400/RC 30.00 9.00
❑ 357 Ian Desmond AU 400/RC 40.00 12.00
❑ 358 Josh Johnson AU 575/RC 12.00 3.60
❑ 359 Garrett Mock AU 600/RC 8.00 2.40
❑ 360 Danny Hill AU 600/RC 8.00 2.40
❑ 361 Cory Dunlap AU 600/RC 25.00 7.50
❑ 362 Grant Hansen AU 600/RC 8.00 2.40
❑ 363 Eric Haberer AU 400/RC 10.00 3.00
❑ 364 E.Morlan AU 400/RC 20.00 6.00
❑ 365 James Happ AU 600/RC 15.00 4.50
❑ 366 M.Tuiasosopo AU 600/RC 60.00 18.00
❑ 367 Jordan Parraz AU 400/RC 20.00 6.00
❑ 368 Andrew Dobies AU 400/RC 15.00 4.50
❑ 369 Mark Reed AU 400/RC 30.00 9.00
❑ 370 Jason Windsor AU 400/RC 20.00 6.00
❑ 371 Gregory Burns AU 600/RC 15.00 4.50
❑ 372 Christian Garcia AU 600/RC 12.00 3.60
❑ 373 John Bowker AU 575/RC 25.00 7.50
❑ 374 J.C. Holt AU 550/RC 12.00 3.60
❑ 375 Daryl Jones AU 400/RC 25.00 7.50
❑ 376 Collin Mahoney AU 400/RC 15.00 4.50
❑ 377 A.Hathaway AU 400/RC 20.00 6.00
❑ 378 Matthew Spring AU 400/RC 10.00 3.00
❑ 379 Joshua Baker AU 400/RC 10.00 3.00
❑ 380 Charles Lofgren AU 400/RC 10.00 3.00
❑ 381 Raf Gonzalez AU 400/RC 10.00 3.00
❑ 382 Brad Bergesen AU 575/RC 8.00 2.40
❑ 383 Brandon Boggs AU 400/RC 15.00 4.50
❑ 384 J.Bauserman AU 400/RC 10.00 3.00
❑ 385 Collin Balester AU 500/RC 25.00 7.50
❑ 386 James Moore AU 400/RC 10.00 3.00
❑ 387 Robert Janssen AU 400/RC 20.00 6.00
❑ 388 Luis Guerra AU 400/RC 15.00 4.50
❑ 389 Lucas Harrell AU 550/RC 8.00 2.40
❑ 390 Donnie Smith AU 500/RC 12.00 3.60
❑ 391 Mark Robinson AU 525/RC 12.00 3.60
❑ 392 Louis Marson AU 550/RC 15.00 4.50
❑ 393 Rob Johnson AU 600/RC 12.00 3.60
❑ 394 L.Santangelo AU 600/RC 12.00 3.60
❑ 395 T.Hottovy AU 400/RC 15.00 4.50
❑ 396 Ryan Webb AU 400/RC 15.00 4.50
❑ 397 Jamar Walton AU 400/RC 20.00 6.00
❑ 398 Jason Jones AU 400/RC 25.00 7.50
❑ 399 Clay Timpner AU 600/RC 12.00 3.60
❑ 400 James Parr AU 400/RC 20.00 6.00
❑ 401 Sean Kazmar AU 400/RC 10.00 3.00
❑ 402 Andrew Kown AU 400/RC 15.00 4.50
❑ 403 Jacob McGee AU 600/RC 8.00 2.40
❑ 404 Michael Butia AU 600/RC 8.00 2.40
❑ 405 Paul Janish AU 500/RC 12.00 3.60
❑ 406 Matthew Macri AU 400/RC 25.00 7.50
❑ 407 Mike Nickeas AU 500/RC 12.00 3.60
❑ 408 Kyle Bloom AU 550/RC 12.00 3.60
❑ 409 Luis Rivera AU 500/RC 12.00 3.60
❑ 410 William Bunn AU 600/RC 25.00 7.50
❑ 411 Enrique Barrera AU 400/RC 25.00 7.50
❑ 412 R.Klosterman AU 400/RC 10.00 3.00
❑ 413 John Raglani AU 515/RC 20.00 6.00
❑ 414 Brandon Allen AU 500/RC 20.00 6.00
❑ 415 A.Baldwin AU 600/RC 8.00 2.40
❑ 416 Mark Lowe AU 400/RC 15.00 4.50
❑ 417 Mitch Einertson AU 400/RC 50.00 15.00
❑ 418 Ryan Schroyer AU 600/RC 12.00 3.60
❑ 419 Bradley Davis AU 400/RC 10.00 3.00
❑ 420 Jesse Hoover AU 500/RC 12.00 3.60
❑ 421 G.Broshuis AU 400/RC 15.00 4.50
❑ 422 Peter Pope AU 400/RC 15.00 4.50

❑ 423 Brent Dlugach AU 400/RC	15.00	4.50
❑ 424 Ryan Coultas AU 400/RC	10.00	3.00
❑ 425 Ryan Royster AU 400/RC	20.00	6.00
❑ 426 S.Chapman AU 400/RC	15.00	4.50
❑ 427 B.Chamberlin AU 400/RC	15.00	4.50
❑ 428 J.Koshansky AU 550/RC	25.00	7.50
❑ 429 William Susdorf AU 400/RC	10.00	3.00
❑ 430 A.J. Johnson AU 400/RC	25.00	7.50
❑ 431 Jeremy Sowers AU 400/RC	25.00	7.50
❑ 432 Justin Pekarek AU 400/RC	15.00	4.50
❑ 433 Brett Smith AU 400/RC	15.00	4.50
❑ 434 Matt Durkin AU 400/RC	20.00	6.00
❑ 435 Daniel Barone AU 400/RC	10.00	3.00
❑ 436 Scott Hyde AU 400/RC	15.00	4.50
❑ 437 T.Everidge AU 400/RC	10.00	3.00
❑ 444 Mark Trumbo AU 400/RC	30.00	9.00
❑ 446 Eric Patterson AU 400/RC	25.00	7.50
❑ 447 Michael Rozier AU 400/RC	15.00	4.50

1986 Sportflics

	Nm-Mt	Ex-Mt
COMP.FACT.SET (200)	25.00	10.00
❑ 1 George Brett	1.50	.60
❑ 2 Don Mattingly	2.00	.80
❑ 3 Wade Boggs	.40	.16
❑ 4 Eddie Murray	.60	.24
❑ 5 Dale Murphy	.40	.16
❑ 6 Rickey Henderson	.60	.24
❑ 7 Harold Baines	.25	.10
❑ 8 Cal Ripken	2.50	1.00
❑ 9 Orel Hershiser	.60	.24
❑ 10 Bret Saberhagen	.25	.10
❑ 11 Tim Raines	.25	.10
❑ 12 Fernando Valenzuela	.25	.10
❑ 13 Tony Gwynn	1.00	.40
❑ 14 Pedro Guerrero	.25	.10
❑ 15 Keith Hernandez	.25	.10
❑ 16 Earnie Riles	.15	.06
❑ 17 Jim Rice	.25	.10
❑ 18 Ron Guidry	.25	.10
❑ 19 Willie McGee	.25	.10
❑ 20 Ryne Sandberg	1.25	.50
❑ 21 Kirk Gibson	.40	.16
❑ 22 Ozzie Guillen	2.00	.80
❑ 23 Dave Parker	.25	.10
❑ 24 Vince Coleman	.40	.16
❑ 25 Tom Seaver	.40	.16
❑ 26 Brett Butler	.25	.10
❑ 27 Steve Carlton	.25	.10
❑ 28 Gary Carter	.25	.10
❑ 29 Cecil Cooper	.25	.10
❑ 30 Jose Cruz	.25	.10
❑ 31 Alvin Davis	.15	.06
❑ 32 Dwight Evans	.40	.16
❑ 33 Julio Franco	.25	.10
❑ 34 Damaso Garcia	.15	.06
❑ 35 Steve Garvey	.25	.10
❑ 36 Kent Hrbek	.25	.10
❑ 37 Reggie Jackson	.40	.16
❑ 38 Fred Lynn	.25	.10
❑ 39 Paul Molitor	.40	.16
❑ 40 Jim Presley	.15	.06
❑ 41 Dave Righetti	.25	.10
❑ 42A Robin Yount ERR New York Yankees	50.00	20.00
❑ 42B Robin Yount COR Milwaukee Brewers	1.00	.40
❑ 43 Nolan Ryan	2.50	1.00
❑ 44 Mike Schmidt	1.50	.60
❑ 45 Lee Smith	.25	.10
❑ 46 Rick Sutcliffe	.25	.10
❑ 47 Bruce Sutter	.25	.10
❑ 48 Lou Whitaker	.25	.10
❑ 49 Dave Winfield	.25	.10
❑ 50 Pete Rose	1.50	.60
❑ 51 Ryne Sandberg Steve Garvey Pete Rose	.60	.24
❑ 52 George Brett Harold Baines Jim Rice	.60	.24
❑ 53 Phil Niekro Jerry Reuss Mike Witt	.15	.06
❑ 54 Don Mattingly Cal Ripken Robin Yount	1.25	.50
❑ 55 Dan Quisenberry Goose Gossage Lee Smith	.15	.06
❑ 56 Darryl Strawberry Steve Sax Pete Rose	.60	.24
❑ 57 Cal Ripken Don Baylor Reggie Jackson	.60	.24
❑ 58 Dave Parker Bill Madlock Pete Rose	.60	.24
❑ 59 LaMarr Hoyt Mike Flanagan Ron Guidry	.15	.06
❑ 60 Fernando Valenzuela Rick Sutcliffe Tom Seaver	.25	.10
❑ 61 Reggie Jackson Jim Rice Tony Armas	.25	.10
❑ 62 Keith Hernandez Dale Murphy Mike Schmidt	.60	.24
❑ 63 Robin Yount George Brett Fred Lynn	.60	.24
❑ 64 Bert Blyleven Jerry Koosman John Denny	.15	.06
❑ 65 Willie Hernandez Rollie Fingers Bruce Sutter	.15	.06
❑ 66 Bob Horner Andre Dawson Gary Matthews	.15	.06
❑ 67 Ron Kittle Carlton Fisk Tom Seaver	.25	.10
❑ 68 Mike Schmidt George Foster Dave Kingman	.60	.24
❑ 69 Cal Ripken Rod Carew Pete Rose	.40	.16
❑ 70 Rick Sutcliffe Steve Carlton Tom Seaver	.25	.10
❑ 71 Reggie Jackson Fred Lynn Robin Yount	.60	.24
❑ 72 Dave Righetti Fernando Valenzuela Rick Sutcliffe	.15	.06
❑ 73 Fred Lynn Eddie Murray Cal Ripken	.60	.24
❑ 74 Alvin Davis Lou Whitaker Rod Carew	.25	.10
❑ 75 Don Mattingly Wade Boggs Carney Lansford	1.00	.40
❑ 76 Jesse Barfield	.25	.10
❑ 77 Phil Bradley	.15	.06
❑ 78 Chris Brown	.00	.00
❑ 79 Tom Browning	.15	.06
❑ 80 Tom Brunansky	.15	.06
❑ 81 Bill Buckner	.25	.10
❑ 82 Chili Davis	.25	.10
❑ 83 Mike Davis	.15	.06
❑ 84 Rich Gedman	.15	.06
❑ 85 Willie Hernandez	.15	.06
❑ 86 Ron Kittle	.15	.06
❑ 87 Lee Lacy	.15	.06
❑ 88 Bill Madlock	.25	.10
❑ 89 Mike Marshall	.15	.06
❑ 90 Keith Moreland	.15	.06
❑ 91 Graig Nettles	.25	.10
❑ 92 Lance Parrish	.25	.10
❑ 93 Kirby Puckett	1.00	.40
❑ 94 Juan Samuel	.15	.06
❑ 95 Steve Sax	.15	.06
❑ 96 Dave Stieb	.25	.10
❑ 97 Darryl Strawberry	.40	.16
❑ 98 Willie Upshaw	.15	.06
❑ 99 Frank Viola	.25	.10
❑ 100 Dwight Gooden	.60	.24
❑ 101 Joaquin Andujar	.25	.10
❑ 102 George Bell	.25	.10
❑ 103 Bert Blyleven	.25	.10
❑ 104 Mike Boddicker	.15	.06
❑ 105 Britt Burns	.15	.06
❑ 106 Rod Carew	.40	.16
❑ 107 Jack Clark	.25	.10
❑ 108 Danny Cox	.15	.06
❑ 109 Ron Darling	.25	.10
❑ 110 Andre Dawson	.25	.10
❑ 111 Leon Durham	.15	.06
❑ 112 Tony Fernandez	.15	.06
❑ 113 Tommy Herr	.15	.06
❑ 114 Teddy Higuera	.25	.10
❑ 115 Bob Horner	.25	.10
❑ 116 Dave Kingman	.25	.10
❑ 117 Jack Morris	.25	.10
❑ 118 Dan Quisenberry	.15	.06
❑ 119 Jeff Reardon	.25	.10
❑ 120 Bryn Smith	.15	.06
❑ 121 Ozzie Smith	1.00	.40
❑ 122 John Tudor	.25	.10
❑ 123 Tim Wallach	.15	.06
❑ 124 Willie Wilson	.25	.10
❑ 125 Carlton Fisk	.40	.16
❑ 126 Gary Carter Al Oliver George Foster	.15	.06
❑ 127 Tim Raines Ryne Sandberg Keith Hernandez	.60	.24
❑ 128 Paul Molitor Cal Ripken Willie Wilson	.60	.24
❑ 129 John Candelaria Dennis Eckersley Bob Forsch	.25	.10
❑ 130 Pete Rose Ron Cey Rollie Fingers	.60	.24
❑ 131 Dave Concepcion George Foster Bill Madlock	.25	.10
❑ 132 John Denny Fernando Valenzuela Vida Blue	.15	.06
❑ 133 Rich Dotson Joaquin Andujar Doyle Alexander	.15	.06
❑ 134 Rick Sutcliffe Tom Seaver John Denny	.25	.10
❑ 135 Tom Seaver Phil Niekro Don Sutton	.25	.10
❑ 136 Dwight Gooden Vince Coleman Alfredo Griffin	.25	.10
❑ 137 Gary Carter Fred Lynn Steve Garvey	.25	.10
❑ 138 Tony Perez Rusty Staub Pete Rose	.60	.24

Card	Nm-Mt	Ex-Mt
❑ 139 Mike Schmidt	.60	.24
Jim Rice		
George Foster		
❑ 140 Tony Gwynn	.40	.16
Al Oliver		
Bill Buckner		
❑ 141 Nolan Ryan	1.00	.40
Jack Morris		
Dave Righetti		
❑ 142 Tom Seaver	.25	.10
Bert Blyleven		
Vida Blue		
❑ 143 Nolan Ryan	1.00	.40
Fernando Valenzuela		
Dwight Gooden		
❑ 144 Tim Raines	.25	.10
Willie Wilson		
Davey Lopes		
❑ 145 Tony Armas	.40	.16
Cecil Cooper		
Eddie Murray		
❑ 146 Rod Carew	.25	.10
Jim Rice		
Rollie Fingers		
❑ 147 Alan Trammell	.25	.10
Rick Dempsey		
Reggie Jackson		
❑ 148 Darrell Porter	.60	.24
Pedro Guerrero		
Mike Schmidt		
❑ 149 Mike Boddicker	.15	.06
Rick Sutcliffe		
Ron Guidry		
❑ 150 Reggie Jackson	.25	.10
Dave Kingman		
Fred Lynn		
❑ 151 Buddy Bell	.25	.10
❑ 152 Dennis Boyd	.15	.06
❑ 153 Dave Concepcion	.25	.10
❑ 154 Brian Downing	.25	.10
❑ 155 Shawon Dunston	.15	.06
❑ 156 John Franco	.25	.10
❑ 157 Scott Garrelts	.15	.06
❑ 158 Bob James	.15	.06
❑ 159 Charlie Leibrandt	.15	.06
❑ 160 Oddibe McDowell	.15	.06
❑ 161 Roger McDowell	.15	.06
❑ 162 Mike Moore	.15	.06
❑ 163 Phil Niekro	.25	.10
❑ 164 Al Oliver	.25	.10
❑ 165 Tony Pena	.15	.06
❑ 166 Ted Power	.15	.06
❑ 167 Mike Scioscia	.25	.10
❑ 168 Mario Soto	.25	.10
❑ 169 Bob Stanley	.15	.06
❑ 170 Garry Templeton	.25	.10
❑ 171 Andre Thornton	.15	.06
❑ 172 Alan Trammell	.25	.10
❑ 173 Doug DeCinces	.15	.06
❑ 174 Greg Walker	.15	.06
❑ 175 Don Sutton	.25	.10
❑ 176 Ozzie Guillen	.60	.24
Bret Saberhagen		
Don Mattingly		
Vince Coleman		
Dwight Gooden		
Willie McGee		
❑ 177 Stew Cliburn	.15	.06
Brian Fisher UER		
(Photo actually		
Mike Pagliarulo)		
Joe Hesketh		
Joe Orsulak		
Mark Salas		
Larry Sheets		
❑ 178 Jose Canseco	8.00	3.20
Mark Funderburk		
Mike Greenwell		
Steve Lombardozzi UER		
(Photo actually		
Mark Salas)		
Billy Joe Robidoux		
Danny Tartabull		
❑ 179 George Brett	1.50	.60
Ron Guidry		
Keith Hernandez		
Don Mattingly		
Willie McGee		
Dale Murphy		
❑ 180 Wade Boggs	1.50	.60
George Brett		
Rod Carew		
Cecil Cooper		
Don Mattingly		
Willie Wilson		
❑ 181 Tony Gwynn	.60	.24
Bill Madlock		
Pedro Guerrero		
Dave Parker		
Pete Rose		
Keith Hernandez		
❑ 182 Rod Carew	.40	.16
Phil Niekro		
Pete Rose		
Nolan Ryan		
Tom Seaver		
Matt Tallman (fan)		
❑ 183 Wade Boggs	1.00	.40
Darrell Evans		
Don Mattingly		
Willie McGee		
Dale Murphy		
Dave Parker		
❑ 184 Wade Boggs	.40	.16
Dwight Gooden		
Rickey Henderson		
Don Mattingly		
Willie McGee		
John Tudor		
❑ 185 Dwight Gooden	.40	.16
Ron Guidry		
John Tudor		
Joaquin Andujar		
Bret Saberhagen		
Tom Browning		
❑ 186 Lonnie Smith	.40	.16
Dane Iorg		
Willie Wilson		
Charlie Leibrandt		
George Brett		
Bret Saberhagen		
Darryl Motley		
Dan Quisenberry		
Danny Jackson		
Jim Sundberg		
Steve Balboni		
Frank White		
❑ 187 Hubie Brooks	.15	.06
❑ 188 Glenn Davis	.15	.06
❑ 189 Darrell Evans	.25	.10
❑ 190 Rich Gossage	.25	.10
❑ 191 Andy Hawkins	.15	.06
❑ 192 Jay Howell	.15	.06
❑ 193 LaMarr Hoyt	.15	.06
❑ 194 Davey Lopes	.25	.10
❑ 195 Mike Scott	.25	.10
❑ 196 Ted Simmons	.25	.10
❑ 197 Gary Ward	.15	.06
❑ 198 Bob Welch	.25	.10
❑ 199 Mike Young	.15	.06
❑ 200 Buddy Biancalana	.15	.06

1986 Sportflics Rookies

	Nm-Mt	Ex-Mt
COMP.FACT.SET (50)	20.00	8.00
❑ 1 John Kruk	.75	.30
❑ 2 Edwin Correa	.10	.04
❑ 3 Pete Incaviglia	.25	.10
❑ 4 Dale Sveum	.10	.04
❑ 5 Juan Nieves	.10	.04
❑ 6 Will Clark	1.50	.60
❑ 7 Wally Joyner	.40	.16
❑ 8 Lance McCullers	.10	.04
❑ 9 Scott Bailes	.10	.04
❑ 10 Dan Plesac	.25	.10
❑ 11 Jose Canseco	3.00	1.20
❑ 12 Bobby Witt	.25	.10
❑ 13 Barry Bonds	15.00	6.00
❑ 14 Andres Thomas	.10	.04
❑ 15 Jim Deshaies	.10	.04
❑ 16 Ruben Sierra	.75	.30
❑ 17 Steve Lombardozzi	.10	.04
❑ 18 Cory Snyder	.10	.04
❑ 19 Reggie Williams	.10	.04
❑ 20 Mitch Williams	.25	.10
❑ 21 Glenn Braggs	.10	.04
❑ 22 Danny Tartabull	.25	.10
❑ 23 Charlie Kerfeld	.10	.04
❑ 24 Paul Assenmacher	.25	.10
❑ 25 Robby Thompson	.25	.10
❑ 26 Bobby Bonilla	.40	.16
❑ 27 Andres Galarraga	.75	.30
❑ 28 Billy Joe Robidoux	.10	.04
❑ 29 Bruce Ruffin	.10	.04
❑ 30 Greg Swindell	.25	.10
❑ 31 John Cangelosi	.10	.04
❑ 32 Jim Traber	.10	.04
❑ 33 Russ Morman	.10	.04
❑ 34 Barry Larkin	1.50	.60
❑ 35 Todd Worrell	.25	.10
❑ 36 John Cerutti	.10	.04
❑ 37 Mike Kingery	.10	.04
❑ 38 Mark Eichhorn	.10	.04
❑ 39 Scott Bankhead	.10	.04
❑ 40 Bo Jackson	5.00	2.00
❑ 41 Greg Mathews	.10	.04
❑ 42 Eric King	.10	.04
❑ 43 Kal Daniels	.25	.10
❑ 44 Calvin Schiraldi	.10	.04
❑ 45 Mickey Brantley	.10	.04
❑ 46 Willie Mays	.75	.30
Pete Rose		
Fred Lynn		
❑ 47 Tom Seaver	.25	.10
Fernando Valenzuela		
Dwight Gooden		
❑ 48 Eddie Murray	.75	.30
Lou Whitaker		
Dave Righetti		
Steve Sax		
Cal Ripken		
Darryl Strawberry		
❑ 49 Kevin Mitchell	.40	.16
❑ 50 Mike Diaz	.10	.04

1994 Sportflics Rookie/Traded

	Nm-Mt	Ex-Mt
COMPLETE SET (150)	25.00	7.50

❑ 1 Will Clark	.75	.23
❑ 2 Sid Fernandez	.25	.07
❑ 3 Joe Magrane	.25	.07
❑ 4 Pete Smith	.25	.07
❑ 5 Roberto Kelly	.25	.07
❑ 6 Delino DeShields	.25	.07
❑ 7 Brian Harper	.25	.07
❑ 8 Darrin Jackson	.25	.07
❑ 9 Omar Vizquel	.75	.23
❑ 10 Luis Polonia	.25	.07
❑ 11 Reggie Jefferson	.25	.07
❑ 12 Geronimo Berroa	.25	.07
❑ 13 Mike Harkey	.25	.07
❑ 14 Bret Boone	.50	.15
❑ 15 Dave Henderson	.25	.07
❑ 16 Pedro Martinez	1.25	.35
❑ 17 Jose Vizcaino	.25	.07
❑ 18 Xavier Hernandez	.25	.07
❑ 19 Eddie Taubensee	.25	.07
❑ 20 Ellis Burks	.50	.15
❑ 21 Turner Ward	.25	.07
❑ 22 Terry Mulholland	.25	.07
❑ 23 Howard Johnson	.25	.07
❑ 24 Vince Coleman	.25	.07
❑ 25 Deion Sanders	.75	.23
❑ 26 Rafael Palmeiro	.75	.23
❑ 27 Dave Weathers	.25	.07
❑ 28 Kent Mercker	.25	.07
❑ 29 Gregg Olson	.25	.07
❑ 30 Cory Bailey RC	.25	.07
❑ 31 Brian L. Hunter	.25	.07
❑ 32 Garey Ingram RC	.25	.07
❑ 33 Daniel Smith	.25	.07
❑ 34 Denny Hocking	.25	.07
❑ 35 Charles Johnson	.50	.15
❑ 36 Otis Nixon	.25	.07
❑ 37 Hector Fajardo	.25	.07
❑ 38 Lee Smith	.50	.15
❑ 39 Phil Stidham	.25	.07
❑ 40 Melvin Nieves	.25	.07
❑ 41 Julio Franco	.50	.15
❑ 42 Greg Gohr	.25	.07
❑ 43 Steve Dunn	.25	.07
❑ 44 Tony Fernandez	.25	.07
❑ 45 Toby Borland RC	.25	.07
❑ 46 Paul Shuey	.25	.07
❑ 47 Shawn Hare	.25	.07
❑ 48 Shawn Green	1.25	.35
❑ 49 Julian Tavarez RC	.50	.15
❑ 50 Ernie Young RC	.50	.15
❑ 51 Chris Sabo	.25	.07
❑ 52 Greg O'Halloran	.25	.07
❑ 53 Donnie Elliott	.25	.07
❑ 54 Jim Converse	.25	.07
❑ 55 Ray Holbert	.25	.07
❑ 56 Keith Lockhart RC	.50	.15
❑ 57 Tony Longmire	.25	.07
❑ 58 Jorge Fabregas	.25	.07
❑ 59 Ravelo Manzanillo	.25	.07
❑ 60 Marcus Moore	.25	.07
❑ 61 Carlos Rodriguez	.25	.07
❑ 62 Mark Portugal	.25	.07
❑ 63 Yorkis Perez	.25	.07
❑ 64 Dan Miceli	.25	.07
❑ 65 Chris Turner	.25	.07
❑ 66 Mike Oquist	.25	.07
❑ 67 Tom Quinlan	.25	.07
❑ 68 Matt Walbeck	.25	.07
❑ 69 Dave Staton	.25	.07
❑ 70 W.VanLandingham RC	.25	.07
❑ 71 Dave Stevens	.25	.07
❑ 72 Domingo Cedeno	.25	.07
❑ 73 Alex Diaz	.25	.07
❑ 74 Darren Bragg RC	.25	.07
❑ 75 James Hurst	.25	.07
❑ 76 Alex Gonzalez	.25	.07
❑ 77 Steve Dreyer	.25	.07
❑ 78 Robert Eenhoorn	.25	.07
❑ 79 Derek Parks	.25	.07
❑ 80 Jose Valentin	.25	.07
❑ 81 Wes Chamberlain	.25	.07
❑ 82 Tony Tarasco	.25	.07
❑ 83 Steve Traschel	.25	.07
❑ 84 Willie Banks	.25	.07
❑ 85 Rob Butler	.25	.07
❑ 86 Miguel Jimenez	.25	.07
❑ 87 Gerald Williams	.25	.07
❑ 88 Aaron Small	.50	.15
❑ 89 Matt Mieske	.25	.07
❑ 90 Tim Hyers RC	.25	.07
❑ 91 Eddie Murray	1.25	.35
❑ 92 Dennis Martinez	.50	.15
❑ 93 Tony Eusebio	.25	.07
❑ 94 Brian Anderson RC	.50	.15
❑ 95 Blaise Ilsley	.25	.07
❑ 96 Johnny Ruffin	.25	.07
❑ 97 Carlos Reyes	.25	.07
❑ 98 Greg Pirkl	.25	.07
❑ 99 Jack Morris	.50	.15
❑ 100 John Mabry RC	.75	.23
❑ 101 Mike Kelly	.25	.07
❑ 102 Rich Becker	.25	.07
❑ 103 Chris Gomez	.25	.07
❑ 104 Jim Edmonds	1.25	.35
❑ 105 Rich Rowland	.25	.07
❑ 106 Damon Buford	.25	.07
❑ 107 Mark Kiefer	.25	.07
❑ 108 Matias Carrillo	.25	.07
❑ 109 James Mouton	.25	.07
❑ 110 Kelly Stinnett RC	.25	.07
❑ 111 Billy Ashley	.25	.07
❑ 112 Fausto Cruz RC	.25	.07
❑ 113 Roberto Petagine	.25	.07
❑ 114 Joe Hall	.25	.07
❑ 115 Brian Johnson RC	.25	.07
❑ 116 Kevin Jarvis	.25	.07
❑ 117 Tim Davis	.25	.07
❑ 118 John Patterson	.25	.07
❑ 119 Stan Royer	.25	.07
❑ 120 Jeff Juden	.25	.07
❑ 121 Bryan Eversgerd	.25	.07
❑ 122 Chan Ho Park RC	.75	.23
❑ 123 Shane Reynolds	.25	.07
❑ 124 Danny Bautista	.25	.07
❑ 125 Rikkert Faneyte RC	.25	.07
❑ 126 Carlos Pulido	.25	.07
❑ 127 Mike Matheny RC	1.25	.35
❑ 128 Hector Carrasco	.25	.07
❑ 129 Eddie Zambrano	.25	.07
❑ 130 Lee Tinsley	.25	.07
❑ 131 Roger Salkeld	.25	.07
❑ 132 Carlos Delgado	.75	.23
❑ 133 Troy O'Leary	.25	.07
❑ 134 Keith Mitchell	.25	.07
❑ 135 Lance Painter	.25	.07
❑ 136 Nate Minchey	.25	.07
❑ 137 Eric Anthony	.25	.07
❑ 138 Rafael Bournigal	.25	.07
❑ 139 Joey Hamilton	.25	.07
❑ 140 Bobby Munoz	.25	.07
❑ 141 Rex Hudler	.25	.07
❑ 142 Alex Cole	.25	.07
❑ 143 Stan Javier	.25	.07
❑ 144 Jose Oliva	.25	.07
❑ 145 Tom Brunansky	.25	.07
❑ 146 Greg Colbrunn	.25	.07
❑ 147 Luis Lopez	.25	.07
❑ 148 Alex Rodriguez RC	20.00	6.00
❑ 149 Darryl Strawberry	.50	.15
❑ 150 Bo Jackson	1.25	.35
❑ R01 Ryan Klesko ROY Manny Ramirez	4.00	1.20

1996 SPx

	Nm-Mt	Ex-Mt
COMPLETE SET (60)	50.00	15.00
❑ 1 Greg Maddux	3.00	.90
❑ 2 Chipper Jones	2.00	.60
❑ 3 Fred McGriff	1.25	.35
❑ 4 Tom Glavine	1.25	.35
❑ 5 Cal Ripken	6.00	1.80
❑ 6 Roberto Alomar	1.25	.35
❑ 7 Rafael Palmeiro	1.25	.35
❑ 8 Jose Canseco	1.25	.35
❑ 9 Roger Clemens	4.00	1.20
❑ 10 Mo Vaughn	.75	.23
❑ 11 Jim Edmonds	.75	.23
❑ 12 Tim Salmon	1.25	.35
❑ 13 Sammy Sosa	2.00	.60
❑ 14 Ryne Sandberg	3.00	.90

❑ 15 Mark Grace	1.25	.35
❑ 16 Frank Thomas	2.00	.60
❑ 17 Barry Larkin	1.25	.35
❑ 18 Kenny Lofton	.75	.23
❑ 19 Albert Belle	.75	.23
❑ 20 Eddie Murray	2.00	.60
❑ 21 Manny Ramirez	1.25	.35
❑ 22 Dante Bichette	.75	.23
❑ 23 Larry Walker	.75	.23
❑ 24 Vinny Castilla	.75	.23
❑ 25 Andres Galarraga	.75	.23
❑ 26 Cecil Fielder	.75	.23
❑ 27 Gary Sheffield	.75	.23
❑ 28 Craig Biggio	1.25	.35
❑ 29 Jeff Bagwell	1.25	.35
❑ 30 Derek Bell	.75	.23
❑ 31 Johnny Damon	1.25	.35
❑ 32 Eric Karros	.75	.23
❑ 33 Mike Piazza	3.00	.90
❑ 34 Raul Mondesi	.75	.23
❑ 35 Hideo Nomo	2.00	.60
❑ 36 Kirby Puckett	2.00	.60
❑ 37 Paul Molitor	1.25	.35
❑ 38 Marty Cordova	.75	.23
❑ 39 Rondell White	.75	.23
❑ 40 Jason Isringhausen	.75	.23
❑ 41 Paul Wilson	.75	.23
❑ 42 Rey Ordonez	.75	.23
❑ 43 Derek Jeter	5.00	1.50
❑ 44 Wade Boggs	1.25	.35
❑ 45 Mark McGwire	5.00	1.50
❑ 46 Jason Kendall	.75	.23
❑ 47 Ron Gant	.75	.23
❑ 48 Ozzie Smith	3.00	.90
❑ 49 Tony Gwynn	2.50	.75
❑ 50 Ken Caminiti	.75	.23
❑ 51 Barry Bonds	5.00	1.50
❑ 52 Matt Williams	.75	.23
❑ 53 Osvaldo Fernandez	.75	.23
❑ 54 Jay Buhner	.75	.23
❑ 55 Ken Griffey Jr.	3.00	.90
❑ 56 Randy Johnson	2.00	.60
❑ 57 Alex Rodriguez	4.00	1.20
❑ 58 Juan Gonzalez	.75	.23
❑ 59 Joe Carter	.75	.23
❑ 60 Carlos Delgado	.75	.23
❑ KG1 K.Griffey Jr. Comm.	5.00	1.50
❑ MP1 Mike Piazza Trib.	5.00	1.50
❑ KGA1 Ken Griffey Jr. Auto.	150.00	45.00
❑ MPA1 Mike Piazza Auto.	200.00	60.00

1998 SPx Finite

	Nm-Mt	Ex-Mt
COMP.YM SER.1 (30)	40.00	12.00
COMMON YM (1-30)	1.50	.45
COMP.PE SER.1 (20)	120.00	36.00
COMMON PE (31-50)	2.50	.75
COMP.BASIC SER.1 (90)	80.00	24.00
COMMON CARD (51-140)	1.00	.30
COMP.SF SER.1 (30)	100.00	30.00
COMMON SF (141-170)	1.25	.35
COMP.HG SER.1 (10)	150.00	45.00
COMMON HG (171-180)	4.00	1.20
COMP.YM SER.2 (30)	60.00	18.00
COMMON YM (181-210)	1.50	.45
COMP.PP SER.2 (30)	80.00	24.00
COMMON PP (211-240)	1.25	.35
COMP.BASIC SER.2 (90)	50.00	15.00

COMMON (241-330)	1.00	.30
COMP.TW SER.2 (20)	30.00	9.00
COMMON TW (331-350)	2.50	.75
COMP.CG SER.2 (10)	150.00	45.00
COMMON CG (351-360)	4.00	1.20

❑ 1	Nomar Garciaparra YM	6.00	1.80
❑ 2	Miguel Tejada YM	4.00	1.20
❑ 3	Mike Cameron YM	1.50	.45
❑ 4	Ken Cloude YM	1.50	.45
❑ 5	Jaret Wright YM	1.50	.45
❑ 6	Mark Kotsay YM	1.50	.45
❑ 7	Craig Counsell YM	1.50	.45
❑ 8	Jose Guillen YM	1.50	.45
❑ 9	Neifi Perez YM	1.50	.45
❑ 10	Jose Cruz Jr. YM	1.50	.45
❑ 11	Brett Tomko YM	1.50	.45
❑ 12	Matt Morris YM	1.50	.45
❑ 13	Justin Thompson YM	1.50	.45
❑ 14	Jeremi Gonzalez YM	1.50	.45
❑ 15	Scott Rolen YM	2.50	.75
❑ 16	Vladimir Guerrero YM	4.00	1.20
❑ 17	Brad Fullmer YM	1.50	.45
❑ 18	Brian Giles YM	1.50	.45
❑ 19	Todd Dunwoody YM	1.50	.45
❑ 20	Ben Grieve YM	1.50	.45
❑ 21	Juan Encarnacion YM	1.50	.45
❑ 22	Aaron Boone YM	1.50	.45
❑ 23	Richie Sexson YM	1.50	.45
❑ 24	Richard Hidalgo YM	1.50	.45
❑ 25	Andruw Jones YM	2.50	.75
❑ 26	Todd Helton YM	2.50	.75
❑ 27	Paul Konerko YM	1.50	.45
❑ 28	Dante Powell YM	1.50	.45
❑ 29	Eli Marrero YM	1.50	.45
❑ 30	Derek Jeter YM	10.00	3.00
❑ 31	Mike Piazza PE	10.00	3.00
❑ 32	Tony Clark PE	2.50	.75
❑ 33	Larry Walker PE	2.50	.75
❑ 34	Jim Thome PE	4.00	1.20
❑ 35	Juan Gonzalez PE	5.00	1.50
❑ 36	Jeff Bagwell PE	4.00	1.20
❑ 37	Jay Buhner PE	2.50	.75
❑ 38	Tim Salmon PE	4.00	1.20
❑ 39	Albert Belle PE	2.50	.75
❑ 40	Mark McGwire PE	15.00	4.50
❑ 41	Sammy Sosa PE	6.00	1.80
❑ 42	Mo Vaughn PE	2.50	.75
❑ 43	Manny Ramirez PE	4.00	1.20
❑ 44	Tino Martinez PE	4.00	1.20
❑ 45	Frank Thomas PE	6.00	1.80
❑ 46	Nomar Garciaparra PE	10.00	3.00
❑ 47	Alex Rodriguez PE	10.00	3.00
❑ 48	Chipper Jones PE	6.00	1.80
❑ 49	Barry Bonds PE	15.00	4.50
❑ 50	Ken Griffey Jr. PE	10.00	3.00
❑ 51	Jason Dickson	1.00	.30
❑ 52	Jim Edmonds	1.00	.30
❑ 53	Darin Erstad	1.00	.30
❑ 54	Tim Salmon	1.50	.45
❑ 55	Chipper Jones	2.50	.75
❑ 56	Ryan Klesko	1.00	.30
❑ 57	Tom Glavine	1.50	.45
❑ 58	Denny Neagle	1.00	.30
❑ 59	John Smoltz	1.50	.45
❑ 60	Javy Lopez	1.00	.30
❑ 61	Roberto Alomar	1.50	.45
❑ 62	Rafael Palmeiro	1.50	.45
❑ 63	Mike Mussina	1.50	.45
❑ 64	Cal Ripken	8.00	2.40
❑ 65	Mo Vaughn	1.00	.30
❑ 66	Tim Naehring	1.00	.30
❑ 67	John Valentin	1.00	.30
❑ 68	Mark Grace	1.50	.45
❑ 69	Kevin Orie	1.00	.30
❑ 70	Sammy Sosa	2.50	.75
❑ 71	Albert Belle	1.00	.30
❑ 72	Frank Thomas	2.50	.75
❑ 73	Robin Ventura	1.00	.30
❑ 74	David Justice	1.00	.30
❑ 75	Kenny Lofton	1.00	.30
❑ 76	Omar Vizquel	1.50	.45
❑ 77	Manny Ramirez	1.50	.45
❑ 78	Jim Thome	1.50	.45
❑ 79	Dante Bichette	1.00	.30
❑ 80	Larry Walker	1.00	.30
❑ 81	Vinny Castilla	1.00	.30
❑ 82	Ellis Burks	1.00	.30
❑ 83	Bobby Higginson	1.00	.30
❑ 84	Brian Hunter	1.00	.30
❑ 85	Tony Clark	1.00	.30
❑ 86	Mike Hampton	1.00	.30
❑ 87	Jeff Bagwell	1.50	.45
❑ 88	Craig Biggio	1.50	.45
❑ 89	Derek Bell	1.00	.30
❑ 90	Mike Piazza	4.00	1.20
❑ 91	Ramon Martinez	1.00	.30
❑ 92	Raul Mondesi	1.00	.30
❑ 93	Hideo Nomo	2.50	.75
❑ 94	Eric Karros	1.00	.30
❑ 95	Paul Molitor	1.50	.45
❑ 96	Marty Cordova	1.00	.30
❑ 97	Brad Radke	1.00	.30
❑ 98	Mark Grudzielanek	1.00	.30
❑ 99	Carlos Perez	1.00	.30
❑ 100	Rondell White	1.00	.30
❑ 101	Todd Hundley	1.00	.30
❑ 102	Edgardo Alfonzo	1.00	.30
❑ 103	John Franco	1.00	.30
❑ 104	John Olerud	1.00	.30
❑ 105	Tino Martinez	1.50	.45
❑ 106	David Cone	1.00	.30
❑ 107	Paul O'Neill	1.50	.45
❑ 108	Andy Pettitte	1.50	.45
❑ 109	Bernie Williams	1.50	.45
❑ 110	Rickey Henderson	4.00	1.20
❑ 111	Jason Giambi	1.00	.30
❑ 112	Matt Stairs	1.00	.30
❑ 113	Gregg Jefferies	1.00	.30
❑ 114	Rico Brogna	1.00	.30
❑ 115	Curt Schilling	1.00	.30
❑ 116	Jason Schmidt	1.00	.30
❑ 117	Jose Guillen	1.00	.30
❑ 118	Kevin Young	1.00	.30
❑ 119	Ray Lankford	1.00	.30
❑ 120	Mark McGwire	6.00	1.80
❑ 121	Delino DeShields	1.00	.30
❑ 122	Ken Caminiti	1.00	.30
❑ 123	Tony Gwynn	3.00	.90
❑ 124	Trevor Hoffman	1.00	.30
❑ 125	Barry Bonds	6.00	1.80
❑ 126	Jeff Kent	1.00	.30
❑ 127	Shawn Estes	1.00	.30
❑ 128	J.T. Snow	1.00	.30
❑ 129	Jay Buhner	1.00	.30
❑ 130	Ken Griffey Jr.	4.00	1.20
❑ 131	Dan Wilson	1.00	.30
❑ 132	Edgar Martinez	1.50	.45
❑ 133	Alex Rodriguez	4.00	1.20
❑ 134	Rusty Greer	1.00	.30
❑ 135	Juan Gonzalez	1.00	.30
❑ 136	Fernando Tatis	1.00	.30
❑ 137	Ivan Rodriguez	1.50	.45
❑ 138	Carlos Delgado	1.00	.30
❑ 139	Pat Hentgen	1.00	.30
❑ 140	Roger Clemens	5.00	1.50
❑ 141	Chipper Jones SF	3.00	.90
❑ 142	Greg Maddux SF	5.00	1.50
❑ 143	Rafael Palmeiro SF	2.00	.60
❑ 144	Mike Mussina SF	2.00	.60
❑ 145	Cal Ripken SF	10.00	3.00
❑ 146	Nomar Garciaparra SF	5.00	1.50
❑ 147	Mo Vaughn SF	1.25	.35
❑ 148	Sammy Sosa SF	3.00	.90
❑ 149	Albert Belle SF	1.25	.35
❑ 150	Frank Thomas SF	3.00	.90
❑ 151	Jim Thome SF	2.00	.60
❑ 152	Kenny Lofton SF	1.25	.35
❑ 153	Manny Ramirez SF	2.00	.60
❑ 154	Larry Walker SF	1.25	.35
❑ 155	Jeff Bagwell SF	2.00	.60
❑ 156	Craig Biggio SF	2.00	.60
❑ 157	Mike Piazza SF	5.00	1.50
❑ 158	Paul Molitor SF	2.00	.60
❑ 159	Derek Jeter SF	8.00	2.40
❑ 160	Tino Martinez SF	2.00	.60
❑ 161	Curt Schilling SF	1.25	.35
❑ 162	Mark McGwire SF	8.00	2.40
❑ 163	Tony Gwynn SF	4.00	1.20
❑ 164	Barry Bonds SF	8.00	2.40
❑ 165	Ken Griffey Jr. SF	5.00	1.50
❑ 166	Randy Johnson SF	3.00	.90
❑ 167	Alex Rodriguez SF	5.00	1.50
❑ 168	Juan Gonzalez SF	1.25	.35
❑ 169	Ivan Rodriguez SF	2.00	.60
❑ 170	Roger Clemens SF	6.00	1.80
❑ 171	Greg Maddux HG	15.00	4.50
❑ 172	Cal Ripken HG	30.00	9.00
❑ 173	Frank Thomas HG	10.00	3.00
❑ 174	Jeff Bagwell HG	6.00	1.80
❑ 175	Mike Piazza HG	15.00	4.50
❑ 176	Mark McGwire HG	25.00	7.50
❑ 177	Barry Bonds HG	25.00	7.50
❑ 178	Ken Griffey Jr. HG	15.00	4.50
❑ 179	Alex Rodriguez HG	15.00	4.50
❑ 180	Roger Clemens HG	20.00	6.00
❑ 181	Mike Caruso YM	1.50	.45
❑ 182	David Ortiz YM	4.00	1.20
❑ 183	Gabe Alvarez YM	1.50	.45
❑ 184	G.Matthews Jr. YM RC	1.50	.45
❑ 185	Kerry Wood YM	2.50	.75
❑ 186	Carl Pavano YM	1.50	.45
❑ 187	Alex Gonzalez YM	1.50	.45
❑ 188	Masato Yoshii YM RC	2.50	.75
❑ 189	Larry Sutton YM	1.50	.45
❑ 190	Russell Branyan YM	1.50	.45
❑ 191	Bruce Chen YM	1.50	.45
❑ 192	R. Arrojo YM RC	1.50	.45
❑ 193	R.Christenson YM RC	1.50	.45
❑ 194	Cliff Politte YM	1.50	.45
❑ 195	A.J. Hinch YM	1.50	.45
❑ 196	Kevin Witt YM	1.50	.45
❑ 197	Daryle Ward YM	1.50	.45
❑ 198	Corey Koskie YM RC	2.50	.75
❑ 199	Mike Lowell YM RC	8.00	2.40
❑ 200	Travis Lee YM	1.50	.45
❑ 201	K.Millwood YM RC	2.50	.75
❑ 202	Robert Smith YM	1.50	.45
❑ 203	M.Ordonez YM RC	10.00	3.00
❑ 204	Eric Milton YM	1.50	.45
❑ 205	Geoff Jenkins YM	1.50	.45
❑ 206	Rich Butler YM RC	1.50	.45
❑ 207	Mike Kinkade YM RC	1.50	.45
❑ 208	Braden Looper YM	1.50	.45
❑ 209	Matt Clement YM	1.50	.45
❑ 210	Derrek Lee YM	2.50	.75
❑ 211	Randy Johnson PP	3.00	.90
❑ 212	John Smoltz PP	2.00	.60
❑ 213	Roger Clemens PP	6.00	1.80
❑ 214	Curt Schilling PP	1.25	.35
❑ 215	Pedro Martinez PP	2.00	.60
❑ 216	Vinny Castilla PP	1.25	.35
❑ 217	Jose Cruz Jr. PP	1.25	.35
❑ 218	Jim Thome PP	2.00	.60
❑ 219	Alex Rodriguez PP	5.00	1.50
❑ 220	Frank Thomas PP	3.00	.90
❑ 221	Tim Salmon PP	2.00	.60
❑ 222	Larry Walker PP	1.25	.35
❑ 223	Albert Belle PP	1.25	.35
❑ 224	Manny Ramirez PP	2.00	.60
❑ 225	Mark McGwire PP	8.00	2.40
❑ 226	Mo Vaughn PP	1.25	.35
❑ 227	Andres Galarraga PP	1.25	.35
❑ 228	Scott Rolen PP	2.00	.60
❑ 229	Travis Lee PP	1.25	.35
❑ 230	Mike Piazza PP	5.00	1.50
❑ 231	N.Garciaparra PP	5.00	1.50
❑ 232	Andruw Jones PP	2.00	.60
❑ 233	Barry Bonds PP	8.00	2.40
❑ 234	Jeff Bagwell PP	2.00	.60
❑ 235	Juan Gonzalez PP	1.25	.35

No.	Player	Nm-Mt	Ex-Mt
236	Tino Martinez PP	2.00	.60
237	Vladimir Guerrero PP	3.00	.90
238	Rafael Palmeiro PP	2.00	.60
239	Russell Branyan PP	1.25	.35
240	Ken Griffey Jr. PP	5.00	1.50
241	Cecil Fielder	1.00	.30
242	Chuck Finley	1.00	.30
243	Jay Bell	1.00	.30
244	Andy Benes	1.00	.30
245	Matt Williams	1.00	.30
246	Brian Anderson	1.00	.30
247	Dave Dellucci RC	1.50	.45
248	Andres Galarraga	1.00	.30
249	Andruw Jones	1.50	.45
250	Greg Maddux	4.00	1.20
251	Brady Anderson	1.00	.30
252	Joe Carter	1.00	.30
253	Eric Davis	1.00	.30
254	Pedro Martinez	1.50	.45
255	Nomar Garciaparra	4.00	1.20
256	Dennis Eckersley	1.00	.30
257	Henry Rodriguez	1.00	.30
258	Jeff Blauser	1.00	.30
259	Jaime Navarro	1.00	.30
260	Ray Durham	1.00	.30
261	Chris Stynes	1.00	.30
262	Willie Greene	1.00	.30
263	Reggie Sanders	1.00	.30
264	Bret Boone	1.00	.30
265	Barry Larkin	1.50	.45
266	Travis Fryman	1.00	.30
267	Charles Nagy	1.00	.30
268	Sandy Alomar Jr.	1.00	.30
269	Darryl Kile	1.00	.30
270	Mike Lansing	1.00	.30
271	Pedro Astacio	1.00	.30
272	Damion Easley	1.00	.30
273	Joe Randa	1.00	.30
274	Luis Gonzalez	1.00	.30
275	Mike Piazza	4.00	1.20
276	Todd Zeile	1.00	.30
277	Edgar Renteria	1.00	.30
278	Livan Hernandez	1.00	.30
279	Cliff Floyd	1.00	.30
280	Moises Alou	1.00	.30
281	Billy Wagner	1.00	.30
282	Jeff King	1.00	.30
283	Hal Morris	1.00	.30
284	Johnny Damon	1.50	.45
285	Dean Palmer	1.00	.30
286	Tim Belcher	1.00	.30
287	Eric Young	1.00	.30
288	Bobby Bonilla	1.00	.30
289	Gary Sheffield	1.00	.30
290	Chan Ho Park	1.00	.30
291	Charles Johnson	1.00	.30
292	Jeff Cirillo	1.00	.30
293	Jeromy Burnitz	1.00	.30
294	Jose Valentin	1.00	.30
295	Marquis Grissom	1.00	.30
296	Todd Walker	1.00	.30
297	Terry Steinbach	1.00	.30
298	Rick Aguilera	1.00	.30
299	Vladimir Guerrero	2.50	.75
300	Rey Ordonez	1.00	.30
301	Butch Huskey	1.00	.30
302	Bernard Gilkey	1.00	.30
303	Mariano Rivera	1.50	.45
304	Chuck Knoblauch	1.00	.30
305	Derek Jeter	6.00	1.80
306	Ricky Bottalico	1.00	.30
307	Bob Abreu	1.00	.30
308	Scott Rolen	1.50	.45
309	Al Martin	1.00	.30
310	Jason Kendall	1.00	.30
311	Brian Jordan	1.00	.30
312	Ron Gant	1.00	.30
313	Todd Stottlemyre	1.00	.30
314	Greg Vaughn	1.00	.30
315	Kevin Brown	1.50	.45
316	Wally Joyner	1.00	.30
317	Robb Nen	1.00	.30
318	Orel Hershiser	1.00	.30
319	Russ Davis	1.00	.30
320	Randy Johnson	2.50	.75
321	Quinton McCracken	1.00	.30
322	Tony Saunders	1.00	.30
323	Wilson Alvarez	1.00	.30
324	Wade Boggs	1.50	.45
325	Fred McGriff	1.50	.45
326	Lee Stevens	1.00	.30
327	John Wetteland	1.00	.30
328	Jose Canseco	1.50	.45
329	Randy Myers	1.00	.30
330	Jose Cruz Jr.	1.00	.30
331	Matt Williams TW	2.50	.75
332	Andres Galarraga TW	2.50	.75
333	Walt Weiss TW	2.50	.75
334	Joe Carter TW	2.50	.75
335	Pedro Martinez TW	4.00	1.20
336	Henry Rodriguez TW	2.50	.75
337	Travis Fryman TW	2.50	.75
338	Darryl Kile TW	2.50	.75
339	Mike Lansing TW	2.50	.75
340	Mike Piazza TW	10.00	3.00
341	Moises Alou TW	2.50	.75
342	Charles Johnson TW	2.50	.75
343	Chuck Knoblauch TW	2.50	.75
344	Rickey Henderson TW	6.00	1.80
345	Kevin Brown TW	4.00	1.20
346	Orel Hershiser TW	2.50	.75
347	Wade Boggs TW	4.00	1.20
348	Fred McGriff TW	4.00	1.20
349	Jose Canseco TW	4.00	1.20
350	Gary Sheffield TW	2.50	.75
351	Travis Lee CG	4.00	1.20
352	N.Garciaparra CG	15.00	4.50
353	Frank Thomas CG	10.00	3.00
354	Cal Ripken CG	30.00	9.00
355	Mark McGwire CG	25.00	7.50
356	Mike Piazza CG	15.00	4.50
357	Alex Rodriguez CG	15.00	4.50
358	Barry Bonds CG	25.00	7.50
359	Tony Gwynn CG	12.00	3.60
360	Ken Griffey Jr. CG	15.00	4.50

1999 SPx

	Nm-Mt	Ex-Mt
COMP.SET w/o SP's (80)	25.00	7.50
COMMON (1-10)	1.50	.45
COMMON CARD (11-80)	.50	.15
COMMON SP (81-120)	10.00	3.00

No.	Player	Nm-Mt	Ex-Mt
1	Mark McGwire 61	3.00	.90
2	Mark McGwire 62	3.00	.90
3	Mark McGwire 63	1.50	.45
4	Mark McGwire 64	1.50	.45
5	Mark McGwire 65	1.50	.45
6	Mark McGwire 66	1.50	.45
7	Mark McGwire 67	1.50	.45
8	Mark McGwire 68	1.50	.45
9	Mark McGwire 69	1.50	.45
10	Mark McGwire 70	4.00	1.20
11	Mo Vaughn	.50	.15
12	Darin Erstad	.50	.15
13	Travis Lee	.50	.15
14	Randy Johnson	1.25	.35
15	Matt Williams	.50	.15
16	Chipper Jones	1.25	.35
17	Greg Maddux	2.00	.60
18	Andruw Jones	.75	.23
19	Andres Galarraga	.50	.15
20	Cal Ripken	4.00	1.20
21	Albert Belle	.50	.15
22	Mike Mussina	.75	.23
23	Nomar Garciaparra	2.00	.60
24	Pedro Martinez	.75	.23
25	John Valentin	.50	.15
26	Kerry Wood	.50	.15
27	Sammy Sosa	1.25	.35
28	Mark Grace	.75	.23
29	Frank Thomas	1.25	.35
30	Mike Caruso	.50	.15
31	Barry Larkin	.75	.23
32	Sean Casey	.75	.23
33	Jim Thome	.75	.23
34	Kenny Lofton	.50	.15
35	Manny Ramirez	.75	.23
36	Larry Walker	.50	.15
37	Todd Helton	.75	.23
38	Vinny Castilla	.50	.15
39	Tony Clark	.50	.15
40	Derrek Lee	.75	.23
41	Mark Kotsay	.50	.15
42	Jeff Bagwell	.75	.23
43	Craig Biggio	.75	.23
44	Moises Alou	.50	.15
45	Larry Sutton	.50	.15
46	Johnny Damon	.75	.23
47	Gary Sheffield	.50	.15
48	Raul Mondesi	.50	.15
49	Jeromy Burnitz	.50	.15
50	Todd Walker	.50	.15
51	David Ortiz	.75	.23
52	Vladimir Guerrero	1.25	.35
53	Rondell White	.50	.15
54	Mike Piazza	2.00	.60
55	Derek Jeter	3.00	.90
56	Tino Martinez	.75	.23
57	Roger Clemens	2.50	.75
58	Ben Grieve	.50	.15
59	A.J. Hinch	.50	.15
60	Scott Rolen	.75	.23
61	Doug Glanville	.50	.15
62	Aramis Ramirez	.50	.15
63	Jose Guillen	.50	.15
64	Tony Gwynn	1.50	.45
65	Greg Vaughn	.50	.15
66	Ruben Rivera	.50	.15
67	Barry Bonds	3.00	.90
68	J.T. Snow	.50	.15
69	Alex Rodriguez	2.00	.60
70	Ken Griffey Jr.	2.00	.60
71	Jay Buhner	.50	.15
72	Mark McGwire	3.00	.90
73	Fernando Tatis	.50	.15
74	Quinton McCracken	.50	.15
75	Wade Boggs	.75	.23
76	Ivan Rodriguez	.75	.23
77	Juan Gonzalez	.50	.15
78	Rafael Palmeiro	.75	.23
79	Jose Cruz Jr.	.50	.15
80	Carlos Delgado	.50	.15
81	Troy Glaus SP	15.00	4.50
82	Vladimir Nunez SP	10.00	3.00
83	George Lombard SP	10.00	3.00
84	Bruce Chen SP	10.00	3.00
85	Ryan Minor SP	10.00	3.00
86	Calvin Pickering SP	10.00	3.00
87	Jin Ho Cho SP	10.00	3.00
88	Russ Branyan SP	10.00	3.00
89	Derrick Gibson SP	10.00	3.00
90	Gabe Kapler SP AU	15.00	4.50
91	Matt Anderson SP	10.00	3.00
92	Robert Fick SP	10.00	3.00
93	Juan Encarnacion SP	10.00	3.00
94	Preston Wilson SP	10.00	3.00
95	Alex Gonzalez SP	10.00	3.00
96	Carlos Beltran SP	15.00	4.50
97	Jeremy Giambi SP	10.00	3.00
98	Dee Brown SP	10.00	3.00
99	Adrian Beltre SP	10.00	3.00
100	Alex Cora SP	10.00	3.00
101	Angel Pena SP	10.00	3.00
102	Geoff Jenkins SP	10.00	3.00
103	Ronnie Belliard SP	10.00	3.00
104	Corey Koskie SP	10.00	3.00
105	A.J. Pierzynski SP	10.00	3.00
106	Michael Barrett SP	10.00	3.00
107	Fern.Seguignol SP	10.00	3.00

Card	Nm-Mt	Ex-Mt
❑ 108 Mike Kinkade SP	10.00	3.00
❑ 109 Mike Lowell SP	10.00	3.00
❑ 110 Ricky Ledee SP	10.00	3.00
❑ 111 Eric Chavez SP	10.00	3.00
❑ 112 Abraham Nunez SP	10.00	3.00
❑ 113 Matt Clement SP	10.00	3.00
❑ 114 Ben Davis SP	10.00	3.00
❑ 115 Mike Darr SP	10.00	3.00
❑ 116 Ramon E.Martinez SP RC	10.00	3.00
❑ 117 Carlos Guillen SP	10.00	3.00
❑ 118 Shane Monahan SP	10.00	3.00
❑ 119 J.D. Drew SP AU	15.00	4.50
❑ 120 Kevin Witt SP	10.00	3.00
❑ 24EAST K.Griffey Jr. SAMP	2.00	.60

2000 SPx

	Nm-Mt	Ex-Mt
COMP.BASIC w/o SP's (90)	25.00	7.50
COMP.UPDATE w/o SP's (30)	10.00	3.00
COMMON CARD (1-90)	.50	.15
COMMON AU/1500 (91-120)	10.00	3.00
COMMON (121-135/182-196)	8.00	2.40
COMMON (136-151)	10.00	3.00
COMMON (152-181)	.75	.23

Card	Nm-Mt	Ex-Mt
❑ 1 Troy Glaus	.50	.15
❑ 2 Mo Vaughn	.50	.15
❑ 3 Ramon Ortiz	.50	.15
❑ 4 Jeff Bagwell	.75	.23
❑ 5 Moises Alou	.50	.15
❑ 6 Craig Biggio	.75	.23
❑ 7 Jose Lima	.50	.15
❑ 8 Jason Giambi	.50	.15
❑ 9 John Jaha	.50	.15
❑ 10 Matt Stairs	.50	.15
❑ 11 Chipper Jones	1.25	.35
❑ 12 Greg Maddux	2.00	.60
❑ 13 Andres Galarraga	.50	.15
❑ 14 Andruw Jones	.75	.23
❑ 15 Jeromy Burnitz	.50	.15
❑ 16 Ron Belliard	.50	.15
❑ 17 Carlos Delgado	.50	.15
❑ 18 David Wells	.50	.15
❑ 19 Tony Batista	.50	.15
❑ 20 Shannon Stewart	.50	.15
❑ 21 Sammy Sosa	1.25	.35
❑ 22 Mark Grace	.75	.23
❑ 23 Henry Rodriguez	.50	.15
❑ 24 Mark McGwire	3.00	.90
❑ 25 J.D. Drew	.50	.15
❑ 26 Luis Gonzalez	.50	.15
❑ 27 Randy Johnson	1.25	.35
❑ 28 Matt Williams	.50	.15
❑ 29 Steve Finley	.50	.15
❑ 30 Shawn Green	.50	.15
❑ 31 Kevin Brown	.75	.23
❑ 32 Gary Sheffield	.50	.15
❑ 33 Jose Canseco	.75	.23
❑ 34 Greg Vaughn	.50	.15
❑ 35 Vladimir Guerrero	1.25	.35
❑ 36 Michael Barrett	.50	.15
❑ 37 Russ Ortiz	.50	.15
❑ 38 Barry Bonds	3.00	.90
❑ 39 Jeff Kent	.50	.15
❑ 40 Richie Sexson	.50	.15
❑ 41 Manny Ramirez	.75	.23
❑ 42 Jim Thome	.75	.23
❑ 43 Roberto Alomar	.75	.23
❑ 44 Edgar Martinez	.75	.23
❑ 45 Alex Rodriguez	2.00	.60
❑ 46 John Olerud	.50	.15
❑ 47 Alex Gonzalez	.50	.15
❑ 48 Cliff Floyd	.50	.15
❑ 49 Mike Piazza	2.00	.60
❑ 50 Al Leiter	.50	.15
❑ 51 Robin Ventura	.75	.23
❑ 52 Edgardo Alfonzo	.50	.15
❑ 53 Albert Belle	.50	.15
❑ 54 Cal Ripken	4.00	1.20
❑ 55 B.J. Surhoff	.50	.15
❑ 56 Tony Gwynn	1.50	.45
❑ 57 Trevor Hoffman	.50	.15
❑ 58 Brian Giles	.50	.15
❑ 59 Jason Kendall	.50	.15
❑ 60 Kris Benson	.50	.15
❑ 61 Bob Abreu	.50	.15
❑ 62 Scott Rolen	.75	.23
❑ 63 Curt Schilling	.50	.15
❑ 64 Mike Lieberthal	.50	.15
❑ 65 Sean Casey	.75	.23
❑ 66 Dante Bichette	.50	.15
❑ 67 Ken Griffey Jr.	2.00	.60
❑ 68 Pokey Reese	.50	.15
❑ 69 Mike Sweeney	.50	.15
❑ 70 Carlos Febles	.50	.15
❑ 71 Ivan Rodriguez	.75	.23
❑ 72 Ruben Mateo	.50	.15
❑ 73 Rafael Palmeiro	.75	.23
❑ 74 Larry Walker	.50	.15
❑ 75 Todd Helton	.75	.23
❑ 76 Nomar Garciaparra	2.00	.60
❑ 77 Pedro Martinez	.75	.23
❑ 78 Troy O'Leary	.50	.15
❑ 79 Jacque Jones	.50	.15
❑ 80 Corey Koskie	.50	.15
❑ 81 Juan Gonzalez	.50	.15
❑ 82 Dean Palmer	.50	.15
❑ 83 Juan Encarnacion	.50	.15
❑ 84 Frank Thomas	1.25	.35
❑ 85 Magglio Ordonez	.50	.15
❑ 86 Paul Konerko	.50	.15
❑ 87 Bernie Williams	.75	.23
❑ 88 Derek Jeter	3.00	.90
❑ 89 Roger Clemens	2.50	.75
❑ 90 Orlando Hernandez	.50	.15
❑ 91 Vernon Wells AU/1500	25.00	7.50
❑ 92 Rick Ankiel AU/1500	10.00	3.00
❑ 93 Eric Chavez AU/1500	25.00	7.50
❑ 94 A.Soriano/1500 AU	60.00	18.00
❑ 95 Eric Gagne AU/1500	60.00	18.00
❑ 96 Rob Bell AU/1500	10.00	3.00
❑ 97 Matt Riley AU/1500	10.00	3.00
❑ 98 Josh Beckett AU/1500	60.00	18.00
❑ 99 Ben Petrick AU/1500	10.00	3.00
❑ 100 Rob Ramsay AU/1500	10.00	3.00
❑ 101 Scott Williamson 1500 AU	10.00	3.00
❑ 102 Doug Davis AU/1500	15.00	4.50
❑ 103 E.Munson/1500 AU*	10.00	3.00
❑ 104 Pat Burrell AU/500	60.00	18.00
❑ 105 Jim Morris AU/1500	25.00	7.50
❑ 106 Gabe Kapler AU/500	40.00	12.00
❑ 107 Lance Berkman/1000	8.00	2.40
❑ 108 E.Durazo/1500 AU	15.00	4.50
❑ 109 Tim Hudson AU/1500	40.00	12.00
❑ 110 Ben Davis AU/1500	10.00	3.00
❑ 111 N.Johnson/1500 AU	15.00	4.50
❑ 112 O.Dotel/1500 AU	10.00	3.00
❑ 113 Jerry Hairston/1000	8.00	2.40
❑ 114 Ruben Mateo/1000	8.00	2.40
❑ 115 Chris Singleton/1000	8.00	2.40
❑ 116 Bruce Chen AU/1500	10.00	3.00
❑ 117 Derrick Gibson/1000	8.00	2.40
❑ 118 Carlos Beltran AU/500	125.00	38.00
❑ 119 F.Garcia/1500 AU	15.00	4.50
❑ 120 P.Wilson/1500 AU	15.00	4.50
❑ 121 B.Wilkerson/1600 RC	10.00	3.00
❑ 122 Roy Oswalt/1600 RC	80.00	24.00
❑ 123 W.Serrano/1600 RC	8.00	2.40
❑ 124 Sean Burnett/1600 RC	10.00	3.00
❑ 125 Alex Cabrera/1600 RC	8.00	2.40
❑ 126 Timo Perez/1600 RC	8.00	2.40
❑ 127 Juan Pierre/1600 RC	10.00	3.00
❑ 128 Daylan Holt/1600 RC	8.00	2.40
❑ 129 T.Ohka/1600 RC	8.00	2.40
❑ 130 K.Sasaki/1600 RC	10.00	3.00
❑ 131 K.Ainsworth/1600 RC	8.00	2.40
❑ 132 B.Abernathy/1600 RC	8.00	2.40
❑ 133 Danys Baez/1600 RC	8.00	2.40
❑ 134 Brad Cresse/1600 RC	8.00	2.40
❑ 135 R.Franklin/1600 RC	8.00	2.40
❑ 136 M.Lamb/1500 AU RC	15.00	4.50
❑ 137 David Espinosa 1500 AU RC	10.00	3.00
❑ 138 Matt Wheatland 1500 AU RC	10.00	3.00
❑ 139 X.Nady/1500 AU RC	25.00	7.50
❑ 140 S.Heard/1500 AU RC	10.00	3.00
❑ 141 P.Coco/1500 AU RC	10.00	3.00
Card erroneously numbered 54 instead of 141		
❑ 142 J.Miller/1500 AU RC	10.00	3.00
❑ 143 Dave Krynzel 1500 AU RC	15.00	4.50
❑ 144 Dane Sardinha 1500 AU RC	10.00	3.00
❑ 145 B.Sheets/1500 AU RC	80.00	24.00
❑ 146 L.Estrella/1500 AU RC	10.00	3.00
❑ 147 Ben Diggins 1500 AU RC	10.00	3.00
❑ 148 B.Zito/1500 AU RC	80.00	24.00
❑ 149 J.Torres/1500 AU RC	10.00	3.00
❑ 150 Mike Meyers 1500 AU RC	10.00	3.00
❑ 151 K.Wilson/1500 AU RC	10.00	3.00
❑ 152 Darin Erstad	.75	.23
❑ 153 Richard Hidalgo	.75	.23
❑ 154 Eric Chavez	.75	.23
❑ 155 B.J. Surhoff	.75	.23
❑ 156 Richie Sexson	.75	.23
❑ 157 Raul Mondesi	.75	.23
❑ 158 Rondell White	.75	.23
❑ 159 Jim Edmonds	.75	.23
❑ 160 Curt Schilling	.75	.23
❑ 161 Tom Goodwin	.75	.23
❑ 162 Fred McGriff	1.25	.35
❑ 163 Jose Vidro	.75	.23
❑ 164 Ellis Burks	.75	.23
❑ 165 David Segui	.75	.23
❑ 166 Aaron Sele	.75	.23
❑ 167 Henry Rodriguez	.75	.23
❑ 168 Mike Bordick	.75	.23
❑ 169 Mike Mussina	1.25	.35
❑ 170 Ryan Klesko	.75	.23
❑ 171 Kevin Young	.75	.23
❑ 172 Travis Lee	.75	.23
❑ 173 Aaron Boone	.75	.23
❑ 174 Jermaine Dye	.75	.23
❑ 175 Ricky Ledee	.75	.23
❑ 176 Jeffrey Hammonds	.75	.23
❑ 177 Carl Everett	.75	.23
❑ 178 Matt Lawton	.75	.23
❑ 179 Bobby Higginson	.75	.23
❑ 180 Charles Johnson	.75	.23
❑ 181 David Justice	.75	.23
❑ 182 Joey Nation/1600 RC	8.00	2.40
❑ 183 Rico Washington 1600 RC	8.00	2.40
❑ 184 Luis Matos/1600 RC	8.00	2.40
❑ 185 C.Wakeland/1600 RC	8.00	2.40
❑ 186 SW Kim/1600 RC	8.00	2.40
❑ 187 Keith Ginter/1600 RC	8.00	2.40
❑ 188 G.Guzman/1600 RC	8.00	2.40
❑ 189 J.Spurgeon/1600 RC	8.00	2.40
❑ 190 Jace Brewer/1600 RC	8.00	2.40
❑ 191 J.Guzman/1600 RC	8.00	2.40
❑ 192 Ross Gload/1600 RC	8.00	2.40
❑ 193 P.Crawford/1600 RC	8.00	2.40
❑ 194 R.Kohlmeier/1600 RC	8.00	2.40
❑ 195 Julio Zuleta/1600 RC	8.00	2.40
❑ 196 Matt Ginter/1600 RC	8.00	2.40

2001 SPx

	Nm-Mt	Ex-Mt
COMP.BASIC w/o SP's (90)	25.00	7.50
COMP.UPDATE w/o SP's (30)	10.00	3.00
COMMON CARD (1-90)	.50	.15
COMMON YS (91-120)	5.00	1.50
COMMON JSY (121-135)	8.00	2.40

COMMON (136-150)	15.00	4.50
COMMON (151-180)	.75	.23
COMMON (181-210)	5.00	1.50

❑ 1 Darin Erstad	.50	.15
❑ 2 Troy Glaus	.50	.15
❑ 3 Mo Vaughn	.50	.15
❑ 4 Johnny Damon	.75	.23
❑ 5 Jason Giambi	.50	.15
❑ 6 Tim Hudson	.50	.15
❑ 7 Miguel Tejada	.50	.15
❑ 8 Carlos Delgado	.50	.15
❑ 9 Raul Mondesi	.50	.15
❑ 10 Tony Batista	.50	.15
❑ 11 Ben Grieve	.50	.15
❑ 12 Greg Vaughn	.50	.15
❑ 13 Juan Gonzalez	.50	.15
❑ 14 Jim Thome	.75	.23
❑ 15 Roberto Alomar	.75	.23
❑ 16 John Olerud	.50	.15
❑ 17 Edgar Martinez	.75	.23
❑ 18 Albert Belle	.50	.15
❑ 19 Cal Ripken	4.00	1.20
❑ 20 Ivan Rodriguez	.75	.23
❑ 21 Rafael Palmeiro	.75	.23
❑ 22 Alex Rodriguez	2.00	.60
❑ 23 Nomar Garciaparra	2.00	.60
❑ 24 Pedro Martinez	.75	.23
❑ 25 Manny Ramirez Sox	.75	.23
❑ 26 Jermaine Dye	.50	.15
❑ 27 Mark Quinn	.50	.15
❑ 28 Carlos Beltran	.50	.15
❑ 29 Tony Clark	.50	.15
❑ 30 Bobby Higginson	.50	.15
❑ 31 Eric Milton	.50	.15
❑ 32 Matt Lawton	.50	.15
❑ 33 Frank Thomas	1.25	.35
❑ 34 Magglio Ordonez	.50	.15
❑ 35 Ray Durham	.50	.15
❑ 36 David Wells	.50	.15
❑ 37 Derek Jeter	3.00	.90
❑ 38 Bernie Williams	.75	.23
❑ 39 Roger Clemens UER Wrong uniform number on card	2.50	.75
❑ 40 David Justice	.50	.15
❑ 41 Jeff Bagwell	.75	.23
❑ 42 Richard Hidalgo	.50	.15
❑ 43 Moises Alou	.50	.15
❑ 44 Chipper Jones	1.25	.35
❑ 45 Andruw Jones	.75	.23
❑ 46 Greg Maddux	2.00	.60
❑ 47 Rafael Furcal	.50	.15
❑ 48 Jeromy Burnitz	.50	.15
❑ 49 Geoff Jenkins	.50	.15
❑ 50 Mark McGwire	3.00	.90
❑ 51 Jim Edmonds	.75	.23
❑ 52 Rick Ankiel	.50	.15
❑ 53 Edgar Renteria	.50	.15
❑ 54 Sammy Sosa	1.25	.35
❑ 55 Kerry Wood	.50	.15
❑ 56 Rondell White	.50	.15
❑ 57 Randy Johnson	1.25	.35
❑ 58 Steve Finley	.50	.15
❑ 59 Matt Williams	.50	.15
❑ 60 Luis Gonzalez	.50	.15
❑ 61 Kevin Brown	.50	.15
❑ 62 Gary Sheffield	.50	.15
❑ 63 Shawn Green	.50	.15
❑ 64 Vladimir Guerrero	1.25	.35
❑ 65 Jose Vidro	.50	.15
❑ 66 Barry Bonds	3.00	.90
❑ 67 Jeff Kent	.50	.15
❑ 68 Livan Hernandez	.50	.15
❑ 69 Preston Wilson	.50	.15
❑ 70 Charles Johnson	.50	.15
❑ 71 Cliff Floyd	.50	.15
❑ 72 Mike Piazza	2.00	.60
❑ 73 Edgardo Alfonzo	.50	.15
❑ 74 Jay Payton	.50	.15
❑ 75 Robin Ventura	.50	.15
❑ 76 Tony Gwynn	1.50	.45
❑ 77 Phil Nevin	.50	.15
❑ 78 Ryan Klesko	.50	.15
❑ 79 Scott Rolen	.75	.23
❑ 80 Pat Burrell	.50	.15
❑ 81 Bob Abreu	.50	.15
❑ 82 Brian Giles	.50	.15
❑ 83 Kris Benson	.50	.15
❑ 84 Jason Kendall	.50	.15
❑ 85 Ken Griffey Jr.	2.00	.60
❑ 86 Barry Larkin	.75	.23
❑ 87 Sean Casey	.75	.23
❑ 88 Todd Helton	.75	.23
❑ 89 Larry Walker	.50	.15
❑ 90 Mike Hampton	.50	.15
❑ 91 Billy Sylvester YS RC	5.00	1.50
❑ 92 Josh Towers YS RC	8.00	2.40
❑ 93 Zach Day YS RC	5.00	1.50
❑ 94 Martin Vargas YS RC	5.00	1.50
❑ 95 Adam Pettyjohn YS RC	5.00	1.50
❑ 96 Andres Torres YS RC	5.00	1.50
❑ 97 Kris Keller YS RC	5.00	1.50
❑ 98 Blaine Neal YS RC	5.00	1.50
❑ 99 Kyle Kessel YS RC	5.00	1.50
❑ 100 Greg Miller YS RC	5.00	1.50
❑ 101 Shawn Sonnier YS	5.00	1.50
❑ 102 Alexis Gomez YS RC	5.00	1.50
❑ 103 Grant Balfour YS RC	5.00	1.50
❑ 104 Henry Mateo YS RC	5.00	1.50
❑ 105 Wilken Ruan YS RC	5.00	1.50
❑ 106 Nick Maness YS RC	5.00	1.50
❑ 107 J. Michaels YS RC	5.00	1.50
❑ 108 Esix Snead YS RC	5.00	1.50
❑ 109 William Ortega YS RC	5.00	1.50
❑ 110 David Elder YS RC	5.00	1.50
❑ 111 J. Melian YS RC	5.00	1.50
❑ 112 Nate Teut YS RC	5.00	1.50
❑ 113 Jason Smith YS RC	5.00	1.50
❑ 114 Mike Penney YS RC	5.00	1.50
❑ 115 Jose Mieses YS RC	5.00	1.50
❑ 116 Juan Pena YS	5.00	1.50
❑ 117 B. Lawrence YS RC	5.00	1.50
❑ 118 Jeremy Owens YS RC	5.00	1.50
❑ 119 C. Valderrama YS RC	5.00	1.50
❑ 120 Rafael Soriano YS RC	5.00	1.50
❑ 121 H. Ramirez JSY RC	10.00	3.00
❑ 122 R. Rodriguez JSY RC	8.00	2.40
❑ 123 Juan Diaz JSY RC	8.00	2.40
❑ 124 Donnie Bridges JSY	8.00	2.40
❑ 125 Tyler Walker JSY RC	8.00	2.40
❑ 126 Erick Almonte JSY RC	8.00	2.40
❑ 127 Jesus Colome JSY	8.00	2.40
❑ 128 Ryan Freel JSY RC	10.00	3.00
❑ 129 Elpidio Guzman JSY RC	8.00	2.40
❑ 130 Jack Cust JSY	8.00	2.40
❑ 131 Eric Hinske JSY RC	10.00	3.00
❑ 132 Josh Fogg JSY RC	8.00	2.40
❑ 133 Juan Uribe JSY RC	10.00	3.00
❑ 134 Bert Snow JSY RC	8.00	2.40
❑ 135 Pedro Feliz JSY	8.00	2.40
❑ 136 W. Betemit JSY AU RC	25.00	7.50
❑ 137 S. Douglass JSY AU RC	15.00	4.50
❑ 138 D. Stenson JSY AU	15.00	4.50
❑ 139 Brandon Inge JSY AU	15.00	4.50
❑ 140 M. Ensberg JSY AU RC	50.00	15.00
❑ 141 Brian Cole JSY AU	15.00	4.50
❑ 142 A. Hernandez JSY AU RC	15.00	4.50
❑ 143 Brandon Duckworth JSY AU RC	15.00	4.50
❑ 144 J. Wilson JSY AU RC	25.00	7.50
❑ 145 T. Hafner JSY AU RC	70.00	21.00
❑ 146 Carlos Pena JSY AU	15.00	4.50
❑ 147 C. Patterson JSY AU	15.00	4.50
❑ 148 Xavier Nady JSY AU	15.00	4.50
❑ 149 Jason Hart JSY AU	15.00	4.50
❑ 150 I.Suzuki JSY AU RC	800.00	240.00
❑ 151 Garret Anderson	.75	.23
❑ 152 Jermaine Dye	.75	.23
❑ 153 Shannon Stewart	.75	.23
❑ 154 Toby Hall	.75	.23
❑ 155 C.C. Sabathia	.75	.23
❑ 156 Bret Boone	.75	.23
❑ 157 Tony Batista	.75	.23
❑ 158 Gabe Kapler	.75	.23
❑ 159 Carl Everett	.75	.23
❑ 160 Mike Sweeney	.75	.23
❑ 161 Dean Palmer	.75	.23
❑ 162 Doug Mientkiewicz	.75	.23
❑ 163 Carlos Lee	.75	.23
❑ 164 Mike Mussina	1.25	.35
❑ 165 Lance Berkman	.75	.23
❑ 166 Ken Caminiti	.75	.23
❑ 167 Ben Sheets	1.25	.35
❑ 168 Matt Morris	.75	.23
❑ 169 Fred McGriff	1.25	.35
❑ 170 Curt Schilling	.75	.23
❑ 171 Paul LoDuca	.75	.23
❑ 172 Javier Vazquez	.75	.23
❑ 173 Rich Aurilia	.75	.23
❑ 174 A.J. Burnett	.75	.23
❑ 175 Al Leiter	.75	.23
❑ 176 Mark Kotsay	.75	.23
❑ 177 Jimmy Rollins	.75	.23
❑ 178 Aramis Ramirez	.75	.23
❑ 179 Aaron Boone	.75	.23
❑ 180 Jeff Cirillo	.75	.23
❑ 181 J.Estrada YS RC	8.00	2.40
❑ 182 Dave Williams YS RC	5.00	1.50
❑ 183 D.Mendez YS RC	5.00	1.50
❑ 184 Junior Spivey YS RC	8.00	2.40
❑ 185 Jay Gibbons YS RC	8.00	2.40
❑ 186 Kyle Lohse YS RC	8.00	2.40
❑ 187 Willie Harris YS RC	5.00	1.50
❑ 188 Juan Cruz YS RC	5.00	1.50
❑ 189 Joe Kennedy YS RC	8.00	2.40
❑ 190 D.Sanchez YS RC	5.00	1.50
❑ 191 Jorge Julio YS RC	5.00	1.50
❑ 192 Cesar Crespo YS RC	5.00	1.50
❑ 193 Casey Fossum YS RC	5.00	1.50
❑ 194 Brian Roberts YS RC	15.00	4.50
❑ 195 Troy Mattes YS RC	5.00	1.50
❑ 196 R.Mackowiak YS RC	8.00	2.40
❑ 197 T.Shinjo YS RC	8.00	2.40
❑ 198 Nick Punto YS RC	5.00	1.50
❑ 199 Wilmy Caceres YS RC	5.00	1.50
❑ 200 Jeremy Affeldt YS RC	5.00	1.50
❑ 201 Bret Prinz YS RC	5.00	1.50
❑ 202 Delvin James YS RC	5.00	1.50
❑ 203 Luis Pineda YS RC	5.00	1.50
❑ 204 Matt White YS RC	5.00	1.50
❑ 205 B.Knight YS RC	5.00	1.50
❑ 206 Albert Pujols YS AU RC	550.00	160.00
❑ 207 M.Teixeira YS AU RC	200.00	60.00
❑ 208 Mark Prior YS AU RC	125.00	38.00
❑ 209 D.Brazelton YS AU RC	15.00	4.50
❑ 210 Bud Smith YS AU RC	15.00	4.50

2002 SPx

	Nm-Mt	Ex-Mt
COMP.LOW w/o SP's (90)	25.00	7.50
COMP.UPDATE w/o SP's (30)	10.00	3.00
COMMON CARD (1-90)	.50	.15

Card		Price	Price
COMMON ROOKIE (91A-		8.00	2.40
COMMON CARD (121-150)		15.00	4.50
COMMON CARD (151-190)		8.00	2.40
COMMON CARD (191-220)		.75	.23
COMMON CARD (221-250)		10.00	3.00
❑ 1	Troy Glaus	.50	.15
❑ 2	Darin Erstad	.50	.15
❑ 3	David Justice	.50	.15
❑ 4	Tim Hudson	.50	.15
❑ 5	Miguel Tejada	.50	.15
❑ 6	Barry Zito	.50	.15
❑ 7	Carlos Delgado	.50	.15
❑ 8	Shannon Stewart	.50	.15
❑ 9	Greg Vaughn	.50	.15
❑ 10	Toby Hall	.50	.15
❑ 11	Jim Thome	.75	.23
❑ 12	C.C. Sabathia	.50	.15
❑ 13	Ichiro Suzuki	2.50	.75
❑ 14	Edgar Martinez	.75	.23
❑ 15	Freddy Garcia	.50	.15
❑ 16	Mike Cameron	.50	.15
❑ 17	Jeff Conine	.50	.15
❑ 18	Tony Batista	.50	.15
❑ 19	Alex Rodriguez	2.00	.60
❑ 20	Rafael Palmeiro	.75	.23
❑ 21	Ivan Rodriguez	.75	.23
❑ 22	Carl Everett	.50	.15
❑ 23	Pedro Martinez	.75	.23
❑ 24	Manny Ramirez	.75	.23
❑ 25	Nomar Garciaparra	2.00	.60
❑ 26	Johnny Damon Sox	.75	.23
❑ 27	Mike Sweeney	.50	.15
❑ 28	Carlos Beltran	.50	.15
❑ 29	Dmitri Young	.50	.15
❑ 30	Joe Mays	.50	.15
❑ 31	Doug Mientkiewicz	.50	.15
❑ 32	Cristian Guzman	.50	.15
❑ 33	Corey Koskie	.50	.15
❑ 34	Frank Thomas	1.25	.35
❑ 35	Magglio Ordonez	.50	.15
❑ 36	Mark Buehrle	.50	.15
❑ 37	Bernie Williams	.75	.23
❑ 38	Roger Clemens	2.50	.75
❑ 39	Derek Jeter	3.00	.90
❑ 40	Jason Giambi	.50	.15
❑ 41	Mike Mussina	.75	.23
❑ 42	Lance Berkman	.50	.15
❑ 43	Jeff Bagwell	.75	.23
❑ 44	Roy Oswalt	.50	.15
❑ 45	Greg Maddux	2.00	.60
❑ 46	Chipper Jones	1.25	.35
❑ 47	Andruw Jones	.75	.23
❑ 48	Gary Sheffield	.50	.15
❑ 49	Geoff Jenkins	.50	.15
❑ 50	Richie Sexson	.50	.15
❑ 51	Ben Sheets	.50	.15
❑ 52	Albert Pujols	2.50	.75
❑ 53	J.D. Drew	.50	.15
❑ 54	Jim Edmonds	.75	.23
❑ 55	Sammy Sosa	1.25	.35
❑ 56	Moises Alou	.50	.15
❑ 57	Kerry Wood	.50	.15
❑ 58	Jon Lieber	.50	.15
❑ 59	Fred McGriff	.75	.23
❑ 60	Randy Johnson	1.25	.35
❑ 61	Luis Gonzalez	.50	.15
❑ 62	Curt Schilling	.50	.15
❑ 63	Kevin Brown	.50	.15
❑ 64	Hideo Nomo	1.25	.35
❑ 65	Shawn Green	.50	.15
❑ 66	Vladimir Guerrero	1.25	.35
❑ 67	Jose Vidro	.50	.15
❑ 68	Barry Bonds	3.00	.90
❑ 69	Jeff Kent	.50	.15
❑ 70	Rich Aurilia	.50	.15
❑ 71	Cliff Floyd	.50	.15
❑ 72	Josh Beckett	.50	.15
❑ 73	Preston Wilson	.50	.15
❑ 74	Mike Piazza	2.00	.60
❑ 75	Mo Vaughn	.50	.15
❑ 76	Jeromy Burnitz	.50	.15
❑ 77	Roberto Alomar	.75	.23
❑ 78	Phil Nevin	.50	.15
❑ 79	Ryan Klesko	.50	.15
❑ 80	Scott Rolen	.75	.23
❑ 81	Bobby Abreu	.50	.15
❑ 82	Jimmy Rollins	.50	.15
❑ 83	Brian Giles	.50	.15
❑ 84	Aramis Ramirez	.50	.15
❑ 85	Ken Griffey Jr.	2.00	.60
❑ 86	Sean Casey	.75	.23
❑ 87	Barry Larkin	.75	.23
❑ 88	Mike Hampton	.50	.15
❑ 89	Larry Walker	.50	.15
❑ 90	Todd Helton	.75	.23
❑ 91A	Ron Calloway YS RC	8.00	2.40
❑ 91P	Ron Calloway YS RC	8.00	2.40
❑ 92A	Joe Orloski YS RC	8.00	2.40
❑ 92P	Joe Orloski YS RC	8.00	2.40
❑ 93A	An. Machado YS RC	8.00	2.40
❑ 93P	An. Machado YS RC	8.00	2.40
❑ 94A	Eric Good YS RC	8.00	2.40
❑ 94P	Eric Good YS RC	8.00	2.40
❑ 95A	Reed Johnson YS RC	10.00	3.00
❑ 95P	Reed Johnson YS RC	10.00	3.00
❑ 96A	Brendan Donnelly YS RC	8.00	2.40
❑ 96P	Brendan Donnelly YS RC	8.00	2.40
❑ 97A	Chris Baker YS RC	8.00	2.40
❑ 97P	Chris Baker YS RC	8.00	2.40
❑ 98A	Wilson Valdez YS RC	8.00	2.40
❑ 98P	Wilson Valdez YS RC	8.00	2.40
❑ 99A	Scotty Layfield YS RC	8.00	2.40
❑ 99P	Scotty Layfield YS RC	8.00	2.40
❑ 100A	P.J. Bevis YS RC	8.00	2.40
❑ 100P	P.J. Bevis YS RC	8.00	2.40
❑ 101A	Edwin Almonte YS RC	8.00	2.40
❑ 101P	Edwin Almonte YS RC	8.00	2.40
❑ 102A	Francis Beltran YS RC	8.00	2.40
❑ 102P	Francis Beltran YS RC	8.00	2.40
❑ 103A	Val Pascucci YS	8.00	2.40
❑ 103P	Val Pascucci YS	8.00	2.40
❑ 104A	Nelson Castro YS RC	8.00	2.40
❑ 104P	Nelson Castro YS RC	8.00	2.40
❑ 105A	Michael Crudale YS RC	8.00	2.40
❑ 105P	Michael Crudale YS RC	8.00	2.40
❑ 106A	Colin Young YS RC	8.00	2.40
❑ 106P	Colin Young YS RC	8.00	2.40
❑ 107A	Todd Donovan YS RC	8.00	2.40
❑ 107P	Todd Donovan YS RC	8.00	2.40
❑ 108A	Felix Escalona YS RC	8.00	2.40
❑ 108P	Felix Escalona YS RC	8.00	2.40
❑ 109A	Brandon Backe YS RC	10.00	3.00
❑ 109P	Brandon Backe YS RC	10.00	3.00
❑ 110A	Corey Thurman YS RC	8.00	2.40
❑ 110P	Corey Thurman YS RC	8.00	2.40
❑ 111A	Kyle Kane YS RC	8.00	2.40
❑ 111P	Kyle Kane YS RC	8.00	2.40
❑ 112A	Allan Simpson YS RC	8.00	2.40
❑ 112P	Allan Simpson YS RC	8.00	2.40
❑ 113A	Jose Valverde YS RC	8.00	2.40
❑ 113P	Jose Valverde YS RC	8.00	2.40
❑ 114A	Chris Booker YS RC	8.00	2.40
❑ 114P	Chris Booker YS RC	8.00	2.40
❑ 115A	Brandon Puffer YS RC	8.00	2.40
❑ 115P	Brandon Puffer YS RC	8.00	2.40
❑ 116A	John Foster YS RC	8.00	2.40
❑ 116P	John Foster YS RC	8.00	2.40
❑ 117A	Cliff Bartosh YS RC	8.00	2.40
❑ 117P	Cliff Bartosh YS RC	8.00	2.40
❑ 118A	Gustavo Chacin YS RC	10.00	3.00
❑ 118P	Gustavo Chacin YS RC	10.00	3.00
❑ 119A	Steve Kent YS RC	8.00	2.40
❑ 119P	Steve Kent YS RC	8.00	2.40
❑ 120A	Nate Field YS RC	8.00	2.40
❑ 120P	Nate Field YS RC	8.00	2.40
❑ 121	Victor Alvarez AU RC	10.00	3.00
❑ 122	Steve Bechler AU RC	10.00	3.00
❑ 123	Adrian Burnside AU RC	10.00	3.00
❑ 124	Marlon Byrd AU	15.00	4.50
❑ 125	Jaime Cerda AU RC	10.00	3.00
❑ 126	Brandon Claussen AU	15.00	4.50
❑ 127	Mark Corey AU RC	10.00	3.00
❑ 128	Doug Devore AU RC	10.00	3.00
❑ 129	Kazuhisa Ishii AU SP RC	80.00	24.00
❑ 130	John Ennis AU RC	10.00	3.00
❑ 131	Kevin Frederick AU RC	10.00	3.00
❑ 132	Josh Hancock AU RC	10.00	3.00
❑ 133	Ben Howard AU RC	10.00	3.00
❑ 134	Orlando Hudson AU	15.00	4.50
❑ 135	Hansel Izquierdo AU RC	10.00	3.00
❑ 136	Eric Junge AU RC	10.00	3.00
❑ 137	Austin Kearns AU	15.00	4.50
❑ 138	Victor Martinez AU	25.00	7.50
❑ 139	Luis Martinez AU RC	10.00	3.00
❑ 140	Danny Mota AU RC	10.00	3.00
❑ 141	Jorge Padilla AU RC	10.00	3.00
❑ 142	Andy Pratt AU RC	10.00	3.00
❑ 143	Rene Reyes AU RC	10.00	3.00
❑ 144	Rodrigo Rosario AU RC	10.00	3.00
❑ 145	Tom Shearn AU RC	10.00	3.00
❑ 146	So Taguchi AU SP RC	40.00	12.00
❑ 147	Dennis Tankersley AU	15.00	4.50
❑ 148	Matt Thornton AU RC	10.00	3.00
❑ 149	Jeremy Ward AU RC	10.00	3.00
❑ 150	Mitch Wylie AU RC	10.00	3.00
❑ 151	Pedro Martinez JSY/800	10.00	3.00
❑ 152	Cal Ripken JSY/800	40.00	12.00
❑ 153	Roger Clemens JSY/800	25.00	7.50
❑ 154	Bernie Williams JSY/800	10.00	3.00
❑ 155	Jason Giambi JSY/700	8.00	2.40
❑ 156	Robin Ventura JSY/800	8.00	2.40
❑ 157	Carlos Delgado JSY/800	8.00	2.40
❑ 158	Frank Thomas JSY/800	10.00	3.00
❑ 159	Mag. Ordonez JSY/800	8.00	2.40
❑ 160	Jim Thome JSY/800	10.00	3.00
❑ 161	Darin Erstad JSY/800	8.00	2.40
❑ 162	Tim Salmon JSY/800	10.00	3.00
❑ 163	Tim Hudson JSY/800	8.00	2.40
❑ 164	Barry Zito JSY/800	8.00	2.40
❑ 165	Ichiro Suzuki JSY/800	40.00	12.00
❑ 166	Edgar Martinez JSY/800	10.00	3.00
❑ 167	Alex Rodriguez JSY/800	20.00	6.00
❑ 168	Ivan Rodriguez JSY/800	10.00	3.00
❑ 169	Juan Gonzalez JSY/800	8.00	2.40
❑ 170	Greg Maddux JSY/800	15.00	4.50
❑ 171	Chipper Jones JSY/800	10.00	3.00
❑ 172	Andruw Jones JSY/800	10.00	3.00
❑ 173	Tom Glavine JSY/800	10.00	3.00
❑ 174	Mike Piazza JSY/800	15.00	4.50
❑ 175	Roberto Alomar JSY/800	10.00	3.00
❑ 176	Scott Rolen JSY/800	10.00	3.00
❑ 177	Sammy Sosa JSY/800	10.00	3.00
❑ 178	Moises Alou JSY/800	8.00	2.40
❑ 179	Ken Griffey Jr. JSY/700	20.00	6.00
❑ 180	Jeff Bagwell JSY/800	10.00	3.00
❑ 181	Jim Edmonds JSY/800	10.00	3.00
❑ 182	J.D. Drew JSY/800	8.00	2.40
❑ 183	Brian Giles JSY/800	8.00	2.40
❑ 184	Randy Johnson JSY/800	10.00	3.00
❑ 185	Curt Schilling JSY/800	8.00	2.40
❑ 186	Luis Gonzalez JSY/800	8.00	2.40
❑ 187	Todd Helton JSY/800	10.00	3.00
❑ 188	Shawn Green JSY/800	8.00	2.40
❑ 189	David Wells JSY/800	8.00	2.40
❑ 190	Jeff Kent JSY/800	8.00	2.40
❑ 191	Tom Glavine	1.25	.35
❑ 192	Cliff Floyd	.75	.23
❑ 193	Mark Prior	2.00	.60
❑ 194	Corey Patterson	.75	.23
❑ 195	Paul Konerko	.75	.23
❑ 196	Adam Dunn	.75	.23
❑ 197	Joe Borchard	.75	.23
❑ 198	Carlos Pena	.75	.23
❑ 199	Juan Encarnacion	.75	.23
❑ 200	Luis Castillo	.75	.23
❑ 201	Torii Hunter	.75	.23
❑ 202	Hee Seop Choi	.75	.23
❑ 203	Bartolo Colon	.75	.23
❑ 204	Raul Mondesi	.75	.23
❑ 205	Jeff Weaver	.75	.23
❑ 206	Eric Munson	.75	.23
❑ 207	Alfonso Soriano	.75	.23
❑ 208	Ray Durham	.75	.23
❑ 209	Eric Chavez	.75	.23
❑ 210	Brett Myers	.75	.23
❑ 211	Jeremy Giambi	.75	.23
❑ 212	Vicente Padilla	.75	.23
❑ 213	Felipe Lopez	.75	.23
❑ 214	Sean Burroughs	.75	.23
❑ 215	Kenny Lofton	.75	.23
❑ 216	Scott Rolen	1.25	.35
❑ 217	Carl Crawford	.75	.23
❑ 218	Juan Gonzalez	.75	.23
❑ 219	Orlando Hudson	.75	.23
❑ 220	Eric Hinske	.75	.23
❑ 221	Adam Walker AU RC	10.00	3.00
❑ 222	Aaron Cook AU RC	10.00	3.00

Card	MINT	NRMT
❑ 223 Cam Esslinger AU RC	10.00	3.00
❑ 224 Kirk Saarloos AU RC	10.00	3.00
❑ 225 Jose Diaz AU RC	10.00	3.00
❑ 226 David Ross AU RC	10.00	3.00
❑ 227 Jayson Durocher AU RC	10.00	3.00
❑ 228 Brian Mallette AU RC	10.00	3.00
❑ 229 Aaron Guiel AU RC	10.00	3.00
❑ 230 Jorge Nunez AU RC	10.00	3.00
❑ 231 Satoru Komiyama AU RC	25.00	7.50
❑ 232 Tyler Yates AU RC	10.00	3.00
❑ 233 Pete Zamora AU RC	10.00	3.00
❑ 234 Mike Gonzalez AU RC	10.00	3.00
❑ 235 Oliver Perez AU RC	40.00	12.00
❑ 236 Julius Matos AU RC	10.00	3.00
❑ 237 Andy Shibilo AU RC	10.00	3.00
❑ 238 J.Simontacchi AU RC	10.00	3.00
❑ 239 Ron Chiavacci AU	10.00	3.00
❑ 240 Deivis Santos AU	10.00	3.00
❑ 241 Travis Driskill AU RC	10.00	3.00
❑ 242 Jorge De La Rosa AU RC	10.00	3.00
❑ 243 An. Martinez AU RC	10.00	3.00
❑ 244 Earl Snyder AU RC	10.00	3.00
❑ 245 Freddy Sanchez AU RC	10.00	3.00
❑ 246 Miguel Asencio AU RC	10.00	3.00
❑ 247 Juan Brito AU RC	10.00	3.00
❑ 248 Franklyn German AU RC	10.00	3.00
❑ 249 Chris Snelling AU RC	25.00	7.50
❑ 250 Ken Huckaby AU RC	10.00	3.00

2003 SPx

	MINT	NRMT
COMP.LO SET w/o SP's (100)	25.00	11.00
COMP.LO SET w/ SP's (125)	100.00	45.00
COMMON CARD (1-125)	.50	.23
COMMON SP (1-125)	4.00	1.80
COMMON CARD (126-160)	8.00	3.60
COMMON CARD (161-178)	15.00	6.75
163-178 PRINT RUN 1224 SERIAL #'d SETS		
126-178 RANDOM INSERTS IN SPx PACKS		
COMMON CARD (179-193)	15.00	6.75
COMMON CARD (381-387)	20.00	9.00

Card	MINT	NRMT
❑ 1 Darin Erstad	.50	.23
❑ 2 Garret Anderson	.50	.23
❑ 3 Tim Salmon	.75	.35
❑ 4 Troy Glaus SP	4.00	1.80
❑ 5 Luis Gonzalez	.50	.23
❑ 6 Randy Johnson	1.25	.55
❑ 7 Curt Schilling	.50	.23
❑ 8 Lyle Overbay	.50	.23
❑ 9 Andruw Jones SP	4.00	1.80
❑ 10 Gary Sheffield	.50	.23
❑ 11 Rafael Furcal	.50	.23
❑ 12 Greg Maddux	2.00	.90
❑ 13 Chipper Jones SP	5.00	2.20
❑ 14 Tony Batista	.50	.23
❑ 15 Rodrigo Lopez	.50	.23
❑ 16 Jay Gibbons	.50	.23
❑ 17 Byung-Hyun Kim	.50	.23
❑ 18 Johnny Damon	.75	.35
❑ 19 Derek Lowe	.50	.23
❑ 20 Nomar Garciaparra SP	8.00	3.60
❑ 21 Pedro Martinez	.75	.35
❑ 22 Manny Ramirez SP	4.00	1.80
❑ 23 Mark Prior	.75	.35
❑ 24 Kerry Wood	.50	.23
❑ 25 Corey Patterson	.50	.23
❑ 26 Sammy Sosa SP	5.00	2.20
❑ 27 Moises Alou	.50	.23
❑ 28 Magglio Ordonez	.50	.23
❑ 29 Frank Thomas	1.25	.55
❑ 30 Paul Konerko	.50	.23
❑ 31 Bartolo Colon	.50	.23
❑ 32 Adam Dunn	.50	.23
❑ 33 Austin Kearns	.50	.23
❑ 34 Aaron Boone	.50	.23
❑ 35 Ken Griffey Jr. SP	8.00	3.60
❑ 36 Omar Vizquel	.75	.35
❑ 37 C.C. Sabathia	.50	.23
❑ 38 Jason Davis	.50	.23
❑ 39 Travis Hafner	.50	.23
❑ 40 Brandon Phillips	.50	.23
❑ 41 Larry Walker	.50	.23
❑ 42 Preston Wilson	.50	.23
❑ 43 Jay Payton	.50	.23
❑ 44 Todd Helton	.75	.35
❑ 45 Carlos Pena	.50	.23
❑ 46 Eric Munson	.50	.23
❑ 47 Ivan Rodriguez	.75	.35
❑ 48 Josh Beckett	.50	.23
❑ 49 Alex Gonzalez	.50	.23
❑ 50 Roy Oswalt	.50	.23
❑ 51 Craig Biggio	.75	.35
❑ 52 Jeff Bagwell	.75	.35
❑ 53 Dontrelle Willis SP	5.00	2.20
❑ 54 Mike Sweeney	.50	.23
❑ 55 Carlos Beltran	.50	.23
❑ 56 Brent Mayne	.50	.23
❑ 57 Hideo Nomo	1.25	.55
❑ 58 Rickey Henderson	1.25	.55
❑ 59 Adrian Beltre	.50	.23
❑ 60 Miguel Cabrera SP	5.00	2.20
❑ 61 Kazuhisa Ishii	.50	.23
❑ 62 Ben Sheets	.50	.23
❑ 63 Richie Sexson	.50	.23
❑ 64 Torii Hunter SP	4.00	1.80
❑ 65 Jacque Jones	.50	.23
❑ 66 Joe Mays	.50	.23
❑ 67 Corey Koskie	.50	.23
❑ 68 A.J. Pierzynski	.50	.23
❑ 69 Jose Vidro	.50	.23
❑ 70 Vladimir Guerrero SP	5.00	2.20
❑ 71 Tom Glavine	.75	.35
❑ 72 Jose Reyes SP	4.00	1.80
❑ 73 Aaron Heilman	.50	.23
❑ 74 Mike Piazza	2.00	.90
❑ 75 Jorge Posada	.75	.35
❑ 76 Mike Mussina	.75	.35
❑ 77 Robin Ventura	.50	.23
❑ 78 Mariano Rivera	.75	.35
❑ 79 Roger Clemens SP	10.00	4.50
❑ 80 Jason Giambi	.50	.23
❑ 81 Bernie Williams	.75	.35
❑ 82 Alfonso Soriano SP	4.00	1.80
❑ 83 Derek Jeter SP	12.00	5.50
❑ 84 Miguel Tejada SP	4.00	1.80
❑ 85 Eric Chavez	.50	.23
❑ 86 Tim Hudson	.50	.23
❑ 87 Barry Zito	.50	.23
❑ 88 Mark Mulder	.50	.23
❑ 89 Erubiel Durazo	.50	.23
❑ 90 Pat Burrell	.50	.23
❑ 91 Jim Thome SP	4.00	1.80
❑ 92 Bobby Abreu	.50	.23
❑ 93 Brian Giles	.50	.23
❑ 94 Reggie Sanders SP	4.00	1.80
❑ 95 Kenny Lofton	.50	.23
❑ 96 Ryan Klesko	.50	.23
❑ 97 Sean Burroughs	.50	.23
❑ 98 Edgardo Alfonzo	.50	.23
❑ 99 Rich Aurilia	.50	.23
❑ 100 Jose Cruz Jr.	.50	.23
❑ 101 Barry Bonds SP	12.00	5.50
❑ 102 Mike Cameron	.50	.23
❑ 103 Kazuhiro Sasaki	.50	.23
❑ 104 Bret Boone	.50	.23
❑ 105 Ichiro Suzuki SP	10.00	4.50
❑ 106 J.D. Drew	.50	.23
❑ 107 Jim Edmonds	.75	.35
❑ 108 Scott Rolen SP	4.00	1.80
❑ 109 Matt Morris	.50	.23
❑ 110 Tino Martinez	.75	.35
❑ 111 Albert Pujols SP	10.00	4.50
❑ 112 Damian Rolls	.50	.23
❑ 113 Carl Crawford	.50	.23
❑ 114 Rocco Baldelli SP	4.00	1.80
❑ 115 Hank Blalock	.50	.23
❑ 116 Alex Rodriguez SP	8.00	3.60
❑ 117 Kevin Mench	.50	.23
❑ 118 Rafael Palmeiro	.75	.35
❑ 119 Mark Teixeira	.75	.35
❑ 120 Shannon Stewart	.50	.23
❑ 121 Vernon Wells	.50	.23
❑ 122 Josh Phelps	.50	.23
❑ 123 Eric Hinske	.50	.23
❑ 124 Orlando Hudson	.50	.23
❑ 125 Carlos Delgado SP	4.00	1.80
❑ 126 Jason Roach ROO RC	8.00	3.60
❑ 127 Dan Haren ROO RC	10.00	4.50
❑ 128 Luis Ayala ROO RC	8.00	3.60
❑ 129 Bo Hart ROO RC	8.00	3.60
❑ 130 Wil. Ledezma ROO RC	8.00	3.60
❑ 131 Rick Roberts ROO RC	8.00	3.60
❑ 132 Miguel Ojeda ROO RC	8.00	3.60
❑ 133 Aquilino Lopez ROO RC	8.00	3.60
❑ 134 Roger Deago ROO RC	8.00	3.60
❑ 135 Arnie Munoz ROO RC	8.00	3.60
❑ 136 Brent Hoard ROO RC	8.00	3.60
❑ 137 Terrmel Sledge ROO RC	8.00	3.60
❑ 138 Ryan Cameron ROO RC	8.00	3.60
❑ 139 Pr. Redman ROO RC	8.00	3.60
❑ 140 Clint Barmes ROO RC	10.00	4.50
❑ 141 Jeremy Griffiths ROO RC	8.00	3.60
❑ 142 Jon Leicester ROO RC	8.00	3.60
❑ 143 Brandon Webb ROO RC	10.00	4.50
❑ 144 T.Wellemeyer ROO RC	8.00	3.60
❑ 145 Felix Sanchez ROO RC	8.00	3.60
❑ 146 Anthony Ferrari ROO RC	8.00	3.60
❑ 147 Ian Ferguson ROO RC	8.00	3.60
❑ 148 Mi. Nakamura ROO RC	8.00	3.60
❑ 149 Lew Ford ROO RC	10.00	4.50
❑ 150 Nate Bland ROO RC	8.00	3.60
❑ 151 David Matranga ROO RC	8.00	3.60
❑ 152 Edgar Gonzalez ROO RC	8.00	3.60
❑ 153 Carlos Mendez ROO RC	8.00	3.60
❑ 154 Jason Gilfillan ROO RC	8.00	3.60
❑ 155 Mike Neu ROO RC	8.00	3.60
❑ 156 Jason Shiell ROO RC	8.00	3.60
❑ 157 Jeff Duncan ROO RC	8.00	3.60
❑ 158 Oscar Villarreal ROO RC	8.00	3.60
❑ 159 D.Markwell ROO RC	8.00	3.60
❑ 160 Joe Valentine ROO RC	8.00	3.60
❑ 161 H.Matsui AU JSY RC	400.00	180.00
❑ 162 Jose Contreras AU RC	30.00	13.50
❑ 163 Willie Eyre AU JSY RC	15.00	6.75
❑ 164 Matt Bruback AU JSY RC	15.00	6.75
❑ 165 Rett Johnson AU JSY RC	15.00	6.75
❑ 166 Jeremy Griffiths AU JSY	15.00	6.75
❑ 167 Fran Cruceta AU JSY RC	15.00	6.75
❑ 168 Fern Cabrera AU JSY RC	15.00	6.75
❑ 169 J.Peralta AU JSY	40.00	18.00
❑ 170 S.Bazzell AU JSY RC	15.00	6.75
❑ 171 B.Madritsch AU JSY RC	25.00	11.00
❑ 172 Phil Seibel AU JSY RC	15.00	6.75
❑ 173 J.Willingham AU JSY RC	25.00	11.00
❑ 174 R.Hammock AU JSY RC	15.00	6.75
❑ 175 A.Machado AU JSY RC	15.00	6.75
❑ 176 D.Sanders AU JSY RC	15.00	6.75
❑ 177 Matt Kata AU JSY RC	15.00	6.75
❑ 178 Heath Bell AU JSY RC	15.00	6.75
❑ 179 Chad Gaudin ROO RC	15.00	6.75
❑ 180 Chris Capuano ROO RC	15.00	6.75
❑ 181 Danny Garcia ROO RC	15.00	6.75
❑ 182 Delmon Young ROO	80.00	36.00
❑ 183 Edwin Jackson ROO RC	20.00	9.00
❑ 184 Greg Jones ROO RC	15.00	6.75
❑ 185 Jeremy Bonderman ROO RC	40.00	18.00
❑ 186 Jorge DePaula ROO	15.00	6.75
❑ 187 Khalil Greene ROO	25.00	11.00
❑ 188 Chad Cordero ROO RC	25.00	11.00
❑ 189 Miguel Cabrera ROO	20.00	9.00
❑ 190 Rich Harden ROO	20.00	9.00
❑ 191 Rickie Weeks ROO	50.00	22.00
❑ 192 Rosman Garcia ROO RC	15.00	6.75
❑ 193 Tom Gregorio ROO RC	15.00	6.75
❑ 381 Andrew Brown AU JSY RC	25.00	11.00
❑ 382 Delm Young AU JSY RC	450.00	200.00
❑ 383 Colin Porter AU JSY RC	20.00	9.00
❑ 385 Rickie Weeks AU JSY RC	200.00	90.00
❑ 386 David Matranga AU JSY RC	20.00	9.00
❑ 387 Bo Hart AU JSY	20.00	9.00

2004 SPx

	Nm-Mt	Ex-Mt
COMP.SET w/o SP's (100)	25.00	7.50
COMMON CARD (1-100)	.50	.15
COMMON CARD (101-110)	8.00	2.40
101-110 STATED ODDS 1:18		
COMMON CARD (111-145)	5.00	1.50
111-145 PRINT RUN 1599 SERIAL #'d SETS		.00
COMMON CARD (146-154)	8.00	2.40
146-154 PRINT RUN 499 SERIAL #'d SETS		
COMMON CARD (155-160)	8.00	2.40
155-160 PRINT RUN 299 SERIAL #'d SETS		
111-160 ODDS W/SPECTRUM 1:9		
161-202 ODDS W/SPECTRUM 1:18		
161-202 PRINT RUN 799 SERIAL #'d SETS		
EXCHANGE DEADLINE 12/03/07		
MASTER PLATE ODDS 1:2500		
MASTER PLATE PRINT RUN 1 #'d SET		
NO PLATE PRICING DUE TO SCARCITY		

Card	Nm-Mt	Ex-Mt
❑ 1 Alfonso Soriano	.50	.15
❑ 2 Todd Helton	.75	.23
❑ 3 Andruw Jones	.75	.23
❑ 4 Eric Gagne	.50	.15
❑ 5 Craig Wilson	.50	.15
❑ 6 Brian Giles	.50	.15
❑ 7 Miguel Tejada	.50	.15
❑ 8 Kevin Brown	.50	.15
❑ 9 Shawn Green	.50	.15
❑ 10 Ben Sheets	.50	.15
❑ 11 John Smoltz	.75	.23
❑ 12 Tim Hudson	.50	.15
❑ 13 Jason Schmidt	.50	.15
❑ 14 Paul Konerko	.50	.15
❑ 15 Randy Johnson	1.25	.35
❑ 16 Roy Oswalt	.50	.15
❑ 17 Mike Lowell	.50	.15
❑ 18 Carlos Lee	.50	.15
❑ 19 Sean Burroughs	.50	.15
❑ 20 Edgar Renteria	.50	.15
❑ 21 Michael Young	.50	.15
❑ 22 Jose Vidro	.50	.15
❑ 23 Scott Rolen	.75	.23
❑ 24 Rafael Furcal	.50	.15
❑ 25 Tom Glavine	.75	.23
❑ 26 Scott Podsednik	.50	.15
❑ 27 Gary Sheffield	.50	.15
❑ 28 Eric Chavez	.50	.15
❑ 29 Mark Prior	.75	.23
❑ 30 Chipper Jones	1.25	.35
❑ 31 Frank Thomas	1.25	.35
❑ 32 Victor Martinez	.50	.15
❑ 33 Jake Peavy	.50	.15
❑ 34 Carlos Beltran	.50	.15
❑ 35 Roy Halladay	.50	.15
❑ 36 Mark Teixeira	.75	.23
❑ 37 Jacque Jones	.50	.15
❑ 38 Mike Sweeney	.50	.15
❑ 39 Troy Glaus	.50	.15
❑ 40 Pat Burrell	.50	.15
❑ 41 Ichiro Suzuki	2.50	.75
❑ 42 Vladimir Guerrero	1.25	.35
❑ 43 Bobby Abreu	.50	.15
❑ 44 Jim Edmonds	.75	.23
❑ 45 Garret Anderson	.50	.15
❑ 46 J.D. Drew	.50	.15
❑ 47 C.C. Sabathia	.50	.15
❑ 48 Joe Mauer	.50	.15
❑ 49 Phil Nevin	.50	.15
❑ 50 Hank Blalock	.50	.15
❑ 51 Carlos Zambrano	.50	.15
❑ 52 Mike Piazza	2.00	.60
❑ 53 Manny Ramirez	.75	.23
❑ 54 Lance Berkman	.50	.15
❑ 55 Delmon Young	.75	.23
❑ 56 Nomar Garciaparra	2.00	.60
❑ 57 Alex Rodriguez	2.00	.60
❑ 58 Rickie Weeks	.75	.23
❑ 59 Adrian Beltre	.50	.15
❑ 60 Albert Pujols	2.50	.75
❑ 61 Richie Sexson	.50	.15
❑ 62 Magglio Ordonez	.50	.15
❑ 63 Derrek Lee	.75	.23
❑ 64 Sammy Sosa	1.25	.35
❑ 65 Jason Giambi	.50	.15
❑ 66 Curt Schilling	.75	.23
❑ 67 Jorge Posada	.75	.23
❑ 68 Rafael Palmeiro	.75	.23
❑ 69 Jeff Kent	.50	.15
❑ 70 Jose Reyes	.50	.15
❑ 71 David Ortiz	1.25	.35
❑ 72 Aubrey Huff	.50	.15
❑ 73 Jim Thome	.75	.23
❑ 74 Andy Pettitte	.75	.23
❑ 75 Barry Zito	.50	.15
❑ 76 Carlos Delgado	.50	.15
❑ 77 Hideki Matsui	2.50	.75
❑ 78 Sean Casey	.75	.23
❑ 79 Luis Gonzalez	.50	.15
❑ 80 Marcus Giles	.50	.15
❑ 81 Preston Wilson	.50	.15
❑ 82 Javy Lopez	.50	.15
❑ 83 Mark Mulder	.50	.15
❑ 84 Derek Jeter	2.50	.75
❑ 85 Miguel Cabrera	.75	.23
❑ 86 Vernon Wells	.50	.15
❑ 87 Roger Clemens	2.50	.75
❑ 88 Lyle Overbay	.50	.15
❑ 89 Bret Boone	.50	.15
❑ 90 Melvin Mora	.50	.15
❑ 91 Greg Maddux	2.00	.60
❑ 92 Kerry Wood	.50	.15
❑ 93 Ivan Rodriguez	.75	.23
❑ 94 Pedro Martinez	.75	.23
❑ 95 Jeff Bagwell	.75	.23
❑ 96 Torii Hunter	.50	.15
❑ 97 Ken Griffey Jr.	2.00	.60
❑ 98 Mike Mussina	.75	.23
❑ 99 Oliver Perez	.50	.15
❑ 100 Josh Beckett	.50	.15
❑ 101 Bob Gibson LGD	8.00	2.40
❑ 102 Cal Ripken LGD	15.00	4.50
❑ 103 Ted Williams LGD	8.00	2.40
❑ 104 Nolan Ryan LGD	10.00	3.00
❑ 105 Mickey Mantle LGD	15.00	4.50
❑ 106 Ernie Banks LGD	8.00	2.40
❑ 107 Joe DiMaggio LGD	8.00	2.40
❑ 108 Stan Musial LGD	8.00	2.40
❑ 109 Tom Seaver LGD	8.00	2.40
❑ 110 Mike Schmidt LGD	10.00	3.00
❑ 111 Jerry Gil T1 RC	5.00	1.50
❑ 112 Dioner Navarro T1 RC	8.00	2.40
❑ 113 Bartolome Fortunato T1 RC	5.00	1.50
❑ 114 Carlos Hines T1 RC	5.00	1.50
❑ 115 Franklyn Gracesqui T1 RC	5.00	1.50
❑ 116 Aarom Baldiris T1 RC	8.00	2.40
❑ 117 Casey Daigle T1 RC	5.00	1.50
❑ 118 Joey Gathright T1 RC	8.00	2.40
❑ 119 William Bergolla T1 RC	5.00	1.50
❑ 120 Jeff Bennett T1 RC	5.00	1.50
❑ 121 Lincoln Holdzkom T1 RC	5.00	1.50
❑ 122 Jorge Vasquez T1 RC	5.00	1.50
❑ 123 Donnie Kelly T1 RC	5.00	1.50
❑ 124 Yadier Molina T1 RC	8.00	2.40
❑ 125 Ryan Wing T1 RC	5.00	1.50
❑ 126 Justin Germano T1 RC	5.00	1.50
❑ 127 Freddy Guzman T1 RC	5.00	1.50
❑ 128 Onil Joseph T1 RC	5.00	1.50
❑ 129 Roman Colon T1 RC	5.00	1.50
❑ 130 Roberto Novoa T1 RC	8.00	2.40
❑ 131 Renyel Pinto T1 RC	8.00	2.40
❑ 132 Evan Rust T1 RC	5.00	1.50
❑ 133 Orlando Rodriguez T1 RC	5.00	1.50
❑ 134 Edwardo Sierra T1 RC	8.00	2.40
❑ 135 Mike Rose T1 RC	5.00	1.50
❑ 136 Phil Stockman T1 RC	5.00	1.50
❑ 137 Greg Dobbs T1 RC	5.00	1.50
❑ 138 Brad Halsey T1 RC	8.00	2.40
❑ 139 David Aardsma T1 RC	8.00	2.40
❑ 140 Joe Hietpas T1 RC	5.00	1.50
❑ 141 Josh Labandeira T1 RC	5.00	1.50
❑ 142 Mariano Gomez T1 RC	5.00	1.50
❑ 143 Jeff Bajenaru T1 RC	5.00	1.50
❑ 144 Travis Blackley T1 RC	5.00	1.50
❑ 145 Abe Alvarez T1 RC	8.00	2.40
❑ 146 Ramon Ramirez T2 RC	8.00	2.40
❑ 147 Edwin Moreno T2 RC	10.00	3.00
❑ 148 Ronny Cedeno T2 RC	10.00	3.00
❑ 149 Hector Gimenez T2 RC	8.00	2.40
❑ 150 Carlos Vasquez T2 RC	10.00	3.00
❑ 151 Jesse Crain T2 RC	15.00	4.50
❑ 152 Logan Kensing T2 RC	8.00	2.40
❑ 153 Sean Henn T2 RC	8.00	2.40
❑ 154 Rusty Tucker T2 RC	10.00	3.00
❑ 155 Justin Lehr T3 RC	8.00	2.40
❑ 156 Ian Snell T3 RC	10.00	3.00
❑ 157 Merkin Valdez T3 RC	10.00	3.00
❑ 158 Scott Proctor T3 RC	10.00	3.00
❑ 159 Jose Capellan T3 RC	10.00	3.00
❑ 160 Kazuo Matsui T3 RC	10.00	3.00
❑ 161 Chris Oxspring AU JSY RC	15.00	4.50
❑ 162 Jimmy Serrano AU JSY RC	15.00	4.50
❑ 163 Jeff Keppinger AU JSY RC	15.00	4.50
❑ 164 B.Medders AU JSY RC	15.00	4.50
❑ 165 Brian Dallimore AU JSY RC	15.00	4.50
❑ 166 Chad Bentz AU JSY RC	15.00	4.50
❑ 167 Chris Aguila AU JSY RC	15.00	4.50
❑ 168 Chris Saenz AU JSY RC	15.00	4.50
❑ 169 Frank Francisco AU JSY RC	15.00	4.50
❑ 170 Colby Miller AU JSY RC	15.00	4.50
❑ 171 D.Crouth AU JSY RC EXCH	15.00	4.50
❑ 172 Charles Thomas AU JSY RC	15.00	4.50
❑ 173 Dennis Sarfate AU JSY RC	15.00	4.50
❑ 174 Lance Cormier AU JSY RC	15.00	4.50
❑ 175 Joe Horgan AU JSY RC	15.00	4.50
❑ 176 Fernando Nieve AU JSY RC	25.00	7.50
❑ 177 Jake Woods AU JSY RC	15.00	4.50
❑ 178 Matt Treanor AU JSY RC	15.00	4.50
❑ 179 Jerome Gamble AU JSY RC	15.00	4.50
❑ 180 John Gall AU JSY RC	25.00	7.50
❑ 181 Jorge Sequea AU JSY RC	15.00	4.50
❑ 182 Justin Hampson AU JSY RC	15.00	4.50
❑ 183 Justin Huisman AU JSY RC	15.00	4.50
❑ 184 Justin Knoedler AU JSY RC	15.00	4.50
❑ 185 Justin Leone AU JSY RC	25.00	7.50
❑ 186 Scott Atchison AU JSY RC	15.00	4.50
❑ 187 Jon Knott AU JSY RC	15.00	4.50
❑ 188 Kevin Cave AU JSY RC	15.00	4.50
❑ 189 Jason Frasor AU JSY RC	15.00	4.50
❑ 190 George Sherrill AU JSY RC	15.00	4.50
❑ 191 Mike Gosling AU JSY RC	15.00	4.50
❑ 192 Mike Johnston AU JSY RC	15.00	4.50
❑ 193 Mike Rouse AU JSY RC	15.00	4.50
❑ 194 Nick Regilio AU JSY RC	15.00	4.50
❑ 195 Ryan Meaux AU JSY RC	15.00	4.50
❑ 196 Scott Dohmann AU JSY RC	15.00	4.50
❑ 197 Shawn Camp AU JSY RC	15.00	4.50
❑ 198 Shawn Hill AU JSY RC	15.00	4.50
❑ 199 Shingo Takatsu AU JSY RC	25.00	7.50
❑ 200 Tim Bausher AU JSY RC	15.00	4.50
❑ 201 Tim Bittner AU JSY RC	15.00	4.50
❑ 202 Scott Kazmir AU JSY RC	50.00	15.00

2005 SPx

	Nm-Mt	Ex-Mt
COMPLETE SET (100)	25.00	7.50
COMMON CARD (1-100)	.40	.12
COMMON RC	.40	.12
ISSUED IN 05 SP COLLECTION PACKS		.00

Card	Nm-Mt	Ex-Mt
❑ 1 Aaron Harang	.40	.12
❑ 2 Aaron Rowand	.40	.12
❑ 3 Aaron Miles	.40	.12
❑ 4 Adrian Gonzalez	.40	.12
❑ 5 Alex Rios	.40	.12
❑ 6 Angel Berroa	.40	.12
❑ 7 B.J. Upton	.40	.12
❑ 8 Brandon Claussen	.40	.12
❑ 9 Andy Marte	.40	.12

❑ 10 Brandon Webb .40 .12
❑ 11 Bronson Arroyo .40 .12
❑ 12 Casey Kotchman .40 .12
❑ 13 Cesar Izturis .40 .12
❑ 14 Chad Cordero .40 .12
❑ 15 Chad Tracy .40 .12
❑ 16 Charles Thomas .40 .12
❑ 17 Chase Utley .40 .12
❑ 18 Chone Figgins .40 .12
❑ 19 Chris Burke .40 .12
❑ 20 Cliff Lee .40 .12
❑ 21 Clint Barmes .40 .12
❑ 22 Coco Crisp .40 .12
❑ 23 Bill Hall .40 .12
❑ 24 Dallas McPherson .40 .12
❑ 25 Brad Halsey .40 .12
❑ 26 Daniel Cabrera .40 .12
❑ 27 Danny Haren .40 .12
❑ 28 Dave Bush .40 .12
❑ 29 David DeJesus .40 .12
❑ 30 D.J. Houlton RC .60 .18
❑ 31 Derek Jeter 2.00 .60
❑ 32 Dewon Brazelton .40 .12
❑ 33 Edwin Jackson .40 .12
❑ 34 Brad Hawpe .40 .12
❑ 35 Brandon Inge .40 .12
❑ 36 Brett Myers .40 .12
❑ 37 Garrett Atkins .40 .12
❑ 38 Gavin Floyd .40 .12
❑ 39 Grady Sizemore .40 .12
❑ 40 Guillermo Mota .40 .12
❑ 41 Carlos Guillen .40 .12
❑ 42 Gustavo Chacin .40 .12
❑ 43 Huston Street .60 .18
❑ 44 Chris Duffy .40 .12
❑ 45 J.D. Closser .40 .12
❑ 46 J.J. Hardy .40 .12
❑ 47 Jason Bartlett .40 .12
❑ 48 Jason DuBois .40 .12
❑ 49 Chris Shelton .40 .12
❑ 50 Jason Lane .40 .12
❑ 51 Jayson Werth .40 .12
❑ 52 Jeff Baker .40 .12
❑ 53 Jeff Francis .40 .12
❑ 54 Jeremy Bonderman .40 .12
❑ 55 Jeremy Reed .40 .12
❑ 56 Jerome Williams .40 .12
❑ 57 Jesse Crain .40 .12
❑ 58 Chris Young .40 .12
❑ 59 Jhonny Peralta .40 .12
❑ 60 Joe Blanton .40 .12
❑ 61 Joe Crede .40 .12
❑ 62 Joel Pineiro .40 .12
❑ 63 Joey Gathright .40 .12
❑ 64 John Buck .40 .12
❑ 65 Jonny Gomes .40 .12
❑ 66 Jorge Cantu .40 .12
❑ 67 Dan Johnson .40 .12
❑ 68 Jose Valverde .40 .12
❑ 69 Ervin Santana .40 .12
❑ 70 Justin Morneau .40 .12
❑ 71 Keiichi Yabu RC .60 .18
❑ 72 Ken Griffey Jr. 1.50 .45
❑ 73 Jason Repko .40 .12
❑ 74 Kevin Youkilis .40 .12
❑ 75 Koyie Hill .40 .12
❑ 76 Laynce Nix .40 .12
❑ 77 Luke Scott RC 1.00 .30
❑ 78 Juan Rivera .40 .12
❑ 79 Justin Duchscherer .40 .12
❑ 80 Mark Teahen .40 .12
❑ 81 Lance Niekro .40 .12
❑ 82 Michael Cuddyer .40 .12
❑ 83 Nick Swisher .40 .12
❑ 84 Noah Lowry .40 .12
❑ 85 Matt Holliday .40 .12
❑ 86 Reed Johnson .40 .12
❑ 87 Rich Harden .40 .12
❑ 88 Robb Quinlan .40 .12
❑ 89 Nick Johnson .40 .12
❑ 90 Ryan Howard .40 .12
❑ 91 Nook Logan .40 .12
❑ 92 Steve Schmoll RC .60 .18
❑ 93 Tadahito Iguchi RC 5.00 1.50
❑ 94 Willy Taveras .40 .12
❑ 95 Wily Mo Pena .40 .12
❑ 96 Xavier Nady .40 .12
❑ 97 Yadier Molina .40 .12
❑ 98 Yhency Brazoban .40 .12
❑ 99 Ryan Freel .40 .12
❑ 100 Zack Greinke .40 .12

1991 Stadium Club

	Nm-Mt	Ex-Mt
COMPLETE SET (600)	60.00	18.00
COMP.SERIES 1 (300)	40.00	12.00
COMP.SERIES 2 (300)	20.00	6.00

❑ 1 Dave Stewart TUX .50 .15
❑ 2 Wally Joyner .50 .15
❑ 3 Shawon Dunston .25 .07
❑ 4 Darren Daulton .50 .15
❑ 5 Will Clark .75 .23
❑ 6 Sammy Sosa 1.25 .35
❑ 7 Dan Plesac .25 .07
❑ 8 Marquis Grissom .50 .15
❑ 9 Erik Hanson .25 .07
❑ 10 Geno Petralli .25 .07
❑ 11 Jose Rijo .25 .07
❑ 12 Carlos Quintana .25 .07
❑ 13 Junior Ortiz .25 .07
❑ 14 Bob Walk .25 .07
❑ 15 Mike Macfarlane .25 .07
❑ 16 Eric Yelding .25 .07
❑ 17 Bryn Smith .25 .07
❑ 18 Bip Roberts .25 .07
❑ 19 Mike Scioscia .25 .07
❑ 20 Mark Williamson .25 .07
❑ 21 Don Mattingly 3.00 .90
❑ 22 John Franco .50 .15
❑ 23 Chet Lemon .25 .07
❑ 24 Tom Henke .25 .07
❑ 25 Jerry Browne .25 .07
❑ 26 Dave Justice .50 .15
❑ 27 Mark Langston .25 .07
❑ 28 Damon Berryhill .25 .07
❑ 29 Kevin Bass .25 .07
❑ 30 Scott Fletcher .25 .07
❑ 31 Moises Alou .50 .15
❑ 32 Dave Valle .25 .07
❑ 33 Jody Reed .25 .07
❑ 34 Dave West .25 .07
❑ 35 Kevin McReynolds .25 .07
❑ 36 Pat Combs .25 .07
❑ 37 Eric Davis .50 .15
❑ 38 Bret Saberhagen .50 .15
❑ 39 Stan Javier .25 .07
❑ 40 Chuck Cary .25 .07
❑ 41 Tony Phillips .25 .07
❑ 42 Lee Smith .50 .15
❑ 43 Tim Teufel .25 .07
❑ 44 Lance Dickson RC .40 .12
❑ 45 Greg Litton .25 .07
❑ 46 Ted Higuera .25 .07
❑ 47 Edgar Martinez .75 .23
❑ 48 Steve Avery .25 .07
❑ 49 Walt Weiss .25 .07
❑ 50 David Segui .25 .07
❑ 51 Andy Benes .25 .07
❑ 52 Karl Rhodes .25 .07
❑ 53 Neal Heaton .25 .07
❑ 54 Danny Gladden .25 .07
❑ 55 Luis Rivera .25 .07
❑ 56 Kevin Brown .50 .15
❑ 57 Frank Thomas 1.25 .35
❑ 58 Terry Mulholland .25 .07
❑ 59 Dick Schofield .25 .07
❑ 60 Ron Darling .25 .07
❑ 61 Sandy Alomar Jr. .25 .07
❑ 62 Dave Stieb .25 .07
❑ 63 Alan Trammell .50 .15
❑ 64 Matt Nokes .25 .07
❑ 65 Lenny Harris .25 .07
❑ 66 Milt Thompson .25 .07
❑ 67 Storm Davis .25 .07
❑ 68 Joe Oliver .25 .07
❑ 69 Andres Galarraga .50 .15
❑ 70 Ozzie Guillen .50 .15
❑ 71 Ken Howell .25 .07
❑ 72 Garry Templeton .25 .07
❑ 73 Derrick May .25 .07
❑ 74 Xavier Hernandez .25 .07
❑ 75 Dave Parker .50 .15
❑ 76 Rick Aguilera .50 .15
❑ 77 Robby Thompson .25 .07
❑ 78 Pete Incaviglia .25 .07
❑ 79 Bob Welch .25 .07
❑ 80 Randy Milligan .25 .07
❑ 81 Chuck Finley .50 .15
❑ 82 Alvin Davis .25 .07
❑ 83 Tim Naehring .25 .07
❑ 84 Jay Bell .50 .15
❑ 85 Joe Magrane .25 .07
❑ 86 Howard Johnson .25 .07
❑ 87 Jack McDowell .25 .07
❑ 88 Kevin Seitzer .25 .07
❑ 89 Bruce Ruffin .25 .07
❑ 90 Fernando Valenzuela .50 .15
❑ 91 Terry Kennedy .25 .07
❑ 92 Barry Larkin .75 .23
❑ 93 Larry Walker 1.25 .35
❑ 94 Luis Salazar .25 .07
❑ 95 Gary Sheffield .50 .15
❑ 96 Bobby Witt .25 .07
❑ 97 Lonnie Smith .25 .07
❑ 98 Bryan Harvey .25 .07
❑ 99 Mookie Wilson .50 .15
❑ 100 Dwight Gooden .50 .15
❑ 101 Lou Whitaker .50 .15
❑ 102 Ron Karkovice .25 .07
❑ 103 Jesse Barfield .25 .07
❑ 104 Jose DeJesus .25 .07
❑ 105 Benito Santiago .50 .15
❑ 106 Brian Holman .25 .07
❑ 107 Rafael Ramirez .25 .07
❑ 108 Ellis Burks .50 .15
❑ 109 Mike Bielecki .25 .07
❑ 110 Kirby Puckett 1.25 .35
❑ 111 Terry Shumpert .25 .07
❑ 112 Chuck Crim .25 .07
❑ 113 Todd Benzinger .25 .07
❑ 114 Brian Barnes RC .40 .12
❑ 115 Carlos Baerga .25 .07
❑ 116 Kal Daniels .25 .07
❑ 117 Dave Johnson .25 .07
❑ 118 Andy Van Slyke .75 .23
❑ 119 John Burkett .25 .07
❑ 120 Rickey Henderson 1.25 .35
❑ 121 Tim Jones .25 .07
❑ 122 Daryl Irvine .25 .07
❑ 123 Ruben Sierra .25 .07
❑ 124 Jim Abbott .75 .23

❏	125	Daryl Boston	.25	.07
❏	126	Greg Maddux	2.00	.60
❏	127	Von Hayes	.25	.07
❏	128	Mike Fitzgerald	.25	.07
❏	129	Wayne Edwards	.25	.07
❏	130	Greg Briley	.25	.07
❏	131	Rob Dibble	.50	.15
❏	132	Gene Larkin	.25	.07
❏	133	David Wells	.50	.15
❏	134	Steve Balboni	.25	.07
❏	135	Greg Vaughn	.25	.07
❏	136	Mark Davis	.25	.07
❏	137	Dave Rhode	.25	.07
❏	138	Eric Show	.25	.07
❏	139	Bobby Bonilla	.50	.15
❏	140	Dana Kiecker	.25	.07
❏	141	Gary Pettis	.25	.07
❏	142	Dennis Boyd	.25	.07
❏	143	Mike Benjamin	.25	.07
❏	144	Luis Polonia	.25	.07
❏	145	Doug Jones	.25	.07
❏	146	Al Newman	.25	.07
❏	147	Alex Fernandez	.25	.07
❏	148	Bill Doran	.25	.07
❏	149	Kevin Elster	.25	.07
❏	150	Len Dykstra	.50	.15
❏	151	Mike Gallego	.25	.07
❏	152	Tim Belcher	.25	.07
❏	153	Jay Buhner	.50	.15
❏	154	Ozzie Smith UER (Rookie card is 1979, but card back says '78)	2.00	.60
❏	155	Jose Canseco	.75	.23
❏	156	Gregg Olson	.25	.07
❏	157	Charlie O'Brien	.25	.07
❏	158	Frank Tanana	.25	.07
❏	159	George Brett	3.00	.90
❏	160	Jeff Huson	.25	.07
❏	161	Kevin Tapani	.25	.07
❏	162	Jerome Walton	.25	.07
❏	163	Charlie Hayes	.25	.07
❏	164	Chris Bosio	.25	.07
❏	165	Chris Sabo	.25	.07
❏	166	Lance Parrish	.50	.15
❏	167	Don Robinson	.25	.07
❏	168	Manny Lee	.25	.07
❏	169	Dennis Rasmussen	.25	.07
❏	170	Wade Boggs	.75	.23
❏	171	Bob Geren	.25	.07
❏	172	Mackey Sasser	.25	.07
❏	173	Julio Franco	.50	.15
❏	174	Otis Nixon	.25	.07
❏	175	Bert Blyleven	.50	.15
❏	176	Craig Biggio	.75	.23
❏	177	Eddie Murray	1.25	.35
❏	178	Randy Tomlin RC	.40	.12
❏	179	Tino Martinez	1.25	.35
❏	180	Carlton Fisk	.75	.23
❏	181	Dwight Smith	.25	.07
❏	182	Scott Garrelts	.25	.07
❏	183	Jim Gantner	.25	.07
❏	184	Dickie Thon	.25	.07
❏	185	John Farrell	.25	.07
❏	186	Cecil Fielder	.50	.15
❏	187	Glenn Braggs	.25	.07
❏	188	Allan Anderson	.25	.07
❏	189	Kurt Stillwell	.25	.07
❏	190	Jose Oquendo	.25	.07
❏	191	Joe Orsulak	.25	.07
❏	192	Ricky Jordan	.25	.07
❏	193	Kelly Downs	.25	.07
❏	194	Delino DeShields	.25	.07
❏	195	Omar Vizquel	.75	.23
❏	196	Mark Carreon	.25	.07
❏	197	Mike Harkey	.25	.07
❏	198	Jack Howell	.25	.07
❏	199	Lance Johnson	.25	.07
❏	200	Nolan Ryan TUX	5.00	1.50
❏	201	John Marzano	.25	.07
❏	202	Doug Drabek	.25	.07
❏	203	Mark Lemke	.25	.07
❏	204	Steve Sax	.25	.07
❏	205	Greg Harris	.25	.07
❏	206	B.J. Surhoff	.50	.15
❏	207	Todd Burns	.25	.07
❏	208	Jose Gonzalez	.25	.07
❏	209	Mike Scott	.25	.07
❏	210	Dave Magadan	.25	.07
❏	211	Dante Bichette	.50	.15
❏	212	Trevor Wilson	.25	.07
❏	213	Hector Villanueva	.25	.07
❏	214	Dan Pasqua	.25	.07
❏	215	Greg Colbrunn RC	.60	.18
❏	216	Mike Jeffcoat	.25	.07
❏	217	Harold Reynolds	.50	.15
❏	218	Paul O'Neill	.75	.23
❏	219	Mark Guthrie	.25	.07
❏	220	Barry Bonds	4.00	1.20
❏	221	Jimmy Key	.50	.15
❏	222	Billy Ripken	.25	.07
❏	223	Tom Pagnozzi	.25	.07
❏	224	Bo Jackson	1.25	.35
❏	225	Sid Fernandez	.25	.07
❏	226	Mike Marshall	.25	.07
❏	227	John Kruk	.50	.15
❏	228	Mike Fetters	.25	.07
❏	229	Eric Anthony	.25	.07
❏	230	Ryne Sandberg	2.00	.60
❏	231	Carney Lansford	.50	.15
❏	232	Melido Perez	.25	.07
❏	233	Jose Lind	.25	.07
❏	234	Darryl Hamilton	.25	.07
❏	235	Tom Browning	.25	.07
❏	236	Spike Owen	.25	.07
❏	237	Juan Gonzalez	1.25	.35
❏	238	Felix Fermin	.25	.07
❏	239	Keith Miller	.25	.07
❏	240	Mark Gubicza	.25	.07
❏	241	Kent Anderson	.25	.07
❏	242	Alvaro Espinoza	.25	.07
❏	243	Dale Murphy	.75	.23
❏	244	Orel Hershiser	.50	.15
❏	245	Paul Molitor	.75	.23
❏	246	Eddie Whitson	.25	.07
❏	247	Joe Girardi	.25	.07
❏	248	Kent Hrbek	.50	.15
❏	249	Bill Sampen	.25	.07
❏	250	Kevin Mitchell	.25	.07
❏	251	Mariano Duncan	.25	.07
❏	252	Scott Bradley	.25	.07
❏	253	Mike Greenwell	.25	.07
❏	254	Tom Gordon	.25	.07
❏	255	Todd Zeile	.25	.07
❏	256	Bobby Thigpen	.25	.07
❏	257	Gregg Jefferies	.25	.07
❏	258	Kenny Rogers	.50	.15
❏	259	Shane Mack	.25	.07
❏	260	Zane Smith	.25	.07
❏	261	Mitch Williams	.25	.07
❏	262	Jim Deshaies	.25	.07
❏	263	Dave Winfield	.50	.15
❏	264	Ben McDonald	.25	.07
❏	265	Randy Ready	.25	.07
❏	266	Pat Borders	.25	.07
❏	267	Jose Uribe	.25	.07
❏	268	Derek Lilliquist	.25	.07
❏	269	Greg Brock	.25	.07
❏	270	Ken Griffey Jr.	2.50	.75
❏	271	Jeff Gray	.25	.07
❏	272	Danny Tartabull	.25	.07
❏	273	Dennis Martinez	.50	.15
❏	274	Robin Ventura	.50	.15
❏	275	Randy Myers	.25	.07
❏	276	Jack Daugherty	.25	.07
❏	277	Greg Gagne	.25	.07
❏	278	Jay Howell	.25	.07
❏	279	Mike LaValliere	.25	.07
❏	280	Rex Hudler	.25	.07
❏	281	Mike Simms	.25	.07
❏	282	Kevin Maas	.25	.07
❏	283	Jeff Ballard	.25	.07
❏	284	Dave Henderson	.25	.07
❏	285	Pete O'Brien	.25	.07
❏	286	Brook Jacoby	.25	.07
❏	287	Mike Henneman	.25	.07
❏	288	Greg Olson	.25	.07
❏	289	Greg Myers	.25	.07
❏	290	Mark Grace	.75	.23
❏	291	Shawn Abner	.25	.07
❏	292	Frank Viola	.50	.15
❏	293	Lee Stevens	.25	.07
❏	294	Jason Grimsley	.25	.07
❏	295	Matt Williams	.50	.15
❏	296	Ron Robinson	.25	.07
❏	297	Tom Brunansky	.25	.07
❏	298	Checklist 1-100	.25	.07
❏	299	Checklist 101-200	.25	.07
❏	300	Checklist 201-300	.25	.07
❏	301	Darryl Strawberry	.50	.15
❏	302	Bud Black	.25	.07
❏	303	Harold Baines	.50	.15
❏	304	Roberto Alomar	.75	.23
❏	305	Norm Charlton	.25	.07
❏	306	Gary Thurman	.25	.07
❏	307	Mike Felder	.25	.07
❏	308	Tony Gwynn	1.50	.45
❏	309	Roger Clemens	2.50	.75
❏	310	Andre Dawson	.50	.15
❏	311	Scott Radinsky	.25	.07
❏	312	Bob Melvin	.25	.07
❏	313	Kirk McCaskill	.25	.07
❏	314	Pedro Guerrero	.50	.15
❏	315	Walt Terrell	.25	.07
❏	316	Sam Horn	.25	.07
❏	317	W.Chamberlain RC UER (Card listed as 1989 Debut card, should be 1990)	.60	.18
❏	318	Pedro Munoz RC	.40	.12
❏	319	Roberto Kelly	.25	.07
❏	320	Mark Portugal	.25	.07
❏	321	Tim McIntosh	.25	.07
❏	322	Jesse Orosco	.25	.07
❏	323	Gary Green	.25	.07
❏	324	Greg Harris	.25	.07
❏	325	Hubie Brooks	.25	.07
❏	326	Chris Nabholz	.25	.07
❏	327	Terry Pendleton	.50	.15
❏	328	Eric King	.25	.07
❏	329	Chili Davis	.50	.15
❏	330	Anthony Telford	.25	.07
❏	331	Kelly Gruber	.25	.07
❏	332	Dennis Eckersley	.50	.15
❏	333	Mel Hall	.25	.07
❏	334	Bob Kipper	.25	.07
❏	335	Willie McGee	.50	.15
❏	336	Steve Olin	.25	.07
❏	337	Steve Buechele	.25	.07
❏	338	Scott Leius	.25	.07
❏	339	Hal Morris	.25	.07
❏	340	Jose Offerman	.25	.07
❏	341	Kent Mercker	.25	.07
❏	342	Ken Griffey Sr.	.50	.15
❏	343	Pete Harnisch	.25	.07
❏	344	Kirk Gibson	.75	.23
❏	345	Dave Smith	.25	.07
❏	346	Dave Martinez	.25	.07
❏	347	Atlee Hammaker	.25	.07
❏	348	Brian Downing	.25	.07
❏	349	Todd Hundley	.25	.07
❏	350	Candy Maldonado	.25	.07
❏	351	Dwight Evans	.75	.23
❏	352	Steve Searcy	.25	.07
❏	353	Gary Gaetti	.50	.15
❏	354	Jeff Reardon	.50	.15
❏	355	Travis Fryman	.50	.15
❏	356	Dave Righetti	.50	.15
❏	357	Fred McGriff	.75	.23
❏	358	Don Slaught	.25	.07
❏	359	Gene Nelson	.25	.07
❏	360	Billy Spiers	.25	.07
❏	361	Lee Guetterman	.25	.07
❏	362	Darren Lewis	.25	.07
❏	363	Duane Ward	.25	.07
❏	364	Lloyd Moseby	.25	.07
❏	365	John Smoltz	.75	.23
❏	366	Felix Jose	.25	.07
❏	367	David Cone	.50	.15
❏	368	Wally Backman	.25	.07
❏	369	Jeff Montgomery	.25	.07
❏	370	Rich Garces RC	.40	.12
❏	371	Billy Hatcher	.25	.07
❏	372	Bill Swift	.25	.07
❏	373	Jim Eisenreich	.25	.07
❏	374	Rob Ducey	.25	.07
❏	375	Tim Crews	.25	.07
❏	376	Steve Finley	.50	.15
❏	377	Jeff Blauser	.25	.07
❏	378	Willie Wilson	.25	.07

❑ 379 Gerald Perry .25 .07
❑ 380 Jose Mesa .25 .07
❑ 381 Pat Kelly RC .60 .18
❑ 382 Matt Merullo .25 .07
❑ 383 Ivan Calderon .25 .07
❑ 384 Scott Chiamparino .25 .07
❑ 385 Lloyd McClendon .25 .07
❑ 386 Dave Bergman .25 .07
❑ 387 Ed Sprague .25 .07
❑ 388 Jeff Bagwell RC 4.00 1.20
❑ 389 Brett Butler .50 .15
❑ 390 Larry Andersen .25 .07
❑ 391 Glenn Davis .25 .07
❑ 392 Alex Cole UER .25 .07
(Front photo actually Otis Nixon)
❑ 393 Mike Heath .25 .07
❑ 394 Danny Darwin .25 .07
❑ 395 Steve Lake .25 .07
❑ 396 Tim Layana .25 .07
❑ 397 Terry Leach .25 .07
❑ 398 Bill Wegman .25 .07
❑ 399 Mark McGwire 3.00 .90
❑ 400 Mike Boddicker .25 .07
❑ 401 Steve Howe .25 .07
❑ 402 Bernard Gilkey .25 .07
❑ 403 Thomas Howard .25 .07
❑ 404 Rafael Belliard .25 .07
❑ 405 Tom Candiotti .25 .07
❑ 406 Rene Gonzales .25 .07
❑ 407 Chuck McElroy .25 .07
❑ 408 Paul Sorrento .25 .07
❑ 409 Randy Johnson 1.50 .45
❑ 410 Brady Anderson .50 .15
❑ 411 Dennis Cook .25 .07
❑ 412 Mickey Tettleton .25 .07
❑ 413 Mike Stanton .25 .07
❑ 414 Ken Oberkfell .25 .07
❑ 415 Rick Honeycutt .25 .07
❑ 416 Nelson Santovenia .25 .07
❑ 417 Bob Tewksbury .25 .07
❑ 418 Brent Mayne .25 .07
❑ 419 Steve Farr .25 .07
❑ 420 Phil Stephenson .25 .07
❑ 421 Jeff Russell .25 .07
❑ 422 Chris James .25 .07
❑ 423 Tim Leary .25 .07
❑ 424 Gary Carter .50 .15
❑ 425 Glenallen Hill .25 .07
❑ 426 Matt Young UER .25 .07
(Card mentions 83T/Tr as RC, but 84T shown)
❑ 427 Sid Bream .25 .07
❑ 428 Greg Swindell .25 .07
❑ 429 Scott Aldred .25 .07
❑ 430 Cal Ripken 4.00 1.20
❑ 431 Bill Landrum .25 .07
❑ 432 Earnest Riles .25 .07
❑ 433 Danny Jackson .25 .07
❑ 434 Casey Candaele .25 .07
❑ 435 Ken Hill .25 .07
❑ 436 Jaime Navarro .25 .07
❑ 437 Lance Blankenship .25 .07
❑ 438 Randy Velarde .25 .07
❑ 439 Frank DiPino .25 .07
❑ 440 Carl Nichols .25 .07
❑ 441 Jeff M. Robinson .25 .07
❑ 442 Deion Sanders .75 .23
❑ 443 Vicente Palacios .25 .07
❑ 444 Devon White .50 .15
❑ 445 John Cerutti .25 .07
❑ 446 Tracy Jones .25 .07
❑ 447 Jack Morris .50 .15
❑ 448 Mitch Webster .25 .07
❑ 449 Bob Ojeda .25 .07
❑ 450 Oscar Azocar .25 .07
❑ 451 Luis Aquino .25 .07
❑ 452 Mark Whiten .25 .07
❑ 453 Stan Belinda .25 .07
❑ 454 Ron Gant .50 .15
❑ 455 Jose DeLeon .25 .07
❑ 456 Mark Salas UER .25 .07
(Back has 85T photo, but calls it 86T)
❑ 457 Junior Felix .25 .07
❑ 458 Wally Whitehurst .25 .07
❑ 459 Phil Plantier RC .60 .18
❑ 460 Juan Berenguer .25 .07
❑ 461 Franklin Stubbs .25 .07
❑ 462 Joe Boever .25 .07
❑ 463 Tim Wallach .25 .07
❑ 464 Mike Moore .25 .07
❑ 465 Albert Belle .50 .15
❑ 466 Mike Witt .25 .07
❑ 467 Craig Worthington .25 .07
❑ 468 Jerald Clark .25 .07
❑ 469 Scott Terry .25 .07
❑ 470 Milt Cuyler .25 .07
❑ 471 John Smiley .25 .07
❑ 472 Charles Nagy .25 .07
❑ 473 Alan Mills .25 .07
❑ 474 John Russell .25 .07
❑ 475 Bruce Hurst .25 .07
❑ 476 Andujar Cedeno .25 .07
❑ 477 Dave Eiland .25 .07
❑ 478 Brian McRae RC .60 .18
❑ 479 Mike LaCoss .25 .07
❑ 480 Chris Gwynn .25 .07
❑ 481 Jamie Moyer .50 .15
❑ 482 John Olerud .50 .15
❑ 483 Efrain Valdez .25 .07
❑ 484 Sil Campusano .25 .07
❑ 485 Pascual Perez .25 .07
❑ 486 Gary Redus .25 .07
❑ 487 Andy Hawkins .25 .07
❑ 488 Cory Snyder .25 .07
❑ 489 Chris Hoiles .25 .07
❑ 490 Ron Hassey .25 .07
❑ 491 Gary Wayne .25 .07
❑ 492 Mark Lewis .25 .07
❑ 493 Scott Coolbaugh .25 .07
❑ 494 Gerald Young .25 .07
❑ 495 Juan Samuel .25 .07
❑ 496 Willie Fraser .25 .07
❑ 497 Jeff Treadway .25 .07
❑ 498 Vince Coleman .25 .07
❑ 499 Cris Carpenter .25 .07
❑ 500 Jack Clark .50 .15
❑ 501 Kevin Appier .50 .15
❑ 502 Rafael Palmeiro .75 .23
❑ 503 Hensley Meulens .25 .07
❑ 504 George Bell .25 .07
❑ 505 Tony Pena .25 .07
❑ 506 Roger McDowell .25 .07
❑ 507 Luis Sojo .25 .07
❑ 508 Mike Schooler .25 .07
❑ 509 Robin Yount 2.00 .60
❑ 510 Jack Armstrong .25 .07
❑ 511 Rick Cerone .25 .07
❑ 512 Curt Wilkerson .25 .07
❑ 513 Joe Carter .50 .15
❑ 514 Tim Burke .25 .07
❑ 515 Tony Fernandez .25 .07
❑ 516 Ramon Martinez .25 .07
❑ 517 Tim Hulett .25 .07
❑ 518 Terry Steinbach .25 .07
❑ 519 Pete Smith .25 .07
❑ 520 Ken Caminiti .50 .15
❑ 521 Shawn Boskie .25 .07
❑ 522 Mike Pagliarulo .25 .07
❑ 523 Tim Raines .50 .15
❑ 524 Alfredo Griffin .25 .07
❑ 525 Henry Cotto .25 .07
❑ 526 Mike Stanley .25 .07
❑ 527 Charlie Leibrandt .25 .07
❑ 528 Jeff King .25 .07
❑ 529 Eric Plunk .25 .07
❑ 530 Tom Lampkin .25 .07
❑ 531 Steve Bedrosian .25 .07
❑ 532 Tom Herr .25 .07
❑ 533 Craig Lefferts .25 .07
❑ 534 Jeff Reed .25 .07
❑ 535 Mickey Morandini .25 .07
❑ 536 Greg Cadaret .25 .07
❑ 537 Ray Lankford .50 .15
❑ 538 John Candelaria .25 .07
❑ 539 Rob Deer .25 .07
❑ 540 Brad Arnsberg .25 .07
❑ 541 Mike Sharperson .25 .07
❑ 542 Jeff D. Robinson .25 .07
❑ 543 Mo Vaughn .50 .15
❑ 544 Jeff Parrett .25 .07
❑ 545 Willie Randolph .50 .15
❑ 546 Herm Winningham .25 .07
❑ 547 Jeff Innis .25 .07
❑ 548 Chuck Knoblauch .50 .15
❑ 549 Tommy Greene UER .25 .07
(Born in North Carolina, not South Carolina)
❑ 550 Jeff Hamilton .25 .07
❑ 551 Barry Jones .25 .07
❑ 552 Ken Dayley .25 .07
❑ 553 Rick Dempsey .25 .07
❑ 554 Greg Smith .25 .07
❑ 555 Mike Devereaux .25 .07
❑ 556 Keith Comstock .25 .07
❑ 557 Paul Faries .25 .07
❑ 558 Tom Glavine .75 .23
❑ 559 Craig Grebeck .25 .07
❑ 560 Scott Erickson .25 .07
❑ 561 Joel Skinner .25 .07
❑ 562 Mike Morgan .25 .07
❑ 563 Dave Gallagher .25 .07
❑ 564 Todd Stottlemyre .25 .07
❑ 565 Rich Rodriguez .25 .07
❑ 566 Craig Wilson .25 .07
❑ 567 Jeff Brantley .25 .07
❑ 568 Scott Kamieniecki RC .60 .18
❑ 569 Steve Decker RC .40 .12
❑ 570 Juan Agosto .25 .07
❑ 571 Tommy Gregg .25 .07
❑ 572 Kevin Wickander .25 .07
❑ 573 Jamie Quirk UER .25 .07
(Rookie card is 1976, but card back is 1990)
❑ 574 Jerry Don Gleaton .25 .07
❑ 575 Chris Hammond .25 .07
❑ 576 Luis Gonzalez RC 1.50 .45
❑ 577 Russ Swan .25 .07
❑ 578 Jeff Conine RC 1.00 .30
❑ 579 Charlie Hough .50 .15
❑ 580 Jeff Kunkel .25 .07
❑ 581 Darrel Akerfelds .25 .07
❑ 582 Jeff Manto .25 .07
❑ 583 Alejandro Pena .25 .07
❑ 584 Mark Davidson .25 .07
❑ 585 Bob MacDonald RC .40 .12
❑ 586 Paul Assenmacher .25 .07
❑ 587 Dan Wilson RC .60 .18
❑ 588 Tom Bolton .25 .07
❑ 589 Brian Harper .25 .07
❑ 590 John Habyan .25 .07
❑ 591 John Orton .25 .07
❑ 592 Mark Gardner .25 .07
❑ 593 Turner Ward RC .60 .18
❑ 594 Bob Patterson .25 .07
❑ 595 Ed Nunez .25 .07
❑ 596 Gary Scott RC UER .40 .12
(Major League Batting Record should be Minor League)
❑ 597 Scott Bankhead .25 .07
❑ 598 Checklist 301-400 .25 .07
❑ 599 Checklist 401-500 .25 .07
❑ 600 Checklist 501-600 .25 .07

1992 Stadium Club Dome

	Nm-Mt	Ex-Mt
COMP.FACT.SET (200)	15.00	4.50
1 Terry Adams RC	.50	.15
2 Tommy Adams RC	.25	.07
3 Rick Aguilera	.15	.04
4 Ron Allen RC	.25	.07
5 Roberto Alomar	.25	.07
6 Sandy Alomar Jr.	.10	.03
7 Greg Anthony RC	.25	.07
8 James Austin RC	.25	.07
9 Steve Avery	.10	.03
10 Harold Baines	.15	.04
11 Brian Barber RC	.25	.07
12 Jon Barnes RC	.25	.07
13 George Bell	.10	.03
14 Doug Bennett RC	.25	.07
15 Sean Bergman RC	.50	.15
16 Craig Biggio	.25	.07
17 Bill Bliss RC	.25	.07
18 Wade Boggs	.25	.07
19 Bobby Bonilla	.15	.04
20 Russell Brock RC	.25	.07
21 Tarrik Brock RC	.25	.07
22 Tom Browning	.10	.03
23 Brett Butler	.15	.04
24 Ivan Calderon	.10	.03
25 Joe Carter	.15	.04
26 Joe Caruso RC	.25	.07
27 Dan Cholowsky RC	.25	.07
28 Will Clark	.25	.07
29 Roger Clemens	1.00	.30
30 Shawn Curran RC	.25	.07
31 Chris Curtis RC	.25	.07
32 Chili Davis	.15	.04
33 Andre Dawson	.15	.04
34 Joe DeBerry RC	.25	.07
35 John Dettmer	.10	.03
36 Rob Dibble	.15	.04
37 John Donati RC	.25	.07
38 Dave Doorneweerd RC	.25	.07
39 Darren Dreifort	.10	.03
40 Mike Durant RC	.25	.07
41 Chris Durkin RC	.25	.07
42 Dennis Eckersley	.15	.04
43 Brian Edmondson RC	.25	.07
44 Vaughn Eshelman RC	.25	.07
45 Shawn Estes RC	.50	.15
46 Jorge Fabregas RC	.50	.15
47 Jon Farrell RC	.25	.07
48 Cecil Fielder	.15	.04
49 Carlton Fisk	.25	.07
50 Tim Flannelly RC	.25	.07
51 Cliff Floyd RC	1.50	.45
52 Julio Franco	.15	.04
53 Greg Gagne	.10	.03
54 Chris Gambs RC	.25	.07
55 Ron Gant	.15	.04
56 Brent Gates RC	.25	.07
57 Dwayne Gerald RC	.25	.07
58 Jason Giambi	1.00	.30
59 Benji Gil RC	.50	.15
60 Mark Gipner RC	.25	.07
61 Danny Gladden	.10	.03
62 Tom Glavine	.25	.07
63 Jimmy Gonzalez RC	.25	.07
64 Jeff Granger	.10	.03
65 Dan Grapenthien RC	.25	.07
66 Dennis Gray RC	.25	.07
67 Shawn Green RC	4.00	1.20
68 Tyler Green RC	.25	.07
69 Todd Greene	.10	.03
70 Ken Griffey Jr.	.75	.23
71 Kelly Gruber	.10	.03
72 Ozzie Guillen	.15	.04
73 Tony Gwynn	.60	.18
74 Shane Halter RC	.25	.07
75 Jeffrey Hammonds	.15	.04
76 Larry Hanlon RC	.25	.07
77 Pete Harnisch	.10	.03
78 Mike Harrison RC	.25	.07
79 Bryan Harvey	.10	.03
80 Scott Hatteberg RC	.50	.15
81 Rick Helling	.10	.03
82 Dave Henderson	.10	.03
83 Rickey Henderson	.50	.15
84 Tyrone Hill RC	.25	.07
85 T.Hollandsworth RC	.50	.15
86 Brian Holliday RC	.25	.07
87 Terry Horn RC	.25	.07
88 Jeff Hostetler RC	.25	.07
89 Kent Hrbek	.15	.04
90 Mark Hubbard RC	.25	.07
91 Charles Johnson	.15	.04
92 Howard Johnson	.10	.03
93 Todd Johnson	.10	.03
94 Bobby Jones RC	.50	.15
95 Dan Jones RC	.25	.07
96 Felix Jose	.10	.03
97 David Justice	.10	.03
98 Jimmy Key	.15	.04
99 Marc Kroon RC	.25	.07
100 John Kruk	.15	.04
101 Mark Langston	.10	.03
102 Barry Larkin	.25	.07
103 Mike LaValliere	.10	.03
104 Scott Leius	.10	.03
105 Mark Lemke	.10	.03
106 Donnie Leshnock	.10	.03
107 Jimmy Lewis RC	.25	.07
108 Shane Livesy RC	.25	.07
109 Ryan Long RC	.25	.07
110 Trevor Mallory RC	.25	.07
111 Dennis Martinez	.15	.04
112 Justin Mashore RC	.25	.07
113 Jason McDonald	.10	.03
114 Jack McDowell	.10	.03
115 Tom McKinnon RC	.25	.07
116 Billy McMillon	.10	.03
117 Buck McNabb RC	.25	.07
118 Jim Mecir RC	.25	.07
119 Dan Melendez	.25	.07
120 Shawn Miller RC	.25	.07
121 Trever Miller RC	.25	.07
122 Paul Molitor	.25	.07
123 Vincent Moore RC	.25	.07
124 Mike Morgan	.10	.03
125 Jack Morris WS	.10	.03
126 Jack Morris AS	.10	.03
127 Sean Mulligan RC	.25	.07
128 Eddie Murray AS	.50	.15
129 Mike Neill RC	.50	.15
130 Phil Nevin	1.00	.30
131 Mark O'Brien RC	.25	.07
132 Alex Ochoa RC	.50	.15
133 Chad Ogea RC	.25	.07
134 Greg Olson	.10	.03
135 Paul O'Neill	.25	.07
136 Jared Osentowski RC	.25	.07
137 Mike Pagliarulo	.10	.03
138 Rafael Palmeiro	.25	.07
139 Rodney Pedraza RC	.25	.07
140 Tony Phillips (P)	.10	.03
141 Scott Pisciotta RC	.25	.07
142 C.Pritchett RC	.25	.07
143 Jason Pruitt RC	.25	.07
144 K.Puckett WS UER (Championship series AB and BA is wrong)	.50	.15
145 Kirby Puckett AS	.50	.15
146 Manny Ramirez RC	8.00	2.40
147 Eddie Ramos RC	.25	.07
148 Mark Ratekin RC	.25	.07
149 Jeff Reardon	.15	.04
150 Sean Rees RC	.25	.07
151 Pokey Reese RC	.75	.23
152 Desmond Relaford RC	.50	.15
153 Eric Richardson RC	.25	.07
154 Cal Ripken	1.50	.45
155 Chris Roberts	.10	.03
156 Mike Robertson RC	.25	.07
157 Steve Rodriguez	.10	.03
158 Mike Rossiter RC	.25	.07
159 Scott Ruffcorn RC	.25	.07
160 Chris Sabo	.10	.03
161 Juan Samuel	.10	.03
162 Ryne Sandberg UER (On 5th line, prior misspelled as prilor)	.75	.23
163 Scott Sanderson	.10	.03
164 Benny Santiago	.15	.04
165 Gene Schall RC	.25	.07
166 Chad Schoenvogel RC	.25	.07
167 Chris Seelbach RC	.25	.07
168 Aaron Sele RC	.75	.23
169 Basil Shabazz RC	.25	.07
170 Al Shirley RC	.25	.07
171 Paul Shuey	.10	.03
172 Ruben Sierra	.10	.03
173 John Smiley	.10	.03
174 Lee Smith	.15	.04
175 Ozzie Smith	.75	.23
176 Tim Smith RC	.25	.07
177 Zane Smith	.10	.03
178 John Smoltz	.25	.07
179 Scott Stahoviak RC	.25	.07
180 Kennie Steenstra	.10	.03
181 Kevin Stocker RC	.25	.07
182 Chris Stynes RC	.50	.15
183 Danny Tartabull	.10	.03
184 Brien Taylor RC	.50	.15
185 Todd Taylor	.10	.03
186 Larry Thomas RC	.25	.07
187 Ozzie Timmons RC (See also 188)	.25	.07
188 David Tuttle UER (Mistakenly numbered as 187 on card)	.10	.03
189 Andy Van Slyke	.25	.07
190 Frank Viola	.15	.04
191 Michael Walkden RC	.25	.07
192 Jeff Ware	.10	.03
193 Allen Watson RC	.25	.07
194 Steve Whitaker RC	.25	.07
195 Jerry Willard	.10	.03
196 Craig Wilson	.10	.03
197 Chris Wimmer	.10	.03
198 S.Wojciechowski RC	.25	.07
199 Joel Wolfe RC	.25	.07
200 Ivan Zweig	.10	.03

1993 Stadium Club Murphy

	Nm-Mt	Ex-Mt
COMP.FACT.SET (212)	50.00	15.00
COMPLETE SET (200)	40.00	12.00
COMMON CARD (1-200)	.15	.04
COMMON RC	.15	.04
1 Dave Winfield	.15	.04
2 Juan Guzman	.15	.04
3 Tony Gwynn	1.00	.30
4 Chris Roberts	.15	.04
5 Benny Santiago	.30	.09
6 Sherard Clinkscales RC	.15	.04
7 Jon Nunnally RC	.50	.15
8 Chuck Knoblauch	.30	.09
9 Bob Wolcott RC	.15	.04
10 Steve Rodriguez	.15	.04
11 Mark Williams RC	.15	.04
12 Danny Clyburn RC	.15	.04
13 Darren Dreifort	.15	.04
14 Andy Van Slyke	.50	.15
15 Wade Boggs	.50	.15
16 Scott Patton RC	.15	.04
17 Gary Sheffield	.30	.09
18 Ron Villone	.15	.04
19 Roberto Alomar	.50	.15
20 Marc Valdes	.15	.04

❑ 21 Daron Kirkreit .15 .04
❑ 22 Jeff Granger .15 .04
❑ 23 Levon Largusa RC .15 .04
❑ 24 Jimmy Key .30 .09
❑ 25 Kevin Pearson RC .15 .04
❑ 26 Michael Moore RC .15 .04
❑ 27 Preston Wilson RC 1.50 .45
❑ 28 Kirby Puckett .75 .23
❑ 29 Tim Crabtree RC .15 .04
❑ 30 Bip Roberts .15 .04
❑ 31 Kelly Gruber .15 .04
❑ 32 Tony Fernandez .15 .04
❑ 33 Jason Angel RC .15 .04
❑ 34 Calvin Murray .15 .04
❑ 35 Chad McConnell .15 .04
❑ 36 Jason Moler .15 .04
❑ 37 Mark Lemke .15 .04
❑ 38 Tom Knauss RC .15 .04
❑ 39 Larry Mitchell RC .15 .04
❑ 40 Doug Mirabelli RC .50 .15
❑ 41 Everett Stull II RC .15 .04
❑ 42 Chris Wimmer .15 .04
❑ 43 Dan Serafini RC .15 .04
❑ 44 Ryne Sandberg 1.25 .35
❑ 45 Steve Lyons RC .15 .04
❑ 46 Ryan Freeburg RC .15 .04
❑ 47 Ruben Sierra .15 .04
❑ 48 David Mysel RC .15 .04
❑ 49 Joe Hamilton RC .15 .04
❑ 50 Steve Rodriguez .15 .04
❑ 51 Tim Wakefield .75 .23
❑ 52 Scott Gentile RC .15 .04
❑ 53 Doug Jones .15 .04
❑ 54 Willie Brown RC .15 .04
❑ 55 Chad Mottola RC .50 .15
❑ 56 Ken Griffey Jr. 1.25 .35
❑ 57 Jon Lieber RC 2.50 .75
❑ 58 Dennis Martinez .30 .09
❑ 59 Joe Petcka RC .15 .04
❑ 60 Benji Simonton RC .15 .04
❑ 61 Brett Backlund RC .15 .04
❑ 62 Damon Berryhill .15 .04
❑ 63 Juan Guzman .15 .04
❑ 64 Doug Hecker RC .15 .04
❑ 65 Jamie Arnold RC .15 .04
❑ 66 Bob Tewksbury .15 .04
❑ 67 Tim Leger RC .15 .04
❑ 68 Todd Etler RC .15 .04
❑ 69 Lloyd McClendon .15 .04
❑ 70 Kurt Ehmann RC .15 .04
❑ 71 Rick Magdaleno RC .15 .04
❑ 72 Tom Pagnozzi .15 .04
❑ 73 Jeffrey Hammonds .15 .04
❑ 74 Joe Carter .30 .09
❑ 75 Chris Holt RC .30 .09
❑ 76 Charles Johnson .30 .09
❑ 77 Bob Walk .15 .04
❑ 78 Fred McGriff .50 .15
❑ 79 Tom Evans RC .15 .04
❑ 80 Scott Klingenbeck RC .15 .04
❑ 81 Chad McConnell .15 .04
❑ 82 Chris Eddy RC .15 .04
❑ 83 Phil Nevin .30 .09
❑ 84 John Kruk .30 .09
❑ 85 Tony Sheffield RC .15 .04
❑ 86 John Smoltz .50 .15
❑ 87 Trevor Humphry RC .15 .04
❑ 88 Charles Nagy .15 .04
❑ 89 Sean Runyan RC .15 .04
❑ 90 Mike Gulan RC .15 .04
❑ 91 Darren Daulton .30 .09
❑ 92 Otis Nixon .15 .04
❑ 93 Nomar Garciaparra 8.00 2.40
❑ 94 Larry Walker .30 .09
❑ 95 Hut Smith RC .15 .04
❑ 96 Rick Helling .15 .04
❑ 97 Roger Clemens 1.50 .45
❑ 98 Ron Gant .30 .09
❑ 99 Kenny Felder RC .15 .04
❑ 100 Steve Murphy RC .15 .04
❑ 101 Mike Smith RC .15 .04
❑ 102 Terry Pendleton .30 .09
❑ 103 Tim Davis .15 .04
❑ 104 Jeff Patzke RC .15 .04
❑ 105 Craig Wilson .15 .04
❑ 106 Tom Glavine .50 .15
❑ 107 Mark Langston .15 .04
❑ 108 Mark Thompson RC .15 .04
❑ 109 Eric Owens RC .50 .15
❑ 110 Keith Johnson RC .15 .04
❑ 111 Robin Ventura .30 .09
❑ 112 Ed Sprague .15 .04
❑ 113 Jeff Schmidt RC .15 .04
❑ 114 Don Wengert RC .15 .04
❑ 115 Craig Biggio .50 .15
❑ 116 Kenny Carlyle RC .15 .04
❑ 117 Derek Jeter RC 30.00 9.00
❑ 118 Manuel Lee .15 .04
❑ 119 Jeff Haas RC .15 .04
❑ 120 Roger Bailey RC .15 .04
❑ 121 Sean Lowe RC .15 .04
❑ 122 Rick Aguilera .15 .04
❑ 123 Sandy Alomar Jr. .15 .04
❑ 124 Derek Wallace RC .15 .04
❑ 125 B.J. Wallace .15 .04
❑ 126 Greg Maddux 1.25 .35
❑ 127 Tim Moore RC .15 .04
❑ 128 Lee Smith .30 .09
❑ 129 Todd Steverson RC .15 .04
❑ 130 Chris Widger RC 1.00 .30
❑ 131 Paul Molitor .50 .15
❑ 132 Chris Smith RC .15 .04
❑ 133 Chris Gomez RC .50 .15
❑ 134 Jimmy Baron RC .15 .04
❑ 135 John Smoltz .50 .15
❑ 136 Pat Borders .15 .04
❑ 137 Donnie Leshnock .15 .04
❑ 138 Gus Gandarillos RC .15 .04
❑ 139 Will Clark .50 .15
❑ 140 Ryan Luzinski RC .15 .04
❑ 141 Cal Ripken 2.50 .75
❑ 142 B.J. Wallace .15 .04
❑ 143 Trey Beamon RC .50 .15
❑ 144 Norm Charlton .15 .04
❑ 145 Mike Mussina .50 .15
❑ 146 Billy Owens RC .15 .04
❑ 147 Ozzie Smith 1.25 .35
❑ 148 Jason Kendall RC 1.50 .45
❑ 149 Mike Matthews RC .15 .04
❑ 150 David Spykstra RC .15 .04
❑ 151 Benji Grigsby RC .15 .04
❑ 152 Sean Smith RC .15 .04
❑ 153 Mark McGwire 2.00 .60
❑ 154 David Cone .30 .09
❑ 155 Shon Walker RC .15 .04
❑ 156 Jason Giambi 1.00 .30
❑ 157 Jack McDowell .15 .04
❑ 158 Paxton Briley RC .15 .04
❑ 159 Edgar Martinez .50 .15
❑ 160 Brian Sackinsky RC .15 .04
❑ 161 Barry Bonds 2.00 .60
❑ 162 Roberto Kelly .15 .04
❑ 163 Jeff Alkire .15 .04
❑ 164 Mike Sharperson .15 .04
❑ 165 Jamie Taylor RC .15 .04
❑ 166 John Saffer UER RC .15 .04
❑ 167 Jerry Browne .15 .04
❑ 168 Travis Fryman .30 .09
❑ 169 Brady Anderson .30 .09
❑ 170 Chris Roberts .15 .04
❑ 171 Lloyd Peever RC .15 .04
❑ 172 Francisco Cabrera .15 .04
❑ 173 Ramiro Martinez RC .15 .04
❑ 174 Jeff Alkire .15 .04
❑ 175 Ivan Rodriguez .50 .15
❑ 176 Kevin Brown .30 .09
❑ 177 Chad Roper RC .15 .04
❑ 178 Rod Henderson RC .15 .04
❑ 179 Dennis Eckersley .30 .09
❑ 180 Shannon Stewart RC 1.50 .45
❑ 181 DeShawn Warren RC .15 .04
❑ 182 Lonnie Smith .15 .04
❑ 183 Willie Adams .15 .04
❑ 184 Jeff Montgomery .15 .04
❑ 185 Damon Hollins RC 1.00 .30
❑ 186 Byron Mathews RC .15 .04
❑ 187 Harold Baines .30 .09
❑ 188 Rick Greene .15 .04
❑ 189 Carlos Baerga .15 .04
❑ 190 Brandon Cromer RC .15 .04
❑ 191 Roberto Alomar .50 .15
❑ 192 Rich Ireland RC .15 .04
❑ 193 S.Montgomery RC .15 .04
❑ 194 Brant Brown RC .15 .04
❑ 195 Ritchie Moody RC .15 .04
❑ 196 Michael Tucker .30 .09
❑ 197 Jason Varitek 5.00 1.50
❑ 198 David Manning RC .15 .04
❑ 199 Marquis Riley RC .15 .04
❑ 200 Jason Giambi 1.00 .30

1994 Stadium Club Draft Picks

	Nm-Mt	Ex-Mt
COMPLETE SET (90)	10.00	3.00
❑ 1 Jacob Shumate XRC	.25	.07
❑ 2 C.J. Nitkowski XRC	.25	.07
❑ 3 Doug Million XRC	.25	.07
❑ 4 Matt Smith XRC	.25	.07
❑ 5 Kevin Lovinger XRC	.25	.07
❑ 6 Alberto Castillo XRC	.25	.07
❑ 7 Mike Russell XRC	.25	.07
❑ 8 Dan Lock XRC	.25	.07
❑ 9 Tom Szimanski XRC	.25	.07
❑ 10 Aaron Boone XRC	.50	.15
❑ 11 Jayson Peterson XRC	.25	.07
❑ 12 Mark Johnson XRC	.25	.07
❑ 13 Cade Gaspar XRC	.25	.07
❑ 14 George Lombard XRC	.25	.07
❑ 15 Russ Johnson	.25	.07
❑ 16 Travis Miller XRC	.25	.07
❑ 17 Jay Payton XRC	.50	.15
❑ 18 Brian Buchanan XRC	.25	.07
❑ 19 Jacob Cruz XRC	.40	.12
❑ 20 Gary Rath XRC	.25	.07
❑ 21 Ramon Castro XRC	.25	.07
❑ 22 Tommy Davis XRC	.25	.07
❑ 23 Tony Terry XRC	.25	.07
❑ 24 Jerry Whittaker XRC	.25	.07
❑ 25 Mike Darr XRC	.40	.12
❑ 26 Doug Webb XRC	.25	.07
❑ 27 Jason Camilli XRC	.25	.07
❑ 28 Brad Rigby XRC	.25	.07
❑ 29 Ryan Nye XRC	.25	.07
❑ 30 Carl Dale XRC	.25	.07
❑ 31 Andy Taulbee XRC	.25	.07
❑ 32 Trey Moore XRC	.25	.07
❑ 33 John Crowther XRC	.25	.07
❑ 34 Joe Giuliano XRC	.25	.07
❑ 35 Brian Rose XRC	.25	.07
❑ 36 Paul Failla XRC	.25	.07
❑ 37 Brian Meadows XRC	.25	.07
❑ 38 Oscar Robles XRC	.40	.12
❑ 39 Mike Metcalfe XRC	.25	.07
❑ 40 Larry Barnes XRC	.25	.07
❑ 41 Paul Ottavinia XRC	.25	.07
❑ 42 Chris McBride XRC	.25	.07
❑ 43 Ricky Stone XRC	.25	.07
❑ 44 Billy Blythe XRC	.25	.07
❑ 45 Eddie Priest XRC	.25	.07
❑ 46 Scott Forster XRC	.25	.07
❑ 47 Eric Pickett XRC	.25	.07
❑ 48 Matt Beaumont	.25	.07
❑ 49 Darrell Nicholas XRC	.25	.07
❑ 50 Mike A. Hampton XRC	.25	.07
❑ 51 Paul O'Malley XRC	.25	.07
❑ 52 Steve Shoemaker XRC	.25	.07
❑ 53 Jason Sikes XRC	.25	.07

❑ 54	Bryan Farson XRC	.25	.07
❑ 55	Yates Hall XRC	.25	.07
❑ 56	Troy Brohawn XRC	.25	.07
❑ 57	Dan Hower XRC	.25	.07
❑ 58	Clay Caruthers XRC	.25	.07
❑ 59	Pepe McNeal XRC	.25	.07
❑ 60	Ray Ricken XRC	.25	.07
❑ 61	Scott Shores XRC	.25	.07
❑ 62	Eddie Brooks XRC	.25	.07
❑ 63	Dave Kauflin XRC	.25	.07
❑ 64	David Meyer XRC	.25	.07
❑ 65	Geoff Blum XRC	1.00	.30
❑ 66	Roy Marsh XRC	.25	.07
❑ 67	Ryan Beeney XRC	.25	.07
❑ 68	Derek Dukart XRC	.25	.07
❑ 69	Nomar Garciaparra	3.00	.90
❑ 70	Jason Kelly XRC	.25	.07
❑ 71	Jesse Ibarra XRC	.25	.07
❑ 72	Bucky Buckles XRC	.25	.07
❑ 73	Mark Little XRC	.25	.07
❑ 74	Heath Murray XRC	.25	.07
❑ 75	Greg Morris XRC	.25	.07
❑ 76	Mike Halperlin XRC	.25	.07
❑ 77	Wes Helms XRC	.50	.15
❑ 78	Ray Brown XRC	.25	.07
❑ 79	Kevin L.Brown XRC	.40	.12
❑ 80	Paul Konerko XRC	5.00	1.50
❑ 81	Mike Thurman XRC	.25	.07
❑ 82	Paul Wilson	.40	.12
❑ 83	Terrence Long XRC	.50	.15
❑ 84	Ben Grieve XRC	.50	.15
❑ 85	Mark Farris XRC	.25	.07
❑ 86	Bret Wagner	.25	.07
❑ 87	Dustin Hermanson	.40	.12
❑ 88	Kevin Witt XRC	.40	.12
❑ 89	Corey Pointer XRC	.25	.07
❑ 90	Tim Grieve XRC	.25	.07

2001 Stadium Club

	Nm-Mt	Ex-Mt
COMPLETE SET (200)	120.00	36.00
COMP.SET w/o SP's (175)	25.00	7.50
COMMON CARD (1-150)	.30	.09
COMMON SP (151-200)	3.00	.90

❑ 1	Nomar Garciaparra	1.25	.35
❑ 2	Chipper Jones	.75	.23
❑ 3	Jeff Bagwell	.50	.15
❑ 4	Chad Kreuter	.30	.09
❑ 5	Randy Johnson	.75	.23
❑ 6	Mike Hampton	.30	.09
❑ 7	Barry Larkin	.50	.15
❑ 8	Bernie Williams	.50	.15
❑ 9	Chris Singleton	.30	.09
❑ 10	Larry Walker	.30	.09
❑ 11	Brad Ausmus	.30	.09
❑ 12	Ron Coomer	.30	.09
❑ 13	Edgardo Alfonzo	.30	.09
❑ 14	Delino DeShields	.30	.09
❑ 15	Tony Gwynn	1.00	.30
❑ 16	Andruw Jones	.50	.15
❑ 17	Raul Mondesi	.30	.09
❑ 18	Troy Glaus	.30	.09
❑ 19	Ben Grieve	.30	.09
❑ 20	Sammy Sosa	.75	.23
❑ 21	Fernando Vina	.30	.09
❑ 22	Jeromy Burnitz	.30	.09
❑ 23	Jay Bell	.30	.09
❑ 24	Pete Harnisch	.30	.09
❑ 25	Barry Bonds	2.00	.60
❑ 26	Eric Karros	.30	.09
❑ 27	Alex Gonzalez	.30	.09
❑ 28	Mike Lieberthal	.30	.09
❑ 29	Juan Encarnacion	.30	.09
❑ 30	Derek Jeter	2.00	.60
❑ 31	Luis Sojo	.30	.09
❑ 32	Eric Milton	.30	.09
❑ 33	Aaron Boone	.30	.09
❑ 34	Roberto Alomar	.50	.15
❑ 35	John Olerud	.30	.09
❑ 36	Orlando Cabrera	.30	.09
❑ 37	Shawn Green	.30	.09
❑ 38	Roger Cedeno	.30	.09
❑ 39	Garret Anderson	.30	.09
❑ 40	Jim Thome	.50	.15
❑ 41	Gabe Kapler	.30	.09
❑ 42	Mo Vaughn	.30	.09
❑ 43	Sean Casey	.50	.15
❑ 44	Preston Wilson	.30	.09
❑ 45	Javy Lopez	.30	.09
❑ 46	Ryan Klesko	.30	.09
❑ 47	Ray Durham	.30	.09
❑ 48	Dean Palmer	.30	.09
❑ 49	Jorge Posada	.50	.15
❑ 50	Alex Rodriguez	1.25	.35
❑ 51	Tom Glavine	.50	.15
❑ 52	Ray Lankford	.30	.09
❑ 53	Jose Canseco	.50	.15
❑ 54	Tim Salmon	.50	.15
❑ 55	Cal Ripken	2.50	.75
❑ 56	Bob Abreu	.30	.09
❑ 57	Robin Ventura	.30	.09
❑ 58	Damion Easley	.30	.09
❑ 59	Paul O'Neill	.50	.15
❑ 60	Ivan Rodriguez	.50	.15
❑ 61	Carl Everett	.30	.09
❑ 62	Doug Glanville	.30	.09
❑ 63	Jeff Kent	.30	.09
❑ 64	Jay Buhner	.30	.09
❑ 65	Cliff Floyd	.30	.09
❑ 66	Rick Ankiel	.30	.09
❑ 67	Mark Grace	.50	.15
❑ 68	Brian Jordan	.30	.09
❑ 69	Craig Biggio	.50	.15
❑ 70	Carlos Delgado	.30	.09
❑ 71	Brad Radke	.30	.09
❑ 72	Greg Maddux	1.25	.35
❑ 73	Al Leiter	.30	.09
❑ 74	Pokey Reese	.30	.09
❑ 75	Todd Helton	.50	.15
❑ 76	Mariano Rivera	.50	.15
❑ 77	Shane Spencer	.30	.09
❑ 78	Jason Kendall	.30	.09
❑ 79	Chuck Knoblauch	.30	.09
❑ 80	Scott Rolen	.50	.15
❑ 81	Jose Offerman	.30	.09
❑ 82	J.T. Snow	.30	.09
❑ 83	Pat Meares	.30	.09
❑ 84	Quilvio Veras	.30	.09
❑ 85	Edgar Renteria	.30	.09
❑ 86	Luis Matos	.30	.09
❑ 87	Adrian Beltre	.30	.09
❑ 88	Luis Gonzalez	.30	.09
❑ 89	Rickey Henderson	.75	.23
❑ 90	Brian Giles	.30	.09
❑ 91	Carlos Febles	.30	.09
❑ 92	Tino Martinez	.50	.15
❑ 93	Magglio Ordonez	.30	.09
❑ 94	Rafael Furcal	.30	.09
❑ 95	Mike Mussina	.50	.15
❑ 96	Gary Sheffield	.30	.09
❑ 97	Kenny Lofton	.30	.09
❑ 98	Fred McGriff	.50	.15
❑ 99	Ken Caminiti	.30	.09
❑ 100	Mark McGwire	2.00	.60
❑ 101	Tom Goodwin	.30	.09
❑ 102	Mark Grudzielanek	.30	.09
❑ 103	Derek Bell	.30	.09
❑ 104	Mike Lowell	.30	.09
❑ 105	Jeff Cirillo	.30	.09
❑ 106	Orlando Hernandez	.30	.09
❑ 107	Jose Valentin	.30	.09
❑ 108	Warren Morris	.30	.09
❑ 109	Mike Williams	.30	.09
❑ 110	Greg Zaun	.30	.09
❑ 111	Jose Vidro	.30	.09
❑ 112	Omar Vizquel	.50	.15
❑ 113	Vinny Castilla	.30	.09
❑ 114	Gregg Jefferies	.30	.09
❑ 115	Kevin Brown	.30	.09
❑ 116	Shannon Stewart	.30	.09
❑ 117	Marquis Grissom	.30	.09
❑ 118	Manny Ramirez	.50	.15
❑ 119	Albert Belle	.30	.09
❑ 120	Bret Boone	.30	.09
❑ 121	Johnny Damon	.50	.15
❑ 122	Juan Gonzalez	.30	.09
❑ 123	David Justice	.30	.09
❑ 124	Jeffrey Hammonds	.30	.09
❑ 125	Ken Griffey Jr.	1.25	.35
❑ 126	Mike Sweeney	.30	.09
❑ 127	Tony Clark	.30	.09
❑ 128	Todd Zeile	.30	.09
❑ 129	Mark Johnson	.30	.09
❑ 130	Matt Williams	.30	.09
❑ 131	Geoff Jenkins	.30	.09
❑ 132	Jason Giambi	.30	.09
❑ 133	Steve Finley	.30	.09
❑ 134	Derrek Lee	.50	.15
❑ 135	Royce Clayton	.30	.09
❑ 136	Joe Randa	.30	.09
❑ 137	Rafael Palmeiro	.50	.15
❑ 138	Kevin Young	.30	.09
❑ 139	Mike Redmond	.30	.09
❑ 140	Vladimir Guerrero	.75	.23
❑ 141	Greg Vaughn	.30	.09
❑ 142	Jermaine Dye	.30	.09
❑ 143	Roger Clemens	1.50	.45
❑ 144	Denny Hocking	.30	.09
❑ 145	Frank Thomas	.75	.23
❑ 146	Carlos Beltran	.30	.09
❑ 147	Eric Young	.30	.09
❑ 148	Pat Burrell	.30	.09
❑ 149	Pedro Martinez	.50	.15
❑ 150	Mike Piazza	1.25	.35
❑ 151	Adrian Gonzalez	.50	.15
❑ 152	Adam Johnson	.50	.15
❑ 153	Luis Montanez SP RC	3.00	.90
❑ 154	Mike Stodolka	.50	.15
❑ 155	Phil Dumatrait	.50	.15
❑ 156	Sean Burnett SP	3.00	.90
❑ 157	Dominic Rich SP RC	3.00	.90
❑ 158	Adam Wainwright	.50	.15
❑ 159	Scott Thorman	.50	.15
❑ 160	Scott Heard SP	3.00	.90
❑ 161	Chad Petty SP RC	3.00	.90
❑ 162	Matt Wheatland	.50	.15
❑ 163	Bryan Digby	.50	.15
❑ 164	Rocco Baldelli	.50	.15
❑ 165	Grady Sizemore	.75	.23
❑ 166	Brian Sellier SP RC	3.00	.90
❑ 167	Rick Brosseau SP RC	3.00	.90
❑ 168	Shawn Fagan SP RC	3.00	.90
❑ 169	Sean Smith SP	3.00	.90
❑ 170	Chris Bass SP RC	3.00	.90
❑ 171	Corey Patterson	.50	.15
❑ 172	Sean Burroughs	.50	.15
❑ 173	Ben Petrick	.50	.15
❑ 174	Mike Glendenning	.50	.15
❑ 175	Barry Zito	.75	.23
❑ 176	Milton Bradley	.50	.15
❑ 177	Bobby Bradley	.50	.15
❑ 178	Jason Hart	.50	.15
❑ 179	Ryan Anderson	.50	.15
❑ 180	Ben Sheets	.75	.23
❑ 181	Adam Everett	.50	.15
❑ 182	Alfonso Soriano	.50	.15
❑ 183	Josh Hamilton	.50	.15
❑ 184	Eric Munson	.50	.15
❑ 185	Chin-Feng Chen	.50	.15
❑ 186	Tim Christman SP RC	3.00	.90
❑ 187	J.R. House SP	3.00	.90
❑ 188	B.Parker SP RC	3.00	.90
❑ 189	Sean Fesh SP RC	3.00	.90
❑ 190	Joel Pineiro SP	3.00	.90
❑ 191	Oscar Ramirez SP RC	3.00	.90
❑ 192	Alex Santos SP RC	3.00	.90
❑ 193	Eddy Reyes SP RC	3.00	.90
❑ 194	Mike Jacobs SP RC	25.00	7.50
❑ 195	Erick Almonte SP RC	3.00	.90

		Nm-Mt	Ex-Mt
❑ 196	B.Claussen SP RC	4.00	1.20
❑ 197	Kris Keller SP RC	3.00	.90
❑ 198	Wilson Betemit SP RC	4.00	1.20
❑ 199	Andy Phillips SP RC	3.00	.90
❑ 200	A.Pettyjohn SP RC	3.00	.90

2001 Sweet Spot

	Nm-Mt	Ex-Mt
COMP.BASIC w/o SP's (60)	20.00	6.00
COMP.UPDATE w/o SP's (30)	10.00	3.00
COMMON CARD (1-60)	.40	.12
COMMON CARD (61-90)	10.00	3.00
COMMON CARD (91-120)	.60	.18
COMMON (121-150)	5.00	1.50

		Nm-Mt	Ex-Mt
❑ 1	Troy Glaus	.40	.12
❑ 2	Darin Erstad	.40	.12
❑ 3	Jason Giambi	.40	.12
❑ 4	Tim Hudson	.40	.12
❑ 5	Ben Grieve	.40	.12
❑ 6	Carlos Delgado	.40	.12
❑ 7	David Wells	.40	.12
❑ 8	Greg Vaughn	.40	.12
❑ 9	Roberto Alomar	.60	.18
❑ 10	Jim Thome	.60	.18
❑ 11	John Olerud	.40	.12
❑ 12	Edgar Martinez	.60	.18
❑ 13	Cal Ripken	3.00	.90
❑ 14	Albert Belle	.40	.12
❑ 15	Ivan Rodriguez	.60	.18
❑ 16	Alex Rodriguez Rangers	3.00	.90
❑ 17	Pedro Martinez	.60	.18
❑ 18	Nomar Garciaparra	1.50	.45
❑ 19	Manny Ramirez	.60	.18
❑ 20	Jermaine Dye	.40	.12
❑ 21	Juan Gonzalez	.40	.12
❑ 22	Dean Palmer	.40	.12
❑ 23	Matt Lawton	.40	.12
❑ 24	Eric Milton	.40	.12
❑ 25	Frank Thomas	1.00	.30
❑ 26	Magglio Ordonez	.40	.12
❑ 27	Derek Jeter	2.50	.75
❑ 28	Bernie Williams	.60	.18
❑ 29	Roger Clemens	2.00	.60
❑ 30	Jeff Bagwell	.60	.18
❑ 31	Richard Hidalgo	.40	.12
❑ 32	Chipper Jones	1.00	.30
❑ 33	Greg Maddux	1.50	.45
❑ 34	Richie Sexson	.40	.12
❑ 35	Jeromy Burnitz	.40	.12
❑ 36	Mark McGwire	2.50	.75
❑ 37	Jim Edmonds	.60	.18
❑ 38	Sammy Sosa	1.00	.30
❑ 39	Randy Johnson	1.00	.30
❑ 40	Steve Finley	.40	.12
❑ 41	Gary Sheffield	.40	.12
❑ 42	Shawn Green	.40	.12
❑ 43	Vladimir Guerrero	1.00	.30
❑ 44	Jose Vidro	.40	.12
❑ 45	Barry Bonds	2.50	.75
❑ 46	Jeff Kent	.40	.12
❑ 47	Preston Wilson	.40	.12
❑ 48	Luis Castillo	.40	.12
❑ 49	Mike Piazza	1.50	.45
❑ 50	Edgardo Alfonzo	.40	.12
❑ 51	Tony Gwynn	1.25	.35
❑ 52	Ryan Klesko	.40	.12
❑ 53	Scott Rolen	.60	.18
❑ 54	Bob Abreu	.40	.12
❑ 55	Jason Kendall	.40	.12
❑ 56	Brian Giles	.40	.12
❑ 57	Ken Griffey Jr.	1.50	.45
❑ 58	Barry Larkin	.60	.18
❑ 59	Todd Helton	.60	.18
❑ 60	Mike Hampton	.40	.12
	Card back has batting header lines UER		
❑ 61	Corey Patterson SB	10.00	3.00
❑ 62	Ichiro Suzuki SB RC	200.00	60.00
❑ 63	Jason Grilli SB	10.00	3.00
❑ 64	Brian Cole SB	10.00	3.00
❑ 65	Juan Pierre SB	10.00	3.00
❑ 66	Matt Ginter SB	10.00	3.00
❑ 67	Jimmy Rollins SB	10.00	3.00
❑ 68	Jason Smith SB RC	10.00	3.00
❑ 69	Israel Alcantara SB	10.00	3.00
❑ 70	Adam Pettyjohn SB RC	10.00	3.00
❑ 71	Luke Prokopec SB	10.00	3.00
❑ 72	Barry Zito SB	12.00	3.60
❑ 73	Keith Ginter SB	10.00	3.00
❑ 74	Sun Woo Kim SB	10.00	3.00
❑ 75	Ross Gload SB	10.00	3.00
❑ 76	Matt Wise SB	10.00	3.00
❑ 77	Aubrey Huff SB	10.00	3.00
❑ 78	Ryan Franklin SB	10.00	3.00
❑ 79	Brandon Inge SB	10.00	3.00
❑ 80	Wes Helms SB	10.00	3.00
❑ 81	Junior Spivey SB RC	12.00	3.60
❑ 82	Ryan Vogelsong SB	10.00	3.00
❑ 83	John Parrish SB	10.00	3.00
❑ 84	Joe Crede SB	12.00	3.60
❑ 85	Damian Rolls SB	10.00	3.00
❑ 86	Esix Snead SB RC	10.00	3.00
❑ 87	Rocky Biddle SB	10.00	3.00
❑ 88	Brady Clark SB	10.00	3.00
❑ 89	Timo Perez SB	10.00	3.00
❑ 90	Jay Spurgeon SB	10.00	3.00
❑ 91	Garret Anderson	.60	.18
❑ 92	Jermaine Dye	.60	.18
❑ 93	Shannon Stewart	.60	.18
❑ 94	Ben Grieve	.60	.18
❑ 95	Juan Gonzalez	.60	.18
❑ 96	Brett Boone	.60	.18
❑ 97	Tony Batista	.60	.18
❑ 98	Rafael Palmeiro	1.00	.30
❑ 99	Carl Everett	.60	.18
❑ 100	Mike Sweeney	.60	.18
❑ 101	Tony Clark	.60	.18
❑ 102	Doug Mientkiewicz	.60	.18
❑ 103	Jose Canseco	1.00	.30
❑ 104	Mike Mussina	1.00	.30
❑ 105	Lance Berkman	.60	.18
❑ 106	Andruw Jones	1.00	.30
❑ 107	Geoff Jenkins	.60	.18
❑ 108	Matt Morris	.60	.18
❑ 109	Fred McGriff	1.00	.30
❑ 110	Luis Gonzalez	.60	.18
❑ 111	Kevin Brown	.60	.18
❑ 112	Tony Armas Jr.	.60	.18
❑ 113	John Vander Wal	.60	.18
❑ 114	Cliff Floyd	.60	.18
❑ 115	Matt Lawton	.60	.18
❑ 116	Phil Nevin	.60	.18
❑ 117	Pat Burrell	.60	.18
❑ 118	Aramis Ramirez	.60	.18
❑ 119	Sean Casey	1.00	.30
❑ 120	Larry Walker	.60	.18
❑ 121	Albert Pujols SB RC	200.00	60.00
❑ 122	J.Estrada SB RC	5.00	1.50
❑ 123	Wilson Betemit SB RC	5.00	1.50
❑ 124	A.Hernandez SB RC	5.00	1.50
❑ 125	M.Ensberg SB RC	12.00	3.60
❑ 126	H.Ramirez SB RC	5.00	1.50
❑ 127	Josh Towers SB RC	5.00	1.50
❑ 128	Juan Uribe SB RC	5.00	1.50
❑ 129	Wilken Ruan SB RC	5.00	1.50
❑ 130	Andres Torres SB RC	5.00	1.50
❑ 131	B.Lawrence SB RC	5.00	1.50
❑ 132	Ryan Freel SB RC	5.00	1.50
❑ 133	B.Duckworth SB RC	5.00	1.50
❑ 134	Juan Diaz SB RC	5.00	1.50
❑ 135	Rafael Soriano SB RC	5.00	1.50
❑ 136	R.Rodriguez SB RC	5.00	1.50
❑ 137	Bud Smith SB RC	5.00	1.50
❑ 138	Mark Teixeira SB RC	50.00	15.00
❑ 139	Mark Prior SB RC	40.00	12.00
❑ 140	J.Melian SB RC	5.00	1.50
❑ 141	D.Brazelton SB RC	5.00	1.50
❑ 142	Greg Miller SB RC	5.00	1.50
❑ 143	Billy Sylvester SB RC	5.00	1.50
❑ 144	E.Guzman SB RC	5.00	1.50
❑ 145	Jack Wilson SB RC	5.00	1.50
❑ 146	Jose Mieses SB RC	5.00	1.50
❑ 147	Brandon Lyon SB RC	5.00	1.50
❑ 148	T.Shinjo SB RC	5.00	1.50
❑ 149	Juan Cruz SB RC	5.00	1.50
❑ 150	Jay Gibbons SB RC	5.00	1.50

2002 Sweet Spot

	Nm-Mt	Ex-Mt
COMP.SET w/o SP's (90)	20.00	6.00
COMMON CARD (1-90)	.40	.12
COMMON CARD (91-130)	4.00	1.20
COMMON TIER 1 AU (131-145)	15.00	4.50
COMMON TIER 2 AU (131-145)	25.00	7.50
COMMON CARD (146-175)	10.00	3.00

		Nm-Mt	Ex-Mt
❑ 1	Troy Glaus	.40	.12
❑ 2	Darin Erstad	.40	.12
❑ 3	Tim Hudson	.40	.12
❑ 4	Eric Chavez	.40	.12
❑ 5	Barry Zito	.40	.12
❑ 6	Miguel Tejada	.40	.12
❑ 7	Carlos Delgado	.40	.12
❑ 8	Eric Hinske	.40	.12
❑ 9	Ben Grieve	.40	.12
❑ 10	Jim Thome	.60	.18
❑ 11	C.C. Sabathia	.40	.12
❑ 12	Omar Vizquel	.60	.18
❑ 13	Ichiro Suzuki	2.00	.60
❑ 14	Edgar Martinez	.60	.18
❑ 15	Bret Boone	.40	.12
❑ 16	Freddy Garcia	.40	.12
❑ 17	Tony Batista	.40	.12
❑ 18	Geronimo Gil	.40	.12
❑ 19	Alex Rodriguez	1.50	.45
❑ 20	Rafael Palmeiro	.60	.18
❑ 21	Ivan Rodriguez	.60	.18
❑ 22	Hank Blalock	.60	.18
❑ 23	Juan Gonzalez	.40	.12
❑ 24	Nomar Garciaparra	1.50	.45
❑ 25	Pedro Martinez	.60	.18
❑ 26	Manny Ramirez	.60	.18
❑ 27	Mike Sweeney	.40	.12
❑ 28	Carlos Beltran	.40	.12
❑ 29	Dmitri Young	.40	.12
❑ 30	Torii Hunter	.40	.12
❑ 31	Eric Milton	.40	.12
❑ 32	Corey Koskie	.40	.12
❑ 33	Frank Thomas	1.00	.30
❑ 34	Mark Buehrle	.40	.12
❑ 35	Magglio Ordonez	.40	.12
❑ 36	Roger Clemens	2.00	.60
❑ 37	Derek Jeter	2.50	.75
❑ 38	Jason Giambi	.40	.12
❑ 39	Alfonso Soriano	.40	.12
❑ 40	Bernie Williams	.60	.18
❑ 41	Jeff Bagwell	.60	.18
❑ 42	Roy Oswalt	.40	.12
❑ 43	Lance Berkman	.40	.12
❑ 44	Greg Maddux	1.50	.45
❑ 45	Chipper Jones	1.00	.30
❑ 46	Gary Sheffield	.40	.12

❑ 47 Andruw Jones .60 .18
❑ 48 Richie Sexson .40 .12
❑ 49 Ben Sheets .40 .12
❑ 50 Albert Pujols 2.00 .60
❑ 51 Matt Morris .40 .12
❑ 52 J.D. Drew .40 .12
❑ 53 Sammy Sosa 1.00 .30
❑ 54 Kerry Wood .40 .12
❑ 55 Mark Prior 1.00 .30
❑ 56 Moises Alou .40 .12
❑ 57 Corey Patterson .40 .12
❑ 58 Randy Johnson 1.00 .30
❑ 59 Luis Gonzalez .40 .12
❑ 60 Curt Schilling .40 .12
❑ 61 Shawn Green .40 .12
❑ 62 Kevin Brown .40 .12
❑ 63 Paul Lo Duca .40 .12
❑ 64 Adrian Beltre .40 .12
❑ 65 Vladimir Guerrero 1.00 .30
❑ 66 Jose Vidro .40 .12
❑ 67 Javier Vazquez .40 .12
❑ 68 Barry Bonds 2.50 .75
❑ 69 Jeff Kent .40 .12
❑ 70 Rich Aurilia .40 .12
❑ 71 Mike Lowell .40 .12
❑ 72 Josh Beckett .40 .12
❑ 73 Brad Penny .40 .12
❑ 74 Roberto Alomar .60 .18
❑ 75 Mike Piazza 1.50 .45
❑ 76 Jeromy Burnitz .40 .12
❑ 77 Mo Vaughn .40 .12
❑ 78 Phil Nevin .40 .12
❑ 79 Sean Burroughs .40 .12
❑ 80 Jeremy Giambi .40 .12
❑ 81 Bobby Abreu .40 .12
❑ 82 Jimmy Rollins .40 .12
❑ 83 Pat Burrell .40 .12
❑ 84 Brian Giles .40 .12
❑ 85 Aramis Ramirez .40 .12
❑ 86 Ken Griffey Jr. 1.50 .45
❑ 87 Adam Dunn .40 .12
❑ 88 Austin Kearns .40 .12
❑ 89 Todd Helton .60 .18
❑ 90 Larry Walker .40 .12
❑ 91 Earl Snyder SB RC 4.00 1.20
❑ 92 Jorge Padilla SB RC 4.00 1.20
❑ 93 Felix Escalona SB RC 4.00 1.20
❑ 94 John Foster SB RC 4.00 1.20
❑ 95 Brandon Puffer SB RC 4.00 1.20
❑ 96 Steve Bechler SB RC 4.00 1.20
❑ 97 Hansel Izquierdo SB RC 4.00 1.20
❑ 98 Chris Baker SB RC 4.00 1.20
❑ 99 Jeremy Ward SB RC 4.00 1.20
❑ 100 Kevin Frederick SB RC 4.00 1.20
❑ 101 Josh Hancock SB RC 4.00 1.20
❑ 102 Allan Simpson SB RC 4.00 1.20
❑ 103 Mitch Wylie SB RC 4.00 1.20
❑ 104 Mark Corey SB RC 4.00 1.20
❑ 105 Victor Alvarez SB RC 4.00 1.20
❑ 106 Todd Donovan SB RC 4.00 1.20
❑ 107 Nelson Castro SB RC 4.00 1.20
❑ 108 Chris Booker SB RC 4.00 1.20
❑ 109 Corey Thurman SB RC 4.00 1.20
❑ 110 Kirk Saarloos SB RC 4.00 1.20
❑ 111 Michael Crudale SB RC 4.00 1.20
❑ 112 J.Simontacchi SB RC 4.00 1.20
❑ 113 Ron Calloway SB RC 4.00 1.20
❑ 114 Brandon Backe SB RC 5.00 1.50
❑ 115 Tom Shearn SB RC 4.00 1.20
❑ 116 Oliver Perez SB RC 6.00 1.80
❑ 117 Kyle Kane SB RC 4.00 1.20
❑ 118 Francis Beltran SB RC 4.00 1.20
❑ 119 So Taguchi SB RC 5.00 1.50
❑ 120 Doug Devore SB RC 4.00 1.20
❑ 121 Juan Brito SB RC 4.00 1.20
❑ 122 Cliff Bartosh SB RC 4.00 1.20
❑ 123 Eric Junge SB RC 4.00 1.20
❑ 124 Joe Orloski SB RC 4.00 1.20
❑ 125 Scotty Layfield SB RC 4.00 1.20
❑ 126 Jorge Sosa SB RC 5.00 1.50
❑ 127 Satoru Komiyama SB RC 4.00 1.20
❑ 128 Edwin Almonte SB RC 4.00 1.20
❑ 129 Takahito Nomura SB RC 4.00 1.20
❑ 130 John Ennis SB RC 4.00 1.20
❑ 131 Kazuhisa Ishii T2 AU RC 100.00 30.00
❑ 132 Ben Howard T2 AU RC 25.00 7.50
❑ 133 Aaron Cook T1 AU RC 15.00 4.50
❑ 134 Andy Machado T1 AU RC 15.00 4.50
❑ 135 Luis Ugueto T1 AU RC 15.00 4.50
❑ 136 Tyler Yates T1 AU RC 15.00 4.50
❑ 137 Rod. Rosario T1 AU RC 15.00 4.50
❑ 138 Jaime Cerda T1 AU RC 15.00 4.50
❑ 139 Luis Martinez T1 AU RC 15.00 4.50
❑ 140 Rene Reyes T1 AU RC 15.00 4.50
❑ 141 Eric Good T1 AU RC 15.00 4.50
❑ 142 Matt Thornton T2 AU RC 25.00 7.50
❑ 143 Steve Kent T1 AU RC 15.00 4.50
❑ 144 Jose Valverde T1 AU RC 15.00 4.50
❑ 145 A.Burnside T1 AU RC 15.00 4.50
❑ 146 Barry Bonds GF 25.00 7.50
❑ 147 Ken Griffey Jr. GF 15.00 4.50
❑ 148 Alex Rodriguez GF 15.00 4.50
❑ 149 Jason Giambi GF 4.00 1.20
❑ 150 Chipper Jones GF 10.00 3.00
❑ 151 Nomar Garciaparra GF 15.00 4.50
❑ 152 Mike Piazza GF 15.00 4.50
❑ 153 Sammy Sosa GF 10.00 3.00
❑ 154 Derek Jeter GF 25.00 7.50
❑ 155 Jeff Bagwell GF 10.00 3.00
❑ 156 Albert Pujols GF 15.00 4.50
❑ 157 Ichiro Suzuki GF 15.00 4.50
❑ 158 Randy Johnson GF 10.00 3.00
❑ 159 Frank Thomas GF 10.00 3.00
❑ 160 Greg Maddux GF 15.00 4.50
❑ 161 Jim Thome GF 10.00 3.00
❑ 162 Scott Rolen GF 10.00 3.00
❑ 163 Shawn Green GF 10.00 3.00
❑ 164 Vladimir Guerrero GF 10.00 3.00
❑ 165 Troy Glaus GF 10.00 3.00
❑ 166 Carlos Delgado GF 10.00 3.00
❑ 167 Luis Gonzalez GF 10.00 3.00
❑ 168 Roger Clemens GF 20.00 6.00
❑ 169 Todd Helton GF 10.00 3.00
❑ 170 Eric Chavez GF 10.00 3.00
❑ 171 Rafael Palmeiro GF 10.00 3.00
❑ 172 Pedro Martinez GF 10.00 3.00
❑ 173 Lance Berkman GF 10.00 3.00
❑ 174 Josh Beckett GF 10.00 3.00
❑ 175 Sean Burroughs GF 10.00 3.00
❑ MM Mark McGwire AU/100 300.00 90.00

2003 Sweet Spot

	MINT	NRMT
COMP.SET w/o SP's (100)	20.00	9.00
COMP.SET w/SP's (130)	120.00	55.00
COMMON CARD (1-130)	.50	.23
COMMON SP (1-130)	3.00	1.35
COMMON CARD (131-190)	3.00	1.35
131-190 PRINT RUN 2003 SERIAL #'d SETS		.00
COMMON P1 (191-232)	4.00	1.80
P1 191-232 PRINT RUN 500 SERIAL #'d SETS		.00
COMMON P2-P3 (191-232)	3.00	1.35
P2 191-232 PRINT RUN 1200 SERIAL #'d SETS		
P3 191-232 PRINT RUN 1430 SERIAL #'d SETS		

❑ 1 Darin Erstad .50 .23
❑ 2 Garret Anderson .50 .23
❑ 3 Tim Salmon .75 .35
❑ 4 Troy Glaus .50 .23
❑ 5 Luis Gonzalez .50 .23
❑ 6 Randy Johnson 1.25 .55
❑ 7 Curt Schilling .50 .23
❑ 8 Lyle Overbay .50 .23
❑ 9 Andruw Jones SP 4.00 1.80
❑ 10 Gary Sheffield SP 3.00 1.35
❑ 11 Rafael Furcal SP 3.00 1.35
❑ 12 Greg Maddux SP 6.00 2.70
❑ 13 Chipper Jones SP 4.00 1.80
❑ 14 Tony Batista .50 .23
❑ 15 Rodrigo Lopez .50 .23
❑ 16 Jay Gibbons .50 .23
❑ 17 Jason Johnson .50 .23
❑ 18 Byung-Hyun Kim SP 3.00 1.35
❑ 19 Johnny Damon SP 4.00 1.80
❑ 20 Derek Lowe SP 3.00 1.35
❑ 21 Nomar Garciaparra SP 6.00 2.70
❑ 22 Pedro Martinez SP 4.00 1.80
❑ 23 Manny Ramirez SP 4.00 1.80
❑ 24 Mark Prior .75 .35
❑ 25 Kerry Wood .50 .23
❑ 26 Corey Patterson .50 .23
❑ 27 Sammy Sosa 1.25 .55
❑ 28 Moises Alou .50 .23
❑ 29 Magglio Ordonez .50 .23
❑ 30 Frank Thomas 1.25 .55
❑ 31 Paul Konerko .50 .23
❑ 32 Roberto Alomar .75 .35
❑ 33 Adam Dunn .50 .23
❑ 34 Austin Kearns .50 .23
❑ 35 Ryan Wagner RC .50 .23
❑ 36 Ken Griffey Jr. 2.00 .90
❑ 37 Sean Casey .75 .35
❑ 38 Omar Vizquel .75 .35
❑ 39 C.C. Sabathia .50 .23
❑ 40 Jason Davis .50 .23
❑ 41 Travis Hafner .50 .23
❑ 42 Brandon Phillips .50 .23
❑ 43 Larry Walker .50 .23
❑ 44 Preston Wilson .50 .23
❑ 45 Jay Payton .50 .23
❑ 46 Todd Helton .75 .35
❑ 47 Carlos Pena .50 .23
❑ 48 Eric Munson .50 .23
❑ 49 Ivan Rodriguez .75 .35
❑ 50 Josh Beckett .50 .23
❑ 51 Alex Gonzalez .50 .23
❑ 52 Roy Oswalt .50 .23
❑ 53 Craig Biggio .75 .35
❑ 54 Jeff Bagwell .75 .35
❑ 55 Lance Berkman .50 .23
❑ 56 Mike Sweeney .50 .23
❑ 57 Carlos Beltran .50 .23
❑ 58 Brent Mayne .50 .23
❑ 59 Mike MacDougal .50 .23
❑ 60 Hideo Nomo 1.25 .55
❑ 61 Dave Roberts .50 .23
❑ 62 Adrian Beltre .50 .23
❑ 63 Shawn Green .50 .23
❑ 64 Kazuhisa Ishii .50 .23
❑ 65 Rickey Henderson 1.25 .55
❑ 66 Richie Sexson .50 .23
❑ 67 Torii Hunter .50 .23
❑ 68 Jacque Jones .50 .23
❑ 69 Joe Mays .50 .23
❑ 70 Corey Koskie .50 .23
❑ 71 A.J. Pierzynski .50 .23
❑ 72 Jose Vidro .50 .23
❑ 73 Vladimir Guerrero 1.25 .55
❑ 74 Tom Glavine .75 .35
❑ 75 Mike Piazza 2.00 .90
❑ 76 Jose Reyes .50 .23
❑ 77 Jae Weong Seo .50 .23
❑ 78 Jorge Posada SP 4.00 1.80
❑ 79 Mike Mussina SP 4.00 1.80
❑ 80 Robin Ventura SP 3.00 1.35
❑ 81 Mariano Rivera SP 4.00 1.80
❑ 82 Roger Clemens SP 8.00 3.60
❑ 83 Jason Giambi SP 3.00 1.35
❑ 84 Bernie Williams SP 4.00 1.80
❑ 85 Alfonso Soriano SP 3.00 1.35
❑ 86 Derek Jeter 3.00 1.35
❑ 87 Miguel Tejada .50 .23
❑ 88 Eric Chavez .50 .23
❑ 89 Tim Hudson .50 .23
❑ 90 Barry Zito .50 .23
❑ 91 Mark Mulder .50 .23
❑ 92 Erubiel Durazo .50 .23
❑ 93 Pat Burrell .50 .23
❑ 94 Jim Thome .75 .35
❑ 95 Bobby Abreu .50 .23

❑ 96 Brian Giles .50 .23
❑ 97 Reggie Sanders .50 .23
❑ 98 Jose Hernandez .50 .23
❑ 99 Ryan Klesko .50 .23
❑ 100 Sean Burroughs .50 .23
❑ 101 Edgardo Alfonzo SP 3.00 1.35
❑ 102 Rich Aurilia SP 3.00 1.35
❑ 103 Jose Cruz Jr. SP 3.00 1.35
❑ 104 Barry Bonds SP 10.00 4.50
❑ 105 Andres Galarraga SP 3.00 1.35
❑ 106 Mike Cameron .50 .23
❑ 107 Kazuhiro Sasaki .50 .23
❑ 108 Bret Boone .50 .23
❑ 109 Ichiro Suzuki 2.50 1.10
❑ 110 John Olerud .50 .23
❑ 111 J.D. Drew SP 3.00 1.35
❑ 112 Jim Edmonds SP 4.00 1.80
❑ 113 Scott Rolen SP 4.00 1.80
❑ 114 Matt Morris SP 3.00 1.35
❑ 115 Tino Martinez SP 4.00 1.80
❑ 116 Albert Pujols SP 8.00 3.60
❑ 117 Jared Sandberg .50 .23
❑ 118 Carl Crawford .50 .23
❑ 119 Rafael Palmeiro .75 .35
❑ 120 Hank Blalock .50 .23
❑ 121 Alex Rodriguez SP 6.00 2.70
❑ 122 Kevin Mench .50 .23
❑ 123 Juan Gonzalez .50 .23
❑ 124 Mark Teixeira .75 .35
❑ 125 Shannon Stewart .50 .23
❑ 126 Vernon Wells .50 .23
❑ 127 Josh Phelps .50 .23
❑ 128 Eric Hinske .50 .23
❑ 129 Orlando Hudson .50 .23
❑ 130 Carlos Delgado .50 .23
❑ 131 Jason Shiell SB RC 3.00 1.35
❑ 132 Kevin Tolar SB RC 3.00 1.35
❑ 133 Nathan Bland SB RC 3.00 1.35
❑ 134 Brent Hoard SB RC 3.00 1.35
❑ 135 Jon Pridie SB RC 3.00 1.35
❑ 136 Mike Ryan SB RC 3.00 1.35
❑ 137 Francisco Rosario SB RC 3.00 1.35
❑ 138 Runelvys Hernandez SB 3.00 1.35
❑ 139 Guillermo Quiroz SB RC 3.00 1.35
❑ 140 Chin-Hui Tsao SB 3.00 1.35
❑ 141 Rett Johnson SB RC 3.00 1.35
❑ 142 Colin Porter SB RC 3.00 1.35
❑ 143 Jose Castillo SB 3.00 1.35
❑ 144 Chris Waters SB RC 3.00 1.35
❑ 145 Jeremy Guthrie SB 3.00 1.35
❑ 146 Pedro Liriano SB 3.00 1.35
❑ 147 Joe Borowski SB 3.00 1.35
❑ 148 Felix Sanchez SB RC 3.00 1.35
❑ 149 Todd Wellemeyer SB RC 3.00 1.35
❑ 150 Gerald Laird SB 3.00 1.35
❑ 151 Brandon Webb SB RC 4.00 1.80
❑ 152 Tommy Whiteman SB 3.00 1.35
❑ 153 Carlos Rivera SB 3.00 1.35
❑ 154 Rick Roberts SB RC 3.00 1.35
❑ 155 Terrmel Sledge SB RC 3.00 1.35
❑ 156 Jeff Duncan SB RC 3.00 1.35
❑ 157 Craig Brazell SB RC 3.00 1.35
❑ 158 Bernie Castro SB RC 3.00 1.35
❑ 159 Cory Stewart SB RC 3.00 1.35
❑ 160 Brandon Villafuerte SB 3.00 1.35
❑ 161 Tommy Phelps SB 3.00 1.35
❑ 162 Josh Hall SB RC 3.00 1.35
❑ 163 Ryan Cameron SB RC 3.00 1.35
❑ 164 Garret Atkins SB 3.00 1.35
❑ 165 Brian Stokes SB RC 3.00 1.35
❑ 166 Rafael Betancourt SB RC 4.00 1.80
❑ 167 Jaime Cerda SB 3.00 1.35
❑ 168 D.J. Carrasco SB RC 3.00 1.35
❑ 169 Ian Ferguson SB RC 3.00 1.35
❑ 170 Jorge Cordova SB RC 3.00 1.35
❑ 171 Eric Munson SB 3.00 1.35
❑ 172 Nook Logan SB RC 4.00 1.80
❑ 173 Jeremy Bonderman SB RC 10.00 4.50
❑ 174 Kyle Snyder SB 3.00 1.35
❑ 175 Rich Harden SB 4.00 1.80
❑ 176 Kevin Ohme SB RC 3.00 1.35
❑ 177 Roger Deago SB RC 3.00 1.35
❑ 178 Marlon Byrd SB 3.00 1.35
❑ 179 Dontrelle Willis SB 4.00 1.80
❑ 180 Bobby Hill SB 3.00 1.35
❑ 181 Jesse Foppert SB 3.00 1.35
❑ 182 Andrew Good SB 3.00 1.35
❑ 183 Chase Utley SB 4.00 1.80
❑ 184 Bo Hart SB RC 3.00 1.35
❑ 185 Dan Haren SB RC 4.00 1.80
❑ 186 Tim Olson SB RC 3.00 1.35
❑ 187 Joe Thurston SB 3.00 1.35
❑ 188 Jason Anderson SB 3.00 1.35
❑ 189 Jason Gilfillan SB RC 3.00 1.35
❑ 190 Rickie Weeks SB RC 10.00 4.50
❑ 191 Hideki Matsui SB P1 RC 25.00 11.00
❑ 192 J.Contreras SB P3 RC 4.00 1.80
❑ 193 Willie Eyre SB P3 RC 3.00 1.35
❑ 194 Matt Bruback SB P3 RC 3.00 1.35
❑ 195 Heath Bell SB P3 RC 3.00 1.35
❑ 196 Lew Ford SB P3 RC 4.00 1.80
❑ 197 J.Griffiths SB P3 RC 3.00 1.35
❑ 198 O.Villarreal SB P1 RC 4.00 1.80
❑ 199 Fr. Cruceta SB P3 RC 3.00 1.35
❑ 200 Fern Cabrera SB P3 RC 3.00 1.35
❑ 201 Jhonny Peralta SB P3 4.00 1.80
❑ 202 Shane Bazzell SB P3 RC 3.00 1.35
❑ 203 B.Madritsch SB P1 RC 5.00 2.20
❑ 204 Phil Seibel SB P3 RC 3.00 1.35
❑ 205 J.Willingham SB P3 RC 4.00 1.80
❑ 206 Rob Hammock SB P1 RC 4.00 1.80
❑ 207 Al. Machado SB P3 RC 3.00 1.35
❑ 208 David Sanders SB P3 RC 3.00 1.35
❑ 209 Mike Neu SB P1 RC 4.00 1.80
❑ 210 Andrew Brown SB P3 RC 4.00 1.80
❑ 211 N. Robertson SB P3 RC 4.00 1.80
❑ 212 Miguel Ojeda SB P3 RC 3.00 1.35
❑ 213 Beau Kemp SB P3 RC 3.00 1.35
❑ 214 Aaron Looper SB P3 RC 3.00 1.35
❑ 215 Alf.Gonzalez SB P3 RC 3.00 1.35
❑ 216 Rich Fischer SB P1 RC 4.00 1.80
❑ 218 Jeremy Wedel SB P3 RC 3.00 1.35
❑ 219 Pr.Redman SB P3 RC 3.00 1.35
❑ 220 Mi.Hernandez SB P3 RC 3.00 1.35
❑ 221 Rocco Baldelli SB P1 4.00 1.80
❑ 222 Luis Ayala SB P3 RC 3.00 1.35
❑ 223 Arnaldo Munoz SB P3 RC 3.00 1.35
❑ 224 Wil.Ledezma SB P3 RC 3.00 1.35
❑ 225 Chris Capuano SB P3 RC 3.00 1.35
❑ 226 Aquilino Lopez SB P3 RC 3.00 1.35
❑ 227 Joe Valentine SB P1 RC 4.00 1.80
❑ 228 Matt Kata SB P2 RC 3.00 1.35
❑ 229 D.Markwell SB P2 RC 3.00 1.35
❑ 230 Clint Barmes SB P2 RC 5.00 2.20
❑ 231 Mike Nicolas SB P1 RC 4.00 1.80
❑ 232 Jon Leicester SB P2 RC 3.00 1.35

2004 Sweet Spot

	Nm-Mt	Ex-Mt
COMP.SET w/o SP's (90)	20.00	6.00
COMMON CARD (1-90)	.50	.15
COMMON (91-170/261-262)	4.00	1.20
91-170/261-262 STATED ODDS 1:12		.00
COMMON CARD (171-230)	4.00	1.20
171-230 PRINT RUN 399 SERIAL #'d SETS		.00
COMMON CARD (231-250)	4.00	1.20
231-250 PRINT RUN 299 SERIAL #'d SETS		.00
COMMON CARD (251-260)	6.00	1.80
251-260 PRINT RUN 199 SERIAL #'d SETS		
171-260/Ltd 10/W99 OVERALL ODDS 1:12		
OVERALL PLATES ODDS 1:360 HOBBY		
PLATES PRINT RUN 1 SET PER COLOR		
BLACK-CYAN-MAGENTA-YELLOW ISSUED		
NO PLATES PRICING DUE TO SACRCITY		.00

❑ 1 Albert Pujols 2.50 .75
❑ 2 Alex Rodriguez 2.00 .60
❑ 3 Alfonso Soriano .50 .15
❑ 4 Andruw Jones .75 .23
❑ 5 Andy Pettitte .75 .23
❑ 6 Aubrey Huff .50 .15
❑ 7 Austin Kearns .50 .15
❑ 8 Barry Zito .50 .15
❑ 9 Bobby Abreu .50 .15
❑ 10 Brandon Webb .50 .15
❑ 11 Bret Boone .50 .15
❑ 12 Brian Giles .50 .15
❑ 13 C.C. Sabathia .50 .15
❑ 14 Carlos Beltran .50 .15
❑ 15 Carlos Delgado .50 .15
❑ 16 Chipper Jones 1.25 .35
❑ 17 Cliff Floyd .50 .15
❑ 18 Curt Schilling .75 .23
❑ 19 Delmon Young .75 .23
❑ 20 Derek Jeter 2.50 .75
❑ 21 Dontrelle Willis .75 .23
❑ 22 Edgar Martinez .75 .23
❑ 23 Edgar Renteria .50 .15
❑ 24 Eric Chavez .50 .15
❑ 25 Eric Gagne .50 .15
❑ 26 Frank Thomas 1.25 .35
❑ 27 Garret Anderson .50 .15
❑ 28 Gary Sheffield .50 .15
❑ 29 Geoff Jenkins .50 .15
❑ 30 Greg Maddux 2.00 .60
❑ 31 Hank Blalock .50 .15
❑ 32 Hideo Nomo 1.25 .35
❑ 33 Ichiro Suzuki 2.50 .75
❑ 34 Ivan Rodriguez .75 .23
❑ 35 Jacque Jones .50 .15
❑ 36 Jason Giambi .50 .15
❑ 37 Jason Schmidt .50 .15
❑ 38 Javier Vazquez .50 .15
❑ 39 Javy Lopez .50 .15
❑ 40 Jeff Bagwell .75 .23
❑ 41 Jim Edmonds .75 .23
❑ 42 Jim Thome .75 .23
❑ 43 Joe Mauer .50 .15
❑ 44 John Smoltz .50 .15
❑ 45 Jose Cruz Jr. .50 .15
❑ 46 Jose Reyes .50 .15
❑ 47 Jose Vidro .50 .15
❑ 48 Josh Beckett .50 .15
❑ 49 Ken Griffey Jr. 2.00 .60
❑ 50 Kerry Wood .50 .15
❑ 51 Kevin Brown .50 .15
❑ 52 Larry Walker .50 .15
❑ 53 Magglio Ordonez .50 .15
❑ 54 Manny Ramirez .75 .23
❑ 55 Mark Mulder .50 .15
❑ 56 Mark Prior .75 .23
❑ 57 Mark Teixeira .75 .23
❑ 58 Miguel Cabrera .75 .23
❑ 59 Miguel Tejada .50 .15
❑ 60 Mike Lowell .50 .15
❑ 61 Mike Mussina .75 .23
❑ 62 Mike Piazza 2.00 .60
❑ 63 Nomar Garciaparra 2.00 .60
❑ 64 Orlando Cabrera .50 .15
❑ 65 Pat Burrell .50 .15
❑ 66 Pedro Martinez .75 .23
❑ 67 Phil Nevin .50 .15
❑ 68 Preston Wilson .50 .15
❑ 69 Rafael Furcal .50 .15
❑ 70 Rafael Palmeiro .75 .23
❑ 71 Randy Johnson 1.25 .35
❑ 72 Craig Wilson .50 .15
❑ 73 Rich Harden .50 .15
❑ 74 Richie Sexson .50 .15
❑ 75 Rickie Weeks .75 .23
❑ 76 Rocco Baldelli .50 .15
❑ 77 Roger Clemens 2.50 .75
❑ 78 Roy Halladay .50 .15
❑ 79 Roy Oswalt .50 .15
❑ 80 Ryan Klesko .50 .15
❑ 81 Sammy Sosa 1.25 .35
❑ 82 Scott Podsednik .50 .15
❑ 83 Scott Rolen .75 .23
❑ 84 Shawn Green .50 .15
❑ 85 Tim Hudson .50 .15
❑ 86 Todd Helton .75 .23

	Card	Nm-Mt	Ex-Mt
❑	87 Torii Hunter	.50	.15
❑	88 Troy Glaus	.50	.15
❑	89 Vernon Wells	.50	.15
❑	90 Vladimir Guerrero	1.25	.35
❑	91 Aarom Baldiris SB RC	5.00	1.50
❑	92 Akinori Otsuka SB RC	4.00	1.20
❑	93 Andres Blanco SB RC	4.00	1.20
❑	94 Angel Chavez SB RC	4.00	1.20
❑	95 Brian Dallimore SB RC	4.00	1.20
❑	96 Carlos Hines SB RC	4.00	1.20
❑	97 Carlos Vasquez SB RC	5.00	1.50
❑	98 Casey Daigle SB RC	4.00	1.20
❑	99 Chad Bentz SB RC	4.00	1.20
❑	100 Chris Aguila SB RC	4.00	1.20
❑	101 Chris Oxspring SB RC	4.00	1.20
❑	102 Chris Saenz SB RC	4.00	1.20
❑	103 Chris Shelton SB RC	6.00	1.80
❑	104 Colby Miller SB RC	4.00	1.20
❑	105 Dave Crouthers SB RC	4.00	1.20
❑	106 David Aardsma SB RC	5.00	1.50
❑	107 Dennis Sarfate SB RC	4.00	1.20
❑	108 Donnie Kelly SB RC	4.00	1.20
❑	109 Eddy Rodriguez SB RC	5.00	1.50
❑	110 Eduardo Villacis SB RC	4.00	1.20
❑	111 Edwin Moreno SB RC	5.00	1.50
❑	112 Enemencio Pacheco SB RC	4.00	1.20
❑	113 Fernando Nieve SB RC	5.00	1.50
❑	114 Franklyn Gracesqui SB RC	4.00	1.20
❑	115 Freddy Guzman SB RC	4.00	1.20
❑	116 Greg Dobbs SB RC	4.00	1.20
❑	117 Hector Gimenez SB RC	4.00	1.20
❑	118 Ian Snell SB RC	5.00	1.50
❑	119 Ivan Ochoa SB RC	4.00	1.20
❑	120 Jake Woods SB RC	4.00	1.20
❑	121 Jamie Brown SB RC	4.00	1.20
❑	122 Jason Bartlett SB RC	5.00	1.50
❑	123 Jason Frasor SB RC	4.00	1.20
❑	124 Jeff Bennett SB RC	4.00	1.20
❑	125 Jerome Gamble SB RC	4.00	1.20
❑	126 Jerry Gil SB RC	4.00	1.20
❑	127 Brandon Medders SB RC	4.00	1.20
❑	128 Ryan Meaux SB RC	4.00	1.20
❑	129 John Gall SB RC	5.00	1.50
❑	130 Jorge Sequea SB RC	4.00	1.20
❑	131 Jorge Vasquez SB RC	4.00	1.20
❑	132 Jose Capellan SB RC	5.00	1.50
❑	133 Josh Labandeira SB RC	4.00	1.20
❑	134 Justin Germano SB RC	4.00	1.20
❑	135 Justin Hampson SB RC	4.00	1.20
❑	136 Justin Huisman SB RC	4.00	1.20
❑	137 Justin Knoedler SB RC	4.00	1.20
❑	138 Justin Leone SB RC	5.00	1.50
❑	139 Kazuhito Tadano SB RC	5.00	1.50
❑	140 Kazuo Matsui SB RC	5.00	1.50
❑	141 Kevin Cave SB RC	4.00	1.20
❑	142 Lincoln Holdzkom SB RC	4.00	1.20
❑	143 Lino Urdaneta SB RC	4.00	1.20
❑	144 Luis A. Gonzalez SB RC	4.00	1.20
❑	145 Mariano Gomez SB RC	4.00	1.20
❑	146 Merkin Valdez SB RC	5.00	1.50
❑	147 Michael Vento SB RC	5.00	1.50
❑	148 Michael Wuertz SB RC	5.00	1.50
❑	149 Mike Gosling SB RC	4.00	1.20
❑	150 Mike Johnston SB RC	4.00	1.20
❑	151 Mike Rouse SB RC	4.00	1.20
❑	152 Nick Regilio SB RC	4.00	1.20
❑	153 Onil Joseph SB RC	4.00	1.20
❑	154 Orlando Rodriguez SB RC	4.00	1.20
❑	155 Ramon Ramirez SB RC	4.00	1.20
❑	156 Renyel Pinto SB RC	5.00	1.50
❑	157 Roberto Novoa SB RC	5.00	1.50
❑	158 Roman Colon SB RC	4.00	1.20
❑	159 Ronald Belisario SB RC	4.00	1.20
❑	160 Ronny Cedeno SB RC	5.00	1.50
❑	161 Rusty Tucker SB RC	5.00	1.50
❑	162 Ryan Wing SB RC	4.00	1.20
❑	163 Scott Dohmann SB RC	4.00	1.20
❑	164 Scott Proctor SB RC	5.00	1.50
❑	165 Sean Henn SB RC	4.00	1.20
❑	166 Shawn Camp SB RC	4.00	1.20
❑	167 Shawn Hill SB RC	4.00	1.20
❑	168 Shingo Takatsu SB RC	5.00	1.50
❑	169 Tim Hamulack SB RC	4.00	1.20
❑	170 William Bergolla SB RC	4.00	1.20
❑	171 Adam Dunn SF	4.00	1.20
❑	172 Albert Pujols SF	10.00	3.00
❑	173 Alex Rodriguez SF	8.00	2.40
❑	174 Alfonso Soriano SF	4.00	1.20
❑	175 Andruw Jones SF	5.00	1.50
❑	176 Bret Boone SF	4.00	1.20
❑	177 Brian Giles SF	4.00	1.20
❑	178 Carlos Delgado SF	4.00	1.20
❑	179 Derrek Lee SF	5.00	1.50
❑	180 Eric Chavez SF	4.00	1.20
❑	181 Frank Thomas SF	5.00	1.50
❑	182 Garret Anderson SF	4.00	1.20
❑	183 Gary Sheffield SF	4.00	1.20
❑	184 Hank Blalock SF	4.00	1.20
❑	185 Jason Giambi SF	4.00	1.20
❑	186 Javy Lopez SF	4.00	1.20
❑	187 Jeff Bagwell SF	5.00	1.50
❑	188 Jim Edmonds SF	5.00	1.50
❑	189 Jim Thome SF	5.00	1.50
❑	190 Ken Griffey Jr. SF	8.00	2.40
❑	191 Lance Berkman SF	4.00	1.20
❑	192 Magglio Ordonez SF	4.00	1.20
❑	193 Manny Ramirez SF	5.00	1.50
❑	194 Mike Lowell SF	4.00	1.20
❑	195 Mike Piazza SF	8.00	2.40
❑	196 Preston Wilson SF	4.00	1.20
❑	197 Rafael Palmeiro SF	5.00	1.50
❑	198 Richie Sexson SF	4.00	1.20
❑	199 Sammy Sosa SF	5.00	1.50
❑	200 Scott Rolen SF	5.00	1.50
❑	201 Shawn Green SF	4.00	1.20
❑	202 Todd Helton SF	5.00	1.50
❑	203 Troy Glaus SF	4.00	1.20
❑	204 Vernon Wells SF	4.00	1.20
❑	205 Vladimir Guerrero SF	5.00	1.50
❑	206 Garret Anderson Vladimir Guerrero SL	5.00	1.50
❑	207 Luis Gonzalez Richie Sexson SL	4.00	1.20
❑	208 Andruw Jones Chipper Jones SL	5.00	1.50
❑	209 Javy Lopez Miguel Tejada SL	4.00	1.20
❑	210 Manny Ramirez David Ortiz SL	5.00	1.50
❑	211 Derrek Lee Sammy Sosa SL	5.00	1.50
❑	212 Frank Thomas Magglio Ordonez SL	5.00	1.50
❑	213 Austin Kearns Ken Griffey Jr. SL	8.00	2.40
❑	214 Preston Wilson Todd Helton SL	5.00	1.50
❑	215 Dmitri Young Ivan Rodriguez SL	5.00	1.50
❑	216 Miguel Cabrera Mike Lowell SL	5.00	1.50
❑	217 Jeff Bagwell Lance Berkman SL	5.00	1.50
❑	218 Lyle Overbay Geoff Jenkins SL	4.00	1.20
❑	219 Adrian Beltre Shawn Green SL	4.00	1.20
❑	220 Jacque Jones Torii Hunter SL	4.00	1.20
❑	221 Jose Vidro Nick Johnson SL	4.00	1.20
❑	222 Kazuo Matsui Mike Piazza SL	8.00	2.40
❑	223 Alex Rodriguez Jason Giambi SL	8.00	2.40
❑	224 Eric Chavez Jermaine Dye SL	4.00	1.20
❑	225 Jim Thome Pat Burrell SL	5.00	1.50
❑	226 Brian Giles Phil Nevin SL	4.00	1.20
❑	227 Bret Boone Ichiro Suzuki SL	10.00	3.00
❑	228 Albert Pujols Scott Rolen SL	10.00	3.00
❑	229 Hank Blalock Mark Teixeira SL	5.00	1.50
❑	230 Carlos Delgado Vernon Wells SL	4.00	1.20
❑	231 Albert Pujols PD	10.00	3.00
❑	232 Alex Rodriguez PD	8.00	2.40
❑	233 Chipper Jones PD	5.00	1.50
❑	234 Craig Biggio PD	5.00	1.50
❑	235 Curt Schilling PD	5.00	1.50
❑	236 Derek Jeter PD	10.00	3.00
❑	237 Ivan Rodriguez PD	5.00	1.50
❑	238 Jeff Bagwell PD	5.00	1.50
❑	239 Jim Edmonds PD	5.00	1.50
❑	240 Jim Thome PD	5.00	1.50
❑	241 Josh Beckett PD	4.00	1.20
❑	242 Kerry Wood PD	4.00	1.20
❑	243 Kevin Brown PD	4.00	1.20
❑	244 Mark Prior PD	5.00	1.50
❑	245 Miguel Tejada PD	4.00	1.20
❑	246 Mike Mussina PD	5.00	1.50
❑	247 Nomar Garciaparra PD	8.00	2.40
❑	248 Pedro Martinez PD	5.00	1.50
❑	249 Randy Johnson PD	5.00	1.50
❑	250 Roger Clemens PD	10.00	3.00
❑	251 Alex Rodriguez Derek Jeter DD	15.00	4.50
❑	252 Alfonso Soriano Hank Blalock DD	6.00	1.80
❑	253 Bobby Abreu Pat Burrell DD	6.00	1.80
❑	254 Edgar Renteria Scott Rolen DD	8.00	2.40
❑	255 Garret Anderson Vladimir Guerrero DD	8.00	2.40
❑	256 Jeff Bagwell Jeff Kent DD	8.00	2.40
❑	257 Jose Reyes Kazuo Matsui DD	8.00	2.40
❑	258 Khalil Greene Sean Burroughs DD	8.00	2.40
❑	259 Marcus Giles Rafael Furcal DD	6.00	1.80
❑	260 Manny Ramirez Johnny Damon DD	8.00	2.40
❑	261 Tim Bausher SB RC	4.00	1.20
❑	262 Tim Bittner SB RC	4.00	1.20

2005 Sweet Spot

		Nm-Mt	Ex-Mt
	COMPLETE SET (90)	20.00	6.00
	COMMON CARD (1-90)	.50	.15
❑	1 Magglio Ordonez	.50	.15
❑	2 Craig Biggio	.75	.23
❑	3 Hank Blalock	.50	.15
❑	4 Nomar Garciaparra	1.25	.35
❑	5 Ken Griffey Jr.	2.00	.60
❑	6 Khalil Greene	.75	.23
❑	7 Andruw Jones	.75	.23
❑	8 Ichiro Suzuki	2.50	.75
❑	9 Philip Humber RC	2.00	.60
❑	10 Vladimir Guerrero	1.25	.35
❑	11 Carlos Delgado	.50	.15
❑	12 Jeff Niemann RC	2.00	.60
❑	13 Chipper Jones	1.25	.35
❑	14 Jose Vidro	.50	.15
❑	15 Miguel Cabrera	.75	.23
❑	16 Albert Pujols	2.50	.75
❑	17 Tadahito Iguchi RC	3.00	.90
❑	18 Norihiro Nakamura RC	3.00	.90
❑	19 Jeff Bagwell	.75	.23
❑	20 Troy Glaus	.50	.15
❑	21 Scott Rolen	.75	.23
❑	22 Derek Lowe	.50	.15
❑	23 Mark Prior	.75	.23

No.	Player	Nm-Mt	Ex-Mt
❑ 24	Bobby Abreu	.50	.15
❑ 25	David Wright	2.00	.60
❑ 26	Barry Zito	.50	.15
❑ 27	Livan Hernandez	.50	.15
❑ 28	Mark Teixeira	.75	.23
❑ 29	Manny Ramirez	.75	.23
❑ 30	Paul Konerko	.50	.15
❑ 31	Victor Martinez	.50	.15
❑ 32	Greg Maddux	2.00	.60
❑ 33	Jim Thome	.75	.23
❑ 34	Miguel Tejada	.50	.15
❑ 35	Ivan Rodriguez	.75	.23
❑ 36	Carlos Beltran	.50	.15
❑ 37	Steve Finley	.50	.15
❑ 38	Torii Hunter	.50	.15
❑ 39	Bobby Crosby	.50	.15
❑ 40	Jorge Posada	.75	.23
❑ 41	Ben Sheets	.50	.15
❑ 42	Mike Piazza	1.25	.35
❑ 43	Luis Gonzalez	.50	.15
❑ 44	Joe Mauer	.50	.15
❑ 45	Shawn Green	.50	.15
❑ 46	Eric Gagne	.50	.15
❑ 47	Kerry Wood	.50	.15
❑ 48	Derek Jeter	3.00	.90
❑ 49	Josh Beckett	.50	.15
❑ 50	Alex Rodriguez	2.00	.60
❑ 51	Aubrey Huff	.50	.15
❑ 52	Eric Chavez	.50	.15
❑ 53	Sammy Sosa	1.25	.35
❑ 54	Roger Clemens	2.00	.60
❑ 55	Mike Mussina	.75	.23
❑ 56	Mike Sweeney	.50	.15
❑ 57	Oliver Perez	.50	.15
❑ 58	Tim Hudson	.50	.15
❑ 59	Justin Verlander RC	2.50	.75
❑ 60	Johan Santana	.75	.23
❑ 61	Hideki Matsui	2.50	.75
❑ 62	Mark Mulder	.50	.15
❑ 63	Jake Peavy	.50	.15
❑ 64	Adam Dunn	.50	.15
❑ 65	Dallas McPherson	.50	.15
❑ 66	Jeff Kent	.50	.15
❑ 67	Pedro Martinez	.75	.23
❑ 68	J.D. Drew	.50	.15
❑ 69	Frank Thomas	1.25	.35
❑ 70	Kazuo Matsui	.50	.15
❑ 71	Travis Hafner	.50	.15
❑ 72	John Smoltz	.75	.23
❑ 73	Jason Schmidt	.50	.15
❑ 74	Carlos Lee	.50	.15
❑ 75	Todd Helton	.75	.23
❑ 76	David Ortiz	1.25	.35
❑ 77	Roy Oswalt	.50	.15
❑ 78	Brian Giles	.50	.15
❑ 79	Gary Sheffield	.50	.15
❑ 80	Jason Bay	.50	.15
❑ 81	Alfonso Soriano	.50	.15
❑ 82	Randy Johnson	1.25	.35
❑ 83	Tom Glavine	.75	.23
❑ 84	Richie Sexson	.50	.15
❑ 85	Curt Schilling	.75	.23
❑ 86	Adrian Beltre	.50	.15
❑ 87	Jim Edmonds	.50	.15
❑ 88	Roy Halladay	.50	.15
❑ 89	Johnny Damon	.75	.23
❑ 90	Lance Berkman	.50	.15

2003 Sweet Spot Classics

	Nm-Mt	Ex-Mt
COMP.SET w/o SP's (89)	40.00	12.00
COMMON (1-74/76-90)	.75	.23
COMMON CARD (91-120)	8.00	2.40
COMMON CARD (121-150)	5.00	1.50

No.	Player	Nm-Mt	Ex-Mt
❑ 1	Al Hrabosky	.75	.23
❑ 2	Al Lopez	.75	.23
❑ 3	Andre Dawson	.75	.23
❑ 4	Bill Buckner	.75	.23
❑ 5	Billy Williams	.75	.23
❑ 6	Bob Feller	.75	.23
❑ 7	Bob Lemon	.75	.23
❑ 8	Bobby Doerr	.75	.23
❑ 9	Cecil Cooper	.75	.23
❑ 10	Cal Ripken	6.00	1.80
❑ 11	Carlton Fisk	1.25	.35
❑ 12	Catfish Hunter	1.25	.35
❑ 13	Chris Chambliss	.75	.23
❑ 14	Dale Murphy	1.25	.35
❑ 15	Gaylord Perry	.75	.23
❑ 16	Dave Kingman	.75	.23
❑ 17	Dave Parker	.75	.23
❑ 18	Dave Stewart	.75	.23
❑ 19	David Cone	.75	.23
❑ 20	Dennis Eckersley	.75	.23
❑ 21	Don Baylor	.75	.23
❑ 22	Don Sutton	.75	.23
❑ 23	Duke Snider	1.25	.35
❑ 24	Dwight Evans	1.25	.35
❑ 25	Dwight Gooden	.75	.23
❑ 26	Earl Weaver MG	.75	.23
❑ 27	Early Wynn	.75	.23
❑ 28	Eddie Mathews	2.00	.60
❑ 29	Enos Slaughter	.75	.23
❑ 30	Ernie Banks	2.00	.60
❑ 31	Fred Lynn	.75	.23
❑ 32	Fred Stanley	.75	.23
❑ 33	Gary Carter	.75	.23
❑ 34	George Foster	.75	.23
❑ 35	Hal Newhouser	.75	.23
❑ 36	George Kell	.75	.23
❑ 37	Harmon Killebrew	2.00	.60
❑ 38	Hoyt Wilhelm	.75	.23
❑ 39	Jack Morris	.75	.23
❑ 40	Jim Bunning	.75	.23
❑ 41	Jim Gilliam	.75	.23
❑ 42	Jim Leyritz	.75	.23
❑ 43	Jimmy Key	.75	.23
❑ 44	Joe Carter	.75	.23
❑ 45	Joe Morgan	.75	.23
❑ 46	John Montefusco	.75	.23
❑ 47	Johnny Bench	2.00	.60
❑ 48	Johnny Podres	.75	.23
❑ 49	Jose Canseco	1.25	.35
❑ 50	Juan Marichal	.75	.23
❑ 51	Keith Hernandez	.75	.23
❑ 52	Ken Griffey Sr.	.75	.23
❑ 53	Kirby Puckett	2.00	.60
❑ 54	Kirk Gibson	1.25	.35
❑ 55	Larry Doby	.75	.23
❑ 56	Lee May	.75	.23
❑ 57	Lee Mazzilli	.75	.23
❑ 58	Lou Boudreau	.75	.23
❑ 59	Mark McGwire	5.00	1.50
❑ 60	Maury Wills	.75	.23
❑ 61	Mike Pagliarulo	.75	.23
❑ 62	Monte Irvin	.75	.23
❑ 63	Nolan Ryan	5.00	1.50
❑ 64	Orlando Cepeda	.75	.23
❑ 65	Ozzie Smith	3.00	.90
❑ 66	Paul O'Neill	1.25	.35
❑ 67	Pee Wee Reese	1.25	.35
❑ 68	Phil Niekro	.75	.23
❑ 69	Ralph Kiner	.75	.23
❑ 70	Red Schoendienst	.75	.23
❑ 71	Richie Ashburn	1.25	.35
❑ 72	Rick Ferrell	.75	.23
❑ 73	Robin Roberts	.75	.23
❑ 74	Robin Yount	2.00	.60
❑ 75	Hideki Matsui/1999 XRC	15.00	4.50
❑ 75B	Rod Carew ERR Not Intended for Public Release	.00	
❑ 76	Rollie Fingers	.75	.23
❑ 77	Ron Cey	.75	.23
❑ 78	Tom Seaver	1.25	.35
❑ 79	Sparky Anderson MG	.75	.23
❑ 80	Stan Musial	3.00	.90
❑ 81	Steve Garvey	.75	.23
❑ 82	Ted Williams	4.00	1.20
❑ 83	Tommy Lasorda	.75	.23
❑ 84	Tony Gwynn	2.50	.75
❑ 85	Tony Perez	.75	.23
❑ 86	Vida Blue	.75	.23
❑ 87	Warren Spahn	1.25	.35
❑ 88	Bob Gibson	1.25	.35
❑ 89	Willie McCovey	.75	.23
❑ 90	Willie Stargell	1.25	.35
❑ 91	Ted Williams TB	8.00	2.40
❑ 92	Ted Williams TB	8.00	2.40
❑ 93	Ted Williams TB	8.00	2.40
❑ 94	Ted Williams TB	8.00	2.40
❑ 95	Ted Williams TB	8.00	2.40
❑ 96	Ted Williams TB	8.00	2.40
❑ 97	Ted Williams TB	8.00	2.40
❑ 98	Ted Williams TB	8.00	2.40
❑ 99	Ted Williams TB	8.00	2.40
❑ 100	Ted Williams TB	8.00	2.40
❑ 101	Ted Williams TB	8.00	2.40
❑ 102	Ted Williams TB	8.00	2.40
❑ 103	Ted Williams TB	8.00	2.40
❑ 104	Ted Williams TB	8.00	2.40
❑ 105	Ted Williams TB	8.00	2.40
❑ 106	Ted Williams TB	8.00	2.40
❑ 106B	Ted Williams TB UER 116	8.00	2.40
❑ 107	Ted Williams TB	8.00	2.40
❑ 108	Ted Williams TB	8.00	2.40
❑ 109	Ted Williams TB	8.00	2.40
❑ 110	Ted Williams TB	8.00	2.40
❑ 111	Ted Williams TB	8.00	2.40
❑ 112	Ted Williams TB	8.00	2.40
❑ 113	Ted Williams TB	8.00	2.40
❑ 114	Ted Williams TB	8.00	2.40
❑ 115	Ted Williams TB	8.00	2.40
❑ 117	Ted Williams TB	8.00	2.40
❑ 118	Ted Williams TB	8.00	2.40
❑ 119	Ted Williams TB	8.00	2.40
❑ 120	Ted Williams TB	8.00	2.40
❑ 121	Babe Ruth YH	15.00	4.50
❑ 122	Bucky Dent YH	5.00	1.50
❑ 123	Casey Stengel YH	5.00	1.50
❑ 124	Dave Righetti YH	5.00	1.50
❑ 125	Dave Winfield YH	5.00	1.50
❑ 126	Dick Tidrow YH	5.00	1.50
❑ 127	Dock Ellis YH	5.00	1.50
❑ 128	Don Mattingly YH	12.00	3.60
❑ 129	Hank Bauer YH	5.00	1.50
❑ 130	Jim Bouton YH	5.00	1.50
❑ 131	Jim Kaat YH	5.00	1.50
❑ 132	Joe DiMaggio YH	10.00	3.00
❑ 133	Joe Torre YH	5.00	1.50
❑ 134	Lou Piniella YH	5.00	1.50
❑ 135	Mel Stottlemyre YH	5.00	1.50
❑ 136	Mickey Mantle YH	20.00	6.00
❑ 137	Mickey Rivers YH	5.00	1.50
❑ 138	Phil Rizzuto YH	5.00	1.50
❑ 139	Ralph Branca YH	5.00	1.50
❑ 140	Ralph Houk YH	5.00	1.50
❑ 141	Roger Maris YH	8.00	2.40
❑ 142	Ron Guidry YH	5.00	1.50
❑ 143	Ruben Amaro Sr. YH	5.00	1.50
❑ 144	Sparky Lyle YH	5.00	1.50
❑ 145	Thurman Munson YH	8.00	2.40
❑ 146	Tommy Henrich YH	5.00	1.50
❑ 147	Tommy John YH	5.00	1.50
❑ 148	Tony Kubek YH	5.00	1.50
❑ 149	Whitey Ford YH	5.00	1.50
❑ 150	Yogi Berra YH	8.00	2.40

2005 Sweet Spot Classic

	Nm-Mt	Ex-Mt
COMPLETE SET (100)	40.00	12.00

No.	Player	Nm-Mt	Ex-Mt
❑ 1	Al Kaline	2.00	.60
❑ 2	Al Rosen	.75	.23
❑ 3	Babe Ruth	6.00	1.80

❑ 4 Bill Mazeroski	1.25	.35
❑ 5 Billy Williams	.75	.23
❑ 6 Bob Feller	1.25	.35
❑ 7 Bob Gibson	1.25	.35
❑ 8 Bobby Doerr	.75	.23
❑ 9 Brooks Robinson	1.25	.35
❑ 10 Cal Ripken	6.00	1.80
❑ 11 Carl Yastrzemski	3.00	.90
❑ 12 Carlton Fisk	1.25	.35
❑ 13 Casey Stengel	1.25	.35
❑ 14 Christy Mathewson	2.00	.60
❑ 15 Cy Young	2.00	.60
❑ 16 Dale Murphy	1.25	.35
❑ 17 Dave Winfield	.75	.23
❑ 18 Dennis Eckersley	.75	.23
❑ 19 Dizzy Dean	1.25	.35
❑ 20 Don Drysdale	1.25	.35
❑ 21 Don Mattingly	4.00	1.20
❑ 22 Don Newcombe	.75	.23
❑ 23 Don Sutton	.75	.23
❑ 24 Duke Snider	1.25	.35
❑ 25 Dwight Evans	1.25	.35
❑ 26 Eddie Mathews	2.00	.60
❑ 27 Eddie Murray	2.00	.60
❑ 28 Enos Slaughter	.75	.23
❑ 29 Ernie Banks	2.00	.60
❑ 30 Frank Howard	.75	.23
❑ 31 Frank Robinson	.75	.23
❑ 32 Gary Carter	.75	.23
❑ 33 Gaylord Perry	.75	.23
❑ 34 George Brett	4.00	1.20
❑ 35 George Kell	.75	.23
❑ 36 George Sisler	.75	.23
❑ 37 Larry Doby	.75	.23
❑ 38 Harmon Killebrew	2.00	.60
❑ 39 Honus Wagner	2.00	.60
❑ 40 Jackie Robinson	2.00	.60
❑ 41 Jim Bunning	.75	.23
❑ 42 Jim Palmer	.75	.23
❑ 43 Jim Rice	.75	.23
❑ 44 Jimmie Foxx	2.00	.60
❑ 45 Joe DiMaggio	4.00	1.20
❑ 46 Joe Morgan	.75	.23
❑ 47 Johnny Bench	2.00	.60
❑ 48 Johnny Mize	.75	.23
❑ 49 Johnny Podres	.75	.23
❑ 50 Juan Marichal	.75	.23
❑ 51 Keith Hernandez	.75	.23
❑ 52 Kirby Puckett	2.00	.60
❑ 53 Lefty Grove	.75	.23
❑ 54 Lou Brock	1.25	.35
❑ 55 Lou Gehrig	4.00	1.20
❑ 56 Luis Aparicio	.75	.23
❑ 57 Fergie Jenkins	.75	.23
❑ 58 Maury Wills	.75	.23
❑ 59 Mel Ott	2.00	.60
❑ 60 Mickey Cochrane	.75	.23
❑ 61 Mickey Mantle	8.00	2.40
❑ 62 Mike Schmidt	4.00	1.20
❑ 63 Monte Irvin	.75	.23
❑ 64 Nolan Ryan	5.00	1.50
❑ 65 Orlando Cepeda	.75	.23
❑ 66 Ozzie Smith	3.00	.90
❑ 67 Paul Molitor	1.25	.35
❑ 68 Pee Wee Reese	1.25	.35
❑ 69 Phil Niekro	.75	.23
❑ 70 Phil Rizzuto	1.25	.35
❑ 71 Ralph Kiner	1.25	.35
❑ 72 Richie Ashburn	1.25	.35
❑ 73 Roberto Clemente	5.00	1.50
❑ 74 Robin Roberts	.75	.23
❑ 75 Robin Yount	2.00	.60
❑ 76 Rocky Colavito	1.25	.35
❑ 77 Rod Carew	1.25	.35
❑ 78 Rogers Hornsby	2.00	.60
❑ 79 Rollie Fingers	.75	.23
❑ 80 Roy Campanella	2.00	.60
❑ 81 Bob Lemon	.75	.23
❑ 82 Red Schoendienst	.75	.23
❑ 83 Satchel Paige	2.00	.60
❑ 84 Stan Musial	3.00	.90
❑ 85 Steve Carlton	.75	.23
❑ 86 Ted Williams	4.00	1.20
❑ 87 Thurman Munson	2.00	.60
❑ 88 Tom Seaver	1.25	.35
❑ 89 Tony Gwynn	2.50	.75
❑ 90 Tony Perez	1.25	.35
❑ 91 Ty Cobb	3.00	.90
❑ 92 Wade Boggs	1.25	.35
❑ 93 Walter Johnson	2.00	.60
❑ 94 Warren Spahn	1.25	.35
❑ 95 Whitey Ford	1.25	.35
❑ 96 Will Clark	1.25	.35
❑ 97 Catfish Hunter	1.25	.35
❑ 98 Willie McCovey	1.25	.35
❑ 99 Willie Stargell	1.25	.35
❑ 100 Yogi Berra	2.00	.60

1911 T205

	Ex-Mt	VG
COMPLETE SET (218)	35000.00	17500.00
COMMON (1-186)	100.00	50.00
COMMON (187-198)	200.00	100.00
❑ 1 Ed Abbaticchio	100.00	50.00
❑ 2 Red Ames	100.00	50.00
❑ 3 Jimmy Archer	100.00	50.00
❑ 4 Jimmy Austin	100.00	50.00
❑ 5 Bill Bailey	100.00	50.00
❑ 6 Frank "Homerun" Baker	400.00	200.00
❑ 7 Neal Ball	100.00	50.00
❑ 8A Cy Barger (Full B)	100.00	50.00
❑ 8B Cy Barger Part B	300.00	150.00
❑ 9 Jack Barry	100.00	50.00
❑ 10 Johnny Bates	100.00	50.00
❑ 11 Fred Beck	100.00	50.00
❑ 12 Beals Becker	100.00	50.00
❑ 13 George Bell	100.00	50.00
❑ 14 Chief Bender	250.00	125.00
❑ 15 Bill Bergen	100.00	50.00
❑ 16 Bob Bescher	100.00	50.00
❑ 17 Joe Birmingham	100.00	50.00
❑ 18 Russ Blackburne	100.00	50.00
❑ 19 Kitty Bransfield	100.00	50.00
❑ 20A Roger Bresnahan (Mouth closed)	250.00	125.00
❑ 20B Roger Bresnahan (Mouth open)	400.00	200.00
❑ 21 Al Bridwell	100.00	50.00
❑ 22 Mordecai Brown	400.00	200.00
❑ 23 Bobby Byrne	100.00	50.00
❑ 24 Howie Camnitz	100.00	50.00
❑ 25 Bill Carrigan	100.00	50.00
❑ 26 Frank Chance	300.00	150.00
❑ 27A Hal Chase (Chase only)	300.00	150.00
❑ 27B Hal Chase (Hal Chase)	150.00	75.00
❑ 28 Eddie Cicotte	200.00	100.00
❑ 29 Fred Clarke	400.00	200.00
❑ 30 Ty Cobb	5000.00	2500.00
❑ 31A Edward T. Collins (Mouth closed)	300.00	150.00
❑ 31B Edward T. Collins (Mouth open)	500.00	250.00
❑ 32 Frank Corridon	100.00	50.00
❑ 33A Otis Crandall T Crossed in name	100.00	50.00
❑ 33B Otis Crandall T Not Crossed in Name	100.00	50.00
❑ 34 Lou Criger	100.00	50.00
❑ 35 Bill Dahlen	150.00	75.00
❑ 36 Jake Daubert	100.00	50.00
❑ 37 Jim Delahanty	100.00	50.00
❑ 38 Art Devlin	100.00	50.00
❑ 39 Josh Devore	100.00	50.00
❑ 40 Walt Dickson	100.00	50.00
❑ 41 Jiggs Donahue UER (Misspelled Donohue on card)	150.00	75.00
❑ 42 Red Dooin	100.00	50.00
❑ 43 Mickey Doolan	100.00	50.00
❑ 44A Patsy Dougherty (White stocking)	150.00	75.00
❑ 44B Patsy Dougherty (Red stocking)	100.00	50.00
❑ 45 Tom Downey	100.00	50.00
❑ 46 Larry Doyle	100.00	50.00
❑ 47 Hugh Duffy	300.00	150.00
❑ 48 Jimmy Dygert	100.00	50.00
❑ 49 Dick Egan	100.00	50.00
❑ 50 Kid Elberfeld	100.00	50.00
❑ 51 Clyde Engle	100.00	50.00
❑ 52 Steve Evans	100.00	50.00
❑ 53 Johnny Evers	250.00	125.00
❑ 54 Bob Ewing	100.00	50.00
❑ 55 George Ferguson	100.00	50.00
❑ 56 Ray Fisher	150.00	75.00
❑ 57 Art Fletcher	100.00	50.00
❑ 58 John Flynn	100.00	50.00
❑ 59A Russell Ford (Dark cap)	100.00	50.00
❑ 59B Russell Ford (Light cap)	150.00	75.00
❑ 60 Bill Foxen	100.00	50.00
❑ 61 Art Fromme	100.00	50.00
❑ 62 Earl Gardner	100.00	50.00
❑ 63 Harry Gaspar	100.00	50.00
❑ 64 George Gibson	100.00	50.00
❑ 65 Wilbur Good	100.00	50.00
❑ 66A George F. Graham (Boston Rustlers)	100.00	50.00
❑ 66B George F. Graham (Chicago Cubs)	400.00	200.00
❑ 67 Eddie Grant	150.00	75.00
❑ 68A Dolly Gray No stats on back	100.00	50.00
❑ 68B Dolly Gray Stats on Back	400.00	200.00
❑ 69 Clark Griffith	300.00	150.00
❑ 70 Bob Groom	100.00	50.00
❑ 71A Robert Harmon (Both ears)	100.00	50.00
❑ 71B Robert Harmon (Left ear only)	300.00	150.00
❑ 72 Topsy Hartsel	100.00	50.00
❑ 73 Arnold Hauser	100.00	50.00
❑ 74 Charlie Hemphill	100.00	50.00
❑ 75 Buck Herzog	100.00	50.00
❑ 76A Dick Hoblitzell No Stats	10000.00	5000.00
❑ 76B Dick Hoblitzell No CIN after second 1908	100.00	50.00
❑ 76C Dick Hoblitzell CIN after second 1908	150.00	75.00
❑ 76D Dick Hoblitzell sic.Hoblitzel	100.00	50.00
❑ 77 Danny Hoffman	100.00	50.00
❑ 78 Miller Huggins	400.00	200.00

❑ 79 John Hummell 100.00 50.00
❑ 80 Fred Jacklitsch 100.00 50.00
❑ 81 Hughie Jennings 300.00 150.00
❑ 82 Walter Johnson 2000.00 1000.00
❑ 83 Davy Jones 100.00 50.00
❑ 84 Tom Jones 100.00 50.00
❑ 85 Addie Joss 700.00 350.00
❑ 86 Ed Karger 150.00 75.00
❑ 87 Ed Killian 100.00 50.00
❑ 88 Red Kleinow 150.00 75.00
❑ 89 John Kling 100.00 50.00
❑ 90 John Knight 100.00 50.00
❑ 91 Ed Konetchy 100.00 50.00
❑ 92 Harry Krause 100.00 50.00
❑ 93 Rube Kroh 100.00 50.00
❑ 94 Frank Lang 100.00 50.00
❑ 95 Frank LaPorte 100.00 50.00
❑ 96A Arlie Latham 100.00 50.00
Back says W.A. Latham
❑ 96B Arlie Latham 100.00 50.00
A. Latham on back
❑ 97 Tommy Leach 100.00 50.00
❑ 98 Sam Leever 100.00 50.00
❑ 99A Lefty Leifield 100.00 50.00
A.Leifield on front
❑ 99B Lefty Leifield 100.00 50.00
A.P.Leifield on front
❑ 100 Ed Lennox 100.00 50.00
❑ 101 Paddy Livingston 100.00 50.00
❑ 102 Hans Lobert 100.00 50.00
❑ 103 Bris Lord 100.00 50.00
❑ 104 Harry Lord 100.00 50.00
❑ 105 John Lush 100.00 50.00
❑ 106 Nick Maddox 100.00 50.00
❑ 107 Sherry Magee 100.00 50.00
❑ 108 Rube Marquard 400.00 200.00
❑ 109 Christy Mathewson 2000.00 1000.00
❑ 110 Al Mattern 100.00 50.00
❑ 111 George McBride 100.00 50.00
❑ 112 Amby McConnell 100.00 50.00
❑ 113 Pryor McElveen 100.00 50.00
❑ 114 John McGraw MG 400.00 200.00
❑ 115 Harry McIntire 100.00 50.00
❑ 116 Matty McIntyre 100.00 50.00
❑ 117 Larry McLean 100.00 50.00
❑ 118 Fred Merkle 100.00 50.00
❑ 119 Chief Meyers 100.00 50.00
❑ 120 Clyde Milan 100.00 50.00
❑ 121 Dots Miller 100.00 50.00
❑ 122 Mike Mitchell 100.00 50.00
❑ 123A Pat Moran 300.00 150.00
Extra Stat Line on Card
❑ 123B Pat Moran 100.00 50.00
❑ 124 George Moriarity 100.00 50.00
❑ 125 George Mullin 100.00 50.00
❑ 126 Danny Murphy 100.00 50.00
❑ 127 Red Murray 100.00 50.00
❑ 128 Tom Needham 100.00 50.00
❑ 129 Rebel Oakes 100.00 50.00
❑ 130 Rube Oldring 100.00 50.00
❑ 131 Charley O'Leary 100.00 50.00
❑ 132 Fred Olmstead 100.00 50.00
❑ 133 Orval Overall 100.00 50.00
❑ 134 Freddy Parent 100.00 50.00
❑ 135 Dode Paskert 100.00 50.00
❑ 136 Fred Payne 100.00 50.00
❑ 137 Barney Pelty 100.00 50.00
❑ 138 Jack Pfiester 100.00 50.00
❑ 139 Ed Phelps 100.00 50.00
❑ 140 Decon Phillippe 100.00 50.00
❑ 141 Jack Quinn 100.00 50.00
❑ 142 Bugs Raymond 150.00 75.00
❑ 143 Ed Reulbach 100.00 50.00
❑ 144 Lewis Richie 100.00 50.00
❑ 145 Jack Rowan 150.00 75.00
❑ 146 Nap Rucker 100.00 50.00
❑ 147 Doc Scanlan 150.00 75.00
❑ 148 Germany Schaefer 100.00 50.00
❑ 149 Admiral Schlei 100.00 50.00
❑ 150 Boss Schmidt 100.00 50.00
❑ 151 Wildfire Schulte 100.00 50.00
❑ 152 Jim Scott 100.00 50.00
❑ 153 Bayard Sharpe 100.00 50.00
❑ 154A David Shean 100.00 50.00
(Boston Rustlers)
❑ 154B David Shean 400.00 200.00
(Chicago Cubs)
❑ 155 Jimmy Sheckard 100.00 50.00
❑ 156 Hack Simmons 100.00 50.00
❑ 157 Tony Smith 100.00 50.00
❑ 158 Fred Snodgrass 100.00 50.00
❑ 159 Tris Speaker 1000.00 500.00
❑ 160 Jake Stahl 100.00 50.00
❑ 161 Oscar Stanage 100.00 50.00
❑ 162 Harry Steinfeldt 100.00 50.00
❑ 163 George Stone 100.00 50.00
❑ 164 George Stovall 100.00 50.00
❑ 165 Gabby Street 100.00 50.00
❑ 166 George Suggs 150.00 75.00
❑ 167 Ed Summers 100.00 50.00
❑ 168 Jeff Sweeney 150.00 75.00
❑ 169 Lee Tannehill 100.00 50.00
❑ 170 Ira Thomas 100.00 50.00
❑ 171 Joe Tinker 600.00 300.00
❑ 172 John Titus 100.00 50.00
❑ 173 Terry Turner 300.00 150.00
❑ 174 Hippo Vaughn 150.00 75.00
❑ 175 Heinie Wagner 150.00 75.00
❑ 176A Bobby Wallace 250.00 125.00
(With cap)
❑ 176B Bobby Wallace 500.00 250.00
(Without cap)
❑ 176C Bobby Wallace 300.00 150.00
no cap 2/1910
❑ 177 Ed Walsh 500.00 250.00
❑ 178 Zach Wheat 300.00 150.00
❑ 179 Doc White 100.00 50.00
❑ 180 Kirby White 150.00 75.00
❑ 181 Kaiser Wilhelm 150.00 75.00
❑ 182 Ed Willett 100.00 50.00
❑ 183A Hooks Wiltse 100.00 50.00
(Both ears)
❑ 183B Hooks Wiltse 300.00 150.00
(Right ear only)
❑ 184 Owen Wilson 100.00 50.00
❑ 185 Harry Wolter 100.00 50.00
❑ 186 Cy Young 2000.00 1000.00
❑ 187 Dr.Merle T. Adkins: 200.00 100.00
Baltimore
❑ 188 Jack Dunn 250.00 125.00
❑ 189 George Merritt 200.00 100.00
❑ 190 Charles Hanford 200.00 100.00
❑ 191 Hick Cady 200.00 100.00
❑ 192 James Frick 200.00 100.00
❑ 193 Wyatt Lee 200.00 100.00
❑ 194 Lewis McAllister 200.00 100.00
❑ 195 John Nee 200.00 100.00
❑ 196 Jimmy Collins 500.00 250.00
❑ 197 James Phelan 200.00 100.00
❑ 198 Emil Batch 200.00 100.00

1909 T206

	Ex-Mt	VG
COMPLETE SET (520)	55000.00	27500.00
COMMON (1-389)	60.00	30.00
COMMON (390-475)	50.00	25.00
COMMON (476-523)	125.00	60.00

❑ 1 Ed Abbaticchio: 60.00 30.00
Pitt
Batting follow thru
❑ 2 Ed Abbaticchio: 75.00 38.00
Pitt.
Batting waiting pitch
❑ 3 Bill Abstein 60.00 30.00
❑ 4 Whitey Alperman 75.00 38.00
❑ 5 Red Ames: N.Y. NL 75.00 38.00
Portrait
❑ 6 Red Ames: N.Y. NL 60.00 30.00
Hands over head
❑ 7 Red Ames: N.Y. NL 75.00 38.00
Hands in front of chest
❑ 8 Frank Arellanes 60.00 30.00
❑ 9 Jake Atz 60.00 30.00
❑ 10 Frank Baker 400.00 200.00
❑ 11 Neal Ball: N.Y. AL 75.00 38.00
❑ 12 Neal Ball: Cleveland 60.00 30.00
❑ 13 Jap Barbeau 60.00 30.00
❑ 14 Jack Barry 60.00 30.00
❑ 15 Johnny Bates 75.00 38.00
❑ 16 Ginger Beaumont 75.00 38.00
❑ 17 Fred Beck 60.00 30.00
❑ 18 Beals Becker 60.00 30.00
❑ 19 George Bell: 60.00 30.00
Brooklyn
pitching follow thru
❑ 20 George Bell: 75.00 38.00
Brooklyn
Hands
over head
❑ 21 Chief Bender 500.00 250.00
Phila. AL
Portrait
❑ 22 Chief Bender 500.00 250.00
Phila. AL
pitching, trees
❑ 23 Chief Bender 400.00 200.00
Phila. AL
pitching, no trees
❑ 24 Bill Bergen: 60.00 30.00
Brooklyn
Catching
❑ 25 Bill Bergen: 75.00 38.00
Brooklyn
Batting
❑ 26 Heinie Berger 60.00 30.00
❑ 27 Bob Bescher: Cinc. 60.00 30.00
Catching fly ball
❑ 28 Bob Bescher: Cinc. 60.00 30.00
Portrait
❑ 29 Joe Birmingham 75.00 38.00
❑ 30 Jack Bliss 60.00 30.00
❑ 31 Frank Bowerman 75.00 38.00
❑ 32 Bill Bradley: 75.00 38.00
Cleveland
Portrait
❑ 33 Bill Bradley: 60.00 30.00
Cleveland
Batting
❑ 34 Kitty Bransfield 75.00 38.00
❑ 35 Roger Bresnahan: 300.00 150.00
St.L. NL
Portrait
❑ 36 Roger Bresnahan: 300.00 150.00
St.L. NL
Batting
❑ 37 Al Bridwell 75.00 38.00
N.Y. NL
Portrait
❑ 38 Al Bridwell 60.00 30.00
N.Y. NL
Wearing sweater
❑ 39 George Brown: 125.00 60.00
Chicago NL
Sic, Browne
❑ 40 George Brown: 400.00 200.00
Washington
Sic, Browne
❑ 41 Mordecai Brown: 500.00 250.00
Chicago NL
Portrait
❑ 42 Mordecai Brown: 500.00 250.00
Chicago NL
Chicago down front of shirt
❑ 43 Mordecai Brown: 500.00 250.00
Chicago NL
Cubs Shirt
❑ 44 Al Burch: Brooklyn 60.00 30.00
Fielding
❑ 45 Al Burch: Brooklyn 125.00 60.00

Batting
❑ 46 Bill Burns 60.00 30.00
❑ 47 Donie Bush 75.00 38.00
❑ 48 Bobby Byrne 60.00 30.00
❑ 49 Howie Camnitz: 75.00 38.00
Pitt
Arms folded over chest
❑ 50 Howie Camnitz: 60.00 30.00
Pitt
Hands over head
❑ 51 Howie Camnitz: 60.00 30.00
Pitt.
Throwing
❑ 52 Billy Campbell 60.00 30.00
❑ 53 Bill Carrigan 60.00 30.00
❑ 54 Frank Chance: 500.00 250.00
Chicago NL
Cubs across chest
❑ 55 Frank Chance: 500.00 250.00
Chicago NL
Chicago down front of shirt
❑ 56 Frank Chance: 400.00 200.00
Chicago NL
Batting
❑ 57 Chappy Charles 60.00 30.00
❑ 58 Hal Chase 125.00 60.00
N.Y. AL
Port. blue bkgd.
❑ 59 Hal Chase 200.00 100.00
N.Y. AL
Port., pink bkgd.
❑ 60 Hal Chase 125.00 60.00
N.Y. AL
Holding cup
❑ 61 Hal Chase 125.00 60.00
N.Y. AL
Throwing, dark cap
❑ 62 Hal Chase 150.00 75.00
N.Y. AL
Throwing, white cap
❑ 63 Jack Chesbro 250.00 125.00
❑ 64 Eddie Cicotte 200.00 100.00
❑ 65 Fred Clarke: Pitt. 200.00 100.00
Portrait
❑ 66 Fred Clarke: Pitt. 200.00 100.00
❑ 67 Nig Clarke 75.00 38.00
❑ 68 Ty Cobb: Detroit 2500.00 1250.00
Port., red bkgd.
❑ 69 Ty Cobb: Detroit 3500.00 1800.00
Port., green background
❑ 70 Ty Cobb: Detroit 2500.00 1250.00
Bat on shoulder
❑ 71 Ty Cobb: Detroit 2500.00 1250.00
Bat away from shoulder
❑ 72 Eddie Collins: 400.00 200.00
Phila. AL
❑ 73 Wid Conroy: 75.00 38.00
Washington
Fielding
❑ 74 Wid Conroy 60.00 30.00
Washington
Bat on shoulder
❑ 75 Harry Covaleski: 75.00 38.00
Phila. NL
❑ 76 Doc Crandall 60.00 30.00
N.Y. NL,
without cap
❑ 77 Doc Crandall 60.00 30.00
N.Y. NL
sweater and cap
❑ 78 Sam Crawford: 500.00 250.00
Detroit, Batting
❑ 79 Sam Crawford: 500.00 250.00
Detroit, Throwing
❑ 80 Birdie Cree 60.00 30.00
❑ 81 Lou Criger 75.00 38.00
❑ 82 Dode Criss 75.00 38.00
❑ 83 Bill Dahlen: 125.00 60.00
Boston NL
❑ 84 Bill Dahlen: 200.00 100.00
Brooklyn
❑ 85 George Davis 200.00 100.00
❑ 86 Harry Davis 60.00 30.00
Phila. AL
Davis on card
❑ 87 Harry Davis 75.00 38.00
Phila. AL
H.Davis on card
❑ 88 Jim Delehanty 75.00 38.00
Sic, Delahanty
❑ 89 Ray Demmitt 5000.00 2500.00
St.L. AL
❑ 90 Ray Demmitt 75.00 38.00
N.Y. AL
❑ 91 Art Devlin 75.00 38.00
❑ 92 Josh Devore 60.00 30.00
❑ 93 Bill Dineen 60.00 30.00
❑ 94 Mike Donlin 125.00 60.00
N.Y. NL
Fielding
❑ 95 Mike Donlin 125.00 60.00
N.Y. NL
Sitting
❑ 96 Mike Donlin 75.00 38.00
N.Y. NL
Batting
❑ 97 Jiggs Donohue 75.00 38.00
❑ 98 Bill Donovan: 75.00 38.00
Detroit
Portrait
❑ 99 Bill Donovan: 60.00 30.00
Detroit
Throwing
❑ 100 Red Dooin 75.00 38.00
❑ 101 Mickey Doolan: 60.00 30.00
Phila. NL
Fielding
❑ 102 Mickey Doolan: 60.00 30.00
Phila. NL
Batting
❑ 103 Mickey Doolin (Sic, 75.00 38.00
Doolan): Phila. NL
❑ 104 Patsy Dougherty: 75.00 38.00
Chicago AL
Portrait
❑ 105 Patsy Dougherty: 60.00 30.00
Chicago AL
Fielding
❑ 106 Tom Downey: Cinc. 60.00 30.00
Batting
❑ 107 Tom Downey: Cinc. 60.00 30.00
Fielding
❑ 108A Joe Doyle: N.Y. 125.00 60.00
Hands over head
❑ 108B Joe Doyle: N.Y. 60000.00 30000.00
NAT'L
hands
over head)
❑ 109 Larry Doyle: N.Y. 75.00 38.00
NL
Sweater
❑ 110 Larry Doyle: N.Y. 125.00 60.00
NL
Throwing
❑ 111 Larry Doyle: N.Y. 75.00 38.00
NL
Bat on shoulder
❑ 112 Jean Dubuc 60.00 30.00
❑ 113 Hugh Duffy 400.00 200.00
❑ 114 Joe Dunn 60.00 30.00
❑ 115 Bull Durham 75.00 38.00
❑ 116 Jimmy Dygert 60.00 30.00
❑ 117 Ted Easterly 60.00 30.00
❑ 118 Dick Egan 60.00 30.00
❑ 119 Kid Elberfeld 60.00 30.00
Wash.
Fielding
❑ 120 Kid Elberfeld 1000.00 500.00
Wash.
Portrait
❑ 121 Kid Elberfeld 75.00 38.00
N.Y. AL
Portrait
❑ 122 Clyde Engle 60.00 30.00
❑ 123 Steve Evans 60.00 30.00
❑ 124 Johnny Evers: 600.00 300.00
Chicago NL
Portrait
❑ 125 Johnny Evers: 500.00 250.00
Chicago NL
Cubs across chest
❑ 126 Johnny Evers: 500.00 250.00
Chicago NL
Chicago down front of shirt
❑ 127 Bob Ewing 75.00 38.00
❑ 128 George Ferguson 60.00 30.00
❑ 129 Hobe Ferris 75.00 38.00
❑ 130 Lou Fiene 60.00 30.00
Chicago AL
Portrait
❑ 131 Lou Fiene 60.00 30.00
Chicago AL
Throwing
❑ 132 Art Fletcher 60.00 30.00
❑ 133 Elmer Flick 300.00 150.00
❑ 134 Russ Ford 60.00 30.00
❑ 135 John Frill 60.00 30.00
❑ 136 Art Fromme 60.00 30.00
❑ 137 Chick Gandil 250.00 125.00
❑ 138 Bob Ganley 75.00 38.00
❑ 139 Harry Gasper 60.00 30.00
❑ 140 Rube Geyer 60.00 30.00
❑ 141 George Gibson 75.00 38.00
❑ 142 Billy Gilbert 75.00 38.00
❑ 143 Wilbur Goode 75.00 38.00
Sic, Good
❑ 144 Bill Graham 60.00 30.00
❑ 145 Peaches Graham 60.00 30.00
❑ 146 Dolly Gray 75.00 38.00
❑ 147 Clark Griffith: 250.00 125.00
Cinc.
Portrait
❑ 148 Clark Griffith: 250.00 125.00
Cinc.
Batting
❑ 149 Bob Groom 60.00 30.00
❑ 150 Ed Hahn 75.00 38.00
❑ 151 Topsy Hartsel 60.00 30.00
❑ 152 Charlie Hemphill 75.00 38.00
❑ 153 Buck Herzog 75.00 38.00
N.Y. NL
❑ 154 Buck Herzog 60.00 30.00
Boston NL
❑ 155 Bill Hinchman 75.00 38.00
❑ 156 Doc Hoblitzell 60.00 30.00
❑ 157 Danny Hoffman 60.00 30.00
❑ 158 Solly Hofman 60.00 30.00
❑ 159 Del Howard 60.00 30.00
❑ 160 Harry Howell 60.00 30.00
St.L. AL
Portrait
❑ 161 Harry Howell 60.00 30.00
St.L. AL
Left hand on hip
❑ 162 Miller Huggins: 400.00 200.00
Cinc.
Portrait
❑ 163 Miller Huggins: 400.00 200.00
Cinc.
Hands to Mouth
❑ 164 Rudy Hulswitt 60.00 30.00
❑ 165 John Hummel 60.00 30.00
❑ 166 George Hunter 60.00 30.00
❑ 167 Frank Isbell 75.00 38.00
❑ 168 Fred Jacklitsch 75.00 38.00
❑ 169 Hughie Jennings MG: 400.00 200.00
Detroit
Portrait
❑ 170 Hughie Jennings MG: 400.00 200.00
Detroit
One
❑ 171 Hughie Jennings MG: 400.00 200.00
Detroit
Both
❑ 172 Walter Johnson: 1500.00 750.00
Washington
Portrait
❑ 173 Walter Johnson: 1200.00 600.00
Washington
Hands at Chest
❑ 174 Davy Jones 60.00 30.00
❑ 175 Fielder Jones 75.00 38.00
Chic. AL
Portrait
❑ 176 Fielder Jones 75.00 38.00
Chic AL
Hands on hips
❑ 177 Tom Jones 75.00 38.00

❑ 178	Tim Jordan: Brooklyn Portrait	75.00	38.00
❑ 179	Tim Jordan: Brooklyn Batting	60.00	30.00
❑ 180	Addie Joss: Cleveland Portrait	600.00	300.00
❑ 181	Addie Joss: Cleveland Ready to pitch	500.00	250.00
❑ 182	Ed Karger	75.00	38.00
❑ 183	Willie Keeler N.Y. AL Portrait	600.00	300.00
❑ 184	Willie Keeler N.Y. AL Batting	500.00	250.00
❑ 185	Ed Killian: Detroit Portrait	75.00	38.00
❑ 186	Ed Killian: Detroit Pitching	60.00	30.00
❑ 187	Red Kleinow N.Y. AL Batting	75.00	38.00
❑ 188	Red Kleinow N.Y. AL Catching	60.00	30.00
❑ 189	Red Kleinow Boston AL Catching	1000.00	500.00
❑ 190	Johnny Kling: Chicago NL	75.00	38.00
❑ 191	Otto Knabe	60.00	30.00
❑ 192	John Knight N.Y. AL Portrait	60.00	30.00
❑ 193	John Knight N.Y. AL Batting	60.00	30.00
❑ 194	Ed Konetchy St.L. NL Awaiting low ball	60.00	30.00
❑ 195	Ed Konetchy St.L. NL Glove above head	75.00	38.00
❑ 196	Harry Krause Phila. AL Portrait	60.00	30.00
❑ 197	Harry Krause Phila. AL Pitching	60.00	30.00
❑ 198	Rube Kroh	60.00	30.00
❑ 199	Nap Lajoie: Cleveland Portrait	800.00	400.00
❑ 200	Nap Lajoie: Cleveland Batting	600.00	300.00
❑ 201	Nap Lajoie: Cleveland Throwing	600.00	300.00
❑ 202	Joe Lake N.Y. AL	75.00	38.00
❑ 203	Joe Lake St.L. AL Hands over head	60.00	30.00
❑ 204	Joe Lake St.L. AL Throwing	60.00	30.00
❑ 205	Frank LaPorte	60.00	30.00
❑ 206	Arlie Latham	75.00	38.00
❑ 207	Tommy Leach: Pitt. Portrait	75.00	38.00
❑ 208	Tommy Leach: Pitt. In fielding position	60.00	30.00
❑ 209	Lefty Leifield: Pitt. Batting	60.00	30.00
❑ 210	Lefty Leifield: Pitt. Hands behind head	75.00	38.00
❑ 211	Ed Lennox	60.00	30.00
❑ 212	Glenn Liebhardt	75.00	38.00
❑ 213	Vive Lindaman	125.00	60.00
❑ 214	Paddy Livingstone	60.00	30.00
❑ 215	Hans Lobert	75.00	38.00
❑ 216	Harry Lord	60.00	30.00
❑ 217	Harry Lumley	75.00	38.00
❑ 218	Carl Lundgren	300.00	150.00
❑ 219	Nick Maddox.	60.00	30.00
❑ 220	Sherry Magee Phila. NL Portrait	125.00	60.00
❑ 221	Sherry Magee Phila. NL Batting	60.00	30.00
❑ 222	Sherry Magie Phila. NL Sic, Magee Portrait, name misspelled	15000.00	7500.00
❑ 223	Rube Manning N.Y. AL Batting	75.00	38.00
❑ 224	Rube Manning N.Y. AL Hands over head	60.00	30.00
❑ 225	Rube Marquard N.Y. NL Portrait	500.00	250.00
❑ 226	Rube Marquard N.Y. NL Pitching	400.00	200.00
❑ 227	Rube Marquard N.Y. NL Standing	400.00	200.00
❑ 228	Doc Marshall	60.00	30.00
❑ 229	Christy Mathewson: N.Y. NL Portrait	2000.00	1000.00
❑ 230	Christy Mathewson: N.Y. NL Pitching, white cap	1500.00	750.00
❑ 231	Christy Mathewson: N.Y. NL Pitching, dark cap	1500.00	750.00
❑ 232	Al Mattern	60.00	30.00
❑ 233	Jack McAleese	60.00	30.00
❑ 234	George McBride	60.00	30.00
❑ 235	Moose McCormick	60.00	30.00
❑ 236	Pryor McElveen	60.00	30.00
❑ 237	John McGraw N.Y. NL Portrait, no cap	500.00	250.00
❑ 238	John McGraw N.Y. NL w/Cap	500.00	250.00
❑ 239	John McGraw N.Y. NL Finger	500.00	250.00
❑ 240	John McGraw N.Y. NL Glove on hip	500.00	250.00
❑ 241	Matty McIntyre: Brooklyn	75.00	38.00
❑ 242	Matty McIntyre: Brooklyn and Chicago NL	60.00	30.00
❑ 243	Mike McIntyre: Detroit	60.00	30.00
❑ 244	Larry McLean	60.00	30.00
❑ 245	George McQuillan: Phila. NL Throwing	75.00	38.00
❑ 246	George McQuillan: Phila. NL Batting	60.00	30.00
❑ 247	Fred Merkle N.Y. NL Portrait	125.00	60.00
❑ 248	Fred Merkle N.Y. NL Throwing	125.00	60.00
❑ 249	Chief Meyers	60.00	30.00
❑ 250	Chief Meyers Sic, Myers) N.Y. NL Fielding	60.00	30.00
❑ 251	Chief Meyers Sic, Myers) N.Y. NL Batting	75.00	38.00
❑ 252	Clyde Milan	60.00	30.00
❑ 253	Dots Miller	60.00	30.00
❑ 254	Mike Mitchell	60.00	30.00
❑ 255	Pat Moran	60.00	30.00
❑ 256	George Moriarty	60.00	30.00
❑ 257	Mike Mowrey	60.00	30.00
❑ 258	George Mullin: Detroit Sic, Mullen	60.00	30.00
❑ 259	George Mullin: Detroit Throwing	75.00	38.00
❑ 260	George Mullin: Detroit Batting	60.00	30.00
❑ 261	Danny Murphy Phila. AL Throwing	75.00	38.00
❑ 262	Danny Murphy Phila. AL Bat on shoulder	60.00	30.00
❑ 263	Red Murray N.Y. NL Sweater	60.00	30.00
❑ 264	Red Murray N.Y. NL Bat on shoulder	60.00	30.00
❑ 265	Tom Needham	60.00	30.00
❑ 266	Simon Nicholls Phila AL	75.00	38.00
❑ 267	Simon Nicholls Sic, Nichols: Phila. AL	60.00	30.00
❑ 268	Harry Niles	75.00	38.00
❑ 269	Rebel Oakes	60.00	30.00
❑ 270	Bill O'Hara: N.Y. NL	60.00	30.00
❑ 271	Bill O'Hara: St. Louis NL	5000.00	2500.00
❑ 272	Rube Oldring Phila. AL Fielding	75.00	38.00
❑ 273	Rube Oldring Phila. AL Bat on shoulder	75.00	38.00
❑ 274	Charley O'Leary: Detroit Portrait	75.00	38.00
❑ 275	Charley O'Leary: Detroit Hands on knees	60.00	30.00
❑ 276	Orval Overall: Chicago NL Portrait	75.00	38.00
❑ 277	Orval Overall: Chicago NL Pitching follow thru	60.00	30.00
❑ 278	Orval Overall: Chicago NL, Pitching hiding ball in glove	60.00	30.00
❑ 279	Frank Owen Chicago AL Sic, Owens)	75.00	38.00
❑ 280	Freddy Parent	75.00	38.00
❑ 281	Dode Paskert	60.00	30.00
❑ 282	Jim Pastorius	75.00	38.00
❑ 283	Harry Pattee	150.00	75.00
❑ 284	Fred Payne	60.00	30.00
❑ 285	Barney Pelty St.L. AL HOR	125.00	60.00
❑ 286	Barney Pelty St.L. AL VERT	60.00	30.00
❑ 287	George Perring	60.00	30.00
❑ 288	Jeff Pfeffer	60.00	30.00
❑ 289	Jack Pfeister Chic. NL Sitting	60.00	30.00
❑ 290	Jack Pfeister Chic. NL Pitching	60.00	30.00
❑ 291	Ed Phelps	60.00	30.00
❑ 292	Deacon Phillippe.	125.00	60.00

❑	293	Eddie Plank	30000.00	15000.00
❑	294	Jack Powell	75.00	38.00
❑	295	Mike Powers	125.00	60.00
❑	296	Billy Purtell	60.00	30.00
❑	297	Jack Quinn	60.00	30.00
❑	298	Bugs Raymond	75.00	38.00
❑	299	Ed Reulbach Chicago NL Pitching	125.00	60.00
❑	300	Ed Reulbach Chicago NL Hands at side	125.00	60.00
❑	301	Bob Rhoades sic,Rhoads Cleveland Hand in air	60.00	30.00
❑	302	Bob Rhoades sic, Rhoads Cleveland Ready to pitch	60.00	30.00
❑	303	Charlie Rhodes	60.00	30.00
❑	304	Claude Ritchey	75.00	38.00
❑	305	Claude Rossman	60.00	30.00
❑	306	Nap Rucker: Brooklyn Portrait	125.00	60.00
❑	307	Nap Rucker: Brooklyn Pitching	75.00	38.00
❑	308	Germany Schaefer: Washington	75.00	38.00
❑	309	Germany Schaefer: Detroit	75.00	38.00
❑	310	Admiral Schlei N.Y. NL Sweater	60.00	30.00
❑	311	Admiral Schlei N.Y. NL Batting	60.00	30.00
❑	312	Admiral Schlei N.Y. NL Fielding	75.00	38.00
❑	313	Boss Schmidt: Detroit Portrait	60.00	30.00
❑	314	Boss Schmidt: Detroit Throwing	75.00	38.00
❑	315	Frank Schulte: Chicago NL Batting, back turned	60.00	30.00
❑	316	Frank Schulte: Chicago NL Batting, front pose	75.00	38.00
❑	317	Jim Scott	60.00	30.00
❑	318	Cy Seymour N.Y. NL Portrait	60.00	30.00
❑	319	Cy Seymour N.Y. NL Throwing	60.00	30.00
❑	320	Cy Seymour N.Y. NL Batting	75.00	38.00
❑	321	Al Shaw	75.00	38.00
❑	322	Jimmy Sheckard: Chicago NL Throwing	60.00	30.00
❑	323	Jimmy Sheckard: Chicago NL Side view	75.00	38.00
❑	324	Bill Shipke	75.00	38.00
❑	325	Frank Smith Chicago AL Listed as Smith	60.00	30.00
❑	326	Frank Smith Chicago and Boston AL	400.00	200.00
❑	327	Frank Smith Chicago AL Listed as F.Smith	75.00	38.00
❑	328	Happy Smith	60.00	30.00
❑	329	Fred Snodgrass N.Y. NL Batting	75.00	38.00
❑	329A	Fred Snodgrass N.Y., Battting Card spelled Nodgrass Due to a printing glitch	3000.00	1500.00
❑	330	Fred Snodgrass N.Y. NL Catching	75.00	38.00
❑	331	Bob Spade	75.00	38.00
❑	332	Tris Speaker	1000.00	500.00
❑	333	Tubby Spencer	75.00	38.00
❑	334	Jake Stahl: Boston AL Catching fly ball	75.00	38.00
❑	335	Jake Stahl: Boston AL Standing, arms down	75.00	38.00
❑	336	Oscar Stanage	60.00	30.00
❑	337	Charlie Starr	60.00	30.00
❑	338	Harry Steinfeldt: Chicago NL Portrait	125.00	60.00
❑	339	Harry Steinfeldt: Chicago NL Batting	75.00	38.00
❑	340	Jim Stephens	60.00	30.00
❑	341	George Stone	75.00	38.00
❑	342	George Stovall: Cleveland Portrait	75.00	38.00
❑	343	George Stovall: Cleveland Batting	60.00	30.00
❑	344	Gabby Street: Washington Portrait	75.00	38.00
❑	345	Gabby Street: Washington Catching	60.00	30.00
❑	346	Billy Sullivan	75.00	38.00
❑	347	Ed Summers	60.00	30.00
❑	348	Jeff Sweeney	60.00	30.00
❑	349	Bill Sweeney	60.00	30.00
❑	350	Jesse Tannehill	60.00	30.00
❑	351	Lee Tannehill: Chicago AL Listed as L.Tannehill	75.00	38.00
❑	352	Lee Tannehill: Chicago AL Listed as Tannehill	60.00	30.00
❑	353	Fred Tenney	75.00	38.00
❑	354	Ira Thomas	60.00	30.00
❑	355	Joe Tinker Chicago NL Bat Off Shoulder	600.00	300.00
❑	356	Joe Tinker Chicago NL Bat on Shoulder	600.00	300.00
❑	357	Joe Tinker Chicago NL Portrait	800.00	400.00
❑	358	Joe Tinker Chicago NL Hands on knees	600.00	300.00
❑	359	John Titus	60.00	30.00
❑	360	Terry Turner	75.00	38.00
❑	361	Bob Unglaub	60.00	30.00
❑	362	Rube Waddell St.L. AL Portrait	600.00	300.00
❑	363	Rube Waddell St.L. AL Pitching	500.00	250.00
❑	364	Heinie Wagner: Boston AL Bat on left shoulder	125.00	60.00
❑	365	Heinie Wagner: Boston AL Bat on right shoulder	75.00	38.00
❑	366	Honus Wagner	500000.00	250000.00
❑	367	Bobby Wallace	400.00	200.00
❑	368	Ed Walsh	600.00	300.00
❑	369	Jack Warhop: N.Y. AL	60.00	30.00
❑	370	Jake Weimer: N.Y. NL	75.00	38.00
❑	371	Zach Wheat	400.00	200.00
❑	372	Doc White Chicago AL Portrait	75.00	38.00
❑	373	Doc White Chicago AL Pitching	60.00	30.00
❑	374	Kaiser Wilhelm: Brooklyn Batting	60.00	30.00
❑	375	Kaiser Wilhelm: Brooklyn Hands to chest	75.00	38.00
❑	376	Ed Willett: Detroit Batting	60.00	30.00
❑	377	Ed Willett Sic, Willetts Detroit Pitching	60.00	30.00
❑	378	Jimmy Williams	75.00	38.00
❑	379	Vic Willis: Pitt.	250.00	125.00
❑	380	Vic Willis St.L. NL Pitching	200.00	100.00
❑	381	Vic Willis St.L. NL Batting	200.00	100.00
❑	382	Chief Wilson	60.00	30.00
❑	383	Hooks Wiltse N.Y. NL Portrait	75.00	38.00
❑	384	Hooks Wiltse N.Y.NL Sweater	60.00	30.00
❑	385	Hooks Wiltse N.Y. NL Pitching	60.00	30.00
❑	386	Cy Young Cleveland Portrait	2000.00	1000.00
❑	387	Cy Young Cleveland Pitch, front view	1500.00	750.00
❑	388	Cy Young Cleveland Pitch, side view	1500.00	750.00
❑	389	Heinie Zimmerman:	60.00	30.00
❑	390	Fred Abbott	50.00	25.00
❑	391	Merle(Doc) Adkins	50.00	25.00
❑	392	John Anderson	50.00	25.00
❑	393	Herman Armbruster	50.00	25.00
❑	394	Harry Arndt	50.00	25.00
❑	395	Cy Barger	60.00	30.00
❑	396	John Barry	50.00	25.00
❑	397	Emil H. Batch	50.00	25.00
❑	398	Jake Beckley	250.00	125.00
❑	399	Lena Blackburne	75.00	38.00
❑	400	David Brain	50.00	25.00
❑	401	Roy Brashear	50.00	25.00
❑	402	Fred Burchell	50.00	25.00
❑	403	Jimmy Burke	50.00	25.00
❑	404	John Butler	50.00	25.00
❑	405	Charles Carr	50.00	25.00
❑	406	Doc Casey	50.00	25.00
❑	407	Peter Cassidy	50.00	25.00
❑	408	Wm. Chappelle	60.00	30.00
❑	409	Wm. Clancy	50.00	25.00
❑	410	Joshua Clarke Sic, Clark	50.00	25.00
❑	411	William Clymer	50.00	25.00
❑	412	Jimmy Collins	400.00	200.00
❑	413	Bunk Congalton	50.00	25.00
❑	414	Gavvy Cravath	125.00	60.00
❑	415	Monte Cross	60.00	30.00
❑	416	Paul Davidson	50.00	25.00
❑	417	Frank Delehanty Sic, Delahanty	75.00	38.00
❑	418	Rube Dessau	50.00	25.00
❑	419	Gus Dorner	50.00	25.00
❑	420	Jerome Downs	50.00	25.00
❑	421	Jack Dunn	75.00	38.00
❑	422	James Flanagan	50.00	25.00
❑	423	James Freeman	50.00	25.00
❑	424	John Ganzel	50.00	25.00
❑	425	Myron Grimshaw	50.00	25.00
❑	426	Robert Hall	50.00	25.00
❑	427	William Hallman	60.00	30.00
❑	428	John Hannifan	50.00	25.00
❑	429	Jack Hayden	50.00	25.00
❑	430	Harry Hinchman	50.00	25.00
❑	431	Harry C. Hoffman	50.00	25.00

❑ 432	James B. Jackson	60.00	30.00
❑ 433	Joe Kelley	250.00	125.00
❑ 434	Rube Kissinger	60.00	30.00
	Sic, Kisinger		
❑ 435	Otto Krueger	50.00	25.00
	Sic, Kruger		
❑ 436	Wm. Lattimore	50.00	25.00
❑ 437	James Lavender	50.00	25.00
❑ 438	Carl Lundgren	50.00	25.00
❑ 439	Wm. Malarkey	60.00	30.00
❑ 440	Wm. Maloney	50.00	25.00
❑ 441	Dennis McGann	50.00	25.00
❑ 442	James McGinley	50.00	25.00
❑ 443	Joe McGinnity	250.00	125.00
❑ 444	Ulysses McGlynn	50.00	25.00
❑ 445	George Merritt	50.00	25.00
❑ 446	Wm. Milligan	50.00	25.00
❑ 447	Fred Mitchell	50.00	25.00
❑ 448	Dan Moeller	50.00	25.00
❑ 449	Joseph H. Moran	50.00	25.00
❑ 450	Wm. Nattress	50.00	25.00
❑ 451	Frank Oberlin	50.00	25.00
❑ 452	Peter O'Brien	50.00	25.00
❑ 453	Wm. O'Neil	50.00	25.00
❑ 454	James Phelan	50.00	25.00
❑ 455	Oliver Pickering	50.00	25.00
❑ 456	Philip Poland	50.00	25.00
❑ 457	Ambrose Puttman	50.00	25.00
❑ 458	Lee Quillen	50.00	25.00
❑ 459	Newton Randall	50.00	25.00
❑ 460	Louis Ritter	50.00	25.00
❑ 461	Dick Rudolph	50.00	25.00
❑ 462	George Schirm	50.00	25.00
❑ 463	Larry Schlafly	50.00	25.00
❑ 464	Ossie Schreckengost	60.00	30.00
	Sic Schreck		
❑ 465	William Shannon	50.00	25.00
❑ 466	Bayard Sharpe	50.00	25.00
❑ 466A	Bayard Sharpe	500.00	250.00
	Name is spelled Shappe on front		
❑ 467	Royal Shaw	50.00	25.00
❑ 468	James Slagle	50.00	25.00
❑ 469	George Henry Smith	50.00	25.00
❑ 470	Samuel Strang	50.00	25.00
❑ 471	Dummy Taylor	125.00	60.00
❑ 472	John Thielman	50.00	25.00
❑ 473	John F. White	50.00	25.00
❑ 474	William Wright	50.00	25.00
❑ 475	Irving M. Young	60.00	30.00
❑ 476	Jack Bastian	125.00	60.00
❑ 477	Harry Bay	125.00	60.00
❑ 478	Wm. Bernhard	125.00	60.00
❑ 479	Ted Breitenstein	125.00	60.00
❑ 480	Scoops Carey	125.00	60.00
❑ 481	Cad Coles	125.00	60.00
❑ 482	Wm. Cranston	125.00	60.00
❑ 483	Roy Ellam	125.00	60.00
❑ 484	Edward Foster	125.00	60.00
❑ 485	Charles Fritz	125.00	60.00
❑ 486	Ed Greminger	125.00	60.00
❑ 487	Guiheen	125.00	60.00
❑ 488	William F. Hart	125.00	60.00
❑ 489	James Henry Hart	125.00	60.00
❑ 490	J.R. Helm	125.00	60.00
❑ 491	Gordon Hickman	125.00	60.00
❑ 492	Buck Hooker	125.00	60.00
❑ 493	Ernie Howard	125.00	60.00
❑ 494	A.O. Jordan	125.00	60.00
❑ 495	J.F. Kiernan	125.00	60.00
❑ 496	Frank King	125.00	60.00
❑ 497	James LaFitte	125.00	60.00
❑ 498	Harry Sentz	125.00	60.00
	Sic, Lentz		
❑ 499	Perry Lipe	125.00	60.00
❑ 500	George Manion	125.00	60.00
❑ 501	McCauley	125.00	60.00
❑ 502	Charles B. Miller	125.00	60.00
❑ 503	Carlton Molesworth	125.00	60.00
❑ 504	Dominic Mullaney	125.00	60.00
❑ 505	Albert Orth	125.00	60.00
❑ 506	William Otey	125.00	60.00
❑ 507	George Paige	125.00	60.00
❑ 508	Hub Perdue	150.00	75.00
❑ 509	Archie Persons	125.00	60.00
❑ 510	Edward Reagan	125.00	60.00
❑ 511	R.H. Revelle	125.00	60.00
❑ 512	Isaac Rockenfeld	125.00	60.00
❑ 513	Ray Ryan	125.00	60.00
❑ 514	Charles Seitz	125.00	60.00
❑ 515	Frank "Shag" Shaughnessy	150.00	75.00
❑ 516	Carlos Smith	125.00	60.00
❑ 517	Sid Smith	125.00	60.00
❑ 518	Dolly Stark	150.00	75.00
❑ 519	Tony Thebo	125.00	60.00
❑ 520	Woodie Thornton	125.00	60.00
❑ 521	Juan Viola	125.00	60.00
	Sic, Violat		
❑ 522	James Westlake	125.00	60.00
❑ 523	Foley White	125.00	60.00

1952 Topps

	NM	Ex
COMP.MASTER SET (487)	80000.00	40000.00
COMPLETE SET (407)	65000.00	32500.00
COMMON CARD (1-80)	60.00	30.00
COMMON CARD (81-250)	40.00	20.00
COMMON (251-310)	50.00	25.00
COMMON (311-407)	250.00	125.00
WRAPPER (1-CENT)	250.00	125.00
WRAPPER (5-CENT)	100.00	50.00

❑ 1	Andy Pafko	5000.00	500.00
❑ 1A	Andy Pafko Black	3000.00	300.00
❑ 2	Pete Runnels RC	250.00	125.00
❑ 2A	Pete Runnels RC Black	250.00	125.00
❑ 3	Hank Thompson	70.00	35.00
❑ 3A	Hank Thompson Black	70.00	35.00
❑ 4	Don Lenhardt	60.00	30.00
❑ 4A	Don Lenhardt Black	60.00	30.00
❑ 5	Larry Jansen	70.00	35.00
❑ 5A	Larry Jansen Black	70.00	35.00
❑ 6	Grady Hatton	60.00	30.00
❑ 6A	Grady Hatton Black	60.00	30.00
❑ 7	Wayne Terwilliger	60.00	30.00
❑ 7A	W. Terwilliger Black	60.00	30.00
❑ 8	Fred Marsh	60.00	30.00
❑ 8A	Fred Marsh Black	60.00	30.00
❑ 9	Robert Hogue	60.00	30.00
❑ 9A	Robert Hogue Black	60.00	30.00
❑ 10	Al Rosen	70.00	35.00
❑ 10A	Al Rosen Black	70.00	35.00
❑ 11	Phil Rizzuto	400.00	200.00
❑ 11A	Phil Rizzuto Black	350.00	180.00
❑ 12	Monty Basgall	60.00	30.00
❑ 12A	Monty Basgall Black	60.00	30.00
❑ 13	Johnny Wyrostek	60.00	30.00
❑ 13A	J. Wyrostek Black	60.00	30.00
❑ 14	Bob Elliott	70.00	35.00
❑ 14A	Bob Elliott Black	70.00	35.00
❑ 15	Johnny Pesky	70.00	35.00
❑ 15A	Johnny Pesky Black	70.00	35.00
❑ 16	Gene Hermanski	60.00	30.00
❑ 16A	G. Hermanski Black	60.00	30.00
❑ 17	Jim Hegan	70.00	35.00
❑ 17A	Jim Hegan Black	70.00	35.00
❑ 18	Merrill Combs	60.00	30.00
❑ 18A	Merrill Combs Black	60.00	30.00
❑ 19	Johnny Bucha	60.00	30.00
❑ 19A	Johnny Bucha Black	60.00	30.00
❑ 20	Billy Loes RC	150.00	75.00
❑ 20A	Billy Loes RC Black	150.00	75.00
❑ 21	Ferris Fain	70.00	35.00
❑ 21A	Ferris Fain Black	70.00	35.00
❑ 22	Dom DiMaggio	125.00	60.00
❑ 22A	Dom DiMaggio Black	100.00	50.00
❑ 23	Billy Goodman	70.00	35.00
❑ 23A	Billy Goodman Black	70.00	35.00
❑ 24	Luke Easter	80.00	40.00
❑ 24A	Luke Easter Black	80.00	40.00
❑ 25	Johnny Groth	60.00	30.00
❑ 25A	Johnny Groth Black	60.00	30.00
❑ 26	Monte Irvin	150.00	75.00
❑ 26A	Monte Irvin Black	150.00	75.00
❑ 27	Sam Jethroe	70.00	35.00
❑ 27A	Sam Jethroe Black	70.00	35.00
❑ 28	Jerry Priddy	60.00	30.00
❑ 28A	Jerry Priddy Black	60.00	30.00
❑ 29	Ted Kluszewski	125.00	60.00
❑ 29A	Ted Kluszewski Black	125.00	60.00
❑ 30	Mel Parnell	70.00	35.00
❑ 30A	Mel Parnell Black	70.00	35.00
❑ 31	Gus Zernial	80.00	40.00
	Posed with seven baseballs		
❑ 31A	Gus Zernial Black	80.00	40.00
	Posed with seven baseballs		
❑ 32	Eddie Robinson	60.00	30.00
❑ 32A	Eddie Robinson Black	60.00	30.00
❑ 33	Warren Spahn	300.00	150.00
❑ 33A	Warren Spahn Black	300.00	150.00
❑ 34	Elmer Valo	60.00	30.00
❑ 34A	Elmer Valo Black	60.00	30.00
❑ 35	Hank Sauer	70.00	35.00
❑ 35A	Hank Sauer Black	70.00	35.00
❑ 36	Gil Hodges	300.00	150.00
❑ 36A	Gil Hodges Black	300.00	150.00
❑ 37	Duke Snider	500.00	250.00
❑ 37A	Duke Snider Black	500.00	250.00
❑ 38	Wally Westlake	60.00	30.00
❑ 38A	Wally Westlake Black	60.00	30.00
❑ 39	Dizzy Trout	70.00	35.00
❑ 39A	Dizzy Trout Black	70.00	35.00
❑ 40	Irv Noren	70.00	35.00
❑ 40A	Irv Noren Black	70.00	35.00
❑ 41	Bob Wellman	60.00	30.00
❑ 41A	Bob Wellman Black	60.00	30.00
❑ 42	Lou Kretlow	60.00	30.00
❑ 42A	Lou Kretlow Black	60.00	30.00
❑ 43	Ray Scarborough	60.00	30.00
❑ 43A	R. Scarbourough Black	60.00	30.00
❑ 44	Con Dempsey	60.00	30.00
❑ 44A	Con Dempsey Black	60.00	30.00
❑ 45	Eddie Joost	60.00	30.00
❑ 45A	Eddie Joost Black	60.00	30.00
❑ 46	Gordon Goldsberry	60.00	30.00
❑ 46A	G. Goldsberry Black	60.00	30.00
❑ 47	Willie Jones	70.00	35.00
❑ 47A	Willie Jones Black	70.00	35.00
❑ 48A	Joe Page ERR	400.00	200.00
	Bio for Sain		
	Black Back		
❑ 48B	Joe Page COR	125.00	60.00
	Black Back		
❑ 48C	Joe Page COR	125.00	60.00
	Red Back		
❑ 49A	John Sain ERR	400.00	200.00
	Bio for Page		
	Black Back		
❑ 49B	John Sain COR	125.00	60.00
	Black Back		
❑ 49C	John Sain COR	125.00	60.00
	Red Back		
❑ 50	Marv Rickert	60.00	30.00
❑ 50A	Marv Rickert Black	60.00	30.00
❑ 51	Jim Russell	60.00	30.00
❑ 51A	Jim Russell Black	60.00	30.00
❑ 52	Don Mueller	70.00	35.00
❑ 52A	Don Mueller Black	70.00	35.00
❑ 53	Chris Van Cuyk	60.00	30.00
❑ 53A	Chris Van Cuyk Black	60.00	30.00
❑ 54	Leo Kiely	60.00	30.00
❑ 54A	Leo Kiely Black	60.00	30.00
❑ 55	Ray Boone	80.00	40.00
❑ 55A	Ray Boone Black	80.00	40.00
❑ 56	Tommy Glaviano	60.00	30.00
❑ 56A	T. Glaviano Black	60.00	30.00
❑ 57	Ed Lopat	100.00	50.00
❑ 57A	Ed Lopat Black	100.00	50.00
❑ 58	Bob Mahoney	60.00	30.00
❑ 58A	Bob Mahoney Black	60.00	30.00
❑ 59	Robin Roberts	175.00	90.00

❑ 59A Robin Roberts Black .. 175.00 90.00
❑ 60 Sid Hudson 60.00 30.00
❑ 60A Sid Hudson Black 60.00 30.00
❑ 61 Tookie Gilbert 60.00 30.00
❑ 61A Tookie Gilbert Black 60.00 30.00
❑ 62 Chuck Stobbs 60.00 30.00
❑ 62A Chuck Stobbs Black 60.00 30.00
❑ 63 Howie Pollet 60.00 30.00
❑ 63A Howie Pollet Black 60.00 30.00
❑ 64 Roy Sievers 70.00 35.00
❑ 64A Roy Sievers Black 70.00 35.00
❑ 65 Enos Slaughter 175.00 90.00
❑ 65A Enos Slaughter Black 175.00 90.00
❑ 66 Preacher Roe 100.00 50.00
❑ 66A Preacher Roe Black 100.00 50.00
❑ 67 Allie Reynolds 125.00 60.00
❑ 67A Allie Reynolds Black .. 125.00 60.00
❑ 68 Cliff Chambers 60.00 30.00
❑ 68A Cliff Chambers Black .. 60.00 30.00
❑ 69 Virgil Stallcup 60.00 30.00
❑ 69A Virgil Stallcup Black 60.00 30.00
❑ 70 Al Zarilla 60.00 30.00
❑ 70A Al Zarilla Black 60.00 30.00
❑ 71 Tom Upton 60.00 30.00
❑ 71A Tom Upton Black 60.00 30.00
❑ 72 Karl Olson 60.00 30.00
❑ 72A Karl Olson Black 60.00 30.00
❑ 73 Bill Werle 60.00 30.00
❑ 73A Bill Werle Black 60.00 30.00
❑ 74 Andy Hansen 60.00 30.00
❑ 74A Andy Hansen Black 60.00 30.00
❑ 75 Wes Westrum 70.00 35.00
❑ 75A Wes Westrum Black 70.00 35.00
❑ 76 Eddie Stanky 70.00 35.00
❑ 76A Eddie Stanky Black 70.00 35.00
❑ 77 Bob Kennedy 70.00 35.00
❑ 77A Bob Kennedy Black 70.00 35.00
❑ 78 Ellis Kinder 60.00 30.00
❑ 78A Ellis Kinder Black 60.00 30.00
❑ 79 Gerry Staley 60.00 30.00
❑ 79A Gerry Staley Black 60.00 30.00
❑ 80 Herman Wehmeier 80.00 40.00
❑ 80A H. Wehmeier Black 80.00 40.00
❑ 81 Vernon Law 80.00 40.00
❑ 82 Duane Pillette 40.00 20.00
❑ 83 Billy Johnson 40.00 20.00
❑ 84 Vern Stephens 50.00 25.00
❑ 85 Bob Kuzava 50.00 25.00
❑ 86 Ted Gray 40.00 20.00
❑ 87 Dale Coogan 40.00 20.00
❑ 88 Bob Feller 250.00 125.00
❑ 89 Johnny Lipon 40.00 20.00
❑ 90 Mickey Grasso 40.00 20.00
❑ 91 Red Schoendienst 150.00 75.00
❑ 92 Dale Mitchell 50.00 25.00
❑ 93 Al Sima 40.00 20.00
❑ 94 Sam Mele 40.00 20.00
❑ 95 Ken Holcombe 40.00 20.00
❑ 96 Willard Marshall 40.00 20.00
❑ 97 Earl Torgeson 40.00 20.00
❑ 98 Billy Pierce 50.00 25.00
❑ 99 Gene Woodling 60.00 30.00
❑ 100 Del Rice 40.00 20.00
❑ 101 Max Lanier 40.00 20.00
❑ 102 Bill Kennedy 40.00 20.00
❑ 103 Cliff Mapes 40.00 20.00
❑ 104 Don Kolloway 40.00 20.00
❑ 105 Johnny Pramesa 40.00 20.00
❑ 106 Mickey Vernon 60.00 30.00
❑ 107 Connie Ryan 40.00 20.00
❑ 108 Jim Konstanty 60.00 30.00
❑ 109 Ted Wilks 40.00 20.00
❑ 110 Dutch Leonard 40.00 20.00
❑ 111 Peanuts Lowrey 40.00 20.00
❑ 112 Hank Majeski 40.00 20.00
❑ 113 Dick Sisler 50.00 25.00
❑ 114 Willard Ramsdell 40.00 20.00
❑ 115 George Munger 40.00 20.00
❑ 116 Carl Scheib 40.00 20.00
❑ 117 Sherm Lollar 50.00 25.00
❑ 118 Ken Raffensberger 40.00 20.00
❑ 119 Mickey McDermott 40.00 20.00
❑ 120 Bob Chakales 40.00 20.00
❑ 121 Gus Niarhos 40.00 20.00
❑ 122 Jackie Jensen 80.00 40.00
❑ 123 Eddie Yost 50.00 25.00
❑ 124 Monte Kennedy 40.00 20.00
❑ 125 Bill Rigney 40.00 20.00
❑ 126 Fred Hutchinson 50.00 25.00
❑ 127 Paul Minner 40.00 20.00
❑ 128 Don Bollweg 40.00 20.00
❑ 129 Johnny Mize 150.00 75.00
❑ 130 Sheldon Jones 40.00 20.00
❑ 131 Morrie Martin 40.00 20.00
❑ 131A Morrie Martin GB .00
❑ 132 Clyde Kluttz 40.00 20.00
❑ 132A Clyde Kluttz GB .00
❑ 133 Al Widmar 40.00 20.00
❑ 133A Al Widmar GB .00
❑ 134 Joe Tipton 40.00 20.00
❑ 134A Joe Tipton GB .00
❑ 135 Dixie Howell 40.00 20.00
❑ 135A Dixie Howell GB .00
❑ 136 Johnny Schmitz 40.00 20.00
❑ 136A Johnny Schmitz GB .00
❑ 137 Roy McMillan RC 50.00 25.00
❑ 137A Roy McMillan RC GB .00
❑ 138 Bill MacDonald 40.00 20.00
❑ 138A Bill MacDonald GB .00
❑ 139 Ken Wood 40.00 20.00
❑ 139A Ken Wood GB .00
❑ 140 Johnny Antonelli 60.00 30.00
❑ 140A Johnny Antonelli GB .00
❑ 141 Clint Hartung 40.00 20.00
❑ 141A Clint Hartung GB .00
❑ 142 Harry Perkowski 40.00 20.00
❑ 142A Harry Perkowski GB .00
❑ 143 Les Moss 40.00 20.00
❑ 143A Les Moss GB .00
❑ 144 Ed Blake 40.00 20.00
❑ 144A Ed Blake GB .00
❑ 145 Joe Haynes 40.00 20.00
❑ 145A Joe Haynes GB .00
❑ 146 Frank House 40.00 20.00
❑ 146A Frank House GB .00
❑ 147 Bob Young 40.00 20.00
❑ 147A Bob Young GB .00
❑ 148 Johnny Klippstein 40.00 20.00
❑ 148A Johnny Klippstein GB .00
❑ 149 Dick Kryhoski 40.00 20.00
❑ 149A Dick Kryhoski GB .00
❑ 150 Ted Beard 40.00 20.00
❑ 150A Ted Beard GB .00
❑ 151 Wally Post RC 50.00 25.00
❑ 151A Wally Post RC GB .00
❑ 152 Al Evans 40.00 20.00
❑ 152A Al Evans GB .00
❑ 153 Bob Rush 40.00 20.00
❑ 153A Bob Rush GB .00
❑ 154 Joe Muir 40.00 20.00
❑ 154A Joe Muir GB .00
❑ 155 Frank Overmire 40.00 20.00
❑ 155A Frank Overmire GB .00
❑ 156 Frank Hiller 40.00 20.00
❑ 156A Frank Hiller GB .00
❑ 157 Bob Usher 40.00 20.00
❑ 157A Bob Usher GB .00
❑ 158 Eddie Waitkus 40.00 20.00
❑ 158A Eddie Waitkus GB .00
❑ 159 Saul Rogovin 40.00 20.00
❑ 159A Saul Rogovin GB .00
❑ 160 Owen Friend 40.00 20.00
❑ 160A Owen Friend GB .00
❑ 161 Bud Byerly RC 40.00 20.00
❑ 161A Bud Byerly RC GB .00
❑ 162 Del Crandall 50.00 25.00
❑ 162A Del Crandall GB .00
❑ 163 Stan Rojek 40.00 20.00
❑ 163A Stan Rojek GB .00
❑ 164 Walt Dubiel 40.00 20.00
❑ 164A Walt Dubiel GB .00
❑ 165 Eddie Kazak 40.00 20.00
❑ 165A Eddie Kazak GB .00
❑ 166 Paul LaPalme 40.00 20.00
❑ 166A Paul LaPalme GB .00
❑ 167 Bill Howerton 40.00 20.00
❑ 167A Bill Howerton GB .00
❑ 168 Charlie Silvera RC 60.00 30.00
❑ 168A Charlie Silvera GB .00
❑ 169 Howie Judson 40.00 20.00
❑ 169A Howie Judson GB .00
❑ 170 Gus Bell 50.00 25.00
❑ 170A Gus Bell GB .00
❑ 171 Ed Erautt 40.00 20.00
❑ 171A Ed Erautt GB .00
❑ 172 Eddie Miksis 40.00 20.00
❑ 172A Eddie Miksis GB .00
❑ 173 Roy Smalley 40.00 20.00
❑ 173A Roy Smalley GB .00
❑ 174 Clarence Marshall 60.00 30.00
❑ 174A Clarence Marshall GB .00
❑ 175 Billy Martin RC 500.00 250.00
❑ 175A Billy Martin RC GB .00
❑ 176 Hank Edwards 40.00 20.00
❑ 176A Hank Edwards GB .00
❑ 177 Bill Wight 40.00 20.00
❑ 177A Bill Wight GB .00
❑ 178 Cass Michaels 40.00 20.00
❑ 178A Cass Michaels GB .00
❑ 179 Frank Smith 40.00 20.00
❑ 179A Frank Smith GB .00
❑ 180 Charlie Maxwell RC 50.00 25.00
❑ 180A Charlie Maxwell GB .00
❑ 181 Bob Swift 40.00 20.00
❑ 181A Bob Swift GB .00
❑ 182 Billy Hitchcock 40.00 20.00
❑ 182A Billy Hitchcock GB .00
❑ 183 Erv Dusak 40.00 20.00
❑ 183A Erv Dusak GB .00
❑ 184 Bob Ramazzotti 40.00 20.00
❑ 184A Bob Ramazzotti GB .00
❑ 185 Bill Nicholson 50.00 25.00
❑ 185A Bill Nicholson GB .00
❑ 186 Walt Masterson 40.00 20.00
❑ 186A Walt Masterson GB .00
❑ 187 Bob Miller 40.00 20.00
❑ 187A Bob Miller GB .00
❑ 188 Clarence Podbielan 40.00 20.00
❑ 188A Clarence Podbielan GB .. .00
❑ 189 Pete Reiser 60.00 30.00
❑ 189A Pete Reiser GB .00
❑ 190 Don Johnson 40.00 20.00
❑ 190A Don Johnson GB .00
❑ 191 Yogi Berra 800.00 400.00
❑ 192 Myron Ginsberg 40.00 20.00
❑ 193 Harry Simpson 50.00 25.00
❑ 194 Joe Hatton 40.00 20.00
❑ 195 Minnie Minoso RC 150.00 75.00
❑ 196 Solly Hemus RC 60.00 30.00
❑ 197 George Strickland 40.00 20.00
❑ 198 Phil Haugstad 40.00 20.00
❑ 199 George Zuverink 40.00 20.00
❑ 200 Ralph Houk RC 80.00 40.00
❑ 201 Alex Kellner 40.00 20.00
❑ 202 Joe Collins RC 60.00 30.00
❑ 203 Curt Simmons 60.00 30.00
❑ 204 Ron Northey 40.00 20.00
❑ 205 Clyde King 60.00 30.00
❑ 206 Joe Ostrowski 40.00 20.00
❑ 207 Mickey Harris 40.00 20.00
❑ 208 Marlin Stuart 40.00 20.00
❑ 209 Howie Fox 40.00 20.00
❑ 210 Dick Fowler 40.00 20.00
❑ 211 Ray Coleman 40.00 20.00
❑ 212 Ned Garver 40.00 20.00
❑ 213 Nippy Jones 40.00 20.00
❑ 214 Johnny Hopp 50.00 25.00
❑ 215 Hank Bauer 100.00 50.00
❑ 216 Richie Ashburn 250.00 125.00
❑ 217 Snuffy Stirnweiss 50.00 25.00
❑ 218 Clyde McCullough 40.00 20.00
❑ 219 Bobby Shantz 60.00 30.00
❑ 220 Joe Presko 40.00 20.00
❑ 221 Granny Hamner 40.00 20.00
❑ 222 Hoot Evers 40.00 20.00
❑ 223 Del Ennis 50.00 25.00
❑ 224 Bruce Edwards 40.00 20.00
❑ 225 Frank Baumholtz 40.00 20.00
❑ 226 Dave Philley 40.00 20.00
❑ 227 Joe Garagiola 80.00 40.00
❑ 228 Al Brazle 40.00 20.00
❑ 229 Gene Bearden UER 40.00 20.00
(Misspelled Beardon)
❑ 230 Matt Batts 40.00 20.00
❑ 231 Sam Zoldak 40.00 20.00
❑ 232 Billy Cox 50.00 25.00
❑ 233 Bob Friend RC 80.00 40.00
❑ 234 Steve Souchock 40.00 20.00

❑ 235 Walt Dropo 40.00 20.00
❑ 236 Ed Fitzgerald 40.00 20.00
❑ 237 Jerry Coleman 60.00 30.00
❑ 238 Art Houtteman 40.00 20.00
❑ 239 Rocky Bridges 50.00 25.00
❑ 240 Jack Phillips 40.00 20.00
❑ 241 Tommy Byrne 40.00 20.00
❑ 242 Tom Poholsky 40.00 20.00
❑ 243 Larry Doby 80.00 40.00
❑ 244 Vic Wertz 40.00 20.00
❑ 245 Sherry Robertson 40.00 20.00
❑ 246 George Kell 80.00 40.00
❑ 247 Randy Gumpert 40.00 20.00
❑ 248 Frank Shea 40.00 20.00
❑ 249 Bobby Adams 40.00 20.00
❑ 250 Carl Erskine 100.00 50.00
❑ 251 Chico Carrasquel 50.00 25.00
❑ 252 Vern Bickford 50.00 25.00
❑ 253 Johnny Berardino 100.00 50.00
❑ 254 Joe Dobson 50.00 25.00
❑ 255 Clyde Vollmer 50.00 25.00
❑ 256 Pete Suder 50.00 25.00
❑ 257 Bobby Avila 60.00 30.00
❑ 258 Steve Gromek 60.00 30.00
❑ 259 Bob Addis 50.00 25.00
❑ 260 Pete Castiglione 50.00 25.00
❑ 261 Willie Mays 3000.00 1500.00
❑ 262 Virgil Trucks 60.00 30.00
❑ 263 Harry Brecheen 60.00 30.00
❑ 264 Roy Hartsfield 50.00 25.00
❑ 265 Chuck Diering 50.00 25.00
❑ 266 Murry Dickson 50.00 25.00
❑ 267 Sid Gordon 60.00 30.00
❑ 268 Bob Lemon 150.00 75.00
❑ 269 Willard Nixon 50.00 25.00
❑ 270 Lou Brissie 50.00 25.00
❑ 271 Jim Delsing 60.00 30.00
❑ 272 Mike Garcia 80.00 40.00
❑ 273 Erv Palica 50.00 25.00
❑ 274 Ralph Branca 125.00 60.00
❑ 275 Pat Mullin 50.00 25.00
❑ 276 Jim Wilson RC 50.00 25.00
❑ 277 Early Wynn 175.00 90.00
❑ 278 Allie Clark 50.00 25.00
❑ 279 Eddie Stewart 50.00 25.00
❑ 280 Cloyd Boyer 80.00 40.00
❑ 281 Tommy Brown SP 80.00 40.00
❑ 282 Birdie Tebbetts SP 80.00 40.00
❑ 283 Phil Masi SP 60.00 30.00
❑ 284 Hank Arft SP 60.00 30.00
❑ 285 Cliff Fannin SP 60.00 30.00
❑ 286 Joe DeMaestri SP 60.00 30.00
❑ 287 Steve Bilko SP 60.00 30.00
❑ 288 Chet Nichols SP 80.00 40.00
❑ 289 Tommy Holmes SP 100.00 50.00
❑ 290 Joe Astroth SP 60.00 30.00
❑ 291 Gil Coan SP 60.00 30.00
❑ 292 Floyd Baker SP 60.00 30.00
❑ 293 Sibby Sisti SP 60.00 30.00
❑ 294 Walker Cooper SP 60.00 30.00
❑ 295 Phil Cavarretta SP 80.00 40.00
❑ 296 Red Rolfe MG SP 60.00 30.00
❑ 297 Andy Seminick SP 60.00 30.00
❑ 298 Bob Ross SP 60.00 30.00
❑ 299 Ray Murray SP 80.00 40.00
❑ 300 Barney McCosky SP 80.00 40.00
❑ 301 Bob Porterfield 50.00 25.00
❑ 302 Max Surkont 50.00 25.00
❑ 303 Harry Dorish 50.00 25.00
❑ 304 Sam Dente 50.00 25.00
❑ 305 Paul Richards MG 60.00 30.00
❑ 306 Lou Sleater 50.00 25.00
❑ 307 Frank Campos 50.00 25.00
❑ 307A Frank Campos .00
Black Star on Back
❑ 308 Luis Aloma 50.00 25.00
❑ 309 Jim Busby 60.00 30.00
❑ 310 George Metkovich 100.00 50.00
❑ 311 Mickey Mantle DP 20000.00 10000.00
❑ 312 Jackie Robinson DP 2000.00 1000.00
❑ 313 Bobby Thomson DP 350.00 180.00
❑ 314 Roy Campanella 2500.00 1250.00
❑ 315 Leo Durocher MG 600.00 300.00
❑ 316 Dave Williams RC 300.00 150.00
❑ 317 Conrado Marrero 300.00 150.00
❑ 318 Harold Gregg 300.00 150.00
❑ 319 Rube Walker 250.00 125.00
❑ 320 John Rutherford RC 300.00 150.00
❑ 321 Joe Black RC 350.00 180.00
❑ 322 Randy Jackson 300.00 150.00
❑ 323 Bubba Church 250.00 125.00
❑ 324 Warren Hacker 250.00 125.00
❑ 325 Bill Serena 300.00 150.00
❑ 326 George Shuba RC 400.00 200.00
❑ 327 Al Wilson 250.00 125.00
❑ 328 Bob Borkowski 300.00 150.00
❑ 329 Ike Delock 300.00 150.00
❑ 330 Turk Lown 300.00 150.00
❑ 331 Tom Morgan 300.00 150.00
❑ 332 Tony Bartirome 300.00 150.00
❑ 333 Pee Wee Reese 1800.00 900.00
❑ 334 Wilmer Mizell RC 300.00 150.00
❑ 335 Ted Lepcio 250.00 125.00
❑ 336 Dave Koslo 250.00 125.00
❑ 337 Jim Hearn 300.00 150.00
❑ 338 Sal Yvars 300.00 150.00
❑ 339 Russ Meyer 300.00 150.00
❑ 340 Bob Hooper 300.00 150.00
❑ 341 Hal Jeffcoat 300.00 150.00
❑ 342 Clem Labine RC 400.00 200.00
❑ 343 Dick Gernert 250.00 125.00
❑ 344 Ewell Blackwell 300.00 150.00
❑ 345 Sammy White 250.00 125.00
❑ 346 George Spencer 250.00 125.00
❑ 347 Joe Adcock 400.00 200.00
❑ 348 Robert Kelly 250.00 125.00
❑ 349 Bob Cain 300.00 150.00
❑ 350 Cal Abrams 300.00 150.00
❑ 351 Alvin Dark 300.00 150.00
❑ 352 Karl Drews 300.00 150.00
❑ 353 Bobby Del Greco 300.00 150.00
❑ 354 Fred Hatfield 300.00 150.00
❑ 355 Bobby Morgan 300.00 150.00
❑ 356 Toby Atwell 300.00 150.00
❑ 357 Smoky Burgess 300.00 150.00
❑ 358 John Kucab 300.00 150.00
❑ 359 Dee Fondy 250.00 125.00
❑ 360 George Crowe RC 300.00 150.00
❑ 361 William Posedel CO 250.00 125.00
❑ 362 Ken Heintzelman 300.00 150.00
❑ 363 Dick Rozek 300.00 150.00
❑ 364 Clyde Sukeforth CO 300.00 150.00
❑ 365 Cookie Lavagetto CO 400.00 200.00
❑ 366 Dave Madison 250.00 125.00
❑ 367 Ben Thorpe 300.00 150.00
❑ 368 Ed Wright 300.00 150.00
❑ 369 Dick Groat RC 400.00 200.00
❑ 370 Billy Hoeft RC 300.00 150.00
❑ 371 Bobby Hofman 250.00 125.00
❑ 372 Gil McDougald RC 500.00 250.00
❑ 373 Jim Turner CO RC 400.00 200.00
❑ 374 Al Benton 250.00 125.00
❑ 375 John Merson 250.00 125.00
❑ 376 Faye Throneberry 250.00 125.00
❑ 377 Chuck Dressen MG 400.00 200.00
❑ 378 Leroy Fusselman 300.00 150.00
❑ 379 Joe Rossi 250.00 125.00
❑ 380 Clem Koshorek 250.00 125.00
❑ 381 Milton Stock CO 300.00 150.00
❑ 382 Sam Jones RC 350.00 180.00
❑ 383 Del Wilber 250.00 125.00
❑ 384 Frank Crosetti CO 500.00 250.00
❑ 385 H.Franks CO RC 250.00 125.00
❑ 386 Ed Yuhas 300.00 150.00
❑ 387 Billy Meyer MG 250.00 125.00
❑ 388 Bob Chipman 250.00 125.00
❑ 389 Ben Wade 300.00 150.00
❑ 390 Rocky Nelson 300.00 150.00
❑ 391 B.Chapman UER CO 250.00 125.00
Photo actually
Sam Chapman
❑ 392 Hoyt Wilhelm RC 800.00 400.00
❑ 393 Ebba St.Claire 300.00 150.00
❑ 394 Billy Herman CO 600.00 300.00
❑ 395 Jake Pitler CO 300.00 150.00
❑ 396 Dick Williams RC 500.00 250.00
❑ 397 Forrest Main 250.00 125.00
❑ 398 Hal Rice 250.00 125.00
❑ 399 Jim Fridley 250.00 125.00
❑ 400 Bill Dickey CO 1000.00 500.00
❑ 401 Bob Schultz 300.00 150.00
❑ 402 Earl Harrist 300.00 150.00
❑ 403 Bill Miller 300.00 150.00
❑ 404 Dick Brodowski 300.00 150.00
❑ 405 Eddie Pellagrini 300.00 150.00
❑ 406 Joe Nuxhall RC 400.00 200.00
❑ 407 Eddie Mathews RC 10000.00 2500.00

1953 Topps

	NM	Ex
COMPLETE SET (274)	15000.00	7500.00
COMMON CARD (1-165)	30.00	15.00
COMMON (166-220)	25.00	12.50
COMMON DP (1-220)	15.00	7.50
COMMON (221-280)	100.00	50.00
NOT ISSUED (253/261/267)		
NOT ISSUED (268/271/275)		
WRAP.(1-CENT, DATED)	200.00	100.00
WRAP.(1-CENT,NO DATE)	300.00	150.00
WRAP.(5-CENT, DATED)	400.00	200.00
WRAP.(5-CENT,NO DATE)	350.00	180.00

❑ 1 Jackie Robinson DP 800.00 220.00
❑ 2 Luke Easter DP 20.00 10.00
❑ 3 George Crowe 40.00 20.00
❑ 4 Ben Wade 30.00 15.00
❑ 5 Joe Dobson 30.00 15.00
❑ 6 Sam Jones 40.00 20.00
❑ 7 Bob Borkowski DP 15.00 7.50
❑ 8 Clem Koshorek DP 15.00 7.50
❑ 9 Joe Collins 60.00 30.00
❑ 10 Smoky Burgess SP 80.00 40.00
❑ 11 Sal Yvars 30.00 15.00
❑ 12 Howie Judson DP 15.00 7.50
❑ 13 Conrado Marrero DP 15.00 7.50
❑ 14 Clem Labine DP 20.00 10.00
❑ 15 Bobo Newsom DP 20.00 10.00
❑ 16 Peanuts Lowrey DP 15.00 7.50
❑ 17 Billy Hitchcock 30.00 15.00
❑ 18 Ted Lepcio DP 15.00 7.50
❑ 19 Mel Parnell DP 20.00 10.00
❑ 20 Hank Thompson 40.00 20.00
❑ 21 Billy Johnson 30.00 15.00
❑ 22 Howie Fox 30.00 15.00
❑ 23 Toby Atwell DP 15.00 7.50
❑ 24 Ferris Fain 40.00 20.00
❑ 25 Ray Boone 40.00 20.00
❑ 26 Dale Mitchell DP 20.00 10.00
❑ 27 Roy Campanella DP 300.00 150.00
❑ 28 Eddie Pellagrini 30.00 15.00
❑ 29 Hal Jeffcoat 30.00 15.00
❑ 30 Willard Nixon 30.00 15.00
❑ 31 Ewell Blackwell 60.00 30.00
❑ 32 Clyde Vollmer 30.00 15.00
❑ 33 Bob Kennedy DP 15.00 7.50
❑ 34 George Shuba 40.00 20.00
❑ 35 Irv Noren DP 15.00 7.50
❑ 36 Johnny Groth DP 15.00 7.50
❑ 37 Eddie Mathews DP 250.00 125.00
❑ 38 Jim Hearn DP 15.00 7.50
❑ 39 Eddie Miksis 30.00 15.00
❑ 40 John Lipon 30.00 15.00
❑ 41 Enos Slaughter 80.00 40.00
❑ 42 Gus Zernial DP 20.00 10.00
❑ 43 Gil McDougald 60.00 30.00
❑ 44 Ellis Kinder SP 60.00 30.00
❑ 45 Grady Hatton DP 15.00 7.50
❑ 46 Johnny Klippstein DP 15.00 7.50
❑ 47 Bubba Church DP 15.00 7.50
❑ 48 Bob Del Greco DP 15.00 7.50

Card	NM	Ex
❑ 49 Faye Throneberry DP	15.00	7.50
❑ 50 Chuck Dressen MG DP	20.00	10.00
❑ 51 Frank Campos DP	15.00	7.50
❑ 52 Ted Gray DP	15.00	7.50
❑ 53 Sherm Lollar DP	20.00	10.00
❑ 54 Bob Feller DP	150.00	75.00
❑ 55 Maurice McDermott DP	15.00	7.50
❑ 56 Gerry Staley DP	15.00	7.50
❑ 57 Carl Scheib	30.00	15.00
❑ 58 George Metkovich	30.00	15.00
❑ 59 Karl Drews DP	15.00	7.50
❑ 60 Cloyd Boyer DP	15.00	7.50
❑ 61 Early Wynn SP	125.00	60.00
❑ 62 Monte Irvin DP	40.00	20.00
❑ 63 Gus Niarhos DP	15.00	7.50
❑ 64 Dave Philley	30.00	15.00
❑ 65 Earl Harrist	30.00	15.00
❑ 66 Minnie Minoso	60.00	30.00
❑ 67 Roy Sievers DP	20.00	10.00
❑ 68 Del Rice	30.00	15.00
❑ 69 Dick Brodowski	30.00	15.00
❑ 70 Ed Yuhas	30.00	15.00
❑ 71 Tony Bartirome	30.00	15.00
❑ 72 F.Hutchinson MG SP	60.00	30.00
❑ 73 Eddie Robinson	30.00	15.00
❑ 74 Joe Rossi	30.00	15.00
❑ 75 Mike Garcia	40.00	20.00
❑ 76 Pee Wee Reese	175.00	90.00
❑ 77 Johnny Mize DP	80.00	40.00
❑ 78 Red Schoendienst	80.00	40.00
❑ 79 Johnny Wyrostek	30.00	15.00
❑ 80 Jim Hegan	40.00	20.00
❑ 81 Joe Black SP	80.00	40.00
❑ 82 Mickey Mantle	3000.00	1500.00
❑ 83 Howie Pollet	30.00	15.00
❑ 84 Bob Hooper DP	15.00	7.50
❑ 85 Bobby Morgan DP	15.00	7.50
❑ 86 Billy Martin	125.00	60.00
❑ 87 Ed Lopat	60.00	30.00
❑ 88 Willie Jones DP	15.00	7.50
❑ 89 Chuck Stobbs DP	15.00	7.50
❑ 90 Hank Edwards DP	15.00	7.50
❑ 91 Ebba St.Claire DP	15.00	7.50
❑ 92 Paul Minner DP	15.00	7.50
❑ 93 Hal Rice DP	15.00	7.50
❑ 94 Bill Kennedy DP	15.00	7.50
❑ 95 Willard Marshall DP	15.00	7.50
❑ 96 Virgil Trucks	40.00	20.00
❑ 97 Don Kolloway DP	15.00	7.50
❑ 98 Cal Abrams DP	15.00	7.50
❑ 99 Dave Madison	30.00	15.00
❑ 100 Bill Miller	30.00	15.00
❑ 101 Ted Wilks	30.00	15.00
❑ 102 Connie Ryan DP	15.00	7.50
❑ 103 Joe Astroth DP	15.00	7.50
❑ 104 Yogi Berra	300.00	150.00
❑ 105 Joe Nuxhall DP	20.00	10.00
❑ 106 Johnny Antonelli	40.00	20.00
❑ 107 Danny O'Connell DP	15.00	7.50
❑ 108 Bob Porterfield DP	15.00	7.50
❑ 109 Alvin Dark	60.00	30.00
❑ 110 Herman Wehmeier DP	15.00	7.50
❑ 111 Hank Sauer DP	15.00	7.50
❑ 112 Ned Garver DP	15.00	7.50
❑ 113 Jerry Priddy	30.00	15.00
❑ 114 Phil Rizzuto	250.00	125.00
❑ 115 George Spencer	30.00	15.00
❑ 116 Frank Smith DP	15.00	7.50
❑ 117 Sid Gordon DP	15.00	7.50
❑ 118 Gus Bell DP	20.00	10.00
❑ 119 Johnny Sain SP	60.00	30.00
❑ 120 Davey Williams	40.00	20.00
❑ 121 Walt Dropo	40.00	20.00
❑ 122 Elmer Valo	30.00	15.00
❑ 123 Tommy Byrne DP	15.00	7.50
❑ 124 Sibby Sisti DP	15.00	7.50
❑ 125 Dick Williams DP	20.00	10.00
❑ 126 Bill Connelly DP	15.00	7.50
❑ 127 Clint Courtney DP	15.00	7.50
❑ 128 Wilmer Mizell DP (Inconsistent design, logo on front with black birds)	20.00	10.00
❑ 129 Keith Thomas	30.00	15.00
❑ 130 Turk Lown DP	15.00	7.50
❑ 131 Harry Byrd DP	15.00	7.50
❑ 132 Tom Morgan	30.00	15.00
❑ 133 Gil Coan	30.00	15.00
❑ 134 Rube Walker	40.00	20.00
❑ 135 Al Rosen DP	20.00	10.00
❑ 136 Ken Heintzelman DP	15.00	7.50
❑ 137 John Rutherford DP	15.00	7.50
❑ 138 George Kell	80.00	40.00
❑ 139 Sammy White	30.00	15.00
❑ 140 Tommy Glaviano	30.00	15.00
❑ 141 Allie Reynolds DP	15.00	7.50
❑ 142 Vic Wertz	40.00	20.00
❑ 143 Billy Pierce	60.00	30.00
❑ 144 Bob Schultz DP	15.00	7.50
❑ 145 Harry Dorish DP	15.00	7.50
❑ 146 Granny Hamner	30.00	15.00
❑ 147 Warren Spahn	175.00	90.00
❑ 148 Mickey Grasso	30.00	15.00
❑ 149 Dom DiMaggio DP	15.00	7.50
❑ 150 Harry Simpson DP	15.00	7.50
❑ 151 Hoyt Wilhelm	100.00	50.00
❑ 152 Bob Adams DP	15.00	7.50
❑ 153 Andy Seminick DP	15.00	7.50
❑ 154 Dick Groat	40.00	20.00
❑ 155 Dutch Leonard	30.00	15.00
❑ 156 Jim Rivera DP	20.00	10.00
❑ 157 Bob Addis DP	15.00	7.50
❑ 158 Johnny Logan RC	40.00	20.00
❑ 159 Wayne Terwilliger DP	15.00	7.50
❑ 160 Bob Young	30.00	15.00
❑ 161 Vern Bickford DP	15.00	7.50
❑ 162 Ted Kluszewski	60.00	30.00
❑ 163 Fred Hatfield DP	15.00	7.50
❑ 164 Frank Shea DP	15.00	7.50
❑ 165 Billy Hoeft	30.00	15.00
❑ 166 Billy Hunter	25.00	12.50
❑ 167 Art Schult	25.00	12.50
❑ 168 Willard Schmidt	25.00	12.50
❑ 169 Dizzy Trout	30.00	15.00
❑ 170 Bill Werle	25.00	12.50
❑ 171 Bill Glynn	25.00	12.50
❑ 172 Rip Repulski	25.00	12.50
❑ 173 Preston Ward	25.00	12.50
❑ 174 Billy Loes	30.00	15.00
❑ 175 Ron Kline	25.00	12.50
❑ 176 Don Hoak RC	40.00	20.00
❑ 177 Jim Dyck	25.00	12.50
❑ 178 Jim Waugh	25.00	12.50
❑ 179 Gene Hermanski	25.00	12.50
❑ 180 Virgil Stallcup	25.00	12.50
❑ 181 Al Zarilla	25.00	12.50
❑ 182 Bobby Hofman	25.00	12.50
❑ 183 Stu Miller RC	40.00	20.00
❑ 184 Hal Brown	25.00	12.50
❑ 185 Jim Pendleton	25.00	12.50
❑ 186 Charlie Bishop	25.00	12.50
❑ 187 Jim Fridley	25.00	12.50
❑ 188 Andy Carey RC	40.00	20.00
❑ 189 Ray Jablonski	25.00	12.50
❑ 190 Dixie Walker CO	30.00	15.00
❑ 191 Ralph Kiner	80.00	40.00
❑ 192 Wally Westlake	25.00	12.50
❑ 193 Mike Clark	25.00	12.50
❑ 194 Eddie Kazak	25.00	12.50
❑ 195 Ed McGhee	25.00	12.50
❑ 196 Bob Keegan	25.00	12.50
❑ 197 Del Crandall	40.00	20.00
❑ 198 Forrest Main	25.00	12.50
❑ 199 Marion Fricano	25.00	12.50
❑ 200 Gordon Goldsberry	25.00	12.50
❑ 201 Paul LaPalme	25.00	12.50
❑ 202 Carl Sawatski	25.00	12.50
❑ 203 Cliff Fannin	25.00	12.50
❑ 204 Dick Bokelman	25.00	12.50
❑ 205 Vern Benson	25.00	12.50
❑ 206 Ed Bailey RC	30.00	15.00
❑ 207 Whitey Ford	300.00	150.00
❑ 208 Jim Wilson	25.00	12.50
❑ 209 Jim Greengrass	25.00	12.50
❑ 210 Bob Cerv RC	40.00	20.00
❑ 211 J.W. Porter	25.00	12.50
❑ 212 Jack Dittmer	25.00	12.50
❑ 213 Ray Scarborough	25.00	12.50
❑ 214 Bill Bruton RC	40.00	20.00
❑ 215 Gene Conley RC	30.00	15.00
❑ 216 Jim Hughes	25.00	12.50
❑ 217 Murray Wall	25.00	12.50
❑ 218 Les Fusselman	25.00	12.50
❑ 219 Pete Runnels UER (Photo actually Don Johnson)	30.00	15.00
❑ 220 Satchel Paige UER (Misspelled Satchell on card front)	600.00	300.00
❑ 221 Bob Milliken	100.00	50.00
❑ 222 Vic Janowicz DP RC	50.00	25.00
❑ 223 Johnny O'Brien DP	50.00	25.00
❑ 224 Lou Sleater DP	50.00	25.00
❑ 225 Bobby Shantz	125.00	60.00
❑ 226 Ed Erautt	100.00	50.00
❑ 227 Morrie Martin	100.00	50.00
❑ 228 Hal Newhouser	150.00	75.00
❑ 229 Rocky Krsnich	100.00	50.00
❑ 230 Johnny Lindell DP	50.00	25.00
❑ 231 Solly Hemus DP	50.00	25.00
❑ 232 Dick Kokos	100.00	50.00
❑ 233 Al Aber	100.00	50.00
❑ 234 Ray Murray DP	50.00	25.00
❑ 235 John Hetki DP	50.00	25.00
❑ 236 Harry Perkowski DP	50.00	25.00
❑ 237 Bud Podbielan DP	50.00	25.00
❑ 238 Cal Hogue DP	50.00	25.00
❑ 239 Jim Delsing	100.00	50.00
❑ 240 Fred Marsh	100.00	50.00
❑ 241 Al Sima DP	50.00	25.00
❑ 242 Charlie Silvera	125.00	60.00
❑ 243 Carlos Bernier DP	50.00	25.00
❑ 244 Willie Mays	2500.00	1250.00
❑ 245 Bill Norman CO	100.00	50.00
❑ 246 Roy Face DP RC	80.00	40.00
❑ 247 Mike Sandlock DP	50.00	25.00
❑ 248 Gene Stephens DP	50.00	25.00
❑ 249 Eddie O'Brien	100.00	50.00
❑ 250 Bob Wilson	100.00	50.00
❑ 251 Sid Hudson	100.00	50.00
❑ 252 Hank Foiles	100.00	50.00
❑ 253 Does not exist	.00	
❑ 254 Preacher Roe DP	80.00	40.00
❑ 255 Dixie Howell	100.00	50.00
❑ 256 Les Peden	100.00	50.00
❑ 257 Bob Boyd	100.00	50.00
❑ 258 Jim Gilliam RC	400.00	200.00
❑ 259 Roy McMillan DP	50.00	25.00
❑ 260 Sam Calderone	100.00	50.00
❑ 261 Does not exist	.00	
❑ 262 Bob Oldis	100.00	50.00
❑ 263 Johnny Podres RC	300.00	150.00
❑ 264 Gene Woodling DP	60.00	30.00
❑ 265 Jackie Jensen	125.00	60.00
❑ 266 Bob Cain	100.00	50.00
❑ 267 Does not exist	.00	
❑ 268 Does not exist	.00	
❑ 269 Duane Pillette	100.00	50.00
❑ 270 Vern Stephens	125.00	60.00
❑ 271 Does not exist	.00	
❑ 272 Bill Antonello	100.00	50.00
❑ 273 Harvey Haddix RC	150.00	75.00
❑ 274 John Riddle CO	100.00	50.00
❑ 275 Does not exist	.00	
❑ 276 Ken Raffensberger	100.00	50.00
❑ 277 Don Lund	100.00	50.00
❑ 278 Willie Miranda	100.00	50.00
❑ 279 Joe Coleman DP	50.00	25.00
❑ 280 Milt Bolling RC	350.00	57.50

1954 Topps

	NM	Ex
COMPLETE SET (250)	8000.00	4000.00
COMMON (1-50/76-250)	15.00	7.50
COMMON CARD (51-75)	25.00	12.50
WRAP.(1-CENT, DATED)	200.00	100.00
WRAP.(1-CENT, UNDAT)	150.00	75.00
WRAP.(5-CENT, DATED)	300.00	150.00
WRAP.(5-CENT, UNDAT)	250.00	125.00

Card	NM	Ex
❑ 1 Ted Williams	800.00	275.00
❑ 2 Gus Zernial	25.00	12.50
❑ 3 Monte Irvin	50.00	25.00
❑ 4 Hank Sauer	25.00	12.50
❑ 5 Ed Lopat	25.00	12.50
❑ 6 Pete Runnels	25.00	12.50
❑ 7 Ted Kluszewski	50.00	25.00

7A	Ted Kluszewski GB	.00	
8	Bob Young	15.00	7.50
9	Harvey Haddix	25.00	12.50
10	Jackie Robinson	400.00	200.00
11	Paul Leslie Smith	15.00	7.50
12	Del Crandall	25.00	12.50
13	Billy Martin	100.00	50.00
14	Preacher Roe UER	25.00	12.50
	February is misspelled		
15	Al Rosen	25.00	12.50
16	Vic Janowicz	25.00	12.50
17	Phil Rizzuto	125.00	60.00
18	Walt Dropo	25.00	12.50
19	Johnny Lipon	15.00	7.50
	Orioles Team Name on Front		
	White Sox team on Back		
	Wearing a Red Sox cap		
20	Warren Spahn	125.00	60.00
21	Bobby Shantz	25.00	12.50
22	Jim Greengrass	15.00	7.50
23	Luke Easter	25.00	12.50
24	Granny Hamner	15.00	7.50
25	Harvey Kuenn RC	40.00	20.00
26	Ray Jablonski	15.00	7.50
27	Ferris Fain	25.00	12.50
28	Paul Minner	15.00	7.50
29	Jim Hegan	25.00	12.50
30	Eddie Mathews	100.00	50.00
31	Johnny Klippstein	15.00	7.50
32	Duke Snider	200.00	100.00
33	Johnny Schmitz	15.00	7.50
34	Jim Rivera	15.00	7.50
35	Jim Gilliam	50.00	25.00
36	Hoyt Wilhelm	50.00	25.00
37	Whitey Ford	200.00	100.00
38	Eddie Stanky MG	25.00	12.50
39	Sherm Lollar	25.00	12.50
40	Mel Parnell	25.00	12.50
41	Willie Jones	15.00	7.50
42	Don Mueller	25.00	12.50
43	Dick Groat	25.00	12.50
44	Ned Garver	15.00	7.50
45	Richie Ashburn	80.00	40.00
46	Ken Raffensberger	15.00	7.50
47	Ellis Kinder	15.00	7.50
48	Billy Hunter	25.00	12.50
49	Ray Murray	15.00	7.50
50	Yogi Berra	250.00	125.00
51	Johnny Lindell	25.00	12.50
52	Vic Power RC	30.00	15.00
53	Jack Dittmer	25.00	12.50
54	Vern Stephens	30.00	15.00
55	Phil Cavarretta MG	30.00	15.00
56	Willie Miranda	25.00	12.50
57	Luis Aloma	25.00	12.50
58	Bob Wilson	25.00	12.50
59	Gene Conley	30.00	15.00
60	Frank Baumholtz	25.00	12.50
61	Bob Cain	25.00	12.50
62	Eddie Robinson	25.00	12.50
63	Johnny Pesky	30.00	15.00
64	Hank Thompson	25.00	12.50
65	Bob Swift CO	25.00	12.50
66	Ted Lepcio	25.00	12.50
67	Jim Willis	25.00	12.50
68	Sam Calderone	25.00	12.50
69	Bud Podbielan	25.00	12.50
70	Larry Doby	60.00	30.00
71	Frank Smith	25.00	12.50
72	Preston Ward	25.00	12.50
73	Wayne Terwilliger	25.00	12.50
74	Bill Taylor	25.00	12.50
75	Fred Haney MG	25.00	12.50
76	Bob Scheffing CO	15.00	7.50
77	Ray Boone	25.00	12.50
78	Ted Kazanski	15.00	7.50
79	Andy Pafko	25.00	12.50
80	Jackie Jensen	25.00	12.50
81	Dave Hoskins	15.00	7.50
82	Milt Bolling	15.00	7.50
83	Joe Collins	25.00	12.50
84	Dick Cole	15.00	7.50
85	Bob Turley RC	40.00	20.00
86	Billy Herman CO	25.00	12.50
87	Roy Face	25.00	12.50
88	Matt Batts	15.00	7.50
89	Howie Pollet	15.00	7.50
90	Willie Mays	800.00	400.00
91	Bob Oldis	15.00	7.50
92	Wally Westlake	15.00	7.50
93	Sid Hudson	15.00	7.50
94	Ernie Banks RC	1200.00	600.00
95	Hal Rice	15.00	7.50
96	Charlie Silvera	25.00	12.50
97	Jerald Hal Lane	15.00	7.50
98	Joe Black	40.00	20.00
99	Bobby Hofman	15.00	7.50
100	Bob Keegan	15.00	7.50
101	Gene Woodling	25.00	12.50
102	Gil Hodges	80.00	40.00
103	Jim Lemon RC	15.00	7.50
104	Mike Sandlock	15.00	7.50
105	Andy Carey	25.00	12.50
106	Dick Kokos	15.00	7.50
107	Duane Pillette	15.00	7.50
108	Thornton Kipper	15.00	7.50
109	Bill Bruton	25.00	12.50
110	Harry Dorish	15.00	7.50
111	Jim Delsing	15.00	7.50
112	Bill Renna	15.00	7.50
113	Bob Boyd	15.00	7.50
114	Dean Stone	15.00	7.50
115	Rip Repulski	15.00	7.50
116	Steve Bilko	15.00	7.50
117	Solly Hemus	15.00	7.50
118	Carl Scheib	15.00	7.50
119	Johnny Antonelli	25.00	12.50
120	Roy McMillan	25.00	12.50
121	Clem Labine	25.00	12.50
122	Johnny Logan	25.00	12.50
123	Bobby Adams	15.00	7.50
124	Marion Fricano	15.00	7.50
125	Harry Perkowski	15.00	7.50
126	Ben Wade	15.00	7.50
127	Steve O'Neill MG	15.00	7.50
128	Hank Aaron RC	1800.00	900.00
129	Forrest Jacobs	15.00	7.50
130	Hank Bauer	25.00	12.50
131	Reno Bertoia	25.00	12.50
132	Tommy Lasorda RC	250.00	125.00
133	Del Baker CO	15.00	7.50
134	Cal Hogue	15.00	7.50
135	Joe Presko	15.00	7.50
136	Connie Ryan	15.00	7.50
137	Wally Moon RC	40.00	20.00
138	Bob Borkowski	15.00	7.50
139	The O'Briens	50.00	25.00
	Johnny O'Brien		
	Eddie O'Brien		
140	Tom Wright	15.00	7.50
141	Joey Jay RC	25.00	12.50
142	Tom Poholsky	15.00	7.50
143	Rollie Hemsley CO	15.00	7.50
144	Bill Werle	15.00	7.50
145	Elmer Valo	15.00	7.50
146	Don Johnson	15.00	7.50
147	Johnny Riddle CO	15.00	7.50
148	Bob Trice	15.00	7.50
149	Al Robertson	15.00	7.50
150	Dick Kryhoski	15.00	7.50
151	Alex Grammas	15.00	7.50
152	Michael Blyzka	15.00	7.50
153	Al Walker	25.00	12.50
154	Mike Fornieles	15.00	7.50
155	Bob Kennedy	25.00	12.50
156	Joe Coleman	25.00	12.50
157	Don Lenhardt	25.00	12.50
158	Peanuts Lowrey	15.00	7.50
159	Dave Philley	15.00	7.50
160	Ralph Kress CO	15.00	7.50
161	John Hetki	15.00	7.50
162	Herman Wehmeier	15.00	7.50
163	Frank House	15.00	7.50
164	Stu Miller	25.00	12.50
165	Jim Pendleton	15.00	7.50
166	Johnny Podres	40.00	20.00
167	Don Lund	15.00	7.50
168	Morrie Martin	25.00	12.50
169	Jim Hughes	40.00	20.00
170	Dusty Rhodes RC	25.00	12.50
171	Leo Kiely	15.00	7.50
172	Harold Brown	15.00	7.50
173	Jack Harshman	15.00	7.50
174	Tom Qualters	15.00	7.50
175	Frank Leja RC	25.00	12.50
176	Robert Keely CO	15.00	7.50
177	Bob Milliken	15.00	7.50
178	Bill Glynn UER	15.00	7.50
	Spelled Gylnn on the front		
179	Gair Allie	15.00	7.50
180	Wes Westrum	25.00	12.50
181	Mel Roach	15.00	7.50
182	Chuck Harmon	15.00	7.50
183	Earle Combs CO	25.00	12.50
184	Ed Bailey	15.00	7.50
185	Chuck Stobbs	15.00	7.50
186	Karl Olson	15.00	7.50
187	Heinie Manush CO	25.00	12.50
188	Dave Jolly	15.00	7.50
189	Bob Ross	15.00	7.50
190	Ray Herbert	15.00	7.50
191	John(Dick) Schofield RC	25.00	12.50
192	Ellis Deal CO	15.00	7.50
193	Johnny Hopp CO	25.00	12.50
194	Bill Sarni	15.00	7.50
195	Billy Consolo RC	15.00	7.50
196	Stan Jok	15.00	7.50
197	Lynwood Rowe CO	25.00	12.50
	("Schoolboy")		
198	Carl Sawatski	15.00	7.50
199	Glenn(Rocky) Nelson	15.00	7.50
200	Larry Jansen	25.00	12.50
201	Al Kaline RC	700.00	350.00
202	Bob Purkey RC	25.00	12.50
203	Harry Brecheen CO	25.00	12.50
204	Angel Scull	15.00	7.50
205	Johnny Sain	40.00	20.00
206	Ray Crone	15.00	7.50
207	Tom Oliver CO	15.00	7.50
208	Grady Hatton	15.00	7.50
209	Chuck Thompson	15.00	7.50
210	Bob Buhl RC	25.00	12.50
211	Don Hoak	25.00	12.50
212	Bob Micelotta	15.00	7.50
213	Johnny Fitzpatrick CO	15.00	7.50
214	Arnie Portocarrero	15.00	7.50
215	Ed McGhee	25.00	12.50
216	Al Sima	15.00	7.50
217	Paul Schreiber CO	15.00	7.50
218	Fred Marsh	15.00	7.50
219	Chuck Kress	15.00	7.50
220	Ruben Gomez	25.00	12.50
221	Dick Brodowski	15.00	7.50
222	Bill Wilson	15.00	7.50
223	Joe Haynes CO	15.00	7.50
224	Dick Weik	15.00	7.50
225	Don Liddle	15.00	7.50
226	Jehosie Heard	25.00	12.50
227	Buster Mills CO	15.00	7.50
228	Gene Hermanski	15.00	7.50
229	Bob Talbot	15.00	7.50
230	Bob Kuzava	25.00	12.50
231	Roy Smalley	15.00	7.50
232	Lou Limmer	15.00	7.50
233	Augie Galan CO	15.00	7.50
234	Jerry Lynch RC	15.00	7.50
235	Vern Law	25.00	12.50
236	Paul Penson	15.00	7.50
237	Mike Ryba CO	15.00	7.50

❑ 238 Al Aber	15.00	7.50
❑ 239 Bill Skowron RC	100.00	50.00
❑ 240 Sam Mele	25.00	12.50
❑ 241 Robert Miller	15.00	7.50
❑ 242 Curt Roberts	15.00	7.50
❑ 243 Ray Blades CO	15.00	7.50
❑ 244 Leroy Wheat	15.00	7.50
❑ 245 Roy Sievers	25.00	12.50
❑ 246 Howie Fox	15.00	7.50
❑ 247 Ed Mayo CO	15.00	7.50
❑ 248 Al Smith RC	25.00	12.50
❑ 249 Wilmer Mizell	25.00	12.50
❑ 250 Ted Williams	800.00	325.00

1955 Topps

	NM	Ex
COMPLETE SET (206)	8000.00	4000.00
COMMON CARD (1-150)	12.00	6.00
COMMON (151-160)	20.00	10.00
COMMON (161-210)	30.00	15.00
NOT ISSUED (175/186/203/209)		.00
WRAP.(1-CENT, DATED)	150.00	75.00
WRAP.(1-CENT, UNDAT)	50.00	25.00
WRAP.(5-CENT, DATED)	150.00	75.00
WRAP.(5-CENT, UNDAT)	100.00	50.00
❑ 1 Dusty Rhodes	125.00	25.00
❑ 2 Ted Williams	600.00	300.00
❑ 3 Art Fowler	15.00	7.50
❑ 4 Al Kaline	150.00	75.00
❑ 5 Jim Gilliam	40.00	20.00
❑ 6 Stan Hack MG	25.00	12.50
❑ 7 Jim Hegan	15.00	7.50
❑ 8 Harold Smith	12.00	6.00
❑ 9 Robert Miller	12.00	6.00
❑ 10 Bob Keegan	12.00	6.00
❑ 11 Ferris Fain	15.00	7.50
❑ 12 Vernon(Jake) Thies	12.00	6.00
❑ 13 Fred Marsh	12.00	6.00
❑ 14 Jim Finigan	12.00	6.00
❑ 15 Jim Pendleton	12.00	6.00
❑ 16 Roy Sievers	15.00	7.50
❑ 17 Bobby Hofman	12.00	6.00
❑ 18 Russ Kemmerer	12.00	6.00
❑ 19 Billy Herman CO	15.00	7.50
❑ 20 Andy Carey	15.00	7.50
❑ 21 Alex Grammas	12.00	6.00
❑ 22 Bill Skowron	40.00	20.00
❑ 23 Jack Parks	12.00	6.00
❑ 24 Hal Newhouser	40.00	20.00
❑ 25 Johnny Podres	25.00	12.50
❑ 26 Dick Groat	15.00	7.50
❑ 27 Billy Gardner RC	15.00	7.50
❑ 28 Ernie Banks	200.00	100.00
❑ 29 Herman Wehmeier	12.00	6.00
❑ 30 Vic Power	15.00	7.50
❑ 31 Warren Spahn	100.00	50.00
❑ 32 Warren McGhee	12.00	6.00
❑ 33 Tom Qualters	12.00	6.00
❑ 34 Wayne Terwilliger	12.00	6.00
❑ 35 Dave Jolly	12.00	6.00
❑ 36 Leo Kiely	12.00	6.00
❑ 37 Joe Cunningham RC	15.00	7.50
❑ 38 Bob Turley	15.00	7.50
❑ 39 Bill Glynn	12.00	6.00
❑ 40 Don Hoak	15.00	7.50
❑ 41 Chuck Stobbs	12.00	6.00
❑ 42 John(Windy) McCall	12.00	6.00

❑ 43 Harvey Haddix	15.00	7.50
❑ 44 Harold Valentine	12.00	6.00
❑ 45 Hank Sauer	15.00	7.50
❑ 46 Ted Kazanski	12.00	6.00
❑ 47 Hank Aaron UER (Birth incorrectly listed as 2/10)	400.00	200.00
❑ 48 Bob Kennedy	15.00	7.50
❑ 49 J.W. Porter	12.00	6.00
❑ 50 Jackie Robinson	500.00	250.00
❑ 51 Jim Hughes	15.00	7.50
❑ 52 Bill Tremel	12.00	6.00
❑ 53 Bill Taylor	12.00	6.00
❑ 54 Lou Limmer	12.00	6.00
❑ 55 Rip Repulski	12.00	6.00
❑ 56 Ray Jablonski	12.00	6.00
❑ 57 Billy O'Dell	12.00	6.00
❑ 58 Jim Rivera	12.00	6.00
❑ 59 Gair Allie	12.00	6.00
❑ 60 Dean Stone	12.00	6.00
❑ 61 Forrest Jacobs	12.00	6.00
❑ 62 Thornton Kipper	12.00	6.00
❑ 63 Joe Collins	15.00	7.50
❑ 64 Gus Triandos RC	15.00	7.50
❑ 65 Ray Boone	15.00	7.50
❑ 66 Ron Jackson RC	12.00	6.00
❑ 67 Wally Moon	15.00	7.50
❑ 68 Jim Davis	12.00	6.00
❑ 69 Ed Bailey	15.00	7.50
❑ 70 Al Rosen	15.00	7.50
❑ 71 Ruben Gomez	12.00	6.00
❑ 72 Karl Olson	12.00	6.00
❑ 73 Jack Shepard	12.00	6.00
❑ 74 Bob Borkowski	12.00	6.00
❑ 75 Sandy Amoros RC	40.00	20.00
❑ 76 Howie Pollet	12.00	6.00
❑ 77 Arnie Portocarrero	12.00	6.00
❑ 78 Gordon Jones	12.00	6.00
❑ 79 Clyde(Danny) Schell	12.00	6.00
❑ 80 Bob Grim RC	15.00	7.50
❑ 81 Gene Conley	15.00	7.50
❑ 82 Chuck Harmon	12.00	6.00
❑ 83 Tom Brewer	12.00	6.00
❑ 84 Camilo Pascual RC	15.00	7.50
❑ 85 Don Mossi RC	25.00	12.50
❑ 86 Bill Wilson	12.00	6.00
❑ 87 Frank House	12.00	6.00
❑ 88 Bob Skinner RC	15.00	7.50
❑ 89 Joe Frazier	15.00	7.50
❑ 90 Karl Spooner RC	15.00	7.50
❑ 91 Milt Bolling	12.00	6.00
❑ 92 Don Zimmer RC	25.00	12.50
❑ 93 Steve Bilko	12.00	6.00
❑ 94 Reno Bertoia	12.00	6.00
❑ 95 Preston Ward	12.00	6.00
❑ 96 Chuck Bishop	12.00	6.00
❑ 97 Carlos Paula	12.00	6.00
❑ 98 John Riddle CO	12.00	6.00
❑ 99 Frank Leja	12.00	6.00
❑ 100 Monte Irvin	40.00	20.00
❑ 101 Johnny Gray	12.00	6.00
❑ 102 Wally Westlake	12.00	6.00
❑ 103 Chuck White	12.00	6.00
❑ 104 Jack Harshman	12.00	6.00
❑ 105 Chuck Diering	12.00	6.00
❑ 106 Frank Sullivan	12.00	6.00
❑ 107 Curt Roberts	12.00	6.00
❑ 108 Rube Walker	15.00	7.50
❑ 109 Ed Lopat	15.00	7.50
❑ 110 Gus Zernial	15.00	7.50
❑ 111 Bob Milliken	15.00	7.50
❑ 112 Nelson King	12.00	6.00
❑ 113 Harry Brecheen CO	15.00	7.50
❑ 114 Louis Ortiz	12.00	6.00
❑ 115 Ellis Kinder	12.00	6.00
❑ 116 Tom Hurd	12.00	6.00
❑ 117 Mel Roach	12.00	6.00
❑ 118 Bob Purkey	12.00	6.00
❑ 119 Bob Lennon	12.00	6.00
❑ 120 Ted Kluszewski	80.00	40.00
❑ 121 Bill Renna	12.00	6.00
❑ 122 Carl Sawatski	12.00	6.00
❑ 123 Sandy Koufax RC	1000.00	500.00
❑ 124 Harmon Killebrew RC	250.00	125.00
❑ 125 Ken Boyer RC	80.00	40.00
❑ 126 Dick Hall	12.00	6.00
❑ 127 Dale Long RC	15.00	7.50
❑ 128 Ted Lepcio	12.00	6.00
❑ 129 Elvin Tappe	15.00	7.50
❑ 130 Mayo Smith MG	12.00	6.00
❑ 131 Grady Hatton	12.00	6.00
❑ 132 Bob Trice	12.00	6.00
❑ 133 Dave Hoskins	12.00	6.00
❑ 134 Joey Jay	15.00	7.50
❑ 135 Johnny O'Brien	15.00	7.50
❑ 136 Veston(Bunky)Stewart	12.00	6.00
❑ 137 Harry Elliott	12.00	6.00
❑ 138 Ray Herbert	12.00	6.00
❑ 139 Steve Kraly	12.00	6.00
❑ 140 Mel Parnell	15.00	7.50
❑ 141 Tom Wright	12.00	6.00
❑ 142 Jerry Lynch	15.00	7.50
❑ 143 John(Dick) Schofield	15.00	7.50
❑ 144 John(Joe) Amalfitano RC	12.00	6.00
❑ 145 Elmer Valo	12.00	6.00
❑ 146 Dick Donovan RC	12.00	6.00
❑ 147 Hugh Pepper	12.00	6.00
❑ 148 Hector Brown	12.00	6.00
❑ 149 Ray Crone	12.00	6.00
❑ 150 Mike Higgins MG	12.00	6.00
❑ 151 Ralph Kress CO	20.00	10.00
❑ 152 Harry Agganis RC	100.00	50.00
❑ 153 Bud Podbielan	25.00	12.50
❑ 154 Willie Miranda	20.00	10.00
❑ 155 Eddie Mathews	200.00	100.00
❑ 156 Joe Black	50.00	25.00
❑ 157 Robert Miller	20.00	10.00
❑ 158 Tommy Carroll	25.00	12.50
❑ 159 Johnny Schmitz	20.00	10.00
❑ 160 Ray Narleski RC	20.00	10.00
❑ 161 Chuck Tanner RC	40.00	20.00
❑ 162 Joe Coleman	30.00	15.00
❑ 163 Faye Throneberry	30.00	15.00
❑ 164 Roberto Clemente RC	2000.00	1000.00
❑ 165 Don Johnson	30.00	15.00
❑ 166 Hank Bauer	80.00	40.00
❑ 167 Tom Casagrande	30.00	15.00
❑ 168 Duane Pillette	30.00	15.00
❑ 169 Bob Oldis	40.00	20.00
❑ 170 Jim Pearce DP	15.00	7.50
❑ 171 Dick Brodowski	30.00	15.00
❑ 172 Frank Baumholtz DP	15.00	7.50
❑ 173 Bob Kline	30.00	15.00
❑ 174 Rudy Minarcin	30.00	15.00
❑ 175 Does not exist	.00	
❑ 176 Norm Zauchin	30.00	15.00
❑ 177 Al Robertson	30.00	15.00
❑ 178 Bobby Adams	30.00	15.00
❑ 179 Jim Bolger	30.00	15.00
❑ 180 Clem Labine	60.00	30.00
❑ 181 Roy McMillan	40.00	20.00
❑ 182 Humberto Robinson	30.00	15.00
❑ 183 Anthony Jacobs	30.00	15.00
❑ 184 Harry Perkowski DP	15.00	7.50
❑ 185 Don Ferrarese	30.00	15.00
❑ 186 Does not exist	.00	
❑ 187 Gil Hodges	175.00	90.00
❑ 188 Charlie Silvera DP	15.00	7.50
❑ 189 Phil Rizzuto	175.00	90.00
❑ 190 Gene Woodling	40.00	20.00
❑ 191 Eddie Stanky MG	40.00	20.00
❑ 192 Jim Delsing	40.00	20.00
❑ 193 Johnny Sain	60.00	30.00
❑ 194 Willie Mays	600.00	300.00
❑ 195 Ed Roebuck RC	60.00	30.00
❑ 196 Gale Wade	30.00	15.00
❑ 197 Al Smith	60.00	30.00
❑ 198 Yogi Berra	300.00	150.00
❑ 199 Bert Hamric	40.00	20.00
❑ 200 Jackie Jensen	60.00	30.00
❑ 201 Sherman Lollar	40.00	20.00
❑ 202 Jim Owens	30.00	15.00
❑ 203 Does not exist	.00	
❑ 204 Frank Smith	30.00	15.00
❑ 205 Gene Freese RC	40.00	20.00
❑ 206 Pete Daley	30.00	15.00
❑ 207 Billy Consolo	30.00	15.00
❑ 208 Ray Moore	40.00	20.00
❑ 209 Does not exist	.00	
❑ 210 Duke Snider	600.00	180.00

1956 Topps

	NM	Ex
COMPLETE SET (340)	8000.00	4000.00
COMMON CARD (1-100)	10.00	5.00
COMMON (101-180)	12.00	6.00
COMMON (261-340)	12.00	6.00
COMMON (181-260)	15.00	7.50
WRAP.(1-CENT)	250.00	125.00
WRAP.(1-CENT, REPEAT)	100.00	50.00
WRAPPER (5-CENT)	200.00	100.00
❑ 1 Will Harridge PRES	125.00	35.00
❑ 2 W. Giles PRES RC DP	50.00	25.00
❑ 3 Elmer Valo	15.00	7.50
❑ 4 Carlos Paula	15.00	7.50
❑ 5 Ted Williams	500.00	250.00
❑ 6 Ray Boone	25.00	12.50
❑ 7 Ron Negray	10.00	5.00
❑ 8 Walter Alston MG RC	40.00	20.00
❑ 9 Ruben Gomez DP	10.00	5.00
❑ 10 Warren Spahn	120.00	60.00
❑ 11A Chicago Cubs (Centered)	30.00	15.00
❑ 11B Cubs Team (Dated 1955)	80.00	40.00
❑ 11C Cubs Team (Name at far left)	30.00	15.00
❑ 12 Andy Carey	15.00	7.50
❑ 13 Roy Face	15.00	7.50
❑ 14 Ken Boyer DP	15.00	7.50
❑ 15 Ernie Banks DP	100.00	50.00
❑ 16 Hector Lopez RC	15.00	7.50
❑ 17 Gene Conley	15.00	7.50
❑ 18 Dick Donovan	10.00	5.00
❑ 19 Chuck Diering DP	10.00	5.00
❑ 20 Al Kaline	125.00	60.00
❑ 21 Joe Collins DP	15.00	7.50
❑ 22 Jim Finigan	10.00	5.00
❑ 23 Fred Marsh	10.00	5.00
❑ 24 Dick Groat	15.00	7.50
❑ 25 Ted Kluszewski	80.00	40.00
❑ 25A Ted Kluszewski GB	.00	
❑ 26 Grady Hatton	10.00	5.00
❑ 27 Nelson Burbrink DP	10.00	5.00
❑ 28 Bobby Hofman	10.00	5.00
❑ 29 Jack Harshman	10.00	5.00
❑ 30 Jackie Robinson DP	250.00	125.00
❑ 31 Hank Aaron UER DP (Small photo actually Willie Mays)	350.00	180.00
❑ 32 Frank House	10.00	5.00
❑ 33 Roberto Clemente	400.00	200.00
❑ 34 Tom Brewer DP	10.00	5.00
❑ 35 Al Rosen	15.00	7.50
❑ 36 Rudy Minarcin	15.00	7.50
❑ 37 Alex Grammas	10.00	5.00
❑ 38 Bob Kennedy	15.00	7.50
❑ 39 Don Mossi	15.00	7.50
❑ 40 Bob Turley	15.00	7.50
❑ 41 Hank Sauer	15.00	7.50
❑ 42 Sandy Amoros	25.00	12.50
❑ 43 Ray Moore	10.00	5.00
❑ 44 Windy McCall	10.00	5.00
❑ 45 Gus Zernial	15.00	7.50
❑ 46 Gene Freese DP	10.00	5.00
❑ 47 Art Fowler	10.00	5.00
❑ 48 Jim Hegan	15.00	7.50
❑ 49 Pedro Ramos	10.00	5.00
❑ 50 Dusty Rhodes DP	15.00	7.50
❑ 51 Ernie Oravetz	10.00	5.00
❑ 52 Bob Grim DP	15.00	7.50
❑ 53 Arnie Portocarrero	10.00	5.00
❑ 54 Bob Keegan	10.00	5.00
❑ 55 Wally Moon	15.00	7.50
❑ 56 Dale Long	15.00	7.50
❑ 57 Duke Maas	10.00	5.00
❑ 58 Ed Roebuck	25.00	12.50
❑ 59 Jose Santiago	10.00	5.00
❑ 60 Mayo Smith MG DP	10.00	5.00
❑ 61 Bill Skowron	25.00	12.50
❑ 62 Hal Smith	15.00	7.50
❑ 63 Roger Craig RC	40.00	20.00
❑ 64 Luis Arroyo RC	10.00	5.00
❑ 65 Johnny O'Brien	15.00	7.50
❑ 66 Bob Speake DP	10.00	5.00
❑ 67 Vic Power	15.00	7.50
❑ 68 Chuck Stobbs	10.00	5.00
❑ 69 Chuck Tanner	15.00	7.50
❑ 70 Jim Rivera	10.00	5.00
❑ 71 Frank Sullivan	10.00	5.00
❑ 72A Phillies Team (Centered)	30.00	15.00
❑ 72B Phillies Team (Dated 1955)	80.00	40.00
❑ 72C Phillies Team DP (Name at far left)	30.00	15.00
❑ 73 Wayne Terwilliger	10.00	5.00
❑ 74 Jim King	10.00	5.00
❑ 75 Roy Sievers DP	15.00	7.50
❑ 76 Ray Crone	10.00	5.00
❑ 77 Harvey Haddix	15.00	7.50
❑ 78 Herman Wehmeier	10.00	5.00
❑ 79 Sandy Koufax	350.00	180.00
❑ 80 Gus Triandos DP	10.00	5.00
❑ 81 Wally Westlake	10.00	5.00
❑ 82 Bill Renna DP	10.00	5.00
❑ 83 Karl Spooner	15.00	7.50
❑ 84 Babe Birrer	10.00	5.00
❑ 85A Cleveland Indians (Centered)	30.00	15.00
❑ 85B Indians Team (Dated 1955)	80.00	40.00
❑ 85C Indians Team (Name at far left)	30.00	15.00
❑ 86 Ray Jablonski DP	10.00	5.00
❑ 87 Dean Stone	10.00	5.00
❑ 88 Johnny Kucks RC	15.00	7.50
❑ 89 Norm Zauchin	10.00	5.00
❑ 90A Cincinnati Redlegs Team (Centered)	30.00	15.00
❑ 90B Reds Team (Dated 1955)	80.00	40.00
❑ 90C Reds Team (Name at far left)	30.00	15.00
❑ 91 Gail Harris	10.00	5.00
❑ 92 Bob(Red) Wilson	10.00	5.00
❑ 93 George Susce	10.00	5.00
❑ 94 Ron Kline	10.00	5.00
❑ 95A Milwaukee Braves Team (Centered)	40.00	20.00
❑ 95B Braves Team (Dated 1955)	80.00	40.00
❑ 95C Braves Team (Name at far left)	40.00	20.00
❑ 96 Bill Tremel	10.00	5.00
❑ 97 Jerry Lynch	15.00	7.50
❑ 98 Camilo Pascual	15.00	7.50
❑ 99 Don Zimmer	25.00	12.50
❑ 100A Baltimore Orioles Team (centered)	40.00	20.00
❑ 100B Orioles Team (Dated 1955)	80.00	40.00
❑ 100C Orioles Team (Name at far left)	40.00	20.00
❑ 101 Roy Campanella	150.00	75.00
❑ 102 Jim Davis	12.00	6.00
❑ 103 Willie Miranda	12.00	6.00
❑ 104 Bob Lennon	12.00	6.00
❑ 105 Al Smith	12.00	6.00
❑ 106 Joe Astroth	12.00	6.00
❑ 107 Eddie Mathews	100.00	50.00
❑ 108 Laurin Pepper	12.00	6.00
❑ 109 Enos Slaughter	40.00	20.00
❑ 110 Yogi Berra	175.00	90.00
❑ 111 Boston Red Sox Team Card	40.00	20.00
❑ 112 Dee Fondy	12.00	6.00
❑ 113 Phil Rizzuto	150.00	75.00
❑ 114 Jim Owens	15.00	7.50
❑ 115 Jackie Jensen	15.00	7.50
❑ 116 Eddie O'Brien	12.00	6.00
❑ 117 Virgil Trucks	15.00	7.50
❑ 118 Nellie Fox	80.00	40.00
❑ 119 Larry Jackson RC	15.00	7.50
❑ 120 Richie Ashburn	60.00	30.00
❑ 121 Pittsburgh Pirates Team Card	40.00	20.00
❑ 122 Willard Nixon	12.00	6.00
❑ 123 Roy McMillan	15.00	7.50
❑ 124 Don Kaiser	12.00	6.00
❑ 125 Minnie Minoso	40.00	20.00
❑ 126 Jim Brady	12.00	6.00
❑ 127 Willie Jones	15.00	7.50
❑ 128 Eddie Yost	15.00	7.50
❑ 129 Jake Martin	12.00	6.00
❑ 130 Willie Mays	300.00	150.00
❑ 131 Bob Roselli	12.00	6.00
❑ 132 Bobby Avila	12.00	6.00
❑ 133 Ray Narleski	12.00	6.00
❑ 134 St. Louis Cardinals Team Card	40.00	20.00
❑ 135 Mickey Mantle	1500.00	750.00
❑ 136 Johnny Logan	15.00	7.50
❑ 137 Al Silvera	12.00	6.00
❑ 138 Johnny Antonelli	15.00	7.50
❑ 139 Tommy Carroll	15.00	7.50
❑ 140 Herb Score RC	60.00	30.00
❑ 141 Joe Frazier	12.00	6.00
❑ 142 Gene Baker	12.00	6.00
❑ 143 Jim Piersall	15.00	7.50
❑ 144 Leroy Powell	12.00	6.00
❑ 145 Gil Hodges	60.00	30.00
❑ 146 Washington Nationals Team Card	40.00	20.00
❑ 147 Earl Torgeson	12.00	6.00
❑ 148 Alvin Dark	15.00	7.50
❑ 149 Dixie Howell	12.00	6.00
❑ 150 Duke Snider	125.00	60.00
❑ 151 Spook Jacobs	15.00	7.50
❑ 152 Billy Hoeft	15.00	7.50
❑ 153 Frank Thomas	15.00	7.50
❑ 154 Dave Pope	12.00	6.00
❑ 155 Harvey Kuenn	15.00	7.50
❑ 156 Wes Westrum	15.00	7.50
❑ 157 Dick Brodowski	12.00	6.00
❑ 158 Wally Post	15.00	7.50
❑ 158A Wally Post WB	.00	
❑ 159 Clint Courtney	12.00	6.00
❑ 160 Billy Pierce	15.00	7.50
❑ 161 Joe DeMaestri	12.00	6.00
❑ 162 Dave(Gus) Bell	15.00	7.50
❑ 163 Gene Woodling	15.00	7.50
❑ 164 Harmon Killebrew	100.00	50.00
❑ 165 Red Schoendienst	40.00	20.00
❑ 166 Brooklyn Dodgers Team Card	200.00	100.00
❑ 167 Harry Dorish	12.00	6.00
❑ 168 Sammy White	12.00	6.00
❑ 169 Bob Nelson	12.00	6.00
❑ 170 Bill Virdon	15.00	7.50
❑ 171 Jim Wilson	12.00	6.00
❑ 172 Frank Torre RC	15.00	7.50
❑ 173 Johnny Podres	25.00	12.50
❑ 174 Glen Gorbous	12.00	6.00
❑ 175 Del Crandall	15.00	7.50
❑ 176 Alex Kellner	12.00	6.00
❑ 177 Hank Bauer	25.00	12.50
❑ 178 Joe Black	15.00	7.50
❑ 179 Harry Chiti	12.00	6.00
❑ 180 Robin Roberts	50.00	25.00
❑ 181 Billy Martin	125.00	60.00
❑ 182 Paul Minner	15.00	7.50
❑ 183 Stan Lopata	20.00	10.00
❑ 184 Don Bessent	20.00	10.00
❑ 185 Bill Bruton	20.00	10.00
❑ 186 Ron Jackson	15.00	7.50
❑ 187 Early Wynn	50.00	25.00
❑ 188 Chicago White Sox Team Card	50.00	25.00
❑ 189 Ned Garver	15.00	7.50

❑ 190 Carl Furillo 30.00 15.00
❑ 191 Frank Lary 20.00 10.00
❑ 192 Smoky Burgess 20.00 10.00
❑ 193 Wilmer Mizell 20.00 10.00
❑ 194 Monte Irvin 30.00 15.00
❑ 195 George Kell 30.00 15.00
❑ 196 Tom Poholsky 15.00 7.50
❑ 197 Granny Hamner 15.00 7.50
❑ 198 Ed Fitzgerald 15.00 7.50
❑ 199 Hank Thompson 20.00 10.00
❑ 200 Bob Feller 125.00 60.00
❑ 201 Rip Repulski 15.00 7.50
❑ 202 Jim Hearn 15.00 7.50
❑ 203 Bill Tuttle 15.00 7.50
❑ 204 Art Swanson 15.00 7.50
❑ 205 Whitey Lockman 20.00 10.00
❑ 206 Erv Palica 15.00 7.50
❑ 207 Jim Small 15.00 7.50
❑ 208 Elston Howard 60.00 30.00
❑ 209 Max Surkont 15.00 7.50
❑ 210 Mike Garcia 20.00 10.00
❑ 211 Murry Dickson 15.00 7.50
❑ 212 Johnny Temple 15.00 7.50
❑ 213 Detroit Tigers 60.00 30.00
Team Card
❑ 214 Bob Rush 15.00 7.50
❑ 215 Tommy Byrne 20.00 10.00
❑ 216 Jerry Schoonmaker 15.00 7.50
❑ 217 Billy Klaus 15.00 7.50
❑ 218 Joe Nuxhall UER 20.00 10.00
(Misspelled Nuxall)
❑ 219 Lew Burdette 20.00 10.00
❑ 220 Del Ennis 20.00 10.00
❑ 221 Bob Friend 20.00 10.00
❑ 222 Dave Philley 15.00 7.50
❑ 223 Randy Jackson 15.00 7.50
❑ 224 Bud Podbielan 15.00 7.50
❑ 225 Gil McDougald 50.00 25.00
❑ 226 New York Giants 80.00 40.00
Team Card
❑ 227 Russ Meyer 15.00 7.50
❑ 228 Mickey Vernon 20.00 10.00
❑ 229 Harry Brecheen CO 20.00 10.00
❑ 230 Chico Carrasquel 15.00 7.50
❑ 231 Bob Hale 15.00 7.50
❑ 232 Toby Atwell 15.00 7.50
❑ 233 Carl Erskine 30.00 15.00
❑ 234 Pete Runnels 15.00 7.50
❑ 235 Don Newcombe 50.00 25.00
❑ 236 Kansas City Athletics 40.00 20.00
Team Card
❑ 237 Jose Valdivielso 15.00 7.50
❑ 238 Walt Dropo 20.00 10.00
❑ 239 Harry Simpson 15.00 7.50
❑ 240 Whitey Ford 125.00 60.00
❑ 241 Don Mueller UER 20.00 10.00
6" tall
❑ 242 Hershell Freeman 15.00 7.50
❑ 243 Sherm Lollar 20.00 10.00
❑ 244 Bob Buhl 30.00 15.00
❑ 245 Billy Goodman 20.00 10.00
❑ 246 Tom Gorman 15.00 7.50
❑ 247 Bill Sarni 15.00 7.50
❑ 248 Bob Porterfield 15.00 7.50
❑ 249 Johnny Klippstein 15.00 7.50
❑ 250 Larry Doby 30.00 15.00
❑ 251 New York Yankees 250.00 125.00
Team Card UER
(Don Larsen misspelled
as Larson on front)
❑ 252 Vern Law 20.00 10.00
❑ 253 Irv Noren 30.00 15.00
❑ 254 George Crowe 15.00 7.50
❑ 255 Bob Lemon 50.00 25.00
❑ 256 Tom Hurd 15.00 7.50
❑ 257 Bobby Thomson 30.00 15.00
❑ 258 Art Ditmar 15.00 7.50
❑ 259 Sam Jones 20.00 10.00
❑ 260 Pee Wee Reese 150.00 75.00
❑ 261 Bobby Shantz 15.00 7.50
❑ 262 Howie Pollet 12.00 6.00
❑ 263 Bob Miller 12.00 6.00
❑ 264 Ray Monzant 12.00 6.00
❑ 265 Sandy Consuegra 12.00 6.00
❑ 266 Don Ferrarese 12.00 6.00
❑ 267 Bob Nieman 12.00 6.00
❑ 268 Dale Mitchell 15.00 7.50
❑ 269 Jack Meyer 12.00 6.00
❑ 270 Billy Loes 15.00 7.50
❑ 271 Foster Castleman 12.00 6.00
❑ 272 Danny O'Connell 12.00 6.00
❑ 273 Walker Cooper 12.00 6.00
❑ 274 Frank Baumholtz 12.00 6.00
❑ 275 Jim Greengrass 12.00 6.00
❑ 276 George Zuverink 12.00 6.00
❑ 277 Daryl Spencer 12.00 6.00
❑ 278 Chet Nichols 12.00 6.00
❑ 279 Johnny Groth 12.00 6.00
❑ 280 Jim Gilliam 40.00 20.00
❑ 281 Art Houtteman 12.00 6.00
❑ 282 Warren Hacker 12.00 6.00
❑ 283 Hal Smith RC 15.00 7.50
❑ 284 Ike Delock 12.00 6.00
❑ 285 Eddie Miksis 12.00 6.00
❑ 286 Bill Wight 12.00 6.00
❑ 287 Bobby Adams 12.00 6.00
❑ 288 Bob Cerv 40.00 20.00
❑ 289 Hal Jeffcoat 12.00 6.00
❑ 290 Curt Simmons 15.00 7.50
❑ 291 Frank Kellert 12.00 6.00
❑ 292 Luis Aparicio RC 150.00 75.00
❑ 293 Stu Miller 25.00 12.50
❑ 294 Ernie Johnson 15.00 7.50
❑ 295 Clem Labine 15.00 7.50
❑ 296 Andy Seminick 12.00 6.00
❑ 297 Bob Skinner 15.00 7.50
❑ 298 Johnny Schmitz 12.00 6.00
❑ 299 Charlie Neal 40.00 20.00
❑ 300 Vic Wertz 15.00 7.50
❑ 301 Marv Grissom 12.00 6.00
❑ 302 Eddie Robinson 12.00 6.00
❑ 303 Jim Dyck 12.00 6.00
❑ 304 Frank Malzone 15.00 7.50
❑ 305 Brooks Lawrence 12.00 6.00
❑ 306 Curt Roberts 12.00 6.00
❑ 307 Hoyt Wilhelm 40.00 20.00
❑ 308 Chuck Harmon 12.00 6.00
❑ 309 Don Blasingame RC 15.00 7.50
❑ 310 Steve Gromek 12.00 6.00
❑ 311 Hal Naragon 12.00 6.00
❑ 312 Andy Pafko 15.00 7.50
❑ 313 Gene Stephens 12.00 6.00
❑ 314 Hobie Landrith 12.00 6.00
❑ 315 Milt Bolling 12.00 6.00
❑ 316 Jerry Coleman 15.00 7.50
❑ 317 Al Aber 12.00 6.00
❑ 318 Fred Hatfield 12.00 6.00
❑ 319 Jack Crimian 12.00 6.00
❑ 320 Joe Adcock 15.00 7.50
❑ 321 Jim Konstanty 15.00 7.50
❑ 322 Karl Olson 12.00 6.00
❑ 323 Willard Schmidt 12.00 6.00
❑ 324 Rocky Bridges 15.00 7.50
❑ 325 Don Liddle 12.00 6.00
❑ 326 Connie Johnson 12.00 6.00
❑ 327 Bob Wiesler 12.00 6.00
❑ 328 Preston Ward 12.00 6.00
❑ 329 Lou Berberet 12.00 6.00
❑ 330 Jim Busby 15.00 7.50
❑ 331 Dick Hall 12.00 6.00
❑ 332 Don Larsen 60.00 30.00
❑ 333 Rube Walker 12.00 6.00
❑ 334 Bob Miller 15.00 7.50
❑ 335 Don Hoak 15.00 7.50
❑ 336 Ellis Kinder 12.00 6.00
❑ 337 Bobby Morgan 12.00 6.00
❑ 338 Jim Delsing 12.00 6.00
❑ 339 Rance Pless 12.00 6.00
❑ 340 Mickey McDermott 60.00 12.00
❑ NNO Checklist 1/3 .... 300.00 95.00
❑ NNO Checklist 2/4 .... 300.00 95.00

1957 Topps

	NM	Ex
COMPLETE SET (407)	10000.00	5000.00
COMMON CARD (1-88)	10.00	5.00
COMMON CARD (89-176)	8.00	4.00
COMMON (177-264)	8.00	4.00
COMMON (265-352)	20.00	10.00
COMMON (353-407)	8.00	4.00
COMMON DP (265-352)	12.00	6.00

WRAPPER (1-CENT) 300.00 150.00
WRAPPER (5-CENT) 200.00 100.00

❑ 1 Ted Williams 600.00 180.00
❑ 2 Yogi Berra 200.00 100.00
❑ 3 Dale Long 20.00 10.00
❑ 4 Johnny Logan 20.00 10.00
❑ 5 Sal Maglie 20.00 10.00
❑ 6 Hector Lopez 15.00 7.50
❑ 7 Luis Aparicio 30.00 15.00
❑ 8 Don Mossi 15.00 7.50
❑ 9 Johnny Temple 15.00 7.50
❑ 10 Willie Mays 400.00 200.00
❑ 11 George Zuverink 10.00 5.00
❑ 12 Dick Groat 20.00 10.00
❑ 13 Wally Burnette 10.00 5.00
❑ 14 Bob Nieman 10.00 5.00
❑ 15 Robin Roberts 30.00 15.00
❑ 16 Walt Moryn 10.00 5.00
❑ 17 Billy Gardner 10.00 5.00
❑ 18 Don Drysdale RC 250.00 125.00
❑ 19 Bob Wilson 10.00 5.00
❑ 20 Hank Aaron UER 300.00 150.00
(Reverse negative
photo on front)
❑ 21 Frank Sullivan 10.00 5.00
❑ 22 Jerry Snyder UER 10.00 5.00
Photo actually Ed Fitzgerald
❑ 23 Sherm Lollar 15.00 7.50
❑ 24 Bill Mazeroski RC 80.00 40.00
❑ 25 Whitey Ford 150.00 75.00
❑ 26 Bob Boyd 10.00 5.00
❑ 27 Ted Kazanski 10.00 5.00
❑ 28 Gene Conley 15.00 7.50
❑ 29 Whitey Herzog RC 30.00 15.00
❑ 30 Pee Wee Reese 80.00 40.00
❑ 31 Ron Northey 10.00 5.00
❑ 32 Hershell Freeman 10.00 5.00
❑ 33 Jim Small 10.00 5.00
❑ 34 Tom Sturdivant 15.00 7.50
❑ 35 Frank Robinson RC 300.00 150.00
❑ 36 Bob Grim 10.00 5.00
❑ 37 Frank Torre 15.00 7.50
❑ 38 Nellie Fox 50.00 25.00
❑ 39 Al Worthington 10.00 5.00
❑ 40 Early Wynn 30.00 15.00
❑ 41 Hal W. Smith 10.00 5.00
❑ 42 Dee Fondy 10.00 5.00
❑ 43 Connie Johnson 10.00 5.00
❑ 44 Joe DeMaestri 10.00 5.00
❑ 45 Carl Furillo 30.00 15.00
❑ 46 Robert J. Miller 10.00 5.00
❑ 47 Don Blasingame 10.00 5.00
❑ 48 Bill Bruton 15.00 7.50
❑ 49 Daryl Spencer 10.00 5.00
❑ 50 Herb Score 30.00 15.00
❑ 51 Clint Courtney 10.00 5.00
❑ 52 Lee Walls 10.00 5.00
❑ 53 Clem Labine 20.00 10.00
❑ 54 Elmer Valo 10.00 5.00
❑ 55 Ernie Banks 125.00 60.00
❑ 56 Dave Sisler 10.00 5.00
❑ 57 Jim Lemon 15.00 7.50
❑ 58 Ruben Gomez 10.00 5.00
❑ 59 Dick Williams 15.00 7.50
❑ 60 Billy Hoeft 15.00 7.50
❑ 61 Dusty Rhodes 15.00 7.50
❑ 62 Billy Martin 60.00 30.00
❑ 63 Ike Delock 10.00 5.00

❑ 64 Pete Runnels 15.00 7.50
❑ 65 Wally Moon 15.00 7.50
❑ 66 Brooks Lawrence 10.00 5.00
❑ 67 Chico Carrasquel 10.00 5.00
❑ 68 Ray Crone 10.00 5.00
❑ 69 Roy McMillan 15.00 7.50
❑ 70 Richie Ashburn 50.00 25.00
❑ 71 Murry Dickson 10.00 5.00
❑ 72 Bill Tuttle 10.00 5.00
❑ 73 George Crowe 10.00 5.00
❑ 74 Vito Valentinetti 10.00 5.00
❑ 75 Jimmy Piersall 15.00 7.50
❑ 76 Roberto Clemente 300.00 150.00
❑ 77 Paul Foytack 10.00 5.00
❑ 78 Vic Wertz 15.00 7.50
❑ 79 Lindy McDaniel RC 15.00 7.50
❑ 80 Gil Hodges 50.00 25.00
❑ 81 Herman Wehmeier 10.00 5.00
❑ 82 Elston Howard 30.00 15.00
❑ 83 Lou Skizas 10.00 5.00
❑ 84 Moe Drabowsky 15.00 7.50
❑ 85 Larry Doby 30.00 15.00
❑ 86 Bill Sarni 10.00 5.00
❑ 87 Tom Gorman 10.00 5.00
❑ 88 Harvey Kuenn 15.00 7.50
❑ 89 Roy Sievers 15.00 7.50
❑ 90 Warren Spahn 80.00 40.00
❑ 91 Mack Burk 8.00 4.00
❑ 92 Mickey Vernon 15.00 7.50
❑ 93 Hal Jeffcoat 8.00 4.00
❑ 94 Bobby Del Greco 8.00 4.00
❑ 95 Mickey Mantle 1000.00 500.00
❑ 96 Hank Aguirre 8.00 4.00
❑ 97 New York Yankees 100.00 50.00
Team Card
❑ 98 Alvin Dark 15.00 7.50
❑ 99 Bob Keegan 8.00 4.00
❑ 100 Warren Giles PRES 15.00 7.50
Will Harridge PRES
❑ 101 Chuck Stobbs 8.00 4.00
❑ 102 Ray Boone 15.00 7.50
❑ 103 Joe Nuxhall 15.00 7.50
❑ 104 Hank Foiles 8.00 4.00
❑ 105 Johnny Antonelli 15.00 7.50
❑ 106 Ray Moore 8.00 4.00
❑ 107 Jim Rivera 8.00 4.00
❑ 108 Tommy Byrne 15.00 7.50
❑ 109 Hank Thompson 8.00 4.00
❑ 110 Bill Virdon 15.00 7.50
❑ 111 Hal R. Smith 8.00 4.00
❑ 112 Tom Brewer 8.00 4.00
❑ 113 Wilmer Mizell 15.00 7.50
❑ 114 Milwaukee Braves 20.00 10.00
Team Card
❑ 115 Jim Gilliam 15.00 7.50
❑ 116 Mike Fornieles 8.00 4.00
❑ 117 Joe Adcock 20.00 10.00
❑ 118 Bob Porterfield 8.00 4.00
❑ 119 Stan Lopata 8.00 4.00
❑ 120 Bob Lemon 30.00 15.00
❑ 121 Clete Boyer RC 30.00 15.00
❑ 122 Ken Boyer 20.00 10.00
❑ 123 Steve Ridzik 8.00 4.00
❑ 124 Dave Philley 8.00 4.00
❑ 125 Al Kaline 100.00 50.00
❑ 126 Bob Wiesler 8.00 4.00
❑ 127 Bob Buhl 15.00 7.50
❑ 128 Ed Bailey 15.00 7.50
❑ 129 Saul Rogovin 8.00 4.00
❑ 130 Don Newcombe 20.00 10.00
❑ 131 Milt Bolling 8.00 4.00
❑ 132 Art Ditmar 15.00 7.50
❑ 133 Del Crandall 15.00 7.50
❑ 134 Don Kaiser 8.00 4.00
❑ 135 Bill Skowron 20.00 10.00
❑ 136 Jim Hegan 15.00 7.50
❑ 137 Bob Rush 8.00 4.00
❑ 138 Minnie Minoso 20.00 10.00
❑ 139 Lou Kretlow 8.00 4.00
❑ 140 Frank Thomas 15.00 7.50
❑ 141 Al Aber 8.00 4.00
❑ 142 Charley Thompson 8.00 4.00
❑ 143 Andy Pafko 15.00 7.50
❑ 144 Ray Narleski 8.00 4.00
❑ 145 Al Smith 8.00 4.00
❑ 146 Don Ferrarese 8.00 4.00
❑ 147 Al Walker 8.00 4.00
❑ 148 Don Mueller 15.00 7.50
❑ 149 Bob Kennedy 15.00 7.50
❑ 150 Bob Friend 15.00 7.50
❑ 151 Willie Miranda 8.00 4.00
❑ 152 Jack Harshman 8.00 4.00
❑ 153 Karl Olson 8.00 4.00
❑ 154 Red Schoendienst 30.00 15.00
❑ 155 Jim Brosnan 15.00 7.50
❑ 156 Gus Triandos 15.00 7.50
❑ 157 Wally Post 15.00 7.50
❑ 158 Curt Simmons 15.00 7.50
❑ 159 Solly Drake 8.00 4.00
❑ 160 Billy Pierce 15.00 7.50
❑ 161 Pittsburgh Pirates 15.00 7.50
Team Card
❑ 162 Jack Meyer 8.00 4.00
❑ 163 Sammy White 8.00 4.00
❑ 164 Tommy Carroll 8.00 4.00
❑ 165 Ted Kluszewski 100.00 50.00
❑ 166 Roy Face 15.00 7.50
❑ 167 Vic Power 15.00 7.50
❑ 168 Frank Lary 15.00 7.50
❑ 169 Herb Plews 8.00 4.00
❑ 170 Duke Snider 125.00 60.00
❑ 171 Boston Red Sox 15.00 7.50
Team Card
❑ 172 Gene Woodling 15.00 7.50
❑ 173 Roger Craig 15.00 7.50
❑ 174 Willie Jones 8.00 4.00
❑ 175 Don Larsen 30.00 15.00
❑ 176A Gene Baker ERR 350.00 180.00
(Misspelled Bakep
on card back)
❑ 176B Gene Baker COR 15.00 7.50
❑ 177 Eddie Yost 15.00 7.50
❑ 178 Don Bessent 8.00 4.00
❑ 179 Ernie Oravetz 8.00 4.00
❑ 180 Gus Bell 15.00 7.50
❑ 181 Dick Donovan 8.00 4.00
❑ 182 Hobie Landrith 8.00 4.00
❑ 183 Chicago Cubs 15.00 7.50
Team Card
❑ 184 Tito Francona RC 8.00 4.00
❑ 185 Johnny Kucks 15.00 7.50
❑ 186 Jim King 15.00 7.50
❑ 187 Virgil Trucks 15.00 7.50
❑ 188 Felix Mantilla RC 15.00 7.50
❑ 189 Willard Nixon 8.00 4.00
❑ 190 Randy Jackson 8.00 4.00
❑ 191 Joe Margoneri 8.00 4.00
❑ 192 Jerry Coleman 15.00 7.50
❑ 193 Del Rice 8.00 4.00
❑ 194 Hal Brown 8.00 4.00
❑ 195 Bobby Avila 8.00 4.00
❑ 196 Larry Jackson 15.00 7.50
❑ 197 Hank Sauer 15.00 7.50
❑ 198 Detroit Tigers 15.00 7.50
Team Card
❑ 199 Vern Law 15.00 7.50
❑ 200 Gil McDougald 15.00 7.50
❑ 201 Sandy Amoros 15.00 7.50
❑ 202 Dick Gernert 8.00 4.00
❑ 203 Hoyt Wilhelm 30.00 15.00
❑ 204 Kansas City Athletics 15.00 7.50
Team Card
❑ 205 Charlie Maxwell 15.00 7.50
❑ 206 Willard Schmidt 8.00 4.00
❑ 207 Gordon(Billy) Hunter 8.00 4.00
❑ 208 Lou Burdette 15.00 7.50
❑ 209 Bob Skinner 15.00 7.50
❑ 210 Roy Campanella 150.00 75.00
❑ 211 Camilo Pascual 15.00 7.50
❑ 212 Rocky Colavito RC 125.00 60.00
❑ 213 Les Moss 8.00 4.00
❑ 214 Philadelphia Phillies 15.00 7.50
Team Card
❑ 215 Enos Slaughter 30.00 15.00
❑ 216 Marv Grissom 8.00 4.00
❑ 217 Gene Stephens 8.00 4.00
❑ 218 Ray Jablonski 8.00 4.00
❑ 219 Tom Acker 8.00 4.00
❑ 220 Jackie Jensen 20.00 10.00
❑ 221 Dixie Howell 8.00 4.00
❑ 222 Alex Grammas 8.00 4.00
❑ 223 Frank House 8.00 4.00
❑ 224 Marv Blaylock 8.00 4.00
❑ 225 Harry Simpson 8.00 4.00
❑ 226 Preston Ward 8.00 4.00
❑ 227 Gerry Staley 8.00 4.00
❑ 228 Smoky Burgess UER 15.00 7.50
(Misspelled Smokey
on card back)
❑ 229 George Susce 8.00 4.00
❑ 230 George Kell 30.00 15.00
❑ 231 Solly Hemus 8.00 4.00
❑ 232 Whitey Lockman 15.00 7.50
❑ 233 Art Fowler 8.00 4.00
❑ 234 Dick Cole 8.00 4.00
❑ 235 Tom Poholsky 8.00 4.00
❑ 236 Joe Ginsberg 8.00 4.00
❑ 237 Foster Castleman 8.00 4.00
❑ 238 Eddie Robinson 8.00 4.00
❑ 239 Tom Morgan 8.00 4.00
❑ 240 Hank Bauer 15.00 7.50
❑ 241 Joe Lonnett 8.00 4.00
❑ 242 Charlie Neal 15.00 7.50
❑ 243 St. Louis Cardinals 15.00 7.50
Team Card
❑ 244 Billy Loes 15.00 7.50
❑ 245 Rip Repulski 8.00 4.00
❑ 246 Jose Valdivielso 8.00 4.00
❑ 247 Turk Lown 8.00 4.00
❑ 248 Jim Finigan 8.00 4.00
❑ 249 Dave Pope 8.00 4.00
❑ 250 Eddie Mathews 50.00 25.00
❑ 251 Baltimore Orioles 15.00 7.50
Team Card
❑ 252 Carl Erskine 15.00 7.50
❑ 253 Gus Zernial 15.00 7.50
❑ 254 Ron Negray 8.00 4.00
❑ 255 Charlie Silvera 15.00 7.50
❑ 256 Ron Kline 8.00 4.00
❑ 257 Walt Dropo 8.00 4.00
❑ 258 Steve Gromek 8.00 4.00
❑ 259 Eddie O'Brien 8.00 4.00
❑ 260 Del Ennis 15.00 7.50
❑ 261 Bob Chakales 8.00 4.00
❑ 262 Bobby Thomson 15.00 7.50
❑ 263 George Strickland 8.00 4.00
❑ 264 Bob Turley 15.00 7.50
❑ 265 Harvey Haddix DP 12.00 6.00
❑ 266 Ken Kuhn DP 12.00 6.00
❑ 267 Danny Kravitz 20.00 10.00
❑ 268 Jack Collum 20.00 10.00
❑ 269 Bob Cerv 30.00 15.00
❑ 270 Washington Senators 60.00 30.00
Team Card
❑ 271 Danny O'Connell DP 12.00 6.00
❑ 272 Bobby Shantz 30.00 15.00
❑ 273 Jim Davis 20.00 10.00
❑ 274 Don Hoak 15.00 7.50
❑ 275 Cleveland Indians 60.00 30.00
Team Card UER
(Text on back credits Tribe
with winning AL title in '28.
The Yankees won that year.)
❑ 276 Jim Pyburn 20.00 10.00
❑ 277 Johnny Podres DP 40.00 20.00
❑ 278 Fred Hatfield DP 12.00 6.00
❑ 279 Bob Thurman 20.00 10.00
❑ 280 Alex Kellner 20.00 10.00
❑ 281 Gail Harris 20.00 10.00
❑ 282 Jack Dittmer DP 12.00 6.00
❑ 283 Wes Covington DP 12.00 6.00
❑ 284 Don Zimmer 40.00 20.00
❑ 285 Ned Garver 20.00 10.00
❑ 286 Bobby Richardson RC 125.00 60.00
❑ 287 Sam Jones 20.00 10.00
❑ 288 Ted Lepcio 20.00 10.00
❑ 289 Jim Bolger DP 12.00 6.00
❑ 290 Andy Carey DP 40.00 20.00
❑ 291 Windy McCall 20.00 10.00
❑ 292 Billy Klaus 20.00 10.00
❑ 293 Ted Abernathy 20.00 10.00
❑ 294 Rocky Bridges DP 12.00 6.00
❑ 295 Joe Collins DP 40.00 20.00
❑ 296 Johnny Klippstein 20.00 10.00
❑ 297 Jack Crimian 20.00 10.00
❑ 298 Irv Noren DP 12.00 6.00
❑ 299 Chuck Harmon 20.00 10.00
❑ 300 Mike Garcia 30.00 15.00

Card	Player	NM	Ex
❑ 301	Sammy Esposito DP	20.00	10.00
❑ 302	Sandy Koufax DP	350.00	180.00
❑ 303	Billy Goodman	30.00	15.00
❑ 304	Joe Cunningham	30.00	15.00
❑ 305	Chico Fernandez	20.00	10.00
❑ 306	Darrell Johnson DP	12.00	6.00
❑ 307	Jack D. Phillips DP	12.00	6.00
❑ 308	Dick Hall	20.00	10.00
❑ 309	Jim Busby DP	12.00	6.00
❑ 310	Max Surkont DP	12.00	6.00
❑ 311	Al Pilarcik DP	12.00	6.00
❑ 312	Tony Kubek DP RC	100.00	50.00
❑ 313	Mel Parnell	15.00	7.50
❑ 314	Ed Bouchee DP	12.00	6.00
❑ 315	Lou Berberet DP	12.00	6.00
❑ 316	Billy O'Dell	20.00	10.00
❑ 317	New York Giants	80.00	40.00
	Team Card		
❑ 318	Mickey McDermott	20.00	10.00
❑ 319	Gino Cimoli RC	20.00	10.00
❑ 320	Neil Chrisley	20.00	10.00
❑ 321	John(Red) Murff	20.00	10.00
❑ 322	Cincinnati Reds	80.00	40.00
	Team Card		
❑ 323	Wes Westrum	30.00	15.00
❑ 324	Brooklyn Dodgers	150.00	75.00
	Team Card		
❑ 325	Frank Bolling	20.00	10.00
❑ 326	Pedro Ramos	20.00	10.00
❑ 327	Jim Pendleton	20.00	10.00
❑ 328	Brooks Robinson RC	400.00	200.00
❑ 329	Chicago White Sox	60.00	30.00
	Team Card		
❑ 330	Jim Wilson	20.00	10.00
❑ 331	Ray Katt	20.00	10.00
❑ 332	Bob Bowman	20.00	10.00
❑ 333	Ernie Johnson	20.00	10.00
❑ 334	Jerry Schoonmaker	20.00	10.00
❑ 335	Granny Hamner	20.00	10.00
❑ 336	Haywood Sullivan RC	40.00	20.00
❑ 337	Rene Valdes	20.00	10.00
❑ 338	Jim Bunning RC	150.00	75.00
❑ 339	Bob Speake	20.00	10.00
❑ 340	Bill Wight	20.00	10.00
❑ 341	Don Gross	20.00	10.00
❑ 342	Gene Mauch	30.00	15.00
❑ 343	Taylor Phillips	15.00	7.50
❑ 344	Paul LaPalme	20.00	10.00
❑ 345	Paul Smith	20.00	10.00
❑ 346	Dick Littlefield	20.00	10.00
❑ 347	Hal Naragon	20.00	10.00
❑ 348	Jim Hearn	20.00	10.00
❑ 349	Nellie King	20.00	10.00
❑ 350	Eddie Miksis	20.00	10.00
❑ 351	Dave Hillman	20.00	10.00
❑ 352	Ellis Kinder	20.00	10.00
❑ 353	Cal Neeman	8.00	4.00
❑ 354	Rip Coleman	8.00	4.00
❑ 355	Frank Malzone	15.00	7.50
❑ 356	Faye Throneberry	8.00	4.00
❑ 357	Earl Torgeson	8.00	4.00
❑ 358	Jerry Lynch	15.00	7.50
❑ 359	Tom Cheney	8.00	4.00
❑ 360	Johnny Groth	8.00	4.00
❑ 361	Curt Barclay	8.00	4.00
❑ 362	Roman Mejias	15.00	7.50
❑ 363	Eddie Kasko	8.00	4.00
❑ 364	Cal McLish	15.00	7.50
❑ 365	Ozzie Virgil	8.00	4.00
❑ 366	Ken Lehman	8.00	4.00
❑ 367	Ed Fitzgerald	8.00	4.00
❑ 368	Bob Purkey	8.00	4.00
❑ 369	Milt Graff	8.00	4.00
❑ 370	Warren Hacker	8.00	4.00
❑ 371	Bob Lennon	8.00	4.00
❑ 372	Norm Zauchin	8.00	4.00
❑ 373	Pete Whisenant	8.00	4.00
❑ 374	Don Cardwell	8.00	4.00
❑ 375	Jim Landis	15.00	7.50
❑ 376	Don Elston	8.00	4.00
❑ 377	Andre Rodgers	8.00	4.00
❑ 378	Elmer Singleton	8.00	4.00
❑ 379	Don Lee	8.00	4.00
❑ 380	Walker Cooper	8.00	4.00
❑ 381	Dean Stone	8.00	4.00
❑ 382	Jim Brideweser	8.00	4.00
❑ 383	Juan Pizarro	8.00	4.00
❑ 384	Bobby G. Smith	8.00	4.00
❑ 385	Art Houtteman	8.00	4.00
❑ 386	Lyle Luttrell	8.00	4.00
❑ 387	Jack Sanford RC	15.00	7.50
❑ 388	Pete Daley	8.00	4.00
❑ 389	Dave Jolly	8.00	4.00
❑ 390	Reno Bertoia	8.00	4.00
❑ 391	Ralph Terry RC	15.00	7.50
❑ 392	Chuck Tanner	15.00	7.50
❑ 393	Raul Sanchez	8.00	4.00
❑ 394	Luis Arroyo	15.00	7.50
❑ 395	Bubba Phillips	8.00	4.00
❑ 396	Casey Wise	8.00	4.00
❑ 397	Roy Smalley	8.00	4.00
❑ 398	Al Cicotte	15.00	7.50
❑ 399	Billy Consolo	8.00	4.00
❑ 400	Carl Furillo	250.00	125.00
	Gil Hodges		
	Roy Campanella		
	Duke Snider		
❑ 401	Earl Battey RC	15.00	7.50
❑ 402	Jim Pisoni	8.00	4.00
❑ 403	Dick Hyde	8.00	4.00
❑ 404	Harry Anderson	8.00	4.00
❑ 405	Duke Maas	8.00	4.00
❑ 406	Bob Hale	8.00	4.00
❑ 407	Mickey Mantle	600.00	180.00
	Yogi Berra		
❑ CC1	Contest Card	100.00	25.00
	Saturday, May 4th		
	Boston Red Sox		
	vs. Cleveland Indians		
	Cincinnati Redlegs		
	vs. New York Giants		
❑ CC2	Contest Card	100.00	25.00
	Saturday, May 25th		
	Detroit Tigers		
	vs. Kansas City Athletics		
	Pittsburgh Pirates		
	vs. Philadelphia Phillies		
❑ CC3	Contest Card	125.00	31.00
	Saturday, June 22nd		
	Brooklyn Dodgers		
	vs. St. Louis Cardinals		
	Chicago White Sox		
	vs. New York Yankees		
❑ CC4	Contest Card	125.00	31.00
	Saturday, July 19th		
	Milwaukee Braves		
	vs. New York Giants		
	Baltimore Orioles		
	vs. Kansas City Athletics		
❑ NNO	Checklist 1/2	250.00	75.00
	Bazooka Back		
❑ NNO	Checklist 1/2	250.00	125.00
	Blony Back		
❑ NNO	Checklist 2/3	400.00	100.00
	Bazooka Back		
❑ NNO	Checklist 2/3	400.00	200.00
	Blony Back		
❑ NNO	Checklist 3/4	800.00	190.00
	Bazooka Back		
❑ NNO	Checklist 3/4	600.00	300.00
	Blony Back		
❑ NNO	Checklist 4/5	1000.00	220.00
	Bazooka Back		
❑ NNO	Checklist 4/5	800.00	400.00
	Blony Back		
❑ NNO	Lucky Penny Charm	100.00	50.00
	and Key Chain		
	offer card		

1958 Topps

	NM	Ex
COMP. MASTER (534)	12000.00	6000.00
COMPLETE SET (494)	6000.00	3000.00
COMMON CARD (1-110)	12.00	6.00
COMMON (111-495)	8.00	4.00
WRAPPER (1-CENT)	100.00	50.00
WRAPPER (5-CENT)	125.00	60.00

Card	Player	NM	Ex
❑ 1	Ted Williams	600.00	210.00
❑ 2A	Bob Lemon	30.00	15.00
❑ 2B	Bob Lemon YT	60.00	30.00
❑ 3	Alex Kellner	12.00	6.00
❑ 4	Hank Foiles	12.00	6.00
❑ 5	Willie Mays	300.00	150.00
❑ 6	George Zuverink	12.00	6.00
❑ 7	Dale Long	15.00	7.50
❑ 8A	Eddie Kasko	12.00	6.00
❑ 8B	Eddie Kasko YN	40.00	20.00
❑ 9	Hank Bauer	20.00	10.00
❑ 10	Lou Burdette	20.00	10.00
❑ 11A	Jim Rivera	12.00	6.00
❑ 11B	Jim Rivera YT	40.00	20.00
❑ 12	George Crowe	12.00	6.00
❑ 13A	Billy Hoeft	12.00	6.00
❑ 13B	Billy Hoeft YN	40.00	20.00
❑ 14	Rip Repulski	12.00	6.00
❑ 15	Jim Lemon	15.00	7.50
❑ 16	Charlie Neal	15.00	7.50
❑ 17	Felix Mantilla	12.00	6.00
❑ 18	Frank Sullivan	12.00	6.00
❑ 19	Giants Team Card CL	40.00	8.00
❑ 20A	Gil McDougald	20.00	10.00
❑ 20B	Gil McDougald YN	60.00	30.00
❑ 21	Curt Barclay	12.00	6.00
❑ 22	Hal Naragon	12.00	6.00
❑ 23A	Bill Tuttle	12.00	6.00
❑ 23B	Bill Tuttle YN	40.00	20.00
❑ 24A	Hobie Landrith	12.00	6.00
❑ 24B	Hobie Landrith YN	40.00	20.00
❑ 25	Don Drysdale	100.00	50.00
❑ 26	Ron Jackson	12.00	6.00
❑ 27	Bud Freeman	12.00	6.00
❑ 28	Jim Busby	12.00	6.00
❑ 29	Ted Lepcio	12.00	6.00
❑ 30A	Hank Aaron	200.00	100.00
❑ 30B	Hank Aaron YN	500.00	250.00
❑ 31	Tex Clevenger	12.00	6.00
❑ 32A	J.W. Porter	12.00	6.00
❑ 32B	J.W. Porter YN	40.00	20.00
❑ 33A	Cal Neeman	12.00	6.00
❑ 33B	Cal Neeman YT	40.00	20.00
❑ 34	Bob Thurman	12.00	6.00
❑ 35A	Don Mossi	15.00	7.50
❑ 35B	Don Mossi YT	40.00	20.00
❑ 36	Ted Kazanski	12.00	6.00
❑ 37	Mike McCormick RC	15.00	7.50
	UER Photo actually		
	Ray Monzant		
❑ 38	Dick Gernert	12.00	6.00
❑ 39	Bob Martyn	12.00	6.00
❑ 40	George Kell	30.00	15.00
❑ 41	Dave Hillman	12.00	6.00
❑ 42	John Roseboro RC	30.00	15.00
❑ 43	Sal Maglie	15.00	7.50
❑ 44	Washington Senators	20.00	4.00
	Team Card CL		
❑ 45	Dick Groat	15.00	7.50
❑ 46A	Lou Sleater	12.00	6.00
❑ 46B	Lou Sleater YN	40.00	20.00
❑ 47	Roger Maris RC	500.00	250.00
❑ 48	Chuck Harmon	12.00	6.00
❑ 49	Smoky Burgess	15.00	7.50
❑ 50A	Billy Pierce	15.00	7.50
❑ 50B	Billy Pierce YT	40.00	20.00
❑ 51	Del Rice	12.00	6.00
❑ 52A	Roberto Clemente	300.00	150.00
❑ 52B	Roberto Clemente YT	500.00	250.00
❑ 53A	Morrie Martin	12.00	6.00
❑ 53B	Morrie Martin YN	40.00	20.00
❑ 54	Norm Siebern RC	20.00	10.00

❑ 55 Chico Carrasquel 12.00 6.00
❑ 56 Bill Fischer 12.00 6.00
❑ 57A Tim Thompson 12.00 6.00
❑ 57B Tim Thompson YN 40.00 20.00
❑ 58A Art Schult 12.00 6.00
❑ 58B Art Schult YT 40.00 20.00
❑ 59 Dave Sisler 12.00 6.00
❑ 60A Del Ennis 15.00 7.50
❑ 60B Del Ennis YN 40.00 20.00
❑ 61A Darrell Johnson 12.00 6.00
❑ 61B Darrell Johnson YN 40.00 20.00
❑ 62 Joe DeMaestri 12.00 6.00
❑ 63 Joe Nuxhall 15.00 7.50
❑ 64 Joe Lonnett 12.00 6.00
❑ 65A Von McDaniel RC 12.00 6.00
❑ 65B Von McDaniel YL RC 40.00 20.00
❑ 66 Lee Walls 12.00 6.00
❑ 67 Joe Ginsberg 12.00 6.00
❑ 68 Daryl Spencer 12.00 6.00
❑ 69 Wally Burnette 12.00 6.00
❑ 70A Al Kaline 100.00 50.00
❑ 70B Al Kaline YN 250.00 125.00
❑ 71 Dodgers Team CL 60.00 12.00
❑ 72 Bud Byerly UER 12.00 6.00
Photo is Hal Griggs
❑ 73 Pete Daley 12.00 6.00
❑ 74 Roy Face 15.00 7.50
❑ 75 Gus Bell 15.00 7.50
❑ 76A Dick Farrell 12.00 6.00
❑ 76B Dick Farrell YT 40.00 20.00
❑ 77A Don Zimmer 15.00 7.50
❑ 77B Don Zimmer YT 40.00 20.00
❑ 78A Ernie Johnson 15.00 7.50
❑ 78B Ernie Johnson YN 40.00 20.00
❑ 79A Dick Williams 15.00 7.50
❑ 79B Dick Williams YT 40.00 20.00
❑ 80 Dick Drott 12.00 6.00
❑ 81A Steve Boros RC 12.00 6.00
❑ 81B Steve Boros YT RC 40.00 20.00
❑ 82 Ron Kline 12.00 6.00
❑ 83 Bob Hazle RC 12.00 6.00
❑ 84 Billy O'Dell 12.00 6.00
❑ 85A Luis Aparicio 30.00 15.00
❑ 85B Luis Aparicio YT 80.00 40.00
❑ 86 Valmy Thomas 12.00 6.00
❑ 87 Johnny Kucks 12.00 6.00
❑ 88 Duke Snider 80.00 40.00
❑ 89 Billy Klaus 12.00 6.00
❑ 90 Robin Roberts 30.00 15.00
❑ 91 Chuck Tanner 15.00 7.50
❑ 92A Clint Courtney 12.00 6.00
❑ 92B Clint Courtney YN 40.00 20.00
❑ 93 Sandy Amoros 15.00 7.50
❑ 94 Bob Skinner 15.00 7.50
❑ 95 Frank Bolling 12.00 6.00
❑ 96 Joe Durham 12.00 6.00
❑ 97A Larry Jackson 12.00 6.00
❑ 97B Larry Jackson YN 40.00 20.00
❑ 98A Billy Hunter 12.00 6.00
❑ 98B Billy Hunter YN 40.00 20.00
❑ 99 Bobby Adams 12.00 6.00
❑ 100A Early Wynn 30.00 15.00
❑ 100B Early Wynn YT 80.00 40.00
❑ 101A Bobby Richardson 30.00 15.00
❑ 101B B.Richardson YN 60.00 30.00
❑ 102 George Strickland 12.00 6.00
❑ 103 Jerry Lynch 15.00 7.50
❑ 104 Jim Pendleton 12.00 6.00
❑ 105 Billy Gardner 12.00 6.00
❑ 106 Dick Schofield 15.00 7.50
❑ 107 Ossie Virgil 12.00 6.00
❑ 108A Jim Landis 12.00 6.00
❑ 108B Jim Landis YT 40.00 20.00
❑ 109 Herb Plews 12.00 6.00
❑ 110 Johnny Logan 15.00 7.50
❑ 111 Stu Miller 10.00 5.00
❑ 112 Gus Zernial 10.00 5.00
❑ 113 Jerry Walker RC 8.00 4.00
❑ 114 Irv Noren 10.00 5.00
❑ 115 Jim Bunning 30.00 15.00
❑ 116 Dave Philley 8.00 4.00
❑ 117 Frank Torre 10.00 5.00
❑ 118 Harvey Haddix 10.00 5.00
❑ 119 Harry Chiti 8.00 4.00
❑ 120 Johnny Podres 10.00 5.00
❑ 121 Eddie Miksis 8.00 4.00
❑ 122 Walt Moryn 8.00 4.00
❑ 123 Dick Tomanek 8.00 4.00
❑ 124 Bobby Usher 8.00 4.00
❑ 125 Alvin Dark 10.00 5.00
❑ 126 Stan Palys 8.00 4.00
❑ 127 Tom Sturdivant 10.00 5.00
❑ 128 Willie Kirkland 8.00 4.00
❑ 129 Jim Derrington 8.00 4.00
❑ 130 Jackie Jensen 10.00 5.00
❑ 131 Bob Henrich 8.00 4.00
❑ 132 Vern Law 10.00 5.00
❑ 133 Russ Nixon RC 8.00 4.00
❑ 134 Philadelphia Phillies 15.00 3.00
Team Card CL
❑ 135 Mike(Moe)Drabowsky 10.00 5.00
❑ 136 Jim Finigan 8.00 4.00
❑ 137 Russ Kemmerer 8.00 4.00
❑ 138 Earl Torgeson 8.00 4.00
❑ 139 George Brunet 8.00 4.00
❑ 140 Wes Covington 10.00 5.00
❑ 141 Ken Lehman 8.00 4.00
❑ 142 Enos Slaughter 25.00 12.50
❑ 143 Billy Muffett RC 8.00 4.00
❑ 144 Bobby Morgan 8.00 4.00
❑ 145 Never issued .00 .00
❑ 146 Dick Gray 8.00 4.00
❑ 147 Don McMahon RC 8.00 4.00
❑ 148 Billy Consolo 8.00 4.00
❑ 149 Tom Acker 8.00 4.00
❑ 150 Mickey Mantle 800.00 400.00
❑ 151 Buddy Pritchard 8.00 4.00
❑ 152 Johnny Antonelli 10.00 5.00
❑ 153 Les Moss 8.00 4.00
❑ 154 Harry Byrd 8.00 4.00
❑ 155 Hector Lopez 10.00 5.00
❑ 156 Dick Hyde 8.00 4.00
❑ 157 Dee Fondy 8.00 4.00
❑ 158 Cleveland Indians 15.00 3.00
Team Card CL
❑ 159 Taylor Phillips 8.00 4.00
❑ 160 Don Hoak 10.00 5.00
❑ 161 Don Larsen 15.00 7.50
❑ 162 Gil Hodges 40.00 20.00
❑ 163 Jim Wilson 8.00 4.00
❑ 164 Bob Taylor 8.00 4.00
❑ 165 Bob Nieman 8.00 4.00
❑ 166 Danny O'Connell 8.00 4.00
❑ 167 Frank Baumann 8.00 4.00
❑ 168 Joe Cunningham 8.00 4.00
❑ 169 Ralph Terry 10.00 5.00
❑ 170 Vic Wertz 10.00 5.00
❑ 171 Harry Anderson 8.00 4.00
❑ 172 Don Gross 8.00 4.00
❑ 173 Eddie Yost 8.00 4.00
❑ 174 K.C. Athletics Team CL 15.00 3.00
❑ 175 Marv Throneberry RC 15.00 7.50
❑ 176 Bob Buhl 10.00 5.00
❑ 177 Al Smith 8.00 4.00
❑ 178 Ted Kluszewski 25.00 12.50
❑ 179 Willie Miranda 8.00 4.00
❑ 180 Lindy McDaniel 10.00 5.00
❑ 181 Willie Jones 8.00 4.00
❑ 182 Joe Caffie 8.00 4.00
❑ 183 Dave Jolly 8.00 4.00
❑ 184 Elvin Tappe 8.00 4.00
❑ 185 Ray Boone 10.00 5.00
❑ 186 Jack Meyer 8.00 4.00
❑ 187 Sandy Koufax 250.00 125.00
❑ 188 Milt Bolling UER 8.00 4.00
(Photo actually
Lou Berberet)
❑ 189 George Susce 8.00 4.00
❑ 190 Red Schoendienst 25.00 12.50
❑ 191 Art Ceccarelli 8.00 4.00
❑ 192 Milt Graff 8.00 4.00
❑ 193 Jerry Lumpe RC 8.00 4.00
❑ 194 Roger Craig 10.00 5.00
❑ 195 Whitey Lockman 10.00 5.00
❑ 196 Mike Garcia 10.00 5.00
❑ 197 Haywood Sullivan 10.00 5.00
❑ 198 Bill Virdon 10.00 5.00
❑ 199 Don Blasingame 8.00 4.00
❑ 200 Bob Keegan 8.00 4.00
❑ 201 Jim Bolger 8.00 4.00
❑ 202 Woody Held RC 8.00 4.00
❑ 203 Al Walker 8.00 4.00
❑ 204 Leo Kiely 8.00 4.00
❑ 205 Johnny Temple 10.00 5.00
❑ 206 Bob Shaw RC 8.00 4.00
❑ 207 Solly Hemus 8.00 4.00
❑ 208 Cal McLish 8.00 4.00
❑ 209 Bob Anderson 8.00 4.00
❑ 210 Wally Moon 10.00 5.00
❑ 211 Pete Burnside 8.00 4.00
❑ 212 Bubba Phillips 8.00 4.00
❑ 213 Red Wilson 8.00 4.00
❑ 214 Willard Schmidt 8.00 4.00
❑ 215 Jim Gilliam 15.00 7.50
❑ 216 St. Louis Cardinals 15.00 3.00
Team Card CL
❑ 217 Jack Harshman 8.00 4.00
❑ 218 Dick Rand 8.00 4.00
❑ 219 Camilo Pascual 10.00 5.00
❑ 220 Tom Brewer 8.00 4.00
❑ 221 Jerry Kindall RC 8.00 4.00
❑ 222 Bud Daley 8.00 4.00
❑ 223 Andy Pafko 10.00 5.00
❑ 224 Bob Grim 10.00 5.00
❑ 225 Billy Goodman 10.00 5.00
❑ 226 Bob Smith 8.00 4.00
❑ 227 Gene Stephens 8.00 4.00
❑ 228 Duke Maas 8.00 4.00
❑ 229 Frank Zupo 8.00 4.00
❑ 230 Richie Ashburn 40.00 20.00
❑ 231 Lloyd Merritt 8.00 4.00
❑ 232 Reno Bertoia 8.00 4.00
❑ 233 Mickey Vernon 10.00 5.00
❑ 234 Carl Sawatski 8.00 4.00
❑ 235 Tom Gorman 8.00 4.00
❑ 236 Ed Fitzgerald 8.00 4.00
❑ 237 Bill Wight 8.00 4.00
❑ 238 Bill Mazeroski 30.00 15.00
❑ 239 Chuck Stobbs 8.00 4.00
❑ 240 Bill Skowron 25.00 12.50
❑ 241 Dick Littlefield 8.00 4.00
❑ 242 Johnny Klippstein 8.00 4.00
❑ 243 Larry Raines 8.00 4.00
❑ 244 Don Demeter 8.00 4.00
❑ 245 Frank Lary 10.00 5.00
❑ 246 New York Yankees 100.00 20.00
Team Card CL
❑ 247 Casey Wise 8.00 4.00
❑ 248 Herman Wehmeier 8.00 4.00
❑ 249 Ray Moore 8.00 4.00
❑ 250 Roy Sievers 10.00 5.00
❑ 251 Warren Hacker 8.00 4.00
❑ 252 Bob Trowbridge 8.00 4.00
❑ 253 Don Mueller 10.00 5.00
❑ 254 Alex Grammas 8.00 4.00
❑ 255 Bob Turley 10.00 5.00
❑ 256 Chicago White Sox 15.00 3.00
Team Card CL
❑ 257 Hal Smith 8.00 4.00
❑ 258 Carl Erskine 15.00 7.50
❑ 259 Al Pilarcik 8.00 4.00
❑ 260 Frank Malzone 10.00 5.00
❑ 261 Turk Lown 8.00 4.00
❑ 262 Johnny Groth 8.00 4.00
❑ 263 Eddie Bressoud 10.00 5.00
❑ 264 Jack Sanford 10.00 5.00
❑ 265 Pete Runnels 10.00 5.00
❑ 266 Connie Johnson 8.00 4.00
❑ 267 Sherm Lollar 10.00 5.00
❑ 268 Granny Hamner 8.00 4.00
❑ 269 Paul Smith 8.00 4.00
❑ 270 Warren Spahn 60.00 30.00
❑ 271 Billy Martin 40.00 20.00
❑ 272 Ray Crone 8.00 4.00
❑ 273 Hal Smith 8.00 4.00
❑ 274 Rocky Bridges 8.00 4.00
❑ 275 Elston Howard 15.00 7.50
❑ 276 Bobby Avila 8.00 4.00
❑ 277 Virgil Trucks 10.00 5.00
❑ 278 Mack Burk 8.00 4.00
❑ 279 Bob Boyd 8.00 4.00
❑ 280 Jim Piersall 10.00 5.00
❑ 281 Sammy Taylor 8.00 4.00
❑ 282 Paul Foytack 8.00 4.00
❑ 283 Ray Shearer 8.00 4.00
❑ 284 Ray Katt 8.00 4.00
❑ 285 Frank Robinson 100.00 50.00
❑ 286 Gino Cimoli 8.00 4.00

❑ 287 Sam Jones 10.00 5.00
❑ 288 Harmon Killebrew 100.00 50.00
❑ 289 Lou Burdette 10.00 5.00
Bobby Shantz
❑ 290 Dick Donovan 8.00 4.00
❑ 291 Don Landrum 8.00 4.00
❑ 292 Ned Garver 8.00 4.00
❑ 293 Gene Freese 8.00 4.00
❑ 294 Hal Jeffcoat 8.00 4.00
❑ 295 Minnie Minoso 25.00 12.50
❑ 296 Ryne Duren RC 15.00 7.50
❑ 297 Don Buddin 8.00 4.00
❑ 298 Jim Hearn 8.00 4.00
❑ 299 Harry Simpson 8.00 4.00
❑ 300 Will Harridge PRES 15.00 7.50
Warren Giles
❑ 301 Randy Jackson 8.00 4.00
❑ 302 Mike Baxes 8.00 4.00
❑ 303 Neil Chrisley 8.00 4.00
❑ 304 Harvey Kuenn 25.00 12.50
Al Kaline
❑ 305 Clem Labine 10.00 5.00
❑ 306 Whammy Douglas 8.00 4.00
❑ 307 Brooks Robinson 100.00 50.00
❑ 308 Paul Giel 10.00 5.00
❑ 309 Gail Harris 8.00 4.00
❑ 310 Ernie Banks 100.00 50.00
❑ 311 Bob Purkey 8.00 4.00
❑ 312 Boston Red Sox 15.00 3.00
Team Card CL
❑ 313 Bob Rush 8.00 4.00
❑ 314 Duke Snider 50.00 25.00
Walt Alston MG
❑ 315 Bob Friend 10.00 5.00
❑ 316 Tito Francona 10.00 5.00
❑ 317 Albie Pearson 10.00 5.00
❑ 318 Frank House 8.00 4.00
❑ 319 Lou Skizas 8.00 4.00
❑ 320 Whitey Ford 60.00 30.00
❑ 321 Ted Kluszewski 100.00 50.00
Ted Williams
❑ 322 Harding Peterson 10.00 5.00
❑ 323 Elmer Valo 8.00 4.00
❑ 324 Hoyt Wilhelm 25.00 12.50
❑ 325 Joe Adcock 10.00 5.00
❑ 326 Bob Miller 8.00 4.00
❑ 327 Chicago Cubs 15.00 3.00
Team Card CL
❑ 328 Ike Delock 8.00 4.00
❑ 329 Bob Cerv 10.00 5.00
❑ 330 Ed Bailey 10.00 5.00
❑ 331 Pedro Ramos 8.00 4.00
❑ 332 Jim King 8.00 4.00
❑ 333 Andy Carey 10.00 5.00
❑ 334 Bob Friend 10.00 5.00
Billy Pierce
❑ 335 Ruben Gomez 8.00 4.00
❑ 336 Bert Hamric 8.00 4.00
❑ 337 Hank Aguirre 8.00 4.00
❑ 338 Walt Dropo 10.00 5.00
❑ 339 Fred Hatfield 8.00 4.00
❑ 340 Don Newcombe 15.00 7.50
❑ 341 Pittsburgh Pirates 15.00 3.00
Team Card CL
❑ 342 Jim Brosnan 10.00 5.00
❑ 343 Orlando Cepeda RC 100.00 50.00
❑ 344 Bob Porterfield 8.00 4.00
❑ 345 Jim Hegan 10.00 5.00
❑ 346 Steve Bilko 8.00 4.00
❑ 347 Don Rudolph 8.00 4.00
❑ 348 Chico Fernandez 8.00 4.00
❑ 349 Murry Dickson 8.00 4.00
❑ 350 Ken Boyer 25.00 12.50
❑ 351 Del Crandall 40.00 20.00
Eddie Mathews
Hank Aaron
Joe Adcock
❑ 352 Herb Score 15.00 7.50
❑ 353 Stan Lopata 8.00 4.00
❑ 354 Art Ditmar 10.00 5.00
❑ 355 Bill Bruton 10.00 5.00
❑ 356 Bob Malkmus 8.00 4.00
❑ 357 Danny McDevitt 8.00 4.00
❑ 358 Gene Baker 8.00 4.00
❑ 359 Billy Loes 10.00 5.00
❑ 360 Roy McMillan 10.00 5.00
❑ 361 Mike Fornieles 8.00 4.00
❑ 362 Ray Jablonski 8.00 4.00
❑ 363 Don Elston 8.00 4.00
❑ 364 Earl Battey 8.00 4.00
❑ 365 Tom Morgan 8.00 4.00
❑ 366 Gene Green 8.00 4.00
❑ 367 Jack Urban 8.00 4.00
❑ 368 Rocky Colavito 50.00 25.00
❑ 369 Ralph Lumenti 8.00 4.00
❑ 370 Yogi Berra 100.00 50.00
❑ 371 Marty Keough 8.00 4.00
❑ 372 Don Cardwell 8.00 4.00
❑ 373 Joe Pignatano 8.00 4.00
❑ 374 Brooks Lawrence 8.00 4.00
❑ 375 Pee Wee Reese 80.00 40.00
❑ 376 Charley Rabe 8.00 4.00
❑ 377A Milwaukee Braves 15.00 7.50
Team Card
(Alphabetical)
❑ 377B Milwaukee Team 100.00 20.00
numerical checklist
❑ 378 Hank Sauer 10.00 5.00
❑ 379 Ray Herbert 8.00 4.00
❑ 380 Charlie Maxwell 10.00 5.00
❑ 381 Hal Brown 8.00 4.00
❑ 382 Al Cicotte 8.00 4.00
❑ 383 Lou Berberet 8.00 4.00
❑ 384 John Goryl 8.00 4.00
❑ 385 Wilmer Mizell 10.00 5.00
❑ 386 Ed Bailey 15.00 7.50
Birdie Tebbetts MG
Frank Robinson
❑ 387 Wally Post 10.00 5.00
❑ 388 Billy Moran 8.00 4.00
❑ 389 Bill Taylor 8.00 4.00
❑ 390 Del Crandall 10.00 5.00
❑ 391 Dave Melton 8.00 4.00
❑ 392 Bennie Daniels 8.00 4.00
❑ 393 Tony Kubek 30.00 15.00
❑ 394 Jim Grant RC 8.00 4.00
❑ 395 Willard Nixon 8.00 4.00
❑ 396 Dutch Dotterer 8.00 4.00
❑ 397A Detroit Tigers 15.00 7.50
Team Card
(Alphabetical)
❑ 397B Detroit Team 100.00 20.00
numerical checklist
❑ 398 Gene Woodling 10.00 5.00
❑ 399 Marv Grissom 8.00 4.00
❑ 400 Nellie Fox 40.00 20.00
❑ 401 Don Bessent 8.00 4.00
❑ 402 Bobby Gene Smith 8.00 4.00
❑ 403 Steve Korcheck 8.00 4.00
❑ 404 Curt Simmons 10.00 5.00
❑ 405 Ken Aspromonte 8.00 4.00
❑ 406 Vic Power 10.00 5.00
❑ 407 Carlton Willey 10.00 5.00
❑ 408A Baltimore Orioles 15.00 7.50
Team Card
(Alphabetical)
❑ 408B Baltimore Team 100.00 20.00
numerical checklist
❑ 409 Frank Thomas 10.00 5.00
❑ 410 Murray Wall 8.00 4.00
❑ 411 Tony Taylor RC 10.00 5.00
❑ 412 Gerry Staley 8.00 4.00
❑ 413 Jim Davenport RC 8.00 4.00
❑ 414 Sammy White 8.00 4.00
❑ 415 Bob Bowman 8.00 4.00
❑ 416 Foster Castleman 8.00 4.00
❑ 417 Carl Furillo 15.00 7.50
❑ 418 Mickey Mantle 400.00 200.00
Hank Aaron
❑ 419 Bobby Shantz 10.00 5.00
❑ 420 Vada Pinson RC 40.00 20.00
❑ 421 Dixie Howell 8.00 4.00
❑ 422 Norm Zauchin 8.00 4.00
❑ 423 Phil Clark 8.00 4.00
❑ 424 Larry Doby 25.00 12.50
❑ 425 Sammy Esposito 8.00 4.00
❑ 426 Johnny O'Brien 10.00 5.00
❑ 427 Al Worthington 8.00 4.00
❑ 428A Cincinnati Reds 15.00 7.50
Team Card
(Alphabetical)
❑ 428B Cincinnati Team 100.00 20.00
numerical checklist
❑ 429 Gus Triandos 10.00 5.00
❑ 430 Bobby Thomson 10.00 5.00
❑ 431 Gene Conley 10.00 5.00
❑ 432 John Powers 8.00 4.00
❑ 433A Pancho Herrer ERR 600.00 300.00
❑ 433B Pancho Herrera COR 10.00 5.00
❑ 434 Harvey Kuenn 10.00 5.00
❑ 435 Ed Roebuck 10.00 5.00
❑ 436 Willie Mays 100.00 50.00
Duke Snider
❑ 437 Bob Speake 8.00 4.00
❑ 438 Whitey Herzog 10.00 5.00
❑ 439 Ray Narleski 8.00 4.00
❑ 440 Eddie Mathews 80.00 40.00
❑ 441 Jim Marshall 10.00 5.00
❑ 442 Phil Paine 8.00 4.00
❑ 443 Billy Harrell SP 20.00 10.00
❑ 444 Danny Kravitz 8.00 4.00
❑ 445 Bob Smith 8.00 4.00
❑ 446 Carroll Hardy SP 20.00 10.00
❑ 447 Ray Monzant 8.00 4.00
❑ 448 Charlie Lau RC 10.00 5.00
❑ 449 Gene Fodge 8.00 4.00
❑ 450 Preston Ward SP 20.00 10.00
❑ 451 Joe Taylor 8.00 4.00
❑ 452 Roman Mejias 8.00 4.00
❑ 453 Tom Qualters 8.00 4.00
❑ 454 Harry Hanebrink 8.00 4.00
❑ 455 Hal Griggs RC 8.00 4.00
❑ 456 Dick Brown 8.00 4.00
❑ 457 Milt Pappas RC 10.00 5.00
❑ 458 Julio Becquer 8.00 4.00
❑ 459 Ron Blackburn 8.00 4.00
❑ 460 Chuck Essegian 8.00 4.00
❑ 461 Ed Mayer 8.00 4.00
❑ 462 Gary Geiger SP 20.00 10.00
❑ 463 Vito Valentinetti 8.00 4.00
❑ 464 Curt Flood RC 30.00 15.00
❑ 465 Arnie Portocarrero 8.00 4.00
❑ 466 Pete Whisenant 8.00 4.00
❑ 467 Glen Hobbie 8.00 4.00
❑ 468 Bob Schmidt 8.00 4.00
❑ 469 Don Ferrarese 8.00 4.00
❑ 470 R.C. Stevens 8.00 4.00
❑ 471 Lenny Green 8.00 4.00
❑ 472 Joey Jay 10.00 5.00
❑ 473 Bill Renna 8.00 4.00
❑ 474 Roman Semproch 8.00 4.00
❑ 475 Fred Haney AS MG 25.00 7.50
Casey Stengel AS MG CL
❑ 476 Stan Musial AS TP 50.00 25.00
❑ 477 Bill Skowron AS 10.00 5.00
❑ 478 J.Temple AS UER 8.00 4.00
Card says record vs American League
Temple was NL AS
❑ 479 Nellie Fox AS 15.00 7.50
❑ 480 Eddie Mathews AS 30.00 15.00
❑ 481 Frank Malzone AS 8.00 4.00
❑ 482 Ernie Banks AS 40.00 20.00
❑ 483 Luis Aparicio AS 15.00 7.50
❑ 484 Frank Robinson AS 40.00 20.00
❑ 485 Ted Williams AS 150.00 75.00
❑ 486 Willie Mays AS 60.00 30.00
❑ 487 Mickey Mantle AS TP 200.00 100.00
❑ 488 Hank Aaron AS 60.00 30.00
❑ 489 Jackie Jensen AS 10.00 5.00
❑ 490 Ed Bailey AS 8.00 4.00
❑ 491 Sherm Lollar AS 8.00 4.00
❑ 492 Bob Friend AS 8.00 4.00
❑ 493 Bob Turley AS 10.00 5.00
❑ 494 Warren Spahn AS 25.00 12.50
❑ 495 Herb Score AS 15.00 3.00
❑ NNO Contest Cards 40.00 20.00

1959 Topps

	NM	Ex
COMPLETE SET (572)	5000.00	2500.00
COMMON CARD (1-110)	6.00	3.00
COMMON (111-506)	4.00	2.00
COMMON (507-572)	15.00	7.50
WRAPPER (1-CENT)	125.00	60.00
WRAPPER (5-CENT)	100.00	50.00

❑ 1 Ford Frick COMM 60.00 16.50

❑	2	Eddie Yost	8.00	4.00
❑	3	Don McMahon	8.00	4.00
❑	4	Albie Pearson	8.00	4.00
❑	5	Dick Donovan	8.00	4.00
❑	6	Alex Grammas	6.00	3.00
❑	7	Al Pilarcik	6.00	3.00
❑	8	Phillies Team CL	80.00	16.00
❑	9	Paul Giel	8.00	4.00
❑	10	Mickey Mantle	800.00	400.00
❑	11	Billy Hunter	8.00	4.00
❑	12	Vern Law	8.00	4.00
❑	13	Dick Gernert	6.00	3.00
❑	14	Pete Whisenant	6.00	3.00
❑	15	Dick Drott	6.00	3.00
❑	16	Joe Pignatano	6.00	3.00
❑	17	Frank Thomas	8.00	4.00
		Danny Murtaugh MG		
		Ted Kluszewski		
❑	18	Jack Urban	6.00	3.00
❑	19	Eddie Bressoud	6.00	3.00
❑	20	Duke Snider	60.00	30.00
❑	21	Connie Johnson	6.00	3.00
❑	22	Al Smith	8.00	4.00
❑	23	Murry Dickson	8.00	4.00
❑	24	Red Wilson	6.00	3.00
❑	25	Don Hoak	8.00	4.00
❑	26	Chuck Stobbs	6.00	3.00
❑	27	Andy Pafko	8.00	4.00
❑	28	Al Worthington	6.00	3.00
❑	29	Jim Bolger	6.00	3.00
❑	30	Nellie Fox	30.00	15.00
❑	31	Ken Lehman	6.00	3.00
❑	32	Don Buddin	6.00	3.00
❑	33	Ed Fitzgerald	6.00	3.00
❑	34	Al Kaline	20.00	10.00
		Charley Maxwell		
❑	35	Ted Kluszewski	12.00	6.00
❑	36	Hank Aguirre	6.00	3.00
❑	37	Gene Green	6.00	3.00
❑	38	Morrie Martin	6.00	3.00
❑	39	Ed Bouchee	6.00	3.00
❑	40A	Warren Spahn ERR	80.00	40.00
		(Born 1931)		
❑	40B	Warren Spahn ERR	100.00	50.00
		(Born 1931, but three is partially obscured)		
❑	40C	Warren Spahn COR	60.00	30.00
		(Born 1921)		
❑	41	Bob Martyn	6.00	3.00
❑	42	Murray Wall	6.00	3.00
❑	43	Steve Bilko	6.00	3.00
❑	44	Vito Valentinetti	6.00	3.00
❑	45	Andy Carey	8.00	4.00
❑	46	Bill R. Henry	6.00	3.00
❑	47	Jim Finigan	6.00	3.00
❑	48	Orioles Team CL	25.00	5.00
❑	49	Bill Hall	6.00	3.00
❑	50	Willie Mays	175.00	90.00
❑	51	Rip Coleman	6.00	3.00
❑	52	Coot Veal	6.00	3.00
❑	53	Stan Williams RC	8.00	4.00
❑	54	Mel Roach	6.00	3.00
❑	55	Tom Brewer	6.00	3.00
❑	56	Carl Sawatski	6.00	3.00
❑	57	Al Cicotte	6.00	3.00
❑	58	Eddie Miksis	6.00	3.00
❑	59	Irv Noren	8.00	4.00
❑	60	Bob Turley	8.00	4.00
❑	61	Dick Brown	6.00	3.00
❑	62	Tony Taylor	8.00	4.00
❑	63	Jim Hearn	6.00	3.00
❑	64	Joe DeMaestri	6.00	3.00
❑	65	Frank Torre	8.00	4.00
❑	66	Joe Ginsberg	6.00	3.00
❑	67	Brooks Lawrence	6.00	3.00
❑	68	Dick Schofield	8.00	4.00
❑	69	Giants Team CL	25.00	5.00
❑	70	Harvey Kuenn	8.00	4.00
❑	71	Don Bessent	6.00	3.00
❑	72	Bill Renna	6.00	3.00
❑	73	Ron Jackson	8.00	4.00
❑	74	Jim Lemon	8.00	4.00
		Cookie Lavagetto MG		
		Roy Sievers		
❑	75	Sam Jones	8.00	4.00
❑	76	Bobby Richardson	20.00	10.00
❑	77	John Goryl	6.00	3.00
❑	78	Pedro Ramos	6.00	3.00
❑	79	Harry Chiti	6.00	3.00
❑	80	Minnie Minoso	12.00	6.00
❑	81	Hal Jeffcoat	6.00	3.00
❑	82	Bob Boyd	6.00	3.00
❑	83	Bob Smith	6.00	3.00
❑	84	Reno Bertoia	6.00	3.00
❑	85	Harry Anderson	6.00	3.00
❑	86	Bob Keegan	8.00	4.00
❑	87	Danny O'Connell	6.00	3.00
❑	88	Herb Score	12.00	6.00
❑	89	Billy Gardner	6.00	3.00
❑	90	Bill Skowron	12.00	6.00
❑	91	Herb Moford	6.00	3.00
❑	92	Dave Philley	6.00	3.00
❑	93	Julio Becquer	6.00	3.00
❑	94	White Sox Team CL	40.00	8.00
❑	95	Carl Willey	6.00	3.00
❑	96	Lou Berberet	6.00	3.00
❑	97	Jerry Lynch	8.00	4.00
❑	98	Arnie Portocarrero	6.00	3.00
❑	99	Ted Kazanski	6.00	3.00
❑	100	Bob Cerv	8.00	4.00
❑	101	Alex Kellner	6.00	3.00
❑	102	Felipe Alou RC	30.00	15.00
❑	103	Billy Goodman	8.00	4.00
❑	104	Del Rice	8.00	4.00
❑	105	Lee Walls	6.00	3.00
❑	106	Hal Woodeshick	6.00	3.00
❑	107	Norm Larker	8.00	4.00
❑	108	Zack Monroe	8.00	4.00
❑	109	Bob Schmidt	6.00	3.00
❑	110	George Witt	8.00	4.00
❑	111	Redlegs Team CL	15.00	3.00
❑	112	Billy Consolo	4.00	2.00
❑	113	Taylor Phillips	4.00	2.00
❑	114	Earl Battey	8.00	4.00
❑	115	Mickey Vernon	8.00	4.00
❑	116	Bob Allison RP RC	12.00	6.00
❑	117	J.Blanchard RP RC	12.00	6.00
❑	118	John Buzhardt RP	5.00	2.50
❑	119	John Callison RP RC	12.00	6.00
❑	120	Chuck Coles RP	5.00	2.50
❑	121	Bob Conley RP	5.00	2.50
❑	122	Bennie Daniels RP	5.00	2.50
❑	123	Don Dillard RP	5.00	2.50
❑	124	Dan Dobbek RP	5.00	2.50
❑	125	Ron Fairly RP RC	12.00	6.00
❑	126	Eddie Haas RP	5.00	2.50
❑	127	Kent Hadley RP	5.00	2.50
❑	128	Bob Hartman RP	5.00	2.50
❑	129	Frank Herrera RP	5.00	2.50
❑	130	Lou Jackson RP	5.00	2.50
❑	131	Deron Johnson RP RC	12.00	6.00
❑	132	Don Lee RP	5.00	2.50
❑	133	Bob Lillis RP RC	5.00	2.50
❑	134	Jim McDaniel RP	5.00	2.50
❑	135	Gene Oliver RP	5.00	2.50
❑	136	Jim O'Toole RP RC	5.00	2.50
❑	137	Dick Ricketts RP	5.00	2.50
❑	138	John Romano RP RC	5.00	2.50
❑	139	Ed Sadowski RP	5.00	2.50
❑	140	Charlie Secrest RP	5.00	2.50
❑	141	Joe Shipley RP	5.00	2.50
❑	142	Dick Stigman RP	5.00	2.50
❑	143	Willie Tasby RP RC	5.00	2.50
❑	144	Jerry Walker RP	5.00	2.50
❑	145	Dom Zanni RP	5.00	2.50
❑	146	Jerry Zimmerman RP	5.00	2.50
❑	147	Dale Long	30.00	15.00
		Ernie Banks		
		Walt Moryn		
❑	148	Mike McCormick	8.00	4.00
❑	149	Jim Bunning	20.00	10.00
❑	150	Stan Musial	125.00	60.00
❑	151	Bob Malkmus	4.00	2.00
❑	152	Johnny Klippstein	4.00	2.00
❑	153	Jim Marshall	4.00	2.00
❑	154	Ray Herbert	4.00	2.00
❑	155	Enos Slaughter	20.00	10.00
❑	156	Billy Pierce	12.00	6.00
		Robin Roberts		
❑	157	Felix Mantilla	4.00	2.00
❑	158	Walt Dropo	4.00	2.00
❑	159	Bob Shaw	8.00	4.00
❑	160	Dick Groat	8.00	4.00
❑	161	Frank Baumann	4.00	2.00
❑	162	Bobby G. Smith	4.00	2.00
❑	163	Sandy Koufax	150.00	75.00
❑	164	Johnny Groth	4.00	2.00
❑	165	Bill Bruton	4.00	2.00
❑	166	Minnie Minoso	30.00	15.00
		Rocky Colavito		
		(Misspelled Colovito on card back)		
		Larry Doby		
❑	167	Duke Maas	4.00	2.00
❑	168	Carroll Hardy	4.00	2.00
❑	169	Ted Abernathy	4.00	2.00
❑	170	Gene Woodling	8.00	4.00
❑	171	Willard Schmidt	4.00	2.00
❑	172	Athletics Team CL	15.00	3.00
❑	173	Bill Monbouquette	8.00	4.00
❑	174	Jim Pendleton	4.00	2.00
❑	175	Dick Farrell	8.00	4.00
❑	176	Preston Ward	4.00	2.00
❑	177	John Briggs	4.00	2.00
❑	178	Ruben Amaro RC	12.00	6.00
❑	179	Don Rudolph	4.00	2.00
❑	180	Yogi Berra	80.00	40.00
❑	181	Bob Porterfield	4.00	2.00
❑	182	Milt Graff	4.00	2.00
❑	183	Stu Miller	8.00	4.00
❑	184	Harvey Haddix	8.00	4.00
❑	185	Jim Busby	4.00	2.00
❑	186	Mudcat Grant	8.00	4.00
❑	187	Bubba Phillips	8.00	4.00
❑	188	Juan Pizarro	4.00	2.00
❑	189	Neil Chrisley	4.00	2.00
❑	190	Bill Virdon	8.00	4.00
❑	191	Russ Kemmerer	4.00	2.00
❑	192	Charlie Beamon	4.00	2.00
❑	193	Sammy Taylor	4.00	2.00
❑	194	Jim Brosnan	8.00	4.00
❑	195	Rip Repulski	4.00	2.00
❑	196	Billy Moran	4.00	2.00
❑	197	Ray Semproch	4.00	2.00
❑	198	Jim Davenport	8.00	4.00
❑	199	Leo Kiely	4.00	2.00
❑	200	W.Giles NL PRES	8.00	4.00
❑	201	Tom Acker	4.00	2.00
❑	202	Roger Maris	125.00	60.00
❑	203	Ossie Virgil	4.00	2.00
❑	204	Casey Wise	4.00	2.00
❑	205	Don Larsen	8.00	4.00
❑	206	Carl Furillo	12.00	6.00
❑	207	George Strickland	4.00	2.00
❑	208	Willie Jones	4.00	2.00
❑	209	Lenny Green	4.00	2.00
❑	210	Ed Bailey	4.00	2.00
❑	211	Bob Blaylock	4.00	2.00
❑	212	Hank Aaron	80.00	40.00
		Eddie Mathews		
❑	213	Jim Rivera	8.00	4.00
❑	214	Marcelino Solis	4.00	2.00
❑	215	Jim Lemon	8.00	4.00
❑	216	Andre Rodgers	4.00	2.00
❑	217	Carl Erskine	12.00	6.00
❑	218	Roman Mejias	4.00	2.00
❑	219	George Zuverink	4.00	2.00
❑	220	Frank Malzone	8.00	4.00
❑	221	Bob Bowman	4.00	2.00
❑	222	Bobby Shantz	8.00	4.00

❑ 223	Cardinals Team CL	15.00	3.00
❑ 224	Claude Osteen RC	8.00	4.00
❑ 225	Johnny Logan	8.00	4.00
❑ 226	Art Ceccarelli	4.00	2.00
❑ 227	Hal W. Smith	4.00	2.00
❑ 228	Don Gross	4.00	2.00
❑ 229	Vic Power	8.00	4.00
❑ 230	Bill Fischer	4.00	2.00
❑ 231	Ellis Burton	4.00	2.00
❑ 232	Eddie Kasko	4.00	2.00
❑ 233	Paul Foytack	4.00	2.00
❑ 234	Chuck Tanner	8.00	4.00
❑ 235	Valmy Thomas	4.00	2.00
❑ 236	Ted Bowsfield	4.00	2.00
❑ 237	Gil McDougald	12.00	6.00
	Bob Turley		
	Bobby Richardson		
❑ 238	Gene Baker	4.00	2.00
❑ 239	Bob Trowbridge	4.00	2.00
❑ 240	Hank Bauer	12.00	6.00
❑ 241	Billy Muffett	4.00	2.00
❑ 242	Ron Samford	4.00	2.00
❑ 243	Marv Grissom	4.00	2.00
❑ 244	Ted Gray	4.00	2.00
❑ 245	Ned Garver	4.00	2.00
❑ 246	J.W. Porter	4.00	2.00
❑ 247	Don Ferrarese	4.00	2.00
❑ 248	Red Sox Team CL	15.00	3.00
❑ 249	Bobby Adams	4.00	2.00
❑ 250	Billy O'Dell	4.00	2.00
❑ 251	Clete Boyer	12.00	6.00
❑ 252	Ray Boone	8.00	4.00
❑ 253	Seth Morehead	4.00	2.00
❑ 254	Zeke Bella	4.00	2.00
❑ 255	Del Ennis	8.00	4.00
❑ 256	Jerry Davie	4.00	2.00
❑ 257	Leon Wagner RC	8.00	4.00
❑ 258	Fred Kipp	4.00	2.00
❑ 259	Jim Pisoni	4.00	2.00
❑ 260	Early Wynn UER	20.00	10.00
	1957 Cleveland		
❑ 261	Gene Stephens	4.00	2.00
❑ 262	Johnny Podres	12.00	6.00
	Clem Labine		
	Don Drysdale		
❑ 263	Bud Daley	4.00	2.00
❑ 264	Chico Carrasquel	4.00	2.00
❑ 265	Ron Kline	4.00	2.00
❑ 266	Woody Held	4.00	2.00
❑ 267	John Romonosky	4.00	2.00
❑ 268	Tito Francona	8.00	4.00
❑ 269	Jack Meyer	4.00	2.00
❑ 270	Gil Hodges	30.00	15.00
❑ 271	Orlando Pena	4.00	2.00
❑ 272	Jerry Lumpe	4.00	2.00
❑ 273	Joey Jay	8.00	4.00
❑ 274	Jerry Kindall	8.00	4.00
❑ 275	Jack Sanford	8.00	4.00
❑ 276	Pete Daley	4.00	2.00
❑ 277	Turk Lown	8.00	4.00
❑ 278	Chuck Essegian	4.00	2.00
❑ 279	Ernie Johnson	4.00	2.00
❑ 280	Frank Bolling	4.00	2.00
❑ 281	Walt Craddock	4.00	2.00
❑ 282	R.C. Stevens	4.00	2.00
❑ 283	Russ Heman	4.00	2.00
❑ 284	Steve Korcheck	4.00	2.00
❑ 285	Joe Cunningham	4.00	2.00
❑ 286	Dean Stone	4.00	2.00
❑ 287	Don Zimmer	12.00	6.00
❑ 288	Dutch Dotterer	4.00	2.00
❑ 289	Johnny Kucks	8.00	4.00
❑ 290	Wes Covington	4.00	2.00
❑ 291	Pedro Ramos	4.00	2.00
	Camilo Pascual		
❑ 292	Dick Williams	8.00	4.00
❑ 293	Ray Moore	4.00	2.00
❑ 294	Hank Foiles	4.00	2.00
❑ 295	Billy Martin	30.00	15.00
❑ 296	Ernie Broglio RC	4.00	2.00
❑ 297	Jackie Brandt	4.00	2.00
❑ 298	Tex Clevenger	4.00	2.00
❑ 299	Billy Klaus	4.00	2.00
❑ 300	Richie Ashburn	30.00	15.00
❑ 301	Earl Averill	4.00	2.00
❑ 302	Don Mossi	8.00	4.00
❑ 303	Marty Keough	4.00	2.00
❑ 304	Cubs Team CL	15.00	3.00
❑ 305	Curt Raydon	4.00	2.00
❑ 306	Jim Gilliam	8.00	4.00
❑ 307	Curt Barclay	4.00	2.00
❑ 308	Norm Siebern	4.00	2.00
❑ 309	Sal Maglie	8.00	4.00
❑ 310	Luis Aparicio	20.00	10.00
❑ 311	Norm Zauchin	4.00	2.00
❑ 312	Don Newcombe	8.00	4.00
❑ 313	Frank House	4.00	2.00
❑ 314	Don Cardwell	4.00	2.00
❑ 315	Joe Adcock	8.00	4.00
❑ 316A	Ralph Lumenti UER	4.00	2.00
	(Option)		
	(Photo actually		
	Camilo Pascual)		
❑ 316B	Ralph Lumenti UER	80.00	40.00
	(No option)		
	(Photo actually		
	Camilo Pascual)		
❑ 317	Willie Mays	80.00	40.00
	Richie Ashburn		
❑ 318	Rocky Bridges	4.00	2.00
❑ 319	Dave Hillman	4.00	2.00
❑ 320	Bob Skinner	8.00	4.00
❑ 321A	Bob Giallombardo	8.00	4.00
	(Option)		
❑ 321B	Bob Giallombardo	80.00	40.00
	(No option)		
❑ 322A	Harry Hanebrink	8.00	4.00
	(Traded)		
❑ 322B	Harry Hanebrink	80.00	40.00
	(No trade)		
❑ 323	Frank Sullivan	4.00	2.00
❑ 324	Don Demeter	4.00	2.00
❑ 325	Ken Boyer	12.00	6.00
❑ 326	Marv Throneberry	8.00	4.00
❑ 327	Gary Bell	4.00	2.00
❑ 328	Lou Skizas	4.00	2.00
❑ 329	Tigers Team CL	15.00	3.00
❑ 330	Gus Triandos	8.00	4.00
❑ 331	Steve Boros	4.00	2.00
❑ 332	Ray Monzant	4.00	2.00
❑ 333	Harry Simpson	4.00	2.00
❑ 334	Glen Hobbie	4.00	2.00
❑ 335	Johnny Temple	8.00	4.00
❑ 336A	Billy Loes	8.00	4.00
	(With traded line)		
❑ 336B	Billy Loes	80.00	40.00
	(No trade)		
❑ 337	George Crowe	4.00	2.00
❑ 338	Sparky Anderson RC	60.00	30.00
❑ 339	Roy Face	8.00	4.00
❑ 340	Roy Sievers	8.00	4.00
❑ 341	Tom Qualters	4.00	2.00
❑ 342	Ray Jablonski	4.00	2.00
❑ 343	Billy Hoeft	4.00	2.00
❑ 344	Russ Nixon	4.00	2.00
❑ 345	Gil McDougald	12.00	6.00
❑ 346	Dave Sisler	4.00	2.00
	Tom Brewer		
❑ 347	Bob Buhl	4.00	2.00
❑ 348	Ted Lepcio	4.00	2.00
❑ 349	Hoyt Wilhelm	20.00	10.00
❑ 350	Ernie Banks	80.00	40.00
❑ 351	Earl Torgeson	4.00	2.00
❑ 352	Robin Roberts	20.00	10.00
❑ 353	Curt Flood	8.00	4.00
❑ 354	Pete Burnside	4.00	2.00
❑ 355	Jimmy Piersall	8.00	4.00
❑ 356	Bob Mabe	4.00	2.00
❑ 357	Dick Stuart RC	8.00	4.00
❑ 358	Ralph Terry	8.00	4.00
❑ 359	Bill White RC	20.00	10.00
❑ 360	Al Kaline	60.00	30.00
❑ 361	Willard Nixon	4.00	2.00
❑ 362A	Dolan Nichols	4.00	2.00
	(With option line)		
❑ 362B	Dolan Nichols	80.00	40.00
	(No option)		
❑ 363	Bobby Avila	4.00	2.00
❑ 364	Danny McDevitt	4.00	2.00
❑ 365	Gus Bell	8.00	4.00
❑ 366	Humberto Robinson	4.00	2.00
❑ 367	Cal Neeman	4.00	2.00
❑ 368	Don Mueller	8.00	4.00
❑ 369	Dick Tomanek	4.00	2.00
❑ 370	Pete Runnels	8.00	4.00
❑ 371	Dick Brodowski	4.00	2.00
❑ 372	Jim Hegan	8.00	4.00
❑ 373	Herb Plews	4.00	2.00
❑ 374	Art Ditmar	8.00	4.00
❑ 375	Bob Nieman	4.00	2.00
❑ 376	Hal Naragon	4.00	2.00
❑ 377	John Antonelli	8.00	4.00
❑ 378	Gail Harris	4.00	2.00
❑ 379	Bob Miller	4.00	2.00
❑ 380	Hank Aaron	150.00	75.00
❑ 381	Mike Baxes	4.00	2.00
❑ 382	Curt Simmons	8.00	4.00
❑ 383	Don Larsen	12.00	6.00
	Casey Stengel MG		
❑ 384	Dave Sisler	4.00	2.00
❑ 385	Sherm Lollar	8.00	4.00
❑ 386	Jim Delsing	4.00	2.00
❑ 387	Don Drysdale	50.00	25.00
❑ 388	Bob Will	4.00	2.00
❑ 389	Joe Nuxhall	8.00	4.00
❑ 390	Orlando Cepeda	20.00	10.00
❑ 391	Milt Pappas	8.00	4.00
❑ 392	Whitey Herzog	8.00	4.00
❑ 393	Frank Lary	8.00	4.00
❑ 394	Randy Jackson	4.00	2.00
❑ 395	Elston Howard	12.00	6.00
❑ 396	Bob Rush	4.00	2.00
❑ 397	Senators Team CL	15.00	3.00
❑ 398	Wally Post	8.00	4.00
❑ 399	Larry Jackson	4.00	2.00
❑ 400	Jackie Jensen	8.00	4.00
❑ 401	Ron Blackburn	4.00	2.00
❑ 402	Hector Lopez	8.00	4.00
❑ 403	Clem Labine	8.00	4.00
❑ 404	Hank Sauer	8.00	4.00
❑ 405	Roy McMillan	8.00	4.00
❑ 406	Solly Drake	4.00	2.00
❑ 407	Moe Drabowsky	8.00	4.00
❑ 408	Nellie Fox	40.00	20.00
	Luis Aparicio		
❑ 409	Gus Zernial	8.00	4.00
❑ 410	Billy Pierce	8.00	4.00
❑ 411	Whitey Lockman	8.00	4.00
❑ 412	Stan Lopata	4.00	2.00
❑ 413	Camilo Pascual UER	8.00	4.00
	(Listed as Camillo		
	on front and Pasqual		
	on back)		
❑ 414	Dale Long	8.00	4.00
❑ 415	Bill Mazeroski	12.00	6.00
❑ 416	Haywood Sullivan	8.00	4.00
❑ 417	Virgil Trucks	8.00	4.00
❑ 418	Gino Cimoli	4.00	2.00
❑ 419	Braves Team CL	15.00	3.00
❑ 420	Rocky Colavito	30.00	15.00
❑ 421	Herman Wehmeier	4.00	2.00
❑ 422	Hobie Landrith	4.00	2.00
❑ 423	Bob Grim	8.00	4.00
❑ 424	Ken Aspromonte	4.00	2.00
❑ 425	Del Crandall	8.00	4.00
❑ 426	Gerry Staley	8.00	4.00
❑ 427	Charlie Neal	8.00	4.00
❑ 428	Ron Kline	4.00	2.00
	Bob Friend		
	Vernon Law		
	Roy Face		
❑ 429	Bobby Thomson	8.00	4.00
❑ 430	Whitey Ford	60.00	30.00
❑ 431	Whammy Douglas	4.00	2.00
❑ 432	Smoky Burgess	8.00	4.00
❑ 433	Billy Harrell	4.00	2.00
❑ 434	Hal Griggs	4.00	2.00
❑ 435	Frank Robinson	50.00	25.00
❑ 436	Granny Hamner	4.00	2.00
❑ 437	Ike Delock	4.00	2.00
❑ 438	Sammy Esposito	4.00	2.00
❑ 439	Brooks Robinson	50.00	25.00
❑ 440	Lou Burdette	8.00	4.00
	(Posing as if		
	lefthanded)		
❑ 441	John Roseboro	8.00	4.00
❑ 442	Ray Narleski	4.00	2.00
❑ 443	Daryl Spencer	4.00	2.00

❑ 444 Ron Hansen RC 8.00 4.00
❑ 445 Cal McLish 4.00 2.00
❑ 446 Rocky Nelson 4.00 2.00
❑ 447 Bob Anderson 4.00 2.00
❑ 448 Vada Pinson UER 12.00 6.00
(Born: 8/8/38
should be 8/11/38)
❑ 449 Tom Gorman 4.00 2.00
❑ 450 Eddie Mathews 40.00 20.00
❑ 451 Jimmy Constable 4.00 2.00
❑ 452 Chico Fernandez 4.00 2.00
❑ 453 Les Moss 4.00 2.00
❑ 454 Phil Clark 4.00 2.00
❑ 455 Larry Doby 12.00 6.00
❑ 456 Jerry Casale 4.00 2.00
❑ 457 Dodgers Team CL 30.00 6.00
❑ 458 Gordon Jones 4.00 2.00
❑ 459 Bill Tuttle 4.00 2.00
❑ 460 Bob Friend 8.00 4.00
❑ 461 Mickey Mantle HL 125.00 60.00
❑ 462 Rocky Colavito HL 12.00 6.00
❑ 463 Al Kaline HL 30.00 15.00
❑ 464 Willie Mays HL 40.00 20.00
54 World Series Catch
❑ 465 Roy Sievers HL 8.00 4.00
❑ 466 Billy Pierce HL 8.00 4.00
❑ 467 Hank Aaron HL 40.00 20.00
❑ 468 Duke Snider HL 20.00 10.00
❑ 469 Ernie Banks HL 20.00 10.00
❑ 470 Stan Musial HL 30.00 15.00
3,000 Hits
❑ 471 Tom Sturdivant 4.00 2.00
❑ 472 Gene Freese 4.00 2.00
❑ 473 Mike Fornieles 4.00 2.00
❑ 474 Moe Thacker 4.00 2.00
❑ 475 Jack Harshman 4.00 2.00
❑ 476 Indians Team CL 15.00 3.00
❑ 477 Barry Latman 4.00 2.00
❑ 478 Roberto Clemente 175.00 90.00
❑ 479 Lindy McDaniel 8.00 4.00
❑ 480 Red Schoendienst 12.00 6.00
❑ 481 Charlie Maxwell 8.00 4.00
❑ 482 Russ Meyer 4.00 2.00
❑ 483 Clint Courtney 4.00 2.00
❑ 484 Willie Kirkland 4.00 2.00
❑ 485 Ryne Duren 8.00 4.00
❑ 486 Sammy White 4.00 2.00
❑ 487 Hal Brown 4.00 2.00
❑ 488 Walt Moryn 4.00 2.00
❑ 489 John Powers 4.00 2.00
❑ 490 Frank Thomas 8.00 4.00
❑ 491 Don Blasingame 4.00 2.00
❑ 492 Gene Conley 8.00 4.00
❑ 493 Jim Landis 8.00 4.00
❑ 494 Don Pavletich 4.00 2.00
❑ 495 Johnny Podres 12.00 6.00
❑ 496 W.Terwilliger UER 4.00 2.00
Athlftics on front
❑ 497 Hal R. Smith 4.00 2.00
❑ 498 Dick Hyde 4.00 2.00
❑ 499 Johnny O'Brien 8.00 4.00
❑ 500 Vic Wertz 8.00 4.00
❑ 501 Bob Tiefenauer 4.00 2.00
❑ 502 Alvin Dark 8.00 4.00
❑ 503 Jim Owens 4.00 2.00
❑ 504 Ossie Alvarez 4.00 2.00
❑ 505 Tony Kubek 12.00 6.00
❑ 506 Bob Purkey 4.00 2.00
❑ 507 Bob Hale 15.00 7.50
❑ 508 Art Fowler 15.00 7.50
❑ 509 Norm Cash RC 80.00 40.00
❑ 510 Yankees Team CL 125.00 25.00
❑ 511 George Susce 15.00 7.50
❑ 512 George Altman 15.00 7.50
❑ 513 Tommy Carroll 15.00 7.50
❑ 514 Bob Gibson RC 300.00 150.00
❑ 515 Harmon Killebrew 125.00 60.00
❑ 516 Mike Garcia 20.00 10.00
❑ 517 Joe Koppe 15.00 7.50
❑ 518 Mike Cueller UER RC 30.00 15.00
Sic, Cuellar
❑ 519 Pete Runnels 20.00 10.00
Dick Gernert
Frank Malzone
❑ 520 Don Elston 15.00 7.50
❑ 521 Gary Geiger 15.00 7.50
❑ 522 Gene Snyder 15.00 7.50
❑ 523 Harry Bright 15.00 7.50
❑ 524 Larry Osborne 15.00 7.50
❑ 525 Jim Coates 20.00 10.00
❑ 526 Bob Speake 15.00 7.50
❑ 527 Solly Hemus 15.00 7.50
❑ 528 Pirates Team CL 80.00 16.00
❑ 529 G.Bamberger RC 20.00 10.00
❑ 530 Wally Moon 20.00 10.00
❑ 531 Ray Webster 15.00 7.50
❑ 532 Mark Freeman 15.00 7.50
❑ 533 Darrell Johnson 20.00 10.00
❑ 534 Faye Throneberry 15.00 7.50
❑ 535 Ruben Gomez 15.00 7.50
❑ 536 Danny Kravitz 15.00 7.50
❑ 537 Rudolph Arias 15.00 7.50
❑ 538 Chick King 15.00 7.50
❑ 539 Gary Blaylock 15.00 7.50
❑ 540 Willie Miranda 15.00 7.50
❑ 541 Bob Thurman 15.00 7.50
❑ 542 Jim Perry RC 30.00 15.00
❑ 543 Bob Skinner 125.00 60.00
Bill Virdon
Roberto Clemente
❑ 544 Lee Tate 15.00 7.50
❑ 545 Tom Morgan 15.00 7.50
❑ 546 Al Schroll 15.00 7.50
❑ 547 Jim Baxes 15.00 7.50
❑ 548 Elmer Singleton 15.00 7.50
❑ 549 Howie Nunn 15.00 7.50
❑ 550 Roy Campanella 150.00 75.00
(Symbol of Courage)
❑ 551 Fred Haney AS MG 15.00 7.50
❑ 552 Casey Stengel AS MG 30.00 15.00
❑ 553 Orlando Cepeda AS 30.00 15.00
❑ 554 Bill Skowron AS 20.00 10.00
❑ 555 Bill Mazeroski AS 30.00 15.00
❑ 556 Nellie Fox AS 40.00 20.00
❑ 557 Ken Boyer AS 30.00 15.00
❑ 558 Frank Malzone AS 15.00 7.50
❑ 559 Ernie Banks AS 60.00 30.00
❑ 560 Luis Aparicio AS 40.00 20.00
❑ 561 Hank Aaron AS 125.00 60.00
❑ 562 Al Kaline AS 60.00 30.00
❑ 563 Willie Mays AS 125.00 60.00
❑ 564 Mickey Mantle AS 300.00 150.00
❑ 565 Wes Covington AS 20.00 10.00
❑ 566 Roy Sievers AS 15.00 7.50
❑ 567 Del Crandall AS 15.00 7.50
❑ 568 Gus Triandos AS 15.00 7.50
❑ 569 Bob Friend AS 15.00 7.50
❑ 570 Bob Turley AS 15.00 7.50
❑ 571 Warren Spahn AS 50.00 25.00
❑ 572 Billy Pierce AS 40.00 13.00

1960 Topps

	NM	Ex
COMPLETE SET (572)	5000.00	2000.00
COMMON CARD (1-440)	4.00	1.60
COMMON (441-506)	8.00	3.20
COMMON (507-572)	15.00	6.00
WRAPPER (1-CENT)	900.00	350.00
WRAP. (1-CENT REPEAT)	500.00	200.00
WRAPPER (5-CENT)	40.00	16.00

❑ 1 Early Wynn 40.00 10.00
❑ 2 Roman Mejias 4.00 1.60
❑ 3 Joe Adcock 6.00 2.40
❑ 4 Bob Purkey 4.00 1.60
❑ 5 Wally Moon 6.00 2.40
❑ 6 Lou Berberet 4.00 1.60
❑ 7 Willie Mays 25.00 10.00
Bill Rigney MG
❑ 8 Bud Daley 4.00 1.60
❑ 9 Faye Throneberry 4.00 1.60
❑ 10 Ernie Banks 50.00 20.00
❑ 11 Norm Siebern 4.00 1.60
❑ 12 Milt Pappas 6.00 2.40
❑ 13 Wally Post 6.00 2.40
❑ 14 Jim Grant 6.00 2.40
❑ 15 Pete Runnels 6.00 2.40
❑ 16 Ernie Broglio 6.00 2.40
❑ 17 Johnny Callison 6.00 2.40
❑ 18 Dodgers Team CL 50.00 10.00
❑ 19 Felix Mantilla 4.00 1.60
❑ 20 Roy Face 6.00 2.40
❑ 21 Dutch Dotterer 4.00 1.60
❑ 22 Rocky Bridges 4.00 1.60
❑ 23 Eddie Fisher 4.00 1.60
❑ 24 Dick Gray 4.00 1.60
❑ 25 Roy Sievers 6.00 2.40
❑ 26 Wayne Terwilliger 4.00 1.60
❑ 27 Dick Drott 4.00 1.60
❑ 28 Brooks Robinson 50.00 20.00
❑ 29 Clem Labine 6.00 2.40
❑ 30 Tito Francona 4.00 1.60
❑ 31 Sammy Esposito 4.00 1.60
❑ 32 Jim O'Toole 4.00 1.60
Vada Pinson
❑ 33 Tom Morgan 4.00 1.60
❑ 34 Sparky Anderson 15.00 6.00
❑ 35 Whitey Ford 50.00 20.00
❑ 36 Russ Nixon 4.00 1.60
❑ 37 Bill Bruton 4.00 1.60
❑ 38 Jerry Casale 4.00 1.60
❑ 39 Earl Averill 4.00 1.60
❑ 40 Joe Cunningham 4.00 1.60
❑ 41 Barry Latman 4.00 1.60
❑ 42 Hobie Landrith 4.00 1.60
❑ 43 Senators Team CL 10.00 2.00
❑ 44 Bobby Locke 4.00 1.60
❑ 45 Roy McMillan 6.00 2.40
❑ 46 Jack Fisher 4.00 1.60
❑ 47 Don Zimmer 6.00 2.40
❑ 48 Hal W. Smith 4.00 1.60
❑ 49 Curt Raydon 4.00 1.60
❑ 50 Al Kaline 50.00 20.00
❑ 51 Jim Coates 6.00 2.40
❑ 52 Dave Philley 4.00 1.60
❑ 53 Jackie Brandt 4.00 1.60
❑ 54 Mike Fornieles 4.00 1.60
❑ 55 Bill Mazeroski 15.00 6.00
❑ 56 Steve Korcheck 4.00 1.60
❑ 57 Turk Lown 4.00 1.60
Gerry Staley
❑ 58 Gino Cimoli 4.00 1.60
❑ 58A Gino Cimoli .... .00
Cardinals Team Logo
❑ 59 Juan Pizarro 4.00 1.60
❑ 60 Gus Triandos 6.00 2.40
❑ 61 Eddie Kasko 4.00 1.60
❑ 62 Roger Craig 6.00 2.40
❑ 63 George Strickland 4.00 1.60
❑ 64 Jack Meyer 4.00 1.60
❑ 65 Elston Howard 6.00 2.40
❑ 66 Bob Trowbridge 4.00 1.60
❑ 67 Jose Pagan 4.00 1.60
❑ 68 Dave Hillman 4.00 1.60
❑ 69 Billy Goodman 6.00 2.40
❑ 70 Lew Burdette 6.00 2.40
Card spelled as Lou on front and back
❑ 71 Marty Keough 4.00 1.60
❑ 72 Tigers Team CL 25.00 5.00
❑ 73 Bob Gibson 50.00 20.00
❑ 74 Walt Moryn 4.00 1.60
❑ 75 Vic Power 6.00 2.40
❑ 76 Bill Fischer 4.00 1.60
❑ 77 Hank Foiles 4.00 1.60
❑ 78 Bob Grim 4.00 1.60
❑ 79 Walt Dropo 4.00 1.60
❑ 80 Johnny Antonelli 6.00 2.40
❑ 81 Russ Snyder 4.00 1.60
❑ 82 Ruben Gomez 4.00 1.60
❑ 83 Tony Kubek 15.00 6.00

❑ 84 Hal R. Smith 4.00 1.60
❑ 85 Frank Lary 6.00 2.40
❑ 86 Dick Gernert 4.00 1.60
❑ 87 John Romonosky 4.00 1.60
❑ 88 John Roseboro 6.00 2.40
❑ 89 Hal Brown 4.00 1.60
❑ 90 Bobby Avila 4.00 1.60
❑ 91 Bennie Daniels 4.00 1.60
❑ 92 Whitey Herzog 6.00 2.40
❑ 93 Art Schult 4.00 1.60
❑ 94 Leo Kiely 4.00 1.60
❑ 95 Frank Thomas 6.00 2.40
❑ 96 Ralph Terry 6.00 2.40
❑ 97 Ted Lepcio 4.00 1.60
❑ 98 Gordon Jones 4.00 1.60
❑ 99 Lenny Green 4.00 1.60
❑ 100 Nellie Fox 20.00 8.00
❑ 101 Bob Miller 4.00 1.60
❑ 102 Kent Hadley 4.00 1.60
❑ 102A Kent Hadley .00
Athletics Team Logo
❑ 103 Dick Farrell 6.00 2.40
❑ 104 Dick Schofield 6.00 2.40
❑ 105 Larry Sherry RC 6.00 2.40
❑ 106 Billy Gardner 4.00 1.60
❑ 107 Carlton Willey 4.00 1.60
❑ 108 Pete Daley 4.00 1.60
❑ 109 Clete Boyer 15.00 6.00
❑ 110 Cal McLish 4.00 1.60
❑ 111 Vic Wertz 6.00 2.40
❑ 112 Jack Harshman 4.00 1.60
❑ 113 Bob Skinner 4.00 1.60
❑ 114 Ken Aspromonte 4.00 1.60
❑ 115 Roy Face 6.00 2.40
Hoyt Wilhelm
❑ 116 Jim Rivera 4.00 1.60
❑ 117 Tom Borland RP 4.00 1.60
❑ 118 Bob Bruce RP 4.00 1.60
❑ 119 Chico Cardenas RP 6.00 2.40
❑ 120 Duke Carmel RP 4.00 1.60
❑ 121 Camilo Carreon RP 4.00 1.60
❑ 122 Don Dillard RP 4.00 1.60
❑ 123 Dan Dobbek RP 4.00 1.60
❑ 124 Jim Donohue RP 4.00 1.60
❑ 125 Dick Ellsworth RP RC 6.00 2.40
❑ 126 Chuck Estrada RP RC 4.00 1.60
❑ 127 Ron Hansen RP 6.00 2.40
❑ 128 Bill Harris RP 4.00 1.60
❑ 129 Bob Hartman RP 4.00 1.60
❑ 130 Frank Herrera RP 4.00 1.60
❑ 131 Ed Hobaugh RP 4.00 1.60
❑ 132 Frank Howard RP RC 25.00 10.00
❑ 133 Manuel Javier RC RP 6.00 2.40
(Sic, Julian)
❑ 134 Deron Johnson RP 6.00 2.40
❑ 135 Ken Johnson RC RP 4.00 1.60
❑ 136 Jim Kaat RP RC 40.00 16.00
❑ 137 Lou Klimchock RP 4.00 1.60
❑ 138 Art Mahaffey RP RC 6.00 2.40
❑ 139 Carl Mathias RP 4.00 1.60
❑ 140 Julio Navarro RP RC 4.00 1.60
❑ 141 Jim Proctor RP 4.00 1.60
❑ 142 Bill Short RP 4.00 1.60
❑ 143 Al Spangler RP 4.00 1.60
❑ 144 Al Stieglitz RP 4.00 1.60
❑ 145 Jim Umbricht RP 4.00 1.60
❑ 146 Ted Wieand RP 4.00 1.60
❑ 147 Bob Will RP 4.00 1.60
❑ 148 C.Yastrzemski RP RC 200.00 80.00
❑ 149 Bob Nieman 4.00 1.60
❑ 150 Billy Pierce 6.00 2.40
❑ 151 Giants Team CL 10.00 2.00
❑ 152 Gail Harris 4.00 1.60
❑ 153 Bobby Thomson 6.00 2.40
❑ 154 Jim Davenport 6.00 2.40
❑ 155 Charlie Neal 6.00 2.40
❑ 156 Art Ceccarelli 4.00 1.60
❑ 157 Rocky Nelson 6.00 2.40
❑ 158 Wes Covington 6.00 2.40
❑ 159 Jim Piersall 6.00 2.40
❑ 160 Mickey Mantle 125.00 50.00
Ken Boyer
❑ 161 Ray Narleski 4.00 1.60
❑ 162 Sammy Taylor 4.00 1.60
❑ 163 Hector Lopez 6.00 2.40
❑ 164 Reds Team CL 10.00 2.00
❑ 165 Jack Sanford 6.00 2.40
❑ 166 Chuck Essegian 4.00 1.60
❑ 167 Valmy Thomas 4.00 1.60
❑ 168 Alex Grammas 4.00 1.60
❑ 169 Jake Striker 4.00 1.60
❑ 170 Del Crandall 6.00 2.40
❑ 171 Johnny Groth 4.00 1.60
❑ 172 Willie Kirkland 4.00 1.60
❑ 173 Billy Martin 20.00 8.00
❑ 174 Indians Team CL 10.00 2.00
❑ 175 Pedro Ramos 4.00 1.60
❑ 176 Vada Pinson 6.00 2.40
❑ 177 Johnny Kucks 4.00 1.60
❑ 178 Woody Held 4.00 1.60
❑ 179 Rip Coleman 4.00 1.60
❑ 180 Harry Simpson 4.00 1.60
❑ 181 Billy Loes 6.00 2.40
❑ 182 Glen Hobbie 4.00 1.60
❑ 183 Eli Grba 4.00 1.60
❑ 184 Gary Geiger 4.00 1.60
❑ 185 Jim Owens 4.00 1.60
❑ 186 Dave Sisler 4.00 1.60
❑ 187 Jay Hook 4.00 1.60
❑ 188 Dick Williams 6.00 2.40
❑ 189 Don McMahon 4.00 1.60
❑ 190 Gene Woodling 6.00 2.40
❑ 191 Johnny Klippstein 4.00 1.60
❑ 192 Danny O'Connell 4.00 1.60
❑ 193 Dick Hyde 4.00 1.60
❑ 194 Bobby Gene Smith 4.00 1.60
❑ 195 Lindy McDaniel 6.00 2.40
❑ 196 Andy Carey 6.00 2.40
❑ 197 Ron Kline 4.00 1.60
❑ 198 Jerry Lynch 6.00 2.40
❑ 199 Dick Donovan 6.00 2.40
❑ 200 Willie Mays 125.00 50.00
❑ 201 Larry Osborne 4.00 1.60
❑ 202 Fred Kipp 4.00 1.60
❑ 203 Sammy White 4.00 1.60
❑ 204 Ryne Duren 6.00 2.40
❑ 205 Johnny Logan 6.00 2.40
❑ 206 Claude Osteen 6.00 2.40
❑ 207 Bob Boyd 4.00 1.60
❑ 208 White Sox Team CL 10.00 2.00
❑ 209 Ron Blackburn 4.00 1.60
❑ 210 Harmon Killebrew 40.00 16.00
❑ 211 Taylor Phillips 4.00 1.60
❑ 212 Walter Alston MG 10.00 4.00
❑ 213 Chuck Dressen MG 6.00 2.40
❑ 214 Jimmy Dykes MG 6.00 2.40
❑ 215 Bob Elliott MG 6.00 2.40
❑ 216 Joe Gordon MG 6.00 2.40
❑ 217 Charlie Grimm MG 6.00 2.40
❑ 218 Solly Hemus MG 4.00 1.60
❑ 219 Fred Hutchinson MG 6.00 2.40
❑ 220 Billy Jurges MG 4.00 1.60
❑ 221 Cookie Lavagetto MG 4.00 1.60
❑ 222 Al Lopez MG 10.00 4.00
❑ 223 Danny Murtaugh MG 6.00 2.40
❑ 224 Paul Richards MG 6.00 2.40
❑ 225 Bill Rigney MG 4.00 1.60
❑ 226 Eddie Sawyer MG 4.00 1.60
❑ 227 Casey Stengel MG 15.00 6.00
❑ 228 Ernie Johnson 6.00 2.40
❑ 229 Joe M. Morgan 4.00 1.60
❑ 230 Lou Burdette 10.00 4.00
Warren Spahn
Bob Buhl
❑ 231 Hal Naragon 4.00 1.60
❑ 232 Jim Busby 4.00 1.60
❑ 233 Don Elston 4.00 1.60
❑ 234 Don Demeter 4.00 1.60
❑ 235 Gus Bell 6.00 2.40
❑ 236 Dick Ricketts 4.00 1.60
❑ 237 Elmer Valo 4.00 1.60
❑ 238 Danny Kravitz 4.00 1.60
❑ 239 Joe Shipley 4.00 1.60
❑ 240 Luis Aparicio 15.00 6.00
❑ 241 Albie Pearson 6.00 2.40
❑ 242 Cardinals Team CL 10.00 2.00
❑ 243 Bubba Phillips 4.00 1.60
❑ 244 Hal Griggs 4.00 1.60
❑ 245 Eddie Yost 6.00 2.40
❑ 246 Lee Maye 6.00 2.40
❑ 247 Gil McDougald 10.00 4.00
❑ 248 Del Rice 4.00 1.60
❑ 249 Earl Wilson RC 6.00 2.40
❑ 250 Stan Musial 100.00 40.00
❑ 251 Bob Malkmus 4.00 1.60
❑ 252 Ray Herbert 4.00 1.60
❑ 253 Eddie Bressoud 4.00 1.60
❑ 254 Arnie Portocarrero 4.00 1.60
❑ 255 Jim Gilliam 6.00 2.40
❑ 256 Dick Brown 4.00 1.60
❑ 257 Gordy Coleman RC 4.00 1.60
❑ 258 Dick Groat 6.00 2.40
❑ 259 George Altman 4.00 1.60
❑ 260 Rocky Colavito 15.00 6.00
Tito Francona
❑ 261 Pete Burnside 4.00 1.60
❑ 262 Hank Bauer 6.00 2.40
❑ 263 Darrell Johnson 4.00 1.60
❑ 264 Robin Roberts 15.00 6.00
❑ 265 Rip Repulski 4.00 1.60
❑ 266 Joey Jay 6.00 2.40
❑ 267 Jim Marshall 4.00 1.60
❑ 268 Al Worthington 4.00 1.60
❑ 269 Gene Green 4.00 1.60
❑ 270 Bob Turley 6.00 2.40
❑ 271 Julio Becquer 4.00 1.60
❑ 272 Fred Green 6.00 2.40
❑ 273 Neil Chrisley 4.00 1.60
❑ 274 Tom Acker 4.00 1.60
❑ 275 Curt Flood 6.00 2.40
❑ 276 Ken McBride 4.00 1.60
❑ 277 Harry Bright 4.00 1.60
❑ 278 Stan Williams 6.00 2.40
❑ 279 Chuck Tanner 6.00 2.40
❑ 280 Frank Sullivan 4.00 1.60
❑ 281 Ray Boone 6.00 2.40
❑ 282 Joe Nuxhall 6.00 2.40
❑ 283 John Blanchard 6.00 2.40
❑ 284 Don Gross 4.00 1.60
❑ 285 Harry Anderson 4.00 1.60
❑ 286 Ray Semproch 4.00 1.60
❑ 287 Felipe Alou 6.00 2.40
❑ 288 Bob Mabe 4.00 1.60
❑ 289 Willie Jones 4.00 1.60
❑ 290 Jerry Lumpe 4.00 1.60
❑ 291 Bob Keegan 4.00 1.60
❑ 292 Joe Pignatano 6.00 2.40
John Roseboro
❑ 293 Gene Conley 6.00 2.40
❑ 294 Tony Taylor 6.00 2.40
❑ 295 Gil Hodges 25.00 10.00
❑ 296 Nelson Chittum 4.00 1.60
❑ 297 Reno Bertoia 4.00 1.60
❑ 298 George Witt 4.00 1.60
❑ 299 Earl Torgeson 4.00 1.60
❑ 300 Hank Aaron 125.00 50.00
❑ 301 Jerry Davie 4.00 1.60
❑ 302 Phillies Team CL 10.00 2.00
❑ 303 Billy O'Dell 4.00 1.60
❑ 304 Joe Ginsberg 4.00 1.60
❑ 305 Richie Ashburn 20.00 8.00
❑ 306 Frank Baumann 4.00 1.60
❑ 307 Gene Oliver 4.00 1.60
❑ 308 Dick Hall 4.00 1.60
❑ 309 Bob Hale 4.00 1.60
❑ 310 Frank Malzone 6.00 2.40
❑ 311 Raul Sanchez 4.00 1.60
❑ 312 Charley Lau 6.00 2.40
❑ 313 Turk Lown 4.00 1.60
❑ 314 Chico Fernandez 4.00 1.60
❑ 315 Bobby Shantz 10.00 4.00
❑ 316 Willie McCovey RC 125.00 50.00
❑ 317 Pumpsie Green 6.00 2.40
❑ 318 Jim Baxes 6.00 2.40
❑ 319 Joe Koppe 6.00 2.40
❑ 320 Bob Allison 6.00 2.40
❑ 321 Ron Fairly 6.00 2.40
❑ 322 Willie Tasby 6.00 2.40
❑ 323 John Romano 6.00 2.40
❑ 324 Jim Perry 6.00 2.40
❑ 325 Jim O'Toole 6.00 2.40
❑ 326 Roberto Clemente 175.00 70.00
❑ 327 Ray Sadecki RC 4.00 1.60
❑ 328 Earl Battey 4.00 1.60
❑ 329 Zack Monroe 4.00 1.60
❑ 330 Harvey Kuenn 6.00 2.40
❑ 331 Henry Mason 4.00 1.60
❑ 332 Yankees Team CL 80.00 16.00

❑ 333 Danny McDevitt 4.00 1.60
❑ 334 Ted Abernathy 4.00 1.60
❑ 335 Red Schoendienst 15.00 6.00
❑ 336 Ike Delock 4.00 1.60
❑ 337 Cal Neeman 4.00 1.60
❑ 338 Ray Monzant 4.00 1.60
❑ 339 Harry Chiti 4.00 1.60
❑ 340 Harvey Haddix 6.00 2.40
❑ 341 Carroll Hardy 4.00 1.60
❑ 342 Casey Wise 4.00 1.60
❑ 343 Sandy Koufax 125.00 50.00
❑ 344 Clint Courtney 4.00 1.60
❑ 345 Don Newcombe 6.00 2.40
❑ 346 J.C. Martin UER 6.00 2.40
(Face actually
Gary Peters)
❑ 347 Ed Bouchee 4.00 1.60
❑ 348 Barry Shetrone 4.00 1.60
❑ 349 Moe Drabowsky 6.00 2.40
❑ 350 Mickey Mantle 500.00 200.00
❑ 351 Don Nottebart 4.00 1.60
❑ 352 Gus Bell 10.00 4.00
Frank Robinson
Jerry Lynch
❑ 353 Don Larsen 6.00 2.40
❑ 354 Bob Lillis 4.00 1.60
❑ 355 Bill White 6.00 2.40
❑ 356 Joe Amalfitano 4.00 1.60
❑ 357 Al Schroll 4.00 1.60
❑ 358 Joe DeMaestri 4.00 1.60
❑ 359 Buddy Gilbert 4.00 1.60
❑ 360 Herb Score 6.00 2.40
❑ 361 Bob Oldis 6.00 2.40
❑ 362 Russ Kemmerer 4.00 1.60
❑ 363 Gene Stephens 4.00 1.60
❑ 364 Paul Foytack 4.00 1.60
❑ 365 Minnie Minoso 10.00 4.00
❑ 366 Dallas Green RC 10.00 4.00
❑ 367 Bill Tuttle 4.00 1.60
❑ 368 Daryl Spencer 4.00 1.60
❑ 369 Billy Hoeft 4.00 1.60
❑ 370 Bill Skowron 10.00 4.00
❑ 371 Bud Byerly 4.00 1.60
❑ 372 Frank House 4.00 1.60
❑ 373 Don Hoak 6.00 2.40
❑ 374 Bob Buhl 6.00 2.40
❑ 375 Dale Long 10.00 4.00
❑ 376 John Briggs 4.00 1.60
❑ 377 Roger Maris 100.00 40.00
❑ 378 Stu Miller 6.00 2.40
❑ 379 Red Wilson 4.00 1.60
❑ 380 Bob Shaw 4.00 1.60
❑ 381 Braves Team CL 10.00 2.00
❑ 382 Ted Bowsfield 4.00 1.60
❑ 383 Leon Wagner 4.00 1.60
❑ 384 Don Cardwell 4.00 1.60
❑ 385 Charlie Neal WS 8.00 3.20
❑ 386 Charlie Neal WS 8.00 3.20
❑ 387 Carl Furillo WS 8.00 3.20
❑ 388 Gil Hodges WS 10.00 4.00
❑ 389 Luis Aparicio WS 10.00 4.00
Maury Wills
❑ 390 World Series Game 6 .... 8.00 3.20
❑ 391 WS Summary 8.00 3.20
The Champs Celebrate
❑ 392 Tex Clevenger 4.00 1.60
❑ 393 Smoky Burgess 6.00 2.40
❑ 394 Norm Larker 6.00 2.40
❑ 395 Hoyt Wilhelm 15.00 6.00
❑ 396 Steve Bilko 4.00 1.60
❑ 397 Don Blasingame 4.00 1.60
❑ 398 Mike Cuellar 6.00 2.40
❑ 399 Milt Pappas 6.00 2.40
Jack Fisher
Jerry Walker
❑ 400 Rocky Colavito 20.00 8.00
❑ 401 Bob Duliba 4.00 1.60
❑ 402 Dick Stuart 15.00 6.00
❑ 403 Ed Sadowski 4.00 1.60
❑ 404 Bob Rush 4.00 1.60
❑ 405 Bobby Richardson 15.00 6.00
❑ 406 Billy Klaus 4.00 1.60
❑ 407 Gary Peters RC UER 6.00 2.40
(Face actually
J.C. Martin)
❑ 408 Carl Furillo 10.00 4.00
❑ 409 Ron Samford 4.00 1.60
❑ 410 Sam Jones 6.00 2.40
❑ 411 Ed Bailey 4.00 1.60
❑ 412 Bob Anderson 4.00 1.60
❑ 413 Athletics Team CL 10.00 2.00
❑ 414 Don Williams 4.00 1.60
❑ 415 Bob Cerv 4.00 1.60
❑ 416 Humberto Robinson 4.00 1.60
❑ 417 Chuck Cottier RC 4.00 1.60
❑ 418 Don Mossi 6.00 2.40
❑ 419 George Crowe 4.00 1.60
❑ 420 Eddie Mathews 40.00 16.00
❑ 421 Duke Maas 4.00 1.60
❑ 422 John Powers 4.00 1.60
❑ 423 Ed Fitzgerald 4.00 1.60
❑ 424 Pete Whisenant 4.00 1.60
❑ 425 Johnny Podres 6.00 2.40
❑ 426 Ron Jackson 4.00 1.60
❑ 427 Al Grunwald 4.00 1.60
❑ 428 Al Smith 4.00 1.60
❑ 429 Nellie Fox 10.00 4.00
Harvey Kuenn
❑ 430 Art Ditmar 4.00 1.60
❑ 431 Andre Rodgers 4.00 1.60
❑ 432 Chuck Stobbs 4.00 1.60
❑ 433 Irv Noren 4.00 1.60
❑ 434 Brooks Lawrence 6.00 2.40
❑ 435 Gene Freese 4.00 1.60
❑ 436 Marv Throneberry 6.00 2.40
❑ 437 Bob Friend 6.00 2.40
❑ 438 Jim Coker 4.00 1.60
❑ 439 Tom Brewer 4.00 1.60
❑ 440 Jim Lemon 6.00 2.40
❑ 441 Gary Bell 10.00 4.00
❑ 442 Joe Pignatano 8.00 3.20
❑ 443 Charlie Maxwell 8.00 3.20
❑ 444 Jerry Kindall 8.00 3.20
❑ 445 Warren Spahn 50.00 20.00
❑ 446 Ellis Burton 8.00 3.20
❑ 447 Ray Moore 8.00 3.20
❑ 448 Jim Gentile RC 15.00 6.00
❑ 449 Jim Brosnan 8.00 3.20
❑ 450 Orlando Cepeda 25.00 10.00
❑ 451 Curt Simmons 8.00 3.20
❑ 452 Ray Webster 8.00 3.20
❑ 453 Vern Law 25.00 10.00
❑ 454 Hal Woodeshick 8.00 3.20
❑ 455 Eddie Robinson CO 8.00 3.20
Harry Brecheen CO
Luman Harris CO
❑ 456 Rudy York CO 10.00 4.00
Billy Herman CO
Sal Maglie CO
Del Baker CO
❑ 457 Charlie Root CO 8.00 3.20
Lou Klein CO
Elvin Tappe CO
❑ 458 Johnny Cooney CO 8.00 3.20
Don Gutteridge CO
Tony Cuccinello CO
Ray Berres CO
❑ 459 Reggie Otero CO 8.00 3.20
Cot Deal CO
Wally Moses CO
❑ 460 Mel Harder CO 15.00 6.00
Jo-Jo White CO
Bob Lemon CO
Ralph(Red) Kress CO
❑ 461 Tom Ferrick CO 10.00 4.00
Luke Appling CO
Billy Hitchcock CO
❑ 462 Fred Fitzsimmons CO 8.00 3.20
Don Heffner CO
Walker Cooper CO
❑ 463 Bobby Bragan CO 8.00 3.20
Pete Reiser CO
Joe Becker CO
Greg Mulleavy CO
❑ 464 Bob Scheffing CO 8.00 3.20
Whitlow Wyatt CO
Andy Pafko CO
George Myatt CO
❑ 465 Bill Dickey CO 25.00 10.00
Ralph Houk CO
Frank Crosetti CO
Ed Lopat CO
❑ 466 Ken Silvestri CO 8.00 3.20
Dick Carter CO
Andy Cohen CO
❑ 467 Mickey Vernon CO 8.00 3.20
Frank Oceak CO
Sam Narron CO
Bill Burwell CO
❑ 468 Johnny Keane CO 8.00 3.20
Howie Pollet CO
Ray Katt CO
Harry Walker CO
❑ 469 Wes Westrum CO 8.00 3.20
Salty Parker CO
Bill Posedel CO
❑ 470 Bob Swift CO 8.00 3.20
Ellis Clary CO
Sam Mele CO
❑ 471 Ned Garver 8.00 3.20
❑ 472 Alvin Dark 8.00 3.20
❑ 473 Al Cicotte 8.00 3.20
❑ 474 Haywood Sullivan 8.00 3.20
❑ 475 Don Drysdale 40.00 16.00
❑ 476 Lou Johnson 8.00 3.20
❑ 477 Don Ferrarese 8.00 3.20
❑ 478 Frank Torre 8.00 3.20
❑ 479 Georges Maranda 8.00 3.20
❑ 480 Yogi Berra 80.00 32.00
❑ 481 Wes Stock 8.00 3.20
❑ 482 Frank Bolling 8.00 3.20
❑ 483 Camilo Pascual 8.00 3.20
❑ 484 Pirates Team CL 40.00 8.00
❑ 485 Ken Boyer 15.00 6.00
❑ 486 Bobby Del Greco 8.00 3.20
❑ 487 Tom Sturdivant 8.00 3.20
❑ 488 Norm Cash 25.00 10.00
Shown with Indians Cap but listed as a Tiger
❑ 489 Steve Ridzik 8.00 3.20
❑ 490 Frank Robinson 50.00 20.00
❑ 491 Mel Roach 8.00 3.20
❑ 492 Larry Jackson 8.00 3.20
❑ 493 Duke Snider 50.00 20.00
❑ 494 Orioles Team CL 25.00 5.00
❑ 495 Sherm Lollar 8.00 3.20
❑ 496 Bill Virdon 10.00 4.00
❑ 497 John Tsitouris 8.00 3.20
❑ 498 Al Pilarcik 8.00 3.20
❑ 499 Johnny James 10.00 4.00
❑ 500 Johnny Temple 8.00 3.20
❑ 501 Bob Schmidt 8.00 3.20
❑ 502 Jim Bunning 25.00 10.00
❑ 503 Don Lee 8.00 3.20
❑ 504 Seth Morehead 8.00 3.20
❑ 505 Ted Kluszewski 25.00 10.00
❑ 506 Lee Walls 8.00 3.20
❑ 507 Dick Stigman 15.00 6.00
❑ 508 Billy Consolo 15.00 6.00
❑ 509 Tommy Davis RC 25.00 10.00
❑ 510 Gerry Staley 15.00 6.00
❑ 511 Ken Walters 15.00 6.00
❑ 512 Joe Gibbon 15.00 6.00
❑ 513 Chicago Cubs 30.00 6.00
Team Card CL
❑ 514 Steve Barber RC 15.00 6.00
❑ 515 Stan Lopata 15.00 6.00
❑ 516 Marty Kutyna 15.00 6.00
❑ 517 Charlie James 25.00 10.00
❑ 518 Tony Gonzalez 15.00 6.00
❑ 519 Ed Roebuck 15.00 6.00
❑ 520 Don Buddin 15.00 6.00
❑ 521 Mike Lee 15.00 6.00
❑ 522 Ken Hunt 30.00 12.00
❑ 523 Clay Dalrymple 15.00 6.00
❑ 524 Bill Henry 15.00 6.00
❑ 525 Marv Breeding 15.00 6.00
❑ 526 Paul Giel 25.00 10.00
❑ 527 Jose Valdivielso 25.00 10.00
❑ 528 Ben Johnson 15.00 6.00
❑ 529 Norm Sherry RC 20.00 8.00
❑ 530 Mike McCormick 15.00 6.00
❑ 531 Sandy Amoros 20.00 8.00
❑ 532 Mike Garcia 20.00 8.00
❑ 533 Lu Clinton 15.00 6.00
❑ 534 Ken MacKenzie 15.00 6.00
❑ 535 Whitey Lockman 15.00 6.00
❑ 536 Wynn Hawkins 15.00 6.00

Card	NM	Ex
❑ 537 Boston Red Sox Team Card CL	30.00	6.00
❑ 538 Frank Barnes	15.00	6.00
❑ 539 Gene Baker	15.00	6.00
❑ 540 Jerry Walker	15.00	6.00
❑ 541 Tony Curry	15.00	6.00
❑ 542 Ken Hamlin	15.00	6.00
❑ 543 Elio Chacon	15.00	6.00
❑ 544 Bill Monbouquette	20.00	8.00
❑ 545 Carl Sawatski	15.00	6.00
❑ 546 Hank Aguirre	15.00	6.00
❑ 547 Bob Aspromonte	20.00	8.00
❑ 548 Don Mincher	15.00	6.00
❑ 549 John Buzhardt	15.00	6.00
❑ 550 Jim Landis	15.00	6.00
❑ 551 Ed Rakow	15.00	6.00
❑ 552 Walt Bond	15.00	6.00
❑ 553 Bill Skowron AS	20.00	8.00
❑ 554 Willie McCovey AS	40.00	16.00
❑ 555 Nellie Fox AS	30.00	12.00
❑ 556 Charlie Neal AS	15.00	6.00
❑ 557 Frank Malzone AS	15.00	6.00
❑ 558 Eddie Mathews AS	40.00	16.00
❑ 559 Luis Aparicio AS	30.00	12.00
❑ 560 Ernie Banks AS	60.00	24.00
❑ 561 Al Kaline AS	60.00	24.00
❑ 562 Joe Cunningham AS	15.00	6.00
❑ 563 Mickey Mantle AS	250.00	100.00
❑ 564 Willie Mays AS	100.00	40.00
❑ 565 Roger Maris AS	100.00	40.00
❑ 566 Hank Aaron AS	100.00	40.00
❑ 567 Sherm Lollar AS	15.00	6.00
❑ 568 Del Crandall AS	15.00	6.00
❑ 569 Camilo Pascual AS	15.00	6.00
❑ 570 Don Drysdale AS	40.00	16.00
❑ 571 Billy Pierce AS	15.00	6.00
❑ 572 Johnny Antonelli AS	30.00	9.00
❑ NNO Iron-on team transfer	5.00	2.00

1961 Topps

	NM	Ex
COMPLETE SET (587)	7000.00	2800.00
COMMON CARD (1-370)	3.00	1.20
COMMON (371-446)	4.00	1.60
COMMON (447-522)	8.00	3.20
COMMON (523-589)	30.00	12.00
NOT ISSUED (587/588)		
WRAPPER (1-CENT)	200.00	80.00
WRAP.(1-CENT, REPEAT)	100.00	40.00
WRAPPER (5-CENT)	40.00	16.00

Card	NM	Ex
❑ 1 Dick Groat	30.00	6.00
❑ 2 Roger Maris	250.00	100.00
❑ 3 John Buzhardt	3.00	1.20
❑ 4 Lenny Green	3.00	1.20
❑ 5 John Romano	3.00	1.20
❑ 6 Ed Roebuck	3.00	1.20
❑ 7 White Sox Team	8.00	3.20
❑ 8 Dick Williams	6.00	2.40
❑ 9 Bob Purkey	3.00	1.20
❑ 10 Brooks Robinson	50.00	20.00
❑ 11 Curt Simmons	6.00	2.40
❑ 12 Moe Thacker	3.00	1.20
❑ 13 Chuck Cottier	3.00	1.20
❑ 14 Don Mossi	6.00	2.40
❑ 15 Willie Kirkland	3.00	1.20
❑ 16 Billy Muffett	3.00	1.20
❑ 17 Checklist 1	10.00	2.00
❑ 18 Jim Grant	6.00	2.40
❑ 19 Clete Boyer	8.00	3.20
❑ 20 Robin Roberts	15.00	6.00
❑ 21 Zorro Versalles UER RC First name should be Zoilo	8.00	3.20
❑ 22 Clem Labine	6.00	2.40
❑ 23 Don Demeter	3.00	1.20
❑ 24 Ken Johnson	6.00	2.40
❑ 25 Vada Pinson Gus Bell Frank Robinson	8.00	3.20
❑ 26 Wes Stock	3.00	1.20
❑ 27 Jerry Kindall	3.00	1.20
❑ 28 Hector Lopez	6.00	2.40
❑ 29 Don Nottebart	3.00	1.20
❑ 30 Nellie Fox	15.00	6.00
❑ 31 Bob Schmidt	3.00	1.20
❑ 32 Ray Sadecki	3.00	1.20
❑ 33 Gary Geiger	3.00	1.20
❑ 34 Wynn Hawkins	3.00	1.20
❑ 35 Ron Santo RC	40.00	16.00
❑ 36 Jack Kralick	3.00	1.20
❑ 37 Charley Maxwell	6.00	2.40
❑ 38 Bob Lillis	3.00	1.20
❑ 39 Leo Posada	3.00	1.20
❑ 40 Bob Turley	6.00	2.40
❑ 41 Dick Groat Norm Larker Willie Mays Roberto Clemente LL	40.00	16.00
❑ 42 Pete Runnels Al Smith Minnie Minoso Bill Skowron LL	8.00	3.20
❑ 43 Ernie Banks Hank Aaron Ed Mathews Ken Boyer LL	30.00	12.00
❑ 44 Mickey Mantle Roger Maris Jim Lemon Rocky Colavito LL	80.00	32.00
❑ 45 Mike McCormick Ernie Broglio Don Drysdale Bob Friend Stan Williams LL	8.00	3.20
❑ 46 Frank Baumann Jim Bunning Art Ditmar Hal Brown LL	8.00	3.20
❑ 47 Ernie Broglio Warren Spahn Vern Law Lou Burdette LL	8.00	3.20
❑ 48 Chuck Estrada Jim Perry UER (Listed as an Oriole) Bud Daley Art Ditmar Frank Lary Milt Pappas LL	8.00	3.20
❑ 49 Don Drysdale Sandy Koufax Sam Jones Ernie Broglio LL	20.00	8.00
❑ 50 Jim Bunning Pedro Ramos Early Wynn Frank Lary LL	8.00	3.20
❑ 51 Detroit Tigers Team Card	8.00	3.20
❑ 52 George Crowe	3.00	1.20
❑ 53 Russ Nixon	3.00	1.20
❑ 54 Earl Francis	3.00	1.20
❑ 55 Jim Davenport	6.00	2.40
❑ 56 Russ Kemmerer	3.00	1.20
❑ 57 Marv Throneberry	6.00	2.40
❑ 58 Joe Schaffernoth	3.00	1.20
❑ 59 Jim Woods	3.00	1.20
❑ 60 Woody Held	3.00	1.20
❑ 61 Ron Piche	3.00	1.20
❑ 62 Al Pilarcik	3.00	1.20
❑ 63 Jim Kaat	8.00	3.20
❑ 64 Alex Grammas	3.00	1.20
❑ 65 Ted Kluszewski	8.00	3.20
❑ 66 Bill Henry	3.00	1.20
❑ 67 Ossie Virgil	3.00	1.20
❑ 68 Deron Johnson	6.00	2.40
❑ 69 Earl Wilson	6.00	2.40
❑ 70 Bill Virdon	6.00	2.40
❑ 71 Jerry Adair	3.00	1.20
❑ 72 Stu Miller	6.00	2.40
❑ 73 Al Spangler	3.00	1.20
❑ 74 Joe Pignatano	3.00	1.20
❑ 75 Lindy McDaniel Larry Jackson	6.00	2.40
❑ 76 Harry Anderson	3.00	1.20
❑ 77 Dick Stigman	3.00	1.20
❑ 78 Lee Walls	6.00	2.40
❑ 79 Joe Ginsberg	3.00	1.20
❑ 80 Harmon Killebrew	20.00	8.00
❑ 81 Tracy Stallard	3.00	1.20
❑ 82 Joe Christopher	3.00	1.20
❑ 83 Bob Bruce	3.00	1.20
❑ 84 Lee Maye	3.00	1.20
❑ 85 Jerry Walker	3.00	1.20
❑ 86 Los Angeles Dodgers Team Card	8.00	3.20
❑ 87 Joe Amalfitano	3.00	1.20
❑ 88 Richie Ashburn	15.00	6.00
❑ 89 Billy Martin	15.00	6.00
❑ 90 Gerry Staley	3.00	1.20
❑ 91 Walt Moryn	3.00	1.20
❑ 92 Hal Naragon	3.00	1.20
❑ 93 Tony Gonzalez	3.00	1.20
❑ 94 Johnny Kucks	3.00	1.20
❑ 95 Norm Cash	8.00	3.20
❑ 96 Billy O'Dell	3.00	1.20
❑ 97 Jerry Lynch	6.00	2.40
❑ 98A Checklist 2 (Red "Checklist" 98 black on white)	10.00	2.00
❑ 98B Checklist 2 (Yellow "Checklist" 98 black on white)	10.00	2.00
❑ 98C Checklist 2 (Yellow "Checklist" 98 white on black no copyright)	10.00	2.00
❑ 99 Don Buddin UER (66 HR's)	3.00	1.20
❑ 100 Harvey Haddix	6.00	2.40
❑ 101 Bubba Phillips	3.00	1.20
❑ 102 Gene Stephens	3.00	1.20
❑ 103 Ruben Amaro	3.00	1.20
❑ 104 John Blanchard	8.00	3.20
❑ 105 Carl Willey	3.00	1.20
❑ 106 Whitey Herzog	3.00	1.20
❑ 107 Seth Morehead	3.00	1.20
❑ 108 Dan Dobbek	3.00	1.20
❑ 109 Johnny Podres	8.00	3.20
❑ 110 Vada Pinson	8.00	3.20
❑ 111 Jack Meyer	3.00	1.20
❑ 112 Chico Fernandez	3.00	1.20
❑ 113 Mike Fornieles	3.00	1.20
❑ 114 Hobie Landrith	3.00	1.20
❑ 115 Johnny Antonelli	6.00	2.40
❑ 116 Joe DeMaestri	3.00	1.20
❑ 117 Dale Long	6.00	2.40
❑ 118 Chris Cannizzaro	3.00	1.20
❑ 119 Norm Siebern Hank Bauer Jerry Lumpe	6.00	2.40
❑ 120 Eddie Mathews	30.00	12.00
❑ 121 Eli Grba	6.00	2.40
❑ 122 Chicago Cubs Team Card	8.00	3.20
❑ 123 Billy Gardner	3.00	1.20
❑ 124 J.C. Martin	3.00	1.20
❑ 125 Steve Barber	3.00	1.20
❑ 126 Dick Stuart	6.00	2.40
❑ 127 Ron Kline	3.00	1.20
❑ 128 Rip Repulski	3.00	1.20
❑ 129 Ed Hobaugh	3.00	1.20
❑ 130 Norm Larker	3.00	1.20
❑ 131 Paul Richards MG	6.00	2.40
❑ 132 Al Lopez MG	8.00	3.20
❑ 133 Ralph Houk MG	6.00	2.40
❑ 134 Mickey Vernon MG	6.00	2.40

❑ 135 Fred Hutchinson MG 6.00 2.40
❑ 136 Walter Alston MG 8.00 3.20
❑ 137 Chuck Dressen MG 6.00 2.40
❑ 138 Danny Murtaugh MG...... 6.00 2.40
❑ 139 Solly Hemus MG........... 6.00 2.40
❑ 140 Gus Triandos................. 6.00 2.40
❑ 141 Billy Williams RC 60.00 24.00
❑ 142 Luis Arroyo 6.00 2.40
❑ 143 Russ Snyder 3.00 1.20
❑ 144 Jim Coker 3.00 1.20
❑ 145 Bob Buhl 6.00 2.40
❑ 146 Marty Keough 3.00 1.20
❑ 147 Ed Rakow 3.00 1.20
❑ 148 Julian Javier 6.00 2.40
❑ 149 Bob Oldis 3.00 1.20
❑ 150 Willie Mays 100.00 40.00
❑ 151 Jim Donohue................... 3.00 1.20
❑ 152 Earl Torgeson 3.00 1.20
❑ 153 Don Lee.......................... 3.00 1.20
❑ 154 Bobby Del Greco 3.00 1.20
❑ 155 Johnny Temple 6.00 2.40
❑ 156 Ken Hunt 6.00 2.40
❑ 157 Cal McLish 3.00 1.20
❑ 158 Pete Daley 3.00 1.20
❑ 159 Orioles Team.................. 8.00 3.20
❑ 160 Whitey Ford UER.......... 50.00 20.00
Incorrectly listed
as 5'0" tall
❑ 161 Sherman Jones RC 3.00 1.20
❑ 162 Jay Hook 3.00 1.20
❑ 163 Ed Sadowski 3.00 1.20
❑ 164 Felix Mantilla 3.00 1.20
❑ 165 Gino Cimoli..................... 3.00 1.20
❑ 166 Danny Kravitz 3.00 1.20
❑ 167 San Francisco Giants 8.00 3.20
Team Card
❑ 168 Tommy Davis 8.00 3.20
❑ 169 Don Elston 3.00 1.20
❑ 170 Al Smith 3.00 1.20
❑ 171 Paul Foytack 3.00 1.20
❑ 172 Don Dillard 3.00 1.20
❑ 173 Frank Malzone................ 6.00 2.40
Vic Wertz
Jackie Jensen
❑ 174 Ray Semproch................ 3.00 1.20
❑ 175 Gene Freese 3.00 1.20
❑ 176 Ken Aspromonte 3.00 1.20
❑ 177 Don Larsen 6.00 2.40
❑ 178 Bob Nieman 3.00 1.20
❑ 179 Joe Koppe 3.00 1.20
❑ 180 Bobby Richardson........ 12.00 4.80
❑ 181 Fred Green 3.00 1.20
❑ 182 Dave Nicholson.............. 3.00 1.20
❑ 183 Andre Rodgers 3.00 1.20
❑ 184 Steve Bilko 6.00 2.40
❑ 185 Herb Score 6.00 2.40
❑ 186 Elmer Valo...................... 6.00 2.40
❑ 187 Billy Klaus...................... 3.00 1.20
❑ 188 Jim Marshall 3.00 1.20
❑ 189A Checklist 3 .... 10.00 2.00
(Copyright symbol
almost adjacent to
263 Ken Hamlin)
❑ 189B Checklist 3 .... 10.00 2.00
(Copyright symbol
adjacent to
264 Glen Hobbie)
❑ 190 Stan Williams 6.00 2.40
❑ 191 Mike de la Hoz 3.00 1.20
❑ 192 Dick Brown 3.00 1.20
❑ 193 Gene Conley 6.00 2.40
❑ 194 Gordy Coleman 6.00 2.40
❑ 195 Jerry Casale 3.00 1.20
❑ 196 Ed Bouchee 3.00 1.20
❑ 197 Dick Hall 3.00 1.20
❑ 198 Carl Sawatski 3.00 1.20
❑ 199 Bob Boyd 3.00 1.20
❑ 200 Warren Spahn 40.00 16.00
❑ 201 Pete Whisenant 3.00 1.20
❑ 202 Al Neiger 3.00 1.20
❑ 203 Eddie Bressoud 3.00 1.20
❑ 204 Bob Skinner 6.00 2.40
❑ 205 Billy Pierce 6.00 2.40
❑ 206 Gene Green 3.00 1.20
❑ 207 Sandy Koufax 30.00 12.00
Johnny Podres
❑ 208 Larry Osborne 3.00 1.20
❑ 209 Ken McBride 3.00 1.20
❑ 210 Pete Runnels.................. 6.00 2.40
❑ 211 Bob Gibson 40.00 16.00
❑ 212 Haywood Sullivan 6.00 2.40
❑ 213 Bill Stafford 3.00 1.20
❑ 214 Danny Murphy 6.00 2.40
❑ 215 Gus Bell 6.00 2.40
❑ 216 Ted Bowsfield 3.00 1.20
❑ 217 Mel Roach....................... 3.00 1.20
❑ 218 Hal Brown 3.00 1.20
❑ 219 Gene Mauch MG............ 6.00 2.40
❑ 220 Alvin Dark MG................ 6.00 2.40
❑ 221 Mike Higgins MG 3.00 1.20
❑ 222 Jimmy Dykes MG 6.00 2.40
❑ 223 Bob Scheffing MG.......... 3.00 1.20
❑ 224 Joe Gordon MG.............. 6.00 2.40
❑ 225 Bill Rigney MG 6.00 2.40
❑ 226 Cookie Lavagetto MG 6.00 2.40
❑ 227 Juan Pizarro 3.00 1.20
❑ 228 New York Yankees....... 60.00 24.00
Team Card
❑ 229 Rudy Hernandez 3.00 1.20
❑ 230 Don Hoak 6.00 2.40
❑ 231 Dick Drott 3.00 1.20
❑ 232 Bill White 6.00 2.40
❑ 233 Joey Jay 6.00 2.40
❑ 234 Ted Lepcio 3.00 1.20
❑ 235 Camilo Pascual 6.00 2.40
❑ 236 Don Gile RC 3.00 1.20
❑ 237 Billy Loes 6.00 2.40
❑ 238 Jim Gilliam 6.00 2.40
❑ 239 Dave Sisler 3.00 1.20
❑ 240 Ron Hansen.................... 3.00 1.20
❑ 241 Al Cicotte 3.00 1.20
❑ 242 Hal Smith 3.00 1.20
❑ 243 Frank Lary 6.00 2.40
❑ 244 Chico Cardenas.............. 6.00 2.40
❑ 245 Joe Adcock 6.00 2.40
❑ 246 Bob Davis 3.00 1.20
❑ 247 Billy Goodman 6.00 2.40
❑ 248 Ed Keegan 3.00 1.20
❑ 249 Cincinnati Reds............. 8.00 3.20
Team Card
❑ 250 Vern Law 6.00 2.40
Roy Face
❑ 251 Bill Bruton...................... 3.00 1.20
❑ 252 Bill Short........................ 3.00 1.20
❑ 253 Sammy Taylor 3.00 1.20
❑ 254 Ted Sadowski 6.00 2.40
❑ 255 Vic Power 6.00 2.40
❑ 256 Billy Hoeft 3.00 1.20
❑ 257 Carroll Hardy.................. 3.00 1.20
❑ 258 Jack Sanford 6.00 2.40
❑ 259 John Schaive.................. 3.00 1.20
❑ 260 Don Drysdale 30.00 12.00
❑ 261 Charlie Lau 6.00 2.40
❑ 262 Tony Curry 3.00 1.20
❑ 263 Ken Hamlin 3.00 1.20
❑ 264 Glen Hobbie 3.00 1.20
❑ 265 Tony Kubek 12.00 4.80
❑ 266 Lindy McDaniel 6.00 2.40
❑ 267 Norm Siebern 3.00 1.20
❑ 268 Ike Delock 3.00 1.20
❑ 269 Harry Chiti...................... 3.00 1.20
❑ 270 Bob Friend 6.00 2.40
❑ 271 Jim Landis 3.00 1.20
❑ 272 Tom Morgan 3.00 1.20
❑ 273A Checklist 4 .... 15.00 3.00
(Copyright symbol
adjacent to
336 Don Mincher)
❑ 273B Checklist 4 .... 10.00 2.00
(Copyright symbol
adjacent to
339 Gene Baker)
❑ 274 Gary Bell 3.00 1.20
❑ 275 Gene Woodling 6.00 2.40
❑ 276 Ray Rippelmeyer 3.00 1.20
❑ 277 Hank Foiles 3.00 1.20
❑ 278 Don McMahon 3.00 1.20
❑ 279 Jose Pagan 3.00 1.20
❑ 280 Frank Howard 8.00 3.20
❑ 281 Frank Sullivan 3.00 1.20
❑ 282 Faye Throneberry 3.00 1.20
❑ 283 Bob Anderson 3.00 1.20
❑ 284 Dick Gernert 3.00 1.20
❑ 285 Sherm Lollar 6.00 2.40
❑ 286 George Witt 3.00 1.20
❑ 287 Carl Yastrzemski 50.00 20.00
❑ 288 Albie Pearson 6.00 2.40
❑ 289 Ray Moore...................... 3.00 1.20
❑ 290 Stan Musial 100.00 40.00
❑ 291 Tex Clevenger 3.00 1.20
❑ 292 Jim Baumer.................... 3.00 1.20
❑ 293 Tom Sturdivant 3.00 1.20
❑ 294 Don Blasingame 3.00 1.20
❑ 295 Milt Pappas.................... 6.00 2.40
❑ 296 Wes Covington 6.00 2.40
❑ 297 Athletics Team.............. 8.00 3.20
❑ 298 Jim Golden 3.00 1.20
❑ 299 Clay Dalrymple 3.00 1.20
❑ 300 Mickey Mantle............ 600.00 240.00
❑ 301 Chet Nichols 3.00 1.20
❑ 302 Al Heist 3.00 1.20
❑ 303 Gary Peters 6.00 2.40
❑ 304 Rocky Nelson 3.00 1.20
❑ 305 Mike McCormick............ 6.00 2.40
❑ 306 Bill Virdon WS 10.00 4.00
❑ 307 Mickey Mantle WS 80.00 32.00
❑ 308 B.Richardson WS 12.00 4.80
❑ 309 Gino Cimoli WS 10.00 4.00
❑ 310 Roy Face WS............... 10.00 4.00
❑ 311 Whitey Ford WS 15.00 6.00
❑ 312 Bill Mazeroski WS....... 20.00 8.00
Mazeroski Homer Wins it
❑ 313 WS Summary 15.00 6.00
Pirates Celebrate
❑ 314 Bob Miller 3.00 1.20
❑ 315 Earl Battey 6.00 2.40
❑ 316 Bobby Gene Smith 3.00 1.20
❑ 317 Jim Brewer 3.00 1.20
❑ 318 Danny O'Connell 3.00 1.20
❑ 319 Valmy Thomas 3.00 1.20
❑ 320 Lou Burdette 6.00 2.40
❑ 321 Marv Breeding................ 3.00 1.20
❑ 322 Bill Kunkel...................... 6.00 2.40
❑ 323 Sammy Esposito 3.00 1.20
❑ 324 Hank Aguirre 3.00 1.20
❑ 325 Wally Moon.................... 6.00 2.40
❑ 326 Dave Hillman.................. 3.00 1.20
❑ 327 Matty Alou RC 12.00 4.80
❑ 328 Jim O'Toole 6.00 2.40
❑ 329 Julio Becquer 3.00 1.20
❑ 330 Rocky Colavito 20.00 8.00
❑ 331 Ned Garver 3.00 1.20
❑ 332 Dutch Dotterer UER 3.00 1.20
(Photo actually
Tommy Dotterer
Dutch's brother)
❑ 333 Fritz Brickell 3.00 1.20
❑ 334 Walt Bond 3.00 1.20
❑ 335 Frank Bolling.................. 3.00 1.20
❑ 336 Don Mincher................... 6.00 2.40
❑ 337 Early Wynn 8.00 3.20
Al Lopez
Herb Score
❑ 338 Don Landrum 3.00 1.20
❑ 339 Gene Baker 3.00 1.20
❑ 340 Vic Wertz........................ 6.00 2.40
❑ 341 Jim Owens 3.00 1.20
❑ 342 Clint Courtney................ 3.00 1.20
❑ 343 Earl Robinson 3.00 1.20
❑ 344 Sandy Koufax 100.00 40.00
❑ 345 Jimmy Piersall 8.00 3.20
❑ 346 Howie Nunn 3.00 1.20
❑ 347 St. Louis Cardinals 8.00 3.20
Team Card
❑ 348 Steve Boros.................... 3.00 1.20
❑ 349 Danny McDevitt.............. 3.00 1.20
❑ 350 Ernie Banks 40.00 16.00
❑ 351 Jim King 3.00 1.20
❑ 352 Bob Shaw 3.00 1.20
❑ 353 Howie Bedell 3.00 1.20
❑ 354 Billy Harrell 6.00 2.40
❑ 355 Bob Allison 8.00 3.20
❑ 356 Ryne Duren 3.00 1.20
❑ 357 Daryl Spencer 3.00 1.20
❑ 358 Earl Averill..................... 6.00 2.40
❑ 359 Dallas Green 3.00 1.20
❑ 360 Frank Robinson............ 40.00 16.00
❑ 361A Checklist 5 .... 15.00 3.00

(No ad on back)
❑ 361B Checklist 5 .... 15.00 3.00
(Special Feature
ad on back)
❑ 362 Frank Funk 3.00 1.20
❑ 363 John Roseboro 6.00 2.40
❑ 364 Moe Drabowsky 6.00 2.40
❑ 365 Jerry Lumpe 3.00 1.20
❑ 366 Eddie Fisher 3.00 1.20
❑ 367 Jim Rivera 3.00 1.20
❑ 368 Bennie Daniels 3.00 1.20
❑ 369 Dave Philley 3.00 1.20
❑ 370 Roy Face 6.00 2.40
❑ 371 Bill Skowron SP 50.00 20.00
❑ 372 Bob Hendley 4.00 1.60
❑ 373 Boston Red Sox 8.00 3.20
Team Card
❑ 374 Paul Giel 4.00 1.60
❑ 375 Ken Boyer 12.00 4.80
❑ 376 Mike Roarke RC 6.00 2.40
❑ 377 Ruben Gomez 4.00 1.60
❑ 378 Wally Post 6.00 2.40
❑ 379 Bobby Shantz 4.00 1.60
❑ 380 Minnie Minoso 8.00 3.20
❑ 381 Dave Wickersham 4.00 1.60
❑ 382 Frank Thomas 6.00 2.40
❑ 383 Mike McCormick 6.00 2.40
Jack Sanford
Billy O'Dell
❑ 384 Chuck Essegian 4.00 1.60
❑ 385 Jim Perry 6.00 2.40
❑ 386 Joe Hicks 4.00 1.60
❑ 387 Duke Maas 4.00 1.60
❑ 388 Roberto Clemente 125.00 50.00
❑ 389 Ralph Terry 6.00 2.40
❑ 390 Del Crandall 8.00 3.20
❑ 391 Winston Brown 4.00 1.60
❑ 392 Reno Bertoia 4.00 1.60
❑ 393 Don Cardwell 4.00 1.60
Glen Hobbie
❑ 394 Ken Walters 4.00 1.60
❑ 395 Chuck Estrada 6.00 2.40
❑ 396 Bob Aspromonte 4.00 1.60
❑ 397 Hal Woodeshick 4.00 1.60
❑ 398 Hank Bauer 6.00 2.40
❑ 399 Cliff Cook 4.00 1.60
❑ 400 Vern Law 6.00 2.40
❑ 401 Babe Ruth HL 60.00 24.00
60th HR
❑ 402 Don Larsen HL SP 25.00 10.00
WS Perfect Game
❑ 403 Joe Oeschger HL 8.00 3.20
Leon Cadore
26 Inning Tie
❑ 404 Rogers Hornsby HL 12.00 4.80
.424 Season BA
❑ 405 Lou Gehrig HL 80.00 32.00
Consecutive Game Streak
❑ 406 Mickey Mantle HL 100.00 40.00
565 foot HR
❑ 407 Jack Chesbro HL 8.00 3.20
41 victories
❑ 408 C. Mathewson HL SP .. 20.00 8.00
267 Strikeouts
❑ 409 Walter Johnson SL 12.00 4.80
3 Shutouts in 4 days
❑ 410 Harvey Haddix HL 8.00 3.20
12 Perfect Innings
❑ 411 Tony Taylor 6.00 2.40
❑ 412 Larry Sherry 6.00 2.40
❑ 413 Eddie Yost 6.00 2.40
❑ 414 Dick Donovan 6.00 2.40
❑ 415 Hank Aaron 125.00 50.00
❑ 416 Dick Howser RC 8.00 3.20
❑ 417 Juan Marichal SP RC 100.00 40.00
❑ 418 Ed Bailey 6.00 2.40
❑ 419 Tom Borland 4.00 1.60
❑ 420 Ernie Broglio 6.00 2.40
❑ 421 Ty Cline SP 20.00 8.00
❑ 422 Bud Daley 4.00 1.60
❑ 423 Charlie Neal SP 20.00 8.00
❑ 424 Turk Lown 4.00 1.60
❑ 425 Yogi Berra 80.00 32.00
❑ 426 Milwaukee Braves 12.00 4.80
Team Card
(Back numbered 463)
❑ 427 Dick Ellsworth 6.00 2.40
❑ 428 Ray Barker SP 20.00 8.00
❑ 429 Al Kaline 50.00 20.00
❑ 430 Bill Mazeroski SP 50.00 20.00
❑ 431 Chuck Stobbs 4.00 1.60
❑ 432 Coot Veal 6.00 2.40
❑ 433 Art Mahaffey 4.00 1.60
❑ 434 Tom Brewer 4.00 1.60
❑ 435 Orlando Cepeda UER 12.00 4.80
(San Francis on
card front)
❑ 436 Jim Maloney SP RC 20.00 8.00
❑ 437A Checklist 6 .... 15.00 3.00
440 Louis Aparicio
❑ 437B Checklist 6 .... 15.00 3.00
440 Luis Aparicio
❑ 438 Curt Flood 8.00 3.20
❑ 439 Phil Regan RC 6.00 2.40
❑ 440 Luis Aparicio 12.00 4.80
❑ 441 Dick Bertell 4.00 1.60
❑ 442 Gordon Jones 4.00 1.60
❑ 443 Duke Snider 50.00 20.00
❑ 444 Joe Nuxhall 6.00 2.40
❑ 445 Frank Malzone 6.00 2.40
❑ 446 Bob Taylor 4.00 1.60
❑ 447 Harry Bright 8.00 3.20
❑ 448 Del Rice 15.00 6.00
❑ 449 Bob Bolin 8.00 3.20
❑ 450 Jim Lemon 8.00 3.20
❑ 451 Daryl Spencer 8.00 3.20
Bill White
Ernie Broglio
❑ 452 Bob Allen 8.00 3.20
❑ 453 Dick Schofield 8.00 3.20
❑ 454 Pumpsie Green 8.00 3.20
❑ 455 Early Wynn 15.00 6.00
❑ 456 Hal Bevan 8.00 3.20
❑ 457 Johnny James 8.00 3.20
(Listed as Angel,
but wearing Yankee
uniform and cap)
❑ 458 Willie Tasby 8.00 3.20
❑ 459 Terry Fox RC 10.00 4.00
❑ 460 Gil Hodges 25.00 10.00
❑ 461 Smoky Burgess 15.00 6.00
❑ 462 Lou Klimchock 8.00 3.20
❑ 463 Jack Fisher 8.00 3.20
(See also 426)
❑ 464 Lee Thomas RC 10.00 4.00
(Pictured with Yankee
cap but listed as
Los Angeles Angel)
❑ 465 Roy McMillan 15.00 6.00
❑ 466 Ron Moeller 8.00 3.20
❑ 467 Cleveland Indians 12.00 4.80
Team Card
❑ 468 John Callison 10.00 4.00
❑ 469 Ralph Lumenti 8.00 3.20
❑ 470 Roy Sievers 10.00 4.00
❑ 471 Phil Rizzuto MVP 25.00 10.00
❑ 472 Yogi Berra MVP 50.00 20.00
❑ 473 Bob Shantz MVP 8.00 3.20
❑ 474 Al Rosen MVP 10.00 4.00
❑ 475 Mickey Mantle MVP .. 200.00 80.00
❑ 476 Jackie Jensen MVP 10.00 4.00
❑ 477 Nellie Fox MVP 15.00 6.00
❑ 478 Roger Maris MVP 60.00 24.00
❑ 479 Jim Konstanty MVP 8.00 3.20
❑ 480 Roy Campanella MVP .. 40.00 16.00
❑ 481 Hank Sauer MVP 8.00 3.20
❑ 482 Willie Mays MVP 50.00 20.00
❑ 483 Don Newcombe MVP .. 10.00 4.00
❑ 484 Hank Aaron MVP 50.00 20.00
❑ 485 Ernie Banks MVP 40.00 16.00
❑ 486 Dick Groat MVP 10.00 4.00
❑ 487 Gene Oliver 8.00 3.20
❑ 488 Joe McClain 10.00 4.00
❑ 489 Walt Dropo 8.00 3.20
❑ 490 Jim Bunning 25.00 10.00
❑ 491 Philadelphia Phillies 12.00 4.80
Team Card
❑ 492 Ron Fairly 10.00 4.00
❑ 493 Don Zimmer UER 10.00 4.00
(Brooklyn A.L.)
❑ 494 Tom Cheney 15.00 6.00
❑ 495 Elston Howard 10.00 4.00
❑ 496 Ken MacKenzie 8.00 3.20
❑ 497 Willie Jones 8.00 3.20
❑ 498 Ray Herbert 8.00 3.20
❑ 499 Chuck Schilling RC 8.00 3.20
❑ 500 Harvey Kuenn 10.00 4.00
❑ 501 John DeMerit 8.00 3.20
❑ 502 Clarence Coleman RC .. 10.00 4.00
❑ 503 Tito Francona 8.00 3.20
❑ 504 Billy Consolo 8.00 3.20
❑ 505 Red Schoendienst 15.00 6.00
❑ 506 Willie Davis RC 15.00 6.00
❑ 507 Pete Burnside 8.00 3.20
❑ 508 Rocky Bridges 8.00 3.20
❑ 509 Camilo Carreon 8.00 3.20
❑ 510 Art Ditmar 8.00 3.20
❑ 511 Joe M. Morgan 8.00 3.20
❑ 512 Bob Will 8.00 3.20
❑ 513 Jim Brosnan 8.00 3.20
❑ 514 Jake Wood 8.00 3.20
❑ 515 Jackie Brandt 8.00 3.20
❑ 516 Checklist 7 .... 15.00 3.00
❑ 517 Willie McCovey 40.00 16.00
❑ 518 Andy Carey 8.00 3.20
❑ 519 Jim Pagliaroni 8.00 3.20
❑ 520 Joe Cunningham 8.00 3.20
❑ 521 Norm Sherry 8.00 3.20
Larry Sherry
❑ 522 Dick Farrell UER 15.00 6.00
(Phillies cap but
listed on Dodgers)
❑ 523 Joe Gibbon 30.00 12.00
❑ 524 Johnny Logan 30.00 12.00
❑ 525 Ron Perranoski RC 60.00 24.00
❑ 526 R.C. Stevens 30.00 12.00
❑ 527 Gene Leek 30.00 12.00
❑ 528 Pedro Ramos 30.00 12.00
❑ 529 Bob Roselli 30.00 12.00
❑ 530 Bob Malkmus 30.00 12.00
❑ 531 Jim Coates 50.00 20.00
❑ 532 Bob Hale 30.00 12.00
❑ 533 Jack Curtis 30.00 12.00
❑ 534 Eddie Kasko 40.00 16.00
❑ 535 Larry Jackson 30.00 12.00
❑ 536 Bill Tuttle 30.00 12.00
❑ 537 Bobby Locke 30.00 12.00
❑ 538 Chuck Hiller 30.00 12.00
❑ 539 Johnny Klippstein 30.00 12.00
❑ 540 Jackie Jensen 40.00 16.00
❑ 541 Roland Sheldon RC 50.00 20.00
❑ 542 Minnesota Twins 60.00 24.00
Team Card
❑ 543 Roger Craig 40.00 16.00
❑ 544 George Thomas 50.00 20.00
❑ 545 Hoyt Wilhelm 60.00 24.00
❑ 546 Marty Kutyna 30.00 12.00
❑ 547 Leon Wagner 30.00 12.00
❑ 548 Ted Wills 30.00 12.00
❑ 549 Hal R. Smith 30.00 12.00
❑ 550 Frank Baumann 30.00 12.00
❑ 551 George Altman 40.00 16.00
❑ 552 Jim Archer 30.00 12.00
❑ 553 Bill Fischer 30.00 12.00
❑ 554 Pittsburgh Pirates 80.00 32.00
Team Card
❑ 555 Sam Jones 30.00 12.00
❑ 556 Ken R. Hunt 30.00 12.00
❑ 557 Jose Valdivielso 30.00 12.00
❑ 558 Don Ferrarese 30.00 12.00
❑ 559 Jim Gentile 60.00 24.00
❑ 560 Barry Latman 40.00 16.00
❑ 561 Charley James 30.00 12.00
❑ 562 Bill Monbouquette 30.00 12.00
❑ 563 Bob Cerv 60.00 24.00
❑ 564 Don Cardwell 30.00 12.00
❑ 565 Felipe Alou 50.00 20.00
❑ 566 Paul Richards AS MG .. 30.00 12.00
❑ 567 D.Murtaugh AS MG 30.00 12.00
❑ 568 Bill Skowron AS 50.00 20.00
❑ 569 Frank Herrera AS 40.00 16.00
❑ 570 Nellie Fox AS 60.00 24.00
❑ 571 Bill Mazeroski AS 60.00 24.00
❑ 572 Brooks Robinson AS 80.00 32.00
❑ 573 Ken Boyer AS 50.00 20.00
❑ 574 Luis Aparicio AS 60.00 24.00
❑ 575 Ernie Banks AS 80.00 32.00
❑ 576 Roger Maris AS 175.00 70.00

❑ 577	Hank Aaron AS	150.00	60.00
❑ 578	Mickey Mantle AS	400.00	160.00
❑ 579	Willie Mays AS	150.00	60.00
❑ 580	Al Kaline AS	80.00	32.00
❑ 581	Frank Robinson AS	80.00	32.00
❑ 582	Earl Battey AS	30.00	12.00
❑ 583	Del Crandall AS	30.00	12.00
❑ 584	Jim Perry AS	30.00	12.00
❑ 585	Bob Friend AS	30.00	12.00
❑ 586	Whitey Ford AS	100.00	40.00
❑ 589	Warren Spahn AS	100.00	30.00

1962 Topps

	NM	Ex
COMP. MASTER (688)	7000.00	2800.00
COMPLETE SET (598)	6000.00	2400.00
COMMON CARD (1-370)	5.00	2.00
COMMON (371-446)	6.00	2.40
COMMON (447-522)	12.00	4.80
COMMON (523-598)	20.00	8.00
WRAPPER (1-CENT)	100.00	40.00
WRAPPER (5-CENT)	30.00	12.00

❑ 1	Roger Maris	500.00	125.00
❑ 2	Jim Brosnan	5.00	2.00
❑ 3	Pete Runnels	5.00	2.00
❑ 4	John DeMerit	8.00	3.20
❑ 5	Sandy Koufax UER	150.00	60.00
	Struck ou 18		
❑ 6	Marv Breeding	5.00	2.00
❑ 7	Frank Thomas	10.00	4.00
❑ 8	Ray Herbert	5.00	2.00
❑ 9	Jim Davenport	8.00	3.20
❑ 10	Roberto Clemente	200.00	80.00
❑ 11	Tom Morgan	5.00	2.00
❑ 12	Harry Craft MG	8.00	3.20
❑ 13	Dick Howser	8.00	3.20
❑ 14	Bill White	8.00	3.20
❑ 15	Dick Donovan	5.00	2.00
❑ 16	Darrell Johnson	5.00	2.00
❑ 17	Johnny Callison	8.00	3.20
❑ 18	Mickey Mantle	175.00	70.00
	Willie Mays		
❑ 19	Ray Washburn	5.00	2.00
❑ 20	Rocky Colavito	15.00	6.00
❑ 21	Jim Kaat	8.00	3.20
❑ 22A	Checklist 1 ERR	12.00	2.40
	(121-176 on back)		
❑ 22B	Checklist 1 COR	12.00	2.40
❑ 23	Norm Larker	5.00	2.00
❑ 24	Tigers Team	10.00	4.00
❑ 25	Ernie Banks	50.00	20.00
❑ 26	Chris Cannizzaro	8.00	3.20
❑ 27	Chuck Cottier	5.00	2.00
❑ 28	Minnie Minoso	10.00	4.00
❑ 29	Casey Stengel MG	20.00	8.00
❑ 30	Eddie Mathews	40.00	16.00
❑ 31	Tom Tresh RC	15.00	6.00
❑ 32	John Roseboro	8.00	3.20
❑ 33	Don Larsen	8.00	3.20
❑ 34	Johnny Temple	8.00	3.20
❑ 35	Don Schwall	10.00	4.00
❑ 36	Don Leppert	5.00	2.00
❑ 37	Barry Latman	5.00	2.00
	Dick Stigman		
	Jim Perry		
❑ 38	Gene Stephens	5.00	2.00
❑ 39	Joe Koppe	5.00	2.00
❑ 40	Orlando Cepeda	15.00	6.00
❑ 41	Cliff Cook	5.00	2.00
❑ 42	Jim King	5.00	2.00
❑ 43	Los Angeles Dodgers	10.00	4.00
	Team Card		
❑ 44	Don Taussig	5.00	2.00
❑ 45	Brooks Robinson	50.00	20.00
❑ 46	Jack Baldschun	5.00	2.00
❑ 47	Bob Will	5.00	2.00
❑ 48	Ralph Terry	8.00	3.20
❑ 49	Hal Jones	5.00	2.00
❑ 50	Stan Musial	100.00	40.00
❑ 51	Norm Cash	8.00	3.20
	Jim Piersall		
	Al Kaline		
	Elston Howard LL		
❑ 52	Roberto Clemente	20.00	8.00
	Vada Pinson		
	Ken Boyer		
	Wally Moon LL		
❑ 53	Roger Maris	100.00	40.00
	Mickey Mantle		
	Jim Gentile		
	Harmon Killebrew LL		
❑ 54	Orlando Cepeda	20.00	8.00
	Willie Mays		
	Frank Robinson LL		
❑ 55	Dick Donovan	8.00	3.20
	Bill Stafford		
	Don Mossi		
	Milt Pappas LL		
❑ 56	Warren Spahn	8.00	3.20
	Jim O'Toole		
	Curt Simmons		
	Mike McCormick LL		
❑ 57	Whitey Ford	8.00	3.20
	Frank Lary		
	Steve Barber		
	Jim Bunning LL		
❑ 58	Warren Spahn	8.00	3.20
	Joe Jay		
	Jim O'Toole LL		
❑ 59	Camilo Pascual	8.00	3.20
	Whitey Ford		
	Jim Bunning		
	Juan Pizzaro LL		
❑ 60	Sandy Koufax	20.00	8.00
	Stan Williams		
	Don Drysdale		
	Jim O'Toole LL		
❑ 61	Cardinals Team	10.00	4.00
❑ 62	Steve Boros	5.00	2.00
❑ 63	Tony Cloninger RC	8.00	3.20
❑ 64	Russ Snyder	5.00	2.00
❑ 65	Bobby Richardson	10.00	4.00
❑ 66	Cuno Barragan	5.00	2.00
❑ 67	Harvey Haddix	8.00	3.20
❑ 68	Ken Hunt	5.00	2.00
❑ 69	Phil Ortega	5.00	2.00
❑ 70	Harmon Killebrew	25.00	10.00
❑ 71	Dick LeMay	5.00	2.00
❑ 72	Steve Boros	5.00	2.00
	Bob Scheffing MG		
	Jake Wood		
❑ 73	Nellie Fox	20.00	8.00
❑ 74	Bob Lillis	8.00	3.20
❑ 75	Milt Pappas	8.00	3.20
❑ 76	Howie Bedell	5.00	2.00
❑ 77	Tony Taylor	8.00	3.20
❑ 78	Gene Green	5.00	2.00
❑ 79	Ed Hobaugh	5.00	2.00
❑ 80	Vada Pinson	8.00	3.20
❑ 81	Jim Pagliaroni	5.00	2.00
❑ 82	Deron Johnson	8.00	3.20
❑ 83	Larry Jackson	5.00	2.00
❑ 84	Lenny Green	5.00	2.00
❑ 85	Gil Hodges	20.00	8.00
❑ 86	Donn Clendenon RC	8.00	3.20
❑ 87	Mike Roarke	5.00	2.00
❑ 88	Ralph Houk MG	8.00	3.20
	(Berra in background)		
❑ 89	Barney Schultz	5.00	2.00
❑ 90	Jimmy Piersall	8.00	3.20
❑ 91	J.C. Martin	5.00	2.00
❑ 92	Sam Jones	5.00	2.00
❑ 93	John Blanchard	8.00	3.20
❑ 94	Jay Hook	8.00	3.20
❑ 95	Don Hoak	8.00	3.20
❑ 96	Eli Grba	5.00	2.00
❑ 97	Tito Francona	5.00	2.00
❑ 98	Checklist 2	12.00	2.40
❑ 99	John (Boog) Powell RC	30.00	12.00
❑ 100	Warren Spahn	40.00	16.00
❑ 101	Carroll Hardy	5.00	2.00
❑ 102	Al Schroll	5.00	2.00
❑ 103	Don Blasingame	5.00	2.00
❑ 104	Ted Savage	5.00	2.00
❑ 105	Don Mossi	8.00	3.20
❑ 106	Carl Sawatski	5.00	2.00
❑ 107	Mike McCormick	8.00	3.20
❑ 108	Willie Davis	8.00	3.20
❑ 109	Bob Shaw	5.00	2.00
❑ 110	Bill Skowron	8.00	3.20
❑ 110A	Bill Skowron	8.00	3.20
	Green Tint		
❑ 111	Dallas Green	8.00	3.20
❑ 111A	Dallas Green	8.00	3.20
	Green Tint		
❑ 112	Hank Foiles	5.00	2.00
❑ 112A	Hank Foiles	5.00	2.00
	Green Tint		
❑ 113	Chicago White Sox	10.00	4.00
	Team Card		
❑ 113A	Chicago White Sox	10.00	4.00
	Team Card		
	Green Tint		
❑ 114	Howie Koplitz	5.00	2.00
❑ 114A	Howie Koplitz	5.00	2.00
	Green Tint		
❑ 115	Bob Skinner	8.00	3.20
❑ 115A	Bob Skinner	8.00	3.20
	Green Tint		
❑ 116	Herb Score	8.00	3.20
❑ 116A	Herb Score	8.00	3.20
	Green Tint		
❑ 117	Gary Geiger	8.00	3.20
❑ 117A	Gary Geiger	8.00	3.20
	Green Tint		
❑ 118	Julian Javier	8.00	3.20
❑ 118A	Julian Javier	8.00	3.20
	Green Tint		
❑ 119	Danny Murphy	5.00	2.00
❑ 119A	Danny Murphy	5.00	2.00
	Green Tint		
❑ 120	Bob Purkey	5.00	2.00
❑ 120A	Bob Purkey	5.00	2.00
	Green Tint		
❑ 121	Billy Hitchcock MG	5.00	2.00
❑ 121A	Billy Hitchcock	5.00	2.00
	Green Tint		
❑ 122	Norm Bass	5.00	2.00
❑ 122A	Norm Bass	5.00	2.00
	Green Tint		
❑ 123	Mike de la Hoz	5.00	2.00
❑ 123A	Mike de la Hoz	5.00	2.00
	Green Tint		
❑ 124	Bill Pleis	5.00	2.00
❑ 124A	Bill Pleis	5.00	2.00
	Green Tint		
❑ 125	Gene Woodling	8.00	3.20
❑ 125A	Gene Woodling	8.00	3.20
	Green Tint		
❑ 126	Al Cicotte	5.00	2.00
❑ 126A	Al Cicotte	5.00	2.00
	Green Tint		
❑ 127	Norm Siebern	5.00	2.00
	Hank Bauer MG		
	Jerry Lumpe		
❑ 127A	Norm Siebern	5.00	2.00
	Hank Bauer MG		
	Jerry Lumpe		
	Green Tint		
❑ 128	Art Fowler	5.00	2.00
❑ 128A	Art Fowler	5.00	2.00
	Green Tint		
❑ 129A	Lee Walls	5.00	2.00
	(Facing right)		
❑ 129B	Lee Walls	30.00	12.00
	(Facing left)		
❑ 130	Frank Bolling	5.00	2.00
❑ 130A	Frank Bolling	5.00	2.00
	Green Tint		

	No.	Card	Price	Price
❑	131	Pete Richert	5.00	2.00
❑	131A	Pete Richert	5.00	2.00
		Green Tint		
❑	132A	Angels Team	10.00	4.00
		(Without photo)		
❑	132B	Angels Team	30.00	12.00
		(With photo)		
❑	133	Felipe Alou	8.00	3.20
❑	133A	Felipe Alou	8.00	3.20
		Green Tint		
❑	134A	Billy Hoeft	5.00	2.00
❑	134B	Billy Hoeft	30.00	12.00
		Green Tint		
❑	135	Babe Ruth Special 1	20.00	8.00
		Babe as a Boy		
❑	135A	Babe Ruth Special	20.00	8.00
		Base as a Boy		
❑	136	Babe Ruth Special 2	20.00	8.00
		Jacob Ruppert OWN		
		Babe Joins Yanks		
❑	136A	Babe Ruth Special	20.00	8.00
		Jacob Ruppert OWN		
		Babe Joins Yanks		
		Green Tint		
❑	137	Babe Ruth Special 3	20.00	8.00
		With Miller Huggins		
❑	137A	Babe Ruth Special	20.00	8.00
		With Miller Huggins		
		Green Tint		
❑	138	Babe Ruth Special 4	20.00	8.00
		Famous Slugger		
❑	138A	Babe Ruth Special	20.00	8.00
		Famous Slugger		
		Green Tint		
❑	139A	Babe Ruth Special 5	30.00	12.00
		Babe Hits 60		
❑	139B	Hal Reniff PORT RC	15.00	6.00
❑	139C	Hal Reniff RC	60.00	24.00
		Pitching		
❑	140	Babe Ruth Special 6	60.00	24.00
		With Lou Gehrig		
❑	140A	Babe Ruth Special	60.00	24.00
		Lou Gehrig		
		Green Tint		
❑	141	Babe Ruth Special 7	20.00	8.00
		Twilight Years		
❑	141A	Babe Ruth Special	20.00	8.00
		Twilight Years		
		Green Tint		
❑	142	Babe Ruth Special 8	20.00	8.00
		Coaching Dodgers		
❑	142A	Babe Ruth Special	20.00	8.00
		Coaching Dodgers		
		Green Tint		
❑	143	Babe Ruth Special 9	20.00	8.00
		Greatest Sports Hero		
❑	143A	Babe Ruth Special	20.00	8.00
		Greatest Sports Hero		
		Green Tint		
❑	144	Babe Ruth Special 10	20.00	8.00
		Farewell Speech		
❑	144A	Babe Ruth Special	20.00	8.00
		Babe Ruth Special		
		Farewell Speech		
❑	145	Barry Latman	5.00	2.00
❑	145A	Barry Latman	5.00	2.00
		Green Tint		
❑	146	Don Demeter	5.00	2.00
❑	146A	Don Demeter	5.00	2.00
		Green Tint		
❑	147A	Bill Kunkel PORT	5.00	2.00
❑	147B	Bill Kunkel	30.00	12.00
		(Pitching pose)		
❑	148	Wally Post	5.00	2.00
❑	148A	Wally Post	5.00	2.00
		Green Tint		
❑	149	Bob Duliba	5.00	2.00
❑	149A	Bob Duliba	5.00	2.00
		Green Tint		
❑	150	Al Kaline	50.00	20.00
❑	150A	Al Kaline	50.00	20.00
		Green Tint		
❑	151	Johnny Klippstein	5.00	2.00
❑	151A	Johnny Klippstein	5.00	2.00
		Green Tint		
❑	152	Mickey Vernon MG	8.00	3.20
❑	152A	Mickey Vernon MG	8.00	3.20
		Green Tint		
❑	153	Pumpsie Green	6.00	2.40
❑	153A	Pumpsie Green	6.00	2.40
		Green Tint		
❑	154	Lee Thomas	6.00	2.40
❑	154A	Lee Thomas	6.00	2.40
		Green Tint		
❑	155	Stu Miller	6.00	2.40
❑	155A	Stu Miller	6.00	2.40
		Green Tint		
❑	156	Merritt Ranew	5.00	2.00
❑	156A	Merritt Ranew	5.00	2.00
		Green Tint		
❑	157	Wes Covington	8.00	3.20
❑	157A	Wes Covington	8.00	3.20
		Green Tint		
❑	158	Braves Team	10.00	4.00
❑	158A	Braves Team	15.00	6.00
		Green Tint		
❑	159	Hal Reniff RC	8.00	3.20
❑	160	Dick Stuart	8.00	3.20
❑	160A	Dick Stuart	8.00	3.20
		Green Tint		
❑	161	Frank Baumann	5.00	2.00
❑	161A	Frank Baumann	5.00	2.00
		Green Tint		
❑	162	Sammy Drake	5.00	2.00
❑	162A	Sammy Drake	5.00	2.00
		Green Tint		
❑	163	Billy Gardner	8.00	3.20
		Cletis Boyer		
❑	163A	Billy Gardner	8.00	3.20
		Clete Boyer		
		Green Tint		
❑	164	Hal Naragon	5.00	2.00
❑	164A	Hal Naragon	5.00	2.00
		Green Tint		
❑	165	Jackie Brandt	5.00	2.00
❑	165A	Jackie Brandt	5.00	2.00
		Green Tint		
❑	166	Don Lee	5.00	2.00
❑	166A	Don Lee	5.00	2.00
		Green Tint		
❑	167	Tim McCarver RC	30.00	12.00
❑	167A	Tim McCarver RC	30.00	12.00
		Green Tint		
❑	168	Leo Posada	5.00	2.00
❑	168A	Leo Posada	5.00	2.00
		Green Tint		
❑	169	Bob Cerv	10.00	4.00
❑	169A	Bob Cerv	10.00	4.00
		Green Tint		
❑	170	Ron Santo	15.00	6.00
❑	170A	Ron Santo	15.00	6.00
		Green Tint		
❑	171	Dave Sisler	5.00	2.00
❑	171A	Dave Sisler	5.00	2.00
		Green Tint		
❑	172	Fred Hutchinson MG	8.00	3.20
❑	172A	Fred Hutchinson MG	8.00	3.20
		Green Tint		
❑	173	Chico Fernandez	5.00	2.00
❑	173A	Chico Fernandez	5.00	2.00
		Green Tint		
❑	174A	Carl Willey	5.00	2.00
		(Capless)		
❑	174B	Carl Willey	30.00	12.00
		(With cap)		
❑	175	Frank Howard	10.00	4.00
❑	175A	Frank Howard	10.00	4.00
		Green Tint		
❑	176A	Eddie Yost PORT	5.00	2.00
❑	176B	Eddie Yost BATTING	30.00	12.00
❑	177	Bobby Shantz	8.00	3.20
❑	177A	Bobby Shantz	8.00	3.20
		Green Tint		
❑	178	Camilo Carreon	5.00	2.00
❑	178A	Camilo Carreon	5.00	2.00
		Green Tint		
❑	179	Tom Sturdivant	5.00	2.00
❑	179A	Tom Sturdivant	5.00	2.00
		Green Tint		
❑	180	Bob Allison	10.00	4.00
❑	180A	Bob Allison	10.00	4.00
		Green Tint		
❑	181	Paul Brown	5.00	2.00
❑	181A	Paul Brown	5.00	2.00
		Green Tint		
❑	182	Bob Nieman	5.00	2.00
❑	182A	Bob Nieman	5.00	2.00
		Green Tint		
❑	183	Roger Craig	8.00	3.20
❑	183A	Roger Craig	8.00	3.20
		Green Tint		
❑	184	Haywood Sullivan	8.00	3.20
❑	184A	Haywood Sullivan	8.00	3.20
		Green Tint		
❑	185	Roland Sheldon	10.00	4.00
❑	185A	Roland Sheldon	10.00	4.00
		Green Tint		
❑	186	Mack Jones	5.00	2.00
❑	186A	Mack Jones	5.00	2.00
		Green Tint		
❑	187	Gene Conley	5.00	2.00
❑	187A	Gene Conley	5.00	2.00
		Green Tint		
❑	188	Chuck Hiller	5.00	2.00
❑	188A	Chuck Hiller	5.00	2.00
		Green Tint		
❑	189	Dick Hall	5.00	2.00
❑	189A	Dick Hall	5.00	2.00
		Green Tint		
❑	190A	Wally Moon PORT	8.00	3.20
❑	190B	W.Moon BATTING	30.00	12.00
❑	191	Jim Brewer	5.00	2.00
❑	191A	Jim Brewer	5.00	2.00
		Green Tint		
❑	192A	Checklist 3	12.00	2.40
		(Without comma)		
❑	192B	Checklist 3	15.00	3.00
		(Comma after		
		Checklist)		
❑	193	Eddie Kasko	5.00	2.00
❑	193A	Eddie Kasko	5.00	2.00
		Green Tint		
❑	194	Dean Chance RC	8.00	3.20
❑	194A	Dean Chance RC	8.00	3.20
		Green Tint		
❑	195	Joe Cunningham	5.00	2.00
❑	195A	Joe Cunningham	5.00	2.00
		Green Tint		
❑	196	Terry Fox	5.00	2.00
❑	196A	Terry Fox	5.00	2.00
		Green Tint		
❑	197	Daryl Spencer	5.00	2.00
❑	198	Johnny Keane MG	5.00	2.00
❑	199	Gaylord Perry RC	80.00	32.00
❑	200	Mickey Mantle	600.00	240.00
❑	201	Ike Delock	5.00	2.00
❑	202	Carl Warwick	5.00	2.00
❑	203	Jack Fisher	5.00	2.00
❑	204	Johnny Weekly	5.00	2.00
❑	205	Gene Freese	5.00	2.00
❑	206	Senators Team	10.00	4.00
❑	207	Pete Burnside	5.00	2.00
❑	208	Billy Martin	20.00	8.00
❑	209	Jim Fregosi RC	15.00	6.00
❑	210	Roy Face	8.00	3.20
❑	211	Frank Bolling	5.00	2.00
		Roy McMillan		
❑	212	Jim Owens	5.00	2.00
❑	213	Richie Ashburn	20.00	8.00
❑	214	Dom Zanni	5.00	2.00
❑	215	Woody Held	5.00	2.00
❑	216	Ron Kline	5.00	2.00
❑	217	Walter Alston MG	10.00	4.00
❑	218	Joe Torre RC	40.00	16.00
❑	219	Al Downing RC	8.00	3.20
❑	220	Roy Sievers	8.00	3.20
❑	221	Bill Short	5.00	2.00
❑	222	Jerry Zimmerman	5.00	2.00
❑	223	Alex Grammas	5.00	2.00
❑	224	Don Rudolph	5.00	2.00
❑	225	Frank Malzone	8.00	3.20
❑	226	San Francisco Giants	10.00	4.00
		Team Card		
❑	227	Bob Tiefenauer	5.00	2.00
❑	228	Dale Long	10.00	4.00
❑	229	Jesus McFarlane	5.00	2.00
❑	230	Camilo Pascual	8.00	3.20
❑	231	Ernie Bowman	5.00	2.00

❑ 232 World Series Game 1 .. 10.00 4.00
Yanks win opener
❑ 233 Joey Jay WS 10.00 4.00
❑ 234 Roger Maris WS 25.00 10.00
❑ 235 Whitey Ford WS 15.00 6.00
sets new mark
❑ 236 World Series Game 5 .. 10.00 4.00
Yanks crush Reds
❑ 237 WS Summary 10.00 4.00
Yanks celebrate
❑ 238 Norm Sherry 5.00 2.00
❑ 239 Cecil Butler 5.00 2.00
❑ 240 George Altman 5.00 2.00
❑ 241 Johnny Kucks 5.00 2.00
❑ 242 Mel McGaha MG 5.00 2.00
❑ 243 Robin Roberts 15.00 6.00
❑ 244 Don Gile 5.00 2.00
❑ 245 Ron Hansen 5.00 2.00
❑ 246 Art Ditmar 5.00 2.00
❑ 247 Joe Pignatano 5.00 2.00
❑ 248 Bob Aspromonte 8.00 3.20
❑ 249 Ed Keegan 5.00 2.00
❑ 250 Norm Cash 10.00 4.00
❑ 251 New York Yankees 50.00 20.00
Team Card
❑ 252 Earl Francis 5.00 2.00
❑ 253 Harry Chiti CO 5.00 2.00
❑ 254 Gordon Windhorn 5.00 2.00
❑ 255 Juan Pizarro 5.00 2.00
❑ 256 Elio Chacon 8.00 3.20
❑ 257 Jack Spring 5.00 2.00
❑ 258 Marty Keough 5.00 2.00
❑ 259 Lou Klimchock 5.00 2.00
❑ 260 Billy Pierce 8.00 3.20
❑ 261 George Alusik 5.00 2.00
❑ 262 Bob Schmidt 5.00 2.00
❑ 263 Bob Purkey 5.00 2.00
Jim Turner CO
Joe Jay
❑ 264 Dick Ellsworth 8.00 3.20
❑ 265 Joe Adcock 8.00 3.20
❑ 266 John Anderson 5.00 2.00
❑ 267 Dan Dobbek 5.00 2.00
❑ 268 Ken McBride 5.00 2.00
❑ 269 Bob Oldis 5.00 2.00
❑ 270 Dick Groat 8.00 3.20
❑ 271 Ray Rippelmeyer 5.00 2.00
❑ 272 Earl Robinson 5.00 2.00
❑ 273 Gary Bell 5.00 2.00
❑ 274 Sammy Taylor 5.00 2.00
❑ 275 Norm Siebern 5.00 2.00
❑ 276 Hal Kolstad 5.00 2.00
❑ 277 Checklist 4 15.00 3.00
❑ 278 Ken Johnson 8.00 3.20
❑ 279 Hobie Landrith UER 8.00 3.20
(Wrong birthdate)
❑ 280 Johnny Podres 8.00 3.20
❑ 281 Jake Gibbs 10.00 4.00
❑ 282 Dave Hillman 5.00 2.00
❑ 283 Charlie Smith 5.00 2.00
❑ 284 Ruben Amaro 5.00 2.00
❑ 285 Curt Simmons 8.00 3.20
❑ 286 Al Lopez MG 10.00 4.00
❑ 287 George Witt 5.00 2.00
❑ 288 Billy Williams 30.00 12.00
❑ 289 Mike Krsnich 5.00 2.00
❑ 290 Jim Gentile 8.00 3.20
❑ 291 Hal Stowe 5.00 2.00
❑ 292 Jerry Kindall 5.00 2.00
❑ 293 Bob Miller 8.00 3.20
❑ 294 Phillies Team 10.00 4.00
❑ 295 Vern Law 8.00 3.20
❑ 296 Ken Hamlin 5.00 2.00
❑ 297 Ron Perranoski 8.00 3.20
❑ 298 Bill Tuttle 5.00 2.00
❑ 299 Don Wert 5.00 2.00
❑ 300 Willie Mays 250.00 100.00
❑ 301 Galen Cisco RC 5.00 2.00
❑ 302 Johnny Edwards 5.00 2.00
❑ 303 Frank Torre 8.00 3.20
❑ 304 Dick Farrell 8.00 3.20
❑ 305 Jerry Lumpe 5.00 2.00
❑ 306 Lindy McDaniel 5.00 2.00
Larry Jackson
❑ 307 Jim Grant 8.00 3.20
❑ 308 Neil Chrisley 8.00 3.20
❑ 309 Moe Morhardt 5.00 2.00
❑ 310 Whitey Ford 50.00 20.00
❑ 311 Tony Kubek IA 8.00 3.20
❑ 312 Warren Spahn IA 15.00 6.00
❑ 313 Roger Maris IA 80.00 32.00
Blasts 61th
❑ 314 Rocky Colavito IA 8.00 3.20
❑ 315 Whitey Ford IA 15.00 6.00
❑ 316 Harmon Killebrew IA 15.00 6.00
❑ 317 Stan Musial IA 20.00 8.00
❑ 318 Mickey Mantle IA 150.00 60.00
❑ 319 Mike McCormick IA 5.00 2.00
❑ 320 Hank Aaron 150.00 60.00
❑ 321 Lee Stange 5.00 2.00
❑ 322 Alvin Dark MG 8.00 3.20
❑ 323 Don Landrum 5.00 2.00
❑ 324 Joe McClain 5.00 2.00
❑ 325 Luis Aparicio 15.00 6.00
❑ 326 Tom Parsons 5.00 2.00
❑ 327 Ozzie Virgil 5.00 2.00
❑ 328 Ken Walters 5.00 2.00
❑ 329 Bob Bolin 5.00 2.00
❑ 330 John Romano 5.00 2.00
❑ 331 Moe Drabowsky 8.00 3.20
❑ 332 Don Buddin 5.00 2.00
❑ 333 Frank Cipriani 5.00 2.00
❑ 334 Boston Red Sox 10.00 4.00
Team Card
❑ 335 Bill Bruton 5.00 2.00
❑ 336 Billy Muffett 5.00 2.00
❑ 337 Jim Marshall 8.00 3.20
❑ 338 Billy Gardner 5.00 2.00
❑ 339 Jose Valdivielso 5.00 2.00
❑ 340 Don Drysdale 50.00 20.00
❑ 341 Mike Hershberger 5.00 2.00
❑ 342 Ed Rakow 5.00 2.00
❑ 343 Albie Pearson 8.00 3.20
❑ 344 Ed Bauta 5.00 2.00
❑ 345 Chuck Schilling 5.00 2.00
❑ 346 Jack Kralick 5.00 2.00
❑ 347 Chuck Hinton 5.00 2.00
❑ 348 Larry Burright 8.00 3.20
❑ 349 Paul Foytack 5.00 2.00
❑ 350 Frank Robinson 50.00 20.00
❑ 351 Joe Torre 8.00 3.20
Del Crandall
❑ 352 Frank Sullivan 5.00 2.00
❑ 353 Bill Mazeroski 15.00 6.00
❑ 354 Roman Mejias 8.00 3.20
❑ 355 Steve Barber 5.00 2.00
❑ 356 Tom Haller RC 5.00 2.00
❑ 357 Jerry Walker 5.00 2.00
❑ 358 Tommy Davis 8.00 3.20
❑ 359 Bobby Locke 5.00 2.00
❑ 360 Yogi Berra 80.00 32.00
❑ 361 Bob Hendley 5.00 2.00
❑ 362 Ty Cline 5.00 2.00
❑ 363 Bob Roselli 5.00 2.00
❑ 364 Ken Hunt 5.00 2.00
❑ 365 Charlie Neal 8.00 3.20
❑ 366 Phil Regan 8.00 3.20
❑ 367 Checklist 5 15.00 3.00
❑ 368 Bob Tillman 5.00 2.00
❑ 369 Ted Bowsfield 5.00 2.00
❑ 370 Ken Boyer 10.00 4.00
❑ 371 Earl Battey 6.00 2.40
❑ 372 Jack Curtis 6.00 2.40
❑ 373 Al Heist 6.00 2.40
❑ 374 Gene Mauch MG 10.00 4.00
❑ 375 Ron Fairly 10.00 4.00
❑ 376 Bud Daley 8.00 3.20
❑ 377 John Orsino 6.00 2.40
❑ 378 Bennie Daniels 6.00 2.40
❑ 379 Chuck Essegian 6.00 2.40
❑ 380 Lou Burdette 10.00 4.00
❑ 381 Chico Cardenas 10.00 4.00
❑ 382 Dick Williams 8.00 3.20
❑ 383 Ray Sadecki 6.00 2.40
❑ 384 K.C. Athletics 10.00 4.00
Team Card
❑ 385 Early Wynn 15.00 6.00
❑ 386 Don Mincher 8.00 3.20
❑ 387 Lou Brock RC 125.00 50.00
❑ 388 Ryne Duren 8.00 3.20
❑ 389 Smoky Burgess 10.00 4.00
❑ 390 Orlando Cepeda AS 10.00 4.00
❑ 391 Bill Mazeroski AS 10.00 4.00
❑ 392 Ken Boyer AS UER 8.00 3.20
Batting Average mistakenly listed as .392
❑ 393 Roy McMillan AS 6.00 2.40
❑ 394 Hank Aaron AS 50.00 20.00
❑ 395 Willie Mays AS 50.00 20.00
❑ 396 Frank Robinson AS 15.00 6.00
❑ 397 John Roseboro AS 6.00 2.40
❑ 398 Don Drysdale AS 15.00 6.00
❑ 399 Warren Spahn AS 15.00 6.00
❑ 400 Elston Howard 10.00 4.00
❑ 401 Roger Maris 60.00 24.00
Orlando Cepeda
❑ 402 Gino Cimoli 6.00 2.40
❑ 403 Chet Nichols 6.00 2.40
❑ 404 Tim Harkness 8.00 3.20
❑ 405 Jim Perry 8.00 3.20
❑ 406 Bob Taylor 6.00 2.40
❑ 407 Hank Aguirre 6.00 2.40
❑ 408 Gus Bell 8.00 3.20
❑ 409 Pittsburgh Pirates 10.00 4.00
Team Card
❑ 410 Al Smith 6.00 2.40
❑ 411 Danny O'Connell 6.00 2.40
❑ 412 Charlie James 6.00 2.40
❑ 413 Matty Alou 10.00 4.00
❑ 414 Joe Gaines 6.00 2.40
❑ 415 Bill Virdon 10.00 4.00
❑ 416 Bob Scheffing MG 6.00 2.40
❑ 417 Joe Azcue 6.00 2.40
❑ 418 Andy Carey 6.00 2.40
❑ 419 Bob Bruce 8.00 3.20
❑ 420 Gus Triandos 8.00 3.20
❑ 421 Ken MacKenzie 8.00 3.20
❑ 422 Steve Bilko 6.00 2.40
❑ 423 Roy Face 10.00 4.00
Hoyt Wilhelm
❑ 424 Al McBean RC 6.00 2.40
❑ 425 Carl Yastrzemski 125.00 50.00
❑ 426 Bob Farley 6.00 2.40
❑ 427 Jake Wood 6.00 2.40
❑ 428 Joe Hicks 6.00 2.40
❑ 429 Billy O'Dell 6.00 2.40
❑ 430 Tony Kubek 15.00 6.00
❑ 431 Bob Rodgers RC 8.00 3.20
❑ 432 Jim Pendleton 6.00 2.40
❑ 433 Jim Archer 6.00 2.40
❑ 434 Clay Dalrymple 6.00 2.40
❑ 435 Larry Sherry 8.00 3.20
❑ 436 Felix Mantilla 8.00 3.20
❑ 437 Ray Moore 6.00 2.40
❑ 438 Dick Brown 6.00 2.40
❑ 439 Jerry Buchek 6.00 2.40
❑ 440 Joey Jay 6.00 2.40
❑ 441 Checklist 6 15.00 6.00
❑ 442 Wes Stock 6.00 2.40
❑ 443 Del Crandall 8.00 3.20
❑ 444 Ted Wills 6.00 2.40
❑ 445 Vic Power 8.00 3.20
❑ 446 Don Elston 6.00 2.40
❑ 447 Willie Kirkland 12.00 4.80
❑ 448 Joe Gibbon 12.00 4.80
❑ 449 Jerry Adair 12.00 4.80
❑ 450 Jim O'Toole 15.00 6.00
❑ 451 Jose Tartabull RC 15.00 6.00
❑ 452 Earl Averill Jr. 12.00 4.80
❑ 453 Cal McLish 12.00 4.80
❑ 454 Floyd Robinson 12.00 4.80
❑ 455 Luis Arroyo 15.00 6.00
❑ 456 Joe Amalfitano 15.00 6.00
❑ 457 Lou Clinton 12.00 4.80
❑ 458A Bob Buhl 15.00 6.00
(Braves emblem on cap)
❑ 458B Bob Buhl 50.00 20.00
(No emblem on cap)
❑ 459 Ed Bailey 12.00 4.80
❑ 460 Jim Bunning 20.00 8.00
❑ 461 Ken Hubbs RC 30.00 12.00
❑ 462A Willie Tasby 12.00 4.80
(Senators emblem on cap)
❑ 462B Willie Tasby 50.00 20.00
(No emblem on cap)
❑ 463 Hank Bauer MG 15.00 6.00

❑ 464 Al Jackson RC 12.00 4.80
❑ 465 Reds Team 20.00 8.00
❑ 466 Norm Cash AS 15.00 6.00
❑ 467 Chuck Schilling AS 12.00 4.80
❑ 468 Brooks Robinson AS 25.00 10.00
❑ 469 Luis Aparicio AS 15.00 6.00
❑ 470 Al Kaline AS 25.00 10.00
❑ 471 Mickey Mantle AS 200.00 80.00
❑ 472 Rocky Colavito AS.......... 15.00 6.00
❑ 473 Elston Howard AS 15.00 6.00
❑ 474 Frank Lary AS 12.00 4.80
❑ 475 Whitey Ford AS 20.00 8.00
❑ 476 Orioles Team.......... 20.00 8.00
❑ 477 Andre Rodgers 12.00 4.80
❑ 478 Don Zimmer 20.00 8.00
Shown with Mets cap,
but listed with Cincinnati
❑ 479 Joel Horlen RC 12.00 4.80
❑ 480 Harvey Kuenn 15.00 6.00
❑ 481 Vic Wertz.......... 15.00 6.00
❑ 482 Sam Mele MG 12.00 4.80
❑ 483 Don McMahon 12.00 4.80
❑ 484 Dick Schofield.......... 12.00 4.80
❑ 485 Pedro Ramos.......... 12.00 4.80
❑ 486 Jim Gilliam 15.00 6.00
❑ 487 Jerry Lynch 12.00 4.80
❑ 488 Hal Brown 12.00 4.80
❑ 489 Julio Gotay 12.00 4.80
❑ 490 Clete Boyer UER 15.00 6.00
Reversed Negative
❑ 491 Leon Wagner.......... 12.00 4.80
❑ 492 Hal W. Smith.......... 15.00 6.00
❑ 493 Danny McDevitt.......... 12.00 4.80
❑ 494 Sammy White 12.00 4.80
❑ 495 Don Cardwell 12.00 4.80
❑ 496 Wayne Causey.......... 12.00 4.80
❑ 497 Ed Bouchee.......... 15.00 6.00
❑ 498 Jim Donohue.......... 12.00 4.80
❑ 499 Zoilo Versalles 15.00 6.00
❑ 500 Duke Snider 60.00 24.00
❑ 501 Claude Osteen 15.00 6.00
❑ 502 Hector Lopez.......... 15.00 6.00
❑ 503 Danny Murtaugh MG.... 15.00 6.00
❑ 504 Eddie Bressoud 12.00 4.80
❑ 505 Juan Marichal 40.00 16.00
❑ 506 Charlie Maxwell 15.00 6.00
❑ 507 Ernie Broglio.......... 15.00 6.00
❑ 508 Gordy Coleman.......... 15.00 6.00
❑ 509 Dave Giusti RC 15.00 6.00
❑ 510 Jim Lemon 12.00 4.80
❑ 511 Bubba Phillips.......... 12.00 4.80
❑ 512 Mike Fornieles 12.00 4.80
❑ 513 Whitey Herzog.......... 15.00 6.00
❑ 514 Sherm Lollar 15.00 6.00
❑ 515 Stan Williams 15.00 6.00
❑ 516A Checklist 7 .... 15.00 3.00
White Boxes
❑ 516B Checklist 7 .... 15.00 6.00
Yellow Boxes
❑ 517 Dave Wickersham 12.00 4.80
❑ 518 Lee Maye.......... 12.00 4.80
❑ 519 Bob Johnson.......... 12.00 4.80
❑ 520 Bob Friend 15.00 6.00
❑ 521 Jacke Davis UER 12.00 4.80
(Listed as OF on
front and P on back)
❑ 522 Lindy McDaniel.......... 15.00 6.00
❑ 523 Russ Nixon SP 30.00 12.00
❑ 524 Howie Nunn SP.......... 30.00 12.00
❑ 525 George Thomas.......... 20.00 8.00
❑ 526 Hal Woodeshick SP...... 30.00 12.00
❑ 527 Dick McAuliffe RC.......... 30.00 12.00
❑ 528 Turk Lown.......... 20.00 8.00
❑ 529 John Schaive SP.......... 30.00 12.00
❑ 530 Bob Gibson SP 125.00 50.00
❑ 531 Bobby G. Smith.......... 20.00 8.00
❑ 532 Dick Stigman.......... 20.00 8.00
❑ 533 Charley Lau SP 30.00 12.00
❑ 534 Tony Gonzalez SP 30.00 12.00
❑ 535 Ed Roebuck.......... 20.00 8.00
❑ 536 Dick Gernert 20.00 8.00
❑ 537 Cleveland Indians 50.00 20.00
Team Card
❑ 538 Jack Sanford.......... 20.00 8.00
❑ 539 Billy Moran 20.00 8.00
❑ 540 Jim Landis SP.......... 30.00 12.00
❑ 541 Don Nottebart SP 30.00 12.00
❑ 542 Dave Philley 20.00 8.00
❑ 543 Bob Allen SP.......... 30.00 12.00
❑ 544 Willie McCovey SP 125.00 50.00
❑ 545 Hoyt Wilhelm SP.......... 50.00 20.00
❑ 546 Moe Thacker SP 30.00 12.00
❑ 547 Don Ferrarese 20.00 8.00
❑ 548 Bobby Del Greco.......... 20.00 8.00
❑ 549 Bill Rigney MG SP 30.00 12.00
❑ 550 Art Mahaffey SP 30.00 12.00
❑ 551 Harry Bright.......... 20.00 8.00
❑ 552 Chicago Cubs SP 50.00 20.00
Team Card
❑ 553 Jim Coates 30.00 12.00
❑ 554 Bubba Morton SP 30.00 12.00
❑ 555 John Buzhardt SP 30.00 12.00
❑ 556 Al Spangler 20.00 8.00
❑ 557 Bob Anderson SP 30.00 12.00
❑ 558 John Goryl 20.00 8.00
❑ 559 Mike Higgins MG 20.00 8.00
❑ 560 Chuck Estrada SP 30.00 12.00
❑ 561 Gene Oliver SP 30.00 12.00
❑ 562 Bill Henry 20.00 8.00
❑ 563 Ken Aspromonte 20.00 8.00
❑ 564 Bob Grim.......... 20.00 8.00
❑ 565 Jose Pagan 20.00 8.00
❑ 566 Marty Kutyna SP 30.00 12.00
❑ 567 Tracy Stallard SP.......... 30.00 12.00
❑ 568 Jim Golden 20.00 8.00
❑ 569 Ed Sadowski SP 30.00 12.00
❑ 570 Bill Stafford SP 30.00 12.00
❑ 571 Billy Klaus SP 30.00 12.00
❑ 572 Bob G. Miller SP 30.00 12.00
❑ 573 Johnny Logan 20.00 8.00
❑ 574 Dean Stone 20.00 8.00
❑ 575 Red Schoendienst SP .. 50.00 20.00
❑ 576 Russ Kemmerer SP 30.00 12.00
❑ 577 Dave Nicholson SP 30.00 12.00
❑ 578 Jim Duffalo 20.00 8.00
❑ 579 Jim Schaffer SP.......... 30.00 12.00
❑ 580 Bill Monbouquette.......... 20.00 8.00
❑ 581 Mel Roach.......... 20.00 8.00
❑ 582 Ron Piche 20.00 8.00
❑ 583 Larry Osborne 20.00 8.00
❑ 584 Minnesota Twins SP 60.00 24.00
Team Card
❑ 585 Glen Hobbie SP.......... 30.00 12.00
❑ 586 Sammy Esposito SP 30.00 12.00
❑ 587 Frank Funk SP.......... 30.00 12.00
❑ 588 Birdie Tebbetts MG 20.00 8.00
❑ 589 Bob Turley.......... 30.00 12.00
❑ 590 Curt Flood.......... 30.00 12.00
❑ 591 Sam McDowell RC 80.00 32.00
Ron Taylor
Ron Nischwitz
Art Quirk
Dick Radatz SP
❑ 592 Dan Pfister 80.00 32.00
Bo Belinsky
Dave Stenhouse
Jim Bouton RC
Joe Bonikowski SP
❑ 593 Jack Lamabe 50.00 20.00
Craig Anderson
Jack Hamilton
Bob Moorhead
Bob Veale SP
❑ 594 Doc Edwards.......... 80.00 32.00
Ken Retzer
Bob Uecker RC
Doug Camilli
Don Pavletich SP
❑ 595 Bob Sadowski 50.00 20.00
Felix Torres
Marlan Coughtry
Ed Charles SP
❑ 596 Bernie Allen.......... 80.00 32.00
Joe Pepitone RC
Phil Linz
Rich Rollins SP
❑ 597 Jim McKnight 50.00 20.00
Rod Kanehl
Amado Samuel
Denis Menke RC SP
❑ 598 Al Luplow 80.00 23.00
Manny Jimenez
Howie Goss
Jim Hickman
Ed Olivares SP

1963 Topps

	NM	Ex
COMPLETE SET (576)	5000.00	2000.00
COMMON CARD (1-196)..........	4.00	1.60
COMMON (197-283)	5.00	2.00
COMMON (284-370)	5.00	2.00
COMMON (371-446)	5.00	2.00
COMMON (447-522)	25.00	10.00
COMMON (523-576)	15.00	6.00
WRAPPER (1-CENT)..........	40.00	16.00
WRAPPER (5-CENT)..........	30.00	12.00

❑ 1 Tommy Davis 40.00 8.00
Frank Robinson
Stan Musial
Hank Aaron
Bill White LL
❑ 2 Pete Runnels.......... 50.00 20.00
Mickey Mantle
Floyd Robinson
Norm Siebern
Chuck Hinton LL
❑ 3 Willie Mays.......... 40.00 16.00
Hank Aaron
Frank Robinson
Orlando Cepeda
Ernie Banks LL
❑ 4 Harmon Killebrew 20.00 8.00
Norm Cash
Rocky Colavito
Roger Maris
Jim Gentile
Leon Wagner LL
❑ 5 Sandy Koufax 25.00 10.00
Bob Shaw
Bob Purkey
Bob Gibson
Don Drysdale LL
❑ 6 Hank Aguirre.......... 10.00 4.00
Robin Roberts
Whitey Ford
Eddie Fisher
Dean Chance LL
❑ 7 Don Drysdale 10.00 4.00
Jack Sanford
Bob Purkey
Billy O'Dell
Art Mahaffey
Joe Jay LL
❑ 8 Ralph Terry 8.00 3.20
Dick Donovan
Ray Herbert
Jim Bunning
Camilo Pascual LL
❑ 9 Don Drysdale 30.00 12.00
Sandy Koufax
Bob Gibson
Billy O'Dell
Dick Farrell LL
❑ 10 Camilo Pascual.......... 8.00 3.20
Jim Bunning
Ralph Terry
Juan Pizarro
Jim Kaat LL

No.	Card	Price 1	Price 2
❑ 11	Lee Walls	4.00	1.60
❑ 12	Steve Barber	4.00	1.60
❑ 13	Philadelphia Phillies	8.00	3.20
	Team Card		
❑ 14	Pedro Ramos	4.00	1.60
❑ 15	Ken Hubbs UER	10.00	4.00
	(No position listed		
	on front of card)		
❑ 16	Al Smith	4.00	1.60
❑ 17	Ryne Duren	8.00	3.20
❑ 18	Smoky Burgess	80.00	32.00
	Dick Stuart		
	Bob Clemente		
	Bob Skinner		
❑ 19	Pete Burnside	4.00	1.60
❑ 20	Tony Kubek	10.00	4.00
❑ 21	Marty Keough	4.00	1.60
❑ 22	Curt Simmons	8.00	3.20
❑ 23	Ed Lopat MG	8.00	3.20
❑ 24	Bob Bruce	4.00	1.60
❑ 25	Al Kaline	50.00	20.00
❑ 26	Ray Moore	4.00	1.60
❑ 27	Choo Choo Coleman	8.00	3.20
❑ 28	Mike Fornieles	4.00	1.60
❑ 29A	1962 Rookie Stars	10.00	4.00
	Sammy Ellis		
	Ray Culp		
	John Boozer		
	Jesse Gonder		
❑ 29B	1963 Rookie Stars	4.00	1.60
	Sammy Ellis		
	Ray Culp		
	John Boozer		
	Jesse Gonder		
❑ 30	Harvey Kuenn	8.00	3.20
❑ 31	Cal Koonce	4.00	1.60
❑ 32	Tony Gonzalez	4.00	1.60
❑ 33	Bo Belinsky	8.00	3.20
❑ 34	Dick Schofield	4.00	1.60
❑ 35	John Buzhardt	4.00	1.60
❑ 36	Jerry Kindall	4.00	1.60
❑ 37	Jerry Lynch	4.00	1.60
❑ 38	Bud Daley	8.00	3.20
❑ 39	Angels Team	8.00	3.20
❑ 40	Vic Power	8.00	3.20
❑ 41	Charley Lau	8.00	3.20
❑ 42	Stan Williams	8.00	3.20
	(Listed as Yankee on		
	card but LA cap)		
❑ 43	Casey Stengel MG	8.00	3.20
	Gene Woodling		
❑ 44	Terry Fox	4.00	1.60
❑ 45	Bob Aspromonte	4.00	1.60
❑ 46	Tommie Aaron RC	8.00	3.20
❑ 47	Don Lock	4.00	1.60
❑ 48	Birdie Tebbetts MG	8.00	3.20
❑ 49	Dal Maxvill RC	8.00	3.20
❑ 50	Billy Pierce	8.00	3.20
❑ 51	George Alusik	4.00	1.60
❑ 52	Chuck Schilling	4.00	1.60
❑ 53	Joe Moeller	8.00	3.20
❑ 54A	1962 Rookie Stars	15.00	6.00
	Nelson Mathews		
	Harry Fanok		
	Jack Cullen		
	Dave DeBusschere RC		
❑ 54B	1963 Rookie Stars	8.00	3.20
	Nelson Mathews		
	Harry Fanok		
	Jack Cullen		
	Dave DeBusschere RC		
❑ 55	Bill Virdon	8.00	3.20
❑ 56	Dennis Bennett	4.00	1.60
❑ 57	Billy Moran	4.00	1.60
❑ 58	Bob Will	4.00	1.60
❑ 59	Craig Anderson	4.00	1.60
❑ 60	Elston Howard	8.00	3.20
❑ 61	Ernie Bowman	4.00	1.60
❑ 62	Bob Hendley	4.00	1.60
❑ 63	Reds Team	8.00	3.20
❑ 64	Dick McAuliffe	8.00	3.20
❑ 65	Jackie Brandt	4.00	1.60
❑ 66	Mike Joyce	4.00	1.60
❑ 67	Ed Charles	4.00	1.60
❑ 68	Duke Snider	25.00	10.00
	Gil Hodges		
❑ 69	Bud Zipfel	4.00	1.60
❑ 70	Jim O'Toole	8.00	3.20
❑ 71	Bobby Wine	8.00	3.20
❑ 72	Johnny Romano	4.00	1.60
❑ 73	Bobby Bragan MG RC	8.00	3.20
❑ 74	Denny Lemaster	4.00	1.60
❑ 75	Bob Allison	8.00	3.20
❑ 76	Earl Wilson	8.00	3.20
❑ 77	Al Spangler	4.00	1.60
❑ 78	Marv Throneberry	8.00	3.20
❑ 79	Checklist 1	12.00	2.40
❑ 80	Jim Gilliam	8.00	3.20
❑ 81	Jim Schaffer	4.00	1.60
❑ 82	Ed Rakow	4.00	1.60
❑ 83	Charley James	4.00	1.60
❑ 84	Ron Kline	4.00	1.60
❑ 85	Tom Haller	8.00	3.20
❑ 86	Charley Maxwell	8.00	3.20
❑ 87	Bob Veale	8.00	3.20
❑ 88	Ron Hansen	4.00	1.60
❑ 89	Dick Stigman	4.00	1.60
❑ 90	Gordy Coleman	8.00	3.20
❑ 91	Dallas Green	8.00	3.20
❑ 92	Hector Lopez	8.00	3.20
❑ 93	Galen Cisco	4.00	1.60
❑ 94	Bob Schmidt	4.00	1.60
❑ 95	Larry Jackson	4.00	1.60
❑ 96	Lou Clinton	4.00	1.60
❑ 97	Bob Duliba	4.00	1.60
❑ 98	George Thomas	4.00	1.60
❑ 99	Jim Umbricht	4.00	1.60
❑ 100	Joe Cunningham	4.00	1.60
❑ 101	Joe Gibbon	4.00	1.60
❑ 102A	Checklist 2	12.00	2.40
	(Red on yellow)		
❑ 102B	Checklist 2	12.00	2.40
	(White on red)		
❑ 103	Chuck Essegian	4.00	1.60
❑ 104	Lew Krausse	4.00	1.60
❑ 105	Ron Fairly	8.00	3.20
❑ 106	Bobby Bolin	4.00	1.60
❑ 107	Jim Hickman	8.00	3.20
❑ 108	Hoyt Wilhelm	10.00	4.00
❑ 109	Lee Maye	4.00	1.60
❑ 110	Rich Rollins	8.00	3.20
❑ 111	Al Jackson	4.00	1.60
❑ 112	Dick Brown	4.00	1.60
❑ 113	Don Landrum UER	4.00	1.60
	(Photo actually		
	Ron Santo)		
❑ 114	Dan Osinski	4.00	1.60
❑ 115	Carl Yastrzemski	40.00	16.00
❑ 116	Jim Brosnan	8.00	3.20
❑ 117	Jacke Davis	4.00	1.60
❑ 118	Sherm Lollar	4.00	1.60
❑ 119	Bob Lillis	4.00	1.60
❑ 120	Roger Maris	80.00	32.00
❑ 121	Jim Hannan	4.00	1.60
❑ 122	Julio Gotay	4.00	1.60
❑ 123	Frank Howard	8.00	3.20
❑ 124	Dick Howser	8.00	3.20
❑ 125	Robin Roberts	15.00	6.00
❑ 126	Bob Uecker	15.00	6.00
❑ 127	Bill Tuttle	4.00	1.60
❑ 128	Matty Alou	8.00	3.20
❑ 129	Gary Bell	4.00	1.60
❑ 130	Dick Groat	8.00	3.20
❑ 131	Washington Senators	8.00	3.20
	Team Card		
❑ 132	Jack Hamilton	4.00	1.60
❑ 133	Gene Freese	4.00	1.60
❑ 134	Bob Scheffing MG	4.00	1.60
❑ 135	Richie Ashburn	20.00	8.00
❑ 136	Ike Delock	4.00	1.60
❑ 137	Mack Jones	4.00	1.60
❑ 138	Willie Mays	80.00	32.00
	Stan Musial		
❑ 139	Earl Averill	4.00	1.60
❑ 140	Frank Lary	8.00	3.20
❑ 141	Manny Mota RC	8.00	3.20
❑ 142	Whitey Ford WS	10.00	4.00
❑ 143	Jack Sanford WS	8.00	3.20
❑ 144	Roger Maris WS	15.00	6.00
❑ 145	Chuck Hiller WS	8.00	3.20
❑ 146	Tom Tresh WS	8.00	3.20
❑ 147	Billy Pierce WS	8.00	3.20
❑ 148	Ralph Terry WS	8.00	3.20
❑ 149	Marv Breeding	4.00	1.60
❑ 150	Johnny Podres	8.00	3.20
❑ 151	Pirates Team	8.00	3.20
❑ 152	Ron Nischwitz	4.00	1.60
❑ 153	Hal Smith	4.00	1.60
❑ 154	Walter Alston MG	8.00	3.20
❑ 155	Bill Stafford	4.00	1.60
❑ 156	Roy McMillan	8.00	3.20
❑ 157	Diego Segui RC	8.00	3.20
❑ 158	Rogelio Alvares	8.00	3.20
	Dave Roberts		
	Tommy Harper RC		
	Bob Saverine		
❑ 159	Jim Pagliaroni	4.00	1.60
❑ 160	Juan Pizarro	4.00	1.60
❑ 161	Frank Torre	8.00	3.20
❑ 162	Twins Team	8.00	3.20
❑ 163	Don Larsen	8.00	3.20
❑ 164	Bubba Morton	4.00	1.60
❑ 165	Jim Kaat	8.00	3.20
❑ 166	Johnny Keane MG	4.00	1.60
❑ 167	Jim Fregosi	8.00	3.20
❑ 168	Russ Nixon	4.00	1.60
❑ 169	Dick Egan	25.00	10.00
	Julio Navarro		
	Tommie Sisk		
	Gaylord Perry		
❑ 170	Joe Adcock	8.00	3.20
❑ 171	Steve Hamilton	4.00	1.60
❑ 172	Gene Oliver	4.00	1.60
❑ 173	Tom Tresh	150.00	60.00
	Mickey Mantle		
	Bobby Richardson		
❑ 174	Larry Burright	4.00	1.60
❑ 175	Bob Buhl	8.00	3.20
❑ 176	Jim King	4.00	1.60
❑ 177	Bubba Phillips	4.00	1.60
❑ 178	Johnny Edwards	4.00	1.60
❑ 179	Ron Piche	4.00	1.60
❑ 180	Bill Skowron	8.00	3.20
❑ 181	Sammy Esposito	4.00	1.60
❑ 182	Albie Pearson	8.00	3.20
❑ 183	Joe Pepitone	8.00	3.20
❑ 184	Vern Law	8.00	3.20
❑ 185	Chuck Hiller	4.00	1.60
❑ 186	Jerry Zimmerman	4.00	1.60
❑ 187	Willie Kirkland	4.00	1.60
❑ 188	Eddie Bressoud	4.00	1.60
❑ 189	Dave Giusti	8.00	3.20
❑ 190	Minnie Minoso	8.00	3.20
❑ 191	Checklist 3	12.00	2.40
❑ 192	Clay Dalrymple	4.00	1.60
❑ 193	Andre Rodgers	4.00	1.60
❑ 194	Joe Nuxhall	8.00	3.20
❑ 195	Manny Jimenez	4.00	1.60
❑ 196	Doug Camilli	4.00	1.60
❑ 197	Roger Craig	8.00	3.20
❑ 198	Lenny Green	5.00	2.00
❑ 199	Joe Amalfitano	5.00	2.00
❑ 200	Mickey Mantle	500.00	200.00
❑ 201	Cecil Butler	5.00	2.00
❑ 202	Boston Red Sox	8.00	3.20
	Team Card		
❑ 203	Chico Cardenas	8.00	3.20
❑ 204	Don Nottebart	5.00	2.00
❑ 205	Luis Aparicio	15.00	6.00
❑ 206	Ray Washburn	5.00	2.00
❑ 207	Ken Hunt	5.00	2.00
❑ 208	Ron Herbel	5.00	2.00
	John Miller		
	Wally Wolf		
	Ron Taylor		
❑ 209	Hobie Landrith	5.00	2.00
❑ 210	Sandy Koufax	150.00	60.00
❑ 211	Fred Whitfield	5.00	2.00
❑ 212	Glen Hobbie	5.00	2.00
❑ 213	Billy Hitchcock MG	5.00	2.00
❑ 214	Orlando Pena	5.00	2.00
❑ 215	Bob Skinner	8.00	3.20
❑ 216	Gene Conley	8.00	3.20
❑ 217	Joe Christopher	5.00	2.00
❑ 218	Frank Lary	8.00	3.20
	Don Mossi		
	Jim Bunning		
❑ 219	Chuck Cottier	5.00	2.00

❑ 220 Camilo Pascual 8.00 3.20
❑ 221 Cookie Rojas RC 8.00 3.20
❑ 222 Cubs Team 8.00 3.20
❑ 223 Eddie Fisher 5.00 2.00
❑ 224 Mike Roarke 5.00 2.00
❑ 225 Joey Jay 5.00 2.00
❑ 226 Julian Javier 8.00 3.20
❑ 227 Jim Grant 8.00 3.20
❑ 228 Max Alvis 50.00 20.00
Bob Bailey
Tony Oliva
(Listed as Pedro)
Ed Kranepool RC
❑ 229 Willie Davis 8.00 3.20
❑ 230 Pete Runnels 8.00 3.20
❑ 231 Eli Grba UER 5.00 2.00
(Large photo is
Ryne Duren)
❑ 232 Frank Malzone 8.00 3.20
❑ 233 Casey Stengel MG 20.00 8.00
❑ 234 Dave Nicholson 5.00 2.00
❑ 235 Billy O'Dell 5.00 2.00
❑ 236 Bill Bryan 5.00 2.00
❑ 237 Jim Coates 8.00 3.20
❑ 238 Lou Johnson 5.00 2.00
❑ 239 Harvey Haddix 8.00 3.20
❑ 240 Rocky Colavito 15.00 6.00
❑ 241 Bob Smith 5.00 2.00
❑ 242 Ernie Banks 60.00 24.00
Hank Aaron
❑ 243 Don Leppert 5.00 2.00
❑ 244 John Tsitouris 5.00 2.00
❑ 245 Gil Hodges 20.00 8.00
❑ 246 Lee Stange 5.00 2.00
❑ 247 Yankees Team 50.00 20.00
❑ 248 Tito Francona 5.00 2.00
❑ 249 Leo Burke 5.00 2.00
❑ 250 Stan Musial 100.00 40.00
❑ 251 Jack Lamabe 5.00 2.00
❑ 252 Ron Santo 10.00 4.00
❑ 253 Len Gabrielson 5.00 2.00
Pete Jernigan
John Wojcik
Deacon Jones
❑ 254 Mike Hershberger 5.00 2.00
❑ 255 Bob Shaw 5.00 2.00
❑ 256 Jerry Lumpe 5.00 2.00
❑ 257 Hank Aguirre 5.00 2.00
❑ 258 Alvin Dark MG 8.00 3.20
❑ 259 Johnny Logan 8.00 3.20
❑ 260 Jim Gentile 8.00 3.20
❑ 261 Bob Miller 5.00 2.00
❑ 262 Ellis Burton 5.00 2.00
❑ 263 Dave Stenhouse 5.00 2.00
❑ 264 Phil Linz 5.00 2.00
❑ 265 Vada Pinson 8.00 3.20
❑ 266 Bob Allen 5.00 2.00
❑ 267 Carl Sawatski 5.00 2.00
❑ 268 Don Demeter 5.00 2.00
❑ 269 Don Mincher 5.00 2.00
❑ 270 Felipe Alou 8.00 3.20
❑ 271 Dean Stone 5.00 2.00
❑ 272 Danny Murphy 5.00 2.00
❑ 273 Sammy Taylor 5.00 2.00
❑ 274 Checklist 4 12.00 2.40
❑ 275 Eddie Mathews 30.00 12.00
❑ 276 Barry Shetrone 5.00 2.00
❑ 277 Dick Farrell 5.00 2.00
❑ 278 Chico Fernandez 5.00 2.00
❑ 279 Wally Moon 8.00 3.20
❑ 280 Bob Rodgers 5.00 2.00
❑ 281 Tom Sturdivant 5.00 2.00
❑ 282 Bobby Del Greco 5.00 2.00
❑ 283 Roy Sievers 8.00 3.20
❑ 284 Dave Sisler 5.00 2.00
❑ 285 Dick Stuart 8.00 3.20
❑ 286 Stu Miller 8.00 3.20
❑ 287 Dick Bertell 5.00 2.00
❑ 288 Chicago White Sox 10.00 4.00
Team Card
❑ 289 Hal Brown 5.00 2.00
❑ 290 Bill White 8.00 3.20
❑ 291 Don Rudolph 5.00 2.00
❑ 292 Pumpsie Green 8.00 3.20
❑ 293 Bill Pleis 5.00 2.00
❑ 294 Bill Rigney MG 5.00 2.00
❑ 295 Ed Roebuck 5.00 2.00
❑ 296 Doc Edwards 5.00 2.00
❑ 297 Jim Golden 5.00 2.00
❑ 298 Don Dillard 5.00 2.00
❑ 299 Dave Morehead 8.00 3.20
Bob Dustal
Tom Butters
Dan Schneider
❑ 300 Willie Mays 150.00 60.00
❑ 301 Bill Fischer 5.00 2.00
❑ 302 Whitey Herzog 8.00 3.20
❑ 303 Earl Francis 5.00 2.00
❑ 304 Harry Bright 5.00 2.00
❑ 305 Don Hoak 5.00 2.00
❑ 306 Earl Battey 10.00 4.00
Elston Howard
❑ 307 Chet Nichols 5.00 2.00
❑ 308 Camilo Carreon 5.00 2.00
❑ 309 Jim Brewer 5.00 2.00
❑ 310 Tommy Davis 8.00 3.20
❑ 311 Joe McClain 5.00 2.00
❑ 312 Houston Colts 25.00 10.00
Team Card
❑ 313 Ernie Broglio 5.00 2.00
❑ 314 John Goryl 5.00 2.00
❑ 315 Ralph Terry 8.00 3.20
❑ 316 Norm Sherry 8.00 3.20
❑ 317 Sam McDowell 8.00 3.20
❑ 318 Gene Mauch MG 8.00 3.20
❑ 319 Joe Gaines 5.00 2.00
❑ 320 Warren Spahn 60.00 24.00
❑ 321 Gino Cimoli 5.00 2.00
❑ 322 Bob Turley 8.00 3.20
❑ 323 Bill Mazeroski 15.00 6.00
❑ 324 George Williams 8.00 3.20
Pete Ward
Phil Roof
Vic Davalillo
❑ 325 Jack Sanford 5.00 2.00
❑ 326 Hank Foiles 5.00 2.00
❑ 327 Paul Foytack 5.00 2.00
❑ 328 Dick Williams 8.00 3.20
❑ 329 Lindy McDaniel 8.00 3.20
❑ 330 Chuck Hinton 5.00 2.00
❑ 331 Bill Stafford 8.00 3.20
Bill Pierce
❑ 332 Joel Horlen 8.00 3.20
❑ 333 Carl Warwick 5.00 2.00
❑ 334 Wynn Hawkins 5.00 2.00
❑ 335 Leon Wagner 5.00 2.00
❑ 336 Ed Bauta 5.00 2.00
❑ 337 Dodgers Team 25.00 10.00
❑ 338 Russ Kemmerer 5.00 2.00
❑ 339 Ted Bowsfield 5.00 2.00
❑ 340 Yogi Berra P/CO 100.00 40.00
❑ 341 Jack Baldschun 5.00 2.00
❑ 342 Gene Woodling 8.00 3.20
❑ 343 Johnny Pesky MG 8.00 3.20
❑ 344 Don Schwall 5.00 2.00
❑ 345 Brooks Robinson 60.00 24.00
❑ 346 Billy Hoeft 5.00 2.00
❑ 347 Joe Torre 15.00 6.00
❑ 348 Vic Wertz 8.00 3.20
❑ 349 Zoilo Versalles 8.00 3.20
❑ 350 Bob Purkey 5.00 2.00
❑ 351 Al Luplow 5.00 2.00
❑ 352 Ken Johnson 5.00 2.00
❑ 353 Billy Williams 30.00 12.00
❑ 354 Dom Zanni 5.00 2.00
❑ 355 Dean Chance 8.00 3.20
❑ 356 John Schaive 5.00 2.00
❑ 357 George Altman 5.00 2.00
❑ 358 Milt Pappas 8.00 3.20
❑ 359 Haywood Sullivan 8.00 3.20
❑ 360 Don Drysdale 60.00 24.00
❑ 361 Clete Boyer 10.00 4.00
❑ 362 Checklist 5 12.00 2.40
❑ 363 Dick Radatz 8.00 3.20
❑ 364 Howie Goss 5.00 2.00
❑ 365 Jim Bunning 20.00 8.00
❑ 366 Tony Taylor 8.00 3.20
❑ 367 Tony Cloninger 5.00 2.00
❑ 368 Ed Bailey 5.00 2.00
❑ 369 Jim Lemon 5.00 2.00
❑ 370 Dick Donovan 5.00 2.00
❑ 371 Rod Kanehl 8.00 3.20
❑ 372 Don Lee 5.00 2.00
❑ 373 Jim Campbell 5.00 2.00
❑ 374 Claude Osteen 8.00 3.20
❑ 375 Ken Boyer 15.00 6.00
❑ 376 John Wyatt 5.00 2.00
❑ 377 Baltimore Orioles 10.00 4.00
Team Card
❑ 378 Bill Henry 5.00 2.00
❑ 379 Bob Anderson 5.00 2.00
❑ 380 Ernie Banks UER 100.00 40.00
(Back has career Major
and Minor, but he
never played in Minors)
❑ 381 Frank Baumann 5.00 2.00
❑ 382 Ralph Houk MG 10.00 4.00
❑ 383 Pete Richert 5.00 2.00
❑ 384 Bob Tillman 5.00 2.00
❑ 385 Art Mahaffey 5.00 2.00
❑ 386 Ed Kirkpatrick 5.00 2.00
John Bateman RC
Larry Bearnarth
Garry Roggenburk
❑ 387 Al McBean 5.00 2.00
❑ 388 Jim Davenport 8.00 3.20
❑ 389 Frank Sullivan 5.00 2.00
❑ 390 Hank Aaron 175.00 70.00
❑ 391 Bill Dailey 5.00 2.00
❑ 392 Johnny Romano 5.00 2.00
Tito Francona
❑ 393 Ken MacKenzie 8.00 3.20
❑ 394 Tim McCarver 15.00 6.00
❑ 395 Don McMahon 5.00 2.00
❑ 396 Joe Koppe 5.00 2.00
❑ 397 Kansas City Athletics 10.00 4.00
Team Card
❑ 398 Boog Powell 25.00 10.00
❑ 399 Dick Ellsworth 5.00 2.00
❑ 400 Frank Robinson 60.00 24.00
❑ 401 Jim Bouton 15.00 6.00
❑ 402 Mickey Vernon MG 8.00 3.20
❑ 403 Ron Perranoski 8.00 3.20
❑ 404 Bob Oldis 5.00 2.00
❑ 405 Floyd Robinson 5.00 2.00
❑ 406 Howie Koplitz 5.00 2.00
❑ 407 Frank Kostro 8.00 3.20
Chico Ruiz
Larry Elliot
Dick Simpson
❑ 408 Billy Gardner 5.00 2.00
❑ 409 Roy Face 8.00 3.20
❑ 410 Earl Battey 5.00 2.00
❑ 411 Jim Constable 5.00 2.00
❑ 412 Johnny Podres 50.00 20.00
Don Drysdale
Sandy Koufax
❑ 413 Jerry Walker 5.00 2.00
❑ 414 Ty Cline 5.00 2.00
❑ 415 Bob Gibson 60.00 24.00
❑ 416 Alex Grammas 5.00 2.00
❑ 417 Giants Team 10.00 4.00
❑ 418 John Orsino 5.00 2.00
❑ 419 Tracy Stallard 5.00 2.00
❑ 420 Bobby Richardson 15.00 6.00
❑ 421 Tom Morgan 5.00 2.00
❑ 422 Fred Hutchinson MG 8.00 3.20
❑ 423 Ed Hobaugh 5.00 2.00
❑ 424 Charlie Smith 5.00 2.00
❑ 425 Smoky Burgess 8.00 3.20
❑ 426 Barry Latman 5.00 2.00
❑ 427 Bernie Allen 5.00 2.00
❑ 428 Carl Boles 5.00 2.00
❑ 429 Lou Burdette 8.00 3.20
❑ 430 Norm Siebern 5.00 2.00
❑ 431A Checklist 6 12.00 2.40
(White on red)
❑ 431B Checklist 6 30.00 6.00
(Black on orange)
❑ 432 Roman Mejias 5.00 2.00
❑ 433 Denis Menke 5.00 2.00
❑ 434 John Callison 8.00 3.20
❑ 435 Woody Held 5.00 2.00
❑ 436 Tim Harkness 8.00 3.20
❑ 437 Bill Bruton 5.00 2.00
❑ 438 Wes Stock 5.00 2.00
❑ 439 Don Zimmer 8.00 3.20
❑ 440 Juan Marichal 30.00 12.00

❑ 441 Lee Thomas 8.00 3.20
❑ 442 J.C. Hartman 5.00 2.00
❑ 443 Jimmy Piersall 8.00 3.20
❑ 444 Jim Maloney 8.00 3.20
❑ 445 Norm Cash 10.00 4.00
❑ 446 Whitey Ford 60.00 24.00
❑ 447 Felix Mantilla 25.00 10.00
❑ 448 Jack Kralick 25.00 10.00
❑ 449 Jose Tartabull 25.00 10.00
❑ 450 Bob Friend 30.00 12.00
❑ 451 Indians Team 40.00 16.00
❑ 452 Barney Schultz 25.00 10.00
❑ 453 Jake Wood 25.00 10.00
❑ 454A Art Fowler 25.00 10.00
(Card number on
white background)
❑ 454B Art Fowler 30.00 12.00
(Card number on
orange background)
❑ 455 Ruben Amaro 25.00 10.00
❑ 456 Jim Coker 25.00 10.00
❑ 457 Tex Clevenger 25.00 10.00
❑ 458 Al Lopez MG 30.00 12.00
❑ 459 Dick LeMay 25.00 10.00
❑ 460 Del Crandall 30.00 12.00
❑ 461 Norm Bass 25.00 10.00
❑ 462 Wally Post 25.00 10.00
❑ 463 Joe Schaffernoth 25.00 10.00
❑ 464 Ken Aspromonte 25.00 10.00
❑ 465 Chuck Estrada 25.00 10.00
❑ 466 Nate Oliver 60.00 24.00
Tony Martinez
Bill Freehan RC
Jerry Robinson SP
❑ 467 Phil Ortega 25.00 10.00
❑ 468 Carroll Hardy 30.00 12.00
❑ 469 Jay Hook 30.00 12.00
❑ 470 Tom Tresh SP 60.00 24.00
❑ 471 Ken Retzer 25.00 10.00
❑ 472 Lou Brock 80.00 32.00
❑ 473 New York Mets 100.00 40.00
Team Card
❑ 474 Jack Fisher 25.00 10.00
❑ 475 Gus Triandos 30.00 12.00
❑ 476 Frank Funk 25.00 10.00
❑ 477 Donn Clendenon 30.00 12.00
❑ 478 Paul Brown 25.00 10.00
❑ 479 Ed Brinkman 25.00 10.00
❑ 480 Bill Monbouquette 25.00 10.00
❑ 481 Bob Taylor 25.00 10.00
❑ 482 Felix Torres 25.00 10.00
❑ 483 Jim Owens UER 25.00 10.00
(Stat column for Wins
has an R instead)
❑ 484 Dale Long SP 30.00 12.00
❑ 485 Jim Landis 25.00 10.00
❑ 486 Ray Sadecki 25.00 10.00
❑ 487 John Roseboro 30.00 12.00
❑ 488 Jerry Adair 25.00 10.00
❑ 489 Paul Toth 25.00 10.00
❑ 490 Willie McCovey 100.00 40.00
❑ 491 Harry Craft MG 25.00 10.00
❑ 492 Dave Wickersham 25.00 10.00
❑ 493 Walt Bond 25.00 10.00
❑ 494 Phil Regan 25.00 10.00
❑ 495 Frank Thomas SP 30.00 12.00
❑ 496 Steve Dalkowski RC 30.00 12.00
Fred Newman
Jack Smith
Carl Bouldin
❑ 497 Bennie Daniels 25.00 10.00
❑ 498 Eddie Kasko 25.00 10.00
❑ 499 J.C. Martin 25.00 10.00
❑ 500 Harmon Killebrew SP 150.00 60.00
❑ 501 Joe Azcue 25.00 10.00
❑ 502 Daryl Spencer 25.00 10.00
❑ 503 Braves Team 40.00 16.00
❑ 504 Bob Johnson 25.00 10.00
❑ 505 Curt Flood 40.00 16.00
❑ 506 Gene Green 25.00 10.00
❑ 507 Roland Sheldon 30.00 12.00
❑ 508 Ted Savage 25.00 10.00
❑ 509A Checklist 7 30.00 6.00
(Copyright centered)
❑ 509B Checklist 7 30.00 6.00
(Copyright to right)
❑ 510 Ken McBride 25.00 10.00
❑ 511 Charlie Neal 30.00 12.00
❑ 512 Cal McLish 25.00 10.00
❑ 513 Gary Geiger 25.00 10.00
❑ 514 Larry Osborne 25.00 10.00
❑ 515 Don Elston 25.00 10.00
❑ 516 Purnell Goldy 25.00 10.00
❑ 517 Hal Woodeshick 25.00 10.00
❑ 518 Don Blasingame 25.00 10.00
❑ 519 Claude Raymond RC 25.00 10.00
❑ 520 Orlando Cepeda 40.00 16.00
❑ 521 Dan Pfister 25.00 10.00
❑ 522 Mel Nelson 30.00 12.00
Gary Peters
Jim Roland
Art Quirk
❑ 523 Bill Kunkel 15.00 6.00
❑ 524 Cardinals Team 30.00 12.00
❑ 525 Nellie Fox 50.00 20.00
❑ 526 Dick Hall 15.00 6.00
❑ 527 Ed Sadowski 15.00 6.00
❑ 528 Carl Willey 15.00 6.00
❑ 529 Wes Covington 15.00 6.00
❑ 530 Don Mossi 20.00 8.00
❑ 531 Sam Mele MG 15.00 6.00
❑ 532 Steve Boros 15.00 6.00
❑ 533 Bobby Shantz 20.00 8.00
❑ 534 Ken Walters 15.00 6.00
❑ 535 Jim Perry 20.00 8.00
❑ 536 Norm Larker 15.00 6.00
❑ 537 Pedro Gonzalez 1000.00 400.00
Ken McMullen
Al Weis
Pete Rose RC
❑ 538 George Brunet 15.00 6.00
❑ 539 Wayne Causey 15.00 6.00
❑ 540 Roberto Clemente 250.00 100.00
❑ 541 Ron Moeller 15.00 6.00
❑ 542 Lou Klimchock 15.00 6.00
❑ 543 Russ Snyder 15.00 6.00
❑ 544 Duke Carmel 50.00 20.00
Bill Haas
Rusty Staub RC
Dick Phillips
❑ 545 Jose Pagan 15.00 6.00
❑ 546 Hal Reniff 20.00 8.00
❑ 547 Gus Bell 15.00 6.00
❑ 548 Tom Satriano 15.00 6.00
❑ 549 Marcelino Lopez 15.00 6.00
Pete Lovrich
Paul Ratliff
Elmo Plaskett
❑ 550 Duke Snider 80.00 32.00
❑ 551 Billy Klaus 15.00 6.00
❑ 552 Detroit Tigers 50.00 20.00
Team Card
❑ 553 Brock Davis 125.00 50.00
Jim Gosger
Willie Stargell RC
John Herrnstein
❑ 554 Hank Fischer 15.00 6.00
❑ 555 John Blanchard 20.00 8.00
❑ 556 Al Worthington 15.00 6.00
❑ 557 Cuno Barragan 15.00 6.00
❑ 558 Bill Faul 20.00 8.00
Ron Hunt RC
Al Moran
Bob Lipski
❑ 559 Danny Murtaugh MG 15.00 6.00
❑ 560 Ray Herbert 15.00 6.00
❑ 561 Mike De La Hoz 15.00 6.00
❑ 562 Randy Cardinal 30.00 12.00
Dave McNally RC
Ken Rowe
Don Rowe
❑ 563 Mike McCormick 15.00 6.00
❑ 564 George Banks 15.00 6.00
❑ 565 Larry Sherry 15.00 6.00
❑ 566 Cliff Cook 15.00 6.00
❑ 567 Jim Duffalo 15.00 6.00
❑ 568 Bob Sadowski 15.00 6.00
❑ 569 Luis Arroyo 20.00 8.00
❑ 570 Frank Bolling 15.00 6.00
❑ 571 Johnny Klippstein 15.00 6.00
❑ 572 Jack Spring 15.00 6.00
❑ 573 Coot Veal 15.00 6.00
❑ 574 Hal Kolstad 15.00 6.00
❑ 575 Don Cardwell 15.00 6.00
❑ 576 Johnny Temple 30.00 11.00

1964 Topps

	NM	Ex
COMPLETE SET (587)	3500.00	1400.00
COMMON CARD (1-196)	3.00	1.20
COMMON (197-370)	4.00	1.60
COMMON (371-522)	8.00	3.20
COMMON (523-587)	15.00	6.00
WRAPPER (1-CENT)	100.00	40.00
WRAP.(1-CENT, REPEAT)	125.00	50.00
WRAPPER (5-CENT)	30.00	12.00
WRAPPER (5-CENT, COIN)	40.00	16.00

❑ 1 Sandy Koufax 30.00 9.00
Dick Ellsworth
Bob Friend LL
❑ 2 Gary Peters 8.00 3.20
Juan Pizarro
Camilo Pascual LL
❑ 3 Sandy Koufax 20.00 8.00
Juan Marichal
Warren Spahn
Jim Maloney LL
❑ 4 Whitey Ford 8.00 3.20
Camilo Pascual
Jim Bouton LL
❑ 5 Sandy Koufax 15.00 6.00
Jim Maloney
Don Drysdale LL
❑ 6 Camilo Pascual 8.00 3.20
Jim Bunning
Dick Stigman LL
❑ 7 Tommy Davis 20.00 8.00
Roberto Clemente
Dick Groat
Hank Aaron LL
❑ 8 Carl Yastrzemski 15.00 6.00
Al Kaline
Rich Rollins LL
❑ 9 Hank Aaron 30.00 12.00
Willie McCovey
Willie Mays
Orlando Cepeda LL
❑ 10 Harmon Killebrew 8.00 3.20
Dick Stuart
Bob Allison LL
❑ 11 Hank Aaron 15.00 6.00
Ken Boyer
Bill White LL
❑ 12 Dick Stuart 8.00 3.20
Al Kaline
Harmon Killebrew LL
❑ 13 Hoyt Wilhelm 12.00 4.80
❑ 14 Dick Nen RC 3.00 1.20
Nick Willhite
❑ 15 Zoilo Versalles 6.00 2.40
❑ 16 John Boozer 3.00 1.20
❑ 17 Willie Kirkland 3.00 1.20
❑ 18 Billy O'Dell 3.00 1.20
❑ 19 Don Wert 3.00 1.20
❑ 20 Bob Friend 6.00 2.40
❑ 21 Yogi Berra MG 40.00 16.00
❑ 22 Jerry Adair 3.00 1.20
❑ 23 Chris Zachary 3.00 1.20
❑ 24 Carl Sawatski 3.00 1.20

❑ 25 Bill Monbouquette 3.00 1.20
❑ 26 Gino Cimoli 3.00 1.20
❑ 27 New York Mets 8.00 3.20
Team Card
❑ 28 Claude Osteen 6.00 2.40
❑ 29 Lou Brock 40.00 16.00
❑ 30 Ron Perranoski 6.00 2.40
❑ 31 Dave Nicholson 3.00 1.20
❑ 32 Dean Chance 6.00 2.40
❑ 33 Sammy Ellis 6.00 2.40
Mel Queen
❑ 34 Jim Perry 6.00 2.40
❑ 35 Eddie Mathews 20.00 8.00
❑ 36 Hal Reniff 3.00 1.20
❑ 37 Smoky Burgess 6.00 2.40
❑ 38 Jim Wynn RC 8.00 3.20
❑ 39 Hank Aguirre 3.00 1.20
❑ 40 Dick Groat 6.00 2.40
❑ 41 Willie McCovey 8.00 3.20
Leon Wagner
❑ 42 Moe Drabowsky 6.00 2.40
❑ 43 Roy Sievers 6.00 2.40
❑ 44 Duke Carmel 3.00 1.20
❑ 45 Milt Pappas 6.00 2.40
❑ 46 Ed Brinkman 3.00 1.20
❑ 47 Jesus Alou RC 6.00 2.40
Ron Herbel
❑ 48 Bob Perry 3.00 1.20
❑ 49 Bill Henry 3.00 1.20
❑ 50 Mickey Mantle 350.00 140.00
❑ 51 Pete Richert 3.00 1.20
❑ 52 Chuck Hinton 3.00 1.20
❑ 53 Denis Menke 3.00 1.20
❑ 54 Sam Mele MG 3.00 1.20
❑ 55 Ernie Banks 40.00 16.00
❑ 56 Hal Brown 3.00 1.20
❑ 57 Tim Harkness 6.00 2.40
❑ 58 Don Demeter 6.00 2.40
❑ 59 Ernie Broglio 3.00 1.20
❑ 60 Frank Malzone 6.00 2.40
❑ 61 Bob Rodgers 6.00 2.40
Ed Sadowski
❑ 62 Ted Savage 3.00 1.20
❑ 63 John Orsino 3.00 1.20
❑ 64 Ted Abernathy 3.00 1.20
❑ 65 Felipe Alou 6.00 2.40
❑ 66 Eddie Fisher 3.00 1.20
❑ 67 Tigers Team 6.00 2.40
❑ 68 Willie Davis 6.00 2.40
❑ 69 Clete Boyer 6.00 2.40
❑ 70 Joe Torre 8.00 3.20
❑ 71 Jack Spring 3.00 1.20
❑ 72 Chico Cardenas 6.00 2.40
❑ 73 Jimmie Hall 8.00 3.20
❑ 74 Bob Priddy 3.00 1.20
Tom Butters
❑ 75 Wayne Causey 3.00 1.20
❑ 76 Checklist 1 10.00 2.00
❑ 77 Jerry Walker 3.00 1.20
❑ 78 Merritt Ranew 3.00 1.20
❑ 79 Bob Heffner 3.00 1.20
❑ 80 Vada Pinson 8.00 3.20
❑ 81 Nellie Fox 12.00 4.80
Harmon Killebrew
❑ 82 Jim Davenport 6.00 2.40
❑ 83 Gus Triandos 6.00 2.40
❑ 84 Carl Willey 3.00 1.20
❑ 85 Pete Ward 3.00 1.20
❑ 86 Al Downing 6.00 2.40
❑ 87 St. Louis Cardinals 6.00 2.40
Team Card
❑ 88 John Roseboro 6.00 2.40
❑ 89 Boog Powell 6.00 2.40
❑ 90 Earl Battey 3.00 1.20
❑ 91 Bob Bailey 6.00 2.40
❑ 92 Steve Ridzik 3.00 1.20
❑ 93 Gary Geiger 3.00 1.20
❑ 94 Jim Britton 3.00 1.20
Larry Maxie
❑ 95 George Altman 3.00 1.20
❑ 96 Bob Buhl 6.00 2.40
❑ 97 Jim Fregosi 6.00 2.40
❑ 98 Bill Bruton 3.00 1.20
❑ 99 Al Stanek 3.00 1.20
❑ 100 Elston Howard 6.00 2.40
❑ 101 Walt Alston MG 8.00 3.20
❑ 102 Checklist 2 10.00 2.00
❑ 103 Curt Flood 6.00 2.40
❑ 104 Art Mahaffey 6.00 2.40
❑ 105 Woody Held 3.00 1.20
❑ 106 Joe Nuxhall 6.00 2.40
❑ 107 Bruce Howard 3.00 1.20
Frank Kreutzer
❑ 108 John Wyatt 3.00 1.20
❑ 109 Rusty Staub 6.00 2.40
❑ 110 Albie Pearson 6.00 2.40
❑ 111 Don Elston 3.00 1.20
❑ 112 Bob Tillman 3.00 1.20
❑ 113 Grover Powell 6.00 2.40
❑ 114 Don Lock 3.00 1.20
❑ 115 Frank Bolling 3.00 1.20
❑ 116 Jay Ward 12.00 4.80
Tony Oliva
❑ 117 Earl Francis 3.00 1.20
❑ 118 John Blanchard 6.00 2.40
❑ 119 Gary Kolb 3.00 1.20
❑ 120 Don Drysdale 20.00 8.00
❑ 121 Pete Runnels 6.00 2.40
❑ 122 Don McMahon 3.00 1.20
❑ 123 Jose Pagan 3.00 1.20
❑ 124 Orlando Pena 3.00 1.20
❑ 125 Pete Rose UER 250.00 100.00
Born in 1942
❑ 126 Russ Snyder 3.00 1.20
❑ 127 Aubrey Gatewood 3.00 1.20
Dick Simpson
❑ 128 Mickey Lolich RC 20.00 8.00
❑ 129 Amado Samuel 3.00 1.20
❑ 130 Gary Peters 6.00 2.40
❑ 131 Steve Boros 3.00 1.20
❑ 132 Braves Team 6.00 2.40
❑ 133 Jim Grant 6.00 2.40
❑ 134 Don Zimmer 6.00 2.40
❑ 135 Johnny Callison 6.00 2.40
❑ 136 Sandy Koufax WS 20.00 8.00
strikes out 15
❑ 137 Willie Davis WS 8.00 3.20
❑ 138 Ron Fairly WS 8.00 3.20
❑ 139 Frank Howard WS 8.00 3.20
❑ 140 WS Summary 8.00 3.20
Dodgers celebrate
❑ 141 Danny Murtaugh MG 6.00 2.40
❑ 142 John Bateman 3.00 1.20
❑ 143 Bubba Phillips 3.00 1.20
❑ 144 Al Worthington 3.00 1.20
❑ 145 Norm Siebern 3.00 1.20
❑ 146 Tommy John RC 30.00 12.00
Bob Chance
❑ 147 Ray Sadecki 3.00 1.20
❑ 148 J.C. Martin 3.00 1.20
❑ 149 Paul Foytack 3.00 1.20
❑ 150 Willie Mays 125.00 50.00
❑ 151 Athletics Team 6.00 2.40
❑ 152 Denny Lemaster 3.00 1.20
❑ 153 Dick Williams 6.00 2.40
❑ 154 Dick Tracewski RC 6.00 2.40
❑ 155 Duke Snider 30.00 12.00
❑ 156 Bill Dailey 3.00 1.20
❑ 157 Gene Mauch MG 6.00 2.40
❑ 158 Ken Johnson 3.00 1.20
❑ 159 Charlie Dees 3.00 1.20
❑ 160 Ken Boyer 6.00 2.40
❑ 161 Dave McNally 6.00 2.40
❑ 162 Dick Sisler CO 6.00 2.40
Vada Pinson
❑ 163 Donn Clendenon 6.00 2.40
❑ 164 Bud Daley 3.00 1.20
❑ 165 Jerry Lumpe 3.00 1.20
❑ 166 Marty Keough 3.00 1.20
❑ 167 Mike Brumley 30.00 12.00
Lou Piniella RC
❑ 168 Al Weis 3.00 1.20
❑ 169 Del Crandall 6.00 2.40
❑ 170 Dick Radatz 6.00 2.40
❑ 171 Ty Cline 3.00 1.20
❑ 172 Indians Team 6.00 2.40
❑ 173 Ryne Duren 6.00 2.40
❑ 174 Doc Edwards 3.00 1.20
❑ 175 Billy Williams 12.00 4.80
❑ 176 Tracy Stallard 3.00 1.20
❑ 177 Harmon Killebrew 20.00 8.00
❑ 178 Hank Bauer MG 6.00 2.40
❑ 179 Carl Warwick 3.00 1.20
❑ 180 Tommy Davis 6.00 2.40
❑ 181 Dave Wickersham 3.00 1.20
❑ 182 Carl Yastrzemski 15.00 6.00
Chuck Schilling
❑ 183 Ron Taylor 3.00 1.20
❑ 184 Al Luplow 3.00 1.20
❑ 185 Jim O'Toole 6.00 2.40
❑ 186 Roman Mejias 3.00 1.20
❑ 187 Ed Roebuck 3.00 1.20
❑ 188 Checklist 3 10.00 2.00
❑ 189 Bob Hendley 3.00 1.20
❑ 190 Bobby Richardson 8.00 3.20
❑ 191 Clay Dalrymple 6.00 2.40
❑ 192 John Boccabella 3.00 1.20
Billy Cowan
❑ 193 Jerry Lynch 3.00 1.20
❑ 194 John Goryl 3.00 1.20
❑ 195 Floyd Robinson 3.00 1.20
❑ 196 Jim Gentile 3.00 1.20
❑ 197 Frank Lary 6.00 2.40
❑ 198 Len Gabrielson 4.00 1.60
❑ 199 Joe Azcue 4.00 1.60
❑ 200 Sandy Koufax 120.00 47.50
❑ 201 Sam Bowens 6.00 2.40
Wally Bunker
❑ 202 Galen Cisco 6.00 2.40
❑ 203 John Kennedy 6.00 2.40
❑ 204 Matty Alou 6.00 2.40
❑ 205 Nellie Fox 12.00 4.80
❑ 206 Steve Hamilton 6.00 2.40
❑ 207 Fred Hutchinson MG 6.00 2.40
❑ 208 Wes Covington 6.00 2.40
❑ 209 Bob Allen 4.00 1.60
❑ 210 Carl Yastrzemski 40.00 16.00
❑ 211 Jim Coker 4.00 1.60
❑ 212 Pete Lovrich 4.00 1.60
❑ 213 Angels Team 6.00 2.40
❑ 214 Ken McMullen 6.00 2.40
❑ 215 Ray Herbert 4.00 1.60
❑ 216 Mike de la Hoz 4.00 1.60
❑ 217 Jim King 4.00 1.60
❑ 218 Hank Fischer 4.00 1.60
❑ 219 Al Downing 6.00 2.40
Jim Bouton
❑ 220 Dick Ellsworth 6.00 2.40
❑ 221 Bob Saverine 4.00 1.60
❑ 222 Billy Pierce 6.00 2.40
❑ 223 George Banks 4.00 1.60
❑ 224 Tommie Sisk 4.00 1.60
❑ 225 Roger Maris 60.00 24.00
❑ 226 Jerry Grote RC 6.00 2.40
Larry Yellen
❑ 227 Barry Latman 4.00 1.60
❑ 228 Felix Mantilla 4.00 1.60
❑ 229 Charley Lau 6.00 2.40
❑ 230 Brooks Robinson 40.00 16.00
❑ 231 Dick Calmus 4.00 1.60
❑ 232 Al Lopez MG 8.00 3.20
❑ 233 Hal Smith 4.00 1.60
❑ 234 Gary Bell 4.00 1.60
❑ 235 Ron Hunt 4.00 1.60
❑ 236 Bill Faul 4.00 1.60
❑ 237 Cubs Team 6.00 2.40
❑ 238 Roy McMillan 6.00 2.40
❑ 239 Herm Starrette 4.00 1.60
❑ 240 Bill White 6.00 2.40
❑ 241 Jim Owens 4.00 1.60
❑ 242 Harvey Kuenn 6.00 2.40
❑ 243 Richie Allen RC 30.00 12.00
John Herrnstein
❑ 244 Tony LaRussa RC 30.00 12.00
❑ 245 Dick Stigman 4.00 1.60
❑ 246 Manny Mota 6.00 2.40
❑ 247 Dave DeBusschere 6.00 2.40
❑ 248 Johnny Pesky MG 6.00 2.40
❑ 249 Doug Camilli 4.00 1.60
❑ 250 Al Kaline 40.00 16.00
❑ 251 Choo Choo Coleman 6.00 2.40
❑ 252 Ken Aspromonte 4.00 1.60
❑ 253 Wally Post 6.00 2.40
❑ 254 Don Hoak 6.00 2.40
❑ 255 Lee Thomas 6.00 2.40
❑ 256 Johnny Weekly 4.00 1.60
❑ 257 San Francisco Giants 6.00 2.40
Team Card

258	Garry Roggenburk	4.00	1.60
259	Harry Bright	4.00	1.60
260	Frank Robinson	40.00	16.00
261	Jim Hannan	4.00	1.60
262	Mike Shannon RC	8.00	3.20
	Harry Fanok		
263	Chuck Estrada	4.00	1.60
264	Jim Landis	4.00	1.60
265	Jim Bunning	12.00	4.80
266	Gene Freese	4.00	1.60
267	Wilbur Wood RC	6.00	2.40
268	Danny Murtaugh MG	6.00	2.40
	Bill Virdon		
269	Ellis Burton	4.00	1.60
270	Rich Rollins	6.00	2.40
271	Bob Sadowski	4.00	1.60
272	Jake Wood	4.00	1.60
273	Mel Nelson	4.00	1.60
274	Checklist 4	10.00	2.00
275	John Tsitouris	4.00	1.60
276	Jose Tartabull	6.00	2.40
277	Ken Retzer	4.00	1.60
278	Bobby Shantz	6.00	2.40
279	Joe Koppe UER	4.00	1.60
	(Glove on wrong hand)		
280	Juan Marichal	15.00	6.00
281	Jake Gibbs	6.00	2.40
	Tom Metcalf		
282	Bob Bruce	4.00	1.60
283	Tom McCraw RC	4.00	1.60
284	Dick Schofield	4.00	1.60
285	Robin Roberts	15.00	6.00
286	Don Landrum	4.00	1.60
287	Tony Conigliaro RC	50.00	20.00
	Bill Spanswick		
288	Al Moran	4.00	1.60
289	Frank Funk	4.00	1.60
290	Bob Allison	6.00	2.40
291	Phil Ortega	4.00	1.60
292	Mike Roarke	4.00	1.60
293	Phillies Team	6.00	2.40
294	Ken L. Hunt	4.00	1.60
295	Roger Craig	6.00	2.40
296	Ed Kirkpatrick	4.00	1.60
297	Ken MacKenzie	4.00	1.60
298	Harry Craft MG	4.00	1.60
299	Bill Stafford	4.00	1.60
300	Hank Aaron	100.00	40.00
301	Larry Brown	4.00	1.60
302	Dan Pfister	4.00	1.60
303	Jim Campbell	4.00	1.60
304	Bob Johnson	4.00	1.60
305	Jack Lamabe	4.00	1.60
306	Willie Mays	40.00	16.00
	Orlando Cepeda		
307	Joe Gibbon	4.00	1.60
308	Gene Stephens	4.00	1.60
309	Paul Toth	4.00	1.60
310	Jim Gilliam	6.00	2.40
311	Tom Brown RC	6.00	2.40
312	Fritz Fisher	4.00	1.60
	Fred Gladding		
313	Chuck Hiller	4.00	1.60
314	Jerry Buchek	4.00	1.60
315	Bo Belinsky	6.00	2.40
316	Gene Oliver	4.00	1.60
317	Al Smith	4.00	1.60
318	Minnesota Twins	6.00	2.40
	Team Card		
319	Paul Brown	4.00	1.60
320	Rocky Colavito	12.00	4.80
321	Bob Lillis	4.00	1.60
322	George Brunet	4.00	1.60
323	John Buzhardt	4.00	1.60
324	Casey Stengel MG	15.00	6.00
325	Hector Lopez	6.00	2.40
326	Ron Brand	4.00	1.60
327	Don Blasingame	4.00	1.60
328	Bob Shaw	4.00	1.60
329	Russ Nixon	4.00	1.60
330	Tommy Harper	6.00	2.40
331	Roger Maris	150.00	60.00
	Norm Cash		
	Mickey Mantle		
	Al Kaline		
332	Ray Washburn	4.00	1.60
333	Billy Moran	4.00	1.60
334	Lew Krausse	4.00	1.60
335	Don Mossi	6.00	2.40
336	Andre Rodgers	4.00	1.60
337	Al Ferrara	6.00	2.40
	Jeff Torborg RC		
338	Jack Kralick	4.00	1.60
339	Walt Bond	4.00	1.60
340	Joe Cunningham	4.00	1.60
341	Jim Roland	4.00	1.60
342	Willie Stargell	30.00	12.00
343	Senators Team	6.00	2.40
344	Phil Linz	6.00	2.40
345	Frank Thomas	8.00	3.20
346	Joey Jay	4.00	1.60
347	Bobby Wine	6.00	2.40
348	Ed Lopat MG	6.00	2.40
349	Art Fowler	4.00	1.60
350	Willie McCovey	25.00	10.00
351	Dan Schneider	4.00	1.60
352	Eddie Bressoud	4.00	1.60
353	Wally Moon	6.00	2.40
354	Dave Giusti	4.00	1.60
355	Vic Power	6.00	2.40
356	Bill McCool	6.00	2.40
	Chico Ruiz		
357	Charley James	4.00	1.60
358	Ron Kline	4.00	1.60
359	Jim Schaffer	4.00	1.60
360	Joe Pepitone	12.00	4.80
361	Jay Hook	4.00	1.60
362	Checklist 5	10.00	2.00
363	Dick McAuliffe	6.00	2.40
364	Joe Gaines	4.00	1.60
365	Cal McLish	6.00	2.40
366	Nelson Mathews	4.00	1.60
367	Fred Whitfield	4.00	1.60
368	Fritz Ackley	6.00	2.40
	Don Buford RC		
369	Jerry Zimmerman	4.00	1.60
370	Hal Woodeshick	4.00	1.60
371	Frank Howard	8.00	3.20
372	Howie Koplitz	8.00	3.20
373	Pirates Team	12.00	4.80
374	Bobby Bolin	8.00	3.20
375	Ron Santo	10.00	4.00
376	Dave Morehead	8.00	3.20
377	Bob Skinner	8.00	3.20
378	Woody Woodward RC	10.00	4.00
	Jack Smith		
379	Tony Gonzalez	8.00	3.20
380	Whitey Ford	40.00	16.00
381	Bob Taylor	8.00	3.20
382	Wes Stock	8.00	3.20
383	Bill Rigney MG	8.00	3.20
384	Ron Hansen	8.00	3.20
385	Curt Simmons	10.00	4.00
386	Lenny Green	8.00	3.20
387	Terry Fox	8.00	3.20
388	John O'Donoghue RC	10.00	4.00
	George Williams		
389	Jim Umbricht	10.00	4.00
	(Card back mentions		
	his death)		
390	Orlando Cepeda	25.00	10.00
391	Sam McDowell	10.00	4.00
392	Jim Pagliaroni	8.00	3.20
393	Casey Stengel MG	15.00	6.00
	Ed Kranepool		
394	Bob Miller	8.00	3.20
395	Tom Tresh	10.00	4.00
396	Dennis Bennett	8.00	3.20
397	Chuck Cottier	8.00	3.20
398	Bill Haas	10.00	4.00
	Dick Smith		
399	Jackie Brandt	8.00	3.20
400	Warren Spahn	40.00	16.00
401	Charlie Maxwell	8.00	3.20
402	Tom Sturdivant	8.00	3.20
403	Reds Team	12.00	4.80
404	Tony Martinez	8.00	3.20
405	Ken McBride	8.00	3.20
406	Al Spangler	8.00	3.20
407	Bill Freehan	10.00	4.00
408	Jim Stewart	8.00	3.20
	Fred Burdette		
409	Bill Fischer	8.00	3.20
410	Dick Stuart	10.00	4.00
411	Lee Walls	8.00	3.20
412	Ray Culp	10.00	4.00
413	Johnny Keane MG	8.00	3.20
414	Jack Sanford	8.00	3.20
415	Tony Kubek	15.00	6.00
416	Lee Maye	8.00	3.20
417	Don Cardwell	8.00	3.20
418	Darold Knowles	10.00	4.00
	Buster Narum		
419	Ken Harrelson RC	15.00	6.00
420	Jim Maloney	10.00	4.00
421	Camilo Carreon	8.00	3.20
422	Jack Fisher	8.00	3.20
423	Hank Aaron	125.00	50.00
	Willie Mays		
424	Dick Bertell	8.00	3.20
425	Norm Cash	10.00	4.00
426	Bob Rodgers	8.00	3.20
427	Don Rudolph	8.00	3.20
428	Archie Skeen	8.00	3.20
	Pete Smith		
	(Back states Archie		
	has retired)		
429	Tim McCarver	10.00	4.00
430	Juan Pizarro	8.00	3.20
431	George Alusik	8.00	3.20
432	Ruben Amaro	10.00	4.00
433	Yankees Team	40.00	16.00
434	Don Nottebart	8.00	3.20
435	Vic Davalillo	8.00	3.20
436	Charlie Neal	10.00	4.00
437	Ed Bailey	8.00	3.20
438	Checklist 6	15.00	3.00
439	Harvey Haddix	10.00	4.00
440	R.Clemente UER	250.00	100.00
	1960 Pittsburfh		
441	Bob Duliba	8.00	3.20
442	Pumpsie Green	10.00	4.00
443	Chuck Dressen MG	10.00	4.00
444	Larry Jackson	8.00	3.20
445	Bill Skowron	10.00	4.00
446	Julian Javier	15.00	6.00
447	Ted Bowsfield	8.00	3.20
448	Cookie Rojas	10.00	4.00
449	Deron Johnson	10.00	4.00
450	Steve Barber	8.00	3.20
451	Joe Amalfitano	8.00	3.20
452	Gil Garrido	10.00	4.00
	Jim Ray Hart RC		
453	Frank Baumann	8.00	3.20
454	Tommie Aaron	10.00	4.00
455	Bernie Allen	8.00	3.20
456	Wes Parker RC	10.00	4.00
	John Werhas		
457	Jesse Gonder	8.00	3.20
458	Ralph Terry	10.00	4.00
459	Pete Charton	8.00	3.20
	Dalton Jones		
460	Bob Gibson	40.00	16.00
461	George Thomas	8.00	3.20
462	Birdie Tebbetts MG	8.00	3.20
463	Don Leppert	8.00	3.20
464	Dallas Green	15.00	6.00
465	Mike Hershberger	8.00	3.20
466	Dick Green	10.00	4.00
	Aurelio Monteagudo		
467	Bob Aspromonte	8.00	3.20
468	Gaylord Perry	40.00	16.00
469	Fred Norman	10.00	4.00
	Sterling Slaughter		
470	Jim Bouton	10.00	4.00
471	Gates Brown RC	10.00	4.00
472	Vern Law	10.00	4.00
473	Baltimore Orioles	12.00	4.80
	Team Card		
474	Larry Sherry	10.00	4.00
475	Ed Charles	8.00	3.20
476	Rico Carty RC	15.00	6.00
	Dick Kelley		
477	Mike Joyce	8.00	3.20
478	Dick Howser	10.00	4.00
479	Dave Bakenhaster	8.00	3.20
	Johnny Lewis		
480	Bob Purkey	8.00	3.20

Card	NM	Ex
❑ 481 Chuck Schilling	8.00	3.20
❑ 482 John Briggs	10.00	4.00
Danny Cater		
❑ 483 Fred Valentine	8.00	3.20
❑ 484 Bill Pleis	8.00	3.20
❑ 485 Tom Haller	8.00	3.20
❑ 486 Bob Kennedy MG	8.00	3.20
❑ 487 Mike McCormick	10.00	4.00
❑ 488 Pete Mikkelsen	15.00	6.00
Bob Meyer		
❑ 489 Julio Navarro	8.00	3.20
❑ 490 Ron Fairly	10.00	4.00
❑ 491 Ed Rakow	8.00	3.20
❑ 492 Jim Beauchamp RC	8.00	3.20
Mike White		
❑ 493 Don Lee	8.00	3.20
❑ 494 Al Jackson	8.00	3.20
❑ 495 Bill Virdon	10.00	4.00
❑ 496 White Sox Team	12.00	4.80
❑ 497 Jeoff Long	8.00	3.20
❑ 498 Dave Stenhouse	8.00	3.20
❑ 499 Chico Salmon	8.00	3.20
Gordon Seyfried		
❑ 500 Camilo Pascual	10.00	4.00
❑ 501 Bob Veale	10.00	4.00
❑ 502 Bobby Knoop RC	8.00	3.20
Bob Lee		
❑ 503 Earl Wilson	8.00	3.20
❑ 504 Claude Raymond	8.00	3.20
❑ 505 Stan Williams	8.00	3.20
❑ 506 Bobby Bragan MG	8.00	3.20
❑ 507 Johnny Edwards	8.00	3.20
❑ 508 Diego Segui	8.00	3.20
❑ 509 Gene Alley RC	10.00	4.00
Orlando McFarlane		
❑ 510 Lindy McDaniel	10.00	4.00
❑ 511 Lou Jackson	10.00	4.00
❑ 512 Willie Horton RC	15.00	6.00
Joe Sparma		
❑ 513 Don Larsen	10.00	4.00
❑ 514 Jim Hickman	10.00	4.00
❑ 515 Johnny Romano	8.00	3.20
❑ 516 Jerry Arrigo	8.00	3.20
Dwight Siebler		
❑ 517A Checklist 7 ERR	25.00	5.00
(Incorrect numbering sequence on back)		
❑ 517B Checklist 7 COR	15.00	3.00
(Correct numbering on back)		
❑ 518 Carl Bouldin	8.00	3.20
❑ 519 Charlie Smith	8.00	3.20
❑ 520 Jack Baldschun	10.00	4.00
❑ 521 Tom Satriano	8.00	3.20
❑ 522 Bob Tiefenauer	8.00	3.20
❑ 523 Lou Burdette UER	20.00	8.00
(Pitching lefty)		
❑ 524 Jim Dickson	15.00	6.00
Bobby Klaus		
❑ 525 Al McBean	15.00	6.00
❑ 526 Lou Clinton	15.00	6.00
❑ 527 Larry Bearnarth	15.00	6.00
❑ 528 Dave Duncan RC	20.00	8.00
Tommie Reynolds		
❑ 529 Alvin Dark MG	20.00	8.00
❑ 530 Leon Wagner	15.00	6.00
❑ 531 Los Angeles Dodgers	25.00	10.00
Team Card		
❑ 532 Bud Bloomfield	15.00	6.00
(Bloomfield photo actually Jay Ward)		
Joe Nossek RC		
❑ 533 Johnny Klippstein	15.00	6.00
❑ 534 Gus Bell	15.00	6.00
❑ 535 Phil Regan	15.00	6.00
❑ 536 Larry Elliot	15.00	6.00
John Stephenson		
❑ 537 Dan Osinski	15.00	6.00
❑ 538 Minnie Minoso	20.00	8.00
❑ 539 Roy Face	20.00	8.00
❑ 540 Luis Aparicio	40.00	16.00
❑ 541 Phil Roof	80.00	32.00
Phil Niekro RC		
❑ 542 Don Mincher	15.00	6.00
❑ 543 Bob Uecker	40.00	16.00
❑ 544 Steve Hertz	15.00	6.00

Card	NM	Ex
Joe Hoerner		
❑ 545 Max Alvis	15.00	6.00
❑ 546 Joe Christopher	15.00	6.00
❑ 547 Gil Hodges MG	30.00	12.00
❑ 548 Wayne Schurr	20.00	8.00
Paul Speckenbach		
❑ 549 Joe Moeller	15.00	6.00
❑ 550 Ken Hubbs MEM	40.00	16.00
❑ 551 Billy Hoeft	15.00	6.00
❑ 552 Tom Kelley	15.00	6.00
Sonny Siebert		
❑ 553 Jim Brewer	15.00	6.00
❑ 554 Hank Foiles	15.00	6.00
❑ 555 Lee Stange	15.00	6.00
❑ 556 Steve Dillon	15.00	6.00
Ron Locke		
❑ 557 Leo Burke	15.00	6.00
❑ 558 Don Schwall	15.00	6.00
❑ 559 Dick Phillips	15.00	6.00
❑ 560 Dick Farrell	15.00	6.00
❑ 561 Dave Bennett UER	20.00	8.00
(19 ... is 18)		
Rick Wise RC		
❑ 562 Pedro Ramos	15.00	6.00
❑ 563 Dal Maxvill	20.00	8.00
❑ 564 Joe McCabe	20.00	8.00
Jerry McNertney		
❑ 565 Stu Miller	15.00	6.00
❑ 566 Ed Kranepool	20.00	8.00
❑ 567 Jim Kaat	20.00	8.00
❑ 568 Phil Gagliano	15.00	6.00
Cap Peterson		
❑ 569 Fred Newman	15.00	6.00
❑ 570 Bill Mazeroski	40.00	16.00
❑ 571 Gene Conley	15.00	6.00
❑ 572 Dave Gray	15.00	6.00
Dick Egan		
❑ 573 Jim Duffalo	15.00	6.00
❑ 574 Manny Jimenez	15.00	6.00
❑ 575 Tony Cloninger	15.00	6.00
❑ 576 Jerry Hinsley	15.00	6.00
Bill Wakefield		
❑ 577 Gordy Coleman	15.00	6.00
❑ 578 Glen Hobbie	15.00	6.00
❑ 579 Red Sox Team	25.00	10.00
❑ 580 Johnny Podres	20.00	8.00
❑ 581 Pedro Gonzalez	20.00	8.00
Archie Moore		
❑ 582 Rod Kanehl	20.00	8.00
❑ 583 Tito Francona	15.00	6.00
❑ 584 Joel Horlen	15.00	6.00
❑ 585 Tony Taylor	20.00	8.00
❑ 586 Jimmy Piersall	20.00	8.00
❑ 587 Bennie Daniels	20.00	8.00

1965 Topps

	NM	Ex
COMPLETE SET (598)	4000.00	1600.00
COMMON CARD (1-196)	2.00	.80
COMMON (197-283)	2.50	1.00
COMMON (284-370)	4.00	1.60
COMMON (371-598)	8.00	3.20
WRAPPER (1-CENT)	125.00	50.00
WRAPPER (5-CENT)	100.00	40.00
❑ 1 Tony Oliva	20.00	6.00
Elston Howard		
Brooks Robinson LL		
❑ 2 Roberto Clemente	25.00	10.00
Hank Aaron		
Rico Carty LL		
❑ 3 Harmon Killebrew	50.00	20.00
Mickey Mantle		
Boog Powell LL		
❑ 4 Willie Mays	15.00	6.00
Billy Williams		
Jim Ray Hart		
Orlando Cepeda		
Johnny Callison LL		
❑ 5 Brooks Robinson	40.00	16.00
Harmon Killebrew		
Mickey Mantle		
Dick Stuart LL		
❑ 6 Ken Boyer	12.00	4.80
Willie Mays		
Ron Santo LL		
❑ 7 Dean Chance	5.00	2.00
Joel Horlen LL		
❑ 8 Sandy Koufax	20.00	8.00
Don Drysdale LL		
❑ 9 Dean Chance	5.00	2.00
Gary Peters		
Dave Wickersham		
Juan Pizarro		
Wally Bunker LL		
❑ 10 Larry Jackson	5.00	2.00
Ray Sadecki		
Juan Marichal LL		
❑ 11 Al Downing	5.00	2.00
Dean Chance		
Camilo Pascual LL		
❑ 12 Bob Veale	10.00	4.00
Don Drysdale		
Bob Gibson LL		
❑ 13 Pedro Ramos	4.00	1.60
❑ 14 Len Gabrielson	2.00	.80
❑ 15 Robin Roberts	10.00	4.00
❑ 16 Joe Morgan RC	60.00	24.00
Sonny Jackson DP		
❑ 17 Johnny Romano	2.00	.80
❑ 18 Bill McCool	2.00	.80
❑ 19 Gates Brown	4.00	1.60
❑ 20 Jim Bunning	10.00	4.00
❑ 21 Don Blasingame	2.00	.80
❑ 22 Charlie Smith	2.00	.80
❑ 23 Bob Tiefenauer	2.00	.80
❑ 24 Minnesota Twins	6.00	2.40
Team Card		
❑ 25 Al McBean	2.00	.80
❑ 26 Bobby Knoop	2.00	.80
❑ 27 Dick Bertell	2.00	.80
❑ 28 Barney Schultz	2.00	.80
❑ 29 Felix Mantilla	2.00	.80
❑ 30 Jim Bouton	6.00	2.40
❑ 31 Mike White	2.00	.80
❑ 32 Herman Franks MG	2.00	.80
❑ 33 Jackie Brandt	2.00	.80
❑ 34 Cal Koonce	2.00	.80
❑ 35 Ed Charles	2.00	.80
❑ 36 Bobby Wine	2.00	.80
❑ 37 Fred Gladding	2.00	.80
❑ 38 Jim King	2.00	.80
❑ 39 Gerry Arrigo	2.00	.80
❑ 40 Frank Howard	6.00	2.40
❑ 41 Bruce Howard	2.00	.80
Marv Staehle		
❑ 42 Earl Wilson	4.00	1.60
❑ 43 Mike Shannon	4.00	1.60
(Name in red, other Cardinals in yellow)		
❑ 44 Wade Blasingame	2.00	.80
❑ 45 Roy McMillan	4.00	1.60
❑ 46 Bob Lee	2.00	.80
❑ 47 Tommy Harper	4.00	1.60
❑ 48 Claude Raymond	4.00	1.60
❑ 49 Curt Blefary RC	4.00	1.60
John Miller		
❑ 50 Juan Marichal	10.00	4.00
❑ 51 Bill Bryan	2.00	.80
❑ 52 Ed Roebuck	2.00	.80
❑ 53 Dick McAuliffe	4.00	1.60
❑ 54 Joe Gibbon	2.00	.80
❑ 55 Tony Conigliaro	15.00	6.00
❑ 56 Ron Kline	2.00	.80

❑ 57 Cardinals Team 6.00 2.40
❑ 58 Fred Talbot 2.00 .80
❑ 59 Nate Oliver 2.00 .80
❑ 60 Jim O'Toole 4.00 1.60
❑ 61 Chris Cannizzaro 2.00 .80
❑ 62 Jim Kaat UER DP 6.00 2.40
(Misspelled Katt)
❑ 63 Ty Cline 2.00 .80
❑ 64 Lou Burdette 4.00 1.60
❑ 65 Tony Kubek 10.00 4.00
❑ 66 Bill Rigney MG 2.00 .80
❑ 67 Harvey Haddix 4.00 1.60
❑ 68 Del Crandall 4.00 1.60
❑ 69 Bill Virdon 4.00 1.60
❑ 70 Bill Skowron 6.00 2.40
❑ 71 John O'Donoghue 2.00 .80
❑ 72 Tony Gonzalez 2.00 .80
❑ 73 Dennis Ribant 2.00 .80
❑ 74 Rico Petrocelli RC 10.00 4.00
Jerry Stephenson
❑ 75 Deron Johnson 4.00 1.60
❑ 76 Sam McDowell 6.00 2.40
❑ 77 Doug Camilli 2.00 .80
❑ 78 Dal Maxvill 2.00 .80
❑ 79A Checklist 1 10.00 2.00
(61 Cannizzaro)
❑ 79B Checklist 1 10.00 2.00
(61 C.Cannizzaro)
❑ 80 Turk Farrell 2.00 .80
❑ 81 Don Buford 4.00 1.60
❑ 82 Santos Alomar RC 6.00 2.40
John Braun
❑ 83 George Thomas 2.00 .80
❑ 84 Ron Herbel 2.00 .80
❑ 85 Willie Smith 2.00 .80
❑ 86 Buster Narum 2.00 .80
❑ 87 Nelson Mathews 2.00 .80
❑ 88 Jack Lamabe 2.00 .80
❑ 89 Mike Hershberger 2.00 .80
❑ 90 Rich Rollins 4.00 1.60
❑ 91 Cubs Team 6.00 2.40
❑ 92 Dick Howser 4.00 1.60
❑ 93 Jack Fisher 2.00 .80
❑ 94 Charlie Lau 4.00 1.60
❑ 95 Bill Mazeroski DP 6.00 2.40
❑ 96 Sonny Siebert 4.00 1.60
❑ 97 Pedro Gonzalez 2.00 .80
❑ 98 Bob Miller 2.00 .80
❑ 99 Gil Hodges MG 6.00 2.40
❑ 100 Ken Boyer 10.00 4.00
❑ 101 Fred Newman 2.00 .80
❑ 102 Steve Boros 2.00 .80
❑ 103 Harvey Kuenn 4.00 1.60
❑ 104 Checklist 2 10.00 2.00
❑ 105 Chico Salmon 2.00 .80
❑ 106 Gene Oliver 2.00 .80
❑ 107 Pat Corrales RC 4.00 1.60
Costen Shockley
❑ 108 Don Mincher 2.00 .80
❑ 109 Walt Bond 2.00 .80
❑ 110 Ron Santo 6.00 2.40
❑ 111 Lee Thomas 4.00 1.60
❑ 112 Derrell Griffith 2.00 .80
❑ 113 Steve Barber 2.00 .80
❑ 114 Jim Hickman 4.00 1.60
❑ 115 Bobby Richardson 10.00 4.00
❑ 116 Dave Dowling 4.00 1.60
Bob Tolan RC
❑ 117 Wes Stock 2.00 .80
❑ 118 Hal Lanier 4.00 1.60
❑ 119 John Kennedy 2.00 .80
❑ 120 Frank Robinson 40.00 16.00
❑ 121 Gene Alley 4.00 1.60
❑ 122 Bill Pleis 2.00 .80
❑ 123 Frank Thomas 4.00 1.60
❑ 124 Tom Satriano 2.00 .80
❑ 125 Juan Pizarro 2.00 .80
❑ 126 Dodgers Team 6.00 2.40
❑ 127 Frank Lary 2.00 .80
❑ 128 Vic Davalillo 2.00 .80
❑ 129 Bennie Daniels 2.00 .80
❑ 130 Al Kaline 40.00 16.00
❑ 131 Johnny Keane MG 2.00 .80
❑ 132 Mike Shannon WS 10.00 4.00
❑ 133 Mel Stottlemyre WS 6.00 2.40
❑ 134 Mickey Mantle WS 80.00 32.00
Mantle's Clutch HR UER
Mantle is shown wearing a road uniform
That game was played in New York
❑ 135 Ken Boyer WS 10.00 4.00
❑ 136 Tim McCarver WS 6.00 2.40
❑ 137 Jim Bouton WS 6.00 2.40
❑ 138 Bob Gibson WS 12.00 4.80
❑ 139 WS Summary 6.00 2.40
Cards celebrate
❑ 140 Dean Chance 4.00 1.60
❑ 141 Charlie James 2.00 .80
❑ 142 Bill Monbouquette 2.00 .80
❑ 143 John Gelnar 2.00 .80
Jerry May
❑ 144 Ed Kranepool 4.00 1.60
❑ 145 Luis Tiant RC 10.00 4.00
❑ 146 Ron Hansen 2.00 .80
❑ 147 Dennis Bennett 2.00 .80
❑ 148 Willie Kirkland 2.00 .80
❑ 149 Wayne Schurr 2.00 .80
❑ 150 Brooks Robinson 40.00 16.00
❑ 151 Athletics Team 6.00 2.40
❑ 152 Phil Ortega 2.00 .80
❑ 153 Norm Cash 6.00 2.40
❑ 154 Bob Humphreys 2.00 .80
❑ 155 Roger Maris 60.00 24.00
❑ 156 Bob Sadowski 2.00 .80
❑ 157 Zoilo Versalles 4.00 1.60
❑ 158 Dick Sisler 2.00 .80
❑ 159 Jim Duffalo 2.00 .80
❑ 160 R.Clemente UER 175.00 70.00
1960 Pittsburfh
❑ 161 Frank Baumann 2.00 .80
❑ 162 Russ Nixon 2.00 .80
❑ 163 Johnny Briggs 2.00 .80
❑ 164 Al Spangler 2.00 .80
❑ 165 Dick Ellsworth 2.00 .80
❑ 166 George Culver 4.00 1.60
Tommie Agee RC
❑ 167 Bill Wakefield 2.00 .80
❑ 168 Dick Green 2.00 .80
❑ 169 Dave Vineyard 2.00 .80
❑ 170 Hank Aaron 150.00 60.00
❑ 171 Jim Roland 2.00 .80
❑ 172 Jimmy Piersall 6.00 2.40
❑ 173 Detroit Tigers 6.00 2.40
Team Card
❑ 174 Joey Jay 2.00 .80
❑ 175 Bob Aspromonte 2.00 .80
❑ 176 Willie McCovey 20.00 8.00
❑ 177 Pete Mikkelsen 2.00 .80
❑ 178 Dalton Jones 2.00 .80
❑ 179 Hal Woodeshick 2.00 .80
❑ 180 Bob Allison 4.00 1.60
❑ 181 Don Loun 2.00 .80
Joe McCabe
❑ 182 Mike de la Hoz 2.00 .80
❑ 183 Dave Nicholson 2.00 .80
❑ 184 John Boozer 2.00 .80
❑ 185 Max Alvis 2.00 .80
❑ 186 Billy Cowan 2.00 .80
❑ 187 Casey Stengel MG 15.00 6.00
❑ 188 Sam Bowens 2.00 .80
❑ 189 Checklist 3 10.00 2.00
❑ 190 Bill White 6.00 2.40
❑ 191 Phil Regan 4.00 1.60
❑ 192 Jim Coker 2.00 .80
❑ 193 Gaylord Perry 15.00 6.00
❑ 194 Bill Kelso 2.00 .80
Rick Reichardt
❑ 195 Bob Veale 4.00 1.60
❑ 196 Ron Fairly 4.00 1.60
❑ 197 Diego Segui 2.50 1.00
❑ 198 Smoky Burgess 4.00 1.60
❑ 199 Bob Heffner 2.50 1.00
❑ 200 Joe Torre 6.00 2.40
❑ 201 Sandy Valdespino 4.00 1.60
Cesar Tovar RC
❑ 202 Leo Burke 2.50 1.00
❑ 203 Dallas Green 4.00 1.60
❑ 204 Russ Snyder 2.50 1.00
❑ 205 Warren Spahn 30.00 12.00
❑ 206 Willie Horton 4.00 1.60
❑ 207 Pete Rose 175.00 70.00
❑ 208 Tommy John 6.00 2.40
❑ 209 Pirates Team 6.00 2.40
❑ 210 Jim Fregosi 4.00 1.60
❑ 211 Steve Ridzik 2.50 1.00
❑ 212 Ron Brand 2.50 1.00
❑ 213 Jim Davenport 2.50 1.00
❑ 214 Bob Purkey 2.50 1.00
❑ 215 Pete Ward 2.50 1.00
❑ 216 Al Worthington 2.50 1.00
❑ 217 Walter Alston MG 6.00 2.40
❑ 218 Dick Schofield 2.50 1.00
❑ 219 Bob Meyer 2.50 1.00
❑ 220 Billy Williams 10.00 4.00
❑ 221 John Tsitouris 2.50 1.00
❑ 222 Bob Tillman 2.50 1.00
❑ 223 Dan Osinski 2.50 1.00
❑ 224 Bob Chance 2.50 1.00
❑ 225 Bo Belinsky 4.00 1.60
❑ 226 Elvio Jimenez 6.00 2.40
Jake Gibbs
❑ 227 Bobby Klaus 2.50 1.00
❑ 228 Jack Sanford 2.50 1.00
❑ 229 Lou Clinton 2.50 1.00
❑ 230 Ray Sadecki 2.50 1.00
❑ 231 Jerry Adair 2.50 1.00
❑ 232 Steve Blass RC 4.00 1.60
❑ 233 Don Zimmer 4.00 1.60
❑ 234 White Sox Team 6.00 2.40
❑ 235 Chuck Hinton 2.50 1.00
❑ 236 Denny McLain RC 25.00 10.00
❑ 237 Bernie Allen 2.50 1.00
❑ 238 Joe Moeller 2.50 1.00
❑ 239 Doc Edwards 2.50 1.00
❑ 240 Bob Bruce 2.50 1.00
❑ 241 Mack Jones 2.50 1.00
❑ 242 George Brunet 2.50 1.00
❑ 243 Ted Davidson 4.00 1.60
Tommy Helms RC
❑ 244 Lindy McDaniel 4.00 1.60
❑ 245 Joe Pepitone 6.00 2.40
❑ 246 Tom Butters 4.00 1.60
❑ 247 Wally Moon 4.00 1.60
❑ 248 Gus Triandos 4.00 1.60
❑ 249 Dave McNally 4.00 1.60
❑ 250 Willie Mays 150.00 60.00
❑ 251 Billy Herman MG 4.00 1.60
❑ 252 Pete Richert 2.50 1.00
❑ 253 Danny Cater 2.50 1.00
❑ 254 Roland Sheldon 2.50 1.00
❑ 255 Camilo Pascual 4.00 1.60
❑ 256 Tito Francona 2.50 1.00
❑ 257 Jim Wynn 4.00 1.60
❑ 258 Larry Bearnarth 2.50 1.00
❑ 259 Jim Northrup RC 6.00 2.40
Ray Oyler
❑ 260 Don Drysdale 20.00 8.00
❑ 261 Duke Carmel 2.50 1.00
❑ 262 Bud Daley 2.50 1.00
❑ 263 Marty Keough 2.50 1.00
❑ 264 Bob Buhl 4.00 1.60
❑ 265 Jim Pagliaroni 2.50 1.00
❑ 266 Bert Campaneris RC 10.00 4.00
❑ 267 Senators Team 6.00 2.40
❑ 268 Ken McBride 2.50 1.00
❑ 269 Frank Bolling 2.50 1.00
❑ 270 Milt Pappas 4.00 1.60
❑ 271 Don Wert 4.00 1.60
❑ 272 Chuck Schilling 2.50 1.00
❑ 273 Checklist 4 10.00 2.00
❑ 274 Lum Harris MG 2.50 1.00
❑ 275 Dick Groat 6.00 2.40
❑ 276 Hoyt Wilhelm 10.00 4.00
❑ 277 Johnny Lewis 2.50 1.00
❑ 278 Ken Retzer 2.50 1.00
❑ 279 Dick Tracewski 2.50 1.00
❑ 280 Dick Stuart 4.00 1.60
❑ 281 Bill Stafford 2.50 1.00
❑ 282 Dick Estelle 40.00 16.00
Masanori Murakami RC
❑ 283 Fred Whitfield 2.50 1.00
❑ 284 Nick Willhite 4.00 1.60
❑ 285 Ron Hunt 4.00 1.60
❑ 286 Jim Dickson 4.00 1.60
Aurelio Monteagudo
❑ 287 Gary Kolb 4.00 1.60
❑ 288 Jack Hamilton 4.00 1.60
❑ 289 Gordy Coleman 6.00 2.40

❑ 290	Wally Bunker	6.00	2.40
❑ 291	Jerry Lynch	4.00	1.60
❑ 292	Larry Yellen	4.00	1.60
❑ 293	Angels Team	6.00	2.40
❑ 294	Tim McCarver	10.00	4.00
❑ 295	Dick Radatz	6.00	2.40
❑ 296	Tony Taylor	6.00	2.40
❑ 297	Dave DeBusschere	10.00	4.00
❑ 298	Jim Stewart	4.00	1.60
❑ 299	Jerry Zimmerman	4.00	1.60
❑ 300	Sandy Koufax	100.00	40.00
❑ 301	Birdie Tebbetts MG	6.00	2.40
❑ 302	Al Stanek	4.00	1.60
❑ 303	John Orsino	4.00	1.60
❑ 304	Dave Stenhouse	4.00	1.60
❑ 305	Rico Carty	6.00	2.40
❑ 306	Bubba Phillips	4.00	1.60
❑ 307	Barry Latman	4.00	1.60
❑ 308	Cleon Jones RC	6.00	2.40
	Tom Parsons		
❑ 309	Steve Hamilton	6.00	2.40
❑ 310	Johnny Callison	6.00	2.40
❑ 311	Orlando Pena	4.00	1.60
❑ 312	Joe Nuxhall	4.00	1.60
❑ 313	Jim Schaffer	4.00	1.60
❑ 314	Sterling Slaughter	4.00	1.60
❑ 315	Frank Malzone	6.00	2.40
❑ 316	Reds Team	6.00	2.40
❑ 317	Don McMahon	4.00	1.60
❑ 318	Matty Alou	6.00	2.40
❑ 319	Ken McMullen	4.00	1.60
❑ 320	Bob Gibson	50.00	20.00
❑ 321	Rusty Staub	10.00	4.00
❑ 322	Rick Wise	6.00	2.40
❑ 323	Hank Bauer MG	6.00	2.40
❑ 324	Bobby Locke	4.00	1.60
❑ 325	Donn Clendenon	6.00	2.40
❑ 326	Dwight Siebler	4.00	1.60
❑ 327	Denis Menke	4.00	1.60
❑ 328	Eddie Fisher	4.00	1.60
❑ 329	Hawk Taylor	4.00	1.60
❑ 330	Whitey Ford	40.00	16.00
❑ 331	Al Ferrara	6.00	2.40
	John Purdin		
❑ 332	Ted Abernathy	4.00	1.60
❑ 333	Tom Reynolds	4.00	1.60
❑ 334	Vic Roznovsky	4.00	1.60
❑ 335	Mickey Lolich	6.00	2.40
❑ 336	Woody Held	4.00	1.60
❑ 337	Mike Cuellar	6.00	2.40
❑ 338	Philadelphia Phillies	6.00	2.40
	Team Card		
❑ 339	Ryne Duren	6.00	2.40
❑ 340	Tony Oliva	20.00	8.00
❑ 341	Bob Bolin	4.00	1.60
❑ 342	Bob Rodgers	6.00	2.40
❑ 343	Mike McCormick	6.00	2.40
❑ 344	Wes Parker	6.00	2.40
❑ 345	Floyd Robinson	4.00	1.60
❑ 346	Bobby Bragan MG	4.00	1.60
❑ 347	Roy Face	6.00	2.40
❑ 348	George Banks	4.00	1.60
❑ 349	Larry Miller	4.00	1.60
❑ 350	Mickey Mantle	500.00	200.00
❑ 351	Jim Perry	6.00	2.40
❑ 352	Alex Johnson RC	6.00	2.40
❑ 353	Jerry Lumpe	4.00	1.60
❑ 354	Billy Ott	4.00	1.60
	Jack Warner		
❑ 355	Vada Pinson	10.00	4.00
❑ 356	Bill Spanswick	4.00	1.60
❑ 357	Carl Warwick	4.00	1.60
❑ 358	Albie Pearson	6.00	2.40
❑ 359	Ken Johnson	4.00	1.60
❑ 360	Orlando Cepeda	15.00	6.00
❑ 361	Checklist 5	12.00	2.40
❑ 362	Don Schwall	4.00	1.60
❑ 363	Bob Johnson	4.00	1.60
❑ 364	Galen Cisco	4.00	1.60
❑ 365	Jim Gentile	6.00	2.40
❑ 366	Dan Schneider	4.00	1.60
❑ 367	Leon Wagner	4.00	1.60
❑ 368	Ken Berry	6.00	2.40
	Joel Gibson		
❑ 369	Phil Linz	6.00	2.40
❑ 370	Tommy Davis	6.00	2.40
❑ 371	Frank Kreutzer	8.00	3.20
❑ 372	Clay Dalrymple	8.00	3.20
❑ 373	Curt Simmons	8.00	3.20
❑ 374	Jose Cardenal RC	8.00	3.20
	Dick Simpson		
❑ 375	Dave Wickersham	8.00	3.20
❑ 376	Jim Landis	8.00	3.20
❑ 377	Willie Stargell	25.00	10.00
❑ 378	Chuck Estrada	8.00	3.20
❑ 379	Giants Team	8.00	3.20
❑ 380	Rocky Colavito	25.00	10.00
❑ 381	Al Jackson	8.00	3.20
❑ 382	J.C. Martin	8.00	3.20
❑ 383	Felipe Alou	15.00	6.00
❑ 384	Johnny Klippstein	8.00	3.20
❑ 385	Carl Yastrzemski	60.00	24.00
❑ 386	Paul Jaeckel	8.00	3.20
	Fred Norman		
❑ 387	Johnny Podres	15.00	6.00
❑ 388	John Blanchard	15.00	6.00
❑ 389	Don Larsen	15.00	6.00
❑ 390	Bill Freehan	15.00	6.00
❑ 391	Mel McGaha MG	8.00	3.20
❑ 392	Bob Friend	15.00	6.00
❑ 393	Ed Kirkpatrick	8.00	3.20
❑ 394	Jim Hannan	8.00	3.20
❑ 395	Jim Ray Hart	8.00	3.20
❑ 396	Frank Bertaina	8.00	3.20
❑ 397	Jerry Buchek	8.00	3.20
❑ 398	Dan Neville	15.00	6.00
	Art Shamsky		
❑ 399	Ray Herbert	8.00	3.20
❑ 400	Harmon Killebrew	50.00	20.00
❑ 401	Carl Willey	8.00	3.20
❑ 402	Joe Amalfitano	8.00	3.20
❑ 403	Boston Red Sox	8.00	3.20
	Team Card		
❑ 404	Stan Williams	8.00	3.20
	(Listed as Indian		
	but Yankee cap)		
❑ 405	John Roseboro	20.00	8.00
❑ 406	Ralph Terry	15.00	6.00
❑ 407	Lee Maye	8.00	3.20
❑ 408	Larry Sherry	8.00	3.20
❑ 409	Jim Beauchamp	15.00	6.00
	Larry Dierker RC		
❑ 410	Luis Aparicio	25.00	10.00
❑ 411	Roger Craig	15.00	6.00
❑ 412	Bob Bailey	8.00	3.20
❑ 413	Hal Reniff	8.00	3.20
❑ 414	Al Lopez MG	15.00	6.00
❑ 415	Curt Flood	15.00	6.00
❑ 416	Jim Brewer	8.00	3.20
❑ 417	Ed Brinkman	8.00	3.20
❑ 418	Johnny Edwards	8.00	3.20
❑ 419	Ruben Amaro	8.00	3.20
❑ 420	Larry Jackson	8.00	3.20
❑ 421	Gary Dotter	8.00	3.20
	Jay Ward		
❑ 422	Aubrey Gatewood	8.00	3.20
❑ 423	Jesse Gonder	8.00	3.20
❑ 424	Gary Bell	8.00	3.20
❑ 425	Wayne Causey	8.00	3.20
❑ 426	Braves Team	8.00	3.20
❑ 427	Bob Saverine	8.00	3.20
❑ 428	Bob Shaw	8.00	3.20
❑ 429	Don Demeter	8.00	3.20
❑ 430	Gary Peters	8.00	3.20
❑ 431	Nelson Briles RC	15.00	6.00
	Wayne Spiezio		
❑ 432	Jim Grant	15.00	6.00
❑ 433	John Bateman	8.00	3.20
❑ 434	Dave Morehead	8.00	3.20
❑ 435	Willie Davis	15.00	6.00
❑ 436	Don Elston	8.00	3.20
❑ 437	Chico Cardenas	15.00	6.00
❑ 438	Harry Walker MG	8.00	3.20
❑ 439	Moe Drabowsky	15.00	6.00
❑ 440	Tom Tresh	15.00	6.00
❑ 441	Denny Lemaster	8.00	3.20
❑ 442	Vic Power	8.00	3.20
❑ 443	Checklist 6	12.00	2.40
❑ 444	Bob Hendley	8.00	3.20
❑ 445	Don Lock	8.00	3.20
❑ 446	Art Mahaffey	8.00	3.20
❑ 447	Julian Javier	15.00	6.00
❑ 448	Lee Stange	8.00	3.20
❑ 449	Jerry Hinsley	15.00	6.00
	Gary Kroll		
❑ 450	Elston Howard	15.00	6.00
❑ 451	Jim Owens	8.00	3.20
❑ 452	Gary Geiger	8.00	3.20
❑ 453	Willie Crawford	15.00	6.00
	John Werhas		
❑ 454	Ed Rakow	8.00	3.20
❑ 455	Norm Siebern	8.00	3.20
❑ 456	Bill Henry	8.00	3.20
❑ 457	Bob Kennedy MG	15.00	6.00
❑ 458	John Buzhardt	8.00	3.20
❑ 459	Frank Kostro	8.00	3.20
❑ 460	Richie Allen	40.00	16.00
❑ 461	Clay Carroll RC	50.00	20.00
	Phil Niekro		
❑ 462	Lew Krausse UER	8.00	3.20
	(Photo actually		
	Pete Lovrich)		
❑ 463	Manny Mota	15.00	6.00
❑ 464	Ron Piche	8.00	3.20
❑ 465	Tom Haller	15.00	6.00
❑ 466	Pete Craig	8.00	3.20
	Dick Nen		
❑ 467	Ray Washburn	8.00	3.20
❑ 468	Larry Brown	8.00	3.20
❑ 469	Don Nottebart	8.00	3.20
❑ 470	Yogi Berra P/CO	50.00	20.00
❑ 471	Billy Hoeft	8.00	3.20
❑ 472	Don Pavletich UER	8.00	3.20
	Listed as a pitcher		
❑ 473	Paul Blair	15.00	6.00
	Davey Johnson RC		
❑ 474	Cookie Rojas	15.00	6.00
❑ 475	Clete Boyer	15.00	6.00
❑ 476	Billy O'Dell	8.00	3.20
❑ 477	Fritz Ackley	175.00	70.00
	Steve Carlton RC		
❑ 478	Wilbur Wood	15.00	6.00
❑ 479	Ken Harrelson	15.00	6.00
❑ 480	Joel Horlen	8.00	3.20
❑ 481	Cleveland Indians	10.00	4.00
	Team Card		
❑ 482	Bob Priddy	8.00	3.20
❑ 483	George Smith	8.00	3.20
❑ 484	Ron Perranoski	20.00	8.00
❑ 485	Nellie Fox P/CO	25.00	10.00
❑ 486	Tom Egan	8.00	3.20
	Pat Rogan		
❑ 487	Woody Woodward	15.00	6.00
❑ 488	Ted Wills	8.00	3.20
❑ 489	Gene Mauch MG	15.00	6.00
❑ 490	Earl Battey	8.00	3.20
❑ 491	Tracy Stallard	8.00	3.20
❑ 492	Gene Freese	8.00	3.20
❑ 493	Bill Roman	8.00	3.20
	Bruce Brubaker		
❑ 494	Jay Ritchie	8.00	3.20
❑ 495	Joe Christopher	8.00	3.20
❑ 496	Joe Cunningham	8.00	3.20
❑ 497	Ken Henderson	15.00	6.00
	Jack Hiatt		
❑ 498	Gene Stephens	8.00	3.20
❑ 499	Stu Miller	15.00	6.00
❑ 500	Eddie Mathews	40.00	16.00
❑ 501	Ralph Gagliano	8.00	3.20
	Jim Rittwage		
❑ 502	Don Cardwell	8.00	3.20
❑ 503	Phil Gagliano	8.00	3.20
❑ 504	Jerry Grote	15.00	6.00
❑ 505	Ray Culp	8.00	3.20
❑ 506	Sam Mele MG	8.00	3.20
❑ 507	Sammy Ellis	8.00	3.20
❑ 508	Checklist 7	12.00	2.40
❑ 509	Bob Guindon	8.00	3.20
	Gerry Vezendy		
❑ 510	Ernie Banks	80.00	32.00
❑ 511	Ron Locke	8.00	3.20
❑ 512	Cap Peterson	8.00	3.20
❑ 513	New York Yankees	40.00	16.00
	Team Card		
❑ 514	Joe Azcue	8.00	3.20
❑ 515	Vern Law	15.00	6.00
❑ 516	Al Weis	8.00	3.20
❑ 517	Paul Schaal	15.00	6.00

Jack Warner
❑ 518 Ken Rowe 8.00 3.20
❑ 519 Bob Uecker UER 30.00 12.00
(Posing as a left-handed batter)
❑ 520 Tony Cloninger 8.00 3.20
❑ 521 Dave Bennett 8.00 3.20
Morrie Stevens
❑ 522 Hank Aguirre 8.00 3.20
❑ 523 Mike Brumley SP 12.00 4.80
❑ 524 Dave Giusti SP 12.00 4.80
❑ 525 Eddie Bressoud 8.00 3.20
❑ 526 Rene Lachemann 80.00 32.00
Johnny Odom
Jim Hunter RC UER
(Tim on back)
Skip Lockwood SP
❑ 527 Jeff Torborg SP 12.00 4.80
❑ 528 George Altman 8.00 3.20
❑ 529 Jerry Fosnow SP 12.00 4.80
❑ 530 Jim Maloney 15.00 6.00
❑ 531 Chuck Hiller 8.00 3.20
❑ 532 Hector Lopez 15.00 6.00
❑ 533 Dan Napoleon 25.00 10.00
Ron Swoboda RC
Tug McGraw RC
Jim Bethke SP
❑ 534 John Herrnstein 8.00 3.20
❑ 535 Jack Kralick SP 12.00 4.80
❑ 536 Andre Rodgers SP 12.00 4.80
❑ 537 Marcelino Lopez 8.00 3.20
Phil Roof
Rudy May RC
❑ 538 C.Dressen SP MG 12.00 4.80
❑ 539 Herm Starrette 8.00 3.20
❑ 540 Lou Brock SP 50.00 20.00
❑ 541 Greg Bollo 8.00 3.20
Bob Locker
❑ 542 Lou Klimchock 8.00 3.20
❑ 543 Ed Connolly SP 12.00 4.80
❑ 544 Howie Reed 8.00 3.20
❑ 545 Jesus Alou SP 15.00 6.00
❑ 546 Bill Davis 8.00 3.20
Mike Hedlund
Ray Barker
Floyd Weaver
❑ 547 Jake Wood SP 12.00 4.80
❑ 548 Dick Stigman 8.00 3.20
❑ 549 Roberto Pena 20.00 8.00
Glenn Beckert RC
❑ 550 Mel Stottlemyre SP RC 30.00 12.00
❑ 551 New York Mets SP 30.00 12.00
Team Card
❑ 552 Julio Gotay 8.00 3.20
❑ 553 Dan Coombs 8.00 3.20
Gene Ratliff
Jack McClure
❑ 554 Chico Ruiz SP 12.00 4.80
❑ 555 Jack Baldschun SP 12.00 4.80
❑ 556 Red Schoendienst 25.00 10.00
SP MG
❑ 557 Jose Santiago 8.00 3.20
❑ 558 Tommie Sisk 8.00 3.20
❑ 559 Ed Bailey SP 12.00 4.80
❑ 560 Boog Powell SP 25.00 10.00
❑ 561 Dennis Daboll 15.00 6.00
Mike Kekich
Hector Valle
Jim Lefebvre RC
❑ 562 Billy Moran 8.00 3.20
❑ 563 Julio Navarro 8.00 3.20
❑ 564 Mel Nelson 8.00 3.20
❑ 565 Ernie Broglio SP 12.00 4.80
❑ 566 Gil Blanco 12.00 4.80
Ross Moschitto
Art Lopez SP
❑ 567 Tommie Aaron 8.00 3.20
❑ 568 Ron Taylor SP 12.00 4.80
❑ 569 Gino Cimoli SP 12.00 4.80
❑ 570 Claude Osteen SP 15.00 6.00
❑ 571 Ossie Virgil SP 12.00 4.80
❑ 572 Baltimore Orioles SP 25.00 10.00
Team Card
❑ 573 Jim Lonborg RC 25.00 10.00
Gerry Moses
Bill Schlesinger
Mike Ryan SP
❑ 574 Roy Sievers 15.00 6.00
❑ 575 Jose Pagan 8.00 3.20
❑ 576 Terry Fox SP 12.00 4.80
❑ 577 Darold Knowles 12.00 4.80
Don Buschhorn
Richie Scheinblum SP
❑ 578 Camilo Carreon SP 12.00 4.80
❑ 579 Dick Smith SP 12.00 4.80
❑ 580 Jimmie Hall SP 12.00 4.80
❑ 581 Tony Perez RC 80.00 32.00
Dave Ricketts
Kevin Collins SP
❑ 582 Bob Schmidt SP 12.00 4.80
❑ 583 Wes Covington SP 12.00 4.80
❑ 584 Harry Bright 15.00 6.00
❑ 585 Hank Fischer 8.00 3.20
❑ 586 Tom McCraw SP 12.00 4.80
❑ 587 Joe Sparma 8.00 3.20
❑ 588 Lenny Green 8.00 3.20
❑ 589 Frank Linzy 12.00 4.80
Bob Schroder SP
❑ 590 John Wyatt 8.00 3.20
❑ 591 Bob Skinner SP 12.00 4.80
❑ 592 Frank Bork SP 12.00 4.80
❑ 593 Jackie Moore RC 12.00 4.80
John Sullivan SP
❑ 594 Joe Gaines 8.00 3.20
❑ 595 Don Lee 8.00 3.20
❑ 596 Don Landrum SP 12.00 4.80
❑ 597 Joe Nossek 8.00 3.20
John Sevcik
Dick Reese
❑ 598 Al Downing SP 25.00 7.50

1966 Topps

	NM	Ex
COMPLETE SET (598)	4000.00	1600.00
COMMON CARD (1-109)	1.50	.60
COMMON (110-283)	2.00	.80
COMMON (284-370)	3.00	1.20
COMMON (371-446)	5.00	2.00
COMMON (447-522)	10.00	4.00
COMMON (523-598)	15.00	6.00
COMMON SP (523-598)	30.00	12.00
WRAPPER (5-CENT)	25.00	10.00

❑ 1 Willie Mays 250.00 80.00
❑ 2 Ted Abernathy .... 1.50 .60
❑ 3 Sam Mele MG .... 1.50 .60
❑ 4 Ray Culp .... 1.50 .60
❑ 5 Jim Fregosi .... 2.00 .80
❑ 6 Chuck Schilling .... 1.50 .60
❑ 7 Tracy Stallard .... 1.50 .60
❑ 8 Floyd Robinson .... 1.50 .60
❑ 9 Clete Boyer .... 2.00 .80
❑ 10 Tony Cloninger .... 1.50 .60
❑ 11 Brant Alyea .... 1.50 .60
Pete Craig
❑ 12 John Tsitouris .... 1.50 .60
❑ 13 Lou Johnson .... 2.00 .80
❑ 14 Norm Siebern .... 1.50 .60
❑ 15 Vern Law .... 2.00 .80
❑ 16 Larry Brown .... 1.50 .60
❑ 17 John Stephenson .... 1.50 .60
❑ 18 Roland Sheldon .... 1.50 .60
❑ 19 San Francisco Giants 5.00 2.00
Team Card
❑ 20 Willie Horton .... 2.00 .80
❑ 21 Don Nottebart .... 1.50 .60
❑ 22 Joe Nossek .... 1.50 .60
❑ 23 Jack Sanford .... 1.50 .60
❑ 24 Don Kessinger RC 4.00 1.60
❑ 25 Pete Ward .... 1.50 .60
❑ 26 Ray Sadecki .... 1.50 .60
❑ 27 Darold Knowles .... 1.50 .60
Andy Etchebarren
❑ 28 Phil Niekro 20.00 8.00
❑ 29 Mike Brumley .... 1.50 .60
❑ 30 Pete Rose DP UER 100.00 40.00
1963 Hit total is wrong
❑ 31 Jack Cullen .... 2.00 .80
❑ 32 Adolfo Phillips .... 1.50 .60
❑ 33 Jim Pagliaroni .... 1.50 .60
❑ 34 Checklist 1 .... 8.00 1.60
❑ 35 Ron Swoboda 4.00 1.60
❑ 36 Jim Hunter UER 20.00 8.00
Stats say 1963 and 1964 should be 1964 and 1965
❑ 37 Billy Herman MG .... 2.00 .80
❑ 38 Ron Nischwitz .... 1.50 .60
❑ 39 Ken Henderson .... 1.50 .60
❑ 40 Jim Grant .... 1.50 .60
❑ 41 Don LeJohn .... 1.50 .60
❑ 42 Aubrey Gatewood .... 1.50 .60
❑ 43A Don Landrum .... 2.00 .80
(Dark button on pants showing)
❑ 43B Don Landrum 20.00 8.00
(Button on pants partially airbrushed)
❑ 43C Don Landrum .... 2.00 .80
(Button on pants not showing)
❑ 44 Bill Davis .... 1.50 .60
Tom Kelley
❑ 45 Jim Gentile .... 2.00 .80
❑ 46 Howie Koplitz .... 1.50 .60
❑ 47 J.C. Martin .... 1.50 .60
❑ 48 Paul Blair .... 2.00 .80
❑ 49 Woody Woodward .... 2.00 .80
❑ 50 Mickey Mantle DP 300.00 120.00
❑ 51 Gordon Richardson .... 1.50 .60
❑ 52 Wes Covington 4.00 1.60
Johnny Callison
❑ 53 Bob Duliba .... 1.50 .60
❑ 54 Jose Pagan .... 1.50 .60
❑ 55 Ken Harrelson .... 2.00 .80
❑ 56 Sandy Valdespino .... 1.50 .60
❑ 57 Jim Lefebvre .... 2.00 .80
❑ 58 Dave Wickersham .... 1.50 .60
❑ 59 Reds Team 5.00 2.00
❑ 60 Curt Flood 4.00 1.60
❑ 61 Bob Bolin .... 1.50 .60
❑ 62A Merritt Ranew .... 2.00 .80
(With sold line)
❑ 62B Merritt Ranew 30.00 12.00
(Without sold line)
❑ 63 Jim Stewart .... 1.50 .60
❑ 64 Bob Bruce .... 1.50 .60
❑ 65 Leon Wagner .... 1.50 .60
❑ 66 Al Weis .... 1.50 .60
❑ 67 Cleon Jones 4.00 1.60
Dick Selma
❑ 68 Hal Reniff .... 1.50 .60
❑ 69 Ken Hamlin .... 1.50 .60
❑ 70 Carl Yastrzemski 30.00 12.00
❑ 71 Frank Carpin .... 1.50 .60
❑ 72 Tony Perez 25.00 10.00
❑ 73 Jerry Zimmerman .... 1.50 .60
❑ 74 Don Mossi .... 2.00 .80
❑ 75 Tommy Davis .... 2.00 .80
❑ 76 Red Schoendienst MG 4.00 1.60
❑ 77 John Orsino .... 1.50 .60
❑ 78 Frank Linzy .... 1.50 .60
❑ 79 Joe Pepitone 4.00 1.60
❑ 80 Richie Allen 6.00 2.40
❑ 81 Ray Oyler .... 1.50 .60
❑ 82 Bob Hendley .... 1.50 .60
❑ 83 Albie Pearson .... 2.00 .80
❑ 84 Jim Beauchamp .... 1.50 .60
Dick Kelley
❑ 85 Eddie Fisher .... 1.50 .60
❑ 86 John Bateman .... 1.50 .60

❑ 87 Dan Napoleon 1.50 .60
❑ 88 Fred Whitfield 1.50 .60
❑ 89 Ted Davidson 1.50 .60
❑ 90 Luis Aparicio 8.00 3.20
❑ 91A Bob Uecker TR 10.00 4.00
❑ 91B Bob Uecker NTR 40.00 16.00
❑ 92 Yankees Team 15.00 6.00
❑ 93 Jim Lonborg 2.00 .80
❑ 94 Matty Alou 2.00 .80
❑ 95 Pete Richert 1.50 .60
❑ 96 Felipe Alou 4.00 1.60
❑ 97 Jim Merritt 1.50 .60
❑ 98 Don Demeter 1.50 .60
❑ 99 Willie Stargell 6.00 2.40
Donn Clendenon
❑ 100 Sandy Koufax 100.00 40.00
❑ 101A Checklist 2 15.00 3.00
(115 W. Spahn) ERR
❑ 101B Checklist 2 10.00 2.00
(115 Bill Henry) COR
❑ 102 Ed Kirkpatrick 1.50 .60
❑ 103A Dick Groat TR 2.00 .80
❑ 103B Dick Groat NTR 40.00 16.00
❑ 104A Alex Johnson TR 2.00 .80
❑ 104B Alex Johnson NTR 30.00 12.00
❑ 105 Milt Pappas 2.00 .80
❑ 106 Rusty Staub 4.00 1.60
❑ 107 Larry Stahl 1.50 .60
Ron Tompkins
❑ 108 Bobby Klaus 1.50 .60
❑ 109 Ralph Terry 2.00 .80
❑ 110 Ernie Banks 30.00 12.00
❑ 111 Gary Peters 2.00 .80
❑ 112 Manny Mota 4.00 1.60
❑ 113 Hank Aguirre 2.00 .80
❑ 114 Jim Gosger 2.00 .80
❑ 115 Bill Henry 2.00 .80
❑ 116 Walter Alston MG 6.00 2.40
❑ 117 Jake Gibbs 2.00 .80
❑ 118 Mike McCormick 2.00 .80
❑ 119 Art Shamsky 2.00 .80
❑ 120 Harmon Killebrew 15.00 6.00
❑ 121 Ray Herbert 2.00 .80
❑ 122 Joe Gaines 2.00 .80
❑ 123 Frank Bork 2.00 .80
Jerry May
❑ 124 Tug McGraw 4.00 1.60
❑ 125 Lou Brock 20.00 8.00
❑ 126 Jim Palmer RC UER 100.00 40.00
Described as a
lefthander on
card back
❑ 127 Ken Berry 2.00 .80
❑ 128 Jim Landis 2.00 .80
❑ 129 Jack Kralick 2.00 .80
❑ 130 Joe Torre 6.00 2.40
❑ 131 Angels Team 5.00 2.00
❑ 132 Orlando Cepeda 8.00 3.20
❑ 133 Don McMahon 2.00 .80
❑ 134 Wes Parker 4.00 1.60
❑ 135 Dave Morehead 2.00 .80
❑ 136 Woody Held 2.00 .80
❑ 137 Pat Corrales 2.00 .80
❑ 138 Roger Repoz 2.00 .80
❑ 139 Byron Browne 2.00 .80
Don Young
❑ 140 Jim Maloney 4.00 1.60
❑ 141 Tom McCraw 2.00 .80
❑ 142 Don Dennis 2.00 .80
❑ 143 Jose Tartabull 4.00 1.60
❑ 144 Don Schwall 2.00 .80
❑ 145 Bill Freehan 4.00 1.60
❑ 146 George Altman 2.00 .80
❑ 147 Lum Harris MG 2.00 .80
❑ 148 Bob Johnson 2.00 .80
❑ 149 Dick Nen 2.00 .80
❑ 150 Rocky Colavito 8.00 3.20
❑ 151 Gary Wagner 2.00 .80
❑ 152 Frank Malzone 4.00 1.60
❑ 153 Rico Carty 4.00 1.60
❑ 154 Chuck Hiller 2.00 .80
❑ 155 Marcelino Lopez 2.00 .80
❑ 156 Dick Schofield 2.00 .80
Hal Lanier
❑ 157 Rene Lachemann 2.00 .80
❑ 158 Jim Brewer 2.00 .80
❑ 159 Chico Ruiz 2.00 .80
❑ 160 Whitey Ford 30.00 12.00
❑ 161 Jerry Lumpe 2.00 .80
❑ 162 Lee Maye 2.00 .80
❑ 163 Tito Francona 2.00 .80
❑ 164 Tommie Agee 4.00 1.60
Marv Staehle
❑ 165 Don Lock 2.00 .80
❑ 166 Chris Krug 2.00 .80
❑ 167 Boog Powell 6.00 2.40
❑ 168 Dan Osinski 2.00 .80
❑ 169 Duke Sims 2.00 .80
❑ 170 Cookie Rojas 4.00 1.60
❑ 171 Nick Willhite 2.00 .80
❑ 172 Mets Team 5.00 2.00
❑ 173 Al Spangler 2.00 .80
❑ 174 Ron Taylor 2.00 .80
❑ 175 Bert Campaneris 4.00 1.60
❑ 176 Jim Davenport 2.00 .80
❑ 177 Hector Lopez 2.00 .80
❑ 178 Bob Tillman 2.00 .80
❑ 179 Dennis Aust 4.00 1.60
Bob Tolan
❑ 180 Vada Pinson 4.00 1.60
❑ 181 Al Worthington 2.00 .80
❑ 182 Jerry Lynch 2.00 .80
❑ 183A Checklist 3 8.00 1.60
(Large print
on front)
❑ 183B Checklist 3 8.00 1.60
(Small print
on front)
❑ 184 Denis Menke 2.00 .80
❑ 185 Bob Buhl 4.00 1.60
❑ 186 Ruben Amaro 2.00 .80
❑ 187 Chuck Dressen MG 4.00 1.60
❑ 188 Al Luplow 2.00 .80
❑ 189 John Roseboro 4.00 1.60
❑ 190 Jimmie Hall 2.00 .80
❑ 191 Darrell Sutherland 2.00 .80
❑ 192 Vic Power 4.00 1.60
❑ 193 Dave McNally 4.00 1.60
❑ 194 Senators Team 5.00 2.00
❑ 195 Joe Morgan 15.00 6.00
❑ 196 Don Pavletich 2.00 .80
❑ 197 Sonny Siebert 2.00 .80
❑ 198 Mickey Stanley RC 6.00 2.40
❑ 199 Bill Skowron 4.00 1.60
Johnny Romano
Floyd Robinson
❑ 200 Eddie Mathews 15.00 6.00
❑ 201 Jim Dickson 2.00 .80
❑ 202 Clay Dalrymple 2.00 .80
❑ 203 Jose Santiago 2.00 .80
❑ 204 Cubs Team 5.00 2.00
❑ 205 Tom Tresh 4.00 1.60
❑ 206 Al Jackson 2.00 .80
❑ 207 Frank Quilici 2.00 .80
❑ 208 Bob Miller 2.00 .80
❑ 209 Fritz Fisher 4.00 1.60
John Hiller RC
❑ 210 Bill Mazeroski 8.00 3.20
❑ 211 Frank Kreutzer 2.00 .80
❑ 212 Ed Kranepool 4.00 1.60
❑ 213 Fred Newman 2.00 .80
❑ 214 Tommy Harper 4.00 1.60
❑ 215 Bob Clemente 50.00 20.00
Hank Aaron
Willie Mays LL
❑ 216 Tony Oliva 5.00 2.00
Carl Yastrzemski
Vic Davalillo LL
❑ 217 Willie Mays 20.00 8.00
Willie McCovey
Billy Williams LL
❑ 218 Tony Conigliaro 5.00 2.00
Norm Cash
Willie Horton LL
❑ 219 Deron Johnson 12.00 4.80
Frank Robinson
Willie Mays LL
❑ 220 Rocky Colavito 5.00 2.00
Willie Horton
Tony Oliva LL
❑ 221 Sandy Koufax 12.00 4.80
Juan Marichal
Vern Law LL
❑ 222 Sam McDowell 5.00 2.00
Eddie Fisher
Sonny Siebert LL
❑ 223 Sandy Koufax 12.00 4.80
Tony Cloninger
Don Drysdale LL
❑ 224 Jim Grant 5.00 2.00
Mel Stottlemyre
Jim Kaat LL
❑ 225 Sandy Koufax 12.00 4.80
Bob Veale
Bob Gibson LL
❑ 226 Sam McDowell 5.00 2.00
Mickey Lolich
Dennis McLain
Sonny Siebert LL
❑ 227 Russ Nixon 2.00 .80
❑ 228 Larry Dierker 4.00 1.60
❑ 229 Hank Bauer MG 4.00 1.60
❑ 230 Johnny Callison 4.00 1.60
❑ 231 Floyd Weaver 2.00 .80
❑ 232 Glenn Beckert 4.00 1.60
❑ 233 Dom Zanni 2.00 .80
❑ 234 Rich Beck 8.00 3.20
Roy White RC
❑ 235 Don Cardwell 2.00 .80
❑ 236 Mike Hershberger 2.00 .80
❑ 237 Billy O'Dell 2.00 .80
❑ 238 Dodgers Team 5.00 2.00
❑ 239 Orlando Pena 2.00 .80
❑ 240 Earl Battey 2.00 .80
❑ 241 Dennis Ribant 2.00 .80
❑ 242 Jesus Alou 2.00 .80
❑ 243 Nelson Briles 4.00 1.60
❑ 244 Chuck Harrison 2.00 .80
Sonny Jackson
❑ 245 John Buzhardt 2.00 .80
❑ 246 Ed Bailey 2.00 .80
❑ 247 Carl Warwick 2.00 .80
❑ 248 Pete Mikkelsen 2.00 .80
❑ 249 Bill Rigney MG 2.00 .80
❑ 250 Sammy Ellis 2.00 .80
❑ 251 Ed Brinkman 2.00 .80
❑ 252 Denny Lemaster 2.00 .80
❑ 253 Don Wert 2.00 .80
❑ 254 Fergie Jenkins RC 60.00 24.00
Bill Sorrell
❑ 255 Willie Stargell 20.00 8.00
❑ 256 Lew Krausse 2.00 .80
❑ 257 Jeff Torborg 4.00 1.60
❑ 258 Dave Giusti 2.00 .80
❑ 259 Boston Red Sox 5.00 2.00
Team Card
❑ 260 Bob Shaw 2.00 .80
❑ 261 Ron Hansen 2.00 .80
❑ 262 Jack Hamilton 2.00 .80
❑ 263 Tom Egan 2.00 .80
❑ 264 Andy Kosco 2.00 .80
Ted Uhlaender
❑ 265 Stu Miller 4.00 1.60
❑ 266 Pedro Gonzalez UER 2.00 .80
(Misspelled Gonzales
on card back)
❑ 267 Joe Sparma 2.00 .80
❑ 268 John Blanchard 2.00 .80
❑ 269 Don Heffner MG 2.00 .80
❑ 270 Claude Osteen 4.00 1.60
❑ 271 Hal Lanier 2.00 .80
❑ 272 Jack Baldschun 2.00 .80
❑ 273 Bob Aspromonte 4.00 1.60
Rusty Staub
❑ 274 Buster Narum 2.00 .80
❑ 275 Tim McCarver 4.00 1.60
❑ 276 Jim Bouton 4.00 1.60
❑ 277 George Thomas 2.00 .80
❑ 278 Cal Koonce 2.00 .80
❑ 279A Checklist 4 8.00 1.60
(Player's cap black)
❑ 279B Checklist 4 8.00 1.60
(Player's cap red)
❑ 280 Bobby Knoop 2.00 .80
❑ 281 Bruce Howard 2.00 .80
❑ 282 Johnny Lewis 2.00 .80
❑ 283 Jim Perry 4.00 1.60
❑ 284 Bobby Wine 3.00 1.20

❑ 285 Luis Tiant 5.00 2.00
❑ 286 Gary Geiger 3.00 1.20
❑ 287 Jack Aker 3.00 1.20
❑ 288 Bill Singer 60.00 24.00
Don Sutton RC
❑ 289 Larry Sherry 3.00 1.20
❑ 290 Ron Santo 5.00 2.00
❑ 291 Moe Drabowsky 5.00 2.00
❑ 292 Jim Coker 3.00 1.20
❑ 293 Mike Shannon 5.00 2.00
❑ 294 Steve Ridzik 3.00 1.20
❑ 295 Jim Ray Hart 5.00 2.00
❑ 296 Johnny Keane MG 5.00 2.00
❑ 297 Jim Owens 3.00 1.20
❑ 298 Rico Petrocelli 5.00 2.00
❑ 299 Lou Burdette 5.00 2.00
❑ 300 Bob Clemente 150.00 60.00
❑ 301 Greg Bollo 3.00 1.20
❑ 302 Ernie Bowman 3.00 1.20
❑ 303 Cleveland Indians 5.00 2.00
Team Card
❑ 304 John Herrnstein 3.00 1.20
❑ 305 Camilo Pascual 5.00 2.00
❑ 306 Ty Cline 3.00 1.20
❑ 307 Clay Carroll 5.00 2.00
❑ 308 Tom Haller 5.00 2.00
❑ 309 Diego Segui 3.00 1.20
❑ 310 Frank Robinson 40.00 16.00
❑ 311 Tommy Helms 5.00 2.00
Dick Simpson
❑ 312 Bob Saverine 3.00 1.20
❑ 313 Chris Zachary 3.00 1.20
❑ 314 Hector Valle 3.00 1.20
❑ 315 Norm Cash 5.00 2.00
❑ 316 Jack Fisher 3.00 1.20
❑ 317 Dalton Jones 3.00 1.20
❑ 318 Harry Walker MG 3.00 1.20
❑ 319 Gene Freese 3.00 1.20
❑ 320 Bob Gibson 25.00 10.00
❑ 321 Rick Reichardt 3.00 1.20
❑ 322 Bill Faul 3.00 1.20
❑ 323 Ray Barker 3.00 1.20
❑ 324 John Boozer 3.00 1.20
❑ 325 Vic Davalillo 3.00 1.20
❑ 326 Braves Team 5.00 2.00
❑ 327 Bernie Allen 3.00 1.20
❑ 328 Jerry Grote 5.00 2.00
❑ 329 Pete Charton 3.00 1.20
❑ 330 Ron Fairly 5.00 2.00
❑ 331 Ron Herbel 3.00 1.20
❑ 332 Bill Bryan 3.00 1.20
❑ 333 Joe Coleman RC 3.00 1.20
Jim French
❑ 334 Marty Keough 3.00 1.20
❑ 335 Juan Pizarro 3.00 1.20
❑ 336 Gene Alley 5.00 2.00
❑ 337 Fred Gladding 3.00 1.20
❑ 338 Dal Maxvill 3.00 1.20
❑ 339 Del Crandall 5.00 2.00
❑ 340 Dean Chance 5.00 2.00
❑ 341 Wes Westrum MG 5.00 2.00
❑ 342 Bob Humphreys 3.00 1.20
❑ 343 Joe Christopher 3.00 1.20
❑ 344 Steve Blass 5.00 2.00
❑ 345 Bob Allison 5.00 2.00
❑ 346 Mike de la Hoz 3.00 1.20
❑ 347 Phil Regan 5.00 2.00
❑ 348 Orioles Team 8.00 3.20
❑ 349 Cap Peterson 3.00 1.20
❑ 350 Mel Stottlemyre 8.00 3.20
❑ 351 Fred Valentine 3.00 1.20
❑ 352 Bob Aspromonte 3.00 1.20
❑ 353 Al McBean 3.00 1.20
❑ 354 Smoky Burgess 5.00 2.00
❑ 355 Wade Blasingame 3.00 1.20
❑ 356 Owen Johnson 3.00 1.20
Ken Sanders
❑ 357 Gerry Arrigo 3.00 1.20
❑ 358 Charlie Smith 3.00 1.20
❑ 359 Johnny Briggs 3.00 1.20
❑ 360 Ron Hunt 3.00 1.20
❑ 361 Tom Satriano 3.00 1.20
❑ 362 Gates Brown 5.00 2.00
❑ 363 Checklist 5 10.00 2.00
❑ 364 Nate Oliver 3.00 1.20
❑ 365 Roger Maris UER 50.00 20.00
Wrong birth year listed on card
❑ 366 Wayne Causey 3.00 1.20
❑ 367 Mel Nelson 3.00 1.20
❑ 368 Charlie Lau 5.00 2.00
❑ 369 Jim King 3.00 1.20
❑ 370 Chico Cardenas 3.00 1.20
❑ 371 Lee Stange 5.00 2.00
❑ 372 Harvey Kuenn 8.00 3.20
❑ 373 Jack Hiatt 8.00 3.20
Dick Estelle
❑ 374 Bob Locker 5.00 2.00
❑ 375 Donn Clendenon 8.00 3.20
❑ 376 Paul Schaal 5.00 2.00
❑ 377 Turk Farrell 5.00 2.00
❑ 378 Dick Tracewski 5.00 2.00
❑ 379 Cardinal Team 10.00 4.00
❑ 380 Tony Conigliaro 10.00 4.00
❑ 381 Hank Fischer 5.00 2.00
❑ 382 Phil Roof 5.00 2.00
❑ 383 Jackie Brandt 5.00 2.00
❑ 384 Al Downing 8.00 3.20
❑ 385 Ken Boyer 10.00 4.00
❑ 386 Gil Hodges MG 8.00 3.20
❑ 387 Howie Reed 5.00 2.00
❑ 388 Don Mincher 5.00 2.00
❑ 389 Jim O'Toole 8.00 3.20
❑ 390 Brooks Robinson 50.00 20.00
❑ 391 Chuck Hinton 5.00 2.00
❑ 392 Bill Hands 8.00 3.20
Randy Hundley RC
❑ 393 George Brunet 5.00 2.00
❑ 394 Ron Brand 5.00 2.00
❑ 395 Len Gabrielson 5.00 2.00
❑ 396 Jerry Stephenson 5.00 2.00
❑ 397 Bill White 8.00 3.20
❑ 398 Danny Cater 5.00 2.00
❑ 399 Ray Washburn 5.00 2.00
❑ 400 Zoilo Versalles 8.00 3.20
❑ 401 Ken McMullen 5.00 2.00
❑ 402 Jim Hickman 5.00 2.00
❑ 403 Fred Talbot 5.00 2.00
❑ 404 Pittsburgh Pirates 10.00 4.00
Team Card
❑ 405 Elston Howard 8.00 3.20
❑ 406 Joey Jay 5.00 2.00
❑ 407 John Kennedy 5.00 2.00
❑ 408 Lee Thomas 8.00 3.20
❑ 409 Billy Hoeft 5.00 2.00
❑ 410 Al Kaline 40.00 16.00
❑ 411 Gene Mauch MG 5.00 2.00
❑ 412 Sam Bowens 5.00 2.00
❑ 413 Johnny Romano 5.00 2.00
❑ 414 Dan Coombs 5.00 2.00
❑ 415 Max Alvis 5.00 2.00
❑ 416 Phil Ortega 5.00 2.00
❑ 417 Jim McGlothlin 5.00 2.00
Ed Sukla
❑ 418 Phil Gagliano 5.00 2.00
❑ 419 Mike Ryan 5.00 2.00
❑ 420 Juan Marichal 15.00 6.00
❑ 421 Roy McMillan 8.00 3.20
❑ 422 Ed Charles 5.00 2.00
❑ 423 Ernie Broglio 5.00 2.00
❑ 424 Lee May RC 10.00 4.00
Darrell Osteen
❑ 425 Bob Veale 8.00 3.20
❑ 426 White Sox Team 10.00 4.00
❑ 427 John Miller 5.00 2.00
❑ 428 Sandy Alomar 5.00 2.00
❑ 429 Bill Monbouquette 5.00 2.00
❑ 430 Don Drysdale 20.00 8.00
❑ 431 Walt Bond 5.00 2.00
❑ 432 Bob Heffner 5.00 2.00
❑ 433 Alvin Dark MG 8.00 3.20
❑ 434 Willie Kirkland 5.00 2.00
❑ 435 Jim Bunning 15.00 6.00
❑ 436 Julian Javier 8.00 3.20
❑ 437 Al Stanek 5.00 2.00
❑ 438 Willie Smith 5.00 2.00
❑ 439 Pedro Ramos 5.00 2.00
❑ 440 Deron Johnson 8.00 3.20
❑ 441 Tommie Sisk 5.00 2.00
❑ 442 Ed Barnowski 5.00 2.00
Eddie Watt
❑ 443 Bill Wakefield 3.00 1.20
❑ 444 Checklist 6 10.00 2.00
❑ 445 Jim Kaat 10.00 4.00
❑ 446 Mack Jones 5.00 2.00
❑ 447 Dick Ellsworth UER 15.00 6.00
(Photo actually
Ken Hubbs)
❑ 448 Eddie Stanky MG 10.00 4.00
❑ 449 Joe Moeller 10.00 4.00
❑ 450 Tony Oliva 15.00 6.00
❑ 451 Barry Latman 10.00 4.00
❑ 452 Joe Azcue 10.00 4.00
❑ 453 Ron Kline 10.00 4.00
❑ 454 Jerry Buchek 10.00 4.00
❑ 455 Mickey Lolich 15.00 6.00
❑ 456 Darrell Brandon 10.00 4.00
Joe Foy
❑ 457 Joe Gibbon 10.00 4.00
❑ 458 Manny Jiminez 10.00 4.00
❑ 459 Bill McCool 10.00 4.00
❑ 460 Curt Blefary 10.00 4.00
❑ 461 Roy Face 15.00 6.00
❑ 462 Bob Rodgers 10.00 4.00
❑ 463 Philadelphia Phillies 15.00 6.00
Team Card
❑ 464 Larry Bearnarth 10.00 4.00
❑ 465 Don Buford 10.00 4.00
❑ 466 Ken Johnson 10.00 4.00
❑ 467 Vic Roznovsky 10.00 4.00
❑ 468 Johnny Podres 15.00 6.00
❑ 469 Bobby Murcer RC 30.00 12.00
Dooley Womack
❑ 470 Sam McDowell 15.00 6.00
❑ 471 Bob Skinner 10.00 4.00
❑ 472 Terry Fox 10.00 4.00
❑ 473 Rich Rollins 10.00 4.00
❑ 474 Dick Schofield 10.00 4.00
❑ 475 Dick Radatz 10.00 4.00
❑ 476 Bobby Bragan MG 10.00 4.00
❑ 477 Steve Barber 10.00 4.00
❑ 478 Tony Gonzalez 10.00 4.00
❑ 479 Jim Hannan 10.00 4.00
❑ 480 Dick Stuart 10.00 4.00
❑ 481 Bob Lee 10.00 4.00
❑ 482 John Boccabella 10.00 4.00
Dave Dowling
❑ 483 Joe Nuxhall 10.00 4.00
❑ 484 Wes Covington 10.00 4.00
❑ 485 Bob Bailey 10.00 4.00
❑ 486 Tommy John 15.00 6.00
❑ 487 Al Ferrara 10.00 4.00
❑ 488 George Banks 10.00 4.00
❑ 489 Curt Simmons 10.00 4.00
❑ 490 Bobby Richardson 25.00 10.00
❑ 491 Dennis Bennett 10.00 4.00
❑ 492 Athletics Team 15.00 6.00
❑ 493 Johnny Klippstein 10.00 4.00
❑ 494 Gordy Coleman 10.00 4.00
❑ 495 Dick McAuliffe 15.00 6.00
❑ 496 Lindy McDaniel 10.00 4.00
❑ 497 Chris Cannizzaro 10.00 4.00
❑ 498 Luke Walker 10.00 4.00
Woody Fryman
❑ 499 Wally Bunker 10.00 4.00
❑ 500 Hank Aaron 125.00 50.00
❑ 501 John O'Donoghue 10.00 4.00
❑ 502 Lenny Green UER 10.00 4.00
Born: aJn. 6, 1933
❑ 503 Steve Hamilton 15.00 6.00
❑ 504 Grady Hatton MG 10.00 4.00
❑ 505 Jose Cardenal 10.00 4.00
❑ 506 Bo Belinsky 15.00 6.00
❑ 507 Johnny Edwards 10.00 4.00
❑ 508 Steve Hargan RC 15.00 6.00
❑ 509 Jake Wood 10.00 4.00
❑ 510 Hoyt Wilhelm 25.00 10.00
❑ 511 Bob Barton 10.00 4.00
Tito Fuentes RC
❑ 512 Dick Stigman 10.00 4.00
❑ 513 Camilo Carreon 10.00 4.00
❑ 514 Hal Woodeshick 10.00 4.00
❑ 515 Frank Howard 15.00 6.00
❑ 516 Eddie Bressoud 10.00 4.00
❑ 517A Checklist 7 15.00 3.00
529 White Sox Rookies
544 Cardinals Rookies
❑ 517B Checklist 7 15.00 3.00
529 W. Sox Rookies

Card	NM	Ex
544 Cards Rookies		
❑ 518 Herb Hippauf	10.00	4.00
Arnie Umbach		
❑ 519 Bob Friend	15.00	6.00
❑ 520 Jim Wynn	15.00	6.00
❑ 521 John Wyatt	10.00	4.00
❑ 522 Phil Linz	10.00	4.00
❑ 523 Bob Sadowski	10.00	4.00
❑ 524 Ollie Brown	30.00	12.00
Don Mason SP		
❑ 525 Gary Bell SP	30.00	12.00
❑ 526 Twins Team SP	100.00	40.00
❑ 527 Julio Navarro	15.00	6.00
❑ 528 Jesse Gonder SP	30.00	12.00
❑ 529 Lee Elia	15.00	6.00
Dennis Higgins		
Bill Voss		
❑ 530 Robin Roberts	50.00	20.00
❑ 531 Joe Cunningham	15.00	6.00
❑ 532 A.Monteagudo SP	30.00	12.00
❑ 533 Jerry Adair SP	30.00	12.00
❑ 534 Dave Eilers	15.00	6.00
Rob Gardner		
❑ 535 Willie Davis SP	40.00	16.00
❑ 536 Dick Egan	15.00	6.00
❑ 537 Herman Franks MG	15.00	6.00
❑ 538 Bob Allen SP	30.00	12.00
❑ 539 Bill Heath	25.00	10.00
Carroll Sembera		
❑ 540 Denny McLain SP	60.00	24.00
❑ 541 Gene Oliver SP	30.00	12.00
❑ 542 George Smith	15.00	6.00
❑ 543 Roger Craig SP	30.00	12.00
❑ 544 Joe Hoerner	30.00	12.00
George Kernek		
Jimy Williams RC UER SP		
(Misspelled Jimmy		
on card)		
❑ 545 Dick Green SP	30.00	12.00
❑ 546 Dwight Siebler	25.00	10.00
❑ 547 Horace Clarke RC SP	40.00	16.00
❑ 548 Gary Kroll SP	30.00	12.00
❑ 549 Al Closter	15.00	6.00
Casey Cox		
❑ 550 Willie McCovey SP	100.00	40.00
❑ 551 Bob Purkey SP	30.00	12.00
❑ 552 Birdie Tebbetts	30.00	12.00
MG SP		
❑ 553 Pat Garrett	15.00	6.00
Jackie Warner		
❑ 554 Jim Northrup SP	30.00	12.00
❑ 555 Ron Perranoski SP	30.00	12.00
❑ 556 Mel Queen SP	30.00	12.00
❑ 557 Felix Mantilla SP	30.00	12.00
❑ 558 Guido Grilli	20.00	8.00
Pete Magrini		
George Scott RC		
❑ 559 Roberto Pena SP	30.00	12.00
❑ 560 Joel Horlen	15.00	6.00
❑ 561 Choo Choo Coleman SP	30.00	12.00
❑ 562 Russ Snyder	25.00	10.00
❑ 563 Pete Cimino	15.00	6.00
Cesar Tovar		
❑ 564 Bob Chance SP	30.00	12.00
❑ 565 Jimmy Piersall SP	40.00	16.00
❑ 566 Mike Cuellar SP	30.00	12.00
❑ 567 Dick Howser SP	40.00	16.00
❑ 568 Paul Lindblad	15.00	6.00
Ron Stone		
❑ 569 Orlando McFarlane SP	30.00	12.00
❑ 570 Art Mahaffey SP	30.00	12.00
❑ 571 Dave Roberts SP	30.00	12.00
❑ 572 Bob Priddy	15.00	6.00
❑ 573 Derrell Griffith	15.00	6.00
❑ 574 Bill Hepler	15.00	6.00
Bill Murphy		
❑ 575 Earl Wilson	15.00	6.00
❑ 576 Dave Nicholson SP	30.00	12.00
❑ 577 Jack Lamabe SP	30.00	12.00
❑ 578 Chi Chi Olivo SP	30.00	12.00
❑ 579 Frank Bertaina	20.00	8.00
Gene Brabender		
Dave Johnson		
❑ 580 Billy Williams SP	60.00	24.00
❑ 581 Tony Martinez	15.00	6.00
❑ 582 Garry Roggenburk	15.00	6.00
❑ 583 Tigers Team SP UER	125.00	50.00
Text on back states Tigers		
finished third in 1965 instead		
of fourth		
❑ 584 Frank Fernandez	15.00	6.00
Fritz Peterson		
❑ 585 Tony Taylor	25.00	10.00
❑ 586 Claude Raymond SP	30.00	12.00
❑ 587 Dick Bertell	15.00	6.00
❑ 588 Chuck Dobson	15.00	6.00
Ken Suarez		
❑ 589 Lou Klimchock SP	30.00	12.00
❑ 590 Bill Skowron SP	40.00	16.00
❑ 591 Bart Shirley	40.00	16.00
Grant Jackson RC SP		
❑ 592 Andre Rodgers	15.00	6.00
❑ 593 Doug Camilli SP	30.00	12.00
❑ 594 Chico Salmon	15.00	6.00
❑ 595 Larry Jackson	15.00	6.00
❑ 596 Nate Colbert RC	30.00	12.00
Greg Sims SP		
❑ 597 John Sullivan	15.00	6.00
❑ 598 Gaylord Perry SP	175.00	50.00

1967 Topps

	NM	Ex
COMPLETE SET (609)	5000.00	2000.00
COMMON CARD (1-109)	1.50	.60
COMMON (110-283)	2.00	.80
COMMON (284-370)	2.50	1.00
COMMON (371-457)	4.00	1.60
COMMON (458-533)	6.00	2.40
COMMON (534-609)	15.00	6.00
COMMON DP (534-609)	8.00	3.20
WRAPPER (5-CENT)	25.00	10.00
❑ 1 Frank Robinson	25.00	7.50
Hank Bauer MG		
Brooks Robinson DP		
❑ 2 Jack Hamilton	1.50	.60
❑ 3 Duke Sims	1.50	.60
❑ 4 Hal Lanier	1.50	.60
❑ 5 Whitey Ford UER	20.00	8.00
(1953 listed as		
1933 in stats on back)		
❑ 6 Dick Simpson	1.50	.60
❑ 7 Don McMahon	1.50	.60
❑ 8 Chuck Harrison	1.50	.60
❑ 9 Ron Hansen	1.50	.60
❑ 10 Matty Alou	4.00	1.60
❑ 11 Barry Moore	1.50	.60
❑ 12 Jim Campanis	4.00	1.60
Bill Singer		
❑ 13 Joe Sparma	1.50	.60
❑ 14 Phil Linz	4.00	1.60
❑ 15 Earl Battey	1.50	.60
❑ 16 Bill Hands	1.50	.60
❑ 17 Jim Gosger	1.50	.60
❑ 18 Gene Oliver	1.50	.60
❑ 19 Jim McGlothlin	1.50	.60
❑ 20 Orlando Cepeda	8.00	3.20
❑ 21 Dave Bristol MG	1.50	.60
❑ 22 Gene Brabender	1.50	.60
❑ 23 Larry Elliot	1.50	.60
❑ 24 Bob Allen	1.50	.60
❑ 25 Elston Howard	4.00	1.60
❑ 26A Bob Priddy NTR	30.00	12.00
❑ 26B Bob Priddy TR	4.00	1.60
❑ 27 Bob Saverine	1.50	.60
❑ 28 Barry Latman	1.50	.60
❑ 29 Tom McCraw	1.50	.60
❑ 30 Al Kaline DP	20.00	8.00
❑ 31 Jim Brewer	1.50	.60
❑ 32 Bob Bailey	4.00	1.60
❑ 33 Sal Bando RC	6.00	2.40
Randy Schwartz		
❑ 34 Pete Cimino	1.50	.60
❑ 35 Rico Carty	4.00	1.60
❑ 36 Bob Tillman	1.50	.60
❑ 37 Rick Wise	4.00	1.60
❑ 38 Bob Johnson	1.50	.60
❑ 39 Curt Simmons	4.00	1.60
❑ 40 Rick Reichardt	1.50	.60
❑ 41 Joe Hoerner	1.50	.60
❑ 42 Mets Team	10.00	4.00
❑ 43 Chico Salmon	1.50	.60
❑ 44 Joe Nuxhall	4.00	1.60
❑ 45 Roger Maris	50.00	20.00
❑ 45A Roger Maris	1000.00	400.00
Yankees listed as team		
Blank Back		
❑ 46 Lindy McDaniel	4.00	1.60
❑ 47 Ken McMullen	1.50	.60
❑ 48 Bill Freehan	4.00	1.60
❑ 49 Roy Face	4.00	1.60
❑ 50 Tony Oliva	6.00	2.40
❑ 51 Dave Adlesh	1.50	.60
Wes Bales		
❑ 52 Dennis Higgins	1.50	.60
❑ 53 Clay Dalrymple	1.50	.60
❑ 54 Dick Green	1.50	.60
❑ 55 Don Drysdale	15.00	6.00
❑ 56 Jose Tartabull	4.00	1.60
❑ 57 Pat Jarvis RC	4.00	1.60
❑ 58A Paul Schaal	20.00	8.00
Green Bat		
❑ 58B Paul Schaal	1.50	.60
Normal Colored Bat		
❑ 59 Ralph Terry	4.00	1.60
❑ 60 Luis Aparicio	8.00	3.20
❑ 61 Gordy Coleman	1.50	.60
❑ 62 Frank Robinson CL	8.00	1.60
❑ 63 Lou Brock	8.00	3.20
Curt Flood		
❑ 64 Fred Valentine	1.50	.60
❑ 65 Tom Haller	4.00	1.60
❑ 66 Manny Mota	4.00	1.60
❑ 67 Ken Berry	1.50	.60
❑ 68 Bob Buhl	4.00	1.60
❑ 69 Vic Davalillo	1.50	.60
❑ 70 Ron Santo	6.00	2.40
❑ 71 Camilo Pascual	4.00	1.60
❑ 72 George Korince	1.50	.60
(Photo actually		
James Murray Brown)		
John (Tom) Matchick		
❑ 73 Rusty Staub	6.00	2.40
❑ 74 Wes Stock	1.50	.60
❑ 75 George Scott	4.00	1.60
❑ 76 Jim Barbieri	1.50	.60
❑ 77 Dooley Womack	4.00	1.60
❑ 78 Pat Corrales	1.50	.60
❑ 79 Bubba Morton	1.50	.60
❑ 80 Jim Maloney	4.00	1.60
❑ 81 Eddie Stanky MG	4.00	1.60
❑ 82 Steve Barber	1.50	.60
❑ 83 Ollie Brown	1.50	.60
❑ 84 Tommie Sisk	1.50	.60
❑ 85 Johnny Callison	4.00	1.60
❑ 86A Mike McCormick NTR	30.00	12.00
(Senators on front		
and Senators on back)		
❑ 86B Mike McCormick TR	4.00	1.60
(Traded line		
at end of bio;		
Senators on front,		
but Giants on back)		
❑ 87 George Altman	1.50	.60
❑ 88 Mickey Lolich	4.00	1.60
❑ 89 Felix Millan	4.00	1.60
❑ 90 Jim Nash	1.50	.60
❑ 91 Johnny Lewis	1.50	.60
❑ 92 Ray Washburn	1.50	.60
❑ 93 Stan Bahnsen RC	4.00	1.60

Bobby Murcer
❑ 94 Ron Fairly 4.00 1.60
❑ 95 Sonny Siebert 1.50 .60
❑ 96 Art Shamsky 1.50 .60
❑ 97 Mike Cuellar 4.00 1.60
❑ 98 Rich Rollins 1.50 .60
❑ 99 Lee Stange 1.50 .60
❑ 100 Frank Robinson DP 15.00 6.00
❑ 101 Ken Johnson 1.50 .60
❑ 102 Philadelphia Phillies 4.00 1.60
Team Card
❑ 103 Mickey Mantle CL 20.00 4.00
❑ 104 Minnie Rojas 1.50 .60
❑ 105 Ken Boyer 6.00 2.40
❑ 106 Randy Hundley 4.00 1.60
❑ 107 Joel Horlen 1.50 .60
❑ 108 Alex Johnson 4.00 1.60
❑ 109 Rocky Colavito 6.00 2.40
Leon Wagner
❑ 110 Jack Aker 4.00 1.60
❑ 111 John Kennedy 2.00 .80
❑ 112 Dave Wickersham 2.00 .80
❑ 113 Dave Nicholson 2.00 .80
❑ 114 Jack Baldschun 2.00 .80
❑ 115 Paul Casanova 2.00 .80
❑ 116 Herman Franks MG 2.00 .80
❑ 117 Darrell Brandon 2.00 .80
❑ 118 Bernie Allen 2.00 .80
❑ 119 Wade Blasingame 2.00 .80
❑ 120 Floyd Robinson 2.00 .80
❑ 121 Eddie Bressoud 2.00 .80
❑ 122 George Brunet 2.00 .80
❑ 123 Jim Price 4.00 1.60
Luke Walker
❑ 124 Jim Stewart 2.00 .80
❑ 125 Moe Drabowsky 4.00 1.60
❑ 126 Tony Taylor 2.00 .80
❑ 127 John O'Donoghue 2.00 .80
❑ 128 Ed Spiezio 2.00 .80
❑ 129 Phil Roof 2.00 .80
❑ 130 Phil Regan 4.00 1.60
❑ 131 Yankees Team 10.00 4.00
❑ 132 Ozzie Virgil 2.00 .80
❑ 133 Ron Kline 2.00 .80
❑ 134 Gates Brown 6.00 2.40
❑ 135 Deron Johnson 4.00 1.60
❑ 136 Carroll Sembera 2.00 .80
❑ 137 Ron Clark 2.00 .80
Jim Ollum
❑ 138 Dick Kelley 2.00 .80
❑ 139 Dalton Jones 4.00 1.60
❑ 140 Willie Stargell 20.00 8.00
❑ 141 John Miller 2.00 .80
❑ 142 Jackie Brandt 2.00 .80
❑ 143 Pete Ward 2.00 .80
Don Buford
❑ 144 Bill Hepler 2.00 .80
❑ 145 Larry Brown 2.00 .80
❑ 146 Steve Carlton 50.00 20.00
❑ 147 Tom Egan 2.00 .80
❑ 148 Adolfo Phillips 2.00 .80
❑ 149 Joe Moeller 2.00 .80
❑ 150 Mickey Mantle 300.00 120.00
❑ 151 Moe Drabowsky WS 5.00 2.00
❑ 152 Jim Palmer WS 8.00 3.20
❑ 153 Paul Blair WS 5.00 2.00
❑ 154 Brooks Robinson WS 5.00 2.00
Dave McNally
❑ 155 WS Summary 5.00 2.00
Winners celebrate
❑ 156 Ron Herbel 2.00 .80
❑ 157 Danny Cater 2.00 .80
❑ 158 Jimmie Coker 2.00 .80
❑ 159 Bruce Howard 2.00 .80
❑ 160 Willie Davis 4.00 1.60
❑ 161 Dick Williams MG 4.00 1.60
❑ 162 Billy O'Dell 2.00 .80
❑ 163 Vic Roznovsky 2.00 .80
❑ 164 Dwight Siebler UER 2.00 .80
(Last line of stats
shows 1960 Minnesota)
❑ 165 Cleon Jones 4.00 1.60
❑ 166 Eddie Mathews 15.00 6.00
❑ 167 Joe Coleman 2.00 .80
Tim Cullen
❑ 168 Ray Culp 2.00 .80
❑ 169 Horace Clarke 4.00 1.60
❑ 170 Dick McAuliffe 4.00 1.60
❑ 171 Cal Koonce 2.00 .80
❑ 172 Bill Heath 2.00 .80
❑ 173 St. Louis Cardinals 4.00 1.60
Team Card
❑ 174 Dick Radatz 4.00 1.60
❑ 175 Bobby Knoop 2.00 .80
❑ 176 Sammy Ellis 2.00 .80
❑ 177 Tito Fuentes 1.50 .60
❑ 178 John Buzhardt 2.00 .80
❑ 179 Charles Vaughan 4.00 1.60
Cecil Upshaw
❑ 180 Curt Blefary 2.00 .80
❑ 181 Terry Fox 2.00 .80
❑ 182 Ed Charles 2.00 .80
❑ 183 Jim Pagliaroni 2.00 .80
❑ 184 George Thomas 2.00 .80
❑ 185 Ken Holtzman RC 4.00 1.60
❑ 186 Ed Kranepool 4.00 1.60
Ron Swoboda
❑ 187 Pedro Ramos 2.00 .80
❑ 188 Ken Harrelson 4.00 1.60
❑ 189 Chuck Hinton 2.00 .80
❑ 190 Turk Farrell 2.00 .80
❑ 191A Willie Mays CL 10.00 2.00
214 Tom Kelley
❑ 191B Willie Mays CL 12.00 2.40
214 Dick Kelley
❑ 192 Fred Gladding 2.00 .80
❑ 193 Jose Cardenal 4.00 1.60
❑ 194 Bob Allison 4.00 1.60
❑ 195 Al Jackson 2.00 .80
❑ 196 Johnny Romano 2.00 .80
❑ 197 Ron Perranoski 4.00 1.60
❑ 198 Chuck Hiller 2.00 .80
❑ 199 Billy Hitchcock MG 2.00 .80
❑ 200 Willie Mays UER 100.00 40.00
('63 San Francisco
on card back stats)
❑ 201 Hal Reniff 4.00 1.60
❑ 202 Johnny Edwards 2.00 .80
❑ 203 Al McBean 2.00 .80
❑ 204 Mike Epstein 6.00 2.40
Tom Phoebus
❑ 205 Dick Groat 4.00 1.60
❑ 206 Dennis Bennett 2.00 .80
❑ 207 John Orsino 2.00 .80
❑ 208 Jack Lamabe 2.00 .80
❑ 209 Joe Nossek 2.00 .80
❑ 210 Bob Gibson 20.00 8.00
❑ 211 Twins Team 4.00 1.60
❑ 212 Chris Zachary 2.00 .80
❑ 213 Jay Johnstone RC 4.00 1.60
❑ 214 Dick Kelley 2.00 .80
❑ 215 Ernie Banks 20.00 8.00
❑ 216 Norm Cash 8.00 3.20
Al Kaline
❑ 217 Rob Gardner 2.00 .80
❑ 218 Wes Parker 4.00 1.60
❑ 219 Clay Carroll 4.00 1.60
❑ 220 Jim Ray Hart 4.00 1.60
❑ 221 Woody Fryman 4.00 1.60
❑ 222 Darrell Osteen 4.00 1.60
Lee May
❑ 223 Mike Ryan 4.00 1.60
❑ 224 Walt Bond 2.00 .80
❑ 225 Mel Stottlemyre 6.00 2.40
❑ 226 Julian Javier 4.00 1.60
❑ 227 Paul Lindblad 2.00 .80
❑ 228 Gil Hodges MG 6.00 2.40
❑ 229 Larry Jackson 2.00 .80
❑ 230 Boog Powell 6.00 2.40
❑ 231 John Bateman 2.00 .80
❑ 232 Don Buford 2.00 .80
❑ 233 Gary Peters 4.00 1.60
Joel Horlen
Steve Hargan LL
❑ 234 Sandy Koufax 15.00 6.00
Mike Cuellar
Juan Marichal LL
❑ 235 Jim Kaat 6.00 2.40
Denny McLain
Earl Wilson LL
❑ 236 Sandy Koufax 25.00 10.00
Juan Marichal
Bob Gibson
Gaylord Perry LL
❑ 237 Sam McDowell 6.00 2.40
Jim Kaat
Earl Wilson LL
❑ 238 Sandy Koufax 12.00 4.80
Jim Bunning
Bob Veale LL
❑ 239 Frank Robinson 10.00 4.00
Tony Oliva
Al Kaline LL
❑ 240 Matty Alou 6.00 2.40
Felipe Alou
Rico Carty LL
❑ 241 Frank Robinson 10.00 4.00
Harmon Killebrew
Boog Powell LL
❑ 242 Hank Aaron 25.00 10.00
Bob Clemente
Richie Allen LL
❑ 243 Frank Robinson 10.00 4.00
Harmon Killebrew
Boog Powell LL
❑ 244 Hank Aaron 20.00 8.00
Richie Allen
Willie Mays LL
❑ 245 Curt Flood 6.00 2.40
❑ 246 Jim Perry 4.00 1.60
❑ 247 Jerry Lumpe 2.00 .80
❑ 248 Gene Mauch MG 4.00 1.60
❑ 249 Nick Willhite 2.00 .80
❑ 250 Hank Aaron UER 80.00 32.00
(Second 1961 in stats
should be 1962)
❑ 251 Woody Held 2.00 .80
❑ 252 Bob Bolin 2.00 .80
❑ 253 Bill Davis 2.00 .80
Gus Gil
❑ 254 Milt Pappas 4.00 1.60
(No facsimile auto-
graph on card front)
❑ 255 Frank Howard 4.00 1.60
❑ 256 Bob Hendley 2.00 .80
❑ 257 Charlie Smith 2.00 .80
❑ 258 Lee Maye 2.00 .80
❑ 259 Don Dennis 2.00 .80
❑ 260 Jim Lefebvre 4.00 1.60
❑ 261 John Wyatt 2.00 .80
❑ 262 Athletics Team 4.00 1.60
❑ 263 Hank Aguirre 2.00 .80
❑ 264 Ron Swoboda 4.00 1.60
❑ 265 Lou Burdette 4.00 1.60
❑ 266 Willie Stargell 4.00 1.60
Donn Clendenon
❑ 267 Don Schwall 2.00 .80
❑ 268 Johnny Briggs 2.00 .80
❑ 269 Don Nottebart 2.00 .80
❑ 270 Zoilo Versalles 2.00 .80
❑ 271 Eddie Watt 2.00 .80
❑ 272 Bill Connors RC 4.00 1.60
Dave Dowling
❑ 273 Dick Lines 2.00 .80
❑ 274 Bob Aspromonte 2.00 .80
❑ 275 Fred Whitfield 2.00 .80
❑ 276 Bruce Brubaker 2.00 .80
❑ 277 Steve Whitaker 6.00 2.40
❑ 278 Jim Kaat CL 8.00 1.60
❑ 279 Frank Linzy 2.00 .80
❑ 280 Tony Conigliaro 8.00 3.20
❑ 281 Bob Rodgers 2.00 .80
❑ 282 John Odom 2.00 .80
❑ 283 Gene Alley 4.00 1.60
❑ 284 Johnny Podres 4.00 1.60
❑ 285 Lou Brock 20.00 8.00
❑ 286 Wayne Causey 2.50 1.00
❑ 287 Greg Goossen 2.50 1.00
Bart Shirley
❑ 288 Denny Lemaster 2.50 1.00
❑ 289 Tom Tresh 5.00 2.00
❑ 290 Bill White 5.00 2.00
❑ 291 Jim Hannan 2.50 1.00
❑ 292 Don Pavletich 2.50 1.00
❑ 293 Ed Kirkpatrick 2.50 1.00
❑ 294 Walter Alston MG 8.00 3.20
❑ 295 Sam McDowell 5.00 2.00
❑ 296 Glenn Beckert 5.00 2.00

❑ 297	Dave Morehead	5.00	2.00
❑ 298	Ron Davis	2.50	1.00
❑ 299	Norm Siebern	2.50	1.00
❑ 300	Jim Kaat	5.00	2.00
❑ 301	Jesse Gonder	2.50	1.00
❑ 302	Orioles Team	8.00	3.20
❑ 303	Gil Blanco	2.50	1.00
❑ 304	Phil Gagliano	2.50	1.00
❑ 305	Earl Wilson	5.00	2.00
❑ 306	Bud Harrelson RC	5.00	2.00
❑ 307	Jim Beauchamp	2.50	1.00
❑ 308	Al Downing	5.00	2.00
❑ 309	Johnny Callison	5.00	2.00
	Richie Allen		
❑ 310	Gary Peters	2.50	1.00
❑ 311	Ed Brinkman	2.50	1.00
❑ 312	Don Mincher	2.50	1.00
❑ 313	Bob Lee	2.50	1.00
❑ 314	Mike Andrews	8.00	3.20
	Reggie Smith RC		
❑ 315	Billy Williams	15.00	6.00
❑ 316	Jack Kralick	2.50	1.00
❑ 317	Cesar Tovar	2.50	1.00
❑ 318	Dave Giusti	2.50	1.00
❑ 319	Paul Blair	5.00	2.00
❑ 320	Gaylord Perry	15.00	6.00
❑ 321	Mayo Smith MG	2.50	1.00
❑ 322	Jose Pagan	2.50	1.00
❑ 323	Mike Hershberger	2.50	1.00
❑ 324	Hal Woodeshick	2.50	1.00
❑ 325	Chico Cardenas	5.00	2.00
❑ 326	Bob Uecker	10.00	4.00
❑ 327	California Angels	8.00	3.20
	Team Card		
❑ 328	Clete Boyer UER	5.00	2.00
	(Stats only go up		
	through 1965)		
❑ 329	Charlie Lau	5.00	2.00
❑ 330	Claude Osteen	5.00	2.00
❑ 331	Joe Foy	5.00	2.00
❑ 332	Jesus Alou	2.50	1.00
❑ 333	Fergie Jenkins	20.00	8.00
❑ 334	Bob Allison	10.00	4.00
	Harmon Killebrew		
❑ 335	Bob Veale	5.00	2.00
❑ 336	Joe Azcue	2.50	1.00
❑ 337	Joe Morgan	15.00	6.00
❑ 338	Bob Locker	2.50	1.00
❑ 339	Chico Ruiz	2.50	1.00
❑ 340	Joe Pepitone	8.00	3.20
❑ 341	Dick Dietz	2.50	1.00
	Bill Sorrell		
❑ 342	Hank Fischer	2.50	1.00
❑ 343	Tom Satriano	2.50	1.00
❑ 344	Ossie Chavarria	2.50	1.00
❑ 345	Stu Miller	5.00	2.00
❑ 346	Jim Hickman	2.50	1.00
❑ 347	Grady Hatton MG	2.50	1.00
❑ 348	Tug McGraw	5.00	2.00
❑ 349	Bob Chance	2.50	1.00
❑ 350	Joe Torre	8.00	3.20
❑ 351	Vern Law	5.00	2.00
❑ 352	Ray Oyler	2.50	1.00
❑ 353	Bill McCool	2.50	1.00
❑ 354	Cubs Team	8.00	3.20
❑ 355	Carl Yastrzemski	60.00	24.00
❑ 356	Larry Jaster	2.50	1.00
❑ 357	Bill Skowron	5.00	2.00
❑ 358	Ruben Amaro	2.50	1.00
❑ 359	Dick Ellsworth	2.50	1.00
❑ 360	Leon Wagner	2.50	1.00
❑ 361	Roberto Clemente CL	15.00	3.00
❑ 362	Darold Knowles	2.50	1.00
❑ 363	Davey Johnson	5.00	2.00
❑ 364	Claude Raymond	2.50	1.00
❑ 365	John Roseboro	5.00	2.00
❑ 366	Andy Kosco	2.50	1.00
❑ 367	Bill Kelso	2.50	1.00
	Don Wallace		
❑ 368	Jack Hiatt	2.50	1.00
❑ 369	Jim Hunter	15.00	6.00
❑ 370	Tommy Davis	5.00	2.00
❑ 371	Jim Lonborg	8.00	3.20
❑ 372	Mike de la Hoz	4.00	1.60
❑ 373	Duane Josephson	4.00	1.60
	Fred Klages DP		
❑ 374A	Mel Queen ERR DP	20.00	8.00
	(Incomplete stat		
	line on back)		
❑ 374B	Mel Queen COR DP	4.00	1.60
	(Complete stat		
	line on back)		
❑ 375	Jake Gibbs	8.00	3.20
❑ 376	Don Lock DP	4.00	1.60
❑ 377	Luis Tiant	8.00	3.20
❑ 378	Detroit Tigers	8.00	3.20
	Team Card UER		
	(Willie Horton with		
	262 RBI's in 1966)		
❑ 379	Jerry May DP	4.00	1.60
❑ 380	Dean Chance DP	4.00	1.60
❑ 381	Dick Schofield DP	4.00	1.60
❑ 382	Dave McNally	8.00	3.20
❑ 383	Ken Henderson DP	4.00	1.60
❑ 384	Jim Cosman	4.00	1.60
	Dick Hughes		
❑ 385	Jim Fregosi	8.00	3.20
	(Batting wrong)		
❑ 386	Dick Selma DP	4.00	1.60
❑ 387	Cap Peterson DP	4.00	1.60
❑ 388	Arnold Earley DP	4.00	1.60
❑ 389	Alvin Dark MG DP	8.00	3.20
❑ 390	Jim Wynn DP	8.00	3.20
❑ 391	Wilbur Wood DP	8.00	3.20
❑ 392	Tommy Harper DP	8.00	3.20
❑ 393	Jim Bouton DP	8.00	3.20
❑ 394	Jake Wood DP	4.00	1.60
❑ 395	Chris Short	8.00	3.20
❑ 396	Denis Menke	4.00	1.60
	Tony Cloninger		
❑ 397	Willie Smith DP	4.00	1.60
❑ 398	Jeff Torborg	8.00	3.20
❑ 399	Al Worthington DP	4.00	1.60
❑ 400	Bob Clemente DP	120.00	47.50
❑ 401	Jim Coates	4.00	1.60
❑ 402A	Phillies Rookies DP	20.00	8.00
	Grant Jackson		
	Billy Wilson		
	Incomplete stat line		
❑ 402B	Phillies Rookies DP	8.00	3.20
	Grant Jackson		
	Billy Wilson		
❑ 403	Dick Nen	4.00	1.60
❑ 404	Nelson Briles	8.00	3.20
❑ 405	Russ Snyder	4.00	1.60
❑ 406	Lee Elia DP	4.00	1.60
❑ 407	Reds Team	8.00	3.20
❑ 408	Jim Northrup DP	8.00	3.20
❑ 409	Ray Sadecki	4.00	1.60
❑ 410	Lou Johnson DP	4.00	1.60
❑ 411	Dick Howser DP	4.00	1.60
❑ 412	Norm Miller	8.00	3.20
	Doug Rader RC		
❑ 413	Jerry Grote	4.00	1.60
❑ 414	Casey Cox	4.00	1.60
❑ 415	Sonny Jackson	4.00	1.60
❑ 416	Roger Repoz	4.00	1.60
❑ 417A	Bob Bruce ERR DP	30.00	12.00
	(RBAVES on back)		
❑ 417B	Bob Bruce COR DP	4.00	1.60
❑ 418	Sam Mele MG	4.00	1.60
❑ 419	Don Kessinger DP	8.00	3.20
❑ 420	Denny McLain	12.00	4.80
❑ 421	Dal Maxvill DP	4.00	1.60
❑ 422	Hoyt Wilhelm	15.00	6.00
❑ 423	Willie Mays	25.00	10.00
	Willie McCovey DP		
❑ 424	Pedro Gonzalez	4.00	1.60
❑ 425	Pete Mikkelsen	4.00	1.60
❑ 426	Lou Clinton	4.00	1.60
❑ 427A	R.Gomez ERR DP	20.00	8.00
	Incomplete stat		
	line on back		
❑ 427B	R.Gomez COR DP	4.00	1.60
	Complete stat		
	line on back		
❑ 428	Tom Hutton RC	8.00	3.20
	Gene Michael DP		
❑ 429	Garry Roggenburk DP	4.00	1.60
❑ 430	Pete Rose	100.00	40.00
❑ 431	Ted Uhlaender	4.00	1.60
❑ 432	Jimmie Hall DP	4.00	1.60
❑ 433	Al Luplow DP	4.00	1.60
❑ 434	Eddie Fisher DP	4.00	1.60
❑ 435	Mack Jones DP	4.00	1.60
❑ 436	Pete Ward	4.00	1.60
❑ 437	Senators Team	8.00	3.20
❑ 438	Chuck Dobson	4.00	1.60
❑ 439	Byron Browne	4.00	1.60
❑ 440	Steve Hargan	4.00	1.60
❑ 441	Jim Davenport	4.00	1.60
❑ 442	Bill Robinson RC	8.00	3.20
	Joe Verbanic DP		
❑ 443	Tito Francona DP	4.00	1.60
❑ 444	George Smith	4.00	1.60
❑ 445	Don Sutton	25.00	10.00
❑ 446	Russ Nixon DP	4.00	1.60
❑ 447A	Bo Belinsky ERR DP	4.00	1.60
	(Incomplete stat		
	line on back)		
❑ 447B	Bo Belinsky COR DP	8.00	3.20
	(Complete stat		
	line on back)		
❑ 448	Harry Walker DP MG	4.00	1.60
❑ 449	Orlando Pena	4.00	1.60
❑ 450	Richie Allen	8.00	3.20
❑ 451	Fred Newman DP	4.00	1.60
❑ 452	Ed Kranepool	8.00	3.20
❑ 453	A.Monteagudo DP	4.00	1.60
❑ 454A	Juan Marichal CL	12.00	2.40
	Missing left ear		
❑ 454B	Juan Marichal CL	12.00	2.40
	left ear showing		
❑ 455	Tommie Agee	8.00	3.20
❑ 456	Phil Niekro	15.00	6.00
❑ 457	Andy Etchebarren DP	8.00	3.20
❑ 458	Lee Thomas	6.00	2.40
❑ 459	Dick Bosman RC	6.00	2.40
	Pete Craig		
❑ 460	Harmon Killebrew	60.00	24.00
❑ 461	Bob Miller	12.00	4.80
❑ 462	Bob Barton	6.00	2.40
❑ 463	Sam McDowell	12.00	4.80
	Sonny Siebert		
❑ 464	Dan Coombs	6.00	2.40
❑ 465	Willie Horton	12.00	4.80
❑ 466	Bobby Wine	6.00	2.40
❑ 467	Jim O'Toole	6.00	2.40
❑ 468	Ralph Houk MG	6.00	2.40
❑ 469	Len Gabrielson	6.00	2.40
❑ 470	Bob Shaw	6.00	2.40
❑ 471	Rene Lachemann	6.00	2.40
❑ 472	John Gelnar	6.00	2.40
	George Spriggs		
❑ 473	Jose Santiago	6.00	2.40
❑ 474	Bob Tolan	6.00	2.40
❑ 475	Jim Palmer	80.00	32.00
❑ 476	Tony Perez SP	60.00	24.00
❑ 477	Braves Team	15.00	6.00
❑ 478	Bob Humphreys	6.00	2.40
❑ 479	Gary Bell	6.00	2.40
❑ 480	Willie McCovey	40.00	16.00
❑ 481	Leo Durocher MG	20.00	8.00
❑ 482	Bill Monbouquette	6.00	2.40
❑ 483	Jim Landis	6.00	2.40
❑ 484	Jerry Adair	6.00	2.40
❑ 485	Tim McCarver	25.00	10.00
❑ 486	Rich Reese	6.00	2.40
	Bill Whitby		
❑ 487	Tommie Reynolds	6.00	2.40
❑ 488	Gerry Arrigo	6.00	2.40
❑ 489	Doug Clemens	6.00	2.40
❑ 490	Tony Cloninger	6.00	2.40
❑ 491	Sam Bowens	6.00	2.40
❑ 492	Pittsburgh Pirates	15.00	6.00
	Team Card		
❑ 493	Phil Ortega	6.00	2.40
❑ 494	Bill Rigney MG	6.00	2.40
❑ 495	Fritz Peterson	6.00	2.40
❑ 496	Orlando McFarlane	6.00	2.40
❑ 497	Ron Campbell	6.00	2.40
❑ 498	Larry Dierker	12.00	4.80
❑ 499	George Culver	6.00	2.40
	Jose Vidal		
❑ 500	Juan Marichal	25.00	10.00
❑ 501	Jerry Zimmerman	6.00	2.40
❑ 502	Derrell Griffith	6.00	2.40
❑ 503	Los Angeles Dodgers	20.00	8.00

Card	NM	Ex
Team Card		
❑ 504 Orlando Martinez	6.00	2.40
❑ 505 Tommy Helms	12.00	4.80
❑ 506 Smoky Burgess	6.00	2.40
❑ 507 Ed Barnowski	6.00	2.40
Larry Haney RC		
❑ 508 Dick Hall	6.00	2.40
❑ 509 Jim King	6.00	2.40
❑ 510 Bill Mazeroski	25.00	10.00
❑ 511 Don Wert	6.00	2.40
❑ 512 Red Schoendienst MG	25.00	10.00
❑ 513 Marcelino Lopez	6.00	2.40
❑ 514 John Werhas	6.00	2.40
❑ 515 Bert Campaneris	12.00	4.80
❑ 516 Giants Team	15.00	6.00
❑ 517 Fred Talbot	12.00	4.80
❑ 518 Denis Menke	6.00	2.40
❑ 519 Ted Davidson	6.00	2.40
❑ 520 Max Alvis	6.00	2.40
❑ 521 Boog Powell	12.00	4.80
Curt Blefary		
❑ 522 John Stephenson	6.00	2.40
❑ 523 Jim Merritt	6.00	2.40
❑ 524 Felix Mantilla	6.00	2.40
❑ 525 Ron Hunt	6.00	2.40
❑ 526 Pat Dobson RC	6.00	2.40
George Korince		
(See 67T-72)		
❑ 527 Dennis Ribant	6.00	2.40
❑ 528 Rico Petrocelli	20.00	8.00
❑ 529 Gary Wagner	6.00	2.40
❑ 530 Felipe Alou	12.00	4.80
❑ 531 Brooks Robinson CL	15.00	3.00
❑ 532 Jim Hicks	6.00	2.40
❑ 533 Jack Fisher	6.00	2.40
❑ 534 Hank Bauer MG DP	8.00	3.20
❑ 535 Donn Clendenon	25.00	10.00
❑ 536 Joe Niekro RC	50.00	20.00
Paul Popovich		
❑ 537 Chuck Estrada DP	8.00	3.20
❑ 538 J.C. Martin	15.00	6.00
❑ 539 Dick Egan DP	8.00	3.20
❑ 540 Norm Cash	50.00	20.00
❑ 541 Joe Gibbon	15.00	6.00
❑ 542 Rick Monday RC	15.00	6.00
Tony Pierce DP		
❑ 543 Dan Schneider	15.00	6.00
❑ 544 Cleveland Indians	30.00	12.00
Team Card		
❑ 545 Jim Grant	25.00	10.00
❑ 546 Woody Woodward	25.00	10.00
❑ 547 Russ Gibson	8.00	3.20
Bill Rohr DP		
❑ 548 Tony Gonzalez DP	8.00	3.20
❑ 549 Jack Sanford	15.00	6.00
❑ 550 Vada Pinson DP	10.00	4.00
❑ 551 Doug Camilli DP	8.00	3.20
❑ 552 Ted Savage	25.00	10.00
❑ 553 Mike Hegan RC	40.00	16.00
Thad Tillotson		
❑ 554 Andre Rodgers DP	8.00	3.20
❑ 555 Don Cardwell	25.00	10.00
❑ 556 Al Weis DP	8.00	3.20
❑ 557 Al Ferrara	25.00	10.00
❑ 558 Mark Belanger RC	50.00	20.00
Bill Dillman		
❑ 559 Dick Tracewski DP	8.00	3.20
❑ 560 Jim Bunning	60.00	24.00
❑ 561 Sandy Alomar	40.00	16.00
❑ 562 Steve Blass DP	8.00	3.20
❑ 563 Joe Adcock	40.00	16.00
❑ 564 Alonzo Harris	8.00	3.20
Aaron Pointer		
❑ 565 Lew Krausse	25.00	10.00
❑ 566 Gary Geiger DP	8.00	3.20
❑ 567 Steve Hamilton	40.00	16.00
❑ 568 John Sullivan	40.00	16.00
❑ 569 Rod Carew RC	250.00	100.00
Hank Allen DP		
❑ 570 Maury Wills	80.00	32.00
❑ 571 Larry Sherry	25.00	10.00
❑ 572 Don Demeter	25.00	10.00
❑ 573 Chicago White Sox	30.00	12.00
Team Card UER		
(Indians team		
stats on back)		
❑ 574 Jerry Buchek	25.00	10.00
❑ 575 Dave Boswell	15.00	6.00
❑ 576 Ramon Hernandez	40.00	16.00
Norm Gigon RC		
❑ 577 Bill Short	15.00	6.00
❑ 578 John Boccabella	15.00	6.00
❑ 579 Bill Henry	15.00	6.00
❑ 580 Rocky Colavito	150.00	60.00
❑ 581 Bill Denehy	500.00	200.00
Tom Seaver RC		
❑ 582 Jim Owens DP	8.00	3.20
❑ 583 Ray Barker	40.00	16.00
❑ 584 Jimmy Piersall	40.00	16.00
❑ 585 Wally Bunker	25.00	10.00
❑ 586 Manny Jimenez	15.00	6.00
❑ 587 Don Shaw	40.00	16.00
Gary Sutherland RC		
❑ 588 Johnny Klippstein DP	8.00	3.20
❑ 589 Dave Ricketts DP	8.00	3.20
❑ 590 Pete Richert	15.00	6.00
❑ 591 Ty Cline	25.00	10.00
❑ 592 Jim Shellenback	25.00	10.00
Ron Willis RC		
❑ 593 Wes Westrum MG	50.00	20.00
❑ 594 Dan Osinski	40.00	16.00
❑ 595 Cookie Rojas	25.00	10.00
❑ 596 Galen Cisco DP	8.00	3.20
❑ 597 Ted Abernathy	15.00	6.00
❑ 598 Walt Williams	25.00	10.00
Ed Stroud		
❑ 599 Bob Duliba DP	8.00	3.20
❑ 600 Brooks Robinson	250.00	100.00
❑ 601 Bill Bryan DP	8.00	3.20
❑ 602 Juan Pizarro	40.00	16.00
❑ 603 Tim Talton	25.00	10.00
Ramon Webster		
❑ 604 Red Sox Team	125.00	50.00
❑ 605 Mike Shannon	50.00	20.00
❑ 606 Ron Taylor	25.00	10.00
❑ 607 Mickey Stanley	50.00	20.00
❑ 608 Rich Nye	8.00	3.20
John Upham DP		
❑ 609 Tommy John	80.00	27.00

1968 Topps

	NM	Ex
COMPLETE SET (598)	3000.00	1200.00
COMMON CARD (1-457)	2.00	.80
COMMON (458-598)	4.00	1.60
WRAPPER (5-CENT)	25.00	10.00
❑ 1 Roberto Clemente	30.00	12.00
Tony Gonzalez		
Matty Alou LL		
❑ 2 Carl Yastrzemski	15.00	6.00
Frank Robinson		
Al Kaline LL		
❑ 3 Orlando Cepeda	20.00	8.00
Roberto Clemente		
Hank Aaron LL		
❑ 4 Carl Yastrzemski	15.00	6.00
Harmon Killebrew		
Frank Robinson LL		
❑ 5 Hank Aaron	8.00	3.20
Jim Wynn		
Ron Santo		
Willie McCovey LL		
❑ 6 Carl Yastrzemski	8.00	3.20
Harmon Killebrew		
Frank Howard LL		
❑ 7 Phil Niekro	4.00	1.60
Jim Bunning		
Chris Short LL		
❑ 8 Joel Horlen	4.00	1.60
Gary Peters		
Sonny Siebert LL		
❑ 9 Mike McCormick	4.00	1.60
Ferguson Jenkins		
Jim Bunning		
Claude Osteen LL		
❑ 10A Jim Lonborg ERR	4.00	1.60
(Misspelled Lonberg		
on card back)		
Earl Wilson		
Dean Chance LL		
❑ 10B Jim Lonborg COR	4.00	1.60
Earl Wilson		
Dean Chance LL		
❑ 11 Jim Bunning	6.00	2.40
Ferguson Jenkins		
Gaylord Perry LL		
❑ 12 Jim Lonborg UER	4.00	1.60
(Misspelled Longberg		
on card back)		
Sam McDowell		
Dean Chance LL		
❑ 13 Chuck Hartenstein	2.00	.80
❑ 14 Jerry McNertney	2.00	.80
❑ 15 Ron Hunt	2.00	.80
❑ 16 Lou Piniella	6.00	2.40
Richie Scheinblum		
❑ 17 Dick Hall	2.00	.80
❑ 18 Mike Hershberger	2.00	.80
❑ 19 Juan Pizarro	2.00	.80
❑ 20 Brooks Robinson	25.00	10.00
❑ 21 Ron Davis	2.00	.80
❑ 22 Pat Dobson	4.00	1.60
❑ 23 Chico Cardenas	4.00	1.60
❑ 24 Bobby Locke	2.00	.80
❑ 25 Julian Javier	4.00	1.60
❑ 26 Darrell Brandon	2.00	.80
❑ 27 Gil Hodges MG	8.00	3.20
❑ 28 Ted Uhlaender	2.00	.80
❑ 29 Joe Verbanic	2.00	.80
❑ 30 Joe Torre	6.00	2.40
❑ 31 Ed Stroud	2.00	.80
❑ 32 Joe Gibbon	2.00	.80
❑ 33 Pete Ward	2.00	.80
❑ 34 Al Ferrara	2.00	.80
❑ 35 Steve Hargan	2.00	.80
❑ 36 Bob Moose	4.00	1.60
Bob Robertson		
❑ 37 Billy Williams	8.00	3.20
❑ 38 Tony Pierce	2.00	.80
❑ 39 Cookie Rojas	2.00	.80
❑ 40 Denny McLain	8.00	3.20
❑ 41 Julio Gotay	2.00	.80
❑ 42 Larry Haney	2.00	.80
❑ 43 Gary Bell	2.00	.80
❑ 44 Frank Kostro	2.00	.80
❑ 45 Tom Seaver	50.00	20.00
❑ 46 Dave Ricketts	2.00	.80
❑ 47 Ralph Houk MG	4.00	1.60
❑ 48 Ted Davidson	2.00	.80
❑ 49A Eddie Brinkman	2.00	.80
(White team name)		
❑ 49B Eddie Brinkman	50.00	20.00
(Yellow team name)		
❑ 50 Willie Mays	60.00	24.00
❑ 51 Bob Locker	2.00	.80
❑ 52 Hawk Taylor	2.00	.80
❑ 53 Gene Alley	4.00	1.60
❑ 54 Stan Williams	2.00	.80
❑ 55 Felipe Alou	4.00	1.60
❑ 56 Dave Leonhard	2.00	.80
Dave May RC		
❑ 57 Dan Schneider	2.00	.80
❑ 58 Eddie Mathews	15.00	6.00
❑ 59 Don Lock	2.00	.80
❑ 60 Ken Holtzman	4.00	1.60
❑ 61 Reggie Smith	4.00	1.60
❑ 62 Chuck Dobson	2.00	.80
❑ 63 Dick Kenworthy	2.00	.80
❑ 64 Jim Merritt	2.00	.80

❑ 65 John Roseboro 4.00 1.60
❑ 66A Casey Cox .... 2.00 .80
(White team name)
❑ 66B Casey Cox 100.00 40.00
(Yellow team name)
❑ 67 Jim Kaat CL 6.00 1.20
❑ 68 Ron Willis .... 2.00 .80
❑ 69 Tom Tresh 4.00 1.60
❑ 70 Bob Veale 4.00 1.60
❑ 71 Vern Fuller .... 2.00 .80
❑ 72 Tommy John 6.00 2.40
❑ 73 Jim Ray Hart 4.00 1.60
❑ 74 Milt Pappas 4.00 1.60
❑ 75 Don Mincher .... 2.00 .80
❑ 76 Jim Britton 4.00 1.60
Ron Reed
❑ 77 Don Wilson 4.00 1.60
❑ 78 Jim Northrup 6.00 2.40
❑ 79 Ted Kubiak .... 2.00 .80
❑ 80 Rod Carew 50.00 20.00
❑ 81 Larry Jackson .... 2.00 .80
❑ 82 Sam Bowens .... 2.00 .80
❑ 83 John Stephenson .... 2.00 .80
❑ 84 Bob Tolan .... 2.00 .80
❑ 85 Gaylord Perry 8.00 3.20
❑ 86 Willie Stargell 8.00 3.20
❑ 87 Dick Williams MG 4.00 1.60
❑ 88 Phil Regan 4.00 1.60
❑ 89 Jake Gibbs 4.00 1.60
❑ 90 Vada Pinson 4.00 1.60
❑ 91 Jim Ollom .... 2.00 .80
❑ 92 Ed Kranepool 4.00 1.60
❑ 93 Tony Cloninger .... 2.00 .80
❑ 94 Lee Maye .... 2.00 .80
❑ 95 Bob Aspromonte .... 2.00 .80
❑ 96 Frank Coggins .... 2.00 .80
Dick Nold
❑ 97 Tom Phoebus .... 2.00 .80
❑ 98 Gary Sutherland .... 2.00 .80
❑ 99 Rocky Colavito 8.00 3.20
❑ 100 Bob Gibson 25.00 10.00
❑ 101 Glenn Beckert 4.00 1.60
❑ 102 Jose Cardenal 4.00 1.60
❑ 103 Don Sutton 8.00 3.20
❑ 104 Dick Dietz .... 2.00 .80
❑ 105 Al Downing 4.00 1.60
❑ 106 Dalton Jones .... 2.00 .80
❑ 107A Juan Marichal CL 6.00 1.20
Tan wide mesh
❑ 107B Juan Marichal CL 6.00 1.20
Brown fine mesh
❑ 108 Don Pavletich .... 2.00 .80
❑ 109 Bert Campaneris 4.00 1.60
❑ 110 Hank Aaron 60.00 24.00
❑ 111 Rich Reese .... 2.00 .80
❑ 112 Woody Fryman .... 2.00 .80
❑ 113 Tom Matchick 4.00 1.60
Daryl Patterson
❑ 114 Ron Swoboda 4.00 1.60
❑ 115 Sam McDowell 4.00 1.60
❑ 116 Ken McMullen .... 2.00 .80
❑ 117 Larry Jaster .... 2.00 .80
❑ 118 Mark Belanger 4.00 1.60
❑ 119 Ted Savage .... 2.00 .80
❑ 120 Mel Stottlemyre 4.00 1.60
❑ 121 Jimmie Hall .... 2.00 .80
❑ 122 Gene Mauch MG 4.00 1.60
❑ 123 Jose Santiago .... 2.00 .80
❑ 124 Nate Oliver .... 2.00 .80
❑ 125 Joel Horlen .... 2.00 .80
❑ 126 Bobby Etheridge .... 2.00 .80
❑ 127 Paul Lindblad .... 2.00 .80
❑ 128 Tom Dukes .... 2.00 .80
Alonzo Harris
❑ 129 Mickey Stanley 6.00 2.40
❑ 130 Tony Perez 8.00 3.20
❑ 131 Frank Bertaina .... 2.00 .80
❑ 132 Bud Harrelson 4.00 1.60
❑ 133 Fred Whitfield .... 2.00 .80
❑ 134 Pat Jarvis .... 2.00 .80
❑ 135 Paul Blair 4.00 1.60
❑ 136 Randy Hundley 4.00 1.60
❑ 137 Twins Team 4.00 1.60
❑ 138 Ruben Amaro .... 2.00 .80
❑ 139 Chris Short .... 2.00 .80
❑ 140 Tony Conigliaro 8.00 3.20
❑ 141 Dal Maxvill .... 2.00 .80
❑ 142 Buddy Bradford .... 2.00 .80
Bill Voss
❑ 143 Pete Cimino .... 2.00 .80
❑ 144 Joe Morgan 12.00 4.80
❑ 145 Don Drysdale 12.00 4.80
❑ 146 Sal Bando 4.00 1.60
❑ 147 Frank Linzy .... 2.00 .80
❑ 148 Dave Bristol MG .... 2.00 .80
❑ 149 Bob Saverine .... 2.00 .80
❑ 150 Roberto Clemente 80.00 32.00
❑ 151 Lou Brock WS 10.00 4.00
❑ 152 Carl Yastrzemski WS 10.00 4.00
❑ 153 Nellie Briles WS 5.00 2.00
❑ 154 Bob Gibson WS 10.00 4.00
❑ 155 Jim Lonborg WS 5.00 2.00
❑ 156 Rico Petrocelli WS 5.00 2.00
❑ 157 World Series Game 7 .... 5.00 2.00
St. Louis wins it
❑ 158 WS Summary 5.00 2.00
Cardinals celebrate
❑ 159 Don Kessinger 4.00 1.60
❑ 160 Earl Wilson 4.00 1.60
❑ 161 Norm Miller .... 2.00 .80
❑ 162 Hal Gilson 4.00 1.60
Mike Torrez
❑ 163 Gene Brabender .... 2.00 .80
❑ 164 Ramon Webster .... 2.00 .80
❑ 165 Tony Oliva 6.00 2.40
❑ 166 Claude Raymond .... 2.00 .80
❑ 167 Elston Howard 6.00 2.40
❑ 168 Dodgers Team 4.00 1.60
❑ 169 Bob Bolin .... 2.00 .80
❑ 170 Jim Fregosi 4.00 1.60
❑ 171 Don Nottebart .... 2.00 .80
❑ 172 Walt Williams .... 2.00 .80
❑ 173 John Boozer .... 2.00 .80
❑ 174 Bob Tillman .... 2.00 .80
❑ 175 Maury Wills 6.00 2.40
❑ 176 Bob Allen .... 2.00 .80
❑ 177 Jerry Koosman RC 500.00 200.00
Nolan Ryan RC
❑ 178 Don Wert 4.00 1.60
❑ 179 Bill Stoneman .... 2.00 .80
❑ 180 Curt Flood 6.00 2.40
❑ 181 Jerry Zimmerman .... 2.00 .80
❑ 182 Dave Giusti .... 2.00 .80
❑ 183 Bob Kennedy MG 4.00 1.60
❑ 184 Lou Johnson .... 2.00 .80
❑ 185 Tom Haller .... 2.00 .80
❑ 186 Eddie Watt .... 2.00 .80
❑ 187 Sonny Jackson .... 2.00 .80
❑ 188 Cap Peterson .... 2.00 .80
❑ 189 Bill Landis .... 2.00 .80
❑ 190 Bill White 4.00 1.60
❑ 191 Dan Frisella .... 2.00 .80
❑ 192A Carl Yastrzemski CL 8.00 1.60
Special Baseball Playing Card
❑ 192B Carl Yastrzemski CL 8.00 1.60
Special Baseball
Playing Card Game
❑ 193 Jack Hamilton .... 2.00 .80
❑ 194 Don Buford .... 2.00 .80
❑ 195 Joe Pepitone 4.00 1.60
❑ 196 Gary Nolan 4.00 1.60
❑ 197 Larry Brown .... 2.00 .80
❑ 198 Roy Face 4.00 1.60
❑ 199 Roberto Rodriquez .... 2.00 .80
Darrell Osteen
❑ 200 Orlando Cepeda 8.00 3.20
❑ 201 Mike Marshall RC 4.00 1.60
❑ 202 Adolfo Phillips .... 2.00 .80
❑ 203 Dick Kelley .... 2.00 .80
❑ 204 Andy Etchebarren .... 2.00 .80
❑ 205 Juan Marichal 8.00 3.20
❑ 206 Cal Ermer MG .... 2.00 .80
❑ 207 Carroll Sembera .... 2.00 .80
❑ 208 Willie Davis 4.00 1.60
❑ 209 Tim Cullen .... 2.00 .80
❑ 210 Gary Peters .... 2.00 .80
❑ 211 J.C. Martin .... 2.00 .80
❑ 212 Dave Morehead .... 2.00 .80
❑ 213 Chico Ruiz .... 2.00 .80
❑ 214 Stan Bahnsen 4.00 1.60
Frank Fernandez
❑ 215 Jim Bunning 8.00 3.20
❑ 216 Bubba Morton .... 2.00 .80
❑ 217 Dick Farrell .... 2.00 .80
❑ 218 Ken Suarez .... 2.00 .80
❑ 219 Rob Gardner .... 2.00 .80
❑ 220 Harmon Killebrew 15.00 6.00
❑ 221 Braves Team 4.00 1.60
❑ 222 Jim Hardin .... 2.00 .80
❑ 223 Ollie Brown .... 2.00 .80
❑ 224 Jack Aker .... 2.00 .80
❑ 225 Richie Allen 6.00 2.40
❑ 226 Jimmie Price .... 2.00 .80
❑ 227 Joe Hoerner .... 2.00 .80
❑ 228 Jack Billingham 4.00 1.60
Jim Fairey
❑ 229 Fred Klages .... 2.00 .80
❑ 230 Pete Rose 60.00 24.00
❑ 231 Dave Baldwin .... 2.00 .80
❑ 232 Denis Menke .... 2.00 .80
❑ 233 George Scott 4.00 1.60
❑ 234 Bill Monbouquette .... 2.00 .80
❑ 235 Ron Santo 8.00 3.20
❑ 236 Tug McGraw 6.00 2.40
❑ 237 Alvin Dark MG 4.00 1.60
❑ 238 Tom Satriano .... 2.00 .80
❑ 239 Bill Henry .... 2.00 .80
❑ 240 Al Kaline 40.00 16.00
❑ 241 Felix Millan .... 2.00 .80
❑ 242 Moe Drabowsky 4.00 1.60
❑ 243 Rich Rollins .... 2.00 .80
❑ 244 John Donaldson .... 2.00 .80
❑ 245 Tony Gonzalez .... 2.00 .80
❑ 246 Fritz Peterson 4.00 1.60
❑ 247 Johnny Bench RC 125.00 50.00
Ron Tompkins
❑ 248 Fred Valentine .... 2.00 .80
❑ 249 Bill Singer .... 2.00 .80
❑ 250 Carl Yastrzemski 30.00 12.00
❑ 251 Manny Sanguillen RC 6.00 2.40
❑ 252 Angels Team 4.00 1.60
❑ 253 Dick Hughes .... 2.00 .80
❑ 254 Cleon Jones 4.00 1.60
❑ 255 Dean Chance 4.00 1.60
❑ 256 Norm Cash 6.00 2.40
❑ 257 Phil Niekro 8.00 3.20
❑ 258 Jose Arcia .... 2.00 .80
Bill Schlesinger
❑ 259 Ken Boyer 6.00 2.40
❑ 260 Jim Wynn 4.00 1.60
❑ 261 Dave Duncan 4.00 1.60
❑ 262 Rick Wise 4.00 1.60
❑ 263 Horace Clarke 4.00 1.60
❑ 264 Ted Abernathy .... 2.00 .80
❑ 265 Tommy Davis 4.00 1.60
❑ 266 Paul Popovich .... 2.00 .80
❑ 267 Herman Franks MG .... 2.00 .80
❑ 268 Bob Humphreys .... 2.00 .80
❑ 269 Bob Tiefenauer .... 2.00 .80
❑ 270 Matty Alou 4.00 1.60
❑ 271 Bobby Knoop .... 2.00 .80
❑ 272 Ray Culp .... 2.00 .80
❑ 273 Dave Johnson 4.00 1.60
❑ 274 Mike Cuellar 4.00 1.60
❑ 275 Tim McCarver 6.00 2.40
❑ 276 Jim Roland .... 2.00 .80
❑ 277 Jerry Buchek .... 2.00 .80
❑ 278 Orlando Cepeda CL 6.00 1.20
❑ 279 Bill Hands .... 2.00 .80
❑ 280 Mickey Mantle 300.00 120.00
❑ 281 Jim Campanis .... 2.00 .80
❑ 282 Rick Monday 4.00 1.60
❑ 283 Mel Queen .... 2.00 .80
❑ 284 Johnny Briggs .... 2.00 .80
❑ 285 Dick McAuliffe 6.00 2.40
❑ 286 Cecil Upshaw .... 2.00 .80
❑ 287 Mickey Abarbanel .... 2.00 .80
Cisco Carlos
❑ 288 Dave Wickersham .... 2.00 .80
❑ 289 Woody Held .... 2.00 .80
❑ 290 Willie McCovey 12.00 4.80
❑ 291 Dick Lines .... 2.00 .80
❑ 292 Art Shamsky .... 2.00 .80
❑ 293 Bruce Howard .... 2.00 .80
❑ 294 Red Schoendienst MG 6.00 2.40
❑ 295 Sonny Siebert .... 2.00 .80
❑ 296 Byron Browne .... 2.00 .80
❑ 297 Russ Gibson .... 2.00 .80

❑ 298 Jim Brewer 2.00 .80
❑ 299 Gene Michael 4.00 1.60
❑ 300 Rusty Staub 4.00 1.60
❑ 301 George Mitterwald 2.00 .80
Rick Renick
❑ 302 Gerry Arrigo 2.00 .80
❑ 303 Dick Green 4.00 1.60
❑ 304 Sandy Valdespino 2.00 .80
❑ 305 Minnie Rojas 2.00 .80
❑ 306 Mike Ryan 2.00 .80
❑ 307 John Hiller 4.00 1.60
❑ 308 Pirates Team 4.00 1.60
❑ 309 Ken Henderson 2.00 .80
❑ 310 Luis Aparicio 8.00 3.20
❑ 311 Jack Lamabe 2.00 .80
❑ 312 Curt Blefary 2.00 .80
❑ 313 Al Weis 2.00 .80
❑ 314 Bill Rohr 2.00 .80
George Spriggs
❑ 315 Zoilo Versalles 2.00 .80
❑ 316 Steve Barber 2.00 .80
❑ 317 Ron Brand 2.00 .80
❑ 318 Chico Salmon 2.00 .80
❑ 319 George Culver 2.00 .80
❑ 320 Frank Howard 4.00 1.60
❑ 321 Leo Durocher MG 6.00 2.40
❑ 322 Dave Boswell 2.00 .80
❑ 323 Deron Johnson 4.00 1.60
❑ 324 Jim Nash 2.00 .80
❑ 325 Manny Mota 4.00 1.60
❑ 326 Dennis Ribant 2.00 .80
❑ 327 Tony Taylor 4.00 1.60
❑ 328 Chuck Vinson 2.00 .80
Jim Weaver
❑ 329 Duane Josephson 2.00 .80
❑ 330 Roger Maris 50.00 20.00
❑ 331 Dan Osinski 2.00 .80
❑ 332 Doug Rader 4.00 1.60
❑ 333 Ron Herbel 2.00 .80
❑ 334 Orioles Team 4.00 1.60
❑ 335 Bob Allison 4.00 1.60
❑ 336 John Purdin 2.00 .80
❑ 337 Bill Robinson 4.00 1.60
❑ 338 Bob Johnson 2.00 .80
❑ 339 Rich Nye 2.00 .80
❑ 340 Max Alvis 2.00 .80
❑ 341 Jim Lemon MG 2.00 .80
❑ 342 Ken Johnson 2.00 .80
❑ 343 Jim Gosger 2.00 .80
❑ 344 Donn Clendenon 4.00 1.60
❑ 345 Bob Hendley 2.00 .80
❑ 346 Jerry Adair 2.00 .80
❑ 347 George Brunet 2.00 .80
❑ 348 Larry Colton 2.00 .80
Dick Thoenen
❑ 349 Ed Spiezio 4.00 1.60
❑ 350 Hoyt Wilhelm 8.00 3.20
❑ 351 Bob Barton 2.00 .80
❑ 352 Jackie Hernandez 2.00 .80
❑ 353 Mack Jones 2.00 .80
❑ 354 Pete Richert 2.00 .80
❑ 355 Ernie Banks 25.00 10.00
❑ 356A Ken Holtzman CL 6.00 1.20
Head centered within circle
❑ 356B Ken Holtzman 6.00 1.20
Head shifted right
within circle
❑ 357 Len Gabrielson 2.00 .80
❑ 358 Mike Epstein 2.00 .80
❑ 359 Joe Moeller 2.00 .80
❑ 360 Willie Horton 6.00 2.40
❑ 361 Harmon Killebrew AS 8.00 3.20
❑ 362 Orlando Cepeda AS 6.00 2.40
❑ 363 Rod Carew AS 8.00 3.20
❑ 364 Joe Morgan AS 8.00 3.20
❑ 365 Brooks Robinson AS 8.00 3.20
❑ 366 Ron Santo AS 6.00 2.40
❑ 367 Jim Fregosi AS 4.00 1.60
❑ 368 Gene Alley AS 4.00 1.60
❑ 369 Carl Yastrzemski AS 10.00 4.00
❑ 370 Hank Aaron AS 20.00 8.00
❑ 371 Tony Oliva AS 6.00 2.40
❑ 372 Lou Brock AS 8.00 3.20
❑ 373 Frank Robinson AS 8.00 3.20
❑ 374 Bob Clemente AS 30.00 12.00
❑ 375 Bill Freehan AS 4.00 1.60
❑ 376 Tim McCarver AS 4.00 1.60
❑ 377 Joel Horlen AS 4.00 1.60
❑ 378 Bob Gibson AS 8.00 3.20
❑ 379 Gary Peters AS 4.00 1.60
❑ 380 Ken Holtzman AS 4.00 1.60
❑ 381 Boog Powell 4.00 1.60
❑ 382 Ramon Hernandez 2.00 .80
❑ 383 Steve Whitaker 2.00 .80
❑ 384 Bill Henry 6.00 2.40
Hal McRae RC
❑ 385 Jim Hunter 10.00 4.00
❑ 386 Greg Goossen 2.00 .80
❑ 387 Joe Foy 2.00 .80
❑ 388 Ray Washburn 2.00 .80
❑ 389 Jay Johnstone 4.00 1.60
❑ 390 Bill Mazeroski 8.00 3.20
❑ 391 Bob Priddy 2.00 .80
❑ 392 Grady Hatton MG 2.00 .80
❑ 393 Jim Perry 4.00 1.60
❑ 394 Tommie Aaron 6.00 2.40
❑ 395 Camilo Pascual 4.00 1.60
❑ 396 Bobby Wine 2.00 .80
❑ 397 Vic Davalillo 2.00 .80
❑ 398 Jim Grant 2.00 .80
❑ 399 Ray Oyler 4.00 1.60
❑ 400A Mike McCormick 4.00 1.60
(Yellow letters)
❑ 400B Mike McCormick 150.00 60.00
(Team name in
white letters)
❑ 401 Mets Team 4.00 1.60
❑ 402 Mike Hegan 4.00 1.60
❑ 403 John Buzhardt 2.00 .80
❑ 404 Floyd Robinson 2.00 .80
❑ 405 Tommy Helms 4.00 1.60
❑ 406 Dick Ellsworth 2.00 .80
❑ 407 Gary Kolb 2.00 .80
❑ 408 Steve Carlton 30.00 12.00
❑ 409 Frank Peters 2.00 .80
Ron Stone
❑ 410 Ferguson Jenkins 10.00 4.00
❑ 411 Ron Hansen 2.00 .80
❑ 412 Clay Carroll 4.00 1.60
❑ 413 Tom McCraw 2.00 .80
❑ 414 Mickey Lolich 8.00 3.20
❑ 415 Johnny Callison 4.00 1.60
❑ 416 Bill Rigney MG 2.00 .80
❑ 417 Willie Crawford 2.00 .80
❑ 418 Eddie Fisher 2.00 .80
❑ 419 Jack Hiatt 2.00 .80
❑ 420 Cesar Tovar 2.00 .80
❑ 421 Ron Taylor 2.00 .80
❑ 422 Rene Lachemann 2.00 .80
❑ 423 Fred Gladding 2.00 .80
❑ 424 Chicago White Sox 4.00 1.60
Team Card
❑ 425 Jim Maloney 4.00 1.60
❑ 426 Hank Allen 2.00 .80
❑ 427 Dick Calmus 2.00 .80
❑ 428 Vic Roznovsky 2.00 .80
❑ 429 Tommie Sisk 2.00 .80
❑ 430 Rico Petrocelli 4.00 1.60
❑ 431 Dooley Womack 2.00 .80
❑ 432 Bill Davis 2.00 .80
Jose Vidal
❑ 433 Bob Rodgers 2.00 .80
❑ 434 Ricardo Joseph 2.00 .80
❑ 435 Ron Perranoski 4.00 1.60
❑ 436 Hal Lanier 2.00 .80
❑ 437 Don Cardwell 2.00 .80
❑ 438 Lee Thomas 4.00 1.60
❑ 439 Lum Harris MG 2.00 .80
❑ 440 Claude Osteen 4.00 1.60
❑ 441 Alex Johnson 4.00 1.60
❑ 442 Dick Bosman 2.00 .80
❑ 443 Joe Azcue 2.00 .80
❑ 444 Jack Fisher 2.00 .80
❑ 445 Mike Shannon 4.00 1.60
❑ 446 Ron Kline 2.00 .80
❑ 447 George Korince 4.00 1.60
Fred Lasher
❑ 448 Gary Wagner 2.00 .80
❑ 449 Gene Oliver 2.00 .80
❑ 450 Jim Kaat 6.00 2.40
❑ 451 Al Spangler 2.00 .80
❑ 452 Jesus Alou 2.00 .80
❑ 453 Sammy Ellis 2.00 .80
❑ 454A Frank Robinson CL 8.00 1.60
Cap complete within circle
❑ 454B Frank Robinson CL 8.00 1.60
Cap partially within circle
❑ 455 Rico Carty 4.00 1.60
❑ 456 John O'Donoghue 2.00 .80
❑ 457 Jim Lefebvre 4.00 1.60
❑ 458 Lew Krausse 6.00 2.40
❑ 459 Dick Simpson 4.00 1.60
❑ 460 Jim Lonborg 6.00 2.40
❑ 461 Chuck Hiller 4.00 1.60
❑ 462 Barry Moore 4.00 1.60
❑ 463 Jim Schaffer 4.00 1.60
❑ 464 Don McMahon 4.00 1.60
❑ 465 Tommie Agee 10.00 4.00
❑ 466 Bill Dillman 4.00 1.60
❑ 467 Dick Howser 10.00 4.00
❑ 468 Larry Sherry 4.00 1.60
❑ 469 Ty Cline 4.00 1.60
❑ 470 Bill Freehan 10.00 4.00
❑ 471 Orlando Pena 4.00 1.60
❑ 472 Walter Alston MG 6.00 2.40
❑ 473 Al Worthington 4.00 1.60
❑ 474 Paul Schaal 4.00 1.60
❑ 475 Joe Niekro 6.00 2.40
❑ 476 Woody Woodward 4.00 1.60
❑ 477 Philadelphia Phillies 8.00 3.20
Team Card
❑ 478 Dave McNally 6.00 2.40
❑ 479 Phil Gagliano 6.00 2.40
❑ 480 Tony Oliva 80.00 32.00
Chico Cardenas
Bob Clemente
❑ 481 John Wyatt 4.00 1.60
❑ 482 Jose Pagan 4.00 1.60
❑ 483 Darold Knowles 4.00 1.60
❑ 484 Phil Roof 4.00 1.60
❑ 485 Ken Berry 6.00 2.40
❑ 486 Cal Koonce 4.00 1.60
❑ 487 Lee May 10.00 4.00
❑ 488 Dick Tracewski 6.00 2.40
❑ 489 Wally Bunker 4.00 1.60
❑ 490 Harmon Killebrew 150.00 60.00
Willie Mays
Mickey Mantle
❑ 491 Denny Lemaster 4.00 1.60
❑ 492 Jeff Torborg 6.00 2.40
❑ 493 Jim McGlothlin 4.00 1.60
❑ 494 Ray Sadecki 4.00 1.60
❑ 495 Leon Wagner 4.00 1.60
❑ 496 Steve Hamilton 6.00 2.40
❑ 497 Cardinals Team 8.00 3.20
❑ 498 Bill Bryan 6.00 2.40
❑ 499 Steve Blass 6.00 2.40
❑ 500 Frank Robinson 30.00 12.00
❑ 501 John Odom 6.00 2.40
❑ 502 Mike Andrews 4.00 1.60
❑ 503 Al Jackson 6.00 2.40
❑ 504 Russ Snyder 4.00 1.60
❑ 505 Joe Sparma 10.00 4.00
❑ 506 Clarence Jones RC 4.00 1.60
❑ 507 Wade Blasingame 4.00 1.60
❑ 508 Duke Sims 4.00 1.60
❑ 509 Dennis Higgins 4.00 1.60
❑ 510 Ron Fairly 10.00 4.00
❑ 511 Bill Kelso 4.00 1.60
❑ 512 Grant Jackson 4.00 1.60
❑ 513 Hank Bauer MG 6.00 2.40
❑ 514 Al McBean 4.00 1.60
❑ 515 Russ Nixon 4.00 1.60
❑ 516 Pete Mikkelsen 4.00 1.60
❑ 517 Diego Segui 6.00 2.40
❑ 518A Clete Boyer CL ERR 12.00 2.40
539 AL Rookies
❑ 518B Clete Boyer CL COR 12.00 2.40
539 ML Rookies
❑ 519 Jerry Stephenson 4.00 1.60
❑ 520 Lou Brock 25.00 10.00
❑ 521 Don Shaw 4.00 1.60
❑ 522 Wayne Causey 4.00 1.60
❑ 523 John Tsitouris 4.00 1.60
❑ 524 Andy Kosco 6.00 2.40
❑ 525 Jim Davenport 4.00 1.60
❑ 526 Bill Denehy 4.00 1.60
❑ 527 Tito Francona 4.00 1.60

❑ 528 Tigers Team 60.00 24.00
❑ 529 Bruce Von Hoff 4.00 1.60
❑ 530 Brooks Robinson 40.00 16.00
Frank Robinson
❑ 531 Chuck Hinton 4.00 1.60
❑ 532 Luis Tiant 6.00 2.40
❑ 533 Wes Parker 6.00 2.40
❑ 534 Bob Miller 6.00 2.40
❑ 535 Danny Cater 6.00 2.40
❑ 536 Bill Short 4.00 1.60
❑ 537 Norm Siebern 6.00 2.40
❑ 538 Manny Jimenez 6.00 2.40
❑ 539 Jim Ray 4.00 1.60
Mike Ferraro
❑ 540 Nelson Briles 6.00 2.40
❑ 541 Sandy Alomar 6.00 2.40
❑ 542 John Boccabella 4.00 1.60
❑ 543 Bob Lee 4.00 1.60
❑ 544 Mayo Smith MG 12.00 4.80
❑ 545 Lindy McDaniel 6.00 2.40
❑ 546 Roy White 6.00 2.40
❑ 547 Dan Coombs 4.00 1.60
❑ 548 Bernie Allen 4.00 1.60
❑ 549 Curt Motton 4.00 1.60
Roger Nelson
❑ 550 Clete Boyer 6.00 2.40
❑ 551 Darrell Sutherland 4.00 1.60
❑ 552 Ed Kirkpatrick 4.00 1.60
❑ 553 Hank Aguirre 4.00 1.60
❑ 554 A's Team 10.00 4.00
❑ 555 Jose Tartabull 6.00 2.40
❑ 556 Dick Selma 4.00 1.60
❑ 557 Frank Quilici 6.00 2.40
❑ 558 Johnny Edwards 4.00 1.60
❑ 559 Carl Taylor 4.00 1.60
Luke Walker
❑ 560 Paul Casanova 4.00 1.60
❑ 561 Lee Elia 4.00 1.60
❑ 562 Jim Bouton 6.00 2.40
❑ 563 Ed Charles 4.00 1.60
❑ 564 Eddie Stanky MG 6.00 2.40
❑ 565 Larry Dierker 6.00 2.40
❑ 566 Ken Harrelson 6.00 2.40
❑ 567 Clay Dalrymple 4.00 1.60
❑ 568 Willie Smith 4.00 1.60
❑ 569 Ivan Murrell 4.00 1.60
Les Rohr
❑ 570 Rick Reichardt 4.00 1.60
❑ 571 Tony LaRussa 12.00 4.80
❑ 572 Don Bosch 4.00 1.60
❑ 573 Joe Coleman 4.00 1.60
❑ 574 Cincinnati Reds 10.00 4.00
Team Card
❑ 575 Jim Palmer 40.00 16.00
❑ 576 Dave Adlesh 4.00 1.60
❑ 577 Fred Talbot 4.00 1.60
❑ 578 Orlando Martinez 4.00 1.60
❑ 579 Larry Hisle RC 10.00 4.00
Mike Lum
❑ 580 Bob Bailey 4.00 1.60
❑ 581 Garry Roggenburk 4.00 1.60
❑ 582 Jerry Grote 10.00 4.00
❑ 583 Gates Brown 10.00 4.00
❑ 584 Larry Shepard MG 4.00 1.60
❑ 585 Wilbur Wood 6.00 2.40
❑ 586 Jim Pagliaroni 6.00 2.40
❑ 587 Roger Repoz 4.00 1.60
❑ 588 Dick Schofield 4.00 1.60
❑ 589 Ron Clark 4.00 1.60
Moe Ogier
❑ 590 Tommy Harper 6.00 2.40
❑ 591 Dick Nen 4.00 1.60
❑ 592 John Bateman 4.00 1.60
❑ 593 Lee Stange 4.00 1.60
❑ 594 Phil Linz 6.00 2.40
❑ 595 Phil Ortega 4.00 1.60
❑ 596 Charlie Smith 4.00 1.60
❑ 597 Bill McCool 4.00 1.60
❑ 598 Jerry May 6.00 1.85

1969 Topps

	NM	Ex
COMP. MASTER (695)	5000.00	2000.00
COMPLETE SET (664)	2800.00	1100.00
COMMON (1-218/328-512)	1.50	.60
COMMON (219-327)	2.50	1.00
COMMON (513-588)	2.00	.80
COMMON (589-664)	3.00	1.20
WRAPPER (5-CENT)	20.00	8.00

❑ 1 Carl Yastrzemski 15.00 5.25
Danny Cater
Tony Oliva LL
❑ 2 Pete Rose 8.00 3.20
Matty Alou
Felipe Alou LL
❑ 3 Ken Harrelson 4.00 1.60
Frank Howard
Jim Northrup LL
❑ 4 Willie McCovey 6.00 2.40
Ron Santo
Billy Williams LL
❑ 5 Frank Howard 4.00 1.60
Willie Horton
Ken Harrelson LL
❑ 6 Willie McCovey 6.00 2.40
Richie Allen
Ernie Banks LL
❑ 7 Luis Tiant 4.00 1.60
Sam McDowell
Dave McNally LL
❑ 8 Bob Gibson 6.00 2.40
Bobby Bolin
Bob Veale LL
❑ 9 Denny McLain 4.00 1.60
Dave McNally
Luis Tiant
Mel Stottlemyre LL
❑ 10 Juan Marichal 8.00 3.20
Bob Gibson
Fergie Jenkins LL
❑ 11 Sam McDowell 4.00 1.60
Denny McLain
Luis Tiant LL
❑ 12 Bob Gibson 4.00 1.60
Fergie Jenkins
Bill Singer LL
❑ 13 Mickey Stanley 2.50 1.00
❑ 14 Al McBean .... 1.50 .60
❑ 15 Boog Powell 4.00 1.60
❑ 16 Cesar Gutierrez .... 1.50 .60
Rich Robertson
❑ 17 Mike Marshall 2.50 1.00
❑ 18 Dick Schofield .... 1.50 .60
❑ 19 Ken Suarez .... 1.50 .60
❑ 20 Ernie Banks 20.00 8.00
❑ 21 Jose Santiago .... 1.50 .60
❑ 22 Jesus Alou 2.50 1.00
❑ 23 Lew Krausse .... 1.50 .60
❑ 24 Walt Alston MG 4.00 1.60
❑ 25 Roy White 2.50 1.00
❑ 26 Clay Carroll 2.50 1.00
❑ 27 Bernie Allen .... 1.50 .60
❑ 28 Mike Ryan .... 1.50 .60
❑ 29 Dave Morehead .... 1.50 .60
❑ 30 Bob Allison 2.50 1.00
❑ 31 Gary Gentry RC 2.50 1.00
Amos Otis RC
❑ 32 Sammy Ellis .... 1.50 .60
❑ 33 Wayne Causey .... 1.50 .60
❑ 34 Gary Peters .... 1.50 .60
❑ 35 Joe Morgan 10.00 4.00
❑ 36 Luke Walker .... 1.50 .60
❑ 37 Curt Motton .... 1.50 .60
❑ 38 Zoilo Versalles 2.50 1.00
❑ 39 Dick Hughes .... 1.50 .60
❑ 40 Mayo Smith MG .... 1.50 .60
❑ 41 Bob Barton .... 1.50 .60
❑ 42 Tommy Harper 2.50 1.00
❑ 43 Joe Niekro 2.50 1.00
❑ 44 Danny Cater .... 1.50 .60
❑ 45 Maury Wills 2.50 1.00
❑ 46 Fritz Peterson 2.50 1.00
❑ 47A Paul Popovich 2.50 1.00
No helmet emblem, thick airbrushing
❑ 47B Paul Popovich 2.50 1.00
No helmet emblem, light airbrushing
❑ 47C Paul Popovich 25.00 10.00
(C emblem on helmet)
❑ 48 Brant Alyea .... 1.50 .60
❑ 49A Royals Rookies ERR 25.00 10.00
Steve Jones
E. Rodriquez
❑ 49B Royals Rookies COR .... 1.50 .60
Steve Jones
E. Rodriguez
❑ 50 Roberto Clemente UER .. 60.00 24.00
Bats Right listed twice
❑ 51 Woody Fryman 2.50 1.00
❑ 52 Mike Andrews .... 1.50 .60
❑ 53 Sonny Jackson .... 1.50 .60
❑ 54 Cisco Carlos .... 1.50 .60
❑ 55 Jerry Grote 2.50 1.00
❑ 56 Rich Reese .... 1.50 .60
❑ 57 Denny McLain CL 6.00 1.20
❑ 58 Fred Gladding .... 1.50 .60
❑ 59 Jay Johnstone 2.50 1.00
❑ 60 Nelson Briles 2.50 1.00
❑ 61 Jimmie Hall .... 1.50 .60
❑ 62 Chico Salmon .... 1.50 .60
❑ 63 Jim Hickman 2.50 1.00
❑ 64 Bill Monbouquette .... 1.50 .60
❑ 65 Willie Davis 2.50 1.00
❑ 66 Mike Adamson .... 1.50 .60
Merv Rettenmund
❑ 67 Bill Stoneman 2.50 1.00
❑ 68 Dave Duncan 2.50 1.00
❑ 69 Steve Hamilton 2.50 1.00
❑ 70 Tommy Helms 2.50 1.00
❑ 71 Steve Whitaker 2.50 1.00
❑ 72 Ron Taylor .... 1.50 .60
❑ 73 Johnny Briggs .... 1.50 .60
❑ 74 Preston Gomez MG 2.50 1.00
❑ 75 Luis Aparicio 6.00 2.40
❑ 76 Norm Miller .... 1.50 .60
❑ 77A Ron Perranoski 2.50 1.00
(No emblem on cap)
❑ 77B Ron Perranoski 25.00 10.00
(LA on cap)
❑ 78 Tom Satriano .... 1.50 .60
❑ 79 Milt Pappas 2.50 1.00
❑ 80 Norm Cash 2.50 1.00
❑ 81 Mel Queen .... 1.50 .60
❑ 82 Rich Hebner RC 8.00 3.20
Al Oliver RC
❑ 83 Mike Ferraro 2.50 1.00
❑ 84 Bob Humphreys .... 1.50 .60
❑ 85 Lou Brock 20.00 8.00
❑ 86 Pete Richert .... 1.50 .60
❑ 87 Horace Clarke 2.50 1.00
❑ 88 Rich Nye .... 1.50 .60
❑ 89 Russ Gibson .... 1.50 .60
❑ 90 Jerry Koosman 2.50 1.00
❑ 91 Alvin Dark MG 2.50 1.00
❑ 92 Jack Billingham 2.50 1.00
❑ 93 Joe Foy 2.50 1.00
❑ 94 Hank Aguirre .... 1.50 .60
❑ 95 Johnny Bench 50.00 20.00
❑ 96 Denny Lemaster .... 1.50 .60
❑ 97 Buddy Bradford .... 1.50 .60
❑ 98 Dave Giusti .... 1.50 .60
❑ 99A Twins Rookies 15.00 6.00
Danny Morris
Graig Nettles RC
(No loop)
❑ 99B Twins Rookies 15.00 6.00
Danny Morris
Graig Nettles RC
(Errant loop in

upper left corner
of obverse)
❑ 100 Hank Aaron 50.00 20.00
❑ 101 Daryl Patterson 1.50 .60
❑ 102 Jim Davenport 1.50 .60
❑ 103 Roger Repoz 1.50 .60
❑ 104 Steve Blass 1.50 .60
❑ 105 Rick Monday 2.50 1.00
❑ 106 Jim Hannan 1.50 .60
❑ 107A Bob Gibson CL ERR 6.00 1.20
161 Jim Purdin
❑ 107B Bob Gibson CL COR 8.00 1.60
161 John Purdin
❑ 108 Tony Taylor 2.50 1.00
❑ 109 Jim Lonborg 2.50 1.00
❑ 110 Mike Shannon 2.50 1.00
❑ 111 John Morris RC 1.50 .60
❑ 112 J.C. Martin 2.50 1.00
❑ 113 Dave May 1.50 .60
❑ 114 Alan Closter 2.50 1.00
John Cumberland
❑ 115 Bill Hands 1.50 .60
❑ 116 Chuck Harrison 1.50 .60
❑ 117 Jim Fairey 2.50 1.00
❑ 118 Stan Williams 1.50 .60
❑ 119 Doug Rader 2.50 1.00
❑ 120 Pete Rose 50.00 20.00
❑ 121 Joe Grzenda 1.50 .60
❑ 122 Ron Fairly 2.50 1.00
❑ 123 Wilbur Wood 2.50 1.00
❑ 124 Hank Bauer MG 2.50 1.00
❑ 125 Ray Sadecki 1.50 .60
❑ 126 Dick Tracewski 1.50 .60
❑ 127 Kevin Collins 2.50 1.00
❑ 128 Tommie Aaron 2.50 1.00
❑ 129 Bill McCool 1.50 .60
❑ 130 Carl Yastrzemski 20.00 8.00
❑ 131 Chris Cannizzaro 1.50 .60
❑ 132 Dave Baldwin 1.50 .60
❑ 133 Johnny Callison 2.50 1.00
❑ 134 Jim Weaver 1.50 .60
❑ 135 Tommy Davis 2.50 1.00
❑ 136 Steve Huntz 1.50 .60
Mike Torrez
❑ 137 Wally Bunker 1.50 .60
❑ 138 John Bateman 1.50 .60
❑ 139 Andy Kosco 1.50 .60
❑ 140 Jim Lefebvre 2.50 1.00
❑ 141 Bill Dillman 1.50 .60
❑ 142 Woody Woodward 1.50 .60
❑ 143 Joe Nossek 1.50 .60
❑ 144 Bob Hendley 2.50 1.00
❑ 145 Max Alvis 1.50 .60
❑ 146 Jim Perry 2.50 1.00
❑ 147 Leo Durocher MG 4.00 1.60
❑ 148 Lee Stange 1.50 .60
❑ 149 Ollie Brown 2.50 1.00
❑ 150 Denny McLain 4.00 1.60
❑ 151A Clay Dalrymple 1.50 .60
Portrait, Orioles
❑ 151B Clay Dalrymple 15.00 6.00
Catching, Phillies
❑ 152 Tommie Sisk 1.50 .60
❑ 153 Ed Brinkman 1.50 .60
❑ 154 Jim Britton 1.50 .60
❑ 155 Pete Ward 1.50 .60
❑ 156 Hal Gilson 1.50 .60
Leon McFadden
❑ 157 Bob Rodgers 2.50 1.00
❑ 158 Joe Gibbon 1.50 .60
❑ 159 Jerry Adair 1.50 .60
❑ 160 Vada Pinson 2.50 1.00
❑ 161 John Purdin 1.50 .60
❑ 162 Bob Gibson WS 8.00 3.20
Fans 17
❑ 163 Willie Horton WS 6.00 2.40
❑ 164 Tim McCarver WS 12.00 4.80
Roger Maris
❑ 165 Lou Brock WS 8.00 3.20
❑ 166 Al Kaline WS 8.00 3.20
❑ 167 Jim Northrup WS 6.00 2.40
❑ 168 Mickey Lolich WS 8.00 3.20
Bob Gibson
❑ 169 Dick McAuliffe WS 6.00 2.40
Denny McLain
Willie Horton
❑ 170 Frank Howard 2.50 1.00
❑ 171 Glenn Beckert 2.50 1.00
❑ 172 Jerry Stephenson 1.50 .60
❑ 173 Bob Christian 1.50 .60
Gerry Nyman
❑ 174 Grant Jackson 1.50 .60
❑ 175 Jim Bunning 6.00 2.40
❑ 176 Joe Azcue 1.50 .60
❑ 177 Ron Reed 1.50 .60
❑ 178 Ray Oyler 2.50 1.00
❑ 179 Don Pavletich 1.50 .60
❑ 180 Willie Horton 2.50 1.00
❑ 181 Mel Nelson 1.50 .60
❑ 182 Bill Rigney MG 1.50 .60
❑ 183 Don Shaw 2.50 1.00
❑ 184 Roberto Pena 1.50 .60
❑ 185 Tom Phoebus 1.50 .60
❑ 186 Johnny Edwards 1.50 .60
❑ 187 Leon Wagner 1.50 .60
❑ 188 Rick Wise 2.50 1.00
❑ 189 Joe Lahoud 1.50 .60
John Thibodeau
❑ 190 Willie Mays 80.00 32.00
❑ 191 Lindy McDaniel 2.50 1.00
❑ 192 Jose Pagan 1.50 .60
❑ 193 Don Cardwell 2.50 1.00
❑ 194 Ted Uhlaender 1.50 .60
❑ 195 John Odom 1.50 .60
❑ 196 Lum Harris MG 1.50 .60
❑ 197 Dick Selma 1.50 .60
❑ 198 Willie Smith 1.50 .60
❑ 199 Jim French 1.50 .60
❑ 200 Bob Gibson 12.00 4.80
❑ 201 Russ Snyder 1.50 .60
❑ 202 Don Wilson 2.50 1.00
❑ 203 Dave Johnson 2.50 1.00
❑ 204 Jack Hiatt 1.50 .60
❑ 205 Rick Reichardt 1.50 .60
❑ 206 Larry Hisle 2.50 1.00
Barry Lersch
❑ 207 Roy Face 2.50 1.00
❑ 208A Donn Clendenon 2.50 1.00
Houston
❑ 208B Donn Clendenon 15.00 6.00
Expos
❑ 209 Larry Haney UER 1.50 .60
(Reverse negative)
❑ 210 Felix Millan 1.50 .60
❑ 211 Galen Cisco 1.50 .60
❑ 212 Tom Tresh 2.50 1.00
❑ 213 Gerry Arrigo 1.50 .60
❑ 214 Checklist 3 6.00 1.20
With 69T deckle CL
on back (no player)
❑ 215 Rico Petrocelli 2.50 1.00
❑ 216 Don Sutton 6.00 2.40
❑ 217 John Donaldson 1.50 .60
❑ 218 John Roseboro 2.50 1.00
❑ 219 Freddie Patek RC 4.00 1.60
❑ 220 Sam McDowell 4.00 1.60
❑ 221 Art Shamsky 4.00 1.60
❑ 222 Duane Josephson 2.50 1.00
❑ 223 Tom Dukes 4.00 1.60
❑ 224 Bill Harrelson 2.50 1.00
Steve Kealey
❑ 225 Don Kessinger 4.00 1.60
❑ 226 Bruce Howard 2.50 1.00
❑ 227 Frank Johnson 2.50 1.00
❑ 228 Dave Leonhard 2.50 1.00
❑ 229 Don Lock 2.50 1.00
❑ 230 Rusty Staub UER 4.00 1.60
For 1966 stats, Houston spelled
Houston
❑ 231 Pat Dobson 4.00 1.60
❑ 232 Dave Ricketts 2.50 1.00
❑ 233 Steve Barber 4.00 1.60
❑ 234 Dave Bristol MG 2.50 1.00
❑ 235 Jim Hunter 10.00 4.00
❑ 236 Manny Mota 4.00 1.60
❑ 237 Bobby Cox RC 10.00 4.00
❑ 238 Ken Johnson 2.50 1.00
❑ 239 Bob Taylor 4.00 1.60
❑ 240 Ken Harrelson 4.00 1.60
❑ 241 Jim Brewer 2.50 1.00
❑ 242 Frank Kostro 2.50 1.00
❑ 243 Ron Kline 2.50 1.00
❑ 244 Ray Fosse RC 4.00 1.60
George Woodson
❑ 245 Ed Charles 4.00 1.60
❑ 246 Joe Coleman 2.50 1.00
❑ 247 Gene Oliver 2.50 1.00
❑ 248 Bob Priddy 2.50 1.00
❑ 249 Ed Spiezio 4.00 1.60
❑ 250 Frank Robinson 20.00 8.00
❑ 251 Ron Herbel 2.50 1.00
❑ 252 Chuck Cottier 2.50 1.00
❑ 253 Jerry Johnson 2.50 1.00
❑ 254 Joe Schultz MG 4.00 1.60
❑ 255 Steve Carlton 30.00 12.00
❑ 256 Gates Brown 4.00 1.60
❑ 257 Jim Ray 2.50 1.00
❑ 258 Jackie Hernandez 4.00 1.60
❑ 259 Bill Short 2.50 1.00
❑ 260 Reggie Jackson RC 250.00 100.00
❑ 261 Bob Johnson 2.50 1.00
❑ 262 Mike Kekich 4.00 1.60
❑ 263 Jerry May 2.50 1.00
❑ 264 Bill Landis 2.50 1.00
❑ 265 Chico Cardenas 4.00 1.60
❑ 266 Tom Hutton 4.00 1.60
Alan Foster
❑ 267 Vicente Romo 2.50 1.00
❑ 268 Al Spangler 2.50 1.00
❑ 269 Al Weis 4.00 1.60
❑ 270 Mickey Lolich 4.00 1.60
❑ 271 Larry Stahl 4.00 1.60
❑ 272 Ed Stroud 2.50 1.00
❑ 273 Ron Willis 2.50 1.00
❑ 274 Clyde King MG 2.50 1.00
❑ 275 Vic Davalillo 2.50 1.00
❑ 276 Gary Wagner 2.50 1.00
❑ 277 Elrod Hendricks RC 2.50 1.00
❑ 278 Gary Geiger UER 2.50 1.00
(Batting wrong)
❑ 279 Roger Nelson 4.00 1.60
❑ 280 Alex Johnson 4.00 1.60
❑ 281 Ted Kubiak 2.50 1.00
❑ 282 Pat Jarvis 2.50 1.00
❑ 283 Sandy Alomar 4.00 1.60
❑ 284 Jerry Robertson 4.00 1.60
Mike Wegener
❑ 285 Don Mincher 4.00 1.60
❑ 286 Dock Ellis RC 4.00 1.60
❑ 287 Jose Tartabull 4.00 1.60
❑ 288 Ken Holtzman 4.00 1.60
❑ 289 Bart Shirley 2.50 1.00
❑ 290 Jim Kaat 4.00 1.60
❑ 291 Vern Fuller 2.50 1.00
❑ 292 Al Downing 4.00 1.60
❑ 293 Dick Dietz 2.50 1.00
❑ 294 Jim Lemon MG 2.50 1.00
❑ 295 Tony Perez 12.00 4.80
❑ 296 Andy Messersmith RC 4.00 1.60
❑ 297 Deron Johnson 2.50 1.00
❑ 298 Dave Nicholson 4.00 1.60
❑ 299 Mark Belanger 4.00 1.60
❑ 300 Felipe Alou 4.00 1.60
❑ 301 Darrell Brandon 4.00 1.60
❑ 302 Jim Pagliaroni 2.50 1.00
❑ 303 Cal Koonce 4.00 1.60
❑ 304 Bill Davis 6.00 2.40
Clarence Gaston RC
❑ 305 Dick McAuliffe 4.00 1.60
❑ 306 Jim Grant 4.00 1.60
❑ 307 Gary Kolb 2.50 1.00
❑ 308 Wade Blasingame 2.50 1.00
❑ 309 Walt Williams 2.50 1.00
❑ 310 Tom Haller 2.50 1.00
❑ 311 Sparky Lyle RC 10.00 4.00
❑ 312 Lee Elia 2.50 1.00
❑ 313 Bill Robinson 4.00 1.60
❑ 314 Don Drysdale CL 6.00 1.20
❑ 315 Eddie Fisher 2.50 1.00
❑ 316 Hal Lanier 2.50 1.00
❑ 317 Bruce Look 2.50 1.00
❑ 318 Jack Fisher 2.50 1.00
❑ 319 Ken McMullen UER 2.50 1.00
(Headings on back
are for a pitcher)
❑ 320 Dal Maxvill 2.50 1.00
❑ 321 Jim McAndrew 4.00 1.60
❑ 322 Jose Vidal 4.00 1.60

❑ 323 Larry Miller 2.50 1.00
❑ 324 Les Cain 4.00 1.60
Dave Campbell RC
❑ 325 Jose Cardenal 4.00 1.60
❑ 326 Gary Sutherland 4.00 1.60
❑ 327 Willie Crawford 2.50 1.00
❑ 328 Joel Horlen 1.50 .60
❑ 329 Rick Joseph 1.50 .60
❑ 330 Tony Conigliaro 4.00 1.60
❑ 331 Gil Garrido 2.50 1.00
Tom House RC
❑ 332 Fred Talbot 1.50 .60
❑ 333 Ivan Murrell 1.50 .60
❑ 334 Phil Roof 1.50 .60
❑ 335 Bill Mazeroski 6.00 2.40
❑ 336 Jim Roland 1.50 .60
❑ 337 Marty Martinez 1.50 .60
❑ 338 Del Unser 1.50 .60
❑ 339 Steve Mingori 1.50 .60
Jose Pena
❑ 340 Dave McNally 2.50 1.00
❑ 341 Dave Adlesh 1.50 .60
❑ 342 Bubba Morton 1.50 .60
❑ 343 Dan Frisella 1.50 .60
❑ 344 Tom Matchick 1.50 .60
❑ 345 Frank Linzy 1.50 .60
❑ 346 Wayne Comer 1.50 .60
❑ 347 Randy Hundley 2.50 1.00
❑ 348 Steve Hargan 1.50 .60
❑ 349 Dick Williams MG 2.50 1.00
❑ 350 Richie Allen 4.00 1.60
❑ 351 Carroll Sembera 1.50 .60
❑ 352 Paul Schaal 2.50 1.00
❑ 353 Jeff Torborg 2.50 1.00
❑ 354 Nate Oliver 1.50 .60
❑ 355 Phil Niekro 6.00 2.40
❑ 356 Frank Quilici 1.50 .60
❑ 357 Carl Taylor 1.50 .60
❑ 358 George Lauzerique 1.50 .60
Roberto Rodriquez
❑ 359 Dick Kelley 1.50 .60
❑ 360 Jim Wynn 2.50 1.00
❑ 361 Gary Holman 1.50 .60
❑ 362 Jim Maloney 2.50 1.00
❑ 363 Russ Nixon 1.50 .60
❑ 364 Tommie Agee 4.00 1.60
❑ 365 Jim Fregosi 2.50 1.00
❑ 366 Bo Belinsky 2.50 1.00
❑ 367 Lou Johnson 2.50 1.00
❑ 368 Vic Roznovsky 1.50 .60
❑ 369 Bob Skinner MG 2.50 1.00
❑ 370 Juan Marichal 8.00 3.20
❑ 371 Sal Bando 2.50 1.00
❑ 372 Adolfo Phillips 1.50 .60
❑ 373 Fred Lasher 1.50 .60
❑ 374 Bob Tillman 1.50 .60
❑ 375 Harmon Killebrew 15.00 6.00
❑ 376 Mike Fiore 1.50 .60
Jim Rooker RC
❑ 377 Gary Bell 2.50 1.00
❑ 378 Jose Herrera 1.50 .60
❑ 379 Ken Boyer 2.50 1.00
❑ 380 Stan Bahnsen 2.50 1.00
❑ 381 Ed Kranepool 2.50 1.00
❑ 382 Pat Corrales 2.50 1.00
❑ 383 Casey Cox 1.50 .60
❑ 384 Larry Shepard MG 1.50 .60
❑ 385 Orlando Cepeda 6.00 2.40
❑ 386 Jim McGlothlin 1.50 .60
❑ 387 Bobby Klaus 1.50 .60
❑ 388 Tom McCraw 1.50 .60
❑ 389 Dan Coombs 1.50 .60
❑ 390 Bill Freehan 2.50 1.00
❑ 391 Ray Culp 1.50 .60
❑ 392 Bob Burda 1.50 .60
❑ 393 Gene Brabender 2.50 1.00
❑ 394 Lou Piniella 6.00 2.40
Marv Staehle
❑ 395 Chris Short 1.50 .60
❑ 396 Jim Campanis 1.50 .60
❑ 397 Chuck Dobson 1.50 .60
❑ 398 Tito Francona 1.50 .60
❑ 399 Bob Bailey 2.50 1.00
❑ 400 Don Drysdale 15.00 6.00
❑ 401 Jake Gibbs 2.50 1.00
❑ 402 Ken Boswell 2.50 1.00
❑ 403 Bob Miller 1.50 .60
❑ 404 Vic LaRose 2.50 1.00
Gary Ross
❑ 405 Lee May 2.50 1.00
❑ 406 Phil Ortega 1.50 .60
❑ 407 Tom Egan 1.50 .60
❑ 408 Nate Colbert 1.50 .60
❑ 409 Bob Moose 1.50 .60
❑ 410 Al Kaline 25.00 10.00
❑ 411 Larry Dierker 2.50 1.00
❑ 412 Mickey Mantle CL DP 15.00 3.00
❑ 413 Roland Sheldon 2.50 1.00
❑ 414 Duke Sims 1.50 .60
❑ 415 Ray Washburn 1.50 .60
❑ 416 Willie McCovey AS 8.00 3.20
❑ 417 Ken Harrelson AS 3.00 1.20
❑ 418 Tommy Helms AS 3.00 1.20
❑ 419 Rod Carew AS 10.00 4.00
❑ 420 Ron Santo AS 4.00 1.60
❑ 421 Brooks Robinson AS 8.00 3.20
❑ 422 Don Kessinger AS 3.00 1.20
❑ 423 Bert Campaneris AS 4.00 1.60
❑ 424 Pete Rose AS 15.00 6.00
❑ 425 Carl Yastrzemski AS 10.00 4.00
❑ 426 Curt Flood AS 4.00 1.60
❑ 427 Tony Oliva AS 4.00 1.60
❑ 428 Lou Brock AS 6.00 2.40
❑ 429 Willie Horton AS 3.00 1.20
❑ 430 Johnny Bench AS 10.00 4.00
❑ 431 Bill Freehan AS 4.00 1.60
❑ 432 Bob Gibson AS 6.00 2.40
❑ 433 Denny McLain AS 3.00 1.20
❑ 434 Jerry Koosman AS 3.00 1.20
❑ 435 Sam McDowell AS 2.50 1.00
❑ 436 Gene Alley 2.50 1.00
❑ 437 Luis Alcaraz 1.50 .60
❑ 438 Gary Waslewski 1.50 .60
❑ 439 Ed Herrmann 1.50 .60
Dan Lazar
❑ 440A Willie McCovey 15.00 6.00
❑ 440B Willie McCovey WL 100.00 40.00
(McCovey white)
❑ 441A Dennis Higgins 1.50 .60
❑ 441B Dennis Higgins WL 25.00 10.00
(Higgins white)
❑ 442 Ty Cline 1.50 .60
❑ 443 Don Wert 1.50 .60
❑ 444A Joe Moeller 1.50 .60
❑ 444B Joe Moeller WL 25.00 10.00
(Moeller white)
❑ 445 Bobby Knoop 1.50 .60
❑ 446 Claude Raymond 1.50 .60
❑ 447A Ralph Houk MG 2.50 1.00
❑ 447B Ralph Houk WL 25.00 10.00
MG (Houk white)
❑ 448 Bob Tolan 2.50 1.00
❑ 449 Paul Lindblad 1.50 .60
❑ 450 Billy Williams 8.00 3.20
❑ 451A Rich Rollins 2.50 1.00
❑ 451B Rich Rollins WL 25.00 10.00
(Rich and 3B white)
❑ 452A Al Ferrara 1.50 .60
❑ 452B Al Ferrara WL 25.00 10.00
(Al and OF white)
❑ 453 Mike Cuellar 2.50 1.00
❑ 454A Phillies Rookies 2.50 1.00
Larry Colton
Don Money
❑ 454B Phillies Rookies WL 25.00 10.00
Larry Colton
Don Money
(Names in white)
❑ 455 Sonny Siebert 1.50 .60
❑ 456 Bud Harrelson 2.50 1.00
❑ 457 Dalton Jones 1.50 .60
❑ 458 Curt Blefary 1.50 .60
❑ 459 Dave Boswell 1.50 .60
❑ 460 Joe Torre 4.00 1.60
❑ 461A Mike Epstein 1.50 .60
❑ 461B Mike Epstein WL 25.00 10.00
(Epstein white)
❑ 462 Red Schoendienst 2.50 1.00
MG
❑ 463 Dennis Ribant 1.50 .60
❑ 464A Dave Marshall 1.50 .60
❑ 464B Dave Marshall WL 25.00 10.00
(Marshall white)
❑ 465 Tommy John 4.00 1.60
❑ 466 John Boccabella 2.50 1.00
❑ 467 Tommie Reynolds 1.50 .60
❑ 468A Pirates Rookies 1.50 .60
Bruce Dal Canton
Bob Robertson
❑ 468B Pirates Rookies WL 25.00 10.00
Bruce Dal Canton
Bob Robertson
(Names in white)
❑ 469 Chico Ruiz 1.50 .60
❑ 470A Mel Stottlemyre 2.50 1.00
❑ 470B Mel Stottlemyre WL 30.00 12.00
(Stottlemyre white)
❑ 471A Ted Savage 1.50 .60
❑ 471B Ted Savage WL 25.00 10.00
(Savage white)
❑ 472 Jim Price 1.50 .60
❑ 473A Jose Arcia 1.50 .60
❑ 473B Jose Arcia WL 25.00 10.00
(Jose and 2B white)
❑ 474 Tom Murphy 1.50 .60
❑ 475 Tim McCarver 4.00 1.60
❑ 476A Boston Rookies 2.50 1.00
Ken Brett RC
Gerry Moses
❑ 476B Boston Rookies WL 30.00 12.00
Ken Brett RC
Gerry Moses
(Names in white)
❑ 477 Jeff James 1.50 .60
❑ 478 Don Buford 1.50 .60
❑ 479 Richie Scheinblum 1.50 .60
❑ 480 Tom Seaver 80.00 32.00
❑ 481 Bill Melton 2.50 1.00
❑ 482A Jim Gosger 1.50 .60
❑ 482B Jim Gosger WL 25.00 10.00
(Jim and OF white)
❑ 483 Ted Abernathy 1.50 .60
❑ 484 Joe Gordon MG 2.50 1.00
❑ 485A Gaylord Perry 10.00 4.00
❑ 485B Gaylord Perry WL 80.00 32.00
(Perry white)
❑ 486A Paul Casanova 1.50 .60
❑ 486B Paul Casanova WL 25.00 10.00
(Casanova white)
❑ 487 Denis Menke 1.50 .60
❑ 488 Joe Sparma 1.50 .60
❑ 489 Clete Boyer 2.50 1.00
❑ 490 Matty Alou 2.50 1.00
❑ 491A Twins Rookies 1.50 .60
Jerry Crider
George Mitterwald
❑ 491B Twins Rookies WL 25.00 10.00
Jerry Crider
George Mitterwald
(Names in white)
❑ 492 Tony Cloninger 1.50 .60
❑ 493A Wes Parker 2.50 1.00
❑ 493B Wes Parker WL 25.00 10.00
(Parker white)
❑ 494 Ken Berry 1.50 .60
❑ 495 Bert Campaneris 2.50 1.00
❑ 496 Larry Jaster 1.50 .60
❑ 497 Julian Javier 2.50 1.00
❑ 498 Juan Pizarro 2.50 1.00
❑ 499 Don Bryant 1.50 .60
Steve Shea
❑ 500A Mickey Mantle UER 350.00 140.00
(No Topps copy-
right on card back)
❑ 500B Mickey Mantle WL 2000.00 800.00
(Mantle in white;
no Topps copyright
on card back) UER
❑ 501A Tony Gonzalez 2.50 1.00
❑ 501B Tony Gonzalez WL 25.00 10.00
(Tony and OF white)
❑ 502 Minnie Rojas 1.50 .60
❑ 503 Larry Brown 1.50 .60
❑ 504 Brooks Robinson CL 8.00 1.60
❑ 505A Bobby Bolin 1.50 .60
❑ 505B Bobby Bolin WL 25.00 10.00
(Bolin white)
❑ 506 Paul Blair 2.50 1.00

❑ 507 Cookie Rojas 2.50 1.00
❑ 508 Moe Drabowsky 2.50 1.00
❑ 509 Manny Sanguillen 2.50 1.00
❑ 510 Rod Carew 40.00 16.00
❑ 511A Diego Segui 2.50 1.00
❑ 511B Diego Segui WL 25.00 10.00
(Diego and P white)
❑ 512 Cleon Jones 2.50 1.00
❑ 513 Camilo Pascual 3.00 1.20
❑ 514 Mike Lum .... 2.00 .80
❑ 515 Dick Green .... 2.00 .80
❑ 516 Earl Weaver RC MG 20.00 8.00
❑ 517 Mike McCormick 3.00 1.20
❑ 518 Fred Whitfield .... 2.00 .80
❑ 519 Jerry Kenney .... 2.00 .80
Len Boehmer
❑ 520 Bob Veale 3.00 1.20
❑ 521 George Thomas .... 2.00 .80
❑ 522 Joe Hoerner .... 2.00 .80
❑ 523 Bob Chance .... 2.00 .80
❑ 524 Jose Laboy 3.00 1.20
Floyd Wicker
❑ 525 Earl Wilson 3.00 1.20
❑ 526 Hector Torres .... 2.00 .80
❑ 527 Al Lopez MG 5.00 2.00
❑ 528 Claude Osteen 3.00 1.20
❑ 529 Ed Kirkpatrick 3.00 1.20
❑ 530 Cesar Tovar .... 2.00 .80
❑ 531 Dick Farrell .... 2.00 .80
❑ 532 Tom Phoebus 3.00 1.20
Jim Hardin
Dave McNally
Mike Cuellar
❑ 533 Nolan Ryan 200.00 80.00
❑ 534 Jerry McNertney 3.00 1.20
❑ 535 Phil Regan 3.00 1.20
❑ 536 Danny Breeden .... 2.00 .80
Dave Roberts
❑ 537 Mike Paul .... 2.00 .80
❑ 538 Charlie Smith .... 2.00 .80
❑ 539 Mike Epstein 12.00 4.80
Ted Williams MG
❑ 540 Curt Flood 3.00 1.20
❑ 541 Joe Verbanic .... 2.00 .80
❑ 542 Bob Aspromonte .... 2.00 .80
❑ 543 Fred Newman .... 2.00 .80
❑ 544 Mike Kilkenny .... 2.00 .80
Ron Woods
❑ 545 Willie Stargell 12.00 4.80
❑ 546 Jim Nash .... 2.00 .80
❑ 547 Billy Martin MG 5.00 2.00
❑ 548 Bob Locker .... 2.00 .80
❑ 549 Ron Brand .... 2.00 .80
❑ 550 Brooks Robinson 30.00 12.00
❑ 551 Wayne Granger .... 2.00 .80
❑ 552 Ted Sizemore RC 3.00 1.20
Bill Sudakis
❑ 553 Ron Davis .... 2.00 .80
❑ 554 Frank Bertaina .... 2.00 .80
❑ 555 Jim Ray Hart 3.00 1.20
❑ 556 Sal Bando 3.00 1.20
Bert Campaneris
Danny Cater
❑ 557 Frank Fernandez .... 2.00 .80
❑ 558 Tom Burgmeier 3.00 1.20
❑ 559 Joe Hague .... 2.00 .80
Jim Hicks
❑ 560 Luis Tiant 3.00 1.20
❑ 561 Ron Clark .... 2.00 .80
❑ 562 Bob Watson RC 8.00 3.20
❑ 563 Marty Pattin 3.00 1.20
❑ 564 Gil Hodges MG 10.00 4.00
❑ 565 Hoyt Wilhelm 8.00 3.20
❑ 566 Ron Hansen .... 2.00 .80
❑ 567 Elvio Jimenez .... 2.00 .80
Jim Shellenback
❑ 568 Cecil Upshaw .... 2.00 .80
❑ 569 Billy Harris .... 1.50 .60
❑ 570 Ron Santo 8.00 3.20
❑ 571 Cap Peterson .... 2.00 .80
❑ 572 Willie McCovey 15.00 6.00
Juan Marichal
❑ 573 Jim Palmer 30.00 12.00
❑ 574 George Scott 3.00 1.20
❑ 575 Bill Singer 3.00 1.20
❑ 576 Ron Stone .... 2.00 .80
Bill Wilson
❑ 577 Mike Hegan 3.00 1.20
❑ 578 Don Bosch .... 2.00 .80
❑ 579 Dave Nelson .... 2.00 .80
❑ 580 Jim Northrup 3.00 1.20
❑ 581 Gary Nolan 3.00 1.20
❑ 582A Tony Oliva CL 6.00 1.20
White circle on back
❑ 582B Tony Oliva CL 8.00 1.60
Red circle on back
❑ 583 Clyde Wright .... 2.00 .80
❑ 584 Don Mason .... 2.00 .80
❑ 585 Ron Swoboda 3.00 1.20
❑ 586 Tim Cullen .... 2.00 .80
❑ 587 Joe Rudi RC 8.00 3.20
❑ 588 Bill White 3.00 1.20
❑ 589 Joe Pepitone 5.00 2.00
❑ 590 Rico Carty 5.00 2.00
❑ 591 Mike Hedlund 3.00 1.20
❑ 592 Rafael Robles 5.00 2.00
Al Santorini
❑ 593 Don Nottebart 3.00 1.20
❑ 594 Dooley Womack 3.00 1.20
❑ 595 Lee Maye 3.00 1.20
❑ 596 Chuck Hartenstein 3.00 1.20
❑ 597 Bob Floyd 40.00 16.00
Larry Burchart
Rollie Fingers RC
❑ 598 Ruben Amaro 3.00 1.20
❑ 599 John Boozer 3.00 1.20
❑ 600 Tony Oliva 8.00 3.20
❑ 601 Tug McGraw 8.00 3.20
❑ 602 Alec Distaso 5.00 2.00
Don Young
Jim Qualls
❑ 603 Joe Keough 3.00 1.20
❑ 604 Bobby Etheridge 3.00 1.20
❑ 605 Dick Ellsworth 3.00 1.20
❑ 606 Gene Mauch MG 5.00 2.00
❑ 607 Dick Bosman 3.00 1.20
❑ 608 Dick Simpson 3.00 1.20
❑ 609 Phil Gagliano 3.00 1.20
❑ 610 Jim Hardin 3.00 1.20
❑ 611 Bob Didier 5.00 2.00
Walt Hriniak RC
Gary Neibauer
❑ 612 Jack Aker 5.00 2.00
❑ 613 Jim Beauchamp 3.00 1.20
❑ 614 Tom Griffin 3.00 1.20
Skip Guinn
❑ 615 Len Gabrielson 3.00 1.20
❑ 616 Don McMahon 3.00 1.20
❑ 617 Jesse Gonder 3.00 1.20
❑ 618 Ramon Webster 3.00 1.20
❑ 619 Bill Butler 5.00 2.00
Pat Kelly
Juan Rios
❑ 620 Dean Chance 5.00 2.00
❑ 621 Bill Voss 3.00 1.20
❑ 622 Dan Osinski 3.00 1.20
❑ 623 Hank Allen 3.00 1.20
❑ 624 Darrel Chaney 5.00 2.00
Duffy Dyer RC
Terry Harmon
❑ 625 Mack Jones UER 5.00 2.00
(Batting wrong)
❑ 626 Gene Michael 5.00 2.00
❑ 627 George Stone 3.00 1.20
❑ 628 Bill Conigliaro RC 5.00 2.00
Syd O'Brien
Fred Wenz
❑ 629 Jack Hamilton 3.00 1.20
❑ 630 Bobby Bonds RC 30.00 12.00
❑ 631 John Kennedy 5.00 2.00
❑ 632 Jon Warden 3.00 1.20
❑ 633 Harry Walker MG 3.00 1.20
❑ 634 Andy Etchebarren 3.00 1.20
❑ 635 George Culver 3.00 1.20
❑ 636 Woody Held 3.00 1.20
❑ 637 Jerry DaVanon 5.00 2.00
Frank Reberger
Clay Kirby
❑ 638 Ed Sprague RC 3.00 1.20
❑ 639 Barry Moore 3.00 1.20
❑ 640 Ferguson Jenkins 20.00 8.00
❑ 641 Bobby Darwin 5.00 2.00
John Miller
Tommy Dean
❑ 642 John Hiller 3.00 1.20
❑ 643 Billy Cowan 3.00 1.20
❑ 644 Chuck Hinton 3.00 1.20
❑ 645 George Brunet 3.00 1.20
❑ 646 Dan McGinn 5.00 2.00
Carl Morton
❑ 647 Dave Wickersham 3.00 1.20
❑ 648 Bobby Wine 5.00 2.00
❑ 649 Al Jackson 3.00 1.20
❑ 650 Ted Williams MG 20.00 8.00
❑ 651 Gus Gil 5.00 2.00
❑ 652 Eddie Watt 3.00 1.20
❑ 653 A.Rodriguez RC UER 5.00 2.00
Photo actually
Angels' batboy
❑ 654 Carlos May RC 5.00 2.00
Don Secrist
Rich Morales
❑ 655 Mike Hershberger 3.00 1.20
❑ 656 Dan Schneider 3.00 1.20
❑ 657 Bobby Murcer 8.00 3.20
❑ 658 Tom Hall 3.00 1.20
Bill Burbach
Jim Miles
❑ 659 Johnny Podres 5.00 2.00
❑ 660 Reggie Smith 5.00 2.00
❑ 661 Jim Merritt 3.00 1.20
❑ 662 Dick Drago 5.00 2.00
George Spriggs
Bob Oliver
❑ 663 Dick Radatz 5.00 2.00
❑ 664 Ron Hunt 5.00 1.35

1970 Topps

	NM	Ex
COMPLETE SET (720)	2000.00	800.00
COMMON CARD (1-132)	.75	.30
COMMON (373-459)	1.00	.40
COMMON CARD (373-459)	1.50	.60
COMMON (460-546)	2.00	.80
COMMON (547-633)	4.00	1.60
COMMON (634-720)	10.00	4.00
WRAPPER (10-CENT)	20.00	8.00

❑ 1 New York Mets 30.00 9.50
Team Card
❑ 2 Diego Segui .... 1.00 .40
❑ 3 Darrel Chaney .... .75 .30
❑ 4 Tom Egan .... .75 .30
❑ 5 Wes Parker .... 1.00 .40
❑ 6 Grant Jackson .... .75 .30
❑ 7 Gary Boyd .... .75 .30
Russ Nagelson
❑ 8 Jose Martinez .... .75 .30
❑ 9 Checklist 1 .... 12.00 2.40
❑ 10 Carl Yastrzemski 20.00 8.00
❑ 11 Nate Colbert .... .75 .30
❑ 12 John Hiller .... .75 .30
❑ 13 Jack Hiatt .... .75 .30
❑ 14 Hank Allen .... .75 .30
❑ 15 Larry Dierker .... .75 .30
❑ 16 Charlie Metro MG .... .75 .30
❑ 17 Hoyt Wilhelm 4.00 1.60
❑ 18 Carlos May .... 1.00 .40
❑ 19 John Boccabella .... .75 .30
❑ 20 Dave McNally .... 1.00 .40

❑ 21 Vida Blue RC 4.00 1.60
Gene Tenace RC
❑ 22 Ray Washburn .75 .30
❑ 23 Bill Robinson 1.00 .40
❑ 24 Dick Selma .75 .30
❑ 25 Cesar Tovar .75 .30
❑ 26 Tug McGraw 2.00 .80
❑ 27 Chuck Hinton .75 .30
❑ 28 Billy Wilson .75 .30
❑ 29 Sandy Alomar 1.00 .40
❑ 30 Matty Alou 1.00 .40
❑ 31 Marty Pattin 1.00 .40
❑ 32 Harry Walker MG .75 .30
❑ 33 Don Wert .75 .30
❑ 34 Willie Crawford .75 .30
❑ 35 Joel Horlen .75 .30
❑ 36 Danny Breeden 1.00 .40
Bernie Carbo
❑ 37 Dick Drago .75 .30
❑ 38 Mack Jones .75 .30
❑ 39 Mike Nagy .75 .30
❑ 40 Rich Allen 2.00 .80
❑ 41 George Lauzerique .75 .30
❑ 42 Tito Fuentes .75 .30
❑ 43 Jack Aker .75 .30
❑ 44 Roberto Pena .75 .30
❑ 45 Dave Johnson 1.00 .40
❑ 46 Ken Rudolph .75 .30
❑ 47 Bob Miller .75 .30
❑ 48 Gil Garrido .75 .30
❑ 49 Tim Cullen .75 .30
❑ 50 Tommie Agee 1.00 .40
❑ 51 Bob Christian .75 .30
❑ 52 Bruce Dal Canton .75 .30
❑ 53 John Kennedy .75 .30
❑ 54 Jeff Torborg 1.00 .40
❑ 55 John Odom .75 .30
❑ 56 Joe Lis .75 .30
Scott Reid
❑ 57 Pat Kelly .75 .30
❑ 58 Dave Marshall .75 .30
❑ 59 Dick Ellsworth .75 .30
❑ 60 Jim Wynn 1.00 .40
❑ 61 Pete Rose 12.00 4.80
Bob Clemente
Cleon Jones LL
❑ 62 Rod Carew 2.00 .80
Reggie Smith
Tony Oliva LL
❑ 63 Willie McCovey 2.00 .80
Ron Santo
Tony Perez LL
❑ 64 Harmon Killebrew 4.00 1.60
Boog Powell
Reggie Jackson LL
❑ 65 Willie McCovey 4.00 1.60
Hank Aaron
Lee May LL
❑ 66 Harmon Killebrew 4.00 1.60
Frank Howard
Reggie Jackson LL
❑ 67 Juan Marichal 4.00 1.60
Steve Carlton
Bob Gibson LL
❑ 68 Dick Bosman 1.00 .40
Jim Palmer
Mike Cuellar LL
❑ 69 Tom Seaver 4.00 1.60
Phil Niekro
Fergie Jenkins
Juan Marichal LL
❑ 70 Dennis McLain 1.00 .40
Mike Cuellar
Dave Boswell
Dave McNally
Jim Perry
Mel Stottlemyre LL
❑ 71 Fergie Jenkins 2.00 .80
Bob Gibson
Bill Singer LL
❑ 72 Sam McDowell 1.00 .40
Mickey Lolich
Andy Messersmith LL
❑ 73 Wayne Granger .75 .30
❑ 74 Greg Washburn .75 .30
Wally Wolf

❑ 75 Jim Kaat 1.00 .40
❑ 76 Carl Taylor .75 .30
❑ 77 Frank Linzy .75 .30
❑ 78 Joe Lahoud .75 .30
❑ 79 Clay Kirby .75 .30
❑ 80 Don Kessinger 1.00 .40
❑ 81 Dave May .75 .30
❑ 82 Frank Fernandez .75 .30
❑ 83 Don Cardwell .75 .30
❑ 84 Paul Casanova .75 .30
❑ 85 Max Alvis .75 .30
❑ 86 Lum Harris MG .75 .30
❑ 87 Steve Renko RC .75 .30
❑ 88 Miguel Fuentes 1.00 .40
Dick Baney
❑ 89 Juan Rios .75 .30
❑ 90 Tim McCarver 1.00 .40
❑ 91 Rich Morales .75 .30
❑ 92 George Culver .75 .30
❑ 93 Rick Renick .75 .30
❑ 94 Freddie Patek 1.00 .40
❑ 95 Earl Wilson 1.00 .40
❑ 96 Leron Lee 1.00 .40
Jerry Reuss RC
❑ 97 Joe Moeller .75 .30
❑ 98 Gates Brown 1.00 .40
❑ 99 Bobby Pfeil .75 .30
❑ 100 Mel Stottlemyre 1.00 .40
❑ 101 Bobby Floyd .75 .30
❑ 102 Joe Rudi 1.00 .40
❑ 103 Frank Reberger .75 .30
❑ 104 Gerry Moses .75 .30
❑ 105 Tony Gonzalez .75 .30
❑ 106 Darold Knowles .75 .30
❑ 107 Bobby Etheridge .75 .30
❑ 108 Tom Burgmeier .75 .30
❑ 109 Garry Jestadt .75 .30
Carl Morton
❑ 110 Bob Moose .75 .30
❑ 111 Mike Hegan 1.00 .40
❑ 112 Dave Nelson .75 .30
❑ 113 Jim Ray .75 .30
❑ 114 Gene Michael 1.00 .40
❑ 115 Alex Johnson 1.00 .40
❑ 116 Sparky Lyle 1.00 .40
❑ 117 Don Young .75 .30
❑ 118 George Mitterwald .75 .30
❑ 119 Chuck Taylor .75 .30
❑ 120 Sal Bando 1.00 .40
❑ 121 Fred Beene .75 .30
Terry Crowley
❑ 122 George Stone .75 .30
❑ 123 Don Gutteridge MG .75 .30
❑ 124 Larry Jaster .75 .30
❑ 125 Deron Johnson .75 .30
❑ 126 Marty Martinez .75 .30
❑ 127 Joe Coleman .75 .30
❑ 128A Checklist 2 ERR 6.00 1.20
(226 R Perranoski)
❑ 128B Checklist 2 COR 6.00 1.20
(226 R. Perranoski)
❑ 129 Jimmie Price .75 .30
❑ 130 Ollie Brown .75 .30
❑ 131 Ray Lamb .75 .30
Bob Stinson
❑ 132 Jim McGlothlin .75 .30
❑ 133 Clay Carroll 1.00 .40
❑ 134 Danny Walton 1.00 .40
❑ 135 Dick Dietz 1.00 .40
❑ 136 Steve Hargan 1.00 .40
❑ 137 Art Shamsky 1.00 .40
❑ 138 Joe Foy 1.00 .40
❑ 139 Rich Nye 1.00 .40
❑ 140 Reggie Jackson 50.00 20.00
❑ 141 Dave Cash RC 1.50 .60
Johnny Jeter
❑ 142 Fritz Peterson 1.00 .40
❑ 143 Phil Gagliano 1.00 .40
❑ 144 Ray Culp 1.00 .40
❑ 145 Rico Carty 1.50 .60
❑ 146 Danny Murphy 1.00 .40
❑ 147 Angel Hermoso 1.00 .40
❑ 148 Earl Weaver MG 3.00 1.20
❑ 149 Billy Champion 1.00 .40
❑ 150 Harmon Killebrew 8.00 3.20
❑ 151 Dave Roberts 1.00 .40

❑ 152 Ike Brown 1.00 .40
❑ 153 Gary Gentry 1.00 .40
❑ 154 Jim Miles 1.00 .40
Jan Dukes
❑ 155 Denis Menke 1.00 .40
❑ 156 Eddie Fisher 1.00 .40
❑ 157 Manny Mota 1.50 .60
❑ 158 Jerry McNertney 1.50 .60
❑ 159 Tommy Helms 1.50 .60
❑ 160 Phil Niekro 5.00 2.00
❑ 161 Richie Scheinblum 1.00 .40
❑ 162 Jerry Johnson 1.00 .40
❑ 163 Syd O'Brien 1.00 .40
❑ 164 Ty Cline 1.00 .40
❑ 165 Ed Kirkpatrick 1.00 .40
❑ 166 Al Oliver 3.00 1.20
❑ 167 Bill Burbach 1.00 .40
❑ 168 Dave Watkins 1.00 .40
❑ 169 Tom Hall 1.00 .40
❑ 170 Billy Williams 5.00 2.00
❑ 171 Jim Nash 1.00 .40
❑ 172 Garry Hill 1.50 .60
Ralph Garr RC
❑ 173 Jim Hicks 1.00 .40
❑ 174 Ted Sizemore 1.50 .60
❑ 175 Dick Bosman 1.00 .40
❑ 176 Jim Ray Hart 1.50 .60
❑ 177 Jim Northrup 1.50 .60
❑ 178 Denny Lemaster 1.00 .40
❑ 179 Ivan Murrell 1.00 .40
❑ 180 Tommy John 1.50 .60
❑ 181 Sparky Anderson MG 5.00 2.00
❑ 182 Dick Hall 1.00 .40
❑ 183 Jerry Grote 1.50 .60
❑ 184 Ray Fosse 1.00 .40
❑ 185 Don Mincher 1.50 .60
❑ 186 Rick Joseph 1.00 .40
❑ 187 Mike Hedlund 1.00 .40
❑ 188 Manny Sanguillen 1.50 .60
❑ 189 Thurman Munson RC 80.00 32.00
Dave McDonald
❑ 190 Joe Torre 3.00 1.20
❑ 191 Vicente Romo 1.00 .40
❑ 192 Jim Qualls 1.00 .40
❑ 193 Mike Wegener 1.00 .40
❑ 194 Chuck Manuel 1.00 .40
❑ 195 Tom Seaver NLCS 15.00 6.00
❑ 196 Ken Boswell NLCS 2.00 .80
❑ 197 Nolan Ryan NLCS 30.00 12.00
❑ 198 NL Playoff Summary 15.00 6.00
Mets celebrate
(Nolan Ryan)
❑ 199 Mike Cuellar ALCS 2.00 .80
❑ 200 Boog Powell ALCS 3.00 1.20
❑ 201 Boog Powell ALCS 2.00 .80
Andy Etchebarren)
❑ 202 AL Playoff Summary 2.00 .80
Orioles celebrate
❑ 203 Rudy May 1.00 .40
❑ 204 Len Gabrielson 1.00 .40
❑ 205 Bert Campaneris 1.50 .60
❑ 206 Clete Boyer 1.50 .60
❑ 207 Norman McRae 1.00 .40
Bob Reed
❑ 208 Fred Gladding 1.00 .40
❑ 209 Ken Suarez 1.00 .40
❑ 210 Juan Marichal 5.00 2.00
❑ 211 Ted Williams MG UER 15.00 6.00
Throwing information on back incorrect
❑ 212 Al Santorini 1.00 .40
❑ 213 Andy Etchebarren 1.00 .40
❑ 214 Ken Boswell 1.00 .40
❑ 215 Reggie Smith 1.50 .60
❑ 216 Chuck Hartenstein 1.00 .40
❑ 217 Ron Hansen 1.00 .40
❑ 218 Ron Stone 1.00 .40
❑ 219 Jerry Kenney 1.00 .40
❑ 220 Steve Carlton 15.00 6.00
❑ 221 Ron Brand 1.00 .40
❑ 222 Jim Rooker 1.00 .40
❑ 223 Nate Oliver 1.00 .40
❑ 224 Steve Barber 1.50 .60
❑ 225 Lee May 1.50 .60
❑ 226 Ron Perranoski 1.00 .40
❑ 227 John Mayberry RC 1.50 .60
Bob Watkins

❑ 228	Aurelio Rodriguez	1.00	.40
❑ 229	Rich Robertson	1.00	.40
❑ 230	Brooks Robinson	15.00	6.00
❑ 231	Luis Tiant	1.50	.60
❑ 232	Bob Didier	1.00	.40
❑ 233	Lew Krausse	1.00	.40
❑ 234	Tommy Dean	1.00	.40
❑ 235	Mike Epstein	1.00	.40
❑ 236	Bob Veale	1.00	.40
❑ 237	Russ Gibson	1.00	.40
❑ 238	Jose Laboy	1.00	.40
❑ 239	Ken Berry	1.00	.40
❑ 240	Ferguson Jenkins	5.00	2.00
❑ 241	Al Fitzmorris	1.00	.40
	Scott Northey		
❑ 242	Walter Alston MG	3.00	1.20
❑ 243	Joe Sparma	1.00	.40
❑ 244A	Checklist 3	6.00	1.20
	(Red bat on front)		
❑ 244B	Checklist 3	6.00	1.20
	(Brown bat on front)		
❑ 245	Leo Cardenas	1.00	.40
❑ 246	Jim McAndrew	1.00	.40
❑ 247	Lou Klimchock	1.00	.40
❑ 248	Jesus Alou	1.00	.40
❑ 249	Bob Locker	1.00	.40
❑ 250	Willie McCovey UER	10.00	4.00
	(1963 San Francisci)		
❑ 251	Dick Schofield	1.00	.40
❑ 252	Lowell Palmer	1.00	.40
❑ 253	Ron Woods	1.00	.40
❑ 254	Camilo Pascual	1.00	.40
❑ 255	Jim Spencer	1.00	.40
❑ 256	Vic Davalillo	1.00	.40
❑ 257	Dennis Higgins	1.00	.40
❑ 258	Paul Popovich	1.00	.40
❑ 259	Tommie Reynolds	1.00	.40
❑ 260	Claude Osteen	1.00	.40
❑ 261	Curt Motton	1.00	.40
❑ 262	Jerry Morales	1.00	.40
	Jim Williams		
❑ 263	Duane Josephson	1.00	.40
❑ 264	Rich Hebner	1.00	.40
❑ 265	Randy Hundley	1.00	.40
❑ 266	Wally Bunker	1.00	.40
❑ 267	Herman Hill	1.00	.40
	Paul Ratliff		
❑ 268	Claude Raymond	1.00	.40
❑ 269	Cesar Gutierrez	1.00	.40
❑ 270	Chris Short	1.00	.40
❑ 271	Greg Goossen	1.50	.60
❑ 272	Hector Torres	1.00	.40
❑ 273	Ralph Houk MG	1.50	.60
❑ 274	Gerry Arrigo	1.00	.40
❑ 275	Duke Sims	1.00	.40
❑ 276	Ron Hunt	1.00	.40
❑ 277	Paul Doyle	1.00	.40
❑ 278	Tommie Aaron	1.00	.40
❑ 279	Bill Lee RC	1.50	.60
❑ 280	Donn Clendenon	1.50	.60
❑ 281	Casey Cox	1.00	.40
❑ 282	Steve Huntz	1.00	.40
❑ 283	Angel Bravo	1.00	.40
❑ 284	Jack Baldschun	1.00	.40
❑ 285	Paul Blair	1.50	.60
❑ 286	Jack Jenkins	5.00	2.00
	Bill Buckner RC		
❑ 287	Fred Talbot	1.00	.40
❑ 288	Larry Hisle	1.50	.60
❑ 289	Gene Brabender	1.00	.40
❑ 290	Rod Carew	15.00	6.00
❑ 291	Leo Durocher MG	3.00	1.20
❑ 292	Eddie Leon	1.00	.40
❑ 293	Bob Bailey	1.50	.60
❑ 294	Jose Azcue	1.00	.40
❑ 295	Cecil Upshaw	1.00	.40
❑ 296	Woody Woodward	1.00	.40
❑ 297	Curt Blefary	1.00	.40
❑ 298	Ken Henderson	1.00	.40
❑ 299	Buddy Bradford	1.00	.40
❑ 300	Tom Seaver	30.00	12.00
❑ 301	Chico Salmon	1.00	.40
❑ 302	Jeff James	1.00	.40
❑ 303	Brant Alyea	1.00	.40
❑ 304	Bill Russell RC	5.00	2.00
❑ 305	Don Buford WS	4.00	1.60
❑ 306	Donn Clendenon WS	4.00	1.60
❑ 307	Tommie Agee WS	4.00	1.60
❑ 308	J.C. Martin WS	4.00	1.60
❑ 309	Jerry Koosman WS	4.00	1.60
❑ 310	WS Summary	5.00	2.00
	Mets whoop it up		
❑ 311	Dick Green	1.00	.40
❑ 312	Mike Torrez	1.00	.40
❑ 313	Mayo Smith MG	1.00	.40
❑ 314	Bill McCool	1.00	.40
❑ 315	Luis Aparicio	5.00	2.00
❑ 316	Skip Guinn	1.00	.40
❑ 317	Billy Conigliaro	1.50	.60
	Luis Alvarado		
❑ 318	Willie Smith	1.00	.40
❑ 319	Clay Dalrymple	1.00	.40
❑ 320	Jim Maloney	1.50	.60
❑ 321	Lou Piniella	1.50	.60
❑ 322	Luke Walker	1.00	.40
❑ 323	Wayne Comer	1.00	.40
❑ 324	Tony Taylor	1.50	.60
❑ 325	Dave Boswell	1.00	.40
❑ 326	Bill Voss	1.00	.40
❑ 327	Hal King	1.00	.40
❑ 328	George Brunet	1.00	.40
❑ 329	Chris Cannizzaro	1.00	.40
❑ 330	Lou Brock	10.00	4.00
❑ 331	Chuck Dobson	1.00	.40
❑ 332	Bobby Wine	1.00	.40
❑ 333	Bobby Murcer	1.50	.60
❑ 334	Phil Regan	1.00	.40
❑ 335	Bill Freehan	1.50	.60
❑ 336	Del Unser	1.00	.40
❑ 337	Mike McCormick	1.50	.60
❑ 338	Paul Schaal	1.00	.40
❑ 339	Johnny Edwards	1.00	.40
❑ 340	Tony Conigliaro	3.00	1.20
❑ 341	Bill Sudakis	1.00	.40
❑ 342	Wilbur Wood	1.50	.60
❑ 343A	Checklist 4	6.00	1.20
	(Red bat on front)		
❑ 343B	Checklist 4	6.00	1.20
	(Brown bat on front)		
❑ 344	Marcelino Lopez	1.00	.40
❑ 345	Al Ferrara	1.00	.40
❑ 346	Red Schoendienst MG	1.50	.60
❑ 347	Russ Snyder	1.00	.40
❑ 348	Mike Jorgensen	1.50	.60
	Jesse Hudson		
❑ 349	Steve Hamilton	1.00	.40
❑ 350	Roberto Clemente	60.00	24.00
❑ 351	Tom Murphy	1.00	.40
❑ 352	Bob Barton	1.00	.40
❑ 353	Stan Williams	1.00	.40
❑ 354	Amos Otis	1.50	.60
❑ 355	Doug Rader	1.00	.40
❑ 356	Fred Lasher	1.00	.40
❑ 357	Bob Burda	1.00	.40
❑ 358	Pedro Borbon RC	1.50	.60
❑ 359	Phil Roof	1.00	.40
❑ 360	Curt Flood	1.50	.60
❑ 361	Ray Jarvis	1.00	.40
❑ 362	Joe Hague	1.00	.40
❑ 363	Tom Shopay	1.00	.40
❑ 364	Dan McGinn	1.00	.40
❑ 365	Zoilo Versalles	1.00	.40
❑ 366	Barry Moore	1.00	.40
❑ 367	Mike Lum	1.00	.40
❑ 368	Ed Herrmann	1.00	.40
❑ 369	Alan Foster	1.00	.40
❑ 370	Tommy Harper	1.50	.60
❑ 371	Rod Gaspar	1.00	.40
❑ 372	Dave Giusti	1.00	.40
❑ 373	Roy White	2.00	.80
❑ 374	Tommie Sisk	1.50	.60
❑ 375	Johnny Callison	2.00	.80
❑ 376	Lefty Phillips MG	1.50	.60
❑ 377	Bill Butler	1.50	.60
❑ 378	Jim Davenport	1.50	.60
❑ 379	Tom Tischinski	1.50	.60
❑ 380	Tony Perez	6.00	2.40
❑ 381	Bobby Brooks	1.50	.60
	Mike Olivo		
❑ 382	Jack DiLauro	1.50	.60
❑ 383	Mickey Stanley	2.00	.80
❑ 384	Gary Neibauer	1.50	.60
❑ 385	George Scott	2.00	.80
❑ 386	Bill Dillman	1.50	.60
❑ 387	Baltimore Orioles	3.00	1.20
	Team Card		
❑ 388	Byron Browne	1.50	.60
❑ 389	Jim Shellenback	1.50	.60
❑ 390	Willie Davis	2.00	.80
❑ 391	Larry Brown	1.50	.60
❑ 392	Walt Hriniak	2.00	.80
❑ 393	John Gelnar	1.50	.60
❑ 394	Gil Hodges MG	4.00	1.60
❑ 395	Walt Williams	1.50	.60
❑ 396	Steve Blass	2.00	.80
❑ 397	Roger Repoz	1.50	.60
❑ 398	Bill Stoneman	1.50	.60
❑ 399	New York Yankees	3.00	1.20
	Team Card		
❑ 400	Denny McLain	4.00	1.60
❑ 401	John Harrell	1.50	.60
	Bernie Williams		
❑ 402	Ellie Rodriguez	1.50	.60
❑ 403	Jim Bunning	6.00	2.40
❑ 404	Rich Reese	1.50	.60
❑ 405	Bill Hands	1.50	.60
❑ 406	Mike Andrews	1.50	.60
❑ 407	Bob Watson	2.00	.80
❑ 408	Paul Lindblad	1.50	.60
❑ 409	Bob Tolan	1.50	.60
❑ 410	Boog Powell	4.00	1.60
❑ 411	Los Angeles Dodgers	3.00	1.20
	Team Card		
❑ 412	Larry Burchart	1.50	.60
❑ 413	Sonny Jackson	1.50	.60
❑ 414	Paul Edmondson	1.50	.60
❑ 415	Julian Javier	2.00	.80
❑ 416	Joe Verbanic	1.50	.60
❑ 417	John Bateman	1.50	.60
❑ 418	John Donaldson	1.50	.60
❑ 419	Ron Taylor	1.50	.60
❑ 420	Ken McMullen	2.00	.80
❑ 421	Pat Dobson	2.00	.80
❑ 422	Royals Team	3.00	1.20
❑ 423	Jerry May	1.50	.60
❑ 424	Mike Kilkenny	1.50	.60
	(Inconsistent design card number in white circle)		
❑ 425	Bobby Bonds	6.00	2.40
❑ 426	Bill Rigney MG	1.50	.60
❑ 427	Fred Norman	1.50	.60
❑ 428	Don Buford	1.50	.60
❑ 429	Randy Bobb	1.50	.60
	Jim Cosman		
❑ 430	Andy Messersmith	2.00	.80
❑ 431	Ron Swoboda	2.00	.80
❑ 432A	Checklist 5	6.00	1.20
	(Baseball in yellow letters)		
❑ 432B	Checklist 5	6.00	1.20
	(Baseball in white letters)		
❑ 433	Ron Bryant	1.50	.60
❑ 434	Felipe Alou	2.00	.80
❑ 435	Nelson Briles	2.00	.80
❑ 436	Philadelphia Phillies	3.00	1.20
	Team Card		
❑ 437	Danny Cater	1.50	.60
❑ 438	Pat Jarvis	1.50	.60
❑ 439	Lee Maye	1.50	.60
❑ 440	Bill Mazeroski	6.00	2.40
❑ 441	John O'Donoghue	1.50	.60
❑ 442	Gene Mauch MG	2.00	.80
❑ 443	Al Jackson	1.50	.60
❑ 444	Billy Farmer	1.50	.60
	John Matias		
❑ 445	Vada Pinson	2.00	.80
❑ 446	Billy Grabarkewitz	1.50	.60
❑ 447	Lee Stange	1.50	.60
❑ 448	Houston Astros	3.00	1.20
	Team Card		
❑ 449	Jim Palmer	12.00	4.80
❑ 450	Willie McCovey AS	6.00	2.40
❑ 451	Boog Powell AS	4.00	1.60
❑ 452	Felix Millan AS	2.00	.80
❑ 453	Rod Carew AS	6.00	2.40
❑ 454	Ron Santo AS	4.00	1.60

❑ 455 Brooks Robinson AS 6.00 2.40
❑ 456 Don Kessinger AS 2.00 .80
❑ 457 Rico Petrocelli AS 4.00 1.60
❑ 458 Pete Rose AS 15.00 6.00
❑ 459 Reggie Jackson AS 12.00 4.80
❑ 460 Matty Alou AS 3.00 1.20
❑ 461 Carl Yastrzemski AS 10.00 4.00
❑ 462 Hank Aaron AS 15.00 6.00
❑ 463 Frank Robinson AS 8.00 3.20
❑ 464 Johnny Bench AS 15.00 6.00
❑ 465 Bill Freehan AS 3.00 1.20
❑ 466 Juan Marichal AS 5.00 2.00
❑ 467 Denny McLain AS 3.00 1.20
❑ 468 Jerry Koosman AS 3.00 1.20
❑ 469 Sam McDowell AS 3.00 1.20
❑ 470 Willie Stargell 10.00 4.00
❑ 471 Chris Zachary 2.00 .80
❑ 472 Braves Team 4.00 1.60
❑ 473 Don Bryant 2.00 .80
❑ 474 Dick Kelley 2.00 .80
❑ 475 Dick McAuliffe 3.00 1.20
❑ 476 Don Shaw 2.00 .80
❑ 477 Al Severinsen 2.00 .80
Roger Freed
❑ 478 Bobby Heise 2.00 .80
❑ 479 Dick Woodson 2.00 .80
❑ 480 Glenn Beckert 3.00 1.20
❑ 481 Jose Tartabull 2.00 .80
❑ 482 Tom Hilgendorf 2.00 .80
❑ 483 Gail Hopkins 2.00 .80
❑ 484 Gary Nolan 3.00 1.20
❑ 485 Jay Johnstone 3.00 1.20
❑ 486 Terry Harmon 2.00 .80
❑ 487 Cisco Carlos 2.00 .80
❑ 488 J.C. Martin 2.00 .80
❑ 489 Eddie Kasko MG 2.00 .80
❑ 490 Bill Singer 3.00 1.20
❑ 491 Graig Nettles 5.00 2.00
❑ 492 Keith Lampard 2.00 .80
Scipio Spinks
❑ 493 Lindy McDaniel 3.00 1.20
❑ 494 Larry Stahl 2.00 .80
❑ 495 Dave Morehead 2.00 .80
❑ 496 Steve Whitaker 2.00 .80
❑ 497 Eddie Watt 2.00 .80
❑ 498 Al Weis 2.00 .80
❑ 499 Skip Lockwood 3.00 1.20
❑ 500 Hank Aaron 50.00 20.00
❑ 501 Chicago White Sox 4.00 1.60
Team Card
❑ 502 Rollie Fingers 10.00 4.00
❑ 503 Dal Maxvill 2.00 .80
❑ 504 Don Pavletich 2.00 .80
❑ 505 Ken Holtzman 3.00 1.20
❑ 506 Ed Stroud 2.00 .80
❑ 507 Pat Corrales 2.00 .80
❑ 508 Joe Niekro 3.00 1.20
❑ 509 Montreal Expos 4.00 1.60
Team Card
❑ 510 Tony Oliva 5.00 2.00
❑ 511 Joe Hoerner 2.00 .80
❑ 512 Billy Harris 2.00 .80
❑ 513 Preston Gomez MG 2.00 .80
❑ 514 Steve Hovley 2.00 .80
❑ 515 Don Wilson 3.00 1.20
❑ 516 John Ellis 2.00 .80
Jim Lyttle
❑ 517 Joe Gibbon 2.00 .80
❑ 518 Bill Melton 2.00 .80
❑ 519 Don McMahon 2.00 .80
❑ 520 Willie Horton 3.00 1.20
❑ 521 Cal Koonce 2.00 .80
❑ 522 Angels Team 4.00 1.60
❑ 523 Jose Pena 2.00 .80
❑ 524 Alvin Dark MG 3.00 1.20
❑ 525 Jerry Adair 2.00 .80
❑ 526 Ron Herbel 2.00 .80
❑ 527 Don Bosch 2.00 .80
❑ 528 Elrod Hendricks 2.00 .80
❑ 529 Bob Aspromonte 2.00 .80
❑ 530 Bob Gibson 15.00 6.00
❑ 531 Ron Clark 2.00 .80
❑ 532 Danny Murtaugh MG 3.00 1.20
❑ 533 Buzz Stephen 2.00 .80
❑ 534 Minnesota Twins 4.00 1.60
Team Card

❑ 535 Andy Kosco 2.00 .80
❑ 536 Mike Kekich 2.00 .80
❑ 537 Joe Morgan 10.00 4.00
❑ 538 Bob Humphreys 2.00 .80
❑ 539 Denny Doyle 8.00 3.20
Larry Bowa RC
❑ 540 Gary Peters 2.00 .80
❑ 541 Bill Heath 2.00 .80
❑ 542 Checklist 6 6.00 1.20
❑ 543 Clyde Wright 2.00 .80
❑ 544 Cincinnati Reds 4.00 1.60
Team Card
❑ 545 Ken Harrelson 3.00 1.20
❑ 546 Ron Reed 2.00 .80
❑ 547 Rick Monday 6.00 2.40
❑ 548 Howie Reed 4.00 1.60
❑ 549 St. Louis Cardinals 6.00 2.40
Team Card
❑ 550 Frank Howard 6.00 2.40
❑ 551 Dock Ellis 6.00 2.40
❑ 552 Don O'Riley 4.00 1.60
Dennis Paepke
Fred Rico
❑ 553 Jim Lefebvre 6.00 2.40
❑ 554 Tom Timmermann 4.00 1.60
❑ 555 Orlando Cepeda 12.00 4.80
❑ 556 Dave Bristol MG 6.00 2.40
❑ 557 Ed Kranepool 6.00 2.40
❑ 558 Vern Fuller 4.00 1.60
❑ 559 Tommy Davis 6.00 2.40
❑ 560 Gaylord Perry 12.00 4.80
❑ 561 Tom McCraw 4.00 1.60
❑ 562 Ted Abernathy 4.00 1.60
❑ 563 Boston Red Sox 6.00 2.40
Team Card
❑ 564 Johnny Briggs 4.00 1.60
❑ 565 Jim Hunter 12.00 4.80
❑ 566 Gene Alley 6.00 2.40
❑ 567 Bob Oliver 4.00 1.60
❑ 568 Stan Bahnsen 6.00 2.40
❑ 569 Cookie Rojas 6.00 2.40
❑ 570 Jim Fregosi 6.00 2.40
White Chevy Pick-Up in Background
❑ 571 Jim Brewer 4.00 1.60
❑ 572 Frank Quilici 4.00 1.60
❑ 573 Mike Corkins 4.00 1.60
Rafael Robles
Ron Slocum
❑ 574 Bobby Bolin 6.00 2.40
❑ 575 Cleon Jones 6.00 2.40
❑ 576 Milt Pappas 6.00 2.40
❑ 577 Bernie Allen 4.00 1.60
❑ 578 Tom Griffin 4.00 1.60
❑ 579 Detroit Tigers 6.00 2.40
Team Card
❑ 580 Pete Rose 60.00 24.00
❑ 581 Tom Satriano 4.00 1.60
❑ 582 Mike Paul 4.00 1.60
❑ 583 Hal Lanier 4.00 1.60
❑ 584 Al Downing 6.00 2.40
❑ 585 Rusty Staub 8.00 3.20
❑ 586 Rickey Clark 4.00 1.60
❑ 587 Jose Arcia 4.00 1.60
❑ 588A Checklist 7 ERR 8.00 1.60
(666 Adollo)
❑ 588B Checklist 7 COR 6.00 1.20
(666 Adolpho)
❑ 589 Joe Keough 4.00 1.60
❑ 590 Mike Cuellar 6.00 2.40
❑ 591 Mike Ryan UER 4.00 1.60
(Pitching Record
header on card back)
❑ 592 Daryl Patterson 4.00 1.60
❑ 593 Chicago Cubs 8.00 3.20
Team Card
❑ 594 Jake Gibbs 4.00 1.60
❑ 595 Maury Wills 8.00 3.20
❑ 596 Mike Hershberger 6.00 2.40
❑ 597 Sonny Siebert 4.00 1.60
❑ 598 Joe Pepitone 6.00 2.40
❑ 599 Dick Stelmaszek 4.00 1.60
Gene Martin
Dick Such
❑ 600 Willie Mays 80.00 32.00
❑ 601 Pete Richert 4.00 1.60
❑ 602 Ted Savage 4.00 1.60

❑ 603 Ray Oyler 4.00 1.60
❑ 604 Clarence Gaston 6.00 2.40
❑ 605 Rick Wise 6.00 2.40
❑ 606 Chico Ruiz 4.00 1.60
❑ 607 Gary Waslewski 4.00 1.60
❑ 608 Pittsburgh Pirates 6.00 2.40
Team Card
❑ 609 Buck Martinez RC 6.00 2.40
(Inconsistent design
card number in
white circle)
❑ 610 Jerry Koosman 8.00 3.20
❑ 611 Norm Cash 6.00 2.40
❑ 612 Jim Hickman 6.00 2.40
❑ 613 Dave Baldwin 6.00 2.40
❑ 614 Mike Shannon 6.00 2.40
❑ 615 Mark Belanger 6.00 2.40
❑ 616 Jim Merritt 4.00 1.60
❑ 617 Jim French 4.00 1.60
❑ 618 Billy Wynne 4.00 1.60
❑ 619 Norm Miller 4.00 1.60
❑ 620 Jim Perry 6.00 2.40
❑ 621 Mike McQueen 12.00 4.80
Darrell Evans RC
Rick Kester
❑ 622 Don Sutton 12.00 4.80
❑ 623 Horace Clarke 6.00 2.40
❑ 624 Clyde King MG 4.00 1.60
❑ 625 Dean Chance 4.00 1.60
❑ 626 Dave Ricketts 4.00 1.60
❑ 627 Gary Wagner 4.00 1.60
❑ 628 Wayne Garrett 4.00 1.60
❑ 629 Merv Rettenmund 4.00 1.60
❑ 630 Ernie Banks 50.00 20.00
❑ 631 Oakland Athletics 6.00 2.40
Team Card
❑ 632 Gary Sutherland 4.00 1.60
❑ 633 Roger Nelson 4.00 1.60
❑ 634 Bud Harrelson 15.00 6.00
❑ 635 Bob Allison 15.00 6.00
❑ 636 Jim Stewart 10.00 4.00
❑ 637 Cleveland Indians 12.00 4.80
Team Card
❑ 638 Frank Bertaina 10.00 4.00
❑ 639 Dave Campbell 15.00 6.00
❑ 640 Al Kaline 50.00 20.00
❑ 641 Al McBean 10.00 4.00
❑ 642 Greg Garrett 10.00 4.00
Gordon Lund
Jarvis Tatum
❑ 643 Jose Pagan 10.00 4.00
❑ 644 Gerry Nyman 10.00 4.00
❑ 645 Don Money 15.00 6.00
❑ 646 Jim Britton 10.00 4.00
❑ 647 Tom Matchick 10.00 4.00
❑ 648 Larry Haney 10.00 4.00
❑ 649 Jimmie Hall 10.00 4.00
❑ 650 Sam McDowell 15.00 6.00
❑ 651 Jim Gosger 10.00 4.00
❑ 652 Rich Rollins 15.00 6.00
❑ 653 Moe Drabowsky 10.00 4.00
❑ 654 Oscar Gamble RC 15.00 6.00
Boots Day
Angel Mangual
❑ 655 John Roseboro 15.00 6.00
❑ 656 Jim Hardin 10.00 4.00
❑ 657 San Diego Padres 12.00 4.80
Team Card
❑ 658 Ken Tatum 10.00 4.00
❑ 659 Pete Ward 10.00 4.00
❑ 660 Johnny Bench 80.00 32.00
❑ 661 Jerry Robertson 10.00 4.00
❑ 662 Frank Lucchesi MG 10.00 4.00
❑ 663 Tito Francona 10.00 4.00
❑ 664 Bob Robertson 10.00 4.00
❑ 665 Jim Lonborg 15.00 6.00
❑ 666 Adolpho Phillips 10.00 4.00
❑ 667 Bob Meyer 15.00 6.00
❑ 668 Bob Tillman 10.00 4.00
❑ 669 Bart Johnson 10.00 4.00
Dan Lazar
Mickey Scott
❑ 670 Ron Santo 15.00 6.00
❑ 671 Jim Campanis 10.00 4.00
❑ 672 Leon McFadden 10.00 4.00
❑ 673 Ted Uhlaender 10.00 4.00

	Card	NM	Ex
❑ 674	Dave Leonhard	10.00	4.00
❑ 675	Jose Cardenal	15.00	6.00
❑ 676	Washington Senators Team Card	12.00	4.80
❑ 677	Woodie Fryman	10.00	4.00
❑ 678	Dave Duncan	15.00	6.00
❑ 679	Ray Sadecki	10.00	4.00
❑ 680	Rico Petrocelli	15.00	6.00
❑ 681	Bob Garibaldi	10.00	4.00
❑ 682	Dalton Jones	10.00	4.00
❑ 683	Vern Geishert / Hal McRae / Wayne Simpson	15.00	6.00
❑ 684	Jack Fisher	10.00	4.00
❑ 685	Tom Haller	10.00	4.00
❑ 686	Jackie Hernandez	10.00	4.00
❑ 687	Bob Priddy	10.00	4.00
❑ 688	Ted Kubiak	15.00	6.00
❑ 689	Frank Tepedino	15.00	6.00
❑ 690	Ron Fairly	15.00	6.00
❑ 691	Joe Grzenda	10.00	4.00
❑ 692	Duffy Dyer	10.00	4.00
❑ 693	Bob Johnson	10.00	4.00
❑ 694	Gary Ross	10.00	4.00
❑ 695	Bobby Knoop	10.00	4.00
❑ 696	San Francisco Giants Team Card	12.00	4.80
❑ 697	Jim Hannan	10.00	4.00
❑ 698	Tom Tresh	15.00	6.00
❑ 699	Hank Aguirre	10.00	4.00
❑ 700	Frank Robinson	50.00	20.00
❑ 701	Jack Billingham	10.00	4.00
❑ 702	Bob Johnson / Ron Klimkowski / Bill Zepp	10.00	4.00
❑ 703	Lou Marone	10.00	4.00
❑ 704	Frank Baker	10.00	4.00
❑ 705	Tony Cloninger UER (Batter headings on card back)	10.00	4.00
❑ 706	John McNamara MG	10.00	4.00
❑ 707	Kevin Collins	10.00	4.00
❑ 708	Jose Santiago	10.00	4.00
❑ 709	Mike Fiore	10.00	4.00
❑ 710	Felix Millan	10.00	4.00
❑ 711	Ed Brinkman	10.00	4.00
❑ 712	Nolan Ryan	200.00	80.00
❑ 713	Seattle Pilots Team Card	25.00	10.00
❑ 714	Al Spangler	10.00	4.00
❑ 715	Mickey Lolich	15.00	6.00
❑ 716	Sal Campisi / Reggie Cleveland / Santiago Guzman	15.00	6.00
❑ 717	Tom Phoebus	10.00	4.00
❑ 718	Ed Spiezio	10.00	4.00
❑ 719	Jim Roland	10.00	4.00
❑ 720	Rick Reichardt	15.00	5.00

1971 Topps

	NM	Ex
COMPLETE SET (752)	2500.00	1000.00
COMMON CARD (1-393)	1.50	.60
COMMON (394-523)	2.50	1.00
COMMON (524-643)	4.00	1.60
COMMON (644-752)	8.00	3.20
COMMON SP (644-752)	12.00	4.80
WRAPPER (10-CENT)	15.00	6.00

	Card	NM	Ex
❑ 1	Baltimore Orioles Team Card	20.00	6.75
❑ 2	Dock Ellis	1.50	.60
❑ 3	Dick McAuliffe	2.00	.80
❑ 4	Vic Davalillo	1.50	.60
❑ 5	Thurman Munson	120.00	47.50
❑ 6	Ed Spiezio	1.50	.60
❑ 7	Jim Holt	1.50	.60
❑ 8	Mike McQueen	1.50	.60
❑ 9	George Scott	2.00	.80
❑ 10	Claude Osteen	2.00	.80
❑ 11	Elliott Maddox	1.50	.60
❑ 12	Johnny Callison	2.00	.80
❑ 13	Charlie Brinkman / Dick Moloney	1.50	.60
❑ 14	Dave Concepcion RC	15.00	6.00
❑ 15	Andy Messersmith	2.00	.80
❑ 16	Ken Singleton RC	4.00	1.60
❑ 17	Billy Sorrell	1.50	.60
❑ 18	Norm Miller	1.50	.60
❑ 19	Skip Pitlock	1.50	.60
❑ 20	Reggie Jackson	50.00	20.00
❑ 21	Dan McGinn	1.50	.60
❑ 22	Phil Roof	1.50	.60
❑ 23	Oscar Gamble	1.50	.60
❑ 24	Rich Hand	1.50	.60
❑ 25	Clarence Gaston	2.00	.80
❑ 26	Bert Blyleven RC	20.00	8.00
❑ 27	Fred Cambria / Gene Clines	1.50	.60
❑ 28	Ron Klimkowski	1.50	.60
❑ 29	Don Buford	1.50	.60
❑ 30	Phil Niekro	6.00	2.40
❑ 31	Eddie Kasko MG	1.50	.60
❑ 32	Jerry DaVanon	1.50	.60
❑ 33	Del Unser	1.50	.60
❑ 34	Sandy Vance	1.50	.60
❑ 35	Lou Piniella	2.00	.80
❑ 36	Dean Chance	2.00	.80
❑ 37	Rich McKinney	1.50	.60
❑ 38	Jim Colborn	1.50	.60
❑ 39	Lerrin LaGrow / Gene Lamont RC	2.00	.80
❑ 40	Lee May	2.00	.80
❑ 41	Rick Austin	1.50	.60
❑ 42	Boots Day	1.50	.60
❑ 43	Steve Kealey	1.50	.60
❑ 44	Johnny Edwards	1.50	.60
❑ 45	Jim Hunter	6.00	2.40
❑ 46	Dave Campbell	2.00	.80
❑ 47	Johnny Jeter	1.50	.60
❑ 48	Dave Baldwin	1.50	.60
❑ 49	Don Money	1.50	.60
❑ 50	Willie McCovey	10.00	4.00
❑ 51	Steve Kline	1.50	.60
❑ 52	Oscar Brown / Earl Williams RC	1.50	.60
❑ 53	Paul Blair	2.00	.80
❑ 54	Checklist 1	10.00	2.00
❑ 55	Steve Carlton	20.00	8.00
❑ 56	Duane Josephson	1.50	.60
❑ 57	Von Joshua	1.50	.60
❑ 58	Bill Lee	2.00	.80
❑ 59	Gene Mauch MG	2.00	.80
❑ 60	Dick Bosman	1.50	.60
❑ 61	Alex Johnson / Carl Yastrzemski / Tony Oliva LL	4.00	1.60
❑ 62	Rico Carty / Joe Torre / Manny Sanguillen LL	2.00	.80
❑ 63	Frank Howard / Tony Conigliaro / Boog Powell LL	4.00	1.60
❑ 64	Johnny Bench / Tony Perez / Billy Williams LL	6.00	2.40
❑ 65	Frank Howard / Harmon Killebrew / Carl Yastrzemski LL	4.00	1.60
❑ 66	Johnny Bench / Billy Williams / Tony Perez LL	6.00	2.40
❑ 67	Diego Segui / Jim Palmer / Clyde Wright LL	4.00	1.60
❑ 68	Tom Seaver / Wayne Simpson / Luke Walker LL	4.00	1.60
❑ 69	Mike Cuellar / Dave McNally / Jim Perry LL	2.00	.80
❑ 70	Bob Gibson / Gaylord Perry / Fergie Jenkins LL	6.00	2.40
❑ 71	Sam McDowell / Mickey Lolich / Bob Johnson LL	2.00	.80
❑ 72	Tom Seaver / Bob Gibson / Fergie Jenkins LL	6.00	2.40
❑ 73	George Brunet	1.50	.60
❑ 74	Pete Hamm / Jim Nettles	1.50	.60
❑ 75	Gary Nolan	2.00	.80
❑ 76	Ted Savage	1.50	.60
❑ 77	Mike Compton	1.50	.60
❑ 78	Jim Spencer	1.50	.60
❑ 79	Wade Blasingame	1.50	.60
❑ 80	Bill Melton	1.50	.60
❑ 81	Felix Millan	1.50	.60
❑ 82	Casey Cox	1.50	.60
❑ 83	Tim Foli RC / Randy Bobb	2.00	.80
❑ 84	Marcel Lachemann RC	1.50	.60
❑ 85	Billy Grabarkewitz	1.50	.60
❑ 86	Mike Kilkenny	1.50	.60
❑ 87	Jack Heidemann	1.50	.60
❑ 88	Hal King	1.50	.60
❑ 89	Ken Brett	1.50	.60
❑ 90	Joe Pepitone	2.00	.80
❑ 91	Bob Lemon MG	2.00	.80
❑ 92	Fred Wenz	1.50	.60
❑ 93	Norm McRae / Denny Riddleberger	1.50	.60
❑ 94	Don Hahn	1.50	.60
❑ 95	Luis Tiant	2.00	.80
❑ 96	Joe Hague	1.50	.60
❑ 97	Floyd Wicker	1.50	.60
❑ 98	Joe Decker	1.50	.60
❑ 99	Mark Belanger	2.00	.80
❑ 100	Pete Rose	80.00	32.00
❑ 101	Les Cain	1.50	.60
❑ 102	Ken Forsch / Larry Howard	2.00	.80
❑ 103	Rich Severson	1.50	.60
❑ 104	Dan Frisella	1.50	.60
❑ 105	Tony Conigliaro	2.00	.80
❑ 106	Tom Dukes	1.50	.60
❑ 107	Roy Foster	1.50	.60
❑ 108	John Cumberland	1.50	.60
❑ 109	Steve Hovley	1.50	.60
❑ 110	Bill Mazeroski	6.00	2.40
❑ 111	Loyd Colson / Bobby Mitchell	1.50	.60
❑ 112	Manny Mota	2.00	.80
❑ 113	Jerry Crider	1.50	.60
❑ 114	Billy Conigliaro	2.00	.80
❑ 115	Donn Clendenon	2.00	.80
❑ 116	Ken Sanders	1.50	.60
❑ 117	Ted Simmons RC	8.00	3.20
❑ 118	Cookie Rojas	2.00	.80
❑ 119	Frank Lucchesi MG	1.50	.60
❑ 120	Willie Horton	2.00	.80
❑ 121	Jim Dunegan / Roe Skidmore	1.50	.60
❑ 122	Eddie Watt	1.50	.60
❑ 123A	Checklist 2 (Card number at bottom right)	10.00	2.00
❑ 123B	Checklist 2 (Card number centered)	10.00	2.00
❑ 124	Don Gullett RC	2.00	.80
❑ 125	Ray Fosse	1.50	.60
❑ 126	Danny Coombs	1.50	.60
❑ 127	Danny Thompson	2.00	.80
❑ 128	Frank Johnson	1.50	.60
❑ 129	Aurelio Monteagudo	1.50	.60
❑ 130	Denis Menke	1.50	.60
❑ 131	Curt Blefary	1.50	.60
❑ 132	Jose Laboy	1.50	.60

❑	133	Mickey Lolich	2.00	.80
❑	134	Jose Arcia	1.50	.60
❑	135	Rick Monday	2.00	.80
❑	136	Duffy Dyer	1.50	.60
❑	137	Marcelino Lopez	1.50	.60
❑	138	Joe Lis	2.00	.80
		Willie Montanez		
❑	139	Paul Casanova	1.50	.60
❑	140	Gaylord Perry	6.00	2.40
❑	141	Frank Quilici	1.50	.60
❑	142	Mack Jones	1.50	.60
❑	143	Steve Blass	2.00	.80
❑	144	Jackie Hernandez	1.50	.60
❑	145	Bill Singer	2.00	.80
❑	146	Ralph Houk MG	2.00	.80
❑	147	Bob Priddy	1.50	.60
❑	148	John Mayberry	2.00	.80
❑	149	Mike Hershberger	1.50	.60
❑	150	Sam McDowell	2.00	.80
❑	151	Tommy Davis	2.00	.80
❑	152	Lloyd Allen	1.50	.60
		Winston Llenas		
❑	153	Gary Ross	1.50	.60
❑	154	Cesar Gutierrez	1.50	.60
❑	155	Ken Henderson	1.50	.60
❑	156	Bart Johnson	1.50	.60
❑	157	Bob Bailey	2.00	.80
❑	158	Jerry Reuss	2.00	.80
❑	159	Jarvis Tatum	1.50	.60
❑	160	Tom Seaver	30.00	12.00
❑	161	Coin Checklist	10.00	2.00
❑	162	Jack Billingham	1.50	.60
❑	163	Buck Martinez	2.00	.80
❑	164	Frank Duffy	2.00	.80
		Milt Wilcox		
❑	165	Cesar Tovar	1.50	.60
❑	166	Joe Hoerner	1.50	.60
❑	167	Tom Grieve RC	2.00	.80
❑	168	Bruce Dal Canton	1.50	.60
❑	169	Ed Herrmann	1.50	.60
❑	170	Mike Cuellar	2.00	.80
❑	171	Bobby Wine	1.50	.60
❑	172	Duke Sims	1.50	.60
❑	173	Gil Garrido	1.50	.60
❑	174	Dave LaRoche	1.50	.60
❑	175	Jim Hickman	1.50	.60
❑	176	Bob Montgomery RC	2.00	.80
		Doug Griffin		
❑	177	Hal McRae	2.00	.80
❑	178	Dave Duncan	2.00	.80
❑	179	Mike Corkins	1.50	.60
❑	180	Al Kaline UER	20.00	8.00
		(Home instead of Birth)		
❑	181	Hal Lanier	1.50	.60
❑	182	Al Downing	2.00	.80
❑	183	Gil Hodges MG	4.00	1.60
❑	184	Stan Bahnsen	1.50	.60
❑	185	Julian Javier	1.50	.60
❑	186	Bob Spence	1.50	.60
❑	187	Ted Abernathy	1.50	.60
❑	188	Bob Valentine RC	6.00	2.40
		Mike Strahler		
❑	189	George Mitterwald	1.50	.60
❑	190	Bob Tolan	1.50	.60
❑	191	Mike Andrews	1.50	.60
❑	192	Billy Wilson	1.50	.60
❑	193	Bob Grich RC	4.00	1.60
❑	194	Mike Lum	1.50	.60
❑	195	Boog Powell ALCS	2.00	.80
❑	196	Dave McNally ALCS	2.00	.80
❑	197	Jim Palmer ALCS	4.00	1.60
❑	198	AL Playoff Summary	2.00	.80
		Orioles celebrate		
❑	199	Ty Cline NLCS	2.00	.80
❑	200	Bobby Tolan NLCS	2.00	.80
❑	201	Ty Cline NLCS	2.00	.80
❑	202	NL Playoff Summary	2.00	.80
		Reds celebrate		
❑	203	Larry Gura	2.00	.80
❑	204	Bernie Smith	1.50	.60
		George Kopacz		
❑	205	Gerry Moses	1.50	.60
❑	206	Checklist 3	10.00	2.00
❑	207	Alan Foster	1.50	.60
❑	208	Billy Martin MG	4.00	1.60
❑	209	Steve Renko	1.50	.60
❑	210	Rod Carew	15.00	6.00
❑	211	Phil Hennigan	1.50	.60
❑	212	Rich Hebner	2.00	.80
❑	213	Frank Baker	1.50	.60
❑	214	Al Ferrara	1.50	.60
❑	215	Diego Segui	1.50	.60
❑	216	Reggie Cleveland	1.50	.60
		Luis Melendez		
❑	217	Ed Stroud	1.50	.60
❑	218	Tony Cloninger	1.50	.60
❑	219	Elrod Hendricks	1.50	.60
❑	220	Ron Santo	4.00	1.60
❑	221	Dave Morehead	1.50	.60
❑	222	Bob Watson	2.00	.80
❑	223	Cecil Upshaw	1.50	.60
❑	224	Alan Gallagher	1.50	.60
❑	225	Gary Peters	1.50	.60
❑	226	Bill Russell	2.00	.80
❑	227	Floyd Weaver	1.50	.60
❑	228	Wayne Garrett	1.50	.60
❑	229	Jim Hannan	1.50	.60
❑	230	Willie Stargell	15.00	6.00
❑	231	Vince Colbert	2.00	.80
		John Lowenstein RC		
❑	232	John Strohmayer	1.50	.60
❑	233	Larry Bowa	2.00	.80
❑	234	Jim Lyttle	1.50	.60
❑	235	Nate Colbert	1.50	.60
❑	236	Bob Humphreys	1.50	.60
❑	237	Cesar Cedeno RC	2.00	.80
❑	238	Chuck Dobson	1.50	.60
❑	239	Red Schoendienst MG	2.00	.80
❑	240	Clyde Wright	1.50	.60
❑	241	Dave Nelson	1.50	.60
❑	242	Jim Ray	1.50	.60
❑	243	Carlos May	1.50	.60
❑	244	Bob Tillman	1.50	.60
❑	245	Jim Kaat	2.00	.80
❑	246	Tony Taylor	1.50	.60
❑	247	Jerry Cram	2.00	.80
		Paul Splittorff		
❑	248	Hoyt Wilhelm	6.00	2.40
❑	249	Chico Salmon	1.50	.60
❑	250	Johnny Bench	50.00	20.00
❑	251	Frank Reberger	1.50	.60
❑	252	Eddie Leon	1.50	.60
❑	253	Bill Sudakis	1.50	.60
❑	254	Cal Koonce	1.50	.60
❑	255	Bob Robertson	2.00	.80
❑	256	Tony Gonzalez	1.50	.60
❑	257	Nelson Briles	2.00	.80
❑	258	Dick Green	1.50	.60
❑	259	Dave Marshall	1.50	.60
❑	260	Tommy Harper	2.00	.80
❑	261	Darold Knowles	1.50	.60
❑	262	Jim Williams	1.50	.60
		Dave Robinson		
❑	263	John Ellis	1.50	.60
❑	264	Joe Morgan	8.00	3.20
❑	265	Jim Northrup	2.00	.80
❑	266	Bill Stoneman	1.50	.60
❑	267	Rich Morales	1.50	.60
❑	268	Philadelphia Phillies	4.00	1.60
		Team Card		
❑	269	Gail Hopkins	1.50	.60
❑	270	Rico Carty	2.00	.80
❑	271	Bill Zepp	1.50	.60
❑	272	Tommy Helms	2.00	.80
❑	273	Pete Richert	1.50	.60
❑	274	Ron Slocum	1.50	.60
❑	275	Vada Pinson	2.00	.80
❑	276	Mike Davison	8.00	3.20
		George Foster RC		
❑	277	Gary Waslewski	1.50	.60
❑	278	Jerry Grote	2.00	.80
❑	279	Lefty Phillips MG	1.50	.60
❑	280	Ferguson Jenkins	6.00	2.40
❑	281	Danny Walton	1.50	.60
❑	282	Jose Pagan	1.50	.60
❑	283	Dick Such	1.50	.60
❑	284	Jim Gosger	1.50	.60
❑	285	Sal Bando	2.00	.80
❑	286	Jerry McNertney	1.50	.60
❑	287	Mike Fiore	1.50	.60
❑	288	Joe Moeller	1.50	.60
❑	289	Chicago White Sox	4.00	1.60
		Team Card		
❑	290	Tony Oliva	4.00	1.60
❑	291	George Culver	1.50	.60
❑	292	Jay Johnstone	2.00	.80
❑	293	Pat Corrales	2.00	.80
❑	294	Steve Dunning	1.50	.60
❑	295	Bobby Bonds	4.00	1.60
❑	296	Tom Timmermann	1.50	.60
❑	297	Johnny Briggs	1.50	.60
❑	298	Jim Nelson	1.50	.60
❑	299	Ed Kirkpatrick	1.50	.60
❑	300	Brooks Robinson	20.00	8.00
❑	301	Earl Wilson	1.50	.60
❑	302	Phil Gagliano	1.50	.60
❑	303	Lindy McDaniel	2.00	.80
❑	304	Ron Brand	1.50	.60
❑	305	Reggie Smith	2.00	.80
❑	306	Jim Nash	1.50	.60
❑	307	Don Wert	1.50	.60
❑	308	St. Louis Cardinals	4.00	1.60
		Team Card		
❑	309	Dick Ellsworth	1.50	.60
❑	310	Tommie Agee	2.00	.80
❑	311	Lee Stange	1.50	.60
❑	312	Harry Walker MG	1.50	.60
❑	313	Tom Hall	1.50	.60
❑	314	Jeff Torborg	2.00	.80
❑	315	Ron Fairly	2.00	.80
❑	316	Fred Scherman	1.50	.60
❑	317	Jim Driscoll	1.50	.60
		Angel Mangual		
❑	318	Rudy May	1.50	.60
❑	319	Ty Cline	1.50	.60
❑	320	Dave McNally	2.00	.80
❑	321	Tom Matchick	1.50	.60
❑	322	Jim Beauchamp	1.50	.60
❑	323	Billy Champion	1.50	.60
❑	324	Graig Nettles	2.00	.80
❑	325	Juan Marichal	8.00	3.20
❑	326	Richie Scheinblum	1.50	.60
❑	327	Boog Powell WS	2.00	.80
❑	328	Don Buford WS	2.00	.80
❑	329	Frank Robinson WS	4.00	1.60
❑	330	World Series Game 4	2.00	.80
		Reds stay alive		
❑	331	Brooks Robinson WS	6.00	2.40
		commits robbery		
❑	332	WS Summary	2.00	.80
		Orioles celebrate		
❑	333	Clay Kirby	1.50	.60
❑	334	Roberto Pena	1.50	.60
❑	335	Jerry Koosman	2.00	.80
❑	336	Detroit Tigers	4.00	1.60
		Team Card		
❑	337	Jesus Alou	1.50	.60
❑	338	Gene Tenace	2.00	.80
❑	339	Wayne Simpson	1.50	.60
❑	340	Rico Petrocelli	2.00	.80
❑	341	Steve Garvey RC	40.00	16.00
❑	342	Frank Tepedino	2.00	.80
❑	343	Ed Acosta	2.00	.80
		Milt May RC		
❑	344	Ellie Rodriguez	1.50	.60
❑	345	Joel Horlen	1.50	.60
❑	346	Lum Harris MG	1.50	.60
❑	347	Ted Uhlaender	1.50	.60
❑	348	Fred Norman	1.50	.60
❑	349	Rich Reese	1.50	.60
❑	350	Billy Williams	6.00	2.40
❑	351	Jim Shellenback	1.50	.60
❑	352	Denny Doyle	1.50	.60
❑	353	Carl Taylor	1.50	.60
❑	354	Don McMahon	1.50	.60
❑	355	Bud Harrelson	4.00	1.60
		(Nolan Ryan in photo)		
❑	356	Bob Locker	1.50	.60
❑	357	Cincinnati Reds	4.00	1.60
		Team Card		
❑	358	Danny Cater	1.50	.60
❑	359	Ron Reed	1.50	.60
❑	360	Jim Fregosi	2.00	.80
❑	361	Don Sutton	6.00	2.40
❑	362	Mike Adamson	1.50	.60
		Roger Freed		
❑	363	Mike Nagy	1.50	.60

❑ 364 Tommy Dean 1.50 .60
❑ 365 Bob Johnson 1.50 .60
❑ 366 Ron Stone 1.50 .60
❑ 367 Dalton Jones 1.50 .60
❑ 368 Bob Veale 2.00 .80
❑ 369 Checklist 4 10.00 2.00
❑ 370 Joe Torre 4.00 1.60
❑ 371 Jack Hiatt 1.50 .60
❑ 372 Lew Krausse 1.50 .60
❑ 373 Tom McCraw 1.50 .60
❑ 374 Clete Boyer 2.00 .80
❑ 375 Steve Hargan 1.50 .60
❑ 376 Clyde Mashore 1.50 .60
Ernie McAnally
❑ 377 Greg Garrett 1.50 .60
❑ 378 Tito Fuentes 1.50 .60
❑ 379 Wayne Granger 1.50 .60
❑ 380 Ted Williams MG 12.00 4.80
❑ 381 Fred Gladding 1.50 .60
❑ 382 Jake Gibbs 1.50 .60
❑ 383 Rod Gaspar 1.50 .60
❑ 384 Rollie Fingers 6.00 2.40
❑ 385 Maury Wills 4.00 1.60
❑ 386 Boston Red Sox 2.00 .80
Team Card
❑ 387 Ron Herbel 1.50 .60
❑ 388 Al Oliver 4.00 1.60
❑ 389 Ed Brinkman 1.50 .60
❑ 390 Glenn Beckert 2.00 .80
❑ 391 Steve Brye 2.00 .80
Cotton Nash
❑ 392 Grant Jackson 1.50 .60
❑ 393 Merv Rettenmund 2.00 .80
❑ 394 Clay Carroll 2.50 1.00
❑ 395 Roy White 4.00 1.60
❑ 396 Dick Schofield 2.50 1.00
❑ 397 Alvin Dark MG 4.00 1.60
❑ 398 Howie Reed 2.50 1.00
❑ 399 Jim French 2.50 1.00
❑ 400 Hank Aaron 60.00 24.00
❑ 401 Tom Murphy 2.50 1.00
❑ 402 Los Angeles Dodgers 6.00 2.40
Team Card
❑ 403 Joe Coleman 2.50 1.00
❑ 404 Buddy Harris 2.50 1.00
Roger Metzger
❑ 405 Leo Cardenas 2.50 1.00
❑ 406 Ray Sadecki 2.50 1.00
❑ 407 Joe Rudi 4.00 1.60
❑ 408 Rafael Robles 2.50 1.00
❑ 409 Don Pavletich 2.50 1.00
❑ 410 Ken Holtzman 4.00 1.60
❑ 411 George Spriggs 2.50 1.00
❑ 412 Jerry Johnson 2.50 1.00
❑ 413 Pat Kelly 2.50 1.00
❑ 414 Woodie Fryman 2.50 1.00
❑ 415 Mike Hegan 2.50 1.00
❑ 416 Gene Alley 2.50 1.00
❑ 417 Dick Hall 2.50 1.00
❑ 418 Adolfo Phillips 2.50 1.00
❑ 419 Ron Hansen 2.50 1.00
❑ 420 Jim Merritt 2.50 1.00
❑ 421 John Stephenson 2.50 1.00
❑ 422 Frank Bertaina 2.50 1.00
❑ 423 Dennis Saunders 2.50 1.00
Tim Marting
❑ 424 Roberto Rodriquez 2.50 1.00
❑ 425 Doug Rader 4.00 1.60
❑ 426 Chris Cannizzaro 2.50 1.00
❑ 427 Bernie Allen 2.50 1.00
❑ 428 Jim McAndrew 2.50 1.00
❑ 429 Chuck Hinton 2.50 1.00
❑ 430 Wes Parker 4.00 1.60
❑ 431 Tom Burgmeier 2.50 1.00
❑ 432 Bob Didier 2.50 1.00
❑ 433 Skip Lockwood 2.50 1.00
❑ 434 Gary Sutherland 2.50 1.00
❑ 435 Jose Cardenal 4.00 1.60
❑ 436 Wilbur Wood 4.00 1.60
❑ 437 Danny Murtaugh MG 4.00 1.60
❑ 438 Mike McCormick 4.00 1.60
❑ 439 Greg Luzinski RC 6.00 2.40
Scott Reid
❑ 440 Bert Campaneris 4.00 1.60
❑ 441 Milt Pappas 4.00 1.60
❑ 442 California Angels 4.00 1.60
Team Card
❑ 443 Rich Robertson 2.50 1.00
❑ 444 Jimmie Price 2.50 1.00
❑ 445 Art Shamsky 2.50 1.00
❑ 446 Bobby Bolin 2.50 1.00
❑ 447 Cesar Geronimo 4.00 1.60
❑ 448 Dave Roberts 2.50 1.00
❑ 449 Brant Alyea 2.50 1.00
❑ 450 Bob Gibson 15.00 6.00
❑ 451 Joe Keough 2.50 1.00
❑ 452 John Boccabella 2.50 1.00
❑ 453 Terry Crowley 2.50 1.00
❑ 454 Mike Paul 2.50 1.00
❑ 455 Don Kessinger 4.00 1.60
❑ 456 Bob Meyer 2.50 1.00
❑ 457 Willie Smith 2.50 1.00
❑ 458 Ron Lolich 2.50 1.00
Dave Lemonds
❑ 459 Jim Lefebvre 2.50 1.00
❑ 460 Fritz Peterson 2.50 1.00
❑ 461 Jim Ray Hart 2.50 1.00
❑ 462 Washington Senators 6.00 2.40
Team Card
❑ 463 Tom Kelley 2.50 1.00
❑ 464 Aurelio Rodriguez 2.50 1.00
❑ 465 Tim McCarver 6.00 2.40
❑ 466 Ken Berry 2.50 1.00
❑ 467 Al Santorini 2.50 1.00
❑ 468 Frank Fernandez 2.50 1.00
❑ 469 Bob Aspromonte 2.50 1.00
❑ 470 Bob Oliver 2.50 1.00
❑ 471 Tom Griffin 2.50 1.00
❑ 472 Ken Rudolph 2.50 1.00
❑ 473 Gary Wagner 2.50 1.00
❑ 474 Jim Fairey 2.50 1.00
❑ 475 Ron Perranoski 2.50 1.00
❑ 476 Dal Maxvill 2.50 1.00
❑ 477 Earl Weaver MG 6.00 2.40
❑ 478 Bernie Carbo 2.50 1.00
❑ 479 Dennis Higgins 2.50 1.00
❑ 480 Manny Sanguillen 4.00 1.60
❑ 481 Daryl Patterson 2.50 1.00
❑ 482 San Diego Padres 6.00 2.40
Team Card
❑ 483 Gene Michael 2.50 1.00
❑ 484 Don Wilson 2.50 1.00
❑ 485 Ken McMullen 2.50 1.00
❑ 486 Steve Huntz 2.50 1.00
❑ 487 Paul Schaal 2.50 1.00
❑ 488 Jerry Stephenson 2.50 1.00
❑ 489 Luis Alvarado 2.50 1.00
❑ 490 Deron Johnson 2.50 1.00
❑ 491 Jim Hardin 2.50 1.00
❑ 492 Ken Boswell 2.50 1.00
❑ 493 Dave May 2.50 1.00
❑ 494 Ralph Garr 4.00 1.60
Rick Kester
❑ 495 Felipe Alou 4.00 1.60
❑ 496 Woody Woodward 2.50 1.00
❑ 497 Horacio Pina 2.50 1.00
❑ 498 John Kennedy 2.50 1.00
❑ 499 Checklist 5 10.00 2.00
❑ 500 Jim Perry 4.00 1.60
❑ 501 Andy Etchebarren 2.50 1.00
❑ 502 Chicago Cubs 6.00 2.40
Team Card
❑ 503 Gates Brown 4.00 1.60
❑ 504 Ken Wright 2.50 1.00
❑ 505 Ollie Brown 2.50 1.00
❑ 506 Bobby Knoop 2.50 1.00
❑ 507 George Stone 2.50 1.00
❑ 508 Roger Repoz 2.50 1.00
❑ 509 Jim Grant 2.50 1.00
❑ 510 Ken Harrelson 4.00 1.60
❑ 511 Chris Short 4.00 1.60
(Pete Rose leading off second)
❑ 512 Dick Mills 2.50 1.00
Mike Garman
❑ 513 Nolan Ryan 150.00 60.00
❑ 514 Ron Woods 2.50 1.00
❑ 515 Carl Morton 2.50 1.00
❑ 516 Ted Kubiak 2.50 1.00
❑ 517 Charlie Fox MG 2.50 1.00
❑ 518 Joe Grzenda 2.50 1.00
❑ 519 Willie Crawford 2.50 1.00
❑ 520 Tommy John 6.00 2.40
❑ 521 Leron Lee 2.50 1.00
❑ 522 Minnesota Twins 6.00 2.40
Team Card
❑ 523 John Odom 2.50 1.00
❑ 524 Mickey Stanley 6.00 2.40
❑ 525 Ernie Banks 50.00 20.00
❑ 526 Ray Jarvis 4.00 1.60
❑ 527 Cleon Jones 6.00 2.40
❑ 528 Wally Bunker 4.00 1.60
❑ 529 Enzo Hernandez 6.00 2.40
Bill Buckner
Marty Perez
❑ 530 Carl Yastrzemski 30.00 12.00
❑ 531 Mike Torrez 4.00 1.60
❑ 532 Bill Rigney MG 4.00 1.60
❑ 533 Mike Ryan 4.00 1.60
❑ 534 Luke Walker 4.00 1.60
❑ 535 Curt Flood 6.00 2.40
❑ 536 Claude Raymond 4.00 1.60
❑ 537 Tom Egan 4.00 1.60
❑ 538 Angel Bravo 4.00 1.60
❑ 539 Larry Brown 4.00 1.60
❑ 540 Larry Dierker 6.00 2.40
❑ 541 Bob Burda 4.00 1.60
❑ 542 Bob Miller 4.00 1.60
❑ 543 New York Yankees 10.00 4.00
Team Card
❑ 544 Vida Blue 6.00 2.40
❑ 545 Dick Dietz 4.00 1.60
❑ 546 John Matias 4.00 1.60
❑ 547 Pat Dobson 6.00 2.40
❑ 548 Don Mason 4.00 1.60
❑ 549 Jim Brewer 6.00 2.40
❑ 550 Harmon Killebrew 25.00 10.00
❑ 551 Frank Linzy 4.00 1.60
❑ 552 Buddy Bradford 4.00 1.60
❑ 553 Kevin Collins 4.00 1.60
❑ 554 Lowell Palmer 4.00 1.60
❑ 555 Walt Williams 4.00 1.60
❑ 556 Jim McGlothlin 4.00 1.60
❑ 557 Tom Satriano 4.00 1.60
❑ 558 Hector Torres 4.00 1.60
❑ 559 Terry Cox 4.00 1.60
Bill Gogolewski
Gary Jones
❑ 560 Rusty Staub 6.00 2.40
❑ 561 Syd O'Brien 4.00 1.60
❑ 562 Dave Giusti 4.00 1.60
❑ 563 San Francisco Giants 8.00 3.20
Team Card
❑ 564 Al Fitzmorris 4.00 1.60
❑ 565 Jim Wynn 6.00 2.40
❑ 566 Tim Cullen 4.00 1.60
❑ 567 Walt Alston MG 8.00 3.20
❑ 568 Sal Campisi 4.00 1.60
❑ 569 Ivan Murrell 4.00 1.60
❑ 570 Jim Palmer 30.00 12.00
❑ 571 Ted Sizemore 4.00 1.60
❑ 572 Jerry Kenney 4.00 1.60
❑ 573 Ed Kranepool 6.00 2.40
❑ 574 Jim Bunning 8.00 3.20
❑ 575 Bill Freehan 6.00 2.40
❑ 576 Adrian Garrett 4.00 1.60
Brock Davis
Garry Jestadt
❑ 577 Jim Lonborg 6.00 2.40
❑ 578 Ron Hunt 4.00 1.60
❑ 579 Marty Pattin 4.00 1.60
❑ 580 Tony Perez 20.00 8.00
❑ 581 Roger Nelson 4.00 1.60
❑ 582 Dave Cash 6.00 2.40
❑ 583 Ron Cook 4.00 1.60
❑ 584 Cleveland Indians 8.00 3.20
Team Card
❑ 585 Willie Davis 6.00 2.40
❑ 586 Dick Woodson 4.00 1.60
❑ 587 Sonny Jackson 4.00 1.60
❑ 588 Tom Bradley 4.00 1.60
❑ 589 Bob Barton 4.00 1.60
❑ 590 Alex Johnson 6.00 2.40
❑ 591 Jackie Brown 4.00 1.60
❑ 592 Randy Hundley 6.00 2.40
❑ 593 Jack Aker 4.00 1.60
❑ 594 Bob Chlupsa 6.00 2.40
Bob Stinson
Al Hrabosky RC

❑ 595 Dave Johnson 6.00 2.40
❑ 596 Mike Jorgensen 4.00 1.60
❑ 597 Ken Suarez 4.00 1.60
❑ 598 Rick Wise 6.00 2.40
❑ 599 Norm Cash 6.00 2.40
❑ 600 Willie Mays 100.00 40.00
❑ 601 Ken Tatum 4.00 1.60
❑ 602 Marty Martinez 4.00 1.60
❑ 603 Pittsburgh Pirates 8.00 3.20
Team Card
❑ 604 John Gelnar 4.00 1.60
❑ 605 Orlando Cepeda 8.00 3.20
❑ 606 Chuck Taylor 4.00 1.60
❑ 607 Paul Ratliff 4.00 1.60
❑ 608 Mike Wegener 4.00 1.60
❑ 609 Leo Durocher MG 8.00 3.20
❑ 610 Amos Otis 6.00 2.40
❑ 611 Tom Phoebus 4.00 1.60
❑ 612 Lou Camilli 4.00 1.60
Ted Ford
Steve Mingori
❑ 613 Pedro Borbon 4.00 1.60
❑ 614 Billy Cowan 4.00 1.60
❑ 615 Mel Stottlemyre 6.00 2.40
❑ 616 Larry Hisle 6.00 2.40
❑ 617 Clay Dalrymple 4.00 1.60
❑ 618 Tug McGraw 6.00 2.40
❑ 619A Checklist 6 ERR 10.00 2.00
(No copyright)
❑ 619B Checklist 6 COR 6.00 1.20
(Copyright on back)
❑ 620 Frank Howard 6.00 2.40
❑ 621 Ron Bryant 4.00 1.60
❑ 622 Joe Lahoud 4.00 1.60
❑ 623 Pat Jarvis 4.00 1.60
❑ 624 Oakland Athletics 8.00 3.20
Team Card
❑ 625 Lou Brock 30.00 12.00
❑ 626 Freddie Patek 6.00 2.40
❑ 627 Steve Hamilton 4.00 1.60
❑ 628 John Bateman 4.00 1.60
❑ 629 John Hiller 6.00 2.40
❑ 630 Roberto Clemente 150.00 60.00
❑ 631 Eddie Fisher 4.00 1.60
❑ 632 Darrel Chaney 4.00 1.60
❑ 633 Bobby Brooks 4.00 1.60
Pete Koegel
Scott Northey
❑ 634 Phil Regan 4.00 1.60
❑ 635 Bobby Murcer 6.00 2.40
❑ 636 Denny Lemaster 4.00 1.60
❑ 637 Dave Bristol MG 4.00 1.60
❑ 638 Stan Williams 4.00 1.60
❑ 639 Tom Haller 4.00 1.60
❑ 640 Frank Robinson 40.00 16.00
❑ 641 New York Mets 15.00 6.00
Team Card
❑ 642 Jim Roland 4.00 1.60
❑ 643 Rick Reichardt 4.00 1.60
❑ 644 Jim Stewart SP 12.00 4.80
❑ 645 Jim Maloney SP 15.00 6.00
❑ 646 Bobby Floyd SP 12.00 4.80
❑ 647 Juan Pizarro 8.00 3.20
❑ 648 Rich Folkers 25.00 10.00
Ted Martinez
John Matlack RC SP
❑ 649 Sparky Lyle SP 15.00 6.00
❑ 650 Rich Allen SP 30.00 12.00
❑ 651 Jerry Robertson SP 12.00 4.80
❑ 652 Atlanta Braves 12.00 4.80
Team Card
❑ 653 Russ Snyder SP 12.00 4.80
❑ 654 Don Shaw SP 12.00 4.80
❑ 655 Mike Epstein SP 12.00 4.80
❑ 656 Gerry Nyman SP 12.00 4.80
❑ 657 Jose Azcue 8.00 3.20
❑ 658 Paul Lindblad SP 12.00 4.80
❑ 659 Byron Browne SP 12.00 4.80
❑ 660 Ray Culp 8.00 3.20
❑ 661 Chuck Tanner MG SP 15.00 6.00
❑ 662 Mike Hedlund SP 12.00 4.80
❑ 663 Marv Staehle 8.00 3.20
❑ 664 Archie Reynolds 12.00 4.80
Bob Reynolds
Ken Reynolds SP
❑ 665 Ron Swoboda SP 15.00 6.00
❑ 666 Gene Brabender SP 12.00 4.80
❑ 667 Pete Ward 8.00 3.20
❑ 668 Gary Neibauer 8.00 3.20
❑ 669 Ike Brown SP 12.00 4.80
❑ 670 Bill Hands 8.00 3.20
❑ 671 Bill Voss SP 12.00 4.80
❑ 672 Ed Crosby SP 12.00 4.80
❑ 673 Gerry Janeski SP 12.00 4.80
❑ 674 Montreal Expos 12.00 4.80
Team Card
❑ 675 Dave Boswell 8.00 3.20
❑ 676 Tommie Reynolds 8.00 3.20
❑ 677 Jack DiLauro SP 12.00 4.80
❑ 678 George Thomas 8.00 3.20
❑ 679 Don O'Riley 8.00 3.20
❑ 680 Don Mincher SP 12.00 4.80
❑ 681 Bill Butler 8.00 3.20
❑ 682 Terry Harmon 8.00 3.20
❑ 683 Bill Burbach SP 12.00 4.80
❑ 684 Curt Motton 8.00 3.20
❑ 685 Moe Drabowsky 8.00 3.20
❑ 686 Chico Ruiz SP 12.00 4.80
❑ 687 Ron Taylor SP 12.00 4.80
❑ 688 S.Anderson MG SP 30.00 12.00
❑ 689 Frank Baker 8.00 3.20
❑ 690 Bob Moose 8.00 3.20
❑ 691 Bobby Heise 8.00 3.20
❑ 692 Hal Haydel 12.00 4.80
Rogelio Moret
Wayne Twitchell SP
❑ 693 Jose Pena SP 12.00 4.80
❑ 694 Rick Renick SP 12.00 4.80
❑ 695 Joe Niekro 12.00 4.80
❑ 696 Jerry Morales 8.00 3.20
❑ 697 Rickey Clark SP 12.00 4.80
❑ 698 M. Brewers SP 20.00 8.00
Team Card
❑ 699 Jim Britton 8.00 3.20
❑ 700 Boog Powell SP 25.00 10.00
❑ 701 Bob Garibaldi 8.00 3.20
❑ 702 Milt Ramirez 8.00 3.20
❑ 703 Mike Kekich 8.00 3.20
❑ 704 J.C. Martin SP 12.00 4.80
❑ 705 Dick Selma SP 12.00 4.80
❑ 706 Joe Foy SP 12.00 4.80
❑ 707 Fred Lasher 8.00 3.20
❑ 708 Russ Nagelson SP 12.00 4.80
❑ 709 Dusty Baker RC 80.00 32.00
Don Baylor RC
Tom Paciorek RC SP
❑ 710 Sonny Siebert 8.00 3.20
❑ 711 Larry Stahl SP 12.00 4.80
❑ 712 Jose Martinez 8.00 3.20
❑ 713 Mike Marshall SP 15.00 6.00
❑ 714 Dick Williams MG SP 15.00 6.00
❑ 715 Horace Clarke SP 15.00 6.00
❑ 716 Dave Leonhard 8.00 3.20
❑ 717 Tommie Aaron SP 12.00 4.80
❑ 718 Billy Wynne 8.00 3.20
❑ 719 Jerry May SP 12.00 4.80
❑ 720 Matty Alou 12.00 4.80
❑ 721 John Morris 8.00 3.20
❑ 722 Houston Astros SP 20.00 8.00
Team Card
❑ 723 Vicente Romo SP 12.00 4.80
❑ 724 Tom Tischinski SP 12.00 4.80
❑ 725 Gary Gentry SP 12.00 4.80
❑ 726 Paul Popovich 8.00 3.20
❑ 727 Ray Lamb SP 12.00 4.80
❑ 728 Wayne Redmond 8.00 3.20
Keith Lampard
Bernie Williams
❑ 729 Dick Billings 8.00 3.20
❑ 730 Jim Rooker 8.00 3.20
❑ 731 Jim Qualls SP 12.00 4.80
❑ 732 Bob Reed 8.00 3.20
❑ 733 Lee Maye SP 12.00 4.80
❑ 734 Rob Gardner SP 12.00 4.80
❑ 735 Mike Shannon SP 15.00 6.00
❑ 736 Mel Queen SP 12.00 4.80
❑ 737 P.Gomez SP MG 12.00 4.80
❑ 738 Russ Gibson SP 12.00 4.80
❑ 739 Barry Lersch SP 12.00 4.80
❑ 740 Luis Aparicio SP UER 30.00 12.00
(Led AL in steals
from 1965 to 1964,
should be 1956 to 1964)
❑ 741 Skip Guinn 8.00 3.20
❑ 742 Kansas City Royals 12.00 4.80
Team Card
❑ 743 John O'Donoghue SP 12.00 4.80
❑ 744 Chuck Manuel SP 12.00 4.80
❑ 745 Sandy Alomar SP 12.00 4.80
❑ 746 Andy Kosco 8.00 3.20
❑ 747 Al Severinsen 8.00 3.20
Scipio Spinks
Balor Moore
❑ 748 John Purdin SP 12.00 4.80
❑ 749 Ken Szotkiewicz 8.00 3.20
❑ 750 Denny McLain SP 25.00 10.00
❑ 751 Al Weis SP 15.00 6.00
❑ 752 Dick Drago 12.00 2.90

1972 Topps

	NM	Ex
COMPLETE SET (787)	1500.00	600.00
COMMON CARD (1-132)	.60	.24
COMMON (133-263)	1.00	.40
COMMON (264-394)	1.25	.50
COMMON (395-525)	1.50	.60
COMMON (526-656)	4.00	1.60
COMMON (657-787)	12.00	4.80
WRAPPER (10-CENT)	15.00	6.00

❑ 1 Pittsburgh Pirates 8.00 2.90
Team Card
❑ 2 Ray Culp .60 .24
❑ 3 Bob Tolan .60 .24
❑ 4 Checklist 1-132 6.00 1.20
❑ 5 John Bateman .60 .24
❑ 6 Fred Scherman .60 .24
❑ 7 Enzo Hernandez .60 .24
❑ 8 Ron Swoboda 1.25 .50
❑ 9 Stan Williams .60 .24
❑ 10 Amos Otis 1.25 .50
❑ 11 Bobby Valentine 1.25 .50
❑ 12 Jose Cardenal .60 .24
❑ 13 Joe Grzenda .60 .24
❑ 14 Pete Koegel .60 .24
Mike Anderson
Wayne Twitchell
❑ 15 Walt Williams .60 .24
❑ 16 Mike Jorgensen .60 .24
❑ 17 Dave Duncan 1.25 .50
❑ 18A Juan Pizarro .60 .24
(Yellow underline
C and S of Cubs)
❑ 18B Juan Pizarro 5.00 2.00
(Green underline
C and S of Cubs)
❑ 19 Billy Cowan .60 .24
❑ 20 Don Wilson .60 .24
❑ 21 Atlanta Braves 1.50 .60
Team Card
❑ 22 Rob Gardner .60 .24
❑ 23 Ted Kubiak .60 .24
❑ 24 Ted Ford .60 .24
❑ 25 Bill Singer .60 .24
❑ 26 Andy Etchebarren .60 .24
❑ 27 Bob Johnson .60 .24
❑ 28 Bob Gebhard .60 .24
Steve Brye
Hal Haydel
❑ 29A Bill Bonham .60 .24

- (Yellow underline C and S of Cubs)
- ❑ 29B Bill Bonham 5.00 2.00 (Green underline C and S of Cubs)
- ❑ 30 Rico Petrocelli 1.25 .50
- ❑ 31 Cleon Jones 1.25 .50
- ❑ 32 Cleon Jones IA .60 .24
- ❑ 33 Billy Martin MG 4.00 1.60
- ❑ 34 Billy Martin IA 2.50 1.00
- ❑ 35 Jerry Johnson .60 .24
- ❑ 36 Jerry Johnson IA .60 .24
- ❑ 37 Carl Yastrzemski 10.00 4.00
- ❑ 38 Carl Yastrzemski IA 8.00 3.20
- ❑ 39 Bob Barton .60 .24
- ❑ 40 Bob Barton IA .60 .24
- ❑ 41 Tommy Davis 1.25 .50
- ❑ 42 Tommy Davis IA .60 .24
- ❑ 43 Rick Wise 1.25 .50
- ❑ 44 Rick Wise IA .60 .24
- ❑ 45A Glenn Beckert 1.25 .50 (Yellow underline C and S of Cubs)
- ❑ 45B Glenn Beckert 5.00 2.00 (Green underline C and S of Cubs)
- ❑ 46 Glenn Beckert IA .60 .24
- ❑ 47 John Ellis .60 .24
- ❑ 48 John Ellis IA .60 .24
- ❑ 49 Willie Mays 40.00 16.00
- ❑ 50 Willie Mays IA 20.00 8.00
- ❑ 51 Harmon Killebrew 8.00 3.20
- ❑ 52 Harmon Killebrew IA 4.00 1.60
- ❑ 53 Bud Harrelson 1.25 .50
- ❑ 54 Bud Harrelson IA .60 .24
- ❑ 55 Clyde Wright .60 .24
- ❑ 56 Rich Chiles .60 .24
- ❑ 57 Bob Oliver .60 .24
- ❑ 58 Ernie McAnally .60 .24
- ❑ 59 Fred Stanley .60 .24
- ❑ 60 Manny Sanguillen 1.25 .50
- ❑ 61 Burt Hooton RC 1.25 .50 Gene Hiser Earl Stephenson
- ❑ 62 Angel Mangual .60 .24
- ❑ 63 Duke Sims .60 .24
- ❑ 64 Pete Broberg .60 .24
- ❑ 65 Cesar Cedeno 1.25 .50
- ❑ 66 Ray Corbin .60 .24
- ❑ 67 Red Schoendienst MG 2.50 1.00
- ❑ 68 Jim York .60 .24
- ❑ 69 Roger Freed .60 .24
- ❑ 70 Mike Cuellar 1.25 .50
- ❑ 71 California Angels 1.50 .60 Team Card
- ❑ 72 Bruce Kison RC .60 .24
- ❑ 73 Steve Huntz .60 .24
- ❑ 74 Cecil Upshaw .60 .24
- ❑ 75 Bert Campaneris 1.25 .50
- ❑ 76 Don Carrithers .60 .24
- ❑ 77 Ron Theobald .60 .24
- ❑ 78 Steve Arlin .60 .24
- ❑ 79 Mike Garman 50.00 20.00 Cecil Cooper RC Carlton Fisk RC
- ❑ 80 Tony Perez 4.00 1.60
- ❑ 81 Mike Hedlund .60 .24
- ❑ 82 Ron Woods .60 .24
- ❑ 83 Dalton Jones .60 .24
- ❑ 84 Vince Colbert .60 .24
- ❑ 85 Joe Torre 2.50 1.00 Ralph Garr Glenn Beckert LL
- ❑ 86 Tony Oliva 2.50 1.00 Bobby Murcer Merv Rettenmund LL
- ❑ 87 Joe Torre 4.00 1.60 Willie Stargell Hank Aaron LL
- ❑ 88 Harmon Killebrew 4.00 1.60 Frank Robinson Reggie Smith LL
- ❑ 89 Willie Stargell 2.50 1.00 Hank Aaron Lee May LL
- ❑ 90 Bill Melton 2.50 1.00 Norm Cash Reggie Jackson LL
- ❑ 91 Tom Seaver 2.50 1.00 Dave Roberts UER (Photo actually Danny Coombs) Don Wilson LL
- ❑ 92 Vida Blue 2.50 1.00 Wilbur Wood Jim Palmer LL
- ❑ 93 Fergie Jenkins 4.00 1.60 Steve Carlton Al Downing Tom Seaver LL
- ❑ 94 Mickey Lolich 2.50 1.00 Vida Blue Wilbur Wood LL
- ❑ 95 Tom Seaver 4.00 1.60 Fergie Jenkins Bill Stoneman LL
- ❑ 96 Mickey Lolich 2.50 1.00 Vida Blue Joe Coleman LL
- ❑ 97 Tom Kelley .60 .24
- ❑ 98 Chuck Tanner MG 1.25 .50
- ❑ 99 Ross Grimsley .60 .24
- ❑ 100 Frank Robinson 8.00 3.20
- ❑ 101 Bill Greif 2.50 1.00 J.R. Richard RC Ray Busse
- ❑ 102 Lloyd Allen .60 .24
- ❑ 103 Checklist 133-263 6.00 1.20
- ❑ 104 Toby Harrah RC 1.25 .50
- ❑ 105 Gary Gentry .60 .24
- ❑ 106 Milwaukee Brewers 1.50 .60 Team Card
- ❑ 107 Jose Cruz RC 1.25 .50
- ❑ 108 Gary Waslewski .60 .24
- ❑ 109 Jerry May .60 .24
- ❑ 110 Ron Hunt .60 .24
- ❑ 111 Jim Grant .60 .24
- ❑ 112 Greg Luzinski 1.25 .50
- ❑ 113 Rogelio Moret .60 .24
- ❑ 114 Bill Buckner 1.25 .50
- ❑ 115 Jim Fregosi 1.25 .50
- ❑ 116 Ed Farmer .60 .24
- ❑ 117A Cleo James .60 .24 (Yellow underline C and S of Cubs)
- ❑ 117B Cleo James 5.00 2.00 (Green underline C and S of Cubs)
- ❑ 118 Skip Lockwood .60 .24
- ❑ 119 Marty Perez .60 .24
- ❑ 120 Bill Freehan 1.25 .50
- ❑ 121 Ed Sprague .60 .24
- ❑ 122 Larry Biittner .60 .24
- ❑ 123 Ed Acosta .60 .24
- ❑ 124 Alan Closter .60 .24 Rusty Torres Roger Hambright
- ❑ 125 Dave Cash 1.25 .50
- ❑ 126 Bart Johnson .60 .24
- ❑ 127 Duffy Dyer .60 .24
- ❑ 128 Eddie Watt .60 .24
- ❑ 129 Charlie Fox MG .60 .24
- ❑ 130 Bob Gibson 8.00 3.20
- ❑ 131 Jim Nettles .60 .24
- ❑ 132 Joe Morgan 6.00 2.40
- ❑ 133 Joe Keough 1.00 .40
- ❑ 134 Carl Morton 1.00 .40
- ❑ 135 Vada Pinson 2.00 .80
- ❑ 136 Darrel Chaney 1.00 .40
- ❑ 137 Dick Williams MG 2.00 .80
- ❑ 138 Mike Kekich 1.00 .40
- ❑ 139 Tim McCarver 2.00 .80
- ❑ 140 Pat Dobson 2.00 .80
- ❑ 141 Buzz Capra 2.00 .80 Lee Stanton Jon Matlack
- ❑ 142 Chris Chambliss RC 4.00 1.60
- ❑ 143 Garry Jestadt 1.00 .40
- ❑ 144 Marty Pattin 1.00 .40
- ❑ 145 Don Kessinger 2.00 .80
- ❑ 146 Steve Kealey 1.00 .40
- ❑ 147 Dave Kingman RC 6.00 2.40
- ❑ 148 Dick Billings 1.00 .40
- ❑ 149 Gary Neibauer 1.00 .40
- ❑ 150 Norm Cash 2.00 .80
- ❑ 151 Jim Brewer 1.00 .40
- ❑ 152 Gene Clines 1.00 .40
- ❑ 153 Rick Auerbach 1.00 .40
- ❑ 154 Ted Simmons 4.00 1.60
- ❑ 155 Larry Dierker 1.00 .40
- ❑ 156 Minnesota Twins 2.00 .80 Team Card
- ❑ 157 Don Gullett 1.00 .40
- ❑ 158 Jerry Kenney 1.00 .40
- ❑ 159 John Boccabella 1.00 .40
- ❑ 160 Andy Messersmith 2.00 .80
- ❑ 161 Brock Davis 1.00 .40
- ❑ 162 Jerry Bell 2.00 .80 Darrell Porter RC Bob Reynolds UER (Porter and Bell photos switched)
- ❑ 163 Tug McGraw 4.00 1.60
- ❑ 164 Tug McGraw IA 2.00 .80
- ❑ 165 Chris Speier RC 2.00 .80
- ❑ 166 Chris Speier IA 1.00 .40
- ❑ 167 Deron Johnson 1.00 .40
- ❑ 168 Deron Johnson IA 1.00 .40
- ❑ 169 Vida Blue 4.00 1.60
- ❑ 170 Vida Blue IA 2.00 .80
- ❑ 171 Darrell Evans 4.00 1.60
- ❑ 172 Darrell Evans IA 2.00 .80
- ❑ 173 Clay Kirby 1.00 .40
- ❑ 174 Clay Kirby IA 1.00 .40
- ❑ 175 Tom Haller 1.00 .40
- ❑ 176 Tom Haller IA 1.00 .40
- ❑ 177 Paul Schaal 1.00 .40
- ❑ 178 Paul Schaal IA 1.00 .40
- ❑ 179 Dock Ellis 1.00 .40
- ❑ 180 Dock Ellis IA 1.00 .40
- ❑ 181 Ed Kranepool 2.00 .80
- ❑ 182 Ed Kranepool IA 1.00 .40
- ❑ 183 Bill Melton 1.00 .40
- ❑ 184 Bill Melton IA 1.00 .40
- ❑ 185 Ron Bryant 1.00 .40
- ❑ 186 Ron Bryant IA 1.00 .40
- ❑ 187 Gates Brown 1.00 .40
- ❑ 188 Frank Lucchesi MG 1.00 .40
- ❑ 189 Gene Tenace 2.00 .80
- ❑ 190 Dave Giusti 1.00 .40
- ❑ 191 Jeff Burroughs RC 4.00 1.60
- ❑ 192 Chicago Cubs 2.00 .80 Team Card
- ❑ 193 Kurt Bevacqua 1.00 .40
- ❑ 194 Fred Norman 1.00 .40
- ❑ 195 Orlando Cepeda 6.00 2.40
- ❑ 196 Mel Queen 1.00 .40
- ❑ 197 Johnny Briggs 1.00 .40
- ❑ 198 Charlie Hough RC 6.00 2.40 Bob O'Brien Mike Strahler
- ❑ 199 Mike Fiore 1.00 .40
- ❑ 200 Lou Brock 8.00 3.20
- ❑ 201 Phil Roof 1.00 .40
- ❑ 202 Scipio Spinks 1.00 .40
- ❑ 203 Ron Blomberg 1.00 .40
- ❑ 204 Tommy Helms 1.00 .40
- ❑ 205 Dick Drago 1.00 .40
- ❑ 206 Dal Maxvill 1.00 .40
- ❑ 207 Tom Egan 1.00 .40
- ❑ 208 Milt Pappas 2.00 .80
- ❑ 209 Joe Rudi 2.00 .80
- ❑ 210 Denny McLain 2.00 .80
- ❑ 211 Gary Sutherland 1.00 .40
- ❑ 212 Grant Jackson 1.00 .40
- ❑ 213 Billy Parker 1.00 .40 Art Kusnyer Tom Silverio
- ❑ 214 Mike McQueen 1.00 .40
- ❑ 215 Alex Johnson 2.00 .80
- ❑ 216 Joe Niekro 2.00 .80
- ❑ 217 Roger Metzger 1.00 .40
- ❑ 218 Eddie Kasko MG 1.00 .40
- ❑ 219 Rennie Stennett 2.00 .80
- ❑ 220 Jim Perry 2.00 .80
- ❑ 221 NL Playoffs 2.00 .80 Bucs champs
- ❑ 222 Br. Robinson ALCS 4.00 1.60

No.	Card	Price	Price
223	Dave McNally WS	2.00	.80
224	Dave Johnson WS	2.00	.80
	Mark Belanger		
225	Manny Sanguillen WS	2.00	.80
226	Roberto Clemente WS	8.00	3.20
227	Nellie Briles WS	2.00	.80
228	Frank Robinson WS	2.00	.80
	Manny Sanguillen		
229	Steve Blass WS	2.00	.80
230	WS Summary	2.00	.80
	Pirates celebrate		
231	Casey Cox	1.00	.40
232	Chris Arnold	1.00	.40
	Jim Barr		
	Dave Rader		
233	Jay Johnstone	2.00	.80
234	Ron Taylor	1.00	.40
235	Merv Rettenmund	1.00	.40
236	Jim McGlothlin	1.00	.40
237	New York Yankees	2.00	.80
	Team Card		
238	Leron Lee	1.00	.40
239	Tom Timmermann	1.00	.40
240	Rich Allen	2.00	.80
241	Rollie Fingers	6.00	2.40
242	Don Mincher	1.00	.40
243	Frank Linzy	1.00	.40
244	Steve Braun	1.00	.40
245	Tommie Agee	2.00	.80
246	Tom Burgmeier	1.00	.40
247	Milt May	1.00	.40
248	Tom Bradley	1.00	.40
249	Harry Walker MG	1.00	.40
250	Boog Powell	2.00	.80
251	Checklist 264-394	6.00	1.20
252	Ken Reynolds	1.00	.40
253	Sandy Alomar	2.00	.80
254	Boots Day	1.00	.40
255	Jim Lonborg	2.00	.80
256	George Foster	2.00	.80
257	Jim Foor	1.00	.40
	Tim Hosley		
	Paul Jata		
258	Randy Hundley	1.00	.40
259	Sparky Lyle	2.00	.80
260	Ralph Garr	2.00	.80
261	Steve Mingori	1.00	.40
262	San Diego Padres	2.00	.80
	Team Card		
263	Felipe Alou	2.00	.80
264	Tommy John	2.00	.80
265	Wes Parker	2.00	.80
266	Bobby Bolin	1.25	.50
267	Dave Concepcion	4.00	1.60
268	Dwain Anderson	1.25	.50
	Chris Floethe		
269	Don Hahn	1.25	.50
270	Jim Palmer	8.00	3.20
271	Ken Rudolph	1.25	.50
272	Mickey Rivers RC	2.00	.80
273	Bobby Floyd	1.25	.50
274	Al Severinsen	1.25	.50
275	Cesar Tovar	1.25	.50
276	Gene Mauch MG	2.00	.80
277	Elliott Maddox	1.25	.50
278	Dennis Higgins	1.25	.50
279	Larry Brown	1.25	.50
280	Willie McCovey	6.00	2.40
281	Bill Parsons	1.25	.50
282	Houston Astros	2.00	.80
	Team Card		
283	Darrell Brandon	1.25	.50
284	Ike Brown	1.25	.50
285	Gaylord Perry	6.00	2.40
286	Gene Alley	1.25	.50
287	Jim Hardin	1.25	.50
288	Johnny Jeter	1.25	.50
289	Syd O'Brien	1.25	.50
290	Sonny Siebert	1.25	.50
291	Hal McRae	2.00	.80
292	Hal McRae IA	1.25	.50
293	Dan Frisella	1.25	.50
294	Dan Frisella IA	1.25	.50
295	Dick Dietz	1.25	.50
296	Dick Dietz IA	1.25	.50
297	Claude Osteen	2.00	.80
298	Claude Osteen IA	1.25	.50
299	Hank Aaron	40.00	16.00
300	Hank Aaron IA	20.00	8.00
301	George Mitterwald	1.25	.50
302	George Mitterwald IA	1.25	.50
303	Joe Pepitone	2.00	.80
304	Joe Pepitone IA	1.25	.50
305	Ken Boswell	1.25	.50
306	Ken Boswell IA	1.25	.50
307	Steve Renko	1.25	.50
308	Steve Renko IA	1.25	.50
309	Roberto Clemente	50.00	20.00
310	Roberto Clemente IA	25.00	10.00
311	Clay Carroll	1.25	.50
312	Clay Carroll IA	1.25	.50
313	Luis Aparicio	6.00	2.40
314	Luis Aparicio IA	2.00	.80
315	Paul Splittorff	1.25	.50
316	Jim Bibby	2.00	.80
	Jorge Roque		
	Santiago Guzman		
317	Rich Hand	1.25	.50
318	Sonny Jackson	1.25	.50
319	Aurelio Rodriguez	1.25	.50
320	Steve Blass	2.00	.80
321	Joe Lahoud	1.25	.50
322	Jose Pena	1.25	.50
323	Earl Weaver MG	4.00	1.60
324	Mike Ryan	1.25	.50
325	Mel Stottlemyre	2.00	.80
326	Pat Kelly	1.25	.50
327	Steve Stone RC	2.00	.80
328	Boston Red Sox	2.00	.80
	Team Card		
329	Roy Foster	1.25	.50
330	Jim Hunter	6.00	2.40
331	Stan Swanson	1.25	.50
332	Buck Martinez	1.25	.50
333	Steve Barber	1.25	.50
334	Bill Fahey	1.25	.50
	Jim Mason		
	Tom Ragland		
335	Bill Hands	1.25	.50
336	Marty Martinez	1.25	.50
337	Mike Kilkenny	1.25	.50
338	Bob Grich	2.00	.80
339	Ron Cook	1.25	.50
340	Roy White	2.00	.80
341	Joe Torre KP	1.25	.50
342	Wilbur Wood KP	1.25	.50
343	Willie Stargell KP	2.00	.80
344	Dave McNally KP	1.25	.50
345	Rick Wise KP	1.25	.50
346	Jim Fregosi KP	1.25	.50
347	Tom Seaver KP	4.00	1.60
348	Sal Bando KP	1.25	.50
349	Al Fitzmorris	1.25	.50
350	Frank Howard	2.00	.80
351	Tom House	2.00	.80
	Rick Kester		
	Jimmy Britton		
352	Dave LaRoche	1.25	.50
353	Art Shamsky	1.25	.50
354	Tom Murphy	1.25	.50
355	Bob Watson	2.00	.80
356	Gerry Moses	1.25	.50
357	Woody Fryman	1.25	.50
358	Sparky Anderson MG	4.00	1.60
359	Don Pavletich	1.25	.50
360	Dave Roberts	1.25	.50
361	Mike Andrews	1.25	.50
362	New York Mets	2.00	.80
	Team Card		
363	Ron Klimkowski	1.25	.50
364	Johnny Callison	2.00	.80
365	Dick Bosman	2.00	.80
366	Jimmy Rosario	1.25	.50
367	Ron Perranoski	1.25	.50
368	Danny Thompson	1.25	.50
369	Jim Lefebvre	2.00	.80
370	Don Buford	1.25	.50
371	Denny Lemaster	1.25	.50
372	Lance Clemons	1.25	.50
	Monty Montgomery		
373	John Mayberry	2.00	.80
374	Jack Heidemann	1.25	.50
375	Reggie Cleveland	1.25	.50
376	Andy Kosco	1.25	.50
377	Terry Harmon	1.25	.50
378	Checklist 395-525	6.00	1.20
379	Ken Berry	1.25	.50
380	Earl Williams	1.25	.50
381	Chicago White Sox	2.00	.80
	Team Card		
382	Joe Gibbon	1.25	.50
383	Brant Alyea	1.25	.50
384	Dave Campbell	2.00	.80
385	Mickey Stanley	2.00	.80
386	Jim Colborn	1.25	.50
387	Horace Clarke	2.00	.80
388	Charlie Williams	1.25	.50
389	Bill Rigney MG	1.25	.50
390	Willie Davis	2.00	.80
391	Ken Sanders	1.25	.50
392	Fred Cambria	2.00	.80
	Richie Zisk RC		
393	Curt Motton	1.25	.50
394	Ken Forsch	2.00	.80
395	Matty Alou	2.00	.80
396	Paul Lindblad	1.50	.60
397	Philadelphia Phillies	2.00	.80
	Team Card		
398	Larry Hisle	2.00	.80
399	Milt Wilcox	2.00	.80
400	Tony Oliva	4.00	1.60
401	Jim Nash	1.50	.60
402	Bobby Heise	1.50	.60
403	John Cumberland	1.50	.60
404	Jeff Torborg	2.00	.80
405	Ron Fairly	2.00	.80
406	George Hendrick RC	2.00	.80
407	Chuck Taylor	1.50	.60
408	Jim Northrup	2.00	.80
409	Frank Baker	1.50	.60
410	Ferguson Jenkins	6.00	2.40
411	Bob Montgomery	1.50	.60
412	Dick Kelley	1.50	.60
413	Don Eddy	1.50	.60
	Dave Lemonds		
414	Bob Miller	1.50	.60
415	Cookie Rojas	2.00	.80
416	Johnny Edwards	1.50	.60
417	Tom Hall	1.50	.60
418	Tom Shopay	1.50	.60
419	Jim Spencer	1.50	.60
420	Steve Carlton	20.00	8.00
421	Ellie Rodriguez	1.50	.60
422	Ray Lamb	1.50	.60
423	Oscar Gamble	2.00	.80
424	Bill Gogolewski	1.50	.60
425	Ken Singleton	2.00	.80
426	Ken Singleton IA	1.50	.60
427	Tito Fuentes	1.50	.60
428	Tito Fuentes IA	1.50	.60
429	Bob Robertson	1.50	.60
430	Bob Robertson IA	1.50	.60
431	Clarence Gaston	2.00	.80
432	Clarence Gaston IA	2.00	.80
433	Johnny Bench	25.00	10.00
434	Johnny Bench IA	15.00	6.00
435	Reggie Jackson	30.00	12.00
436	Reggie Jackson IA	12.00	4.80
437	Maury Wills	2.00	.80
438	Maury Wills IA	2.00	.80
439	Billy Williams	6.00	2.40
440	Billy Williams IA	4.00	1.60
441	Thurman Munson	15.00	6.00
442	Thurman Munson IA	8.00	3.20
443	Ken Henderson	1.50	.60
444	Ken Henderson IA	1.50	.60
445	Tom Seaver	30.00	12.00
446	Tom Seaver IA	15.00	6.00
447	Willie Stargell	8.00	3.20
448	Willie Stargell IA	4.00	1.60
449	Bob Lemon MG	2.00	.80
450	Mickey Lolich	2.00	.80
451	Tony LaRussa	4.00	1.60
452	Ed Herrmann	1.50	.60
453	Barry Lersch	1.50	.60
454	Oakland A's	2.00	.80
	Team Card		
455	Tommy Harper	2.00	.80

❑	456	Mark Belanger	2.00	.80
❑	457	Darcy Fast	1.50	.60
		Derrel Thomas		
		Mike Ivie		
❑	458	Aurelio Monteagudo	1.50	.60
❑	459	Rick Renick	1.50	.60
❑	460	Al Downing	1.50	.60
❑	461	Tim Cullen	1.50	.60
❑	462	Rickey Clark	1.50	.60
❑	463	Bernie Carbo	1.50	.60
❑	464	Jim Roland	1.50	.60
❑	465	Gil Hodges MG	4.00	1.60
❑	466	Norm Miller	1.50	.60
❑	467	Steve Kline	1.50	.60
❑	468	Richie Scheinblum	1.50	.60
❑	469	Ron Herbel	1.50	.60
❑	470	Ray Fosse	1.50	.60
❑	471	Luke Walker	1.50	.60
❑	472	Phil Gagliano	1.50	.60
❑	473	Dan McGinn	1.50	.60
❑	474	Don Baylor	15.00	6.00
		Roric Harrison		
		Johnny Oates RC		
❑	475	Gary Nolan	2.00	.80
❑	476	Lee Richard	1.50	.60
❑	477	Tom Phoebus	1.50	.60
❑	478	Checklist 526-656	6.00	1.20
❑	479	Don Shaw	1.50	.60
❑	480	Lee May	2.00	.80
❑	481	Billy Conigliaro	2.00	.80
❑	482	Joe Hoerner	1.50	.60
❑	483	Ken Suarez	1.50	.60
❑	484	Lum Harris MG	1.50	.60
❑	485	Phil Regan	2.00	.80
❑	486	John Lowenstein	1.50	.60
❑	487	Detroit Tigers	2.00	.80
		Team Card		
❑	488	Mike Nagy	1.50	.60
❑	489	Terry Humphrey	1.50	.60
		Keith Lampard		
❑	490	Dave McNally	2.00	.80
❑	491	Lou Piniella KP	2.00	.80
❑	492	Mel Stottlemyre KP	2.00	.80
❑	493	Bob Bailey KP	2.00	.80
❑	494	Willie Horton KP	2.00	.80
❑	495	Bill Melton KP	2.00	.80
❑	496	Bud Harrelson KP	2.00	.80
❑	497	Jim Perry KP	2.00	.80
❑	498	Brooks Robinson KP	4.00	1.60
❑	499	Vicente Romo	1.50	.60
❑	500	Joe Torre	4.00	1.60
❑	501	Pete Hamm	1.50	.60
❑	502	Jackie Hernandez	1.50	.60
❑	503	Gary Peters	1.50	.60
❑	504	Ed Spiezio	1.50	.60
❑	505	Mike Marshall	2.00	.80
❑	506	Terry Ley	1.50	.60
		Jim Moyer		
		Dick Tidrow RC		
❑	507	Fred Gladding	1.50	.60
❑	508	Elrod Hendricks	1.50	.60
❑	509	Don McMahon	1.50	.60
❑	510	Ted Williams MG	12.00	4.80
❑	511	Tony Taylor	2.00	.80
❑	512	Paul Popovich	1.50	.60
❑	513	Lindy McDaniel	2.00	.80
❑	514	Ted Sizemore	1.50	.60
❑	515	Bert Blyleven	4.00	1.60
❑	516	Oscar Brown	1.50	.60
❑	517	Ken Brett	1.50	.60
❑	518	Wayne Garrett	1.50	.60
❑	519	Ted Abernathy	1.50	.60
❑	520	Larry Bowa	2.00	.80
❑	521	Alan Foster	1.50	.60
❑	522	Los Angeles Dodgers	2.00	.80
		Team Card		
❑	523	Chuck Dobson	1.50	.60
❑	524	Ed Armbrister	1.50	.60
		Mel Behney		
❑	525	Carlos May	2.00	.80
❑	526	Bob Bailey	6.00	2.40
❑	527	Dave Leonhard	4.00	1.60
❑	528	Ron Stone	4.00	1.60
❑	529	Dave Nelson	6.00	2.40
❑	530	Don Sutton	12.00	4.80
❑	531	Freddie Patek	6.00	2.40
❑	532	Fred Kendall	4.00	1.60
❑	533	Ralph Houk MG	6.00	2.40
❑	534	Jim Hickman	6.00	2.40
❑	535	Ed Brinkman	4.00	1.60
❑	536	Doug Rader	6.00	2.40
❑	537	Bob Locker	4.00	1.60
❑	538	Charlie Sands	4.00	1.60
❑	539	Terry Forster RC	6.00	2.40
❑	540	Felix Millan	4.00	1.60
❑	541	Roger Repoz	4.00	1.60
❑	542	Jack Billingham	4.00	1.60
❑	543	Duane Josephson	4.00	1.60
❑	544	Ted Martinez	4.00	1.60
❑	545	Wayne Granger	4.00	1.60
❑	546	Joe Hague	4.00	1.60
❑	547	Cleveland Indians	8.00	3.20
		Team Card		
❑	548	Frank Reberger	4.00	1.60
❑	549	Dave May	4.00	1.60
❑	550	Brooks Robinson	25.00	10.00
❑	551	Ollie Brown	4.00	1.60
❑	552	Ollie Brown IA	4.00	1.60
❑	553	Wilbur Wood	6.00	2.40
❑	554	Wilbur Wood IA	4.00	1.60
❑	555	Ron Santo	8.00	3.20
❑	556	Ron Santo IA	6.00	2.40
❑	557	John Odom	4.00	1.60
❑	558	John Odom IA	4.00	1.60
❑	559	Pete Rose	50.00	20.00
❑	560	Pete Rose IA	25.00	10.00
❑	561	Leo Cardenas	4.00	1.60
❑	562	Leo Cardenas IA	4.00	1.60
❑	563	Ray Sadecki	4.00	1.60
❑	564	Ray Sadecki IA	4.00	1.60
❑	565	Reggie Smith	6.00	2.40
❑	566	Reggie Smith IA	4.00	1.60
❑	567	Juan Marichal	12.00	4.80
❑	568	Juan Marichal IA	6.00	2.40
❑	569	Ed Kirkpatrick	4.00	1.60
❑	570	Ed Kirkpatrick IA	4.00	1.60
❑	571	Nate Colbert	4.00	1.60
❑	572	Nate Colbert IA	4.00	1.60
❑	573	Fritz Peterson	4.00	1.60
❑	574	Fritz Peterson IA	4.00	1.60
❑	575	Al Oliver	8.00	3.20
❑	576	Leo Durocher MG	6.00	2.40
❑	577	Mike Paul	6.00	2.40
❑	578	Billy Grabarkewitz	4.00	1.60
❑	579	Doyle Alexander RC	6.00	2.40
❑	580	Lou Piniella	6.00	2.40
❑	581	Wade Blasingame	4.00	1.60
❑	582	Montreal Expos	8.00	3.20
		Team Card		
❑	583	Darold Knowles	4.00	1.60
❑	584	Jerry McNertney	4.00	1.60
❑	585	George Scott	6.00	2.40
❑	586	Denis Menke	4.00	1.60
❑	587	Billy Wilson	4.00	1.60
❑	588	Jim Holt	4.00	1.60
❑	589	Hal Lanier	4.00	1.60
❑	590	Graig Nettles	8.00	3.20
❑	591	Paul Casanova	4.00	1.60
❑	592	Lew Krausse	4.00	1.60
❑	593	Rich Morales	4.00	1.60
❑	594	Jim Beauchamp	4.00	1.60
❑	595	Nolan Ryan	80.00	32.00
❑	596	Manny Mota	6.00	2.40
❑	597	Jim Magnuson	4.00	1.60
❑	598	Hal King	6.00	2.40
❑	599	Billy Champion	4.00	1.60
❑	600	Al Kaline	25.00	10.00
❑	601	George Stone	4.00	1.60
❑	602	Dave Bristol MG	4.00	1.60
❑	603	Jim Ray	4.00	1.60
❑	604A	Checklist 657-787	12.00	2.40
		(Copyright on back bottom right)		
❑	604B	Checklist 657-787	12.00	2.40
		(Copyright on back bottom left)		
❑	605	Nelson Briles	6.00	2.40
❑	606	Luis Melendez	4.00	1.60
❑	607	Frank Duffy	4.00	1.60
❑	608	Mike Corkins	4.00	1.60
❑	609	Tom Grieve	6.00	2.40
❑	610	Bill Stoneman	6.00	2.40
❑	611	Rich Reese	4.00	1.60
❑	612	Joe Decker	4.00	1.60
❑	613	Mike Ferraro	4.00	1.60
❑	614	Ted Uhlaender	4.00	1.60
❑	615	Steve Hargan	4.00	1.60
❑	616	Joe Ferguson RC	6.00	2.40
❑	617	Kansas City Royals	8.00	3.20
		Team Card		
❑	618	Rich Robertson	4.00	1.60
❑	619	Rich McKinney	4.00	1.60
❑	620	Phil Niekro	12.00	4.80
❑	621	Comm. Award	8.00	3.20
❑	622	MVP Award	8.00	3.20
❑	623	Cy Young Award	8.00	3.20
❑	624	Minor League Player	8.00	3.20
		of the Year		
❑	625	Rookie of the Year	8.00	3.20
❑	626	Babe Ruth Award	8.00	3.20
❑	627	Moe Drabowsky	4.00	1.60
❑	628	Terry Crowley	4.00	1.60
❑	629	Paul Doyle	4.00	1.60
❑	630	Rich Hebner	6.00	2.40
❑	631	John Strohmayer	4.00	1.60
❑	632	Mike Hegan	4.00	1.60
❑	633	Jack Hiatt	4.00	1.60
❑	634	Dick Woodson	4.00	1.60
❑	635	Don Money	6.00	2.40
❑	636	Bill Lee	6.00	2.40
❑	637	Preston Gomez MG	4.00	1.60
❑	638	Ken Wright	4.00	1.60
❑	639	J.C. Martin	4.00	1.60
❑	640	Joe Coleman	4.00	1.60
❑	641	Mike Lum	4.00	1.60
❑	642	Dennis Riddleberger	4.00	1.60
❑	643	Russ Gibson	4.00	1.60
❑	644	Bernie Allen	4.00	1.60
❑	645	Jim Maloney	6.00	2.40
❑	646	Chico Salmon	4.00	1.60
❑	647	Bob Moose	4.00	1.60
❑	648	Jim Lyttle	4.00	1.60
❑	649	Pete Richert	4.00	1.60
❑	650	Sal Bando	6.00	2.40
❑	651	Cincinnati Reds	8.00	3.20
		Team Card		
❑	652	Marcelino Lopez	4.00	1.60
❑	653	Jim Fairey	4.00	1.60
❑	654	Horacio Pina	6.00	2.40
❑	655	Jerry Grote	4.00	1.60
❑	656	Rudy May	4.00	1.60
❑	657	Bobby Wine	12.00	4.80
❑	658	Steve Dunning	12.00	4.80
❑	659	Bob Aspromonte	12.00	4.80
❑	660	Paul Blair	15.00	6.00
❑	661	Bill Virdon MG	12.00	4.80
❑	662	Stan Bahnsen	12.00	4.80
❑	663	Fran Healy	15.00	6.00
❑	664	Bobby Knoop	12.00	4.80
❑	665	Chris Short	12.00	4.80
❑	666	Hector Torres	12.00	4.80
❑	667	Ray Newman	12.00	4.80
❑	668	Texas Rangers	30.00	12.00
		Team Card		
❑	669	Willie Crawford	12.00	4.80
❑	670	Ken Holtzman	15.00	6.00
❑	671	Donn Clendenon	15.00	6.00
❑	672	Archie Reynolds	12.00	4.80
❑	673	Dave Marshall	12.00	4.80
❑	674	John Kennedy	12.00	4.80
❑	675	Pat Jarvis	12.00	4.80
❑	676	Danny Cater	12.00	4.80
❑	677	Ivan Murrell	12.00	4.80
❑	678	Steve Luebber	12.00	4.80
❑	679	Bob Fenwick	12.00	4.80
		Bob Stinson		
❑	680	Dave Johnson	15.00	6.00
❑	681	Bobby Pfeil	12.00	4.80
❑	682	Mike McCormick	15.00	6.00
❑	683	Steve Hovley	12.00	4.80
❑	684	Hal Breeden	12.00	4.80
❑	685	Joel Horlen	12.00	4.80
❑	686	Steve Garvey	40.00	16.00
❑	687	Del Unser	12.00	4.80
❑	688	St. Louis Cardinals	20.00	8.00
		Team Card		
❑	689	Eddie Fisher	12.00	4.80
❑	690	Willie Montanez	15.00	6.00

❑ 691 Curt Blefary	12.00	4.80
❑ 692 Curt Blefary IA	12.00	4.80
❑ 693 Alan Gallagher	12.00	4.80
❑ 694 Alan Gallagher IA	12.00	4.80
❑ 695 Rod Carew	50.00	20.00
❑ 696 Rod Carew IA	30.00	12.00
❑ 697 Jerry Koosman	15.00	6.00
❑ 698 Jerry Koosman IA	15.00	6.00
❑ 699 Bobby Murcer	15.00	6.00
❑ 700 Bobby Murcer IA	15.00	6.00
❑ 701 Jose Pagan	12.00	4.80
❑ 702 Jose Pagan IA	12.00	4.80
❑ 703 Doug Griffin	12.00	4.80
❑ 704 Doug Griffin IA	12.00	4.80
❑ 705 Pat Corrales	15.00	6.00
❑ 706 Pat Corrales IA	12.00	4.80
❑ 707 Tim Foli	12.00	4.80
❑ 708 Tim Foli IA	12.00	4.80
❑ 709 Jim Kaat	15.00	6.00
❑ 710 Jim Kaat IA	15.00	6.00
❑ 711 Bobby Bonds	20.00	8.00
❑ 712 Bobby Bonds IA	15.00	6.00
❑ 713 Gene Michael	20.00	8.00
❑ 714 Gene Michael IA	15.00	6.00
❑ 715 Mike Epstein	12.00	4.80
❑ 716 Jesus Alou	12.00	4.80
❑ 717 Bruce Dal Canton	12.00	4.80
❑ 718 Del Rice MG	12.00	4.80
❑ 719 Cesar Geronimo	12.00	4.80
❑ 720 Sam McDowell	15.00	6.00
❑ 721 Eddie Leon	12.00	4.80
❑ 722 Bill Sudakis	12.00	4.80
❑ 723 Al Santorini	12.00	4.80
❑ 724 John Curtis	12.00	4.80
Rich Hinton		
Mickey Scott RC		
❑ 725 Dick McAuliffe	15.00	6.00
❑ 726 Dick Selma	12.00	4.80
❑ 727 Jose Laboy	12.00	4.80
❑ 728 Gail Hopkins	12.00	4.80
❑ 729 Bob Veale	15.00	6.00
❑ 730 Rick Monday	15.00	6.00
❑ 731 Baltimore Orioles	20.00	8.00
Team Card		
❑ 732 George Culver	12.00	4.80
❑ 733 Jim Ray Hart	15.00	6.00
❑ 734 Bob Burda	12.00	4.80
❑ 735 Diego Segui	12.00	4.80
❑ 736 Bill Russell	15.00	6.00
❑ 737 Len Randle	15.00	6.00
❑ 738 Jim Merritt	12.00	4.80
❑ 739 Don Mason	12.00	4.80
❑ 740 Rico Carty	15.00	6.00
❑ 741 Tom Hutton	15.00	6.00
John Milner		
Rick Miller RC		
❑ 742 Jim Rooker	12.00	4.80
❑ 743 Cesar Gutierrez	12.00	4.80
❑ 744 Jim Slaton	12.00	4.80
❑ 745 Julian Javier	15.00	6.00
❑ 746 Lowell Palmer	12.00	4.80
❑ 747 Jim Stewart	12.00	4.80
❑ 748 Phil Hennigan	12.00	4.80
❑ 749 Walter Alston MG	20.00	8.00
❑ 750 Willie Horton	15.00	6.00
❑ 751 Steve Carlton TR	40.00	16.00
❑ 752 Joe Morgan TR	40.00	16.00
❑ 753 Denny McLain TR	20.00	8.00
❑ 754 Frank Robinson TR	40.00	16.00
❑ 755 Jim Fregosi TR	15.00	6.00
❑ 756 Rick Wise TR	15.00	6.00
❑ 757 Jose Cardenal TR	15.00	6.00
❑ 758 Gil Garrido	12.00	4.80
❑ 759 Chris Cannizzaro	12.00	4.80
❑ 760 Bill Mazeroski	25.00	10.00
❑ 761 Ben Oglivie RC	25.00	10.00
Ron Cey RC		
Bernie Williams		
❑ 762 Wayne Simpson	12.00	4.80
❑ 763 Ron Hansen	12.00	4.80
❑ 764 Dusty Baker	20.00	8.00
❑ 765 Ken McMullen	12.00	4.80
❑ 766 Steve Hamilton	12.00	4.80
❑ 767 Tom McCraw	15.00	6.00
❑ 768 Denny Doyle	12.00	4.80
❑ 769 Jack Aker	12.00	4.80
❑ 770 Jim Wynn	15.00	6.00
❑ 771 San Francisco Giants	20.00	8.00
Team Card		
❑ 772 Ken Tatum	12.00	4.80
❑ 773 Ron Brand	12.00	4.80
❑ 774 Luis Alvarado	12.00	4.80
❑ 775 Jerry Reuss	15.00	6.00
❑ 776 Bill Voss	12.00	4.80
❑ 777 Hoyt Wilhelm	25.00	10.00
❑ 778 Vic Albury	20.00	8.00
Rick Dempsey RC		
Jim Strickland		
❑ 779 Tony Cloninger	12.00	4.80
❑ 780 Dick Green	12.00	4.80
❑ 781 Jim McAndrew	12.00	4.80
❑ 782 Larry Stahl	12.00	4.80
❑ 783 Les Cain	12.00	4.80
❑ 784 Ken Aspromonte	12.00	4.80
❑ 785 Vic Davalillo	12.00	4.80
❑ 786 Chuck Brinkman	12.00	4.80
❑ 787 Ron Reed	15.00	5.25

1973 Topps

	NM	Ex
COMPLETE SET (660)	700.00	275.00
COMMON CARD (1-264)	.50	.20
COMMON (265-396)	.75	.30
COMMON (397-528)	1.25	.50
COMMON (529-660)	3.00	1.20
WRAPPER (10-CENT, BAT)	15.00	6.00
WRAPPER (10-CENT)	15.00	6.00
❑ 1 Babe Ruth 714	40.00	11.50
Hank Aaron 673		
Willie Mays 654 ATL		
❑ 2 Rich Hebner	1.50	.60
❑ 3 Jim Lonborg	1.50	.60
❑ 4 John Milner	.50	.20
❑ 5 Ed Brinkman	.50	.20
❑ 6 Mac Scarce	.50	.20
❑ 7 Texas Rangers	2.00	.80
Team Card		
❑ 8 Tom Hall	.50	.20
❑ 9 Johnny Oates	1.50	.60
❑ 10 Don Sutton	4.00	1.60
❑ 11 Chris Chambliss	1.50	.60
❑ 12A Don Zimmer MG	3.00	1.20
Dave Garcia CO		
Johnny Podres CO		
Bob Skinner CO		
Whitey Wietelmann CO		
(Podres no right ear)		
❑ 12B Padres Leaders	.75	.30
(Podres has right ear)		
❑ 13 George Hendrick	1.50	.60
❑ 14 Sonny Siebert	.50	.20
❑ 15 Ralph Garr	1.50	.60
❑ 16 Steve Braun	.50	.20
❑ 17 Fred Gladding	.50	.20
❑ 18 Leroy Stanton	.50	.20
❑ 19 Tim Foli	.50	.20
❑ 20 Stan Bahnsen	.50	.20
❑ 21 Randy Hundley	1.50	.60
❑ 22 Ted Abernathy	.50	.20
❑ 23 Dave Kingman	1.50	.60
❑ 24 Al Santorini	.50	.20
❑ 25 Roy White	1.50	.60
❑ 26 Pittsburgh Pirates	2.00	.80
Team Card		
❑ 27 Bill Gogolewski	.50	.20
❑ 28 Hal McRae	1.50	.60
❑ 29 Tony Taylor	1.50	.60
❑ 30 Tug McGraw	1.50	.60
❑ 31 Buddy Bell RC	2.50	1.00
❑ 32 Fred Norman	.50	.20
❑ 33 Jim Breazeale	.50	.20
❑ 34 Pat Dobson	.50	.20
❑ 35 Willie Davis	1.50	.60
❑ 36 Steve Barber	.50	.20
❑ 37 Bill Robinson	1.50	.60
❑ 38 Mike Epstein	.50	.20
❑ 39 Dave Roberts	.50	.20
❑ 40 Reggie Smith	1.50	.60
❑ 41 Tom Walker	.50	.20
❑ 42 Mike Andrews	.50	.20
❑ 43 Randy Moffitt	.50	.20
❑ 44 Rick Monday	1.50	.60
❑ 45 Ellie Rodriguez UER	.50	.20
(Photo is either John Felske or Paul Ratliff		
❑ 46 Lindy McDaniel	1.50	.60
❑ 47 Luis Melendez	.50	.20
❑ 48 Paul Splittorff	.50	.20
❑ 49A Frank Quilici MG	3.00	1.20
Vern Morgan CO		
Bob Rodgers CO		
Ralph Rowe CO		
Al Worthington CO		
(Solid backgrounds)		
❑ 49B Twins Leaders	.75	.30
(Natural backgrounds)		
❑ 50 Roberto Clemente	40.00	16.00
❑ 51 Chuck Seelbach	.50	.20
❑ 52 Denis Menke	.50	.20
❑ 53 Steve Dunning	.50	.20
❑ 54 Checklist 1-132	3.00	.60
❑ 55 Jon Matlack	1.50	.60
❑ 56 Merv Rettenmund	.50	.20
❑ 57 Derrel Thomas	.50	.20
❑ 58 Mike Paul	.50	.20
❑ 59 Steve Yeager RC	1.50	.60
❑ 60 Ken Holtzman	1.50	.60
❑ 61 Billy Williams	2.50	1.00
Rod Carew LL		
❑ 62 Johnny Bench	2.50	1.00
Dick Allen LL		
Home Run Leaders		
❑ 63 Johnny Bench	2.50	1.00
Dick Allen		
RBI Leaders		
❑ 64 Lou Brock	1.50	.60
Bert Campaneris LL		
❑ 65 Steve Carlton	1.50	.60
Luis Tiant LL		
❑ 66 Steve Carlton	1.50	.60
Gaylord Perry		
Wilbur Wood LL		
❑ 67 Steve Carlton	25.00	10.00
Nolan Ryan LL		
❑ 68 Clay Carroll	1.50	.60
Sparky Lyle LL		
❑ 69 Phil Gagliano	.50	.20
❑ 70 Milt Pappas	1.50	.60
❑ 71 Johnny Briggs	.50	.20
❑ 72 Ron Reed	.50	.20
❑ 73 Ed Herrmann	.50	.20
❑ 74 Billy Champion	.50	.20
❑ 75 Vada Pinson	1.50	.60
❑ 76 Doug Rader	.50	.20
❑ 77 Mike Torrez	1.50	.60
❑ 78 Richie Scheinblum	.50	.20
❑ 79 Jim Willoughby	.50	.20
❑ 80 Tony Oliva UER	2.50	1.00
(Minnseota on front)		
❑ 81A Whitey Lockman MG	1.50	.60
Hank Aguirre CO		
Ernie Banks CO		
Larry Jansen CO		
Pete Reiser CO		
(Solid backgrounds)		
❑ 81B Cubs Leaders	1.50	.60
(Natural backgrounds)		
❑ 82 Fritz Peterson	.50	.20
❑ 83 Leron Lee	.50	.20

❑ 84 Rollie Fingers 4.00 1.60
❑ 85 Ted Simmons 1.50 .60
❑ 86 Tom McCraw .50 .20
❑ 87 Ken Boswell .50 .20
❑ 88 Mickey Stanley 1.50 .60
❑ 89 Jack Billingham .50 .20
❑ 90 Brooks Robinson 8.00 3.20
❑ 91 Los Angeles Dodgers 2.00 .80
Team Card
❑ 92 Jerry Bell .50 .20
❑ 93 Jesus Alou .50 .20
❑ 94 Dick Billings .50 .20
❑ 95 Steve Blass 1.50 .60
❑ 96 Doug Griffin .50 .20
❑ 97 Willie Montanez 1.50 .60
❑ 98 Dick Woodson .50 .20
❑ 99 Carl Taylor .50 .20
❑ 100 Hank Aaron 40.00 16.00
❑ 101 Ken Henderson .50 .20
❑ 102 Rudy May .50 .20
❑ 103 Celerino Sanchez .50 .20
❑ 104 Reggie Cleveland .50 .20
❑ 105 Carlos May .50 .20
❑ 106 Terry Humphrey .50 .20
❑ 107 Phil Hennigan .50 .20
❑ 108 Bill Russell 1.50 .60
❑ 109 Doyle Alexander 1.50 .60
❑ 110 Bob Watson 1.50 .60
❑ 111 Dave Nelson .50 .20
❑ 112 Gary Ross .50 .20
❑ 113 Jerry Grote 1.50 .60
❑ 114 Lynn McGlothen .50 .20
❑ 115 Ron Santo 1.50 .60
❑ 116A Ralph Houk MG 3.00 1.20
Jim Hegan CO
Elston Howard CO
Dick Howser CO
Jim Turner CO
(Solid backgrounds)
❑ 116B Yankees Leaders .75 .30
(Natural backgrounds)
❑ 117 Ramon Hernandez .50 .20
❑ 118 John Mayberry 1.50 .60
❑ 119 Larry Bowa 1.50 .60
❑ 120 Joe Coleman .50 .20
❑ 121 Dave Rader .50 .20
❑ 122 Jim Strickland .50 .20
❑ 123 Sandy Alomar 1.50 .60
❑ 124 Jim Hardin .50 .20
❑ 125 Ron Fairly 1.50 .60
❑ 126 Jim Brewer .50 .20
❑ 127 Milwaukee Brewers 2.00 .80
Team Card
❑ 128 Ted Sizemore .50 .20
❑ 129 Terry Forster 1.50 .60
❑ 130 Pete Rose 30.00 12.00
❑ 131A Eddie Kasko MG 3.00 1.20
Doug Camilli CO
Don Lenhardt CO
Eddie Popowski CO
(No right ear)
Lee Stange CO
❑ 131B Red Sox Leaders 1.50 .60
(Popowski has right
ear showing)
❑ 132 Matty Alou 1.50 .60
❑ 133 Dave Roberts RC .50 .20
❑ 134 Milt Wilcox .50 .20
❑ 135 Lee May UER 1.50 .60
(Career average .000)
❑ 136A Earl Weaver MG 1.50 .60
George Bamberger CO
Jim Frey CO
Billy Hunter CO
George Staller CO
(Orange backgrounds)
❑ 136B Orioles Leaders 3.00 1.20
(Dark pale
backgrounds)
❑ 137 Jim Beauchamp .50 .20
❑ 138 Horacio Pina .50 .20
❑ 139 Carmen Fanzone .50 .20
❑ 140 Lou Piniella 2.50 1.00
❑ 141 Bruce Kison .50 .20
❑ 142 Thurman Munson 8.00 3.20
❑ 143 John Curtis .50 .20
❑ 144 Marty Perez .50 .20
❑ 145 Bobby Bonds 2.50 1.00
❑ 146 Woodie Fryman .50 .20
❑ 147 Mike Anderson .50 .20
❑ 148 Dave Goltz .50 .20
❑ 149 Ron Hunt .50 .20
❑ 150 Wilbur Wood 1.50 .60
❑ 151 Wes Parker 1.50 .60
❑ 152 Dave May .50 .20
❑ 153 Al Hrabosky 1.50 .60
❑ 154 Jeff Torborg 1.50 .60
❑ 155 Sal Bando 1.50 .60
❑ 156 Cesar Geronimo .50 .20
❑ 157 Denny Riddleberger .50 .20
❑ 158 Houston Astros 2.00 .80
Team Card
❑ 159 Clarence Gaston 1.50 .60
❑ 160 Jim Palmer 6.00 2.40
❑ 161 Ted Martinez .50 .20
❑ 162 Pete Broberg .50 .20
❑ 163 Vic Davalillo .50 .20
❑ 164 Monty Montgomery .50 .20
❑ 165 Luis Aparicio 4.00 1.60
❑ 166 Terry Harmon .50 .20
❑ 167 Steve Stone 1.50 .60
❑ 168 Jim Northrup 1.50 .60
❑ 169 Ron Schueler RC 1.50 .60
❑ 170 Harmon Killebrew 5.00 2.00
❑ 171 Bernie Carbo .50 .20
❑ 172 Steve Kline .50 .20
❑ 173 Hal Breeden .50 .20
❑ 174 Goose Gossage RC 6.00 2.40
❑ 175 Frank Robinson 6.00 2.40
❑ 176 Chuck Taylor .50 .20
❑ 177 Bill Plummer .50 .20
❑ 178 Don Rose .50 .20
❑ 179A Dick Williams MG 4.00 1.60
Jerry Adair CO
Vern Hoscheit CO
Irv Noren CO
Wes Stock CO
(Hoscheit left ear
showing)
❑ 179B A's Leaders 1.50 .60
(Hoscheit left ear
not showing)
❑ 180 Ferguson Jenkins 4.00 1.60
❑ 181 Jack Brohamer .50 .20
❑ 182 Mike Caldwell RC 1.50 .60
❑ 183 Don Buford .50 .20
❑ 184 Jerry Koosman 1.50 .60
❑ 185 Jim Wynn 1.50 .60
❑ 186 Bill Fahey .50 .20
❑ 187 Luke Walker .50 .20
❑ 188 Cookie Rojas 1.50 .60
❑ 189 Greg Luzinski 2.50 1.00
❑ 190 Bob Gibson 8.00 3.20
❑ 191 Detroit Tigers 2.50 1.00
Team Card
❑ 192 Pat Jarvis .50 .20
❑ 193 Carlton Fisk 10.00 4.00
❑ 194 Jorge Orta .50 .20
❑ 195 Clay Carroll .50 .20
❑ 196 Ken McMullen .50 .20
❑ 197 Ed Goodson .50 .20
❑ 198 Horace Clarke .50 .20
❑ 199 Bert Blyleven 2.50 1.00
❑ 200 Billy Williams 4.00 1.60
❑ 201 G. Hendrick ALCS 1.50 .60
❑ 202 George Foster NLCS 1.50 .60
❑ 203 Gene Tenace WS 1.50 .60
❑ 204 World Series Game 2 1.50 .60
A's two straight
❑ 205 Tony Perez WS 2.50 1.00
❑ 206 Gene Tenace WS 1.50 .60
❑ 207 Blue Moon Odom WS 1.50 .60
❑ 208 Johnny Bench WS6 5.00 2.00
❑ 209 Bert Campaneris WS 1.50 .60
❑ 210 W.S. Summary .50 .20
World champions:
A's Win
❑ 211 Balor Moore .50 .20
❑ 212 Joe Lahoud .50 .20
❑ 213 Steve Garvey 5.00 2.00
❑ 214 Dave Hamilton .50 .20
❑ 215 Dusty Baker 2.50 1.00
❑ 216 Toby Harrah 1.50 .60
❑ 217 Don Wilson .50 .20
❑ 218 Aurelio Rodriguez .50 .20
❑ 219 St. Louis Cardinals 2.50 1.00
Team Card
❑ 220 Nolan Ryan 50.00 20.00
❑ 221 Fred Kendall .50 .20
❑ 222 Rob Gardner .50 .20
❑ 223 Bud Harrelson 1.50 .60
❑ 224 Bill Lee 1.50 .60
❑ 225 Al Oliver 1.50 .60
❑ 226 Ray Fosse .50 .20
❑ 227 Wayne Twitchell .50 .20
❑ 228 Bobby Darwin .50 .20
❑ 229 Roric Harrison .50 .20
❑ 230 Joe Morgan 6.00 2.40
❑ 231 Bill Parsons .50 .20
❑ 232 Ken Singleton 1.50 .60
❑ 233 Ed Kirkpatrick .50 .20
❑ 234 Bill North .50 .20
❑ 235 Jim Hunter 4.00 1.60
❑ 236 Tito Fuentes .50 .20
❑ 237A Eddie Mathews MG 1.50 .60
Lew Burdette CO
Jim Busby CO
Roy Hartsfield CO
Ken Silvestri CO
(Burdette right ear
showing)
❑ 237B Braves Leaders 3.00 1.20
(Burdette right ear
not showing)
❑ 238 Tony Muser .50 .20
❑ 239 Pete Richert .50 .20
❑ 240 Bobby Murcer 1.50 .60
❑ 241 Dwain Anderson .50 .20
❑ 242 George Culver .50 .20
❑ 243 California Angels 2.50 1.00
Team Card
❑ 244 Ed Acosta .50 .20
❑ 245 Carl Yastrzemski 10.00 4.00
❑ 246 Ken Sanders .50 .20
❑ 247 Del Unser .50 .20
❑ 248 Jerry Johnson .50 .20
❑ 249 Larry Biittner .50 .20
❑ 250 Manny Sanguillen 1.50 .60
❑ 251 Roger Nelson .50 .20
❑ 252A Charlie Fox MG 4.00 1.60
Joe Amalfitano CO
Andy Gilbert CO
Don McMahon CO
John McNamara CO
(Orange backgrounds)
❑ 252B Giants Leaders 1.50 .60
(Dark pale
backgrounds)
❑ 253 Mark Belanger 1.50 .60
❑ 254 Bill Stoneman .50 .20
❑ 255 Reggie Jackson 15.00 6.00
❑ 256 Chris Zachary .50 .20
❑ 257A Yogi Berra MG 3.00 1.20
Roy McMillan CO
Joe Pignatano CO
Rube Walker CO
Eddie Yost CO
(Orange backgrounds)
❑ 257B Mets Leaders 5.00 2.00
(Dark pale
backgrounds)
❑ 258 Tommy John 1.50 .60
❑ 259 Jim Holt .50 .20
❑ 260 Gary Nolan 1.50 .60
❑ 261 Pat Kelly .50 .20
❑ 262 Jack Aker .50 .20
❑ 263 George Scott 1.50 .60
❑ 264 Checklist 133-264 3.00 .60
❑ 265 Gene Michael 1.50 .60
❑ 266 Mike Lum .75 .30
❑ 267 Lloyd Allen .75 .30
❑ 268 Jerry Morales .75 .30
❑ 269 Tim McCarver 1.50 .60
❑ 270 Luis Tiant 1.50 .60
❑ 271 Tom Hutton .75 .30
❑ 272 Ed Farmer .75 .30
❑ 273 Chris Speier .75 .30
❑ 274 Darold Knowles .75 .30

❑ 275 Tony Perez 4.00 1.60
❑ 276 Joe Lovitto .75 .30
❑ 277 Bob Miller .75 .30
❑ 278 Baltimore Orioles 1.50 .60
Team Card
❑ 279 Mike Strahler .75 .30
❑ 280 Al Kaline 8.00 3.20
❑ 281 Mike Jorgensen .75 .30
❑ 282 Steve Hovley .75 .30
❑ 283 Ray Sadecki .75 .30
❑ 284 Glenn Borgmann .75 .30
❑ 285 Don Kessinger 1.50 .60
❑ 286 Frank Linzy .75 .30
❑ 287 Eddie Leon .75 .30
❑ 288 Gary Gentry .75 .30
❑ 289 Bob Oliver .75 .30
❑ 290 Cesar Cedeno 1.50 .60
❑ 291 Rogelio Moret .75 .30
❑ 292 Jose Cruz 1.50 .60
❑ 293 Bernie Allen .75 .30
❑ 294 Steve Arlin .75 .30
❑ 295 Bert Campaneris 1.50 .60
❑ 296 Sparky Anderson MG 2.50 1.00
Alex Grammas CO
Ted Kluszewski CO
George Scherger CO
Larry Shepard CO
❑ 297 Walt Williams .75 .30
❑ 298 Ron Bryant .75 .30
❑ 299 Ted Ford .75 .30
❑ 300 Steve Carlton 10.00 4.00
❑ 301 Billy Grabarkewitz .75 .30
❑ 302 Terry Crowley .75 .30
❑ 303 Nelson Briles .75 .30
❑ 304 Duke Sims .75 .30
❑ 305 Willie Mays 40.00 16.00
❑ 306 Tom Burgmeier .75 .30
❑ 307 Boots Day .75 .30
❑ 308 Skip Lockwood .75 .30
❑ 309 Paul Popovich .75 .30
❑ 310 Dick Allen 1.50 .60
❑ 311 Joe Decker .75 .30
❑ 312 Oscar Brown .75 .30
❑ 313 Jim Ray .75 .30
❑ 314 Ron Swoboda 1.50 .60
❑ 315 John Odom .75 .30
❑ 316 San Diego Padres 1.50 .60
Team Card
❑ 317 Danny Cater .75 .30
❑ 318 Jim McGlothlin .75 .30
❑ 319 Jim Spencer .75 .30
❑ 320 Lou Brock 8.00 3.20
❑ 321 Rich Hinton .75 .30
❑ 322 Garry Maddox RC 1.50 .60
❑ 323 Billy Martin MG 1.50 .60
Art Fowler CO
Charlie Silvera CO
Dick Tracewski CO
Joe Schultz CO ERR
Schult's name not printed on card
❑ 324 Al Downing .75 .30
❑ 325 Boog Powell 1.50 .60
❑ 326 Darrell Brandon .75 .30
❑ 327 John Lowenstein .75 .30
❑ 328 Bill Bonham .75 .30
❑ 329 Ed Kranepool 1.50 .60
❑ 330 Rod Carew 8.00 3.20
❑ 331 Carl Morton .75 .30
❑ 332 John Felske .75 .30
❑ 333 Gene Clines .75 .30
❑ 334 Freddie Patek .75 .30
❑ 335 Bob Tolan .75 .30
❑ 336 Tom Bradley .75 .30
❑ 337 Dave Duncan 1.50 .60
❑ 338 Checklist 265-396 3.00 .60
❑ 339 Dick Tidrow .75 .30
❑ 340 Nate Colbert .75 .30
❑ 341 Jim Palmer KP 2.50 1.00
❑ 342 Sam McDowell KP .75 .30
❑ 343 Bobby Murcer KP .75 .30
❑ 344 Jim Hunter KP 2.50 1.00
❑ 345 Chris Speier KP .75 .30
❑ 346 Gaylord Perry KP 1.50 .60
❑ 347 Kansas City Royals 1.50 .60
Team Card
❑ 348 Rennie Stennett .75 .30

❑ 349 Dick McAuliffe .75 .30
❑ 350 Tom Seaver 12.00 4.80
❑ 351 Jimmy Stewart .75 .30
❑ 352 Don Stanhouse .75 .30
❑ 353 Steve Brye .75 .30
❑ 354 Billy Parker .75 .30
❑ 355 Mike Marshall 1.50 .60
❑ 356 Chuck Tanner MG 4.00 1.60
Joe Lonnett CO
Jim Mahoney CO
Al Monchak CO
Johnny Sain CO
❑ 357 Ross Grimsley .75 .30
❑ 358 Jim Nettles .75 .30
❑ 359 Cecil Upshaw .75 .30
❑ 360 Joe Rudi UER 1.50 .60
(Photo actually
Gene Tenace)
❑ 361 Fran Healy .75 .30
❑ 362 Eddie Watt .75 .30
❑ 363 Jackie Hernandez .75 .30
❑ 364 Rick Wise .75 .30
❑ 365 Rico Petrocelli 1.50 .60
❑ 366 Brock Davis .75 .30
❑ 367 Burt Hooton 1.50 .60
❑ 368 Bill Buckner 1.50 .60
❑ 369 Lerrin LaGrow .75 .30
❑ 370 Willie Stargell 5.00 2.00
❑ 371 Mike Kekich .75 .30
❑ 372 Oscar Gamble .75 .30
❑ 373 Clyde Wright .75 .30
❑ 374 Darrell Evans 1.50 .60
❑ 375 Larry Dierker 1.50 .60
❑ 376 Frank Duffy .75 .30
❑ 377 Gene Mauch MG 4.00 1.60
Dave Bristol CO
Larry Doby CO
Cal McLish CO
Jerry Zimmerman CO
❑ 378 Len Randle .75 .30
❑ 379 Cy Acosta .75 .30
❑ 380 Johnny Bench 12.00 4.80
❑ 381 Vicente Romo .75 .30
❑ 382 Mike Hegan .75 .30
❑ 383 Diego Segui .75 .30
❑ 384 Don Baylor 4.00 1.60
❑ 385 Jim Perry 1.50 .60
❑ 386 Don Money .75 .30
❑ 387 Jim Barr .75 .30
❑ 388 Ben Oglivie 1.50 .60
❑ 389 New York Mets 4.00 1.60
Team Card
❑ 390 Mickey Lolich 1.50 .60
❑ 391 Lee Lacy RC 1.50 .60
❑ 392 Dick Drago .75 .30
❑ 393 Jose Cardenal .75 .30
❑ 394 Sparky Lyle 1.50 .60
❑ 395 Roger Metzger .75 .30
❑ 396 Grant Jackson .75 .30
❑ 397 Dave Cash 1.25 .50
❑ 398 Rich Hand 1.25 .50
❑ 399 George Foster 2.00 .80
❑ 400 Gaylord Perry 5.00 2.00
❑ 401 Clyde Mashore 1.25 .50
❑ 402 Jack Hiatt 1.25 .50
❑ 403 Sonny Jackson 1.25 .50
❑ 404 Chuck Brinkman 1.25 .50
❑ 405 Cesar Tovar 1.25 .50
❑ 406 Paul Lindblad 1.25 .50
❑ 407 Felix Millan 1.25 .50
❑ 408 Jim Colborn 1.25 .50
❑ 409 Ivan Murrell 1.25 .50
❑ 410 Willie McCovey 6.00 2.40
(Bench behind plate)
❑ 411 Ray Corbin 1.25 .50
❑ 412 Manny Mota 2.00 .80
❑ 413 Tom Timmermann 1.25 .50
❑ 414 Ken Rudolph 1.25 .50
❑ 415 Marty Pattin 1.25 .50
❑ 416 Paul Schaal 1.25 .50
❑ 417 Scipio Spinks 1.25 .50
❑ 418 Bob Grich 2.00 .80
❑ 419 Casey Cox 1.25 .50
❑ 420 Tommie Agee 1.25 .50
❑ 421A Bobby Winkles MG 1.50 .60
Tom Morgan CO
Salty Parker CO
Jimmie Reese CO
John Roseboro CO
(Orange backgrounds)
❑ 421B Angels Leaders 3.00 1.20
(Dark pale
backgrounds)
❑ 422 Bob Robertson 1.25 .50
❑ 423 Johnny Jeter 1.25 .50
❑ 424 Denny Doyle 1.25 .50
❑ 425 Alex Johnson 1.25 .50
❑ 426 Dave LaRoche 1.25 .50
❑ 427 Rick Auerbach 1.25 .50
❑ 428 Wayne Simpson 1.25 .50
❑ 429 Jim Fairey 1.25 .50
❑ 430 Vida Blue 2.00 .80
❑ 431 Gerry Moses 1.25 .50
❑ 432 Dan Frisella 1.25 .50
❑ 433 Willie Horton 2.00 .80
❑ 434 San Francisco Giants 3.00 1.20
Team Card
❑ 435 Rico Carty 2.00 .80
❑ 436 Jim McAndrew 1.25 .50
❑ 437 John Kennedy 1.25 .50
❑ 438 Enzo Hernandez 1.25 .50
❑ 439 Eddie Fisher 1.25 .50
❑ 440 Glenn Beckert 1.25 .50
❑ 441 Gail Hopkins 1.25 .50
❑ 442 Dick Dietz 1.25 .50
❑ 443 Danny Thompson 1.25 .50
❑ 444 Ken Brett 1.25 .50
❑ 445 Ken Berry 1.25 .50
❑ 446 Jerry Reuss 2.00 .80
❑ 447 Joe Hague 1.25 .50
❑ 448 John Hiller 1.25 .50
❑ 449A Ken Aspromonte MG 4.00 1.60
Rocky Colavito CO
Joe Lutz CO
Warren Spahn CO
(Spahn's right
ear pointed)
❑ 449B Indians Leaders 4.00 1.60
(Spahn's right
ear round)
❑ 450 Joe Torre 3.00 1.20
❑ 451 John Vukovich 1.25 .50
❑ 452 Paul Casanova 1.25 .50
❑ 453 Checklist 397-528 3.00 .60
❑ 454 Tom Haller 1.25 .50
❑ 455 Bill Melton 1.25 .50
❑ 456 Dick Green 1.25 .50
❑ 457 John Strohmayer 1.25 .50
❑ 458 Jim Mason 1.25 .50
❑ 459 Jimmy Howarth 1.25 .50
❑ 460 Bill Freehan 2.00 .80
❑ 461 Mike Corkins 1.25 .50
❑ 462 Ron Blomberg 1.25 .50
❑ 463 Ken Tatum 1.25 .50
❑ 464 Chicago Cubs 3.00 1.20
Team Card
❑ 465 Dave Giusti 1.25 .50
❑ 466 Jose Arcia 1.25 .50
❑ 467 Mike Ryan 1.25 .50
❑ 468 Tom Griffin 1.25 .50
❑ 469 Dan Monzon 1.25 .50
❑ 470 Mike Cuellar 2.00 .80
❑ 471 Ty Cobb ATL 10.00 4.00
4191 Hits
❑ 472 Lou Gehrig ATL 15.00 6.00
23 Grand Slams
❑ 473 Hank Aaron ATL 10.00 4.00
6172 Total Bases
❑ 474 Babe Ruth ATL 20.00 8.00
2209 RBI
❑ 475 Ty Cobb ATL 8.00 3.20
.367 Batting Average
❑ 476 Walter Johnson ATL 3.00 1.20
113 Shutouts
❑ 477 Cy Young ATL 3.00 1.20
511 Victories
❑ 478 Walter Johnson ATL 3.00 1.20
3508 Strikeouts
❑ 479 Hal Lanier 1.25 .50
❑ 480 Juan Marichal 5.00 2.00
❑ 481 Chicago White Sox 3.00 1.20
Team Card

❑ 482 Rick Reuschel RC 3.00 1.20
❑ 483 Dal Maxvill .... 1.25 .50
❑ 484 Ernie McAnally .... 1.25 .50
❑ 485 Norm Cash .... 2.00 .80
❑ 486A Danny Ozark MG .... 1.50 .60
Carroll Beringer CO
Billy DeMars CO
Ray Rippelmeyer CO
Bobby Wine CO
(Orange backgrounds)
❑ 486B Phillies Leaders 3.00 1.20
(Dark pale
backgrounds)
❑ 487 Bruce Dal Canton .... 1.25 .50
❑ 488 Dave Campbell .... 2.00 .80
❑ 489 Jeff Burroughs .... 2.00 .80
❑ 490 Claude Osteen .... 2.00 .80
❑ 491 Bob Montgomery .... 1.25 .50
❑ 492 Pedro Borbon .... 1.25 .50
❑ 493 Duffy Dyer .... 1.25 .50
❑ 494 Rich Morales .... 1.25 .50
❑ 495 Tommy Helms .... 1.25 .50
❑ 496 Ray Lamb .... 1.25 .50
❑ 497A Red Schoendienst MG 2.00 .80
Vern Benson CO
George Kissell CO
Barney Schultz CO
(Orange backgrounds)
❑ 497B Cardinals Leaders 3.00 1.20
(Dark pale
backgrounds)
❑ 498 Graig Nettles 3.00 1.20
❑ 499 Bob Moose .... 1.25 .50
❑ 500 Oakland A's 3.00 1.20
Team Card
❑ 501 Larry Gura .... 1.25 .50
❑ 502 Bobby Valentine 3.00 1.20
❑ 503 Phil Niekro 5.00 2.00
❑ 504 Earl Williams .... 1.25 .50
❑ 505 Bob Bailey .... 1.25 .50
❑ 506 Bart Johnson .... 1.25 .50
❑ 507 Darrel Chaney .... 1.25 .50
❑ 508 Gates Brown .... 1.25 .50
❑ 509 Jim Nash .... 1.25 .50
❑ 510 Amos Otis .... 2.00 .80
❑ 511 Sam McDowell .... 2.00 .80
❑ 512 Dalton Jones .... 1.25 .50
❑ 513 Dave Marshall .... 1.25 .50
❑ 514 Jerry Kenney .... 1.25 .50
❑ 515 Andy Messersmith .... 2.00 .80
❑ 516 Danny Walton .... 1.25 .50
❑ 517A Bill Virdon MG .... 1.50 .60
Don Leppert CO
Bill Mazeroski CO
Dave Ricketts CO
Mel Wright CO
(Mazeroski has
no right ear)
❑ 517B Pirates Leaders 3.00 1.20
(Mazeroski has
right ear)
❑ 518 Bob Veale .... 1.25 .50
❑ 519 Johnny Edwards .... 1.25 .50
❑ 520 Mel Stottlemyre .... 2.00 .80
❑ 521 Atlanta Braves 3.00 1.20
Team Card
❑ 522 Leo Cardenas .... 1.25 .50
❑ 523 Wayne Granger .... 1.25 .50
❑ 524 Gene Tenace .... 2.00 .80
❑ 525 Jim Fregosi .... 2.00 .80
❑ 526 Ollie Brown .... 1.25 .50
❑ 527 Dan McGinn .... 1.25 .50
❑ 528 Paul Blair .... 1.25 .50
❑ 529 Milt May 3.00 1.20
❑ 530 Jim Kaat 5.00 2.00
❑ 531 Ron Woods 3.00 1.20
❑ 532 Steve Mingori 3.00 1.20
❑ 533 Larry Stahl 3.00 1.20
❑ 534 Dave Lemonds 3.00 1.20
❑ 535 Johnny Callison 5.00 2.00
❑ 536 Philadelphia Phillies 6.00 2.40
Team Card
❑ 537 Bill Slayback 3.00 1.20
❑ 538 Jim Ray Hart 5.00 2.00
❑ 539 Tom Murphy 3.00 1.20
❑ 540 Cleon Jones 5.00 2.00
❑ 541 Bob Bolin 3.00 1.20
❑ 542 Pat Corrales 5.00 2.00
❑ 543 Alan Foster 3.00 1.20
❑ 544 Von Joshua 3.00 1.20
❑ 545 Orlando Cepeda 8.00 3.20
❑ 546 Jim York 3.00 1.20
❑ 547 Bobby Heise 3.00 1.20
❑ 548 Don Durham 3.00 1.20
❑ 549 Whitey Herzog MG 5.00 2.00
Chuck Estrada CO
Chuck Hiller CO
Jackie Moore CO
❑ 550 Dave Johnson 5.00 2.00
❑ 551 Mike Kilkenny 3.00 1.20
❑ 552 J.C. Martin 3.00 1.20
❑ 553 Mickey Scott 3.00 1.20
❑ 554 Dave Concepcion 5.00 2.00
❑ 555 Bill Hands 3.00 1.20
❑ 556 New York Yankees 8.00 3.20
Team Card
❑ 557 Bernie Williams 3.00 1.20
❑ 558 Jerry May 3.00 1.20
❑ 559 Barry Lersch 3.00 1.20
❑ 560 Frank Howard 5.00 2.00
❑ 561 Jim Geddes 3.00 1.20
❑ 562 Wayne Garrett 3.00 1.20
❑ 563 Larry Haney 3.00 1.20
❑ 564 Mike Thompson 3.00 1.20
❑ 565 Jim Hickman 3.00 1.20
❑ 566 Lew Krausse 3.00 1.20
❑ 567 Bob Fenwick 3.00 1.20
❑ 568 Ray Newman 3.00 1.20
❑ 569 Walt Alston MG 8.00 3.20
Red Adams CO
Monty Basgall CO
Jim Gilliam CO
Tom Lasorda CO
❑ 570 Bill Singer 5.00 2.00
❑ 571 Rusty Torres 3.00 1.20
❑ 572 Gary Sutherland 3.00 1.20
❑ 573 Fred Beene 3.00 1.20
❑ 574 Bob Didier 3.00 1.20
❑ 575 Dock Ellis 3.00 1.20
❑ 576 Montreal Expos 6.00 2.40
Team Card
❑ 577 Eric Soderholm 3.00 1.20
❑ 578 Ken Wright 3.00 1.20
❑ 579 Tom Grieve 5.00 2.00
❑ 580 Joe Pepitone 5.00 2.00
❑ 581 Steve Kealey 3.00 1.20
❑ 582 Darrell Porter 5.00 2.00
❑ 583 Bill Grief 3.00 1.20
❑ 584 Chris Arnold 3.00 1.20
❑ 585 Joe Niekro 5.00 2.00
❑ 586 Bill Sudakis 3.00 1.20
❑ 587 Rich McKinney 3.00 1.20
❑ 588 Checklist 529-660 .... 20.00 4.00
❑ 589 Ken Forsch 3.00 1.20
❑ 590 Deron Johnson 3.00 1.20
❑ 591 Mike Hedlund 3.00 1.20
❑ 592 John Boccabella 3.00 1.20
❑ 593 Jack McKeon MG 4.00 1.60
Galen Cisco CO
Harry Dunlop CO
Charlie Lau CO
❑ 594 Vic Harris 3.00 1.20
❑ 595 Don Gullett 5.00 2.00
❑ 596 Boston Red Sox 6.00 2.40
Team Card
❑ 597 Mickey Rivers 5.00 2.00
❑ 598 Phil Roof 3.00 1.20
❑ 599 Ed Crosby 3.00 1.20
❑ 600 Dave McNally 5.00 2.00
❑ 601 Sergio Robles 5.00 2.00
George Pena
Rick Stelmaszek
❑ 602 Mel Behney 5.00 2.00
Ralph Garcia
Doug Rau
❑ 603 Terry Hughes 5.00 2.00
Bill McNulty
Ken Reitz RC
❑ 604 Jesse Jefferson 5.00 2.00
Dennis O'Toole
Bob Strampe
❑ 605 Enos Cabell RC 5.00 2.00
Pat Bourque
Gonzalo Marquez
❑ 606 Gary Matthews RC 5.00 2.00
Tom Paciorek
Jorge Roque
❑ 607 Pepe Frias 5.00 2.00
Ray Busse
Mario Guerrero
❑ 608 Steve Busby RC 5.00 2.00
Dick Colpaert
George Medich RC
❑ 609 Larvell Blanks 5.00 2.00
Pedro Garcia
Dave Lopes RC
❑ 610 Jimmy Freeman 5.00 2.00
Charlie Hough
Hank Webb
❑ 611 Rich Coggins 5.00 2.00
Jim Wohlford
Richie Zisk
❑ 612 Steve Lawson 5.00 2.00
Bob Reynolds
Brent Strom
❑ 613 Bob Boone RC 15.00 6.00
Skip Jutze
Mike Ivie
❑ 614 Al Bumbry RC 20.00 8.00
Dwight Evans RC
Charlie Spikes
❑ 615 Ron Cey 150.00 60.00
John Hilton
Mike Schmidt RC
❑ 616 Norm Angelini 5.00 2.00
Steve Blateric
Mike Garman
❑ 617 Rich Chiles 3.00 1.20
❑ 618 Andy Etchebarren 3.00 1.20
❑ 619 Billy Wilson 3.00 1.20
❑ 620 Tommy Harper 5.00 2.00
❑ 621 Joe Ferguson 5.00 2.00
❑ 622 Larry Hisle 5.00 2.00
❑ 623 Steve Renko 3.00 1.20
❑ 624 Leo Durocher MG 5.00 2.00
Preston Gomez CO
Grady Hatton CO
Hub Kittle CO
Jim Owens CO
❑ 625 Angel Mangual 3.00 1.20
❑ 626 Bob Barton 3.00 1.20
❑ 627 Luis Alvarado 3.00 1.20
❑ 628 Jim Slaton 3.00 1.20
❑ 629 Cleveland Indians 6.00 2.40
Team Card
❑ 630 Denny McLain 8.00 3.20
❑ 631 Tom Matchick 3.00 1.20
❑ 632 Dick Selma 3.00 1.20
❑ 633 Ike Brown 3.00 1.20
❑ 634 Alan Closter 3.00 1.20
❑ 635 Gene Alley 5.00 2.00
❑ 636 Rickey Clark 3.00 1.20
❑ 637 Norm Miller 3.00 1.20
❑ 638 Ken Reynolds 3.00 1.20
❑ 639 Willie Crawford 3.00 1.20
❑ 640 Dick Bosman 3.00 1.20
❑ 641 Cincinnati Reds 6.00 2.40
Team Card
❑ 642 Jose Laboy 3.00 1.20
❑ 643 Al Fitzmorris 3.00 1.20
❑ 644 Jack Heidemann 3.00 1.20
❑ 645 Bob Locker 3.00 1.20
❑ 646 Del Crandall MG 4.00 1.60
Harvey Kuenn CO
Joe Nossek CO
Bob Shaw CO
Jim Walton CO
❑ 647 George Stone 3.00 1.20
❑ 648 Tom Egan 3.00 1.20
❑ 649 Rich Folkers 3.00 1.20
❑ 650 Felipe Alou 5.00 2.00
❑ 651 Don Carrithers 3.00 1.20
❑ 652 Ted Kubiak 3.00 1.20
❑ 653 Joe Hoerner 3.00 1.20
❑ 654 Minnesota Twins 6.00 2.40
Team Card
❑ 655 Clay Kirby 3.00 1.20
❑ 656 John Ellis 3.00 1.20

❑ 657 Bob Johnson 3.00 1.20
❑ 658 Elliott Maddox 3.00 1.20
❑ 659 Jose Pagan 3.00 1.20
❑ 660 Fred Scherman 5.00 1.95

1974 Topps

	NM	Ex
COMPLETE SET (660)	400.00	160.00
COMP.FACT.SET (660)	600.00	240.00
WRAPPERS (10-CENTS)	10.00	4.00

❑ 1 Hank Aaron 715 40.00 12.00
❑ 2 Hank Aaron 54-57 8.00 3.20
❑ 3 Hank Aaron 58-61 8.00 3.20
❑ 4 Hank Aaron 62-65 8.00 3.20
❑ 5 Hank Aaron 66-69 8.00 3.20
❑ 6 Hank Aaron 70-73 8.00 3.20
❑ 7 Jim Hunter 4.00 1.60
❑ 8 George Theodore .50 .20
❑ 9 Mickey Lolich 1.00 .40
❑ 10 Johnny Bench 15.00 6.00
❑ 11 Jim Bibby .50 .20
❑ 12 Dave May .50 .20
❑ 13 Tom Hilgendorf .50 .20
❑ 14 Paul Popovich .50 .20
❑ 15 Joe Torre 2.00 .80
❑ 16 Baltimore Orioles 1.00 .40
Team Card
❑ 17 Doug Bird .50 .20
❑ 18 Gary Thomasson .50 .20
❑ 19 Gerry Moses .50 .20
❑ 20 Nolan Ryan 40.00 16.00
❑ 21 Bob Gallagher .50 .20
❑ 22 Cy Acosta .50 .20
❑ 23 Craig Robinson .50 .20
❑ 24 John Hiller 1.00 .40
❑ 25 Ken Singleton 1.00 .40
❑ 26 Bill Campbell .50 .20
❑ 27 George Scott 1.00 .40
❑ 28 Manny Sanguillen 1.00 .40
❑ 29 Phil Niekro 3.00 1.20
❑ 30 Bobby Bonds 2.00 .80
❑ 31 Preston Gomez MG 1.00 .40
Roger Craig CO
Hub Kittle CO
Grady Hatton CO
Bob Lillis CO
❑ 32A Johnny Grubb SD 1.00 .40
❑ 32B Johnny Grubb WASH 4.00 1.60
❑ 33 Don Newhauser .50 .20
❑ 34 Andy Kosco .50 .20
❑ 35 Gaylord Perry 3.00 1.20
❑ 36 St. Louis Cardinals 1.00 .40
Team Card
❑ 37 Dave Sells .50 .20
❑ 38 Don Kessinger 1.00 .40
❑ 39 Ken Suarez .50 .20
❑ 40 Jim Palmer 8.00 3.20
❑ 41 Bobby Floyd .50 .20
❑ 42 Claude Osteen 1.00 .40
❑ 43 Jim Wynn 1.00 .40
❑ 44 Mel Stottlemyre 1.00 .40
❑ 45 Dave Johnson 1.00 .40
❑ 46 Pat Kelly .50 .20
❑ 47 Dick Ruthven .50 .20
❑ 48 Dick Sharon .50 .20
❑ 49 Steve Renko .50 .20
❑ 50 Rod Carew 8.00 3.20
❑ 51 Bobby Heise .50 .20
❑ 52 Al Oliver 1.00 .40
❑ 53A Fred Kendall SD 1.00 .40
❑ 53B Fred Kendall WASH 4.00 1.60
❑ 54 Elias Sosa .50 .20
❑ 55 Frank Robinson 8.00 3.20
❑ 56 New York Mets 1.00 .40
Team Card
❑ 57 Darold Knowles .50 .20
❑ 58 Charlie Spikes .50 .20
❑ 59 Ross Grimsley .50 .20
❑ 60 Lou Brock 6.00 2.40
❑ 61 Luis Aparicio 3.00 1.20
❑ 62 Bob Locker .50 .20
❑ 63 Bill Sudakis .50 .20
❑ 64 Doug Rau .50 .20
❑ 65 Amos Otis 1.00 .40
❑ 66 Sparky Lyle 1.00 .40
❑ 67 Tommy Helms .50 .20
❑ 68 Grant Jackson .50 .20
❑ 69 Del Unser .50 .20
❑ 70 Dick Allen 2.00 .80
❑ 71 Dan Frisella .50 .20
❑ 72 Aurelio Rodriguez .50 .20
❑ 73 Mike Marshall 2.00 .80
❑ 74 Minnesota Twins 1.00 .40
Team Card
❑ 75 Jim Colborn .50 .20
❑ 76 Mickey Rivers 1.00 .40
❑ 77A Rich Troedson SD 1.00 .40
❑ 77B Rich Troedson WASH 4.00 1.60
❑ 78 Charlie Fox MG 1.00 .40
John McNamara CO
Joe Amalfitano CO
Andy Gilbert CO
Don McMahon CO
❑ 79 Gene Tenace 1.00 .40
❑ 80 Tom Seaver 12.00 4.80
❑ 81 Frank Duffy .50 .20
❑ 82 Dave Giusti .50 .20
❑ 83 Orlando Cepeda 3.00 1.20
❑ 84 Rick Wise .50 .20
❑ 85 Joe Morgan 8.00 3.20
❑ 86 Joe Ferguson 1.00 .40
❑ 87 Fergie Jenkins 3.00 1.20
❑ 88 Freddie Patek 1.00 .40
❑ 89 Jackie Brown .50 .20
❑ 90 Bobby Murcer 1.00 .40
❑ 91 Ken Forsch .50 .20
❑ 92 Paul Blair 1.00 .40
❑ 93 Rod Gilbreath .50 .20
❑ 94 Detroit Tigers 1.00 .40
Team Card
❑ 95 Steve Carlton 8.00 3.20
❑ 96 Jerry Hairston .50 .20
❑ 97 Bob Bailey .50 .20
❑ 98 Bert Blyleven 2.00 .80
❑ 99 Del Crandall MG 1.00 .40
Harvey Kuenn CO
Joe Nossek CO
Jim Walton CO
Al Widmar CO
❑ 100 Willie Stargell 6.00 2.40
❑ 101 Bobby Valentine 1.00 .40
❑ 102A Bill Greif SD 1.00 .40
❑ 102B Bill Greif WASH 4.00 1.60
❑ 103 Sal Bando 1.00 .40
❑ 104 Ron Bryant .50 .20
❑ 105 Carlton Fisk 12.00 4.80
❑ 106 Harry Parker .50 .20
❑ 107 Alex Johnson .50 .20
❑ 108 Al Hrabosky 1.00 .40
❑ 109 Bob Grich 1.00 .40
❑ 110 Billy Williams 3.00 1.20
❑ 111 Clay Carroll .50 .20
❑ 112 Dave Lopes 2.00 .80
❑ 113 Dick Drago .50 .20
❑ 114 Angels Team 1.00 .40
❑ 115 Willie Horton 1.00 .40
❑ 116 Jerry Reuss 1.00 .40
❑ 117 Ron Blomberg .50 .20
❑ 118 Bill Lee 1.00 .40
❑ 119 Danny Ozark MG 1.00 .40
Ray Ripplemeyer CO
Bobby Wine CO
Carroll Beringer CO
Billy DeMars CO
❑ 120 Wilbur Wood .50 .20
❑ 121 Larry Lintz .50 .20
❑ 122 Jim Holt .50 .20
❑ 123 Nelson Briles 1.00 .40
❑ 124 Bobby Coluccio .50 .20
❑ 125A Nate Colbert SD 1.00 .40
❑ 125B Nate Colbert WASH 4.00 1.60
❑ 126 Checklist 1-132 3.00 .60
❑ 127 Tom Paciorek 1.00 .40
❑ 128 John Ellis .50 .20
❑ 129 Chris Speier .50 .20
❑ 130 Reggie Jackson 15.00 6.00
❑ 131 Bob Boone 2.00 .80
❑ 132 Felix Millan .50 .20
❑ 133 David Clyde 1.00 .40
❑ 134 Denis Menke .50 .20
❑ 135 Roy White 1.00 .40
❑ 136 Rick Reuschel 1.00 .40
❑ 137 Al Bumbry 1.00 .40
❑ 138 Eddie Brinkman .50 .20
❑ 139 Aurelio Monteagudo .50 .20
❑ 140 Darrell Evans 2.00 .80
❑ 141 Pat Bourque .50 .20
❑ 142 Pedro Garcia .50 .20
❑ 143 Dick Woodson .50 .20
❑ 144 Walter Alston MG 3.00 1.20
Tom Lasorda CO
Jim Gilliam CO
Red Adams CO
Monty Basgall CO
❑ 145 Dock Ellis .50 .20
❑ 146 Ron Fairly 1.00 .40
❑ 147 Bart Johnson .50 .20
❑ 148A Dave Hilton SD 1.00 .40
❑ 148B Dave Hilton WASH 4.00 1.60
❑ 149 Mac Scarce .50 .20
❑ 150 John Mayberry 1.00 .40
❑ 151 Diego Segui .50 .20
❑ 152 Oscar Gamble 1.00 .40
❑ 153 Jon Matlack 1.00 .40
❑ 154 Houston Astros 1.00 .40
Team Card
❑ 155 Bert Campaneris 1.00 .40
❑ 156 Randy Moffitt .50 .20
❑ 157 Vic Harris .50 .20
❑ 158 Jack Billingham .50 .20
❑ 159 Jim Ray Hart .50 .20
❑ 160 Brooks Robinson 8.00 3.20
❑ 161 Ray Burris UER 1.00 .40
(Card number is
printed sideways)
❑ 162 Bill Freehan 1.00 .40
❑ 163 Ken Berry .50 .20
❑ 164 Tom House .50 .20
❑ 165 Willie Davis 1.00 .40
❑ 166 Jack McKeon MG 1.00 .40
Charlie Lau CO
Harry Dunlop CO
Galen Cisco CO
❑ 167 Luis Tiant 2.00 .80
❑ 168 Danny Thompson .50 .20
❑ 169 Steve Rogers RC 2.00 .80
❑ 170 Bill Melton .50 .20
❑ 171 Eduardo Rodriguez .50 .20
❑ 172 Gene Clines .50 .20
❑ 173A Randy Jones SD RC 2.00 .80
❑ 173B Randy Jones WASH 5.00 2.00
❑ 174 Bill Robinson 1.00 .40
❑ 175 Reggie Cleveland .50 .20
❑ 176 John Lowenstein .50 .20
❑ 177 Dave Roberts .50 .20
❑ 178 Garry Maddox 1.00 .40
❑ 179 Yogi Berra MG 5.00 2.00
Rube Walker CO
Eddie Yost CO
Roy McMillan CO
Joe Pignatano CO
❑ 180 Ken Holtzman 1.00 .40
❑ 181 Cesar Geronimo .50 .20
❑ 182 Lindy McDaniel 1.00 .40
❑ 183 Johnny Oates 1.00 .40
❑ 184 Texas Rangers 1.00 .40
Team Card
❑ 185 Jose Cardenal .50 .20
❑ 186 Fred Scherman .50 .20

❑ 187 Don Baylor 2.00 .80
❑ 188 Rudy Meoli .50 .20
❑ 189 Jim Brewer .50 .20
❑ 190 Tony Oliva 2.00 .80
❑ 191 Al Fitzmorris .50 .20
❑ 192 Mario Guerrero .50 .20
❑ 193 Tom Walker .50 .20
❑ 194 Darrell Porter 1.00 .40
❑ 195 Carlos May .50 .20
❑ 196 Jim Fregosi 1.00 .40
❑ 197A Vicente Romo SD 1.00 .40
❑ 197B V.Romo WASH 4.00 1.60
❑ 198 Dave Cash .50 .20
❑ 199 Mike Kekich .50 .20
❑ 200 Cesar Cedeno 1.00 .40
❑ 201 Rod Carew 6.00 2.40
Pete Rose LL
❑ 202 Reggie Jackson 5.00 2.00
Willie Stargell LL
❑ 203 Reggie Jackson 5.00 2.00
Willie Stargell LL
❑ 204 Tommy Harper 2.00 .80
Lou Brock LL
❑ 205 Wilbur Wood 1.00 .40
Ron Bryant LL
❑ 206 Jim Palmer 5.00 2.00
Tom Seaver LL
❑ 207 Nolan Ryan 12.00 4.80
Tom Seaver LL
❑ 208 John Hiller 1.00 .40
Mike Marshall LL
❑ 209 Ted Sizemore .50 .20
❑ 210 Bill Singer .50 .20
❑ 211 Chicago Cubs 1.00 .40
Team Card
❑ 212 Rollie Fingers 3.00 1.20
❑ 213 Dave Rader .50 .20
❑ 214 Billy Grabarkewitz .50 .20
❑ 215 Al Kaline UER 10.00 4.00
(No copyright on back)
❑ 216 Ray Sadecki .50 .20
❑ 217 Tim Foli .50 .20
❑ 218 Johnny Briggs .50 .20
❑ 219 Doug Griffin .50 .20
❑ 220 Don Sutton 3.00 1.20
❑ 221 Chuck Tanner MG 1.00 .40
Jim Mahoney CO
Alex Monchak CO
Johnny Sain CO
Joe Lonnett CO
❑ 222 Ramon Hernandez .50 .20
❑ 223 Jeff Burroughs 2.00 .80
❑ 224 Roger Metzger .50 .20
❑ 225 Paul Splittorff .50 .20
❑ 226A San Diego Padres 2.00 .80
Team Card San Diego Variation
❑ 226B San Diego Padres 8.00 3.20
Team Card Washington Variation
❑ 227 Mike Lum .50 .20
❑ 228 Ted Kubiak .50 .20
❑ 229 Fritz Peterson .50 .20
❑ 230 Tony Perez 4.00 1.60
❑ 231 Dick Tidrow .50 .20
❑ 232 Steve Brye .50 .20
❑ 233 Jim Barr .50 .20
❑ 234 John Milner .50 .20
❑ 235 Dave McNally 1.00 .40
❑ 236 Red Schoendienst MG 3.00 1.20
Barney Schultz CO
George Kissell CO
Johnny Lewis CO
Vern Benson CO
❑ 237 Ken Brett .50 .20
❑ 238 Fran Healy HOR .50 .20
(Munson sliding
in background)
❑ 239 Bill Russell 1.00 .40
❑ 240 Joe Coleman .50 .20
❑ 241A Glenn Beckert SD 1.00 .40
❑ 241B G.Beckert WASH 4.00 1.60
❑ 242 Bill Gogolewski .50 .20
❑ 243 Bob Oliver .50 .20
❑ 244 Carl Morton .50 .20
❑ 245 Cleon Jones .50 .20
❑ 246 Oakland Athletics 2.00 .80
Team Card

❑ 247 Rick Miller .50 .20
❑ 248 Tom Hall .50 .20
❑ 249 George Mitterwald .50 .20
❑ 250A Willie McCovey SD 8.00 3.20
❑ 250B W.McCovey WASH 25.00 10.00
❑ 251 Graig Nettles 2.00 .80
❑ 252 Dave Parker RC 10.00 4.00
❑ 253 John Boccabella .50 .20
❑ 254 Stan Bahnsen .50 .20
❑ 255 Larry Bowa 1.00 .40
❑ 256 Tom Griffin .50 .20
❑ 257 Buddy Bell 2.00 .80
❑ 258 Jerry Morales .50 .20
❑ 259 Bob Reynolds .50 .20
❑ 260 Ted Simmons 2.00 .80
❑ 261 Jerry Bell .50 .20
❑ 262 Ed Kirkpatrick .50 .20
❑ 263 Checklist 133-264 3.00 .60
❑ 264 Joe Rudi 1.00 .40
❑ 265 Tug McGraw 2.00 .80
❑ 266 Jim Northrup 1.00 .40
❑ 267 Andy Messersmith 1.00 .40
❑ 268 Tom Grieve 1.00 .40
❑ 269 Bob Johnson .50 .20
❑ 270 Ron Santo 2.00 .80
❑ 271 Bill Hands .50 .20
❑ 272 Paul Casanova .50 .20
❑ 273 Checklist 265-396 3.00 .60
❑ 274 Fred Beene .50 .20
❑ 275 Ron Hunt .50 .20
❑ 276 Bobby Winkles MG 1.00 .40
John Roseboro CO
Tom Morgan CO
Jimmie Reese CO
Salty Parker CO
❑ 277 Gary Nolan 1.00 .40
❑ 278 Cookie Rojas 1.00 .40
❑ 279 Jim Crawford .50 .20
❑ 280 Carl Yastrzemski 12.00 4.80
❑ 281 San Francisco Giants 1.00 .40
Team Card
❑ 282 Doyle Alexander 1.00 .40
❑ 283 Mike Schmidt 20.00 8.00
❑ 284 Dave Duncan 1.00 .40
❑ 285 Reggie Smith 1.00 .40
❑ 286 Tony Muser .50 .20
❑ 287 Clay Kirby .50 .20
❑ 288 Gorman Thomas RC 2.00 .80
❑ 289 Rick Auerbach .50 .20
❑ 290 Vida Blue 1.00 .40
❑ 291 Don Hahn .50 .20
❑ 292 Chuck Seelbach .50 .20
❑ 293 Milt May .50 .20
❑ 294 Steve Foucault .50 .20
❑ 295 Rick Monday 1.00 .40
❑ 296 Ray Corbin .50 .20
❑ 297 Hal Breeden .50 .20
❑ 298 Roric Harrison .50 .20
❑ 299 Gene Michael .50 .20
❑ 300 Pete Rose 25.00 10.00
❑ 301 Bob Montgomery .50 .20
❑ 302 Rudy May .50 .20
❑ 303 George Hendrick 1.00 .40
❑ 304 Don Wilson .50 .20
❑ 305 Tito Fuentes .50 .20
❑ 306 Earl Weaver MG 3.00 1.20
Jim Frey CO
George Bamberger CO
Billy Hunter CO
George Staller CO
❑ 307 Luis Melendez .50 .20
❑ 308 Bruce Dal Canton .50 .20
❑ 309A Dave Roberts SD 1.00 .40
❑ 309B Dave Roberts WASH 6.00 2.40
❑ 310 Terry Forster 1.00 .40
❑ 311 Jerry Grote 1.00 .40
❑ 312 Deron Johnson .50 .20
❑ 313 Barry Lersch .50 .20
❑ 314 Milwaukee Brewers 1.00 .40
Team Card
❑ 315 Ron Cey 2.00 .80
❑ 316 Jim Perry 1.00 .40
❑ 317 Richie Zisk 1.00 .40
❑ 318 Jim Merritt .50 .20
❑ 319 Randy Hundley .50 .20
❑ 320 Dusty Baker 2.00 .80

❑ 321 Steve Braun .50 .20
❑ 322 Ernie McAnally .50 .20
❑ 323 Richie Scheinblum .50 .20
❑ 324 Steve Kline .50 .20
❑ 325 Tommy Harper 1.00 .40
❑ 326 Sparky Anderson MG 3.00 1.20
Larry Shepard CO
George Scherger CO
Alex Grammas CO
Ted Kluszewski CO
❑ 327 Tom Timmermann .50 .20
❑ 328 Skip Jutze .50 .20
❑ 329 Mark Belanger 1.00 .40
❑ 330 Juan Marichal 5.00 2.00
❑ 331 Carlton Fisk 5.00 2.00
Johnny Bench AS
❑ 332 Dick Allen 8.00 3.20
Hank Aaron AS
❑ 333 Rod Carew 4.00 1.60
Joe Morgan AS
❑ 334 Brooks Robinson 2.00 .80
Ron Santo AS
❑ 335 Bert Campaneris 1.00 .40
Chris Speier AS
❑ 336 Bobby Murcer 5.00 2.00
Pete Rose AS
❑ 337 Amos Otis 1.00 .40
Cesar Cedeno AS
❑ 338 Reggie Jackson 5.00 2.00
Billy Williams AS
❑ 339 Jim Hunter 3.00 1.20
Rick Wise AS
❑ 340 Thurman Munson 8.00 3.20
❑ 341 Dan Driessen RC 1.00 .40
❑ 342 Jim Lonborg 1.00 .40
❑ 343 Royals Team 1.00 .40
❑ 344 Mike Caldwell .50 .20
❑ 345 Bill North .50 .20
❑ 346 Ron Reed .50 .20
❑ 347 Sandy Alomar 1.00 .40
❑ 348 Pete Richert .50 .20
❑ 349 John Vukovich .50 .20
❑ 350 Bob Gibson 8.00 3.20
❑ 351 Dwight Evans 3.00 1.20
❑ 352 Bill Stoneman .50 .20
❑ 353 Rich Coggins .50 .20
❑ 354 Whitey Lockman MG 1.00 .40
J.C. Martin CO
Hank Aguirre CO
Al Spangler CO
Jim Marshall CO
❑ 355 Dave Nelson .50 .20
❑ 356 Jerry Koosman 1.00 .40
❑ 357 Buddy Bradford .50 .20
❑ 358 Dal Maxvill .50 .20
❑ 359 Brent Strom .50 .20
❑ 360 Greg Luzinski 2.00 .80
❑ 361 Don Carrithers .50 .20
❑ 362 Hal King .50 .20
❑ 363 New York Yankees 2.00 .80
Team Card
❑ 364A Cito Gaston SD 2.00 .80
❑ 364B Cito Gaston WASH 8.00 3.20
❑ 365 Steve Busby 1.00 .40
❑ 366 Larry Hisle 1.00 .40
❑ 367 Norm Cash 2.00 .80
❑ 368 Manny Mota 1.00 .40
❑ 369 Paul Lindblad .50 .20
❑ 370 Bob Watson 1.00 .40
❑ 371 Jim Slaton .50 .20
❑ 372 Ken Reitz .50 .20
❑ 373 John Curtis .50 .20
❑ 374 Marty Perez .50 .20
❑ 375 Earl Williams .50 .20
❑ 376 Jorge Orta .50 .20
❑ 377 Ron Woods .50 .20
❑ 378 Burt Hooton 1.00 .40
❑ 379 Billy Martin MG 2.00 .80
Frank Lucchesi CO
Art Fowler CO
Charlie Silvera CO
Jackie Moore CO
❑ 380 Bud Harrelson 1.00 .40
❑ 381 Charlie Sands .50 .20
❑ 382 Bob Moose .50 .20
❑ 383 Philadelphia Phillies 1.00 .40

	No.	Player	Price 1	Price 2
		Team Card		
❑	384	Chris Chambliss	1.00	.40
❑	385	Don Gullett	1.00	.40
❑	386	Gary Matthews	2.00	.80
❑	387A	Rich Morales SD	1.00	.40
❑	387B	Rich Morales WASH	6.00	2.40
❑	388	Phil Roof	.50	.20
❑	389	Gates Brown	.50	.20
❑	390	Lou Piniella	2.00	.80
❑	391	Billy Champion	.50	.20
❑	392	Dick Green	.50	.20
❑	393	Orlando Pena	.50	.20
❑	394	Ken Henderson	.50	.20
❑	395	Doug Rader	.50	.20
❑	396	Tommy Davis	1.00	.40
❑	397	George Stone	.50	.20
❑	398	Duke Sims	.50	.20
❑	399	Mike Paul	.50	.20
❑	400	Harmon Killebrew	6.00	2.40
❑	401	Elliott Maddox	.50	.20
❑	402	Jim Rooker	.50	.20
❑	403	Darrell Johnson MG	1.00	.40
		Eddie Popowski CO		
		Lee Stange CO		
		Don Zimmer CO		
		Don Bryant CO		
❑	404	Jim Howarth	.50	.20
❑	405	Ellie Rodriguez	.50	.20
❑	406	Steve Arlin	.50	.20
❑	407	Jim Wohlford	.50	.20
❑	408	Charlie Hough	1.00	.40
❑	409	Ike Brown	.50	.20
❑	410	Pedro Borbon	.50	.20
❑	411	Frank Baker	.50	.20
❑	412	Chuck Taylor	.50	.20
❑	413	Don Money	1.00	.40
❑	414	Checklist 397-528	3.00	.60
❑	415	Gary Gentry	.50	.20
❑	416	Chicago White Sox	1.00	.40
		Team Card		
❑	417	Rich Folkers	.50	.20
❑	418	Walt Williams	.50	.20
❑	419	Wayne Twitchell	.50	.20
❑	420	Ray Fosse	.50	.20
❑	421	Dan Fife	.50	.20
❑	422	Gonzalo Marquez	.50	.20
❑	423	Fred Stanley	.50	.20
❑	424	Jim Beauchamp	.50	.20
❑	425	Pete Broberg	.50	.20
❑	426	Rennie Stennett	.50	.20
❑	427	Bobby Bolin	.50	.20
❑	428	Gary Sutherland	.50	.20
❑	429	Dick Lange	.50	.20
❑	430	Matty Alou	1.00	.40
❑	431	Gene Garber RC	1.00	.40
❑	432	Chris Arnold	.50	.20
❑	433	Lerrin LaGrow	.50	.20
❑	434	Ken McMullen	.50	.20
❑	435	Dave Concepcion	2.00	.80
❑	436	Don Hood	.50	.20
❑	437	Jim Lyttle	.50	.20
❑	438	Ed Herrmann	.50	.20
❑	439	Norm Miller	.50	.20
❑	440	Jim Kaat	2.00	.80
❑	441	Tom Ragland	.50	.20
❑	442	Alan Foster	.50	.20
❑	443	Tom Hutton	.50	.20
❑	444	Vic Davalillo	.50	.20
❑	445	George Medich	.50	.20
❑	446	Len Randle	.50	.20
❑	447	Frank Quilici MG	1.00	.40
		Ralph Rowe CO		
		Bob Rodgers CO		
		Vern Morgan CO		
❑	448	Ron Hodges	.50	.20
❑	449	Tom McCraw	.50	.20
❑	450	Rich Hebner	1.00	.40
❑	451	Tommy John	2.00	.80
❑	452	Gene Hiser	.50	.20
❑	453	Balor Moore	.50	.20
❑	454	Kurt Bevacqua	.50	.20
❑	455	Tom Bradley	.50	.20
❑	456	Dave Winfield RC	40.00	16.00
❑	457	Chuck Goggin	.50	.20
❑	458	Jim Ray	.50	.20
❑	459	Cincinnati Reds	2.00	.80
		Team Card		
❑	460	Boog Powell	2.00	.80
❑	461	John Odom	.50	.20
❑	462	Luis Alvarado	.50	.20
❑	463	Pat Dobson	.50	.20
❑	464	Jose Cruz	2.00	.80
❑	465	Dick Bosman	.50	.20
❑	466	Dick Billings	.50	.20
❑	467	Winston Llenas	.50	.20
❑	468	Pepe Frias	.50	.20
❑	469	Joe Decker	.50	.20
❑	470	Reggie Jackson ALCS	5.00	2.00
❑	471	Jon Matlack NLCS	1.00	.40
❑	472	Darold Knowles WS1	1.00	.40
❑	473	Willie Mays WS	8.00	3.20
❑	474	Bert Campaneris WS3	1.00	.40
❑	475	Rusty Staub WS4	1.00	.40
❑	476	Cleon Jones WS5	1.00	.40
❑	477	Reggie Jackson WS	5.00	2.00
❑	478	Bert Campaneris WS7	1.00	.40
❑	479	WS Summary	1.00	.40
		A's celebrate; win		
		2nd consecutive		
		championship		
❑	480	Willie Crawford	.50	.20
❑	481	Jerry Terrell	.50	.20
❑	482	Bob Didier	.50	.20
❑	483	Atlanta Braves	1.00	.40
		Team Card		
❑	484	Carmen Fanzone	.50	.20
❑	485	Felipe Alou	2.00	.80
❑	486	Steve Stone	1.00	.40
❑	487	Ted Martinez	.50	.20
❑	488	Andy Etchebarren	.50	.20
❑	489	Danny Murtaugh MG	1.00	.40
		Don Osborn CO		
		Don Leppert CO		
		Bill Mazeroski CO		
		Bob Skinner CO		
❑	490	Vada Pinson	2.00	.80
❑	491	Roger Nelson	.50	.20
❑	492	Mike Rogodzinski	.50	.20
❑	493	Joe Hoerner	.50	.20
❑	494	Ed Goodson	.50	.20
❑	495	Dick McAuliffe	1.00	.40
❑	496	Tom Murphy	.50	.20
❑	497	Bobby Mitchell	.50	.20
❑	498	Pat Corrales	.50	.20
❑	499	Rusty Torres	.50	.20
❑	500	Lee May	1.00	.40
❑	501	Eddie Leon	.50	.20
❑	502	Dave LaRoche	.50	.20
❑	503	Eric Soderholm	.50	.20
❑	504	Joe Niekro	1.00	.40
❑	505	Bill Buckner	1.00	.40
❑	506	Ed Farmer	.50	.20
❑	507	Larry Stahl	.50	.20
❑	508	Montreal Expos	1.00	.40
		Team Card		
❑	509	Jesse Jefferson	.50	.20
❑	510	Wayne Garrett	.50	.20
❑	511	Toby Harrah	1.00	.40
❑	512	Joe Lahoud	.50	.20
❑	513	Jim Campanis	.50	.20
❑	514	Paul Schaal	.50	.20
❑	515	Willie Montanez	.50	.20
❑	516	Horacio Pina	.50	.20
❑	517	Mike Hegan	.50	.20
❑	518	Derrel Thomas	.50	.20
❑	519	Bill Sharp	.50	.20
❑	520	Tim McCarver	2.00	.80
❑	521	Ken Aspromonte MG	1.00	.40
		Clay Bryant CO		
		Tony Pacheco CO		
❑	522	J.R. Richard	2.00	.80
❑	523	Cecil Cooper	2.00	.80
❑	524	Bill Plummer	.50	.20
❑	525	Clyde Wright	.50	.20
❑	526	Frank Tepedino	1.00	.40
❑	527	Bobby Darwin	.50	.20
❑	528	Bill Bonham	.50	.20
❑	529	Horace Clarke	1.00	.40
❑	530	Mickey Stanley	1.00	.40
❑	531	Gene Mauch MG	1.00	.40
		Dave Bristol CO		
		Cal McLish CO		
		Larry Doby CO		
		Jerry Zimmerman CO		
❑	532	Skip Lockwood	.50	.20
❑	533	Mike Phillips	.50	.20
❑	534	Eddie Watt	.50	.20
❑	535	Bob Tolan	.50	.20
❑	536	Duffy Dyer	.50	.20
❑	537	Steve Mingori	.50	.20
❑	538	Cesar Tovar	.50	.20
❑	539	Lloyd Allen	.50	.20
❑	540	Bob Robertson	.50	.20
❑	541	Cleveland Indians	1.00	.40
		Team Card		
❑	542	Goose Gossage	2.00	.80
❑	543	Danny Cater	.50	.20
❑	544	Ron Schueler	.50	.20
❑	545	Billy Conigliaro	1.00	.40
❑	546	Mike Corkins	.50	.20
❑	547	Glenn Borgmann	.50	.20
❑	548	Sonny Siebert	.50	.20
❑	549	Mike Jorgensen	.50	.20
❑	550	Sam McDowell	1.00	.40
❑	551	Von Joshua	.50	.20
❑	552	Denny Doyle	.50	.20
❑	553	Jim Willoughby	.50	.20
❑	554	Tim Johnson	.50	.20
❑	555	Woodie Fryman	.50	.20
❑	556	Dave Campbell	1.00	.40
❑	557	Jim McGlothlin	.50	.20
❑	558	Bill Fahey	.50	.20
❑	559	Darrel Chaney	.50	.20
❑	560	Mike Cuellar	1.00	.40
❑	561	Ed Kranepool	1.00	.40
❑	562	Jack Aker	.50	.20
❑	563	Hal McRae	1.00	.40
❑	564	Mike Ryan	.50	.20
❑	565	Milt Wilcox	.50	.20
❑	566	Jackie Hernandez	.50	.20
❑	567	Boston Red Sox	1.00	.40
		Team Card		
❑	568	Mike Torrez	1.00	.40
❑	569	Rick Dempsey	1.00	.40
❑	570	Ralph Garr	1.00	.40
❑	571	Rich Hand	.50	.20
❑	572	Enzo Hernandez	.50	.20
❑	573	Mike Adams	.50	.20
❑	574	Bill Parsons	.50	.20
❑	575	Steve Garvey	3.00	1.20
❑	576	Scipio Spinks	.50	.20
❑	577	Mike Sadek	.50	.20
❑	578	Ralph Houk MG	1.00	.40
❑	579	Cecil Upshaw	.50	.20
❑	580	Jim Spencer	.50	.20
❑	581	Fred Norman	.50	.20
❑	582	Bucky Dent RC	5.00	2.00
❑	583	Marty Pattin	.50	.20
❑	584	Ken Rudolph	.50	.20
❑	585	Merv Rettenmund	.50	.20
❑	586	Jack Brohamer	.50	.20
❑	587	Larry Christenson	.50	.20
❑	588	Hal Lanier	.50	.20
❑	589	Boots Day	.50	.20
❑	590	Roger Moret	.50	.20
❑	591	Sonny Jackson	.50	.20
❑	592	Ed Bane	.50	.20
❑	593	Steve Yeager	1.00	.40
❑	594	Leroy Stanton	.50	.20
❑	595	Steve Blass	1.00	.40
❑	596	Wayne Garland	.50	.20
		Fred Holdsworth		
		Mark Littell		
		Dick Pole		
❑	597	Dave Chalk	1.00	.40
		John Gamble		
		Pete MacKanin		
		Manny Trillo RC		
❑	598	Dave Augustine	12.00	4.80
		Ken Griffey RC		
		Steve Ontiveros		
		Jim Tyrone		
❑	599A	Rookie Pitchers WAS	2.00	.80
		Ron Diorio		
		Dave Freisleben		
		Frank Riccelli		
		Greg Shanahan		
❑	599B	Rookie Pitchers SD	3.00	1.20

	No.	Card	NM	Ex
		(SD in large print)		
❑	599C	Rookie Pitchers SD	6.00	2.40
		(SD in small print)		
❑	600	Ron Cash	5.00	2.00
		Jim Cox		
		Bill Madlock RC		
		Reggie Sanders		
❑	601	Ed Armbrister	3.00	1.20
		Rich Bladt		
		Brian Downing RC		
		Bake McBride RC		
❑	602	Glen Abbott	1.00	.40
		Rick Henninger		
		Craig Swan		
		Dan Vossler		
❑	603	Barry Foote	1.00	.40
		Tom Lundstedt		
		Charlie Moore RC		
		Sergio Robles		
❑	604	Terry Hughes	5.00	2.00
		John Knox		
		Andre Thornton RC		
		Frank White RC		
❑	605	Vic Albury	4.00	1.60
		Ken Frailing		
		Kevin Kobel		
		Frank Tanana RC		
❑	606	Jim Fuller	1.00	.40
		Wilbur Howard		
		Tommy Smith		
		Otto Velez		
❑	607	Leo Foster	1.00	.40
		Tom Heintzelman		
		Dave Rosello		
		Frank Taveras RC		
❑	608A	Rookie Pitchers ERR	2.00	.80
		Bob Apodaco (sic)		
		Dick Baney		
		John D'Acquisto		
		Mike Wallace		
❑	608B	Rookie Pitchers COR	1.00	.40
		Bob Apodaca		
		Dick Baney		
		John D'Acquisto		
		Mike Wallace		
❑	609	Rico Petrocelli	1.00	.40
❑	610	Dave Kingman	2.00	.80
❑	611	Rich Stelmaszek	.50	.20
❑	612	Luke Walker	.50	.20
❑	613	Dan Monzon	.50	.20
❑	614	Adrian Devine	.50	.20
❑	615	Johnny Jeter UER	.50	.20
		(Misspelled Johnnie on card back)		
❑	616	Larry Gura	.50	.20
❑	617	Ted Ford	.50	.20
❑	618	Jim Mason	.50	.20
❑	619	Mike Anderson	.50	.20
❑	620	Al Downing	.50	.20
❑	621	Bernie Carbo	.50	.20
❑	622	Phil Gagliano	.50	.20
❑	623	Celerino Sanchez	.50	.20
❑	624	Bob Miller	.50	.20
❑	625	Ollie Brown	.50	.20
❑	626	Pittsburgh Pirates Team Card	1.00	.40
❑	627	Carl Taylor	.50	.20
❑	628	Ivan Murrell	.50	.20
❑	629	Rusty Staub	2.00	.80
❑	630	Tommie Agee	1.00	.40
❑	631	Steve Barber	.50	.20
❑	632	George Culver	.50	.20
❑	633	Dave Hamilton	.50	.20
❑	634	Eddie Mathews MG	3.00	1.20
		Herm Starrette CO		
		Connie Ryan CO		
		Jim Busby CO		
		Ken Silvestri CO		
❑	635	Johnny Edwards	.50	.20
❑	636	Dave Goltz	.50	.20
❑	637	Checklist 529-660	3.00	.60
❑	638	Ken Sanders	.50	.20
❑	639	Joe Lovitto	.50	.20
❑	640	Milt Pappas	1.00	.40
❑	641	Chuck Brinkman	.50	.20
❑	642	Terry Harmon	.50	.20
❑	643	Dodgers Team	1.00	.40
❑	644	Wayne Granger	.50	.20
❑	645	Ken Boswell	.50	.20
❑	646	George Foster	2.00	.80
❑	647	Juan Beniquez	.50	.20
❑	648	Terry Crowley	.50	.20
❑	649	Fernando Gonzalez RC	.50	.20
❑	650	Mike Epstein	.50	.20
❑	651	Leron Lee	.50	.20
❑	652	Gail Hopkins	.50	.20
❑	653	Bob Stinson	.50	.20
❑	654A	Jesus Alou ERR	4.00	1.60
		(No position)		
❑	654B	Jesus Alou COR	1.00	.40
		(Outfield)		
❑	655	Mike Tyson	.50	.20
❑	656	Adrian Garrett	.50	.20
❑	657	Jim Shellenback	.50	.20
❑	658	Lee Lacy	.50	.20
❑	659	Joe Lis	.50	.20
❑	660	Larry Dierker	2.00	.50

1975 Topps

	No.	Card	NM	Ex
		COMPLETE SET (660)	500.00	200.00
		WRAPPER (15-CENT)	8.00	3.20
❑	1	Hank Aaron HL	30.00	10.00
❑	2	Lou Brock HL	3.00	1.20
❑	3	Bob Gibson HL	3.00	1.20
❑	4	Al Kaline HL	6.00	2.40
❑	5	Nolan Ryan HL	15.00	6.00
❑	6	Mike Marshall HL	1.00	.40
❑	7	Steve Busby HL	8.00	3.20
		Dick Bosman		
		Nolan Ryan		
❑	8	Rogelio Moret	.50	.20
❑	9	Frank Tepedino	1.00	.40
❑	10	Willie Davis	1.00	.40
❑	11	Bill Melton	.50	.20
❑	12	David Clyde	.50	.20
❑	13	Gene Locklear RC	1.00	.40
❑	14	Milt Wilcox	.50	.20
❑	15	Jose Cardenal	1.00	.40
❑	16	Frank Tanana	2.00	.80
❑	17	Dave Concepcion	2.00	.80
❑	18	Tigers Team CL	2.00	.40
		Ralph Houk MG		
❑	19	Jerry Koosman	1.00	.40
❑	20	Thurman Munson	8.00	3.20
❑	21	Rollie Fingers	3.00	1.20
❑	22	Dave Cash	.50	.20
❑	23	Bill Russell	1.00	.40
❑	24	Al Fitzmorris	.50	.20
❑	25	Lee May	1.00	.40
❑	26	Dave McNally	1.00	.40
❑	27	Ken Reitz	.50	.20
❑	28	Tom Murphy	.50	.20
❑	29	Dave Parker	3.00	1.20
❑	30	Bert Blyleven	2.00	.80
❑	31	Dave Rader	.50	.20
❑	32	Reggie Cleveland	.50	.20
❑	33	Dusty Baker	2.00	.80
❑	34	Steve Renko	.50	.20
❑	35	Ron Santo	1.00	.40
❑	36	Joe Lovitto	.50	.20
❑	37	Dave Freisleben	.50	.20
❑	38	Buddy Bell	2.00	.80
❑	39	Andre Thornton	1.00	.40
❑	40	Bill Singer	.50	.20
❑	41	Cesar Geronimo	1.00	.40
❑	42	Joe Coleman	.50	.20
❑	43	Cleon Jones	1.00	.40
❑	44	Pat Dobson	.50	.20
❑	45	Joe Rudi	1.00	.40
❑	46	Phillies Team CL	2.00	.40
		Danny Ozark MG UER		
		Terry Harmon listed as 339 instead of 399		
❑	47	Tommy John	2.00	.80
❑	48	Freddie Patek	1.00	.40
❑	49	Larry Dierker	1.00	.40
❑	50	Brooks Robinson	8.00	3.20
❑	51	Bob Forsch RC	1.00	.40
❑	52	Darrell Porter	1.00	.40
❑	53	Dave Giusti	.50	.20
❑	54	Eric Soderholm	.50	.20
❑	55	Bobby Bonds	2.00	.80
❑	56	Rick Wise	1.00	.40
❑	57	Dave Johnson	1.00	.40
❑	58	Chuck Taylor	.50	.20
❑	59	Ken Henderson	.50	.20
❑	60	Fergie Jenkins	3.00	1.20
❑	61	Dave Winfield	15.00	6.00
❑	62	Fritz Peterson	.50	.20
❑	63	Steve Swisher	.50	.20
❑	64	Dave Chalk	.50	.20
❑	65	Don Gullett	1.00	.40
❑	66	Willie Horton	1.00	.40
❑	67	Tug McGraw	1.00	.40
❑	68	Ron Blomberg	.50	.20
❑	69	John Odom	.50	.20
❑	70	Mike Schmidt	20.00	8.00
❑	71	Charlie Hough	1.00	.40
❑	72	Royals Team CL	2.00	.40
		Jack McKeon MG		
❑	73	J.R. Richard	1.00	.40
❑	74	Mark Belanger	1.00	.40
❑	75	Ted Simmons	2.00	.80
❑	76	Ed Sprague	.50	.20
❑	77	Richie Zisk	1.00	.40
❑	78	Ray Corbin	.50	.20
❑	79	Gary Matthews	1.00	.40
❑	80	Carlton Fisk	8.00	3.20
❑	81	Ron Reed	.50	.20
❑	82	Pat Kelly	.50	.20
❑	83	Jim Merritt	.50	.20
❑	84	Enzo Hernandez	.50	.20
❑	85	Bill Bonham	.50	.20
❑	86	Joe Lis	.50	.20
❑	87	George Foster	2.00	.80
❑	88	Tom Egan	.50	.20
❑	89	Jim Ray	.50	.20
❑	90	Rusty Staub	2.00	.80
❑	91	Dick Green	.50	.20
❑	92	Cecil Upshaw	.50	.20
❑	93	Dave Lopes	2.00	.80
❑	94	Jim Lonborg	1.00	.40
❑	95	John Mayberry	1.00	.40
❑	96	Mike Cosgrove	.50	.20
❑	97	Earl Williams	.50	.20
❑	98	Rich Folkers	.50	.20
❑	99	Mike Hegan	.50	.20
❑	100	Willie Stargell	4.00	1.60
❑	101	Expos Team CL	2.00	.40
		Gene Mauch MG		
❑	102	Joe Decker	.50	.20
❑	103	Rick Miller	.50	.20
❑	104	Bill Madlock	2.00	.80
❑	105	Buzz Capra	.50	.20
❑	106	M. Hargrove RC UER	3.00	1.20
		Gastonia At-bats are wrong		
❑	107	Jim Barr	.50	.20
❑	108	Tom Hall	.50	.20
❑	109	George Hendrick	1.00	.40
❑	110	Wilbur Wood	.50	.20
❑	111	Wayne Garrett	.50	.20
❑	112	Larry Hardy	.50	.20
❑	113	Elliott Maddox	.50	.20
❑	114	Dick Lange	.50	.20
❑	115	Joe Ferguson	.50	.20
❑	116	Lerrin LaGrow	.50	.20
❑	117	Orioles Team CL	3.00	.60
		Earl Weaver MG		

❑ 118 Mike Anderson .50 .20
❑ 119 Tommy Helms .50 .20
❑ 120 Steve Busby UER 1.00 .40
(Photo actually
Fran Healy)
❑ 121 Bill North .50 .20
❑ 122 Al Hrabosky 1.00 .40
❑ 123 Johnny Briggs .50 .20
❑ 124 Jerry Reuss 1.00 .40
❑ 125 Ken Singleton 1.00 .40
❑ 126 Checklist 1-132 3.00 .60
❑ 127 Glenn Borgmann .50 .20
❑ 128 Bill Lee 1.00 .40
❑ 129 Rick Monday 1.00 .40
❑ 130 Phil Niekro 3.00 1.20
❑ 131 Toby Harrah 1.00 .40
❑ 132 Randy Moffitt .50 .20
❑ 133 Dan Driessen 1.00 .40
❑ 134 Ron Hodges .50 .20
❑ 135 Charlie Spikes .50 .20
❑ 136 Jim Mason .50 .20
❑ 137 Terry Forster 1.00 .40
❑ 138 Del Unser .50 .20
❑ 139 Horacio Pina .50 .20
❑ 140 Steve Garvey 3.00 1.20
❑ 141 Mickey Stanley 1.00 .40
❑ 142 Bob Reynolds .50 .20
❑ 143 Cliff Johnson 1.00 .40
❑ 144 Jim Wohlford .50 .20
❑ 145 Ken Holtzman 1.00 .40
❑ 146 Padres Team CL 2.00 .40
John McNamara MG
❑ 147 Pedro Garcia .50 .20
❑ 148 Jim Rooker .50 .20
❑ 149 Tim Foli .50 .20
❑ 150 Bob Gibson 6.00 2.40
❑ 151 Steve Brye .50 .20
❑ 152 Mario Guerrero .50 .20
❑ 153 Rick Reuschel 1.00 .40
❑ 154 Mike Lum .50 .20
❑ 155 Jim Bibby .50 .20
❑ 156 Dave Kingman 2.00 .80
❑ 157 Pedro Borbon 1.00 .40
❑ 158 Jerry Grote .50 .20
❑ 159 Steve Arlin .50 .20
❑ 160 Graig Nettles 2.00 .80
❑ 161 Stan Bahnsen .50 .20
❑ 162 Willie Montanez .50 .20
❑ 163 Jim Brewer .50 .20
❑ 164 Mickey Rivers 1.00 .40
❑ 165 Doug Rader 1.00 .40
❑ 166 Woodie Fryman .50 .20
❑ 167 Rich Coggins .50 .20
❑ 168 Bill Greif .50 .20
❑ 169 Cookie Rojas .50 .20
❑ 170 Bert Campaneris 1.00 .40
❑ 171 Ed Kirkpatrick .50 .20
❑ 172 Red Sox Team CL 3.00 .60
Darrell Johnson MG
❑ 173 Steve Rogers 1.00 .40
❑ 174 Bake McBride 1.00 .40
❑ 175 Don Money 1.00 .40
❑ 176 Burt Hooton 1.00 .40
❑ 177 Vic Correll .50 .20
❑ 178 Cesar Tovar .50 .20
❑ 179 Tom Bradley .50 .20
❑ 180 Joe Morgan 6.00 2.40
❑ 181 Fred Beene .50 .20
❑ 182 Don Hahn .50 .20
❑ 183 Mel Stottlemyre 1.00 .40
❑ 184 Jorge Orta .50 .20
❑ 185 Steve Carlton 8.00 3.20
❑ 186 Willie Crawford .50 .20
❑ 187 Denny Doyle .50 .20
❑ 188 Tom Griffin .50 .20
❑ 189 Larry (Yogi) Berra 4.00 1.60
Roy Campanella MVP
Campanella card never issued
❑ 190 Bobby Shantz 2.00 .80
Hank Sauer MVP
❑ 191 Al Rosen 2.00 .80
Roy Campanella MVP
❑ 192 Yogi Berra 4.00 1.60
Willie Mays MVP
❑ 193 Yogi Berra 3.00 1.20
Roy Campanella MVP
Campanella card never issued
he is pictured with LA cap
❑ 194 Mickey Mantle 10.00 4.00
Don Newcombe MVP
❑ 195 Mickey Mantle 12.00 4.80
Hank Aaron MVP
❑ 196 Jackie Jensen 3.00 1.20
Ernie Banks MVP
❑ 197 Nellie Fox 2.00 .80
Ernie Banks MVP
❑ 198 Roger Maris 2.00 .80
Dick Groat MVP
❑ 199 Roger Maris 3.00 1.20
Frank Robinson MVP
❑ 200 Mickey Mantle 10.00 4.00
Maury Wills MVP
(Wills card never issued)
❑ 201 Elston Howard 2.00 .80
Sandy Koufax MVP
❑ 202 Brooks Robinson 1.00 .40
Ken Boyer MVP
❑ 203 Zoilo Versalles 2.00 .80
Willie Mays MVP
❑ 204 Frank Robinson 6.00 2.40
Bob Clemente MVP
❑ 205 Carl Yastrzemski 2.00 .80
Orlando Cepeda MVP
❑ 206 Denny McLain UER 2.00 .80
Bob Gibson MVP
On the back McLain is spelled McClain
❑ 207 Harmon Killebrew 1.00 .40
Willie McCovey MVP
❑ 208 Boog Powell 2.00 .80
Johnny Bench MVP
❑ 209 Vida Blue 2.00 .80
Joe Torre MVP
❑ 210 Rich Allen 2.00 .80
Johnny Bench MVP
❑ 211 Reggie Jackson 5.00 2.00
Pete Rose MVP
❑ 212 Jeff Burroughs 2.00 .80
Steve Garvey MVP
❑ 213 Oscar Gamble 1.00 .40
❑ 214 Harry Parker .50 .20
❑ 215 Bobby Valentine 1.00 .40
❑ 216 Giants Team CL 2.00 .40
Wes Westrum MG
❑ 217 Lou Piniella 2.00 .80
❑ 218 Jerry Johnson .50 .20
❑ 219 Ed Herrmann .50 .20
❑ 220 Don Sutton 3.00 1.20
❑ 221 Aurelio Rodriguez .50 .20
❑ 222 Dan Spillner .50 .20
❑ 223 Robin Yount RC 50.00 20.00
❑ 224 Ramon Hernandez .50 .20
❑ 225 Bob Grich 1.00 .40
❑ 226 Bill Campbell .50 .20
❑ 227 Bob Watson 1.00 .40
❑ 228 George Brett RC 80.00 32.00
❑ 229 Barry Foote .50 .20
❑ 230 Jim Hunter 4.00 1.60
❑ 231 Mike Tyson .50 .20
❑ 232 Diego Segui .50 .20
❑ 233 Billy Grabarkewitz .50 .20
❑ 234 Tom Grieve 1.00 .40
❑ 235 Jack Billingham 1.00 .40
❑ 236 Angels Team CL 2.00 .40
Dick Williams MG
❑ 237 Carl Morton 1.00 .40
❑ 238 Dave Duncan 1.00 .40
❑ 239 George Stone .50 .20
❑ 240 Garry Maddox 1.00 .40
❑ 241 Dick Tidrow .50 .20
❑ 242 Jay Johnstone 1.00 .40
❑ 243 Jim Kaat 2.00 .80
❑ 244 Bill Buckner 1.00 .40
❑ 245 Mickey Lolich 2.00 .80
❑ 246 Cardinals Team CL 2.00 .40
Red Schoendienst MG
❑ 247 Enos Cabell .50 .20
❑ 248 Randy Jones 2.00 .80
❑ 249 Danny Thompson .50 .20
❑ 250 Ken Brett .50 .20
❑ 251 Fran Healy .50 .20
❑ 252 Fred Scherman .50 .20
❑ 253 Jesus Alou .50 .20
❑ 254 Mike Torrez 1.00 .40
❑ 255 Dwight Evans 2.00 .80
❑ 256 Billy Champion .50 .20
❑ 257 Checklist: 133-264 3.00 .60
❑ 258 Dave LaRoche .50 .20
❑ 259 Len Randle .50 .20
❑ 260 Johnny Bench 15.00 6.00
❑ 261 Andy Hassler .50 .20
❑ 262 Rowland Office .50 .20
❑ 263 Jim Perry 1.00 .40
❑ 264 John Milner .50 .20
❑ 265 Ron Bryant .50 .20
❑ 266 Sandy Alomar 1.00 .40
❑ 267 Dick Ruthven .50 .20
❑ 268 Hal McRae 1.00 .40
❑ 269 Doug Rau .50 .20
❑ 270 Ron Fairly 1.00 .40
❑ 271 Gerry Moses .50 .20
❑ 272 Lynn McGlothen .50 .20
❑ 273 Steve Braun .50 .20
❑ 274 Vicente Romo .50 .20
❑ 275 Paul Blair 1.00 .40
❑ 276 White Sox Team CL 2.00 .40
Chuck Tanner MG
❑ 277 Frank Taveras .50 .20
❑ 278 Paul Lindblad .50 .20
❑ 279 Milt May .50 .20
❑ 280 Carl Yastrzemski 12.00 4.80
❑ 281 Jim Slaton .50 .20
❑ 282 Jerry Morales .50 .20
❑ 283 Steve Foucault .50 .20
❑ 284 Ken Griffey 4.00 1.60
❑ 285 Ellie Rodriguez .50 .20
❑ 286 Mike Jorgensen .50 .20
❑ 287 Roric Harrison .50 .20
❑ 288 Bruce Ellingsen .50 .20
❑ 289 Ken Rudolph .50 .20
❑ 290 Jon Matlack .50 .20
❑ 291 Bill Sudakis .50 .20
❑ 292 Ron Schueler .50 .20
❑ 293 Dick Sharon .50 .20
❑ 294 Geoff Zahn .50 .20
❑ 295 Vada Pinson 2.00 .80
❑ 296 Alan Foster .50 .20
❑ 297 Craig Kusick .50 .20
❑ 298 Johnny Grubb .50 .20
❑ 299 Bucky Dent 2.00 .80
❑ 300 Reggie Jackson 15.00 6.00
❑ 301 Dave Roberts .50 .20
❑ 302 Rick Burleson 1.00 .40
❑ 303 Grant Jackson .50 .20
❑ 304 Pirates Team CL 2.00 .40
Danny Murtaugh MG
❑ 305 Jim Colborn .50 .20
❑ 306 Rod Carew 2.00 .80
Ralph Garr LL
❑ 307 Dick Allen 4.00 1.60
Mike Schmidt LL
❑ 308 Jeff Burroughs 2.00 .80
Johnny Bench LL
❑ 309 Bill North 2.00 .80
Lou Brock LL
❑ 310 Jim Hunter 2.00 .80
Fergie Jenkins
Andy Messersmith
Phil Niekro LL
❑ 311 Jim Hunter 2.00 .80
Buzz Capra LL
❑ 312 Nolan Ryan 12.00 4.80
Steve Carlton LL
❑ 313 Terry Forster 1.00 .40
Mike Marshall LL
❑ 314 Buck Martinez .50 .20
❑ 315 Don Kessinger 1.00 .40
❑ 316 Jackie Brown .50 .20
❑ 317 Joe Lahoud .50 .20
❑ 318 Ernie McAnally .50 .20
❑ 319 Johnny Oates 1.00 .40
❑ 320 Pete Rose 30.00 12.00
❑ 321 Rudy May .50 .20
❑ 322 Ed Goodson .50 .20
❑ 323 Fred Holdsworth .50 .20
❑ 324 Ed Kranepool 1.00 .40
❑ 325 Tony Oliva 2.00 .80
❑ 326 Wayne Twitchell .50 .20
❑ 327 Jerry Hairston .50 .20

❑	328	Sonny Siebert	.50	.20
❑	329	Ted Kubiak	.50	.20
❑	330	Mike Marshall	1.00	.40
❑	331	Indians Team CL	2.00	.40
		Frank Robinson MG		
❑	332	Fred Kendall	.50	.20
❑	333	Dick Drago	.50	.20
❑	334	Greg Gross	.50	.20
❑	335	Jim Palmer	6.00	2.40
❑	336	Rennie Stennett	.50	.20
❑	337	Kevin Kobel	.50	.20
❑	338	Rich Stelmaszek	.50	.20
❑	339	Jim Fregosi	1.00	.40
❑	340	Paul Splittorff	.50	.20
❑	341	Hal Breeden	.50	.20
❑	342	Leroy Stanton	.50	.20
❑	343	Danny Frisella	.50	.20
❑	344	Ben Oglivie	1.00	.40
❑	345	Clay Carroll	1.00	.40
❑	346	Bobby Darwin	.50	.20
❑	347	Mike Caldwell	.50	.20
❑	348	Tony Muser	.50	.20
❑	349	Ray Sadecki	.50	.20
❑	350	Bobby Murcer	1.00	.40
❑	351	Bob Boone	2.00	.80
❑	352	Darold Knowles	.50	.20
❑	353	Luis Melendez	.50	.20
❑	354	Dick Bosman	.50	.20
❑	355	Chris Cannizzaro	.50	.20
❑	356	Rico Petrocelli	1.00	.40
❑	357	Ken Forsch UER	.50	.20
		Forsch is misspelled in blurb		
❑	358	Al Bumbry	1.00	.40
❑	359	Paul Popovich	.50	.20
❑	360	George Scott	1.00	.40
❑	361	Dodgers Team CL	2.00	.40
		Walter Alston MG		
❑	362	Steve Hargan	.50	.20
❑	363	Carmen Fanzone	.50	.20
❑	364	Doug Bird	.50	.20
❑	365	Bob Bailey	.50	.20
❑	366	Ken Sanders	.50	.20
❑	367	Craig Robinson	.50	.20
❑	368	Vic Albury	.50	.20
❑	369	Merv Rettenmund	.50	.20
❑	370	Tom Seaver	12.00	4.80
❑	371	Gates Brown	.50	.20
❑	372	John D'Acquisto	.50	.20
❑	373	Bill Sharp	.50	.20
❑	374	Eddie Watt	.50	.20
❑	375	Roy White	1.00	.40
❑	376	Steve Yeager	1.00	.40
❑	377	Tom Hilgendorf	.50	.20
❑	378	Derrel Thomas	.50	.20
❑	379	Bernie Carbo	.50	.20
❑	380	Sal Bando	1.00	.40
❑	381	John Curtis	.50	.20
❑	382	Don Baylor	2.00	.80
❑	383	Jim York	.50	.20
❑	384	Brewers Team	2.00	.40
		Del Crandall MG		
❑	385	Dock Ellis	.50	.20
❑	386	Checklist: 265-396 UER	3.00	.60
		Dick Sharon's name is misspelled		
❑	387	Jim Spencer	.50	.20
❑	388	Steve Stone	1.00	.40
❑	389	Tony Solaita	.50	.20
❑	390	Ron Cey	2.00	.80
❑	391	Don DeMola	.50	.20
❑	392	Bruce Bochte RC	1.00	.40
❑	393	Gary Gentry	.50	.20
❑	394	Larvell Blanks	.50	.20
❑	395	Bud Harrelson	1.00	.40
❑	396	Fred Norman	1.00	.40
❑	397	Bill Freehan	1.00	.40
❑	398	Elias Sosa	.50	.20
❑	399	Terry Harmon	.50	.20
❑	400	Dick Allen	2.00	.80
❑	401	Mike Wallace	.50	.20
❑	402	Bob Tolan	.50	.20
❑	403	Tom Buskey	.50	.20
❑	404	Ted Sizemore	.50	.20
❑	405	John Montague	.50	.20
❑	406	Bob Gallagher	.50	.20
❑	407	Herb Washington RC	2.00	.80
❑	408	Clyde Wright UER	.50	.20
		Listed with wrong 1974 team		
❑	409	Bob Robertson	.50	.20
❑	410	Mike Cueller UER	1.00	.40
		Sic, Cuellar		
❑	411	George Mitterwald	.50	.20
❑	412	Bill Hands	.50	.20
❑	413	Marty Pattin	.50	.20
❑	414	Manny Mota	1.00	.40
❑	415	John Hiller	1.00	.40
❑	416	Larry Lintz	.50	.20
❑	417	Skip Lockwood	.50	.20
❑	418	Leo Foster	.50	.20
❑	419	Dave Goltz	.50	.20
❑	420	Larry Bowa	2.00	.80
❑	421	Mets Team CL	3.00	.60
		Yogi Berra MG		
❑	422	Brian Downing	1.00	.40
❑	423	Clay Kirby	.50	.20
❑	424	John Lowenstein	.50	.20
❑	425	Tito Fuentes	.50	.20
❑	426	George Medich	.50	.20
❑	427	Clarence Gaston	1.00	.40
❑	428	Dave Hamilton	.50	.20
❑	429	Jim Dwyer	.50	.20
❑	430	Luis Tiant	2.00	.80
❑	431	Rod Gilbreath	.50	.20
❑	432	Ken Berry	.50	.20
❑	433	Larry Demery	.50	.20
❑	434	Bob Locker	.50	.20
❑	435	Dave Nelson	.50	.20
❑	436	Ken Frailing	.50	.20
❑	437	Al Cowens	1.00	.40
❑	438	Don Carrithers	.50	.20
❑	439	Ed Brinkman	.50	.20
❑	440	Andy Messersmith	1.00	.40
❑	441	Bobby Heise	.50	.20
❑	442	Maximino Leon	.50	.20
❑	443	Twins Team CL	2.00	.40
		Frank Quilici MG		
❑	444	Gene Garber	1.00	.40
❑	445	Felix Millan	.50	.20
❑	446	Bart Johnson	.50	.20
❑	447	Terry Crowley	.50	.20
❑	448	Frank Duffy	.50	.20
❑	449	Charlie Williams	.50	.20
❑	450	Willie McCovey	6.00	2.40
❑	451	Rick Dempsey	1.00	.40
❑	452	Angel Mangual	.50	.20
❑	453	Claude Osteen	1.00	.40
❑	454	Doug Griffin	.50	.20
❑	455	Don Wilson	.50	.20
❑	456	Bob Coluccio	.50	.20
❑	457	Mario Mendoza	.50	.20
❑	458	Ross Grimsley	.50	.20
❑	459	1974 AL Champs	1.00	.40
		A's over Orioles (Second base action pictured)		
❑	460	Steve Garvey NLCS	2.00	.80
		Frank Taveras		
❑	461	Reggie Jackson WS	5.00	2.00
❑	462	World Series Game 2	1.00	.40
		(Dodger dugout)		
❑	463	Rollie Fingers WS	2.00	.80
❑	464	World Series Game 4	1.00	.40
		(A's batter)		
❑	465	Joe Rudi WS5	1.00	.40
❑	466	WS Summary	2.00	.80
		A's do it again; win third straight A's group picture		
❑	467	Ed Halicki	.50	.20
❑	468	Bobby Mitchell	.50	.20
❑	469	Tom Dettore	.50	.20
❑	470	Jeff Burroughs	1.00	.40
❑	471	Bob Stinson	.50	.20
❑	472	Bruce Dal Canton	.50	.20
❑	473	Ken McMullen	.50	.20
❑	474	Luke Walker	.50	.20
❑	475	Darrell Evans	1.00	.40
❑	476	Ed Figueroa	.50	.20
❑	477	Tom Hutton	.50	.20
❑	478	Tom Burgmeier	.50	.20
❑	479	Ken Boswell	.50	.20
❑	480	Carlos May	.50	.20
❑	481	Will McEnaney	1.00	.40
❑	482	Tom McCraw	.50	.20
❑	483	Steve Ontiveros	.50	.20
❑	484	Glenn Beckert	1.00	.40
❑	485	Sparky Lyle	1.00	.40
❑	486	Ray Fosse	.50	.20
❑	487	Astros Team CL	2.00	.40
		Preston Gomez MG		
❑	488	Bill Travers	.50	.20
❑	489	Cecil Cooper	2.00	.80
❑	490	Reggie Smith	1.00	.40
❑	491	Doyle Alexander	1.00	.40
❑	492	Rich Hebner	1.00	.40
❑	493	Don Stanhouse	.50	.20
❑	494	Pete LaCock	.50	.20
❑	495	Nelson Briles	1.00	.40
❑	496	Pepe Frias	.50	.20
❑	497	Jim Nettles	.50	.20
❑	498	Al Downing	.50	.20
❑	499	Marty Perez	.50	.20
❑	500	Nolan Ryan	50.00	20.00
❑	501	Bill Robinson	1.00	.40
❑	502	Pat Bourque	.50	.20
❑	503	Fred Stanley	.50	.20
❑	504	Buddy Bradford	.50	.20
❑	505	Chris Speier	.50	.20
❑	506	Leron Lee	.50	.20
❑	507	Tom Carroll	.50	.20
❑	508	Bob Hansen	.50	.20
❑	509	Dave Hilton	.50	.20
❑	510	Vida Blue	1.00	.40
❑	511	Rangers Team CL	2.00	.40
		Billy Martin MG		
❑	512	Larry Milbourne	.50	.20
❑	513	Dick Pole	.50	.20
❑	514	Jose Cruz	2.00	.80
❑	515	Manny Sanguillen	1.00	.40
❑	516	Don Hood	.50	.20
❑	517	Checklist: 397-528	3.00	.60
❑	518	Leo Cardenas	.50	.20
❑	519	Jim Todd	.50	.20
❑	520	Amos Otis	1.00	.40
❑	521	Dennis Blair	.50	.20
❑	522	Gary Sutherland	.50	.20
❑	523	Tom Paciorek	1.00	.40
❑	524	John Doherty	.50	.20
❑	525	Tom House	.50	.20
❑	526	Larry Hisle	1.00	.40
❑	527	Mac Scarce	.50	.20
❑	528	Eddie Leon	.50	.20
❑	529	Gary Thomasson	.50	.20
❑	530	Gaylord Perry	3.00	1.20
❑	531	Reds Team CL	5.00	1.00
		Sparky Anderson MG		
❑	532	Gorman Thomas	1.00	.40
❑	533	Rudy Meoli	.50	.20
❑	534	Alex Johnson	.50	.20
❑	535	Gene Tenace	1.00	.40
❑	536	Bob Moose	.50	.20
❑	537	Tommy Harper	1.00	.40
❑	538	Duffy Dyer	.50	.20
❑	539	Jesse Jefferson	.50	.20
❑	540	Lou Brock	6.00	2.40
❑	541	Roger Metzger	.50	.20
❑	542	Pete Broberg	.50	.20
❑	543	Larry Biittner	.50	.20
❑	544	Steve Mingori	.50	.20
❑	545	Billy Williams	3.00	1.20
❑	546	John Knox	.50	.20
❑	547	Von Joshua	.50	.20
❑	548	Charlie Sands	.50	.20
❑	549	Bill Butler	.50	.20
❑	550	Ralph Garr	1.00	.40
❑	551	Larry Christenson	.50	.20
❑	552	Jack Brohamer	.50	.20
❑	553	John Boccabella	.50	.20
❑	554	Goose Gossage	2.00	.80
❑	555	Al Oliver	2.00	.80
❑	556	Tim Johnson	.50	.20
❑	557	Larry Gura	.50	.20
❑	558	Dave Roberts	.50	.20
❑	559	Bob Montgomery	.50	.20
❑	560	Tony Perez	4.00	1.60
❑	561	A's Team CL	2.00	.40
		Alvin Dark MG		
❑	562	Gary Nolan	1.00	.40
❑	563	Wilbur Howard	.50	.20

❑ 564 Tommy Davis .... 1.00 .40
❑ 565 Joe Torre........................ 2.00 .80
❑ 566 Ray Burris .... .50 .20
❑ 567 Jim Sundberg RC .... 2.00 .80
❑ 568 Dale Murray .... .50 .20
❑ 569 Frank White...................... 1.00 .40
❑ 570 Jim Wynn .... 1.00 .40
❑ 571 Dave Lemanczyk .... .50 .20
❑ 572 Roger Nelson .... .50 .20
❑ 573 Orlando Pena .... .50 .20
❑ 574 Tony Taylor .... .50 .20
❑ 575 Gene Clines...................... .50 .20
❑ 576 Phil Roof.......................... .50 .20
❑ 577 John Morris .... .50 .20
❑ 578 Dave Tomlin .... .50 .20
❑ 579 Skip Pitlock...................... .50 .20
❑ 580 Frank Robinson.............. 6.00 2.40
❑ 581 Darrel Chaney .... .50 .20
❑ 582 Eduardo Rodriguez .... .50 .20
❑ 583 Andy Etchebarren .... .50 .20
❑ 584 Mike Garman.................... .50 .20
❑ 585 Chris Chambliss .... 1.00 .40
❑ 586 Tim McCarver .... 2.00 .80
❑ 587 Chris Ward .... .50 .20
❑ 588 Rick Auerbach .... .50 .20
❑ 589 Braves Team CL .... 2.00 .40
Clyde King MG
❑ 590 Cesar Cedeno .... 1.00 .40
❑ 591 Glenn Abbott .... .50 .20
❑ 592 Balor Moore .... .50 .20
❑ 593 Gene Lamont...................... .50 .20
❑ 594 Jim Fuller .... .50 .20
❑ 595 Joe Niekro...................... 1.00 .40
❑ 596 Ollie Brown .... .50 .20
❑ 597 Winston Llenas .... .50 .20
❑ 598 Bruce Kison...................... .50 .20
❑ 599 Nate Colbert .... .50 .20
❑ 600 Rod Carew...................... 8.00 3.20
❑ 601 Juan Beniquez.................. .50 .20
❑ 602 John Vukovich .... .50 .20
❑ 603 Lew Krausse .... .50 .20
❑ 604 Oscar Zamora .... .50 .20
❑ 605 John Ellis .... .50 .20
❑ 606 Bruce Miller .... .50 .20
❑ 607 Jim Holt .... .50 .20
❑ 608 Gene Michael .... .50 .20
❑ 609 Elrod Hendricks.................. .50 .20
❑ 610 Ron Hunt............................ .50 .20
❑ 611 Yankees Team CL .... 2.00 .40
Bill Virdon MG
❑ 612 Terry Hughes...................... .50 .20
❑ 613 Bill Parsons........................ .50 .20
❑ 614 Jack Kucek .... 1.00 .40
Dyar Miller
Vern Ruhle
Paul Siebert
❑ 615 Pat Darcy.......................... 2.00 .80
Dennis Leonard RC
Tom Underwood
Hank Webb
❑ 616 Dave Augustine 15.00 6.00
Pepe Mangual
Jim Rice RC
John Scott
❑ 617 Mike Cubbage.................. 2.00 .80
Doug DeCinces RC
Reggie Sanders
Manny Trillo
❑ 618 Jamie Easterly .... 1.00 .40
Tom Johnson
Scott McGregor RC
Rick Rhoden RC
❑ 619 Benny Ayala .... 1.00 .40
Nyls Nyman
Tommy Smith
Jerry Turner
❑ 620 Gary Carter RC 15.00 6.00
Marc Hill
Danny Meyer
Leon Roberts
❑ 621 John Denny RC.............. 2.00 .80
Rawly Eastwick
Jim Kern
Juan Veintidos
❑ 622 Ed Armbrister 8.00 3.20
Fred Lynn RC
Tom Poquette
Terry Whitfield UER
(Listed as Ney York)
❑ 623 Phil Garner 10.00 4.00
Keith Hernandez RC UER
(Sic, bats right)
Bob Sheldon
Tom Veryzer
❑ 624 Doug Konieczny .... 1.00 .40
Gary Lavelle
Jim Otten
Eddie Solomon
❑ 625 Boog Powell .... 2.00 .80
❑ 626 Larry Haney UER.............. .50 .20
Photo actually
Dave Duncan
❑ 627 Tom Walker........................ .50 .20
❑ 628 Ron LeFlore RC.............. 1.00 .40
❑ 629 Joe Hoerner........................ .50 .20
❑ 630 Greg Luzinski .... 2.00 .80
❑ 631 Lee Lacy .... .50 .20
❑ 632 Morris Nettles .... .50 .20
❑ 633 Paul Casanova .... .50 .20
❑ 634 Cy Acosta .... .50 .20
❑ 635 Chuck Dobson .... .50 .20
❑ 636 Charlie Moore.................... .50 .20
❑ 637 Ted Martinez...................... .50 .20
❑ 638 Cubs Team CL .... 2.00 .40
Jim Marshall MG
❑ 639 Steve Kline .... .50 .20
❑ 640 Harmon Killebrew 6.00 2.40
❑ 641 Jim Northrup.................. 1.00 .40
❑ 642 Mike Phillips...................... .50 .20
❑ 643 Brent Strom........................ .50 .20
❑ 644 Bill Fahey .... .50 .20
❑ 645 Danny Cater .... .50 .20
❑ 646 Checklist: 529-660 .... 3.00 .60
❑ 647 Cl. Washington RC .... 2.00 .80
❑ 648 Dave Pagan........................ .50 .20
❑ 649 Jack Heidemann .... .50 .20
❑ 650 Dave May .... .50 .20
❑ 651 John Morlan .... .50 .20
❑ 652 Lindy McDaniel.............. 1.00 .40
❑ 653 Lee Richard UER .... .50 .20
(Listed as Richards
on card front)
❑ 654 Jerry Terrell........................ .50 .20
❑ 655 Rico Carty...................... 1.00 .40
❑ 656 Bill Plummer...................... .50 .20
❑ 657 Bob Oliver.......................... .50 .20
❑ 658 Vic Harris .... .50 .20
❑ 659 Bob Apodaca...................... .50 .20
❑ 660 Hank Aaron.................. 30.00 9.00

1976 Topps

	NM	Ex
COMPLETE SET (660)	250.00	100.00

❑ 1 Hank Aaron RB 15.00 4.70
❑ 2 Bobby Bonds RB.............. 1.50 .60
❑ 3 Mickey Lolich RB .... .75 .30
❑ 4 Dave Lopes RB .... .75 .30
❑ 5 Tom Seaver RB 5.00 2.00
❑ 6 Rennie Stennett RB .... .75 .30
❑ 7 Jim Umbarger .... .40 .16
❑ 8 Tito Fuentes .... .40 .16
❑ 9 Paul Lindblad .... .40 .16
❑ 10 Lou Brock 5.00 2.00
❑ 11 Jim Hughes........................ .40 .16
❑ 12 Richie Zisk .... .75 .30
❑ 13 John Wockenfuss .... .40 .16
❑ 14 Gene Garber .... .75 .30
❑ 15 George Scott...................... .75 .30
❑ 16 Bob Apodaca...................... .40 .16
❑ 17 New York Yankees.......... 1.50 .30
Team Card CL
Billy Martin MG
❑ 18 Dale Murray .... .40 .16
❑ 19 George Brett 30.00 12.00
❑ 20 Bob Watson........................ .75 .30
❑ 21 Dave LaRoche .... .40 .16
❑ 22 Bill Russell .... .75 .30
❑ 23 Brian Downing .... .40 .16
❑ 24 Cesar Geronimo .... .75 .30
❑ 25 Mike Torrez........................ .75 .30
❑ 26 Andre Thornton.................. .75 .30
❑ 27 Ed Figueroa........................ .40 .16
❑ 28 Dusty Baker.................... 1.50 .60
❑ 29 Rick Burleson .... .75 .30
❑ 30 John Montefusco .... .75 .30
❑ 31 Len Randle .... .40 .16
❑ 32 Danny Frisella.................... .40 .16
❑ 33 Bill North............................ .40 .16
❑ 34 Mike Garman...................... .40 .16
❑ 35 Tony Oliva...................... 1.50 .60
❑ 36 Frank Taveras .... .40 .16
❑ 37 John Hiller .... .75 .30
❑ 38 Garry Maddox .... .75 .30
❑ 39 Pete Broberg .... .40 .16
❑ 40 Dave Kingman.................. 1.50 .60
❑ 41 Tippy Martinez .... .75 .30
❑ 42 Barry Foote .... .40 .16
❑ 43 Paul Splittorff .... .40 .16
❑ 44 Doug Rader........................ .75 .30
❑ 45 Boog Powell .... 1.50 .60
❑ 46 Los Angeles Dodgers ...... 1.50 .30
Team Card CL
Walter Alston MG
❑ 47 Jesse Jefferson .... .40 .16
❑ 48 Dave Concepcion .... 1.50 .60
❑ 49 Dave Duncan...................... .75 .30
❑ 50 Fred Lynn .... 1.50 .60
❑ 51 Ray Burris .... .40 .16
❑ 52 Dave Chalk .... .40 .16
❑ 53 Mike Beard .... .40 .16
❑ 54 Dave Rader .... .40 .16
❑ 55 Gaylord Perry 2.50 1.00
❑ 56 Bob Tolan .... .40 .16
❑ 57 Phil Garner .... .75 .30
❑ 58 Ron Reed............................ .40 .16
❑ 59 Larry Hisle.......................... .75 .30
❑ 60 Jerry Reuss .... .75 .30
❑ 61 Ron LeFlore........................ .75 .30
❑ 62 Johnny Oates .... .75 .30
❑ 63 Bobby Darwin .... .40 .16
❑ 64 Jerry Koosman .... .75 .30
❑ 65 Chris Chambliss .... .75 .30
❑ 66 Gus Bell FS........................ .75 .30
Buddy Bell
❑ 67 Ray Boone FS .... .75 .30
Bob Boone
❑ 68 Joe Coleman FS .... .40 .16
Joe Coleman Jr.
❑ 69 Jim Hegan FS .... .40 .16
Mike Hegan
❑ 70 Roy Smalley FS.................. .75 .30
Roy Smalley Jr.
❑ 71 Steve Rogers...................... .75 .30
❑ 72 Hal McRae.......................... .75 .30
❑ 73 Baltimore Orioles .... 1.50 .30
Team Card CL
Earl Weaver MG
❑ 74 Oscar Gamble .... .75 .30
❑ 75 Larry Dierker .... .75 .30
❑ 76 Willie Crawford .... .40 .16
❑ 77 Pedro Borbon .... .75 .30
❑ 78 Cecil Cooper...................... .75 .30
❑ 79 Jerry Morales .... .40 .16
❑ 80 Jim Kaat .... 1.50 .60
❑ 81 Darrell Evans...................... .75 .30
❑ 82 Von Joshua .... .40 .16
❑ 83 Jim Spencer .... .40 .16
❑ 84 Brent Strom........................ .40 .16
❑ 85 Mickey Rivers .... .75 .30

❑ 86 Mike Tyson .40 .16
❑ 87 Tom Burgmeier .40 .16
❑ 88 Duffy Dyer .40 .16
❑ 89 Vern Ruhle .40 .16
❑ 90 Sal Bando .75 .30
❑ 91 Tom Hutton .40 .16
❑ 92 Eduardo Rodriguez .40 .16
❑ 93 Mike Phillips .40 .16
❑ 94 Jim Dwyer .40 .16
❑ 95 Brooks Robinson 6.00 2.40
❑ 96 Doug Bird .40 .16
❑ 97 Wilbur Howard .40 .16
❑ 98 Dennis Eckersley RC 25.00 10.00
❑ 99 Lee Lacy .40 .16
❑ 100 Jim Hunter 3.00 1.20
❑ 101 Pete LaCock .40 .16
❑ 102 Jim Willoughby .40 .16
❑ 103 Biff Pocoroba .40 .16
❑ 104 Cincinnati Reds 2.50 .50
Team Card CL
Sparky Anderson MG
❑ 105 Gary Lavelle .40 .16
❑ 106 Tom Grieve .75 .30
❑ 107 Dave Roberts .40 .16
❑ 108 Don Kirkwood .40 .16
❑ 109 Larry Lintz .40 .16
❑ 110 Carlos May .40 .16
❑ 111 Danny Thompson .40 .16
❑ 112 Kent Tekulve RC 1.50 .60
❑ 113 Gary Sutherland .40 .16
❑ 114 Jay Johnstone .75 .30
❑ 115 Ken Holtzman .75 .30
❑ 116 Charlie Moore .40 .16
❑ 117 Mike Jorgensen .40 .16
❑ 118 Boston Red Sox 1.50 .30
Team Card CL
Darrell Johnson MG
❑ 119 Checklist 1-132 1.50 .30
❑ 120 Rusty Staub .75 .30
❑ 121 Tony Solaita .40 .16
❑ 122 Mike Cosgrove .40 .16
❑ 123 Walt Williams .40 .16
❑ 124 Doug Rau .40 .16
❑ 125 Don Baylor 1.50 .60
❑ 126 Tom Dettore .40 .16
❑ 127 Larvell Blanks .40 .16
❑ 128 Ken Griffey Sr. 2.50 1.00
❑ 129 Andy Etchebarren .40 .16
❑ 130 Luis Tiant 1.50 .60
❑ 131 Bill Stein .40 .16
❑ 132 Don Hood .40 .16
❑ 133 Gary Matthews .75 .30
❑ 134 Mike Ivie .40 .16
❑ 135 Bake McBride .75 .30
❑ 136 Dave Goltz .40 .16
❑ 137 Bill Robinson .75 .30
❑ 138 Lerrin LaGrow .40 .16
❑ 139 Gorman Thomas .75 .30
❑ 140 Vida Blue .75 .30
❑ 141 Larry Parrish RC 1.50 .60
❑ 142 Dick Drago .40 .16
❑ 143 Jerry Grote .40 .16
❑ 144 Al Fitzmorris .40 .16
❑ 145 Larry Bowa .75 .30
❑ 146 George Medich .40 .16
❑ 147 Houston Astros 1.50 .30
Team Card CL
Bill Virdon MG
❑ 148 Stan Thomas .40 .16
❑ 149 Tommy Davis .75 .30
❑ 150 Steve Garvey 2.50 1.00
❑ 151 Bill Bonham .40 .16
❑ 152 Leroy Stanton .40 .16
❑ 153 Buzz Capra .40 .16
❑ 154 Bucky Dent .75 .30
❑ 155 Jack Billingham .75 .30
❑ 156 Rico Carty .75 .30
❑ 157 Mike Caldwell .40 .16
❑ 158 Ken Reitz .40 .16
❑ 159 Jerry Terrell .40 .16
❑ 160 Dave Winfield 10.00 4.00
❑ 161 Bruce Kison .40 .16
❑ 162 Jack Pierce .40 .16
❑ 163 Jim Slaton .40 .16
❑ 164 Pepe Mangual .40 .16
❑ 165 Gene Tenace .75 .30
❑ 166 Skip Lockwood .40 .16
❑ 167 Freddie Patek .75 .30
❑ 168 Tom Hilgendorf .40 .16
❑ 169 Graig Nettles 1.50 .60
❑ 170 Rick Wise .40 .16
❑ 171 Greg Gross .40 .16
❑ 172 Texas Rangers 1.50 .30
Team Card CL
Frank Lucchesi MG
❑ 173 Steve Swisher .40 .16
❑ 174 Charlie Hough .75 .30
❑ 175 Ken Singleton .75 .30
❑ 176 Dick Lange .40 .16
❑ 177 Marty Perez .40 .16
❑ 178 Tom Buskey .40 .16
❑ 179 George Foster 1.50 .60
❑ 180 Goose Gossage 1.50 .60
❑ 181 Willie Montanez .40 .16
❑ 182 Harry Rasmussen .40 .16
❑ 183 Steve Braun .40 .16
❑ 184 Bill Greif .40 .16
❑ 185 Dave Parker 1.50 .60
❑ 186 Tom Walker .40 .16
❑ 187 Pedro Garcia .40 .16
❑ 188 Fred Scherman .40 .16
❑ 189 Claudell Washington .75 .30
❑ 190 Jon Matlack .40 .16
❑ 191 Bill Madlock .75 .30
Ted Simmons
Manny Sanguillen LL
❑ 192 Rod Carew 2.50 1.00
Fred Lynn
Thurman Munson LL
❑ 193 Mike Schmidt 3.00 1.20
Dave Kingman
Greg Luzinski LL
❑ 194 Reggie Jackson 3.00 1.20
George Scott
John Mayberry LL
❑ 195 Greg Luzinski 1.50 .60
Johnny Bench
Tony Perez LL
❑ 196 George Scott .75 .30
John Mayberry
Fred Lynn LL
❑ 197 Dave Lopes 1.50 .60
Joe Morgan
Lou Brock LL
❑ 198 Mickey Rivers .75 .30
Claudell Washington
Amos Otis LL
❑ 199 Tom Seaver 2.50 1.00
Randy Jones
Andy Messersmith LL
❑ 200 Jim Hunter 1.50 .60
Jim Palmer
Vida Blue LL
❑ 201 Randy Jones 1.50 .60
Andy Messersmith
Tom Seaver LL
❑ 202 Jim Palmer 3.00 1.20
Jim Hunter
Dennis Eckersley LL
❑ 203 Tom Seaver 2.50 1.00
John Montefusco
Andy Messersmith LL
❑ 204 Frank Tanana .75 .30
Bert Blyleven
Gaylord Perry LL
❑ 205 Al Hrabosky .75 .30
Rich Gossage LL
❑ 206 Manny Trillo .40 .16
❑ 207 Andy Hassler .40 .16
❑ 208 Mike Lum .40 .16
❑ 209 Alan Ashby .75 .30
❑ 210 Lee May .75 .30
❑ 211 Clay Carroll .75 .30
❑ 212 Pat Kelly .40 .16
❑ 213 Dave Heaverlo .40 .16
❑ 214 Eric Soderholm .40 .16
❑ 215 Reggie Smith .75 .30
❑ 216 Montreal Expos 1.50 .30
Team Card CL
Karl Kuehl MG
❑ 217 Dave Freisleben .40 .16
❑ 218 John Knox .40 .16
❑ 219 Tom Murphy .40 .16
❑ 220 Manny Sanguillen .75 .30
❑ 221 Jim Todd .40 .16
❑ 222 Wayne Garrett .40 .16
❑ 223 Ollie Brown .40 .16
❑ 224 Jim York .40 .16
❑ 225 Roy White .75 .30
❑ 226 Jim Sundberg .75 .30
❑ 227 Oscar Zamora .40 .16
❑ 228 John Hale .40 .16
❑ 229 Jerry Remy .40 .16
❑ 230 Carl Yastrzemski 10.00 4.00
❑ 231 Tom House .40 .16
❑ 232 Frank Duffy .40 .16
❑ 233 Grant Jackson .40 .16
❑ 234 Mike Sadek .40 .16
❑ 235 Bert Blyleven 1.50 .60
❑ 236 Kansas City Royals 1.50 .30
Team Card CL
Whitey Herzog MG
❑ 237 Dave Hamilton .40 .16
❑ 238 Larry Biittner .40 .16
❑ 239 John Curtis .40 .16
❑ 240 Pete Rose 25.00 10.00
❑ 241 Hector Torres .40 .16
❑ 242 Dan Meyer .40 .16
❑ 243 Jim Rooker .40 .16
❑ 244 Bill Sharp .40 .16
❑ 245 Felix Millan .40 .16
❑ 246 Cesar Tovar .40 .16
❑ 247 Terry Harmon .40 .16
❑ 248 Dick Tidrow .40 .16
❑ 249 Cliff Johnson .75 .30
❑ 250 Fergie Jenkins 2.50 1.00
❑ 251 Rick Monday .75 .30
❑ 252 Tim Nordbrook .40 .16
❑ 253 Bill Buckner .75 .30
❑ 254 Rudy Meoli .40 .16
❑ 255 Fritz Peterson .40 .16
❑ 256 Rowland Office .40 .16
❑ 257 Ross Grimsley .40 .16
❑ 258 Nyls Nyman .40 .16
❑ 259 Darrel Chaney .40 .16
❑ 260 Steve Busby .40 .16
❑ 261 Gary Thomasson .40 .16
❑ 262 Checklist 133-264 1.50 .30
❑ 263 Lyman Bostock RC 1.50 .60
❑ 264 Steve Renko .40 .16
❑ 265 Willie Davis .75 .30
❑ 266 Alan Foster .40 .16
❑ 267 Aurelio Rodriguez .40 .16
❑ 268 Del Unser .40 .16
❑ 269 Rick Austin .40 .16
❑ 270 Willie Stargell 3.00 1.20
❑ 271 Jim Lonborg .75 .30
❑ 272 Rick Dempsey .75 .30
❑ 273 Joe Niekro .75 .30
❑ 274 Tommy Harper .75 .30
❑ 275 Rick Manning .40 .16
❑ 276 Mickey Scott .40 .16
❑ 277 Chicago Cubs 1.50 .30
Team Card CL
Jim Marshall MG
❑ 278 Bernie Carbo .40 .16
❑ 279 Roy Howell .40 .16
❑ 280 Burt Hooton .75 .30
❑ 281 Dave May .40 .16
❑ 282 Dan Osborn .40 .16
❑ 283 Merv Rettenmund .40 .16
❑ 284 Steve Ontiveros .40 .16
❑ 285 Mike Cuellar .75 .30
❑ 286 Jim Wohlford .40 .16
❑ 287 Pete Mackanin .40 .16
❑ 288 Bill Campbell .40 .16
❑ 289 Enzo Hernandez .40 .16
❑ 290 Ted Simmons .75 .30
❑ 291 Ken Sanders .40 .16
❑ 292 Leon Roberts .40 .16
❑ 293 Bill Castro .40 .16
❑ 294 Ed Kirkpatrick .40 .16
❑ 295 Dave Cash .40 .16
❑ 296 Pat Dobson .40 .16
❑ 297 Roger Metzger .40 .16
❑ 298 Dick Bosman .40 .16
❑ 299 Champ Summers .40 .16
❑ 300 Johnny Bench 12.00 4.80

❑ 301 Jackie Brown .40 .16
❑ 302 Rick Miller .40 .16
❑ 303 Steve Foucault .40 .16
❑ 304 California Angels 1.50 .30
Team Card CL
Dick Williams MG
❑ 305 Andy Messersmith .75 .30
❑ 306 Rod Gilbreath .40 .16
❑ 307 Al Bumbry .75 .30
❑ 308 Jim Barr .40 .16
❑ 309 Bill Melton .40 .16
❑ 310 Randy Jones .75 .30
❑ 311 Cookie Rojas .40 .16
❑ 312 Don Carrithers .40 .16
❑ 313 Dan Ford .40 .16
❑ 314 Ed Kranepool .40 .16
❑ 315 Al Hrabosky .75 .30
❑ 316 Robin Yount 15.00 6.00
❑ 317 John Candelaria RC 1.50 .60
❑ 318 Bob Boone 1.50 .60
❑ 319 Larry Gura .40 .16
❑ 320 Willie Horton .75 .30
❑ 321 Jose Cruz 1.50 .60
❑ 322 Glenn Abbott .40 .16
❑ 323 Rob Sperring .40 .16
❑ 324 Jim Bibby .40 .16
❑ 325 Tony Perez 3.00 1.20
❑ 326 Dick Pole .40 .16
❑ 327 Dave Moates .40 .16
❑ 328 Carl Morton .40 .16
❑ 329 Joe Ferguson .40 .16
❑ 330 Nolan Ryan 25.00 10.00
❑ 331 San Diego Padres 1.50 .30
Team Card CL
John McNamara MG
❑ 332 Charlie Williams .40 .16
❑ 333 Bob Coluccio .40 .16
❑ 334 Dennis Leonard .75 .30
❑ 335 Bob Grich .75 .30
❑ 336 Vic Albury .40 .16
❑ 337 Bud Harrelson .75 .30
❑ 338 Bob Bailey .40 .16
❑ 339 John Denny .75 .30
❑ 340 Jim Rice 4.00 1.60
❑ 341 Lou Gehrig ATG 12.00 4.80
❑ 342 Rogers Hornsby ATG 3.00 1.20
❑ 343 Pie Traynor ATG 1.50 .60
❑ 344 Honus Wagner ATG 5.00 2.00
❑ 345 Babe Ruth ATG 15.00 6.00
❑ 346 Ty Cobb ATG 12.00 4.80
❑ 347 Ted Williams ATG 12.00 4.80
❑ 348 Mickey Cochrane ATG 1.50 .60
❑ 349 Walter Johnson ATG 5.00 2.00
❑ 350 Lefty Grove ATG 1.50 .60
❑ 351 Randy Hundley .75 .30
❑ 352 Dave Giusti .40 .16
❑ 353 Sixto Lezcano .75 .30
❑ 354 Ron Blomberg .40 .16
❑ 355 Steve Carlton 6.00 2.40
❑ 356 Ted Martinez .40 .16
❑ 357 Ken Forsch .40 .16
❑ 358 Buddy Bell .75 .30
❑ 359 Rick Reuschel .75 .30
❑ 360 Jeff Burroughs .75 .30
❑ 361 Detroit Tigers 1.50 .30
Team Card CL
Ralph Houk MG
❑ 362 Will McEnaney .75 .30
❑ 363 Dave Collins RC .75 .30
❑ 364 Elias Sosa .40 .16
❑ 365 Carlton Fisk 6.00 2.40
❑ 366 Bobby Valentine .75 .30
❑ 367 Bruce Miller .40 .16
❑ 368 Wilbur Wood .40 .16
❑ 369 Frank White .75 .30
❑ 370 Ron Cey .75 .30
❑ 371 Elrod Hendricks .40 .16
❑ 372 Rick Baldwin .40 .16
❑ 373 Johnny Briggs .40 .16
❑ 374 Dan Warthen .40 .16
❑ 375 Ron Fairly .75 .30
❑ 376 Rich Hebner .75 .30
❑ 377 Mike Hegan .40 .16
❑ 378 Steve Stone .75 .30
❑ 379 Ken Boswell .40 .16
❑ 380 Bobby Bonds 1.50 .60
❑ 381 Denny Doyle .40 .16
❑ 382 Matt Alexander .40 .16
❑ 383 John Ellis .40 .16
❑ 384 Philadelphia Phillies 1.50 .30
Team Card CL
Danny Ozark MG
❑ 385 Mickey Lolich .75 .30
❑ 386 Ed Goodson .40 .16
❑ 387 Mike Miley .40 .16
❑ 388 Stan Perzanowski .40 .16
❑ 389 Glenn Adams .40 .16
❑ 390 Don Gullett .75 .30
❑ 391 Jerry Hairston .40 .16
❑ 392 Checklist 265-396 1.50 .30
❑ 393 Paul Mitchell .40 .16
❑ 394 Fran Healy .40 .16
❑ 395 Jim Wynn .75 .30
❑ 396 Bill Lee .40 .16
❑ 397 Tim Foli .40 .16
❑ 398 Dave Tomlin .40 .16
❑ 399 Luis Melendez .40 .16
❑ 400 Rod Carew 6.00 2.40
❑ 401 Ken Brett .40 .16
❑ 402 Don Money .75 .30
❑ 403 Geoff Zahn .40 .16
❑ 404 Enos Cabell .40 .16
❑ 405 Rollie Fingers 2.50 1.00
❑ 406 Ed Herrmann .40 .16
❑ 407 Tom Underwood .40 .16
❑ 408 Charlie Spikes .40 .16
❑ 409 Dave Lemanczyk .40 .16
❑ 410 Ralph Garr .75 .30
❑ 411 Bill Singer .40 .16
❑ 412 Toby Harrah .75 .30
❑ 413 Pete Varney .40 .16
❑ 414 Wayne Garland .40 .16
❑ 415 Vada Pinson 1.50 .60
❑ 416 Tommy John 1.50 .60
❑ 417 Gene Clines .40 .16
❑ 418 Jose Morales RC .40 .16
❑ 419 Reggie Cleveland .40 .16
❑ 420 Joe Morgan 5.00 2.00
❑ 421 Oakland A's 1.50 .30
Team Card CL
(No MG on front)
❑ 422 Johnny Grubb .40 .16
❑ 423 Ed Halicki .40 .16
❑ 424 Phil Roof .40 .16
❑ 425 Rennie Stennett .40 .16
❑ 426 Bob Forsch .40 .16
❑ 427 Kurt Bevacqua .40 .16
❑ 428 Jim Crawford .40 .16
❑ 429 Fred Stanley .40 .16
❑ 430 Jose Cardenal .75 .30
❑ 431 Dick Ruthven .40 .16
❑ 432 Tom Veryzer .40 .16
❑ 433 Rick Waits .40 .16
❑ 434 Morris Nettles .40 .16
❑ 435 Phil Niekro 2.50 1.00
❑ 436 Bill Fahey .40 .16
❑ 437 Terry Forster .40 .16
❑ 438 Doug DeCinces .75 .30
❑ 439 Rick Rhoden .75 .30
❑ 440 John Mayberry .75 .30
❑ 441 Gary Carter 4.00 1.60
❑ 442 Hank Webb .40 .16
❑ 443 San Francisco Giants 1.50 .30
Team Card CL
(No MG on front)
❑ 444 Gary Nolan .75 .30
❑ 445 Rico Petrocelli .75 .30
❑ 446 Larry Haney .40 .16
❑ 447 Gene Locklear .75 .30
❑ 448 Tom Johnson .40 .16
❑ 449 Bob Robertson .40 .16
❑ 450 Jim Palmer 5.00 2.00
❑ 451 Buddy Bradford .40 .16
❑ 452 Tom Hausman .40 .16
❑ 453 Lou Piniella 1.50 .60
❑ 454 Tom Griffin .40 .16
❑ 455 Dick Allen 1.50 .60
❑ 456 Joe Coleman .40 .16
❑ 457 Ed Crosby .40 .16
❑ 458 Earl Williams .40 .16
❑ 459 Jim Brewer .40 .16
❑ 460 Cesar Cedeno .75 .30
❑ 461 NL and AL Champs .75 .30
Reds sweep Bucs,
Bosox surprise A's
❑ 462 '75 World Series .75 .30
Reds Champs
❑ 463 Steve Hargan .40 .16
❑ 464 Ken Henderson .40 .16
❑ 465 Mike Marshall .75 .30
❑ 466 Bob Stinson .40 .16
❑ 467 Woodie Fryman .40 .16
❑ 468 Jesus Alou .40 .16
❑ 469 Rawly Eastwick .75 .30
❑ 470 Bobby Murcer .75 .30
❑ 471 Jim Burton .40 .16
❑ 472 Bob Davis .40 .16
❑ 473 Paul Blair .75 .30
❑ 474 Ray Corbin .40 .16
❑ 475 Joe Rudi .75 .30
❑ 476 Bob Moose .40 .16
❑ 477 Cleveland Indians 1.50 .30
Team Card CL
Frank Robinson MG
❑ 478 Lynn McGlothen .40 .16
❑ 479 Bobby Mitchell .40 .16
❑ 480 Mike Schmidt 15.00 6.00
❑ 481 Rudy May .40 .16
❑ 482 Tim Hosley .40 .16
❑ 483 Mickey Stanley .40 .16
❑ 484 Eric Raich .40 .16
❑ 485 Mike Hargrove .75 .30
❑ 486 Bruce Dal Canton .40 .16
❑ 487 Leron Lee .40 .16
❑ 488 Claude Osteen .75 .30
❑ 489 Skip Jutze .40 .16
❑ 490 Frank Tanana .75 .30
❑ 491 Terry Crowley .40 .16
❑ 492 Marty Pattin .40 .16
❑ 493 Derrel Thomas .40 .16
❑ 494 Craig Swan .75 .30
❑ 495 Nate Colbert .40 .16
❑ 496 Juan Beniquez .40 .16
❑ 497 Joe McIntosh .40 .16
❑ 498 Glenn Borgmann .40 .16
❑ 499 Mario Guerrero .40 .16
❑ 500 Reggie Jackson 12.00 4.80
❑ 501 Billy Champion .40 .16
❑ 502 Tim McCarver 1.50 .60
❑ 503 Elliott Maddox .40 .16
❑ 504 Pittsburgh Pirates 1.50 .30
Team Card CL
Danny Murtaugh MG
❑ 505 Mark Belanger .75 .30
❑ 506 George Mitterwald .40 .16
❑ 507 Ray Bare .40 .16
❑ 508 Duane Kuiper .40 .16
❑ 509 Bill Hands .40 .16
❑ 510 Amos Otis .75 .30
❑ 511 Jamie Easterley .40 .16
❑ 512 Ellie Rodriguez .40 .16
❑ 513 Bart Johnson .40 .16
❑ 514 Dan Driessen .75 .30
❑ 515 Steve Yeager .75 .30
❑ 516 Wayne Granger .40 .16
❑ 517 John Milner .40 .16
❑ 518 Doug Flynn .40 .16
❑ 519 Steve Brye .40 .16
❑ 520 Willie McCovey 5.00 2.00
❑ 521 Jim Colborn .40 .16
❑ 522 Ted Sizemore .40 .16
❑ 523 Bob Montgomery .40 .16
❑ 524 Pete Falcone .40 .16
❑ 525 Billy Williams 2.50 1.00
❑ 526 Checklist 397-528 1.50 .30
❑ 527 Mike Anderson .40 .16
❑ 528 Dock Ellis .40 .16
❑ 529 Deron Johnson .40 .16
❑ 530 Don Sutton 2.50 1.00
❑ 531 New York Mets 1.50 .30
Team Card CL
Joe Frazier MG
❑ 532 Milt May .40 .16
❑ 533 Lee Richard .40 .16
❑ 534 Stan Bahnsen .40 .16
❑ 535 Dave Nelson .40 .16
❑ 536 Mike Thompson .40 .16
❑ 537 Tony Muser .40 .16

Card	Player	NM	Ex
❑ 538	Pat Darcy	.40	.16
❑ 539	John Balaz	.40	.16
❑ 540	Bill Freehan	.75	.30
❑ 541	Steve Mingori	.40	.16
❑ 542	Keith Hernandez	.75	.30
❑ 543	Wayne Twitchell	.40	.16
❑ 544	Pepe Frias	.40	.16
❑ 545	Sparky Lyle	.75	.30
❑ 546	Dave Rosello	.40	.16
❑ 547	Roric Harrison	.40	.16
❑ 548	Manny Mota	.75	.30
❑ 549	Randy Tate	.40	.16
❑ 550	Hank Aaron	25.00	10.00
❑ 551	Jerry DaVanon	.40	.16
❑ 552	Terry Humphrey	.40	.16
❑ 553	Randy Moffitt	.40	.16
❑ 554	Ray Fosse	.40	.16
❑ 555	Dyar Miller	.40	.16
❑ 556	Minnesota Twins	1.50	.30
	Team Card CL		
	Gene Mauch MG		
❑ 557	Dan Spillner	.40	.16
❑ 558	Clarence Gaston	.75	.30
❑ 559	Clyde Wright	.40	.16
❑ 560	Jorge Orta	.40	.16
❑ 561	Tom Carroll	.40	.16
❑ 562	Adrian Garrett	.40	.16
❑ 563	Larry Demery	.40	.16
❑ 564	Bubble Gum Champ	1.50	.60
	Kurt Bevacqua		
❑ 565	Tug McGraw	.75	.30
❑ 566	Ken McMullen	.40	.16
❑ 567	George Stone	.40	.16
❑ 568	Rob Andrews	.40	.16
❑ 569	Nelson Briles	.75	.30
❑ 570	George Hendrick	.75	.30
❑ 571	Don DeMola	.40	.16
❑ 572	Rich Coggins	.40	.16
❑ 573	Bill Travers	.40	.16
❑ 574	Don Kessinger	.75	.30
❑ 575	Dwight Evans	1.50	.60
❑ 576	Maximino Leon	.40	.16
❑ 577	Marc Hill	.40	.16
❑ 578	Ted Kubiak	.40	.16
❑ 579	Clay Kirby	.40	.16
❑ 580	Bert Campaneris	.75	.30
❑ 581	St. Louis Cardinals	1.50	.30
	Team Card CL		
	Red Schoendienst MG		
❑ 582	Mike Kekich	.40	.16
❑ 583	Tommy Helms	.40	.16
❑ 584	Stan Wall	.40	.16
❑ 585	Joe Torre	1.50	.60
❑ 586	Ron Schueler	.40	.16
❑ 587	Leo Cardenas	.40	.16
❑ 588	Kevin Kobel	.40	.16
❑ 589	Santo Alcala	1.50	.60
	Mike Flanagan RC		
	Joe Pactwa		
	Pablo Torrealba		
❑ 590	Henry Cruz	.75	.30
	Chet Lemon RC		
	Ellis Valentine		
	Terry Whitfield		
❑ 591	Steve Grilli	.75	.30
	Craig Mitchell		
	Jose Sosa		
	George Throop		
❑ 592	Willie Randolph RC	5.00	2.00
	Dave McKay		
	Jerry Royster		
	Roy Staiger		
❑ 593	Larry Anderson	.75	.30
	Ken Crosby		
	Mark Littell		
	Butch Metzger		
❑ 594	Andy Merchant	.75	.30
	Ed Ott		
	Royle Stillman		
	Jerry White		
❑ 595	Art DeFillipis	.75	.30
	Randy Lerch		
	Sid Monge		
	Steve Barr		
❑ 596	Craig Reynolds	.75	.30
	Lamar Johnson		
	Johnnie LeMaster		
	Jerry Manuel RC		
❑ 597	Don Aase	.75	.30
	Jack Kucek		
	Frank LaCorte		
	Mike Pazik		
❑ 598	Hector Cruz	.75	.30
	Jamie Quirk		
	Jerry Turner		
	Joe Wallis		
❑ 599	Rob Dressler	8.00	3.20
	Ron Guidry RC		
	Bob McClure		
	Pat Zachry		
❑ 600	Tom Seaver	10.00	4.00
❑ 601	Ken Rudolph	.40	.16
❑ 602	Doug Konieczny	.40	.16
❑ 603	Jim Holt	.40	.16
❑ 604	Joe Lovitto	.40	.16
❑ 605	Al Downing	.40	.16
❑ 606	Milwaukee Brewers	1.50	.30
	Team Card CL		
	Alex Grammas MG		
❑ 607	Rich Hinton	.40	.16
❑ 608	Vic Correll	.40	.16
❑ 609	Fred Norman	.40	.16
❑ 610	Greg Luzinski	1.50	.60
❑ 611	Rich Folkers	.40	.16
❑ 612	Joe Lahoud	.40	.16
❑ 613	Tim Johnson	.40	.16
❑ 614	Fernando Arroyo	.40	.16
❑ 615	Mike Cubbage	.40	.16
❑ 616	Buck Martinez	.40	.16
❑ 617	Darold Knowles	.40	.16
❑ 618	Jack Brohamer	.40	.16
❑ 619	Bill Butler	.40	.16
❑ 620	Al Oliver	.75	.30
❑ 621	Tom Hall	.40	.16
❑ 622	Rick Auerbach	.40	.16
❑ 623	Bob Allietta	.40	.16
❑ 624	Tony Taylor	.40	.16
❑ 625	J.R. Richard	.75	.30
❑ 626	Bob Sheldon	.40	.16
❑ 627	Bill Plummer	.40	.16
❑ 628	John D'Acquisto	.40	.16
❑ 629	Sandy Alomar	.75	.30
❑ 630	Chris Speier	.40	.16
❑ 631	Atlanta Braves	1.50	.30
	Team Card CL		
	Dave Bristol MG		
❑ 632	Rogelio Moret	.40	.16
❑ 633	John Stearns RC	.75	.30
❑ 634	Larry Christenson	.40	.16
❑ 635	Jim Fregosi	.75	.30
❑ 636	Joe Decker	.40	.16
❑ 637	Bruce Bochte	.40	.16
❑ 638	Doyle Alexander	.75	.30
❑ 639	Fred Kendall	.40	.16
❑ 640	Bill Madlock	1.50	.60
❑ 641	Tom Paciorek	.75	.30
❑ 642	Dennis Blair	.40	.16
❑ 643	Checklist 529-660	1.50	.30
❑ 644	Tom Bradley	.40	.16
❑ 645	Darrell Porter	.75	.30
❑ 646	John Lowenstein	.40	.16
❑ 647	Ramon Hernandez	.40	.16
❑ 648	Al Cowens	.40	.16
❑ 649	Dave Roberts	.40	.16
❑ 650	Thurman Munson	6.00	2.40
❑ 651	John Odom	.40	.16
❑ 652	Ed Armbrister	.40	.16
❑ 653	Mike Norris RC	.75	.30
❑ 654	Doug Griffin	.40	.16
❑ 655	Mike Vail	.40	.16
❑ 656	Chicago White Sox	1.50	.30
	Team Card CL		
	Chuck Tanner MG		
❑ 657	Roy Smalley RC	.75	.30
❑ 658	Jerry Johnson	.40	.16
❑ 659	Ben Oglivie	.75	.30
❑ 660	Dave Lopes	1.50	.30

1977 Topps

Card	Player	NM	Ex
	COMPLETE SET (660)	225.00	90.00
❑ 1	George Brett	8.00	2.30
	Bill Madlock LL		
❑ 2	Graig Nettles	2.50	1.00
	Mike Schmidt LL		
❑ 3	Lee May	1.50	.60
	George Foster LL		
❑ 4	Bill North	.75	.30
	Dave Lopes LL		
❑ 5	Jim Palmer	1.50	.60
	Randy Jones LL		
❑ 6	Nolan Ryan	15.00	6.00
	Tom Seaver LL		
❑ 7	Mark Fidrych	.75	.30
	John Denny LL		
❑ 8	Bill Campbell	.75	.30
	Rawly Eastwick LL		
❑ 9	Doug Rader	.30	.12
❑ 10	Reggie Jackson	10.00	4.00
❑ 11	Rob Dressler	.30	.12
❑ 12	Larry Haney	.30	.12
❑ 13	Luis Gomez	.30	.12
❑ 14	Tommy Smith	.30	.12
❑ 15	Don Gullett	.75	.30
❑ 16	Bob Jones	.30	.12
❑ 17	Steve Stone	.75	.30
❑ 18	Indians Team CL	1.50	.30
	Frank Robinson MG		
❑ 19	John D'Acquisto	.30	.12
❑ 20	Graig Nettles	1.50	.60
❑ 21	Ken Forsch	.30	.12
❑ 22	Bill Freehan	.75	.30
❑ 23	Dan Driessen	.30	.12
❑ 24	Carl Morton	.30	.12
❑ 25	Dwight Evans	1.50	.60
❑ 26	Ray Sadecki	.30	.12
❑ 27	Bill Buckner	.75	.30
❑ 28	Woodie Fryman	.30	.12
❑ 29	Bucky Dent	.75	.30
❑ 30	Greg Luzinski	1.50	.60
❑ 31	Jim Todd	.30	.12
❑ 32	Checklist 1-132	1.50	.30
❑ 33	Wayne Garland	.30	.12
❑ 34	Angels Team CL	1.50	.30
	Norm Sherry MG		
❑ 35	Rennie Stennett	.30	.12
❑ 36	John Ellis	.30	.12
❑ 37	Steve Hargan	.30	.12
❑ 38	Craig Kusick	.30	.12
❑ 39	Tom Griffin	.30	.12
❑ 40	Bobby Murcer	.75	.30
❑ 41	Jim Kern	.30	.12
❑ 42	Jose Cruz	.75	.30
❑ 43	Ray Bare	.30	.12
❑ 44	Bud Harrelson	.75	.30
❑ 45	Rawly Eastwick	.30	.12
❑ 46	Buck Martinez	.30	.12
❑ 47	Lynn McGlothen	.30	.12
❑ 48	Tom Paciorek	.75	.30
❑ 49	Grant Jackson	.30	.12
❑ 50	Ron Cey	.75	.30
❑ 51	Brewers Team CL	1.50	.30
	Alex Grammas MG		
❑ 52	Ellis Valentine	.30	.12
❑ 53	Paul Mitchell	.30	.12
❑ 54	Sandy Alomar	.75	.30
❑ 55	Jeff Burroughs	.75	.30
❑ 56	Rudy May	.30	.12
❑ 57	Marc Hill	.30	.12
❑ 58	Chet Lemon	.75	.30

❑ 59	Larry Christenson	.30	.12
❑ 60	Jim Rice	2.50	1.00
❑ 61	Manny Sanguillen	.75	.30
❑ 62	Eric Raich	.30	.12
❑ 63	Tito Fuentes	.30	.12
❑ 64	Larry Biittner	.30	.12
❑ 65	Skip Lockwood	.30	.12
❑ 66	Roy Smalley	.75	.30
❑ 67	Joaquin Andujar RC	.75	.30
❑ 68	Bruce Bochte	.30	.12
❑ 69	Jim Crawford	.30	.12
❑ 70	Johnny Bench	10.00	4.00
❑ 71	Dock Ellis	.30	.12
❑ 72	Mike Anderson	.30	.12
❑ 73	Charlie Williams	.30	.12
❑ 74	A's Team CL Jack McKeon MG	1.50	.30
❑ 75	Dennis Leonard	.75	.30
❑ 76	Tim Foli	.30	.12
❑ 77	Dyar Miller	.30	.12
❑ 78	Bob Davis	.30	.12
❑ 79	Don Money	.75	.30
❑ 80	Andy Messersmith	.75	.30
❑ 81	Juan Beniquez	.30	.12
❑ 82	Jim Rooker	.30	.12
❑ 83	Kevin Bell	.30	.12
❑ 84	Ollie Brown	.30	.12
❑ 85	Duane Kuiper	.30	.12
❑ 86	Pat Zachry	.30	.12
❑ 87	Glenn Borgmann	.30	.12
❑ 88	Stan Wall	.30	.12
❑ 89	Butch Hobson RC	.75	.30
❑ 90	Cesar Cedeno	.75	.30
❑ 91	John Verhoeven	.30	.12
❑ 92	Dave Rosello	.30	.12
❑ 93	Tom Poquette	.30	.12
❑ 94	Craig Swan	.30	.12
❑ 95	Keith Hernandez	.75	.30
❑ 96	Lou Piniella	.75	.30
❑ 97	Dave Heaverlo	.30	.12
❑ 98	Milt May	.30	.12
❑ 99	Tom Hausman	.30	.12
❑ 100	Joe Morgan	4.00	1.60
❑ 101	Dick Bosman	.30	.12
❑ 102	Jose Morales	.30	.12
❑ 103	Mike Bacsik	.30	.12
❑ 104	Omar Moreno	.75	.30
❑ 105	Steve Yeager	.75	.30
❑ 106	Mike Flanagan	.75	.30
❑ 107	Bill Melton	.30	.12
❑ 108	Alan Foster	.30	.12
❑ 109	Jorge Orta	.30	.12
❑ 110	Steve Carlton	5.00	2.00
❑ 111	Rico Petrocelli	.75	.30
❑ 112	Bill Greif	.30	.12
❑ 113	Blue Jays Leaders Roy Hartsfield MG Don Leppert CO Bob Miller CO Jackie Moore CO Harry Warner CO	1.50	.30
❑ 114	Bruce Dal Canton	.30	.12
❑ 115	Rick Manning	.30	.12
❑ 116	Joe Niekro	.75	.30
❑ 117	Frank White	.75	.30
❑ 118	Rick Jones	.30	.12
❑ 119	John Stearns	.30	.12
❑ 120	Rod Carew	5.00	2.00
❑ 121	Gary Nolan	.30	.12
❑ 122	Ben Oglivie	.75	.30
❑ 123	Fred Stanley	.30	.12
❑ 124	George Mitterwald	.30	.12
❑ 125	Bill Travers	.30	.12
❑ 126	Rod Gilbreath	.30	.12
❑ 127	Ron Fairly	.75	.30
❑ 128	Tommy John	1.50	.60
❑ 129	Mike Sadek	.30	.12
❑ 130	Al Oliver	.75	.30
❑ 131	Orlando Ramirez	.30	.12
❑ 132	Chip Lang	.30	.12
❑ 133	Ralph Garr	.75	.30
❑ 134	Padres Team CL John McNamara MG	1.50	.30
❑ 135	Mark Belanger	.75	.30
❑ 136	Jerry Mumphrey	.75	.30
❑ 137	Jeff Terpko	.30	.12
❑ 138	Bob Stinson	.30	.12
❑ 139	Fred Norman	.30	.12
❑ 140	Mike Schmidt	12.00	4.80
❑ 141	Mark Littell	.30	.12
❑ 142	Steve Dillard	.30	.12
❑ 143	Ed Herrmann	.30	.12
❑ 144	Bruce Sutter RC	5.00	2.00
❑ 145	Tom Veryzer	.30	.12
❑ 146	Dusty Baker	1.50	.60
❑ 147	Jackie Brown	.30	.12
❑ 148	Fran Healy	.30	.12
❑ 149	Mike Cubbage	.30	.12
❑ 150	Tom Seaver	8.00	3.20
❑ 151	Johnny LeMaster	.30	.12
❑ 152	Gaylord Perry	2.50	1.00
❑ 153	Ron Jackson RC	.30	.12
❑ 154	Dave Giusti	.30	.12
❑ 155	Joe Rudi	.75	.30
❑ 156	Pete Mackanin	.30	.12
❑ 157	Ken Brett	.30	.12
❑ 158	Ted Kubiak	.30	.12
❑ 159	Bernie Carbo	.30	.12
❑ 160	Will McEnaney	.30	.12
❑ 161	Garry Templeton RC	1.50	.60
❑ 162	Mike Cuellar	.75	.30
❑ 163	Dave Hilton	.30	.12
❑ 164	Tug McGraw	.75	.30
❑ 165	Jim Wynn	.75	.30
❑ 166	Bill Campbell	.30	.12
❑ 167	Rich Hebner	.75	.30
❑ 168	Charlie Spikes	.30	.12
❑ 169	Darold Knowles	.30	.12
❑ 170	Thurman Munson	5.00	2.00
❑ 171	Ken Sanders	.30	.12
❑ 172	John Milner	.30	.12
❑ 173	Chuck Scrivener	.30	.12
❑ 174	Nelson Briles	.75	.30
❑ 175	Butch Wynegar	.75	.30
❑ 176	Bob Robertson	.30	.12
❑ 177	Bart Johnson	.30	.12
❑ 178	Bombo Rivera	.30	.12
❑ 179	Paul Hartzell	.30	.12
❑ 180	Dave Lopes	.75	.30
❑ 181	Ken McMullen	.30	.12
❑ 182	Dan Spillner	.30	.12
❑ 183	Cardinals Team CL Vern Rapp MG	1.50	.30
❑ 184	Bo McLaughlin	.30	.12
❑ 185	Sixto Lezcano	.30	.12
❑ 186	Doug Flynn	.30	.12
❑ 187	Dick Pole	.30	.12
❑ 188	Bob Tolan	.30	.12
❑ 189	Rick Dempsey	.75	.30
❑ 190	Ray Burris	.30	.12
❑ 191	Doug Griffin	.30	.12
❑ 192	Clarence Gaston	.75	.30
❑ 193	Larry Gura	.30	.12
❑ 194	Gary Matthews	.75	.30
❑ 195	Ed Figueroa	.30	.12
❑ 196	Len Randle	.30	.12
❑ 197	Ed Ott	.30	.12
❑ 198	Wilbur Wood	.30	.12
❑ 199	Pepe Frias	.30	.12
❑ 200	Frank Tanana	.75	.30
❑ 201	Ed Kranepool	.30	.12
❑ 202	Tom Johnson	.30	.12
❑ 203	Ed Armbrister	.30	.12
❑ 204	Jeff Newman	.30	.12
❑ 205	Pete Falcone	.30	.12
❑ 206	Boog Powell	1.50	.60
❑ 207	Glenn Abbott	.30	.12
❑ 208	Checklist 133-264	1.50	.30
❑ 209	Rob Andrews	.30	.12
❑ 210	Fred Lynn	.75	.15
❑ 211	Giants Team CL Joe Altobelli MG	1.50	.60
❑ 212	Jim Mason	.30	.12
❑ 213	Maximino Leon	.30	.12
❑ 214	Darrell Porter	.75	.30
❑ 215	Butch Metzger	.30	.12
❑ 216	Doug DeCinces	.75	.30
❑ 217	Tom Underwood	.30	.12
❑ 218	John Wathan RC	.75	.30
❑ 219	Joe Coleman	.30	.12
❑ 220	Chris Chambliss	.75	.30
❑ 221	Bob Bailey	.30	.12
❑ 222	Francisco Barrios	.30	.12
❑ 223	Earl Williams	.30	.12
❑ 224	Rusty Torres	.30	.12
❑ 225	Bob Apodaca	.30	.12
❑ 226	Leroy Stanton	.75	.30
❑ 227	Joe Sambito	.30	.12
❑ 228	Twins Team CL Gene Mauch MG	1.50	.30
❑ 229	Don Kessinger	.75	.30
❑ 230	Vida Blue	.75	.30
❑ 231	George Brett RB	8.00	3.20
❑ 232	Minnie Minoso RB	.75	.30
❑ 233	Jose Morales RB	.30	.12
❑ 234	Nolan Ryan RB	15.00	6.00
❑ 235	Cecil Cooper	.75	.30
❑ 236	Tom Buskey	.30	.12
❑ 237	Gene Clines	.30	.12
❑ 238	Tippy Martinez	.30	.12
❑ 239	Bill Plummer	.30	.12
❑ 240	Ron LeFlore	.75	.30
❑ 241	Dave Tomlin	.30	.12
❑ 242	Ken Henderson	.30	.12
❑ 243	Ron Reed	.30	.12
❑ 244	John Mayberry (Cartoon mentions T206 Wagner)	.75	.30
❑ 245	Rick Rhoden	.75	.30
❑ 246	Mike Vail	.30	.12
❑ 247	Chris Knapp	.30	.12
❑ 248	Wilbur Howard	.30	.12
❑ 249	Pete Redfern	.30	.12
❑ 250	Bill Madlock	.75	.30
❑ 251	Tony Muser	.30	.12
❑ 252	Dale Murray	.30	.12
❑ 253	John Hale	.30	.12
❑ 254	Doyle Alexander	.30	.12
❑ 255	George Scott	.75	.30
❑ 256	Joe Hoerner	.30	.12
❑ 257	Mike Miley	.30	.12
❑ 258	Luis Tiant	.75	.30
❑ 259	Mets Team CL Joe Frazier MG	1.50	.30
❑ 260	J.R. Richard	.75	.30
❑ 261	Phil Garner	.75	.30
❑ 262	Al Cowens	.30	.12
❑ 263	Mike Marshall	.75	.30
❑ 264	Tom Hutton	.30	.12
❑ 265	Mark Fidrych RC	3.00	1.20
❑ 266	Derrel Thomas	.30	.12
❑ 267	Ray Fosse	.30	.12
❑ 268	Rick Sawyer	.30	.12
❑ 269	Joe Lis	.30	.12
❑ 270	Dave Parker	1.50	.60
❑ 271	Terry Forster	.30	.12
❑ 272	Lee Lacy	.30	.12
❑ 273	Eric Soderholm	.30	.12
❑ 274	Don Stanhouse	.30	.12
❑ 275	Mike Hargrove	.75	.30
❑ 276	C.Chambliss ALCS homer decides it	1.50	.60
❑ 277	Pete Rose NLCS	5.00	2.00
❑ 278	Danny Frisella	.30	.12
❑ 279	Joe Wallis	.30	.12
❑ 280	Jim Hunter	2.50	1.00
❑ 281	Roy Staiger	.30	.12
❑ 282	Sid Monge	.30	.12
❑ 283	Jerry DaVanon	.30	.12
❑ 284	Mike Norris	.30	.12
❑ 285	Brooks Robinson	5.00	2.00
❑ 286	Johnny Grubb	.30	.06
❑ 287	Reds Team CL Sparky Anderson MG	1.50	.60
❑ 288	Bob Montgomery	.30	.12
❑ 289	Gene Garber	.75	.30
❑ 290	Amos Otis	.75	.30
❑ 291	Jason Thompson RC	.75	.30
❑ 292	Rogelio Moret	.30	.12
❑ 293	Jack Brohamer	.30	.12
❑ 294	George Medich	.30	.12
❑ 295	Gary Carter	2.50	1.00
❑ 296	Don Hood	.30	.12
❑ 297	Ken Reitz	.30	.12
❑ 298	Charlie Hough	.75	.30
❑ 299	Otto Velez	.75	.30
❑ 300	Jerry Koosman	.75	.30
❑ 301	Toby Harrah	.75	.30

❑ 302 Mike Garman .30 .12
❑ 303 Gene Tenace .75 .30
❑ 304 Jim Hughes .30 .12
❑ 305 Mickey Rivers .75 .30
❑ 306 Rick Waits .30 .12
❑ 307 Gary Sutherland .30 .12
❑ 308 Gene Pentz .30 .12
❑ 309 Red Sox Team CL 1.50 .30
Don Zimmer MG
❑ 310 Larry Bowa .75 .30
❑ 311 Vern Ruhle .30 .12
❑ 312 Rob Belloir .30 .12
❑ 313 Paul Blair .75 .30
❑ 314 Steve Mingori .30 .12
❑ 315 Dave Chalk .30 .12
❑ 316 Steve Rogers .30 .12
❑ 317 Kurt Bevacqua .30 .12
❑ 318 Duffy Dyer .30 .12
❑ 319 Goose Gossage 1.50 .60
❑ 320 Ken Griffey Sr. 1.50 .60
❑ 321 Dave Goltz .30 .12
❑ 322 Bill Russell .75 .30
❑ 323 Larry Lintz .30 .12
❑ 324 John Curtis .30 .12
❑ 325 Mike Ivie .30 .12
❑ 326 Jesse Jefferson .30 .12
❑ 327 Astros Team CL 1.50 .30
Bill Virdon MG
❑ 328 Tommy Boggs .30 .12
❑ 329 Ron Hodges .30 .12
❑ 330 George Hendrick .75 .30
❑ 331 Jim Colborn .30 .12
❑ 332 Elliott Maddox .30 .12
❑ 333 Paul Reuschel .30 .12
❑ 334 Bill Stein .30 .12
❑ 335 Bill Robinson .75 .30
❑ 336 Denny Doyle .30 .12
❑ 337 Ron Schueler .30 .12
❑ 338 Dave Duncan .75 .30
❑ 339 Adrian Devine .30 .12
❑ 340 Hal McRae .75 .30
❑ 341 Joe Kerrigan .30 .12
❑ 342 Jerry Remy .30 .12
❑ 343 Ed Halicki .30 .12
❑ 344 Brian Downing .75 .30
❑ 345 Reggie Smith .75 .30
❑ 346 Bill Singer .30 .12
❑ 347 George Foster 1.50 .60
❑ 348 Brent Strom .30 .12
❑ 349 Jim Holt .30 .12
❑ 350 Larry Dierker .75 .30
❑ 351 Jim Sundberg .75 .30
❑ 352 Mike Phillips .30 .12
❑ 353 Stan Thomas .30 .12
❑ 354 Pirates Team CL 1.50 .30
Chuck Tanner MG
❑ 355 Lou Brock 4.00 1.60
❑ 356 Checklist 265-396 1.50 .30
❑ 357 Tim McCarver 1.50 .60
❑ 358 Tom House .30 .12
❑ 359 Willie Randolph 1.50 .60
❑ 360 Rick Monday .75 .30
❑ 361 Eduardo Rodriguez .30 .12
❑ 362 Tommy Davis .75 .30
❑ 363 Dave Roberts .30 .12
❑ 364 Vic Correll .30 .12
❑ 365 Mike Torrez .75 .30
❑ 366 Ted Sizemore .30 .12
❑ 367 Dave Hamilton .30 .12
❑ 368 Mike Jorgensen .30 .12
❑ 369 Terry Humphrey .30 .12
❑ 370 John Montefusco .30 .12
❑ 371 Royals Team CL 1.50 .30
Whitey Herzog MG
❑ 372 Rich Folkers .30 .12
❑ 373 Bert Campaneris .75 .30
❑ 374 Kent Tekulve .75 .30
❑ 375 Larry Hisle .75 .30
❑ 376 Nino Espinosa .30 .12
❑ 377 Dave McKay .30 .12
❑ 378 Jim Umbarger .30 .12
❑ 379 Larry Cox .30 .12
❑ 380 Lee May .75 .30
❑ 381 Bob Forsch .30 .12
❑ 382 Charlie Moore .30 .12
❑ 383 Stan Bahnsen .30 .12
❑ 384 Darrel Chaney .30 .12
❑ 385 Dave LaRoche .30 .12
❑ 386 Manny Mota .75 .30
❑ 387 Yankees Team CL 2.50 .50
Billy Martin MG
❑ 388 Terry Harmon .30 .12
❑ 389 Ken Kravec .30 .12
❑ 390 Dave Winfield 6.00 2.40
❑ 391 Dan Warthen .30 .12
❑ 392 Phil Roof .30 .12
❑ 393 John Lowenstein .30 .12
❑ 394 Bill Laxton .30 .12
❑ 395 Manny Trillo .30 .12
❑ 396 Tom Murphy .30 .12
❑ 397 Larry Herndon RC .75 .30
❑ 398 Tom Burgmeier .30 .12
❑ 399 Bruce Boisclair .30 .12
❑ 400 Steve Garvey 2.50 1.00
❑ 401 Mickey Scott .30 .12
❑ 402 Tommy Helms .30 .12
❑ 403 Tom Grieve .75 .30
❑ 404 Eric Rasmussen .30 .12
❑ 405 Claudell Washington .75 .30
❑ 406 Tim Johnson .30 .12
❑ 407 Dave Freisleben .30 .12
❑ 408 Cesar Tovar .30 .12
❑ 409 Pete Broberg .30 .12
❑ 410 Willie Montanez .30 .12
❑ 411 Joe Morgan WS 2.50 1.00
Johnny Bench
❑ 412 Johnny Bench WS 2.50 1.00
❑ 413 WS Summary .75 .30
Cincy wins 2nd
straight series
❑ 414 Tommy Harper .75 .30
❑ 415 Jay Johnstone .75 .30
❑ 416 Chuck Hartenstein .30 .12
❑ 417 Wayne Garrett .30 .12
❑ 418 White Sox Team CL 1.50 .30
Bob Lemon MG
❑ 419 Steve Swisher .30 .12
❑ 420 Rusty Staub 1.50 .60
❑ 421 Doug Rau .30 .12
❑ 422 Freddie Patek .75 .30
❑ 423 Gary Lavelle .30 .12
❑ 424 Steve Brye .30 .12
❑ 425 Joe Torre 1.50 .60
❑ 426 Dick Drago .30 .12
❑ 427 Dave Rader .30 .12
❑ 428 Rangers Team CL 1.50 .30
Frank Lucchesi
❑ 429 Ken Boswell .30 .12
❑ 430 Fergie Jenkins 2.50 1.00
❑ 431 Dave Collins UER .75 .30
(Photo actually
Bobby Jones)
❑ 432 Buzz Capra .30 .12
❑ 433 Nate Colbert TBC .30 .12
(5 HR, 13 RBI)
❑ 434 Carl Yastrzemski TBC 1.50 .60
'67 Triple Crown
❑ 435 Maury Wills TBC .75 .30
104 steals
❑ 436 Bob Keegan TBC .30 .12
Majors' only no-hitter
❑ 437 Ralph Kiner TBC 1.50 .60
Leads NL in HR's
7th straight year
❑ 438 Marty Perez .30 .12
❑ 439 Gorman Thomas .75 .30
❑ 440 Jon Matlack .30 .12
❑ 441 Larvell Blanks .30 .12
❑ 442 Braves Team CL 1.50 .30
Dave Bristol MG
❑ 443 Lamar Johnson .30 .12
❑ 444 Wayne Twitchell .30 .12
❑ 445 Ken Singleton .75 .30
❑ 446 Bill Bonham .30 .12
❑ 447 Jerry Turner .30 .12
❑ 448 Ellie Rodriguez .30 .12
❑ 449 Al Fitzmorris .30 .12
❑ 450 Pete Rose 20.00 8.00
❑ 451 Checklist 397-528 1.50 .30
❑ 452 Mike Caldwell .30 .12
❑ 453 Pedro Garcia .30 .12
❑ 454 Andy Etchebarren .30 .12
❑ 455 Rick Wise .30 .12
❑ 456 Leon Roberts .30 .12
❑ 457 Steve Luebber .30 .12
❑ 458 Leo Foster .30 .12
❑ 459 Steve Foucault .30 .12
❑ 460 Willie Stargell 2.50 1.00
❑ 461 Dick Tidrow .30 .12
❑ 462 Don Baylor 1.50 .60
❑ 463 Jamie Quirk .30 .12
❑ 464 Randy Moffitt .30 .12
❑ 465 Rico Carty .75 .30
❑ 466 Fred Holdsworth .30 .12
❑ 467 Phillies Team CL 1.50 .30
Danny Ozark MG
❑ 468 Ramon Hernandez .30 .12
❑ 469 Pat Kelly .30 .12
❑ 470 Ted Simmons .75 .30
❑ 471 Del Unser .30 .12
❑ 472 Don Aase .30 .12
Bob McClure
Gil Patterson
Dave Wehrmeister
Sheldon Gill pictured instead of Gil
Patterson
❑ 473 Andre Dawson RC 20.00 8.00
Gene Richards
John Scott
Denny Walling
❑ 474 Bob Bailor .75 .30
Kiko Garcia
Craig Reynolds
Alex Taveras
❑ 475 Chris Batton .75 .30
Rick Camp
Scott McGregor
Manny Sarmiento
❑ 476 Gary Alexander 20.00 8.00
Rick Cerone
Dale Murphy RC
Kevin Pasley
❑ 477 Doug Ault .75 .30
Rich Dauer
Orlando Gonzalez
Phil Mankowski
❑ 478 Jim Gideon .75 .30
Leon Hooten
Dave Johnson
Mark Lemongello
❑ 479 Brian Asselstine .75 .30
Wayne Gross
Sam Mejias
Alvis Woods
❑ 480 Carl Yastrzemski 8.00 3.20
❑ 481 Roger Metzger .30 .12
❑ 482 Tony Solaita .30 .12
❑ 483 Richie Zisk .30 .12
❑ 484 Burt Hooton .75 .30
❑ 485 Roy White .75 .30
❑ 486 Ed Bane .30 .12
❑ 487 Larry Anderson .75 .30
Ed Glynn
Joe Henderson
Greg Terlecky
❑ 488 Jack Clark RC 3.00 1.20
Ruppert Jones RC
Lee Mazzilli RC
Dan Thomas
❑ 489 Len Barker RC .75 .30
Randy Lerch
Greg Minton
Mike Overy
❑ 490 Billy Almon .75 .30
Mickey Klutts
Tommy McMillan
Mark Wagner
❑ 491 Mike Dupree 3.00 1.20
Dennis Martinez RC
Craig Mitchell
Bob Sykes
❑ 492 Tony Armas RC .75 .30
Steve Kemp RC
Carlos Lopez
Gary Woods
❑ 493 Mike Krukow .75 .30
Jim Otten
Gary Wheelock

Mike Willis
❑ 494 Juan Bernhardt 1.50 .60
Mike Champion
Jim Gantner RC
Bump Wills
❑ 495 Al Hrabosky .30 .12
❑ 496 Gary Thomasson .30 .12
❑ 497 Clay Carroll .30 .12
❑ 498 Sal Bando .75 .30
❑ 499 Pablo Torrealba .30 .12
❑ 500 Dave Kingman 1.50 .60
❑ 501 Jim Bibby .30 .12
❑ 502 Randy Hundley .30 .12
❑ 503 Bill Lee .30 .12
❑ 504 Dodgers Team CL 1.50 .30
Tom Lasorda MG
❑ 505 Oscar Gamble .75 .30
❑ 506 Steve Grilli .30 .12
❑ 507 Mike Hegan .30 .12
❑ 508 Dave Pagan .30 .12
❑ 509 Cookie Rojas .75 .30
❑ 510 John Candelaria .30 .12
❑ 511 Bill Fahey .30 .12
❑ 512 Jack Billingham .30 .12
❑ 513 Jerry Terrell .30 .12
❑ 514 Cliff Johnson .30 .12
❑ 515 Chris Speier .30 .12
❑ 516 Bake McBride .75 .30
❑ 517 Pete Vuckovich RC .75 .30
❑ 518 Cubs Team CL 1.50 .30
Herman Franks MG
❑ 519 Don Kirkwood .30 .12
❑ 520 Garry Maddox .30 .12
❑ 521 Bob Grich .75 .30
Only card in set with no date of birth
❑ 522 Enzo Hernandez .30 .12
❑ 523 Rollie Fingers 2.50 1.00
❑ 524 Rowland Office .30 .12
❑ 525 Dennis Eckersley 5.00 2.00
❑ 526 Larry Parrish .75 .30
❑ 527 Dan Meyer .75 .30
❑ 528 Bill Castro .30 .12
❑ 529 Jim Essian .30 .12
❑ 530 Rick Reuschel .75 .30
❑ 531 Lyman Bostock .75 .30
❑ 532 Jim Willoughby .30 .12
❑ 533 Mickey Stanley .30 .12
❑ 534 Paul Splittorff .30 .12
❑ 535 Cesar Geronimo .30 .12
❑ 536 Vic Albury .30 .12
❑ 537 Dave Roberts .30 .12
❑ 538 Frank Taveras .30 .12
❑ 539 Mike Wallace .30 .12
❑ 540 Bob Watson .75 .30
❑ 541 John Denny .75 .30
❑ 542 Frank Duffy .30 .12
❑ 543 Ron Blomberg .30 .12
❑ 544 Gary Ross .30 .12
❑ 545 Bob Boone .75 .30
❑ 546 Oriole Team CL 1.50 .30
Earl Weaver MG
❑ 547 Willie McCovey 4.00 1.60
❑ 548 Joel Youngblood .30 .12
❑ 549 Jerry Royster .30 .12
❑ 550 Randy Jones .30 .12
❑ 551 Bill North .30 .12
❑ 552 Pepe Mangual .30 .12
❑ 553 Jack Heidemann .30 .12
❑ 554 Bruce Kimm .30 .12
❑ 555 Dan Ford .30 .12
❑ 556 Doug Bird .30 .12
❑ 557 Jerry White .30 .12
❑ 558 Elias Sosa .30 .12
❑ 559 Alan Bannister .30 .12
❑ 560 Dave Concepcion 1.50 .60
❑ 561 Pete LaCock .30 .12
❑ 562 Checklist 529-660 1.50 .30
❑ 563 Bruce Kison .30 .12
❑ 564 Alan Ashby .75 .30
❑ 565 Mickey Lolich .75 .30
❑ 566 Rick Miller .30 .12
❑ 567 Enos Cabell .30 .12
❑ 568 Carlos May .30 .12
❑ 569 Jim Lonborg .75 .30
❑ 570 Bobby Bonds 1.50 .60
❑ 571 Darrell Evans .75 .30
❑ 572 Ross Grimsley .30 .12
❑ 573 Joe Ferguson .30 .12
❑ 574 Aurelio Rodriguez .30 .12
❑ 575 Dick Ruthven .30 .12
❑ 576 Fred Kendall .30 .12
❑ 577 Jerry Augustine .30 .12
❑ 578 Bob Randall .30 .12
❑ 579 Don Carrithers .30 .12
❑ 580 George Brett 15.00 6.00
❑ 581 Pedro Borbon .30 .12
❑ 582 Ed Kirkpatrick .30 .12
❑ 583 Paul Lindblad .30 .12
❑ 584 Ed Goodson .30 .12
❑ 585 Rick Burleson .75 .30
❑ 586 Steve Renko .30 .12
❑ 587 Rick Baldwin .30 .12
❑ 588 Dave Moates .30 .12
❑ 589 Mike Cosgrove .30 .12
❑ 590 Buddy Bell .75 .30
❑ 591 Chris Arnold .30 .12
❑ 592 Dan Briggs .30 .12
❑ 593 Dennis Blair .30 .12
❑ 594 Biff Pocoroba .30 .12
❑ 595 John Hiller .30 .12
❑ 596 Jerry Martin .30 .12
❑ 597 Mariners Leaders CL 1.50 .30
Darrell Johnson MG
Don Bryant CO
Jim Busby CO
Vada Pinson CO
Wes Stock CO
❑ 598 Sparky Lyle .75 .30
❑ 599 Mike Tyson .30 .12
❑ 600 Jim Palmer 4.00 1.60
❑ 601 Mike Lum .30 .12
❑ 602 Andy Hassler .30 .12
❑ 603 Willie Davis .75 .30
❑ 604 Jim Slaton .30 .12
❑ 605 Felix Millan .30 .12
❑ 606 Steve Braun .30 .12
❑ 607 Larry Demery .30 .12
❑ 608 Roy Howell .30 .12
❑ 609 Jim Barr .30 .12
❑ 610 Jose Cardenal .75 .30
❑ 611 Dave Lemanczyk .30 .12
❑ 612 Barry Foote .30 .12
❑ 613 Reggie Cleveland .30 .12
❑ 614 Greg Gross .30 .12
❑ 615 Phil Niekro 2.50 1.00
❑ 616 Tommy Sandt .30 .12
❑ 617 Bobby Darwin .30 .12
❑ 618 Pat Dobson .30 .12
❑ 619 Johnny Oates .75 .30
❑ 620 Don Sutton 2.50 1.00
❑ 621 Tigers Team CL 1.50 .30
Ralph Houk MG
❑ 622 Jim Wohlford .30 .12
❑ 623 Jack Kucek .30 .12
❑ 624 Hector Cruz .30 .12
❑ 625 Ken Holtzman .75 .30
❑ 626 Al Bumbry .75 .30
❑ 627 Bob Myrick .30 .12
❑ 628 Mario Guerrero .30 .12
❑ 629 Bobby Valentine .75 .30
❑ 630 Bert Blyleven 1.50 .60
❑ 631 George Brett 6.00 2.40
Ken Brett
❑ 632 Bob Forsch .75 .30
Ken Forsch
❑ 633 Lee May .75 .30
Carlos May
❑ 634 Paul Reuschel .75 .30
Rick Reuschel UER
(Photos switched)
❑ 635 Robin Yount 8.00 3.20
❑ 636 Santo Alcala .30 .12
❑ 637 Alex Johnson .30 .12
❑ 638 Jim Kaat 1.50 .60
❑ 639 Jerry Morales .30 .12
❑ 640 Carlton Fisk 5.00 2.00
❑ 641 Dan Larson .30 .12
❑ 642 Willie Crawford .30 .12
❑ 643 Mike Pazik .30 .12
❑ 644 Matt Alexander .30 .12
❑ 645 Jerry Reuss .75 .30
❑ 646 Andres Mora .30 .12
❑ 647 Expos Team CL 1.50 .30
Dick Williams MG
❑ 648 Jim Spencer .30 .12
❑ 649 Dave Cash .30 .12
❑ 650 Nolan Ryan 30.00 12.00
❑ 651 Von Joshua .30 .12
❑ 652 Tom Walker .30 .12
❑ 653 Diego Segui .75 .30
❑ 654 Ron Pruitt .30 .12
❑ 655 Tony Perez 2.50 1.00
❑ 656 Ron Guidry 1.50 .60
❑ 657 Mick Kelleher .30 .12
❑ 658 Marty Pattin .30 .12
❑ 659 Merv Rettenmund .30 .12
❑ 660 Willie Horton 1.50 .30

1978 Topps

	NM	Ex
COMPLETE SET (726)	200.00	80.00
COMMON CARD (1-726)	.25	.10
COMMON CARD DP	.15	.06

❑ 1 Lou Brock RB 3.00 .90
❑ 2 Sparky Lyle RB .60 .24
❑ 3 Willie McCovey RB 2.50 1.00
❑ 4 Brooks Robinson RB 1.25 .50
❑ 5 Pete Rose RB 8.00 3.20
❑ 6 Nolan Ryan RB 15.00 6.00
❑ 7 Reggie Jackson RB 4.00 1.60
❑ 8 Mike Sadek .25 .10
❑ 9 Doug DeCinces .60 .24
❑ 10 Phil Niekro 2.50 1.00
❑ 11 Rick Manning .25 .10
❑ 12 Don Aase .25 .10
❑ 13 Art Howe RC .60 .24
❑ 14 Lerrin LaGrow .25 .10
❑ 15 Tony Perez DP 1.25 .50
❑ 16 Roy White .60 .24
❑ 17 Mike Krukow .25 .10
❑ 18 Bob Grich .60 .24
❑ 19 Darrell Porter .60 .24
❑ 20 Pete Rose DP 12.00 4.80
❑ 21 Steve Kemp .25 .10
❑ 22 Charlie Hough .60 .24
❑ 23 Bump Wills .25 .10
❑ 24 Don Money DP .15 .06
❑ 25 Jon Matlack .25 .10
❑ 26 Rich Hebner .60 .24
❑ 27 Geoff Zahn .25 .10
❑ 28 Ed Ott .25 .10
❑ 29 Bob Lacey .25 .10
❑ 30 George Hendrick .60 .24
❑ 31 Glenn Abbott .25 .10
❑ 32 Garry Templeton .60 .24
❑ 33 Dave Lemanczyk .25 .10
❑ 34 Willie McCovey 3.00 1.20
❑ 35 Sparky Lyle .60 .24
❑ 36 Eddie Murray RC 60.00 24.00
❑ 37 Rick Waits .25 .10
❑ 38 Willie Montanez .25 .10
❑ 39 Floyd Bannister RC .25 .10
❑ 40 Carl Yastrzemski 6.00 2.40
❑ 41 Burt Hooton .60 .24
❑ 42 Jorge Orta .25 .10
❑ 43 Bill Atkinson .25 .10
❑ 44 Toby Harrah .60 .24
❑ 45 Mark Fidrych 2.50 1.00
❑ 46 Al Cowens .25 .10

❑ 47 Jack Billingham .25 .10
❑ 48 Don Baylor 1.25 .50
❑ 49 Ed Kranepool .60 .24
❑ 50 Rick Reuschel .60 .24
❑ 51 Charlie Moore DP .15 .06
❑ 52 Jim Lonborg .60 .24
❑ 53 Phil Garner DP .25 .10
❑ 54 Tom Johnson .25 .10
❑ 55 Mitchell Page .25 .10
❑ 56 Randy Jones .25 .10
❑ 57 Dan Meyer .25 .10
❑ 58 Bob Forsch .25 .10
❑ 59 Otto Velez .25 .10
❑ 60 Thurman Munson 4.00 1.60
❑ 61 Larvell Blanks .25 .10
❑ 62 Jim Barr .25 .10
❑ 63 Don Zimmer MG .60 .24
❑ 64 Gene Pentz .25 .10
❑ 65 Ken Singleton .60 .24
❑ 66 Chicago White Sox 1.25 .25
Team Card CL
❑ 67 Claudell Washington .60 .24
❑ 68 Steve Foucault DP .15 .06
❑ 69 Mike Vail .25 .10
❑ 70 Goose Gossage 1.25 .50
❑ 71 Terry Humphrey .25 .10
❑ 72 Andre Dawson 4.00 1.60
❑ 73 Andy Hassler .25 .10
❑ 74 Checklist 1-121 1.25 .25
❑ 75 Dick Ruthven .25 .10
❑ 76 Steve Ontiveros .25 .10
❑ 77 Ed Kirkpatrick .25 .10
❑ 78 Pablo Torrealba .25 .10
❑ 79 Da.Johnson DP MG .15 .06
❑ 80 Ken Griffey Sr. 1.25 .50
❑ 81 Pete Redfern .25 .10
❑ 82 San Francisco Giants 1.25 .25
Team Card CL
❑ 83 Bob Montgomery .25 .10
❑ 84 Kent Tekulve .60 .24
❑ 85 Ron Fairly .60 .24
❑ 86 Dave Tomlin .25 .10
❑ 87 John Lowenstein .25 .10
❑ 88 Mike Phillips .25 .10
❑ 89 Ken Clay .25 .10
❑ 90 Larry Bowa 1.25 .50
❑ 91 Oscar Zamora .25 .10
❑ 92 Adrian Devine .25 .10
❑ 93 Bobby Cox DP .15 .06
❑ 94 Chuck Scrivener .25 .10
❑ 95 Jamie Quirk .25 .10
❑ 96 Baltimore Orioles 1.25 .25
Team Card CL
❑ 97 Stan Bahnsen .25 .10
❑ 98 Jim Essian .60 .24
❑ 99 Willie Hernandez RC 1.25 .50
❑ 100 George Brett 15.00 6.00
❑ 101 Sid Monge .25 .10
❑ 102 Matt Alexander .25 .10
❑ 103 Tom Murphy .25 .10
❑ 104 Lee Lacy .25 .10
❑ 105 Reggie Cleveland .25 .10
❑ 106 Bill Plummer .25 .10
❑ 107 Ed Halicki .25 .10
❑ 108 Von Joshua .25 .10
❑ 109 Joe Torre MG .60 .24
❑ 110 Richie Zisk .25 .10
❑ 111 Mike Tyson .25 .10
❑ 112 Houston Astros 1.25 .25
Team Card CL
❑ 113 Don Carrithers .25 .10
❑ 114 Paul Blair .60 .24
❑ 115 Gary Nolan .25 .10
❑ 116 Tucker Ashford .25 .10
❑ 117 John Montague .25 .10
❑ 118 Terry Harmon .25 .10
❑ 119 Dennis Martinez 2.50 1.00
❑ 120 Gary Carter 2.50 1.00
❑ 121 Alvis Woods .25 .10
❑ 122 Dennis Eckersley 3.00 1.20
❑ 123 Manny Trillo .25 .10
❑ 124 Dave Rozema RC .25 .10
❑ 125 George Scott .60 .24
❑ 126 Paul Moskau .25 .10
❑ 127 Chet Lemon .60 .24
❑ 128 Bill Russell .60 .24
❑ 129 Jim Colborn .25 .10
❑ 130 Jeff Burroughs .60 .24
❑ 131 Bert Blyleven 1.25 .50
❑ 132 Enos Cabell .25 .10
❑ 133 Jerry Augustine .25 .10
❑ 134 Steve Henderson .25 .10
❑ 135 Ron Guidry DP 1.25 .50
❑ 136 Ted Sizemore .25 .10
❑ 137 Craig Kusick .25 .10
❑ 138 Larry Demery .25 .10
❑ 139 Wayne Gross .25 .10
❑ 140 Rollie Fingers 2.50 1.00
❑ 141 Ruppert Jones .25 .10
❑ 142 John Montefusco .25 .10
❑ 143 Keith Hernandez .60 .24
❑ 144 Jesse Jefferson .25 .10
❑ 145 Rick Monday .60 .24
❑ 146 Doyle Alexander .60 .24
❑ 147 Lee Mazzilli .25 .10
❑ 148 Andre Thornton .60 .24
❑ 149 Dale Murray .25 .10
❑ 150 Bobby Bonds 1.25 .50
❑ 151 Milt Wilcox .25 .10
❑ 152 Ivan DeJesus .25 .10
❑ 153 Steve Stone .60 .24
❑ 154 Cecil Cooper DP .25 .10
❑ 155 Butch Hobson .25 .10
❑ 156 Andy Messersmith .60 .24
❑ 157 Pete LaCock DP .15 .06
❑ 158 Joaquin Andujar .60 .24
❑ 159 Lou Piniella .60 .24
❑ 160 Jim Palmer 3.00 1.20
❑ 161 Bob Boone 1.25 .50
❑ 162 Paul Thormodsgard .25 .10
❑ 163 Bill North .25 .10
❑ 164 Bob Owchinko .25 .10
❑ 165 Rennie Stennett .25 .10
❑ 166 Carlos Lopez .25 .10
❑ 167 Tim Foli .25 .10
❑ 168 Reggie Smith .60 .24
❑ 169 Jerry Johnson .25 .10
❑ 170 Lou Brock 3.00 1.20
❑ 171 Pat Zachry .25 .10
❑ 172 Mike Hargrove .60 .24
❑ 173 Robin Yount UER 5.00 2.00
(Played for Newark
in 1973, not 1971)
❑ 174 Wayne Garland .25 .10
❑ 175 Jerry Morales .25 .10
❑ 176 Milt May .25 .10
❑ 177 Gene Garber DP .25 .10
❑ 178 Dave Chalk .25 .10
❑ 179 Dick Tidrow .25 .10
❑ 180 Dave Concepcion 1.25 .50
❑ 181 Ken Forsch .25 .10
❑ 182 Jim Spencer .25 .10
❑ 183 Doug Bird .25 .10
❑ 184 Checklist 122-242 1.25 .25
❑ 185 Ellis Valentine .25 .10
❑ 186 Bob Stanley DP .15 .06
❑ 187 Jerry Royster DP .15 .06
❑ 188 Al Bumbry .60 .24
❑ 189 Tom Lasorda MG 2.50 1.00
❑ 190 John Candelaria .60 .24
❑ 191 Rodney Scott .25 .10
❑ 192 San Diego Padres 1.25 .25
Team Card CL
❑ 193 Rich Chiles .25 .10
❑ 194 Derrel Thomas .25 .10
❑ 195 Larry Dierker .60 .24
❑ 196 Bob Bailor .25 .10
❑ 197 Nino Espinosa .25 .10
❑ 198 Ron Pruitt .25 .10
❑ 199 Craig Reynolds .25 .10
❑ 200 Reggie Jackson 8.00 3.20
❑ 201 Dave Parker 1.25 .50
Rod Carew LL
❑ 202 George Foster .60 .24
Jim Rice LL DP
❑ 203 George Foster .60 .24
Larry Hisle LL
❑ 204 Frank Taveras .25 .10
Freddie Patek LL DP
❑ 205 Steve Carlton 2.50 1.00
Dave Goltz
Dennis Leonard
Jim Palmer LL
❑ 206 Phil Niekro 6.00 2.40
Nolan Ryan LL DP
❑ 207 John Candelaria .60 .24
Frank Tanana LL DP
❑ 208 Rollie Fingers 1.25 .50
Bill Campbell LL
❑ 209 Dock Ellis .25 .10
❑ 210 Jose Cardenal .25 .10
❑ 211 Earl Weaver MG DP 1.25 .50
❑ 212 Mike Caldwell .25 .10
❑ 213 Alan Bannister .25 .10
❑ 214 California Angels 1.25 .25
Team Card CL
❑ 215 Darrell Evans .60 .24
❑ 216 Mike Paxton .25 .10
❑ 217 Rod Gilbreath .25 .10
❑ 218 Marty Pattin .25 .10
❑ 219 Mike Cubbage .25 .10
❑ 220 Pedro Borbon .25 .10
❑ 221 Chris Speier .25 .10
❑ 222 Jerry Martin .25 .10
❑ 223 Bruce Kison .25 .10
❑ 224 Jerry Tabb .25 .10
❑ 225 Don Gullett DP .25 .10
❑ 226 Joe Ferguson .25 .10
❑ 227 Al Fitzmorris .25 .10
❑ 228 Manny Mota DP .25 .10
❑ 229 Leo Foster .25 .10
❑ 230 Al Hrabosky .25 .10
❑ 231 Wayne Nordhagen .25 .10
❑ 232 Mickey Stanley .25 .10
❑ 233 Dick Pole .25 .10
❑ 234 Herman Franks MG .25 .10
❑ 235 Tim McCarver .60 .24
❑ 236 Terry Whitfield .25 .10
❑ 237 Rich Dauer .25 .10
❑ 238 Juan Beniquez .25 .10
❑ 239 Dyar Miller .25 .10
❑ 240 Gene Tenace .60 .24
❑ 241 Pete Vuckovich .60 .24
❑ 242 Barry Bonnell DP .15 .06
❑ 243 Bob McClure .25 .10
❑ 244 Montreal Expos .60 .12
Team Card CL DP
❑ 245 Rick Burleson .60 .24
❑ 246 Dan Driessen .25 .10
❑ 247 Larry Christenson .25 .10
❑ 248 Frank White DP .60 .24
❑ 249 Dave Goltz DP .15 .06
❑ 250 Graig Nettles DP .60 .24
❑ 251 Don Kirkwood .25 .10
❑ 252 Steve Swisher DP .15 .06
❑ 253 Jim Kern .25 .10
❑ 254 Dave Collins .60 .24
❑ 255 Jerry Reuss .60 .24
❑ 256 Joe Altobelli MG .25 .10
❑ 257 Hector Cruz .25 .10
❑ 258 John Hiller .25 .10
❑ 259 Los Angeles Dodgers 1.25 .25
Team Card CL
❑ 260 Bert Campaneris .60 .24
❑ 261 Tim Hosley .25 .10
❑ 262 Rudy May .25 .10
❑ 263 Danny Walton .25 .10
❑ 264 Jamie Easterly .25 .10
❑ 265 Sal Bando DP .60 .24
❑ 266 Bob Shirley .25 .10
❑ 267 Doug Ault .25 .10
❑ 268 Gil Flores .25 .10
❑ 269 Wayne Twitchell .25 .10
❑ 270 Carlton Fisk 4.00 1.60
❑ 271 Randy Lerch DP .15 .06
❑ 272 Royle Stillman .25 .10
❑ 273 Fred Norman .25 .10
❑ 274 Freddie Patek .60 .24
❑ 275 Dan Ford .25 .10
❑ 276 Bill Bonham DP .15 .06
❑ 277 Bruce Boisclair .25 .10
❑ 278 Enrique Romo .25 .10
❑ 279 Bill Virdon MG .25 .10
❑ 280 Buddy Bell .60 .24
❑ 281 Eric Rasmussen DP .15 .06
❑ 282 New York Yankees 2.50 .50
Team Card CL
❑ 283 Omar Moreno .25 .10

❑ 284 Randy Moffitt .25 .10
❑ 285 Steve Yeager DP .60 .24
❑ 286 Ben Oglivie .60 .24
❑ 287 Kiko Garcia .25 .10
❑ 288 Dave Hamilton .25 .10
❑ 289 Checklist 243-363 1.25 .25
❑ 290 Willie Horton .60 .24
❑ 291 Gary Ross .25 .10
❑ 292 Gene Richards .25 .10
❑ 293 Mike Willis .25 .10
❑ 294 Larry Parrish .60 .24
❑ 295 Bill Lee .25 .10
❑ 296 Biff Pocoroba .25 .10
❑ 297 Warren Brusstar DP .15 .06
❑ 298 Tony Armas .60 .24
❑ 299 Whitey Herzog MG .60 .24
❑ 300 Joe Morgan 3.00 1.20
❑ 301 Buddy Schultz .25 .10
❑ 302 Chicago Cubs 1.25 .25
Team Card CL
❑ 303 Sam Hinds .25 .10
❑ 304 John Milner .25 .10
❑ 305 Rico Carty .60 .24
❑ 306 Joe Niekro .60 .24
❑ 307 Glenn Borgmann .25 .10
❑ 308 Jim Rooker .25 .10
❑ 309 Cliff Johnson .25 .10
❑ 310 Don Sutton 2.50 1.00
❑ 311 Jose Baez DP .15 .06
❑ 312 Greg Minton .25 .10
❑ 313 Andy Etchebarren .25 .10
❑ 314 Paul Lindblad .25 .10
❑ 315 Mark Belanger .60 .24
❑ 316 Henry Cruz DP .15 .06
❑ 317 Dave Johnson .25 .10
❑ 318 Tom Griffin .25 .10
❑ 319 Alan Ashby .25 .10
❑ 320 Fred Lynn .60 .24
❑ 321 Santo Alcala .25 .10
❑ 322 Tom Paciorek .60 .24
❑ 323 Jim Fregosi DP .25 .10
❑ 324 Vern Rapp MG .25 .10
❑ 325 Bruce Sutter 1.25 .50
❑ 326 Mike Lum DP .15 .06
❑ 327 Rick Langford DP .15 .06
❑ 328 Milwaukee Brewers 1.25 .25
Team Card CL
❑ 329 John Verhoeven .25 .10
❑ 330 Bob Watson .60 .24
❑ 331 Mark Littell .25 .10
❑ 332 Duane Kuiper .25 .10
❑ 333 Jim Todd .25 .10
❑ 334 John Stearns .25 .10
❑ 335 Bucky Dent .60 .24
❑ 336 Steve Busby .25 .10
❑ 337 Tom Grieve .60 .24
❑ 338 Dave Heaverlo .25 .10
❑ 339 Mario Guerrero .25 .10
❑ 340 Bake McBride .60 .24
❑ 341 Mike Flanagan .60 .24
❑ 342 Aurelio Rodriguez .25 .10
❑ 343 John Wathan DP .15 .06
❑ 344 Sam Ewing .25 .10
❑ 345 Luis Tiant .60 .24
❑ 346 Larry Biittner .25 .10
❑ 347 Terry Forster .25 .10
❑ 348 Del Unser .25 .10
❑ 349 Rick Camp DP .15 .06
❑ 350 Steve Garvey 2.50 1.00
❑ 351 Jeff Torborg .60 .24
❑ 352 Tony Scott .25 .10
❑ 353 Doug Bair .25 .10
❑ 354 Cesar Geronimo .25 .10
❑ 355 Bill Travers .25 .10
❑ 356 New York Mets 1.25 .25
Team Card CL
❑ 357 Tom Poquette .25 .10
❑ 358 Mark Lemongello .25 .10
❑ 359 Marc Hill .25 .10
❑ 360 Mike Schmidt 10.00 4.00
❑ 361 Chris Knapp .25 .10
❑ 362 Dave May .25 .10
❑ 363 Bob Randall .25 .10
❑ 364 Jerry Turner .25 .10
❑ 365 Ed Figueroa .25 .10
❑ 366 Larry Milbourne DP .15 .06
❑ 367 Rick Dempsey .60 .24
❑ 368 Balor Moore .25 .10
❑ 369 Tim Nordbrook .25 .10
❑ 370 Rusty Staub 1.25 .50
❑ 371 Ray Burris .25 .10
❑ 372 Brian Asselstine .25 .10
❑ 373 Jim Willoughby .25 .10
❑ 374 Jose Morales .25 .10
❑ 375 Tommy John 1.25 .50
❑ 376 Jim Wohlford .25 .10
❑ 377 Manny Sarmiento .25 .10
❑ 378 Bobby Winkles MG .25 .10
❑ 379 Skip Lockwood .25 .10
❑ 380 Ted Simmons .60 .24
❑ 381 Philadelphia Phillies 1.25 .25
Team Card CL
❑ 382 Joe Lahoud .25 .10
❑ 383 Mario Mendoza .25 .10
❑ 384 Jack Clark 1.25 .50
❑ 385 Tito Fuentes .25 .10
❑ 386 Bob Gorinski .25 .10
❑ 387 Ken Holtzman .60 .24
❑ 388 Bill Fahey DP .15 .06
❑ 389 Julio Gonzalez .25 .10
❑ 390 Oscar Gamble .60 .24
❑ 391 Larry Haney .25 .10
❑ 392 Billy Almon .25 .10
❑ 393 Tippy Martinez .60 .24
❑ 394 Roy Howell DP .15 .06
❑ 395 Jim Hughes .25 .10
❑ 396 Bob Stinson DP .15 .06
❑ 397 Greg Gross .25 .10
❑ 398 Don Hood .25 .10
❑ 399 Pete Mackanin .25 .10
❑ 400 Nolan Ryan 25.00 10.00
❑ 401 Sparky Anderson MG .60 .24
❑ 402 Dave Campbell .25 .10
❑ 403 Bud Harrelson .60 .24
❑ 404 Detroit Tigers 1.25 .25
Team Card CL
❑ 405 Rawly Eastwick .25 .10
❑ 406 Mike Jorgensen .25 .10
❑ 407 Odell Jones .25 .10
❑ 408 Joe Zdeb .25 .10
❑ 409 Ron Schueler .25 .10
❑ 410 Bill Madlock .60 .24
❑ 411 Mickey Rivers ALCS .60 .24
❑ 412 Davey Lopes NLCS .60 .24
❑ 413 Reggie Jackson WS 4.00 1.60
❑ 414 Darold Knowles DP .15 .06
❑ 415 Ray Fosse .25 .10
❑ 416 Jack Brohamer .25 .10
❑ 417 Mike Garman DP .15 .06
❑ 418 Tony Muser .25 .10
❑ 419 Jerry Garvin .25 .10
❑ 420 Greg Luzinski 1.25 .50
❑ 421 Junior Moore .25 .10
❑ 422 Steve Braun .25 .10
❑ 423 Dave Rosello .25 .10
❑ 424 Boston Red Sox 1.25 .25
Team Card CL
❑ 425 Steve Rogers DP .25 .10
❑ 426 Fred Kendall .25 .10
❑ 427 Mario Soto RC .60 .24
❑ 428 Joel Youngblood .25 .10
❑ 429 Mike Barlow .25 .10
❑ 430 Al Oliver .60 .24
❑ 431 Butch Metzger .25 .10
❑ 432 Terry Bulling .25 .10
❑ 433 Fernando Gonzalez .25 .10
❑ 434 Mike Norris .25 .10
❑ 435 Checklist 364-484 1.25 .25
❑ 436 Vic Harris DP .15 .06
❑ 437 Bo McLaughlin .25 .10
❑ 438 John Ellis .25 .10
❑ 439 Ken Kravec .25 .10
❑ 440 Dave Lopes .60 .24
❑ 441 Larry Gura .25 .10
❑ 442 Elliott Maddox .25 .10
❑ 443 Darrel Chaney .25 .10
❑ 444 Roy Hartsfield MG .25 .10
❑ 445 Mike Ivie .25 .10
❑ 446 Tug McGraw .60 .24
❑ 447 Leroy Stanton .25 .10
❑ 448 Bill Castro .25 .10
❑ 449 Tim Blackwell DP .15 .06
❑ 450 Tom Seaver 6.00 2.40
❑ 451 Minnesota Twins 1.25 .25
Team Card CL
❑ 452 Jerry Mumphrey .25 .10
❑ 453 Doug Flynn .25 .10
❑ 454 Dave LaRoche .25 .10
❑ 455 Bill Robinson .60 .24
❑ 456 Vern Ruhle .25 .10
❑ 457 Bob Bailey .25 .10
❑ 458 Jeff Newman .25 .10
❑ 459 Charlie Spikes .25 .10
❑ 460 Jim Hunter 2.50 1.00
❑ 461 Rob Andrews DP .15 .06
❑ 462 Rogelio Moret .25 .10
❑ 463 Kevin Bell .25 .10
❑ 464 Jerry Grote .25 .10
❑ 465 Hal McRae .60 .24
❑ 466 Dennis Blair .25 .10
❑ 467 Alvin Dark MG .60 .24
❑ 468 Warren Cromartie RC .60 .24
❑ 469 Rick Cerone .60 .24
❑ 470 J.R. Richard .60 .24
❑ 471 Roy Smalley .60 .24
❑ 472 Ron Reed .25 .10
❑ 473 Bill Buckner .60 .24
❑ 474 Jim Slaton .25 .10
❑ 475 Gary Matthews .60 .24
❑ 476 Bill Stein .25 .10
❑ 477 Doug Capilla .25 .10
❑ 478 Jerry Remy .25 .10
❑ 479 St. Louis Cardinals 1.25 .25
Team Card CL
❑ 480 Ron LeFlore .60 .24
❑ 481 Jackson Todd .25 .10
❑ 482 Rick Miller .25 .10
❑ 483 Ken Macha RC .25 .10
❑ 484 Jim Norris .25 .10
❑ 485 Chris Chambliss .60 .24
❑ 486 John Curtis .25 .10
❑ 487 Jim Tyrone .25 .10
❑ 488 Dan Spillner .25 .10
❑ 489 Rudy Meoli .25 .10
❑ 490 Amos Otis .60 .24
❑ 491 Scott McGregor .60 .24
❑ 492 Jim Sundberg .60 .24
❑ 493 Steve Renko .25 .10
❑ 494 Chuck Tanner MG .60 .24
❑ 495 Dave Cash .25 .10
❑ 496 Jim Clancy DP .15 .06
❑ 497 Glenn Adams .25 .10
❑ 498 Joe Sambito .25 .10
❑ 499 Seattle Mariners 1.25 .25
Team Card CL
❑ 500 George Foster 1.25 .50
❑ 501 Dave Roberts .25 .10
❑ 502 Pat Rockett .25 .10
❑ 503 Ike Hampton .25 .10
❑ 504 Roger Freed .25 .10
❑ 505 Felix Millan .25 .10
❑ 506 Ron Blomberg .25 .10
❑ 507 Willie Crawford .25 .10
❑ 508 Johnny Oates .60 .24
❑ 509 Brent Strom .25 .10
❑ 510 Willie Stargell 2.50 1.00
❑ 511 Frank Duffy .25 .10
❑ 512 Larry Herndon .25 .10
❑ 513 Barry Foote .25 .10
❑ 514 Rob Sperring .25 .10
❑ 515 Tim Corcoran .25 .10
❑ 516 Gary Beare .25 .10
❑ 517 Andres Mora .25 .10
❑ 518 Tommy Boggs DP .15 .06
❑ 519 Brian Downing .60 .24
❑ 520 Larry Hisle .25 .10
❑ 521 Steve Staggs .25 .10
❑ 522 Dick Williams MG .60 .24
❑ 523 Donnie Moore RC .25 .10
❑ 524 Bernie Carbo .25 .10
❑ 525 Jerry Terrell .25 .10
❑ 526 Cincinnati Reds 1.25 .25
Team Card CL
❑ 527 Vic Correll .25 .10
❑ 528 Rob Picciolo .25 .10
❑ 529 Paul Hartzell .25 .10
❑ 530 Dave Winfield 4.00 1.60
❑ 531 Tom Underwood .25 .10

Card	NM	Ex
❑ 532 Skip Jutze	.25	.10
❑ 533 Sandy Alomar	.60	.24
❑ 534 Wilbur Howard	.25	.10
❑ 535 Checklist 485-605	1.25	.25
❑ 536 Roric Harrison	.25	.10
❑ 537 Bruce Bochte	.25	.10
❑ 538 Johnny LeMaster	.25	.10
❑ 539 Vic Davalillo DP	.15	.06
❑ 540 Steve Carlton	4.00	1.60
❑ 541 Larry Cox	.25	.10
❑ 542 Tim Johnson	.25	.10
❑ 543 Larry Harlow DP	.15	.06
❑ 544 Len Randle DP	.15	.06
❑ 545 Bill Campbell	.25	.10
❑ 546 Ted Martinez	.25	.10
❑ 547 John Scott	.25	.10
❑ 548 Billy Hunter DP MG	.15	.06
❑ 549 Joe Kerrigan	.25	.10
❑ 550 John Mayberry	.60	.24
❑ 551 Atlanta Braves	1.25	.25
Team Card CL		
❑ 552 Francisco Barrios	.25	.10
❑ 553 Terry Puhl	.60	.24
❑ 554 Joe Coleman	.25	.10
❑ 555 Butch Wynegar	.25	.10
❑ 556 Ed Armbrister	.25	.10
❑ 557 Tony Solaita	.25	.10
❑ 558 Paul Mitchell	.25	.10
❑ 559 Phil Mankowski	.25	.10
❑ 560 Dave Parker	1.25	.50
❑ 561 Charlie Williams	.25	.10
❑ 562 Glenn Burke	.25	.10
❑ 563 Dave Rader	.25	.10
❑ 564 Mick Kelleher	.25	.10
❑ 565 Jerry Koosman	.60	.24
❑ 566 Merv Rettenmund	.25	.10
❑ 567 Dick Drago	.25	.10
❑ 568 Tom Hutton	.25	.10
❑ 569 Lary Sorensen	.25	.10
❑ 570 Dave Kingman	1.25	.50
❑ 571 Buck Martinez	.25	.10
❑ 572 Rick Wise	.25	.10
❑ 573 Luis Gomez	.25	.10
❑ 574 Bob Lemon MG	1.25	.50
❑ 575 Pat Dobson	.25	.10
❑ 576 Sam Mejias	.25	.10
❑ 577 Oakland A's	1.25	.25
Team Card CL		
❑ 578 Buzz Capra	.25	.10
❑ 579 Rance Mulliniks	.25	.10
❑ 580 Rod Carew	4.00	1.60
❑ 581 Lynn McGlothen	.25	.10
❑ 582 Fran Healy	.25	.10
❑ 583 George Medich	.25	.10
❑ 584 John Hale	.25	.10
❑ 585 Woodie Fryman DP	.15	.06
❑ 586 Ed Goodson	.25	.10
❑ 587 John Urrea	.25	.10
❑ 588 Jim Mason	.25	.10
❑ 589 Bob Knepper	.25	.10
❑ 590 Bobby Murcer	.60	.24
❑ 591 George Zeber	.25	.10
❑ 592 Bob Apodaca	.25	.10
❑ 593 Dave Skaggs	.25	.10
❑ 594 Dave Freisleben	.25	.10
❑ 595 Sixto Lezcano	.25	.10
❑ 596 Gary Wheelock	.25	.10
❑ 597 Steve Dillard	.25	.10
❑ 598 Eddie Solomon	.25	.10
❑ 599 Gary Woods	.25	.10
❑ 600 Frank Tanana	.60	.24
❑ 601 Gene Mauch MG	.60	.24
❑ 602 Eric Soderholm	.25	.10
❑ 603 Will McEnaney	.25	.10
❑ 604 Earl Williams	.25	.10
❑ 605 Rick Rhoden	.60	.24
❑ 606 Pittsburgh Pirates	1.25	.25
Team Card CL		
❑ 607 Fernando Arroyo	.25	.10
❑ 608 Johnny Grubb	.25	.10
❑ 609 John Denny	.25	.10
❑ 610 Garry Maddox	.60	.24
❑ 611 Pat Scanlon	.25	.10
❑ 612 Ken Henderson	.25	.10
❑ 613 Marty Perez	.25	.10
❑ 614 Joe Wallis	.25	.10
❑ 615 Clay Carroll	.25	.10
❑ 616 Pat Kelly	.25	.10
❑ 617 Joe Nolan	.25	.10
❑ 618 Tommy Helms	.25	.10
❑ 619 Thad Bosley DP	.15	.06
❑ 620 Willie Randolph	1.25	.50
❑ 621 Craig Swan DP	.15	.06
❑ 622 Champ Summers	.25	.10
❑ 623 Eduardo Rodriguez	.25	.10
❑ 624 Gary Alexander DP	.15	.06
❑ 625 Jose Cruz	.60	.24
❑ 626 Toronto Blue Jays	1.25	.25
Team Card CL DP		
❑ 627 David Johnson	.25	.10
❑ 628 Ralph Garr	.60	.24
❑ 629 Don Stanhouse	.25	.10
❑ 630 Ron Cey	1.25	.50
❑ 631 Danny Ozark MG	.25	.10
❑ 632 Rowland Office	.25	.10
❑ 633 Tom Veryzer	.25	.10
❑ 634 Len Barker	.25	.10
❑ 635 Joe Rudi	.60	.24
❑ 636 Jim Bibby	.25	.10
❑ 637 Duffy Dyer	.25	.10
❑ 638 Paul Splittorff	.25	.10
❑ 639 Gene Clines	.25	.10
❑ 640 Lee May DP	.25	.10
❑ 641 Doug Rau	.25	.10
❑ 642 Denny Doyle	.25	.10
❑ 643 Tom House	.25	.10
❑ 644 Jim Dwyer	.25	.10
❑ 645 Mike Torrez	.60	.24
❑ 646 Rick Auerbach DP	.15	.06
❑ 647 Steve Dunning	.25	.10
❑ 648 Gary Thomasson	.25	.10
❑ 649 Moose Haas	.25	.10
❑ 650 Cesar Cedeno	.60	.24
❑ 651 Doug Rader	.25	.10
❑ 652 Checklist 606-726	1.25	.25
❑ 653 Ron Hodges DP	.15	.06
❑ 654 Pepe Frias	.25	.10
❑ 655 Lyman Bostock	.60	.24
❑ 656 Dave Garcia MG	.25	.10
❑ 657 Bombo Rivera	.25	.10
❑ 658 Manny Sanguillen	.60	.24
❑ 659 Texas Rangers	1.25	.25
Team Card CL		
❑ 660 Jason Thompson	.60	.24
❑ 661 Grant Jackson	.25	.10
❑ 662 Paul Dade	.25	.10
❑ 663 Paul Reuschel	.25	.10
❑ 664 Fred Stanley	.25	.10
❑ 665 Dennis Leonard	.60	.24
❑ 666 Billy Smith RC	.25	.10
❑ 667 Jeff Byrd	.25	.10
❑ 668 Dusty Baker	1.25	.50
❑ 669 Pete Falcone	.25	.10
❑ 670 Jim Rice	1.25	.50
❑ 671 Gary Lavelle	.25	.10
❑ 672 Don Kessinger	.60	.24
❑ 673 Steve Brye	.25	.10
❑ 674 Ray Knight RC	2.50	1.00
❑ 675 Jay Johnstone	.60	.24
❑ 676 Bob Myrick	.25	.10
❑ 677 Ed Herrmann	.25	.10
❑ 678 Tom Burgmeier	.25	.10
❑ 679 Wayne Garrett	.25	.10
❑ 680 Vida Blue	.60	.24
❑ 681 Rob Belloir	.25	.10
❑ 682 Ken Brett	.25	.10
❑ 683 Mike Champion	.25	.10
❑ 684 Ralph Houk MG	.60	.24
❑ 685 Frank Taveras	.25	.10
❑ 686 Gaylord Perry	2.50	1.00
❑ 687 Julio Cruz RC	.25	.10
❑ 688 George Mitterwald	.25	.10
❑ 689 Cleveland Indians	1.25	.25
Team Card CL		
❑ 690 Mickey Rivers	.60	.24
❑ 691 Ross Grimsley	.25	.10
❑ 692 Ken Reitz	.25	.10
❑ 693 Lamar Johnson	.25	.10
❑ 694 Elias Sosa	.25	.10
❑ 695 Dwight Evans	1.25	.50
❑ 696 Steve Mingori	.25	.10
❑ 697 Roger Metzger	.25	.10
❑ 698 Juan Bernhardt	.25	.10
❑ 699 Jackie Brown	.25	.10
❑ 700 Johnny Bench	8.00	3.20
❑ 701 Tom Hume	.60	.24
Larry Landreth		
Steve McCatty		
Bruce Taylor		
❑ 702 Bill Nahorodny	.60	.24
Kevin Pasley		
Rick Sweet		
Don Werner		
❑ 703 Larry Andersen	5.00	2.00
Tim Jones		
Mickey Mahler		
Jack Morris RC DP		
❑ 704 Garth Iorg	8.00	3.20
Dave Oliver		
Sam Perlozzo		
Lou Whitaker RC		
❑ 705 Dave Bergman	1.25	.50
Miguel Dilone		
Clint Hurdle		
Willie Norwood		
❑ 706 Wayne Cage	.60	.24
Ted Cox		
Pat Putnam		
Dave Revering		
❑ 707 Mickey Klutts	50.00	20.00
Paul Molitor RC		
Alan Trammell RC		
U.L. Washington		
❑ 708 Bo Diaz	4.00	1.60
Dale Murphy		
Lance Parrish RC		
Ernie Whitt		
❑ 709 Steve Burke	.60	.24
Matt Keough		
Lance Rautzhan		
Dan Schatzeder		
❑ 710 Dell Alston	1.25	.50
Rick Bosetti		
Mike Easler RC		
Keith Smith		
❑ 711 Cardell Camper	.25	.10
Dennis Lamp		
Craig Mitchell		
Roy Thomas DP		
❑ 712 Bobby Valentine	.60	.24
❑ 713 Bob Davis	.25	.10
❑ 714 Mike Anderson	.25	.10
❑ 715 Jim Kaat	1.25	.50
❑ 716 Clarence Gaston	.60	.24
❑ 717 Nelson Briles	.25	.10
❑ 718 Ron Jackson	.25	.10
❑ 719 Randy Elliott	.25	.10
❑ 720 Fergie Jenkins	2.50	1.00
❑ 721 Billy Martin MG	1.25	.50
❑ 722 Pete Broberg	.25	.10
❑ 723 John Wockenfuss	.25	.10
❑ 724 Kansas City Royals	1.25	.25
Team Card CL		
❑ 725 Kurt Bevacqua	.25	.10
❑ 726 Wilbur Wood	1.25	.30

1979 Topps

	NM	Ex
COMPLETE SET (726)	175.00	70.00

COMMON CARD (1-726) .25 .10
COMMON CARD DP .15 .06

❑ 1 Rod Carew 2.50 .50
Dave Parker LL
❑ 2 Jim Rice 1.00 .40
George Foster LL
❑ 3 Jim Rice 1.00 .40
George Foster LL
❑ 4 Ron LeFlore .50 .20
Omar Moreno LL
❑ 5 Ron Guidry .50 .20
Gaylord Perry LL
❑ 6 Nolan Ryan 5.00 2.00
J.R. Richard LL
❑ 7 Ron Guidry .50 .20
Craig Swan LL
❑ 8 Rich Gossage 1.00 .40
Rollie Fingers LL
❑ 9 Dave Campbell .25 .10
❑ 10 Lee May .50 .20
❑ 11 Marc Hill .25 .10
❑ 12 Dick Drago .25 .10
❑ 13 Paul Dade .25 .10
❑ 14 Rafael Landestoy .25 .10
❑ 15 Ross Grimsley .25 .10
❑ 16 Fred Stanley .25 .10
❑ 17 Donnie Moore .25 .10
❑ 18 Tony Solaita .25 .10
❑ 19 Larry Gura DP .15 .06
❑ 20 Joe Morgan DP 2.00 .80
❑ 21 Kevin Kobel .25 .10
❑ 22 Mike Jorgensen .25 .10
❑ 23 Terry Forster .25 .10
❑ 24 Paul Molitor 10.00 4.00
❑ 25 Steve Carlton 3.00 1.20
❑ 26 Jamie Quirk .25 .10
❑ 27 Dave Goltz .25 .10
❑ 28 Steve Brye .25 .10
❑ 29 Rick Langford .25 .10
❑ 30 Dave Winfield 4.00 1.60
❑ 31 Tom House DP .15 .06
❑ 32 Jerry Mumphrey .25 .10
❑ 33 Dave Rozema .25 .10
❑ 34 Rob Andrews .25 .10
❑ 35 Ed Figueroa .25 .10
❑ 36 Alan Ashby .25 .10
❑ 37 Joe Kerrigan DP .15 .06
❑ 38 Bernie Carbo .25 .10
❑ 39 Dale Murphy 3.00 1.20
❑ 40 Dennis Eckersley 2.00 .80
❑ 41 Twins Team CL 1.00 .20
Gene Mauch MG
❑ 42 Ron Blomberg .25 .10
❑ 43 Wayne Twitchell .25 .10
❑ 44 Kurt Bevacqua .25 .10
❑ 45 Al Hrabosky .25 .10
❑ 46 Ron Hodges .25 .10
❑ 47 Fred Norman .25 .10
❑ 48 Merv Rettenmund .25 .10
❑ 49 Vern Ruhle .25 .10
❑ 50 Steve Garvey DP 1.00 .40
❑ 51 Ray Fosse DP .15 .06
❑ 52 Randy Lerch .25 .10
❑ 53 Mick Kelleher .25 .10
❑ 54 Dell Alston DP .15 .06
❑ 55 Willie Stargell 2.00 .80
❑ 56 John Hale .25 .10
❑ 57 Eric Rasmussen .25 .10
❑ 58 Bob Randall DP .15 .06
❑ 59 John Denny DP .25 .10
❑ 60 Mickey Rivers .50 .20
❑ 61 Bo Diaz .25 .10
❑ 62 Randy Moffitt .25 .10
❑ 63 Jack Brohamer .25 .10
❑ 64 Tom Underwood .25 .10
❑ 65 Mark Belanger .50 .20
❑ 66 Tigers Team CL 1.00 .20
Les Moss MG
❑ 67 Jim Mason DP .15 .06
❑ 68 Joe Niekro DP .25 .10
❑ 69 Elliott Maddox .25 .10
❑ 70 John Candelaria .50 .20
❑ 71 Brian Downing .50 .20
❑ 72 Steve Mingori .25 .10
❑ 73 Ken Henderson .25 .10
❑ 74 Shane Rawley .25 .10
❑ 75 Steve Yeager .50 .20
❑ 76 Warren Cromartie .50 .20
❑ 77 Dan Briggs DP .15 .06
❑ 78 Elias Sosa .25 .10
❑ 79 Ted Cox .25 .10
❑ 80 Jason Thompson .50 .20
❑ 81 Roger Erickson .25 .10
❑ 82 Mets Team CL 1.00 .20
Joe Torre MG
❑ 83 Fred Kendall .25 .10
❑ 84 Greg Minton .25 .10
❑ 85 Gary Matthews .50 .20
❑ 86 Rodney Scott .25 .10
❑ 87 Pete Falcone .25 .10
❑ 88 Bob Molinaro .25 .10
❑ 89 Dick Tidrow .25 .10
❑ 90 Bob Boone 1.00 .40
❑ 91 Terry Crowley .25 .10
❑ 92 Jim Bibby .25 .10
❑ 93 Phil Mankowski .25 .10
❑ 94 Len Barker .25 .10
❑ 95 Robin Yount 5.00 2.00
❑ 96 Indians Team CL 1.00 .20
Jeff Torborg
❑ 97 Sam Mejias .25 .10
❑ 98 Ray Burris .25 .10
❑ 99 John Wathan .50 .20
❑ 100 Tom Seaver DP 4.00 1.60
❑ 101 Roy Howell .25 .10
❑ 102 Mike Anderson .25 .10
❑ 103 Jim Todd .25 .10
❑ 104 Johnny Oates DP .25 .10
❑ 105 Rick Camp DP .15 .06
❑ 106 Frank Duffy .25 .10
❑ 107 Jesus Alou DP .15 .06
❑ 108 Eduardo Rodriguez .25 .10
❑ 109 Joel Youngblood .25 .10
❑ 110 Vida Blue .50 .20
❑ 111 Roger Freed .25 .10
❑ 112 Phillies Team 1.00 .20
Danny Ozark MG
❑ 113 Pete Redfern .25 .10
❑ 114 Cliff Johnson .25 .10
❑ 115 Nolan Ryan 20.00 8.00
❑ 116 Ozzie Smith RC 60.00 24.00
❑ 117 Grant Jackson .25 .10
❑ 118 Bud Harrelson .50 .20
❑ 119 Don Stanhouse .25 .10
❑ 120 Jim Sundberg .50 .20
❑ 121 Checklist 1-121 DP .50 .10
❑ 122 Mike Paxton .25 .10
❑ 123 Lou Whitaker 2.50 1.00
❑ 124 Dan Schatzeder .25 .10
❑ 125 Rick Burleson .25 .10
❑ 126 Doug Bair .25 .10
❑ 127 Thad Bosley .25 .10
❑ 128 Ted Martinez .25 .10
❑ 129 Marty Pattin DP .15 .06
❑ 130 Bob Watson DP .25 .10
❑ 131 Jim Clancy .25 .10
❑ 132 Rowland Office .25 .10
❑ 133 Bill Castro .25 .10
❑ 134 Alan Bannister .25 .10
❑ 135 Bobby Murcer .50 .20
❑ 136 Jim Kaat .50 .20
❑ 137 Larry Wolfe DP .15 .06
❑ 138 Mark Lee RC .25 .10
❑ 139 Luis Pujols .25 .10
❑ 140 Don Gullett .50 .20
❑ 141 Tom Paciorek .50 .20
❑ 142 Charlie Williams .25 .10
❑ 143 Tony Scott .25 .10
❑ 144 Sandy Alomar .25 .10
❑ 145 Rick Rhoden .25 .10
❑ 146 Duane Kuiper .25 .10
❑ 147 Dave Hamilton .25 .10
❑ 148 Bruce Boisclair .25 .10
❑ 149 Manny Sarmiento .25 .10
❑ 150 Wayne Cage .25 .10
❑ 151 John Hiller .25 .10
❑ 152 Rick Cerone .25 .10
❑ 153 Dennis Lamp .25 .10
❑ 154 Jim Gantner DP .25 .10
❑ 155 Dwight Evans 1.00 .40
❑ 156 Buddy Solomon .25 .10
❑ 157 U.L. Washington UER .25 .10
(Sic, bats left,
should be right)
❑ 158 Joe Sambito .25 .10
❑ 159 Roy White .50 .20
❑ 160 Mike Flanagan 1.00 .40
❑ 161 Barry Foote .25 .10
❑ 162 Tom Johnson .25 .10
❑ 163 Glenn Burke .25 .10
❑ 164 Mickey Lolich .50 .20
❑ 165 Frank Taveras .25 .10
❑ 166 Leon Roberts .25 .10
❑ 167 Roger Metzger DP .15 .06
❑ 168 Dave Freisleben .25 .10
❑ 169 Bill Nahorodny .25 .10
❑ 170 Don Sutton 2.00 .80
❑ 171 Gene Clines .25 .10
❑ 172 Mike Bruhert .25 .10
❑ 173 John Lowenstein .25 .10
❑ 174 Rick Auerbach .25 .10
❑ 175 George Hendrick 1.00 .40
❑ 176 Aurelio Rodriguez .25 .10
❑ 177 Ron Reed .25 .10
❑ 178 Alvis Woods .25 .10
❑ 179 Jim Beattie DP .15 .06
❑ 180 Larry Hisle .25 .10
❑ 181 Mike Garman .25 .10
❑ 182 Tim Johnson .25 .10
❑ 183 Paul Splittorff .25 .10
❑ 184 Darrel Chaney .25 .10
❑ 185 Mike Torrez .50 .20
❑ 186 Eric Soderholm .25 .10
❑ 187 Mark Lemongello .25 .10
❑ 188 Pat Kelly .25 .10
❑ 189 Eddie Whitson RC .25 .10
❑ 190 Ron Cey .50 .20
❑ 191 Mike Norris .25 .10
❑ 192 Cardinals Team CL 1.00 .20
Ken Boyer MG
❑ 193 Glenn Adams .25 .10
❑ 194 Randy Jones .25 .10
❑ 195 Bill Madlock .50 .20
❑ 196 Steve Kemp DP .25 .10
❑ 197 Bob Apodaca .25 .10
❑ 198 Johnny Grubb .25 .10
❑ 199 Larry Milbourne .25 .10
❑ 200 Johnny Bench DP 5.00 2.00
❑ 201 Mike Edwards RB .25 .10
❑ 202 Ron Guidry RB .50 .20
❑ 203 J.R. Richard RB .25 .10
❑ 204 Pete Rose RB 5.00 2.00
❑ 205 John Stearns RB .25 .10
❑ 206 Sammy Stewart RB .25 .10
❑ 207 Dave Lemanczyk .25 .10
❑ 208 Clarence Gaston .25 .10
❑ 209 Reggie Cleveland .25 .10
❑ 210 Larry Bowa .50 .20
❑ 211 Denny Martinez 2.00 .80
❑ 212 Carney Lansford RC 1.00 .40
❑ 213 Bill Travers .25 .10
❑ 214 Red Sox Team CL 1.00 .20
Don Zimmer MG
❑ 215 Willie McCovey 2.50 1.00
❑ 216 Wilbur Wood .25 .10
❑ 217 Steve Dillard .25 .10
❑ 218 Dennis Leonard .50 .20
❑ 219 Roy Smalley .50 .20
❑ 220 Cesar Geronimo .25 .10
❑ 221 Jesse Jefferson .25 .10
❑ 222 Bob Beall .25 .10
❑ 223 Kent Tekulve .50 .20
❑ 224 Dave Revering .25 .10
❑ 225 Goose Gossage 1.00 .40
❑ 226 Ron Pruitt .25 .10
❑ 227 Steve Stone .50 .20
❑ 228 Vic Davalillo .25 .10
❑ 229 Doug Flynn .25 .10
❑ 230 Bob Forsch .25 .10
❑ 231 John Wockenfuss .25 .10
❑ 232 Jimmy Sexton .25 .10
❑ 233 Paul Mitchell .25 .10
❑ 234 Toby Harrah .50 .20
❑ 235 Steve Rogers .25 .10
❑ 236 Jim Dwyer .25 .10
❑ 237 Billy Smith .25 .10
❑ 238 Balor Moore .25 .10

❑	239	Willie Horton	.50	.20
❑	240	Rick Reuschel	.50	.20
❑	241	Checklist 122-242 DP	.50	.10
❑	242	Pablo Torrealba	.25	.10
❑	243	Buck Martinez DP	.15	.06
❑	244	Pirates Team CL	1.00	.20
		Chuck Tanner MG		
❑	245	Jeff Burroughs	.50	.20
❑	246	Darrell Jackson	.25	.10
❑	247	Tucker Ashford DP	.15	.06
❑	248	Pete LaCock	.25	.10
❑	249	Paul Thormodsgard	.25	.10
❑	250	Willie Randolph	.50	.20
❑	251	Jack Morris	2.00	.80
❑	252	Bob Stinson	.25	.10
❑	253	Rick Wise	.25	.10
❑	254	Luis Gomez	.25	.10
❑	255	Tommy John	1.00	.40
❑	256	Mike Sadek	.25	.10
❑	257	Adrian Devine	.25	.10
❑	258	Mike Phillips	.25	.10
❑	259	Reds Team CL	1.00	.20
		Sparky Anderson MG		
❑	260	Richie Zisk	.25	.10
❑	261	Mario Guerrero	.25	.10
❑	262	Nelson Briles	.25	.10
❑	263	Oscar Gamble	.50	.20
❑	264	Don Robinson RC	.25	.10
❑	265	Don Money	.25	.10
❑	266	Jim Willoughby	.25	.10
❑	267	Joe Rudi	.50	.20
❑	268	Julio Gonzalez	.25	.10
❑	269	Woodie Fryman	.25	.10
❑	270	Butch Hobson	.50	.20
❑	271	Rawly Eastwick	.25	.10
❑	272	Tim Corcoran	.25	.10
❑	273	Jerry Terrell	.25	.10
❑	274	Willie Norwood	.25	.10
❑	275	Junior Moore	.25	.10
❑	276	Jim Colborn	.25	.10
❑	277	Tom Grieve	.50	.20
❑	278	Andy Messersmith	.50	.20
❑	279	Jerry Grote DP	.15	.06
❑	280	Andre Thornton	.50	.20
❑	281	Vic Correll DP	.15	.06
❑	282	Blue Jays Team CL	.50	.10
		Roy Hartsfield MG		
❑	283	Ken Kravec	.25	.10
❑	284	Johnnie LeMaster	.25	.10
❑	285	Bobby Bonds	1.00	.40
❑	286	Duffy Dyer	.25	.10
❑	287	Andres Mora	.25	.10
❑	288	Milt Wilcox	.25	.10
❑	289	Jose Cruz	1.00	.40
❑	290	Dave Lopes	.50	.20
❑	291	Tom Griffin	.25	.10
❑	292	Don Reynolds	.25	.10
❑	293	Jerry Garvin	.25	.10
❑	294	Pepe Frias	.25	.10
❑	295	Mitchell Page	.25	.10
❑	296	Preston Hanna	.25	.10
❑	297	Ted Sizemore	.25	.10
❑	298	Rich Gale	.25	.10
❑	299	Steve Ontiveros	.25	.10
❑	300	Rod Carew	3.00	1.20
❑	301	Tom Hume	.25	.10
❑	302	Braves Team CL	1.00	.20
		Bobby Cox MG		
❑	303	Lary Sorensen DP	.15	.06
❑	304	Steve Swisher	.25	.10
❑	305	Willie Montanez	.25	.10
❑	306	Floyd Bannister	.25	.10
❑	307	Larvell Blanks	.25	.10
❑	308	Bert Blyleven	1.00	.40
❑	309	Ralph Garr	.50	.20
❑	310	Thurman Munson	3.00	1.20
❑	311	Gary Lavelle	.25	.10
❑	312	Bob Robertson	.25	.10
❑	313	Dyar Miller	.25	.10
❑	314	Larry Harlow	.25	.10
❑	315	Jon Matlack	.25	.10
❑	316	Milt May	.25	.10
❑	317	Jose Cardenal	.50	.20
❑	318	Bob Welch RC	2.00	.80
❑	319	Wayne Garrett	.25	.10
❑	320	Carl Yastrzemski	5.00	2.00
❑	321	Gaylord Perry	2.00	.80
❑	322	Danny Goodwin	.25	.10
❑	323	Lynn McGlothen	.25	.10
❑	324	Mike Tyson	.25	.10
❑	325	Cecil Cooper	.50	.20
❑	326	Pedro Borbon	.25	.10
❑	327	Art Howe DP	.25	.10
❑	328	A's Team CL	1.00	.20
		Jack McKeon MG		
❑	329	Joe Coleman	.25	.10
❑	330	George Brett	10.00	4.00
❑	331	Mickey Mahler	.25	.10
❑	332	Gary Alexander	.25	.10
❑	333	Chet Lemon	.50	.20
❑	334	Craig Swan	.25	.10
❑	335	Chris Chambliss	.50	.20
❑	336	Bobby Thompson	.25	.10
❑	337	John Montague	.25	.10
❑	338	Vic Harris	.25	.10
❑	339	Ron Jackson	.25	.10
❑	340	Jim Palmer	2.50	1.00
❑	341	Willie Upshaw	.50	.20
❑	342	Dave Roberts	.25	.10
❑	343	Ed Glynn	.25	.10
❑	344	Jerry Royster	.25	.10
❑	345	Tug McGraw	.50	.20
❑	346	Bill Buckner	.50	.20
❑	347	Doug Rau	.25	.10
❑	348	Andre Dawson	3.00	1.20
❑	349	Jim Wright	.25	.10
❑	350	Garry Templeton	.50	.20
❑	351	Wayne Nordhagen DP	.15	.06
❑	352	Steve Renko	.25	.10
❑	353	Checklist 243-363	1.00	.20
❑	354	Bill Bonham	.25	.10
❑	355	Lee Mazzilli	.25	.10
❑	356	Giants Team CL	1.00	.20
		Joe Altobelli MG		
❑	357	Jerry Augustine	.25	.10
❑	358	Alan Trammell	3.00	1.20
❑	359	Dan Spillner DP	.15	.06
❑	360	Amos Otis	.50	.20
❑	361	Tom Dixon	.25	.10
❑	362	Mike Cubbage	.25	.10
❑	363	Craig Skok	.25	.10
❑	364	Gene Richards	.25	.10
❑	365	Sparky Lyle	.50	.20
❑	366	Juan Bernhardt	.25	.10
❑	367	Dave Skaggs	.25	.10
❑	368	Don Aase	.25	.10
❑	369A	Bump Wills ERR	3.00	1.20
		(Blue Jays)		
❑	369B	Bump Wills COR	3.00	1.20
		(Rangers)		
❑	370	Dave Kingman	1.00	.40
❑	371	Jeff Holly	.25	.10
❑	372	Lamar Johnson	.25	.10
❑	373	Lance Rautzhan	.25	.10
❑	374	Ed Herrmann	.25	.10
❑	375	Bill Campbell	.25	.10
❑	376	Gorman Thomas	.50	.20
❑	377	Paul Moskau	.25	.10
❑	378	Rob Picciolo DP	.15	.06
❑	379	Dale Murray	.25	.10
❑	380	John Mayberry	.50	.20
❑	381	Astros Team CL	1.00	.20
		Bill Virdon MG		
❑	382	Jerry Martin	.25	.10
❑	383	Phil Garner	.50	.20
❑	384	Tommy Boggs	.25	.10
❑	385	Dan Ford	.25	.10
❑	386	Francisco Barrios	.25	.10
❑	387	Gary Thomasson	.25	.10
❑	388	Jack Billingham	.25	.10
❑	389	Joe Zdeb	.25	.10
❑	390	Rollie Fingers	2.00	.80
❑	391	Al Oliver	.50	.20
❑	392	Doug Ault	.25	.10
❑	393	Scott McGregor	.50	.20
❑	394	Randy Stein	.25	.10
❑	395	Dave Cash	.25	.10
❑	396	Bill Plummer	.25	.10
❑	397	Sergio Ferrer	.25	.10
❑	398	Ivan DeJesus	.25	.10
❑	399	David Clyde	.25	.10
❑	400	Jim Rice	1.00	.40
❑	401	Ray Knight	.50	.20
❑	402	Paul Hartzell	.25	.10
❑	403	Tim Foli	.25	.10
❑	404	White Sox Team CL	1.00	.20
		Don Kessinger MG		
❑	405	Butch Wynegar DP	.15	.06
❑	406	Joe Wallis DP	.15	.06
❑	407	Pete Vuckovich	.50	.20
❑	408	Charlie Moore DP	.15	.06
❑	409	Willie Wilson RC	1.00	.40
❑	410	Darrell Evans	1.00	.40
❑	411	George Sisler ATL	2.50	1.00
		Ty Cobb		
❑	412	Hack Wilson ATL	2.50	1.00
		Hank Aaron		
❑	413	Roger Maris ATL	4.00	1.60
		Hank Aaron		
❑	414	Rogers Hornsby ATL	2.50	1.00
		Ty Cobb		
❑	415	Lou Brock ATL	1.00	.40
❑	416	Jack Chesbro ATL	.50	.20
		Cy Young		
❑	417	Nolan Ryan ATL DP	5.00	2.00
		Walter Johnson		
❑	418	D.Leonard ATL DP	.25	.10
		Walter Johnson		
❑	419	Dick Ruthven	.25	.10
❑	420	Ken Griffey Sr.	.50	.20
❑	421	Doug DeCinces	.50	.20
❑	422	Ruppert Jones	.25	.10
❑	423	Bob Montgomery	.25	.10
❑	424	Angels Team CL	1.00	.20
		Jim Fregosi MG		
❑	425	Rick Manning	.25	.10
❑	426	Chris Speier	.25	.10
❑	427	Andy Replogle	.25	.10
❑	428	Bobby Valentine	.50	.20
❑	429	John Urrea DP	.15	.06
❑	430	Dave Parker	.50	.20
❑	431	Glenn Borgmann	.25	.10
❑	432	Dave Heaverlo	.25	.10
❑	433	Larry Biittner	.25	.10
❑	434	Ken Clay	.25	.10
❑	435	Gene Tenace	.50	.20
❑	436	Hector Cruz	.25	.10
❑	437	Rick Williams	.25	.10
❑	438	Horace Speed	.25	.10
❑	439	Frank White	.50	.20
❑	440	Rusty Staub	1.00	.40
❑	441	Lee Lacy	.25	.10
❑	442	Doyle Alexander	.25	.10
❑	443	Bruce Bochte	.25	.10
❑	444	Aurelio Lopez	.25	.10
❑	445	Steve Henderson	.25	.10
❑	446	Jim Lonborg	.50	.20
❑	447	Manny Sanguillen	.50	.20
❑	448	Moose Haas	.25	.10
❑	449	Bombo Rivera	.25	.10
❑	450	Dave Concepcion	1.00	.40
❑	451	Royals Team CL	1.00	.20
		Whitey Herzog MG		
❑	452	Jerry Morales	.25	.10
❑	453	Chris Knapp	.25	.10
❑	454	Len Randle	.25	.10
❑	455	Bill Lee DP	.15	.06
❑	456	Chuck Baker	.25	.10
❑	457	Bruce Sutter	.50	.20
❑	458	Jim Essian	.25	.10
❑	459	Sid Monge	.25	.10
❑	460	Graig Nettles	1.00	.40
❑	461	Jim Barr DP	.15	.06
❑	462	Otto Velez	.25	.10
❑	463	Steve Comer	.25	.10
❑	464	Joe Nolan	.25	.10
❑	465	Reggie Smith	.50	.20
❑	466	Mark Littell	.25	.10
❑	467	Don Kessinger DP	.25	.10
❑	468	Stan Bahnsen DP	.15	.06
❑	469	Lance Parrish	1.00	.40
❑	470	Garry Maddox DP	.25	.10
❑	471	Joaquin Andujar	.50	.20
❑	472	Craig Kusick	.25	.10
❑	473	Dave Roberts	.25	.10
❑	474	Dick Davis	.25	.10
❑	475	Dan Driessen	.25	.10
❑	476	Tom Poquette	.25	.10

477	Bob Grich	.50	.20
478	Juan Beniquez	.25	.10
479	Padres Team CL	1.00	.20
	Roger Craig MG		
480	Fred Lynn	.50	.20
481	Skip Lockwood	.25	.10
482	Craig Reynolds	.25	.10
483	Checklist 364-484 DP	.50	.10
484	Rick Waits	.25	.10
485	Bucky Dent	.50	.20
486	Bob Knepper	.25	.10
487	Miguel Dilone	.25	.10
488	Bob Owchinko	.25	.10
489	Larry Cox UER	.25	.10
	(Photo actually		
	Dave Rader)		
490	Al Cowens	.25	.10
491	Tippy Martinez	.25	.10
492	Bob Bailor	.25	.10
493	Larry Christenson	.25	.10
494	Jerry White	.25	.10
495	Tony Perez	2.00	.80
496	Barry Bonnell DP	.15	.06
497	Glenn Abbott	.25	.10
498	Rich Chiles	.25	.10
499	Rangers Team CL	1.00	.20
	Pat Corrales MG		
500	Ron Guidry	.50	.20
501	Junior Kennedy	.25	.10
502	Steve Braun	.25	.10
503	Terry Humphrey	.25	.10
504	Larry McWilliams	.25	.10
505	Ed Kranepool	.25	.10
506	John D'Acquisto	.25	.10
507	Tony Armas	.50	.20
508	Charlie Hough	.50	.20
509	Mario Mendoza UER	.25	.10
	(Career BA .278,		
	should say .204)		
510	Ted Simmons	1.00	.40
511	Paul Reuschel DP	.15	.06
512	Jack Clark	.50	.20
513	Dave Johnson	.50	.20
514	Mike Proly	.25	.10
515	Enos Cabell	.25	.10
516	Champ Summers DP	.15	.06
517	Al Bumbry	.50	.20
518	Jim Umbarger	.25	.10
519	Ben Oglivie	.50	.20
520	Gary Carter	1.00	.40
521	Sam Ewing	.25	.10
522	Ken Holtzman	.50	.20
523	John Milner	.25	.10
524	Tom Burgmeier	.25	.10
525	Freddie Patek	.25	.10
526	Dodgers Team CL	1.00	.20
	Tom Lasorda MG		
527	Lerrin LaGrow	.25	.10
528	Wayne Gross DP	.15	.06
529	Brian Asselstine	.25	.10
530	Frank Tanana	.50	.20
531	Fernando Gonzalez	.25	.10
532	Buddy Schultz	.25	.10
533	Leroy Stanton	.25	.10
534	Ken Forsch	.25	.10
535	Ellis Valentine	.25	.10
536	Jerry Reuss	.50	.20
537	Tom Veryzer	.25	.10
538	Mike Ivie DP	.15	.06
539	John Ellis	.25	.10
540	Greg Luzinski	.50	.20
541	Jim Slaton	.25	.10
542	Rick Bosetti	.25	.10
543	Kiko Garcia	.25	.10
544	Fergie Jenkins	2.00	.80
545	John Stearns	.25	.10
546	Bill Russell	.50	.20
547	Clint Hurdle	.25	.10
548	Enrique Romo	.25	.10
549	Bob Bailey	.25	.10
550	Sal Bando	.50	.20
551	Cubs Team CL	1.00	.20
	Herman Franks MG		
552	Jose Morales	.25	.10
553	Denny Walling	.25	.10
554	Matt Keough	.25	.10
555	Biff Pocoroba	.25	.10
556	Mike Lum	.25	.10
557	Ken Brett	.25	.10
558	Jay Johnstone	.50	.20
559	Greg Pryor	.25	.10
560	John Montefusco	.25	.10
561	Ed Ott	.25	.10
562	Dusty Baker	1.00	.40
563	Roy Thomas	.25	.10
564	Jerry Turner	.25	.10
565	Rico Carty	.50	.20
566	Nino Espinosa	.25	.10
567	Richie Hebner	.50	.20
568	Carlos Lopez	.25	.10
569	Bob Sykes	.25	.10
570	Cesar Cedeno	.50	.20
571	Darrell Porter	.50	.20
572	Rod Gilbreath	.25	.10
573	Jim Kern	.25	.10
574	Claudell Washington	.50	.20
575	Luis Tiant	.50	.20
576	Mike Parrott	.25	.10
577	Brewers Team CL	1.00	.20
	George Bamberger MG		
578	Pete Broberg	.25	.10
579	Greg Gross	.25	.10
580	Ron Fairly	.50	.20
581	Darold Knowles	.25	.10
582	Paul Blair	.50	.20
583	Julio Cruz	.25	.10
584	Jim Rooker	.25	.10
585	Hal McRae	1.00	.40
586	Bob Horner RC	1.00	.40
587	Ken Reitz	.25	.10
588	Tom Murphy	.25	.10
589	Terry Whitfield	.25	.10
590	J.R. Richard	.50	.20
591	Mike Hargrove	.50	.20
592	Mike Krukow	.25	.10
593	Rick Dempsey	.50	.20
594	Bob Shirley	.25	.10
595	Phil Niekro	2.00	.80
596	Jim Wohlford	.25	.10
597	Bob Stanley	.25	.10
598	Mark Wagner	.25	.10
599	Jim Spencer	.25	.10
600	George Foster	.50	.20
601	Dave LaRoche	.25	.10
602	Checklist 485-605	1.00	.20
603	Rudy May	.25	.10
604	Jeff Newman	.25	.10
605	Rick Monday DP	.25	.10
606	Expos Team CL	1.00	.20
	Dick Williams MG		
607	Omar Moreno	.25	.10
608	Dave McKay	.25	.10
609	Silvio Martinez	.25	.10
610	Mike Schmidt	8.00	3.20
611	Jim Norris	.25	.10
612	Rick Honeycutt RC	.50	.20
613	Mike Edwards	.25	.10
614	Willie Hernandez	.50	.20
615	Ken Singleton	.50	.20
616	Billy Almon	.25	.10
617	Terry Puhl	.25	.10
618	Jerry Remy	.25	.10
619	Ken Landreaux	.50	.20
620	Bert Campaneris	.50	.20
621	Pat Zachry	.25	.10
622	Dave Collins	.50	.20
623	Bob McClure	.25	.10
624	Larry Herndon	.25	.10
625	Mark Fidrych	2.00	.80
626	Yankees Team CL	1.00	.20
	Bob Lemon MG		
627	Gary Serum	.25	.10
628	Del Unser	.25	.10
629	Gene Garber	.50	.20
630	Bake McBride	.50	.20
631	Jorge Orta	.25	.10
632	Don Kirkwood	.25	.10
633	Rob Wilfong DP	.15	.06
634	Paul Lindblad	.25	.10
635	Don Baylor	1.00	.40
636	Wayne Garland	.25	.10
637	Bill Robinson	.50	.20
638	Al Fitzmorris	.25	.10
639	Manny Trillo	.25	.10
640	Eddie Murray	12.00	4.80
641	Bobby Castillo	.25	.10
642	Wilbur Howard DP	.15	.06
643	Tom Hausman	.25	.10
644	Manny Mota	.50	.20
645	George Scott DP	.25	.10
646	Rick Sweet	.25	.10
647	Bob Lacey	.25	.10
648	Lou Piniella	.50	.20
649	John Curtis	.25	.10
650	Pete Rose	12.00	4.80
651	Mike Caldwell	.25	.10
652	Stan Papi	.25	.10
653	Warren Brusstar DP	.15	.06
654	Rick Miller	.25	.10
655	Jerry Koosman	.50	.20
656	Hosken Powell	.25	.10
657	George Medich	.25	.10
658	Taylor Duncan	.25	.10
659	Mariners Team CL	1.00	.20
	Darrell Johnson MG		
660	Ron LeFlore DP	.25	.10
661	Bruce Kison	.25	.10
662	Kevin Bell	.25	.10
663	Mike Vail	.25	.10
664	Doug Bird	.25	.10
665	Lou Brock	2.50	1.00
666	Rich Dauer	.25	.10
667	Don Hood	.25	.10
668	Bill North	.25	.10
669	Checklist 606-726	1.00	.20
670	Jim Hunter DP	1.00	.40
671	Joe Ferguson DP	.15	.06
672	Ed Halicki	.25	.10
673	Tom Hutton	.25	.10
674	Dave Tomlin	.25	.10
675	Tim McCarver	1.00	.40
676	Johnny Sutton	.25	.10
677	Larry Parrish	.50	.20
678	Geoff Zahn	.25	.10
679	Derrel Thomas	.25	.10
680	Carlton Fisk	3.00	1.20
681	John Henry Johnson	.25	.10
682	Dave Chalk	.25	.10
683	Dan Meyer DP	.15	.06
684	Jamie Easterly DP	.15	.06
685	Sixto Lezcano	.25	.10
686	Ron Schueler DP	.15	.06
687	Rennie Stennett	.25	.10
688	Mike Willis	.25	.10
689	Orioles Team CL	1.00	.20
	Earl Weaver MG		
690	Buddy Bell DP	.25	.10
691	Dock Ellis DP	.15	.06
692	Mickey Stanley	.25	.10
693	Dave Rader	.25	.10
694	Burt Hooton	.50	.20
695	Keith Hernandez	.50	.20
696	Andy Hassler	.25	.10
697	Dave Bergman	.25	.10
698	Bill Stein	.25	.10
699	Hal Dues	.25	.10
700	Reggie Jackson DP	5.00	2.00
701	Mark Corey	.50	.20
	John Flinn		
	Sammy Stewart		
702	Joel Finch	.50	.20
	Garry Hancock		
	Allen Ripley		
703	Jim Anderson	.50	.20
	Dave Frost		
	Bob Slater		
704	Ross Baumgarten	.50	.20
	Mike Colbern		
	Mike Squires		
705	Alfredo Griffin RC	1.00	.40
	Tim Norrid		
	Dave Oliver		
706	Dave Stegman	.50	.20
	Dave Tobik		
	Kip Young		
707	Randy Bass RC	1.00	.40
	Jim Gaudet		
	Randy McGilberry		

		NM	Ex
❑ 708	Kevin Bass RC Eddie Romero Ned Yost RC	1.00	.40
❑ 709	Sam Perlozzo Rick Sofield Kevin Stanfield	.50	.20
❑ 710	Brian Doyle Mike Heath Dave Rajsich	.50	.20
❑ 711	Dwayne Murphy RC Bruce Robinson Alan Wirth	1.00	.40
❑ 712	Bud Anderson Greg Biercevicz Byron McLaughlin	.50	.20
❑ 713	Danny Darwin RC Pat Putnam Billy Sample	1.00	.40
❑ 714	Victor Cruz Pat Kelly Ernie Whitt	.50	.20
❑ 715	Bruce Benedict Glenn Hubbard RC Larry Whisenton	1.00	.40
❑ 716	Dave Geisel Karl Pagel Scot Thompson	.50	.20
❑ 717	Mike LaCoss Ron Oester RC Harry Spilman	.50	.20
❑ 718	Bruce Bochy Mike Fischlin Don Pisker	.50	.20
❑ 719	Pedro Guerrero RC Rudy Law Joe Simpson	1.00	.40
❑ 720	Jerry Fry Jerry Pirtle Scott Sanderson RC	1.00	.40
❑ 721	Juan Berenguer Dwight Bernard Dan Norman	.50	.20
❑ 722	Jim Morrison Lonnie Smith RC Jim Wright	1.00	.40
❑ 723	Dale Berra RC Eugenio Cotes Ben Wiltbank	.50	.20
❑ 724	Tom Bruno George Frazier Terry Kennedy RC	1.00	.40
❑ 725	Jim Beswick Steve Mura Broderick Perkins	.50	.20
❑ 726	Greg Johnston Joe Strain John Tamargo	.50	.10

1980 Topps

	NM	Ex
COMPLETE SET (726)	120.00	47.50
COMMON CARD (1-726)	.25	.10
COMMON DP	.25	.10

		NM	Ex
❑ 1	Lou Brock HL Carl Yastrzemski	2.50	.50
❑ 2	Willie McCovey HL	.75	.30
❑ 3	Manny Mota HL	.25	.10
❑ 4	Pete Rose HL	3.00	1.20
❑ 5	Garry Templeton HL	.25	.10
❑ 6	Del Unser HL	.25	.10
❑ 7	Mike Lum	.25	.10
❑ 8	Craig Swan	.25	.10
❑ 9	Steve Braun	.25	.10
❑ 10	Dennis Martinez	.75	.30
❑ 11	Jimmy Sexton	.25	.10
❑ 12	John Curtis DP	.25	.10
❑ 13	Ron Pruitt	.25	.10
❑ 14	Dave Cash	.75	.30
❑ 15	Bill Campbell	.25	.10
❑ 16	Jerry Narron	.25	.10
❑ 17	Bruce Sutter	.75	.30
❑ 18	Ron Jackson	.25	.10
❑ 19	Balor Moore	.25	.10
❑ 20	Dan Ford	.25	.10
❑ 21	Manny Sarmiento	.25	.10
❑ 22	Pat Putnam	.25	.10
❑ 23	Derrel Thomas	.25	.10
❑ 24	Jim Slaton	.25	.10
❑ 25	Lee Mazzilli	.75	.30
❑ 26	Marty Pattin	.25	.10
❑ 27	Del Unser	.25	.10
❑ 28	Bruce Kison	.25	.10
❑ 29	Mark Wagner	.25	.10
❑ 30	Vida Blue	.75	.30
❑ 31	Jay Johnstone	.25	.10
❑ 32	Julio Cruz DP	.25	.10
❑ 33	Tony Scott	.25	.10
❑ 34	Jeff Newman DP	.25	.10
❑ 35	Luis Tiant	.75	.30
❑ 36	Rusty Torres	.25	.10
❑ 37	Kiko Garcia	.25	.10
❑ 38	Dan Spillner DP	.25	.10
❑ 39	Rowland Office	.25	.10
❑ 40	Carlton Fisk	2.50	1.00
❑ 41	Rangers Team CL Pat Corrales MG	.75	.15
❑ 42	David Palmer	.25	.10
❑ 43	Bombo Rivera	.25	.10
❑ 44	Bill Fahey	.25	.10
❑ 45	Frank White	.75	.30
❑ 46	Rico Carty	.75	.30
❑ 47	Bill Bonham DP	.25	.10
❑ 48	Rick Miller	.25	.10
❑ 49	Mario Guerrero	.25	.10
❑ 50	J.R. Richard	.75	.30
❑ 51	Joe Ferguson DP	.25	.10
❑ 52	Warren Brusstar	.25	.10
❑ 53	Ben Oglivie	.75	.30
❑ 54	Dennis Lamp	.25	.10
❑ 55	Bill Madlock	.75	.30
❑ 56	Bobby Valentine	.75	.30
❑ 57	Pete Vuckovich	.25	.10
❑ 58	Doug Flynn	.25	.10
❑ 59	Eddy Putman	.25	.10
❑ 60	Bucky Dent	.75	.30
❑ 61	Gary Serum	.25	.10
❑ 62	Mike Ivie	.25	.10
❑ 63	Bob Stanley	.25	.10
❑ 64	Joe Nolan	.25	.10
❑ 65	Al Bumbry	.75	.30
❑ 66	Royals Team CL Jim Frey MG	.75	.15
❑ 67	Doyle Alexander	.25	.10
❑ 68	Larry Harlow	.25	.10
❑ 69	Rick Williams	.25	.10
❑ 70	Gary Carter	1.50	.60
❑ 71	John Milner DP	.25	.10
❑ 72	Fred Howard DP	.25	.10
❑ 73	Dave Collins	.25	.10
❑ 74	Sid Monge	.25	.10
❑ 75	Bill Russell	.75	.30
❑ 76	John Stearns	.25	.10
❑ 77	Dave Stieb RC	1.50	.60
❑ 78	Ruppert Jones	.25	.10
❑ 79	Bob Owchinko	.25	.10
❑ 80	Ron LeFlore	.75	.30
❑ 81	Ted Sizemore	.25	.10
❑ 82	Astros Team CL Bill Virdon MG	.75	.15
❑ 83	Steve Trout	.25	.10
❑ 84	Gary Lavelle	.25	.10
❑ 85	Ted Simmons	.75	.30
❑ 86	Dave Hamilton	.25	.10
❑ 87	Pepe Frias	.25	.10
❑ 88	Ken Landreaux	.25	.10
❑ 89	Don Hood	.25	.10
❑ 90	Manny Trillo	.75	.30
❑ 91	Rick Dempsey	.75	.30
❑ 92	Rick Rhoden	.25	.10
❑ 93	Dave Roberts DP	.25	.10
❑ 94	Neil Allen	.25	.10
❑ 95	Cecil Cooper	.75	.30
❑ 96	A's Team CL Jim Marshall MG	.75	.15
❑ 97	Bill Lee	.75	.30
❑ 98	Jerry Terrell	.25	.10
❑ 99	Victor Cruz	.25	.10
❑ 100	Johnny Bench	3.00	1.20
❑ 101	Aurelio Lopez	.25	.10
❑ 102	Rich Dauer	.25	.10
❑ 103	Bill Caudill	.25	.10
❑ 104	Manny Mota	.75	.30
❑ 105	Frank Tanana	.75	.30
❑ 106	Jeff Leonard RC	1.50	.60
❑ 107	Francisco Barrios	.25	.10
❑ 108	Bob Horner	.75	.30
❑ 109	Bill Travers	.25	.10
❑ 110	Fred Lynn DP	.50	.20
❑ 111	Bob Knepper	.25	.10
❑ 112	White Sox Team CL Tony LaRussa MG	.75	.15
❑ 113	Geoff Zahn	.25	.10
❑ 114	Juan Beniquez	.25	.10
❑ 115	Sparky Lyle	.75	.30
❑ 116	Larry Cox	.25	.10
❑ 117	Dock Ellis	.75	.30
❑ 118	Phil Garner	.75	.30
❑ 119	Sammy Stewart	.25	.10
❑ 120	Greg Luzinski	.75	.30
❑ 121	Checklist 1-121	.75	.15
❑ 122	Dave Rosello DP	.25	.10
❑ 123	Lynn Jones	.25	.10
❑ 124	Dave Lemanczyk	.25	.10
❑ 125	Tony Perez	.75	.30
❑ 126	Dave Tomlin	.25	.10
❑ 127	Gary Thomasson	.25	.10
❑ 128	Tom Burgmeier	.25	.10
❑ 129	Craig Reynolds	.25	.10
❑ 130	Amos Otis	.75	.30
❑ 131	Paul Mitchell	.25	.10
❑ 132	Biff Pocoroba	.25	.10
❑ 133	Jerry Turner	.25	.10
❑ 134	Matt Keough	.25	.10
❑ 135	Bill Buckner	.75	.30
❑ 136	Dick Ruthven	.25	.10
❑ 137	John Castino	.25	.10
❑ 138	Ross Baumgarten	.25	.10
❑ 139	Dane Iorg	.25	.10
❑ 140	Rich Gossage	.75	.30
❑ 141	Gary Alexander	.25	.10
❑ 142	Phil Huffman	.25	.10
❑ 143	Bruce Bochte DP	.25	.10
❑ 144	Steve Comer	.25	.10
❑ 145	Darrell Evans	.75	.30
❑ 146	Bob Welch	.75	.30
❑ 147	Terry Puhl	.25	.10
❑ 148	Manny Sanguillen	.75	.30
❑ 149	Tom Hume	.25	.10
❑ 150	Jason Thompson	.25	.10
❑ 151	Tom Hausman DP	.25	.10
❑ 152	John Fulgham	.25	.10
❑ 153	Tim Blackwell	.25	.10
❑ 154	Lary Sorensen	.25	.10
❑ 155	Jerry Remy	.25	.10
❑ 156	Tony Brizzolara	.25	.10
❑ 157	Willie Wilson DP	.50	.20
❑ 158	Rob Picciolo DP	.25	.10
❑ 159	Ken Clay	.25	.10
❑ 160	Eddie Murray	5.00	2.00
❑ 161	Larry Christenson	.25	.10
❑ 162	Bob Randall	.25	.10
❑ 163	Steve Swisher	.25	.10
❑ 164	Greg Pryor	.25	.10
❑ 165	Omar Moreno	.25	.10
❑ 166	Glenn Abbott	.25	.10
❑ 167	Jack Clark	.75	.30
❑ 168	Rick Waits	.25	.10
❑ 169	Luis Gomez	.25	.10
❑ 170	Burt Hooton	.75	.30

❑ 171 Fernando Gonzalez .25 .10
❑ 172 Ron Hodges .25 .10
❑ 173 John Henry Johnson .25 .10
❑ 174 Ray Knight .75 .30
❑ 175 Rick Reuschel .75 .30
❑ 176 Champ Summers .25 .10
❑ 177 Dave Heaverlo .25 .10
❑ 178 Tim McCarver .75 .30
❑ 179 Ron Davis .25 .10
❑ 180 Warren Cromartie .25 .10
❑ 181 Moose Haas .25 .10
❑ 182 Ken Reitz .25 .10
❑ 183 Jim Anderson DP .25 .10
❑ 184 Steve Renko DP .25 .10
❑ 185 Hal McRae .75 .30
❑ 186 Junior Moore .25 .10
❑ 187 Alan Ashby .25 .10
❑ 188 Terry Crowley .25 .10
❑ 189 Kevin Kobel .25 .10
❑ 190 Buddy Bell .75 .30
❑ 191 Ted Martinez .25 .10
❑ 192 Braves Team CL .75 .15
Bobby Cox MG
❑ 193 Dave Goltz .25 .10
❑ 194 Mike Easler .25 .10
❑ 195 John Montefusco .75 .30
❑ 196 Lance Parrish .75 .30
❑ 197 Byron McLaughlin .25 .10
❑ 198 Dell Alston DP .25 .10
❑ 199 Mike LaCoss .25 .10
❑ 200 Jim Rice .75 .30
❑ 201 Keith Hernandez .75 .30
Fred Lynn LL
❑ 202 Dave Kingman 1.50 .60
Gorman Thomas LL
❑ 203 Dave Winfield 1.50 .60
Don Baylor LL
❑ 204 Omar Moreno .75 .30
Willie Wilson LL
❑ 205 Joe Niekro .75 .30
Phil Niekro
Mike Flanagan LL
❑ 206 J.R. Richard 5.00 2.00
Nolan Ryan LL
❑ 207 J.R. Richard .75 .30
Ron Guidry LL
❑ 208 Wayne Cage .25 .10
❑ 209 Von Joshua .25 .10
❑ 210 Steve Carlton 1.50 .60
❑ 211 Dave Skaggs DP .25 .10
❑ 212 Dave Roberts .25 .10
❑ 213 Mike Jorgensen DP .25 .10
❑ 214 Angels Team CL .75 .15
Jim Fregosi MG
❑ 215 Sixto Lezcano .25 .10
❑ 216 Phil Mankowski .25 .10
❑ 217 Ed Halicki .25 .10
❑ 218 Jose Morales .25 .10
❑ 219 Steve Mingori .25 .10
❑ 220 Dave Concepcion .75 .30
❑ 221 Joe Cannon .25 .10
❑ 222 Ron Hassey .25 .10
❑ 223 Bob Sykes .25 .10
❑ 224 Willie Montanez .25 .10
❑ 225 Lou Piniella .75 .30
❑ 226 Bill Stein .25 .10
❑ 227 Len Barker .75 .30
❑ 228 Johnny Oates .75 .30
❑ 229 Jim Bibby .25 .10
❑ 230 Dave Winfield 1.50 .60
❑ 231 Steve McCatty .25 .10
❑ 232 Alan Trammell 1.50 .60
❑ 233 LaRue Washington .25 .10
❑ 234 Vern Ruhle .25 .10
❑ 235 Andre Dawson 1.50 .60
❑ 236 Marc Hill .25 .10
❑ 237 Scott McGregor .75 .30
❑ 238 Rob Wilfong .25 .10
❑ 239 Don Aase .25 .10
❑ 240 Dave Kingman .75 .30
❑ 241 Checklist 122-242 .75 .15
❑ 242 Lamar Johnson .25 .10
❑ 243 Jerry Augustine .25 .10
❑ 244 Cardinals Team CL .75 .15
Ken Boyer MG
❑ 245 Phil Niekro .75 .30
❑ 246 Tim Foli DP .25 .10
❑ 247 Frank Riccelli .25 .10
❑ 248 Jamie Quirk .25 .10
❑ 249 Jim Clancy .25 .10
❑ 250 Jim Kaat .75 .30
❑ 251 Kip Young .25 .10
❑ 252 Ted Cox .25 .10
❑ 253 John Montague .25 .10
❑ 254 Paul Dade DP .25 .10
❑ 255 Dusty Baker DP .50 .20
❑ 256 Roger Erickson .25 .10
❑ 257 Larry Herndon .25 .10
❑ 258 Paul Moskau .25 .10
❑ 259 Mets Team CL 1.50 .30
Joe Torre MG
❑ 260 Al Oliver .75 .30
❑ 261 Dave Chalk .25 .10
❑ 262 Benny Ayala .25 .10
❑ 263 Dave LaRoche DP .25 .10
❑ 264 Bill Robinson .25 .10
❑ 265 Robin Yount 3.00 1.20
❑ 266 Bernie Carbo .25 .10
❑ 267 Dan Schatzeder .25 .10
❑ 268 Rafael Landestoy .25 .10
❑ 269 Dave Tobik .25 .10
❑ 270 Mike Schmidt DP 3.00 1.20
❑ 271 Dick Drago DP .25 .10
❑ 272 Ralph Garr .75 .30
❑ 273 Eduardo Rodriguez .25 .10
❑ 274 Dale Murphy 2.50 1.00
❑ 275 Jerry Koosman .75 .30
❑ 276 Tom Veryzer .25 .10
❑ 277 Rick Bosetti .25 .10
❑ 278 Jim Spencer .25 .10
❑ 279 Rob Andrews .25 .10
❑ 280 Gaylord Perry .75 .30
❑ 281 Paul Blair .75 .30
❑ 282 Mariners Team CL .75 .15
Darrell Johnson MG
❑ 283 John Ellis .25 .10
❑ 284 Larry Murray DP .25 .10
❑ 285 Don Baylor .75 .30
❑ 286 Darold Knowles DP .25 .10
❑ 287 John Lowenstein .25 .10
❑ 288 Dave Rozema .25 .10
❑ 289 Bruce Bochy .25 .10
❑ 290 Steve Garvey 1.50 .60
❑ 291 Randy Scarberry .25 .10
❑ 292 Dale Berra .25 .10
❑ 293 Elias Sosa .25 .10
❑ 294 Charlie Spikes .25 .10
❑ 295 Larry Gura .25 .10
❑ 296 Dave Rader .25 .10
❑ 297 Tim Johnson .25 .10
❑ 298 Ken Holtzman .75 .30
❑ 299 Steve Henderson .25 .10
❑ 300 Ron Guidry .75 .30
❑ 301 Mike Edwards .25 .10
❑ 302 Dodgers Team CL 1.50 .30
Tom Lasorda MG
❑ 303 Bill Castro .25 .10
❑ 304 Butch Wynegar .25 .10
❑ 305 Randy Jones .75 .30
❑ 306 Denny Walling .25 .10
❑ 307 Rick Honeycutt .25 .10
❑ 308 Mike Hargrove .75 .30
❑ 309 Larry McWilliams .25 .10
❑ 310 Dave Parker .75 .30
❑ 311 Roger Metzger .25 .10
❑ 312 Mike Barlow .25 .10
❑ 313 Johnny Grubb .25 .10
❑ 314 Tim Stoddard .25 .10
❑ 315 Steve Kemp .75 .30
❑ 316 Bob Lacey .25 .10
❑ 317 Mike Anderson DP .25 .10
❑ 318 Jerry Reuss .75 .30
❑ 319 Chris Speier .25 .10
❑ 320 Dennis Eckersley 1.50 .60
❑ 321 Keith Hernandez .75 .30
❑ 322 Claudell Washington .25 .10
❑ 323 Mick Kelleher .25 .10
❑ 324 Tom Underwood .25 .10
❑ 325 Dan Driessen .25 .10
❑ 326 Bo McLaughlin .25 .10
❑ 327 Ray Fosse DP .50 .20
❑ 328 Twins Team CL .75 .15
Gene Mauch MG
❑ 329 Bert Roberge .25 .10
❑ 330 Al Cowens .25 .10
❑ 331 Richie Hebner .25 .10
❑ 332 Enrique Romo .25 .10
❑ 333 Jim Norris DP .25 .10
❑ 334 Jim Beattie .25 .10
❑ 335 Willie McCovey 1.50 .60
❑ 336 George Medich .25 .10
❑ 337 Carney Lansford .75 .30
❑ 338 John Wockenfuss .25 .10
❑ 339 John D'Acquisto .25 .10
❑ 340 Ken Singleton .75 .30
❑ 341 Jim Essian .25 .10
❑ 342 Odell Jones .25 .10
❑ 343 Mike Vail .25 .10
❑ 344 Randy Lerch .25 .10
❑ 345 Larry Parrish .75 .30
❑ 346 Buddy Solomon .25 .10
❑ 347 Harry Chappas .25 .10
❑ 348 Checklist 243-363 .75 .15
❑ 349 Jack Brohamer .25 .10
❑ 350 George Hendrick .75 .30
❑ 351 Bob Davis .25 .10
❑ 352 Dan Briggs .25 .10
❑ 353 Andy Hassler .25 .10
❑ 354 Rick Auerbach .25 .10
❑ 355 Gary Matthews .75 .30
❑ 356 Padres Team CL .75 .15
Jerry Coleman MG
❑ 357 Bob McClure .25 .10
❑ 358 Lou Whitaker .75 .30
❑ 359 Randy Moffitt .25 .10
❑ 360 Darrell Porter DP .50 .20
❑ 361 Wayne Garland .25 .10
❑ 362 Danny Goodwin .25 .10
❑ 363 Wayne Gross .25 .10
❑ 364 Ray Burris .25 .10
❑ 365 Bobby Murcer .75 .30
❑ 366 Rob Dressler .25 .10
❑ 367 Billy Smith .25 .10
❑ 368 Willie Aikens .25 .10
❑ 369 Jim Kern .25 .10
❑ 370 Cesar Cedeno .75 .30
❑ 371 Jack Morris .75 .30
❑ 372 Joel Youngblood .25 .10
❑ 373 Dan Petry DP RC .75 .30
❑ 374 Jim Gantner .75 .30
❑ 375 Ross Grimsley .25 .10
❑ 376 Gary Allenson .25 .10
❑ 377 Junior Kennedy .25 .10
❑ 378 Jerry Mumphrey .25 .10
❑ 379 Kevin Bell .25 .10
❑ 380 Garry Maddox .75 .30
❑ 381 Cubs Team CL .75 .15
Preston Gomez MG
❑ 382 Dave Freisleben .25 .10
❑ 383 Ed Ott .25 .10
❑ 384 Joey McLaughlin .25 .10
❑ 385 Enos Cabell .25 .10
❑ 386 Darrell Jackson .25 .10
❑ 387A Fred Stanley YL 2.00 .80
❑ 387B Fred Stanley .25 .10
(Red name on front)
❑ 388 Mike Paxton .25 .10
❑ 389 Pete LaCock .25 .10
❑ 390 Fergie Jenkins .75 .30
❑ 391 Tony Armas DP .50 .20
❑ 392 Milt Wilcox .25 .10
❑ 393 Ozzie Smith 10.00 4.00
❑ 394 Reggie Cleveland .25 .10
❑ 395 Ellis Valentine .25 .10
❑ 396 Dan Meyer .25 .10
❑ 397 Roy Thomas DP .25 .10
❑ 398 Barry Foote .25 .10
❑ 399 Mike Proly DP .25 .10
❑ 400 George Foster .75 .30
❑ 401 Pete Falcone .25 .10
❑ 402 Merv Rettenmund .25 .10
❑ 403 Pete Redfern DP .25 .10
❑ 404 Orioles Team CL .75 .15
Earl Weaver MG
❑ 405 Dwight Evans 1.50 .60
❑ 406 Paul Molitor 4.00 1.60
❑ 407 Tony Solaita .25 .10
❑ 408 Bill North .25 .10

❑ 409 Paul Splittorff .25 .10
❑ 410 Bobby Bonds .75 .30
❑ 411 Frank LaCorte .25 .10
❑ 412 Thad Bosley .25 .10
❑ 413 Allen Ripley .25 .10
❑ 414 George Scott .75 .30
❑ 415 Bill Atkinson .25 .10
❑ 416 Tom Brookens .25 .10
❑ 417 Craig Chamberlain DP .25 .10
❑ 418 Roger Freed DP .25 .10
❑ 419 Vic Correll .25 .10
❑ 420 Butch Hobson .25 .10
❑ 421 Doug Bird .25 .10
❑ 422 Larry Milbourne .25 .10
❑ 423 Dave Frost .25 .10
❑ 424 Yankees Team CL .75 .15
Dick Howser MG
❑ 424A Yankees Team CL .00
Billy Martin MG
Card is believed to be a pre-production issue
❑ 425 Mark Belanger .75 .30
❑ 426 Grant Jackson .25 .10
❑ 427 Tom Hutton DP .25 .10
❑ 428 Pat Zachry .25 .10
❑ 429 Duane Kuiper .25 .10
❑ 430 Larry Hisle DP .25 .10
❑ 431 Mike Krukow .25 .10
❑ 432 Willie Norwood .25 .10
❑ 433 Rich Gale .25 .10
❑ 434 Johnnie LeMaster .25 .10
❑ 435 Don Gullett .75 .30
❑ 436 Billy Almon .25 .10
❑ 437 Joe Niekro .75 .30
❑ 438 Dave Revering .25 .10
❑ 439 Mike Phillips .25 .10
❑ 440 Don Sutton .75 .30
❑ 441 Eric Soderholm .25 .10
❑ 442 Jorge Orta .25 .10
❑ 443 Mike Parrott .25 .10
❑ 444 Alvis Woods .25 .10
❑ 445 Mark Fidrych .75 .30
❑ 446 Duffy Dyer .25 .10
❑ 447 Nino Espinosa .25 .10
❑ 448 Jim Wohlford .25 .10
❑ 449 Doug Bair .25 .10
❑ 450 George Brett 8.00 3.20
❑ 451 Indians Team CL .75 .15
Dave Garcia MG
❑ 452 Steve Dillard .25 .10
❑ 453 Mike Bacsik .25 .10
❑ 454 Tom Donohue .25 .10
❑ 455 Mike Torrez .75 .30
❑ 456 Frank Taveras .25 .10
❑ 457 Bert Blyleven .75 .30
❑ 458 Billy Sample .25 .10
❑ 459 Mickey Lolich DP .50 .20
❑ 460 Willie Randolph .75 .30
❑ 461 Dwayne Murphy .25 .10
❑ 462 Mike Sadek DP .25 .10
❑ 463 Jerry Royster .25 .10
❑ 464 John Denny .75 .30
❑ 465 Rick Monday .75 .30
❑ 466 Mike Squires .25 .10
❑ 467 Jesse Jefferson .25 .10
❑ 468 Aurelio Rodriguez .25 .10
❑ 469 Randy Niemann DP .25 .10
❑ 470 Bob Boone .75 .30
❑ 471 Hosken Powell DP .25 .10
❑ 472 Willie Hernandez .75 .30
❑ 473 Bump Wills .25 .10
❑ 474 Steve Busby .25 .10
❑ 475 Cesar Geronimo .75 .30
❑ 476 Bob Shirley .25 .10
❑ 477 Buck Martinez .25 .10
❑ 478 Gil Flores .25 .10
❑ 479 Expos Team CL .75 .15
Dick Williams MG
❑ 480 Bob Watson .75 .30
❑ 481 Tom Paciorek .75 .30
❑ 482 R.Henderson RC UER .. 60.00 24.00
7 steals at Modesto, should be at Fresno
❑ 483 Bo Diaz .25 .10
❑ 484 Checklist 364-484 .75 .15
❑ 485 Mickey Rivers .75 .30
❑ 486 Mike Tyson DP .25 .10
❑ 487 Wayne Nordhagen .25 .10
❑ 488 Roy Howell .25 .10
❑ 489 Preston Hanna DP .25 .10
❑ 490 Lee May .75 .30
❑ 491 Steve Mura DP .25 .10
❑ 492 Todd Cruz .25 .10
❑ 493 Jerry Martin .25 .10
❑ 494 Craig Minetto .25 .10
❑ 495 Bake McBride .75 .30
❑ 496 Silvio Martinez .25 .10
❑ 497 Jim Mason .25 .10
❑ 498 Danny Darwin .25 .10
❑ 499 Giants Team CL .75 .15
Dave Bristol MG
❑ 500 Tom Seaver 3.00 1.20
❑ 501 Rennie Stennett .25 .10
❑ 502 Rich Wortham DP .25 .10
❑ 503 Mike Cubbage .25 .10
❑ 504 Gene Garber .25 .10
❑ 505 Bert Campaneris .75 .30
❑ 506 Tom Buskey .25 .10
❑ 507 Leon Roberts .25 .10
❑ 508 U.L. Washington .25 .10
❑ 509 Ed Glynn .25 .10
❑ 510 Ron Cey .75 .30
❑ 511 Eric Wilkins .25 .10
❑ 512 Jose Cardenal .25 .10
❑ 513 Tom Dixon DP .25 .10
❑ 514 Steve Ontiveros .25 .10
❑ 515 Mike Caldwell UER .25 .10
1979 loss total reads 96 instead of 6
❑ 516 Hector Cruz .25 .10
❑ 517 Don Stanhouse .25 .10
❑ 518 Nelson Norman .25 .10
❑ 519 Steve Nicosia .25 .10
❑ 520 Steve Rogers .75 .30
❑ 521 Ken Brett .25 .10
❑ 522 Jim Morrison .25 .10
❑ 523 Ken Henderson .25 .10
❑ 524 Jim Wright DP .25 .10
❑ 525 Clint Hurdle .25 .10
❑ 526 Phillies Team CL .75 .15
Dallas Green MG
❑ 527 Doug Rau DP .25 .10
❑ 528 Adrian Devine .25 .10
❑ 529 Jim Barr .25 .10
❑ 530 Jim Sundberg DP .50 .20
❑ 531 Eric Rasmussen .25 .10
❑ 532 Willie Horton .75 .30
❑ 533 Checklist 485-605 .75 .15
❑ 534 Andre Thornton .75 .30
❑ 535 Bob Forsch .25 .10
❑ 536 Lee Lacy .25 .10
❑ 537 Alex Trevino .25 .10
❑ 538 Joe Strain .25 .10
❑ 539 Rudy May .25 .10
❑ 540 Pete Rose 8.00 3.20
❑ 541 Miguel Dilone .25 .10
❑ 542 Joe Coleman .25 .10
❑ 543 Pat Kelly .25 .10
❑ 544 Rick Sutcliffe RC 1.50 .60
❑ 545 Jeff Burroughs .75 .30
❑ 546 Rick Langford .25 .10
❑ 547 John Wathan .25 .10
❑ 548 Dave Rajsich .25 .10
❑ 549 Larry Wolfe .25 .10
❑ 550 Ken Griffey Sr. .75 .30
❑ 551 Pirates Team CL .75 .15
Chuck Tanner MG
❑ 552 Bill Nahorodny .25 .10
❑ 553 Dick Davis .25 .10
❑ 554 Art Howe .75 .30
❑ 555 Ed Figueroa .25 .10
❑ 556 Joe Rudi .75 .30
❑ 557 Mark Lee .25 .10
❑ 558 Alfredo Griffin .25 .10
❑ 559 Dale Murray .25 .10
❑ 560 Dave Lopes .75 .30
❑ 561 Eddie Whitson .25 .10
❑ 562 Joe Wallis .25 .10
❑ 563 Will McEnaney .25 .10
❑ 564 Rick Manning .25 .10
❑ 565 Dennis Leonard .25 .10
❑ 566 Bud Harrelson .75 .30
❑ 567 Skip Lockwood .25 .10
❑ 568 Gary Roenicke .25 .10
❑ 569 Terry Kennedy .25 .10
❑ 570 Roy Smalley .75 .30
❑ 571 Joe Sambito .25 .10
❑ 572 Jerry Morales DP .25 .10
❑ 573 Kent Tekulve .75 .30
❑ 574 Scot Thompson .25 .10
❑ 575 Ken Kravec .25 .10
❑ 576 Jim Dwyer .25 .10
❑ 577 Blue Jays Team CL .75 .15
Bobby Mattick MG
❑ 578 Scott Sanderson .25 .10
❑ 579 Charlie Moore .25 .10
❑ 580 Nolan Ryan 15.00 6.00
❑ 581 Bob Bailor .25 .10
❑ 582 Brian Doyle .25 .10
❑ 583 Bob Stinson .25 .10
❑ 584 Kurt Bevacqua .25 .10
❑ 585 Al Hrabosky .75 .30
❑ 586 Mitchell Page .25 .10
❑ 587 Garry Templeton .75 .30
❑ 588 Greg Minton .25 .10
❑ 589 Chet Lemon .75 .30
❑ 590 Jim Palmer 1.50 .60
❑ 591 Rick Cerone .25 .10
❑ 592 Jon Matlack .75 .30
❑ 593 Jesus Alou .25 .10
❑ 594 Dick Tidrow .25 .10
❑ 595 Don Money .25 .10
❑ 596 Rick Matula .25 .10
❑ 597 Tom Poquette .25 .10
❑ 598 Fred Kendall DP .25 .10
❑ 599 Mike Norris .25 .10
❑ 600 Reggie Jackson 3.00 1.20
❑ 601 Buddy Schultz .25 .10
❑ 602 Brian Downing .75 .30
❑ 603 Jack Billingham DP .25 .10
❑ 604 Glenn Adams .25 .10
❑ 605 Terry Forster .75 .30
❑ 606 Reds Team CL .75 .15
John McNamara MG
❑ 607 Woodie Fryman .25 .10
❑ 608 Alan Bannister .25 .10
❑ 609 Ron Reed .25 .10
❑ 610 Willie Stargell 1.50 .60
❑ 611 Jerry Garvin DP .25 .10
❑ 612 Cliff Johnson .25 .10
❑ 613 Randy Stein .25 .10
❑ 614 John Hiller .25 .10
❑ 615 Doug DeCinces .75 .30
❑ 616 Gene Richards .25 .10
❑ 617 Joaquin Andujar .75 .30
❑ 618 Bob Montgomery DP .25 .10
❑ 619 Sergio Ferrer .25 .10
❑ 620 Richie Zisk .75 .30
❑ 621 Bob Grich .75 .30
❑ 622 Mario Soto .75 .30
❑ 623 Gorman Thomas .75 .30
❑ 624 Lerrin LaGrow .25 .10
❑ 625 Chris Chambliss .75 .30
❑ 626 Tigers Team CL .75 .15
Sparky Anderson MG
❑ 627 Pedro Borbon .25 .10
❑ 628 Doug Capilla .25 .10
❑ 629 Jim Todd .25 .10
❑ 630 Larry Bowa .75 .30
❑ 631 Mark Littell .25 .10
❑ 632 Barry Bonnell .25 .10
❑ 633 Bob Apodaca .25 .10
❑ 634 Glenn Borgmann DP .25 .10
❑ 635 John Candelaria .75 .30
❑ 636 Toby Harrah .75 .30
❑ 637 Joe Simpson .25 .10
❑ 638 Mark Clear .25 .10
❑ 639 Larry Biittner .25 .10
❑ 640 Mike Flanagan .75 .30
❑ 641 Ed Kranepool .75 .30
❑ 642 Ken Forsch DP .25 .10
❑ 643 John Mayberry .75 .30
❑ 644 Charlie Hough .75 .30
❑ 645 Rick Burleson .75 .30
❑ 646 Checklist 606-726 .75 .15
❑ 647 Milt May .25 .10
❑ 648 Roy White .75 .30
❑ 649 Tom Griffin .25 .10

Card	Nm-Mt	Ex-Mt
❑ 650 Joe Morgan	1.50	.60
❑ 651 Rollie Fingers	.75	.30
❑ 652 Mario Mendoza	.25	.10
❑ 653 Stan Bahnsen	.25	.10
❑ 654 Bruce Boisclair DP	.25	.10
❑ 655 Tug McGraw	.75	.30
❑ 656 Larvell Blanks	.25	.10
❑ 657 Dave Edwards	.25	.10
❑ 658 Chris Knapp	.25	.10
❑ 659 Brewers Team CL	.75	.15
George Bamberger MG		
❑ 660 Rusty Staub	.75	.30
❑ 661 Mark Corey	.25	.10
Dave Ford		
Wayne Krenchicki		
❑ 662 Joel Finch	.25	.10
Mike O'Berry		
Chuck Rainey		
❑ 663 Ralph Botting	.75	.30
Bob Clark		
Dickie Thon RC		
❑ 664 Mike Colbern	.25	.10
Guy Hoffman		
Dewey Robinson		
❑ 665 Larry Andersen	.25	.10
Bobby Cuellar		
Sandy Wihtol		
❑ 666 Mike Chris	.25	.10
Al Greene		
Bruce Robbins		
❑ 667 Renie Martin	.75	.30
Bill Paschall		
Dan Quisenberry RC		
❑ 668 Danny Boitano	.25	.10
Willie Mueller		
Lenn Sakata		
❑ 669 Dan Graham	.75	.30
Rick Sofield		
Gary Ward RC		
❑ 670 Bobby Brown	.25	.10
Brad Gulden		
Darryl Jones		
❑ 671 Derek Bryant	.75	.30
Brian Kingman		
Mike Morgan RC		
❑ 672 Charlie Beamon	.25	.10
Rodney Craig		
Rafael Vasquez		
❑ 673 Brian Allard	.25	.10
Jerry Don Gleaton		
Greg Mahlberg		
❑ 674 Butch Edge	.25	.10
Pat Kelly		
Ted Wilborn		
❑ 675 Bruce Benedict	.25	.10
Larry Bradford		
Eddie Miller		
❑ 676 Dave Geisel	.25	.10
Steve Macko		
Karl Pagel		
❑ 677 Art DeFreites	.25	.10
Frank Pastore		
Harry Spilman		
❑ 678 Reggie Baldwin	.25	.10
Alan Knicely		
Pete Ladd		
❑ 679 Joe Beckwith	.75	.30
Mickey Hatcher RC		
Dave Patterson		
❑ 680 Tony Bernazard	.25	.10
Randy Miller		
John Tamargo		
❑ 681 Dan Norman	1.50	.60
Jesse Orosco RC		
Mike Scott RC		
❑ 682 Ramon Aviles	.25	.10
Dickie Noles		
Kevin Saucier		
❑ 683 Dorian Boyland	.25	.10
Alberto Lois		
Harry Saferight		
❑ 684 George Frazier	.75	.30
Tom Herr RC		
Dan O'Brien		
❑ 685 Tim Flannery	.25	.10
Brian Greer		
Jim Wilhelm		
❑ 686 Greg Johnston	.25	.10
Dennis Littlejohn		
Phil Nastu		
❑ 687 Mike Heath DP	.25	.10
❑ 688 Steve Stone	.75	.30
❑ 689 Red Sox Team CL	.75	.15
Don Zimmer MG		
❑ 690 Tommy John	.75	.30
❑ 691 Ivan DeJesus	.25	.10
❑ 692 Rawly Eastwick DP	.50	.20
❑ 693 Craig Kusick	.25	.10
❑ 694 Jim Rooker	.25	.10
❑ 695 Reggie Smith	.75	.30
❑ 696 Julio Gonzalez	.25	.10
❑ 697 David Clyde	.25	.10
❑ 698 Oscar Gamble	.75	.30
❑ 699 Floyd Bannister	.25	.10
❑ 700 Rod Carew DP	.75	.30
❑ 701 Ken Oberkfell	.25	.10
❑ 702 Ed Farmer	.25	.10
❑ 703 Otto Velez	.25	.10
❑ 704 Gene Tenace	.75	.30
❑ 705 Freddie Patek	.75	.30
❑ 706 Tippy Martinez	.25	.10
❑ 707 Elliott Maddox	.25	.10
❑ 708 Bob Tolan	.25	.10
❑ 709 Pat Underwood	.25	.10
❑ 710 Graig Nettles	.75	.30
❑ 711 Bob Galasso	.25	.10
❑ 712 Rodney Scott	.25	.10
❑ 713 Terry Whitfield	.25	.10
❑ 714 Fred Norman	.25	.10
❑ 715 Sal Bando	.75	.30
❑ 716 Lynn McGlothen	.25	.10
❑ 717 Mickey Klutts DP	.25	.10
❑ 718 Greg Gross	.25	.10
❑ 719 Don Robinson	.75	.30
❑ 720 Carl Yastrzemski DP	2.00	.80
❑ 721 Paul Hartzell	.25	.10
❑ 722 Jose Cruz	.75	.30
❑ 723 Shane Rawley	.25	.10
❑ 724 Jerry White	.25	.10
❑ 725 Rick Wise	.25	.10
❑ 726 Steve Yeager	.75	.15

1981 Topps

	Nm-Mt	Ex-Mt
COMPLETE SET (726)	50.00	20.00
COMMON CARD (1-726)	.15	.06
COMMON CARD DP	.15	.06
❑ 1 George Brett	3.00	1.20
Bill Buckner LL		
❑ 2 Reggie Jackson	1.50	.60
Ben Oglivie		
Mike Schmidt LL		
❑ 3 Cecil Cooper	1.50	.60
Mike Schmidt LL		
❑ 4 Rickey Henderson	3.00	1.20
Ron LeFlore LL		
❑ 5 Steve Stone	.40	.16
Steve Carlton LL		
❑ 6 Len Barker	.40	.16
Steve Carlton LL		
❑ 7 Rudy May	.40	.16
Don Sutton LL		
❑ 8 Dan Quisenberry	.40	.16
Rollie Fingers		
Tom Hume LL		
❑ 9 Pete LaCock DP	.15	.06
❑ 10 Mike Flanagan	.15	.06
❑ 11 Jim Wohlford DP	.15	.06
❑ 12 Mark Clear	.15	.06
❑ 13 Joe Charboneau RC	1.50	.60
❑ 14 John Tudor RC	1.50	.60
❑ 15 Larry Parrish	.15	.06
❑ 16 Ron Davis	.15	.06
❑ 17 Cliff Johnson	.15	.06
❑ 18 Glenn Adams	.15	.06
❑ 19 Jim Clancy	.15	.06
❑ 20 Jeff Burroughs	.40	.16
❑ 21 Ron Oester	.15	.06
❑ 22 Danny Darwin	.15	.06
❑ 23 Alex Trevino	.15	.06
❑ 24 Don Stanhouse	.15	.06
❑ 25 Sixto Lezcano	.15	.06
❑ 26 U.L. Washington	.15	.06
❑ 27 Champ Summers DP	.15	.06
❑ 28 Enrique Romo	.15	.06
❑ 29 Gene Tenace	.40	.16
❑ 30 Jack Clark	.40	.16
❑ 31 Checklist 1-121 DP	.25	.10
❑ 32 Ken Oberkfell	.15	.06
❑ 33 Rick Honeycutt	.15	.06
❑ 34 Aurelio Rodriguez	.15	.06
❑ 35 Mitchell Page	.15	.06
❑ 36 Ed Farmer	.15	.06
❑ 37 Gary Roenicke	.15	.06
❑ 38 Win Remmerswaal	.15	.06
❑ 39 Tom Veryzer	.15	.06
❑ 40 Tug McGraw	.40	.16
❑ 41 Bob Babcock	.25	.10
John Butcher		
Jerry Don Gleaton		
❑ 42 Jerry White DP	.15	.06
❑ 43 Jose Morales	.15	.06
❑ 44 Larry McWilliams	.15	.06
❑ 45 Enos Cabell	.15	.06
❑ 46 Rick Bosetti	.15	.06
❑ 47 Ken Brett	.15	.06
❑ 48 Dave Skaggs	.15	.06
❑ 49 Bob Shirley	.15	.06
❑ 50 Dave Lopes	.40	.16
❑ 51 Bill Robinson DP	.15	.06
❑ 52 Hector Cruz	.15	.06
❑ 53 Kevin Saucier	.15	.06
❑ 54 Ivan DeJesus	.15	.06
❑ 55 Mike Norris	.15	.06
❑ 56 Buck Martinez	.15	.06
❑ 57 Dave Roberts	.15	.06
❑ 58 Joel Youngblood	.15	.06
❑ 59 Dan Petry	.15	.06
❑ 60 Willie Randolph	.40	.16
❑ 61 Butch Wynegar	.15	.06
❑ 62 Joe Pettini	.15	.06
❑ 63 Steve Renko DP	.15	.06
❑ 64 Brian Asselstine	.15	.06
❑ 65 Scott McGregor	.15	.06
❑ 66 Manny Castillo	.25	.10
Tim Ireland		
Mike Jones		
❑ 67 Ken Kravec	.15	.06
❑ 68 Matt Alexander DP	.15	.06
❑ 69 Ed Halicki	.15	.06
❑ 70 Al Oliver DP	.25	.10
❑ 71 Hal Dues	.15	.06
❑ 72 Barry Evans DP	.15	.06
❑ 73 Doug Bair	.15	.06
❑ 74 Mike Hargrove	.15	.06
❑ 75 Reggie Smith	.40	.16
❑ 76 Mario Mendoza	.15	.06
❑ 77 Mike Barlow	.15	.06
❑ 78 Steve Dillard	.15	.06
❑ 79 Bruce Robbins	.15	.06
❑ 80 Rusty Staub	.40	.16
❑ 81 Dave Stapleton	.15	.06
❑ 82 Danny Heep	.25	.10
Alan Knicely		
Bobby Sprowl		
❑ 83 Mike Proly	.15	.06
❑ 84 Johnnie LeMaster	.15	.06
❑ 85 Mike Caldwell	.15	.06
❑ 86 Wayne Gross	.15	.06

❑ 87 Rick Camp .15 .06
❑ 88 Joe Lefebvre .15 .06
❑ 89 Darrell Jackson .15 .06
❑ 90 Bake McBride .40 .16
❑ 91 Tim Stoddard DP .15 .06
❑ 92 Mike Easler .15 .06
❑ 93 Ed Glynn DP .15 .06
❑ 94 Harry Spilman DP .15 .06
❑ 95 Jim Sundberg .40 .16
❑ 96 Dave Beard .25 .10
Ernie Camacho
Pat Dempsey
❑ 97 Chris Speier .15 .06
❑ 98 Clint Hurdle .15 .06
❑ 99 Eric Wilkins .15 .06
❑ 100 Rod Carew .75 .30
❑ 101 Benny Ayala .15 .06
❑ 102 Dave Tobik .15 .06
❑ 103 Jerry Martin .15 .06
❑ 104 Terry Forster .40 .16
❑ 105 Jose Cruz .40 .16
❑ 106 Don Money .15 .06
❑ 107 Rich Wortham .15 .06
❑ 108 Bruce Benedict .15 .06
❑ 109 Mike Scott .40 .16
❑ 110 Carl Yastrzemski 2.50 1.00
❑ 111 Greg Minton .15 .06
❑ 112 Rusty Kuntz .25 .10
Fran Mullins
Leo Sutherland
❑ 113 Mike Phillips .15 .06
❑ 114 Tom Underwood .15 .06
❑ 115 Roy Smalley .40 .16
❑ 116 Joe Simpson .15 .06
❑ 117 Pete Falcone .15 .06
❑ 118 Kurt Bevacqua .15 .06
❑ 119 Tippy Martinez .15 .06
❑ 120 Larry Bowa .40 .16
❑ 121 Larry Harlow .15 .06
❑ 122 John Denny .15 .06
❑ 123 Al Cowens .15 .06
❑ 124 Jerry Garvin .15 .06
❑ 125 Andre Dawson .75 .30
❑ 126 Charlie Leibrandt RC .75 .30
❑ 127 Rudy Law .15 .06
❑ 128 Gary Allenson DP .15 .06
❑ 129 Art Howe .15 .06
❑ 130 Larry Gura .15 .06
❑ 131 Keith Moreland .15 .06
❑ 132 Tommy Boggs .15 .06
❑ 133 Jeff Cox .15 .06
❑ 134 Steve Mura .15 .06
❑ 135 Gorman Thomas .40 .16
❑ 136 Doug Capilla .15 .06
❑ 137 Hosken Powell .15 .06
❑ 138 Rich Dotson DP .15 .06
❑ 139 Oscar Gamble .15 .06
❑ 140 Bob Forsch .15 .06
❑ 141 Miguel Dilone .15 .06
❑ 142 Jackson Todd .15 .06
❑ 143 Dan Meyer .15 .06
❑ 144 Allen Ripley .15 .06
❑ 145 Mickey Rivers .15 .06
❑ 146 Bobby Castillo .15 .06
❑ 147 Dale Berra .15 .06
❑ 148 Randy Niemann .15 .06
❑ 149 Joe Nolan .15 .06
❑ 150 Mark Fidrych .40 .16
❑ 151 Claudell Washington .15 .06
❑ 152 John Urrea .15 .06
❑ 153 Tom Poquette .15 .06
❑ 154 Rick Langford .15 .06
❑ 155 Chris Chambliss .40 .16
❑ 156 Bob McClure .15 .06
❑ 157 John Wathan .15 .06
❑ 158 Fergie Jenkins .40 .16
❑ 159 Brian Doyle .15 .06
❑ 160 Garry Maddox .15 .06
❑ 161 Dan Graham .15 .06
❑ 162 Doug Corbett .15 .06
❑ 163 Bill Almon .15 .06
❑ 164 LaMarr Hoyt RC .75 .30
❑ 165 Tony Scott .15 .06
❑ 166 Floyd Bannister .15 .06
❑ 167 Terry Whitfield .15 .06
❑ 168 Don Robinson DP .15 .06
❑ 169 John Mayberry .15 .06
❑ 170 Ross Grimsley .15 .06
❑ 171 Gene Richards .15 .06
❑ 172 Gary Woods .15 .06
❑ 173 Bump Wills .15 .06
❑ 174 Doug Rau .15 .06
❑ 175 Dave Collins .15 .06
❑ 176 Mike Krukow .15 .06
❑ 177 Rick Peters .15 .06
❑ 178 Jim Essian DP .15 .06
❑ 179 Rudy May .15 .06
❑ 180 Pete Rose 5.00 2.00
❑ 181 Elias Sosa .15 .06
❑ 182 Bob Grich .40 .16
❑ 183 Dick Davis DP .15 .06
❑ 184 Jim Dwyer .15 .06
❑ 185 Dennis Leonard .15 .06
❑ 186 Wayne Nordhagen .15 .06
❑ 187 Mike Parrott .15 .06
❑ 188 Doug DeCinces .15 .06
❑ 189 Craig Swan .15 .06
❑ 190 Cesar Cedeno .40 .16
❑ 191 Rick Sutcliffe .40 .16
❑ 192 Terry Harper .25 .10
Ed Miller
Rafael Ramirez
❑ 193 Pete Vuckovich .15 .06
❑ 194 Rod Scurry .15 .06
❑ 195 Rich Murray .15 .06
❑ 196 Duffy Dyer .15 .06
❑ 197 Jim Kern .15 .06
❑ 198 Jerry Dybzinski .15 .06
❑ 199 Chuck Rainey .15 .06
❑ 200 George Foster .40 .16
❑ 201 Johnny Bench RB .75 .30
❑ 202 Steve Carlton RB .40 .16
❑ 203 Bill Gullickson RB .15 .06
❑ 204 Ron LeFlore RB .40 .16
Rodney Scott
❑ 205 Pete Rose RB 1.50 .60
❑ 206 Mike Schmidt RB 1.50 .60
❑ 207 Ozzie Smith RB 2.00 .80
❑ 208 Willie Wilson RB .15 .06
❑ 209 Dickie Thon DP .15 .06
❑ 210 Jim Palmer .75 .30
❑ 211 Derrel Thomas .15 .06
❑ 212 Steve Nicosia .15 .06
❑ 213 Al Holland .15 .06
❑ 214 Ralph Botting .25 .10
Jim Dorsey
John Harris
❑ 215 Larry Hisle .15 .06
❑ 216 John Henry Johnson .15 .06
❑ 217 Rich Hebner .15 .06
❑ 218 Paul Splittorff .15 .06
❑ 219 Ken Landreaux .15 .06
❑ 220 Tom Seaver 1.50 .60
❑ 221 Bob Davis .15 .06
❑ 222 Jorge Orta .15 .06
❑ 223 Roy Lee Jackson .15 .06
❑ 224 Pat Zachry .15 .06
❑ 225 Ruppert Jones .15 .06
❑ 226 Manny Sanguillen DP .25 .10
❑ 227 Fred Martinez .15 .06
❑ 228 Tom Paciorek .15 .06
❑ 229 Rollie Fingers .40 .16
❑ 230 George Hendrick .40 .16
❑ 231 Joe Beckwith .15 .06
❑ 232 Mickey Klutts .15 .06
❑ 233 Skip Lockwood .15 .06
❑ 234 Lou Whitaker .75 .30
❑ 235 Scott Sanderson .15 .06
❑ 236 Mike Ivie .15 .06
❑ 237 Charlie Moore .15 .06
❑ 238 Willie Hernandez .15 .06
❑ 239 Rick Miller DP .15 .06
❑ 240 Nolan Ryan 8.00 3.20
❑ 241 Checklist 122-242 DP .25 .10
❑ 242 Chet Lemon .40 .16
❑ 243 Sal Butera .15 .06
❑ 244 Tito Landrum .25 .10
Al Olmsted
Andy Rincon
❑ 245 Ed Figueroa .15 .06
❑ 246 Ed Ott DP .15 .06
❑ 247 Glenn Hubbard DP .15 .06
❑ 248 Joey McLaughlin .15 .06
❑ 249 Larry Cox .15 .06
❑ 250 Ron Guidry .40 .16
❑ 251 Tom Brookens .15 .06
❑ 252 Victor Cruz .15 .06
❑ 253 Dave Bergman .15 .06
❑ 254 Ozzie Smith 5.00 2.00
❑ 255 Mark Littell .15 .06
❑ 256 Bombo Rivera .15 .06
❑ 257 Rennie Stennett .15 .06
❑ 258 Joe Price .15 .06
❑ 259 Juan Berenguer 5.00 2.00
Hubie Brooks RC
Mookie Wilson
❑ 260 Ron Cey .40 .16
❑ 261 Rickey Henderson 10.00 4.00
❑ 262 Sammy Stewart .15 .06
❑ 263 Brian Downing .40 .16
❑ 264 Jim Norris .15 .06
❑ 265 John Candelaria .40 .16
❑ 266 Tom Herr .15 .06
❑ 267 Stan Bahnsen .15 .06
❑ 268 Jerry Royster .15 .06
❑ 269 Ken Forsch .15 .06
❑ 270 Greg Luzinski .40 .16
❑ 271 Bill Castro .15 .06
❑ 272 Bruce Kimm .15 .06
❑ 273 Stan Papi .15 .06
❑ 274 Craig Chamberlain .15 .06
❑ 275 Dwight Evans .75 .30
❑ 276 Dan Spillner .15 .06
❑ 277 Alfredo Griffin .15 .06
❑ 278 Rick Sofield .15 .06
❑ 279 Bob Knepper .15 .06
❑ 280 Ken Griffey .40 .16
❑ 281 Fred Stanley .15 .06
❑ 282 Rick Anderson .25 .10
Greg Biercevicz
Rodney Craig
❑ 283 Billy Sample .15 .06
❑ 284 Brian Kingman .15 .06
❑ 285 Jerry Turner .15 .06
❑ 286 Dave Frost .15 .06
❑ 287 Lenn Sakata .15 .06
❑ 288 Bob Clark .15 .06
❑ 289 Mickey Hatcher .15 .06
❑ 290 Bob Boone DP .25 .10
❑ 291 Aurelio Lopez .15 .06
❑ 292 Mike Squires .15 .06
❑ 293 Charlie Lea .15 .06
❑ 294 Mike Tyson DP .15 .06
❑ 295 Hal McRae .40 .16
❑ 296 Bill Nahorodny DP .15 .06
❑ 297 Bob Bailor .15 .06
❑ 298 Buddy Solomon .15 .06
❑ 299 Elliott Maddox .15 .06
❑ 300 Paul Molitor 1.50 .60
❑ 301 Matt Keough .15 .06
❑ 302 Jack Perconte 8.00 3.20
Mike Scioscia RC
Fernando Valenzuela RC
❑ 303 Johnny Oates .40 .16
❑ 304 John Castino .15 .06
❑ 305 Ken Clay .15 .06
❑ 306 Juan Beniquez DP .15 .06
❑ 307 Gene Garber .15 .06
❑ 308 Rick Manning .15 .06
❑ 309 Luis Salazar RC .75 .30
❑ 310 Vida Blue DP .25 .10
❑ 311 Freddie Patek .15 .06
❑ 312 Rick Rhoden .15 .06
❑ 313 Luis Pujols .15 .06
❑ 314 Rich Dauer .15 .06
❑ 315 Kirk Gibson RC 8.00 3.20
❑ 316 Craig Minetto .15 .06
❑ 317 Lonnie Smith .40 .16
❑ 318 Steve Yeager .40 .16
❑ 319 Rowland Office .15 .06
❑ 320 Tom Burgmeier .15 .06
❑ 321 Leon Durham RC .75 .30
❑ 322 Neil Allen .15 .06
❑ 323 Jim Morrison DP .15 .06
❑ 324 Mike Willis .15 .06
❑ 325 Ray Knight .40 .16
❑ 326 Biff Pocoroba .15 .06
❑ 327 Moose Haas .15 .06

❑ 328 Dave Engle .25 .10
Greg Johnston
Gary Ward
❑ 329 Joaquin Andujar .40 .16
❑ 330 Frank White .40 .16
❑ 331 Dennis Lamp .15 .06
❑ 332 Lee Lacy DP .15 .06
❑ 333 Sid Monge .15 .06
❑ 334 Dane Iorg .15 .06
❑ 335 Rick Cerone .15 .06
❑ 336 Eddie Whitson .15 .06
❑ 337 Lynn Jones .15 .06
❑ 338 Checklist 243-363 .40 .16
❑ 339 John Ellis .15 .06
❑ 340 Bruce Kison .15 .06
❑ 341 Dwayne Murphy .15 .06
❑ 342 Eric Rasmussen DP .15 .06
❑ 343 Frank Taveras .15 .06
❑ 344 Byron McLaughlin .15 .06
❑ 345 Warren Cromartie .15 .06
❑ 346 Larry Christenson DP .15 .06
❑ 347 Harold Baines RC 3.00 1.20
❑ 348 Bob Sykes .15 .06
❑ 349 Glenn Hoffman .15 .06
❑ 350 J.R. Richard .40 .16
❑ 351 Otto Velez .15 .06
❑ 352 Dick Tidrow DP .15 .06
❑ 353 Terry Kennedy .15 .06
❑ 354 Mario Soto .40 .16
❑ 355 Bob Horner .40 .16
❑ 356 George Stablein .25 .10
Craig Stimac
Tom Tellmann
❑ 357 Jim Slaton .15 .06
❑ 358 Mark Wagner .15 .06
❑ 359 Tom Hausman .15 .06
❑ 360 Willie Wilson .40 .16
❑ 361 Joe Strain .15 .06
❑ 362 Bo Diaz .15 .06
❑ 363 Geoff Zahn .15 .06
❑ 364 Mike Davis RC .25 .10
❑ 365 Graig Nettles DP .25 .10
❑ 366 Mike Ramsey RC .25 .10
❑ 367 Dennis Martinez .40 .16
❑ 368 Leon Roberts .15 .06
❑ 369 Frank Tanana .40 .16
❑ 370 Dave Winfield .75 .30
❑ 371 Charlie Hough .40 .16
❑ 372 Jay Johnstone .15 .06
❑ 373 Pat Underwood .15 .06
❑ 374 Tommy Hutton .15 .06
❑ 375 Dave Concepcion .40 .16
❑ 376 Ron Reed .15 .06
❑ 377 Jerry Morales .15 .06
❑ 378 Dave Rader .15 .06
❑ 379 Lary Sorensen .15 .06
❑ 380 Willie Stargell .75 .30
❑ 381 Carlos Lezcano .25 .10
Steve Macko
Randy Martz
❑ 382 Paul Mirabella .15 .06
❑ 383 Eric Soderholm DP .15 .06
❑ 384 Mike Sadek .15 .06
❑ 385 Joe Sambito .15 .06
❑ 386 Dave Edwards .15 .06
❑ 387 Phil Niekro .40 .16
❑ 388 Andre Thornton .40 .16
❑ 389 Marty Pattin .15 .06
❑ 390 Cesar Geronimo .15 .06
❑ 391 Dave Lemanczyk DP .15 .06
❑ 392 Lance Parrish .40 .16
❑ 393 Broderick Perkins .15 .06
❑ 394 Woodie Fryman .15 .06
❑ 395 Scot Thompson .15 .06
❑ 396 Bill Campbell .15 .06
❑ 397 Julio Cruz .15 .06
❑ 398 Ross Baumgarten .15 .06
❑ 399 Mike Boddicker RC .75 .30
Mark Corey
Floyd Rayford
❑ 400 Reggie Jackson 1.50 .60
❑ 401 George Brett ALCS 2.50 1.00
❑ 402 NL Champs .75 .30
Phillies squeak
past Astros
(Phillies celebrating)
❑ 403 Larry Bowa WS .75 .30
❑ 404 Tug McGraw WS .75 .30
❑ 405 Nino Espinosa .15 .06
❑ 406 Dickie Noles .15 .06
❑ 407 Ernie Whitt .15 .06
❑ 408 Fernando Arroyo .15 .06
❑ 409 Larry Herndon .15 .06
❑ 410 Bert Campaneris .40 .16
❑ 411 Terry Puhl .15 .06
❑ 412 Britt Burns .15 .06
❑ 413 Tony Bernazard .15 .06
❑ 414 John Pacella DP .15 .06
❑ 415 Ben Oglivie .40 .16
❑ 416 Gary Alexander .15 .06
❑ 417 Dan Schatzeder .15 .06
❑ 418 Bobby Brown .15 .06
❑ 419 Tom Hume .15 .06
❑ 420 Keith Hernandez .40 .16
❑ 421 Bob Stanley .15 .06
❑ 422 Dan Ford .15 .06
❑ 423 Shane Rawley .15 .06
❑ 424 Tim Lollar .25 .10
Bruce Robinson
Dennis Werth
❑ 425 Al Bumbry .15 .06
❑ 426 Warren Brusstar .15 .06
❑ 427 John D'Acquisto .15 .06
❑ 428 John Stearns .15 .06
❑ 429 Mick Kelleher .15 .06
❑ 430 Jim Bibby .15 .06
❑ 431 Dave Roberts .15 .06
❑ 432 Len Barker .40 .16
❑ 433 Rance Mulliniks .15 .06
❑ 434 Roger Erickson .15 .06
❑ 435 Jim Spencer .15 .06
❑ 436 Gary Lucas .15 .06
❑ 437 Mike Heath DP .15 .06
❑ 438 John Montefusco .15 .06
❑ 439 Denny Walling .15 .06
❑ 440 Jerry Reuss .15 .06
❑ 441 Ken Reitz .15 .06
❑ 442 Ron Pruitt .15 .06
❑ 443 Jim Beattie DP .15 .06
❑ 444 Garth Iorg .15 .06
❑ 445 Ellis Valentine .15 .06
❑ 446 Checklist 364-484 .40 .16
❑ 447 Junior Kennedy DP .15 .06
❑ 448 Tim Corcoran .15 .06
❑ 449 Paul Mitchell .15 .06
❑ 450 Dave Kingman DP .25 .10
❑ 451 Chris Bando .25 .10
Tom Brennan
Sandy Wihtol
❑ 452 Renie Martin .15 .06
❑ 453 Rob Wilfong DP .15 .06
❑ 454 Andy Hassler .15 .06
❑ 455 Rick Burleson .15 .06
❑ 456 Jeff Reardon RC 1.50 .60
❑ 457 Mike Lum .15 .06
❑ 458 Randy Jones .40 .16
❑ 459 Greg Gross .15 .06
❑ 460 Rich Gossage .40 .16
❑ 461 Dave McKay .15 .06
❑ 462 Jack Brohamer .15 .06
❑ 463 Milt May .15 .06
❑ 464 Adrian Devine .15 .06
❑ 465 Bill Russell .40 .16
❑ 466 Bob Molinaro .15 .06
❑ 467 Dave Stieb .40 .16
❑ 468 John Wockenfuss .15 .06
❑ 469 Jeff Leonard .40 .16
❑ 470 Manny Trillo .15 .06
❑ 471 Mike Vail .15 .06
❑ 472 Dyar Miller DP .15 .06
❑ 473 Jose Cardenal .15 .06
❑ 474 Mike LaCoss .15 .06
❑ 475 Buddy Bell .40 .16
❑ 476 Jerry Koosman .40 .16
❑ 477 Luis Gomez .15 .06
❑ 478 Juan Eichelberger .15 .06
❑ 479 Tim Raines RC 4.00 1.60
Roberto Ramos
Bobby Pate
❑ 480 Carlton Fisk .75 .30
❑ 481 Bob Lacey DP .15 .06
❑ 482 Jim Gantner .15 .06
❑ 483 Mike Griffin RC .25 .10
❑ 484 Max Venable DP .15 .06
❑ 485 Garry Templeton .40 .16
❑ 486 Marc Hill .15 .06
❑ 487 Dewey Robinson .15 .06
❑ 488 Damaso Garcia .15 .06
❑ 489 John Littlefield .15 .06
Photo on card believed to be Mark
Riggins
❑ 490 Eddie Murray 2.50 1.00
❑ 491 Gordy Pladson .15 .06
❑ 492 Barry Foote .15 .06
❑ 493 Dan Quisenberry .15 .06
❑ 494 Bob Walk RC .75 .30
❑ 495 Dusty Baker .40 .16
❑ 496 Paul Dade .15 .06
❑ 497 Fred Norman .15 .06
❑ 498 Pat Putnam .15 .06
❑ 499 Frank Pastore .15 .06
❑ 500 Jim Rice .40 .16
❑ 501 Tim Foli DP .15 .06
❑ 502 Chris Bourjos .25 .10
Al Hargesheimer
Mike Rowland
❑ 503 Steve McCatty .15 .06
❑ 504 Dale Murphy .75 .30
❑ 505 Jason Thompson .15 .06
❑ 506 Phil Huffman .15 .06
❑ 507 Jamie Quirk .15 .06
❑ 508 Rob Dressler .15 .06
❑ 509 Pete Mackanin .15 .06
❑ 510 Lee Mazzilli .40 .16
❑ 511 Wayne Garland .15 .06
❑ 512 Gary Thomasson .15 .06
❑ 513 Frank LaCorte .15 .06
❑ 514 George Riley .15 .06
❑ 515 Robin Yount 2.50 1.00
❑ 516 Doug Bird .15 .06
❑ 517 Richie Zisk .15 .06
❑ 518 Grant Jackson .15 .06
❑ 519 John Tamargo DP .15 .06
❑ 520 Steve Stone .15 .06
❑ 521 Sam Mejias .15 .06
❑ 522 Mike Colbern .15 .06
❑ 523 John Fulgham .15 .06
❑ 524 Willie Aikens .15 .06
❑ 525 Mike Torrez .15 .06
❑ 526 Marty Bystrom .25 .10
Jay Loviglio
Jim Wright
❑ 527 Danny Goodwin .15 .06
❑ 528 Gary Matthews .40 .16
❑ 529 Dave LaRoche .15 .06
❑ 530 Steve Garvey .75 .30
❑ 531 John Curtis .15 .06
❑ 532 Bill Stein .15 .06
❑ 533 Jesus Figueroa .15 .06
❑ 534 Dave Smith RC .75 .30
❑ 535 Omar Moreno .15 .06
❑ 536 Bob Owchinko DP .15 .06
❑ 537 Ron Hodges .15 .06
❑ 538 Tom Griffin .15 .06
❑ 539 Rodney Scott .15 .06
❑ 540 Mike Schmidt DP 2.00 .80
❑ 541 Steve Swisher .15 .06
❑ 542 Larry Bradford DP .15 .06
❑ 543 Terry Crowley .15 .06
❑ 544 Rich Gale .15 .06
❑ 545 Johnny Grubb .15 .06
❑ 546 Paul Moskau .15 .06
❑ 547 Mario Guerrero .15 .06
❑ 548 Dave Goltz .15 .06
❑ 549 Jerry Remy .15 .06
❑ 550 Tommy John .40 .16
❑ 551 Vance Law .75 .30
Tony Pena RC
Pascual Perez RC
❑ 552 Steve Trout .15 .06
❑ 553 Tim Blackwell .15 .06
❑ 554 Bert Blyleven UER .40 .16
(1 is missing from
1980 on card back)
❑ 555 Cecil Cooper .40 .16
❑ 556 Jerry Mumphrey .15 .06
❑ 557 Chris Knapp .15 .06
❑ 558 Barry Bonnell .15 .06

- ❑ 559 Willie Montanez .15 .06
- ❑ 560 Joe Morgan .75 .30
- ❑ 561 Dennis Littlejohn .15 .06
- ❑ 562 Checklist 485-605 .40 .16
- ❑ 563 Jim Kaat .40 .16
- ❑ 564 Ron Hassey DP .15 .06
- ❑ 565 Burt Hooton .15 .06
- ❑ 566 Del Unser .15 .06
- ❑ 567 Mark Bomback .15 .06
- ❑ 568 Dave Revering .15 .06
- ❑ 569 Al Williams DP .15 .06
- ❑ 570 Ken Singleton .40 .16
- ❑ 571 Todd Cruz .15 .06
- ❑ 572 Jack Morris .75 .30
- ❑ 573 Phil Garner .40 .16
- ❑ 574 Bill Caudill .15 .06
- ❑ 575 Tony Perez .75 .30
- ❑ 576 Reggie Cleveland .15 .06
- ❑ 577 Luis Leal .25 .10
  Brian Milner
  Ken Schrom
- ❑ 578 Bill Gullickson RC .75 .30
- ❑ 579 Tim Flannery .15 .06
- ❑ 580 Don Baylor .40 .16
- ❑ 581 Roy Howell .15 .06
- ❑ 582 Gaylord Perry .40 .16
- ❑ 583 Larry Milbourne .15 .06
- ❑ 584 Randy Lerch .15 .06
- ❑ 585 Amos Otis .40 .16
- ❑ 586 Silvio Martinez .15 .06
- ❑ 587 Jeff Newman .15 .06
- ❑ 588 Gary Lavelle .15 .06
- ❑ 589 Lamar Johnson .15 .06
- ❑ 590 Bruce Sutter .40 .16
- ❑ 591 John Lowenstein .15 .06
- ❑ 592 Steve Comer .15 .06
- ❑ 593 Steve Kemp .15 .06
- ❑ 594 Preston Hanna DP .15 .06
- ❑ 595 Butch Hobson .15 .06
- ❑ 596 Jerry Augustine .15 .06
- ❑ 597 Rafael Landestoy .15 .06
- ❑ 598 George Vukovich DP .15 .06
- ❑ 599 Dennis Kinney .15 .06
- ❑ 600 Johnny Bench 1.50 .60
- ❑ 601 Don Aase .15 .06
- ❑ 602 Bobby Murcer .40 .16
- ❑ 603 John Verhoeven .15 .06
- ❑ 604 Rob Picciolo .15 .06
- ❑ 605 Don Sutton .40 .16
- ❑ 606 Bruce Berenyi .25 .10
  Geoff Combe
  Paul Householder
- ❑ 607 David Palmer .15 .06
- ❑ 608 Greg Pryor .15 .06
- ❑ 609 Lynn McGlothen .15 .06
- ❑ 610 Darrell Porter .15 .06
- ❑ 611 Rick Matula DP .15 .06
- ❑ 612 Duane Kuiper .15 .06
- ❑ 613 Jim Anderson .15 .06
- ❑ 614 Dave Rozema .15 .06
- ❑ 615 Rick Dempsey .15 .06
- ❑ 616 Rick Wise .15 .06
- ❑ 617 Craig Reynolds .15 .06
- ❑ 618 John Milner .15 .06
- ❑ 619 Steve Henderson .15 .06
- ❑ 620 Dennis Eckersley .75 .30
- ❑ 621 Tom Donohue .15 .06
- ❑ 622 Randy Moffitt .15 .06
- ❑ 623 Sal Bando .40 .16
- ❑ 624 Bob Welch .40 .16
- ❑ 625 Bill Buckner .40 .16
- ❑ 626 Dave Steffen .25 .10
  Jerry Ujdur
  Roger Weaver
- ❑ 627 Luis Tiant .40 .16
- ❑ 628 Vic Correll .15 .06
- ❑ 629 Tony Armas .40 .16
- ❑ 630 Steve Carlton .75 .30
- ❑ 631 Ron Jackson .15 .06
- ❑ 632 Alan Bannister .15 .06
- ❑ 633 Bill Lee .40 .16
- ❑ 634 Doug Flynn .15 .06
- ❑ 635 Bobby Bonds .40 .16
- ❑ 636 Al Hrabosky .40 .16
- ❑ 637 Jerry Narron .15 .06
- ❑ 638 Checklist 606-726 .40 .16
- ❑ 639 Carney Lansford .40 .16
- ❑ 640 Dave Parker .40 .16
- ❑ 641 Mark Belanger .15 .06
- ❑ 642 Vern Ruhle .15 .06
- ❑ 643 Lloyd Moseby RC .75 .30
- ❑ 644 Ramon Aviles DP .15 .06
- ❑ 645 Rick Reuschel .40 .16
- ❑ 646 Marvis Foley .15 .06
- ❑ 647 Dick Drago .15 .06
- ❑ 648 Darrell Evans .40 .16
- ❑ 649 Manny Sarmiento .15 .06
- ❑ 650 Bucky Dent .40 .16
- ❑ 651 Pedro Guerrero .40 .16
- ❑ 652 John Montague .15 .06
- ❑ 653 Bill Fahey .15 .06
- ❑ 654 Ray Burris .15 .06
- ❑ 655 Dan Driessen .15 .06
- ❑ 656 Jon Matlack .15 .06
- ❑ 657 Mike Cubbage DP .15 .06
- ❑ 658 Milt Wilcox .15 .06
- ❑ 659 John Flinn .75 .30
  Ed Romero
  Ned Yost
- ❑ 660 Gary Carter .75 .30
- ❑ 661 Orioles Team CL .40 .16
  Earl Weaver MG
- ❑ 662 Red Sox Team CL .40 .16
  Ralph Houk MG
- ❑ 663 Angels Team CL .40 .16
  Jim Fregosi MG
- ❑ 664 White Sox CL .40 .16
  Tony LaRussa MG
- ❑ 665 Indians Team CL .40 .16
  Dave Garcia MG
- ❑ 666 Tigers Team CL .40 .16
  Sparky Anderson MG
- ❑ 667 Royals Team CL .40 .16
  Jim Frey MG
- ❑ 668 Brewers Team CL .40 .16
  Bob Rodgers MG
- ❑ 669 Twins Team CL .40 .16
  John Goryl MG
- ❑ 670 Yankees Team CL .40 .16
  Gene Michael MG
- ❑ 671 A's Team CL .75 .30
  Billy Martin MG
- ❑ 672 Mariners Team CL .40 .16
  Maury Wills MG
- ❑ 673 Rangers Team CL .40 .16
  Don Zimmer MG
- ❑ 674 Blue Jays Team CL .40 .16
  Bobby Mattick MG
- ❑ 675 Braves Team CL .40 .16
  Bobby Cox MG
- ❑ 676 Cubs Team CL .40 .16
  Joe Amalfitano MG
- ❑ 677 Reds Team CL .40 .16
  John McNamara MG
- ❑ 678 Astros Team CL .40 .16
  Bill Virdon MG
- ❑ 679 Dodgers Team CL .75 .30
  Tom Lasorda MG
- ❑ 680 Expos Team CL .40 .16
  Dick Williams MG
- ❑ 681 Mets Team CL .75 .30
  Joe Torre MG
- ❑ 682 Phillies Team CL .40 .16
  Dallas Green MG
- ❑ 683 Pirates Team CL .40 .16
  Chuck Tanner MG
- ❑ 684 Cardinals Team CL .40 .16
  Whitey Herzog MG
- ❑ 685 Padres Team CL .40 .16
  Frank Howard MG
- ❑ 686 Giants Team CL .40 .16
  Dave Bristol MG
- ❑ 687 Jeff Jones .15 .06
- ❑ 688 Kiko Garcia .15 .06
- ❑ 689 Bruce Hurst RC .75 .30
  Keith MacWhorter
  Reid Nichols
- ❑ 690 Bob Watson .15 .06
- ❑ 691 Dick Ruthven .15 .06
- ❑ 692 Lenny Randle .15 .06
- ❑ 693 Steve Howe RC .25 .10
- ❑ 694 Bud Harrelson DP .25 .10
- ❑ 695 Kent Tekulve .15 .06
- ❑ 696 Alan Ashby .15 .06
- ❑ 697 Rick Waits .15 .06
- ❑ 698 Mike Jorgensen .15 .06
- ❑ 699 Glenn Abbott .15 .06
- ❑ 700 George Brett 4.00 1.60
- ❑ 701 Joe Rudi .40 .16
- ❑ 702 George Medich .15 .06
- ❑ 703 Alvis Woods .15 .06
- ❑ 704 Bill Travers DP .15 .06
- ❑ 705 Ted Simmons .40 .16
- ❑ 706 Dave Ford .15 .06
- ❑ 707 Dave Cash .15 .06
- ❑ 708 Doyle Alexander .15 .06
- ❑ 709 Alan Trammell DP .50 .20
- ❑ 710 Ron LeFlore DP .25 .10
- ❑ 711 Joe Ferguson .15 .06
- ❑ 712 Bill Bonham .15 .06
- ❑ 713 Bill North .15 .06
- ❑ 714 Pete Redfern .15 .06
- ❑ 715 Bill Madlock .40 .16
- ❑ 716 Glenn Borgmann .15 .06
- ❑ 717 Jim Barr DP .15 .06
- ❑ 718 Larry Biittner .15 .06
- ❑ 719 Sparky Lyle .40 .16
- ❑ 720 Fred Lynn .40 .16
- ❑ 721 Toby Harrah .40 .16
- ❑ 722 Joe Niekro .15 .06
- ❑ 723 Bruce Bochte .15 .06
- ❑ 724 Lou Piniella .40 .16
- ❑ 725 Steve Rogers .40 .16
- ❑ 726 Rick Monday .40 .16

1981 Topps Traded

	Nm-Mt	Ex-Mt
COMP.FACT.SET (132)	25.00	10.00

- ❑ 727 Danny Ainge XRC 5.00 2.00
- ❑ 728 Doyle Alexander .25 .10
- ❑ 729 Gary Alexander .25 .10
- ❑ 730 Bill Almon .25 .10
- ❑ 731 Joaquin Andujar 1.00 .40
- ❑ 732 Bob Bailor .25 .10
- ❑ 733 Juan Beniquez .25 .10
- ❑ 734 Dave Bergman .25 .10
- ❑ 735 Tony Bernazard .25 .10
- ❑ 736 Larry Biittner .25 .10
- ❑ 737 Doug Bird .25 .10
- ❑ 738 Bert Blyleven 1.00 .40
- ❑ 739 Mark Bomback .25 .10
- ❑ 740 Bobby Bonds 1.00 .40
- ❑ 741 Rick Bosetti .25 .10
- ❑ 742 Hubie Brooks 2.00 .80
- ❑ 743 Rick Burleson .25 .10
- ❑ 744 Ray Burris .25 .10
- ❑ 745 Jeff Burroughs 1.00 .40
- ❑ 746 Enos Cabell .25 .10
- ❑ 747 Ken Clay .25 .10
- ❑ 748 Mark Clear .25 .10
- ❑ 749 Larry Cox .25 .10
- ❑ 750 Hector Cruz .25 .10
- ❑ 751 Victor Cruz .25 .10
- ❑ 752 Mike Cubbage .25 .10
- ❑ 753 Dick Davis .25 .10
- ❑ 754 Brian Doyle .25 .10
- ❑ 755 Dick Drago .25 .10
- ❑ 756 Leon Durham 1.00 .40
- ❑ 757 Jim Dwyer .25 .10

	Nm-Mt	Ex-Mt
❑ 758 Dave Edwards UER	.25	.10
No birthdate on card		
❑ 759 Jim Essian	.25	.10
❑ 760 Bill Fahey	.25	.10
❑ 761 Rollie Fingers	1.00	.40
❑ 762 Carlton Fisk	2.00	.80
❑ 763 Barry Foote	.25	.10
❑ 764 Ken Forsch	.25	.10
❑ 765 Kiko Garcia	.25	.10
❑ 766 Cesar Geronimo	.25	.10
❑ 767 Gary Gray	.25	.10
❑ 768 Mickey Hatcher	.25	.10
❑ 769 Steve Henderson	.25	.10
❑ 770 Marc Hill	.25	.10
❑ 771 Butch Hobson	.25	.10
❑ 772 Rick Honeycutt	.25	.10
❑ 773 Roy Howell	.25	.10
❑ 774 Mike Ivie	.25	.10
❑ 775 Roy Lee Jackson	.25	.10
❑ 776 Cliff Johnson	.25	.10
❑ 777 Randy Jones	1.00	.40
❑ 778 Ruppert Jones	.25	.10
❑ 779 Mick Kelleher	.25	.10
❑ 780 Terry Kennedy	.25	.10
❑ 781 Dave Kingman	1.00	.40
❑ 782 Bob Knepper	.25	.10
❑ 783 Ken Kravec	.25	.10
❑ 784 Bob Lacey	.25	.10
❑ 785 Dennis Lamp	.25	.10
❑ 786 Rafael Landestoy	.25	.10
❑ 787 Ken Landreaux	.25	.10
❑ 788 Carney Lansford	1.00	.40
❑ 789 Dave LaRoche	.25	.10
❑ 790 Joe Lefebvre	.25	.10
❑ 791 Ron LeFlore	1.00	.40
❑ 792 Randy Lerch	.25	.10
❑ 793 Sixto Lezcano	.25	.10
❑ 794 John Littlefield	.25	.10
❑ 795 Mike Lum	.25	.10
❑ 796 Greg Luzinski	1.00	.40
❑ 797 Fred Lynn	1.00	.40
❑ 798 Jerry Martin	.25	.10
❑ 799 Buck Martinez	.25	.10
❑ 800 Gary Matthews	1.00	.40
❑ 801 Mario Mendoza	.25	.10
❑ 802 Larry Milbourne	.25	.10
❑ 803 Rick Miller	.25	.10
❑ 804 John Montefusco	.25	.10
❑ 805 Jerry Morales	.25	.10
❑ 806 Jose Morales	.25	.10
❑ 807 Joe Morgan	2.00	.80
❑ 808 Jerry Mumphrey	.25	.10
❑ 809 Gene Nelson	.25	.10
❑ 810 Ed Ott	.25	.10
❑ 811 Bob Owchinko	.25	.10
❑ 812 Gaylord Perry	1.00	.40
❑ 813 Mike Phillips	.25	.10
❑ 814 Darrell Porter	.25	.10
❑ 815 Mike Proly	.25	.10
❑ 816 Tim Raines	5.00	2.00
❑ 817 Lenny Randle	.25	.10
❑ 818 Doug Rau	.25	.10
❑ 819 Jeff Reardon	2.00	.80
❑ 820 Ken Reitz	.25	.10
❑ 821 Steve Renko	.25	.10
❑ 822 Rick Reuschel	1.00	.40
❑ 823 Dave Revering	.25	.10
❑ 824 Dave Roberts	.25	.10
❑ 825 Leon Roberts	.25	.10
❑ 826 Joe Rudi	1.00	.40
❑ 827 Kevin Saucier	.25	.10
❑ 828 Tony Scott	.25	.10
❑ 829 Bob Shirley	.25	.10
❑ 830 Ted Simmons	1.00	.40
❑ 831 Lary Sorensen	.25	.10
❑ 832 Jim Spencer	.25	.10
❑ 833 Harry Spilman	.25	.10
❑ 834 Fred Stanley	.25	.10
❑ 835 Rusty Staub	1.00	.40
❑ 836 Bill Stein	.25	.10
❑ 837 Joe Strain	.25	.10
❑ 838 Bruce Sutter	1.00	.40
❑ 839 Don Sutton	1.00	.40
❑ 840 Steve Swisher	.25	.10
❑ 841 Frank Tanana	1.00	.40
❑ 842 Gene Tenace	1.00	.40
❑ 843 Jason Thompson	.25	.10
❑ 844 Dickie Thon	.25	.10
❑ 845 Bill Travers	.25	.10
❑ 846 Tom Underwood	.25	.10
❑ 847 John Urrea	.25	.10
❑ 848 Mike Vail	.25	.10
❑ 849 Ellis Valentine	.25	.10
❑ 850 Fernando Valenzuela	10.00	4.00
❑ 851 Pete Vuckovich	.25	.10
❑ 852 Mark Wagner	.25	.10
❑ 853 Bob Walk	1.00	.40
❑ 854 Claudell Washington	.25	.10
❑ 855 Dave Winfield	2.00	.80
❑ 856 Geoff Zahn	.25	.10
❑ 857 Richie Zisk	.25	.10
❑ 858 Checklist 727-858	.25	.10

1982 Topps

	Nm-Mt	Ex-Mt
COMPLETE SET (792)	80.00	32.00
❑ 1 Steve Carlton HL	.30	.12
❑ 2 Ron Davis HL	.15	.06
❑ 3 Tim Raines HL	.30	.12
❑ 4 Pete Rose HL	.60	.24
❑ 5 Nolan Ryan HL	3.00	1.20
❑ 6 Fernando Valenzuela HL	.60	.24
❑ 7 Scott Sanderson	.15	.06
❑ 8 Rich Dauer	.15	.06
❑ 9 Ron Guidry	.30	.12
❑ 10 Ron Guidry SA	.15	.06
❑ 11 Gary Alexander	.15	.06
❑ 12 Moose Haas	.15	.06
❑ 13 Lamar Johnson	.15	.06
❑ 14 Steve Howe	.15	.06
❑ 15 Ellis Valentine	.15	.06
❑ 16 Steve Comer	.15	.06
❑ 17 Darrell Evans	.30	.12
❑ 18 Fernando Arroyo	.15	.06
❑ 19 Ernie Whitt	.15	.06
❑ 20 Garry Maddox	.15	.06
❑ 21 Bob Bonner	50.00	20.00
Cal Ripken RC		
Jeff Schneider		
Birthdate for Jeff Scheider is wrong		
❑ 22 Jim Beattie	.15	.06
❑ 23 Willie Hernandez	.15	.06
❑ 24 Dave Frost	.15	.06
❑ 25 Jerry Remy	.15	.06
❑ 26 Jorge Orta	.15	.06
❑ 27 Tom Herr	.15	.06
❑ 28 John Urrea	.15	.06
❑ 29 Dwayne Murphy	.15	.06
❑ 30 Tom Seaver	1.25	.50
❑ 31 Tom Seaver SA	.30	.12
❑ 32 Gene Garber	.15	.06
❑ 33 Jerry Morales	.15	.06
❑ 34 Joe Sambito	.15	.06
❑ 35 Willie Aikens	.15	.06
❑ 36 Al Oliver	.60	.24
Doc Medich TL		
❑ 37 Dan Graham	.15	.06
❑ 38 Charlie Lea	.15	.06
❑ 39 Lou Whitaker	.30	.12
❑ 40 Dave Parker	.30	.12
❑ 41 Dave Parker SA	.15	.06
❑ 42 Rick Sofield	.15	.06
❑ 43 Mike Cubbage	.15	.06
❑ 44 Britt Burns	.15	.06
❑ 45 Rick Cerone	.15	.06
❑ 46 Jerry Augustine	.15	.06
❑ 47 Jeff Leonard	.15	.06
❑ 48 Bobby Castillo	.15	.06
❑ 49 Alvis Woods	.15	.06
❑ 50 Buddy Bell	.30	.12
❑ 51 Jay Howell RC	.75	.30
Carlos Lezcano		
Ty Waller		
❑ 52 Larry Andersen	.15	.06
❑ 53 Greg Gross	.15	.06
❑ 54 Ron Hassey	.15	.06
❑ 55 Rick Burleson	.15	.06
❑ 56 Mark Littell	.15	.06
❑ 57 Craig Reynolds	.15	.06
❑ 58 John D'Acquisto	.15	.06
❑ 59 Rich Gedman	.75	.30
❑ 60 Tony Armas	.30	.12
❑ 61 Tommy Boggs	.15	.06
❑ 62 Mike Tyson	.15	.06
❑ 63 Mario Soto	.30	.12
❑ 64 Lynn Jones	.15	.06
❑ 65 Terry Kennedy	.15	.06
❑ 66 Art Howe	2.00	.80
Nolan Ryan TL		
❑ 67 Rich Gale	.15	.06
❑ 68 Roy Howell	.15	.06
❑ 69 Al Williams	.15	.06
❑ 70 Tim Raines	.60	.24
❑ 71 Roy Lee Jackson	.15	.06
❑ 72 Rick Auerbach	.15	.06
❑ 73 Buddy Solomon	.15	.06
❑ 74 Bob Clark	.15	.06
❑ 75 Tommy John	.30	.12
❑ 76 Greg Pryor	.15	.06
❑ 77 Miguel Dilone	.15	.06
❑ 78 George Medich	.15	.06
❑ 79 Bob Bailor	.15	.06
❑ 80 Jim Palmer	.30	.12
❑ 81 Jim Palmer SA	.15	.06
❑ 82 Bob Welch	.30	.12
❑ 83 Steve Balboni RC	.75	.30
Andy McGaffigan		
Andre Robertson		
❑ 84 Rennie Stennett	.15	.06
❑ 85 Lynn McGlothen	.15	.06
❑ 86 Dane Iorg	.15	.06
❑ 87 Matt Keough	.15	.06
❑ 88 Biff Pocoroba	.15	.06
❑ 89 Steve Henderson	.15	.06
❑ 90 Nolan Ryan	6.00	2.40
❑ 91 Carney Lansford	.30	.12
❑ 92 Brad Havens	.15	.06
❑ 93 Larry Hisle	.15	.06
❑ 94 Andy Hassler	.15	.06
❑ 95 Ozzie Smith	2.50	1.00
❑ 96 George Brett	1.25	.50
Larry Gura TL		
❑ 97 Paul Moskau	.15	.06
❑ 98 Terry Bulling	.15	.06
❑ 99 Barry Bonnell	.15	.06
❑ 100 Mike Schmidt	3.00	1.20
❑ 101 Mike Schmidt SA	1.25	.50
❑ 102 Dan Briggs	.15	.06
❑ 103 Bob Lacey	.15	.06
❑ 104 Rance Mulliniks	.15	.06
❑ 105 Kirk Gibson	1.25	.50
❑ 106 Enrique Romo	.15	.06
❑ 107 Wayne Krenchicki	.15	.06
❑ 108 Bob Sykes	.15	.06
❑ 109 Dave Revering	.15	.06
❑ 110 Carlton Fisk	.60	.24
❑ 111 Carlton Fisk SA	.30	.12
❑ 112 Billy Sample	.15	.06
❑ 113 Steve McCatty	.15	.06
❑ 114 Ken Landreaux	.15	.06
❑ 115 Gaylord Perry	.30	.12
❑ 116 Jim Wohlford	.15	.06
❑ 117 Rawly Eastwick	.30	.12
❑ 118 Terry Francona RC	5.00	2.00
Brad Mills		
Bryn Smith RC		
❑ 119 Joe Pittman	.15	.06
❑ 120 Gary Lucas	.15	.06
❑ 121 Ed Lynch	.15	.06

❑ 122 Jamie Easterly UER .15 .06
(Photo actually
Reggie Cleveland)
❑ 123 Danny Goodwin .15 .06
❑ 124 Reid Nichols .15 .06
❑ 125 Danny Ainge .30 .12
❑ 126 Claudell Washington .60 .24
Rick Mahler TL
❑ 127 Lonnie Smith .15 .06
❑ 128 Frank Pastore .15 .06
❑ 129 Checklist 1-132 .30 .12
❑ 130 Julio Cruz .15 .06
❑ 131 Stan Bahnsen .15 .06
❑ 132 Lee May .15 .06
❑ 133 Pat Underwood .15 .06
❑ 134 Dan Ford .15 .06
❑ 135 Andy Rincon .15 .06
❑ 136 Lenn Sakata .15 .06
❑ 137 George Cappuzzello .15 .06
❑ 138 Tony Pena .30 .12
❑ 139 Jeff Jones .15 .06
❑ 140 Ron LeFlore .30 .12
❑ 141 Chris Bando .75 .30
Tom Brennan
Von Hayes RC
❑ 142 Dave LaRoche .15 .06
❑ 143 Mookie Wilson .30 .12
❑ 144 Fred Breining .15 .06
❑ 145 Bob Horner .30 .12
❑ 146 Mike Griffin .15 .06
❑ 147 Denny Walling .15 .06
❑ 148 Mickey Klutts .15 .06
❑ 149 Pat Putnam .15 .06
❑ 150 Ted Simmons .30 .12
❑ 151 Dave Edwards .15 .06
❑ 152 Ramon Aviles .15 .06
❑ 153 Roger Erickson .15 .06
❑ 154 Dennis Werth .15 .06
❑ 155 Otto Velez .15 .06
❑ 156 Rickey Henderson 1.25 .50
Steve McCatty TL
❑ 157 Steve Crawford .15 .06
❑ 158 Brian Downing .30 .12
❑ 159 Larry Biittner .15 .06
❑ 160 Luis Tiant .30 .12
❑ 161 Bill Madlock .30 .12
Carney Lansford LL
❑ 162 Mike Schmidt 1.25 .50
Tony Armas
Dwight Evans
Bobby Grich
Eddie Murray LL
❑ 163 Mike Schmidt 1.25 .50
Eddie Murray LL
❑ 164 Tim Raines 1.25 .50
Rickey Henderson LL
❑ 165 Tom Seaver .30 .12
Denny Martinez
Steve McCatty
Jack Morris
Pete Vuckovich LL
❑ 166 Fernando Valenzuela .30 .12
Len Barker LL
❑ 167 Nolan Ryan 2.00 .80
Steve McCatty LL
❑ 168 Bruce Sutter .30 .12
Rollie Fingers LL
❑ 169 Charlie Leibrandt .15 .06
❑ 170 Jim Bibby .15 .06
❑ 171 Bob Brenly RC 1.50 .60
Chili Davis RC
Bob Tufts
❑ 172 Bill Gullickson .15 .06
❑ 173 Jamie Quirk .15 .06
❑ 174 Dave Ford .15 .06
❑ 175 Jerry Mumphrey .15 .06
❑ 176 Dewey Robinson .15 .06
❑ 177 John Ellis .15 .06
❑ 178 Dyar Miller .15 .06
❑ 179 Steve Garvey .30 .12
❑ 180 Steve Garvey SA .15 .06
❑ 181 Silvio Martinez .15 .06
❑ 182 Larry Herndon .15 .06
❑ 183 Mike Proly .15 .06
❑ 184 Mick Kelleher .15 .06
❑ 185 Phil Niekro .30 .12
❑ 186 Keith Hernandez .30 .12
Bob Forsch TL
❑ 187 Jeff Newman .15 .06
❑ 188 Randy Martz .15 .06
❑ 189 Glenn Hoffman .15 .06
❑ 190 J.R. Richard .30 .12
❑ 191 Tim Wallach RC 1.50 .60
❑ 192 Broderick Perkins .15 .06
❑ 193 Darrell Jackson .15 .06
❑ 194 Mike Vail .15 .06
❑ 195 Paul Molitor .60 .24
❑ 196 Willie Upshaw .75 .30
❑ 197 Shane Rawley .15 .06
❑ 198 Chris Speier .15 .06
❑ 199 Don Aase .15 .06
❑ 200 George Brett 3.00 1.20
❑ 201 George Brett SA 1.50 .60
❑ 202 Rick Manning .15 .06
❑ 203 Jesse Barfield RC 1.50 .60
Brian Milner
Boomer Wells
❑ 204 Gary Roenicke .15 .06
❑ 205 Neil Allen .15 .06
❑ 206 Tony Bernazard .15 .06
❑ 207 Rod Scurry .15 .06
❑ 208 Bobby Murcer .30 .12
❑ 209 Gary Lavelle .15 .06
❑ 210 Keith Hernandez .30 .12
❑ 211 Dan Petry .15 .06
❑ 212 Mario Mendoza .15 .06
❑ 213 Dave Stewart RC 2.50 1.00
❑ 214 Brian Asselstine .15 .06
❑ 215 Mike Krukow .15 .06
❑ 216 Chet Lemon .60 .24
Dennis Lamp TL
❑ 217 Bo McLaughlin .15 .06
❑ 218 Dave Roberts .15 .06
❑ 219 John Curtis .15 .06
❑ 220 Manny Trillo .15 .06
❑ 221 Jim Slaton .15 .06
❑ 222 Butch Wynegar .15 .06
❑ 223 Lloyd Moseby .15 .06
❑ 224 Bruce Bochte .15 .06
❑ 225 Mike Torrez .15 .06
❑ 226 Checklist 133-264 .60 .24
❑ 227 Ray Burris .15 .06
❑ 228 Sam Mejias .15 .06
❑ 229 Geoff Zahn .15 .06
❑ 230 Willie Wilson .30 .12
❑ 231 Mark Davis RC .75 .30
Bob Dernier
Ozzie Virgil
❑ 232 Terry Crowley .15 .06
❑ 233 Duane Kuiper .15 .06
❑ 234 Ron Hodges .15 .06
❑ 235 Mike Easler .15 .06
❑ 236 John Martin RC .25 .10
❑ 237 Rusty Kuntz .15 .06
❑ 238 Kevin Saucier .15 .06
❑ 239 Jon Matlack .15 .06
❑ 240 Bucky Dent .30 .12
❑ 241 Bucky Dent SA .15 .06
❑ 242 Milt May .15 .06
❑ 243 Bob Owchinko .15 .06
❑ 244 Rufino Linares .15 .06
❑ 245 Ken Reitz .15 .06
❑ 246 Hubie Brooks .60 .24
Mike Scott TL
❑ 247 Pedro Guerrero .30 .12
❑ 248 Frank LaCorte .15 .06
❑ 249 Tim Flannery .15 .06
❑ 250 Tug McGraw .30 .12
❑ 251 Fred Lynn .30 .12
❑ 252 Fred Lynn SA .15 .06
❑ 253 Chuck Baker .15 .06
❑ 254 Jorge Bell RC 1.50 .60
❑ 255 Tony Perez .60 .24
❑ 256 Tony Perez SA .30 .12
❑ 257 Larry Harlow .15 .06
❑ 258 Bo Diaz .15 .06
❑ 259 Rodney Scott .15 .06
❑ 260 Bruce Sutter .30 .12
❑ 261 Howard Bailey .15 .06
Marty Castillo
Dave Rucker UER
(Rucker photo actually Roger Weaver)
❑ 262 Doug Bair .15 .06
❑ 263 Victor Cruz .15 .06
❑ 264 Dan Quisenberry .15 .06
❑ 265 Al Bumbry .15 .06
❑ 266 Rick Leach .15 .06
❑ 267 Kurt Bevacqua .15 .06
❑ 268 Rickey Keeton .15 .06
❑ 269 Jim Essian .15 .06
❑ 270 Rusty Staub .30 .12
❑ 271 Larry Bradford .15 .06
❑ 272 Bump Wills .15 .06
❑ 273 Doug Bird .15 .06
❑ 274 Bob Ojeda RC .75 .30
❑ 275 Bob Watson .15 .06
❑ 276 Rod Carew .60 .24
Ken Forsch TL
❑ 277 Terry Puhl .15 .06
❑ 278 John Littlefield .15 .06
❑ 279 Bill Russell .30 .12
❑ 280 Ben Oglivie .30 .12
❑ 281 John Verhoeven .15 .06
❑ 282 Ken Macha .15 .06
❑ 283 Brian Allard .15 .06
❑ 284 Bobby Grich .30 .12
❑ 285 Sparky Lyle .30 .12
❑ 286 Bill Fahey .15 .06
❑ 287 Alan Bannister .15 .06
❑ 288 Garry Templeton .30 .12
❑ 289 Bob Stanley .15 .06
❑ 290 Ken Singleton .30 .12
❑ 291 Vance Law .30 .12
Bob Long
Johnny Ray RC
❑ 292 David Palmer .15 .06
❑ 293 Rob Picciolo .15 .06
❑ 294 Mike LaCoss .15 .06
❑ 295 Jason Thompson .15 .06
❑ 296 Bob Walk .15 .06
❑ 297 Clint Hurdle .15 .06
❑ 298 Danny Darwin .15 .06
❑ 299 Steve Trout .15 .06
❑ 300 Reggie Jackson .60 .24
❑ 301 Reggie Jackson SA .30 .12
❑ 302 Doug Flynn .15 .06
❑ 303 Bill Caudill .15 .06
❑ 304 Johnnie LeMaster .15 .06
❑ 305 Don Sutton .30 .12
❑ 306 Don Sutton SA .15 .06
❑ 307 Randy Bass RC .75 .30
❑ 308 Charlie Moore .15 .06
❑ 309 Pete Redfern .15 .06
❑ 310 Mike Hargrove .15 .06
❑ 311 Dusty Baker .30 .12
Burt Hooton TL
❑ 312 Lenny Randle .15 .06
❑ 313 John Harris .15 .06
❑ 314 Buck Martinez .15 .06
❑ 315 Burt Hooton .15 .06
❑ 316 Steve Braun .15 .06
❑ 317 Dick Ruthven .15 .06
❑ 318 Mike Heath .15 .06
❑ 319 Dave Rozema .15 .06
❑ 320 Chris Chambliss .30 .12
❑ 321 Chris Chambliss SA .15 .06
❑ 322 Garry Hancock .15 .06
❑ 323 Bill Lee .30 .12
❑ 324 Steve Dillard .15 .06
❑ 325 Jose Cruz .30 .12
❑ 326 Pete Falcone .15 .06
❑ 327 Joe Nolan .15 .06
❑ 328 Ed Farmer .15 .06
❑ 329 U.L. Washington .15 .06
❑ 330 Rick Wise .15 .06
❑ 331 Benny Ayala .15 .06
❑ 332 Don Robinson .15 .06
❑ 333 Frank DiPino .15 .06
Marshall Edwards
Chuck Porter
❑ 334 Aurelio Rodriguez .15 .06
❑ 335 Jim Sundberg .30 .12
❑ 336 Tom Paciorek .60 .24
Glenn Abbott TL
❑ 337 Pete Rose AS .60 .24
❑ 338 Dave Lopes AS .15 .06
❑ 339 Mike Schmidt AS 1.25 .50

❑ 340 Dave Concepcion AS .15 .06
❑ 341 Andre Dawson AS .15 .06
❑ 342A George Foster AS .30 .12
(With autograph)
❑ 342B George Foster AS 1.25 .50
(W/o autograph)
❑ 343 Dave Parker AS .15 .06
❑ 344 Gary Carter AS .15 .06
❑ 345 F. Valenzuela AS .60 .24
❑ 346 Tom Seaver AS ERR .30 .12
("t ed")
❑ 346B Tom Seaver AS COR .30 .12
("tied")
❑ 347 Bruce Sutter AS .15 .06
❑ 348 Derrel Thomas .15 .06
❑ 349 George Frazier .15 .06
❑ 350 Thad Bosley .15 .06
❑ 351 Scott Brown .15 .06
Geoff Combe
Paul Householder
❑ 352 Dick Davis .15 .06
❑ 353 Jack O'Connor .15 .06
❑ 354 Roberto Ramos .15 .06
❑ 355 Dwight Evans .60 .24
❑ 356 Denny Lewallyn .15 .06
❑ 357 Butch Hobson .15 .06
❑ 358 Mike Parrott .15 .06
❑ 359 Jim Dwyer .15 .06
❑ 360 Len Barker .15 .06
❑ 361 Rafael Landestoy .15 .06
❑ 362 Jim Wright UER .15 .06
(Wrong Jim Wright
pictured)
❑ 363 Bob Molinaro .15 .06
❑ 364 Doyle Alexander .15 .06
❑ 365 Bill Madlock .30 .12
❑ 366 Luis Salazar .60 .24
Juan Eichelberger TL
❑ 367 Jim Kaat .30 .12
❑ 368 Alex Trevino .15 .06
❑ 369 Champ Summers .15 .06
❑ 370 Mike Norris .15 .06
❑ 371 Jerry Don Gleaton .15 .06
❑ 372 Luis Gomez .15 .06
❑ 373 Gene Nelson .15 .06
❑ 374 Tim Blackwell .15 .06
❑ 375 Dusty Baker .30 .12
❑ 376 Chris Welsh .15 .06
❑ 377 Kiko Garcia .15 .06
❑ 378 Mike Caldwell .15 .06
❑ 379 Rob Wilfong .15 .06
❑ 380 Dave Stieb .30 .12
❑ 381 Bruce Hurst .15 .06
Dave Schmidt
Julio Valdez
❑ 382 Joe Simpson .15 .06
❑ 383A Pascual Perez ERR 40.00 16.00
(No position
on front)
❑ 383B Pascual Perez COR .30 .12
❑ 384 Keith Moreland .15 .06
❑ 385 Ken Forsch .15 .06
❑ 386 Jerry White .15 .06
❑ 387 Tom Veryzer .15 .06
❑ 388 Joe Rudi .30 .12
❑ 389 George Vukovich .15 .06
❑ 390 Eddie Murray 1.25 .50
❑ 391 Dave Tobik .15 .06
❑ 392 Rick Bosetti .15 .06
❑ 393 Al Hrabosky .15 .06
❑ 394 Checklist 265-396 .60 .24
❑ 395 Omar Moreno .15 .06
❑ 396 John Castino .60 .24
Fernando Arroyo TL
❑ 397 Ken Brett .15 .06
❑ 398 Mike Squires .15 .06
❑ 399 Pat Zachry .15 .06
❑ 400 Johnny Bench 1.25 .50
❑ 401 Johnny Bench SA .60 .24
❑ 402 Bill Stein .15 .06
❑ 403 Jim Tracy .30 .12
❑ 404 Dickie Thon .15 .06
❑ 405 Rick Reuschel .30 .12
❑ 406 Al Holland .15 .06
❑ 407 Danny Boone .15 .06
❑ 408 Ed Romero .15 .06
❑ 409 Don Cooper .15 .06
❑ 410 Ron Cey .30 .12
❑ 411 Ron Cey SA .15 .06
❑ 412 Luis Leal .15 .06
❑ 413 Dan Meyer .15 .06
❑ 414 Elias Sosa .15 .06
❑ 415 Don Baylor .30 .12
❑ 416 Marty Bystrom .15 .06
❑ 417 Pat Kelly .15 .06
❑ 418 John Butcher .15 .06
Bobby Johnson
Dave Schmidt
❑ 419 Steve Stone .15 .06
❑ 420 George Hendrick .30 .12
❑ 421 Mark Clear .15 .06
❑ 422 Cliff Johnson .15 .06
❑ 423 Stan Papi .15 .06
❑ 424 Bruce Benedict .15 .06
❑ 425 John Candelaria .15 .06
❑ 426 Eddie Murray .60 .24
Sammy Stewart
❑ 427 Ron Oester .15 .06
❑ 428 LaMarr Hoyt .15 .06
❑ 429 John Wathan .15 .06
❑ 430 Vida Blue .30 .12
❑ 431 Vida Blue SA .15 .06
❑ 432 Mike Scott .30 .12
❑ 433 Alan Ashby .15 .06
❑ 434 Joe Lefebvre .15 .06
❑ 435 Robin Yount 2.00 .80
❑ 436 Joe Strain .15 .06
❑ 437 Juan Berenguer .15 .06
❑ 438 Pete Mackanin .15 .06
❑ 439 Dave Righetti RC 2.50 1.00
❑ 440 Jeff Burroughs .15 .06
❑ 441 Danny Heep .15 .06
Billy Smith
Bobby Sprowl
❑ 442 Bruce Kison .15 .06
❑ 443 Mark Wagner .15 .06
❑ 444 Terry Forster .30 .12
❑ 445 Larry Parrish .15 .06
❑ 446 Wayne Garland .15 .06
❑ 447 Darrell Porter .15 .06
❑ 448 Darrell Porter SA .15 .06
❑ 449 Luis Aguayo .15 .06
❑ 450 Jack Morris .30 .12
❑ 451 Ed Miller .15 .06
❑ 452 Lee Smith RC 3.00 1.20
❑ 453 Art Howe .15 .06
❑ 454 Rick Langford .15 .06
❑ 455 Tom Burgmeier .15 .06
❑ 456 Bill Buckner .30 .12
Randy Martz TL
❑ 457 Tim Stoddard .15 .06
❑ 458 Willie Montanez .15 .06
❑ 459 Bruce Berenyi .15 .06
❑ 460 Jack Clark .30 .12
❑ 461 Rich Dotson .15 .06
❑ 462 Dave Chalk .15 .06
❑ 463 Jim Kern .15 .06
❑ 464 Juan Bonilla RC .25 .10
❑ 465 Lee Mazzilli .30 .12
❑ 466 Randy Lerch .15 .06
❑ 467 Mickey Hatcher .15 .06
❑ 468 Floyd Bannister .15 .06
❑ 469 Ed Ott .15 .06
❑ 470 John Mayberry .15 .06
❑ 471 Atlee Hammaker .15 .06
Mike Jones
Darryl Motley
❑ 472 Oscar Gamble .15 .06
❑ 473 Mike Stanton .15 .06
❑ 474 Ken Oberkfell .15 .06
❑ 475 Alan Trammell .30 .12
❑ 476 Brian Kingman .15 .06
❑ 477 Steve Yeager .30 .12
❑ 478 Ray Searage .15 .06
❑ 479 Rowland Office .15 .06
❑ 480 Steve Carlton .60 .24
❑ 481 Steve Carlton SA .30 .12
❑ 482 Glenn Hubbard .15 .06
❑ 483 Gary Woods .15 .06
❑ 484 Ivan DeJesus .15 .06
❑ 485 Kent Tekulve .15 .06
❑ 486 Jerry Mumphrey .30 .12
Tommy John TL
❑ 487 Bob McClure .15 .06
❑ 488 Ron Jackson .15 .06
❑ 489 Rick Dempsey .15 .06
❑ 490 Dennis Eckersley .60 .24
❑ 491 Checklist 397-528 .60 .24
❑ 492 Joe Price .15 .06
❑ 493 Chet Lemon .30 .12
❑ 494 Hubie Brooks .15 .06
❑ 495 Dennis Leonard .15 .06
❑ 496 Johnny Grubb .15 .06
❑ 497 Jim Anderson .15 .06
❑ 498 Dave Bergman .15 .06
❑ 499 Paul Mirabella .15 .06
❑ 500 Rod Carew .60 .24
❑ 501 Rod Carew SA .30 .12
❑ 502 Steve Bedrosian RC UER 1.50 .60
Photo actually Larry Owen)
Brett Butler RC
Larry Owen
❑ 503 Julio Gonzalez .15 .06
❑ 504 Rick Peters .15 .06
❑ 505 Graig Nettles .30 .12
❑ 506 Graig Nettles SA .15 .06
❑ 507 Terry Harper .15 .06
❑ 508 Jody Davis .15 .06
❑ 509 Harry Spilman .15 .06
❑ 510 Fernando Valenzuela 1.25 .50
❑ 511 Ruppert Jones .15 .06
❑ 512 Jerry Dybzinski .15 .06
❑ 513 Rick Rhoden .15 .06
❑ 514 Joe Ferguson .15 .06
❑ 515 Larry Bowa .30 .12
❑ 516 Larry Bowa SA .15 .06
❑ 517 Mark Brouhard .15 .06
❑ 518 Garth Iorg .15 .06
❑ 519 Glenn Adams .15 .06
❑ 520 Mike Flanagan .15 .06
❑ 521 Bill Almon .15 .06
❑ 522 Chuck Rainey .15 .06
❑ 523 Gary Gray .15 .06
❑ 524 Tom Hausman .15 .06
❑ 525 Ray Knight .30 .12
❑ 526 Warren Cromartie .60 .24
Bill Gullickson TL
❑ 527 John Henry Johnson .15 .06
❑ 528 Matt Alexander .15 .06
❑ 529 Allen Ripley .15 .06
❑ 530 Dickie Noles .15 .06
❑ 531 Rich Bordi .15 .06
Mark Budaska
Kelvin Moore
❑ 532 Toby Harrah .30 .12
❑ 533 Joaquin Andujar .30 .12
❑ 534 Dave McKay .15 .06
❑ 535 Lance Parrish .30 .12
❑ 536 Rafael Ramirez .15 .06
❑ 537 Doug Capilla .15 .06
❑ 538 Lou Piniella .30 .12
❑ 539 Vern Ruhle .15 .06
❑ 540 Andre Dawson .30 .12
❑ 541 Barry Evans .15 .06
❑ 542 Ned Yost .15 .06
❑ 543 Bill Robinson .15 .06
❑ 544 Larry Christenson .15 .06
❑ 545 Reggie Smith .30 .12
❑ 546 Reggie Smith SA .15 .06
❑ 547 Rod Carew AS .30 .12
❑ 548 Willie Randolph AS .15 .06
❑ 549 George Brett AS 1.50 .60
❑ 550 Bucky Dent AS .15 .06
❑ 551 Reggie Jackson AS .30 .12
❑ 552 Ken Singleton AS .15 .06
❑ 553 Dave Winfield AS .15 .06
❑ 554 Carlton Fisk AS .30 .12
❑ 555 Scott McGregor AS .15 .06
❑ 556 Jack Morris AS .15 .06
❑ 557 Rich Gossage AS .15 .06
❑ 558 John Tudor .30 .12
❑ 559 Mike Hargrove .30 .12
Bert Blyleven TL
❑ 560 Doug Corbett .15 .06
❑ 561 Glenn Brummer .15 .06
Luis DeLeon
Gene Roof
❑ 562 Mike O'Berry .15 .06

Card	Player	Nm-Mt	Ex-Mt
❑ 563	Ross Baumgarten	.15	.06
❑ 564	Doug DeCinces	.15	.06
❑ 565	Jackson Todd	.15	.06
❑ 566	Mike Jorgensen	.15	.06
❑ 567	Bob Babcock	.15	.06
❑ 568	Joe Pettini	.15	.06
❑ 569	Willie Randolph	.30	.12
❑ 570	Willie Randolph SA	.15	.06
❑ 571	Glenn Abbott	.15	.06
❑ 572	Juan Beniquez	.15	.06
❑ 573	Rick Waits	.15	.06
❑ 574	Mike Ramsey	.15	.06
❑ 575	Al Cowens	.15	.06
❑ 576	Milt May	.60	.24
	Vida Blue TL		
❑ 577	Rick Monday	.30	.12
❑ 578	Shooty Babitt	.15	.06
❑ 579	Rick Mahler	.15	.06
❑ 580	Bobby Bonds	.30	.12
❑ 581	Ron Reed	.15	.06
❑ 582	Luis Pujols	.15	.06
❑ 583	Tippy Martinez	.15	.06
❑ 584	Hosken Powell	.15	.06
❑ 585	Rollie Fingers	.30	.12
❑ 586	Rollie Fingers SA	.15	.06
❑ 587	Tim Lollar	.15	.06
❑ 588	Dale Berra	.15	.06
❑ 589	Dave Stapleton	.15	.06
❑ 590	Al Oliver	.30	.12
❑ 591	Al Oliver SA	.15	.06
❑ 592	Craig Swan	.15	.06
❑ 593	Billy Smith	.15	.06
❑ 594	Renie Martin	.15	.06
❑ 595	Dave Collins	.15	.06
❑ 596	Damaso Garcia	.15	.06
❑ 597	Wayne Nordhagen	.15	.06
❑ 598	Bob Galasso	.15	.06
❑ 599	Jay Loviglio	.15	.06
	Reggie Patterson		
	Leo Sutherland		
❑ 600	Dave Winfield	.30	.12
❑ 601	Sid Monge	.15	.06
❑ 602	Freddie Patek	.15	.06
❑ 603	Rich Hebner	.15	.06
❑ 604	Orlando Sanchez	.15	.06
❑ 605	Steve Rogers	.30	.12
❑ 606	John Mayberry	.30	.12
	Dave Stieb TL		
❑ 607	Leon Durham	.15	.06
❑ 608	Jerry Royster	.15	.06
❑ 609	Rick Sutcliffe	.30	.12
❑ 610	Rickey Henderson	4.00	1.60
❑ 611	Joe Niekro	.15	.06
❑ 612	Gary Ward	.15	.06
❑ 613	Jim Gantner	.15	.06
❑ 614	Juan Eichelberger	.15	.06
❑ 615	Bob Boone	.30	.12
❑ 616	Bob Boone SA	.15	.06
❑ 617	Scott McGregor	.15	.06
❑ 618	Tim Foli	.15	.06
❑ 619	Bill Campbell	.15	.06
❑ 620	Ken Griffey	.30	.12
❑ 621	Ken Griffey SA	.15	.06
❑ 622	Dennis Lamp	.15	.06
❑ 623	Ron Gardenhire RC	.75	.30
	Terry Leach		
	Tim Leary RC		
❑ 624	Fergie Jenkins	.30	.12
❑ 625	Hal McRae	.30	.12
❑ 626	Randy Jones	.15	.06
❑ 627	Enos Cabell	.15	.06
❑ 628	Bill Travers	.15	.06
❑ 629	John Wockenfuss	.15	.06
❑ 630	Joe Charboneau	.30	.12
❑ 631	Gene Tenace	.30	.12
❑ 632	Bryan Clark RC	.25	.10
❑ 633	Mitchell Page	.15	.06
❑ 634	Checklist 529-660	.60	.24
❑ 635	Ron Davis	.15	.06
❑ 636	Pete Rose	1.25	.50
	Steve Carlton TL		
❑ 637	Rick Camp	.15	.06
❑ 638	John Milner	.15	.06
❑ 639	Ken Kravec	.15	.06
❑ 640	Cesar Cedeno	.30	.12
❑ 641	Steve Mura	.15	.06
❑ 642	Mike Scioscia	.30	.12
❑ 643	Pete Vuckovich	.15	.06
❑ 644	John Castino	.15	.06
❑ 645	Frank White	.30	.12
❑ 646	Frank White SA	.15	.06
❑ 647	Warren Brusstar	.15	.06
❑ 648	Jose Morales	.15	.06
❑ 649	Ken Clay	.15	.06
❑ 650	Carl Yastrzemski	2.00	.80
❑ 651	Carl Yastrzemski SA	1.25	.50
❑ 652	Steve Nicosia	.15	.06
❑ 653	Tom Brunansky RC	1.50	.60
	Luis Sanchez		
	Daryl Sconiers		
❑ 654	Jim Morrison	.15	.06
❑ 655	Joel Youngblood	.15	.06
❑ 656	Eddie Whitson	.15	.06
❑ 657	Tom Poquette	.15	.06
❑ 658	Tito Landrum	.15	.06
❑ 659	Fred Martinez	.15	.06
❑ 660	Dave Concepcion	.30	.12
❑ 661	Dave Concepcion SA	.15	.06
❑ 662	Luis Salazar	.15	.06
❑ 663	Hector Cruz	.15	.06
❑ 664	Dan Spillner	.15	.06
❑ 665	Jim Clancy	.15	.06
❑ 666	Steve Kemp	.60	.24
	Dan Petry TL		
❑ 667	Jeff Reardon	.30	.12
❑ 668	Dale Murphy	.60	.24
❑ 669	Larry Milbourne	.15	.06
❑ 670	Steve Kemp	.15	.06
❑ 671	Mike Davis	.15	.06
❑ 672	Bob Knepper	.15	.06
❑ 673	Keith Drumwright	.15	.06
❑ 674	Dave Goltz	.15	.06
❑ 675	Cecil Cooper	.30	.12
❑ 676	Sal Butera	.15	.06
❑ 677	Alfredo Griffin	.15	.06
❑ 678	Tom Paciorek	.15	.06
❑ 679	Sammy Stewart	.15	.06
❑ 680	Gary Matthews	.30	.12
❑ 681	Mike Marshall RC	1.50	.60
	Ron Roenicke		
	Steve Sax RC		
❑ 682	Jesse Jefferson	.15	.06
❑ 683	Phil Garner	.30	.12
❑ 684	Harold Baines	.30	.12
❑ 685	Bert Blyleven	.30	.12
❑ 686	Gary Allenson	.15	.06
❑ 687	Greg Minton	.15	.06
❑ 688	Leon Roberts	.15	.06
❑ 689	Lary Sorensen	.15	.06
❑ 690	Dave Kingman	.30	.12
❑ 691	Dan Schatzeder	.15	.06
❑ 692	Wayne Gross	.15	.06
❑ 693	Cesar Geronimo	.15	.06
❑ 694	Dave Wehrmeister	.15	.06
❑ 695	Warren Cromartie	.15	.06
❑ 696	Bill Madlock	.60	.24
	Eddie Solomon TL		
❑ 697	John Montefusco	.15	.06
❑ 698	Tony Scott	.15	.06
❑ 699	Dick Tidrow	.15	.06
❑ 700	George Foster	.30	.12
❑ 701	George Foster SA	.15	.06
❑ 702	Steve Renko	.15	.06
❑ 703	Cecil Cooper	.60	.24
	Pete Vuckovich TL		
❑ 704	Mickey Rivers	.15	.06
❑ 705	Mickey Rivers SA	.15	.06
❑ 706	Barry Foote	.15	.06
❑ 707	Mark Bomback	.15	.06
❑ 708	Gene Richards	.15	.06
❑ 709	Don Money	.15	.06
❑ 710	Jerry Reuss	.15	.06
❑ 711	Dave Edler	.75	.30
	Dave Henderson RC		
	Reggie Walton		
❑ 712	Dennis Martinez	.30	.12
❑ 713	Del Unser	.15	.06
❑ 714	Jerry Koosman	.30	.12
❑ 715	Willie Stargell	.60	.24
❑ 716	Willie Stargell SA	.30	.12
❑ 717	Rick Miller	.15	.06
❑ 718	Charlie Hough	.30	.12
❑ 719	Jerry Narron	.15	.06
❑ 720	Greg Luzinski	.30	.12
❑ 721	Greg Luzinski SA	.15	.06
❑ 722	Jerry Martin	.15	.06
❑ 723	Junior Kennedy	.15	.06
❑ 724	Dave Rosello	.15	.06
❑ 725	Amos Otis	.30	.12
❑ 726	Amos Otis SA	.15	.06
❑ 727	Sixto Lezcano	.15	.06
❑ 728	Aurelio Lopez	.15	.06
❑ 729	Jim Spencer	.15	.06
❑ 730	Gary Carter	.30	.12
❑ 731	Mike Armstrong	.15	.06
	Doug Gwosdz		
	Fred Kuhaulua		
❑ 732	Mike Lum	.15	.06
❑ 733	Larry McWilliams	.15	.06
❑ 734	Mike Ivie	.15	.06
❑ 735	Rudy May	.15	.06
❑ 736	Jerry Turner	.15	.06
❑ 737	Reggie Cleveland	.15	.06
❑ 738	Dave Engle	.15	.06
❑ 739	Joey McLaughlin	.15	.06
❑ 740	Dave Lopes	.30	.12
❑ 741	Dave Lopes SA	.15	.06
❑ 742	Dick Drago	.15	.06
❑ 743	John Stearns	.15	.06
❑ 744	Mike Witt	.75	.30
❑ 745	Bake McBride	.30	.12
❑ 746	Andre Thornton	.15	.06
❑ 747	John Lowenstein	.15	.06
❑ 748	Marc Hill	.15	.06
❑ 749	Bob Shirley	.15	.06
❑ 750	Jim Rice	.30	.12
❑ 751	Rick Honeycutt	.15	.06
❑ 752	Lee Lacy	.15	.06
❑ 753	Tom Brookens	.15	.06
❑ 754	Joe Morgan	.30	.12
❑ 755	Joe Morgan SA	.15	.06
❑ 756	Ken Griffey	.30	.12
	Tom Seaver TL		
❑ 757	Tom Underwood	.15	.06
❑ 758	Claudell Washington	.15	.06
❑ 759	Paul Splittorff	.15	.06
❑ 760	Bill Buckner	.30	.12
❑ 761	Dave Smith	.15	.06
❑ 762	Mike Phillips	.15	.06
❑ 763	Tom Hume	.15	.06
❑ 764	Steve Swisher	.15	.06
❑ 765	Gorman Thomas	.30	.12
❑ 766	Lenny Faedo	1.50	.60
	Kent Hrbek RC		
	Tim Laudner		
❑ 767	Roy Smalley	.15	.06
❑ 768	Jerry Garvin	.15	.06
❑ 769	Richie Zisk	.15	.06
❑ 770	Rich Gossage	.30	.12
❑ 771	Rich Gossage SA	.15	.06
❑ 772	Bert Campaneris	.30	.12
❑ 773	John Denny	.15	.06
❑ 774	Jay Johnstone	.15	.06
❑ 775	Bob Forsch	.15	.06
❑ 776	Mark Belanger	.15	.06
❑ 777	Tom Griffin	.15	.06
❑ 778	Kevin Hickey RC	.25	.10
❑ 779	Grant Jackson	.15	.06
❑ 780	Pete Rose	4.00	1.60
❑ 781	Pete Rose SA	1.25	.50
❑ 782	Frank Taveras	.15	.06
❑ 783	Greg Harris RC	.25	.10
❑ 784	Milt Wilcox	.15	.06
❑ 785	Dan Driessen	.15	.06
❑ 786	Carney Lansford	.60	.24
	Mike Torrez TL		
❑ 787	Fred Stanley	.15	.06
❑ 788	Woodie Fryman	.15	.06
❑ 789	Checklist 661-792	.60	.24
❑ 790	Larry Gura	.15	.06
❑ 791	Bobby Brown	.15	.06
❑ 792	Frank Tanana	.30	.12

1982 Topps Traded

	Nm-Mt	Ex-Mt
COMP.FACT.SET (132)	175.00	70.00

❑ 1T Doyle Alexander .50 .20
❑ 2T Jesse Barfield 3.00 1.20
❑ 3T Ross Baumgarten .50 .20
❑ 4T Steve Bedrosian 1.50 .60
❑ 5T Mark Belanger .50 .20
❑ 6T Kurt Bevacqua .50 .20
❑ 7T Tim Blackwell .50 .20
❑ 8T Vida Blue 1.00 .40
❑ 9T Bob Boone 1.00 .40
❑ 10T Larry Bowa 1.00 .40
❑ 11T Dan Briggs .50 .20
❑ 12T Bobby Brown .50 .20
❑ 13T Tom Brunansky 3.00 1.20
❑ 14T Jeff Burroughs .50 .20
❑ 15T Enos Cabell .50 .20
❑ 16T Bill Campbell .50 .20
❑ 17T Bobby Castillo .50 .20
❑ 18T Bill Caudill .50 .20
❑ 19T Cesar Cedeno 1.00 .40
❑ 20T Dave Collins .50 .20
❑ 21T Doug Corbett .50 .20
❑ 22T Al Cowens .50 .20
❑ 23T Chili Davis 3.00 1.20
❑ 24T Dick Davis .50 .20
❑ 25T Ron Davis .50 .20
❑ 26T Doug DeCinces .50 .20
❑ 27T Ivan DeJesus .50 .20
❑ 28T Bob Dernier .50 .20
❑ 29T Bo Diaz .50 .20
❑ 30T Roger Erickson .50 .20
❑ 31T Jim Essian .50 .20
❑ 32T Ed Farmer .50 .20
❑ 33T Doug Flynn .50 .20
❑ 34T Tim Foli .50 .20
❑ 35T Dan Ford .50 .20
❑ 36T George Foster 1.00 .40
❑ 37T Dave Frost .50 .20
❑ 38T Rich Gale .50 .20
❑ 39T Ron Gardenhire 1.50 .60
❑ 40T Ken Griffey 1.00 .40
❑ 41T Greg Harris .50 .20
❑ 42T Von Hayes 1.50 .60
❑ 43T Larry Herndon .50 .20
❑ 44T Kent Hrbek 3.00 1.20
❑ 45T Mike Ivie .50 .20
❑ 46T Grant Jackson .50 .20
❑ 47T Reggie Jackson 2.00 .80
❑ 48T Ron Jackson .50 .20
❑ 49T Fergie Jenkins 1.00 .40
❑ 50T Lamar Johnson .50 .20
❑ 51T Randy Johnson .50 .20
❑ 52T Jay Johnstone .50 .20
❑ 53T Mick Kelleher .50 .20
❑ 54T Steve Kemp .50 .20
❑ 55T Junior Kennedy .50 .20
❑ 56T Jim Kern .50 .20
❑ 57T Ray Knight 1.00 .40
❑ 58T Wayne Krenchicki .50 .20
❑ 59T Mike Krukow .50 .20
❑ 60T Duane Kuiper .50 .20
❑ 61T Mike LaCoss .50 .20
❑ 62T Chet Lemon 1.00 .40
❑ 63T Sixto Lezcano .50 .20
❑ 64T Dave Lopes 1.00 .40
❑ 65T Jerry Martin .50 .20
❑ 66T Renie Martin .50 .20
❑ 67T John Mayberry .50 .20
❑ 68T Lee Mazzilli 1.00 .40
❑ 69T Bake McBride 1.00 .40
❑ 70T Dan Meyer .50 .20
❑ 71T Larry Milbourne .50 .20
❑ 72T Eddie Milner .50 .20
❑ 73T Sid Monge .50 .20
❑ 74T John Montefusco .50 .20
❑ 75T Jose Morales .50 .20
❑ 76T Keith Moreland .50 .20
❑ 77T Jim Morrison .50 .20
❑ 78T Rance Mulliniks .50 .20
❑ 79T Steve Mura .50 .20
❑ 80T Gene Nelson .50 .20
❑ 81T Joe Nolan .50 .20
❑ 82T Dickie Noles .50 .20
❑ 83T Al Oliver 1.00 .40
❑ 84T Jorge Orta .50 .20
❑ 85T Tom Paciorek .50 .20
❑ 86T Larry Parrish .50 .20
❑ 87T Jack Perconte .50 .20
❑ 88T Gaylord Perry 1.00 .40
❑ 89T Rob Picciolo .50 .20
❑ 90T Joe Pittman .50 .20
❑ 91T Hosken Powell .50 .20
❑ 92T Mike Proly .50 .20
❑ 93T Greg Pryor .50 .20
❑ 94T Charlie Puleo .50 .20
❑ 95T Shane Rawley .50 .20
❑ 96T Johnny Ray XRC 1.50 .60
❑ 97T Dave Revering .50 .20
❑ 98T Cal Ripken 125.00 50.00
❑ 99T Allen Ripley .50 .20
❑ 100T Bill Robinson .50 .20
❑ 101T Aurelio Rodriguez .50 .20
❑ 102T Joe Rudi 1.00 .40
❑ 103T Steve Sax 3.00 1.20
❑ 104T Dan Schatzeder .50 .20
❑ 105T Bob Shirley .50 .20
❑ 106T Eric Show XRC 1.50 .60
❑ 107T Roy Smalley .50 .20
❑ 108T Lonnie Smith .50 .20
❑ 109T Ozzie Smith 15.00 6.00
❑ 110T Reggie Smith 1.00 .40
❑ 111T Lary Sorensen .50 .20
❑ 112T Elias Sosa .50 .20
❑ 113T Mike Stanton .50 .20
❑ 114T Steve Stroughter .50 .20
❑ 115T Champ Summers .50 .20
❑ 116T Rick Sutcliffe 1.00 .40
❑ 117T Frank Tanana 1.00 .40
❑ 118T Frank Taveras .50 .20
❑ 119T Garry Templeton 1.00 .40
❑ 120T Alex Trevino .50 .20
❑ 121T Jerry Turner .50 .20
❑ 122T Ed VandeBerg .50 .20
❑ 123T Tom Veryzer .50 .20
❑ 124T Ron Washington .50 .20
❑ 125T Bob Watson .50 .20
❑ 126T Dennis Werth .50 .20
❑ 127T Eddie Whitson .50 .20
❑ 128T Rob Wilfong .50 .20
❑ 129T Bump Wills .50 .20
❑ 130T Gary Woods .50 .20
❑ 131T Butch Wynegar .50 .20
❑ 132T Checklist: 1-132 .50 .20

1983 Topps

	Nm-Mt	Ex-Mt
COMPLETE SET (792)	80.00	32.00

❑ 1 Tony Armas RB .30 .12
❑ 2 Rickey Henderson RB 1.25 .50
❑ 3 Greg Minton RB .15 .06
❑ 4 Lance Parrish RB .15 .06
❑ 5 Manny Trillo RB .15 .06
❑ 6 John Wathan RB .15 .06
❑ 7 Gene Richards .15 .06
❑ 8 Steve Balboni .15 .06
❑ 9 Joey McLaughlin .15 .06
❑ 10 Gorman Thomas .30 .12
❑ 11 Billy Gardner MG .15 .06
❑ 12 Paul Mirabella .15 .06
❑ 13 Larry Herndon .15 .06
❑ 14 Frank LaCorte .15 .06
❑ 15 Ron Cey .30 .12
❑ 16 George Vukovich .15 .06
❑ 17 Kent Tekulve .15 .06
❑ 18 Kent Tekulve SV .15 .06
❑ 19 Oscar Gamble .15 .06
❑ 20 Carlton Fisk .60 .24
❑ 21 Eddie Murray .60 .24
Jim Palmer TL
❑ 22 Randy Martz .15 .06
❑ 23 Mike Heath .15 .06
❑ 24 Steve Mura .15 .06
❑ 25 Hal McRae .30 .12
❑ 26 Jerry Royster .15 .06
❑ 27 Doug Corbett .15 .06
❑ 28 Bruce Bochte .15 .06
❑ 29 Randy Jones .15 .06
❑ 30 Jim Rice .30 .12
❑ 31 Bill Gullickson .15 .06
❑ 32 Dave Bergman .15 .06
❑ 33 Jack O'Connor .15 .06
❑ 34 Paul Householder .15 .06
❑ 35 Rollie Fingers .30 .12
❑ 36 Rollie Fingers SV .15 .06
❑ 37 Darrell Johnson MG .15 .06
❑ 38 Tim Flannery .15 .06
❑ 39 Terry Puhl .15 .06
❑ 40 Fernando Valenzuela .30 .12
❑ 41 Jerry Turner .15 .06
❑ 42 Dale Murray .15 .06
❑ 43 Bob Dernier .15 .06
❑ 44 Don Robinson .15 .06
❑ 45 John Mayberry .15 .06
❑ 46 Richard Dotson .15 .06
❑ 47 Dave McKay .15 .06
❑ 48 Lary Sorensen .15 .06
❑ 49 Willie McGee RC 2.50 1.00
❑ 50 Bob Horner UER .30 .12
('82 RBI total 7)
❑ 51 Leon Durham .15 .06
Fergie Jenkins TL
❑ 52 Onix Concepcion .15 .06
❑ 53 Mike Witt .15 .06
❑ 54 Jim Maler .15 .06
❑ 55 Mookie Wilson .30 .12
❑ 56 Chuck Rainey .15 .06
❑ 57 Tim Blackwell .15 .06
❑ 58 Al Holland .15 .06
❑ 59 Benny Ayala .15 .06
❑ 60 Johnny Bench 1.25 .50
❑ 61 Johnny Bench SV .60 .24
❑ 62 Bob McClure .15 .06
❑ 63 Rick Monday .30 .12
❑ 64 Bill Stein .15 .06
❑ 65 Jack Morris .30 .12
❑ 66 Bob Lillis MG .15 .06
❑ 67 Sal Butera .15 .06
❑ 68 Eric Show RC .75 .30
❑ 69 Lee Lacy .15 .06
❑ 70 Steve Carlton .60 .24
❑ 71 Steve Carlton SV .30 .12
❑ 72 Tom Paciorek .15 .06
❑ 73 Allen Ripley .15 .06
❑ 74 Julio Gonzalez .15 .06
❑ 75 Amos Otis .30 .12
❑ 76 Rick Mahler .15 .06
❑ 77 Hosken Powell .15 .06
❑ 78 Bill Caudill .15 .06
❑ 79 Mick Kelleher .15 .06
❑ 80 George Foster .30 .12
❑ 81 Jerry Mumphrey .30 .12
Dave Righetti TL
❑ 82 Bruce Hurst .15 .06

❏	83	Ryne Sandberg RC	15.00	6.00
❏	84	Milt May	.15	.06
❏	85	Ken Singleton	.30	.12
❏	86	Tom Hume	.15	.06
❏	87	Joe Rudi	.30	.12
❏	88	Jim Gantner	.15	.06
❏	89	Leon Roberts	.15	.06
❏	90	Jerry Reuss	.15	.06
❏	91	Larry Milbourne	.15	.06
❏	92	Mike LaCoss	.15	.06
❏	93	John Castino	.15	.06
❏	94	Dave Edwards	.15	.06
❏	95	Alan Trammell	.30	.12
❏	96	Dick Howser MG	.15	.06
❏	97	Ross Baumgarten	.15	.06
❏	98	Vance Law	.15	.06
❏	99	Dickie Noles	.15	.06
❏	100	Pete Rose	4.00	1.60
❏	101	Pete Rose SV	1.25	.50
❏	102	Dave Beard	.15	.06
❏	103	Darrell Porter	.15	.06
❏	104	Bob Walk	.15	.06
❏	105	Don Baylor	.30	.12
❏	106	Gene Nelson	.15	.06
❏	107	Mike Jorgensen	.15	.06
❏	108	Glenn Hoffman	.15	.06
❏	109	Luis Leal	.15	.06
❏	110	Ken Griffey	.30	.12
❏	111	Al Oliver	.30	.12
		Steve Rogers TL		
❏	112	Bob Shirley	.15	.06
❏	113	Ron Roenicke	.15	.06
❏	114	Jim Slaton	.15	.06
❏	115	Chili Davis	.30	.12
❏	116	Dave Schmidt	.15	.06
❏	117	Alan Knicely	.15	.06
❏	118	Chris Welsh	.15	.06
❏	119	Tom Brookens	.15	.06
❏	120	Len Barker	.15	.06
❏	121	Mickey Hatcher	.15	.06
❏	122	Jimmy Smith	.15	.06
❏	123	George Frazier	.15	.06
❏	124	Marc Hill	.15	.06
❏	125	Leon Durham	.15	.06
❏	126	Joe Torre MG	.30	.12
❏	127	Preston Hanna	.15	.06
❏	128	Mike Ramsey	.15	.06
❏	129	Checklist: 1-132	.30	.12
❏	130	Dave Stieb	.30	.12
❏	131	Ed Ott	.15	.06
❏	132	Todd Cruz	.15	.06
❏	133	Jim Barr	.15	.06
❏	134	Hubie Brooks	.15	.06
❏	135	Dwight Evans	.60	.24
❏	136	Willie Aikens	.15	.06
❏	137	Woodie Fryman	.15	.06
❏	138	Rick Dempsey	.15	.06
❏	139	Bruce Berenyi	.15	.06
❏	140	Willie Randolph	.30	.12
❏	141	Toby Harrah	.30	.12
		Rick Sutcliffe TL		
❏	142	Mike Caldwell	.15	.06
❏	143	Joe Pettini	.15	.06
❏	144	Mark Wagner	.15	.06
❏	145	Don Sutton	.30	.12
❏	146	Don Sutton SV	.15	.06
❏	147	Rick Leach	.15	.06
❏	148	Dave Roberts	.15	.06
❏	149	Johnny Ray	.15	.06
❏	150	Bruce Sutter	.30	.12
❏	151	Bruce Sutter SV	.15	.06
❏	152	Jay Johnstone	.15	.06
❏	153	Jerry Koosman	.30	.12
❏	154	Johnnie LeMaster	.15	.06
❏	155	Dan Quisenberry	.15	.06
❏	156	Billy Martin MG	.60	.24
❏	157	Steve Bedrosian	.15	.06
❏	158	Rob Wilfong	.15	.06
❏	159	Mike Stanton	.15	.06
❏	160	Dave Kingman	.30	.12
❏	161	Dave Kingman SV	.15	.06
❏	162	Mark Clear	.15	.06
❏	163	Cal Ripken	10.00	4.00
❏	164	David Palmer	.15	.06
❏	165	Dan Driessen	.15	.06
❏	166	John Pacella	.15	.06
❏	167	Mark Brouhard	.15	.06
❏	168	Juan Eichelberger	.15	.06
❏	169	Doug Flynn	.15	.06
❏	170	Steve Howe	.15	.06
❏	171	Joe Morgan	.30	.12
		Bill Laskey TL		
❏	172	Vern Ruhle	.15	.06
❏	173	Jim Morrison	.15	.06
❏	174	Jerry Ujdur	.15	.06
❏	175	Bo Diaz	.15	.06
❏	176	Dave Righetti	.30	.12
❏	177	Harold Baines	.30	.12
❏	178	Luis Tiant	.30	.12
❏	179	Luis Tiant SV	.15	.06
❏	180	Rickey Henderson	2.50	1.00
❏	181	Terry Felton	.15	.06
❏	182	Mike Fischlin	.15	.06
❏	183	Ed VandeBerg	.15	.06
❏	184	Bob Clark	.15	.06
❏	185	Tim Lollar	.15	.06
❏	186	Whitey Herzog MG	.30	.12
❏	187	Terry Leach	.15	.06
❏	188	Rick Miller	.15	.06
❏	189	Dan Schatzeder	.15	.06
❏	190	Cecil Cooper	.30	.12
❏	191	Joe Price	.15	.06
❏	192	Floyd Rayford	.15	.06
❏	193	Harry Spilman	.15	.06
❏	194	Cesar Geronimo	.15	.06
❏	195	Bob Stoddard	.15	.06
❏	196	Bill Fahey	.15	.06
❏	197	Jim Eisenreich RC	.75	.30
❏	198	Kiko Garcia	.15	.06
❏	199	Marty Bystrom	.15	.06
❏	200	Rod Carew	.60	.24
❏	201	Rod Carew SV	.30	.12
❏	202	Damaso Garcia	.30	.12
		Dave Stieb TL		
❏	203	Mike Morgan	.15	.06
❏	204	Junior Kennedy	.15	.06
❏	205	Dave Parker	.30	.12
❏	206	Ken Oberkfell	.15	.06
❏	207	Rick Camp	.15	.06
❏	208	Dan Meyer	.15	.06
❏	209	Mike Moore RC	.75	.30
❏	210	Jack Clark	.30	.12
❏	211	John Denny	.15	.06
❏	212	John Stearns	.15	.06
❏	213	Tom Burgmeier	.15	.06
❏	214	Jerry White	.15	.06
❏	215	Mario Soto	.30	.12
❏	216	Tony LaRussa MG	.30	.12
❏	217	Tim Stoddard	.15	.06
❏	218	Roy Howell	.15	.06
❏	219	Mike Armstrong	.15	.06
❏	220	Dusty Baker	.30	.12
❏	221	Joe Niekro	.15	.06
❏	222	Damaso Garcia	.15	.06
❏	223	John Montefusco	.15	.06
❏	224	Mickey Rivers	.15	.06
❏	225	Enos Cabell	.15	.06
❏	226	Enrique Romo	.15	.06
❏	227	Chris Bando	.15	.06
❏	228	Joaquin Andujar	.30	.12
❏	229	Bo Diaz	.15	.06
		Steve Carlton TL		
❏	230	Fergie Jenkins	.30	.12
❏	231	Fergie Jenkins SV	.15	.06
❏	232	Tom Brunansky	.30	.12
❏	233	Wayne Gross	.15	.06
❏	234	Larry Andersen	.15	.06
❏	235	Claudell Washington	.15	.06
❏	236	Steve Renko	.15	.06
❏	237	Dan Norman	.15	.06
❏	238	Bud Black RC	.75	.30
❏	239	Dave Stapleton	.15	.06
❏	240	Rich Gossage	.30	.12
❏	241	Rich Gossage SV	.15	.06
❏	242	Joe Nolan	.15	.06
❏	243	Duane Walker	.15	.06
❏	244	Dwight Bernard	.15	.06
❏	245	Steve Sax	.30	.12
❏	246	G.Bamberger MG	.15	.06
❏	247	Dave Smith	.15	.06
❏	248	Bake McBride	.30	.12
❏	249	Checklist: 133-264	.30	.12
❏	250	Bill Buckner	.30	.12
❏	251	Alan Wiggins	.15	.06
❏	252	Luis Aguayo	.15	.06
❏	253	Larry McWilliams	.15	.06
❏	254	Rick Cerone	.15	.06
❏	255	Gene Garber	.15	.06
❏	256	Gene Garber SV	.15	.06
❏	257	Jesse Barfield	.30	.12
❏	258	Manny Castillo	.15	.06
❏	259	Jeff Jones	.15	.06
❏	260	Steve Kemp	.15	.06
❏	261	Larry Herndon	.30	.12
		Dan Petry TL		
❏	262	Ron Jackson	.15	.06
❏	263	Renie Martin	.15	.06
❏	264	Jamie Quirk	.15	.06
❏	265	Joel Youngblood	.15	.06
❏	266	Paul Boris	.15	.06
❏	267	Terry Francona	.30	.12
❏	268	Storm Davis RC	.75	.30
❏	269	Ron Oester	.15	.06
❏	270	Dennis Eckersley	.60	.24
❏	271	Ed Romero	.15	.06
❏	272	Frank Tanana	.30	.12
❏	273	Mark Belanger	.15	.06
❏	274	Terry Kennedy	.15	.06
❏	275	Ray Knight	.30	.12
❏	276	Gene Mauch MG	.15	.06
❏	277	Rance Mulliniks	.15	.06
❏	278	Kevin Hickey	.15	.06
❏	279	Greg Gross	.15	.06
❏	280	Bert Blyleven	.30	.12
❏	281	Andre Robertson	.15	.06
❏	282	Reggie Smith	1.25	.50
		(Ryne Sandberg ducking back)		
❏	283	Reggie Smith SV	.15	.06
❏	284	Jeff Lahti	.15	.06
❏	285	Lance Parrish	.30	.12
❏	286	Rick Langford	.15	.06
❏	287	Bobby Brown	.15	.06
❏	288	Joe Cowley	.15	.06
❏	289	Jerry Dybzinski	.15	.06
❏	290	Jeff Reardon	.30	.12
❏	291	Bill Madlock	.30	.12
		John Candelaria TL		
❏	292	Craig Swan	.15	.06
❏	293	Glenn Gulliver	.15	.06
❏	294	Dave Engle	.15	.06
❏	295	Jerry Remy	.15	.06
❏	296	Greg Harris	.15	.06
❏	297	Ned Yost	.15	.06
❏	298	Floyd Chiffer	.15	.06
❏	299	George Wright RC	.75	.30
❏	300	Mike Schmidt	3.00	1.20
❏	301	Mike Schmidt SV	1.25	.50
❏	302	Ernie Whitt	.15	.06
❏	303	Miguel Dilone	.15	.06
❏	304	Dave Rucker	.15	.06
❏	305	Larry Bowa	.30	.12
❏	306	Tom Lasorda MG	.60	.24
❏	307	Lou Piniella	.30	.12
❏	308	Jesus Vega	.15	.06
❏	309	Jeff Leonard	.15	.06
❏	310	Greg Luzinski	.30	.12
❏	311	Glenn Brummer	.15	.06
❏	312	Brian Kingman	.15	.06
❏	313	Gary Gray	.15	.06
❏	314	Ken Dayley	.15	.06
❏	315	Rick Burleson	.15	.06
❏	316	Paul Splittorff	.15	.06
❏	317	Gary Rajsich	.15	.06
❏	318	John Tudor	.30	.12
❏	319	Lenn Sakata	.15	.06
❏	320	Steve Rogers	.30	.12
❏	321	Robin Yount	1.25	.50
		Pete Vuckovich TL		
❏	322	Dave Van Gorder	.15	.06
❏	323	Luis DeLeon	.15	.06
❏	324	Mike Marshall	.15	.06
❏	325	Von Hayes	.15	.06
❏	326	Garth Iorg	.15	.06
❏	327	Bobby Castillo	.15	.06
❏	328	Craig Reynolds	.15	.06
❏	329	Randy Niemann	.15	.06
❏	330	Buddy Bell	.30	.12

❑ 331 Mike Krukow .15 .06
❑ 332 Glenn Wilson .75 .30
❑ 333 Dave LaRoche .15 .06
❑ 334 Dave LaRoche SV .15 .06
❑ 335 Steve Henderson .15 .06
❑ 336 Rene Lachemann MG .15 .06
❑ 337 Tito Landrum .15 .06
❑ 338 Bob Owchinko .15 .06
❑ 339 Terry Harper .15 .06
❑ 340 Larry Gura .15 .06
❑ 341 Doug DeCinces .15 .06
❑ 342 Atlee Hammaker .15 .06
❑ 343 Bob Bailor .15 .06
❑ 344 Roger LaFrancois .15 .06
❑ 345 Jim Clancy .15 .06
❑ 346 Joe Pittman .15 .06
❑ 347 Sammy Stewart .15 .06
❑ 348 Alan Bannister .15 .06
❑ 349 Checklist: 265-396 .30 .12
❑ 350 Robin Yount 2.00 .80
❑ 351 Cesar Cedeno .30 .12
Mario Soto TL
❑ 352 Mike Scioscia .30 .12
❑ 353 Steve Comer .15 .06
❑ 354 Randy Johnson .15 .06
❑ 355 Jim Bibby .15 .06
❑ 356 Gary Woods .15 .06
❑ 357 Len Matuszek .15 .06
❑ 358 Jerry Garvin .15 .06
❑ 359 Dave Collins .15 .06
❑ 360 Nolan Ryan 6.00 2.40
❑ 361 Nolan Ryan SV 3.00 1.20
❑ 362 Bill Almon .15 .06
❑ 363 John Stuper .15 .06
❑ 364 Brett Butler .30 .12
❑ 365 Dave Lopes .30 .12
❑ 366 Dick Williams MG .15 .06
❑ 367 Bud Anderson .15 .06
❑ 368 Richie Zisk .15 .06
❑ 369 Jesse Orosco .15 .06
❑ 370 Gary Carter .30 .12
❑ 371 Mike Richardt .15 .06
❑ 372 Terry Crowley .15 .06
❑ 373 Kevin Saucier .15 .06
❑ 374 Wayne Krenchicki .15 .06
❑ 375 Pete Vuckovich .15 .06
❑ 376 Ken Landreaux .15 .06
❑ 377 Lee May .15 .06
❑ 378 Lee May SV .15 .06
❑ 379 Guy Sularz .15 .06
❑ 380 Ron Davis .15 .06
❑ 381 Jim Rice .30 .12
Bob Stanley TL
❑ 382 Bob Knepper .15 .06
❑ 383 Ozzie Virgil .15 .06
❑ 384 Dave Dravecky RC 1.50 .60
❑ 385 Mike Easler .15 .06
❑ 386 Rod Carew AS .30 .12
❑ 387 Bob Grich AS .15 .06
❑ 388 George Brett AS 1.50 .60
❑ 389 Robin Yount AS 1.25 .50
❑ 390 Reggie Jackson AS .30 .12
❑ 391 Rickey Henderson AS 1.25 .50
❑ 392 Fred Lynn AS .15 .06
❑ 393 Carlton Fisk AS .30 .12
❑ 394 Pete Vuckovich AS .15 .06
❑ 395 Larry Gura AS .15 .06
❑ 396 Dan Quisenberry AS .15 .06
❑ 397 Pete Rose AS .60 .24
❑ 398 Manny Trillo AS .15 .06
❑ 399 Mike Schmidt AS 1.25 .50
❑ 400 Dave Concepcion AS .15 .06
❑ 401 Dale Murphy AS .30 .12
❑ 402 Andre Dawson AS .15 .06
❑ 403 Tim Raines AS .15 .06
❑ 404 Gary Carter AS .15 .06
❑ 405 Steve Rogers AS .15 .06
❑ 406 Steve Carlton AS .30 .12
❑ 407 Bruce Sutter AS .15 .06
❑ 408 Rudy May .15 .06
❑ 409 Marvis Foley .15 .06
❑ 410 Phil Niekro .30 .12
❑ 411 Phil Niekro SV .15 .06
❑ 412 Buddy Bell .30 .12
Charlie Hough TL
❑ 413 Matt Keough .15 .06
❑ 414 Julio Cruz .15 .06
❑ 415 Bob Forsch .15 .06
❑ 416 Joe Ferguson .15 .06
❑ 417 Tom Hausman .15 .06
❑ 418 Greg Pryor .15 .06
❑ 419 Steve Crawford .15 .06
❑ 420 Al Oliver .30 .12
❑ 421 Al Oliver SV .15 .06
❑ 422 George Cappuzzello .15 .06
❑ 423 Tom Lawless .15 .06
❑ 424 Jerry Augustine .15 .06
❑ 425 Pedro Guerrero .30 .12
❑ 426 Earl Weaver MG .30 .12
❑ 427 Roy Lee Jackson .15 .06
❑ 428 Champ Summers .15 .06
❑ 429 Eddie Whitson .15 .06
❑ 430 Kirk Gibson .60 .24
❑ 431 Gary Gaetti RC 1.50 .60
❑ 432 Porfirio Altamirano .15 .06
❑ 433 Dale Berra .15 .06
❑ 434 Dennis Lamp .15 .06
❑ 435 Tony Armas .30 .12
❑ 436 Bill Campbell .15 .06
❑ 437 Rick Sweet .15 .06
❑ 438 Dave LaPoint .15 .06
❑ 439 Rafael Ramirez .15 .06
❑ 440 Ron Guidry .30 .12
❑ 441 Ray Knight .30 .12
Joe Niekro TL
❑ 442 Brian Downing .30 .12
❑ 443 Don Hood .15 .06
❑ 444 Wally Backman .15 .06
❑ 445 Mike Flanagan .15 .06
❑ 446 Reid Nichols .15 .06
❑ 447 Bryn Smith .15 .06
❑ 448 Darrell Evans .30 .12
❑ 449 Eddie Milner .15 .06
❑ 450 Ted Simmons .30 .12
❑ 451 Ted Simmons SV .15 .06
❑ 452 Lloyd Moseby .15 .06
❑ 453 Lamar Johnson .15 .06
❑ 454 Bob Welch .30 .12
❑ 455 Sixto Lezcano .15 .06
❑ 456 Lee Elia MG .15 .06
❑ 457 Milt Wilcox .15 .06
❑ 458 Ron Washington .15 .06
❑ 459 Ed Farmer .15 .06
❑ 460 Roy Smalley .15 .06
❑ 461 Steve Trout .15 .06
❑ 462 Steve Nicosia .15 .06
❑ 463 Gaylord Perry .30 .12
❑ 464 Gaylord Perry SV .15 .06
❑ 465 Lonnie Smith .15 .06
❑ 466 Tom Underwood .15 .06
❑ 467 Rufino Linares .15 .06
❑ 468 Dave Goltz .15 .06
❑ 469 Ron Gardenhire .15 .06
❑ 470 Greg Minton .15 .06
❑ 471 Willie Wilson .30 .12
Vida Blue TL
❑ 472 Gary Allenson .15 .06
❑ 473 John Lowenstein .15 .06
❑ 474 Ray Burris .15 .06
❑ 475 Cesar Cedeno .30 .12
❑ 476 Rob Picciolo .15 .06
❑ 477 Tom Niedenfuer .15 .06
❑ 478 Phil Garner .30 .12
❑ 479 Charlie Hough .30 .12
❑ 480 Toby Harrah .30 .12
❑ 481 Scot Thompson .15 .06
❑ 482 Tony Gwynn UER RC 25.00 10.00
No Topps logo under
card number on back
❑ 483 Lynn Jones .15 .06
❑ 484 Dick Ruthven .15 .06
❑ 485 Omar Moreno .15 .06
❑ 486 Clyde King MG .15 .06
❑ 487 Jerry Hairston .15 .06
❑ 488 Alfredo Griffin .15 .06
❑ 489 Tom Herr .15 .06
❑ 490 Jim Palmer .30 .12
❑ 491 Jim Palmer SV .15 .06
❑ 492 Paul Serna .15 .06
❑ 493 Steve McCatty .15 .06
❑ 494 Bob Brenly .15 .06
❑ 495 Warren Cromartie .15 .06
❑ 496 Tom Veryzer .15 .06
❑ 497 Rick Sutcliffe .30 .12
❑ 498 Wade Boggs RC 15.00 6.00
❑ 499 Jeff Little .15 .06
❑ 500 Reggie Jackson .60 .24
❑ 501 Reggie Jackson SV .30 .12
❑ 502 Dale Murphy .60 .24
Phil Niekro TL
❑ 503 Moose Haas .15 .06
❑ 504 Don Werner .15 .06
❑ 505 Garry Templeton .30 .12
❑ 506 Jim Gott RC .75 .30
❑ 507 Tony Scott .15 .06
❑ 508 Tom Filer .15 .06
❑ 509 Lou Whitaker .30 .12
❑ 510 Tug McGraw .30 .12
❑ 511 Tug McGraw SV .15 .06
❑ 512 Doyle Alexander .15 .06
❑ 513 Fred Stanley .15 .06
❑ 514 Rudy Law .15 .06
❑ 515 Gene Tenace .30 .12
❑ 516 Bill Virdon MG .15 .06
❑ 517 Gary Ward .15 .06
❑ 518 Bill Laskey .15 .06
❑ 519 Terry Bulling .15 .06
❑ 520 Fred Lynn .30 .12
❑ 521 Bruce Benedict .15 .06
❑ 522 Pat Zachry .15 .06
❑ 523 Carney Lansford .30 .12
❑ 524 Tom Brennan .15 .06
❑ 525 Frank White .30 .12
❑ 526 Checklist: 397-528 .30 .12
❑ 527 Larry Biittner .15 .06
❑ 528 Jamie Easterly .15 .06
❑ 529 Tim Laudner .15 .06
❑ 530 Eddie Murray 1.25 .50
❑ 531 Rickey Henderson 1.25 .50
Rick Langford TL
❑ 532 Dave Stewart .30 .12
❑ 533 Luis Salazar .15 .06
❑ 534 John Butcher .15 .06
❑ 535 Manny Trillo .15 .06
❑ 536 John Wockenfuss .15 .06
❑ 537 Rod Scurry .15 .06
❑ 538 Danny Heep .15 .06
❑ 539 Roger Erickson .15 .06
❑ 540 Ozzie Smith 2.00 .80
❑ 541 Britt Burns .15 .06
❑ 542 Jody Davis .15 .06
❑ 543 Alan Fowlkes .15 .06
❑ 544 Larry Whisenton .15 .06
❑ 545 Floyd Bannister .15 .06
❑ 546 Dave Garcia MG .15 .06
❑ 547 Geoff Zahn .15 .06
❑ 548 Brian Giles .15 .06
❑ 549 Charlie Puleo .15 .06
❑ 550 Carl Yastrzemski 2.00 .80
❑ 551 Carl Yastrzemski SV 1.25 .50
❑ 552 Tim Wallach .30 .12
❑ 553 Dennis Martinez .30 .12
❑ 554 Mike Vail .15 .06
❑ 555 Steve Yeager .30 .12
❑ 556 Willie Upshaw .15 .06
❑ 557 Rick Honeycutt .15 .06
❑ 558 Dickie Thon .15 .06
❑ 559 Pete Redfern .15 .06
❑ 560 Ron LeFlore .30 .12
❑ 561 Lonnie Smith .30 .12
Joaquin Andujar TL
❑ 562 Dave Rozema .15 .06
❑ 563 Juan Bonilla .15 .06
❑ 564 Sid Monge .15 .06
❑ 565 Bucky Dent .30 .12
❑ 566 Manny Sarmiento .15 .06
❑ 567 Joe Simpson .15 .06
❑ 568 Willie Hernandez .15 .06
❑ 569 Jack Perconte .15 .06
❑ 570 Vida Blue .30 .12
❑ 571 Mickey Klutts .15 .06
❑ 572 Bob Watson .15 .06
❑ 573 Andy Hassler .15 .06
❑ 574 Glenn Adams .15 .06
❑ 575 Neil Allen .15 .06
❑ 576 Frank Robinson MG .60 .24
❑ 577 Luis Aponte .15 .06
❑ 578 David Green RC .75 .30

❑ 579 Rich Dauer .15 .06
❑ 580 Tom Seaver 1.25 .50
❑ 581 Tom Seaver SV .30 .12
❑ 582 Marshall Edwards .15 .06
❑ 583 Terry Forster .30 .12
❑ 584 Dave Hostetler .15 .06
❑ 585 Jose Cruz .30 .12
❑ 586 Frank Viola RC 2.50 1.00
❑ 587 Ivan DeJesus .15 .06
❑ 588 Pat Underwood .15 .06
❑ 589 Alvis Woods .15 .06
❑ 590 Tony Pena .15 .06
❑ 591 Greg Luzinski .30 .12
LaMarr Hoyt TL
❑ 592 Shane Rawley .15 .06
❑ 593 Broderick Perkins .15 .06
❑ 594 Eric Rasmussen .15 .06
❑ 595 Tim Raines .30 .12
❑ 596 Randy Johnson .15 .06
❑ 597 Mike Proly .15 .06
❑ 598 Dwayne Murphy .15 .06
❑ 599 Don Aase .15 .06
❑ 600 George Brett 3.00 1.20
❑ 601 Ed Lynch .15 .06
❑ 602 Rich Gedman .15 .06
❑ 603 Joe Morgan .30 .12
❑ 604 Joe Morgan SV .15 .06
❑ 605 Gary Roenicke .15 .06
❑ 606 Bobby Cox MG .30 .12
❑ 607 Charlie Leibrandt .15 .06
❑ 608 Don Money .15 .06
❑ 609 Danny Darwin .15 .06
❑ 610 Steve Garvey .30 .12
❑ 611 Bert Roberge .15 .06
❑ 612 Steve Swisher .15 .06
❑ 613 Mike Ivie .15 .06
❑ 614 Ed Glynn .15 .06
❑ 615 Garry Maddox .15 .06
❑ 616 Bill Nahorodny .15 .06
❑ 617 Butch Wynegar .15 .06
❑ 618 LaMarr Hoyt .15 .06
❑ 619 Keith Moreland .15 .06
❑ 620 Mike Norris .15 .06
❑ 621 Mookie Wilson .30 .12
Craig Swan TL
❑ 622 Dave Edler .15 .06
❑ 623 Luis Sanchez .15 .06
❑ 624 Glenn Hubbard .15 .06
❑ 625 Ken Forsch .15 .06
❑ 626 Jerry Martin .15 .06
❑ 627 Doug Bair .15 .06
❑ 628 Julio Valdez .15 .06
❑ 629 Charlie Lea .15 .06
❑ 630 Paul Molitor .60 .24
❑ 631 Tippy Martinez .15 .06
❑ 632 Alex Trevino .15 .06
❑ 633 Vicente Romo .15 .06
❑ 634 Max Venable .15 .06
❑ 635 Graig Nettles .30 .12
❑ 636 Graig Nettles SV .15 .06
❑ 637 Pat Corrales MG .15 .06
❑ 638 Dan Petry .15 .06
❑ 639 Art Howe .15 .06
❑ 640 Andre Thornton .15 .06
❑ 641 Billy Sample .15 .06
❑ 642 Checklist: 529-660 .30 .12
❑ 643 Bump Wills .15 .06
❑ 644 Joe Lefebvre .15 .06
❑ 645 Bill Madlock .30 .12
❑ 646 Jim Essian .15 .06
❑ 647 Bobby Mitchell .15 .06
❑ 648 Jeff Burroughs .15 .06
❑ 649 Tommy Boggs .15 .06
❑ 650 George Hendrick .30 .12
❑ 651 Rod Carew .30 .12
Mike Witt TL
❑ 652 Butch Hobson .15 .06
❑ 653 Ellis Valentine .15 .06
❑ 654 Bob Ojeda .15 .06
❑ 655 Al Bumbry .15 .06
❑ 656 Dave Frost .15 .06
❑ 657 Mike Gates .15 .06
❑ 658 Frank Pastore .15 .06
❑ 659 Charlie Moore .15 .06
❑ 660 Mike Hargrove .15 .06
❑ 661 Bill Russell .30 .12
❑ 662 Joe Sambito .15 .06
❑ 663 Tom O'Malley .15 .06
❑ 664 Bob Molinaro .15 .06
❑ 665 Jim Sundberg .30 .12
❑ 666 Sparky Anderson MG .30 .12
❑ 667 Dick Davis .15 .06
❑ 668 Larry Christenson .15 .06
❑ 669 Mike Squires .15 .06
❑ 670 Jerry Mumphrey .15 .06
❑ 671 Lenny Faedo .15 .06
❑ 672 Jim Kaat .30 .12
❑ 673 Jim Kaat SV .15 .06
❑ 674 Kurt Bevacqua .15 .06
❑ 675 Jim Beattie .15 .06
❑ 676 Biff Pocoroba .15 .06
❑ 677 Dave Revering .15 .06
❑ 678 Juan Beniquez .15 .06
❑ 679 Mike Scott .30 .12
❑ 680 Andre Dawson .30 .12
❑ 681 Pedro Guerrero .30 .12
Fernando Valenzuela TL
❑ 682 Bob Stanley .15 .06
❑ 683 Dan Ford .15 .06
❑ 684 Rafael Landestoy .15 .06
❑ 685 Lee Mazzilli .30 .12
❑ 686 Randy Lerch .15 .06
❑ 687 U.L. Washington .15 .06
❑ 688 Jim Wohlford .15 .06
❑ 689 Ron Hassey .15 .06
❑ 690 Kent Hrbek .30 .12
❑ 691 Dave Tobik .15 .06
❑ 692 Denny Walling .15 .06
❑ 693 Sparky Lyle .30 .12
❑ 694 Sparky Lyle SV .15 .06
❑ 695 Ruppert Jones .15 .06
❑ 696 Chuck Tanner MG .15 .06
❑ 697 Barry Foote .15 .06
❑ 698 Tony Bernazard .15 .06
❑ 699 Lee Smith .60 .24
❑ 700 Keith Hernandez .30 .12
❑ 701 Willie Wilson .30 .12
Al Oliver LL
❑ 702 Reggie Jackson .30 .12
Gorman Thomas
Dave Kingman LL
❑ 703 Hal McRae .60 .24
Dale Murphy
Al Oliver LL
❑ 704 Rickey Henderson 1.25 .50
Tim Raines LL
❑ 705 LaMarr Hoyt .30 .12
Steve Carlton LL
❑ 706 Floyd Bannister .30 .12
Steve Carlton LL
❑ 707 Rick Sutcliffe .30 .12
Steve Rogers LL
❑ 708 Dan Quisenberry .30 .12
Bruce Sutter LL
❑ 709 Jimmy Sexton .15 .06
❑ 710 Willie Wilson .30 .12
❑ 711 Bruce Bochte .30 .12
Jim Beattie TL
❑ 712 Bruce Kison .15 .06
❑ 713 Ron Hodges .15 .06
❑ 714 Wayne Nordhagen .15 .06
❑ 715 Tony Perez .60 .24
❑ 716 Tony Perez SV .30 .12
❑ 717 Scott Sanderson .15 .06
❑ 718 Jim Dwyer .15 .06
❑ 719 Rich Gale .15 .06
❑ 720 Dave Concepcion .30 .12
❑ 721 John Martin .15 .06
❑ 722 Jorge Orta .15 .06
❑ 723 Randy Moffitt .15 .06
❑ 724 Johnny Grubb .15 .06
❑ 725 Dan Spillner .15 .06
❑ 726 Harvey Kuenn MG .15 .06
❑ 727 Chet Lemon .30 .12
❑ 728 Ron Reed .15 .06
❑ 729 Jerry Morales .15 .06
❑ 730 Jason Thompson .15 .06
❑ 731 Al Williams .15 .06
❑ 732 Dave Henderson .15 .06
❑ 733 Buck Martinez .15 .06
❑ 734 Steve Braun .15 .06
❑ 735 Tommy John .30 .12
❑ 736 Tommy John SV .15 .06
❑ 737 Mitchell Page .15 .06
❑ 738 Tim Foli .15 .06
❑ 739 Rick Ownbey .15 .06
❑ 740 Rusty Staub .30 .12
❑ 741 Rusty Staub SV .15 .06
❑ 742 Terry Kennedy .30 .12
Tim Lollar
❑ 743 Mike Torrez .15 .06
❑ 744 Brad Mills .15 .06
❑ 745 Scott McGregor .15 .06
❑ 746 John Wathan .15 .06
❑ 747 Fred Breining .15 .06
❑ 748 Derrel Thomas .15 .06
❑ 749 Jon Matlack .15 .06
❑ 750 Ben Oglivie .30 .12
❑ 751 Brad Havens .15 .06
❑ 752 Luis Pujols .15 .06
❑ 753 Elias Sosa .15 .06
❑ 754 Bill Robinson .15 .06
❑ 755 John Candelaria .15 .06
❑ 756 Russ Nixon MG .15 .06
❑ 757 Rick Manning .15 .06
❑ 758 Aurelio Rodriguez .15 .06
❑ 759 Doug Bird .15 .06
❑ 760 Dale Murphy .60 .24
❑ 761 Gary Lucas .15 .06
❑ 762 Cliff Johnson .15 .06
❑ 763 Al Cowens .15 .06
❑ 764 Pete Falcone .15 .06
❑ 765 Bob Boone .30 .12
❑ 766 Barry Bonnell .15 .06
❑ 767 Duane Kuiper .15 .06
❑ 768 Chris Speier .15 .06
❑ 769 Checklist: 661-792 .30 .12
❑ 770 Dave Winfield .30 .12
❑ 771 Kent Hrbek .30 .12
Bobby Castillo TL
❑ 772 Jim Kern .15 .06
❑ 773 Larry Hisle .15 .06
❑ 774 Alan Ashby .15 .06
❑ 775 Burt Hooton .15 .06
❑ 776 Larry Parrish .15 .06
❑ 777 John Curtis .15 .06
❑ 778 Rich Hebner .15 .06
❑ 779 Rick Waits .15 .06
❑ 780 Gary Matthews .30 .12
❑ 781 Rick Rhoden .15 .06
❑ 782 Bobby Murcer .30 .12
❑ 783 Bobby Murcer SV .15 .06
❑ 784 Jeff Newman .15 .06
❑ 785 Dennis Leonard .15 .06
❑ 786 Ralph Houk MG .15 .06
❑ 787 Dick Tidrow .15 .06
❑ 788 Dane Iorg .15 .06
❑ 789 Bryan Clark .15 .06
❑ 790 Bob Grich .30 .12
❑ 791 Gary Lavelle .15 .06
❑ 792 Chris Chambliss .30 .12
❑ XX Game Insert Card .10 .04

1983 Topps Traded

	Nm-Mt	Ex-Mt
COMP.FACT.SET (132)	40.00	16.00
❑ 1T Neil Allen	.25	.10
❑ 2T Bill Almon	.25	.10
❑ 3T Joe Altobelli MG	.25	.10

❑ 4T Tony Armas 1.00 .40
❑ 5T Doug Bair .25 .10
❑ 6T Steve Baker .25 .10
❑ 7T Floyd Bannister .25 .10
❑ 8T Don Baylor 1.00 .40
❑ 9T Tony Bernazard .25 .10
❑ 10T Larry Biittner .25 .10
❑ 11T Dann Bilardello .25 .10
❑ 12T Doug Bird .25 .10
❑ 13T Steve Boros MG .25 .10
❑ 14T Greg Brock .25 .10
❑ 15T Mike C. Brown .25 .10
❑ 16T Tom Burgmeier .25 .10
❑ 17T Randy Bush .25 .10
❑ 18T Bert Campaneris 1.00 .40
❑ 19T Ron Cey 1.00 .40
❑ 20T Chris Codiroli .25 .10
❑ 21T Dave Collins .25 .10
❑ 22T Terry Crowley .25 .10
❑ 23T Julio Cruz .25 .10
❑ 24T Mike Davis .25 .10
❑ 25T Frank DiPino .25 .10
❑ 26T Bill Doran XRC 1.00 .40
❑ 27T Jerry Dybzinski .25 .10
❑ 28T Jamie Easterly .25 .10
❑ 29T Juan Eichelberger .25 .10
❑ 30T Jim Essian .25 .10
❑ 31T Pete Falcone .25 .10
❑ 32T Mike Ferraro MG .25 .10
❑ 33T Terry Forster 1.00 .40
❑ 34T Julio Franco XRC 8.00 3.20
❑ 35T Rich Gale .25 .10
❑ 36T Kiko Garcia .25 .10
❑ 37T Steve Garvey 1.00 .40
❑ 38T Johnny Grubb .25 .10
❑ 39T Mel Hall XRC* 1.00 .40
❑ 40T Von Hayes .25 .10
❑ 41T Danny Heep .25 .10
❑ 42T Steve Henderson .25 .10
❑ 43T Keith Hernandez 1.00 .40
❑ 44T Leo Hernandez .25 .10
❑ 45T Willie Hernandez .25 .10
❑ 46T Al Holland .25 .10
❑ 47T Frank Howard MG 1.00 .40
❑ 48T Bobby Johnson .25 .10
❑ 49T Cliff Johnson .25 .10
❑ 50T Odell Jones .25 .10
❑ 51T Mike Jorgensen .25 .10
❑ 52T Bob Kearney .25 .10
❑ 53T Steve Kemp .25 .10
❑ 54T Matt Keough .25 .10
❑ 55T Ron Kittle XRC* 2.00 .80
❑ 56T Mickey Klutts .25 .10
❑ 57T Alan Knicely .25 .10
❑ 58T Mike Krukow .25 .10
❑ 59T Rafael Landestoy .25 .10
❑ 60T Carney Lansford 1.00 .40
❑ 61T Joe Lefebvre .25 .10
❑ 62T Bryan Little .25 .10
❑ 63T Aurelio Lopez .25 .10
❑ 64T Mike Madden .25 .10
❑ 65T Rick Manning .25 .10
❑ 66T Billy Martin MG 2.00 .80
❑ 67T Lee Mazzilli 1.00 .40
❑ 68T Andy McGaffigan .25 .10
❑ 69T Craig McMurtry .25 .10
❑ 70T John McNamara MG .25 .10
❑ 71T Orlando Mercado .25 .10
❑ 72T Larry Milbourne .25 .10
❑ 73T Randy Moffitt .25 .10
❑ 74T Sid Monge .25 .10
❑ 75T Jose Morales .25 .10
❑ 76T Omar Moreno .25 .10
❑ 77T Joe Morgan 1.00 .40
❑ 78T Mike Morgan .25 .10
❑ 79T Dale Murray .25 .10
❑ 80T Jeff Newman .25 .10
❑ 81T Pete O'Brien XRC 1.00 .40
❑ 82T Jorge Orta .25 .10
❑ 83T Alejandro Pena XRC 2.00 .80
❑ 84T Pascual Perez .25 .10
❑ 85T Tony Perez 2.00 .80
❑ 86T Broderick Perkins .25 .10
❑ 87T Tony Phillips XRC 2.00 .80
❑ 88T Charlie Puleo .25 .10
❑ 89T Pat Putnam .25 .10
❑ 90T Jamie Quirk .25 .10
❑ 91T Doug Rader MG .25 .10
❑ 92T Chuck Rainey .25 .10
❑ 93T Bobby Ramos .25 .10
❑ 94T Gary Redus XRC 1.00 .40
❑ 95T Steve Renko .25 .10
❑ 96T Leon Roberts .25 .10
❑ 97T Aurelio Rodriguez .25 .10
❑ 98T Dick Ruthven .25 .10
❑ 99T Daryl Sconiers .25 .10
❑ 100T Mike Scott 1.00 .40
❑ 101T Tom Seaver 2.00 .80
❑ 102T John Shelby .25 .10
❑ 103T Bob Shirley .25 .10
❑ 104T Joe Simpson .25 .10
❑ 105T Doug Sisk .25 .10
❑ 106T Mike Smithson .25 .10
❑ 107T Elias Sosa .25 .10
❑ 108T D.Strawberry XRC 20.00 8.00
❑ 109T Tom Tellmann .25 .10
❑ 110T Gene Tenace 1.00 .40
❑ 111T Gorman Thomas 1.00 .40
❑ 112T Dick Tidrow .25 .10
❑ 113T Dave Tobik .25 .10
❑ 114T Wayne Tolleson .25 .10
❑ 115T Mike Torrez .25 .10
❑ 116T Manny Trillo .25 .10
❑ 117T Steve Trout .25 .10
❑ 118T Lee Tunnell .25 .10
❑ 119T Mike Vail .25 .10
❑ 120T Ellis Valentine .25 .10
❑ 121T Tom Veryzer .25 .10
❑ 122T George Vukovich .25 .10
❑ 123T Rick Waits .25 .10
❑ 124T Greg Walker 1.00 .40
❑ 125T Chris Welsh .25 .10
❑ 126T Len Whitehouse .25 .10
❑ 127T Eddie Whitson .25 .10
❑ 128T Jim Wohlford .25 .10
❑ 129T Matt Young XRC 1.00 .40
❑ 130T Joel Youngblood .25 .10
❑ 131T Pat Zachry .25 .10
❑ 132T Checklist 1T-132T .25 .10

1984 Topps

	Nm-Mt	Ex-Mt
COMPLETE SET (792)	50.00	20.00

❑ 1 Steve Carlton HL .25 .10
❑ 2 Rickey Henderson HL .60 .24
❑ 3 Dan Quisenberry HL .15 .06
❑ 4 Nolan Ryan HL 1.00 .40
Steve Carlton
Gaylord Perry
❑ 5 Dave Righetti HL .25 .10
Bob Forsch
Mike Warren
❑ 6 Johnny Bench HL .40 .16
Gaylord Perry
Carl Yastrzemski
❑ 7 Gary Lucas .15 .06
❑ 8 Don Mattingly RC 15.00 6.00
❑ 9 Jim Gott .15 .06
❑ 10 Robin Yount 1.00 .40
❑ 11 Kent Hrbek .25 .10
Ken Schrom TL
❑ 12 Billy Sample .15 .06
❑ 13 Scott Holman .15 .06
❑ 14 Tom Brookens .25 .10
❑ 15 Burt Hooton .15 .06
❑ 16 Omar Moreno .15 .06
❑ 17 John Denny .15 .06
❑ 18 Dale Berra .15 .06
❑ 19 Ray Fontenot .15 .06
❑ 20 Greg Luzinski .25 .10
❑ 21 Joe Altobelli MG .15 .06
❑ 22 Bryan Clark .15 .06
❑ 23 Keith Moreland .15 .06
❑ 24 John Martin .15 .06
❑ 25 Glenn Hubbard .15 .06
❑ 26 Bud Black .15 .06
❑ 27 Daryl Sconiers .15 .06
❑ 28 Frank Viola .40 .16
❑ 29 Danny Heep .15 .06
❑ 30 Wade Boggs 1.50 .60
❑ 31 Andy McGaffigan .15 .06
❑ 32 Bobby Ramos .15 .06
❑ 33 Tom Burgmeier .15 .06
❑ 34 Eddie Milner .15 .06
❑ 35 Don Sutton .25 .10
❑ 36 Denny Walling .15 .06
❑ 37 Buddy Bell .25 .10
Rick Honeycutt TL
❑ 38 Luis DeLeon .15 .06
❑ 39 Garth Iorg .15 .06
❑ 40 Dusty Baker .25 .10
❑ 41 Tony Bernazard .15 .06
❑ 42 Johnny Grubb .15 .06
❑ 43 Ron Reed .15 .06
❑ 44 Jim Morrison .15 .06
❑ 45 Jerry Mumphrey .15 .06
❑ 46 Ray Smith .15 .06
❑ 47 Rudy Law .15 .06
❑ 48 Julio Franco .25 .10
❑ 49 John Stuper .15 .06
❑ 50 Chris Chambliss .25 .10
❑ 51 Jim Frey MG .15 .06
❑ 52 Paul Splittorff .15 .06
❑ 53 Juan Beniquez .15 .06
❑ 54 Jesse Orosco .15 .06
❑ 55 Dave Concepcion .25 .10
❑ 56 Gary Allenson .15 .06
❑ 57 Dan Schatzeder .15 .06
❑ 58 Max Venable .15 .06
❑ 59 Sammy Stewart .15 .06
❑ 60 Paul Molitor UER .40 .16
('83 stats .272, 613,
167; should be .270,
608, 164)
❑ 61 Chris Codiroli .15 .06
❑ 62 Dave Hostetler .15 .06
❑ 63 Ed VandeBerg .15 .06
❑ 64 Mike Scioscia .25 .10
❑ 65 Kirk Gibson .60 .24
❑ 66 Jose Cruz 1.00 .40
Nolan Ryan TL
❑ 67 Gary Ward .15 .06
❑ 68 Luis Salazar .15 .06
❑ 69 Rod Scurry .15 .06
❑ 70 Gary Matthews .25 .10
❑ 71 Leo Hernandez .15 .06
❑ 72 Mike Squires .15 .06
❑ 73 Jody Davis .15 .06
❑ 74 Jerry Martin .15 .06
❑ 75 Bob Forsch .15 .06
❑ 76 Alfredo Griffin .15 .06
❑ 77 Brett Butler .25 .10
❑ 78 Mike Torrez .15 .06
❑ 79 Rob Wilfong .15 .06
❑ 80 Steve Rogers .25 .10
❑ 81 Billy Martin MG .40 .16
❑ 82 Doug Bird .15 .06
❑ 83 Richie Zisk .15 .06
❑ 84 Lenny Faedo .15 .06
❑ 85 Atlee Hammaker .15 .06
❑ 86 John Shelby .15 .06
❑ 87 Frank Pastore .15 .06
❑ 88 Rob Picciolo .15 .06
❑ 89 Mike Smithson .15 .06
❑ 90 Pedro Guerrero .25 .10
❑ 91 Dan Spillner .15 .06
❑ 92 Lloyd Moseby .15 .06
❑ 93 Bob Knepper .15 .06
❑ 94 Mario Ramirez .15 .06

- ❑ 95 Aurelio Lopez .25 .10
- ❑ 96 Hal McRae .25 .10
  Larry Gura TL
- ❑ 97 LaMarr Hoyt .15 .06
- ❑ 98 Steve Nicosia .15 .06
- ❑ 99 Craig Lefferts RC .15 .06
- ❑ 100 Reggie Jackson .40 .16
- ❑ 101 Porfirio Altamirano .15 .06
- ❑ 102 Ken Oberkfell .15 .06
- ❑ 103 Dwayne Murphy .15 .06
- ❑ 104 Ken Dayley .15 .06
- ❑ 105 Tony Armas .25 .10
- ❑ 106 Tim Stoddard .15 .06
- ❑ 107 Ned Yost .15 .06
- ❑ 108 Randy Moffitt .15 .06
- ❑ 109 Brad Wellman .15 .06
- ❑ 110 Ron Guidry .25 .10
- ❑ 111 Bill Virdon MG .15 .06
- ❑ 112 Tom Niedenfuer .15 .06
- ❑ 113 Kelly Paris .15 .06
- ❑ 114 Checklist 1-132 .25 .10
- ❑ 115 Andre Thornton .15 .06
- ❑ 116 George Bjorkman .15 .06
- ❑ 117 Tom Veryzer .15 .06
- ❑ 118 Charlie Hough .25 .10
- ❑ 119 John Wockenfuss .15 .06
- ❑ 120 Keith Hernandez .25 .10
- ❑ 121 Pat Sheridan .15 .06
- ❑ 122 Cecilio Guante .15 .06
- ❑ 123 Butch Wynegar .15 .06
- ❑ 124 Damaso Garcia .15 .06
- ❑ 125 Britt Burns .15 .06
- ❑ 126 Dale Murphy .40 .16
  Craig McMurtry TL
- ❑ 127 Mike Madden .15 .06
- ❑ 128 Rick Manning .15 .06
- ❑ 129 Bill Laskey .15 .06
- ❑ 130 Ozzie Smith 1.00 .40
- ❑ 131 Bill Madlock .60 .24
  Wade Boggs LL
- ❑ 132 Mike Schmidt .60 .24
  Jim Rice LL
- ❑ 133 Dale Murphy .40 .16
  Cecil Cooper
  Jim Rice LL
- ❑ 134 Tim Raines .60 .24
  Rickey Henderson LL
- ❑ 135 John Denny .60 .24
  LaMarr Hoyt LL
- ❑ 136 Steve Carlton .25 .10
  Jack Morris LL
- ❑ 137 Atlee Hammaker .25 .10
  Rick Honeycutt LL
- ❑ 138 Al Holland .25 .10
  Dan Quisenberry LL
- ❑ 139 Bert Campaneris .25 .10
- ❑ 140 Storm Davis .15 .06
- ❑ 141 Pat Corrales MG .15 .06
- ❑ 142 Rich Gale .15 .06
- ❑ 143 Jose Morales .15 .06
- ❑ 144 Brian Harper RC .40 .16
- ❑ 145 Gary Lavelle .15 .06
- ❑ 146 Ed Romero .15 .06
- ❑ 147 Dan Petry .25 .10
- ❑ 148 Joe Lefebvre .15 .06
- ❑ 149 Jon Matlack .15 .06
- ❑ 150 Dale Murphy .40 .16
- ❑ 151 Steve Trout .15 .06
- ❑ 152 Glenn Brummer .15 .06
- ❑ 153 Dick Tidrow .15 .06
- ❑ 154 Dave Henderson .25 .10
- ❑ 155 Frank White .25 .10
- ❑ 156 Rickey Henderson .60 .24
  Tim Conroy TL
- ❑ 157 Gary Gaetti .40 .16
- ❑ 158 John Curtis .15 .06
- ❑ 159 Darryl Cias .15 .06
- ❑ 160 Mario Soto .25 .10
- ❑ 161 Junior Ortiz .15 .06
- ❑ 162 Bob Ojeda .15 .06
- ❑ 163 Lorenzo Gray .15 .06
- ❑ 164 Scott Sanderson .15 .06
- ❑ 165 Ken Singleton .25 .10
- ❑ 166 Jamie Nelson .15 .06
- ❑ 167 Marshall Edwards .15 .06
- ❑ 168 Juan Bonilla .15 .06
- ❑ 169 Larry Parrish .15 .06
- ❑ 170 Jerry Reuss .15 .06
- ❑ 171 Frank Robinson MG .40 .16
- ❑ 172 Frank DiPino .15 .06
- ❑ 173 Marvell Wynne .40 .16
- ❑ 174 Juan Berenguer .15 .06
- ❑ 175 Graig Nettles .25 .10
- ❑ 176 Lee Smith .25 .10
- ❑ 177 Jerry Hairston .15 .06
- ❑ 178 Bill Krueger RC .15 .06
- ❑ 179 Buck Martinez .15 .06
- ❑ 180 Manny Trillo .15 .06
- ❑ 181 Roy Thomas .15 .06
- ❑ 182 Darryl Strawberry RC 3.00 1.20
- ❑ 183 Al Williams .15 .06
- ❑ 184 Mike O'Berry .15 .06
- ❑ 185 Sixto Lezcano .15 .06
- ❑ 186 Lonnie Smith .25 .10
  John Stuper TL
- ❑ 187 Luis Aponte .15 .06
- ❑ 188 Bryan Little .15 .06
- ❑ 189 Tim Conroy .15 .06
- ❑ 190 Ben Oglivie .25 .10
- ❑ 191 Mike Boddicker .15 .06
- ❑ 192 Nick Esasky .15 .06
- ❑ 193 Darrell Brown .15 .06
- ❑ 194 Domingo Ramos .15 .06
- ❑ 195 Jack Morris .25 .10
- ❑ 196 Don Slaught .25 .10
- ❑ 197 Garry Hancock .15 .06
- ❑ 198 Bill Doran RC* .40 .16
- ❑ 199 Willie Hernandez .15 .06
- ❑ 200 Andre Dawson .25 .10
- ❑ 201 Bruce Kison .15 .06
- ❑ 202 Bobby Cox MG .25 .10
- ❑ 203 Matt Keough .15 .06
- ❑ 204 Bobby Meacham .15 .06
- ❑ 205 Greg Minton .15 .06
- ❑ 206 Andy Van Slyke RC 1.50 .60
- ❑ 207 Donnie Moore .15 .06
- ❑ 208 Jose Oquendo RC .40 .16
- ❑ 209 Manny Sarmiento .15 .06
- ❑ 210 Joe Morgan .25 .10
- ❑ 211 Rick Sweet .15 .06
- ❑ 212 Broderick Perkins .15 .06
- ❑ 213 Bruce Hurst .15 .06
- ❑ 214 Paul Householder .15 .06
- ❑ 215 Tippy Martinez .15 .06
- ❑ 216 Carlton Fisk .25 .10
  Richard Dotson TL
- ❑ 217 Alan Ashby .15 .06
- ❑ 218 Rick Waits .15 .06
- ❑ 219 Joe Simpson .15 .06
- ❑ 220 Fernando Valenzuela .25 .10
- ❑ 221 Cliff Johnson .15 .06
- ❑ 222 Rick Honeycutt .15 .06
- ❑ 223 Wayne Krenchicki .15 .06
- ❑ 224 Sid Monge .15 .06
- ❑ 225 Lee Mazzilli .25 .10
- ❑ 226 Juan Eichelberger .15 .06
- ❑ 227 Steve Braun .15 .06
- ❑ 228 John Rabb .15 .06
- ❑ 229 Paul Owens MG .15 .06
- ❑ 230 Rickey Henderson 1.00 .40
- ❑ 231 Gary Woods .15 .06
- ❑ 232 Tim Wallach .15 .06
- ❑ 233 Checklist 133-264 .25 .10
- ❑ 234 Rafael Ramirez .15 .06
- ❑ 235 Matt Young RC .40 .16
- ❑ 236 Ellis Valentine .15 .06
- ❑ 237 John Castino .15 .06
- ❑ 238 Reid Nichols .15 .06
- ❑ 239 Jay Howell .15 .06
- ❑ 240 Eddie Murray .60 .24
- ❑ 241 Bill Almon .15 .06
- ❑ 242 Alex Trevino .15 .06
- ❑ 243 Pete Ladd .15 .06
- ❑ 244 Candy Maldonado .15 .06
- ❑ 245 Rick Sutcliffe .25 .10
- ❑ 246 Mookie Wilson .25 .10
  Tom Seaver TL
- ❑ 247 Onix Concepcion .15 .06
- ❑ 248 Bill Dawley .15 .06
- ❑ 249 Jay Johnstone .15 .06
- ❑ 250 Bill Madlock .25 .10
- ❑ 251 Tony Gwynn 2.50 1.00
- ❑ 252 Larry Christenson .15 .06
- ❑ 253 Jim Wohlford .15 .06
- ❑ 254 Shane Rawley .15 .06
- ❑ 255 Bruce Benedict .15 .06
- ❑ 256 Dave Geisel .15 .06
- ❑ 257 Julio Cruz .15 .06
- ❑ 258 Luis Sanchez .15 .06
- ❑ 259 Sparky Anderson MG .25 .10
- ❑ 260 Scott McGregor .15 .06
- ❑ 261 Bobby Brown .15 .06
- ❑ 262 Tom Candiotti RC .75 .30
- ❑ 263 Jack Fimple .15 .06
- ❑ 264 Doug Frobel RC .15 .06
- ❑ 265 Donnie Hill .15 .06
- ❑ 266 Steve Lubratich .15 .06
- ❑ 267 Carmelo Martinez .15 .06
- ❑ 268 Jack O'Connor .15 .06
- ❑ 269 Aurelio Rodriguez .15 .06
- ❑ 270 Jeff Russell RC .40 .16
- ❑ 271 Moose Haas .15 .06
- ❑ 272 Rick Dempsey .15 .06
- ❑ 273 Charlie Puleo .15 .06
- ❑ 274 Rick Monday .25 .10
- ❑ 275 Len Matuszek .15 .06
- ❑ 276 Rod Carew .25 .10
  Geoff Zahn TL
- ❑ 277 Eddie Whitson .15 .06
- ❑ 278 Jorge Bell .25 .10
- ❑ 279 Ivan DeJesus .15 .06
- ❑ 280 Floyd Bannister .15 .06
- ❑ 281 Larry Milbourne .15 .06
- ❑ 282 Jim Barr .15 .06
- ❑ 283 Larry Biittner .15 .06
- ❑ 284 Howard Bailey .15 .06
- ❑ 285 Darrell Porter .15 .06
- ❑ 286 Lary Sorensen .15 .06
- ❑ 287 Warren Cromartie .15 .06
- ❑ 288 Jim Beattie .15 .06
- ❑ 289 Randy Johnson .15 .06
- ❑ 290 Dave Dravecky .15 .06
- ❑ 291 Chuck Tanner MG .15 .06
- ❑ 292 Tony Scott .15 .06
- ❑ 293 Ed Lynch .15 .06
- ❑ 294 U.L. Washington .15 .06
- ❑ 295 Mike Flanagan .15 .06
- ❑ 296 Jeff Newman .15 .06
- ❑ 297 Bruce Berenyi .15 .06
- ❑ 298 Jim Gantner .15 .06
- ❑ 299 John Butcher .15 .06
- ❑ 300 Pete Rose 2.00 .80
- ❑ 301 Frank LaCorte .15 .06
- ❑ 302 Barry Bonnell .15 .06
- ❑ 303 Marty Castillo .15 .06
- ❑ 304 Warren Brusstar .15 .06
- ❑ 305 Roy Smalley .15 .06
- ❑ 306 Pedro Guerrero .25 .10
  Bob Welch TL
- ❑ 307 Bobby Mitchell .15 .06
- ❑ 308 Ron Hassey .15 .06
- ❑ 309 Tony Phillips RC .75 .30
- ❑ 310 Willie McGee .25 .10
- ❑ 311 Jerry Koosman .25 .10
- ❑ 312 Jorge Orta .15 .06
- ❑ 313 Mike Jorgensen .15 .06
- ❑ 314 Orlando Mercado .15 .06
- ❑ 315 Bobby Grich .25 .10
- ❑ 316 Mark Bradley .15 .06
- ❑ 317 Greg Pryor .15 .06
- ❑ 318 Bill Gullickson .15 .06
- ❑ 319 Al Bumbry .15 .06
- ❑ 320 Bob Stanley .15 .06
- ❑ 321 Harvey Kuenn MG .15 .06
- ❑ 322 Ken Schrom .15 .06
- ❑ 323 Alan Knicely .15 .06
- ❑ 324 Alejandro Pena RC* .75 .30
- ❑ 325 Darrell Evans .25 .10
- ❑ 326 Bob Kearney .15 .06
- ❑ 327 Ruppert Jones .15 .06
- ❑ 328 Vern Ruhle .15 .06
- ❑ 329 Pat Tabler .15 .06
- ❑ 330 John Candelaria .15 .06
- ❑ 331 Bucky Dent .25 .10
- ❑ 332 Kevin Gross RC .40 .16
- ❑ 333 Larry Herndon .25 .10
- ❑ 334 Chuck Rainey .15 .06
- ❑ 335 Don Baylor .25 .10

❑ 336 Pat Putnam .25 .10
Matt Young TL
❑ 337 Kevin Hagen .15 .06
❑ 338 Mike Warren .15 .06
❑ 339 Roy Lee Jackson .15 .06
❑ 340 Hal McRae .25 .10
❑ 341 Dave Tobik .15 .06
❑ 342 Tim Foli .15 .06
❑ 343 Mark Davis .15 .06
❑ 344 Rick Miller .15 .06
❑ 345 Kent Hrbek .25 .10
❑ 346 Kurt Bevacqua .15 .06
❑ 347 Allan Ramirez .15 .06
❑ 348 Toby Harrah .25 .10
❑ 349 Bob L. Gibson RC .15 .06
❑ 350 George Foster .25 .10
❑ 351 Russ Nixon MG .15 .06
❑ 352 Dave Stewart .25 .10
❑ 353 Jim Anderson .15 .06
❑ 354 Jeff Burroughs .15 .06
❑ 355 Jason Thompson .15 .06
❑ 356 Glenn Abbott .15 .06
❑ 357 Ron Cey .25 .10
❑ 358 Bob Dernier .15 .06
❑ 359 Jim Acker .15 .06
❑ 360 Willie Randolph .25 .10
❑ 361 Dave Smith .15 .06
❑ 362 David Green .15 .06
❑ 363 Tim Laudner .15 .06
❑ 364 Scott Fletcher .15 .06
❑ 365 Steve Bedrosian .15 .06
❑ 366 Terry Kennedy .25 .10
Dave Dravecky TL
❑ 367 Jamie Easterly .15 .06
❑ 368 Hubie Brooks .15 .06
❑ 369 Steve McCatty .15 .06
❑ 370 Tim Raines .25 .10
❑ 371 Dave Gumpert .15 .06
❑ 372 Gary Roenicke .15 .06
❑ 373 Bill Scherrer .15 .06
❑ 374 Don Money .15 .06
❑ 375 Dennis Leonard .15 .06
❑ 376 Dave Anderson RC .15 .06
❑ 377 Danny Darwin .15 .06
❑ 378 Bob Brenly .15 .06
❑ 379 Checklist 265-396 .25 .10
❑ 380 Steve Garvey .25 .10
❑ 381 Ralph Houk MG .15 .06
❑ 382 Chris Nyman .15 .06
❑ 383 Terry Puhl .15 .06
❑ 384 Lee Tunnell .15 .06
❑ 385 Tony Perez .40 .16
❑ 386 George Hendrick AS .15 .06
❑ 387 Johnny Ray AS .15 .06
❑ 388 Mike Schmidt AS .60 .24
❑ 389 Ozzie Smith AS .60 .24
❑ 390 Tim Raines AS .15 .06
❑ 391 Dale Murphy AS .25 .10
❑ 392 Andre Dawson AS .15 .06
❑ 393 Gary Carter AS .15 .06
❑ 394 Steve Rogers AS .15 .06
❑ 395 Steve Carlton AS .25 .10
❑ 396 Jesse Orosco AS .15 .06
❑ 397 Eddie Murray AS .40 .16
❑ 398 Lou Whitaker AS .15 .06
❑ 399 George Brett AS .60 .24
❑ 400 Cal Ripken AS 2.00 .80
❑ 401 Jim Rice AS .15 .06
❑ 402 Dave Winfield AS .15 .06
❑ 403 Lloyd Moseby AS .15 .06
❑ 404 Ted Simmons AS .15 .06
❑ 405 LaMarr Hoyt AS .15 .06
❑ 406 Ron Guidry AS .15 .06
❑ 407 Dan Quisenberry AS .15 .06
❑ 408 Lou Piniella .25 .10
❑ 409 Juan Agosto .15 .06
❑ 410 Claudell Washington .15 .06
❑ 411 Houston Jimenez .15 .06
❑ 412 Doug Rader MG .15 .06
❑ 413 Spike Owen RC .40 .16
❑ 414 Mitchell Page .15 .06
❑ 415 Tommy John .25 .10
❑ 416 Dane Iorg .15 .06
❑ 417 Mike Armstrong .15 .06
❑ 418 Ron Hodges .15 .06
❑ 419 John Henry Johnson .15 .06
❑ 420 Cecil Cooper .25 .10
❑ 421 Charlie Lea .15 .06
❑ 422 Jose Cruz .25 .10
❑ 423 Mike Morgan .15 .06
❑ 424 Dann Bilardello .15 .06
❑ 425 Steve Howe .15 .06
❑ 426 Cal Ripken 1.50 .60
Mike Boddicker TL
❑ 427 Rick Leach .15 .06
❑ 428 Fred Breining .15 .06
❑ 429 Randy Bush .15 .06
❑ 430 Rusty Staub .25 .10
❑ 431 Chris Bando .15 .06
❑ 432 Charles Hudson .15 .06
❑ 433 Rich Hebner .15 .06
❑ 434 Harold Baines .25 .10
❑ 435 Neil Allen .15 .06
❑ 436 Rick Peters .15 .06
❑ 437 Mike Proly .15 .06
❑ 438 Biff Pocoroba .15 .06
❑ 439 Bob Stoddard .15 .06
❑ 440 Steve Kemp .15 .06
❑ 441 Bob Lillis MG .15 .06
❑ 442 Byron McLaughlin .15 .06
❑ 443 Benny Ayala .15 .06
❑ 444 Steve Renko .15 .06
❑ 445 Jerry Remy .15 .06
❑ 446 Luis Pujols .15 .06
❑ 447 Tom Brunansky .15 .06
❑ 448 Ben Hayes .15 .06
❑ 449 Joe Pettini .15 .06
❑ 450 Gary Carter .25 .10
❑ 451 Bob Jones .15 .06
❑ 452 Chuck Porter .15 .06
❑ 453 Willie Upshaw .15 .06
❑ 454 Joe Beckwith .15 .06
❑ 455 Terry Kennedy .15 .06
❑ 456 Keith Moreland .15 .06
Fergie Jenkins TL
❑ 457 Dave Rozema .15 .06
❑ 458 Kiko Garcia .15 .06
❑ 459 Kevin Hickey .15 .06
❑ 460 Dave Winfield .25 .10
❑ 461 Jim Maler .15 .06
❑ 462 Lee Lacy .15 .06
❑ 463 Dave Engle .15 .06
❑ 464 Jeff A. Jones .15 .06
❑ 465 Mookie Wilson .25 .10
❑ 466 Gene Garber .15 .06
❑ 467 Mike Ramsey .15 .06
❑ 468 Geoff Zahn .15 .06
❑ 469 Tom O'Malley .15 .06
❑ 470 Nolan Ryan 3.00 1.20
❑ 471 Dick Howser MG .15 .06
❑ 472 Mike G. Brown RC .15 .06
❑ 473 Jim Dwyer .15 .06
❑ 474 Greg Bargar .15 .06
❑ 475 Gary Redus RC* .40 .16
❑ 476 Tom Tellmann .15 .06
❑ 477 Rafael Landestoy .15 .06
❑ 478 Alan Bannister .15 .06
❑ 479 Frank Tanana .25 .10
❑ 480 Ron Kittle .15 .06
❑ 481 Mark Thurmond .15 .06
❑ 482 Enos Cabell .15 .06
❑ 483 Fergie Jenkins .25 .10
❑ 484 Ozzie Virgil .15 .06
❑ 485 Rick Rhoden .15 .06
❑ 486 Don Baylor .25 .10
Ron Guidry TL
❑ 487 Ricky Adams .15 .06
❑ 488 Jesse Barfield .25 .10
❑ 489 Dave Von Ohlen .15 .06
❑ 490 Cal Ripken 4.00 1.60
❑ 491 Bobby Castillo .15 .06
❑ 492 Tucker Ashford .15 .06
❑ 493 Mike Norris .15 .06
❑ 494 Chili Davis .25 .10
❑ 495 Rollie Fingers .25 .10
❑ 496 Terry Francona .25 .10
❑ 497 Bud Anderson .15 .06
❑ 498 Rich Gedman .15 .06
❑ 499 Mike Witt .15 .06
❑ 500 George Brett 1.50 .60
❑ 501 Steve Henderson .15 .06
❑ 502 Joe Torre MG .25 .10
❑ 503 Elias Sosa .15 .06
❑ 504 Mickey Rivers .15 .06
❑ 505 Pete Vuckovich .15 .06
❑ 506 Ernie Whitt .15 .06
❑ 507 Mike LaCoss .15 .06
❑ 508 Mel Hall .25 .10
❑ 509 Brad Havens .15 .06
❑ 510 Alan Trammell .25 .10
❑ 511 Marty Bystrom .15 .06
❑ 512 Oscar Gamble .15 .06
❑ 513 Dave Beard .15 .06
❑ 514 Floyd Rayford .15 .06
❑ 515 Gorman Thomas .25 .10
❑ 516 Al Oliver .25 .10
Charlie Lea TL
❑ 517 John Moses .15 .06
❑ 518 Greg Walker .40 .16
❑ 519 Ron Davis .15 .06
❑ 520 Bob Boone .25 .10
❑ 521 Pete Falcone .15 .06
❑ 522 Dave Bergman .15 .06
❑ 523 Glenn Hoffman .15 .06
❑ 524 Carlos Diaz .15 .06
❑ 525 Willie Wilson .25 .10
❑ 526 Ron Oester .15 .06
❑ 527 Checklist 397-528 .25 .10
❑ 528 Mark Brouhard .15 .06
❑ 529 Keith Atherton .15 .06
❑ 530 Dan Ford .15 .06
❑ 531 Steve Boros MG .15 .06
❑ 532 Eric Show .15 .06
❑ 533 Ken Landreaux .15 .06
❑ 534 Pete O'Brien RC* .40 .16
❑ 535 Bo Diaz .15 .06
❑ 536 Doug Bair .15 .06
❑ 537 Johnny Ray .15 .06
❑ 538 Kevin Bass .15 .06
❑ 539 George Frazier .15 .06
❑ 540 George Hendrick .25 .10
❑ 541 Dennis Lamp .15 .06
❑ 542 Duane Kuiper .15 .06
❑ 543 Craig McMurtry .15 .06
❑ 544 Cesar Geronimo .15 .06
❑ 545 Bill Buckner .25 .10
❑ 546 Mike Hargrove .25 .10
Lary Sorensen TL
❑ 547 Mike Moore .15 .06
❑ 548 Ron Jackson .15 .06
❑ 549 Walt Terrell .15 .06
❑ 550 Jim Rice .25 .10
❑ 551 Scott Ullger .15 .06
❑ 552 Ray Burris .15 .06
❑ 553 Joe Nolan .15 .06
❑ 554 Ted Power .15 .06
❑ 555 Greg Brock .15 .06
❑ 556 Joey McLaughlin .15 .06
❑ 557 Wayne Tolleson .15 .06
❑ 558 Mike Davis .15 .06
❑ 559 Mike Scott .25 .10
❑ 560 Carlton Fisk .40 .16
❑ 561 Whitey Herzog MG .25 .10
❑ 562 Manny Castillo .15 .06
❑ 563 Glenn Wilson .25 .10
❑ 564 Al Holland .15 .06
❑ 565 Leon Durham .15 .06
❑ 566 Jim Bibby .15 .06
❑ 567 Mike Heath .15 .06
❑ 568 Pete Filson .15 .06
❑ 569 Bake McBride .25 .10
❑ 570 Dan Quisenberry .15 .06
❑ 571 Bruce Bochy .15 .06
❑ 572 Jerry Royster .15 .06
❑ 573 Dave Kingman .25 .10
❑ 574 Brian Downing .25 .10
❑ 575 Jim Clancy .15 .06
❑ 576 Jeff Leonard .25 .10
Atlee Hammaker TL
❑ 577 Mark Clear .15 .06
❑ 578 Lenn Sakata .15 .06
❑ 579 Bob James .15 .06
❑ 580 Lonnie Smith .15 .06
❑ 581 Jose DeLeon RC .40 .16
❑ 582 Bob McClure .15 .06
❑ 583 Derrel Thomas .15 .06
❑ 584 Dave Schmidt .15 .06
❑ 585 Dan Driessen .15 .06

❑ 586 Joe Niekro .15 .06
❑ 587 Von Hayes .15 .06
❑ 588 Milt Wilcox .15 .06
❑ 589 Mike Easler .15 .06
❑ 590 Dave Stieb .25 .10
❑ 591 Tony LaRussa MG .25 .10
❑ 592 Andre Robertson .15 .06
❑ 593 Jeff Lahti .15 .06
❑ 594 Gene Richards .15 .06
❑ 595 Jeff Reardon .25 .10
❑ 596 Ryne Sandberg 2.50 1.00
❑ 597 Rick Camp .15 .06
❑ 598 Rusty Kuntz .15 .06
❑ 599 Doug Sisk .15 .06
❑ 600 Rod Carew .40 .16
❑ 601 John Tudor .25 .10
❑ 602 John Wathan .15 .06
❑ 603 Renie Martin .15 .06
❑ 604 John Lowenstein .15 .06
❑ 605 Mike Caldwell .15 .06
❑ 606 Lloyd Moseby .25 .10
Dave Stieb TL
❑ 607 Tom Hume .15 .06
❑ 608 Bobby Johnson .15 .06
❑ 609 Dan Meyer .15 .06
❑ 610 Steve Sax .15 .06
❑ 611 Chet Lemon .25 .10
❑ 612 Harry Spilman .15 .06
❑ 613 Greg Gross .15 .06
❑ 614 Len Barker .15 .06
❑ 615 Garry Templeton .25 .10
❑ 616 Don Robinson .15 .06
❑ 617 Rick Cerone .15 .06
❑ 618 Dickie Noles .15 .06
❑ 619 Jerry Dybzinski .15 .06
❑ 620 Al Oliver .25 .10
❑ 621 Frank Howard MG .25 .10
❑ 622 Al Cowens .15 .06
❑ 623 Ron Washington .15 .06
❑ 624 Terry Harper .15 .06
❑ 625 Larry Gura .15 .06
❑ 626 Bob Clark .15 .06
❑ 627 Dave LaPoint .15 .06
❑ 628 Ed Jurak .15 .06
❑ 629 Rick Langford .15 .06
❑ 630 Ted Simmons .25 .10
❑ 631 Dennis Martinez .25 .10
❑ 632 Tom Foley .15 .06
❑ 633 Mike Krukow .15 .06
❑ 634 Mike Marshall .15 .06
❑ 635 Dave Righetti .25 .10
❑ 636 Pat Putnam .15 .06
❑ 637 Gary Matthews .25 .10
John Denny TL
❑ 638 George Vukovich .15 .06
❑ 639 Rick Lysander .15 .06
❑ 640 Lance Parrish .40 .16
❑ 641 Mike Richardt .15 .06
❑ 642 Tom Underwood .15 .06
❑ 643 Mike C. Brown .15 .06
❑ 644 Tim Lollar .15 .06
❑ 645 Tony Pena .15 .06
❑ 646 Checklist 529-660 .25 .10
❑ 647 Ron Roenicke .15 .06
❑ 648 Len Whitehouse .15 .06
❑ 649 Tom Herr .15 .06
❑ 650 Phil Niekro .25 .10
❑ 651 John McNamara MG .15 .06
❑ 652 Rudy May .15 .06
❑ 653 Dave Stapleton .15 .06
❑ 654 Bob Bailor .15 .06
❑ 655 Amos Otis .25 .10
❑ 656 Bryn Smith .15 .06
❑ 657 Thad Bosley .15 .06
❑ 658 Jerry Augustine .15 .06
❑ 659 Duane Walker .15 .06
❑ 660 Ray Knight .25 .10
❑ 661 Steve Yeager .25 .10
❑ 662 Tom Brennan .15 .06
❑ 663 Johnnie LeMaster .15 .06
❑ 664 Dave Stegman .15 .06
❑ 665 Buddy Bell .25 .10
❑ 666 Lou Whitaker .25 .10
Jack Morris TL
❑ 667 Vance Law .15 .06
❑ 668 Larry McWilliams .15 .06
❑ 669 Dave Lopes .25 .10
❑ 670 Rich Gossage .25 .10
❑ 671 Jamie Quirk .15 .06
❑ 672 Ricky Nelson .15 .06
❑ 673 Mike Walters .15 .06
❑ 674 Tim Flannery .15 .06
❑ 675 Pascual Perez .15 .06
❑ 676 Brian Giles .15 .06
❑ 677 Doyle Alexander .15 .06
❑ 678 Chris Speier .15 .06
❑ 679 Art Howe .15 .06
❑ 680 Fred Lynn .25 .10
❑ 681 Tom Lasorda MG .40 .16
❑ 682 Dan Morogiello .15 .06
❑ 683 Marty Barrett RC .40 .16
❑ 684 Bob Shirley .15 .06
❑ 685 Willie Aikens .15 .06
❑ 686 Joe Price .15 .06
❑ 687 Roy Howell .15 .06
❑ 688 George Wright .15 .06
❑ 689 Mike Fischlin .15 .06
❑ 690 Jack Clark .25 .10
❑ 691 Steve Lake .15 .06
❑ 692 Dickie Thon .15 .06
❑ 693 Alan Wiggins .15 .06
❑ 694 Mike Stanton .15 .06
❑ 695 Lou Whitaker .25 .10
❑ 696 Bill Madlock .25 .10
Rick Rhoden TL
❑ 697 Dale Murray .15 .06
❑ 698 Marc Hill .15 .06
❑ 699 Dave Rucker .15 .06
❑ 700 Mike Schmidt 1.50 .60
❑ 701 Bill Madlock .60 .24
Pete Rose
Dave Parker LL
❑ 702 Pete Rose .60 .24
Rusty Staub
Tony Perez LL
❑ 703 Mike Schmidt .60 .24
Tony Perez
Dave Kingman LL
❑ 704 Tony Perez .25 .10
Rusty Staub
Al Oliver LL
❑ 705 Joe Morgan .40 .16
Cesar Cedeno
Larry Bowa LL
❑ 706 Steve Carlton .25 .10
Fergie Jenkins
Tom Seaver LL
❑ 707 Steve Carlton 1.50 .60
Nolan Ryan
Tom Seaver LL
❑ 708 Tom Seaver .25 .10
Steve Carlton
Steve Rogers LL
❑ 709 Bruce Sutter .25 .10
Tug McGraw
Gene Garber LL
❑ 710 Rod Carew .40 .16
George Brett
Cecil Cooper LL
❑ 711 Rod Carew .25 .10
Bert Campaneris
Reggie Jackson LL
❑ 712 Reggie Jackson .25 .10
Graig Nettles
Greg Luzinski LL
❑ 713 Reggie Jackson .25 .10
Ted Simmons
Graig Nettles LL
❑ 714 Bert Campaneris .25 .10
Dave Lopes
Omar Moreno LL
❑ 715 Jim Palmer .25 .10
Don Sutton
Tommy John LL
❑ 716 Don Sutton .40 .16
Bert Blyleven
Jerry Koosman LL
❑ 717 Jim Palmer .25 .10
Rollie Fingers
Ron Guidry LL
❑ 718 Rollie Fingers .25 .10
Rich Gossage
Dan Quisenberry LL
❑ 719 Andy Hassler .15 .06
❑ 720 Dwight Evans .40 .16
❑ 721 Del Crandall MG .15 .06
❑ 722 Bob Welch .25 .10
❑ 723 Rich Dauer .15 .06
❑ 724 Eric Rasmussen .15 .06
❑ 725 Cesar Cedeno .25 .10
❑ 726 Ted Simmons .25 .10
Moose Haas TL
❑ 727 Joel Youngblood .15 .06
❑ 728 Tug McGraw .25 .10
❑ 729 Gene Tenace .25 .10
❑ 730 Bruce Sutter .25 .10
❑ 731 Lynn Jones .15 .06
❑ 732 Terry Crowley .15 .06
❑ 733 Dave Collins .15 .06
❑ 734 Odell Jones .15 .06
❑ 735 Rick Burleson .15 .06
❑ 736 Dick Ruthven .15 .06
❑ 737 Jim Essian .15 .06
❑ 738 Bill Schroeder .15 .06
❑ 739 Bob Watson .15 .06
❑ 740 Tom Seaver .60 .24
❑ 741 Wayne Gross .15 .06
❑ 742 Dick Williams MG .15 .06
❑ 743 Don Hood .15 .06
❑ 744 Jamie Allen .15 .06
❑ 745 Dennis Eckersley .40 .16
❑ 746 Mickey Hatcher .15 .06
❑ 747 Pat Zachry .15 .06
❑ 748 Jeff Leonard .15 .06
❑ 749 Doug Flynn .15 .06
❑ 750 Jim Palmer .25 .10
❑ 751 Charlie Moore .15 .06
❑ 752 Phil Garner .25 .10
❑ 753 Doug Gwosdz .15 .06
❑ 754 Kent Tekulve .15 .06
❑ 755 Garry Maddox .15 .06
❑ 756 Ron Oester .25 .10
Mario Soto TL
❑ 757 Larry Bowa .25 .10
❑ 758 Bill Stein .15 .06
❑ 759 Richard Dotson .15 .06
❑ 760 Bob Horner .25 .10
❑ 761 John Montefusco .15 .06
❑ 762 Rance Mulliniks .15 .06
❑ 763 Craig Swan .15 .06
❑ 764 Mike Hargrove .15 .06
❑ 765 Ken Forsch .15 .06
❑ 766 Mike Vail .15 .06
❑ 767 Carney Lansford .25 .10
❑ 768 Champ Summers .15 .06
❑ 769 Bill Caudill .15 .06
❑ 770 Ken Griffey .25 .10
❑ 771 Billy Gardner MG .15 .06
❑ 772 Jim Slaton .15 .06
❑ 773 Todd Cruz .15 .06
❑ 774 Tom Gorman .15 .06
❑ 775 Dave Parker .25 .10
❑ 776 Craig Reynolds .15 .06
❑ 777 Tom Paciorek .15 .06
❑ 778 Andy Hawkins .15 .06
❑ 779 Jim Sundberg .25 .10
❑ 780 Steve Carlton .40 .16
❑ 781 Checklist 661-792 .25 .10
❑ 782 Steve Balboni .15 .06
❑ 783 Luis Leal .15 .06
❑ 784 Leon Roberts .15 .06
❑ 785 Joaquin Andujar .25 .10
❑ 786 Wade Boggs .40 .16
Bob Ojeda TL
❑ 787 Bill Campbell .15 .06
❑ 788 Milt May .15 .06
❑ 789 Bert Blyleven .25 .10
❑ 790 Doug DeCinces .15 .06
❑ 791 Terry Forster .25 .10
❑ 792 Bill Russell .25 .10

1984 Topps Traded

	Nm-Mt	Ex-Mt
COMP.FACT.SET (132)	30.00	12.00

❑ 1T Willie Aikens .40 .16
❑ 2T Luis Aponte .40 .16

❑ 3T Mike Armstrong .40 .16
❑ 4T Bob Bailor .40 .16
❑ 5T Dusty Baker .60 .24
❑ 6T Steve Balboni .40 .16
❑ 7T Alan Bannister .40 .16
❑ 8T Dave Beard .40 .16
❑ 9T Joe Beckwith .40 .16
❑ 10T Bruce Berenyi .40 .16
❑ 11T Dave Bergman .40 .16
❑ 12T Tony Bernazard .40 .16
❑ 13T Yogi Berra MG 1.50 .60
❑ 14T Barry Bonnell .40 .16
❑ 15T Phil Bradley 1.00 .40
❑ 16T Fred Breining .40 .16
❑ 17T Bill Buckner .60 .24
❑ 18T Ray Burris .40 .16
❑ 19T John Butcher .40 .16
❑ 20T Brett Butler .60 .24
❑ 21T Enos Cabell .40 .16
❑ 22T Bill Campbell .40 .16
❑ 23T Bill Caudill .40 .16
❑ 24T Bob Clark .40 .16
❑ 25T Bryan Clark .40 .16
❑ 26T Jaime Cocanower .40 .16
❑ 27T Ron Darling XRC* 2.00 .80
❑ 28T Alvin Davis XRC 1.00 .40
❑ 29T Ken Dayley .40 .16
❑ 30T Jeff Dedmon .40 .16
❑ 31T Bob Dernier .40 .16
❑ 32T Carlos Diaz .40 .16
❑ 33T Mike Easler .40 .16
❑ 34T Dennis Eckersley 1.00 .40
❑ 35T Jim Essian .40 .16
❑ 36T Darrell Evans .60 .24
❑ 37T Mike Fitzgerald .40 .16
❑ 38T Tim Foli .40 .16
❑ 39T George Frazier .40 .16
❑ 40T Rich Gale .40 .16
❑ 41T Barbaro Garbey .40 .16
❑ 42T Dwight Gooden XRC 10.00 4.00
❑ 43T Rich Gossage .60 .24
❑ 44T Wayne Gross .40 .16
❑ 45T Mark Gubicza XRC 1.00 .40
❑ 46T Jackie Gutierrez .40 .16
❑ 47T Mel Hall .60 .24
❑ 48T Toby Harrah .60 .24
❑ 49T Ron Hassey .40 .16
❑ 50T Rich Hebner .40 .16
❑ 51T Willie Hernandez .40 .16
❑ 52T Ricky Horton .40 .16
❑ 53T Art Howe .40 .16
❑ 54T Dane Iorg .40 .16
❑ 55T Brook Jacoby 1.00 .40
❑ 56T Mike Jeffcoat XRC .50 .20
❑ 57T Dave Johnson MG .40 .16
❑ 58T Lynn Jones .40 .16
❑ 59T Ruppert Jones .40 .16
❑ 60T Mike Jorgensen .40 .16
❑ 61T Bob Kearney .40 .16
❑ 62T Jimmy Key XRC 2.00 .80
❑ 63T Dave Kingman .60 .24
❑ 64T Jerry Koosman .60 .24
❑ 65T Wayne Krenchicki .40 .16
❑ 66T Rusty Kuntz .40 .16
❑ 67T Rene Lachemann MG .40 .16
❑ 68T Frank LaCorte .40 .16
❑ 69T Dennis Lamp .40 .16
❑ 70T Mark Langston XRC 2.00 .80
❑ 71T Rick Leach .40 .16
❑ 72T Craig Lefferts .50 .20
❑ 73T Gary Lucas .40 .16
❑ 74T Jerry Martin .40 .16
❑ 75T Carmelo Martinez .40 .16
❑ 76T Mike Mason XRC .50 .20
❑ 77T Gary Matthews .60 .24
❑ 78T Andy McGaffigan .40 .16
❑ 79T Larry Milbourne .40 .16
❑ 80T Sid Monge .40 .16
❑ 81T Jackie Moore MG .40 .16
❑ 82T Joe Morgan .60 .24
❑ 83T Graig Nettles .60 .24
❑ 84T Phil Niekro .60 .24
❑ 85T Ken Oberkfell .40 .16
❑ 86T Mike O'Berry .40 .16
❑ 87T Al Oliver .60 .24
❑ 88T Jorge Orta .40 .16
❑ 89T Amos Otis .60 .24
❑ 90T Dave Parker .60 .24
❑ 91T Tony Perez 1.00 .40
❑ 92T Gerald Perry 1.00 .40
❑ 93T Gary Pettis .40 .16
❑ 94T Rob Picciolo .40 .16
❑ 95T Vern Rapp MG .40 .16
❑ 96T Floyd Rayford .40 .16
❑ 97T Randy Ready XRC 1.00 .40
❑ 98T Ron Reed .40 .16
❑ 99T Gene Richards .40 .16
❑ 100T Jose Rijo XRC 2.00 .80
❑ 101T Jeff D. Robinson .40 .16
❑ 102T Ron Romanick .40 .16
❑ 103T Pete Rose 5.00 2.00
❑ 104T B.Saberhagen XRC 4.00 1.60
❑ 105T Juan Samuel XRC* 2.00 .80
❑ 106T Scott Sanderson .40 .16
❑ 107T Dick Schofield XRC* 1.00 .40
❑ 108T Tom Seaver 1.50 .60
❑ 109T Jim Slaton .40 .16
❑ 110T Mike Smithson .40 .16
❑ 111T Lary Sorensen .40 .16
❑ 112T Tim Stoddard .40 .16
❑ 113T Champ Summers .40 .16
❑ 114T Jim Sundberg .60 .24
❑ 115T Rick Sutcliffe .60 .24
❑ 116T Craig Swan .40 .16
❑ 117T Tim Teufel XRC* 1.00 .40
❑ 118T Derrel Thomas .40 .16
❑ 119T Gorman Thomas .60 .24
❑ 120T Alex Trevino .40 .16
❑ 121T Manny Trillo .40 .16
❑ 122T John Tudor .60 .24
❑ 123T Tom Underwood .40 .16
❑ 124T Mike Vail .40 .16
❑ 125T Tom Waddell .40 .16
❑ 126T Gary Ward .40 .16
❑ 127T Curtis Wilkerson .40 .16
❑ 128T Frank Williams .40 .16
❑ 129T Glenn Wilson .60 .24
❑ 130T John Wockenfuss .40 .16
❑ 131T Ned Yost .40 .16
❑ 132T Checklist 1T-132T .40 .16

1985 Topps

	Nm-Mt	Ex-Mt
COMPLETE SET (792)	80.00	32.00
COMP.FACT.SET (792)	150.00	60.00

❑ 1 Carlton Fisk RB .25 .10
❑ 2 Steve Garvey RB .15 .06
❑ 3 Dwight Gooden RB .60 .24
❑ 4 Cliff Johnson RB .15 .06
❑ 5 Joe Morgan RB .15 .06
❑ 6 Pete Rose RB .40 .16
❑ 7 Nolan Ryan RB 1.50 .60
❑ 8 Juan Samuel RB .15 .06
❑ 9 Bruce Sutter RB .15 .06
❑ 10 Don Sutton RB .15 .06
❑ 11 Ralph Houk MG .15 .06
❑ 12 Dave Lopes .25 .10
❑ 13 Tim Lollar .15 .06
❑ 14 Chris Bando .15 .06
❑ 15 Jerry Koosman .25 .10
❑ 16 Bobby Meacham .15 .06
❑ 17 Mike Scott .25 .10
❑ 18 Mickey Hatcher .15 .06
❑ 19 George Frazier .15 .06
❑ 20 Chet Lemon .25 .10
❑ 21 Lee Tunnell .15 .06
❑ 22 Duane Kuiper .15 .06
❑ 23 Bret Saberhagen RC 1.00 .40
❑ 24 Jesse Barfield .25 .10
❑ 25 Steve Bedrosian .15 .06
❑ 26 Roy Smalley .15 .06
❑ 27 Bruce Berenyi .15 .06
❑ 28 Dann Bilardello .15 .06
❑ 29 Odell Jones .15 .06
❑ 30 Cal Ripken 2.50 1.00
❑ 31 Terry Whitfield .15 .06
❑ 32 Chuck Porter .15 .06
❑ 33 Tito Landrum .15 .06
❑ 34 Ed Nunez .15 .06
❑ 35 Graig Nettles .25 .10
❑ 36 Fred Breining .15 .06
❑ 37 Reid Nichols .15 .06
❑ 38 Jackie Moore MG .15 .06
❑ 39 John Wockenfuss .15 .06
❑ 40 Phil Niekro .25 .10
❑ 41 Mike Fischlin .15 .06
❑ 42 Luis Sanchez .15 .06
❑ 43 Andre David .15 .06
❑ 44 Dickie Thon .15 .06
❑ 45 Greg Minton .15 .06
❑ 46 Gary Woods .15 .06
❑ 47 Dave Rozema .15 .06
❑ 48 Tony Fernandez .25 .10
❑ 49 Butch Davis .15 .06
❑ 50 John Candelaria .15 .06
❑ 51 Bob Watson .15 .06
❑ 52 Jerry Dybzinski .15 .06
❑ 53 Tom Gorman .15 .06
❑ 54 Cesar Cedeno .25 .10
❑ 55 Frank Tanana .25 .10
❑ 56 Jim Dwyer .15 .06
❑ 57 Pat Zachry .15 .06
❑ 58 Orlando Mercado .15 .06
❑ 59 Rick Waits .15 .06
❑ 60 George Hendrick .25 .10
❑ 61 Curt Kaufman .15 .06
❑ 62 Mike Ramsey .15 .06
❑ 63 Steve McCatty .15 .06
❑ 64 Mark Bailey .15 .06
❑ 65 Bill Buckner .25 .10
❑ 66 Dick Williams MG .15 .06
❑ 67 Rafael Santana .15 .06
❑ 68 Von Hayes .15 .06
❑ 69 Jim Winn .15 .06
❑ 70 Don Baylor .25 .10
❑ 71 Tim Laudner .15 .06
❑ 72 Rick Sutcliffe .25 .10
❑ 73 Rusty Kuntz .15 .06
❑ 74 Mike Krukow .15 .06
❑ 75 Willie Upshaw .15 .06
❑ 76 Alan Bannister .15 .06
❑ 77 Joe Beckwith .15 .06
❑ 78 Scott Fletcher .15 .06
❑ 79 Rick Mahler .15 .06
❑ 80 Keith Hernandez .25 .10
❑ 81 Lenn Sakata .15 .06
❑ 82 Joe Price .15 .06
❑ 83 Charlie Moore .15 .06
❑ 84 Spike Owen .15 .06
❑ 85 Mike Marshall .15 .06

❑ 86 Don Aase .15 .06
❑ 87 David Green .15 .06
❑ 88 Bryn Smith .15 .06
❑ 89 Jackie Gutierrez .15 .06
❑ 90 Rich Gossage .25 .10
❑ 91 Jeff Burroughs .15 .06
❑ 92 Paul Owens MG .15 .06
❑ 93 Don Schulze .15 .06
❑ 94 Toby Harrah .25 .10
❑ 95 Jose Cruz .25 .10
❑ 96 Johnny Ray .15 .06
❑ 97 Pete Filson .15 .06
❑ 98 Steve Lake .15 .06
❑ 99 Milt Wilcox .15 .06
❑ 100 George Brett 1.50 .60
❑ 101 Jim Acker .15 .06
❑ 102 Tommy Dunbar .15 .06
❑ 103 Randy Lerch .15 .06
❑ 104 Mike Fitzgerald .15 .06
❑ 105 Ron Kittle .15 .06
❑ 106 Pascual Perez .15 .06
❑ 107 Tom Foley .15 .06
❑ 108 Darnell Coles .15 .06
❑ 109 Gary Roenicke .15 .06
❑ 110 Alejandro Pena .15 .06
❑ 111 Doug DeCinces .15 .06
❑ 112 Tom Tellmann .15 .06
❑ 113 Tom Herr .15 .06
❑ 114 Bob James .15 .06
❑ 115 Rickey Henderson .75 .30
❑ 116 Dennis Boyd .15 .06
❑ 117 Greg Gross .15 .06
❑ 118 Eric Show .15 .06
❑ 119 Pat Corrales MG .15 .06
❑ 120 Steve Kemp .15 .06
❑ 121 Checklist: 1-132 .15 .06
❑ 122 Tom Brunansky .15 .06
❑ 123 Dave Smith .15 .06
❑ 124 Rich Hebner .15 .06
❑ 125 Kent Tekulve .15 .06
❑ 126 Ruppert Jones .15 .06
❑ 127 Mark Gubicza RC* .40 .16
❑ 128 Ernie Whitt .15 .06
❑ 129 Gene Garber .15 .06
❑ 130 Al Oliver .25 .10
❑ 131 Buddy Bell FS .25 .10
Gus Bell
❑ 132 Dale Berra FS .60 .24
Yogi Berra
❑ 133 Bob Boone FS .15 .06
Ray Boone
❑ 134 Terry Francona FS .25 .10
Tito Francona
❑ 135 Terry Kennedy FS .15 .06
Bob Kennedy
❑ 136 Jeff Kunkel FS .15 .06
Bill Kunkel
❑ 137 Vance Law FS .25 .10
Vern Law
❑ 138 Dick Schofield FS .15 .06
Dick Schofield
❑ 139 Joel Skinner FS .15 .06
Bob Skinner
❑ 140 Roy Smalley Jr. FS .15 .06
Roy Smalley
❑ 141 Mike Stenhouse FS .15 .06
Dave Stenhouse
❑ 142 Steve Trout FS .15 .06
Dizzy Trout
❑ 143 Ozzie Virgil FS .15 .06
Ossie Virgil
❑ 144 Ron Gardenhire .15 .06
❑ 145 Alvin Davis RC* .40 .16
❑ 146 Gary Redus .15 .06
❑ 147 Bill Swaggerty .15 .06
❑ 148 Steve Yeager .25 .10
❑ 149 Dickie Noles .15 .06
❑ 150 Jim Rice .25 .10
❑ 151 Moose Haas .15 .06
❑ 152 Steve Braun .15 .06
❑ 153 Frank LaCorte .15 .06
❑ 154 Angel Salazar .15 .06
❑ 155 Yogi Berra MG .60 .24
❑ 156 Craig Reynolds .15 .06
❑ 157 Tug McGraw .25 .10
❑ 158 Pat Tabler .15 .06
❑ 159 Carlos Diaz .15 .06
❑ 160 Lance Parrish .25 .10
❑ 161 Ken Schrom .15 .06
❑ 162 Benny Distefano .15 .06
❑ 163 Dennis Eckersley .40 .16
❑ 164 Jorge Orta .15 .06
❑ 165 Dusty Baker .25 .10
❑ 166 Keith Atherton .15 .06
❑ 167 Rufino Linares .15 .06
❑ 168 Garth Iorg .15 .06
❑ 169 Dan Spillner .15 .06
❑ 170 George Foster .25 .10
❑ 171 Bill Stein .15 .06
❑ 172 Jack Perconte .15 .06
❑ 173 Mike Young .15 .06
❑ 174 Rick Honeycutt .15 .06
❑ 175 Dave Parker .25 .10
❑ 176 Bill Schroeder .15 .06
❑ 177 Dave Von Ohlen .15 .06
❑ 178 Miguel Dilone .15 .06
❑ 179 Tommy John .25 .10
❑ 180 Dave Winfield .25 .10
❑ 181 Roger Clemens RC 30.00 12.00
❑ 182 Tim Flannery .15 .06
❑ 183 Larry McWilliams .15 .06
❑ 184 Carmen Castillo .15 .06
❑ 185 Al Holland .15 .06
❑ 186 Bob Lillis MG .15 .06
❑ 187 Mike Walters .15 .06
❑ 188 Greg Pryor .15 .06
❑ 189 Warren Brusstar .15 .06
❑ 190 Rusty Staub .25 .10
❑ 191 Steve Nicosia .15 .06
❑ 192 Howard Johnson .25 .10
❑ 193 Jimmy Key RC .75 .30
❑ 194 Dave Stegman .15 .06
❑ 195 Glenn Hubbard .15 .06
❑ 196 Pete O'Brien .15 .06
❑ 197 Mike Warren .15 .06
❑ 198 Eddie Milner .15 .06
❑ 199 Dennis Martinez .25 .10
❑ 200 Reggie Jackson .40 .16
❑ 201 Burt Hooton .15 .06
❑ 202 Gorman Thomas .25 .10
❑ 203 Bob McClure .15 .06
❑ 204 Art Howe .15 .06
❑ 205 Steve Rogers .25 .10
❑ 206 Phil Garner .25 .10
❑ 207 Mark Clear .15 .06
❑ 208 Champ Summers .15 .06
❑ 209 Bill Campbell .15 .06
❑ 210 Gary Matthews .25 .10
❑ 211 Clay Christiansen .15 .06
❑ 212 George Vukovich .15 .06
❑ 213 Billy Gardner MG .15 .06
❑ 214 John Tudor .25 .10
❑ 215 Bob Brenly .15 .06
❑ 216 Jerry Don Gleaton .15 .06
❑ 217 Leon Roberts .15 .06
❑ 218 Doyle Alexander .15 .06
❑ 219 Gerald Perry .15 .06
❑ 220 Fred Lynn .25 .10
❑ 221 Ron Reed .15 .06
❑ 222 Hubie Brooks .15 .06
❑ 223 Tom Hume .15 .06
❑ 224 Al Cowens .15 .06
❑ 225 Mike Boddicker .15 .06
❑ 226 Juan Beniquez .15 .06
❑ 227 Danny Darwin .15 .06
❑ 228 Dion James .15 .06
❑ 229 Dave LaPoint .15 .06
❑ 230 Gary Carter .25 .10
❑ 231 Dwayne Murphy .15 .06
❑ 232 Dave Beard .15 .06
❑ 233 Ed Jurak .15 .06
❑ 234 Jerry Narron .15 .06
❑ 235 Garry Maddox .15 .06
❑ 236 Mark Thurmond .15 .06
❑ 237 Julio Franco .25 .10
❑ 238 Jose Rijo RC .75 .30
❑ 239 Tim Teufel .15 .06
❑ 240 Dave Stieb .25 .10
❑ 241 Jim Frey MG .15 .06
❑ 242 Greg Harris .15 .06
❑ 243 Barbaro Garbey .15 .06
❑ 244 Mike Jones .15 .06
❑ 245 Chili Davis .25 .10
❑ 246 Mike Norris .15 .06
❑ 247 Wayne Tolleson .15 .06
❑ 248 Terry Forster .25 .10
❑ 249 Harold Baines .25 .10
❑ 250 Jesse Orosco .15 .06
❑ 251 Brad Gulden .15 .06
❑ 252 Dan Ford .15 .06
❑ 253 Sid Bream RC .40 .16
❑ 254 Pete Vuckovich .15 .06
❑ 255 Lonnie Smith .15 .06
❑ 256 Mike Stanton .15 .06
❑ 257 Bryan Little UER .15 .06
Name spelled Brian on front
❑ 258 Mike C. Brown .15 .06
❑ 259 Gary Allenson .15 .06
❑ 260 Dave Righetti .25 .10
❑ 261 Checklist: 133-264 .15 .06
❑ 262 Greg Booker .15 .06
❑ 263 Mel Hall .15 .06
❑ 264 Joe Sambito .15 .06
❑ 265 Juan Samuel .15 .06
❑ 266 Frank Viola .25 .10
❑ 267 Henry Cotto RC .15 .06
❑ 268 Chuck Tanner MG .15 .06
❑ 269 Doug Baker .15 .06
❑ 270 Dan Quisenberry .15 .06
❑ 271 Tim Foli FDP .15 .06
❑ 272 Jeff Burroughs FDP .15 .06
❑ 273 Bill Almon FDP .15 .06
❑ 274 F.Bannister FDP76 .15 .06
❑ 275 Harold Baines FDP77 .15 .06
❑ 276 Bob Horner FDP .15 .06
❑ 277 Al Chambers FDP .15 .06
❑ 278 Darryl Strawberry FDP80 .40 .16
❑ 279 Mike Moore FDP .15 .06
❑ 280 S.Dunston FDP82 RC .75 .30
❑ 281 T.Belcher RC FDP83 .40 .16
❑ 282 Shawn Abner FDP RC .15 .06
❑ 283 Fran Mullins .15 .06
❑ 284 Marty Bystrom .15 .06
❑ 285 Dan Driessen .15 .06
❑ 286 Rudy Law .15 .06
❑ 287 Walt Terrell .15 .06
❑ 288 Jeff Kunkel .15 .06
❑ 289 Tom Underwood .15 .06
❑ 290 Cecil Cooper .25 .10
❑ 291 Bob Welch .25 .10
❑ 292 Brad Komminsk .15 .06
❑ 293 Curt Young .15 .06
❑ 294 Tom Nieto .15 .06
❑ 295 Joe Niekro .15 .06
❑ 296 Ricky Nelson .15 .06
❑ 297 Gary Lucas .15 .06
❑ 298 Marty Barrett .15 .06
❑ 299 Andy Hawkins .15 .06
❑ 300 Rod Carew .40 .16
❑ 301 John Montefusco .15 .06
❑ 302 Tim Corcoran .15 .06
❑ 303 Mike Jeffcoat .15 .06
❑ 304 Gary Gaetti .25 .10
❑ 305 Dale Berra .15 .06
❑ 306 Rick Reuschel .25 .10
❑ 307 Sparky Anderson MG .25 .10
❑ 308 John Wathan .15 .06
❑ 309 Mike Witt .15 .06
❑ 310 Manny Trillo .15 .06
❑ 311 Jim Gott .15 .06
❑ 312 Marc Hill .15 .06
❑ 313 Dave Schmidt .15 .06
❑ 314 Ron Oester .15 .06
❑ 315 Doug Sisk .15 .06
❑ 316 John Lowenstein .15 .06
❑ 317 Jack Lazorko .15 .06
❑ 318 Ted Simmons .25 .10
❑ 319 Jeff Jones .15 .06
❑ 320 Dale Murphy .40 .16
❑ 321 Ricky Horton .15 .06
❑ 322 Dave Stapleton .15 .06
❑ 323 Andy McGaffigan .15 .06
❑ 324 Bruce Bochy .15 .06
❑ 325 John Denny .15 .06
❑ 326 Kevin Bass .15 .06
❑ 327 Brook Jacoby .15 .06
❑ 328 Bob Shirley .15 .06

- ❑ 329 Ron Washington .15 .06
- ❑ 330 Leon Durham .15 .06
- ❑ 331 Bill Laskey .15 .06
- ❑ 332 Brian Harper .15 .06
- ❑ 333 Willie Hernandez .15 .06
- ❑ 334 Dick Howser MG .15 .06
- ❑ 335 Bruce Benedict .15 .06
- ❑ 336 Rance Mulliniks .15 .06
- ❑ 337 Billy Sample .15 .06
- ❑ 338 Britt Burns .15 .06
- ❑ 339 Danny Heep .15 .06
- ❑ 340 Robin Yount 1.00 .40
- ❑ 341 Floyd Rayford .15 .06
- ❑ 342 Ted Power .15 .06
- ❑ 343 Bill Russell .25 .10
- ❑ 344 Dave Henderson .15 .06
- ❑ 345 Charlie Lea .15 .06
- ❑ 346 Terry Pendleton RC .75 .30
- ❑ 347 Rick Langford .15 .06
- ❑ 348 Bob Boone .25 .10
- ❑ 349 Domingo Ramos .15 .06
- ❑ 350 Wade Boggs .60 .24
- ❑ 351 Juan Agosto .15 .06
- ❑ 352 Joe Morgan .25 .10
- ❑ 353 Julio Solano .15 .06
- ❑ 354 Andre Robertson .15 .06
- ❑ 355 Bert Blyleven .25 .10
- ❑ 356 Dave Meier .15 .06
- ❑ 357 Rich Bordi .15 .06
- ❑ 358 Tony Pena .15 .06
- ❑ 359 Pat Sheridan .15 .06
- ❑ 360 Steve Carlton .25 .10
- ❑ 361 Alfredo Griffin .15 .06
- ❑ 362 Craig McMurtry .15 .06
- ❑ 363 Ron Hodges .15 .06
- ❑ 364 Richard Dotson .15 .06
- ❑ 365 Danny Ozark MG .15 .06
- ❑ 366 Todd Cruz .15 .06
- ❑ 367 Keefe Cato .15 .06
- ❑ 368 Dave Bergman .15 .06
- ❑ 369 R.J. Reynolds .15 .06
- ❑ 370 Bruce Sutter .25 .10
- ❑ 371 Mickey Rivers .15 .06
- ❑ 372 Roy Howell .15 .06
- ❑ 373 Mike Moore .15 .06
- ❑ 374 Brian Downing .25 .10
- ❑ 375 Jeff Reardon .25 .10
- ❑ 376 Jeff Newman .15 .06
- ❑ 377 Checklist: 265-396 .15 .06
- ❑ 378 Alan Wiggins .15 .06
- ❑ 379 Charles Hudson .15 .06
- ❑ 380 Ken Griffey .25 .10
- ❑ 381 Roy Smith .15 .06
- ❑ 382 Denny Walling .15 .06
- ❑ 383 Rick Lysander .15 .06
- ❑ 384 Jody Davis .15 .06
- ❑ 385 Jose DeLeon .15 .06
- ❑ 386 Dan Gladden RC .40 .16
- ❑ 387 Buddy Biancalana .15 .06
- ❑ 388 Bert Roberge .15 .06
- ❑ 389 Rod Dedeaux OLY CO .25 .10
- ❑ 390 Sid Akins OLY RC .15 .06
- ❑ 391 Flavio Alfaro OLY RC .15 .06
- ❑ 392 Don August OLY RC .15 .06
- ❑ 393 S.Bankhead RC OLY .15 .06
- ❑ 394 Bob Caffrey OLY RC .15 .06
- ❑ 395 Mike Dunne OLY RC .15 .06
- ❑ 396 Gary Green OLY RC .15 .06
- ❑ 397 John Hoover OLY RC .15 .06
- ❑ 398 Shane Mack RC OLY .40 .16
- ❑ 399 John Marzano OLY RC .15 .06
- ❑ 400 O.McDowell RC OLY .40 .16
- ❑ 401 M.McGwire OLY RC 30.00 12.00
- ❑ 402 Pat Pacillo OLY RC .15 .06
- ❑ 403 Cory Snyder OLY RC .75 .30
- ❑ 404 Billy Swift OLY RC .40 .16
- ❑ 405 Tom Veryzer .15 .06
- ❑ 406 Len Whitehouse .15 .06
- ❑ 407 Bobby Ramos .15 .06
- ❑ 408 Sid Monge .15 .06
- ❑ 409 Brad Wellman .15 .06
- ❑ 410 Bob Horner .25 .10
- ❑ 411 Bobby Cox MG .25 .10
- ❑ 412 Bud Black .15 .06
- ❑ 413 Vance Law .15 .06
- ❑ 414 Gary Ward .15 .06
- ❑ 415 Ron Darling UER (No trivia answer) .25 .10
- ❑ 416 Wayne Gross .15 .06
- ❑ 417 John Franco RC .75 .30
- ❑ 418 Ken Landreaux .15 .06
- ❑ 419 Mike Caldwell .15 .06
- ❑ 420 Andre Dawson .25 .10
- ❑ 421 Dave Rucker .15 .06
- ❑ 422 Carney Lansford .25 .10
- ❑ 423 Barry Bonnell .15 .06
- ❑ 424 Al Nipper .15 .06
- ❑ 425 Mike Hargrove .15 .06
- ❑ 426 Vern Ruhle .15 .06
- ❑ 427 Mario Ramirez .15 .06
- ❑ 428 Larry Andersen .15 .06
- ❑ 429 Rick Cerone .15 .06
- ❑ 430 Ron Davis .15 .06
- ❑ 431 U.L. Washington .15 .06
- ❑ 432 Thad Bosley .15 .06
- ❑ 433 Jim Morrison .15 .06
- ❑ 434 Gene Richards .15 .06
- ❑ 435 Dan Petry .15 .06
- ❑ 436 Willie Aikens .15 .06
- ❑ 437 Al Jones .15 .06
- ❑ 438 Joe Torre MG .25 .10
- ❑ 439 Junior Ortiz .15 .06
- ❑ 440 Fernando Valenzuela .25 .10
- ❑ 441 Duane Walker .15 .06
- ❑ 442 Ken Forsch .15 .06
- ❑ 443 George Wright .15 .06
- ❑ 444 Tony Phillips .15 .06
- ❑ 445 Tippy Martinez .15 .06
- ❑ 446 Jim Sundberg .25 .10
- ❑ 447 Jeff Lahti .15 .06
- ❑ 448 Derrel Thomas .15 .06
- ❑ 449 Phil Bradley .40 .16
- ❑ 450 Steve Garvey .25 .10
- ❑ 451 Bruce Hurst .15 .06
- ❑ 452 John Castino .15 .06
- ❑ 453 Tom Waddell .15 .06
- ❑ 454 Glenn Wilson .15 .06
- ❑ 455 Bob Knepper .15 .06
- ❑ 456 Tim Foli .15 .06
- ❑ 457 Cecilio Guante .15 .06
- ❑ 458 Randy Johnson .15 .06
- ❑ 459 Charlie Leibrandt .15 .06
- ❑ 460 Ryne Sandberg 1.25 .50
- ❑ 461 Marty Castillo .15 .06
- ❑ 462 Gary Lavelle .15 .06
- ❑ 463 Dave Collins .15 .06
- ❑ 464 Mike Mason RC .15 .06
- ❑ 465 Bobby Grich .25 .10
- ❑ 466 Tony LaRussa MG .25 .10
- ❑ 467 Ed Lynch .15 .06
- ❑ 468 Wayne Krenchicki .15 .06
- ❑ 469 Sammy Stewart .15 .06
- ❑ 470 Steve Sax .15 .06
- ❑ 471 Pete Ladd .15 .06
- ❑ 472 Jim Essian .15 .06
- ❑ 473 Tim Wallach .15 .06
- ❑ 474 Kurt Kepshire .15 .06
- ❑ 475 Andre Thornton .15 .06
- ❑ 476 Jeff Stone .15 .06
- ❑ 477 Bob Ojeda .15 .06
- ❑ 478 Kurt Bevacqua .15 .06
- ❑ 479 Mike Madden .15 .06
- ❑ 480 Lou Whitaker .25 .10
- ❑ 481 Dale Murray .15 .06
- ❑ 482 Harry Spilman .15 .06
- ❑ 483 Mike Smithson .15 .06
- ❑ 484 Larry Bowa .25 .10
- ❑ 485 Matt Young .15 .06
- ❑ 486 Steve Balboni .15 .06
- ❑ 487 Frank Williams .15 .06
- ❑ 488 Joel Skinner .15 .06
- ❑ 489 Bryan Clark .15 .06
- ❑ 490 Jason Thompson .15 .06
- ❑ 491 Rick Camp .15 .06
- ❑ 492 Dave Johnson MG .15 .06
- ❑ 493 Orel Hershiser RC 2.00 .80
- ❑ 494 Rich Dauer .15 .06
- ❑ 495 Mario Soto .25 .10
- ❑ 496 Donnie Scott .15 .06
- ❑ 497 Gary Pettis UER (Photo actually Gary's little brother Lynn) .15 .06
- ❑ 498 Ed Romero .15 .06
- ❑ 499 Danny Cox .15 .06
- ❑ 500 Mike Schmidt 1.50 .60
- ❑ 501 Dan Schatzeder .15 .06
- ❑ 502 Rick Miller .15 .06
- ❑ 503 Tim Conroy .15 .06
- ❑ 504 Jerry Willard .15 .06
- ❑ 505 Jim Beattie .15 .06
- ❑ 506 Franklin Stubbs .15 .06
- ❑ 507 Ray Fontenot .15 .06
- ❑ 508 John Shelby .15 .06
- ❑ 509 Milt May .15 .06
- ❑ 510 Kent Hrbek .25 .10
- ❑ 511 Lee Smith .25 .10
- ❑ 512 Tom Brookens .15 .06
- ❑ 513 Lynn Jones .15 .06
- ❑ 514 Jeff Cornell .15 .06
- ❑ 515 Dave Concepcion .25 .10
- ❑ 516 Roy Lee Jackson .15 .06
- ❑ 517 Jerry Martin .15 .06
- ❑ 518 Chris Chambliss .25 .10
- ❑ 519 Doug Rader MG .15 .06
- ❑ 520 LaMarr Hoyt .15 .06
- ❑ 521 Rick Dempsey .15 .06
- ❑ 522 Paul Molitor .40 .16
- ❑ 523 Candy Maldonado .15 .06
- ❑ 524 Rob Wilfong .15 .06
- ❑ 525 Darrell Porter .15 .06
- ❑ 526 David Palmer .15 .06
- ❑ 527 Checklist: 397-528 .15 .06
- ❑ 528 Bill Krueger .15 .06
- ❑ 529 Rich Gedman .15 .06
- ❑ 530 Dave Dravecky .15 .06
- ❑ 531 Joe Lefebvre .15 .06
- ❑ 532 Frank DiPino .15 .06
- ❑ 533 Tony Bernazard .15 .06
- ❑ 534 Brian Dayett .15 .06
- ❑ 535 Pat Putnam .15 .06
- ❑ 536 Kirby Puckett RC 8.00 3.20
- ❑ 537 Don Robinson .15 .06
- ❑ 538 Keith Moreland .15 .06
- ❑ 539 Aurelio Lopez .15 .06
- ❑ 540 Claudell Washington .15 .06
- ❑ 541 Mark Davis .15 .06
- ❑ 542 Don Slaught .15 .06
- ❑ 543 Mike Squires .15 .06
- ❑ 544 Bruce Kison .15 .06
- ❑ 545 Lloyd Moseby .15 .06
- ❑ 546 Brent Gaff .15 .06
- ❑ 547 Pete Rose MG .40 .16
- ❑ 548 Larry Parrish .15 .06
- ❑ 549 Mike Scioscia .25 .10
- ❑ 550 Scott McGregor .15 .06
- ❑ 551 Andy Van Slyke .40 .16
- ❑ 552 Chris Codiroli .15 .06
- ❑ 553 Bob Clark .15 .06
- ❑ 554 Doug Flynn .15 .06
- ❑ 555 Bob Stanley .15 .06
- ❑ 556 Sixto Lezcano .15 .06
- ❑ 557 Len Barker .15 .06
- ❑ 558 Carmelo Martinez .15 .06
- ❑ 559 Jay Howell .15 .06
- ❑ 560 Bill Madlock .25 .10
- ❑ 561 Darryl Motley .15 .06
- ❑ 562 Houston Jimenez .15 .06
- ❑ 563 Dick Ruthven .15 .06
- ❑ 564 Alan Ashby .15 .06
- ❑ 565 Kirk Gibson .40 .16
- ❑ 566 Ed VandeBerg .15 .06
- ❑ 567 Joel Youngblood .15 .06
- ❑ 568 Cliff Johnson .15 .06
- ❑ 569 Ken Oberkfell .15 .06
- ❑ 570 Darryl Strawberry .60 .24
- ❑ 571 Charlie Hough .25 .10
- ❑ 572 Tom Paciorek .15 .06
- ❑ 573 Jay Tibbs .15 .06
- ❑ 574 Joe Altobelli MG .15 .06
- ❑ 575 Pedro Guerrero .25 .10
- ❑ 576 Jaime Cocanower .15 .06
- ❑ 577 Chris Speier .15 .06
- ❑ 578 Terry Francona .25 .10
- ❑ 579 Ron Romanick .15 .06
- ❑ 580 Dwight Evans .40 .16
- ❑ 581 Mark Wagner .15 .06
- ❑ 582 Ken Phelps .15 .06

❑ 583 Bobby Brown .15 .06
❑ 584 Kevin Gross .15 .06
❑ 585 Butch Wynegar .15 .06
❑ 586 Bill Scherrer .15 .06
❑ 587 Doug Frobel .15 .06
❑ 588 Bobby Castillo .15 .06
❑ 589 Bob Dernier .15 .06
❑ 590 Ray Knight .25 .10
❑ 591 Larry Herndon .15 .06
❑ 592 Jeff D. Robinson .15 .06
❑ 593 Rick Leach .15 .06
❑ 594 Curt Wilkerson .15 .06
❑ 595 Larry Gura .15 .06
❑ 596 Jerry Hairston .15 .06
❑ 597 Brad Lesley .15 .06
❑ 598 Jose Oquendo .15 .06
❑ 599 Storm Davis .15 .06
❑ 600 Pete Rose 1.50 .60
❑ 601 Tom Lasorda MG .40 .16
❑ 602 Jeff Dedmon .15 .06
❑ 603 Rick Manning .15 .06
❑ 604 Daryl Sconiers .15 .06
❑ 605 Ozzie Smith 1.00 .40
❑ 606 Rich Gale .15 .06
❑ 607 Bill Almon .15 .06
❑ 608 Craig Lefferts .15 .06
❑ 609 Broderick Perkins .15 .06
❑ 610 Jack Morris .25 .10
❑ 611 Ozzie Virgil .15 .06
❑ 612 Mike Armstrong .15 .06
❑ 613 Terry Puhl .15 .06
❑ 614 Al Williams .15 .06
❑ 615 Marvell Wynne .15 .06
❑ 616 Scott Sanderson .15 .06
❑ 617 Willie Wilson .25 .10
❑ 618 Pete Falcone .15 .06
❑ 619 Jeff Leonard .15 .06
❑ 620 Dwight Gooden RC 2.00 .80
❑ 621 Marvis Foley .15 .06
❑ 622 Luis Leal .15 .06
❑ 623 Greg Walker .15 .06
❑ 624 Benny Ayala .15 .06
❑ 625 Mark Langston RC .75 .30
❑ 626 German Rivera .15 .06
❑ 627 Eric Davis RC 2.00 .80
❑ 628 Rene Lachemann MG .15 .06
❑ 629 Dick Schofield .15 .06
❑ 630 Tim Raines .25 .10
❑ 631 Bob Forsch .15 .06
❑ 632 Bruce Bochte .15 .06
❑ 633 Glenn Hoffman .15 .06
❑ 634 Bill Dawley .15 .06
❑ 635 Terry Kennedy .15 .06
❑ 636 Shane Rawley .15 .06
❑ 637 Brett Butler .25 .10
❑ 638 Mike Pagliarulo .15 .06
❑ 639 Ed Hodge .15 .06
❑ 640 Steve Henderson .15 .06
❑ 641 Rod Scurry .15 .06
❑ 642 Dave Owen .15 .06
❑ 643 Johnny Grubb .15 .06
❑ 644 Mark Huismann .15 .06
❑ 645 Damaso Garcia .15 .06
❑ 646 Scot Thompson .15 .06
❑ 647 Rafael Ramirez .15 .06
❑ 648 Bob Jones .15 .06
❑ 649 Sid Fernandez .25 .10
❑ 650 Greg Luzinski .25 .10
❑ 651 Jeff Russell .15 .06
❑ 652 Joe Nolan .15 .06
❑ 653 Mark Brouhard .15 .06
❑ 654 Dave Anderson .15 .06
❑ 655 Joaquin Andujar .25 .10
❑ 656 Chuck Cottier MG .15 .06
❑ 657 Jim Slaton .15 .06
❑ 658 Mike Stenhouse .15 .06
❑ 659 Checklist: 529-660 .15 .06
❑ 660 Tony Gwynn 1.25 .50
❑ 661 Steve Crawford .15 .06
❑ 662 Mike Heath .15 .06
❑ 663 Luis Aguayo .15 .06
❑ 664 Steve Farr RC .40 .16
❑ 665 Don Mattingly 2.50 1.00
❑ 666 Mike LaCoss .15 .06
❑ 667 Dave Engle .15 .06
❑ 668 Steve Trout .15 .06
❑ 669 Lee Lacy .15 .06
❑ 670 Tom Seaver .40 .16
❑ 671 Dane Iorg .15 .06
❑ 672 Juan Berenguer .15 .06
❑ 673 Buck Martinez .15 .06
❑ 674 Atlee Hammaker .15 .06
❑ 675 Tony Perez .40 .16
❑ 676 Albert Hall .15 .06
❑ 677 Wally Backman .15 .06
❑ 678 Joey McLaughlin .15 .06
❑ 679 Bob Kearney .15 .06
❑ 680 Jerry Reuss .15 .06
❑ 681 Ben Oglivie .25 .10
❑ 682 Doug Corbett .15 .06
❑ 683 Whitey Herzog MG .25 .10
❑ 684 Bill Doran .15 .06
❑ 685 Bill Caudill .15 .06
❑ 686 Mike Easler .15 .06
❑ 687 Bill Gullickson .15 .06
❑ 688 Len Matuszek .15 .06
❑ 689 Luis DeLeon .15 .06
❑ 690 Alan Trammell .25 .10
❑ 691 Dennis Rasmussen .15 .06
❑ 692 Randy Bush .15 .06
❑ 693 Tim Stoddard .15 .06
❑ 694 Joe Carter .60 .24
❑ 695 Rick Rhoden .15 .06
❑ 696 John Rabb .15 .06
❑ 697 Onix Concepcion .15 .06
❑ 698 Jorge Bell .25 .10
❑ 699 Donnie Moore .15 .06
❑ 700 Eddie Murray .60 .24
❑ 701 Eddie Murray AS .40 .16
❑ 702 Damaso Garcia AS .15 .06
❑ 703 George Brett AS .60 .24
❑ 704 Cal Ripken AS 1.50 .60
❑ 705 Dave Winfield AS .15 .06
❑ 706 Rickey Henderson AS .40 .16
❑ 707 Tony Armas AS .15 .06
❑ 708 Lance Parrish AS .15 .06
❑ 709 Mike Boddicker AS .15 .06
❑ 710 Frank Viola AS .15 .06
❑ 711 Dan Quisenberry AS .15 .06
❑ 712 Keith Hernandez AS .15 .06
❑ 713 Ryne Sandberg AS .60 .24
❑ 714 Mike Schmidt AS .60 .24
❑ 715 Ozzie Smith AS .60 .24
❑ 716 Dale Murphy AS .25 .10
❑ 717 Tony Gwynn AS 1.00 .40
❑ 718 Jeff Leonard AS .15 .06
❑ 719 Gary Carter AS .15 .06
❑ 720 Rick Sutcliffe AS .15 .06
❑ 721 Bob Knepper AS .15 .06
❑ 722 Bruce Sutter AS .15 .06
❑ 723 Dave Stewart .25 .10
❑ 724 Oscar Gamble .15 .06
❑ 725 Floyd Bannister .15 .06
❑ 726 Al Bumbry .15 .06
❑ 727 Frank Pastore .15 .06
❑ 728 Bob Bailor .15 .06
❑ 729 Don Sutton .25 .10
❑ 730 Dave Kingman .25 .10
❑ 731 Neil Allen .15 .06
❑ 732 John McNamara MG .15 .06
❑ 733 Tony Scott .15 .06
❑ 734 John Henry Johnson .15 .06
❑ 735 Garry Templeton .25 .10
❑ 736 Jerry Mumphrey .15 .06
❑ 737 Bo Diaz .15 .06
❑ 738 Omar Moreno .15 .06
❑ 739 Ernie Camacho .15 .06
❑ 740 Jack Clark .25 .10
❑ 741 John Butcher .15 .06
❑ 742 Ron Hassey .15 .06
❑ 743 Frank White .25 .10
❑ 744 Doug Bair .15 .06
❑ 745 Buddy Bell .25 .10
❑ 746 Jim Clancy .15 .06
❑ 747 Alex Trevino .15 .06
❑ 748 Lee Mazzilli .25 .10
❑ 749 Julio Cruz .15 .06
❑ 750 Rollie Fingers .25 .10
❑ 751 Kelvin Chapman .15 .06
❑ 752 Bob Owchinko .15 .06
❑ 753 Greg Brock .15 .06
❑ 754 Larry Milbourne .15 .06
❑ 755 Ken Singleton .25 .10
❑ 756 Rob Picciolo .15 .06
❑ 757 Willie McGee .25 .10
❑ 758 Ray Burris .15 .06
❑ 759 Jim Fanning MG .15 .06
❑ 760 Nolan Ryan 3.00 1.20
❑ 761 Jerry Remy .15 .06
❑ 762 Eddie Whitson .15 .06
❑ 763 Kiko Garcia .15 .06
❑ 764 Jamie Easterly .15 .06
❑ 765 Willie Randolph .25 .10
❑ 766 Paul Mirabella .15 .06
❑ 767 Darrell Brown .15 .06
❑ 768 Ron Cey .25 .10
❑ 769 Joe Cowley .15 .06
❑ 770 Carlton Fisk .40 .16
❑ 771 Geoff Zahn .15 .06
❑ 772 Johnnie LeMaster .15 .06
❑ 773 Hal McRae .25 .10
❑ 774 Dennis Lamp .15 .06
❑ 775 Mookie Wilson .25 .10
❑ 776 Jerry Royster .15 .06
❑ 777 Ned Yost .15 .06
❑ 778 Mike Davis .15 .06
❑ 779 Nick Esasky .15 .06
❑ 780 Mike Flanagan .15 .06
❑ 781 Jim Gantner .15 .06
❑ 782 Tom Niedenfuer .15 .06
❑ 783 Mike Jorgensen .15 .06
❑ 784 Checklist: 661-792 .15 .06
❑ 785 Tony Armas .25 .10
❑ 786 Enos Cabell .15 .06
❑ 787 Jim Wohlford .15 .06
❑ 788 Steve Comer .15 .06
❑ 789 Luis Salazar .15 .06
❑ 790 Ron Guidry .25 .10
❑ 791 Ivan DeJesus .15 .06
❑ 792 Darrell Evans .25 .10

1985 Topps Traded

	Nm-Mt	Ex-Mt
COMP.FACT.SET (132)	8.00	3.20

❑ 1T Don Aase .15 .06
❑ 2T Bill Almon .15 .06
❑ 3T Benny Ayala .15 .06
❑ 4T Dusty Baker .40 .16
❑ 5T George Bamberger MG .15 .06
❑ 6T Dale Berra .15 .06
❑ 7T Rich Bordi .15 .06
❑ 8T Daryl Boston XRC* .25 .10
❑ 9T Hubie Brooks .15 .06
❑ 10T Chris Brown .25 .10
❑ 11T Tom Browning XRC* .50 .20
❑ 12T Al Bumbry .15 .06
❑ 13T Ray Burris .15 .06
❑ 14T Jeff Burroughs .15 .06
❑ 15T Bill Campbell .15 .06
❑ 16T Don Carman .15 .06
❑ 17T Gary Carter .40 .16
❑ 18T Bobby Castillo .15 .06
❑ 19T Bill Caudill .15 .06
❑ 20T Rick Cerone .15 .06
❑ 21T Bryan Clark .15 .06
❑ 22T Jack Clark .40 .16
❑ 23T Pat Clements .15 .06
❑ 24T Vince Coleman XRC 1.00 .40
❑ 25T Dave Collins .15 .06

❑ 26T Danny Darwin .15 .06
❑ 27T Jim Davenport MG .15 .06
❑ 28T Jerry Davis .15 .06
❑ 29T Brian Dayett .15 .06
❑ 30T Ivan DeJesus .15 .06
❑ 31T Ken Dixon .15 .06
❑ 32T Mariano Duncan XRC .50 .20
❑ 33T John Felske MG .15 .06
❑ 34T Mike Fitzgerald .15 .06
❑ 35T Ray Fontenot .15 .06
❑ 36T Greg Gagne XRC* .50 .20
❑ 37T Oscar Gamble .15 .06
❑ 38T Scott Garrelts .15 .06
❑ 39T Bob L. Gibson .15 .06
❑ 40T Jim Gott .15 .06
❑ 41T David Green .15 .06
❑ 42T Alfredo Griffin .15 .06
❑ 43T Ozzie Guillen XRC 4.00 1.60
❑ 44T Eddie Haas MG .15 .06
❑ 45T Terry Harper .15 .06
❑ 46T Toby Harrah .40 .16
❑ 47T Greg Harris .15 .06
❑ 48T Ron Hassey .15 .06
❑ 49T Rickey Henderson 2.50 1.00
❑ 50T Steve Henderson .15 .06
❑ 51T George Hendrick .40 .16
❑ 52T Joe Hesketh .15 .06
❑ 53T Teddy Higuera XRC .50 .20
❑ 54T Donnie Hill .15 .06
❑ 55T Al Holland .15 .06
❑ 56T Burt Hooton .15 .06
❑ 57T Jay Howell .15 .06
❑ 58T Ken Howell .15 .06
❑ 59T LaMarr Hoyt .15 .06
❑ 60T Tim Hulett XRC* .25 .10
❑ 61T Bob James .15 .06
❑ 62T Steve Jeltz XRC .25 .10
❑ 63T Cliff Johnson .15 .06
❑ 64T Howard Johnson .40 .16
❑ 65T Ruppert Jones .15 .06
❑ 66T Steve Kemp .15 .06
❑ 67T Bruce Kison .15 .06
❑ 68T Alan Knicely .15 .06
❑ 69T Mike LaCoss .15 .06
❑ 70T Lee Lacy .15 .06
❑ 71T Dave LaPoint .15 .06
❑ 72T Gary Lavelle .15 .06
❑ 73T Vance Law .15 .06
❑ 74T Johnnie LeMaster .15 .06
❑ 75T Sixto Lezcano .15 .06
❑ 76T Tim Lollar .15 .06
❑ 77T Fred Lynn .40 .16
❑ 78T Billy Martin MG .75 .30
❑ 79T Ron Mathis .15 .06
❑ 80T Len Matuszek .15 .06
❑ 81T Gene Mauch MG .15 .06
❑ 82T Oddibe McDowell .50 .20
❑ 83T Roger McDowell XRC .50 .20
❑ 84T John McNamara MG .15 .06
❑ 85T Donnie Moore .15 .06
❑ 86T Gene Nelson .15 .06
❑ 87T Steve Nicosia .15 .06
❑ 88T Al Oliver .40 .16
❑ 89T Joe Orsulak XRC .50 .20
❑ 90T Rob Picciolo .15 .06
❑ 91T Chris Pittaro .15 .06
❑ 92T Jim Presley .50 .20
❑ 93T Rick Reuschel .40 .16
❑ 94T Bert Roberge .15 .06
❑ 95T Bob Rodgers MG .15 .06
❑ 96T Jerry Royster .15 .06
❑ 97T Dave Rozema .15 .06
❑ 98T Dave Rucker .15 .06
❑ 99T Vern Ruhle .15 .06
❑ 100T Paul Runge XRC .25 .10
❑ 101T Mark Salas .15 .06
❑ 102T Luis Salazar .15 .06
❑ 103T Joe Sambito .15 .06
❑ 104T Rick Schu .15 .06
❑ 105T Donnie Scott .15 .06
❑ 106T Larry Sheets XRC .25 .10
❑ 107T Don Slaught .15 .06
❑ 108T Roy Smalley .15 .06
❑ 109T Lonnie Smith .15 .06
❑ 110T Nate Snell UER .15 .06
(Headings on back for a batter)
❑ 111T Chris Speier .15 .06
❑ 112T Mike Stenhouse .15 .06
❑ 113T Tim Stoddard .15 .06
❑ 114T Jim Sundberg .40 .16
❑ 115T Bruce Sutter .40 .16
❑ 116T Don Sutton .40 .16
❑ 117T Kent Tekulve .15 .06
❑ 118T Tom Tellmann .15 .06
❑ 119T Walt Terrell .15 .06
❑ 120T M.Tettleton XRC .50 .20
❑ 121T Derrel Thomas .15 .06
❑ 122T Rich Thompson .15 .06
❑ 123T Alex Trevino .15 .06
❑ 124T John Tudor .40 .16
❑ 125T Jose Uribe .15 .06
❑ 126T Bobby Valentine MG .40 .16
❑ 127T Dave Von Ohlen .15 .06
❑ 128T U.L. Washington .15 .06
❑ 129T Earl Weaver MG .40 .16
❑ 130T Eddie Whitson .15 .06
❑ 131T Herm Winningham .15 .06
❑ 132T Checklist 1-132 .15 .06

1986 Topps

VINCE COLEMAN

	Nm-Mt	Ex-Mt
COMPLETE SET (792)	25.00	10.00
COMP.X-MAS.SET (792)	150.00	60.00

❑ 1 Pete Rose 2.00 .80
❑ 2 Pete Rose 63-66 .25 .10
❑ 3 Pete Rose 67-70 .25 .10
❑ 4 Pete Rose 71-74 .25 .10
❑ 5 Pete Rose 75-78 .25 .10
❑ 6 Pete Rose 79-82 .25 .10
❑ 7 Pete Rose 83-85 .25 .10
❑ 8 Dwayne Murphy .10 .04
❑ 9 Roy Smith .10 .04
❑ 10 Tony Gwynn .60 .24
❑ 11 Bob Ojeda .10 .04
❑ 12 Jose Uribe .10 .04
❑ 13 Bob Kearney .10 .04
❑ 14 Julio Cruz .10 .04
❑ 15 Eddie Whitson .10 .04
❑ 16 Rick Schu .10 .04
❑ 17 Mike Stenhouse .10 .04
❑ 18 Brent Gaff .10 .04
❑ 19 Rich Hebner .10 .04
❑ 20 Lou Whitaker .15 .06
❑ 21 George Bamberger MG .10 .04
❑ 22 Duane Walker .10 .04
❑ 23 Manny Lee RC* .10 .04
❑ 24 Len Barker .10 .04
❑ 25 Willie Wilson .15 .06
❑ 26 Frank DiPino .10 .04
❑ 27 Ray Knight .15 .06
❑ 28 Eric Davis .40 .16
❑ 29 Tony Phillips .10 .04
❑ 30 Eddie Murray .40 .16
❑ 31 Jamie Easterly .10 .04
❑ 32 Steve Yeager .15 .06
❑ 33 Jeff Lahti .10 .04
❑ 34 Ken Phelps .10 .04
❑ 35 Jeff Reardon .15 .06
❑ 36 Lance Parrish TL .15 .06
❑ 37 Mark Thurmond .10 .04
❑ 38 Glenn Hoffman .10 .04
❑ 39 Dave Rucker .10 .04
❑ 40 Ken Griffey .15 .06
❑ 41 Brad Wellman .10 .04
❑ 42 Geoff Zahn .10 .04
❑ 43 Dave Engle .10 .04
❑ 44 Lance McCullers .10 .04
❑ 45 Damaso Garcia .10 .04
❑ 46 Billy Hatcher .10 .04
❑ 47 Juan Berenguer .10 .04
❑ 48 Bill Almon .10 .04
❑ 49 Rick Manning .10 .04
❑ 50 Dan Quisenberry .10 .04
❑ 51 Bobby Wine MG ERR .10 .04
(Number of card on back is actually 57)
❑ 52 Chris Welsh .10 .04
❑ 53 Len Dykstra RC .75 .30
❑ 54 John Franco .15 .06
❑ 55 Fred Lynn .15 .06
❑ 56 Tom Niedenfuer .10 .04
❑ 57 Bill Doran .10 .04
(See also 51)
❑ 58 Bill Krueger .10 .04
❑ 59 Andre Thornton .10 .04
❑ 60 Dwight Evans .25 .10
❑ 61 Karl Best .10 .04
❑ 62 Bob Boone .15 .06
❑ 63 Ron Roenicke .10 .04
❑ 64 Floyd Bannister .10 .04
❑ 65 Dan Driessen .10 .04
❑ 66 Bob Forsch TL .10 .04
❑ 67 Carmelo Martinez .10 .04
❑ 68 Ed Lynch .10 .04
❑ 69 Luis Aguayo .10 .04
❑ 70 Dave Winfield .15 .06
❑ 71 Ken Schrom .10 .04
❑ 72 Shawon Dunston .15 .06
❑ 73 Randy O'Neal .10 .04
❑ 74 Rance Mulliniks .10 .04
❑ 75 Jose DeLeon .10 .04
❑ 76 Dion James .10 .04
❑ 77 Charlie Leibrandt .10 .04
❑ 78 Bruce Benedict .10 .04
❑ 79 Dave Schmidt .10 .04
❑ 80 Darryl Strawberry .25 .10
❑ 81 Gene Mauch MG .10 .04
❑ 82 Tippy Martinez .10 .04
❑ 83 Phil Garner .15 .06
❑ 84 Curt Young .10 .04
❑ 85 Tony Perez .15 .06
(Eric Davis also shown on card)
❑ 86 Tom Waddell .10 .04
❑ 87 Candy Maldonado .10 .04
❑ 88 Tom Nieto .10 .04
❑ 89 Randy St.Claire .10 .04
❑ 90 Garry Templeton .15 .06
❑ 91 Steve Crawford .10 .04
❑ 92 Al Cowens .10 .04
❑ 93 Scot Thompson .10 .04
❑ 94 Rich Bordi .10 .04
❑ 95 Ozzie Virgil .10 .04
❑ 96 Jim Clancy TL .10 .04
❑ 97 Gary Gaetti .15 .06
❑ 98 Dick Ruthven .10 .04
❑ 99 Buddy Biancalana .10 .04
❑ 100 Nolan Ryan 2.00 .80
❑ 101 Dave Bergman .10 .04
❑ 102 Joe Orsulak RC* .25 .10
❑ 103 Luis Salazar .10 .04
❑ 104 Sid Fernandez .10 .04
❑ 105 Gary Ward .10 .04
❑ 106 Ray Burris .10 .04
❑ 107 Rafael Ramirez .10 .04
❑ 108 Ted Power .10 .04
❑ 109 Len Matuszek .10 .04
❑ 110 Scott McGregor .10 .04
❑ 111 Roger Craig MG .15 .06
❑ 112 Bill Campbell .10 .04
❑ 113 U.L. Washington .10 .04
❑ 114 Mike C. Brown .10 .04
❑ 115 Jay Howell .10 .04
❑ 116 Brook Jacoby .10 .04
❑ 117 Bruce Kison .10 .04
❑ 118 Jerry Royster .10 .04
❑ 119 Barry Bonnell .10 .04
❑ 120 Steve Carlton .15 .06

❑ 121 Nelson Simmons .10 .04
❑ 122 Pete Filson .10 .04
❑ 123 Greg Walker .10 .04
❑ 124 Luis Sanchez .10 .04
❑ 125 Dave Lopes .15 .06
❑ 126 Mookie Wilson TL .10 .04
❑ 127 Jack Howell .10 .04
❑ 128 John Wathan .10 .04
❑ 129 Jeff Dedmon .10 .04
❑ 130 Alan Trammell .15 .06
❑ 131 Checklist: 1-132 .15 .06
❑ 132 Razor Shines .10 .04
❑ 133 Andy McGaffigan .10 .04
❑ 134 Carney Lansford .15 .06
❑ 135 Joe Niekro .10 .04
❑ 136 Mike Hargrove .10 .04
❑ 137 Charlie Moore .10 .04
❑ 138 Mark Davis .10 .04
❑ 139 Daryl Boston .10 .04
❑ 140 John Candelaria .10 .04
❑ 141 Chuck Cottier MG .10 .04
See also 171
❑ 142 Bob Jones .10 .04
❑ 143 Dave Van Gorder .10 .04
❑ 144 Doug Sisk .10 .04
❑ 145 Pedro Guerrero .15 .06
❑ 146 Jack Perconte .10 .04
❑ 147 Larry Sheets .10 .04
❑ 148 Mike Heath .10 .04
❑ 149 Brett Butler .15 .06
❑ 150 Joaquin Andujar .15 .06
❑ 151 Dave Stapleton .10 .04
❑ 152 Mike Morgan .10 .04
❑ 153 Ricky Adams .10 .04
❑ 154 Bert Roberge .10 .04
❑ 155 Bobby Grich .15 .06
❑ 156 Richard Dotson TL .10 .04
❑ 157 Ron Hassey .10 .04
❑ 158 Derrel Thomas .10 .04
❑ 159 Orel Hershiser UER .40 .16
(82 Alburquerque)
❑ 160 Chet Lemon .15 .06
❑ 161 Lee Tunnell .10 .04
❑ 162 Greg Gagne .10 .04
❑ 163 Pete Ladd .10 .04
❑ 164 Steve Balboni .10 .04
❑ 165 Mike Davis .10 .04
❑ 166 Dickie Thon .10 .04
❑ 167 Zane Smith .10 .04
❑ 168 Jeff Burroughs .10 .04
❑ 169 George Wright .10 .04
❑ 170 Gary Carter .15 .06
❑ 171 Bob Rodgers MG ERR .10 .04
Number of card on
back actually 141)
❑ 172 Jerry Reed .10 .04
❑ 173 Wayne Gross .10 .04
❑ 174 Brian Snyder .10 .04
❑ 175 Steve Sax .10 .04
❑ 176 Jay Tibbs .10 .04
❑ 177 Joel Youngblood .10 .04
❑ 178 Ivan DeJesus .10 .04
❑ 179 Stu Cliburn .10 .04
❑ 180 Don Mattingly 1.25 .50
❑ 181 Al Nipper .10 .04
❑ 182 Bobby Brown .10 .04
❑ 183 Larry Andersen .10 .04
❑ 184 Tim Laudner .10 .04
❑ 185 Rollie Fingers .15 .06
❑ 186 Jose Cruz TL .10 .04
❑ 187 Scott Fletcher .10 .04
❑ 188 Bob Dernier .10 .04
❑ 189 Mike Mason .10 .04
❑ 190 George Hendrick .15 .06
❑ 191 Wally Backman .10 .04
❑ 192 Milt Wilcox .10 .04
❑ 193 Daryl Sconiers .10 .04
❑ 194 Craig McMurtry .10 .04
❑ 195 Dave Concepcion .15 .06
❑ 196 Doyle Alexander .10 .04
❑ 197 Enos Cabell .10 .04
❑ 198 Ken Dixon .10 .04
❑ 199 Dick Howser MG .10 .04
❑ 200 Mike Schmidt 1.00 .40
❑ 201 Vince Coleman RB .15 .06
❑ 202 Dwight Gooden RB .25 .10
❑ 203 Keith Hernandez RB .10 .04
❑ 204 Phil Niekro RB .15 .06
❑ 205 Tony Perez RB .15 .06
❑ 206 Pete Rose RB .40 .16
❑ 207 F. Valenzuela RB .10 .04
❑ 208 Ramon Romero .10 .04
❑ 209 Randy Ready .10 .04
❑ 210 Calvin Schiraldi .10 .04
❑ 211 Ed Wojna .10 .04
❑ 212 Chris Speier .10 .04
❑ 213 Bob Shirley .10 .04
❑ 214 Randy Bush .10 .04
❑ 215 Frank White .15 .06
❑ 216 Dwayne Murphy TL .10 .04
❑ 217 Bill Scherrer .10 .04
❑ 218 Randy Hunt .10 .04
❑ 219 Dennis Lamp .10 .04
❑ 220 Bob Horner .15 .06
❑ 221 Dave Henderson .10 .04
❑ 222 Craig Gerber .10 .04
❑ 223 Atlee Hammaker .10 .04
❑ 224 Cesar Cedeno .15 .06
❑ 225 Ron Darling .15 .06
❑ 226 Lee Lacy .10 .04
❑ 227 Al Jones .10 .04
❑ 228 Tom Lawless .10 .04
❑ 229 Bill Gullickson .10 .04
❑ 230 Terry Kennedy .10 .04
❑ 231 Jim Frey MG .10 .04
❑ 232 Rick Rhoden .10 .04
❑ 233 Steve Lyons .10 .04
❑ 234 Doug Corbett .10 .04
❑ 235 Butch Wynegar .10 .04
❑ 236 Frank Eufemia .10 .04
❑ 237 Ted Simmons .15 .06
❑ 238 Larry Parrish .10 .04
❑ 239 Joel Skinner .10 .04
❑ 240 Tommy John .15 .06
❑ 241 Tony Fernandez .10 .04
❑ 242 Rich Thompson .10 .04
❑ 243 Johnny Grubb .10 .04
❑ 244 Craig Lefferts .10 .04
❑ 245 Jim Sundberg .15 .06
❑ 246 Steve Carlton TL .10 .04
❑ 247 Terry Harper .10 .04
❑ 248 Spike Owen .10 .04
❑ 249 Rob Deer .10 .04
❑ 250 Dwight Gooden .40 .16
❑ 251 Rich Dauer .10 .04
❑ 252 Bobby Castillo .10 .04
❑ 253 Dann Bilardello .10 .04
❑ 254 Ozzie Guillen RC 1.50 .60
❑ 255 Tony Armas .15 .06
❑ 256 Kurt Kepshire .10 .04
❑ 257 Doug DeCinces .10 .04
❑ 258 Tim Burke .10 .04
❑ 259 Dan Pasqua .10 .04
❑ 260 Tony Pena .10 .04
❑ 261 Bobby Valentine MG .15 .06
❑ 262 Mario Ramirez .10 .04
❑ 263 Checklist: 133-264 .15 .06
❑ 264 Darren Daulton RC .50 .20
❑ 265 Ron Davis .10 .04
❑ 266 Keith Moreland .10 .04
❑ 267 Paul Molitor .25 .10
❑ 268 Mike Scott .15 .06
❑ 269 Dane Iorg .10 .04
❑ 270 Jack Morris .15 .06
❑ 271 Dave Collins .10 .04
❑ 272 Tim Tolman .10 .04
❑ 273 Jerry Willard .10 .04
❑ 274 Ron Gardenhire .10 .04
❑ 275 Charlie Hough .15 .06
❑ 276 Willie Randolph TL .15 .06
❑ 277 Jaime Cocanower .10 .04
❑ 278 Sixto Lezcano .10 .04
❑ 279 Al Pardo .10 .04
❑ 280 Tim Raines .15 .06
❑ 281 Steve Mura .10 .04
❑ 282 Jerry Mumphrey .10 .04
❑ 283 Mike Fischlin .10 .04
❑ 284 Brian Dayett .10 .04
❑ 285 Buddy Bell .15 .06
❑ 286 Luis DeLeon .10 .04
❑ 287 John Christensen .10 .04
❑ 288 Don Aase .10 .04
❑ 289 Johnnie LeMaster .10 .04
❑ 290 Carlton Fisk .25 .10
❑ 291 Tom Lasorda MG .25 .10
❑ 292 Chuck Porter .10 .04
❑ 293 Chris Chambliss .15 .06
❑ 294 Danny Cox .10 .04
❑ 295 Kirk Gibson .25 .10
❑ 296 Geno Petralli .10 .04
❑ 297 Tim Lollar .10 .04
❑ 298 Craig Reynolds .10 .04
❑ 299 Bryn Smith .10 .04
❑ 300 George Brett 1.00 .40
❑ 301 Dennis Rasmussen .10 .04
❑ 302 Greg Gross .10 .04
❑ 303 Curt Wardle .10 .04
❑ 304 Mike Gallego RC .10 .04
❑ 305 Phil Bradley .10 .04
❑ 306 Terry Kennedy TL .10 .04
❑ 307 Dave Sax .10 .04
❑ 308 Ray Fontenot .10 .04
❑ 309 John Shelby .10 .04
❑ 310 Greg Minton .10 .04
❑ 311 Dick Schofield .10 .04
❑ 312 Tom Filer .10 .04
❑ 313 Joe DeSa .10 .04
❑ 314 Frank Pastore .10 .04
❑ 315 Mookie Wilson .15 .06
❑ 316 Sammy Khalifa .10 .04
❑ 317 Ed Romero .10 .04
❑ 318 Terry Whitfield .10 .04
❑ 319 Rick Camp .10 .04
❑ 320 Jim Rice .15 .06
❑ 321 Earl Weaver MG .15 .06
❑ 322 Bob Forsch .10 .04
❑ 323 Jerry Davis .10 .04
❑ 324 Dan Schatzeder .10 .04
❑ 325 Juan Beniquez .10 .04
❑ 326 Kent Tekulve .10 .04
❑ 327 Mike Pagliarulo .10 .04
❑ 328 Pete O'Brien .10 .04
❑ 329 Kirby Puckett .75 .30
❑ 330 Rick Sutcliffe .15 .06
❑ 331 Alan Ashby .10 .04
❑ 332 Darryl Motley .10 .04
❑ 333 Tom Henke .15 .06
❑ 334 Ken Oberkfell .10 .04
❑ 335 Don Sutton .15 .06
❑ 336 Andre Thornton TL .15 .06
❑ 337 Darnell Coles .10 .04
❑ 338 Jorge Bell .15 .06
❑ 339 Bruce Berenyi .10 .04
❑ 340 Cal Ripken 1.50 .60
❑ 341 Frank Williams .10 .04
❑ 342 Gary Redus .10 .04
❑ 343 Carlos Diaz .10 .04
❑ 344 Jim Wohlford .10 .04
❑ 345 Donnie Moore .10 .04
❑ 346 Bryan Little .10 .04
❑ 347 Teddy Higuera RC* .25 .10
❑ 348 Cliff Johnson .10 .04
❑ 349 Mark Clear .10 .04
❑ 350 Jack Clark .15 .06
❑ 351 Chuck Tanner MG .10 .04
❑ 352 Harry Spilman .10 .04
❑ 353 Keith Atherton .10 .04
❑ 354 Tony Bernazard .10 .04
❑ 355 Lee Smith .15 .06
❑ 356 Mickey Hatcher .10 .04
❑ 357 Ed VandeBerg .10 .04
❑ 358 Rick Dempsey .10 .04
❑ 359 Mike LaCoss .10 .04
❑ 360 Lloyd Moseby .10 .04
❑ 361 Shane Rawley .10 .04
❑ 362 Tom Paciorek .10 .04
❑ 363 Terry Forster .15 .06
❑ 364 Reid Nichols .10 .04
❑ 365 Mike Flanagan .10 .04
❑ 366 Dave Concepcion TL .15 .06
❑ 367 Aurelio Lopez .10 .04
❑ 368 Greg Brock .10 .04
❑ 369 Al Holland .10 .04
❑ 370 Vince Coleman RC* .50 .20
❑ 371 Bill Stein .10 .04
❑ 372 Ben Oglivie .15 .06
❑ 373 Urbano Lugo .10 .04
❑ 374 Terry Francona .15 .06

❑ 375 Rich Gedman .10 .04
❑ 376 Bill Dawley .10 .04
❑ 377 Joe Carter .15 .06
❑ 378 Bruce Bochte .10 .04
❑ 379 Bobby Meacham .10 .04
❑ 380 LaMarr Hoyt .10 .04
❑ 381 Ray Miller MG .10 .04
❑ 382 Ivan Calderon RC* .25 .10
❑ 383 Chris Brown .10 .04
❑ 384 Steve Trout .10 .04
❑ 385 Cecil Cooper .15 .06
❑ 386 Cecil Fielder RC 1.00 .40
❑ 387 Steve Kemp .10 .04
❑ 388 Dickie Noles .10 .04
❑ 389 Glenn Davis .10 .04
❑ 390 Tom Seaver .25 .10
❑ 391 Julio Franco .15 .06
❑ 392 John Russell .10 .04
❑ 393 Chris Pittaro .10 .04
❑ 394 Checklist: 265-396 .15 .06
❑ 395 Scott Garrelts .10 .04
❑ 396 Dwight Evans TL .25 .10
❑ 397 Steve Buechele RC .25 .10
❑ 398 Earnie Riles .10 .04
❑ 399 Bill Swift .10 .04
❑ 400 Rod Carew .25 .10
❑ 401 Fernando Valenzuela TBC '81 .10 .04
❑ 402 Tom Seaver TBC '76 .15 .06
❑ 403 Willie Mays TBC '71 .40 .16
❑ 404 Frank Robinson TBC '66 .15 .06
❑ 405 Roger Maris TBC '61 .40 .16
❑ 406 Scott Sanderson .10 .04
❑ 407 Sal Butera .10 .04
❑ 408 Dave Smith .10 .04
❑ 409 Paul Runge RC .10 .04
❑ 410 Dave Kingman .15 .06
❑ 411 Sparky Anderson MG .15 .06
❑ 412 Jim Clancy .10 .04
❑ 413 Tim Flannery .10 .04
❑ 414 Tom Gorman .10 .04
❑ 415 Hal McRae .15 .06
❑ 416 Dennis Martinez .15 .06
❑ 417 R.J. Reynolds .10 .04
❑ 418 Alan Knicely .10 .04
❑ 419 Frank Wills .10 .04
❑ 420 Von Hayes .10 .04
❑ 421 David Palmer .10 .04
❑ 422 Mike Jorgensen .10 .04
❑ 423 Dan Spillner .10 .04
❑ 424 Rick Miller .10 .04
❑ 425 Larry McWilliams .10 .04
❑ 426 Charlie Moore TL .10 .04
❑ 427 Joe Cowley .10 .04
❑ 428 Max Venable .10 .04
❑ 429 Greg Booker .10 .04
❑ 430 Kent Hrbek .15 .06
❑ 431 George Frazier .10 .04
❑ 432 Mark Bailey .10 .04
❑ 433 Chris Codiroli .10 .04
❑ 434 Curt Wilkerson .10 .04
❑ 435 Bill Caudill .10 .04
❑ 436 Doug Flynn .10 .04
❑ 437 Rick Mahler .10 .04
❑ 438 Clint Hurdle .10 .04
❑ 439 Rick Honeycutt .10 .04
❑ 440 Alvin Davis .10 .04
❑ 441 Whitey Herzog MG .25 .10
❑ 442 Ron Robinson .10 .04
❑ 443 Bill Buckner .15 .06
❑ 444 Alex Trevino .10 .04
❑ 445 Bert Blyleven .15 .06
❑ 446 Lenn Sakata .10 .04
❑ 447 Jerry Don Gleaton .10 .04
❑ 448 Herm Winningham .10 .04
❑ 449 Rod Scurry .10 .04
❑ 450 Graig Nettles .15 .06
❑ 451 Mark Brown .10 .04
❑ 452 Bob Clark .10 .04
❑ 453 Steve Jeltz .10 .04
❑ 454 Burt Hooton .10 .04
❑ 455 Willie Randolph .15 .06
❑ 456 Dale Murphy TL .25 .10
❑ 457 Mickey Tettleton RC .25 .10
❑ 458 Kevin Bass .10 .04
❑ 459 Luis Leal .10 .04
❑ 460 Leon Durham .10 .04
❑ 461 Walt Terrell .10 .04
❑ 462 Domingo Ramos .10 .04
❑ 463 Jim Gott .10 .04
❑ 464 Ruppert Jones .10 .04
❑ 465 Jesse Orosco .10 .04
❑ 466 Tom Foley .10 .04
❑ 467 Bob James .10 .04
❑ 468 Mike Scioscia .15 .06
❑ 469 Storm Davis .10 .04
❑ 470 Bill Madlock .15 .06
❑ 471 Bobby Cox MG .15 .06
❑ 472 Joe Hesketh .10 .04
❑ 473 Mark Brouhard .10 .04
❑ 474 John Tudor .15 .06
❑ 475 Juan Samuel .10 .04
❑ 476 Ron Mathis .10 .04
❑ 477 Mike Easler .10 .04
❑ 478 Andy Hawkins .10 .04
❑ 479 Bob Melvin .10 .04
❑ 480 Oddibe McDowell .10 .04
❑ 481 Scott Bradley .10 .04
❑ 482 Rick Lysander .10 .04
❑ 483 George Vukovich .10 .04
❑ 484 Donnie Hill .10 .04
❑ 485 Gary Matthews .15 .06
❑ 486 Bobby Grich TL .10 .04
❑ 487 Bret Saberhagen .15 .06
❑ 488 Lou Thornton .10 .04
❑ 489 Jim Winn .10 .04
❑ 490 Jeff Leonard .10 .04
❑ 491 Pascual Perez .10 .04
❑ 492 Kelvin Chapman .10 .04
❑ 493 Gene Nelson .10 .04
❑ 494 Gary Roenicke .10 .04
❑ 495 Mark Langston .15 .06
❑ 496 Jay Johnstone .10 .04
❑ 497 John Stuper .10 .04
❑ 498 Tito Landrum .10 .04
❑ 499 Bob L. Gibson .10 .04
❑ 500 Rickey Henderson .40 .16
❑ 501 Dave Johnson MG .10 .04
❑ 502 Glen Cook .10 .04
❑ 503 Mike Fitzgerald .10 .04
❑ 504 Denny Walling .10 .04
❑ 505 Jerry Koosman .15 .06
❑ 506 Bill Russell .15 .06
❑ 507 Steve Ontiveros RC .10 .04
❑ 508 Alan Wiggins .10 .04
❑ 509 Ernie Camacho .10 .04
❑ 510 Wade Boggs .25 .10
❑ 511 Ed Nunez .10 .04
❑ 512 Thad Bosley .10 .04
❑ 513 Ron Washington .10 .04
❑ 514 Mike Jones .10 .04
❑ 515 Darrell Evans .15 .06
❑ 516 Greg Minton TL .10 .04
❑ 517 Milt Thompson RC .25 .10
❑ 518 Buck Martinez .10 .04
❑ 519 Danny Darwin .10 .04
❑ 520 Keith Hernandez .15 .06
❑ 521 Nate Snell .10 .04
❑ 522 Bob Bailor .10 .04
❑ 523 Joe Price .10 .04
❑ 524 Darrell Miller .10 .04
❑ 525 Marvell Wynne .10 .04
❑ 526 Charlie Lea .10 .04
❑ 527 Checklist: 397-528 .15 .06
❑ 528 Terry Pendleton .15 .06
❑ 529 Marc Sullivan .10 .04
❑ 530 Rich Gossage .15 .06
❑ 531 Tony LaRussa MG .15 .06
❑ 532 Don Carman .10 .04
❑ 533 Billy Sample .10 .04
❑ 534 Jeff Calhoun .10 .04
❑ 535 Toby Harrah .15 .06
❑ 536 Jose Rijo .15 .06
❑ 537 Mark Salas .10 .04
❑ 538 Dennis Eckersley .25 .10
❑ 539 Glenn Hubbard .10 .04
❑ 540 Dan Petry .10 .04
❑ 541 Jorge Orta .10 .04
❑ 542 Don Schulze .10 .04
❑ 543 Jerry Narron .10 .04
❑ 544 Eddie Milner .10 .04
❑ 545 Jimmy Key .15 .06
❑ 546 Dave Henderson TL .10 .04
❑ 547 Roger McDowell RC* .25 .10
❑ 548 Mike Young .10 .04
❑ 549 Bob Welch .15 .06
❑ 550 Tom Herr .10 .04
❑ 551 Dave LaPoint .10 .04
❑ 552 Marc Hill .10 .04
❑ 553 Jim Morrison .10 .04
❑ 554 Paul Householder .10 .04
❑ 555 Hubie Brooks .10 .04
❑ 556 John Denny .10 .04
❑ 557 Gerald Perry .10 .04
❑ 558 Tim Stoddard .10 .04
❑ 559 Tommy Dunbar .10 .04
❑ 560 Dave Righetti .15 .06
❑ 561 Bob Lillis MG .10 .04
❑ 562 Joe Beckwith .10 .04
❑ 563 Alejandro Sanchez .10 .04
❑ 564 Warren Brusstar .10 .04
❑ 565 Tom Brunansky .10 .04
❑ 566 Alfredo Griffin .10 .04
❑ 567 Jeff Barkley .10 .04
❑ 568 Donnie Scott .10 .04
❑ 569 Jim Acker .10 .04
❑ 570 Rusty Staub .15 .06
❑ 571 Mike Jeffcoat .10 .04
❑ 572 Paul Zuvella .10 .04
❑ 573 Tom Hume .10 .04
❑ 574 Ron Kittle .10 .04
❑ 575 Mike Boddicker .10 .04
❑ 576 Andre Dawson TL .10 .04
❑ 577 Jerry Reuss .10 .04
❑ 578 Lee Mazzilli .15 .06
❑ 579 Jim Slaton .10 .04
❑ 580 Willie McGee .15 .06
❑ 581 Bruce Hurst .10 .04
❑ 582 Jim Gantner .10 .04
❑ 583 Al Bumbry .10 .04
❑ 584 Brian Fisher RC .10 .04
❑ 585 Garry Maddox .10 .04
❑ 586 Greg Harris .10 .04
❑ 587 Rafael Santana .10 .04
❑ 588 Steve Lake .10 .04
❑ 589 Sid Bream .10 .04
❑ 590 Bob Knepper .10 .04
❑ 591 Jackie Moore MG .10 .04
❑ 592 Frank Tanana .15 .06
❑ 593 Jesse Barfield .15 .06
❑ 594 Chris Bando .10 .04
❑ 595 Dave Parker .15 .06
❑ 596 Onix Concepcion .10 .04
❑ 597 Sammy Stewart .10 .04
❑ 598 Jim Presley .10 .04
❑ 599 Rick Aguilera RC .25 .10
❑ 600 Dale Murphy .25 .10
❑ 601 Gary Lucas .10 .04
❑ 602 Mariano Duncan RC* .25 .10
❑ 603 Bill Laskey .10 .04
❑ 604 Gary Pettis .10 .04
❑ 605 Dennis Boyd .10 .04
❑ 606 Hal McRae TL .15 .06
❑ 607 Ken Dayley .10 .04
❑ 608 Bruce Bochy .10 .04
❑ 609 Barbaro Garbey .10 .04
❑ 610 Ron Guidry .15 .06
❑ 611 Gary Woods .10 .04
❑ 612 Richard Dotson .10 .04
❑ 613 Roy Smalley .10 .04
❑ 614 Rick Waits .10 .04
❑ 615 Johnny Ray .10 .04
❑ 616 Glenn Brummer .10 .04
❑ 617 Lonnie Smith .10 .04
❑ 618 Jim Pankovits .10 .04
❑ 619 Danny Heep .10 .04
❑ 620 Bruce Sutter .15 .06
❑ 621 John Felske MG .10 .04
❑ 622 Gary Lavelle .10 .04
❑ 623 Floyd Rayford .10 .04
❑ 624 Steve McCatty .10 .04
❑ 625 Bob Brenly .10 .04
❑ 626 Roy Thomas .10 .04
❑ 627 Ron Oester .10 .04
❑ 628 Kirk McCaskill RC .25 .10
❑ 629 Mitch Webster .10 .04
❑ 630 Fernando Valenzuela .15 .06

- ❑ 631 Steve Braun .10 .04
- ❑ 632 Dave Von Ohlen .10 .04
- ❑ 633 Jackie Gutierrez .10 .04
- ❑ 634 Roy Lee Jackson .10 .04
- ❑ 635 Jason Thompson .10 .04
- ❑ 636 Lee Smith TL .10 .04
- ❑ 637 Rudy Law .10 .04
- ❑ 638 John Butcher .10 .04
- ❑ 639 Bo Diaz .10 .04
- ❑ 640 Jose Cruz .15 .06
- ❑ 641 Wayne Tolleson .10 .04
- ❑ 642 Ray Searage .10 .04
- ❑ 643 Tom Brookens .10 .04
- ❑ 644 Mark Gubicza .10 .04
- ❑ 645 Dusty Baker .15 .06
- ❑ 646 Mike Moore .10 .04
- ❑ 647 Mel Hall .10 .04
- ❑ 648 Steve Bedrosian .10 .04
- ❑ 649 Ronn Reynolds .10 .04
- ❑ 650 Dave Stieb .15 .06
- ❑ 651 Billy Martin MG .25 .10
- ❑ 652 Tom Browning .10 .04
- ❑ 653 Jim Dwyer .10 .04
- ❑ 654 Ken Howell .10 .04
- ❑ 655 Manny Trillo .10 .04
- ❑ 656 Brian Harper .10 .04
- ❑ 657 Juan Agosto .10 .04
- ❑ 658 Rob Wilfong .10 .04
- ❑ 659 Checklist: 529-660 .15 .06
- ❑ 660 Steve Garvey .15 .06
- ❑ 661 Roger Clemens 3.00 1.20
- ❑ 662 Bill Schroeder .10 .04
- ❑ 663 Neil Allen .10 .04
- ❑ 664 Tim Corcoran .10 .04
- ❑ 665 Alejandro Pena .10 .04
- ❑ 666 Charlie Hough TL .15 .06
- ❑ 667 Tim Teufel .10 .04
- ❑ 668 Cecilio Guante .10 .04
- ❑ 669 Ron Cey .15 .06
- ❑ 670 Willie Hernandez .10 .04
- ❑ 671 Lynn Jones .10 .04
- ❑ 672 Rob Picciolo .10 .04
- ❑ 673 Ernie Whitt .10 .04
- ❑ 674 Pat Tabler .10 .04
- ❑ 675 Claudell Washington .10 .04
- ❑ 676 Matt Young .10 .04
- ❑ 677 Nick Esasky .10 .04
- ❑ 678 Dan Gladden .10 .04
- ❑ 679 Britt Burns .10 .04
- ❑ 680 George Foster .15 .06
- ❑ 681 Dick Williams MG .10 .04
- ❑ 682 Junior Ortiz .10 .04
- ❑ 683 Andy Van Slyke .25 .10
- ❑ 684 Bob McClure .10 .04
- ❑ 685 Tim Wallach .10 .04
- ❑ 686 Jeff Stone .10 .04
- ❑ 687 Mike Trujillo .10 .04
- ❑ 688 Larry Herndon .10 .04
- ❑ 689 Dave Stewart .15 .06
- ❑ 690 Ryne Sandberg UER .75 .30 (No Topps logo on front)
- ❑ 691 Mike Madden .10 .04
- ❑ 692 Dale Berra .10 .04
- ❑ 693 Tom Tellmann .10 .04
- ❑ 694 Garth Iorg .10 .04
- ❑ 695 Mike Smithson .10 .04
- ❑ 696 Bill Russell TL .15 .06
- ❑ 697 Bud Black .10 .04
- ❑ 698 Brad Komminsk .10 .04
- ❑ 699 Pat Corrales MG .10 .04
- ❑ 700 Reggie Jackson .25 .10
- ❑ 701 Keith Hernandez AS .10 .04
- ❑ 702 Tom Herr AS .10 .04
- ❑ 703 Tim Wallach AS .10 .04
- ❑ 704 Ozzie Smith AS .40 .16
- ❑ 705 Dale Murphy AS .15 .06
- ❑ 706 Pedro Guerrero AS .10 .04
- ❑ 707 Willie McGee AS .10 .04
- ❑ 708 Gary Carter AS .10 .04
- ❑ 709 Dwight Gooden AS .25 .10
- ❑ 710 John Tudor AS .10 .04
- ❑ 711 Jeff Reardon AS .10 .04
- ❑ 712 Don Mattingly AS .60 .24
- ❑ 713 Damaso Garcia AS .10 .04
- ❑ 714 George Brett AS .40 .16
- ❑ 715 Cal Ripken AS .40 .16
- ❑ 716 Rickey Henderson AS .25 .10
- ❑ 717 Dave Winfield AS .10 .04
- ❑ 718 George Bell AS .10 .04
- ❑ 719 Carlton Fisk AS .15 .06
- ❑ 720 Bret Saberhagen AS .10 .04
- ❑ 721 Ron Guidry AS .10 .04
- ❑ 722 Dan Quisenberry AS .10 .04
- ❑ 723 Marty Bystrom .10 .04
- ❑ 724 Tim Hulett .10 .04
- ❑ 725 Mario Soto .15 .06
- ❑ 726 Rick Dempsey TL .15 .06
- ❑ 727 David Green .10 .04
- ❑ 728 Mike Marshall .10 .04
- ❑ 729 Jim Beattie .10 .04
- ❑ 730 Ozzie Smith .60 .24
- ❑ 731 Don Robinson .10 .04
- ❑ 732 Floyd Youmans .10 .04
- ❑ 733 Ron Romanick .10 .04
- ❑ 734 Marty Barrett .10 .04
- ❑ 735 Dave Dravecky .10 .04
- ❑ 736 Glenn Wilson .10 .04
- ❑ 737 Pete Vuckovich .10 .04
- ❑ 738 Andre Robertson .10 .04
- ❑ 739 Dave Rozema .10 .04
- ❑ 740 Lance Parrish .15 .06
- ❑ 741 Pete Rose MG .40 .16
- ❑ 742 Frank Viola .15 .06
- ❑ 743 Pat Sheridan .10 .04
- ❑ 744 Lary Sorensen .10 .04
- ❑ 745 Willie Upshaw .10 .04
- ❑ 746 Denny Gonzalez .10 .04
- ❑ 747 Rick Cerone .10 .04
- ❑ 748 Steve Henderson .10 .04
- ❑ 749 Ed Jurak .10 .04
- ❑ 750 Gorman Thomas .15 .06
- ❑ 751 Howard Johnson .15 .06
- ❑ 752 Mike Krukow .10 .04
- ❑ 753 Dan Ford .10 .04
- ❑ 754 Pat Clements .10 .04
- ❑ 755 Harold Baines .15 .06
- ❑ 756 Rick Rhoden TL .10 .04
- ❑ 757 Darrell Porter .10 .04
- ❑ 758 Dave Anderson .10 .04
- ❑ 759 Moose Haas .10 .04
- ❑ 760 Andre Dawson .15 .06
- ❑ 761 Don Slaught .10 .04
- ❑ 762 Eric Show .10 .04
- ❑ 763 Terry Puhl .10 .04
- ❑ 764 Kevin Gross .10 .04
- ❑ 765 Don Baylor .15 .06
- ❑ 766 Rick Langford .10 .04
- ❑ 767 Jody Davis .10 .04
- ❑ 768 Vern Ruhle .10 .04
- ❑ 769 Harold Reynolds RC .75 .30
- ❑ 770 Vida Blue .15 .06
- ❑ 771 John McNamara MG .10 .04
- ❑ 772 Brian Downing .15 .06
- ❑ 773 Greg Pryor .10 .04
- ❑ 774 Terry Leach .10 .04
- ❑ 775 Al Oliver .15 .06
- ❑ 776 Gene Garber .10 .04
- ❑ 777 Wayne Krenchicki .10 .04
- ❑ 778 Jerry Hairston .10 .04
- ❑ 779 Rick Reuschel .15 .06
- ❑ 780 Robin Yount .60 .24
- ❑ 781 Joe Nolan .10 .04
- ❑ 782 Ken Landreaux .10 .04
- ❑ 783 Ricky Horton .10 .04
- ❑ 784 Alan Bannister .10 .04
- ❑ 785 Bob Stanley .10 .04
- ❑ 786 Mickey Hatcher TL .10 .04
- ❑ 787 Vance Law .10 .04
- ❑ 788 Marty Castillo .10 .04
- ❑ 789 Kurt Bevacqua .10 .04
- ❑ 790 Phil Niekro .15 .06
- ❑ 791 Checklist: 661-792 .15 .06
- ❑ 792 Charles Hudson .10 .04

1986 Topps Traded

	Nm-Mt	Ex-Mt
COMP.FACT.SET (132)	40.00	16.00

- ❑ 1T Andy Allanson .10 .04
- ❑ 2T Neil Allen .10 .04

- ❑ 3T Joaquin Andujar .15 .06
- ❑ 4T Paul Assenmacher .40 .16
- ❑ 5T Scott Bailes .10 .04
- ❑ 6T Don Baylor .15 .06
- ❑ 7T Steve Bedrosian .10 .04
- ❑ 8T Juan Beniquez .10 .04
- ❑ 9T Juan Berenguer .10 .04
- ❑ 10T Mike Bielecki .10 .04
- ❑ 11T Barry Bonds XRC 30.00 12.00
- ❑ 12T Bobby Bonilla XRC .75 .30
- ❑ 13T Juan Bonilla .10 .04
- ❑ 14T Rich Bordi .10 .04
- ❑ 15T Steve Boros MG .10 .04
- ❑ 16T Rick Burleson .10 .04
- ❑ 17T Bill Campbell .10 .04
- ❑ 18T Tom Candiotti .10 .04
- ❑ 19T John Cangelosi .10 .04
- ❑ 20T Jose Canseco XRC 4.00 1.60
- ❑ 21T Carmen Castillo .10 .04
- ❑ 22T Rick Cerone .10 .04
- ❑ 23T John Cerutti .10 .04
- ❑ 24T Will Clark XRC 1.50 .60
- ❑ 25T Mark Clear .10 .04
- ❑ 26T Darnell Coles .10 .04
- ❑ 27T Dave Collins .10 .04
- ❑ 28T Tim Conroy .10 .04
- ❑ 29T Joe Cowley .10 .04
- ❑ 30T Joel Davis .10 .04
- ❑ 31T Rob Deer .10 .04
- ❑ 32T John Denny .10 .04
- ❑ 33T Mike Easler .10 .04
- ❑ 34T Mark Eichhorn .10 .04
- ❑ 35T Steve Farr .10 .04
- ❑ 36T Scott Fletcher .10 .04
- ❑ 37T Terry Forster .15 .06
- ❑ 38T Terry Francona .15 .06
- ❑ 39T Jim Fregosi MG .10 .04
- ❑ 40T Andres Galarraga XRC 1.00 .40
- ❑ 41T Ken Griffey .15 .06
- ❑ 42T Bill Gullickson .10 .04
- ❑ 43T Jose Guzman XRC * .10 .04
- ❑ 44T Moose Haas .10 .04
- ❑ 45T Billy Hatcher .10 .04
- ❑ 46T Mike Heath .10 .04
- ❑ 47T Tom Hume .10 .04
- ❑ 48T Pete Incaviglia XRC .40 .16
- ❑ 49T Dane Iorg .10 .04
- ❑ 50T Bo Jackson XRC 5.00 2.00
- ❑ 51T Wally Joyner XRC .75 .30
- ❑ 52T Charlie Kerfeld .10 .04
- ❑ 53T Eric King .10 .04
- ❑ 54T Bob Kipper .10 .04
- ❑ 55T Wayne Krenchicki .10 .04
- ❑ 56T John Kruk XRC 1.25 .50
- ❑ 57T Mike LaCoss .10 .04
- ❑ 58T Pete Ladd .10 .04
- ❑ 59T Mike Laga .10 .04
- ❑ 60T Hal Lanier MG .10 .04
- ❑ 61T Dave LaPoint .10 .04
- ❑ 62T Rudy Law .10 .04
- ❑ 63T Rick Leach .10 .04
- ❑ 64T Tim Leary .10 .04
- ❑ 65T Dennis Leonard .10 .04
- ❑ 66T Jim Leyland MG XRC .40 .16
- ❑ 67T Steve Lyons .10 .04
- ❑ 68T Mickey Mahler .10 .04
- ❑ 69T Candy Maldonado .10 .04
- ❑ 70T Roger Mason XRC * .10 .04

Card	Player	Nm-Mt	Ex-Mt
❑ 71T	Bob McClure	.10	.04
❑ 72T	Andy McGaffigan	.10	.04
❑ 73T	Gene Michael MG	.10	.04
❑ 74T	Kevin Mitchell XRC	.75	.30
❑ 75T	Omar Moreno	.10	.04
❑ 76T	Jerry Mumphrey	.10	.04
❑ 77T	Phil Niekro	.15	.06
❑ 78T	Randy Niemann	.10	.04
❑ 79T	Juan Nieves	.10	.04
❑ 80T	Otis Nixon XRC*	.75	.30
❑ 81T	Bob Ojeda	.10	.04
❑ 82T	Jose Oquendo	.10	.04
❑ 83T	Tom Paciorek	.10	.04
❑ 84T	David Palmer	.10	.04
❑ 85T	Frank Pastore	.10	.04
❑ 86T	Lou Piniella MG	.15	.06
❑ 87T	Dan Plesac	.40	.16
❑ 88T	Darrell Porter	.10	.04
❑ 89T	Rey Quinones	.10	.04
❑ 90T	Gary Redus	.10	.04
❑ 91T	Bip Roberts XRC	.40	.16
❑ 92T	Billy Joe Robidoux	.10	.04
❑ 93T	Jeff D. Robinson	.10	.04
❑ 94T	Gary Roenicke	.10	.04
❑ 95T	Ed Romero	.10	.04
❑ 96T	Angel Salazar	.10	.04
❑ 97T	Joe Sambito	.10	.04
❑ 98T	Billy Sample	.10	.04
❑ 99T	Dave Schmidt	.10	.04
❑ 100T	Ken Schrom	.10	.04
❑ 101T	Tom Seaver	.25	.10
❑ 102T	Ted Simmons	.15	.06
❑ 103T	Sammy Stewart	.10	.04
❑ 104T	Kurt Stillwell	.10	.04
❑ 105T	Franklin Stubbs	.10	.04
❑ 106T	Dale Sveum	.10	.04
❑ 107T	Chuck Tanner MG	.10	.04
❑ 108T	Danny Tartabull	.15	.06
❑ 109T	Tim Teufel	.10	.04
❑ 110T	Bob Tewksbury XRC	.40	.16
❑ 111T	Andres Thomas	.10	.04
❑ 112T	Milt Thompson	.40	.16
❑ 113T	R.Thompson XRC	.40	.16
❑ 114T	Jay Tibbs	.10	.04
❑ 115T	Wayne Tolleson	.10	.04
❑ 116T	Alex Trevino	.10	.04
❑ 117T	Manny Trillo	.10	.04
❑ 118T	Ed VandeBerg	.10	.04
❑ 119T	Ozzie Virgil	.10	.04
❑ 120T	Bob Walk	.10	.04
❑ 121T	Gene Walter	.10	.04
❑ 122T	Claudell Washington	.10	.04
❑ 123T	Bill Wegman XRC *	.10	.04
❑ 124T	Dick Williams MG	.10	.04
❑ 125T	Mitch Williams XRC	.40	.16
❑ 126T	Bobby Witt XRC	.40	.16
❑ 127T	Todd Worrell XRC *	.40	.16
❑ 128T	George Wright	.10	.04
❑ 129T	Ricky Wright	.10	.04
❑ 130T	Steve Yeager	.15	.06
❑ 131T	Paul Zuvella	.10	.04
❑ 132T	Checklist 1T-132T	.10	.04

1987 Topps

	Nm-Mt	Ex-Mt
COMPLETE SET (792)	25.00	10.00
COMP.FACT SET (792)	25.00	10.00
COMP.HOBBY SET (792)	40.00	16.00
COMP.X-MAS.SET (792)	40.00	16.00

Card	Player	Nm-Mt	Ex-Mt
❑ 1	Roger Clemens RB	.25	.10
❑ 2	Jim Deshaies RB	.05	.02
❑ 3	Dwight Evans RB	.15	.06
❑ 4	Davey Lopes RB	.05	.02
❑ 5	Dave Righetti RB	.05	.02
❑ 6	Ruben Sierra RB	.25	.10
❑ 7	Todd Worrell RB	.05	.02
❑ 8	Terry Pendleton	.10	.04
❑ 9	Jay Tibbs	.05	.02
❑ 10	Cecil Cooper	.10	.04
❑ 11	Indians Team (Mound conference)	.05	.02
❑ 12	Jeff Sellers	.05	.02
❑ 13	Nick Esasky	.05	.02
❑ 14	Dave Stewart	.10	.04
❑ 15	Claudell Washington	.05	.02
❑ 16	Pat Clements	.05	.02
❑ 17	Pete O'Brien	.05	.02
❑ 18	Dick Howser MG	.05	.02
❑ 19	Matt Young	.05	.02
❑ 20	Gary Carter	.10	.04
❑ 21	Mark Davis	.05	.02
❑ 22	Doug DeCinces	.05	.02
❑ 23	Lee Smith	.10	.04
❑ 24	Tony Walker	.05	.02
❑ 25	Bert Blyleven	.10	.04
❑ 26	Greg Brock	.05	.02
❑ 27	Joe Cowley	.05	.02
❑ 28	Rick Dempsey	.05	.02
❑ 29	Jimmy Key	.10	.04
❑ 30	Tim Raines	.10	.04
❑ 31	Braves Team (Glenn Hubbard and Rafael Ramirez)	.05	.02
❑ 32	Tim Leary	.05	.02
❑ 33	Andy Van Slyke	.15	.06
❑ 34	Jose Rijo	.10	.04
❑ 35	Sid Bream	.05	.02
❑ 36	Eric King	.05	.02
❑ 37	Marvell Wynne	.05	.02
❑ 38	Dennis Leonard	.05	.02
❑ 39	Marty Barrett	.05	.02
❑ 40	Dave Righetti	.10	.04
❑ 41	Bo Diaz	.05	.02
❑ 42	Gary Redus	.05	.02
❑ 43	Gene Michael MG	.05	.02
❑ 44	Greg Harris	.05	.02
❑ 45	Jim Presley	.05	.02
❑ 46	Dan Gladden	.05	.02
❑ 47	Dennis Powell	.05	.02
❑ 48	Wally Backman	.05	.02
❑ 49	Terry Harper	.05	.02
❑ 50	Dave Smith	.05	.02
❑ 51	Mel Hall	.05	.02
❑ 52	Keith Atherton	.05	.02
❑ 53	Ruppert Jones	.05	.02
❑ 54	Bill Dawley	.05	.02
❑ 55	Tim Wallach	.05	.02
❑ 56	Brewers Team (Mound conference)	.05	.02
❑ 57	Scott Nielsen	.05	.02
❑ 58	Thad Bosley	.05	.02
❑ 59	Ken Dayley	.05	.02
❑ 60	Tony Pena	.05	.02
❑ 61	Bobby Thigpen RC	.25	.10
❑ 62	Bobby Meacham	.05	.02
❑ 63	Fred Toliver	.05	.02
❑ 64	Harry Spilman	.05	.02
❑ 65	Tom Browning	.05	.02
❑ 66	Marc Sullivan	.05	.02
❑ 67	Bill Swift	.05	.02
❑ 68	Tony LaRussa MG	.10	.04
❑ 69	Lonnie Smith	.05	.02
❑ 70	Charlie Hough	.10	.04
❑ 71	Mike Aldrete	.05	.02
❑ 72	Walt Terrell	.05	.02
❑ 73	Dave Anderson	.05	.02
❑ 74	Dan Pasqua	.05	.02
❑ 75	Ron Darling	.10	.04
❑ 76	Rafael Ramirez	.05	.02
❑ 77	Bryan Oelkers	.05	.02
❑ 78	Tom Foley	.05	.02
❑ 79	Juan Nieves	.05	.02
❑ 80	Wally Joyner RC	.40	.16
❑ 81	Padres Team (Andy Hawkins and Terry Kennedy)	.05	.02
❑ 82	Rob Murphy	.05	.02
❑ 83	Mike Davis	.05	.02
❑ 84	Steve Lake	.05	.02
❑ 85	Kevin Bass	.05	.02
❑ 86	Nate Snell	.05	.02
❑ 87	Mark Salas	.05	.02
❑ 88	Ed Wojna	.05	.02
❑ 89	Ozzie Guillen	.15	.06
❑ 90	Dave Stieb	.10	.04
❑ 91	Harold Reynolds	.10	.04
❑ 92A	Urbano Lugo ERR (no trademark)	.15	.06
❑ 92B	Urbano Lugo COR	.05	.02
❑ 93	Jim Leyland MG/TC RC*	.25	.10
❑ 94	Calvin Schiraldi	.05	.02
❑ 95	Oddibe McDowell	.05	.02
❑ 96	Frank Williams	.05	.02
❑ 97	Glenn Wilson	.05	.02
❑ 98	Bill Scherrer	.05	.02
❑ 99	Darryl Motley (Now with Braves on card front)	.05	.02
❑ 100	Steve Garvey	.10	.04
❑ 101	Carl Willis RC	.10	.04
❑ 102	Paul Zuvella	.05	.02
❑ 103	Rick Aguilera	.05	.02
❑ 104	Billy Sample	.05	.02
❑ 105	Floyd Youmans	.05	.02
❑ 106	Blue Jays Team (George Bell and Jesse Barfield)	.05	.02
❑ 107	John Butcher	.05	.02
❑ 108	Jim Gantner UER (Brewers logo reversed)	.05	.02
❑ 109	R.J. Reynolds	.05	.02
❑ 110	John Tudor	.10	.04
❑ 111	Alfredo Griffin	.05	.02
❑ 112	Alan Ashby	.05	.02
❑ 113	Neil Allen	.05	.02
❑ 114	Billy Beane	.10	.04
❑ 115	Donnie Moore	.05	.02
❑ 116	Bill Russell	.10	.04
❑ 117	Jim Beattie	.05	.02
❑ 118	Bobby Valentine MG	.10	.04
❑ 119	Ron Robinson	.05	.02
❑ 120	Eddie Murray	.25	.10
❑ 121	Kevin Romine	.05	.02
❑ 122	Jim Clancy	.05	.02
❑ 123	John Kruk RC*	.75	.30
❑ 124	Ray Fontenot	.05	.02
❑ 125	Bob Brenly	.05	.02
❑ 126	Mike Loynd RC	.10	.04
❑ 127	Vance Law	.05	.02
❑ 128	Checklist 1-132	.05	.02
❑ 129	Rick Cerone	.05	.02
❑ 130	Dwight Gooden	.15	.06
❑ 131	Pirates Team (Sid Bream and Tony Pena)	.05	.02
❑ 132	Paul Assenmacher	.25	.10
❑ 133	Jose Oquendo	.05	.02
❑ 134	Rich Yett	.05	.02
❑ 135	Mike Easler	.05	.02
❑ 136	Ron Romanick	.05	.02
❑ 137	Jerry Willard	.05	.02
❑ 138	Roy Lee Jackson	.05	.02
❑ 139	Devon White RC	.40	.16
❑ 140	Bret Saberhagen	.10	.04
❑ 141	Herm Winningham	.05	.02
❑ 142	Rick Sutcliffe	.10	.04
❑ 143	Steve Boros MG	.05	.02
❑ 144	Mike Scioscia	.10	.04
❑ 145	Charlie Kerfeld	.05	.02
❑ 146	Tracy Jones	.05	.02
❑ 147	Randy Niemann	.05	.02
❑ 148	Dave Collins	.05	.02
❑ 149	Ray Searage	.05	.02
❑ 150	Wade Boggs	.15	.06
❑ 151	Mike LaCoss	.05	.02
❑ 152	Toby Harrah	.10	.04
❑ 153	Duane Ward RC *	.25	.10
❑ 154	Tom O'Malley	.05	.02

❑ 155 Eddie Whitson .05 .02
❑ 156 Mariners Team .05 .02
(Mound conference)
❑ 157 Danny Darwin .05 .02
❑ 158 Tim Teufel .05 .02
❑ 159 Ed Olwine .05 .02
❑ 160 Julio Franco .10 .04
❑ 161 Steve Ontiveros .05 .02
❑ 162 Mike LaValliere RC * .25 .10
❑ 163 Kevin Gross .05 .02
❑ 164 Sammy Khalifa .05 .02
❑ 165 Jeff Reardon .10 .04
❑ 166 Bob Boone .10 .04
❑ 167 Jim Deshaies RC * .10 .04
❑ 168 Lou Piniella MG .10 .04
❑ 169 Ron Washington .05 .02
❑ 170 Bo Jackson RC 3.00 1.20
❑ 171 Chuck Cary .05 .02
❑ 172 Ron Oester .05 .02
❑ 173 Alex Trevino .05 .02
❑ 174 Henry Cotto .05 .02
❑ 175 Bob Stanley .05 .02
❑ 176 Steve Buechele .05 .02
❑ 177 Keith Moreland .05 .02
❑ 178 Cecil Fielder .10 .04
❑ 179 Bill Wegman .05 .02
❑ 180 Chris Brown .05 .02
❑ 181 Cardinals Team .05 .02
(Mound conference)
❑ 182 Lee Lacy .05 .02
❑ 183 Andy Hawkins .05 .02
❑ 184 Bobby Bonilla RC .40 .16
❑ 185 Roger McDowell .05 .02
❑ 186 Bruce Benedict .05 .02
❑ 187 Mark Huismann .05 .02
❑ 188 Tony Phillips .05 .02
❑ 189 Joe Hesketh .05 .02
❑ 190 Jim Sundberg .10 .04
❑ 191 Charles Hudson .05 .02
❑ 192 Cory Snyder .05 .02
❑ 193 Roger Craig MG .10 .04
❑ 194 Kirk McCaskill .05 .02
❑ 195 Mike Pagliarulo .05 .02
❑ 196 Randy O'Neal UER .05 .02
(Wrong ML career
W-L totals)
❑ 197 Mark Bailey .05 .02
❑ 198 Lee Mazzilli .10 .04
❑ 199 Mariano Duncan .05 .02
❑ 200 Pete Rose .60 .24
❑ 201 John Cangelosi .05 .02
❑ 202 Ricky Wright .05 .02
❑ 203 Mike Kingery RC .10 .04
❑ 204 Sammy Stewart .05 .02
❑ 205 Graig Nettles .10 .04
❑ 206 Twins Team .05 .02
(Frank Viola and
Tim Laudner)
❑ 207 George Frazier .05 .02
❑ 208 John Shelby .05 .02
❑ 209 Rick Schu .05 .02
❑ 210 Lloyd Moseby .05 .02
❑ 211 John Morris .05 .02
❑ 212 Mike Fitzgerald .05 .02
❑ 213 Randy Myers RC .40 .16
❑ 214 Omar Moreno .05 .02
❑ 215 Mark Langston .05 .02
❑ 216 B.J. Surhoff RC .40 .16
❑ 217 Chris Codiroli .05 .02
❑ 218 Sparky Anderson MG .10 .04
❑ 219 Cecilio Guante .05 .02
❑ 220 Joe Carter .10 .04
❑ 221 Vern Ruhle .05 .02
❑ 222 Denny Walling .05 .02
❑ 223 Charlie Leibrandt .05 .02
❑ 224 Wayne Tolleson .05 .02
❑ 225 Mike Smithson .05 .02
❑ 226 Max Venable .05 .02
❑ 227 Jamie Moyer RC .50 .20
❑ 228 Curt Wilkerson .05 .02
❑ 229 Mike Birkbeck .10 .04
❑ 230 Don Baylor .10 .04
❑ 231 Giants Team .05 .02
(Bob Brenly and
Jim Gott)
❑ 232 Reggie Williams .05 .02
❑ 233 Russ Morman .05 .02
❑ 234 Pat Sheridan .05 .02
❑ 235 Alvin Davis .05 .02
❑ 236 Tommy John .10 .04
❑ 237 Jim Morrison .05 .02
❑ 238 Bill Krueger .05 .02
❑ 239 Juan Espino .05 .02
❑ 240 Steve Balboni .05 .02
❑ 241 Danny Heep .05 .02
❑ 242 Rick Mahler .05 .02
❑ 243 Whitey Herzog MG .10 .04
❑ 244 Dickie Noles .05 .02
❑ 245 Willie Upshaw .05 .02
❑ 246 Jim Dwyer .05 .02
❑ 247 Jeff Reed .05 .02
❑ 248 Gene Walter .05 .02
❑ 249 Jim Pankovits .05 .02
❑ 250 Teddy Higuera .05 .02
❑ 251 Rob Wilfong .05 .02
❑ 252 Dennis Martinez .10 .04
❑ 253 Eddie Milner .05 .02
❑ 254 Bob Tewksbury RC * .25 .10
❑ 255 Juan Samuel .05 .02
❑ 256 Royals Team .15 .06
(George Brett and
Frank White)
❑ 257 Bob Forsch .05 .02
❑ 258 Steve Yeager .10 .04
❑ 259 Mike Greenwell RC .25 .10
❑ 260 Vida Blue .10 .04
❑ 261 Ruben Sierra RC .50 .20
❑ 262 Jim Winn .05 .02
❑ 263 Stan Javier .05 .02
❑ 264 Checklist 133-264 .05 .02
❑ 265 Darrell Evans .10 .04
❑ 266 Jeff Hamilton .05 .02
❑ 267 Howard Johnson .10 .04
❑ 268 Pat Corrales MG .05 .02
❑ 269 Cliff Speck .05 .02
❑ 270 Jody Davis .05 .02
❑ 271 Mike G. Brown .05 .02
❑ 272 Andres Galarraga .10 .04
❑ 273 Gene Nelson .05 .02
❑ 274 Jeff Hearron UER .05 .02
(Duplicate 1986
stat line on back)
❑ 275 LaMarr Hoyt .05 .02
❑ 276 Jackie Gutierrez .05 .02
❑ 277 Juan Agosto .05 .02
❑ 278 Gary Pettis .05 .02
❑ 279 Dan Plesac .05 .02
❑ 280 Jeff Leonard .05 .02
❑ 281 Reds Team .25 .10
Pete Rose, Bo Diaz
and Bill Gullickson
❑ 282 Jeff Calhoun .05 .02
❑ 283 Doug Drabek RC* .40 .16
❑ 284 John Moses .05 .02
❑ 285 Dennis Boyd .05 .02
❑ 286 Mike Woodard .05 .02
❑ 287 Dave Von Ohlen .05 .02
❑ 288 Tito Landrum .05 .02
❑ 289 Bob Kipper .05 .02
❑ 290 Leon Durham .05 .02
❑ 291 Mitch Williams RC * .25 .10
❑ 292 Franklin Stubbs .05 .02
❑ 293 Bob Rodgers MG .05 .02
❑ 294 Steve Jeltz .05 .02
❑ 295 Len Dykstra .10 .04
❑ 296 Andres Thomas .05 .02
❑ 297 Don Schulze .05 .02
❑ 298 Larry Herndon .05 .02
❑ 299 Joel Davis .05 .02
❑ 300 Reggie Jackson .15 .06
❑ 301 Luis Aquino UER .05 .02
(No trademark
never corrected)
❑ 302 Bill Schroeder .05 .02
❑ 303 Juan Berenguer .05 .02
❑ 304 Phil Garner .10 .04
❑ 305 John Franco .10 .04
❑ 306 Red Sox Team .10 .04
(Tom Seaver,
John McNamara MG,
and Rich Gedman)
❑ 307 Lee Guetterman .05 .02
❑ 308 Don Slaught .05 .02
❑ 309 Mike Young .05 .02
❑ 310 Frank Viola .10 .04
❑ 311 Rickey Henderson .15 .06
TBC '82
❑ 312 Reggie Jackson .10 .04
TBC '77
❑ 313 Roberto Clemente .25 .10
TBC '72
❑ 314 Carl Yastrzemski UER .25 .10
TBC '67 (Sic, 112
RBI's on back)
❑ 315 Maury Wills TBC '62 .10 .04
❑ 316 Brian Fisher .05 .02
❑ 317 Clint Hurdle .05 .02
❑ 318 Jim Fregosi MG .05 .02
❑ 319 Greg Swindell RC .25 .10
❑ 320 Barry Bonds RC 10.00 4.00
❑ 321 Mike Laga .05 .02
❑ 322 Chris Bando .05 .02
❑ 323 Al Newman .05 .02
❑ 324 David Palmer .05 .02
❑ 325 Garry Templeton .10 .04
❑ 326 Mark Gubicza .05 .02
❑ 327 Dale Sveum .05 .02
❑ 328 Bob Welch .10 .04
❑ 329 Ron Roenicke .05 .02
❑ 330 Mike Scott .10 .04
❑ 331 Mets Team .10 .04
(Gary Carter and
Darryl Strawberry)
❑ 332 Joe Price .05 .02
❑ 333 Ken Phelps .05 .02
❑ 334 Ed Correa .05 .02
❑ 335 Candy Maldonado .05 .02
❑ 336 Allan Anderson .05 .02
❑ 337 Darrell Miller .05 .02
❑ 338 Tim Conroy .05 .02
❑ 339 Donnie Hill .05 .02
❑ 340 Roger Clemens .50 .20
❑ 341 Mike C. Brown .05 .02
❑ 342 Bob James .05 .02
❑ 343 Hal Lanier MG .05 .02
❑ 344A Joe Niekro .05 .02
(Copyright inside
righthand border)
❑ 344B Joe Niekro .05 .02
(Copyright outside
righthand border)
❑ 345 Andre Dawson .10 .04
❑ 346 Shawon Dunston .05 .02
❑ 347 Mickey Brantley .05 .02
❑ 348 Carmelo Martinez .05 .02
❑ 349 Storm Davis .05 .02
❑ 350 Keith Hernandez .10 .04
❑ 351 Gene Garber .05 .02
❑ 352 Mike Felder .05 .02
❑ 353 Ernie Camacho .05 .02
❑ 354 Jamie Quirk .05 .02
❑ 355 Don Carman .05 .02
❑ 356 White Sox Team .05 .02
(Mound conference)
❑ 357 Steve Fireovid .05 .02
❑ 358 Sal Butera .05 .02
❑ 359 Doug Corbett .05 .02
❑ 360 Pedro Guerrero .10 .04
❑ 361 Mark Thurmond .05 .02
❑ 362 Luis Quinones .05 .02
❑ 363 Jose Guzman .05 .02
❑ 364 Randy Bush .05 .02
❑ 365 Rick Rhoden .05 .02
❑ 366 Mark McGwire 4.00 1.60
❑ 367 Jeff Lahti .05 .02
❑ 368 John McNamara MG .05 .02
❑ 369 Brian Dayett .05 .02
❑ 370 Fred Lynn .10 .04
❑ 371 Mark Eichhorn .05 .02
❑ 372 Jerry Mumphrey .05 .02
❑ 373 Jeff Dedmon .05 .02
❑ 374 Glenn Hoffman .05 .02
❑ 375 Ron Guidry .10 .04
❑ 376 Scott Bradley .05 .02
❑ 377 John Henry Johnson .05 .02
❑ 378 Rafael Santana .05 .02
❑ 379 John Russell .05 .02
❑ 380 Rich Gossage .10 .04

381	Expos Team (Mound conference)	.05	.02
382	Rudy Law	.05	.02
383	Ron Davis	.05	.02
384	Johnny Grubb	.05	.02
385	Orel Hershiser	.15	.06
386	Dickie Thon	.05	.02
387	T.R. Bryden	.05	.02
388	Geno Petralli	.05	.02
389	Jeff D. Robinson	.05	.02
390	Gary Matthews	.10	.04
391	Jay Howell	.05	.02
392	Checklist 265-396	.05	.02
393	Pete Rose MG	.15	.06
394	Mike Bielecki	.05	.02
395	Damaso Garcia	.05	.02
396	Tim Lollar	.05	.02
397	Greg Walker	.05	.02
398	Brad Havens	.05	.02
399	Curt Ford	.05	.02
400	George Brett	.60	.24
401	Billy Joe Robidoux	.05	.02
402	Mike Trujillo	.05	.02
403	Jerry Royster	.05	.02
404	Doug Sisk	.05	.02
405	Brook Jacoby	.05	.02
406	Yankees Team (Rickey Henderson and Don Mattingly)	.50	.20
407	Jim Acker	.05	.02
408	John Mizerock	.05	.02
409	Milt Thompson	.05	.02
410	Fernando Valenzuela	.10	.04
411	Darnell Coles	.05	.02
412	Eric Davis	.15	.06
413	Moose Haas	.05	.02
414	Joe Orsulak	.05	.02
415	Bobby Witt RC	.25	.10
416	Tom Nieto	.05	.02
417	Pat Perry	.05	.02
418	Dick Williams MG	.05	.02
419	Mark Portugal RC *	.25	.10
420	Will Clark RC	1.00	.40
421	Jose DeLeon	.05	.02
422	Jack Howell	.05	.02
423	Jaime Cocanower	.05	.02
424	Chris Speier	.05	.02
425	Tom Seaver UER Earned Runs amount is wrong For 86 Red Sox and Career Also the ERA is wrong for 86 and career	.15	.06
426	Floyd Rayford	.05	.02
427	Edwin Nunez	.05	.02
428	Bruce Bochy	.05	.02
429	Tim Pyznarski	.05	.02
430	Mike Schmidt	.50	.20
431	Dodgers Team (Mound conference)	.05	.02
432	Jim Slaton	.05	.02
433	Ed Hearn	.05	.02
434	Mike Fischlin	.05	.02
435	Bruce Sutter	.10	.04
436	Andy Allanson	.05	.02
437	Ted Power	.05	.02
438	Kelly Downs RC	.10	.04
439	Karl Best	.05	.02
440	Willie McGee	.10	.04
441	Dave Leiper	.05	.02
442	Mitch Webster	.05	.02
443	John Felske MG	.05	.02
444	Jeff Russell	.05	.02
445	Dave Lopes	.10	.04
446	Chuck Finley RC	.40	.16
447	Bill Almon	.05	.02
448	Chris Bosio RC	.25	.10
449	Pat Dodson	.10	.04
450	Kirby Puckett	.25	.10
451	Joe Sambito	.05	.02
452	Dave Henderson	.05	.02
453	Scott Terry RC	.10	.04
454	Luis Salazar	.05	.02
455	Mike Boddicker	.05	.02
456	A's Team (Mound conference)	.05	.02
457	Len Matuszek	.05	.02
458	Kelly Gruber	.05	.02
459	Dennis Eckersley	.15	.06
460	Darryl Strawberry	.10	.04
461	Craig McMurtry	.05	.02
462	Scott Fletcher	.05	.02
463	Tom Candiotti	.05	.02
464	Butch Wynegar	.05	.02
465	Todd Worrell	.05	.02
466	Kal Daniels	.05	.02
467	Randy St.Claire	.05	.02
468	G.Bamberger MG	.05	.02
469	Mike Diaz	.05	.02
470	Dave Dravecky	.05	.02
471	Ronn Reynolds	.05	.02
472	Bill Doran	.05	.02
473	Steve Farr	.05	.02
474	Jerry Narron	.05	.02
475	Scott Garrelts	.05	.02
476	Danny Tartabull	.05	.02
477	Ken Howell	.05	.02
478	Tim Laudner	.05	.02
479	Bob Sebra	.05	.02
480	Jim Rice	.10	.04
481	Phillies Team (Glenn Wilson Juan Samuel and Von Hayes)	.05	.02
482	Daryl Boston	.05	.02
483	Dwight Lowry	.05	.02
484	Jim Traber	.05	.02
485	Tony Fernandez	.05	.02
486	Otis Nixon	.05	.02
487	Dave Gumpert	.05	.02
488	Ray Knight	.10	.04
489	Bill Gullickson	.05	.02
490	Dale Murphy	.15	.06
491	Ron Karkovice RC	.25	.10
492	Mike Heath	.05	.02
493	Tom Lasorda MG	.15	.06
494	Barry Jones	.05	.02
495	Gorman Thomas	.10	.04
496	Bruce Bochte	.05	.02
497	Dale Mohorcic	.05	.02
498	Bob Kearney	.05	.02
499	Bruce Ruffin RC	.10	.04
500	Don Mattingly	.60	.24
501	Craig Lefferts	.05	.02
502	Dick Schofield	.05	.02
503	Larry Andersen	.05	.02
504	Mickey Hatcher	.05	.02
505	Bryn Smith	.05	.02
506	Orioles Team (Mound conference)	.05	.02
507	Dave L. Stapleton	.05	.02
508	Scott Bankhead	.05	.02
509	Enos Cabell	.05	.02
510	Tom Henke	.05	.02
511	Steve Lyons	.05	.02
512	Dave Magadan RC	.25	.10
513	Carmen Castillo	.05	.02
514	Orlando Mercado	.05	.02
515	Willie Hernandez	.05	.02
516	Ted Simmons	.10	.04
517	Mario Soto	.10	.04
518	Gene Mauch MG	.05	.02
519	Curt Young	.05	.02
520	Jack Clark	.10	.04
521	Rick Reuschel	.10	.04
522	Checklist 397-528	.05	.02
523	Earnie Riles	.05	.02
524	Bob Shirley	.05	.02
525	Phil Bradley	.05	.02
526	Roger Mason	.05	.02
527	Jim Wohlford	.05	.02
528	Ken Dixon	.05	.02
529	Alvaro Espinoza RC	.10	.04
530	Tony Gwynn	.30	.12
531	Astros Team (Yogi Berra conference)	.10	.04
532	Jeff Stone	.05	.02
533	Angel Salazar	.05	.02
534	Scott Sanderson	.05	.02
535	Tony Armas	.10	.04
536	Terry Mulholland RC	.25	.10
537	Rance Mulliniks	.05	.02
538	Tom Niedenfuer	.05	.02
539	Reid Nichols	.05	.02
540	Terry Kennedy	.05	.02
541	Rafael Belliard RC	.25	.10
542	Ricky Horton	.05	.02
543	Dave Johnson MG	.05	.02
544	Zane Smith	.05	.02
545	Buddy Bell	.10	.04
546	Mike Morgan	.05	.02
547	Rob Deer	.05	.02
548	Bill Mooneyham	.05	.02
549	Bob Melvin	.05	.02
550	Pete Incaviglia RC *	.25	.10
551	Frank Wills	.05	.02
552	Larry Sheets	.05	.02
553	Mike Maddux	.05	.02
554	Buddy Biancalana	.05	.02
555	Dennis Rasmussen	.05	.02
556	Angels Team (Rene Lachemann CO, Mike Witt, and Bob Boone)	.05	.02
557	John Cerutti	.05	.02
558	Greg Gagne	.05	.02
559	Lance McCullers	.05	.02
560	Glenn Davis	.05	.02
561	Rey Quinones	.05	.02
562	Bryan Clutterbuck	.05	.02
563	John Stefero	.05	.02
564	Larry McWilliams	.05	.02
565	Dusty Baker	.10	.04
566	Tim Hulett	.05	.02
567	Greg Mathews	.05	.02
568	Earl Weaver MG	.10	.04
569	Wade Rowdon	.05	.02
570	Sid Fernandez	.05	.02
571	Ozzie Virgil	.05	.02
572	Pete Ladd	.05	.02
573	Hal McRae	.10	.04
574	Manny Lee	.05	.02
575	Pat Tabler	.05	.02
576	Frank Pastore	.05	.02
577	Dann Bilardello	.05	.02
578	Billy Hatcher	.05	.02
579	Rick Burleson	.05	.02
580	Mike Krukow	.05	.02
581	Cubs Team (Ron Cey and Steve Trout)	.05	.02
582	Bruce Berenyi	.05	.02
583	Junior Ortiz	.05	.02
584	Ron Kittle	.05	.02
585	Scott Bailes	.05	.02
586	Ben Oglivie	.10	.04
587	Eric Plunk	.05	.02
588	Wallace Johnson	.05	.02
589	Steve Crawford	.05	.02
590	Vince Coleman	.05	.02
591	Spike Owen	.05	.02
592	Chris Welsh	.05	.02
593	Chuck Tanner MG	.05	.02
594	Rick Anderson	.05	.02
595	Keith Hernandez AS	.05	.02
596	Steve Sax AS	.05	.02
597	Mike Schmidt AS	.25	.10
598	Ozzie Smith AS	.25	.10
599	Tony Gwynn AS	.15	.06
600	Dave Parker AS	.05	.02
601	Darryl Strawberry AS	.05	.02
602	Gary Carter AS	.05	.02
603A	D.Gooden AS ERR no trademark	.10	.04
603B	D.Gooden AS COR	.10	.04
604	F.Valenzuela AS	.05	.02
605	Todd Worrell AS	.05	.02
606	D.Mattingly AS COR	.30	.12
606A	Don Mattingly AS ERR (no trademark)	1.00	.40
607	Tony Bernazard AS	.05	.02
608	Wade Boggs AS	.10	.04
609	Cal Ripken AS	.25	.10
610	Jim Rice AS	.05	.02
611	Kirby Puckett AS	.15	.06
612	George Bell AS	.05	.02
613	Lance Parrish AS UER (Pitcher heading on back)	.05	.02

❑ 614 Roger Clemens AS .25 .10
❑ 615 Teddy Higuera AS .05 .02
❑ 616 Dave Righetti AS .05 .02
❑ 617 Al Nipper .05 .02
❑ 618 Tom Kelly MG .05 .02
❑ 619 Jerry Reed .05 .02
❑ 620 Jose Canseco 1.00 .40
❑ 621 Danny Cox .05 .02
❑ 622 Glenn Braggs RC .10 .04
❑ 623 Kurt Stillwell .05 .02
❑ 624 Tim Burke .05 .02
❑ 625 Mookie Wilson .10 .04
❑ 626 Joel Skinner .05 .02
❑ 627 Ken Oberkfell .05 .02
❑ 628 Bob Walk .05 .02
❑ 629 Larry Parrish .05 .02
❑ 630 John Candelaria .05 .02
❑ 631 Tigers Team .05 .02
(Mound conference)
❑ 632 Rob Woodward .05 .02
❑ 633 Jose Uribe .05 .02
❑ 634 Rafael Palmeiro RC 2.00 .80
❑ 635 Ken Schrom .05 .02
❑ 636 Darren Daulton .10 .04
❑ 637 Bip Roberts RC* .25 .10
❑ 638 Rich Bordi .05 .02
❑ 639 Gerald Perry .05 .02
❑ 640 Mark Clear .05 .02
❑ 641 Domingo Ramos .05 .02
❑ 642 Al Pulido .05 .02
❑ 643 Ron Shepherd .05 .02
❑ 644 John Denny .05 .02
❑ 645 Dwight Evans .15 .06
❑ 646 Mike Mason .05 .02
❑ 647 Tom Lawless .05 .02
❑ 648 Barry Larkin RC 1.00 .40
❑ 649 Mickey Tettleton .05 .02
❑ 650 Hubie Brooks .05 .02
❑ 651 Benny Distefano .05 .02
❑ 652 Terry Forster .10 .04
❑ 653 Kevin Mitchell RC * .40 .16
❑ 654 Checklist 529-660 .10 .04
❑ 655 Jesse Barfield .10 .04
❑ 656 Rangers Team .05 .02
(Bobby Valentine MG
and Ricky Wright)
❑ 657 Tom Waddell .05 .02
❑ 658 R.Thompson RC* .25 .10
❑ 659 Aurelio Lopez .05 .02
❑ 660 Bob Horner .10 .04
❑ 661 Lou Whitaker .10 .04
❑ 662 Frank DiPino .05 .02
❑ 663 Cliff Johnson .05 .02
❑ 664 Mike Marshall .05 .02
❑ 665 Rod Scurry .05 .02
❑ 666 Von Hayes .05 .02
❑ 667 Ron Hassey .05 .02
❑ 668 Juan Bonilla .05 .02
❑ 669 Bud Black .05 .02
❑ 670 Jose Cruz .10 .04
❑ 671A Ray Soff ERR .05 .02
(No D* before
copyright line)
❑ 671B Ray Soff COR .05 .02
(D* before
copyright line)
❑ 672 Chili Davis .10 .04
❑ 673 Don Sutton .10 .04
❑ 674 Bill Campbell .05 .02
❑ 675 Ed Romero .05 .02
❑ 676 Charlie Moore .05 .02
❑ 677 Bob Grich .10 .04
❑ 678 Carney Lansford .10 .04
❑ 679 Kent Hrbek .10 .04
❑ 680 Ryne Sandberg .40 .16
❑ 681 George Bell .10 .04
❑ 682 Jerry Reuss .05 .02
❑ 683 Gary Roenicke .05 .02
❑ 684 Kent Tekulve .05 .02
❑ 685 Jerry Hairston .05 .02
❑ 686 Doyle Alexander .05 .02
❑ 687 Alan Trammell .10 .04
❑ 688 Juan Beniquez .05 .02
❑ 689 Darrell Porter .05 .02
❑ 690 Dane Iorg .05 .02
❑ 691 Dave Parker .10 .04
❑ 692 Frank White .10 .04
❑ 693 Terry Puhl .05 .02
❑ 694 Phil Niekro .10 .04
❑ 695 Chico Walker .05 .02
❑ 696 Gary Lucas .05 .02
❑ 697 Ed Lynch .05 .02
❑ 698 Ernie Whitt .05 .02
❑ 699 Ken Landreaux .05 .02
❑ 700 Dave Bergman .05 .02
❑ 701 Willie Randolph .10 .04
❑ 702 Greg Gross .05 .02
❑ 703 Dave Schmidt .05 .02
❑ 704 Jesse Orosco .05 .02
❑ 705 Bruce Hurst .05 .02
❑ 706 Rick Manning .05 .02
❑ 707 Bob McClure .05 .02
❑ 708 Scott McGregor .05 .02
❑ 709 Dave Kingman .10 .04
❑ 710 Gary Gaetti .10 .04
❑ 711 Ken Griffey .10 .04
❑ 712 Don Robinson .05 .02
❑ 713 Tom Brookens .05 .02
❑ 714 Dan Quisenberry .05 .02
❑ 715 Bob Dernier .05 .02
❑ 716 Rick Leach .05 .02
❑ 717 Ed VandeBerg .05 .02
❑ 718 Steve Carlton .10 .04
❑ 719 Tom Hume .05 .02
❑ 720 Richard Dotson .05 .02
❑ 721 Tom Herr .05 .02
❑ 722 Bob Knepper .05 .02
❑ 723 Brett Butler .10 .04
❑ 724 Greg Minton .05 .02
❑ 725 George Hendrick .10 .04
❑ 726 Frank Tanana .10 .04
❑ 727 Mike Moore .05 .02
❑ 728 Tippy Martinez .05 .02
❑ 729 Tom Paciorek .05 .02
❑ 730 Eric Show .05 .02
❑ 731 Dave Concepcion .10 .04
❑ 732 Manny Trillo .05 .02
❑ 733 Bill Caudill .05 .02
❑ 734 Bill Madlock .10 .04
❑ 735 Rickey Henderson .25 .10
❑ 736 Steve Bedrosian .05 .02
❑ 737 Floyd Bannister .05 .02
❑ 738 Jorge Orta .05 .02
❑ 739 Chet Lemon .10 .04
❑ 740 Rich Gedman .05 .02
❑ 741 Paul Molitor .15 .06
❑ 742 Andy McGaffigan .05 .02
❑ 743 Dwayne Murphy .05 .02
❑ 744 Roy Smalley .05 .02
❑ 745 Glenn Hubbard .05 .02
❑ 746 Bob Ojeda .05 .02
❑ 747 Johnny Ray .05 .02
❑ 748 Mike Flanagan .05 .02
❑ 749 Ozzie Smith .40 .16
❑ 750 Steve Trout .05 .02
❑ 751 Garth Iorg .05 .02
❑ 752 Dan Petry .05 .02
❑ 753 Rick Honeycutt .05 .02
❑ 754 Dave LaPoint .05 .02
❑ 755 Luis Aguayo .05 .02
❑ 756 Carlton Fisk .15 .06
❑ 757 Nolan Ryan 1.00 .40
❑ 758 Tony Bernazard .05 .02
❑ 759 Joel Youngblood .05 .02
❑ 760 Mike Witt .05 .02
❑ 761 Greg Pryor .05 .02
❑ 762 Gary Ward .05 .02
❑ 763 Tim Flannery .05 .02
❑ 764 Bill Buckner .10 .04
❑ 765 Kirk Gibson .15 .06
❑ 766 Don Aase .05 .02
❑ 767 Ron Cey .10 .04
❑ 768 Dennis Lamp .05 .02
❑ 769 Steve Sax .05 .02
❑ 770 Dave Winfield .10 .04
❑ 771 Shane Rawley .05 .02
❑ 772 Harold Baines .10 .04
❑ 773 Robin Yount .40 .16
❑ 774 Wayne Krenchicki .05 .02
❑ 775 Joaquin Andujar .10 .04
❑ 776 Tom Brunansky .05 .02
❑ 777 Chris Chambliss .10 .04
❑ 778 Jack Morris .10 .04
❑ 779 Craig Reynolds .05 .02
❑ 780 Andre Thornton .05 .02
❑ 781 Atlee Hammaker .05 .02
❑ 782 Brian Downing .10 .04
❑ 783 Willie Wilson .10 .04
❑ 784 Cal Ripken .75 .30
❑ 785 Terry Francona .10 .04
❑ 786 Jimy Williams MG .05 .02
❑ 787 Alejandro Pena .05 .02
❑ 788 Tim Stoddard .05 .02
❑ 789 Dan Schatzeder .05 .02
❑ 790 Julio Cruz .05 .02
❑ 791 Lance Parrish .10 .04
❑ 792 Checklist 661-792 .05 .02

1987 Topps Traded

	Nm-Mt	Ex-Mt
COMP.FACT.SET (132)	10.00	4.00

❑ 1T Bill Almon .05 .02
❑ 2T Scott Bankhead .05 .02
❑ 3T Eric Bell .10 .04
❑ 4T Juan Beniquez .05 .02
❑ 5T Juan Berenguer .05 .02
❑ 6T Greg Booker .05 .02
❑ 7T Thad Bosley .05 .02
❑ 8T Larry Bowa MG .10 .04
❑ 9T Greg Brock .05 .02
❑ 10T Bob Brower .05 .02
❑ 11T Jerry Browne .10 .04
❑ 12T Ralph Bryant .05 .02
❑ 13T DeWayne Buice .05 .02
❑ 14T Ellis Burks XRC .50 .20
❑ 15T Ivan Calderon .05 .02
❑ 16T Jeff Calhoun .05 .02
❑ 17T Casey Candaele .05 .02
❑ 18T John Cangelosi .05 .02
❑ 19T Steve Carlton .10 .04
❑ 20T Juan Castillo .10 .04
❑ 21T Rick Cerone .05 .02
❑ 22T Ron Cey .10 .04
❑ 23T John Christensen .05 .02
❑ 24T David Cone XRC .75 .30
❑ 25T Chuck Crim .05 .02
❑ 26T Storm Davis .05 .02
❑ 27T Andre Dawson .10 .04
❑ 28T Rick Dempsey .05 .02
❑ 29T Doug Drabek .50 .20
❑ 30T Mike Dunne .05 .02
❑ 31T Dennis Eckersley .15 .06
❑ 32T Lee Elia MG .05 .02
❑ 33T Brian Fisher .05 .02
❑ 34T Terry Francona .10 .04
❑ 35T Willie Fraser .10 .04
❑ 36T Billy Gardner MG .05 .02
❑ 37T Ken Gerhart .05 .02
❑ 38T Dan Gladden .05 .02
❑ 39T Jim Gott .05 .02
❑ 40T Cecilio Guante .05 .02
❑ 41T Albert Hall .05 .02
❑ 42T Terry Harper .05 .02
❑ 43T Mickey Hatcher .05 .02
❑ 44T Brad Havens .05 .02
❑ 45T Neal Heaton .05 .02
❑ 46T Mike Henneman XRC .25 .10
❑ 47T Donnie Hill .05 .02

❑ 48T Guy Hoffman .05 .02
❑ 49T Brian Holton .05 .02
❑ 50T Charles Hudson .05 .02
❑ 51T Danny Jackson .05 .02
❑ 52T Reggie Jackson .15 .06
❑ 53T Chris James XRC * .10 .04
❑ 54T Dion James .05 .02
❑ 55T Stan Jefferson .05 .02
❑ 56T Joe Johnson .05 .02
❑ 57T Terry Kennedy .05 .02
❑ 58T Mike Kingery .10 .04
❑ 59T Ray Knight .10 .04
❑ 60T Gene Larkin XRC .25 .10
❑ 61T Mike LaValliere .25 .10
❑ 62T Jack Lazorko .05 .02
❑ 63T Terry Leach .05 .02
❑ 64T Tim Leary .05 .02
❑ 65T Jim Lindeman .10 .04
❑ 66T Steve Lombardozzi .05 .02
❑ 67T Bill Long .05 .02
❑ 68T Barry Lyons .05 .02
❑ 69T Shane Mack .05 .02
❑ 70T Greg Maddux XRC 5.00 2.00
❑ 71T Bill Madlock .10 .04
❑ 72T Joe Magrane XRC .10 .04
❑ 73T Dave Martinez XRC * .25 .10
❑ 74T Fred McGriff .60 .24
❑ 75T Mark McLemore .10 .04
❑ 76T Kevin McReynolds .05 .02
❑ 77T Dave Meads .05 .02
❑ 78T Eddie Milner .05 .02
❑ 79T Greg Minton .05 .02
❑ 80T John Mitchell XRC .10 .04
❑ 81T Kevin Mitchell .15 .06
❑ 82T Charlie Moore .05 .02
❑ 83T Jeff Musselman .05 .02
❑ 84T Gene Nelson .05 .02
❑ 85T Graig Nettles .10 .04
❑ 86T Al Newman .05 .02
❑ 87T Reid Nichols .05 .02
❑ 88T Tom Niedenfuer .05 .02
❑ 89T Joe Niekro .05 .02
❑ 90T Tom Nieto .05 .02
❑ 91T Matt Nokes XRC .25 .10
❑ 92T Dickie Noles .05 .02
❑ 93T Pat Pacillo .05 .02
❑ 94T Lance Parrish .10 .04
❑ 95T Tony Pena .05 .02
❑ 96T Luis Polonia XRC .25 .10
❑ 97T Randy Ready .05 .02
❑ 98T Jeff Reardon .10 .04
❑ 99T Gary Redus .05 .02
❑ 100T Jeff Reed .05 .02
❑ 101T Rick Rhoden .05 .02
❑ 102T Cal Ripken Sr. MG .05 .02
❑ 103T Wally Ritchie .05 .02
❑ 104T Jeff M. Robinson .05 .02
❑ 105T Gary Roenicke .05 .02
❑ 106T Jerry Royster .05 .02
❑ 107T Mark Salas .05 .02
❑ 108T Luis Salazar .05 .02
❑ 109T Benny Santiago .10 .04
❑ 110T Dave Schmidt .05 .02
❑ 111T Kevin Seitzer XRC* .25 .10
❑ 112T John Shelby .05 .02
❑ 113T Steve Shields .05 .02
❑ 114T John Smiley XRC .25 .10
❑ 115T Chris Speier .05 .02
❑ 116T Mike Stanley XRC* .25 .10
❑ 117T Terry Steinbach XRC .50 .20
❑ 118T Les Straker .05 .02
❑ 119T Jim Sundberg .10 .04
❑ 120T Danny Tartabull .05 .02
❑ 121T Tom Trebelhorn MG .05 .02
❑ 122T Dave Valle XRC ** .10 .04
❑ 123T Ed VandeBerg .05 .02
❑ 124T Andy Van Slyke .15 .06
❑ 125T Gary Ward .05 .02
❑ 126T Alan Wiggins .05 .02
❑ 127T Bill Wilkinson .05 .02
❑ 128T Frank Williams .05 .02
❑ 129T Matt Williams XRC 1.00 .40
❑ 130T Jim Winn .05 .02
❑ 131T Matt Young .05 .02
❑ 132T Checklist 1T-132T .05 .02

1988 Topps

	Nm-Mt	Ex-Mt
COMPLETE SET (792)	15.00	6.00
COMP.FACT SET (792)	15.00	6.00
COMP.X-MAS.SET (792)	40.00	16.00

❑ 1 Vince Coleman RB .05 .02
❑ 2 Don Mattingly RB .30 .12
❑ 3 Mark McGwire RB .75 .30
Rookie Homer Record
(No white spot)
❑ 3A Mark McGwire RB .20 .08
Rookie Homer Record
(White spot behind
left foot)
❑ 4 Eddie Murray RB .15 .06
Switch Home Runs,
Two Straight Games
(No caption on front)
❑ 4A Eddie Murray RB .50 .20
Switch Home Runs,
Two Straight Games
(Caption in box
on card front)
❑ 5 Phil Niekro .10 .04
Joe Niekro RB
❑ 6 Nolan Ryan RB .40 .16
❑ 7 Benito Santiago RB .05 .02
❑ 8 Kevin Elster .05 .02
❑ 9 Andy Hawkins .05 .02
❑ 10 Ryne Sandberg .40 .16
❑ 11 Mike Young .05 .02
❑ 12 Bill Schroeder .05 .02
❑ 13 Andres Thomas .05 .02
❑ 14 Sparky Anderson MG .10 .04
❑ 15 Chili Davis .10 .04
❑ 16 Kirk McCaskill .05 .02
❑ 17 Ron Oester .05 .02
❑ 18A Al Leiter RC ERR .50 .20
(Photo actually
Steve George,
right ear visible)
❑ 18B Al Leiter RC COR .50 .20
(Left ear visible)
❑ 19 Mark Davidson .05 .02
❑ 20 Kevin Gross .05 .02
❑ 21 Wade Boggs .10 .04
Spike Owen TL
❑ 22 Greg Swindell .05 .02
❑ 23 Ken Landreaux .05 .02
❑ 24 Jim Deshaies .05 .02
❑ 25 Andres Galarraga .10 .04
❑ 26 Mitch Williams .05 .02
❑ 27 R.J. Reynolds .05 .02
❑ 28 Jose Nunez .05 .02
❑ 29 Angel Salazar .05 .02
❑ 30 Sid Fernandez .05 .02
❑ 31 Bruce Bochy .05 .02
❑ 32 Mike Morgan .05 .02
❑ 33 Rob Deer .05 .02
❑ 34 Ricky Horton .05 .02
❑ 35 Harold Baines .10 .04
❑ 36 Jamie Moyer .10 .04
❑ 37 Ed Romero .05 .02
❑ 38 Jeff Calhoun .05 .02
❑ 39 Gerald Perry .05 .02
❑ 40 Orel Hershiser .10 .04
❑ 41 Bob Melvin .05 .02

❑ 42 Bill Landrum .05 .02
❑ 43 Dick Schofield .05 .02
❑ 44 Lou Piniella MG .10 .04
❑ 45 Kent Hrbek .10 .04
❑ 46 Darnell Coles .05 .02
❑ 47 Joaquin Andujar .10 .04
❑ 48 Alan Ashby .05 .02
❑ 49 Dave Clark .05 .02
❑ 50 Hubie Brooks .05 .02
❑ 51 Eddie Murray .40 .16
Cal Ripken TL
❑ 52 Don Robinson .05 .02
❑ 53 Curt Wilkerson .05 .02
❑ 54 Jim Clancy .05 .02
❑ 55 Phil Bradley .05 .02
❑ 56 Ed Hearn .05 .02
❑ 57 Tim Crews RC .25 .10
❑ 58 Dave Magadan .05 .02
❑ 59 Danny Cox .05 .02
❑ 60 Rickey Henderson .20 .08
❑ 61 Mark Knudson .05 .02
❑ 62 Jeff Hamilton .05 .02
❑ 63 Jimmy Jones .05 .02
❑ 64 Ken Caminiti RC 2.00 .80
❑ 65 Leon Durham .05 .02
❑ 66 Shane Rawley .05 .02
❑ 67 Ken Oberkfell .05 .02
❑ 68 Dave Dravecky .05 .02
❑ 69 Mike Hart .05 .02
❑ 70 Roger Clemens .50 .20
❑ 71 Gary Pettis .05 .02
❑ 72 Dennis Eckersley .15 .06
❑ 73 Randy Bush .05 .02
❑ 74 Tom Lasorda MG .15 .06
❑ 75 Joe Carter .10 .04
❑ 76 Dennis Martinez .10 .04
❑ 77 Tom O'Malley .05 .02
❑ 78 Dan Petry .05 .02
❑ 79 Ernie Whitt .05 .02
❑ 80 Mark Langston .05 .02
❑ 81 Ron Robinson .05 .02
John Franco TL
❑ 82 Darrel Akerfelds .05 .02
❑ 83 Jose Oquendo .05 .02
❑ 84 Cecilio Guante .05 .02
❑ 85 Howard Johnson .10 .04
❑ 86 Ron Karkovice .05 .02
❑ 87 Mike Mason .05 .02
❑ 88 Earnie Riles .05 .02
❑ 89 Gary Thurman .05 .02
❑ 90 Dale Murphy .15 .06
❑ 91 Joey Cora RC .25 .10
❑ 92 Len Matuszek .05 .02
❑ 93 Bob Sebra .05 .02
❑ 94 Chuck Jackson .05 .02
❑ 95 Lance Parrish .10 .04
❑ 96 Todd Benzinger RC* .25 .10
❑ 97 Scott Garrelts .05 .02
❑ 98 Rene Gonzales RC .10 .04
❑ 99 Chuck Finley .10 .04
❑ 100 Jack Clark .10 .04
❑ 101 Allan Anderson .05 .02
❑ 102 Barry Larkin .15 .06
❑ 103 Curt Young .05 .02
❑ 104 Dick Williams MG .05 .02
❑ 105 Jesse Orosco .05 .02
❑ 106 Jim Walewander .05 .02
❑ 107 Scott Bailes .05 .02
❑ 108 Steve Lyons .05 .02
❑ 109 Joel Skinner .05 .02
❑ 110 Teddy Higuera .05 .02
❑ 111 Hubie Brooks .05 .02
Vance Law TL
❑ 112 Les Lancaster .05 .02
❑ 113 Kelly Gruber .05 .02
❑ 114 Jeff Russell .05 .02
❑ 115 Johnny Ray .05 .02
❑ 116 Jerry Don Gleaton .05 .02
❑ 117 James Steels .05 .02
❑ 118 Bob Welch .10 .04
❑ 119 Robbie Wine .05 .02
❑ 120 Kirby Puckett .20 .08
❑ 121 Checklist 1-132 .05 .02
❑ 122 Tony Bernazard .05 .02
❑ 123 Tom Candiotti .05 .02
❑ 124 Ray Knight .10 .04

❑ 125 Bruce Hurst .05 .02
❑ 126 Steve Jeltz .05 .02
❑ 127 Jim Gott .05 .02
❑ 128 Johnny Grubb .05 .02
❑ 129 Greg Minton .05 .02
❑ 130 Buddy Bell .10 .04
❑ 131 Don Schulze .05 .02
❑ 132 Donnie Hill .05 .02
❑ 133 Greg Mathews .05 .02
❑ 134 Chuck Tanner MG .05 .02
❑ 135 Dennis Rasmussen .05 .02
❑ 136 Brian Dayett .05 .02
❑ 137 Chris Bosio .05 .02
❑ 138 Mitch Webster .05 .02
❑ 139 Jerry Browne .05 .02
❑ 140 Jesse Barfield .10 .04
❑ 141 George Brett .20 .08
Bret Saberhagen TL
❑ 142 Andy Van Slyke .15 .06
❑ 143 Mickey Tettleton .05 .02
❑ 144 Don Gordon .05 .02
❑ 145 Bill Madlock .10 .04
❑ 146 Donell Nixon .05 .02
❑ 147 Bill Buckner .10 .04
❑ 148 Carmelo Martinez .05 .02
❑ 149 Ken Howell .05 .02
❑ 150 Eric Davis .10 .04
❑ 151 Bob Knepper .05 .02
❑ 152 Jody Reed RC .25 .10
❑ 153 John Habyan .05 .02
❑ 154 Jeff Stone .05 .02
❑ 155 Bruce Sutter .10 .04
❑ 156 Gary Matthews .10 .04
❑ 157 Atlee Hammaker .05 .02
❑ 158 Tim Hulett .05 .02
❑ 159 Brad Arnsberg .05 .02
❑ 160 Willie McGee .10 .04
❑ 161 Bryn Smith .05 .02
❑ 162 Mark McLemore .05 .02
❑ 163 Dale Mohorcic .05 .02
❑ 164 Dave Johnson MG .05 .02
❑ 165 Robin Yount .30 .12
❑ 166 Rick Rodriquez .05 .02
❑ 167 Rance Mulliniks .05 .02
❑ 168 Barry Jones .05 .02
❑ 169 Ross Jones .05 .02
❑ 170 Rich Gossage .10 .04
❑ 171 Shawon Dunston .05 .02
Manny Trillo TL
❑ 172 Lloyd McClendon RC .25 .10
❑ 173 Eric Plunk .05 .02
❑ 174 Phil Garner .10 .04
❑ 175 Kevin Bass .05 .02
❑ 176 Jeff Reed .05 .02
❑ 177 Frank Tanana .10 .04
❑ 178 Dwayne Henry .05 .02
❑ 179 Charlie Puleo .05 .02
❑ 180 Terry Kennedy .05 .02
❑ 181 David Cone .10 .04
❑ 182 Ken Phelps .05 .02
❑ 183 Tom Lawless .05 .02
❑ 184 Ivan Calderon .05 .02
❑ 185 Rick Rhoden .05 .02
❑ 186 Rafael Palmeiro .40 .16
❑ 187 Steve Kiefer .05 .02
❑ 188 John Russell .05 .02
❑ 189 Wes Gardner .05 .02
❑ 190 Candy Maldonado .05 .02
❑ 191 John Cerutti .05 .02
❑ 192 Devon White .10 .04
❑ 193 Brian Fisher .05 .02
❑ 194 Tom Kelly MG .05 .02
❑ 195 Dan Quisenberry .05 .02
❑ 196 Dave Engle .05 .02
❑ 197 Lance McCullers .05 .02
❑ 198 Franklin Stubbs .05 .02
❑ 199 Dave Meads .05 .02
❑ 200 Wade Boggs .15 .06
❑ 201 Bobby Valentine MG .05 .02
Pete O'Brien
Pete Incaviglia
Steve Buechele TL
❑ 202 Glenn Hoffman .05 .02
❑ 203 Fred Toliver .05 .02
❑ 204 Paul O'Neill .15 .06
❑ 205 Nelson Liriano .05 .02
❑ 206 Domingo Ramos .05 .02
❑ 207 John Mitchell RC .10 .04
❑ 208 Steve Lake .05 .02
❑ 209 Richard Dotson .05 .02
❑ 210 Willie Randolph .10 .04
❑ 211 Frank DiPino .05 .02
❑ 212 Greg Brock .05 .02
❑ 213 Albert Hall .05 .02
❑ 214 Dave Schmidt .05 .02
❑ 215 Von Hayes .05 .02
❑ 216 Jerry Reuss .05 .02
❑ 217 Harry Spilman .05 .02
❑ 218 Dan Schatzeder .05 .02
❑ 219 Mike Stanley .05 .02
❑ 220 Tom Henke .05 .02
❑ 221 Rafael Belliard .05 .02
❑ 222 Steve Farr .05 .02
❑ 223 Stan Jefferson .05 .02
❑ 224 Tom Trebelhorn MG .05 .02
❑ 225 Mike Scioscia .10 .04
❑ 226 Dave Lopes .10 .04
❑ 227 Ed Correa .05 .02
❑ 228 Wallace Johnson .05 .02
❑ 229 Jeff Musselman .05 .02
❑ 230 Pat Tabler .05 .02
❑ 231 Barry Bonds 1.00 .40
Bobby Bonilla TL
❑ 232 Bob James .05 .02
❑ 233 Rafael Santana .05 .02
❑ 234 Ken Dayley .05 .02
❑ 235 Gary Ward .05 .02
❑ 236 Ted Power .05 .02
❑ 237 Mike Heath .05 .02
❑ 238 Luis Polonia RC* .25 .10
❑ 239 Roy Smalley .05 .02
❑ 240 Lee Smith .10 .04
❑ 241 Damaso Garcia .05 .02
❑ 242 Tom Niedenfuer .05 .02
❑ 243 Mark Ryal .05 .02
❑ 244 Jeff D. Robinson .05 .02
❑ 245 Rich Gedman .05 .02
❑ 246 Mike Campbell .05 .02
❑ 247 Thad Bosley .05 .02
❑ 248 Storm Davis .05 .02
❑ 249 Mike Marshall .05 .02
❑ 250 Nolan Ryan 1.00 .40
❑ 251 Tom Foley .05 .02
❑ 252 Bob Brower .05 .02
❑ 253 Checklist 133-264 .05 .02
❑ 254 Lee Elia MG .05 .02
❑ 255 Mookie Wilson .10 .04
❑ 256 Ken Schrom .05 .02
❑ 257 Jerry Royster .05 .02
❑ 258 Ed Nunez .05 .02
❑ 259 Ron Kittle .05 .02
❑ 260 Vince Coleman .05 .02
❑ 261 Giants TL .05 .02
(Five players)
❑ 262 Drew Hall .05 .02
❑ 263 Glenn Braggs .05 .02
❑ 264 Les Straker .05 .02
❑ 265 Bo Diaz .05 .02
❑ 266 Paul Assenmacher .05 .02
❑ 267 Billy Bean RC .10 .04
❑ 268 Bruce Ruffin .05 .02
❑ 269 Ellis Burks RC .40 .16
❑ 270 Mike Witt .05 .02
❑ 271 Ken Gerhart .05 .02
❑ 272 Steve Ontiveros .05 .02
❑ 273 Garth Iorg .05 .02
❑ 274 Junior Ortiz .05 .02
❑ 275 Kevin Seitzer .05 .02
❑ 276 Luis Salazar .05 .02
❑ 277 Alejandro Pena .05 .02
❑ 278 Jose Cruz .10 .04
❑ 279 Randy St.Claire .05 .02
❑ 280 Pete Incaviglia .05 .02
❑ 281 Jerry Hairston .05 .02
❑ 282 Pat Perry .05 .02
❑ 283 Phil Lombardi .05 .02
❑ 284 Larry Bowa MG .10 .04
❑ 285 Jim Presley .05 .02
❑ 286 Chuck Crim .05 .02
❑ 287 Manny Trillo .05 .02
❑ 288 Pat Pacillo .05 .02
(Chris Sabo in
background of photo)
❑ 289 Dave Bergman .05 .02
❑ 290 Tony Fernandez .05 .02
❑ 291 Billy Hatcher .05 .02
Kevin Bass TL
❑ 292 Carney Lansford .10 .04
❑ 293 Doug Jones RC .25 .10
❑ 294 Al Pedrique .05 .02
❑ 295 Bert Blyleven .10 .04
❑ 296 Floyd Rayford .05 .02
❑ 297 Zane Smith .05 .02
❑ 298 Milt Thompson .05 .02
❑ 299 Steve Crawford .05 .02
❑ 300 Don Mattingly .60 .24
❑ 301 Bud Black .05 .02
❑ 302 Jose Uribe .05 .02
❑ 303 Eric Show .05 .02
❑ 304 George Hendrick .10 .04
❑ 305 Steve Sax .05 .02
❑ 306 Billy Hatcher .05 .02
❑ 307 Mike Trujillo .05 .02
❑ 308 Lee Mazzilli .10 .04
❑ 309 Bill Long .05 .02
❑ 310 Tom Herr .05 .02
❑ 311 Scott Sanderson .05 .02
❑ 312 Joey Meyer .05 .02
❑ 313 Bob McClure .05 .02
❑ 314 Jimy Williams MG .05 .02
❑ 315 Dave Parker .10 .04
❑ 316 Jose Rijo .10 .04
❑ 317 Tom Nieto .05 .02
❑ 318 Mel Hall .05 .02
❑ 319 Mike Loynd .05 .02
❑ 320 Alan Trammell .10 .04
❑ 321 Harold Baines .10 .04
Carlton Fisk TL
❑ 322 Vicente Palacios .05 .02
❑ 323 Rick Leach .05 .02
❑ 324 Danny Jackson .05 .02
❑ 325 Glenn Hubbard .05 .02
❑ 326 Al Nipper .05 .02
❑ 327 Larry Sheets .05 .02
❑ 328 Greg Cadaret .05 .02
❑ 329 Chris Speier .05 .02
❑ 330 Eddie Whitson .05 .02
❑ 331 Brian Downing .10 .04
❑ 332 Jerry Reed .05 .02
❑ 333 Wally Backman .05 .02
❑ 334 Dave LaPoint .05 .02
❑ 335 Claudell Washington .05 .02
❑ 336 Ed Lynch .05 .02
❑ 337 Jim Gantner .05 .02
❑ 338 Brian Holton UER .05 .02
1987 ERA .389,
should be 3.89
❑ 339 Kurt Stillwell .05 .02
❑ 340 Jack Morris .10 .04
❑ 341 Carmen Castillo .05 .02
❑ 342 Larry Andersen .05 .02
❑ 343 Greg Gagne .05 .02
❑ 344 Tony LaRussa MG .10 .04
❑ 345 Scott Fletcher .05 .02
❑ 346 Vance Law .05 .02
❑ 347 Joe Johnson .05 .02
❑ 348 Jim Eisenreich .05 .02
❑ 349 Bob Walk .05 .02
❑ 350 Will Clark .20 .08
❑ 351 Red Schoendienst CO .10 .04
Tony Pena TL
❑ 352 Bill Ripken RC* .05 .02
❑ 353 Ed Olwine .05 .02
❑ 354 Marc Sullivan .05 .02
❑ 355 Roger McDowell .05 .02
❑ 356 Luis Aguayo .05 .02
❑ 357 Floyd Bannister .05 .02
❑ 358 Rey Quinones .05 .02
❑ 359 Tim Stoddard .05 .02
❑ 360 Tony Gwynn .30 .12
❑ 361 Greg Maddux 1.00 .40
❑ 362 Juan Castillo .05 .02
❑ 363 Willie Fraser .05 .02
❑ 364 Nick Esasky .05 .02
❑ 365 Floyd Youmans .05 .02
❑ 366 Chet Lemon .10 .04
❑ 367 Tim Leary .05 .02
❑ 368 Gerald Young .05 .02

❑ 369 Greg Harris .05 .02
❑ 370 Jose Canseco .50 .20
❑ 371 Joe Hesketh .05 .02
❑ 372 Matt Williams RC .75 .30
❑ 373 Checklist 265-396 .05 .02
❑ 374 Doc Edwards MG .05 .02
❑ 375 Tom Brunansky .05 .02
❑ 376 Bill Wilkinson .05 .02
❑ 377 Sam Horn RC .10 .04
❑ 378 Todd Frohwirth .05 .02
❑ 379 Rafael Ramirez .05 .02
❑ 380 Joe Magrane RC* .05 .02
❑ 381 Wally Joyner .10 .04
Jack Howell TL
❑ 382 Keith A. Miller RC .25 .10
❑ 383 Eric Bell .05 .02
❑ 384 Neil Allen .05 .02
❑ 385 Carlton Fisk .15 .06
❑ 386 Don Mattingly AS .30 .12
❑ 387 Willie Randolph AS .05 .02
❑ 388 Wade Boggs AS .10 .04
❑ 389 Alan Trammell AS .05 .02
❑ 390 George Bell AS .05 .02
❑ 391 Kirby Puckett AS .15 .06
❑ 392 Dave Winfield AS .05 .02
❑ 393 Matt Nokes AS .05 .02
❑ 394 Roger Clemens AS .20 .08
❑ 395 Jimmy Key AS .05 .02
❑ 396 Tom Henke AS .05 .02
❑ 397 Jack Clark AS .05 .02
❑ 398 Juan Samuel AS .05 .02
❑ 399 Tim Wallach AS .05 .02
❑ 400 Ozzie Smith AS .20 .08
❑ 401 Andre Dawson AS .05 .02
❑ 402 Tony Gwynn AS .15 .06
❑ 403 Tim Raines AS .05 .02
❑ 404 Benny Santiago AS .05 .02
❑ 405 Dwight Gooden AS .05 .02
❑ 406 Shane Rawley AS .05 .02
❑ 407 Steve Bedrosian AS .05 .02
❑ 408 Dion James .05 .02
❑ 409 Joel McKeon .05 .02
❑ 410 Tony Pena .05 .02
❑ 411 Wayne Tolleson .05 .02
❑ 412 Randy Myers .10 .04
❑ 413 John Christensen .05 .02
❑ 414 John McNamara MG .05 .02
❑ 415 Don Carman .05 .02
❑ 416 Keith Moreland .05 .02
❑ 417 Mark Ciardi .05 .02
❑ 418 Joel Youngblood .05 .02
❑ 419 Scott McGregor .05 .02
❑ 420 Wally Joyner .10 .04
❑ 421 Ed VandeBerg .05 .02
❑ 422 Dave Concepcion .10 .04
❑ 423 John Smiley RC* .25 .10
❑ 424 Dwayne Murphy .05 .02
❑ 425 Jeff Reardon .10 .04
❑ 426 Randy Ready .05 .02
❑ 427 Paul Kilgus .05 .02
❑ 428 John Shelby .05 .02
❑ 429 Alan Trammell .10 .04
Kirk Gibson TL
❑ 430 Glenn Davis .05 .02
❑ 431 Casey Candaele .05 .02
❑ 432 Mike Moore .05 .02
❑ 433 Bill Pecota RC* .05 .02
❑ 434 Rick Aguilera .05 .02
❑ 435 Mike Pagliarulo .05 .02
❑ 436 Mike Bielecki .05 .02
❑ 437 Fred Manrique .05 .02
❑ 438 Rob Ducey .05 .02
❑ 439 Dave Martinez .05 .02
❑ 440 Steve Bedrosian .05 .02
❑ 441 Rick Manning .05 .02
❑ 442 Tom Bolton .05 .02
❑ 443 Ken Griffey .10 .04
❑ 444 C.Ripken Sr. MG UER .05 .02
two copyrights
❑ 445 Mike Krukow .05 .02
❑ 446 Doug DeCinces .05 .02
(Now with Cardinals
on card front)
❑ 447 Jeff Montgomery RC .25 .10
❑ 448 Mike Davis .05 .02
❑ 449 Jeff M. Robinson .05 .02
❑ 450 Barry Bonds 2.00 .80
❑ 451 Keith Atherton .05 .02
❑ 452 Willie Wilson .10 .04
❑ 453 Dennis Powell .05 .02
❑ 454 Marvell Wynne .05 .02
❑ 455 Shawn Hillegas .05 .02
❑ 456 Dave Anderson .05 .02
❑ 457 Terry Leach .05 .02
❑ 458 Ron Hassey .05 .02
❑ 459 Dave Winfield .05 .02
Willie Randolph TL
❑ 460 Ozzie Smith .30 .12
❑ 461 Danny Darwin .05 .02
❑ 462 Don Slaught .05 .02
❑ 463 Fred McGriff .20 .08
❑ 464 Jay Tibbs .05 .02
❑ 465 Paul Molitor .15 .06
❑ 466 Jerry Mumphrey .05 .02
❑ 467 Don Aase .05 .02
❑ 468 Darren Daulton .10 .04
❑ 469 Jeff Dedmon .05 .02
❑ 470 Dwight Evans .15 .06
❑ 471 Donnie Moore .05 .02
❑ 472 Robby Thompson .05 .02
❑ 473 Joe Niekro .05 .02
❑ 474 Tom Brookens .05 .02
❑ 475 Pete Rose MG .50 .20
❑ 476 Dave Stewart .10 .04
❑ 477 Jamie Quirk .05 .02
❑ 478 Sid Bream .05 .02
❑ 479 Brett Butler .10 .04
❑ 480 Dwight Gooden .10 .04
❑ 481 Mariano Duncan .05 .02
❑ 482 Mark Davis .05 .02
❑ 483 Rod Booker .05 .02
❑ 484 Pat Clements .05 .02
❑ 485 Harold Reynolds .10 .04
❑ 486 Pat Keedy .05 .02
❑ 487 Jim Pankovits .05 .02
❑ 488 Andy McGaffigan .05 .02
❑ 489 Pedro Guerrero .05 .02
Fernando Valenzuela TL
❑ 490 Larry Parrish .05 .02
❑ 491 B.J. Surhoff .10 .04
❑ 492 Doyle Alexander .05 .02
❑ 493 Mike Greenwell .05 .02
❑ 494 Wally Ritchie .05 .02
❑ 495 Eddie Murray .20 .08
❑ 496 Guy Hoffman .05 .02
❑ 497 Kevin Mitchell .10 .04
❑ 498 Bob Boone .10 .04
❑ 499 Eric King .05 .02
❑ 500 Andre Dawson .10 .04
❑ 501 Tim Birtsas .05 .02
❑ 502 Dan Gladden .05 .02
❑ 503 Junior Noboa .05 .02
❑ 504 Bob Rodgers MG .05 .02
❑ 505 Willie Upshaw .05 .02
❑ 506 John Cangelosi .05 .02
❑ 507 Mark Gubicza .05 .02
❑ 508 Tim Teufel .05 .02
❑ 509 Bill Dawley .05 .02
❑ 510 Dave Winfield .10 .04
❑ 511 Joel Davis .05 .02
❑ 512 Alex Trevino .05 .02
❑ 513 Tim Flannery .05 .02
❑ 514 Pat Sheridan .05 .02
❑ 515 Juan Nieves .05 .02
❑ 516 Jim Sundberg .10 .04
❑ 517 Ron Robinson .05 .02
❑ 518 Greg Gross .05 .02
❑ 519 Harold Reynolds .05 .02
Phil Bradley TL
❑ 520 Dave Smith .05 .02
❑ 521 Jim Dwyer .05 .02
❑ 522 Bob Patterson .05 .02
❑ 523 Gary Roenicke .05 .02
❑ 524 Gary Lucas .05 .02
❑ 525 Marty Barrett .05 .02
❑ 526 Juan Berenguer .05 .02
❑ 527 Steve Henderson .05 .02
❑ 528A Checklist 397-528 .15 .06
ERR (455 S. Carlton)
❑ 528B Checklist 397-528 .10 .04
COR (455 S. Hillegas)
❑ 529 Tim Burke .05 .02
❑ 530 Gary Carter .10 .04
❑ 531 Rich Yett .05 .02
❑ 532 Mike Kingery .05 .02
❑ 533 John Farrell RC .10 .04
❑ 534 John Wathan MG .05 .02
❑ 535 Ron Guidry .10 .04
❑ 536 John Morris .05 .02
❑ 537 Steve Buechele .05 .02
❑ 538 Bill Wegman .05 .02
❑ 539 Mike LaValliere .05 .02
❑ 540 Bret Saberhagen .10 .04
❑ 541 Juan Beniquez .05 .02
❑ 542 Paul Noce .05 .02
❑ 543 Kent Tekulve .05 .02
❑ 544 Jim Traber .05 .02
❑ 545 Don Baylor .10 .04
❑ 546 John Candelaria .05 .02
❑ 547 Felix Fermin .05 .02
❑ 548 Shane Mack .05 .02
❑ 549 Albert Hall .10 .04
Dale Murphy
Ken Griffey
Dion James TL
❑ 550 Pedro Guerrero .10 .04
❑ 551 Terry Steinbach .10 .04
❑ 552 Mark Thurmond .05 .02
❑ 553 Tracy Jones .05 .02
❑ 554 Mike Smithson .05 .02
❑ 555 Brook Jacoby .05 .02
❑ 556 Stan Clarke .05 .02
❑ 557 Craig Reynolds .05 .02
❑ 558 Bob Ojeda .05 .02
❑ 559 Ken Williams RC .05 .02
❑ 560 Tim Wallach .05 .02
❑ 561 Rick Cerone .05 .02
❑ 562 Jim Lindeman .05 .02
❑ 563 Jose Guzman .05 .02
❑ 564 Frank Lucchesi MG .05 .02
❑ 565 Lloyd Moseby .05 .02
❑ 566 Charlie O'Brien .05 .02
❑ 567 Mike Diaz .05 .02
❑ 568 Chris Brown .05 .02
❑ 569 Charlie Leibrandt .05 .02
❑ 570 Jeffrey Leonard .05 .02
❑ 571 Mark Williamson .05 .02
❑ 572 Chris James .05 .02
❑ 573 Bob Stanley .05 .02
❑ 574 Graig Nettles .10 .04
❑ 575 Don Sutton .10 .04
❑ 576 Tommy Hinzo .05 .02
❑ 577 Tom Browning .05 .02
❑ 578 Gary Gaetti .10 .04
❑ 579 Gary Carter .05 .02
Kevin McReynolds TL
❑ 580 Mark McGwire 1.50 .60
❑ 581 Tito Landrum .05 .02
❑ 582 Mike Henneman RC* .25 .10
❑ 583 Dave Valle .05 .02
❑ 584 Steve Trout .05 .02
❑ 585 Ozzie Guillen .10 .04
❑ 586 Bob Forsch .05 .02
❑ 587 Terry Puhl .05 .02
❑ 588 Jeff Parrett .05 .02
❑ 589 Geno Petralli .05 .02
❑ 590 George Bell .10 .04
❑ 591 Doug Drabek .05 .02
❑ 592 Dale Sveum .05 .02
❑ 593 Bob Tewksbury .05 .02
❑ 594 Bobby Valentine MG .10 .04
❑ 595 Frank White .10 .04
❑ 596 John Kruk .10 .04
❑ 597 Gene Garber .05 .02
❑ 598 Lee Lacy .05 .02
❑ 599 Calvin Schiraldi .05 .02
❑ 600 Mike Schmidt .50 .20
❑ 601 Jack Lazorko .05 .02
❑ 602 Mike Aldrete .05 .02
❑ 603 Rob Murphy .05 .02
❑ 604 Chris Bando .05 .02
❑ 605 Kirk Gibson .20 .08
❑ 606 Moose Haas .05 .02
❑ 607 Mickey Hatcher .05 .02
❑ 608 Charlie Kerfeld .05 .02
❑ 609 Gary Gaetti .10 .04
Kent Hrbek TL
❑ 610 Keith Hernandez .10 .04

❑ 611 Tommy John .10 .04
❑ 612 Curt Ford .05 .02
❑ 613 Bobby Thigpen .05 .02
❑ 614 Herm Winningham .05 .02
❑ 615 Jody Davis .05 .02
❑ 616 Jay Aldrich .05 .02
❑ 617 Oddibe McDowell .05 .02
❑ 618 Cecil Fielder .10 .04
❑ 619 Mike Dunne .05 .02
(Inconsistent design, black name on front)
❑ 620 Cory Snyder .05 .02
❑ 621 Gene Nelson .05 .02
❑ 622 Kal Daniels .05 .02
❑ 623 Mike Flanagan .05 .02
❑ 624 Jim Leyland MG .10 .04
❑ 625 Frank Viola .10 .04
❑ 626 Glenn Wilson .05 .02
❑ 627 Joe Boever .05 .02
❑ 628 Dave Henderson .05 .02
❑ 629 Kelly Downs .05 .02
❑ 630 Darrell Evans .10 .04
❑ 631 Jack Howell .05 .02
❑ 632 Steve Shields .05 .02
❑ 633 Barry Lyons .05 .02
❑ 634 Jose DeLeon .05 .02
❑ 635 Terry Pendleton .10 .04
❑ 636 Charles Hudson .05 .02
❑ 637 Jay Bell RC .40 .16
❑ 638 Steve Balboni .05 .02
❑ 639 Glenn Braggs .05 .02
Tony Muser CO TL
❑ 640 Garry Templeton .10 .04
(Inconsistent design, green border)
❑ 641 Rick Honeycutt .05 .02
❑ 642 Bob Dernier .05 .02
❑ 643 Rocky Childress .05 .02
❑ 644 Terry McGriff .05 .02
❑ 645 Matt Nokes RC* .25 .10
❑ 646 Checklist 529-660 .05 .02
❑ 647 Pascual Perez .05 .02
❑ 648 Al Newman .05 .02
❑ 649 DeWayne Buice .05 .02
❑ 650 Cal Ripken .75 .30
❑ 651 Mike Jackson RC* .25 .10
❑ 652 Bruce Benedict .05 .02
❑ 653 Jeff Sellers .05 .02
❑ 654 Roger Craig MG .10 .04
❑ 655 Len Dykstra .10 .04
❑ 656 Lee Guetterman .05 .02
❑ 657 Gary Redus .05 .02
❑ 658 Tim Conroy .05 .02
(Inconsistent design, name in white)
❑ 659 Bobby Meacham .05 .02
❑ 660 Rick Reuschel .10 .04
❑ 661 Nolan Ryan TBC '83 .50 .20
❑ 662 Jim Rice TBC .05 .02
❑ 663 Ron Blomberg TBC .05 .02
❑ 664 Bob Gibson TBC '68 .25 .10
❑ 665 Stan Musial TBC '63 .20 .08
❑ 666 Mario Soto .10 .04
❑ 667 Luis Quinones .05 .02
❑ 668 Walt Terrell .05 .02
❑ 669 Lance Parrish .05 .02
Mike Ryan CO TL
❑ 670 Dan Plesac .05 .02
❑ 671 Tim Laudner .05 .02
❑ 672 John Davis .05 .02
❑ 673 Tony Phillips .05 .02
❑ 674 Mike Fitzgerald .05 .02
❑ 675 Jim Rice .10 .04
❑ 676 Ken Dixon .05 .02
❑ 677 Eddie Milner .05 .02
❑ 678 Jim Acker .05 .02
❑ 679 Darrell Miller .05 .02
❑ 680 Charlie Hough .10 .04
❑ 681 Bobby Bonilla .10 .04
❑ 682 Jimmy Key .10 .04
❑ 683 Julio Franco .10 .04
❑ 684 Hal Lanier MG .05 .02
❑ 685 Ron Darling .10 .04
❑ 686 Terry Francona .10 .04
❑ 687 Mickey Brantley .05 .02
❑ 688 Jim Winn .05 .02
❑ 689 Tom Pagnozzi RC .10 .04
❑ 690 Jay Howell .05 .02
❑ 691 Dan Pasqua .05 .02
❑ 692 Mike Birkbeck .05 .02
❑ 693 Benito Santiago .10 .04
❑ 694 Eric Nolte .05 .02
❑ 695 Shawon Dunston .05 .02
❑ 696 Duane Ward .05 .02
❑ 697 Steve Lombardozzi .05 .02
❑ 698 Brad Havens .05 .02
❑ 699 Benito Santiago .10 .04
Tony Gwynn TL
❑ 700 George Brett .50 .20
❑ 701 Sammy Stewart .05 .02
❑ 702 Mike Gallego .05 .02
❑ 703 Bob Brenly .05 .02
❑ 704 Dennis Boyd .05 .02
❑ 705 Juan Samuel .05 .02
❑ 706 Rick Mahler .05 .02
❑ 707 Fred Lynn .10 .04
❑ 708 Gus Polidor .05 .02
❑ 709 George Frazier .05 .02
❑ 710 Darryl Strawberry .10 .04
❑ 711 Bill Gullickson .05 .02
❑ 712 John Moses .05 .02
❑ 713 Willie Hernandez .05 .02
❑ 714 Jim Fregosi MG .05 .02
❑ 715 Todd Worrell .05 .02
❑ 716 Lenn Sakata .05 .02
❑ 717 Jay Baller .05 .02
❑ 718 Mike Felder .05 .02
❑ 719 Denny Walling .05 .02
❑ 720 Tim Raines .10 .04
❑ 721 Pete O'Brien .05 .02
❑ 722 Manny Lee .05 .02
❑ 723 Bob Kipper .05 .02
❑ 724 Danny Tartabull .05 .02
❑ 725 Mike Boddicker .05 .02
❑ 726 Alfredo Griffin .05 .02
❑ 727 Greg Booker .05 .02
❑ 728 Andy Allanson .05 .02
❑ 729 George Bell .10 .04
Fred McGriff TL
❑ 730 John Franco .10 .04
❑ 731 Rick Schu .05 .02
❑ 732 David Palmer .05 .02
❑ 733 Spike Owen .05 .02
❑ 734 Craig Lefferts .05 .02
❑ 735 Kevin McReynolds .05 .02
❑ 736 Matt Young .05 .02
❑ 737 Butch Wynegar .05 .02
❑ 738 Scott Bankhead .05 .02
❑ 739 Daryl Boston .05 .02
❑ 740 Rick Sutcliffe .10 .04
❑ 741 Mike Easler .05 .02
❑ 742 Mark Clear .05 .02
❑ 743 Larry Herndon .05 .02
❑ 744 Whitey Herzog MG .10 .04
❑ 745 Bill Doran .05 .02
❑ 746 Gene Larkin RC* .25 .10
❑ 747 Bobby Witt .05 .02
❑ 748 Reid Nichols .05 .02
❑ 749 Mark Eichhorn .05 .02
❑ 750 Bo Jackson .20 .08
❑ 751 Jim Morrison .05 .02
❑ 752 Mark Grant .05 .02
❑ 753 Danny Heep .05 .02
❑ 754 Mike LaCoss .05 .02
❑ 755 Ozzie Virgil .05 .02
❑ 756 Mike Maddux .05 .02
❑ 757 John Marzano .05 .02
❑ 758 Eddie Williams RC .10 .04
❑ 759 Mark McGwire 1.00 .40
Jose Canseco TL UER (two copyrights)
❑ 760 Mike Scott .10 .04
❑ 761 Tony Armas .10 .04
❑ 762 Scott Bradley .05 .02
❑ 763 Doug Sisk .05 .02
❑ 764 Greg Walker .05 .02
❑ 765 Neal Heaton .05 .02
❑ 766 Henry Cotto .05 .02
❑ 767 Jose Lind RC .25 .10
❑ 768 Dickie Noles .05 .02
(Now with Tigers on card front)
❑ 769 Cecil Cooper .10 .04
❑ 770 Lou Whitaker .10 .04
❑ 771 Ruben Sierra .10 .04
❑ 772 Sal Butera .05 .02
❑ 773 Frank Williams .05 .02
❑ 774 Gene Mauch MG .05 .02
❑ 775 Dave Stieb .10 .04
❑ 776 Checklist 661-792 .05 .02
❑ 777 Lonnie Smith .05 .02
❑ 778A Keith Comstock ERR 2.00 .80
(White "Padres")
❑ 778B Keith Comstock COR .05 .02
(Blue "Padres")
❑ 779 Tom Glavine RC 2.00 .80
❑ 780 Fernando Valenzuela .10 .04
❑ 781 Keith Hughes .05 .02
❑ 782 Jeff Ballard .05 .02
❑ 783 Ron Roenicke .05 .02
❑ 784 Joe Sambito .05 .02
❑ 785 Alvin Davis .05 .02
❑ 786 Joe Price .05 .02
Inconsistent design, orange team name
❑ 787 Bill Almon .05 .02
❑ 788 Ray Searage .05 .02
❑ 789 Joe Carter .05 .02
Cory Snyder TL
❑ 790 Dave Righetti .10 .04
❑ 791 Ted Simmons .10 .04
❑ 792 John Tudor .10 .04

1988 Topps Traded

	Nm-Mt	Ex-Mt
COMP.FACT.SET (132)	10.00	4.00

❑ 1T Jim Abbott OLY XRC 2.00 .80
❑ 2T Juan Agosto .10 .04
❑ 3T Luis Alicea XRC .50 .20
❑ 4T Roberto Alomar XRC 2.00 .80
❑ 5T Brady Anderson XRC .75 .30
❑ 6T Jack Armstrong XRC .50 .20
❑ 7T Don August .10 .04
❑ 8T Floyd Bannister .10 .04
❑ 9T Bret Barberie OLY XRC .25 .10
❑ 10T Jose Bautista XRC .25 .10
❑ 11T Don Baylor .20 .08
❑ 12T Tim Belcher .10 .04
❑ 13T Buddy Bell .20 .08
❑ 14T Andy Benes OLY XRC .75 .30
❑ 15T Damon Berryhill XRC .50 .20
❑ 16T Bud Black .10 .04
❑ 17T Pat Borders XRC .50 .20
❑ 18T Phil Bradley .10 .04
❑ 19T J.Branson XRC OLY .50 .20
❑ 20T Tom Brunansky .10 .04
❑ 21T Jay Buhner XRC 1.00 .40
❑ 22T Brett Butler .20 .08
❑ 23T Jim Campanis OLY .10 .04
❑ 24T Sil Campusano .10 .04
❑ 25T John Candelaria .10 .04
❑ 26T Jose Cecena .10 .04
❑ 27T Rick Cerone .10 .04
❑ 28T Jack Clark .20 .08
❑ 29T Kevin Coffman .10 .04
❑ 30T Pat Combs OLY XRC .25 .10
❑ 31T Henry Cotto .10 .04
❑ 32T Chili Davis .20 .08
❑ 33T Mike Davis .10 .04

❑ 34T Jose DeLeon .10 .04
❑ 35T Richard Dotson .10 .04
❑ 36T Cecil Espy .10 .04
❑ 37T Tom Filer .10 .04
❑ 38T Mike Fiore OLY .10 .04
❑ 39T Ron Gant XRC .75 .30
❑ 40T Kirk Gibson .50 .20
❑ 41T Rich Gossage .20 .08
❑ 42T Mark Grace XRC 2.00 .80
❑ 43T Alfredo Griffin .10 .04
❑ 44T Ty Griffin OLY .10 .04
❑ 45T Bryan Harvey XRC .50 .20
❑ 46T Ron Hassey .10 .04
❑ 47T Ray Hayward .10 .04
❑ 48T Dave Henderson .10 .04
❑ 49T Tom Herr .10 .04
❑ 50T Bob Horner .20 .08
❑ 51T Ricky Horton .10 .04
❑ 52T Jay Howell .10 .04
❑ 53T Glenn Hubbard .10 .04
❑ 54T Jeff Innis .10 .04
❑ 55T Danny Jackson .10 .04
❑ 56T Darrin Jackson XRC* .25 .10
❑ 57T Roberto Kelly XRC* .50 .20
❑ 58T Ron Kittle .10 .04
❑ 59T Ray Knight .20 .08
❑ 60T Vance Law .10 .04
❑ 61T Jeffrey Leonard .10 .04
❑ 62T Mike Macfarlane XRC .50 .20
❑ 63T Scotti Madison .10 .04
❑ 64T Kirt Manwaring .10 .04
❑ 65T M.Marquess OLY CO .10 .04
❑ 66T T.Martinez OLY XRC 3.00 1.20
❑ 67T Billy Masse OLY XRC .25 .10
❑ 68T Jack McDowell XRC .75 .30
❑ 69T Jack McKeon MG .20 .08
❑ 70T Larry McWilliams .10 .04
❑ 71T M.Morandini OLY XRC .50 .20
❑ 72T Keith Moreland .10 .04
❑ 73T Mike Morgan .10 .04
❑ 74T C.Nagy OLY XRC .50 .20
❑ 75T Al Nipper .10 .04
❑ 76T Russ Nixon MG .10 .04
❑ 77T Jesse Orosco .10 .04
❑ 78T Joe Orsulak .10 .04
❑ 79T Dave Palmer .10 .04
❑ 80T Mark Parent .10 .04
❑ 81T Dave Parker .20 .08
❑ 82T Dan Pasqua .10 .04
❑ 83T Melido Perez XRC* .50 .20
❑ 84T Steve Peters .10 .04
❑ 85T Dan Petry .10 .04
❑ 86T Gary Pettis .10 .04
❑ 87T Jeff Pico .10 .04
❑ 88T Jim Poole OLY XRC .25 .10
❑ 89T Ted Power .10 .04
❑ 90T Rafael Ramirez .10 .04
❑ 91T Dennis Rasmussen .10 .04
❑ 92T Jose Rijo .20 .08
❑ 93T Ernie Riles .10 .04
❑ 94T Luis Rivera .10 .04
❑ 95T D.Robbins XRC OLY .25 .10
❑ 96T Frank Robinson MG .30 .12
❑ 97T Cookie Rojas MG .10 .04
❑ 98T Chris Sabo XRC .75 .30
❑ 99T Mark Salas .10 .04
❑ 100T Luis Salazar .10 .04
❑ 101T Rafael Santana .10 .04
❑ 102T Nelson Santovenia .10 .04
❑ 103T Mackey Sasser XRC .50 .20
❑ 104T Calvin Schiraldi .10 .04
❑ 105T Mike Schooler .10 .04
❑ 106T S.Servais XRC OLY .50 .20
❑ 107T D.Silvestri XRC OLY .25 .10
❑ 108T Don Slaught .10 .04
❑ 109T J.Slusarski XRC OLY .25 .10
❑ 110T Lee Smith .20 .08
❑ 111T Pete Smith XRC* .25 .10
❑ 112T Jim Snyder MG .10 .04
❑ 113T E.Sprague OLY XRC .50 .20
❑ 114T Pete Stanicek .10 .04
❑ 115T Kurt Stillwell .10 .04
❑ 116T T.Stottlemyre XRC .50 .20
❑ 117T Bill Swift .10 .04
❑ 118T Pat Tabler .10 .04
❑ 119T Scott Terry .10 .04
❑ 120T Mickey Tettleton .10 .04
❑ 121T Dickie Thon .10 .04
❑ 122T Jeff Treadway XRC* .50 .20
❑ 123T Willie Upshaw .10 .04
❑ 124T R.Ventura OLY XRC 1.50 .60
❑ 125T Ron Washington .10 .04
❑ 126T Walt Weiss XRC* .75 .30
❑ 127T Bob Welch .20 .08
❑ 128T David Wells XRC 1.50 .60
❑ 129T Glenn Wilson .10 .04
❑ 130T Ted Wood OLY XRC .25 .10
❑ 131T Don Zimmer MG .20 .08
❑ 132T Checklist 1T-132T .10 .04

1989 Topps

	Nm-Mt	Ex-Mt
COMPLETE SET (792)	20.00	8.00
COMP.FACT SET (792)	25.00	10.00
COMP.X-MAS.SET (792)	25.00	10.00
FS SUBSET VARIATIONS EXIST	.00	
FS PHOTOS ARE PLACED HIGHER/LOWER		.00

❑ 1 George Bell RB .05 .02
Slams 3 HR on
Opening Day
❑ 2 Wade Boggs RB .10 .04
❑ 3 Gary Carter RB .05 .02
Sets Record for
Career Putouts
❑ 4 Andre Dawson RB .05 .02
Logs Double Figures
in HR and SB
❑ 5 Orel Hershiser RB .05 .02
Pitches 59
Scoreless Innings
❑ 6 Doug Jones RB UER .05 .02
Earns His 15th
Straight Save
Photo actually Chris Codiroli
❑ 7 Kevin McReynolds RB .05 .02
Steals 21 Without
Being Caught
❑ 8 Dave Eiland .05 .02
❑ 9 Tim Teufel .05 .02
❑ 10 Andre Dawson .10 .04
❑ 11 Bruce Sutter .10 .04
❑ 12 Dale Sveum .05 .02
❑ 13 Doug Sisk .05 .02
❑ 14 Tom Kelly MG .05 .02
❑ 15 Robby Thompson .05 .02
❑ 16 Ron Robinson .05 .02
❑ 17 Brian Downing .10 .04
❑ 18 Rick Rhoden .05 .02
❑ 19 Greg Gagne .05 .02
❑ 20 Steve Bedrosian .05 .02
❑ 21 Greg Walker TL .05 .02
❑ 22 Tim Crews .05 .02
❑ 23 Mike Fitzgerald .05 .02
❑ 24 Larry Andersen .05 .02
❑ 25 Frank White .10 .04
❑ 26 Dale Mohorcic .05 .02
❑ 27A Orestes Destrade .10 .04
(F* next to copyright) RC*
❑ 27B Orestes Destrade .10 .04
(E*F* next to
copyright) RC*
❑ 28 Mike Moore .05 .02
❑ 29 Kelly Gruber .05 .02
❑ 30 Dwight Gooden .10 .04
❑ 31 Terry Francona .10 .04
❑ 32 Dennis Rasmussen .05 .02
❑ 33 B.J. Surhoff .10 .04
❑ 34 Ken Williams .05 .02
❑ 35 John Tudor UER .10 .04
(With Red Sox in '84,should be Pirates)
❑ 36 Mitch Webster .05 .02
❑ 37 Bob Stanley .05 .02
❑ 38 Paul Runge .05 .02
❑ 39 Mike Maddux .05 .02
❑ 40 Steve Sax .05 .02
❑ 41 Terry Mulholland .05 .02
❑ 42 Jim Eppard .05 .02
❑ 43 Guillermo Hernandez .05 .02
❑ 44 Jim Snyder MG .05 .02
❑ 45 Kal Daniels .05 .02
❑ 46 Mark Portugal .05 .02
❑ 47 Carney Lansford .10 .04
❑ 48 Tim Burke .05 .02
❑ 49 Craig Biggio RC 1.50 .60
❑ 50 George Bell .10 .04
❑ 51 Mark McLemore TL .05 .02
❑ 52 Bob Brenly .05 .02
❑ 53 Ruben Sierra .05 .02
❑ 54 Steve Trout .05 .02
❑ 55 Julio Franco .10 .04
❑ 56 Pat Tabler .05 .02
❑ 57 Alejandro Pena .05 .02
❑ 58 Lee Mazzilli .10 .04
❑ 59 Mark Davis .05 .02
❑ 60 Tom Brunansky .05 .02
❑ 61 Neil Allen .05 .02
❑ 62 Alfredo Griffin .05 .02
❑ 63 Mark Clear .05 .02
❑ 64 Alex Trevino .05 .02
❑ 65 Rick Reuschel .10 .04
❑ 66 Manny Trillo .05 .02
❑ 67 Dave Palmer .05 .02
❑ 68 Darrell Miller .05 .02
❑ 69 Jeff Ballard .05 .02
❑ 70 Mark McGwire 1.00 .40
❑ 71 Mike Boddicker .05 .02
❑ 72 John Moses .05 .02
❑ 73 Pascual Perez .05 .02
❑ 74 Nick Leyva MG .05 .02
❑ 75 Tom Henke .05 .02
❑ 76 Terry Blocker .05 .02
❑ 77 Doyle Alexander .05 .02
❑ 78 Jim Sundberg .10 .04
❑ 79 Scott Bankhead .05 .02
❑ 80 Cory Snyder .05 .02
❑ 81 Tim Raines TL .05 .02
❑ 82 Dave Leiper .05 .02
❑ 83 Jeff Blauser .05 .02
❑ 84 Bill Bene FDP .05 .02
❑ 85 Kevin McReynolds .05 .02
❑ 86 Al Nipper .05 .02
❑ 87 Larry Owen .05 .02
❑ 88 Darryl Hamilton RC * .25 .10
❑ 89 Dave LaPoint .05 .02
❑ 90 Vince Coleman UER .05 .02
(Wrong birth year)
❑ 91 Floyd Youmans .05 .02
❑ 92 Jeff Kunkel .05 .02
❑ 93 Ken Howell .05 .02
❑ 94 Chris Speier .05 .02
❑ 95 Gerald Young .05 .02
❑ 96 Rick Cerone .05 .02
❑ 97 Greg Mathews .05 .02
❑ 98 Larry Sheets .05 .02
❑ 99 Sherman Corbett .05 .02
❑ 100 Mike Schmidt .50 .20
❑ 101 Les Straker .05 .02
❑ 102 Mike Gallego .05 .02
❑ 103 Tim Birtsas .05 .02
❑ 104 Dallas Green MG .05 .02
❑ 105 Ron Darling .10 .04
❑ 106 Willie Upshaw .05 .02
❑ 107 Jose DeLeon .05 .02
❑ 108 Fred Manrique .05 .02
❑ 109 Hipolito Pena .05 .02
❑ 110 Paul Molitor .15 .06
❑ 111 Eric Davis TL .05 .02
❑ 112 Jim Presley .05 .02

No.	Player	Price	Price
❑ 113	Lloyd Moseby	.05	.02
❑ 114	Bob Kipper	.05	.02
❑ 115	Jody Davis	.05	.02
❑ 116	Jeff Montgomery	.05	.02
❑ 117	Dave Anderson	.05	.02
❑ 118	Checklist 1-132	.05	.02
❑ 119	Terry Puhl	.05	.02
❑ 120	Frank Viola	.10	.04
❑ 121	Garry Templeton	.10	.04
❑ 122	Lance Johnson	.05	.02
❑ 123	Spike Owen	.05	.02
❑ 124	Jim Traber	.05	.02
❑ 125	Mike Krukow	.05	.02
❑ 126	Sid Bream	.05	.02
❑ 127	Walt Terrell	.05	.02
❑ 128	Milt Thompson	.05	.02
❑ 129	Terry Clark	.05	.02
❑ 130	Gerald Perry	.05	.02
❑ 131	Dave Otto	.05	.02
❑ 132	Curt Ford	.05	.02
❑ 133	Bill Long	.05	.02
❑ 134	Don Zimmer MG	.10	.04
❑ 135	Jose Rijo	.10	.04
❑ 136	Joey Meyer	.05	.02
❑ 137	Geno Petralli	.05	.02
❑ 138	Wallace Johnson	.05	.02
❑ 139	Mike Flanagan	.05	.02
❑ 140	Shawon Dunston	.05	.02
❑ 141	Brook Jacoby TL	.05	.02
❑ 142	Mike Diaz	.05	.02
❑ 143	Mike Campbell	.05	.02
❑ 144	Jay Bell	.10	.04
❑ 145	Dave Stewart	.10	.04
❑ 146	Gary Pettis	.05	.02
❑ 147	DeWayne Buice	.05	.02
❑ 148	Bill Pecota	.05	.02
❑ 149	Doug Dascenzo	.05	.02
❑ 150	Fernando Valenzuela	.10	.04
❑ 151	Terry McGriff	.05	.02
❑ 152	Mark Thurmond	.05	.02
❑ 153	Jim Pankovits	.05	.02
❑ 154	Don Carman	.05	.02
❑ 155	Marty Barrett	.05	.02
❑ 156	Dave Gallagher	.05	.02
❑ 157	Tom Glavine	.25	.10
❑ 158	Mike Aldrete	.05	.02
❑ 159	Pat Clements	.05	.02
❑ 160	Jeffrey Leonard	.05	.02
❑ 161	G. Olson RC FDP UER	.25	.10
	Born Scribner, NE,		
	should be Omaha, NE		
❑ 162	John Davis	.05	.02
❑ 163	Bob Forsch	.05	.02
❑ 164	Hal Lanier MG	.05	.02
❑ 165	Mike Dunne	.05	.02
❑ 166	Doug Jennings	.05	.02
❑ 167	Steve Searcy FS	.05	.02
❑ 168	Willie Wilson	.10	.04
❑ 169	Mike Jackson	.05	.02
❑ 170	Tony Fernandez	.05	.02
❑ 171	Andres Thomas TL	.05	.02
❑ 172	Frank Williams	.05	.02
❑ 173	Mel Hall	.05	.02
❑ 174	Todd Burns	.05	.02
❑ 175	John Shelby	.05	.02
❑ 176	Jeff Parrett	.05	.02
❑ 177	Monty Fariss FDP	.05	.02
❑ 178	Mark Grant	.05	.02
❑ 179	Ozzie Virgil	.05	.02
❑ 180	Mike Scott	.10	.04
❑ 181	Craig Worthington	.05	.02
❑ 182	Bob McClure	.05	.02
❑ 183	Oddibe McDowell	.05	.02
❑ 184	John Costello	.05	.02
❑ 185	Claudell Washington	.05	.02
❑ 186	Pat Perry	.05	.02
❑ 187	Darren Daulton	.10	.04
❑ 188	Dennis Lamp	.05	.02
❑ 189	Kevin Mitchell	.10	.04
❑ 190	Mike Witt	.05	.02
❑ 191	Sil Campusano	.05	.02
❑ 192	Paul Mirabella	.05	.02
❑ 193	Sparky Anderson MG	.10	.04
	UER (553 Salazer)		
❑ 194	Greg W. Harris RC	.10	.04
❑ 195	Ozzie Guillen	.10	.04
❑ 196	Denny Walling	.05	.02
❑ 197	Neal Heaton	.05	.02
❑ 198	Danny Heep	.05	.02
❑ 199	Mike Schooler RC *	.10	.04
❑ 200	George Brett	.60	.24
❑ 201	Kelly Gruber TL	.05	.02
❑ 202	Brad Moore	.05	.02
❑ 203	Rob Ducey	.05	.02
❑ 204	Brad Havens	.05	.02
❑ 205	Dwight Evans	.15	.06
❑ 206	Roberto Alomar	.25	.10
❑ 207	Terry Leach	.05	.02
❑ 208	Tom Pagnozzi	.05	.02
❑ 209	Jeff Bittiger	.05	.02
❑ 210	Dale Murphy	.15	.06
❑ 211	Mike Pagliarulo	.05	.02
❑ 212	Scott Sanderson	.05	.02
❑ 213	Rene Gonzales	.05	.02
❑ 214	Charlie O'Brien	.05	.02
❑ 215	Kevin Gross	.05	.02
❑ 216	Jack Howell	.05	.02
❑ 217	Joe Price	.05	.02
❑ 218	Mike LaValliere	.05	.02
❑ 219	Jim Clancy	.05	.02
❑ 220	Gary Gaetti	.10	.04
❑ 221	Cecil Espy	.05	.02
❑ 222	Mark Lewis FDP RC	.25	.10
❑ 223	Jay Buhner	.10	.04
❑ 224	Tony LaRussa MG	.10	.04
❑ 225	Ramon Martinez RC	.25	.10
❑ 226	Bill Doran	.05	.02
❑ 227	John Farrell	.05	.02
❑ 228	Nelson Santovenia	.05	.02
❑ 229	Jimmy Key	.10	.04
❑ 230	Ozzie Smith	.40	.16
❑ 231	Roberto Alomar TL	.25	.10
	(Gary Carter at plate)		
❑ 232	Ricky Horton	.05	.02
❑ 233	Gregg Jefferies FS	.05	.02
❑ 234	Tom Browning	.05	.02
❑ 235	John Kruk	.10	.04
❑ 236	Charles Hudson	.05	.02
❑ 237	Glenn Hubbard	.05	.02
❑ 238	Eric King	.05	.02
❑ 239	Tim Laudner	.05	.02
❑ 240	Greg Maddux	.50	.20
❑ 241	Brett Butler	.10	.04
❑ 242	Ed VandeBerg	.05	.02
❑ 243	Bob Boone	.10	.04
❑ 244	Jim Acker	.05	.02
❑ 245	Jim Rice	.10	.04
❑ 246	Rey Quinones	.05	.02
❑ 247	Shawn Hillegas	.05	.02
❑ 248	Tony Phillips	.05	.02
❑ 249	Tim Leary	.05	.02
❑ 250	Cal Ripken	.75	.30
❑ 251	John Dopson	.05	.02
❑ 252	Billy Hatcher	.05	.02
❑ 253	Jose Alvarez RC	.10	.04
❑ 254	Tom Lasorda MG	.15	.06
❑ 255	Ron Guidry	.10	.04
❑ 256	Benny Santiago	.10	.04
❑ 257	Rick Aguilera	.05	.02
❑ 258	Checklist 133-264	.05	.02
❑ 259	Larry McWilliams	.05	.02
❑ 260	Dave Winfield	.10	.04
❑ 261	Tom Brunansky	.05	.02
	Luis Alicea TL		
❑ 262	Jeff Pico	.05	.02
❑ 263	Mike Felder	.05	.02
❑ 264	Rob Dibble RC	.50	.20
❑ 265	Kent Hrbek	.10	.04
❑ 266	Luis Aquino	.05	.02
❑ 267	Jeff M. Robinson	.05	.02
❑ 268	Keith Miller RC	.25	.10
❑ 269	Tom Bolton	.05	.02
❑ 270	Wally Joyner	.10	.04
❑ 271	Jay Tibbs	.05	.02
❑ 272	Ron Hassey	.05	.02
❑ 273	Jose Lind	.05	.02
❑ 274	Mark Eichhorn	.05	.02
❑ 275	Danny Tartabull UER	.05	.02
	(Born San Juan, PR		
	should be Miami, FL)		
❑ 276	Paul Kilgus	.05	.02
❑ 277	Mike Davis	.05	.02
❑ 278	Andy McGaffigan	.05	.02
❑ 279	Scott Bradley	.05	.02
❑ 280	Bob Knepper	.05	.02
❑ 281	Gary Redus	.05	.02
❑ 282	Cris Carpenter RC *	.10	.04
❑ 283	Andy Allanson	.05	.02
❑ 284	Jim Leyland MG	.10	.04
❑ 285	John Candelaria	.05	.02
❑ 286	Darrin Jackson	.10	.04
❑ 287	Juan Nieves	.05	.02
❑ 288	Pat Sheridan	.05	.02
❑ 289	Ernie Whitt	.05	.02
❑ 290	John Franco	.10	.04
❑ 291	Darryl Strawberry	.05	.02
	Keith Hernandez		
	Kevin McReynolds TL		
❑ 292	Jim Corsi	.05	.02
❑ 293	Glenn Wilson	.05	.02
❑ 294	Juan Berenguer	.05	.02
❑ 295	Scott Fletcher	.05	.02
❑ 296	Ron Gant	.10	.04
❑ 297	Oswald Peraza	.05	.02
❑ 298	Chris James	.05	.02
❑ 299	Steve Ellsworth	.05	.02
❑ 300	Darryl Strawberry	.10	.04
❑ 301	Charlie Leibrandt	.05	.02
❑ 302	Gary Ward	.05	.02
❑ 303	Felix Fermin	.05	.02
❑ 304	Joel Youngblood	.05	.02
❑ 305	Dave Smith	.05	.02
❑ 306	Tracy Woodson	.05	.02
❑ 307	Lance McCullers	.05	.02
❑ 308	Ron Karkovice	.05	.02
❑ 309	Mario Diaz	.05	.02
❑ 310	Rafael Palmeiro	.25	.10
❑ 311	Chris Bosio	.05	.02
❑ 312	Tom Lawless	.05	.02
❑ 313	Dennis Martinez	.10	.04
❑ 314	Bobby Valentine MG	.10	.04
❑ 315	Greg Swindell	.05	.02
❑ 316	Walt Weiss	.05	.02
❑ 317	Jack Armstrong RC *	.25	.10
❑ 318	Gene Larkin	.05	.02
❑ 319	Greg Booker	.05	.02
❑ 320	Lou Whitaker	.10	.04
❑ 321	Jody Reed TL	.05	.02
❑ 322	John Smiley	.05	.02
❑ 323	Gary Thurman	.05	.02
❑ 324	Bob Milacki	.05	.02
❑ 325	Jesse Barfield	.10	.04
❑ 326	Dennis Boyd	.05	.02
❑ 327	Mark Lemke RC	.40	.16
❑ 328	Rick Honeycutt	.05	.02
❑ 329	Bob Melvin	.05	.02
❑ 330	Eric Davis	.10	.04
❑ 331	Curt Wilkerson	.05	.02
❑ 332	Tony Armas	.10	.04
❑ 333	Bob Ojeda	.05	.02
❑ 334	Steve Lyons	.05	.02
❑ 335	Dave Righetti	.10	.04
❑ 336	Steve Balboni	.05	.02
❑ 337	Calvin Schiraldi	.05	.02
❑ 338	Jim Adduci	.05	.02
❑ 339	Scott Bailes	.05	.02
❑ 340	Kirk Gibson	.15	.06
❑ 341	Jim Deshaies	.05	.02
❑ 342	Tom Brookens	.05	.02
❑ 343	Gary Sheffield FS RC	2.00	.80
❑ 344	Tom Trebelhorn MG	.05	.02
❑ 345	Charlie Hough	.10	.04
❑ 346	Rex Hudler	.05	.02
❑ 347	John Cerutti	.05	.02
❑ 348	Ed Hearn	.05	.02
❑ 349	Ron Jones	.10	.04
❑ 350	Andy Van Slyke	.15	.06
❑ 351	Bob Melvin	.05	.02
	Bill Fahey CO TL		
❑ 352	Rick Schu	.05	.02
❑ 353	Marvell Wynne	.05	.02
❑ 354	Larry Parrish	.05	.02
❑ 355	Mark Langston	.05	.02
❑ 356	Kevin Elster	.05	.02
❑ 357	Jerry Reuss	.05	.02
❑ 358	Ricky Jordan RC *	.25	.10
❑ 359	Tommy John	.10	.04
❑ 360	Ryne Sandberg	.40	.16

❑ 361 Kelly Downs .05 .02
❑ 362 Jack Lazorko .05 .02
❑ 363 Rich Yett .05 .02
❑ 364 Rob Deer .05 .02
❑ 365 Mike Henneman .05 .02
❑ 366 Herm Winningham .05 .02
❑ 367 Johnny Paredes .05 .02
❑ 368 Brian Holton .05 .02
❑ 369 Ken Caminiti .15 .06
❑ 370 Dennis Eckersley .15 .06
❑ 371 Manny Lee .05 .02
❑ 372 Craig Lefferts .05 .02
❑ 373 Tracy Jones .05 .02
❑ 374 John Wathan MG .05 .02
❑ 375 Terry Pendleton .10 .04
❑ 376 Steve Lombardozzi .05 .02
❑ 377 Mike Smithson .05 .02
❑ 378 Checklist 265-396 .05 .02
❑ 379 Tim Flannery .05 .02
❑ 380 Rickey Henderson .25 .10
❑ 381 Larry Sheets TL .05 .02
❑ 382 John Smoltz RC 2.00 .80
❑ 383 Howard Johnson .10 .04
❑ 384 Mark Salas .05 .02
❑ 385 Von Hayes .05 .02
❑ 386 Andres Galarraga AS .05 .02
❑ 387 Ryne Sandberg AS .25 .10
❑ 388 Bobby Bonilla AS .05 .02
❑ 389 Ozzie Smith AS .25 .10
❑ 390 Darryl Strawberry AS .05 .02
❑ 391 Andre Dawson AS .05 .02
❑ 392 Andy Van Slyke AS .10 .04
❑ 393 Gary Carter AS .05 .02
❑ 394 Orel Hershiser AS .05 .02
❑ 395 Danny Jackson AS .05 .02
❑ 396 Kirk Gibson AS .10 .04
❑ 397 Don Mattingly AS .30 .12
❑ 398 Julio Franco AS .05 .02
❑ 399 Wade Boggs AS .10 .04
❑ 400 Alan Trammell AS .05 .02
❑ 401 Jose Canseco AS .15 .06
❑ 402 Mike Greenwell AS .05 .02
❑ 403 Kirby Puckett AS .15 .06
❑ 404 Bob Boone AS .05 .02
❑ 405 Roger Clemens AS .25 .10
❑ 406 Frank Viola AS .05 .02
❑ 407 Dave Winfield AS .05 .02
❑ 408 Greg Walker .05 .02
❑ 409 Ken Dayley .05 .02
❑ 410 Jack Clark .10 .04
❑ 411 Mitch Williams .05 .02
❑ 412 Barry Lyons .05 .02
❑ 413 Mike Kingery .05 .02
❑ 414 Jim Fregosi MG .05 .02
❑ 415 Rich Gossage .10 .04
❑ 416 Fred Lynn .10 .04
❑ 417 Mike LaCoss .05 .02
❑ 418 Bob Dernier .05 .02
❑ 419 Tom Filer .05 .02
❑ 420 Joe Carter .10 .04
❑ 421 Kirk McCaskill .05 .02
❑ 422 Bo Diaz .05 .02
❑ 423 Brian Fisher .05 .02
❑ 424 Luis Polonia UER .05 .02
(Wrong birthdate)
❑ 425 Jay Howell .05 .02
❑ 426 Dan Gladden .05 .02
❑ 427 Eric Show .05 .02
❑ 428 Craig Reynolds .05 .02
❑ 429 Greg Gagne TL .05 .02
❑ 430 Mark Gubicza .05 .02
❑ 431 Luis Rivera .05 .02
❑ 432 Chad Kreuter RC .25 .10
❑ 433 Albert Hall .05 .02
❑ 434 Ken Patterson .05 .02
❑ 435 Len Dykstra .10 .04
❑ 436 Bobby Meacham .05 .02
❑ 437 Andy Benes FDP RC .40 .16
❑ 438 Greg Gross .05 .02
❑ 439 Frank DiPino .05 .02
❑ 440 Bobby Bonilla .10 .04
❑ 441 Jerry Reed .05 .02
❑ 442 Jose Oquendo .05 .02
❑ 443 Rod Nichols .05 .02
❑ 444 Moose Stubing MG .05 .02
❑ 445 Matt Nokes .05 .02
❑ 446 Rob Murphy .05 .02
❑ 447 Donell Nixon .05 .02
❑ 448 Eric Plunk .05 .02
❑ 449 Carmelo Martinez .05 .02
❑ 450 Roger Clemens .50 .20
❑ 451 Mark Davidson .05 .02
❑ 452 Israel Sanchez .05 .02
❑ 453 Tom Prince .05 .02
❑ 454 Paul Assenmacher .05 .02
❑ 455 Johnny Ray .05 .02
❑ 456 Tim Belcher .05 .02
❑ 457 Mackey Sasser .05 .02
❑ 458 Donn Pall .05 .02
❑ 459 Dave Valle TL .05 .02
❑ 460 Dave Stieb .10 .04
❑ 461 Buddy Bell .10 .04
❑ 462 Jose Guzman .05 .02
❑ 463 Steve Lake .05 .02
❑ 464 Bryn Smith .05 .02
❑ 465 Mark Grace .25 .10
❑ 466 Chuck Crim .05 .02
❑ 467 Jim Walewander .05 .02
❑ 468 Henry Cotto .05 .02
❑ 469 Jose Bautista RC .10 .04
❑ 470 Lance Parrish .10 .04
❑ 471 Steve Curry .05 .02
❑ 472 Brian Harper .05 .02
❑ 473 Don Robinson .05 .02
❑ 474 Bob Rodgers MG .05 .02
❑ 475 Dave Parker .10 .04
❑ 476 Jon Perlman .05 .02
❑ 477 Dick Schofield .05 .02
❑ 478 Doug Drabek .05 .02
❑ 479 Mike Macfarlane RC * .25 .10
❑ 480 Keith Hernandez .10 .04
❑ 481 Chris Brown .05 .02
❑ 482 Steve Peters .05 .02
❑ 483 Mickey Hatcher .05 .02
❑ 484 Steve Shields .05 .02
❑ 485 Hubie Brooks .05 .02
❑ 486 Jack McDowell .10 .04
❑ 487 Scott Lusader .05 .02
❑ 488 Kevin Coffman .05 .02
Now with Cubs
❑ 489 Mike Schmidt TL .15 .06
❑ 490 Chris Sabo RC * .40 .16
❑ 491 Mike Birkbeck .05 .02
❑ 492 Alan Ashby .05 .02
❑ 493 Todd Benzinger .05 .02
❑ 494 Shane Rawley .05 .02
❑ 495 Candy Maldonado .05 .02
❑ 496 Dwayne Henry .05 .02
❑ 497 Pete Stanicek .05 .02
❑ 498 Dave Valle .05 .02
❑ 499 Don Heinkel .05 .02
❑ 500 Jose Canseco .25 .10
❑ 501 Vance Law .05 .02
❑ 502 Duane Ward .05 .02
❑ 503 Al Newman .05 .02
❑ 504 Bob Walk .05 .02
❑ 505 Pete Rose MG .50 .20
❑ 506 Kirt Manwaring .05 .02
❑ 507 Steve Farr .05 .02
❑ 508 Wally Backman .05 .02
❑ 509 Bud Black .05 .02
❑ 510 Bob Horner .10 .04
❑ 511 Richard Dotson .05 .02
❑ 512 Donnie Hill .05 .02
❑ 513 Jesse Orosco .05 .02
❑ 514 Chet Lemon .10 .04
❑ 515 Barry Larkin .15 .06
❑ 516 Eddie Whitson .05 .02
❑ 517 Greg Brock .05 .02
❑ 518 Bruce Ruffin .05 .02
❑ 519 Willie Randolph TL .05 .02
❑ 520 Rick Sutcliffe .10 .04
❑ 521 Mickey Tettleton .05 .02
❑ 522 Randy Kramer .05 .02
❑ 523 Andres Thomas .05 .02
❑ 524 Checklist 397-528 .05 .02
❑ 525 Chili Davis .10 .04
❑ 526 Wes Gardner .05 .02
❑ 527 Dave Henderson .05 .02
❑ 528 Luis Medina .05 .02
(Lower left front
has white triangle)
❑ 529 Tom Foley .05 .02
❑ 530 Nolan Ryan 1.00 .40
❑ 531 Dave Hengel .05 .02
❑ 532 Jerry Browne .05 .02
❑ 533 Andy Hawkins .05 .02
❑ 534 Doc Edwards MG .05 .02
❑ 535 Todd Worrell UER .05 .02
(4 wins in '88,
should be 5)
❑ 536 Joel Skinner .05 .02
❑ 537 Pete Smith .05 .02
❑ 538 Juan Castillo .05 .02
❑ 539 Barry Jones .05 .02
❑ 540 Bo Jackson .25 .10
❑ 541 Cecil Fielder .10 .04
❑ 542 Todd Frohwirth .05 .02
❑ 543 Damon Berryhill .05 .02
❑ 544 Jeff Sellers .05 .02
❑ 545 Mookie Wilson .10 .04
❑ 546 Mark Williamson .05 .02
❑ 547 Mark McLemore .05 .02
❑ 548 Bobby Witt .05 .02
❑ 549 Jamie Moyer TL .05 .02
❑ 550 Orel Hershiser .10 .04
❑ 551 Randy Ready .05 .02
❑ 552 Greg Cadaret .05 .02
❑ 553 Luis Salazar .05 .02
❑ 554 Nick Esasky .05 .02
❑ 555 Bert Blyleven .10 .04
❑ 556 Bruce Fields .05 .02
❑ 557 Keith A. Miller .05 .02
❑ 558 Dan Pasqua .05 .02
❑ 559 Juan Agosto .05 .02
❑ 560 Tim Raines .10 .04
❑ 561 Luis Aguayo .05 .02
❑ 562 Danny Cox .05 .02
❑ 563 Bill Schroeder .05 .02
❑ 564 Russ Nixon MG .05 .02
❑ 565 Jeff Russell .05 .02
❑ 566 Al Pedrique .05 .02
❑ 567 David Wells UER .10 .04
(Complete Pitching
Recor)
❑ 568 Mickey Brantley .05 .02
❑ 569 German Jimenez .05 .02
❑ 570 Tony Gwynn UER .30 .12
('88 average should
be italicized as
league leader)
❑ 571 Billy Ripken .05 .02
❑ 572 Atlee Hammaker .05 .02
❑ 573 Jim Abbott FDP RC* 1.00 .40
❑ 574 Dave Clark .05 .02
❑ 575 Juan Samuel .05 .02
❑ 576 Greg Minton .05 .02
❑ 577 Randy Bush .05 .02
❑ 578 John Morris .05 .02
❑ 579 Glenn Davis TL .05 .02
❑ 580 Harold Reynolds .10 .04
❑ 581 Gene Nelson .05 .02
❑ 582 Mike Marshall .05 .02
❑ 583 Paul Gibson .05 .02
❑ 584 Randy Velarde UER .05 .02
(Signed 1935,
should be 1985)
❑ 585 Harold Baines .10 .04
❑ 586 Joe Boever .05 .02
❑ 587 Mike Stanley .05 .02
❑ 588 Luis Alicea RC * .25 .10
❑ 589 Dave Meads .05 .02
❑ 590 Andres Galarraga .10 .04
❑ 591 Jeff Musselman .05 .02
❑ 592 John Cangelosi .05 .02
❑ 593 Drew Hall .05 .02
❑ 594 Jimy Williams MG .05 .02
❑ 595 Teddy Higuera .05 .02
❑ 596 Kurt Stillwell .05 .02
❑ 597 Terry Taylor RC .10 .04
❑ 598 Ken Gerhart .05 .02
❑ 599 Tom Candiotti .05 .02
❑ 600 Wade Boggs .15 .06
❑ 601 Dave Dravecky .05 .02
❑ 602 Devon White .10 .04
❑ 603 Frank Tanana .10 .04
❑ 604 Paul O'Neill .15 .06
❑ 605A Bob Welch ERR 10.00 4.00

(Missing line on back
Complete M.L. Pitching Record
❏ 605B Bob Welch COR .10 .04
❏ 606 Rick Dempsey .05 .02
❏ 607 Willie Ansley FDP RC .10 .04
❏ 608 Phil Bradley .05 .02
❏ 609 Frank Tanana .05 .02
Alan Trammell
Mike Heath TL
❏ 610 Randy Myers .10 .04
❏ 611 Don Slaught .05 .02
❏ 612 Dan Quisenberry .05 .02
❏ 613 Gary Varsho .05 .02
❏ 614 Joe Hesketh .05 .02
❏ 615 Robin Yount .40 .16
❏ 616 Steve Rosenberg .05 .02
❏ 617 Mark Parent .05 .02
❏ 618 Rance Mulliniks .05 .02
❏ 619 Checklist 529-660 .05 .02
❏ 620 Barry Bonds 1.50 .60
❏ 621 Rick Mahler .05 .02
❏ 622 Stan Javier .05 .02
❏ 623 Fred Toliver .05 .02
❏ 624 Jack McKeon MG .10 .04
❏ 625 Eddie Murray .25 .10
❏ 626 Jeff Reed .05 .02
❏ 627 Greg A. Harris .05 .02
❏ 628 Matt Williams .25 .10
❏ 629 Pete O'Brien .05 .02
❏ 630 Mike Greenwell .05 .02
❏ 631 Dave Bergman .05 .02
❏ 632 Bryan Harvey RC * .25 .10
❏ 633 Daryl Boston .05 .02
❏ 634 Marvin Freeman .05 .02
❏ 635 Willie Randolph .10 .04
❏ 636 Bill Wilkinson .05 .02
❏ 637 Carmen Castillo .05 .02
❏ 638 Floyd Bannister .05 .02
❏ 639 Walt Weiss TL .05 .02
❏ 640 Willie McGee .10 .04
❏ 641 Curt Young .05 .02
❏ 642 Angel Salazar .05 .02
❏ 643 Louie Meadows .05 .02
❏ 644 Lloyd McClendon .05 .02
❏ 645 Jack Morris .10 .04
❏ 646 Kevin Bass .05 .02
❏ 647 Randy Johnson RC 5.00 2.00
❏ 648 Sandy Alomar FS RC .40 .16
❏ 649 Stu Cliburn .05 .02
❏ 650 Kirby Puckett .25 .10
❏ 651 Tom Niedenfuer .05 .02
❏ 652 Rich Gedman .05 .02
❏ 653 Tommy Barrett .05 .02
❏ 654 Whitey Herzog MG .10 .04
❏ 655 Dave Magadan .05 .02
❏ 656 Ivan Calderon .05 .02
❏ 657 Joe Magrane .05 .02
❏ 658 R.J. Reynolds .05 .02
❏ 659 Al Leiter .25 .10
❏ 660 Will Clark .15 .06
❏ 661 D.Gooden TBC84 .05 .02
❏ 662 Lou Brock TBC79 .10 .04
❏ 663 Hank Aaron TBC74 .25 .10
❏ 664 Gil Hodges TBC 69 .10 .04
❏ 665A Tony Oliva TBC64 .00 .00
ERR (fabricated card
is enlarged version
of Oliva's 64T card;
Topps copyright
missing)
❏ 665B Tony Oliva TBC 64 .10 .04
COR (fabricated
card)
❏ 666 Randy St.Claire .05 .02
❏ 667 Dwayne Murphy .05 .02
❏ 668 Mike Bielecki .05 .02
❏ 669 Orel Hershiser .10 .04
Mike Scioscia TL
❏ 670 Kevin Seitzer .05 .02
❏ 671 Jim Gantner .05 .02
❏ 672 Allan Anderson .05 .02
❏ 673 Don Baylor .10 .04
❏ 674 Otis Nixon .05 .02
❏ 675 Bruce Hurst .05 .02
❏ 676 Ernie Riles .05 .02
❏ 677 Dave Schmidt .05 .02
❏ 678 Dion James .05 .02
❏ 679 Willie Fraser .05 .02
❏ 680 Gary Carter .10 .04
❏ 681 Jeff D. Robinson .05 .02
❏ 682 Rick Leach .05 .02
❏ 683 Jose Cecena .05 .02
❏ 684 Dave Johnson MG .05 .02
❏ 685 Jeff Treadway .05 .02
❏ 686 Scott Terry .05 .02
❏ 687 Alvin Davis .05 .02
❏ 688 Zane Smith .05 .02
❏ 689A Stan Jefferson 10.00 4.00
(Pink triangle on
front bottom left)
❏ 689B Stan Jefferson .05 .02
(Violet triangle on
front bottom left)
❏ 690 Doug Jones .05 .02
❏ 691 Roberto Kelly UER .05 .02
(83 Oneonita)
❏ 692 Steve Ontiveros .05 .02
❏ 693 Pat Borders RC * .25 .10
❏ 694 Les Lancaster .05 .02
❏ 695 Carlton Fisk .15 .06
❏ 696 Don August .05 .02
❏ 697A Franklin Stubbs ERR .. 10.00 4.00
(Team name on front
in white)
❏ 697B Franklin Stubbs .05 .02
(Team name on front
in gray)
❏ 698 Keith Atherton .05 .02
❏ 699 Al Pedrique TL .05 .02
Tony Gwynn sliding
❏ 700 Don Mattingly .60 .24
❏ 701 Storm Davis .05 .02
❏ 702 Jamie Quirk .05 .02
❏ 703 Scott Garrelts .05 .02
❏ 704 Carlos Quintana RC .10 .04
❏ 705 Terry Kennedy .05 .02
❏ 706 Pete Incaviglia .05 .02
❏ 707 Steve Jeltz .05 .02
❏ 708 Chuck Finley .10 .04
❏ 709 Tom Herr .05 .02
❏ 710 David Cone .10 .04
❏ 711 Candy Sierra .05 .02
❏ 712 Bill Swift .05 .02
❏ 713 Ty Griffin FDP .05 .02
❏ 714 Joe Morgan MG .10 .04
❏ 715 Tony Pena .05 .02
❏ 716 Wayne Tolleson .05 .02
❏ 717 Jamie Moyer .10 .04
❏ 718 Glenn Braggs .05 .02
❏ 719 Danny Darwin .05 .02
❏ 720 Tim Wallach .05 .02
❏ 721 Ron Tingley .05 .02
❏ 722 Todd Stottlemyre .05 .02
❏ 723 Rafael Belliard .05 .02
❏ 724 Jerry Don Gleaton .05 .02
❏ 725 Terry Steinbach .10 .04
❏ 726 Dickie Thon .05 .02
❏ 727 Joe Orsulak .05 .02
❏ 728 Charlie Puleo .05 .02
❏ 729 Steve Buechele TL .05 .02
(Inconsistent design,
team name on front
surrounded by black,
should be white)
❏ 730 Danny Jackson .05 .02
❏ 731 Mike Young .05 .02
❏ 732 Steve Buechele .05 .02
❏ 733 Randy Bockus .05 .02
❏ 734 Jody Reed .05 .02
❏ 735 Roger McDowell .05 .02
❏ 736 Jeff Hamilton .05 .02
❏ 737 Norm Charlton RC .25 .10
❏ 738 Darnell Coles .05 .02
❏ 739 Brook Jacoby .05 .02
❏ 740 Dan Plesac .05 .02
❏ 741 Ken Phelps .05 .02
❏ 742 Mike Harkey FS RC .10 .04
❏ 743 Mike Heath .05 .02
❏ 744 Roger Craig MG .10 .04
❏ 745 Fred McGriff .15 .06
❏ 746 G.Gonzalez UER .05 .02
Wrong birthdate
❏ 747 Wil Tejada .05 .02
❏ 748 Jimmy Jones .05 .02
❏ 749 Rafael Ramirez .05 .02
❏ 750 Bret Saberhagen .10 .04
❏ 751 Ken Oberkfell .05 .02
❏ 752 Jim Gott .05 .02
❏ 753 Jose Uribe .05 .02
❏ 754 Bob Brower .05 .02
❏ 755 Mike Scioscia .10 .04
❏ 756 Scott Medvin .05 .02
❏ 757 Brady Anderson RC .40 .16
❏ 758 Gene Walter .05 .02
❏ 759 Rob Deer TL .05 .02
❏ 760 Lee Smith .10 .04
❏ 761 Dante Bichette RC .40 .16
❏ 762 Bobby Thigpen .05 .02
❏ 763 Dave Martinez .05 .02
❏ 764 Robin Ventura FDP RC .75 .30
❏ 765 Glenn Davis .05 .02
❏ 766 Cecilio Guante .05 .02
❏ 767 Mike Capel .05 .02
❏ 768 Bill Wegman .05 .02
❏ 769 Junior Ortiz .05 .02
❏ 770 Alan Trammell .10 .04
❏ 771 Ron Kittle .05 .02
❏ 772 Ron Oester .05 .02
❏ 773 Keith Moreland .05 .02
❏ 774 Frank Robinson MG .15 .06
❏ 775 Jeff Reardon .10 .04
❏ 776 Nelson Liriano .05 .02
❏ 777 Ted Power .05 .02
❏ 778 Bruce Benedict .05 .02
❏ 779 Craig McMurtry .05 .02
❏ 780 Pedro Guerrero .10 .04
❏ 781 Greg Briley .10 .04
❏ 782 Checklist 661-792 .05 .02
❏ 783 Trevor Wilson RC .10 .04
❏ 784 Steve Avery FDP RC .25 .10
❏ 785 Ellis Burks .10 .04
❏ 786 Melido Perez .05 .02
❏ 787 Dave West RC .10 .04
❏ 788 Mike Morgan .05 .02
❏ 789 Bo Jackson TL .25 .10
❏ 790 Sid Fernandez .05 .02
❏ 791 Jim Lindeman .05 .02
❏ 792 Rafael Santana .05 .02

1989 Topps Traded

	Nm-Mt	Ex-Mt
COMP.FACT.SET (132)	15.00	6.00

❏ 1T Don Aase .05 .02
❏ 2T Jim Abbott .50 .20
❏ 3T Kent Anderson .05 .02
❏ 4T Keith Atherton .05 .02
❏ 5T Wally Backman .05 .02
❏ 6T Steve Balboni .05 .02
❏ 7T Jesse Barfield .10 .04
❏ 8T Steve Bedrosian .05 .02
❏ 9T Todd Benzinger .05 .02
❏ 10T Geronimo Berroa .05 .02
❏ 11T Bert Blyleven .10 .04
❏ 12T Bob Boone .10 .04
❏ 13T Phil Bradley .05 .02
❏ 14T Jeff Brantley RC .25 .10
❏ 15T Kevin Brown .25 .10
❏ 16T Jerry Browne .05 .02
❏ 17T Chuck Cary .05 .02

❑ 18T Carmen Castillo .05 .02
❑ 19T Jim Clancy .05 .02
❑ 20T Jack Clark .10 .04
❑ 21T Bryan Clutterbuck .05 .02
❑ 22T Jody Davis .05 .02
❑ 23T Mike Devereaux .05 .02
❑ 24T Frank DiPino .05 .02
❑ 25T Benny Distefano .05 .02
❑ 26T John Dopson .05 .02
❑ 27T Len Dykstra .10 .04
❑ 28T Jim Eisenreich .05 .02
❑ 29T Nick Esasky .05 .02
❑ 30T Alvaro Espinoza .05 .02
❑ 31T Darrell Evans UER .10 .04
(Stat headings on back are for a pitcher)
❑ 32T Junior Felix RC .10 .04
❑ 33T Felix Fermin .05 .02
❑ 34T Julio Franco .10 .04
❑ 35T Terry Francona .10 .04
❑ 36T Cito Gaston MG .05 .02
❑ 37T Bob Geren RC UER .05 .02
(Photo actually Mike Fennell)
❑ 38T Tom Gordon RC .40 .16
❑ 39T Tommy Gregg .05 .02
❑ 40T Ken Griffey Sr. .10 .04
❑ 41T Ken Griffey Jr. RC 8.00 3.20
❑ 42T Kevin Gross .05 .02
❑ 43T Lee Guetterman .05 .02
❑ 44T Mel Hall .05 .02
❑ 45T Erik Hanson RC .25 .10
❑ 46T Gene Harris RC .10 .04
❑ 47T Andy Hawkins .05 .02
❑ 48T Rickey Henderson .25 .10
❑ 49T Tom Herr .05 .02
❑ 50T Ken Hill RC .25 .10
❑ 51T Brian Holman RC * .10 .04
❑ 52T Brian Holton .05 .02
❑ 53T Art Howe MG .05 .02
❑ 54T Ken Howell .05 .02
❑ 55T Bruce Hurst .05 .02
❑ 56T Chris James .05 .02
❑ 57T Randy Johnson 3.00 1.20
❑ 58T Jimmy Jones .05 .02
❑ 59T Terry Kennedy .05 .02
❑ 60T Paul Kilgus .05 .02
❑ 61T Eric King .05 .02
❑ 62T Ron Kittle .05 .02
❑ 63T John Kruk .10 .04
❑ 64T Randy Kutcher .05 .02
❑ 65T Steve Lake .05 .02
❑ 66T Mark Langston .05 .02
❑ 67T Dave LaPoint .05 .02
❑ 68T Rick Leach .05 .02
❑ 69T Terry Leach .05 .02
❑ 70T Jim Lefebvre MG .05 .02
❑ 71T Al Leiter .25 .10
❑ 72T Jeffrey Leonard .05 .02
❑ 73T Derek Lilliquist RC .10 .04
❑ 74T Rick Mahler .05 .02
❑ 75T Tom McCarthy .05 .02
❑ 76T Lloyd McClendon .05 .02
❑ 77T Lance McCullers .05 .02
❑ 78T Oddibe McDowell .05 .02
❑ 79T Roger McDowell .05 .02
❑ 80T Larry McWilliams .05 .02
❑ 81T Randy Milligan .05 .02
❑ 82T Mike Moore .05 .02
❑ 83T Keith Moreland .05 .02
❑ 84T Mike Morgan .05 .02
❑ 85T Jamie Moyer .10 .04
❑ 86T Rob Murphy .05 .02
❑ 87T Eddie Murray .25 .10
❑ 88T Pete O'Brien .05 .02
❑ 89T Gregg Olson .25 .10
❑ 90T Steve Ontiveros .05 .02
❑ 91T Jesse Orosco .05 .02
❑ 92T Spike Owen .05 .02
❑ 93T Rafael Palmeiro .25 .10
❑ 94T Clay Parker .05 .02
❑ 95T Jeff Parrett .05 .02
❑ 96T Lance Parrish .10 .04
❑ 97T Dennis Powell .05 .02
❑ 98T Rey Quinones .05 .02
❑ 99T Doug Rader MG .05 .02
❑ 100T Willie Randolph .10 .04
❑ 101T Shane Rawley .05 .02
❑ 102T Randy Ready .05 .02
❑ 103T Bip Roberts .05 .02
❑ 104T Kenny Rogers RC 1.00 .40
❑ 105T Ed Romero .05 .02
❑ 106T Nolan Ryan 1.50 .60
❑ 107T Luis Salazar .05 .02
❑ 108T Juan Samuel .05 .02
❑ 109T Alex Sanchez .05 .02
❑ 110T Deion Sanders RC 1.50 .60
❑ 111T Steve Sax .05 .02
❑ 112T Rick Schu .05 .02
❑ 113T Dwight Smith RC .25 .10
❑ 114T Lonnie Smith .05 .02
❑ 115T Billy Spiers RC .25 .10
❑ 116T Kent Tekulve .05 .02
❑ 117T Walt Terrell .05 .02
❑ 118T Milt Thompson .05 .02
❑ 119T Dickie Thon .05 .02
❑ 120T Jeff Torborg MG .05 .02
❑ 121T Jeff Treadway .05 .02
❑ 122T Omar Vizquel RC 1.00 .40
❑ 123T Jerome Walton RC .25 .10
❑ 124T Gary Ward .05 .02
❑ 125T Claudell Washington .05 .02
❑ 126T Curt Wilkerson .05 .02
❑ 127T Eddie Williams .05 .02
❑ 128T Frank Williams .05 .02
❑ 129T Ken Williams .05 .02
❑ 130T Mitch Williams .05 .02
❑ 131T Steve Wilson RC .10 .04
❑ 132T Checklist 1T-132T .05 .02

1990 Topps

	Nm-Mt	Ex-Mt
COMPLETE SET (792)	20.00	6.00
COMP.FACT.SET (792)	25.00	7.50
COMP.X-MAS.SET (792)	40.00	12.00

❑ 1 Nolan Ryan 1.00 .30
❑ 2 Nolan Ryan Mets .50 .15
❑ 3 Nolan Ryan Angels .50 .15
❑ 4 Nolan Ryan Astros .50 .15
❑ 5 N.Ryan Rangers UER .50 .15
(Says Texas Stadium rather than Arlington Stadium)
❑ 6 Vince Coleman RB .05 .02
❑ 7 Rickey Henderson RB .15 .04
❑ 8 Cal Ripken RB .25 .07
❑ 9 Eric Plunk .05 .02
❑ 10 Barry Larkin .15 .04
❑ 11 Paul Gibson .05 .02
❑ 12 Joe Girardi .15 .04
❑ 13 Mark Williamson .05 .02
❑ 14 Mike Fetters RC .25 .07
❑ 15 Teddy Higuera .05 .02
❑ 16 Kent Anderson .05 .02
❑ 17 Kelly Downs .05 .02
❑ 18 Carlos Quintana .05 .02
❑ 19 Al Newman .05 .02
❑ 20 Mark Gubicza .05 .02
❑ 21 Jeff Torborg MG .05 .02
❑ 22 Bruce Ruffin .05 .02
❑ 23 Randy Velarde .05 .02
❑ 24 Joe Hesketh .05 .02
❑ 25 Willie Randolph .10 .03
❑ 26 Don Slaught .05 .02
❑ 27 Rick Leach .05 .02
❑ 28 Duane Ward .05 .02
❑ 29 John Cangelosi .05 .02
❑ 30 David Cone .10 .03
❑ 31 Henry Cotto .05 .02
❑ 32 John Farrell .05 .02
❑ 33 Greg Walker .05 .02
❑ 34 Tony Fossas .05 .02
❑ 35 Benito Santiago .10 .03
❑ 36 John Costello .05 .02
❑ 37 Domingo Ramos .05 .02
❑ 38 Wes Gardner .05 .02
❑ 39 Curt Ford .05 .02
❑ 40 Jay Howell .05 .02
❑ 41 Matt Williams .10 .03
❑ 42 Jeff M. Robinson .05 .02
❑ 43 Dante Bichette .10 .03
❑ 44 Roger Salkeld FDP RC .10 .03
❑ 45 Dave Parker UER .10 .03
(Born in Jackson, not Calhoun)
❑ 46 Rob Dibble .10 .03
❑ 47 Brian Harper .05 .02
❑ 48 Zane Smith .05 .02
❑ 49 Tom Lawless .05 .02
❑ 50 Glenn Davis .05 .02
❑ 51 Doug Rader MG .05 .02
❑ 52 Jack Daugherty .05 .02
❑ 53 Mike LaCoss .05 .02
❑ 54 Joel Skinner .05 .02
❑ 55 Darrell Evans UER .10 .03
(HR total should be 414, not 424)
❑ 56 Franklin Stubbs .05 .02
❑ 57 Greg Vaughn .05 .02
❑ 58 Keith Miller .05 .02
❑ 59 Ted Power .05 .02
❑ 60 George Brett .60 .18
❑ 61 Deion Sanders .25 .07
❑ 62 Ramon Martinez .05 .02
❑ 63 Mike Pagliarulo .05 .02
❑ 64 Danny Darwin .05 .02
❑ 65 Devon White .10 .03
❑ 66 Greg Litton .05 .02
❑ 67 Scott Sanderson .05 .02
❑ 68 Dave Henderson .05 .02
❑ 69 Todd Frohwirth .05 .02
❑ 70 Mike Greenwell .05 .02
❑ 71 Allan Anderson .05 .02
❑ 72 Jeff Huson RC .10 .03
❑ 73 Bob Milacki .05 .02
❑ 74 Jeff Jackson FDP RC .10 .03
❑ 75 Doug Jones .05 .02
❑ 76 Dave Valle .05 .02
❑ 77 Dave Bergman .05 .02
❑ 78 Mike Flanagan .05 .02
❑ 79 Ron Kittle .05 .02
❑ 80 Jeff Russell .05 .02
❑ 81 Bob Rodgers MG .05 .02
❑ 82 Scott Terry .05 .02
❑ 83 Hensley Meulens .05 .02
❑ 84 Ray Searage .05 .02
❑ 85 Juan Samuel .05 .02
❑ 86 Paul Kilgus .05 .02
❑ 87 Rick Luecken .05 .02
❑ 88 Glenn Braggs .05 .02
❑ 89 Clint Zavaras .05 .02
❑ 90 Jack Clark .10 .03
❑ 91 Steve Frey .05 .02
❑ 92 Mike Stanley .05 .02
❑ 93 Shawn Hillegas .05 .02
❑ 94 Herm Winningham .05 .02
❑ 95 Todd Worrell .05 .02
❑ 96 Jody Reed .05 .02
❑ 97 Curt Schilling 1.00 .30
❑ 98 Jose Gonzalez .05 .02
❑ 99 Rich Monteleone .05 .02
❑ 100 Will Clark .15 .04
❑ 101 Shane Rawley .05 .02
❑ 102 Stan Javier .05 .02
❑ 103 Marvin Freeman .05 .02
❑ 104 Bob Knepper .05 .02
❑ 105 Randy Myers .10 .03
❑ 106 Charlie O'Brien .05 .02
❑ 107 Fred Lynn .05 .02

- ❑ 108 Rod Nichols .05 .02
- ❑ 109 Roberto Kelly .05 .02
- ❑ 110 Tommy Helms MG .05 .02
- ❑ 111 Ed Whited .05 .02
- ❑ 112 Glenn Wilson .05 .02
- ❑ 113 Manny Lee .05 .02
- ❑ 114 Mike Bielecki .05 .02
- ❑ 115 Tony Pena .05 .02
- ❑ 116 Floyd Bannister .05 .02
- ❑ 117 Mike Sharperson .05 .02
- ❑ 118 Erik Hanson .05 .02
- ❑ 119 Billy Hatcher .05 .02
- ❑ 120 John Franco .10 .03
- ❑ 121 Robin Ventura .25 .07
- ❑ 122 Shawn Abner .05 .02
- ❑ 123 Rich Gedman .05 .02
- ❑ 124 Dave Dravecky .10 .03
- ❑ 125 Kent Hrbek .10 .03
- ❑ 126 Randy Kramer .05 .02
- ❑ 127 Mike Devereaux .05 .02
- ❑ 128 Checklist 1 .05 .02
- ❑ 129 Ron Jones .05 .02
- ❑ 130 Bert Blyleven .10 .03
- ❑ 131 Matt Nokes .05 .02
- ❑ 132 Lance Blankenship .05 .02
- ❑ 133 Ricky Horton .05 .02
- ❑ 134 E.Cunningham FDP RC .10 .03
- ❑ 135 Dave Magadan .05 .02
- ❑ 136 Kevin Brown .10 .03
- ❑ 137 Marty Pevey .05 .02
- ❑ 138 Al Leiter .25 .07
- ❑ 139 Greg Brock .05 .02
- ❑ 140 Andre Dawson .10 .03
- ❑ 141 John Hart MG .05 .02
- ❑ 142 Jeff Wetherby .05 .02
- ❑ 143 Rafael Belliard .05 .02
- ❑ 144 Bud Black .05 .02
- ❑ 145 Terry Steinbach .05 .02
- ❑ 146 Rob Richie .05 .02
- ❑ 147 Chuck Finley .10 .03
- ❑ 148 Edgar Martinez .15 .04
- ❑ 149 Steve Farr .05 .02
- ❑ 150 Kirk Gibson .15 .04
- ❑ 151 Rick Mahler .05 .02
- ❑ 152 Lonnie Smith .05 .02
- ❑ 153 Randy Milligan .05 .02
- ❑ 154 Mike Maddux .05 .02
- ❑ 155 Ellis Burks .15 .04
- ❑ 156 Ken Patterson .05 .02
- ❑ 157 Craig Biggio .25 .07
- ❑ 158 Craig Lefferts .05 .02
- ❑ 159 Mike Felder .05 .02
- ❑ 160 Dave Righetti .05 .02
- ❑ 161 Harold Reynolds .10 .03
- ❑ 162 Todd Zeile .10 .03
- ❑ 163 Phil Bradley .05 .02
- ❑ 164 Jeff Juden FDP RC .10 .03
- ❑ 165 Walt Weiss .05 .02
- ❑ 166 Bobby Witt .05 .02
- ❑ 167 Kevin Appier .10 .03
- ❑ 168 Jose Lind .05 .02
- ❑ 169 Richard Dotson .05 .02
- ❑ 170 George Bell .05 .02
- ❑ 171 Russ Nixon MG .05 .02
- ❑ 172 Tom Lampkin .05 .02
- ❑ 173 Tim Belcher .05 .02
- ❑ 174 Jeff Kunkel .05 .02
- ❑ 175 Mike Moore .05 .02
- ❑ 176 Luis Quinones .05 .02
- ❑ 177 Mike Henneman .05 .02
- ❑ 178 Chris James .05 .02
- ❑ 179 Brian Holton .05 .02
- ❑ 180 Tim Raines .10 .03
- ❑ 181 Juan Agosto .05 .02
- ❑ 182 Mookie Wilson .10 .03
- ❑ 183 Steve Lake .05 .02
- ❑ 184 Danny Cox .05 .02
- ❑ 185 Ruben Sierra .05 .02
- ❑ 186 Dave LaPoint .05 .02
- ❑ 187 Rick Wrona .05 .02
- ❑ 188 Mike Smithson .05 .02
- ❑ 189 Dick Schofield .05 .02
- ❑ 190 Rick Reuschel .05 .02
- ❑ 191 Pat Borders .05 .02
- ❑ 192 Don August .05 .02
- ❑ 193 Andy Benes .10 .03
- ❑ 194 Glenallen Hill .05 .02
- ❑ 195 Tim Burke .05 .02
- ❑ 196 Gerald Young .05 .02
- ❑ 197 Doug Drabek .05 .02
- ❑ 198 Mike Marshall .05 .02
- ❑ 199 Sergio Valdez .05 .02
- ❑ 200 Don Mattingly .60 .18
- ❑ 201 Cito Gaston MG .05 .02
- ❑ 202 Mike Macfarlane .05 .02
- ❑ 203 Mike Roesler .05 .02
- ❑ 204 Bob Dernier .05 .02
- ❑ 205 Mark Davis .05 .02
- ❑ 206 Nick Esasky .05 .02
- ❑ 207 Bob Ojeda .05 .02
- ❑ 208 Brook Jacoby .05 .02
- ❑ 209 Greg Mathews .05 .02
- ❑ 210 Ryne Sandberg .40 .12
- ❑ 211 John Cerutti .05 .02
- ❑ 212 Joe Orsulak .05 .02
- ❑ 213 Scott Bankhead .05 .02
- ❑ 214 Terry Francona .10 .03
- ❑ 215 Kirk McCaskill .05 .02
- ❑ 216 Ricky Jordan .05 .02
- ❑ 217 Don Robinson .05 .02
- ❑ 218 Wally Backman .05 .02
- ❑ 219 Donn Pall .05 .02
- ❑ 220 Barry Bonds 1.00 .30
- ❑ 221 Gary Mielke .05 .02
- ❑ 222 Kurt Stillwell UER .05 .02
  (Graduate misspelled as gradute)
- ❑ 223 Tommy Gregg .05 .02
- ❑ 224 Delino DeShields RC .25 .07
- ❑ 225 Jim Deshaies .05 .02
- ❑ 226 Mickey Hatcher .05 .02
- ❑ 227 Kevin Tapani RC .25 .07
- ❑ 228 Dave Martinez .05 .02
- ❑ 229 David Wells .10 .03
- ❑ 230 Keith Hernandez .10 .03
- ❑ 231 Jack McKeon MG .05 .02
- ❑ 232 Darnell Coles .05 .02
- ❑ 233 Ken Hill .10 .03
- ❑ 234 Mariano Duncan .05 .02
- ❑ 235 Jeff Reardon .10 .03
- ❑ 236 Hal Morris .05 .02
- ❑ 237 Kevin Ritz .05 .02
- ❑ 238 Felix Jose .05 .02
- ❑ 239 Eric Show .05 .02
- ❑ 240 Mark Grace .15 .04
- ❑ 241 Mike Krukow .05 .02
- ❑ 242 Fred Manrique .05 .02
- ❑ 243 Barry Jones .05 .02
- ❑ 244 Bill Schroeder .05 .02
- ❑ 245 Roger Clemens .50 .15
- ❑ 246 Jim Eisenreich .05 .02
- ❑ 247 Jerry Reed .05 .02
- ❑ 248 Dave Anderson .05 .02
- ❑ 249 Mike (Texas) Smith .05 .02
- ❑ 250 Jose Canseco .15 .04
- ❑ 251 Jeff Blauser .05 .02
- ❑ 252 Otis Nixon .05 .02
- ❑ 253 Mark Portugal .05 .02
- ❑ 254 Francisco Cabrera .05 .02
- ❑ 255 Bobby Thigpen .05 .02
- ❑ 256 Marvell Wynne .05 .02
- ❑ 257 Jose DeLeon .05 .02
- ❑ 258 Barry Lyons .05 .02
- ❑ 259 Lance McCullers .05 .02
- ❑ 260 Eric Davis .10 .03
- ❑ 261 Whitey Herzog MG .10 .03
- ❑ 262 Checklist 2 .05 .02
- ❑ 263 Mel Stottlemyre Jr. .05 .02
- ❑ 264 Bryan Clutterbuck .05 .02
- ❑ 265 Pete O'Brien .05 .02
- ❑ 266 German Gonzalez .05 .02
- ❑ 267 Mark Davidson .05 .02
- ❑ 268 Rob Murphy .05 .02
- ❑ 269 Dickie Thon .05 .02
- ❑ 270 Dave Stewart .10 .03
- ❑ 271 Chet Lemon .05 .02
- ❑ 272 Bryan Harvey .05 .02
- ❑ 273 Bobby Bonilla .10 .03
- ❑ 274 Mauro Gozzo .05 .02
- ❑ 275 Mickey Tettleton .05 .02
- ❑ 276 Gary Thurman .05 .02
- ❑ 277 Lenny Harris .05 .02
- ❑ 278 Pascual Perez .05 .02
- ❑ 279 Steve Buechele .05 .02
- ❑ 280 Lou Whitaker .10 .03
- ❑ 281 Kevin Bass .05 .02
- ❑ 282 Derek Lilliquist .05 .02
- ❑ 283 Joey Belle .25 .07
- ❑ 284 Mark Gardner RC .10 .03
- ❑ 285 Willie McGee .10 .03
- ❑ 286 Lee Guetterman .05 .02
- ❑ 287 Vance Law .05 .02
- ❑ 288 Greg Briley .05 .02
- ❑ 289 Norm Charlton .05 .02
- ❑ 290 Robin Yount .40 .12
- ❑ 291 Dave Johnson MG .10 .03
- ❑ 292 Jim Gott .05 .02
- ❑ 293 Mike Gallego .05 .02
- ❑ 294 Craig McMurtry .05 .02
- ❑ 295 Fred McGriff .25 .07
- ❑ 296 Jeff Ballard .05 .02
- ❑ 297 Tommy Herr .05 .02
- ❑ 298 Dan Gladden .05 .02
- ❑ 299 Adam Peterson .05 .02
- ❑ 300 Bo Jackson .25 .07
- ❑ 301 Don Aase .05 .02
- ❑ 302 Marcus Lawton .05 .02
- ❑ 303 Rick Cerone .05 .02
- ❑ 304 Marty Clary .05 .02
- ❑ 305 Eddie Murray .25 .07
- ❑ 306 Tom Niedenfuer .05 .02
- ❑ 307 Bip Roberts .05 .02
- ❑ 308 Jose Guzman .05 .02
- ❑ 309 Eric Yelding .05 .02
- ❑ 310 Steve Bedrosian .05 .02
- ❑ 311 Dwight Smith .05 .02
- ❑ 312 Dan Quisenberry .05 .02
- ❑ 313 Gus Polidor .05 .02
- ❑ 314 Donald Harris FDP .05 .02
- ❑ 315 Bruce Hurst .05 .02
- ❑ 316 Carney Lansford .10 .03
- ❑ 317 Mark Guthrie .05 .02
- ❑ 318 Wallace Johnson .05 .02
- ❑ 319 Dion James .05 .02
- ❑ 320 Dave Stieb .10 .03
- ❑ 321 Joe Morgan MG .05 .02
- ❑ 322 Junior Ortiz .05 .02
- ❑ 323 Willie Wilson .05 .02
- ❑ 324 Pete Harnisch .05 .02
- ❑ 325 Robby Thompson .05 .02
- ❑ 326 Tom McCarthy .05 .02
- ❑ 327 Ken Williams .05 .02
- ❑ 328 Curt Young .05 .02
- ❑ 329 Oddibe McDowell .05 .02
- ❑ 330 Ron Darling .05 .02
- ❑ 331 Juan Gonzalez RC 1.00 .30
- ❑ 332 Paul O'Neill .15 .04
- ❑ 333 Bill Wegman .05 .02
- ❑ 334 Johnny Ray .05 .02
- ❑ 335 Andy Hawkins .05 .02
- ❑ 336 Ken Griffey Jr. .75 .23
- ❑ 337 Lloyd McClendon .05 .02
- ❑ 338 Dennis Lamp .05 .02
- ❑ 339 Dave Clark .05 .02
- ❑ 340 Fernando Valenzuela .10 .03
- ❑ 341 Tom Foley .05 .02
- ❑ 342 Alex Trevino .05 .02
- ❑ 343 Frank Tanana .05 .02
- ❑ 344 George Canale .05 .02
- ❑ 345 Harold Baines .10 .03
- ❑ 346 Jim Presley .05 .02
- ❑ 347 Junior Felix .05 .02
- ❑ 348 Gary Wayne .05 .02
- ❑ 349 Steve Finley .10 .03
- ❑ 350 Bret Saberhagen .10 .03
- ❑ 351 Roger Craig MG .05 .02
- ❑ 352 Bryn Smith .05 .02
- ❑ 353 Sandy Alomar Jr. .10 .03
  (Not listed as Jr. on card front)
- ❑ 354 Stan Belinda RC .10 .03
- ❑ 355 Marty Barrett .05 .02
- ❑ 356 Randy Ready .05 .02
- ❑ 357 Dave West .05 .02
- ❑ 358 Andres Thomas .05 .02
- ❑ 359 Jimmy Jones .05 .02
- ❑ 360 Paul Molitor .15 .04
- ❑ 361 Randy McCament .05 .02

❑ 362 Damon Berryhill .05 .02
❑ 363 Dan Petry .05 .02
❑ 364 Rolando Roomes .05 .02
❑ 365 Ozzie Guillen .10 .03
❑ 366 Mike Heath .05 .02
❑ 367 Mike Morgan .05 .02
❑ 368 Bill Doran .05 .02
❑ 369 Todd Burns .05 .02
❑ 370 Tim Wallach .05 .02
❑ 371 Jimmy Key .10 .03
❑ 372 Terry Kennedy .05 .02
❑ 373 Alvin Davis .05 .02
❑ 374 Steve Cummings RC .05 .02
❑ 375 Dwight Evans .15 .04
❑ 376 Checklist 3 UER .05 .02
(Higuera misalphabetized in Brewer list)
❑ 377 Mickey Weston .05 .02
❑ 378 Luis Salazar .05 .02
❑ 379 Steve Rosenberg .05 .02
❑ 380 Dave Winfield .10 .03
❑ 381 Frank Robinson MG .15 .04
❑ 382 Jeff Musselman .05 .02
❑ 383 John Morris .05 .02
❑ 384 Pat Combs .05 .02
❑ 385 Fred McGriff AS .10 .03
❑ 386 Julio Franco AS .05 .02
❑ 387 Wade Boggs AS .10 .03
❑ 388 Cal Ripken AS .40 .12
❑ 389 Robin Yount AS .25 .07
❑ 390 Ruben Sierra AS .05 .02
❑ 391 Kirby Puckett AS .15 .04
❑ 392 Carlton Fisk AS .10 .03
❑ 393 Bret Saberhagen AS .05 .02
❑ 394 Jeff Ballard AS .05 .02
❑ 395 Jeff Russell AS .05 .02
❑ 396 A.Bartlett Giamatti .25 .07
COMM MEM
❑ 397 Will Clark AS .10 .03
❑ 398 Ryne Sandberg AS .25 .07
❑ 399 Howard Johnson AS .05 .02
❑ 400 Ozzie Smith AS .25 .07
❑ 401 Kevin Mitchell AS .05 .02
❑ 402 Eric Davis AS .05 .02
❑ 403 Tony Gwynn AS .15 .04
❑ 404 Craig Biggio AS .25 .07
❑ 405 Mike Scott AS .05 .02
❑ 406 Joe Magrane AS .05 .02
❑ 407 Mark Davis AS .05 .02
❑ 408 Trevor Wilson .05 .02
❑ 409 Tom Brunansky .05 .02
❑ 410 Joe Boever .05 .02
❑ 411 Ken Phelps .05 .02
❑ 412 Jamie Moyer .10 .03
❑ 413 Brian DuBois .05 .02
❑ 414A Frank Thomas FDP .. 500.00 150.00
ERR (Name missing on card front)
❑ 414B F.Thomas COR RC 2.00 .60
❑ 415 Shawon Dunston .05 .02
❑ 416 Dave Johnson (P) .05 .02
❑ 417 Jim Gantner .05 .02
❑ 418 Tom Browning .05 .02
❑ 419 Beau Allred RC .05 .02
❑ 420 Carlton Fisk .15 .04
❑ 421 Greg Minton .05 .02
❑ 422 Pat Sheridan .05 .02
❑ 423 Fred Toliver .05 .02
❑ 424 Jerry Reuss .05 .02
❑ 425 Bill Landrum .05 .02
❑ 426 Jeff Hamilton UER .05 .02
(Stats say he fanned 197 times in 1987, but he only had 147 at bats)
❑ 427 Carmen Castillo .05 .02
❑ 428 Steve Davis .05 .02
❑ 429 Tom Kelly MG .05 .02
❑ 430 Pete Incaviglia .05 .02
❑ 431 Randy Johnson .50 .15
❑ 432 Damaso Garcia .05 .02
❑ 433 Steve Olin RC .25 .07
❑ 434 Mark Carreon .05 .02
❑ 435 Kevin Seitzer .05 .02
❑ 436 Mel Hall .05 .02
❑ 437 Les Lancaster .05 .02
❑ 438 Greg Myers .05 .02
❑ 439 Jeff Parrett .05 .02
❑ 440 Alan Trammell .10 .03
❑ 441 Bob Kipper .05 .02
❑ 442 Jerry Browne .05 .02
❑ 443 Cris Carpenter .05 .02
❑ 444 Kyle Abbott FDP .05 .02
❑ 445 Danny Jackson .05 .02
❑ 446 Dan Pasqua .05 .02
❑ 447 Atlee Hammaker .05 .02
❑ 448 Greg Gagne .05 .02
❑ 449 Dennis Rasmussen .05 .02
❑ 450 Rickey Henderson .25 .07
❑ 451 Mark Lemke .05 .02
❑ 452 Luis DeLosSantos .05 .02
❑ 453 Jody Davis .05 .02
❑ 454 Jeff King .05 .02
❑ 455 Jeffrey Leonard .05 .02
❑ 456 Chris Gwynn .05 .02
❑ 457 Gregg Jefferies .10 .03
❑ 458 Bob McClure .05 .02
❑ 459 Jim Lefebvre MG .05 .02
❑ 460 Mike Scott .05 .02
❑ 461 Carlos Martinez .05 .02
❑ 462 Denny Walling .05 .02
❑ 463 Drew Hall .05 .02
❑ 464 Jerome Walton .05 .02
❑ 465 Kevin Gross .05 .02
❑ 466 Rance Mulliniks .05 .02
❑ 467 Juan Nieves .05 .02
❑ 468 Bill Ripken .05 .02
❑ 469 John Kruk .10 .03
❑ 470 Frank Viola .05 .02
❑ 471 Mike Brumley .05 .02
❑ 472 Jose Uribe .05 .02
❑ 473 Joe Price .05 .02
❑ 474 Rich Thompson .05 .02
❑ 475 Bob Welch .05 .02
❑ 476 Brad Komminsk .05 .02
❑ 477 Willie Fraser .05 .02
❑ 478 Mike LaValliere .05 .02
❑ 479 Frank White .10 .03
❑ 480 Sid Fernandez .05 .02
❑ 481 Garry Templeton .05 .02
❑ 482 Steve Carter .05 .02
❑ 483 Alejandro Pena .05 .02
❑ 484 Mike Fitzgerald .05 .02
❑ 485 John Candelaria .05 .02
❑ 486 Jeff Treadway .05 .02
❑ 487 Steve Searcy .05 .02
❑ 488 Ken Oberkfell .05 .02
❑ 489 Nick Leyva MG .05 .02
❑ 490 Dan Plesac .05 .02
❑ 491 Dave Cochrane RC .05 .02
❑ 492 Ron Oester .05 .02
❑ 493 Jason Grimsley RC .10 .03
❑ 494 Terry Puhl .05 .02
❑ 495 Lee Smith .10 .03
❑ 496 Cecil Espy UER .05 .02
('88 stats have 3 SB's, should be 33)
❑ 497 Dave Schmidt .05 .02
❑ 498 Rick Schu .05 .02
❑ 499 Bill Long .05 .02
❑ 500 Kevin Mitchell .05 .02
❑ 501 Matt Young .05 .02
❑ 502 Mitch Webster .05 .02
❑ 503 Randy St.Claire .05 .02
❑ 504 Tom O'Malley .05 .02
❑ 505 Kelly Gruber .05 .02
❑ 506 Tom Glavine .15 .04
❑ 507 Gary Redus .05 .02
❑ 508 Terry Leach .05 .02
❑ 509 Tom Pagnozzi .05 .02
❑ 510 Dwight Gooden .10 .03
❑ 511 Clay Parker .05 .02
❑ 512 Gary Pettis .05 .02
❑ 513 Mark Eichhorn .05 .02
❑ 514 Andy Allanson .05 .02
❑ 515 Len Dykstra .10 .03
❑ 516 Tim Leary .05 .02
❑ 517 Roberto Alomar .15 .04
❑ 518 Bill Krueger .05 .02
❑ 519 Bucky Dent MG .05 .02
❑ 520 Mitch Williams .05 .02
❑ 521 Craig Worthington .05 .02
❑ 522 Mike Dunne .05 .02
❑ 523 Jay Bell .10 .03
❑ 524 Daryl Boston .05 .02
❑ 525 Wally Joyner .10 .03
❑ 526 Checklist 4 .05 .02
❑ 527 Ron Hassey .05 .02
❑ 528 Kevin Wickander UER .05 .02
(Monthly scoreboard strikeout total was 2.2, that was his innings pitched total)
❑ 529 Greg A. Harris .05 .02
❑ 530 Mark Langston .05 .02
❑ 531 Ken Caminiti .10 .03
❑ 532 Cecilio Guante .05 .02
❑ 533 Tim Jones .05 .02
❑ 534 Louie Meadows .05 .02
❑ 535 John Smoltz .25 .07
❑ 536 Bob Geren .05 .02
❑ 537 Mark Grant .05 .02
❑ 538 Bill Spiers UER .05 .02
(Photo actually George Canale)
❑ 539 Neal Heaton .05 .02
❑ 540 Danny Tartabull .05 .02
❑ 541 Pat Perry .05 .02
❑ 542 Darren Daulton .10 .03
❑ 543 Nelson Liriano .05 .02
❑ 544 Dennis Boyd .05 .02
❑ 545 Kevin McReynolds .05 .02
❑ 546 Kevin Hickey .05 .02
❑ 547 Jack Howell .05 .02
❑ 548 Pat Clements .05 .02
❑ 549 Don Zimmer MG .05 .02
❑ 550 Julio Franco .10 .03
❑ 551 Tim Crews .05 .02
❑ 552 Mike(Miss.) Smith .05 .02
❑ 553 Scott Scudder UER .05 .02
(Cedar Rap1ds)
❑ 554 Jay Buhner .10 .03
❑ 555 Jack Morris .10 .03
❑ 556 Gene Larkin .05 .02
❑ 557 Jeff Innis .05 .02
❑ 558 Rafael Ramirez .05 .02
❑ 559 Andy McGaffigan .05 .02
❑ 560 Steve Sax .05 .02
❑ 561 Ken Dayley .05 .02
❑ 562 Chad Kreuter .05 .02
❑ 563 Alex Sanchez .05 .02
❑ 564 T.Houston FDP RC .25 .07
❑ 565 Scott Fletcher .05 .02
❑ 566 Mark Knudson .05 .02
❑ 567 Ron Gant .10 .03
❑ 568 John Smiley .05 .02
❑ 569 Ivan Calderon .05 .02
❑ 570 Cal Ripken .75 .23
❑ 571 Brett Butler .10 .03
❑ 572 Greg W. Harris .05 .02
❑ 573 Danny Heep .05 .02
❑ 574 Bill Swift .05 .02
❑ 575 Lance Parrish .05 .02
❑ 576 Mike Dyer RC .05 .02
❑ 577 Charlie Hayes .05 .02
❑ 578 Joe Magrane .05 .02
❑ 579 Art Howe MG .05 .02
❑ 580 Joe Carter .10 .03
❑ 581 Ken Griffey Sr. .10 .03
❑ 582 Rick Honeycutt .05 .02
❑ 583 Bruce Benedict .05 .02
❑ 584 Phil Stephenson .05 .02
❑ 585 Kal Daniels .05 .02
❑ 586 Edwin Nunez .05 .02
❑ 587 Lance Johnson .05 .02
❑ 588 Rick Rhoden .05 .02
❑ 589 Mike Aldrete .05 .02
❑ 590 Ozzie Smith .40 .12
❑ 591 Todd Stottlemyre .10 .03
❑ 592 R.J. Reynolds .05 .02
❑ 593 Scott Bradley .05 .02
❑ 594 Luis Sojo .05 .02
❑ 595 Greg Swindell .05 .02
❑ 596 Jose DeJesus .05 .02
❑ 597 Chris Bosio .05 .02
❑ 598 Brady Anderson .10 .03
❑ 599 Frank Williams .05 .02
❑ 600 Darryl Strawberry .10 .03
❑ 601 Luis Rivera .05 .02

❑ 602 Scott Garrelts .05 .02
❑ 603 Tony Armas .05 .02
❑ 604 Ron Robinson .05 .02
❑ 605 Mike Scioscia .05 .02
❑ 606 Storm Davis .05 .02
❑ 607 Steve Jeltz .05 .02
❑ 608 Eric Anthony RC .10 .03
❑ 609 Sparky Anderson MG .10 .03
❑ 610 Pedro Guerrero .05 .02
❑ 611 Walt Terrell .05 .02
❑ 612 Dave Gallagher .05 .02
❑ 613 Jeff Pico .05 .02
❑ 614 Nelson Santovenia .05 .02
❑ 615 Rob Deer .05 .02
❑ 616 Brian Holman .05 .02
❑ 617 Geronimo Berroa .05 .02
❑ 618 Ed Whitson .05 .02
❑ 619 Rob Ducey .05 .02
❑ 620 Tony Castillo .05 .02
❑ 621 Melido Perez .05 .02
❑ 622 Sid Bream .05 .02
❑ 623 Jim Corsi .05 .02
❑ 624 Darrin Jackson .05 .02
❑ 625 Roger McDowell .05 .02
❑ 626 Bob Melvin .05 .02
❑ 627 Jose Rijo .05 .02
❑ 628 Candy Maldonado .05 .02
❑ 629 Eric Hetzel .05 .02
❑ 630 Gary Gaetti .10 .03
❑ 631 John Wetteland .25 .07
❑ 632 Scott Lusader .05 .02
❑ 633 Dennis Cook .05 .02
❑ 634 Luis Polonia .05 .02
❑ 635 Brian Downing .05 .02
❑ 636 Jesse Orosco .05 .02
❑ 637 Craig Reynolds .05 .02
❑ 638 Jeff Montgomery .10 .03
❑ 639 Tony LaRussa MG .10 .03
❑ 640 Rick Sutcliffe .10 .03
❑ 641 Doug Strange .05 .02
❑ 642 Jack Armstrong .05 .02
❑ 643 Alfredo Griffin .05 .02
❑ 644 Paul Assenmacher .05 .02
❑ 645 Jose Oquendo .05 .02
❑ 646 Checklist 5 .05 .02
❑ 647 Rex Hudler .05 .02
❑ 648 Jim Clancy .05 .02
❑ 649 Dan Murphy RC .10 .03
❑ 650 Mike Witt .05 .02
❑ 651 Rafael Santana .05 .02
❑ 652 Mike Boddicker .05 .02
❑ 653 John Moses .05 .02
❑ 654 Paul Coleman FDP RC .10 .03
❑ 655 Gregg Olson .10 .03
❑ 656 Mackey Sasser .05 .02
❑ 657 Terry Mulholland .05 .02
❑ 658 Donell Nixon .05 .02
❑ 659 Greg Cadaret .05 .02
❑ 660 Vince Coleman .05 .02
❑ 661 Dick Howser TBC'85 .05 .02
UER (Seaver's 300th on 7/11/85, should be 8/4/85)
❑ 662 Mike Schmidt TBC'80 .25 .07
❑ 663 Fred Lynn TBC'75 .05 .02
❑ 664 Johnny Bench TBC'70 .15 .04
❑ 665 Sandy Koufax TBC'65 .50 .15
❑ 666 Brian Fisher .05 .02
❑ 667 Curt Wilkerson .05 .02
❑ 668 Joe Oliver .05 .02
❑ 669 Tom Lasorda MG .25 .07
❑ 670 Dennis Eckersley .10 .03
❑ 671 Bob Boone .10 .03
❑ 672 Roy Smith .05 .02
❑ 673 Joey Meyer .05 .02
❑ 674 Spike Owen .05 .02
❑ 675 Jim Abbott .15 .04
❑ 676 Randy Kutcher .05 .02
❑ 677 Jay Tibbs .05 .02
❑ 678 Kirt Manwaring UER .05 .02
('88 Phoenix stats repeated)
❑ 679 Gary Ward .05 .02
❑ 680 Howard Johnson .05 .02
❑ 681 Mike Schooler .05 .02
❑ 682 Dann Bilardello .05 .02
❑ 683 Kenny Rogers .10 .03
❑ 684 Julio Machado .05 .02
❑ 685 Tony Fernandez .05 .02
❑ 686 Carmelo Martinez .05 .02
❑ 687 Tim Birtsas .05 .02
❑ 688 Milt Thompson .05 .02
❑ 689 Rich Yett .05 .02
❑ 690 Mark McGwire .60 .18
❑ 691 Chuck Cary .05 .02
❑ 692 Sammy Sosa RC 3.00 .90
❑ 693 Calvin Schiraldi .05 .02
❑ 694 Mike Stanton RC .25 .07
❑ 695 Tom Henke .05 .02
❑ 696 B.J. Surhoff .10 .03
❑ 697 Mike Davis .05 .02
❑ 698 Omar Vizquel .25 .07
❑ 699 Jim Leyland MG .05 .02
❑ 700 Kirby Puckett .25 .07
❑ 701 Bernie Williams RC 1.50 .45
❑ 702 Tony Phillips .05 .02
❑ 703 Jeff Brantley .05 .02
❑ 704 Chip Hale .05 .02
❑ 705 Claudell Washington .05 .02
❑ 706 Geno Petralli .05 .02
❑ 707 Luis Aquino .05 .02
❑ 708 Larry Sheets .05 .02
❑ 709 Juan Berenguer .05 .02
❑ 710 Von Hayes .05 .02
❑ 711 Rick Aguilera .10 .03
❑ 712 Todd Benzinger .05 .02
❑ 713 Tim Drummond .05 .02
❑ 714 Marquis Grissom RC .40 .12
❑ 715 Greg Maddux .40 .12
❑ 716 Steve Balboni .05 .02
❑ 717 Ron Karkovice .05 .02
❑ 718 Gary Sheffield .25 .07
❑ 719 Wally Whitehurst .05 .02
❑ 720 Andres Galarraga .10 .03
❑ 721 Lee Mazzilli .05 .02
❑ 722 Felix Fermin .05 .02
❑ 723 Jeff D. Robinson .05 .02
❑ 724 Juan Bell .05 .02
❑ 725 Terry Pendleton .10 .03
❑ 726 Gene Nelson .05 .02
❑ 727 Pat Tabler .05 .02
❑ 728 Jim Acker .05 .02
❑ 729 Bobby Valentine MG .05 .02
❑ 730 Tony Gwynn .30 .09
❑ 731 Don Carman .05 .02
❑ 732 Ernest Riles .05 .02
❑ 733 John Dopson .05 .02
❑ 734 Kevin Elster .05 .02
❑ 735 Charlie Hough .10 .03
❑ 736 Rick Dempsey .05 .02
❑ 737 Chris Sabo .05 .02
❑ 738 Gene Harris .05 .02
❑ 739 Dale Sveum .05 .02
❑ 740 Jesse Barfield .05 .02
❑ 741 Steve Wilson .05 .02
❑ 742 Ernie Whitt .05 .02
❑ 743 Tom Candiotti .05 .02
❑ 744 Kelly Mann .05 .02
❑ 745 Hubie Brooks .05 .02
❑ 746 Dave Smith .05 .02
❑ 747 Randy Bush .05 .02
❑ 748 Doyle Alexander .05 .02
❑ 749 Mark Parent UER .05 .02
('87 BA .80, should be .080)
❑ 750 Dale Murphy .15 .04
❑ 751 Steve Lyons .05 .02
❑ 752 Tom Gordon .10 .03
❑ 753 Chris Speier .05 .02
❑ 754 Bob Walk .05 .02
❑ 755 Rafael Palmeiro .15 .04
❑ 756 Ken Howell .05 .02
❑ 757 Larry Walker RC 1.00 .30
❑ 758 Mark Thurmond .05 .02
❑ 759 Tom Trebelhorn MG .05 .02
❑ 760 Wade Boggs .15 .04
❑ 761 Mike Jackson .05 .02
❑ 762 Doug Dascenzo .05 .02
❑ 763 Dennis Martinez .10 .03
❑ 764 Tim Teufel .05 .02
❑ 765 Chili Davis .10 .03
❑ 766 Brian Meyer .05 .02
❑ 767 Tracy Jones .05 .02
❑ 768 Chuck Crim .05 .02
❑ 769 Greg Hibbard RC .10 .03
❑ 770 Cory Snyder .05 .02
❑ 771 Pete Smith .05 .02
❑ 772 Jeff Reed .05 .02
❑ 773 Dave Leiper .05 .02
❑ 774 Ben McDonald RC .25 .07
❑ 775 Andy Van Slyke .15 .04
❑ 776 Charlie Leibrandt .05 .02
❑ 777 Tim Laudner .05 .02
❑ 778 Mike Jeffcoat .05 .02
❑ 779 Lloyd Moseby .05 .02
❑ 780 Orel Hershiser .10 .03
❑ 781 Mario Diaz .05 .02
❑ 782 Jose Alvarez .05 .02
❑ 783 Checklist 6 .05 .02
❑ 784 Scott Bailes .05 .02
❑ 785 Jim Rice .10 .03
❑ 786 Eric King .05 .02
❑ 787 Rene Gonzales .05 .02
❑ 788 Frank DiPino .05 .02
❑ 789 John Wathan MG .05 .02
❑ 790 Gary Carter .10 .03
❑ 791 Alvaro Espinoza .05 .02
❑ 792 Gerald Perry .05 .02
❑ XX George Bush PRES .00

1990 Topps Debut '89

	Nm-Mt	Ex-Mt
COMP.FACT.SET (152)	15.00	4.50

❑ 1 Jim Abbott .50 .15
❑ 2 Beau Allred .15 .04
❑ 3 Wilson Alvarez .25 .07
❑ 4 Kent Anderson .15 .04
❑ 5 Eric Anthony .15 .04
❑ 6 Kevin Appier .25 .07
❑ 7 Larry Arndt .15 .04
❑ 8 John Barfield .15 .04
❑ 9 Billy Bates .15 .04
❑ 10 Kevin Batiste .15 .04
❑ 11 Blaine Beatty .15 .04
❑ 12 Stan Belinda .15 .04
❑ 13 Juan Bell .15 .04
❑ 14 Joey Belle .75 .23
(Now known as Albert)
❑ 15 Andy Benes .25 .07
❑ 16 Mike Benjamin .15 .04
❑ 17 Geronimo Berroa .15 .04
❑ 18 Mike Blowers .25 .07
❑ 19 Brian Brady .15 .04
❑ 20 Francisco Cabrera .15 .04
❑ 21 George Canale .15 .04
❑ 22 Jose Cano .15 .04
❑ 23 Steve Carter .15 .04
❑ 24 Pat Combs .15 .04
❑ 25 Scott Coolbaugh .15 .04
❑ 26 Steve Cummings .15 .04
❑ 27 Pete Dalena .15 .04
❑ 28 Jeff Datz .15 .04
❑ 29 Bobby Davidson .15 .04
❑ 30 Drew Denson .15 .04
❑ 31 Gary DiSarcina .25 .07
❑ 32 Brian DuBois .15 .04
❑ 33 Mike Dyer .15 .04
❑ 34 Wayne Edwards .15 .04
❑ 35 Junior Felix .15 .04

	Card	Nm-Mt	Ex-Mt
❑	36 Mike Fetters	.15	.04
❑	37 Steve Finley	.25	.07
❑	38 Darrin Fletcher	.25	.07
❑	39 LaVel Freeman	.15	.04
❑	40 Steve Frey	.15	.04
❑	41 Mark Gardner	.15	.04
❑	42 Joe Girardi	.25	.07
❑	43 Juan Gonzalez	2.50	.75
❑	44 Goose Gozzo	.15	.04
❑	45 Tommy Greene	.15	.04
❑	46 Ken Griffey Jr.	5.00	1.50
❑	47 Jason Grimsley	.15	.04
❑	48 Marquis Grissom	.75	.23
❑	49 Mark Guthrie	.15	.04
❑	50 Chip Hale	.15	.04
❑	51 Jack Hardy	.15	.04
❑	52 Gene Harris	.15	.04
❑	53 Mike Hartley	.15	.04
❑	54 Scott Hemond	.15	.04
❑	55 Xavier Hernandez	.15	.04
❑	56 Eric Hetzel	.15	.04
❑	57 Greg Hibbard	.15	.04
❑	58 Mark Higgins	.15	.04
❑	59 Glenallen Hill	.15	.04
❑	60 Chris Hoiles	.25	.07
❑	61 Shawn Holman	.15	.04
❑	62 Dann Howitt	.15	.04
❑	63 Mike Huff	.15	.04
❑	64 Terry Jorgensen	.15	.04
❑	65 David Justice	1.00	.30
❑	66 Jeff King	.15	.04
❑	67 Matt Kinzer	.15	.04
❑	68 Joe Kraemer	.15	.04
❑	69 Marcus Lawton	.15	.04
❑	70 Derek Lilliquist	.15	.04
❑	71 Scott Little	.15	.04
❑	72 Greg Litton	.15	.04
❑	73 Rick Luecken	.15	.04
❑	74 Julio Machado	.15	.04
❑	75 Tom Magrann	.15	.04
❑	76 Kelly Mann	.15	.04
❑	77 Randy McCament	.15	.04
❑	78 Ben McDonald	.15	.04
❑	79 Chuck McElroy	.15	.04
❑	80 Jeff McKnight	.15	.04
❑	81 Kent Mercker	.15	.04
❑	82 Matt Merullo	.15	.04
❑	83 Hensley Meulens	.15	.04
❑	84 Kevin Mmahat	.15	.04
❑	85 Mike Munoz	.15	.04
❑	86 Dan Murphy	.15	.04
❑	87 Jaime Navarro	.15	.04
❑	88 Randy Nosek	.15	.04
❑	89 John Olerud	1.00	.30
❑	90 Steve Olin	.25	.07
❑	91 Joe Oliver	.15	.04
❑	92 Francisco Oliveras	.15	.04
❑	93 Gregg Olson	.25	.07
❑	94 John Orton	.15	.04
❑	95 Dean Palmer	.50	.15
❑	96 Ramon Pena	.15	.04
❑	97 Jeff Peterek	.15	.04
❑	98 Marty Pevey	.15	.04
❑	99 Rusty Richards	.15	.04
❑	100 Jeff Richardson	.15	.04
❑	101 Rob Richie	.15	.04
❑	102 Kevin Ritz	.15	.04
❑	103 Rosario Rodriguez	.15	.04
❑	104 Mike Roesler	.15	.04
❑	105 Kenny Rogers	.25	.07
❑	106 Bobby Rose	.15	.04
❑	107 Alex Sanchez	.15	.04
❑	108 Deion Sanders	.75	.23
❑	109 Jeff Schaefer	.15	.04
❑	110 Jeff Schulz	.15	.04
❑	111 Mike Schwabe	.15	.04
❑	112 Dick Scott	.15	.04
❑	113 Scott Scudder	.15	.04
❑	114 Rudy Seanez	.15	.04
❑	115 Joe Skalski	.15	.04
❑	116 Dwight Smith	.15	.04
❑	117 Greg Smith	.15	.04
❑	118 Mike Smith	.15	.04
❑	119 Paul Sorrento	.25	.07
❑	120 Sammy Sosa	5.00	1.50
❑	121 Billy Spiers	.15	.04
❑	122 Mike Stanton	.15	.04
❑	123 Phil Stephenson	.15	.04
❑	124 Doug Strange	.15	.04
❑	125 Russ Swan	.15	.04
❑	126 Kevin Tapani	.25	.07
❑	127 Stu Tate	.15	.04
❑	128 Greg Vaughn	.15	.04
❑	129 Robin Ventura	.75	.23
❑	130 Randy Veres	.15	.04
❑	131 Jose Vizcaino	.25	.07
❑	132 Omar Vizquel	.75	.23
❑	133 Larry Walker	2.50	.75
❑	134 Jerome Walton	.15	.04
❑	135 Gary Wayne	.15	.04
❑	136 Lenny Webster	.15	.04
❑	137 Mickey Weston	.15	.04
❑	138 Jeff Wetherby	.15	.04
❑	139 John Wetteland	.50	.15
❑	140 Ed Whited	.15	.04
❑	141 Wally Whitehurst	.15	.04
❑	142 Kevin Wickander	.15	.04
❑	143 Dean Wilkins	.15	.04
❑	144 Dana Williams	.15	.04
❑	145 Paul Wilmet	.15	.04
❑	146 Craig Wilson	.15	.04
❑	147 Matt Winters	.15	.04
❑	148 Eric Yelding	.15	.04
❑	149 Clint Zavaras	.15	.04
❑	150 Todd Zeile	.50	.15
❑	151 Checklist Card	.15	.04
❑	152 Checklist Card	.15	.04

1991 Topps

	Card	Nm-Mt	Ex-Mt
	COMPLETE SET (792)	20.00	6.00
	COMP.FACT.SET (792)	25.00	7.50
❑	1 Nolan Ryan	1.50	.45
❑	2 George Brett RB	.30	.09
❑	3 Carlton Fisk RB	.10	.03
❑	4 Kevin Maas RB	.05	.02
❑	5 Cal Ripken RB	.40	.12
❑	6 Nolan Ryan RB	.50	.15
❑	7 Ryne Sandberg RB	.25	.07
❑	8 Bobby Thigpen RB	.05	.02
❑	9 Darrin Fletcher	.05	.02
❑	10 Gregg Olson	.05	.02
❑	11 Roberto Kelly	.05	.02
❑	12 Paul Assenmacher	.05	.02
❑	13 Mariano Duncan	.05	.02
❑	14 Dennis Lamp	.05	.02
❑	15 Von Hayes	.05	.02
❑	16 Mike Heath	.05	.02
❑	17 Jeff Brantley	.05	.02
❑	18 Nelson Liriano	.05	.02
❑	19 Jeff D. Robinson	.05	.02
❑	20 Pedro Guerrero	.10	.03
❑	21 Joe Morgan MG	.05	.02
❑	22 Storm Davis	.05	.02
❑	23 Jim Gantner	.05	.02
❑	24 Dave Martinez	.05	.02
❑	25 Tim Belcher	.05	.02
❑	26 Luis Sojo UER (Born in Barquisimento, not Carquis)	.05	.02
❑	27 Bobby Witt	.05	.02
❑	28 Alvaro Espinoza	.05	.02
❑	29 Bob Walk	.05	.02
❑	30 Gregg Jefferies	.05	.02
❑	31 Colby Ward	.05	.02
❑	32 Mike Simms	.05	.02
❑	33 Barry Jones	.05	.02
❑	34 Atlee Hammaker	.05	.02
❑	35 Greg Maddux	.40	.12
❑	36 Donnie Hill	.05	.02
❑	37 Tom Bolton	.05	.02
❑	38 Scott Bradley	.05	.02
❑	39 Jim Neidlinger	.05	.02
❑	40 Kevin Mitchell	.05	.02
❑	41 Ken Dayley	.05	.02
❑	42 Chris Hoiles	.05	.02
❑	43 Roger McDowell	.05	.02
❑	44 Mike Felder	.05	.02
❑	45 Chris Sabo	.05	.02
❑	46 Tim Drummond	.05	.02
❑	47 Brook Jacoby	.05	.02
❑	48 Dennis Boyd	.05	.02
❑	49A Pat Borders ERR (40 steals at Kinston in '86)	.25	.07
❑	49B Pat Borders COR (0 steals at Kinston in '86)	.05	.02
❑	50 Bob Welch	.05	.02
❑	51 Art Howe MG	.05	.02
❑	52 Francisco Oliveras	.05	.02
❑	53 Mike Sharperson UER (Born in 1961, not 1960)	.05	.02
❑	54 Gary Mielke	.05	.02
❑	55 Jeffrey Leonard	.05	.02
❑	56 Jeff Parrett	.05	.02
❑	57 Jack Howell	.05	.02
❑	58 Mel Stottlemyre Jr.	.05	.02
❑	59 Eric Yelding	.05	.02
❑	60 Frank Viola	.10	.03
❑	61 Stan Javier	.05	.02
❑	62 Lee Guetterman	.05	.02
❑	63 Milt Thompson	.05	.02
❑	64 Tom Herr	.05	.02
❑	65 Bruce Hurst	.05	.02
❑	66 Terry Kennedy	.05	.02
❑	67 Rick Honeycutt	.05	.02
❑	68 Gary Sheffield	.10	.03
❑	69 Steve Wilson	.05	.02
❑	70 Ellis Burks	.10	.03
❑	71 Jim Acker	.05	.02
❑	72 Junior Ortiz	.05	.02
❑	73 Craig Worthington	.05	.02
❑	74 Shane Andrews RC	.25	.07
❑	75 Jack Morris	.10	.03
❑	76 Jerry Browne	.05	.02
❑	77 Drew Hall	.05	.02
❑	78 Geno Petralli	.05	.02
❑	79 Frank Thomas	.25	.07
❑	80A Fernando Valenzuela ERR (104 earned runs in '90 tied for league lead)	.40	.12
❑	80B Fernando Valenzuela COR (104 earned runs in '90 led league, 20 CG's in 1986 now italicized)	.10	.03
❑	81 Cito Gaston MG	.05	.02
❑	82 Tom Glavine	.15	.04
❑	83 Daryl Boston	.05	.02
❑	84 Bob McClure	.05	.02
❑	85 Jesse Barfield	.05	.02
❑	86 Les Lancaster	.05	.02
❑	87 Tracy Jones	.05	.02
❑	88 Bob Tewksbury	.05	.02
❑	89 Darren Daulton	.10	.03
❑	90 Danny Tartabull	.05	.02
❑	91 Greg Colbrunn RC	.25	.07
❑	92 Danny Jackson	.05	.02
❑	93 Ivan Calderon	.05	.02
❑	94 John Dopson	.05	.02
❑	95 Paul Molitor	.15	.04
❑	96 Trevor Wilson	.05	.02
❑	97A Brady Anderson ERR (September, 2 RBI and 3 hits, should be 3 RBI and 14 hits	.40	.12
❑	97B Brady Anderson COR	.10	.03

No.	Player		
❑ 98	Sergio Valdez	.05	.02
❑ 99	Chris Gwynn	.05	.02
❑ 100	Don Mattingly COR	.60	.18
	(101 hits in 1990)		
❑ 100A	Don Mattingly ERR	2.00	.60
	(10 hits in 1990)		
❑ 101	Rob Ducey	.05	.02
❑ 102	Gene Larkin	.05	.02
❑ 103	Tim Costo RC	.05	.02
❑ 104	Don Robinson	.05	.02
❑ 105	Kevin McReynolds	.05	.02
❑ 106	Ed Nunez	.05	.02
❑ 107	Luis Polonia	.05	.02
❑ 108	Matt Young	.05	.02
❑ 109	Greg Riddoch MG	.05	.02
❑ 110	Tom Henke	.05	.02
❑ 111	Andres Thomas	.05	.02
❑ 112	Frank DiPino	.05	.02
❑ 113	Carl Everett RC	.50	.15
❑ 114	Lance Dickson RC	.10	.03
❑ 115	Hubie Brooks	.05	.02
❑ 116	Mark Davis	.05	.02
❑ 117	Dion James	.05	.02
❑ 118	Tom Edens	.05	.02
❑ 119	Carl Nichols	.05	.02
❑ 120	Joe Carter	.10	.03
❑ 121	Eric King	.05	.02
❑ 122	Paul O'Neill	.15	.04
❑ 123	Greg A. Harris	.05	.02
❑ 124	Randy Bush	.05	.02
❑ 125	Steve Bedrosian	.05	.02
❑ 126	Bernard Gilkey	.05	.02
❑ 127	Joe Price	.05	.02
❑ 128	Travis Fryman	.10	.03
	(Front has SS back has SS-3B)		
❑ 129	Mark Eichhorn	.05	.02
❑ 130	Ozzie Smith	.40	.12
❑ 131A	Checklist 1 ERR	.25	.07
	727 Phil Bradley		
❑ 131B	Checklist 1 COR	.05	.02
	717 Phil Bradley		
❑ 132	Jamie Quirk	.05	.02
❑ 133	Greg Briley	.05	.02
❑ 134	Kevin Elster	.05	.02
❑ 135	Jerome Walton	.05	.02
❑ 136	Dave Schmidt	.05	.02
❑ 137	Randy Ready	.05	.02
❑ 138	Jamie Moyer	.10	.03
❑ 139	Jeff Treadway	.05	.02
❑ 140	Fred McGriff	.15	.04
❑ 141	Nick Leyva MG	.05	.02
❑ 142	Curt Wilkerson	.05	.02
❑ 143	John Smiley	.05	.02
❑ 144	Dave Henderson	.05	.02
❑ 145	Lou Whitaker	.10	.03
❑ 146	Dan Plesac	.05	.02
❑ 147	Carlos Baerga	.05	.02
❑ 148	Rey Palacios	.05	.02
❑ 149	Al Osuna UER	.10	.03
	(Shown throwing right, but bio says lefty)		
❑ 150	Cal Ripken	.75	.23
❑ 151	Tom Browning	.05	.02
❑ 152	Mickey Hatcher	.05	.02
❑ 153	Bryan Harvey	.05	.02
❑ 154	Jay Buhner	.10	.03
❑ 155A	Dwight Evans ERR	.50	.15
	(Led league with 162 games in '82)		
❑ 155B	Dwight Evans COR	.15	.04
	(Tied for lead with 162 games in '82)		
❑ 156	Carlos Martinez	.05	.02
❑ 157	John Smoltz	.15	.04
❑ 158	Jose Uribe	.05	.02
❑ 159	Joe Boever	.05	.02
❑ 160	Vince Coleman UER	.05	.02
	(Wrong birth year, born 9/22/60)		
❑ 161	Tim Leary	.05	.02
❑ 162	Ozzie Canseco	.05	.02
❑ 163	Dave Johnson	.05	.02
❑ 164	Edgar Diaz	.05	.02
❑ 165	Sandy Alomar Jr.	.05	.02
❑ 166	Harold Baines	.10	.03
❑ 167A	R.Tomlin RC ERR	.25	.07
	Harriburg		
❑ 167B	R.Tomlin RC COR	.10	.03
	Harrisburg		
❑ 168	John Olerud	.10	.03
❑ 169	Luis Aquino	.05	.02
❑ 170	Carlton Fisk	.15	.04
❑ 171	Tony LaRussa MG	.10	.03
❑ 172	Pete Incaviglia	.05	.02
❑ 173	Jason Grimsley	.05	.02
❑ 174	Ken Caminiti	.10	.03
❑ 175	Jack Armstrong	.05	.02
❑ 176	John Orton	.05	.02
❑ 177	Reggie Harris	.05	.02
❑ 178	Dave Valle	.05	.02
❑ 179	Pete Harnisch	.05	.02
❑ 180	Tony Gwynn	.30	.09
❑ 181	Duane Ward	.05	.02
❑ 182	Junior Noboa	.05	.02
❑ 183	Clay Parker	.05	.02
❑ 184	Gary Green	.05	.02
❑ 185	Joe Magrane	.05	.02
❑ 186	Rod Booker	.05	.02
❑ 187	Greg Cadaret	.05	.02
❑ 188	Damon Berryhill	.05	.02
❑ 189	Daryl Irvine	.05	.02
❑ 190	Matt Williams	.10	.03
❑ 191	Willie Blair	.05	.02
❑ 192	Rob Deer	.05	.02
❑ 193	Felix Fermin	.05	.02
❑ 194	Xavier Hernandez	.05	.02
❑ 195	Wally Joyner	.10	.03
❑ 196	Jim Vatcher	.05	.02
❑ 197	Chris Nabholz	.05	.02
❑ 198	R.J. Reynolds	.05	.02
❑ 199	Mike Hartley	.05	.02
❑ 200	Darryl Strawberry	.10	.03
❑ 201	Tom Kelly MG	.05	.02
❑ 202	Jim Leyritz	.05	.02
❑ 203	Gene Harris	.05	.02
❑ 204	Herm Winningham	.05	.02
❑ 205	Mike Perez RC	.10	.03
❑ 206	Carlos Quintana	.05	.02
❑ 207	Gary Wayne	.05	.02
❑ 208	Willie Wilson	.05	.02
❑ 209	Ken Howell	.05	.02
❑ 210	Lance Parrish	.10	.03
❑ 211	Brian Barnes RC	.05	.02
❑ 212	Steve Finley	.10	.03
❑ 213	Frank Wills	.05	.02
❑ 214	Joe Girardi	.05	.02
❑ 215	Dave Smith	.05	.02
❑ 216	Greg Gagne	.05	.02
❑ 217	Chris Bosio	.05	.02
❑ 218	Rick Parker	.05	.02
❑ 219	Jack McDowell	.05	.02
❑ 220	Tim Wallach	.05	.02
❑ 221	Don Slaught	.05	.02
❑ 222	Brian McRae RC	.25	.07
❑ 223	Allan Anderson	.05	.02
❑ 224	Juan Gonzalez	.25	.07
❑ 225	Randy Johnson	.30	.09
❑ 226	Alfredo Griffin	.05	.02
❑ 227	Steve Avery UER	.05	.02
	(Pitched 13 games for Durham in 1989, not 2)		
❑ 228	Rex Hudler	.05	.02
❑ 229	Rance Mulliniks	.05	.02
❑ 230	Sid Fernandez	.05	.02
❑ 231	Doug Rader MG	.05	.02
❑ 232	Jose DeJesus	.05	.02
❑ 233	Al Leiter	.10	.03
❑ 234	Scott Erickson	.05	.02
❑ 235	Dave Parker	.10	.03
❑ 236A	Frank Tanana ERR	.25	.07
	(Tied for lead with 269 K's in '75)		
❑ 236B	Frank Tanana COR	.05	.02
	(Led league with 269 K's in '75)		
❑ 237	Rick Cerone	.05	.02
❑ 238	Mike Dunne	.05	.02
❑ 239	Darren Lewis	.05	.02
❑ 240	Mike Scott	.05	.02
❑ 241	Dave Clark UER	.05	.02
	(Career totals 19 HR and 5 3B, should be 22 and 3)		
❑ 242	Mike LaCoss	.05	.02
❑ 243	Lance Johnson	.05	.02
❑ 244	Mike Jeffcoat	.05	.02
❑ 245	Kal Daniels	.05	.02
❑ 246	Kevin Wickander	.05	.02
❑ 247	Jody Reed	.05	.02
❑ 248	Tom Gordon	.05	.02
❑ 249	Bob Melvin	.05	.02
❑ 250	Dennis Eckersley	.10	.03
❑ 251	Mark Lemke	.05	.02
❑ 252	Mel Rojas	.05	.02
❑ 253	Garry Templeton	.05	.02
❑ 254	Shawn Boskie	.05	.02
❑ 255	Brian Downing	.05	.02
❑ 256	Greg Hibbard	.05	.02
❑ 257	Tom O'Malley	.05	.02
❑ 258	Chris Hammond	.05	.02
❑ 259	Hensley Meulens	.05	.02
❑ 260	Harold Reynolds	.10	.03
❑ 261	Bud Harrelson MG	.05	.02
❑ 262	Tim Jones	.05	.02
❑ 263	Checklist 2	.05	.02
❑ 264	Dave Hollins	.05	.02
❑ 265	Mark Gubicza	.05	.02
❑ 266	Carmelo Castillo	.05	.02
❑ 267	Mark Knudson	.05	.02
❑ 268	Tom Brookens	.05	.02
❑ 269	Joe Hesketh	.05	.02
❑ 270	Mark McGwire COR	.60	.18
	(1987 Slugging Pctg. listed as .618)		
❑ 270A	Mark McGwire ERR	2.00	.60
	(1987 Slugging Pctg. listed as 618)		
❑ 271	Omar Olivares RC	.10	.03
❑ 272	Jeff King	.05	.02
❑ 273	Johnny Ray	.05	.02
❑ 274	Ken Williams	.05	.02
❑ 275	Alan Trammell	.10	.03
❑ 276	Bill Swift	.05	.02
❑ 277	Scott Coolbaugh	.05	.02
❑ 278	Alex Fernandez UER	.05	.02
	(No '90 White Sox stats)		
❑ 279A	Jose Gonzalez ERR	.25	.07
	(Photo actually Billy Bean)		
❑ 279B	Jose Gonzalez COR	.05	.02
❑ 280	Bret Saberhagen	.10	.03
❑ 281	Larry Sheets	.05	.02
❑ 282	Don Carman	.05	.02
❑ 283	Marquis Grissom	.10	.03
❑ 284	Billy Spiers	.05	.02
❑ 285	Jim Abbott	.15	.04
❑ 286	Ken Oberkfell	.05	.02
❑ 287	Mark Grant	.05	.02
❑ 288	Derrick May	.05	.02
❑ 289	Tim Birtsas	.05	.02
❑ 290	Steve Sax	.05	.02
❑ 291	John Wathan MG	.05	.02
❑ 292	Bud Black	.05	.02
❑ 293	Jay Bell	.10	.03
❑ 294	Mike Moore	.05	.02
❑ 295	Rafael Palmeiro	.15	.04
❑ 296	Mark Williamson	.05	.02
❑ 297	Manny Lee	.05	.02
❑ 298	Omar Vizquel	.15	.04
❑ 299	Scott Radinsky	.05	.02
❑ 300	Kirby Puckett	.25	.07
❑ 301	Steve Farr	.05	.02
❑ 302	Tim Teufel	.05	.02
❑ 303	Mike Boddicker	.05	.02
❑ 304	Kevin Reimer	.05	.02
❑ 305	Mike Scioscia	.05	.02
❑ 306A	Lonnie Smith ERR	.40	.12
	(136 games in '90)		
❑ 306B	Lonnie Smith COR	.05	.02
	(135 games in '90)		
❑ 307	Andy Benes	.05	.02
❑ 308	Tom Pagnozzi	.05	.02
❑ 309	Norm Charlton	.05	.02
❑ 310	Gary Carter	.10	.03
❑ 311	Jeff Pico	.05	.02
❑ 312	Charlie Hayes	.05	.02
❑ 313	Ron Robinson	.05	.02

	No.	Player		
❑	314	Gary Pettis	.05	.02
❑	315	Roberto Alomar	.15	.04
❑	316	Gene Nelson	.05	.02
❑	317	Mike Fitzgerald	.05	.02
❑	318	Rick Aguilera	.10	.03
❑	319	Jeff McKnight	.05	.02
❑	320	Tony Fernandez	.05	.02
❑	321	Bob Rodgers MG	.05	.02
❑	322	Terry Shumpert	.05	.02
❑	323	Cory Snyder	.05	.02
❑	324A	Ron Kittle ERR (Set another standard ...)	.40	.12
❑	324B	Ron Kittle COR (Tied another standard ...)	.05	.02
❑	325	Brett Butler	.10	.03
❑	326	Ken Patterson	.05	.02
❑	327	Ron Hassey	.05	.02
❑	328	Walt Terrell	.05	.02
❑	329	Dave Justice UER (Drafted third round on card, should say fourth pick)	.10	.03
❑	330	Dwight Gooden	.10	.03
❑	331	Eric Anthony	.05	.02
❑	332	Kenny Rogers	.10	.03
❑	333	C.Jones FDP RC	4.00	1.20
❑	334	Todd Benzinger	.05	.02
❑	335	Mitch Williams	.05	.02
❑	336	Matt Nokes	.05	.02
❑	337A	Keith Comstock ERR (Cubs logo on front)	.25	.07
❑	337B	Keith Comstock COR (Mariners logo on front)	.05	.02
❑	338	Luis Rivera	.05	.02
❑	339	Larry Walker	.25	.07
❑	340	Ramon Martinez	.05	.02
❑	341	John Moses	.05	.02
❑	342	Mickey Morandini	.05	.02
❑	343	Jose Oquendo	.05	.02
❑	344	Jeff Russell	.05	.02
❑	345	Len Dykstra	.10	.03
❑	346	Jesse Orosco	.05	.02
❑	347	Greg Vaughn	.05	.02
❑	348	Todd Stottlemyre	.05	.02
❑	349	Dave Gallagher	.05	.02
❑	350	Glenn Davis	.05	.02
❑	351	Joe Torre MG	.10	.03
❑	352	Frank White	.10	.03
❑	353	Tony Castillo	.05	.02
❑	354	Sid Bream	.05	.02
❑	355	Chili Davis	.10	.03
❑	356	Mike Marshall	.05	.02
❑	357	Jack Savage	.05	.02
❑	358	Mark Parent	.05	.02
❑	359	Chuck Cary	.05	.02
❑	360	Tim Raines	.10	.03
❑	361	Scott Garrelts	.05	.02
❑	362	Hector Villenueva	.05	.02
❑	363	Rick Mahler	.05	.02
❑	364	Dan Pasqua	.05	.02
❑	365	Mike Schooler	.05	.02
❑	366A	Checklist 3 ERR 19 Carl Nichols	.25	.07
❑	366B	Checklist 3 COR 119 Carl Nichols	.05	.02
❑	367	Dave Walsh RC	.05	.02
❑	368	Felix Jose	.05	.02
❑	369	Steve Searcy	.05	.02
❑	370	Kelly Gruber	.05	.02
❑	371	Jeff Montgomery	.05	.02
❑	372	Spike Owen	.05	.02
❑	373	Darrin Jackson	.05	.02
❑	374	Larry Casian	.05	.02
❑	375	Tony Pena	.05	.02
❑	376	Mike Harkey	.05	.02
❑	377	Rene Gonzales	.05	.02
❑	378A	Wilson Alvarez ERR ('89 Port Charlotte and '90 Birmingham stat lines omitted)	.25	.07
❑	378B	Wilson Alvarez COR Text still says 143 K's in 1988, whereas stats say 134	.05	.02
❑	379	Randy Velarde	.05	.02
❑	380	Willie McGee	.10	.03
❑	381	Jim Leyland MG	.05	.02
❑	382	Mackey Sasser	.05	.02
❑	383	Pete Smith	.05	.02
❑	384	Gerald Perry	.05	.02
❑	385	Mickey Tettleton	.05	.02
❑	386	Cecil Fielder AS	.05	.02
❑	387	Julio Franco AS	.05	.02
❑	388	Kelly Gruber AS	.05	.02
❑	389	Alan Trammell AS	.10	.03
❑	390	Jose Canseco AS	.10	.03
❑	391	Rickey Henderson AS	.15	.04
❑	392	Ken Griffey Jr. AS	.40	.12
❑	393	Carlton Fisk AS	.10	.03
❑	394	Bob Welch AS	.05	.02
❑	395	Chuck Finley AS	.05	.02
❑	396	Bobby Thigpen AS	.05	.02
❑	397	Eddie Murray AS	.15	.04
❑	398	Ryne Sandberg AS	.25	.07
❑	399	Matt Williams AS	.05	.02
❑	400	Barry Larkin AS	.10	.03
❑	401	Barry Bonds AS	.50	.15
❑	402	Darryl Strawbery AS	.05	.02
❑	403	Bobby Bonilla AS	.05	.02
❑	404	Mike Scioscia AS	.05	.02
❑	405	Doug Drabek AS	.05	.02
❑	406	Frank Viola AS	.05	.02
❑	407	John Franco AS	.05	.02
❑	408	Earnest Riles	.05	.02
❑	409	Mike Stanley	.05	.02
❑	410	Dave Righetti	.10	.03
❑	411	Lance Blankenship	.05	.02
❑	412	Dave Bergman	.05	.02
❑	413	Terry Mulholland	.05	.02
❑	414	Sammy Sosa	.25	.07
❑	415	Rick Sutcliffe	.10	.03
❑	416	Randy Milligan	.05	.02
❑	417	Bill Krueger	.05	.02
❑	418	Nick Esasky	.05	.02
❑	419	Jeff Reed	.05	.02
❑	420	Bobby Thigpen	.05	.02
❑	421	Alex Cole	.05	.02
❑	422	Rick Reuschel	.05	.02
❑	423	Rafael Ramirez UER (Born 1959, not 1958)	.05	.02
❑	424	Calvin Schiraldi	.05	.02
❑	425	Andy Van Slyke	.15	.04
❑	426	Joe Grahe RC	.10	.03
❑	427	Rick Dempsey	.05	.02
❑	428	John Barfield	.05	.02
❑	429	Stump Merrill MG	.05	.02
❑	430	Gary Gaetti	.10	.03
❑	431	Paul Gibson	.05	.02
❑	432	Delino DeShields	.10	.03
❑	433	Pat Tabler	.05	.02
❑	434	Julio Machado	.05	.02
❑	435	Kevin Maas	.05	.02
❑	436	Scott Bankhead	.05	.02
❑	437	Doug Dascenzo	.05	.02
❑	438	Vicente Palacios	.05	.02
❑	439	Dickie Thon	.05	.02
❑	440	George Bell	.05	.02
❑	441	Zane Smith	.05	.02
❑	442	Charlie O'Brien	.05	.02
❑	443	Jeff Innis	.05	.02
❑	444	Glenn Braggs	.05	.02
❑	445	Greg Swindell	.05	.02
❑	446	Craig Grebeck	.05	.02
❑	447	John Burkett	.05	.02
❑	448	Craig Lefferts	.05	.02
❑	449	Juan Berenguer	.05	.02
❑	450	Wade Boggs	.15	.04
❑	451	Neal Heaton	.05	.02
❑	452	Bill Schroeder	.05	.02
❑	453	Lenny Harris	.05	.02
❑	454A	Kevin Appier ERR ('90 Omaha stat line omitted)	.40	.12
❑	454B	Kevin Appier COR	.10	.03
❑	455	Walt Weiss	.05	.02
❑	456	Charlie Leibrandt	.05	.02
❑	457	Todd Hundley	.05	.02
❑	458	Brian Holman	.05	.02
❑	459	T.Trebelhorn MG UER Pitching and batting columns switched	.05	.02
❑	460	Dave Stieb	.05	.02
❑	461	Robin Ventura	.10	.03
❑	462	Steve Frey	.05	.02
❑	463	Dwight Smith	.05	.02
❑	464	Steve Buechele	.05	.02
❑	465	Ken Griffey Sr.	.10	.03
❑	466	Charles Nagy	.05	.02
❑	467	Dennis Cook	.05	.02
❑	468	Tim Hulett	.05	.02
❑	469	Chet Lemon	.05	.02
❑	470	Howard Johnson	.05	.02
❑	471	Mike Lieberthal RC	.40	.12
❑	472	Kirt Manwaring	.05	.02
❑	473	Curt Young	.05	.02
❑	474	Phil Plantier RC	.10	.03
❑	475	Ted Higuera	.05	.02
❑	476	Glenn Wilson	.05	.02
❑	477	Mike Fetters	.05	.02
❑	478	Kurt Stillwell	.05	.02
❑	479	Bob Patterson UER (Has a decimal point between 7 and 9)	.05	.02
❑	480	Dave Magadan	.05	.02
❑	481	Eddie Whitson	.05	.02
❑	482	Tino Martinez	.25	.07
❑	483	Mike Aldrete	.05	.02
❑	484	Dave LaPoint	.05	.02
❑	485	Terry Pendleton	.10	.03
❑	486	Tommy Greene	.05	.02
❑	487	Rafael Belliard	.05	.02
❑	488	Jeff Manto	.05	.02
❑	489	Bobby Valentine MG	.05	.02
❑	490	Kirk Gibson	.15	.04
❑	491	Kurt Miller RC	.05	.02
❑	492	Ernie Whitt	.05	.02
❑	493	Jose Rijo	.05	.02
❑	494	Chris James	.05	.02
❑	495	Charlie Hough	.10	.03
❑	496	Marty Barrett	.05	.02
❑	497	Ben McDonald	.05	.02
❑	498	Mark Salas	.05	.02
❑	499	Melido Perez	.05	.02
❑	500	Will Clark	.15	.04
❑	501	Mike Bielecki	.05	.02
❑	502	Carney Lansford	.10	.03
❑	503	Roy Smith	.05	.02
❑	504	Julio Valera	.05	.02
❑	505	Chuck Finley	.10	.03
❑	506	Darnell Coles	.05	.02
❑	507	Steve Jeltz	.05	.02
❑	508	Mike York	.05	.02
❑	509	Glenallen Hill	.05	.02
❑	510	John Franco	.10	.03
❑	511	Steve Balboni	.05	.02
❑	512	Jose Mesa	.05	.02
❑	513	Jerald Clark	.05	.02
❑	514	Mike Stanton	.05	.02
❑	515	Alvin Davis	.05	.02
❑	516	Karl Rhodes	.05	.02
❑	517	Joe Oliver	.05	.02
❑	518	Cris Carpenter	.05	.02
❑	519	Sparky Anderson MG	.10	.03
❑	520	Mark Grace	.15	.04
❑	521	Joe Orsulak	.05	.02
❑	522	Stan Belinda	.05	.02
❑	523	Rodney McCray	.05	.02
❑	524	Darrel Akerfelds	.05	.02
❑	525	Willie Randolph	.10	.03
❑	526A	Moises Alou ERR (37 runs in 2 games for '90 Pirates)	.40	.12
❑	526B	Moises Alou COR (0 runs in 2 games for '90 Pirates)	.10	.03
❑	527A	Checklist 4 ERR 105 Keith Miller 719 Kevin McReynolds	.25	.07
❑	527B	Checklist 4 COR 105 Kevin McReynolds 719 Keith Miller	.05	.02
❑	528	Dennis Martinez	.10	.03
❑	529	Marc Newfield RC	.10	.03
❑	530	Roger Clemens	.50	.15
❑	531	Dave Rohde	.05	.02
❑	532	Kirk McCaskill	.05	.02

❑ 533 Oddibe McDowell .05 .02
❑ 534 Mike Jackson .05 .02
❑ 535 Ruben Sierra UER .05 .02
(Back reads 100 Runs
amd 100 RBI's)
❑ 536 Mike Witt .05 .02
❑ 537 Jose Lind .05 .02
❑ 538 Bip Roberts .05 .02
❑ 539 Scott Terry .05 .02
❑ 540 George Brett .60 .18
❑ 541 Domingo Ramos .05 .02
❑ 542 Rob Murphy .05 .02
❑ 543 Junior Felix .05 .02
❑ 544 Alejandro Pena .05 .02
❑ 545 Dale Murphy .15 .04
❑ 546 Jeff Ballard .05 .02
❑ 547 Mike Pagliarulo .05 .02
❑ 548 Jaime Navarro .05 .02
❑ 549 John McNamara MG .05 .02
❑ 550 Eric Davis .10 .03
❑ 551 Bob Kipper .05 .02
❑ 552 Jeff Hamilton .05 .02
❑ 553 Joe Klink .05 .02
❑ 554 Brian Harper .05 .02
❑ 555 Turner Ward RC .10 .03
❑ 556 Gary Ward .05 .02
❑ 557 Wally Whitehurst .05 .02
❑ 558 Otis Nixon .05 .02
❑ 559 Adam Peterson .05 .02
❑ 560 Greg Smith .05 .02
❑ 561 Tim McIntosh .05 .02
❑ 562 Jeff Kunkel .05 .02
❑ 563 Brent Knackert .05 .02
❑ 564 Dante Bichette .10 .03
❑ 565 Craig Biggio .15 .04
❑ 566 Craig Wilson .05 .02
❑ 567 Dwayne Henry .05 .02
❑ 568 Ron Karkovice .05 .02
❑ 569 Curt Schilling .25 .07
❑ 570 Barry Bonds 1.00 .30
❑ 571 Pat Combs .05 .02
❑ 572 Dave Anderson .05 .02
❑ 573 Rich Rodriguez UER .05 .02
(Stats say drafted 4th,
but bio says 9th round)
❑ 574 John Marzano .05 .02
❑ 575 Robin Yount .40 .12
❑ 576 Jeff Kaiser .05 .02
❑ 577 Bill Doran .05 .02
❑ 578 Dave West .05 .02
❑ 579 Roger Craig MG .05 .02
❑ 580 Dave Stewart .10 .03
❑ 581 Luis Quinones .05 .02
❑ 582 Marty Clary .05 .02
❑ 583 Tony Phillips .05 .02
❑ 584 Kevin Brown .10 .03
❑ 585 Pete O'Brien .05 .02
❑ 586 Fred Lynn .05 .02
❑ 587 Jose Offerman UER .05 .02
(Text says he signed
7/24/86, but bio
says 1988)
❑ 588 Mark Whiten .05 .02
❑ 589 Scott Ruskin .05 .02
❑ 590 Eddie Murray .25 .07
❑ 591 Ken Hill .05 .02
❑ 592 B.J. Surhoff .10 .03
❑ 593A Mike Walker ERR .25 .07
('90 Canton-Akron
stat line omitted)
❑ 593B Mike Walker COR .05 .02
❑ 594 Rich Garces RC .10 .03
❑ 595 Bill Landrum .05 .02
❑ 596 Ronnie Walden RC .10 .03
❑ 597 Jerry Don Gleaton .05 .02
❑ 598 Sam Horn .05 .02
❑ 599A Greg Myers ERR .25 .07
('90 Syracuse
stat line omitted)
❑ 599B Greg Myers COR .05 .02
❑ 600 Bo Jackson .25 .07
❑ 601 Bob Ojeda .05 .02
❑ 602 Casey Candaele .05 .02
❑ 603A W.Chamberlain RC ERR .40 .12
Photo actually
Louie Meadows
❑ 603B Wes Chamberlain RC COR .10 .03
❑ 604 Billy Hatcher .05 .02
❑ 605 Jeff Reardon .10 .03
❑ 606 Jim Gott .05 .02
❑ 607 Edgar Martinez .15 .04
❑ 608 Todd Burns .05 .02
❑ 609 Jeff Torborg MG .05 .02
❑ 610 Andres Galarraga .10 .03
❑ 611 Dave Eiland .05 .02
❑ 612 Steve Lyons .05 .02
❑ 613 Eric Show .05 .02
❑ 614 Luis Salazar .05 .02
❑ 615 Bert Blyleven .10 .03
❑ 616 Todd Zeile .05 .02
❑ 617 Bill Wegman .05 .02
❑ 618 Sil Campusano .05 .02
❑ 619 David Wells .10 .03
❑ 620 Ozzie Guillen .10 .03
❑ 621 Ted Power .05 .02
❑ 622 Jack Daugherty .05 .02
❑ 623 Jeff Blauser .05 .02
❑ 624 Tom Candiotti .05 .02
❑ 625 Terry Steinbach .05 .02
❑ 626 Gerald Young .05 .02
❑ 627 Tim Layana .05 .02
❑ 628 Greg Litton .05 .02
❑ 629 Wes Gardner .05 .02
❑ 630 Dave Winfield .10 .03
❑ 631 Mike Morgan .05 .02
❑ 632 Lloyd Moseby .05 .02
❑ 633 Kevin Tapani .05 .02
❑ 634 Henry Cotto .05 .02
❑ 635 Andy Hawkins .05 .02
❑ 636 Geronimo Pena .05 .02
❑ 637 Bruce Ruffin .05 .02
❑ 638 Mike Macfarlane .05 .02
❑ 639 Frank Robinson MG .15 .04
❑ 640 Andre Dawson .10 .03
❑ 641 Mike Henneman .05 .02
❑ 642 Hal Morris .05 .02
❑ 643 Jim Presley .05 .02
❑ 644 Chuck Crim .05 .02
❑ 645 Juan Samuel .05 .02
❑ 646 Andujar Cedeno .05 .02
❑ 647 Mark Portugal .05 .02
❑ 648 Lee Stevens .05 .02
❑ 649 Bill Sampen .05 .02
❑ 650 Jack Clark .10 .03
❑ 651 Alan Mills .05 .02
❑ 652 Kevin Romine .05 .02
❑ 653 Anthony Telford .05 .02
❑ 654 Paul Sorrento .05 .02
❑ 655 Erik Hanson .05 .02
❑ 656A Checklist 5 ERR .25 .07
348 Vicente Palacios
381 Jose Lind
537 Mike LaValliere
665 Jim Leyland
❑ 656B Checklist 5 ERR .25 .07
433 Vicente Palacios
(Palacios should be 438)
537 Jose Lind
665 Mike LaValliere
381 Jim Leyland
❑ 656C Checklist 5 COR .05 .02
438 Vicente Palacios
537 Jose Lind
665 Mike LaValliere
381 Jim Leyland
❑ 657 Mike Kingery .05 .02
❑ 658 Scott Aldred .05 .02
❑ 659 Oscar Azocar .05 .02
❑ 660 Lee Smith .10 .03
❑ 661 Steve Lake .05 .02
❑ 662 Ron Dibble .10 .03
❑ 663 Greg Brock .05 .02
❑ 664 John Farrell .05 .02
❑ 665 Mike LaValliere .05 .02
❑ 666 Danny Darwin .05 .02
❑ 667 Kent Anderson .05 .02
❑ 668 Bill Long .05 .02
❑ 669 Lou Piniella MG .10 .03
❑ 670 Rickey Henderson .25 .07
❑ 671 Andy McGaffigan .05 .02
❑ 672 Shane Mack .05 .02
❑ 673 Greg Olson UER .05 .02
(6 RBI in '88 at Tidewater
and 2 RBI in '87,
should be 48 and 15)
❑ 674A Kevin Gross ERR .25 .07
(89 BB with Phillies
in '88 tied for
league lead)
❑ 674B Kevin Gross COR .05 .02
(89 BB with Phillies
in '88 led league)
❑ 675 Tom Brunansky .05 .02
❑ 676 Scott Chiamparino .05 .02
❑ 677 Billy Ripken .05 .02
❑ 678 Mark Davidson .05 .02
❑ 679 Bill Bathe .05 .02
❑ 680 David Cone .10 .03
❑ 681 Jeff Schaefer .05 .02
❑ 682 Ray Lankford .10 .03
❑ 683 Derek Lilliquist .05 .02
❑ 684 Milt Cuyler .05 .02
❑ 685 Doug Drabek .05 .02
❑ 686 Mike Gallego .05 .02
❑ 687A John Cerutti ERR .25 .07
(4.46 ERA in '90)
❑ 687B John Cerutti COR .05 .02
(4.76 ERA in '90)
❑ 688 Rosario Rodriguez .05 .02
❑ 689 John Kruk .10 .03
❑ 690 Orel Hershiser .10 .03
❑ 691 Mike Blowers .05 .02
❑ 692A Efrain Valdez ERR .25 .07
(Born 6/11/66)
❑ 692B Efrain Valdez COR .05 .02
(Born 7/11/66 and two
lines of text added)
❑ 693 Francisco Cabrera .05 .02
❑ 694 Randy Veres .05 .02
❑ 695 Kevin Seitzer .05 .02
❑ 696 Steve Olin .05 .02
❑ 697 Shawn Abner .05 .02
❑ 698 Mark Guthrie .05 .02
❑ 699 Jim Lefebvre MG .05 .02
❑ 700 Jose Canseco .15 .04
❑ 701 Pascual Perez .05 .02
❑ 702 Tim Naehring .05 .02
❑ 703 Juan Agosto .05 .02
❑ 704 Devon White .10 .03
❑ 705 Robby Thompson .05 .02
❑ 706A Brad Arnsberg ERR .25 .07
(68.2 IP in '90)
❑ 706B Brad Arnsberg COR .05 .02
(62.2 IP in '90)
❑ 707 Jim Eisenreich .05 .02
❑ 708 John Mitchell .05 .02
❑ 709 Matt Sinatro .05 .02
❑ 710 Kent Hrbek .10 .03
❑ 711 Jose DeLeon .05 .02
❑ 712 Ricky Jordan .05 .02
❑ 713 Scott Scudder .05 .02
❑ 714 Marvell Wynne .05 .02
❑ 715 Tim Burke .05 .02
❑ 716 Bob Geren .05 .02
❑ 717 Phil Bradley .05 .02
❑ 718 Steve Crawford .05 .02
❑ 719 Keith Miller .05 .02
❑ 720 Cecil Fielder .10 .03
❑ 721 Mark Lee RC .05 .02
❑ 722 Wally Backman .05 .02
❑ 723 Candy Maldonado .05 .02
❑ 724 David Segui .05 .02
❑ 725 Ron Gant .10 .03
❑ 726 Phil Stephenson .05 .02
❑ 727 Mookie Wilson .10 .03
❑ 728 Scott Sanderson .05 .02
❑ 729 Don Zimmer MG .10 .03
❑ 730 Barry Larkin .15 .04
❑ 731 Jeff Gray .05 .02
❑ 732 Franklin Stubbs .05 .02
❑ 733 Kelly Downs .05 .02
❑ 734 John Russell .05 .02
❑ 735 Ron Darling .05 .02
❑ 736 Dick Schofield .05 .02
❑ 737 Tim Crews .05 .02
❑ 738 Mel Hall .05 .02
❑ 739 Russ Swan .05 .02
❑ 740 Ryne Sandberg .40 .12

	Card	Nm-Mt	Ex-Mt
❑	741 Jimmy Key	.10	.03
❑	742 Tommy Gregg	.05	.02
❑	743 Bryn Smith	.05	.02
❑	744 Nelson Santovenia	.05	.02
❑	745 Doug Jones	.05	.02
❑	746 John Shelby	.05	.02
❑	747 Tony Fossas	.05	.02
❑	748 Al Newman	.05	.02
❑	749 Greg W. Harris	.05	.02
❑	750 Bobby Bonilla	.10	.03
❑	751 Wayne Edwards	.05	.02
❑	752 Kevin Bass	.05	.02
❑	753 Paul Marak UER (Stats say drafted in Jan. but bio says May)	.05	.02
❑	754 Bill Pecota	.05	.02
❑	755 Mark Langston	.05	.02
❑	756 Jeff Huson	.05	.02
❑	757 Mark Gardner	.05	.02
❑	758 Mike Devereaux	.05	.02
❑	759 Bobby Cox MG	.05	.02
❑	760 Benny Santiago	.10	.03
❑	761 Larry Andersen	.05	.02
❑	762 Mitch Webster	.05	.02
❑	763 Dana Kiecker	.05	.02
❑	764 Mark Carreon	.05	.02
❑	765 Shawon Dunston	.05	.02
❑	766 Jeff Robinson	.05	.02
❑	767 Dan Wilson RC	.25	.07
❑	768 Don Pall	.05	.02
❑	769 Tim Sherrill	.05	.02
❑	770 Jay Howell	.05	.02
❑	771 Gary Redus UER (Born in Tanner, should say Athens)	.05	.02
❑	772 Kent Mercker UER (Born in Indianapolis, should say Dublin, Ohio)	.05	.02
❑	773 Tom Foley	.05	.02
❑	774 Dennis Rasmussen	.05	.02
❑	775 Julio Franco	.10	.03
❑	776 Brent Mayne	.05	.02
❑	777 John Candelaria	.05	.02
❑	778 Dan Gladden	.05	.02
❑	779 Carmelo Martinez	.05	.02
❑	780A Randy Myers ERR (15 career losses)	.40	.12
❑	780B Randy Myers COR (19 career losses)	.05	.02
❑	781 Darryl Hamilton	.05	.02
❑	782 Jim Deshaies	.05	.02
❑	783 Joel Skinner	.05	.02
❑	784 Willie Fraser	.05	.02
❑	785 Scott Fletcher	.05	.02
❑	786 Eric Plunk	.05	.02
❑	787 Checklist 6	.05	.02
❑	788 Bob Milacki	.05	.02
❑	789 Tom Lasorda MG	.25	.07
❑	790 Ken Griffey Jr.	.75	.23
❑	791 Mike Benjamin	.05	.02
❑	792 Mike Greenwell	.05	.02

1991 Topps Traded

	Nm-Mt	Ex-Mt
COMPLETE SET (132)	10.00	3.00
COMP.FACT.SET (132)	10.00	3.00

	Card	Nm-Mt	Ex-Mt
❑	1T Juan Agosto	.05	.02
❑	2T Roberto Alomar	.15	.04
❑	3T Wally Backman	.05	.02
❑	4T Jeff Bagwell RC	2.00	.60
❑	5T Skeeter Barnes	.05	.02
❑	6T Steve Bedrosian	.05	.02
❑	7T Derek Bell	.10	.03
❑	8T George Bell	.05	.02
❑	9T Rafael Belliard	.05	.02
❑	10T Dante Bichette	.10	.03
❑	11T Bud Black	.05	.02
❑	12T Mike Boddicker	.05	.02
❑	13T Sid Bream	.05	.02
❑	14T Hubie Brooks	.05	.02
❑	15T Brett Butler	.10	.03
❑	16T Ivan Calderon	.05	.02
❑	17T John Candelaria	.05	.02
❑	18T Tom Candiotti	.05	.02
❑	19T Gary Carter	.10	.03
❑	20T Joe Carter	.10	.03
❑	21T Rick Cerone	.05	.02
❑	22T Jack Clark	.10	.03
❑	23T Vince Coleman	.05	.02
❑	24T Scott Coolbaugh	.05	.02
❑	25T Danny Cox	.05	.02
❑	26T Danny Darwin	.05	.02
❑	27T Chili Davis	.10	.03
❑	28T Glenn Davis	.05	.02
❑	29T Steve Decker	.05	.02
❑	30T Rob Deer	.05	.02
❑	31T Rich DeLucia	.05	.02
❑	32T John Dettmer USA RC	.25	.07
❑	33T Brian Downing	.05	.02
❑	34T D.Dreifort USA RC	.50	.15
❑	35T K.Dressendorfer RC	.05	.02
❑	36T Jim Essian MG	.05	.02
❑	37T Dwight Evans	.15	.04
❑	38T Steve Farr	.05	.02
❑	39T Jeff Fassero RC	.25	.07
❑	40T Junior Felix	.05	.02
❑	41T Tony Fernandez	.05	.02
❑	42T Steve Finley	.10	.03
❑	43T Jim Fregosi MG	.05	.02
❑	44T Gary Gaetti	.10	.03
❑	45T Jason Giambi USA RC	4.00	1.20
❑	46T Kirk Gibson	.15	.04
❑	47T Leo Gomez	.05	.02
❑	48T Luis Gonzalez RC	.50	.15
❑	49T Jeff Granger USA RC	.25	.07
❑	50T Todd Greene USA RC	.50	.15
❑	51T J.Hammonds USA RC	.50	.15
❑	52T Mike Hargrove MG	.05	.02
❑	53T Pete Harnisch	.05	.02
❑	54T Rick Helling RC USA UER Misspelled Hellings on card back	.50	.15
❑	55T Glenallen Hill	.05	.02
❑	56T Charlie Hough	.10	.03
❑	57T Pete Incaviglia	.05	.02
❑	58T Bo Jackson	.25	.07
❑	59T Danny Jackson	.05	.02
❑	60T Reggie Jefferson	.05	.02
❑	61T C.Johnson USA RC	.75	.23
❑	62T Jeff Johnson	.05	.02
❑	63T T.Johnson USA RC	.25	.07
❑	64T Barry Jones	.05	.02
❑	65T Chris Jones RC	.10	.03
❑	66T Scott Kamieniecki RC	.10	.03
❑	67T Pat Kelly RC	.10	.03
❑	68T Darryl Kile	.10	.03
❑	69T Chuck Knoblauch	.10	.03
❑	70T Bill Krueger	.05	.02
❑	71T Scott Leius	.05	.02
❑	72T D.Leshnock USA RC	.25	.07
❑	73T Mark Lewis	.05	.02
❑	74T Candy Maldonado	.05	.02
❑	75T J.McDonald USA RC	.25	.07
❑	76T Willie McGee	.10	.03
❑	77T Fred McGriff	.15	.04
❑	78T B.McMillon USA RC	.25	.07
❑	79T Hal McRae MG	.10	.03
❑	80T D.Melendez USA RC	.25	.07
❑	81T Orlando Merced RC	.10	.03
❑	82T Jack Morris	.10	.03
❑	83T Phil Nevin USA RC	1.00	.30
❑	84T Otis Nixon	.05	.02
❑	85T Johnny Oates MG	.05	.02
❑	86T Bob Ojeda	.05	.02
❑	87T Mike Pagliarulo	.05	.02
❑	88T Dean Palmer	.10	.03
❑	89T Dave Parker	.10	.03
❑	90T Terry Pendleton	.10	.03
❑	91T T.Phillips (P) USA RC	.25	.07
❑	92T Doug Piatt	.05	.02
❑	93T Ron Polk USA CO	.25	.07
❑	94T Tim Raines	.10	.03
❑	95T Willie Randolph	.10	.03
❑	96T Dave Righetti	.10	.03
❑	97T Ernie Riles	.05	.02
❑	98T C.Roberts USA RC	.25	.07
❑	99T Jeff D. Robinson	.05	.02
❑	100T Jeff M. Robinson	.05	.02
❑	101T Ivan Rodriguez RC	2.00	.60
❑	102T S.Rodriguez USA RC	.25	.07
❑	103T Tom Runnells MG	.05	.02
❑	104T Scott Sanderson	.05	.02
❑	105T Bob Scanlan	.05	.02
❑	106T Pete Schourek RC	.10	.03
❑	107T Gary Scott	.05	.02
❑	108T Paul Shuey USA RC	.50	.15
❑	109T Doug Simons	.05	.02
❑	110T Dave Smith	.05	.02
❑	111T Cory Snyder	.05	.02
❑	112T Luis Sojo	.05	.02
❑	113T K.Steenstra USA RC	.25	.07
❑	114T Darryl Strawberry	.10	.03
❑	115T Franklin Stubbs	.05	.02
❑	116T Todd Taylor USA RC	.25	.07
❑	117T Wade Taylor	.05	.02
❑	118T Garry Templeton	.05	.02
❑	119T Mickey Tettleton	.05	.02
❑	120T Tim Teufel	.05	.02
❑	121T Mike Timlin RC	.40	.12
❑	122T David Tuttle USA RC	.25	.07
❑	123T Mo Vaughn	.10	.03
❑	124T Jeff Ware USA RC	.25	.07
❑	125T Devon White	.10	.03
❑	126T Mark Whiten	.05	.02
❑	127T Mitch Williams	.05	.02
❑	128T C.Wilson USA RC	.25	.07
❑	129T Willie Wilson	.05	.02
❑	130T C.Wimmer USA RC	.25	.07
❑	131T Ivan Zweig USA RC	.25	.07
❑	132T Checklist 1T-132T	.05	.02

1992 Topps

	Nm-Mt	Ex-Mt
COMPLETE SET (792)	25.00	7.50
COMP.FACT.SET (802)	25.00	7.50
COMP.HOLIDAY (811)	40.00	12.00

	Card	Nm-Mt	Ex-Mt
❑	1 Nolan Ryan	1.00	.30
❑	2 Ricky Henderson RB Most career SB's (Some cards have print marks that show 1.991 on the front)	.15	.04
❑	3 Jeff Reardon RB	.05	.02
❑	4 Nolan Ryan RB	.50	.15
❑	5 Dave Winfield RB	.05	.02
❑	6 Brien Taylor RC	.25	.07
❑	7 Jim Olander	.05	.02
❑	8 Bryan Hickerson RC	.10	.03
❑	9 Jon Farrell RC	.10	.03
❑	10 Wade Boggs	.15	.04

❑ 11 Jack McDowell .05 .02
❑ 12 Luis Gonzalez .10 .03
❑ 13 Mike Scioscia .05 .02
❑ 14 Wes Chamberlain .05 .02
❑ 15 Dennis Martinez .10 .03
❑ 16 Jeff Montgomery .05 .02
❑ 17 Randy Milligan .05 .02
❑ 18 Greg Cadaret .05 .02
❑ 19 Jamie Quirk .05 .02
❑ 20 Bip Roberts .05 .02
❑ 21 Buck Rodgers MG .05 .02
❑ 22 Bill Wegman .05 .02
❑ 23 Chuck Knoblauch .10 .03
❑ 24 Randy Myers .05 .02
❑ 25 Ron Gant .10 .03
❑ 26 Mike Bielecki .05 .02
❑ 27 Juan Gonzalez .15 .04
❑ 28 Mike Schooler .05 .02
❑ 29 Mickey Tettleton .05 .02
❑ 30 John Kruk .10 .03
❑ 31 Bryn Smith .05 .02
❑ 32 Chris Nabholz .05 .02
❑ 33 Carlos Baerga .05 .02
❑ 34 Jeff Juden .05 .02
❑ 35 Dave Righetti .10 .03
❑ 36 Scott Ruffcorn RC .10 .03
❑ 37 Luis Polonia .05 .02
❑ 38 Tom Candiotti .05 .02
❑ 39 Greg Olson .05 .02
❑ 40 Cal Ripken 2.00 .60
❑ 41 Craig Lefferts .05 .02
❑ 42 Mike Macfarlane .05 .02
❑ 43 Jose Lind .05 .02
❑ 44 Rick Aguilera .10 .03
❑ 45 Gary Carter .10 .03
❑ 46 Steve Farr .05 .02
❑ 47 Rex Hudler .05 .02
❑ 48 Scott Scudder .05 .02
❑ 49 Damon Berryhill .05 .02
❑ 50 Ken Griffey Jr. .40 .12
❑ 51 Tom Runnells MG .05 .02
❑ 52 Juan Bell .05 .02
❑ 53 Tommy Gregg .05 .02
❑ 54 David Wells .10 .03
❑ 55 Rafael Palmeiro .15 .04
❑ 56 Charlie O'Brien .05 .02
❑ 57 Donn Pall .05 .02
❑ 58 Brad Ausmus RC 1.00 .30
Jim Campanis Jr.
Dave Nilsson
Doug Robbins
❑ 59 Mo Vaughn .10 .03
❑ 60 Tony Fernandez .05 .02
❑ 61 Paul O'Neill .15 .04
❑ 62 Gene Nelson .05 .02
❑ 63 Randy Ready .05 .02
❑ 64 Bob Kipper .05 .02
❑ 65 Willie McGee .10 .03
❑ 66 Scott Stahoviak RC .10 .03
❑ 67 Luis Salazar .05 .02
❑ 68 Marvin Freeman .05 .02
❑ 69 Kenny Lofton .15 .04
❑ 70 Gary Gaetti .10 .03
❑ 71 Erik Hanson .05 .02
❑ 72 Eddie Zosky .05 .02
❑ 73 Brian Barnes .05 .02
❑ 74 Scott Leius .05 .02
❑ 75 Bret Saberhagen .10 .03
❑ 76 Mike Gallego .05 .02
❑ 77 Jack Armstrong .05 .02
❑ 78 Ivan Rodriguez .25 .07
❑ 79 Jesse Orosco .05 .02
❑ 80 David Justice .10 .03
❑ 81 Ced Landrum .05 .02
❑ 82 Doug Simons .05 .02
❑ 83 Tommy Greene .05 .02
❑ 84 Leo Gomez .05 .02
❑ 85 Jose DeLeon .05 .02
❑ 86 Steve Finley .10 .03
❑ 87 Bob MacDonald .05 .02
❑ 88 Darrin Jackson .05 .02
❑ 89 Neal Heaton .05 .02
❑ 90 Robin Yount .40 .12
❑ 91 Jeff Reed .05 .02
❑ 92 Lenny Harris .05 .02
❑ 93 Reggie Jefferson .05 .02
❑ 94 Sammy Sosa .25 .07
❑ 95 Scott Bailes .05 .02
❑ 96 Tom McKinnon RC .10 .03
❑ 97 Luis Rivera .05 .02
❑ 98 Mike Harkey .05 .02
❑ 99 Jeff Treadway .05 .02
❑ 100 Jose Canseco .15 .04
❑ 101 Omar Vizquel .15 .04
❑ 102 Scott Kamieniecki .05 .02
❑ 103 Ricky Jordan .05 .02
❑ 104 Jeff Ballard .05 .02
❑ 105 Felix Jose .05 .02
❑ 106 Mike Boddicker .05 .02
❑ 107 Dan Pasqua .05 .02
❑ 108 Mike Timlin .05 .02
❑ 109 Roger Craig MG .05 .02
❑ 110 Ryne Sandberg .40 .12
❑ 111 Mark Carreon .05 .02
❑ 112 Oscar Azocar .05 .02
❑ 113 Mike Greenwell .05 .02
❑ 114 Mark Portugal .05 .02
❑ 115 Terry Pendleton .10 .03
❑ 116 Willie Randolph .10 .03
❑ 117 Scott Terry .05 .02
❑ 118 Chili Davis .10 .03
❑ 119 Mark Gardner .05 .02
❑ 120 Alan Trammell .10 .03
❑ 121 Derek Bell .10 .03
❑ 122 Gary Varsho .05 .02
❑ 123 Bob Ojeda .05 .02
❑ 124 Shawn Livsey RC .10 .03
❑ 125 Chris Hoiles .05 .02
❑ 126 Ryan Klesko .25 .07
John Jaha RC
Rico Brogna
Dave Staton
❑ 127 Carlos Quintana .05 .02
❑ 128 Kurt Stillwell .05 .02
❑ 129 Melido Perez .05 .02
❑ 130 Alvin Davis .05 .02
❑ 131 Checklist 1-132 .05 .02
❑ 132 Eric Show .05 .02
❑ 133 Rance Mulliniks .05 .02
❑ 134 Darryl Kile .10 .03
❑ 135 Von Hayes .05 .02
❑ 136 Bill Doran .05 .02
❑ 137 Jeff D. Robinson .05 .02
❑ 138 Monty Fariss .05 .02
❑ 139 Jeff Innis .05 .02
❑ 140 Mark Grace UER .15 .04
Home Calie., should
be Calif.
❑ 141 Jim Leyland MG UER .10 .03
(No closed parenthesis
after East in 1991)
❑ 142 Todd Van Poppel .05 .02
❑ 143 Paul Gibson .05 .02
❑ 144 Bill Swift .05 .02
❑ 145 Danny Tartabull .05 .02
❑ 146 Al Newman .05 .02
❑ 147 Cris Carpenter .05 .02
❑ 148 Anthony Young .05 .02
❑ 149 Brian Bohanon .05 .02
❑ 150 Roger Clemens UER .50 .15
(League leading ERA in
1990 not italicized)
❑ 151 Jeff Hamilton .05 .02
❑ 152 Charlie Leibrandt .05 .02
❑ 153 Ron Karkovice .05 .02
❑ 154 Hensley Meulens .05 .02
❑ 155 Scott Bankhead .05 .02
❑ 156 Manny Ramirez RC 4.00 1.20
❑ 157 Keith Miller .05 .02
❑ 158 Todd Frohwirth .05 .02
❑ 159 Darrin Fletcher .05 .02
❑ 160 Bobby Bonilla .10 .03
❑ 161 Casey Candaele .05 .02
❑ 162 Paul Faries .05 .02
❑ 163 Dana Kiecker .05 .02
❑ 164 Shane Mack .05 .02
❑ 165 Mark Langston .05 .02
❑ 166 Geronimo Pena .05 .02
❑ 167 Andy Allanson .05 .02
❑ 168 Dwight Smith .05 .02
❑ 169 Chuck Crim .05 .02
❑ 170 Alex Cole .05 .02
❑ 171 Bill Plummer MG .05 .02
❑ 172 Juan Berenguer .05 .02
❑ 173 Brian Downing .05 .02
❑ 174 Steve Frey .05 .02
❑ 175 Orel Hershiser .10 .03
❑ 176 Ramon Garcia .05 .02
❑ 177 Dan Gladden .05 .02
❑ 178 Jim Acker .05 .02
❑ 179 Bobby DeJardin .05 .02
Cesar Bernhardt
Armando Moreno
Andy Stankiewicz
❑ 180 Kevin Mitchell .05 .02
❑ 181 Hector Villanueva .05 .02
❑ 182 Jeff Reardon .10 .03
❑ 183 Brent Mayne .05 .02
❑ 184 Jimmy Jones .05 .02
❑ 185 Benito Santiago .10 .03
❑ 186 Cliff Floyd RC 1.00 .30
❑ 187 Ernie Riles .05 .02
❑ 188 Jose Guzman .05 .02
❑ 189 Junior Felix .05 .02
❑ 190 Glenn Davis .05 .02
❑ 191 Charlie Hough .10 .03
❑ 192 Dave Fleming .05 .02
❑ 193 Omar Olivares .05 .02
❑ 194 Eric Karros .10 .03
❑ 195 David Cone .10 .03
❑ 196 Frank Castillo .05 .02
❑ 197 Glenn Braggs .05 .02
❑ 198 Scott Aldred .05 .02
❑ 199 Jeff Blauser .05 .02
❑ 200 Len Dykstra .10 .03
❑ 201 B.Showalter RC MG .25 .07
❑ 202 Rick Honeycutt .05 .02
❑ 203 Greg Myers .05 .02
❑ 204 Trevor Wilson .05 .02
❑ 205 Jay Howell .05 .02
❑ 206 Luis Sojo .05 .02
❑ 207 Jack Clark .10 .03
❑ 208 Julio Machado .05 .02
❑ 209 Lloyd McClendon .05 .02
❑ 210 Ozzie Guillen .10 .03
❑ 211 Jeremy Hernandez RC .10 .03
❑ 212 Randy Velarde .05 .02
❑ 213 Les Lancaster .05 .02
❑ 214 Andy Mota .05 .02
❑ 215 Rich Gossage .10 .03
❑ 216 Brent Gates RC .10 .03
❑ 217 Brian Harper .05 .02
❑ 218 Mike Flanagan .05 .02
❑ 219 Jerry Browne .05 .02
❑ 220 Jose Rijo .05 .02
❑ 221 Skeeter Barnes .05 .02
❑ 222 Jaime Navarro .05 .02
❑ 223 Mel Hall .05 .02
❑ 224 Bret Barberie .05 .02
❑ 225 Roberto Alomar .15 .04
❑ 226 Pete Smith .05 .02
❑ 227 Daryl Boston .05 .02
❑ 228 Eddie Whitson .05 .02
❑ 229 Shawn Boskie .05 .02
❑ 230 Dick Schofield .05 .02
❑ 231 Brian Drahman .05 .02
❑ 232 John Smiley .05 .02
❑ 233 Mitch Webster .05 .02
❑ 234 Terry Steinbach .05 .02
❑ 235 Jack Morris .10 .03
❑ 236 Bill Pecota .05 .02
❑ 237 Jose Hernandez RC .40 .12
❑ 238 Greg Litton .05 .02
❑ 239 Brian Holman .05 .02
❑ 240 Andres Galarraga .10 .03
❑ 241 Gerald Young .05 .02
❑ 242 Mike Mussina .25 .07
❑ 243 Alvaro Espinoza .05 .02
❑ 244 Darren Daulton .10 .03
❑ 245 John Smoltz .15 .04
❑ 246 Jason Pruitt RC .10 .03
❑ 247 Chuck Finley .10 .03
❑ 248 Jim Gantner .05 .02
❑ 249 Tony Fossas .05 .02
❑ 250 Ken Griffey Sr. .10 .03
❑ 251 Kevin Elster .05 .02
❑ 252 Dennis Rasmussen .05 .02
❑ 253 Terry Kennedy .05 .02

❑ 254	Ryan Bowen	.05	.02
❑ 255	Robin Ventura	.10	.03
❑ 256	Mike Aldrete	.05	.02
❑ 257	Jeff Russell	.05	.02
❑ 258	Jim Lindeman	.05	.02
❑ 259	Ron Darling	.05	.02
❑ 260	Devon White	.10	.03
❑ 261	Tom Lasorda MG	.10	.03
❑ 262	Terry Lee	.05	.02
❑ 263	Bob Patterson	.05	.02
❑ 264	Checklist 133-264	.05	.02
❑ 265	Teddy Higuera	.05	.02
❑ 266	Roberto Kelly	.05	.02
❑ 267	Steve Bedrosian	.05	.02
❑ 268	Brady Anderson	.10	.03
❑ 269	Ruben Amaro	.05	.02
❑ 270	Tony Gwynn	.30	.09
❑ 271	Tracy Jones	.05	.02
❑ 272	Jerry Don Gleaton	.05	.02
❑ 273	Craig Grebeck	.05	.02
❑ 274	Bob Scanlan	.05	.02
❑ 275	Todd Zeile	.05	.02
❑ 276	Shawn Green RC	1.50	.45
❑ 277	Scott Chiamparino	.05	.02
❑ 278	Darryl Hamilton	.05	.02
❑ 279	Jim Clancy	.05	.02
❑ 280	Carlos Martinez	.05	.02
❑ 281	Kevin Appier	.10	.03
❑ 282	John Wehner	.05	.02
❑ 283	Reggie Sanders	.10	.03
❑ 284	Gene Larkin	.05	.02
❑ 285	Bob Welch	.05	.02
❑ 286	Gilberto Reyes	.05	.02
❑ 287	Pete Schourek	.05	.02
❑ 288	Andujar Cedeno	.05	.02
❑ 289	Mike Morgan	.05	.02
❑ 290	Bo Jackson	.25	.07
❑ 291	Phil Garner MG	.10	.03
❑ 292	Ray Lankford	.10	.03
❑ 293	Mike Henneman	.05	.02
❑ 294	Dave Valle	.05	.02
❑ 295	Alonzo Powell	.05	.02
❑ 296	Tom Brunansky	.05	.02
❑ 297	Kevin Brown	.10	.03
❑ 298	Kelly Gruber	.05	.02
❑ 299	Charles Nagy	.05	.02
❑ 300	Don Mattingly	.60	.18
❑ 301	Kirk McCaskill	.05	.02
❑ 302	Joey Cora	.05	.02
❑ 303	Dan Plesac	.05	.02
❑ 304	Joe Oliver	.05	.02
❑ 305	Tom Glavine	.15	.04
❑ 306	Al Shirley RC	.10	.03
❑ 307	Bruce Ruffin	.05	.02
❑ 308	Craig Shipley	.05	.02
❑ 309	Dave Martinez	.05	.02
❑ 310	Jose Mesa	.05	.02
❑ 311	Henry Cotto	.05	.02
❑ 312	Mike LaValliere	.05	.02
❑ 313	Kevin Tapani	.05	.02
❑ 314	Jeff Huson (Shows Jose Canseco sliding into second)	.05	.02
❑ 315	Juan Samuel	.05	.02
❑ 316	Curt Schilling	.15	.04
❑ 317	Mike Bordick	.05	.02
❑ 318	Steve Howe	.05	.02
❑ 319	Tony Phillips	.05	.02
❑ 320	George Bell	.05	.02
❑ 321	Lou Piniella MG	.10	.03
❑ 322	Tim Burke	.05	.02
❑ 323	Milt Thompson	.05	.02
❑ 324	Danny Darwin	.05	.02
❑ 325	Joe Orsulak	.05	.02
❑ 326	Eric King	.05	.02
❑ 327	Jay Buhner	.10	.03
❑ 328	Joel Johnston	.05	.02
❑ 329	Franklin Stubbs	.05	.02
❑ 330	Will Clark	.15	.04
❑ 331	Steve Lake	.05	.02
❑ 332	Chris Jones	.05	.02
❑ 333	Pat Tabler	.05	.02
❑ 334	Kevin Gross	.05	.02
❑ 335	Dave Henderson	.05	.02
❑ 336	Greg Anthony RC	.10	.03
❑ 337	Alejandro Pena	.05	.02
❑ 338	Shawn Abner	.05	.02
❑ 339	Tom Browning	.05	.02
❑ 340	Otis Nixon	.05	.02
❑ 341	Bob Geren	.05	.02
❑ 342	Tim Spehr	.05	.02
❑ 343	John Vander Wal	.05	.02
❑ 344	Jack Daugherty	.05	.02
❑ 345	Zane Smith	.05	.02
❑ 346	Rheal Cormier	.05	.02
❑ 347	Kent Hrbek	.10	.03
❑ 348	Rick Wilkins	.05	.02
❑ 349	Steve Lyons	.05	.02
❑ 350	Gregg Olson	.05	.02
❑ 351	Greg Riddoch MG	.05	.02
❑ 352	Ed Nunez	.05	.02
❑ 353	Braulio Castillo	.05	.02
❑ 354	Dave Bergman	.05	.02
❑ 355	Warren Newson	.05	.02
❑ 356	Luis Quinones	.05	.02
❑ 357	Mike Witt	.05	.02
❑ 358	Ted Wood	.05	.02
❑ 359	Mike Moore	.05	.02
❑ 360	Lance Parrish	.10	.03
❑ 361	Barry Jones	.05	.02
❑ 362	Javier Ortiz	.05	.02
❑ 363	John Candelaria	.05	.02
❑ 364	Glenallen Hill	.05	.02
❑ 365	Duane Ward	.05	.02
❑ 366	Checklist 265-396	.05	.02
❑ 367	Rafael Belliard	.05	.02
❑ 368	Bill Krueger	.05	.02
❑ 369	Steve Whitaker RC	.10	.03
❑ 370	Shawon Dunston	.05	.02
❑ 371	Dante Bichette	.10	.03
❑ 372	Kip Gross	.05	.02
❑ 373	Don Robinson	.05	.02
❑ 374	Bernie Williams	.15	.04
❑ 375	Bert Blyleven	.10	.03
❑ 376	Chris Donnels	.05	.02
❑ 377	Bob Zupcic RC	.10	.03
❑ 378	Joel Skinner	.05	.02
❑ 379	Steve Chitren	.05	.02
❑ 380	Barry Bonds	1.00	.30
❑ 381	Sparky Anderson MG	.10	.03
❑ 382	Sid Fernandez	.05	.02
❑ 383	Dave Hollins	.05	.02
❑ 384	Mark Lee	.05	.02
❑ 385	Tim Wallach	.05	.02
❑ 386	Will Clark AS	.10	.03
❑ 387	Ryne Sandberg AS	.25	.07
❑ 388	Howard Johnson AS	.05	.02
❑ 389	Barry Larkin AS	.10	.03
❑ 390	Barry Bonds AS	.50	.15
❑ 391	Ron Gant AS	.05	.02
❑ 392	Bobby Bonilla AS	.05	.02
❑ 393	Craig Biggio AS	.10	.03
❑ 394	Dennis Martinez AS	.05	.02
❑ 395	Tom Glavine AS	.10	.03
❑ 396	Lee Smith AS	.05	.02
❑ 397	Cecil Fielder AS	.05	.02
❑ 398	Julio Franco AS	.05	.02
❑ 399	Wade Boggs AS	.10	.03
❑ 400	Cal Ripken AS	.40	.12
❑ 401	Jose Canseco AS	.15	.04
❑ 402	Joe Carter AS	.05	.02
❑ 403	Ruben Sierra AS	.05	.02
❑ 404	Matt Nokes AS	.05	.02
❑ 405	Roger Clemens AS	.25	.07
❑ 406	Jim Abbott AS	.10	.03
❑ 407	Bryan Harvey AS	.05	.02
❑ 408	Bob Milacki	.05	.02
❑ 409	Geno Petralli	.05	.02
❑ 410	Dave Stewart	.10	.03
❑ 411	Mike Jackson	.05	.02
❑ 412	Luis Aquino	.05	.02
❑ 413	Tim Teufel	.05	.02
❑ 414	Jeff Ware	.05	.02
❑ 415	Jim Deshaies	.05	.02
❑ 416	Ellis Burks	.10	.03
❑ 417	Allan Anderson	.05	.02
❑ 418	Alfredo Griffin	.05	.02
❑ 419	Wally Whitehurst	.05	.02
❑ 420	Sandy Alomar Jr.	.05	.02
❑ 421	Juan Agosto	.05	.02
❑ 422	Sam Horn	.05	.02
❑ 423	Jeff Fassero	.05	.02
❑ 424	Paul McClellan	.05	.02
❑ 425	Cecil Fielder	.10	.03
❑ 426	Tim Raines	.10	.03
❑ 427	Eddie Taubensee RC	.25	.07
❑ 428	Dennis Boyd	.05	.02
❑ 429	Tony LaRussa MG	.10	.03
❑ 430	Steve Sax	.05	.02
❑ 431	Tom Gordon	.05	.02
❑ 432	Billy Hatcher	.05	.02
❑ 433	Cal Eldred	.05	.02
❑ 434	Wally Backman	.05	.02
❑ 435	Mark Eichhorn	.05	.02
❑ 436	Mookie Wilson	.10	.03
❑ 437	Scott Servais	.05	.02
❑ 438	Mike Maddux	.05	.02
❑ 439	Chico Walker	.05	.02
❑ 440	Doug Drabek	.05	.02
❑ 441	Rob Deer	.05	.02
❑ 442	Dave West	.05	.02
❑ 443	Spike Owen	.05	.02
❑ 444	Tyrone Hill RC	.10	.03
❑ 445	Matt Williams	.10	.03
❑ 446	Mark Lewis	.05	.02
❑ 447	David Segui	.05	.02
❑ 448	Tom Pagnozzi	.05	.02
❑ 449	Jeff Johnson	.05	.02
❑ 450	Mark McGwire	.60	.18
❑ 451	Tom Henke	.05	.02
❑ 452	Wilson Alvarez	.05	.02
❑ 453	Gary Redus	.05	.02
❑ 454	Darren Holmes	.05	.02
❑ 455	Pete O'Brien	.05	.02
❑ 456	Pat Combs	.05	.02
❑ 457	Hubie Brooks	.05	.02
❑ 458	Frank Tanana	.05	.02
❑ 459	Tom Kelly MG	.05	.02
❑ 460	Andre Dawson	.10	.03
❑ 461	Doug Jones	.05	.02
❑ 462	Rich Rodriguez	.05	.02
❑ 463	Mike Simms	.05	.02
❑ 464	Mike Jeffcoat	.05	.02
❑ 465	Barry Larkin	.15	.04
❑ 466	Stan Belinda	.05	.02
❑ 467	Lonnie Smith	.05	.02
❑ 468	Greg Harris	.05	.02
❑ 469	Jim Eisenreich	.05	.02
❑ 470	Pedro Guerrero	.10	.03
❑ 471	Jose DeJesus	.05	.02
❑ 472	Rich Rowland RC	.10	.03
❑ 473	Frank Bolick Craig Paquette Tom Redington Paul Russo UER (Line around top border)	.05	.02
❑ 474	Mike Rossiter RC	.10	.03
❑ 475	Robby Thompson	.05	.02
❑ 476	Randy Bush	.05	.02
❑ 477	Greg Hibbard	.05	.02
❑ 478	Dale Sveum	.05	.02
❑ 479	Chito Martinez	.05	.02
❑ 480	Scott Sanderson	.05	.02
❑ 481	Tino Martinez	.15	.04
❑ 482	Jimmy Key	.10	.03
❑ 483	Terry Shumpert	.05	.02
❑ 484	Mike Hartley	.05	.02
❑ 485	Chris Sabo	.05	.02
❑ 486	Bob Walk	.05	.02
❑ 487	John Cerutti	.05	.02
❑ 488	Scott Cooper	.05	.02
❑ 489	Bobby Cox MG	.10	.03
❑ 490	Julio Franco	.10	.03
❑ 491	Jeff Brantley	.05	.02
❑ 492	Mike Devereaux	.05	.02
❑ 493	Jose Offerman	.05	.02
❑ 494	Gary Thurman	.05	.02
❑ 495	Carney Lansford	.10	.03
❑ 496	Joe Grahe	.05	.02
❑ 497	Andy Ashby	.05	.02
❑ 498	Gerald Perry	.05	.02
❑ 499	Dave Otto	.05	.02
❑ 500	Vince Coleman	.05	.02
❑ 501	Rob Mallicoat	.05	.02
❑ 502	Greg Briley	.05	.02
❑ 503	Pascual Perez	.05	.02
❑ 504	Aaron Sele RC	.40	.12
❑ 505	Bobby Thigpen	.05	.02

❑ 506 Todd Benzinger .05 .02
❑ 507 Candy Maldonado .05 .02
❑ 508 Bill Gullickson .05 .02
❑ 509 Doug Dascenzo .05 .02
❑ 510 Frank Viola .10 .03
❑ 511 Kenny Rogers .10 .03
❑ 512 Mike Heath .05 .02
❑ 513 Kevin Bass .05 .02
❑ 514 Kim Batiste .05 .02
❑ 515 Delino DeShields .05 .02
❑ 516 Ed Sprague .05 .02
❑ 517 Jim Gott .05 .02
❑ 518 Jose Melendez .05 .02
❑ 519 Hal McRae MG .10 .03
❑ 520 Jeff Bagwell .25 .07
❑ 521 Joe Hesketh .05 .02
❑ 522 Milt Cuyler .05 .02
❑ 523 Shawn Hillegas .05 .02
❑ 524 Don Slaught .05 .02
❑ 525 Randy Johnson .25 .07
❑ 526 Doug Piatt .05 .02
❑ 527 Checklist 397-528 .05 .02
❑ 528 Steve Foster .05 .02
❑ 529 Joe Girardi .05 .02
❑ 530 Jim Abbott .15 .04
❑ 531 Larry Walker .15 .04
❑ 532 Mike Huff .05 .02
❑ 533 Mackey Sasser .05 .02
❑ 534 Benji Gil RC .25 .07
❑ 535 Dave Stieb .05 .02
❑ 536 Willie Wilson .05 .02
❑ 537 Mark Leiter .05 .02
❑ 538 Jose Uribe .05 .02
❑ 539 Thomas Howard .05 .02
❑ 540 Ben McDonald .05 .02
❑ 541 Jose Tolentino .05 .02
❑ 542 Keith Mitchell .05 .02
❑ 543 Jerome Walton .05 .02
❑ 544 Cliff Brantley .05 .02
❑ 545 Andy Van Slyke .15 .04
❑ 546 Paul Sorrento .05 .02
❑ 547 Herm Winningham .05 .02
❑ 548 Mark Guthrie .05 .02
❑ 549 Joe Torre MG .10 .03
❑ 550 Darryl Strawberry .10 .03
❑ 551 Wilfredo Cordero .25 .07
Chipper Jones
Manny Alexander
Alex Arias UER
(No line around
top border)
❑ 552 Dave Gallagher .05 .02
❑ 553 Edgar Martinez .15 .04
❑ 554 Donald Harris .05 .02
❑ 555 Frank Thomas .25 .07
❑ 556 Storm Davis .05 .02
❑ 557 Dickie Thon .05 .02
❑ 558 Scott Garrelts .05 .02
❑ 559 Steve Olin .05 .02
❑ 560 Rickey Henderson .25 .07
❑ 561 Jose Vizcaino .05 .02
❑ 562 Wade Taylor .05 .02
❑ 563 Pat Borders .05 .02
❑ 564 Jimmy Gonzalez RC .10 .03
❑ 565 Lee Smith .10 .03
❑ 566 Bill Sampen .05 .02
❑ 567 Dean Palmer .10 .03
❑ 568 Bryan Harvey .05 .02
❑ 569 Tony Pena .05 .02
❑ 570 Lou Whitaker .10 .03
❑ 571 Randy Tomlin .05 .02
❑ 572 Greg Vaughn .05 .02
❑ 573 Kelly Downs .05 .02
❑ 574 Steve Avery UER .05 .02
(Should be 13 games
for Durham in 1989)
❑ 575 Kirby Puckett .25 .07
❑ 576 Heathcliff Slocumb .05 .02
❑ 577 Kevin Seitzer .05 .02
❑ 578 Lee Guetterman .05 .02
❑ 579 Johnny Oates MG .05 .02
❑ 580 Greg Maddux .40 .12
❑ 581 Stan Javier .05 .02
❑ 582 Vicente Palacios .05 .02
❑ 583 Mel Rojas .05 .02
❑ 584 Wayne Rosenthal RC .10 .03
❑ 585 Lenny Webster .05 .02
❑ 586 Rod Nichols .05 .02
❑ 587 Mickey Morandini .05 .02
❑ 588 Russ Swan .05 .02
❑ 589 Mariano Duncan .05 .02
❑ 590 Howard Johnson .05 .02
❑ 591 Jeromy Burnitz .10 .03
Jacob Brumfield
Alan Cockrell
D.J. Dozier
❑ 592 Denny Neagle .10 .03
❑ 593 Steve Decker .05 .02
❑ 594 Brian Barber RC .10 .03
❑ 595 Bruce Hurst .05 .02
❑ 596 Kent Mercker .05 .02
❑ 597 Mike Magnante RC .10 .03
❑ 598 Jody Reed .05 .02
❑ 599 Steve Searcy .05 .02
❑ 600 Paul Molitor .15 .04
❑ 601 Dave Smith .05 .02
❑ 602 Mike Fetters .05 .02
❑ 603 Luis Mercedes .05 .02
❑ 604 Chris Gwynn .05 .02
❑ 605 Scott Erickson .05 .02
❑ 606 Brook Jacoby .05 .02
❑ 607 Todd Stottlemyre .05 .02
❑ 608 Scott Bradley .05 .02
❑ 609 Mike Hargrove MG .10 .03
❑ 610 Eric Davis .10 .03
❑ 611 Brian Hunter .05 .02
❑ 612 Pat Kelly .05 .02
❑ 613 Pedro Munoz .05 .02
❑ 614 Al Osuna .05 .02
❑ 615 Matt Merullo .05 .02
❑ 616 Larry Andersen .05 .02
❑ 617 Junior Ortiz .05 .02
❑ 618 Cesar Hernandez .05 .02
Steve Hosey
Jeff McNeely
Dan Peltier
❑ 619 Danny Jackson .05 .02
❑ 620 George Brett .60 .18
❑ 621 Dan Gakeler .05 .02
❑ 622 Steve Buechele .05 .02
❑ 623 Bob Tewksbury .05 .02
❑ 624 Shawn Estes RC .25 .07
❑ 625 Kevin McReynolds .05 .02
❑ 626 Chris Haney .05 .02
❑ 627 Mike Sharperson .05 .02
❑ 628 Mark Williamson .05 .02
❑ 629 Wally Joyner .10 .03
❑ 630 Carlton Fisk .15 .04
❑ 631 Armando Reynoso RC .25 .07
❑ 632 Felix Fermin .05 .02
❑ 633 Mitch Williams .05 .02
❑ 634 Manuel Lee .05 .02
❑ 635 Harold Baines .10 .03
❑ 636 Greg Harris .05 .02
❑ 637 Orlando Merced .05 .02
❑ 638 Chris Bosio .05 .02
❑ 639 Wayne Housie .05 .02
❑ 640 Xavier Hernandez .05 .02
❑ 641 David Howard .05 .02
❑ 642 Tim Crews .05 .02
❑ 643 Rick Cerone .05 .02
❑ 644 Terry Leach .05 .02
❑ 645 Deion Sanders .15 .04
❑ 646 Craig Wilson .05 .02
❑ 647 Marquis Grissom .10 .03
❑ 648 Scott Fletcher .05 .02
❑ 649 Norm Charlton .05 .02
❑ 650 Jesse Barfield .05 .02
❑ 651 Joe Slusarski .05 .02
❑ 652 Bobby Rose .05 .02
❑ 653 Dennis Lamp .05 .02
❑ 654 Allen Watson RC .10 .03
❑ 655 Brett Butler .10 .03
❑ 656 Rudy Pemberton .10 .03
Henry Rodriguez
Lee Tinsley RC
Gerald Williams
❑ 657 Dave Johnson .05 .02
❑ 658 Checklist 529-660 .05 .02
❑ 659 Brian McRae .05 .02
❑ 660 Fred McGriff .15 .04
❑ 661 Bill Landrum .05 .02
❑ 662 Juan Guzman .05 .02
❑ 663 Greg Gagne .05 .02
❑ 664 Ken Hill .05 .02
❑ 665 Dave Haas .05 .02
❑ 666 Tom Foley .05 .02
❑ 667 Roberto Hernandez .05 .02
❑ 668 Dwayne Henry .05 .02
❑ 669 Jim Fregosi MG .05 .02
❑ 670 Harold Reynolds .10 .03
❑ 671 Mark Whiten .05 .02
❑ 672 Eric Plunk .05 .02
❑ 673 Todd Hundley .05 .02
❑ 674 Mo Sanford .05 .02
❑ 675 Bobby Witt .05 .02
❑ 676 Sam Militello .25 .07
Pat Mahomes RC
Turk Wendell
Roger Salkeld
❑ 677 John Marzano .05 .02
❑ 678 Joe Klink .05 .02
❑ 679 Pete Incaviglia .05 .02
❑ 680 Dale Murphy .15 .04
❑ 681 Rene Gonzales .05 .02
❑ 682 Andy Benes .05 .02
❑ 683 Jim Poole .05 .02
❑ 684 Trever Miller RC .10 .03
❑ 685 Scott Livingstone .05 .02
❑ 686 Rich DeLucia .05 .02
❑ 687 Harvey Pulliam .05 .02
❑ 688 Tim Belcher .05 .02
❑ 689 Mark Lemke .05 .02
❑ 690 John Franco .10 .03
❑ 691 Walt Weiss .05 .02
❑ 692 Scott Ruskin .05 .02
❑ 693 Jeff King .05 .02
❑ 694 Mike Gardiner .05 .02
❑ 695 Gary Sheffield .10 .03
❑ 696 Joe Boever .05 .02
❑ 697 Mike Felder .05 .02
❑ 698 John Habyan .05 .02
❑ 699 Cito Gaston MG .05 .02
❑ 700 Ruben Sierra .05 .02
❑ 701 Scott Radinsky .05 .02
❑ 702 Lee Stevens .05 .02
❑ 703 Mark Wohlers .05 .02
❑ 704 Curt Young .05 .02
❑ 705 Dwight Evans .15 .04
❑ 706 Rob Murphy .05 .02
❑ 707 Gregg Jefferies .05 .02
❑ 708 Tom Bolton .05 .02
❑ 709 Chris James .05 .02
❑ 710 Kevin Maas .05 .02
❑ 711 Ricky Bones .05 .02
❑ 712 Curt Wilkerson .05 .02
❑ 713 Roger McDowell .05 .02
❑ 714 Pokey Reese RC .40 .12
❑ 715 Craig Biggio .15 .04
❑ 716 Kirk Dressendorfer .05 .02
❑ 717 Ken Dayley .05 .02
❑ 718 B.J. Surhoff .10 .03
❑ 719 Terry Mulholland .05 .02
❑ 720 Kirk Gibson .15 .04
❑ 721 Mike Pagliarulo .05 .02
❑ 722 Walt Terrell .05 .02
❑ 723 Jose Oquendo .05 .02
❑ 724 Kevin Morton .05 .02
❑ 725 Dwight Gooden .10 .03
❑ 726 Kirt Manwaring .05 .02
❑ 727 Chuck McElroy .05 .02
❑ 728 Dave Burba .05 .02
❑ 729 Art Howe MG .05 .02
❑ 730 Ramon Martinez .05 .02
❑ 731 Donnie Hill .05 .02
❑ 732 Nelson Santovenia .05 .02
❑ 733 Bob Melvin .05 .02
❑ 734 Scott Hatteberg RC .25 .07
❑ 735 Greg Swindell .05 .02
❑ 736 Lance Johnson .05 .02
❑ 737 Kevin Reimer .05 .02
❑ 738 Dennis Eckersley .10 .03
❑ 739 Rob Ducey .05 .02
❑ 740 Ken Caminiti .10 .03
❑ 741 Mark Gubicza .05 .02
❑ 742 Bill Spiers .05 .02
❑ 743 Darren Lewis .05 .02
❑ 744 Chris Hammond .05 .02

❑ 745 Dave Magadan .05 .02
❑ 746 Bernard Gilkey .05 .02
❑ 747 Willie Banks .05 .02
❑ 748 Matt Nokes .05 .02
❑ 749 Jerald Clark .05 .02
❑ 750 Travis Fryman .10 .03
❑ 751 Steve Wilson .05 .02
❑ 752 Billy Ripken .05 .02
❑ 753 Paul Assenmacher .05 .02
❑ 754 Charlie Hayes .05 .02
❑ 755 Alex Fernandez .05 .02
❑ 756 Gary Pettis .05 .02
❑ 757 Rob Dibble .10 .03
❑ 758 Tim Naehring .05 .02
❑ 759 Jeff Torborg MG .05 .02
❑ 760 Ozzie Smith .40 .12
❑ 761 Mike Fitzgerald .05 .02
❑ 762 John Burkett .05 .02
❑ 763 Kyle Abbott .05 .02
❑ 764 Tyler Green RC .10 .03
❑ 765 Pete Harnisch .05 .02
❑ 766 Mark Davis .05 .02
❑ 767 Kal Daniels .05 .02
❑ 768 Jim Thome .25 .07
❑ 769 Jack Howell .05 .02
❑ 770 Sid Bream .05 .02
❑ 771 Arthur Rhodes .05 .02
❑ 772 Garry Templeton UER .05 .02
(Stat heading in for pitchers)
❑ 773 Hal Morris .05 .02
❑ 774 Bud Black .05 .02
❑ 775 Ivan Calderon .05 .02
❑ 776 Doug Henry RC .10 .03
❑ 777 John Olerud .10 .03
❑ 778 Tim Leary .05 .02
❑ 779 Jay Bell .10 .03
❑ 780 Eddie Murray .25 .07
❑ 781 Paul Abbott .05 .02
❑ 782 Phil Plantier .05 .02
❑ 783 Joe Magrane .05 .02
❑ 784 Ken Patterson .05 .02
❑ 785 Albert Belle .10 .03
❑ 786 Royce Clayton .05 .02
❑ 787 Checklist 661-792 .05 .02
❑ 788 Mike Stanton .05 .02
❑ 789 Bobby Valentine MG .05 .02
❑ 790 Joe Carter .10 .03
❑ 791 Danny Cox .05 .02
❑ 792 Dave Winfield .10 .03

1992 Topps Traded

	Nm-Mt	Ex-Mt
COMP.FACT.SET (132)	50.00	15.00

❑ 1T Willie Adams USA RC .25 .07
❑ 2T Jeff Alkire USA RC .25 .07
❑ 3T Felipe Alou MG .20 .06
❑ 4T Moises Alou .20 .06
❑ 5T Ruben Amaro .10 .03
❑ 6T Jack Armstrong .10 .03
❑ 7T Scott Bankhead .10 .03
❑ 8T Tim Belcher .10 .03
❑ 9T George Bell .10 .03
❑ 10T Freddie Benavides .10 .03
❑ 11T Todd Benzinger .10 .03
❑ 12T Joe Boever .10 .03
❑ 13T Ricky Bones .10 .03
❑ 14T Bobby Bonilla .20 .06
❑ 15T Hubie Brooks .10 .03
❑ 16T Jerry Browne .10 .03
❑ 17T Jim Bullinger .10 .03
❑ 18T Dave Burba .10 .03
❑ 19T Kevin Campbell .10 .03
❑ 20T Tom Candiotti .10 .03
❑ 21T Mark Carreon .10 .03
❑ 22T Gary Carter .20 .06
❑ 23T Archi Cianfrocco RC .10 .03
❑ 24T Phil Clark .10 .03
❑ 25T Chad Curtis RC .40 .12
❑ 26T Eric Davis .20 .06
❑ 27T Tim Davis USA RC .25 .07
❑ 28T Gary DiSarcina .10 .03
❑ 29T Darren Dreifort USA .10 .03
❑ 30T Mariano Duncan .10 .03
❑ 31T Mike Fitzgerald .10 .03
❑ 32T John Flaherty .10 .03
❑ 33T Darrin Fletcher .10 .03
❑ 34T Scott Fletcher .10 .03
❑ 35T R.Fraser CO USA RC .25 .07
❑ 36T Andres Galarraga .20 .06
❑ 37T Dave Gallagher .10 .03
❑ 38T Mike Gallego .10 .03
❑ 39T Nomar Garciaparra USA RC 30.00 9.00
❑ 40T Jason Giambi USA 1.00 .30
❑ 41T Danny Gladden .10 .03
❑ 42T Rene Gonzales .10 .03
❑ 43T Jeff Granger USA .10 .03
❑ 44T Rick Greene USA RC .25 .07
❑ 45T J.Hammonds USA .20 .06
❑ 46T Charlie Hayes .10 .03
❑ 47T Von Hayes .10 .03
❑ 48T Rick Helling USA .10 .03
❑ 49T Butch Henry RC .10 .03
❑ 50T Carlos Hernandez .10 .03
❑ 51T Ken Hill .10 .03
❑ 52T Butch Hobson .10 .03
❑ 53T Vince Horsman .10 .03
❑ 54T Pete Incaviglia .10 .03
❑ 55T Gregg Jefferies .10 .03
❑ 56T Charles Johnson USA .20 .06
❑ 57T Doug Jones .10 .03
❑ 58T Brian Jordan RC .75 .23
❑ 59T Wally Joyner .20 .06
❑ 60T D.Kirkreit USA RC .25 .07
❑ 61T Bill Krueger .10 .03
❑ 62T Gene Lamont MG .10 .03
❑ 63T Jim Lefebvre MG .10 .03
❑ 64T Danny Leon .10 .03
❑ 65T Pat Listach RC .40 .12
❑ 66T Kenny Lofton .30 .09
❑ 67T Dave Martinez .10 .03
❑ 68T Derrick May .10 .03
❑ 69T Kirk McCaskill .10 .03
❑ 70T C.McConnell USA RC .25 .07
❑ 71T Kevin McReynolds .10 .03
❑ 72T Rusty Meacham .10 .03
❑ 73T Keith Miller .10 .03
❑ 74T Kevin Mitchell .10 .03
❑ 75T Jason Moler USA RC .25 .07
❑ 76T Mike Morgan .10 .03
❑ 77T Jack Morris .20 .06
❑ 78T C.Murray USA RC .75 .23
❑ 79T Eddie Murray .50 .15
❑ 80T Randy Myers .10 .03
❑ 81T Denny Neagle .20 .06
❑ 82T Phil Nevin USA .30 .09
❑ 83T Dave Nilsson .10 .03
❑ 84T Junior Ortiz .10 .03
❑ 85T Donovan Osborne .10 .03
❑ 86T Bill Pecota .10 .03
❑ 87T Melido Perez .10 .03
❑ 88T Mike Perez .10 .03
❑ 89T Hipolito Pichardo RC .10 .03
❑ 90T Willie Randolph .20 .06
❑ 91T Darren Reed .10 .03
❑ 92T Bip Roberts .10 .03
❑ 93T Chris Roberts USA .10 .03
❑ 94T Steve Rodriguez USA .10 .03
❑ 95T Bruce Ruffin .10 .03
❑ 96T Scott Ruskin .10 .03
❑ 97T Bret Saberhagen .20 .06
❑ 98T Rey Sanchez RC .40 .12
❑ 99T Steve Sax .10 .03
❑ 100T Curt Schilling .30 .09
❑ 101T Dick Schofield .10 .03
❑ 102T Gary Scott .10 .03
❑ 103T Kevin Seitzer .10 .03
❑ 104T Frank Seminara RC .10 .03
❑ 105T Gary Sheffield .20 .06
❑ 106T John Smiley .10 .03
❑ 107T Cory Snyder .10 .03
❑ 108T Paul Sorrento .10 .03
❑ 109T Sammy Sosa 1.50 .45
❑ 110T Matt Stairs RC .50 .15
❑ 111T Andy Stankiewicz .10 .03
❑ 112T Kurt Stillwell .10 .03
❑ 113T Rick Sutcliffe .20 .06
❑ 114T Bill Swift .10 .03
❑ 115T Jeff Tackett .10 .03
❑ 116T Danny Tartabull .10 .03
❑ 117T Eddie Taubensee .20 .06
❑ 118T Dickie Thon .10 .03
❑ 119T M.Tucker USA RC 1.50 .45
❑ 120T Scooter Tucker .10 .03
❑ 121T Marc Valdes USA RC .25 .07
❑ 122T Julio Valera .10 .03
❑ 123T J.Varitek USA RC 20.00 6.00
❑ 124T Ron Villone USA RC .25 .07
❑ 125T Frank Viola .20 .06
❑ 126T B.J. Wallace USA RC .25 .07
❑ 127T Dan Walters .10 .03
❑ 128T Craig Wilson USA .10 .03
❑ 129T Chris Wimmer USA .10 .03
❑ 130T Dave Winfield .20 .06
❑ 131T Herm Winningham .10 .03
❑ 132T Checklist 1T-132T .10 .03

1993 Topps

	Nm-Mt	Ex-Mt
COMPLETE SET (825)	50.00	15.00
COMP.HOBBY.SET (847)	80.00	24.00
COMP.RETAIL.SET (838)	60.00	18.00
COMP. SERIES 1 (396)	25.00	7.50
COMP.SERIES 2 (429)	25.00	7.50

❑ 1 Robin Yount .75 .23
❑ 2 Barry Bonds 1.50 .45
❑ 3 Ryne Sandberg .75 .23
❑ 4 Roger Clemens 1.00 .30
❑ 5 Tony Gwynn .60 .18
❑ 6 Jeff Tackett .10 .03
❑ 7 Pete Incaviglia .10 .03
❑ 8 Mark Wohlers .10 .03
❑ 9 Kent Hrbek .20 .06
❑ 10 Will Clark .30 .09
❑ 11 Eric Karros .20 .06
❑ 12 Lee Smith .20 .06
❑ 13 Esteban Beltre .10 .03
❑ 14 Greg Briley .10 .03
❑ 15 Marquis Grissom .20 .06
❑ 16 Dan Plesac .10 .03
❑ 17 Dave Hollins .10 .03
❑ 18 Terry Steinbach .10 .03
❑ 19 Ed Nunez .10 .03
❑ 20 Tim Salmon .30 .09
❑ 21 Luis Salazar .10 .03
❑ 22 Jim Eisenreich .10 .03
❑ 23 Todd Stottlemyre .10 .03
❑ 24 Tim Naehring .10 .03
❑ 25 John Franco .20 .06
❑ 26 Skeeter Barnes .10 .03

❑ 27 Carlos Garcia .10 .03
❑ 28 Joe Orsulak .10 .03
❑ 29 Dwayne Henry .10 .03
❑ 30 Fred McGriff .30 .09
❑ 31 Derek Lilliquist .10 .03
❑ 32 Don Mattingly 1.25 .35
❑ 33 B.J. Wallace .10 .03
❑ 34 Juan Gonzalez .20 .06
❑ 35 John Smoltz .30 .09
❑ 36 Scott Servais .10 .03
❑ 37 Lenny Webster .10 .03
❑ 38 Chris James .10 .03
❑ 39 Roger McDowell .10 .03
❑ 40 Ozzie Smith .75 .23
❑ 41 Alex Fernandez .10 .03
❑ 42 Spike Owen .10 .03
❑ 43 Ruben Amaro .10 .03
❑ 44 Kevin Seitzer .10 .03
❑ 45 Dave Fleming .10 .03
❑ 46 Eric Fox .10 .03
❑ 47 Bob Scanlan .10 .03
❑ 48 Bert Blyleven .20 .06
❑ 49 Brian McRae .10 .03
❑ 50 Roberto Alomar .30 .09
❑ 51 Mo Vaughn .20 .06
❑ 52 Bobby Bonilla .20 .06
❑ 53 Frank Tanana .10 .03
❑ 54 Mike LaValliere .10 .03
❑ 55 Mark McLemore .10 .03
❑ 56 Chad Mottola RC .10 .03
❑ 57 Norm Charlton .10 .03
❑ 58 Jose Melendez .10 .03
❑ 59 Carlos Martinez .10 .03
❑ 60 Roberto Kelly .10 .03
❑ 61 Gene Larkin .10 .03
❑ 62 Rafael Belliard .10 .03
❑ 63 Al Osuna .10 .03
❑ 64 Scott Chiamparino .10 .03
❑ 65 Brett Butler .20 .06
❑ 66 John Burkett .10 .03
❑ 67 Felix Jose .10 .03
❑ 68 Omar Vizquel .30 .09
❑ 69 John Vander Wal .10 .03
❑ 70 Roberto Hernandez .10 .03
❑ 71 Ricky Bones .10 .03
❑ 72 Jeff Grotewold .10 .03
❑ 73 Mike Moore .10 .03
❑ 74 Steve Buechele .10 .03
❑ 75 Juan Guzman .10 .03
❑ 76 Kevin Appier .20 .06
❑ 77 Junior Felix .10 .03
❑ 78 Greg W. Harris .10 .03
❑ 79 Dick Schofield .10 .03
❑ 80 Cecil Fielder .20 .06
❑ 81 Lloyd McClendon .10 .03
❑ 82 David Segui .10 .03
❑ 83 Reggie Sanders .20 .06
❑ 84 Kurt Stillwell .10 .03
❑ 85 Sandy Alomar Jr. .10 .03
❑ 86 John Habyan .10 .03
❑ 87 Kevin Reimer .10 .03
❑ 88 Mike Stanton .10 .03
❑ 89 Eric Anthony .10 .03
❑ 90 Scott Erickson .10 .03
❑ 91 Craig Colbert .10 .03
❑ 92 Tom Pagnozzi .10 .03
❑ 93 Pedro Astacio .10 .03
❑ 94 Lance Johnson .10 .03
❑ 95 Larry Walker .20 .06
❑ 96 Russ Swan .10 .03
❑ 97 Scott Fletcher .10 .03
❑ 98 Derek Jeter RC 10.00 3.00
❑ 99 Mike Williams .10 .03
❑ 100 Mark McGwire 1.25 .35
❑ 101 Jim Bullinger .10 .03
❑ 102 Brian Hunter .10 .03
❑ 103 Jody Reed .10 .03
❑ 104 Mike Butcher .10 .03
❑ 105 Gregg Jefferies .10 .03
❑ 106 Howard Johnson .10 .03
❑ 107 John Kiely .10 .03
❑ 108 Jose Lind .10 .03
❑ 109 Sam Horn .10 .03
❑ 110 Barry Larkin .30 .09
❑ 111 Bruce Hurst .10 .03
❑ 112 Brian Barnes .10 .03
❑ 113 Thomas Howard .10 .03
❑ 114 Mel Hall .10 .03
❑ 115 Robby Thompson .10 .03
❑ 116 Mark Lemke .10 .03
❑ 117 Eddie Taubensee .10 .03
❑ 118 David Hulse RC .10 .03
❑ 119 Pedro Munoz .10 .03
❑ 120 Ramon Martinez .10 .03
❑ 121 Todd Worrell .10 .03
❑ 122 Joey Cora .10 .03
❑ 123 Moises Alou .20 .06
❑ 124 Franklin Stubbs .10 .03
❑ 125 Pete O'Brien .10 .03
❑ 126 Bob Ayrault .10 .03
❑ 127 Carney Lansford .20 .06
❑ 128 Kal Daniels .10 .03
❑ 129 Joe Grahe .10 .03
❑ 130 Jeff Montgomery .10 .03
❑ 131 Dave Winfield .20 .06
❑ 132 Preston Wilson RC .50 .15
❑ 133 Steve Wilson .10 .03
❑ 134 Lee Guetterman .10 .03
❑ 135 Mickey Tettleton .10 .03
❑ 136 Jeff King .10 .03
❑ 137 Alan Mills .10 .03
❑ 138 Joe Oliver .10 .03
❑ 139 Gary Gaetti .20 .06
❑ 140 Gary Sheffield .20 .06
❑ 141 Dennis Cook .10 .03
❑ 142 Charlie Hayes .10 .03
❑ 143 Jeff Huson .10 .03
❑ 144 Kent Mercker .10 .03
❑ 145 Eric Young .10 .03
❑ 146 Scott Leius .10 .03
❑ 147 Bryan Hickerson .10 .03
❑ 148 Steve Finley .20 .06
❑ 149 Rheal Cormier .10 .03
❑ 150 Frank Thomas UER .50 .15
(Categories leading league are italicized but not printed in red)
❑ 151 Archi Cianfrocco .10 .03
❑ 152 Rich DeLucia .10 .03
❑ 153 Greg Vaughn .10 .03
❑ 154 Wes Chamberlain .10 .03
❑ 155 Dennis Eckersley .20 .06
❑ 156 Sammy Sosa .50 .15
❑ 157 Gary DiSarcina .10 .03
❑ 158 Kevin Koslofski .10 .03
❑ 159 Doug Linton .10 .03
❑ 160 Lou Whitaker .20 .06
❑ 161 Chad McConnell .10 .03
❑ 162 Joe Hesketh .10 .03
❑ 163 Tim Wakefield .50 .15
❑ 164 Leo Gomez .10 .03
❑ 165 Jose Rijo .10 .03
❑ 166 Tim Scott .10 .03
❑ 167 Steve Olin UER .10 .03
(Born 10/4/65 should say 10/10/65)
❑ 168 Kevin Maas .10 .03
❑ 169 Kenny Rogers .20 .06
❑ 170 David Justice .20 .06
❑ 171 Doug Jones .10 .03
❑ 172 Jeff Reboulet .10 .03
❑ 173 Andres Galarraga .20 .06
❑ 174 Randy Velarde .10 .03
❑ 175 Kirk McCaskill .10 .03
❑ 176 Darren Lewis .10 .03
❑ 177 Lenny Harris .10 .03
❑ 178 Jeff Fassero .10 .03
❑ 179 Ken Griffey Jr. .75 .23
❑ 180 Darren Daulton .20 .06
❑ 181 John Jaha .10 .03
❑ 182 Ron Darling .10 .03
❑ 183 Greg Maddux .75 .23
❑ 184 Damion Easley .10 .03
❑ 185 Jack Morris .20 .06
❑ 186 Mike Magnante .10 .03
❑ 187 John Dopson .10 .03
❑ 188 Sid Fernandez .10 .03
❑ 189 Tony Phillips .10 .03
❑ 190 Doug Drabek .10 .03
❑ 191 Sean Lowe RC .10 .03
❑ 192 Bob Milacki .10 .03
❑ 193 Steve Foster .10 .03
❑ 194 Jerald Clark .10 .03
❑ 195 Pete Harnisch .10 .03
❑ 196 Pat Kelly .10 .03
❑ 197 Jeff Frye .10 .03
❑ 198 Alejandro Pena .10 .03
❑ 199 Junior Ortiz .10 .03
❑ 200 Kirby Puckett .50 .15
❑ 201 Jose Uribe .10 .03
❑ 202 Mike Scioscia .10 .03
❑ 203 Bernard Gilkey .10 .03
❑ 204 Dan Pasqua .10 .03
❑ 205 Gary Carter .20 .06
❑ 206 Henry Cotto .10 .03
❑ 207 Paul Molitor .30 .09
❑ 208 Mike Hartley .10 .03
❑ 209 Jeff Parrett .10 .03
❑ 210 Mark Langston .10 .03
❑ 211 Doug Dascenzo .10 .03
❑ 212 Rick Reed .10 .03
❑ 213 Candy Maldonado .10 .03
❑ 214 Danny Darwin .10 .03
❑ 215 Pat Howell .10 .03
❑ 216 Mark Leiter .10 .03
❑ 217 Kevin Mitchell .10 .03
❑ 218 Ben McDonald .10 .03
❑ 219 Bip Roberts .10 .03
❑ 220 Benny Santiago .20 .06
❑ 221 Carlos Baerga .10 .03
❑ 222 Bernie Williams .30 .09
❑ 223 Roger Pavlik .10 .03
❑ 224 Sid Bream .10 .03
❑ 225 Matt Williams .20 .06
❑ 226 Willie Banks .10 .03
❑ 227 Jeff Bagwell .30 .09
❑ 228 Tom Goodwin .10 .03
❑ 229 Mike Perez .10 .03
❑ 230 Carlton Fisk .30 .09
❑ 231 John Wetteland .20 .06
❑ 232 Tino Martinez .30 .09
❑ 233 Rick Greene .10 .03
❑ 234 Tim McIntosh .10 .03
❑ 235 Mitch Williams .10 .03
❑ 236 Kevin Campbell .10 .03
❑ 237 Jose Vizcaino .10 .03
❑ 238 Chris Donnels .10 .03
❑ 239 Mike Boddicker .10 .03
❑ 240 John Olerud .20 .06
❑ 241 Mike Gardiner .10 .03
❑ 242 Charlie O'Brien .10 .03
❑ 243 Rob Deer .10 .03
❑ 244 Denny Neagle .20 .06
❑ 245 Chris Sabo .10 .03
❑ 246 Gregg Olson .10 .03
❑ 247 Frank Seminara UER .10 .03
(Acquired 12/3/98)
❑ 248 Scott Scudder .10 .03
❑ 249 Tim Burke .10 .03
❑ 250 Chuck Knoblauch .20 .06
❑ 251 Mike Bielecki .10 .03
❑ 252 Xavier Hernandez .10 .03
❑ 253 Jose Guzman .10 .03
❑ 254 Cory Snyder .10 .03
❑ 255 Orel Hershiser .20 .06
❑ 256 Wil Cordero .10 .03
❑ 257 Luis Alicea .10 .03
❑ 258 Mike Schooler .10 .03
❑ 259 Craig Grebeck .10 .03
❑ 260 Duane Ward .10 .03
❑ 261 Bill Wegman .10 .03
❑ 262 Mickey Morandini .10 .03
❑ 263 Vince Horsman .10 .03
❑ 264 Paul Sorrento .10 .03
❑ 265 Andre Dawson .20 .06
❑ 266 Rene Gonzales .10 .03
❑ 267 Keith Miller .10 .03
❑ 268 Derek Bell .10 .03
❑ 269 Todd Steverson RC .10 .03
❑ 270 Frank Viola .20 .06
❑ 271 Wally Whitehurst .10 .03
❑ 272 Kurt Knudsen .10 .03
❑ 273 Dan Walters .10 .03
❑ 274 Rick Sutcliffe .20 .06
❑ 275 Andy Van Slyke .30 .09
❑ 276 Paul O'Neill .30 .09
❑ 277 Mark Whiten .10 .03
❑ 278 Chris Nabholz .10 .03

279	Todd Burns	.10	.03
280	Tom Glavine	.30	.09
281	Butch Henry	.10	.03
282	Shane Mack	.10	.03
283	Mike Jackson	.10	.03
284	Henry Rodriguez	.10	.03
285	Bob Tewksbury	.10	.03
286	Ron Karkovice	.10	.03
287	Mike Gallego	.10	.03
288	Dave Cochrane	.10	.03
289	Jesse Orosco	.10	.03
290	Dave Stewart	.20	.06
291	Tommy Greene	.10	.03
292	Rey Sanchez	.10	.03
293	Rob Ducey	.10	.03
294	Brent Mayne	.10	.03
295	Dave Stieb	.10	.03
296	Luis Rivera	.10	.03
297	Jeff Innis	.10	.03
298	Scott Livingstone	.10	.03
299	Bob Patterson	.10	.03
300	Cal Ripken	1.50	.45
301	Cesar Hernandez	.10	.03
302	Randy Myers	.10	.03
303	Brook Jacoby	.10	.03
304	Melido Perez	.10	.03
305	Rafael Palmeiro	.30	.09
306	Damon Berryhill	.10	.03
307	Dan Serafini RC	.10	.03
308	Darryl Kile	.20	.06
309	J.T. Bruett	.10	.03
310	Dave Righetti	.20	.06
311	Jay Howell	.10	.03
312	Geronimo Pena	.10	.03
313	Greg Hibbard	.10	.03
314	Mark Gardner	.10	.03
315	Edgar Martinez	.30	.09
316	Dave Nilsson	.10	.03
317	Kyle Abbott	.10	.03
318	Willie Wilson	.10	.03
319	Paul Assenmacher	.10	.03
320	Tim Fortugno	.10	.03
321	Rusty Meacham	.10	.03
322	Pat Borders	.10	.03
323	Mike Greenwell	.10	.03
324	Willie Randolph	.20	.06
325	Bill Gullickson	.10	.03
326	Gary Varsho	.10	.03
327	Tim Hulett	.10	.03
328	Scott Ruskin	.10	.03
329	Mike Maddux	.10	.03
330	Danny Tartabull	.10	.03
331	Kenny Lofton	.20	.06
332	Geno Petralli	.10	.03
333	Otis Nixon	.10	.03
334	Jason Kendall RC	.50	.15
335	Mark Portugal	.10	.03
336	Mike Pagliarulo	.10	.03
337	Kirt Manwaring	.10	.03
338	Bob Ojeda	.10	.03
339	Mark Clark	.10	.03
340	John Kruk	.20	.06
341	Mel Rojas	.10	.03
342	Erik Hanson	.10	.03
343	Doug Henry	.10	.03
344	Jack McDowell	.10	.03
345	Harold Baines	.20	.06
346	Chuck McElroy	.10	.03
347	Luis Sojo	.10	.03
348	Andy Stankiewicz	.10	.03
349	Hipolito Pichardo	.10	.03
350	Joe Carter	.20	.06
351	Ellis Burks	.20	.06
352	Pete Schourek	.10	.03
353	Buddy Groom	.10	.03
354	Jay Bell	.20	.06
355	Brady Anderson	.20	.06
356	Freddie Benavides	.10	.03
357	Phil Stephenson	.10	.03
358	Kevin Wickander	.10	.03
359	Mike Stanley	.10	.03
360	Ivan Rodriguez	.30	.09
361	Scott Bankhead	.10	.03
362	Luis Gonzalez	.20	.06
363	John Smiley	.10	.03
364	Trevor Wilson	.10	.03
365	Tom Candiotti	.10	.03
366	Craig Wilson	.10	.03
367	Steve Sax	.10	.03
368	Delino DeShields	.10	.03
369	Jaime Navarro	.10	.03
370	Dave Valle	.10	.03
371	Mariano Duncan	.10	.03
372	Rod Nichols	.10	.03
373	Mike Morgan	.10	.03
374	Julio Valera	.10	.03
375	Wally Joyner	.20	.06
376	Tom Henke	.10	.03
377	Herm Winningham	.10	.03
378	Orlando Merced	.10	.03
379	Mike Munoz	.10	.03
380	Todd Hundley	.10	.03
381	Mike Flanagan	.10	.03
382	Tim Belcher	.10	.03
383	Jerry Browne	.10	.03
384	Mike Benjamin	.10	.03
385	Jim Leyritz	.10	.03
386	Ray Lankford	.20	.06
387	Devon White	.20	.06
388	Jeremy Hernandez	.10	.03
389	Brian Harper	.10	.03
390	Wade Boggs	.30	.09
391	Derrick May	.10	.03
392	Travis Fryman	.20	.06
393	Ron Gant	.20	.06
394	Checklist 1-132	.10	.03
395	CL 133-264 UER	.10	.03
	Eckerlsey		
396	Checklist 265-396	.10	.03
397	George Brett	1.25	.35
398	Bobby Witt	.10	.03
399	Daryl Boston	.10	.03
400	Bo Jackson	.50	.15
401	Fred McGriff	.30	.09
	Frank Thomas AS		
402	Ryne Sandberg	.50	.15
	Carlos Baerga AS		
403	Gary Sheffield	.20	.06
	Edgar Martinez AS		
404	Barry Larkin	.20	.06
	Travis Fryman AS		
405	Andy Van Slyke	.50	.15
	Ken Griffey Jr. AS		
406	Larry Walker	.30	.09
	Kirby Puckett AS		
407	Barry Bonds	.75	.23
	Joe Carter AS		
408	Darren Daulton	.20	.06
	Brian Harper AS		
409	Greg Maddux	.50	.15
	Roger Clemens AS		
410	Tom Glavine	.20	.06
	Dave Fleming AS		
411	Lee Smith	.20	.06
	Dennis Eckersley AS		
412	Jamie McAndrew	.10	.03
413	Pete Smith	.10	.03
414	Juan Guerrero	.10	.03
415	Todd Frohwirth	.10	.03
416	Randy Tomlin	.10	.03
417	B.J. Surhoff	.20	.06
418	Jim Gott	.10	.03
419	Mark Thompson RC	.10	.03
420	Kevin Tapani	.10	.03
421	Curt Schilling	.20	.06
422	J.T. Snow RC	.40	.12
423	Ryan Klesko	.20	.06
	Ivan Cruz		
	Bubba Smith		
	Larry Sutton RC		
424	John Valentin	.10	.03
425	Joe Girardi	.10	.03
426	Nigel Wilson	.10	.03
427	Bob MacDonald	.10	.03
428	Todd Zeile	.10	.03
429	Milt Cuyler	.10	.03
430	Eddie Murray	.50	.15
431	Rich Amaral	.10	.03
432	Pete Young	.10	.03
433	Roger Bailey RC	.10	.03
	Tom Schmidt		
434	Jack Armstrong	.10	.03
435	Willie McGee	.20	.06
436	Greg W. Harris	.10	.03
437	Chris Hammond	.10	.03
438	Ritchie Moody RC	.10	.03
439	Bryan Harvey	.10	.03
440	Ruben Sierra	.10	.03
441	Don Lemon	.10	.03
	Todd Pridy RC		
442	Kevin McReynolds	.10	.03
443	Terry Leach	.10	.03
444	David Nied	.10	.03
445	Dale Murphy	.30	.09
446	Luis Mercedes	.10	.03
447	Keith Shepherd RC	.10	.03
448	Ken Caminiti	.20	.06
449	Jim Austin	.10	.03
450	Darryl Strawberry	.20	.06
451	Ramon Caraballo	.25	.07
	Jon Shave RC		
	Brent Gates		
	Quinton McCracken		
452	Bob Wickman	.10	.03
453	Victor Cole	.10	.03
454	John Johnstone RC	.10	.03
455	Chili Davis	.20	.06
456	Scott Taylor	.10	.03
457	Tracy Woodson	.10	.03
458	David Wells	.20	.06
459	Derek Wallace RC	.10	.03
460	Randy Johnson	.50	.15
461	Steve Reed RC	.10	.03
462	Felix Fermin	.10	.03
463	Scott Aldred	.10	.03
464	Greg Colbrunn	.10	.03
465	Tony Fernandez	.10	.03
466	Mike Felder	.10	.03
467	Lee Stevens	.10	.03
468	Matt Whiteside RC	.10	.03
469	Dave Hansen	.10	.03
470	Rob Dibble	.20	.06
471	Dave Gallagher	.10	.03
472	Chris Gwynn	.10	.03
473	Dave Henderson	.10	.03
474	Ozzie Guillen	.20	.06
475	Jeff Reardon	.20	.06
476	Mark Voisard	.10	.03
	Will Scalzitti RC		
477	Jimmy Jones	.10	.03
478	Greg Cadaret	.10	.03
479	Todd Pratt RC	.10	.03
480	Pat Listach	.10	.03
481	Ryan Luzinski RC	.10	.03
482	Darren Reed	.10	.03
483	Brian Griffiths RC	.10	.03
484	John Wehner	.10	.03
485	Glenn Davis	.10	.03
486	Eric Wedge RC	.10	.03
487	Jesse Hollins	.10	.03
488	Manuel Lee	.10	.03
489	Scott Fredrickson RC	.10	.03
490	Omar Olivares	.10	.03
491	Shawn Hare	.10	.03
492	Tom Lampkin	.10	.03
493	Jeff Nelson	.10	.03
494	Kevin Young	.10	.03
	Adell Davenport		
	Eduardo Perez		
	Lou Lucca RC		
495	Ken Hill	.10	.03
496	Reggie Jefferson	.10	.03
497	Matt Petersen	.10	.03
	Willie Brown RC		
498	Bud Black	.10	.03
499	Chuck Crim	.10	.03
500	Jose Canseco	.30	.09
501	Johnny Oates MG	.20	.06
	Bobby Cox MG		
502	Butch Hobson MG	.10	.03
	Jim Lefebvre MG		
503	Buck Rodgers MG	.20	.06
	Tony Perez MG		
504	Gene Lamont MG	.20	.06
	Don Baylor MG		
505	Mike Hargrove MG	.20	.06
	Rene Lachemann MG		
506	Sparky Anderson MG	.20	.06

Art Howe MG
❑ 507 Hal McRae MG .20 .06
Tom Lasorda MG
❑ 508 Phil Garner MG .20 .06
Felipe Alou MG
❑ 509 Tom Kelly MG .10 .03
Jeff Torborg MG
❑ 510 Buck Showalter MG .20 .06
Jim Fregosi MG
❑ 511 Tony LaRussa MG .20 .06
Jim Leyland MG
❑ 512 Lou Piniella MG .20 .06
Joe Torre MG
❑ 513 Kevin Kennedy MG .10 .03
Jim Riggleman MG
❑ 514 Cito Gaston MG .20 .06
Dusty Baker MG
❑ 515 Greg Swindell .10 .03
❑ 516 Alex Arias .10 .03
❑ 517 Bill Pecota .10 .03
❑ 518 Benji Grigsby RC UER .10 .03
(Misspelled Bengi
on card front)
❑ 519 David Howard .10 .03
❑ 520 Charlie Hough .20 .06
❑ 521 Kevin Flora .10 .03
❑ 522 Shane Reynolds .10 .03
❑ 523 Doug Bochtler RC .10 .03
❑ 524 Chris Hoiles .10 .03
❑ 525 Scott Sanderson .10 .03
❑ 526 Mike Sharperson .10 .03
❑ 527 Mike Fetters .10 .03
❑ 528 Paul Quantrill .10 .03
❑ 529 Dave Silvestri .50 .15
Chipper Jones
Benji Gil
Jeff Patzke
❑ 530 Sterling Hitchcock RC .25 .07
❑ 531 Joe Millette .10 .03
❑ 532 Tom Brunansky .10 .03
❑ 533 Frank Castillo .10 .03
❑ 534 Randy Knorr .10 .03
❑ 535 Jose Oquendo .10 .03
❑ 536 Dave Haas .10 .03
❑ 537 Jason Hutchins RC .10 .03
Ryan Turner
❑ 538 Jimmy Baron RC .10 .03
❑ 539 Kerry Woodson .10 .03
❑ 540 Ivan Calderon .10 .03
❑ 541 Denis Boucher .10 .03
❑ 542 Royce Clayton .10 .03
❑ 543 Reggie Williams .10 .03
❑ 544 Steve Decker .10 .03
❑ 545 Dean Palmer .20 .06
❑ 546 Hal Morris .10 .03
❑ 547 Ryan Thompson .10 .03
❑ 548 Lance Blankenship .10 .03
❑ 549 Hensley Meulens .10 .03
❑ 550 Scott Radinsky .10 .03
❑ 551 Eric Young .10 .03
❑ 552 Jeff Blauser .10 .03
❑ 553 Andujar Cedeno .10 .03
❑ 554 Arthur Rhodes .10 .03
❑ 555 Terry Mulholland .10 .03
❑ 556 Darryl Hamilton .10 .03
❑ 557 Pedro Martinez 1.00 .30
❑ 558 Ryan Whitman RC .10 .03
Mark Skeels
❑ 559 Jamie Arnold RC .10 .03
❑ 560 Zane Smith .10 .03
❑ 561 Matt Nokes .10 .03
❑ 562 Bob Zupcic .10 .03
❑ 563 Shawn Boskie .10 .03
❑ 564 Mike Timlin .10 .03
❑ 565 Jerald Clark .10 .03
❑ 566 Rod Brewer .10 .03
❑ 567 Mark Carreon .10 .03
❑ 568 Andy Benes .10 .03
❑ 569 Shawn Barton RC .10 .03
❑ 570 Tim Wallach .10 .03
❑ 571 Dave Mlicki .10 .03
❑ 572 Trevor Hoffman .50 .15
❑ 573 John Patterson .10 .03
❑ 574 De Shawn Warren RC .10 .03
❑ 575 Monty Fariss .10 .03
❑ 576 Darrell Sherman .20 .06
Damon Buford
Cliff Floyd
Michael Moore
❑ 577 Tim Costo .10 .03
❑ 578 Dave Magadan .10 .03
❑ 579 Neil Garret .10 .03
Jason Bates RC
❑ 580 Walt Weiss .10 .03
❑ 581 Chris Haney .10 .03
❑ 582 Shawn Abner .10 .03
❑ 583 Marvin Freeman .10 .03
❑ 584 Casey Candaele .10 .03
❑ 585 Ricky Jordan .10 .03
❑ 586 Jeff Tabaka RC .10 .03
❑ 587 Manny Alexander .10 .03
❑ 588 Mike Trombley .10 .03
❑ 589 Carlos Hernandez .10 .03
❑ 590 Cal Eldred .10 .03
❑ 591 Alex Cole .10 .03
❑ 592 Phil Plantier .10 .03
❑ 593 Brett Merriman RC .10 .03
❑ 594 Jerry Nielsen .10 .03
❑ 595 Shawon Dunston .10 .03
❑ 596 Jimmy Key .20 .06
❑ 597 Gerald Perry .10 .03
❑ 598 Rico Brogna .10 .03
❑ 599 Clemente Nunez .10 .03
Daniel Robinson
❑ 600 Bret Saberhagen .20 .06
❑ 601 Craig Shipley .10 .03
❑ 602 Henry Mercedes .10 .03
❑ 603 Jim Thome .30 .09
❑ 604 Rod Beck .10 .03
❑ 605 Chuck Finley .20 .06
❑ 606 J. Owens RC .10 .03
❑ 607 Dan Smith .10 .03
❑ 608 Bill Doran .10 .03
❑ 609 Lance Parrish .20 .06
❑ 610 Dennis Martinez .20 .06
❑ 611 Tom Gordon .10 .03
❑ 612 Byron Mathews RC .10 .03
❑ 613 Joel Adamson RC .10 .03
❑ 614 Brian Williams .10 .03
❑ 615 Steve Avery .10 .03
❑ 616 Matt Mieske .10 .03
Tracy Sanders
Midre Cummings RC
Ryan Freeburg
❑ 617 Craig Lefferts .10 .03
❑ 618 Tony Pena .10 .03
❑ 619 Billy Spiers .10 .03
❑ 620 Todd Benzinger .10 .03
❑ 621 Mike Kotarski .10 .03
Greg Boyd RC
❑ 622 Ben Rivera .10 .03
❑ 623 Al Martin .10 .03
❑ 624 Sam Militello UER .10 .03
(Profile says drafted
in 1988, bio says
drafted in 1990)
❑ 625 Rick Aguilera .10 .03
❑ 626 Dan Gladden .10 .03
❑ 627 Andres Berumen RC .10 .03
❑ 628 Kelly Gruber .10 .03
❑ 629 Cris Carpenter .10 .03
❑ 630 Mark Grace .30 .09
❑ 631 Jeff Brantley .10 .03
❑ 632 Chris Widger RC .40 .12
❑ 633 Three Russians UER .10 .03
Rudolf Razjigaev
Eugneyi Puchkov
Ilya Bogatyrev
Bogatyrev is a shortstop,
card has pitching header
❑ 634 Mo Sanford .10 .03
❑ 635 Albert Belle .20 .06
❑ 636 Tim Teufel .10 .03
❑ 637 Greg Myers .10 .03
❑ 638 Brian Bohanon .10 .03
❑ 639 Mike Bordick .10 .03
❑ 640 Dwight Gooden .20 .06
❑ 641 Pat Leahy .10 .03
Gavin Baugh RC
❑ 642 Milt Hill .10 .03
❑ 643 Luis Aquino .10 .03
❑ 644 Dante Bichette .20 .06
❑ 645 Bobby Thigpen .10 .03
❑ 646 Rich Scheid RC .10 .03
❑ 647 Brian Sackinsky RC .10 .03
❑ 648 Ryan Hawblitzel .10 .03
❑ 649 Tom Marsh .10 .03
❑ 650 Terry Pendleton .20 .06
❑ 651 Rafael Bournigal .10 .03
❑ 652 Dave West .10 .03
❑ 653 Steve Hosey .10 .03
❑ 654 Gerald Williams .10 .03
❑ 655 Scott Cooper .10 .03
❑ 656 Gary Scott .10 .03
❑ 657 Mike Harkey .10 .03
❑ 658 Jeromy Burnitz .20 .06
Melvin Nieves
Rich Becker
Shon Walker RC
❑ 659 Ed Sprague .10 .03
❑ 660 Alan Trammell .20 .06
❑ 661 Garvin Alston RC .10 .03
Michael Case
❑ 662 Donovan Osborne .10 .03
❑ 663 Jeff Gardner .10 .03
❑ 664 Calvin Jones .10 .03
❑ 665 Darrin Fletcher .10 .03
❑ 666 Glenallen Hill .10 .03
❑ 667 Jim Rosenbohm RC .10 .03
❑ 668 Scott Lewis .10 .03
❑ 669 Kip Yaughn RC .10 .03
❑ 670 Julio Franco .20 .06
❑ 671 Dave Martinez .10 .03
❑ 672 Kevin Bass .10 .03
❑ 673 Todd Van Poppel .10 .03
❑ 674 Mark Gubicza .10 .03
❑ 675 Tim Raines .20 .06
❑ 676 Rudy Seanez .10 .03
❑ 677 Charlie Leibrandt .10 .03
❑ 678 Randy Milligan .10 .03
❑ 679 Kim Batiste .10 .03
❑ 680 Craig Biggio .30 .09
❑ 681 Darren Holmes .10 .03
❑ 682 John Candelaria .10 .03
❑ 683 Jerry Stafford .10 .03
Eddie Christian RC
❑ 684 Pat Mahomes .10 .03
❑ 685 Bob Walk .10 .03
❑ 686 Russ Springer .10 .03
❑ 687 Tony Sheffield RC .10 .03
❑ 688 Dwight Smith .10 .03
❑ 689 Eddie Zosky .10 .03
❑ 690 Bien Figueroa .10 .03
❑ 691 Jim Tatum RC .10 .03
❑ 692 Chad Kreuter .10 .03
❑ 693 Rich Rodriguez .10 .03
❑ 694 Shane Turner .10 .03
❑ 695 Kent Bottenfield .10 .03
❑ 696 Jose Mesa .10 .03
❑ 697 Darrell Whitmore RC .10 .03
❑ 698 Ted Wood .10 .03
❑ 699 Chad Curtis .10 .03
❑ 700 Nolan Ryan 2.00 .60
❑ 701 Mike Piazza 3.00 .90
Brook Fordyce
Carlos Delgado
Donnie Leshnock
❑ 702 Tim Pugh RC .10 .03
❑ 703 Jeff Kent .50 .15
❑ 704 Jon Goodrich .10 .03
Danny Figueroa RC
❑ 705 Bob Welch .10 .03
❑ 706 S.Clinkscales RC .10 .03
❑ 707 Donn Pall .10 .03
❑ 708 Greg Olson .10 .03
❑ 709 Jeff Juden .10 .03
❑ 710 Mike Mussina .30 .09
❑ 711 Scott Chiamparino .10 .03
❑ 712 Stan Javier .10 .03
❑ 713 John Doherty .10 .03
❑ 714 Kevin Gross .10 .03
❑ 715 Greg Gagne .10 .03
❑ 716 Steve Cooke .10 .03
❑ 717 Steve Farr .10 .03
❑ 718 Jay Buhner .20 .06
❑ 719 Butch Henry .10 .03
❑ 720 David Cone .20 .06
❑ 721 Rick Wilkins .10 .03

❑ 722 Chuck Carr .10 .03
❑ 723 Kenny Felder RC .10 .03
❑ 724 Guillermo Velasquez .10 .03
❑ 725 Billy Hatcher .10 .03
❑ 726 Mike Veneziale RC .10 .03
Ken Kendrena
❑ 727 Jonathan Hurst .10 .03
❑ 728 Steve Frey .10 .03
❑ 729 Mark Leonard .10 .03
❑ 730 Charles Nagy .10 .03
❑ 731 Donald Harris .10 .03
❑ 732 Travis Buckley RC .10 .03
❑ 733 Tom Browning .10 .03
❑ 734 Anthony Young .10 .03
❑ 735 Steve Shifflett .10 .03
❑ 736 Jeff Russell .10 .03
❑ 737 Wilson Alvarez .10 .03
❑ 738 Lance Painter RC .10 .03
❑ 739 Dave Weathers .10 .03
❑ 740 Len Dykstra .20 .06
❑ 741 Mike Devereaux .10 .03
❑ 742 Rene Arocha .25 .07
Alan Embree
Brien Taylor
Tim Crabtree
❑ 743 Dave Landaker RC .10 .03
❑ 744 Chris George .10 .03
❑ 745 Eric Davis .20 .06
❑ 746 Mark Strittmatter .10 .03
Lamarr Rogers RC
❑ 747 Carl Willis .10 .03
❑ 748 Stan Belinda .10 .03
❑ 749 Scott Kamieniecki .10 .03
❑ 750 Rickey Henderson .50 .15
❑ 751 Eric Hillman .10 .03
❑ 752 Pat Hentgen .10 .03
❑ 753 Jim Corsi .10 .03
❑ 754 Brian Jordan .20 .06
❑ 755 Bill Swift .10 .03
❑ 756 Mike Henneman .10 .03
❑ 757 Harold Reynolds .20 .06
❑ 758 Sean Berry .10 .03
❑ 759 Charlie Hayes .10 .03
❑ 760 Luis Polonia .10 .03
❑ 761 Darrin Jackson .10 .03
❑ 762 Mark Lewis .10 .03
❑ 763 Rob Maurer .10 .03
❑ 764 Willie Greene .10 .03
❑ 765 Vince Coleman .10 .03
❑ 766 Todd Revenig .10 .03
❑ 767 Rich Ireland RC .10 .03
❑ 768 Mike Macfarlane .10 .03
❑ 769 Francisco Cabrera .10 .03
❑ 770 Robin Ventura .20 .06
❑ 771 Kevin Ritz .10 .03
❑ 772 Chito Martinez .10 .03
❑ 773 Cliff Brantley .10 .03
❑ 774 Curt Leskanic RC .40 .12
❑ 775 Chris Bosio .10 .03
❑ 776 Jose Offerman .10 .03
❑ 777 Mark Guthrie .10 .03
❑ 778 Don Slaught .10 .03
❑ 779 Rich Monteleone .10 .03
❑ 780 Jim Abbott .30 .09
❑ 781 Jack Clark .20 .06
❑ 782 Reynol Mendoza .10 .03
Dan Roman RC
❑ 783 Heathcliff Slocumb .10 .03
❑ 784 Jeff Branson .10 .03
❑ 785 Kevin Brown .20 .06
❑ 786 Mike Christopher .10 .03
Ken Ryan
Aaron Taylor
Gus Gandarillas RC
❑ 787 Mike Matthews RC .10 .03
❑ 788 Mackey Sasser .10 .03
❑ 789 Jeff Conine UER .20 .06
No inclusion of 1990
RBI stats in career total
❑ 790 George Bell .10 .03
❑ 791 Pat Rapp .10 .03
❑ 792 Joe Boever .10 .03
❑ 793 Jim Poole .10 .03
❑ 794 Andy Ashby .10 .03
❑ 795 Deion Sanders .30 .09
❑ 796 Scott Brosius .20 .06
❑ 797 Brad Pennington .10 .03
❑ 798 Greg Blosser .10 .03
❑ 799 Jim Edmonds RC 3.00 .90
❑ 800 Shawn Jeter .10 .03
❑ 801 Jesse Levis .10 .03
❑ 802 Phil Clark UER .10 .03
(Word "a" is missing in
sentence beginning
with "In 1992 ...")
❑ 803 Ed Pierce RC .10 .03
❑ 804 Jose Valentin RC .40 .12
❑ 805 Terry Jorgensen .10 .03
❑ 806 Mark Hutton .10 .03
❑ 807 Troy Neel .10 .03
❑ 808 Bret Boone .30 .09
❑ 809 Cris Colon .10 .03
❑ 810 Domingo Martinez RC .10 .03
❑ 811 Javier Lopez .30 .09
❑ 812 Matt Walbeck RC .10 .03
❑ 813 Dan Wilson .20 .06
❑ 814 Scooter Tucker .10 .03
❑ 815 Billy Ashley .10 .03
❑ 816 Tim Laker RC .10 .03
❑ 817 Bobby Jones .20 .06
❑ 818 Brad Brink .10 .03
❑ 819 William Pennyfeather .10 .03
❑ 820 Stan Royer .10 .03
❑ 821 Doug Brocail .10 .03
❑ 822 Kevin Rogers .10 .03
❑ 823 Checklist 397-540 .10 .03
❑ 824 Checklist 541-691 .10 .03
❑ 825 Checklist 692-825 .10 .03

1993 Topps Traded

Nm-Mt Ex-Mt
COMP.FACT.SET (132) 25.00 7.50

❑ 1T Barry Bonds 1.50 .45
❑ 2T Rich Renteria .10 .03
❑ 3T Aaron Sele .10 .03
❑ 4T C.Loewer USA RC .25 .07
❑ 5T Erik Pappas .10 .03
❑ 6T Greg McMichael RC .25 .07
❑ 7T Freddie Benavides .10 .03
❑ 8T Kirk Gibson .30 .09
❑ 9T Tony Fernandez .10 .03
❑ 10T Jay Gainer RC .25 .07
❑ 11T Orestes Destrade .10 .03
❑ 12T A.J. Hinch USA RC .50 .15
❑ 13T Bobby Munoz .10 .03
❑ 14T Tom Henke .10 .03
❑ 15T Rob Butler .10 .03
❑ 16T Gary Wayne .10 .03
❑ 17T David McCarty .10 .03
❑ 18T Walt Weiss .10 .03
❑ 19T Todd Helton USA RC 15.00 4.50
❑ 20T Mark Whiten .10 .03
❑ 21T Ricky Gutierrez .10 .03
❑ 22T D.Hermanson USA RC 1.50 .45
❑ 23T Sherman Obando RC .25 .07
❑ 24T Mike Piazza 3.00 .90
❑ 25T Jeff Russell .10 .03
❑ 26T Jason Bere .10 .03
❑ 27T Jack Voigt RC .25 .07
❑ 28T Chris Bosio .10 .03
❑ 29T Phil Hiatt .10 .03
❑ 30T M.Beaumont USA RC .25 .07
❑ 31T Andres Galarraga .20 .06
❑ 32T Greg Swindell .10 .03
❑ 33T Vinny Castilla .50 .15
❑ 34T P.Clougherty RC USA .25 .07
❑ 35T Greg Briley .10 .03
❑ 36T Dallas Green MG .10 .03
Davey Johnson MG
❑ 37T Tyler Green .10 .03
❑ 38T Craig Paquette .10 .03
❑ 39T Danny Sheaffer RC .25 .07
❑ 40T Jim Converse RC .25 .07
❑ 41T Terry Harvey USA RC .25 .07
❑ 42T Phil Plantier .10 .03
❑ 43T Doug Saunders RC .25 .07
❑ 44T Benny Santiago .20 .06
❑ 45T Dante Powell USA RC .25 .07
❑ 46T Jeff Parrett .10 .03
❑ 47T Wade Boggs .30 .09
❑ 48T Paul Molitor .30 .09
❑ 49T Turk Wendell .10 .03
❑ 50T David Wells .20 .06
❑ 51T Gary Sheffield .20 .06
❑ 52T Kevin Young .20 .06
❑ 53T Nelson Liriano .10 .03
❑ 54T Greg Maddux .75 .23
❑ 55T Derek Bell .10 .03
❑ 56T Matt Turner RC .25 .07
❑ 57T C.Nelson RC USA .25 .07
❑ 58T Mike Hampton .20 .06
❑ 59T Troy O'Leary RC .50 .15
❑ 60T Benji Gil .10 .03
❑ 61T Mitch Lyden RC .25 .07
❑ 62T J.T. Snow .30 .09
❑ 63T Damon Buford .10 .03
❑ 64T Gene Harris .10 .03
❑ 65T Randy Myers .10 .03
❑ 66T Felix Jose .10 .03
❑ 67T Todd Dunn USA RC .25 .07
❑ 68T Jimmy Key .20 .06
❑ 69T Pedro Castellano .10 .03
❑ 70T Mark Merila USA RC .25 .07
❑ 71T Rich Rodriguez .10 .03
❑ 72T Matt Mieske .10 .03
❑ 73T Pete Incaviglia .10 .03
❑ 74T Carl Everett .20 .06
❑ 75T Jim Abbott .30 .09
❑ 76T Luis Aquino .10 .03
❑ 77T Rene Arocha .20 .06
❑ 78T Jon Shave .10 .03
❑ 79T Todd Walker USA RC 1.00 .30
❑ 80T Jack Armstrong .10 .03
❑ 81T Jeff Richardson .10 .03
❑ 82T Blas Minor .10 .03
❑ 83T Dave Winfield .20 .06
❑ 84T Paul O'Neill .30 .09
❑ 85T Steve Reich USA RC .25 .07
❑ 86T Chris Hammond .10 .03
❑ 87T Hilly Hathaway RC .25 .07
❑ 88T Fred McGriff .30 .09
❑ 89T Dave Telgheder RC .25 .07
❑ 90T Richie Lewis RC .25 .07
❑ 91T Brent Gates .10 .03
❑ 92T Andre Dawson .20 .06
❑ 93T Andy Barkett USA RC .25 .07
❑ 94T Doug Drabek .10 .03
❑ 95T Joe Klink .10 .03
❑ 96T Willie Blair .10 .03
❑ 97T D.Graves USA RC .50 .15
❑ 98T Pat Meares RC .50 .15
❑ 99T Mike Lansing RC .50 .15
❑ 100T Marcos Armas RC .25 .07
❑ 101T D.Grass RC USA .25 .07
❑ 102T Chris Jones .10 .03
❑ 103T Ken Ryan RC .25 .07
❑ 104T Ellis Burks .20 .06
❑ 105T Roberto Kelly .10 .03
❑ 106T Dave Magadan .10 .03
❑ 107T Paul Wilson USA RC 1.00 .30
❑ 108T Rob Natal .10 .03
❑ 109T Paul Wagner .10 .03
❑ 110T Jeromy Burnitz .20 .06
❑ 111T Monty Fariss .10 .03
❑ 112T Kevin Mitchell .10 .03
❑ 113T Scott Pose RC .25 .07
❑ 114T Dave Stewart .20 .06
❑ 115T R.Johnson USA RC .25 .07
❑ 116T Armando Reynoso .10 .03

❑ 117T Geronimo Berroa	.10	.03
❑ 118T Woody Williams RC	1.00	.30
❑ 119T Tim Bogar RC	.25	.07
❑ 120T Bob Scafa USA RC	.25	.07
❑ 121T Henry Cotto	.10	.03
❑ 122T Gregg Jefferies	.10	.03
❑ 123T Norm Charlton	.10	.03
❑ 124T B.Wagner USA RC	.25	.07
❑ 125T David Cone	.20	.06
❑ 126T Daryl Boston	.10	.03
❑ 127T Tim Wallach	.10	.03
❑ 128T Mike Martin USA RC	.25	.07
❑ 129T John Cummings RC	.25	.07
❑ 130T Ryan Bowen	.10	.03
❑ 131T John Powell USA RC	.25	.07
❑ 132T Checklist 1-132	.10	.03

1994 Topps

	Nm-Mt	Ex-Mt
COMPLETE SET (792)	50.00	15.00
COMP.FACT.SET (808)	80.00	24.00
COMP.BAKER SET (818)	80.00	24.00
COMP. SERIES 1 (396)	25.00	7.50
COMP. SERIES 2 (396)	25.00	7.50

Card	Nm-Mt	Ex-Mt
❑ 1 Mike Piazza	1.00	.30
❑ 2 Bernie Williams	.30	.09
❑ 3 Kevin Rogers	.10	.03
❑ 4 Paul Carey	.10	.03
❑ 5 Ozzie Guillen	.20	.06
❑ 6 Derrick May	.10	.03
❑ 7 Jose Mesa	.10	.03
❑ 8 Todd Hundley	.10	.03
❑ 9 Chris Haney	.10	.03
❑ 10 John Olerud	.20	.06
❑ 11 Andujar Cedeno	.10	.03
❑ 12 John Smiley	.10	.03
❑ 13 Phil Plantier	.10	.03
❑ 14 Willie Banks	.10	.03
❑ 15 Jay Bell	.20	.06
❑ 16 Doug Henry	.10	.03
❑ 17 Lance Blankenship	.10	.03
❑ 18 Greg W. Harris	.10	.03
❑ 19 Scott Livingstone	.10	.03
❑ 20 Bryan Harvey	.10	.03
❑ 21 Wil Cordero	.10	.03
❑ 22 Roger Pavlik	.10	.03
❑ 23 Mark Lemke	.10	.03
❑ 24 Jeff Nelson	.10	.03
❑ 25 Todd Zeile	.10	.03
❑ 26 Billy Hatcher	.10	.03
❑ 27 Joe Magrane	.10	.03
❑ 28 Tony Longmire	.10	.03
❑ 29 Omar Daal	.10	.03
❑ 30 Kirt Manwaring	.10	.03
❑ 31 Melido Perez	.10	.03
❑ 32 Tim Hulett	.10	.03
❑ 33 Jeff Schwarz	.10	.03
❑ 34 Nolan Ryan	2.00	.60
❑ 35 Jose Guzman	.10	.03
❑ 36 Felix Fermin	.10	.03
❑ 37 Jeff Innis	.10	.03
❑ 38 Brett Mayne	.10	.03
❑ 39 Huck Flener RC	.10	.03
❑ 40 Jeff Bagwell	.30	.09
❑ 41 Kevin Wickander	.10	.03
❑ 42 Ricky Gutierrez	.10	.03
❑ 43 Pat Mahomes	.10	.03
❑ 44 Jeff King	.10	.03
❑ 45 Cal Eldred	.10	.03
❑ 46 Craig Paquette	.10	.03
❑ 47 Richie Lewis	.10	.03
❑ 48 Tony Phillips	.10	.03
❑ 49 Armando Reynoso	.10	.03
❑ 50 Moises Alou	.20	.06
❑ 51 Manuel Lee	.10	.03
❑ 52 Otis Nixon	.10	.03
❑ 53 Billy Ashley	.10	.03
❑ 54 Mark Whiten	.10	.03
❑ 55 Jeff Russell	.10	.03
❑ 56 Chad Curtis	.10	.03
❑ 57 Kevin Stocker	.10	.03
❑ 58 Mike Jackson	.10	.03
❑ 59 Matt Nokes	.10	.03
❑ 60 Chris Bosio	.10	.03
❑ 61 Damon Buford	.10	.03
❑ 62 Tim Belcher	.10	.03
❑ 63 Glenallen Hill	.10	.03
❑ 64 Bill Wertz	.10	.03
❑ 65 Eddie Murray	.50	.15
❑ 66 Tom Gordon	.10	.03
❑ 67 Alex Gonzalez	.10	.03
❑ 68 Eddie Taubensee	.10	.03
❑ 69 Jacob Brumfield	.10	.03
❑ 70 Andy Benes	.10	.03
❑ 71 Rich Becker	.10	.03
❑ 72 Steve Cooke	.10	.03
❑ 73 Billy Spiers	.10	.03
❑ 74 Scott Brosius	.20	.06
❑ 75 Alan Trammell	.20	.06
❑ 76 Luis Aquino	.10	.03
❑ 77 Jerald Clark	.10	.03
❑ 78 Mel Rojas	.10	.03
❑ 79 Billy Masse Stanton Cameron Tim Clark Craig McClure RC	.10	.03
❑ 80 Jose Canseco	.30	.09
❑ 81 Greg McMichael	.10	.03
❑ 82 Brian Turang RC	.10	.03
❑ 83 Tom Urbani	.10	.03
❑ 84 Garret Anderson	.50	.15
❑ 85 Tony Pena	.10	.03
❑ 86 Ricky Jordan	.10	.03
❑ 87 Jim Gott	.10	.03
❑ 88 Pat Kelly	.10	.03
❑ 89 Bud Black	.10	.03
❑ 90 Robin Ventura	.20	.06
❑ 91 Rick Sutcliffe	.20	.06
❑ 92 Jose Bautista	.10	.03
❑ 93 Bob Ojeda	.10	.03
❑ 94 Phil Hiatt	.10	.03
❑ 95 Tim Pugh	.10	.03
❑ 96 Randy Knorr	.10	.03
❑ 97 Todd Jones	.10	.03
❑ 98 Ryan Thompson	.10	.03
❑ 99 Tim Mauser	.10	.03
❑ 100 Kirby Puckett	.50	.15
❑ 101 Mark Dewey	.10	.03
❑ 102 B.J. Surhoff	.20	.06
❑ 103 Sterling Hitchcock	.10	.03
❑ 104 Alex Arias	.10	.03
❑ 105 David Wells	.20	.06
❑ 106 Daryl Boston	.10	.03
❑ 107 Mike Stanton	.10	.03
❑ 108 Gary Redus	.10	.03
❑ 109 Delino DeShields	.10	.03
❑ 110 Lee Smith	.20	.06
❑ 111 Greg Litton	.10	.03
❑ 112 Frankie Rodriguez	.10	.03
❑ 113 Russ Springer	.10	.03
❑ 114 Mitch Williams	.10	.03
❑ 115 Eric Karros	.20	.06
❑ 116 Jeff Brantley	.10	.03
❑ 117 Jack Voigt	.10	.03
❑ 118 Jason Bere	.10	.03
❑ 119 Kevin Roberson	.10	.03
❑ 120 Jimmy Key	.20	.06
❑ 121 Reggie Jefferson	.10	.03
❑ 122 Jeromy Burnitz	.20	.06
❑ 123 Billy Brewer	.10	.03
❑ 124 Willie Canate	.10	.03
❑ 125 Greg Swindell	.10	.03
❑ 126 Hal Morris	.10	.03
❑ 127 Brad Ausmus	.20	.06
❑ 128 George Tsamis	.10	.03
❑ 129 Denny Neagle	.20	.06
❑ 130 Pat Listach	.10	.03
❑ 131 Steve Karsay	.10	.03
❑ 132 Bret Barberie	.10	.03
❑ 133 Mark Leiter	.10	.03
❑ 134 Greg Colbrunn	.10	.03
❑ 135 David Nied	.10	.03
❑ 136 Dean Palmer	.20	.06
❑ 137 Steve Avery	.10	.03
❑ 138 Bill Haselman	.10	.03
❑ 139 Tripp Cromer	.10	.03
❑ 140 Frank Viola	.20	.06
❑ 141 Rene Gonzales	.10	.03
❑ 142 Curt Schilling	.20	.06
❑ 143 Tim Wallach	.10	.03
❑ 144 Bobby Munoz	.10	.03
❑ 145 Brady Anderson	.20	.06
❑ 146 Rod Beck	.10	.03
❑ 147 Mike LaValliere	.10	.03
❑ 148 Greg Hibbard	.10	.03
❑ 149 Kenny Lofton	.20	.06
❑ 150 Dwight Gooden	.20	.06
❑ 151 Greg Gagne	.10	.03
❑ 152 Ray McDavid	.10	.03
❑ 153 Chris Donnels	.10	.03
❑ 154 Dan Wilson	.10	.03
❑ 155 Todd Stottlemyre	.10	.03
❑ 156 David McCarty	.10	.03
❑ 157 Paul Wagner	.10	.03
❑ 158 Orlando Miller Brandon Wilson Derek Jeter Mike Neal	1.50	.45
❑ 159 Mike Fetters	.10	.03
❑ 160 Scott Lydy	.10	.03
❑ 161 Darrell Whitmore	.10	.03
❑ 162 Bob MacDonald	.10	.03
❑ 163 Vinny Castilla	.20	.06
❑ 164 Denis Boucher	.10	.03
❑ 165 Ivan Rodriguez	.30	.09
❑ 166 Ron Gant	.20	.06
❑ 167 Tim Davis	.10	.03
❑ 168 Steve Dixon	.10	.03
❑ 169 Scott Fletcher	.10	.03
❑ 170 Terry Mulholland	.10	.03
❑ 171 Greg Myers	.10	.03
❑ 172 Brett Butler	.20	.06
❑ 173 Bob Wickman	.10	.03
❑ 174 Dave Martinez	.10	.03
❑ 175 Fernando Valenzuela	.20	.06
❑ 176 Craig Grebeck	.10	.03
❑ 177 Shawn Boskie	.10	.03
❑ 178 Albie Lopez	.10	.03
❑ 179 Butch Huskey	.10	.03
❑ 180 George Brett	1.25	.35
❑ 181 Juan Guzman	.10	.03
❑ 182 Eric Anthony	.10	.03
❑ 183 Rob Dibble	.20	.06
❑ 184 Craig Shipley	.10	.03
❑ 185 Kevin Tapani	.10	.03
❑ 186 Marcus Moore	.10	.03
❑ 187 Graeme Lloyd	.10	.03
❑ 188 Mike Bordick	.10	.03
❑ 189 Chris Hammond	.10	.03
❑ 190 Cecil Fielder	.20	.06
❑ 191 Curt Leskanic	.10	.03
❑ 192 Lou Frazier	.10	.03
❑ 193 Steve Dreyer RC	.10	.03
❑ 194 Javier Lopez	.20	.06
❑ 195 Edgar Martinez	.30	.09
❑ 196 Allen Watson	.10	.03
❑ 197 John Flaherty	.10	.03
❑ 198 Kurt Stillwell	.10	.03
❑ 199 Danny Jackson	.10	.03
❑ 200 Cal Ripken	1.50	.45
❑ 201 Mike Bell FDP RC	.10	.03
❑ 202 Alan Benes FDP RC	.25	.07
❑ 203 Matt Farner FDP RC	.10	.03
❑ 204 Jeff Granger	.10	.03
❑ 205 B.Kieschnick FDP RC	.25	.07
❑ 206 Jeremy Lee FDP RC	.10	.03
❑ 207 C.Peterson FDP RC	.10	.03
❑ 208 Alan Rice FDP RC	.10	.03
❑ 209 Billy Wagner FDP RC	1.00	.30

- ❑ 210 Kelly Wunsch FDP RC .25 .07
- ❑ 211 Tom Candiotti .10 .03
- ❑ 212 Domingo Jean .10 .03
- ❑ 213 John Burkett .10 .03
- ❑ 214 George Bell .10 .03
- ❑ 215 Dan Plesac .10 .03
- ❑ 216 Manny Ramirez .50 .15
- ❑ 217 Mike Maddux .10 .03
- ❑ 218 Kevin McReynolds .10 .03
- ❑ 219 Pat Borders .10 .03
- ❑ 220 Doug Drabek .10 .03
- ❑ 221 Larry Luebbers RC .10 .03
- ❑ 222 Trevor Hoffman .30 .09
- ❑ 223 Pat Meares .10 .03
- ❑ 224 Danny Miceli .10 .03
- ❑ 225 Greg Vaughn .10 .03
- ❑ 226 Scott Hemond .10 .03
- ❑ 227 Pat Rapp .10 .03
- ❑ 228 Kirk Gibson .30 .09
- ❑ 229 Lance Painter .10 .03
- ❑ 230 Larry Walker .20 .06
- ❑ 231 Benji Gil .10 .03
- ❑ 232 Mark Wohlers .10 .03
- ❑ 233 Rich Amaral .10 .03
- ❑ 234 Eric Pappas .10 .03
- ❑ 235 Scott Cooper .10 .03
- ❑ 236 Mike Butcher .10 .03
- ❑ 237 Curtis Pride RC .50 .15
  Shawn Green
  Mark Sweeney RC
  Eddie Davis RC
- ❑ 238 Kim Batiste .10 .03
- ❑ 239 Paul Assenmacher .10 .03
- ❑ 240 Will Clark .30 .09
- ❑ 241 Jose Offerman .10 .03
- ❑ 242 Todd Frohwirth .10 .03
- ❑ 243 Tim Raines .20 .06
- ❑ 244 Rick Wilkins .10 .03
- ❑ 245 Bret Saberhagen .20 .06
- ❑ 246 Thomas Howard .10 .03
- ❑ 247 Stan Belinda .10 .03
- ❑ 248 Rickey Henderson .50 .15
- ❑ 249 Brian Williams .10 .03
- ❑ 250 Barry Larkin .30 .09
- ❑ 251 Jose Valentin .10 .03
- ❑ 252 Lenny Webster .10 .03
- ❑ 253 Blas Minor .10 .03
- ❑ 254 Tim Teufel .10 .03
- ❑ 255 Bobby Witt .10 .03
- ❑ 256 Walt Weiss .10 .03
- ❑ 257 Chad Kreuter .10 .03
- ❑ 258 Roberto Mejia .10 .03
- ❑ 259 Cliff Floyd .20 .06
- ❑ 260 Julio Franco .20 .06
- ❑ 261 Rafael Belliard .10 .03
- ❑ 262 Marc Newfield .10 .03
- ❑ 263 Gerald Perry .10 .03
- ❑ 264 Ken Ryan .10 .03
- ❑ 265 Chili Davis .20 .06
- ❑ 266 Dave West .10 .03
- ❑ 267 Royce Clayton .10 .03
- ❑ 268 Pedro Martinez .50 .15
- ❑ 269 Mark Hutton .10 .03
- ❑ 270 Frank Thomas .50 .15
- ❑ 271 Brad Pennington .10 .03
- ❑ 272 Mike Harkey .10 .03
- ❑ 273 Sandy Alomar Jr. .10 .03
- ❑ 274 Dave Gallagher .10 .03
- ❑ 275 Wally Joyner .20 .06
- ❑ 276 Ricky Trlicek .10 .03
- ❑ 277 Al Osuna .10 .03
- ❑ 278 Pokey Reese .10 .03
- ❑ 279 Kevin Higgins .10 .03
- ❑ 280 Rick Aguilera .10 .03
- ❑ 281 Orlando Merced .10 .03
- ❑ 282 Mike Mohler .10 .03
- ❑ 283 John Jaha .10 .03
- ❑ 284 Robb Nen .20 .06
- ❑ 285 Travis Fryman .20 .06
- ❑ 286 Mark Thompson .10 .03
- ❑ 287 Mike Lansing .10 .03
- ❑ 288 Craig Lefferts .10 .03
- ❑ 289 Damon Berryhill .10 .03
- ❑ 290 Randy Johnson .50 .15
- ❑ 291 Jeff Reed .10 .03
- ❑ 292 Danny Darwin .10 .03
- ❑ 293 J.T. Snow .20 .06
- ❑ 294 Tyler Green .10 .03
- ❑ 295 Chris Hoiles .10 .03
- ❑ 296 Roger McDowell .10 .03
- ❑ 297 Spike Owen .10 .03
- ❑ 298 Salomon Torres .10 .03
- ❑ 299 Wilson Alvarez .10 .03
- ❑ 300 Ryne Sandberg .75 .23
- ❑ 301 Derek Lilliquist .10 .03
- ❑ 302 Howard Johnson .10 .03
- ❑ 303 Greg Cadaret .10 .03
- ❑ 304 Pat Hentgen .10 .03
- ❑ 305 Craig Biggio .30 .09
- ❑ 306 Scott Service .10 .03
- ❑ 307 Melvin Nieves .10 .03
- ❑ 308 Mike Trombley .10 .03
- ❑ 309 Carlos Garcia .10 .03
- ❑ 310 Robin Yount UER .75 .23
  (listed with 111 triples in
  1988; should be 11)
- ❑ 311 Marcos Armas .10 .03
- ❑ 312 Rich Rodriguez .10 .03
- ❑ 313 Justin Thompson .10 .03
- ❑ 314 Danny Sheaffer .10 .03
- ❑ 315 Ken Hill .10 .03
- ❑ 316 Chad Ogea .10 .03
  Duff Brumley
  Terrell Wade RC
  Chris Michalak
- ❑ 317 Cris Carpenter .10 .03
- ❑ 318 Jeff Blauser .10 .03
- ❑ 319 Ted Power .10 .03
- ❑ 320 Ozzie Smith .75 .23
- ❑ 321 John Dopson .10 .03
- ❑ 322 Chris Turner .10 .03
- ❑ 323 Pete Incaviglia .10 .03
- ❑ 324 Alan Mills .10 .03
- ❑ 325 Jody Reed .10 .03
- ❑ 326 Rich Monteleone .10 .03
- ❑ 327 Mark Carreon .10 .03
- ❑ 328 Donn Pall .10 .03
- ❑ 329 Matt Walbeck .10 .03
- ❑ 330 Charles Nagy .10 .03
- ❑ 331 Jeff McKnight .10 .03
- ❑ 332 Jose Lind .10 .03
- ❑ 333 Mike Timlin .10 .03
- ❑ 334 Doug Jones .10 .03
- ❑ 335 Kevin Mitchell .10 .03
- ❑ 336 Luis Lopez .10 .03
- ❑ 337 Shane Mack .10 .03
- ❑ 338 Randy Tomlin .10 .03
- ❑ 339 Matt Mieske .10 .03
- ❑ 340 Mark McGwire 1.25 .35
- ❑ 341 Nigel Wilson .10 .03
- ❑ 342 Danny Gladden .10 .03
- ❑ 343 Mo Sanford .10 .03
- ❑ 344 Sean Berry .10 .03
- ❑ 345 Kevin Brown .20 .06
- ❑ 346 Greg Olson .10 .03
- ❑ 347 Dave Magadan .10 .03
- ❑ 348 Rene Arocha .10 .03
- ❑ 349 Carlos Quintana .10 .03
- ❑ 350 Jim Abbott .30 .09
- ❑ 351 Gary DiSarcina .10 .03
- ❑ 352 Ben Rivera .10 .03
- ❑ 353 Carlos Hernandez .10 .03
- ❑ 354 Darren Lewis .10 .03
- ❑ 355 Harold Reynolds .20 .06
- ❑ 356 Scott Ruffcorn .10 .03
- ❑ 357 Mark Gubicza .10 .03
- ❑ 358 Paul Sorrento .10 .03
- ❑ 359 Anthony Young .10 .03
- ❑ 360 Mark Grace .30 .09
- ❑ 361 Rob Butler .10 .03
- ❑ 362 Kevin Bass .10 .03
- ❑ 363 Eric Helfand .10 .03
- ❑ 364 Derek Bell .10 .03
- ❑ 365 Scott Erickson .10 .03
- ❑ 366 Al Martin .10 .03
- ❑ 367 Ricky Bones .10 .03
- ❑ 368 Jeff Branson .10 .03
- ❑ 369 Luis Ortiz .50 .15
  David Bell RC
  Jason Giambi
  George Arias
- ❑ 370 Benito Santiago .20 .06
  (See also 379)
- ❑ 371 John Doherty .10 .03
- ❑ 372 Joe Girardi .10 .03
- ❑ 373 Tim Scott .10 .03
- ❑ 374 Marvin Freeman .10 .03
- ❑ 375 Deion Sanders .30 .09
- ❑ 376 Roger Salkeld .10 .03
- ❑ 377 Bernard Gilkey .10 .03
- ❑ 378 Tony Fossas .10 .03
- ❑ 379 Mark McLemore UER .10 .03
  (Card number is 370)
- ❑ 380 Darren Daulton .20 .06
- ❑ 381 Chuck Finley .20 .06
- ❑ 382 Mitch Webster .10 .03
- ❑ 383 Gerald Williams .10 .03
- ❑ 384 Frank Thomas AS .30 .09
  Fred McGriff AS
- ❑ 385 Roberto Alomar AS .20 .06
  Robby Thompson AS
- ❑ 386 Wade Boggs AS .20 .06
  Matt Williams AS
- ❑ 387 Cal Ripken AS .50 .15
  Jeff Blauser AS
- ❑ 388 Ken Griffey Jr. AS .50 .15
  Len Dykstra AS
- ❑ 389 Juan Gonzalez AS .20 .06
  David Justice AS
- ❑ 390 George Belle AS .75 .23
  Bobby Bonds AS
- ❑ 391 Mike Stanley AS .50 .15
  Mike Piazza AS
- ❑ 392 Jack McDowell AS .30 .09
  Greg Maddux AS
- ❑ 393 Jimmy Key AS .20 .06
  Tom Glavine AS
- ❑ 394 Jeff Montgomery AS .10 .03
  Randy Myers AS
- ❑ 395 Checklist 1-198 .10 .03
- ❑ 396 Checklist 199-396 .10 .03
- ❑ 397 Tim Salmon .30 .09
- ❑ 398 Todd Benzinger .10 .03
- ❑ 399 Frank Castillo .10 .03
- ❑ 400 Ken Griffey Jr. .75 .23
- ❑ 401 John Kruk .20 .06
- ❑ 402 Dave Telgheder .10 .03
- ❑ 403 Gary Gaetti .20 .06
- ❑ 404 Jim Edmonds .50 .15
- ❑ 405 Don Slaught .10 .03
- ❑ 406 Jose Oquendo .10 .03
- ❑ 407 Bruce Ruffin .10 .03
- ❑ 408 Phil Clark .10 .03
- ❑ 409 Joe Klink .10 .03
- ❑ 410 Lou Whitaker .20 .06
- ❑ 411 Kevin Seitzer .10 .03
- ❑ 412 Darrin Fletcher .10 .03
- ❑ 413 Kenny Rogers .20 .06
- ❑ 414 Bill Pecota .10 .03
- ❑ 415 Dave Fleming .10 .03
- ❑ 416 Luis Alicea .10 .03
- ❑ 417 Paul Quantrill .10 .03
- ❑ 418 Damion Easley .10 .03
- ❑ 419 Wes Chamberlain .10 .03
- ❑ 420 Harold Baines .20 .06
- ❑ 421 Scott Radinsky .10 .03
- ❑ 422 Rey Sanchez .10 .03
- ❑ 423 Junior Ortiz .10 .03
- ❑ 424 Jeff Kent .30 .09
- ❑ 425 Brian McRae .10 .03
- ❑ 426 Ed Sprague .10 .03
- ❑ 427 Tom Edens .10 .03
- ❑ 428 Willie Greene .10 .03
- ❑ 429 Bryan Hickerson .10 .03
- ❑ 430 Dave Winfield .20 .06
- ❑ 431 Pedro Astacio .10 .03
- ❑ 432 Mike Gallego .10 .03
- ❑ 433 Dave Burba .10 .03
- ❑ 434 Bob Walk .10 .03
- ❑ 435 Darryl Hamilton .10 .03
- ❑ 436 Vince Horsman .10 .03
- ❑ 437 Bob Natal .10 .03
- ❑ 438 Mike Henneman .10 .03
- ❑ 439 Willie Blair .10 .03
- ❑ 440 Dennis Martinez .20 .06
- ❑ 441 Dan Peltier .10 .03
- ❑ 442 Tony Tarasco .10 .03
- ❑ 443 John Cummings .10 .03

❑ 444 Geronimo Pena .10 .03
❑ 445 Aaron Sele .10 .03
❑ 446 Stan Javier .10 .03
❑ 447 Mike Williams .10 .03
❑ 448 Greg Pirkl .10 .03
Roberto Petagine
D.J.Boston
Shawn Wooten RC
❑ 449 Jim Poole .10 .03
❑ 450 Carlos Baerga .10 .03
❑ 451 Bob Scanlan .10 .03
❑ 452 Lance Johnson .10 .03
❑ 453 Eric Hillman .10 .03
❑ 454 Keith Miller .10 .03
❑ 455 Dave Stewart .20 .06
❑ 456 Pete Harnisch .10 .03
❑ 457 Roberto Kelly .10 .03
❑ 458 Tim Worrell .10 .03
❑ 459 Pedro Munoz .10 .03
❑ 460 Orel Hershiser .20 .06
❑ 461 Randy Velarde .10 .03
❑ 462 Trevor Wilson .10 .03
❑ 463 Jerry Goff .10 .03
❑ 464 Bill Wegman .10 .03
❑ 465 Dennis Eckersley .20 .06
❑ 466 Jeff Conine .20 .06
❑ 467 Joe Boever .10 .03
❑ 468 Dante Bichette .20 .06
❑ 469 Jeff Shaw .10 .03
❑ 470 Rafael Palmeiro .30 .09
❑ 471 Phil Leftwich RC .10 .03
❑ 472 Jay Buhner .20 .06
❑ 473 Bob Tewksbury .10 .03
❑ 474 Tim Naehring .10 .03
❑ 475 Tom Glavine .30 .09
❑ 476 Dave Hollins .10 .03
❑ 477 Arthur Rhodes .10 .03
❑ 478 Joey Cora .10 .03
❑ 479 Mike Morgan .10 .03
❑ 480 Albert Belle .20 .06
❑ 481 John Franco .20 .06
❑ 482 Hipolito Pichardo .10 .03
❑ 483 Duane Ward .10 .03
❑ 484 Luis Gonzalez .20 .06
❑ 485 Joe Oliver .10 .03
❑ 486 Wally Whitehurst .10 .03
❑ 487 Mike Benjamin .10 .03
❑ 488 Eric Davis .20 .06
❑ 489 Scott Kamieniecki .10 .03
❑ 490 Kent Hrbek .20 .06
❑ 491 John Hope RC .10 .03
❑ 492 Jesse Orosco .10 .03
❑ 493 Troy Neel .10 .03
❑ 494 Ryan Bowen .10 .03
❑ 495 Mickey Tettleton .10 .03
❑ 496 Chris Jones .10 .03
❑ 497 John Wetteland .20 .06
❑ 498 David Hulse .10 .03
❑ 499 Greg Maddux .75 .23
❑ 500 Bo Jackson .50 .15
❑ 501 Donovan Osborne .10 .03
❑ 502 Mike Greenwell .10 .03
❑ 503 Steve Frey .10 .03
❑ 504 Jim Eisenreich .10 .03
❑ 505 Robby Thompson .10 .03
❑ 506 Leo Gomez .10 .03
❑ 507 Dave Staton .10 .03
❑ 508 Wayne Kirby .10 .03
❑ 509 Tim Bogar .10 .03
❑ 510 David Cone .20 .06
❑ 511 Devon White .20 .06
❑ 512 Xavier Hernandez .10 .03
❑ 513 Tim Costo .10 .03
❑ 514 Gene Harris .10 .03
❑ 515 Jack McDowell .10 .03
❑ 516 Kevin Gross .10 .03
❑ 517 Scott Leius .10 .03
❑ 518 Lloyd McClendon .10 .03
❑ 519 Alex Diaz RC .10 .03
❑ 520 Wade Boggs .30 .09
❑ 521 Bob Welch .10 .03
❑ 522 Henry Cotto .10 .03
❑ 523 Mike Moore .10 .03
❑ 524 Tim Laker .10 .03
❑ 525 Andres Galarraga .20 .06
❑ 526 Jamie Moyer .20 .06
❑ 527 Norberto Martin .10 .03
Ruben Santana
Jason Hardtke
Chris Sexton RC
❑ 528 Sid Bream .10 .03
❑ 529 Erik Hanson .10 .03
❑ 530 Ray Lankford .20 .06
❑ 531 Rob Deer .10 .03
❑ 532 Rod Correia .10 .03
❑ 533 Roger Mason .10 .03
❑ 534 Mike Devereaux .10 .03
❑ 535 Jeff Montgomery .10 .03
❑ 536 Dwight Smith .10 .03
❑ 537 Jeremy Hernandez .10 .03
❑ 538 Ellis Burks .20 .06
❑ 539 Bobby Jones .10 .03
❑ 540 Paul Molitor .30 .09
❑ 541 Jeff Juden .10 .03
❑ 542 Chris Sabo .10 .03
❑ 543 Larry Casian .10 .03
❑ 544 Jeff Gardner .10 .03
❑ 545 Ramon Martinez .10 .03
❑ 546 Paul O'Neill .30 .09
❑ 547 Steve Hosey .10 .03
❑ 548 Dave Nilsson .10 .03
❑ 549 Ron Darling .10 .03
❑ 550 Matt Williams .20 .06
❑ 551 Jack Armstrong .10 .03
❑ 552 Bill Krueger .10 .03
❑ 553 Freddie Benavides .10 .03
❑ 554 Jeff Fassero .10 .03
❑ 555 Chuck Knoblauch .20 .06
❑ 556 Guillermo Velasquez .10 .03
❑ 557 Joel Johnston .10 .03
❑ 558 Tom Lampkin .10 .03
❑ 559 Todd Van Poppel .10 .03
❑ 560 Gary Sheffield .20 .06
❑ 561 Skeeter Barnes .10 .03
❑ 562 Darren Holmes .10 .03
❑ 563 John Vander Wal .10 .03
❑ 564 Mike Ignasiak .10 .03
❑ 565 Fred McGriff .30 .09
❑ 566 Luis Polonia .10 .03
❑ 567 Mike Perez .10 .03
❑ 568 John Valentin .10 .03
❑ 569 Mike Felder .10 .03
❑ 570 Tommy Greene .10 .03
❑ 571 David Segui .10 .03
❑ 572 Roberto Hernandez .10 .03
❑ 573 Steve Wilson .10 .03
❑ 574 Willie McGee .20 .06
❑ 575 Randy Myers .10 .03
❑ 576 Darrin Jackson .10 .03
❑ 577 Eric Plunk .10 .03
❑ 578 Mike Macfarlane .10 .03
❑ 579 Doug Brocail .10 .03
❑ 580 Steve Finley .20 .06
❑ 581 John Roper .10 .03
❑ 582 Danny Cox .10 .03
❑ 583 Chip Hale .10 .03
❑ 584 Scott Bullett .10 .03
❑ 585 Kevin Reimer .10 .03
❑ 586 Brent Gates .10 .03
❑ 587 Matt Turner .10 .03
❑ 588 Rich Rowland .10 .03
❑ 589 Kent Bottenfield .10 .03
❑ 590 Marquis Grissom .20 .06
❑ 591 Doug Strange .10 .03
❑ 592 Jay Howell .10 .03
❑ 593 Omar Vizquel .30 .09
❑ 594 Rheal Cormier .10 .03
❑ 595 Andre Dawson .20 .06
❑ 596 Hilly Hathaway .10 .03
❑ 597 Todd Pratt .10 .03
❑ 598 Mike Mussina .30 .09
❑ 599 Alex Fernandez .10 .03
❑ 600 Don Mattingly 1.25 .35
❑ 601 Frank Thomas MOG .30 .09
❑ 602 Ryne Sandberg MOG .50 .15
❑ 603 Wade Boggs MOG .20 .06
❑ 604 Cal Ripken MOG .75 .23
❑ 605 Barry Bonds MOG .75 .23
❑ 606 Ken Griffey Jr. MOG .50 .15
❑ 607 Kirby Puckett MOG .30 .09
❑ 608 Darren Daulton MOG .10 .03
❑ 609 Paul Molitor MOG .20 .06
❑ 610 Terry Steinbach .10 .03
❑ 611 Todd Worrell .10 .03
❑ 612 Jim Thome .30 .09
❑ 613 Chuck McElroy .10 .03
❑ 614 John Habyan .10 .03
❑ 615 Sid Fernandez .10 .03
❑ 616 Eddie Zambrano .10 .03
Glenn Murray
Chad Mottola
Jermaine Allensworth RC
❑ 617 Steve Bedrosian .10 .03
❑ 618 Rob Ducey .10 .03
❑ 619 Tom Browning .10 .03
❑ 620 Tony Gwynn .60 .18
❑ 621 Carl Willis .10 .03
❑ 622 Kevin Young .10 .03
❑ 623 Rafael Novoa .10 .03
❑ 624 Jerry Browne .10 .03
❑ 625 Charlie Hough .20 .06
❑ 626 Chris Gomez .10 .03
❑ 627 Steve Reed .10 .03
❑ 628 Kirk Rueter .20 .06
❑ 629 Matt Whiteside .10 .03
❑ 630 David Justice .20 .06
❑ 631 Brad Holman .10 .03
❑ 632 Brian Jordan .20 .06
❑ 633 Scott Bankhead .10 .03
❑ 634 Torey Lovullo .10 .03
❑ 635 Len Dykstra .20 .06
❑ 636 Ben McDonald .10 .03
❑ 637 Steve Howe .10 .03
❑ 638 Jose Vizcaino .10 .03
❑ 639 Bill Swift .10 .03
❑ 640 Darryl Strawberry .20 .06
❑ 641 Steve Farr .10 .03
❑ 642 Tom Kramer .10 .03
❑ 643 Joe Orsulak .10 .03
❑ 644 Tom Henke .10 .03
❑ 645 Joe Carter .20 .06
❑ 646 Ken Caminiti .20 .06
❑ 647 Reggie Sanders .20 .06
❑ 648 Andy Ashby .10 .03
❑ 649 Derek Parks .10 .03
❑ 650 Andy Van Slyke .30 .09
❑ 651 Juan Bell .10 .03
❑ 652 Roger Smithberg .10 .03
❑ 653 Chuck Carr .10 .03
❑ 654 Bill Gullickson .10 .03
❑ 655 Charlie Hayes .10 .03
❑ 656 Chris Nabholz .10 .03
❑ 657 Karl Rhodes .10 .03
❑ 658 Pete Smith .10 .03
❑ 659 Bret Boone .20 .06
❑ 660 Gregg Jefferies .10 .03
❑ 661 Bob Zupcic .10 .03
❑ 662 Steve Sax .10 .03
❑ 663 Mariano Duncan .10 .03
❑ 664 Jeff Tackett .10 .03
❑ 665 Mark Langston .10 .03
❑ 666 Steve Buechele .10 .03
❑ 667 Candy Maldonado .10 .03
❑ 668 Woody Williams .20 .06
❑ 669 Tim Wakefield .30 .09
❑ 670 Danny Tartabull .10 .03
❑ 671 Charlie O'Brien .10 .03
❑ 672 Felix Jose .10 .03
❑ 673 Bobby Ayala .10 .03
❑ 674 Scott Servais .10 .03
❑ 675 Roberto Alomar .30 .09
❑ 676 Pedro A.Martinez RC .10 .03
❑ 677 Eddie Guardado .10 .03
❑ 678 Mark Lewis .10 .03
❑ 679 Jaime Navarro .10 .03
❑ 680 Ruben Sierra .10 .03
❑ 681 Rick Renteria .10 .03
❑ 682 Storm Davis .10 .03
❑ 683 Cory Snyder .10 .03
❑ 684 Ron Karkovice .10 .03
❑ 685 Juan Gonzalez .20 .06
❑ 686 Chris Howard .30 .09
Carlos Delgado
Jason Kendall
Paul Bako
❑ 687 John Smoltz .30 .09
❑ 688 Brian Dorsett .10 .03
❑ 689 Omar Olivares .10 .03

❑ 690 Mo Vaughn .20 .06
❑ 691 Joe Grahe .10 .03
❑ 692 Mickey Morandini .10 .03
❑ 693 Tino Martinez .30 .09
❑ 694 Brian Barnes .10 .03
❑ 695 Mike Stanley .10 .03
❑ 696 Mark Clark .10 .03
❑ 697 Dave Hansen .10 .03
❑ 698 Willie Wilson .10 .03
❑ 699 Pete Schourek .10 .03
❑ 700 Barry Bonds 1.50 .45
❑ 701 Kevin Appier .20 .06
❑ 702 Tony Fernandez .10 .03
❑ 703 Darryl Kile .20 .06
❑ 704 Archi Cianfrocco .10 .03
❑ 705 Jose Rijo .10 .03
❑ 706 Brian Harper .10 .03
❑ 707 Zane Smith .10 .03
❑ 708 Dave Henderson .10 .03
❑ 709 Angel Miranda UER .10 .03
(no Topps logo on back)
❑ 710 Orestes Destrade .10 .03
❑ 711 Greg Gohr .10 .03
❑ 712 Eric Young .10 .03
❑ 713 Todd Williams .10 .03
Ron Watson
Kirk Bullinger
Mike Welch
❑ 714 Tim Spehr .10 .03
❑ 715 Hank Aaron 715 HR .50 .15
❑ 716 Nate Minchey .10 .03
❑ 717 Mike Blowers .10 .03
❑ 718 Kent Mercker .10 .03
❑ 719 Tom Pagnozzi .10 .03
❑ 720 Roger Clemens 1.00 .30
❑ 721 Eduardo Perez .10 .03
❑ 722 Milt Thompson .10 .03
❑ 723 Gregg Olson .10 .03
❑ 724 Kirk McCaskill .10 .03
❑ 725 Sammy Sosa .50 .15
❑ 726 Alvaro Espinoza .10 .03
❑ 727 Henry Rodriguez .10 .03
❑ 728 Jim Leyritz .10 .03
❑ 729 Steve Scarsone .10 .03
❑ 730 Bobby Bonilla .20 .06
❑ 731 Chris Gwynn .10 .03
❑ 732 Al Leiter .20 .06
❑ 733 Bip Roberts .10 .03
❑ 734 Mark Portugal .10 .03
❑ 735 Terry Pendleton .20 .06
❑ 736 Dave Valle .10 .03
❑ 737 Paul Kilgus .10 .03
❑ 738 Greg A. Harris .10 .03
❑ 739 Jon Ratliff DP RC .10 .03
❑ 740 Kirk Presley DP RC .10 .03
❑ 741 Josue Estrada DP RC .10 .03
❑ 742 Wayne Gomes DP RC .10 .03
❑ 743 Pat Watkins DP RC .10 .03
❑ 744 Jamey Wright DP RC .25 .07
❑ 745 Jay Powell DP RC .10 .03
❑ 746 Ryan McGuire DP RC .10 .03
❑ 747 Marc Barcelo DP RC .10 .03
❑ 748 Sloan Smith DP RC .10 .03
❑ 749 John Wasdin DP RC .10 .03
❑ 750 Marc Vlades DP .10 .03
❑ 751 Dan Ehler DP RC .10 .03
❑ 752 Andre King DP RC .10 .03
❑ 753 Greg Keagle DP RC .10 .03
❑ 754 Jason Myers DP RC .10 .03
❑ 755 Dax Winslett DP RC .10 .03
❑ 756 Casey Whitten DP RC .10 .03
❑ 757 Tony Fuduric DP RC .10 .03
❑ 758 Greg Norton DP RC .25 .07
❑ 759 Jeff D'Amico DP RC .25 .07
❑ 760 Ryan Hancock DP RC .10 .03
❑ 761 David Cooper DP RC .10 .03
❑ 762 Kevin Orie DP RC .10 .03
❑ 763 John O'Donoghue .10 .03
Mike Oquist
❑ 764 Cory Bailey RC .10 .03
Scott Hatteberg
❑ 765 Mark Holzemer .10 .03
Paul Swingle RC
❑ 766 James Baldwin .10 .03
Rod Bolton
❑ 767 Jerry Di Poto .25 .07
Julian Tavarez RC
❑ 768 Danny Bautista .10 .03
Sean Bergman
❑ 769 Bob Hamelin .10 .03
Joe Vitiello
❑ 770 Mark Kiefer .10 .03
Troy O'Leary
❑ 771 Denny Hocking .10 .03
Oscar Munoz RC
❑ 772 Russ Davis .10 .03
Brien Taylor
❑ 773 Kyle Abbott RC .25 .07
Miguel Jimenez
❑ 774 Kevin King .10 .03
Eric Plantenberg RC
❑ 775 Jon Shave .10 .03
Desi Wilson
❑ 776 Domingo Cedeno .10 .03
Paul Spoljaric
❑ 777 Chipper Jones .50 .15
Ryan Klesko
❑ 778 Steve Trachsel .10 .03
Turk Wendell
❑ 779 Johnny Ruffin .10 .03
Jerry Spradlin RC
❑ 780 Jason Bates .10 .03
John Burke
❑ 781 Carl Everett .20 .06
Dave Weathers
❑ 782 Gary Mota .10 .03
James Mouton
❑ 783 Raul Mondesi .20 .06
Ben Van Ryn
❑ 784 Gabe White .20 .06
Rondell White
❑ 785 Brook Fordyce .20 .06
Bill Pulsipher
❑ 786 Kevin Foster RC .10 .03
Gene Schall
❑ 787 Rich Aude RC .10 .03
Midre Cummings
❑ 788 Brian Barber .10 .03
Rich Batchelor
❑ 789 Brian Johnson RC .10 .03
Scott Sanders
❑ 790 Ricky Faneyte .10 .03
J.R. Phillips
❑ 791 Checklist 3 .10 .03
❑ 792 Checklist 4 .10 .03

1994 Topps Traded

	Nm-Mt	Ex-Mt
COMP.FACT.SET (140)	40.00	12.00

❑ 1T Paul Wilson .20 .06
❑ 2T Bill Taylor RC 1.00 .30
❑ 3T Dan Wilson .10 .03
❑ 4T Mark Smith .10 .03
❑ 5T Toby Borland RC .25 .07
❑ 6T Dave Clark .10 .03
❑ 7T Dennis Martinez .20 .06
❑ 8T Dave Gallagher .10 .03
❑ 9T Josias Manzanillo .10 .03
❑ 10T Brian Anderson RC 1.00 .30
❑ 11T Damon Berryhill .10 .03
❑ 12T Alex Cole .10 .03
❑ 13T Jacob Shumate RC .25 .07
❑ 14T Oddibe McDowell .10 .03
❑ 15T Willie Banks .10 .03
❑ 16T Jerry Browne .10 .03
❑ 17T Donnie Elliott .10 .03
❑ 18T Ellis Burks .20 .06
❑ 19T Chuck McElroy .10 .03
❑ 20T Luis Polonia .10 .03
❑ 21T Brian Harper .10 .03
❑ 22T Mark Portugal .10 .03
❑ 23T Dave Henderson .10 .03
❑ 24T Mark Acre RC .25 .07
❑ 25T Julio Franco .20 .06
❑ 26T Darren Hall RC .25 .07
❑ 27T Eric Anthony .10 .03
❑ 28T Sid Fernandez .10 .03
❑ 29T Rusty Greer RC 1.50 .45
❑ 30T Riccardo Ingram RC .25 .07
❑ 31T Gabe White .10 .03
❑ 32T Tim Belcher .10 .03
❑ 33T Terrence Long RC 1.50 .45
❑ 34T Mark Dalesandro RC .25 .07
❑ 35T Mike Kelly .10 .03
❑ 36T Jack Morris .20 .06
❑ 37T Jeff Brantley .10 .03
❑ 38T Larry Barnes RC .25 .07
❑ 39T Brian R. Hunter .10 .03
❑ 40T Otis Nixon .10 .03
❑ 41T Bret Wagner .10 .03
❑ 42T Pedro Martinez TR .50 .15
Delino Deshields
❑ 43T Heathcliff Slocumb .10 .03
❑ 44T Ben Grieve RC 1.50 .45
❑ 45T John Hudek RC .25 .07
❑ 46T Shawon Dunston .10 .03
❑ 47T Greg Colbrunn .10 .03
❑ 48T Joey Hamilton .10 .03
❑ 49T Marvin Freeman .10 .03
❑ 50T Terry Mulholland .10 .03
❑ 51T Keith Mitchell .10 .03
❑ 52T Dwight Smith .10 .03
❑ 53T Shawn Boskie .10 .03
❑ 54T Kevin Witt RC 1.00 .30
❑ 55T Ron Gant .20 .06
❑ 56T Trenidad Hubbard RC .. 10.00 3.00
Jason Schmidt RC
Larry Sutton
Stephen Larkin RC
❑ 57T Jody Reed .10 .03
❑ 58T Rick Helling .10 .03
❑ 59T John Powell .10 .03
❑ 60T Eddie Murray .50 .15
❑ 61T Joe Hall RC .25 .07
❑ 62T Jorge Fabregas .10 .03
❑ 63T Mike Mordecai RC .25 .07
❑ 64T Ed Vosberg .10 .03
❑ 65T Rickey Henderson .50 .15
❑ 66T Tim Grieve RC .25 .07
❑ 67T Jon Lieber .20 .06
❑ 68T Chris Howard .10 .03
❑ 69T Matt Walbeck .10 .03
❑ 70T Chan Ho Park RC 1.50 .45
❑ 71T Bryan Eversgerd RC .25 .07
❑ 72T John Dettmer .10 .03
❑ 73T Erik Hanson .10 .03
❑ 74T Mike Thurman RC .25 .07
❑ 75T Bobby Ayala .10 .03
❑ 76T Rafael Palmeiro .30 .09
❑ 77T Bret Boone .20 .06
❑ 78T Paul Shuey .10 .03
❑ 79T Kevin Foster RC .25 .07
❑ 80T Dave Magadan .10 .03
❑ 81T Bip Roberts .10 .03
❑ 82T Howard Johnson .10 .03
❑ 83T Xavier Hernandez .10 .03
❑ 84T Ross Powell RC .25 .07
❑ 85T Doug Million RC .25 .07
❑ 86T Geronimo Berroa .10 .03
❑ 87T Mark Farris RC .25 .07
❑ 88T Butch Henry .10 .03
❑ 89T Junior Felix .10 .03
❑ 90T Bo Jackson .50 .15
❑ 91T Hector Carrasco .10 .03
❑ 92T Charlie O'Brien .10 .03
❑ 93T Omar Vizquel .30 .09
❑ 94T David Segui .10 .03
❑ 95T Dustin Hermanson .20 .06
❑ 96T Gar Finnvold RC .25 .07

- ❑ 97T Dave Stevens .10 .03
- ❑ 98T Corey Pointer RC .25 .07
- ❑ 99T Felix Fermin .10 .03
- ❑ 100T Lee Smith .20 .06
- ❑ 101T Reid Ryan RC 1.00 .30
- ❑ 102T Bobby Munoz .10 .03
- ❑ 103T Deion Sanders TR .30 .09
  Roberto Kelly
- ❑ 104T Turner Ward .10 .03
- ❑ 105T W.VanLandingham RC .25 .07
- ❑ 106T Vince Coleman .10 .03
- ❑ 107T Stan Javier .10 .03
- ❑ 108T Darrin Jackson .10 .03
- ❑ 109T C.J. Nitkowski RC .25 .07
- ❑ 110T Anthony Young .10 .03
- ❑ 111T Kurt Miller .10 .03
- ❑ 112T Paul Konerko RC 15.00 4.50
- ❑ 113T Walt Weiss .10 .03
- ❑ 114T Daryl Boston .10 .03
- ❑ 115T Will Clark .30 .09
- ❑ 116T Matt Smith RC .25 .07
- ❑ 117T Mark Leiter .10 .03
- ❑ 118T Gregg Olson .10 .03
- ❑ 119T Tony Pena .10 .03
- ❑ 120T Jose Vizcaino .10 .03
- ❑ 121T Rick White RC .25 .07
- ❑ 122T Rich Rowland .10 .03
- ❑ 123T Jeff Reboulet .10 .03
- ❑ 124T Greg Hibbard .10 .03
- ❑ 125T Chris Sabo .10 .03
- ❑ 126T Doug Jones .10 .03
- ❑ 127T Tony Fernandez .10 .03
- ❑ 128T Carlos Reyes RC .25 .07
- ❑ 129T Kevin L.Brown RC 1.00 .30
- ❑ 130T Ryne Sandberg 1.25 .35
  Farewell
- ❑ 131T Ryne Sandberg 1.25 .35
  Farewell
- ❑ 132T Checklist 1-132 .10 .03

1995 Topps

	Nm-Mt	Ex-Mt
COMPLETE SET (660)	80.00	24.00
COMP.HOBBY SET (677)	120.00	36.00
COMP.RETAIL SET (677)	120.00	36.00
COMP.SERIES 1 (396)	40.00	12.00
COMP.SERIES 2 (264)	40.00	12.00

- ❑ 1 Frank Thomas .75 .23
- ❑ 2 Mickey Morandini .15 .04
- ❑ 3 Babe Ruth 100th B-Day 2.00 .60
- ❑ 4 Scott Cooper .15 .04
- ❑ 5 David Cone .30 .09
- ❑ 6 Jacob Shumate .15 .04
- ❑ 7 Trevor Hoffman .30 .09
- ❑ 8 Shane Mack .15 .04
- ❑ 9 Delino DeShields .15 .04
- ❑ 10 Matt Williams .30 .09
- ❑ 11 Sammy Sosa .75 .23
- ❑ 12 Gary DiSarcina .15 .04
- ❑ 13 Kenny Rogers .30 .09
- ❑ 14 Jose Vizcaino .15 .04
- ❑ 15 Lou Whitaker .30 .09
- ❑ 16 Ron Darling .15 .04
- ❑ 17 Dave Nilsson .15 .04
- ❑ 18 Chris Hammond .15 .04
- ❑ 19 Sid Bream .15 .04
- ❑ 20 Denny Martinez .30 .09
- ❑ 21 Orlando Merced .15 .04
- ❑ 22 John Wetteland .30 .09
- ❑ 23 Mike Devereaux .15 .04
- ❑ 24 Rene Arocha .15 .04
- ❑ 25 Jay Buhner .30 .09
- ❑ 26 Darren Holmes .15 .04
- ❑ 27 Hal Morris .15 .04
- ❑ 28 Brian Buchanan RC .15 .04
- ❑ 29 Keith Miller .15 .04
- ❑ 30 Paul Molitor .50 .15
- ❑ 31 Dave West .15 .04
- ❑ 32 Tony Tarasco .15 .04
- ❑ 33 Scott Sanders .15 .04
- ❑ 34 Eddie Zambrano .15 .04
- ❑ 35 Ricky Bones .15 .04
- ❑ 36 John Valentin .15 .04
- ❑ 37 Kevin Tapani .15 .04
- ❑ 38 Tim Wallach .15 .04
- ❑ 39 Darren Lewis .15 .04
- ❑ 40 Travis Fryman .30 .09
- ❑ 41 Mark Leiter .15 .04
- ❑ 42 Jose Bautista .15 .04
- ❑ 43 Pete Smith .15 .04
- ❑ 44 Bret Barberie .15 .04
- ❑ 45 Dennis Eckersley .30 .09
- ❑ 46 Ken Hill .15 .04
- ❑ 47 Chad Ogea .15 .04
- ❑ 48 Pete Harnisch .15 .04
- ❑ 49 James Baldwin .15 .04
- ❑ 50 Mike Mussina .50 .15
- ❑ 51 Al Martin .15 .04
- ❑ 52 Mark Thompson .15 .04
- ❑ 53 Matt Smith .15 .04
- ❑ 54 Joey Hamilton .15 .04
- ❑ 55 Edgar Martinez .50 .15
- ❑ 56 John Smiley .15 .04
- ❑ 57 Rey Sanchez .15 .04
- ❑ 58 Mike Timlin .15 .04
- ❑ 59 Ricky Bottalico .15 .04
- ❑ 60 Jim Abbott .50 .15
- ❑ 61 Mike Kelly .15 .04
- ❑ 62 Brian Jordan .30 .09
- ❑ 63 Ken Ryan .15 .04
- ❑ 64 Matt Mieske .15 .04
- ❑ 65 Rick Aguilera .15 .04
- ❑ 66 Ismael Valdes .15 .04
- ❑ 67 Royce Clayton .15 .04
- ❑ 68 Junior Felix .15 .04
- ❑ 69 Harold Reynolds .30 .09
- ❑ 70 Juan Gonzalez .30 .09
- ❑ 71 Kelly Stinnett .15 .04
- ❑ 72 Carlos Reyes .15 .04
- ❑ 73 Dave Weathers .15 .04
- ❑ 74 Mel Rojas .15 .04
- ❑ 75 Doug Drabek .15 .04
- ❑ 76 Charles Nagy .15 .04
- ❑ 77 Tim Raines .30 .09
- ❑ 78 Midre Cummings .15 .04
- ❑ 79 Gene Schall .15 .04
  Scott Talanoa
  Harold Williams
  Ray Brown RC
- ❑ 80 Rafael Palmeiro .50 .15
- ❑ 81 Charlie Hayes .15 .04
- ❑ 82 Ray Lankford .30 .09
- ❑ 83 Tim Davis .15 .04
- ❑ 84 C.J. Nitkowski .15 .04
- ❑ 85 Andy Ashby .15 .04
- ❑ 86 Gerald Williams .15 .04
- ❑ 87 Terry Shumpert .15 .04
- ❑ 88 Heathcliff Slocumb .15 .04
- ❑ 89 Domingo Cedeno .15 .04
- ❑ 90 Mark Grace .50 .15
- ❑ 91 Brad Woodall RC .15 .04
- ❑ 92 Gar Finnvold .15 .04
- ❑ 93 Jaime Navarro .15 .04
- ❑ 94 Carlos Hernandez .15 .04
- ❑ 95 Mark Langston .15 .04
- ❑ 96 Chuck Carr .15 .04
- ❑ 97 Mike Gardiner .15 .04
- ❑ 98 Dave McCarty .15 .04
- ❑ 99 Cris Carpenter .15 .04
- ❑ 100 Barry Bonds 2.00 .60
- ❑ 101 David Segui .15 .04
- ❑ 102 Scott Brosius .30 .09
- ❑ 103 Mariano Duncan .15 .04
- ❑ 104 Kenny Lofton .30 .09
- ❑ 105 Ken Caminiti .30 .09
- ❑ 106 Darrin Jackson .15 .04
- ❑ 107 Jim Poole .15 .04
- ❑ 108 Wil Cordero .15 .04
- ❑ 109 Danny Miceli .15 .04
- ❑ 110 Walt Weiss .15 .04
- ❑ 111 Tom Pagnozzi .15 .04
- ❑ 112 Terrence Long .30 .09
- ❑ 113 Bret Boone .30 .09
- ❑ 114 Daryl Boston .15 .04
- ❑ 115 Wally Joyner .30 .09
- ❑ 116 Rob Butler .15 .04
- ❑ 117 Rafael Belliard .15 .04
- ❑ 118 Luis Lopez .15 .04
- ❑ 119 Tony Fossas .15 .04
- ❑ 120 Len Dykstra .30 .09
- ❑ 121 Mike Morgan .15 .04
- ❑ 122 Denny Hocking .15 .04
- ❑ 123 Kevin Gross .15 .04
- ❑ 124 Todd Benzinger .15 .04
- ❑ 125 John Doherty .15 .04
- ❑ 126 Eduardo Perez .15 .04
- ❑ 127 Dan Smith .15 .04
- ❑ 128 Joe Orsulak .15 .04
- ❑ 129 Brent Gates .15 .04
- ❑ 130 Jeff Conine .30 .09
- ❑ 131 Doug Henry .15 .04
- ❑ 132 Paul Sorrento .15 .04
- ❑ 133 Mike Hampton .30 .09
- ❑ 134 Tim Spehr .15 .04
- ❑ 135 Julio Franco .30 .09
- ❑ 136 Mike Dyer .15 .04
- ❑ 137 Chris Sabo .15 .04
- ❑ 138 Rheal Cormier .15 .04
- ❑ 139 Paul Konerko 1.00 .30
- ❑ 140 Dante Bichette .30 .09
- ❑ 141 Chuck McElroy .15 .04
- ❑ 142 Mike Stanley .15 .04
- ❑ 143 Bob Hamelin .15 .04
- ❑ 144 Tommy Greene .15 .04
- ❑ 145 John Smoltz .50 .15
- ❑ 146 Ed Sprague .15 .04
- ❑ 147 Ray McDavid .15 .04
- ❑ 148 Otis Nixon .15 .04
- ❑ 149 Turk Wendell .15 .04
- ❑ 150 Chris James .15 .04
- ❑ 151 Derek Parks .15 .04
- ❑ 152 Jose Offerman .15 .04
- ❑ 153 Tony Clark .15 .04
- ❑ 154 Chad Curtis .15 .04
- ❑ 155 Mark Portugal .15 .04
- ❑ 156 Bill Pulsipher .15 .04
- ❑ 157 Troy Neel .15 .04
- ❑ 158 Dave Winfield .30 .09
- ❑ 159 Bill Wegman .15 .04
- ❑ 160 Benito Santiago .30 .09
- ❑ 161 Jose Mesa .15 .04
- ❑ 162 Luis Gonzalez .30 .09
- ❑ 163 Alex Fernandez .15 .04
- ❑ 164 Freddie Benavides .15 .04
- ❑ 165 Ben McDonald .15 .04
- ❑ 166 Blas Minor .15 .04
- ❑ 167 Bret Wagner .15 .04
- ❑ 168 Mac Suzuki .15 .04
- ❑ 169 Roberto Mejia .15 .04
- ❑ 170 Wade Boggs .50 .15
- ❑ 171 Pokey Reese .15 .04
- ❑ 172 Hipolito Pichardo .15 .04
- ❑ 173 Kim Batiste .15 .04
- ❑ 174 Darren Hall .15 .04
- ❑ 175 Tom Glavine .50 .15
- ❑ 176 Phil Plantier .15 .04
- ❑ 177 Chris Howard .15 .04
- ❑ 178 Karl Rhodes .15 .04
- ❑ 179 LaTroy Hawkins .15 .04
- ❑ 180 Raul Mondesi .30 .09
- ❑ 181 Jeff Reed .15 .04
- ❑ 182 Milt Cuyler .15 .04
- ❑ 183 Jim Edmonds .50 .15
- ❑ 184 Hector Fajardo .15 .04
- ❑ 185 Jeff Kent .30 .09
- ❑ 186 Wilson Alvarez .15 .04
- ❑ 187 Geronimo Berroa .15 .04
- ❑ 188 Billy Spiers .15 .04
- ❑ 189 Derek Lilliquist .15 .04

Card	Player	Price	Price
❑ 190	Craig Biggio	.50	.15
❑ 191	Roberto Hernandez	.15	.04
❑ 192	Bob Natal	.15	.04
❑ 193	Bobby Ayala	.15	.04
❑ 194	Travis Miller RC	.15	.04
❑ 195	Bob Tewksbury	.15	.04
❑ 196	Rondell White	.30	.09
❑ 197	Steve Cooke	.15	.04
❑ 198	Jeff Branson	.15	.04
❑ 199	Derek Jeter	2.00	.60
❑ 200	Tim Salmon	.50	.15
❑ 201	Steve Frey	.15	.04
❑ 202	Kent Mercker	.15	.04
❑ 203	Randy Johnson	.75	.23
❑ 204	Todd Worrell	.15	.04
❑ 205	Mo Vaughn	.30	.09
❑ 206	Howard Johnson	.15	.04
❑ 207	John Wasdin	.15	.04
❑ 208	Eddie Williams	.15	.04
❑ 209	Tim Belcher	.15	.04
❑ 210	Jeff Montgomery	.15	.04
❑ 211	Kirt Manwaring	.15	.04
❑ 212	Ben Grieve	.30	.09
❑ 213	Pat Hentgen	.15	.04
❑ 214	Shawon Dunston	.15	.04
❑ 215	Mike Greenwell	.15	.04
❑ 216	Alex Diaz	.15	.04
❑ 217	Pat Mahomes	.15	.04
❑ 218	Dave Hansen	.15	.04
❑ 219	Kevin Rogers	.15	.04
❑ 220	Cecil Fielder	.30	.09
❑ 221	Andrew Lorraine	.15	.04
❑ 222	Jack Armstrong	.15	.04
❑ 223	Todd Hundley	.15	.04
❑ 224	Mark Acre	.15	.04
❑ 225	Darrell Whitmore	.15	.04
❑ 226	Randy Milligan	.15	.04
❑ 227	Wayne Kirby	.15	.04
❑ 228	Darryl Kile	.30	.09
❑ 229	Bob Zupcic	.15	.04
❑ 230	Jay Bell	.30	.09
❑ 231	Dustin Hermanson	.15	.04
❑ 232	Harold Baines	.30	.09
❑ 233	Alan Benes	.15	.04
❑ 234	Felix Fermin	.15	.04
❑ 235	Ellis Burks	.30	.09
❑ 236	Jeff Brantley	.15	.04
❑ 237	Brian Hunter Jose Malave Karim Garcia RC Shane Pullen	.40	.12
❑ 238	Matt Nokes	.15	.04
❑ 239	Ben Rivera	.15	.04
❑ 240	Joe Carter	.30	.09
❑ 241	Jeff Granger	.15	.04
❑ 242	Terry Pendleton	.30	.09
❑ 243	Melvin Nieves	.15	.04
❑ 244	Frankie Rodriguez	.15	.04
❑ 245	Darryl Hamilton	.15	.04
❑ 246	Brooks Kieschnick	.15	.04
❑ 247	Todd Hollandsworth	.15	.04
❑ 248	Joe Rosselli	.15	.04
❑ 249	Bill Gullickson	.15	.04
❑ 250	Chuck Knoblauch	.30	.09
❑ 251	Kurt Miller	.15	.04
❑ 252	Bobby Jones	.15	.04
❑ 253	Lance Blankenship	.15	.04
❑ 254	Matt Whiteside	.15	.04
❑ 255	Darrin Fletcher	.15	.04
❑ 256	Eric Plunk	.15	.04
❑ 257	Shane Reynolds	.15	.04
❑ 258	Norberto Martin	.15	.04
❑ 259	Mike Thurman	.15	.04
❑ 260	Andy Van Slyke	.50	.15
❑ 261	Dwight Smith	.15	.04
❑ 262	Allen Watson	.15	.04
❑ 263	Dan Wilson	.15	.04
❑ 264	Brent Mayne	.15	.04
❑ 265	Bip Roberts	.15	.04
❑ 266	Sterling Hitchcock	.15	.04
❑ 267	Alex Gonzalez	.15	.04
❑ 268	Greg Harris	.15	.04
❑ 269	Ricky Jordan	.15	.04
❑ 270	Johnny Ruffin	.15	.04
❑ 271	Mike Stanton	.15	.04
❑ 272	Rich Rowland	.15	.04
❑ 273	Steve Trachsel	.15	.04
❑ 274	Pedro Munoz	.15	.04
❑ 275	Ramon Martinez	.15	.04
❑ 276	Dave Henderson	.15	.04
❑ 277	Chris Gomez	.15	.04
❑ 278	Joe Grahe	.15	.04
❑ 279	Rusty Greer	.30	.09
❑ 280	John Franco	.30	.09
❑ 281	Mike Bordick	.15	.04
❑ 282	Jeff D'Amico	.15	.04
❑ 283	Dave Magadan	.15	.04
❑ 284	Tony Pena	.15	.04
❑ 285	Greg Swindell	.15	.04
❑ 286	Doug Million	.15	.04
❑ 287	Gabe White	.15	.04
❑ 288	Trey Beamon	.15	.04
❑ 289	Arthur Rhodes	.15	.04
❑ 290	Juan Guzman	.15	.04
❑ 291	Jose Oquendo	.15	.04
❑ 292	Willie Blair	.15	.04
❑ 293	Eddie Taubensee	.15	.04
❑ 294	Steve Howe	.15	.04
❑ 295	Greg Maddux	1.25	.35
❑ 296	Mike Macfarlane	.15	.04
❑ 297	Curt Schilling	.30	.09
❑ 298	Phil Clark	.15	.04
❑ 299	Woody Williams	.15	.04
❑ 300	Jose Canseco	.50	.15
❑ 301	Aaron Sele	.15	.04
❑ 302	Carl Willis	.15	.04
❑ 303	Steve Buechele	.15	.04
❑ 304	Dave Burba	.15	.04
❑ 305	Orel Hershiser	.30	.09
❑ 306	Damion Easley	.15	.04
❑ 307	Mike Henneman	.15	.04
❑ 308	Josias Manzanillo	.15	.04
❑ 309	Kevin Seitzer	.15	.04
❑ 310	Ruben Sierra	.15	.04
❑ 311	Bryan Harvey	.15	.04
❑ 312	Jim Thome	.50	.15
❑ 313	Ramon Castro RC	.40	.12
❑ 314	Lance Johnson	.15	.04
❑ 315	Marquis Grissom	.30	.09
❑ 316	Terrell Wade Juan Acevedo Matt Arrandale Eddie Priest RC	.15	.04
❑ 317	Paul Wagner	.15	.04
❑ 318	Jamie Moyer	.30	.09
❑ 319	Todd Zeile	.15	.04
❑ 320	Chris Bosio	.15	.04
❑ 321	Steve Reed	.15	.04
❑ 322	Erik Hanson	.15	.04
❑ 323	Luis Polonia	.15	.04
❑ 324	Ryan Klesko	.30	.09
❑ 325	Kevin Appier	.30	.09
❑ 326	Jim Eisenreich	.15	.04
❑ 327	Randy Knorr	.15	.04
❑ 328	Craig Shipley	.15	.04
❑ 329	Tim Naehring	.15	.04
❑ 330	Randy Myers	.15	.04
❑ 331	Alex Cole	.15	.04
❑ 332	Jim Gott	.15	.04
❑ 333	Mike Jackson	.15	.04
❑ 334	John Flaherty	.15	.04
❑ 335	Chili Davis	.30	.09
❑ 336	Benji Gil	.15	.04
❑ 337	Jason Jacome	.15	.04
❑ 338	Stan Javier	.15	.04
❑ 339	Mike Fetters	.15	.04
❑ 340	Rich Renteria	.15	.04
❑ 341	Kevin Witt	.15	.04
❑ 342	Scott Servais	.15	.04
❑ 343	Craig Grebeck	.15	.04
❑ 344	Kirk Rueter	.15	.04
❑ 345	Don Slaught	.15	.04
❑ 346	Armando Benitez	.30	.09
❑ 347	Ozzie Smith	1.25	.35
❑ 348	Mike Blowers	.15	.04
❑ 349	Armando Reynoso	.15	.04
❑ 350	Barry Larkin	.50	.15
❑ 351	Mike Williams	.15	.04
❑ 352	Scott Kamieniecki	.15	.04
❑ 353	Gary Gaetti	.30	.09
❑ 354	Todd Stottlemyre	.15	.04
❑ 355	Fred McGriff	.50	.15
❑ 356	Tim Mauser	.15	.04
❑ 357	Chris Gwynn	.15	.04
❑ 358	Frank Castillo	.15	.04
❑ 359	Jeff Reboulet	.15	.04
❑ 360	Roger Clemens	1.50	.45
❑ 361	Mark Carreon	.15	.04
❑ 362	Chad Kreuter	.15	.04
❑ 363	Mark Farris	.15	.04
❑ 364	Bob Welch	.15	.04
❑ 365	Dean Palmer	.30	.09
❑ 366	Jeromy Burnitz	.30	.09
❑ 367	B.J. Surhoff	.30	.09
❑ 368	Mike Butcher	.15	.04
❑ 369	Brad Clontz Steve Phoenix Scott Gentile Bucky Buckles RC	.15	.04
❑ 370	Eddie Murray	.75	.23
❑ 371	Orlando Miller	.15	.04
❑ 372	Ron Karkovice	.15	.04
❑ 373	Richie Lewis	.15	.04
❑ 374	Lenny Webster	.15	.04
❑ 375	Jeff Tackett	.15	.04
❑ 376	Tom Urbani	.15	.04
❑ 377	Tino Martinez	.50	.15
❑ 378	Mark Dewey	.15	.04
❑ 379	Charles O'Brien	.15	.04
❑ 380	Terry Mulholland	.15	.04
❑ 381	Thomas Howard	.15	.04
❑ 382	Chris Haney	.15	.04
❑ 383	Billy Hatcher	.15	.04
❑ 384	Jeff Bagwell AS Frank Thomas AS	.50	.15
❑ 385	Bret Boone AS Carlos Baerga AS	.30	.09
❑ 386	Matt Williams AS Wade Boggs AS	.30	.09
❑ 387	Wil Cordero AS Cal Ripken AS	.75	.23
❑ 388	Barry Bonds AS Ken Griffey AS	1.00	.30
❑ 389	Tony Gwynn AS Albert Belle AS	.30	.09
❑ 390	Dante Bichette AS Kirby Puckett AS	.50	.15
❑ 391	Mike Piazza AS Mike Stanley AS	.75	.23
❑ 392	Greg Maddux AS David Cone AS	.75	.23
❑ 393	Danny Jackson AS Jimmy Key AS	.15	.04
❑ 394	John Franco AS Lee Smith AS	.15	.04
❑ 395	Checklist 1-198	.15	.04
❑ 396	Checklist 199-396	.15	.04
❑ 397	Ken Griffey Jr.	1.25	.35
❑ 398	Rick Heiserman RC	.15	.04
❑ 399	Don Mattingly	2.00	.60
❑ 400	Henry Rodriguez	.15	.04
❑ 401	Lenny Harris	.15	.04
❑ 402	Ryan Thompson	.15	.04
❑ 403	Darren Oliver	.15	.04
❑ 404	Omar Vizquel	.50	.15
❑ 405	Jeff Bagwell	.50	.15
❑ 406	Doug Webb RC	.15	.04
❑ 407	Todd Van Poppel	.15	.04
❑ 408	Leo Gomez	.15	.04
❑ 409	Mark Whiten	.15	.04
❑ 410	Pedro A.Martinez	.15	.04
❑ 411	Reggie Sanders	.30	.09
❑ 412	Kevin Foster	.15	.04
❑ 413	Danny Tartabull	.15	.04
❑ 414	Jeff Blauser	.15	.04
❑ 415	Mike Magnante	.15	.04
❑ 416	Tom Candiotti	.15	.04
❑ 417	Rod Beck	.15	.04
❑ 418	Jody Reed	.15	.04
❑ 419	Vince Coleman	.15	.04
❑ 420	Danny Jackson	.15	.04
❑ 421	Ryan Nye RC	.15	.04
❑ 422	Larry Walker	.30	.09
❑ 423	Russ Johnson DP	.15	.04
❑ 424	Pat Borders	.15	.04
❑ 425	Lee Smith	.30	.09
❑ 426	Paul O'Neill	.50	.15
❑ 427	Devon White	.30	.09

❑ 428	Jim Bullinger	.15	.04
❑ 429	Greg Hansell	.15	.04
	Brian Sackinsky		
	Carey Paige		
	Rob Welch RC		
❑ 430	Steve Avery	.15	.04
❑ 431	Tony Gwynn	1.00	.30
❑ 432	Pat Meares	.15	.04
❑ 433	Bill Swift	.15	.04
❑ 434	David Wells	.30	.09
❑ 435	John Briscoe	.15	.04
❑ 436	Roger Pavlik	.15	.04
❑ 437	Jayson Peterson RC	.15	.04
❑ 438	Roberto Alomar	.50	.15
❑ 439	Billy Brewer	.15	.04
❑ 440	Gary Sheffield	.30	.09
❑ 441	Lou Frazier	.15	.04
❑ 442	Terry Steinbach	.15	.04
❑ 443	Jay Payton RC	.75	.23
❑ 444	Jason Bere	.15	.04
❑ 445	Denny Neagle	.30	.09
❑ 446	Andres Galarraga	.30	.09
❑ 447	Hector Carrasco	.15	.04
❑ 448	Bill Risley	.15	.04
❑ 449	Andy Benes	.15	.04
❑ 450	Jim Leyritz	.15	.04
❑ 451	Jose Oliva	.15	.04
❑ 452	Greg Vaughn	.15	.04
❑ 453	Rich Monteleone	.15	.04
❑ 454	Tony Eusebio	.15	.04
❑ 455	Chuck Finley	.30	.09
❑ 456	Kevin Brown	.30	.09
❑ 457	Joe Boever	.15	.04
❑ 458	Bobby Munoz	.15	.04
❑ 459	Bret Saberhagen	.30	.09
❑ 460	Kurt Abbott	.15	.04
❑ 461	Bobby Witt	.15	.04
❑ 462	Cliff Floyd	.30	.09
❑ 463	Mark Clark	.15	.04
❑ 464	Andujar Cedeno	.15	.04
❑ 465	Marvin Freeman	.15	.04
❑ 466	Mike Piazza	1.25	.35
❑ 467	Willie Greene	.15	.04
❑ 468	Pat Kelly	.15	.04
❑ 469	Carlos Delgado	.30	.09
❑ 470	Willie Banks	.15	.04
❑ 471	Matt Walbeck	.15	.04
❑ 472	Mark McGwire	2.00	.60
❑ 473	M.Christensen RC	.15	.04
❑ 474	Alan Trammell	.30	.09
❑ 475	Tom Gordon	.15	.04
❑ 476	Greg Colbrunn	.15	.04
❑ 477	Darren Daulton	.30	.09
❑ 478	Albie Lopez	.15	.04
❑ 479	Robin Ventura	.30	.09
❑ 480	Eddie Perez RC	.40	.12
	Jason Kendall		
	Einar Diaz		
	Bret Hemphill		
❑ 481	Bryan Eversgerd	.15	.04
❑ 482	Dave Fleming	.15	.04
❑ 483	Scott Livingstone	.15	.04
❑ 484	Pete Schourek	.15	.04
❑ 485	Bernie Williams	.50	.15
❑ 486	Mark Lemke	.15	.04
❑ 487	Eric Karros	.30	.09
❑ 488	Scott Ruffcorn	.15	.04
❑ 489	Billy Ashley	.15	.04
❑ 490	Rico Brogna	.15	.04
❑ 491	John Burkett	.15	.04
❑ 492	Cade Gaspar RC	.15	.04
❑ 493	Jorge Fabregas	.15	.04
❑ 494	Greg Gagne	.15	.04
❑ 495	Doug Jones	.15	.04
❑ 496	Troy O'Leary	.15	.04
❑ 497	Pat Rapp	.15	.04
❑ 498	Butch Henry	.15	.04
❑ 499	John Olerud	.30	.09
❑ 500	John Hudek	.15	.04
❑ 501	Jeff King	.15	.04
❑ 502	Bobby Bonilla	.30	.09
❑ 503	Albert Belle	.30	.09
❑ 504	Rick Wilkins	.15	.04
❑ 505	John Jaha	.15	.04
❑ 506	Nigel Wilson	.15	.04
❑ 507	Sid Fernandez	.15	.04
❑ 508	Deion Sanders	.50	.15
❑ 509	Gil Heredia	.15	.04
❑ 510	Scott Elarton RC	.40	.12
❑ 511	Melido Perez	.15	.04
❑ 512	Greg McMichael	.15	.04
❑ 513	Rusty Meacham	.15	.04
❑ 514	Shawn Green	.30	.09
❑ 515	Carlos Garcia	.15	.04
❑ 516	Dave Stevens	.15	.04
❑ 517	Eric Young	.15	.04
❑ 518	Omar Daal	.15	.04
❑ 519	Kirk Gibson	.50	.15
❑ 520	Spike Owen	.15	.04
❑ 521	Jacob Cruz RC	.30	.09
❑ 522	Sandy Alomar Jr.	.15	.04
❑ 523	Steve Bedrosian	.15	.04
❑ 524	Ricky Gutierrez	.15	.04
❑ 525	Dave Veres	.15	.04
❑ 526	Gregg Jefferies	.15	.04
❑ 527	Jose Valentin	.15	.04
❑ 528	Robb Nen	.30	.09
❑ 529	Jose Rijo	.15	.04
❑ 530	Sean Berry	.15	.04
❑ 531	Mike Gallego	.15	.04
❑ 532	Roberto Kelly	.15	.04
❑ 533	Kevin Stocker	.15	.04
❑ 534	Kirby Puckett	.75	.23
❑ 535	Chipper Jones	.75	.23
❑ 536	Russ Davis	.15	.04
❑ 537	Jon Lieber	.15	.04
❑ 538	Trey Moore RC	.15	.04
❑ 539	Joe Girardi	.15	.04
❑ 540	Quilvio Veras	.40	.12
	Arquimedez Pozo		
	Miguel Cairo RC		
	Jason Camilli		
❑ 541	Tony Phillips	.15	.04
❑ 542	Brian Anderson	.15	.04
❑ 543	Ivan Rodriguez	.50	.15
❑ 544	Jeff Cirillo	.30	.09
❑ 545	Joey Cora	.15	.04
❑ 546	Chris Hoiles	.15	.04
❑ 547	Bernard Gilkey	.15	.04
❑ 548	Mike Lansing	.15	.04
❑ 549	Jimmy Key	.30	.09
❑ 550	Mark Wohlers	.15	.04
❑ 551	Chris Clemons RC	.15	.04
❑ 552	Vinny Castilla	.30	.09
❑ 553	Mark Guthrie	.15	.04
❑ 554	Mike Lieberthal	.15	.04
❑ 555	Tommy Davis RC	.15	.04
❑ 556	Robby Thompson	.15	.04
❑ 557	Danny Bautista	.15	.04
❑ 558	Will Clark	.50	.15
❑ 559	Rickey Henderson	.75	.23
❑ 560	Todd Jones	.15	.04
❑ 561	Jack McDowell	.15	.04
❑ 562	Carlos Rodriguez	.15	.04
❑ 563	Mark Eichhorn	.15	.04
❑ 564	Jeff Nelson	.15	.04
❑ 565	Eric Anthony	.15	.04
❑ 566	Randy Velarde	.15	.04
❑ 567	Javier Lopez	.30	.09
❑ 568	Kevin Mitchell	.15	.04
❑ 569	Steve Karsay	.15	.04
❑ 570	Brian Meadows RC	.15	.04
❑ 571	Rey Ordonez RC	.75	.23
	Mike Metcalfe		
	Kevin Orie		
	Ray Holbert		
❑ 572	John Kruk	.30	.09
❑ 573	Scott Leius	.15	.04
❑ 574	John Patterson	.15	.04
❑ 575	Kevin Brown	.30	.09
❑ 576	Mike Moore	.15	.04
❑ 577	Manny Ramirez	.50	.15
❑ 578	Jose Lind	.15	.04
❑ 579	Derrick May	.15	.04
❑ 580	Cal Eldred	.15	.04
❑ 581	David Bell	.75	.23
	Joel Chelmis		
	Lino Diaz		
	Aaron Boone RC		
❑ 582	J.T. Snow	.30	.09
❑ 583	Luis Sojo	.15	.04
❑ 584	Moises Alou	.30	.09
❑ 585	Dave Clark	.15	.04
❑ 586	Dave Hollins	.15	.04
❑ 587	Nomar Garciaparra	2.00	.60
❑ 588	Cal Ripken	2.50	.75
❑ 589	Pedro Astacio	.15	.04
❑ 590	J.R. Phillips	.15	.04
❑ 591	Jeff Frye	.15	.04
❑ 592	Bo Jackson	.75	.23
❑ 593	Steve Ontiveros	.15	.04
❑ 594	David Nied	.15	.04
❑ 595	Brad Ausmus	.30	.09
❑ 596	Carlos Baerga	.15	.04
❑ 597	James Mouton	.15	.04
❑ 598	Ozzie Guillen	.30	.09
❑ 599	Ozzie Timmons	.75	.23
	Curtis Goodwin		
	Johnny Damon		
	Jeff Abbott RC		
❑ 600	Yorkis Perez	.15	.04
❑ 601	Rich Rodriguez	.15	.04
❑ 602	Mark McLemore	.15	.04
❑ 603	Jeff Fassero	.15	.04
❑ 604	John Roper	.15	.04
❑ 605	Mark Johnson RC	.40	.12
❑ 606	Wes Chamberlain	.15	.04
❑ 607	Felix Jose	.15	.04
❑ 608	Tony Longmire	.15	.04
❑ 609	Duane Ward	.15	.04
❑ 610	Brett Butler	.30	.09
❑ 611	W.VanLandingham	.15	.04
❑ 612	Mickey Tettleton	.15	.04
❑ 613	Brady Anderson	.30	.09
❑ 614	Reggie Jefferson	.15	.04
❑ 615	Mike Kingery	.15	.04
❑ 616	Derek Bell	.15	.04
❑ 617	Scott Erickson	.15	.04
❑ 618	Bob Wickman	.15	.04
❑ 619	Phil Leftwich	.15	.04
❑ 620	David Justice	.30	.09
❑ 621	Paul Wilson	.15	.04
❑ 622	Pedro Martinez	.50	.15
❑ 623	Terry Mathews	.15	.04
❑ 624	Brian McRae	.15	.04
❑ 625	Bruce Ruffin	.15	.04
❑ 626	Steve Finley	.30	.09
❑ 627	Ron Gant	.30	.09
❑ 628	Rafael Bournigal	.15	.04
❑ 629	Darryl Strawberry	.30	.09
❑ 630	Luis Alicea	.15	.04
❑ 631	Mark Smith	.15	.04
	Scott Klingenbeck		
❑ 632	Cory Bailey	.15	.04
	Scott Hatteberg		
❑ 633	Todd Greene	.30	.09
	Troy Percival		
❑ 634	Rod Bolton	.15	.04
	Olmedo Saenz		
❑ 635	Steve Kline	.15	.04
	Herb Perry		
❑ 636	Sean Bergman	.15	.04
	Shannon Penn		
❑ 637	Joe Randa	.15	.04
	Joe Vitiello		
❑ 638	Jose Mercedes	.15	.04
	Duane Singleton		
❑ 639	Marc Barcelo	.15	.04
	Marty Cordova		
❑ 640	Andy Pettitte	.30	.09
	Ruben Rivera		
❑ 641	Willie Adams	.15	.04
	Scott Spiezio		
❑ 642	Eddy Diaz RC	.15	.04
	Desi Relaford		
❑ 643	Terrell Lowery	.15	.04
	Jon Shave		
❑ 644	Angel Martinez	.15	.04
	Paul Spoljaric		
❑ 645	Tony Graffanino	.15	.04
	Damon Hollins		
❑ 646	Darron Cox	.15	.04
	Doug Glanville		
❑ 647	Tim Belk	.15	.04
	Pat Watkins		
❑ 648	Rod Pedraza	.15	.04
	Phil Schneider		
❑ 649	Vic Darensbourg	.15	.04

	Marc Valdes		
❑ 650	Rick Huisman	.15	.04
	Roberto Petagine		
❑ 651	Roger Cedeno	.40	.12
	Ron Coomer RC		
❑ 652	Shane Andrews	.40	.12
	Carlos Perez RC		
❑ 653	Jason Isringhausen	.30	.09
	Chris Roberts		
❑ 654	Wayne Gomes	.15	.04
	Kevin Jordan		
❑ 655	Esteban Loiaza	.15	.04
	Steve Pegues		
❑ 656	Terry Bradshaw	.15	.04
	John Frascatore		
❑ 657	Andres Berumen	.15	.04
	Bryce Florie		
❑ 658	Dan Carlson	.15	.04
	Keith Williams		
❑ 659	Checklist	.15	.04
❑ 660	Checklist	.15	.04

1995 Topps Traded

		Nm-Mt	Ex-Mt
COMPLETE SET (165)		50.00	15.00
❑ 1T	Frank Thomas ATB	.60	.18
❑ 2T	Ken Griffey Jr. ATB	1.00	.30
❑ 3T	Barry Bonds ATB	1.25	.35
❑ 4T	Albert Belle ATB	.40	.12
❑ 5T	Cal Ripken ATB	1.50	.45
❑ 6T	Mike Piazza ATB	1.00	.30
❑ 7T	Tony Gwynn ATB	.60	.18
❑ 8T	Jeff Bagwell ATB	.40	.12
❑ 9T	Mo Vaughn ATB	.20	.06
❑ 10T	Matt Williams ATB	.20	.06
❑ 11T	Ray Durham	.40	.12
❑ 12T	Juan LeBron	5.00	1.50
	Card pictures Carlos Beltran instead of Juan LeBron RC		
❑ 13T	Shawn Green	.40	.12
❑ 14T	Kevin Gross	.20	.06
❑ 15T	Jon Nunnally	.20	.06
❑ 16T	Brian Maxcy RC	.25	.07
❑ 17T	Mark Kiefer	.20	.06
❑ 18T	Carlos Beltran UER	15.00	4.50
	Card pictures Juan LeBron instead of Carlos Beltran RC.		
❑ 19T	Mike Mimbs RC	.25	.07
❑ 20T	Larry Walker	.40	.12
❑ 21T	Chad Curtis	.20	.06
❑ 22T	Jeff Barry	.20	.06
❑ 23T	Joe Oliver	.20	.06
❑ 24T	Tomas Perez RC	.25	.07
❑ 25T	Michael Barrett RC	1.00	.30
❑ 26T	Brian McRae	.20	.06
❑ 27T	Derek Bell	.20	.06
❑ 28T	Ray Durham	.40	.12
❑ 29T	Todd Williams	.20	.06
❑ 30T	Ryan Jaroncyk RC	.25	.07
❑ 31T	Todd Steverson	.20	.06
❑ 32T	Mike Devereaux	.20	.06
❑ 33T	Rheal Cormier	.20	.06
❑ 34T	Benny Santiago	.40	.12
❑ 35T	Bobby Higginson RC	1.00	.30
❑ 36T	Jack McDowell	.20	.06
❑ 37T	Mike Macfarlane	.20	.06
❑ 38T	Tony McKnight RC	.25	.07
❑ 39T	Brian Hunter	.20	.06
❑ 40T	Hideo Nomo RC	4.00	1.20
❑ 41T	Brett Butler	.40	.12
❑ 42T	Donovan Osborne	.20	.06
❑ 43T	Scott Karl	.20	.06
❑ 44T	Tony Phillips	.20	.06
❑ 45T	Marty Cordova	.20	.06
❑ 46T	Dave Mlicki	.20	.06
❑ 47T	Bronson Arroyo RC	8.00	2.40
❑ 48T	John Burkett	.20	.06
❑ 49T	J.D. Smart RC	.25	.07
❑ 50T	Mickey Tettleton	.20	.06
❑ 51T	Todd Stottlemyre	.20	.06
❑ 52T	Mike Perez	.20	.06
❑ 53T	Terry Mulholland	.20	.06
❑ 54T	Edgardo Alfonzo	.20	.06
❑ 55T	Zane Smith	.20	.06
❑ 56T	Jacob Brumfield	.20	.06
❑ 57T	Andujar Cedeno	.20	.06
❑ 58T	Jose Parra	.20	.06
❑ 59T	Manny Alexander	.20	.06
❑ 60T	Tony Tarasco	.20	.06
❑ 61T	Orel Hershiser	.40	.12
❑ 62T	Tim Scott	.20	.06
❑ 63T	Felix Rodriguez RC	.50	.15
❑ 64T	Ken Hill	.20	.06
❑ 65T	Marquis Grissom	.40	.12
❑ 66T	Lee Smith	.40	.12
❑ 67T	Jason Bates	.20	.06
❑ 68T	Felipe Lira	.20	.06
❑ 69T	Alex Hernandez RC	.25	.07
❑ 70T	Tony Fernandez	.20	.06
❑ 71T	Scott Radinsky	.20	.06
❑ 72T	Jose Canseco	.60	.18
❑ 73T	Mark Grudzielanek RC	1.00	.30
❑ 74T	Ben Davis RC	.50	.15
❑ 75T	Jim Abbott	.60	.18
❑ 76T	Roger Bailey	.20	.06
❑ 77T	Gregg Jefferies	.20	.06
❑ 78T	Erik Hanson	.20	.06
❑ 79T	Brad Radke RC	1.00	.30
❑ 80T	Jaime Navarro	.20	.06
❑ 81T	John Wetteland	.40	.12
❑ 82T	Chad Fonville RC	.25	.07
❑ 83T	John Mabry	.40	.12
❑ 84T	Glenallen Hill	.20	.06
❑ 85T	Ken Caminiti	.40	.12
❑ 86T	Tom Goodwin	.20	.06
❑ 87T	Darren Bragg	.20	.06
❑ 88T	Pat Ahearne	.25	.07
	Gary Rath		
	Larry Wimberly		
	Robbie Bell RC		
❑ 89T	Jeff Russell	.20	.06
❑ 90T	Dave Gallagher	.20	.06
❑ 91T	Steve Finley	.40	.12
❑ 92T	Vaughn Eshelman	.20	.06
❑ 93T	Kevin Jarvis	.20	.06
❑ 94T	Mark Gubicza	.20	.06
❑ 95T	Tim Wakefield	.40	.12
❑ 96T	Bob Tewksbury	.20	.06
❑ 97T	Sid Roberson RC	.25	.07
❑ 98T	Tom Henke	.20	.06
❑ 99T	Michael Tucker	.20	.06
❑ 100T	Jason Bates	.20	.06
❑ 101T	Otis Nixon	.20	.06
❑ 102T	Mark Whiten	.20	.06
❑ 103T	Dilson Torres RC	.25	.07
❑ 104T	Melvin Bunch RC	.25	.07
❑ 105T	Terry Pendleton	.40	.12
❑ 106T	Corey Jenkins RC	.25	.07
❑ 107T	Glenn Dishman RC	.25	.07
	Rob Grable		
❑ 108T	Reggie Taylor RC	.50	.15
❑ 109T	Curtis Goodwin	.20	.06
❑ 110T	David Cone	.40	.12
❑ 111T	Antonio Osuna	.20	.06
❑ 112T	Paul Shuey	.20	.06
❑ 113T	Doug Jones	.20	.06
❑ 114T	Mark McLemore	.20	.06
❑ 115T	Kevin Ritz	.20	.06
❑ 116T	John Kruk	.40	.12
❑ 117T	Trevor Wilson	.20	.06
❑ 118T	Jerald Clark	.20	.06
❑ 119T	Julian Tavarez	.20	.06
❑ 120T	Tim Pugh	.20	.06
❑ 121T	Todd Zeile	.20	.06
❑ 122T	Mark Sweeney UER	4.00	1.20
	George Arias		
	Richie Sexson RC		
	Brian Schneider		
❑ 123T	Bobby Witt	.20	.06
❑ 124T	Hideo Nomo	1.50	.45
❑ 125T	Joey Cora	.20	.06
❑ 126T	Jim Scharrer RC	.25	.07
❑ 127T	Paul Quantrill	.20	.06
❑ 128T	Chipper Jones ROY	.60	.18
❑ 129T	Kenny James RC	.25	.07
❑ 130T	Lyle Mouton	1.00	.30
	Mariano Rivera		
❑ 131T	Tyler Green	.20	.06
❑ 132T	Brad Clontz	.20	.06
❑ 133T	Jon Nunnally	.20	.06
❑ 134T	Dave Magadan	.20	.06
❑ 135T	Al Leiter	.40	.12
❑ 136T	Bret Barberie	.20	.06
❑ 137T	Bill Swift	.20	.06
❑ 138T	Scott Cooper	.20	.06
❑ 139T	Roberto Kelly	.20	.06
❑ 140T	Charlie Hayes	.20	.06
❑ 141T	Pete Harnisch	.20	.06
❑ 142T	Rich Amaral	.20	.06
❑ 143T	Rudy Seanez	.20	.06
❑ 144T	Pat Listach	.20	.06
❑ 145T	Quilvio Veras	.20	.06
❑ 146T	Jose Olmeda RC	.25	.07
❑ 147T	Roberto Petagine	.20	.06
❑ 148T	Kevin Brown	.40	.12
❑ 149T	Phil Plantier	.20	.06
❑ 150T	Carlos Perez	.40	.12
❑ 151T	Pat Borders	.20	.06
❑ 152T	Tyler Green	.20	.06
❑ 153T	Stan Belinda	.20	.06
❑ 154T	Dave Stewart	.40	.12
❑ 155T	Andre Dawson	.40	.12
❑ 156T	Frank Thomas AS	.60	.18
	Fred McGriff UER		
	(McGriff's team shown as Blue Jays)		
❑ 157T	Carlos Baerga AS	.40	.12
	Craig Biggio		
❑ 158T	Wade Boggs AS	.40	.12
	Matt Williams		
❑ 159T	Cal Ripken AS	1.00	.30
	Ozzie Smith		
❑ 160T	Ken Griffey Jr. AS	1.00	.30
	Tony Gwynn		
❑ 161T	Albert Belle AS	1.25	.35
	Barry Bonds		
❑ 162T	Kirby Puckett	.60	.18
	Len Dykstra		
❑ 163T	Ivan Rodriguez AS	1.00	.30
	Mike Piazza		
❑ 164T	Randy Johnson AS	1.50	.45
	Hideo Nomo		
❑ 165T	Checklist	.20	.06

1996 Topps

	Nm-Mt	Ex-Mt
COMPLETE SET (440)	40.00	12.00
COMP.HOBBY SET (449)	40.00	12.00
COMP.CEREAL SET (444)	60.00	18.00
COMP.SERIES 1 (220)	20.00	6.00
COMP.SERIES 2 (220)	20.00	6.00

COMMON CARD (1-440)	.20	.06
COMMON RC	.25	.07
❑ 1 Tony Gwynn STP	.30	.09
❑ 2 Mike Piazza STP	.50	.15
❑ 3 Greg Maddux STP	.50	.15
❑ 4 Jeff Bagwell STP	.20	.06
❑ 5 Larry Walker STP	.20	.06
❑ 6 Barry Larkin STP	.20	.06
❑ 7 Mickey Mantle	4.00	1.20
❑ 8 Tom Glavine STP UER	.20	.06
Won 21 games in June 95		
❑ 9 Craig Biggio STP	.20	.06
❑ 10 Barry Bonds STP	.75	.23
❑ 11 H.Slocumb STP	.20	.06
❑ 12 Matt Williams STP	.20	.06
❑ 13 Todd Helton	1.00	.30
❑ 14 Mark Redman	.25	.07
❑ 15 Michael Barrett	.25	.07
❑ 16 Ben Davis	.25	.07
❑ 17 Juan LeBron	.25	.07
❑ 18 Tony McKnight	.25	.07
❑ 19 Ryan Jaroncyk	.25	.07
❑ 20 Corey Jenkins	.25	.07
❑ 21 Jim Scharrer	.25	.07
❑ 22 Mark Bellhorn RC	2.50	.75
❑ 23 Jarrod Washburn RC	.60	.18
❑ 24 Geoff Jenkins RC	.60	.18
❑ 25 Sean Casey RC	4.00	1.20
❑ 26 Brett Tomko RC	.40	.12
❑ 27 Tony Fernandez	.20	.06
❑ 28 Rich Becker	.20	.06
❑ 29 Andujar Cedeno	.20	.06
❑ 30 Paul Molitor	.30	.09
❑ 31 Brent Gates	.20	.06
❑ 32 Glenallen Hill	.20	.06
❑ 33 Mike Macfarlane	.20	.06
❑ 34 Manny Alexander	.20	.06
❑ 35 Todd Zeile	.20	.06
❑ 36 Joe Girardi	.20	.06
❑ 37 Tony Tarasco	.20	.06
❑ 38 Tim Belcher	.20	.06
❑ 39 Tom Goodwin	.20	.06
❑ 40 Orel Hershiser	.20	.06
❑ 41 Tripp Cromer	.20	.06
❑ 42 Sean Bergman	.20	.06
❑ 43 Troy Percival	.20	.06
❑ 44 Kevin Stocker	.20	.06
❑ 45 Albert Belle	.20	.06
❑ 46 Tony Eusebio	.20	.06
❑ 47 Sid Roberson	.20	.06
❑ 48 Todd Hollandsworth	.20	.06
❑ 49 Mark Wohlers	.20	.06
❑ 50 Kirby Puckett	.50	.15
❑ 51 Darren Holmes	.20	.06
❑ 52 Ron Karkovice	.20	.06
❑ 53 Al Martin	.20	.06
❑ 54 Pat Rapp	.20	.06
❑ 55 Mark Grace	.30	.09
❑ 56 Greg Gagne	.20	.06
❑ 57 Stan Javier	.20	.06
❑ 58 Scott Sanders	.20	.06
❑ 59 J.T. Snow	.20	.06
❑ 60 David Justice	.20	.06
❑ 61 Royce Clayton	.20	.06
❑ 62 Kevin Foster	.20	.06
❑ 63 Tim Naehring	.20	.06
❑ 64 Orlando Miller	.20	.06
❑ 65 Mike Mussina	.30	.09
❑ 66 Jim Eisenreich	.20	.06
❑ 67 Felix Fermin	.20	.06
❑ 68 Bernie Williams	.30	.09
❑ 69 Robb Nen	.20	.06
❑ 70 Ron Gant	.20	.06
❑ 71 Felipe Lira	.20	.06
❑ 72 Jacob Brumfield	.20	.06
❑ 73 John Mabry	.20	.06
❑ 74 Mark Carreon	.20	.06
❑ 75 Carlos Baerga	.20	.06
❑ 76 Jim Dougherty	.20	.06
❑ 77 Ryan Thompson	.20	.06
❑ 78 Scott Leius	.20	.06
❑ 79 Roger Pavlik	.20	.06
❑ 80 Gary Sheffield	.20	.06
❑ 81 Julian Tavarez	.20	.06
❑ 82 Andy Ashby	.20	.06
❑ 83 Mark Lemke	.20	.06
❑ 84 Omar Vizquel	.30	.09
❑ 85 Darren Daulton	.20	.06
❑ 86 Mike Lansing	.20	.06
❑ 87 Rusty Greer	.20	.06
❑ 88 Dave Stevens	.20	.06
❑ 89 Jose Offerman	.20	.06
❑ 90 Tom Henke	.20	.06
❑ 91 Troy O'Leary	.20	.06
❑ 92 Michael Tucker	.20	.06
❑ 93 Marvin Freeman	.20	.06
❑ 94 Alex Diaz	.20	.06
❑ 95 John Wetteland	.20	.06
❑ 96 Cal Ripken 2131	2.00	.60
❑ 97 Mike Mimbs	.20	.06
❑ 98 Bobby Higginson	.20	.06
❑ 99 Edgardo Alfonzo	.20	.06
❑ 100 Frank Thomas	.50	.15
❑ 101 Steve Gibralter	.50	.15
Bob Abreu		
❑ 102 Brian Givens	.25	.07
T.J. Mathews		
❑ 103 Chris Pritchett	.25	.07
Trenidad Hubbard		
❑ 104 Eric Owens	.25	.07
Butch Huskey		
❑ 105 Doug Drabek	.20	.06
❑ 106 Tomas Perez	.20	.06
❑ 107 Mark Leiter	.20	.06
❑ 108 Joe Oliver	.20	.06
❑ 109 Tony Castillo	.20	.06
❑ 110 Checklist (1-110)	.20	.06
❑ 111 Kevin Seitzer	.20	.06
❑ 112 Pete Schourek	.20	.06
❑ 113 Sean Berry	.20	.06
❑ 114 Todd Stottlemyre	.20	.06
❑ 115 Joe Carter	.20	.06
❑ 116 Jeff King	.20	.06
❑ 117 Dan Wilson	.20	.06
❑ 118 Kurt Abbott	.20	.06
❑ 119 Lyle Mouton	.20	.06
❑ 120 Jose Rijo	.20	.06
❑ 121 Curtis Goodwin	.20	.06
❑ 122 Jose Valentin	.20	.06
❑ 123 Ellis Burks	.20	.06
❑ 124 David Cone	.20	.06
❑ 125 Eddie Murray	.50	.15
❑ 126 Brian Jordan	.20	.06
❑ 127 Darrin Fletcher	.20	.06
❑ 128 Curt Schilling	.20	.06
❑ 129 Ozzie Guillen	.20	.06
❑ 130 Kenny Rogers	.20	.06
❑ 131 Tom Pagnozzi	.20	.06
❑ 132 Garret Anderson	.20	.06
❑ 133 Bobby Jones	.20	.06
❑ 134 Chris Gomez	.20	.06
❑ 135 Mike Stanley	.20	.06
❑ 136 Hideo Nomo	.50	.15
❑ 137 Jon Nunnally	.20	.06
❑ 138 Tim Wakefield	.20	.06
❑ 139 Steve Finley	.20	.06
❑ 140 Ivan Rodriguez	.30	.09
❑ 141 Quilvio Veras	.20	.06
❑ 142 Mike Fetters	.20	.06
❑ 143 Mike Greenwell	.20	.06
❑ 144 Bill Pulsipher	.20	.06
❑ 145 Mark McGwire	1.25	.35
❑ 146 Frank Castillo	.20	.06
❑ 147 Greg Vaughn	.20	.06
❑ 148 Pat Hentgen	.20	.06
❑ 149 Walt Weiss	.20	.06
❑ 150 Randy Johnson	.50	.15
❑ 151 David Segui	.20	.06
❑ 152 Benji Gil	.20	.06
❑ 153 Tom Candiotti	.20	.06
❑ 154 Geronimo Berroa	.20	.06
❑ 155 John Franco	.20	.06
❑ 156 Jay Bell	.20	.06
❑ 157 Mark Gubicza	.20	.06
❑ 158 Hal Morris	.20	.06
❑ 159 Wilson Alvarez	.20	.06
❑ 160 Derek Bell	.20	.06
❑ 161 Ricky Bottalico	.20	.06
❑ 162 Bret Boone	.20	.06
❑ 163 Brad Radke	.20	.06
❑ 164 John Valentin	.20	.06
❑ 165 Steve Avery	.20	.06
❑ 166 Mark McLemore	.20	.06
❑ 167 Danny Jackson	.20	.06
❑ 168 Tino Martinez	.30	.09
❑ 169 Shane Reynolds	.20	.06
❑ 170 Terry Pendleton	.20	.06
❑ 171 Jim Edmonds	.20	.06
❑ 172 Esteban Loaiza	.20	.06
❑ 173 Ray Durham	.20	.06
❑ 174 Carlos Perez	.20	.06
❑ 175 Raul Mondesi	.20	.06
❑ 176 Steve Ontiveros	.20	.06
❑ 177 Chipper Jones	.50	.15
❑ 178 Otis Nixon	.20	.06
❑ 179 John Burkett	.20	.06
❑ 180 Gregg Jefferies	.20	.06
❑ 181 Denny Martinez	.20	.06
❑ 182 Ken Caminiti	.20	.06
❑ 183 Doug Jones	.20	.06
❑ 184 Brian McRae	.20	.06
❑ 185 Don Mattingly	1.25	.35
❑ 186 Mel Rojas	.20	.06
❑ 187 Marty Cordova	.20	.06
❑ 188 Vinny Castilla	.20	.06
❑ 189 John Smoltz	.30	.09
❑ 190 Travis Fryman	.20	.06
❑ 191 Chris Hoiles	.20	.06
❑ 192 Chuck Finley	.20	.06
❑ 193 Ryan Klesko	.20	.06
❑ 194 Alex Fernandez	.20	.06
❑ 195 Dante Bichette	.20	.06
❑ 196 Eric Karros	.20	.06
❑ 197 Roger Clemens	1.00	.30
❑ 198 Randy Myers	.20	.06
❑ 199 Tony Phillips	.20	.06
❑ 200 Cal Ripken	1.50	.45
❑ 201 Rod Beck	.20	.06
❑ 202 Chad Curtis	.20	.06
❑ 203 Jack McDowell	.20	.06
❑ 204 Gary Gaetti	.20	.06
❑ 205 Ken Griffey Jr.	.75	.23
❑ 206 Ramon Martinez	.20	.06
❑ 207 Jeff Kent	.20	.06
❑ 208 Brad Ausmus	.20	.06
❑ 209 Devon White	.20	.06
❑ 210 Jason Giambi	.20	.06
❑ 211 Nomar Garciaparra	.75	.23
❑ 212 Billy Wagner	.20	.06
❑ 213 Todd Greene	.20	.06
❑ 214 Paul Wilson	.20	.06
❑ 215 Johnny Damon	.30	.09
❑ 216 Alan Benes	.20	.06
❑ 217 Karim Garcia	.20	.06
❑ 218 Dustin Hermanson	.20	.06
❑ 219 Derek Jeter	1.25	.35
❑ 220 Checklist (111-220)	.20	.06
❑ 221 Kirby Puckett STP	.30	.09
❑ 222 Cal Ripken STP	.75	.23
❑ 223 Albert Belle STP	.20	.06
❑ 224 Randy Johnson STP	.30	.09
❑ 225 Wade Boggs STP	.20	.06
❑ 226 Carlos Baerga STP	.20	.06
❑ 227 Ivan Rodriguez STP	.20	.06
❑ 228 Mike Mussina STP	.20	.06
❑ 229 Frank Thomas STP	.30	.09
❑ 230 Ken Griffey Jr. STP	.50	.15
❑ 231 Jose Mesa STP	.20	.06
❑ 232 Matt Morris RC	1.50	.45
❑ 233 Craig Wilson RC	1.00	.30
❑ 234 Alvie Shepherd	.25	.07
❑ 235 Randy Winn RC	.60	.18
❑ 236 David Yocum RC	.25	.07
❑ 237 Jason Brester RC	.25	.07
❑ 238 Shane Monahan RC	.25	.07
❑ 239 Brian McNichol RC	.25	.07
❑ 240 Reggie Taylor	.25	.07
❑ 241 Garrett Long	.25	.07
❑ 242 Jonathan Johnson	.25	.07
❑ 243 Jeff Liefer RC	.25	.07
❑ 244 Brian Powell	.25	.07
❑ 245 Brian Buchanan RC	.25	.07
❑ 246 Mike Piazza	.75	.23
❑ 247 Edgar Martinez	.30	.09
❑ 248 Chuck Knoblauch	.20	.06
❑ 249 Andres Galarraga	.20	.06
❑ 250 Tony Gwynn	.60	.18

❑ 251 Lee Smith .20 .06
❑ 252 Sammy Sosa .50 .15
❑ 253 Jim Thome .30 .09
❑ 254 Frank Rodriguez .20 .06
❑ 255 Charlie Hayes .20 .06
❑ 256 Bernard Gilkey .20 .06
❑ 257 John Smiley .20 .06
❑ 258 Brady Anderson .20 .06
❑ 259 Rico Brogna .20 .06
❑ 260 Kirt Manwaring .20 .06
❑ 261 Len Dykstra .20 .06
❑ 262 Tom Glavine .30 .09
❑ 263 Vince Coleman .20 .06
❑ 264 John Olerud .20 .06
❑ 265 Orlando Merced .20 .06
❑ 266 Kent Mercker .20 .06
❑ 267 Terry Steinbach .20 .06
❑ 268 Brian L. Hunter .20 .06
❑ 269 Jeff Fassero .20 .06
❑ 270 Jay Buhner .20 .06
❑ 271 Jeff Brantley .20 .06
❑ 272 Tim Raines .20 .06
❑ 273 Jimmy Key .20 .06
❑ 274 Mo Vaughn .20 .06
❑ 275 Andre Dawson .20 .06
❑ 276 Jose Mesa .20 .06
❑ 277 Brett Butler .20 .06
❑ 278 Luis Gonzalez .20 .06
❑ 279 Steve Sparks .20 .06
❑ 280 Chili Davis .20 .06
❑ 281 Carl Everett .20 .06
❑ 282 Jeff Cirillo .20 .06
❑ 283 Thomas Howard .20 .06
❑ 284 Paul O'Neill .30 .09
❑ 285 Pat Meares .20 .06
❑ 286 Mickey Tettleton .20 .06
❑ 287 Rey Sanchez .20 .06
❑ 288 Bip Roberts .20 .06
❑ 289 Roberto Alomar .30 .09
❑ 290 Ruben Sierra .20 .06
❑ 291 John Flaherty .20 .06
❑ 292 Bret Saberhagen .20 .06
❑ 293 Barry Larkin .30 .09
❑ 294 Sandy Alomar Jr. .20 .06
❑ 295 Ed Sprague .20 .06
❑ 296 Gary DiSarcina .20 .06
❑ 297 Marquis Grissom .20 .06
❑ 298 John Frascatore .20 .06
❑ 299 Will Clark .30 .09
❑ 300 Barry Bonds 1.50 .45
❑ 301 Ozzie Smith UER .75 .23
Padres is listed as Padre
❑ 302 Dave Nilsson .20 .06
❑ 303 Pedro Martinez .30 .09
❑ 304 Joey Cora .20 .06
❑ 305 Rick Aguilera .20 .06
❑ 306 Craig Biggio .30 .09
❑ 307 Jose Vizcaino .20 .06
❑ 308 Jeff Montgomery .20 .06
❑ 309 Moises Alou .20 .06
❑ 310 Robin Ventura .20 .06
❑ 311 David Wells .20 .06
❑ 312 Delino DeShields .20 .06
❑ 313 Trevor Hoffman .20 .06
❑ 314 Andy Benes .20 .06
❑ 315 Deion Sanders .30 .09
❑ 316 Jim Bullinger .20 .06
❑ 317 John Jaha .20 .06
❑ 318 Greg Maddux .75 .23
❑ 319 Tim Salmon .30 .09
❑ 320 Ben McDonald .20 .06
❑ 321 Sandy Martinez .20 .06
❑ 322 Dan Miceli .20 .06
❑ 323 Wade Boggs .30 .09
❑ 324 Ismael Valdes .20 .06
❑ 325 Juan Gonzalez .20 .06
❑ 326 Charles Nagy .20 .06
❑ 327 Ray Lankford .20 .06
❑ 328 Mark Portugal .20 .06
❑ 329 Bobby Bonilla .20 .06
❑ 330 Reggie Sanders .20 .06
❑ 331 Jamie Brewington RC .25 .07
❑ 332 Aaron Sele .20 .06
❑ 333 Pete Harnisch .20 .06
❑ 334 Cliff Floyd .20 .06
❑ 335 Cal Eldred .20 .06
❑ 336 Jason Bates .20 .06
❑ 337 Tony Clark .20 .06
❑ 338 Jose Herrera .20 .06
❑ 339 Alex Ochoa .20 .06
❑ 340 Mark Loretta .20 .06
❑ 341 Donne Wall .20 .06
❑ 342 Jason Kendall .20 .06
❑ 343 Shannon Stewart .20 .06
❑ 344 Brooks Kieschnick .20 .06
❑ 345 Chris Snopek .20 .06
❑ 346 Ruben Rivera .20 .06
❑ 347 Jeff Suppan .20 .06
❑ 348 Phil Nevin .20 .06
❑ 349 John Wasdin .20 .06
❑ 350 Jay Payton .20 .06
❑ 351 Tim Crabtree .20 .06
❑ 352 Rick Krivda .20 .06
❑ 353 Bob Wolcott .20 .06
❑ 354 Jimmy Haynes .20 .06
❑ 355 Herb Perry .20 .06
❑ 356 Ryne Sandberg .75 .23
❑ 357 Harold Baines .20 .06
❑ 358 Chad Ogea .20 .06
❑ 359 Lee Tinsley .20 .06
❑ 360 Matt Williams .20 .06
❑ 361 Randy Velarde .20 .06
❑ 362 Jose Canseco .30 .09
❑ 363 Larry Walker .20 .06
❑ 364 Kevin Appier .20 .06
❑ 365 Darryl Hamilton .20 .06
❑ 366 Jose Lima .20 .06
❑ 367 Javy Lopez .20 .06
❑ 368 Dennis Eckersley .20 .06
❑ 369 Jason Isringhausen .20 .06
❑ 370 Mickey Morandini .20 .06
❑ 371 Scott Cooper .20 .06
❑ 372 Jim Abbott .30 .09
❑ 373 Paul Sorrento .20 .06
❑ 374 Chris Hammond .20 .06
❑ 375 Lance Johnson .20 .06
❑ 376 Kevin Brown .20 .06
❑ 377 Luis Alicea .20 .06
❑ 378 Andy Pettitte .30 .09
❑ 379 Dean Palmer .20 .06
❑ 380 Jeff Bagwell .30 .09
❑ 381 Jaime Navarro .20 .06
❑ 382 Rondell White .20 .06
❑ 383 Erik Hanson .20 .06
❑ 384 Pedro Munoz .20 .06
❑ 385 Heathcliff Slocumb .20 .06
❑ 386 Wally Joyner .20 .06
❑ 387 Bob Tewksbury .20 .06
❑ 388 David Bell .20 .06
❑ 389 Fred McGriff .30 .09
❑ 390 Mike Henneman .20 .06
❑ 391 Robby Thompson .20 .06
❑ 392 Norm Charlton .20 .06
❑ 393 Cecil Fielder .20 .06
❑ 394 Benito Santiago .20 .06
❑ 395 Rafael Palmeiro .30 .09
❑ 396 Ricky Bones .20 .06
❑ 397 Rickey Henderson .50 .15
❑ 398 C.J. Nitkowski .20 .06
❑ 399 Shawon Dunston .20 .06
❑ 400 Manny Ramirez .30 .09
❑ 401 Bill Swift .20 .06
❑ 402 Chad Fonville .20 .06
❑ 403 Joey Hamilton .20 .06
❑ 404 Alex Gonzalez .20 .06
❑ 405 Roberto Hernandez .20 .06
❑ 406 Jeff Blauser .20 .06
❑ 407 LaTroy Hawkins .20 .06
❑ 408 Greg Colbrunn .20 .06
❑ 409 Todd Hundley .20 .06
❑ 410 Glenn Dishman .20 .06
❑ 411 Joe Vitiello .20 .06
❑ 412 Todd Worrell .20 .06
❑ 413 Wil Cordero .20 .06
❑ 414 Ken Hill .20 .06
❑ 415 Carlos Garcia .20 .06
❑ 416 Bryan Rekar .20 .06
❑ 417 Shawn Green .20 .06
❑ 418 Tyler Green .20 .06
❑ 419 Mike Blowers .20 .06
❑ 420 Kenny Lofton .20 .06
❑ 421 Denny Neagle .20 .06
❑ 422 Jeff Conine .20 .06
❑ 423 Mark Langston .20 .06
❑ 424 Steve Cox .60 .18
Jesse Ibarra
Derrek Lee
Ron Wright RC
❑ 425 Jim Bonnici 1.00 .30
Billy Owens
Richie Sexson
Daryle Ward RC
❑ 426 Kevin Jordan .25 .07
Bobby Morris
Desi Relaford
Adam Riggs RC
❑ 427 Tim Harkrider .25 .07
Rey Ordonez
Neifi Perez
Enrique Wilson
❑ 428 Bartolo Colon .50 .15
Doug Million
Rafael Orellano
Ray Ricken
❑ 429 Jeff D'Amico .25 .07
Marty Janzen RC
Gary Rath
Clint Sodowsky
❑ 430 Matt Drews .25 .07
Rich Hunter RC
Matt Ruebel
Bret Wagner
❑ 431 Jaime Bluma .25 .07
David Coggin
Steve Montgomery
Brandon Reed RC
❑ 432 Mike Figga 1.00 .30
Raul Ibanez
Paul Konerko
Julio Mosquera
❑ 433 Brian Barber .20 .06
Marc Kroon
Marc Valdes
Don Wengert
❑ 434 George Arias .50 .15
Chris Haas RC
Scott Rolen
Scott Spiezio
❑ 435 Brian Banks 2.50 .75
Vladimir Guerrero
Andruw Jones
Billy McMillon
❑ 436 Roger Cedeno .60 .18
Derrick Gibson
Ben Grieve
Shane Spencer RC
❑ 437 Anton French .25 .07
Demond Smith
DaRond Stovall RC
Keith Williams
❑ 438 Michael Coleman RC .25 .07
Jacob Cruz
Richard Hidalgo
Charles Peterson
❑ 439 Trey Beamon .20 .06
Yamil Benitez
Jermaine Dye
Angel Echevarria
❑ 440 Checklist .20 .06
❑ F7 M.Mantle Last Day 5.00 1.50
❑ NNO Mickey Mantle TRIB. 3.00 .90
Promotes the Mantle Foundation
Black and White Photo

1997 Topps

	Nm-Mt	Ex-Mt
COMPLETE SET (495)	80.00	24.00
COMP.SERIES 1 (275)	40.00	12.00
COMP.SERIES 2 (220)	40.00	12.00

❑ 1 Barry Bonds 1.50 .45
❑ 2 Tom Pagnozzi .20 .06
❑ 3 Terrell Wade .20 .06
❑ 4 Jose Valentin .20 .06
❑ 5 Mark Clark .20 .06
❑ 6 Brady Anderson .20 .06
❑ 8 Wade Boggs .30 .09

❑ 9 Scott Stahoviak .20 .06
❑ 10 Andres Galarraga .20 .06
❑ 11 Steve Avery .20 .06
❑ 12 Rusty Greer .20 .06
❑ 13 Derek Jeter 1.25 .35
❑ 14 Ricky Bottalico .20 .06
❑ 15 Andy Ashby .20 .06
❑ 16 Paul Shuey .20 .06
❑ 17 F.P. Santangelo .20 .06
❑ 18 Royce Clayton .20 .06
❑ 19 Mike Mohler .20 .06
❑ 20 Mike Piazza .75 .23
❑ 21 Jaime Navarro .20 .06
❑ 22 Billy Wagner .20 .06
❑ 23 Mike Timlin .20 .06
❑ 24 Garret Anderson .20 .06
❑ 25 Ben McDonald .20 .06
❑ 26 Mel Rojas .20 .06
❑ 27 John Burkett .20 .06
❑ 28 Jeff King .20 .06
❑ 29 Reggie Jefferson .20 .06
❑ 30 Kevin Appier .20 .06
❑ 31 Felipe Lira .20 .06
❑ 32 Kevin Tapani .20 .06
❑ 33 Mark Portugal .20 .06
❑ 34 Carlos Garcia .20 .06
❑ 35 Joey Cora .20 .06
❑ 36 David Segui .20 .06
❑ 37 Mark Grace .30 .09
❑ 38 Erik Hanson .20 .06
❑ 39 Jeff D'Amico .20 .06
❑ 40 Jay Buhner .20 .06
❑ 41 B.J. Surhoff .20 .06
❑ 42 Jackie Robinson TRIB .50 .15
❑ 43 Roger Pavlik .20 .06
❑ 44 Hal Morris .20 .06
❑ 45 Mariano Duncan .20 .06
❑ 46 Harold Baines .20 .06
❑ 47 Jorge Fabregas .20 .06
❑ 48 Jose Herrera .20 .06
❑ 49 Jeff Cirillo .20 .06
❑ 50 Tom Glavine .30 .09
❑ 51 Pedro Astacio .20 .06
❑ 52 Mark Gardner .20 .06
❑ 53 Arthur Rhodes .20 .06
❑ 54 Troy O'Leary .20 .06
❑ 55 Bip Roberts .20 .06
❑ 56 Mike Lieberthal .20 .06
❑ 57 Shane Andrews .20 .06
❑ 58 Scott Karl .20 .06
❑ 59 Gary DiSarcina .20 .06
❑ 60 Andy Pettitte .30 .09
❑ 61 Kevin Elster .20 .06
❑ 61B Mike Fetters UER .20 .06
Card was intended as number 84
❑ 62 Mark McGwire 1.25 .35
❑ 63 Dan Wilson .20 .06
❑ 64 Mickey Morandini .20 .06
❑ 65 Chuck Knoblauch .20 .06
❑ 66 Tim Wakefield .20 .06
❑ 67 Raul Mondesi .20 .06
❑ 68 Todd Jones .20 .06
❑ 69 Albert Belle .20 .06
❑ 70 Trevor Hoffman .20 .06
❑ 71 Eric Young .20 .06
❑ 72 Robert Perez .20 .06
❑ 73 Butch Huskey .20 .06
❑ 74 Brian McRae .20 .06
❑ 75 Jim Edmonds .20 .06
❑ 76 Mike Henneman .20 .06
❑ 77 Frank Rodriguez .20 .06
❑ 78 Danny Tartabull .20 .06
❑ 79 Robb Nen .20 .06
❑ 80 Reggie Sanders .20 .06
❑ 81 Ron Karkovice .20 .06
❑ 82 Benito Santiago .20 .06
❑ 83 Mike Lansing .20 .06
❑ 85 Craig Biggio .30 .09
❑ 86 Mike Bordick .20 .06
❑ 87 Ray Lankford .20 .06
❑ 88 Charles Nagy .20 .06
❑ 89 Paul Wilson .20 .06
❑ 90 John Wetteland .20 .06
❑ 91 Tom Candiotti .20 .06
❑ 92 Carlos Delgado .20 .06
❑ 93 Derek Bell .20 .06
❑ 94 Mark Lemke .20 .06
❑ 95 Edgar Martinez .30 .09
❑ 96 Rickey Henderson .50 .15
❑ 97 Greg Myers .20 .06
❑ 98 Jim Leyritz .20 .06
❑ 99 Mark Johnson .20 .06
❑ 100 Dwight Gooden HL .20 .06
❑ 101 Al Leiter HL .20 .06
❑ 102 John Mabry HL .20 .06
❑ 103 Alex Ochoa HL .20 .06
❑ 104 Mike Piazza HL .50 .15
❑ 105 Jim Thome .30 .09
❑ 106 Ricky Otero .20 .06
❑ 107 Jamey Wright .20 .06
❑ 108 Frank Thomas .50 .15
❑ 109 Jody Reed .20 .06
❑ 110 Orel Hershiser .20 .06
❑ 111 Terry Steinbach .20 .06
❑ 112 Mark Loretta .20 .06
❑ 113 Turk Wendell .20 .06
❑ 114 Marvin Benard .20 .06
❑ 115 Kevin Brown .20 .06
❑ 116 Robert Person .20 .06
❑ 117 Joey Hamilton .20 .06
❑ 118 Francisco Cordova .20 .06
❑ 119 John Smiley .20 .06
❑ 120 Travis Fryman .20 .06
❑ 121 Jimmy Key .20 .06
❑ 122 Tom Goodwin .20 .06
❑ 123 Mike Greenwell .20 .06
❑ 124 Juan Gonzalez .20 .06
❑ 125 Pete Harnisch .20 .06
❑ 126 Roger Cedeno .20 .06
❑ 127 Ron Gant .20 .06
❑ 128 Mark Langston .20 .06
❑ 129 Tim Crabtree .20 .06
❑ 130 Greg Maddux .75 .23
❑ 131 W.VanLandingham .20 .06
❑ 132 Wally Joyner .20 .06
❑ 133 Randy Myers .20 .06
❑ 134 John Valentin .20 .06
❑ 135 Bret Boone .20 .06
❑ 136 Bruce Ruffin .20 .06
❑ 137 Chris Snopek .20 .06
❑ 138 Paul Molitor .30 .09
❑ 139 Mark McLemore .20 .06
❑ 140 Rafael Palmeiro .30 .09
❑ 141 Herb Perry .20 .06
❑ 142 Luis Gonzalez .20 .06
❑ 143 Doug Drabek .20 .06
❑ 144 Ken Ryan .20 .06
❑ 145 Todd Hundley .20 .06
❑ 146 Ellis Burks .20 .06
❑ 147 Ozzie Guillen .20 .06
❑ 148 Rich Becker .20 .06
❑ 149 Sterling Hitchcock .20 .06
❑ 150 Bernie Williams .30 .09
❑ 151 Mike Stanley .20 .06
❑ 152 Roberto Alomar .30 .09
❑ 153 Jose Mesa .20 .06
❑ 154 Steve Trachsel .20 .06
❑ 155 Alex Gonzalez .20 .06
❑ 156 Troy Percival .20 .06
❑ 157 John Smoltz .30 .09
❑ 158 Pedro Martinez .30 .09
❑ 159 Jeff Conine .20 .06
❑ 160 Bernard Gilkey .20 .06
❑ 161 Jim Eisenreich .20 .06
❑ 162 Mickey Tettleton .20 .06
❑ 163 Justin Thompson .20 .06
❑ 164 Jose Offerman .20 .06
❑ 165 Tony Phillips .20 .06
❑ 166 Ismael Valdes .20 .06
❑ 167 Ryne Sandberg UER .75 .23
Card has him with 252 homers in 1996
❑ 168 Matt Mieske .20 .06
❑ 169 Geronimo Berroa .20 .06
❑ 170 Otis Nixon .20 .06
❑ 171 John Mabry .20 .06
❑ 172 Shawon Dunston .20 .06
❑ 173 Omar Vizquel .30 .09
❑ 174 Chris Hoiles .20 .06
❑ 175 Dwight Gooden .20 .06
❑ 176 Wilson Alvarez .20 .06
❑ 177 Todd Hollandsworth .20 .06
❑ 178 Roger Salkeld .20 .06
❑ 179 Rey Sanchez .20 .06
❑ 180 Rey Ordonez .20 .06
❑ 181 Denny Martinez .20 .06
❑ 182 Ramon Martinez .20 .06
❑ 183 Dave Nilsson .20 .06
❑ 184 Marquis Grissom .20 .06
❑ 185 Randy Velarde .20 .06
❑ 186 Ron Coomer .20 .06
❑ 187 Tino Martinez .30 .09
❑ 188 Jeff Brantley .20 .06
❑ 189 Steve Finley .20 .06
❑ 190 Andy Benes .20 .06
❑ 191 Terry Adams .20 .06
❑ 192 Mike Blowers .20 .06
❑ 193 Russ Davis .20 .06
❑ 194 Darryl Hamilton .20 .06
❑ 195 Jason Kendall .20 .06
❑ 196 Johnny Damon .30 .09
❑ 197 Dave Martinez .20 .06
❑ 198 Mike Macfarlane .20 .06
❑ 199 Norm Charlton .20 .06
❑ 200 Doug Million RC .25 .07
Damian Moss
Bobby Rodgers
❑ 201 Geoff Jenkins .20 .06
Raul Ibanez
Mike Cameron
❑ 202 Sean Casey .30 .09
Jim Bonnici
Dmitri Young
❑ 203 Jed Hansen .20 .06
Homer Bush
Felipe Crespo
❑ 204 Kevin Orie .20 .06
Gabe Alvarez
Aaron Boone
❑ 205 Ben Davis .20 .06
Kevin Brown
Bobby Estalella
❑ 206 Billy McMillon RC .40 .12
Bubba Trammell
Dante Powell
❑ 207 Jarrod Washburn .20 .06
Marc Wilkins RC
Glendon Rusch
❑ 208 Brian Hunter .20 .06
❑ 209 Jason Giambi .20 .06
❑ 210 Henry Rodriguez .20 .06
❑ 211 Edgar Renteria .20 .06
❑ 212 Edgardo Alfonzo .20 .06
❑ 213 Fernando Vina .20 .06
❑ 214 Shawn Green .20 .06
❑ 215 Ray Durham .20 .06
❑ 216 Joe Randa .20 .06
❑ 217 Armando Reynoso .20 .06
❑ 218 Eric Davis .20 .06
❑ 219 Bob Tewksbury .20 .06
❑ 220 Jacob Cruz .20 .06
❑ 221 Glenallen Hill .20 .06
❑ 222 Gary Gaetti .20 .06
❑ 223 Donne Wall .20 .06
❑ 224 Brad Clontz .20 .06
❑ 225 Marty Janzen .20 .06
❑ 226 Todd Worrell .20 .06
❑ 227 John Franco .20 .06
❑ 228 David Wells .20 .06
❑ 229 Gregg Jefferies .20 .06
❑ 230 Tim Naehring .20 .06

❑ 231 Thomas Howard .20 .06
❑ 232 Roberto Hernandez .20 .06
❑ 233 Kevin Ritz .20 .06
❑ 234 Julian Tavarez .20 .06
❑ 235 Ken Hill .20 .06
❑ 236 Greg Gagne .20 .06
❑ 237 Bobby Chouinard .20 .06
❑ 238 Joe Carter .20 .06
❑ 239 Jermaine Dye .20 .06
❑ 240 Antonio Osuna .20 .06
❑ 241 Julio Franco .20 .06
❑ 242 Mike Grace .20 .06
❑ 243 Aaron Sele .20 .06
❑ 244 David Justice .20 .06
❑ 245 Sandy Alomar Jr. .20 .06
❑ 246 Jose Canseco .30 .09
❑ 247 Paul O'Neill .30 .09
❑ 248 Sean Berry .20 .06
❑ 249 Nick Bierbrodt .25 .07
Kevin Sweeney RC
❑ 250 Larry Rodriguez RC .25 .07
Vladimir Nunez RC
❑ 251 Ron Hartman .25 .07
David Hayman RC
❑ 252 Alex Sanchez .40 .12
Matthew Quatraro RC
❑ 253 Ronni Seberino RC .25 .07
Pablo Ortego RC
❑ 254 Rex Hudler .20 .06
❑ 255 Orlando Miller .20 .06
❑ 256 Mariano Rivera .30 .09
❑ 257 Brad Radke .20 .06
❑ 258 Bobby Higginson .20 .06
❑ 259 Jay Bell .20 .06
❑ 260 Mark Grudzielanek .20 .06
❑ 261 Lance Johnson .20 .06
❑ 262 Ken Caminiti .20 .06
❑ 263 J.T. Snow .20 .06
❑ 264 Gary Sheffield .20 .06
❑ 265 Darrin Fletcher .20 .06
❑ 266 Eric Owens .20 .06
❑ 267 Luis Castillo .20 .06
❑ 268 Scott Rolen .30 .09
❑ 269 Todd Noel .25 .07
John Oliver RC
❑ 270 Robert Stratton RC .40 .12
Corey Lee RC
❑ 271 Gil Meche RC 1.00 .30
Matt Halloran RC
❑ 272 Eric Milton RC .50 .15
Dee Brown RC
❑ 273 Josh Garrett .40 .12
Chris Reitsma RC
❑ 274 A.J.Zapp RC .50 .15
Jason Marquis
❑ 275 Checklist .20 .06
❑ 276 Checklist .20 .06
❑ 277 Chipper Jones UER .50 .15
incorrectly numbered 276
❑ 278 Orlando Merced .20 .06
❑ 279 Ariel Prieto .20 .06
❑ 280 Al Leiter .20 .06
❑ 281 Pat Meares .20 .06
❑ 282 Darryl Strawberry .20 .06
❑ 283 Jamie Moyer .20 .06
❑ 284 Scott Servais .20 .06
❑ 285 Delino DeShields .20 .06
❑ 286 Danny Graves .20 .06
❑ 287 Gerald Williams .20 .06
❑ 288 Todd Greene .20 .06
❑ 289 Rico Brogna .20 .06
❑ 290 Derrick Gibson .20 .06
❑ 291 Joe Girardi .20 .06
❑ 292 Darren Lewis .20 .06
❑ 293 Nomar Garciaparra .75 .23
❑ 294 Greg Colbrunn .20 .06
❑ 295 Jeff Bagwell .30 .09
❑ 296 Brent Gates .20 .06
❑ 297 Jose Vizcaino .20 .06
❑ 298 Alex Ochoa .20 .06
❑ 299 Sid Fernandez .20 .06
❑ 300 Ken Griffey Jr. .75 .23
❑ 301 Chris Gomez .20 .06
❑ 302 Wendell Magee .20 .06
❑ 303 Darren Oliver .20 .06
❑ 304 Mel Nieves .20 .06
❑ 305 Sammy Sosa .50 .15
❑ 306 George Arias .20 .06
❑ 307 Jack McDowell .20 .06
❑ 308 Stan Javier .20 .06
❑ 309 Kimera Bartee .20 .06
❑ 310 James Baldwin .20 .06
❑ 311 Rocky Coppinger .20 .06
❑ 312 Keith Lockhart .20 .06
❑ 313 C.J. Nitkowski .20 .06
❑ 314 Allen Watson .20 .06
❑ 315 Darryl Kile .20 .06
❑ 316 Amaury Telemaco .20 .06
❑ 317 Jason Isringhausen .20 .06
❑ 318 Manny Ramirez .30 .09
❑ 319 Terry Pendleton .20 .06
❑ 320 Tim Salmon .30 .09
❑ 321 Eric Karros .20 .06
❑ 322 Mark Whiten .20 .06
❑ 323 Rick Krivda .20 .06
❑ 324 Brett Butler .20 .06
❑ 325 Randy Johnson .50 .15
❑ 326 Eddie Taubensee .20 .06
❑ 327 Mark Leiter .20 .06
❑ 328 Kevin Gross .20 .06
❑ 329 Ernie Young .20 .06
❑ 330 Pat Hentgen .20 .06
❑ 331 Rondell White .20 .06
❑ 332 Bobby Witt .20 .06
❑ 333 Eddie Murray .50 .15
❑ 334 Tim Raines .20 .06
❑ 335 Jeff Fassero .20 .06
❑ 336 Chuck Finley .20 .06
❑ 337 Willie Adams .20 .06
❑ 338 Chan Ho Park .20 .06
❑ 339 Jay Powell .20 .06
❑ 340 Ivan Rodriguez .30 .09
❑ 341 Jermaine Allensworth .20 .06
❑ 342 Jay Payton .20 .06
❑ 343 T.J. Mathews .20 .06
❑ 344 Tony Batista .20 .06
❑ 345 Ed Sprague .20 .06
❑ 346 Jeff Kent .20 .06
❑ 347 Scott Erickson .20 .06
❑ 348 Jeff Suppan .20 .06
❑ 349 Pete Schourek .20 .06
❑ 350 Kenny Lofton .20 .06
❑ 351 Alan Benes .20 .06
❑ 352 Fred McGriff .30 .09
❑ 353 Charlie O'Brien .20 .06
❑ 354 Darren Bragg .20 .06
❑ 355 Alex Fernandez .20 .06
❑ 356 Al Martin .20 .06
❑ 357 Bob Wells .20 .06
❑ 358 Chad Mottola .20 .06
❑ 359 Devon White .20 .06
❑ 360 David Cone .20 .06
❑ 361 Bobby Jones .20 .06
❑ 362 Scott Sanders .20 .06
❑ 363 Karim Garcia .20 .06
❑ 364 Kirt Manwaring .20 .06
❑ 365 Chili Davis .20 .06
❑ 366 Mike Hampton .20 .06
❑ 367 Chad Ogea .20 .06
❑ 368 Curt Schilling .20 .06
❑ 369 Phil Nevin .20 .06
❑ 370 Roger Clemens 1.00 .30
❑ 371 Willie Greene .20 .06
❑ 372 Kenny Rogers .20 .06
❑ 373 Jose Rijo .20 .06
❑ 374 Bobby Bonilla .20 .06
❑ 375 Mike Mussina .30 .09
❑ 376 Curtis Pride .20 .06
❑ 377 Todd Walker .20 .06
❑ 378 Jason Bere .20 .06
❑ 379 Heathcliff Slocumb .20 .06
❑ 380 Dante Bichette .20 .06
❑ 381 Carlos Baerga .20 .06
❑ 382 Livan Hernandez .20 .06
❑ 383 Jason Schmidt .20 .06
❑ 384 Kevin Stocker .20 .06
❑ 385 Matt Williams .20 .06
❑ 386 Bartolo Colon .20 .06
❑ 387 Will Clark .30 .09
❑ 388 Dennis Eckersley .20 .06
❑ 389 Brooks Kieschnick .20 .06
❑ 390 Ryan Klesko .20 .06
❑ 391 Mark Carreon .20 .06
❑ 392 Tim Worrell .20 .06
❑ 393 Dean Palmer .20 .06
❑ 394 Wil Cordero .20 .06
❑ 395 Javy Lopez .20 .06
❑ 396 Rich Aurilia .20 .06
❑ 397 Greg Vaughn .20 .06
❑ 398 Vinny Castilla .20 .06
❑ 399 Jeff Montgomery .20 .06
❑ 400 Cal Ripken 1.50 .45
❑ 401 Walt Weiss .20 .06
❑ 402 Brad Ausmus .20 .06
❑ 403 Ruben Rivera .20 .06
❑ 404 Mark Wohlers .20 .06
❑ 405 Rick Aguilera .20 .06
❑ 406 Tony Clark .20 .06
❑ 407 Lyle Mouton .20 .06
❑ 408 Bill Pulsipher .20 .06
❑ 409 Jose Rosado .20 .06
❑ 410 Tony Gwynn .60 .18
❑ 411 Cecil Fielder .20 .06
❑ 412 John Flaherty .20 .06
❑ 413 Lenny Dykstra .20 .06
❑ 414 Ugueth Urbina .20 .06
❑ 415 Brian Jordan .20 .06
❑ 416 Bob Abreu .30 .09
❑ 417 Craig Paquette .20 .06
❑ 418 Sandy Martinez .20 .06
❑ 419 Jeff Blauser .20 .06
❑ 420 Barry Larkin .30 .09
❑ 421 Kevin Seitzer .20 .06
❑ 422 Tim Belcher .20 .06
❑ 423 Paul Sorrento .20 .06
❑ 424 Cal Eldred .20 .06
❑ 425 Robin Ventura .20 .06
❑ 426 John Olerud .20 .06
❑ 427 Bob Wolcott .20 .06
❑ 428 Matt Lawton .20 .06
❑ 429 Rod Beck .20 .06
❑ 430 Shane Reynolds .20 .06
❑ 431 Mike James .20 .06
❑ 432 Steve Wojciechowski .20 .06
❑ 433 Vladimir Guerrero .50 .15
❑ 434 Dustin Hermanson .20 .06
❑ 435 Marty Cordova .20 .06
❑ 436 Marc Newfield .20 .06
❑ 437 Todd Stottlemyre .20 .06
❑ 438 Jeffrey Hammonds .20 .06
❑ 439 Dave Stevens .20 .06
❑ 440 Hideo Nomo .50 .15
❑ 441 Mark Thompson .20 .06
❑ 442 Mark Lewis .20 .06
❑ 443 Quinton McCracken .20 .06
❑ 444 Cliff Floyd .20 .06
❑ 445 Denny Neagle .20 .06
❑ 446 John Jaha .20 .06
❑ 447 Mike Sweeney .20 .06
❑ 448 John Wasdin .20 .06
❑ 449 Chad Curtis .20 .06
❑ 450 Mo Vaughn .20 .06
❑ 451 Donovan Osborne .20 .06
❑ 452 Ruben Sierra .20 .06
❑ 453 Michael Tucker .20 .06
❑ 454 Kurt Abbott .20 .06
❑ 455 Andruw Jones UER .30 .09
Birthdate is incorrectly listed
as 1-22-67, should be 1-22-77
❑ 456 Shannon Stewart .20 .06
❑ 457 Scott Brosius .20 .06
❑ 458 Juan Guzman .20 .06
❑ 459 Ron Villone .20 .06
❑ 460 Moises Alou .20 .06
❑ 461 Larry Walker .20 .06
❑ 462 Eddie Murray SH .30 .09
❑ 463 Paul Molitor SH .20 .06
❑ 464 Hideo Nomo SH .20 .06
❑ 465 Barry Bonds SH .75 .23
❑ 466 Todd Hundley SH .20 .06
❑ 467 Rheal Cormier .20 .06
❑ 468 Jason Conti RC .25 .07
Jhensy Sandoval
❑ 469 Rod Barajas 1.50 .45
Jackie Rexrode RC
❑ 470 Cedric Bowers RC .25 .07
Jared Sandberg RC
❑ 471 Chei Gunner RC .25 .07

Paul Wilder
❑ 472 Mike Decelle .25 .07
Marcus McCain RC
❑ 473 Todd Zeile .20 .06
❑ 474 Neifi Perez .20 .06
❑ 475 Jeromy Burnitz .20 .06
❑ 476 Trey Beamon .20 .06
❑ 477 Braden Looper RC 1.00 .30
John Patterson
❑ 478 Danny Peoples .50 .15
Jake Westbrook RC
❑ 479 Eric Chavez 2.00 .60
Adam Eaton RC
❑ 480 Joe Lawrence RC .25 .07
Pete Tucci
❑ 481 Kris Benson .50 .15
Billy Koch RC
❑ 482 John Nicholson .25 .07
Andy Prater RC
❑ 483 Mark Johnson RC .75 .23
Mark Kotsay
❑ 484 Armando Benitez .20 .06
❑ 485 Mike Matheny .20 .06
❑ 486 Jeff Reed .20 .06
❑ 487 Mark Bellhorn .20 .06
Russ Johnson
Enrique Wilson
❑ 488 Ben Grieve .20 .06
Richard Hidalgo
Scott Morgan RC
❑ 489 Paul Konerko .30 .09
Derrek Lee UER
spelled Derek on back
Ron Wright
❑ 490 Wes Helms RC 1.50 .45
Bill Mueller
Brad Seitzer
❑ 491 Jeff Abbott .20 .06
Shane Monahan
Edgard Velazquez
❑ 492 Jimmy Anderson RC .25 .07
Ron Blazier
Gerald Witasick
❑ 493 Darin Blood .20 .06
Heath Murray
Carl Pavano
❑ 494 Nelson Figueroa RC .25 .07
Mark Redman
Mike Villano
❑ 495 Checklist .20 .06
❑ 496 Checklist .20 .06
❑ NNO Derek Jeter AU 150.00 45.00

1998 Topps

	Nm-Mt	Ex-Mt
COMPLETE SET (503)	80.00	24.00
COMP.HOBBY SET (511)	120.00	36.00
COMP.RETAIL SET (511)	120.00	36.00
COMP.SERIES 1 (282)	40.00	12.00
COMP.SERIES 2 (221)	40.00	12.00

❑ 1 Tony Gwynn .60 .18
❑ 2 Larry Walker .20 .06
❑ 3 Billy Wagner .20 .06
❑ 4 Denny Neagle .20 .06
❑ 5 Vladimir Guerrero .50 .15
❑ 6 Kevin Brown .30 .09
❑ 8 Mariano Rivera .30 .09
❑ 9 Tony Clark .20 .06
❑ 10 Deion Sanders .30 .09
❑ 11 Francisco Cordova .20 .06
❑ 12 Matt Williams .20 .06
❑ 13 Carlos Baerga .20 .06
❑ 14 Mo Vaughn .20 .06
❑ 15 Bobby Witt .20 .06
❑ 16 Matt Stairs .20 .06
❑ 17 Chan Ho Park .20 .06
❑ 18 Mike Bordick .20 .06
❑ 19 Michael Tucker .20 .06
❑ 20 Frank Thomas .50 .15
❑ 21 Roberto Clemente 1.00 .30
❑ 22 Dmitri Young .20 .06
❑ 23 Steve Trachsel .20 .06
❑ 24 Jeff Kent .20 .06
❑ 25 Scott Rolen .30 .09
❑ 26 John Thomson .20 .06
❑ 27 Joe Vitiello .20 .06
❑ 28 Eddie Guardado .20 .06
❑ 29 Charlie Hayes .20 .06
❑ 30 Juan Gonzalez .20 .06
❑ 31 Garret Anderson .20 .06
❑ 32 John Jaha .20 .06
❑ 33 Omar Vizquel .30 .09
❑ 34 Brian Hunter .20 .06
❑ 35 Jeff Bagwell .30 .09
❑ 36 Mark Lemke .20 .06
❑ 37 Doug Glanville .20 .06
❑ 38 Dan Wilson .20 .06
❑ 39 Steve Cooke .20 .06
❑ 40 Chili Davis .20 .06
❑ 41 Mike Cameron .20 .06
❑ 42 F.P. Santangelo .20 .06
❑ 43 Brad Ausmus .20 .06
❑ 44 Gary DiSarcina .20 .06
❑ 45 Pat Hentgen .20 .06
❑ 46 Wilton Guerrero .20 .06
❑ 47 Devon White .20 .06
❑ 48 Danny Patterson .20 .06
❑ 49 Pat Meares .20 .06
❑ 50 Rafael Palmeiro .30 .09
❑ 51 Mark Gardner .20 .06
❑ 52 Jeff Blauser .20 .06
❑ 53 Dave Hollins .20 .06
❑ 54 Carlos Garcia .20 .06
❑ 55 Ben McDonald .20 .06
❑ 56 John Mabry .20 .06
❑ 57 Trevor Hoffman .20 .06
❑ 58 Tony Fernandez .20 .06
❑ 59 Rich Loiselle .20 .06
❑ 60 Mark Leiter .20 .06
❑ 61 Pat Kelly .20 .06
❑ 62 John Flaherty .20 .06
❑ 63 Roger Bailey .20 .06
❑ 64 Tom Gordon .20 .06
❑ 65 Ryan Klesko .20 .06
❑ 66 Darryl Hamilton .20 .06
❑ 67 Jim Eisenreich .20 .06
❑ 68 Butch Huskey .20 .06
❑ 69 Mark Grudzielanek .20 .06
❑ 70 Marquis Grissom .20 .06
❑ 71 Mark McLemore .20 .06
❑ 72 Gary Gaetti .20 .06
❑ 73 Greg Gagne .20 .06
❑ 74 Lyle Mouton .20 .06
❑ 75 Jim Edmonds .20 .06
❑ 76 Shawn Green .20 .06
❑ 77 Greg Vaughn .20 .06
❑ 78 Terry Adams .20 .06
❑ 79 Kevin Polcovich .20 .06
❑ 80 Troy O'Leary .20 .06
❑ 81 Jeff Shaw .20 .06
❑ 82 Rich Becker .20 .06
❑ 83 David Wells .20 .06
❑ 84 Steve Karsay .20 .06
❑ 85 Charles Nagy .20 .06
❑ 86 B.J. Surhoff .20 .06
❑ 87 Jamey Wright .20 .06
❑ 88 James Baldwin .20 .06
❑ 89 Edgardo Alfonzo .20 .06
❑ 90 Jay Buhner .20 .06
❑ 91 Brady Anderson .20 .06
❑ 92 Scott Servais .20 .06
❑ 93 Edgar Renteria .20 .06
❑ 94 Mike Lieberthal .20 .06
❑ 95 Rick Aguilera .20 .06
❑ 96 Walt Weiss .20 .06
❑ 97 Deivi Cruz .20 .06
❑ 98 Kurt Abbott .20 .06
❑ 99 Henry Rodriguez .20 .06
❑ 100 Mike Piazza .75 .23
❑ 101 Bill Taylor .20 .06
❑ 102 Todd Zeile .20 .06
❑ 103 Rey Ordonez .20 .06
❑ 104 Willie Greene .20 .06
❑ 105 Tony Womack .20 .06
❑ 106 Mike Sweeney .20 .06
❑ 107 Jeffrey Hammonds .20 .06
❑ 108 Kevin Orie .20 .06
❑ 109 Alex Gonzalez .20 .06
❑ 110 Jose Canseco .30 .09
❑ 111 Paul Sorrento .20 .06
❑ 112 Joey Hamilton .20 .06
❑ 113 Brad Radke .20 .06
❑ 114 Steve Avery .20 .06
❑ 115 Esteban Loaiza .20 .06
❑ 116 Stan Javier .20 .06
❑ 117 Chris Gomez .20 .06
❑ 118 Royce Clayton .20 .06
❑ 119 Orlando Merced .20 .06
❑ 120 Kevin Appier .20 .06
❑ 121 Mel Nieves .20 .06
❑ 122 Joe Girardi .20 .06
❑ 123 Rico Brogna .20 .06
❑ 124 Kent Mercker .20 .06
❑ 125 Manny Ramirez .30 .09
❑ 126 Jeromy Burnitz .20 .06
❑ 127 Kevin Foster .20 .06
❑ 128 Matt Morris .20 .06
❑ 129 Jason Dickson .20 .06
❑ 130 Tom Glavine .30 .09
❑ 131 Wally Joyner .20 .06
❑ 132 Rick Reed .20 .06
❑ 133 Todd Jones .20 .06
❑ 134 Dave Martinez .20 .06
❑ 135 Sandy Alomar Jr. .20 .06
❑ 136 Mike Lansing .20 .06
❑ 137 Sean Berry .20 .06
❑ 138 Doug Jones .20 .06
❑ 139 Todd Stottlemyre .20 .06
❑ 140 Jay Bell .20 .06
❑ 141 Jaime Navarro .20 .06
❑ 142 Chris Hoiles .20 .06
❑ 143 Joey Cora .20 .06
❑ 144 Scott Spiezio .20 .06
❑ 145 Joe Carter .20 .06
❑ 146 Jose Guillen .20 .06
❑ 147 Damion Easley .20 .06
❑ 148 Lee Stevens .20 .06
❑ 149 Alex Fernandez .20 .06
❑ 150 Randy Johnson .50 .15
❑ 151 J.T. Snow .20 .06
❑ 152 Chuck Finley .20 .06
❑ 153 Bernard Gilkey .20 .06
❑ 154 David Segui .20 .06
❑ 155 Dante Bichette .20 .06
❑ 156 Kevin Stocker .20 .06
❑ 157 Carl Everett .20 .06
❑ 158 Jose Valentin .20 .06
❑ 159 Pokey Reese .20 .06
❑ 160 Derek Jeter 1.25 .35
❑ 161 Roger Pavlik .20 .06
❑ 162 Mark Wohlers .20 .06
❑ 163 Ricky Bottalico .20 .06
❑ 164 Ozzie Guillen .20 .06
❑ 165 Mike Mussina .30 .09
❑ 166 Gary Sheffield .20 .06
❑ 167 Hideo Nomo .50 .15
❑ 168 Mark Grace .30 .09
❑ 169 Aaron Sele .20 .06
❑ 170 Darryl Kile .20 .06
❑ 171 Shawn Estes .20 .06
❑ 172 Vinny Castilla .20 .06
❑ 173 Ron Coomer .20 .06
❑ 174 Jose Rosado .20 .06
❑ 175 Kenny Lofton .20 .06
❑ 176 Jason Giambi .20 .06
❑ 177 Hal Morris .20 .06
❑ 178 Darren Bragg .20 .06
❑ 179 Orel Hershiser .20 .06
❑ 180 Ray Lankford .20 .06

❑ 181 Hideki Irabu .20 .06
❑ 182 Kevin Young .20 .06
❑ 183 Javy Lopez .20 .06
❑ 184 Jeff Montgomery .20 .06
❑ 185 Mike Holtz .20 .06
❑ 186 George Williams .20 .06
❑ 187 Cal Eldred .20 .06
❑ 188 Tom Candiotti .20 .06
❑ 189 Glenallen Hill .20 .06
❑ 190 Brian Giles .20 .06
❑ 191 Dave Mlicki .20 .06
❑ 192 Garrett Stephenson .20 .06
❑ 193 Jeff Frye .20 .06
❑ 194 Joe Oliver .20 .06
❑ 195 Bob Hamelin .20 .06
❑ 196 Luis Sojo .20 .06
❑ 197 LaTroy Hawkins .20 .06
❑ 198 Kevin Elster .20 .06
❑ 199 Jeff Reed .20 .06
❑ 200 Dennis Eckersley .20 .06
❑ 201 Bill Mueller .20 .06
❑ 202 Russ Davis .20 .06
❑ 203 Armando Benitez .20 .06
❑ 204 Quilvio Veras .20 .06
❑ 205 Tim Naehring .20 .06
❑ 206 Quinton McCracken .20 .06
❑ 207 Raul Casanova .20 .06
❑ 208 Matt Lawton .20 .06
❑ 209 Luis Alicea .20 .06
❑ 210 Luis Gonzalez .20 .06
❑ 211 Allen Watson .20 .06
❑ 212 Gerald Williams .20 .06
❑ 213 David Bell .20 .06
❑ 214 Todd Hollandsworth .20 .06
❑ 215 Wade Boggs .30 .09
❑ 216 Jose Mesa .20 .06
❑ 217 Jamie Moyer .20 .06
❑ 218 Darren Daulton .20 .06
❑ 219 Mickey Morandini .20 .06
❑ 220 Rusty Greer .20 .06
❑ 221 Jim Bullinger .20 .06
❑ 222 Jose Offerman .20 .06
❑ 223 Matt Karchner .20 .06
❑ 224 Woody Williams .20 .06
❑ 225 Mark Loretta .20 .06
❑ 226 Mike Hampton .20 .06
❑ 227 Willie Adams .20 .06
❑ 228 Scott Hatteberg .20 .06
❑ 229 Rich Amaral .20 .06
❑ 230 Terry Steinbach .20 .06
❑ 231 Glendon Rusch .20 .06
❑ 232 Bret Boone .20 .06
❑ 233 Robert Person .20 .06
❑ 234 Jose Hernandez .20 .06
❑ 235 Doug Drabek .20 .06
❑ 236 Jason McDonald .20 .06
❑ 237 Chris Widger .20 .06
❑ 238 Tom Martin .20 .06
❑ 239 Dave Burba .20 .06
❑ 240 Pete Rose Jr. .20 .06
❑ 241 Bobby Ayala .20 .06
❑ 242 Tim Wakefield .20 .06
❑ 243 Dennis Springer .20 .06
❑ 244 Tim Belcher .20 .06
❑ 245 Jon Garland .30 .09
Geoff Goetz
❑ 246 Glenn Davis .30 .09
Lance Berkman
❑ 247 Vernon Wells .30 .09
Aaron Akin
❑ 248 Adam Kennedy .20 .06
Jason Romano
❑ 249 Jason Dellaero .20 .06
Troy Cameron
❑ 250 Alex Sanchez .20 .06
Jared Sandberg
❑ 251 Pablo Ortega .20 .06
James Manias
❑ 252 Jason Conti RC .20 .06
Mike Stoner
❑ 253 John Patterson .20 .06
Larry Rodriguez
❑ 254 Adrian Beltre .30 .09
Ryan Minor RC
Aaron Boone
❑ 255 Ben Grieve .20 .06
Brian Buchanan
Dermal Brown
❑ 256 Kerry Wood .30 .09
Carl Pavano
Gil Meche
❑ 257 David Ortiz 2.00 .60
Daryle Ward
Richie Sexson
❑ 258 Randy Winn .20 .06
Juan Encarnacion
Andrew Vessel
❑ 259 Kris Benson .20 .06
Travis Smith
Courtney Duncan RC
❑ 260 Chad Hermansen .20 .06
Brent Butler
Warren Morris RC
❑ 261 Ben Davis .20 .06
Eli Marrero
Ramon Hernandez
❑ 262 Eric Chavez .30 .09
Russell Branyan
Russ Johnson
❑ 263 Todd Dunwoody RC .20 .06
John Barnes
Ryan Jackson
❑ 264 Matt Clement .30 .09
Roy Halladay
Brian Fuentes RC
❑ 265 Randy Johnson SH .30 .09
❑ 266 Kevin Brown SH .20 .06
❑ 267 Ricardo Rincon SH .20 .06
Francisco Cordova
❑ 268 N.Garciaparra SH .50 .15
❑ 269 Tino Martinez SH .20 .06
❑ 270 Chuck Knoblauch IL .20 .06
❑ 271 Pedro Martinez IL .30 .09
❑ 272 Denny Neagle IL .20 .06
❑ 273 Juan Gonzalez IL .20 .06
❑ 274 Andres Galarraga IL .20 .06
❑ 275 Checklist .20 .06
❑ 276 Checklist .20 .06
❑ 277 Moises Alou WS .20 .06
❑ 278 Sandy Alomar Jr. WS .20 .06
❑ 279 Gary Sheffield WS .20 .06
❑ 280 Matt Williams WS .20 .06
❑ 281 Livan Hernandez WS .20 .06
❑ 282 Chad Ogea WS .20 .06
❑ 283 Marlins Champs .20 .06
❑ 284 Tino Martinez .30 .09
❑ 285 Roberto Alomar .30 .09
❑ 286 Jeff King .20 .06
❑ 287 Brian Jordan .20 .06
❑ 288 Darin Erstad .20 .06
❑ 289 Ken Caminiti .20 .06
❑ 290 Jim Thome .30 .09
❑ 291 Paul Molitor .30 .09
❑ 292 Ivan Rodriguez .30 .09
❑ 293 Bernie Williams .30 .09
❑ 294 Todd Hundley .20 .06
❑ 295 Andres Galarraga .20 .06
❑ 296 Greg Maddux .75 .23
❑ 297 Edgar Martinez .30 .09
❑ 298 Ron Gant .20 .06
❑ 299 Derek Bell .20 .06
❑ 300 Roger Clemens 1.00 .30
❑ 301 Rondell White .20 .06
❑ 302 Barry Larkin .30 .09
❑ 303 Robin Ventura .20 .06
❑ 304 Jason Kendall .20 .06
❑ 305 Chipper Jones .50 .15
❑ 306 John Franco .20 .06
❑ 307 Sammy Sosa .50 .15
❑ 308 Troy Percival .20 .06
❑ 309 Chuck Knoblauch .20 .06
❑ 310 Ellis Burks .20 .06
❑ 311 Al Martin .20 .06
❑ 312 Tim Salmon .30 .09
❑ 313 Moises Alou .20 .06
❑ 314 Lance Johnson .20 .06
❑ 315 Justin Thompson .20 .06
❑ 316 Will Clark .30 .09
❑ 317 Barry Bonds 1.50 .45
❑ 318 Craig Biggio .30 .09
❑ 319 John Smoltz .30 .09
❑ 320 Cal Ripken 1.50 .45
❑ 321 Ken Griffey Jr. .75 .23
❑ 322 Paul O'Neill .30 .09
❑ 323 Todd Helton .30 .09
❑ 324 John Olerud .20 .06
❑ 325 Mark McGwire 1.25 .35
❑ 326 Jose Cruz Jr. .20 .06
❑ 327 Jeff Cirillo .20 .06
❑ 328 Dean Palmer .20 .06
❑ 329 John Wetteland .20 .06
❑ 330 Steve Finley .20 .06
❑ 331 Albert Belle .20 .06
❑ 332 Curt Schilling .20 .06
❑ 333 Raul Mondesi .20 .06
❑ 334 Andruw Jones .30 .09
❑ 335 Nomar Garciaparra .75 .23
❑ 336 David Justice .20 .06
❑ 337 Andy Pettitte .30 .09
❑ 338 Pedro Martinez .30 .09
❑ 339 Travis Miller .20 .06
❑ 340 Chris Stynes .20 .06
❑ 341 Gregg Jefferies .20 .06
❑ 342 Jeff Fassero .20 .06
❑ 343 Craig Counsell .20 .06
❑ 344 Wilson Alvarez .20 .06
❑ 345 Bip Roberts .20 .06
❑ 346 Kelvim Escobar .20 .06
❑ 347 Mark Bellhorn .20 .06
❑ 348 Cory Lidle RC .30 .09
❑ 349 Fred McGriff .30 .09
❑ 350 Chuck Carr .20 .06
❑ 351 Bob Abreu .20 .06
❑ 352 Juan Guzman .20 .06
❑ 353 Fernando Vina .20 .06
❑ 354 Andy Benes .20 .06
❑ 355 Dave Nilsson .20 .06
❑ 356 Bobby Bonilla .20 .06
❑ 357 Ismael Valdes .20 .06
❑ 358 Carlos Perez .20 .06
❑ 359 Kirk Rueter .20 .06
❑ 360 Bartolo Colon .20 .06
❑ 361 Mel Rojas .20 .06
❑ 362 Johnny Damon .30 .09
❑ 363 Geronimo Berroa .20 .06
❑ 364 Reggie Sanders .20 .06
❑ 365 Jermaine Allensworth .20 .06
❑ 366 Orlando Cabrera .20 .06
❑ 367 Jorge Fabregas .20 .06
❑ 368 Scott Stahoviak .20 .06
❑ 369 Ken Cloude .20 .06
❑ 370 Donovan Osborne .20 .06
❑ 371 Roger Cedeno .20 .06
❑ 372 Neifi Perez .20 .06
❑ 373 Chris Holt .20 .06
❑ 374 Cecil Fielder .20 .06
❑ 375 Marty Cordova .20 .06
❑ 376 Tom Goodwin .20 .06
❑ 377 Jeff Suppan .20 .06
❑ 378 Jeff Brantley .20 .06
❑ 379 Mark Langston .20 .06
❑ 380 Shane Reynolds .20 .06
❑ 381 Mike Fetters .20 .06
❑ 382 Todd Greene .20 .06
❑ 383 Ray Durham .20 .06
❑ 384 Carlos Delgado .20 .06
❑ 385 Jeff D'Amico .20 .06
❑ 386 Brian McRae .20 .06
❑ 387 Alan Benes .20 .06
❑ 388 Heathcliff Slocumb .20 .06
❑ 389 Eric Young .20 .06
❑ 390 Travis Fryman .20 .06
❑ 391 David Cone .20 .06
❑ 392 Otis Nixon .20 .06
❑ 393 Jeremi Gonzalez .20 .06
❑ 394 Jeff Juden .20 .06
❑ 395 Jose Vizcaino .20 .06
❑ 396 Ugueth Urbina .20 .06
❑ 397 Ramon Martinez .20 .06
❑ 398 Robb Nen .20 .06
❑ 399 Harold Baines .20 .06
❑ 400 Delino DeShields .20 .06
❑ 401 John Burkett .20 .06
❑ 402 Sterling Hitchcock .20 .06
❑ 403 Mark Clark .20 .06
❑ 404 Terrell Wade .20 .06
❑ 405 Scott Brosius .20 .06
❑ 406 Chad Curtis .20 .06

❑ 407 Brian Johnson .20 .06
❑ 408 Roberto Kelly .20 .06
❑ 409 Dave Dellucci RC .40 .12
❑ 410 Michael Tucker .20 .06
❑ 411 Mark Kotsay .20 .06
❑ 412 Mark Lewis .20 .06
❑ 413 Ryan McGuire .20 .06
❑ 414 Shawon Dunston .20 .06
❑ 415 Brad Rigby .20 .06
❑ 416 Scott Erickson .20 .06
❑ 417 Bobby Jones .20 .06
❑ 418 Darren Oliver .20 .06
❑ 419 John Smiley .20 .06
❑ 420 T.J. Mathews .20 .06
❑ 421 Dustin Hermanson .20 .06
❑ 422 Mike Timlin .20 .06
❑ 423 Willie Blair .20 .06
❑ 424 Manny Alexander .20 .06
❑ 425 Bob Tewksbury .20 .06
❑ 426 Pete Schourek .20 .06
❑ 427 Reggie Jefferson .20 .06
❑ 428 Ed Sprague .20 .06
❑ 429 Jeff Conine .20 .06
❑ 430 Roberto Hernandez .20 .06
❑ 431 Tom Pagnozzi .20 .06
❑ 432 Jaret Wright .20 .06
❑ 433 Livan Hernandez .20 .06
❑ 434 Andy Ashby .20 .06
❑ 435 Todd Dunn .20 .06
❑ 436 Bobby Higginson .20 .06
❑ 437 Rod Beck .20 .06
❑ 438 Jim Leyritz .20 .06
❑ 439 Matt Williams .20 .06
❑ 440 Brett Tomko .20 .06
❑ 441 Joe Randa .20 .06
❑ 442 Chris Carpenter .20 .06
❑ 443 Dennis Reyes .20 .06
❑ 444 Al Leiter .20 .06
❑ 445 Jason Schmidt .20 .06
❑ 446 Ken Hill .20 .06
❑ 447 Shannon Stewart .20 .06
❑ 448 Enrique Wilson .20 .06
❑ 449 Fernando Tatis .20 .06
❑ 450 Jimmy Key .20 .06
❑ 451 Darrin Fletcher .20 .06
❑ 452 John Valentin .20 .06
❑ 453 Kevin Tapani .20 .06
❑ 454 Eric Karros .20 .06
❑ 455 Jay Bell .20 .06
❑ 456 Walt Weiss .20 .06
❑ 457 Devon White .20 .06
❑ 458 Carl Pavano .20 .06
❑ 459 Mike Lansing .20 .06
❑ 460 John Flaherty .20 .06
❑ 461 Richard Hidalgo .20 .06
❑ 462 Quinton McCracken .20 .06
❑ 463 Karim Garcia .20 .06
❑ 464 Miguel Cairo .20 .06
❑ 465 Edwin Diaz .20 .06
❑ 466 Bobby Smith .20 .06
❑ 467 Yamil Benitez .20 .06
❑ 468 Rich Butler .20 .06
❑ 469 Ben Ford RC .20 .06
❑ 470 Bubba Trammell .20 .06
❑ 471 Brent Brede .20 .06
❑ 472 Brooks Kieschnick .20 .06
❑ 473 Carlos Castillo .20 .06
❑ 474 Brad Radke SH .20 .06
❑ 475 Roger Clemens SH .50 .15
❑ 476 Curt Schilling SH .20 .06
❑ 477 John Olerud SH .20 .06
❑ 478 Mark McGwire SH .60 .18
❑ 479 Mike Piazza .50 .15
Ken Griffey Jr. IL
❑ 480 Jeff Bagwell .30 .09
Frank Thomas IL
❑ 481 Chipper Jones .30 .09
Nomar Garciaparra IL
❑ 482 Larry Walker .20 .06
Juan Gonzalez IL
❑ 483 Gary Sheffield .20 .06
Tino Martinez IL
❑ 484 Derrick Gibson .20 .06
Michael Coleman
Norm Hutchins
❑ 485 Braden Looper .20 .06
Cliff Politte
Brian Rose
❑ 486 Eric Milton .20 .06
Jason Marquis
Corey Lee
❑ 487 A.J.Hinch .30 .09
Mark Osborne
Robert Fick RC
❑ 488 Aramis Ramirez .40 .12
Alex Gonzalez
Sean Casey
❑ 489 Donnie Bridges .20 .06
Tim Drew RC
❑ 490 Ntema Ndungidi RC .20 .06
Darnell McDonald
❑ 491 Ryan Anderson RC .30 .09
Mark Mangum
❑ 492 J.J.Davis 2.00 .60
Troy Glaus RC
❑ 493 Jayson Werth RC .20 .06
Dan Reichert
❑ 494 John Curtice RC .40 .12
Michael Cuddyer RC
❑ 495 Jack Cust RC .30 .09
Jason Standridge
❑ 496 Brian Anderson .20 .06
❑ 497 Tony Saunders .20 .06
❑ 498 Vladimir Nunez .20 .06
Jhensy Sandoval
❑ 499 Brad Penny .30 .09
Nick Bierbrodt
❑ 500 Dustin Carr .20 .06
Luis Cruz RC
❑ 501 Cedric Bowers .20 .06
Marcus McCain
❑ 502 Checklist .20 .06
❑ 503 Checklist .20 .06
❑ 504 Alex Rodriguez 2.00 .60

1999 Topps

	Nm-Mt	Ex-Mt
COMPLETE SET (462)	80.00	24.00
COMP.HOBBY SET (462)	80.00	24.00
COMP.X-MAS SET (463)	80.00	24.00
COMP. SERIES 1 (241)	40.00	12.00
COMP. SERIES 2 (221)	40.00	12.00
COMP.MAC HR SET (70)	500.00	150.00
COMP.SOSA HR SET (66)	200.00	60.00

❑ 1 Roger Clemens 1.00 .30
❑ 2 Andres Galarraga .20 .06
❑ 3 Scott Brosius .20 .06
❑ 4 John Flaherty .20 .06
❑ 5 Jim Leyritz .20 .06
❑ 6 Ray Durham .20 .06
❑ 8 Jose Vizcaino .20 .06
❑ 9 Will Clark .30 .09
❑ 10 David Wells .20 .06
❑ 11 Jose Guillen .20 .06
❑ 12 Scott Hatteberg .20 .06
❑ 13 Edgardo Alfonzo .20 .06
❑ 14 Mike Bordick .20 .06
❑ 15 Manny Ramirez .30 .09
❑ 16 Greg Maddux .75 .23
❑ 17 David Segui .20 .06
❑ 18 Darryl Strawberry .20 .06
❑ 19 Brad Radke .20 .06
❑ 20 Kerry Wood .20 .06
❑ 21 Matt Anderson .20 .06
❑ 22 Derrek Lee .30 .09
❑ 23 Mickey Morandini .20 .06
❑ 24 Paul Konerko .20 .06
❑ 25 Travis Lee .20 .06
❑ 26 Ken Hill .20 .06
❑ 27 Kenny Rogers .20 .06
❑ 28 Paul Sorrento .20 .06
❑ 29 Quilvio Veras .20 .06
❑ 30 Todd Walker .20 .06
❑ 31 Ryan Jackson .20 .06
❑ 32 John Olerud .20 .06
❑ 33 Doug Glanville .20 .06
❑ 34 Nolan Ryan 2.00 .60
❑ 35 Ray Lankford .20 .06
❑ 36 Mark Loretta .20 .06
❑ 37 Jason Dickson .20 .06
❑ 38 Sean Bergman .20 .06
❑ 39 Quinton McCracken .20 .06
❑ 40 Bartolo Colon .20 .06
❑ 41 Brady Anderson .20 .06
❑ 42 Chris Stynes .20 .06
❑ 43 Jorge Posada .30 .09
❑ 44 Justin Thompson .20 .06
❑ 45 Johnny Damon .30 .09
❑ 46 Armando Benitez .20 .06
❑ 47 Brant Brown .20 .06
❑ 48 Charlie Hayes .20 .06
❑ 49 Darren Dreifort .20 .06
❑ 50 Juan Gonzalez .20 .06
❑ 51 Chuck Knoblauch .20 .06
❑ 52 Todd Helton .30 .09
❑ 53 Rick Reed .20 .06
❑ 54 Chris Gomez .20 .06
❑ 55 Gary Sheffield .20 .06
❑ 56 Rod Beck .20 .06
❑ 57 Rey Sanchez .20 .06
❑ 58 Garret Anderson .20 .06
❑ 59 Jimmy Haynes .20 .06
❑ 60 Steve Woodard .20 .06
❑ 61 Rondell White .20 .06
❑ 62 Vladimir Guerrero .50 .15
❑ 63 Eric Karros .20 .06
❑ 64 Russ Davis .20 .06
❑ 65 Mo Vaughn .20 .06
❑ 66 Sammy Sosa .50 .15
❑ 67 Troy Percival .20 .06
❑ 68 Kenny Lofton .20 .06
❑ 69 Bill Taylor .20 .06
❑ 70 Mark McGwire 1.25 .35
❑ 71 Roger Cedeno .20 .06
❑ 72 Javy Lopez .20 .06
❑ 73 Damion Easley .20 .06
❑ 74 Andy Pettitte .30 .09
❑ 75 Tony Gwynn .60 .18
❑ 76 Ricardo Rincon .20 .06
❑ 77 F.P. Santangelo .20 .06
❑ 78 Jay Bell .20 .06
❑ 79 Scott Servais .20 .06
❑ 80 Jose Canseco .30 .09
❑ 81 Roberto Hernandez .20 .06
❑ 82 Todd Dunwoody .20 .06
❑ 83 John Wetteland .20 .06
❑ 84 Mike Caruso .20 .06
❑ 85 Derek Jeter 1.25 .35
❑ 86 Aaron Sele .20 .06
❑ 87 Jose Lima .20 .06
❑ 88 Ryan Christenson .20 .06
❑ 89 Jeff Cirillo .20 .06
❑ 90 Jose Hernandez .20 .06
❑ 91 Mark Kotsay .20 .06
❑ 92 Darren Bragg .20 .06
❑ 93 Albert Belle .20 .06
❑ 94 Matt Lawton .20 .06
❑ 95 Pedro Martinez .30 .09
❑ 96 Greg Vaughn .20 .06
❑ 97 Neifi Perez .20 .06
❑ 98 Gerald Williams .20 .06
❑ 99 Derek Bell .20 .06
❑ 100 Ken Griffey Jr. .75 .23
❑ 101 David Cone .20 .06
❑ 102 Brian Johnson .20 .06
❑ 103 Dean Palmer .20 .06
❑ 104 Javier Valentin .20 .06
❑ 105 Trevor Hoffman .20 .06
❑ 106 Butch Huskey .20 .06

❑ 107 Dave Martinez .20 .06
❑ 108 Billy Wagner .20 .06
❑ 109 Shawn Green .20 .06
❑ 110 Ben Grieve .20 .06
❑ 111 Tom Goodwin .20 .06
❑ 112 Jaret Wright .20 .06
❑ 113 Aramis Ramirez .20 .06
❑ 114 Dmitri Young .20 .06
❑ 115 Hideki Irabu .20 .06
❑ 116 Roberto Kelly .20 .06
❑ 117 Jeff Fassero .20 .06
❑ 118 Mark Clark UER .20 .06
1997 and Career Victory totals are wrong
❑ 119 Jason McDonald .20 .06
❑ 120 Matt Williams .20 .06
❑ 121 Dave Burba .20 .06
❑ 122 Bret Saberhagen .20 .06
❑ 123 Deivi Cruz .20 .06
❑ 124 Chad Curtis .20 .06
❑ 125 Scott Rolen .30 .09
❑ 126 Lee Stevens .20 .06
❑ 127 J.T. Snow .20 .06
❑ 128 Rusty Greer .20 .06
❑ 129 Brian Meadows .20 .06
❑ 130 Jim Edmonds .20 .06
❑ 131 Ron Gant .20 .06
❑ 132 A.J. Hinch UER .20 .06
Photo is a reverse negative
❑ 133 Shannon Stewart .20 .06
❑ 134 Brad Fullmer .20 .06
❑ 135 Cal Eldred .20 .06
❑ 136 Matt Walbeck .20 .06
❑ 137 Carl Everett .20 .06
❑ 138 Walt Weiss .20 .06
❑ 139 Fred McGriff .30 .09
❑ 140 Darin Erstad .20 .06
❑ 141 Dave Nilsson .20 .06
❑ 142 Eric Young .20 .06
❑ 143 Dan Wilson .20 .06
❑ 144 Jeff Reed .20 .06
❑ 145 Brett Tomko .20 .06
❑ 146 Terry Steinbach .20 .06
❑ 147 Seth Greisinger .20 .06
❑ 148 Pat Meares .20 .06
❑ 149 Livan Hernandez .20 .06
❑ 150 Jeff Bagwell .30 .09
❑ 151 Bob Wickman .20 .06
❑ 152 Omar Vizquel .30 .09
❑ 153 Eric Davis .20 .06
❑ 154 Larry Sutton .20 .06
❑ 155 Magglio Ordonez .20 .06
❑ 156 Eric Milton .20 .06
❑ 157 Darren Lewis .20 .06
❑ 158 Rick Aguilera .20 .06
❑ 159 Mike Lieberthal .20 .06
❑ 160 Robb Nen .20 .06
❑ 161 Brian Giles .20 .06
❑ 162 Jeff Brantley .20 .06
❑ 163 Gary DiSarcina .20 .06
❑ 164 John Valentin .20 .06
❑ 165 David Dellucci .20 .06
❑ 166 Chan Ho Park .20 .06
❑ 167 Masato Yoshii .20 .06
❑ 168 Jason Schmidt .20 .06
❑ 169 LaTroy Hawkins .20 .06
❑ 170 Bret Boone .20 .06
❑ 171 Jerry DiPoto .20 .06
❑ 172 Mariano Rivera .30 .09
❑ 173 Mike Cameron .20 .06
❑ 174 Scott Erickson .20 .06
❑ 175 Charles Johnson .20 .06
❑ 176 Bobby Jones .20 .06
❑ 177 Francisco Cordova .20 .06
❑ 178 Todd Jones .20 .06
❑ 179 Jeff Montgomery .20 .06
❑ 180 Mike Mussina .30 .09
❑ 181 Bob Abreu .20 .06
❑ 182 Ismael Valdes .20 .06
❑ 183 Andy Fox .20 .06
❑ 184 Woody Williams .20 .06
❑ 185 Denny Neagle .20 .06
❑ 186 Jose Valentin .20 .06
❑ 187 Darrin Fletcher .20 .06
❑ 188 Gabe Alvarez .20 .06
❑ 189 Eddie Taubensee .20 .06
❑ 190 Edgar Martinez .30 .09
❑ 191 Jason Kendall .20 .06
❑ 192 Darryl Kile .20 .06
❑ 193 Jeff King .20 .06
❑ 194 Rey Ordonez .20 .06
❑ 195 Andruw Jones .30 .09
❑ 196 Tony Fernandez .20 .06
❑ 197 Jamey Wright .20 .06
❑ 198 B.J. Surhoff .20 .06
❑ 199 Vinny Castilla .20 .06
❑ 200 David Wells HL .20 .06
❑ 201 Mark McGwire HL .60 .18
❑ 202 Sammy Sosa HL .30 .09
❑ 203 Roger Clemens HL .50 .15
❑ 204 Kerry Wood HL .20 .06
❑ 205 Lance Berkman .40 .12
Mike Frank
Gabe Kapler
❑ 206 Alex Escobar RC .40 .12
Ricky Ledee
Mike Stoner
❑ 207 Peter Bergeron RC .40 .12
Jeremy Giambi
George Lombard
❑ 208 Michael Barrett .25 .07
Ben Davis
Robert Fick
❑ 209 Pat Cline .25 .07
Ramon Hernandez
Jayson Werth
❑ 210 Bruce Chen .25 .07
Chris Enochs
Ryan Anderson
❑ 211 Mike Lincoln .25 .07
Octavio Dotel
Brad Penny
❑ 212 Chuck Abbott RC .25 .07
Brent Butler
Danny Klassen
❑ 213 Chris C.Jones .25 .07
Jeff Urban RC
❑ 214 Arturo McDowell RC .25 .07
Tony Torcato
❑ 215 Josh McKinley RC .40 .12
Jason Tyner
❑ 216 Matt Burch .25 .07
Seth Etheron RC
UER back Etherton
❑ 217 Mamon Tucker RC .40 .12
Rick Elder
❑ 218 J.M.Gold .25 .07
Ryan Mills RC
❑ 219 Adam Brown .25 .07
Choo Freeman RC
❑ 220A Mark McGwire HR 1 40.00 12.00
❑ 220B Mark McGwire HR 2 15.00 4.50
❑ 220C Mark McGwire HR 3 15.00 4.50
❑ 220D Mark McGwire HR 4 15.00 4.50
❑ 220E Mark McGwire HR 5 15.00 4.50
❑ 220F Mark McGwire HR 6 15.00 4.50
❑ 220G Mark McGwire HR 7 15.00 4.50
❑ 220H Mark McGwire HR 8 15.00 4.50
❑ 220I Mark McGwire HR 9 15.00 4.50
❑ 220J M.McGwire HR 10 15.00 4.50
❑ 220K M.McGwire HR 11 15.00 4.50
❑ 220L M.McGwire HR 12 15.00 4.50
❑ 220M M.McGwire HR 13 15.00 4.50
❑ 220N M.McGwire HR 14 15.00 4.50
❑ 220O M.McGwire HR 15 15.00 4.50
❑ 220P M.McGwire HR 16 15.00 4.50
❑ 220Q M.McGwire HR 17 15.00 4.50
❑ 220R M.McGwire HR 18 15.00 4.50
❑ 220S M.McGwire HR 19 15.00 4.50
❑ 220T M.McGwire HR 20 15.00 4.50
❑ 220U M.McGwire HR 21 15.00 4.50
❑ 220V M.McGwire HR 22 15.00 4.50
❑ 220W M.McGwire HR 23 15.00 4.50
❑ 220X M.McGwire HR 24 15.00 4.50
❑ 220Y M.McGwire HR 25 15.00 4.50
❑ 220Z M.McGwire HR 26 15.00 4.50
❑ 220AA M.McGwire HR 27 15.00 4.50
❑ 220AB M.McGwire HR 28 15.00 4.50
❑ 220AC M.McGwire HR 29 15.00 4.50
❑ 220AD M.McGwire HR 30 15.00 4.50
❑ 220AE M.McGwire HR 31 15.00 4.50
❑ 220AF M.McGwire HR 32 15.00 4.50
❑ 220AG M.McGwire HR 33 15.00 4.50
❑ 220AH M.McGwire HR 34 15.00 4.50
❑ 220AI M.McGwire HR 35 15.00 4.50
❑ 220AJ M.McGwire HR 36 15.00 4.50
❑ 220AK M.McGwire HR 37 15.00 4.50
❑ 220AL M.McGwire HR 38 15.00 4.50
❑ 220AM M.McGwire HR 39 15.00 4.50
❑ 220AN M.McGwire HR 40 15.00 4.50
❑ 220AO M.McGwire HR 41 15.00 4.50
❑ 220AP M.McGwire HR 42 15.00 4.50
❑ 220AQ M.McGwire HR 43 15.00 4.50
❑ 220AR M.McGwire HR 44 15.00 4.50
❑ 220AS M.McGwire HR 45 15.00 4.50
❑ 220AT M.McGwire HR 46 15.00 4.50
❑ 220AU M.McGwire HR 47 15.00 4.50
❑ 220AV M.McGwire HR 48 15.00 4.50
❑ 220AW M.McGwire HR 49 15.00 4.50
❑ 220AX M.McGwire HR 50 15.00 4.50
❑ 220AY M.McGwire HR 51 15.00 4.50
❑ 220AZ M.McGwire HR 52 15.00 4.50
❑ 220BB M.McGwire HR 53 15.00 4.50
❑ 220CC M.McGwire HR 54 15.00 4.50
❑ 220DD M.McGwire HR 55 15.00 4.50
❑ 220EE M.McGwire HR 56 15.00 4.50
❑ 220FF M.McGwire HR 57 15.00 4.50
❑ 220GG M.McGwire HR 58 15.00 4.50
❑ 220HH M.McGwire HR 59 15.00 4.50
❑ 220II M.McGwire HR 60 15.00 4.50
❑ 220JJ M.McGwire HR 61 30.00 9.00
❑ 220KK M.McGwire HR 62 40.00 12.00
❑ 220LL M.McGwire HR 63 15.00 4.50
❑ 220MM M.McGwire HR 64 15.00 4.50
❑ 220NN M.McGwire HR 65 15.00 4.50
❑ 220OO M.McGwire HR 66 15.00 4.50
❑ 220PP M.McGwire HR 67 15.00 4.50
❑ 220QQ M.McGwire HR 68 15.00 4.50
❑ 220RR M.McGwire HR 69 15.00 4.50
❑ 220SS M.McGwire HR 70 100.00 30.00
❑ 221 Larry Walker LL .20 .06
❑ 222 Bernie Williams LL .20 .06
❑ 223 Mark McGwire LL .60 .18
❑ 224 Ken Griffey Jr. LL .50 .15
❑ 225 Sammy Sosa LL .30 .09
❑ 226 Juan Gonzalez LL .20 .06
❑ 227 Dante Bichette LL .20 .06
❑ 228 Alex Rodriguez LL .50 .15
❑ 229 Sammy Sosa LL .30 .09
❑ 230 Derek Jeter LL .60 .18
❑ 231 Greg Maddux LL .50 .15
❑ 232 Roger Clemens LL .50 .15
❑ 233 Ricky Ledee WS .20 .06
❑ 234 Chuck Knoblauch WS .20 .06
❑ 235 Bernie Williams WS .20 .06
❑ 236 Tino Martinez WS .20 .06
❑ 237 Orl. Hernandez WS .20 .06
❑ 238 Scott Brosius WS .20 .06
❑ 239 Andy Pettitte WS .20 .06
❑ 240 Mariano Rivera WS .20 .06
❑ 241 Checklist 1 .20 .06
❑ 242 Checklist 2 .20 .06
❑ 243 Tom Glavine .30 .09
❑ 244 Andy Benes .20 .06
❑ 245 Sandy Alomar Jr. .20 .06
❑ 246 Wilton Guerrero .20 .06
❑ 247 Alex Gonzalez .20 .06
❑ 248 Roberto Alomar .30 .09
❑ 249 Ruben Rivera .20 .06
❑ 250 Eric Chavez .20 .06
❑ 251 Ellis Burks .20 .06
❑ 252 Richie Sexson .20 .06
❑ 253 Steve Finley .20 .06
❑ 254 Dwight Gooden .20 .06
❑ 255 Dustin Hermanson .20 .06
❑ 256 Kirk Rueter .20 .06
❑ 257 Steve Trachsel .20 .06
❑ 258 Gregg Jefferies .20 .06
❑ 259 Matt Stairs .20 .06
❑ 260 Shane Reynolds .20 .06
❑ 261 Gregg Olson .20 .06
❑ 262 Kevin Tapani .20 .06
❑ 263 Matt Morris .20 .06
❑ 264 Carl Pavano .20 .06
❑ 265 Nomar Garciaparra .75 .23
❑ 266 Kevin Young .20 .06
❑ 267 Rick Helling .20 .06
❑ 268 Matt Franco .20 .06

❏	269	Brian McRae	.20	.06
❏	270	Cal Ripken	1.50	.45
❏	271	Jeff Abbott	.20	.06
❏	272	Tony Batista	.20	.06
❏	273	Bill Simas	.20	.06
❏	274	Brian Hunter	.20	.06
❏	275	John Franco	.20	.06
❏	276	Devon White	.20	.06
❏	277	Rickey Henderson	.50	.15
❏	278	Chuck Finley	.20	.06
❏	279	Mike Blowers	.20	.06
❏	280	Mark Grace	.30	.09
❏	281	Randy Winn	.20	.06
❏	282	Bobby Bonilla	.20	.06
❏	283	David Justice	.20	.06
❏	284	Shane Monahan	.20	.06
❏	285	Kevin Brown	.30	.09
❏	286	Todd Zeile	.20	.06
❏	287	Al Martin	.20	.06
❏	288	Troy O'Leary	.20	.06
❏	289	Darryl Hamilton	.20	.06
❏	290	Tino Martinez	.30	.09
❏	291	David Ortiz	.30	.09
❏	292	Tony Clark	.20	.06
❏	293	Ryan Minor	.20	.06
❏	294	Mark Leiter	.20	.06
❏	295	Wally Joyner	.20	.06
❏	296	Cliff Floyd	.20	.06
❏	297	Shawn Estes	.20	.06
❏	298	Pat Hentgen	.20	.06
❏	299	Scott Elarton	.20	.06
❏	300	Alex Rodriguez	.75	.23
❏	301	Ozzie Guillen	.20	.06
❏	302	Hideo Nomo	.50	.15
❏	303	Ryan McGuire	.20	.06
❏	304	Brad Ausmus	.20	.06
❏	305	Alex Gonzalez	.20	.06
❏	306	Brian Jordan	.20	.06
❏	307	John Jaha	.20	.06
❏	308	Mark Grudzielanek	.20	.06
❏	309	Juan Guzman	.20	.06
❏	310	Tony Womack	.20	.06
❏	311	Dennis Reyes	.20	.06
❏	312	Marty Cordova	.20	.06
❏	313	Ramiro Mendoza	.20	.06
❏	314	Robin Ventura	.20	.06
❏	315	Rafael Palmeiro	.30	.09
❏	316	Ramon Martinez	.20	.06
❏	317	Pedro Astacio	.20	.06
❏	318	Dave Hollins	.20	.06
❏	319	Tom Candiotti	.20	.06
❏	320	Al Leiter	.20	.06
❏	321	Rico Brogna	.20	.06
❏	322	Reggie Jefferson	.20	.06
❏	323	Bernard Gilkey	.20	.06
❏	324	Jason Giambi	.20	.06
❏	325	Craig Biggio	.30	.09
❏	326	Troy Glaus	.30	.09
❏	327	Delino DeShields	.20	.06
❏	328	Fernando Vina	.20	.06
❏	329	John Smoltz	.30	.09
❏	330	Jeff Kent	.20	.06
❏	331	Roy Halladay	.20	.06
❏	332	Andy Ashby	.20	.06
❏	333	Tim Wakefield	.20	.06
❏	334	Roger Clemens	1.00	.30
❏	335	Bernie Williams	.30	.09
❏	336	Desi Relaford	.20	.06
❏	337	John Burkett	.20	.06
❏	338	Mike Hampton	.20	.06
❏	339	Royce Clayton	.20	.06
❏	340	Mike Piazza	.75	.23
❏	341	Jeremi Gonzalez	.20	.06
❏	342	Mike Lansing	.20	.06
❏	343	Jamie Moyer	.20	.06
❏	344	Ron Coomer	.20	.06
❏	345	Barry Larkin	.30	.09
❏	346	Fernando Tatis	.20	.06
❏	347	Chili Davis	.20	.06
❏	348	Bobby Higginson	.20	.06
❏	349	Hal Morris	.20	.06
❏	350	Larry Walker	.20	.06
❏	351	Carlos Guillen	.20	.06
❏	352	Miguel Tejada	.20	.06
❏	353	Travis Fryman	.20	.06
❏	354	Jarrod Washburn	.20	.06
❏	355	Chipper Jones	.50	.15
❏	356	Todd Stottlemyre	.20	.06
❏	357	Henry Rodriguez	.20	.06
❏	358	Eli Marrero	.20	.06
❏	359	Alan Benes	.20	.06
❏	360	Tim Salmon	.30	.09
❏	361	Luis Gonzalez	.20	.06
❏	362	Scott Spiezio	.20	.06
❏	363	Chris Carpenter	.20	.06
❏	364	Bobby Howry	.20	.06
❏	365	Raul Mondesi	.20	.06
❏	366	Ugueth Urbina	.20	.06
❏	367	Tom Evans	.20	.06
❏	368	Kerry Ligtenberg RC	.25	.07
❏	369	Adrian Beltre	.20	.06
❏	370	Ryan Klesko	.20	.06
❏	371	Wilson Alvarez	.20	.06
❏	372	John Thomson	.20	.06
❏	373	Tony Saunders	.20	.06
❏	374	Dave Mlicki	.20	.06
❏	375	Ken Caminiti	.20	.06
❏	376	Jay Buhner	.20	.06
❏	377	Bill Mueller	.20	.06
❏	378	Jeff Blauser	.20	.06
❏	379	Edgar Renteria	.20	.06
❏	380	Jim Thome	.30	.09
❏	381	Joey Hamilton	.20	.06
❏	382	Calvin Pickering	.20	.06
❏	383	Marquis Grissom	.20	.06
❏	384	Omar Daal	.20	.06
❏	385	Curt Schilling	.20	.06
❏	386	Jose Cruz Jr.	.20	.06
❏	387	Chris Widger	.20	.06
❏	388	Pete Harnisch	.20	.06
❏	389	Charles Nagy	.20	.06
❏	390	Tom Gordon	.20	.06
❏	391	Bobby Smith	.20	.06
❏	392	Derrick Gibson	.20	.06
❏	393	Jeff Conine	.20	.06
❏	394	Carlos Perez	.20	.06
❏	395	Barry Bonds	1.50	.45
❏	396	Mark McLemore	.20	.06
❏	397	Juan Encarnacion	.20	.06
❏	398	Wade Boggs	.30	.09
❏	399	Ivan Rodriguez	.30	.09
❏	400	Moises Alou	.20	.06
❏	401	Jeromy Burnitz	.20	.06
❏	402	Sean Casey	.30	.09
❏	403	Jose Offerman	.20	.06
❏	404	Joe Fontenot	.20	.06
❏	405	Kevin Millwood	.20	.06
❏	406	Lance Johnson	.20	.06
❏	407	Richard Hidalgo	.20	.06
❏	408	Mike Jackson	.20	.06
❏	409	Brian Anderson	.20	.06
❏	410	Jeff Shaw	.20	.06
❏	411	Preston Wilson	.20	.06
❏	412	Todd Hundley	.20	.06
❏	413	Jim Parque	.20	.06
❏	414	Justin Baughman	.20	.06
❏	415	Dante Bichette	.20	.06
❏	416	Paul O'Neill	.30	.09
❏	417	Miguel Cairo	.20	.06
❏	418	Randy Johnson	.50	.15
❏	419	Jesus Sanchez	.20	.06
❏	420	Carlos Delgado	.20	.06
❏	421	Ricky Ledee	.20	.06
❏	422	Orlando Hernandez	.20	.06
❏	423	Frank Thomas	.50	.15
❏	424	Pokey Reese	.20	.06
❏	425	Carlos Lee	.40	.12
		Mike Lowell		
		Kit Pellow RC		
❏	426	Michael Cuddyer	.25	.07
		Mark DeRosa		
		Jerry Hairston Jr.		
❏	427	Marlon Anderson	.40	.12
		Ron Belliard		
		Orlando Cabrera		
❏	428	Micah Bowie	.25	.07
		Phil Norton RC		
		Randy Wolf		
❏	429	Jack Cressend RC	.40	.12
		Jason Rakers		
		John Rocker		
❏	430	Ruben Mateo	.25	.07
		Scott Morgan		
		Mike Zywica RC		
❏	431	Jason LaRue	.25	.07
		Matt LeCroy		
		Mitch Meluskey		
❏	432	Gabe Kapler	.40	.12
		Armando Rios		
		Fernando Seguignol		
❏	433	Adam Kennedy	.25	.07
		Mickey Lopez RC		
		Jackie Rexrode		
❏	434	Jose Fernandez RC	.25	.07
		Jeff Liefer		
		Chris Truby		
❏	435	Corey Koskie	.50	.15
		Doug Mientkiewicz RC		
		Damon Minor		
❏	436	Roosevelt Brown RC	.40	.12
		Dernell Stenson		
		Vernon Wells		
❏	437	A.J. Burnett RC	1.00	.30
		Billy Koch		
		John Nicholson		
❏	438	Matt Belisle	.25	.07
		Matt Roney RC		
❏	439	Austin Kearns	1.00	.30
		Chris George RC		
❏	440	Nate Bump RC	.40	.12
		Nate Cornejo		
❏	441	Brad Lidge	2.00	.60
		Mike Nannini RC		
❏	442	Matt Holliday	.50	.15
		Jeff Winchester RC		
❏	443	Adam Everett	.50	.15
		Chip Ambres RC		
❏	444	Pat Burrell	1.50	.45
		Eric Valent RC		
❏	445	Roger Clemens SK	.50	.15
❏	446	Kerry Wood SK	.20	.06
❏	447	Curt Schilling SK	.20	.06
❏	448	Randy Johnson SK	.30	.09
❏	449	Pedro Martinez SK	.30	.09
❏	450	Jeff Bagwell AT	.50	.15
		Andres Galarraga		
		Mark McGwire		
❏	451	John Olerud AT	.20	.06
		Jim Thome		
		Tino Martinez		
❏	452	Alex Rodriguez AT	.60	.18
		Nomar Garciaparra		
		Derek Jeter		
❏	453	Vinny Castilla AT	.30	.09
		Chipper Jones		
		Scott Rolen		
❏	454	Sammy Sosa AT	.50	.15
		Ken Griffey Jr.		
		Juan Gonzalez		
❏	455	Barry Bonds AT	.75	.23
		Manny Ramirez		
		Larry Walker		
❏	456	Frank Thomas AT	.50	.15
		Tim Salmon		
		David Justice		
❏	457	Travis Lee AT	.20	.06
		Todd Helton		
		Ben Grieve		
❏	458	Vladimir Guerrero AT	.20	.06
		Greg Vaughn		
		Bernie Williams		
❏	459	Mike Piazza AT	.50	.15
		Ivan Rodriguez		
		Jason Kendall		
❏	460	Roger Clemens AT	.50	.15
		Kerry Wood		
		Greg Maddux		
❏	461A	Sammy Sosa HR 1	15.00	4.50
❏	461B	Sammy Sosa HR 2	6.00	1.80
❏	461C	Sammy Sosa HR 3	6.00	1.80
❏	461D	Sammy Sosa HR 4	6.00	1.80
❏	461E	Sammy Sosa HR 5	6.00	1.80
❏	461F	Sammy Sosa HR 6	6.00	1.80
❏	461G	Sammy Sosa HR 7	6.00	6.50
❏	461H	Sammy Sosa HR 8	6.00	1.80
❏	461I	Sammy Sosa HR 9	6.00	1.80
❏	461J	Sammy Sosa HR 10	6.00	1.80
❏	461K	Sammy Sosa HR 11	6.00	1.80

Card	Nm-Mt	Ex-Mt
❑ 461L Sammy Sosa HR 12	6.00	1.80
❑ 461M Sammy Sosa HR 13	6.00	1.80
❑ 461N Sammy Sosa HR 14	6.00	1.80
❑ 461O Sammy Sosa HR 15	6.00	1.80
❑ 461P Sammy Sosa HR 16	6.00	1.80
❑ 461Q Sammy Sosa HR 17	6.00	1.80
❑ 461R Sammy Sosa HR 18	6.00	1.80
❑ 461S Sammy Sosa HR 19	6.00	1.80
❑ 461T Sammy Sosa HR 20	6.00	1.80
❑ 461U Sammy Sosa HR 21	6.00	1.80
❑ 461V Sammy Sosa HR 22	6.00	1.80
❑ 461W Sammy Sosa HR 23	6.00	1.80
❑ 461X Sammy Sosa HR 24	6.00	1.80
❑ 461Y Sammy Sosa HR 25	6.00	1.80
❑ 461Z Sammy Sosa HR 26	6.00	1.80
❑ 461AA S.Sosa HR 27	6.00	1.80
❑ 461AB S.Sosa HR 28	6.00	1.80
❑ 461AC S.Sosa HR 29	6.00	1.80
❑ 461AD S.Sosa HR 30	6.00	1.80
❑ 461AE S.Sosa HR 31	6.00	1.80
❑ 461AF S.Sosa HR 32	6.00	1.80
❑ 461AG S.Sosa HR 33	6.00	1.80
❑ 461AH S.Sosa HR 34	6.00	1.80
❑ 461AI S.Sosa HR 35	6.00	1.80
❑ 461AJ S.Sosa HR 36	6.00	1.80
❑ 461AK S.Sosa HR 37	6.00	1.80
❑ 461AL S.Sosa HR 38	6.00	1.80
❑ 461AM S.Sosa HR 39	6.00	1.80
❑ 461AN S.Sosa HR 40	6.00	1.80
❑ 461AO S.Sosa HR 41	6.00	1.80
❑ 461AP S.Sosa HR 42	6.00	1.80
❑ 461AR S.Sosa HR 43	6.00	1.80
❑ 461AS S.Sosa HR 44	6.00	1.80
❑ 461AT S.Sosa HR 45	6.00	1.80
❑ 461AU S.Sosa HR 46	6.00	1.80
❑ 461AV S.Sosa HR 47	6.00	1.80
❑ 461AW S.Sosa HR 48	6.00	1.80
❑ 461AX S.Sosa HR 49	6.00	1.80
❑ 461AY S.Sosa HR 50	6.00	1.80
❑ 461AZ S.Sosa HR 51	6.00	1.80
❑ 461BB S.Sosa HR 52	6.00	1.80
❑ 461CC S.Sosa HR 53	6.00	1.80
❑ 461DD S.Sosa HR 54	6.00	1.80
❑ 461EE S.Sosa HR 55	6.00	1.80
❑ 461FF S.Sosa HR 56	6.00	1.80
❑ 461GG S.Sosa HR 57	6.00	1.80
❑ 461HH S.Sosa HR 58	6.00	1.80
❑ 461II S.Sosa HR 59	6.00	1.80
❑ 461JJ S.Sosa HR 60	6.00	1.80
❑ 461KK S.Sosa HR 61	15.00	4.50
❑ 461LL S.Sosa HR 62	20.00	6.00
❑ 461MM S.Sosa HR 63	8.00	2.40
❑ 461NN S.Sosa HR 64	8.00	2.40
❑ 461OO S.Sosa HR 65	8.00	2.40
❑ 461PP S.Sosa HR 66	25.00	7.50
❑ 462 Checklist	.20	.06
❑ 463 Checklist	.20	.06

1999 Topps Traded

	Nm-Mt	Ex-Mt
COMP.FACT.SET (122)	40.00	12.00
COMPLETE SET (121)	25.00	7.50

Card	Nm-Mt	Ex-Mt
❑ T1 Seth Etherton	.20	.06
❑ T2 Mark Harriger RC	.25	.07
❑ T3 Matt Wise RC	.25	.07
❑ T4 Carlos E. Hernandez RC	.40	.12
❑ T5 Julio Lugo RC	.60	.18
❑ T6 Mike Nannini	.20	.06
❑ T7 Justin Bowles RC	.25	.07
❑ T8 Mark Mulder RC	2.00	.60
❑ T9 Roberto Vaz RC	.25	.07
❑ T10 Felipe Lopez RC	1.25	.35
❑ T11 Matt Belisle	.20	.06
❑ T12 Micah Bowie	.20	.06
❑ T13 Ruben Quevedo RC	.25	.07
❑ T14 Jose Garcia RC	.25	.07
❑ T15 David Kelton RC	.40	.12
❑ T16 Phil Norton	.20	.06
❑ T17 Corey Patterson RC	.60	.18
❑ T18 Ron Walker RC	.25	.07
❑ T19 Paul Hoover RC	.25	.07
❑ T20 Ryan Rupe RC	.25	.07
❑ T21 J.D. Closser RC	.60	.18
❑ T22 Rob Ryan RC	.25	.07
❑ T23 Steve Colyer RC	.40	.12
❑ T24 Bubba Crosby RC	.60	.18
❑ T25 Luke Prokopec RC	.25	.07
❑ T26 Matt Blank RC	.25	.07
❑ T27 Josh McKinley	.20	.06
❑ T28 Nate Bump	.20	.06
❑ T29 G.Chiaramonte RC	.25	.07
❑ T30 Arturo McDowell	.20	.06
❑ T31 Tony Torcato	.20	.06
❑ T32 Dave Roberts RC	.60	.18
❑ T33 C.C. Sabathia RC	1.00	.30
❑ T34 Sean Spencer RC	.25	.07
❑ T35 Chip Ambres	.20	.06
❑ T36 A.J. Burnett	1.00	.30
❑ T37 Mo Bruce RC	.25	.07
❑ T38 Jason Tyner	.20	.06
❑ T39 Mamon Tucker	.20	.06
❑ T40 Sean Burroughs RC	.60	.18
❑ T41 Kevin Eberwein RC	.25	.07
❑ T42 Junior Herndon RC	.40	.12
❑ T43 Bryan Wolff RC	.25	.07
❑ T44 Pat Burrell	1.25	.35
❑ T45 Eric Valent	.20	.06
❑ T46 Carlos Pena RC	.40	.12
❑ T47 Mike Zywica	.20	.06
❑ T48 Adam Everett	.30	.09
❑ T49 Juan Pena RC	.40	.12
❑ T50 Adam Dunn RC	5.00	1.50
❑ T51 Austin Kearns	.60	.18
❑ T52 Jacobo Sequea RC	.25	.07
❑ T53 Choo Freeman	.20	.06
❑ T54 Jeff Winchester	.20	.06
❑ T55 Matt Burch	.20	.06
❑ T56 Chris George	.20	.06
❑ T57 Scott Mullen RC	.25	.07
❑ T58 Kit Pellow	.20	.06
❑ T59 Mark Quinn RC	.40	.12
❑ T60 Nate Cornejo	.40	.12
❑ T61 Ryan Mills	.20	.06
❑ T62 Kevin Beirne RC	.40	.12
❑ T63 Kip Wells RC	.60	.18
❑ T64 Juan Rivera RC	.60	.18
❑ T65 Alfonso Soriano RC	5.00	1.50
❑ T66 Josh Hamilton RC	.60	.18
❑ T67 Josh Girdley RC	.25	.07
❑ T68 Kyle Snyder RC	.25	.07
❑ T69 Mike Paradis RC	.25	.07
❑ T70 Jason Jennings RC	.60	.18
❑ T71 David Walling RC	.25	.07
❑ T72 Omar Ortiz RC	.25	.07
❑ T73 Jay Gehrke RC	.40	.12
❑ T74 Casey Burns RC	.40	.12
❑ T75 Carl Crawford RC	2.00	.60
❑ T76 Reggie Sanders	.20	.06
❑ T77 Will Clark	.30	.09
❑ T78 David Wells	.20	.06
❑ T79 Paul Konerko	.20	.06
❑ T80 Armando Benitez	.20	.06
❑ T81 Brant Brown	.20	.06
❑ T82 Mo Vaughn	.20	.06
❑ T83 Jose Canseco	.30	.09
❑ T84 Albert Belle	.20	.06
❑ T85 Dean Palmer	.20	.06
❑ T86 Greg Vaughn	.20	.06
❑ T87 Mark Clark	.20	.06
❑ T88 Pat Meares	.20	.06
❑ T89 Eric Davis	.20	.06
❑ T90 Brian Giles	.20	.06
❑ T91 Jeff Brantley	.20	.06
❑ T92 Bret Boone	.20	.06
❑ T93 Ron Gant	.20	.06
❑ T94 Mike Cameron	.20	.06
❑ T95 Charles Johnson	.20	.06
❑ T96 Denny Neagle	.20	.06
❑ T97 Brian Hunter	.20	.06
❑ T98 Jose Hernandez	.20	.06
❑ T99 Rick Aguilera	.20	.06
❑ T100 Tony Batista	.20	.06
❑ T101 Roger Cedeno	.20	.06
❑ T102 C.Gubanich RC	.25	.07
❑ T103 Tim Belcher	.20	.06
❑ T104 Bruce Aven	.20	.06
❑ T105 Brian Daubach RC	.40	.12
❑ T106 Ed Sprague	.20	.06
❑ T107 Michael Tucker	.20	.06
❑ T108 Homer Bush	.20	.06
❑ T109 Armando Reynoso	.20	.06
❑ T110 Brook Fordyce	.20	.06
❑ T111 Matt Mantei	.20	.06
❑ T112 Dave Mlicki	.20	.06
❑ T113 Kenny Rogers	.20	.06
❑ T114 Livan Hernandez	.20	.06
❑ T115 Butch Huskey	.20	.06
❑ T116 David Segui	.20	.06
❑ T117 Darryl Hamilton	.20	.06
❑ T118 Terry Mulholland	.20	.06
❑ T119 Randy Velarde	.20	.06
❑ T120 Bill Taylor	.20	.06
❑ T121 Kevin Appier	.20	.06

2000 Topps

	Nm-Mt	Ex-Mt
COMPLETE SET (478)	50.00	15.00
COMP.HOBBY SET (478)	50.00	15.00
COMP. SERIES 1 (239)	25.00	7.50
COMP. SERIES 2 (240)	25.00	7.50
MCGWIRE MM SET (5)	12.00	3.60
AARON MM SET (5)	10.00	3.00
RIPKEN MM SET (5)	15.00	4.50
BOGGS MM SET (5)	3.00	.90
GWYNN MM SET (5)	6.00	1.80
GRIFFEY MM SET (5)	8.00	2.40
BONDS MM SET (5)	12.00	3.60
SOSA MM SET (5)	8.00	2.40
JETER MM SET (5)	12.00	3.60
A.ROD MM SET (5)	8.00	2.40

Card	Nm-Mt	Ex-Mt
❑ 1 Mark McGwire	1.25	.35
❑ 2 Tony Gwynn	.60	.18
❑ 3 Wade Boggs	.30	.09
❑ 4 Cal Ripken	1.50	.45
❑ 5 Matt Williams	.20	.06
❑ 6 Jay Buhner	.20	.06
❑ 8 Jeff Conine	.20	.06
❑ 9 Todd Greene	.20	.06
❑ 10 Mike Lieberthal	.20	.06
❑ 11 Steve Avery	.20	.06
❑ 12 Bret Saberhagen	.20	.06
❑ 13 Magglio Ordonez	.20	.06
❑ 14 Brad Radke	.20	.06
❑ 15 Derek Jeter	1.25	.35
❑ 16 Javy Lopez	.20	.06
❑ 17 Russ Davis	.20	.06
❑ 18 Armando Benitez	.20	.06
❑ 19 B.J. Surhoff	.20	.06
❑ 20 Darryl Kile	.20	.06
❑ 21 Mark Lewis	.20	.06

❑ 22 Mike Williams .20 .06
❑ 23 Mark McLemore .20 .06
❑ 24 Sterling Hitchcock .20 .06
❑ 25 Darin Erstad .20 .06
❑ 26 Ricky Gutierrez .20 .06
❑ 27 John Jaha .20 .06
❑ 28 Homer Bush .20 .06
❑ 29 Darrin Fletcher .20 .06
❑ 30 Mark Grace .30 .09
❑ 31 Fred McGriff .30 .09
❑ 32 Omar Daal .20 .06
❑ 33 Eric Karros .20 .06
❑ 34 Orlando Cabrera .20 .06
❑ 35 J.T. Snow .20 .06
❑ 36 Luis Castillo .20 .06
❑ 37 Rey Ordonez .20 .06
❑ 38 Bob Abreu .20 .06
❑ 39 Warren Morris .20 .06
❑ 40 Juan Gonzalez .20 .06
❑ 41 Mike Lansing .20 .06
❑ 42 Chili Davis .20 .06
❑ 43 Dean Palmer .20 .06
❑ 44 Hank Aaron .75 .23
❑ 45 Jeff Bagwell .30 .09
❑ 46 Jose Valentin .20 .06
❑ 47 Shannon Stewart .20 .06
❑ 48 Kent Bottenfield .20 .06
❑ 49 Jeff Shaw .20 .06
❑ 50 Sammy Sosa .50 .15
❑ 51 Randy Johnson .50 .15
❑ 52 Benny Agbayani .20 .06
❑ 53 Dante Bichette .20 .06
❑ 54 Pete Harnisch .20 .06
❑ 55 Frank Thomas .50 .15
❑ 56 Jorge Posada .30 .09
❑ 57 Todd Walker .20 .06
❑ 58 Juan Encarnacion .20 .06
❑ 59 Mike Sweeney .20 .06
❑ 60 Pedro Martinez .30 .09
❑ 61 Lee Stevens .20 .06
❑ 62 Brian Giles .20 .06
❑ 63 Chad Ogea .20 .06
❑ 64 Ivan Rodriguez .30 .09
❑ 65 Roger Cedeno .20 .06
❑ 66 David Justice .20 .06
❑ 67 Steve Trachsel .20 .06
❑ 68 Eli Marrero .20 .06
❑ 69 Dave Nilsson .20 .06
❑ 70 Ken Caminiti .20 .06
❑ 71 Tim Raines .20 .06
❑ 72 Brian Jordan .20 .06
❑ 73 Jeff Blauser .20 .06
❑ 74 Bernard Gilkey .20 .06
❑ 75 John Flaherty .20 .06
❑ 76 Brent Mayne .20 .06
❑ 77 Jose Vidro .20 .06
❑ 78 David Bell .20 .06
❑ 79 Bruce Aven .20 .06
❑ 80 John Olerud .20 .06
❑ 81 Pokey Reese .20 .06
❑ 82 Woody Williams .20 .06
❑ 83 Ed Sprague .20 .06
❑ 84 Joe Girardi .20 .06
❑ 85 Barry Larkin .30 .09
❑ 86 Mike Caruso .20 .06
❑ 87 Bobby Higginson .20 .06
❑ 88 Roberto Kelly .20 .06
❑ 89 Edgar Martinez .30 .09
❑ 90 Mark Kotsay .20 .06
❑ 91 Paul Sorrento .20 .06
❑ 92 Eric Young .20 .06
❑ 93 Carlos Delgado .20 .06
❑ 94 Troy Glaus .20 .06
❑ 95 Ben Grieve .20 .06
❑ 96 Jose Lima .20 .06
❑ 97 Garret Anderson .20 .06
❑ 98 Luis Gonzalez .20 .06
❑ 99 Carl Pavano .20 .06
❑ 100 Alex Rodriguez .75 .23
❑ 101 Preston Wilson .20 .06
❑ 102 Ron Gant .20 .06
❑ 103 Brady Anderson .20 .06
❑ 104 Rickey Henderson .50 .15
❑ 105 Gary Sheffield .20 .06
❑ 106 Mickey Morandini .20 .06
❑ 107 Jim Edmonds .20 .06
❑ 108 Kris Benson .20 .06
❑ 109 Adrian Beltre .20 .06
❑ 110 Alex Fernandez .20 .06
❑ 111 Dan Wilson .20 .06
❑ 112 Mark Clark .20 .06
❑ 113 Greg Vaughn .20 .06
❑ 114 Neifi Perez .20 .06
❑ 115 Paul O'Neill .30 .09
❑ 116 Jermaine Dye .20 .06
❑ 117 Todd Jones .20 .06
❑ 118 Terry Steinbach .20 .06
❑ 119 Greg Norton .20 .06
❑ 120 Curt Schilling .20 .06
❑ 121 Todd Zeile .20 .06
❑ 122 Edgardo Alfonzo .20 .06
❑ 123 Ryan McGuire .20 .06
❑ 124 Rich Aurilia .20 .06
❑ 125 John Smoltz .30 .09
❑ 126 Bob Wickman .20 .06
❑ 127 Richard Hidalgo .20 .06
❑ 128 Chuck Finley .20 .06
❑ 129 Billy Wagner .20 .06
❑ 130 Todd Hundley .20 .06
❑ 131 Dwight Gooden .20 .06
❑ 132 Russ Ortiz .20 .06
❑ 133 Mike Lowell .20 .06
❑ 134 Reggie Sanders .20 .06
❑ 135 John Valentin .20 .06
❑ 136 Brad Ausmus .20 .06
❑ 137 Chad Kreuter .20 .06
❑ 138 David Cone .20 .06
❑ 139 Brook Fordyce .20 .06
❑ 140 Roberto Alomar .30 .09
❑ 141 Charles Nagy .20 .06
❑ 142 Brian Hunter .20 .06
❑ 143 Mike Mussina .30 .09
❑ 144 Robin Ventura .30 .09
❑ 145 Kevin Brown .30 .09
❑ 146 Pat Hentgen .20 .06
❑ 147 Ryan Klesko .20 .06
❑ 148 Derek Bell .20 .06
❑ 149 Andy Sheets .20 .06
❑ 150 Larry Walker .20 .06
❑ 151 Scott Williamson .20 .06
❑ 152 Jose Offerman .20 .06
❑ 153 Doug Mientkiewicz .20 .06
❑ 154 John Snyder RC .40 .12
❑ 155 Sandy Alomar Jr. .20 .06
❑ 156 Joe Nathan .20 .06
❑ 157 Lance Johnson .20 .06
❑ 158 Odalis Perez .20 .06
❑ 159 Hideo Nomo .50 .15
❑ 160 Steve Finley .20 .06
❑ 161 Dave Martinez .20 .06
❑ 162 Matt Walbeck .20 .06
❑ 163 Bill Spiers .20 .06
❑ 164 Fernando Tatis .20 .06
❑ 165 Kenny Lofton .20 .06
❑ 166 Paul Byrd .20 .06
❑ 167 Aaron Sele .20 .06
❑ 168 Eddie Taubensee .20 .06
❑ 169 Reggie Jefferson .20 .06
❑ 170 Roger Clemens 1.00 .30
❑ 171 Francisco Cordova .20 .06
❑ 172 Mike Bordick .20 .06
❑ 173 Wally Joyner .20 .06
❑ 174 Marvin Benard .20 .06
❑ 175 Jason Kendall .20 .06
❑ 176 Mike Stanley .20 .06
❑ 177 Chad Allen .20 .06
❑ 178 Carlos Beltran .20 .06
❑ 179 Deivi Cruz .20 .06
❑ 180 Chipper Jones .50 .15
❑ 181 Vladimir Guerrero .50 .15
❑ 182 Dave Burba .20 .06
❑ 183 Tom Goodwin .20 .06
❑ 184 Brian Daubach .20 .06
❑ 185 Jay Bell .20 .06
❑ 186 Roy Halladay .20 .06
❑ 187 Miguel Tejada .20 .06
❑ 188 Armando Rios .20 .06
❑ 189 Fernando Vina .20 .06
❑ 190 Eric Davis .20 .06
❑ 191 Henry Rodriguez .20 .06
❑ 192 Joe McEwing .20 .06
❑ 193 Jeff Kent .20 .06
❑ 194 Mike Jackson .20 .06
❑ 195 Mike Morgan .20 .06
❑ 196 Jeff Montgomery .20 .06
❑ 197 Jeff Zimmerman .20 .06
❑ 198 Tony Fernandez .20 .06
❑ 199 Jason Giambi .20 .06
❑ 200 Jose Canseco .30 .09
❑ 201 Alex Gonzalez .20 .06
❑ 202 Jack Cust .40 .12
Mike Colangelo
Dee Brown
❑ 203 Felipe Lopez .50 .15
Alfonso Soriano
Pablo Ozuna
❑ 204 Erubiel Durazo .40 .12
Pat Burrell
Nick Johnson
❑ 205 John Sneed RC .40 .12
Kip Wells
Matt Blank
❑ 206 Josh Kalinowski .40 .12
Michael Tejera
Chris Mears RC
❑ 207 Roosevelt Brown .40 .12
Corey Patterson
Lance Berkman
❑ 208 Kit Pellow .40 .12
Kevin Barker
Russ Branyan
❑ 209 B.J. Garbe .50 .15
Larry Bigbie RC
❑ 210 Eric Munson .40 .12
Bobby Bradley RC
❑ 211 Josh Girdley .40 .12
Kyle Snyder
❑ 212 Chance Caple RC .40 .12
Jason Jennings
❑ 213 Ryan Christianson 1.25 .35
Brett Myers RC
❑ 214 Jason Stumm .40 .12
Rob Purvis RC
❑ 215 David Walling .40 .12
Mike Paradis
❑ 216 Omar Ortiz .40 .12
Jay Gehrke
❑ 217 David Cone HL .20 .06
❑ 218 Jose Jimenez HL .20 .06
❑ 219 Chris Singleton HL .20 .06
❑ 220 Fernando Tatis HL .20 .06
❑ 221 Todd Helton HL .20 .06
❑ 222 Kevin Millwood DIV .20 .06
❑ 223 Todd Pratt DIV .20 .06
❑ 224 Orl.Hernandez DIV .20 .06
❑ 225 Pedro Martinez DIV .30 .09
❑ 226 Tom Glavine LCS .20 .06
❑ 227 Bernie Williams LCS .20 .06
❑ 228 Mariano Rivera WS .20 .06
❑ 229 Tony Gwynn 20CB .60 .18
❑ 230 Wade Boggs 20CB .30 .09
❑ 231 Lance Johnson CB .20 .06
❑ 232 Mark McGwire 20CB 1.25 .35
❑ 233 R.Henderson 20CB .50 .15
❑ 234 R.Henderson 20CB .50 .15
❑ 235 Roger Clemens 20CB 1.00 .30
❑ 236A M.McGwire MM .00 .00
1st HR
❑ 236B M.McGwire MM .00 .00
1987 ROY
❑ 236C M.McGwire MM .00 .00
62nd HR
❑ 236D M.McGwire MM .00 .00
70th HR
❑ 236E M.McGwire MM .00 .00
500th HR
❑ 237A H.Aaron MM 2.00 .60
1st Career HR
❑ 237B H.Aaron MM 2.00 .60
1957 MVP
❑ 237C H.Aaron MM 2.00 .60
3000th Hit
❑ 237D H.Aaron MM 2.00 .60
715th HR
❑ 237E H.Aaron MM 2.00 .60
755th HR
❑ 238A C.Ripken MM 4.00 1.20
1982 ROY

❑ 238B C.Ripken MM 4.00 1.20
1991 MVP
❑ 238C C.Ripken MM 4.00 1.20
2131 Game
❑ 238D C.Ripken MM 4.00 1.20
Streak Ends
❑ 238E C.Ripken MM 4.00 1.20
400th HR
❑ 239A W.Boggs MM .... .75 .23
1983 Batting
❑ 239B W.Boggs MM .... .75 .23
1988 Batting
❑ 239C W.Boggs MM .... .75 .23
2000th Hit
❑ 239D W.Boggs MM .... .75 .23
1996 Champs
❑ 239E W.Boggs MM .... .75 .23
3000th Hit
❑ 240A T.Gwynn MM .... 1.50 .45
1984 Batting
❑ 240B T.Gwynn MM .... 1.50 .45
1984 NLCS
❑ 240C T.Gwynn MM .... 1.50 .45
1995 Batting
❑ 240D T.Gwynn MM .... 1.50 .45
1998 NLCS
❑ 240E T.Gwynn MM .... 1.50 .45
3000th Hit
❑ 241 Tom Glavine .... .30 .09
❑ 242 David Wells .... .20 .06
❑ 243 Kevin Appier .... .20 .06
❑ 244 Troy Percival .... .20 .06
❑ 245 Ray Lankford .... .20 .06
❑ 246 Marquis Grissom .... .20 .06
❑ 247 Randy Winn .... .20 .06
❑ 248 Miguel Batista .... .20 .06
❑ 249 Darren Dreifort .... .20 .06
❑ 250 Barry Bonds .... 1.50 .45
❑ 251 Harold Baines .... .20 .06
❑ 252 Cliff Floyd .... .20 .06
❑ 253 Freddy Garcia .... .20 .06
❑ 254 Kenny Rogers .... .20 .06
❑ 255 Ben Davis .... .20 .06
❑ 256 Charles Johnson .... .20 .06
❑ 257 Bubba Trammell .... .20 .06
❑ 258 Desi Relaford .... .20 .06
❑ 259 Al Martin .... .20 .06
❑ 260 Andy Pettitte .... .30 .09
❑ 261 Carlos Lee .... .20 .06
❑ 262 Matt Lawton .... .20 .06
❑ 263 Andy Fox .... .20 .06
❑ 264 Chan Ho Park .... .20 .06
❑ 265 Billy Koch .... .20 .06
❑ 266 Dave Roberts .... .20 .06
❑ 267 Carl Everett .... .20 .06
❑ 268 Orel Hershiser .... .20 .06
❑ 269 Trot Nixon .... .20 .06
❑ 270 Rusty Greer .... .20 .06
❑ 271 Will Clark .... .30 .09
❑ 272 Quilvio Veras .... .20 .06
❑ 273 Rico Brogna .... .20 .06
❑ 274 Devon White .... .20 .06
❑ 275 Tim Hudson .... .20 .06
❑ 276 Mike Hampton .... .20 .06
❑ 277 Miguel Cairo .... .20 .06
❑ 278 Darren Oliver .... .20 .06
❑ 279 Jeff Cirillo .... .20 .06
❑ 280 Al Leiter .... .20 .06
❑ 281 Shane Andrews .... .20 .06
❑ 282 Carlos Febles .... .20 .06
❑ 283 Pedro Astacio .... .20 .06
❑ 284 Juan Guzman .... .20 .06
❑ 285 Orlando Hernandez .... .20 .06
❑ 286 Paul Konerko .... .20 .06
❑ 287 Tony Clark .... .20 .06
❑ 288 Aaron Boone .... .20 .06
❑ 289 Ismael Valdes .... .20 .06
❑ 290 Moises Alou .... .20 .06
❑ 291 Kevin Tapani .... .20 .06
❑ 292 John Franco .... .20 .06
❑ 293 Todd Zeile .... .20 .06
❑ 294 Jason Schmidt .... .20 .06
❑ 295 Johnny Damon .... .30 .09
❑ 296 Scott Brosius .... .20 .06
❑ 297 Travis Fryman .... .20 .06
❑ 298 Jose Vizcaino .... .20 .06
❑ 299 Eric Chavez .... .20 .06
❑ 300 Mike Piazza .... .75 .23
❑ 301 Matt Clement .... .20 .06
❑ 302 Cristian Guzman .... .20 .06
❑ 303 C.J. Nitkowski .... .20 .06
❑ 304 Michael Tucker .... .20 .06
❑ 305 Brett Tomko .... .20 .06
❑ 306 Mike Lansing .... .20 .06
❑ 307 Eric Owens .... .20 .06
❑ 308 Livan Hernandez .... .20 .06
❑ 309 Rondell White .... .20 .06
❑ 310 Todd Stottlemyre .... .20 .06
❑ 311 Chris Carpenter .... .20 .06
❑ 312 Ken Hill .... .20 .06
❑ 313 Mark Loretta .... .20 .06
❑ 314 John Rocker .... .20 .06
❑ 315 Richie Sexson .... .20 .06
❑ 316 Ruben Mateo .... .20 .06
❑ 317 Joe Randa .... .20 .06
❑ 318 Mike Sirotka .... .20 .06
❑ 319 Jose Rosado .... .20 .06
❑ 320 Matt Mantei .... .20 .06
❑ 321 Kevin Millwood .... .20 .06
❑ 322 Gary DiSarcina .... .20 .06
❑ 323 Dustin Hermanson .... .20 .06
❑ 324 Mike Stanton .... .20 .06
❑ 325 Kirk Rueter .... .20 .06
❑ 326 Damian Miller RC .... .40 .12
❑ 327 Doug Glanville .... .20 .06
❑ 328 Scott Rolen .... .30 .09
❑ 329 Ray Durham .... .20 .06
❑ 330 Butch Huskey .... .20 .06
❑ 331 Mariano Rivera .... .30 .09
❑ 332 Darren Lewis .... .20 .06
❑ 333 Mike Timlin .... .20 .06
❑ 334 Mark Grudzielanek .... .20 .06
❑ 335 Mike Cameron .... .20 .06
❑ 336 Kelvim Escobar .... .20 .06
❑ 337 Bret Boone .... .20 .06
❑ 338 Mo Vaughn .... .20 .06
❑ 339 Craig Biggio .... .30 .09
❑ 340 Michael Barrett .... .20 .06
❑ 341 Marlon Anderson .... .20 .06
❑ 342 Bobby Jones .... .20 .06
❑ 343 John Halama .... .20 .06
❑ 344 Todd Ritchie .... .20 .06
❑ 345 Chuck Knoblauch .... .20 .06
❑ 346 Rick Reed .... .20 .06
❑ 347 Kelly Stinnett .... .20 .06
❑ 348 Tim Salmon .... .30 .09
❑ 349 A.J. Hinch .... .20 .06
❑ 350 Jose Cruz Jr. .... .20 .06
❑ 351 Roberto Hernandez .... .20 .06
❑ 352 Edgar Renteria .... .20 .06
❑ 353 Jose Hernandez .... .20 .06
❑ 354 Brad Fullmer .... .20 .06
❑ 355 Trevor Hoffman .... .20 .06
❑ 356 Troy O'Leary .... .20 .06
❑ 357 Justin Thompson .... .20 .06
❑ 358 Kevin Young .... .20 .06
❑ 359 Hideki Irabu .... .20 .06
❑ 360 Jim Thome .... .30 .09
❑ 361 Steve Karsay .... .20 .06
❑ 362 Octavio Dotel .... .20 .06
❑ 363 Omar Vizquel .... .30 .09
❑ 364 Raul Mondesi .... .20 .06
❑ 365 Shane Reynolds .... .20 .06
❑ 366 Bartolo Colon .... .20 .06
❑ 367 Chris Widger .... .20 .06
❑ 368 Gabe Kapler .... .20 .06
❑ 369 Bill Simas .... .20 .06
❑ 370 Tino Martinez .... .30 .09
❑ 371 John Thomson .... .20 .06
❑ 372 Delino DeShields .... .20 .06
❑ 373 Carlos Perez .... .20 .06
❑ 374 Eddie Perez .... .20 .06
❑ 375 Jeromy Burnitz .... .20 .06
❑ 376 Jimmy Haynes .... .20 .06
❑ 377 Travis Lee .... .20 .06
❑ 378 Darryl Hamilton .... .20 .06
❑ 379 Jamie Moyer .... .20 .06
❑ 380 Alex Gonzalez .... .20 .06
❑ 381 John Wetteland .... .20 .06
❑ 382 Vinny Castilla .... .20 .06
❑ 383 Jeff Suppan .... .20 .06
❑ 384 Jim Leyritz .... .20 .06
❑ 385 Robb Nen .... .20 .06
❑ 386 Wilson Alvarez .... .20 .06
❑ 387 Andres Galarraga .... .20 .06
❑ 388 Mike Remlinger .... .20 .06
❑ 389 Geoff Jenkins .... .20 .06
❑ 390 Matt Stairs .... .20 .06
❑ 391 Bill Mueller .... .20 .06
❑ 392 Mike Lowell .... .20 .06
❑ 393 Andy Ashby .... .20 .06
❑ 394 Ruben Rivera .... .20 .06
❑ 395 Todd Helton .... .30 .09
❑ 396 Bernie Williams .... .30 .09
❑ 397 Royce Clayton .... .20 .06
❑ 398 Manny Ramirez .... .30 .09
❑ 399 Kerry Wood .... .20 .06
❑ 400 Ken Griffey Jr. .... .75 .23
❑ 401 Enrique Wilson .... .20 .06
❑ 402 Joey Hamilton .... .20 .06
❑ 403 Shawn Estes .... .20 .06
❑ 404 Ugueth Urbina .... .20 .06
❑ 405 Albert Belle .... .20 .06
❑ 406 Rick Helling .... .20 .06
❑ 407 Steve Parris .... .20 .06
❑ 408 Eric Milton .... .20 .06
❑ 409 Dave Mlicki .... .20 .06
❑ 410 Shawn Green .... .20 .06
❑ 411 Jaret Wright .... .20 .06
❑ 412 Tony Womack .... .20 .06
❑ 413 Vernon Wells .... .20 .06
❑ 414 Ron Belliard .... .20 .06
❑ 415 Ellis Burks .... .20 .06
❑ 416 Scott Erickson .... .20 .06
❑ 417 Rafael Palmeiro .... .30 .09
❑ 418 Damion Easley .... .20 .06
❑ 419 Jamey Wright .... .20 .06
❑ 420 Corey Koskie .... .20 .06
❑ 421 Bobby Howry .... .20 .06
❑ 422 Ricky Ledee .... .20 .06
❑ 423 Dmitri Young .... .20 .06
❑ 424 Sidney Ponson .... .20 .06
❑ 425 Greg Maddux .... .75 .23
❑ 426 Jose Guillen .... .20 .06
❑ 427 Jon Lieber .... .20 .06
❑ 428 Andy Benes .... .20 .06
❑ 429 Randy Velarde .... .20 .06
❑ 430 Sean Casey .... .30 .09
❑ 431 Torii Hunter .... .20 .06
❑ 432 Ryan Rupe .... .20 .06
❑ 433 David Segui .... .20 .06
❑ 434 Todd Pratt .... .20 .06
❑ 435 Nomar Garciaparra .... .75 .23
❑ 436 Denny Neagle .... .20 .06
❑ 437 Ron Coomer .... .20 .06
❑ 438 Chris Singleton .... .20 .06
❑ 439 Tony Batista .... .20 .06
❑ 440 Andruw Jones .... .30 .09
❑ 441 Aubrey Huff .... .20 .06
Sean Burroughs
Adam Piatt
❑ 442 Rafael Furcal .... .40 .12
Travis Dawkins
Jason Dellaero
❑ 443 Mike Lamb RC .... 1.00 .30
Joe Crede
Wilton Veras
❑ 444 Julio Zuleta RC .... .40 .12
Jorge Toca
Dernell Stenson
❑ 445 Garry Maddox Jr. RC .... .40 .12
Gary Matthews Jr.
Tim Raines Jr.
❑ 446 Mark Mulder .... .40 .12
C.C. Sabathia
Matt Riley
❑ 447 Scott Downs RC .... .40 .12
Chris George
Matt Belisle
❑ 448 Doug Mirabelli .... .40 .12
Ben Petrick
Jayson Werth
❑ 449 Josh Hamilton .... .40 .12
Corey Myers RC
❑ 450 Ben Christensen RC .... .40 .12
Richard Stahl RC
❑ 451 Ben Sheets RC .... 2.00 .60
Barry Zito

Card	Player	Nm-Mt	Ex-Mt
❑ 452	Kurt Ainsworth Ty Howington RC	.40	.12
❑ 453	Vince Faison RC Rick Asadoorian	.40	.12
❑ 454	Keith Reed RC Jeff Heaverlo	.40	.12
❑ 455	Mike MacDougal Brad Baker RC	.40	.12
❑ 456	Mark McGwire SH	.60	.18
❑ 457	Cal Ripken SH	.75	.23
❑ 458	Wade Boggs SH	.20	.06
❑ 459	Tony Gwynn SH	.30	.09
❑ 460	Jesse Orosco SH	.20	.06
❑ 461	Larry Walker Nomar Garciaparra LL	.30	.09
❑ 462	Ken Griffey Jr. Mark McGwire LL	.50	.15
❑ 463	Manny Ramirez Mark McGwire LL	.50	.15
❑ 464	Pedro Martinez Randy Johnson LL	.30	.09
❑ 465	Pedro Martinez Randy Johnson LL	.30	.09
❑ 466	Derek Jeter Luis Gonzalez LL	.50	.15
❑ 467	Larry Walker Manny Ramirez LL	.30	.09
❑ 468	Tony Gwynn 20CB	.60	.18
❑ 469	Mark McGwire 20CB	1.25	.35
❑ 470	Frank Thomas 20CB	.30	.09
❑ 471	Harold Baines 20CB	.20	.06
❑ 472	Roger Clemens 20CB	1.00	.30
❑ 473	John Franco 20CB	.20	.06
❑ 474	John Franco 20CB	.20	.06
❑ 475A	K.Griffey Jr. MM 350th HR	2.00	.60
❑ 475B	K.Griffey Jr. MM 1997 MVP	2.00	.60
❑ 475C	K.Griffey Jr. MM HR Dad	2.00	.60
❑ 475D	K.Griffey Jr. MM 1992 AS MVP	2.00	.60
❑ 475E	K.Griffey Jr. MM 50 HR 1997	2.00	.60
❑ 476A	B.Bonds MM 400HR/400SB	3.00	.90
❑ 476B	B.Bonds MM 40HR/40SB	3.00	.90
❑ 476C	B.Bonds MM 1993 MVP	3.00	.90
❑ 476D	B.Bonds MM 1990 MVP	3.00	.90
❑ 476E	B.Bonds MM 1992 MVP	3.00	.90
❑ 477A	S.Sosa MM 20 HR June	2.00	.60
❑ 477B	S.Sosa MM 66 HR 1998	2.00	.60
❑ 477C	S.Sosa MM 60 HR 1999	2.00	.60
❑ 477D	S.Sosa MM 1998 MVP	2.00	.60
❑ 477E	S.Sosa MM HR's 61/62	2.00	.60
❑ 478A	D.Jeter MM 1996 ROY	3.00	.90
❑ 478B	D.Jeter MM Wins 1999 WS	3.00	.90
❑ 478C	D.Jeter MM Wins 1998 WS	3.00	.90
❑ 478D	D.Jeter MM Wins 1996 WS	3.00	.90
❑ 478E	D.Jeter MM 17 GM Hit Streak	3.00	.90
❑ 479A	A.Rodriguez MM 40HR/40SB	2.00	.60
❑ 479B	A.Rodriguez MM 100th HR	2.00	.60
❑ 479C	A.Rodriguez MM 1996 POY	2.00	.60
❑ 479D	A.Rodriguez MM Wins 1 Million	2.00	.60
❑ 479E	A.Rodriguez MM 1996 Batting Leader	2.00	.60
❑ NNO	M. McGwire 85 Reprint	5.00	1.50

2000 Topps Traded

	Nm-Mt	Ex-Mt
COMP.FACT.SET (136)	50.00	15.00
COMPLETE SET (135)	30.00	9.00
FACT.SET PRICE IS FOR SEALED SETS		.00

Card	Player	Nm-Mt	Ex-Mt
❑ T1	Mike MacDougal	.30	.09
❑ T2	Andy Tracy RC	.30	.09
❑ T3	Brandon Phillips RC	.50	.15
❑ T4	Brandon Inge RC	.75	.23
❑ T5	Robbie Morrison RC	.30	.09
❑ T6	Josh Pressley RC	.30	.09
❑ T7	Todd Moser RC	.30	.09
❑ T8	Rob Purvis	.30	.09
❑ T9	Chance Caple	.20	.06
❑ T10	Ben Sheets	1.25	.35
❑ T11	Russ Jacobson RC	.30	.09
❑ T12	Brian Cole RC	.30	.09
❑ T13	Brad Baker	.30	.09
❑ T14	Alex Cintron RC	.30	.09
❑ T15	Lyle Overbay RC	.75	.23
❑ T16	Mike Edwards RC	.30	.09
❑ T17	Sean McGowan RC	.30	.09
❑ T18	Jose Molina	.20	.06
❑ T19	Marcos Castillo RC	.30	.09
❑ T20	Josue Espada RC	.30	.09
❑ T21	Alex Gordon RC	.30	.09
❑ T22	Rob Pugmire RC	.30	.09
❑ T23	Jason Stumm	.20	.06
❑ T24	Ty Howington	.30	.09
❑ T25	Brett Myers	.75	.23
❑ T26	Maicer Izturis RC	.50	.15
❑ T27	John McDonald	.20	.06
❑ T28	W.Rodriguez RC	.30	.09
❑ T29	Carlos Zambrano RC	2.50	.75
❑ T30	Alejandro Diaz RC	.30	.09
❑ T31	Geraldo Guzman RC	.30	.09
❑ T32	J.R. House RC	.30	.09
❑ T33	Elvin Nina RC	.30	.09
❑ T34	Juan Pierre RC	.75	.23
❑ T35	Ben Johnson RC	.30	.09
❑ T36	Jeff Bailey RC	.30	.09
❑ T37	Miguel Olivo RC	.50	.15
❑ T38	F.Rodriguez RC	1.50	.45
❑ T39	Tony Pena Jr. RC	.30	.09
❑ T40	Miguel Cabrera RC	20.00	6.00
❑ T41	Asdrubal Oropeza RC	.30	.09
❑ T42	Junior Zamora RC	.30	.09
❑ T43	Jovanny Cedeno RC	.30	.09
❑ T44	John Sneed	.30	.09
❑ T45	Josh Kalinowski	.30	.09
❑ T46	Mike Young RC	3.00	.90
❑ T47	Rico Washington RC	.30	.09
❑ T48	Chad Durbin RC	.30	.09
❑ T49	Junior Brignac RC	.30	.09
❑ T50	Carlos Hernandez RC	.30	.09
❑ T51	Cesar Izturis RC	1.00	.30
❑ T52	Oscar Salazar RC	.30	.09
❑ T53	Pat Strange RC	.30	.09
❑ T54	Rick Asadoorian	.30	.09
❑ T55	Keith Reed	.30	.09
❑ T56	Leo Estrella RC	.30	.09
❑ T57	Wascar Serrano RC	.30	.09
❑ T58	Richard Gomez RC	.30	.09
❑ T59	Ramon Santiago RC	.30	.09
❑ T60	Jovanny Sosa RC	.30	.09
❑ T61	Aaron Rowand RC	1.25	.35
❑ T62	Junior Guerrero RC	.30	.09
❑ T63	Luis Terrero RC	.50	.15
❑ T64	Brian Sanches RC	.30	.09
❑ T65	Scott Sobkowiak RC	.30	.09
❑ T66	Gary Majewski RC	.50	.15
❑ T67	Barry Zito	1.25	.35
❑ T68	Ryan Christianson	.30	.09
❑ T69	Cristian Guerrero RC	.30	.09
❑ T70	T.De La Rosa RC	.30	.09
❑ T71	Andrew Beinbrink RC	.30	.09
❑ T72	Ryan Knox RC	.30	.09
❑ T73	Alex Graman RC	.30	.09
❑ T74	Juan Guzman RC	.30	.09
❑ T75	Ruben Salazar RC	.30	.09
❑ T76	Luis Matos RC	.30	.09
❑ T77	Tony Mota RC	.30	.09
❑ T78	Doug Davis	.30	.09
❑ T79	Ben Christensen	.20	.06
❑ T80	Mike Lamb	.50	.15
❑ T81	Adrian Gonzalez RC	.50	.15
❑ T82	Mike Stodolka RC	.30	.09
❑ T83	Adam Johnson RC	.30	.09
❑ T84	Matt Wheatland RC	.30	.09
❑ T85	Corey Smith RC	.30	.09
❑ T86	Rocco Baldelli RC	1.50	.45
❑ T87	Keith Bucktrot RC	.30	.09
❑ T88	Adam Wainwright RC	.50	.15
❑ T89	Scott Thorman RC	.30	.09
❑ T90	Tripper Johnson RC	.30	.09
❑ T91	Jim Edmonds Cards	.50	.15
❑ T92	Masato Yoshii	.20	.06
❑ T93	Adam Kennedy	.20	.06
❑ T94	Darryl Kile	.30	.09
❑ T95	Mark McLemore	.20	.06
❑ T96	Ricky Gutierrez	.20	.06
❑ T97	Juan Gonzalez	.30	.09
❑ T98	Melvin Mora	.30	.09
❑ T99	Dante Bichette	.30	.09
❑ T100	Lee Stevens	.20	.06
❑ T101	Roger Cedeno	.20	.06
❑ T102	John Olerud	.30	.09
❑ T103	Eric Young	.20	.06
❑ T104	Mickey Morandini	.20	.06
❑ T105	Travis Lee	.20	.06
❑ T106	Greg Vaughn	.20	.06
❑ T107	Todd Zeile	.30	.09
❑ T108	Chuck Finley	.30	.09
❑ T109	Ismael Valdes	.20	.06
❑ T110	Reggie Sanders	.30	.09
❑ T111	Pat Hentgen	.20	.06
❑ T112	Ryan Klesko	.30	.09
❑ T113	Derek Bell	.20	.06
❑ T114	Hideo Nomo	.75	.23
❑ T115	Aaron Sele	.20	.06
❑ T116	Fernando Vina	.20	.06
❑ T117	Wally Joyner	.30	.09
❑ T118	Brian Hunter	.20	.06
❑ T119	Joe Girardi	.20	.06
❑ T120	Omar Daal	.20	.06
❑ T121	Brook Fordyce	.20	.06
❑ T122	Jose Valentin	.20	.06
❑ T123	Curt Schilling	.30	.09
❑ T124	B.J. Surhoff	.30	.09
❑ T125	Henry Rodriguez	.20	.06
❑ T126	Mike Bordick	.20	.06
❑ T127	David Justice	.30	.09
❑ T128	Charles Johnson	.30	.09
❑ T129	Will Clark	.50	.15
❑ T130	Dwight Gooden	.30	.09
❑ T131	David Segui	.20	.06
❑ T132	Denny Neagle	.30	.09
❑ T133	Jose Canseco	.50	.15
❑ T134	Bruce Chen	.20	.06
❑ T135	Jason Bere	.20	.06

2001 Topps

	Nm-Mt	Ex-Mt
COMPLETE SET (790)	80.00	24.00
COMP.FACT.BLUE SET (795)	120.00	36.00
COMP.SERIES 1 (405)	40.00	12.00
COMP. SERIES 2 (385)	40.00	12.00
COMMON (1-6/8-791)	.20	.06
COMMON (352-376/727-751)	.25	.07

Card	Player	Nm-Mt	Ex-Mt
❑ 1	Cal Ripken	1.50	.45
❑ 2	Chipper Jones	.50	.15

❑	3	Roger Cedeno	.20	.06
❑	4	Garret Anderson	.20	.06
❑	5	Robin Ventura	.20	.06
❑	6	Daryle Ward	.20	.06
❑	7	Does Not Exist	.00	
❑	8	Craig Paquette	.20	.06
❑	9	Phil Nevin	.20	.06
❑	10	Jermaine Dye	.20	.06
❑	11	Chris Singleton	.20	.06
❑	12	Mike Stanton	.20	.06
❑	13	Brian Hunter	.20	.06
❑	14	Mike Redmond	.20	.06
❑	15	Jim Thome	.30	.09
❑	16	Brian Jordan	.20	.06
❑	17	Joe Girardi	.20	.06
❑	18	Steve Woodard	.20	.06
❑	19	Dustin Hermanson	.20	.06
❑	20	Shawn Green	.20	.06
❑	21	Todd Stottlemyre	.20	.06
❑	22	Dan Wilson	.20	.06
❑	23	Todd Pratt	.20	.06
❑	24	Derek Lowe	.20	.06
❑	25	Juan Gonzalez	.20	.06
❑	26	Clay Bellinger	.20	.06
❑	27	Jeff Fassero	.20	.06
❑	28	Pat Meares	.20	.06
❑	29	Eddie Taubensee	.20	.06
❑	30	Paul O'Neill	.30	.09
❑	31	Jeffrey Hammonds	.20	.06
❑	32	Pokey Reese	.20	.06
❑	33	Mike Mussina	.30	.09
❑	34	Rico Brogna	.20	.06
❑	35	Jay Buhner	.20	.06
❑	36	Steve Cox	.20	.06
❑	37	Quilvio Veras	.20	.06
❑	38	Marquis Grissom	.20	.06
❑	39	Shigetoshi Hasegawa	.20	.06
❑	40	Shane Reynolds	.20	.06
❑	41	Adam Piatt	.20	.06
❑	42	Luis Polonia	.20	.06
❑	43	Brook Fordyce	.20	.06
❑	44	Preston Wilson	.20	.06
❑	45	Ellis Burks	.20	.06
❑	46	Armando Rios	.20	.06
❑	47	Chuck Finley	.20	.06
❑	48	Dan Plesac	.20	.06
❑	49	Shannon Stewart	.20	.06
❑	50	Mark McGwire	1.25	.35
❑	51	Mark Loretta	.20	.06
❑	52	Gerald Williams	.20	.06
❑	53	Eric Young	.20	.06
❑	54	Peter Bergeron	.20	.06
❑	55	Dave Hansen	.20	.06
❑	56	Arthur Rhodes	.20	.06
❑	57	Bobby Jones	.20	.06
❑	58	Matt Clement	.20	.06
❑	59	Mike Benjamin	.20	.06
❑	60	Pedro Martinez	.30	.09
❑	61	Jose Canseco	.30	.09
❑	62	Matt Anderson	.20	.06
❑	63	Torii Hunter	.20	.06
❑	64	Carlos Lee UER 1999 Charlotte Games Played are wrong	.20	.06
❑	65	David Cone	.20	.06
❑	66	Rey Sanchez	.20	.06
❑	67	Eric Chavez	.20	.06
❑	68	Rick Helling	.20	.06
❑	69	Manny Alexander	.20	.06
❑	70	John Franco	.20	.06
❑	71	Mike Bordick	.20	.06
❑	72	Andres Galarraga	.20	.06
❑	73	Jose Cruz Jr.	.20	.06
❑	74	Mike Matheny	.20	.06
❑	75	Randy Johnson	.50	.15
❑	76	Richie Sexson	.20	.06
❑	77	Vladimir Nunez	.20	.06
❑	78	Harold Baines	.20	.06
❑	79	Aaron Boone	.20	.06
❑	80	Darin Erstad	.20	.06
❑	81	Alex Gonzalez	.20	.06
❑	82	Gil Heredia	.20	.06
❑	83	Shane Andrews	.20	.06
❑	84	Todd Hundley	.20	.06
❑	85	Bill Mueller	.20	.06
❑	86	Mark McLemore	.20	.06
❑	87	Scott Spiezio	.20	.06
❑	88	Kevin McGlinchy	.20	.06
❑	89	Bubba Trammell	.20	.06
❑	90	Manny Ramirez	.30	.09
❑	91	Mike Lamb	.20	.06
❑	92	Scott Karl	.20	.06
❑	93	Brian Buchanan	.20	.06
❑	94	Chris Turner	.20	.06
❑	95	Mike Sweeney	.20	.06
❑	96	John Wetteland	.20	.06
❑	97	Rob Bell	.20	.06
❑	98	Pat Rapp	.20	.06
❑	99	John Burkett	.20	.06
❑	100	Derek Jeter	1.25	.35
❑	101	J.D. Drew	.20	.06
❑	102	Jose Offerman	.20	.06
❑	103	Rick Reed	.20	.06
❑	104	Will Clark	.30	.09
❑	105	Rickey Henderson	.50	.15
❑	106	Dave Berg	.20	.06
❑	107	Kirk Rueter	.20	.06
❑	108	Lee Stevens	.20	.06
❑	109	Jay Bell	.20	.06
❑	110	Fred McGriff	.30	.09
❑	111	Julio Zuleta	.20	.06
❑	112	Brian Anderson	.20	.06
❑	113	Orlando Cabrera	.20	.06
❑	114	Alex Fernandez	.20	.06
❑	115	Derek Bell	.20	.06
❑	116	Eric Owens	.20	.06
❑	117	Brian Bohanon	.20	.06
❑	118	Dennys Reyes	.20	.06
❑	119	Mike Stanley	.20	.06
❑	120	Jorge Posada	.30	.09
❑	121	Rich Becker	.20	.06
❑	122	Paul Konerko	.20	.06
❑	123	Mike Remlinger	.20	.06
❑	124	Travis Lee	.20	.06
❑	125	Ken Caminiti	.20	.06
❑	126	Kevin Barker	.20	.06
❑	127	Paul Quantrill	.20	.06
❑	128	Ozzie Guillen	.20	.06
❑	129	Kevin Tapani	.20	.06
❑	130	Mark Johnson	.20	.06
❑	131	Randy Wolf	.20	.06
❑	132	Michael Tucker	.20	.06
❑	133	Darren Lewis	.20	.06
❑	134	Joe Randa	.20	.06
❑	135	Jeff Cirillo	.20	.06
❑	136	David Ortiz	.30	.09
❑	137	Herb Perry	.20	.06
❑	138	Jeff Nelson	.20	.06
❑	139	Chris Stynes	.20	.06
❑	140	Johnny Damon	.30	.09
❑	141	Jeff Reboulet	.20	.06
❑	142	Jason Schmidt	.20	.06
❑	143	Charles Johnson	.20	.06
❑	144	Pat Burrell	.20	.06
❑	145	Gary Sheffield	.20	.06
❑	146	Tom Glavine	.30	.09
❑	147	Jason Isringhausen	.20	.06
❑	148	Chris Carpenter	.20	.06
❑	149	Jeff Suppan	.20	.06
❑	150	Ivan Rodriguez	.30	.09
❑	151	Luis Sojo	.20	.06
❑	152	Ron Villone	.20	.06
❑	153	Mike Sirotka	.20	.06
❑	154	Chuck Knoblauch	.20	.06
❑	155	Jason Kendall	.20	.06
❑	156	Dennis Cook	.20	.06
❑	157	Bobby Estalella	.20	.06
❑	158	Jose Guillen	.20	.06
❑	159	Thomas Howard	.20	.06
❑	160	Carlos Delgado	.20	.06
❑	161	Benji Gil	.20	.06
❑	162	Tim Bogar	.20	.06
❑	163	Kevin Elster	.20	.06
❑	164	Einar Diaz	.20	.06
❑	165	Andy Benes	.20	.06
❑	166	Adrian Beltre	.20	.06
❑	167	David Bell	.20	.06
❑	168	Turk Wendell	.20	.06
❑	169	Pete Harnisch	.20	.06
❑	170	Roger Clemens	1.00	.30
❑	171	Scott Williamson	.20	.06
❑	172	Kevin Jordan	.20	.06
❑	173	Brad Penny	.20	.06
❑	174	John Flaherty	.20	.06
❑	175	Troy Glaus	.20	.06
❑	176	Kevin Appier	.20	.06
❑	177	Walt Weiss	.20	.06
❑	178	Tyler Houston	.20	.06
❑	179	Michael Barrett	.20	.06
❑	180	Mike Hampton	.20	.06
❑	181	Francisco Cordova	.20	.06
❑	182	Mike Jackson	.20	.06
❑	183	David Segui	.20	.06
❑	184	Carlos Febles	.20	.06
❑	185	Roy Halladay	.20	.06
❑	186	Seth Etherton	.20	.06
❑	187	Charlie Hayes	.20	.06
❑	188	Fernando Tatis	.20	.06
❑	189	Steve Trachsel	.20	.06
❑	190	Livan Hernandez	.20	.06
❑	191	Joe Oliver	.20	.06
❑	192	Stan Javier	.20	.06
❑	193	B.J. Surhoff	.20	.06
❑	194	Rob Ducey	.20	.06
❑	195	Barry Larkin	.30	.09
❑	196	Danny Patterson	.20	.06
❑	197	Bobby Howry	.20	.06
❑	198	Dmitri Young	.20	.06
❑	199	Brian Hunter	.20	.06
❑	200	Alex Rodriguez	.75	.23
❑	201	Hideo Nomo	.50	.15
❑	202	Luis Alicea	.20	.06
❑	203	Warren Morris	.20	.06
❑	204	Antonio Alfonseca	.20	.06
❑	205	Edgardo Alfonzo	.20	.06
❑	206	Mark Grudzielanek	.20	.06
❑	207	Fernando Vina	.20	.06
❑	208	Willie Greene	.20	.06
❑	209	Homer Bush	.20	.06
❑	210	Jason Giambi	.20	.06
❑	211	Mike Morgan	.20	.06
❑	212	Steve Karsay	.20	.06
❑	213	Matt Lawton	.20	.06
❑	214	Wendell Magee Jr.	.20	.06
❑	215	Rusty Greer	.20	.06
❑	216	Keith Lockhart	.20	.06
❑	217	Billy Koch	.20	.06
❑	218	Todd Hollandsworth	.20	.06
❑	219	Raul Ibanez	.20	.06
❑	220	Tony Gwynn	.60	.18
❑	221	Carl Everett	.20	.06
❑	222	Hector Carrasco	.20	.06
❑	223	Jose Valentin	.20	.06
❑	224	Deivi Cruz	.20	.06
❑	225	Bret Boone	.20	.06
❑	226	Kurt Abbott	.20	.06
❑	227	Melvin Mora	.20	.06
❑	228	Danny Graves	.20	.06
❑	229	Jose Jimenez	.20	.06
❑	230	James Baldwin	.20	.06
❑	231	C.J. Nitkowski	.20	.06
❑	232	Jeff Zimmerman	.20	.06
❑	233	Mike Lowell	.20	.06
❑	234	Hideki Irabu	.20	.06
❑	235	Greg Vaughn	.20	.06
❑	236	Omar Daal	.20	.06
❑	237	Darren Dreifort	.20	.06
❑	238	Gil Meche	.20	.06
❑	239	Damian Jackson	.20	.06
❑	240	Frank Thomas	.50	.15

❑ 241 Travis Miller .20 .06
❑ 242 Jeff Frye .20 .06
❑ 243 Dave Magadan .20 .06
❑ 244 Luis Castillo .20 .06
❑ 245 Bartolo Colon .20 .06
❑ 246 Steve Kline .20 .06
❑ 247 Shawon Dunston .20 .06
❑ 248 Rick Aguilera .20 .06
❑ 249 Omar Olivares .20 .06
❑ 250 Craig Biggio .30 .09
❑ 251 Scott Schoeneweis .20 .06
❑ 252 Dave Veres .20 .06
❑ 253 Ramon Martinez .20 .06
❑ 254 Jose Vidro .20 .06
❑ 255 Todd Helton .30 .09
❑ 256 Greg Norton .20 .06
❑ 257 Jacque Jones .20 .06
❑ 258 Jason Grimsley .20 .06
❑ 259 Dan Reichert .20 .06
❑ 260 Robb Nen .20 .06
❑ 261 Mark Clark .20 .06
❑ 262 Scott Hatteberg .20 .06
❑ 263 Doug Brocail .20 .06
❑ 264 Mark Johnson .20 .06
❑ 265 Eric Davis .20 .06
❑ 266 Terry Shumpert .20 .06
❑ 267 Kevin Millar .20 .06
❑ 268 Ismael Valdes .20 .06
❑ 269 Richard Hidalgo .20 .06
❑ 270 Randy Velarde .20 .06
❑ 271 Bengie Molina .20 .06
❑ 272 Tony Womack .20 .06
❑ 273 Enrique Wilson .20 .06
❑ 274 Jeff Brantley .20 .06
❑ 275 Rick Ankiel .20 .06
❑ 276 Terry Mulholland .20 .06
❑ 277 Ron Belliard .20 .06
❑ 278 Terrence Long .20 .06
❑ 279 Alberto Castillo .20 .06
❑ 280 Royce Clayton .20 .06
❑ 281 Joe McEwing .20 .06
❑ 282 Jason McDonald .20 .06
❑ 283 Ricky Bottalico .20 .06
❑ 284 Keith Foulke .20 .06
❑ 285 Brad Radke .20 .06
❑ 286 Gabe Kapler .20 .06
❑ 287 Pedro Astacio .20 .06
❑ 288 Armando Reynoso .20 .06
❑ 289 Darryl Kile .20 .06
❑ 290 Reggie Sanders .20 .06
❑ 291 Esteban Yan .20 .06
❑ 292 Joe Nathan .20 .06
❑ 293 Jay Payton .20 .06
❑ 294 Francisco Cordero .20 .06
❑ 295 Gregg Jefferies .20 .06
❑ 296 LaTroy Hawkins .20 .06
❑ 297 Jeff Tam RC .40 .12
❑ 298 Jacob Cruz .20 .06
❑ 299 Chris Holt .20 .06
❑ 300 Vladimir Guerrero .50 .15
❑ 301 Marvin Benard .20 .06
❑ 302 Alex Ramirez .20 .06
❑ 303 Mike Williams .20 .06
❑ 304 Sean Bergman .20 .06
❑ 305 Juan Encarnacion .20 .06
❑ 306 Russ Davis .20 .06
❑ 307 Hanley Frias .20 .06
❑ 308 Ramon Hernandez .20 .06
❑ 309 Matt Walbeck .20 .06
❑ 310 Bill Spiers .20 .06
❑ 311 Bob Wickman .20 .06
❑ 312 Sandy Alomar Jr. .20 .06
❑ 313 Eddie Guardado .20 .06
❑ 314 Shane Halter .20 .06
❑ 315 Geoff Jenkins .20 .06
❑ 316 Brian Meadows .20 .06
❑ 317 Damian Miller .20 .06
❑ 318 Darrin Fletcher .20 .06
❑ 319 Rafael Furcal .20 .06
❑ 320 Mark Grace .30 .09
❑ 321 Mark Mulder .20 .06
❑ 322 Joe Torre MG .30 .09
❑ 323 Bobby Cox MG .20 .06
❑ 324 Mike Scioscia MG .20 .06
❑ 325 Mike Hargrove MG .20 .06
❑ 326 Jimy Williams MG .20 .06
❑ 327 Jerry Manuel MG .20 .06
❑ 328 Buck Showalter MG .20 .06
❑ 329 Charlie Manuel MG .20 .06
❑ 330 Don Baylor MG .20 .06
❑ 331 Phil Garner MG .20 .06
❑ 332 Jack McKeon MG .20 .06
❑ 333 Tony Muser MG .20 .06
❑ 334 Buddy Bell MG .20 .06
❑ 335 Tom Kelly MG .20 .06
❑ 336 John Boles MG .20 .06
❑ 337 Art Howe MG .20 .06
❑ 338 Larry Dierker MG .20 .06
❑ 339 Lou Piniella MG .20 .06
❑ 340 Davey Johnson MG .20 .06
❑ 341 Larry Rothschild MG .20 .06
❑ 342 Davey Lopes MG .20 .06
❑ 343 Johnny Oates MG .20 .06
❑ 344 Felipe Alou MG .20 .06
❑ 345 Jim Fregosi MG .20 .06
❑ 346 Bobby Valentine MG .20 .06
❑ 347 Terry Francona MG .20 .06
❑ 348 Gene Lamont MG .20 .06
❑ 349 Tony LaRussa MG .20 .06
❑ 350 Bruce Bochy MG .20 .06
❑ 351 Dusty Baker MG .20 .06
❑ 352 Adrian Gonzalez .25 .07
Adam Johnson
❑ 353 Matt Wheatland .25 .07
Bryan Digby
❑ 354 Tripper Johnson .25 .07
Scott Thorman
❑ 355 Phil Dumatrait .25 .07
Adam Wainwright
❑ 356 Scott Heard .40 .12
David Parrish RC
❑ 357 Rocco Baldelli .40 .12
Mark Folsom RC
❑ 358 Dominic Rich RC .40 .12
Aaron Herr
❑ 359 Mike Stodolka .25 .07
Sean Burnett
❑ 360 Derek Thompson .25 .07
Corey Smith
❑ 361 Danny Borrell RC .40 .12
Jason Bourgeois RC
❑ 362 Chin-Feng Chen .25 .07
Corey Patterson
Josh Hamilton
❑ 363 Ryan Anderson .50 .15
Barry Zito
C.C. Sabathia
❑ 364 Scott Sobkowiak .50 .15
David Walling
Ben Sheets
❑ 365 Ty Howington .25 .07
Josh Kalinowski
Josh Girdley
❑ 366 Hee Seop Choi RC .75 .23
Aaron McNeal
Jason Hart
❑ 367 Bobby Bradley .40 .12
Kurt Ainsworth
Chin-Hui Tsao
❑ 368 Mike Glendenning .25 .07
Kenny Kelly
Juan Silvestre
❑ 369 J.R. House .25 .07
Ramon Castro
Ben Davis
❑ 370 Chance Caple .40 .12
Rafael Soriano RC
Pasqual Coco
❑ 371 Travis Hafner RC 3.00 .90
Eric Munson
Bucky Jacobsen
❑ 372 Jason Conti .25 .07
Chris Wakeland
Brian Cole
❑ 373 Scott Seabol .75 .23
Aubrey Huff
Joe Crede
❑ 374 Adam Everett .25 .07
Jose Ortiz
Keith Ginter
❑ 375 Carlos Hernandez .25 .07
Geraldo Guzman
Adam Eaton
❑ 376 Bobby Kielty .40 .12
Milton Bradley
Juan Rivera
❑ 377 Mark McGwire GM .60 .18
❑ 378 Don Larsen GM .20 .06
❑ 379 Bobby Thomson GM .20 .06
❑ 380 Bill Mazeroski GM .20 .06
❑ 381 Reggie Jackson GM .30 .09
❑ 382 Kirk Gibson GM .30 .09
❑ 383 Roger Maris GM .30 .09
❑ 384 Cal Ripken GM .75 .23
❑ 385 Hank Aaron GM .50 .15
❑ 386 Joe Carter GM .20 .06
❑ 387 Cal Ripken SH 1.50 .45
❑ 388 Randy Johnson SH .30 .09
❑ 389 Ken Griffey Jr. SH .75 .23
❑ 390 Troy Glaus SH .20 .06
❑ 391 Kazuhiro Sasaki SH .20 .06
❑ 392 Sammy Sosa LL .30 .09
Troy Glaus
❑ 393 Todd Helton LL .20 .06
Edgar Martinez
❑ 394 Todd Helton LL .50 .15
Nomar Garicaparra
❑ 395 Barry Bonds LL .75 .23
Jason Giambi
❑ 396 Todd Helton LL .20 .06
Manny Ramirez
❑ 397 Todd Helton LL .20 .06
Darin Erstad
❑ 398 Kevin Brown LL .30 .09
Pedro Martinez
❑ 399 Randy Johnson LL .30 .09
Pedro Martinez
❑ 400 Will Clark HL .30 .09
❑ 401 New York Mets HL .50 .15
❑ 402 New York Yankees HL .75 .23
❑ 403 Seattle Mariners HL .20 .06
❑ 404 Mike Hampton HL .20 .06
❑ 405 New York Yankees HL 1.00 .30
❑ 406 N.Y. Yankees Champs 2.00 .60
❑ 407 Jeff Bagwell .30 .09
❑ 408 Brant Brown .20 .06
❑ 409 Brad Fullmer .20 .06
❑ 410 Dean Palmer .20 .06
❑ 411 Greg Zaun .20 .06
❑ 412 Jose Vizcaino .20 .06
❑ 413 Jeff Abbott .20 .06
❑ 414 Travis Fryman .20 .06
❑ 415 Mike Cameron .20 .06
❑ 416 Matt Mantei .20 .06
❑ 417 Alan Benes .20 .06
❑ 418 Mickey Morandini .20 .06
❑ 419 Troy Percival .20 .06
❑ 420 Eddie Perez .20 .06
❑ 421 Vernon Wells .20 .06
❑ 422 Ricky Gutierrez .20 .06
❑ 423 Carlos Hernandez .20 .06
❑ 424 Chan Ho Park .20 .06
❑ 425 Armando Benitez .20 .06
❑ 426 Sidney Ponson .20 .06
❑ 427 Adrian Brown .20 .06
❑ 428 Ruben Mateo .20 .06
❑ 429 Alex Ochoa .20 .06
❑ 430 Jose Rosado .20 .06
❑ 431 Masato Yoshii .20 .06
❑ 432 Corey Koskie .20 .06
❑ 433 Andy Pettitte .30 .09
❑ 434 Brian Daubach .20 .06
❑ 435 Sterling Hitchcock .20 .06
❑ 436 Timo Perez .20 .06
❑ 437 Shawn Estes .20 .06
❑ 438 Tony Armas Jr. .20 .06
❑ 439 Danny Bautista .20 .06
❑ 440 Randy Winn .20 .06
❑ 441 Wilson Alvarez .20 .06
❑ 442 Rondell White .20 .06
❑ 443 Jeromy Burnitz .20 .06
❑ 444 Kelvim Escobar .20 .06
❑ 445 Paul Bako .20 .06
❑ 446 Javier Vazquez .20 .06
❑ 447 Eric Gagne .20 .06
❑ 448 Kenny Lofton .20 .06
❑ 449 Mark Kotsay .20 .06
❑ 450 Jamie Moyer .20 .06

❑ 451 Delino DeShields .20 .06
❑ 452 Rey Ordonez .20 .06
❑ 453 Russ Ortiz .20 .06
❑ 454 Dave Burba .20 .06
❑ 455 Eric Karros .20 .06
❑ 456 Felix Martinez .20 .06
❑ 457 Tony Batista .20 .06
❑ 458 Bobby Higginson .20 .06
❑ 459 Jeff D'Amico .20 .06
❑ 460 Shane Spencer .20 .06
❑ 461 Brent Mayne .20 .06
❑ 462 Glendon Rusch .20 .06
❑ 463 Chris Gomez .20 .06
❑ 464 Jeff Shaw .20 .06
❑ 465 Damon Buford .20 .06
❑ 466 Mike DiFelice .20 .06
❑ 467 Jimmy Haynes .20 .06
❑ 468 Billy Wagner .20 .06
❑ 469 A.J. Hinch .20 .06
❑ 470 Gary DiSarcina .20 .06
❑ 471 Tom Lampkin .20 .06
❑ 472 Adam Eaton .20 .06
❑ 473 Brian Giles .20 .06
❑ 474 John Thomson .20 .06
❑ 475 Cal Eldred .20 .06
❑ 476 Ramiro Mendoza .20 .06
❑ 477 Scott Sullivan .20 .06
❑ 478 Scott Rolen .30 .09
❑ 479 Todd Ritchie .20 .06
❑ 480 Pablo Ozuna .20 .06
❑ 481 Carl Pavano .20 .06
❑ 482 Matt Morris .20 .06
❑ 483 Matt Stairs .20 .06
❑ 484 Tim Belcher .20 .06
❑ 485 Lance Berkman .20 .06
❑ 486 Brian Meadows .20 .06
❑ 487 Bob Abreu .20 .06
❑ 488 John VanderWal .20 .06
❑ 489 Donnie Sadler .20 .06
❑ 490 Damion Easley .20 .06
❑ 491 David Justice .20 .06
❑ 492 Ray Durham .20 .06
❑ 493 Todd Zeile .20 .06
❑ 494 Desi Relaford .20 .06
❑ 495 Cliff Floyd .20 .06
❑ 496 Scott Downs .20 .06
❑ 497 Barry Bonds 1.25 .35
❑ 498 Jeff D'Amico .20 .06
❑ 499 Octavio Dotel .20 .06
❑ 500 Kent Mercker .20 .06
❑ 501 Craig Grebeck .20 .06
❑ 502 Roberto Hernandez .20 .06
❑ 503 Matt Williams .20 .06
❑ 504 Bruce Aven .20 .06
❑ 505 Brett Tomko .20 .06
❑ 506 Kris Benson .20 .06
❑ 507 Neifi Perez .20 .06
❑ 508 Alfonso Soriano .30 .09
❑ 509 Keith Osik .20 .06
❑ 510 Matt Franco .20 .06
❑ 511 Steve Finley .20 .06
❑ 512 Olmedo Saenz .20 .06
❑ 513 Esteban Loaiza .20 .06
❑ 514 Adam Kennedy .20 .06
❑ 515 Scott Elarton .20 .06
❑ 516 Moises Alou .20 .06
❑ 517 Bryan Rekar .20 .06
❑ 518 Darryl Hamilton .20 .06
❑ 519 Osvaldo Fernandez .20 .06
❑ 520 Kip Wells .20 .06
❑ 521 Bernie Williams .30 .09
❑ 522 Mike Darr .20 .06
❑ 523 Marlon Anderson .20 .06
❑ 524 Derrek Lee .30 .09
❑ 525 Ugueth Urbina .20 .06
❑ 526 Vinny Castilla .20 .06
❑ 527 David Wells .20 .06
❑ 528 Jason Marquis .20 .06
❑ 529 Orlando Palmeiro .20 .06
❑ 530 Carlos Perez .20 .06
❑ 531 J.T. Snow .20 .06
❑ 532 Al Leiter .20 .06
❑ 533 Jimmy Anderson .20 .06
❑ 534 Brett Laxton .20 .06
❑ 535 Butch Huskey .20 .06
❑ 536 Orlando Hernandez .20 .06
❑ 537 Magglio Ordonez .20 .06
❑ 538 Willie Blair .20 .06
❑ 539 Kevin Sefcik .20 .06
❑ 540 Chad Curtis .20 .06
❑ 541 John Halama .20 .06
❑ 542 Andy Fox .20 .06
❑ 543 Juan Guzman .20 .06
❑ 544 Frank Menechino RC .20 .06
❑ 545 Raul Mondesi .20 .06
❑ 546 Tim Salmon .30 .09
❑ 547 Ryan Rupe .20 .06
❑ 548 Jeff Reed .20 .06
❑ 549 Mike Mordecai .20 .06
❑ 550 Jeff Kent .20 .06
❑ 551 Wiki Gonzalez .20 .06
❑ 552 Kenny Rogers .20 .06
❑ 553 Kevin Young .20 .06
❑ 554 Brian Johnson .20 .06
❑ 555 Tom Goodwin .20 .06
❑ 556 Tony Clark UER .20 .06
0 games, 208 At-Bats
❑ 557 Mac Suzuki .20 .06
❑ 558 Brian Moehler .20 .06
❑ 559 Jim Parque .20 .06
❑ 560 Mariano Rivera .30 .09
❑ 561 Trot Nixon .20 .06
❑ 562 Mike Mussina .30 .09
❑ 563 Nelson Figueroa .20 .06
❑ 564 Alex Gonzalez .20 .06
❑ 565 Benny Agbayani .20 .06
❑ 566 Ed Sprague .20 .06
❑ 567 Scott Erickson .20 .06
❑ 568 Abraham Nunez .20 .06
❑ 569 Jerry DiPoto .20 .06
❑ 570 Sean Casey .30 .09
❑ 571 Wilton Veras .20 .06
❑ 572 Joe Mays .20 .06
❑ 573 Bill Simas .20 .06
❑ 574 Doug Glanville .20 .06
❑ 575 Scott Sauerbeck .20 .06
❑ 576 Ben Davis .20 .06
❑ 577 Jesus Sanchez .20 .06
❑ 578 Ricardo Rincon .20 .06
❑ 579 John Olerud .20 .06
❑ 580 Curt Schilling .20 .06
❑ 581 Alex Cora .20 .06
❑ 582 Pat Hentgen .20 .06
❑ 583 Javy Lopez .20 .06
❑ 584 Ben Grieve .20 .06
❑ 585 Frank Castillo .20 .06
❑ 586 Kevin Stocker .20 .06
❑ 587 Mark Sweeney .20 .06
❑ 588 Ray Lankford .20 .06
❑ 589 Turner Ward .20 .06
❑ 590 Felipe Crespo .20 .06
❑ 591 Omar Vizquel .30 .09
❑ 592 Mike Lieberthal .20 .06
❑ 593 Ken Griffey Jr. .75 .23
❑ 594 Troy O'Leary .20 .06
❑ 595 Dave Mlicki .20 .06
❑ 596 Manny Ramirez Sox .30 .09
❑ 597 Mike Lansing .20 .06
❑ 598 Rich Aurilia .20 .06
❑ 599 Russell Branyan .20 .06
❑ 600 Russ Johnson .20 .06
❑ 601 Greg Colbrunn .20 .06
❑ 602 Andruw Jones .30 .09
❑ 603 Henry Blanco .20 .06
❑ 604 Jarrod Washburn .20 .06
❑ 605 Tony Eusebio .20 .06
❑ 606 Aaron Sele .20 .06
❑ 607 Charles Nagy .20 .06
❑ 608 Ryan Klesko .20 .06
❑ 609 Dante Bichette .20 .06
❑ 610 Bill Haselman .20 .06
❑ 611 Jerry Spradlin .20 .06
❑ 612 A. Rodriguez Rangers .75 .23
❑ 613 Jose Silva .20 .06
❑ 614 Darren Oliver .20 .06
❑ 615 Pat Mahomes .20 .06
❑ 616 Roberto Alomar .30 .09
❑ 617 Edgar Renteria .20 .06
❑ 618 Jon Lieber .20 .06
❑ 619 John Rocker .20 .06
❑ 620 Miguel Tejada .20 .06
❑ 621 Mo Vaughn .20 .06
❑ 622 Jose Lima .20 .06
❑ 623 Kerry Wood .20 .06
❑ 624 Mike Timlin .20 .06
❑ 625 Wil Cordero .20 .06
❑ 626 Albert Belle .20 .06
❑ 627 Bobby Jones .20 .06
❑ 628 Doug Mirabelli .20 .06
❑ 629 Jason Tyner .20 .06
❑ 630 Andy Ashby .20 .06
❑ 631 Jose Hernandez .20 .06
❑ 632 Devon White .20 .06
❑ 633 Ruben Rivera .20 .06
❑ 634 Steve Parris .20 .06
❑ 635 David McCarty .20 .06
❑ 636 Jose Canseco .30 .09
❑ 637 Todd Walker .20 .06
❑ 638 Stan Spencer .20 .06
❑ 639 Wayne Gomes .20 .06
❑ 640 Freddy Garcia .20 .06
❑ 641 Jeremy Giambi .20 .06
❑ 642 Luis Lopez .20 .06
❑ 643 John Smoltz .30 .09
❑ 644 Kelly Stinnett .20 .06
❑ 645 Kevin Brown .20 .06
❑ 646 Wilton Guerrero .20 .06
❑ 647 Al Martin .20 .06
❑ 648 Woody Williams .20 .06
❑ 649 Brian Rose .20 .06
❑ 650 Rafael Palmeiro .30 .09
❑ 651 Pete Schourek .20 .06
❑ 652 Kevin Jarvis .20 .06
❑ 653 Mark Redman .20 .06
❑ 654 Ricky Ledee .20 .06
❑ 655 Larry Walker .20 .06
❑ 656 Paul Byrd .20 .06
❑ 657 Jason Bere .20 .06
❑ 658 Rick White .20 .06
❑ 659 Calvin Murray .20 .06
❑ 660 Greg Maddux .75 .23
❑ 661 Ron Gant .20 .06
❑ 662 Eli Marrero .20 .06
❑ 663 Graeme Lloyd .20 .06
❑ 664 Trevor Hoffman .20 .06
❑ 665 Nomar Garciaparra .75 .23
❑ 666 Glenallen Hill .20 .06
❑ 667 Matt LeCroy .20 .06
❑ 668 Justin Thompson .20 .06
❑ 669 Brady Anderson .20 .06
❑ 670 Miguel Batista .20 .06
❑ 671 Erubiel Durazo .20 .06
❑ 672 Kevin Millwood .20 .06
❑ 673 Mitch Meluskey .20 .06
❑ 674 Luis Gonzalez .20 .06
❑ 675 Edgar Martinez .30 .09
❑ 676 Robert Person .20 .06
❑ 677 Benito Santiago .20 .06
❑ 678 Todd Jones .20 .06
❑ 679 Tino Martinez .30 .09
❑ 680 Carlos Beltran .20 .06
❑ 681 Gabe White .20 .06
❑ 682 Bret Saberhagen .20 .06
❑ 683 Jeff Conine .20 .06
❑ 684 Jaret Wright .20 .06
❑ 685 Bernard Gilkey .20 .06
❑ 686 Garrett Stephenson .20 .06
❑ 687 Jamey Wright .20 .06
❑ 688 Sammy Sosa .50 .15
❑ 689 John Jaha .20 .06
❑ 690 Ramon Martinez .20 .06
❑ 691 Robert Fick .20 .06
❑ 692 Eric Milton .20 .06
❑ 693 Denny Neagle .20 .06
❑ 694 Ron Coomer .20 .06
❑ 695 John Valentin .20 .06
❑ 696 Placido Polanco .20 .06
❑ 697 Tim Hudson .20 .06
❑ 698 Marty Cordova .20 .06
❑ 699 Chad Kreuter .20 .06
❑ 700 Frank Catalanotto .20 .06
❑ 701 Tim Wakefield .20 .06
❑ 702 Jim Edmonds .30 .09
❑ 703 Michael Tucker .20 .06
❑ 704 Cristian Guzman .20 .06
❑ 705 Joey Hamilton .20 .06
❑ 706 Mike Piazza .75 .23
❑ 707 Dave Martinez .20 .06

❑ 708	Mike Hampton	.20	.06
❑ 709	Bobby Bonilla	.20	.06
❑ 710	Juan Pierre	.20	.06
❑ 711	John Parrish	.20	.06
❑ 712	Kory DeHaan	.20	.06
❑ 713	Brian Tollberg	.20	.06
❑ 714	Chris Truby	.20	.06
❑ 715	Emil Brown	.20	.06
❑ 716	Ryan Dempster	.20	.06
❑ 717	Rich Garces	.20	.06
❑ 718	Mike Myers	.20	.06
❑ 719	Luis Ordaz	.20	.06
❑ 720	Kazuhiro Sasaki	.20	.06
❑ 721	Mark Quinn	.20	.06
❑ 722	Ramon Ortiz	.20	.06
❑ 723	Kerry Ligtenberg	.20	.06
❑ 724	Rolando Arrojo	.20	.06
❑ 725	Tsuyoshi Shinjo RC	.50	.15
❑ 726	Ichiro Suzuki RC	15.00	4.50
❑ 727	Roy Oswalt	.50	.15
	Pat Strange		
	Jon Rauch		
❑ 728	Phil Wilson RC	4.00	1.20
	Jake Peavy RC		
	Darwin Cubillan RC UER		
	Sic, Peavey		
❑ 729	Steve Smyth RC	.25	.07
	Mike Bynum		
	Nathan Haynes		
❑ 730	Michael Cuddyer	.25	.07
	Joe Lawrence		
	Choo Freeman		
❑ 731	Carlos Pena	.25	.07
	Larry Barnes		
	DeWayne Wise		
❑ 732	Travis Dawkins	.40	.12
	Erick Almonte		
	Felipe Lopez		
❑ 733	Alex Escobar	.25	.07
	Eric Valent		
	Brad Wilkerson		
❑ 734	Toby Hall	.25	.07
	Rod Barajas		
	Jeff Goldbach		
❑ 735	Jason Romano	.40	.12
	Marcus Giles		
	Pablo Ozuna		
❑ 736	Dee Brown	.40	.12
	Jack Cust		
	Vernon Wells		
❑ 737	David Espinosa	.40	.12
	Luis Montanez RC		
❑ 738	Anthony Pluta RC	.40	.12
	Justin Wayne RC		
❑ 739	Josh Axelson RC	.40	.12
	Carmen Cali RC		
❑ 740	Shaun Boyd RC	.40	.12
	Chris Morris RC		
❑ 741	Tommy Arko RC	.40	.12
	Dan Moylan RC		
❑ 742	Luis Cotto RC	.25	.07
	Luis Escobar		
❑ 743	Brandon Mims RC	.40	.12
	Blake Williams RC		
❑ 744	Chris Russ RC	.25	.07
	Bryan Edwards		
❑ 745	Joe Torres	.25	.07
	Ben Diggins		
❑ 746	Hugh Quattlebaum RC	2.00	.60
	Edwin Encarnacion RC		
❑ 747	Brian Bass RC	.40	.12
	Odannis Ayala RC		
❑ 748	Jason Kaanoi	.25	.07
	Michael Matthews RC UER		
	name misspelled Mathews		
❑ 749	Stuart McFarland RC	.40	.12
	Adam Sterrett RC		
❑ 750	David Krynzel	.50	.15
	Grady Sizemore		
❑ 751	Keith Bucktrot	.25	.07
	Dane Sardinha		
❑ 752	Anaheim Angels TC	.20	.06
❑ 753	Ariz. Diamondbacks TC	.20	.06
❑ 754	Atlanta Braves TC	.20	.06
❑ 755	Baltimore Orioles TC	.20	.06
❑ 756	Boston Red Sox TC	.20	.06
❑ 757	Chicago Cubs TC	.20	.06
❑ 758	Chicago White Sox TC	.20	.06
❑ 759	Cincinnati Reds TC	.20	.06
❑ 760	Cleveland Indians TC	.20	.06
❑ 761	Colorado Rockies TC	.20	.06
❑ 762	Detroit Tigers TC	.20	.06
❑ 763	Florida Marlins TC	.20	.06
❑ 764	Houston Astros TC	.20	.06
❑ 765	K.C. Royals TC	.20	.06
❑ 766	L.A. Dodgers TC	.20	.06
❑ 767	Milw. Brewers TC	.20	.06
❑ 768	Minnesota Twins TC	.20	.06
❑ 769	Montreal Expos TC	.20	.06
❑ 770	New York Mets TC	.20	.06
❑ 771	New York Yankees TC	1.00	.30
❑ 772	Oakland Athletics TC	.20	.06
❑ 773	Phil. Phillies TC	.20	.06
❑ 774	Pittsburgh Pirates TC	.20	.06
❑ 775	San Diego Padres TC	.20	.06
❑ 776	San Francisco Giants TC	.20	.06
❑ 777	Seattle Mariners TC	.20	.06
❑ 778	St. Louis Cardinals TC	.20	.06
❑ 779	T.B. Devil Rays TC	.20	.06
❑ 780	Texas Rangers TC	.20	.06
❑ 781	Toronto Blue Jays TC	.20	.06
❑ 782	Bucky Dent GM	.20	.06
❑ 783	Jackie Robinson GM	.50	.15
❑ 784	Roberto Clemente GM	.60	.18
❑ 785	Nolan Ryan GM	.75	.23
❑ 786	Kerry Wood GM	.20	.06
❑ 787	Rickey Henderson GM	.20	.06
❑ 788	Lou Brock GM	.30	.09
❑ 789	David Wells GM	.20	.06
❑ 790	Andruw Jones GM	.20	.06
❑ 791	Carlton Fisk GM	.20	.06
❑ TK	Bo Jackson	120.00	36.00
	Deion Sanders Bat		
❑ NNO	Bobby Thomson	50.00	15.00
	Ralph Branca		
	1991 Bowman Autograph		

2001 Topps Traded

	Nm-Mt	Ex-Mt
COMPLETE SET (265)	150.00	45.00
COMMON (T1-T99/T145-T265)	.40	.12
COMMON (100-144)	1.00	.30

❑ T1	Sandy Alomar Jr.	.40	.12
❑ T2	Kevin Appier	.50	.15
❑ T3	Brad Ausmus	.50	.15
❑ T4	Derek Bell	.40	.12
❑ T5	Bret Boone	.50	.15
❑ T6	Rico Brogna	.40	.12
❑ T7	Ellis Burks	.50	.15
❑ T8	Ken Caminiti	.50	.15
❑ T9	Roger Cedeno	.40	.12
❑ T10	Royce Clayton	.40	.12
❑ T11	Enrique Wilson	.40	.12
❑ T12	Rheal Cormier	.40	.12
❑ T13	Eric Davis	.50	.15
❑ T14	Shawon Dunston	.40	.12
❑ T15	Andres Galarraga	.50	.15
❑ T16	Tom Gordon	.40	.12
❑ T17	Mark Grace	.75	.23
❑ T18	Jeffrey Hammonds	.40	.12
❑ T19	Dustin Hermanson	.40	.12
❑ T20	Quinton McCracken	.40	.12
❑ T21	Todd Hundley	.40	.12
❑ T22	Charles Johnson	.50	.15
❑ T23	Marquis Grissom	.50	.15
❑ T24	Jose Mesa	.40	.12
❑ T25	Brian Boehringer	.40	.12
❑ T26	John Rocker	.50	.15
❑ T27	Jeff Frye	.40	.12
❑ T28	Reggie Sanders	.50	.15
❑ T29	David Segui	.40	.12
❑ T30	Mike Sirotka	.40	.12
❑ T31	Fernando Tatis	.40	.12
❑ T32	Steve Trachsel	.40	.12
❑ T33	Ismael Valdes	.40	.12
❑ T34	Randy Velarde	.40	.12
❑ T35	Ryan Kohlmeier	.40	.12
❑ T36	Mike Bordick	.50	.15
❑ T37	Kent Bottenfield	.40	.12
❑ T38	Pat Rapp	.40	.12
❑ T39	Jeff Nelson	.40	.12
❑ T40	Ricky Bottalico	.40	.12
❑ T41	Luke Prokopec	.40	.12
❑ T42	Hideo Nomo	1.25	.35
❑ T43	Bill Mueller	.50	.15
❑ T44	Roberto Kelly	.40	.12
❑ T45	Chris Holt	.40	.12
❑ T46	Mike Jackson	.40	.12
❑ T47	Devon White	.50	.15
❑ T48	Gerald Williams	.40	.12
❑ T49	Eddie Taubensee	.40	.12
❑ T50	Brian Hunter UER	.40	.12
	Brian R Hunter pictured		
	Brian L Hunter stats		
❑ T51	Nelson Cruz	.40	.12
❑ T52	Jeff Fassero	.40	.12
❑ T53	Bubba Trammell	.40	.12
❑ T54	Bo Porter	.40	.12
❑ T55	Greg Norton	.40	.12
❑ T56	Benito Santiago	.50	.15
❑ T57	Ruben Rivera	.40	.12
❑ T58	Dee Brown	.40	.12
❑ T59	Jose Canseco UER	.75	.23
	2000 strikeout totals are wrong		
❑ T60	Chris Michalak	.40	.12
❑ T61	Tim Worrell	.40	.12
❑ T62	Matt Clement	.50	.15
❑ T63	Bill Pulsipher	.40	.12
❑ T64	Troy Brohawn RC	.40	.12
❑ T65	Mark Kotsay	.50	.15
❑ T66	Jimmy Rollins	.50	.15
❑ T67	Shea Hillenbrand	.50	.15
❑ T68	Ted Lilly	.40	.12
❑ T69	Jermaine Dye	.50	.15
❑ T70	Jerry Hairston Jr.	.40	.12
❑ T71	John Mabry	.40	.12
❑ T72	Kurt Abbott	.40	.12
❑ T73	Eric Owens	.40	.12
❑ T74	Jeff Brantley	.40	.12
❑ T75	Roy Oswalt	.75	.23
❑ T76	Doug Mientkiewicz	.50	.15
❑ T77	Rickey Henderson	1.25	.35
❑ T78	Jason Grimsley	.40	.12
❑ T79	Christian Parker RC	.40	.12
❑ T80	Donne Wall	.40	.12
❑ T81	Alex Arias	.40	.12
❑ T82	Willis Roberts	.40	.12
❑ T83	Ryan Minor	.40	.12
❑ T84	Jason LaRue	.40	.12
❑ T85	Ruben Sierra	.40	.12
❑ T86	Johnny Damon	.75	.23
❑ T87	Juan Gonzalez	.50	.15
❑ T88	C.C. Sabathia	.50	.15
❑ T89	Tony Batista	.40	.12
❑ T90	Jay Witasick	.40	.12
❑ T91	Brent Abernathy	.40	.12
❑ T92	Paul LoDuca	.50	.15
❑ T93	Wes Helms	.40	.12
❑ T94	Mark Wohlers	.40	.12
❑ T95	Rob Bell	.40	.12
❑ T96	Tim Redding	.40	.12
❑ T97	Bud Smith RC	.40	.12
❑ T98	Adam Dunn	.75	.23
❑ T99	Ichiro Suzuki	20.00	6.00
	Albert Pujols ROY		
❑ T100	Carlton Fisk 81	1.25	.35
❑ T101	Tim Raines 81	1.00	.30
❑ T102	Juan Marichal 74	1.00	.30
❑ T103	Dave Winfield 81	1.00	.30

❑ T104 Reggie Jackson 82 1.25 .35
❑ T105 Cal Ripken 82 6.00 1.80
❑ T106 Ozzie Smith 82 3.00 .90
❑ T107 Tom Seaver 83 1.25 .35
❑ T108 Lou Piniella 74 1.00 .30
❑ T109 Dwight Gooden 84 1.00 .30
❑ T110 Bret Saberhagen 84 1.00 .30
❑ T111 Gary Carter 85 1.00 .30
❑ T112 Jack Clark 85 1.00 .30
❑ T113 R. Henderson 85 2.00 .60
❑ T114 Barry Bonds 86 5.00 1.50
❑ T115 Bobby Bonilla 86 1.00 .30
❑ T116 Jose Canseco 86 1.25 .35
❑ T117 Will Clark 86 1.25 .35
❑ T118 Andres Galarraga 86 1.00 .30
❑ T119 Bo Jackson 86 2.00 .60
❑ T120 Wally Joyner 86 1.00 .30
❑ T121 Ellis Burks 87 1.00 .30
❑ T122 David Cone 87 1.00 .30
❑ T123 Greg Maddux 87 3.00 .90
❑ T124 Willie Randolph 76 1.00 .30
❑ T125 Dennis Eckersley 87 1.00 .30
❑ T126 Matt Williams 87 1.00 .30
❑ T127 Joe Morgan 81 1.00 .30
❑ T128 Fred McGriff 87 1.25 .35
❑ T129 Roberto Alomar 88 1.25 .35
❑ T130 Lee Smith 88 1.00 .30
❑ T131 David Wells 88 1.00 .30
❑ T132 Ken Griffey Jr. 89 3.00 .90
❑ T133 Deion Sanders 89 1.25 .35
❑ T134 Nolan Ryan 89 4.00 1.20
❑ T135 David Justice 90 1.00 .30
❑ T136 Joe Carter 91 1.00 .30
❑ T137 Jack Morris 92 1.00 .30
❑ T138 Mike Piazza 93 3.00 .90
❑ T139 Barry Bonds 93 5.00 1.50
❑ T140 Terrence Long 94 1.00 .30
❑ T141 Ben Grieve 94 1.00 .30
❑ T142 Richie Sexson 95 1.00 .30
George Arias
Mark Sweeney
Brian Schneider
❑ T143 Sean Burroughs 99 1.00 .30
❑ T144 Alfonso Soriano 99 1.25 .35
❑ T145 Bob Boone MG .50 .15
❑ T146 Larry Bowa MG .50 .15
❑ T147 Bob Brenly MG .40 .12
❑ T148 Buck Martinez MG .40 .12
❑ T149 L. McClendon MG .40 .12
❑ T150 Jim Tracy MG .40 .12
❑ T151 Jared Abruzzo RC .40 .12
❑ T152 Kurt Ainsworth .40 .12
❑ T153 Willie Bloomquist .50 .15
❑ T154 Ben Broussard .40 .12
❑ T155 Bobby Bradley .40 .12
❑ T156 Mike Bynum .40 .12
❑ T157 A.J. Hinch .40 .12
❑ T158 Ryan Christianson .40 .12
❑ T159 Carlos Silva .40 .12
❑ T160 Joe Crede 1.25 .35
❑ T161 Jack Cust .40 .12
❑ T162 Ben Diggins .40 .12
❑ T163 Phil Dumatrait .40 .12
❑ T164 Alex Escobar .40 .12
❑ T165 Miguel Olivo .40 .12
❑ T166 Chris George .40 .12
❑ T167 Marcus Giles .50 .15
❑ T168 Keith Ginter .40 .12
❑ T169 Josh Girdley .40 .12
❑ T170 Tony Alvarez .40 .12
❑ T171 Scott Seabol .40 .12
❑ T172 Josh Hamilton .40 .12
❑ T173 Jason Hart .40 .12
❑ T174 Israel Alcantara .40 .12
❑ T175 Jake Peavy 2.00 .60
❑ T176 Stubby Clapp RC .40 .12
❑ T177 D'Angelo Jimenez .40 .12
❑ T178 Nick Johnson .50 .15
❑ T179 Ben Johnson .40 .12
❑ T180 Larry Bigbie .40 .12
❑ T181 Allen Levrault .40 .12
❑ T182 Felipe Lopez .50 .15
❑ T183 Sean Burnett .40 .12
❑ T184 Nick Neugebauer .40 .12
❑ T185 Austin Kearns .50 .15
❑ T186 Corey Patterson .40 .12
❑ T187 Carlos Pena .40 .12
❑ T188 R. Rodriguez RC .40 .12
❑ T189 Juan Rivera .40 .12
❑ T190 Grant Roberts .40 .12
❑ T191 Adam Pettyjohn RC .40 .12
❑ T192 Jared Sandberg .40 .12
❑ T193 Xavier Nady .40 .12
❑ T194 Dane Sardinha .40 .12
❑ T195 Shawn Sonnier .40 .12
❑ T196 Rafael Soriano .40 .12
❑ T197 Brian Specht RC .40 .12
❑ T198 Aaron Myette .40 .12
❑ T199 Juan Uribe RC .50 .15
❑ T200 Jayson Werth .40 .12
❑ T201 Brad Wilkerson .40 .12
❑ T202 Horacio Estrada .40 .12
❑ T203 Joel Pineiro .50 .15
❑ T204 Matt LeCroy .40 .12
❑ T205 Michael Coleman .40 .12
❑ T206 Ben Sheets .75 .23
❑ T207 Eric Byrnes .40 .12
❑ T208 Sean Burroughs .40 .12
❑ T209 Ken Harvey .40 .12
❑ T210 Travis Hafner 1.50 .45
❑ T211 Erick Almonte .40 .12
❑ T212 Jason Belcher RC .40 .12
❑ T213 Wilson Betemit RC .50 .15
❑ T214 Hank Blalock RC 4.00 1.20
❑ T215 Danny Borrell .40 .12
❑ T216 John Buck RC .50 .15
❑ T217 Freddie Bynum RC .40 .12
❑ T218 Noel Devarez RC .40 .12
❑ T219 Juan Diaz RC .40 .12
❑ T220 Felix Diaz RC .40 .12
❑ T221 Josh Fogg RC .40 .12
❑ T222 Matt Ford RC .40 .12
❑ T223 Scott Heard .40 .12
❑ T224 Ben Hendrickson RC .40 .12
❑ T225 Cody Ross RC .40 .12
❑ T226 A. Hernandez RC .40 .12
❑ T227 Alfredo Amezaga RC .40 .12
❑ T228 Bob Keppel RC .40 .12
❑ T229 Ryan Madson RC .40 .12
❑ T230 Octavio Martinez RC .40 .12
❑ T231 Hee Seop Choi .75 .23
❑ T232 Thomas Mitchell .40 .12
❑ T233 Luis Montanez .40 .12
❑ T234 Andy Morales RC .40 .12
❑ T235 Justin Morneau RC 2.50 .75
❑ T236 Toe Nash RC .40 .12
❑ T237 V. Pascucci RC .40 .12
❑ T238 Roy Smith RC .40 .12
❑ T239 Antonio Perez RC .50 .15
❑ T240 Chad Petty RC .40 .12
❑ T241 Steve Smyth .40 .12
❑ T242 Jose Reyes RC 4.00 1.20
❑ T243 Eric Reynolds RC .40 .12
❑ T244 Dominic Rich .40 .12
❑ T245 J. Richardson RC .40 .12
❑ T246 Ed Rogers RC .40 .12
❑ T247 Albert Pujols RC 50.00 15.00
❑ T248 Esix Snead RC .40 .12
❑ T249 Luis Torres RC .40 .12
❑ T250 Matt White RC .40 .12
❑ T251 Blake Williams .40 .12
❑ T252 Chris Russ .40 .12
❑ T253 Joe Kennedy RC .50 .15
❑ T254 Jeff Randazzo RC .40 .12
❑ T255 Beau Hale RC .40 .12
❑ T256 Brad Hennessey RC 1.25 .35
❑ T257 Jake Gautreau RC .40 .12
❑ T258 Jeff Mathis RC .50 .15
❑ T259 Aaron Heilman RC .40 .12
❑ T260 B. Sardinha RC .40 .12
❑ T261 Irvin Guzman RC 6.00 1.80
❑ T262 Gabe Gross RC .50 .15
❑ T263 J.D. Martin RC .40 .12
❑ T264 Chris Smith RC .40 .12
❑ T265 Kenny Baugh RC .40 .12

2002 Topps

	Nm-Mt	Ex-Mt
COMPLETE SET (718)	80.00	24.00
COMP.FACT.BROWN SET (723)	80.00	24.00
COMP.FACT.GREEN SET (723)	80.00	24.00
COMP. SERIES 1 (365)	40.00	12.00
COMPLETE SERIES 2 (354)	40.00	12.00
COMMON CARD (1-6/8-719)	.20	.06
COMMON (307-331)	.50	.15
COMMON CARD (332-364)	.50	.15

❑ 1 Pedro Martinez .30 .09
❑ 2 Mike Stanton .20 .06
❑ 3 Brad Penny .20 .06
❑ 4 Mike Matheny .20 .06
❑ 5 Johnny Damon .30 .09
❑ 6 Bret Boone .20 .06
❑ 7 Does Not Exist .00
❑ 8 Chris Truby .20 .06
❑ 9 B.J. Surhoff .20 .06
❑ 10 Mike Hampton .20 .06
❑ 11 Juan Pierre .20 .06
❑ 12 Mark Buehrle .20 .06
❑ 13 Bob Abreu .20 .06
❑ 14 David Cone .20 .06
❑ 15 Aaron Sele UER .20 .06
Card lists him as being born in New Mexico
He was born in Minnesota
❑ 16 Fernando Tatis .20 .06
❑ 17 Bobby Jones .20 .06
❑ 18 Rick Helling .20 .06
❑ 19 Dmitri Young .20 .06
❑ 20 Mike Mussina UER .30 .09
Career win total is wrong
❑ 21 Mike Sweeney .20 .06
❑ 22 Cristian Guzman .20 .06
❑ 23 Ryan Kohlmeier .20 .06
❑ 24 Adam Kennedy .20 .06
❑ 25 Larry Walker .20 .06
❑ 26 Eric Davis UER .20 .06
2000 Stolen Base totals are wrong
❑ 27 Jason Tyner .20 .06
❑ 28 Eric Young .20 .06
❑ 29 Jason Marquis .20 .06
❑ 30 Luis Gonzalez .20 .06
❑ 31 Kevin Tapani .20 .06
❑ 32 Orlando Cabrera .20 .06
❑ 33 Marty Cordova UER .20 .06
Career homer total, 1003
❑ 34 Brad Ausmus .20 .06
❑ 35 Livan Hernandez .20 .06
❑ 36 Alex Gonzalez .20 .06
❑ 37 Edgar Renteria .20 .06
❑ 38 Bengie Molina .20 .06
❑ 39 Frank Menechino .20 .06
❑ 40 Rafael Palmeiro .30 .09
❑ 41 Brad Fullmer .20 .06
❑ 42 Julio Zuleta .20 .06
❑ 43 Darren Dreifort .20 .06
❑ 44 Trot Nixon .20 .06
❑ 45 Trevor Hoffman .20 .06
❑ 46 Vladimir Nunez .20 .06
❑ 47 Mark Kotsay .20 .06
❑ 48 Kenny Rogers .20 .06
❑ 49 Ben Petrick .20 .06
❑ 50 Jeff Bagwell .30 .09
❑ 51 Juan Encarnacion .20 .06
❑ 52 Ramiro Mendoza .20 .06
❑ 53 Brian Meadows .20 .06
❑ 54 Chad Curtis .20 .06
❑ 55 Aramis Ramirez .20 .06
❑ 56 Mark McLemore .20 .06
❑ 57 Dante Bichette .20 .06

❑ 58 Scott Schoeneweis .20 .06
❑ 59 Jose Cruz Jr. .20 .06
❑ 60 Roger Clemens 1.00 .30
❑ 61 Jose Guillen .20 .06
❑ 62 Darren Oliver .20 .06
❑ 63 Chris Reitsma .20 .06
❑ 64 Jeff Abbott .20 .06
❑ 65 Robin Ventura .20 .06
❑ 66 Denny Neagle .20 .06
❑ 67 Al Martin .20 .06
❑ 68 Benito Santiago .20 .06
❑ 69 Roy Oswalt .20 .06
❑ 70 Juan Gonzalez .20 .06
❑ 71 Garret Anderson .20 .06
❑ 72 Bobby Bonilla .20 .06
❑ 73 Danny Bautista .20 .06
❑ 74 J.T. Snow .20 .06
❑ 75 Derek Jeter 1.25 .35
❑ 76 John Olerud .20 .06
❑ 77 Kevin Appier .20 .06
❑ 78 Phil Nevin .20 .06
❑ 79 Sean Casey .30 .09
❑ 80 Troy Glaus .20 .06
❑ 81 Joe Randa .20 .06
❑ 82 Jose Valentin .20 .06
❑ 83 Ricky Bottalico .20 .06
❑ 84 Todd Zeile .20 .06
❑ 85 Barry Larkin .30 .09
❑ 86 Bob Wickman .20 .06
❑ 87 Jeff Shaw .20 .06
❑ 88 Greg Vaughn .20 .06
❑ 89 Fernando Vina .20 .06
❑ 90 Mark Mulder .20 .06
❑ 91 Paul Bako .20 .06
❑ 92 Aaron Boone .20 .06
❑ 93 Esteban Loaiza .20 .06
❑ 94 Richie Sexson .20 .06
❑ 95 Alfonso Soriano .20 .06
❑ 96 Tony Womack .20 .06
❑ 97 Paul Shuey .20 .06
❑ 98 Melvin Mora .20 .06
❑ 99 Tony Gwynn .60 .18
❑ 100 Vladimir Guerrero .50 .15
❑ 101 Keith Osik .20 .06
❑ 102 Bud Smith .20 .06
❑ 103 Scott Williamson .20 .06
❑ 104 Daryle Ward .20 .06
❑ 105 Doug Mientkiewicz .20 .06
❑ 106 Stan Javier .20 .06
❑ 107 Russ Ortiz .20 .06
❑ 108 Wade Miller .20 .06
❑ 109 Luke Prokopec .20 .06
❑ 110 Andruw Jones UER .30 .09
Careel SB total, 1442
❑ 111 Ron Coomer .20 .06
❑ 112 Dan Wilson UER .20 .06
Career SB total, 1245
❑ 113 Luis Castillo .20 .06
❑ 114 Derek Bell .20 .06
❑ 115 Gary Sheffield .20 .06
❑ 116 Ruben Rivera .20 .06
❑ 117 Paul O'Neill .30 .09
❑ 118 Craig Paquette .20 .06
❑ 119 Kelvin Escobar .20 .06
❑ 120 Brad Radke .20 .06
❑ 121 Jorge Fabregas .20 .06
❑ 122 Randy Winn .20 .06
❑ 123 Tom Goodwin .20 .06
❑ 124 Jaret Wright .20 .06
❑ 125 Manny Ramirez .30 .09
❑ 126 Al Leiter .20 .06
❑ 127 Ben Davis .20 .06
❑ 128 Frank Catalanotto .20 .06
❑ 129 Jose Cabrera .20 .06
❑ 130 Magglio Ordonez .20 .06
❑ 131 Jose Macias .20 .06
❑ 132 Ted Lilly .20 .06
❑ 133 Chris Holt .20 .06
❑ 134 Eric Milton .20 .06
❑ 135 Shannon Stewart .20 .06
❑ 136 Omar Olivares .20 .06
❑ 137 David Segui .20 .06
❑ 138 Jeff Nelson .20 .06
❑ 139 Matt Williams .20 .06
❑ 140 Ellis Burks .20 .06
❑ 141 Jason Bere .20 .06
❑ 142 Jimmy Haynes .20 .06
❑ 143 Ramon Hernandez .20 .06
❑ 144 Craig Counsell UER .20 .06
Card pictures Greg Colbrunn
Some vital stats are wrong as well
❑ 145 John Smoltz .30 .09
❑ 146 Homer Bush .20 .06
❑ 147 Quilvio Veras .20 .06
❑ 148 Esteban Yan .20 .06
❑ 149 Ramon Ortiz .20 .06
❑ 150 Carlos Delgado .20 .06
❑ 151 Lee Stevens .20 .06
❑ 152 Wil Cordero .20 .06
❑ 153 Mike Bordick .20 .06
❑ 154 John Flaherty .20 .06
❑ 155 Omar Daal .20 .06
❑ 156 Todd Ritchie .20 .06
❑ 157 Carl Everett .20 .06
❑ 158 Scott Sullivan .20 .06
❑ 159 Deivi Cruz .20 .06
❑ 160 Albert Pujols UER 1.00 .30
Placido Polanco pictured on back
❑ 160A Albert Pujols COR .00
Pujols correctly pictured on back
❑ 161 Royce Clayton .20 .06
❑ 162 Jeff Suppan .20 .06
❑ 163 C.C. Sabathia .20 .06
❑ 164 Jimmy Rollins .20 .06
❑ 165 Rickey Henderson .50 .15
❑ 166 Rey Ordonez .20 .06
❑ 167 Shawn Estes .20 .06
❑ 168 Reggie Sanders .20 .06
❑ 169 Jon Lieber .20 .06
❑ 170 Armando Benitez .20 .06
❑ 171 Mike Remlinger .20 .06
❑ 172 Billy Wagner .20 .06
❑ 173 Troy Percival .20 .06
❑ 174 Devon White .20 .06
❑ 175 Ivan Rodriguez .30 .09
❑ 176 Dustin Hermanson .20 .06
❑ 177 Brian Anderson .20 .06
❑ 178 Graeme Lloyd .20 .06
❑ 179 Russel Branyan .20 .06
❑ 180 Bobby Higginson .20 .06
❑ 181 Alex Gonzalez .20 .06
❑ 182 John Franco .20 .06
❑ 183 Sidney Ponson .20 .06
❑ 184 Jose Mesa .20 .06
❑ 185 Todd Hollandsworth .20 .06
❑ 186 Kevin Young .20 .06
❑ 187 Tim Wakefield .20 .06
❑ 188 Craig Biggio .30 .09
❑ 189 Jason Isringhausen .20 .06
❑ 190 Mark Quinn .20 .06
❑ 191 Glendon Rusch .20 .06
❑ 192 Damian Miller .20 .06
❑ 193 Sandy Alomar Jr. .20 .06
❑ 194 Scott Brosius .20 .06
❑ 195 Dave Martinez .20 .06
❑ 196 Danny Graves .20 .06
❑ 197 Shea Hillenbrand .20 .06
❑ 198 Jimmy Anderson .20 .06
❑ 199 Travis Lee .20 .06
❑ 200 Randy Johnson .50 .15
❑ 201 Carlos Beltran .20 .06
❑ 202 Jerry Hairston .20 .06
❑ 203 Jesus Sanchez .20 .06
❑ 204 Eddie Taubensee .20 .06
❑ 205 David Wells .20 .06
❑ 206 Russ Davis .20 .06
❑ 207 Michael Barrett .20 .06
❑ 208 Marquis Grissom .20 .06
❑ 209 Byung-Hyun Kim .20 .06
❑ 210 Hideo Nomo .50 .15
❑ 211 Ryan Rupe .20 .06
❑ 212 Ricky Gutierrez .20 .06
❑ 213 Darryl Kile .20 .06
❑ 214 Rico Brogna .20 .06
❑ 215 Terrence Long .20 .06
❑ 216 Mike Jackson .20 .06
❑ 217 Jamey Wright .20 .06
❑ 218 Adrian Beltre .20 .06
❑ 219 Benny Agbayani .20 .06
❑ 220 Chuck Knoblauch .20 .06
❑ 221 Randy Wolf .20 .06
❑ 222 Andy Ashby .20 .06
❑ 223 Corey Koskie .20 .06
❑ 224 Roger Cedeno .20 .06
❑ 225 Ichiro Suzuki 1.00 .30
❑ 226 Keith Foulke .20 .06
❑ 227 Ryan Minor .20 .06
❑ 228 Shawon Dunston .20 .06
❑ 229 Alex Cora .20 .06
❑ 230 Jeromy Burnitz .20 .06
❑ 231 Mark Grace .30 .09
❑ 232 Aubrey Huff .20 .06
❑ 233 Jeffrey Hammonds .20 .06
❑ 234 Olmedo Saenz .20 .06
❑ 235 Brian Jordan .20 .06
❑ 236 Jeremy Giambi .20 .06
❑ 237 Joe Girardi .20 .06
❑ 238 Eric Gagne .20 .06
❑ 239 Masato Yoshii .20 .06
❑ 240 Greg Maddux .75 .23
❑ 241 Bryan Rekar .20 .06
❑ 242 Ray Durham .20 .06
❑ 243 Torii Hunter .20 .06
❑ 244 Derrek Lee .30 .09
❑ 245 Jim Edmonds .30 .09
❑ 246 Einar Diaz .20 .06
❑ 247 Brian Bohanon .20 .06
❑ 248 Ron Belliard .20 .06
❑ 249 Mike Lowell .20 .06
❑ 250 Sammy Sosa .50 .15
❑ 251 Richard Hidalgo .20 .06
❑ 252 Bartolo Colon .20 .06
❑ 253 Jorge Posada .30 .09
❑ 254 LaTroy Hawkins .20 .06
❑ 255 Paul LoDuca .20 .06
❑ 256 Carlos Febles .20 .06
❑ 257 Nelson Cruz .20 .06
❑ 258 Edgardo Alfonzo .20 .06
❑ 259 Joey Hamilton .20 .06
❑ 260 Cliff Floyd .20 .06
❑ 261 Wes Helms .20 .06
❑ 262 Jay Bell .20 .06
❑ 263 Mike Cameron .20 .06
❑ 264 Paul Konerko .20 .06
❑ 265 Jeff Kent .20 .06
❑ 266 Robert Fick .20 .06
❑ 267 Allen Levrault .20 .06
❑ 268 Placido Polanco .20 .06
❑ 269 Marlon Anderson .20 .06
❑ 270 Mariano Rivera .30 .09
❑ 271 Chan Ho Park .20 .06
❑ 272 Jose Vizcaino .20 .06
❑ 273 Jeff D'Amico .20 .06
❑ 274 Mark Gardner .20 .06
❑ 275 Travis Fryman .20 .06
❑ 276 Darren Lewis .20 .06
❑ 277 Bruce Bochy MG .20 .06
❑ 278 Jerry Manuel MG .20 .06
❑ 279 Bob Brenly MG .20 .06
❑ 280 Don Baylor MG .20 .06
❑ 281 Davey Lopes MG .20 .06
❑ 282 Jerry Narron MG .20 .06
❑ 283 Tony Muser MG .20 .06
❑ 284 Hal McRae MG .20 .06
❑ 285 Bobby Cox MG .20 .06
❑ 286 Larry Dierker MG .20 .06
❑ 287 Phil Garner MG .20 .06
❑ 288 Joe Kerrigan MG .20 .06
❑ 289 Bobby Valentine MG .20 .06
❑ 290 Dusty Baker MG .20 .06
❑ 291 Lloyd McClendon MG .20 .06
❑ 292 Mike Scioscia MG .20 .06
❑ 293 Buck Martinez MG .20 .06
❑ 294 Larry Bowa MG .20 .06
❑ 295 Tony LaRussa MG .20 .06
❑ 296 Jeff Torborg MG .20 .06
❑ 297 Tom Kelly MG .20 .06
❑ 298 Mike Hargrove MG .20 .06
❑ 299 Art Howe MG .20 .06
❑ 300 Lou Piniella MG .20 .06
❑ 301 Charlie Manuel MG .20 .06
❑ 302 Buddy Bell MG .20 .06
❑ 303 Tony Perez MG .20 .06
❑ 304 Bob Boone MG .20 .06
❑ 305 Joe Torre MG .30 .09
❑ 306 Jim Tracy MG .20 .06
❑ 307 Jason Lane PROS .50 .15
❑ 308 Chris George PROS .50 .15

❑ 309 Hank Blalock PROS UER 1.00 .30
Bio has him throwing lefty
❑ 310 Joe Borchard PROS .50 .15
❑ 311 Marlon Byrd PROS .50 .15
❑ 312 R. Cabrera PROS RC .50 .15
❑ 313 F. Sanchez PROS RC .50 .15
❑ 314 S. Wiggins PROS RC .50 .15
❑ 315 J. Maule PROS RC .50 .15
❑ 316 D. Cesar PROS RC .50 .15
❑ 317 Boof Bonser PROS .50 .15
❑ 318 J. Tolentino PROS RC .50 .15
❑ 319 Earl Snyder PROS RC .50 .15
❑ 320 T. Wade PROS RC .50 .15
❑ 321 N. Calzado PROS RC .50 .15
❑ 322 Eric Glaser PROS RC .50 .15
❑ 323 C. Kuzmic PROS RC .50 .15
❑ 324 Nic Jackson PROS RC .50 .15
❑ 325 Mike Rivera PROS .50 .15
❑ 326 Jason Bay PROS RC 4.00 1.20
❑ 327 Chris Smith DP .50 .15
❑ 328 Jake Gautreau DP .50 .15
❑ 329 Gabe Gross DP .50 .15
❑ 330 Kenny Baugh DP .50 .15
❑ 331 J.D. Martin DP .50 .15
❑ 332 Barry Bonds HL 1.25 .35
500th Homer
❑ 333 Rickey Henderson HL .50 .15
Sets record for career walks
❑ 334 Bud Smith HL .50 .15
❑ 335 R. Henderson HL 3000 .50 .15
❑ 336 Barry Bonds HL 1.25 .35
73 homers in a season
❑ 337 Ichiro Suzuki .50 .15
Jason Giambi
Roberto Alomar LL
❑ 338 Alex Rodriguez .50 .15
Ichiro Suzuki
Bret Boone LL
❑ 339 Alex Rodriguez .50 .15
Jim Thome
Rafael Palmeiro LL
❑ 340 Bret Boone .50 .15
Juan Gonzalez
Alex Rodriguez LL
❑ 341 Freddy Garcia .50 .15
Mike Mussina
Joe Mays LL
❑ 342 Hideo Nomo .50 .15
Mike Mussina
Roger Clemens LL
❑ 343 Larry Walker .50 .15
Todd Helton
Moises Alou
Lance Berkman LL
❑ 344 Sammy Sosa .75 .23
Todd Helton
Barry Bonds LL
❑ 345 Barry Bonds .75 .23
Sammy Sosa
Luis Gonzalez LL
❑ 346 Sammy Sosa .50 .15
Todd Helton
Luis Gonzalez LL
❑ 347 Randy Johnson .50 .15
Curt Schilling
John Burkett LL
❑ 348 Randy Johnson .50 .15
Curt Schilling
Chan Ho Park LL
❑ 349 Seattle Mariners PB .50 .15
❑ 350 Oakland Athletics PB .50 .15
❑ 351 New York Yankees PB .50 .15
❑ 352 Cleveland Indians PB .50 .15
❑ 353 Ariz. Diamondbacks PB .50 .15
❑ 354 Atlanta Braves PB .50 .15
❑ 355 St. Louis Cardinals PB .50 .15
❑ 356 Houston Astros PB .50 .15
❑ 357 Ariz.Diamondbacks .50 .15
Colorado Rockies UWS
❑ 358 Mike Piazza UWS .50 .15
❑ 359 Braves-Phillies UWS .50 .15
❑ 360 Curt Schilling UWS .50 .15
❑ 361 Roger Clemens .50 .15
Lee Mazzilli UWS
❑ 362 Sammy Sosa UWS .30 .09
❑ 363 Tom Lampkin .50 .15
Ichiro Suzuki
Bret Boone UWS
❑ 364 Barry Bonds .75 .23
Jeff Bagwell UWS
❑ 365 Barry Bonds HR 1 15.00 4.50
❑ 365 Barry Bonds HR 2 10.00 3.00
❑ 365 Barry Bonds HR 3 10.00 3.00
❑ 365 Barry Bonds HR 4 10.00 3.00
❑ 365 Barry Bonds HR 5 10.00 3.00
❑ 365 Barry Bonds HR 6 10.00 3.00
❑ 365 Barry Bonds HR 7 10.00 3.00
❑ 365 Barry Bonds HR 8 10.00 3.00
❑ 365 Barry Bonds HR 9 10.00 3.00
❑ 365 Barry Bonds HR 10 10.00 3.00
❑ 365 Barry Bonds HR 11 10.00 3.00
❑ 365 Barry Bonds HR 12 10.00 3.00
❑ 365 Barry Bonds HR 13 10.00 3.00
❑ 365 Barry Bonds HR 14 10.00 3.00
❑ 365 Barry Bonds HR 15 10.00 3.00
❑ 365 Barry Bonds HR 16 10.00 3.00
❑ 365 Barry Bonds HR 17 10.00 3.00
❑ 365 Barry Bonds HR 18 10.00 3.00
❑ 365 Barry Bonds HR 19 10.00 3.00
❑ 365 Barry Bonds HR 20 10.00 3.00
❑ 365 Barry Bonds HR 21 10.00 3.00
❑ 365 Barry Bonds HR 22 10.00 3.00
❑ 365 Barry Bonds HR 23 10.00 3.00
❑ 365 Barry Bonds HR 24 10.00 3.00
❑ 365 Barry Bonds HR 25 10.00 3.00
❑ 365 Barry Bonds HR 26 10.00 3.00
❑ 365 Barry Bonds HR 27 10.00 3.00
❑ 365 Barry Bonds HR 28 10.00 3.00
❑ 365 Barry Bonds HR 29 10.00 3.00
❑ 365 Barry Bonds HR 30 10.00 3.00
❑ 365 Barry Bonds HR 31 10.00 3.00
❑ 365 Barry Bonds HR 32 UER 10.00 3.00
No pitcher is listed on this card
❑ 365 Barry Bonds HR 33 10.00 3.00
❑ 365 Barry Bonds HR 34 10.00 3.00
❑ 365 Barry Bonds HR 35 10.00 3.00
❑ 365 Barry Bonds HR 36 10.00 3.00
❑ 365 Barry Bonds HR 37 10.00 3.00
❑ 365 Barry Bonds HR 38 10.00 3.00
❑ 365 Barry Bonds HR 39 10.00 3.00
❑ 365 Barry Bonds HR 40 10.00 3.00
❑ 365 Barry Bonds HR 41 10.00 3.00
❑ 365 Barry Bonds HR 42 10.00 3.00
❑ 365 Barry Bonds HR 43 10.00 3.00
❑ 365 Barry Bonds HR 44 10.00 3.00
❑ 365 Barry Bonds HR 45 10.00 3.00
❑ 365 Barry Bonds HR 46 10.00 3.00
❑ 365 Barry Bonds HR 47 10.00 3.00
❑ 365 Barry Bonds HR 48 10.00 3.00
❑ 365 Barry Bonds HR 49 10.00 3.00
❑ 365 Barry Bonds HR 50 10.00 3.00
❑ 365 Barry Bonds HR 51 10.00 3.00
❑ 365 Barry Bonds HR 52 10.00 3.00
❑ 365 Barry Bonds HR 53 10.00 3.00
❑ 365 Barry Bonds HR 54 10.00 3.00
❑ 365 Barry Bonds HR 55 10.00 3.00
❑ 365 Barry Bonds HR 56 10.00 3.00
❑ 365 Barry Bonds HR 57 10.00 3.00
❑ 365 Barry Bonds HR 58 10.00 3.00
❑ 365 Barry Bonds HR 59 10.00 3.00
❑ 365 Barry Bonds HR 60 10.00 3.00
❑ 365 Barry Bonds HR 61 15.00 4.50
❑ 365 Barry Bonds HR 62 10.00 3.00
❑ 365 Barry Bonds HR 63 10.00 3.00
❑ 365 Barry Bonds HR 64 10.00 3.00
❑ 365 Barry Bonds HR 65 10.00 3.00
❑ 365 Barry Bonds HR 66 10.00 3.00
❑ 365 Barry Bonds HR 67 10.00 3.00
❑ 365 Barry Bonds HR 68 10.00 3.00
❑ 365 Barry Bonds HR 69 10.00 3.00
❑ 365 Barry Bonds HR 70 15.00 4.50
❑ 365 Barry Bonds HR 71 10.00 3.00
❑ 365 Barry Bonds HR 72 10.00 3.00
❑ 365 Barry Bonds HR 73 50.00 15.00
❑ 366 Pat Meares .20 .06
❑ 367 Mike Lieberthal .20 .06
❑ 368 Larry Bigbie .20 .06
❑ 369 Ron Gant .20 .06
❑ 370 Moises Alou .20 .06
❑ 371 Chad Kreuter .20 .06
❑ 372 Willis Roberts .20 .06
❑ 373 Toby Hall .20 .06
❑ 374 Miguel Batista .20 .06
❑ 375 John Burkett .20 .06
❑ 376 Cory Lidle .20 .06
❑ 377 Nick Neugebauer .20 .06
❑ 378 Jay Payton .20 .06
❑ 379 Steve Karsay .20 .06
❑ 380 Eric Chavez .20 .06
❑ 381 Kelly Stinnett .20 .06
❑ 382 Jarrod Washburn .20 .06
❑ 383 Rick White .20 .06
❑ 384 Jeff Conine .20 .06
❑ 385 Fred McGriff .30 .09
❑ 386 Marvin Benard .20 .06
❑ 387 Joe Crede .20 .06
❑ 388 Dennis Cook .20 .06
❑ 389 Rick Reed .20 .06
❑ 390 Tom Glavine .30 .09
❑ 391 Rondell White .20 .06
❑ 392 Matt Morris .20 .06
❑ 393 Pat Rapp .20 .06
❑ 394 Robert Person .20 .06
❑ 395 Omar Vizquel .30 .09
❑ 396 Jeff Cirillo .20 .06
❑ 397 Dave Mlicki .20 .06
❑ 398 Jose Ortiz .20 .06
❑ 399 Ryan Dempster .20 .06
❑ 400 Curt Schilling .20 .06
❑ 401 Peter Bergeron .20 .06
❑ 402 Kyle Lohse .20 .06
❑ 403 Craig Wilson UER .20 .06
Homer totals are wrong
❑ 404 David Justice .20 .06
❑ 405 Darin Erstad .20 .06
❑ 406 Jose Mercedes .20 .06
❑ 407 Carl Pavano .20 .06
❑ 408 Albie Lopez .20 .06
❑ 409 Alex Ochoa .20 .06
❑ 410 Chipper Jones .50 .15
❑ 411 Tyler Houston .20 .06
❑ 412 Dean Palmer .20 .06
❑ 413 Damian Jackson .20 .06
❑ 414 Josh Towers .20 .06
❑ 415 Rafael Furcal .20 .06
❑ 416 Mike Morgan .20 .06
❑ 417 Herb Perry .20 .06
❑ 418 Mike Sirotka .20 .06
❑ 419 Mark Wohlers .20 .06
❑ 420 Nomar Garciaparra .75 .23
❑ 421 Felipe Lopez .20 .06
❑ 422 Joe McEwing .20 .06
❑ 423 Jacque Jones .20 .06
❑ 424 Julio Franco .20 .06
❑ 425 Frank Thomas .50 .15
❑ 426 So Taguchi RC .75 .23
❑ 427 Kazuhisa Ishii RC .50 .15
❑ 428 D'Angelo Jimenez .20 .06
❑ 429 Chris Stynes .20 .06
❑ 430 Kerry Wood .20 .06
❑ 431 Chris Singleton .20 .06
❑ 432 Erubiel Durazo .20 .06
❑ 433 Matt Lawton .20 .06
❑ 434 Bill Mueller .20 .06
❑ 435 Jose Canseco .30 .09
❑ 436 Ben Grieve .20 .06
❑ 437 Terry Mulholland .20 .06
❑ 438 David Bell .20 .06
❑ 439 A.J. Pierzynski .20 .06
❑ 440 Adam Dunn .20 .06
❑ 441 Jon Garland .20 .06
❑ 442 Jeff Fassero .20 .06
❑ 443 Julio Lugo .20 .06
❑ 444 Carlos Guillen .20 .06
❑ 445 Orlando Hernandez .20 .06
❑ 446 Mark Loretta UER .20 .06
Photo is Curtis Leskanic
❑ 447 Scott Spiezio .20 .06
❑ 448 Kevin Millwood .20 .06
❑ 449 Jamie Moyer .20 .06
❑ 450 Todd Helton .30 .09
❑ 451 Todd Walker .20 .06
❑ 452 Jose Lima .20 .06
❑ 453 Brook Fordyce .20 .06
❑ 454 Aaron Rowand .20 .06
❑ 455 Barry Zito .20 .06
❑ 456 Eric Owens .20 .06
❑ 457 Charles Nagy .20 .06

❑ 458 Raul Ibanez .20 .06
❑ 459 Joe Mays .20 .06
❑ 460 Jim Thome .30 .09
❑ 461 Adam Eaton .20 .06
❑ 462 Felix Martinez .20 .06
❑ 463 Vernon Wells .20 .06
❑ 464 Donnie Sadler .20 .06
❑ 465 Tony Clark .20 .06
❑ 466 Jose Hernandez .20 .06
❑ 467 Ramon Martinez .20 .06
❑ 468 Rusty Greer .20 .06
❑ 469 Rod Barajas .20 .06
❑ 470 Lance Berkman .20 .06
❑ 471 Brady Anderson .20 .06
❑ 472 Pedro Astacio .20 .06
❑ 473 Shane Halter .20 .06
❑ 474 Bret Prinz .20 .06
❑ 475 Edgar Martinez .30 .09
❑ 476 Steve Trachsel .20 .06
❑ 477 Gary Matthews Jr. .20 .06
❑ 478 Ismael Valdes .20 .06
❑ 479 Juan Uribe .20 .06
❑ 480 Shawn Green .20 .06
❑ 481 Kirk Rueter .20 .06
❑ 482 Damion Easley .20 .06
❑ 483 Chris Carpenter .20 .06
❑ 484 Kris Benson .20 .06
❑ 485 Antonio Alfonseca .20 .06
❑ 486 Kyle Farnsworth .20 .06
❑ 487 Brandon Lyon .20 .06
❑ 488 Hideki Irabu .20 .06
❑ 489 David Ortiz .30 .09
❑ 490 Mike Piazza .75 .23
❑ 491 Derek Lowe .20 .06
❑ 492 Chris Gomez .20 .06
❑ 493 Mark Johnson .20 .06
❑ 494 John Rocker .20 .06
❑ 495 Eric Karros .20 .06
❑ 496 Bill Haselman .20 .06
❑ 497 Dave Veres .20 .06
❑ 498 Pete Harnisch .20 .06
❑ 499 Tomokazu Ohka .20 .06
❑ 500 Barry Bonds 1.25 .35
❑ 501 David Dellucci .20 .06
❑ 502 Wendell Magee .20 .06
❑ 503 Tom Gordon .20 .06
❑ 504 Javier Vazquez .20 .06
❑ 505 Ben Sheets .20 .06
❑ 506 Wilton Guerrero .20 .06
❑ 507 John Halama .20 .06
❑ 508 Mark Redman .20 .06
❑ 509 Jack Wilson .20 .06
❑ 510 Bernie Williams .30 .09
❑ 511 Miguel Cairo .20 .06
❑ 512 Denny Hocking .20 .06
❑ 513 Tony Batista .20 .06
❑ 514 Mark Grudzielanek .20 .06
❑ 515 Jose Vidro .20 .06
❑ 516 Sterling Hitchcock .20 .06
❑ 517 Billy Koch .20 .06
❑ 518 Matt Clement .20 .06
❑ 519 Bruce Chen .20 .06
❑ 520 Roberto Alomar .30 .09
❑ 521 Orlando Palmeiro .20 .06
❑ 522 Steve Finley .20 .06
❑ 523 Danny Patterson .20 .06
❑ 524 Terry Adams .20 .06
❑ 525 Tino Martinez .30 .09
❑ 526 Tony Armas Jr. .20 .06
❑ 527 Geoff Jenkins .20 .06
❑ 528 Kerry Robinson .20 .06
❑ 529 Corey Patterson .20 .06
❑ 530 Brian Giles .20 .06
❑ 531 Jose Jimenez .20 .06
❑ 532 Joe Kennedy .20 .06
❑ 533 Armando Rios .20 .06
❑ 534 Osvaldo Fernandez .20 .06
❑ 535 Ruben Sierra .20 .06
❑ 536 Octavio Dotel .20 .06
❑ 537 Luis Sojo .20 .06
❑ 538 Brent Butler .20 .06
❑ 539 Pablo Ozuna UER .20 .06
Games played for Portland is wrong for 2002
❑ 540 Freddy Garcia .20 .06
❑ 541 Chad Durbin .20 .06
❑ 542 Orlando Merced .20 .06
❑ 543 Michael Tucker .20 .06
❑ 544 Roberto Hernandez .20 .06
❑ 545 Pat Burrell .20 .06
❑ 546 A.J. Burnett .20 .06
❑ 547 Bubba Trammell .20 .06
❑ 548 Scott Elarton .20 .06
❑ 549 Mike Darr .20 .06
❑ 550 Ken Griffey Jr. .75 .23
❑ 551 Ugueth Urbina .20 .06
❑ 552 Todd Jones .20 .06
❑ 553 Delino Deshields .20 .06
❑ 554 Adam Piatt .20 .06
❑ 555 Jason Kendall .20 .06
❑ 556 Hector Ortiz .20 .06
❑ 557 Turk Wendell .20 .06
❑ 558 Rob Bell .20 .06
❑ 559 Sun Woo Kim .20 .06
❑ 560 Raul Mondesi .20 .06
❑ 561 Brent Abernathy .20 .06
❑ 562 Seth Etherton .20 .06
❑ 563 Shawn Wooten .20 .06
❑ 564 Jay Buhner .20 .06
❑ 565 Andres Galarraga .20 .06
❑ 566 Shane Reynolds .20 .06
❑ 567 Rod Beck .20 .06
❑ 568 Dee Brown .20 .06
❑ 569 Pedro Feliz .20 .06
❑ 570 Ryan Klesko .20 .06
❑ 571 John Vander Wal UER .20 .06
Home Run Total in 1999 was 64
❑ 572 Nick Bierbrodt .20 .06
❑ 573 Joe Nathan .20 .06
❑ 574 James Baldwin .20 .06
❑ 575 J.D. Drew .20 .06
❑ 576 Greg Colbrunn .20 .06
❑ 577 Doug Glanville .20 .06
❑ 578 Brandon Duckworth .20 .06
❑ 579 Shawn Chacon .20 .06
❑ 580 Rich Aurilia .20 .06
❑ 581 Chuck Finley .20 .06
❑ 582 Abraham Nunez .20 .06
❑ 583 Kenny Lofton .20 .06
❑ 584 Brian Daubach .20 .06
❑ 585 Miguel Tejada .20 .06
❑ 586 Nate Cornejo .20 .06
❑ 587 Kazuhiro Sasaki .20 .06
❑ 588 Chris Richard .20 .06
❑ 589 Armando Reynoso .20 .06
❑ 590 Tim Hudson .20 .06
❑ 591 Neifi Perez .20 .06
❑ 592 Steve Cox .20 .06
❑ 593 Henry Blanco .20 .06
❑ 594 Ricky Ledee .20 .06
❑ 595 Tim Salmon .30 .09
❑ 596 Luis Rivas .20 .06
❑ 597 Jeff Zimmerman .20 .06
❑ 598 Matt Stairs .20 .06
❑ 599 Preston Wilson .20 .06
❑ 600 Mark McGwire 1.25 .35
❑ 601 Timo Perez UER .20 .06
Biographical Information is that of Aaron Rowand's
❑ 602 Matt Anderson .20 .06
❑ 603 Todd Hundley .20 .06
❑ 604 Rick Ankiel .20 .06
❑ 605 Tsuyoshi Shinjo .20 .06
❑ 606 Woody Williams .20 .06
❑ 607 Jason LaRue .20 .06
❑ 608 Carlos Lee .20 .06
❑ 609 Russ Johnson .20 .06
❑ 610 Scott Rolen .30 .09
❑ 611 Brent Mayne .20 .06
❑ 612 Darrin Fletcher .20 .06
❑ 613 Ray Lankford .20 .06
❑ 614 Troy O'Leary .20 .06
❑ 615 Javier Lopez .20 .06
❑ 616 Randy Velarde .20 .06
❑ 617 Vinny Castilla .20 .06
❑ 618 Milton Bradley .20 .06
❑ 619 Ruben Mateo .20 .06
❑ 620 Jason Giambi Yankees .20 .06
❑ 621 Andy Benes .20 .06
❑ 622 Joe Mauer RC 4.00 1.20
❑ 623 Andy Pettitte .30 .09
❑ 624 Jose Offerman .20 .06
❑ 625 Mo Vaughn .20 .06
❑ 626 Steve Sparks .20 .06
❑ 627 Mike Matthews .20 .06
❑ 628 Robb Nen .20 .06
❑ 629 Kip Wells .20 .06
❑ 630 Kevin Brown .20 .06
❑ 631 Arthur Rhodes .20 .06
❑ 632 Gabe Kapler .20 .06
❑ 633 Jermaine Dye .20 .06
❑ 634 Josh Beckett .20 .06
❑ 635 Pokey Reese .20 .06
❑ 636 Benji Gil .20 .06
❑ 637 Marcus Giles .20 .06
❑ 638 Julian Tavarez .20 .06
❑ 639 Jason Schmidt .20 .06
❑ 640 Alex Rodriguez .75 .23
❑ 641 Anaheim Angels TC .20 .06
❑ 642 Arizona Diamondbacks TC .30 .09
❑ 643 Atlanta Braves TC .20 .06
❑ 644 Baltimore Orioles TC .20 .06
❑ 645 Boston Red Sox TC .20 .06
❑ 646 Chicago Cubs TC .20 .06
❑ 647 Chicago White Sox TC .20 .06
❑ 648 Cincinnati Reds TC .20 .06
❑ 649 Cleveland Indians TC .20 .06
❑ 650 Colorado Rockies TC .20 .06
❑ 651 Detroit Tigers TC .20 .06
❑ 652 Florida Marlins TC .20 .06
❑ 653 Houston Astros TC .20 .06
❑ 654 Kansas City Royals TC .20 .06
❑ 655 Los Angeles Dodgers TC .20 .06
❑ 656 Milwaukee Brewers TC .20 .06
❑ 657 Minnesota Twins TC .20 .06
❑ 658 Montreal Expos TC .20 .06
❑ 659 New York Mets TC .20 .06
❑ 660 New York Yankees TC .50 .15
❑ 661 Oakland Athletics TC .20 .06
❑ 662 Philadelphia Phillies TC .20 .06
❑ 663 Pittsburgh Pirates TC .20 .06
❑ 664 San Diego Padres TC .20 .06
❑ 665 San Francisco Giants TC .20 .06
❑ 666 Seattle Mariners TC .30 .09
❑ 667 St. Louis Cardinals TC .20 .06
❑ 668 T.B. Devil Rays TC .20 .06
❑ 669 Texas Rangers TC .20 .06
❑ 670 Toronto Blue Jays TC .20 .06
❑ 671 Juan Cruz PROS .50 .15
❑ 672 Kevin Cash PROS RC .50 .15
❑ 673 Jimmy Gobble PROS RC .50 .15
❑ 674 Mike Hill PROS RC .50 .15
❑ 675 T.Buchholz PROS RC .50 .15
❑ 676 Bill Hall PROS .50 .15
❑ 677 B.Roneberg PROS RC .50 .15
❑ 678 R.Huffman PROS RC .50 .15
❑ 679 Chris Tritle PROS RC .50 .15
❑ 680 Nate Espy PROS RC .50 .15
❑ 681 Nick Alvarez PROS RC .50 .15
❑ 682 Jason Botts PROS RC .75 .23
❑ 683 Ryan Gripp PROS RC .50 .15
❑ 684 Dan Phillips PROS RC .50 .15
❑ 685 Pablo Arias PROS RC .50 .15
❑ 686 J.Rodriguez PROS RC .50 .15
❑ 687 Rich Harden PROS RC 5.00 1.50
❑ 688 Neal Frendling PROS RC .50 .15
❑ 689 Rich Thompson PROS RC .50 .15
❑ 690 G.Montalbano PROS RC .50 .15
❑ 691 Len Dinardo DP RC .50 .15
❑ 692 Ryan Raburn DP RC .50 .15
❑ 693 Josh Barfield DP RC 1.25 .35
❑ 694 David Bacani DP RC .50 .15
❑ 695 Dan Johnson DP RC 4.00 1.20
❑ 696 Mike Mussina GG .20 .06
❑ 697 Ivan Rodriguez GG .30 .09
❑ 698 Doug Mientkiewicz GG .20 .06
❑ 699 Roberto Alomar GG .20 .06
❑ 700 Eric Chavez GG .20 .06
❑ 701 Omar Vizquel GG .20 .06
❑ 702 Mike Cameron GG .20 .06
❑ 703 Torii Hunter GG .20 .06
❑ 704 Ichiro Suzuki GG .50 .15
❑ 705 Greg Maddux GG .50 .15
❑ 706 Brad Ausmus GG .20 .06
❑ 707 Todd Helton GG .20 .06
❑ 708 Fernando Vina GG .20 .06
❑ 709 Scott Rolen GG .20 .06
❑ 710 Orlando Cabrera GG .20 .06

Card	Player	Nm-Mt	Ex-Mt
❑ 711	Andruw Jones GG	.20	.06
❑ 712	Jim Edmonds GG	.20	.06
❑ 713	Larry Walker GG	.20	.06
❑ 714	Roger Clemens CY	.50	.15
❑ 715	Randy Johnson CY	.30	.09
❑ 716	Ichiro Suzuki MVP	.50	.15
❑ 717	Barry Bonds MVP	.75	.23
❑ 718	Ichiro Suzuki ROY	.50	.15
❑ 719	Albert Pujols ROY	.50	.15

2002 Topps Traded

	Nm-Mt	Ex-Mt
COMPLETE SET (275)	200.00	60.00
COMMON CARD (T1-T110)	2.00	.60
COMMON CARD (T111-T275)	.40	.12

Card	Player	Nm-Mt	Ex-Mt
❑ T1	Jeff Weaver	2.00	.60
❑ T2	Jay Powell	2.00	.60
❑ T3	Alex Gonzalez	2.00	.60
❑ T4	Jason Isringhausen	2.00	.60
❑ T5	Tyler Houston	2.00	.60
❑ T6	Ben Broussard	2.00	.60
❑ T7	Chuck Knoblauch	2.00	.60
❑ T8	Brian L. Hunter	2.00	.60
❑ T9	Dustan Mohr	2.00	.60
❑ T10	Eric Hinske	2.00	.60
❑ T11	Roger Cedeno	2.00	.60
❑ T12	Eddie Perez	2.00	.60
❑ T13	Jeromy Burnitz	2.00	.60
❑ T14	Bartolo Colon	2.00	.60
❑ T15	Rick Helling	2.00	.60
❑ T16	Dan Plesac	2.00	.60
❑ T17	Scott Strickland	2.00	.60
❑ T18	Antonio Alfonseca	2.00	.60
❑ T19	Ricky Gutierrez	2.00	.60
❑ T20	John Valentin	2.00	.60
❑ T21	Raul Mondesi	2.00	.60
❑ T22	Ben Davis	2.00	.60
❑ T23	Nelson Figueroa	2.00	.60
❑ T24	Earl Snyder	2.00	.60
❑ T25	Robin Ventura	2.00	.60
❑ T26	Jimmy Haynes	2.00	.60
❑ T27	Kenny Kelly	2.00	.60
❑ T28	Morgan Ensberg	2.00	.60
❑ T29	Reggie Sanders	2.00	.60
❑ T30	Shigetoshi Hasegawa	2.00	.60
❑ T31	Mike Timlin	2.00	.60
❑ T32	Russell Branyan	2.00	.60
❑ T33	Alan Embree	2.00	.60
❑ T34	D'Angelo Jimenez	2.00	.60
❑ T35	Kent Mercker	2.00	.60
❑ T36	Jesse Orosco	2.00	.60
❑ T37	Gregg Zaun	2.00	.60
❑ T38	Reggie Taylor	2.00	.60
❑ T39	Andres Galarraga	2.00	.60
❑ T40	Chris Truby	2.00	.60
❑ T41	Bruce Chen	2.00	.60
❑ T42	Darren Lewis	2.00	.60
❑ T43	Ryan Kohlmeier	2.00	.60
❑ T44	John McDonald	2.00	.60
❑ T45	Omar Daal	2.00	.60
❑ T46	Matt Clement	2.00	.60
❑ T47	Glendon Rusch	2.00	.60
❑ T48	Chan Ho Park	2.00	.60
❑ T49	Benny Agbayani	2.00	.60
❑ T50	Juan Gonzalez	2.00	.60
❑ T51	Carlos Baerga	2.00	.60
❑ T52	Tim Raines	2.00	.60
❑ T53	Kevin Appier	2.00	.60
❑ T54	Marty Cordova	2.00	.60
❑ T55	Jeff D'Amico	2.00	.60
❑ T56	Dmitri Young	2.00	.60
❑ T57	Roosevelt Brown	2.00	.60
❑ T58	Dustin Hermanson	2.00	.60
❑ T59	Jose Rijo	2.00	.60
❑ T60	Todd Ritchie	2.00	.60
❑ T61	Lee Stevens	2.00	.60
❑ T62	Placido Polanco	2.00	.60
❑ T63	Eric Young	2.00	.60
❑ T64	Chuck Finley	2.00	.60
❑ T65	Dicky Gonzalez	2.00	.60
❑ T66	Jose Macias	2.00	.60
❑ T67	Gabe Kapler	2.00	.60
❑ T68	Sandy Alomar Jr.	2.00	.60
❑ T69	Henry Blanco	2.00	.60
❑ T70	Julian Tavarez	2.00	.60
❑ T71	Paul Bako	2.00	.60
❑ T72	Scott Rolen	3.00	.90
❑ T73	Brian Jordan	2.00	.60
❑ T74	Rickey Henderson	4.00	1.20
❑ T75	Kevin Mench	2.00	.60
❑ T76	Hideo Nomo	4.00	1.20
❑ T77	Jeremy Giambi	2.00	.60
❑ T78	Brad Fullmer	2.00	.60
❑ T79	Carl Everett	2.00	.60
❑ T80	David Wells	2.00	.60
❑ T81	Aaron Sele	2.00	.60
❑ T82	Todd Hollandsworth	2.00	.60
❑ T83	Vicente Padilla	2.00	.60
❑ T84	Kenny Lofton	2.00	.60
❑ T85	Corky Miller	2.00	.60
❑ T86	Josh Fogg	2.00	.60
❑ T87	Cliff Floyd	2.00	.60
❑ T88	Craig Paquette	2.00	.60
❑ T89	Jay Payton	2.00	.60
❑ T90	Carlos Pena	2.00	.60
❑ T91	Juan Encarnacion	2.00	.60
❑ T92	Rey Sanchez	2.00	.60
❑ T93	Ryan Dempster	2.00	.60
❑ T94	Mario Encarnacion	2.00	.60
❑ T95	Jorge Julio	2.00	.60
❑ T96	John Mabry	2.00	.60
❑ T97	Todd Zeile	2.00	.60
❑ T98	Johnny Damon Sox	3.00	.90
❑ T99	Deivi Cruz	2.00	.60
❑ T100	Gary Sheffield	2.00	.60
❑ T101	Ted Lilly	2.00	.60
❑ T102	Todd Van Poppel	2.00	.60
❑ T103	Shawn Estes	2.00	.60
❑ T104	Cesar Izturis	2.00	.60
❑ T105	Ron Coomer	2.00	.60
❑ T106	Grady Little MG RC	2.00	.60
❑ T107	Jimy Williams MG	2.00	.60
❑ T108	Tony Pena MG	2.00	.60
❑ T109	Frank Robinson MG	3.00	.90
❑ T110	Ron Gardenhire MG	2.00	.60
❑ T111	Dennis Tankersley	.40	.12
❑ T112	Alejandro Cadena RC	.40	.12
❑ T113	Justin Reid RC	.40	.12
❑ T114	Nate Field RC	.40	.12
❑ T115	Rene Reyes RC	.40	.12
❑ T116	Nelson Castro RC	.40	.12
❑ T117	Miguel Olivo	.40	.12
❑ T118	David Espinosa	.40	.12
❑ T119	Chris Bootcheck RC	.40	.12
❑ T120	Rob Henkel RC	.40	.12
❑ T121	Steve Bechler RC	.40	.12
❑ T122	Mark Outlaw RC	.40	.12
❑ T123	Henry Pichardo RC	.40	.12
❑ T124	Michael Floyd RC	.40	.12
❑ T125	Richard Lane RC	.40	.12
❑ T126	Pete Zamora RC	.40	.12
❑ T127	Javier Colina	.40	.12
❑ T128	Greg Sain RC	.40	.12
❑ T129	Ronnie Merrill	.40	.12
❑ T130	Gavin Floyd RC	1.00	.30
❑ T131	Josh Bonifay RC	.40	.12
❑ T132	Tommy Marx RC	.40	.12
❑ T133	Gary Cates Jr. RC	.40	.12
❑ T134	Neal Cotts RC	1.00	.30
❑ T135	Angel Berroa	.40	.12
❑ T136	Elio Serrano RC	.40	.12
❑ T137	J.J. Putz RC	.40	.12
❑ T138	Ruben Gotay RC	.50	.15
❑ T139	Eddie Rogers	.40	.12
❑ T140	Wily Mo Pena	.40	.12
❑ T141	Tyler Yates RC	.40	.12
❑ T142	Colin Young RC	.40	.12
❑ T143	Chance Caple	.40	.12
❑ T144	Ben Howard RC	.40	.12
❑ T145	Ryan Bukvich RC	.40	.12
❑ T146	Cliff Bartosh RC	.40	.12
❑ T147	Brandon Claussen	.40	.12
❑ T148	Cristian Guerrero	.40	.12
❑ T149	Derrick Lewis	.40	.12
❑ T150	Eric Miller RC	.40	.12
❑ T151	Justin Huber RC	.75	.23
❑ T152	Adrian Gonzalez	.40	.12
❑ T153	Brian West RC	.40	.12
❑ T154	Chris Baker RC	.40	.12
❑ T155	Drew Henson	.40	.12
❑ T156	Scott Hairston RC	.50	.15
❑ T157	Jason Simontacchi RC	.40	.12
❑ T158	Jason Arnold RC	.40	.12
❑ T159	Brandon Phillips	.40	.12
❑ T160	Adam Roller RC	.40	.12
❑ T161	Scotty Layfield RC	.40	.12
❑ T162	Freddie Money RC	.40	.12
❑ T163	Noochie Varner RC	.40	.12
❑ T164	Terrance Hill RC	.40	.12
❑ T165	Jeremy Hill RC	.40	.12
❑ T166	Carlos Cabrera RC	.40	.12
❑ T167	Jose Morban RC	.40	.12
❑ T168	Kevin Frederick RC	.40	.12
❑ T169	Mark Teixeira	1.50	.45
❑ T170	Brian Rogers	.40	.12
❑ T171	Anastacio Martinez RC	.40	.12
❑ T172	Bobby Jenks RC	1.50	.45
❑ T173	David Gil RC	.40	.12
❑ T174	Andres Torres	.40	.12
❑ T175	James Barrett RC	.40	.12
❑ T176	Jimmy Journell	.40	.12
❑ T177	Brett Kay RC	.40	.12
❑ T178	Jason Young RC	.40	.12
❑ T179	Mark Hamilton RC	.40	.12
❑ T180	Jose Bautista RC	.50	.15
❑ T181	Blake McGinley RC	.40	.12
❑ T182	Ryan Mottl RC	.40	.12
❑ T183	Jeff Austin RC	.40	.12
❑ T184	Xavier Nady	.40	.12
❑ T185	Kyle Kane RC	.40	.12
❑ T186	Travis Foley RC	.40	.12
❑ T187	Nathan Kaup RC	.40	.12
❑ T188	Eric Cyr	.40	.12
❑ T189	Josh Cisneros RC	.40	.12
❑ T190	Brad Nelson RC	.50	.15
❑ T191	Clint Weibl RC	.40	.12
❑ T192	Ron Calloway RC	.40	.12
❑ T193	Jung Bong	.40	.12
❑ T194	Rolando Viera RC	.40	.12
❑ T195	Jason Bulger RC	.40	.12
❑ T196	Chone Figgins RC	.75	.23
❑ T197	Jimmy Alvarez RC	.40	.12
❑ T198	Joel Crump RC	.40	.12
❑ T199	Ryan Doumit RC	1.25	.35
❑ T200	Demetrius Heath RC	.40	.12
❑ T201	John Ennis RC	.40	.12
❑ T202	Doug Sessions RC	.40	.12
❑ T203	Clinton Hosford RC	.40	.12
❑ T204	Chris Narveson RC	.40	.12
❑ T205	Ross Peeples RC	.40	.12
❑ T206	Alex Requena RC	.40	.12
❑ T207	Matt Erickson RC	.40	.12
❑ T208	Brian Forystek RC	.40	.12
❑ T209	Dewon Brazelton	.40	.12
❑ T210	Nathan Haynes	.40	.12
❑ T211	Jack Cust	.40	.12
❑ T212	Jesse Foppert RC	.50	.15
❑ T213	Jesus Cota RC	.40	.12
❑ T214	Juan M. Gonzalez RC	.40	.12
❑ T215	Tim Kalita RC	.40	.12
❑ T216	Manny Delcarmen RC	.50	.15
❑ T217	Jim Kavourias RC	.40	.12
❑ T218	C.J. Wilson RC	.40	.12
❑ T219	Edwin Yan RC	.40	.12
❑ T220	Andy Van Hekken	.40	.12
❑ T221	Michael Cuddyer	.40	.12
❑ T222	Jeff Verplancke RC	.40	.12
❑ T223	Mike Wilson RC	.40	.12

Card	Nm-Mt	Ex-Mt
❑ T224 Corwin Malone RC	.40	.12
❑ T225 Chris Snelling RC	.75	.23
❑ T226 Joe Rogers RC	.40	.12
❑ T227 Jason Bay	4.00	1.20
❑ T228 Ezequiel Astacio RC	.40	.12
❑ T229 Joey Hammond RC	.40	.12
❑ T230 Chris Duffy RC	1.00	.30
❑ T231 Mark Prior	1.50	.45
❑ T232 Hansel Izquierdo RC	.40	.12
❑ T233 Franklyn German RC	.40	.12
❑ T234 Alexis Gomez	.40	.12
❑ T235 Jorge Padilla RC	.40	.12
❑ T236 Ryan Snare RC	.40	.12
❑ T237 Deivis Santos	.40	.12
❑ T238 Taggert Bozied RC	.50	.15
❑ T239 Mike Peeples RC	.40	.12
❑ T240 Ronald Acuna RC	.40	.12
❑ T241 Koyie Hill	.40	.12
❑ T242 Garrett Guzman RC	.40	.12
❑ T243 Ryan Church RC	1.50	.45
❑ T244 Tony Fontana RC	.40	.12
❑ T245 Keto Anderson RC	.40	.12
❑ T246 Brad Bouras RC	.40	.12
❑ T247 Jason Dubois RC	.50	.15
❑ T248 Angel Guzman RC	.75	.23
❑ T249 Joel Hanrahan RC	.40	.12
❑ T250 Joe Jiannetti RC	.40	.12
❑ T251 Sean Pierce RC	.40	.12
❑ T252 Jake Mauer RC	.40	.12
❑ T253 Marshall McDougall RC	.40	.12
❑ T254 Edwin Almonte RC	.40	.12
❑ T255 Shawn Riggans RC	.40	.12
❑ T256 Steven Shell RC	.40	.12
❑ T257 Kevin Hooper RC	.40	.12
❑ T258 Michael Frick RC	.40	.12
❑ T259 Travis Chapman RC	.40	.12
❑ T260 Tim Hummel RC	.40	.12
❑ T261 Adam Morrissey RC	.40	.12
❑ T262 Dontrelle Willis RC	8.00	2.40
❑ T263 Justin Sherrod RC	.40	.12
❑ T264 Gerald Smiley RC	.40	.12
❑ T265 Tony Miller RC	.40	.12
❑ T266 Nolan Ryan WW	2.50	.75
❑ T267 Reggie Jackson WW	.60	.18
❑ T268 Steve Garvey WW	.40	.12
❑ T269 Wade Boggs WW	.60	.18
❑ T270 Sammy Sosa WW	1.00	.30
❑ T271 Curt Schilling WW	.40	.12
❑ T272 Mark Grace WW	.60	.18
❑ T273 Jason Giambi WW	.40	.12
❑ T274 Ken Griffey Jr. WW	1.50	.45
❑ T275 Roberto Alomar WW	.60	.18

2003 Topps

	Nm-Mt	Ex-Mt
COMPLETE SET (720)	80.00	24.00
COMPLETE SERIES 1 (366)	40.00	12.00
COMPLETE SERIES 2 (354)	40.00	12.00
COMMON CARD (1-6/8-721)	.20	.06
COMMON (292-331/660-684)	.50	.15

Card	Nm-Mt	Ex-Mt
❑ 1 Alex Rodriguez	.75	.23
❑ 2 Dan Wilson	.20	.06
❑ 3 Jimmy Rollins	.20	.06
❑ 4 Jermaine Dye	.20	.06
❑ 5 Steve Karsay	.20	.06
❑ 6 Timo Perez	.20	.06
❑ 7 Does Not Exist	.00	
❑ 8 Jose Vidro	.20	.06
❑ 9 Eddie Guardado	.20	.06
❑ 10 Mark Prior	.30	.09
❑ 11 Curt Schilling	.20	.06
❑ 12 Dennis Cook	.20	.06
❑ 13 Andruw Jones	.30	.09
❑ 14 David Segui	.20	.06
❑ 15 Trot Nixon	.20	.06
❑ 16 Kerry Wood	.20	.06
❑ 17 Magglio Ordonez	.20	.06
❑ 18 Jason LaRue	.20	.06
❑ 19 Danys Baez	.20	.06
❑ 20 Todd Helton	.30	.09
❑ 21 Denny Neagle	.20	.06
❑ 22 Dave Mlicki	.20	.06
❑ 23 Roberto Hernandez	.20	.06
❑ 24 Odalis Perez	.20	.06
❑ 25 Nick Neugebauer	.20	.06
❑ 26 David Ortiz	.30	.09
❑ 27 Andres Galarraga	.20	.06
❑ 28 Edgardo Alfonzo	.20	.06
❑ 29 Chad Bradford	.20	.06
❑ 30 Jason Giambi	.20	.06
❑ 31 Brian Giles	.20	.06
❑ 32 Deivi Cruz	.20	.06
❑ 33 Robb Nen	.20	.06
❑ 34 Jeff Nelson	.20	.06
❑ 35 Edgar Renteria	.20	.06
❑ 36 Aubrey Huff	.20	.06
❑ 37 Brandon Duckworth	.20	.06
❑ 38 Juan Gonzalez	.20	.06
❑ 39 Sidney Ponson	.20	.06
❑ 40 Eric Hinske	.20	.06
❑ 41 Kevin Appier	.20	.06
❑ 42 Danny Bautista	.20	.06
❑ 43 Javier Lopez	.20	.06
❑ 44 Jeff Conine	.20	.06
❑ 45 Carlos Baerga	.20	.06
❑ 46 Ugueth Urbina	.20	.06
❑ 47 Mark Buehrle	.20	.06
❑ 48 Aaron Boone	.20	.06
❑ 49 Jason Simontacchi	.20	.06
❑ 50 Sammy Sosa	.50	.15
❑ 51 Jose Jimenez	.20	.06
❑ 52 Bobby Higginson	.20	.06
❑ 53 Luis Castillo	.20	.06
❑ 54 Orlando Merced	.20	.06
❑ 55 Brian Jordan	.20	.06
❑ 56 Eric Young	.20	.06
❑ 57 Bobby Kielty	.20	.06
❑ 58 Luis Rivas	.20	.06
❑ 59 Brad Wilkerson	.20	.06
❑ 60 Roberto Alomar	.30	.09
❑ 61 Roger Clemens	1.00	.30
❑ 62 Scott Hatteberg	.20	.06
❑ 63 Andy Ashby	.20	.06
❑ 64 Mike Williams	.20	.06
❑ 65 Ron Gant	.20	.06
❑ 66 Benito Santiago	.20	.06
❑ 67 Bret Boone	.20	.06
❑ 68 Matt Morris	.20	.06
❑ 69 Troy Glaus	.20	.06
❑ 70 Austin Kearns	.20	.06
❑ 71 Jim Thome	.30	.09
❑ 72 Rickey Henderson	.50	.15
❑ 73 Luis Gonzalez	.20	.06
❑ 74 Brad Fullmer	.20	.06
❑ 75 Herbert Perry	.20	.06
❑ 76 Randy Wolf	.20	.06
❑ 77 Miguel Tejada	.20	.06
❑ 78 Jimmy Anderson	.20	.06
❑ 79 Ramon Martinez	.20	.06
❑ 80 Ivan Rodriguez	.30	.09
❑ 81 John Flaherty	.20	.06
❑ 82 Shannon Stewart	.20	.06
❑ 83 Orlando Palmeiro	.20	.06
❑ 84 Rafael Furcal	.20	.06
❑ 85 Kenny Rogers	.20	.06
❑ 86 Terry Adams	.20	.06
❑ 87 Mo Vaughn	.20	.06
❑ 88 Jose Cruz Jr.	.20	.06
❑ 89 Mike Matheny	.20	.06
❑ 90 Alfonso Soriano	.20	.06
❑ 91 Orlando Cabrera	.20	.06
❑ 92 Jeffrey Hammonds	.20	.06
❑ 93 Hideo Nomo	.50	.15
❑ 94 Carlos Febles	.20	.06
❑ 95 Billy Wagner	.20	.06
❑ 96 Alex Gonzalez	.20	.06
❑ 97 Todd Zeile	.20	.06
❑ 98 Omar Vizquel	.30	.09
❑ 99 Jose Rijo	.20	.06
❑ 100 Ichiro Suzuki	1.00	.30
❑ 101 Steve Cox	.20	.06
❑ 102 Hideki Irabu	.20	.06
❑ 103 Roy Halladay	.20	.06
❑ 104 David Eckstein	.20	.06
❑ 105 Greg Maddux	.75	.23
❑ 106 Jay Gibbons	.20	.06
❑ 107 Travis Driskill	.20	.06
❑ 108 Fred McGriff	.30	.09
❑ 109 Frank Thomas	.50	.15
❑ 110 Shawn Green	.20	.06
❑ 111 Ruben Quevedo	.20	.06
❑ 112 Jacque Jones	.20	.06
❑ 113 Tomo Ohka	.20	.06
❑ 114 Joe McEwing	.20	.06
❑ 115 Ramiro Mendoza	.20	.06
❑ 116 Mark Mulder	.20	.06
❑ 117 Mike Lieberthal	.20	.06
❑ 118 Jack Wilson	.20	.06
❑ 119 Randall Simon	.20	.06
❑ 120 Bernie Williams	.30	.09
❑ 121 Marvin Benard	.20	.06
❑ 122 Jamie Moyer	.20	.06
❑ 123 Andy Benes	.20	.06
❑ 124 Tino Martinez	.30	.09
❑ 125 Esteban Yan	.20	.06
❑ 126 Juan Uribe	.20	.06
❑ 127 Jason Isringhausen	.20	.06
❑ 128 Chris Carpenter	.20	.06
❑ 129 Mike Cameron	.20	.06
❑ 130 Gary Sheffield	.20	.06
❑ 131 Geronimo Gil	.20	.06
❑ 132 Brian Daubach	.20	.06
❑ 133 Corey Patterson	.20	.06
❑ 134 Aaron Rowand	.20	.06
❑ 135 Chris Reitsma	.20	.06
❑ 136 Bob Wickman	.20	.06
❑ 137 Cesar Izturis	.20	.06
❑ 138 Jason Jennings	.20	.06
❑ 139 Brandon Inge	.20	.06
❑ 140 Larry Walker	.20	.06
❑ 141 Ramon Santiago	.20	.06
❑ 142 Vladimir Nunez	.20	.06
❑ 143 Jose Vizcaino	.20	.06
❑ 144 Mark Quinn	.20	.06
❑ 145 Michael Tucker	.20	.06
❑ 146 Darren Dreifort	.20	.06
❑ 147 Ben Sheets	.20	.06
❑ 148 Corey Koskie	.20	.06
❑ 149 Tony Armas Jr.	.20	.06
❑ 150 Kazuhisa Ishii	.20	.06
❑ 151 Al Leiter	.20	.06
❑ 152 Steve Trachsel	.20	.06
❑ 153 Mike Stanton	.20	.06
❑ 154 David Justice	.20	.06
❑ 155 Marlon Anderson	.20	.06
❑ 156 Jason Kendall	.20	.06
❑ 157 Brian Lawrence	.20	.06
❑ 158 J.T. Snow	.20	.06
❑ 159 Edgar Martinez	.30	.09
❑ 160 Pat Burrell	.20	.06
❑ 161 Kerry Robinson	.20	.06
❑ 162 Greg Vaughn	.20	.06
❑ 163 Carl Everett	.20	.06
❑ 164 Vernon Wells	.20	.06
❑ 165 Jose Mesa	.20	.06
❑ 166 Troy Percival	.20	.06
❑ 167 Erubiel Durazo	.20	.06
❑ 168 Jason Marquis	.20	.06
❑ 169 Jerry Hairston Jr.	.20	.06
❑ 170 Vladimir Guerrero	.50	.15
❑ 171 Byung-Hyun Kim	.20	.06
❑ 172 Marcus Giles	.20	.06
❑ 173 Johnny Damon	.30	.09
❑ 174 Jon Lieber	.20	.06
❑ 175 Terrence Long	.20	.06
❑ 176 Sean Casey	.30	.09
❑ 177 Adam Dunn	.20	.06
❑ 178 Juan Pierre	.20	.06
❑ 179 Wendell Magee	.20	.06

❑ 180 Barry Zito .20 .06
❑ 181 Aramis Ramirez .20 .06
❑ 182 Pokey Reese .20 .06
❑ 183 Jeff Kent .20 .06
❑ 184 Russ Ortiz .20 .06
❑ 185 Ruben Sierra .20 .06
❑ 186 Brent Abernathy .20 .06
❑ 187 Ismael Valdes UER .20 .06
Card does not include 2002 Rangers stats
❑ 188 Tom Wilson .20 .06
❑ 189 Craig Counsell .20 .06
❑ 190 Mike Mussina .30 .09
❑ 191 Ramon Hernandez .20 .06
❑ 192 Adam Kennedy .20 .06
❑ 193 Tony Womack .20 .06
❑ 194 Wes Helms .20 .06
❑ 195 Tony Batista .20 .06
❑ 196 Rolando Arrojo .20 .06
❑ 197 Kyle Farnsworth .20 .06
❑ 198 Gary Bennett .20 .06
❑ 199 Scott Sullivan .20 .06
❑ 200 Albert Pujols 1.00 .30
❑ 201 Kirk Rueter .20 .06
❑ 202 Phil Nevin .20 .06
❑ 203 Kip Wells .20 .06
❑ 204 Ron Coomer .20 .06
❑ 205 Jeromy Burnitz .20 .06
❑ 206 Kyle Lohse .20 .06
❑ 207 Mike DeJean .20 .06
❑ 208 Paul Lo Duca .20 .06
❑ 209 Carlos Beltran .20 .06
❑ 210 Roy Oswalt .20 .06
❑ 211 Mike Lowell .20 .06
❑ 212 Robert Fick .20 .06
❑ 213 Todd Jones .20 .06
❑ 214 C.C. Sabathia .20 .06
❑ 215 Danny Graves .20 .06
❑ 216 Todd Hundley .20 .06
❑ 217 Tim Wakefield .20 .06
❑ 218 Derek Lowe .20 .06
❑ 219 Kevin Millwood .20 .06
❑ 220 Jorge Posada .30 .09
❑ 221 Bobby J. Jones .20 .06
❑ 222 Carlos Guillen .20 .06
❑ 223 Fernando Vina .20 .06
❑ 224 Ryan Rupe .20 .06
❑ 225 Kelvim Escobar .20 .06
❑ 226 Ramon Ortiz .20 .06
❑ 227 Junior Spivey .20 .06
❑ 228 Juan Cruz .20 .06
❑ 229 Melvin Mora .20 .06
❑ 230 Lance Berkman .20 .06
❑ 231 Brent Butler .20 .06
❑ 232 Shane Halter .20 .06
❑ 233 Derrek Lee .30 .09
❑ 234 Matt Lawton .20 .06
❑ 235 Chuck Knoblauch .20 .06
❑ 236 Eric Gagne .20 .06
❑ 237 Alex Sanchez .20 .06
❑ 238 Denny Hocking .20 .06
❑ 239 Eric Milton .20 .06
❑ 240 Rey Ordonez .20 .06
❑ 241 Orlando Hernandez .20 .06
❑ 242 Robert Person .20 .06
❑ 243 Sean Burroughs .20 .06
❑ 244 Jeff Cirillo .20 .06
❑ 245 Mike Lamb .20 .06
❑ 246 Jose Valentin .20 .06
❑ 247 Ellis Burks .20 .06
❑ 248 Shawn Chacon .20 .06
❑ 249 Josh Beckett .20 .06
❑ 250 Nomar Garciaparra .75 .23
❑ 251 Craig Biggio .30 .09
❑ 252 Joe Randa .20 .06
❑ 253 Mark Grudzielanek .20 .06
❑ 254 Glendon Rusch .20 .06
❑ 255 Michael Barrett .20 .06
❑ 256 Omar Daal .20 .06
❑ 257 Elmer Dessens .20 .06
❑ 258 Wade Miller .20 .06
❑ 259 Adrian Beltre .20 .06
❑ 260 Vicente Padilla .20 .06
❑ 261 Kazuhiro Sasaki .20 .06
❑ 262 Mike Scioscia MG .20 .06
❑ 263 Bobby Cox MG .20 .06
❑ 264 Mike Hargrove MG .20 .06
❑ 265 Grady Little MG RC .20 .06
❑ 266 Alex Gonzalez UER .20 .06
2002 stats are listed as all zero's
❑ 267 Jerry Manuel MG .20 .06
❑ 268 Bob Boone MG .20 .06
❑ 269 Joel Skinner MG .20 .06
❑ 270 Clint Hurdle MG .20 .06
❑ 271 Miguel Batista UER .20 .06
All 2002 Stats are 0's
❑ 272 Bob Brenly MG .20 .06
❑ 273 Jeff Torborg MG .20 .06
❑ 274 Jimy Williams MG UER .20 .06
Career managerial record is wrong
❑ 275 Tony Pena MG .20 .06
❑ 276 Jim Tracy MG .20 .06
❑ 277 Jerry Royster MG .20 .06
❑ 278 Ron Gardenhire MG .20 .06
❑ 279 Frank Robinson MG .30 .09
❑ 280 John Halama .20 .06
❑ 281 Joe Torre MG .30 .09
❑ 282 Art Howe MG .20 .06
❑ 283 Larry Bowa MG .20 .06
❑ 284 Lloyd McClendon MG .20 .06
❑ 285 Bruce Bochy MG .20 .06
❑ 286 Dusty Baker MG .20 .06
❑ 287 Lou Piniella MG .20 .06
❑ 288 Tony LaRussa MG .20 .06
❑ 289 Todd Walker .20 .06
❑ 290 Jerry Narron MG .20 .06
❑ 291 Carlos Tosca MG .20 .06
❑ 292 Chris Duncan FY RC .50 .15
❑ 293 Franklin Gutierrez FY RC 1.00 .30
❑ 294 Adam LaRoche FY .50 .15
❑ 295 Manuel Ramirez FY RC .50 .15
❑ 296 Il Kim FY RC .50 .15
❑ 297 Wayne Lydon FY RC .50 .15
❑ 298 Daryl Clark FY RC .50 .15
❑ 299 Sean Pierce FY .50 .15
❑ 300 Andy Marte FY RC 3.00 .90
❑ 301 Matthew Peterson FY RC .50 .15
❑ 302 Gonzalo Lopez FY RC .50 .15
❑ 303 Bernie Castro FY RC .50 .15
❑ 304 Cliff Lee FY .50 .15
❑ 305 Jason Perry FY RC .50 .15
❑ 306 Jaime Bubela FY RC .50 .15
❑ 307 Alexis Rios FY .50 .15
❑ 308 Brendan Harris FY RC .50 .15
❑ 309 R.Nivar-Martinez FY RC .50 .15
❑ 310 Terry Tiffee FY RC .50 .15
❑ 311 Kevin Youkilis FY RC .75 .23
❑ 312 Ruddy Lugo FY RC .50 .15
❑ 313 C.J. Wilson FY .50 .15
❑ 314 Mike McNutt FY RC .50 .15
❑ 315 Jeff Clark FY RC .50 .15
❑ 316 Mark Malaska FY RC .50 .15
❑ 317 Doug Waechter FY RC .50 .15
❑ 318 Derell McCall FY RC .50 .15
❑ 319 Scott Tyler FY RC .50 .15
❑ 320 Craig Brazell FY RC .50 .15
❑ 321 Walter Young FY .50 .15
❑ 322 Marlon Byrd .50 .15
Jorge Padilla FS
❑ 323 Chris Snelling .50 .15
Shin-Soo Choo FS
❑ 324 Hank Blalock .50 .15
Mark Teixeira FS
❑ 325 Josh Hamilton .50 .15
Carl Crawford FS
❑ 326 Orlando Hudson .50 .15
Josh Phelps FS
❑ 327 Jack Cust .50 .15
Rene Reyes FS
❑ 328 Angel Berroa .50 .15
Alexis Gomez FS
❑ 329 Michael Cuddyer .50 .15
Michael Restovich FS
❑ 330 Juan Rivera .50 .15
Marcus Thames FS
❑ 331 Brandon Puffer .50 .15
Jung Bong FS
❑ 332 Mike Cameron SH .20 .06
❑ 333 Shawn Green SH .20 .06
❑ 334 Oakland A's SH .20 .06
❑ 335 Jason Giambi SH .20 .06
❑ 336 Derek Lowe SH .20 .06
❑ 337 Manny Ramirez .30 .09
Mike Sweeney
Bernie Williams LL
❑ 338 Alfonso Soriano .20 .06
Alex Rodriguez
Derek Jeter LL
❑ 339 Alex Rodriguez .30 .09
Jim Thome
Rafael Palmeiro LL
❑ 340 Alex Rodriguez .50 .15
Magglio Ordonez
Miguel Tejada LL
❑ 341 Pedro Martinez .20 .06
Derek Lowe
Barry Zito LL
❑ 342 Pedro Martinez .30 .09
Roger Clemens
Mike Mussina LL
❑ 343 Larry Walker .50 .15
Vladimir Guerrero
Todd Helton LL
❑ 344 Sammy Sosa .50 .15
Albert Pujols
Shawn Green LL
❑ 345 Sammy Sosa .50 .15
Lance Berkman
Shawn Green LL
❑ 346 Lance Berkman .20 .06
Albert Pujols
Pat Burrell LL
❑ 347 Randy Johnson .30 .09
Greg Maddux
Tom Glavine LL
❑ 348 Randy Johnson .30 .09
Curt Schilling
Kerry Wood LL
❑ 349 Francisco Rodriguez .20 .06
Darin Erstad
Tim Salmon
AL Division Series
❑ 350 Minnesota Twins .30 .09
St Louis Cardinals
AL and NL Division Series
❑ 351 Anaheim Angels .30 .09
San Francisco Giants
AL and NL Division Series
❑ 352 Jim Edmonds .30 .09
Scott Rolen
NL Division Series
❑ 353 Adam Kennedy ALCS .20 .06
❑ 354 J.T. Snow WS .30 .09
❑ 355 David Bell NLCS .30 .09
❑ 356 Jason Giambi AS .20 .06
❑ 357 Alfonso Soriano AS .20 .06
❑ 358 Alex Rodriguez AS .50 .15
❑ 359 Eric Chavez AS .20 .06
❑ 360 Torii Hunter AS .20 .06
❑ 361 Bernie Williams AS .20 .06
❑ 362 Garret Anderson AS .20 .06
❑ 363 Jorge Posada AS .20 .06
❑ 364 Derek Lowe AS .20 .06
❑ 365 Barry Zito AS .20 .06
❑ 366 Manny Ramirez AS .30 .09
❑ 367 Mike Scioscia AS .20 .06
❑ 368 Francisco Rodriguez .20 .06
❑ 369 Chris Hammond .20 .06
❑ 370 Chipper Jones .50 .15
❑ 371 Chris Singleton .20 .06
❑ 372 Cliff Floyd .20 .06
❑ 373 Bobby Hill .20 .06
❑ 374 Antonio Osuna .20 .06
❑ 375 Barry Larkin .30 .09
❑ 376 Charles Nagy .20 .06
❑ 377 Denny Stark .20 .06
❑ 378 Dean Palmer .20 .06
❑ 379 Eric Owens .20 .06
❑ 380 Randy Johnson .50 .15
❑ 381 Jeff Suppan .20 .06
❑ 382 Eric Karros .20 .06
❑ 383 Luis Vizcaino .20 .06
❑ 384 Johan Santana .30 .09
❑ 385 Javier Vazquez .20 .06
❑ 386 John Thomson .20 .06
❑ 387 Nick Johnson .20 .06
❑ 388 Mark Ellis .20 .06
❑ 389 Doug Glanville .20 .06

390	Ken Griffey Jr.	.75	.23
391	Bubba Trammell	.20	.06
392	Livan Hernandez	.20	.06
393	Desi Relaford	.20	.06
394	Eli Marrero	.20	.06
395	Jared Sandberg	.20	.06
396	Barry Bonds	1.25	.35
397	Esteban Loaiza	.20	.06
398	Aaron Sele	.20	.06
399	Geoff Blum	.20	.06
400	Derek Jeter	1.25	.35
401	Eric Byrnes	.20	.06
402	Mike Timlin	.20	.06
403	Mark Kotsay	.20	.06
404	Rich Aurilia	.20	.06
405	Joel Pineiro	.20	.06
406	Chuck Finley	.20	.06
407	Bengie Molina	.20	.06
408	Steve Finley	.20	.06
409	Julio Franco	.20	.06
410	Marty Cordova	.20	.06
411	Shea Hillenbrand	.20	.06
412	Mark Bellhorn	.20	.06
413	Jon Garland	.20	.06
414	Reggie Taylor	.20	.06
415	Milton Bradley	.20	.06
416	Carlos Pena	.20	.06
417	Andy Fox	.20	.06
418	Brad Ausmus	.20	.06
419	Brent Mayne	.20	.06
420	Paul Quantrill	.20	.06
421	Carlos Delgado	.20	.06
422	Kevin Mench	.20	.06
423	Joe Kennedy	.20	.06
424	Mike Crudale	.20	.06
425	Mark McLemore	.20	.06
426	Bill Mueller	.20	.06
427	Rob Mackowiak	.20	.06
428	Ricky Ledee	.20	.06
429	Ted Lilly	.20	.06
430	Sterling Hitchcock	.20	.06
431	Scott Strickland	.20	.06
432	Damion Easley	.20	.06
433	Torii Hunter	.20	.06
434	Brad Radke	.20	.06
435	Geoff Jenkins	.20	.06
436	Paul Byrd	.20	.06
437	Morgan Ensberg	.20	.06
438	Mike Maroth	.20	.06
439	Mike Hampton	.20	.06
440	Adam Hyzdu	.20	.06
441	Vance Wilson	.20	.06
442	Todd Ritchie	.20	.06
443	Tom Gordon	.20	.06
444	John Burkett	.20	.06
445	Rodrigo Lopez	.20	.06
446	Tim Spooneybarger	.20	.06
447	Quinton Mccracken	.20	.06
448	Tim Salmon	.30	.09
449	Jarrod Washburn	.20	.06
450	Pedro Martinez	.30	.09
451	Dustan Mohr	.20	.06
452	Julio Lugo	.20	.06
453	Scott Stewart	.20	.06
454	Armando Benitez	.20	.06
455	Raul Mondesi	.20	.06
456	Robin Ventura	.20	.06
457	Bobby Abreu	.20	.06
458	Josh Fogg	.20	.06
459	Ryan Klesko	.20	.06
460	Tsuyoshi Shinjo	.20	.06
461	Jim Edmonds	.30	.09
462	Cliff Politte	.20	.06
463	Chan Ho Park	.20	.06
464	John Mabry	.20	.06
465	Woody Williams	.20	.06
466	Jason Michaels	.20	.06
467	Scott Schoeneweis	.20	.06
468	Brian Anderson	.20	.06
469	Brett Tomko	.20	.06
470	Scott Erickson	.20	.06
471	Kevin Millar Sox	.20	.06
472	Danny Wright	.20	.06
473	Jason Schmidt	.20	.06
474	Scott Williamson	.20	.06
475	Einar Diaz	.20	.06
476	Jay Payton	.20	.06
477	Juan Acevedo	.20	.06
478	Ben Grieve	.20	.06
479	Raul Ibanez	.20	.06
480	Richie Sexson	.20	.06
481	Rick Reed	.20	.06
482	Pedro Astacio	.20	.06
483	Adam Piatt	.20	.06
484	Bud Smith	.20	.06
485	Tomas Perez	.20	.06
486	Adam Eaton	.20	.06
487	Rafael Palmeiro	.30	.09
488	Jason Tyner	.20	.06
489	Scott Rolen	.30	.09
490	Randy Winn	.20	.06
491	Ryan Jensen	.20	.06
492	Trevor Hoffman	.20	.06
493	Craig Wilson	.20	.06
494	Jeremy Giambi	.20	.06
495	Daryle Ward	.20	.06
496	Shane Spencer	.20	.06
497	Andy Pettitte	.30	.09
498	John Franco	.20	.06
499	Felipe Lopez	.20	.06
500	Mike Piazza	.75	.23
501	Cristian Guzman	.20	.06
502	Jose Hernandez	.20	.06
503	Octavio Dotel	.20	.06
504	Brad Penny	.20	.06
505	Dave Veres	.20	.06
506	Ryan Dempster	.20	.06
507	Joe Crede	.20	.06
508	Chad Hermansen	.20	.06
509	Gary Matthews Jr.	.20	.06
510	Matt Franco	.20	.06
511	Ben Weber	.20	.06
512	Dave Berg	.20	.06
513	Michael Young	.30	.09
514	Frank Catalanotto	.20	.06
515	Darin Erstad	.20	.06
516	Matt Williams	.20	.06
517	B.J. Surhoff	.20	.06
518	Kerry Ligtenberg	.20	.06
519	Mike Bordick	.20	.06
520	Arthur Rhodes	.20	.06
521	Joe Girardi	.20	.06
522	D'Angelo Jimenez	.20	.06
523	Paul Konerko	.20	.06
524	Jose Macias	.20	.06
525	Joe Mays	.20	.06
526	Marquis Grissom	.20	.06
527	Neifi Perez	.20	.06
528	Preston Wilson	.20	.06
529	Jeff Weaver	.20	.06
530	Eric Chavez	.20	.06
531	Placido Polanco	.20	.06
532	Matt Mantei	.20	.06
533	James Baldwin	.20	.06
534	Toby Hall	.20	.06
535	Brendan Donnelly	.20	.06
536	Benji Gil	.20	.06
537	Damian Moss	.20	.06
538	Jorge Julio	.20	.06
539	Matt Clement	.20	.06
540	Brian Moehler	.20	.06
541	Lee Stevens	.20	.06
542	Jimmy Haynes	.20	.06
543	Terry Mulholland	.20	.06
544	Dave Roberts	.20	.06
545	J.C. Romero	.20	.06
546	Bartolo Colon	.20	.06
547	Roger Cedeno	.20	.06
548	Mariano Rivera	.30	.09
549	Billy Koch	.20	.06
550	Manny Ramirez	.30	.09
551	Travis Lee	.20	.06
552	Oliver Perez	.20	.06
553	Tim Worrell	.20	.06
554	Rafael Soriano	.20	.06
555	Damian Miller	.20	.06
556	John Smoltz	.30	.09
557	Willis Roberts	.20	.06
558	Tim Hudson	.20	.06
559	Moises Alou	.20	.06
560	Gary Glover	.20	.06
561	Corky Miller	.20	.06
562	Ben Broussard	.20	.06
563	Gabe Kapler	.20	.06
564	Chris Woodward	.20	.06
565	Paul Wilson	.20	.06
566	Todd Hollandsworth	.20	.06
567	So Taguchi	.20	.06
568	John Olerud	.20	.06
569	Reggie Sanders	.20	.06
570	Jake Peavy	.20	.06
571	Kris Benson	.20	.06
572	Todd Pratt	.20	.06
573	Ray Durham	.20	.06
574	Boomer Wells	.20	.06
575	Chris Widger	.20	.06
576	Shawn Wooten	.20	.06
577	Tom Glavine	.30	.09
578	Antonio Alfonseca	.20	.06
579	Keith Foulke	.20	.06
580	Shawn Estes	.20	.06
581	Mark Grace	.30	.09
582	Dmitri Young	.20	.06
583	A.J. Burnett	.20	.06
584	Richard Hidalgo	.20	.06
585	Mike Sweeney	.20	.06
586	Alex Cora	.20	.06
587	Matt Stairs	.20	.06
588	Doug Mientkiewicz	.20	.06
589	Fernando Tatis	.20	.06
590	David Weathers	.20	.06
591	Cory Lidle	.20	.06
592	Dan Plesac	.20	.06
593	Jeff Bagwell	.30	.09
594	Steve Sparks	.20	.06
595	Sandy Alomar Jr.	.20	.06
596	John Lackey	.20	.06
597	Rick Helling	.20	.06
598	Mark DeRosa	.20	.06
599	Carlos Lee	.20	.06
600	Garret Anderson	.20	.06
601	Vinny Castilla	.20	.06
602	Ryan Drese	.20	.06
603	LaTroy Hawkins	.20	.06
604	David Bell	.20	.06
605	Freddy Garcia	.20	.06
606	Miguel Cairo	.20	.06
607	Scott Spiezio	.20	.06
608	Mike Remlinger	.20	.06
609	Tony Graffanino	.20	.06
610	Russell Branyan	.20	.06
611	Chris Magruder	.20	.06
612	Jose Contreras RC	1.00	.30
613	Carl Pavano	.20	.06
614	Kevin Brown	.20	.06
615	Tyler Houston	.20	.06
616	A.J. Pierzynski	.20	.06
617	Tony Fiore	.20	.06
618	Peter Bergeron	.20	.06
619	Rondell White	.20	.06
620	Brett Myers	.20	.06
621	Kevin Young	.20	.06
622	Kenny Lofton	.20	.06
623	Ben Davis	.20	.06
624	J.D. Drew	.20	.06
625	Chris Gomez	.20	.06
626	Karim Garcia	.20	.06
627	Ricky Gutierrez	.20	.06
628	Mark Redman	.20	.06
629	Juan Encarnacion	.20	.06
630	Anaheim Angels TC	.30	.09
631	Ariz.Diamondbacks TC	.20	.06
632	Atlanta Braves TC	.20	.06
633	Baltimore Orioles TC	.20	.06
634	Boston Red Sox TC	.20	.06
635	Chicago Cubs TC	.20	.06
636	Chicago White Sox TC	.20	.06
637	Cincinnati Reds TC	.20	.06
638	Cleveland Indians TC	.20	.06
639	Colorado Rockies TC	.20	.06
640	Detroit Tigers TC	.20	.06
641	Florida Marlins TC	.20	.06
642	Houston Astros TC	.20	.06
643	Kansas City Royals TC	.20	.06
644	Los Angeles Dodgers TC	.20	.06
645	Milwaukee Brewers TC	.20	.06
646	Minnesota Twins TC	.20	.06
647	Montreal Expos TC	.20	.06

❑ 648	New York Mets TC	.20	.06
❑ 649	New York Yankees TC	.30	.09
❑ 650	Oakland Athletics TC	.20	.06
❑ 651	Philadelphia Phillies TC	.20	.06
❑ 652	Pittsburgh Pirates TC	.20	.06
❑ 653	San Diego Padres TC	.20	.06
❑ 654	San Francisco Giants TC	.20	.06
❑ 655	Seattle Mariners TC	.20	.06
❑ 656	St. Louis Cardinals TC	.20	.06
❑ 657	T.B. Devil Rays TC	.20	.06
❑ 658	Texas Rangers TC	.20	.06
❑ 659	Toronto Blue Jays TC	.20	.06
❑ 660	Bryan Bullington DP RC	.50	.15
❑ 661	Jeremy Guthrie DP	.50	.15
❑ 662	Joey Gomes DP RC	.50	.15
❑ 663	E.Bastida-Martinez DP RC	.50	.15
❑ 664	Brian Wright DP RC	.50	.15
❑ 665	B.J. Upton DP	.75	.23
❑ 666	Jeff Francis DP	.50	.15
❑ 667	Drew Meyer DP	.50	.15
❑ 668	Jeremy Hermida DP	.50	.15
❑ 669	Khalil Greene DP	1.50	.45
❑ 670	Darrell Rasner DP RC	.50	.15
❑ 671	Cole Hamels DP	.50	.15
❑ 672	James Loney DP	.50	.15
❑ 673	Sergio Santos DP	.50	.15
❑ 674	Jason Pridie DP	.50	.15
❑ 675	Brandon Phillips Victor Martinez	.50	.15
❑ 676	Hee Seop Choi Nic Jackson	.50	.15
❑ 677	Dontrelle Willis Jason Stokes	.75	.23
❑ 678	Chad Tracy Lyle Overbay	.50	.15
❑ 679	Joe Borchard Corwin Malone	.50	.15
❑ 680	Joe Mauer Justin Morneau	.50	.15
❑ 681	Drew Henson Brandon Claussen	.50	.15
❑ 682	Chase Utley Gavin Floyd	.75	.23
❑ 683	Taggert Bozied Xavier Nady	.50	.15
❑ 684	Aaron Heilman Jose Reyes	.50	.15
❑ 685	Kenny Rogers AW	.20	.06
❑ 686	Bengie Molina AW	.20	.06
❑ 687	John Olerud AW	.20	.06
❑ 688	Bret Boone AW	.20	.06
❑ 689	Eric Chavez AW	.20	.06
❑ 690	Alex Rodriguez AW	.50	.15
❑ 691	Darin Erstad AW	.20	.06
❑ 692	Ichiro Suzuki AW	.50	.15
❑ 693	Torii Hunter AW	.20	.06
❑ 694	Greg Maddux AW	.50	.15
❑ 695	Brad Ausmus AW	.20	.06
❑ 696	Todd Helton AW	.20	.06
❑ 697	Fernando Vina AW	.20	.06
❑ 698	Scott Rolen AW	.20	.06
❑ 699	Edgar Renteria AW	.20	.06
❑ 700	Andruw Jones AW	.20	.06
❑ 701	Larry Walker AW	.20	.06
❑ 702	Jim Edmonds AW	.20	.06
❑ 703	Barry Zito AW	.20	.06
❑ 704	Randy Johnson AW	.30	.09
❑ 705	Miguel Tejada AW	.20	.06
❑ 706	Barry Bonds AW	.75	.23
❑ 707	Eric Hinske AW	.20	.06
❑ 708	Jason Jennings AW	.20	.06
❑ 709	Todd Helton AS	.20	.06
❑ 710	Jeff Kent AS	.20	.06
❑ 711	Edgar Renteria AS	.20	.06
❑ 712	Scott Rolen AS	.20	.06
❑ 713	Barry Bonds AS	.75	.23
❑ 714	Sammy Sosa AS	.30	.09
❑ 715	Vladimir Guerrero AS	.30	.09
❑ 716	Mike Piazza AS	.50	.15
❑ 717	Curt Schilling AS	.20	.06
❑ 718	Randy Johnson AS	.30	.09
❑ 719	Bobby Cox AS	.20	.06
❑ 720	Anaheim Angels WS	.30	.09
❑ 721	Anaheim Angels WS	.50	.15

2003 Topps Traded

	MINT	NRMT
COMPLETE SET (275)	50.00	22.00
COMMON CARD (T1-T120)	.20	.09
COMMON CARD (121-165)	.40	.18

❑ T1	Juan Pierre	.20	.09
❑ T2	Mark Grudzielanek	.20	.09
❑ T3	Tanyon Sturtze	.20	.09
❑ T4	Greg Vaughn	.20	.09
❑ T5	Greg Myers	.20	.09
❑ T6	Randall Simon	.20	.09
❑ T7	Todd Hundley	.20	.09
❑ T8	Marlon Anderson	.20	.09
❑ T9	Jeff Reboulet	.20	.09
❑ T10	Alex Sanchez	.20	.09
❑ T11	Mike Rivera	.20	.09
❑ T12	Todd Walker	.20	.09
❑ T13	Ray King	.20	.09
❑ T14	Shawn Estes	.20	.09
❑ T15	Gary Matthews Jr.	.20	.09
❑ T16	Jaret Wright	.20	.09
❑ T17	Edgardo Alfonzo	.20	.09
❑ T18	Omar Daal	.20	.09
❑ T19	Ryan Rupe	.20	.09
❑ T20	Tony Clark	.20	.09
❑ T21	Jeff Suppan	.20	.09
❑ T22	Mike Stanton	.20	.09
❑ T23	Ramon Martinez	.20	.09
❑ T24	Armando Rios	.20	.09
❑ T25	Johnny Estrada	.20	.09
❑ T26	Joe Girardi	.20	.09
❑ T27	Ivan Rodriguez	.30	.14
❑ T28	Robert Fick	.20	.09
❑ T29	Rick White	.20	.09
❑ T30	Robert Person	.20	.09
❑ T31	Alan Benes	.20	.09
❑ T32	Chris Carpenter	.20	.09
❑ T33	Chris Widger	.20	.09
❑ T34	Travis Hafner	.20	.09
❑ T35	Mike Venafro	.20	.09
❑ T36	Jon Lieber	.20	.09
❑ T37	Orlando Hernandez	.20	.09
❑ T38	Aaron Myette	.20	.09
❑ T39	Paul Bako	.20	.09
❑ T40	Erubiel Durazo	.20	.09
❑ T41	Mark Guthrie	.20	.09
❑ T42	Steve Avery	.20	.09
❑ T43	Damian Jackson	.20	.09
❑ T44	Rey Ordonez	.20	.09
❑ T45	John Flaherty	.20	.09
❑ T46	Byung-Hyun Kim	.20	.09
❑ T47	Tom Goodwin	.20	.09
❑ T48	Elmer Dessens	.20	.09
❑ T49	Al Martin	.20	.09
❑ T50	Gene Kingsale	.20	.09
❑ T51	Lenny Harris	.20	.09
❑ T52	David Ortiz Sox	.50	.23
❑ T53	Jose Lima	.20	.09
❑ T54	Mike Difelice	.20	.09
❑ T55	Jose Hernandez	.20	.09
❑ T56	Todd Zeile	.20	.09
❑ T57	Roberto Hernandez	.20	.09
❑ T58	Albie Lopez	.20	.09
❑ T59	Roberto Alomar	.30	.14
❑ T60	Russ Ortiz	.20	.09
❑ T61	Brian Daubach	.20	.09
❑ T62	Carl Everett	.20	.09
❑ T63	Jeromy Burnitz	.20	.09
❑ T64	Mark Bellhorn	.20	.09
❑ T65	Ruben Sierra	.20	.09
❑ T66	Mike Fetters	.20	.09
❑ T67	Armando Benitez	.20	.09
❑ T68	Deivi Cruz	.20	.09
❑ T69	Jose Cruz Jr.	.20	.09
❑ T70	Jeremy Fikac	.20	.09
❑ T71	Jeff Kent	.20	.09
❑ T72	Andres Galarraga	.20	.09
❑ T73	Rickey Henderson	.50	.23
❑ T74	Royce Clayton	.20	.09
❑ T75	Troy O'Leary	.20	.09
❑ T76	Ron Coomer	.20	.09
❑ T77	Greg Colbrunn	.20	.09
❑ T78	Wes Helms	.20	.09
❑ T79	Kevin Millwood	.20	.09
❑ T80	Damion Easley	.20	.09
❑ T81	Bobby Kielty	.20	.09
❑ T82	Keith Osik	.20	.09
❑ T83	Ramiro Mendoza	.20	.09
❑ T84	Shea Hillenbrand	.20	.09
❑ T85	Shannon Stewart	.20	.09
❑ T86	Eddie Perez	.20	.09
❑ T87	Ugueth Urbina	.20	.09
❑ T88	Orlando Palmeiro	.20	.09
❑ T89	Graeme Lloyd	.20	.09
❑ T90	John Vander Wal	.20	.09
❑ T91	Gary Bennett	.20	.09
❑ T92	Shane Reynolds	.20	.09
❑ T93	Steve Parris	.20	.09
❑ T94	Julio Lugo	.20	.09
❑ T95	John Halama	.20	.09
❑ T96	Carlos Baerga	.20	.09
❑ T97	Jim Parque	.20	.09
❑ T98	Mike Williams	.20	.09
❑ T99	Fred McGriff	.30	.14
❑ T100	Kenny Rogers	.20	.09
❑ T101	Matt Herges	.20	.09
❑ T102	Jay Bell	.20	.09
❑ T103	Esteban Yan	.20	.09
❑ T104	Eric Owens	.20	.09
❑ T105	Aaron Fultz	.20	.09
❑ T106	Rey Sanchez	.20	.09
❑ T107	Jim Thome	.30	.14
❑ T108	Aaron Boone	.20	.09
❑ T109	Raul Mondesi	.20	.09
❑ T110	Kenny Lofton	.20	.09
❑ T111	Jose Guillen	.20	.09
❑ T112	Aramis Ramirez	.20	.09
❑ T113	Sidney Ponson	.20	.09
❑ T114	Scott Williamson	.20	.09
❑ T115	Robin Ventura	.20	.09
❑ T116	Dusty Baker MG	.20	.09
❑ T117	Felipe Alou MG	.20	.09
❑ T118	Buck Showalter MG	.20	.09
❑ T119	Jack McKeon MG	.20	.09
❑ T120	Art Howe MG	.20	.09
❑ T121	Bobby Crosby PROS	.60	.25
❑ T122	Adrian Gonzalez PROS	.40	.18
❑ T123	Kevin Cash PROS	.40	.18
❑ T124	Shin-Soo Choo PROS	.40	.18
❑ T125	Chin-Feng Chen PROS	1.00	.45
❑ T126	Miguel Cabrera PROS	1.00	.45
❑ T127	Jason Young PROS	.40	.18
❑ T128	Alex Herrera PROS	.40	.18
❑ T129	Jason Dubois PROS	.40	.18
❑ T130	Jeff Mathis PROS	.40	.18
❑ T131	Casey Kotchman PROS	.40	.18
❑ T132	Ed Rogers PROS	.40	.18
❑ T133	Wilson Betemit PROS	.40	.18
❑ T134	Jim Kavourias PROS	.40	.18
❑ T135	Taylor Buchholz PROS	.40	.18
❑ T136	Adam LaRoche PROS	.40	.18
❑ T137	D.McPherson PROS	.40	.18
❑ T138	Jesus Cota PROS	.40	.18
❑ T139	Clint Nageotte PROS	.40	.18
❑ T140	Boof Bonser PROS	.40	.18
❑ T141	Walter Young PROS	.40	.18
❑ T142	Joe Crede PROS	.40	.18
❑ T143	Denny Bautista PROS	.40	.18
❑ T144	Victor Diaz PROS	.40	.18
❑ T145	Chris Narveson PROS	.40	.18
❑ T146	Gabe Gross PROS	.40	.18
❑ T147	Jimmy Journell PROS	.40	.18
❑ T148	Rafael Soriano PROS	.40	.18

- ❑ T149 Jerome Williams PROS .40 .18
- ❑ T150 Aaron Cook PROS .40 .18
- ❑ T151 An. Martinez PROS .40 .18
- ❑ T152 Scott Hairston PROS .40 .18
- ❑ T153 John Buck PROS .40 .18
- ❑ T154 Ryan Ludwick PROS .40 .18
- ❑ T155 Chris Bootcheck PROS .40 .18
- ❑ T156 John Rheinecker PROS .40 .18
- ❑ T157 Jason Lane PROS .40 .18
- ❑ T158 Shelley Duncan PROS .40 .18
- ❑ T159 Adam Wainwright PROS .40 .18
- ❑ T160 Jason Arnold PROS .40 .18
- ❑ T161 Jonny Gomes PROS .60 .25
- ❑ T162 James Loney PROS .40 .18
- ❑ T163 Mike Fontenot PROS .40 .18
- ❑ T164 Khalil Greene PROS 1.50 .70
- ❑ T165 Sean Burnett PROS .40 .18
- ❑ T166 David Martinez FY RC .40 .18
- ❑ T167 Felix Pie FY RC 4.00 1.80
- ❑ T168 Joe Valentine FY RC .40 .18
- ❑ T169 Brandon Webb FY RC .75 .35
- ❑ T170 Matt Diaz FY RC .50 .23
- ❑ T171 Lew Ford FY RC .50 .23
- ❑ T172 Jeremy Griffiths FY RC .40 .18
- ❑ T173 Matt Hensley FY RC .40 .18
- ❑ T174 Charlie Manning FY RC .40 .18
- ❑ T175 Elizardo Ramirez FY RC .50 .23
- ❑ T176 Greg Aquino FY RC .40 .18
- ❑ T177 Felix Sanchez FY RC .40 .18
- ❑ T178 Kelly Shoppach FY RC .75 .35
- ❑ T179 Bubba Nelson FY RC .50 .23
- ❑ T180 Mike O'Keefe FY RC .40 .18
- ❑ T181 Hanley Ramirez FY RC 2.50 1.10
- ❑ T182 T.Wellemeyer FY RC .40 .18
- ❑ T183 Dustin Moseley FY RC .40 .18
- ❑ T184 Eric Crozier FY RC .50 .23
- ❑ T185 Ryan Shealy FY RC .75 .35
- ❑ T186 Jer. Bonderman FY RC 2.50 1.10
- ❑ T187 T.Story-Harden FY RC .40 .18
- ❑ T188 Dusty Brown FY RC .40 .18
- ❑ T189 Rob Hammock FY RC .40 .18
- ❑ T190 Jorge Piedra FY RC .50 .23
- ❑ T191 Chris De La Cruz FY RC .40 .18
- ❑ T192 Eli Whiteside FY RC .40 .18
- ❑ T193 Jason Kubel FY RC .75 .35
- ❑ T194 Jon Schuerholz FY RC .40 .18
- ❑ T195 St. Randolph FY RC .40 .18
- ❑ T196 Andy Sisco FY RC .50 .23
- ❑ T197 Sean Smith FY RC .50 .23
- ❑ T198 Jon-Mark Sprowl FY RC .40 .18
- ❑ T199 Matt Kata FY RC .40 .18
- ❑ T200 Robinson Cano FY RC 5.00 2.20
- ❑ T201 Nook Logan FY RC .50 .23
- ❑ T202 Ben Francisco FY RC .40 .18
- ❑ T203 Arnie Munoz FY RC .40 .18
- ❑ T204 Ozzie Chavez FY RC .40 .18
- ❑ T205 Eric Riggs FY RC .50 .23
- ❑ T206 Beau Kemp FY RC .40 .18
- ❑ T207 Travis Wong FY RC .50 .23
- ❑ T208 Dustin Yount FY RC .50 .23
- ❑ T209 Brian McCann FY RC 3.00 1.35
- ❑ T210 Wilton Reynolds FY RC .50 .23
- ❑ T211 Matt Bruback FY RC .40 .18
- ❑ T212 Andrew Brown FY RC .50 .23
- ❑ T213 Edgar Gonzalez FY RC .40 .18
- ❑ T214 Eider Torres FY RC .40 .18
- ❑ T215 Aquilino Lopez FY RC .40 .18
- ❑ T216 Bobby Basham FY RC .50 .23
- ❑ T217 Tim Olson FY RC .40 .18
- ❑ T218 Nathan Panther FY RC .40 .18
- ❑ T219 Bryan Grace FY RC .40 .18
- ❑ T220 Dusty Gomon FY RC .50 .23
- ❑ T221 Wil Ledezma FY RC .40 .18
- ❑ T222 Josh Willingham FY RC .50 .23
- ❑ T223 David Cash FY RC .40 .18
- ❑ T224 Oscar Villarreal FY RC .40 .18
- ❑ T225 Jeff Duncan FY RC .40 .18
- ❑ T226 Kade Johnson FY RC .40 .18
- ❑ T227 L.Steidlmayer FY RC .40 .18
- ❑ T228 Brandon Watson FY RC .40 .18
- ❑ T229 Jose Morales FY RC .40 .18
- ❑ T230 Mike Gallo FY RC .40 .18
- ❑ T231 Tyler Adamczyk FY RC .40 .18
- ❑ T232 Adam Stern FY RC .40 .18
- ❑ T233 Brennan King FY RC .40 .18
- ❑ T234 Dan Haren FY RC .75 .35
- ❑ T235 Mi. Hernandez FY RC .40 .18
- ❑ T236 Ben Fritz FY RC .40 .18
- ❑ T237 Clay Hensley FY RC .40 .18
- ❑ T238 Tyler Johnson FY RC .40 .18
- ❑ T239 Pete LaForest FY RC .40 .18
- ❑ T240 Tyler Martin FY RC .40 .18
- ❑ T241 J.D. Durbin FY RC .40 .18
- ❑ T242 Shane Victorino FY RC .50 .23
- ❑ T243 Rajai Davis FY RC .40 .18
- ❑ T244 Ismael Castro FY RC .40 .18
- ❑ T245 C.Wang FY RC 2.50 1.10
- ❑ T246 Travis Ishikawa FY RC .40 .18
- ❑ T247 Corey Shafer FY RC .40 .18
- ❑ T248 G.Schneidmiller FY RC .40 .18
- ❑ T249 Dave Pember FY RC .40 .18
- ❑ T250 Keith Stamler FY RC .40 .18
- ❑ T251 Tyson Graham FY RC .40 .18
- ❑ T252 Ryan Cameron FY RC .40 .18
- ❑ T253 E.Eckenstahler FY RC .40 .18
- ❑ T254 Ma. Peterson FY RC .40 .18
- ❑ T255 D. McGowan FY RC .40 .18
- ❑ T256 Pr. Redman FY RC .40 .18
- ❑ T257 Haj Turay FY RC .50 .23
- ❑ T258 Carlos Guzman FY RC .50 .23
- ❑ T259 Matt DeMarco FY RC .40 .18
- ❑ T260 Derek Michaelis FY RC .40 .18
- ❑ T261 Brian Burgamy FY RC .40 .18
- ❑ T262 Jay Sitzman FY RC .40 .18
- ❑ T263 Chris Fallon FY RC .40 .18
- ❑ T264 Mike Adams FY RC .40 .18
- ❑ T265 Clint Barmes FY RC 1.50 .70
- ❑ T266 Eric Reed FY RC .40 .18
- ❑ T267 Willie Eyre FY RC .40 .18
- ❑ T268 Carlos Duran FY RC .40 .18
- ❑ T269 Nick Trzesniak FY RC .40 .18
- ❑ T270 Ferdin Tejeda FY RC .40 .18
- ❑ T271 Mi. Garciaparra FY RC .40 .18
- ❑ T272 Michael Hinckley FY RC .50 .23
- ❑ T273 Br. Florence FY RC .40 .18
- ❑ T274 Trent Oeltjen FY RC .50 .23
- ❑ T275 Mike Neu FY RC .40 .18

2004 Topps

	MINT	NRMT
COMP.HOBBY SET (737)	80.00	36.00
COMP.HOLIDAY SET (742)	80.00	36.00
COMP.RETAIL SET (737)	80.00	36.00
COMP.ASTROS SET (737)	80.00	36.00
COMP.CUBS SET (737)	80.00	36.00
COMP.RED SOX SET (737)	80.00	36.00
COMP.YANKEES SET (737)	80.00	36.00
COMPLETE SET (732)	80.00	36.00
COMPLETE SERIES 1 (366)	40.00	18.00
COMPLETE SERIES 2 (366)	40.00	18.00
COMMON CARD (1-6/8-732)	.20	.09
COMMON (297-326/668-687)	.50	.23
COMMON (327-331/688-692)	.50	.23

- ❑ 1 Jim Thome .30 .14
- ❑ 2 Reggie Sanders .20 .09
- ❑ 3 Mark Kotsay .20 .09
- ❑ 4 Edgardo Alfonzo .20 .09
- ❑ 5 Ben Davis .20 .09
- ❑ 6 Mike Matheny .20 .09
- ❑ 8 Marlon Anderson .20 .09
- ❑ 9 Chan Ho Park .20 .09
- ❑ 10 Ichiro Suzuki 1.00 .45
- ❑ 11 Kevin Millwood .20 .09
- ❑ 12 Bengie Molina .20 .09
- ❑ 13 Tom Glavine .30 .14
- ❑ 14 Junior Spivey .20 .09
- ❑ 15 Marcus Giles .20 .09
- ❑ 16 David Segui .20 .09
- ❑ 17 Kevin Millar .20 .09
- ❑ 18 Corey Patterson .20 .09
- ❑ 19 Aaron Rowand .20 .09
- ❑ 20 Derek Jeter 1.00 .45
- ❑ 21 Jason LaRue .20 .09
- ❑ 22 Chris Hammond .20 .09
- ❑ 23 Jay Payton .20 .09
- ❑ 24 Bobby Higginson .20 .09
- ❑ 25 Lance Berkman .20 .09
- ❑ 26 Juan Pierre .20 .09
- ❑ 27 Brent Mayne .20 .09
- ❑ 28 Fred McGriff .30 .14
- ❑ 29 Richie Sexson .20 .09
- ❑ 30 Tim Hudson .20 .09
- ❑ 31 Mike Piazza .75 .35
- ❑ 32 Brad Radke .20 .09
- ❑ 33 Jeff Weaver .20 .09
- ❑ 34 Ramon Hernandez .20 .09
- ❑ 35 David Bell .20 .09
- ❑ 36 Craig Wilson .20 .09
- ❑ 37 Jake Peavy .20 .09
- ❑ 38 Tim Worrell .20 .09
- ❑ 39 Gil Meche .20 .09
- ❑ 40 Albert Pujols 1.00 .45
- ❑ 41 Michael Young .20 .09
- ❑ 42 Josh Phelps .20 .09
- ❑ 43 Brendan Donnelly .20 .09
- ❑ 44 Steve Finley .20 .09
- ❑ 45 John Smoltz .30 .14
- ❑ 46 Jay Gibbons .20 .09
- ❑ 47 Trot Nixon .20 .09
- ❑ 48 Carl Pavano .20 .09
- ❑ 49 Frank Thomas .50 .23
- ❑ 50 Mark Prior .30 .14
- ❑ 51 Danny Graves .20 .09
- ❑ 52 Milton Bradley UER .20 .09
- ❑ 53 Jose Jimenez .20 .09
- ❑ 54 Shane Halter .20 .09
- ❑ 55 Mike Lowell .20 .09
- ❑ 56 Geoff Blum .20 .09
- ❑ 57 Michael Tucker UER .20 .09
  Dee Brown pictured
- ❑ 58 Paul Lo Duca .20 .09
- ❑ 59 Vicente Padilla .20 .09
- ❑ 60 Jacque Jones .20 .09
- ❑ 61 Fernando Tatis .20 .09
- ❑ 62 Ty Wigginton .20 .09
- ❑ 63 Pedro Astacio .20 .09
- ❑ 64 Andy Pettitte .30 .14
- ❑ 65 Terrence Long .20 .09
- ❑ 66 Cliff Floyd .20 .09
- ❑ 67 Mariano Rivera .30 .14
- ❑ 68 Carlos Silva .20 .09
- ❑ 69 Marlon Byrd .20 .09
- ❑ 70 Mark Mulder .20 .09
- ❑ 71 Kerry Ligtenberg .20 .09
- ❑ 72 Carlos Guillen .20 .09
- ❑ 73 Fernando Vina .20 .09
- ❑ 74 Lance Carter .20 .09
- ❑ 75 Hank Blalock .20 .09
- ❑ 76 Jimmy Rollins .20 .09
- ❑ 77 Francisco Rodriguez .20 .09
- ❑ 78 Javy Lopez .20 .09
- ❑ 79 Jerry Hairston Jr. .20 .09
- ❑ 80 Andruw Jones .30 .14
- ❑ 81 Rodrigo Lopez .20 .09
- ❑ 82 Johnny Damon .30 .14
- ❑ 83 Hee Seop Choi .20 .09
- ❑ 84 Miguel Olivo .20 .09
- ❑ 85 Jon Garland .20 .09
- ❑ 86 Matt Lawton .20 .09
- ❑ 87 Juan Uribe .20 .09
- ❑ 88 Steve Sparks .20 .09
- ❑ 89 Tim Spooneybarger .20 .09
- ❑ 90 Jose Vidro .20 .09
- ❑ 91 Luis Rivas .20 .09
- ❑ 92 Hideo Nomo .50 .23
- ❑ 93 Javier Vazquez .20 .09
- ❑ 94 Al Leiter .20 .09
- ❑ 95 Darren Dreifort .20 .09
- ❑ 96 Alex Cintron .20 .09

❑ 97 Zach Day .20 .09
❑ 98 Jorge Posada .30 .14
❑ 99 John Halama .20 .09
❑ 100 Alex Rodriguez .75 .35
❑ 101 Orlando Palmeiro .20 .09
❑ 102 Dave Berg .20 .09
❑ 103 Brad Fullmer .20 .09
❑ 104 Mike Hampton .20 .09
❑ 105 Willis Roberts .20 .09
❑ 106 Ramiro Mendoza .20 .09
❑ 107 Juan Cruz .20 .09
❑ 108 Esteban Loaiza .20 .09
❑ 109 Russell Branyan .20 .09
❑ 110 Todd Helton .30 .14
❑ 111 Braden Looper .20 .09
❑ 112 Octavio Dotel .20 .09
❑ 113 Mike MacDougal .20 .09
❑ 114 Cesar Izturis .20 .09
❑ 115 Johan Santana .30 .14
❑ 116 Jose Contreras .20 .09
❑ 117 Placido Polanco .20 .09
❑ 118 Jason Phillips .20 .09
❑ 119 Adam Eaton .20 .09
❑ 120 Vernon Wells .20 .09
❑ 121 Ben Grieve .20 .09
❑ 122 Randy Winn .20 .09
❑ 123 Ismael Valdes .20 .09
❑ 124 Eric Owens .20 .09
❑ 125 Curt Schilling .20 .09
❑ 126 Russ Ortiz .20 .09
❑ 127 Mark Buehrle .20 .09
❑ 128 Danys Baez .20 .09
❑ 129 Dmitri Young .20 .09
❑ 130 Kazuhisa Ishii .20 .09
❑ 131 A.J. Pierzynski .20 .09
❑ 132 Michael Barrett .20 .09
❑ 133 Joe McEwing .20 .09
❑ 134 Alex Cora .20 .09
❑ 135 Tom Wilson .20 .09
❑ 136 Carlos Zambrano .20 .09
❑ 137 Brett Tomko .20 .09
❑ 138 Shigetoshi Hasegawa .20 .09
❑ 139 Jarrod Washburn .20 .09
❑ 140 Greg Maddux .75 .35
❑ 141 Craig Counsell .20 .09
❑ 142 Reggie Taylor .20 .09
❑ 143 Omar Vizquel .30 .14
❑ 144 Alex Gonzalez .20 .09
❑ 145 Billy Wagner .20 .09
❑ 146 Brian Jordan .20 .09
❑ 147 Wes Helms .20 .09
❑ 148 Kyle Lohse .20 .09
❑ 149 Timo Perez .20 .09
❑ 150 Jason Giambi .20 .09
❑ 151 Erubiel Durazo .20 .09
❑ 152 Mike Lieberthal .20 .09
❑ 153 Jason Kendall .20 .09
❑ 154 Xavier Nady .20 .09
❑ 155 Kirk Rueter .20 .09
❑ 156 Mike Cameron .20 .09
❑ 157 Miguel Cairo .20 .09
❑ 158 Woody Williams .20 .09
❑ 159 Toby Hall .20 .09
❑ 160 Bernie Williams .30 .14
❑ 161 Darin Erstad .20 .09
❑ 162 Matt Mantei .20 .09
❑ 163 Geronimo Gil .20 .09
❑ 164 Bill Mueller .20 .09
❑ 165 Damian Miller .20 .09
❑ 166 Tony Graffanino .20 .09
❑ 167 Sean Casey .30 .14
❑ 168 Brandon Phillips .20 .09
❑ 169 Mike Remlinger .20 .09
❑ 170 Adam Dunn .20 .09
❑ 171 Carlos Lee .20 .09
❑ 172 Juan Encarnacion .20 .09
❑ 173 Angel Berroa .20 .09
❑ 174 Desi Relaford .20 .09
❑ 175 Paul Quantrill .20 .09
❑ 176 Ben Sheets .20 .09
❑ 177 Eddie Guardado .20 .09
❑ 178 Rocky Biddle .20 .09
❑ 179 Mike Stanton .20 .09
❑ 180 Eric Chavez .20 .09
❑ 181 Jason Michaels .20 .09
❑ 182 Terry Adams .20 .09
❑ 183 Kip Wells .20 .09
❑ 184 Brian Lawrence .20 .09
❑ 185 Bret Boone .20 .09
❑ 186 Tino Martinez .30 .14
❑ 187 Aubrey Huff .20 .09
❑ 188 Kevin Mench .20 .09
❑ 189 Tim Salmon .30 .14
❑ 190 Carlos Delgado .20 .09
❑ 191 John Lackey .20 .09
❑ 192 Oscar Villarreal .20 .09
❑ 193 Luis Matos .20 .09
❑ 194 Derek Lowe .20 .09
❑ 195 Mark Grudzielanek .20 .09
❑ 196 Tom Gordon .20 .09
❑ 197 Matt Clement .20 .09
❑ 198 Byung-Hyun Kim .20 .09
❑ 199 Brandon Inge .20 .09
❑ 200 Nomar Garciaparra .75 .35
❑ 201 Antonio Osuna .20 .09
❑ 202 Jose Mesa .20 .09
❑ 203 Bo Hart .20 .09
❑ 204 Jack Wilson .20 .09
❑ 205 Ray Durham .20 .09
❑ 206 Freddy Garcia .20 .09
❑ 207 J.D. Drew .20 .09
❑ 208 Einar Diaz .20 .09
❑ 209 Roy Halladay .20 .09
❑ 210 David Eckstein UER .20 .09
Adam Kennedy pictured
❑ 211 Jason Marquis .20 .09
❑ 212 Jorge Julio .20 .09
❑ 213 Tim Wakefield .20 .09
❑ 214 Moises Alou .20 .09
❑ 215 Bartolo Colon .20 .09
❑ 216 Jimmy Haynes .20 .09
❑ 217 Preston Wilson .20 .09
❑ 218 Luis Castillo .20 .09
❑ 219 Richard Hidalgo .20 .09
❑ 220 Manny Ramirez .30 .14
❑ 221 Mike Mussina .30 .14
❑ 222 Randy Wolf .20 .09
❑ 223 Kris Benson .20 .09
❑ 224 Ryan Klesko .20 .09
❑ 225 Rich Aurilia .20 .09
❑ 226 Kelvim Escobar .20 .09
❑ 227 Francisco Cordero .20 .09
❑ 228 Kazuhiro Sasaki .20 .09
❑ 229 Danny Bautista .20 .09
❑ 230 Rafael Furcal .20 .09
❑ 231 Travis Driskill .20 .09
❑ 232 Kyle Farnsworth .20 .09
❑ 233 Jose Valentin .20 .09
❑ 234 Felipe Lopez .20 .09
❑ 235 C.C. Sabathia .20 .09
❑ 236 Brad Penny .20 .09
❑ 237 Brad Ausmus .20 .09
❑ 238 Raul Ibanez .20 .09
❑ 239 Adrian Beltre .20 .09
❑ 240 Rocco Baldelli .20 .09
❑ 241 Orlando Hudson .20 .09
❑ 242 Dave Roberts .20 .09
❑ 243 Doug Mientkiewicz .20 .09
❑ 244 Brad Wilkerson .20 .09
❑ 245 Scott Strickland .20 .09
❑ 246 Ryan Franklin .20 .09
❑ 247 Chad Bradford .20 .09
❑ 248 Gary Bennett .20 .09
❑ 249 Jose Cruz Jr. .20 .09
❑ 250 Jeff Kent .20 .09
❑ 251 Josh Beckett .20 .09
❑ 252 Ramon Ortiz .20 .09
❑ 253 Miguel Batista .20 .09
❑ 254 Jung Bong .20 .09
❑ 255 Deivi Cruz .20 .09
❑ 256 Alex Gonzalez .20 .09
❑ 257 Shawn Chacon .20 .09
❑ 258 Runelvys Hernandez .20 .09
❑ 259 Joe Mays .20 .09
❑ 260 Eric Gagne .20 .09
❑ 261 Dustan Mohr UER .20 .09
1998 Kinston stats are wrong
❑ 262 Tomokazu Ohka .20 .09
❑ 263 Eric Byrnes .20 .09
❑ 264 Frank Catalanotto .20 .09
❑ 265 Cristian Guzman .20 .09
❑ 266 Orlando Cabrera .20 .09
❑ 267A Juan Castro .20 .09
❑ 267B M.Scioscia MG UER 274 .20 .09
❑ 268 Bob Brenly MG .20 .09
❑ 269 Bobby Cox MG .20 .09
❑ 270 Mike Hargrove MG .20 .09
❑ 271 Grady Little MG .20 .09
❑ 272 Dusty Baker MG .20 .09
❑ 273 Jerry Manuel MG .20 .09
❑ 275 Eric Wedge MG .20 .09
❑ 276 Clint Hurdle MG .20 .09
❑ 277 Alan Trammell MG .20 .09
❑ 278 Jack McKeon MG .20 .09
❑ 279 Jimy Williams MG .20 .09
❑ 280 Tony Pena MG .20 .09
❑ 281 Jim Tracy MG .20 .09
❑ 282 Ned Yost MG .20 .09
❑ 283 Ron Gardenhire MG .20 .09
❑ 284 Frank Robinson MG .20 .09
❑ 285 Art Howe MG .20 .09
❑ 286 Joe Torre MG .30 .14
❑ 287 Ken Macha MG .20 .09
❑ 288 Larry Bowa MG .20 .09
❑ 289 Lloyd McClendon MG .20 .09
❑ 290 Bruce Bochy MG .20 .09
❑ 291 Felipe Alou MG .20 .09
❑ 292 Bob Melvin MG .20 .09
❑ 293 Tony LaRussa MG .20 .09
❑ 294 Lou Piniella MG .20 .09
❑ 295 Buck Showalter MG .20 .09
❑ 296 Carlos Tosca MG .20 .09
❑ 297 Anthony Acevedo FY RC .50 .23
❑ 298 Anthony Lerew FY RC .50 .23
❑ 299 Blake Hawksworth FY RC .50 .23
❑ 300 Brayan Pena FY RC .50 .23
❑ 301 Casey Myers FY RC .50 .23
❑ 302 Craig Ansman FY RC .50 .23
❑ 303 David Murphy FY RC 1.00 .45
❑ 304 Dave Crouthers FY RC .50 .23
❑ 305 Dioner Navarro FY RC 1.50 .70
❑ 306 Donald Levinski FY RC .50 .23
❑ 307 Jesse Roman FY RC .50 .23
❑ 308 Sung Jung FY RC .50 .23
❑ 309 Jon Knott FY RC .50 .23
❑ 310 Josh Labandeira FY RC .50 .23
❑ 311 Kenny Perez FY RC .50 .23
❑ 312 Khalid Ballouli FY RC .50 .23
❑ 313 Kyle Davies FY RC 2.50 1.10
❑ 314 Marcus McBeth FY RC .50 .23
❑ 315 Matt Creighton FY RC .50 .23
❑ 316 Chris O'Riordan FY RC .50 .23
❑ 317 Mike Gosling FY RC .50 .23
❑ 318 Nic Ungs FY RC .50 .23
❑ 319 Omar Falcon FY RC .50 .23
❑ 320 Rodney Choy Foo FY RC .50 .23
❑ 321 Tim Frend FY RC .50 .23
❑ 322 Todd Self FY RC .50 .23
❑ 323 Tydus Meadows FY RC .50 .23
❑ 324 Yadier Molina FY RC 2.00 .90
❑ 325 Zach Duke FY RC 4.00 1.80
❑ 326 Zach Miner FY RC .50 .23
❑ 327 Bernie Castro .50 .23
Khalil Greene FS
❑ 328 Ryan Madson .50 .23
Elizardo Ramirez FS
❑ 329 Rich Harden .50 .23
Bobby Crosby FS
❑ 330 Zack Greinke .50 .23
Jimmy Gobble FS
❑ 331 Bobby Jenks .50 .23
Casey Kotchman FS
❑ 332 Sammy Sosa HL .30 .14
❑ 333 Kevin Millwood HL .20 .09
❑ 334 Rafael Palmeiro HL .20 .09
❑ 335 Roger Clemens HL .50 .23
❑ 336 Eric Gagne HL .20 .09
❑ 337 Bill Mueller .30 .14
Manny Ramirez
Derek Jeter
AL Batting Avg LL
❑ 338 Vernon Wells .50 .23
Ichiro Suzuki
Michael Young
AL Hits LL
❑ 339 Alex Rodriguez .50 .23
Frank Thomas
Carlos Delgado

AL Home Runs LL		
❑ 340 Carlos Delgado	.50	.23
Alex Rodriguez		
Bret Boone		
AL RBI's LL		
❑ 341 Pedro Martinez	.30	.14
Tim Hudson		
Esteban Loaiza		
AL ERA LL		
❑ 342 Esteban Loaiza	.30	.14
Pedro Martinez		
Roy Halladay		
AL Strikeouts LL		
❑ 343 Albert Pujols	.50	.23
Todd Helton		
Edgar Renteria		
NL Batting Avg LL		
❑ 344 Albert Pujols	.50	.23
Todd Helton		
Juan Pierre		
NL Hits LL		
❑ 345 Jim Thome	.20	.09
Richie Sexson		
Javy Lopez		
NL Home Runs LL		
❑ 346 Preston Wilson	.20	.09
Gary Sheffield		
Jim Thome		
NL RBI's LL		
❑ 347 Jason Schmidt	.30	.14
Kevin Brown		
Mark Prior		
NL ERA LL		
❑ 348 Kerry Wood	.30	.14
Mark Prior		
Javier Vazquez		
NL Strikeouts LL		
❑ 349 Roger Clemens	.50	.23
David Wells ALDS		
❑ 350 Kerry Wood	.30	.14
Mark Prior NLDS		
❑ 351 Josh Beckett	.50	.23
Miguel Cabrera		
Ivan Rodriguez NLCS		
❑ 352 Jason Giambi	.50	.23
Mariano Rivera		
Aaron Boone ALCS		
❑ 353 Derek Lowe	.50	.23
Ivan Rodriguez AL/NLDS		
❑ 354 Pedro Martinez	.50	.23
Jorge Posada		
Roger Clemens ALCS		
❑ 355 Juan Pierre WS	.20	.09
❑ 356 Carlos Delgado AS	.20	.09
❑ 357 Bret Boone AS	.20	.09
❑ 358 Alex Rodriguez AS	.50	.23
❑ 359 Bill Mueller AS	.20	.09
❑ 360 Vernon Wells AS	.20	.09
❑ 361 Garret Anderson AS	.20	.09
❑ 362 Magglio Ordonez AS	.20	.09
❑ 363 Jorge Posada AS	.20	.09
❑ 364 Roy Halladay AS	.20	.09
❑ 365 Andy Pettitte AS	.20	.09
❑ 366 Frank Thomas AS	.30	.14
❑ 367 Jody Gerut AS	.20	.09
❑ 368 Sammy Sosa	.50	.23
❑ 369 Joe Crede	.20	.09
❑ 370 Gary Sheffield	.20	.09
❑ 371 Coco Crisp	.20	.09
❑ 372 Torii Hunter	.20	.09
❑ 373 Derrek Lee	.30	.14
❑ 374 Adam Everett	.20	.09
❑ 375 Miguel Tejada	.20	.09
❑ 376 Jeremy Affeldt	.20	.09
❑ 377 Robin Ventura	.20	.09
❑ 378 Scott Podsednik	.20	.09
❑ 379 Matthew LeCroy	.20	.09
❑ 380 Vladimir Guerrero	.50	.23
❑ 381 Tike Redman	.20	.09
❑ 382 Jeff Nelson	.20	.09
❑ 383 Cliff Lee	.20	.09
❑ 384 Bobby Abreu	.20	.09
❑ 385 Josh Fogg	.20	.09
❑ 386 Trevor Hoffman	.20	.09
❑ 387 Jesse Foppert	.20	.09
❑ 388 Edgar Martinez	.30	.14
❑ 389 Edgar Renteria	.20	.09
❑ 390 Chipper Jones	.50	.23
❑ 391 Eric Munson	.20	.09
❑ 392 Dewon Brazelton	.20	.09
❑ 393 John Thomson	.20	.09
❑ 394 Chris Woodward	.20	.09
❑ 395 Adam LaRoche	.20	.09
❑ 396 Elmer Dessens	.20	.09
❑ 397 Johnny Estrada	.20	.09
❑ 398 Damian Moss	.20	.09
❑ 399 Gabe Kapler	.20	.09
❑ 400 Dontrelle Willis	.30	.14
❑ 401 Troy Glaus	.20	.09
❑ 402 Raul Mondesi	.20	.09
❑ 403 Shane Reynolds	.20	.09
❑ 404 Kurt Ainsworth	.20	.09
❑ 405 Pedro Martinez	.30	.14
❑ 406 Eric Karros	.20	.09
❑ 407 Billy Koch	.20	.09
❑ 408 Scott Schoeneweis	.20	.09
❑ 409 Paul Wilson	.20	.09
❑ 410 Mike Sweeney	.20	.09
❑ 411 Jason Bay	.20	.09
❑ 412 Mark Redman	.20	.09
❑ 413 Jason Jennings	.20	.09
❑ 414 Rondell White	.20	.09
❑ 415 Todd Hundley	.20	.09
❑ 416 Shannon Stewart	.20	.09
❑ 417 Jae Weong Seo	.20	.09
❑ 418 Livan Hernandez	.20	.09
❑ 419 Mark Ellis	.20	.09
❑ 420 Pat Burrell	.20	.09
❑ 421 Mark Loretta	.20	.09
❑ 422 Robb Nen	.20	.09
❑ 423 Joel Pineiro	.20	.09
❑ 424 Jason Simontacchi	.20	.09
❑ 425 Sterling Hitchcock	.20	.09
❑ 426 Rey Ordonez	.20	.09
❑ 427 Greg Myers	.20	.09
❑ 428 Shane Spencer	.20	.09
❑ 429 Carlos Baerga	.20	.09
❑ 430 Garret Anderson	.20	.09
❑ 431 Horacio Ramirez	.20	.09
❑ 432 Brian Roberts	.20	.09
❑ 433 Damian Jackson	.20	.09
❑ 434 Doug Glanville	.20	.09
❑ 435 Brian Daubach	.20	.09
❑ 436 Alex Escobar	.20	.09
❑ 437 Alex Sanchez	.20	.09
❑ 438 Jeff Bagwell	.30	.14
❑ 439 Darrell May	.20	.09
❑ 440 Shawn Green	.20	.09
❑ 441 Geoff Jenkins	.20	.09
❑ 442 Endy Chavez	.20	.09
❑ 443 Nick Johnson	.20	.09
❑ 444 Jose Guillen	.20	.09
❑ 445 Tomas Perez	.20	.09
❑ 446 Phil Nevin	.20	.09
❑ 447 Jason Schmidt	.20	.09
❑ 448 Julio Mateo	.20	.09
❑ 449 So Taguchi	.20	.09
❑ 450 Randy Johnson	.50	.23
❑ 451 Paul Byrd	.20	.09
❑ 452 Chone Figgins	.20	.09
❑ 453 Larry Bigbie	.20	.09
❑ 454 Scott Williamson	.20	.09
❑ 455 Ramon Martinez	.20	.09
❑ 456 Roberto Alomar	.30	.14
❑ 457 Ryan Dempster	.20	.09
❑ 458 Ryan Ludwick	.20	.09
❑ 459 Ramon Santiago	.20	.09
❑ 460 Jeff Conine	.20	.09
❑ 461 Brad Lidge	.20	.09
❑ 462 Ken Harvey	.20	.09
❑ 463 Guillermo Mota	.20	.09
❑ 464 Rick Reed	.20	.09
❑ 465 Joey Eischen	.20	.09
❑ 466 Wade Miller	.20	.09
❑ 467 Steve Karsay	.20	.09
❑ 468 Chase Utley	.30	.14
❑ 469 Matt Stairs	.20	.09
❑ 470 Yorvit Torrealba	.20	.09
❑ 471 Joe Kennedy	.20	.09
❑ 472 Reed Johnson	.20	.09
❑ 473 Victor Zambrano	.20	.09
❑ 474 Jeff Davanon	.20	.09
❑ 475 Luis Gonzalez	.20	.09
❑ 476 Eli Marrero	.20	.09
❑ 477 Ray King	.20	.09
❑ 478 Jack Cust	.20	.09
❑ 479 Omar Daal	.20	.09
❑ 480 Todd Walker	.20	.09
❑ 481 Shawn Estes	.20	.09
❑ 482 Chris Reitsma	.20	.09
❑ 483 Jake Westbrook	.20	.09
❑ 484 Jeremy Bonderman	.20	.09
❑ 485 A.J. Burnett	.20	.09
❑ 486 Roy Oswalt	.20	.09
❑ 487 Kevin Brown	.20	.09
❑ 488 Eric Milton	.20	.09
❑ 489 Claudio Vargas	.20	.09
❑ 490 Roger Cedeno	.20	.09
❑ 491 David Wells	.20	.09
❑ 492 Scott Hatteberg	.20	.09
❑ 493 Ricky Ledee	.20	.09
❑ 494 Eric Young	.20	.09
❑ 495 Armando Benitez	.20	.09
❑ 496 Dan Haren	.20	.09
❑ 497 Carl Crawford	.20	.09
❑ 498 Laynce Nix	.20	.09
❑ 499 Eric Hinske	.20	.09
❑ 500 Ivan Rodriguez	.30	.14
❑ 501 Scot Shields	.20	.09
❑ 502 Brandon Webb	.20	.09
❑ 503 Mark DeRosa	.20	.09
❑ 504 Jhonny Peralta	.20	.09
❑ 505 Adam Kennedy	.20	.09
❑ 506 Tony Batista	.20	.09
❑ 507 Jeff Suppan	.20	.09
❑ 508 Kenny Lofton	.20	.09
❑ 509 Scott Sullivan	.20	.09
❑ 510 Ken Griffey Jr.	.75	.35
❑ 511 Billy Traber	.20	.09
❑ 512 Larry Walker	.20	.09
❑ 513 Mike Maroth	.20	.09
❑ 514 Todd Hollandsworth	.20	.09
❑ 515 Kirk Saarloos	.20	.09
❑ 516 Carlos Beltran	.20	.09
❑ 517 Juan Rivera	.20	.09
❑ 518 Roger Clemens	1.00	.45
❑ 519 Karim Garcia	.20	.09
❑ 520 Jose Reyes	.20	.09
❑ 521 Brandon Duckworth	.20	.09
❑ 522 Brian Giles	.20	.09
❑ 523 J.T. Snow	.20	.09
❑ 524 Jamie Moyer	.20	.09
❑ 525 Jason Isringhausen	.20	.09
❑ 526 Julio Lugo	.20	.09
❑ 527 Mark Teixeira	.30	.14
❑ 528 Cory Lidle	.20	.09
❑ 529 Lyle Overbay	.20	.09
❑ 530 Troy Percival	.20	.09
❑ 531 Robby Hammock	.20	.09
❑ 532 Robert Fick	.20	.09
❑ 533 Jason Johnson	.20	.09
❑ 534 Brandon Lyon	.20	.09
❑ 535 Antonio Alfonseca	.20	.09
❑ 536 Tom Goodwin	.20	.09
❑ 537 Paul Konerko	.20	.09
❑ 538 D'Angelo Jimenez	.20	.09
❑ 539 Ben Broussard	.20	.09
❑ 540 Magglio Ordonez	.20	.09
❑ 541 Ellis Burks	.20	.09
❑ 542 Carlos Pena	.20	.09
❑ 543 Chad Fox	.20	.09
❑ 544 Jeriome Robertson	.20	.09
❑ 545 Travis Hafner	.20	.09
❑ 546 Joe Randa	.20	.09
❑ 547 Wil Cordero	.20	.09
❑ 548 Brady Clark	.20	.09
❑ 549 Ruben Sierra	.20	.09
❑ 550 Barry Zito	.20	.09
❑ 551 Brett Myers	.20	.09
❑ 552 Oliver Perez	.20	.09
❑ 553 Trey Hodges	.20	.09
❑ 554 Benito Santiago	.20	.09
❑ 555 David Ross	.20	.09
❑ 556 Ramon Vazquez	.20	.09
❑ 557 Joe Nathan	.20	.09
❑ 558 Dan Wilson	.20	.09
❑ 559 Joe Mauer	.20	.09
❑ 560 Jim Edmonds	.30	.14

❑ 561 Shawn Wooten .20 .09
❑ 562 Matt Kata .20 .09
❑ 563 Vinny Castilla .20 .09
❑ 564 Marty Cordova .20 .09
❑ 565 Aramis Ramirez .20 .09
❑ 566 Carl Everett .20 .09
❑ 567 Ryan Freel .20 .09
❑ 568 Jason Davis .20 .09
❑ 569 Mark Bellhorn Sox .20 .09
❑ 570 Craig Monroe .20 .09
❑ 571 Roberto Hernandez .20 .09
❑ 572 Tim Redding .20 .09
❑ 573 Kevin Appier .20 .09
❑ 574 Jeromy Burnitz .20 .09
❑ 575 Miguel Cabrera .30 .14
❑ 576 Ramon Nivar .20 .09
❑ 577 Casey Blake .20 .09
❑ 578 Aaron Boone .20 .09
❑ 579 Jermaine Dye .20 .09
❑ 580 Jerome Williams .20 .09
❑ 581 John Olerud .20 .09
❑ 582 Scott Rolen .30 .14
❑ 583 Bobby Kielty .20 .09
❑ 584 Travis Lee .20 .09
❑ 585 Jeff Cirillo .20 .09
❑ 586 Scott Spiezio .20 .09
❑ 587 Stephen Randolph .20 .09
❑ 588 Melvin Mora .20 .09
❑ 589 Mike Timlin .20 .09
❑ 590 Kerry Wood .20 .09
❑ 591 Tony Womack .20 .09
❑ 592 Jody Gerut .20 .09
❑ 593 Franklyn German .20 .09
❑ 594 Morgan Ensberg .20 .09
❑ 595 Odalis Perez .20 .09
❑ 596 Michael Cuddyer .20 .09
❑ 597 Jon Lieber .20 .09
❑ 598 Mike Williams .20 .09
❑ 599 Jose Hernandez .20 .09
❑ 600 Alfonso Soriano .20 .09
❑ 601 Marquis Grissom .20 .09
❑ 602 Matt Morris .20 .09
❑ 603 Damian Rolls .20 .09
❑ 604 Juan Gonzalez .20 .09
❑ 605 Aquilino Lopez .20 .09
❑ 606 Jose Valverde .20 .09
❑ 607 Kenny Rogers .20 .09
❑ 608 Joe Borowski .20 .09
❑ 609 Josh Bard .20 .09
❑ 610 Austin Kearns .20 .09
❑ 611 Chin-Hui Tsao .20 .09
❑ 612 Wil Ledezma .20 .09
❑ 613 Aaron Guiel .20 .09
❑ 614 LaTroy Hawkins .20 .09
❑ 615 Tony Armas Jr. .20 .09
❑ 616 Steve Trachsel .20 .09
❑ 617 Ted Lilly .20 .09
❑ 618 Todd Pratt .20 .09
❑ 619 Sean Burroughs .20 .09
❑ 620 Rafael Palmeiro .30 .14
❑ 621 Jeremi Gonzalez .20 .09
❑ 622 Quinton McCracken .20 .09
❑ 623 David Ortiz .50 .23
❑ 624 Randall Simon .20 .09
❑ 625 Wily Mo Pena .20 .09
❑ 626 Nate Cornejo .20 .09
❑ 627 Brian Anderson .20 .09
❑ 628 Corey Koskie .20 .09
❑ 629 Keith Foulke Sox .20 .09
❑ 630 Rheal Cormier .20 .09
❑ 631 Sidney Ponson .20 .09
❑ 632 Gary Matthews Jr. .20 .09
❑ 633 Herbert Perry .20 .09
❑ 634 Shea Hillenbrand .20 .09
❑ 635 Craig Biggio .30 .14
❑ 636 Barry Larkin .30 .14
❑ 637 Arthur Rhodes .20 .09
❑ 638 Anaheim Angels TC .20 .09
❑ 639 Arizona Diamondbacks TC .20 .09
❑ 640 Atlanta Braves TC .20 .09
❑ 641 Baltimore Orioles TC .20 .09
❑ 642 Boston Red Sox TC .30 .14
❑ 643 Chicago Cubs TC .20 .09
❑ 644 Chicago White Sox TC .20 .09
❑ 645 Cincinnati Reds TC .20 .09
❑ 646 Cleveland Indians TC .20 .09
❑ 647 Colorado Rockies TC .20 .09
❑ 648 Detroit Tigers TC .20 .09
❑ 649 Florida Marlins TC .20 .09
❑ 650 Houston Astros TC .20 .09
❑ 651 Kansas City Royals TC .20 .09
❑ 652 Los Angeles Dodgers TC .20 .09
❑ 653 Milwaukee Brewers TC .20 .09
❑ 654 Minnesota Twins TC .20 .09
❑ 655 Montreal Expos TC .20 .09
❑ 656 New York Mets TC .20 .09
❑ 657 New York Yankees TC .50 .23
❑ 658 Oakland Athletics TC .20 .09
❑ 659 Philadelphia Phillies TC .20 .09
❑ 660 Pittsburgh Pirates TC .20 .09
❑ 661 San Diego Padres TC .20 .09
❑ 662 San Francisco Giants TC .20 .09
❑ 663 Seattle Mariners TC .20 .09
❑ 664 St. Louis Cardinals TC .20 .09
❑ 665 Tampa Bay Devil Rays TC .20 .09
❑ 666 Texas Rangers TC .20 .09
❑ 667 Toronto Blue Jays TC .20 .09
❑ 668 Kyle Sleeth DP RC .75 .35
❑ 669 Bradley Sullivan DP RC .50 .23
❑ 670 Carlos Quentin DP RC 2.50 1.10
❑ 671 Conor Jackson DP RC 3.00 1.35
❑ 672 Jeffrey Allison DP RC .50 .23
❑ 673 Matthew Moses DP RC 1.25 .55
❑ 674 Tim Stauffer DP RC 1.00 .45
❑ 675 Estee Harris DP RC .50 .23
❑ 676 David Aardsma DP RC .50 .23
❑ 677 Omar Quintanilla DP RC .75 .35
❑ 678 Aaron Hill DP .50 .23
❑ 679 Tony Richie DP RC .50 .23
❑ 680 Lastings Milledge DP RC 2.50 1.10
❑ 681 Brad Snyder DP RC 1.25 .55
❑ 682 Jason Hirsh DP RC .75 .35
❑ 683 Logan Kensing DP RC .50 .23
❑ 684 Chris Lubanski DP .50 .23
❑ 685 Ryan Harvey DP .50 .23
❑ 686 Ryan Wagner DP .50 .23
❑ 687 Rickie Weeks DP .50 .23
❑ 688 Grady Sizemore .50 .23
Jeremy Guthrie
❑ 689 Edwin Jackson .50 .23
Greg Miller
❑ 690 Jeremy Reed .50 .23
Neal Cotts
❑ 691 Adam Loewen .50 .23
Nick Markakis
❑ 692 B.J. Upton .50 .23
Delmon Young
❑ 693 Kings of New York 1.50 .70
Alex Rodriguez
Derek Jeter
❑ 694 Fan Favorites 1.00 .45
Ichiro Suzuki
Albert Pujols
❑ 695 South Philly Sluggers 1.00 .45
Jim Thome
Mike Schmidt
❑ 696 Mike Mussina GG .20 .09
❑ 697 Bengie Molina GG .20 .09
❑ 698 John Olerud GG .20 .09
❑ 699 Bret Boone GG .20 .09
❑ 700 Eric Chavez GG .20 .09
❑ 701 Alex Rodriguez GG .50 .23
❑ 702 Mike Cameron GG UER .20 .09
Pictures Randy Winn
❑ 703 Ichiro Suzuki GG .50 .23
❑ 704 Torii Hunter GG .20 .09
❑ 705 Mike Hampton GG .20 .09
❑ 706 Mike Matheny GG .20 .09
❑ 707 Derrek Lee GG .20 .09
❑ 708 Luis Castillo GG .20 .09
❑ 709 Scott Rolen GG .20 .09
❑ 710 Edgar Renteria GG .20 .09
❑ 711 Andruw Jones GG .20 .09
❑ 712 Jose Cruz Jr. GG .20 .09
❑ 713 Jim Edmonds GG .20 .09
❑ 714 Roy Halladay CY .20 .09
❑ 715 Eric Gagne CY .20 .09
❑ 716 Alex Rodriguez MVP .50 .23
❑ 717 Angel Berroa ROY .20 .09
❑ 718 Dontrelle Willis ROY .20 .09
❑ 719 Todd Helton AS .20 .09
❑ 720 Marcus Giles AS .20 .09
❑ 721 Edgar Renteria AS .20 .09
❑ 722 Scott Rolen AS .20 .09
❑ 723 Albert Pujols AS .50 .23
❑ 724 Gary Sheffield AS .20 .09
❑ 725 Javy Lopez AS .20 .09
❑ 726 Eric Gagne AS .20 .09
❑ 727 Randy Wolf AS .20 .09
❑ 728 Bobby Cox AS .20 .09
❑ 729 Scott Podsednik AS .20 .09
❑ 730 Alex Gonzalez WS .30 .14
❑ 731 Brad Penny WS .30 .14
❑ 732 Josh Beckett .30 .14
Ivan Rodriguez
Alex Gonzalez WS
❑ 733 Josh Beckett WS MVP .30 .14

2004 Topps Traded

	Nm-Mt	Ex-Mt
COMPLETE SET (220)	50.00	15.00
COMMON CARD (1-70)	.20	.06
COMMON CARD (71-90)	.50	.15
COMMON CARD (91-110)	.40	.12
COMMON CARD (111-220)	.40	.12
BONDS AVAIL VIA HTA SHOP EXCHANGE		.00
PLATE ODDS 1:1151 H, 1:1173 R, 1:327 HTA		.00
PLATE PRINT RUN 1 SET PER COLOR		.00
BLACK-CYAN-MAGENTA-YELLOW ISSUED		.00
NO PLATE PRICING DUE TO SCARCITY		.00

❑ T1 Pokey Reese .20 .06
❑ T2 Tony Womack .20 .06
❑ T3 Richard Hidalgo .20 .06
❑ T4 Juan Uribe .20 .06
❑ T5 J.D. Drew .20 .06
❑ T6 Alex Gonzalez .20 .06
❑ T7 Carlos Guillen .20 .06
❑ T8 Doug Mientkiewicz .20 .06
❑ T9 Fernando Vina .20 .06
❑ T10 Milton Bradley .20 .06
❑ T11 Kelvim Escobar .20 .06
❑ T12 Ben Grieve .20 .06
❑ T13 Brian Jordan .20 .06
❑ T14 A.J. Pierzynski .20 .06
❑ T15 Billy Wagner .20 .06
❑ T16 Terrence Long .20 .06
❑ T17 Carlos Beltran .20 .06
❑ T18 Carl Everett .20 .06
❑ T19 Reggie Sanders .20 .06
❑ T20 Javy Lopez .20 .06
❑ T21 Jay Payton .20 .06
❑ T22 Octavio Dotel .20 .06
❑ T23 Eddie Guardado .20 .06
❑ T24 Andy Pettitte .30 .09
❑ T25 Richie Sexson .20 .06
❑ T26 Ronnie Belliard .20 .06
❑ T27 Michael Tucker .20 .06
❑ T28 Brad Fullmer .20 .06
❑ T29 Freddy Garcia .20 .06
❑ T30 Bartolo Colon .20 .06
❑ T31 Larry Walker Cards .30 .09
❑ T32 Mark Kotsay .20 .06
❑ T33 Jason Marquis .20 .06
❑ T34 Dustan Mohr .20 .06
❑ T35 Javier Vazquez .20 .06
❑ T36 Nomar Garciaparra .75 .23
❑ T37 Tino Martinez .30 .09
❑ T38 Hee Seop Choi .20 .06
❑ T39 Damian Miller .20 .06

❑ T40 Jose Lima .20 .06
❑ T41 Ty Wigginton .20 .06
❑ T42 Raul Ibanez .20 .06
❑ T43 Danys Baez .20 .06
❑ T44 Tony Clark .20 .06
❑ T45 Greg Maddux .75 .23
❑ T46 Victor Zambrano .20 .06
❑ T47 Orlando Cabrera Sox .20 .06
❑ T48 Jose Cruz Jr. .20 .06
❑ T49 Kris Benson .20 .06
❑ T50 Alex Rodriguez 1.00 .30
❑ T51 Steve Finley .20 .06
❑ T52 Ramon Hernandez .20 .06
❑ T53 Esteban Loaiza .20 .06
❑ T54 Ugueth Urbina .20 .06
❑ T55 Jeff Weaver .20 .06
❑ T56 Flash Gordon .20 .06
❑ T57 Jose Contreras .20 .06
❑ T58 Paul Lo Duca .20 .06
❑ T59 Junior Spivey .20 .06
❑ T60 Curt Schilling .30 .09
❑ T61 Brad Penny .20 .06
❑ T62 Braden Looper .20 .06
❑ T63 Miguel Cairo .20 .06
❑ T64 Juan Encarnacion .20 .06
❑ T65 Miguel Batista .20 .06
❑ T66 Terry Francona MG .20 .06
❑ T67 Lee Mazzilli MG .20 .06
❑ T68 Al Pedrique MG .20 .06
❑ T69 Ozzie Guillen MG .50 .15
❑ T70 Phil Garner MG .20 .06
❑ T71 Matt Bush DP RC 2.00 .60
❑ T72 Homer Bailey DP RC 1.50 .45
❑ T73 Greg Golson DP RC 1.50 .45
❑ T74 Kyle Waldrop DP RC 1.25 .35
❑ T75 Richie Robnett DP RC 1.25 .35
❑ T76 Jay Rainville DP RC 1.50 .45
❑ T77 Bill Bray DP RC .50 .15
❑ T78 Phillip Hughes DP RC 2.00 .60
❑ T79 Scott Elbert DP RC 1.25 .35
❑ T80 Josh Fields DP RC 1.50 .45
❑ T81 Justin Orenduff DP RC 1.00 .30
❑ T82 Dan Putnam DP RC 1.00 .30
❑ T83 Chris Nelson DP RC 2.00 .60
❑ T84 Blake DeWitt DP RC 2.00 .60
❑ T85 J.P. Howell DP RC 1.25 .35
❑ T86 Huston Street DP RC 2.50 .75
❑ T87 Kurt Suzuki DP RC 1.50 .45
❑ T88 Erick San Pedro DP RC .50 .15
❑ T89 Matt Tuiasosopo DP RC 3.00 .90
❑ T90 Matt Macri DP RC 1.25 .35
❑ T91 Chad Tracy PROS .40 .12
❑ T92 Scott Hairston PROS .40 .12
❑ T93 Jonny Gomes PROS .40 .12
❑ T94 Chin-Feng Chen PROS .40 .12
❑ T95 Chien-Ming Wang PROS .40 .12
❑ T96 Dustin McGowan PROS .40 .12
❑ T97 Chris Burke PROS .40 .12
❑ T98 Denny Bautista PROS .40 .12
❑ T99 Preston Larrison PROS .40 .12
❑ T100 Kevin Youkilis PROS .40 .12
❑ T101 John Maine PROS .40 .12
❑ T102 Guillermo Quiroz PROS .40 .12
❑ T103 Dave Krynzel PROS .40 .12
❑ T104 David Kelton PROS .40 .12
❑ T105 Edwin Encarnacion PROS .40 .12
❑ T106 Chad Gaudin PROS .40 .12
❑ T107 Sergio Mitre PROS .40 .12
❑ T108 Laynce Nix PROS .40 .12
❑ T109 David Parrish PROS .40 .12
❑ T110 Brandon Claussen PROS .40 .12
❑ T111 Frank Francisco FY RC .40 .12
❑ T112 Brian Dallimore FY RC .40 .12
❑ T113 Jim Crowell FY RC .50 .15
❑ T114 Andres Blanco FY RC .40 .12
❑ T115 Eduardo Villacis FY RC .40 .12
❑ T116 Kazuhito Tadano FY RC .50 .15
❑ T117 Aarom Baldiris FY RC .50 .15
❑ T118 Justin Germano FY RC .40 .12
❑ T119 Joey Gathright FY RC 1.25 .35
❑ T120 Franklyn Gracesqui FY RC .40 .12
❑ T121 Chin-Lung Hu FY RC 1.00 .30
❑ T122 Scott Olsen FY RC 1.25 .35
❑ T123 Tyler Davidson FY RC .50 .15
❑ T124 Fausto Carmona FY RC .75 .23
❑ T125 Tim Hutting FY RC .40 .12
❑ T126 Ryan Meaux FY RC .40 .12
❑ T127 Jon Connolly FY RC 1.00 .30
❑ T128 Hector Made FY RC .75 .23
❑ T129 Jamie Brown FY RC .40 .12
❑ T130 Paul McAnulty FY RC .75 .23
❑ T131 Chris Saenz FY RC .40 .12
❑ T132 Marland Williams FY RC .50 .15
❑ T133 Mike Huggins FY RC .40 .12
❑ T134 Jesse Crain FY RC .75 .23
❑ T135 Chad Bentz FY RC .40 .12
❑ T136 Kazuo Matsui FY RC .75 .23
❑ T137 Paul Maholm FY RC 1.25 .35
❑ T138 Brock Jacobsen FY RC .40 .12
❑ T139 Casey Daigle FY RC .40 .12
❑ T140 Nyjer Morgan FY RC .40 .12
❑ T141 Tom Mastny FY RC .40 .12
❑ T142 Kody Kirkland FY RC .50 .15
❑ T143 Jose Capellan FY RC .50 .15
❑ T144 Felix Hernandez FY RC 10.00 3.00
❑ T145 Shawn Hill FY RC .40 .12
❑ T146 Danny Gonzalez FY RC .40 .12
❑ T147 Scott Dohmann FY RC .40 .12
❑ T148 Tommy Murphy FY RC .40 .12
❑ T149 Akinori Otsuka FY RC .40 .12
❑ T150 Miguel Perez FY RC .40 .12
❑ T151 Mike Rouse FY RC .40 .12
❑ T152 Ramon Ramirez FY RC .40 .12
❑ T153 Luke Hughes FY RC .40 .12
❑ T154 Howie Kendrick FY RC 6.00 1.80
❑ T155 Ryan Budde FY RC .40 .12
❑ T156 Charlie Zink FY RC .40 .12
❑ T157 Warner Madrigal FY RC .75 .23
❑ T158 Jason Szuminski FY RC .40 .12
❑ T159 Chad Chop FY RC .40 .12
❑ T160 Shingo Takatsu FY RC .75 .23
❑ T161 Matt Lemanczyk FY RC .40 .12
❑ T162 Wardell Starling FY RC .40 .12
❑ T163 Nick Gorneault FY RC .50 .15
❑ T164 Scott Proctor FY RC .50 .15
❑ T165 Brooks Conrad FY RC .50 .15
❑ T166 Hector Gimenez FY RC .40 .12
❑ T167 Kevin Howard FY RC .50 .15
❑ T168 Vince Perkins FY RC .50 .15
❑ T169 Brock Peterson FY RC .40 .12
❑ T170 Chris Shelton FY RC 1.50 .45
❑ T171 Erick Aybar FY RC 1.25 .35
❑ T172 Paul Bacot FY RC .50 .15
❑ T173 Matt Capps FY RC .40 .12
❑ T174 Kory Casto FY RC .50 .15
❑ T175 Juan Cedeno FY RC .40 .12
❑ T176 Vito Chiaravalloti FY RC .40 .12
❑ T177 Alec Zumwalt FY RC .40 .12
❑ T178 J.J. Furmaniak FY RC .75 .23
❑ T179 Lee Gwaltney FY RC .40 .12
❑ T180 Donald Kelly FY RC .40 .12
❑ T181 Benji DeQuin FY RC .40 .12
❑ T182 Brant Colamarino FY RC .75 .23
❑ T183 Juan Gutierrez FY RC .40 .12
❑ T184 Carl Loadenthal FY RC .50 .15
❑ T185 Ricky Nolasco FY RC .75 .23
❑ T186 Jeff Salazar FY RC 1.00 .30
❑ T187 Rob Tejeda FY RC .75 .23
❑ T188 Alex Romero FY RC .40 .12
❑ T189 Yoann Torrealba FY RC .40 .12
❑ T190 Carlos Sosa FY RC .40 .12
❑ T191 Tim Bittner FY RC .40 .12
❑ T192 Chris Aguila FY RC .40 .12
❑ T193 Jason Frasor FY RC .40 .12
❑ T194 Reid Gorecki FY RC .40 .12
❑ T195 Dustin Nippert FY RC .50 .15
❑ T196 Javier Guzman FY RC .50 .15
❑ T197 Harvey Garcia FY RC .40 .12
❑ T198 Ivan Ochoa FY RC .40 .12
❑ T199 David Wallace FY RC .50 .15
❑ T200 Joel Zumaya FY RC 1.50 .45
❑ T201 Casey Kopitzke FY RC .40 .12
❑ T202 Lincoln Holdzkom FY RC .40 .12
❑ T203 Chad Santos FY RC .40 .12
❑ T204 Brian Pilkington FY RC .40 .12
❑ T205 Terry Jones FY RC .50 .15
❑ T206 Jerome Gamble FY RC .40 .12
❑ T207 Brad Eldred FY RC 2.00 .60
❑ T208 David Pauley FY RC .40 .12
❑ T209 Kevin Davidson FY RC .40 .12
❑ T210 Damaso Espino FY RC .40 .12
❑ T211 Tom Farmer FY RC .40 .12
❑ T212 Michael Mooney FY RC .40 .12
❑ T213 James Tomlin FY RC .40 .12
❑ T214 Greg Thissen FY RC .40 .12
❑ T215 Calvin Hayes FY RC .50 .15
❑ T216 Fernando Cortez FY RC .40 .12
❑ T217 Sergio Silva FY RC .40 .12
❑ T218 Jon de Vries FY RC .40 .12
❑ T219 Don Sutton FY RC 1.00 .30
❑ T220 Leo Nunez FY RC .40 .12
❑ T221 Barry Bonds HTA EXCH 8.00 2.40

2005 Topps

	Nm-Mt	Ex-Mt
COMP.HOBBY SET (737)	80.00	24.00
COMP.HOLIDAY SET (742)	80.00	24.00
COMP.CUBS SET (737)	80.00	24.00
COMP.GIANTS SET (737)	80.00	24.00
COMP.NATIONALS SET (737)	80.00	24.00
COMP.RED SOX SET (737)	80.00	24.00
COMP.TIGERS SET (737)	80.00	24.00
COMP.YANKEES SET (737)	80.00	24.00
COMPLETE SET (732)	80.00	24.00
COMPLETE SERIES 1 (366)	40.00	12.00
COMPLETE SERIES 2 (366)	40.00	12.00
COMMON CARD (1-6/8-734)	.20	.06
COMMON (297-326/668-687)	.50	.15
COMMON (327-331/688-692)	.50	.15
COM (349-355/368/731-734)	1.00	.30
CARD NUMBER 7 DOES NOT EXIST		.00
OVERALL PLATE SER.1 ODDS 1:154 HTA		.00
OVERALL PLATE SER.2 ODDS 1:112 HTA		.00
PLATE PRINT RUN 1 SET PER COLOR		.00
BLACK-CYAN-MAGENTA-YELLOW ISSUED		.00
NO PLATE PRICING DUE TO SCARCITY		.00

❑ 1 Alex Rodriguez 1.00 .30
❑ 2 Placido Polanco .20 .06
❑ 3 Torii Hunter .20 .06
❑ 4 Lyle Overbay .20 .06
❑ 5 Johnny Damon .30 .09
❑ 6 Johnny Estrada .20 .06
❑ 7 Does Not Exist .00
❑ 8 Francisco Rodriguez .20 .06
❑ 9 Jason LaRue .20 .06
❑ 10 Sammy Sosa .50 .15
❑ 11 Randy Wolf .20 .06
❑ 12 Jason Bay .20 .06
❑ 13 Tom Glavine .30 .09
❑ 14 Michael Tucker .20 .06
❑ 15 Brian Giles .20 .06
❑ 16 Dan Wilson .20 .06
❑ 17 Jim Edmonds .30 .09
❑ 18 Danys Baez .20 .06
❑ 19 Roy Halladay .20 .06
❑ 20 Hank Blalock .20 .06
❑ 21 Darin Erstad .20 .06
❑ 22 Robby Hammock .20 .06
❑ 23 Mike Hampton .20 .06
❑ 24 Mark Bellhorn .20 .06
❑ 25 Jim Thome .30 .09
❑ 26 Scott Schoeneweis .20 .06
❑ 27 Jody Gerut .20 .06
❑ 28 Vinny Castilla .20 .06
❑ 29 Luis Castillo .20 .06
❑ 30 Ivan Rodriguez .30 .09
❑ 31 Craig Biggio .30 .09
❑ 32 Joe Randa .20 .06
❑ 33 Adrian Beltre .20 .06

❑ 34 Scott Podsednik .20 .06
❑ 35 Cliff Floyd .20 .06
❑ 36 Livan Hernandez .20 .06
❑ 37 Eric Byrnes .20 .06
❑ 38 Gabe Kapler .20 .06
❑ 39 Jack Wilson .20 .06
❑ 40 Gary Sheffield .20 .06
❑ 41 Chan Ho Park .20 .06
❑ 42 Carl Crawford .20 .06
❑ 43 Miguel Batista .20 .06
❑ 44 David Bell .20 .06
❑ 45 Jeff DaVanon .20 .06
❑ 46 Brandon Webb .20 .06
❑ 47 Bronson Arroyo .20 .06
❑ 48 Melvin Mora .20 .06
❑ 49 David Ortiz .50 .15
❑ 50 Andruw Jones .30 .09
❑ 51 Chone Figgins .20 .06
❑ 52 Danny Graves .20 .06
❑ 53 Preston Wilson .20 .06
❑ 54 Jeremy Bonderman .20 .06
❑ 55 Chad Fox .20 .06
❑ 56 Dan Miceli .20 .06
❑ 57 Jimmy Gobble .20 .06
❑ 58 Darren Dreifort .20 .06
❑ 59 Matt LeCroy .20 .06
❑ 60 Jose Vidro .20 .06
❑ 61 Al Leiter .20 .06
❑ 62 Javier Vazquez .20 .06
❑ 63 Erubiel Durazo .20 .06
❑ 64 Doug Glanville .20 .06
❑ 65 Scot Shields .20 .06
❑ 66 Edgardo Alfonzo .20 .06
❑ 67 Ryan Franklin .20 .06
❑ 68 Francisco Cordero .20 .06
❑ 69 Brett Myers .20 .06
❑ 70 Curt Schilling .30 .09
❑ 71 Matt Kata .20 .06
❑ 72 Mark DeRosa .20 .06
❑ 73 Rodrigo Lopez .20 .06
❑ 74 Tim Wakefield .30 .09
❑ 75 Frank Thomas .50 .15
❑ 76 Jimmy Rollins .20 .06
❑ 77 Barry Zito .20 .06
❑ 78 Hideo Nomo .50 .15
❑ 79 Brad Wilkerson .20 .06
❑ 80 Adam Dunn .20 .06
❑ 81 Billy Traber .20 .06
❑ 82 Fernando Vina .20 .06
❑ 83 Nate Robertson .20 .06
❑ 84 Brad Ausmus .20 .06
❑ 85 Mike Sweeney .20 .06
❑ 86 Kip Wells .20 .06
❑ 87 Chris Reitsma .20 .06
❑ 88 Zach Day .20 .06
❑ 89 Tony Clark .20 .06
❑ 90 Bret Boone .20 .06
❑ 91 Mark Loretta .20 .06
❑ 92 Jerome Williams .20 .06
❑ 93 Randy Winn .20 .06
❑ 94 Marlon Anderson .20 .06
❑ 95 Aubrey Huff .20 .06
❑ 96 Kevin Mench .20 .06
❑ 97 Frank Catalanotto .20 .06
❑ 98 Flash Gordon .20 .06
❑ 99 Scott Hatteberg .20 .06
❑ 100 Albert Pujols 1.00 .30
❑ 101 Jose/Bengie Molina .50 .15
❑ 102 Oscar Villarreal .20 .06
❑ 103 Jay Gibbons .20 .06
❑ 104 Byung-Hyun Kim .20 .06
❑ 105 Joe Borowski .20 .06
❑ 106 Mark Grudzielanek .20 .06
❑ 107 Mark Buehrle .20 .06
❑ 108 Paul Wilson .20 .06
❑ 109 Ronnie Belliard .20 .06
❑ 110 Reggie Sanders .20 .06
❑ 111 Tim Redding .20 .06
❑ 112 Brian Lawrence .20 .06
❑ 113 Darrell May .20 .06
❑ 114 Jose Hernandez .20 .06
❑ 115 Ben Sheets .20 .06
❑ 116 Johan Santana .30 .09
❑ 117 Billy Wagner .20 .06
❑ 118 Mariano Rivera .30 .09
❑ 119 Steve Trachsel .20 .06
❑ 120 Akinori Otsuka .20 .06
❑ 121 Bobby Kielty .20 .06
❑ 122 Orlando Hernandez .20 .06
❑ 123 Raul Ibanez .20 .06
❑ 124 Mike Matheny .20 .06
❑ 125 Vernon Wells .20 .06
❑ 126 Jason Isringhausen .20 .06
❑ 127 Jose Guillen .20 .06
❑ 128 Danny Bautista .20 .06
❑ 129 Marcus Giles .20 .06
❑ 130 Javy Lopez .20 .06
❑ 131 Kevin Millar .20 .06
❑ 132 Kyle Farnsworth .20 .06
❑ 133 Carl Pavano .20 .06
❑ 134 D'Angelo Jimenez .20 .06
❑ 135 Casey Blake .20 .06
❑ 136 Matt Holliday .20 .06
❑ 137 Bobby Higginson .20 .06
❑ 138 Nate Field .20 .06
❑ 139 Alex Gonzalez .20 .06
❑ 140 Jeff Kent .20 .06
❑ 141 Aaron Guiel .20 .06
❑ 142 Shawn Green .20 .06
❑ 143 Bill Hall .20 .06
❑ 144 Shannon Stewart .20 .06
❑ 145 Juan Rivera .20 .06
❑ 146 Coco Crisp .20 .06
❑ 147 Mike Mussina .30 .09
❑ 148 Eric Chavez .20 .06
❑ 149 Jon Lieber .20 .06
❑ 150 Vladimir Guerrero .50 .15
❑ 151 Alex Cintron .20 .06
❑ 152 Horacio Ramirez .20 .06
❑ 153 Sidney Ponson .20 .06
❑ 154 Trot Nixon .30 .09
❑ 155 Greg Maddux .75 .23
❑ 156 Edgar Renteria .20 .06
❑ 157 Ryan Freel .20 .06
❑ 158 Matt Lawton .20 .06
❑ 159 Shawn Chacon .20 .06
❑ 160 Josh Beckett .20 .06
❑ 161 Ken Harvey .20 .06
❑ 162 Juan Cruz .20 .06
❑ 163 Juan Encarnacion .20 .06
❑ 164 Wes Helms .20 .06
❑ 165 Brad Radke .20 .06
❑ 166 Claudio Vargas .20 .06
❑ 167 Mike Cameron .20 .06
❑ 168 Billy Koch .20 .06
❑ 169 Bobby Crosby .20 .06
❑ 170 Mike Lieberthal .20 .06
❑ 171 Rob Mackowiak .20 .06
❑ 172 Sean Burroughs .20 .06
❑ 173 J.T. Snow Jr. .20 .06
❑ 174 Paul Konerko .20 .06
❑ 175 Luis Gonzalez .20 .06
❑ 176 John Lackey .20 .06
❑ 177 Antonio Alfonseca .20 .06
❑ 178 Brian Roberts .20 .06
❑ 179 Bill Mueller .20 .06
❑ 180 Carlos Lee .20 .06
❑ 181 Corey Patterson .20 .06
❑ 182 Sean Casey .30 .09
❑ 183 Cliff Lee .20 .06
❑ 184 Jason Jennings .20 .06
❑ 185 Dmitri Young .20 .06
❑ 186 Juan Uribe .20 .06
❑ 187 Andy Pettitte .30 .09
❑ 188 Juan Gonzalez .20 .06
❑ 189 Pokey Reese .20 .06
❑ 190 Jason Phillips .20 .06
❑ 191 Rocky Biddle .20 .06
❑ 192 Lew Ford .20 .06
❑ 193 Mark Mulder .20 .06
❑ 194 Bobby Abreu .20 .06
❑ 195 Jason Kendall .20 .06
❑ 196 Terrence Long .20 .06
❑ 197 A.J. Pierzynski .20 .06
❑ 198 Eddie Guardado .20 .06
❑ 199 So Taguchi .20 .06
❑ 200 Jason Giambi .20 .06
❑ 201 Tony Batista .20 .06
❑ 202 Kyle Lohse .20 .06
❑ 203 Trevor Hoffman .20 .06
❑ 204 Tike Redman .20 .06
❑ 205 Matt Herges .20 .06
❑ 206 Gil Meche .20 .06
❑ 207 Chris Carpenter .20 .06
❑ 208 Ben Broussard .20 .06
❑ 209 Eric Young .20 .06
❑ 210 Doug Waechter .20 .06
❑ 211 Jarrod Washburn .20 .06
❑ 212 Chad Tracy .20 .06
❑ 213 John Smoltz .30 .09
❑ 214 Jorge Julio .20 .06
❑ 215 Todd Walker .20 .06
❑ 216 Shingo Takatsu .20 .06
❑ 217 Jose Acevedo .20 .06
❑ 218 David Riske .20 .06
❑ 219 Shawn Estes .20 .06
❑ 220 Lance Berkman .20 .06
❑ 221 Carlos Guillen .20 .06
❑ 222 Jeremy Affeldt .20 .06
❑ 223 Cesar Izturis .20 .06
❑ 224 Scott Sullivan .20 .06
❑ 225 Kazuo Matsui .20 .06
❑ 226 Josh Fogg .20 .06
❑ 227 Jason Schmidt .20 .06
❑ 228 Jason Marquis .20 .06
❑ 229 Scott Spiezio .20 .06
❑ 230 Miguel Tejada .20 .06
❑ 231 Bartolo Colon .20 .06
❑ 232 Jose Valverde .20 .06
❑ 233 Derrek Lee .30 .09
❑ 234 Scott Williamson .20 .06
❑ 235 Joe Crede .20 .06
❑ 236 John Thomson .20 .06
❑ 237 Mike MacDougal .20 .06
❑ 238 Eric Gagne .20 .06
❑ 239 Alex Sanchez .20 .06
❑ 240 Miguel Cabrera .30 .09
❑ 241 Luis Rivas .20 .06
❑ 242 Adam Everett .20 .06
❑ 243 Jason Johnson .20 .06
❑ 244 Travis Hafner .20 .06
❑ 245 Jose Valentin .20 .06
❑ 246 Stephen Randolph .20 .06
❑ 247 Rafael Furcal .20 .06
❑ 248 Adam Kennedy .20 .06
❑ 249 Luis Matos .20 .06
❑ 250 Mark Prior .30 .09
❑ 251 Angel Berroa .20 .06
❑ 252 Phil Nevin .20 .06
❑ 253 Oliver Perez .20 .06
❑ 254 Orlando Hudson .20 .06
❑ 255 Braden Looper .20 .06
❑ 256 Khalil Greene .30 .09
❑ 257 Tim Worrell .20 .06
❑ 258 Carlos Zambrano .20 .06
❑ 259 Odalis Perez .20 .06
❑ 260 Gerald Laird .20 .06
❑ 261 Jose Cruz Jr. .20 .06
❑ 262 Michael Barrett .20 .06
❑ 263 Michael Young .20 .06
❑ 264 Toby Hall .20 .06
❑ 265 Woody Williams .20 .06
❑ 266 Rich Harden .20 .06
❑ 267 Mike Scioscia MG .20 .06
❑ 268 Al Pedrique MG .20 .06
❑ 269 Bobby Cox MG .20 .06
❑ 270 Lee Mazzilli MG .20 .06
❑ 271 Terry Francona MG .30 .09
❑ 272 Dusty Baker MG .20 .06
❑ 273 Ozzie Guillen MG .50 .15
❑ 274 Dave Miley MG .20 .06
❑ 275 Eric Wedge MG .20 .06
❑ 276 Clint Hurdle MG .20 .06
❑ 277 Alan Trammell MG .20 .06
❑ 278 Jack McKeon MG .20 .06
❑ 279 Phil Garner MG .20 .06
❑ 280 Tony Pena MG .20 .06
❑ 281 Jim Tracy MG .20 .06
❑ 282 Ned Yost MG .20 .06
❑ 283 Ron Gardenhire MG .20 .06
❑ 284 Frank Robinson MG .20 .06
❑ 285 Art Howe MG .20 .06
❑ 286 Joe Torre MG .30 .09
❑ 287 Ken Macha MG .20 .06
❑ 288 Larry Bowa MG .20 .06
❑ 289 Lloyd McClendon MG .20 .06
❑ 290 Bruce Bochy MG .20 .06
❑ 291 Felipe Alou MG .20 .06

❑ 292 Bob Melvin MG .20 .06
❑ 293 Tony LaRussa MG .20 .06
❑ 294 Lou Piniella MG .20 .06
❑ 295 Buck Showalter MG .20 .06
❑ 296 John Gibbons MG .20 .06
❑ 297 Steve Doetsch FY RC .75 .23
❑ 298 Melky Cabrera FY RC 1.00 .30
❑ 299 Luis Ramirez FY RC .50 .15
❑ 300 Chris Seddon FY RC .50 .15
❑ 301 Nate Schierholtz FY .75 .23
❑ 302 Ian Kinsler FY RC 1.00 .30
❑ 303 Brandon Moss FY RC 1.50 .45
❑ 304 Chadd Blasko FY RC .75 .23
❑ 305 Jeremy West FY RC .75 .23
❑ 306 Sean Marshall FY RC .75 .23
❑ 307 Matt DeSalvo FY RC .75 .23
❑ 308 Ryan Sweeney FY RC 1.00 .30
❑ 309 Matthew Lindstrom FY RC .50 .15
❑ 310 Ryan Goleski FY RC .75 .23
❑ 311 Brett Harper FY RC .75 .23
❑ 312 Chris Roberson FY RC .50 .15
❑ 313 Andre Ethier FY RC 1.25 .35
❑ 314 Chris Denorfia FY RC .75 .23
❑ 315 Ian Bladergroen FY RC .75 .23
❑ 316 Darren Fenster FY RC .50 .15
❑ 317 Kevin West FY RC .50 .15
❑ 318 Chaz Lytle FY RC .75 .23
❑ 319 James Jurries FY RC .75 .23
❑ 320 Matt Rogelstad FY RC .50 .15
❑ 321 Wade Robinson FY RC .50 .15
❑ 322 Jake Dittler FY .50 .15
❑ 323 Brian Stavisky FY RC .50 .15
❑ 324 Kole Strayhorn FY RC .50 .15
❑ 325 Jose Vaquedano FY RC .50 .15
❑ 326 Elvys Quezada FY RC .50 .15
❑ 327 John Maine .50 .15
Val Majewski FS
❑ 328 Rickie Weeks .50 .15
J.J. Hardy FS
❑ 329 Gabe Gross .50 .15
Guillermo Quiroz FS
❑ 330 David Wright 3.00 .90
Craig Brazell FS
❑ 331 Dallas McPherson .50 .15
Jeff Mathis FS
❑ 332 Randy Johnson SH .30 .09
❑ 333 Randy Johnson SH .30 .09
❑ 334 Ichiro Suzuki SH .50 .15
❑ 335 Ken Griffey Jr. SH .50 .15
❑ 336 Greg Maddux SH .50 .15
❑ 337 Ichiro Suzuki .50 .15
Melvin Mora
Vladimir Guerrero LL
❑ 338 Ichiro Suzuki .50 .15
Michael Young
Vladimir Guerrero LL
❑ 339 Manny Ramirez .30 .09
Paul Konerko
David Ortiz LL
❑ 340 Miguel Tejada .30 .09
David Ortiz
Manny Ramirez LL
❑ 341 Johan Santana .20 .06
Curt Schilling
Jake Westbrook LL
❑ 342 Johan Santana .20 .06
Pedro Martinez
Curt Schilling LL
❑ 343 Todd Helton .20 .06
Mark Loretta
Adrian Beltre LL
❑ 344 Juan Pierre .20 .06
Mark Loretta
Jack Wilson LL
❑ 345 Adrian Beltre .50 .15
Adam Dunn
Albert Pujols LL
❑ 346 Vinny Castilla .50 .15
Scott Rolen
Albert Pujols LL
❑ 347 Jake Peavy .30 .09
Randy Johnson
Ben Sheets LL
❑ 348 Randy Johnson .30 .09
Ben Sheets
Jason Schmidt LL
❑ 349 Alex Rodriguez 1.00 .30
Ruben Sierra ALDS
❑ 350 Larry Walker 1.00 .30
Albert Pujols NLDS
❑ 351 Curt Schilling 1.00 .30
David Ortiz ALDS
❑ 352 Curt Schilling WS2 1.00 .30
❑ 353 Sox Celebration 1.00 .30
David Ortiz
Curt Schilling ALCS
❑ 354 Cards Celebration 1.00 .30
Albert Pujols
Jim Edmonds NLCS
❑ 355 Mark Bellhorn WS1 1.00 .30
❑ 356 Paul Konerko AS .20 .06
❑ 357 Alfonso Soriano AS .20 .06
❑ 358 Miguel Tejada AS .20 .06
❑ 359 Melvin Mora AS .20 .06
❑ 360 Vladimir Guerrero AS .30 .09
❑ 361 Ichiro Suzuki AS .50 .15
❑ 362 Manny Ramirez AS .30 .09
❑ 363 Ivan Rodriguez AS .20 .06
❑ 364 Johan Santana AS .20 .06
❑ 365 Paul Konerko AS .20 .06
❑ 366 David Ortiz AS .30 .09
❑ 367 Bobby Crosby AS .20 .06
❑ 368 Sox Celebration 1.50 .45
Manny Ramirez
Derek Lowe WS4
❑ 369 Garret Anderson .20 .06
❑ 370 Randy Johnson .50 .15
❑ 371 Charles Thomas .20 .06
❑ 372 Rafael Palmeiro .30 .09
❑ 373 Kevin Youkilis .20 .06
❑ 374 Freddy Garcia .20 .06
❑ 375 Magglio Ordonez .20 .06
❑ 376 Aaron Harang .20 .06
❑ 377 Grady Sizemore .20 .06
❑ 378 Chin-Hui Tsao .20 .06
❑ 379 Eric Munson .20 .06
❑ 380 Juan Pierre .20 .06
❑ 381 Brad Lidge .20 .06
❑ 382 Brian Anderson .20 .06
❑ 383 Alex Cora .20 .06
❑ 384 Brady Clark .20 .06
❑ 385 Todd Helton .30 .09
❑ 386 Chad Cordero .20 .06
❑ 387 Kris Benson .20 .06
❑ 388 Brad Halsey .20 .06
❑ 389 Jermaine Dye .20 .06
❑ 390 Manny Ramirez .30 .09
❑ 391 Daryle Ward .20 .06
❑ 392 Adam Eaton .20 .06
❑ 393 Brett Tomko .20 .06
❑ 394 Bucky Jacobsen .20 .06
❑ 395 Dontrelle Willis .20 .06
❑ 396 B.J. Upton .20 .06
❑ 397 Rocco Baldelli .20 .06
❑ 398 Ted Lilly .20 .06
❑ 399 Ryan Drese .20 .06
❑ 400 Ichiro Suzuki 1.00 .30
❑ 401 Brendan Donnelly .20 .06
❑ 402 Brandon Lyon .20 .06
❑ 403 Nick Green .20 .06
❑ 404 Jerry Hairston Jr. .20 .06
❑ 405 Mike Lowell .20 .06
❑ 406 Kerry Wood .20 .06
❑ 407 Carl Everett .20 .06
❑ 408 Hideki Matsui 1.00 .30
❑ 409 Omar Vizquel .30 .09
❑ 410 Joe Kennedy .20 .06
❑ 411 Carlos Pena .20 .06
❑ 412 Armando Benitez .20 .06
❑ 413 Carlos Beltran .20 .06
❑ 414 Kevin Appier .20 .06
❑ 415 Jeff Weaver .20 .06
❑ 416 Chad Moeller .20 .06
❑ 417 Joe Mays .20 .06
❑ 418 Terrmel Sledge .20 .06
❑ 419 Richard Hidalgo .20 .06
❑ 420 Kenny Lofton .20 .06
❑ 421 Justin Duchscherer .20 .06
❑ 422 Eric Milton .20 .06
❑ 423 Jose Mesa .20 .06
❑ 424 Ramon Hernandez .20 .06
❑ 425 Jose Reyes .20 .06
❑ 426 Joel Pineiro .20 .06
❑ 427 Matt Morris .20 .06
❑ 428 John Halama .20 .06
❑ 429 Gary Matthews Jr. .20 .06
❑ 430 Ryan Madson .20 .06
❑ 431 Mark Kotsay .20 .06
❑ 432 Carlos Delgado .20 .06
❑ 433 Casey Kotchman .20 .06
❑ 434 Greg Aquino .20 .06
❑ 435 Eli Marrero .20 .06
❑ 436 David Newhan .20 .06
❑ 437 Mike Timlin .20 .06
❑ 438 LaTroy Hawkins .20 .06
❑ 439 Jose Contreras .20 .06
❑ 440 Ken Griffey Jr. .75 .23
❑ 441 C.C. Sabathia .20 .06
❑ 442 Brandon Inge .20 .06
❑ 443 Pete Munro .20 .06
❑ 444 John Buck .20 .06
❑ 445 Hee Seop Choi .20 .06
❑ 446 Chris Capuano .20 .06
❑ 447 Jesse Crain .20 .06
❑ 448 Geoff Jenkins .20 .06
❑ 449 Brian Schneider .20 .06
❑ 450 Mike Piazza .50 .15
❑ 451 Jorge Posada .30 .09
❑ 452 Nick Swisher .20 .06
❑ 453 Kevin Millwood .20 .06
❑ 454 Mike Gonzalez .20 .06
❑ 455 Jake Peavy .20 .06
❑ 456 Dustin Hermanson .20 .06
❑ 457 Jeremy Reed .20 .06
❑ 458 Julian Tavarez .20 .06
❑ 459 Geoff Blum .20 .06
❑ 460 Alfonso Soriano .20 .06
❑ 461 Alexis Rios .20 .06
❑ 462 David Eckstein .20 .06
❑ 463 Shea Hillenbrand .20 .06
❑ 464 Russ Ortiz .20 .06
❑ 465 Kurt Ainsworth .20 .06
❑ 466 Orlando Cabrera .20 .06
❑ 467 Carlos Silva .20 .06
❑ 468 Ross Gload .20 .06
❑ 469 Josh Phelps .20 .06
❑ 470 Marquis Grissom .20 .06
❑ 471 Mike Maroth .20 .06
❑ 472 Guillermo Mota .20 .06
❑ 473 Chris Burke .20 .06
❑ 474 David DeJesus .20 .06
❑ 475 Jose Lima .20 .06
❑ 476 Cristian Guzman .20 .06
❑ 477 Nick Johnson .20 .06
❑ 478 Victor Zambrano .20 .06
❑ 479 Rod Barajas .20 .06
❑ 480 Damian Miller .20 .06
❑ 481 Chase Utley .20 .06
❑ 482 Todd Pratt .20 .06
❑ 483 Sean Burnett .20 .06
❑ 484 Boomer Wells .20 .06
❑ 485 Dustan Mohr .20 .06
❑ 486 Bobby Madritsch .20 .06
❑ 487 Ray King .20 .06
❑ 488 Reed Johnson .20 .06
❑ 489 R.A. Dickey .20 .06
❑ 490 Scott Kazmir .20 .06
❑ 491 Tony Womack .20 .06
❑ 492 Tomas Perez .20 .06
❑ 493 Esteban Loaiza .20 .06
❑ 494 Tomo Ohka .20 .06
❑ 495 Mike Lamb .20 .06
❑ 496 Ramon Ortiz .20 .06
❑ 497 Richie Sexson .20 .06
❑ 498 J.D. Drew .20 .06
❑ 499 David Segui .20 .06
❑ 500 Barry Bonds 2.00 .60
❑ 501 Aramis Ramirez .20 .06
❑ 502 Wily Mo Pena .20 .06
❑ 503 Jeromy Burnitz .20 .06
❑ 504 Craig Monroe .20 .06
❑ 505 Nomar Garciaparra .50 .15
❑ 506 Brandon Backe .20 .06
❑ 507 Marcus Thames .20 .06
❑ 508 Derek Lowe .20 .06
❑ 509 Doug Davis .20 .06
❑ 510 Joe Mauer .20 .06
❑ 511 Endy Chavez .20 .06

❑ 512 Bernie Williams .30 .09
❑ 513 Mark Redman .20 .06
❑ 514 Jason Michaels .20 .06
❑ 515 Craig Wilson .20 .06
❑ 516 Ryan Klesko .20 .06
❑ 517 Ray Durham .20 .06
❑ 518 Jose Lopez .20 .06
❑ 519 Jeff Suppan .20 .06
❑ 520 Julio Lugo .20 .06
❑ 521 Mike Wood .20 .06
❑ 522 David Bush .20 .06
❑ 523 Juan Rincon .20 .06
❑ 524 Paul Quantrill .20 .06
❑ 525 Marlon Byrd .20 .06
❑ 526 Roy Oswalt .20 .06
❑ 527 Rondell White .20 .06
❑ 528 Troy Glaus .20 .06
❑ 529 Scott Hairston .20 .06
❑ 530 Chipper Jones .50 .15
❑ 531 Daniel Cabrera .20 .06
❑ 532 Doug Mientkiewicz .20 .06
❑ 533 Glendon Rusch .20 .06
❑ 534 Jon Garland .20 .06
❑ 535 Austin Kearns .20 .06
❑ 536 Jake Westbrook .20 .06
❑ 537 Aaron Miles .20 .06
❑ 538 Omar Infante .20 .06
❑ 539 Paul Lo Duca .20 .06
❑ 540 Morgan Ensberg .20 .06
❑ 541 Tony Graffanino .20 .06
❑ 542 Milton Bradley .20 .06
❑ 543 Keith Ginter .20 .06
❑ 544 Justin Morneau .20 .06
❑ 545 Tony Armas Jr. .20 .06
❑ 546 Mike Stanton .20 .06
❑ 547 Kevin Brown .20 .06
❑ 548 Marco Scutaro .20 .06
❑ 549 Tim Hudson .20 .06
❑ 550 Pat Burrell .20 .06
❑ 551 Ty Wigginton .20 .06
❑ 552 Jeff Cirillo .20 .06
❑ 553 Jim Brower .20 .06
❑ 554 Jamie Moyer .20 .06
❑ 555 Larry Walker .30 .09
❑ 556 Dewon Brazelton .20 .06
❑ 557 Brian Jordan .20 .06
❑ 558 Josh Towers .20 .06
❑ 559 Shigetoshi Hasegawa .20 .06
❑ 560 Octavio Dotel .20 .06
❑ 561 Travis Lee .20 .06
❑ 562 Michael Cuddyer .20 .06
❑ 563 Junior Spivey .20 .06
❑ 564 Zack Greinke .20 .06
❑ 565 Roger Clemens .75 .23
❑ 566 Chris Shelton .20 .06
❑ 567 Ugueth Urbina .20 .06
❑ 568 Rafael Betancourt .20 .06
❑ 569 Willie Harris .20 .06
❑ 570 Todd Hollandsworth .20 .06
❑ 571 Keith Foulke .20 .06
❑ 572 Larry Bigbie .20 .06
❑ 573 Paul Byrd .20 .06
❑ 574 Troy Percival .20 .06
❑ 575 Pedro Martinez .30 .09
❑ 576 Matt Clement .20 .06
❑ 577 Ryan Wagner .20 .06
❑ 578 Jeff Francis .20 .06
❑ 579 Jeff Conine .20 .06
❑ 580 Wade Miller .20 .06
❑ 581 Matt Stairs .20 .06
❑ 582 Gavin Floyd .20 .06
❑ 583 Kazuhisa Ishii .20 .06
❑ 584 Victor Santos .20 .06
❑ 585 Jacque Jones .20 .06
❑ 586 Sunny Kim .20 .06
❑ 587 Dan Kolb .20 .06
❑ 588 Cory Lidle .20 .06
❑ 589 Jose Castillo .20 .06
❑ 590 Alex Gonzalez .20 .06
❑ 591 Kirk Rueter .20 .06
❑ 592 Jolbert Cabrera .20 .06
❑ 593 Erik Bedard .20 .06
❑ 594 Ben Grieve .20 .06
❑ 595 Ricky Ledee .20 .06
❑ 596 Mark Hendrickson .20 .06
❑ 597 Laynce Nix .20 .06
❑ 598 Jason Frasor .20 .06
❑ 599 Kevin Gregg .20 .06
❑ 600 Derek Jeter 1.00 .30
❑ 601 Luis Terrero .20 .06
❑ 602 Jaret Wright .20 .06
❑ 603 Edwin Jackson .20 .06
❑ 604 Dave Roberts .20 .06
❑ 605 Moises Alou .20 .06
❑ 606 Aaron Rowand .20 .06
❑ 607 Kazuhito Tadano .20 .06
❑ 608 Luis A. Gonzalez .20 .06
❑ 609 A.J. Burnett .20 .06
❑ 610 Jeff Bagwell .30 .09
❑ 611 Brad Penny .20 .06
❑ 612 Craig Counsell .20 .06
❑ 613 Corey Koskie .20 .06
❑ 614 Mark Ellis .20 .06
❑ 615 Felix Rodriguez .20 .06
❑ 616 Jay Payton .20 .06
❑ 617 Hector Luna .20 .06
❑ 618 Miguel Olivo .20 .06
❑ 619 Rob Bell .20 .06
❑ 620 Scott Rolen .30 .09
❑ 621 Ricardo Rodriguez .20 .06
❑ 622 Eric Hinske .20 .06
❑ 623 Tim Salmon .30 .09
❑ 624 Adam LaRoche .20 .06
❑ 625 B.J. Ryan .20 .06
❑ 626 Roberto Alomar .30 .09
❑ 627 Steve Finley .20 .06
❑ 628 Joe Nathan .20 .06
❑ 629 Scott Linebrink .20 .06
❑ 630 Vicente Padilla .20 .06
❑ 631 Raul Mondesi .20 .06
❑ 632 Yadier Molina .20 .06
❑ 633 Tino Martinez .30 .09
❑ 634 Mark Teixeira .30 .09
❑ 635 Kelvim Escobar .20 .06
❑ 636 Pedro Feliz .20 .06
❑ 637 Rich Aurilia .20 .06
❑ 638 Los Angeles Angels TC .20 .06
❑ 639 Arizona Diamondbacks TC .20 .06
❑ 640 Atlanta Braves TC .30 .09
❑ 641 Baltimore Orioles TC .20 .06
❑ 642 Boston Red Sox TC .50 .15
❑ 643 Chicago Cubs TC .30 .09
❑ 644 Chicago White Sox TC .20 .06
❑ 645 Cincinnati Reds TC .20 .06
❑ 646 Cleveland Indians TC .20 .06
❑ 647 Colorado Rockies TC .20 .06
❑ 648 Detroit Tigers TC .20 .06
❑ 649 Florida Marlins TC .20 .06
❑ 650 Houston Astros TC .20 .06
❑ 651 Kansas City Royals TC .20 .06
❑ 652 Los Angeles Dodgers TC .20 .06
❑ 653 Milwaukee Brewers TC .20 .06
❑ 654 Minnesota Twins TC .20 .06
❑ 655 Montreal Expos TC .20 .06
❑ 656 New York Mets TC .20 .06
❑ 657 New York Yankees TC .50 .15
❑ 658 Oakland Athletics TC .20 .06
❑ 659 Philadelphia Phillies TC .20 .06
❑ 660 Pittsburgh Pirates TC .20 .06
❑ 661 San Diego Padres TC .20 .06
❑ 662 San Francisco Giants TC .20 .06
❑ 663 Seattle Mariners TC .20 .06
❑ 664 St. Louis Cardinals TC .30 .09
❑ 665 Tampa Bay Devil Rays TC .20 .06
❑ 666 Texas Rangers TC .20 .06
❑ 667 Toronto Blue Jays TC .20 .06
❑ 668 Billy Butler FY RC 3.00 .90
❑ 669 Wes Swackhamer FY RC .50 .15
❑ 670 Matt Campbell FY RC .50 .15
❑ 671 Ryan Webb FY .50 .15
❑ 672 Glen Perkins FY RC .75 .23
❑ 673 Michael Rogers FY RC .50 .15
❑ 674 Kevin Melillo FY RC .75 .23
❑ 675 Erik Cordier FY RC .50 .15
❑ 676 Landon Powell FY RC .75 .23
❑ 677 Justin Verlander FY RC 1.50 .45
❑ 678 Eric Nielsen FY RC .50 .15
❑ 679 Alexander Smit FY RC .50 .15
❑ 680 Ryan Garko FY RC 1.25 .35
❑ 681 Bobby Livingston FY RC .50 .15
❑ 682 Jeff Niemann FY RC 1.00 .30
❑ 683 Wladimir Balentien FY RC 1.00 .30
❑ 684 Chip Cannon FY RC .50 .15
❑ 685 Yorman Bazardo FY RC .50 .15
❑ 686 Mike Bourn FY RC .75 .23
❑ 687 Andy LaRoche FY RC 3.00 .90
❑ 688 Felix Hernandez .50 .15
Justin Leone
❑ 689 Ryan Howard .50 .15
Cole Hamels
❑ 690 Matt Cain 1.00 .30
Merkin Valdez
❑ 691 Andy Marte 5.00 1.50
Jeff Francoeur
❑ 692 Chad Billingsley .50 .15
Joel Guzman
❑ 693 Jerry Hairston Jr. .20 .06
Scott Hairston
❑ 694 Miguel Tejada .30 .09
Lance Berkman
❑ 695 Kenny Rogers GG .20 .06
❑ 696 Ivan Rodriguez GG .20 .06
❑ 697 Darin Erstad GG .20 .06
❑ 698 Bret Boone GG .20 .06
❑ 699 Eric Chavez GG .20 .06
❑ 700 Derek Jeter GG .50 .15
❑ 701 Vernon Wells GG .20 .06
❑ 702 Ichiro Suzuki GG .50 .15
❑ 703 Torii Hunter GG .20 .06
❑ 704 Greg Maddux GG .50 .15
❑ 705 Mike Matheny GG .20 .06
❑ 706 Todd Helton GG .20 .06
❑ 707 Luis Castillo GG .20 .06
❑ 708 Scott Rolen GG .20 .06
❑ 709 Cesar Izturis GG .20 .06
❑ 710 Jim Edmonds GG .20 .06
❑ 711 Andruw Jones GG .20 .06
❑ 712 Steve Finley GG .20 .06
❑ 713 Johan Santana CY .20 .06
❑ 714 Roger Clemens CY .50 .15
❑ 715 Vladimir Guerrero MVP .30 .09
❑ 716 Barry Bonds MVP 1.00 .30
❑ 717 Bobby Crosby ROY .20 .06
❑ 718 Jason Bay ROY .20 .06
❑ 719 Albert Pujols AS .50 .15
❑ 720 Mark Loretta AS .20 .06
❑ 721 Edgar Renteria AS .20 .06
❑ 722 Scott Rolen AS .20 .06
❑ 723 J.D. Drew AS .20 .06
❑ 724 Jim Edmonds AS .20 .06
❑ 725 Johnny Estrada AS .20 .06
❑ 726 Jason Schmidt AS .20 .06
❑ 727 Chris Carpenter AS .20 .06
❑ 728 Eric Gagne AS .20 .06
❑ 729 Jason Bay AS .20 .06
❑ 730 Bobby Cox MG AS .20 .06
❑ 731 David Ortiz 1.00 .30
Mark Bellhorn WS1
❑ 732 Curt Schilling WS2 1.00 .30
❑ 733 Manny Ramirez 1.00 .30
Pedro Martinez WS3
❑ 734 Red Sox Win 1.50 .45
Johnny Damon
Derek Lowe WS4

2005 Topps Update

	Nm-Mt	Ex-Mt
COMPLETE SET (330)	40.00	12.00
COMP.FACT.SET (330)	40.00	15.00
COMMON CARD (1-330)	.20	.06

COM (90-110/203-220)	.50	.15
COMMON (116-134)	.50	.15
COM (14/66/221-310)	.50	.15
COMMON (311-330)	.50	.15

PLATE ODDS 1:2009 H, 1:582 HTA, 1:2009 R
PLATE PRINT RUN 1 SET PER COLOR
BLACK-CYAN-MAGENTA-YELLOW ISSUED
NO PLATE PRICING DUE TO SCARCITY

❑ 1	Sammy Sosa	.50	.15
❑ 2	Jeff Francoeur	3.00	.90
❑ 3	Tony Clark	.20	.06
❑ 4	Michael Tucker	.20	.06
❑ 5	Mike Matheny	.20	.06
❑ 6	Eric Young	.20	.06
❑ 7	Jose Valentin	.20	.06
❑ 8	Matt Lawton	.20	.06
❑ 9	Juan Rivera	.20	.06
❑ 10	Shawn Green	.20	.06
❑ 11	Aaron Boone	.20	.06
❑ 12	Woody Williams	.20	.06
❑ 13	Brad Wilkerson	.20	.06
❑ 14	Anthony Reyes RC	1.00	.30
❑ 15	Russ Adams	.20	.06
❑ 16	Gustavo Chacin	.20	.06
❑ 17	Michael Restovich	.20	.06
❑ 18	Humberto Quintero	.20	.06
❑ 19	Matt Ginter	.20	.06
❑ 20	Scott Podsednik	.20	.06
❑ 21	Byung-Hyun Kim	.20	.06
❑ 22	Orlando Hernandez	.20	.06
❑ 23	Mark Grudzielanek	.20	.06
❑ 24	Jody Gerut	.20	.06
❑ 25	Adrian Beltre	.20	.06
❑ 26	Scott Schoeneweis	.20	.06
❑ 27	Marlon Anderson	.20	.06
❑ 28	Jason Vargas	.20	.06
❑ 29	Claudio Vargas	.20	.06
❑ 30	Jason Kendall	.20	.06
❑ 31	Aaron Small	.20	.06
❑ 32	Juan Cruz	.20	.06
❑ 33	Placido Polanco	.20	.06
❑ 34	Jorge Sosa	.20	.06
❑ 35	John Olerud	.20	.06
❑ 36	Ryan Langerhans	.20	.06
❑ 37	Randy Winn	.20	.06
❑ 38	Zach Duke	.30	.09
❑ 39	Garrett Atkins	.20	.06
❑ 40	Al Leiter	.20	.06
❑ 41	Shawn Chacon	.20	.06
❑ 42	Mark DeRosa	.20	.06
❑ 43	Miguel Ojeda	.20	.06
❑ 44	A.J. Pierzynski	.20	.06
❑ 45	Carlos Lee	.20	.06
❑ 46	LaTroy Hawkins	.20	.06
❑ 47	Nick Green	.20	.06
❑ 48	Shawn Estes	.20	.06
❑ 49	Eli Marrero	.20	.06
❑ 50	Jeff Kent	.20	.06
❑ 51	Joe Randa	.20	.06
❑ 52	Jose Hernandez	.20	.06
❑ 53	Joe Blanton	.20	.06
❑ 54	Huston Street	.30	.09
❑ 55	Marlon Byrd	.20	.06
❑ 56	Alex Sanchez	.20	.06
❑ 57	Livan Hernandez	.20	.06
❑ 58	Chris Young	.20	.06
❑ 59	Brad Eldred	.20	.06
❑ 60	Terrence Long	.20	.06
❑ 61	Phil Nevin	.20	.06
❑ 62	Kyle Farnsworth	.20	.06
❑ 63	Jon Lieber	.20	.06
❑ 64	Antonio Alfonseca	.20	.06
❑ 65	Tony Graffanino	.20	.06
❑ 66	Tadahito Iguchi RC	1.50	.45
❑ 67	Brad Thompson	.20	.06
❑ 68	Jose Vidro	.20	.06
❑ 69	Jason Phillips	.20	.06
❑ 70	Carl Pavano	.20	.06
❑ 71	Pokey Reese	.20	.06
❑ 72	Jerome Williams	.20	.06
❑ 73	Kazuhisa Ishii	.20	.06
❑ 74	Zach Day	.20	.06
❑ 75	Edgar Renteria	.20	.06
❑ 76	Mike Myers	.20	.06
❑ 77	Jeff Cirillo	.20	.06
❑ 78	Endy Chavez	.20	.06
❑ 79	Jose Guillen	.20	.06
❑ 80	Ugueth Urbina	.20	.06
❑ 81	Vinny Castilla	.20	.06
❑ 82	Javier Vazquez	.20	.06
❑ 83	Willy Taveras	.20	.06
❑ 84	Mark Mulder	.20	.06
❑ 85	Mike Hargrove MG	.20	.06
❑ 86	Buddy Bell MG	.20	.06
❑ 87	Charlie Manuel MG	.20	.06
❑ 88	Willie Randolph MG	.20	.06
❑ 89	Bob Melvin MG	.20	.06
❑ 90	Chris Lambert PROS	.50	.15
❑ 91	Homer Bailey PROS	.50	.15
❑ 92	Ervin Santana PROS	.50	.15
❑ 93	Bill Bray PROS	.50	.15
❑ 94	Thomas Diamond PROS	.50	.15
❑ 95	Trevor Plouffe PROS	.50	.15
❑ 96	James Houser PROS	.50	.15
❑ 97	Jake Stevens PROS	.50	.15
❑ 98	Anthony Whittington PROS	.50	.15
❑ 99	Philip Hughes PROS	.50	.15
❑ 100	Greg Golson PROS	.50	.15
❑ 101	Paul Maholm PROS	.50	.15
❑ 102	Carlos Quentin PROS	.50	.15
❑ 103	Dan Johnson PROS	.50	.15
❑ 104	Mark Rogers PROS	.50	.15
❑ 105	Neil Walker PROS	.50	.15
❑ 106	Omar Quintanilla PROS	.50	.15
❑ 107	Blake DeWitt PROS	.50	.15
❑ 108	Taylor Tankersley PROS	.50	.15
❑ 109	David Murphy PROS	.50	.15
❑ 110	Felix Hernandez PROS	1.00	.30
❑ 111	Craig Biggio HL	.20	.06
❑ 112	Greg Maddux HL	.50	.15
❑ 113	Bobby Abreu HL	.20	.06
❑ 114	Alex Rodriguez HL	.50	.15
❑ 115	Trevor Hoffman HL	.20	.06
❑ 116	A.J. Pierzynski Tadahito Iguchi ALDS	.75	.23
❑ 117	Reggie Sanders NLDS	.50	.15
❑ 118	Bengie Molina Ervin Santana ALDS	.50	.15
❑ 119	Chris Burke Lance Berkman Adam LaRoche NLDS	.50	.15
❑ 120	Garret Anderson ALCS	.50	.15
❑ 121	A.J. Pierzynski ALCS	.50	.15
❑ 122	Paul Konerko ALCS	.50	.15
❑ 123	Joe Crede ALCS	.50	.15
❑ 124	Mark Buehrle Jon Garland ALCS	.50	.15
❑ 125	Freddy Garcia Jose Contreras ALCS	.50	.15
❑ 126	Reggie Sanders NLCS	.50	.15
❑ 127	Roy Oswalt NLCS	.50	.15
❑ 128	Roger Clemens NLCS	1.00	.30
❑ 129	Albert Pujols NLCS	1.00	.30
❑ 130	Roy Oswalt NLCS	.50	.15
❑ 131	Joe Crede Bobby Jenks WS	.75	.23
❑ 132	Paul Konerko Scott Podsednik WS	.75	.23
❑ 133	Geoff Blum WS	.50	.15
❑ 134	White Sox Sweep WS	1.00	.30
❑ 135	Alex Rodriguez David Ortiz Manny Ramirez AL HR	.50	.15
❑ 136	Michael Young Alex Rodriguez Vladimir Guerrero AL BA	.30	.09
❑ 137	David Ortiz Mark Teixeira Manny Ramirez AL RBI	.30	.09
❑ 138	Bartolo Colon Jon Garland Cliff Lee AL Wins	.20	.06
❑ 139	Kevin Millwood Johan Santana Mark Buehrle AL ERA	.20	.06
❑ 140	Johan Santana Randy Johnson John Lackey AL K's	.30	.09
❑ 141	Andruw Jones Derrek Lee Albert Pujols NL HR	.50	.15
❑ 142	Derrek Lee Albert Pujols Miguel Cabrera NL BA	.50	.15
❑ 143	Andruw Jones Albert Pujols Pat Burrell NL RBI	.50	.15
❑ 144	Dontrelle Willis Chris Carpenter Roy Oswalt NL Wins	.20	.06
❑ 145	Roger Clemens Andy Pettitte Dontrelle Willis NL ERA	.50	.15
❑ 146	Jake Peavy Chris Carpenter Pedro Martinez NL K's	.20	.06
❑ 147	Mark Teixeira AS	.20	.06
❑ 148	Brian Roberts AS	.20	.06
❑ 149	Michael Young AS	.20	.06
❑ 150	Alex Rodriguez AS	.50	.15
❑ 151	Johnny Damon AS	.20	.06
❑ 152	Vladimir Guerrero AS	.30	.09
❑ 153	Manny Ramirez AS	.20	.06
❑ 154	David Ortiz AS	.30	.09
❑ 155	Mariano Rivera AS	.20	.06
❑ 156	Joe Nathan AS	.20	.06
❑ 157	Albert Pujols AS	.50	.15
❑ 158	Jeff Kent AS	.20	.06
❑ 159	Felipe Lopez AS	.20	.06
❑ 160	Morgan Ensberg AS	.20	.06
❑ 161	Miguel Cabrera AS	.20	.06
❑ 162	Ken Griffey Jr. AS	.50	.15
❑ 163	Andruw Jones AS	.20	.06
❑ 164	Paul Lo Duca AS	.20	.06
❑ 165	Chad Cordero AS	.20	.06
❑ 166	Ken Griffey Jr. Comeback	.50	.15
❑ 167	Jason Giambi Comeback	.20	.06
❑ 168	Willy Taveras ROY	.20	.06
❑ 169	Huston Street ROY	.20	.06
❑ 170	Chris Carpenter AS	.20	.06
❑ 171	Bartolo Colon AS	.20	.06
❑ 172	Bobby Cox AS MG	.20	.06
❑ 173	Ozzie Guillen AS MG	.50	.15
❑ 174	Andruw Jones POY	.20	.06
❑ 175	Johnny Damon AS	.20	.06
❑ 176	Alex Rodriguez AS	.50	.15
❑ 177	David Ortiz AS	.30	.09
❑ 178	Manny Ramirez AS	.20	.06
❑ 179	Miguel Tejada AS	.20	.06
❑ 180	Vladimir Guerrero AS	.30	.09
❑ 181	Mark Teixeira AS	.20	.06
❑ 182	Ivan Rodriguez AS	.20	.06
❑ 183	Brian Roberts AS	.20	.06
❑ 184	Mark Buehrle AS	.20	.06
❑ 185	Bobby Abreu AS	.20	.06
❑ 186	Carlos Beltran AS	.20	.06
❑ 187	Albert Pujols AS	.50	.15
❑ 188	Derrek Lee AS	.20	.06
❑ 189	Jim Edmonds AS	.20	.06
❑ 190	Aramis Ramirez AS	.20	.06
❑ 191	Mike Piazza AS	.30	.09
❑ 192	Jeff Kent AS	.20	.06
❑ 193	David Eckstein AS	.20	.06
❑ 194	Chris Carpenter AS	.20	.06
❑ 195	Bobby Abreu HR	.20	.06
❑ 196	Ivan Rodriguez HR	.20	.06
❑ 197	Carlos Lee HR	.20	.06
❑ 198	David Ortiz HR	.30	.09
❑ 199	Hee-Seop Choi HR	.20	.06
❑ 200	Andruw Jones HR	.20	.06
❑ 201	Mark Teixeira HR	.20	.06
❑ 202	Jason Bay HR	.20	.06
❑ 203	Hanley Ramirez FUT	.50	.15
❑ 204	Shin-Soo Choo FUT	.50	.15
❑ 205	Justin Huber FUT	.50	.15
❑ 206	Nelson Cruz FUT RC	.50	.15
❑ 207	Edwin Encarnacion FUT	.50	.15
❑ 208	Miguel Montero FUT RC	1.25	.35
❑ 209	William Bergolla FUT	.50	.15
❑ 210	Luis Montanez FUT	.50	.15
❑ 211	Francisco Liriano FUT	.50	.15
❑ 212	Kevin Thompson FUT	.50	.15
❑ 213	B.J. Upton FUT	.50	.15
❑ 214	Conor Jackson FUT	.50	.15
❑ 215	Delmon Young FUT	.50	.15
❑ 216	Andy LaRoche FUT	1.00	.30
❑ 217	Ryan Garko FUT	.50	.15

❑ 218 Josh Barfield FUT .50 .15
❑ 219 Chris B.Young FUT .50 .15
❑ 220 Justin Verlander FUT .50 .15
❑ 221 Drew Anderson FY RC .50 .15
❑ 222 Luis Hernandez FY RC .50 .15
❑ 223 Jim Burt FY RC .50 .15
❑ 224 Mike Morse FY RC .75 .23
❑ 225 Elliot Johnson FY RC .50 .15
❑ 226 C.J. Smith FY RC .50 .15
❑ 227 Casey McGehee FY RC .50 .15
❑ 228 Brian Miller FY RC .50 .15
❑ 229 Chris Vines FY RC .50 .15
❑ 230 D.J. Houlton FY RC .50 .15
❑ 231 Chuck Tiffany FY RC 1.00 .30
❑ 232 Humberto Sanchez FY RC .50 .15
❑ 233 Baltazar Lopez FY RC .50 .15
❑ 234 Russ Martin FY RC .75 .23
❑ 235 Dana Eveland FY RC .50 .15
❑ 236 Johan Silva FY RC .50 .15
❑ 237 Adam Harben FY RC .75 .23
❑ 238 Brian Bannister FY RC .50 .15
❑ 239 Adam Boeve FY RC .50 .15
❑ 240 Thomas Oldham FY RC .50 .15
❑ 241 Cody Haerther FY RC .50 .15
❑ 242 Dan Santin FY RC .50 .15
❑ 243 Daniel Haigwood FY RC 1.00 .30
❑ 244 Craig Tatum FY RC .50 .15
❑ 245 Martin Prado FY RC .50 .15
❑ 246 Errol Simonitsch FY RC .75 .23
❑ 247 Lorenzo Scott FY RC .50 .15
❑ 248 Hayden Penn FY RC .75 .23
❑ 249 Heath Totten FY RC .50 .15
❑ 250 Nick Masset FY RC .50 .15
❑ 251 Pedro Lopez FY RC .50 .15
❑ 252 Ben Harrison FY .50 .15
❑ 253 Mike Spidale FY RC .50 .15
❑ 254 Jeremy Harts FY RC .50 .15
❑ 255 Danny Zell FY RC .50 .15
❑ 256 Kevin Collins FY RC .50 .15
❑ 257 Tony Americh FY RC .50 .15
❑ 258 Matt Albers FY RC .50 .15
❑ 259 Ricky Barrett FY RC .50 .15
❑ 260 Hernan Iribarren FY RC .75 .23
❑ 261 Sean Tracey FY RC .50 .15
❑ 262 Jerry Owens FY RC .75 .23
❑ 263 Steve Nelson FY RC .50 .15
❑ 264 Brandon McCarthy FY RC 1.00 .30
❑ 265 David Shepard FY RC .50 .15
❑ 266 Steven Bondurant FY RC .50 .15
❑ 267 Billy Sadler FY RC .50 .15
❑ 268 Ryan Feierabend FY RC .50 .15
❑ 269 Stuart Pomeranz FY RC .50 .15
❑ 270 Shaun Marcum FY .50 .15
❑ 271 Erik Schindewolf FY RC .50 .15
❑ 272 Stefan Bailie FY RC .50 .15
❑ 273 Mike Esposito FY RC .50 .15
❑ 274 Buck Coats FY RC .50 .15
❑ 275 Andy Sides FY RC .50 .15
❑ 276 Micah Schnurstein FY RC .50 .15
❑ 277 Jesse Gutierrez FY RC .50 .15
❑ 278 Jake Postlewait FY RC .50 .15
❑ 279 Willy Mota FY RC .50 .15
❑ 280 Ryan Speier FY RC .50 .15
❑ 281 Frank Mata FY RC .50 .15
❑ 282 Jair Jurrjens FY RC .75 .23
❑ 283 Nick Touchstone FY RC .50 .15
❑ 284 Matthew Kemp FY RC 1.00 .30
❑ 285 Vinny Rottino FY RC .50 .15
❑ 286 J.B. Thurmond FY RC .50 .15
❑ 287 Kelvin Pichardo FY RC .50 .15
❑ 288 Scott Mitchinson FY RC .50 .15
❑ 289 Darwinson Salazar FY RC .50 .15
❑ 290 George Kottaras FY RC .75 .23
❑ 291 Kenny Durost FY RC .50 .15
❑ 292 Jonathan Sanchez FY RC .50 .15
❑ 293 Brandon Moorhead FY RC .50 .15
❑ 294 Kennard Bibbs FY RC .50 .15
❑ 295 David Gassner FY RC .50 .15
❑ 296 Micah Furtado FY RC .50 .15
❑ 297 Ismael Ramirez FY RC .50 .15
❑ 298 Carlos Gonzalez FY RC 2.00 .60
❑ 299 Brandon Sing FY RC .75 .23
❑ 300 Jason Motte FY RC .50 .15
❑ 301 Chuck James FY RC 1.00 .30
❑ 302 Andy Santana FY RC .50 .15
❑ 303 Manny Parra FY RC .50 .15
❑ 304 Chris B.Young FY RC 1.00 .30
❑ 305 Juan Senreiso FY RC .50 .15
❑ 306 Franklin Morales FY RC .50 .15
❑ 307 Jared Gothreaux FY RC .50 .15
❑ 308 Jayce Tingler FY RC .50 .15
❑ 309 Matt Brown FY RC .50 .15
❑ 310 Frank Diaz FY RC .50 .15
❑ 311 Stephen Drew DP RC 5.00 1.50
❑ 312 Jered Weaver DP RC 2.50 .75
❑ 313 Ryan Braun DP RC 2.00 .60
❑ 314 John Mayberry DP RC 1.00 .30
❑ 315 Aaron Thompson DP RC .75 .23
❑ 316 Cesar Carrillo DP RC 1.00 .30
❑ 317 Jacoby Ellsbury DP RC 1.00 .30
❑ 318 Matt Garza DP RC .75 .23
❑ 319 Cliff Pennington DP RC .75 .23
❑ 320 Colby Rasmus DP RC 2.00 .60
❑ 321 Chris Volstad DP RC 1.00 .30
❑ 322 Ricky Romero DP RC .50 .15
❑ 323 Ryan Zimmerman DP RC 5.00 1.50
❑ 324 C.J. Henry DP RC 1.50 .45
❑ 325 Jay Bruce DP RC 2.50 .75
❑ 326 Beau Jones DP RC 1.00 .30
❑ 327 Mark McCormick DP RC .75 .23
❑ 328 Eli Iorg DP RC 1.00 .30
❑ 329 Andrew McCutchen DP RC 1.50 .45
❑ 330 Mike Costanzo DP RC 1.00 .30

2003 Topps 205

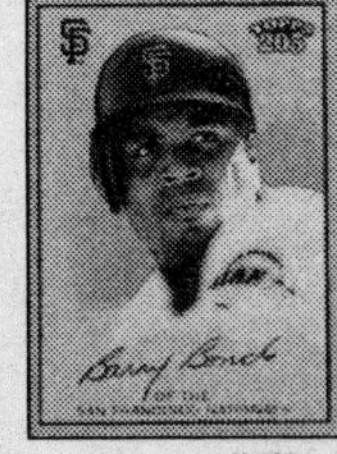

	Nm-Mt	Ex-Mt
COMPLETE SERIES 1 (165)	40.00	12.00
COMPLETE SERIES 2 (175)	125.00	38.00
COMP.SERIES 2 w/o SP's (155)	40.00	12.00
COM (1-130/161-169/193-315)	.50	.15
COMMON (131-145/170-192)	.50	.15
COMMON (146-150)	1.00	.30
COMMON SP	2.50	.75
SERIES 2 SP STATED ODDS 1:5		

❑ 1A Barry Bonds w/Cap 3.00 .90
❑ 1B Barry Bonds w/Helmet 3.00 .90
❑ 2 Bret Boone .50 .15
❑ 3A Albert Pujols Clear Logo 2.50 .75
❑ 3B Albert Pujols White Logo 2.50 .75
❑ 4 Carl Crawford .50 .15
❑ 5 Bartolo Colon .50 .15
❑ 6 Cliff Floyd .50 .15
❑ 7 John Olerud .50 .15
❑ 8A Jason Giambi Full Jkt .50 .15
❑ 8B Jason Giambi Partial Jkt .50 .15
❑ 9 Edgardo Alfonzo .50 .15
❑ 10 Ivan Rodriguez .75 .23
❑ 11 Jim Edmonds .75 .23
❑ 12A Mike Piazza Orange 2.00 .60
❑ 12B Mike Piazza Yellow 2.00 .60
❑ 13 Greg Maddux 2.00 .60
❑ 14 Jose Vidro .50 .15
❑ 15A Vlad Guerrero Clear Logo 1.25 .35
❑ 15B V.Guerrero White Logo 1.25 .35
❑ 16 Bernie Williams .75 .23
❑ 17 Roger Clemens 2.50 .75
❑ 18A Miguel Tejada Blue .50 .15
❑ 18B Miguel Tejada Green .50 .15
❑ 19 Carlos Delgado .50 .15
❑ 20A Alfonso Soriano w/Bat .50 .15
❑ 20B Alf. Soriano Sunglasses .50 .15
❑ 21 Bobby Cox MG .50 .15
❑ 22 Mike Scioscia .50 .15
❑ 23 John Smoltz .75 .23
❑ 24 Luis Gonzalez .50 .15
❑ 25 Shawn Green .50 .15
❑ 26 Raul Ibanez .50 .15
❑ 27 Andruw Jones .75 .23
❑ 28 Josh Beckett .50 .15
❑ 29 Derek Lowe .50 .15
❑ 30 Todd Helton .75 .23
❑ 31 Barry Larkin .75 .23
❑ 32 Jason Jennings .50 .15
❑ 33 Darin Erstad .50 .15
❑ 34 Magglio Ordonez .50 .15
❑ 35 Mike Sweeney .50 .15
❑ 36 Kazuhisa Ishii .50 .15
❑ 37 Ron Gardenhire MG .50 .15
❑ 38 Tim Hudson .50 .15
❑ 39 Tim Salmon .75 .23
❑ 40A Pat Burrell Black Bat .50 .15
❑ 40B Pat Burrell Brown Bat .50 .15
❑ 41 Manny Ramirez .75 .23
❑ 42 Nick Johnson .50 .15
❑ 43 Tom Glavine .75 .23
❑ 44 Mark Mulder .50 .15
❑ 45 Brian Jordan .50 .15
❑ 46 Rafael Palmeiro .75 .23
❑ 47 Vernon Wells .50 .15
❑ 48 Bob Brenly MG .50 .15
❑ 49 C.C. Sabathia .50 .15
❑ 50A A.Rodriguez Look Ahead 2.00 .60
❑ 50B A.Rodriguez Look Away 2.00 .60
❑ 51A Sammy Sosa Head Duck 1.25 .35
❑ 51B Sammy Sosa Head Left 1.25 .35
❑ 52 Paul Konerko .50 .15
❑ 53 Craig Biggio .75 .23
❑ 54 Moises Alou .50 .15
❑ 55 Johnny Damon .75 .23
❑ 56 Torii Hunter .50 .15
❑ 57 Omar Vizquel .75 .23
❑ 58 Orlando Hernandez .50 .15
❑ 59 Barry Zito .50 .15
❑ 60 Lance Berkman .50 .15
❑ 61 Carlos Beltran .50 .15
❑ 62 Edgar Renteria .50 .15
❑ 63 Ben Sheets .50 .15
❑ 64 Doug Mientkiewicz .50 .15
❑ 65 Troy Glaus .50 .15
❑ 66 Preston Wilson .50 .15
❑ 67 Kerry Wood .50 .15
❑ 68 Frank Thomas 1.25 .35
❑ 69 Jimmy Rollins .50 .15
❑ 70 Brian Giles .50 .15
❑ 71 Bobby Higginson .50 .15
❑ 72 Larry Walker .50 .15
❑ 73 Randy Johnson 1.25 .35
❑ 74 Tony LaRussa MG .50 .15
❑ 75A Derek Jeter w/Gold Trim 3.00 .90
❑ 75B D.Jeter w/o Gold Trim 3.00 .90
❑ 76 Bobby Abreu .50 .15
❑ 77A A.Dunn Closed Mouth .50 .15
❑ 77B Adam Dunn Open Mouth .50 .15
❑ 78 Ryan Klesko .50 .15
❑ 79 Francisco Rodriguez .50 .15
❑ 80 Scott Rolen .75 .23
❑ 81 Roberto Alomar .75 .23
❑ 82 Joe Torre MG .75 .23
❑ 83 Jim Thome .75 .23
❑ 84 Kevin Millwood .50 .15
❑ 85 J.T. Snow .50 .15
❑ 86 Trevor Hoffman .50 .15
❑ 87 Jay Gibbons .50 .15
❑ 88A Mark Prior New Logo .75 .23
❑ 88B Mark Prior Old Logo .75 .23
❑ 89 Rich Aurilia .50 .15
❑ 90 Chipper Jones 1.25 .35
❑ 91 Richie Sexson .50 .15
❑ 92 Gary Sheffield .50 .15
❑ 93 Pedro Martinez .75 .23
❑ 94 Rodrigo Lopez .50 .15
❑ 95 Al Leiter .50 .15
❑ 96 Jorge Posada .75 .23
❑ 97 Luis Castillo .50 .15
❑ 98 Aubrey Huff .50 .15
❑ 99 A.J. Pierzynski .50 .15
❑ 100A I.Suzuki Look Ahead 2.50 .75
❑ 100B Ichiro Suzuki Look Right 2.50 .75
❑ 101 Eric Chavez .50 .15

Card	Nm-Mt	Ex-Mt
❑ 102 Brett Myers	.50	.15
❑ 103 Jason Kendall	.50	.15
❑ 104 Jeff Kent	.50	.15
❑ 105 Eric Hinske	.50	.15
❑ 106 Jacque Jones	.50	.15
❑ 107 Phil Nevin	.50	.15
❑ 108 Roy Oswalt	.50	.15
❑ 109 Curt Schilling	.50	.15
❑ 110A N.Garciaparra w/Gold Trim	2.00	.60
❑ 110B N.Garciaparra w/o Gold Trim	2.00	.60
❑ 111 Garret Anderson	.50	.15
❑ 112 Eric Gagne	.50	.15
❑ 113 Javier Vazquez	.50	.15
❑ 114 Jeff Bagwell	.75	.23
❑ 115 Mike Lowell	.50	.15
❑ 116 Carlos Pena	.50	.15
❑ 117 Ken Griffey Jr.	2.00	.60
❑ 118 Tony Batista	.50	.15
❑ 119 Edgar Martinez	.75	.23
❑ 120 Austin Kearns	.50	.15
❑ 121 Jason Stokes PROS	.50	.15
❑ 122 Jose Reyes PROS	.50	.15
❑ 123 Rocco Baldelli PROS	.50	.15
❑ 124 Joe Borchard PROS	.50	.15
❑ 125 Joe Mauer PROS	.75	.23
❑ 126 Gavin Floyd PROS	.50	.15
❑ 127 Mark Teixeira PROS	.75	.23
❑ 128 Jeremy Guthrie PROS	.50	.15
❑ 129 B.J. Upton PROS	1.25	.35
❑ 130 Khalil Greene PROS	2.00	.60
❑ 131 Hanley Ramirez FY RC	3.00	.90
❑ 132 Andy Marte FY RC	4.00	1.20
❑ 133 J.D. Durbin FY RC	.50	.15
❑ 134 Jason Kubel FY RC	1.00	.30
❑ 135 Craig Brazell FY RC	.50	.15
❑ 136 Bryan Bullington FY RC	.50	.15
❑ 137 Jose Contreras FY RC	1.00	.30
❑ 138 Brian Burgamy FY RC	.50	.15
❑ 139 E.Bastida-Martinez FY RC	.50	.15
❑ 140 Joey Gomes FY RC	.50	.15
❑ 141 Ismael Castro FY RC	.60	.18
❑ 142 Travis Wong FY RC	.60	.18
❑ 143 Mi.Garciaparra FY RC	.50	.15
❑ 144 Arnaldo Munoz FY RC	.50	.15
❑ 145 Louis Sockalexis FY XRC	.50	.15
❑ 146 Richard Hoblitzell REP	1.00	.30
❑ 147 George Graham REP	1.00	.30
❑ 148 Hal Chase REP	1.00	.30
❑ 149 John McGraw REP	1.50	.45
❑ 150 Bobby Wallace REP	1.00	.30
❑ 151 David Shean REP	1.00	.30
❑ 152 Richard Hoblitzell REP SP	2.50	.75
❑ 153 Hal Chase REP	1.00	.30
❑ 154 Hooks Wiltse REP	1.00	.30
❑ 155 George Brett RET	3.00	.90
❑ 156 Willie Mays RET	3.00	.90
❑ 157 Honus Wagner RET SP	10.00	3.00
❑ 158 Nolan Ryan RET	4.00	1.20
❑ 159 Reggie Jackson RET	1.50	.45
❑ 160 Mike Schmidt RET	3.00	.90
❑ 161 Josh Barfield PROS	.50	.15
❑ 162 Grady Sizemore PROS	.50	.15
❑ 163 Justin Morneau PROS	.50	.15
❑ 164 Laynce Nix PROS	.50	.15
❑ 165 Zack Greinke PROS	.50	.15
❑ 166 Victor Martinez PROS	.75	.23
❑ 167 Jeff Mathis PROS	.50	.15
❑ 168 Casey Kotchman PROS	.50	.15
❑ 169 Gabe Gross PROS	.50	.15
❑ 170 Edwin Jackson FY RC	.60	.18
❑ 171 Delmon Young FY SP RC	10.00	3.00
❑ 172 Eric Duncan FY SP RC	8.00	2.40
❑ 173 Brian Snyder FY SP RC	5.00	1.50
❑ 174 Chris Lubanski FY SP RC	5.00	1.50
❑ 175 Ryan Harvey FY SP RC	6.00	1.80
❑ 176 Nick Markakis FY SP RC	6.00	1.80
❑ 177 Chad Billingsley FY SP RC	8.00	2.40
❑ 178 Elizardo Ramirez FY RC	.60	.18
❑ 179 Ben Francisco FY RC	.50	.15
❑ 180 Franklin Gutierrez FY SP RC	5.00	1.50
❑ 181 Aaron Hill FY SP RC	5.00	1.50
❑ 182 Kevin Correia FY RC	.50	.15
❑ 183 Kelly Shoppach FY RC	1.00	.30
❑ 184 Felix Pie FY SP RC	10.00	3.00
❑ 185 Adam Loewen FY SP RC	5.00	1.50
❑ 186 Danny Garcia FY RC	.50	.15
❑ 187 Rickie Weeks FY SP RC	8.00	2.40
❑ 188 Robby Hammock FY SP RC	4.00	1.20
❑ 189 Ryan Wagner FY SP RC	4.00	1.20
❑ 190 Matt Kata FY SP RC	4.00	1.20
❑ 191 Bo Hart FY SP RC	4.00	1.20
❑ 192 Brandon Webb FY SP RC	5.00	1.50
❑ 193 Bengie Molina	.50	.15
❑ 194 Junior Spivey	.50	.15
❑ 195 Gary Sheffield	.50	.15
❑ 196 Jason Johnson	.50	.15
❑ 197 David Ortiz	.75	.23
❑ 198 Roberto Alomar	.75	.23
❑ 199 Wily Mo Pena	.50	.15
❑ 200 Sammy Sosa	1.25	.35
❑ 201 Jay Payton	.50	.15
❑ 202 Dmitri Young	.50	.15
❑ 203 Derrek Lee	.75	.23
❑ 204A Jeff Bagwell w/Hat	.75	.23
❑ 204B Jeff Bagwell w/o Hat	.75	.23
❑ 205 Runelvys Hernandez	.50	.15
❑ 206 Kevin Brown	.50	.15
❑ 207 Wes Helms	.50	.15
❑ 208 Eddie Guardado	.50	.15
❑ 209 Orlando Cabrera	.50	.15
❑ 210 Alfonso Soriano	.50	.15
❑ 211 Ty Wigginton	.50	.15
❑ 212A Rich Harden Look Left	.75	.23
❑ 212B Rich Harden Look Right	.75	.23
❑ 213 Mike Lieberthal	.50	.15
❑ 214 Brian Giles	.50	.15
❑ 215 Jason Schmidt	.50	.15
❑ 216 Jamie Moyer	.50	.15
❑ 217 Matt Morris	.50	.15
❑ 218 Victor Zambrano	.50	.15
❑ 219 Roy Halladay	.50	.15
❑ 220 Mike Hampton	.50	.15
❑ 221 Kevin Millar Sox	.50	.15
❑ 222 Hideo Nomo	1.25	.35
❑ 223 Milton Bradley	.50	.15
❑ 224 Jose Guillen	.50	.15
❑ 225 Derek Jeter	3.00	.90
❑ 226 Rondell White	.50	.15
❑ 227A Hank Blalock Blue Jsy	.50	.15
❑ 227B Hank Blalock White Jsy	.50	.15
❑ 228 Shigetoshi Hasegawa	.50	.15
❑ 229 Mike Mussina	.75	.23
❑ 230 Cristian Guzman	.50	.15
❑ 231A Todd Helton Blue	.75	.23
❑ 231B Todd Helton Green	.75	.23
❑ 232 Kenny Lofton	.50	.15
❑ 233 Carl Everett	.50	.15
❑ 234 Shea Hillenbrand	.50	.15
❑ 235 Brad Fullmer	.50	.15
❑ 236 Bernie Williams	.75	.23
❑ 237 Vicente Padilla	.50	.15
❑ 238 Tim Worrell	.50	.15
❑ 239 Juan Gonzalez	.50	.15
❑ 240 Ichiro Suzuki	2.50	.75
❑ 241 Aaron Boone	.50	.15
❑ 242 Shannon Stewart	.50	.15
❑ 243A Barry Zito Blue	.50	.15
❑ 243B Barry Zito Green	.50	.15
❑ 244 Reggie Sanders	.50	.15
❑ 245 Scott Podsednik	.50	.15
❑ 246 Miguel Cabrera	1.25	.35
❑ 247 Angel Berroa	.50	.15
❑ 248 Carlos Zambrano	.50	.15
❑ 249 Marlon Byrd	.50	.15
❑ 250 Mark Prior	.75	.23
❑ 251 Esteban Loaiza	.50	.15
❑ 252 David Eckstein	.50	.15
❑ 253 Alex Cintron	.50	.15
❑ 254 Melvin Mora	.50	.15
❑ 255 Russ Ortiz	.50	.15
❑ 256 Carlos Lee	.50	.15
❑ 257 Tino Martinez	.75	.23
❑ 258 Randy Wolf	.50	.15
❑ 259 Jason Phillips	.50	.15
❑ 260 Vladimir Guerrero	1.25	.35
❑ 261 Brad Wilkerson	.50	.15
❑ 262 Ivan Rodriguez	.75	.23
❑ 263 Matt Lawton	.50	.15
❑ 264 Adam Dunn	.50	.15
❑ 265 Joe Borowski	.50	.15
❑ 266 Jody Gerut	.50	.15
❑ 267 Alex Rodriguez	2.00	.60
❑ 268 Brendan Donnelly	.50	.15
❑ 269A Randy Johnson Grey	1.25	.35
❑ 269B Randy Johnson Pink	1.25	.35
❑ 270 Nomar Garciaparra	2.00	.60
❑ 271 Javy Lopez	.50	.15
❑ 272 Travis Hafner	.50	.15
❑ 273 Juan Pierre	.50	.15
❑ 274 Morgan Ensberg	.50	.15
❑ 275 Albert Pujols	2.50	.75
❑ 276 Jason LaRue	.50	.15
❑ 277 Paul Lo Duca	.50	.15
❑ 278 Andy Pettitte	.75	.23
❑ 279 Mike Piazza	2.00	.60
❑ 280A Jim Thome Blue	.75	.23
❑ 280B Jim Thome Green	.75	.23
❑ 281 Marquis Grissom	.50	.15
❑ 282 Woody Williams	.50	.15
❑ 283A Curt Schilling Look Ahead	.50	.15
❑ 283B Curt Schilling Look Right	.50	.15
❑ 284A Chipper Jones Blue	1.25	.35
❑ 284B Chipper Jones Yellow	1.25	.35
❑ 285 Deivi Cruz	.50	.15
❑ 286 Johnny Damon	.75	.23
❑ 287 Chin-Hui Tsao	.50	.15
❑ 288 Alex Gonzalez	.50	.15
❑ 289 Billy Wagner	.50	.15
❑ 290 Jason Giambi	.50	.15
❑ 291 Keith Foulke	.50	.15
❑ 292 Jerome Williams	.50	.15
❑ 293 Livan Hernandez	.50	.15
❑ 294 Aaron Guiel	.50	.15
❑ 295 Randall Simon	.50	.15
❑ 296 Byung-Hyun Kim	.50	.15
❑ 297 Jorge Julio	.50	.15
❑ 298 Miguel Batista	.50	.15
❑ 299 Rafael Furcal	.50	.15
❑ 300A Dontrelle Willis No Smile	1.25	.35
❑ 300B Dontrelle Willis Smile SP	4.00	1.20
❑ 301 Alex Sanchez	.50	.15
❑ 302 Shawn Chacon	.50	.15
❑ 303 Matt Clement	.50	.15
❑ 304 Luis Matos	.50	.15
❑ 305 Steve Finley	.50	.15
❑ 306 Marcus Giles	.50	.15
❑ 307 Boomer Wells	.50	.15
❑ 308 Jeromy Burnitz	.50	.15
❑ 309 Mike MacDougal	.50	.15
❑ 310 Mariano Rivera	.75	.23
❑ 311 Adrian Beltre	.50	.15
❑ 312 Mark Loretta	.50	.15
❑ 313 Ugueth Urbina	.50	.15
❑ 314 Bill Mueller	.50	.15
❑ 315 Johan Santana	.75	.23
❑ NNO Vintage Buyback	.00	

2002 Topps 206

	Nm-Mt	Ex-Mt
COMPLETE SET (525)	220.00	65.00
COMPLETE SERIES 1 (180)	60.00	18.00
COMPLETE SERIES 2 (180)	60.00	18.00
COMPLETE SERIES 3 (165)	100.00	30.00
COM(1-140/181-270/308-418)	.50	.15
COMMON (141-155/271-285)	.50	.15
COMMON RC (308-418)	.50	.15
COMMON SP (308-398)	2.00	.60
COMMON FYP SP (	1.00	.30
COMMON RET SP (433-447)	2.00	.60

Card	Nm-Mt	Ex-Mt
❑ 1 Vladimir Guerrero	1.25	.35

❑	2	Sammy Sosa	1.25	.35
❑	3	Garret Anderson	.50	.15
❑	4	Rafael Palmeiro	.75	.23
❑	5	Juan Gonzalez	.50	.15
❑	6	John Smoltz	.75	.23
❑	7	Mark Mulder	.50	.15
❑	8	Jon Lieber	.50	.15
❑	9	Greg Maddux	2.00	.60
❑	10	Moises Alou	.50	.15
❑	11	Joe Randa	.50	.15
❑	12	Bobby Abreu	.50	.15
❑	13	Juan Pierre	.50	.15
❑	14	Kerry Wood	.50	.15
❑	15	Craig Biggio	.75	.23
❑	16	Curt Schilling	.50	.15
❑	17	Brian Jordan	.50	.15
❑	18	Edgardo Alfonzo	.50	.15
❑	19	Darren Dreifort	.50	.15
❑	20	Todd Helton	.75	.23
❑	21	Ramon Ortiz	.50	.15
❑	22	Ichiro Suzuki	2.50	.75
❑	23	Jimmy Rollins	.50	.15
❑	24	Darin Erstad	.50	.15
❑	25	Shawn Green	.50	.15
❑	26	Tino Martinez	.75	.23
❑	27	Bret Boone	.50	.15
❑	28	Alfonso Soriano	.50	.15
❑	29	Chan Ho Park	.50	.15
❑	30	Roger Clemens	2.50	.75
❑	31	Cliff Floyd	.50	.15
❑	32	Johnny Damon	.75	.23
❑	33	Frank Thomas	1.25	.35
❑	34	Barry Bonds	3.00	.90
❑	35	Luis Gonzalez	.50	.15
❑	36	Carlos Lee	.50	.15
❑	37	Roberto Alomar	.75	.23
❑	38	Carlos Delgado	.50	.15
❑	39	Nomar Garciaparra	2.00	.60
❑	40	Jason Kendall	.50	.15
❑	41	Scott Rolen	.75	.23
❑	42	Tom Glavine	.75	.23
❑	43	Ryan Klesko	.50	.15
❑	44	Brian Giles	.50	.15
❑	45	Bud Smith	.50	.15
❑	46	Charles Nagy	.50	.15
❑	47	Tony Gwynn	1.50	.45
❑	48	C.C. Sabathia UER Credited with incorrect victory total in 2001	.50	.15
❑	49	Frank Catalanotto	.50	.15
❑	50	Jerry Hairston	.50	.15
❑	51	Jeromy Burnitz	.50	.15
❑	52	David Justice	.50	.15
❑	53	Bartolo Colon	.50	.15
❑	54	Andres Galarraga	.50	.15
❑	55	Jeff Weaver	.50	.15
❑	56	Terrence Long	.50	.15
❑	57	Tsuyoshi Shinjo	.50	.15
❑	58	Barry Zito	.50	.15
❑	59	Mariano Rivera	.75	.23
❑	60	John Olerud	.50	.15
❑	61	Randy Johnson	1.25	.35
❑	62	Kenny Lofton	.50	.15
❑	63	Jermaine Dye	.50	.15
❑	64	Troy Glaus	.50	.15
❑	65	Larry Walker	.50	.15
❑	66	Hideo Nomo	1.25	.35
❑	67	Mike Mussina	.75	.23
❑	68	Paul LoDuca	.50	.15
❑	69	Magglio Ordonez	.50	.15
❑	70	Paul O'Neill	.75	.23
❑	71	Sean Casey	.75	.23
❑	72	Lance Berkman	.50	.15
❑	73	Adam Dunn	.50	.15
❑	74	Aramis Ramirez	.50	.15
❑	75	Rafael Furcal	.50	.15
❑	76	Gary Sheffield	.50	.15
❑	77	Todd Hollandsworth	.50	.15
❑	78	Chipper Jones	1.25	.35
❑	79	Bernie Williams	.75	.23
❑	80	Richard Hidalgo	.50	.15
❑	81	Eric Chavez	.50	.15
❑	82	Mike Piazza	2.00	.60
❑	83	J.D. Drew	.50	.15
❑	84	Ken Griffey Jr.	2.00	.60
❑	85	Joe Kennedy	.50	.15
❑	86	Joel Pineiro	.50	.15
❑	87	Josh Towers	.50	.15
❑	88	Andruw Jones	.75	.23
❑	89	Carlos Beltran	.50	.15
❑	90	Mike Cameron	.50	.15
❑	91	Albert Pujols	2.50	.75
❑	92	Alex Rodriguez	2.00	.60
❑	93	Omar Vizquel	.75	.23
❑	94	Juan Encarnacion	.50	.15
❑	95	Jeff Bagwell	.75	.23
❑	96	Jose Canseco	.75	.23
❑	97	Ben Sheets	.50	.15
❑	98	Mark Grace	.75	.23
❑	99	Mike Sweeney	.50	.15
❑	100	Mark McGwire	3.00	.90
❑	101	Ivan Rodriguez	.75	.23
❑	102	Rich Aurilia	.50	.15
❑	103	Cristian Guzman	.50	.15
❑	104	Roy Oswalt	.50	.15
❑	105	Tim Hudson	.50	.15
❑	106	Brent Abernathy	.50	.15
❑	107	Mike Hampton	.50	.15
❑	108	Miguel Tejada	.50	.15
❑	109	Bobby Higginson	.50	.15
❑	110	Edgar Martinez	.75	.23
❑	111	Jorge Posada	.75	.23
❑	112	Jason Giambi Yankees	.50	.15
❑	113	Pedro Astacio	.50	.15
❑	114	Kazuhiro Sasaki	.50	.15
❑	115	Preston Wilson	.50	.15
❑	116	Jason Bere	.50	.15
❑	117	Mark Quinn	.50	.15
❑	118	Pokey Reese	.50	.15
❑	119	Derek Jeter	3.00	.90
❑	120	Shannon Stewart	.50	.15
❑	121	Jeff Kent	.50	.15
❑	122	Jeremy Giambi	.50	.15
❑	123	Pat Burrell	.50	.15
❑	124	Jim Edmonds	.75	.23
❑	125	Mark Buehrle	.50	.15
❑	126	Kevin Brown	.50	.15
❑	127	Raul Mondesi	.50	.15
❑	128	Pedro Martinez	.75	.23
❑	129	Jim Thome	.75	.23
❑	130	Russ Ortiz	.50	.15
❑	131	Br.Duckworth PROS	.50	.15
❑	132	Ryan Jamison PROS	.50	.15
❑	133	Brandon Inge PROS	.50	.15
❑	134	Felipe Lopez PROS	.50	.15
❑	135	Jason Lane PROS	.50	.15
❑	136	F.Johnson PROS RC	.50	.15
❑	137	Greg Nash PROS	.50	.15
❑	138	Covelli Crisp PROS	.75	.23
❑	139	Nick Neugebauer PROS	.50	.15
❑	140	Dustan Mohr PROS	.50	.15
❑	141	Freddy Sanchez FYP RC	.50	.15
❑	142	Justin Backsmeyer FYP RC	.50	.15
❑	143	Jorge Julio FYP	.50	.15
❑	144	Ryan Mottl FYP RC	.50	.15
❑	145	Chris Tritle FYP RC	.50	.15
❑	146	Noochie Varner FYP RC	.50	.15
❑	147	Brian Rogers FYP	.50	.15
❑	148	Michael Hill FYP RC	.50	.15
❑	149	Luis Pineda FYP	.50	.15
❑	150	Rich Thompson FYP RC	.50	.15
❑	151	Bill Hall FYP	.50	.15
❑	152	Juan Dominguez FYP RC	.50	.15
❑	153	Justin Woodrow FYP	.50	.15
❑	154	Nic Jackson FYP RC	.50	.15
❑	155	Laynce Nix FYP RC	2.00	.60
❑	156	Hank Aaron RET	5.00	1.50
❑	157	Ernie Banks RET	2.50	.75
❑	158	Johnny Bench RET	2.50	.75
❑	159	George Brett RET	5.00	1.50
❑	160	Carlton Fisk RET	1.50	.45
❑	161	Bob Gibson RET	1.50	.45
❑	162	Reggie Jackson RET	1.50	.45
❑	163	Don Mattingly RET	5.00	1.50
❑	164	Kirby Puckett RET	2.50	.75
❑	165	Frank Robinson RET	1.50	.45
❑	166	Nolan Ryan RET	6.00	1.80
❑	167	Tom Seaver RET	1.50	.45
❑	168	Mike Schmidt RET	5.00	1.50
❑	169	Dave Winfield RET	1.00	.30
❑	170	Carl Yastrzemski RET	3.00	.90
❑	171	Frank Chance REP	1.00	.30
❑	172	Ty Cobb REP	5.00	1.50
❑	173	Sam Crawford REP	1.00	.30
❑	174	Johnny Evers REP	1.00	.30
❑	175	John McGraw REP	1.50	.45
❑	176	Eddie Plank REP	2.50	.75
❑	177	Tris Speaker REP	2.50	.75
❑	178	Joe Tinker REP	1.00	.30
❑	179	H.Wagner Orange REP	8.00	2.40
❑	180	Cy Young REP	2.50	.75
❑	181	Javier Vazquez	.50	.15
❑	182A	Mark Mulder Green Jsy	.50	.15
❑	182B	Mark Mulder White Jsy	.50	.15
❑	183A	R.Clemens Blue Jsy	2.50	.75
❑	183B	R.Clemens Pinstripes	2.50	.75
❑	184	Kazuhisa Ishii RC	.75	.23
❑	185	Roberto Alomar	.75	.23
❑	186	Lance Berkman	.50	.15
❑	187A	A.Dunn Arms Folded	.50	.15
❑	187B	Adam Dunn w/Bat	.50	.15
❑	188A	Aramis Ramirez w/Bat	.50	.15
❑	188B	Aramis Ramirez w/o Bat	.50	.15
❑	189	Chuck Knoblauch	.50	.15
❑	190	Nomar Garciaparra	2.00	.60
❑	191	Brad Penny	.50	.15
❑	192A	Gary Sheffield w/Bat	.50	.15
❑	192B	Gary Sheffield w/o Bat	.50	.15
❑	193	Alfonso Soriano	.50	.15
❑	194	Andruw Jones	.75	.23
❑	195A	R.Johnson Black Jsy	1.25	.35
❑	195B	R.Johnson Purple Jsy	1.25	.35
❑	196A	C.Patterson Blue Jsy	.50	.15
❑	196B	C.Patterson Pinstripes	.50	.15
❑	197	Milton Bradley	.50	.15
❑	198A	J.Damon Blue Jsy/Cap	.75	.23
❑	198B	J.Damon Blue Jsy/Hlmt	.75	.23
❑	198C	J.Damon White Jsy	.75	.23
❑	199A	Paul Lo Duca Blue Jsy	.50	.15
❑	199B	Paul Lo Duca White Jsy	.50	.15
❑	200A	Albert Pujols Red Jsy	2.50	.75
❑	200B	Albert Pujols Running	2.50	.75
❑	200C	Albert Pujols w/Bat	2.50	.75
❑	201	Scott Rolen	.75	.23
❑	202A	J.D. Drew Running	.50	.15
❑	202B	J.D. Drew w/Bat	.50	.15
❑	202C	J.D. Drew White Jsy	.50	.15
❑	203	Vladimir Guerrero	1.25	.35
❑	204A	Jason Giambi Blue Jsy	.50	.15
❑	204B	Jason Giambi Grey Jsy	.50	.15
❑	204C	Jason Giambi Pinstripes	.50	.15
❑	205A	Moises Alou Grey Jsy	.50	.15
❑	205B	Moises Alou Pinstripes	.50	.15
❑	206A	Mag. Ordonez Signing	.50	.15
❑	206B	Magglio Ordonez w/Bat	.50	.15
❑	207	Carlos Febles	.50	.15
❑	208	So Taguchi RC	.75	.23
❑	209A	Raf. Palmeiro One Hand	.75	.23
❑	209B	Raf. Palmeiro Two Hands	.75	.23
❑	210	David Wells	.50	.15
❑	211	Orlando Cabrera	.50	.15
❑	212	Sammy Sosa	1.25	.35
❑	213	Armando Benitez	.50	.15
❑	214	Wes Helms	.50	.15
❑	215A	Mar. Rivera Arms Folded	.75	.23
❑	215B	Mar. Rivera Holding Ball	.75	.23
❑	216	Jimmy Rollins	.50	.15
❑	217	Matt Lawton	.50	.15
❑	218A	Shawn Green w/Bat	.50	.15
❑	218B	Shawn Green w/o Bat	.50	.15
❑	219A	Bernie Williams w/Bat	.75	.23
❑	219B	Bernie Williams w/o Bat	.75	.23
❑	220A	Bret Boone Blue Jsy	.50	.15
❑	220B	Bret Boone White Jsy	.50	.15
❑	221A	Alex Rodriguez Blue Jsy	2.00	.60
❑	221B	Alex Rodriguez One Hand	2.00	.60
❑	221C	Alex Rodriguez Two Hands	2.00	.60
❑	222	Roger Cedeno	.50	.15
❑	223	Marty Cordova	.50	.15
❑	224	Fred McGriff	.75	.23
❑	225A	Chipper Jones Batting	1.25	.35
❑	225B	Chipper Jones Running	1.25	.35
❑	226	Kerry Wood	.50	.15
❑	227A	Larry Walker Grey Jsy	.50	.15
❑	227B	Larry Walker Purple Jsy	.50	.15
❑	228	Robin Ventura	.50	.15
❑	229	Robert Fick	.50	.15
❑	230A	Tino Martinez Black Glove	.75	.23

❑ 230B Tino Martinez Throwing .75 .23
❑ 230C Tino Martinez w/Bat .75 .23
❑ 231 Ben Petrick .50 .15
❑ 232 Neifi Perez .50 .15
❑ 233 Pedro Martinez .75 .23
❑ 234A Brian Jordan Grey Jsy .50 .15
❑ 234B Brian Jordan White Jsy .50 .15
❑ 235 Freddy Garcia .50 .15
❑ 236A Derek Jeter Batting 3.00 .90
❑ 236B Derek Jeter Blue Jsy 3.00 .90
❑ 236C Derek Jeter Kneeling 3.00 .90
❑ 237 Ben Grieve .50 .15
❑ 238A Barry Bonds Black Jsy 3.00 .90
❑ 238B B.Bonds w/Wrist Band 3.00 .90
❑ 238C B.Bonds w/o Wrist Band 3.00 .90
❑ 239 Luis Gonzalez .50 .15
❑ 240 Shane Halter .50 .15
❑ 241A Brian Giles Black Jsy .50 .15
❑ 241B Brian Giles Grey Jsy .50 .15
❑ 242 Bud Smith .50 .15
❑ 243 Richie Sexson .50 .15
❑ 244A Barry Zito Green Jsy .50 .15
❑ 244B Barry Zito White Jsy .50 .15
❑ 245 Eric Milton .50 .15
❑ 246A Ivan Rodriguez Blue Jsy .75 .23
❑ 246B I.Rodriguez Grey Jsy .75 .23
❑ 246C I.Rodriguez White Jsy .75 .23
❑ 247 Toby Hall .50 .15
❑ 248A Mike Piazza Black Jsy 2.00 .60
❑ 248B Mike Piazza Grey Jsy 2.00 .60
❑ 249 Ruben Sierra .50 .15
❑ 250A Tsuyoshi Shinjo Cap .50 .15
❑ 250B Tsuyoshi Shinjo Helmet .50 .15
❑ 251A Jer. Dye Green Jsy .50 .15
❑ 251B Jermaine Dye White Jsy .50 .15
❑ 252 Roy Oswalt .50 .15
❑ 253 Todd Helton .75 .23
❑ 254 Adrian Beltre .50 .15
❑ 255 Doug Mientkiewicz .50 .15
❑ 256A Ichiro Suzuki Blue Jsy 2.50 .75
❑ 256B Ichiro Suzuki w/Bat 2.50 .75
❑ 256C Ichiro Suzuki White Jsy 2.50 .75
❑ 257A C.C. Sabathia Blue Jsy .50 .15
❑ 257B C.C. Sabathia White Jsy .50 .15
❑ 258 Paul Konerko .50 .15
❑ 259 Ken Griffey Jr. 2.00 .60
❑ 260A Jeromy Burnitz w/Bat .50 .15
❑ 260B Jeromy Burnitz w/o Bat .50 .15
❑ 261 Hank Blalock PROS .75 .23
❑ 262 Mark Prior PROS 1.25 .35
❑ 263 Josh Beckett PROS .50 .15
❑ 264 Carlos Pena PROS .50 .15
❑ 265 Sean Burroughs PROS .50 .15
❑ 266 Austin Kearns PROS .50 .15
❑ 267 Chin-Hui Tsao PROS .50 .15
❑ 268 Dewon Brazelton PROS .50 .15
❑ 269 J.D. Martin PROS .50 .15
❑ 270 Marlon Byrd PROS .50 .15
❑ 271 Joe Mauer FYP RC 4.00 1.20
❑ 272 Jason Botts FYP RC .75 .23
❑ 273 Mauricio Lara FYP RC .50 .15
❑ 274 Jonny Gomes FYP RC 3.00 .90
❑ 275 Gavin Floyd FYP RC 1.00 .30
❑ 276 Alex Requena FYP RC .50 .15
❑ 277 Jimmy Gobble FYP RC .50 .15
❑ 278 Chris Duffy FYP RC 1.00 .30
❑ 279 Colt Griffin FYP RC .50 .15
❑ 280 Ryan Church FYP RC 1.50 .45
❑ 281 Beltran Perez FYP RC .50 .15
❑ 282 Clint Nageotte FYP RC .75 .23
❑ 283 Justin Schuda FYP RC .50 .15
❑ 284 Scott Hairston FYP RC .75 .23
❑ 285 Mario Ramos FYP RC .50 .15
❑ 286 Tom Seaver White Sox RET 1.50 .45
❑ 286 Tom Seaver Mets RET 1.50 .45
❑ 287 H.Aaron White Jsy RET 5.00 1.50
❑ 287 H.Aaron Blue Jsy RET 5.00 1.50
❑ 288 Mike Schmidt RET 5.00 1.50
❑ 289A R.Yount Blue Jsy RET 2.50 .75
❑ 289B R.Yount P'stripes RET 2.50 .75
❑ 290 Joe Morgan RET 1.00 .30
❑ 291 Frank Robinson RET 1.50 .45
❑ 292A Reggie Jackson A's RET 1.50 .45
❑ 292B Reggie Jackson Yanks RET 1.50 .45
❑ 293A Nolan Ryan Astros RET 6.00 1.80
❑ 293B N.Ryan Rangers RET 6.00 1.80
❑ 294 Dave Winfield RET 1.00 .30
❑ 295 Willie Mays RET 5.00 1.50
❑ 296 Brooks Robinson RET 1.50 .45
❑ 297A Mark McGwire A's RET 6.00 1.80
❑ 297B M.McGwire Cards RET 6.00 1.80
❑ 298 Honus Wagner RET 2.50 .75
❑ 299A Sherry Magee REP 1.00 .30
❑ 299B Sherry Magie UER REP 1.00 .30
❑ 300 Frank Chance REP 1.00 .30
❑ 301A Joe Doyle NY REP 1.00 .30
❑ 301B Joe Doyle NY Nat'l REP 1.00 .30
❑ 302 John McGraw REP 1.50 .45
❑ 303 Jimmy Collins REP 1.00 .30
❑ 304 Buck Herzog REP 1.00 .30
❑ 305 Sam Crawford REP 1.00 .30
❑ 306 Cy Young REP 2.50 .75
❑ 307 Honus Wagner Blue REP 8.00 2.40
❑ 308A A.Rodriguez Blue Jsy SP 4.00 1.20
❑ 308B A.Rodriguez White Jsy 2.00 .60
❑ 309 Vernon Wells .50 .15
❑ 310A B.Bonds w/Elbow Pad 3.00 .90
❑ 310B B.Bonds w/o Elbow Pad SP 6.00 1.80
❑ 311 Vicente Padilla .50 .15
❑ 312A A.Soriano w/Wristband .50 .15
❑ 312B A.Soriano w/o Wristband SP 2.00 .60
❑ 313 Mike Piazza 2.00 .60
❑ 314 Jacque Jones .50 .15
❑ 315 Shawn Green SP 2.00 .60
❑ 316 Paul Byrd .50 .15
❑ 317 Lance Berkman .50 .15
❑ 318 Larry Walker .50 .15
❑ 319 Ken Griffey Jr. SP 4.00 1.20
❑ 320 Shea Hillenbrand .50 .15
❑ 321 Jay Gibbons .50 .15
❑ 322 Andruw Jones .75 .23
❑ 323 Luis Gonzalez SP 2.00 .60
❑ 324 Garret Anderson .50 .15
❑ 325 Roy Halladay .50 .15
❑ 326 Randy Winn .50 .15
❑ 327 Matt Morris .50 .15
❑ 328 Robb Nen .50 .15
❑ 329 Trevor Hoffman .50 .15
❑ 330 Kip Wells .50 .15
❑ 331 Orlando Hernandez .50 .15
❑ 332 Rey Ordonez .50 .15
❑ 333 Torii Hunter .50 .15
❑ 334 Geoff Jenkins .50 .15
❑ 335 Eric Karros .50 .15
❑ 336 Mike Lowell .50 .15
❑ 337 Nick Johnson .50 .15
❑ 338 Randall Simon .50 .15
❑ 339 Ellis Burks .50 .15
❑ 340A S.Sosa Blue Jsy SP 2.50 .75
❑ 340B Sammy Sosa White Jsy 1.25 .35
❑ 341 Pedro Martinez .75 .23
❑ 342 Junior Spivey .50 .15
❑ 343 Vinny Castilla .50 .15
❑ 344 Randy Johnson SP 2.50 .75
❑ 345 Chipper Jones SP 2.50 .75
❑ 346 Orlando Hudson .50 .15
❑ 347 Albert Pujols SP 5.00 1.50
❑ 348 Rondell White .50 .15
❑ 349 Vladimir Guerrero 1.25 .35
❑ 350A Mark Prior Red SP 2.50 .75
❑ 350B Mark Prior Yellow 1.25 .35
❑ 351 Eric Gagne .50 .15
❑ 352 Todd Zeile .50 .15
❑ 353 Manny Ramirez SP 2.00 .60
❑ 354 Kevin Millwood .50 .15
❑ 355 Troy Percival .50 .15
❑ 356A Jason Giambi Batting SP 2.00 .60
❑ 356B Jason Giambi Throwing .50 .15
❑ 357 Bartolo Colon .50 .15
❑ 358 Jeremy Giambi .50 .15
❑ 359 Jose Cruz Jr. .50 .15
❑ 360A I.Suzuki Blue Jsy SP 5.00 1.50
❑ 360B I.Suzuki White Jsy 2.50 .75
❑ 361 Eddie Guardado .50 .15
❑ 362 Ivan Rodriguez .75 .23
❑ 363 Carl Crawford .50 .15
❑ 364 Jason Simontacchi RC .50 .15
❑ 365 Kenny Lofton .50 .15
❑ 366 Raul Mondesi .50 .15
❑ 367 A.J. Pierzynski .50 .15
❑ 368 Ugueth Urbina .50 .15
❑ 369 Rodrigo Lopez .50 .15
❑ 370A N.Garciaparra One Bat SP 4.00 1.20
❑ 370B N.Garciaparra Two Bats 2.00 .60
❑ 371 Craig Counsell .50 .15
❑ 372 Barry Larkin .75 .23
❑ 373 Carlos Pena .50 .15
❑ 374 Luis Castillo .50 .15
❑ 375 Raul Ibanez .50 .15
❑ 376 Kazuhisa Ishii SP 2.00 .60
❑ 377 Derek Lowe .50 .15
❑ 378 Curt Schilling .50 .15
❑ 379 Jim Thome Phillies .75 .23
❑ 380A Derek Jeter Blue SP 6.00 1.80
❑ 380B Derek Jeter Seats 3.00 .90
❑ 381 Pat Burrell .50 .15
❑ 382 Jamie Moyer .50 .15
❑ 383 Eric Hinske .50 .15
❑ 384 Scott Rolen .75 .23
❑ 385 Miguel Tejada SP 2.00 .60
❑ 386 Andy Pettitte .75 .23
❑ 387 Mike Lieberthal .50 .15
❑ 388 Al Leiter .50 .15
❑ 389 Todd Helton SP 2.00 .60
❑ 390A Adam Dunn Bat SP 2.00 .60
❑ 390B Adam Dunn Glove .50 .15
❑ 391 Cliff Floyd .50 .15
❑ 392 Tim Salmon .75 .23
❑ 393 Joe Torre MG .75 .23
❑ 394 Bobby Cox MG .50 .15
❑ 395 Tony LaRussa MG .50 .15
❑ 396 Art Howe MG .50 .15
❑ 397 Bob Brenly MG .50 .15
❑ 398 Ron Gardenhire MG .50 .15
❑ 399 Mike Cuddyer PROS .50 .15
❑ 400 Joe Mauer PROS 4.00 1.20
❑ 401 Mark Teixeira PROS 1.25 .35
❑ 402 Hee Seop Choi PROS .50 .15
❑ 403 Angel Berroa PROS .50 .15
❑ 404 Jesse Foppert PROS RC .75 .23
❑ 405 Bobby Crosby PROS 1.25 .35
❑ 406 Jose Reyes PROS .75 .23
❑ 407 C.Kotchman PROS RC 2.50 .75
❑ 408 Aaron Heilman PROS .50 .15
❑ 409 Adrian Gonzalez PROS .50 .15
❑ 410 Delwyn Young PROS RC 1.00 .30
❑ 411 Brett Myers PROS .50 .15
❑ 412 Justin Huber PROS RC .75 .23
❑ 413 Drew Henson PROS .50 .15
❑ 414 T.Bozied PROS RC .75 .23
❑ 415 Dontrelle Willis PROS RC 8.00 2.40
❑ 416 Rocco Baldelli PROS .50 .15
❑ 417 Jason Stokes PROS RC 1.25 .35
❑ 418 Brandon Phillips PROS .50 .15
❑ 419 Jake Blalock FYP RC 1.00 .30
❑ 420 Micah Schilling FYP RC 1.00 .30
❑ 421 Denard Span FYP RC 1.00 .30
❑ 422A J.Loney Red FYP RC 1.50 .45
❑ 422B J.Loney w/Sky FYP RC 1.50 .45
❑ 423A W.Bankston Blue FYP RC 1.50 .45
❑ 423B W.Bankston w/Sky FYP RC 1.50 .45
❑ 424 Jeremy Hermida FYP RC 4.00 1.20
❑ 425 C.Granderson FYP RC 1.50 .45
❑ 426A J.Pridie Red FYP RC 1.00 .30
❑ 426B J.Pridie w/Sky FYP RC 1.00 .30
❑ 427 Larry Broadway FYP RC 1.00 .30
❑ 428A K.Greene Green FYP RC 10.00 3.00
❑ 428B K.Greene Red FYP RC 10.00 3.00
❑ 429 Joey Votto FYP RC 1.00 .30
❑ 430A B.Upton Grey FYP RC 5.00 1.50
❑ 430B B.Upton w/People FYP RC 5.00 1.50
❑ 431A S.Santos Gold FYP RC 1.00 .30
❑ 431B S.Santos Grey FYP RC 1.00 .30
❑ 432 Brian Dopirak FYP RC 1.50 .45
❑ 433 Ozzie Smith RET SP 4.00 1.20
❑ 434 Wade Boggs RET SP 2.50 .75
❑ 435 Yogi Berra RET SP 4.00 1.20
❑ 436 Al Kaline RET SP 4.00 1.20
❑ 437 Robin Roberts RET SP 2.00 .60
❑ 438 Rob. Clemente RET SP 8.00 2.40
❑ 439 Gary Carter RET SP 2.00 .60
❑ 440 Fergie Jenkins RET SP 2.00 .60
❑ 441 Orlando Cepeda RET SP 2.00 .60
❑ 442 Rod Carew RET SP 2.50 .75
❑ 443 Ha. Killebrew RET SP 4.00 1.20
❑ 444 Duke Snider RET SP 2.50 .75
❑ 445 Stan Musial RET SP 6.00 1.80
❑ 446 Hank Greenberg RET SP 4.00 1.20

	Card	Nm-Mt	Ex-Mt
❑ 447	Lou Brock RET SP	2.50	.75
❑ 448	Jim Palmer RET	1.00	.30
❑ 449	John McGraw REP	1.50	.45
❑ 450	Mordecai Brown REP	1.00	.30
❑ 451	Christy Mathewson REP	1.50	.45
❑ 452	Sam Crawford REP	1.00	.30
❑ 453	Bill O'Hara REP	1.00	.30
❑ 454	Joe Tinker REP	1.00	.30
❑ 455	Nap Lajoie REP	1.50	.45
❑ 456	Honus Wagner Red REP	8.00	2.40
❑ NNO	Repurchased Tobacco Card		

2004 Topps All-Time Fan Favorites

		Nm-Mt	Ex-Mt
COMPLETE SET (150)		50.00	15.00
❑ 1	Willie Mays	3.00	.90
❑ 2	Bob Gibson	1.00	.30
❑ 3	Dave Stieb	.60	.18
❑ 4	Tim McCarver	.60	.18
❑ 5	Reggie Jackson	1.00	.30
❑ 6	John Candelaria	.60	.18
❑ 7	Lenny Dykstra	.60	.18
❑ 8	Tony Oliva	.60	.18
❑ 9	Frank Viola	.60	.18
❑ 10	Don Mattingly	3.00	.90
❑ 11	Garry Maddox	.60	.18
❑ 12	Randy Jones	.40	.12
❑ 13	Joe Carter	.60	.18
❑ 14	Orlando Cepeda	.60	.18
❑ 15	Bob Sheppard ANC	1.00	.30
❑ 16	Bobby Grich	.60	.18
❑ 17	George Scott	.40	.12
❑ 18	Mickey Rivers	.40	.12
❑ 19	Ron Santo	1.00	.30
❑ 20	Mike Schmidt	3.00	.90
❑ 21	Luis Aparicio	.60	.18
❑ 22	Cesar Geronimo	.40	.12
❑ 23	Jack Morris	.60	.18
❑ 24	Jeffrey Loria OWNER	.40	.12
❑ 25	George Brett	3.00	.90
❑ 26	Paul O'Neill	1.00	.30
❑ 27	Reggie Smith	.60	.18
❑ 28	Robin Yount	1.50	.45
❑ 29	Andre Dawson	.60	.18
❑ 30	Whitey Ford	1.00	.30
❑ 31	Ralph Kiner	.60	.18
❑ 32	Will Clark	1.00	.30
❑ 33	Keith Hernandez	.60	.18
❑ 34	Tony Fernandez	.40	.12
❑ 35	Willie McGee	.60	.18
❑ 36	Harmon Killebrew	1.50	.45
❑ 37	Dave Kingman	.60	.18
❑ 38	Kirk Gibson	1.00	.30
❑ 39	Terry Steinbach	.40	.12
❑ 40	Frank Robinson	.60	.18
❑ 41	Chet Lemon	.60	.18
❑ 42	Mike Cuellar	.60	.18
❑ 43	Darrell Evans	.60	.18
❑ 44	Don Kessinger	.40	.12
❑ 45	Dave Concepcion	.60	.18
❑ 46	Sparky Anderson	.60	.18
❑ 47	Bret Saberhagen	.60	.18
❑ 48	Brett Butler	.60	.18
❑ 49	Kent Hrbek	.60	.18
❑ 50	Hank Aaron	3.00	.90
❑ 51	Rudolph Giuliani	1.50	.45
❑ 52	Clete Boyer	.60	.18
❑ 53	Mookie Wilson	.60	.18
❑ 54	Dave Stewart	.60	.18
❑ 55	Gary Matthews Sr.	.60	.18
❑ 56	Roy Face	.60	.18
❑ 57	Vida Blue	.60	.18
❑ 58	Jimmy Key	1.00	.30
❑ 59	Al Hrabosky	.60	.18
❑ 60	Al Kaline	1.50	.45
❑ 61	Mike Scott	.60	.18
❑ 62	Jack McDowell	.60	.18
❑ 63	Reggie Jackson	1.00	.30
❑ 64	Earl Weaver	.60	.18
❑ 65	Ernie Harwell ANC	1.00	.30
❑ 66	David Justice	.60	.18
❑ 67	Wilbur Wood	.60	.18
❑ 68	Mike Boddicker	.60	.18
❑ 69	Don Zimmer	.60	.18
❑ 70	Jim Palmer	.60	.18
❑ 71	Doug DeCinces	.60	.18
❑ 72	Ryne Sandberg	3.00	.90
❑ 73	Don Newcombe	.60	.18
❑ 74	Denny Martinez	.60	.18
❑ 75	Carl Yastrzemski	2.50	.75
❑ 76	Bake McBride	.60	.18
❑ 77	Andy Van Slyke	1.00	.30
❑ 78	Bruce Sutter	.60	.18
❑ 79	Bobby Valentine	.60	.18
❑ 80	Johnny Bench	1.50	.45
❑ 81	Orel Hershiser	.60	.18
❑ 82	Cecil Fielder	.60	.18
❑ 83	Lou Whitaker	.60	.18
❑ 84	Alan Trammell	.60	.18
❑ 85	Sam McDowell	.60	.18
❑ 86	Ray Knight	.60	.18
❑ 87	Gregg Jefferies	.40	.12
❑ 88	Ben Oglivie	.40	.12
❑ 89	Billy Beane	.40	.12
❑ 90	Yogi Berra	1.50	.45
❑ 91	Jose Canseco	1.00	.30
❑ 92	Bobby Bonilla	.60	.18
❑ 93	Darren Daulton	.60	.18
❑ 94	Harold Reynolds	.60	.18
❑ 95	Lou Brock	1.00	.30
❑ 96	Pete Incaviglia	.40	.12
❑ 97	Eric Gregg UMP	.40	.12
❑ 98	Devon White	.40	.12
❑ 99	Kelly Gruber	.40	.12
❑ 100	Nolan Ryan	4.00	1.20
❑ 101	Carlton Fisk	1.00	.30
❑ 102	George Foster	.60	.18
❑ 103	Dennis Eckersley	1.00	.30
❑ 104	Rick Sutcliffe	.60	.18
❑ 105	Cal Ripken	5.00	1.50
❑ 106	Norm Cash	.60	.18
❑ 107	Charlie Hough	.40	.12
❑ 108	Paul Molitor	1.00	.30
❑ 109	Maury Wills	.60	.18
❑ 110	Tom Seaver	1.00	.30
❑ 111	Brooks Robinson	1.00	.30
❑ 112	Jim Rice	.60	.18
❑ 113	Dwight Gooden	.60	.18
❑ 114	Harold Baines	.60	.18
❑ 115	Tim Raines	.60	.18
❑ 116	Roy Smalley	.40	.12
❑ 117	Richie Allen	.60	.18
❑ 118	Ron Swoboda	.60	.18
❑ 119	Ron Guidry	1.00	.30
❑ 120	Duke Snider	1.00	.30
❑ 121	Ferguson Jenkins	.60	.18
❑ 122	Mark Fidrych UER Posing as a lefty	.60	.18
❑ 123	Buddy Bell	.60	.18
❑ 124	Bo Jackson	1.50	.45
❑ 125	Stan Musial	2.50	.75
❑ 126	Jesse Barfield	.40	.12
❑ 127	Tony Gwynn	2.00	.60
❑ 128	Phil Garner	.60	.18
❑ 129	Dale Murphy	1.00	.30
❑ 130	Wade Boggs	1.00	.30
❑ 131	Sid Fernandez	.60	.18
❑ 132	Monte Irvin	.60	.18
❑ 133	Peter Ueberroth COM	.40	.12
❑ 134	Gary Gaetti	.60	.18
❑ 135	Gorman Thomas	.60	.18
❑ 136	Dave Lopes	.60	.18
❑ 137	Sy Berger	.60	.18
❑ 138	Buck O'Neil UER Wrong birth year on back	.60	.18
❑ 139	Herb Score	.60	.18
❑ 140	Rod Carew	1.00	.30
❑ 141	Joe Buck ANC	1.00	.30
❑ 142	Willie Horton	.60	.18
❑ 143	Hal McRae	.60	.18
❑ 144	Rollie Fingers	.60	.18
❑ 145	Tom Brunansky	.40	.12
❑ 146	Fay Vincent COM	.40	.12
❑ 147	Gary Carter	.60	.18
❑ 148	Bobby Richardson	.60	.18
❑ 149	Steve Garvey	.60	.18
❑ 150	Don Larsen	.60	.18

2005 Topps All-Time Fan Favorites

		Nm-Mt	Ex-Mt
COMPLETE SET (142)		50.00	15.00
COMMON CARD (1-142)		.50	.15
OVERALL PLATE ODDS 1:1414 HOB/RET			.00
PLATE PRINT RUN 1 SET PER COLOR			
BLACK-CYAN-MAGENTA-YELLOW ISSUED			
NO PLATE PRICING DUE TO SCARCITY			
❑ 1	Andy Van Slyke	.75	.23
❑ 2	Bill Freehan	.75	.23
❑ 3	Bo Jackson	2.00	.60
❑ 4	Mark Grace	1.25	.35
❑ 5	Chuck Knoblauch	.75	.23
❑ 6	Candy Maldonado	.50	.15
❑ 7	David Cone	.75	.23
❑ 8	Don Mattingly	4.00	1.20
❑ 9	Darryl Strawberry	.75	.23
❑ 10	Dick Williams	.50	.15
❑ 11	Frank Robinson	1.25	.35
❑ 12	Glenn Hubbard	.50	.15
❑ 13	Jim Abbott	.75	.23
❑ 14	Jeff Brantley	.50	.15
❑ 15	John Elway UER Back has him drafted by wrong Football team	5.00	1.50
❑ 16	Jim Leyland	.50	.15
❑ 17	Jesse Orosco	.50	.15
❑ 18	Joe Pepitone	.75	.23
❑ 19	J.R. Richard	.75	.23
❑ 20	Jerome Walton	.50	.15
❑ 21	Kevin Maas	.50	.15
❑ 22	Lou Brock	1.25	.35
❑ 23	Lou Whitaker	.75	.23
❑ 24	Carl Erskine	.75	.23
❑ 25	John Candelaria	.75	.23
❑ 26	Mike Norris	.50	.15
❑ 27	Nolan Ryan	5.00	1.50
❑ 28	Pedro Guerrero	.75	.23
❑ 29	Roger Craig	.75	.23
❑ 30	Ron Gant	.75	.23
❑ 31	Sid Bream	.50	.15
❑ 32	Sid Fernandez	.50	.15
❑ 33	Tony LaRussa	.75	.23
❑ 34	Tom Seaver	1.25	.35
❑ 35	Yogi Berra	2.00	.60
❑ 36	Andre Dawson	.75	.23
❑ 37	Al Kaline	2.00	.60
❑ 38	Brett Butler	.75	.23
❑ 39	Bob Gibson	1.25	.35

❑ 40 Bill Mazeroski 1.25 .35
❑ 41 Matty Alou .50 .15
❑ 42 Chet Lemon .75 .23
❑ 43 Cal Ripken 6.00 1.80
❑ 44 Dusty Baker .75 .23
❑ 45 Dwight Gooden .75 .23
❑ 46 Dave Winfield .75 .23
❑ 47 Ernie Banks 2.00 .60
❑ 48 Gary Carter .75 .23
❑ 49 Howard Johnson .75 .23
❑ 50 Mike Schmidt 4.00 1.20
❑ 51 Matt Williams .75 .23
❑ 52 Ozzie Smith 3.00 .90
❑ 53 Atlee Hammaker .50 .15
❑ 54 Cleon Jones .50 .15
❑ 55 Dave Johnson .50 .15
❑ 56 Denny McLain .75 .23
❑ 57 Don Zimmer .75 .23
❑ 58 Gregg Jefferies .50 .15
❑ 59 Jay Buhner .75 .23
❑ 60 Johnny Bench 2.00 .60
❑ 61 George Brett 4.00 1.20
❑ 62 Dale Murphy 1.25 .35
❑ 63 Bob Welch .75 .23
❑ 64 Paul O'Neill 1.25 .35
❑ 65 Mark Lemke .50 .15
❑ 66 Kevin McReynolds .75 .23
❑ 67 Jesus Alou .50 .15
❑ 68 Joe Pignatano .50 .15
❑ 69 Jim Lonborg .75 .23
❑ 70 Jerry Grote .50 .15
❑ 71 Joaquin Andujar .75 .23
❑ 72 Gary Gaetti .75 .23
❑ 73 Edgar Martinez 1.25 .35
❑ 74 Ron Darling .75 .23
❑ 75 Duke Snider 1.25 .35
❑ 76 Dave Magadan .50 .15
❑ 77 Doug Drabek .75 .23
❑ 78 Carl Yastrzemski 3.00 .90
❑ 79 Mitch Williams .75 .23
❑ 80 Marvin Miller PA .50 .15
❑ 81 Michael Kay ANC .50 .15
❑ 82 Lonnie Smith .50 .15
❑ 83 John Wetteland .75 .23
❑ 84 Johnny Podres .75 .23
❑ 85 Joe Morgan .75 .23
❑ 86 Juan Marichal .75 .23
❑ 87 Jeffrey Leonard .50 .15
❑ 88 Bob Feller 1.25 .35
❑ 89 Brooks Robinson 1.25 .35
❑ 90 Clem Labine .50 .15
❑ 91 Barry Lyons .50 .15
❑ 92 Harmon Killebrew 2.00 .60
❑ 93 Jim Frey .50 .15
❑ 94 John Kruk 1.25 .35
❑ 95 Ed Kranepool .50 .15
❑ 96 Jose Oquendo .50 .15
❑ 97 Johnny Pesky .75 .23
❑ 98 John Tudor .50 .15
❑ 99 Keith Hernandez .75 .23
❑ 100 Monte Irvin .75 .23
❑ 101 Marty Barrett .50 .15
❑ 102 Oscar Gamble .50 .15
❑ 103 Hank Bauer .75 .23
❑ 104 Ron Blomberg .50 .15
❑ 105 Rod Carew 1.25 .35
❑ 106 Rick Dempsey .50 .15
❑ 107 Walt Jocketty GM .50 .15
❑ 108 Tom Kelly .50 .15
❑ 109 Steve Carlton .75 .23
❑ 110 Rick Monday .75 .23
❑ 111 Rob Dibble .75 .23
❑ 112 Shawon Dunston .50 .15
❑ 113 Tony Gwynn 2.50 .75
❑ 114 Tom Niedenfuer .50 .15
❑ 115 Bob Dernier .50 .15
❑ 116 Anthony Young .50 .15
❑ 117 Reggie Jackson 1.25 .35
❑ 118 Steve Garvey .75 .23
❑ 119 Tim Raines .75 .23
❑ 120 Whitey Ford 1.25 .35
❑ 121 Rafael Santana .50 .15
❑ 122 Scott Brosius .75 .23
❑ 123 Stan Musial 3.00 .90
❑ 124 Ron Santo 1.25 .35
❑ 125 Wade Boggs 1.25 .35
❑ 126 Jose Canseco 2.00 .60
❑ 127 Brady Anderson .75 .23
❑ 128 Vida Blue .75 .23
❑ 129 Charlie Hough .50 .15
❑ 130 Jim Kaat .75 .23
❑ 131 Zane Smith .50 .15
❑ 132 Bob Boone .75 .23
❑ 133 Travis Fryman .75 .23
❑ 134 Harold Baines .75 .23
❑ 135 Orlando Cepeda .75 .23
❑ 136 Mike Cuellar .75 .23
❑ 137 Tito Fuentes .50 .15
❑ 138 Daryl Boston .50 .15
❑ 139 Jim Leyritz .50 .15
❑ 140 Moose Skowron .75 .23
❑ 141 Theo Epstein GM .50 .15
❑ 142 Barry Bonds 5.00 1.50

1998 Topps Chrome

	Nm-Mt	Ex-Mt
COMPLETE SET (503)	150.00	45.00
COMP. SERIES 1 (282)	80.00	24.00
COMP. SERIES 2 (221)	80.00	24.00

❑ 1 Tony Gwynn 2.50 .75
❑ 2 Larry Walker .75 .23
❑ 3 Billy Wagner .75 .23
❑ 4 Denny Neagle .75 .23
❑ 5 Vladimir Guerrero 2.00 .60
❑ 6 Kevin Brown 1.25 .35
❑ 8 Mariano Rivera 1.25 .35
❑ 9 Tony Clark .75 .23
❑ 10 Deion Sanders 1.25 .35
❑ 11 Francisco Cordova .75 .23
❑ 12 Matt Williams .75 .23
❑ 13 Carlos Baerga .75 .23
❑ 14 Mo Vaughn .75 .23
❑ 15 Bobby Witt .75 .23
❑ 16 Matt Stairs .75 .23
❑ 17 Chan Ho Park .75 .23
❑ 18 Mike Bordick .75 .23
❑ 19 Michael Tucker .75 .23
❑ 20 Frank Thomas 2.00 .60
❑ 21 Roberto Clemente 5.00 1.50
❑ 22 Dmitri Young .75 .23
❑ 23 Steve Trachsel .75 .23
❑ 24 Jeff Kent .75 .23
❑ 25 Scott Rolen 1.25 .35
❑ 26 John Thomson .75 .23
❑ 27 Joe Vitiello .75 .23
❑ 28 Eddie Guardado .75 .23
❑ 29 Charlie Hayes .75 .23
❑ 30 Juan Gonzalez .75 .23
❑ 31 Garret Anderson .75 .23
❑ 32 John Jaha .75 .23
❑ 33 Omar Vizquel 1.25 .35
❑ 34 Brian Hunter .75 .23
❑ 35 Jeff Bagwell 1.25 .35
❑ 36 Mark Lemke .75 .23
❑ 37 Doug Glanville .75 .23
❑ 38 Dan Wilson .75 .23
❑ 39 Steve Cooke .75 .23
❑ 40 Chili Davis .75 .23
❑ 41 Mike Cameron .75 .23
❑ 42 F.P. Santangelo .75 .23
❑ 43 Brad Ausmus .75 .23
❑ 44 Gary DiSarcina .75 .23
❑ 45 Pat Hentgen .75 .23
❑ 46 Wilton Guerrero .75 .23
❑ 47 Devon White .75 .23
❑ 48 Danny Patterson .75 .23
❑ 49 Pat Meares .75 .23
❑ 50 Rafael Palmeiro 1.25 .35
❑ 51 Mark Gardner .75 .23
❑ 52 Jeff Blauser .75 .23
❑ 53 Dave Hollins .75 .23
❑ 54 Carlos Garcia .75 .23
❑ 55 Ben McDonald .75 .23
❑ 56 John Mabry .75 .23
❑ 57 Trevor Hoffman .75 .23
❑ 58 Tony Fernandez .75 .23
❑ 59 Rich Loiselle RC .75 .23
❑ 60 Mark Leiter .75 .23
❑ 61 Pat Kelly .75 .23
❑ 62 John Flaherty .75 .23
❑ 63 Roger Bailey .75 .23
❑ 64 Tom Gordon .75 .23
❑ 65 Ryan Klesko .75 .23
❑ 66 Darryl Hamilton .75 .23
❑ 67 Jim Eisenreich .75 .23
❑ 68 Butch Huskey .75 .23
❑ 69 Mark Grudzielanek .75 .23
❑ 70 Marquis Grissom .75 .23
❑ 71 Mark McLemore .75 .23
❑ 72 Gary Gaetti .75 .23
❑ 73 Greg Gagne .75 .23
❑ 74 Lyle Mouton .75 .23
❑ 75 Jim Edmonds .75 .23
❑ 76 Shawn Green .75 .23
❑ 77 Greg Vaughn .75 .23
❑ 78 Terry Adams .75 .23
❑ 79 Kevin Polcovich .75 .23
❑ 80 Troy O'Leary .75 .23
❑ 81 Jeff Shaw .75 .23
❑ 82 Rich Becker .75 .23
❑ 83 David Wells .75 .23
❑ 84 Steve Karsay .75 .23
❑ 85 Charles Nagy .75 .23
❑ 86 B.J. Surhoff .75 .23
❑ 87 Jamey Wright .75 .23
❑ 88 James Baldwin .75 .23
❑ 89 Edgardo Alfonzo .75 .23
❑ 90 Jay Buhner .75 .23
❑ 91 Brady Anderson .75 .23
❑ 92 Scott Servais .75 .23
❑ 93 Edgar Renteria .75 .23
❑ 94 Mike Lieberthal .75 .23
❑ 95 Rick Aguilera .75 .23
❑ 96 Walt Weiss .75 .23
❑ 97 Deivi Cruz .75 .23
❑ 98 Kurt Abbott .75 .23
❑ 99 Henry Rodriguez .75 .23
❑ 100 Mike Piazza 3.00 .90
❑ 101 Billy Taylor .75 .23
❑ 102 Todd Zeile .75 .23
❑ 103 Rey Ordonez .75 .23
❑ 104 Willie Greene .75 .23
❑ 105 Tony Womack .75 .23
❑ 106 Mike Sweeney .75 .23
❑ 107 Jeffrey Hammonds .75 .23
❑ 108 Kevin Orie .75 .23
❑ 109 Alex Gonzalez .75 .23
❑ 110 Jose Canseco 1.25 .35
❑ 111 Paul Sorrento .75 .23
❑ 112 Joey Hamilton .75 .23
❑ 113 Brad Radke .75 .23
❑ 114 Steve Avery .75 .23
❑ 115 Esteban Loaiza .75 .23
❑ 116 Stan Javier .75 .23
❑ 117 Chris Gomez .75 .23
❑ 118 Royce Clayton .75 .23
❑ 119 Orlando Merced .75 .23
❑ 120 Kevin Appier .75 .23
❑ 121 Mel Nieves .75 .23
❑ 122 Joe Girardi .75 .23
❑ 123 Rico Brogna .75 .23
❑ 124 Kent Mercker .75 .23
❑ 125 Manny Ramirez 1.25 .35
❑ 126 Jeromy Burnitz .75 .23
❑ 127 Kevin Foster .75 .23
❑ 128 Matt Morris .75 .23
❑ 129 Jason Dickson .75 .23
❑ 130 Tom Glavine 1.25 .35
❑ 131 Wally Joyner .75 .23

❑	132 Rick Reed	.75	.23
❑	133 Todd Jones	.75	.23
❑	134 Dave Martinez	.75	.23
❑	135 Sandy Alomar Jr.	.75	.23
❑	136 Mike Lansing	.75	.23
❑	137 Sean Berry	.75	.23
❑	138 Doug Jones	.75	.23
❑	139 Todd Stottlemyre	.75	.23
❑	140 Jay Bell	.75	.23
❑	141 Jaime Navarro	.75	.23
❑	142 Chris Hoiles	.75	.23
❑	143 Joey Cora	.75	.23
❑	144 Scott Spiezio	.75	.23
❑	145 Joe Carter	.75	.23
❑	146 Jose Guillen	.75	.23
❑	147 Damion Easley	.75	.23
❑	148 Lee Stevens	.75	.23
❑	149 Alex Fernandez	.75	.23
❑	150 Randy Johnson	2.00	.60
❑	151 J.T. Snow	.75	.23
❑	152 Chuck Finley	.75	.23
❑	153 Bernard Gilkey	.75	.23
❑	154 David Segui	.75	.23
❑	155 Dante Bichette	.75	.23
❑	156 Kevin Stocker	.75	.23
❑	157 Carl Everett	.75	.23
❑	158 Jose Valentin	.75	.23
❑	159 Pokey Reese	.75	.23
❑	160 Derek Jeter	5.00	1.50
❑	161 Roger Pavlik	.75	.23
❑	162 Mark Wohlers	.75	.23
❑	163 Ricky Bottalico	.75	.23
❑	164 Ozzie Guillen	.75	.23
❑	165 Mike Mussina	1.25	.35
❑	166 Gary Sheffield	.75	.23
❑	167 Hideo Nomo	2.00	.60
❑	168 Mark Grace	1.25	.35
❑	169 Aaron Sele	.75	.23
❑	170 Darryl Kile	.75	.23
❑	171 Shawn Estes	.75	.23
❑	172 Vinny Castilla	.75	.23
❑	173 Ron Coomer	.75	.23
❑	174 Jose Rosado	.75	.23
❑	175 Kenny Lofton	.75	.23
❑	176 Jason Giambi	.75	.23
❑	177 Hal Morris	.75	.23
❑	178 Darren Bragg	.75	.23
❑	179 Orel Hershiser	.75	.23
❑	180 Ray Lankford	.75	.23
❑	181 Hideki Irabu	.75	.23
❑	182 Kevin Young	.75	.23
❑	183 Javy Lopez	.75	.23
❑	184 Jeff Montgomery	.75	.23
❑	185 Mike Holtz	.75	.23
❑	186 George Williams	.75	.23
❑	187 Cal Eldred	.75	.23
❑	188 Tom Candiotti	.75	.23
❑	189 Glenallen Hill	.75	.23
❑	190 Brian Giles	.75	.23
❑	191 Dave Mlicki	.75	.23
❑	192 Garrett Stephenson	.75	.23
❑	193 Jeff Frye	.75	.23
❑	194 Joe Oliver	.75	.23
❑	195 Bob Hamelin	.75	.23
❑	196 Luis Sojo	.75	.23
❑	197 LaTroy Hawkins	.75	.23
❑	198 Kevin Elster	.75	.23
❑	199 Jeff Reed	.75	.23
❑	200 Dennis Eckersley	.75	.23
❑	201 Bill Mueller	.75	.23
❑	202 Russ Davis	.75	.23
❑	203 Armando Benitez	.75	.23
❑	204 Quilvio Veras	.75	.23
❑	205 Tim Naehring	.75	.23
❑	206 Quinton McCracken	.75	.23
❑	207 Raul Casanova	.75	.23
❑	208 Matt Lawton	.75	.23
❑	209 Luis Alicea	.75	.23
❑	210 Luis Gonzalez	.75	.23
❑	211 Allen Watson	.75	.23
❑	212 Gerald Williams	.75	.23
❑	213 David Bell	.75	.23
❑	214 Todd Hollandsworth	.75	.23
❑	215 Wade Boggs	1.25	.35
❑	216 Jose Mesa	.75	.23
❑	217 Jamie Moyer	.75	.23
❑	218 Darren Daulton	.75	.23
❑	219 Mickey Morandini	.75	.23
❑	220 Rusty Greer	.75	.23
❑	221 Jim Bullinger	.75	.23
❑	222 Jose Offerman	.75	.23
❑	223 Matt Karchner	.75	.23
❑	224 Woody Williams	.75	.23
❑	225 Mark Loretta	.75	.23
❑	226 Mike Hampton	.75	.23
❑	227 Willie Adams	.75	.23
❑	228 Scott Hatteberg	.75	.23
❑	229 Rich Amaral	.75	.23
❑	230 Terry Steinbach	.75	.23
❑	231 Glendon Rusch	.75	.23
❑	232 Bret Boone	.75	.23
❑	233 Robert Person	.75	.23
❑	234 Jose Hernandez	.75	.23
❑	235 Doug Drabek	.75	.23
❑	236 Jason McDonald	.75	.23
❑	237 Chris Widger	.75	.23
❑	238 Tom Martin	.75	.23
❑	239 Dave Burba	.75	.23
❑	240 Pete Rose Jr. RC	.75	.23
❑	241 Bobby Ayala	.75	.23
❑	242 Tim Wakefield	.75	.23
❑	243 Dennis Springer	.75	.23
❑	244 Tim Belcher	.75	.23
❑	245 Jon Garland Geoff Goetz	1.00	.30
❑	246 Glenn Davis Lance Berkman	1.00	.30
❑	247 Vernon Wells Aaron Akin	1.00	.30
❑	248 Adam Kennedy Jason Romano	1.00	.30
❑	249 Jason Dellaero Troy Cameron	1.00	.30
❑	250 Alex Sanchez Jared Sandberg	1.00	.30
❑	251 Pablo Ortega James Manias	1.00	.30
❑	252 Jason Conti RC Mike Stoner	1.00	.30
❑	253 John Patterson Larry Rodriguez	1.00	.30
❑	254 Adrian Beltre Ryan Minor RC Aaron Boone	1.00	.30
❑	255 Ben Grieve Brian Buchanan Dermal Brown	1.00	.30
❑	256 Kerrry Wood Carl Pavano Gil Meche	1.25	.35
❑	257 David Ortiz Daryle Ward Richie Sexson	4.00	1.20
❑	258 Randy Winn Juan Encarnacion Andrew Vessel	1.00	.30
❑	259 Kris Benson Travis Smith Courtney Duncan RC	1.00	.30
❑	260 Chad Hermansen RC Brent Butler Warren Morris	1.00	.30
❑	261 Ben Davis Eli Marrero Ramon Hernandez	1.00	.30
❑	262 Eric Chavez Russell Branyan Russ Johnson	1.00	.30
❑	263 Todd Dunwoody RC John Barnes Ryan Jackson	1.00	.30
❑	264 Matt Clement Roy Halladay Brian Fuentes RC	1.00	.30
❑	265 Randy Johnson SH	1.25	.35
❑	266 Kevin Brown SH	.75	.23
❑	267 Ricardo Rincon SH	.75	.23
❑	268 N.Garciaparra SH	2.00	.60
❑	269 Tino Martinez SH	.75	.23
❑	270 Chuck Knoblauch IL	.75	.23
❑	271 Pedro Martinez IL	1.25	.35
❑	272 Denny Neagle IL	.75	.23
❑	273 Juan Gonzalez IL	.75	.23
❑	274 Andres Galarraga IL	.75	.23
❑	275 Checklist	.75	.23
❑	276 Checklist	.75	.23
❑	277 Moises Alou WS	.75	.23
❑	278 Sandy Alomar Jr. WS	.75	.23
❑	279 Gary Sheffield WS	.75	.23
❑	280 Matt Williams WS	.75	.23
❑	281 Livan Hernandez WS	.75	.23
❑	282 Chad Ogea WS	.75	.23
❑	283 Marlins Champs	.75	.23
❑	284 Tino Martinez	1.25	.35
❑	285 Roberto Alomar	1.25	.35
❑	286 Jeff King	.75	.23
❑	287 Brian Jordan	.75	.23
❑	288 Darin Erstad	.75	.23
❑	289 Ken Caminiti	.75	.23
❑	290 Jim Thome	1.25	.35
❑	291 Paul Molitor	1.25	.35
❑	292 Ivan Rodriguez	1.25	.35
❑	293 Bernie Williams	1.25	.35
❑	294 Todd Hundley	.75	.23
❑	295 Andres Galarraga	.75	.23
❑	296 Greg Maddux	3.00	.90
❑	297 Edgar Martinez	1.25	.35
❑	298 Ron Gant	.75	.23
❑	299 Derek Bell	.75	.23
❑	300 Roger Clemens	4.00	1.20
❑	301 Rondell White	.75	.23
❑	302 Barry Larkin	1.25	.35
❑	303 Robin Ventura	.75	.23
❑	304 Jason Kendall	.75	.23
❑	305 Chipper Jones	2.00	.60
❑	306 John Franco	.75	.23
❑	307 Sammy Sosa	2.00	.60
❑	308 Troy Percival	.75	.23
❑	309 Chuck Knoblauch	.75	.23
❑	310 Ellis Burks	.75	.23
❑	311 Al Martin	.75	.23
❑	312 Tim Salmon	1.25	.35
❑	313 Moises Alou	.75	.23
❑	314 Lance Johnson	.75	.23
❑	315 Justin Thompson	.75	.23
❑	316 Will Clark	1.25	.35
❑	317 Barry Bonds	5.00	1.50
❑	318 Craig Biggio	1.25	.35
❑	319 John Smoltz	1.25	.35
❑	320 Cal Ripken	6.00	1.80
❑	321 Ken Griffey Jr.	3.00	.90
❑	322 Paul O'Neill	1.25	.35
❑	323 Todd Helton	1.25	.35
❑	324 John Olerud	.75	.23
❑	325 Mark McGwire	5.00	1.50
❑	326 Jose Cruz Jr.	.75	.23
❑	327 Jeff Cirillo	.75	.23
❑	328 Dean Palmer	.75	.23
❑	329 John Wetteland	.75	.23
❑	330 Steve Finley	.75	.23
❑	331 Albert Belle	.75	.23
❑	332 Curt Schilling	.75	.23
❑	333 Raul Mondesi	.75	.23
❑	334 Andruw Jones	1.25	.35
❑	335 Nomar Garciaparra	3.00	.90
❑	336 David Justice	.75	.23
❑	337 Andy Pettitte	1.25	.35
❑	338 Pedro Martinez	1.25	.35
❑	339 Travis Miller	.75	.23
❑	340 Chris Stynes	.75	.23
❑	341 Gregg Jefferies	.75	.23
❑	342 Jeff Fassero	.75	.23
❑	343 Craig Counsell	.75	.23
❑	344 Wilson Alvarez	.75	.23
❑	345 Bip Roberts	.75	.23
❑	346 Kelvim Escobar	.75	.23
❑	347 Mark Bellhorn	.75	.23
❑	348 Cory Lidle RC	1.00	.30
❑	349 Fred McGriff	1.25	.35
❑	350 Chuck Carr	.75	.23
❑	351 Bob Abreu	.75	.23
❑	352 Juan Guzman	.75	.23
❑	353 Fernando Vina	.75	.23
❑	354 Andy Benes	.75	.23
❑	355 Dave Nilsson	.75	.23
❑	356 Bobby Bonilla	.75	.23
❑	357 Ismael Valdes	.75	.23
❑	358 Carlos Perez	.75	.23

No.	Player	Nm-Mt	Ex-Mt
❑ 359	Kirk Rueter	.75	.23
❑ 360	Bartolo Colon	.75	.23
❑ 361	Mel Rojas	.75	.23
❑ 362	Johnny Damon	1.25	.35
❑ 363	Geronimo Berroa	.75	.23
❑ 364	Reggie Sanders	.75	.23
❑ 365	Jermaine Allensworth	.75	.23
❑ 366	Orlando Cabrera	.75	.23
❑ 367	Jorge Fabregas	.75	.23
❑ 368	Scott Stahoviak	.75	.23
❑ 369	Ken Cloude	.75	.23
❑ 370	Donovan Osborne	.75	.23
❑ 371	Roger Cedeno	.75	.23
❑ 372	Neifi Perez	.75	.23
❑ 373	Chris Holt	.75	.23
❑ 374	Cecil Fielder	.75	.23
❑ 375	Marty Cordova	.75	.23
❑ 376	Tom Goodwin	.75	.23
❑ 377	Jeff Suppan	.75	.23
❑ 378	Jeff Brantley	.75	.23
❑ 379	Mark Langston	.75	.23
❑ 380	Shane Reynolds	.75	.23
❑ 381	Mike Fetters	.75	.23
❑ 382	Todd Greene	.75	.23
❑ 383	Ray Durham	.75	.23
❑ 384	Carlos Delgado	.75	.23
❑ 385	Jeff D'Amico	.75	.23
❑ 386	Brian McRae	.75	.23
❑ 387	Alan Benes	.75	.23
❑ 388	Heathcliff Slocumb	.75	.23
❑ 389	Eric Young	.75	.23
❑ 390	Travis Fryman	.75	.23
❑ 391	David Cone	.75	.23
❑ 392	Otis Nixon	.75	.23
❑ 393	Jeremi Gonzalez	.75	.23
❑ 394	Jeff Juden	.75	.23
❑ 395	Jose Vizcaino	.75	.23
❑ 396	Ugueth Urbina	.75	.23
❑ 397	Ramon Martinez	.75	.23
❑ 398	Robb Nen	.75	.23
❑ 399	Harold Baines	.75	.23
❑ 400	Delino DeShields	.75	.23
❑ 401	John Burkett	.75	.23
❑ 402	Sterling Hitchcock	.75	.23
❑ 403	Mark Clark	.75	.23
❑ 404	Terrell Wade	.75	.23
❑ 405	Scott Brosius	.75	.23
❑ 406	Chad Curtis	.75	.23
❑ 407	Brian Johnson	.75	.23
❑ 408	Roberto Kelly	.75	.23
❑ 409	Dave Dellucci RC	1.25	.35
❑ 410	Michael Tucker	.75	.23
❑ 411	Mark Kotsay	.75	.23
❑ 412	Mark Lewis	.75	.23
❑ 413	Ryan McGuire	.75	.23
❑ 414	Shawon Dunston	.75	.23
❑ 415	Brad Rigby	.75	.23
❑ 416	Scott Erickson	.75	.23
❑ 417	Bobby Jones	.75	.23
❑ 418	Darren Oliver	.75	.23
❑ 419	John Smiley	.75	.23
❑ 420	T.J. Mathews	.75	.23
❑ 421	Dustin Hermanson	.75	.23
❑ 422	Mike Timlin	.75	.23
❑ 423	Willie Blair	.75	.23
❑ 424	Manny Alexander	.75	.23
❑ 425	Bob Tewksbury	.75	.23
❑ 426	Pete Schourek	.75	.23
❑ 427	Reggie Jefferson	.75	.23
❑ 428	Ed Sprague	.75	.23
❑ 429	Jeff Conine	.75	.23
❑ 430	Roberto Hernandez	.75	.23
❑ 431	Tom Pagnozzi	.75	.23
❑ 432	Jaret Wright	.75	.23
❑ 433	Livan Hernandez	.75	.23
❑ 434	Andy Ashby	.75	.23
❑ 435	Todd Dunn	.75	.23
❑ 436	Bobby Higginson	.75	.23
❑ 437	Rod Beck	.75	.23
❑ 438	Jim Leyritz	.75	.23
❑ 439	Matt Williams	.75	.23
❑ 440	Brett Tomko	.75	.23
❑ 441	Joe Randa	.75	.23
❑ 442	Chris Carpenter	.75	.23
❑ 443	Dennis Reyes	.75	.23
❑ 444	Al Leiter	.75	.23
❑ 445	Jason Schmidt	.75	.23
❑ 446	Ken Hill	.75	.23
❑ 447	Shannon Stewart	.75	.23
❑ 448	Enrique Wilson	.75	.23
❑ 449	Fernando Tatis	.75	.23
❑ 450	Jimmy Key	.75	.23
❑ 451	Darrin Fletcher	.75	.23
❑ 452	John Valentin	.75	.23
❑ 453	Kevin Tapani	.75	.23
❑ 454	Eric Karros	.75	.23
❑ 455	Jay Bell	.75	.23
❑ 456	Walt Weiss	.75	.23
❑ 457	Devon White	.75	.23
❑ 458	Carl Pavano	.75	.23
❑ 459	Mike Lansing	.75	.23
❑ 460	John Flaherty	.75	.23
❑ 461	Richard Hidalgo	.75	.23
❑ 462	Quinton McCracken	.75	.23
❑ 463	Karim Garcia	.75	.23
❑ 464	Miguel Cairo	.75	.23
❑ 465	Edwin Diaz	.75	.23
❑ 466	Bobby Smith	.75	.23
❑ 467	Yamil Benitez	.75	.23
❑ 468	Rich Butler RC	.75	.23
❑ 469	Ben Ford RC	.75	.23
❑ 470	Bubba Trammell	.75	.23
❑ 471	Brent Brede	.75	.23
❑ 472	Brooks Kieschnick	.75	.23
❑ 473	Carlos Castillo	.75	.23
❑ 474	Brad Radke SH	.75	.23
❑ 475	Roger Clemens SH	2.00	.60
❑ 476	Curt Schilling SH	.75	.23
❑ 477	John Olerud SH	.75	.23
❑ 478	Mark McGwire SH	2.50	.75
❑ 479	Mike Piazza IL	2.00	.60
	Ken Griffey Jr.		
❑ 480	Jeff Bagwell	1.25	.35
	Frank Thomas		
❑ 481	Chipper Jones	1.25	.35
	Nomar Garciaparra IL		
❑ 482	Larry Walker IL	.75	.23
	Juan Gonzalez IL		
❑ 483	Gary Sheffield IL	.75	.23
	Tino Martinez IL		
❑ 484	Derrick Gibson	1.00	.30
	Michael Coleman		
	Norm Hutchins		
❑ 485	Braden Looper	1.00	.30
	Cliff Politte		
	Brian Rose		
❑ 486	Eric Milton	1.00	.30
	Jason Marquis		
	Corey Lee		
❑ 487	A.J.Hinch	1.00	.30
	Mark Osborne RC		
	Robert Fick		
❑ 488	Aramis Ramirez	1.25	.35
	Alex Gonzalez		
	Sean Casey		
❑ 489	Donnie Bridges	1.00	.30
	Tim Drew RC		
❑ 490	Ntema Ndungidi RC	1.00	.30
	Darnell McDonald		
❑ 491	Ryan Anderson RC	1.00	.30
	Mark Mangum		
❑ 492	J.J.Davis	6.00	1.80
	Troy Glaus RC		
❑ 493	Jayson Werth RC	1.00	.30
	Dan Reichert		
❑ 494	John Curtice RC	1.25	.35
	Michael Cuddyer RC		
❑ 495	Jack Cust RC	1.00	.30
	Jason Standridge		
❑ 496	Brian Anderson	1.00	.30
❑ 497	Tony Saunders	1.00	.30
❑ 498	Vladimir Nunez	1.00	.30
	Jhensy Sandoval		
❑ 499	Brad Penny	1.00	.30
	Nick Bierbrodt		
❑ 500	Dustin Carr	1.00	.30
	Luis Cruz RC		
❑ 501	Cedric Bowers	1.00	.30
	Marcus McCain		
❑ 502	Checklist	.75	.23
❑ 503	Checklist	.75	.23
❑ 504	Alex Rodriguez	4.00	1.20

1999 Topps Chrome

	Nm-Mt	Ex-Mt
COMPLETE SET (462)	120.00	36.00
COMP. SERIES 1 (241)	60.00	18.00
COMP. SERIES 2 (221)	60.00	18.00
COMMON (1-6/8-463)	.50	.15
COMMON (205-212/425-437)	1.00	.30

No.	Player	Nm-Mt	Ex-Mt
❑ 1	Roger Clemens	4.00	1.20
❑ 2	Andres Galarraga	.75	.23
❑ 3	Scott Brosius	.75	.23
❑ 4	John Flaherty	.50	.15
❑ 5	Jim Leyritz	.50	.15
❑ 6	Ray Durham	.75	.23
❑ 8	Jose Vizcaino	.50	.15
❑ 9	Will Clark	1.25	.35
❑ 10	David Wells	.75	.23
❑ 11	Jose Guillen	.75	.23
❑ 12	Scott Hatteberg	.50	.15
❑ 13	Edgardo Alfonzo	.50	.15
❑ 14	Mike Bordick	.50	.15
❑ 15	Manny Ramirez	1.25	.35
❑ 16	Greg Maddux	3.00	.90
❑ 17	David Segui	.50	.15
❑ 18	Darryl Strawberry	.75	.23
❑ 19	Brad Radke	.75	.23
❑ 20	Kerry Wood	.75	.23
❑ 21	Matt Anderson	.50	.15
❑ 22	Derrek Lee	1.25	.35
❑ 23	Mickey Morandini	.50	.15
❑ 24	Paul Konerko	.75	.23
❑ 25	Travis Lee	.50	.15
❑ 26	Ken Hill	.50	.15
❑ 27	Kenny Rogers	.75	.23
❑ 28	Paul Sorrento	.50	.15
❑ 29	Quilvio Veras	.50	.15
❑ 30	Todd Walker	.50	.15
❑ 31	Ryan Jackson	.50	.15
❑ 32	John Olerud	.75	.23
❑ 33	Doug Glanville	.50	.15
❑ 34	Nolan Ryan	6.00	1.80
❑ 35	Ray Lankford	.75	.23
❑ 36	Mark Loretta	.75	.23
❑ 37	Jason Dickson	.50	.15
❑ 38	Sean Bergman	.50	.15
❑ 39	Quinton McCracken	.50	.15
❑ 40	Bartolo Colon	.75	.23
❑ 41	Brady Anderson	.75	.23
❑ 42	Chris Stynes	.50	.15
❑ 43	Jorge Posada	1.25	.35
❑ 44	Justin Thompson	.50	.15
❑ 45	Johnny Damon	1.25	.35
❑ 46	Armando Benitez	.50	.15
❑ 47	Brant Brown	.50	.15
❑ 48	Charlie Hayes	.50	.15
❑ 49	Darren Dreifort	.50	.15
❑ 50	Juan Gonzalez	.75	.23
❑ 51	Chuck Knoblauch	.75	.23
❑ 52	Todd Helton	1.25	.35
❑ 53	Rick Reed	.50	.15
❑ 54	Chris Gomez	.50	.15
❑ 55	Gary Sheffield	.75	.23
❑ 56	Rod Beck	.50	.15
❑ 57	Rey Sanchez	.50	.15
❑ 58	Garret Anderson	.75	.23
❑ 59	Jimmy Haynes	.50	.15
❑ 60	Steve Woodard	.50	.15
❑ 61	Rondell White	.75	.23

No.	Player	Mint	Nrmt
❑ 62	Vladimir Guerrero	2.00	.60
❑ 63	Eric Karros	.75	.23
❑ 64	Russ Davis	.50	.15
❑ 65	Mo Vaughn	.75	.23
❑ 66	Sammy Sosa	2.00	.60
❑ 67	Troy Percival	.75	.23
❑ 68	Kenny Lofton	.75	.23
❑ 69	Bill Taylor	.50	.15
❑ 70	Mark McGwire	5.00	1.50
❑ 71	Roger Cedeno	.50	.15
❑ 72	Javy Lopez	.75	.23
❑ 73	Damion Easley	.50	.15
❑ 74	Andy Pettitte	1.25	.35
❑ 75	Tony Gwynn	2.50	.75
❑ 76	Ricardo Rincon	.50	.15
❑ 77	F.P. Santangelo	.50	.15
❑ 78	Jay Bell	.75	.23
❑ 79	Scott Servais	.50	.15
❑ 80	Jose Canseco	1.25	.35
❑ 81	Roberto Hernandez	.50	.15
❑ 82	Todd Dunwoody	.50	.15
❑ 83	John Wetteland	.75	.23
❑ 84	Mike Caruso	.50	.15
❑ 85	Derek Jeter	5.00	1.50
❑ 86	Aaron Sele	.50	.15
❑ 87	Jose Lima	.50	.15
❑ 88	Ryan Christenson	.50	.15
❑ 89	Jeff Cirillo	.50	.15
❑ 90	Jose Hernandez	.50	.15
❑ 91	Mark Kotsay	.75	.23
❑ 92	Darren Bragg	.50	.15
❑ 93	Albert Belle	.75	.23
❑ 94	Matt Lawton	.50	.15
❑ 95	Pedro Martinez	1.25	.35
❑ 96	Greg Vaughn	.50	.15
❑ 97	Neifi Perez	.50	.15
❑ 98	Gerald Williams	.50	.15
❑ 99	Derek Bell	.50	.15
❑ 100	Ken Griffey Jr.	3.00	.90
❑ 101	David Cone	.75	.23
❑ 102	Brian Johnson	.50	.15
❑ 103	Dean Palmer	.75	.23
❑ 104	Javier Valentin	.50	.15
❑ 105	Trevor Hoffman	.75	.23
❑ 106	Butch Huskey	.50	.15
❑ 107	Dave Martinez	.50	.15
❑ 108	Billy Wagner	.75	.23
❑ 109	Shawn Green	.75	.23
❑ 110	Ben Grieve	.50	.15
❑ 111	Tom Goodwin	.50	.15
❑ 112	Jaret Wright	.50	.15
❑ 113	Aramis Ramirez	.75	.23
❑ 114	Dmitri Young	.75	.23
❑ 115	Hideki Irabu	.50	.15
❑ 116	Roberto Kelly	.50	.15
❑ 117	Jeff Fassero	.50	.15
❑ 118	Mark Clark	.50	.15
❑ 119	Jason McDonald	.50	.15
❑ 120	Matt Williams	.75	.23
❑ 121	Dave Burba	.50	.15
❑ 122	Bret Saberhagen	.75	.23
❑ 123	Deivi Cruz	.50	.15
❑ 124	Chad Curtis	.50	.15
❑ 125	Scott Rolen	1.25	.35
❑ 126	Lee Stevens	.50	.15
❑ 127	J.T. Snow	.75	.23
❑ 128	Rusty Greer	.75	.23
❑ 129	Brian Meadows	.50	.15
❑ 130	Jim Edmonds	.75	.23
❑ 131	Ron Gant	.75	.23
❑ 132	A.J. Hinch	.50	.15
❑ 133	Shannon Stewart	.75	.23
❑ 134	Brad Fullmer	.50	.15
❑ 135	Cal Eldred	.50	.15
❑ 136	Matt Walbeck	.50	.15
❑ 137	Carl Everett	.75	.23
❑ 138	Walt Weiss	.50	.15
❑ 139	Fred McGriff	1.25	.35
❑ 140	Darin Erstad	.75	.23
❑ 141	Dave Nilsson	.50	.15
❑ 142	Eric Young	.50	.15
❑ 143	Dan Wilson	.50	.15
❑ 144	Jeff Reed	.50	.15
❑ 145	Brett Tomko	.50	.15
❑ 146	Terry Steinbach	.50	.15
❑ 147	Seth Greisinger	.50	.15
❑ 148	Pat Meares	.50	.15
❑ 149	Livan Hernandez	.75	.23
❑ 150	Jeff Bagwell	1.25	.35
❑ 151	Bob Wickman	.50	.15
❑ 152	Omar Vizquel	1.25	.35
❑ 153	Eric Davis	.75	.23
❑ 154	Larry Sutton	.50	.15
❑ 155	Magglio Ordonez	.75	.23
❑ 156	Eric Milton	.50	.15
❑ 157	Darren Lewis	.50	.15
❑ 158	Rick Aguilera	.50	.15
❑ 159	Mike Lieberthal	.50	.15
❑ 160	Robb Nen	.75	.23
❑ 161	Brian Giles	.75	.23
❑ 162	Jeff Brantley	.50	.15
❑ 163	Gary DiSarcina	.50	.15
❑ 164	John Valentin	.50	.15
❑ 165	Dave Dellucci	.50	.15
❑ 166	Chan Ho Park	.75	.23
❑ 167	Masato Yoshii	.50	.15
❑ 168	Jason Schmidt	.75	.23
❑ 169	LaTroy Hawkins	.50	.15
❑ 170	Bret Boone	.75	.23
❑ 171	Jerry DiPoto	.50	.15
❑ 172	Mariano Rivera	1.25	.35
❑ 173	Mike Cameron	.50	.15
❑ 174	Scott Erickson	.50	.15
❑ 175	Charles Johnson	.75	.23
❑ 176	Bobby Jones	.50	.15
❑ 177	Francisco Cordova	.50	.15
❑ 178	Todd Jones	.50	.15
❑ 179	Jeff Montgomery	.50	.15
❑ 180	Mike Mussina	1.25	.35
❑ 181	Bob Abreu	.75	.23
❑ 182	Ismael Valdes	.50	.15
❑ 183	Andy Fox	.50	.15
❑ 184	Woody Williams	.50	.15
❑ 185	Denny Neagle	.50	.15
❑ 186	Jose Valentin	.50	.15
❑ 187	Darrin Fletcher	.50	.15
❑ 188	Gabe Alvarez	.50	.15
❑ 189	Eddie Taubensee	.50	.15
❑ 190	Edgar Martinez	1.25	.35
❑ 191	Jason Kendall	.75	.23
❑ 192	Darryl Kile	.75	.23
❑ 193	Jeff King	.50	.15
❑ 194	Rey Ordonez	.50	.15
❑ 195	Andruw Jones	1.25	.35
❑ 196	Tony Fernandez	.50	.15
❑ 197	Jamey Wright	.50	.15
❑ 198	B.J. Surhoff	.75	.23
❑ 199	Vinny Castilla	.75	.23
❑ 200	David Wells HL	.50	.15
❑ 201	Mark McGwire HL	2.50	.75
❑ 202	Sammy Sosa HL	1.25	.35
❑ 203	Roger Clemens HL	2.00	.60
❑ 204	Kerry Wood HL	.50	.15
❑ 205	Gabe Kapler	1.00	.30
	Lance Berkman		
	Mike Frank		
❑ 206	Alex Escobar RC	1.00	.30
	Ricky Ledee		
	Mike Stoner		
❑ 207	Peter Bergeron RC	1.00	.30
	Jeremy Giambi		
	George Lombard		
❑ 208	Michael Barrett	1.00	.30
	Ben Davis		
	Robert Fick		
❑ 209	Jayson Werth	1.00	.30
	Ramon Hernandez		
	Pat Cline		
❑ 210	Ryan Anderson	1.00	.30
	Bruce Chen		
	Chris Enochs		
❑ 211	Brad Penny	1.00	.30
	Octavio Dotel		
	Mike Lincoln		
❑ 212	Chuck Abbott RC	1.00	.30
	Brent Butler		
	Danny Klassen		
❑ 213	Chris C.Jones	1.00	.30
	Jeff Urban RC		
❑ 214	Arturo McDowell RC	1.00	.30
	Tony Torcato		
❑ 215	Josh McKinley RC	1.00	.30
	Jason Tyner		
❑ 216	Matt Burch	1.00	.30
	Seth Etheron RC		
❑ 217	Mamon Tucker RC	1.00	.30
	Rick Elder		
❑ 218	J.M.Gold	1.00	.30
	Ryan Mills RC		
❑ 219	Andy Brown	1.00	.30
	Choo Freeman RC		
❑ 220A	Mark McGwire HR 1	50.00	15.00
❑ 220B	Mark McGwire HR 2	30.00	9.00
❑ 220C	Mark McGwire HR 3	30.00	9.00
❑ 220D	Mark McGwire HR 4	30.00	9.00
❑ 220E	Mark McGwire HR 5	30.00	9.00
❑ 220F	Mark McGwire HR 6	30.00	9.00
❑ 220G	Mark McGwire HR 7	30.00	9.00
❑ 220H	Mark McGwire HR 8	30.00	9.00
❑ 220I	Mark McGwire HR 9	30.00	9.00
❑ 220J	M.McGwire HR 10	30.00	9.00
❑ 220K	M.McGwire HR 11	30.00	9.00
❑ 220L	M.McGwire HR 12	30.00	9.00
❑ 220M	M.McGwire HR 13	30.00	9.00
❑ 220N	M.McGwire HR 14	30.00	9.00
❑ 220O	M.McGwire HR 15	30.00	9.00
❑ 220P	M.McGwire HR 16	30.00	9.00
❑ 220Q	M.McGwire HR 17	30.00	9.00
❑ 220R	M.McGwire HR 18	30.00	9.00
❑ 220S	M.McGwire HR 19	30.00	9.00
❑ 220T	M.McGwire HR 20	30.00	9.00
❑ 220U	M.McGwire HR 21	30.00	9.00
❑ 220V	M.McGwire HR 22	30.00	9.00
❑ 220W	M.McGwire HR 23	30.00	9.00
❑ 220X	M.McGwire HR 24	30.00	9.00
❑ 220Y	M.McGwire HR 25	30.00	9.00
❑ 220Z	M.McGwire HR 26	30.00	9.00
❑ 220AA	M.McGwire HR 27	30.00	9.00
❑ 220AB	M.McGwire HR 28	30.00	9.00
❑ 220AC	M.McGwire HR 29	30.00	9.00
❑ 220AD	M.McGwire HR 30	30.00	9.00
❑ 220AE	M.McGwire HR 31	30.00	9.00
❑ 220AF	M.McGwire HR 32	30.00	9.00
❑ 220AG	M.McGwire HR 33	30.00	9.00
❑ 220AH	M.McGwire HR 34	30.00	9.00
❑ 220AI	M.McGwire HR 35	30.00	9.00
❑ 220AJ	M.McGwire HR 36	30.00	9.00
❑ 220AK	M.McGwire HR 37	30.00	9.00
❑ 220AL	M.McGwire HR 38	30.00	9.00
❑ 220AM	M.McGwire HR 39	30.00	9.00
❑ 220AN	M.McGwire HR 40	30.00	9.00
❑ 220AO	M.McGwire HR 41	30.00	9.00
❑ 220AP	M.McGwire HR 42	30.00	9.00
❑ 220AQ	M.McGwire HR 43	30.00	9.00
❑ 220AR	M.McGwire HR 44	30.00	9.00
❑ 220AS	M.McGwire HR 45	30.00	9.00
❑ 220AT	M.McGwire HR 46	30.00	9.00
❑ 220AU	M.McGwire HR 47	30.00	9.00
❑ 220AV	M.McGwire HR 48	30.00	9.00
❑ 220AW	M.McGwire HR 49	30.00	9.00
❑ 220AX	M.McGwire HR 50	30.00	9.00
❑ 220AY	M.McGwire HR 51	30.00	9.00
❑ 220AZ	M.McGwire HR 52	30.00	9.00
❑ 220BB	M.McGwire HR 53	30.00	9.00
❑ 220CC	M.McGwire HR 54	30.00	9.00
❑ 220DD	M.McGwire HR 55	30.00	9.00
❑ 220EE	M.McGwire HR 56	30.00	9.00
❑ 220FF	M.McGwire HR 57	30.00	9.00
❑ 220GG	M.McGwire HR 58	30.00	9.00
❑ 220HH	M.McGwire HR 59	30.00	9.00
❑ 220II	M.McGwire HR 60	30.00	9.00
❑ 220JJ	M.McGwire HR 61	50.00	15.00
❑ 220KK	M.McGwire HR 62	80.00	24.00
❑ 220LL	M.McGwire HR 63	50.00	15.00
❑ 220MM	M.McGwire HR 64	50.00	15.00
❑ 220NN	M.McGwire HR 65	50.00	15.00
❑ 220OO	M.McGwire HR 66	50.00	15.00
❑ 220PP	M.McGwire HR 67	50.00	15.00
❑ 220QQ	M.McGwire HR 68	50.00	15.00
❑ 220RR	M.McGwire HR 69	50.00	15.00
❑ 220SS	M.McGwire HR 70	120.00	36.00
❑ 221	Larry Walker LL	.50	.15
❑ 222	Bernie Williams LL	.75	.23
❑ 223	Mark McGwire LL	2.50	.75
❑ 224	Ken Griffey Jr. LL	2.00	.60
❑ 225	Sammy Sosa LL	1.25	.35
❑ 226	Juan Gonzalez LL	.50	.15
❑ 227	Dante Bichette LL	.50	.15

	No.	Player	Price	Price
❑	228	Alex Rodriguez LL	2.00	.60
❑	229	Sammy Sosa LL	1.25	.35
❑	230	Derek Jeter LL	2.50	.75
❑	231	Greg Maddux LL	2.00	.60
❑	232	Roger Clemens LL	2.00	.60
❑	233	Ricky Ledee WS	.50	.15
❑	234	Chuck Knoblauch WS	.50	.15
❑	235	Bernie Williams WS	.75	.23
❑	236	Tino Martinez WS	.75	.23
❑	237	Orl. Hernandez WS	.75	.23
❑	238	Scott Brosius WS	.50	.15
❑	239	Andy Pettitte WS	.75	.23
❑	240	Mariano Rivera WS	.75	.23
❑	241	Checklist	.50	.15
❑	242	Checklist	.50	.15
❑	243	Tom Glavine	1.25	.35
❑	244	Andy Benes	.50	.15
❑	245	Sandy Alomar Jr.	.50	.15
❑	246	Wilton Guerrero	.50	.15
❑	247	Alex Gonzalez	.50	.15
❑	248	Roberto Alomar	1.25	.35
❑	249	Ruben Rivera	.50	.15
❑	250	Eric Chavez	.75	.23
❑	251	Ellis Burks	.75	.23
❑	252	Richie Sexson	.75	.23
❑	253	Steve Finley	.75	.23
❑	254	Dwight Gooden	.75	.23
❑	255	Dustin Hermanson	.50	.15
❑	256	Kirk Rueter	.50	.15
❑	257	Steve Trachsel	.50	.15
❑	258	Gregg Jefferies	.50	.15
❑	259	Matt Stairs	.50	.15
❑	260	Shane Reynolds	.50	.15
❑	261	Gregg Olson	.50	.15
❑	262	Kevin Tapani	.50	.15
❑	263	Matt Morris	.75	.23
❑	264	Carl Pavano	.75	.23
❑	265	Nomar Garciaparra	3.00	.90
❑	266	Kevin Young	.75	.23
❑	267	Rick Helling	.50	.15
❑	268	Matt Franco	.50	.15
❑	269	Brian McRae	.50	.15
❑	270	Cal Ripken	6.00	1.80
❑	271	Jeff Abbott	.50	.15
❑	272	Tony Batista	.50	.15
❑	273	Bill Simas	.50	.15
❑	274	Brian Hunter	.50	.15
❑	275	John Franco	.75	.23
❑	276	Devon White	.75	.23
❑	277	Rickey Henderson	2.00	.60
❑	278	Chuck Finley	.75	.23
❑	279	Mike Blowers	.50	.15
❑	280	Mark Grace	1.25	.35
❑	281	Randy Winn	.50	.15
❑	282	Bobby Bonilla	.75	.23
❑	283	David Justice	.75	.23
❑	284	Shane Monahan	.50	.15
❑	285	Kevin Brown	1.25	.35
❑	286	Todd Zeile	.75	.23
❑	287	Al Martin	.50	.15
❑	288	Troy O'Leary	.50	.15
❑	289	Darryl Hamilton	.50	.15
❑	290	Tino Martinez	1.25	.35
❑	291	David Ortiz	1.25	.35
❑	292	Tony Clark	.50	.15
❑	293	Ryan Minor	.50	.15
❑	294	Mark Leiter	.50	.15
❑	295	Wally Joyner	.75	.23
❑	296	Cliff Floyd	.75	.23
❑	297	Shawn Estes	.50	.15
❑	298	Pat Hentgen	.50	.15
❑	299	Scott Elarton	.50	.15
❑	300	Alex Rodriguez	3.00	.90
❑	301	Ozzie Guillen	.75	.23
❑	302	Hideo Nomo	2.00	.60
❑	303	Ryan McGuire	.50	.15
❑	304	Brad Ausmus	.75	.23
❑	305	Alex Gonzalez	.50	.15
❑	306	Brian Jordan	.75	.23
❑	307	John Jaha	.50	.15
❑	308	Mark Grudzielanek	.50	.15
❑	309	Juan Guzman	.50	.15
❑	310	Tony Womack	.50	.15
❑	311	Dennis Reyes	.50	.15
❑	312	Marty Cordova	.50	.15
❑	313	Ramiro Mendoza	.50	.15
❑	314	Robin Ventura	.75	.23
❑	315	Rafael Palmeiro	1.25	.35
❑	316	Ramon Martinez	.50	.15
❑	317	Pedro Astacio	.50	.15
❑	318	Dave Hollins	.50	.15
❑	319	Tom Candiotti	.50	.15
❑	320	Al Leiter	.75	.23
❑	321	Rico Brogna	.50	.15
❑	322	Reggie Jefferson	.50	.15
❑	323	Bernard Gilkey	.50	.15
❑	324	Jason Giambi	.75	.23
❑	325	Craig Biggio	1.25	.35
❑	326	Troy Glaus	1.25	.35
❑	327	Delino DeShields	.50	.15
❑	328	Fernando Vina	.50	.15
❑	329	John Smoltz	1.25	.35
❑	330	Jeff Kent	.75	.23
❑	331	Roy Halladay	.75	.23
❑	332	Andy Ashby	.50	.15
❑	333	Tim Wakefield	.75	.23
❑	334	Roger Clemens	4.00	1.20
❑	335	Bernie Williams	1.25	.35
❑	336	Desi Relaford	.50	.15
❑	337	John Burkett	.50	.15
❑	338	Mike Hampton	.75	.23
❑	339	Royce Clayton	.50	.15
❑	340	Mike Piazza	3.00	.90
❑	341	Jeremi Gonzalez	.50	.15
❑	342	Mike Lansing	.50	.15
❑	343	Jamie Moyer	.75	.23
❑	344	Ron Coomer	.50	.15
❑	345	Barry Larkin	1.25	.35
❑	346	Fernando Tatis	.50	.15
❑	347	Chili Davis	.75	.23
❑	348	Bobby Higginson	.75	.23
❑	349	Hal Morris	.50	.15
❑	350	Larry Walker	.75	.23
❑	351	Carlos Guillen	.75	.23
❑	352	Miguel Tejada	.75	.23
❑	353	Travis Fryman	.75	.23
❑	354	Jarrod Washburn	.50	.15
❑	355	Chipper Jones	2.00	.60
❑	356	Todd Stottlemyre	.50	.15
❑	357	Henry Rodriguez	.50	.15
❑	358	Eli Marrero	.50	.15
❑	359	Alan Benes	.50	.15
❑	360	Tim Salmon	1.25	.35
❑	361	Luis Gonzalez	.75	.23
❑	362	Scott Spiezio	.50	.15
❑	363	Chris Carpenter	.75	.23
❑	364	Bobby Howry	.50	.15
❑	365	Raul Mondesi	.75	.23
❑	366	Ugueth Urbina	.50	.15
❑	367	Tom Evans	.50	.15
❑	368	Kerry Ligtenberg RC	.75	.23
❑	369	Adrian Beltre	.75	.23
❑	370	Ryan Klesko	.75	.23
❑	371	Wilson Alvarez	.50	.15
❑	372	John Thomson	.50	.15
❑	373	Tony Saunders	.50	.15
❑	374	Dave Mlicki	.50	.15
❑	375	Ken Caminiti	.75	.23
❑	376	Jay Buhner	.75	.23
❑	377	Bill Mueller	.75	.23
❑	378	Jeff Blauser	.50	.15
❑	379	Edgar Renteria	.75	.23
❑	380	Jim Thome	1.25	.35
❑	381	Joey Hamilton	.50	.15
❑	382	Calvin Pickering	.50	.15
❑	383	Marquis Grissom	.75	.23
❑	384	Omar Daal	.50	.15
❑	385	Curt Schilling	.75	.23
❑	386	Jose Cruz Jr.	.50	.15
❑	387	Chris Widger	.50	.15
❑	388	Pete Harnisch	.50	.15
❑	389	Charles Nagy	.50	.15
❑	390	Tom Gordon	.50	.15
❑	391	Bobby Smith	.50	.15
❑	392	Derrick Gibson	.50	.15
❑	393	Jeff Conine	.75	.23
❑	394	Carlos Perez	.50	.15
❑	395	Barry Bonds	5.00	1.50
❑	396	Mark McLemore	.50	.15
❑	397	Juan Encarnacion	.50	.15
❑	398	Wade Boggs	1.25	.35
❑	399	Ivan Rodriguez	1.25	.35
❑	400	Moises Alou	.75	.23
❑	401	Jeromy Burnitz	.75	.23
❑	402	Sean Casey	1.25	.35
❑	403	Jose Offerman	.50	.15
❑	404	Joe Fontenot	.50	.15
❑	405	Kevin Millwood	.50	.15
❑	406	Lance Johnson	.50	.15
❑	407	Richard Hidalgo	.50	.15
❑	408	Mike Jackson	.50	.15
❑	409	Brian Anderson	.50	.15
❑	410	Jeff Shaw	.50	.15
❑	411	Preston Wilson	.75	.23
❑	412	Todd Hundley	.50	.15
❑	413	Jim Parque	.50	.15
❑	414	Justin Baughman	.50	.15
❑	415	Dante Bichette	.75	.23
❑	416	Paul O'Neill	1.25	.35
❑	417	Miguel Cairo	.50	.15
❑	418	Randy Johnson	2.00	.60
❑	419	Jesus Sanchez	.50	.15
❑	420	Carlos Delgado	.75	.23
❑	421	Ricky Ledee	.50	.15
❑	422	Orlando Hernandez	.75	.23
❑	423	Frank Thomas	2.00	.60
❑	424	Pokey Reese	.50	.15
❑	425	Carlos Lee Mike Lowell Kit Pellow RC	1.00	.30
❑	426	Michael Cuddyer Mark DeRosa Jerry Hairston Jr.	1.00	.30
❑	427	Marlon Anderson Ron Belliard Orlando Cabrera	1.00	.30
❑	428	Micah Bowie Phil Norton RC Randy Wolf	1.00	.30
❑	429	Jack Cressend RC Jason Rakers John Rocker	1.00	.30
❑	430	Ruben Mateo Scott Morgan Mike Zywica RC	1.00	.30
❑	431	Jason LaRue Matt LeCroy Mitch Meluskey	1.00	.30
❑	432	Gabe Kapler Armando Rios Fernando Seguignol	1.00	.30
❑	433	Adam Kennedy Mickey Lopez RC Jackie Rexrode	1.00	.30
❑	434	Jose Fernandez RC Jeff Liefer Chris Truby	1.00	.30
❑	435	Corey Koskie Doug Mientkiewicz RC Damon Minor	1.50	.45
❑	436	Roosevelt Brown RC Dernell Stenson Vernon Wells	1.00	.30
❑	437	A.J. Burnett RC Billy Koch John Nicholson	2.50	.75
❑	438	Matt Belisle Matt Roney RC	1.00	.30
❑	439	Austin Kearns Chris George RC	2.00	.60
❑	440	Nate Bump RC Nate Cornejo	1.00	.30
❑	441	Brad Lidge Mike Nannini RC	5.00	1.50
❑	442	Matt Holliday Jeff Winchester RC	1.50	.45
❑	443	Adam Everett Chip Ambres RC	1.50	.45
❑	444	Pat Burrell Eric Valent RC	4.00	1.20
❑	445	Roger Clemens SK	2.00	.60
❑	446	Kerry Wood SK	.50	.15
❑	447	Curt Schilling SK	.50	.15
❑	448	Randy Johnson SK	1.25	.35
❑	449	Pedro Martinez SK	1.25	.35
❑	450	Jeff Bagwell AT Andres Galarraga Mark McGwire	2.00	.60

❑ 451 John Olerud AT .75 .23
Jim Thome
Tino Martinez
❑ 452 Alex Rodriguez AT 2.50 .75
Nomar Garciaparra
Derek Jeter
❑ 453 Vinny Castilla AT 1.25 .35
Chipper Jones
Scott Rolen
❑ 454 Sammy Sosa AT 2.00 .60
Ken Griffey Jr.
Juan Gonzalez
❑ 455 Barry Bonds AT 2.50 .75
Manny Ramirez
Larry Walker
❑ 456 Frank Thomas AT 2.00 .60
Tim Salmon
David Justice
❑ 457 Travis Lee AT .75 .23
Todd Helton
Ben Grieve
❑ 458 Vladimir Guerrero AT .75 .23
Greg Vaughn
Bernie Williams
❑ 459 Mike Piazza AT 2.00 .60
Ivan Rodriguez
Jason Kendall
❑ 460 Roger Clemens AT 2.00 .60
Kerry Wood
Greg Maddux
❑ 461A Sammy Sosa HR 1 20.00 6.00
❑ 461B Sammy Sosa HR 2 12.00 3.60
❑ 461C Sammy Sosa HR 3 12.00 3.60
❑ 461D Sammy Sosa HR 4 12.00 3.60
❑ 461E Sammy Sosa HR 5 12.00 3.60
❑ 461F Sammy Sosa HR 6 12.00 3.60
❑ 461G Sammy Sosa HR 7 12.00 3.60
❑ 461H Sammy Sosa HR 8 12.00 3.60
❑ 461I Sammy Sosa HR 9 12.00 3.60
❑ 461J Sammy Sosa HR 10 12.00 3.60
❑ 461K Sammy Sosa HR 11 12.00 3.60
❑ 461L Sammy Sosa HR 12 12.00 3.60
❑ 461M Sammy Sosa HR 13 12.00 3.60
❑ 461N Sammy Sosa HR 14 12.00 3.60
❑ 461O Sammy Sosa HR 15 12.00 3.60
❑ 461P Sammy Sosa HR 16 12.00 3.60
❑ 461Q Sammy Sosa HR 17 12.00 3.60
❑ 461R Sammy Sosa HR 18 12.00 3.60
❑ 461S Sammy Sosa HR 19 12.00 3.60
❑ 461T Sammy Sosa HR 20 12.00 3.60
❑ 461U Sammy Sosa HR 21 12.00 3.60
❑ 461V Sammy Sosa HR 22 12.00 3.60
❑ 461W Sammy Sosa HR 23 12.00 3.60
❑ 461X Sammy Sosa HR 24 12.00 3.60
❑ 461Y Sammy Sosa HR 25 12.00 3.60
❑ 461Z Sammy Sosa HR 26 12.00 3.60
❑ 461AA S.Sosa HR 27 12.00 3.60
❑ 461AB S.Sosa HR 28 12.00 3.60
❑ 461AC S.Sosa HR 29 12.00 3.60
❑ 461AD S.Sosa HR 30 12.00 3.60
❑ 461AE S.Sosa HR 31 12.00 3.60
❑ 461AF S.Sosa HR 32 12.00 3.60
❑ 461AG S.Sosa HR 33 12.00 3.60
❑ 461AH S.Sosa HR 34 12.00 3.60
❑ 461AI S.Sosa HR 35 12.00 3.60
❑ 461AJ S.Sosa HR 36 12.00 3.60
❑ 461AK S.Sosa HR 37 12.00 3.60
❑ 461AL S.Sosa HR 38 12.00 3.60
❑ 461AM S.Sosa HR 39 12.00 3.60
❑ 461AN S.Sosa HR 40 12.00 3.60
❑ 461AO S.Sosa HR 41 12.00 3.60
❑ 461AP S.Sosa HR 42 12.00 3.60
❑ 461AR S.Sosa HR 43 12.00 3.60
❑ 461AS S.Sosa HR 44 12.00 3.60
❑ 461AT S.Sosa HR 45 12.00 3.60
❑ 461AU S.Sosa HR 46 12.00 3.60
❑ 461AV S.Sosa HR 47 12.00 3.60
❑ 461AW S.Sosa HR 48 12.00 3.60
❑ 461AX S.Sosa HR 49 12.00 3.60
❑ 461AY S.Sosa HR 50 12.00 3.60
❑ 461AZ S.Sosa HR 51 12.00 3.60
❑ 461BB S.Sosa HR 52 12.00 3.60
❑ 461CC S.Sosa HR 53 12.00 3.60
❑ 461DD S.Sosa HR 54 12.00 3.60
❑ 461EE S.Sosa HR 55 12.00 3.60
❑ 461FF S.Sosa HR 56 12.00 3.60
❑ 461GG S.Sosa HR 57 12.00 3.60
❑ 461HH S.Sosa HR 58 12.00 3.60
❑ 461II S.Sosa HR 59 12.00 3.60
❑ 461JJ S.Sosa HR 60 12.00 3.60
❑ 461KK S.Sosa HR 61 20.00 6.00
❑ 461LL S.Sosa HR 62 30.00 9.00
❑ 461MM S.Sosa HR 63 20.00 6.00
❑ 461NN S.Sosa HR 64 20.00 6.00
❑ 461OO S.Sosa HR 65 20.00 6.00
❑ 461PP S.Sosa HR 66 60.00 18.00
❑ 462 Checklist .50 .15
❑ 463 Checklist .50 .15

1999 Topps Chrome Traded

	Nm-Mt	Ex-Mt
COMP.FACT SET (121)	80.00	24.00
❑ T1 Seth Etherton	.40	.12
❑ T2 Mark Harriger RC	.50	.15
❑ T3 Matt Wise RC	.50	.15
❑ T4 Carlos E. Hernandez RC	.75	.23
❑ T5 Julio Lugo RC	1.25	.35
❑ T6 Mike Nannini	.40	.12
❑ T7 Justin Bowles RC	.50	.15
❑ T8 Mark Mulder RC	4.00	1.20
❑ T9 Roberto Vaz RC	.50	.15
❑ T10 Felipe Lopez RC	2.50	.75
❑ T11 Matt Belisle	.40	.12
❑ T12 Micah Bowie	.40	.12
❑ T13 Ruben Quevedo RC	.50	.15
❑ T14 Jose Garcia RC	.50	.15
❑ T15 David Kelton RC	.75	.23
❑ T16 Phil Norton	.40	.12
❑ T17 Corey Patterson RC	1.25	.35
❑ T18 Ron Walker RC	.50	.15
❑ T19 Paul Hoover RC	.50	.15
❑ T20 Ryan Rupe RC	.50	.15
❑ T21 J.D. Closser RC	1.25	.35
❑ T22 Rob Ryan RC	.50	.15
❑ T23 Steve Colyer RC	.75	.23
❑ T24 Bubba Crosby RC	1.25	.35
❑ T25 Luke Prokopec RC	.50	.15
❑ T26 Matt Blank RC	.50	.15
❑ T27 Josh McKinley	.60	.18
❑ T28 Nate Bump	.50	.15
❑ T29 G.Chiaramonte RC	.50	.15
❑ T30 Arturo McDowell	.40	.12
❑ T31 Tony Torcato	.60	.18
❑ T32 Dave Roberts RC	1.25	.35
❑ T33 C.C. Sabathia RC	2.00	.60
❑ T34 Sean Spencer RC	.50	.15
❑ T35 Chip Ambres	.40	.12
❑ T36 A.J. Burnett	2.00	.60
❑ T37 Mo Bruce RC	.50	.15
❑ T38 Jason Tyner	.40	.12
❑ T39 Mamon Tucker	.40	.12
❑ T40 Sean Burroughs RC	1.25	.35
❑ T41 Kevin Eberwein RC	.50	.15
❑ T42 Junior Herndon RC	.75	.23
❑ T43 Bryan Wolff RC	.50	.15
❑ T44 Pat Burrell	3.00	.90
❑ T45 Eric Valent	.75	.23
❑ T46 Carlos Pena RC	.75	.23
❑ T47 Mike Zywica	.40	.12
❑ T48 Adam Everett	1.00	.30
❑ T49 Juan Pena RC	.50	.15
❑ T50 Adam Dunn RC	10.00	3.00
❑ T51 Austin Kearns	1.25	.35
❑ T52 Jacobo Sequea RC	.50	.15
❑ T53 Choo Freeman	.60	.18
❑ T54 Jeff Winchester	.40	.12
❑ T55 Matt Burch	.50	.15
❑ T56 Chris George	.60	.18
❑ T57 Scott Mullen RC	.50	.15
❑ T58 Kit Pellow	.50	.15
❑ T59 Mark Quinn RC	.75	.23
❑ T60 Nate Cornejo	.75	.23
❑ T61 Ryan Mills	.40	.12
❑ T62 Kevin Beirne RC	.75	.23
❑ T63 Kip Wells RC	1.25	.35
❑ T64 Juan Rivera RC	1.25	.35
❑ T65 Alfonso Soriano RC	10.00	3.00
❑ T66 Josh Hamilton RC	1.25	.35
❑ T67 Josh Girdley RC	.50	.15
❑ T68 Kyle Snyder RC	.50	.15
❑ T69 Mike Paradis RC	.50	.15
❑ T70 Jason Jennings RC	1.25	.35
❑ T71 David Walling RC	.50	.15
❑ T72 Omar Ortiz RC	.50	.15
❑ T73 Jay Gehrke RC	.50	.15
❑ T74 Casey Burns RC	.50	.15
❑ T75 Carl Crawford RC	4.00	1.20
❑ T76 Reggie Sanders	.60	.18
❑ T77 Will Clark	1.00	.30
❑ T78 David Wells	.60	.18
❑ T79 Paul Konerko	.60	.18
❑ T80 Armando Benitez	.40	.12
❑ T81 Brant Brown	.40	.12
❑ T82 Mo Vaughn	.60	.18
❑ T83 Jose Canseco	1.00	.30
❑ T84 Albert Belle	.60	.18
❑ T85 Dean Palmer	.60	.18
❑ T86 Greg Vaughn	.40	.12
❑ T87 Mark Clark	.40	.12
❑ T88 Pat Meares	.40	.12
❑ T89 Eric Davis	.60	.18
❑ T90 Brian Giles	.60	.18
❑ T91 Jeff Brantley	.40	.12
❑ T92 Bret Boone	.60	.18
❑ T93 Ron Gant	.60	.18
❑ T94 Mike Cameron	.40	.12
❑ T95 Charles Johnson	.60	.18
❑ T96 Denny Neagle	.40	.12
❑ T97 Brian Hunter	.40	.12
❑ T98 Jose Hernandez	.40	.12
❑ T99 Rick Aguilera	.40	.12
❑ T100 Tony Batista	.40	.12
❑ T101 Roger Cedeno	.40	.12
❑ T102 C.Gubanich RC	.50	.15
❑ T103 Tim Belcher	.40	.12
❑ T104 Bruce Aven	.40	.12
❑ T105 Brian Daubach RC	.75	.23
❑ T106 Ed Sprague	.40	.12
❑ T107 Michael Tucker	.40	.12
❑ T108 Homer Bush	.40	.12
❑ T109 Armando Reynoso	.40	.12
❑ T110 Brook Fordyce	.40	.12
❑ T111 Matt Mantei	.40	.12
❑ T112 Dave Mlicki	.40	.12
❑ T113 Kenny Rogers	.60	.18
❑ T114 Livan Hernandez	.60	.18
❑ T115 Butch Huskey	.40	.12
❑ T116 David Segui	.40	.12
❑ T117 Darryl Hamilton	.40	.12
❑ T118 Terry Mulholland	.40	.12
❑ T119 Randy Velarde	.40	.12
❑ T120 Bill Taylor	.40	.12
❑ T121 Kevin Appier	.60	.18

2000 Topps Chrome Traded

	Nm-Mt	Ex-Mt
COMP.FACT.SET (135)	80.00	24.00
❑ T1 Mike MacDougal	.75	.23
❑ T2 Andy Tracy RC	.50	.15
❑ T3 Brandon Phillips RC	1.25	.35
❑ T4 Brandon Inge RC	2.00	.60
❑ T5 Robbie Morrison RC	.50	.15
❑ T6 Josh Pressley RC	.50	.15
❑ T7 Todd Moser RC	.50	.15

❑ T8 Rob Purvis .60 .18
❑ T9 Chance Caple .40 .12
❑ T10 Ben Sheets 3.00 .90
❑ T11 Russ Jacobson RC .50 .15
❑ T12 Brian Cole RC .50 .15
❑ T13 Brad Baker .60 .18
❑ T14 Alex Cintron RC .75 .23
❑ T15 Lyle Overbay RC 2.00 .60
❑ T16 Mike Edwards RC .50 .15
❑ T17 Sean McGowan RC .50 .15
❑ T18 Jose Molina .40 .12
❑ T19 Marcos Castillo RC .50 .15
❑ T20 Josue Espada RC .50 .15
❑ T21 Alex Gordon RC .50 .15
❑ T22 Rob Pugmire RC .50 .15
❑ T23 Jason Stumm .50 .15
❑ T24 Ty Howington .60 .18
❑ T25 Brett Myers 2.00 .60
❑ T26 Maicer Izturis RC 1.25 .35
❑ T27 John McDonald .40 .12
❑ T28 W.Rodriguez RC .50 .15
❑ T29 Carlos Zambrano RC 6.00 1.80
❑ T30 Alejandro Diaz RC .50 .15
❑ T31 Geraldo Guzman RC .50 .15
❑ T32 J.R. House RC .75 .23
❑ T33 Elvin Nina RC .50 .15
❑ T34 Juan Pierre RC 2.00 .60
❑ T35 Ben Johnson RC .50 .15
❑ T36 Jeff Bailey RC .50 .15
❑ T37 Miguel Olivo RC 1.25 .35
❑ T38 F.Rodriguez RC 4.00 1.20
❑ T39 Tony Pena Jr. RC .75 .23
❑ T40 Miguel Cabrera RC 50.00 15.00
❑ T41 Asdrubal Oropeza RC .50 .15
❑ T42 Junior Zamora RC .75 .23
❑ T43 Jovanny Cedeno RC .50 .15
❑ T44 John Sneed .60 .18
❑ T45 Josh Kalinowski .60 .18
❑ T46 Mike Young RC 8.00 2.40
❑ T47 Rico Washington RC .50 .15
❑ T48 Chad Durbin RC .50 .15
❑ T49 Junior Brignac RC .50 .15
❑ T50 Carlos Hernandez RC .75 .23
❑ T51 Cesar Izturis RC 2.50 .75
❑ T52 Oscar Salazar RC .50 .15
❑ T53 Pat Strange RC .50 .15
❑ T54 Rick Asadoorian .75 .23
❑ T55 Keith Reed .60 .18
❑ T56 Leo Estrella RC .50 .15
❑ T57 Wascar Serrano RC .50 .15
❑ T58 Richard Gomez RC .50 .15
❑ T59 Ramon Santiago RC .75 .23
❑ T60 Jovanny Sosa RC .75 .23
❑ T61 Aaron Rowand RC 3.00 .90
❑ T62 Junior Guerrero RC .50 .15
❑ T63 Luis Terrero RC 1.25 .35
❑ T64 Brian Sanches RC .50 .15
❑ T65 Scott Sobkowiak RC .50 .15
❑ T66 Gary Majewski RC 1.25 .35
❑ T67 Barry Zito 3.00 .90
❑ T68 Ryan Christianson .75 .23
❑ T69 Cristian Guerrero RC .75 .23
❑ T70 T.De La Rosa RC .50 .15
❑ T71 Andrew Beinbrink RC .50 .15
❑ T72 Ryan Knox RC .50 .15
❑ T73 Alex Graman RC .50 .15
❑ T74 Juan Guzman RC .50 .15
❑ T75 Ruben Salazar RC .50 .15
❑ T76 Luis Matos RC .75 .23
❑ T77 Tony Mota RC .50 .15
❑ T78 Doug Davis .60 .18
❑ T79 Ben Christensen .40 .12
❑ T80 Mike Lamb 1.25 .35
❑ T81 Adrian Gonzalez RC 1.25 .35
❑ T82 Mike Stodolka RC .50 .15
❑ T83 Adam Johnson RC .75 .23
❑ T84 Matt Wheatland RC .50 .15
❑ T85 Corey Smith RC .75 .23
❑ T86 Rocco Baldelli RC 4.00 1.20
❑ T87 Keith Bucktrot RC .50 .15
❑ T88 Adam Wainwright RC 1.25 .35
❑ T89 Scott Thorman RC .75 .23
❑ T90 Tripper Johnson RC .75 .23
❑ T91 Jim Edmonds Cards 1.00 .30
❑ T92 Masato Yoshii .40 .12
❑ T93 Adam Kennedy .40 .12
❑ T94 Darryl Kile .60 .18
❑ T95 Mark McLemore .40 .12
❑ T96 Ricky Gutierrez .40 .12
❑ T97 Juan Gonzalez .60 .18
❑ T98 Melvin Mora .60 .18
❑ T99 Dante Bichette .60 .18
❑ T100 Lee Stevens .40 .12
❑ T101 Roger Cedeno .40 .12
❑ T102 John Olerud .60 .18
❑ T103 Eric Young .40 .12
❑ T104 Mickey Morandini .40 .12
❑ T105 Travis Lee .40 .12
❑ T106 Greg Vaughn .40 .12
❑ T107 Todd Zeile .60 .18
❑ T108 Chuck Finley .60 .18
❑ T109 Ismael Valdes .40 .12
❑ T110 Reggie Sanders .60 .18
❑ T111 Pat Hentgen .40 .12
❑ T112 Ryan Klesko .60 .18
❑ T113 Derek Bell .40 .12
❑ T114 Hideo Nomo 1.50 .45
❑ T115 Aaron Sele .40 .12
❑ T116 Fernando Vina .40 .12
❑ T117 Wally Joyner .60 .18
❑ T118 Brian Hunter .40 .12
❑ T119 Joe Girardi .40 .12
❑ T120 Omar Daal .40 .12
❑ T121 Brook Fordyce .40 .12
❑ T122 Jose Valentin .40 .12
❑ T123 Curt Schilling .60 .18
❑ T124 B.J. Surhoff .60 .18
❑ T125 Henry Rodriguez .40 .12
❑ T126 Mike Bordick .40 .12
❑ T127 David Justice .60 .18
❑ T128 Charles Johnson .60 .18
❑ T129 Will Clark 1.00 .30
❑ T130 Dwight Gooden .60 .18
❑ T131 David Segui .40 .12
❑ T132 Denny Neagle .60 .18
❑ T133 Jose Canseco 1.00 .30
❑ T134 Bruce Chen .40 .12
❑ T135 Jason Bere .40 .12

2001 Topps Chrome

	Nm-Mt	Ex-Mt
COMPLETE SET (661)	300.00	90.00
COMP. SERIES 1 (331)	150.00	45.00
COMP. SERIES 2 (330)	150.00	45.00

❑ 1 Cal Ripken 6.00 1.80
❑ 2 Chipper Jones 2.00 .60
❑ 3 Roger Cedeno .50 .15
❑ 4 Garret Anderson .75 .23
❑ 5 Robin Ventura .75 .23
❑ 6 Daryle Ward .50 .15
❑ 7 Does Not Exist .00
❑ 8 Phil Nevin .75 .23
❑ 9 Jermaine Dye .75 .23
❑ 10 Chris Singleton .50 .15
❑ 11 Mike Redmond .50 .15
❑ 12 Jim Thome 1.25 .35
❑ 13 Brian Jordan .75 .23
❑ 14 Dustin Hermanson .50 .15
❑ 15 Shawn Green .75 .23
❑ 16 Todd Stottlemyre .50 .15
❑ 17 Dan Wilson .50 .15
❑ 18 Derek Lowe .75 .23
❑ 19 Juan Gonzalez .75 .23
❑ 20 Pat Meares .50 .15
❑ 21 Paul O'Neill 1.25 .35
❑ 22 Jeffrey Hammonds .50 .15
❑ 23 Pokey Reese .50 .15
❑ 24 Mike Mussina 1.25 .35
❑ 25 Rico Brogna .50 .15
❑ 26 Jay Buhner .75 .23
❑ 27 Steve Cox .50 .15
❑ 28 Quilvio Veras .50 .15
❑ 29 Marquis Grissom .75 .23
❑ 30 Shigetoshi Hasegawa .75 .23
❑ 31 Shane Reynolds .50 .15
❑ 32 Adam Piatt .50 .15
❑ 33 Preston Wilson .75 .23
❑ 34 Ellis Burks .75 .23
❑ 35 Armando Rios .50 .15
❑ 36 Chuck Finley .75 .23
❑ 37 Shannon Stewart .75 .23
❑ 38 Mark McGwire 5.00 1.50
❑ 39 Gerald Williams .50 .15
❑ 40 Eric Young .50 .15
❑ 41 Peter Bergeron .50 .15
❑ 42 Arthur Rhodes .50 .15
❑ 43 Bobby Jones .50 .15
❑ 44 Matt Clement .75 .23
❑ 45 Pedro Martinez 1.25 .35
❑ 46 Jose Canseco 1.25 .35
❑ 47 Matt Anderson .50 .15
❑ 48 Torii Hunter .75 .23
❑ 49 Carlos Lee .75 .23
❑ 50 Eric Chavez .75 .23
❑ 51 Rick Helling .50 .15
❑ 52 John Franco .75 .23
❑ 53 Mike Bordick .75 .23
❑ 54 Andres Galarraga .75 .23
❑ 55 Jose Cruz Jr. .50 .15
❑ 56 Mike Matheny .50 .15
❑ 57 Randy Johnson 2.00 .60
❑ 58 Richie Sexson .75 .23
❑ 59 Vladimir Nunez .50 .15
❑ 60 Aaron Boone .75 .23
❑ 61 Darin Erstad .75 .23
❑ 62 Alex Gonzalez .50 .15
❑ 63 Gil Heredia .50 .15
❑ 64 Shane Andrews .50 .15
❑ 65 Todd Hundley .50 .15
❑ 66 Bill Mueller .75 .23
❑ 67 Mark McLemore .50 .15
❑ 68 Scott Spiezio .50 .15
❑ 69 Kevin McGlinchy .50 .15
❑ 70 Manny Ramirez 1.25 .35
❑ 71 Mike Lamb .50 .15
❑ 72 Brian Buchanan .50 .15
❑ 73 Mike Sweeney .75 .23
❑ 74 John Wetteland .75 .23
❑ 75 Rob Bell .50 .15
❑ 76 John Burkett .50 .15
❑ 77 Derek Jeter 5.00 1.50
❑ 78 J.D. Drew .75 .23
❑ 79 Jose Offerman .50 .15
❑ 80 Rick Reed .50 .15
❑ 81 Will Clark 1.25 .35
❑ 82 Rickey Henderson 2.00 .60
❑ 83 Kirk Rueter .50 .15
❑ 84 Lee Stevens .50 .15
❑ 85 Jay Bell .75 .23
❑ 86 Fred McGriff 1.25 .35
❑ 87 Julio Zuleta .50 .15

❑ 88 Brian Anderson .50 .15
❑ 89 Orlando Cabrera .75 .23
❑ 90 Alex Fernandez .50 .15
❑ 91 Derek Bell .50 .15
❑ 92 Eric Owens .50 .15
❑ 93 Dennys Reyes .50 .15
❑ 94 Mike Stanley .50 .15
❑ 95 Jorge Posada 1.25 .35
❑ 96 Paul Konerko .75 .23
❑ 97 Mike Remlinger .50 .15
❑ 98 Travis Lee .50 .15
❑ 99 Ken Caminiti .75 .23
❑ 100 Kevin Barker .50 .15
❑ 101 Ozzie Guillen .75 .23
❑ 102 Randy Wolf .50 .15
❑ 103 Michael Tucker .50 .15
❑ 104 Darren Lewis .50 .15
❑ 105 Joe Randa .50 .15
❑ 106 Jeff Cirillo .50 .15
❑ 107 David Ortiz 1.25 .35
❑ 108 Herb Perry .50 .15
❑ 109 Jeff Nelson .50 .15
❑ 110 Chris Stynes .50 .15
❑ 111 Johnny Damon 1.25 .35
❑ 112 Jason Schmidt .75 .23
❑ 113 Charles Johnson .50 .15
❑ 114 Pat Burrell .75 .23
❑ 115 Gary Sheffield .75 .23
❑ 116 Tom Glavine 1.25 .35
❑ 117 Jason Isringhausen .75 .23
❑ 118 Chris Carpenter .75 .23
❑ 119 Jeff Suppan .50 .15
❑ 120 Ivan Rodriguez 1.25 .35
❑ 121 Luis Sojo .50 .15
❑ 122 Ron Villone .50 .15
❑ 123 Mike Sirotka .50 .15
❑ 124 Chuck Knoblauch .75 .23
❑ 125 Jason Kendall .75 .23
❑ 126 Bobby Estalella .50 .15
❑ 127 Jose Guillen .75 .23
❑ 128 Carlos Delgado .75 .23
❑ 129 Benji Gil .50 .15
❑ 130 Einar Diaz .50 .15
❑ 131 Andy Benes .50 .15
❑ 132 Adrian Beltre .75 .23
❑ 133 Roger Clemens 4.00 1.20
❑ 134 Scott Williamson .50 .15
❑ 135 Brad Penny .50 .15
❑ 136 Troy Glaus .75 .23
❑ 137 Kevin Appier .75 .23
❑ 138 Walt Weiss .50 .15
❑ 139 Michael Barrett .50 .15
❑ 140 Mike Hampton .75 .23
❑ 141 Francisco Cordova .50 .15
❑ 142 David Segui .50 .15
❑ 143 Carlos Febles .50 .15
❑ 144 Roy Halladay .75 .23
❑ 145 Seth Etherton .50 .15
❑ 146 Fernando Tatis .50 .15
❑ 147 Livan Hernandez .75 .23
❑ 148 B.J. Surhoff .75 .23
❑ 149 Barry Larkin 1.25 .35
❑ 150 Bobby Howry .50 .15
❑ 151 Dmitri Young .75 .23
❑ 152 Brian Hunter .50 .15
❑ 153 A.Rodriguez Rangers 3.00 .90
❑ 154 Hideo Nomo 2.00 .60
❑ 155 Warren Morris .50 .15
❑ 156 Antonio Alfonseca .50 .15
❑ 157 Edgardo Alfonzo .50 .15
❑ 158 Mark Grudzielanek .50 .15
❑ 159 Fernando Vina .50 .15
❑ 160 Homer Bush .50 .15
❑ 161 Jason Giambi .75 .23
❑ 162 Steve Karsay .50 .15
❑ 163 Matt Lawton .50 .15
❑ 164 Rusty Greer .75 .23
❑ 165 Billy Koch .50 .15
❑ 166 Todd Hollandsworth .50 .15
❑ 167 Raul Ibanez .50 .15
❑ 168 Tony Gwynn 2.50 .75
❑ 169 Carl Everett .75 .23
❑ 170 Hector Carrasco .50 .15
❑ 171 Jose Valentin .50 .15
❑ 172 Deivi Cruz .50 .15
❑ 173 Bret Boone .75 .23
❑ 174 Melvin Mora .75 .23
❑ 175 Danny Graves .50 .15
❑ 176 Jose Jimenez .50 .15
❑ 177 James Baldwin .50 .15
❑ 178 C.J. Nitkowski .50 .15
❑ 179 Jeff Zimmerman .50 .15
❑ 180 Mike Lowell .75 .23
❑ 181 Hideki Irabu .50 .15
❑ 182 Greg Vaughn .50 .15
❑ 183 Omar Daal .50 .15
❑ 184 Darren Dreifort .50 .15
❑ 185 Gil Meche .50 .15
❑ 186 Damian Jackson .50 .15
❑ 187 Frank Thomas 2.00 .60
❑ 188 Luis Castillo .50 .15
❑ 189 Bartolo Colon .75 .23
❑ 190 Craig Biggio 1.25 .35
❑ 191 Scott Schoeneweis .50 .15
❑ 192 Dave Veres .50 .15
❑ 193 Ramon Martinez .50 .15
❑ 194 Jose Vidro .50 .15
❑ 195 Todd Helton 1.25 .35
❑ 196 Greg Norton .50 .15
❑ 197 Jacque Jones .75 .23
❑ 198 Jason Grimsley .50 .15
❑ 199 Dan Reichert .50 .15
❑ 200 Robb Nen .75 .23
❑ 201 Scott Hatteberg .50 .15
❑ 202 Terry Shumpert .50 .15
❑ 203 Kevin Millar .75 .23
❑ 204 Ismael Valdes .50 .15
❑ 205 Richard Hidalgo .50 .15
❑ 206 Randy Velarde .50 .15
❑ 207 Bengie Molina .50 .15
❑ 208 Tony Womack .50 .15
❑ 209 Enrique Wilson .50 .15
❑ 210 Jeff Brantley .50 .15
❑ 211 Rick Ankiel .50 .15
❑ 212 Terry Mulholland .50 .15
❑ 213 Ron Belliard .50 .15
❑ 214 Terrence Long .50 .15
❑ 215 Alberto Castillo .50 .15
❑ 216 Royce Clayton .50 .15
❑ 217 Joe McEwing .50 .15
❑ 218 Jason McDonald .50 .15
❑ 219 Ricky Bottalico .50 .15
❑ 220 Keith Foulke .75 .23
❑ 221 Brad Radke .75 .23
❑ 222 Gabe Kapler .75 .23
❑ 223 Pedro Astacio .50 .15
❑ 224 Armando Reynoso .50 .15
❑ 225 Darryl Kile .75 .23
❑ 226 Reggie Sanders .75 .23
❑ 227 Esteban Yan .50 .15
❑ 228 Joe Nathan .75 .23
❑ 229 Jay Payton .50 .15
❑ 230 Francisco Cordero .50 .15
❑ 231 Gregg Jefferies .50 .15
❑ 232 LaTroy Hawkins .50 .15
❑ 233 Jacob Cruz .50 .15
❑ 234 Chris Holt .50 .15
❑ 235 Vladimir Guerrero 2.00 .60
❑ 236 Marvin Benard .50 .15
❑ 237 Alex Ramirez .50 .15
❑ 238 Mike Williams .50 .15
❑ 239 Sean Bergman .50 .15
❑ 240 Juan Encarnacion .50 .15
❑ 241 Russ Davis .50 .15
❑ 242 Ramon Hernandez .50 .15
❑ 243 Sandy Alomar Jr. .50 .15
❑ 244 Eddie Guardado .50 .15
❑ 245 Shane Halter .50 .15
❑ 246 Geoff Jenkins .50 .15
❑ 247 Brian Meadows .50 .15
❑ 248 Damian Miller .50 .15
❑ 249 Darrin Fletcher .50 .15
❑ 250 Rafael Furcal .75 .23
❑ 251 Mark Grace 1.25 .35
❑ 252 Mark Mulder .75 .23
❑ 253 Joe Torre MG 1.25 .35
❑ 254 Bobby Cox MG .50 .15
❑ 255 Mike Scioscia MG .50 .15
❑ 256 Mike Hargrove MG .50 .15
❑ 257 Jimy Williams MG .50 .15
❑ 258 Jerry Manuel MG .50 .15
❑ 259 Charlie Manuel MG .50 .15
❑ 260 Don Baylor MG .75 .23
❑ 261 Phil Garner MG .75 .23
❑ 262 Tony Muser MG .50 .15
❑ 263 Buddy Bell MG .75 .23
❑ 264 Tom Kelly MG .50 .15
❑ 265 John Boles MG .50 .15
❑ 266 Art Howe MG .50 .15
❑ 267 Larry Dierker MG .50 .15
❑ 268 Lou Piniella MG .75 .23
❑ 269 Larry Rothschild MG .50 .15
❑ 270 Davey Lopes MG .75 .23
❑ 271 Johnny Oates MG .50 .15
❑ 272 Felipe Alou MG .50 .15
❑ 273 Bobby Valentine MG .50 .15
❑ 274 Tony LaRussa MG .50 .15
❑ 275 Bruce Bochy MG .50 .15
❑ 276 Dusty Baker MG .75 .23
❑ 277 Adrian Gonzalez 1.00 .30
Adam Johnson
❑ 278 Matt Wheatland 1.00 .30
Bryan Digby
❑ 279 Tripper Johnson 1.00 .30
Scott Thorman
❑ 280 Phil Dumatrait 1.00 .30
Adam Wainwright
❑ 281 Scott Heard 1.50 .45
David Parrish RC
❑ 282 Rocco Baldelli 1.50 .45
Mark Folsom
❑ 283 Dominic Rich RC 1.50 .45
Aaron Herr
❑ 284 Mike Stodolka 1.00 .30
Sean Burnett
❑ 285 Derek Thompson 1.00 .30
Corey Smith
❑ 286 Danny Borrell 1.50 .45
Jason Bourgeois RC
❑ 287 Chin-Feng Chen 1.00 .30
Corey Patterson
Josh Hamilton
❑ 288 Ryan Anderson 2.00 .60
Barry Zito
C.C. Sabathia
❑ 289 Scott Sobkowiak 2.00 .60
David Walling
Ben Sheets
❑ 290 Ty Howington 1.00 .30
Josh Kalinowski
Josh Girdley
❑ 291 Hee Seop Choi 2.50 .75
Aaron McNeal
Jason Hart
❑ 292 Bobby Bradley 1.50 .45
Kurt Ainsworth
Chin-Hui Tsao
❑ 293 Mike Glendenning 1.00 .30
Kenny Kelly
Juan Silvestre
❑ 294 J.R. House 1.00 .30
Ramon Castro
Ben Davis
❑ 295 Chance Caple 1.50 .45
Rafael Soriano
Pasqual Coco
❑ 296 Travis Hafner RC 8.00 2.40
Eric Munson
Bucky Jacobsen
❑ 297 Jason Conti 1.00 .30
Chris Wakeland
Brian Cole
❑ 298 Scott Seabol 2.50 .75
Aubrey Huff
Joe Crede
❑ 299 Adam Everett 1.00 .30
Jose Ortiz
Keith Ginter
❑ 300 Carlos Hernandez 1.00 .30
Geraldo Guzman
Adam Eaton
❑ 301 Bobby Kielty 1.50 .45
Milton Bradley
Juan Rivera
❑ 302 Mark McGwire GM 2.50 .75
❑ 303 Don Larsen GM .75 .23
❑ 304 Bobby Thomson GM .75 .23
❑ 305 Bill Mazeroski GM .75 .23

☐ 306 Reggie Jackson GM ...... 1.25 .35
☐ 307 Kirk Gibson GM .... 1.25 .35
☐ 308 Roger Maris GM .... 1.25 .35
☐ 309 Cal Ripken GM .... 3.00 .90
☐ 310 Hank Aaron GM............. 2.00 .60
☐ 311 Joe Carter GM................ .75 .23
☐ 312 Cal Ripken SH .... 3.00 .90
☐ 313 Randy Johnson SH .... 1.25 .35
☐ 314 Ken Griffey Jr. SH .... 2.00 .60
☐ 315 Troy Glaus SH................. .75 .23
☐ 316 Kazuhiro Sasaki SH......... .75 .23
☐ 317 Sammy Sosa .... 1.25 .35
Troy Glaus LL
☐ 318 Todd Helton .... .75 .23
Edgar Martinez LL
☐ 319 Todd Helton .... 2.00 .60
Nomar Garicaparra LL
☐ 320 Barry Bonds .... 2.00 .60
Jason Giambi LL
☐ 321 Todd Helton .... .75 .23
Manny Ramirez LL
☐ 322 Todd Helton .... .75 .23
Darin Erstad LL
☐ 323 Kevin Brown .... 1.25 .35
Pedro Martinez LL
☐ 324 Randy Johnson .... 1.25 .35
Pedro Martinez LL
☐ 325 Will Clark HL.................. 1.25 .35
☐ 326 New York Mets HL .... 2.00 .60
☐ 327 New York Yankees HL.... 3.00 .90
☐ 328 Seattle Mariners HL.......... .75 .23
☐ 329 Mike Hampton HL .... .75 .23
☐ 330 New York Yankees HL 4.00 1.20
☐ 331 N.Y. Yankees Champs.... 8.00 2.40
☐ 332 Jeff Bagwell................... 1.25 .35
☐ 333 Andy Pettitte .... 1.25 .35
☐ 334 Tony Armas Jr. .... .50 .15
☐ 335 Jeromy Burnitz .... .75 .23
☐ 336 Javier Vazquez................. .75 .23
☐ 337 Eric Karros .... .75 .23
☐ 338 Brian Giles .... .75 .23
☐ 339 Scott Rolen .... 1.25 .35
☐ 340 David Justice.................... .75 .23
☐ 341 Ray Durham .... .75 .23
☐ 342 Todd Zeile .... .75 .23
☐ 343 Cliff Floyd .... .75 .23
☐ 344 Barry Bonds 5.00 1.50
☐ 345 Matt Williams .... .75 .23
☐ 346 Steve Finley...................... .75 .23
☐ 347 Scott Elarton .... .50 .15
☐ 348 Bernie Williams............. 1.25 .35
☐ 349 David Wells....................... .75 .23
☐ 350 J.T. Snow .... .75 .23
☐ 351 Al Leiter............................ .75 .23
☐ 352 Magglio Ordonez.............. .75 .23
☐ 353 Raul Mondesi .... .75 .23
☐ 354 Tim Salmon.................... 1.25 .35
☐ 355 Jeff Kent .... .75 .23
☐ 356 Mariano Rivera .... 1.25 .35
☐ 357 John Olerud .... .75 .23
☐ 358 Javy Lopez .... .75 .23
☐ 359 Ben Grieve........................ .50 .15
☐ 360 Ray Lankford .... .75 .23
☐ 361 Ken Griffey Jr. .... 3.00 .90
☐ 362 Rich Aurilia .... .50 .15
☐ 363 Andruw Jones .... 1.25 .35
☐ 364 Ryan Klesko .... .75 .23
☐ 365 Roberto Alomar............. 1.25 .35
☐ 366 Miguel Tejada .... .75 .23
☐ 367 Mo Vaughn .... .75 .23
☐ 368 Albert Belle .... .75 .23
☐ 369 Jose Canseco .... 1.25 .35
☐ 370 Kevin Brown .... .75 .23
☐ 371 Rafael Palmeiro............. 1.25 .35
☐ 372 Mark Redman .... .50 .15
☐ 373 Larry Walker .... .75 .23
☐ 374 Greg Maddux .... 3.00 .90
☐ 375 Nomar Garciaparra .... 3.00 .90
☐ 376 Kevin Millwood .... .50 .15
☐ 377 Edgar Martinez .... 1.25 .35
☐ 378 Sammy Sosa.................. 2.00 .60
☐ 379 Tim Hudson .... .75 .23
☐ 380 Jim Edmonds .... 1.25 .35
☐ 381 Mike Piazza................... 3.00 .90
☐ 382 Brant Brown .... .50 .15
☐ 383 Brad Fullmer .... .50 .15
☐ 384 Alan Benes .... .50 .15
☐ 385 Mickey Morandini .... .50 .15
☐ 386 Troy Percival .... .75 .23
☐ 387 Eddie Perez .... .50 .15
☐ 388 Vernon Wells.................... .75 .23
☐ 389 Ricky Gutierrez .... .50 .15
☐ 390 Rondell White .... .75 .23
☐ 391 Kelvim Escobar .... .50 .15
☐ 392 Tony Batista .... .50 .15
☐ 393 Jimmy Haynes.................. .50 .15
☐ 394 Billy Wagner .... .75 .23
☐ 395 A.J. Hinch .... .50 .15
☐ 396 Matt Morris....................... .75 .23
☐ 397 Lance Berkman .... .75 .23
☐ 398 Jeff D'Amico .... .50 .15
☐ 399 Octavio Dotel.................... .50 .15
☐ 400 Olmedo Saenz .... .50 .15
☐ 401 Esteban Loaiza .... .50 .15
☐ 402 Adam Kennedy .... .50 .15
☐ 403 Moises Alou .... .75 .23
☐ 404 Orlando Palmeiro .... .50 .15
☐ 405 Kevin Young .... .50 .15
☐ 406 Tom Goodwin .... .50 .15
☐ 407 Mac Suzuki .... .75 .23
☐ 408 Pat Hentgen...................... .50 .15
☐ 409 Kevin Stocker .... .50 .15
☐ 410 Mark Sweeney .... .50 .15
☐ 411 Tony Eusebio .... .50 .15
☐ 412 Edgar Renteria.................. .75 .23
☐ 413 John Rocker .... .75 .23
☐ 414 Jose Lima .... .50 .15
☐ 415 Kerry Wood .... .75 .23
☐ 416 Mike Timlin....................... .50 .15
☐ 417 Jose Hernandez................. .50 .15
☐ 418 Jeremy Giambi .... .50 .15
☐ 419 Luis Lopez......................... .50 .15
☐ 420 Mitch Meluskey................. .50 .15
☐ 421 Garrett Stephenson .... .50 .15
☐ 422 Jamey Wright .... .50 .15
☐ 423 John Jaha .... .50 .15
☐ 424 Placido Polanco .... .50 .15
☐ 425 Marty Cordova .... .50 .15
☐ 426 Joey Hamilton .... .50 .15
☐ 427 Travis Fryman .... .75 .23
☐ 428 Mike Cameron................... .50 .15
☐ 429 Matt Mantei .... .50 .15
☐ 430 Chan Ho Park .... .75 .23
☐ 431 Shawn Estes .... .50 .15
☐ 432 Danny Bautista .... .50 .15
☐ 433 Wilson Alvarez .... .50 .15
☐ 434 Kenny Lofton..................... .75 .23
☐ 435 Russ Ortiz .... .75 .23
☐ 436 Dave Burba .... .50 .15
☐ 437 Felix Martinez .... .50 .15
☐ 438 Jeff Shaw........................... .50 .15
☐ 439 Mike DiFelice .... .50 .15
☐ 440 Roberto Hernandez .... .50 .15
☐ 441 Bryan Rekar...................... .50 .15
☐ 442 Ugueth Urbina................... .50 .15
☐ 443 Vinny Castilla .... .75 .23
☐ 444 Carlos Perez .... .50 .15
☐ 445 Juan Guzman .... .50 .15
☐ 446 Ryan Rupe......................... .50 .15
☐ 447 Mike Mordecai .... .50 .15
☐ 448 Ricardo Rincon .... .50 .15
☐ 449 Curt Schilling .... .75 .23
☐ 450 Alex Cora .... .50 .15
☐ 451 Turner Ward .... .50 .15
☐ 452 Omar Vizquel................. 1.25 .35
☐ 453 Russ Branyan .... .50 .15
☐ 454 Russ Johnson .... .50 .15
☐ 455 Greg Colbrunn .... .50 .15
☐ 456 Charles Nagy..................... .50 .15
☐ 457 Wil Cordero....................... .50 .15
☐ 458 Jason Tyner....................... .50 .15
☐ 459 Devon White .... .75 .23
☐ 460 Kelly Stinnett..................... .50 .15
☐ 461 Wilton Guerrero................ .50 .15
☐ 462 Jason Bere .... .50 .15
☐ 463 Calvin Murray .... .50 .15
☐ 464 Miguel Batista................... .50 .15
☐ 466 Luis Gonzalez .... .75 .23
☐ 467 Jaret Wright...................... .50 .15
☐ 468 Chad Kreuter.................... .50 .15
☐ 469 Armando Benitez.............. .75 .23
☐ 470 Erubiel Durazo.................. .50 .15
☐ 470 Sidney Ponson .... .50 .15
☐ 471 Adrian Brown .... .50 .15
☐ 472 Sterling Hitchcock............ .50 .15
☐ 473 Timo Perez .... .50 .15
☐ 474 Jamie Moyer .... .75 .23
☐ 475 Delino DeShields .... .50 .15
☐ 476 Glendon Rusch .... .50 .15
☐ 477 Chris Gomez .... .50 .15
☐ 478 Adam Eaton....................... .50 .15
☐ 479 Pablo Ozuna .... .50 .15
☐ 480 Bob Abreu......................... .75 .23
☐ 481 Kris Benson....................... .50 .15
☐ 482 Keith Osik .... .50 .15
☐ 483 Darryl Hamilton................. .50 .15
☐ 484 Marlon Anderson .... .50 .15
☐ 485 Jimmy Anderson............... .50 .15
☐ 486 John Halama..................... .50 .15
☐ 487 Nelson Figueroa .... .50 .15
☐ 488 Alex Gonzalez .... .50 .15
☐ 489 Benny Agbayani .... .50 .15
☐ 490 Ed Sprague .... .50 .15
☐ 491 Scott Erickson................... .50 .15
☐ 492 Doug Glanville .... .50 .15
☐ 493 Jesus Sanchez................... .50 .15
☐ 494 Mike Lieberthal .... .50 .15
☐ 495 Aaron Sele......................... .50 .15
☐ 496 Pat Mahomes.................... .50 .15
☐ 497 Ruben Rivera.................... .50 .15
☐ 498 Wayne Gomes................... .50 .15
☐ 499 Freddy Garcia .... .75 .23
☐ 500 Al Martin........................... .50 .15
☐ 501 Woody Williams .... .50 .15
☐ 502 Paul Byrd .... .50 .15
☐ 503 Rick White......................... .50 .15
☐ 504 Trevor Hoffman .... .75 .23
☐ 505 Brady Anderson................ .75 .23
☐ 506 Robert Person .... .50 .15
☐ 507 Jeff Conine .... .75 .23
☐ 508 Chris Truby .... .50 .15
☐ 509 Emil Brown .... .50 .15
☐ 510 Ryan Dempster .... .50 .15
☐ 511 Ruben Mateo..................... .50 .15
☐ 512 Alex Ochoa .... .50 .15
☐ 513 Jose Rosado .... .50 .15
☐ 514 Masato Yoshii .... .50 .15
☐ 515 Brian Daubach................... .50 .15
☐ 516 Jeff D'Amico .... .50 .15
☐ 517 Brent Mayne .... .50 .15
☐ 518 John Thomson .... .50 .15
☐ 519 Todd Ritchie .... .50 .15
☐ 520 John VanderWal .... .50 .15
☐ 521 Neifi Perez......................... .50 .15
☐ 522 Chad Curtis....................... .50 .15
☐ 523 Kenny Rogers .... .75 .23
☐ 524 Trot Nixon......................... .75 .23
☐ 525 Sean Casey .... 1.25 .35
☐ 526 Wilton Veras .... .50 .15
☐ 527 Troy O'Leary .... .50 .15
☐ 528 Dante Bichette .... .75 .23
☐ 529 Jose Silva .... .50 .15
☐ 530 Darren Oliver.................... .50 .15
☐ 531 Steve Parris....................... .50 .15
☐ 532 David McCarty .... .50 .15
☐ 533 Todd Walker .... .50 .15
☐ 534 Brian Rose......................... .50 .15
☐ 535 Pete Schourek................... .50 .15
☐ 536 Ricky Ledee....................... .50 .15
☐ 537 Justin Thompson .... .50 .15
☐ 538 Benito Santiago................ .75 .23
☐ 539 Carlos Beltran................... .75 .23
☐ 540 Gabe White .... .50 .15
☐ 541 Bret Saberhagen .... .75 .23
☐ 542 Ramon Martinez .... .50 .15
☐ 543 John Valentin .... .50 .15
☐ 544 Frank Catalanotto .... .50 .15
☐ 545 Tim Wakefield .... .75 .23
☐ 546 Michael Tucker .... .50 .15
☐ 547 Juan Pierre .... .75 .23
☐ 548 Rich Garces....................... .50 .15
☐ 549 Luis Ordaz......................... .50 .15
☐ 550 Jerry Spradlin .... .50 .15
☐ 551 Corey Koskie..................... .50 .15
☐ 552 Cal Eldred .... .50 .15
☐ 553 Alfonso Soriano .... 1.25 .35
☐ 554 Kip Wells........................... .50 .15
☐ 555 Orlando Hernandez .... .75 .23

❑ 556 Bill Simas .50 .15
❑ 557 Jim Parque .50 .15
❑ 558 Joe Mays .50 .15
❑ 559 Tim Belcher .50 .15
❑ 560 Shane Spencer .50 .15
❑ 561 Glenallen Hill .50 .15
❑ 562 Matt LeCroy .50 .15
❑ 563 Tino Martinez 1.25 .35
❑ 564 Eric Milton .50 .15
❑ 565 Ron Coomer .50 .15
❑ 566 Cristian Guzman .50 .15
❑ 567 Kazuhiro Sasaki .75 .23
❑ 568 Mark Quinn .50 .15
❑ 569 Eric Gagne .75 .23
❑ 570 Kerry Ligtenberg .50 .15
❑ 571 Rolando Arrojo .50 .15
❑ 572 Jon Lieber .50 .15
❑ 573 Jose Vizcaino .50 .15
❑ 574 Jeff Abbott .50 .15
❑ 575 Carlos Hernandez .50 .15
❑ 576 Scott Sullivan .50 .15
❑ 577 Matt Stairs .50 .15
❑ 578 Tom Lampkin .50 .15
❑ 579 Donnie Sadler .50 .15
❑ 580 Desi Relaford .50 .15
❑ 581 Scott Downs .50 .15
❑ 582 Mike Mussina 1.25 .35
❑ 583 Ramon Ortiz .50 .15
❑ 584 Mike Myers .50 .15
❑ 585 Frank Castillo .50 .15
❑ 586 Manny Ramirez Sox 1.25 .35
❑ 587 Alex Rodriguez 3.00 .90
❑ 588 Andy Ashby .50 .15
❑ 589 Felipe Crespo .50 .15
❑ 590 Bobby Bonilla .75 .23
❑ 591 Denny Neagle .50 .15
❑ 592 Dave Martinez .50 .15
❑ 593 Mike Hampton .75 .23
❑ 594 Gary DiSarcina .50 .15
❑ 595 Tsuyoshi Shinjo RC 2.00 .60
❑ 596 Albert Pujols RC 60.00 18.00
❑ 597 Roy Oswalt 2.00 .60
Pat Strange
Jon Rauch
❑ 598 Phil Wilson RC 10.00 3.00
Jake Peavy RC
Darwin Cubillan RC UER
Peavy is spelled incorrectly
❑ 599 Nathan Haynes 1.00 .30
Steve Smyth RC
Mike Bynum
❑ 600 Joe Lawrence 1.00 .30
Choo Freeman
Michael Cuddyer
❑ 601 Larry Barnes 1.00 .30
DeWayne Wise
Carlos Pena
❑ 602 Feilpe Lopez 1.50 .45
Gookie Dawkins
Eric Almonte RC
❑ 603 Brad Wilkerson 1.00 .30
Alex Escobar
Eric Valent
❑ 604 Jeff Goldbach 1.00 .30
Toby Hall
Rod Barajas
❑ 605 Marcus Giles 1.50 .45
Pablo Ozuna
Jason Romano
❑ 606 Vernon Wells 1.50 .45
Jack Cust
Dee Brown
❑ 607 Luis Montanez RC 1.50 .45
David Espinosa
❑ 608 Anthony Pluta RC 1.50 .45
Justin Wayne RC
❑ 609 Josh Axelson RC 1.50 .45
Carmen Cali RC
❑ 610 Shaun Boyd RC 1.50 .45
Chris Morris RC
❑ 611 Dan Moylan RC 1.50 .45
Tommy Arko RC
❑ 612 Luis Cotto RC 1.00 .30
Luis Escobar
❑ 613 Blake Williams RC 1.50 .45
Brandon Mims RC
❑ 614 Chris Russ RC 1.00 .30
Bryan Edwards
❑ 615 Joe Torres 1.00 .30
Ben Diggins
❑ 616 Hugh Quattlebaum RC 5.00 1.50
Edwin Encarnacion RC
❑ 617 Brian Bass RC 1.50 .45
Odannis Ayala RC
❑ 618 Jason Kaanoi 1.00 .30
Michael Matthews RC UER
name misspelled Mathews
❑ 619 Stuart McFarland RC 1.50 .45
Adam Sterrett RC
❑ 620 David Krynzel 2.00 .60
Grady Sizemore
❑ 621 Keith Bucktrot 1.00 .30
Dane Sardinha
❑ 622 Anaheim Angels TC .75 .23
❑ 623 Ariz. Diamondbacks TC .75 .23
❑ 624 Atlanta Braves TC .75 .23
❑ 625 Baltimore Orioles TC .75 .23
❑ 626 Boston Red Sox TC .75 .23
❑ 627 Chicago Cubs TC .75 .23
❑ 628 Chicago White Sox TC .75 .23
❑ 629 Cincinnati Reds TC .75 .23
❑ 630 Cleveland Indians TC .75 .23
❑ 631 Colorado Rockies TC .75 .23
❑ 632 Detroit Tigers TC .75 .23
❑ 633 Florida Marlins TC .75 .23
❑ 634 Houston Astros TC .75 .23
❑ 635 K.C. Royals TC .75 .23
❑ 636 L.A. Dodgers TC .75 .23
❑ 637 Milw. Brewers TC .75 .23
❑ 638 Minnesota Twins TC .75 .23
❑ 639 Montreal Expos TC .75 .23
❑ 640 New York Mets TC .75 .23
❑ 641 New York Yankees TC 4.00 1.20
❑ 642 Oakland Athletics TC .75 .23
❑ 643 Phil. Phillies TC .75 .23
❑ 644 Pittsburgh Pirates TC .75 .23
❑ 645 San Diego Padres TC .75 .23
❑ 646 S.F. Giants TC .75 .23
❑ 647 Seattle Mariners TC .75 .23
❑ 648 St. Louis Cardinals TC .75 .23
❑ 649 T. Bay Devil Rays TC .75 .23
❑ 650 Texas Rangers TC .75 .23
❑ 651 Toronto Blue Jays TC .75 .23
❑ 652 Bucky Dent GM .50 .15
❑ 653 Jackie Robinson GM 2.00 .60
❑ 654 Roberto Clemente GM 2.50 .75
❑ 655 Nolan Ryan GM 3.00 .90
❑ 656 Kerry Wood GM .75 .23
❑ 657 Rickey Henderson GM 2.00 .60
❑ 658 Lou Brock GM 1.25 .35
❑ 659 David Wells GM .50 .15
❑ 660 Andruw Jones GM .75 .23
❑ 661 Carlton Fisk GM .75 .23

2001 Topps Chrome Traded

	Nm-Mt	Ex-Mt
COMPLETE SET (266)	150.00	45.00
COMMON (1-99/145-266)	.75	.23
COMMON (100-144)	1.25	.35

❑ T1 Sandy Alomar Jr. .75 .23
❑ T2 Kevin Appier 1.25 .35
❑ T3 Brad Ausmus 1.25 .35
❑ T4 Derek Bell .75 .23
❑ T5 Bret Boone 1.25 .35
❑ T6 Rico Brogna .75 .23
❑ T7 Ellis Burks 1.25 .35
❑ T8 Ken Caminiti 1.25 .35
❑ T9 Roger Cedeno .75 .23
❑ T10 Royce Clayton .75 .23
❑ T11 Enrique Wilson .75 .23
❑ T12 Rheal Cormier .75 .23
❑ T13 Eric Davis 1.25 .35
❑ T14 Shawon Dunston .75 .23
❑ T15 Andres Galarraga 1.25 .35
❑ T16 Tom Gordon .75 .23
❑ T17 Mark Grace 2.00 .60
❑ T18 Jeffrey Hammonds .75 .23
❑ T19 Dustin Hermanson .75 .23
❑ T20 Quinton McCracken .75 .23
❑ T21 Todd Hundley .75 .23
❑ T22 Charles Johnson 1.25 .35
❑ T23 Marquis Grissom 1.25 .35
❑ T24 Jose Mesa .75 .23
❑ T25 Brian Boehringer .75 .23
❑ T26 John Rocker 1.25 .35
❑ T27 Jeff Frye .75 .23
❑ T28 Reggie Sanders 1.25 .35
❑ T29 David Segui .75 .23
❑ T30 Mike Sirotka .75 .23
❑ T31 Fernando Tatis .75 .23
❑ T32 Steve Trachsel .75 .23
❑ T33 Ismael Valdes .75 .23
❑ T34 Randy Velarde .75 .23
❑ T35 Ryan Kohlmeier .75 .23
❑ T36 Mike Bordick 1.25 .35
❑ T37 Kent Bottenfield .75 .23
❑ T38 Pat Rapp .75 .23
❑ T39 Jeff Nelson .75 .23
❑ T40 Ricky Bottalico .75 .23
❑ T41 Luke Prokopec .75 .23
❑ T42 Hideo Nomo 3.00 .90
❑ T43 Bill Mueller 1.25 .35
❑ T44 Roberto Kelly .75 .23
❑ T45 Chris Holt .75 .23
❑ T46 Mike Jackson .75 .23
❑ T47 Devon White 1.25 .35
❑ T48 Gerald Williams .75 .23
❑ T49 Eddie Taubensee .75 .23
❑ T50 Brian Hunter UER .75 .23
Brian R Hunter pictured
Brian L Hunter stats
❑ T51 Nelson Cruz .75 .23
❑ T52 Jeff Fassero .75 .23
❑ T53 Bubba Trammell .75 .23
❑ T54 Bo Porter .75 .23
❑ T55 Greg Norton .75 .23
❑ T56 Benito Santiago 1.25 .35
❑ T57 Ruben Rivera .75 .23
❑ T58 Dee Brown .75 .23
❑ T59 Jose Canseco 2.00 .60
❑ T60 Chris Michalak .75 .23
❑ T61 Tim Worrell .75 .23
❑ T62 Matt Clement 1.25 .35
❑ T63 Bill Pulsipher .75 .23
❑ T64 Troy Brohawn RC 1.00 .30
❑ T65 Mark Kotsay 1.25 .35
❑ T66 Jimmy Rollins 1.25 .35
❑ T67 Shea Hillenbrand 1.25 .35
❑ T68 Ted Lilly .75 .23
❑ T69 Jermaine Dye 1.25 .35
❑ T70 Jerry Hairston Jr. .75 .23
❑ T71 John Mabry .75 .23
❑ T72 Kurt Abbott .75 .23
❑ T73 Eric Owens .75 .23
❑ T74 Jeff Brantley .75 .23
❑ T75 Roy Oswalt 2.00 .60
❑ T76 Doug Mientkiewicz 1.25 .35
❑ T77 Rickey Henderson 3.00 .90
❑ T78 Jason Grimsley .75 .23
❑ T79 Christian Parker RC 1.00 .30
❑ T80 Donne Wall .75 .23
❑ T81 Alex Arias .75 .23
❑ T82 Willis Roberts .75 .23
❑ T83 Ryan Minor .75 .23
❑ T84 Jason LaRue .75 .23
❑ T85 Ruben Sierra .75 .23
❑ T86 Johnny Damon 2.00 .60

❑ T87 Juan Gonzalez 1.25 .35
❑ T88 C.C. Sabathia 1.25 .35
❑ T89 Tony Batista .75 .23
❑ T90 Jay Witasick .75 .23
❑ T91 Brent Abernathy .75 .23
❑ T92 Paul LoDuca 1.25 .35
❑ T93 Wes Helms .75 .23
❑ T94 Mark Wohlers .75 .23
❑ T95 Rob Bell .75 .23
❑ T96 Tim Redding .75 .23
❑ T97 Bud Smith RC 1.00 .30
❑ T98 Adam Dunn 2.00 .60
❑ T99 Ichiro Suzuki 25.00 7.50
Albert Pujols ROY
❑ T100 Carlton Fisk 81 2.00 .60
❑ T101 Tim Raines 81 1.25 .35
❑ T102 Juan Marichal 74 1.25 .35
❑ T103 Dave Winfield 81 1.25 .35
❑ T104 Reggie Jackson 82 2.00 .60
❑ T105 Cal Ripken 82 10.00 3.00
❑ T106 Ozzie Smith 82 5.00 1.50
❑ T107 Tom Seaver 83 2.00 .60
❑ T108 Lou Piniella 74 1.25 .35
❑ T109 Dwight Gooden 84 1.25 .35
❑ T110 Bret Saberhagen 84 1.25 .35
❑ T111 Gary Carter 85 1.25 .35
❑ T112 Jack Clark 85 1.25 .35
❑ T113 Rickey Henderson 85 3.00 .90
❑ T114 Barry Bonds 86 8.00 2.40
❑ T115 Bobby Bonilla 86 1.25 .35
❑ T116 Jose Canseco 86 2.00 .60
❑ T117 Will Clark 86 2.00 .60
❑ T118 Andres Galarraga 86 1.25 .35
❑ T119 Bo Jackson 86 3.00 .90
❑ T120 Wally Joyner 86 1.25 .35
❑ T121 Ellis Burks 87 1.25 .35
❑ T122 David Cone 87 1.25 .35
❑ T123 Greg Maddux 87 5.00 1.50
❑ T124 Willie Randolph 76 1.25 .35
❑ T125 Dennis Eckersley 87 1.25 .35
❑ T126 Matt Williams 87 1.25 .35
❑ T127 Joe Morgan 81 1.25 .35
❑ T128 Fred McGriff 87 2.00 .60
❑ T129 Roberto Alomar 88 2.00 .60
❑ T130 Lee Smith 88 1.25 .35
❑ T131 David Wells 88 1.25 .35
❑ T132 Ken Griffey Jr. 89 5.00 1.50
❑ T133 Deion Sanders 89 2.00 .60
❑ T134 Nolan Ryan 89 8.00 2.40
❑ T135 David Justice 90 1.25 .35
❑ T136 Joe Carter 91 1.25 .35
❑ T137 Jack Morris 92 1.25 .35
❑ T138 Mike Piazza 93 5.00 1.50
❑ T139 Barry Bonds 93 8.00 2.40
❑ T140 Terrence Long 94 1.25 .35
❑ T141 Ben Grieve 94 1.25 .35
❑ T142 Richie Sexson 95 1.25 .35
George Arias
Mark Sweeney
Brian Schneider
❑ T143 Sean Burroughs 99 1.25 .35
❑ T144 Alfonso Soriano 99 2.00 .60
❑ T145 Bob Boone MG 1.25 .35
❑ T146 Larry Bowa MG 1.25 .35
❑ T147 Bob Brenly MG .75 .23
❑ T148 Buck Martinez MG .75 .23
❑ T149 L. McClendon MG .75 .23
❑ T150 Jim Tracy MG .75 .23
❑ T151 Jared Abruzzo RC 1.00 .30
❑ T152 Kurt Ainsworth .75 .23
❑ T153 Willie Bloomquist 1.25 .35
❑ T154 Ben Broussard .75 .23
❑ T155 Bobby Bradley .75 .23
❑ T156 Mike Bynum .75 .23
❑ T157 A.J. Hinch .75 .23
❑ T158 Ryan Christianson .75 .23
❑ T159 Carlos Silva .75 .23
❑ T160 Joe Crede 3.00 .90
❑ T161 Jack Cust .75 .23
❑ T162 Ben Diggins .75 .23
❑ T163 Phil Dumatrait .75 .23
❑ T164 Alex Escobar .75 .23
❑ T165 Miguel Olivo .75 .23
❑ T166 Chris George .75 .23
❑ T167 Marcus Giles 1.25 .35
❑ T168 Keith Ginter .75 .23
❑ T169 Josh Girdley .75 .23
❑ T170 Tony Alvarez .75 .23
❑ T171 Scott Seabol .75 .23
❑ T172 Josh Hamilton .75 .23
❑ T173 Jason Hart .75 .23
❑ T174 Israel Alcantara .75 .23
❑ T175 Jake Peavy 8.00 2.40
❑ T176 Stubby Clapp RC 1.00 .30
❑ T177 D'Angelo Jimenez .75 .23
❑ T178 Nick Johnson 1.25 .35
❑ T179 Ben Johnson .75 .23
❑ T180 Larry Bigbie .75 .23
❑ T181 Allen Levrault .75 .23
❑ T182 Felipe Lopez 1.25 .35
❑ T183 Sean Burnett .75 .23
❑ T184 Nick Neugebauer .75 .23
❑ T185 Austin Kearns 1.25 .35
❑ T186 Corey Patterson .75 .23
❑ T187 Carlos Pena .75 .23
❑ T188 R. Rodriguez RC 1.00 .30
❑ T189 Juan Rivera .75 .23
❑ T190 Grant Roberts .75 .23
❑ T191 Adam Pettyjohn RC 1.00 .30
❑ T192 Jared Sandberg .75 .23
❑ T193 Xavier Nady .75 .23
❑ T194 Dane Sardinha .75 .23
❑ T195 Shawn Sonnier .75 .23
❑ T196 Rafael Soriano 1.00 .30
❑ T197 Brian Specht RC 1.00 .30
❑ T198 Aaron Myette .75 .23
❑ T199 Juan Uribe RC 1.25 .35
❑ T200 Jayson Werth .75 .23
❑ T201 Brad Wilkerson .75 .23
❑ T202 Horacio Estrada .75 .23
❑ T203 Joel Pineiro 1.25 .35
❑ T204 Matt LeCroy .75 .23
❑ T205 Michael Coleman .75 .23
❑ T206 Ben Sheets 2.00 .60
❑ T207 Eric Byrnes .75 .23
❑ T208 Sean Burroughs .75 .23
❑ T209 Ken Harvey .75 .23
❑ T210 Travis Hafner 6.00 1.80
❑ T211 Erick Almonte 1.00 .30
❑ T212 Jason Belcher RC 1.00 .30
❑ T213 Wilson Betemit RC 1.25 .35
❑ T214 Hank Blalock RC 8.00 2.40
❑ T215 Danny Borrell 1.00 .30
❑ T216 John Buck RC 1.25 .35
❑ T217 Freddie Bynum RC 1.00 .30
❑ T218 Noel Devarez RC 1.00 .30
❑ T219 Juan Diaz RC 1.00 .30
❑ T220 Felix Diaz RC 1.00 .30
❑ T221 Josh Fogg RC 1.00 .30
❑ T222 Matt Ford RC 1.00 .30
❑ T223 Scott Heard .75 .23
❑ T224 Ben Hendrickson RC 1.00 .30
❑ T225 Cody Ross RC 1.00 .30
❑ T226 A. Hernandez RC 1.00 .30
❑ T227 Alfredo Amezaga RC 1.00 .30
❑ T228 Bob Keppel RC 1.00 .30
❑ T229 Ryan Madson RC 1.00 .30
❑ T230 Octavio Martinez RC 1.00 .30
❑ T231 Hee Seop Choi 2.00 .60
❑ T232 Thomas Mitchell .75 .23
❑ T233 Luis Montanez 1.00 .30
❑ T234 Andy Morales RC 1.00 .30
❑ T235 Justin Morneau RC 6.00 1.80
❑ T236 Toe Nash RC 1.00 .30
❑ T237 V. Pascucci RC 1.00 .30
❑ T238 Roy Smith RC 1.00 .30
❑ T239 Antonio Perez RC 1.25 .35
❑ T240 Chad Petty RC 1.00 .30
❑ T241 Steve Smyth 1.00 .30
❑ T242 Jose Reyes RC 10.00 3.00
❑ T243 Eric Reynolds RC 1.00 .30
❑ T244 Dominic Rich 1.00 .30
❑ T245 J. Richardson RC 1.00 .30
❑ T246 Ed Rogers RC 1.00 .30
❑ T247 Albert Pujols 60.00 18.00
❑ T248 Esix Snead RC 1.00 .30
❑ T249 Luis Torres RC 1.00 .30
❑ T250 Matt White RC 1.00 .30
❑ T251 Blake Williams 1.00 .30
❑ T252 Chris Russ 1.00 .30
❑ T253 Joe Kennedy RC 1.25 .35
❑ T254 Jeff Randazzo RC 1.00 .30
❑ T255 Beau Hale RC 1.00 .30
❑ T256 Brad Hennessey RC 2.00 .60
❑ T257 Jake Gautreau RC 1.00 .30
❑ T258 Jeff Mathis RC 1.25 .35
❑ T259 Aaron Heilman RC 1.00 .30
❑ T260 B. Sardinha RC 1.00 .30
❑ T261 Irvin Guzman RC 15.00 4.50
❑ T262 Gabe Gross RC 1.25 .35
❑ T263 J.D. Martin RC 1.00 .30
❑ T264 Chris Smith RC 1.00 .30
❑ T265 Kenny Baugh RC 1.00 .30
❑ T266 Ichiro Suzuki RC 30.00 9.00

2002 Topps Chrome

	Nm-Mt	Ex-Mt
COMPLETE SET (660)	300.00	90.00
COMPLETE SERIES 1 (330)	150.00	45.00
COMPLETE SERIES 2 (330)	150.00	45.00
COMMON (1-331/366-695)	.50	.15
COMMON (307-326/671-690)	1.50	.45
COMMON (327-331/691-695)	1.50	.45

❑ 1 Pedro Martinez 1.50 .45
❑ 2 Mike Stanton .50 .15
❑ 3 Brad Penny .50 .15
❑ 4 Mike Matheny .50 .15
❑ 5 Johnny Damon 1.50 .45
❑ 6 Bret Boone 1.00 .30
❑ 7 Does Not Exist .00
❑ 8 Chris Truby .50 .15
❑ 9 B.J. Surhoff 1.00 .30
❑ 10 Mike Hampton 1.00 .30
❑ 11 Juan Pierre 1.00 .30
❑ 12 Mark Buehrle 1.00 .30
❑ 13 Bob Abreu 1.00 .30
❑ 14 David Cone 1.00 .30
❑ 15 Aaron Sele .50 .15
❑ 16 Fernando Tatis .50 .15
❑ 17 Bobby Jones .50 .15
❑ 18 Rick Helling .50 .15
❑ 19 Dmitri Young 1.00 .30
❑ 20 Mike Mussina 1.50 .45
❑ 21 Mike Sweeney 1.00 .30
❑ 22 Cristian Guzman .50 .15
❑ 23 Ryan Kohlmeier .50 .15
❑ 24 Adam Kennedy .50 .15
❑ 25 Larry Walker 1.00 .30
❑ 26 Eric Davis 1.00 .30
❑ 27 Jason Tyner .50 .15
❑ 28 Eric Young .50 .15
❑ 29 Jason Marquis .50 .15
❑ 30 Luis Gonzalez 1.00 .30
❑ 31 Kevin Tapani .50 .15
❑ 32 Orlando Cabrera 1.00 .30
❑ 33 Marty Cordova .50 .15
❑ 34 Brad Ausmus 1.00 .30
❑ 35 Livan Hernandez 1.00 .30
❑ 36 Alex Gonzalez .50 .15
❑ 37 Edgar Renteria 1.00 .30
❑ 38 Bengie Molina .50 .15
❑ 39 Frank Menechino .50 .15
❑ 40 Rafael Palmeiro 1.50 .45
❑ 41 Brad Fullmer .50 .15
❑ 42 Julio Zuleta .50 .15
❑ 43 Darren Dreifort .50 .15
❑ 44 Trot Nixon 1.00 .30
❑ 45 Trevor Hoffman 1.00 .30
❑ 46 Vladimir Nunez .50 .15

❑ 47 Mark Kotsay 1.00 .30
❑ 48 Kenny Rogers 1.00 .30
❑ 49 Ben Petrick .50 .15
❑ 50 Jeff Bagwell 1.50 .45
❑ 51 Juan Encarnacion .50 .15
❑ 52 Ramiro Mendoza .50 .15
❑ 53 Brian Meadows .50 .15
❑ 54 Chad Curtis .50 .15
❑ 55 Aramis Ramirez 1.00 .30
❑ 56 Mark McLemore .50 .15
❑ 57 Dante Bichette 1.00 .30
❑ 58 Scott Schoeneweis .50 .15
❑ 59 Jose Cruz Jr. .50 .15
❑ 60 Roger Clemens 5.00 1.50
❑ 61 Jose Guillen 1.00 .30
❑ 62 Darren Oliver .50 .15
❑ 63 Chris Reitsma .50 .15
❑ 64 Jeff Abbott .50 .15
❑ 65 Robin Ventura 1.00 .30
❑ 66 Denny Neagle .50 .15
❑ 67 Al Martin .50 .15
❑ 68 Benito Santiago 1.00 .30
❑ 69 Roy Oswalt 1.00 .30
❑ 70 Juan Gonzalez 1.00 .30
❑ 71 Garret Anderson 1.00 .30
❑ 72 Bobby Bonilla 1.00 .30
❑ 73 Danny Bautista .50 .15
❑ 74 J.T. Snow 1.00 .30
❑ 75 Derek Jeter 6.00 1.80
❑ 76 John Olerud 1.00 .30
❑ 77 Kevin Appier 1.00 .30
❑ 78 Phil Nevin 1.00 .30
❑ 79 Sean Casey 1.50 .45
❑ 80 Troy Glaus 1.00 .30
❑ 81 Joe Randa .50 .15
❑ 82 Jose Valentin .50 .15
❑ 83 Ricky Bottalico .50 .15
❑ 84 Todd Zeile 1.00 .30
❑ 85 Barry Larkin 1.50 .45
❑ 86 Bob Wickman .50 .15
❑ 87 Jeff Shaw .50 .15
❑ 88 Greg Vaughn .50 .15
❑ 89 Fernando Vina .50 .15
❑ 90 Mark Mulder 1.00 .30
❑ 91 Paul Bako .50 .15
❑ 92 Aaron Boone 1.00 .30
❑ 93 Esteban Loaiza .50 .15
❑ 94 Richie Sexson 1.00 .30
❑ 95 Alfonso Soriano 1.00 .30
❑ 96 Tony Womack .50 .15
❑ 97 Paul Shuey .50 .15
❑ 98 Melvin Mora 1.00 .30
❑ 99 Tony Gwynn 3.00 .90
❑ 100 Vladimir Guerrero 2.50 .75
❑ 101 Keith Osik .50 .15
❑ 102 Bud Smith .50 .15
❑ 103 Scott Williamson .50 .15
❑ 104 Daryle Ward .50 .15
❑ 105 Doug Mientkiewicz 1.00 .30
❑ 106 Stan Javier .50 .15
❑ 107 Russ Ortiz 1.00 .30
❑ 108 Wade Miller .50 .15
❑ 109 Luke Prokopec .50 .15
❑ 110 Andruw Jones 1.50 .45
❑ 111 Ron Coomer .50 .15
❑ 112 Dan Wilson .50 .15
❑ 113 Luis Castillo .50 .15
❑ 114 Derek Bell .50 .15
❑ 115 Gary Sheffield 1.00 .30
❑ 116 Ruben Rivera .50 .15
❑ 117 Paul O'Neill 1.50 .45
❑ 118 Craig Paquette .50 .15
❑ 119 Kelvim Escobar .50 .15
❑ 120 Brad Radke 1.00 .30
❑ 121 Jorge Fabregas .50 .15
❑ 122 Randy Winn .50 .15
❑ 123 Tom Goodwin .50 .15
❑ 124 Jaret Wright .50 .15
❑ 125 Barry Bonds HR 73 40.00 12.00
❑ 126 Al Leiter .50 .15
❑ 127 Ben Davis .50 .15
❑ 128 Frank Catalanotto .50 .15
❑ 129 Jose Cabrera .50 .15
❑ 130 Magglio Ordonez 1.00 .30
❑ 131 Jose Macias .50 .15
❑ 132 Ted Lilly .50 .15
❑ 133 Chris Holt .50 .15
❑ 134 Eric Milton .50 .15
❑ 135 Shannon Stewart 1.00 .30
❑ 136 Omar Olivares .50 .15
❑ 137 David Segui .50 .15
❑ 138 Jeff Nelson .50 .15
❑ 139 Matt Williams 1.00 .30
❑ 140 Ellis Burks 1.00 .30
❑ 141 Jason Bere .50 .15
❑ 142 Jimmy Haynes .50 .15
❑ 143 Ramon Hernandez .50 .15
❑ 144 Craig Counsell .50 .15
❑ 145 John Smoltz 1.50 .45
❑ 146 Homer Bush .50 .15
❑ 147 Quilvio Veras .50 .15
❑ 148 Esteban Yan .50 .15
❑ 149 Ramon Ortiz .50 .15
❑ 150 Carlos Delgado 1.00 .30
❑ 151 Lee Stevens .50 .15
❑ 152 Wil Cordero .50 .15
❑ 153 Mike Bordick 1.00 .30
❑ 154 John Flaherty .50 .15
❑ 155 Omar Daal .50 .15
❑ 156 Todd Ritchie .50 .15
❑ 157 Carl Everett 1.00 .30
❑ 158 Scott Sullivan .50 .15
❑ 159 Deivi Cruz .50 .15
❑ 160 Albert Pujols 5.00 1.50
❑ 161 Royce Clayton .50 .15
❑ 162 Jeff Suppan .50 .15
❑ 163 C.C. Sabathia 1.00 .30
❑ 164 Jimmy Rollins 1.00 .30
❑ 165 Rickey Henderson 2.50 .75
❑ 166 Rey Ordonez .50 .15
❑ 167 Shawn Estes .50 .15
❑ 168 Reggie Sanders 1.00 .30
❑ 169 Jon Lieber .50 .15
❑ 170 Armando Benitez 1.00 .30
❑ 171 Mike Remlinger .50 .15
❑ 172 Billy Wagner 1.00 .30
❑ 173 Troy Percival 1.00 .30
❑ 174 Devon White 1.00 .30
❑ 175 Ivan Rodriguez 1.50 .45
❑ 176 Dustin Hermanson .50 .15
❑ 177 Brian Anderson .50 .15
❑ 178 Graeme Lloyd .50 .15
❑ 179 Russell Branyan .50 .15
❑ 180 Bobby Higginson 1.00 .30
❑ 181 Alex Gonzalez .50 .15
❑ 182 John Franco 1.00 .30
❑ 183 Sidney Ponson .50 .15
❑ 184 Jose Mesa .50 .15
❑ 185 Todd Hollandsworth .50 .15
❑ 186 Kevin Young .50 .15
❑ 187 Tim Wakefield 1.00 .30
❑ 188 Craig Biggio 1.50 .45
❑ 189 Jason Isringhausen 1.00 .30
❑ 190 Mark Quinn .50 .15
❑ 191 Glendon Rusch .50 .15
❑ 192 Damian Miller .50 .15
❑ 193 Sandy Alomar Jr. .50 .15
❑ 194 Scott Brosius 1.00 .30
❑ 195 Dave Martinez .50 .15
❑ 196 Danny Graves .50 .15
❑ 197 Shea Hillenbrand 1.00 .30
❑ 198 Jimmy Anderson .50 .15
❑ 199 Travis Lee .50 .15
❑ 200 Randy Johnson 2.50 .75
❑ 201 Carlos Beltran 1.00 .30
❑ 202 Jerry Hairston .50 .15
❑ 203 Jesus Sanchez .50 .15
❑ 204 Eddie Taubensee .50 .15
❑ 205 David Wells 1.00 .30
❑ 206 Russ Davis .50 .15
❑ 207 Michael Barrett .50 .15
❑ 208 Marquis Grissom 1.00 .30
❑ 209 Byung-Hyun Kim 1.00 .30
❑ 210 Hideo Nomo 2.50 .75
❑ 211 Ryan Rupe .50 .15
❑ 212 Ricky Gutierrez .50 .15
❑ 213 Darryl Kile 1.00 .30
❑ 214 Rico Brogna .50 .15
❑ 215 Terrence Long .50 .15
❑ 216 Mike Jackson .50 .15
❑ 217 Jamey Wright .50 .15
❑ 218 Adrian Beltre 1.00 .30
❑ 219 Benny Agbayani .50 .15
❑ 220 Chuck Knoblauch 1.00 .30
❑ 221 Randy Wolf .50 .15
❑ 222 Andy Ashby .50 .15
❑ 223 Corey Koskie .50 .15
❑ 224 Roger Cedeno .50 .15
❑ 225 Ichiro Suzuki 5.00 1.50
❑ 226 Keith Foulke 1.00 .30
❑ 227 Ryan Minor .50 .15
❑ 228 Shawon Dunston .50 .15
❑ 229 Alex Cora .50 .15
❑ 230 Jeromy Burnitz 1.00 .30
❑ 231 Mark Grace 1.50 .45
❑ 232 Aubrey Huff 1.00 .30
❑ 233 Jeffrey Hammonds .50 .15
❑ 234 Olmedo Saenz .50 .15
❑ 235 Brian Jordan 1.00 .30
❑ 236 Jeremy Giambi .50 .15
❑ 237 Joe Girardi .50 .15
❑ 238 Eric Gagne 1.00 .30
❑ 239 Masato Yoshii .50 .15
❑ 240 Greg Maddux 4.00 1.20
❑ 241 Bryan Rekar .50 .15
❑ 242 Ray Durham 1.00 .30
❑ 243 Torii Hunter 1.00 .30
❑ 244 Derrek Lee 1.50 .45
❑ 245 Jim Edmonds 1.50 .45
❑ 246 Einar Diaz .50 .15
❑ 247 Brian Bohanon .50 .15
❑ 248 Ron Belliard .50 .15
❑ 249 Mike Lowell 1.00 .30
❑ 250 Sammy Sosa 2.50 .75
❑ 251 Richard Hidalgo .50 .15
❑ 252 Bartolo Colon 1.00 .30
❑ 253 Jorge Posada 1.50 .45
❑ 254 Latroy Hawkins .50 .15
❑ 255 Paul LoDuca 1.00 .30
❑ 256 Carlos Febles .50 .15
❑ 257 Nelson Cruz .50 .15
❑ 258 Edgardo Alfonzo .50 .15
❑ 259 Joey Hamilton .50 .15
❑ 260 Cliff Floyd 1.00 .30
❑ 261 Wes Helms .50 .15
❑ 262 Jay Bell 1.00 .30
❑ 263 Mike Cameron .50 .15
❑ 264 Paul Konerko 1.00 .30
❑ 265 Jeff Kent 1.00 .30
❑ 266 Robert Fick .50 .15
❑ 267 Allen Levrault .50 .15
❑ 268 Placido Polanco .50 .15
❑ 269 Marlon Anderson .50 .15
❑ 270 Mariano Rivera 1.50 .45
❑ 271 Chan Ho Park 1.00 .30
❑ 272 Jose Vizcaino .50 .15
❑ 273 Jeff D'Amico .50 .15
❑ 274 Mark Gardner .50 .15
❑ 275 Travis Fryman 1.00 .30
❑ 276 Darren Lewis .50 .15
❑ 277 Bruce Bochy MG .50 .15
❑ 278 Jerry Manuel MG .50 .15
❑ 279 Bob Brenly MG .50 .15
❑ 280 Don Baylor MG 1.00 .30
❑ 281 Davey Lopes MG 1.00 .30
❑ 282 Jerry Narron MG .50 .15
❑ 283 Tony Muser MG .50 .15
❑ 284 Hal McRae MG 1.00 .30
❑ 285 Bobby Cox MG .50 .15
❑ 286 Larry Dierker MG .50 .15
❑ 287 Phil Garner MG 1.00 .30
❑ 288 Joe Kerrigan MG .50 .15
❑ 289 Bobby Valentine MG .50 .15
❑ 290 Dusty Baker MG 1.00 .30
❑ 291 Lloyd McClendon MG .50 .15
❑ 292 Mike Scioscia MG .50 .15
❑ 293 Buck Martinez MG .50 .15
❑ 294 Larry Bowa MG 1.00 .30
❑ 295 Tony LaRussa MG 1.00 .30
❑ 296 Jeff Torborg MG .50 .15
❑ 297 Tom Kelly MG .50 .15
❑ 298 Mike Hargrove MG .50 .15
❑ 299 Art Howe MG .50 .15
❑ 300 Lou Piniella MG 1.00 .30
❑ 301 Charlie Manuel MG .50 .15
❑ 302 Buddy Bell MG 1.00 .30
❑ 303 Tony Perez MG 1.00 .30
❑ 304 Bob Boone MG 1.00 .30

❑ 305 Joe Torre MG 1.50 .45
❑ 306 Jim Tracy MG .50 .15
❑ 307 Jason Lane PROS 1.50 .45
❑ 308 Chris George PROS 1.50 .45
❑ 309 Hank Blalock PROS 2.50 .75
❑ 310 Joe Borchard PROS 1.50 .45
❑ 311 Marlon Byrd PROS 1.50 .45
❑ 312 Ray. Cabrera PROS RC 1.50 .45
❑ 313 Fr. Sanchez PROS RC 1.50 .45
❑ 314 Scott Wiggins PROS RC 1.50 .45
❑ 315 Jason Maule PROS RC 1.50 .45
❑ 316 Dionys Cesar PROS RC 1.50 .45
❑ 317 Boof Bonser PROS 1.50 .45
❑ 318 Juan Tolentino PROS RC 1.50 .45
❑ 319 Earl Snyder PROS RC 1.50 .45
❑ 320 Travis Wade PROS RC 1.50 .45
❑ 321 Nap. Calzado PROS RC 1.50 .45
❑ 322 Eric Glaser PROS 1.50 .45
❑ 323 Craig Kuzmic PROS RC 1.50 .45
❑ 324 Nic Jackson PROS RC 1.50 .45
❑ 325 Mike Rivera PROS 1.50 .45
❑ 326 Jason Bay PROS RC 8.00 2.40
❑ 327 Chris Smith DP 1.50 .45
❑ 328 Jake Gautreau DP 1.50 .45
❑ 329 Gabe Gross DP 1.50 .45
❑ 330 Kenny Baugh DP 1.50 .45
❑ 331 J.D. Martin DP 1.50 .45
❑ 366 Pat Meares .50 .15
❑ 367 Mike Lieberthal .50 .15
❑ 368 Larry Bigbie .50 .15
❑ 369 Ron Gant 1.00 .30
❑ 370 Moises Alou 1.00 .30
❑ 371 Chad Kreuter .50 .15
❑ 372 Willis Roberts .50 .15
❑ 373 Toby Hall .50 .15
❑ 374 Miguel Batista .50 .15
❑ 375 John Burkett .50 .15
❑ 376 Cory Lidle .50 .15
❑ 377 Nick Neugebauer .50 .15
❑ 378 Jay Payton .50 .15
❑ 379 Steve Karsay .50 .15
❑ 380 Eric Chavez 1.00 .30
❑ 381 Kelly Stinnett .50 .15
❑ 382 Jarrod Washburn .50 .15
❑ 383 Rick White .50 .15
❑ 384 Jeff Conine 1.00 .30
❑ 385 Fred McGriff 1.50 .45
❑ 386 Marvin Benard .50 .15
❑ 387 Joe Crede 1.00 .30
❑ 388 Dennis Cook .50 .15
❑ 389 Rick Reed .50 .15
❑ 390 Tom Glavine 1.50 .45
❑ 391 Rondell White 1.00 .30
❑ 392 Matt Morris 1.00 .30
❑ 393 Pat Rapp .50 .15
❑ 394 Robert Person .50 .15
❑ 395 Omar Vizquel 1.50 .45
❑ 396 Jeff Cirillo .50 .15
❑ 397 Dave Mlicki .50 .15
❑ 398 Jose Ortiz .50 .15
❑ 399 Ryan Dempster .50 .15
❑ 400 Curt Schilling 1.00 .30
❑ 401 Peter Bergeron .50 .15
❑ 402 Kyle Lohse .50 .15
❑ 403 Craig Wilson 1.00 .30
❑ 404 David Justice 1.00 .30
❑ 405 Darin Erstad 1.00 .30
❑ 406 Jose Mercedes .50 .15
❑ 407 Carl Pavano 1.00 .30
❑ 408 Albie Lopez .50 .15
❑ 409 Alex Ochoa .50 .15
❑ 410 Chipper Jones 2.50 .75
❑ 411 Tyler Houston .50 .15
❑ 412 Dean Palmer 1.00 .30
❑ 413 Damian Jackson .50 .15
❑ 414 Josh Towers .50 .15
❑ 415 Rafael Furcal 1.00 .30
❑ 416 Mike Morgan .50 .15
❑ 417 Herb Perry .50 .15
❑ 418 Mike Sirotka .50 .15
❑ 419 Mark Wohlers .50 .15
❑ 420 Nomar Garciaparra 4.00 1.20
❑ 421 Felipe Lopez .50 .15
❑ 422 Joe McEwing .50 .15
❑ 423 Jacque Jones 1.00 .30
❑ 424 Julio Franco 1.00 .30
❑ 425 Frank Thomas 2.50 .75
❑ 426 So Taguchi RC 2.50 .75
❑ 427 Kazuhisa Ishii RC 2.50 .75
❑ 428 D'Angelo Jimenez .50 .15
❑ 429 Chris Stynes .50 .15
❑ 430 Kerry Wood 1.00 .30
❑ 431 Chris Singleton .50 .15
❑ 432 Erubiel Durazo .50 .15
❑ 433 Matt Lawton .50 .15
❑ 434 Bill Mueller 1.00 .30
❑ 435 Jose Canseco 1.50 .45
❑ 436 Ben Grieve .50 .15
❑ 437 Terry Mulholland .50 .15
❑ 438 David Bell .50 .15
❑ 439 A.J. Pierzynski 1.00 .30
❑ 440 Adam Dunn 1.00 .30
❑ 441 Jon Garland 1.00 .30
❑ 442 Jeff Fassero .50 .15
❑ 443 Julio Lugo .50 .15
❑ 444 Carlos Guillen 1.00 .30
❑ 445 Orlando Hernandez 1.00 .30
❑ 446 Mark Loretta 1.00 .30
❑ 447 Scott Spiezio .50 .15
❑ 448 Kevin Millwood .50 .15
❑ 449 Jamie Moyer 1.00 .30
❑ 450 Todd Helton 1.50 .45
❑ 451 Todd Walker .50 .15
❑ 452 Jose Lima .50 .15
❑ 453 Brook Fordyce .50 .15
❑ 454 Aaron Rowand 1.00 .30
❑ 455 Barry Zito 1.00 .30
❑ 456 Eric Owens .50 .15
❑ 457 Charles Nagy .50 .15
❑ 458 Raul Ibanez .50 .15
❑ 459 Joe Mays .50 .15
❑ 460 Jim Thome 1.50 .45
❑ 461 Adam Eaton .50 .15
❑ 462 Felix Martinez .50 .15
❑ 463 Vernon Wells 1.00 .30
❑ 464 Donnie Sadler .50 .15
❑ 465 Tony Clark .50 .15
❑ 466 Jose Hernandez .50 .15
❑ 467 Ramon Martinez .50 .15
❑ 468 Rusty Greer 1.00 .30
❑ 469 Rod Barajas .50 .15
❑ 470 Lance Berkman 1.00 .30
❑ 471 Brady Anderson 1.00 .30
❑ 472 Pedro Astacio .50 .15
❑ 473 Shane Halter .50 .15
❑ 474 Bret Prinz .50 .15
❑ 475 Edgar Martinez 1.50 .45
❑ 476 Steve Trachsel .50 .15
❑ 477 Gary Matthews Jr. .50 .15
❑ 478 Ismael Valdes .50 .15
❑ 479 Juan Uribe .50 .15
❑ 480 Shawn Green 1.00 .30
❑ 481 Kirk Rueter .50 .15
❑ 482 Damion Easley .50 .15
❑ 483 Chris Carpenter 1.00 .30
❑ 484 Kris Benson .50 .15
❑ 485 Antonio Alfonseca .50 .15
❑ 486 Kyle Farnsworth .50 .15
❑ 487 Brandon Lyon .50 .15
❑ 488 Hideki Irabu .50 .15
❑ 489 David Ortiz 1.50 .45
❑ 490 Mike Piazza 4.00 1.20
❑ 491 Derek Lowe 1.00 .30
❑ 492 Chris Gomez .50 .15
❑ 493 Mark Johnson .50 .15
❑ 494 John Rocker 1.00 .30
❑ 495 Eric Karros 1.00 .30
❑ 496 Bill Haselman .50 .15
❑ 497 Dave Veres .50 .15
❑ 498 Pete Harnisch .50 .15
❑ 499 Tomokazu Ohka .50 .15
❑ 500 Barry Bonds 6.00 1.80
❑ 501 David Dellucci .50 .15
❑ 502 Wendell Magee .50 .15
❑ 503 Tom Gordon .50 .15
❑ 504 Javier Vazquez 1.00 .30
❑ 505 Ben Sheets 1.00 .30
❑ 506 Wilton Guerrero .50 .15
❑ 507 John Halama .50 .15
❑ 508 Mark Redman .50 .15
❑ 509 Jack Wilson .50 .15
❑ 510 Bernie Williams 1.50 .45
❑ 511 Miguel Cairo .50 .15
❑ 512 Denny Hocking .50 .15
❑ 513 Tony Batista .50 .15
❑ 514 Mark Grudzielanek .50 .15
❑ 515 Jose Vidro .50 .15
❑ 516 Sterling Hitchcock .50 .15
❑ 517 Billy Koch .50 .15
❑ 518 Matt Clement 1.00 .30
❑ 519 Bruce Chen .50 .15
❑ 520 Roberto Alomar 1.50 .45
❑ 521 Orlando Palmeiro .50 .15
❑ 522 Steve Finley 1.00 .30
❑ 523 Danny Patterson .50 .15
❑ 524 Terry Adams .50 .15
❑ 525 Tino Martinez 1.50 .45
❑ 526 Tony Armas Jr. UER .50 .15
Career stats do not include pre-2001
❑ 527 Geoff Jenkins .50 .15
❑ 528 Kerry Robinson .50 .15
❑ 529 Corey Patterson .50 .15
❑ 530 Brian Giles 1.00 .30
❑ 531 Jose Jimenez .50 .15
❑ 532 Joe Kennedy .50 .15
❑ 533 Armando Rios .50 .15
❑ 534 Osvaldo Fernandez .50 .15
❑ 535 Ruben Sierra .50 .15
❑ 536 Octavio Dotel .50 .15
❑ 537 Luis Sojo .50 .15
❑ 538 Brent Butler .50 .15
❑ 539 Pablo Ozuna .50 .15
❑ 540 Freddy Garcia 1.00 .30
❑ 541 Chad Durbin .50 .15
❑ 542 Orlando Merced .50 .15
❑ 543 Michael Tucker .50 .15
❑ 544 Roberto Hernandez .50 .15
❑ 545 Pat Burrell 1.00 .30
❑ 546 A.J. Burnett 1.00 .30
❑ 547 Bubba Trammell .50 .15
❑ 548 Scott Elarton .50 .15
❑ 549 Mike Darr .50 .15
❑ 550 Ken Griffey Jr. 4.00 1.20
❑ 551 Ugueth Urbina .50 .15
❑ 552 Todd Jones .50 .15
❑ 553 Delino Deshields .50 .15
❑ 554 Adam Piatt .50 .15
❑ 555 Jason Kendall 1.00 .30
❑ 556 Hector Ortiz .50 .15
❑ 557 Turk Wendell .50 .15
❑ 558 Rob Bell .50 .15
❑ 559 Sun Woo Kim .50 .15
❑ 560 Raul Mondesi 1.00 .30
❑ 561 Brent Abernathy .50 .15
❑ 562 Seth Etherton .50 .15
❑ 563 Shawn Wooten .50 .15
❑ 564 Jay Buhner 1.00 .30
❑ 565 Andres Galarraga 1.00 .30
❑ 566 Shane Reynolds .50 .15
❑ 567 Rod Beck .50 .15
❑ 568 Dee Brown .50 .15
❑ 569 Pedro Feliz .50 .15
❑ 570 Ryan Klesko 1.00 .30
❑ 571 John Vander Wal .50 .15
❑ 572 Nick Bierbrodt .50 .15
❑ 573 Joe Nathan 1.00 .30
❑ 574 James Baldwin .50 .15
❑ 575 J.D. Drew 1.00 .30
❑ 576 Greg Colbrunn .50 .15
❑ 577 Doug Glanville .50 .15
❑ 578 Brandon Duckworth .50 .15
❑ 579 Shawn Chacon .50 .15
❑ 580 Rich Aurilia .50 .15
❑ 581 Chuck Finley 1.00 .30
❑ 582 Abraham Nunez .50 .15
❑ 583 Kenny Lofton 1.00 .30
❑ 584 Brian Daubach .50 .15
❑ 585 Miguel Tejada 1.00 .30
❑ 586 Nate Cornejo .50 .15
❑ 587 Kazuhiro Sasaki 1.00 .30
❑ 588 Chris Richard .50 .15
❑ 589 Armando Reynoso .50 .15
❑ 590 Tim Hudson 1.00 .30
❑ 591 Neifi Perez .50 .15
❑ 592 Steve Cox .50 .15
❑ 593 Henry Blanco .50 .15
❑ 594 Ricky Ledee .50 .15
❑ 595 Tim Salmon 1.50 .45

❑ 596	Luis Rivas	.50	.15
❑ 597	Jeff Zimmerman	.50	.15
❑ 598	Matt Stairs	.50	.15
❑ 599	Preston Wilson	1.00	.30
❑ 600	Mark McGwire	6.00	1.80
❑ 601	Timo Perez	.50	.15
❑ 602	Matt Anderson	.50	.15
❑ 603	Todd Hundley	.50	.15
❑ 604	Rick Ankiel	.50	.15
❑ 605	Tsuyoshi Shinjo	1.00	.30
❑ 606	Woody Williams	.50	.15
❑ 607	Jason LaRue	.50	.15
❑ 608	Carlos Lee	1.00	.30
❑ 609	Russ Johnson	.50	.15
❑ 610	Scott Rolen	1.50	.45
❑ 611	Brent Mayne	.50	.15
❑ 612	Darrin Fletcher	.50	.15
❑ 613	Ray Lankford	1.00	.30
❑ 614	Troy O'Leary	.50	.15
❑ 615	Javier Lopez	1.00	.30
❑ 616	Randy Velarde	.50	.15
❑ 617	Vinny Castilla	1.00	.30
❑ 618	Milton Bradley	1.00	.30
❑ 619	Ruben Mateo	.50	.15
❑ 620	Jason Giambi Yankees	1.00	.30
❑ 621	Andy Benes	.50	.15
❑ 622	Joe Mauer RC	8.00	2.40
❑ 623	Andy Pettitte	1.50	.45
❑ 624	Jose Offerman	.50	.15
❑ 625	Mo Vaughn	1.00	.30
❑ 626	Steve Sparks UER No 2001 Stats listed	.50	.15
❑ 627	Mike Matthews	.50	.15
❑ 628	Robb Nen	1.00	.30
❑ 629	Kip Wells	.50	.15
❑ 630	Kevin Brown	1.00	.30
❑ 631	Arthur Rhodes	.50	.15
❑ 632	Gabe Kapler	1.00	.30
❑ 633	Jermaine Dye	1.00	.30
❑ 634	Josh Beckett	1.00	.30
❑ 635	Pokey Reese	.50	.15
❑ 636	Benji Gil	.50	.15
❑ 637	Marcus Giles	1.00	.30
❑ 638	Julian Tavarez	.50	.15
❑ 639	Jason Schmidt	1.00	.30
❑ 640	Alex Rodriguez	4.00	1.20
❑ 641	Anaheim Angels TC	1.00	.30
❑ 642	Ariz. Diamondbacks TC	1.50	.45
❑ 643	Atlanta Braves TC	1.00	.30
❑ 644	Baltimore Orioles TC	1.00	.30
❑ 645	Boston Red Sox TC	1.00	.30
❑ 646	Chicago Cubs TC	1.00	.30
❑ 647	Chicago White Sox TC	1.00	.30
❑ 648	Cincinnati Reds TC	1.00	.30
❑ 649	Cleveland Indians TC	1.00	.30
❑ 650	Colorado Rockies TC	1.00	.30
❑ 651	Detroit Tigers TC	1.00	.30
❑ 652	Florida Marlins TC	1.00	.30
❑ 653	Houston Astros TC	1.00	.30
❑ 654	Kansas City Royals TC	1.00	.30
❑ 655	Los Angeles Dodgers TC	1.00	.30
❑ 656	Milwaukee Brewers TC	1.00	.30
❑ 657	Minnesota Twins TC	1.00	.30
❑ 658	Montreal Expos TC	1.00	.30
❑ 659	New York Mets TC	1.00	.30
❑ 660	New York Yankees TC	2.50	.75
❑ 661	Oakland Athletics TC	1.00	.30
❑ 662	Philadelphia Phillies TC	1.00	.30
❑ 663	Pittsburgh Pirates TC	1.00	.30
❑ 664	San Diego Padres TC	1.00	.30
❑ 665	San Francisco Giants TC	1.00	.30
❑ 666	Seattle Mariners TC	1.50	.45
❑ 667	St. Louis Cardinals TC	1.00	.30
❑ 668	T.B. Devil Rays TC	1.00	.30
❑ 669	Texas Rangers TC	1.00	.30
❑ 670	Toronto Blue Jays TC	1.00	.30
❑ 671	Juan Cruz PROS	1.50	.45
❑ 672	Kevin Cash PROS RC	1.50	.45
❑ 673	Jimmy Gobble PROS RC	1.50	.45
❑ 674	Mike Hill PROS RC	1.50	.45
❑ 675	T.Buchholz PROS RC	1.50	.45
❑ 676	Bill Hall PROS	1.50	.45
❑ 677	B.Roneberg PROS RC	1.50	.45
❑ 678	R.Huffman PROS RC	1.50	.45
❑ 679	Chris Tritle PROS RC	1.50	.45
❑ 680	Nate Espy PROS	1.50	.45
❑ 681	Nick Alvarez PROS RC	1.50	.45
❑ 682	Jason Botts PROS RC	2.50	.75
❑ 683	Ryan Gripp PROS RC	1.50	.45
❑ 684	Dan Phillips PROS RC	1.50	.45
❑ 685	Pablo Arias PROS RC	1.50	.45
❑ 686	J.Rodriguez PROS RC	2.50	.75
❑ 687	Rich Harden PROS RC	10.00	3.00
❑ 688	Neal Frendling PROS RC	1.50	.45
❑ 689	R.Thompson PROS RC	1.50	.45
❑ 690	G.Montalbano PROS RC	1.50	.45
❑ 691	Len Dinardo DP RC	1.50	.45
❑ 692	Ryan Raburn DP RC	1.50	.45
❑ 693	Josh Barfield DP RC	3.00	.90
❑ 694	David Bacani DP RC	1.50	.45
❑ 695	Dan Johnson DP RC	8.00	2.40

2002 Topps Chrome Traded

		Nm-Mt	Ex-Mt
COMPLETE SET (275)		120.00	36.00
❑ T1	Jeff Weaver	.50	.15
❑ T2	Jay Powell	.50	.15
❑ T3	Alex Gonzalez	.50	.15
❑ T4	Jason Isringhausen	.75	.23
❑ T5	Tyler Houston	.50	.15
❑ T6	Ben Broussard	.50	.15
❑ T7	Chuck Knoblauch	.75	.23
❑ T8	Brian L. Hunter	.50	.15
❑ T9	Dustan Mohr	.50	.15
❑ T10	Eric Hinske	.50	.15
❑ T11	Roger Cedeno	.50	.15
❑ T12	Eddie Perez	.50	.15
❑ T13	Jeromy Burnitz	.75	.23
❑ T14	Bartolo Colon	.75	.23
❑ T15	Rick Helling	.50	.15
❑ T16	Dan Plesac	.50	.15
❑ T17	Scott Strickland	.50	.15
❑ T18	Antonio Alfonseca	.50	.15
❑ T19	Ricky Gutierrez	.50	.15
❑ T20	John Valentin	.50	.15
❑ T21	Raul Mondesi	.75	.23
❑ T22	Ben Davis	.50	.15
❑ T23	Nelson Figueroa	.50	.15
❑ T24	Earl Snyder	.50	.15
❑ T25	Robin Ventura	.75	.23
❑ T26	Jimmy Haynes	.50	.15
❑ T27	Kenny Kelly	.50	.15
❑ T28	Morgan Ensberg	.75	.23
❑ T29	Reggie Sanders	.75	.23
❑ T30	Shigetoshi Hasegawa	.75	.23
❑ T31	Mike Timlin	.50	.15
❑ T32	Russell Branyan	.50	.15
❑ T33	Alan Embree	.50	.15
❑ T34	D'Angelo Jimenez	.50	.15
❑ T35	Kent Mercker	.50	.15
❑ T36	Jesse Orosco	.50	.15
❑ T37	Gregg Zaun	.50	.15
❑ T38	Reggie Taylor	.50	.15
❑ T39	Andres Galarraga	.75	.23
❑ T40	Chris Truby	.50	.15
❑ T41	Bruce Chen	.50	.15
❑ T42	Darren Lewis	.50	.15
❑ T43	Ryan Kohlmeier	.50	.15
❑ T44	John McDonald	.50	.15
❑ T45	Omar Daal	.50	.15
❑ T46	Matt Clement	.75	.23
❑ T47	Glendon Rusch	.50	.15
❑ T48	Chan Ho Park	.75	.23
❑ T49	Benny Agbayani	.50	.15
❑ T50	Juan Gonzalez	.75	.23
❑ T51	Carlos Baerga	.50	.15
❑ T52	Tim Raines	.75	.23
❑ T53	Kevin Appier	.75	.23
❑ T54	Marty Cordova	.50	.15
❑ T55	Jeff D'Amico	.50	.15
❑ T56	Dmitri Young	.75	.23
❑ T57	Roosevelt Brown	.50	.15
❑ T58	Dustin Hermanson	.50	.15
❑ T59	Jose Rijo	.50	.15
❑ T60	Todd Ritchie	.50	.15
❑ T61	Lee Stevens	.50	.15
❑ T62	Placido Polanco	.50	.15
❑ T63	Eric Young	.50	.15
❑ T64	Chuck Finley	.75	.23
❑ T65	Dicky Gonzalez	.50	.15
❑ T66	Jose Macias	.50	.15
❑ T67	Gabe Kapler	.75	.23
❑ T68	Sandy Alomar Jr.	.50	.15
❑ T69	Henry Blanco	.50	.15
❑ T70	Julian Tavarez	.50	.15
❑ T71	Paul Bako	.50	.15
❑ T72	Scott Rolen	1.25	.35
❑ T73	Brian Jordan	.75	.23
❑ T74	Rickey Henderson	2.00	.60
❑ T75	Kevin Mench	.50	.15
❑ T76	Hideo Nomo	2.00	.60
❑ T77	Jeremy Giambi	.50	.15
❑ T78	Brad Fullmer	.50	.15
❑ T79	Carl Everett	.75	.23
❑ T80	David Wells	.75	.23
❑ T81	Aaron Sele	.50	.15
❑ T82	Todd Hollandsworth	.50	.15
❑ T83	Vicente Padilla	.50	.15
❑ T84	Kenny Lofton	.75	.23
❑ T85	Corky Miller	.50	.15
❑ T86	Josh Fogg	.50	.15
❑ T87	Cliff Floyd	.75	.23
❑ T88	Craig Paquette	.50	.15
❑ T89	Jay Payton	.50	.15
❑ T90	Carlos Pena	.50	.15
❑ T91	Juan Encarnacion	.50	.15
❑ T92	Rey Sanchez	.50	.15
❑ T93	Ryan Dempster	.50	.15
❑ T94	Mario Encarnacion	.50	.15
❑ T95	Jorge Julio	.50	.15
❑ T96	John Mabry	.50	.15
❑ T97	Todd Zeile	.75	.23
❑ T98	Johnny Damon	1.25	.35
❑ T99	Deivi Cruz	.50	.15
❑ T100	Gary Sheffield	.75	.23
❑ T101	Ted Lilly	.50	.15
❑ T102	Todd Van Poppel	.50	.15
❑ T103	Shawn Estes	.50	.15
❑ T104	Cesar Izturis	.50	.15
❑ T105	Ron Coomer	.50	.15
❑ T106	Grady Little MG RC	.50	.15
❑ T107	Jimy Williams MGR	.50	.15
❑ T108	Tony Pena MGR	.50	.15
❑ T109	Frank Robinson MGR	1.25	.35
❑ T110	Ron Gardenhire MGR	.50	.15
❑ T111	Dennis Tankersley	.50	.15
❑ T112	Alejandro Cadena RC	1.00	.30
❑ T113	Justin Reid RC	1.00	.30
❑ T114	Nate Field RC	1.00	.30
❑ T115	Rene Reyes RC	1.00	.30
❑ T116	Nelson Castro RC	1.00	.30
❑ T117	Miguel Olivo	.50	.15
❑ T118	David Espinosa	.50	.15
❑ T119	Chris Bootcheck RC	1.00	.30
❑ T120	Rob Henkel RC	1.00	.30
❑ T121	Steve Bechler RC	1.00	.30
❑ T122	Mark Outlaw RC	1.00	.30
❑ T123	Henry Pichardo RC	1.00	.30
❑ T124	Michael Floyd RC	1.00	.30
❑ T125	Richard Lane RC	1.00	.30
❑ T126	Pete Zamora RC	1.00	.30
❑ T127	Javier Colina	.50	.15
❑ T128	Greg Sain RC	1.00	.30
❑ T129	Ronnie Merrill	.50	.15
❑ T130	Gavin Floyd RC	2.50	.75
❑ T131	Josh Bonifay RC	1.00	.30
❑ T132	Tommy Marx RC	1.00	.30

❑ T133 Gary Cates Jr. RC 1.00 .30
❑ T134 Neal Cotts RC 2.00 .60
❑ T135 Angel Berroa .50 .15
❑ T136 Elio Serrano RC 1.00 .30
❑ T137 J.J. Putz RC 1.00 .30
❑ T138 Ruben Gotay RC 1.25 .35
❑ T139 Eddie Rogers .50 .15
❑ T140 Wily Mo Pena .75 .23
❑ T141 Tyler Yates RC 1.00 .30
❑ T142 Colin Young RC .75 .23
❑ T143 Chance Caple .50 .15
❑ T144 Ben Howard RC 1.00 .30
❑ T145 Ryan Bukvich RC 1.00 .30
❑ T146 Cliff Bartosh RC 1.00 .30
❑ T147 Brandon Claussen .50 .15
❑ T148 Cristian Guerrero .50 .15
❑ T149 Derrick Lewis .50 .15
❑ T150 Eric Miller RC 1.00 .30
❑ T151 Justin Huber RC 2.00 .60
❑ T152 Adrian Gonzalez .50 .15
❑ T153 Brian West RC 1.00 .30
❑ T154 Chris Baker RC 1.00 .30
❑ T155 Drew Henson .75 .23
❑ T156 Scott Hairston RC 1.25 .35
❑ T157 Jason Simontacchi RC 1.00 .30
❑ T158 Jason Arnold RC 1.00 .30
❑ T159 Brandon Phillips .50 .15
❑ T160 Adam Roller RC 1.00 .30
❑ T161 Scotty Layfield RC 1.00 .30
❑ T162 Freddie Money RC 1.00 .30
❑ T163 Noochie Varner RC 1.00 .30
❑ T164 Terrance Hill RC 1.00 .30
❑ T165 Jeremy Hill RC 1.00 .30
❑ T166 Carlos Cabrera RC 1.00 .30
❑ T167 Jose Morban RC 1.00 .30
❑ T168 Kevin Frederick RC 1.00 .30
❑ T169 Mark Teixeira 4.00 1.20
❑ T170 Brian Rogers .50 .15
❑ T171 Anastacio Martinez RC 1.00 .30
❑ T172 Bobby Jenks RC 4.00 1.20
❑ T173 David Gil RC 1.00 .30
❑ T174 Andres Torres .50 .15
❑ T175 James Barrett RC 1.00 .30
❑ T176 Jimmy Journell .50 .15
❑ T177 Brett Kay RC 1.00 .30
❑ T178 Jason Young RC 1.00 .30
❑ T179 Mark Hamilton RC 1.00 .30
❑ T180 Jose Bautista RC .00 .00
❑ T181 Blake McGinley RC 1.00 .30
❑ T182 Ryan Mottl RC 1.00 .30
❑ T183 Jeff Austin RC 1.00 .30
❑ T184 Xavier Nady .50 .15
❑ T185 Kyle Kane RC 1.00 .30
❑ T186 Travis Foley RC 1.00 .30
❑ T187 Nathan Kaup RC 1.00 .30
❑ T188 Eric Cyr .50 .15
❑ T189 Josh Cisneros RC 1.00 .30
❑ T190 Brad Nelson RC 1.25 .35
❑ T191 Clint Weibl RC 1.00 .30
❑ T192 Ron Calloway RC 1.00 .30
❑ T193 Jung Bong .50 .15
❑ T194 Rolando Viera RC 1.00 .30
❑ T195 Jason Bulger RC 1.00 .30
❑ T196 Chone Figgins RC 2.00 .60
❑ T197 Jimmy Alvarez RC 1.00 .30
❑ T198 Joel Crump RC 1.00 .30
❑ T199 Ryan Doumit RC 3.00 .90
❑ T200 Demetrius Heath RC 1.00 .30
❑ T201 John Ennis RC 1.00 .30
❑ T202 Doug Sessions RC 1.00 .30
❑ T203 Clinton Hosford RC 1.00 .30
❑ T204 Chris Narveson RC 1.00 .30
❑ T205 Ross Peeples RC 1.00 .30
❑ T206 Alex Requena RC 1.00 .30
❑ T207 Matt Erickson RC 1.00 .30
❑ T208 Brian Forystek RC 1.00 .30
❑ T209 Dewon Brazelton .50 .15
❑ T210 Nathan Haynes .50 .15
❑ T211 Jack Cust .50 .15
❑ T212 Jesse Foppert RC 1.25 .35
❑ T213 Jesus Cota RC 1.00 .30
❑ T214 Juan M. Gonzalez RC 1.00 .30
❑ T215 Tim Kalita RC 1.00 .30
❑ T216 Manny Delcarmen RC 1.25 .35
❑ T217 Jim Kavourias RC 1.00 .30
❑ T218 C.J. Wilson RC 1.00 .30
❑ T219 Edwin Yan RC 1.00 .30
❑ T220 Andy Van Hekken .50 .15
❑ T221 Michael Cuddyer .50 .15
❑ T222 Jeff Verplancke RC 1.00 .30
❑ T223 Mike Wilson RC 1.00 .30
❑ T224 Corwin Malone RC 1.00 .30
❑ T225 Chris Snelling RC 2.00 .60
❑ T226 Joe Rogers RC 1.00 .30
❑ T227 Jason Bay 8.00 2.40
❑ T228 Ezequiel Astacio RC 1.00 .30
❑ T229 Joey Hammond RC 1.00 .30
❑ T230 Chris Duffy RC 2.00 .60
❑ T231 Mark Prior 4.00 1.20
❑ T232 Hansel Izquierdo RC 1.00 .30
❑ T233 Franklyn German RC 1.00 .30
❑ T234 Alexis Gomez .50 .15
❑ T235 Jorge Padilla RC 1.00 .30
❑ T236 Ryan Snare RC 1.00 .30
❑ T237 Deivis Santos .50 .15
❑ T238 Taggert Bozied RC 1.25 .35
❑ T239 Mike Peeples RC 1.00 .30
❑ T240 Ronald Acuna RC 1.00 .30
❑ T241 Koyie Hill .50 .15
❑ T242 Garrett Guzman RC 1.00 .30
❑ T243 Ryan Church RC 4.00 1.20
❑ T244 Tony Fontana RC 1.00 .30
❑ T245 Keto Anderson RC 1.00 .30
❑ T246 Brad Bouras RC 1.00 .30
❑ T247 Jason Dubois RC 1.25 .35
❑ T248 Angel Guzman RC 2.00 .60
❑ T249 Joel Hanrahan RC 1.00 .30
❑ T250 Joe Jiannetti RC 1.00 .30
❑ T251 Sean Pierce RC 1.00 .30
❑ T252 Jake Mauer RC 1.00 .30
❑ T253 Marshall McDougall RC 1.00 .30
❑ T254 Edwin Almonte RC 1.00 .30
❑ T255 Shawn Riggans RC 1.00 .30
❑ T256 Steven Shell RC 1.00 .30
❑ T257 Kevin Hooper RC 1.00 .30
❑ T258 Michael Frick RC 1.00 .30
❑ T259 Travis Chapman RC 1.00 .30
❑ T260 Tim Hummel RC 1.00 .30
❑ T261 Adam Morrissey RC 1.00 .30
❑ T262 Dontrelle Willis RC 15.00 4.50
❑ T263 Justin Sherrod RC 1.00 .30
❑ T264 Gerald Smiley RC 1.00 .30
❑ T265 Tony Miller RC 1.00 .30
❑ T266 Nolan Ryan WW 5.00 1.50
❑ T267 Reggie Jackson WW 1.25 .35
❑ T268 Steve Garvey WW .75 .23
❑ T269 Wade Boggs WW 1.25 .35
❑ T270 Sammy Sosa WW 2.00 .60
❑ T271 Curt Schilling WW .75 .23
❑ T272 Mark Grace WW 1.25 .35
❑ T273 Jason Giambi WW .50 .15
❑ T274 Ken Griffey Jr. WW 3.00 .90
❑ T275 Roberto Alomar WW 1.25 .35

2003 Topps Chrome

	Nm-Mt	Ex-Mt
COMPLETE SET (440)	200.00	60.00
COMPLETE SERIES 1 (220)	100.00	30.00
COMPLETE SERIES 2 (220)	100.00	30.00
COMMON (1-200/221-420)	1.00	.30
COMMON (201-220/421-440)	1.50	.45

❑ 1 Alex Rodriguez 4.00 1.20
❑ 2 Eddie Guardado 1.00 .30
❑ 3 Curt Schilling 1.00 .30
❑ 4 Andruw Jones 1.50 .45
❑ 5 Magglio Ordonez 1.00 .30
❑ 6 Todd Helton 1.50 .45
❑ 7 Odalis Perez 1.00 .30
❑ 8 Edgardo Alfonzo 1.00 .30
❑ 9 Eric Hinske 1.00 .30
❑ 10 Danny Bautista 1.00 .30
❑ 11 Sammy Sosa 2.50 .75
❑ 12 Roberto Alomar 1.50 .45
❑ 13 Roger Clemens 5.00 1.50
❑ 14 Austin Kearns 1.00 .30
❑ 15 Luis Gonzalez 1.00 .30
❑ 16 Mo Vaughn 1.00 .30
❑ 17 Alfonso Soriano 1.00 .30
❑ 18 Orlando Cabrera 1.00 .30
❑ 19 Hideo Nomo 2.50 .75
❑ 20 Omar Vizquel 1.50 .45
❑ 21 Greg Maddux 4.00 1.20
❑ 22 Fred McGriff 1.50 .45
❑ 23 Frank Thomas 2.50 .75
❑ 24 Shawn Green 1.00 .30
❑ 25 Jacque Jones 1.00 .30
❑ 26 Bernie Williams 1.50 .45
❑ 27 Corey Patterson 1.00 .30
❑ 28 Cesar Izturis 1.00 .30
❑ 29 Larry Walker 1.00 .30
❑ 30 Darren Dreifort 1.00 .30
❑ 31 Al Leiter 1.00 .30
❑ 32 Jason Marquis 1.00 .30
❑ 33 Sean Casey 1.50 .45
❑ 34 Craig Counsell 1.00 .30
❑ 35 Albert Pujols 5.00 1.50
❑ 36 Kyle Lohse 1.00 .30
❑ 37 Paul Lo Duca 1.00 .30
❑ 38 Roy Oswalt 1.00 .30
❑ 39 Danny Graves 1.00 .30
❑ 40 Kevin Millwood 1.00 .30
❑ 41 Lance Berkman 1.00 .30
❑ 42 Denny Hocking 1.00 .30
❑ 43 Jose Valentin 1.00 .30
❑ 44 Josh Beckett 1.00 .30
❑ 45 Nomar Garciaparra 4.00 1.20
❑ 46 Craig Biggio 1.50 .45
❑ 47 Omar Daal 1.00 .30
❑ 48 Jimmy Rollins 1.00 .30
❑ 49 Jermaine Dye 1.00 .30
❑ 50 Edgar Renteria 1.00 .30
❑ 51 Brandon Duckworth 1.00 .30
❑ 52 Luis Castillo 1.00 .30
❑ 53 Andy Ashby 1.00 .30
❑ 54 Mike Williams 1.00 .30
❑ 55 Benito Santiago 1.00 .30
❑ 56 Bret Boone 1.00 .30
❑ 57 Randy Wolf 1.00 .30
❑ 58 Ivan Rodriguez 1.50 .45
❑ 59 Shannon Stewart 1.00 .30
❑ 60 Jose Cruz Jr. 1.00 .30
❑ 61 Billy Wagner 1.00 .30
❑ 62 Alex Gonzalez 1.00 .30
❑ 63 Ichiro Suzuki 5.00 1.50
❑ 64 Joe McEwing 1.00 .30
❑ 65 Mark Mulder 1.00 .30
❑ 66 Mike Cameron 1.00 .30
❑ 67 Corey Koskie 1.00 .30
❑ 68 Marlon Anderson 1.00 .30
❑ 69 Jason Kendall 1.00 .30
❑ 70 J.T. Snow 1.00 .30
❑ 71 Edgar Martinez 1.50 .45
❑ 72 Vernon Wells 1.00 .30
❑ 73 Vladimir Guerrero 2.50 .75
❑ 74 Adam Dunn 1.00 .30
❑ 75 Barry Zito 1.00 .30
❑ 76 Jeff Kent 1.00 .30
❑ 77 Russ Ortiz 1.00 .30
❑ 78 Phil Nevin 1.00 .30
❑ 79 Carlos Beltran 1.00 .30
❑ 80 Mike Lowell 1.00 .30
❑ 81 Bob Wickman 1.00 .30
❑ 82 Junior Spivey 1.00 .30
❑ 83 Melvin Mora 1.00 .30
❑ 84 Derrek Lee 1.50 .45
❑ 85 Chuck Knoblauch 1.00 .30
❑ 86 Eric Gagne 1.00 .30
❑ 87 Orlando Hernandez 1.00 .30
❑ 88 Robert Person 1.00 .30

❑ 89 Elmer Dessens	1.00	.30
❑ 90 Wade Miller	1.00	.30
❑ 91 Adrian Beltre	1.00	.30
❑ 92 Kazuhiro Sasaki	1.00	.30
❑ 93 Timo Perez	1.00	.30
❑ 94 Jose Vidro	1.00	.30
❑ 95 Geronimo Gil	1.00	.30
❑ 96 Trot Nixon	1.00	.30
❑ 97 Denny Neagle	1.00	.30
❑ 98 Roberto Hernandez	1.00	.30
❑ 99 David Ortiz	1.50	.45
❑ 100 Robb Nen	1.00	.30
❑ 101 Sidney Ponson	1.00	.30
❑ 102 Kevin Appier	1.00	.30
❑ 103 Javier Lopez	1.00	.30
❑ 104 Jeff Conine	1.00	.30
❑ 105 Mark Buehrle	1.00	.30
❑ 106 Jason Simontacchi	1.00	.30
❑ 107 Jose Jimenez	1.00	.30
❑ 108 Brian Jordan	1.00	.30
❑ 109 Brad Wilkerson	1.00	.30
❑ 110 Scott Hatteberg	1.00	.30
❑ 111 Matt Morris	1.00	.30
❑ 112 Miguel Tejada	1.00	.30
❑ 113 Rafael Furcal	1.00	.30
❑ 114 Steve Cox	1.00	.30
❑ 115 Roy Halladay	1.00	.30
❑ 116 David Eckstein	1.00	.30
❑ 117 Tomo Ohka	1.00	.30
❑ 118 Jack Wilson	1.00	.30
❑ 119 Randall Simon	1.00	.30
❑ 120 Jamie Moyer	1.00	.30
❑ 121 Andy Benes	1.00	.30
❑ 122 Tino Martinez	1.50	.45
❑ 123 Esteban Yan	1.00	.30
❑ 124 Jason Isringhausen	1.00	.30
❑ 125 Chris Carpenter	1.00	.30
❑ 126 Aaron Rowand	1.00	.30
❑ 127 Brandon Inge	1.00	.30
❑ 128 Jose Vizcaino	1.00	.30
❑ 129 Jose Mesa	1.00	.30
❑ 130 Troy Percival	1.00	.30
❑ 131 Jon Lieber	1.00	.30
❑ 132 Brian Giles	1.00	.30
❑ 133 Aaron Boone	1.00	.30
❑ 134 Bobby Higginson	1.00	.30
❑ 135 Luis Rivas	1.00	.30
❑ 136 Troy Glaus	1.00	.30
❑ 137 Jim Thome	1.50	.45
❑ 138 Ramon Martinez	1.00	.30
❑ 139 Jay Gibbons	1.00	.30
❑ 140 Mike Lieberthal	1.00	.30
❑ 141 Juan Uribe	1.00	.30
❑ 142 Gary Sheffield	1.00	.30
❑ 143 Ramon Santiago	1.00	.30
❑ 144 Ben Sheets	1.00	.30
❑ 145 Tony Armas Jr.	1.00	.30
❑ 146 Kazuhisa Ishii	1.00	.30
❑ 147 Erubiel Durazo	1.00	.30
❑ 148 Jerry Hairston Jr.	1.00	.30
❑ 149 Byung-Hyun Kim	1.00	.30
❑ 150 Marcus Giles	1.00	.30
❑ 151 Johnny Damon	1.50	.45
❑ 152 Terrence Long	1.00	.30
❑ 153 Juan Pierre	1.00	.30
❑ 154 Aramis Ramirez	1.00	.30
❑ 155 Brent Abernathy	1.00	.30
❑ 156 Ismael Valdes	1.00	.30
❑ 157 Mike Mussina	1.50	.45
❑ 158 Ramon Hernandez	1.00	.30
❑ 159 Adam Kennedy	1.00	.30
❑ 160 Tony Womack	1.00	.30
❑ 161 Tony Batista	1.00	.30
❑ 162 Kip Wells	1.00	.30
❑ 163 Jeromy Burnitz	1.00	.30
❑ 164 Todd Hundley	1.00	.30
❑ 165 Tim Wakefield	1.00	.30
❑ 166 Derek Lowe	1.00	.30
❑ 167 Jorge Posada	1.50	.45
❑ 168 Ramon Ortiz	1.00	.30
❑ 169 Brent Butler	1.00	.30
❑ 170 Shane Halter	1.00	.30
❑ 171 Matt Lawton	1.00	.30
❑ 172 Alex Sanchez	1.00	.30
❑ 173 Eric Milton	1.00	.30
❑ 174 Vicente Padilla	1.00	.30
❑ 175 Steve Karsay	1.00	.30
❑ 176 Mark Prior	1.50	.45
❑ 177 Kerry Wood	1.00	.30
❑ 178 Jason LaRue	1.00	.30
❑ 179 Danys Baez	1.00	.30
❑ 180 Nick Neugebauer	1.00	.30
❑ 181 Andres Galarraga	1.00	.30
❑ 182 Jason Giambi	1.00	.30
❑ 183 Aubrey Huff	1.00	.30
❑ 184 Juan Gonzalez	1.00	.30
❑ 185 Ugueth Urbina	1.00	.30
❑ 186 Rickey Henderson	2.50	.75
❑ 187 Brad Fullmer	1.00	.30
❑ 188 Todd Zeile	1.00	.30
❑ 189 Jason Jennings	1.00	.30
❑ 190 Vladimir Nunez	1.00	.30
❑ 191 David Justice	1.00	.30
❑ 192 Brian Lawrence	1.00	.30
❑ 193 Pat Burrell	1.00	.30
❑ 194 Pokey Reese	1.00	.30
❑ 195 Robert Fick	1.00	.30
❑ 196 C.C. Sabathia	1.00	.30
❑ 197 Fernando Vina	1.00	.30
❑ 198 Sean Burroughs	1.00	.30
❑ 199 Ellis Burks	1.00	.30
❑ 200 Joe Randa	1.00	.30
❑ 201 Chris Duncan FY RC	1.50	.45
❑ 202 Franklin Gutierrez FY RC	2.50	.75
❑ 203 Adam LaRoche FY	1.50	.45
❑ 204 Manuel Ramirez FY RC	2.50	.75
❑ 205 Il Kim FY RC	1.50	.45
❑ 206 Daryl Clark FY RC	1.50	.45
❑ 207 Sean Pierce FY	1.50	.45
❑ 208 Andy Marte FY RC	8.00	2.40
❑ 209 Bernie Castro FY RC	1.50	.45
❑ 210 Jason Perry FY RC	2.50	.75
❑ 211 Jaime Bubela FY RC	1.50	.45
❑ 212 Alexis Rios FY	1.50	.45
❑ 213 Brendan Harris FY RC	2.50	.75
❑ 214 R.Nivar-Martinez FY RC	1.50	.45
❑ 215 Terry Tiffee FY RC	1.50	.45
❑ 216 Kevin Youkilis FY RC	2.50	.75
❑ 217 Derell McCall FY RC	1.50	.45
❑ 218 Scott Tyler FY RC	2.50	.75
❑ 219 Craig Brazell FY RC	1.50	.45
❑ 220 Walter Young FY	1.50	.45
❑ 221 Francisco Rodriguez	1.00	.30
❑ 222 Chipper Jones	2.50	.75
❑ 223 Chris Singleton	1.00	.30
❑ 224 Cliff Floyd	1.00	.30
❑ 225 Bobby Hill	1.00	.30
❑ 226 Antonio Osuna	1.00	.30
❑ 227 Barry Larkin	1.50	.45
❑ 228 Dean Palmer	1.00	.30
❑ 229 Eric Owens	1.00	.30
❑ 230 Randy Johnson	2.50	.75
❑ 231 Jeff Suppan	1.00	.30
❑ 232 Eric Karros	1.00	.30
❑ 233 Johan Santana	1.50	.45
❑ 234 Javier Vazquez	1.00	.30
❑ 235 John Thomson	1.00	.30
❑ 236 Nick Johnson	1.00	.30
❑ 237 Mark Ellis	1.00	.30
❑ 238 Doug Glanville	1.00	.30
❑ 239 Ken Griffey Jr.	4.00	1.20
❑ 240 Bubba Trammell	1.00	.30
❑ 241 Livan Hernandez	1.00	.30
❑ 242 Desi Relaford	1.00	.30
❑ 243 Eli Marrero	1.00	.30
❑ 244 Jared Sandberg	1.00	.30
❑ 245 Barry Bonds	6.00	1.80
❑ 246 Aaron Sele	1.00	.30
❑ 247 Derek Jeter	6.00	1.80
❑ 248 Eric Byrnes	1.00	.30
❑ 249 Rich Aurilia	1.00	.30
❑ 250 Joel Pineiro	1.00	.30
❑ 251 Chuck Finley	1.00	.30
❑ 252 Bengie Molina	1.00	.30
❑ 253 Steve Finley	1.00	.30
❑ 254 Marty Cordova	1.00	.30
❑ 255 Shea Hillenbrand	1.00	.30
❑ 256 Milton Bradley	1.00	.30
❑ 257 Carlos Pena	1.00	.30
❑ 258 Brad Ausmus	1.00	.30
❑ 259 Carlos Delgado	1.00	.30
❑ 260 Kevin Mench	1.00	.30
❑ 261 Joe Kennedy	1.00	.30
❑ 262 Mark McLemore	1.00	.30
❑ 263 Bill Mueller	1.00	.30
❑ 264 Ricky Ledee	1.00	.30
❑ 265 Ted Lilly	1.00	.30
❑ 266 Sterling Hitchcock	1.00	.30
❑ 267 Scott Strickland	1.00	.30
❑ 268 Damion Easley	1.00	.30
❑ 269 Torii Hunter	1.00	.30
❑ 270 Brad Radke	1.00	.30
❑ 271 Geoff Jenkins	1.00	.30
❑ 272 Paul Byrd	1.00	.30
❑ 273 Morgan Ensberg	1.00	.30
❑ 274 Mike Maroth	1.00	.30
❑ 275 Mike Hampton	1.00	.30
❑ 276 Flash Gordon	1.00	.30
❑ 277 John Burkett	1.00	.30
❑ 278 Rodrigo Lopez	1.00	.30
❑ 279 Tim Spooneybarger	1.00	.30
❑ 280 Quinton McCracken	1.00	.30
❑ 281 Tim Salmon	1.50	.45
❑ 282 Jarrod Washburn	1.00	.30
❑ 283 Pedro Martinez	1.50	.45
❑ 284 Julio Lugo	1.00	.30
❑ 285 Armando Benitez	1.00	.30
❑ 286 Raul Mondesi	1.00	.30
❑ 287 Robin Ventura	1.00	.30
❑ 288 Bobby Abreu	1.00	.30
❑ 289 Josh Fogg	1.00	.30
❑ 290 Ryan Klesko	1.00	.30
❑ 291 Tsuyoshi Shinjo	1.00	.30
❑ 292 Jim Edmonds	1.50	.45
❑ 293 Chan Ho Park	1.00	.30
❑ 294 John Mabry	1.00	.30
❑ 295 Woody Williams	1.00	.30
❑ 296 Scott Schoeneweis	1.00	.30
❑ 297 Brian Anderson	1.00	.30
❑ 298 Brett Tomko	1.00	.30
❑ 299 Scott Erickson	1.00	.30
❑ 300 Kevin Millar Sox	1.00	.30
❑ 301 Danny Wright	1.00	.30
❑ 302 Jason Schmidt	1.00	.30
❑ 303 Scott Williamson	1.00	.30
❑ 304 Einar Diaz	1.00	.30
❑ 305 Jay Payton	1.00	.30
❑ 306 Juan Acevedo	1.00	.30
❑ 307 Ben Grieve	1.00	.30
❑ 308 Raul Ibanez	1.00	.30
❑ 309 Richie Sexson	1.00	.30
❑ 310 Rick Reed	1.00	.30
❑ 311 Pedro Astacio	1.00	.30
❑ 312 Bud Smith	1.00	.30
❑ 313 Tomas Perez	1.00	.30
❑ 314 Rafael Palmeiro	1.50	.45
❑ 315 Jason Tyner	1.00	.30
❑ 316 Scott Rolen	1.50	.45
❑ 317 Randy Winn	1.00	.30
❑ 318 Ryan Jensen	1.00	.30
❑ 319 Trevor Hoffman	1.00	.30
❑ 320 Craig Wilson	1.00	.30
❑ 321 Jeremy Giambi	1.00	.30
❑ 322 Andy Pettitte	1.50	.45
❑ 323 John Franco	1.00	.30
❑ 324 Felipe Lopez	1.00	.30
❑ 325 Mike Piazza	4.00	1.20
❑ 326 Cristian Guzman	1.00	.30
❑ 327 Jose Hernandez	1.00	.30
❑ 328 Octavio Dotel	1.00	.30
❑ 329 Brad Penny	1.00	.30
❑ 330 Dave Veres	1.00	.30
❑ 331 Ryan Dempster	1.00	.30
❑ 332 Joe Crede	1.00	.30
❑ 333 Chad Hermansen	1.00	.30
❑ 334 Gary Matthews Jr.	1.00	.30
❑ 335 Frank Catalanotto	1.00	.30
❑ 336 Darin Erstad	1.00	.30
❑ 337 Matt Williams	1.00	.30
❑ 338 B.J. Surhoff	1.00	.30
❑ 339 Kerry Ligtenberg	1.00	.30
❑ 340 Mike Bordick	1.00	.30
❑ 341 Joe Girardi	1.00	.30
❑ 342 D'Angelo Jimenez	1.00	.30
❑ 343 Paul Konerko	1.00	.30
❑ 344 Joe Mays	1.00	.30
❑ 345 Marquis Grissom	1.00	.30
❑ 346 Neifi Perez	1.00	.30

Card	MINT	NRMT
❑ 347 Preston Wilson	1.00	.30
❑ 348 Jeff Weaver	1.00	.30
❑ 349 Eric Chavez	1.00	.30
❑ 350 Placido Polanco	1.00	.30
❑ 351 Matt Mantei	1.00	.30
❑ 352 James Baldwin	1.00	.30
❑ 353 Toby Hall	1.00	.30
❑ 354 Benji Gil	1.00	.30
❑ 355 Damian Moss	1.00	.30
❑ 356 Jorge Julio	1.00	.30
❑ 357 Matt Clement	1.00	.30
❑ 358 Lee Stevens	1.00	.30
❑ 359 Dave Roberts	1.00	.30
❑ 360 J.C. Romero	1.00	.30
❑ 361 Bartolo Colon	1.00	.30
❑ 362 Roger Cedeno	1.00	.30
❑ 363 Mariano Rivera	1.50	.45
❑ 364 Billy Koch	1.00	.30
❑ 365 Manny Ramirez	1.50	.45
❑ 366 Travis Lee	1.00	.30
❑ 367 Oliver Perez	1.00	.30
❑ 368 Tim Worrell	1.00	.30
❑ 369 Damian Miller	1.00	.30
❑ 370 John Smoltz	1.50	.45
❑ 371 Willis Roberts	1.00	.30
❑ 372 Tim Hudson	1.00	.30
❑ 373 Moises Alou	1.00	.30
❑ 374 Corky Miller	1.00	.30
❑ 375 Ben Broussard	1.00	.30
❑ 376 Gabe Kapler	1.00	.30
❑ 377 Chris Woodward	1.00	.30
❑ 378 Todd Hollandsworth	1.00	.30
❑ 379 So Taguchi	1.00	.30
❑ 380 John Olerud	1.00	.30
❑ 381 Reggie Sanders	1.00	.30
❑ 382 Jake Peavy	1.00	.30
❑ 383 Kris Benson	1.00	.30
❑ 384 Ray Durham	1.00	.30
❑ 385 Boomer Wells	1.00	.30
❑ 386 Tom Glavine	1.50	.45
❑ 387 Antonio Alfonseca	1.00	.30
❑ 388 Keith Foulke	1.00	.30
❑ 389 Shawn Estes	1.00	.30
❑ 390 Mark Grace	1.50	.45
❑ 391 Dmitri Young	1.00	.30
❑ 392 A.J. Burnett	1.00	.30
❑ 393 Richard Hidalgo	1.00	.30
❑ 394 Mike Sweeney	1.00	.30
❑ 395 Doug Mientkiewicz	1.00	.30
❑ 396 Cory Lidle	1.00	.30
❑ 397 Jeff Bagwell	1.50	.45
❑ 398 Steve Sparks	1.00	.30
❑ 399 Sandy Alomar Jr.	1.00	.30
❑ 400 John Lackey	1.00	.30
❑ 401 Rick Helling	1.00	.30
❑ 402 Carlos Lee	1.00	.30
❑ 403 Garret Anderson	1.00	.30
❑ 404 Vinny Castilla	1.00	.30
❑ 405 David Bell	1.00	.30
❑ 406 Freddy Garcia	1.00	.30
❑ 407 Scott Spiezio	1.00	.30
❑ 408 Russell Branyan	1.00	.30
❑ 409 Jose Contreras RC	3.00	.90
❑ 410 Kevin Brown	1.00	.30
❑ 411 Tyler Houston	1.00	.30
❑ 412 A.J. Pierzynski	1.00	.30
❑ 413 Peter Bergeron	1.00	.30
❑ 414 Brett Myers	1.00	.30
❑ 415 Kenny Lofton	1.00	.30
❑ 416 Ben Davis	1.00	.30
❑ 417 J.D. Drew	1.00	.30
❑ 418 Ricky Gutierrez	1.00	.30
❑ 419 Mark Redman	1.00	.30
❑ 420 Juan Encarnacion	1.00	.30
❑ 421 Bryan Bullington DP RC	1.50	.45
❑ 422 Jeremy Guthrie DP	1.50	.45
❑ 423 Joey Gomes DP RC	1.50	.45
❑ 424 E.Bastida-Martinez DP RC	1.50	.45
❑ 425 Brian Wright DP RC	1.50	.45
❑ 426 B.J. Upton DP	2.50	.75
❑ 427 Jeff Francis DP	1.50	.45
❑ 428 Jeremy Hermida DP	1.50	.45
❑ 429 Khalil Greene DP	4.00	1.20
❑ 430 Darrell Rasner DP RC	1.50	.45
❑ 431 Brandon Phillips	2.50	.75
Victor Martinez		
❑ 432 Hee Seop Choi	1.50	.45
Nic Jackson		
❑ 433 Dontrelle Willis	2.50	.75
Jason Stokes		
❑ 434 Chad Tracy	1.50	.45
Lyle Overbay		
❑ 435 Joe Borchard	1.50	.45
Corwin Malone		
❑ 436 Joe Mauer	1.50	.45
Justin Morneau		
❑ 437 Drew Henson	1.50	.45
Brandon Claussen		
❑ 438 Chase Utley	2.50	.75
Gavin Floyd		
❑ 439 Taggert Bozied	1.50	.45
Xavier Nady		
❑ 440 Aaron Heilman	1.50	.45
Jose Reyes		

2003 Topps Chrome Traded

	MINT	NRMT
COMPLETE SET (275)	120.00	55.00
COMMON CARD (1-120)	.75	.35
COMMON CARD (121-165)	1.00	.45
COMMON CARD (166-275)	1.00	.45
2 PER 2003 TOPPS TRADED HOBBY PACK		.00
2 PER 2003 TOPPS TRADED HTA PACK		.00
2 PER 2003 TOPPS TRADED RETAIL PACK		.00

Card	MINT	NRMT
❑ T1 Juan Pierre	.75	.35
❑ T2 Mark Grudzielanek	.75	.35
❑ T3 Tanyon Sturtze	.75	.35
❑ T4 Greg Vaughn	.75	.35
❑ T5 Greg Myers	.75	.35
❑ T6 Randall Simon	.75	.35
❑ T7 Todd Hundley	.75	.35
❑ T8 Marlon Anderson	.75	.35
❑ T9 Jeff Reboulet	.75	.35
❑ T10 Alex Sanchez	.75	.35
❑ T11 Mike Rivera	.75	.35
❑ T12 Todd Walker	.75	.35
❑ T13 Ray King	.75	.35
❑ T14 Shawn Estes	.75	.35
❑ T15 Gary Matthews Jr.	.75	.35
❑ T16 Jaret Wright	.75	.35
❑ T17 Edgardo Alfonzo	.75	.35
❑ T18 Omar Daal	.75	.35
❑ T19 Ryan Rupe	.75	.35
❑ T20 Tony Clark	.75	.35
❑ T21 Jeff Suppan	.75	.35
❑ T22 Mike Stanton	.75	.35
❑ T23 Ramon Martinez	.75	.35
❑ T24 Armando Rios	.75	.35
❑ T25 Johnny Estrada	.75	.35
❑ T26 Joe Girardi	.75	.35
❑ T27 Ivan Rodriguez	1.25	.55
❑ T28 Robert Fick	.75	.35
❑ T29 Rick White	.75	.35
❑ T30 Robert Person	.75	.35
❑ T31 Alan Benes	.75	.35
❑ T32 Chris Carpenter	.75	.35
❑ T33 Chris Widger	.75	.35
❑ T34 Travis Hafner	.75	.35
❑ T35 Mike Venafro	.75	.35
❑ T36 Jon Lieber	.75	.35
❑ T37 Orlando Hernandez	.75	.35
❑ T38 Aaron Myette	.75	.35
❑ T39 Paul Bako	.75	.35
❑ T40 Erubiel Durazo	.75	.35
❑ T41 Mark Guthrie	.75	.35
❑ T42 Steve Avery	.75	.35
❑ T43 Damian Jackson	.75	.35
❑ T44 Rey Ordonez	.75	.35
❑ T45 John Flaherty	.75	.35
❑ T46 Byung-Hyun Kim	.75	.35
❑ T47 Tom Goodwin	.75	.35
❑ T48 Elmer Dessens	.75	.35
❑ T49 Al Martin	.75	.35
❑ T50 Gene Kingsale	.75	.35
❑ T51 Lenny Harris	.75	.35
❑ T52 David Ortiz Sox	2.00	.90
❑ T53 Jose Lima	.75	.35
❑ T54 Mike Difelice	.75	.35
❑ T55 Jose Hernandez	.75	.35
❑ T56 Todd Zeile	.75	.35
❑ T57 Roberto Hernandez	.75	.35
❑ T58 Albie Lopez	.75	.35
❑ T59 Roberto Alomar	1.25	.55
❑ T60 Russ Ortiz	.75	.35
❑ T61 Brian Daubach	.75	.35
❑ T62 Carl Everett	.75	.35
❑ T63 Jeromy Burnitz	.75	.35
❑ T64 Mark Bellhorn	.75	.35
❑ T65 Ruben Sierra	.75	.35
❑ T66 Mike Fetters	.75	.35
❑ T67 Armando Benitez	.75	.35
❑ T68 Deivi Cruz	.75	.35
❑ T69 Jose Cruz Jr.	.75	.35
❑ T70 Jeremy Fikac	.75	.35
❑ T71 Jeff Kent	.75	.35
❑ T72 Andres Galarraga	.75	.35
❑ T73 Rickey Henderson	2.00	.90
❑ T74 Royce Clayton	.75	.35
❑ T75 Troy O'Leary	.75	.35
❑ T76 Ron Coomer	.75	.35
❑ T77 Greg Colbrunn	.75	.35
❑ T78 Wes Helms	.75	.35
❑ T79 Kevin Millwood	.75	.35
❑ T80 Damion Easley	.75	.35
❑ T81 Bobby Kielty	.75	.35
❑ T82 Keith Osik	.75	.35
❑ T83 Ramiro Mendoza	.75	.35
❑ T84 Shea Hillenbrand	.75	.35
❑ T85 Shannon Stewart	.75	.35
❑ T86 Eddie Perez	.75	.35
❑ T87 Ugueth Urbina	.75	.35
❑ T88 Orlando Palmeiro	.75	.35
❑ T89 Graeme Lloyd	.75	.35
❑ T90 John Vander Wal	.75	.35
❑ T91 Gary Bennett	.75	.35
❑ T92 Shane Reynolds	.75	.35
❑ T93 Steve Parris	.75	.35
❑ T94 Julio Lugo	.75	.35
❑ T95 John Halama	.75	.35
❑ T96 Carlos Baerga	.75	.35
❑ T97 Jim Parque	.75	.35
❑ T98 Mike Williams	.75	.35
❑ T99 Fred McGriff	1.25	.55
❑ T100 Kenny Rogers	.75	.35
❑ T101 Matt Herges	.75	.35
❑ T102 Jay Bell	.75	.35
❑ T103 Esteban Yan	.75	.35
❑ T104 Eric Owens	.75	.35
❑ T105 Aaron Fultz	.75	.35
❑ T106 Rey Sanchez	.75	.35
❑ T107 Jim Thome	1.25	.55
❑ T108 Aaron Boone	.75	.35
❑ T109 Raul Mondesi	.75	.35
❑ T110 Kenny Lofton	.75	.35
❑ T111 Jose Guillen	.75	.35
❑ T112 Aramis Ramirez	.75	.35
❑ T113 Sidney Ponson	.75	.35
❑ T114 Scott Williamson	.75	.35
❑ T115 Robin Ventura	.75	.35
❑ T116 Dusty Baker MG	.75	.35
❑ T117 Felipe Alou MG	.75	.35
❑ T118 Buck Showalter MG	.75	.35
❑ T119 Jack McKeon MG	.75	.35
❑ T120 Art Howe MG	.75	.35
❑ T121 Bobby Crosby PROS	1.50	.70
❑ T122 Adrian Gonzalez PROS	1.00	.45
❑ T123 Kevin Cash PROS	1.00	.45

Card	Nm-Mt	Ex-Mt
❑ T124 Shin-Soo Choo PROS	1.00	.45
❑ T125 Chin-Feng Chen PROS	2.50	1.10
❑ T126 Miguel Cabrera PROS	2.50	1.10
❑ T127 Jason Young PROS	1.00	.45
❑ T128 Alex Herrera PROS	1.00	.45
❑ T129 Jason Dubois PROS	1.00	.45
❑ T130 Jeff Mathis PROS	1.00	.45
❑ T131 Casey Kotchman PROS	1.00	.45
❑ T132 Ed Rogers PROS	1.00	.45
❑ T133 Wilson Betemit PROS	1.00	.45
❑ T134 Jim Kavourias PROS	1.00	.45
❑ T135 Taylor Buchholz PROS	1.00	.45
❑ T136 Adam LaRoche PROS	1.00	.45
❑ T137 D.McPherson PROS	1.00	.45
❑ T138 Jesus Cota PROS	1.00	.45
❑ T139 Clint Nageotte PROS	1.00	.45
❑ T140 Boof Bonser PROS	1.00	.45
❑ T141 Walter Young PROS	1.00	.45
❑ T142 Joe Crede PROS	1.00	.45
❑ T143 Denny Bautista PROS	1.00	.45
❑ T144 Victor Diaz PROS	1.00	.45
❑ T145 Chris Narveson PROS	1.00	.45
❑ T146 Gabe Gross PROS	1.00	.45
❑ T147 Jimmy Journell PROS	1.00	.45
❑ T148 Rafael Soriano PROS	1.00	.45
❑ T149 Jerome Williams PROS	1.00	.45
❑ T150 Aaron Cook PROS	1.00	.45
❑ T151 An. Martinez PROS	1.00	.45
❑ T152 Scott Hairston PROS	1.00	.45
❑ T153 John Buck PROS	1.00	.45
❑ T154 Ryan Ludwick PROS	1.00	.45
❑ T155 Chris Bootcheck PROS	1.00	.45
❑ T156 John Rheinecker PROS	1.00	.45
❑ T157 Jason Lane PROS	1.00	.45
❑ T158 Shelley Duncan PROS	1.00	.45
❑ T159 Adam Wainwright PROS	1.00	.45
❑ T160 Jason Arnold PROS	1.00	.45
❑ T161 Jonny Gomes PROS	1.50	.70
❑ T162 James Loney PROS	1.00	.45
❑ T163 Mike Fontenot PROS	1.00	.45
❑ T164 Khalil Greene PROS	4.00	1.80
❑ T165 Sean Burnett PROS	1.00	.45
❑ T166 David Martinez FY RC	1.00	.45
❑ T167 Felix Pie FY RC	10.00	4.50
❑ T168 Joe Valentine FY RC	1.00	.45
❑ T169 Brandon Webb FY RC	2.00	.90
❑ T170 Matt Diaz FY RC	1.25	.55
❑ T171 Lew Ford FY RC	1.25	.55
❑ T172 Jeremy Griffiths FY RC	1.00	.45
❑ T173 Matt Hensley FY RC	1.00	.45
❑ T174 Charlie Manning FY RC	1.00	.45
❑ T175 Elizardo Ramirez FY RC	1.25	.55
❑ T176 Greg Aquino FY RC	1.00	.45
❑ T177 Felix Sanchez FY RC	1.00	.45
❑ T178 Kelly Shoppach FY RC	2.00	.90
❑ T179 Bubba Nelson FY RC	1.25	.55
❑ T180 Mike O'Keefe FY RC	1.00	.45
❑ T181 Hanley Ramirez FY RC	5.00	2.20
❑ T182 T.Wellemeyer FY RC	1.00	.45
❑ T183 Dustin Moseley FY RC	1.00	.45
❑ T184 Eric Crozier FY RC	1.25	.55
❑ T185 Ryan Shealy FY RC	2.00	.90
❑ T186 Jer. Bonderman FY RC	6.00	2.70
❑ T187 T.Story-Harden FY RC	1.00	.45
❑ T188 Dusty Brown FY RC	1.00	.45
❑ T189 Rob Hammock FY RC	1.00	.45
❑ T190 Jorge Piedra FY RC	1.25	.55
❑ T191 Chris De La Cruz FY RC	1.00	.45
❑ T192 Eli Whiteside FY RC	1.00	.45
❑ T193 Jason Kubel FY RC	2.00	.90
❑ T194 Jon Schuerholz FY RC	1.00	.45
❑ T195 St. Randolph FY RC	1.00	.45
❑ T196 Andy Sisco FY RC	1.25	.55
❑ T197 Sean Smith FY RC	1.25	.55
❑ T198 Jon-Mark Sprowl FY RC	1.00	.45
❑ T199 Matt Kata FY RC	1.00	.45
❑ T200 Robinson Cano FY RC	12.00	5.50
❑ T201 Nook Logan FY RC	1.25	.55
❑ T202 Ben Francisco FY RC	1.00	.45
❑ T203 Arnie Munoz FY RC	1.00	.45
❑ T204 Ozzie Chavez FY RC	1.00	.45
❑ T205 Eric Riggs FY RC	1.25	.55
❑ T206 Beau Kemp FY RC	1.00	.45
❑ T207 Travis Wong FY RC	1.25	.55
❑ T208 Dustin Yount FY RC	1.25	.55
❑ T209 Brian McCann FY RC	8.00	3.60
❑ T210 Wilton Reynolds FY RC	1.25	.55
❑ T211 Matt Bruback FY RC	1.00	.45
❑ T212 Andrew Brown FY RC	1.25	.55
❑ T213 Edgar Gonzalez FY RC	1.00	.45
❑ T214 Eider Torres FY RC	1.00	.45
❑ T215 Aquilino Lopez FY RC	1.00	.45
❑ T216 Bobby Basham FY RC	1.25	.55
❑ T217 Tim Olson FY RC	1.00	.45
❑ T218 Nathan Panther FY RC	1.00	.45
❑ T219 Bryan Grace FY RC	1.00	.45
❑ T220 Dusty Gomon FY RC	1.25	.55
❑ T221 Wil Ledezma FY RC	1.00	.45
❑ T222 Josh Willingham FY RC	1.25	.55
❑ T223 David Cash FY RC	1.00	.45
❑ T224 Oscar Villarreal FY RC	1.00	.45
❑ T225 Jeff Duncan FY RC	1.00	.45
❑ T226 Kade Johnson FY RC	1.00	.45
❑ T227 L.Steidlmayer FY RC	1.00	.45
❑ T228 Brandon Watson FY RC	1.00	.45
❑ T229 Jose Morales FY RC	1.00	.45
❑ T230 Mike Gallo FY RC	1.00	.45
❑ T231 Tyler Adamczyk FY RC	1.00	.45
❑ T232 Adam Stern FY RC	1.00	.45
❑ T233 Brennan King FY RC	1.00	.45
❑ T234 Dan Haren FY RC	2.00	.90
❑ T235 Mi. Hernandez FY RC	1.00	.45
❑ T236 Ben Fritz FY RC	1.00	.45
❑ T237 Clay Hensley FY RC	1.00	.45
❑ T238 Tyler Johnson FY RC	1.00	.45
❑ T239 Pete LaForest FY RC	1.00	.45
❑ T240 Tyler Martin FY RC	1.00	.45
❑ T241 J.D. Durbin FY RC	1.00	.45
❑ T242 Shane Victorino FY RC	1.25	.55
❑ T243 Rajai Davis FY RC	1.00	.45
❑ T244 Ismael Castro FY RC	1.00	.45
❑ T245 C.Wang FY RC	6.00	2.70
❑ T246 Travis Ishikawa FY RC	1.00	.45
❑ T247 Corey Shafer FY RC	1.00	.45
❑ T248 G.Schneidmiller FY RC	1.00	.45
❑ T249 Dave Pember FY RC	1.00	.45
❑ T250 Keith Stamler FY RC	1.00	.45
❑ T251 Tyson Graham FY RC	1.00	.45
❑ T252 Ryan Cameron FY RC	1.00	.45
❑ T253 Eric Eckenstahler FY	1.00	.45
❑ T254 Ma. Peterson FY RC	1.00	.45
❑ T255 Dustin McGowan FY RC	1.00	.45
❑ T256 Pr. Redman FY RC	1.00	.45
❑ T257 Haj Turay FY RC	1.25	.55
❑ T258 Carlos Guzman FY RC	1.25	.55
❑ T259 Matt DeMarco FY RC	1.00	.45
❑ T260 Derek Michaelis FY RC	1.00	.45
❑ T261 Brian Burgamy FY RC	1.00	.45
❑ T262 Jay Sitzman FY RC	1.00	.45
❑ T263 Chris Fallon FY RC	1.00	.45
❑ T264 Mike Adams FY RC	1.00	.45
❑ T265 Clint Barmes FY RC	4.00	1.80
❑ T266 Eric Reed FY RC	1.00	.45
❑ T267 Willie Eyre FY RC	1.00	.45
❑ T268 Carlos Duran FY RC	1.00	.45
❑ T269 Nick Trzesniak FY RC	1.00	.45
❑ T270 Ferdin Tejeda FY RC	1.00	.45
❑ T271 Mi. Garciaparra FY RC	1.00	.45
❑ T272 Michael Hinckley FY RC	1.25	.55
❑ T273 Br. Florence FY RC	1.00	.45
❑ T274 Trent Oeltjen FY RC	1.25	.55
❑ T275 Mike Neu FY RC	1.00	.45

2004 Topps Chrome

	Nm-Mt	Ex-Mt
COMP.SERIES 1 w/o SP's (220)	80.00	24.00
COMP.SERIES 2 w/o SP's (220)	80.00	24.00
COMMON (1-210/257-466)	1.00	.30
COMMON (211-220/247-256)	2.00	.60
COMMON AU (221-233)	10.00	3.00

Card	Nm-Mt	Ex-Mt
❑ 1 Jim Thome	1.50	.45
❑ 2 Reggie Sanders	1.00	.30
❑ 3 Mark Kotsay	1.00	.30
❑ 4 Edgardo Alfonzo	1.00	.30
❑ 5 Tim Wakefield	1.00	.30
❑ 6 Moises Alou	1.00	.30
❑ 7 Jorge Julio	1.00	.30
❑ 8 Bartolo Colon	1.00	.30
❑ 9 Chan Ho Park	1.00	.30
❑ 10 Ichiro Suzuki	5.00	1.50

Card	Nm-Mt	Ex-Mt
❑ 11 Kevin Millwood	1.00	.30
❑ 12 Preston Wilson	1.00	.30
❑ 13 Tom Glavine	1.50	.45
❑ 14 Junior Spivey	1.00	.30
❑ 15 Marcus Giles	1.00	.30
❑ 16 David Segui	1.00	.30
❑ 17 Kevin Millar	1.00	.30
❑ 18 Corey Patterson	1.00	.30
❑ 19 Aaron Rowand	1.00	.30
❑ 20 Derek Jeter	5.00	1.50
❑ 21 Luis Castillo	1.00	.30
❑ 22 Manny Ramirez	1.50	.45
❑ 23 Jay Payton	1.00	.30
❑ 24 Bobby Higginson	1.00	.30
❑ 25 Lance Berkman	1.00	.30
❑ 26 Juan Pierre	1.00	.30
❑ 27 Mike Mussina	1.50	.45
❑ 28 Fred McGriff	1.50	.45
❑ 29 Richie Sexson	1.00	.30
❑ 30 Tim Hudson	1.00	.30
❑ 31 Mike Piazza	4.00	1.20
❑ 32 Brad Radke	1.00	.30
❑ 33 Jeff Weaver	1.00	.30
❑ 34 Ramon Hernandez	1.00	.30
❑ 35 David Bell	1.00	.30
❑ 36 Randy Wolf	1.00	.30
❑ 37 Jake Peavy	1.00	.30
❑ 38 Tim Worrell	1.00	.30
❑ 39 Gil Meche	1.00	.30
❑ 40 Albert Pujols	5.00	1.50
❑ 41 Michael Young	1.00	.30
❑ 42 Josh Phelps	1.00	.30
❑ 43 Brendan Donnelly	1.00	.30
❑ 44 Steve Finley	1.00	.30
❑ 45 John Smoltz	1.50	.45
❑ 46 Jay Gibbons	1.00	.30
❑ 47 Trot Nixon	1.00	.30
❑ 48 Carl Pavano	1.00	.30
❑ 49 Frank Thomas	2.50	.75
❑ 50 Mark Prior	1.50	.45
❑ 51 Danny Graves	1.00	.30
❑ 52 Milton Bradley	1.00	.30
❑ 53 Kris Benson	1.00	.30
❑ 54 Ryan Klesko	1.00	.30
❑ 55 Mike Lowell	1.00	.30
❑ 56 Geoff Blum	1.00	.30
❑ 57 Michael Tucker	1.00	.30
❑ 58 Paul Lo Duca	1.00	.30
❑ 59 Vicente Padilla	1.00	.30
❑ 60 Jacque Jones	1.00	.30
❑ 61 Fernando Tatis	1.00	.30
❑ 62 Ty Wigginton	1.00	.30
❑ 63 Rich Aurilia	1.00	.30
❑ 64 Andy Pettitte	1.50	.45
❑ 65 Terrence Long	1.00	.30
❑ 66 Cliff Floyd	1.00	.30
❑ 67 Mariano Rivera	1.50	.45
❑ 68 Kelvim Escobar	1.00	.30
❑ 69 Marlon Byrd	1.00	.30
❑ 70 Mark Mulder	1.00	.30
❑ 71 Francisco Cordero	1.00	.30
❑ 72 Carlos Guillen	1.00	.30
❑ 73 Fernando Vina	1.00	.30
❑ 74 Lance Carter	1.00	.30
❑ 75 Hank Blalock	1.00	.30
❑ 76 Jimmy Rollins	1.00	.30
❑ 77 Francisco Rodriguez	1.00	.30
❑ 78 Javy Lopez	1.00	.30

❑ 79 Jerry Hairston Jr. 1.00 .30
❑ 80 Andruw Jones 1.50 .45
❑ 81 Rodrigo Lopez 1.00 .30
❑ 82 Johnny Damon 1.50 .45
❑ 83 Hee Seop Choi 1.00 .30
❑ 84 Kazuhiro Sasaki 1.00 .30
❑ 85 Danny Bautista 1.00 .30
❑ 86 Matt Lawton 1.00 .30
❑ 87 Juan Uribe 1.00 .30
❑ 88 Rafael Furcal 1.00 .30
❑ 89 Kyle Farnsworth 1.00 .30
❑ 90 Jose Vidro 1.00 .30
❑ 91 Luis Rivas 1.00 .30
❑ 92 Hideo Nomo 2.50 .75
❑ 93 Javier Vazquez 1.00 .30
❑ 94 Al Leiter 1.00 .30
❑ 95 Jose Valentin 1.00 .30
❑ 96 Alex Cintron 1.00 .30
❑ 97 Zach Day 1.00 .30
❑ 98 Jorge Posada 1.50 .45
❑ 99 C.C. Sabathia 1.00 .30
❑ 100 Alex Rodriguez 4.00 1.20
❑ 101 Brad Penny 1.00 .30
❑ 102 Brad Ausmus 1.00 .30
❑ 103 Raul Ibanez 1.00 .30
❑ 104 Mike Hampton 1.00 .30
❑ 105 Adrian Beltre 1.00 .30
❑ 106 Ramiro Mendoza 1.00 .30
❑ 107 Rocco Baldelli 1.00 .30
❑ 108 Esteban Loaiza 1.00 .30
❑ 109 Russell Branyan 1.00 .30
❑ 110 Todd Helton 1.50 .45
❑ 111 Braden Looper 1.00 .30
❑ 112 Octavio Dotel 1.00 .30
❑ 113 Mike MacDougal 1.00 .30
❑ 114 Cesar Izturis 1.00 .30
❑ 115 Johan Santana 1.50 .45
❑ 116 Jose Contreras 1.00 .30
❑ 117 Placido Polanco 1.00 .30
❑ 118 Jason Phillips 1.00 .30
❑ 119 Orlando Hudson 1.00 .30
❑ 120 Vernon Wells 1.00 .30
❑ 121 Ben Grieve 1.00 .30
❑ 122 Dave Roberts 1.00 .30
❑ 123 Ismael Valdes 1.00 .30
❑ 124 Eric Owens 1.00 .30
❑ 125 Curt Schilling 1.00 .30
❑ 126 Russ Ortiz 1.00 .30
❑ 127 Mark Buehrle 1.00 .30
❑ 128 Doug Mientkiewicz 1.00 .30
❑ 129 Dmitri Young 1.00 .30
❑ 130 Kazuhisa Ishii 1.00 .30
❑ 131 A.J. Pierzynski 1.00 .30
❑ 132 Brad Wilkerson 1.00 .30
❑ 133 Joe McEwing 1.00 .30
❑ 134 Alex Cora 1.00 .30
❑ 135 Jose Cruz Jr. 1.00 .30
❑ 136 Carlos Zambrano 1.00 .30
❑ 137 Jeff Kent 1.00 .30
❑ 138 Shigetoshi Hasegawa 1.00 .30
❑ 139 Jarrod Washburn 1.00 .30
❑ 140 Greg Maddux 4.00 1.20
❑ 141 Josh Beckett 1.00 .30
❑ 142 Miguel Batista 1.00 .30
❑ 143 Omar Vizquel 1.50 .45
❑ 144 Alex Gonzalez 1.00 .30
❑ 145 Billy Wagner 1.00 .30
❑ 146 Brian Jordan 1.00 .30
❑ 147 Wes Helms 1.00 .30
❑ 148 Deivi Cruz 1.00 .30
❑ 149 Alex Gonzalez 1.00 .30
❑ 150 Jason Giambi 1.00 .30
❑ 151 Erubiel Durazo 1.00 .30
❑ 152 Mike Lieberthal 1.00 .30
❑ 153 Jason Kendall 1.00 .30
❑ 154 Xavier Nady 1.00 .30
❑ 155 Kirk Rueter 1.00 .30
❑ 156 Mike Cameron 1.00 .30
❑ 157 Miguel Cairo 1.00 .30
❑ 158 Woody Williams 1.00 .30
❑ 159 Toby Hall 1.00 .30
❑ 160 Bernie Williams 1.50 .45
❑ 161 Darin Erstad 1.00 .30
❑ 162 Matt Mantei 1.00 .30
❑ 163 Shawn Chacon 1.00 .30
❑ 164 Bill Mueller 1.00 .30
❑ 165 Damian Miller 1.00 .30
❑ 166 Tony Graffanino 1.00 .30
❑ 167 Sean Casey 1.50 .45
❑ 168 Brandon Phillips 1.00 .30
❑ 169 Runelvys Hernandez 1.00 .30
❑ 170 Adam Dunn 1.00 .30
❑ 171 Carlos Lee 1.00 .30
❑ 172 Juan Encarnacion 1.00 .30
❑ 173 Angel Berroa 1.00 .30
❑ 174 Desi Relaford 1.00 .30
❑ 175 Joe Mays 1.00 .30
❑ 176 Ben Sheets 1.00 .30
❑ 177 Eddie Guardado 1.00 .30
❑ 178 Rocky Biddle 1.00 .30
❑ 179 Eric Gagne 1.00 .30
❑ 180 Eric Chavez 1.00 .30
❑ 181 Jason Michaels 1.00 .30
❑ 182 Dustan Mohr 1.00 .30
❑ 183 Kip Wells 1.00 .30
❑ 184 Brian Lawrence 1.00 .30
❑ 185 Bret Boone 1.00 .30
❑ 186 Tino Martinez 1.50 .45
❑ 187 Aubrey Huff 1.00 .30
❑ 188 Kevin Mench 1.00 .30
❑ 189 Tim Salmon 1.50 .45
❑ 190 Carlos Delgado 1.00 .30
❑ 191 John Lackey 1.00 .30
❑ 192 Eric Byrnes 1.00 .30
❑ 193 Luis Matos 1.00 .30
❑ 194 Derek Lowe 1.00 .30
❑ 195 Mark Grudzielanek 1.00 .30
❑ 196 Tom Gordon 1.00 .30
❑ 197 Matt Clement 1.00 .30
❑ 198 Byung-Hyun Kim 1.00 .30
❑ 199 Brandon Inge 1.00 .30
❑ 200 Nomar Garciaparra 4.00 1.20
❑ 201 Frank Catalanotto 1.00 .30
❑ 202 Cristian Guzman 1.00 .30
❑ 203 Bo Hart 1.00 .30
❑ 204 Jack Wilson 1.00 .30
❑ 205 Ray Durham 1.00 .30
❑ 206 Freddy Garcia 1.00 .30
❑ 207 J.D. Drew 1.00 .30
❑ 208 Orlando Cabrera 1.00 .30
❑ 209 Roy Halladay 1.00 .30
❑ 210 David Eckstein 1.00 .30
❑ 211 Omar Falcon FY RC 2.00 .60
❑ 212 Todd Self FY RC 3.00 .90
❑ 213 David Murphy FY RC 3.00 .90
❑ 214 Dioner Navarro FY RC 4.00 1.20
❑ 215 Marcus McBeth FY RC 2.00 .60
❑ 216 Chris O'Riordan FY RC 2.00 .60
❑ 217 Rodney Choy Foo FY RC 2.00 .60
❑ 218 Tim Frend FY RC 2.00 .60
❑ 219 Yadier Molina FY RC 5.00 1.50
❑ 220 Zach Duke FY RC 10.00 3.00
❑ 221 Anthony Lerew FY AU RC 15.00 4.50
❑ 222 B.Hawksworth FY AU RC 15.00 4.50
❑ 223 Brayan Pena FY AU RC 10.00 3.00
❑ 224 Craig Ansman FY AU RC 10.00 3.00
❑ 225 Jon Knott FY AU RC 10.00 3.00
❑ 226 Josh Labandeira FY AU RC 10.00 3.00
❑ 227 Khalid Ballouli FY AU RC 10.00 3.00
❑ 228 Kyle Davies FY AU RC 40.00 12.00
❑ 229 Matt Creighton FY AU RC 10.00 3.00
❑ 230 Mike Gosling FY AU RC 10.00 3.00
❑ 231 Nic Ungs FY AU RC 10.00 3.00
❑ 232 Zach Miner FY AU RC 15.00 4.50
❑ 233 Donald Levinski FY AU RC 10.00 3.00
❑ 234A Bradley Sullivan FY AU RC 15.00 4.50
❑ 234B B.Sullivan FY AU ERR 345 25.00 7.50
❑ 235 Carlos Quentin FY AU RC 40.00 12.00
❑ 236 Conor Jackson FY AU RC 60.00 18.00
❑ 237 Estee Harris FY AU RC 15.00 4.50
❑ 238 Jeffrey Allison FY AU RC 10.00 3.00
❑ 239 Kyle Sleeth FY AU RC 20.00 6.00
❑ 240 Matthew Moses FY AU RC 25.00 7.50
❑ 241 Tim Stauffer FY AU RC 20.00 6.00
❑ 242 Brad Snyder FY AU RC 20.00 6.00
❑ 243 Jason Hirsh FY AU RC 20.00 6.00
❑ 244 L.Milledge FY AU RC 40.00 12.00
❑ 245 Logan Kensing FY AU RC 10.00 3.00
❑ 246 Kory Casto FY AU RC 15.00 4.50
❑ 247 David Aardsma FY RC 3.00 .90
❑ 248 Omar Quintanilla FY RC 3.00 .90
❑ 249 Ervin Santana FY RC 5.00 1.50
❑ 250 Merkin Valdez FY RC 3.00 .90
❑ 251 Vito Chiaravalloti FY RC 2.00 .60
❑ 252 Travis Blackley FY RC 2.00 .60
❑ 253 Chris Shelton FY RC 4.00 1.20
❑ 254 Rudy Guillen FY RC 3.00 .90
❑ 255 Bobby Brownlie FY RC 3.00 .90
❑ 256 Paul Maholm FY RC 4.00 1.20
❑ 257 Roger Clemens 5.00 1.50
❑ 258 Laynce Nix 1.00 .30
❑ 259 Eric Hinske 1.00 .30
❑ 260 Ivan Rodriguez 1.50 .45
❑ 261 Brandon Webb 1.00 .30
❑ 262 Jhonny Peralta 1.00 .30
❑ 263 Adam Kennedy 1.00 .30
❑ 264 Tony Batista 1.00 .30
❑ 265 Jeff Suppan 1.00 .30
❑ 266 Kenny Lofton 1.00 .30
❑ 267 Scott Sullivan 1.00 .30
❑ 268 Ken Griffey Jr. 4.00 1.20
❑ 269 Juan Rivera 1.00 .30
❑ 270 Larry Walker 1.00 .30
❑ 271 Todd Hollandsworth 1.00 .30
❑ 272 Carlos Beltran 1.00 .30
❑ 273 Carl Crawford 1.00 .30
❑ 274 Karim Garcia 1.00 .30
❑ 275 Jose Reyes 1.00 .30
❑ 276 Brandon Duckworth 1.00 .30
❑ 277 Brian Giles 1.00 .30
❑ 278 J.T. Snow 1.00 .30
❑ 279 Jamie Moyer 1.00 .30
❑ 280 Julio Lugo 1.00 .30
❑ 281 Mark Teixeira 1.50 .45
❑ 282 Cory Lidle 1.00 .30
❑ 283 Lyle Overbay 1.00 .30
❑ 284 Troy Percival 1.00 .30
❑ 285 Robby Hammock 1.00 .30
❑ 286 Jason Johnson 1.00 .30
❑ 287 Damian Rolls 1.00 .30
❑ 288 Antonio Alfonseca 1.00 .30
❑ 289 Tom Goodwin 1.00 .30
❑ 290 Paul Konerko 1.00 .30
❑ 291 D'Angelo Jimenez 1.00 .30
❑ 292 Ben Broussard 1.00 .30
❑ 293 Magglio Ordonez 1.00 .30
❑ 294 Carlos Pena 1.00 .30
❑ 295 Chad Fox 1.00 .30
❑ 296 Jeriome Robertson 1.00 .30
❑ 297 Travis Hafner 1.00 .30
❑ 298 Joe Randa 1.00 .30
❑ 299 Brady Clark 1.00 .30
❑ 300 Barry Zito 1.00 .30
❑ 301 Ruben Sierra 1.00 .30
❑ 302 Brett Myers 1.00 .30
❑ 303 Oliver Perez 1.00 .30
❑ 304 Benito Santiago 1.00 .30
❑ 305 David Ross 1.00 .30
❑ 306 Joe Nathan 1.00 .30
❑ 307 Jim Edmonds 1.50 .45
❑ 308 Matt Kata 1.00 .30
❑ 309 Vinny Castilla 1.00 .30
❑ 310 Marty Cordova 1.00 .30
❑ 311 Aramis Ramirez 1.00 .30
❑ 312 Carl Everett 1.00 .30
❑ 313 Ryan Freel 1.00 .30
❑ 314 Mark Bellhorn Sox 1.00 .30
❑ 315 Joe Mauer 1.00 .30
❑ 316 Tim Redding 1.00 .30
❑ 317 Jeromy Burnitz 1.00 .30
❑ 318 Miguel Cabrera 1.50 .45
❑ 319 Ramon Nivar 1.00 .30
❑ 320 Casey Blake 1.00 .30
❑ 321 Adam LaRoche 1.00 .30
❑ 322 Jermaine Dye 1.00 .30
❑ 323 Jerome Williams 1.00 .30
❑ 324 John Olerud 1.00 .30
❑ 325 Scott Rolen 1.50 .45
❑ 326 Bobby Kielty 1.00 .30
❑ 327 Travis Lee 1.00 .30
❑ 328 Jeff Cirillo 1.00 .30
❑ 329 Scott Spiezio 1.00 .30
❑ 330 Melvin Mora 1.00 .30
❑ 331 Mike Timlin 1.00 .30
❑ 332 Kerry Wood 1.00 .30
❑ 333 Tony Womack 1.00 .30

❑ 334 Jody Gerut 1.00 .30
❑ 335 Morgan Ensberg 1.00 .30
❑ 336 Odalis Perez 1.00 .30
❑ 337 Michael Cuddyer 1.00 .30
❑ 338 Jose Hernandez 1.00 .30
❑ 339 LaTroy Hawkins 1.00 .30
❑ 340 Marquis Grissom 1.00 .30
❑ 341 Matt Morris 1.00 .30
❑ 342 Juan Gonzalez 1.00 .30
❑ 343 Jose Valverde 1.00 .30
❑ 344 Joe Borowski 1.00 .30
❑ 345 Josh Bard 1.00 .30
❑ 346 Austin Kearns 1.00 .30
❑ 347 Chin-Hui Tsao 1.00 .30
❑ 348 Wil Ledezma 1.00 .30
❑ 349 Aaron Guiel 1.00 .30
❑ 350 Alfonso Soriano 1.00 .30
❑ 351 Ted Lilly 1.00 .30
❑ 352 Sean Burroughs 1.00 .30
❑ 353 Rafael Palmeiro 1.50 .45
❑ 354 Quinton McCracken 1.00 .30
❑ 355 David Ortiz 2.50 .75
❑ 356 Randall Simon 1.00 .30
❑ 357 Wily Mo Pena 1.00 .30
❑ 358 Brian Anderson 1.00 .30
❑ 359 Corey Koskie 1.00 .30
❑ 360 Keith Foulke Sox 1.00 .30
❑ 361 Sidney Ponson 1.00 .30
❑ 362 Gary Matthews Jr. 1.00 .30
❑ 363 Herbert Perry 1.00 .30
❑ 364 Shea Hillenbrand 1.00 .30
❑ 365 Craig Biggio 1.50 .45
❑ 366 Barry Larkin 1.50 .45
❑ 367 Arthur Rhodes 1.00 .30
❑ 368 Sammy Sosa 2.50 .75
❑ 369 Joe Crede 1.00 .30
❑ 370 Gary Sheffield 1.00 .30
❑ 371 Coco Crisp 1.00 .30
❑ 372 Torii Hunter 1.00 .30
❑ 373 Derrek Lee 1.50 .45
❑ 374 Adam Everett 1.00 .30
❑ 375 Miguel Tejada 1.00 .30
❑ 376 Jeremy Affeldt 1.00 .30
❑ 377 Robin Ventura 1.00 .30
❑ 378 Scott Podsednik 1.00 .30
❑ 379 Matthew LeCroy 1.00 .30
❑ 380 Vladimir Guerrero 2.50 .75
❑ 381 Steve Karsay 1.00 .30
❑ 382 Jeff Nelson 1.00 .30
❑ 383 Chase Utley 1.50 .45
❑ 384 Bobby Abreu 1.00 .30
❑ 385 Josh Fogg 1.00 .30
❑ 386 Trevor Hoffman 1.00 .30
❑ 387 Matt Stairs 1.00 .30
❑ 388 Edgar Martinez 1.50 .45
❑ 389 Edgar Renteria 1.00 .30
❑ 390 Chipper Jones 2.50 .75
❑ 391 Eric Munson 1.00 .30
❑ 392 Dewon Brazelton 1.00 .30
❑ 393 John Thomson 1.00 .30
❑ 394 Chris Woodward 1.00 .30
❑ 395 Joe Kennedy 1.00 .30
❑ 396 Reed Johnson 1.00 .30
❑ 397 Johnny Estrada 1.00 .30
❑ 398 Damian Moss 1.00 .30
❑ 399 Victor Zambrano 1.00 .30
❑ 400 Dontrelle Willis 1.50 .45
❑ 401 Troy Glaus 1.00 .30
❑ 402 Raul Mondesi 1.00 .30
❑ 403 Jeff Davanon 1.00 .30
❑ 404 Kurt Ainsworth 1.00 .30
❑ 405 Pedro Martinez 1.50 .45
❑ 406 Eric Karros 1.00 .30
❑ 407 Billy Koch 1.00 .30
❑ 408 Luis Gonzalez 1.00 .30
❑ 409 Jack Cust 1.00 .30
❑ 410 Mike Sweeney 1.00 .30
❑ 411 Jason Bay 1.00 .30
❑ 412 Mark Redman 1.00 .30
❑ 413 Jason Jennings 1.00 .30
❑ 414 Rondell White 1.00 .30
❑ 415 Todd Hundley 1.00 .30
❑ 416 Shannon Stewart 1.00 .30
❑ 417 Jae Weong Seo 1.00 .30
❑ 418 Livan Hernandez 1.00 .30
❑ 419 Mark Ellis 1.00 .30
❑ 420 Pat Burrell 1.00 .30
❑ 421 Mark Loretta 1.00 .30
❑ 422 Robb Nen 1.00 .30
❑ 423 Joel Pineiro 1.00 .30
❑ 424 Todd Walker 1.00 .30
❑ 425 Jeremy Bonderman 1.00 .30
❑ 426 A.J. Burnett 1.00 .30
❑ 427 Greg Myers 1.00 .30
❑ 428 Roy Oswalt 1.00 .30
❑ 429 Carlos Baerga 1.00 .30
❑ 430 Garret Anderson 1.00 .30
❑ 431 Horacio Ramirez 1.00 .30
❑ 432 Brian Roberts 1.00 .30
❑ 433 Kevin Brown 1.00 .30
❑ 434 Eric Milton 1.00 .30
❑ 435 Ramon Vazquez 1.00 .30
❑ 436 Alex Escobar 1.00 .30
❑ 437 Alex Sanchez 1.00 .30
❑ 438 Jeff Bagwell 1.50 .45
❑ 439 Claudio Vargas 1.00 .30
❑ 440 Shawn Green 1.00 .30
❑ 441 Geoff Jenkins 1.00 .30
❑ 442 David Wells 1.00 .30
❑ 443 Nick Johnson 1.00 .30
❑ 444 Jose Guillen 1.00 .30
❑ 445 Scott Hatteberg 1.00 .30
❑ 446 Phil Nevin 1.00 .30
❑ 447 Jason Schmidt 1.00 .30
❑ 448 Ricky Ledee 1.00 .30
❑ 449 So Taguchi 1.00 .30
❑ 450 Randy Johnson 2.50 .75
❑ 451 Eric Young 1.00 .30
❑ 452 Chone Figgins 1.00 .30
❑ 453 Larry Bigbie 1.00 .30
❑ 454 Scott Williamson 1.00 .30
❑ 455 Ramon Martinez 1.00 .30
❑ 456 Roberto Alomar 1.50 .45
❑ 457 Ryan Dempster 1.00 .30
❑ 458 Ryan Ludwick 1.00 .30
❑ 459 Ramon Santiago 1.00 .30
❑ 460 Jeff Conine 1.00 .30
❑ 461 Brad Lidge 1.00 .30
❑ 462 Ken Harvey 1.00 .30
❑ 463 Guillermo Mota 1.00 .30
❑ 464 Rick Reed 1.00 .30
❑ 465 Armando Benitez 1.00 .30
❑ 466 Wade Miller 1.00 .30

2004 Topps Chrome Traded

	Nm-Mt	Ex-Mt
COMPLETE SET (220)	120.00	36.00
COMMON CARD (1-70)	.75	.23
COMMON CARD (71-90)	1.00	.30
COMMON CARD (91-110)	1.00	.30
COMMON CARD (111-220)	1.00	.30
2 PER 2004 TOPPS TRADED HOBBY PACK		.00
2 PER 2004 TOPPS TRADED HTA PACK		.00
2 PER 2004 TOPPS TRADED RETAIL PACK		.00
PLATE ODDS 1:1151 H, 1:1173 R, 1:327 HTA		.00
PLATE PRINT RUN 1 SET PER COLOR		.00
BLACK-CYAN-MAGENTA-YELLOW ISSUED		.00
NO PLATE PRICING DUE TO SCARCITY		.00

❑ T1 Pokey Reese .75 .23
❑ T2 Tony Womack .75 .23
❑ T3 Richard Hidalgo .75 .23
❑ T4 Juan Uribe .75 .23
❑ T5 J.D. Drew .75 .23
❑ T6 Alex Gonzalez .75 .23
❑ T7 Carlos Guillen .75 .23
❑ T8 Doug Mientkiewicz .75 .23
❑ T9 Fernando Vina .75 .23
❑ T10 Milton Bradley .75 .23
❑ T11 Kelvim Escobar .75 .23
❑ T12 Ben Grieve .75 .23
❑ T13 Brian Jordan .75 .23
❑ T14 A.J. Pierzynski .75 .23
❑ T15 Billy Wagner .75 .23
❑ T16 Terrence Long .75 .23
❑ T17 Carlos Beltran .75 .23
❑ T18 Carl Everett .75 .23
❑ T19 Reggie Sanders .75 .23
❑ T20 Javy Lopez .75 .23
❑ T21 Jay Payton .75 .23
❑ T22 Octavio Dotel .75 .23
❑ T23 Eddie Guardado .75 .23
❑ T24 Andy Pettitte 1.25 .35
❑ T25 Richie Sexson .75 .23
❑ T26 Ronnie Belliard .75 .23
❑ T27 Michael Tucker .75 .23
❑ T28 Brad Fullmer .75 .23
❑ T29 Freddy Garcia .75 .23
❑ T30 Bartolo Colon .75 .23
❑ T31 Larry Walker Cards 1.25 .35
❑ T32 Mark Kotsay .75 .23
❑ T33 Jason Marquis .75 .23
❑ T34 Dustan Mohr .75 .23
❑ T35 Javier Vazquez .75 .23
❑ T36 Nomar Garciaparra 3.00 .90
❑ T37 Tino Martinez 1.25 .35
❑ T38 Hee Seop Choi .75 .23
❑ T39 Damian Miller .75 .23
❑ T40 Jose Lima .75 .23
❑ T41 Ty Wigginton .75 .23
❑ T42 Raul Ibanez .75 .23
❑ T43 Danys Baez .75 .23
❑ T44 Tony Clark .75 .23
❑ T45 Greg Maddux 3.00 .90
❑ T46 Victor Zambrano .75 .23
❑ T47 Orlando Cabrera Sox .75 .23
❑ T48 Jose Cruz Jr. .75 .23
❑ T49 Kris Benson .75 .23
❑ T50 Alex Rodriguez 4.00 1.20
❑ T51 Steve Finley .75 .23
❑ T52 Ramon Hernandez .75 .23
❑ T53 Esteban Loaiza .75 .23
❑ T54 Ugueth Urbina .75 .23
❑ T55 Jeff Weaver .75 .23
❑ T56 Flash Gordon .75 .23
❑ T57 Jose Contreras .75 .23
❑ T58 Paul Lo Duca .75 .23
❑ T59 Junior Spivey .75 .23
❑ T60 Curt Schilling 1.25 .35
❑ T61 Brad Penny .75 .23
❑ T62 Braden Looper .75 .23
❑ T63 Miguel Cairo .75 .23
❑ T64 Juan Encarnacion .75 .23
❑ T65 Miguel Batista .75 .23
❑ T66 Terry Francona MG .75 .23
❑ T67 Lee Mazzilli MG .75 .23
❑ T68 Al Pedrique MG .75 .23
❑ T69 Ozzie Guillen MG 2.00 .60
❑ T70 Phil Garner MG .75 .23
❑ T71 Matt Bush DP RC 5.00 1.50
❑ T72 Homer Bailey DP RC 3.00 .90
❑ T73 Greg Golson DP RC 3.00 .90
❑ T74 Kyle Waldrop DP RC 2.50 .75
❑ T75 Richie Robnett DP RC 3.00 .90
❑ T76 Jay Rainville DP RC 4.00 1.20
❑ T77 Bill Bray DP RC 1.00 .30
❑ T78 Phillip Hughes DP RC 4.00 1.20
❑ T79 Scott Elbert DP RC 2.50 .75
❑ T80 Josh Fields DP RC 4.00 1.20
❑ T81 Justin Orenduff DP RC 2.50 .75
❑ T82 Dan Putnam DP RC 2.50 .75
❑ T83 Chris Nelson DP RC 5.00 1.50
❑ T84 Blake DeWitt DP RC 4.00 1.20
❑ T85 J.P. Howell DP RC 2.50 .75
❑ T86 Huston Street DP RC 6.00 1.80
❑ T87 Kurt Suzuki DP RC 4.00 1.20
❑ T88 Erick San Pedro DP RC 1.00 .30
❑ T89 Matt Tuiasosopo DP RC 8.00 2.40

- ❑ T90 Matt Macri DP RC 3.00 .90
- ❑ T91 Chad Tracy PROS 1.00 .30
- ❑ T92 Scott Hairston PROS 1.00 .30
- ❑ T93 Jonny Gomes PROS 1.00 .30
- ❑ T94 Chin-Feng Chen PROS 1.00 .30
- ❑ T95 Chien-Ming Wang PROS 1.00 .30
- ❑ T96 Dustin McGowan PROS 1.00 .30
- ❑ T97 Chris Burke PROS 1.00 .30
- ❑ T98 Denny Bautista PROS 1.00 .30
- ❑ T99 Preston Larrison PROS 1.00 .30
- ❑ T100 Kevin Youkilis PROS 1.00 .30
- ❑ T101 John Maine PROS 1.00 .30
- ❑ T102 Guillermo Quiroz PROS 1.00 .30
- ❑ T103 Dave Krynzel PROS 1.00 .30
- ❑ T104 David Kelton PROS 1.00 .30
- ❑ T105 Edwin Encarnacion PROS 1.00 .30
- ❑ T106 Chad Gaudin PROS 1.00 .30
- ❑ T107 Sergio Mitre PROS 1.00 .30
- ❑ T108 Laynce Nix PROS 1.00 .30
- ❑ T109 David Parrish PROS 1.00 .30
- ❑ T110 Brandon Claussen PROS 1.00 .30
- ❑ T111 Frank Francisco FY RC 1.00 .30
- ❑ T112 Brian Dallimore FY RC 1.00 .30
- ❑ T113 Jim Crowell FY RC 1.25 .35
- ❑ T114 Andres Blanco FY RC 1.00 .30
- ❑ T115 Eduardo Villacis FY RC 1.00 .30
- ❑ T116 Kazuhito Tadano FY RC 1.25 .35
- ❑ T117 Aarom Baldiris FY RC 1.25 .35
- ❑ T118 Justin Germano FY RC 1.00 .30
- ❑ T119 Joey Gathright FY RC 3.00 .90
- ❑ T120 Franklyn Gracesqui FY RC 1.00 .30
- ❑ T121 Chin-Lung Hu FY RC 2.50 .75
- ❑ T122 Scott Olsen FY RC 3.00 .90
- ❑ T123 Tyler Davidson FY RC 1.25 .35
- ❑ T124 Fausto Carmona FY RC 2.00 .60
- ❑ T125 Tim Hutting FY RC 1.00 .30
- ❑ T126 Ryan Meaux FY RC 1.00 .30
- ❑ T127 Jon Connolly FY RC 2.50 .75
- ❑ T128 Hector Made FY RC 2.00 .60
- ❑ T129 Jamie Brown FY RC 1.00 .30
- ❑ T130 Paul McAnulty FY RC 2.00 .60
- ❑ T131 Chris Saenz FY RC 1.00 .30
- ❑ T132 Marland Williams FY RC 1.25 .35
- ❑ T133 Mike Huggins FY RC 1.00 .30
- ❑ T134 Jesse Crain FY RC 2.00 .60
- ❑ T135 Chad Bentz FY RC 1.00 .30
- ❑ T136 Kazuo Matsui FY RC 2.00 .60
- ❑ T137 Paul Maholm FY 2.50 .75
- ❑ T138 Brock Jacobsen FY RC 1.00 .30
- ❑ T139 Casey Daigle FY RC 1.00 .30
- ❑ T140 Nyjer Morgan FY RC 1.00 .30
- ❑ T141 Tom Mastny FY RC 1.00 .30
- ❑ T142 Kody Kirkland FY RC 1.25 .35
- ❑ T143 Jose Capellan FY RC 1.25 .35
- ❑ T144 Felix Hernandez FY RC 25.00 7.50
- ❑ T145 Shawn Hill FY RC 1.00 .30
- ❑ T146 Danny Gonzalez FY RC 1.00 .30
- ❑ T147 Scott Dohmann FY RC 1.00 .30
- ❑ T148 Tommy Murphy FY RC 1.00 .30
- ❑ T149 Akinori Otsuka FY RC 1.00 .30
- ❑ T150 Miguel Perez FY RC 1.00 .30
- ❑ T151 Mike Rouse FY RC 1.00 .30
- ❑ T152 Ramon Ramirez FY RC 1.00 .30
- ❑ T153 Luke Hughes FY RC 1.00 .30
- ❑ T154 Howie Kendrick FY RC 20.00 6.00
- ❑ T155 Ryan Budde FY RC 1.00 .30
- ❑ T156 Charlie Zink FY RC 1.00 .30
- ❑ T157 Warner Madrigal FY RC 2.00 .60
- ❑ T158 Jason Szuminski FY RC 1.00 .30
- ❑ T159 Chad Chop FY RC 1.00 .30
- ❑ T160 Shingo Takatsu FY RC 2.00 .60
- ❑ T161 Matt Lemanczyk FY RC 1.00 .30
- ❑ T162 Wardell Starling FY RC 1.00 .30
- ❑ T163 Nick Gorneault FY RC 1.25 .35
- ❑ T164 Scott Proctor FY RC 1.25 .35
- ❑ T165 Brooks Conrad FY RC 1.25 .35
- ❑ T166 Hector Gimenez FY RC 1.00 .30
- ❑ T167 Kevin Howard FY RC 1.25 .35
- ❑ T168 Vince Perkins FY RC 1.25 .35
- ❑ T169 Brock Peterson FY RC 1.00 .30
- ❑ T170 Chris Shelton FY 2.50 .75
- ❑ T171 Erick Aybar FY RC 3.00 .90
- ❑ T172 Paul Bacot FY RC 1.25 .35
- ❑ T173 Matt Capps FY RC 1.00 .30
- ❑ T174 Kory Casto FY 1.25 .35
- ❑ T175 Juan Cedeno FY RC 1.00 .30
- ❑ T176 Vito Chiaravalloti FY 1.00 .30
- ❑ T177 Alec Zumwalt FY RC 1.00 .30
- ❑ T178 J.J. Furmaniak FY RC 2.00 .60
- ❑ T179 Lee Gwaltney FY RC 1.00 .30
- ❑ T180 Donald Kelly FY RC 1.00 .30
- ❑ T181 Benji DeQuin FY RC 1.00 .30
- ❑ T182 Brant Colamarino FY RC 2.00 .60
- ❑ T183 Juan Gutierrez FY RC 1.00 .30
- ❑ T184 Carl Loadenthal FY RC 1.25 .35
- ❑ T185 Ricky Nolasco FY RC 2.00 .60
- ❑ T186 Jeff Salazar FY RC 2.50 .75
- ❑ T187 Rob Tejeda FY RC 2.00 .60
- ❑ T188 Alex Romero FY RC 1.00 .30
- ❑ T189 Yoann Torrealba FY RC 1.00 .30
- ❑ T190 Carlos Sosa FY RC 1.00 .30
- ❑ T191 Tim Bittner FY RC 1.00 .30
- ❑ T192 Chris Aguila FY RC 1.00 .30
- ❑ T193 Jason Frasor FY RC 1.00 .30
- ❑ T194 Reid Gorecki FY RC 1.00 .30
- ❑ T195 Dustin Nippert FY RC 1.25 .35
- ❑ T196 Javier Guzman FY RC 1.25 .35
- ❑ T197 Harvey Garcia FY RC 1.00 .30
- ❑ T198 Ivan Ochoa FY RC 1.00 .30
- ❑ T199 David Wallace FY RC 1.25 .35
- ❑ T200 Joel Zumaya FY RC 4.00 1.20
- ❑ T201 Casey Kopitzke FY RC 1.00 .30
- ❑ T202 Lincoln Holdzkom FY RC 1.00 .30
- ❑ T203 Chad Santos FY RC 1.00 .30
- ❑ T204 Brian Pilkington FY RC 1.00 .30
- ❑ T205 Terry Jones FY RC 1.25 .35
- ❑ T206 Jerome Gamble FY RC 1.00 .30
- ❑ T207 Brad Eldred FY RC 6.00 1.80
- ❑ T208 David Pauley FY RC 1.00 .30
- ❑ T209 Kevin Davidson FY RC 1.00 .30
- ❑ T210 Damaso Espino FY RC 1.00 .30
- ❑ T211 Tom Farmer FY RC 1.00 .30
- ❑ T212 Michael Mooney FY RC 1.00 .30
- ❑ T213 James Tomlin FY RC 1.00 .30
- ❑ T214 Greg Thissen FY RC 1.00 .30
- ❑ T215 Calvin Hayes FY RC 1.25 .35
- ❑ T216 Fernando Cortez FY RC 1.00 .30
- ❑ T217 Sergio Silva FY RC 1.00 .30
- ❑ T218 Jon de Vries FY RC 1.00 .30
- ❑ T219 Don Sutton FY RC 2.50 .75
- ❑ T220 Leo Nunez FY RC 1.00 .30

2005 Topps Chrome

	Nm-Mt	Ex-Mt
COMP.SET w/o AU'S (440)	160.00	47.50
COMP.SERIES 1 w/o AU's (220)	80.00	24.00
COMP.SERIES 2 w/o AU's (220)	80.00	24.00
COMMON (1-210/253-467)	1.00	.30
COMMON (211-220/468-472)	2.00	.60
221-252 PRINT RUN PROVIDED BY TOPPS		.00
EXCHANGE DEADLINE 05/31/07	.00	
1-234 PLATE ODDS 1:310 SER.1 HOBBY		.00
235-252 PLATE ODDS 1:350 SER.2 MINI BOX		.00
253-472 PLATE ODDS 1:29 SER.2 MINI BOX		.00
PLATE PRINT RUN 1 SET PER COLOR		.00
BLACK-CYAN-MAGENTA-YELLOW ISSUED		.00
NO PLATE PRICING DUE TO SCARCITY		.00

- ❑ 1 Alex Rodriguez 4.00 1.20
- ❑ 2 Placido Polanco 1.00 .30
- ❑ 3 Torii Hunter 1.00 .30
- ❑ 4 Lyle Overbay 1.00 .30
- ❑ 5 Johnny Damon 1.50 .45
- ❑ 6 Johnny Estrada 1.00 .30
- ❑ 7 Rich Harden 1.00 .30
- ❑ 8 Francisco Rodriguez 1.00 .30
- ❑ 9 Jarrod Washburn 1.00 .30
- ❑ 10 Sammy Sosa 2.50 .75
- ❑ 11 Randy Wolf 1.00 .30
- ❑ 12 Jason Bay 1.00 .30
- ❑ 13 Tom Glavine 1.50 .45
- ❑ 14 Michael Tucker 1.00 .30
- ❑ 15 Brian Giles 1.00 .30
- ❑ 16 Chad Tracy 1.00 .30
- ❑ 17 Jim Edmonds 1.50 .45
- ❑ 18 John Smoltz 1.50 .45
- ❑ 19 Roy Halladay 1.00 .30
- ❑ 20 Hank Blalock 1.00 .30
- ❑ 21 Darin Erstad 1.00 .30
- ❑ 22 Todd Walker 1.00 .30
- ❑ 23 Mike Hampton 1.00 .30
- ❑ 24 Mark Bellhorn 1.00 .30
- ❑ 25 Jim Thome 1.50 .45
- ❑ 26 Shingo Takatsu 1.00 .30
- ❑ 27 Jody Gerut 1.00 .30
- ❑ 28 Vinny Castilla 1.00 .30
- ❑ 29 Luis Castillo 1.00 .30
- ❑ 30 Ivan Rodriguez 1.50 .45
- ❑ 31 Craig Biggio 1.50 .45
- ❑ 32 Joe Randa 1.00 .30
- ❑ 33 Adrian Beltre 1.00 .30
- ❑ 34 Scott Podsednik 1.00 .30
- ❑ 35 Cliff Floyd 1.00 .30
- ❑ 36 Livan Hernandez 1.00 .30
- ❑ 37 Eric Byrnes 1.00 .30
- ❑ 38 Jose Acevedo 1.00 .30
- ❑ 39 Jack Wilson 1.00 .30
- ❑ 40 Gary Sheffield 1.00 .30
- ❑ 41 Chan Ho Park 1.00 .30
- ❑ 42 Carl Crawford 1.00 .30
- ❑ 43 Shawn Estes 1.00 .30
- ❑ 44 David Bell 1.00 .30
- ❑ 45 Jeff DaVanon 1.00 .30
- ❑ 46 Brandon Webb 1.00 .30
- ❑ 47 Lance Berkman 1.00 .30
- ❑ 48 Melvin Mora 1.00 .30
- ❑ 49 David Ortiz 2.50 .75
- ❑ 50 Andruw Jones 1.50 .45
- ❑ 51 Chone Figgins 1.00 .30
- ❑ 52 Danny Graves 1.00 .30
- ❑ 53 Preston Wilson 1.00 .30
- ❑ 54 Jeremy Bonderman 1.00 .30
- ❑ 55 Carlos Guillen 1.00 .30
- ❑ 56 Cesar Izturis 1.00 .30
- ❑ 57 Kazuo Matsui 1.00 .30
- ❑ 58 Jason Schmidt 1.00 .30
- ❑ 59 Jason Marquis 1.00 .30
- ❑ 60 Jose Vidro 1.00 .30
- ❑ 61 Al Leiter 1.00 .30
- ❑ 62 Javier Vazquez 1.00 .30
- ❑ 63 Erubiel Durazo 1.00 .30
- ❑ 64 Scott Spiezio 1.00 .30
- ❑ 65 Scot Shields 1.00 .30
- ❑ 66 Edgardo Alfonzo 1.00 .30
- ❑ 67 Miguel Tejada 1.00 .30
- ❑ 68 Francisco Cordero 1.00 .30
- ❑ 69 Brett Myers 1.00 .30
- ❑ 70 Curt Schilling 1.50 .45
- ❑ 71 Matt Kata 1.00 .30
- ❑ 72 Bartolo Colon 1.00 .30
- ❑ 73 Rodrigo Lopez 1.00 .30
- ❑ 74 Tim Wakefield 1.00 .30
- ❑ 75 Frank Thomas 2.50 .75
- ❑ 76 Jimmy Rollins 1.00 .30
- ❑ 77 Barry Zito 1.00 .30
- ❑ 78 Hideo Nomo 2.50 .75
- ❑ 79 Brad Wilkerson 1.00 .30
- ❑ 80 Adam Dunn 1.00 .30
- ❑ 81 Derrek Lee 1.50 .45
- ❑ 82 Joe Crede 1.00 .30
- ❑ 83 Nate Robertson 1.00 .30
- ❑ 84 John Thomson 1.00 .30
- ❑ 85 Mike Sweeney 1.00 .30
- ❑ 86 Kip Wells 1.00 .30
- ❑ 87 Eric Gagne 1.00 .30
- ❑ 88 Zach Day 1.00 .30
- ❑ 89 Alex Sanchez 1.00 .30
- ❑ 90 Bret Boone 1.00 .30
- ❑ 91 Mark Loretta 1.00 .30
- ❑ 92 Miguel Cabrera 1.50 .45

❑ 93 Randy Winn 1.00 .30
❑ 94 Adam Everett 1.00 .30
❑ 95 Aubrey Huff 1.00 .30
❑ 96 Kevin Mench 1.00 .30
❑ 97 Frank Catalanotto 1.00 .30
❑ 98 Flash Gordon 1.00 .30
❑ 99 Scott Hatteberg 1.00 .30
❑ 100 Albert Pujols 5.00 1.50
❑ 101 Jose Molina 1.00 .30
Bengie Molina
❑ 102 Jason Johnson 1.00 .30
❑ 103 Jay Gibbons 1.00 .30
❑ 104 Byung-Hyun Kim 1.00 .30
❑ 105 Joe Borowski 1.00 .30
❑ 106 Mark Grudzielanek 1.00 .30
❑ 107 Mark Buehrle 1.00 .30
❑ 108 Paul Wilson 1.00 .30
❑ 109 Ronnie Belliard 1.00 .30
❑ 110 Reggie Sanders 1.00 .30
❑ 111 Tim Redding 1.00 .30
❑ 112 Brian Lawrence 1.00 .30
❑ 113 Travis Hafner 1.00 .30
❑ 114 Jose Hernandez 1.00 .30
❑ 115 Ben Sheets 1.00 .30
❑ 116 Johan Santana 1.50 .45
❑ 117 Billy Wagner 1.00 .30
❑ 118 Mariano Rivera 1.50 .45
❑ 119 Steve Trachsel 1.00 .30
❑ 120 Akinori Otsuka 1.00 .30
❑ 121 Jose Valentin 1.00 .30
❑ 122 Orlando Hernandez 1.00 .30
❑ 123 Raul Ibanez 1.00 .30
❑ 124 Mike Matheny 1.00 .30
❑ 125 Vernon Wells 1.00 .30
❑ 126 Jason Isringhausen 1.00 .30
❑ 127 Jose Guillen 1.00 .30
❑ 128 Danny Bautista 1.00 .30
❑ 129 Marcus Giles 1.00 .30
❑ 130 Javy Lopez 1.00 .30
❑ 131 Kevin Millar 1.00 .30
❑ 132 Kyle Farnsworth 1.00 .30
❑ 133 Carl Pavano 1.00 .30
❑ 134 Rafael Furcal 1.00 .30
❑ 135 Casey Blake 1.00 .30
❑ 136 Matt Holliday 1.00 .30
❑ 137 Bobby Higginson 1.00 .30
❑ 138 Adam Kennedy 1.00 .30
❑ 139 Alex Gonzalez 1.00 .30
❑ 140 Jeff Kent 1.00 .30
❑ 141 Aaron Guiel 1.00 .30
❑ 142 Shawn Green 1.00 .30
❑ 143 Bill Hall 1.00 .30
❑ 144 Shannon Stewart 1.00 .30
❑ 145 Juan Rivera 1.00 .30
❑ 146 Coco Crisp 1.00 .30
❑ 147 Mike Mussina 1.50 .45
❑ 148 Eric Chavez 1.00 .30
❑ 149 Jon Lieber 1.00 .30
❑ 150 Vladimir Guerrero 2.50 .75
❑ 151 Alex Cintron 1.00 .30
❑ 152 Luis Matos 1.00 .30
❑ 153 Sidney Ponson 1.00 .30
❑ 154 Trot Nixon 1.00 .30
❑ 155 Greg Maddux 4.00 1.20
❑ 156 Edgar Renteria 1.00 .30
❑ 157 Ryan Freel 1.00 .30
❑ 158 Matt Lawton 1.00 .30
❑ 159 Mark Prior 1.50 .45
❑ 160 Josh Beckett 1.00 .30
❑ 161 Ken Harvey 1.00 .30
❑ 162 Angel Berroa 1.00 .30
❑ 163 Juan Encarnacion 1.00 .30
❑ 164 Wes Helms 1.00 .30
❑ 165 Brad Radke 1.00 .30
❑ 166 Phil Nevin 1.00 .30
❑ 167 Mike Cameron 1.00 .30
❑ 168 Billy Koch 1.00 .30
❑ 169 Bobby Crosby 1.00 .30
❑ 170 Mike Lieberthal 1.00 .30
❑ 171 Rob Mackowiak 1.00 .30
❑ 172 Sean Burroughs 1.00 .30
❑ 173 J.T. Snow 1.00 .30
❑ 174 Paul Konerko 1.00 .30
❑ 175 Luis Gonzalez 1.00 .30
❑ 176 John Lackey 1.00 .30
❑ 177 Oliver Perez 1.00 .30
❑ 178 Brian Roberts 1.00 .30
❑ 179 Bill Mueller 1.00 .30
❑ 180 Carlos Lee 1.00 .30
❑ 181 Corey Patterson 1.00 .30
❑ 182 Sean Casey 1.50 .45
❑ 183 Cliff Lee 1.00 .30
❑ 184 Jason Jennings 1.00 .30
❑ 185 Dmitri Young 1.00 .30
❑ 186 Juan Uribe 1.00 .30
❑ 187 Andy Pettitte 1.50 .45
❑ 188 Juan Gonzalez 1.00 .30
❑ 189 Orlando Hudson 1.00 .30
❑ 190 Jason Phillips 1.00 .30
❑ 191 Braden Looper 1.00 .30
❑ 192 Lew Ford 1.00 .30
❑ 193 Mark Mulder 1.00 .30
❑ 194 Bobby Abreu 1.00 .30
❑ 195 Jason Kendall 1.00 .30
❑ 196 Khalil Greene 1.50 .45
❑ 197 A.J. Pierzynski 1.00 .30
❑ 198 Tim Worrell 1.00 .30
❑ 199 So Taguchi 1.00 .30
❑ 200 Jason Giambi 1.00 .30
❑ 201 Tony Batista 1.00 .30
❑ 202 Carlos Zambrano 1.00 .30
❑ 203 Trevor Hoffman 1.00 .30
❑ 204 Odalis Perez 1.00 .30
❑ 205 Jose Cruz Jr. 1.00 .30
❑ 206 Michael Barrett 1.00 .30
❑ 207 Chris Carpenter 1.00 .30
❑ 208 Michael Young 1.00 .30
❑ 209 Toby Hall 1.00 .30
❑ 210 Woody Williams 1.00 .30
❑ 211 Chris Denorfia FY RC 3.00 .90
❑ 212 Darren Fenster FY RC 2.00 .60
❑ 213 Elvys Quezada FY RC 2.00 .60
❑ 214 Ian Kinsler FY RC 4.00 1.20
❑ 215 Matthew Lindstrom FY RC 2.00 .60
❑ 216 Ryan Goleski FY RC 3.00 .90
❑ 217 Ryan Sweeney FY RC 3.00 .90
❑ 218 Sean Marshall FY RC 3.00 .90
❑ 219 Steve Doetsch FY RC 3.00 .90
❑ 220 Wade Robinson FY RC 2.00 .60
❑ 221 Andre Ethier FY AU RC 25.00 7.50
❑ 222 Brandon Moss FY AU RC 30.00 9.00
❑ 223 Chadd Blasko FY AU RC 15.00 4.50
❑ 224 Chris Roberson FY AU RC 10.00 3.00
❑ 225 Chris Seddon FY AU RC 10.00 3.00
❑ 226 Ian Bladergroen FY AU RC 15.00 4.50
❑ 227 Jake Dittler FY AU 10.00 3.00
❑ 228 Jose Vaquedano FY AU RC 10.00 3.00
❑ 229 Jeremy West FY AU RC 15.00 4.50
❑ 230 Kole Strayhorn FY AU RC 10.00 3.00
❑ 231 Kevin West FY AU RC 10.00 3.00
❑ 232 Luis Ramirez FY AU RC 10.00 3.00
❑ 233 Melky Cabrera FY AU RC 25.00 7.50
❑ 234 Nate Schierholtz FY AU 15.00 4.50
❑ 235 Billy Butler FY AU RC 50.00 15.00
❑ 236 B.Szymanski FY AU EXCH 10.00 3.00
❑ 237 Chad Orvella FY AU RC 10.00 3.00
❑ 238 Chip Cannon FY AU RC 15.00 4.50
❑ 239 Eric Nielsen FY AU RC 10.00 3.00
❑ 240 Erik Cordier FY AU RC 10.00 3.00
❑ 241 Glen Perkins FY AU RC 20.00 6.00
❑ 242 Justin Verlander FY AU RC 25.00 7.50
❑ 243 Kevin Melillo FY AU RC 20.00 6.00
❑ 244 Landon Powell FY AU RC 15.00 4.50
❑ 245 Matt Campbell FY AU RC 10.00 3.00
❑ 246 Michael Rogers FY AU RC 10.00 3.00
❑ 247 Nate McLouth FY AU RC 15.00 4.50
❑ 248 Scott Mathieson FY AU RC 20.00 6.00
❑ 249 Shane Costa FY AU RC 10.00 3.00
❑ 250 Tony Giarratano FY AU RC 10.00 3.00
❑ 251 Tyler Pelland FY AU RC 15.00 4.50
❑ 252 Wes Swackhamer FY AU RC 10.00 3.00
❑ 253 Garret Anderson 1.00 .30
❑ 254 Randy Johnson 2.50 .75
❑ 255 Charles Thomas 1.00 .30
❑ 256 Rafael Palmeiro 1.50 .45
❑ 257 Kevin Youkilis 1.00 .30
❑ 258 Freddy Garcia 1.00 .30
❑ 259 Magglio Ordonez 1.00 .30
❑ 260 Aaron Harang 1.00 .30
❑ 261 Grady Sizemore 1.00 .30
❑ 262 Chin-hui Tsao 1.00 .30
❑ 263 Eric Munson 1.00 .30
❑ 264 Juan Pierre 1.00 .30
❑ 265 Brad Lidge 1.00 .30
❑ 266 Brian Anderson 1.00 .30
❑ 267 Todd Helton 1.50 .45
❑ 268 Chad Cordero 1.00 .30
❑ 269 Kris Benson 1.00 .30
❑ 270 Brad Halsey 1.00 .30
❑ 271 Jermaine Dye 1.00 .30
❑ 272 Manny Ramirez 1.50 .45
❑ 273 Adam Eaton 1.00 .30
❑ 274 Brett Tomko 1.00 .30
❑ 275 Bucky Jacobsen 1.00 .30
❑ 276 Dontrelle Willis 1.00 .30
❑ 277 B.J. Upton 1.00 .30
❑ 278 Rocco Baldelli 1.00 .30
❑ 279 Ryan Drese 1.00 .30
❑ 280 Ichiro Suzuki 5.00 1.50
❑ 281 Brandon Lyon 1.00 .30
❑ 282 Nick Green 1.00 .30
❑ 283 Jerry Hairston Jr. 1.00 .30
❑ 284 Mike Lowell 1.00 .30
❑ 285 Kerry Wood 1.00 .30
❑ 286 Omar Vizquel 1.50 .45
❑ 287 Carlos Beltran 1.00 .30
❑ 288 Carlos Pena 1.00 .30
❑ 289 Jeff Weaver 1.00 .30
❑ 290 Chad Moeller 1.00 .30
❑ 291 Joe Mays 1.00 .30
❑ 292 Termel Sledge 1.00 .30
❑ 293 Richard Hidalgo 1.00 .30
❑ 294 Justin Duchscherer 1.00 .30
❑ 295 Eric Milton 1.00 .30
❑ 296 Ramon Hernandez 1.00 .30
❑ 297 Jose Reyes 1.00 .30
❑ 298 Joel Pineiro 1.00 .30
❑ 299 Matt Morris 1.00 .30
❑ 300 John Halama 1.00 .30
❑ 301 Gary Matthews Jr. 1.00 .30
❑ 302 Ryan Madson 1.00 .30
❑ 303 Mark Kotsay 1.00 .30
❑ 304 Carlos Delgado 1.00 .30
❑ 305 Casey Kotchman 1.00 .30
❑ 306 Greg Aquino 1.00 .30
❑ 307 LaTroy Hawkins 1.00 .30
❑ 308 Jose Contreras 1.00 .30
❑ 309 Ken Griffey Jr. 4.00 1.20
❑ 310 C.C. Sabathia 1.00 .30
❑ 311 Brandon Inge 1.00 .30
❑ 312 John Buck 1.00 .30
❑ 313 Hee Seop Choi 1.00 .30
❑ 314 Chris Capuano 1.00 .30
❑ 315 Jesse Crain 1.00 .30
❑ 316 Geoff Jenkins 1.00 .30
❑ 317 Mike Piazza 2.50 .75
❑ 318 Jorge Posada 1.50 .45
❑ 319 Nick Swisher 1.00 .30
❑ 320 Kevin Millwood 1.00 .30
❑ 321 Mike Gonzalez 1.00 .30
❑ 322 Jake Peavy 1.00 .30
❑ 323 Dustin Hermanson 1.00 .30
❑ 324 Jeremy Reed 1.00 .30
❑ 325 Alfonso Soriano 1.00 .30
❑ 326 Alexis Rios 1.00 .30
❑ 327 David Eckstein 1.00 .30
❑ 328 Shea Hillenbrand 1.00 .30
❑ 329 Russ Ortiz 1.00 .30
❑ 330 Kurt Ainsworth 1.00 .30
❑ 331 Orlando Cabrera 1.00 .30
❑ 332 Carlos Silva 1.00 .30
❑ 333 Ross Gload 1.00 .30
❑ 334 Josh Phelps 1.00 .30
❑ 335 Mike Maroth 1.00 .30
❑ 336 Guillermo Mota 1.00 .30
❑ 337 Chris Burke 1.00 .30
❑ 338 David DeJesus 1.00 .30
❑ 339 Jose Lima 1.00 .30
❑ 340 Cristian Guzman 1.00 .30
❑ 341 Nick Johnson 1.00 .30
❑ 342 Victor Zambrano 1.00 .30
❑ 343 Rod Barajas 1.00 .30
❑ 344 Damian Miller 1.00 .30
❑ 345 Chase Utley 1.00 .30
❑ 346 Sean Burnett 1.00 .30
❑ 347 David Wells 1.00 .30
❑ 348 Dustan Mohr 1.00 .30
❑ 349 Bobby Madritsch 1.00 .30

❑ 350 Reed Johnson	1.00	.30
❑ 351 R.A. Dickey	1.00	.30
❑ 352 Scott Kazmir	1.00	.30
❑ 353 Tony Womack	1.00	.30
❑ 354 Tomas Perez	1.00	.30
❑ 355 Esteban Loaiza	1.00	.30
❑ 356 Tomokazu Ohka	1.00	.30
❑ 357 Ramon Ortiz	1.00	.30
❑ 358 Richie Sexson	1.00	.30
❑ 359 J.D. Drew	1.00	.30
❑ 360 Barry Bonds	6.00	1.80
❑ 361 Aramis Ramirez	1.00	.30
❑ 362 Wily Mo Pena	1.00	.30
❑ 363 Jeromy Burnitz	1.00	.30
❑ 364 Nomar Garciaparra	2.50	.75
❑ 365 Brandon Backe	1.00	.30
❑ 366 Derek Lowe	1.00	.30
❑ 367 Doug Davis	1.00	.30
❑ 368 Joe Mauer	1.00	.30
❑ 369 Endy Chavez	1.00	.30
❑ 370 Bernie Williams	1.50	.45
❑ 371 Jason Michaels	1.00	.30
❑ 372 Craig Wilson	1.00	.30
❑ 373 Ryan Klesko	1.00	.30
❑ 374 Ray Durham	1.00	.30
❑ 375 Jose Lopez	1.00	.30
❑ 376 Jeff Suppan	1.00	.30
❑ 377 David Bush	1.00	.30
❑ 378 Marlon Byrd	1.00	.30
❑ 379 Roy Oswalt	1.00	.30
❑ 380 Rondell White	1.00	.30
❑ 381 Troy Glaus	1.00	.30
❑ 382 Scott Hairston	1.00	.30
❑ 383 Chipper Jones	2.50	.75
❑ 384 Daniel Cabrera	1.00	.30
❑ 385 Jon Garland	1.00	.30
❑ 386 Austin Kearns	1.00	.30
❑ 387 Jake Westbrook	1.00	.30
❑ 388 Aaron Miles	1.00	.30
❑ 389 Omar Infante	1.00	.30
❑ 390 Paul Lo Duca	1.00	.30
❑ 391 Morgan Ensberg	1.00	.30
❑ 392 Tony Graffanino	1.00	.30
❑ 393 Milton Bradley	1.00	.30
❑ 394 Keith Ginter	1.00	.30
❑ 395 Justin Morneau	1.00	.30
❑ 396 Tony Armas Jr.	1.00	.30
❑ 397 Kevin Brown	1.00	.30
❑ 398 Marco Scutaro	1.00	.30
❑ 399 Tim Hudson	1.00	.30
❑ 400 Pat Burrell	1.00	.30
❑ 401 Jeff Cirillo	1.00	.30
❑ 402 Larry Walker	1.50	.45
❑ 403 Dewon Brazelton	1.00	.30
❑ 404 Shigetoshi Hasegawa	1.00	.30
❑ 405 Octavio Dotel	1.00	.30
❑ 406 Michael Cuddyer	1.00	.30
❑ 407 Junior Spivey	1.00	.30
❑ 408 Zack Greinke	1.00	.30
❑ 409 Roger Clemens	4.00	1.20
❑ 410 Chris Shelton	1.00	.30
❑ 411 Ugueth Urbina	1.00	.30
❑ 412 Rafael Betancourt	1.00	.30
❑ 413 Willie Harris	1.00	.30
❑ 414 Keith Foulke	1.00	.30
❑ 415 Larry Bigbie	1.00	.30
❑ 416 Paul Byrd	1.00	.30
❑ 417 Troy Percival	1.00	.30
❑ 418 Pedro Martinez	1.50	.45
❑ 419 Matt Clement	1.00	.30
❑ 420 Ryan Wagner	1.00	.30
❑ 421 Jeff Francis	1.00	.30
❑ 422 Jeff Conine	1.00	.30
❑ 423 Wade Miller	1.00	.30
❑ 424 Gavin Floyd	1.00	.30
❑ 425 Kazuhisa Ishii	1.00	.30
❑ 426 Victor Santos	1.00	.30
❑ 427 Jacque Jones	1.00	.30
❑ 428 Hideki Matsui	5.00	1.50
❑ 429 Cory Lidle	1.00	.30
❑ 430 Jose Castillo	1.00	.30
❑ 431 Alex Gonzalez	1.00	.30
❑ 432 Kirk Rueter	1.00	.30
❑ 433 Jolbert Cabrera	1.00	.30
❑ 434 Erik Bedard	1.00	.30
❑ 435 Ricky Ledee	1.00	.30
❑ 436 Mark Hendrickson	1.00	.30
❑ 437 Laynce Nix	1.00	.30
❑ 438 Jason Frasor	1.00	.30
❑ 439 Kevin Gregg	1.00	.30
❑ 440 Derek Jeter	5.00	1.50
❑ 441 Jaret Wright	1.00	.30
❑ 442 Edwin Jackson	1.00	.30
❑ 443 Moises Alou	1.00	.30
❑ 444 Aaron Rowand	1.00	.30
❑ 445 Kazuhito Tadano	1.00	.30
❑ 446 Luis Gonzalez	1.00	.30
❑ 447 A.J. Burnett	1.00	.30
❑ 448 Jeff Bagwell	1.50	.45
❑ 449 Brad Penny	1.00	.30
❑ 450 Corey Koskie	1.00	.30
❑ 451 Mark Ellis	1.00	.30
❑ 452 Hector Luna	1.00	.30
❑ 453 Miguel Olivo	1.00	.30
❑ 454 Scott Rolen	1.50	.45
❑ 455 Ricardo Rodriguez	1.00	.30
❑ 456 Eric Hinske	1.00	.30
❑ 457 Tim Salmon	1.50	.45
❑ 458 Adam LaRoche	1.00	.30
❑ 459 B.J. Ryan	1.00	.30
❑ 460 Steve Finley	1.00	.30
❑ 461 Joe Nathan	1.00	.30
❑ 462 Vicente Padilla	1.00	.30
❑ 463 Yadier Molina	1.00	.30
❑ 464 Tino Martinez	1.50	.45
❑ 465 Mark Teixeira	1.50	.45
❑ 466 Kelvim Escobar	1.00	.30
❑ 467 Pedro Feliz	1.00	.30
❑ 468 Ryan Garko FY RC	4.00	1.20
❑ 469 Bobby Livingston FY RC	2.00	.60
❑ 470 Yorman Bazardo FY RC	2.00	.60
❑ 471 Mike Bourn FY RC	3.00	.90
❑ 472 Andy LaRoche FY RC	8.00	2.40

2004 Topps Cracker Jack

	Nm-Mt	Ex-Mt
COMPLETE SET (250)	200.00	60.00
COMP.SET w/o SP's (200)	40.00	12.00
COMMON CARD	.40	.12
COMMON SP	4.00	1.20
COMMON SP RC	4.00	1.20
SP STATED ODDS 1:3	.00	
SP CL: 226/229B/232/236A-236B	.00	

❑ 1 Jose Reyes SP	4.00	1.20
❑ 2 Edgar Renteria	.40	.12
❑ 3A Albert Pujols Portrait	2.00	.60
❑ 3B Albert Pujols Swinging SP	8.00	2.40
❑ 4 Garret Anderson	.40	.12
❑ 5 Bobby Abreu	.40	.12
❑ 6 Andruw Jones	.60	.18
❑ 7 Jeff Kent	.40	.12
❑ 8 Magglio Ordonez	.40	.12
❑ 9 Kris Benson	.40	.12
❑ 10 Luis Gonzalez	.40	.12
❑ 11 Corey Patterson	.40	.12
❑ 12 Connie Mack MG	.40	.12
❑ 13 Vernon Wells SP	4.00	1.20
❑ 14 Jim Edmonds	.60	.18
❑ 15 Bret Boone	.40	.12
❑ 16 Travis Lee	.40	.12
❑ 17 Alex Rodriguez Yanks SP	8.00	2.40
❑ 18 Erubiel Durazo	.40	.12
❑ 19 Brett Myers	.40	.12
❑ 20 Scott Rolen SP	5.00	1.50
❑ 21 Paul Lo Duca	.40	.12
❑ 22 Geoff Jenkins	.40	.12
❑ 23 Charles Comiskey	.40	.12
❑ 24 Cliff Floyd	.40	.12
❑ 25A Jim Thome Batting	.60	.18
❑ 25B Jim Thome Fielding SP	5.00	1.50
❑ 26 Russ Ortiz	.40	.12
❑ 27 Bill Mueller	.40	.12
❑ 28 Kenny Lofton	.40	.12
❑ 29 Jay Gibbons	.40	.12
❑ 30 Ken Griffey Jr.	1.50	.45
❑ 31 Jeff Bagwell	.60	.18
❑ 32 Jose Lima	.40	.12
❑ 33 Brad Radke	.40	.12
❑ 34 Ramon Hernandez	.40	.12
❑ 35 Brian Giles SP	4.00	1.20
❑ 36 Jeremy Bonderman	.40	.12
❑ 37 Jerome Williams	.40	.12
❑ 38 Rafael Palmeiro	.60	.18
❑ 39 Scott Podsednik	.40	.12
❑ 40 Rafael Furcal	.40	.12
❑ 41 Roy Oswalt	.40	.12
❑ 42 Orlando Hudson	.40	.12
❑ 43 Todd Helton	.60	.18
❑ 44 Kerry Wood	.40	.12
❑ 45 Tom Glavine	.60	.18
❑ 46 David Eckstein	.40	.12
❑ 47 Trot Nixon	.40	.12
❑ 48 Preston Wilson	.40	.12
❑ 49 Bernie Williams	.60	.18
❑ 50 Eric Gagne SP	4.00	1.20
❑ 51 Ichiro Suzuki SP	8.00	2.40
❑ 52 Juan Gonzalez	.40	.12
❑ 53 Torii Hunter	.40	.12
❑ 54 Bartolo Colon	.40	.12
❑ 55A Dick Hoblitzel ERR	.40	.12
❑ 55B Dick Hoblitzell COR	.40	.12
❑ 56 Al Leiter	.40	.12
❑ 57 Johnny Damon	.60	.18
❑ 58 Larry Walker	.40	.12
❑ 59 Brian Jordan	.40	.12
❑ 60 Richie Sexson SP	4.00	1.20
❑ 61 Orlando Cabrera	.40	.12
❑ 62 Jason Phillips	.40	.12
❑ 63 Phil Nevin	.40	.12
❑ 64 John Olerud	.40	.12
❑ 65 Miguel Tejada	.40	.12
❑ 66A Nap La Joie ERR	1.00	.30
❑ 66B Nap Lajoie COR	1.00	.30
❑ 67 C.C. Sabathia	.40	.12
❑ 68 Ty Wigginton	.40	.12
❑ 69 Troy Glaus	.40	.12
❑ 70 Mike Piazza	1.50	.45
❑ 71 Craig Biggio	.60	.18
❑ 72 Cristian Guzman	.40	.12
❑ 73 Dmitri Young	.40	.12
❑ 74 Roger Clemens	1.50	.45
❑ 75 Runelvys Hernandez	.40	.12
❑ 76 Nomar Garciaparra	1.50	.45
❑ 77 Mark Mulder	.40	.12
❑ 78 Derek Lowe	.40	.12
❑ 79 Paul Konerko	.40	.12
❑ 80A Sammy Sosa SP	5.00	1.50
❑ 80B Felix Pie SP	5.00	1.50
❑ 81 Vladimir Guerrero	1.00	.30
❑ 82 Xavier Nady	.40	.12
❑ 83 Joel Pineiro	.40	.12
❑ 84 Chipper Jones	1.00	.30
❑ 85 Manny Ramirez	.60	.18
❑ 86A Burt Shotten ERR	.40	.12
❑ 86B Burt Shotton COR UER	.40	.12
Began his playing career in 1997; should be 1907		
❑ 87 Raul Ibanez SP	4.00	1.20
❑ 88 Eric Chavez	.40	.12
❑ 89 Frank Catalanotto	.40	.12
❑ 90 Dontrelle Willis	.60	.18
❑ 91 Roy Halladay	.40	.12
❑ 92 Jermaine Dye	.40	.12
❑ 93 Jason Kendall	.40	.12
❑ 94 Jacque Jones	.40	.12
❑ 95A Gary Sheffield Braves	.40	.12
❑ 95B Gary Sheffield Yanks SP	5.00	1.50
❑ 96 Mike Lieberthal	.40	.12

	Nm-Mt	Ex-Mt
❑ 97 Adam Dunn	.40	.12
❑ 98 Carl Crawford	.40	.12
❑ 99 Reggie Sanders	.40	.12
❑ 100 Mark Prior SP	5.00	1.50
❑ 101 Luis Matos	.40	.12
❑ 102 Barry Zito	.40	.12
❑ 103 Randy Johnson	1.00	.30
❑ 104A Kevin Brown	.40	.12
❑ 104B Edwin Jackson SP	4.00	1.20
❑ 105 Pat Burrell	.40	.12
❑ 106 Steve Finley	.40	.12
❑ 107 Moises Alou	.40	.12
❑ 108 David Ortiz SP	5.00	1.50
❑ 109 Austin Kearns SP	4.00	1.20
❑ 110 Carlos Beltran	.40	.12
❑ 111 Shawn Green	.40	.12
❑ 112 Javier Vazquez	.40	.12
❑ 113 Hideo Nomo	1.00	.30
❑ 114 Kazuhisa Ishii	.40	.12
❑ 115 Corey Koskie	.40	.12
❑ 116 Kevin Millwood	.40	.12
❑ 117 Randy Wolf	.40	.12
❑ 118 Darin Erstad	.40	.12
❑ 119 Fernando Vina	.40	.12
❑ 120 Pedro Martinez	.60	.18
❑ 121 Melvin Mora	.40	.12
❑ 122 Carl Everett	.40	.12
❑ 123 Matt Morris	.40	.12
❑ 124 Greg Maddux	1.50	.45
❑ 125 Jason Schmidt	.40	.12
❑ 126 Mark Teixeira SP	5.00	1.50
❑ 127 Randy Winn	.40	.12
❑ 128 Rich Aurilia	.40	.12
❑ 129 Vicente Padilla	.40	.12
❑ 130 Tim Hudson	.40	.12
❑ 131 Marlon Byrd	.40	.12
❑ 132 Jae Weong Seo	.40	.12
❑ 133 Branch Rickey MG	.40	.12
❑ 134 A.J. Pierzynski	.40	.12
❑ 135 Ryan Klesko	.40	.12
❑ 136 Eric Hinske	.40	.12
❑ 137 Mike Cameron	.40	.12
❑ 138 Roberto Alomar	.60	.18
❑ 139 Jarrod Washburn	.40	.12
❑ 140A Curt Schilling D'backs	.40	.12
❑ 140B Curt Schilling Sox SP	5.00	1.50
❑ 141 Omar Vizquel	.60	.18
❑ 142 Mike Sweeney	.40	.12
❑ 143 Wade Miller	.40	.12
❑ 144 Jose Vidro	.40	.12
❑ 145 Rich Harden SP	4.00	1.20
❑ 146 Eric Munson	.40	.12
❑ 147 Lance Berkman	.40	.12
❑ 148 Mark Buehrle	.40	.12
❑ 149 Carlos Delgado	.40	.12
❑ 150 Sean Burroughs	.40	.12
❑ 151 Kevin Millar	.40	.12
❑ 152 Frank Thomas	1.00	.30
❑ 153 Adrian Beltre	.40	.12
❑ 154 Shannon Stewart	.40	.12
❑ 155 Johan Santana	.60	.18
❑ 156 Edgardo Alfonzo	.40	.12
❑ 157 Jose Cruz Jr.	.40	.12
❑ 158 Sidney Ponson	.40	.12
❑ 159 Edgar Martinez	.60	.18
❑ 160 Jamie Moyer	.40	.12
❑ 161 Tony Batista	.40	.12
❑ 162 Wes Helms	.40	.12
❑ 163 Brandon Webb SP	4.00	1.20
❑ 164 Gil Meche	.40	.12
❑ 165 Marcus Giles SP	4.00	1.20
❑ 166 Angel Berroa SP	4.00	1.20
❑ 167 Rocco Baldelli SP	4.00	1.20
❑ 168 Michael Young	.40	.12
❑ 169 Esteban Loaiza	.40	.12
❑ 170 Casey Blake	.40	.12
❑ 171 Jody Gerut	.40	.12
❑ 172 Bo Hart SP	4.00	1.20
❑ 173 Kelvim Escobar	.40	.12
❑ 174 Aaron Guiel	.40	.12
❑ 175 Javy Lopez SP	4.00	1.20
❑ 176 Aubrey Huff	.40	.12
❑ 177 Hank Blalock	.40	.12
❑ 178 Edwin Jackson	.40	.12
❑ 179 Delmon Young SP	5.00	1.50
❑ 180 Bobby Jenks	.40	.12
❑ 181 Felix Pie	.60	.18
❑ 182 Jeremy Reed SP	4.00	1.20
❑ 183 Aaron Hill	.40	.12
❑ 184 Casey Kotchman SP	4.00	1.20
❑ 185 Grady Sizemore	.40	.12
❑ 186 Joe Mauer SP	4.00	1.20
❑ 187 Ryan Harvey	.40	.12
❑ 188 Neal Cotts	.40	.12
❑ 189 Victor Martinez	.40	.12
❑ 190 Rene Reyes	.40	.12
❑ 191 Eric Duncan	.40	.12
❑ 192 B.J. Upton SP	5.00	1.50
❑ 193 Khalil Greene SP	5.00	1.50
❑ 194 Bobby Crosby	.40	.12
❑ 195 Rickie Weeks SP	5.00	1.50
❑ 196 Zack Greinke SP	4.00	1.20
❑ 197 Laynce Nix	.40	.12
❑ 198 Vito Chiaravalloti SP RC	4.00	1.20
❑ 199 Estee Harris RC	1.00	.30
❑ 200 Jon Knott SP RC	4.00	1.20
❑ 201 Dioner Navarro RC	1.50	.45
❑ 202 Craig Ansman RC	.75	.23
❑ 203 Travis Blackley RC	.75	.23
❑ 204 Yadier Molina RC	2.00	.60
❑ 205 Rodney Choy Foo RC	.50	.15
❑ 206 Kyle Sleeth SP RC	5.00	1.50
❑ 207 Jeff Allison RC	.75	.23
❑ 208 Josh Labandeira RC	.75	.23
❑ 209 Lastings Milledge SP RC	8.00	2.40
❑ 210 Rudy Guillen SP RC	5.00	1.50
❑ 211 Blake Hawksworth SP RC	5.00	1.50
❑ 212 David Aardsma RC	1.00	.30
❑ 213 Shawn Hill RC	.75	.23
❑ 214 Erick Aybar SP RC	5.00	1.50
❑ 215 Ervin Santana RC	2.00	.60
❑ 216 Tim Stauffer SP RC	8.00	2.40
❑ 217 Merkin Valdez RC	1.00	.30
❑ 218 Jack McKeon MG	.40	.12
❑ 219 Jeff Conine	.40	.12
❑ 220 Josh Beckett SP	4.00	1.20
❑ 221 Luis Castillo	.40	.12
❑ 222 Mike Lowell	.40	.12
❑ 223 Juan Pierre	.40	.12
❑ 224A Ivan Rodriguez Marlins	.60	.18
❑ 224B Ivan Rodriguez Tigers SP	5.00	1.50
❑ 225 A.J. Burnett	.40	.12
❑ 226 Miguel Cabrera SP	5.00	1.50
❑ 227 Jeffrey Loria	.40	.12
❑ 228 Joe Torre MG	.60	.18
❑ 229A Jason Giambi Portrait	.40	.12
❑ 229B Jason Giambi Fielding SP	4.00	1.20
❑ 230 Aaron Boone	.40	.12
❑ 231 Jose Contreras	.40	.12
❑ 232 Derek Jeter SP	8.00	2.40
❑ 233 Ruben Sierra	.40	.12
❑ 234 Mike Mussina	.60	.18
❑ 235 Mariano Rivera	.60	.18
❑ 236A Jorge Posada SP	5.00	1.50
❑ 236B Dioner Navarro SP	5.00	1.50
❑ 237 Alfonso Soriano	.40	.12
❑ NNO Alex Rodriguez Yanks	3.00	.90
❑ VB Vintage Buyback	.00	

2005 Topps Cracker Jack

	Nm-Mt	Ex-Mt
COMPLETE SET (250)	200.00	60.00
COMP.SET w/o SP'S (200)	40.00	12.00
SP STATED ODDS 1:3 HOBBY/RETAIL		.00
SP CL: 1/3B/4/6/11/13/21/26/30/31/41/51		.00
SP CL: 56/60B/71/75A/75B/84/85B/106/110		.00
SP CL: 111/112/126/135A/135B/146/151/156		.00
SP CL: 164B/166/176/181/186/191/196/201		.00
SP CL: 211/216/221A/221B/225/226/228B		.00
SP CL: 231/235/236A/236B	.00	

	Nm-Mt	Ex-Mt
❑ 1 David Wright SP	8.00	2.40
❑ 2 Rafael Furcal	.40	.12
❑ 3A Alex Rodriguez Portrait	1.50	.45
❑ 3B Alex Rodriguez Fielding SP	6.00	1.80
❑ 4 Victor Martinez SP	4.00	1.20
❑ 5 Ken Griffey Jr.	1.50	.45
❑ 6 Bobby Crosby SP	4.00	1.20
❑ 7 Ivan Rodriguez	.60	.18
❑ 8 Darin Erstad	.40	.12
❑ 9 Javy Lopez	.40	.12
❑ 10 Brian Giles	.40	.12
❑ 11 Aaron Rowand SP	4.00	1.20
❑ 12 Joe Torre MG	.60	.18
❑ 13 Zack Greinke SP	4.00	1.20
❑ 14 Shannon Stewart	.40	.12
❑ 15 Jack Wilson	.40	.12
❑ 16 Jose Vidro	.40	.12
❑ 17 Josh Beckett	.40	.12
❑ 18 Barry Zito	.40	.12
❑ 19 Bret Boone	.40	.12
❑ 20 Greg Maddux	1.50	.45
❑ 21 Carl Crawford SP	4.00	1.20
❑ 22 Mark Teixeira	.60	.18
❑ 23 Jason Schmidt	.40	.12
❑ 24 Kazuhisa Ishii	.40	.12
❑ 25 Mike Piazza	1.00	.30
❑ 26 Daniel Cabrera SP	4.00	1.20
❑ 27 Mike Lieberthal	.40	.12
❑ 28 Gil Meche	.40	.12
❑ 29 Phil Nevin	.40	.12
❑ 30 Adrian Beltre SP	4.00	1.20
❑ 31 Chipper Jones SP	5.00	1.50
❑ 32 Zach Day	.40	.12
❑ 33 Ben Sheets	.40	.12
❑ 34 Carlos Zambrano	.40	.12
❑ 35 Melvin Mora	.40	.12
❑ 36 Joe Mauer	.40	.12
❑ 37 Ken Harvey	.40	.12
❑ 38 Bernie Williams	.40	.12
❑ 39 Mike Maroth	.40	.12
❑ 40 Eric Chavez	.40	.12
❑ 41 Matt Lawton SP	4.00	1.20
❑ 42 Ray Durham	.40	.12
❑ 43 Vernon Wells	.40	.12
❑ 44 Mike Lowell	.40	.12
❑ 45 Jim Thome	.60	.18
❑ 46 Joel Pineiro	.40	.12
❑ 47 Lance Berkman	.40	.12
❑ 48 Ryan Klesko	.40	.12
❑ 49 Adam Dunn	.40	.12
❑ 50 Vladimir Guerrero	1.00	.30
❑ 51 Eric Gagne SP	4.00	1.20
❑ 52 Richie Sexson	.40	.12
❑ 53 Javier Vazquez	.40	.12
❑ 54 Roy Oswalt	.40	.12
❑ 55 Carlos Delgado	.40	.12
❑ 56 John Buck SP	4.00	1.20
❑ 57 Kenny Rogers	.40	.12
❑ 58 Sidney Ponson	.40	.12
❑ 59 Vicente Padilla	.40	.12
❑ 60A Mark Prior Leg Up	.60	.18
❑ 60B Mark Prior Portrait SP	5.00	1.50
❑ 61 A.J. Pierzynski	.40	.12
❑ 62 Aubrey Huff	.40	.12
❑ 63 Shea Hillenbrand	.40	.12
❑ 64 Carlos Guillen	.40	.12
❑ 65 Lyle Overbay	.40	.12
❑ 66 Al Leiter	.40	.12
❑ 67 Eric Hinske	.40	.12
❑ 68 Laynce Nix	.40	.12
❑ 69 Scott Hairston	.40	.12
❑ 70 Roger Clemens	1.50	.45
❑ 71 Cesar Izturis SP	4.00	1.20
❑ 72 Shawn Green	.40	.12
❑ 73 Marcus Giles	.40	.12
❑ 74 Rafael Palmeiro	.60	.18
❑ 75A Gary Sheffield SP	4.00	1.20
❑ 75B Melky Cabrera SP	5.00	1.50

	Card	Nm-Mt	Ex-Mt
❑	76 Juan Pierre	.40	.12
❑	77 Pat Burrell	.40	.12
❑	78 Sean Burroughs	.40	.12
❑	79 Frank Thomas	1.00	.30
❑	80 Andruw Jones	.60	.18
❑	81 C.C. Sabathia	.40	.12
❑	82 Jeff Bagwell	.60	.18
❑	83 Tom Glavine	.60	.18
❑	84 Craig Wilson SP	4.00	1.20
❑	85A Johan Santana Throwing	.60	.18
❑	85B Johan Santana Portrait SP	5.00	1.50
❑	86 Raul Ibanez	.40	.12
❑	87 Sean Casey	.60	.18
❑	88 Bucky Jacobsen	.40	.12
❑	89 B.J. Upton	.60	.18
❑	90 Bobby Abreu	.40	.12
❑	91 Geoff Jenkins	.40	.12
❑	92 Troy Glaus	.40	.12
❑	93 Dontrelle Willis	.40	.12
❑	94 Jose Lima	.40	.12
❑	95 Rocco Baldelli	.40	.12
❑	96 Aramis Ramirez	.40	.12
❑	97 Paul Lo Duca	.40	.12
❑	98 Torii Hunter	.40	.12
❑	99 Jay Payton	.40	.12
❑	100 Carlos Beltran	.40	.12
❑	101 Jaret Wright	.40	.12
❑	102 Jason Bay	.40	.12
❑	103 Cliff Floyd	.40	.12
❑	104 Mike Sweeney	.40	.12
❑	105 Sammy Sosa	1.00	.30
❑	106 Khalil Greene SP	5.00	1.50
❑	107 David DeJesus	.40	.12
❑	108 Jermaine Dye	.40	.12
❑	109 Miguel Cabrera	.60	.18
❑	110 Miguel Tejada SP	4.00	1.20
❑	111 Johnny Estrada SP	4.00	1.20
❑	112 Ronnie Belliard SP	4.00	1.20
❑	113 Austin Kearns	.40	.12
❑	114 Erubiel Durazo	.40	.12
❑	115 Preston Wilson	.40	.12
❑	116 Hideo Nomo	1.00	.30
❑	117 Dmitri Young	.40	.12
❑	118 Jon Lieber	.40	.12
❑	119 Derrek Lee	.60	.18
❑	120 Todd Helton	.60	.18
❑	121 Omar Vizquel	.60	.18
❑	122 Wily Mo Pena	.40	.12
❑	123 J.D. Drew	.40	.12
❑	124 Matt Holliday	.40	.12
❑	125 Ichiro Suzuki	2.00	.60
❑	126 Mark Buehrle SP	4.00	1.20
❑	127 Barry Bonds	2.50	.75
❑	128 Jeff Kent	.40	.12
❑	129 Kerry Wood	.40	.12
❑	130 Mariano Rivera	.60	.18
❑	131 Nick Johnson	.40	.12
❑	132 Randy Winn	.40	.12
❑	133 Phil Garner MG	.40	.12
❑	134 Jose Reyes	.40	.12
❑	135A Michael Young SP	4.00	1.20
❑	135B Ian Kinsler SP	6.00	1.80
❑	136 Jose Contreras	.40	.12
❑	137 Oliver Perez	.40	.12
❑	138 Roy Halladay	.40	.12
❑	139 Kevin Millwood	.40	.12
❑	140 Jorge Posada	.60	.18
❑	141 Mike Cameron	.40	.12
❑	142 Edgardo Alfonzo	.40	.12
❑	143 Chris Shelton	.40	.12
❑	144 Luis Castillo	.40	.12
❑	145 Alfonso Soriano	.40	.12
❑	146 Ryan Drese SP	4.00	1.20
❑	147 Mark Mulder	.40	.12
❑	148 Jason Giambi	.40	.12
❑	149 Travis Hafner	.40	.12
❑	150 Randy Johnson	1.00	.30
❑	151 Paul Konerko SP	4.00	1.20
❑	152 Mike Mussina	.60	.18
❑	153 Brad Wilkerson	.40	.12
❑	154 Tim Hudson	.40	.12
❑	155 Garret Anderson	.40	.12
❑	156 Chase Utley SP	4.00	1.20
❑	157 Jamie Moyer	.40	.12
❑	158 Scott Kazmir	.40	.12
❑	159 Brett Myers	.40	.12
❑	160 Kazuo Matsui	.40	.12
❑	161 Orlando Hudson	.40	.12
❑	162 Luis Gonzalez	.40	.12
❑	163 Kevin Youkilis	.40	.12
❑	164A Jason Kendall	.40	.12
❑	164B Landon Powell SP	5.00	1.50
❑	165 Hank Blalock	.40	.12
❑	166 Mark Loretta SP	4.00	1.20
❑	167 Miguel Cairo	.40	.12
❑	168 Corey Patterson	.40	.12
❑	169 Victor Zambrano	.40	.12
❑	170 Magglio Ordonez	.40	.12
❑	171 J.T. Snow	.40	.12
❑	172 Randy Wolf	.40	.12
❑	173 Rich Harden	.40	.12
❑	174 Bartolo Colon	.40	.12
❑	175 Derek Jeter	2.00	.60
❑	176 Casey Kotchman SP	4.00	1.20
❑	177 Val Majewski	.40	.12
❑	178 Grady Sizemore	.40	.12
❑	179 Rickie Weeks	.40	.12
❑	180 Robinson Cano	.60	.18
❑	181 Nick Swisher SP	4.00	1.20
❑	182 Ryan Howard	.40	.12
❑	183 John Van Benschoten	.40	.12
❑	184 Delmon Young	.40	.12
❑	185 Aaron Hill	.40	.12
❑	186 Chris Burke SP	4.00	1.20
❑	187 Merkin Valdez	.40	.12
❑	188 Jeremy Reed	.40	.12
❑	189 Conor Jackson	.60	.18
❑	190 Mark Teahen	.40	.12
❑	191 Joey Gathright SP	4.00	1.20
❑	192 Gavin Floyd	.40	.12
❑	193 Joe Blanton	.40	.12
❑	194 Jason Kubel	.40	.12
❑	195 Jeff Francis	.40	.12
❑	196 Angel Guzman SP	4.00	1.20
❑	197 Dallas McPherson	.40	.12
❑	198 Melky Cabrera RC	1.25	.35
❑	199 Jake Dittler	.50	.15
❑	200 Elvys Quezada RC	.75	.23
❑	201 Ian Kinsler SP RC	6.00	1.80
❑	202 Nate McLouth RC	1.00	.30
❑	203 Chris Seddon RC	.75	.23
❑	204 Chad Orvella RC	.75	.23
❑	205 Ian Bladergroen RC	1.00	.30
❑	206 James Jurries SP RC	5.00	1.50
❑	207 Landon Powell RC	1.00	.30
❑	208 Eric Nielsen RC	.75	.23
❑	209 Chris Roberson RC	.75	.23
❑	210 Andre Ethier RC	1.25	.35
❑	211 Chris Denorfia SP RC	5.00	1.50
❑	212 Darren Fenster RC	.75	.23
❑	213 Jeremy West RC	1.00	.30
❑	214 Sean Marshall RC	1.00	.30
❑	215 Ryan Sweeney RC	1.25	.35
❑	216 Steve Doetsch SP RC	5.00	1.50
❑	217 Kevin Melillo RC	1.00	.30
❑	218 Chip Cannon RC	.75	.23
❑	219 Tony La Russa MG	.40	.12
❑	220 Chris Carpenter	.40	.12
❑	221A Edgar Renteria Sox SP	4.00	1.20
❑	221B Edgar Renteria Cards SP	4.00	1.20
❑	222 Albert Pujols	2.00	.60
❑	223 Jim Edmonds	.60	.18
❑	224 Jason Marquis	.40	.12
❑	225 Scott Rolen SP	5.00	1.50
❑	226 Larry Walker SP	5.00	1.50
❑	227 Matt Morris	.40	.12
❑	228A Mike Matheny Giants	.40	.12
❑	228B Mike Matheny Cards SP	4.00	1.20
❑	229 Jeromy Burnitz	.40	.12
❑	230 Terry Francona MG	.60	.18
❑	231 Johnny Damon SP	5.00	1.50
❑	232 Keith Foulke	.40	.12
❑	233 Trot Nixon	.40	.12
❑	234 Manny Ramirez	.60	.18
❑	235 David Ortiz SP	5.00	1.50
❑	236A Pedro Martinez Sox SP	5.00	1.50
❑	236B Pedro Martinez Mets SP	5.00	1.50
❑	237 Curt Schilling	.60	.18
❑	238 Kevin Millar	.40	.12
❑	239 Bill Mueller	.40	.12
❑	240 Mark Bellhorn	.40	.12
❑	NNO Josh Beckett NNO SP	4.00	1.20

2001 Topps Gallery

	Nm-Mt	Ex-Mt
COMPLETE SET (150)	80.00	24.00
COMP.SET w/o SP's (100)	40.00	12.00
COMMON (1-49/51-101)	.50	.15
COMMON (102-150)	3.00	.90

	Card	Nm-Mt	Ex-Mt
❑	1 Darin Erstad	.50	.15
❑	2 Chipper Jones	1.25	.35
❑	3 Nomar Garciaparra	2.00	.60
❑	4 Fernando Vina	.50	.15
❑	5 Bartolo Colon	.50	.15
❑	6 Bobby Higginson	.50	.15
❑	7 Antonio Alfonseca	.50	.15
❑	8 Mike Sweeney	.50	.15
❑	9 Kevin Brown	.50	.15
❑	10 Jose Vidro	.50	.15
❑	11 Derek Jeter	3.00	.90
❑	12 Jason Giambi	.50	.15
❑	13 Pat Burrell	.50	.15
❑	14 Jeff Kent	.50	.15
❑	15 Alex Rodriguez	2.00	.60
❑	16 Rafael Palmeiro	.75	.23
❑	17 Garret Anderson	.50	.15
❑	18 Brad Fullmer	.50	.15
❑	19 Doug Glanville	.50	.15
❑	20 Mark Quinn	.50	.15
❑	21 Mo Vaughn	.50	.15
❑	22 Andruw Jones	.75	.23
❑	23 Pedro Martinez	.75	.23
❑	24 Ken Griffey Jr.	2.00	.60
❑	25 Roberto Alomar	.75	.23
❑	26 Dean Palmer	.50	.15
❑	27 Jeff Bagwell	.75	.23
❑	28 Jermaine Dye	.50	.15
❑	29 Chan Ho Park	.50	.15
❑	30 Vladimir Guerrero	1.25	.35
❑	31 Bernie Williams	.75	.23
❑	32 Ben Grieve	.50	.15
❑	33 Jason Kendall	.50	.15
❑	34 Barry Bonds	3.00	.90
❑	35 Jim Edmonds	.75	.23
❑	36 Ivan Rodriguez	.75	.23
❑	37 Javy Lopez	.50	.15
❑	38 J.T. Snow	.50	.15
❑	39 Erubiel Durazo	.50	.15
❑	40 Terrence Long	.50	.15
❑	41 Tim Salmon	.75	.23
❑	42 Greg Maddux	2.00	.60
❑	43 Sammy Sosa	1.25	.35
❑	44 Sean Casey	.75	.23
❑	45 Jeff Cirillo	.50	.15
❑	46 Juan Gonzalez	.50	.15
❑	47 Richard Hidalgo	.50	.15
❑	48 Shawn Green	.50	.15
❑	49 Jeromy Burnitz	.50	.15
❑	50 Willie Mays HTA N.Y. Giants	15.00	4.50
❑	50 Willie Mays RETAIL S.F. Giants	40.00	12.00
❑	51 David Justice	.50	.15
❑	52 Tim Hudson	.50	.15
❑	53 Brian Giles	.50	.15
❑	54 Robb Nen	.50	.15
❑	55 Fernando Tatis	.50	.15
❑	56 Tony Batista	.50	.15
❑	57 Pokey Reese	.50	.15
❑	58 Ray Durham	.50	.15

❑ 59 Greg Vaughn .50 .15
❑ 60 Kazuhiro Sasaki .50 .15
❑ 61 Troy Glaus .50 .15
❑ 62 Rafael Furcal .50 .15
❑ 63 Magglio Ordonez .50 .15
❑ 64 Jim Thome .75 .23
❑ 65 Todd Helton .75 .23
❑ 66 Preston Wilson .50 .15
❑ 67 Moises Alou .50 .15
❑ 68 Gary Sheffield .50 .15
❑ 69 Geoff Jenkins .50 .15
❑ 70 Mike Piazza 2.00 .60
❑ 71 Jorge Posada .75 .23
❑ 72 Bobby Abreu .50 .15
❑ 73 Phil Nevin .50 .15
❑ 74 John Olerud .50 .15
❑ 75 Mark McGwire 3.00 .90
❑ 76 Jose Cruz Jr. .50 .15
❑ 77 David Segui .50 .15
❑ 78 Neifi Perez .50 .15
❑ 79 Omar Vizquel .75 .23
❑ 80 Rick Ankiel .50 .15
❑ 81 Randy Johnson 1.25 .35
❑ 82 Albert Belle .50 .15
❑ 83 Frank Thomas 1.25 .35
❑ 84 Manny Ramirez Sox .75 .23
❑ 85 Larry Walker .50 .15
❑ 86 Luis Castillo .50 .15
❑ 87 Johnny Damon .75 .23
❑ 88 Adrian Beltre .50 .15
❑ 89 Cristian Guzman .50 .15
❑ 90 Jay Payton .50 .15
❑ 91 Miguel Tejada .50 .15
❑ 92 Scott Rolen .75 .23
❑ 93 Ryan Klesko .50 .15
❑ 94 Edgar Martinez .75 .23
❑ 95 Fred McGriff .75 .23
❑ 96 Carlos Delgado .50 .15
❑ 97 Barry Zito .75 .23
❑ 98 Mike Lieberthal .50 .15
❑ 99 Trevor Hoffman .50 .15
❑ 100 Gabe Kapler .50 .15
❑ 101 Edgardo Alfonzo .50 .15
❑ 102 Corey Patterson 3.00 .90
❑ 103 Alfonso Soriano .75 .23
❑ 104 Keith Ginter 3.00 .90
❑ 105 Keith Reed 3.00 .90
❑ 106 Nick Johnson 3.00 .90
❑ 107 Carlos Pena 3.00 .90
❑ 108 Vernon Wells 3.00 .90
❑ 109 Roy Oswalt 4.00 1.20
❑ 110 Alex Escobar 3.00 .90
❑ 111 Adam Everett 3.00 .90
❑ 112 Jimmy Rollins 3.00 .90
❑ 113 Marcus Giles 3.00 .90
❑ 114 Jack Cust 3.00 .90
❑ 115 Chin-Feng Chen 3.00 .90
❑ 116 Pablo Ozuna 3.00 .90
❑ 117 Ben Sheets 4.00 1.20
❑ 118 Adrian Gonzalez 3.00 .90
❑ 119 Ben Davis 3.00 .90
❑ 120 Eric Valent 3.00 .90
❑ 121 Scott Heard 3.00 .90
❑ 122 David Parrish RC 3.00 .90
❑ 123 Sean Burnett 3.00 .90
❑ 124 Derek Thompson 3.00 .90
❑ 125 Tim Christman RC 3.00 .90
❑ 126 Mike Jacobs RC 15.00 4.50
❑ 127 Luis Montanez RC 3.00 .90
❑ 128 Chris Bass RC 3.00 .90
❑ 129 Willi Smith RC 3.00 .90
❑ 130 Justin Wayne RC 3.00 .90
❑ 131 Shawn Fagan RC 3.00 .90
❑ 132 Chad Petty RC 3.00 .90
❑ 133 J.R. House 3.00 .90
❑ 134 Joel Pineiro 3.00 .90
❑ 135 Albert Pujols RC 60.00 18.00
❑ 136 Carmen Cali RC 3.00 .90
❑ 137 Steve Smyth RC 3.00 .90
❑ 138 John Lackey 3.00 .90
❑ 139 Bob Keppel RC 3.00 .90
❑ 140 Dominic Rich RC 3.00 .90
❑ 141 Josh Hamilton 3.00 .90
❑ 142 Nolan Ryan 6.00 1.80
❑ 143 Tom Seaver 4.00 1.20
❑ 144 Reggie Jackson 4.00 1.20
❑ 145 Johnny Bench 4.00 1.20
❑ 146 Warren Spahn 4.00 1.20
❑ 147 Brooks Robinson 4.00 1.20
❑ 148 Carl Yastrzemski 5.00 1.50
❑ 149 Al Kaline 4.00 1.20
❑ 150 Bob Feller 3.00 .90
❑ 151A I. Suzuki English RC 25.00 7.50
❑ 151B I.Suzuki Japan RC 25.00 7.50

2005 Topps Gallery

	Nm-Mt	Ex-Mt
COMP.SET w/o SP'S (150)	60.00	18.00
COMMON CARD (1-150)	.75	.23
COMMON CARD (151-170)	5.00	1.50
COMMON CARD (171-185)	5.00	1.50
COMMON CARD (186-195)	5.00	1.50
151-195 ODDS FIVE PER MINI-BOX		.00

VARIATION ODDS 1:8 MINI-BOXES.00
VARIATION STATED PRINT RUN 517 SETS
VARIATIONS ARE NOT SERIAL-NUMBERED
PRINT RUN INFO PROVIDED BY TOPPS
VAR CL: 1/40/100/154-155/157/165
VAR CL: 167-168/187
SEE BECKETT.COM FOR VARIATION INFO
PLATE ODDS 1:48 MINI-BOXES
PLATE PRINT RUN 1 SET PER COLOR
BLACK-CYAN-MAGENTA-YELLOW ISSUED
NO PLATE PRICING DUE TO SCARCITY

❑ 1A A.Rodriguez White Glv 3.00 .90
❑ 1B A.Rodriguez Blk Glv SP 8.00 2.40
❑ 2 Eric Chavez .75 .23
❑ 3 Mike Piazza 2.00 .60
❑ 4 Bret Boone .75 .23
❑ 5 Albert Pujols 4.00 1.20
❑ 6 Vernon Wells .75 .23
❑ 7 Andruw Jones 1.25 .35
❑ 8 Miguel Tejada .75 .23
❑ 9 Johnny Damon 1.25 .35
❑ 10 Nomar Garciaparra 2.00 .60
❑ 11 Pat Burrell .75 .23
❑ 12 Bartolo Colon .75 .23
❑ 13 Johnny Estrada .75 .23
❑ 14 Luis Gonzalez .75 .23
❑ 15 Jay Gibbons .75 .23
❑ 16 Curt Schilling 1.25 .35
❑ 17 Aramis Ramirez .75 .23
❑ 18 Frank Thomas 2.00 .60
❑ 19 Adam Dunn .75 .23
❑ 20 Sammy Sosa 2.00 .60
❑ 21 Matt Lawton .75 .23
❑ 22 Preston Wilson .75 .23
❑ 23 Carlos Pena .75 .23
❑ 24 Josh Beckett .75 .23
❑ 25 Carlos Beltran .75 .23
❑ 26 Juan Gonzalez .75 .23
❑ 27 Adrian Beltre .75 .23
❑ 28 Lyle Overbay .75 .23
❑ 29 Justin Morneau .75 .23
❑ 30 Derek Jeter 4.00 1.20
❑ 31 Barry Zito .75 .23
❑ 32 Bobby Abreu .75 .23
❑ 33 Jason Bay .75 .23
❑ 34 Jose Reyes .75 .23
❑ 35 Nick Johnson .75 .23
❑ 36 Lew Ford .75 .23
❑ 37 Scott Podsednik .75 .23
❑ 38 Rocco Baldelli .75 .23
❑ 39 Eric Hinske .75 .23
❑ 40A Ichiro Black Wall 4.00 1.20
❑ 40B Ichiro Writing on Wall SP 10.00 3.00
❑ 41 Larry Walker 1.25 .35
❑ 42 Mark Teixeira 1.25 .35
❑ 43 Khalil Greene 1.25 .35
❑ 44 Edgardo Alfonzo .75 .23
❑ 45 Javier Vazquez .75 .23
❑ 46 Cliff Floyd .75 .23
❑ 47 Geoff Jenkins .75 .23
❑ 48 Ken Griffey Jr. 3.00 .90
❑ 49 Vinny Castilla .75 .23
❑ 50 Mark Prior 1.25 .35
❑ 51 Jose Guillen .75 .23
❑ 52 J.D. Drew .75 .23
❑ 53 Rafael Palmeiro 1.25 .35
❑ 54 Kevin Youkilis .75 .23
❑ 55 Derrek Lee 1.25 .35
❑ 56 Freddy Garcia .75 .23
❑ 57 Wily Mo Pena .75 .23
❑ 58 C.C. Sabathia .75 .23
❑ 59 Craig Biggio 1.25 .35
❑ 60 Ivan Rodriguez 1.25 .35
❑ 61 Angel Berroa .75 .23
❑ 62 Ben Sheets .75 .23
❑ 63 Johan Santana 1.25 .35
❑ 64 Al Leiter .75 .23
❑ 65 Bernie Williams 1.25 .35
❑ 66 Bobby Crosby .75 .23
❑ 67 Jack Wilson .75 .23
❑ 68 A.J. Pierzynski .75 .23
❑ 69 Jimmy Rollins .75 .23
❑ 70 Jason Giambi .75 .23
❑ 71 Tom Glavine 1.25 .35
❑ 72 Kevin Brown .75 .23
❑ 73 B.J. Upton 1.25 .35
❑ 74 Edgar Renteria .75 .23
❑ 75 Alfonso Soriano .75 .23
❑ 76 Mike Lieberthal .75 .23
❑ 77 Kazuo Matsui .75 .23
❑ 78 Phil Nevin .75 .23
❑ 79 Shawn Green .75 .23
❑ 80 Miguel Cabrera 1.25 .35
❑ 81 Todd Helton 1.25 .35
❑ 82 Magglio Ordonez .75 .23
❑ 83 Manny Ramirez 1.25 .35
❑ 84 Bill Mueller .75 .23
❑ 85 Troy Glaus .75 .23
❑ 86 Richie Sexson .75 .23
❑ 87 Javy Lopez .75 .23
❑ 88 David Ortiz 2.00 .60
❑ 89 Greg Maddux 3.00 .90
❑ 90 Vladimir Guerrero 2.00 .60
❑ 91 Jeromy Burnitz .75 .23
❑ 92 Jeff Kent .75 .23
❑ 93 Travis Hafner .75 .23
❑ 94 Mark Buehrle .75 .23
❑ 95 Paul Lo Duca .75 .23
❑ 96 Roy Oswalt .75 .23
❑ 97 Torii Hunter .75 .23
❑ 98 Gary Sheffield .75 .23
❑ 99 Erubiel Durazo .75 .23
❑ 100A J.Thome Kid's Shirt Blue 1.25 .35
❑ 100B J.Thome Kid's Shirt Red SP 8.00 2.40
❑ 101 Ken Harvey .75 .23
❑ 102 Shannon Stewart .75 .23
❑ 103 Dmitri Young .75 .23
❑ 104 Kevin Millar .75 .23
❑ 105 Kerry Wood .75 .23
❑ 106 Paul Konerko .75 .23
❑ 107 Ronnie Belliard .75 .23
❑ 108 Mike Lowell .75 .23
❑ 109 Hee Seop Choi .75 .23
❑ 110 Joe Mauer .75 .23
❑ 111 David Wright 3.00 .90
❑ 112 Jorge Posada 1.25 .35
❑ 113 Tim Hudson .75 .23
❑ 114 Brian Giles .75 .23
❑ 115 Jason Schmidt .75 .23
❑ 116 Aubrey Huff .75 .23
❑ 117 Hank Blalock .75 .23
❑ 118 Jim Edmonds 1.25 .35
❑ 119 Raul Ibanez .75 .23
❑ 120 Carlos Delgado .75 .23
❑ 121 Craig Wilson .75 .23
❑ 122 Ryan Klesko .75 .23

❑ 123 Mark Mulder .75 .23
❑ 124 Jose Vidro .75 .23
❑ 125 Mike Sweeney .75 .23
❑ 126 Lance Berkman .75 .23
❑ 127 Juan Pierre .75 .23
❑ 128 Austin Kearns .75 .23
❑ 129 Moises Alou .75 .23
❑ 130 Garret Anderson .75 .23
❑ 131 Pedro Martinez 1.25 .35
❑ 132 Melvin Mora .75 .23
❑ 133 Marcus Giles .75 .23
❑ 134 Corey Patterson .75 .23
❑ 135 Carlos Lee .75 .23
❑ 136 Sean Casey 1.25 .35
❑ 137 Jody Gerut .75 .23
❑ 138 Jose Valentin .75 .23
❑ 139 Aaron Miles .75 .23
❑ 140 Randy Johnson 2.00 .60
❑ 141 Carlos Guillen .75 .23
❑ 142 Dontrelle Willis .75 .23
❑ 143 Jeff Bagwell 1.25 .35
❑ 144 Jason Kendall .75 .23
❑ 145 Mark Loretta .75 .23
❑ 146 Scott Rolen 1.25 .35
❑ 147 Carl Crawford .75 .23
❑ 148 Michael Young .75 .23
❑ 149 Jermaine Dye .75 .23
❑ 150 Chipper Jones 2.00 .60
❑ 151 Melky Cabrera FY RC 8.00 2.40
❑ 152 Chris Seddon FY RC 5.00 1.50
❑ 153 Nate Schierholtz FY 5.00 1.50
❑ 154A Ian Kinsler FY Green RC 6.00 1.80
❑ 154B Ian Kinsler FY Gold SP 10.00 3.00
❑ 155A B.Moss FY Black Hat RC 8.00 2.40
❑ 155B B.Moss FY Red Hat SP 10.00 3.00
❑ 156 Chadd Blasko FY RC 5.00 1.50
❑ 157A J.West FY Red Jsy RC 5.00 1.50
❑ 157B J.West FY Navy Jsy SP 8.00 2.40
❑ 158 Sean Marshall FY RC 5.00 1.50
❑ 159 Ryan Sweeney FY RC 8.00 2.40
❑ 160 Matthew Lindstrom FY RC 5.00 1.50
❑ 161 Ryan Goleski FY RC 5.00 1.50
❑ 162 Brett Harper FY RC 5.00 1.50
❑ 163 Chris Roberson FY RC 5.00 1.50
❑ 164 Andre Ethier FY RC 8.00 2.40
❑ 165A I.Bladergroen FY Pose RC 5.00 1.50
❑ 165B I.Bladergroen FY Swing SP 8.00 2.40
❑ 166 James Jurries FY RC 5.00 1.50
❑ 167A Billy Butler FY Vest RC 15.00 4.50
❑ 167B B.Butler FY Black Uni SP 20.00 6.00
❑ 168A M.Rogers FY Ball/Air RC 5.00 1.50
❑ 168B M.Rogers FY Ball/Hand SP 8.00 2.40
❑ 169 Tyler Clippard FY RC 8.00 2.40
❑ 170 Luis Ramirez FY RC 5.00 1.50
❑ 171 Casey Kotchman PROS 5.00 1.50
❑ 172 Chris Burke PROS 5.00 1.50
❑ 173 Dallas McPherson PROS 5.00 1.50
❑ 174 Edwin Jackson PROS 5.00 1.50
❑ 175 Felix Hernandez PROS 10.00 3.00
❑ 176 Gavin Floyd PROS 5.00 1.50
❑ 177 Guillermo Quiroz PROS 5.00 1.50
❑ 178 Jason Kubel PROS 5.00 1.50
❑ 179 Jeff Mathis PROS 5.00 1.50
❑ 180 Rickie Weeks PROS 5.00 1.50
❑ 181 Ryan Howard PROS 5.00 1.50
❑ 182 Franklin Gutierrez PROS 5.00 1.50
❑ 183 Jeremy Reed PROS 5.00 1.50
❑ 184 Carlos Quentin PROS 5.00 1.50
❑ 185 Jeff Francis PROS 5.00 1.50
❑ 186 Nolan Ryan RET 15.00 4.50
❑ 187A Hank Aaron RET w/o 755 10.00 3.00
❑ 187B Hank Aaron RET w/755 SP 15.00 4.50
❑ 188 Duke Snider RET 8.00 2.40
❑ 189 Mike Schmidt RET 10.00 3.00
❑ 190 Ernie Banks RET 8.00 2.40
❑ 191 Frank Robinson RET 5.00 1.50
❑ 192 Harmon Killebrew RET 8.00 2.40
❑ 193 Al Kaline RET 8.00 2.40
❑ 194 Rod Carew RET 8.00 2.40
❑ 195 Johnny Bench RET 8.00 2.40

2001 Topps Heritage

	Nm-Mt	Ex-Mt
COMP.MASTER SET (487)	400.00	120.00
COMPLETE SET (407)	300.00	90.00

COMP.SET w/o SP's (230)	80.00	24.00
COMMON CARD (81-310)	.50	.15
COMMON CARD (1-80)	2.50	.75
COMMON (311-407)	5.00	1.50

❑ 1 Kris Benson 2.50 .75
❑ 1 Kris Benson Black 2.50 .75
❑ 2 Brian Jordan 2.50 .75
❑ 2 Brian Jordan Black 2.50 .75
❑ 3 Fernando Vina 2.50 .75
❑ 3 Fernando Vina Black 2.50 .75
❑ 4 Mike Sweeney 2.50 .75
❑ 4 Mike Sweeney Black 2.50 .75
❑ 5 Rafael Palmeiro 2.50 .75
❑ 5 Rafael Palmeiro Black 2.50 .75
❑ 6 Paul O'Neill 2.50 .75
❑ 6 Paul O'Neill Black 2.50 .75
❑ 7 Todd Helton 2.50 .75
❑ 7 Todd Helton Black 2.50 .75
❑ 8 Ramiro Mendoza 2.50 .75
❑ 8 Ramiro Mendoza Black 2.50 .75
❑ 9 Kevin Millwood 2.50 .75
❑ 9 Kevin Millwood Black 2.50 .75
❑ 10 Chuck Knoblauch 2.50 .75
❑ 10 Chuck Knoblauch Black 2.50 .75
❑ 11 Derek Jeter 10.00 3.00
❑ 11 Derek Jeter Black 10.00 3.00
❑ 12 A.Rodriguez Rangers 6.00 1.80
❑ 12 A.Rod Black Rangers 6.00 1.80
❑ 13 Geoff Jenkins 2.50 .75
❑ 13 Geoff Jenkins Black 2.50 .75
❑ 14 David Justice 2.50 .75
❑ 14 David Justice Black 2.50 .75
❑ 15 David Cone 2.50 .75
❑ 15 David Cone Black 2.50 .75
❑ 16 Andres Galarraga 2.50 .75
❑ 16 Andres Galarraga Black 2.50 .75
❑ 17 Garret Anderson 2.50 .75
❑ 17 Garret Anderson Black 2.50 .75
❑ 18 Roger Cedeno 2.50 .75
❑ 18 Roger Cedeno Black 2.50 .75
❑ 19 Randy Velarde 2.50 .75
❑ 19 Randy Velarde Black 2.50 .75
❑ 20 Carlos Delgado 2.50 .75
❑ 20 Carlos Delgado Black 2.50 .75
❑ 21 Quilvio Veras 2.50 .75
❑ 21 Quilvio Veras Black 2.50 .75
❑ 22 Jose Vidro 2.50 .75
❑ 22 Jose Vidro Black 2.50 .75
❑ 23 Corey Patterson 2.50 .75
❑ 23 Corey Patterson Black 2.50 .75
❑ 24 Jorge Posada 2.50 .75
❑ 24 Jorge Posada Black 2.50 .75
❑ 25 Eddie Perez 2.50 .75
❑ 25 Eddie Perez Black 2.50 .75
❑ 26 Jack Cust 2.50 .75
❑ 26 Jack Cust Black 2.50 .75
❑ 27 Sean Burroughs 2.50 .75
❑ 27 Sean Burroughs Black 2.50 .75
❑ 28 Randy Wolf 2.50 .75
❑ 28 Randy Wolf Black 2.50 .75
❑ 29 Mike Lamb 2.50 .75
❑ 29 Mike Lamb Black 2.50 .75
❑ 30 Rafael Furcal 2.50 .75
❑ 30 Rafael Furcal Black 2.50 .75
❑ 31 Barry Bonds 10.00 3.00
❑ 31 Barry Bonds Black 10.00 3.00
❑ 32 Tim Hudson 2.50 .75
❑ 32 Tim Hudson Black 2.50 .75
❑ 33 Tom Glavine 2.50 .75
❑ 33 Tom Glavine Black 2.50 .75
❑ 34 Javy Lopez 2.50 .75
❑ 34 Javy Lopez Black 2.50 .75
❑ 35 Aubrey Huff 2.50 .75
❑ 35 Aubrey Huff Black 2.50 .75
❑ 36 Wally Joyner 2.50 .75
❑ 36 Wally Joyner Black 2.50 .75
❑ 37 Magglio Ordonez 2.50 .75
❑ 37 Magglio Ordonez Black 2.50 .75
❑ 38 Matt Lawton 2.50 .75
❑ 38 Matt Lawton Black 2.50 .75
❑ 39 Mariano Rivera 2.50 .75
❑ 39 Mariano Rivera Black 2.50 .75
❑ 40 Andy Ashby 2.50 .75
❑ 40 Andy Ashby Black 2.50 .75
❑ 41 Mark Buehrle 2.50 .75
❑ 41 Mark Buehrle Black 2.50 .75
❑ 42 Esteban Loaiza 2.50 .75
❑ 42 Esteban Loaiza Black 2.50 .75
❑ 43 Mark Redman 2.50 .75
❑ 43 Mark Redman Black 2.50 .75
❑ 44 Mark Quinn 2.50 .75
❑ 44 Mark Quinn Black 2.50 .75
❑ 45 Tino Martinez 2.50 .75
❑ 45 Tino Martinez Black 2.50 .75
❑ 46 Joe Mays 2.50 .75
❑ 46 Joe Mays Black 2.50 .75
❑ 47 Walt Weiss 2.50 .75
❑ 47 Walt Weiss Black 2.50 .75
❑ 48 Roger Clemens 8.00 2.40
❑ 48 Roger Clemens Black 8.00 2.40
❑ 49 Greg Maddux 6.00 1.80
❑ 49 Greg Maddux Black 6.00 1.80
❑ 50 Richard Hidalgo 2.50 .75
❑ 50 Richard Hidalgo Black 2.50 .75
❑ 51 Orlando Hernandez 2.50 .75
❑ 51 O.Hernandez Black 2.50 .75
❑ 52 Chipper Jones 4.00 1.20
❑ 52 Chipper Jones Black 4.00 1.20
❑ 53 Ben Grieve 2.50 .75
❑ 53 Ben Grieve Black 2.50 .75
❑ 54 Jimmy Haynes 2.50 .75
❑ 54 Jimmy Haynes Black 2.50 .75
❑ 55 Ken Caminiti 2.50 .75
❑ 55 Ken Caminiti Black 2.50 .75
❑ 56 Tim Salmon 2.50 .75
❑ 56 Tim Salmon Black 2.50 .75
❑ 57 Andy Pettitte 2.50 .75
❑ 57 Andy Pettitte Black 2.50 .75
❑ 58 Darin Erstad 2.50 .75
❑ 58 Darin Erstad Black 2.50 .75
❑ 59 Marquis Grissom 2.50 .75
❑ 59 Marquis Grissom Black 2.50 .75
❑ 60 Raul Mondesi 2.50 .75
❑ 60 Raul Mondesi Black 2.50 .75
❑ 61 Bengie Molina 2.50 .75
❑ 61 Bengie Molina Black 2.50 .75
❑ 62 Miguel Tejada 2.50 .75
❑ 62 Miguel Tejada Black 2.50 .75
❑ 63 Jose Cruz Jr. 2.50 .75
❑ 63 Jose Cruz Jr. Black 2.50 .75
❑ 64 Billy Koch 2.50 .75
❑ 64 Billy Koch Black 2.50 .75
❑ 65 Troy Glaus 2.50 .75
❑ 65 Troy Glaus Black 2.50 .75
❑ 66 Cliff Floyd 2.50 .75
❑ 66 Cliff Floyd Black 2.50 .75
❑ 67 Tony Batista 2.50 .75
❑ 67 Tony Batista Black 2.50 .75
❑ 68 Jeff Bagwell 2.50 .75
❑ 68 Jeff Bagwell Black 2.50 .75
❑ 69 Billy Wagner 2.50 .75
❑ 69 Billy Wagner Black 2.50 .75
❑ 70 Eric Chavez 2.50 .75
❑ 70 Eric Chavez Black 2.50 .75
❑ 71 Troy Percival 2.50 .75
❑ 71 Troy Percival Black 2.50 .75
❑ 72 Andruw Jones 2.50 .75
❑ 72 Andruw Jones Black 2.50 .75
❑ 73 Shane Reynolds 2.50 .75
❑ 73 Shane Reynolds Black 2.50 .75
❑ 74 Barry Zito 2.50 .75
❑ 74 Barry Zito Black 2.50 .75
❑ 75 Roy Halladay 2.50 .75
❑ 75 Roy Halladay Black 2.50 .75

❑ 76 David Wells 2.50 .75
❑ 76 David Wells Black 2.50 .75
❑ 77 Jason Giambi 2.50 .75
❑ 77 Jason Giambi Black 2.50 .75
❑ 78 Scott Elarton 2.50 .75
❑ 78 Scott Elarton Black 2.50 .75
❑ 79 Moises Alou 2.50 .75
❑ 79 Moises Alou Black 2.50 .75
❑ 80 Adam Piatt 2.50 .75
❑ 80 Adam Piatt Black 2.50 .75
❑ 81 Wilton Veras .50 .15
❑ 82 Darryl Kile .60 .18
❑ 83 Johnny Damon 1.00 .30
❑ 84 Tony Armas Jr. .50 .15
❑ 85 Ellis Burks .60 .18
❑ 86 Jamey Wright .50 .15
❑ 87 Jose Vizcaino .50 .15
❑ 88 Bartolo Colon .60 .18
❑ 89 Carmen Cali RC .60 .18
❑ 90 Kevin Brown .60 .18
❑ 91 Josh Hamilton .50 .15
❑ 92 Jay Buhner .60 .18
❑ 93 Scott Pratt RC .60 .18
❑ 94 Alex Cora .50 .15
❑ 95 Luis Montanez RC .60 .18
❑ 96 Dmitri Young .60 .18
❑ 97 J.T. Snow .60 .18
❑ 98 Damion Easley .50 .15
❑ 99 Greg Norton .50 .15
❑ 100 Matt Wheatland .50 .15
❑ 101 Chin-Feng Chen .60 .18
❑ 102 Tony Womack .50 .15
❑ 103 Adam Kennedy Black .50 .15
❑ 104 J.D. Drew .60 .18
❑ 105 Carlos Febles .50 .15
❑ 106 Jim Thome 1.00 .30
❑ 107 Danny Graves .50 .15
❑ 108 Dave Mlicki .50 .15
❑ 109 Ron Coomer .50 .15
❑ 110 James Baldwin .50 .15
❑ 111 Shaun Boyd RC .60 .18
❑ 112 Brian Bohanon .50 .15
❑ 113 Jacque Jones .60 .18
❑ 114 Alfonso Soriano 1.00 .30
❑ 115 Tony Clark .50 .15
❑ 116 Terrence Long .50 .15
❑ 117 Todd Hundley .50 .15
❑ 118 Kazuhiro Sasaki .60 .18
❑ 119 Brian Sellier RC .60 .18
❑ 120 John Olerud .60 .18
❑ 121 Javier Vazquez .60 .18
❑ 122 Sean Burnett .50 .15
❑ 123 Matt LeCroy .50 .15
❑ 124 Erubiel Durazo .50 .15
❑ 125 Juan Encarnacion .50 .15
❑ 126 Pablo Ozuna .50 .15
❑ 127 Russ Ortiz .60 .18
❑ 128 David Segui .50 .15
❑ 129 Mark McGwire 4.00 1.20
❑ 130 Mark Grace 1.00 .30
❑ 131 Fred McGriff 1.00 .30
❑ 132 Carl Pavano .60 .18
❑ 133 Derek Thompson .50 .15
❑ 134 Shawn Green .60 .18
❑ 135 B.J. Surhoff .60 .18
❑ 136 Michael Tucker .50 .15
❑ 137 Jason Isringhausen .60 .18
❑ 138 Eric Milton .50 .15
❑ 139 Mike Stodolka .50 .15
❑ 140 Milton Bradley .60 .18
❑ 141 Curt Schilling .60 .18
❑ 142 Sandy Alomar Jr. .50 .15
❑ 143 Brent Mayne .50 .15
❑ 144 Todd Jones .50 .15
❑ 145 Charles Johnson .60 .18
❑ 146 Dean Palmer .60 .18
❑ 147 Masato Yoshii .50 .15
❑ 148 Edgar Renteria .60 .18
❑ 149 Joe Randa .50 .15
❑ 150 Adam Johnson .50 .15
❑ 151 Greg Vaughn .50 .15
❑ 152 Adrian Beltre .60 .18
❑ 153 Glenallen Hill .50 .15
❑ 154 David Parrish RC .60 .18
❑ 155 Neifi Perez .50 .15
❑ 156 Pete Harnisch .50 .15
❑ 157 Paul Konerko .60 .18
❑ 158 Dennys Reyes .50 .15
❑ 159 Jose Lima Black .50 .15
❑ 160 Eddie Taubensee .50 .15
❑ 161 Miguel Cairo .50 .15
❑ 162 Jeff Kent .60 .18
❑ 163 Dustin Hermanson .50 .15
❑ 164 Alex Gonzalez .50 .15
❑ 165 Hideo Nomo 1.50 .45
❑ 166 Sammy Sosa 1.50 .45
❑ 167 C.J. Nitkowski .50 .15
❑ 168 Cal Eldred .50 .15
❑ 169 Jeff Abbott .50 .15
❑ 170 Jim Edmonds 1.00 .30
❑ 171 Mark Mulder Black .60 .18
❑ 172 Dominic Rich RC .60 .18
❑ 173 Ray Lankford .60 .18
❑ 174 Danny Borrell RC .60 .18
❑ 175 Rick Aguilera .50 .15
❑ 176 S.Stewart Black .60 .18
❑ 177 Steve Finley .60 .18
❑ 178 Jim Parque .50 .15
❑ 179 Kevin Appier Black .60 .18
❑ 180 Adrian Gonzalez .50 .15
❑ 181 Tom Goodwin .50 .15
❑ 182 Kevin Tapani .50 .15
❑ 183 Fernando Tatis .50 .15
❑ 184 Mark Grudzielanek .50 .15
❑ 185 Ryan Anderson .50 .15
❑ 186 Jeffrey Hammonds .50 .15
❑ 187 Corey Koskie .50 .15
❑ 188 Brad Fullmer Black .50 .15
❑ 189 Rey Sanchez .50 .15
❑ 190 Michael Barrett .50 .15
❑ 191 Rickey Henderson 1.50 .45
❑ 192 Jermaine Dye .60 .18
❑ 193 Scott Brosius .60 .18
❑ 194 Matt Anderson .50 .15
❑ 195 Brian Buchanan .50 .15
❑ 196 Derrek Lee 1.00 .30
❑ 197 Larry Walker .60 .18
❑ 198 Dan Moylan RC .60 .18
❑ 199 Vinny Castilla .60 .18
❑ 200 Ken Griffey Jr. 2.50 .75
❑ 201 Matt Stairs Black .50 .15
❑ 202 Ty Howington .50 .15
❑ 203 Andy Benes .50 .15
❑ 204 Luis Gonzalez .60 .18
❑ 205 Brian Moehler .50 .15
❑ 206 Harold Baines .60 .18
❑ 207 Pedro Astacio .50 .15
❑ 208 Cristian Guzman .50 .15
❑ 209 Kip Wells .50 .15
❑ 210 Frank Thomas 1.50 .45
❑ 211 Jose Rosado .50 .15
❑ 212 Vernon Wells Black .60 .18
❑ 213 Bobby Higginson .60 .18
❑ 214 Juan Gonzalez .60 .18
❑ 215 Omar Vizquel 1.00 .30
❑ 216 Bernie Williams 1.00 .30
❑ 217 Aaron Sele .50 .15
❑ 218 Shawn Estes .50 .15
❑ 219 Roberto Alomar 1.00 .30
❑ 220 Rick Ankiel .50 .15
❑ 221 Josh Kalinowski .50 .15
❑ 222 David Bell .50 .15
❑ 223 Keith Foulke .60 .18
❑ 224 Craig Biggio Black 1.00 .30
❑ 225 Josh Axelson RC .60 .18
❑ 226 Scott Williamson .50 .15
❑ 227 Ron Belliard .50 .15
❑ 228 Chris Singleton .50 .15
❑ 229 Alex Serrano RC .60 .18
❑ 230 Deivi Cruz .50 .15
❑ 231 Eric Munson .50 .15
❑ 232 Luis Castillo .50 .15
❑ 233 Edgar Martinez 1.00 .30
❑ 234 Jeff Shaw .50 .15
❑ 235 Jeromy Burnitz .60 .18
❑ 236 Richie Sexson .60 .18
❑ 237 Will Clark 1.00 .30
❑ 238 Ron Villone .50 .15
❑ 239 Kerry Wood .60 .18
❑ 240 Rich Aurilia .50 .15
❑ 241 Mo Vaughn Black .60 .18
❑ 242 Travis Fryman .60 .18
❑ 243 M. Ramirez Sox 1.00 .30
❑ 244 Chris Stynes .50 .15
❑ 245 Ray Durham .60 .18
❑ 246 Juan Uribe RC 1.00 .30
❑ 247 Juan Guzman .50 .15
❑ 248 Lee Stevens .50 .15
❑ 249 Devon White .60 .18
❑ 250 Kyle Lohse RC 1.00 .30
❑ 251 Bryan Wolff .50 .15
❑ 252 Matt Galante RC .60 .18
❑ 253 Eric Young .50 .15
❑ 254 Freddy Garcia .60 .18
❑ 255 Jay Bell .60 .18
❑ 256 Steve Cox .50 .15
❑ 257 Torii Hunter .60 .18
❑ 258 Jose Canseco 1.00 .30
❑ 259 Brad Ausmus .60 .18
❑ 260 Jeff Cirillo .50 .15
❑ 261 Brad Penny .50 .15
❑ 262 Antonio Alfonseca .50 .15
❑ 263 Russ Branyan .50 .15
❑ 264 Chris Morris RC .60 .18
❑ 265 John Lackey .50 .15
❑ 266 Justin Wayne RC .60 .18
❑ 267 Brad Radke .60 .18
❑ 268 Todd Stottlemyre .50 .15
❑ 269 Mark Loretta .60 .18
❑ 270 Matt Williams .60 .18
❑ 271 Kenny Lofton .60 .18
❑ 272 Jeff D'Amico .50 .15
❑ 273 Jamie Moyer .60 .18
❑ 274 Darren Dreifort .50 .15
❑ 275 Denny Neagle .50 .15
❑ 276 Orlando Cabrera .60 .18
❑ 277 Chuck Finley .60 .18
❑ 278 Miguel Batista .60 .18
❑ 279 Carlos Beltran .60 .18
❑ 280 Eric Karros .60 .18
❑ 281 Mark Kotsay .60 .18
❑ 282 Ryan Dempster .50 .15
❑ 283 Barry Larkin 1.00 .30
❑ 284 Jeff Suppan .50 .15
❑ 285 Gary Sheffield .60 .18
❑ 286 Jose Valentin .50 .15
❑ 287 Robb Nen .60 .18
❑ 288 Chan Ho Park .60 .18
❑ 289 John Halama .50 .15
❑ 290 Steve Smyth RC .60 .18
❑ 291 Gerald Williams .50 .15
❑ 292 Preston Wilson .60 .18
❑ 293 Victor Hall RC .60 .18
❑ 294 Ben Sheets 1.00 .30
❑ 295 Eric Davis .60 .18
❑ 296 Kirk Rueter .50 .15
❑ 297 Chad Petty RC .60 .18
❑ 298 Kevin Millar .60 .18
❑ 299 Marvin Benard .50 .15
❑ 300 Vladimir Guerrero 1.50 .45
❑ 301 Livan Hernandez .60 .18
❑ 302 Travis Baptist RC .50 .15
❑ 303 Bill Mueller .60 .18
❑ 304 Mike Cameron .50 .15
❑ 305 Randy Johnson 1.50 .45
❑ 306 Alan Mahaffey RC .50 .15
❑ 307 Timo Perez UER .50 .15
No facsimile autograph on card
❑ 308 Pokey Reese .50 .15
❑ 309 Ryan Rupe .50 .15
❑ 310 Carlos Lee .60 .18
❑ 311 Doug Glanville SP 5.00 1.50
❑ 312 Jay Payton SP 5.00 1.50
❑ 313 Troy O'Leary SP 5.00 1.50
❑ 314 Francisco Cordero SP 5.00 1.50
❑ 315 Rusty Greer SP 5.00 1.50
❑ 316 Cal Ripken SP 25.00 7.50
❑ 317 Ricky Ledee SP 5.00 1.50
❑ 318 Brian Daubach SP 5.00 1.50
❑ 319 Robin Ventura SP 5.00 1.50
❑ 320 Todd Zeile SP 5.00 1.50
❑ 321 Francisco Cordova SP 5.00 1.50
❑ 322 Henry Rodriguez SP 5.00 1.50
❑ 323 Pat Meares SP 5.00 1.50
❑ 324 Glendon Rusch SP 5.00 1.50
❑ 325 Keith Osik SP 5.00 1.50
❑ 326 Robert Keppel SP RC 5.00 1.50
❑ 327 Bobby Jones SP 5.00 1.50

❑ 328 Alex Ramirez SP	5.00	1.50
❑ 329 Robert Person SP	5.00	1.50
❑ 330 Ruben Mateo SP	5.00	1.50
❑ 331 Rob Bell SP	5.00	1.50
❑ 332 Carl Everett SP	5.00	1.50
❑ 333 Jason Schmidt SP	5.00	1.50
❑ 334 Scott Rolen SP	8.00	2.40
❑ 335 Jimmy Anderson SP	5.00	1.50
❑ 336 Bret Boone SP	5.00	1.50
❑ 337 Delino DeShields SP	5.00	1.50
❑ 338 Trevor Hoffman SP	5.00	1.50
❑ 339 Bob Abreu SP	5.00	1.50
❑ 340 Mike Williams SP	5.00	1.50
❑ 341 Mike Hampton SP	5.00	1.50
❑ 342 John Wetteland SP	5.00	1.50
❑ 343 Scott Erickson SP	5.00	1.50
❑ 344 Enrique Wilson SP	5.00	1.50
❑ 345 Tim Wakefield SP	5.00	1.50
❑ 346 Mike Lowell SP	5.00	1.50
❑ 347 Todd Pratt SP	5.00	1.50
❑ 348 Brook Fordyce SP	5.00	1.50
❑ 349 Benny Agbayani SP	5.00	1.50
❑ 350 Gabe Kapler SP	5.00	1.50
❑ 351 Sean Casey SP	8.00	2.40
❑ 352 Darren Oliver SP	5.00	1.50
❑ 353 Todd Ritchie SP	5.00	1.50
❑ 354 Kenny Rogers SP	5.00	1.50
❑ 355 Jason Kendall SP	5.00	1.50
❑ 356 John Vander Wal SP	5.00	1.50
❑ 357 Ramon Martinez SP	5.00	1.50
❑ 358 Edgardo Alfonzo SP	5.00	1.50
❑ 359 Phil Nevin SP	5.00	1.50
❑ 360 Albert Belle SP	5.00	1.50
❑ 361 Ruben Rivera SP	5.00	1.50
❑ 362 Pedro Martinez SP	8.00	2.40
❑ 363 Derek Lowe SP	5.00	1.50
❑ 364 Pat Burrell SP	5.00	1.50
❑ 365 Mike Mussina SP	8.00	2.40
❑ 366 Brady Anderson SP	5.00	1.50
❑ 367 Darren Lewis SP	5.00	1.50
❑ 368 Sidney Ponson SP	5.00	1.50
❑ 369 Adam Eaton SP	5.00	1.50
❑ 370 Eric Owens SP	5.00	1.50
❑ 371 Aaron Boone SP	5.00	1.50
❑ 372 Matt Clement SP	5.00	1.50
❑ 373 Derek Bell SP	5.00	1.50
❑ 374 Trot Nixon SP	5.00	1.50
❑ 375 Travis Lee SP	5.00	1.50
❑ 376 Mike Benjamin SP	5.00	1.50
❑ 377 Jeff Zimmerman SP	5.00	1.50
❑ 378 Mike Lieberthal SP	5.00	1.50
❑ 379 Rick Reed SP	5.00	1.50
❑ 380 N.Garciaparra SP	12.00	3.60
❑ 381 Omar Daal SP	5.00	1.50
❑ 382 Ryan Klesko SP	5.00	1.50
❑ 383 Rey Ordonez SP	5.00	1.50
❑ 384 Kevin Young SP	5.00	1.50
❑ 385 Rick Helling SP	5.00	1.50
❑ 386 Brian Giles SP	5.00	1.50
❑ 387 Tony Gwynn SP	10.00	3.00
❑ 388 Ed Sprague SP	5.00	1.50
❑ 389 J.R. House SP	5.00	1.50
❑ 390 Scott Hatteberg SP	5.00	1.50
❑ 391 John Valentin SP	5.00	1.50
❑ 392 Melvin Mora SP	5.00	1.50
❑ 393 Royce Clayton SP	5.00	1.50
❑ 394 Jeff Fassero SP	5.00	1.50
❑ 395 Manny Alexander SP	5.00	1.50
❑ 396 John Franco SP	5.00	1.50
❑ 397 Luis Alicea SP	5.00	1.50
❑ 398 Ivan Rodriguez SP	8.00	2.40
❑ 399 Kevin Jordan SP	5.00	1.50
❑ 400 Jose Offerman SP	5.00	1.50
❑ 401 Jeff Conine SP	5.00	1.50
❑ 402 Seth Etherton SP	5.00	1.50
❑ 403 Mike Bordick SP	5.00	1.50
❑ 404 Al Leiter SP	5.00	1.50
❑ 405 Mike Piazza SP	12.00	3.60
❑ 406 Armando Benitez SP	5.00	1.50
❑ 407 Warren Morris SP	5.00	1.50
❑ NNO 1952 Card Redemption EXCH		
❑ NNO Replica Hat-Jsy EXCH		

2002 Topps Heritage

	Nm-Mt	Ex-Mt
COMPLETE SET (440)	300.00	90.00
COMP.SET w/o SP's (350)	80.00	24.00
COMMON CARD (1-363)	.50	.15
COMMON SP (364-446)	5.00	1.50
❑ 1 Ichiro Suzuki SP	15.00	4.50
❑ 2 Darin Erstad	.60	.18
❑ 3 Rod Beck	.60	.18
❑ 4 Doug Mientkiewicz	.60	.18
❑ 5 Mike Sweeney	.60	.18
❑ 6 Roger Clemens	3.00	.90
❑ 7 Jason Tyner	.50	.15
❑ 8 Alex Gonzalez	.50	.15
❑ 9 Eric Young	.50	.15
❑ 10 Randy Johnson	1.50	.45
❑ 10N Randy Johnson Night SP	8.00	2.40
❑ 11 Aaron Sele	.50	.15
❑ 12 Tony Clark	.50	.15
❑ 13 C.C. Sabathia	.60	.18
❑ 14 Melvin Mora	.60	.18
❑ 15 Tim Hudson	.60	.18
❑ 16 Ben Petrick	.50	.15
❑ 17 Tom Glavine	1.00	.30
❑ 18 Jason Lane	.60	.18
❑ 19 Larry Walker	.60	.18
❑ 20 Mark Mulder	.60	.18
❑ 21 Steve Finley	.60	.18
❑ 22 Bengie Molina	.50	.15
❑ 23 Rob Bell	.50	.15
❑ 24 Nathan Haynes	.50	.15
❑ 25 Rafael Furcal	.60	.18
❑ 25N Rafael Furcal Night SP	5.00	1.50
❑ 26 Mike Mussina	1.00	.30
❑ 27 Paul LoDuca	.60	.18
❑ 28 Torii Hunter	.60	.18
❑ 29 Carlos Lee	.60	.18
❑ 30 Jimmy Rollins	.60	.18
❑ 31 Arthur Rhodes	.50	.15
❑ 32 Ivan Rodriguez	1.00	.30
❑ 33 Wes Helms	.50	.15
❑ 34 Cliff Floyd	.60	.18
❑ 35 Julian Tavarez	.50	.15
❑ 36 Mark McGwire	4.00	1.20
❑ 37 Chipper Jones SP	8.00	2.40
❑ 38 Denny Neagle	.50	.15
❑ 39 Odalis Perez	.50	.15
❑ 40 Antonio Alfonseca	.50	.15
❑ 41 Edgar Renteria	.60	.18
❑ 42 Troy Glaus	.60	.18
❑ 43 Scott Brosius	.60	.18
❑ 44 Abraham Nunez	.50	.15
❑ 45 Jamey Wright	.50	.15
❑ 46 Bobby Bonilla	.60	.18
❑ 47 Ismael Valdes	.50	.15
❑ 48 Chris Reitsma	.50	.15
❑ 49 Neifi Perez	.50	.15
❑ 50 Juan Cruz	.50	.15
❑ 51 Kevin Brown	.60	.18
❑ 52 Ben Grieve	.50	.15
❑ 53 Alex Rodriguez SP	12.00	3.60
❑ 54 Charles Nagy	.50	.15
❑ 55 Reggie Sanders	.60	.18
❑ 56 Nelson Figueroa	.50	.15
❑ 57 Felipe Lopez	.50	.15
❑ 58 Bill Ortega	.50	.15
❑ 59 Jeffrey Hammonds	.60	.18
❑ 60 Johnny Estrada	.50	.15
❑ 61 Bob Wickman	.50	.15
❑ 62 Doug Glanville	.50	.15
❑ 63 Jeff Cirillo	.50	.15
❑ 63N Jeff Cirillo Night SP	5.00	1.50
❑ 64 Corey Patterson	.50	.15
❑ 65 Aaron Myette	.50	.15
❑ 66 Magglio Ordonez	.60	.18
❑ 67 Ellis Burks	.60	.18
❑ 68 Miguel Tejada	.60	.18
❑ 69 John Olerud	.60	.18
❑ 69N John Olerud Night SP	5.00	1.50
❑ 70 Greg Vaughn	.50	.15
❑ 71 Andy Pettitte	1.00	.30
❑ 72 Mike Matheny	.50	.15
❑ 73 Brandon Duckworth	.50	.15
❑ 74 Scott Schoeneweis	.50	.15
❑ 75 Mike Lowell	.60	.18
❑ 76 Einar Diaz	.50	.15
❑ 77 Tino Martinez	1.00	.30
❑ 78 Matt Williams	.60	.18
❑ 79 Jason Young RC	1.00	.30
❑ 80 Nate Cornejo	.50	.15
❑ 81 Andres Galarraga	.60	.18
❑ 82 Bernie Williams SP	8.00	2.40
❑ 83 Ryan Klesko	.60	.18
❑ 84 Dan Wilson	.50	.15
❑ 85 Henry Pichardo RC	1.00	.30
❑ 86 Ray Durham	.60	.18
❑ 87 Omar Daal	.50	.15
❑ 88 Derrek Lee	1.00	.30
❑ 89 Al Leiter	.60	.18
❑ 90 Darrin Fletcher	.50	.15
❑ 91 Josh Beckett	.60	.18
❑ 92 Johnny Damon	1.00	.30
❑ 92N Johnny Damon Night SP	8.00	2.40
❑ 93 Abraham Nunez	.50	.15
❑ 94 Ricky Ledee	.50	.15
❑ 95 Richie Sexson	.60	.18
❑ 96 Adam Kennedy	.50	.15
❑ 97 Raul Mondesi	.60	.18
❑ 98 John Burkett	.60	.18
❑ 99 Ben Sheets	.60	.18
❑ 99N Ben Sheets Night SP	5.00	1.50
❑ 100 Preston Wilson	.60	.18
❑ 100N Pr. Wilson Night SP	5.00	1.50
❑ 101 Boof Bonser	.50	.15
❑ 102 Shigetoshi Hasegawa	.60	.18
❑ 103 Carlos Febles	.50	.15
❑ 104 Jorge Posada SP	8.00	2.40
❑ 105 Michael Tucker	.50	.15
❑ 106 Roberto Hernandez	.60	.18
❑ 107 John Rodriguez RC	1.00	.30
❑ 108 Danny Graves	.50	.15
❑ 109 Rich Aurilia	.50	.15
❑ 110 Jon Lieber	.50	.15
❑ 111 Tim Hummel RC	1.00	.30
❑ 112 J.T. Snow	.60	.18
❑ 113 Kris Benson	.50	.15
❑ 114 Derek Jeter	4.00	1.20
❑ 115 John Franco	.60	.18
❑ 116 Matt Stairs	.50	.15
❑ 117 Ben Davis	.50	.15
❑ 118 Darryl Kile	.60	.18
❑ 119 Mike Peeples RC	1.00	.30
❑ 120 Kevin Tapani	.50	.15
❑ 121 Armando Benitez	.60	.18
❑ 122 Damian Miller	.50	.15
❑ 123 Jose Jimenez	.50	.15
❑ 124 Pedro Astacio	.50	.15
❑ 125 Marlyn Tisdale RC	1.00	.30
❑ 126 Deivi Cruz	.50	.15
❑ 127 Paul O'Neill	1.00	.30
❑ 128 Jermaine Dye	.60	.18
❑ 129 Marcus Giles	.60	.18
❑ 130 Mark Loretta	.60	.18
❑ 131 Garret Anderson	.60	.18
❑ 132 Todd Ritchie	.50	.15
❑ 133 Joe Crede	.60	.18
❑ 134 Kevin Millwood	.50	.15
❑ 135 Shane Reynolds	.50	.15
❑ 136 Mark Grace	1.00	.30
❑ 137 Shannon Stewart	.60	.18
❑ 138 Nick Neugebauer	.50	.15
❑ 139 Nic Jackson RC	1.00	.30
❑ 140 Robb Nen UER	.60	.18

Name spelled Rob on front

❑ 141 Dmitri Young .60 .18
❑ 142 Kevin Appier .60 .18
❑ 143 Jack Cust .50 .15
❑ 144 Andres Torres .50 .15
❑ 145 Frank Thomas 1.50 .45
❑ 146 Jason Kendall .60 .18
❑ 147 Greg Maddux 2.50 .75
❑ 148 David Justice .60 .18
❑ 149 Hideo Nomo 1.50 .45
❑ 150 Bret Boone .60 .18
❑ 151 Wade Miller .50 .15
❑ 152 Jeff Kent .60 .18
❑ 153 Scott Williamson .50 .15
❑ 154 Julio Lugo .50 .15
❑ 155 Bobby Higginson .60 .18
❑ 156 Geoff Jenkins .50 .15
❑ 157 Darren Dreifort .50 .15
❑ 158 Freddy Sanchez RC 1.00 .30
❑ 159 Bud Smith .50 .15
❑ 160 Phil Nevin .60 .18
❑ 161 Cesar Izturis .50 .15
❑ 162 Sean Casey 1.00 .30
❑ 163 Jose Ortiz .50 .15
❑ 164 Brent Abernathy .50 .15
❑ 165 Kevin Young .50 .15
❑ 166 Daryle Ward .50 .15
❑ 167 Trevor Hoffman .60 .18
❑ 168 Rondell White .60 .18
❑ 169 Kip Wells .50 .15
❑ 170 John Vander Wal .50 .15
❑ 171 Jose Lima .50 .15
❑ 172 Wilton Guerrero .50 .15
❑ 173 Aaron Dean RC 1.00 .30
❑ 174 Rick Helling .50 .15
❑ 175 Juan Pierre .60 .18
❑ 176 Jay Bell .60 .18
❑ 177 Craig House .50 .15
❑ 178 David Bell .50 .15
❑ 179 Pat Burrell .60 .18
❑ 180 Eric Gagne .60 .18
❑ 181 Adam Pettyjohn .50 .15
❑ 182 Ugueth Urbina .50 .15
❑ 183 Peter Bergeron .50 .15
❑ 184 Adrian Gonzalez UER .50 .15
Birthdate is wrong
❑ 184N Adrian Gonzalez 5.00 1.50
Night SP UER
Birthdate is wrong
❑ 185 Damion Easley .50 .15
❑ 186 Gookie Dawkins .50 .15
❑ 187 Matt Lawton .50 .15
❑ 188 Frank Catalanotto .50 .15
❑ 189 David Wells .60 .18
❑ 190 Roger Cedeno .50 .15
❑ 191 Brian Giles .60 .18
❑ 192 Julio Zuleta .50 .15
❑ 193 Timo Perez .50 .15
❑ 194 Billy Wagner .60 .18
❑ 195 Craig Counsell .50 .15
❑ 196 Bart Miadich .50 .15
❑ 197 Gary Sheffield .60 .18
❑ 198 Richard Hidalgo .50 .15
❑ 199 Juan Uribe .50 .15
❑ 200 Curt Schilling .60 .18
❑ 201 Javy Lopez .60 .18
❑ 202 Jimmy Haynes .50 .15
❑ 203 Jim Edmonds 1.00 .30
❑ 204 Pokey Reese .50 .15
❑ 204N Pokey Reese Night SP 5.00 1.50
❑ 205 Matt Clement .60 .18
❑ 206 Dean Palmer .60 .18
❑ 207 Nick Johnson .60 .18
❑ 208 Nate Espy RC 1.00 .30
❑ 209 Pedro Feliz .50 .15
❑ 210 Aaron Rowand .60 .18
❑ 211 Masato Yoshii .50 .15
❑ 212 Jose Cruz Jr. .50 .15
❑ 213 Paul Byrd .50 .15
❑ 214 Mark Phillips RC 1.00 .30
❑ 215 Benny Agbayani .50 .15
❑ 216 Frank Menechino .50 .15
❑ 217 John Flaherty .50 .15
❑ 218 Brian Boehringer .50 .15
❑ 219 Todd Hollandsworth .50 .15
❑ 220 Sammy Sosa SP 8.00 2.40
❑ 221 Steve Sparks .50 .15
❑ 222 Homer Bush .50 .15
❑ 223 Mike Hampton .60 .18
❑ 224 Bobby Abreu .60 .18
❑ 225 Barry Larkin 1.00 .30
❑ 226 Ryan Rupe .50 .15
❑ 227 Bubba Trammell .50 .15
❑ 228 Todd Zeile .60 .18
❑ 229 Jeff Shaw .50 .15
❑ 230 Alex Ochoa .50 .15
❑ 231 Orlando Cabrera .60 .18
❑ 232 Jeremy Giambi .50 .15
❑ 233 Tomo Ohka .50 .15
❑ 234 Luis Castillo .50 .15
❑ 235 Chris Holt .50 .15
❑ 236 Shawn Green .60 .18
❑ 237 Sidney Ponson .50 .15
❑ 238 Lee Stevens .50 .15
❑ 239 Hank Blalock 1.00 .30
❑ 240 Randy Winn .50 .15
❑ 241 Pedro Martinez 1.00 .30
❑ 242 Vinny Castilla .60 .18
❑ 243 Steve Karsay .50 .15
❑ 244 Barry Bonds SP 20.00 6.00
❑ 245 Jason Bere .50 .15
❑ 246 Scott Rolen 1.00 .30
❑ 246N Scott Rolen Night SP 8.00 2.40
❑ 247 Ryan Kohlmeier .50 .15
❑ 248 Kerry Wood .60 .18
❑ 249 Aramis Ramirez .60 .18
❑ 250 Lance Berkman .60 .18
❑ 251 Omar Vizquel 1.00 .30
❑ 252 Juan Encarnacion .50 .15
❑ 253 Does Not Exist .00
❑ 254 David Segui .50 .15
❑ 255 Brian Anderson .50 .15
❑ 256 Jay Payton .50 .15
❑ 257 Mark Grudzielanek .50 .15
❑ 258 Jimmy Anderson .50 .15
❑ 259 Eric Valent .50 .15
❑ 260 Chad Durbin .50 .15
❑ 261 Does Not Exist .00
❑ 262 Alex Gonzalez .50 .15
❑ 263 Scott Dunn .50 .15
❑ 264 Scott Elarton .50 .15
❑ 265 Tom Gordon .50 .15
❑ 266 Moises Alou .60 .18
❑ 267 Does Not Exist .00
❑ 268 Does Not Exist .00
❑ 269 Mark Buehrle .60 .18
❑ 270 Jerry Hairston .50 .15
❑ 271 Does Not Exist .00
❑ 272 Luke Prokopec .50 .15
❑ 273 Graeme Lloyd .50 .15
❑ 274 Bret Prinz .50 .15
❑ 275 Does Not Exist .00
❑ 276 Chris Carpenter .60 .18
❑ 277 Ryan Minor .50 .15
❑ 278 Jeff D'Amico .50 .15
❑ 279 Raul Ibanez .50 .15
❑ 280 Joe Mays .50 .15
❑ 281 Livan Hernandez .60 .18
❑ 282 Robin Ventura .60 .18
❑ 283 Gabe Kapler .60 .18
❑ 284 Tony Batista .50 .15
❑ 285 Ramon Hernandez .50 .15
❑ 286 Craig Paquette .50 .15
❑ 287 Mark Kotsay .60 .18
❑ 288 Mike Lieberthal .50 .15
❑ 289 Joe Borchard .50 .15
❑ 290 Cristian Guzman .50 .15
❑ 291 Craig Biggio 1.00 .30
❑ 292 Joaquin Benoit .50 .15
❑ 293 Ken Caminiti .60 .18
❑ 294 Sean Burroughs .50 .15
❑ 295 Eric Karros .60 .18
❑ 296 Eric Chavez .60 .18
❑ 297 LaTroy Hawkins .50 .15
❑ 298 Alfonso Soriano .60 .18
❑ 299 John Smoltz 1.00 .30
❑ 300 Adam Dunn .60 .18
❑ 301 Ryan Dempster .50 .15
❑ 302 Travis Hafner .60 .18
❑ 303 Russell Branyan .50 .15
❑ 304 Dustin Hermanson .50 .15
❑ 305 Jim Thome 1.00 .30
❑ 306 Carlos Beltran .60 .18
❑ 307 Jason Botts RC 1.00 .30
❑ 308 David Cone .60 .18
❑ 309 Ivanon Coffie .50 .15
❑ 310 Brian Jordan .60 .18
❑ 311 Todd Walker .50 .15
❑ 312 Jeromy Burnitz .60 .18
❑ 313 Tony Armas Jr. .50 .15
❑ 314 Jeff Conine .60 .18
❑ 315 Todd Jones .50 .15
❑ 316 Roy Oswalt .60 .18
❑ 317 Aubrey Huff .60 .18
❑ 318 Josh Fogg .50 .15
❑ 319 Jose Vidro .50 .15
❑ 320 Jace Brewer .50 .15
❑ 321 Mike Redmond .50 .15
❑ 322 Noochie Varner RC 1.00 .30
❑ 323 Russ Ortiz .60 .18
❑ 324 Edgardo Alfonzo .50 .15
❑ 325 Ruben Sierra .50 .15
❑ 326 Calvin Murray .50 .15
❑ 327 Marlon Anderson .50 .15
❑ 328 Albie Lopez .50 .15
❑ 329 Chris Gomez .50 .15
❑ 330 Fernando Tatis .50 .15
❑ 331 Stubby Clapp .50 .15
❑ 332 Rickey Henderson 1.50 .45
❑ 333 Brad Radke .60 .18
❑ 334 Brent Mayne .50 .15
❑ 335 Cory Lidle .50 .15
❑ 336 Edgar Martinez 1.00 .30
❑ 337 Aaron Boone .60 .18
❑ 338 Jay Witasick .50 .15
❑ 339 Benito Santiago .60 .18
❑ 340 Jose Mercedes .50 .15
❑ 341 Fernando Vina .50 .15
❑ 342 A.J. Pierzynski .60 .18
❑ 343 Jeff Bagwell 1.00 .30
❑ 344 Brian Bohanon .50 .15
❑ 345 Adrian Beltre .60 .18
❑ 346 Troy Percival .60 .18
❑ 347 Napoleon Calzado RC 1.00 .30
❑ 348 Ruben Rivera .50 .15
❑ 349 Rafael Soriano .50 .15
❑ 350 Damian Jackson .50 .15
❑ 351 Joe Randa .50 .15
❑ 352 Chan Ho Park .60 .18
❑ 353 Dante Bichette .60 .18
❑ 354 Bartolo Colon .60 .18
❑ 355 Jason Bay RC 5.00 1.50
❑ 356 Shea Hillenbrand .60 .18
❑ 357 Matt Morris .60 .18
❑ 358 Brad Penny .50 .15
❑ 359 Mark Quinn .50 .15
❑ 360 Marquis Grissom .60 .18
❑ 361 Henry Blanco .50 .15
❑ 362 Billy Koch .50 .15
❑ 363 Mike Cameron .50 .15
❑ 364 Albert Pujols SP 15.00 4.50
❑ 365 Paul Konerko SP 5.00 1.50
❑ 366 Eric Milton SP 5.00 1.50
❑ 367 Nick Bierbrodt SP 5.00 1.50
❑ 368 Rafael Palmeiro SP 8.00 2.40
❑ 369 Jorge Padilla SP RC 5.00 1.50
❑ 370 Jason Giambi 5.00 1.50
Yankees SP
Stats on back are Jeremy Giambi's
❑ 371 Mike Piazza SP 12.00 3.60
❑ 372 Alex Cora SP 5.00 1.50
❑ 373 Todd Helton SP 8.00 2.40
❑ 374 Juan Gonzalez SP 5.00 1.50
❑ 375 Mariano Rivera SP 8.00 2.40
❑ 376 Jason LaRue SP 5.00 1.50
❑ 377 Tony Gwynn SP 10.00 3.00
❑ 378 Wilson Betemit SP 5.00 1.50
❑ 379 J.J. Trujillo SP RC 5.00 1.50
❑ 380 Brad Ausmus SP 5.00 1.50
❑ 381 Chris George SP 5.00 1.50
❑ 382 Jose Canseco SP 8.00 2.40
❑ 383 Ramon Ortiz SP 5.00 1.50
❑ 384 John Rocker SP 5.00 1.50
❑ 385 Rey Ordonez SP 5.00 1.50
❑ 386 Ken Griffey Jr. SP 12.00 3.60
❑ 387 Juan Pena SP 5.00 1.50
❑ 388 Michael Barrett SP 5.00 1.50
❑ 389 J.D. Drew SP 5.00 1.50

Card	Nm-Mt	Ex-Mt
❑ 390 Corey Koskie SP	5.00	1.50
❑ 391 Vernon Wells SP	5.00	1.50
❑ 392 Juan Tolentino SP RC	5.00	1.50
❑ 393 Luis Gonzalez SP	5.00	1.50
❑ 394 Terrence Long SP	5.00	1.50
❑ 395 Travis Lee SP	5.00	1.50
❑ 396 Earl Snyder SP RC	5.00	1.50
❑ 397 Nomar Garciaparra SP	12.00	3.60
❑ 398 Jason Schmidt SP	5.00	1.50
❑ 399 David Espinosa SP	5.00	1.50
❑ 400 Steve Green SP	5.00	1.50
❑ 401 Jack Wilson SP	5.00	1.50
❑ 402 Chris Tritle SP RC	5.00	1.50
❑ 403 Angel Berroa SP	5.00	1.50
❑ 404 Josh Towers SP	5.00	1.50
❑ 405 Andruw Jones SP	8.00	2.40
❑ 406 Brent Butler SP	5.00	1.50
❑ 407 Craig Kuzmic SP	5.00	1.50
❑ 408 Derek Bell SP	5.00	1.50
❑ 409 Eric Glaser SP RC	5.00	1.50
❑ 410 Joel Pineiro SP	5.00	1.50
❑ 411 Alexis Gomez SP	5.00	1.50
❑ 412 Mike Rivera SP	5.00	1.50
❑ 413 Shawn Estes SP	5.00	1.50
❑ 414 Milton Bradley SP	5.00	1.50
❑ 415 Carl Everett SP	5.00	1.50
❑ 416 Kazuhiro Sasaki SP	5.00	1.50
❑ 417 Tony Fontana SP RC	5.00	1.50
❑ 418 Josh Pearce SP	5.00	1.50
❑ 419 Gary Matthews Jr. SP	5.00	1.50
❑ 420 Raymond Cabrera SP RC	5.00	1.50
❑ 421 Joe Kennedy SP	5.00	1.50
❑ 422 Jason Maule SP RC	5.00	1.50
❑ 423 Casey Fossum SP	5.00	1.50
❑ 424 Christian Parker SP	5.00	1.50
❑ 425 Laynce Nix SP RC	15.00	4.50
❑ 426 Byung-Hyun Kim SP	5.00	1.50
❑ 427 Freddy Garcia SP	5.00	1.50
❑ 428 Herbert Perry SP	5.00	1.50
❑ 429 Jason Marquis SP	5.00	1.50
❑ 430 Sandy Alomar Jr. SP	5.00	1.50
❑ 431 Roberto Alomar SP	8.00	2.40
❑ 432 Tsuyoshi Shinjo SP	5.00	1.50
❑ 433 Tim Wakefield SP	5.00	1.50
❑ 434 Robert Fick SP	5.00	1.50
❑ 435 Vladimir Guerrero SP	8.00	2.40
❑ 436 Jose Mesa SP	5.00	1.50
❑ 437 Scott Spiezio SP	5.00	1.50
❑ 438 Jose Hernandez SP	5.00	1.50
❑ 439 Jose Acevedo SP	5.00	1.50
❑ 440 Brian West SP RC	5.00	1.50
❑ 441 Barry Zito SP	5.00	1.50
❑ 442 Luis Maza SP	5.00	1.50
❑ 443 Marlon Byrd SP	5.00	1.50
❑ 444 A.J. Burnett SP	5.00	1.50
❑ 445 Dee Brown SP	5.00	1.50
❑ 446 Carlos Delgado SP	5.00	1.50
❑ NNO 1953 Repurchased EXCH.	.00	

2003 Topps Heritage

	Nm-Mt	Ex-Mt
COMPLETE SET (450)	300.00	90.00
COMP.SET w/o SP's (350)	80.00	24.00
COMMON CARD	.50	.15
COMMON RC	1.00	.30
COMMON SP	5.00	1.50
COMMON SP RC	5.00	1.50

Card	Nm-Mt	Ex-Mt
❑ 1A Alex Rodriguez Red	2.50	.75
❑ 1B Alex Rodriguez Black SP	12.00	3.60
❑ 2 Jose Cruz Jr.	.50	.15
❑ 3 Ichiro Suzuki SP	15.00	4.50
❑ 4 Rich Aurilia	.50	.15
❑ 5 Trevor Hoffman	.60	.18
❑ 6A Brian Giles New Logo	.60	.18
❑ 6B Brian Giles Old Logo SP	5.00	1.50
❑ 7A Albert Pujols Orange	3.00	.90
❑ 7B Albert Pujols Black SP	15.00	4.50
❑ 8 Vicente Padilla	.50	.15
❑ 9 Bobby Crosby	1.00	.30
❑ 10A Derek Jeter New Logo	4.00	1.20
❑ 10B Derek Jeter Old Logo SP	15.00	4.50
❑ 11A Pat Burrell New Logo	.60	.18
❑ 11B Pat Burrell Old Logo SP	5.00	1.50
❑ 12 Armando Benitez	.60	.18
❑ 13 Javier Vazquez	.60	.18
❑ 14 Justin Morneau	.60	.18
❑ 15 Doug Mientkiewicz	.60	.18
❑ 16 Kevin Brown	.60	.18
❑ 17 Alexis Gomez	.50	.15
❑ 18A Lance Berkman Blue	.60	.18
❑ 18B Lance Berkman Black SP	5.00	1.50
❑ 19 Adrian Gonzalez	.50	.15
❑ 20A Todd Helton Green	1.00	.30
❑ 20B Todd Helton Black SP	8.00	2.40
❑ 21 Carlos Pena	.50	.15
❑ 22 Matt Lawton	.50	.15
❑ 23 Elmer Dessens	.50	.15
❑ 24 Hee Seop Choi	.60	.18
❑ 25 Chris Duncan SP RC	5.00	1.50
❑ 26 Ugueth Urbina	.50	.15
❑ 27A Rodrigo Lopez New Logo	.50	.15
❑ 27B Ro. Lopez Old Logo SP	5.00	1.50
❑ 28 Damian Moss	.50	.15
❑ 29 Steve Finley	.60	.18
❑ 30A Sammy Sosa New Logo	1.50	.45
❑ 30B S.Sosa Old Logo SP	8.00	2.40
❑ 31 Kevin Cash	.50	.15
❑ 32 Kenny Rogers	.60	.18
❑ 33 Ben Grieve	.50	.15
❑ 34 Jason Simontacchi	.50	.15
❑ 35 Shin-Soo Choo	.50	.15
❑ 36 Freddy Garcia	.60	.18
❑ 37 Jesse Foppert	.50	.15
❑ 38 Tony LaRussa MG	.60	.18
❑ 39 Mark Kotsay	.60	.18
❑ 40 Barry Zito	.60	.18
❑ 41 Josh Fogg	.50	.15
❑ 42 Marlon Byrd	.50	.15
❑ 43 Marcus Thames	.50	.15
❑ 44 Al Leiter	.60	.18
❑ 45 Michael Barrett	.50	.15
❑ 46 Jake Peavy	.60	.18
❑ 47 Dustan Mohr	.50	.15
❑ 48 Alex Sanchez	.50	.15
❑ 49 Chin-Feng Chen	.60	.18
❑ 50A Kazuhisa Ishii Blue	.60	.18
❑ 50B Kazuhisa Ishii Black SP	5.00	1.50
❑ 51 Carlos Beltran	.60	.18
❑ 52 Franklin Gutierrez RC	1.25	.35
❑ 53 Miguel Cabrera	1.50	.45
❑ 54 Roger Clemens	3.00	.90
❑ 55 Juan Cruz	.50	.15
❑ 56 Jason Young	.50	.15
❑ 57 Alex Herrera	.50	.15
❑ 58 Aaron Boone	.60	.18
❑ 59 Mark Buehrle	.60	.18
❑ 60 Larry Walker	.60	.18
❑ 61 Morgan Ensberg	.60	.18
❑ 62 Barry Larkin	1.00	.30
❑ 63 Joe Borchard	.50	.15
❑ 64 Jason Dubois	.50	.15
❑ 65 Shea Hillenbrand	.60	.18
❑ 66 Jay Gibbons	.50	.15
❑ 67 Vinny Castilla	.60	.18
❑ 68 Jeff Mathis	.50	.15
❑ 69 Curt Schilling	.60	.18
❑ 70 Garret Anderson	.60	.18
❑ 71 Josh Phelps	.50	.15
❑ 72 Chan Ho Park	.60	.18
❑ 73 Edgar Renteria	.60	.18
❑ 74 Kazuhiro Sasaki	.60	.18
❑ 75 Lloyd McClendon MG	.50	.15
❑ 76 Jon Lieber	.50	.15
❑ 77 Rolando Viera	.50	.15
❑ 78 Jeff Conine	.60	.18
❑ 79 Kevin Millwood	.50	.15
❑ 80A Randy Johnson Green	1.50	.45
❑ 80B Randy Johnson Black SP	12.00	3.60
❑ 81 Troy Percival	.60	.18
❑ 82 Cliff Floyd	.60	.18
❑ 83 Tony Graffanino	.50	.15
❑ 84 Austin Kearns	.50	.15
❑ 85 Manuel Ramirez SP RC	8.00	2.40
❑ 86 Jim Tracy MG	.50	.15
❑ 87 Rondell White	.60	.18
❑ 88 Trot Nixon	.60	.18
❑ 89 Carlos Lee	.60	.18
❑ 90 Mike Lowell	.60	.18
❑ 91 Raul Ibanez	.50	.15
❑ 92 Ricardo Rodriguez	.50	.15
❑ 93 Ben Sheets	.60	.18
❑ 94 Jason Perry SP RC	8.00	2.40
❑ 95 Mark Teixeira	1.00	.30
❑ 96 Brad Fullmer	.50	.15
❑ 97 Casey Kotchman	.60	.18
❑ 98 Craig Counsell	.50	.15
❑ 99 Jason Marquis	.50	.15
❑ 100A N.Garciaparra New Logo	2.50	.75
❑ 100B N.Garciaparra Old Logo SP	12.00	3.60
❑ 101 Ed Rogers	.50	.15
❑ 102 Wilson Betemit	.50	.15
❑ 103 Wayne Lydon RC	1.00	.30
❑ 104 Jack Cust	.50	.15
❑ 105 Derrek Lee	1.00	.30
❑ 106 Jim Kavourias	.50	.15
❑ 107 Joe Randa	.50	.15
❑ 108 Taylor Buchholz	.50	.15
❑ 109 Gabe Kapler	.60	.18
❑ 110 Preston Wilson	.60	.18
❑ 111 Craig Biggio	1.00	.30
❑ 112 Paul Lo Duca	.60	.18
❑ 113 Eddie Guardado	.50	.15
❑ 114 Andres Galarraga	1.00	.30
❑ 115 Edgardo Alfonzo	.50	.15
❑ 116 Robin Ventura	.60	.18
❑ 117 Jeremy Giambi	.50	.15
❑ 118 Ray Durham	.60	.18
❑ 119 Mariano Rivera	1.00	.30
❑ 120 Jimmy Rollins	.60	.18
❑ 121 Dennis Tankersley	.50	.15
❑ 122 Jason Schmidt	.60	.18
❑ 123 Bret Boone	.60	.18
❑ 124 Josh Hamilton	.50	.15
❑ 125 Scott Rolen	1.00	.30
❑ 126 Steve Cox	.50	.15
❑ 127 Larry Bowa MG	.60	.18
❑ 128 Adam LaRoche SP	5.00	1.50
❑ 129 Ryan Klesko	.60	.18
❑ 130 Tim Hudson	.60	.18
❑ 131 Brandon Claussen	.50	.15
❑ 132 Craig Brazell SP RC	5.00	1.50
❑ 133 Grady Little MG	.50	.15
❑ 134 Jarrod Washburn	.50	.15
❑ 135 Lyle Overbay	.50	.15
❑ 136 John Burkett	.50	.15
❑ 137 Daryl Clark RC	1.00	.30
❑ 138 Kirk Rueter	.50	.15
❑ 139A Joe Mauer Jake Mauer Green	1.00	.30
❑ 139B Joe Mauer Jake Mauer Black SP	8.00	2.40
❑ 140 Troy Glaus	.60	.18
❑ 141 Trey Hodges SP	5.00	1.50
❑ 142 Dallas McPherson	.60	.18
❑ 143 Art Howe MG	.50	.15
❑ 144 Jesus Cota	.50	.15
❑ 145 J.R. House	.50	.15
❑ 146 Reggie Sanders	.60	.18
❑ 147 Clint Nageotte	.50	.15
❑ 148 Jim Edmonds	1.00	.30
❑ 149 Carl Crawford	.60	.18
❑ 150A Mike Piazza Blue	2.50	.75
❑ 150B Mike Piazza Black SP	12.00	3.60
❑ 151 Seung Song	.50	.15
❑ 152 Roberto Hernandez	.60	.18
❑ 153 Marquis Grissom	.60	.18
❑ 154 Billy Wagner	.60	.18
❑ 155 Josh Beckett	.60	.18
❑ 156A R.Simon New Logo	.50	.15

❑ 156B	R.Simon Old Logo SP	5.00	1.50
❑ 157	Ben Broussard	.50	.15
❑ 158	Russell Branyan	.50	.15
❑ 159	Frank Thomas	1.50	.45
❑ 160	Alex Escobar	.50	.15
❑ 161	Mark Bellhorn	.60	.18
❑ 162	Melvin Mora	.60	.18
❑ 163	Andruw Jones	1.00	.30
❑ 164	Danny Bautista	.50	.15
❑ 165	Ramon Ortiz	.50	.15
❑ 166	Wily Mo Pena	.60	.18
❑ 167	Jose Jimenez	.50	.15
❑ 168	Mark Redman	.50	.15
❑ 169	Angel Berroa	.50	.15
❑ 170	Andy Marte SP RC	15.00	4.50
❑ 171	Juan Gonzalez	.60	.18
❑ 172	Fernando Vina	.50	.15
❑ 173	Joel Pineiro	.50	.15
❑ 174	Boof Bonser	.50	.15
❑ 175	Bernie Castro SP RC	5.00	1.50
❑ 176	Bobby Cox MG	.50	.15
❑ 177	Jeff Kent	.60	.18
❑ 178	Oliver Perez	.60	.18
❑ 179	Chase Utley	1.50	.45
❑ 180	Mark Mulder	.60	.18
❑ 181	Bobby Abreu	.60	.18
❑ 182	Ramiro Mendoza	.50	.15
❑ 183	Aaron Heilman	.50	.15
❑ 184	A.J. Pierzynski	.60	.18
❑ 185	Eric Gagne	.60	.18
❑ 186	Kirk Saarloos	.50	.15
❑ 187	Ron Gardenhire MG	.50	.15
❑ 188	Dmitri Young	.60	.18
❑ 189	Todd Zeile	.60	.18
❑ 190A	Jim Thome New Logo	1.00	.30
❑ 190B	Jim Thome Old Logo SP	8.00	2.40
❑ 191	Cliff Lee	.50	.15
❑ 192	Matt Morris	.60	.18
❑ 193	Robert Fick	.50	.15
❑ 194	C.C. Sabathia	.60	.18
❑ 195	Alexis Rios	.60	.18
❑ 196	D'Angelo Jimenez	.50	.15
❑ 197	Edgar Martinez	1.00	.30
❑ 198	Robb Nen	.60	.18
❑ 199	Taggert Bozied	.50	.15
❑ 200	Vladimir Guerrero SP	8.00	2.40
❑ 201	Walter Young SP	5.00	1.50
❑ 202	Brendan Harris RC	1.00	.30
❑ 203	Mike Hargrove MG	.50	.15
❑ 204	Vernon Wells	.60	.18
❑ 205	Hank Blalock	.60	.18
❑ 206	Mike Cameron	.50	.15
❑ 207	Tony Batista	.50	.15
❑ 208	Matt Williams	.60	.18
❑ 209	Tony Womack	.50	.15
❑ 210	R.Nivar-Martinez RC	1.00	.30
❑ 211	Aaron Sele	.50	.15
❑ 212	Mark Grace	1.00	.30
❑ 213	Joe Crede	.60	.18
❑ 214	Ryan Dempster	.50	.15
❑ 215	Omar Vizquel	1.00	.30
❑ 216	Juan Pierre	.60	.18
❑ 217	Denny Bautista	.50	.15
❑ 218	Chuck Knoblauch	.60	.18
❑ 219	Eric Karros	.60	.18
❑ 220	Victor Diaz	.60	.18
❑ 221	Jacque Jones	.60	.18
❑ 222	Jose Vidro	.50	.15
❑ 223	Joe McEwing	.50	.15
❑ 224	Nick Johnson	.60	.18
❑ 225	Eric Chavez	.60	.18
❑ 226	Jose Mesa	.50	.15
❑ 227	Aramis Ramirez	.60	.18
❑ 228	John Lackey	.50	.15
❑ 229	David Bell	.50	.15
❑ 230	John Olerud	.60	.18
❑ 231	Tino Martinez	1.00	.30
❑ 232	Randy Winn	.50	.15
❑ 233	Todd Hollandsworth	.50	.15
❑ 234	Ruddy Lugo RC	1.00	.30
❑ 235	Carlos Delgado	.60	.18
❑ 236	Chris Narveson	.50	.15
❑ 237	Tim Salmon	1.00	.30
❑ 238	Orlando Palmeiro	.50	.15
❑ 239	Jeff Clark SP RC	5.00	1.50
❑ 240	Byung-Hyun Kim	.60	.18
❑ 241	Mike Remlinger	.50	.15
❑ 242	Johnny Damon	1.00	.30
❑ 243	Corey Patterson	.50	.15
❑ 244	Paul Konerko	.60	.18
❑ 245	Danny Graves	.50	.15
❑ 246	Ellis Burks	.60	.18
❑ 247	Gavin Floyd	.50	.15
❑ 248	Jaime Bubela RC	1.00	.30
❑ 249	Sean Burroughs	.50	.15
❑ 250	Alex Rodriguez SP	12.00	3.60
❑ 251	Gabe Gross	.50	.15
❑ 252	Rafael Palmeiro	1.00	.30
❑ 253	Dewon Brazelton	.50	.15
❑ 254	Jimmy Journell	.50	.15
❑ 255	Rafael Soriano	.50	.15
❑ 256	Jerome Williams	.50	.15
❑ 257	Xavier Nady	.50	.15
❑ 258	Mike Williams	.50	.15
❑ 259	Randy Wolf	.50	.15
❑ 260A	Miguel Tejada Orange	.60	.18
❑ 260B	Miguel Tejada Black SP	5.00	1.50
❑ 261	Juan Rivera	.50	.15
❑ 262	Rey Ordonez	.50	.15
❑ 263	Bartolo Colon	.60	.18
❑ 264	Eric Milton	.50	.15
❑ 265	Jeffrey Hammonds	.50	.15
❑ 266	Odalis Perez	.50	.15
❑ 267	Mike Sweeney	.60	.18
❑ 268	Richard Hidalgo	.50	.15
❑ 269	Alex Gonzalez	.50	.15
❑ 270	Aaron Cook	.50	.15
❑ 271	Earl Snyder	.50	.15
❑ 272	Todd Walker	.50	.15
❑ 273	Aaron Rowand	.60	.18
❑ 274	Matt Clement	.60	.18
❑ 275	Anastacio Martinez	.50	.15
❑ 276	Mike Bordick	.60	.18
❑ 277	John Smoltz	1.00	.30
❑ 278	Scott Hairston	.50	.15
❑ 279	David Eckstein	.60	.18
❑ 280	Shannon Stewart	.60	.18
❑ 281	Carl Everett	.60	.18
❑ 282	Aubrey Huff	.60	.18
❑ 283	Mike Mussina	1.00	.30
❑ 284	Ruben Sierra	.50	.15
❑ 285	Russ Ortiz	.60	.18
❑ 286	Brian Lawrence	.50	.15
❑ 287	Kip Wells	.50	.15
❑ 288	Placido Polanco	.50	.15
❑ 289	Ted Lilly	.50	.15
❑ 290	Andy Pettitte	1.00	.30
❑ 291	John Buck	.50	.15
❑ 292	Orlando Cabrera	.60	.18
❑ 293	Cristian Guzman	.50	.15
❑ 294	Ruben Quevedo	.50	.15
❑ 295	Cesar Izturis	.50	.15
❑ 296	Ryan Ludwick	.50	.15
❑ 297	Roy Oswalt	.60	.18
❑ 298	Jason Stokes	.60	.18
❑ 299	Mike Hampton	.60	.18
❑ 300	Pedro Martinez	1.00	.30
❑ 301	Nic Jackson	.50	.15
❑ 302A	Mag. Ordonez New Logo	.60	.18
❑ 302B	Mag. Ordonez Old Logo SP	5.00	1.50
❑ 303	Manny Ramirez	1.00	.30
❑ 304	Jorge Julio	.50	.15
❑ 305	Javy Lopez	.60	.18
❑ 306	Roy Halladay	.60	.18
❑ 307	Kevin Mench	.50	.15
❑ 308	Jason Isringhausen	.60	.18
❑ 309	Carlos Guillen	.60	.18
❑ 310	Tsuyoshi Shinjo	.60	.18
❑ 311	Phil Nevin	.60	.18
❑ 312	Pokey Reese	.50	.15
❑ 313	Jorge Padilla	.50	.15
❑ 314	Jermaine Dye	.60	.18
❑ 315	David Wells	.60	.18
❑ 316	Mo Vaughn	.60	.18
❑ 317	Bernie Williams	1.00	.30
❑ 318	Michael Restovich	.50	.15
❑ 319	Jose Hernandez	.50	.15
❑ 320	Richie Sexson	.60	.18
❑ 321	Daryle Ward	.50	.15
❑ 322	Luis Castillo	.50	.15
❑ 323	Rene Reyes	.50	.15
❑ 324	Victor Martinez	1.00	.30
❑ 325A	Adam Dunn New Logo	.60	.18
❑ 325B	Adam Dunn Old Logo SP	5.00	1.50
❑ 326	Corwin Malone	.50	.15
❑ 327	Kerry Wood	.60	.18
❑ 328	Rickey Henderson	1.50	.45
❑ 329	Marty Cordova	.50	.15
❑ 330	Greg Maddux	2.50	.75
❑ 331	Miguel Batista	.50	.15
❑ 332	Chris Bootcheck	.50	.15
❑ 333	Carlos Baerga	.50	.15
❑ 334	Antonio Alfonseca	.50	.15
❑ 335	Shane Halter	.50	.15
❑ 336	Juan Encarnacion	.50	.15
❑ 337	Tom Gordon	.50	.15
❑ 338	Hideo Nomo	1.50	.45
❑ 339	Torii Hunter	.60	.18
❑ 340A	Alfonso Soriano Yellow	.60	.18
❑ 340B	Alf. Soriano Black SP	5.00	1.50
❑ 341	Roberto Alomar	1.00	.30
❑ 342	David Justice	.60	.18
❑ 343	Mike Lieberthal	.50	.15
❑ 344	Jeff Weaver	.50	.15
❑ 345	Timo Perez	.50	.15
❑ 346	Travis Lee	.50	.15
❑ 347	Sean Casey	1.00	.30
❑ 348	Willie Harris	.50	.15
❑ 349	Derek Lowe	.60	.18
❑ 350	Tom Glavine	1.00	.30
❑ 351	Eric Hinske	.50	.15
❑ 352	Rocco Baldelli	.60	.18
❑ 353	J.D. Drew	.60	.18
❑ 354	Jamie Moyer	.60	.18
❑ 355	Todd Linden	.50	.15
❑ 356	Benito Santiago	.60	.18
❑ 357	Brad Baker	.50	.15
❑ 358	Alex Gonzalez	.50	.15
❑ 359	Brandon Duckworth	.50	.15
❑ 360	John Rheinecker	.50	.15
❑ 361	Orlando Hernandez	.60	.18
❑ 362	Pedro Astacio	.50	.15
❑ 363	Brad Wilkerson	.50	.15
❑ 364	David Ortiz SP	8.00	2.40
❑ 365	Geoff Jenkins SP	5.00	1.50
❑ 366	Brian Jordan SP	5.00	1.50
❑ 367	Paul Byrd SP	5.00	1.50
❑ 368	Jason Lane SP	5.00	1.50
❑ 369	Jeff Bagwell SP	8.00	2.40
❑ 370	Bobby Higginson SP	5.00	1.50
❑ 371	Juan Uribe SP	5.00	1.50
❑ 372	Lee Stevens SP	5.00	1.50
❑ 373	Jimmy Haynes SP	5.00	1.50
❑ 374	Jose Valentin SP	5.00	1.50
❑ 375	Ken Griffey Jr. SP	12.00	3.60
❑ 376	Barry Bonds SP	20.00	6.00
❑ 377	Gary Matthews Jr. SP	5.00	1.50
❑ 378	Gary Sheffield SP	5.00	1.50
❑ 379	Rick Helling SP	5.00	1.50
❑ 380	Junior Spivey SP	5.00	1.50
❑ 381	Francisco Rodriguez SP	5.00	1.50
❑ 382	Chipper Jones SP	8.00	2.40
❑ 383	Orlando Hudson SP	5.00	1.50
❑ 384	Ivan Rodriguez SP	8.00	2.40
❑ 385	Chris Snelling SP	5.00	1.50
❑ 386	Kenny Lofton SP	5.00	1.50
❑ 387	Eric Cyr SP	5.00	1.50
❑ 388	Jason Kendall SP	5.00	1.50
❑ 389	Marlon Anderson SP	5.00	1.50
❑ 390	Billy Koch SP	5.00	1.50
❑ 391	Shelley Duncan SP	5.00	1.50
❑ 392	Jose Reyes SP	5.00	1.50
❑ 393	Fernando Tatis SP	5.00	1.50
❑ 394	Michael Cuddyer SP	5.00	1.50
❑ 395	Mark Prior SP	8.00	2.40
❑ 396	Dontrelle Willis SP	8.00	2.40
❑ 397	Jay Payton SP	5.00	1.50
❑ 398	Brandon Phillips SP	5.00	1.50
❑ 399	Dustin Moseley SP RC	5.00	1.50
❑ 400	Jason Giambi SP	5.00	1.50
❑ 401	John Mabry SP	5.00	1.50
❑ 402	Ron Gant SP	5.00	1.50
❑ 403	J.T. Snow SP	5.00	1.50
❑ 404	Jeff Cirillo SP	5.00	1.50
❑ 405	Darin Erstad SP	5.00	1.50
❑ 406	Luis Gonzalez SP	5.00	1.50
❑ 407	Marcus Giles SP	5.00	1.50
❑ 408	Brian Daubach SP	5.00	1.50

❑ 409 Moises Alou SP	5.00	1.50
❑ 410 Raul Mondesi SP	5.00	1.50
❑ 411 Adrian Beltre SP	5.00	1.50
❑ 412 A.J. Burnett SP	5.00	1.50
❑ 413 Jason Jennings SP	5.00	1.50
❑ 414 Edwin Almonte SP	5.00	1.50
❑ 415 Fred McGriff SP	8.00	2.40
❑ 416 Tim Raines Jr. SP	5.00	1.50
❑ 417 Rafael Furcal SP	5.00	1.50
❑ 418 Erubiel Durazo SP	5.00	1.50
❑ 419 Drew Henson SP	5.00	1.50
❑ 420 Kevin Appier SP	5.00	1.50
❑ 421 Chad Tracy SP	5.00	1.50
❑ 422 Adam Wainwright SP	5.00	1.50
❑ 423 Choo Freeman SP	5.00	1.50
❑ 424 Sandy Alomar Jr. SP	5.00	1.50
❑ 425 Corey Koskie SP	5.00	1.50
❑ 426 Jeromy Burnitz SP	5.00	1.50
❑ 427 Jorge Posada SP	8.00	2.40
❑ 428 Jason Arnold SP	5.00	1.50
❑ 429 Brett Myers SP	5.00	1.50
❑ 430 Shawn Green SP	5.00	1.50

2004 Topps Heritage

	Nm-Mt	Ex-Mt
COMPLETE SET (495)	350.00	105.00
COMP.SET w/o SP's (385)	60.00	18.00
❑ 1A Jim Thome Fielding	1.00	.30
❑ 1B Jim Thome Hitting SP	8.00	2.40
❑ 2 Nomar Garciaparra SP	10.00	3.00
❑ 3 Aramis Ramirez	.60	.18
❑ 4 Rafael Palmeiro SP	8.00	2.40
❑ 5 Danny Graves	.50	.15
❑ 6 Casey Blake	.50	.15
❑ 7 Juan Uribe	.50	.15
❑ 8A Dmitri Young New Logo	.60	.18
❑ 8B Dmitri Young Old Logo SP	5.00	1.50
❑ 9 Billy Wagner	.60	.18
❑ 10A Jason Giambi Swinging	.60	.18
❑ 10B Jason Giambi Btg Stance SP	5.00	1.50
❑ 11 Carlos Beltran	.60	.18
❑ 12 Chad Hermansen	.50	.15
❑ 13 B.J. Upton	1.00	.30
❑ 14 Dustan Mohr	.50	.15
❑ 15 Endy Chavez	.50	.15
❑ 16 Cliff Floyd	.60	.18
❑ 17 Bernie Williams	1.00	.30
❑ 18 Eric Chavez	.60	.18
❑ 19 Chase Utley	1.00	.30
❑ 20 Randy Johnson	1.50	.45
❑ 21 Vernon Wells	.60	.18
❑ 22 Juan Gonzalez	.60	.18
❑ 23 Joe Kennedy	.50	.15
❑ 24 Bengie Molina	.50	.15
❑ 25 Carlos Lee	.60	.18
❑ 26 Horacio Ramirez	.50	.15
❑ 27 Anthony Acevedo RC	.75	.23
❑ 28 Sammy Sosa SP	8.00	2.40
❑ 29 Jon Garland	.60	.18
❑ 30A Adam Dunn Fielding	.60	.18
❑ 30B Adam Dunn Hitting SP	5.00	1.50
❑ 31 Aaron Rowand	.60	.18
❑ 32 Jody Gerut	.50	.15
❑ 33 Chin-Hui Tsao	.60	.18
❑ 34 Alex Sanchez	.50	.15
❑ 35 A.J. Burnett	.60	.18
❑ 36 Brad Ausmus	.60	.18
❑ 37 Blake Hawksworth RC	1.00	.30
❑ 38 Francisco Rodriguez	.60	.18
❑ 39 Alex Cintron	.50	.15
❑ 40A Chipper Jones Pointing	1.50	.45
❑ 40B Chipper Jones Fielding SP	8.00	2.40
❑ 41 Deivi Cruz	.50	.15
❑ 42 Bill Mueller	.60	.18
❑ 43 Joe Borowski	.50	.15
❑ 44 Jimmy Haynes	.50	.15
❑ 45 Mark Loretta	.60	.18
❑ 46 Jerome Williams	.50	.15
❑ 47 Gary Sheffield Yanks SP	8.00	2.40
❑ 48 Richard Hidalgo	.50	.15
❑ 49A Jason Kendall New Logo	.60	.18
❑ 49B Jason Kendall Old Logo SP	5.00	1.50
❑ 50 Ichiro Suzuki SP	12.00	3.60
❑ 51 Jim Edmonds	1.00	.30
❑ 52 Frank Catalanotto	.50	.15
❑ 53 Jose Contreras	.50	.15
❑ 54 Mo Vaughn	.60	.18
❑ 55 Brendan Donnelly	.50	.15
❑ 56 Luis Gonzalez	.60	.18
❑ 57 Robert Fick	.50	.15
❑ 58 Laynce Nix	.50	.15
❑ 59 Johnny Damon	1.00	.30
❑ 60A Magglio Ordonez Running	.60	.18
❑ 60B Magglio Ordonez Hitting SP	5.00	1.50
❑ 61 Matt Clement	.60	.18
❑ 62 Ryan Ludwick	.50	.15
❑ 63 Luis Castillo	.50	.15
❑ 64 Dave Crouthers RC	.75	.23
❑ 65 Dave Berg	.50	.15
❑ 66 Kyle Davies RC	4.00	1.20
❑ 67 Tim Salmon	1.00	.30
❑ 68 Marcus Giles	.60	.18
❑ 69 Marty Cordova	.50	.15
❑ 70A Todd Helton White Jsy	1.00	.30
❑ 70B Todd Helton Purple Jsy SP	8.00	2.40
❑ 71 Jeff Kent	.60	.18
❑ 72 Michael Tucker	.50	.15
❑ 73 Cesar Izturis	.50	.15
❑ 74 Paul Quantrill	.50	.15
❑ 75 Conor Jackson RC	3.00	.90
❑ 76 Placido Polanco	.50	.15
❑ 77 Adam Eaton	.50	.15
❑ 78 Ramon Hernandez	.60	.18
❑ 79 Edgardo Alfonzo	.50	.15
❑ 80 Dioner Navarro RC	2.00	.60
❑ 81 Woody Williams	.50	.15
❑ 82 Rey Ordonez	.50	.15
❑ 83 Randy Winn	.50	.15
❑ 84 Casey Myers RC	.75	.23
❑ 85A R.Choy Foo New Logo RC	.75	.23
❑ 85B R.Choy Foo Old Logo SP	5.00	1.50
❑ 86 Ray Durham	.60	.18
❑ 87 Sean Burroughs	.50	.15
❑ 88 Tim Frend RC	.75	.23
❑ 89 Shigetoshi Hasegawa	.60	.18
❑ 90 Jeffrey Allison RC	.75	.23
❑ 91 Orlando Hudson	.50	.15
❑ 92 Matt Creighton SP RC	5.00	1.50
❑ 93 Tim Worrell	.50	.15
❑ 94 Kris Benson	.50	.15
❑ 95 Mike Lieberthal	.50	.15
❑ 96 David Wells	.60	.18
❑ 97 Jason Phillips	.50	.15
❑ 98 Bobby Cox MGR	.50	.15
❑ 99 Johan Santana	1.00	.30
❑ 100A Alex Rodriguez Hitting	2.50	.75
❑ 100B Alex Rodriguez Throwing SP	10.00	3.00
❑ 101 John Vander Wal	.50	.15
❑ 102 Orlando Cabrera	.60	.18
❑ 103 Hideo Nomo	1.50	.45
❑ 104 Todd Walker	.50	.15
❑ 105 Jason Johnson	.50	.15
❑ 106 Matt Mantei	.50	.15
❑ 107 Jarrod Washburn	.50	.15
❑ 108 Preston Wilson	.60	.18
❑ 109 Carl Pavano	.60	.18
❑ 110 Geoff Blum	.50	.15
❑ 111 Eric Gagne	.60	.18
❑ 112 Geoff Jenkins	.50	.15
❑ 113 Joe Torre MG	1.00	.30
❑ 114 Jon Knott RC	.75	.23
❑ 115 Hank Blalock	.60	.18
❑ 116 John Olerud	.60	.18
❑ 117A Pat Burrell New Logo	.60	.18
❑ 117B Pat Burrell Old Logo SP	5.00	1.50
❑ 118 Aaron Boone	.60	.18
❑ 119 Zach Day	.50	.15
❑ 120A Frank Thomas New Logo	1.50	.45
❑ 120B Frank Thomas Old Logo SP	8.00	2.40
❑ 121 Kyle Farnsworth	.50	.15
❑ 122 Derek Lowe	.60	.18
❑ 123 Zach Miner SP RC	8.00	2.40
❑ 124 Matthew Moses SP RC	8.00	2.40
❑ 125 Jesse Roman RC	.75	.23
❑ 126 Josh Phelps	.50	.15
❑ 127 Nic Ungs RC	.75	.23
❑ 128 Dan Haren	.50	.15
❑ 129 Kirk Rueter	.50	.15
❑ 130 Jack McKeon MGR	.60	.18
❑ 131 Keith Foulke	.60	.18
❑ 132 Garrett Stephenson	.50	.15
❑ 133 Wes Helms	.50	.15
❑ 134 Raul Ibanez	.50	.15
❑ 135 Morgan Ensberg	.60	.18
❑ 136 Jay Payton	.60	.18
❑ 137 Billy Koch	.50	.15
❑ 138 Mark Grudzielanek	.50	.15
❑ 139 Rodrigo Lopez	.50	.15
❑ 140 Corey Patterson	.50	.15
❑ 141 Troy Percival	.60	.18
❑ 142 Shea Hillenbrand	.60	.18
❑ 143 Brad Fullmer	.60	.18
❑ 144 Ricky Nolasco RC	1.00	.30
❑ 145 Mark Teixeira	1.00	.30
❑ 146 Tydus Meadows RC	.75	.23
❑ 147 Toby Hall	.50	.15
❑ 148 Orlando Palmeiro	.50	.15
❑ 149 Khalid Ballouli RC	.75	.23
❑ 150 Grady Little MGR	.50	.15
❑ 151 David Eckstein	.60	.18
❑ 152 Kenny Perez RC	.75	.23
❑ 153 Ben Grieve	.50	.15
❑ 154 Ismael Valdes	.50	.15
❑ 155 Bret Boone	.60	.18
❑ 156 Jesse Foppert	.50	.15
❑ 157 Vicente Padilla	.50	.15
❑ 158 Bobby Abreu	.60	.18
❑ 159 Scott Hatteberg	.50	.15
❑ 160 Carlos Quentin RC	2.50	.75
❑ 161 Anthony Lerew RC	1.00	.30
❑ 162 Lance Carter	.50	.15
❑ 163 Robb Nen	.60	.18
❑ 164 Zach Duke SP RC	20.00	6.00
❑ 165 Xavier Nady	.50	.15
❑ 166 Kip Wells	.50	.15
❑ 167 Kevin Millwood	.50	.15
❑ 168 Jon Lieber	.50	.15
❑ 169 Jose Reyes	.60	.18
❑ 170 Eric Byrnes	.50	.15
❑ 171 Paul Konerko	.60	.18
❑ 172 Chris Lubanski	.60	.18
❑ 173 Jae Weong Seo	.50	.15
❑ 174 Corey Koskie	.50	.15
❑ 175 Tim Stauffer RC	1.25	.35
❑ 176 John Lackey	.50	.15
❑ 177 Danny Bautista	.50	.15
❑ 178 Shane Reynolds	.50	.15
❑ 179 Jorge Julio	.50	.15
❑ 180A Manny Ramirez New Logo	1.00	.30
❑ 180B Manny Ramirez Old Logo SP	8.00	2.40
❑ 181 Alex Gonzalez	.50	.15
❑ 182A Moises Alou New Logo	.60	.18
❑ 182B Moises Alou Old Logo SP	5.00	1.50
❑ 183 Mark Buehrle	.60	.18
❑ 184 Carlos Guillen	.60	.18
❑ 185 Nate Cornejo	.50	.15
❑ 186 Billy Traber	.50	.15
❑ 187 Jason Jennings	.50	.15
❑ 188 Eric Munson	.50	.15
❑ 189 Braden Looper	.50	.15
❑ 190 Juan Encarnacion	.50	.15
❑ 191 Dusty Baker MGR	.60	.18
❑ 192 Travis Lee	.50	.15
❑ 193 Miguel Cairo	.50	.15
❑ 194 Rich Aurilia SP	5.00	1.50
❑ 195 Tom Gordon	.50	.15
❑ 196 Freddy Garcia	.60	.18
❑ 197 Brian Lawrence	.50	.15
❑ 198 Jorge Posada SP	8.00	2.40

❑	199 Javier Vazquez	.60	.18
❑	200A Albert Pujols New Logo	3.00	.90
❑	200B Albert Pujols Old Logo SP	12.00	3.60
❑	201 Victor Zambrano	.50	.15
❑	202 Eli Marrero	.50	.15
❑	203 Joel Pineiro	.50	.15
❑	204 Rondell White	.60	.18
❑	205 Craig Ansman RC	.75	.23
❑	206 Michael Young	.60	.18
❑	207 Carlos Baerga	.50	.15
❑	208 Andruw Jones	1.00	.30
❑	209 Jerry Hairston Jr.	.50	.15
❑	210 Shawn Green SP	5.00	1.50
❑	211 Ron Gardenhire MGR	.50	.15
❑	212 Darin Erstad	.60	.18
❑	213A Brandon Webb Glove Chest	.50	.15
❑	213B Brandon Webb Glove Out SP	5.00	1.50
❑	214 Greg Maddux	2.50	.75
❑	215 Reed Johnson	.50	.15
❑	216 John Thomson	.50	.15
❑	217 Tino Martinez	1.00	.30
❑	218 Mike Cameron UER	.50	.15
	Card has facsimile autograph of Troy Cameron		
❑	219 Edgar Martinez	1.00	.30
❑	220 Eric Young	.50	.15
❑	221 Reggie Sanders	.60	.18
❑	222 Randy Wolf	.50	.15
❑	223 Erubiel Durazo	.50	.15
❑	224 Mike Mussina	1.00	.30
❑	225 Tom Glavine	1.00	.30
❑	226 Troy Glaus	.60	.18
❑	227 Oscar Villarreal	.50	.15
❑	228 David Segui	.50	.15
❑	229 Jeff Suppan	.50	.15
❑	230 Kenny Lofton	.60	.18
❑	231 Esteban Loaiza	.50	.15
❑	232 Felipe Lopez	.50	.15
❑	233 Matt Lawton	.50	.15
❑	234 Mark Bellhorn	.60	.18
❑	235 Wil Ledezma	.50	.15
❑	236 Todd Hollandsworth	.50	.15
❑	237 Octavio Dotel	.50	.15
❑	238 Darren Dreifort	.50	.15
❑	239 Paul Lo Duca	.60	.18
❑	240 Richie Sexson	.60	.18
❑	241 Doug Mientkiewicz	.60	.18
❑	242 Luis Rivas	.50	.15
❑	243 Claudio Vargas	.50	.15
❑	244 Mark Ellis	.50	.15
❑	245 Brett Myers	.60	.18
❑	246 Jake Peavy	.60	.18
❑	247 Marquis Grissom	.60	.18
❑	248 Armando Benitez	.60	.18
❑	249 Ryan Franklin	.50	.15
❑	250A Alfonso Soriano Throwing	.60	.18
❑	250B Alfonso Soriano Fielding SP	5.00	1.50
❑	251 Tim Hudson	.60	.18
❑	252 Shannon Stewart	.60	.18
❑	253 A.J. Pierzynski	.60	.18
❑	254 Runelvys Hernandez	.50	.15
❑	255 Roy Oswalt	.60	.18
❑	256 Shawn Chacon	.50	.15
❑	257 Tony Graffanino	.50	.15
❑	258 Tim Wakefield	.60	.18
❑	259 Damian Miller	.50	.15
❑	260 Joe Crede	.60	.18
❑	261 Jason LaRue	.50	.15
❑	262 Jose Jimenez	.50	.15
❑	263 Juan Pierre	.60	.18
❑	264 Wade Miller	.50	.15
❑	265 Odalis Perez	.50	.15
❑	266 Eddie Guardado	.50	.15
❑	267 Rocky Biddle	.50	.15
❑	268 Jeff Nelson	.50	.15
❑	269 Terrence Long	.50	.15
❑	270 Ramon Ortiz	.50	.15
❑	271 Raul Mondesi	.60	.18
❑	272 Ugueth Urbina	.50	.15
❑	273 Jeromy Burnitz	.60	.18
❑	274 Brad Radke	.60	.18
❑	275 Jose Vidro	.50	.15
❑	276 Bobby Jenks	.60	.18
❑	277 Ty Wigginton	.50	.15
❑	278 Jose Guillen	.60	.18
❑	279 Delmon Young	1.00	.30
❑	280 Brian Giles	.60	.18
❑	281 Jason Schmidt	.60	.18
❑	282 Nick Markakis	.60	.18
❑	283 Felipe Alou MGR	.60	.18
❑	284 Carl Crawford	.60	.18
❑	285 Neifi Perez	.50	.15
❑	286 Miguel Tejada	.60	.18
❑	287 Victor Martinez	.60	.18
❑	288 Adam Kennedy	.50	.15
❑	289 Kerry Ligtenberg	.50	.15
❑	290 Scott Williamson	.50	.15
❑	291 Tony Womack	.50	.15
❑	292 Travis Hafner	.60	.18
❑	293 Bobby Crosby	.60	.18
❑	294 Chad Billingsley	.60	.18
❑	295 Russ Ortiz	.60	.18
❑	296 John Burkett	.50	.15
❑	297 Carlos Zambrano	.60	.18
❑	298 Randall Simon	.50	.15
❑	299 Juan Castro	.50	.15
❑	300 Mike Lowell	.60	.18
❑	301 Fred McGriff	1.00	.30
❑	302 Glendon Rusch	.50	.15
❑	303 Sung Jung RC	.75	.23
❑	304 Rocco Baldelli	.60	.18
❑	305 Fernando Vina	.50	.15
❑	306 Gil Meche	.50	.15
❑	307 Jose Cruz Jr.	.50	.15
❑	308 Bernie Castro	.50	.15
❑	309 Scott Spiezio	.50	.15
❑	310 Paul Byrd	.50	.15
❑	311A Jay Gibbons New Logo	.50	.15
❑	311B Jay Gibbons Old Logo SP	5.00	1.50
❑	312 Trot Nixon	.60	.18
❑	313 Chris O'Riordan RC	.75	.23
❑	314 Julio Lugo	.50	.15
❑	315 Ben Davis	.50	.15
❑	316 Mike Williams	.50	.15
❑	317 Trevor Hoffman	.60	.18
❑	318 Andy Pettitte	1.00	.30
❑	319 Orlando Hernandez	.60	.18
❑	320 Juan Rivera	.50	.15
❑	321 Elizardo Ramirez	.50	.15
❑	322 Junior Spivey	.50	.15
❑	323 Tony Batista	.50	.15
❑	324 Mike Remlinger	.50	.15
❑	325 Alex Gonzalez	.50	.15
❑	326 Aaron Hill	.50	.15
❑	327 Steve Finley	.60	.18
❑	328 Vinny Castilla	.60	.18
❑	329 Eric Duncan	.60	.18
❑	330 Mike Gosling RC	.75	.23
❑	331 Eric Hinske	.50	.15
❑	332 Scott Rolen	1.00	.30
❑	333 Benito Santiago	.60	.18
❑	334 Jimmy Gobble	.50	.15
❑	335 Bobby Higginson	.60	.18
❑	336 Kelvim Escobar	.50	.15
❑	337 Mike DeJean	.50	.15
❑	338 Sidney Ponson	.50	.15
❑	339 Todd Self RC	1.00	.30
❑	340 Jeff Cirillo	.50	.15
❑	341 Jimmy Rollins	.60	.18
❑	342A Barry Zito White Jsy	.60	.18
❑	342B Barry Zito Green Jsy SP	5.00	1.50
❑	343 Felix Pie	1.00	.30
❑	344 Matt Morris	.60	.18
❑	345 Kazuhiro Sasaki	.60	.18
❑	346 Jack Wilson	.50	.15
❑	347 Nick Johnson	.60	.18
❑	348 Wil Cordero	.50	.15
❑	349 Ryan Madson	.50	.15
❑	350 Torii Hunter	.60	.18
❑	351 Andy Ashby	.50	.15
❑	352 Aubrey Huff	.60	.18
❑	353 Brad Lidge	.60	.18
❑	354 Derrek Lee	1.00	.30
❑	355 Yadier Molina RC	2.50	.75
❑	356 Paul Wilson	.50	.15
❑	357 Omar Vizquel	1.00	.30
❑	358 Rene Reyes	.50	.15
❑	359 Marlon Anderson	.50	.15
❑	360 Bobby Kielty	.50	.15
❑	361A Ryan Wagner New Logo	.50	.15
❑	361B Ryan Wagner Old Logo SP	5.00	1.50
❑	362 Justin Morneau	.60	.18
❑	363 Shane Spencer	.50	.15
❑	364 David Bell	.50	.15
❑	365 Matt Stairs	.50	.15
❑	366 Joe Borchard	.50	.15
❑	367 Mark Redman	.50	.15
❑	368 Dave Roberts	.50	.15
❑	369 Desi Relaford	.50	.15
❑	370 Rich Harden	.60	.18
❑	371 Fernando Tatis	.50	.15
❑	372 Eric Karros	.60	.18
❑	373 Eric Milton	.60	.18
❑	374 Mike Sweeney	.60	.18
❑	375 Brian Daubach	.50	.15
❑	376 Brian Snyder	.50	.15
❑	377 Chris Reitsma	.50	.15
❑	378 Kyle Lohse	.50	.15
❑	379 Livan Hernandez	.60	.18
❑	380 Robin Ventura	.60	.18
❑	381 Jacque Jones	.60	.18
❑	382 Danny Kolb	.50	.15
❑	383 Casey Kotchman	.60	.18
❑	384 Cristian Guzman	.50	.15
❑	385 Josh Beckett	.60	.18
❑	386 Khalil Greene	1.50	.45
❑	387 Greg Myers	.50	.15
❑	388 Francisco Cordero	.50	.15
❑	389 Donald Levinski RC	.75	.23
❑	390 Roy Halladay	.60	.18
❑	391 J.D. Drew	.60	.18
❑	392 Jamie Moyer	.60	.18
❑	393 Ken Macha MGR	.50	.15
❑	394 Jeff Davanon	.50	.15
❑	395 Matt Kata	.50	.15
❑	396 Jack Cust	.50	.15
❑	397 Mike Timlin	.50	.15
❑	398 Zack Greinke SP	5.00	1.50
❑	399 Byung-Hyun Kim SP	5.00	1.50
❑	400 Kazuhisa Ishii SP	5.00	1.50
❑	401 Brayan Pena SP RC	5.00	1.50
❑	402 Garret Anderson SP	5.00	1.50
❑	403 Kyle Sleeth SP RC	8.00	2.40
❑	404 Javy Lopez SP	5.00	1.50
❑	405 Damian Moss SP	5.00	1.50
❑	406 David Ortiz SP	8.00	2.40
❑	407 Pedro Martinez SP	8.00	2.40
❑	408 Hee Seop Choi SP	5.00	1.50
❑	409 Carl Everett SP	5.00	1.50
❑	410 Dontrelle Willis SP	8.00	2.40
❑	411 Ryan Harvey SP	5.00	1.50
❑	412 Russell Branyan SP	5.00	1.50
❑	413 Milton Bradley SP	5.00	1.50
❑	414 Marcus McBeth SP RC	5.00	1.50
❑	415 Carlos Pena SP	5.00	1.50
❑	416 Ivan Rodriguez SP	8.00	2.40
❑	417 Craig Biggio SP	8.00	2.40
❑	418 Angel Berroa SP	5.00	1.50
❑	419 Brian Jordan SP	5.00	1.50
❑	420 Scott Podsednik SP	5.00	1.50
❑	421 Omar Falcon SP RC	5.00	1.50
❑	422 Joe Mays SP	5.00	1.50
❑	423 Brad Wilkerson SP	5.00	1.50
❑	424 Al Leiter SP	5.00	1.50
❑	425 Derek Jeter SP	12.00	3.60
❑	426 Mark Mulder SP	5.00	1.50
❑	427 Marlon Byrd SP	5.00	1.50
❑	428 David Murphy SP RC	8.00	2.40
❑	429 Phil Nevin SP	5.00	1.50
❑	430 J.T. Snow SP	5.00	1.50
❑	431 Brad Sullivan SP RC	8.00	2.40
❑	432 Bo Hart SP	5.00	1.50
❑	433 Josh Labandeira SP RC	5.00	1.50
❑	434 Chan Ho Park SP	5.00	1.50
❑	435 Carlos Delgado SP	5.00	1.50
❑	436 Curt Schilling Sox SP	8.00	2.40
❑	437 John Smoltz SP	8.00	2.40
❑	438 Luis Matos SP	5.00	1.50
❑	439 Mark Prior SP	8.00	2.40
❑	440 Roberto Alomar SP	8.00	2.40
❑	441 Coco Crisp SP	5.00	1.50
❑	442 Austin Kearns SP	5.00	1.50
❑	443 Larry Walker SP	5.00	1.50
❑	444 Neal Cotts SP	5.00	1.50
❑	445 Jeff Bagwell SP	8.00	2.40
❑	446 Adrian Beltre SP	5.00	1.50
❑	447 Grady Sizemore SP	5.00	1.50
❑	448 Keith Ginter SP	5.00	1.50

		Nm-Mt	Ex-Mt
❑ 449	Vladimir Guerrero SP	8.00	2.40
❑ 450	Lyle Overbay SP	5.00	1.50
❑ 451	Rafael Furcal SP	5.00	1.50
❑ 452	Melvin Mora SP	5.00	1.50
❑ 453	Kerry Wood SP	5.00	1.50
❑ 454	Jose Valentin SP	5.00	1.50
❑ 455	Ken Griffey Jr. SP	10.00	3.00
❑ 456	Brandon Phillips SP	5.00	1.50
❑ 457	Miguel Cabrera SP	8.00	2.40
❑ 458	Edwin Jackson SP	5.00	1.50
❑ 459	Eric Owens SP	5.00	1.50
❑ 460	Miguel Batista SP	5.00	1.50
❑ 461	Mike Hampton SP	5.00	1.50
❑ 462	Kevin Millar SP	5.00	1.50
❑ 463	Bartolo Colon SP	5.00	1.50
❑ 464	Sean Casey SP	8.00	2.40
❑ 465	C.C. Sabathia SP	5.00	1.50
❑ 466	Rickie Weeks SP	8.00	2.40
❑ 467	Brad Penny SP	5.00	1.50
❑ 468	Mike MacDougal SP	5.00	1.50
❑ 469	Kevin Brown SP	5.00	1.50
❑ 470	Lance Berkman SP	5.00	1.50
❑ 471	Ben Sheets SP	5.00	1.50
❑ 472	Mariano Rivera SP	8.00	2.40
❑ 473	Mike Piazza SP	10.00	3.00
❑ 474	Ryan Klesko SP	5.00	1.50
❑ 475	Edgar Renteria SP	5.00	1.50

2005 Topps Heritage

	Nm-Mt	Ex-Mt
COMPLETE SET (495)	400.00	120.00
COMP.SET w/o SP's (385)	60.00	18.00

SP STATED ODDS 1:2 HOBBY/RETAIL
BASIC SP: 5/20/30/31/33/79/101/110/130
BASIC SP: 135/260/292/398-475 ..
VARIATION SP: 3/6/7/31/50/69/78/82/118
VARIATION SP: 125/135/155/261/273/286
VARIATION SP: 296/300/312/353/389
SEE BECKETT.COM FOR VAR.DESCRIPTIONS

		Nm-Mt	Ex-Mt
❑ 1	Will Harridge	.50	.15
❑ 2	Warren Giles	.50	.15
❑ 3A	Alfonso Soriano Fldg	.50	.15
❑ 3B	Alfonso Soriano Running SP	8.00	2.40
❑ 4	Mark Mulder	.50	.15
❑ 5	Todd Helton SP	8.00	2.40
❑ 6A	Jason Bay Black Cap	.50	.15
❑ 6B	Jason Bay Yellow Cap SP	8.00	2.40
❑ 7A	Ichiro Suzuki Running	2.00	.60
❑ 7B	Ichiro Suzuki Crouch SP	12.00	3.60
❑ 8	Jim Tracy MG	.50	.15
❑ 9	Gavin Floyd	.50	.15
❑ 10	John Smoltz	.75	.23
❑ 11	Chicago Cubs TC	1.00	.30
❑ 12	Darin Erstad	.50	.15
❑ 13	Chad Tracy	.50	.15
❑ 14	Charles Thomas	.50	.15
❑ 15	Miguel Tejada	.50	.15
❑ 16	Andre Ethier RC	1.50	.45
❑ 17	Jeff Francis	.50	.15
❑ 18	Derrek Lee	.75	.23
❑ 19	Juan Uribe	.50	.15
❑ 20	Jim Edmonds SP	8.00	2.40
❑ 21	Kenny Lofton	.50	.15
❑ 22	Brad Ausmus	.50	.15
❑ 23	Jon Garland	.50	.15
❑ 24	Edwin Jackson	.50	.15
❑ 25	Joe Mauer	.50	.15
❑ 26	Wes Helms	.50	.15
❑ 27	Brian Schneider	.50	.15
❑ 28	Kazuo Matsui	.50	.15
❑ 29	Flash Gordon	.50	.15
❑ 30	Hideo Nomo SP	8.00	2.40
❑ 31A	Albert Pujols Red Hat SP	12.00	3.60
❑ 31B	Albert Pujols Blue Hat SP	12.00	3.60
❑ 32	Carl Crawford	.50	.15
❑ 33	Vladimir Guerrero SP	8.00	2.40
❑ 34	Nick Green	.50	.15
❑ 35	Jay Gibbons	.50	.15
❑ 36	Kevin Youkilis	.50	.15
❑ 37	Billy Wagner	.50	.15
❑ 38	Terrence Long	.50	.15
❑ 39	Kevin Mench	.50	.15
❑ 40	Garret Anderson	.50	.15
❑ 41	Reed Johnson	.50	.15
❑ 42	Reggie Sanders	.50	.15
❑ 43	Kirk Rueter	.50	.15
❑ 44	Jay Payton	.50	.15
❑ 45	Tike Redman	.50	.15
❑ 46	Mike Lieberthal	.50	.15
❑ 47	Damian Miller	.50	.15
❑ 48	Zach Day	.50	.15
❑ 49	Juan Rincon	.50	.15
❑ 50A	Jim Thome At Bat	.75	.23
❑ 50B	Jim Thome Fldg SP	8.00	2.40
❑ 51	Jose Guillen	.50	.15
❑ 52	Richie Sexson	.50	.15
❑ 53	Juan Cruz	.50	.15
❑ 54	Byung-Hyun Kim	.50	.15
❑ 55	Carlos Zambrano	.50	.15
❑ 56	Carlos Lee	.50	.15
❑ 57	Adam Dunn	.50	.15
❑ 58	David Riske	.50	.15
❑ 59	Carlos Guillen	.50	.15
❑ 60	Larry Bowa MG	.50	.15
❑ 61	Barry Bonds	8.00	2.40
❑ 62	Chris Woodward	.50	.15
❑ 63	Matt DeSalvo RC	1.00	.30
❑ 64	Brian Slavisky RC	.75	.23
❑ 65	Scot Shields	.50	.15
❑ 66	J.D. Drew	.50	.15
❑ 67	Erik Bedard	.50	.15
❑ 68	Scott Williamson	.50	.15
❑ 69A	M.Prior New C on Cap	.75	.23
❑ 69B	M.Prior Old C on Cap SP	8.00	2.40
❑ 70	Ken Griffey Jr.	1.50	.45
❑ 71	Kazuhito Tadano	.50	.15
❑ 72	Philadelphia Phillies TC	.50	.15
❑ 73	Jeremy Reed	.50	.15
❑ 74	Ricardo Rodriguez	.50	.15
❑ 75	Carlos Delgado	.50	.15
❑ 76	Eric Milton	.50	.15
❑ 77	Miguel Olivo	.50	.15
❑ 78A	E.Alfonzo No Socks	.50	.15
❑ 78B	E.Alfonzo Black Socks SP	8.00	2.40
❑ 79	Kazuhisa Ishii SP	8.00	2.40
❑ 80	Jason Giambi	.50	.15
❑ 81	Cliff Floyd	.50	.15
❑ 82A	Torii Hunter Twins Cap	.50	.15
❑ 82B	Torii Hunter Wash Cap SP	8.00	2.40
❑ 83	Odalis Perez	.50	.15
❑ 84	Scott Podsednik	.50	.15
❑ 85	Cleveland Indians TC	.50	.15
❑ 86	Jeff Suppan	.50	.15
❑ 87	Ray Durham	.50	.15
❑ 88	Tyler Clippard RC	1.00	.30
❑ 89	Ryan Howard	.50	.15
❑ 90	Cincinnati Reds TC	.50	.15
❑ 91	Bengie Molina	.50	.15
❑ 92	Danny Bautista	.50	.15
❑ 93	Eli Marrero	.50	.15
❑ 94	Larry Bigbie	.50	.15
❑ 95	Atlanta Braves TC	.75	.23
❑ 96	Merkin Valdez	.50	.15
❑ 97	Rocco Baldelli	.50	.15
❑ 98	Woody Williams	.50	.15
❑ 99	Jason Frasor	.50	.15
❑ 100	Baltimore Orioles TC	.50	.15
❑ 101	Ivan Rodriguez SP	8.00	2.40
❑ 102	Joe Kennedy	.50	.15
❑ 103	Mike Lowell	.50	.15
❑ 104	Armando Benitez	.50	.15
❑ 105	Craig Biggio	.75	.23
❑ 106	David DeJesus	.50	.15
❑ 107	Adrian Beltre	.50	.15
❑ 108	Phil Nevin	.50	.15
❑ 109	Cristian Guzman	.50	.15
❑ 110	Jorge Posada SP	8.00	2.40
❑ 111	Boston Red Sox TC	1.50	.45
❑ 112	Jeff Mathis	.50	.15
❑ 113	Bartolo Colon	.50	.15
❑ 114	Alex Cintron	.50	.15
❑ 115	Russ Ortiz	.50	.15
❑ 116	Doug Mientkiewicz	.50	.15
❑ 117	Placido Polanco	.50	.15
❑ 118A	M.Ordonez Black Uni	.50	.15
❑ 118B	M.Ordonez White Uni SP	8.00	2.40
❑ 119	Chris Seddon RC	.75	.23
❑ 120	Bobby Abreu	.50	.15
❑ 121	Pittsburgh Pirates TC	.50	.15
❑ 122	Dallas McPherson	.50	.15
❑ 123	Rodrigo Lopez	.50	.15
❑ 124	Mark Bellhorn	.50	.15
❑ 125A	N.Garciaparra Red Cap	1.00	.30
❑ 125B	N.Garciaparra Blue Cap SP	8.00	2.40
❑ 126	Sean Casey	.75	.23
❑ 127	Ronnie Belliard	.50	.15
❑ 128	Tom Goodwin	.50	.15
❑ 129	Preston Wilson	.50	.15
❑ 130	Andruw Jones SP	8.00	2.40
❑ 131	Roberto Alomar	.75	.23
❑ 132	John Buck	.50	.15
❑ 133	Jason LaRue	.50	.15
❑ 134	St. Louis Cardinals TC	1.00	.30
❑ 135A	Alex Rodriguez Fldg SP	12.00	3.60
❑ 135B	Alex Rodriguez At Bat SP	12.00	3.60
❑ 136	Nate Robertson	.50	.15
❑ 137	Juan Pierre	.50	.15
❑ 138	Morgan Ensberg	.50	.15
❑ 139	Vinny Castilla	.50	.15
❑ 140	Jake Dittler	.50	.15
❑ 141	Chan Ho Park	.50	.15
❑ 142	Felix Hernandez	3.00	.90
❑ 143	Jason Isringhausen	.50	.15
❑ 144	Dustan Mohr	.50	.15
❑ 145	Khalil Greene	.75	.23
❑ 146	Minnesota Twins TC	.50	.15
❑ 147	Vicente Padilla	.50	.15
❑ 148	Oliver Perez	.50	.15
❑ 149	Brian Giles	.50	.15
❑ 150	Shawn Green	.50	.15
❑ 151	Matt Lawton	.50	.15
❑ 152	Casey Blake	.50	.15
❑ 153	Frank Thomas	1.00	.30
❑ 154	Orlando Hernandez	.50	.15
❑ 155A	Eric Chavez Green Cap	.50	.15
❑ 155B	Eric Chavez Blue Cap SP	8.00	2.40
❑ 156	Chase Utley	.50	.15
❑ 157	John Olerud	.50	.15
❑ 158	Adam Eaton	.50	.15
❑ 159	Josh Fogg	.50	.15
❑ 160	Michael Tucker	.50	.15
❑ 161	Kevin Brown	.50	.15
❑ 162	Bobby Crosby	.50	.15
❑ 163	Jason Schmidt	.50	.15
❑ 164	Shannon Stewart	.50	.15
❑ 165	Tony Womack	.50	.15
❑ 166	Los Angeles Dodgers TC	1.00	.30
❑ 167	Franklin Gutierrez	.50	.15
❑ 168	Ted Lilly	.50	.15
❑ 169	Mark Teixeira	.75	.23
❑ 170	Matt Morris	.50	.15
❑ 171	Bucky Jacobsen	.50	.15
❑ 172	Steve Doetsch RC	1.00	.30
❑ 173	Jeff Weaver	.50	.15
❑ 174	Tony Graffanino	.50	.15
❑ 175	Jeff Bagwell	.75	.23
❑ 176	Carl Pavano	.50	.15
❑ 177	Junior Spivey	.50	.15
❑ 178	Carlos Silva	.50	.15
❑ 179	Tim Redding	.50	.15
❑ 180	Brett Myers	.50	.15
❑ 181	Mike Mussina	.75	.23
❑ 182	Richard Hidalgo	.50	.15
❑ 183	Nick Johnson	.50	.15
❑ 184	Lew Ford	.50	.15
❑ 185	Barry Zito	.50	.15
❑ 186	Jimmy Rollins	.50	.15
❑ 187	Jack Wilson	.50	.15
❑ 188	Chicago White Sox TC	.50	.15

❑ 189 Guillermo Quiroz .50 .15
❑ 190 Mark Hendrickson .50 .15
❑ 191 Jeremy Bonderman .50 .15
❑ 192 Jason Jennings .50 .15
❑ 193 Paul Lo Duca .50 .15
❑ 194 A.J. Burnett .50 .15
❑ 195 Ken Harvey .50 .15
❑ 196 Geoff Jenkins .50 .15
❑ 197 Joe Mays .50 .15
❑ 198 Jose Vidro .50 .15
❑ 199 David Wright 2.00 .60
❑ 200 Randy Johnson 1.00 .30
❑ 201 Jeff DaVanon .50 .15
❑ 202 Paul Byrd .50 .15
❑ 203 David Ortiz 1.00 .30
❑ 204 Kyle Farnsworth .50 .15
❑ 205 Keith Foulke .50 .15
❑ 206 Joe Crede .50 .15
❑ 207 Austin Kearns .50 .15
❑ 208 Jody Gerut .50 .15
❑ 209 Shawn Chacon .50 .15
❑ 210 Carlos Pena .50 .15
❑ 211 Luis Castillo .50 .15
❑ 212 Chris Denorfia RC 1.00 .30
❑ 213 Detroit Tigers TC .50 .15
❑ 214 Aubrey Huff .50 .15
❑ 215 Brad Fullmer .50 .15
❑ 216 Frank Catalanotto .50 .15
❑ 217 Raul Ibanez .50 .15
❑ 218 Ryan Klesko .50 .15
❑ 219 Octavio Dotel .50 .15
❑ 220 Rob Mackowiak .50 .15
❑ 221 Scott Hatteberg .50 .15
❑ 222 Pat Burrell .50 .15
❑ 223 Bernie Williams .75 .23
❑ 224 Kris Benson .50 .15
❑ 225 Eric Gagne .50 .15
❑ 226 San Francisco Giants TC 1.00 .30
❑ 227 Roy Oswalt .50 .15
❑ 228 Josh Beckett .50 .15
❑ 229 Lee Mazzilli MG .50 .15
❑ 230 Rickie Weeks .50 .15
❑ 231 Troy Glaus .50 .15
❑ 232 Chone Figgins .50 .15
❑ 233 John Thomson .50 .15
❑ 234 Trot Nixon .50 .15
❑ 235 Brad Penny .50 .15
❑ 236 Oakland A's TC .50 .15
❑ 237 Miguel Batista .50 .15
❑ 238 Ryan Drese .50 .15
❑ 239 Aaron Miles .50 .15
❑ 240 Randy Wolf .50 .15
❑ 241 Brian Lawrence .50 .15
❑ 242 A.J. Pierzynski .50 .15
❑ 243 Jamie Moyer .50 .15
❑ 244 Chris Carpenter .50 .15
❑ 245 So Taguchi .50 .15
❑ 246 Rob Bell .50 .15
❑ 247 Francisco Cordero .50 .15
❑ 248 Tom Glavine .75 .23
❑ 249 Jermaine Dye .50 .15
❑ 250 Cliff Lee .50 .15
❑ 251 New York Yankees TC 1.50 .45
❑ 252 Vernon Wells .50 .15
❑ 253 R.A. Dickey .50 .15
❑ 254 Larry Walker .75 .23
❑ 255 Randy Winn .50 .15
❑ 256 Pedro Feliz .50 .15
❑ 257 Mark Loretta .50 .15
❑ 258 Tim Worrell .50 .15
❑ 259 Kip Wells .50 .15
❑ 260 Cesar Izturis SP 8.00 2.40
❑ 261A Carlos Beltran Fldg .50 .15
❑ 261B Carlos Beltran At Bat SP 8.00 2.40
❑ 262 Juan Encarnacion .50 .15
❑ 263 Luis A. Gonzalez .50 .15
❑ 264 Grady Sizemore .50 .15
❑ 265 Paul Wilson .50 .15
❑ 266 Mark Buehrle .50 .15
❑ 267 Todd Hollandsworth .50 .15
❑ 268 Orlando Cabrera .50 .15
❑ 269 Sidney Ponson .50 .15
❑ 270 Mike Hampton .50 .15
❑ 271 Luis Gonzalez .50 .15
❑ 272 Brendan Donnelly .50 .15
❑ 273A Chipper Jones Slide 1.00 .30
❑ 273B Chipper Jones Fldg SP 8.00 2.40
❑ 274 Brandon Webb .50 .15
❑ 275 Marty Cordova .50 .15
❑ 276 Greg Maddux 1.50 .45
❑ 277 Jose Contreras .50 .15
❑ 278 Aaron Harang .50 .15
❑ 279 Coco Crisp .50 .15
❑ 280 Bobby Higginson .50 .15
❑ 281 Guillermo Mota .50 .15
❑ 282 Andy Pettitte .75 .23
❑ 283 Jeremy West RC 1.00 .30
❑ 284 Craig Brazell .50 .15
❑ 285 Eric Hinske .50 .15
❑ 286A Hank Blalock Hitting .50 .15
❑ 286B Hank Blalock Fldg SP 8.00 2.40
❑ 287 B.J. Upton .75 .23
❑ 288 Jason Marquis .50 .15
❑ 289 Matt Herges .50 .15
❑ 290 Ramon Hernandez .50 .15
❑ 291 Marlon Byrd .50 .15
❑ 292 Ryan Sweeney SP RC 8.00 2.40
❑ 293 Esteban Loaiza .50 .15
❑ 294 Al Leiter .50 .15
❑ 295 Alex Gonzalez .50 .15
❑ 296A J.Santana Twins Cap .75 .23
❑ 296B J.Santana Wash Cap SP 8.00 2.40
❑ 297 Milton Bradley .50 .15
❑ 298 Mike Sweeney .50 .15
❑ 299 Wade Miller .50 .15
❑ 300A Sammy Sosa Hitting 1.00 .30
❑ 300B Sammy Sosa Standing SP 8.00 2.40
❑ 301 Wily Mo Pena .50 .15
❑ 302 Tim Wakefield .50 .15
❑ 303 Rafael Palmeiro .75 .23
❑ 304 Rafael Furcal .50 .15
❑ 305 David Eckstein .50 .15
❑ 306 David Segui .50 .15
❑ 307 Kevin Millar .50 .15
❑ 308 Matt Clement .50 .15
❑ 309 Wade Robinson RC .75 .23
❑ 310 Brad Radke .50 .15
❑ 311 Steve Finley .50 .15
❑ 312A Lance Berkman Hitting .50 .15
❑ 312B Lance Berkman Fldg SP 8.00 2.40
❑ 313 Joe Randa .50 .15
❑ 314 Miguel Cabrera .75 .23
❑ 315 Billy Koch .50 .15
❑ 316 Alex Sanchez .50 .15
❑ 317 Chin-Hui Tsao .50 .15
❑ 318 Omar Vizquel .75 .23
❑ 319 Ryan Freel .50 .15
❑ 320 LaTroy Hawkins .50 .15
❑ 321 Aaron Rowand .50 .15
❑ 322 Paul Konerko .50 .15
❑ 323 Joe Borowski .50 .15
❑ 324 Jarrod Washburn .50 .15
❑ 325 Jaret Wright .50 .15
❑ 326 Johnny Damon .75 .23
❑ 327 Corey Patterson .50 .15
❑ 328 Travis Hafner .50 .15
❑ 329 Shingo Takatsu .50 .15
❑ 330 Dmitri Young .50 .15
❑ 331 Matt Holliday .50 .15
❑ 332 Jeff Kent .50 .15
❑ 333 Desi Relaford .50 .15
❑ 334 Jose Hernandez .50 .15
❑ 335 Lyle Overbay .50 .15
❑ 336 Jacque Jones .50 .15
❑ 337 Termel Sledge .50 .15
❑ 338 Victor Zambrano .50 .15
❑ 339 Gary Sheffield .50 .15
❑ 340 Brad Wilkerson .50 .15
❑ 341 Ian Kinsler RC 1.25 .35
❑ 342 Jesse Crain .50 .15
❑ 343 Orlando Hudson .50 .15
❑ 344 Laynce Nix .50 .15
❑ 345 Jose Cruz Jr. .50 .15
❑ 346 Edgar Renteria .50 .15
❑ 347 Eddie Guardado .50 .15
❑ 348 Jerome Williams .50 .15
❑ 349 Trevor Hoffman .50 .15
❑ 350 Mike Piazza 1.00 .30
❑ 351 Jason Kendall .50 .15
❑ 352 Kevin Millwood .50 .15
❑ 353A Tim Hudson Atl Cap .50 .15
❑ 353B Tim Hudson Milw Cap SP 8.00 2.40
❑ 354 Paul Quantrill .50 .15
❑ 355 Jon Lieber .50 .15
❑ 356 Braden Looper .50 .15
❑ 357 Chad Cordero .50 .15
❑ 358 Joe Nathan .50 .15
❑ 359 Doug Davis .50 .15
❑ 360 Ian Bladergroen RC 1.00 .30
❑ 361 Val Majewski .50 .15
❑ 362 Francisco Rodriguez .50 .15
❑ 363 Kelvim Escobar .50 .15
❑ 364 Marcus Giles .50 .15
❑ 365 Darren Fenster RC .75 .23
❑ 366 David Bell .50 .15
❑ 367 Shea Hillenbrand .50 .15
❑ 368 Manny Ramirez .75 .23
❑ 369 Ben Broussard .50 .15
❑ 370 Luis Ramirez RC .75 .23
❑ 371 Dustin Hermanson .50 .15
❑ 372 Akinori Otsuka .50 .15
❑ 373 Chadd Blasko RC 1.00 .30
❑ 374 Delmon Young .50 .15
❑ 375 Michael Young .50 .15
❑ 376 Bret Boone .50 .15
❑ 377 Jake Peavy .50 .15
❑ 378 Matthew Lindstrom RC .75 .23
❑ 379 Sean Burroughs .50 .15
❑ 380 Rich Harden .50 .15
❑ 381 Chris Roberson RC .75 .23
❑ 382 John Lackey .50 .15
❑ 383 Johnny Estrada .50 .15
❑ 384 Matt Rogelstad RC .75 .23
❑ 385 Toby Hall .50 .15
❑ 386 Adam LaRoche .50 .15
❑ 387 Bill Hall .50 .15
❑ 388 Tim Salmon .50 .15
❑ 389A Curt Schilling Throw .75 .23
❑ 389B Curt Schilling Glove Up SP 8.00 2.40
❑ 390 Michael Barrett .50 .15
❑ 391 Jose Acevedo .50 .15
❑ 392 Nate Schierholtz .75 .23
❑ 393 J.T. Snow Jr. .50 .15
❑ 394 Mark Redman .50 .15
❑ 395 Ryan Madson .50 .15
❑ 396 Kevin West RC .75 .23
❑ 397 Ramon Ortiz .50 .15
❑ 398 Derek Lowe SP 8.00 2.40
❑ 399 Kerry Wood SP 8.00 2.40
❑ 400 Derek Jeter SP 15.00 4.50
❑ 401 Livan Hernandez SP 8.00 2.40
❑ 402 Casey Kotchman SP 8.00 2.40
❑ 403 Chaz Lytle SP RC 8.00 2.40
❑ 404 Alexis Rios SP 8.00 2.40
❑ 405 Scott Spiezio SP 8.00 2.40
❑ 406 Craig Wilson SP 8.00 2.40
❑ 407 Felix Rodriguez SP 8.00 2.40
❑ 408 D'Angelo Jimenez SP 8.00 2.40
❑ 409 Rondell White SP 8.00 2.40
❑ 410 Shawn Estes SP 8.00 2.40
❑ 411 Troy Percival SP 8.00 2.40
❑ 412 Melvin Mora SP 8.00 2.40
❑ 413 Aramis Ramirez SP 8.00 2.40
❑ 414 Carl Everett SP 8.00 2.40
❑ 415 Elvys Quezada SP RC 8.00 2.40
❑ 416 Ben Sheets SP 8.00 2.40
❑ 417 Matt Stairs SP 8.00 2.40
❑ 418 Adam Everett SP 8.00 2.40
❑ 419 Jason Johnson SP 8.00 2.40
❑ 420 Billy Butler SP RC 10.00 3.00
❑ 421 Justin Morneau SP 8.00 2.40
❑ 422 Jose Reyes SP 8.00 2.40
❑ 423 Mariano Rivera SP 8.00 2.40
❑ 424 Jose Vaquedano SP RC 8.00 2.40
❑ 425 Gabe Gross SP 8.00 2.40
❑ 426 Scott Rolen SP 8.00 2.40
❑ 427 Ty Wigginton SP 8.00 2.40
❑ 428 James Jurries SP RC 8.00 2.40
❑ 429 Pedro Martinez SP 8.00 2.40
❑ 430 Mark Grudzielanek SP 8.00 2.40
❑ 431 Josh Phelps SP 8.00 2.40
❑ 432 Ryan Goleski SP RC 8.00 2.40
❑ 433 Mike Matheny SP 8.00 2.40
❑ 434 Bobby Kielty SP 8.00 2.40
❑ 435 Tony Batista SP 8.00 2.40
❑ 436 Corey Koskie SP 8.00 2.40
❑ 437 Brad Lidge SP 8.00 2.40
❑ 438 Dontrelle Willis SP 8.00 2.40

❑ 439 Angel Berroa SP 8.00 2.40
❑ 440 Jason Kubel SP 8.00 2.40
❑ 441 Roy Halladay SP 8.00 2.40
❑ 442 Brian Roberts SP 8.00 2.40
❑ 443 Bill Mueller SP 8.00 2.40
❑ 444 Adam Kennedy SP 8.00 2.40
❑ 445 Brandon Moss SP RC 8.00 2.40
❑ 446 Sean Burnett SP 8.00 2.40
❑ 447 Eric Byrnes SP 8.00 2.40
❑ 448 Matt Campbell SP RC 8.00 2.40
❑ 449 Ryan Webb SP 8.00 2.40
❑ 450 Jose Valentin SP 8.00 2.40
❑ 451 Jake Westbrook SP 8.00 2.40
❑ 452 Glen Perkins SP RC 8.00 2.40
❑ 453 Alex Gonzalez SP 8.00 2.40
❑ 454 Jeromy Burnitz SP 8.00 2.40
❑ 455 Zack Greinke SP 8.00 2.40
❑ 456 Sean Marshall SP RC 8.00 2.40
❑ 457 Erubiel Durazo SP 8.00 2.40
❑ 458 Michael Cuddyer SP 8.00 2.40
❑ 459 Hee Seop Choi SP 8.00 2.40
❑ 460 Melky Cabrera SP RC 8.00 2.40
❑ 461 Jerry Hairston Jr. SP 8.00 2.40
❑ 462 Moises Alou SP 8.00 2.40
❑ 463 Michael Rogers SP RC .. 8.00 2.40
❑ 464 Javy Lopez SP 8.00 2.40
❑ 465 Freddy Garcia SP 8.00 2.40
❑ 466 Brett Harper SP RC 8.00 2.40
❑ 467 Juan Gonzalez SP 8.00 2.40
❑ 468 Kevin Melillo SP RC 8.00 2.40
❑ 469 Todd Walker SP 8.00 2.40
❑ 470 C.C. Sabathia SP 8.00 2.40
❑ 471 Kole Strayhorn SP RC 8.00 2.40
❑ 472 Mark Kotsay SP 8.00 2.40
❑ 473 Javier Vazquez SP 8.00 2.40
❑ 474 Mike Cameron SP 8.00 2.40
❑ 475 Wes Swackhamer SP RC 8.00 2.40

2005 Topps Opening Day

	Nm-Mt	Ex-Mt
COMPLETE SET (165)	40.00	12.00
COMMON CARD (1-165)	.40	.12

ISSUED IN OPENING DAY PACKS..

❑ 1 Alex Rodriguez .... 1.50 .45
❑ 2 Placido Polanco .... .40 .12
❑ 3 Torii Hunter .... .40 .12
❑ 4 Lyle Overbay .... .40 .12
❑ 5 Johnny Damon .... .60 .18
❑ 6 Mike Cameron .... .40 .12
❑ 7 Ichiro Suzuki .... 2.00 .60
❑ 8 Francisco Rodriguez .... .40 .12
❑ 9 Bobby Crosby .... .40 .12
❑ 10 Sammy Sosa .... 1.00 .30
❑ 11 Randy Wolf .... .40 .12
❑ 12 Jason Bay .... .40 .12
❑ 13 Mike Lieberthal .... .40 .12
❑ 14 Paul Konerko .... .40 .12
❑ 15 Brian Giles .... .40 .12
❑ 16 Luis Gonzalez .... .40 .12
❑ 17 Jim Edmonds .... .60 .18
❑ 18 Carlos Lee .... .40 .12
❑ 19 Corey Patterson .... .40 .12
❑ 20 Hank Blalock .... .40 .12
❑ 21 Sean Casey .... .60 .18
❑ 22 Dmitri Young .... .40 .12
❑ 23 Mark Mulder .... .40 .12
❑ 24 Bobby Abreu .... .40 .12
❑ 25 Jim Thome .... .60 .18
❑ 26 Jason Kendall .... .40 .12
❑ 27 Jason Giambi .... .40 .12
❑ 28 Vinny Castilla .... .40 .12
❑ 29 Tony Batista .... .40 .12
❑ 30 Ivan Rodriguez .... .60 .18
❑ 31 Craig Biggio .... .60 .18
❑ 32 Chris Carpenter .... .40 .12
❑ 33 Adrian Beltre .... .40 .12
❑ 34 Scott Podsednik .... .40 .12
❑ 35 Cliff Floyd .... .40 .12
❑ 36 Chad Tracy .... .40 .12
❑ 37 John Smoltz .... .60 .18
❑ 38 Shingo Takatsu .... .40 .12
❑ 39 Jack Wilson .... .40 .12
❑ 40 Gary Sheffield .... .40 .12
❑ 41 Lance Berkman .... .40 .12
❑ 42 Carl Crawford .... .40 .12
❑ 43 Carlos Guillen .... .40 .12
❑ 44 David Bell .... .40 .12
❑ 45 Kazuo Matsui .... .40 .12
❑ 46 Jason Schmidt .... .40 .12
❑ 47 Jason Marquis .... .40 .12
❑ 48 Melvin Mora .... .40 .12
❑ 49 David Ortiz .... 1.00 .30
❑ 50 Andruw Jones .... .60 .18
❑ 51 Miguel Tejada .... .40 .12
❑ 52 Bartolo Colon .... .40 .12
❑ 53 Derrek Lee .... .60 .18
❑ 54 Eric Gagne .... .40 .12
❑ 55 Miguel Cabrera .... .60 .18
❑ 56 Travis Hafner .... .40 .12
❑ 57 Jose Valentin .... .40 .12
❑ 58 Mark Prior .... .60 .18
❑ 59 Phil Nevin .... .40 .12
❑ 60 Jose Vidro .... .40 .12
❑ 61 Khalil Greene .... .60 .18
❑ 62 Carlos Zambrano .... .40 .12
❑ 63 Erubiel Durazo .... .40 .12
❑ 64 Michael Young .... .40 .12
❑ 65 Woody Williams .... .40 .12
❑ 66 Edgardo Alfonzo .... .40 .12
❑ 67 Troy Glaus .... .40 .12
❑ 68 Garret Anderson .... .40 .12
❑ 69 Richie Sexson .... .40 .12
❑ 70 Curt Schilling .... .60 .18
❑ 71 Randy Johnson .... 1.00 .30
❑ 72 Chipper Jones .... 1.00 .30
❑ 73 J.D. Drew .... .40 .12
❑ 74 Russ Ortiz .... .40 .12
❑ 75 Frank Thomas .... 1.00 .30
❑ 76 Jimmy Rollins .... .40 .12
❑ 77 Barry Zito .... .40 .12
❑ 78 Rafael Palmeiro .... .60 .18
❑ 79 Brad Wilkerson .... .40 .12
❑ 80 Adam Dunn .... .40 .12
❑ 81 Doug Mientkiewicz .... .40 .12
❑ 82 Manny Ramirez .... .60 .18
❑ 83 Pedro Martinez .... .60 .18
❑ 84 Moises Alou .... .40 .12
❑ 85 Mike Sweeney .... .40 .12
❑ 86 Boston Red Sox WC .... 1.00 .30
❑ 87 Matt Clement .... .40 .12
❑ 88 Nomar Garciaparra .... 1.00 .30
❑ 89 Magglio Ordonez .... .40 .12
❑ 90 Bret Boone .... .40 .12
❑ 91 Mark Loretta .... .40 .12
❑ 92 Jose Contreras .... .40 .12
❑ 93 Randy Winn .... .40 .12
❑ 94 Austin Kearns .... .40 .12
❑ 95 Ken Griffey Jr. .... 1.50 .45
❑ 96 Jake Westbrook .... .40 .12
❑ 97 Kazuhito Tadano .... .40 .12
❑ 98 C.C. Sabathia .... .40 .12
❑ 99 Todd Helton .... .60 .18
❑ 100 Albert Pujols .... 2.00 .60
❑ 101 Jose Molina .... .40 .12
Bengie Molina
❑ 102 Aaron Miles .... .40 .12
❑ 103 Mike Lowell .... .40 .12
❑ 104 Paul Lo Duca .... .40 .12
❑ 105 Juan Pierre .... .40 .12
❑ 106 Dontrelle Willis .... .40 .12
❑ 107 Jeff Bagwell .... .60 .18
❑ 108 Carlos Beltran .... .40 .12
❑ 109 Ronnie Belliard .... .40 .12
❑ 110 Roy Oswalt .... .40 .12
❑ 111 Zack Greinke .... .60 .18
❑ 112 Steve Finley .... .40 .12
❑ 113 Kazuhisa Ishii .... .40 .12
❑ 114 Justin Morneau .... .40 .12
❑ 115 Ben Sheets .... .40 .12
❑ 116 Johan Santana .... .60 .18
❑ 117 Billy Wagner .... .40 .12
❑ 118 Mariano Rivera .... .60 .18
❑ 119 Corey Koskie .... .40 .12
❑ 120 Akinori Otsuka .... .40 .12
❑ 121 Joe Mauer .... .40 .12
❑ 122 Jacque Jones .... .40 .12
❑ 123 Joe Nathan .... .40 .12
❑ 124 Nick Johnson .... .40 .12
❑ 125 Vernon Wells .... .40 .12
❑ 126 Mike Piazza .... 1.00 .30
❑ 127 Jose Guillen .... .40 .12
❑ 128 Jose Reyes .... .40 .12
❑ 129 Marcus Giles .... .40 .12
❑ 130 Javy Lopez .... .40 .12
❑ 131 Kevin Millar .... .40 .12
❑ 132 Jorge Posada .... .60 .18
❑ 133 Carl Pavano .... .40 .12
❑ 134 Bernie Williams .... .60 .18
❑ 135 Kerry Wood .... .40 .12
❑ 136 Matt Holliday .... .40 .12
❑ 137 Kevin Brown .... .40 .12
❑ 138 Derek Jeter .... 2.00 .60
❑ 139 Barry Bonds .... 2.50 .75
❑ 140 Jeff Kent .... .40 .12
❑ 141 Mark Kotsay .... .40 .12
❑ 142 Shawn Green .... .40 .12
❑ 143 Tim Hudson .... .40 .12
❑ 144 Shannon Stewart .... .40 .12
❑ 145 Pat Burrell .... .40 .12
❑ 146 Gavin Floyd .... .40 .12
❑ 147 Mike Mussina .... .60 .18
❑ 148 Eric Chavez .... .40 .12
❑ 149 Jon Lieber .... .40 .12
❑ 150 Vladimir Guerrero .... 1.00 .30
❑ 151 Vicente Padilla .... .40 .12
❑ 152 Ryan Klesko .... .40 .12
❑ 153 Jake Peavy .... .40 .12
❑ 154 Scott Rolen .... .60 .18
❑ 155 Greg Maddux .... 1.50 .45
❑ 156 Edgar Renteria .... .40 .12
❑ 157 Larry Walker .... .60 .18
❑ 158 Scott Kazmir .... .40 .12
❑ 159 B.J. Upton .... .60 .18
❑ 160 Mark Teixeira .... .60 .18
❑ 161 Ken Harvey .... .40 .12
❑ 162 Alfonso Soriano .... .40 .12
❑ 163 Carlos Delgado .... .40 .12
❑ 164 Alexis Rios .... .40 .12
❑ 165 Checklist .... .40 .12

2002 Topps Pristine

	Nm-Mt	Ex-Mt
COMMON CARD (1-140)	1.25	.35
COMMON CARD (141-150)	2.00	.60
COMMON C CARD (151-210)	1.25	.35
COMMON U CARD (151-210)	2.50	.75
COMMON R CARD (151-210)	4.00	1.20

❑ 1 Alex Rodriguez 5.00 1.50
❑ 2 Carlos Delgado .... 1.25 .35

❑ 3 Jimmy Rollins	1.25	.35
❑ 4 Jason Kendall	1.25	.35
❑ 5 John Olerud	1.25	.35
❑ 6 Albert Pujols	6.00	1.80
❑ 7 Curt Schilling	1.25	.35
❑ 8 Gary Sheffield	1.25	.35
❑ 9 Johnny Damon Sox	2.00	.60
❑ 10 Ichiro Suzuki	6.00	1.80
❑ 11 Pat Burrell	1.25	.35
❑ 12 Garret Anderson	1.25	.35
❑ 13 Andruw Jones	2.00	.60
❑ 14 Kerry Wood	1.25	.35
❑ 15 Kenny Lofton	1.25	.35
❑ 16 Adam Dunn	1.25	.35
❑ 17 Juan Pierre	1.25	.35
❑ 18 Josh Beckett	1.25	.35
❑ 19 Roy Oswalt	1.25	.35
❑ 20 Derek Jeter	8.00	2.40
❑ 21 Jose Vidro	1.25	.35
❑ 22 Richie Sexson	1.25	.35
❑ 23 Mike Sweeney	1.25	.35
❑ 24 Jeff Kent	1.25	.35
❑ 25 Jason Giambi	1.25	.35
❑ 26 Bret Boone	1.25	.35
❑ 27 J.D. Drew	1.25	.35
❑ 28 Shannon Stewart	1.25	.35
❑ 29 Miguel Tejada	1.25	.35
❑ 30 Barry Bonds	8.00	2.40
❑ 31 Randy Johnson	3.00	.90
❑ 32 Pedro Martinez	2.00	.60
❑ 33 Magglio Ordonez	1.25	.35
❑ 34 Todd Helton	2.00	.60
❑ 35 Craig Biggio	2.00	.60
❑ 36 Shawn Green	1.25	.35
❑ 37 Vladimir Guerrero	3.00	.90
❑ 38 Mo Vaughn	1.25	.35
❑ 39 Alfonso Soriano	1.25	.35
❑ 40 Barry Zito	1.25	.35
❑ 41 Aramis Ramirez	1.25	.35
❑ 42 Ryan Klesko	1.25	.35
❑ 43 Ruben Sierra	1.25	.35
❑ 44 Tino Martinez	2.00	.60
❑ 45 Toby Hall	1.25	.35
❑ 46 Ivan Rodriguez	2.00	.60
❑ 47 Raul Mondesi	1.25	.35
❑ 48 Carlos Pena	1.25	.35
❑ 49 Darin Erstad	1.25	.35
❑ 50 Sammy Sosa	3.00	.90
❑ 51 Bartolo Colon	1.25	.35
❑ 52 Robert Fick	1.25	.35
❑ 53 Cliff Floyd	1.25	.35
❑ 54 Brian Jordan	1.25	.35
❑ 55 Torii Hunter	1.25	.35
❑ 56 Roberto Alomar	2.00	.60
❑ 57 Roger Clemens	6.00	1.80
❑ 58 Mark Mulder	1.25	.35
❑ 59 Brian Giles	1.25	.35
❑ 60 Mike Piazza	5.00	1.50
❑ 61 Rich Aurilia	1.25	.35
❑ 62 Freddy Garcia	1.25	.35
❑ 63 Jim Edmonds	2.00	.60
❑ 64 Eric Hinske	1.25	.35
❑ 65 Vicente Padilla	1.25	.35
❑ 66 Javier Vazquez	1.25	.35
❑ 67 Cristian Guzman	1.25	.35
❑ 68 Paul Lo Duca	1.25	.35
❑ 69 Bobby Abreu	1.25	.35
❑ 70 Nomar Garciaparra	5.00	1.50
❑ 71 Troy Glaus	1.25	.35
❑ 72 Chipper Jones	3.00	.90
❑ 73 Scott Rolen	2.00	.60
❑ 74 Lance Berkman	1.25	.35
❑ 75 C.C. Sabathia	1.25	.35
❑ 76 Bernie Williams	2.00	.60
❑ 77 Rafael Palmeiro	2.00	.60
❑ 78 Phil Nevin	1.25	.35
❑ 79 Kazuhiro Sasaki	1.25	.35
❑ 80 Eric Chavez	1.25	.35
❑ 81 Jorge Posada	2.00	.60
❑ 82 Edgardo Alfonzo	1.25	.35
❑ 83 Geoff Jenkins	1.25	.35
❑ 84 Preston Wilson	1.25	.35
❑ 85 Jim Thome	2.00	.60
❑ 86 Frank Thomas	3.00	.90
❑ 87 Jeff Bagwell	2.00	.60
❑ 88 Greg Maddux	5.00	1.50
❑ 89 Mark Prior	3.00	.90
❑ 90 Larry Walker	1.25	.35
❑ 91 Luis Gonzalez	1.25	.35
❑ 92 Tim Hudson	1.25	.35
❑ 93 Tsuyoshi Shinjo	1.25	.35
❑ 94 Juan Gonzalez	1.25	.35
❑ 95 Shea Hillenbrand	1.25	.35
❑ 96 Paul Konerko	1.25	.35
❑ 97 Tom Glavine	2.00	.60
❑ 98 Marty Cordova	1.25	.35
❑ 99 Moises Alou	1.25	.35
❑ 100 Ken Griffey Jr.	5.00	1.50
❑ 101 Hank Blalock	2.00	.60
❑ 102 Matt Morris	1.25	.35
❑ 103 Robb Nen	1.25	.35
❑ 104 Mike Cameron	1.25	.35
❑ 105 Mark Buehrle	1.25	.35
❑ 106 Sean Burroughs	1.25	.35
❑ 107 Orlando Cabrera	1.25	.35
❑ 108 Jeromy Burnitz	1.25	.35
❑ 109 Juan Uribe	1.25	.35
❑ 110 Eric Milton	1.25	.35
❑ 111 Carlos Lee	1.25	.35
❑ 112 Jose Mesa	1.25	.35
❑ 113 Morgan Ensberg	1.25	.35
❑ 114 Derek Lowe	1.25	.35
❑ 115 Juan Cruz	1.25	.35
❑ 116 Mike Lieberthal	1.25	.35
❑ 117 Armando Benitez	1.25	.35
❑ 118 Vinny Castilla	1.25	.35
❑ 119 Russ Ortiz	1.25	.35
❑ 120 Mike Lowell	1.25	.35
❑ 121 Corey Patterson	1.25	.35
❑ 122 Mike Mussina	2.00	.60
❑ 123 Rafael Furcal	1.25	.35
❑ 124 Mark Grace	2.00	.60
❑ 125 Ben Sheets	1.25	.35
❑ 126 John Smoltz	2.00	.60
❑ 127 Fred McGriff	2.00	.60
❑ 128 Nick Johnson	1.25	.35
❑ 129 J.T. Snow	1.25	.35
❑ 130 Jeff Cirillo	1.25	.35
❑ 131 Trevor Hoffman	1.25	.35
❑ 132 Kevin Brown	1.25	.35
❑ 133 Mariano Rivera	2.00	.60
❑ 134 Marlon Anderson	1.25	.35
❑ 135 Al Leiter	1.25	.35
❑ 136 Doug Mientkiewicz	1.25	.35
❑ 137 Eric Karros	1.25	.35
❑ 138 Bobby Higginson	1.25	.35
❑ 139 Sean Casey	2.00	.60
❑ 140 Troy Percival	1.25	.35
❑ 141 Willie Mays	6.00	1.80
❑ 142 Carl Yastrzemski	5.00	1.50
❑ 143 Stan Musial	5.00	1.50
❑ 144 Harmon Killebrew	3.00	.90
❑ 145 Mike Schmidt	6.00	1.80
❑ 146 Duke Snider	2.00	.60
❑ 147 Brooks Robinson	2.00	.60
❑ 148 Frank Robinson	2.00	.60
❑ 149 Nolan Ryan	8.00	2.40
❑ 150 Reggie Jackson	2.00	.60
❑ 151 Joe Mauer C RC	8.00	2.40
❑ 152 Joe Mauer U	15.00	4.50
❑ 153 Joe Mauer R	25.00	7.50
❑ 154 Colt Griffin C RC	1.25	.35
❑ 155 Colt Griffin U	2.50	.75
❑ 156 Colt Griffin R	4.00	1.20
❑ 157 Jason Simontacchi C RC	1.25	.35
❑ 158 Jason Simontacchi U	2.50	.75
❑ 159 Jason Simontacchi R	4.00	1.20
❑ 160 Casey Kotchman C RC	5.00	1.50
❑ 161 Casey Kotchman U	10.00	3.00
❑ 162 Casey Kotchman R	15.00	4.50
❑ 163 Greg Sain C RC	1.25	.35
❑ 164 Greg Sain U	2.50	.75
❑ 165 Greg Sain R	4.00	1.20
❑ 166 David Wright C RC	20.00	6.00
❑ 167 David Wright U	30.00	9.00
❑ 168 David Wright R	40.00	12.00
❑ 169 Scott Hairston C RC	2.00	.60
❑ 170 Scott Hairston U	4.00	1.20
❑ 171 Scott Hairston R	6.00	1.80
❑ 172 Rolando Viera C RC	1.25	.35
❑ 173 Rolando Viera U	2.50	.75
❑ 174 Rolando Viera R	4.00	1.20
❑ 175 Tyrell Godwin C RC	1.25	.35
❑ 176 Tyrell Godwin U	2.50	.75
❑ 177 Tyrell Godwin R	4.00	1.20
❑ 178 Jesus Cota C RC	1.25	.35
❑ 179 Jesus Cota U	2.50	.75
❑ 180 Jesus Cota R	4.00	1.20
❑ 181 Dan Johnson C RC	8.00	2.40
❑ 182 Dan Johnson U	15.00	4.50
❑ 183 Dan Johnson R	25.00	7.50
❑ 184 Mario Ramos C RC	1.25	.35
❑ 185 Mario Ramos U	2.50	.75
❑ 186 Mario Ramos R	4.00	1.20
❑ 187 Jason Dubois C RC	2.00	.60
❑ 188 Jason Dubois U	4.00	1.20
❑ 189 Jason Dubois R	6.00	1.80
❑ 190 Jonny Gomes C RC	6.00	1.80
❑ 191 Jonny Gomes U	12.00	3.60
❑ 192 Jonny Gomes R	20.00	6.00
❑ 193 Chris Snelling C RC	2.00	.60
❑ 194 Chris Snelling U	4.00	1.20
❑ 195 Chris Snelling R	6.00	1.80
❑ 196 Hansel Izquierdo C RC	1.25	.35
❑ 197 Hansel Izquierdo U	2.50	.75
❑ 198 Hansel Izquierdo R	4.00	1.20
❑ 199 So Taguchi C RC	2.00	.60
❑ 200 So Taguchi U	4.00	1.20
❑ 201 So Taguchi R	6.00	1.80
❑ 202 Kazuhisa Ishii C RC	2.00	.60
❑ 203 Kazuhisa Ishii U	4.00	1.20
❑ 204 Kazuhisa Ishii R	6.00	1.80
❑ 205 Jorge Padilla C RC	1.25	.35
❑ 206 Jorge Padilla U	2.50	.75
❑ 207 Jorge Padilla R	4.00	1.20
❑ 208 Earl Snyder C RC	1.25	.35
❑ 209 Earl Snyder U	2.50	.75
❑ 210 Earl Snyder R	4.00	1.20

2003 Topps Pristine

	MINT	NRMT
COMMON CARD (1-100)	1.50	.70
COMMON C (101-190)	1.25	.55
C 101-190 APPX. 2X EASIER THAN 1-100		.00
COMMON U (101-190)	2.50	1.10
UNCOMMON 101-190 STATED ODDS 1:2		.00
UNCOMMON PRINT 1499 SERIAL #'d SETS		.00
COMMON R (101-190)	5.00	2.20
RARE 101-190 STATED ODDS 1:6	.00	
RARE PRINT RUN 499 SERIAL #'d SETS		.00

❑ 1 Pedro Martinez	2.50	1.10
❑ 2 Derek Jeter	10.00	4.50
❑ 3 Alex Rodriguez	6.00	2.70
❑ 4 Miguel Tejada	1.50	.70
❑ 5 Nomar Garciaparra	6.00	2.70
❑ 6 Austin Kearns	1.50	.70
❑ 7 Jose Vidro	1.50	.70
❑ 8 Bret Boone	1.50	.70
❑ 9 Scott Rolen	2.50	1.10
❑ 10 Mike Sweeney	1.50	.70
❑ 11 Jason Schmidt	1.50	.70
❑ 12 Alfonso Soriano	1.50	.70
❑ 13 Tim Hudson	1.50	.70
❑ 14 A.J. Pierzynski	1.50	.70
❑ 15 Lance Berkman	1.50	.70
❑ 16 Frank Thomas	4.00	1.80
❑ 17 Gary Sheffield	1.50	.70
❑ 18 Jarrod Washburn	1.50	.70
❑ 19 Hideo Nomo	4.00	1.80

❑ 20 Barry Zito 1.50 .70
❑ 21 Kevin Millwood 1.50 .70
❑ 22 Matt Morris 1.50 .70
❑ 23 Carl Crawford 1.50 .70
❑ 24 Carlos Delgado 1.50 .70
❑ 25 Mike Piazza 6.00 2.70
❑ 26 Brad Radke 1.50 .70
❑ 27 Richie Sexson 1.50 .70
❑ 28 Kevin Brown 1.50 .70
❑ 29 Carlos Beltran 1.50 .70
❑ 30 Curt Schilling 1.50 .70
❑ 31 Chipper Jones 4.00 1.80
❑ 32 Paul Konerko 1.50 .70
❑ 33 Larry Walker 1.50 .70
❑ 34 Jeff Bagwell 2.50 1.10
❑ 35 Jason Giambi 1.50 .70
❑ 36 Mark Mulder 1.50 .70
❑ 37 Vicente Padilla 1.50 .70
❑ 38 Kris Benson 1.50 .70
❑ 39 Bernie Williams 2.50 1.10
❑ 40 Jim Thome 2.50 1.10
❑ 41 Roger Clemens 8.00 3.60
❑ 42 Roberto Alomar 2.50 1.10
❑ 43 Torii Hunter 1.50 .70
❑ 44 Bobby Abreu 1.50 .70
❑ 45 Jeff Kent 1.50 .70
❑ 46 Roy Oswalt 1.50 .70
❑ 47 Bartolo Colon 1.50 .70
❑ 48 Greg Maddux 6.00 2.70
❑ 49 Tom Glavine 2.50 1.10
❑ 50 Sammy Sosa 4.00 1.80
❑ 51 Ichiro Suzuki 8.00 3.60
❑ 52 Mark Prior 2.50 1.10
❑ 53 Manny Ramirez 2.50 1.10
❑ 54 Andruw Jones 2.50 1.10
❑ 55 Randy Johnson 4.00 1.80
❑ 56 Garret Anderson 1.50 .70
❑ 57 Roy Halladay 1.50 .70
❑ 58 Rafael Palmeiro 2.50 1.10
❑ 59 Rocco Baldelli 1.50 .70
❑ 60 Albert Pujols 8.00 3.60
❑ 61 Edgar Renteria 1.50 .70
❑ 62 John Olerud 1.50 .70
❑ 63 Rich Aurilia 1.50 .70
❑ 64 Ryan Klesko 1.50 .70
❑ 65 Brian Giles 1.50 .70
❑ 66 Eric Chavez 1.50 .70
❑ 67 Jorge Posada 2.50 1.10
❑ 68 Cliff Floyd 1.50 .70
❑ 69 Vladimir Guerrero 4.00 1.80
❑ 70 Cristian Guzman 1.50 .70
❑ 71 Raul Ibanez 1.50 .70
❑ 72 Paul Lo Duca 1.50 .70
❑ 73 A.J. Burnett 1.50 .70
❑ 74 Ken Griffey Jr. 6.00 2.70
❑ 75 Mark Buehrle 1.50 .70
❑ 76 Moises Alou 1.50 .70
❑ 77 Adam Dunn 1.50 .70
❑ 78 Tony Batista 1.50 .70
❑ 79 Troy Glaus 1.50 .70
❑ 80 Luis Gonzalez 1.50 .70
❑ 81 Shea Hillenbrand 1.50 .70
❑ 82 Kerry Wood 1.50 .70
❑ 83 Magglio Ordonez 1.50 .70
❑ 84 Omar Vizquel 2.50 1.10
❑ 85 Bobby Higginson 1.50 .70
❑ 86 Mike Lowell 1.50 .70
❑ 87 Runelvys Hernandez 1.50 .70
❑ 88 Shawn Green 1.50 .70
❑ 89 Erubiel Durazo 1.50 .70
❑ 90 Pat Burrell 1.50 .70
❑ 91 Todd Helton 2.50 1.10
❑ 92 Jim Edmonds 2.50 1.10
❑ 93 Aubrey Huff 1.50 .70
❑ 94 Eric Hinske 1.50 .70
❑ 95 Barry Bonds 10.00 4.50
❑ 96 Willie Mays 8.00 3.60
❑ 97 Bo Jackson 4.00 1.80
❑ 98 Carl Yastrzemski 6.00 2.70
❑ 99 Don Mattingly 8.00 3.60
❑ 100 Gary Carter 2.50 1.10
❑ 101 Jose Contreras C RC 2.00 .90
❑ 102 Jose Contreras U 4.00 1.80
❑ 103 Jose Contreras R 8.00 3.60
❑ 104 Dan Haren C RC 2.00 .90
❑ 105 Dan Haren U 4.00 1.80
❑ 106 Dan Haren R 8.00 3.60
❑ 107 Michel Hernandez C RC 1.25 .55
❑ 108 Michel Hernandez U 2.50 1.10
❑ 109 Michel Hernandez R 5.00 2.20
❑ 110 Bobby Basham C RC 1.25 .55
❑ 111 Bobby Basham U 2.50 1.10
❑ 112 Bobby Basham R 5.00 2.20
❑ 113 Bryan Bullington C RC 1.25 .55
❑ 114 Bryan Bullington U 2.50 1.10
❑ 115 Bryan Bullington R 5.00 2.20
❑ 116 Bernie Castro C RC 1.25 .55
❑ 117 Bernie Castro U 2.50 1.10
❑ 118 Bernie Castro R 5.00 2.20
❑ 119 Chien-Ming Wang C RC 4.00 1.80
❑ 120 Chien-Ming Wang U 8.00 3.60
❑ 121 Chien-Ming Wang R 15.00 6.75
❑ 122 Eric Crozier C RC 1.25 .55
❑ 123 Eric Crozier U 2.50 1.10
❑ 124 Eric Crozier R 5.00 2.20
❑ 125 Mi. Garciaparra C RC 1.25 .55
❑ 126 Michael Garciaparra U 2.50 1.10
❑ 127 Michael Garciaparra R 5.00 2.20
❑ 128 Joey Gomes C RC 1.25 .55
❑ 129 Joey Gomes U 2.50 1.10
❑ 130 Joey Gomes R 5.00 2.20
❑ 131 Wil Ledezma C RC 1.25 .55
❑ 132 Wil Ledezma U 2.50 1.10
❑ 133 Wil Ledezma R 5.00 2.20
❑ 134 Branden Florence C RC 1.25 .55
❑ 135 Branden Florence U 2.50 1.10
❑ 136 Branden Florence R 5.00 2.20
❑ 137 Jeremy Bonderman C RC 4.00 1.80
❑ 138 Jeremy Bonderman U 8.00 3.60
❑ 139 Jeremy Bonderman R 15.00 6.75
❑ 140 Travis Ishikawa C RC 1.25 .55
❑ 141 Travis Ishikawa U 2.50 1.10
❑ 142 Travis Ishikawa R 5.00 2.20
❑ 143 Ben Francisco C RC 1.25 .55
❑ 144 Ben Francisco U 2.50 1.10
❑ 145 Ben Francisco R 5.00 2.20
❑ 146 Jason Kubel C RC 2.00 .90
❑ 147 Jason Kubel U 4.00 1.80
❑ 148 Jason Kubel R 8.00 3.60
❑ 149 Tyler Martin C RC 1.25 .55
❑ 150 Tyler Martin U 2.50 1.10
❑ 151 Tyler Martin R 5.00 2.20
❑ 152 Jason Perry C RC 1.25 .55
❑ 153 Jason Perry U 2.50 1.10
❑ 154 Jason Perry R 5.00 2.20
❑ 155 Ryan Shealy C RC 2.00 .90
❑ 156 Ryan Shealy U 4.00 1.80
❑ 157 Ryan Shealy R 8.00 3.60
❑ 158 Hanley Ramirez C RC 4.00 1.80
❑ 159 Hanley Ramirez U 8.00 3.60
❑ 160 Hanley Ramirez R 15.00 6.75
❑ 161 Rajai Davis C RC 1.25 .55
❑ 162 Rajai Davis U 2.50 1.10
❑ 163 Rajai Davis R 5.00 2.20
❑ 164 Gary Schneidmiller C RC 1.25 .55
❑ 165 Gary Schneidmiller U 2.50 1.10
❑ 166 Gary Schneidmiller R 5.00 2.20
❑ 167 Haj Turay C RC 1.25 .55
❑ 168 Haj Turay U 2.50 1.10
❑ 169 Haj Turay R 5.00 2.20
❑ 170 Kevin Youkilis C RC 2.00 .90
❑ 171 Kevin Youkilis U 4.00 1.80
❑ 172 Kevin Youkilis R 8.00 3.60
❑ 173 Shane Bazzell C RC 1.25 .55
❑ 174 Shane Bazzell U 2.50 1.10
❑ 175 Shane Bazzell R 5.00 2.20
❑ 176 Elizardo Ramirez C RC 1.25 .55
❑ 177 Elizardo Ramirez U 2.50 1.10
❑ 178 Elizardo Ramirez R 5.00 2.20
❑ 179 Robinson Cano C RC 8.00 3.60
❑ 180 Robinson Cano U 15.00 6.75
❑ 181 Robinson Cano R 30.00 13.50
❑ 182 Nook Logan C RC 1.25 .55
❑ 183 Nook Logan U 2.50 1.10
❑ 184 Nook Logan R 5.00 2.20
❑ 185 Dustin McGowan C RC 1.25 .55
❑ 186 Dustin McGowan U 2.50 1.10
❑ 187 Dustin McGowan R 5.00 2.20
❑ 188 Ryan Howard C RC 8.00 3.60
❑ 189 Ryan Howard U 15.00 6.75
❑ 190 Ryan Howard R 30.00 13.50

2004 Topps Pristine

	Nm-Mt	Ex-Mt
COMMON CARD (1-100)	1.50	.45
COMMON C (101-190)	2.00	.60
C 101-190 APPROX.EQUAL TO 1-100		.00
COMMON U (101-190)	3.00	.90
UNCOMMON 101-190 STATED ODDS 1:2		.00
UNCOMMON 101-190 PRINT 999 #'d SETS		.00
COMMON R (101-190)	5.00	1.50
RARE 101-190 STATED ODDS 1:4	.00	
RARE 101-190 PRINT RUN 499 #'d SETS		.00
OVERALL PLATES ODDS 1:52 HOBBY		.00
PLATE PRINT RUN 1 SET PER COLOR		.00
BLACK-CYAN-MAGENTA-YELLOW ISSUED		.00
NO PLATE PRICING DUE TO SCARCITY		.00

❑ 1 Jim Thome 2.50 .75
❑ 2 Ryan Klesko 1.50 .45
❑ 3 Ichiro Suzuki 8.00 2.40
❑ 4 Rocco Baldelli 1.50 .45
❑ 5 Vernon Wells 1.50 .45
❑ 6 Javier Vazquez 1.50 .45
❑ 7 Billy Wagner 1.50 .45
❑ 8 Jose Reyes 1.50 .45
❑ 9 Lance Berkman 1.50 .45
❑ 10 Alex Rodriguez 6.00 1.80
❑ 11 Pat Burrell 1.50 .45
❑ 12 Mark Mulder 1.50 .45
❑ 13 Mike Piazza 6.00 1.80
❑ 14 Miguel Cabrera 2.50 .75
❑ 15 Larry Walker 1.50 .45
❑ 16 Carlos Lee 1.50 .45
❑ 17 Mark Prior 2.50 .75
❑ 18 Pedro Martinez 2.50 .75
❑ 19 Melvin Mora 1.50 .45
❑ 20 Sammy Sosa 4.00 1.20
❑ 21 Bartolo Colon 1.50 .45
❑ 22 Luis Gonzalez 1.50 .45
❑ 23 Marcus Giles 1.50 .45
❑ 24 Ken Griffey Jr. 6.00 1.80
❑ 25 Ivan Rodriguez 2.50 .75
❑ 26 Carlos Beltran 1.50 .45
❑ 27 Geoff Jenkins 1.50 .45
❑ 28 Nick Johnson 1.50 .45
❑ 29 Gary Sheffield 1.50 .45
❑ 30 Alfonso Soriano 1.50 .45
❑ 31 Scott Rolen 2.50 .75
❑ 32 Garret Anderson 1.50 .45
❑ 33 Richie Sexson 1.50 .45
❑ 34 Curt Schilling 2.50 .75
❑ 35 Greg Maddux 6.00 1.80
❑ 36 Adam Dunn 1.50 .45
❑ 37 Preston Wilson 1.50 .45
❑ 38 Josh Beckett 1.50 .45
❑ 39 Roy Oswalt 1.50 .45
❑ 40 Derek Jeter 8.00 2.40
❑ 41 Jason Kendall 1.50 .45
❑ 42 Bret Boone 1.50 .45
❑ 43 Torii Hunter 1.50 .45
❑ 44 Roy Halladay 1.50 .45
❑ 45 Edgar Renteria 1.50 .45
❑ 46 Troy Glaus 1.50 .45
❑ 47 Chipper Jones 4.00 1.20
❑ 48 Manny Ramirez 2.50 .75
❑ 49 C.C. Sabathia 1.50 .45
❑ 50 Albert Pujols 8.00 2.40
❑ 51 Randy Wolf 1.50 .45

Card	Nm-Mt	Ex-Mt
❑ 52 Eric Chavez	1.50	.45
❑ 53 Kevin Brown	1.50	.45
❑ 54 Cliff Floyd	1.50	.45
❑ 55 Jeff Bagwell	2.50	.75
❑ 56 Frank Thomas	4.00	1.20
❑ 57 David Ortiz	4.00	1.20
❑ 58 Rafael Palmeiro	2.50	.75
❑ 59 Randy Johnson	4.00	1.20
❑ 60 Vladimir Guerrero	4.00	1.20
❑ 61 Carlos Delgado	1.50	.45
❑ 62 Hank Blalock	1.50	.45
❑ 63 Jim Edmonds	2.50	.75
❑ 64 Jason Schmidt	1.50	.45
❑ 65 Mike Lieberthal	1.50	.45
❑ 66 Tim Hudson	1.50	.45
❑ 67 Jorge Posada	2.50	.75
❑ 68 Jose Vidro	1.50	.45
❑ 69 Eric Gagne	1.50	.45
❑ 70 Roger Clemens	8.00	2.40
❑ 71 Mike Lowell	1.50	.45
❑ 72 Dontrelle Willis	2.50	.75
❑ 73 Austin Kearns	1.50	.45
❑ 74 Kerry Wood	1.50	.45
❑ 75 Miguel Tejada	1.50	.45
❑ 76 Bobby Abreu	1.50	.45
❑ 77 Edgar Martinez	2.50	.75
❑ 78 Joe Mauer	1.50	.45
❑ 79 Mike Sweeney	1.50	.45
❑ 80 Jason Giambi	1.50	.45
❑ 81 Mark Teixeira	2.50	.75
❑ 82 Aubrey Huff	1.50	.45
❑ 83 Brian Giles	1.50	.45
❑ 84 Barry Zito	1.50	.45
❑ 85 Mike Mussina	2.50	.75
❑ 86 Brandon Webb	1.50	.45
❑ 87 Andruw Jones	2.50	.75
❑ 88 Javy Lopez	1.50	.45
❑ 89 Bill Mueller	1.50	.45
❑ 90 Scott Podsednik	1.50	.45
❑ 91 Moises Alou	1.50	.45
❑ 92 Esteban Loaiza	1.50	.45
❑ 93 Magglio Ordonez	1.50	.45
❑ 94 Jeff Kent	1.50	.45
❑ 95 Todd Helton	2.50	.75
❑ 96 Juan Pierre	1.50	.45
❑ 97 Jody Gerut	1.50	.45
❑ 98 Angel Berroa	1.50	.45
❑ 99 Shawn Green	1.50	.45
❑ 100 Nomar Garciaparra	6.00	1.80
❑ 101 David Aardsma C RC	2.00	.60
❑ 102 David Aardsma U	3.00	.90
❑ 103 David Aardsma R	5.00	1.50
❑ 104 Erick Aybar C RC	3.00	.90
❑ 105 Erick Aybar U	5.00	1.50
❑ 106 Erick Aybar R	8.00	2.40
❑ 107 Chad Bentz C RC	2.00	.60
❑ 108 Chad Bentz U	3.00	.90
❑ 109 Chad Bentz R	5.00	1.50
❑ 110 Travis Blackley C RC	2.00	.60
❑ 111 Travis Blackley U	3.00	.90
❑ 112 Travis Blackley R	5.00	1.50
❑ 113 Bobby Brownlie C RC	3.00	.90
❑ 114 Bobby Brownlie U	5.00	1.50
❑ 115 Bobby Brownlie R	8.00	2.40
❑ 116 Alberto Callaspo C RC	3.00	.90
❑ 117 Alberto Callaspo U	5.00	1.50
❑ 118 Alberto Callaspo R	8.00	2.40
❑ 119 Kazuo Matsui C RC	3.00	.90
❑ 120 Kazuo Matsui U	5.00	1.50
❑ 121 Kazuo Matsui R	8.00	2.40
❑ 122 Jesse Crain C RC	3.00	.90
❑ 123 Jesse Crain U	5.00	1.50
❑ 124 Jesse Crain R	8.00	2.40
❑ 125 Howie Kendrick C RC	15.00	4.50
❑ 126 Howie Kendrick U	25.00	7.50
❑ 127 Howie Kendrick R	40.00	12.00
❑ 128 Blake Hawksworth C RC	2.00	.60
❑ 129 Blake Hawksworth U	3.00	.90
❑ 130 Blake Hawksworth R	5.00	1.50
❑ 131 Conor Jackson C RC	8.00	2.40
❑ 132 Conor Jackson U	12.00	3.60
❑ 133 Conor Jackson R	20.00	6.00
❑ 134 Paul Maholm C RC	4.00	1.20
❑ 135 Paul Maholm U	6.00	1.80
❑ 136 Paul Maholm R	10.00	3.00
❑ 137 Lastings Milledge C RC	5.00	1.50
❑ 138 Lastings Milledge U	8.00	2.40
❑ 139 Lastings Milledge R	12.00	3.60
❑ 140 Matt Moses C RC	3.00	.90
❑ 141 Matt Moses U	5.00	1.50
❑ 142 Matt Moses R	8.00	2.40
❑ 143 David Murphy C RC	3.00	.90
❑ 144 David Murphy U	5.00	1.50
❑ 145 David Murphy R	8.00	2.40
❑ 146 Dioner Navarro C RC	4.00	1.20
❑ 147 Dioner Navarro U	6.00	1.80
❑ 148 Dioner Navarro R	10.00	3.00
❑ 149 Dustin Nippert C RC	2.00	.60
❑ 150 Dustin Nippert U	3.00	.90
❑ 151 Dustin Nippert R	5.00	1.50
❑ 152 Vito Chiaravalloti C RC	2.00	.60
❑ 153 Vito Chiaravalloti U	3.00	.90
❑ 154 Vito Chiaravalloti R	5.00	1.50
❑ 155 Akinori Otsuka C RC	2.00	.60
❑ 156 Akinori Otsuka U	3.00	.90
❑ 157 Akinori Otsuka R	5.00	1.50
❑ 158 Casey Daigle C RC	2.00	.60
❑ 159 Casey Daigle U	3.00	.90
❑ 160 Casey Daigle R	5.00	1.50
❑ 161 Carlos Quentin C RC	6.00	1.80
❑ 162 Carlos Quentin U	10.00	3.00
❑ 163 Carlos Quentin R	15.00	4.50
❑ 164 Omar Quintanilla C RC	3.00	.90
❑ 165 Omar Quintanilla U	5.00	1.50
❑ 166 Omar Quintanilla R	8.00	2.40
❑ 167 Chris Saenz C RC	2.00	.60
❑ 168 Chris Saenz U	.00	.00
❑ 169 Chris Saenz R	.00	.00
❑ 170 Ervin Santana C RC	5.00	1.50
❑ 171 Ervin Santana U	8.00	2.40
❑ 172 Ervin Santana R	12.00	3.60
❑ 173 Chris Shelton C RC	4.00	1.20
❑ 174 Chris Shelton U	6.00	1.80
❑ 175 Chris Shelton R	10.00	3.00
❑ 176 Kyle Sleeth C RC	3.00	.90
❑ 177 Kyle Sleeth U	5.00	1.50
❑ 178 Kyle Sleeth R	8.00	2.40
❑ 179 Brad Snyder C RC	3.00	.90
❑ 180 Brad Snyder U	5.00	1.50
❑ 181 Brad Snyder R	8.00	2.40
❑ 182 Tim Stauffer C RC	2.50	.75
❑ 183 Tim Stauffer U	4.00	1.20
❑ 184 Tim Stauffer R	6.00	1.80
❑ 185 Shingo Takatsu C RC	3.00	.90
❑ 186 Shingo Takatsu U	5.00	1.50
❑ 187 Shingo Takatsu R	8.00	2.40
❑ 188 Merkin Valdez C RC	2.00	.60
❑ 189 Merkin Valdez U	3.00	.90
❑ 190 Merkin Valdez R	5.00	1.50

2005 Topps Pristine

	Nm-Mt	Ex-Mt
COMMON CARD (1-100)	1.00	.30
COMMON RC (101-130)	1.50	.45

OVERALL PLATE ODDS 1:53 HOBBY
PLATE PRINT RUN 1 SET PER COLOR
BLACK-CYAN-MAGENTA-YELLOW ISSUED
NO PLATE PRICING DUE TO SCARCITY

Card	Nm-Mt	Ex-Mt
❑ 1 Alex Rodriguez	4.00	1.20
❑ 2 Jake Peavy	1.00	.30
❑ 3 Bobby Crosby	1.00	.30
❑ 4 J.D. Drew	1.00	.30
❑ 5 Scott Rolen	1.50	.45
❑ 6 Bobby Abreu	1.00	.30
❑ 7 Ken Griffey Jr.	4.00	1.20
❑ 8 Jeremy Bonderman	1.00	.30
❑ 9 Mike Sweeney	1.00	.30
❑ 10 Mark Prior	1.50	.45
❑ 11 Tim Hudson	1.00	.30
❑ 12 Clint Barmes	1.00	.30
❑ 13 Jeff Bagwell	1.50	.45
❑ 14 Andruw Jones	1.50	.45
❑ 15 Carlos Delgado	1.00	.30
❑ 16 Rocco Baldelli	1.00	.30
❑ 17 Adam Dunn	1.00	.30
❑ 18 Greg Maddux	4.00	1.20
❑ 19 Torii Hunter	1.00	.30
❑ 20 Miguel Tejada	1.00	.30
❑ 21 Lyle Overbay	1.00	.30
❑ 22 Craig Wilson	1.00	.30
❑ 23 Scott Kazmir	1.00	.30
❑ 24 Alex Rios	1.00	.30
❑ 25 Ichiro Suzuki	5.00	1.50
❑ 26 Jorge Posada	1.50	.45
❑ 27 Jose Reyes	1.00	.30
❑ 28 Hank Blalock	1.00	.30
❑ 29 Troy Glaus	1.00	.30
❑ 30 Todd Helton	1.50	.45
❑ 31 Javy Lopez	1.00	.30
❑ 32 Barry Zito	1.00	.30
❑ 33 Jimmy Rollins	1.00	.30
❑ 34 Mark Loretta	1.00	.30
❑ 35 Richie Sexson	1.00	.30
❑ 36 Nick Johnson	1.00	.30
❑ 37 Ivan Rodriguez	1.50	.45
❑ 38 Jeff Kent	1.00	.30
❑ 39 Jake Westbrook	1.00	.30
❑ 40 Carlos Beltran	1.00	.30
❑ 41 Rich Harden	1.00	.30
❑ 42 Joe Mauer	1.00	.30
❑ 43 Luis Gonzalez	1.00	.30
❑ 44 Frank Thomas	2.50	.75
❑ 45 Michael Young	1.00	.30
❑ 46 Jason Schmidt	1.00	.30
❑ 47 Eric Chavez	1.00	.30
❑ 48 Vinny Castilla	1.00	.30
❑ 49 John Smoltz	1.50	.45
❑ 50 Barry Bonds	6.00	1.80
❑ 51 Jim Edmonds	1.50	.45
❑ 52 Edgar Renteria	1.00	.30
❑ 53 Jose Vidro	1.00	.30
❑ 54 Chipper Jones	2.50	.75
❑ 55 Curt Schilling	1.50	.45
❑ 56 Victor Martinez	1.00	.30
❑ 57 Josh Beckett	1.00	.30
❑ 58 Derrek Lee	1.50	.45
❑ 59 Shawn Green	1.00	.30
❑ 60 Roger Clemens	4.00	1.20
❑ 61 Orlando Cabrera	1.00	.30
❑ 62 Mike Piazza	2.50	.75
❑ 63 Gary Sheffield	1.00	.30
❑ 64 Carl Crawford	1.00	.30
❑ 65 Johan Santana	1.50	.45
❑ 66 Oliver Perez	1.00	.30
❑ 67 Manny Ramirez	1.50	.45
❑ 68 Paul Konerko	1.00	.30
❑ 69 Preston Wilson	1.00	.30
❑ 70 Sammy Sosa	2.50	.75
❑ 71 Eric Gagne	1.00	.30
❑ 72 Geoff Jenkins	1.00	.30
❑ 73 Magglio Ordonez	1.00	.30
❑ 74 Kerry Wood	1.00	.30
❑ 75 Albert Pujols	5.00	1.50
❑ 76 Roy Halladay	1.00	.30
❑ 77 Aubrey Huff	1.00	.30
❑ 78 Nomar Garciaparra	2.50	.75
❑ 79 Brian Roberts	1.00	.30
❑ 80 Randy Johnson	2.50	.75
❑ 81 Pat Burrell	1.00	.30
❑ 82 Brian Giles	1.00	.30
❑ 83 Mike Mussina	1.50	.45
❑ 84 Mark Teixeira	1.50	.45
❑ 85 Pedro Martinez	1.50	.45
❑ 86 Jason Bay	1.00	.30
❑ 87 Mark Buehrle	1.00	.30
❑ 88 Rafael Furcal	1.00	.30
❑ 89 Juan Pierre	1.00	.30
❑ 90 Jim Thome	1.50	.45
❑ 91 Ben Sheets	1.00	.30

❑ 92 Alfonso Soriano 1.00 .30
❑ 93 Adrian Beltre 1.00 .30
❑ 94 Miguel Cabrera 1.50 .45
❑ 95 Derek Jeter 5.00 1.50
❑ 96 Vernon Wells 1.00 .30
❑ 97 Lance Berkman 1.00 .30
❑ 98 Hideki Matsui 5.00 1.50
❑ 99 David Ortiz 2.50 .75
❑ 100 Vladimir Guerrero 2.50 .75
❑ 101 Justin Verlander FY RC 4.00 1.20
❑ 102 Billy Butler FY RC 10.00 3.00
❑ 103 Wladimir Balentien FY RC 3.00 .90
❑ 104 Jeremy West FY RC 3.00 .90
❑ 105 Philip Humber FY RC 3.00 .90
❑ 106 Tyler Pelland FY RC 2.00 .60
❑ 107 Andy LaRoche FY RC 8.00 2.40
❑ 108 Hernan Iribarren FY RC 3.00 .90
❑ 109 Luke Scott FY RC 2.00 .60
❑ 110 Landon Powell FY RC 2.00 .60
❑ 111 Alexander Smit FY RC 1.50 .45
❑ 112 Ryan Garko FY RC 3.00 .90
❑ 113 Bear Bay FY RC 2.00 .60
❑ 114 Ian Bladergroen FY RC 2.00 .60
❑ 115 Manny Parra FY RC 1.50 .45
❑ 116 Andy Sides FY RC 1.50 .45
❑ 117 Travis Chick FY RC 2.00 .60
❑ 118 Stefan Bailie FY RC 1.50 .45
❑ 119 Chuck Tiffany FY RC 3.00 .90
❑ 120 Buck Coats FY RC 1.50 .45
❑ 121 Jeff Niemann FY RC 3.00 .90
❑ 122 Jake Postlewait FY RC 1.50 .45
❑ 123 Matt Campbell FY RC 1.50 .45
❑ 124 Kevin Melillo FY RC 3.00 .90
❑ 125 Mike Morse FY RC 3.00 .90
❑ 126 Anthony Reyes FY RC 5.00 1.50
❑ 127 Casey McGehee FY RC 1.50 .45
❑ 128 Cody Haerther FY RC 1.50 .45
❑ 129 Brandon McCarthy FY RC 4.00 1.20
❑ 130 Glen Perkins FY RC 3.00 .90
❑ 131 Moises Alou Bat 5.00 1.50
❑ 132 Nomar Garciaparra Bat 10.00 3.00
❑ 133 Scott Rolen Jsy 8.00 2.40
❑ 134 Miguel Tejada Uni 5.00 1.50
❑ 135 Alex Rodriguez Bat 15.00 4.50
❑ 136 Michael Young Jsy 5.00 1.50
❑ 137 Tim Hudson Uni 5.00 1.50
❑ 138 Troy Glaus Bat 5.00 1.50
❑ 139 Eric Chavez Uni 5.00 1.50
❑ 140 David Ortiz Bat 10.00 3.00
❑ 141 Andruw Jones Jsy 8.00 2.40
❑ 142 Richie Sexson Bat 5.00 1.50
❑ 143 Jim Thome Bat 8.00 2.40
❑ 144 Javy Lopez Bat 5.00 1.50
❑ 145 Lance Berkman Jsy 5.00 1.50
❑ 146 Gary Sheffield Bat 5.00 1.50
❑ 147 Dontrelle Willis Jsy 5.00 1.50
❑ 148 Curt Schilling Jsy 8.00 2.40
❑ 149 Jorge Posada Jsy 8.00 2.40
❑ 150 Vladimir Guerrero Bat 10.00 3.00
❑ 151 Adam Dunn Jsy 5.00 1.50
❑ 152 Ryan Drese Jsy 5.00 1.50
❑ 153 Hank Blalock Uni 5.00 1.50
❑ 154 Kerry Wood Jsy 5.00 1.50
❑ 155 Alfonso Soriano Bat 5.00 1.50
❑ 156 Aramis Ramirez Bat 5.00 1.50
❑ 157 Mark Mulder Uni 5.00 1.50
❑ 158 Paul Konerko Bat 5.00 1.50
❑ 159 Jim Edmonds Jsy 8.00 2.40
❑ 160 Roger Clemens Jsy 12.00 3.60
❑ 161 Mariano Rivera Jsy 8.00 2.40
❑ 162 Rafael Palmeiro Bat 8.00 2.40
❑ 163 Mark Teixeira Bat 8.00 2.40
❑ 164 Eric Gagne Jsy 5.00 1.50
❑ 165 Sammy Sosa Bat 10.00 3.00
❑ 166 Brett Myers Jsy 5.00 1.50
❑ 167 Kazuhisa Ishii Uni 5.00 1.50
❑ 168 Ken Harvey Bat 5.00 1.50
❑ 169 Johnny Estrada Jsy 5.00 1.50
❑ 170 Todd Helton Jsy 8.00 2.40
❑ 171 Rich Harden Jsy 5.00 1.50
❑ 172 Johnny Damon Bat 8.00 2.40
❑ 173 Manny Ramirez Bat 8.00 2.40
❑ 174 Benito Santiago Bat 5.00 1.50
❑ 175 Albert Pujols Jsy 15.00 4.50
❑ 176 Chipper Jones Jsy 10.00 3.00
❑ 177 Miguel Cabrera Bat 8.00 2.40
❑ 178 Jeff Bagwell Uni 8.00 2.40
❑ 179 Ivan Rodriguez Jsy 8.00 2.40
❑ 180 Mike Piazza Uni 10.00 3.00
❑ 181 Chip Cannon FY AU RC 25.00 7.50
❑ 182 Erik Cordier FY AU RC 25.00 7.50
❑ 183 Billy Butler FY AU 80.00 24.00
❑ 184 C.J. Smith FY AU RC 25.00 7.50
❑ 185 Alfonso Soriano AU 30.00 9.00
❑ 186 Bobby Livingston FY AU RC 25.00 7.50
❑ 187 Wladimir Balentien FY AU 40.00 12.00
❑ 188 Mike Morse FY AU 50.00 15.00
❑ 189 W.Swackhamer FY AU RC 25.00 7.50
❑ 190 Justin Verlander FY AU 40.00 12.00
❑ 191 Jake Postlewait FY AU 25.00 7.50
❑ 192 Michael Rogers FY AU RC 25.00 7.50
❑ 193 Matt Campbell FY AU 25.00 7.50
❑ 194 Eric Nielsen FY AU RC 25.00 7.50
❑ 195 Gary Sheffield AU 50.00 15.00
❑ 196 Glen Perkins FY AU 40.00 12.00
❑ 197 Kevin Melillo FY AU 40.00 12.00
❑ 198 Chad Orvella FY AU RC 25.00 7.50
❑ 199 Jeff Niemann FY AU 40.00 12.00
❑ 200 Alex Rodriguez AU 200.00 60.00
❑ 201 Brian Stavisky FY AU RC 25.00 7.50
❑ 202 Brian Miller FY AU RC 25.00 7.50
❑ 203 Landon Powell FY AU 40.00 12.00
❑ 204 Philip Humber FY AU 40.00 12.00
❑ 205 Mariano Rivera AU 125.00 38.00
❑ 206 Curt Schilling AU Jsy EXCH 100.00 30.00
❑ 207 Nolan Ryan AU Jsy 120.00 36.00
❑ 208 Albert Pujols AU Jsy 300.00 90.00
❑ 209 Stan Musial AU Bat 120.00 36.00
❑ 210 B.Bonds AU Jsy * EXCH 400.00 120.00

2005 Topps Pristine Legends

	Nm-Mt	Ex-Mt
COMP. SET w/o SP's (100)	120.00	36.00
COMMON C (1-100)	1.50	.45
COMMON U (101-125)	3.00	.90
COMMON R (126-135)	4.00	1.20
COMMON S (136-140)	5.00	1.50

OVERALL PLATE ODDS 1:82 HOBBY
PLATE PRINT RUN 1 SET PER COLOR
BLACK-CYAN-MAGENTA-YELLOW ISSUED
NO PLATE PRICING DUE TO SCARCITY

❑ 1 Vida Blue C 1.50 .45
❑ 2 Bert Blyleven C 1.50 .45
❑ 3 Joe Carter C 1.50 .45
❑ 4 Bill Buckner C 1.50 .45
❑ 5 Luis Aparicio C 1.50 .45
❑ 6 Ernie Banks C 3.00 .90
❑ 7 Wade Boggs C 2.00 .60
❑ 8 George Brett C 5.00 1.50
❑ 9 Lou Brock C 2.00 .60
❑ 10 Rod Carew C 2.00 .60
❑ 11 Gary Carter C 1.50 .45
❑ 12 Andre Dawson C 1.50 .45
❑ 13 Dennis Eckersley C 1.50 .45
❑ 14 Rollie Fingers C 1.50 .45
❑ 15 Steve Garvey C 1.50 .45
❑ 16 Dwight Gooden C 1.50 .45
❑ 17 Goose Gossage C 1.50 .45
❑ 18 Ron Guidry C 1.50 .45
❑ 19 Keith Hernandez C 1.50 .45
❑ 20 Charlie Hough C 1.50 .45
❑ 21 Bo Jackson C 3.00 .90
❑ 22 Monte Irvin C 1.50 .45
❑ 23 Reggie Jackson C 2.00 .60
❑ 24 Ferguson Jenkins C 1.50 .45
❑ 25 Ralph Kiner C 1.50 .45
❑ 26 Juan Marichal C 1.50 .45
❑ 27 Stan Musial C 4.00 1.20
❑ 28 Tony Oliva C 1.50 .45
❑ 29 Jim Palmer C 1.50 .45
❑ 30 Dave Parker C 1.50 .45
❑ 31 Gaylord Perry C 1.50 .45
❑ 32 Jimmy Piersall C 1.50 .45
❑ 33 Johnny Podres C 1.50 .45
❑ 34 Brooks Robinson C 2.00 .60
❑ 35 Frank Robinson C 1.50 .45
❑ 36 Nolan Ryan C 6.00 1.80
❑ 37 Tom Seaver C 2.00 .60
❑ 38 Ozzie Smith C 4.00 1.20
❑ 39 Duke Snider C 2.00 .60
❑ 40 Bobby Thomson C 1.50 .45
❑ 41 Carl Yastrzemski C 3.00 .90
❑ 42 Maury Wills C 1.50 .45
❑ 43 Robin Yount C 3.00 .90
❑ 44 Matt Williams C 2.00 .60
❑ 45 Orel Hershiser C 1.50 .45
❑ 46 Tim McCarver C 1.50 .45
❑ 47 Don Newcombe C 1.50 .45
❑ 48 Paul O'Neill C 2.00 .60
❑ 49 Al Kaline C 3.00 .90
❑ 50 Harmon Killebrew C 3.00 .90
❑ 51 Dave Kingman C 1.50 .45
❑ 52 Ken Griffey Sr. C 1.50 .45
❑ 53 George Foster C 1.50 .45
❑ 54 Mark Fidrych C 1.50 .45
❑ 55 Orlando Cepeda C 1.50 .45
❑ 56 Don Larsen C 1.50 .45
❑ 57 Bill Madlock C 1.50 .45
❑ 58 Dale Murphy C 2.00 .60
❑ 59 Graig Nettles C 1.50 .45
❑ 60 Phil Niekro C 1.50 .45
❑ 61 Al Oliver C 1.50 .45
❑ 62 Harold Reynolds C 1.50 .45
❑ 63 Bobby Richardson C 2.00 .60
❑ 64 Mike Scott C 1.50 .45
❑ 65 Dave Stewart C 1.50 .45
❑ 66 Rick Sutcliffe C 1.50 .45
❑ 67 Bruce Sutter C 1.50 .45
❑ 68 Luis Tiant C 1.50 .45
❑ 69 Bob Watson C 1.50 .45
❑ 70 Walt Weiss C 1.50 .45
❑ 71 Don Zimmer C 1.50 .45
❑ 72 Tommy John C 1.50 .45
❑ 73 Ray Knight C 1.50 .45
❑ 74 Jack Morris C 1.50 .45
❑ 75 Mickey Rivers C 1.50 .45
❑ 76 Lee Smith C 1.50 .45
❑ 77 Darryl Strawberry C 1.50 .45
❑ 78 Dave Justice C 2.00 .60
❑ 79 Wally Joyner C 1.50 .45
❑ 80 Jimmy Key C 1.50 .45
❑ 81 John Kruk C 1.50 .45
❑ 82 Greg Luzinski C 1.50 .45
❑ 83 Mookie Wilson C 1.50 .45
❑ 84 Wilbur Wood C 1.50 .45
❑ 85 Tim Raines C 1.50 .45
❑ 86 Jim Rice C 1.50 .45
❑ 87 Tony Armas C 1.50 .45
❑ 88 Harold Baines C 1.50 .45
❑ 89 Bucky Dent C 1.50 .45
❑ 90 Darrell Evans C 1.50 .45
❑ 91 Cecil Fielder C 1.50 .45
❑ 92 Jose Cruz C 1.50 .45
❑ 93 Dave Concepcion C 1.50 .45
❑ 94 Ron Cey C 1.50 .45
❑ 95 Davey Lopes C 1.50 .45
❑ 96 Boog Powell C 1.50 .45
❑ 97 Buddy Bell C 1.50 .45
❑ 98 George Bell C 1.50 .45
❑ 99 Bert Campaneris C 1.50 .45
❑ 100 Chet Lemon C 1.50 .45
❑ 101 Bo Jackson U 8.00 2.40
❑ 102 Will Clark U 5.00 1.50
❑ 103 Cecil Fielder U 3.00 .90
❑ 104 Ron Cey U 3.00 .90
❑ 105 Tony Gwynn U 5.00 1.50
❑ 106 Orel Hershiser U 3.00 .90

❑ 107 Jimmy Key U 3.00 .90
❑ 108 Paul Molitor U 5.00 1.50
❑ 109 Pete Incaviglia U 3.00 .90
❑ 110 Wally Joyner U 3.00 .90
❑ 111 Dave Kingman U 3.00 .90
❑ 112 Ron Guidry U 3.00 .90
❑ 113 Ron Darling U 3.00 .90
❑ 114 Mookie Wilson U 3.00 .90
❑ 115 Reggie Jackson U 5.00 1.50
❑ 116 Walt Weiss U 3.00 .90
❑ 117 Joe Carter U 3.00 .90
❑ 118 Cory Snyder U 3.00 .90
❑ 119 Dave Winfield U 3.00 .90
❑ 120 Terry Steinbach U 3.00 .90
❑ 121 Matt Williams U 5.00 1.50
❑ 122 Ozzie Smith U 6.00 1.80
❑ 123 Jack McDowell U 3.00 .90
❑ 124 Bob Horner U 3.00 .90
❑ 125 Don Kessinger U 3.00 .90
❑ 126 Minnie Minoso R 4.00 1.20
❑ 127 Josh Gibson R 6.00 1.80
❑ 128 Buck O'Neil R 4.00 1.20
❑ 129 Monte Irvin R 4.00 1.20
❑ 130 Jim Gilliam R 4.00 1.20
❑ 131 Josh Gibson R 6.00 1.80
❑ 132 Ernie Banks R 8.00 2.40
❑ 133 Don Newcombe R 4.00 1.20
❑ 134 Josh Gibson R 6.00 1.80
❑ 135 Josh Gibson R 6.00 1.80
❑ 136 Gary Carter S 5.00 1.50
❑ 137 Bo Jackson S 8.00 2.40
❑ 138 George Brett S 15.00 4.50
❑ 139 Joe Carter S 5.00 1.50
❑ 140 Nolan Ryan S 15.00 4.50

2001 Topps Reserve

	Nm-Mt	Ex-Mt
COMP.SET w/o SP's (100)	100.00	30.00
COMMON CARD (1-100)	1.00	.30
COMMON (101-151)	8.00	2.40

❑ 1 Darin Erstad 1.00 .30
❑ 2 Moises Alou 1.00 .30
❑ 3 Tony Batista 1.00 .30
❑ 4 Andruw Jones 1.50 .45
❑ 5 Edgar Renteria 1.00 .30
❑ 6 Eric Young 1.00 .30
❑ 7 Steve Finley 1.00 .30
❑ 8 Adrian Beltre 1.00 .30
❑ 9 Vladimir Guerrero 2.50 .75
❑ 10 Barry Bonds 6.00 1.80
❑ 11 Juan Gonzalez 1.00 .30
❑ 12 Jay Buhner 1.00 .30
❑ 13 Luis Castillo 1.00 .30
❑ 14 Cal Ripken 8.00 2.40
❑ 15 Bob Abreu 1.00 .30
❑ 16 Ivan Rodriguez 1.50 .45
❑ 17 Nomar Garciaparra 4.00 1.20
❑ 18 Todd Helton 1.50 .45
❑ 19 Bobby Higginson 1.00 .30
❑ 20 Jorge Posada 1.50 .45
❑ 21 Tim Salmon 1.50 .45
❑ 22 Jason Giambi 1.00 .30
❑ 23 Jose Cruz Jr. 1.00 .30
❑ 24 Chipper Jones 2.50 .75
❑ 25 Jim Edmonds 1.50 .45
❑ 26 Gerald Williams 1.00 .30
❑ 27 Randy Johnson 2.50 .75
❑ 28 Gary Sheffield 1.00 .30
❑ 29 Jeff Kent 1.00 .30
❑ 30 Jim Thome 1.50 .45
❑ 31 John Olerud 1.00 .30
❑ 32 Cliff Floyd 1.00 .30
❑ 33 Mike Lowell 1.00 .30
❑ 34 Phil Nevin 1.00 .30
❑ 35 Scott Rolen 1.50 .45
❑ 36 Alex Rodriguez 4.00 1.20
❑ 37 Ken Griffey Jr. 4.00 1.20
❑ 38 Neifi Perez 1.00 .30
❑ 39 Cristian Guzman 1.00 .30
❑ 40 Mariano Rivera 1.50 .45
❑ 41 Troy Glaus 1.00 .30
❑ 42 Johnny Damon 1.50 .45
❑ 43 Rafael Furcal 1.00 .30
❑ 44 Jeromy Burnitz 1.00 .30
❑ 45 Mark McGwire 6.00 1.80
❑ 46 Fred McGriff 1.50 .45
❑ 47 Matt Williams 1.00 .30
❑ 48 Kevin Brown 1.00 .30
❑ 49 J.T. Snow 1.00 .30
❑ 50 Kenny Lofton 1.00 .30
❑ 51 Al Martin 1.00 .30
❑ 52 Antonio Alfonseca 1.00 .30
❑ 53 Edgardo Alfonzo 1.00 .30
❑ 54 Ryan Klesko 1.00 .30
❑ 55 Pat Burrell 1.00 .30
❑ 56 Rafael Palmeiro 1.50 .45
❑ 57 Sean Casey 1.50 .45
❑ 58 Jeff Cirillo 1.00 .30
❑ 59 Ray Durham 1.00 .30
❑ 60 Derek Jeter 6.00 1.80
❑ 61 Jeff Bagwell 1.50 .45
❑ 62 Carlos Delgado 1.00 .30
❑ 63 Tom Glavine 1.50 .45
❑ 64 Richie Sexson 1.00 .30
❑ 65 J.D. Drew 1.00 .30
❑ 66 Ben Grieve 1.00 .30
❑ 67 Mark Grace 1.50 .45
❑ 68 Shawn Green 1.00 .30
❑ 69 Robb Nen 1.00 .30
❑ 70 Omar Vizquel 1.50 .45
❑ 71 Edgar Martinez 1.50 .45
❑ 72 Preston Wilson 1.00 .30
❑ 73 Mike Piazza 4.00 1.20
❑ 74 Tony Gwynn 3.00 .90
❑ 75 Jason Kendall 1.00 .30
❑ 76 Manny Ramirez Sox 1.50 .45
❑ 77 Pokey Reese 1.00 .30
❑ 78 Mike Sweeney 1.00 .30
❑ 79 Magglio Ordonez 1.00 .30
❑ 80 Bernie Williams 1.50 .45
❑ 81 Richard Hidalgo 1.00 .30
❑ 82 Brad Fullmer 1.00 .30
❑ 83 Greg Maddux 4.00 1.20
❑ 84 Geoff Jenkins 1.00 .30
❑ 85 Sammy Sosa 2.50 .75
❑ 86 Luis Gonzalez 1.00 .30
❑ 87 Eric Karros 1.00 .30
❑ 88 Jose Vidro 1.00 .30
❑ 89 Rich Aurilia 1.00 .30
❑ 90 Roberto Alomar 1.50 .45
❑ 91 Mike Cameron 1.00 .30
❑ 92 Mike Mussina 1.50 .45
❑ 93 Barry Zito 1.50 .45
❑ 94 Mike Lieberthal 1.00 .30
❑ 95 Brian Giles 1.00 .30
❑ 96 Pedro Martinez 1.50 .45
❑ 97 Barry Larkin 1.50 .45
❑ 98 Jermaine Dye 1.00 .30
❑ 99 Frank Thomas 2.50 .75
❑ 100 David Justice 1.00 .30
❑ 101 Gary Johnson RC 8.00 2.40
❑ 102 Matt Ford RC 8.00 2.40
❑ 103 Albert Pujols RC 80.00 24.00
❑ 104 Brad Cresse 8.00 2.40
❑ 105 V. Pascucci RC 8.00 2.40
❑ 106 Bob Keppel RC 8.00 2.40
❑ 107 Luis Torres RC 8.00 2.40
❑ 108 Tony Blanco RC 8.00 2.40
❑ 109 Ronnie Corona RC 8.00 2.40
❑ 110 Phil Wilson RC 8.00 2.40
❑ 111 John Buck RC 10.00 3.00
❑ 112 Jim Journell RC 8.00 2.40
❑ 113 Victor Hall RC 8.00 2.40
❑ 114 Jeff Andra RC 8.00 2.40
❑ 115 Greg Nash RC 8.00 2.40
❑ 116 Travis Hafner RC 15.00 4.50
❑ 117 Casey Fossum RC 8.00 2.40
❑ 118 Miguel Olivo 8.00 2.40
❑ 119 Elpidio Guzman RC 8.00 2.40
❑ 120 Jason Belcher RC 8.00 2.40
❑ 121 Esix Snead RC 8.00 2.40
❑ 122 Joe Thurston RC 8.00 2.40
❑ 123 Rafael Soriano RC 8.00 2.40
❑ 124 Ed Rogers RC 8.00 2.40
❑ 125 Omar Beltre RC 8.00 2.40
❑ 126 Brett Gray RC 8.00 2.40
❑ 127 Deivi Mendez RC 8.00 2.40
❑ 128 Freddie Bynum RC 8.00 2.40
❑ 129 David Krynzel 8.00 2.40
❑ 130 Blake Williams RC 8.00 2.40
❑ 131 R. Abercrombie RC 8.00 2.40
❑ 132 Miguel Villilo RC 8.00 2.40
❑ 133 Ryan Madson RC 8.00 2.40
❑ 134 Matt Thompson RC 8.00 2.40
❑ 135 Mark Burnett RC 8.00 2.40
❑ 136 Andy Beal RC 8.00 2.40
❑ 137 Ryan Ludwick RC 8.00 2.40
❑ 138 Roberto Miniel RC 8.00 2.40
❑ 139 Steve Smyth RC 8.00 2.40
❑ 140 Ben Washburn RC 8.00 2.40
❑ 141 Marvin Seale RC 8.00 2.40
❑ 142 Reggie Griggs RC 8.00 2.40
❑ 143 Seung Song RC 8.00 2.40
❑ 144 Chad Petty RC 8.00 2.40
❑ 145 Noel Devarez RC 8.00 2.40
❑ 146 Matt Butler RC 8.00 2.40
❑ 147 Brett Evert RC 8.00 2.40
❑ 148 Cesar Izturis 8.00 2.40
❑ 149 Troy Farnsworth RC 8.00 2.40
❑ 150 Brian Schmitt RC 8.00 2.40
❑ 151 Ichiro Suzuki RC 50.00 15.00

2002 Topps Reserve

	Nm-Mt	Ex-Mt
COMP.SET w/o SP's (135)	100.00	30.00
COMMON CARD (1-135)	1.00	.30
COMMON CARD (136-150)	4.00	1.20

❑ 1 Alex Rodriguez 4.00 1.20
❑ 2 Tsuyoshi Shinjo 1.00 .30
❑ 3 Craig Biggio 1.50 .45
❑ 4 Troy Glaus 1.00 .30
❑ 5 Mike Rivera 1.00 .30
❑ 6 Curt Schilling 1.00 .30
❑ 7 Garret Anderson 1.00 .30
❑ 8 Ben Sheets 1.00 .30
❑ 9 Todd Helton 1.50 .45
❑ 10 Paul Konerko 1.00 .30
❑ 11 Sammy Sosa 2.50 .75
❑ 12 Bud Smith 1.00 .30
❑ 13 Jeff Bagwell 1.50 .45
❑ 14 Albert Pujols 5.00 1.50
❑ 15 Jose Vidro 1.00 .30
❑ 16 Carlos Delgado 1.00 .30
❑ 17 Torii Hunter 1.00 .30
❑ 18 Jerry Hairston 1.00 .30
❑ 19 Troy Percival 1.00 .30
❑ 20 Vladimir Guerrero 2.50 .75
❑ 21 Geoff Jenkins 1.00 .30
❑ 22 Carlos Pena 1.00 .30
❑ 23 Juan Gonzalez 1.00 .30

❑ 24 Raul Mondesi 1.00 .30
❑ 25 Jimmy Rollins 1.00 .30
❑ 26 Mariano Rivera 1.50 .45
❑ 27 Jorge Posada 1.50 .45
❑ 28 Magglio Ordonez 1.00 .30
❑ 29 Roberto Alomar 1.50 .45
❑ 30 Randy Johnson 2.50 .75
❑ 31 Xavier Nady 1.00 .30
❑ 32 Terrence Long 1.00 .30
❑ 33 Chipper Jones 2.50 .75
❑ 34 Rich Aurilia 1.00 .30
❑ 35 Aramis Ramirez 1.00 .30
❑ 36 Jim Thome 1.50 .45
❑ 37 Bret Boone 1.00 .30
❑ 38 Angel Berroa 1.00 .30
❑ 39 Jeff Conine 1.00 .30
❑ 40 Cliff Floyd 1.00 .30
❑ 41 Pedro Martinez 1.50 .45
❑ 42 J.D. Drew 1.00 .30
❑ 43 Kazuhiro Sasaki 1.00 .30
❑ 44 Jon Rauch 1.00 .30
❑ 45 Orlando Hudson 1.00 .30
❑ 46 Scott Rolen 1.50 .45
❑ 47 Rafael Furcal 1.00 .30
❑ 48 Brad Penny 1.00 .30
❑ 49 Miguel Tejada 1.00 .30
❑ 50 Orlando Cabrera 1.00 .30
❑ 51 Bob Abreu 1.00 .30
❑ 52 Darin Erstad 1.00 .30
❑ 53 Edgar Martinez 1.50 .45
❑ 54 Ben Grieve 1.00 .30
❑ 55 Shawn Green 1.00 .30
❑ 56 Ivan Rodriguez 1.50 .45
❑ 57 Josh Beckett 1.00 .30
❑ 58 Ray Durham 1.00 .30
❑ 59 Jason Hart 1.00 .30
❑ 60 Nathan Haynes 1.00 .30
❑ 61 Jason Giambi 1.00 .30
❑ 62 Eric Chavez 1.00 .30
❑ 63 Matt Morris 1.00 .30
❑ 64 Lance Berkman 1.00 .30
❑ 65 Jeff Kent 1.00 .30
❑ 66 Andruw Jones 1.50 .45
❑ 67 Brian Giles 1.00 .30
❑ 68 Morgan Ensberg 1.00 .30
❑ 69 Pat Burrell 1.00 .30
❑ 70 Ken Griffey Jr. 4.00 1.20
❑ 71 Carlos Beltran 1.00 .30
❑ 72 Ichiro Suzuki 5.00 1.50
❑ 73 Larry Walker 1.00 .30
❑ 74 J.J. Putz RC 1.00 .30
❑ 75 Mike Piazza 4.00 1.20
❑ 76 Rafael Palmeiro 1.50 .45
❑ 77 Mark Prior 2.50 .75
❑ 78 Toby Hall 1.00 .30
❑ 79 Pokey Reese 1.00 .30
❑ 80 Mike Mussina 1.50 .45
❑ 81 Omar Vizquel 1.50 .45
❑ 82 Shannon Stewart 1.00 .30
❑ 83 Jeromy Burnitz 1.00 .30
❑ 84 Bernie Williams 1.50 .45
❑ 85 C.C. Sabathia 1.00 .30
❑ 86 Mike Hampton 1.00 .30
❑ 87 Kevin Brown 1.00 .30
❑ 88 Juan Cruz 1.00 .30
❑ 89 Jeff Weaver 1.00 .30
❑ 90 Jason Lane 1.00 .30
❑ 91 Adam Dunn 1.00 .30
❑ 92 Jose Cruz Jr. 1.00 .30
❑ 93 Marlon Anderson 1.00 .30
❑ 94 Jeff Cirillo 1.00 .30
❑ 95 Mark Buehrle 1.00 .30
❑ 96 Austin Kearns 1.00 .30
❑ 97 Tim Hudson 1.00 .30
❑ 98 Brian Jordan 1.00 .30
❑ 99 Phil Nevin 1.00 .30
❑ 100 Barry Bonds 6.00 1.80
❑ 101 Derek Jeter 6.00 1.80
❑ 102 Javier Vazquez 1.00 .30
❑ 103 Jason Kendall 1.00 .30
❑ 104 Jim Edmonds 1.50 .45
❑ 105 Kenny Kelly 1.00 .30
❑ 106 Juan Pena 1.00 .30
❑ 107 Mark Grace 1.50 .45
❑ 108 Roger Clemens 5.00 1.50
❑ 109 Barry Zito 1.00 .30
❑ 110 Greg Vaughn 1.00 .30
❑ 111 Greg Maddux 4.00 1.20
❑ 112 Richie Sexson 1.00 .30
❑ 113 Jermaine Dye 1.00 .30
❑ 114 Kerry Wood 1.00 .30
❑ 115 Matt Lawton 1.00 .30
❑ 116 Sean Casey 1.50 .45
❑ 117 Gary Sheffield 1.00 .30
❑ 118 Preston Wilson 1.00 .30
❑ 119 Cristian Guzman 1.00 .30
❑ 120 Mike Sweeney 1.00 .30
❑ 121 Neifi Perez 1.00 .30
❑ 122 Paul LoDuca 1.00 .30
❑ 123 Luis Gonzalez 1.00 .30
❑ 124 Ryan Klesko 1.00 .30
❑ 125 Alfonso Soriano 1.00 .30
❑ 126 Bobby Higginson 1.00 .30
❑ 127 Juan Pierre 1.00 .30
❑ 128 Moises Alou 1.00 .30
❑ 129 Roy Oswalt 1.00 .30
❑ 130 Nomar Garciaparra 4.00 1.20
❑ 131 Fred McGriff 1.50 .45
❑ 132 Edgardo Alfonzo 1.00 .30
❑ 133 Johnny Damon Sox 1.50 .45
❑ 134 Dewon Brazelton 1.00 .30
❑ 135 Mark Mulder 1.00 .30
❑ 136 So Taguchi FYP RC 5.00 1.50
❑ 137 Mario Ramos FYP RC 4.00 1.20
❑ 138 Dan Johnson FYP RC 15.00 4.50
❑ 139 Hansel Izquierdo FYP RC 4.00 1.20
❑ 140 Kazuhisa Ishii FYP RC 5.00 1.50
❑ 141 Jon Switzer FYP RC 4.00 1.20
❑ 142 Chris Tritle FYP RC 4.00 1.20
❑ 143 Chris Snelling FYP RC 5.00 1.50
❑ 144 Chone Figgins FYP RC 5.00 1.50
❑ 145 Dan Phillips FYP RC 4.00 1.20
❑ 146 John Rodriguez FYP RC 5.00 1.50
❑ 147 Colt Griffin FYP RC 4.00 1.20
❑ 148 Jonny Gomes FYP RC 12.00 3.60
❑ 149 Josh Barfield FYP RC 6.00 1.80
❑ 150 Joe Mauer FYP RC 15.00 4.50

2003 Topps Retired Signature

	MINT	NRMT
COMPLETE SET (110)	200.00	90.00

❑ 1 Willie Mays 6.00 2.70
❑ 2 Tony Perez 1.25 .55
❑ 3 Tom Seaver 2.00 .90
❑ 4 Johnny Bench 3.00 1.35
❑ 5 Rod Carew 2.00 .90
❑ 6 Red Schoendienst 1.25 .55
❑ 7 Phil Rizzuto 2.00 .90
❑ 8 Ozzie Smith 5.00 2.20
❑ 9 Maury Wills 1.25 .55
❑ 10 Hank Aaron 6.00 2.70
❑ 11 Jim Palmer 1.25 .55
❑ 12 Jose Cruz Sr. 1.25 .55
❑ 13 Dave Parker 1.25 .55
❑ 14 Don Sutton 1.25 .55
❑ 15 Brooks Robinson 2.00 .90
❑ 16 Bo Jackson 3.00 1.35
❑ 17 Andre Dawson 1.25 .55
❑ 18 Fergie Jenkins 1.25 .55
❑ 19 George Foster 1.25 .55
❑ 20 George Brett 6.00 2.70
❑ 21 Jerry Koosman 1.25 .55
❑ 22 John Kruk 1.25 .55
❑ 23 Kent Tekulve 1.25 .55
❑ 24 Lee Smith 1.25 .55
❑ 25 Nolan Ryan 8.00 3.60
❑ 26 Paul O'Neill 1.25 .55
❑ 27 Rich Gossage 1.25 .55
❑ 28 Ron Santo 1.25 .55
❑ 29 Tom Lasorda 1.25 .55
❑ 30 Tony Gwynn 4.00 1.80
❑ 31 Vida Blue 1.25 .55
❑ 32 Whitey Herzog 1.25 .55
❑ 33 Willie McGee 1.25 .55
❑ 34 Bill Mazeroski 1.25 .55
❑ 35 Al Kaline 3.00 1.35
❑ 36 Bobby Richardson 1.25 .55
❑ 37 Carlton Fisk 2.00 .90
❑ 38 Darrell Evans 1.25 .55
❑ 39 Dave Concepcion 1.25 .55
❑ 40 Cal Ripken 10.00 4.50
❑ 41 Dwight Evans 2.00 .90
❑ 42 Earl Weaver 1.25 .55
❑ 43 Fred Lynn 1.25 .55
❑ 44 Greg Luzinski 1.25 .55
❑ 45 Duke Snider 2.00 .90
❑ 46 Hank Bauer 1.25 .55
❑ 47 Jim Rice 1.25 .55
❑ 48 Johnny Sain 1.25 .55
❑ 49 Lenny Dykstra 1.25 .55
❑ 50 Mike Schmidt 6.00 2.70
❑ 51 Orlando Cepeda 1.25 .55
❑ 52 Ralph Kiner 1.25 .55
❑ 53 Robin Roberts 1.25 .55
❑ 54 Ron Guidry 1.25 .55
❑ 55 Steve Garvey 1.25 .55
❑ 56 Tony Oliva 1.25 .55
❑ 57 Whitey Ford 2.00 .90
❑ 58 Willie McCovey 1.25 .55
❑ 59 Phil Niekro 1.25 .55
❑ 60 Stan Musial 5.00 2.20
❑ 61 Rollie Fingers 1.25 .55
❑ 62 Robin Yount 3.00 1.35
❑ 63 Alan Trammell 1.25 .55
❑ 64 Bill Buckner 1.25 .55
❑ 65 Bob Feller 1.25 .55
❑ 66 Bruce Sutter 1.25 .55
❑ 67 Dale Murphy 2.00 .90
❑ 68 Dennis Eckersley 1.25 .55
❑ 69 Don Newcombe 1.25 .55
❑ 70 Don Mattingly 6.00 2.70
❑ 71 Dwight Gooden 1.25 .55
❑ 72 Frank Robinson 2.00 .90
❑ 73 Gary Carter 1.25 .55
❑ 74 Graig Nettles 1.25 .55
❑ 75 Harmon Killebrew 3.00 1.35
❑ 76 Jim Bunning 1.25 .55
❑ 77 Joe Morgan 1.25 .55
❑ 78 Joe Rudi 1.25 .55
❑ 79 Jose Canseco 2.00 .90
❑ 80 Ernie Banks 3.00 1.35
❑ 81 Luis Aparicio 1.25 .55
❑ 82 Luis Tiant 1.25 .55
❑ 83 Mark Fidrych 1.25 .55
❑ 84 Kirk Gibson 2.00 .90
❑ 85 Lou Brock 2.00 .90
❑ 86 Juan Marichal 1.25 .55
❑ 87 Monte Irvin 1.25 .55
❑ 88 Paul Molitor 2.00 .90
❑ 89 Tommy John 1.25 .55
❑ 90 Warren Spahn 2.00 .90
❑ 91 Wade Boggs 2.00 .90
❑ 92 Reggie Jackson 2.00 .90
❑ 93 Kirby Puckett 3.00 1.35
❑ 94 Boog Powell 2.00 .90
❑ 95 Carl Yastrzemski 5.00 2.20
❑ 96 Bobby Thomson 1.25 .55
❑ 97 Bill Skowron 1.25 .55
❑ 98 Bill Madlock 1.25 .55
❑ 99 Sparky Anderson 1.25 .55
❑ 100 Yogi Berra 3.00 1.35
❑ 101 Bobby Doerr 1.25 .55
❑ 102 Gaylord Perry 1.25 .55
❑ 103 George Kell 1.25 .55
❑ 104 Harold Reynolds 1.25 .55
❑ 105 Joe Carter 1.25 .55
❑ 106 Johnny Podres 1.25 .55

		Nm-Mt	Ex-Mt
❑ 107	Ron Cey	1.25	.55
❑ 108	Tim McCarver	1.25	.55
❑ 109	Tug McGraw	1.25	.55
❑ 110	Don Larsen	1.25	.55

2004 Topps Retired Signature

		Nm-Mt	Ex-Mt
COMPLETE SET (110)		200.00	60.00
❑ 1	Willie Mays	6.00	1.80
❑ 2	Tony Gwynn	5.00	1.50
❑ 3	Dale Murphy	2.00	.60
❑ 4	Lenny Dykstra	1.25	.35
❑ 5	Johnny Bench	3.00	.90
❑ 6	Bill Buckner	1.25	.35
❑ 7	Ferguson Jenkins	1.25	.35
❑ 8	George Brett	6.00	1.80
❑ 9	Ralph Kiner	2.00	.60
❑ 10	Ernie Banks	3.00	.90
❑ 11	Hal McRae	1.25	.35
❑ 12	Lou Brock	2.00	.60
❑ 13	Keith Hernandez	1.25	.35
❑ 14	Jose Canseco	2.00	.60
❑ 15	Whitey Ford	2.00	.60
❑ 16	Dave Kingman	1.25	.35
❑ 17	Tim Raines	1.25	.35
❑ 18	Paul O'Neill	2.00	.60
❑ 19	Lou Whitaker	1.25	.35
❑ 20	Mike Schmidt	6.00	1.80
❑ 21	Wally Joyner	1.00	.30
❑ 22	Kirk Gibson	2.00	.60
❑ 23	Ryne Sandberg	6.00	1.80
❑ 24	Luis Tiant	1.25	.35
❑ 25	Al Kaline	3.00	.90
❑ 26	Brooks Robinson	2.00	.60
❑ 27	Don Zimmer	1.25	.35
❑ 28	Nolan Ryan	8.00	2.40
❑ 29	Maury Wills	1.25	.35
❑ 30	Stan Musial	5.00	1.50
❑ 31	Garry Maddox	1.00	.30
❑ 32	Tom Brunansky	1.00	.30
❑ 33	Don Mattingly	6.00	1.80
❑ 34	Earl Weaver	1.25	.35
❑ 35	Bobby Grich	1.25	.35
❑ 36	Orlando Cepeda	1.25	.35
❑ 37	Alan Trammell	1.25	.35
❑ 38	Al Hrabosky	1.00	.30
❑ 39	Dave Lopes	1.00	.30
❑ 40	Rod Carew	2.00	.60
❑ 41	Robin Yount	3.00	.90
❑ 42	Dwight Gooden	1.25	.35
❑ 43	Andre Dawson	1.25	.35
❑ 44	Hank Aaron	6.00	1.80
❑ 45	Norm Cash	2.00	.60
❑ 46	Reggie Jackson	2.00	.60
❑ 47	Jim Rice	1.25	.35
❑ 48	Carlton Fisk	2.00	.60
❑ 49	Dave Parker	1.25	.35
❑ 50	Cal Ripken	10.00	3.00
❑ 51	Roy Face	1.00	.30
❑ 52	Bob Gibson	2.00	.60
❑ 53	Jimmy Key	1.25	.35
❑ 54	Al Oliver	1.00	.30
❑ 55	Don Larsen	1.25	.35
❑ 56	Tom Seaver	2.00	.60
❑ 57	Tony Armas	1.00	.30
❑ 58	Dave Stieb	1.25	.35
❑ 59	Will Clark	2.00	.60
❑ 60	Duke Snider	2.00	.60
❑ 61	Cesar Geronimo	1.00	.30
❑ 62	Ron Kittle	1.00	.30
❑ 63	Ron Santo	2.00	.60
❑ 64	Mickey Rivers	1.00	.30
❑ 65	Jim Piersall	1.25	.35
❑ 66	Ron Swoboda	1.25	.35
❑ 67	Kent Hrbek	1.25	.35
❑ 68	Dennis Eckersley	2.00	.60
❑ 69	Greg Luzinski	1.25	.35
❑ 70	Harmon Killebrew	3.00	.90
❑ 71	Ron Guidry	1.25	.35
❑ 72	Steve Garvey	1.25	.35
❑ 73	Andy Van Slyke	2.00	.60
❑ 74	Goose Gossage	1.25	.35
❑ 75	Ozzie Smith	5.00	1.50
❑ 76	Richie Allen	1.25	.35
❑ 77	Vida Blue	1.00	.30
❑ 78	Tony Oliva	1.25	.35
❑ 79	Darryl Strawberry	1.25	.35
❑ 80	Frank Robinson	1.25	.35
❑ 81	Bruce Sutter	1.25	.35
❑ 82	Dave Concepcion	1.25	.35
❑ 83	Darrell Evans	1.00	.30
❑ 84	Jack Morris	1.25	.35
❑ 85	Bo Jackson	3.00	.90
❑ 86	Orel Hershiser	1.25	.35
❑ 87	Rob Dibble	1.25	.35
❑ 88	Wade Boggs	2.00	.60
❑ 89	Fernando Valenzuela	1.25	.35
❑ 90	Jim Palmer	1.25	.35
❑ 91	George Foster	1.25	.35
❑ 92	Mike Scott	1.00	.30
❑ 93	Paul Molitor	2.00	.60
❑ 94	Gary Carter	1.25	.35
❑ 95	Bobby Richardson	1.25	.35
❑ 96	Rollie Fingers	1.25	.35
❑ 97	Tim McCarver	1.25	.35
❑ 98	John Candelaria	1.00	.30
❑ 99	Dave Winfield	1.25	.35
❑ 100	Yogi Berra	3.00	.90
❑ 101	Bill Madlock	1.25	.35
❑ 102	Jack McDowell	1.00	.30
❑ 103	Luis Aparicio	1.25	.35
❑ 104	Graig Nettles	1.25	.35
❑ 105	Dave Stewart	1.25	.35
❑ 106	Darren Daulton	1.25	.35
❑ 107	Gary Gaetti	1.25	.35
❑ 108	Tony Fernandez	1.00	.30
❑ 109	Buddy Bell	1.00	.30
❑ 110	Carl Yastrzemski	5.00	1.50

2005 Topps Retired Signature

PLATE ODDS 1:126 HOBBY, 1:127 RETAIL
PLATE PRINT RUN 1 SET PER COLOR
BLACK-CYAN-MAGENTA-YELLOW ISSUED
NO PLATE PRICING DUE TO SCARCITY

		Nm-Mt	Ex-Mt
❑ 1	Josh Gibson	5.00	1.50
❑ 2	Andre Dawson	2.00	.60
❑ 3	Al Kaline	5.00	1.50
❑ 4	Andy Van Slyke	3.00	.90
❑ 5	Brett Butler	2.00	.60
❑ 6	Bob Gibson	3.00	.90
❑ 7	Bo Jackson	5.00	1.50
❑ 8	Carlton Fisk	3.00	.90
❑ 9	Chuck Knoblauch	2.00	.60
❑ 10	Cal Ripken	15.00	4.50
❑ 11	Carl Yastrzemski	6.00	1.80
❑ 12	Tom Niedenfuer	2.00	.60
❑ 13	Dennis Eckersley	2.00	.60
❑ 14	Darryl Strawberry	2.00	.60
❑ 15	Dwight Gooden	2.00	.60
❑ 16	Davey Johnson	2.00	.60
❑ 17	Don Mattingly	10.00	3.00
❑ 18	Dave Winfield	2.00	.60
❑ 19	Don Zimmer	2.00	.60
❑ 20	Ernie Banks	5.00	1.50
❑ 21	George Brett	10.00	3.00
❑ 22	Gary Carter	2.00	.60
❑ 23	Gregg Jefferies	2.00	.60
❑ 24	Harold Baines	2.00	.60
❑ 25	Ryne Sandberg	10.00	3.00
❑ 26	Howard Johnson	2.00	.60
❑ 27	Jim Abbott	2.00	.60
❑ 28	Johnny Bench	5.00	1.50
❑ 29	Jay Buhner	2.00	.60
❑ 30	Johnny Podres	2.00	.60
❑ 31	Jose Canseco	3.00	.90
❑ 32	Keith Hernandez	2.00	.60
❑ 33	Lou Brock Cubs	5.00	1.50
❑ 34	Lou Whitaker	2.00	.60
❑ 35	Mark Fidrych	2.00	.60
❑ 36	Orlando Cepeda	2.00	.60
❑ 37	Ozzie Smith	8.00	2.40
❑ 38	Paul O'Neill	3.00	.90
❑ 39	Reggie Jackson	3.00	.90
❑ 40	Sid Fernandez	2.00	.60
❑ 41	Tony Gwynn	6.00	1.80
❑ 42	Tim Raines	2.00	.60
❑ 43	Tom Seaver	3.00	.90
❑ 44	Vida Blue	2.00	.60
❑ 45	Brady Anderson	2.00	.60
❑ 46	Bob Brenly	2.00	.60
❑ 47	Bob Feller	2.00	.60
❑ 48	Bill Mazeroski	3.00	.90
❑ 49	Brooks Robinson	3.00	.90
❑ 50	Harmon Killebrew	5.00	1.50
❑ 51	Bob Welch	2.00	.60
❑ 52	Carl Erskine	2.00	.60
❑ 53	Dale Murphy	3.00	.90
❑ 54	Denny McLain	2.00	.60
❑ 55	Dave Magadan	2.00	.60
❑ 56	Duke Snider	3.00	.90
❑ 57	Ed Kranepool	2.00	.60
❑ 58	Frank Robinson	2.00	.60
❑ 59	Jesus Alou	2.00	.60
❑ 60	Joe Girardi	2.00	.60
❑ 61	John Kruk	3.00	.90
❑ 62	Jimmy Leyland MG	2.00	.60
❑ 63	Juan Marichal	2.00	.60
❑ 64	Johnny Pesky	2.00	.60
❑ 65	Jesse Orosco	2.00	.60
❑ 66	Ken Singleton	2.00	.60
❑ 67	Matty Alou	2.00	.60
❑ 68	Monte Irvin	2.00	.60
❑ 69	Matt Williams	3.00	.90
❑ 70	Pedro Guerrero	2.00	.60
❑ 71	Ron Blomberg	2.00	.60
❑ 72	Rod Carew	3.00	.90
❑ 73	Rafael Santana	2.00	.60
❑ 74	Ralph Kiner	2.00	.60
❑ 75	Wade Boggs	3.00	.90
❑ 76	Roger Craig	2.00	.60
❑ 77	Robin Yount	5.00	1.50
❑ 78	Steve Carlton	2.00	.60
❑ 79	Shawon Dunston	2.00	.60
❑ 80	Steve Garvey	2.00	.60
❑ 81	Stan Musial	8.00	2.40
❑ 82	Travis Fryman	2.00	.60
❑ 83	Tito Fuentes	2.00	.60
❑ 84	Mike Cuellar	2.00	.60
❑ 85	Roberto Clemente	12.00	3.60
❑ 86	Whitey Ford	3.00	.90
❑ 87	Yogi Berra	5.00	1.50
❑ 88	Atlee Hammaker	2.00	.60
❑ 89	Bill Freehan	2.00	.60
❑ 90	Brian Cashman GM	2.00	.60
❑ 91	Bobby Richardson	3.00	.90
❑ 92	Bob Boone	2.00	.60
❑ 93	Charlie Hough	2.00	.60

		Nm-Mt	Ex-Mt
❑ 94	Glenn Hubbard	2.00	.60
❑ 95	Grady Little MG	2.00	.60
❑ 96	Jimmy Piersall	2.00	.60
❑ 97	Jim Frey MG	2.00	.60
❑ 98	Jerry Grote	2.00	.60
❑ 99	Jim Leyritz	2.00	.60
❑ 100	Nolan Ryan	10.00	3.00
❑ 101	Jim Kaat	2.00	.60
❑ 102	Joe Pepitone	2.00	.60
❑ 103	J.R. Richard	2.00	.60
❑ 104	John Candelaria	2.00	.60
❑ 105	Moose Skowron	2.00	.60
❑ 106	Rick Cerone	2.00	.60
❑ 107	Ron Santo	3.00	.90
❑ 108	Rick Dempsey	2.00	.60
❑ 109	Roy White	2.00	.60
❑ 110	Tippy Martinez	2.00	.60

1997 Topps Stars

		Nm-Mt	Ex-Mt
COMPLETE SET (125)		30.00	9.00
❑ 1	Larry Walker	.30	.09
❑ 2	Tino Martinez	.50	.15
❑ 3	Cal Ripken	2.50	.75
❑ 4	Ken Griffey Jr.	1.25	.35
❑ 5	Chipper Jones	.75	.23
❑ 6	David Justice	.30	.09
❑ 7	Mike Piazza	1.25	.35
❑ 8	Jeff Bagwell	.50	.15
❑ 9	Ron Gant	.30	.09
❑ 10	Sammy Sosa	.75	.23
❑ 11	Tony Gwynn	1.00	.30
❑ 12	Carlos Baerga	.30	.09
❑ 13	Frank Thomas	.75	.23
❑ 14	Moises Alou	.30	.09
❑ 15	Barry Larkin	.50	.15
❑ 16	Ivan Rodriguez	.50	.15
❑ 17	Greg Maddux	1.25	.35
❑ 18	Jim Edmonds	.30	.09
❑ 19	Jose Canseco	.50	.15
❑ 20	Rafael Palmeiro	.50	.15
❑ 21	Paul Molitor	.50	.15
❑ 22	Kevin Appier	.30	.09
❑ 23	Raul Mondesi	.30	.09
❑ 24	Lance Johnson	.30	.09
❑ 25	Edgar Martinez	.50	.15
❑ 26	Andres Galarraga	.30	.09
❑ 27	Mo Vaughn	.30	.09
❑ 28	Ken Caminiti	.30	.09
❑ 29	Cecil Fielder	.30	.09
❑ 30	Harold Baines	.30	.09
❑ 31	Roberto Alomar	.50	.15
❑ 32	Shawn Estes	.30	.09
❑ 33	Tom Glavine	.50	.15
❑ 34	Dennis Eckersley	.30	.09
❑ 35	Manny Ramirez	.50	.15
❑ 36	John Olerud	.30	.09
❑ 37	Juan Gonzalez	.30	.09
❑ 38	Chuck Knoblauch	.30	.09
❑ 39	Albert Belle	.30	.09
❑ 40	Vinny Castilla	.30	.09
❑ 41	John Smoltz	.50	.15
❑ 42	Barry Bonds	2.00	.60
❑ 43	Randy Johnson	.75	.23
❑ 44	Brady Anderson	.30	.09
❑ 45	Jeff Blauser	.30	.09
❑ 46	Craig Biggio	.50	.15
❑ 47	Jeff Conine	.30	.09
❑ 48	Marquis Grissom	.30	.09
❑ 49	Mark Grace	.50	.15
❑ 50	Roger Clemens	1.50	.45
❑ 51	Mark McGwire	2.00	.60
❑ 52	Fred McGriff	.50	.15
❑ 53	Gary Sheffield	.30	.09
❑ 54	Bobby Jones	.30	.09
❑ 55	Eric Young	.30	.09
❑ 56	Robin Ventura	.30	.09
❑ 57	Wade Boggs	.50	.15
❑ 58	Joe Carter	.30	.09
❑ 59	Ryne Sandberg	1.25	.35
❑ 60	Matt Williams	.30	.09
❑ 61	Todd Hundley	.30	.09
❑ 62	Dante Bichette	.30	.09
❑ 63	Chili Davis	.30	.09
❑ 64	Kenny Lofton	.30	.09
❑ 65	Jay Buhner	.30	.09
❑ 66	Will Clark	.50	.15
❑ 67	Travis Fryman	.30	.09
❑ 68	Pat Hentgen	.30	.09
❑ 69	Ellis Burks	.30	.09
❑ 70	Mike Mussina	.50	.15
❑ 71	Hideo Nomo	.75	.23
❑ 72	Sandy Alomar Jr.	.30	.09
❑ 73	Bobby Bonilla	.30	.09
❑ 74	Rickey Henderson	.75	.23
❑ 75	David Cone	.30	.09
❑ 76	Terry Steinbach	.30	.09
❑ 77	Pedro Martinez	.50	.15
❑ 78	Jim Thome	.50	.15
❑ 79	Rod Beck	.30	.09
❑ 80	Randy Myers	.30	.09
❑ 81	Charles Nagy	.30	.09
❑ 82	Mark Wohlers	.30	.09
❑ 83	Paul O'Neill	.50	.15
❑ 84	Curt Schilling	.30	.09
❑ 85	Joey Cora	.30	.09
❑ 86	John Franco	.30	.09
❑ 87	Kevin Brown	.30	.09
❑ 88	Benito Santiago	.30	.09
❑ 89	Ray Lankford	.30	.09
❑ 90	Bernie Williams	.50	.15
❑ 91	Jason Dickson	.30	.09
❑ 92	Jeff Cirillo	.30	.09
❑ 93	Nomar Garciaparra	1.25	.35
❑ 94	Mariano Rivera	.50	.15
❑ 95	Javy Lopez	.30	.09
❑ 96	Tony Womack RC	.75	.23
❑ 97	Jose Rosado	.30	.09
❑ 98	Denny Neagle	.30	.09
❑ 99	Darryl Kile	.30	.09
❑ 100	Justin Thompson	.30	.09
❑ 101	Juan Encarnacion	.30	.09
❑ 102	Brad Fullmer	.30	.09
❑ 103	Kris Benson RC	.75	.23
❑ 104	Todd Helton	.75	.23
❑ 105	Paul Konerko	.50	.15
❑ 106	Travis Lee RC	.50	.15
❑ 107	Todd Greene	.30	.09
❑ 108	Mark Kotsay RC	1.25	.35
❑ 109	Carl Pavano	.30	.09
❑ 110	Kerry Wood RC	8.00	2.40
❑ 111	Jason Romano RC	.30	.09
❑ 112	Geoff Goetz RC	.30	.09
❑ 113	Scott Hodges RC	.30	.09
❑ 114	Aaron Akin RC	.30	.09
❑ 115	Vernon Wells RC	2.00	.60
❑ 116	Chris Stowe RC	.30	.09
❑ 117	Brett Caradonna RC	.30	.09
❑ 118	Adam Kennedy RC	.75	.23
❑ 119	Jayson Werth RC	.75	.23
❑ 120	Glenn Davis RC	.30	.09
❑ 121	Troy Cameron RC	.30	.09
❑ 122	J.J. Davis RC	.50	.15
❑ 123	Jason Dellaero RC	.30	.09
❑ 124	Jason Standridge RC	.50	.15
❑ 125	Lance Berkman RC	5.00	1.50
❑ NNO	Checklist	.30	.09

2001 Topps Stars

		Nm-Mt	Ex-Mt
COMPLETE SET (200)		50.00	15.00
❑ 1	Darin Erstad	.50	.15
❑ 2	Luis Gonzalez	.50	.15
❑ 3	Rafael Furcal	.50	.15
❑ 4	Dante Bichette	.50	.15
❑ 5	Sammy Sosa	1.25	.35
❑ 6	Ken Griffey Jr.	2.00	.60
❑ 7	Jim Thome	.75	.23
❑ 8	Bobby Higginson	.50	.15
❑ 9	Cliff Floyd	.50	.15
❑ 10	Lance Berkman	.50	.15
❑ 11	Eric Karros	.50	.15
❑ 12	Jeromy Burnitz	.50	.15
❑ 13	Jose Vidro	.40	.12
❑ 14	Benny Agbayani	.40	.12
❑ 15	Jorge Posada	.75	.23
❑ 16	Ramon Hernandez	.40	.12
❑ 17	Jason Kendall	.50	.15
❑ 18	Jeff Kent	.50	.15
❑ 19	John Olerud	.50	.15
❑ 20	Al Martin	.40	.12
❑ 21	Gerald Williams	.40	.12
❑ 22	Gabe Kapler	.50	.15
❑ 23	Carlos Delgado	.50	.15
❑ 24	Mariano Rivera	.75	.23
❑ 25	Javy Lopez	.50	.15
❑ 26	Paul Konerko	.50	.15
❑ 27	Daryle Ward	.40	.12
❑ 28	Mike Lieberthal	.40	.12
❑ 29	Tom Goodwin	.40	.12
❑ 30	Garret Anderson	.50	.15
❑ 31	Steve Finley	.50	.15
❑ 32	Brian Jordan	.50	.15
❑ 33	Nomar Garciaparra	2.00	.60
❑ 34	Ray Durham	.50	.15
❑ 35	Sean Casey	.75	.23
❑ 36	Kenny Lofton	.50	.15
❑ 37	Dean Palmer	.50	.15
❑ 38	Jeff Bagwell	.75	.23
❑ 39	Mike Sweeney	.50	.15
❑ 40	Adrian Beltre	.50	.15
❑ 41	Richie Sexson	.50	.15
❑ 42	Vladimir Guerrero	1.25	.35
❑ 43	Derek Jeter	3.00	.90
❑ 44	Miguel Tejada	.50	.15
❑ 45	Doug Glanville	.40	.12
❑ 46	Brian Giles	.50	.15
❑ 47	Marvin Benard	.40	.12
❑ 48	Edgar Martinez	.75	.23
❑ 49	Edgar Renteria	.50	.15
❑ 50	Fred McGriff	.75	.23
❑ 51	Ivan Rodriguez	.75	.23
❑ 52	Brad Fullmer	.40	.12
❑ 53	Antonio Alfonseca	.40	.12
❑ 54	Tom Glavine	.75	.23
❑ 55	Warren Morris	.40	.12
❑ 56	Johnny Damon	.75	.23
❑ 57	Dmitri Young	.50	.15
❑ 58	Mo Vaughn	.50	.15
❑ 59	Randy Johnson	1.25	.35
❑ 60	Greg Maddux	2.00	.60
❑ 61	Carl Everett	.50	.15
❑ 62	Magglio Ordonez	.50	.15
❑ 63	Pokey Reese	.40	.12
❑ 64	Todd Helton	.75	.23
❑ 65	Preston Wilson	.50	.15
❑ 66	Richard Hidalgo	.40	.12
❑ 67	Jermaine Dye	.50	.15
❑ 68	Gary Sheffield	.50	.15
❑ 69	Geoff Jenkins	.40	.12
❑ 70	Edgardo Alfonzo	.40	.12

Card	Nm-Mt	Ex-Mt
❑ 71 Paul O'Neill	.75	.23
❑ 72 Terrence Long	.40	.12
❑ 73 Bob Abreu	.50	.15
❑ 74 Kevin Young	.40	.12
❑ 75 J.T. Snow	.50	.15
❑ 76 Alex Rodriguez	2.00	.60
❑ 77 Jim Edmonds	.75	.23
❑ 78 Mark McGwire	3.00	.90
❑ 79 Tony Batista	.40	.12
❑ 80 Darrin Fletcher	.40	.12
❑ 81 Robb Nen	.50	.15
❑ 82 Jose Offerman	.40	.12
❑ 83 Travis Fryman	.50	.15
❑ 84 Joe Randa	.40	.12
❑ 85 Omar Vizquel	.75	.23
❑ 86 Tim Salmon	.75	.23
❑ 87 Andruw Jones	.75	.23
❑ 88 Albert Belle	.50	.15
❑ 89 Manny Ramirez Sox	.75	.23
❑ 90 Frank Thomas	1.25	.35
❑ 91 Barry Larkin	.75	.23
❑ 92 Neifi Perez	.40	.12
❑ 93 Luis Castillo	.40	.12
❑ 94 Moises Alou	.50	.15
❑ 95 Mark Quinn	.40	.12
❑ 96 Kevin Brown	.50	.15
❑ 97 Cristian Guzman	.40	.12
❑ 98 Mike Piazza	2.00	.60
❑ 99 Bernie Williams	.75	.23
❑ 100 Jason Giambi	.50	.15
❑ 101 Scott Rolen	.75	.23
❑ 102 Phil Nevin	.50	.15
❑ 103 Rich Aurilia	.40	.12
❑ 104 Mike Cameron	.40	.12
❑ 105 Fernando Vina	.40	.12
❑ 106 Greg Vaughn	.40	.12
❑ 107 Jose Cruz Jr.	.40	.12
❑ 108 Raul Mondesi	.50	.15
❑ 109 Ben Molina	.40	.12
❑ 110 Pedro Martinez	.75	.23
❑ 111 Todd Hollandsworth	.40	.12
❑ 112 Jacque Jones	.50	.15
❑ 113 Rickey Henderson	1.25	.35
❑ 114 Troy Glaus	.50	.15
❑ 115 Chipper Jones	1.25	.35
❑ 116 Delino DeShields	.40	.12
❑ 117 Eric Young	.40	.12
❑ 118 Jose Valentin	.40	.12
❑ 119 Roberto Alomar	.75	.23
❑ 120 Jeff Cirillo	.40	.12
❑ 121 Mike Lowell	.50	.15
❑ 122 Julio Lugo	.40	.12
❑ 123 Shawn Green	.50	.15
❑ 124 Marquis Grissom	.50	.15
❑ 125 Matt Lawton	.40	.12
❑ 126 Jay Payton	.40	.12
❑ 127 David Justice	.50	.15
❑ 128 Eric Chavez	.50	.15
❑ 129 Pat Burrell	.50	.15
❑ 130 Ryan Klesko	.50	.15
❑ 131 Barry Bonds	3.00	.90
❑ 132 Jay Buhner	.50	.15
❑ 133 J.D. Drew	.50	.15
❑ 134 Rafael Palmeiro	.75	.23
❑ 135 Shannon Stewart	.50	.15
❑ 136 Juan Gonzalez	.50	.15
❑ 137 Tony Womack	.40	.12
❑ 138 Carlos Lee	.50	.15
❑ 139 Derrek Lee	.75	.23
❑ 140 Ben Grieve	.40	.12
❑ 141 Ron Belliard	.40	.12
❑ 142 Stan Musial	2.00	.60
❑ 143 Ernie Banks	1.25	.35
❑ 144 Jim Palmer	.50	.15
❑ 145 Tony Perez	.50	.15
❑ 146 Duke Snider	.75	.23
❑ 147 Rod Carew	.75	.23
❑ 148 Warren Spahn	.75	.23
❑ 149 Yogi Berra	1.50	.45
❑ 150 Juan Marichal	.50	.15
❑ 151 Eric Munson	.40	.12
❑ 152 Carlos Pena	.40	.12
❑ 153 Joe Crede	1.25	.35
❑ 154 Ryan Anderson	.40	.12
❑ 155 Milton Bradley	.50	.15
❑ 156 Sean Burroughs	.40	.12
❑ 157 Corey Patterson	.40	.12
❑ 158 C.C. Sabathia	.50	.15
❑ 159 Ben Petrick	.40	.12
❑ 160 Aubrey Huff	.50	.15
❑ 161 Gookie Dawkins	.40	.12
❑ 162 Ben Sheets	.75	.23
❑ 163 Pablo Ozuna	.40	.12
❑ 164 Eric Valent	.40	.12
❑ 165 Rod Barajas	.40	.12
❑ 166 Chin-Feng Chen	.50	.15
❑ 167 Josh Hamilton	.40	.12
❑ 168 Keith Ginter	.40	.12
❑ 169 Vernon Wells	.50	.15
❑ 170 Dernell Stenson	.40	.12
❑ 171 Alfonso Soriano	.75	.23
❑ 172 Jason Marquis	.40	.12
❑ 173 Nick Johnson	.50	.15
❑ 174 Adam Everett	.40	.12
❑ 175 Jimmy Rollins	.50	.15
❑ 176 Ben Diggins	.40	.12
❑ 177 John Lackey	.40	.12
❑ 178 Scott Heard	.40	.12
❑ 179 Brian Hitchcox RC	.40	.12
❑ 180 Odannis Ayala RC	.40	.12
❑ 181 Scott Pratt RC	.40	.12
❑ 182 Greg Runser RC	.40	.12
❑ 183 Chris Russ RC	.40	.12
❑ 184 Derek Thompson	.40	.12
❑ 185 Jason Jones RC	.40	.12
❑ 186 Dominic Rich RC	.40	.12
❑ 187 Chad Petty RC	.40	.12
❑ 188 Steve Smyth RC	.40	.12
❑ 189 Bryan Hebson RC	.40	.12
❑ 190 Danny Borrell RC	.40	.12
❑ 191 Bob Keppel RC	.40	.12
❑ 192 Justin Wayne RC	.40	.12
❑ 193 R. Abercrombie RC	.40	.12
❑ 194 Travis Baptist RC	.40	.12
❑ 195 Shawn Fagan RC	.40	.12
❑ 196 Jose Reyes RC	5.00	1.50
❑ 197 Chris Bass RC	.40	.12
❑ 198 Albert Pujols RC	50.00	15.00
❑ 199 Luis Cotto RC	.40	.12
❑ 200 Jake Peavy RC	5.00	1.50

2004 Topps Total

	Nm-Mt	Ex-Mt
COMPLETE SET (880)	150.00	45.00
OVERALL PRESS PLATES ODDS 1:159		.00
PLATES PRINT RUN 1 #'d SET PER COLOR		.00

PLATES: BLACK, CYAN, MAGENTA & YELLOW
NO PLATES PRICING DUE TO SCARCITY

Card	Nm-Mt	Ex-Mt
❑ 1 Kevin Brown	.30	.09
❑ 2 Mike Mordecai	.30	.09
❑ 3 Seung Song	.30	.09
❑ 4 Mike Maroth	.30	.09
❑ 5 Mike Lieberthal	.30	.09
❑ 6 Billy Koch	.30	.09
❑ 7 Mike Stanton	.30	.09
❑ 8 Brad Penny	.30	.09
❑ 9 Brooks Kieschnick	.30	.09
❑ 10 Carlos Delgado	.30	.09
❑ 11 Brady Clark	.30	.09
❑ 12 Ramon Martinez	.30	.09
❑ 13 Dan Wilson	.30	.09
❑ 14 Guillermo Mota	.30	.09
❑ 15 Trevor Hoffman	.30	.09
❑ 16 Tony Batista	.30	.09
❑ 17 Rusty Greer	.30	.09
❑ 18 David Weathers	.30	.09
❑ 19 Horacio Ramirez	.30	.09
❑ 20 Aubrey Huff	.30	.09
❑ 21 Casey Blake	.30	.09
❑ 22 Ryan Bukvich	.30	.09
❑ 23 Garrett Atkins	.30	.09
❑ 24 Jose Contreras	.30	.09
❑ 25 Chipper Jones	.75	.23
❑ 26 Neifi Perez	.30	.09
❑ 27 Scott Linebrink	.30	.09
❑ 28 Matt Kinney	.30	.09
❑ 29 Michael Restovich	.30	.09
❑ 30 Scott Rolen	.50	.15
❑ 31 John Franco	.30	.09
❑ 32 Toby Hall	.30	.09
❑ 33 Wily Mo Pena	.30	.09
❑ 34 Dennis Tankersley	.30	.09
❑ 35 Robb Nen	.30	.09
❑ 36 Jose Valverde	.30	.09
❑ 37 Chin-Feng Chen	.30	.09
❑ 38 Gary Knotts	.30	.09
❑ 39 Mark Sweeney	.30	.09
❑ 40 Bret Boone	.30	.09
❑ 41 Josh Phelps	.30	.09
❑ 42 Jason LaRue	.30	.09
❑ 43 Tim Redding	.30	.09
❑ 44 Greg Myers	.30	.09
❑ 45 Darin Erstad	.30	.09
❑ 46 Kip Wells	.30	.09
❑ 47 Matt Ford	.30	.09
❑ 48 Jerome Williams	.30	.09
❑ 49 Brian Meadows	.30	.09
❑ 50 Albert Pujols	1.50	.45
❑ 51 Kirk Saarloos	.30	.09
❑ 52 Scott Eyre	.30	.09
❑ 53 John Flaherty	.30	.09
❑ 54 Rafael Soriano	.30	.09
❑ 55 Shea Hillenbrand	.30	.09
❑ 56 Kyle Farnsworth	.30	.09
❑ 57 Nate Cornejo	.30	.09
❑ 58 Julian Tavarez	.30	.09
❑ 59 Ryan Vogelsong	.30	.09
❑ 60 Ryan Klesko	.30	.09
❑ 61 Luke Hudson	.30	.09
❑ 62 Justin Morneau	.30	.09
❑ 63 Frank Catalanotto	.30	.09
❑ 64 Derrick Turnbow	.30	.09
❑ 65 Marcus Giles	.30	.09
❑ 66 Mark Mulder	.30	.09
❑ 67 Matt Anderson	.30	.09
❑ 68 Mike Matheny	.30	.09
❑ 69 Brian Lawrence	.30	.09
❑ 70 Bobby Abreu	.30	.09
❑ 71 Damian Moss	.30	.09
❑ 72 Richard Hidalgo	.30	.09
❑ 73 Mark Kotsay	.30	.09
❑ 74 Mike Cameron	.30	.09
❑ 75 Troy Glaus	.30	.09
❑ 76 Matt Holliday	.30	.09
❑ 77 Byung-Hyun Kim	.30	.09
❑ 78 Aaron Sele	.30	.09
❑ 79 Danny Graves	.30	.09
❑ 80 Barry Zito	.30	.09
❑ 81 Matt LeCroy	.30	.09
❑ 82 Jason Isringhausen	.30	.09
❑ 83 Colby Lewis	.30	.09
❑ 84 Franklyn German	.30	.09
❑ 85 Luis Matos	.30	.09
❑ 86 Mike Timlin	.30	.09
❑ 87 Miguel Batista	.30	.09
❑ 88 John McDonald	.30	.09
❑ 89 Joey Eischen	.30	.09
❑ 90 Mike Mussina	.50	.15
❑ 91 Jack Wilson	.30	.09
❑ 92 Aaron Cook	.30	.09
❑ 93 John Parrish	.30	.09
❑ 94 Jose Valentin	.30	.09
❑ 95 Johnny Damon	.50	.15
❑ 96 Pat Burrell	.30	.09
❑ 97 Brendan Donnelly	.30	.09
❑ 98 Lance Carter	.30	.09
❑ 99 Omar Daal	.30	.09
❑ 100 Ichiro Suzuki	1.50	.45
❑ 101 Robin Ventura	.30	.09

❑	102	Brian Shouse	.30	.09
❑	103	Kevin Jarvis	.30	.09
❑	104	Jason Young	.30	.09
❑	105	Moises Alou	.30	.09
❑	106	Wes Obermueller	.30	.09
❑	107	David Segui	.30	.09
❑	108	Mike MacDougal	.30	.09
❑	109	John Buck	.30	.09
❑	110	Gary Sheffield	.30	.09
❑	111	Yorvit Torrealba	.30	.09
❑	112	Matt Kata	.30	.09
❑	113	David Bell	.30	.09
❑	114	Juan Gonzalez	.30	.09
❑	115	Kelvim Escobar	.30	.09
❑	116	Ruben Sierra	.30	.09
❑	117	Todd Wellemeyer	.30	.09
❑	118	Jamie Walker	.30	.09
❑	119	Will Cunnane	.30	.09
❑	120	Cliff Floyd	.30	.09
❑	121	Aramis Ramirez	.30	.09
❑	122	Damaso Marte	.30	.09
❑	123	Juan Castro	.30	.09
❑	124	Chris Woodward	.30	.09
❑	125	Andruw Jones	.50	.15
❑	126	Ben Weber	.30	.09
❑	127	Dee Brown	.30	.09
❑	128	Steve Reed	.30	.09
❑	129	Gabe Kapler	.30	.09
❑	130	Miguel Cabrera	.50	.15
❑	131	Billy McMillon	.30	.09
❑	132	Julio Mateo	.30	.09
❑	133	Preston Wilson	.30	.09
❑	134	Tony Clark	.30	.09
❑	135	Carlos Lee	.30	.09
❑	136	Carlos Baerga	.30	.09
❑	137	Mike Crudale	.30	.09
❑	138	David Ross	.30	.09
❑	139	Josh Fogg	.30	.09
❑	140	Dmitri Young	.30	.09
❑	141	Cliff Lee	.30	.09
❑	142	Mike Lowell	.30	.09
❑	143	Jason Lane	.30	.09
❑	144	Pedro Feliz	.30	.09
❑	145	Ken Griffey Jr.	1.25	.35
❑	146	Dustin Hermanson	.30	.09
❑	147	Scott Hodges	.30	.09
❑	148	Aquilino Lopez	.30	.09
❑	149	Wes Helms	.30	.09
❑	150	Jason Giambi	.30	.09
❑	151	Erasmo Ramirez	.30	.09
❑	152	Sean Burroughs	.30	.09
❑	153	J.T. Snow	.30	.09
❑	154	Eddie Guardado	.30	.09
❑	155	C.C. Sabathia	.30	.09
❑	156	Kyle Lohse	.30	.09
❑	157	Roberto Hernandez	.30	.09
❑	158	Jason Simontacchi	.30	.09
❑	159	Tim Spooneybarger	.30	.09
❑	160	Alfonso Soriano	.30	.09
❑	161	Mike Gonzalez	.30	.09
❑	162	Alex Cora	.30	.09
❑	163	Kevin Gryboski	.30	.09
❑	164	Mike Lincoln	.30	.09
❑	165	Luis Castillo	.30	.09
❑	166	Odalis Perez	.30	.09
❑	167	Alex Sanchez	.30	.09
❑	168	Rob Mackowiak	.30	.09
❑	169	Francisco Rodriguez	.30	.09
❑	170	Roy Oswalt	.30	.09
❑	171	Omar Infante	.30	.09
❑	172	Ryan Jensen	.30	.09
❑	173	Ben Broussard	.30	.09
❑	174	Mark Hendrickson	.30	.09
❑	175	Manny Ramirez	.50	.15
❑	176	Rob Bell	.30	.09
❑	177	Adam Everett	.30	.09
❑	178	Chris George	.30	.09
❑	179	Ronnie Belliard	.30	.09
❑	180	Eric Gagne	.30	.09
❑	181	Scott Schoeneweis	.30	.09
❑	182	Kris Benson	.30	.09
❑	183	Amaury Telemaco	.30	.09
❑	184	John Riedling	.30	.09
❑	185	Juan Pierre	.30	.09
❑	186	Ramon Ortiz	.30	.09
❑	187	Luis Rivas	.30	.09
❑	188	Larry Bigbie	.30	.09
❑	189	Robby Hammock	.30	.09
❑	190	Geoff Jenkins	.30	.09
❑	191	Chad Cordero	.30	.09
❑	192	Mark Ellis	.30	.09
❑	193	Mark Loretta	.30	.09
❑	194	Ryan Drese	.30	.09
❑	195	Lance Berkman	.30	.09
❑	196	Kevin Appier	.30	.09
❑	197	Kiko Calero	.30	.09
❑	198	Mickey Callaway	.30	.09
❑	199	Chase Utley	.50	.15
❑	200	Nomar Garciaparra	1.25	.35
❑	201	Kevin Cash	.30	.09
❑	202	Ramiro Mendoza	.30	.09
❑	203	Shane Reynolds	.30	.09
❑	204	Chris Spurling	.30	.09
❑	205	Aaron Guiel	.30	.09
❑	206	Mark DeRosa	.30	.09
❑	207	Adam Kennedy	.30	.09
❑	208	Andy Pettitte	.50	.15
❑	209	Rafael Palmeiro	.50	.15
❑	210	Luis Gonzalez	.30	.09
❑	211	Ryan Franklin	.30	.09
❑	212	Bob Wickman	.30	.09
❑	213	Ron Calloway	.30	.09
❑	214	Jae Weong Seo	.30	.09
❑	215	Kazuhisa Ishii	.30	.09
❑	216	Sterling Hitchcock	.30	.09
❑	217	Jimmy Gobble	.30	.09
❑	218	Chad Moeller	.30	.09
❑	219	Jake Peavy	.30	.09
❑	220	John Smoltz	.50	.15
❑	221	Donovan Osborne	.30	.09
❑	222	David Wells	.30	.09
❑	223	Brad Lidge	.30	.09
❑	224	Carlos Zambrano	.30	.09
❑	225	Kerry Wood	.30	.09
❑	226	Alex Cintron	.30	.09
❑	227	Javier A. Lopez	.30	.09
❑	228	Jeremy Griffiths	.30	.09
❑	229	Jon Garland	.30	.09
❑	230	Curt Schilling	.50	.15
❑	231	Alex Scott Gonzalez	.30	.09
❑	232	Jay Gibbons	.30	.09
❑	233	Aaron Miles	.30	.09
❑	234	Mike Gallo	.30	.09
❑	235	Johan Santana	.50	.15
❑	236	Jose Guillen	.30	.09
❑	237	Jeff Conine	.30	.09
❑	238	Matt Roney	.30	.09
❑	239	Desi Relaford	.30	.09
❑	240	Frank Thomas	.75	.23
❑	241	Danny Patterson	.30	.09
❑	242	Kevin Mench	.30	.09
❑	243	Mike Redmond	.30	.09
❑	244	Jeff Suppan	.30	.09
❑	245	Carl Everett	.30	.09
❑	246	Jack Cressend	.30	.09
❑	247	Matt Mantei	.30	.09
❑	248	Enrique Wilson	.30	.09
❑	249	Craig Counsell	.30	.09
❑	250	Mark Prior	.50	.15
❑	251	Jared Sandberg	.30	.09
❑	252	Scott Strickland	.30	.09
❑	253	Lew Ford	.30	.09
❑	254	Hee Seop Choi	.30	.09
❑	255	Jason Phillips	.30	.09
❑	256	Jason Jennings	.30	.09
❑	257	Todd Pratt	.30	.09
❑	258	Matt Herges	.30	.09
❑	259	Kerry Ligtenberg	.30	.09
❑	260	Austin Kearns	.30	.09
❑	261	Jay Witasick	.30	.09
❑	262	Tony Armas Jr.	.30	.09
❑	263	Tom Martin	.30	.09
❑	264	Oliver Perez	.30	.09
❑	265	Jorge Posada	.50	.15
❑	266	Jason Boyd	.30	.09
❑	267	Ben Hendrickson	.30	.09
❑	268	Reggie Sanders	.30	.09
❑	269	Julio Lugo	.30	.09
❑	270	Pedro Martinez	.50	.15
❑	271	Kyle Snyder	.30	.09
❑	272	Felipe Lopez	.30	.09
❑	273	Kevin Millar	.30	.09
❑	274	Travis Hafner	.30	.09
❑	275	Magglio Ordonez	.30	.09
❑	276	Marlon Byrd	.30	.09
❑	277	Scott Spiezio	.30	.09
❑	278	Mark Corey	.30	.09
❑	279	Tim Salmon	.50	.15
❑	280	Alex Gonzalez	.30	.09
❑	281	Marquis Grissom	.30	.09
❑	282	Miguel Olivo	.30	.09
❑	283	Orlando Hudson	.30	.09
❑	284	Rondell White	.30	.09
❑	285	Jermaine Dye	.30	.09
❑	286	Paul Shuey	.30	.09
❑	287	Brandon Inge	.30	.09
❑	288	B.J. Surhoff	.30	.09
❑	289	Edgar Gonzalez	.30	.09
❑	290	Angel Berroa	.30	.09
❑	291	Claudio Vargas	.30	.09
❑	292	Cesar Izturis	.30	.09
❑	293	Brandon Phillips	.30	.09
❑	294	Jeff Duncan	.30	.09
❑	295	Randy Wolf	.30	.09
❑	296	Barry Larkin	.50	.15
❑	297	Felix Rodriguez	.30	.09
❑	298	Robb Quinlan	.30	.09
❑	299	Brian Jordan	.30	.09
❑	300	Dontrelle Willis	.50	.15
❑	301	Doug Davis	.30	.09
❑	302	Ricky Stone	.30	.09
❑	303	Travis Harper	.30	.09
❑	304	Jaret Wright	.30	.09
❑	305	Edgardo Alfonzo	.30	.09
❑	306	Quinton McCracken	.30	.09
❑	307	Jason Bay	.30	.09
❑	308	Joe Randa	.30	.09
❑	309	Steve Sparks	.30	.09
❑	310	Roy Halladay	.30	.09
❑	311	Antonio Alfonseca	.30	.09
❑	312	Michael Cuddyer	.30	.09
❑	313	John Patterson	.30	.09
❑	314	Chris Widger	.30	.09
❑	315	Shigetoshi Hasegawa	.30	.09
❑	316	Tim Wakefield	.30	.09
❑	317	Scott Hatteberg	.30	.09
❑	318	Mike Remlinger	.30	.09
❑	319	Jose Vizcaino	.30	.09
❑	320	Rocco Baldelli	.30	.09
❑	321	David Riske	.30	.09
❑	322	Steve Karsay	.30	.09
❑	323	Peter Bergeron	.30	.09
❑	324	Jeff Weaver	.30	.09
❑	325	Larry Walker	.30	.09
❑	326	Jack Cust	.30	.09
❑	327	Bo Hart	.30	.09
❑	328	Rod Beck	.30	.09
❑	329	Jose Acevedo	.30	.09
❑	330	Hank Blalock	.30	.09
❑	331	Tom Gordon	.30	.09
❑	332	Brian Fuentes	.30	.09
❑	333	Tomas Perez	.30	.09
❑	334	Lenny Harris	.30	.09
❑	335	Matt Morris	.30	.09
❑	336	Jeremi Gonzalez	.30	.09
❑	337	David Eckstein	.30	.09
❑	338	Aaron Rowand	.30	.09
❑	339	Rick Bauer	.30	.09
❑	340	Jim Edmonds	.50	.15
❑	341	Joe Borowski	.30	.09
❑	342	Eric DuBose	.30	.09
❑	343	D'Angelo Jimenez	.30	.09
❑	344	Tomo Ohka	.30	.09
❑	345	Victor Zambrano	.30	.09
❑	346	Joe McEwing	.30	.09
❑	347	Jorge Sosa	.30	.09
❑	348	Keith Ginter	.30	.09
❑	349	A.J. Pierzynski	.30	.09
❑	350	Mike Sweeney	.30	.09
❑	351	Shawn Chacon	.30	.09
❑	352	Matt Clement	.30	.09
❑	353	Vance Wilson	.30	.09
❑	354	Benito Santiago	.30	.09
❑	355	Eric Hinske	.30	.09
❑	356	Vladimir Guerrero	.75	.23
❑	357	Kenny Rogers	.30	.09
❑	358	Travis Lee	.30	.09
❑	359	Jay Powell	.30	.09

❑ 360 Phil Nevin .30 .09
❑ 361 Willie Harris .30 .09
❑ 362 Ty Wigginton .30 .09
❑ 363 Chad Fox .30 .09
❑ 364 Junior Spivey .30 .09
❑ 365 Brandon Webb .30 .09
❑ 366 Brett Myers .30 .09
❑ 367 Alexis Gomez .30 .09
❑ 368 Dave Roberts .30 .09
❑ 369 LaTroy Hawkins .30 .09
❑ 370 Kevin Millwood .30 .09
❑ 371 Brian Schneider .30 .09
❑ 372 Blaine Neal .30 .09
❑ 373 Jeromy Burnitz .30 .09
❑ 374 Ted Lilly .30 .09
❑ 375 Shawn Green .30 .09
❑ 376 Carlos Pena .30 .09
❑ 377 Gil Meche .30 .09
❑ 378 Jeff Bagwell .50 .15
❑ 379 Alex Escobar .30 .09
❑ 380 Erubiel Durazo .30 .09
❑ 381 Cristian Guzman .30 .09
❑ 382 Rocky Biddle .30 .09
❑ 383 Craig Wilson .30 .09
❑ 384 Rey Sanchez .30 .09
❑ 385 Russ Ortiz .30 .09
❑ 386 Freddy Garcia .30 .09
❑ 387 Luis Vizcaino .30 .09
❑ 388 David Ortiz .75 .23
❑ 389 Jose Molina .30 .09
❑ 390 Edgar Martinez .50 .15
❑ 391 Nate Bump .30 .09
❑ 392 Brent Mayne .30 .09
❑ 393 Ray King .30 .09
❑ 394 Paul Wilson .30 .09
❑ 395 Melvin Mora .30 .09
❑ 396 Morgan Ensberg .30 .09
❑ 397 Ramon Hernandez .30 .09
❑ 398 Juan Rincon .30 .09
❑ 399 Ron Mahay .30 .09
❑ 400 Jeff Kent .30 .09
❑ 401 Cal Eldred .30 .09
❑ 402 Mike Difelice .30 .09
❑ 403 Valerio De Los Santos .30 .09
❑ 404 Steve Finley .30 .09
❑ 405 Trot Nixon .30 .09
❑ 406 Akinori Otsuka RC .40 .12
❑ 407 Ryan Freel .30 .09
❑ 408 Ray Durham .30 .09
❑ 409 Aaron Heilman .30 .09
❑ 410 Edgar Renteria .30 .09
❑ 411 Mike Hampton .30 .09
❑ 412 Kirk Rueter .30 .09
❑ 413 Jim Mecir .30 .09
❑ 414 Brian Roberts .30 .09
❑ 415 Paul Konerko .30 .09
❑ 416 Reed Johnson .30 .09
❑ 417 Roger Clemens 1.50 .45
❑ 418 Coco Crisp .30 .09
❑ 419 Carlos Hernandez .30 .09
❑ 420 Scott Podsednik .30 .09
❑ 421 Miguel Cairo .30 .09
❑ 422 Abraham Nunez .30 .09
❑ 423 Endy Chavez .30 .09
❑ 424 Eric Munson .30 .09
❑ 425 Torii Hunter .30 .09
❑ 426 Ben Howard .30 .09
❑ 427 Chris Gomez .30 .09
❑ 428 Francisco Cordero .30 .09
❑ 429 Jeffrey Hammonds .30 .09
❑ 430 Shannon Stewart .30 .09
❑ 431 Einar Diaz .30 .09
❑ 432 Eric Byrnes .30 .09
❑ 433 Marty Cordova .30 .09
❑ 434 Matt Ginter .30 .09
❑ 435 Victor Martinez .30 .09
❑ 436 Geronimo Gil .30 .09
❑ 437 Grant Balfour .30 .09
❑ 438 Ramon Vazquez .30 .09
❑ 439 Jose Cruz Jr. .30 .09
❑ 440 Orlando Cabrera .30 .09
❑ 441 Joe Kennedy .30 .09
❑ 442 Scott Williamson .30 .09
❑ 443 Troy Percival .30 .09
❑ 444 Derrek Lee .50 .15
❑ 445 Runelvys Hernandez .30 .09
❑ 446 Mark Grudzielanek .30 .09
❑ 447 Trey Hodges .30 .09
❑ 448 Jimmy Haynes .30 .09
❑ 449 Eric Milton .30 .09
❑ 450 Todd Helton .50 .15
❑ 451 Greg Zaun .30 .09
❑ 452 Woody Williams .30 .09
❑ 453 Todd Walker .30 .09
❑ 454 Juan Cruz .30 .09
❑ 455 Fernando Vina .30 .09
❑ 456 Omar Vizquel .50 .15
❑ 457 Roberto Alomar .50 .15
❑ 458 Bill Hall .30 .09
❑ 459 Juan Rivera .30 .09
❑ 460 Tom Glavine .50 .15
❑ 461 Ramon Castro .30 .09
❑ 462 Cory Vance .30 .09
❑ 463 Dan Miceli .30 .09
❑ 464 Lyle Overbay .30 .09
❑ 465 Craig Biggio .50 .15
❑ 466 Ricky Ledee .30 .09
❑ 467 Michael Barrett .30 .09
❑ 468 Jason Anderson .30 .09
❑ 469 Matt Stairs .30 .09
❑ 470 Jarrod Washburn .30 .09
❑ 471 Todd Hundley .30 .09
❑ 472 Grant Roberts .30 .09
❑ 473 Randy Winn .30 .09
❑ 474 Pat Hentgen .30 .09
❑ 475 Jose Vidro .30 .09
❑ 476 Tony Torcato .30 .09
❑ 477 Jeremy Affeldt .30 .09
❑ 478 Carlos Guillen .30 .09
❑ 479 Paul Quantrill .30 .09
❑ 480 Rafael Furcal .30 .09
❑ 481 Adam Melhuse .30 .09
❑ 482 Jerry Hairston Jr. .30 .09
❑ 483 Adam Bernero .30 .09
❑ 484 Terrence Long .30 .09
❑ 485 Paul Lo Duca .30 .09
❑ 486 Corey Koskie .30 .09
❑ 487 John Lackey .30 .09
❑ 488 Chad Zerbe .30 .09
❑ 489 Vinny Castilla .30 .09
❑ 490 Corey Patterson .30 .09
❑ 491 John Olerud .30 .09
❑ 492 Josh Bard .30 .09
❑ 493 Darren Dreifort .30 .09
❑ 494 Jason Standridge .30 .09
❑ 495 Ben Sheets .30 .09
❑ 496 Jose Castillo .30 .09
❑ 497 Jay Payton .30 .09
❑ 498 Rob Bowen .30 .09
❑ 499 Bobby Higginson .30 .09
❑ 500 Alex Rodriguez Yanks 1.25 .35
❑ 501 Octavio Dotel .30 .09
❑ 502 Rheal Cormier .30 .09
❑ 503 Felix Heredia .30 .09
❑ 504 Dan Wright .30 .09
❑ 505 Michael Young .30 .09
❑ 506 Wilfredo Ledezma .30 .09
❑ 507 Sun Woo Kim .30 .09
❑ 508 Michael Tejera .30 .09
❑ 509 Herbert Perry .30 .09
❑ 510 Esteban Loaiza .30 .09
❑ 511 Alan Embree .30 .09
❑ 512 Ben Davis .30 .09
❑ 513 Greg Colbrunn .30 .09
❑ 514 Josh Hall .30 .09
❑ 515 Raul Ibanez .30 .09
❑ 516 Jason Kershner .30 .09
❑ 517 Corky Miller .30 .09
❑ 518 Jason Marquis .30 .09
❑ 519 Roger Cedeno .30 .09
❑ 520 Adam Dunn .30 .09
❑ 521 Paul Byrd .30 .09
❑ 522 Sandy Alomar Jr. .30 .09
❑ 523 Salomon Torres .30 .09
❑ 524 John Halama .30 .09
❑ 525 Mike Piazza 1.25 .35
❑ 526 Buddy Groom .30 .09
❑ 527 Adrian Beltre .30 .09
❑ 528 Chad Harville .30 .09
❑ 529 Javier Vazquez .30 .09
❑ 530 Jody Gerut .30 .09
❑ 531 Elmer Dessens .30 .09
❑ 532 B.J. Ryan .30 .09
❑ 533 Chad Durbin .30 .09
❑ 534 Doug Mirabelli .30 .09
❑ 535 Bernie Williams .50 .15
❑ 536 Jeff DaVanon .30 .09
❑ 537 Dave Berg .30 .09
❑ 538 Geoff Blum .30 .09
❑ 539 John Thomson .30 .09
❑ 540 Jeremy Bonderman .30 .09
❑ 541 Jeff Zimmerman .30 .09
❑ 542 Derek Lowe .30 .09
❑ 543 Scot Shields .30 .09
❑ 544 Michael Tucker .30 .09
❑ 545 Tim Hudson .30 .09
❑ 546 Ryan Ludwick .30 .09
❑ 547 Rick Reed .30 .09
❑ 548 Placido Polanco .30 .09
❑ 549 Tony Graffanino .30 .09
❑ 550 Garret Anderson .30 .09
❑ 551 Timo Perez .30 .09
❑ 552 Jesus Colome .30 .09
❑ 553 R.A. Dickey .30 .09
❑ 554 Tim Worrell .30 .09
❑ 555 Jason Kendall .30 .09
❑ 556 Tom Goodwin .30 .09
❑ 557 Joaquin Benoit .30 .09
❑ 558 Stephen Randolph .30 .09
❑ 559 Miguel Tejada .30 .09
❑ 560 A.J. Burnett .30 .09
❑ 561 Ben Diggins .30 .09
❑ 562 Kent Mercker .30 .09
❑ 563 Zach Day .30 .09
❑ 564 Antonio Perez .30 .09
❑ 565 Jason Schmidt .30 .09
❑ 566 Armando Benitez .30 .09
❑ 567 Denny Neagle .30 .09
❑ 568 Eric Eckenstahler .30 .09
❑ 569 Chan Ho Park .30 .09
❑ 570 Carlos Beltran .30 .09
❑ 571 Brett Tomko .30 .09
❑ 572 Henry Mateo .30 .09
❑ 573 Ken Harvey .30 .09
❑ 574 Matt Lawton .30 .09
❑ 575 Mariano Rivera .50 .15
❑ 576 Darrell May .30 .09
❑ 577 Jamie Moyer .30 .09
❑ 578 Paul Bako .30 .09
❑ 579 Cory Lidle .30 .09
❑ 580 Jacque Jones .30 .09
❑ 581 Jolbert Cabrera .30 .09
❑ 582 Jason Grimsley .30 .09
❑ 583 Danny Kolb .30 .09
❑ 584 Billy Wagner .30 .09
❑ 585 Rich Aurilia .30 .09
❑ 586 Vicente Padilla .30 .09
❑ 587 Oscar Villarreal .30 .09
❑ 588 Rene Reyes .30 .09
❑ 589 Jon Lieber .30 .09
❑ 590 Nick Johnson .30 .09
❑ 591 Bobby Crosby .30 .09
❑ 592 Steve Trachsel .30 .09
❑ 593 Brian Boehringer .30 .09
❑ 594 Juan Uribe .30 .09
❑ 595 Bartolo Colon .30 .09
❑ 596 Bobby Hill .30 .09
❑ 597 Chris Shelton RC 1.50 .45
❑ 598 Carl Pavano .30 .09
❑ 599 Kurt Ainsworth .30 .09
❑ 600 Derek Jeter 1.50 .45
❑ 601 Doug Mientkiewicz .30 .09
❑ 602 Orlando Palmeiro .30 .09
❑ 603 J.C. Romero .30 .09
❑ 604 Scott Sullivan .30 .09
❑ 605 Brad Radke .30 .09
❑ 606 Fernando Rodney .30 .09
❑ 607 Jim Brower .30 .09
❑ 608 Josh Towers .30 .09
❑ 609 Brad Fullmer .30 .09
❑ 610 Jose Reyes .30 .09
❑ 611 Ryan Wagner .30 .09
❑ 612 Joe Mays .30 .09
❑ 613 Jung Bong .30 .09
❑ 614 Curtis Leskanic .30 .09
❑ 615 Al Leiter .30 .09
❑ 616 Wade Miller .30 .09
❑ 617 Keith Foulke Sox .30 .09

- ❑ 618 Casey Fossum .30 .09
- ❑ 619 Craig Monroe .30 .09
- ❑ 620 Hideo Nomo .75 .23
- ❑ 621 Bob File .30 .09
- ❑ 622 Steve Kline .30 .09
- ❑ 623 Bobby Kielty .30 .09
- ❑ 624 Dewon Brazelton .30 .09
- ❑ 625 Eric Chavez .30 .09
- ❑ 626 Chris Carpenter .30 .09
- ❑ 627 Alexis Rios .30 .09
- ❑ 628 Jason Davis .30 .09
- ❑ 629 Jose Jimenez .30 .09
- ❑ 630 Vernon Wells .30 .09
- ❑ 631 Kenny Lofton .30 .09
- ❑ 632 Chad Bradford .30 .09
- ❑ 633 Brad Wilkerson .30 .09
- ❑ 634 Pokey Reese .30 .09
- ❑ 635 Richie Sexson .30 .09
- ❑ 636 Chin-Hui Tsao .30 .09
- ❑ 637 Eli Marrero .30 .09
- ❑ 638 Chris Reitsma .30 .09
- ❑ 639 Daryle Ward .30 .09
- ❑ 640 Mark Teixeira .50 .15
- ❑ 641 Corwin Malone .30 .09
- ❑ 642 Adam Eaton .30 .09
- ❑ 643 Jimmy Rollins .30 .09
- ❑ 644 Brian Anderson .30 .09
- ❑ 645 Bill Mueller .30 .09
- ❑ 646 Jake Westbrook .30 .09
- ❑ 647 Bengie Molina .30 .09
- ❑ 648 Jorge Julio .30 .09
- ❑ 649 Billy Traber .30 .09
- ❑ 650 Randy Johnson .75 .23
- ❑ 651 Javy Lopez .30 .09
- ❑ 652 Doug Glanville .30 .09
- ❑ 653 Jeff Cirillo .30 .09
- ❑ 654 Tino Martinez .50 .15
- ❑ 655 Mark Buehrle .30 .09
- ❑ 656 Jason Michaels .30 .09
- ❑ 657 Damian Rolls .30 .09
- ❑ 658 Rosman Garcia .30 .09
- ❑ 659 Scott Hairston .30 .09
- ❑ 660 Carl Crawford .30 .09
- ❑ 661 Livan Hernandez .30 .09
- ❑ 662 Danny Bautista .30 .09
- ❑ 663 Brad Ausmus .30 .09
- ❑ 664 Juan Acevedo .30 .09
- ❑ 665 Sean Casey .50 .15
- ❑ 666 Josh Beckett .30 .09
- ❑ 667 Milton Bradley .30 .09
- ❑ 668 Braden Looper .30 .09
- ❑ 669 Paul Abbott .30 .09
- ❑ 670 Joel Pineiro .30 .09
- ❑ 671 Luis Terrero .30 .09
- ❑ 672 Rodrigo Lopez .30 .09
- ❑ 673 Joe Crede .30 .09
- ❑ 674 Mike Koplove .30 .09
- ❑ 675 Brian Giles .30 .09
- ❑ 676 Jeff Nelson .30 .09
- ❑ 677 Russell Branyan .30 .09
- ❑ 678 Mike DeJean .30 .09
- ❑ 679 Brian Daubach .30 .09
- ❑ 680 Ellis Burks .30 .09
- ❑ 681 Ryan Dempster .30 .09
- ❑ 682 Cliff Politte .30 .09
- ❑ 683 Brian Reith .30 .09
- ❑ 684 Scott Stewart .30 .09
- ❑ 685 Allan Simpson .30 .09
- ❑ 686 Shawn Estes .30 .09
- ❑ 687 Jason Johnson .30 .09
- ❑ 688 Wil Cordero .30 .09
- ❑ 689 Kelly Stinnett .30 .09
- ❑ 690 Jose Lima .30 .09
- ❑ 691 Gary Bennett .30 .09
- ❑ 692 T.J. Tucker .30 .09
- ❑ 693 Shane Spencer .30 .09
- ❑ 694 Chris Hammond .30 .09
- ❑ 695 Raul Mondesi .30 .09
- ❑ 696 Xavier Nady .30 .09
- ❑ 697 Cody Ransom .30 .09
- ❑ 698 Ron Villone .30 .09
- ❑ 699 Brook Fordyce .30 .09
- ❑ 700 Sammy Sosa .75 .23
- ❑ 701 Terry Adams .30 .09
- ❑ 702 Ricardo Rincon .30 .09
- ❑ 703 Tike Redman .30 .09
- ❑ 704 Chris Stynes .30 .09
- ❑ 705 Mark Redman .30 .09
- ❑ 706 Juan Encarnacion .30 .09
- ❑ 707 Jhonny Peralta .30 .09
- ❑ 708 Denny Hocking .30 .09
- ❑ 709 Ivan Rodriguez .50 .15
- ❑ 710 Jose Hernandez .30 .09
- ❑ 711 Brandon Duckworth .30 .09
- ❑ 712 Dave Burba .30 .09
- ❑ 713 Joe Nathan .30 .09
- ❑ 714 Dan Smith .30 .09
- ❑ 715 Karim Garcia .30 .09
- ❑ 716 Arthur Rhodes .30 .09
- ❑ 717 Shawn Wooten .30 .09
- ❑ 718 Ramon Santiago .30 .09
- ❑ 719 Luis Ugueto .30 .09
- ❑ 720 Danys Baez .30 .09
- ❑ 721 Alfredo Amezaga PROS .30 .09
- ❑ 722 Sidney Ponson .30 .09
- ❑ 723 Joe Mauer PROS .30 .09
- ❑ 724 Jesse Foppert PROS .30 .09
- ❑ 725 Todd Greene .30 .09
- ❑ 726 Dan Haren PROS .30 .09
- ❑ 727 Brandon Larson PROS .30 .09
- ❑ 728 Bobby Jenks PROS .30 .09
- ❑ 729 Grady Sizemore PROS .30 .09
- ❑ 730 Ben Grieve .30 .09
- ❑ 731 Khalil Greene PROS .75 .23
- ❑ 732 Chad Gaudin PROS .30 .09
- ❑ 733 Johnny Estrada PROS .30 .09
- ❑ 734 Joe Valentine PROS .30 .09
- ❑ 735 Tim Raines Jr. PROS .30 .09
- ❑ 736 Brandon Claussen PROS .30 .09
- ❑ 737 Sam Marsonek PROS .30 .09
- ❑ 738 Delmon Young PROS .50 .15
- ❑ 739 David Dellucci .30 .09
- ❑ 740 Sergio Mitre PROS .30 .09
- ❑ 741 Nick Neugebauer PROS .30 .09
- ❑ 742 Laynce Nix PROS .30 .09
- ❑ 743 Joe Thurston PROS .30 .09
- ❑ 744 Ryan Langerhans PROS .30 .09
- ❑ 745 Pete LaForest PROS .30 .09
- ❑ 746 Arnie Munoz PROS .30 .09
- ❑ 747 Rickie Weeks PROS .50 .15
- ❑ 748 Neal Cotts PROS .30 .09
- ❑ 749 Jonny Gomes PROS .30 .09
- ❑ 750 Jim Thome .50 .15
- ❑ 751 Jon Rauch PROS .30 .09
- ❑ 752 Edwin Jackson PROS .30 .09
- ❑ 753 Ryan Madson PROS .30 .09
- ❑ 754 Andrew Good PROS .30 .09
- ❑ 755 Eddie Perez .30 .09
- ❑ 756 Joe Borchard PROS .30 .09
- ❑ 757 Jeremy Guthrie PROS .30 .09
- ❑ 758 Jose Mesa .30 .09
- ❑ 759 Doug Waechter PROS .30 .09
- ❑ 760 J.D. Drew .30 .09
- ❑ 761 Adam LaRoche PROS .30 .09
- ❑ 762 Rich Harden PROS .30 .09
- ❑ 763 Justin Speier .30 .09
- ❑ 764 Todd Zeile .30 .09
- ❑ 765 Turk Wendell .30 .09
- ❑ 766 Mark Bellhorn Sox .30 .09
- ❑ 767 Mike Jackson .30 .09
- ❑ 768 Chone Figgins .30 .09
- ❑ 769 Mike Neu .30 .09
- ❑ 770 Greg Maddux 1.25 .35
- ❑ 771 Frank Menechino .30 .09
- ❑ 772 Alec Zumwalt RC .30 .09
- ❑ 773 Eric Young .30 .09
- ❑ 774 Dustan Mohr .30 .09
- ❑ 775 Shane Halter .30 .09
- ❑ 776 Brian Buchanan .30 .09
- ❑ 777 So Taguchi .30 .09
- ❑ 778 Eric Karros .30 .09
- ❑ 779 Ramon Nivar .30 .09
- ❑ 780 Marlon Anderson .30 .09
- ❑ 781 Brayan Pena FY RC .40 .12
- ❑ 782 Chris O'Riordan FY RC .40 .12
- ❑ 783 Dioner Navarro FY RC 1.50 .45
- ❑ 784 Alberto Callaspo FY RC .75 .23
- ❑ 785 Hector Gimenez FY RC .30 .09
- ❑ 786 Yadier Molina FY RC 2.00 .60
- ❑ 787 Kevin Richardson FY RC .30 .09
- ❑ 788 Brian Pilkington FY RC .40 .12
- ❑ 789 Adam Greenberg FY RC .75 .23
- ❑ 790 Ervin Santana FY RC 2.00 .60
- ❑ 791 Brant Colamarino FY RC .75 .23
- ❑ 792 Ben Himes FY RC .30 .09
- ❑ 793 Todd Self FY RC .50 .15
- ❑ 794 Brad Vericker FY RC .40 .12
- ❑ 795 Donald Kelly FY RC .40 .12
- ❑ 796 Brock Jacobsen FY RC .30 .09
- ❑ 797 Brock Peterson FY RC .40 .12
- ❑ 798 Carlos Sosa FY RC .40 .12
- ❑ 799 Chad Chop FY RC .40 .12
- ❑ 800 Matt Moses FY RC 1.25 .35
- ❑ 801 Chris Aguila FY RC .40 .12
- ❑ 802 David Murphy FY RC 1.00 .30
- ❑ 803 Don Sutton FY RC 1.00 .30
- ❑ 804 Jereme Milons FY RC .50 .15
- ❑ 805 Jon Coutlangus FY RC .30 .09
- ❑ 806 Greg Thissen FY RC .40 .12
- ❑ 807 Jose Capellan FY RC .50 .15
- ❑ 808 Chad Santos FY RC .40 .12
- ❑ 809 Wardell Starling FY RC .40 .12
- ❑ 810 Kevin Kouzmanoff FY RC .75 .23
- ❑ 811 Kevin Davidson FY RC .30 .09
- ❑ 812 Michael Mooney FY RC .40 .12
- ❑ 813 Rodney Choy Foo FY RC .30 .09
- ❑ 814 Reid Gorecki FY RC .40 .12
- ❑ 815 Rudy Guillen FY RC .75 .23
- ❑ 816 Harvey Garcia FY RC .30 .09
- ❑ 817 Warner Madrigal FY RC .75 .23
- ❑ 818 Kenny Perez FY RC .40 .12
- ❑ 819 Joaquin Arias FY RC .75 .23
- ❑ 820 Benji DeQuin FY RC .30 .09
- ❑ 821 Lastings Milledge FY RC 2.00 .60
- ❑ 822 Blake Hawksworth FY RC .50 .15
- ❑ 823 Estee Harris FY RC .50 .15
- ❑ 824 Bobby Brownlie FY RC 1.25 .35
- ❑ 825 Wanell Severino FY RC .30 .09
- ❑ 826 Bobby Madritsch FY .30 .09
- ❑ 827 Travis Hanson FY RC .40 .12
- ❑ 828 Brandon Medders FY RC .40 .12
- ❑ 829 Kevin Howard FY RC .50 .15
- ❑ 830 Brian Steffek FY RC .30 .09
- ❑ 831 Terry Jones FY RC .50 .15
- ❑ 832 Anthony Acevedo FY RC .40 .12
- ❑ 833 Kory Casto FY RC .50 .15
- ❑ 834 Brooks Conrad FY RC UER .40 .12
  Anthony Acevedo Pictured on front
- ❑ 835 Juan Gutierrez FY RC .40 .12
- ❑ 836 Charlie Zink FY RC .30 .09
- ❑ 837 David Aardsma FY RC .50 .15
- ❑ 838 Carl Loadenthal FY RC .50 .15
- ❑ 839 Donald Levinski FY RC .30 .09
- ❑ 840 Dustin Nippert FY RC .50 .15
- ❑ 841 Calvin Hayes FY RC .50 .15
- ❑ 842 Felix Hernandez FY RC 12.00 3.60
- ❑ 843 Tyler Davidson FY RC .50 .15
- ❑ 844 George Sherrill FY RC .40 .12
- ❑ 845 Craig Ansman FY RC .40 .12
- ❑ 846 Jeff Allison FY RC .40 .12
- ❑ 847 Tommy Murphy FY RC .40 .12
- ❑ 848 Jerome Gamble FY RC .30 .09
- ❑ 849 Jesse English FY RC .40 .12
- ❑ 850 Alex Romero FY RC .40 .12
- ❑ 851 Joel Zumaya FY RC 1.50 .45
- ❑ 852 Carlos Quentin FY RC 2.50 .75
- ❑ 853 Jose Valdez FY RC .40 .12
- ❑ 854 J.J. Furmaniak FY RC .75 .23
- ❑ 855 Juan Cedeno FY RC .40 .12
- ❑ 856 Kyle Sleeth FY RC .75 .23
- ❑ 857 Josh Labandeira FY RC .40 .12
- ❑ 858 Lee Gwaltney FY RC .30 .09
- ❑ 859 Lincoln Holdzkom FY RC .40 .12
- ❑ 860 Ivan Ochoa FY RC .40 .12
- ❑ 861 Luke Anderson FY RC .30 .09
- ❑ 862 Conor Jackson FY RC 3.00 .90
- ❑ 863 Matt Capps FY RC .40 .12
- ❑ 864 Merkin Valdez FY RC .50 .15
- ❑ 865 Paul Bacot FY RC .50 .15
- ❑ 866 Erick Aybar FY RC 1.25 .35
- ❑ 867 Scott Proctor FY RC .50 .15
- ❑ 868 Tim Stauffer FY RC 1.00 .30
- ❑ 869 Matt Creighton FY RC .40 .12
- ❑ 870 Zach Miner FY RC .50 .15
- ❑ 871 Danny Gonzalez FY RC .30 .09
- ❑ 872 Tom Farmer FY RC .40 .12
- ❑ 873 John Santor FY RC .30 .09
- ❑ 874 Logan Kensing FY RC .40 .12

❑ 875 Vito Chiaravalloti FY RC .. .40 .12
❑ 876 Checklist .30 .09
❑ 877 Checklist .30 .09
❑ 878 Checklist .30 .09
❑ 879 Checklist .30 .09
❑ 880 Checklist .30 .09

2005 Topps Total

	Nm-Mt	Ex-Mt
COMPLETE SET (770)	150.00	45.00
COMMON (1-575/666)	.30	.09
COMMON CARD (576-690)	.30	.09
COM (269/588/691-765)	.50	.15
COMMON CL (766-770)	.30	.09
OVERALL PLATE ODDS 1:85 HOBBY		.00
PLATE PRINT RUN 1 SET PER COLOR		.00
BLACK-CYAN-MAGENTA-YELLOW ISSUED		.00
FRONT AND BACK PLATES PRODUCED		.00
NO PLATE PRICING DUE TO SCARCITY		.00

❑ 1 Rafael Furcal .30 .09
❑ 2 Tony Clark .30 .09
❑ 3 Hideki Matsui 1.50 .45
❑ 4 Zach Day .30 .09
❑ 5 Garret Anderson .30 .09
❑ 6 B.J. Surhoff .30 .09
❑ 7 Trevor Hoffman .30 .09
❑ 8 Kenny Lofton .30 .09
❑ 9 Ross Gload .30 .09
❑ 10 Jorge Cantu .30 .09
❑ 11 Joel Pineiro .30 .09
❑ 12 Alex Cintron .30 .09
❑ 13 Mike Matheny .30 .09
❑ 14 Rod Barajas .30 .09
❑ 15 Ray Durham .30 .09
❑ 16 Danys Baez .30 .09
❑ 17 Brian Schneider .30 .09
❑ 18 Tike Redman .30 .09
❑ 19 Ricardo Rodriguez .30 .09
❑ 20 Mike Sweeney .30 .09
❑ 21 Greg Myers .30 .09
❑ 22 Chone Figgins .30 .09
❑ 23 Brian Lawrence .30 .09
❑ 24 Joe Nathan .30 .09
❑ 25 Placido Polanco .30 .09
❑ 26 Yadier Molina .30 .09
❑ 27 Gary Bennett .30 .09
❑ 28 Yorvit Torrealba .30 .09
❑ 29 Javier Valentin .30 .09
❑ 30 Jason Giambi .30 .09
❑ 31 Brandon Claussen .30 .09
❑ 32 Miguel Olivo .30 .09
❑ 33 Josh Bard .30 .09
❑ 34 Ramon Hernandez .30 .09
❑ 35 Geoff Jenkins .30 .09
❑ 36 Bobby Kielty .30 .09
❑ 37 Luis A. Gonzalez .30 .09
❑ 38 Benito Santiago .30 .09
❑ 39 Brandon Inge .30 .09
❑ 40 Mark Prior .50 .15
❑ 41 Mike Lieberthal .30 .09
❑ 42 Toby Hall .30 .09
❑ 43 Brad Ausmus .30 .09
❑ 44 Damian Miller .30 .09
❑ 45 Mark Kotsay .30 .09
❑ 46 John Buck .30 .09
❑ 47 Oliver Perez .30 .09
❑ 48 Matt Morris .30 .09
❑ 49 Raul Chavez .30 .09
❑ 50 Randy Johnson .75 .23
❑ 51 Dave Bush .30 .09
❑ 52 Jose Macias .30 .09
❑ 53 Paul Wilson .30 .09
❑ 54 Wilfredo Ledezma .30 .09
❑ 55 J.D. Drew .30 .09
❑ 56 Pedro Martinez .50 .15
❑ 57 Josh Towers .30 .09
❑ 58 Jamie Moyer .30 .09
❑ 59 Scott Elarton .30 .09
❑ 60 Ken Griffey Jr. 1.25 .35
❑ 61 Steve Trachsel .30 .09
❑ 62 Bubba Crosby .30 .09
❑ 63 Michael Barrett .30 .09
❑ 64 Odalis Perez .30 .09
❑ 65 B.J. Upton .30 .09
❑ 66 Eric Bruntlett .30 .09
❑ 67 Victor Zambrano .30 .09
❑ 68 Brandon League .30 .09
❑ 69 Carlos Silva .30 .09
❑ 70 Lyle Overbay .30 .09
❑ 71 Runelvys Hernandez .30 .09
❑ 72 Brad Penny .30 .09
❑ 73 Ty Wigginton .30 .09
❑ 74 Orlando Hudson .30 .09
❑ 75 Roy Oswalt .30 .09
❑ 76 Jason LaRue .30 .09
❑ 77 Ismael Valdez .30 .09
❑ 78 Calvin Pickering .30 .09
❑ 79 Bill Hall .30 .09
❑ 80 Carl Crawford .30 .09
❑ 81 Tomas Perez .30 .09
❑ 82 Joe Kennedy .30 .09
❑ 83 Chris Woodward .30 .09
❑ 84 Jason Lane .30 .09
❑ 85 Steve Finley .30 .09
❑ 86 Jeff Francis .30 .09
❑ 87 Felipe Lopez .30 .09
❑ 88 Chan Ho Park .30 .09
❑ 89 Joe Crede .30 .09
❑ 90 Jose Vidro .30 .09
❑ 91 Casey Kotchman .30 .09
❑ 92 Brandon Backe .30 .09
❑ 93 Mike Hampton .30 .09
❑ 94 Ryan Dempster .30 .09
❑ 95 Wily Mo Pena .30 .09
❑ 96 Matt Holliday .30 .09
❑ 97 A.J. Pierzynski .30 .09
❑ 98 Jason Jennings .30 .09
❑ 99 Eli Marrero .30 .09
❑ 100 Carlos Beltran .30 .09
❑ 101 Scott Kazmir .30 .09
❑ 102 Kenny Rogers .30 .09
❑ 103 Roy Halladay .30 .09
❑ 104 Alex Cora .30 .09
❑ 105 Richie Sexson .30 .09
❑ 106 Ben Sheets .30 .09
❑ 107 Bartolo Colon .30 .09
❑ 108 Eddie Perez .30 .09
❑ 109 Vicente Padilla .30 .09
❑ 110 Sammy Sosa .75 .23
❑ 111 Mark Ellis .30 .09
❑ 112 Woody Williams .30 .09
❑ 113 Todd Greene .30 .09
❑ 114 Nook Logan .30 .09
❑ 115 Francisco Rodriguez .30 .09
❑ 116 Miguel Batista .30 .09
❑ 117 Livan Hernandez .30 .09
❑ 118 Chris Aguila .30 .09
❑ 119 Coco Crisp .30 .09
❑ 120 Jose Reyes .30 .09
❑ 121 Ricky Ledee .30 .09
❑ 122 Brad Radke .30 .09
❑ 123 Carlos Guillen .30 .09
❑ 124 Paul Bako .30 .09
❑ 125 Tom Glavine .50 .15
❑ 126 Chad Moeller .30 .09
❑ 127 Mark Buehrle .30 .09
❑ 128 Casey Blake .30 .09
❑ 129 Juan Rivera .30 .09
❑ 130 Preston Wilson .30 .09
❑ 131 Nate Robertson .30 .09
❑ 132 Julio Franco .30 .09
❑ 133 Derek Lowe .30 .09
❑ 134 Rob Bell .30 .09
❑ 135 Javy Lopez .30 .09
❑ 136 Javier Vazquez .30 .09
❑ 137 Desi Relaford .30 .09
❑ 138 Danny Graves .30 .09
❑ 139 Josh Fogg .30 .09
❑ 140 Bobby Crosby .30 .09
❑ 141 Ramon Castro .30 .09
❑ 142 Jerry Hairston Jr. .30 .09
❑ 143 Morgan Ensberg .30 .09
❑ 144 Brandon Webb .30 .09
❑ 145 Jack Wilson .30 .09
❑ 146 Bill Mueller .30 .09
❑ 147 Troy Glaus .30 .09
❑ 148 Armando Benitez .30 .09
❑ 149 Adam LaRoche .30 .09
❑ 150 Hank Blalock .30 .09
❑ 151 Ryan Franklin .30 .09
❑ 152 Kevin Millwood .30 .09
❑ 153 Jason Marquis .30 .09
❑ 154 Dewon Brazelton .30 .09
❑ 155 Al Leiter .30 .09
❑ 156 Garrett Atkins .30 .09
❑ 157 Todd Walker .30 .09
❑ 158 Kris Benson .30 .09
❑ 159 Eric Milton .30 .09
❑ 160 Bret Boone .30 .09
❑ 161 Matt LeCroy .30 .09
❑ 162 Chris Widger .30 .09
❑ 163 Ruben Gotay .30 .09
❑ 164 Craig Monroe .30 .09
❑ 165 Travis Hafner .30 .09
❑ 166 Vance Wilson .30 .09
❑ 167 Jason Grabowski .30 .09
❑ 168 Tim Salmon .50 .15
❑ 169 Henry Blanco .30 .09
❑ 170 Josh Beckett .30 .09
❑ 171 Jake Westbrook .30 .09
❑ 172 Paul Lo Duca .30 .09
❑ 173 Julio Lugo .30 .09
❑ 174 Juan Cruz .30 .09
❑ 175 Mark Mulder .30 .09
❑ 176 Juan Castro .30 .09
❑ 177 Damion Easley .30 .09
❑ 178 LaTroy Hawkins .30 .09
❑ 179 Jon Lieber .30 .09
❑ 180 Vernon Wells .30 .09
❑ 181 Jeff DaVanon .30 .09
❑ 182 Dustan Mohr .30 .09
❑ 183 Ryan Freel .30 .09
❑ 184 Doug Davis .30 .09
❑ 185 Sean Casey .30 .09
❑ 186 Robb Quinlan .30 .09
❑ 187 J.D. Closser .30 .09
❑ 188 Tim Wakefield .30 .09
❑ 189 Brian Jordan .30 .09
❑ 190 Adam Dunn .30 .09
❑ 191 Antonio Perez .30 .09
❑ 192 Brett Tomko .30 .09
❑ 193 John Flaherty .30 .09
❑ 194 Michael Cuddyer .30 .09
❑ 195 Ronnie Belliard .30 .09
❑ 196 Tony Womack .30 .09
❑ 197 Jason Johnson .30 .09
❑ 198 Victor Santos .30 .09
❑ 199 Danny Haren .30 .09
❑ 200 Derek Jeter 1.50 .45
❑ 201 Brian Anderson .30 .09
❑ 202 Carlos Pena .30 .09
❑ 203 Jaret Wright .30 .09
❑ 204 Paul Byrd .30 .09
❑ 205 Shannon Stewart .30 .09
❑ 206 Chris Carpenter .30 .09
❑ 207 Matt Stairs .30 .09
❑ 208 Brad Hawpe .30 .09
❑ 209 Bobby Higginson .30 .09
❑ 210 Torii Hunter .30 .09
❑ 211 Shawn Green .30 .09
❑ 212 Todd Hollandsworth .30 .09
❑ 213 Scott Erickson .30 .09
❑ 214 C.C. Sabathia .30 .09
❑ 215 Mike Mussina .50 .15
❑ 216 Jason Kendall .30 .09
❑ 217 Todd Pratt .30 .09
❑ 218 Danny Kolb .30 .09
❑ 219 Tony Armas .30 .09
❑ 220 Edgar Renteria .30 .09

❑ 221 Dave Roberts .30 .09
❑ 222 Luis Rivas .30 .09
❑ 223 Adam Everett .30 .09
❑ 224 Jeff Cirillo .30 .09
❑ 225 Orlando Hernandez .30 .09
❑ 226 Ken Harvey .30 .09
❑ 227 Corey Patterson .30 .09
❑ 228 Humberto Cota .30 .09
❑ 229 A.J. Burnett .30 .09
❑ 230 Roger Clemens 1.25 .35
❑ 231 Joe Randa .30 .09
❑ 232 David Dellucci .30 .09
❑ 233 Troy Percival .30 .09
❑ 234 Dustin Hermanson .30 .09
❑ 235 Eric Gagne .30 .09
❑ 236 Terry Tiffee .30 .09
❑ 237 Tony Graffanino .30 .09
❑ 238 Jayson Werth .30 .09
❑ 239 Mark Sweeney .30 .09
❑ 240 Chipper Jones .75 .23
❑ 241 Aramis Ramirez .30 .09
❑ 242 Frank Catalanotto .30 .09
❑ 243 Mike Maroth .30 .09
❑ 244 Kelvim Escobar .30 .09
❑ 245 Bobby Abreu .30 .09
❑ 246 Kyle Lohse .30 .09
❑ 247 Jason Isringhausen .30 .09
❑ 248 Jose Lima .30 .09
❑ 249 Adrian Gonzalez .30 .09
❑ 250 Alex Rodriguez 1.25 .35
❑ 251 Ramon Ortiz .30 .09
❑ 252 Frank Menechino .30 .09
❑ 253 Keith Ginter .30 .09
❑ 254 Kip Wells .30 .09
❑ 255 Dmitri Young .30 .09
❑ 256 Craig Biggio .50 .15
❑ 257 Ramon E. Martinez .30 .09
❑ 258 Jason Bartlett .30 .09
❑ 259 Brad Lidge .30 .09
❑ 260 Brian Giles .30 .09
❑ 261 Luis Terrero .30 .09
❑ 262 Miguel Ojeda .30 .09
❑ 263 Rich Harden .30 .09
❑ 264 Jacque Jones .30 .09
❑ 265 Marcus Giles .30 .09
❑ 266 Carlos Zambrano .30 .09
❑ 267 Michael Tucker .30 .09
❑ 268 Wes Obermueller .30 .09
❑ 269 Pete Orr RC .50 .15
❑ 270 Jim Thome .50 .15
❑ 271 Omar Vizquel .50 .15
❑ 272 Jose Valentin .30 .09
❑ 273 Juan Uribe .30 .09
❑ 274 Doug Mirabelli .30 .09
❑ 275 Jeff Kent .30 .09
❑ 276 Brad Wilkerson .30 .09
❑ 277 Chris Burke .30 .09
❑ 278 Endy Chavez .30 .09
❑ 279 Richard Hidalgo .30 .09
❑ 280 John Smoltz .50 .15
❑ 281 Jarrod Washburn .30 .09
❑ 282 Larry Bigbie .30 .09
❑ 283 Edgardo Alfonzo .30 .09
❑ 284 Cliff Lee .30 .09
❑ 285 Carlos Lee .30 .09
❑ 286 Olmedo Saenz .30 .09
❑ 287 Tomo Ohka .30 .09
❑ 288 Ruben Sierra .30 .09
❑ 289 Nick Swisher .30 .09
❑ 290 Frank Thomas .75 .23
❑ 291 Aaron Cook .30 .09
❑ 292 Cody McKay .30 .09
❑ 293 Hee-Seop Choi .30 .09
❑ 294 Carl Pavano .30 .09
❑ 295 Scott Rolen .50 .15
❑ 296 Matt Kata .30 .09
❑ 297 Terrence Long .30 .09
❑ 298 Jimmy Gobble .30 .09
❑ 299 Jason Repko .30 .09
❑ 300 Manny Ramirez .50 .15
❑ 301 Dan Wilson .30 .09
❑ 302 Jhonny Peralta .30 .09
❑ 303 John Mabry .30 .09
❑ 304 Adam Melhuse .30 .09
❑ 305 Kerry Wood .30 .09
❑ 306 Ryan Langerhans .30 .09
❑ 307 Antonio Alfonseca .30 .09
❑ 308 Marco Scutaro .30 .09
❑ 309 Jamey Carroll .30 .09
❑ 310 Lance Berkman .30 .09
❑ 311 Willie Harris .30 .09
❑ 312 Phil Nevin .30 .09
❑ 313 Gregg Zaun .30 .09
❑ 314 Michael Ryan .30 .09
❑ 315 Zack Greinke .30 .09
❑ 316 Ted Lilly .30 .09
❑ 317 David Eckstein .30 .09
❑ 318 Tony Torcato .30 .09
❑ 319 Rob Mackowiak .30 .09
❑ 320 Mark Teixeira .50 .15
❑ 321 Jason Phillips .30 .09
❑ 322 Jeremy Reed .30 .09
❑ 323 Bengie Molina .30 .09
❑ 324 Terrmel Sledge .30 .09
❑ 325 Justin Morneau .30 .09
❑ 326 Sandy Alomar Jr. .30 .09
❑ 327 Jon Garland .30 .09
❑ 328 Jay Payton .30 .09
❑ 329 Tino Martinez .50 .15
❑ 330 Jason Bay .30 .09
❑ 331 Jeff Conine .30 .09
❑ 332 Shawn Chacon .30 .09
❑ 333 Angel Berroa .30 .09
❑ 334 Reggie Sanders .30 .09
❑ 335 Kevin Brown .30 .09
❑ 336 Brady Clark .30 .09
❑ 337 Casey Fossum .30 .09
❑ 338 Raul Ibanez .30 .09
❑ 339 Derrek Lee .50 .15
❑ 340 Victor Martinez .30 .09
❑ 341 Kazuhisa Ishii .30 .09
❑ 342 Royce Clayton .30 .09
❑ 343 Trot Nixon .30 .09
❑ 344 Eric Young .30 .09
❑ 345 Aubrey Huff .30 .09
❑ 346 Brett Myers .30 .09
❑ 347 Joey Gathright .30 .09
❑ 348 Mark Grudzielanek .30 .09
❑ 349 Scott Spiezio .30 .09
❑ 350 Eric Chavez .30 .09
❑ 351 Einar Diaz .30 .09
❑ 352 Dallas McPherson .30 .09
❑ 353 John Thomson .30 .09
❑ 354 Neifi Perez .30 .09
❑ 355 Larry Walker .50 .15
❑ 356 Billy Wagner .30 .09
❑ 357 Mike Cameron .30 .09
❑ 358 Jimmy Rollins .30 .09
❑ 359 Kevin Mench .30 .09
❑ 360 Joe Mauer .30 .09
❑ 361 Jose Molina .30 .09
❑ 362 Joe Borchard .30 .09
❑ 363 Kevin Cash .30 .09
❑ 364 Jay Gibbons .30 .09
❑ 365 Khalil Greene .50 .15
❑ 366 Justin Leone .30 .09
❑ 367 Eddie Guardado .30 .09
❑ 368 Mike Lamb .30 .09
❑ 369 Matt Riley .30 .09
❑ 370 Luis Gonzalez .30 .09
❑ 371 Alfredo Amezaga .30 .09
❑ 372 J.J. Hardy .30 .09
❑ 373 Hector Luna .30 .09
❑ 374 Greg Aquino .30 .09
❑ 375 Jim Edmonds .50 .15
❑ 376 Joe Blanton .30 .09
❑ 377 Russell Branyan .30 .09
❑ 378 J.T. Snow .30 .09
❑ 379 Magglio Ordonez .30 .09
❑ 380 Rafael Palmeiro .50 .15
❑ 381 Andruw Jones .50 .15
❑ 382 David DeJesus .30 .09
❑ 383 Marquis Grissom .30 .09
❑ 384 Bobby Hill .30 .09
❑ 385 Kazuo Matsui .30 .09
❑ 386 Mark Loretta .30 .09
❑ 387 Chris Shelton .30 .09
❑ 388 Johnny Estrada .30 .09
❑ 389 Adam Hyzdu .30 .09
❑ 390 Nomar Garciaparra .75 .23
❑ 391 Mark Teahen .30 .09
❑ 392 Chris Capuano .30 .09
❑ 393 Ben Broussard .30 .09
❑ 394 Daniel Cabrera .30 .09
❑ 395 Jeremy Bonderman .30 .09
❑ 396 Darin Erstad .30 .09
❑ 397 Alex S. Gonzalez .30 .09
❑ 398 Kevin Millar .30 .09
❑ 399 Freddy Garcia .30 .09
❑ 400 Alfonso Soriano .30 .09
❑ 401 Koyie Hill .30 .09
❑ 402 Omar Infante .30 .09
❑ 403 Alex Gonzalez .30 .09
❑ 404 Pat Burrell .30 .09
❑ 405 Wes Helms .30 .09
❑ 406 Junior Spivey .30 .09
❑ 407 Joe Mays .30 .09
❑ 408 Jason Stanford .30 .09
❑ 409 Gil Meche .30 .09
❑ 410 Tim Hudson .30 .09
❑ 411 Chase Utley .30 .09
❑ 412 Matt Clement .30 .09
❑ 413 Nick Green .30 .09
❑ 414 Jose Vizcaino .30 .09
❑ 415 Ryan Klesko .30 .09
❑ 416 Vinny Castilla .30 .09
❑ 417 Brian Roberts .30 .09
❑ 418 Geronimo Gil .30 .09
❑ 419 Gary Matthews .30 .09
❑ 420 Jeff Weaver .30 .09
❑ 421 Jerome Williams .30 .09
❑ 422 Andy Pettitte .50 .15
❑ 423 Randy Wolf .30 .09
❑ 424 D'Angelo Jimenez .30 .09
❑ 425 Moises Alou .30 .09
❑ 426 Eric Byrnes .30 .09
❑ 427 Mark Redman .30 .09
❑ 428 Jermaine Dye .30 .09
❑ 429 Cory Lidle .30 .09
❑ 430 Jason Schmidt .30 .09
❑ 431 Jason W. Smith .30 .09
❑ 432 Jose Castillo .30 .09
❑ 433 Pokey Reese .30 .09
❑ 434 Matt Lawton .30 .09
❑ 435 Jose Guillen .30 .09
❑ 436 Craig Counsell .30 .09
❑ 437 Jose Hernandez .30 .09
❑ 438 Braden Looper .30 .09
❑ 439 Scott Hatteberg .30 .09
❑ 440 Gary Sheffield .30 .09
❑ 441 Gabe Gross .30 .09
❑ 442 Chris Gomez .30 .09
❑ 443 Dontrelle Willis .30 .09
❑ 444 Jamey Wright .30 .09
❑ 445 Rocco Baldelli .30 .09
❑ 446 Bernie Williams .50 .15
❑ 447 Sean Burroughs .30 .09
❑ 448 Willie Bloomquist .30 .09
❑ 449 Luis Castillo .30 .09
❑ 450 Mike Piazza .75 .23
❑ 451 Ryan Drese .30 .09
❑ 452 Pedro Feliz .30 .09
❑ 453 Horacio Ramirez .30 .09
❑ 454 Luis Matos .30 .09
❑ 455 Craig Wilson .30 .09
❑ 456 Russ Ortiz .30 .09
❑ 457 Xavier Nady .30 .09
❑ 458 Hideo Nomo .75 .23
❑ 459 Miguel Cairo .30 .09
❑ 460 Mike Lowell .30 .09
❑ 461 Corky Miller .30 .09
❑ 462 Bobby Madritsch .30 .09
❑ 463 Jose Contreras .30 .09
❑ 464 Johnny Damon .50 .15
❑ 465 Miguel Cabrera .50 .15
❑ 466 Eric Hinske .30 .09
❑ 467 Marlon Byrd .30 .09
❑ 468 Aaron Miles .30 .09
❑ 469 Ramon Vazquez .30 .09
❑ 470 Michael Young .30 .09
❑ 471 Alex Sanchez .30 .09
❑ 472 Shea Hillenbrand .30 .09
❑ 473 Jeff Bagwell .50 .15
❑ 474 Erik Bedard .30 .09
❑ 475 Jake Peavy .30 .09
❑ 476 Jody Gerut .30 .09
❑ 477 Randy Winn .30 .09
❑ 478 Kevin Youkilis .30 .09

❑	479	Eric Dubose	.30	.09
❑	480	David Wright	1.25	.35
❑	481	Wilson Valdez	.30	.09
❑	482	Cliff Floyd	.30	.09
❑	483	Jose Mesa	.30	.09
❑	484	Doug Mientkiewicz	.30	.09
❑	485	Jorge Posada	.50	.15
❑	486	Sidney Ponson	.30	.09
❑	487	Dave Krynzel	.30	.09
❑	488	Octavio Dotel	.30	.09
❑	489	Matt Treanor	.30	.09
❑	490	Johan Santana	.50	.15
❑	491	John Patterson	.30	.09
❑	492	So Taguchi	.30	.09
❑	493	Carl Everett	.30	.09
❑	494	Jason Dubois	.30	.09
❑	495	Albert Pujols	1.50	.45
❑	496	Kirk Rueter	.30	.09
❑	497	Geoff Blum	.30	.09
❑	498	Juan Encarnacion	.30	.09
❑	499	Mark Hendrickson	.30	.09
❑	500	Barry Bonds	2.00	.60
❑	501	Cesar Izturis	.30	.09
❑	502	David Wells	.30	.09
❑	503	Jorge Julio	.30	.09
❑	504	Cristian Guzman	.30	.09
❑	505	Juan Pierre	.30	.09
❑	506	Adam Eaton	.30	.09
❑	507	Nick Johnson	.30	.09
❑	508	Mike Redmond	.30	.09
❑	509	Daryle Ward	.30	.09
❑	510	Adrian Beltre	.30	.09
❑	511	Laynce Nix	.30	.09
❑	512	Reed Johnson	.30	.09
❑	513	Jeremy Affeldt	.30	.09
❑	514	R.A. Dickey	.30	.09
❑	515	Alex Rios	.30	.09
❑	516	Orlando Palmeiro	.30	.09
❑	517	Mark Bellhorn	.30	.09
❑	518	Adam Kennedy	.30	.09
❑	519	Curtis Granderson	.30	.09
❑	520	Todd Helton	.50	.15
❑	521	Aaron Boone	.30	.09
❑	522	Milton Bradley	.30	.09
❑	523	Timo Perez	.30	.09
❑	524	Jeff Suppan	.30	.09
❑	525	Austin Kearns	.30	.09
❑	526	Charles Thomas	.30	.09
❑	527	Bronson Arroyo	.30	.09
❑	528	Roger Cedeno	.30	.09
❑	529	Russ Adams	.30	.09
❑	530	Barry Zito	.30	.09
❑	531	Bob Wickman	.30	.09
❑	532	Deivi Cruz	.30	.09
❑	533	Mariano Rivera	.50	.15
❑	534	J.J. Davis	.30	.09
❑	535	Greg Maddux	1.25	.35
❑	536	Ryan Vogelsong	.30	.09
❑	537	Josh Phelps	.30	.09
❑	538	Scott Hairston	.30	.09
❑	539	Vladimir Guerrero	.75	.23
❑	540	Ivan Rodriguez	.50	.15
❑	541	David Newhan	.30	.09
❑	542	David Bell	.30	.09
❑	543	Lew Ford	.30	.09
❑	544	Grady Sizemore	.30	.09
❑	545	David Ortiz	.75	.23
❑	546	Jose Cruz Jr.	.30	.09
❑	547	Aaron Rowand	.30	.09
❑	548	Marcus Thames	.30	.09
❑	549	Scott Podsednik	.30	.09
❑	550	Ichiro Suzuki	1.50	.45
❑	551	Eduardo Perez	.30	.09
❑	552	Chris Snyder	.30	.09
❑	553	Corey Koskie	.30	.09
❑	554	Miguel Tejada	.30	.09
❑	555	Orlando Cabrera	.30	.09
❑	556	Rondell White	.30	.09
❑	557	Wade Miller	.30	.09
❑	558	Rodrigo Lopez	.30	.09
❑	559	Chad Tracy	.30	.09
❑	560	Paul Konerko	.30	.09
❑	561	Wil Cordero	.30	.09
❑	562	John McDonald	.30	.09
❑	563	Jason Ellison	.30	.09
❑	564	Jason Michaels	.30	.09
❑	565	Melvin Mora	.30	.09
❑	566	Ryan Church	.30	.09
❑	567	Ryan Ludwick	.30	.09
❑	568	Erubiel Durazo	.30	.09
❑	569	Noah Lowry	.30	.09
❑	570	Curt Schilling	.50	.15
❑	571	Esteban Loaiza	.30	.09
❑	572	Freddy Sanchez	.30	.09
❑	573	Rich Aurilia	.30	.09
❑	574	Travis Lee	.30	.09
❑	575	Nick Punto	.30	.09
❑	576	Jason Christiansen	.30	.09
		Kevin Correia		
❑	577	Brad Baker	.30	.09
		Tim Redding		
❑	578	Terry Adams	.30	.09
		Gavin Floyd		
❑	579	Seth Etherton	.30	.09
		Dan Meyer		
❑	580	Justin Lehr	.30	.09
		Derrick Turnbow		
❑	581	Mike Gosling	.30	.09
		Brad Halsey		
❑	582	Jim Mecir	.30	.09
		Logan Kensing		
❑	583	Brad Hennessey	.30	.09
		Jeff Fassero		
❑	584	Jon Adkins	.30	.09
		Felix Diaz		
❑	585	Jesse Crain	.30	.09
		Juan Rincon		
❑	586	Jamie Cerda	.30	.09
		Nate Field		
❑	587	Bartolome Fortunato	.30	.09
		Jae Weong Seo		
❑	588	Steve Schmoll RC	.50	.15
		Yhency Brazoban		
❑	589	Ugueth Urbina	.30	.09
		Jamie Walker		
❑	590	Jorge De Paula	.30	.09
		Scott Proctor		
❑	591	Jason Davis	.30	.09
		Bob Howry		
❑	592	Tim Worrell	.30	.09
		Pedro Liriano		
❑	593	Jose Acevedo	.30	.09
		Kent Mercker		
❑	594	Chris Hammond	.30	.09
		Scott Linebrink		
❑	595	Fernando Nieve	.30	.09
		John Franco		
❑	596	Randy Flores	.30	.09
		Mike Lincoln		
❑	597	Joe Borowski	.30	.09
		Sergio Mitre		
❑	598	Lance Carter	.30	.09
		Jesus Colome		
❑	599	John Halama	.30	.09
		Lenny DiNardo		
❑	600	Chad Bradford	.30	.09
		Kiko Calero		
❑	601	David Aardsma	.30	.09
		Jim Brower		
❑	602	Geoff Geary	.30	.09
		Ryan Madson		
❑	603	Brian Moehler	.30	.09
		Nate Bump		
❑	604	Chin-Hui Tsao	.30	.09
		Ryan Speier		
❑	605	Ryan Wagner	.30	.09
		Aaron Harang		
❑	606	Steve Kline	.30	.09
		Rick Bauer		
❑	607	Lance Cormier	.30	.09
		Randy Choate		
❑	608	Jon Leicester	.30	.09
		Todd Wellemeyer		
❑	609	Vinnie Chulk	.30	.09
		Jason Frasor		
❑	610	Scott Dohmann	.30	.09
		Brian Fuentes		
❑	611	Steve Colyer	.30	.09
		Roberto Hernandez		
❑	612	Ian Snell	.30	.09
		Salomon Torres		
❑	613	Cal Eldred	.30	.09
		Adam Wainwright		
❑	614	Ryan Bukvich	.30	.09
		Doug Brocail		
❑	615	J.J. Putz	.30	.09
		Aaron Sele		
❑	616	Bruce Chen	.30	.09
		Todd Williams		
❑	617	David Weathers	.30	.09
		Ben Weber		
❑	618	Dennys Reyes	.30	.09
		Rudy Seanez		
❑	619	Tim Harikkala	.30	.09
		Ricardo Rincon		
❑	620	Shawn Camp	.30	.09
		Denny Bautista		
❑	621	Javier A. Lopez	.30	.09
		Allan Simpson		
❑	622	Mike Remlinger	.30	.09
		Glendon Rusch		
❑	623	Roman Colon	.30	.09
		Kevin Gryboski		
❑	624	Tom Martin	.30	.09
		Chris Reitsma		
❑	625	Chad Qualls	.30	.09
		Dan Wheeler		
❑	626	Tommy Phelps	.30	.09
		Matt Wise		
❑	627	Scott Schoeneweis	.30	.09
		Justin Speier		
❑	628	Francisco Cordero	.30	.09
		Frank Francisco		
❑	629	Rafael Soriano	.30	.09
		Matt Thornton		
❑	630	Mike Stanton	.30	.09
		Steve Karsay		
❑	631	Mike MacDougal	.30	.09
		Scott Sullivan		
❑	632	Brian Bruney	.30	.09
		Oscar Villarreal		
❑	633	Mike Adams	.30	.09
		Ricky Bottalico		
❑	634	Eddy Rodriguez	.30	.09
		Dave Borkowski		
❑	635	Rafael Betancourt	.30	.09
		David Riske		
❑	636	Jorge De La Rosa	.30	.09
		Gary Glover		
❑	637	Matt Perisho	.30	.09
		Ben Howard		
❑	638	Jeff Bajenaru	.30	.09
		Luis Vizcaino		
❑	639	Ron Mahay	.30	.09
		Erasmo Ramirez		
❑	640	John Grabow	.30	.09
		Mike Gonzalez		
❑	641	J.C. Romero	.30	.09
		Matt Guerrier		
❑	642	Carlos Hernandez	.30	.09
		Brandon Duckworth UER Tim Redding is referred to in the Hernandez" informational blurb		
❑	643	Travis Harper	.30	.09
		Seth McClung		
❑	644	Matt Herges	.30	.09
		Tyler Walker		
❑	645	Kelly Wunsch	.30	.09
		Elmer Dessens		
❑	646	Mark Malaska	.30	.09
		Mike Myers		
❑	647	Kyle Farnsworth	.30	.09
		Gary Knotts		
❑	648	Justin Duchscherer	.30	.09
		Jairo Garcia		
❑	649	Aaron Rakers	.30	.09
		Steve Reed		
❑	650	Tom Gordon	.30	.09
		Paul Quantrill		
❑	651	Brandon Lyon	.30	.09
		Shawn Estes		
❑	652	Pete Walker	.30	.09
		Gustavo Chacin		
❑	653	John Lackey	.30	.09
		Scot Shields		
❑	654	Doug Waechter	.30	.09
		Trever Miller		
❑	655	Luis Ayala	.30	.09

Chad Cordero
❑ 656 Ron Villone .30 .09
Julio Mateo
❑ 657 Matt Mantei .30 .09
Blaine Neal
❑ 658 Damaso Marte .30 .09
Cliff Politte
❑ 659 Joe Valentine .30 .09
Luke Hudson
❑ 660 Todd Jones .30 .09
John Riedling
❑ 661 Heath Bell .30 .09
Aaron Heilman
❑ 662 Darrell May .30 .09
Akinori Otsuka
❑ 663 Joey Eischen .30 .09
Joe Horgan
❑ 664 Andy Sisco .30 .09
Mike Wood
❑ 665 Alan Embree .30 .09
Mike Timlin
❑ 666 Keith Foulke .30 .09
❑ 667 Rheal Cormier .30 .09
Aaron Fultz
❑ 668 Jake Woods .30 .09
Kevin Gregg
❑ 669 Matt Ginter .30 .09
Franklyn German
❑ 670 Scott Eyre .30 .09
Merkin Valdez
❑ 671 Brian Meadows .30 .09
Rick White
❑ 672 Guillermo Mota .30 .09
Tim Spooneybarger
❑ 673 Jason Grimsley .30 .09
B.J. Ryan
❑ 674 Neal Cotts .30 .09
Shingo Takatsu
❑ 675 Mike DeJean .30 .09
Felix Heredia
❑ 676 Matt Belisle .30 .09
Josh Hancock
❑ 677 Jon Rauch .30 .09
T.J. Tucker
❑ 678 Nick Regilio .30 .09
Brian Shouse
❑ 679 Julian Tavarez .30 .09
Ray King
❑ 680 Chad Fox .30 .09
Michael Wuertz
❑ 681 Jorge Sosa .30 .09
Adam Bernero
❑ 682 Jose Valverde .30 .09
Mike Koplove
❑ 683 Arthur Rhodes .30 .09
Scott Sauerbeck
❑ 684 Felix Rodriguez .30 .09
Tanyon Sturtze
❑ 685 Giovanni Carrara .30 .09
Duaner Sanchez
❑ 686 Mike Gallo .30 .09
Chad Harville
❑ 687 Mike Johnston .30 .09
Sean Burnett
❑ 688 Jeff Nelson .30 .09
Shigetoshi Hasegawa
❑ 689 Claudio Vargas .30 .09
Antonio Osuna
❑ 690 Brendan Donnelly .30 .09
Esteban Yan
❑ 691 Jeff Mathis .50 .15
Ervin Santana
❑ 692 Clint Everts .50 .15
Bill Bray
❑ 693 Jason Kubel .50 .15
Trevor Plouffe
❑ 694 Jake Stevens .50 .15
Andy Marte
❑ 695 Aaron Hill .50 .15
Chad Gaudin
❑ 696 Carlos Quentin .50 .15
Jesus Cota
❑ 697 Thomas Diamond .50 .15
Chris Young
❑ 698 Omar Quintanilla .50 .15
Dan Johnson
❑ 699 John Maine .50 .15
Val Majewski
❑ 700 James Houser .50 .15
Jonny Gomes
❑ 701 David Murphy .50 .15
Hanley Ramirez
❑ 702 Chris Lambert .50 .15
Rick Ankiel
❑ 703 Felix Pie .50 .15
Angel Guzman
❑ 704 Fred Lewis .50 .15
Nate Schierholtz
❑ 705 Arnie Munoz .50 .15
Gio Gonzalez
❑ 706 Felix Hernandez 1.50 .45
Travis Blackley
❑ 707 Ray Olmedo .50 .15
Edwin Encarnacion UER
Photos Reversed
❑ 708 Tim Stauffer .50 .15
Justin Germano
❑ 709 Jeremy Guthrie .50 .15
Jeremy Sowers
❑ 710 Jorge Cortes .50 .15
Tom Gorzelanny
❑ 711 Taylor Tankersley .50 .15
Eric Reed
❑ 712 Neil Walker .50 .15
Paul Maholm
❑ 713 Willy Taveras .50 .15
Luke Scott RC
❑ 714 Ryan Howard .50 .15
Greg Golson
❑ 715 Blake DeWitt .50 .15
Edwin Jackson
❑ 716 Huston Street .50 .15
Dan Putnam
❑ 717 Rickie Weeks .50 .15
Mark Rogers
❑ 718 Robinson Cano .50 .15
Philip Hughes
❑ 719 Kyle Waldrop .50 .15
Jay Rainville
❑ 720 Craig Brazell .50 .15
Yusmeiro Petit
❑ 721 Baltazar Lopez RC .50 .15
Matt Brown RC
❑ 722 Daryl Thompson RC .50 .15
Ender Chavez RC
❑ 723 Dan Uggla RC .75 .23
Erik Schindewolf RC
❑ 724 Ismael Ramirez RC .50 .15
Jayce Tingler RC
❑ 725 Tony Giarratano RC .50 .15
Eulogio de la Cruz RC
❑ 726 Matt Campbell RC .50 .15
Shane Costa RC
❑ 727 Martin Prado RC .50 .15
Bill McCarthy RC
❑ 728 Ian Kinsler RC .60 .18
Juan Senreiso RC UER
Kinsler photo is Edison Volquez
❑ 729 Luis Ramirez RC .50 .15
Lorenzo Scott RC
❑ 730 Chris Seddon RC .50 .15
Elliot Johnson RC
❑ 731 Craig Tatum RC .50 .15
Javon Moran RC
❑ 732 Stuart Pomeranz RC .50 .15
Jason Motte RC
❑ 733 Jose Vaquedano RC .50 .15
Stefan Bailie RC
❑ 734 Matt Albers RC .50 .15
Wade Robinson RC
❑ 735 Matt DeSalvo RC 1.00 .30
Melky Cabrera RC
❑ 736 Brian Stavisky RC .50 .15
Landon Powell RC
❑ 737 Scott Mathieson RC .75 .23
Scott Mitchinson RC
❑ 738 Sean Marshall RC .50 .15
Bear Bay RC
❑ 739 Brandon McCarthy RC 1.25 .35
Pedro Lopez RC
❑ 740 Alexander Smit RC .50 .15
Ricky Barrett RC
❑ 741 Matt Rogelstad RC .50 .15
Ryan Feierabend RC
❑ 742 Nate McLouth RC .50 .15
Adam Boeve RC
❑ 743 Kevin Melillo RC .75 .23
Michael Rogers RC
❑ 744 Matthew Kemp RC 1.50 .45
Heath Totten RC
❑ 745 Jai Miller RC .50 .15
Tony Arnerich RC
❑ 746 Tyler Pelland RC .50 .15
Jesse Gutierrez RC
❑ 747 Jeremy West RC .50 .15
Willy Mota RC
❑ 748 Ryan Goleski RC .50 .15
Ryan Garko RC
❑ 749 Bryan Triplett RC .50 .15
Jared Gothreaux RC
❑ 750 Kevin West RC .75 .23
Glen Perkins RC
❑ 751 Mike Esposito RC .50 .15
Zach Parker RC
❑ 752 Ryan Sweeney RC 1.00 .30
Brian Miller RC
❑ 753 Casey McGehee RC .50 .15
Buck Coats RC
❑ 754 Mike Bourn RC .75 .23
Kelvin Pichardo RC
❑ 755 Mike Morse RC .75 .23
Bobby Livingston RC
❑ 756 Wes Swackhamer RC .50 .15
Brendan Ryan RC
❑ 757 Micah Furtado RC .50 .15
Nick Masset RC
❑ 758 Peeter Ramos RC .75 .23
George Kottaras RC
❑ 759 Elvys Quezada RC .75 .23
T.J. Beam RC
❑ 760 Dana Eveland RC .50 .15
Travis Hinton RC
❑ 761 James Jurries RC .50 .15
Chris Vines RC
❑ 762 Humberto Sanchez RC 1.50 .45
Justin Verlander RC
❑ 763 Philip Humber RC 1.00 .30
Shawn Bowman RC
❑ 764 Pat Misch RC .50 .15
J.B. Thurmond RC
❑ 765 Christian Colonel RC .50 .15
Neil Wilson RC
❑ 766 Checklist 1 .30 .09
❑ 767 Checklist 2 .30 .09
❑ 768 Checklist 3 .30 .09
❑ 769 Checklist 4 .30 .09
❑ 770 Checklist 5 .30 .09

2001 Topps Tribute

	Nm-Mt	Ex-Mt
COMPLETE SET (90)	200.00	60.00
❑ 1 Pee Wee Reese	6.00	1.80
❑ 2 Babe Ruth	20.00	6.00
❑ 3 Ralph Kiner	5.00	1.50
❑ 4 Brooks Robinson	5.00	1.50
❑ 5 Don Sutton	5.00	1.50
❑ 6 Carl Yastrzemski	10.00	3.00
❑ 7 Roger Maris	6.00	1.80
❑ 8 Andre Dawson	5.00	1.50

❑ 9 Luis Aparicio	5.00	1.50
❑ 10 Wade Boggs	5.00	1.50
❑ 11 Johnny Bench	6.00	1.80
❑ 12 Ernie Banks	6.00	1.80
❑ 13 Thurman Munson	6.00	1.80
❑ 14 Harmon Killebrew	6.00	1.80
❑ 15 Ted Kluszewski	5.00	1.50
❑ 16 Bob Feller	5.00	1.50
❑ 17 Mike Schmidt	12.00	3.60
❑ 18 Warren Spahn	5.00	1.50
❑ 19 Jim Palmer	5.00	1.50
❑ 20 Don Mattingly	12.00	3.60
❑ 21 Willie Mays	12.00	3.60
❑ 22 Gil Hodges	6.00	1.80
❑ 23 Juan Marichal	5.00	1.50
❑ 24 Robin Yount	6.00	1.80
❑ 25 Nolan Ryan Angels	15.00	4.50
❑ 26 Dave Winfield	5.00	1.50
❑ 27 Hank Greenberg	6.00	1.80
❑ 28 Honus Wagner	8.00	2.40
❑ 29 Nolan Ryan Rangers	15.00	4.50
❑ 30 Phil Niekro	5.00	1.50
❑ 31 Robin Roberts	5.00	1.50
❑ 32 Casey Stengel Yankees	5.00	1.50
❑ 33 Willie McCovey	5.00	1.50
❑ 34 Roy Campanella	6.00	1.80
❑ 35 Rollie Fingers A's	5.00	1.50
❑ 36 Tom Seaver	5.00	1.50
❑ 37 Jackie Robinson	6.00	1.80
❑ 38 Hank Aaron Braves	12.00	3.60
❑ 39 Bob Gibson	5.00	1.50
❑ 40 Carlton Fisk Red Sox	5.00	1.50
❑ 41 Hank Aaron Brewers	12.00	3.60
❑ 42 George Brett	12.00	3.60
❑ 43 Orlando Cepeda	5.00	1.50
❑ 44 Red Schoendienst	5.00	1.50
❑ 45 Don Drysdale	5.00	1.50
❑ 46 Mel Ott	6.00	1.80
❑ 47 Casey Stengel Mets	6.00	1.80
❑ 48 Al Kaline	6.00	1.80
❑ 49 Reggie Jackson	5.00	1.50
❑ 50 Tony Perez	5.00	1.50
❑ 51 Ozzie Smith	10.00	3.00
❑ 52 Billy Martin	5.00	1.50
❑ 53 Bill Dickey	5.00	1.50
❑ 54 Catfish Hunter	5.00	1.50
❑ 55 Duke Snider	5.00	1.50
❑ 56 Dale Murphy	5.00	1.50
❑ 57 Bobby Doerr	5.00	1.50
❑ 58 Earl Averill UER Card pictures Earl Averill Jr.	5.00	1.50
❑ 59 Carlton Fisk White Sox	5.00	1.50
❑ 60 Tom Lasorda	5.00	1.50
❑ 61 Lou Gehrig	12.00	3.60
❑ 62 Enos Slaughter	5.00	1.50
❑ 63 Jim Bunning	5.00	1.50
❑ 64 Rollie Fingers Brewers	5.00	1.50
❑ 65 Frank Robinson Reds	5.00	1.50
❑ 66 Earl Weaver	5.00	1.50
❑ 67 Eddie Mathews	6.00	1.80
❑ 68 Kirby Puckett	6.00	1.80
❑ 69 Phil Rizzuto	6.00	1.80
❑ 70 Lou Brock	5.00	1.50
❑ 71 Walt Alston	5.00	1.50
❑ 72 Billy Pierce	5.00	1.50
❑ 73 Joe Morgan	5.00	1.50
❑ 74 Roberto Clemente	15.00	4.50
❑ 75 Whitey Ford	5.00	1.50
❑ 76 Richie Ashburn	5.00	1.50
❑ 77 Elston Howard	5.00	1.50
❑ 78 Gary Carter	5.00	1.50
❑ 79 Carl Hubbell	5.00	1.50
❑ 80 Yogi Berra	6.00	1.80
❑ 81 Ken Boyer	5.00	1.50
❑ 82 Nolan Ryan Astros	15.00	4.50
❑ 83 Bill Mazeroski	5.00	1.50
❑ 84 Dizzy Dean	6.00	1.80
❑ 85 Nellie Fox	5.00	1.50
❑ 86 Stan Musial	10.00	3.00
❑ 87 Steve Carlton	5.00	1.50
❑ 88 Willie Stargell	5.00	1.50
❑ 89 Hal Newhouser	5.00	1.50
❑ 90 Frank Robinson Orioles	5.00	1.50
❑ NNO Mickey Mantle PSA Redemption	.00	.00
❑ NNO Mickey Mantle Buyback EXCH	.00	
❑ NNO Jackie Robinson Buyback EXCH	.00	
❑ NNO Ted Williams Buyback EXCH	.00	

2003 Topps Tribute Contemporary

	MINT	NRMT
COMMON CARD (1-90)	2.00	.90
COMMON CARD (91-100)	2.00	.90
COMMON CARD (101-110)	10.00	4.50

Card	MINT	NRMT
❑ 1 Jim Thome	2.50	1.10
❑ 2 Edgardo Alfonzo	2.00	.90
❑ 3 Edgar Martinez	2.50	1.10
❑ 4 Scott Rolen	2.50	1.10
❑ 5 Eric Hinske	2.00	.90
❑ 6 Mark Mulder	2.00	.90
❑ 7 Jason Giambi	2.00	.90
❑ 8 Bernie Williams	2.50	1.10
❑ 9 Cliff Floyd	2.00	.90
❑ 10 Ichiro Suzuki	8.00	3.60
❑ 11 Pat Burrell	2.00	.90
❑ 12 Garret Anderson	2.00	.90
❑ 13 Gary Sheffield	2.00	.90
❑ 14 Johnny Damon	2.50	1.10
❑ 15 Kerry Wood	2.00	.90
❑ 16 Bartolo Colon	2.00	.90
❑ 17 Adam Dunn	2.00	.90
❑ 18 Omar Vizquel	2.50	1.10
❑ 19 Todd Helton	2.50	1.10
❑ 20 Nomar Garciaparra	6.00	2.70
❑ 21 A.J. Burnett	2.00	.90
❑ 22 Craig Biggio	2.50	1.10
❑ 23 Carlos Beltran	2.00	.90
❑ 24 Kazuhisa Ishii	2.00	.90
❑ 25 Vladimir Guerrero	4.00	1.80
❑ 26 Roberto Alomar	2.50	1.10
❑ 27 Roger Clemens	8.00	3.60
❑ 28 Tim Hudson	2.00	.90
❑ 29 Brian Giles	2.00	.90
❑ 30 Barry Bonds	10.00	4.50
❑ 31 Jim Edmonds	2.50	1.10
❑ 32 Rafael Palmeiro	2.50	1.10
❑ 33 Francisco Rodriguez	2.00	.90
❑ 34 Andruw Jones	2.50	1.10
❑ 35 Shea Hillenbrand	2.00	.90
❑ 36 Moises Alou	2.00	.90
❑ 37 Luis Gonzalez	2.00	.90
❑ 38 Darin Erstad	2.00	.90
❑ 39 John Smoltz	2.50	1.10
❑ 40 Derek Jeter	10.00	4.50
❑ 41 Aubrey Huff	2.00	.90
❑ 42 Eric Chavez	2.00	.90
❑ 43 Doug Mientkiewicz	2.00	.90
❑ 44 Lance Berkman	2.00	.90
❑ 45 Josh Beckett	2.00	.90
❑ 46 Austin Kearns	2.00	.90
❑ 47 Frank Thomas	4.00	1.80
❑ 48 Pedro Martinez	2.50	1.10
❑ 49 Tim Salmon	2.00	.90
❑ 50 Alex Rodriguez	6.00	2.70
❑ 51 Ryan Klesko	2.00	.90
❑ 52 Tom Glavine	2.50	1.10
❑ 53 Shawn Green	2.00	.90
❑ 54 Jeff Kent	2.00	.90
❑ 55 Carlos Pena	2.00	.90
❑ 56 Paul Konerko	2.00	.90
❑ 57 Troy Glaus	2.00	.90
❑ 58 Manny Ramirez	2.50	1.10
❑ 59 Jason Jennings	2.00	.90
❑ 60 Randy Johnson	4.00	1.80
❑ 61 Ivan Rodriguez	2.50	1.10
❑ 62 Roy Oswalt	2.00	.90
❑ 63 Kevin Brown	2.00	.90
❑ 64 Jose Vidro	2.00	.90
❑ 65 Jorge Posada	2.50	1.10
❑ 66 Mike Piazza	6.00	2.70
❑ 67 Bret Boone	2.00	.90
❑ 68 Carlos Delgado	2.00	.90
❑ 69 Jimmy Rollins	2.00	.90
❑ 70 Alfonso Soriano	2.00	.90
❑ 71 Greg Maddux	6.00	2.70
❑ 72 Mark Prior	2.50	1.10
❑ 73 Jeff Bagwell	2.50	1.10
❑ 74 Richie Sexson	2.00	.90
❑ 75 Sammy Sosa	4.00	1.80
❑ 76 Curt Schilling	2.00	.90
❑ 77 Mike Sweeney	2.00	.90
❑ 78 Torii Hunter	2.00	.90
❑ 79 Larry Walker	2.00	.90
❑ 80 Miguel Tejada	2.00	.90
❑ 81 Rich Aurilia	2.00	.90
❑ 82 Bobby Abreu	2.00	.90
❑ 83 Phil Nevin	2.00	.90
❑ 84 Rodrigo Lopez	2.00	.90
❑ 85 Chipper Jones	4.00	1.80
❑ 86 Ken Griffey Jr.	6.00	2.70
❑ 87 Mike Lowell	2.00	.90
❑ 88 Maggio Ordonez	2.00	.90
❑ 89 Barry Zito	2.00	.90
❑ 90 Albert Pujols	8.00	3.60
❑ 91 Corey Shafer FY RC	2.00	.90
❑ 92 Dan Haren FY RC	3.00	1.35
❑ 93 Jeremy Bonderman FY RC	6.00	2.70
❑ 94 Branden Florence FY RC	2.00	.90
❑ 95 E.Bastida-Martinez FY RC	2.00	.90
❑ 96 Brian Wright FY RC	2.00	.90
❑ 97 Elizardo Ramirez FY RC	3.00	1.35
❑ 98 Mi.Garciaparra FY RC	2.00	.90
❑ 99 Clay Hensley FY RC	2.00	.90
❑ 100 Bobby Basham FY RC	3.00	1.35
❑ 101 Jose Contreras FY AU RC	15.00	6.75
❑ 102 Br. Bullington FY AU RC	10.00	4.50
❑ 103 Joey Gomes FY AU RC	10.00	4.50
❑ 104 Craig Brazell FY AU RC	10.00	4.50
❑ 105 Andy Marte FY AU RC	80.00	36.00
❑ 106 Han. Ramirez FY AU RC	60.00	27.00
❑ 107 Ryan Shealy FY AU RC	15.00	6.75
❑ 108 Daryl Clark FY AU RC	10.00	4.50
❑ 109 Tyler Johnson FY AU RC	10.00	4.50
❑ 110 Ben Francisco FY AU RC	10.00	4.50

2004 Topps Tribute HOF

	Nm-Mt	Ex-Mt
COMPLETE SET (80)	150.00	45.00
COMMON CARD (1-80)	4.00	1.20

Card	Nm-Mt	Ex-Mt
❑ 1 Willie Mays	10.00	3.00
❑ 2 Richie Ashburn	5.00	1.50
❑ 3 Babe Ruth	15.00	4.50
❑ 4 Lou Gehrig	10.00	3.00
❑ 5 Carl Yastrzemski	8.00	2.40
❑ 6 Fergie Jenkins	4.00	1.20

	Nm-Mt	Ex-Mt
❑ 7 Cool Papa Bell	5.00	1.50
❑ 8 Johnny Bench	5.00	1.50
❑ 9 Satchel Paige	5.00	1.50
❑ 10 Ty Cobb	8.00	2.40
❑ 11 Robin Roberts	4.00	1.20
❑ 12 Eddie Mathews	5.00	1.50
❑ 13 Tom Seaver	5.00	1.50
❑ 14 Kirby Puckett	5.00	1.50
❑ 15 Stan Musial	8.00	2.40
❑ 16 Ralph Kiner	5.00	1.50
❑ 17 Reggie Jackson	5.00	1.50
❑ 18 Walter Johnson	5.00	1.50
❑ 19 Phil Niekro	4.00	1.20
❑ 20 Mike Schmidt	10.00	3.00
❑ 21 Brooks Robinson	5.00	1.50
❑ 22 Jimmie Foxx	5.00	1.50
❑ 23 Nellie Fox	5.00	1.50
❑ 24 Joe Morgan	4.00	1.20
❑ 25 Cy Young	5.00	1.50
❑ 26 Hank Greenberg	5.00	1.50
❑ 27 Josh Gibson	5.00	1.50
❑ 28 Robin Yount	5.00	1.50
❑ 29 Hoyt Wilhelm	4.00	1.20
❑ 30 Yogi Berra	5.00	1.50
❑ 31 Rollie Fingers	4.00	1.20
❑ 32 Gaylord Perry	4.00	1.20
❑ 33 Ozzie Smith	8.00	2.40
❑ 34 Jim Palmer	4.00	1.20
❑ 35 Harmon Killebrew	5.00	1.50
❑ 36 Bob Feller	4.00	1.20
❑ 37 Chuck Klein	4.00	1.20
❑ 38 Mordecai Brown	4.00	1.20
❑ 39 Napoleon Lajoie	5.00	1.50
❑ 40 Al Kaline	5.00	1.50
❑ 41 Paul Molitor	5.00	1.50
❑ 42 Jackie Robinson	5.00	1.50
❑ 43 Mel Ott	5.00	1.50
❑ 44 Hank Aaron	10.00	3.00
❑ 45 Rod Carew	5.00	1.50
❑ 46 Rogers Hornsby	5.00	1.50
❑ 47 Bob Gibson	5.00	1.50
❑ 48 Juan Marichal	4.00	1.20
❑ 49 Bill Mazeroski	5.00	1.50
❑ 50 Roberto Clemente	12.00	3.60
❑ 51 Willie McCovey	5.00	1.50
❑ 52 Red Schoendienst	4.00	1.20
❑ 53 Nolan Ryan	12.00	3.60
❑ 54 Dennis Eckersley	4.00	1.20
❑ 55 Monte Irvin	4.00	1.20
❑ 56 George Kell	4.00	1.20
❑ 57 Gary Carter	4.00	1.20
❑ 58 Tony Perez	4.00	1.20
❑ 59 Carlton Fisk	5.00	1.50
❑ 60 Duke Snider	5.00	1.50
❑ 61 Bobby Doerr	4.00	1.20
❑ 62 John McGraw	5.00	1.50
❑ 63 George Sisler	5.00	1.50
❑ 64 Orlando Cepeda	4.00	1.20
❑ 65 Earl Weaver	4.00	1.20
❑ 66 Roy Campanella	5.00	1.50
❑ 67 Tris Speaker	5.00	1.50
❑ 68 Sparky Anderson	4.00	1.20
❑ 69 Willie Stargell	5.00	1.50
❑ 70 Honus Wagner	5.00	1.50
❑ 71 Lou Brock	5.00	1.50
❑ 72 Whitey Ford	5.00	1.50
❑ 73 George Brett	10.00	3.00
❑ 74 Luis Aparicio	4.00	1.20
❑ 75 Ernie Banks	5.00	1.50
❑ 76 Jim Bunning	4.00	1.20
❑ 77 Warren Spahn	5.00	1.50
❑ 78 Catfish Hunter	5.00	1.50
❑ 79 Pee Wee Reese	5.00	1.50
❑ 80 Frank Robinson	4.00	1.20

2005 Topps Turkey Red

	Nm-Mt	Ex-Mt
COMPLETE SET (330)	300.00	90.00
COMP.SET w/o SP's (275)	50.00	15.00
COMMON CARD (1-270)	.40	.12
COMMON SP (1-270)	8.00	2.40
SP CL: 160A/160B/170/175/181/184/185/193.00		
COMMON REPRINT	.75	.23
COMMON RC (271-300)	1.00	.30
COMMON RET (301-315)	1.00	.30

VAR CL: 1/5/10/16/75/83/100/102/120/125
VAR CL: 130/160/225/230/270
TWO VERSIONS OF EACH VARIATION EXIST

	Nm-Mt	Ex-Mt
❑ 1A B.Bonds Grey Uni SP	15.00	4.50
❑ 1B B.Bonds White Uni	2.50	.75
❑ 2 Michael Young	.40	.12
❑ 3 Jim Edmonds	.40	.12
❑ 4 Cliff Floyd	.40	.12
❑ 5A R.Clemens Blue Sky SP	10.00	3.00
❑ 5B R.Clemens Yellow Sky SP	10.00	3.00
❑ 6 Hal Chase REP	.75	.23
❑ 7 Shannon Stewart	.40	.12
❑ 8 Fred Clarke REP	.75	.23
❑ 9 Travis Hafner	.40	.12
❑ 10A S.Sosa w/Name SP	8.00	2.40
❑ 10B S.Sosa w/o Name SP	8.00	2.40
❑ 11 Jermaine Dye	.40	.12
❑ 12 Lyle Overbay	.40	.12
❑ 13 Oliver Perez	.40	.12
❑ 14 Red Dooin REP	.75	.23
❑ 15 Kid Elberfeld REP	.75	.23
❑ 16A M.Piazza Blue Uni SP	8.00	2.40
❑ 16B M.Piazza Pinstripe	1.00	.30
❑ 17 Bret Boone	.40	.12
❑ 18 Hughie Jennings REP	.75	.23
❑ 19 Jeff Francis	.40	.12
❑ 20 Manny Ramirez SP	8.00	2.40
❑ 21 Russ Ortiz	.40	.12
❑ 22 Carlos Zambrano	.40	.12
❑ 23 Luis Castillo	.40	.12
❑ 24 David DeJesus	.40	.12
❑ 25 Carlos Beltran SP	8.00	2.40
❑ 26 Doug Davis	.40	.12
❑ 27 Bobby Abreu	.40	.12
❑ 28 Rich Harden SP	8.00	2.40
❑ 29 Brian Giles	.40	.12
❑ 30 Richie Sexson SP	8.00	2.40
❑ 31 Nick Johnson	.40	.12
❑ 32 Roy Halladay	.40	.12
❑ 33 Andy Pettitte	.60	.18
❑ 34 Miguel Cabrera	.60	.18
❑ 35 Jeff Kent	.40	.12
❑ 36 Chone Figgins	.40	.12
❑ 37 Carlos Lee	.40	.12
❑ 38 Greg Maddux	1.50	.45
❑ 39 Preston Wilson	.40	.12
❑ 40 Chipper Jones	1.00	.30
❑ 41 Coco Crisp	.40	.12
❑ 42 Adam Dunn	.40	.12
❑ 43 Out At Second M.Tejada CL	.40	.12
❑ 44 Sheffield At Bat CL	.40	.12
❑ 45 Play At the Plate J.Lopez CL	.40	.12
❑ 46 Rolen Diggin' In CL	.40	.12
❑ 47 Helton With the Slap Tag CL	.40	.12
❑ 48 Clemens Bringing Heat CL	1.00	.30
❑ 49 A Close Play J.Rollins CL	.40	.12
❑ 50 Ichiro At Bat CL	1.00	.30
❑ 51 Can of Corn C.Floyd CL	.40	.12
❑ 52 Pulling String J.Santana CL	.40	.12
❑ 53 Mark Teixeira	.60	.18
❑ 54 Chris Carpenter	.40	.12
❑ 55 Roy Oswalt SP	8.00	2.40
❑ 56 Casey Kotchman	.40	.12
❑ 57 Torii Hunter	.40	.12
❑ 58 Jose Reyes	.40	.12
❑ 59 Wily Mo Pena SP	8.00	2.40
❑ 60 Magglio Ordonez SP	8.00	2.40
❑ 61 Aaron Miles	.40	.12
❑ 62 Dallas McPherson	.40	.12
❑ 63 Javy Lopez	.40	.12
❑ 64 Luis Gonzalez	.40	.12
❑ 65 David Ortiz	1.00	.30
❑ 66 Jorge Posada	.60	.18
❑ 67 Xavier Nady	.40	.12
❑ 68 Larry Walker	.60	.18
❑ 69 Mark Loretta	.40	.12
❑ 70 Jim Thome SP	8.00	2.40
❑ 71 Livan Hernandez	.40	.12
❑ 72 Garrett Atkins	.40	.12
❑ 73 Milton Bradley	.40	.12
❑ 74 B.J. Upton	.40	.12
❑ 75A I.Suzuki w/Name SP	10.00	3.00
❑ 75B I.Suzuki w/o Name SP	10.00	3.00
❑ 76 Aramis Ramirez	.40	.12
❑ 77 Eric Milton	.40	.12
❑ 78 Troy Glaus SP	8.00	2.40
❑ 79 David Newhan	.40	.12
❑ 80 Delmon Young	.40	.12
❑ 81 Justin Morneau	.40	.12
❑ 82 Ramon Ortiz	.40	.12
❑ 83A E.Chavez Blue Sky	.40	.12
❑ 83B E.Chavez Purple Sky SP	8.00	2.40
❑ 84 Sean Burroughs	.40	.12
❑ 85 Scott Rolen SP	8.00	2.40
❑ 86 Rocco Baldelli	.40	.12
❑ 87 Joe Mauer SP	8.00	2.40
❑ 88 Tony Womack	.40	.12
❑ 89 Ken Griffey Jr.	1.50	.45
❑ 90 Alfonso Soriano SP	8.00	2.40
❑ 91 Paul Konerko	.40	.12
❑ 92 Guillermo Mota	.40	.12
❑ 93 Lance Berkman	.40	.12
❑ 94 Mark Buehrle	.40	.12
❑ 95 Matt Clement	.40	.12
❑ 96 Melvin Mora	.40	.12
❑ 97 Khalil Greene	.60	.18
❑ 98 David Wright	1.50	.45
❑ 99 Jack Wilson	.40	.12
❑ 100A A.Rodriguez w/Bat SP	10.00	3.00
❑ 100B A.Rodriguez w/Glove SP	10.00	3.00
❑ 101 Joe Nathan	.40	.12
❑ 102A A.Beltre Grey Uni SP	8.00	2.40
❑ 102B A.Beltre White Uni	.40	.12
❑ 103 Mike Sweeney	.40	.12
❑ 104 Brad Lidge	.40	.12
❑ 105 Shawn Green	.40	.12
❑ 106 Miguel Tejada SP	8.00	2.40
❑ 107 Derrek Lee	.60	.18
❑ 108 Eric Hinske	.40	.12
❑ 109 Eric Byrnes	.40	.12
❑ 110 Hideki Matsui SP	10.00	3.00
❑ 111 Tom Glavine	.60	.18
❑ 112 Jimmy Rollins	.40	.12
❑ 113 Ryan Drese	.40	.12
❑ 114 Josh Beckett	.40	.12
❑ 115 Curt Schilling SP	8.00	2.40
❑ 116 Jeremy Bonderman	.40	.12
❑ 117 Kazuo Matsui	.40	.12
❑ 118 Chase Utley	.40	.12
❑ 119 Troy Percival	.40	.12
❑ 120A V.Guerrero w/Bat SP	8.00	2.40
❑ 120B V.Guerrero w/Glove SP	8.00	2.40
❑ 121 Gary Sheffield	.40	.12
❑ 122 Jeromy Burnitz	.40	.12
❑ 123 Javier Vazquez	.40	.12
❑ 124 Kevin Millar	.40	.12
❑ 125A R.Johnson Blue Sky	1.00	.30
❑ 125B R.Johnson Purple Sky SP	8.00	2.40
❑ 126 Pat Burrell	.40	.12
❑ 127 Jason Schmidt	.40	.12
❑ 128 Jose Vidro	.40	.12
❑ 129 Kip Wells	.40	.12
❑ 130A I.Rodriguez w/Cap	.60	.18
❑ 130B I.Rodriguez w/Helmet SP	8.00	2.40
❑ 131 C.C. Sabathia	.40	.12
❑ 132 Carlos Delgado SP	8.00	2.40
❑ 133 Bartolo Colon	.40	.12
❑ 134 Andruw Jones	.60	.18
❑ 135 Kerry Wood	.40	.12
❑ 136 Sidney Ponson	.40	.12
❑ 137 Eric Gagne	.40	.12
❑ 138 Rickie Weeks	.40	.12
❑ 139 Mariano Rivera	.60	.18
❑ 140 Bobby Crosby	.40	.12

❑ 141 Jamie Moyer .40 .12
❑ 142 Corey Koskie .40 .12
❑ 143 John Smoltz .60 .18
❑ 144 Frank Thomas 1.00 .30
❑ 145 Cristian Guzman .40 .12
❑ 146 Paul Lo Duca .40 .12
❑ 147 Geoff Jenkins .40 .12
❑ 148 Nick Swisher .40 .12
❑ 149 Jason Bay SP 8.00 2.40
❑ 150 Albert Pujols SP 15.00 4.50
❑ 151 Edwin Jackson .40 .12
❑ 152 Carl Crawford .40 .12
❑ 153 Mark Mulder .40 .12
❑ 154 Rafael Palmeiro .60 .18
❑ 155 Pedro Martinez SP 8.00 2.40
❑ 156 Jake Westbrook .40 .12
❑ 157 Sean Casey .40 .12
❑ 158 Aaron Rowand .40 .12
❑ 159 J.D. Drew .40 .12
❑ 160A J.Sant Glove on Knee SP 8.00 2.40
❑ 160B J.Santana Throwing SP 8.00 2.40
❑ 161 Gavin Floyd .40 .12
❑ 162 Vernon Wells .40 .12
❑ 163 Aubrey Huff .40 .12
❑ 164 Jeff Bagwell .60 .18
❑ 165 Boomer Wells .40 .12
❑ 166 Brad Penny .40 .12
❑ 167 Austin Kearns .40 .12
❑ 168 Mike Mussina .60 .18
❑ 169 Randy Wolf .40 .12
❑ 170 Tim Hudson SP 8.00 2.40
❑ 171 Casey Blake .40 .12
❑ 172 Edgar Renteria .40 .12
❑ 173 Ben Sheets .40 .12
❑ 174 Kevin Brown .40 .12
❑ 175 Nomar Garciaparra SP 8.00 2.40
❑ 176 Armando Benitez .40 .12
❑ 177 Jody Gerut .40 .12
❑ 178 Craig Biggio .60 .18
❑ 179 Omar Vizquel .60 .18
❑ 180 Jake Peavy .40 .12
❑ 181 Gustavo Chacin SP 8.00 2.40
❑ 182 Johnny Damon .60 .18
❑ 183 Mike Lieberthal .40 .12
❑ 184 Felix Hernandez SP 15.00 4.50
❑ 185 Zach Day SP 8.00 2.40
❑ 186 Matt Cain .40 .12
❑ 187 Erubiel Durazo .40 .12
❑ 188 Zack Greinke .40 .12
❑ 189 Matt Morris .40 .12
❑ 190 Billy Wagner .40 .12
❑ 191 Al Leiter .40 .12
❑ 192 Miguel Olivo .40 .12
❑ 193 Jose Capellan SP 8.00 2.40
❑ 194 Adam Eaton .40 .12
❑ 195 Steven White SP RC 8.00 2.40
❑ 196 Joe Randa .40 .12
❑ 197 Richard Hidalgo .40 .12
❑ 198 Orlando Cabrera .40 .12
❑ 199 Joel Guzman SP 8.00 2.40
❑ 200 Garret Anderson .40 .12
❑ 201 Endy Chavez .40 .12
❑ 202 Andy Marte .40 .12
❑ 203 Jose Guillen .40 .12
❑ 204 Victor Martinez .40 .12
❑ 205 Johnny Estrada .40 .12
❑ 206 Damian Miller .40 .12
❑ 207 Ken Harvey .40 .12
❑ 208 Ronnie Belliard .40 .12
❑ 209 Chan Ho Park .40 .12
❑ 210 Laynce Nix .40 .12
❑ 211 Lew Ford .40 .12
❑ 212 Moises Alou .40 .12
❑ 213 Kris Benson .40 .12
❑ 214 Mike Gonzalez SP 8.00 2.40
❑ 215 Chris Burke .40 .12
❑ 216 Juan Pierre .40 .12
❑ 217 Phil Nevin .40 .12
❑ 218 Jerry Hairston Jr. .40 .12
❑ 219 Jeremy Reed .40 .12
❑ 220 Scott Kazmir SP 8.00 2.40
❑ 221 Mike Maroth .40 .12
❑ 222 Alex Rios .40 .12
❑ 223 Esteban Loaiza .40 .12
❑ 224 Termel Sledge .40 .12
❑ 225A M.Prior Blue Sky SP 8.00 2.40
❑ 225B M.Prior Yellow Sky SP 8.00 2.40
❑ 226 Hank Blalock .40 .12
❑ 227 Craig Wilson .40 .12
❑ 228 Cesar Izturis .40 .12
❑ 229 Dmitri Young .40 .12
❑ 230A D.Jeter Blue Sky SP 15.00 4.50
❑ 230B D.Jeter Purple Sky SP 15.00 4.50
❑ 231 Mark Kotsay .40 .12
❑ 232 Darin Erstad .40 .12
❑ 233 Brandon Backe SP 8.00 2.40
❑ 234 Mike Lowell .40 .12
❑ 235 Scott Podsednik .40 .12
❑ 236 Michael Barrett .40 .12
❑ 237 Chad Tracy .40 .12
❑ 238 David Dellucci .40 .12
❑ 239 Brady Clark .40 .12
❑ 240 Jorge Cantu .40 .12
❑ 241 Wil Ledezma .40 .12
❑ 242 Morgan Ensberg .40 .12
❑ 243 Omar Infante .40 .12
❑ 244 Corey Patterson .40 .12
❑ 245 Matt Holliday .40 .12
❑ 246 Vinny Castilla .40 .12
❑ 247 Jason Bartlett .40 .12
❑ 248 Noah Lowry .40 .12
❑ 249 Huston Street .60 .18
❑ 250 Russell Branyan .40 .12
❑ 251 Juan Uribe .40 .12
❑ 252 Larry Bigbie .40 .12
❑ 253 Grady Sizemore .40 .12
❑ 254 Pedro Feliz .40 .12
❑ 255 Brad Wilkerson .40 .12
❑ 256 Brandon Inge .40 .12
❑ 257 Dewon Brazelton .40 .12
❑ 258 Rodrigo Lopez .40 .12
❑ 259 Jacque Jones .40 .12
❑ 260 Jason Giambi .40 .12
❑ 261 Clint Barmes .40 .12
❑ 262 Willy Taveras .40 .12
❑ 263 Marcus Giles .40 .12
❑ 264 Joe Blanton .40 .12
❑ 265 John Thomson .40 .12
❑ 266 Steve Finley SP 8.00 2.40
❑ 267 Kevin Millwood .40 .12
❑ 268 David Eckstein .40 .12
❑ 269 Barry Zito .40 .12
❑ 270A T.Helton Purple Sky SP 8.00 2.40
❑ 270B T.Helton Yellow Sky SP 8.00 2.40
❑ 271 Landon Powell RC 1.00 .30
❑ 272 Justin Verlander RC 1.50 .45
❑ 273 Wes Swackhamer RC 1.00 .30
❑ 274 Wladimir Balentien RC 1.00 .30
❑ 275 Philip Humber RC 1.00 .30
❑ 276 Kevin Melillo RC 1.00 .30
❑ 277 Billy Butler RC 4.00 1.20
❑ 278 Michael Rogers RC 1.00 .30
❑ 279 Bobby Livingston RC 1.00 .30
❑ 280 Glen Perkins RC 1.00 .30
❑ 281 Mike Bourn RC 1.00 .30
❑ 282 Tyler Pelland RC 1.00 .30
❑ 283 Jeremy West RC 1.00 .30
❑ 284 Brandon McCarthy RC 1.50 .45
❑ 285 Ian Kinsler RC 1.25 .35
❑ 286 Chris Roberson RC 1.00 .30
❑ 287 Melky Cabrera RC 1.00 .30
❑ 288 Ryan Sweeney RC 1.00 .30
❑ 289 Chip Cannon RC 1.00 .30
❑ 290 Andy LaRoche RC 4.00 1.20
❑ 291 Chuck Tiffany RC 1.25 .35
❑ 292 Ian Bladergroen RC 1.00 .30
❑ 293 Bear Bay RC 1.00 .30
❑ 294 Hernan Iribarren RC 1.25 .35
❑ 295 Stuart Pomeranz RC 1.00 .30
❑ 296 Luke Scott RC 1.00 .30
❑ 297 Chuck James RC 2.50 .75
❑ 298 Kennard Bibbs RC 1.00 .30
❑ 299 Steven Bondurant RC 1.00 .30
❑ 300 Thomas Oldham RC 1.00 .30
❑ 301 Nolan Ryan RET 5.00 1.50
❑ 302 Reggie Jackson RET 1.25 .35
❑ 303 Tom Seaver RET 1.25 .35
❑ 304 Al Kaline RET 2.00 .60
❑ 305 Cal Ripken RET 6.00 1.80
❑ 306 Josh Gibson RET 2.00 .60
❑ 307 Frank Robinson RET 1.00 .30
❑ 308 Duke Snider RET 1.25 .35
❑ 309 Wade Boggs RET 1.25 .35
❑ 310 Tony Gwynn RET 2.50 .75
❑ 311 Carl Yastrzemski RET 2.00 .60
❑ 312 Ryne Sandberg RET 3.00 .90
❑ 313 Gary Carter RET 1.00 .30
❑ 314 Brooks Robinson RET 1.25 .35
❑ 315 Ernie Banks RET 2.00 .60

2005 UD All-Star Classics

	Nm-Mt	Ex-Mt
COMPLETE SET (100)	25.00	7.50
COMMON CARD (76-100)	.30	.09

51-100 ARE NOT SHORT PRINTS

❑ 1 Albert Pujols 1.50 .45
❑ 2 Alex Rodriguez 1.25 .35
❑ 3 Alfonso Soriano .30 .09
❑ 4 Barry Zito .30 .09
❑ 5 Bobby Abreu .30 .09
❑ 6 Carlos Beltran .30 .09
❑ 7 Carlos Delgado .30 .09
❑ 8 Chipper Jones .75 .23
❑ 9 Curt Schilling .50 .15
❑ 10 David Ortiz .75 .23
❑ 11 Derek Jeter 1.50 .45
❑ 12 Edgar Renteria .30 .09
❑ 13 Eric Gagne .30 .09
❑ 14 Frank Thomas .75 .23
❑ 15 Gary Sheffield .30 .09
❑ 16 Greg Maddux 1.25 .35
❑ 17 Hank Blalock .30 .09
❑ 18 Hideki Matsui 1.50 .45
❑ 19 Ichiro Suzuki 1.50 .45
❑ 20 Ivan Rodriguez .50 .15
❑ 21 Jason Schmidt .30 .09
❑ 22 Jason Varitek .75 .23
❑ 23 Jeff Kent .30 .09
❑ 24 Jim Thome .50 .15
❑ 25 Jorge Posada .50 .15
❑ 26 Ken Griffey Jr. 1.25 .35
❑ 27 Kerry Wood .30 .09
❑ 28 Lance Berkman .30 .09
❑ 29 Manny Ramirez .50 .15
❑ 30 Mariano Rivera .50 .15
❑ 31 Mark Mulder .30 .09
❑ 32 Mark Prior .50 .15
❑ 33 Miguel Cabrera .50 .15
❑ 34 Miguel Tejada .30 .09
❑ 35 Mike Piazza .75 .23
❑ 36 Nomar Garciaparra .75 .23
❑ 37 Pedro Martinez .50 .15
❑ 38 Randy Johnson .75 .23
❑ 39 Richie Sexson .30 .09
❑ 40 Roger Clemens UER 1.25 .35
Clemens is misspelled
❑ 41 Roy Halladay .30 .09
❑ 42 Sammy Sosa .75 .23
❑ 43 Scott Rolen .50 .15
❑ 44 Sean Casey .30 .09
❑ 45 Tim Hudson .30 .09
❑ 46 Todd Helton .50 .15
❑ 47 Tom Glavine .50 .15
❑ 48 Torii Hunter .30 .09
❑ 49 Troy Glaus .30 .09
❑ 50 Vladimir Guerrero .75 .23
❑ 51 Adrian Beltre FUT .30 .09

❑ 52 Alexis Rios FUT	.30	.09
❑ 53 Aubrey Huff FUT	.30	.09
❑ 54 Brandon Webb FUT	.30	.09
❑ 55 Dallas McPherson FUT	.30	.09
❑ 56 David Wright FUT	1.25	.35
❑ 57 Edwin Jackson FUT	.30	.09
❑ 58 Grady Sizemore FUT	.30	.09
❑ 59 Tadahito Iguchi FUT RC	1.50	.45
❑ 60 Jake Peavy FUT	.30	.09
❑ 61 Jake Westbrook FUT	.30	.09
❑ 62 Jason Bay FUT	.30	.09
❑ 63 Jeff Francis FUT	.30	.09
❑ 64 Jeremy Reed FUT	.30	.09
❑ 65 Joe Mauer FUT	.30	.09
❑ 66 Johan Santana FUT	.50	.15
❑ 67 Jose Capellan FUT	.30	.09
❑ 68 Jose Reyes FUT	.30	.09
❑ 69 Justin Morneau FUT	.30	.09
❑ 70 Mark Teixeira FUT	.50	.15
❑ 71 Oliver Perez FUT	.30	.09
❑ 72 Rich Harden FUT	.30	.09
❑ 73 Rickie Weeks FUT	.30	.09
❑ 74 Ryan Howard FUT	.30	.09
❑ 75 Scott Kazmir FUT	.30	.09
❑ 76 Al Kaline LGD	.75	.23
❑ 77 Bill Mazeroski LGD	.50	.15
❑ 78 Bob Feller LGD	.50	.15
❑ 79 Bob Gibson LGD	.50	.15
❑ 80 Brooks Robinson LGD	.50	.15
❑ 81 Cal Ripken LGD	2.50	.75
❑ 82 Carlton Fisk LGD	.50	.15
❑ 83 Eddie Murray LGD	.75	.23
❑ 84 Gaylord Perry LGD	.30	.09
❑ 85 Harmon Killebrew LGD	.75	.23
❑ 86 Jim Palmer LGD	.30	.09
❑ 87 Joe DiMaggio LGD	1.50	.45
❑ 88 Joe Morgan LGD	.30	.09
❑ 89 Johnny Bench LGD	.75	.23
❑ 90 Juan Marichal LGD	.30	.09
❑ 91 Lou Brock LGD	.50	.15
❑ 92 Mike Schmidt LGD	1.50	.45
❑ 93 Nolan Ryan LGD	2.00	.60
❑ 94 Ozzie Smith LGD	1.25	.35
❑ 95 Phil Niekro LGD	.30	.09
❑ 96 Robin Yount LGD	.75	.23
❑ 97 Rollie Fingers LGD	.30	.09
❑ 98 Tom Seaver LGD	.50	.15
❑ 99 Willie McCovey LGD	.50	.15
❑ 100 Yogi Berra LGD	.75	.23

2003 UD Authentics

	MINT	NRMT
COMP.SET w/o SP's (100)	40.00	18.00
COMMON ACTIVE (1-100)	.40	.18
COMMON RETIRED (1-100)	.50	.23
COMMON CARD (101-130)	4.00	1.80
101-130 RANDOM INSERTS IN PACKS	.00	
101-130 PRINT RUN 999 SERIAL #'d SETS	.00	
COMMON CARD (131-140)	8.00	3.60
131-140 RANDOM IN FINITE BONUS PACKS	.00	
131-140 PRINT RUN 150 SERIAL #'d SETS	.00	

❑ 1 Pee Wee Reese	.75	.35
❑ 2 Richie Ashburn	.75	.35
❑ 3 Derek Jeter	2.50	1.10
❑ 4 Alex Rodriguez	1.50	.70
❑ 5 Jose Vidro	.40	.18
❑ 6 Miguel Tejada	.40	.18
❑ 7 Nomar Garciaparra	1.50	.70
❑ 8 Pat Burrell	.40	.18
❑ 9 Albert Pujols	2.00	.90
❑ 10 Jeff Bagwell	.60	.25
❑ 11 Stan Musial	2.00	.90
❑ 12 Mickey Mantle	5.00	2.20
❑ 13 J.D. Drew	.40	.18
❑ 14 Ivan Rodriguez	.60	.25
❑ 15 Joe Morgan	.50	.23
❑ 16 Ted Williams	2.50	1.10
❑ 17 Travis Hafner	.40	.18
❑ 18 Chipper Jones	1.00	.45
❑ 19 Hideo Nomo	1.00	.45
❑ 20 Gary Sheffield	.40	.18
❑ 21 Jacque Jones	.40	.18
❑ 22 Alfonso Soriano	.40	.18
❑ 23 Roberto Alomar	.60	.25
❑ 24 Jeff Kent	.40	.18
❑ 25 Omar Vizquel	.60	.25
❑ 26 Ernie Banks	1.25	.55
❑ 27 Shawn Green	.40	.18
❑ 28 Tim Hudson	.40	.18
❑ 29 Jim Edmonds	.60	.25
❑ 30 Brandon Larson	.40	.18
❑ 31 Doug Mientkiewicz	.40	.18
❑ 32 Darin Erstad	.40	.18
❑ 33 Bobby Hill	.40	.18
❑ 34 Todd Helton	.60	.25
❑ 35 Kazuhisa Ishii	.40	.18
❑ 36 Lance Berkman	.40	.18
❑ 37 Eric Hinske	.40	.18
❑ 38 Jason Kendall	.40	.18
❑ 39 Bob Feller	.50	.23
❑ 40 Luis Gonzalez	.40	.18
❑ 41 Sammy Sosa	1.00	.45
❑ 42 Mike Piazza	1.50	.70
❑ 43 Roger Clemens	2.00	.90
❑ 44 Jose Cruz Jr.	.40	.18
❑ 45 Mark Prior	.60	.25
❑ 46 Mark Teixeira	.60	.25
❑ 47 Phil Nevin	.40	.18
❑ 48 Lyle Overbay	.40	.18
❑ 49 Manny Ramirez	.60	.25
❑ 50 Brian Giles	.40	.18
❑ 51 Preston Wilson	.40	.18
❑ 52 Jermaine Dye	.40	.18
❑ 53 Troy Glaus	.40	.18
❑ 54 Frank Thomas	1.00	.45
❑ 55 Jim Thome	.60	.25
❑ 56 Barry Bonds	2.50	1.10
❑ 57 Carlos Delgado	.40	.18
❑ 58 Jason Giambi	.40	.18
❑ 59 Joe Mays	.40	.18
❑ 60 Andruw Jones	.60	.25
❑ 61 Billy Williams	.50	.23
❑ 62 Vladimir Guerrero	1.00	.45
❑ 63 Scott Rolen	.60	.25
❑ 64 Juan Marichal	.50	.23
❑ 65 Austin Kearns	.40	.18
❑ 66 Kerry Wood	.40	.18
❑ 67 Bret Boone	.40	.18
❑ 68 Shea Hillenbrand	.40	.18
❑ 69 Mike Sweeney	.40	.18
❑ 70 Rocco Baldelli	.40	.18
❑ 71 Ken Griffey Jr.	1.50	.70
❑ 72 Cliff Floyd	.40	.18
❑ 73 Greg Maddux	1.50	.70
❑ 74 Mike Hampton	.40	.18
❑ 75 Larry Walker	.40	.18
❑ 76 Nolan Ryan	3.00	1.35
❑ 77 Rollie Fingers	.50	.23
❑ 78 Mike Mussina	.60	.25
❑ 79 Matt Morris	.40	.18
❑ 80 Robin Roberts	.50	.23
❑ 81 Barry Zito	.40	.18
❑ 82 Curt Schilling	.40	.18
❑ 83 Ken Harvey	.40	.18
❑ 84 Troy Percival	.40	.18
❑ 85 Tom Seaver	.75	.35
❑ 86 Mariano Rivera	.60	.25
❑ 87 Raul Mondesi	.40	.18
❑ 88 Adam Dunn	.40	.18
❑ 89 Roy Oswalt	.40	.18
❑ 90 Pedro Martinez	.60	.25
❑ 91 Andy Pettitte	.60	.25
❑ 92 Tom Glavine	.60	.25
❑ 93 Torii Hunter	.40	.18
❑ 94 Joe Thurston	.40	.18
❑ 95 Runelvys Hernandez	.40	.18
❑ 96 Randy Johnson	1.00	.45
❑ 97 Bernie Williams	.60	.25
❑ 98 Ichiro Suzuki	2.00	.90
❑ 99 C.C. Sabathia	.40	.18
❑ 100 Bobby Abreu	.40	.18
❑ 101 Jose Contreras RH RC	5.00	2.20
❑ 102 Hideki Matsui RH RC	15.00	6.75
❑ 103 Chris Capuano RH RC	4.00	1.80
❑ 104 Willie Eyre RH RC	4.00	1.80
❑ 105 Lew Ford RH RC	5.00	2.20
❑ 106 Shane Bazzell RH RC	4.00	1.80
❑ 107 Guillermo Quiroz RH RC	4.00	1.80
❑ 108 Fern. Cabrera RH RC	4.00	1.80
❑ 109 Francisco Cruceta RH RC	4.00	1.80
❑ 110 Jhonny Peralta RH	5.00	2.20
❑ 111 Bobby Madritsch RH RC	5.00	2.20
❑ 112 Diego Markwell RH RC	4.00	1.80
❑ 113 Matt Bruback RH RC	4.00	1.80
❑ 114 Matt Kata RH RC	4.00	1.80
❑ 115 Rob Hammock RH RC	4.00	1.80
❑ 116 Brandon Webb RH RC	5.00	2.20
❑ 117 Jon Leicester RH RC	4.00	1.80
❑ 118 Josh Willingham RH RC	5.00	2.20
❑ 119 Prentice Redman RH RC	4.00	1.80
❑ 120 Jeff Duncan RH RC	4.00	1.80
❑ 121 Craig Brazell RH RC	4.00	1.80
❑ 122 Jeremy Griffiths RH RC	4.00	1.80
❑ 123 Phil Seibel RH RC	4.00	1.80
❑ 124 Luis Ayala RH RC	4.00	1.80
❑ 125 Miguel Ojeda RH RC	4.00	1.80
❑ 126 Jeremy Wedel RH RC	4.00	1.80
❑ 127 Josh Hall RH RC	4.00	1.80
❑ 128 Oscar Villarreal RH RC	4.00	1.80
❑ 129 Clint Barmes RH RC	5.00	2.20
❑ 130 Nook Logan RH RC	5.00	2.20
❑ 131 Dan Haren RH RC	12.00	5.50
❑ 132 Delmon Young RH RC	50.00	22.00
❑ 133 Dontrelle Willis RH	5.00	2.20
❑ 134 Edwin Jackson RH RC	12.00	5.50
❑ 135 Jeremy Bonderman RH RC	25.00	11.00
❑ 136 Khalil Greene RH	25.00	11.00
❑ 137 Rich Harden RH	12.00	5.50
❑ 138 Rickie Weeks RH RC	40.00	18.00
❑ 139 Rosman Garcia RH RC	8.00	3.60
❑ 140 Ryan Wagner RH RC	8.00	3.60

2004 UD Diamond Pro Sigs

	Nm-Mt	Ex-Mt
COMP.SET w/o SP's (90)	15.00	4.50
COMMON CARD (1-90)	.30	.09
COMMON CARD (91-150)	4.00	1.20
91-150 STATED ODDS 1:6	.00	
COMMON CARD (151-240)	10.00	3.00
151-240 STATED ODDS 1:24	.00	
CARDS 160/169/174-175/177 DO NOT EXIST	.00	
CARDS 220/224/226-228 DO NOT EXIST	.00	
INSTANT WIN EXCH.ODDS 1:60,000	.00	

❑ 1 Alfonso Soriano	.30	.09
❑ 2 Josh Beckett	.30	.09
❑ 3 Kerry Wood	.30	.09
❑ 4 Brandon Webb	.30	.09
❑ 5 Shannon Stewart	.30	.09
❑ 6 Larry Walker	.30	.09

❑ 7 Tim Hudson .30 .09
❑ 8 Carlos Lee .30 .09
❑ 9 Austin Kearns .30 .09
❑ 10 Vernon Wells .30 .09
❑ 11 Jeff Bagwell .50 .15
❑ 12 Hideo Nomo .75 .23
❑ 13 Jerome Williams .30 .09
❑ 14 Kevin Brown .30 .09
❑ 15 Jose Vidro .30 .09
❑ 16 Rocco Baldelli .30 .09
❑ 17 Frank Thomas .75 .23
❑ 18 Albert Pujols 1.50 .45
❑ 19 Bartolo Colon .30 .09
❑ 20 C.C. Sabathia .30 .09
❑ 21 Andruw Jones .50 .15
❑ 22 Reggie Sanders .30 .09
❑ 23 Carlos Beltran .30 .09
❑ 24 Curt Schilling .50 .15
❑ 25 Miguel Tejada .30 .09
❑ 26 Barry Zito .30 .09
❑ 27 Pedro Martinez .50 .15
❑ 28 Sean Burroughs .30 .09
❑ 29 Sammy Sosa .75 .23
❑ 30 Eric Chavez .30 .09
❑ 31 Roy Halladay .30 .09
❑ 32 Todd Helton .50 .15
❑ 33 Mark Prior .50 .15
❑ 34 Mike Mussina .50 .15
❑ 35 Alex Rodriguez Yanks 1.25 .35
❑ 36 Ivan Rodriguez .50 .15
❑ 37 Mike Piazza 1.25 .35
❑ 38 Angel Berroa .30 .09
❑ 39 Orlando Cabrera .30 .09
❑ 40 Jim Thome .50 .15
❑ 41 Brian Giles .30 .09
❑ 42 Ichiro Suzuki 1.50 .45
❑ 43 Edgar Renteria .30 .09
❑ 44 Eric Gagne .30 .09
❑ 45 Gary Sheffield .30 .09
❑ 46 Torii Hunter .30 .09
❑ 47 Roger Clemens UER 1.50 .45
Photo on back in Curt Schilling
❑ 48 Scott Rolen .50 .15
❑ 49 Johan Santana .50 .15
❑ 50 Jacque Jones .30 .09
❑ 51 Hank Blalock .30 .09
❑ 52 Rafael Palmeiro .50 .15
❑ 53 Dmitri Young .30 .09
❑ 54 Ryan Klesko .30 .09
❑ 55 Mark Teixeira .50 .15
❑ 56 Nomar Garciaparra 1.25 .35
❑ 57 Jose Reyes .30 .09
❑ 58 Vladimir Guerrero .75 .23
❑ 59 Mike Sweeney .30 .09
❑ 60 Jorge Posada .50 .15
❑ 61 Derek Jeter 1.50 .45
❑ 62 Milton Bradley .30 .09
❑ 63 Bobby Abreu .30 .09
❑ 64 Greg Maddux 1.25 .35
❑ 65 Adam Dunn .30 .09
❑ 66 Troy Glaus .30 .09
❑ 67 Luis Gonzalez .30 .09
❑ 68 Shawn Green .30 .09
❑ 69 Bret Boone .30 .09
❑ 70 Mark Mulder .30 .09
❑ 71 Lance Berkman .30 .09
❑ 72 Preston Wilson .30 .09
❑ 73 Phil Nevin .30 .09
❑ 74 Chipper Jones .75 .23
❑ 75 Garret Anderson .30 .09
❑ 76 Jason Giambi .30 .09
❑ 77 Magglio Ordonez .30 .09
❑ 78 Jeff Kent .30 .09
❑ 79 Richie Sexson .30 .09
❑ 80 Mike Lowell .30 .09
❑ 81 Ben Sheets .30 .09
❑ 82 Randy Johnson .75 .23
❑ 83 Dontrelle Willis .50 .15
❑ 84 Javier Vazquez .30 .09
❑ 85 Geoff Jenkins .30 .09
❑ 86 Manny Ramirez .50 .15
❑ 87 Jim Edmonds .50 .15
❑ 88 Roy Oswalt .30 .09
❑ 89 Edgar Martinez .50 .15
❑ 90 Carlos Delgado .30 .09
❑ 91 Chris Saenz FC RC 4.00 1.20
❑ 92 Justin Leone FC RC 5.00 1.50
❑ 93 Shawn Hill FC RC 4.00 1.20
❑ 94 Chad Bentz FC RC 4.00 1.20
❑ 95 Jesse Harper FC RC 4.00 1.20
❑ 96 Dave Crouthers FC RC 4.00 1.20
❑ 97 Justin Germano FC RC 4.00 1.20
❑ 98 Tim Bausher FC RC 4.00 1.20
❑ 99 Greg Dobbs FC RC 4.00 1.20
❑ 100 Enemencio Pacheco FC RC 4.00 1.20
❑ 101 Dennis Sarfate FC RC 4.00 1.20
❑ 102 Edwin Moreno FC RC 4.00 1.20
❑ 103 Colby Miller FC RC 4.00 1.20
❑ 104 Mike Rouse FC RC 4.00 1.20
❑ 105 Fernando Nieve FC RC 5.00 1.50
❑ 106 Tim Hamulack FC RC 4.00 1.20
❑ 107 Jason Frasor FC RC 4.00 1.20
❑ 108 Jose Capellan FC RC 5.00 1.50
❑ 109 Jamie Brown FC RC 4.00 1.20
❑ 110 Mariano Gomez FC RC 4.00 1.20
❑ 111 Mike Vento FC RC 5.00 1.50
❑ 112 Josh Labandeira FC RC 4.00 1.20
❑ 113 Mike Gosling FC RC 4.00 1.20
❑ 114 Shingo Takatsu FC RC 5.00 1.50
❑ 115 Justin Hampson FC RC 4.00 1.20
❑ 116 Tim Bittner FC RC 4.00 1.20
❑ 117 Jerry Gil FC RC 4.00 1.20
❑ 118 Carlos Vasquez FC RC 5.00 1.50
❑ 119 Lincoln Holdzkom FC RC 4.00 1.20
❑ 120 Mike Johnston FC RC 4.00 1.20
❑ 121 William Bergolla FC RC 4.00 1.20
❑ 122 Luis A. Gonzalez FC RC 5.00 1.50
❑ 123 Ivan Ochoa FC RC 4.00 1.20
❑ 124 Roman Colon FC RC 4.00 1.20
❑ 125 Renyel Pinto FC RC 5.00 1.50
❑ 126 Donnie Kelly FC RC 4.00 1.20
❑ 127 Chris Oxspring FC RC 4.00 1.20
❑ 128 Sean Henn FC RC 4.00 1.20
❑ 129 Ryan Meaux FC RC 4.00 1.20
❑ 130 Shawn Camp FC RC 4.00 1.20
❑ 131 Brandon Medders FC RC 4.00 1.20
❑ 132 Rusty Tucker FC RC 5.00 1.50
❑ 133 Kazuo Matsui FC RC 5.00 1.50
❑ 134 Jorge Sequea FC RC 4.00 1.20
❑ 135 Hector Gimenez FC RC 4.00 1.20
❑ 136 Casey Daigle FC RC 4.00 1.20
❑ 137 Ian Snell FC RC 5.00 1.50
❑ 138 Scott Dohmann FC RC 4.00 1.20
❑ 139 Ronny Cedeno FC RC 5.00 1.50
❑ 140 Jorge Vasquez FC RC 4.00 1.20
❑ 141 David Aardsma FC RC 5.00 1.50
❑ 142 Carlos Hines FC RC 4.00 1.20
❑ 143 Scott Proctor FC RC 5.00 1.50
❑ 144 Jerome Gamble FC RC 4.00 1.20
❑ 145 Jason Bartlett FC RC 5.00 1.50
❑ 146 Akinori Otsuka FC RC 4.00 1.20
❑ 147 Merkin Valdez FC RC 5.00 1.50
❑ 148 Jake Woods FC RC 4.00 1.20
❑ 149 Chris Aguila FC RC 4.00 1.20
❑ 150 John Gall FC RC 5.00 1.50
❑ 151 Aaron Miles AU 10.00 3.00
❑ 152 Aquilino Lopez AU 10.00 3.00
❑ 153 Bill Hall AU 10.00 3.00
❑ 154 Billy Traber AU 10.00 3.00
❑ 155 Brad Lidge AU 40.00 12.00
❑ 156 Brady Clark AU 15.00 4.50
❑ 157 Brandon Duckworth AU 10.00 3.00
❑ 158 Brett Tomko AU 10.00 3.00
❑ 159 Brian Fuentes AU 10.00 3.00
❑ 160 Does Not Exist .00 .00
❑ 161 Brooks Kieshnick AU 10.00 3.00
❑ 162 Carlos Rivera AU 10.00 3.00
❑ 163 Chad Cordero AU 15.00 4.50
❑ 164 Chad Tracy AU 10.00 3.00
❑ 165 Claudio Vargas AU 10.00 3.00
❑ 166 D.J. Carrasco AU 10.00 3.00
❑ 167 Damian Rolls AU 10.00 3.00
❑ 168 David Sanders AU 10.00 3.00
❑ 169 Does Not Exist .00 .00
❑ 170 Derrick Turnbow AU 15.00 4.50
❑ 171 Desi Relaford AU 10.00 3.00
❑ 172 Doug Davis AU 10.00 3.00
❑ 173 Dustan Mohr AU 10.00 3.00
❑ 174 Does Not Exist .00 .00
❑ 175 Does Not Exist .00 .00
❑ 176 Frank Catalanotto AU 10.00 3.00
❑ 177 Does Not Exist .00 .00
❑ 178 Franklyn German AU 10.00 3.00
❑ 179 Ron Belliard AU 10.00 3.00
❑ 180 Geoff Geary AU 10.00 3.00
❑ 181 Greg Colbrunn AU 10.00 3.00
❑ 182 Henry Mateo AU 10.00 3.00
❑ 183 Brent Mayne AU 10.00 3.00
❑ 184 Horacio Ramirez AU 10.00 3.00
❑ 185 J.C. Romero AU 10.00 3.00
❑ 186 J.J. Putz AU 10.00 3.00
❑ 187 Ferdin Tejeda AU 10.00 3.00
❑ 188 Jaime Cerda AU 10.00 3.00
❑ 189 Jason Michaels AU 10.00 3.00
❑ 190 Jason Simontacchi AU 10.00 3.00
❑ 191 Jay Witasick AU 10.00 3.00
❑ 192 Joe Valentine AU 10.00 3.00
❑ 193 Joey Eischen AU 10.00 3.00
❑ 194 Johnny Estrada AU 10.00 3.00
❑ 195 Jon Garland AU 40.00 12.00
❑ 196 Jon Switzer AU 10.00 3.00
❑ 197 Jorge Julio AU 10.00 3.00
❑ 198 Jorge Sosa AU 10.00 3.00
❑ 199 Jose Castillo AU 10.00 3.00
❑ 200 Jose Macias AU 10.00 3.00
❑ 201 Josh Bard AU 10.00 3.00
❑ 202 Juan Cruz AU 10.00 3.00
❑ 203 Juan Rivera AU 10.00 3.00
❑ 204 Ken Griffey Jr. AU 120.00 36.00
❑ 205 Kevin Hooper AU 10.00 3.00
❑ 206 Kiko Calero AU 10.00 3.00
❑ 207 Chad Gaudin AU 10.00 3.00
❑ 208 Luis Rivas AU 10.00 3.00
❑ 209 Mark Corey AU 10.00 3.00
❑ 210 Matt Ford AU 10.00 3.00
❑ 211 Matt Herges AU 10.00 3.00
❑ 212 Miguel Cairo AU 10.00 3.00
❑ 213 Fernando Cabrera AU 10.00 3.00
❑ 214 Mike MacDougal AU 10.00 3.00
❑ 215 Mike Neu AU 10.00 3.00
❑ 216 Lew Ford AU 10.00 3.00
❑ 217 Mike Wood AU 10.00 3.00
❑ 218 Nate Robertson AU 10.00 3.00
❑ 219 Nick Punto AU 10.00 3.00
❑ 220 Does Not Exist .00 .00
❑ 221 Oscar Villarreal AU 10.00 3.00
❑ 222 Ramon Vazquez AU 10.00 3.00
❑ 223 Randall Simon AU 10.00 3.00
❑ 224 Does Not Exist .00 .00
❑ 225 Ricky Stone AU 10.00 3.00
❑ 226 Does Not Exist .00 .00
❑ 227 Does Not Exist .00 .00
❑ 228 Does Not Exist .00 .00
❑ 229 Ryan Drese AU 10.00 3.00
❑ 230 Ryan Ludwick AU 10.00 3.00
❑ 231 Scot Shields AU 10.00 3.00
❑ 232 Shane Nance AU 10.00 3.00
❑ 233 Steve Colyer AU 10.00 3.00
❑ 234 Tony Armas Jr. AU 10.00 3.00
❑ 235 Robby Hammock AU 10.00 3.00
❑ 236 Travis Hafner AU 15.00 4.50
❑ 237 Victor Martinez AU 15.00 4.50
❑ 238 Wilfredo Ledezma AU 10.00 3.00
❑ 239 Willie Bloomquist AU 10.00 3.00
❑ 240 Yorvit Torrealba AU 10.00 3.00
❑ NNO Instant Win Exchange .00

2005 UD Mini Jersey Collection

	Nm-Mt	Ex-Mt
COMMON CARD (1-70)	.75	.23
COMMON CARD (71-85)	.75	.23
COMMON CARD (86-100)	.75	.23
❑ 1 Garret Anderson	.75	.23
❑ 2 Vladimir Guerrero	2.00	.60
❑ 3 Luis Gonzalez	.75	.23
❑ 4 Shawn Green	.75	.23
❑ 5 Troy Glaus	.75	.23
❑ 6 Andruw Jones	1.25	.35
❑ 7 Chipper Jones	2.00	.60
❑ 8 John Smoltz	1.25	.35
❑ 9 Tim Hudson	.75	.23
❑ 10 Miguel Tejada	.75	.23
❑ 11 Sammy Sosa	2.00	.60
❑ 12 Curt Schilling	1.25	.35
❑ 13 David Ortiz	2.00	.60
❑ 14 Johnny Damon	1.25	.35
❑ 15 Manny Ramirez	1.25	.35
❑ 16 Greg Maddux	3.00	.90
❑ 17 Kerry Wood	.75	.23
❑ 18 Mark Prior	1.25	.35
❑ 19 Nomar Garciaparra	2.00	.60
❑ 20 Frank Thomas	2.00	.60
❑ 21 Adam Dunn	.75	.23
❑ 22 Ken Griffey Jr.	3.00	.90
❑ 23 Travis Hafner	.75	.23
❑ 24 Victor Martinez	.75	.23
❑ 25 Todd Helton	1.25	.35
❑ 26 Ivan Rodriguez	1.25	.35
❑ 27 Magglio Ordonez	.75	.23
❑ 28 Carlos Delgado	.75	.23
❑ 29 Miguel Cabrera	1.25	.35
❑ 30 Jeff Bagwell	1.25	.35
❑ 31 Lance Berkman	.75	.23
❑ 32 Roger Clemens	3.00	.90
❑ 33 Roy Oswalt	.75	.23
❑ 34 Mike Sweeney	.75	.23
❑ 35 Eric Gagne	.75	.23
❑ 36 J.D. Drew	.75	.23
❑ 37 Ben Sheets	.75	.23
❑ 38 Johan Santana	1.25	.35
❑ 39 Torii Hunter	.75	.23
❑ 40 Carlos Beltran	.75	.23
❑ 41 Mike Piazza	2.00	.60
❑ 42 Pedro Martinez	1.25	.35
❑ 43 Alex Rodriguez	3.00	.90
❑ 44 Derek Jeter	4.00	1.20
❑ 45 Hideki Matsui	4.00	1.20
❑ 46 Mike Mussina	1.25	.35
❑ 47 Randy Johnson	2.00	.60
❑ 48 Bobby Crosby	.75	.23
❑ 49 Eric Chavez	.75	.23
❑ 50 Bobby Abreu	.75	.23
❑ 51 Jim Thome	1.25	.35
❑ 52 Jason Bay	.75	.23
❑ 53 Oliver Perez	.75	.23
❑ 54 Jake Peavy	.75	.23
❑ 55 Khalil Greene	1.25	.35
❑ 56 Jason Schmidt	.75	.23
❑ 57 Moises Alou	.75	.23
❑ 58 Adrian Beltre	.75	.23
❑ 59 Ichiro Suzuki	4.00	1.20
❑ 60 Albert Pujols	4.00	1.20
❑ 61 Jim Edmonds	1.25	.35
❑ 62 Mark Mulder	.75	.23
❑ 63 Scott Rolen	1.25	.35
❑ 64 Aubrey Huff	.75	.23
❑ 65 Alfonso Soriano	.75	.23
❑ 66 Hank Blalock	.75	.23
❑ 67 Mark Teixeira	1.25	.35
❑ 68 Roy Halladay	.75	.23
❑ 69 Jose Vidro	.75	.23
❑ 70 Livan Hernandez	.75	.23
❑ 71 Andruw Jones JE	1.25	.35
❑ 72 Mark Prior JE	1.25	.35
❑ 73 Frank Thomas JE	2.00	.60
❑ 74 Ken Griffey Jr. JE	3.00	.90
❑ 75 C.C. Sabathia JE	.75	.23
❑ 76 Jeff Bagwell JE	1.25	.35
❑ 77 Garret Anderson JE	.75	.23
❑ 78 Eric Gagne JE	.75	.23
❑ 79 Derek Jeter JE	4.00	1.20
❑ 80 Eric Chavez JE	.75	.23
❑ 81 Bobby Abreu JE	.75	.23
❑ 82 Jason Bay JE	.75	.23
❑ 83 Khalil Greene JE	1.25	.35
❑ 84 Jason Schmidt JE	.75	.23
❑ 85 Michael Young JE	.75	.23
❑ 86 Cal Ripken MCM	6.00	1.80
❑ 87 Derek Jeter MCM	4.00	1.20
❑ 88 Hank Blalock MCM	.75	.23
❑ 89 Hideo Nomo MCM	2.00	.60
❑ 90 Joe DiMaggio MCM	3.00	.90
❑ 91 Joe Morgan MCM	.75	.23
❑ 92 Ken Griffey Jr. MCM	3.00	.90
❑ 93 Larry Doby MCM	.75	.23
❑ 94 Pedro Martinez MCM	1.25	.35
❑ 95 Randy Johnson MCM	2.00	.60
❑ 96 Rick Ferrell MCM	.75	.23
❑ 97 Roger Clemens MCM	3.00	.90
❑ 98 Stan Musial MCM	2.50	.75
❑ 99 Ted Williams MCM	3.00	.90
❑ 100 Torii Hunter MCM	.75	.23

2005 UD Past Time Pennants

	Nm-Mt	Ex-Mt
COMPLETE SET (90)	25.00	7.50
❑ 1 Al Kaline	1.50	.45
❑ 2 Al Rosen	.50	.15
❑ 3 Bert Blyleven	.50	.15
❑ 4 Bill Mazeroski	.75	.23
❑ 5 Billy Williams	.50	.15
❑ 6 Bob Feller UER Feller never pitched a perfect game	.75	.23
❑ 7 Bob Gibson	.75	.23
❑ 8 Bob Lemon	.50	.15
❑ 9 Bobby Doerr	.50	.15
❑ 10 Brooks Robinson	.75	.23
❑ 11 Bruce Sutter	.50	.15
❑ 12 Bucky Dent	.50	.15
❑ 13 Cal Ripken	5.00	1.50
❑ 14 Carl Yastrzemski	2.50	.75
❑ 15 Carlton Fisk	.75	.23
❑ 16 Catfish Hunter	.75	.23
❑ 17 Dale Murphy	.75	.23
❑ 18 Dave Parker	.50	.15
❑ 19 Don Larsen	.75	.23
❑ 20 Don Mattingly	3.00	.90
❑ 21 Don Newcombe	.50	.15
❑ 22 Duke Snider	.75	.23
❑ 23 Early Wynn	.50	.15
❑ 24 Eddie Mathews	1.50	.45
❑ 25 Eddie Murray	1.50	.45
❑ 26 Enos Slaughter	.50	.15
❑ 27 Ernie Banks	1.50	.45
❑ 28 Fergie Jenkins UER Wrong year for Jenkins' Cy Young award	.50	.15
❑ 29 Frank Howard	.50	.15
❑ 30 Frank Robinson	.50	.15
❑ 31 Fred Lynn	.50	.15
❑ 32 Gary Carter	.50	.15
❑ 33 Gaylord Perry	.50	.15
❑ 34 George Brett	3.00	.90
❑ 35 George Kell	.50	.15
❑ 36 Goose Gossage	.50	.15
❑ 37 Graig Nettles	.50	.15
❑ 38 Harmon Killebrew	1.50	.45
❑ 39 Jack Morris	.50	.15
❑ 40 Jim Bunning	.50	.15
❑ 41 Felipe Alou	.50	.15
❑ 42 Jim Palmer	.50	.15
❑ 43 Jim Rice	.50	.15
❑ 44 Joe DiMaggio	3.00	.90
❑ 45 Joe Morgan	.50	.15
❑ 46 Johnny Bench	1.50	.45
❑ 47 Johnny Podres	.50	.15
❑ 48 Juan Marichal	.50	.15
❑ 49 Keith Hernandez	.50	.15
❑ 50 Kirby Puckett	1.50	.45
❑ 51 Larry Doby	.50	.15
❑ 52 Lou Brock	.75	.23
❑ 53 Luis Aparicio	.50	.15
❑ 54 Luis Tiant	.50	.15
❑ 55 Maury Wills	.50	.15
❑ 56 Mickey Mantle	8.00	2.40
❑ 57 Mike Schmidt	3.00	.90
❑ 58 Monte Irvin	.50	.15
❑ 59 Nolan Ryan	4.00	1.20
❑ 60 Orlando Cepeda	.50	.15
❑ 61 Ozzie Smith	2.50	.75
❑ 62 Paul Molitor	.75	.23
❑ 63 Pee Wee Reese	.75	.23
❑ 64 Phil Niekro	.50	.15
❑ 65 Phil Rizzuto	.75	.23
❑ 66 Ralph Kiner	.75	.23
❑ 67 Richie Ashburn	.75	.23
❑ 68 Rico Petrocelli	.50	.15
❑ 69 Robin Roberts	.50	.15
❑ 70 Robin Yount	1.50	.45
❑ 71 Rocky Colavito	.75	.23
❑ 72 Rod Carew	.75	.23
❑ 73 Rollie Fingers	.50	.15
❑ 74 Ron Guidry	.50	.15
❑ 75 Ron Santo	.75	.23
❑ 76 Tony Gwynn	2.00	.60
❑ 77 Sparky Lyle	.50	.15
❑ 78 Stan Musial	2.50	.75
❑ 79 Steve Carlton	.50	.15
❑ 80 Rick Ferrell	.50	.15
❑ 81 Tom Seaver	.75	.23
❑ 82 Tommy John	.50	.15
❑ 83 Tony Perez	.50	.15
❑ 84 Wade Boggs	.75	.23
❑ 85 Warren Spahn	.75	.23
❑ 86 Whitey Ford	.75	.23
❑ 87 Will Clark	.75	.23
❑ 88 Willie McCovey	.75	.23
❑ 89 Willie Stargell	.75	.23
❑ 90 Yogi Berra	1.50	.45

2005 UD Portraits

	Nm-Mt	Ex-Mt
COMMON CARD (1-100)	2.00	.60
COMMON RETIRED	2.00	.60
❑ 1 Dallas McPherson	2.00	.60
❑ 2 Steve Finley	2.00	.60
❑ 3 Vladimir Guerrero	4.00	1.20
❑ 4 Troy Glaus	2.00	.60
❑ 5 Andruw Jones	3.00	.90
❑ 6 Chipper Jones	4.00	1.20
❑ 7 John Smoltz	3.00	.90
❑ 8 Marcus Giles	2.00	.60
❑ 9 Tim Hudson	2.00	.60
❑ 10 Cal Ripken	15.00	4.50
❑ 11 Miguel Tejada	2.00	.60

❑ 12 Curt Schilling 3.00 .90
❑ 13 David Ortiz 4.00 1.20
❑ 14 Edgar Renteria 2.00 .60
❑ 15 Jason Varitek 4.00 1.20
❑ 16 Jim Rice 2.00 .60
❑ 17 Johnny Damon 3.00 .90
❑ 18 Matt Clement 2.00 .60
❑ 19 Wade Boggs 3.00 .90
❑ 20 Aramis Ramirez 2.00 .60
❑ 21 Carlos Zambrano 2.00 .60
❑ 22 Corey Patterson 2.00 .60
❑ 23 Fergie Jenkins 2.00 .60
❑ 24 Greg Maddux 6.00 1.80
❑ 25 Kerry Wood 2.00 .60
❑ 26 Mark Prior 3.00 .90
❑ 27 Nomar Garciaparra 4.00 1.20
❑ 28 Ryne Sandberg 8.00 2.40
❑ 29 Frank Thomas 4.00 1.20
❑ 30 Adam Dunn 2.00 .60
❑ 31 Barry Larkin 3.00 .90
❑ 32 Ken Griffey Jr. 6.00 1.80
❑ 33 Sean Casey 2.00 .60
❑ 34 Travis Hafner 2.00 .60
❑ 35 Victor Martinez 2.00 .60
❑ 36 Todd Helton 3.00 .90
❑ 37 Ivan Rodriguez 3.00 .90
❑ 38 Magglio Ordonez 2.00 .60
❑ 39 Josh Beckett 2.00 .60
❑ 40 Miguel Cabrera 3.00 .90
❑ 41 Mike Lowell 2.00 .60
❑ 42 Craig Biggio 3.00 .90
❑ 43 Jeff Bagwell 3.00 .90
❑ 44 Roger Clemens 6.00 1.80
❑ 45 Roy Oswalt 2.00 .60
❑ 46 Bo Jackson 4.00 1.20
❑ 47 Prince Fielder RC 10.00 3.00
❑ 48 Eric Gagne 2.00 .60
❑ 49 J.D. Drew 2.00 .60
❑ 50 Ben Sheets 2.00 .60
❑ 51 Robin Yount 4.00 1.20
❑ 52 Jacque Jones 2.00 .60
❑ 53 Joe Mauer 2.00 .60
❑ 54 Johan Santana 3.00 .90
❑ 55 Justin Morneau 2.00 .60
❑ 56 Torii Hunter 2.00 .60
❑ 57 Dontrelle Willis 2.00 .60
❑ 58 David Wright 6.00 1.80
❑ 59 Gary Carter 2.00 .60
❑ 60 Jose Reyes 2.00 .60
❑ 61 Keith Hernandez 2.00 .60
❑ 62 Mike Piazza 4.00 1.20
❑ 63 Pedro Martinez 3.00 .90
❑ 64 Tom Glavine 3.00 .90
❑ 65 Carl Pavano 2.00 .60
❑ 66 Derek Jeter 8.00 2.40
❑ 67 Don Mattingly 8.00 2.40
❑ 68 Mike Mussina 3.00 .90
❑ 69 Randy Johnson 4.00 1.20
❑ 70 Bobby Crosby 2.00 .60
❑ 71 Eric Chavez 2.00 .60
❑ 72 Rich Harden 2.00 .60
❑ 73 Bobby Abreu 2.00 .60
❑ 74 Mike Schmidt 8.00 2.40
❑ 75 Jason Bay 2.00 .60
❑ 76 Oliver Perez 2.00 .60
❑ 77 Brian Giles 2.00 .60
❑ 78 Jake Peavy 2.00 .60
❑ 79 Khalil Greene 3.00 .90
❑ 80 Tony Gwynn 5.00 1.50
❑ 81 Jason Schmidt 2.00 .60
❑ 82 Will Clark 3.00 .90
❑ 83 Adrian Beltre 2.00 .60
❑ 84 Justin Verlander RC 6.00 1.80
❑ 85 Albert Pujols 8.00 2.40
❑ 86 Jim Edmonds 3.00 .90
❑ 87 Mark Mulder 2.00 .60
❑ 88 Scott Rolen 3.00 .90
❑ 89 Aubrey Huff 2.00 .60
❑ 90 B.J. Upton 2.00 .60
❑ 91 Carl Crawford 2.00 .60
❑ 92 Tadahito Iguchi RC 8.00 2.40
❑ 93 Scott Kazmir 2.00 .60
❑ 94 Alfonso Soriano 2.00 .60
❑ 95 Hank Blalock 2.00 .60
❑ 96 Mark Teixeira 3.00 .90
❑ 97 Michael Young 2.00 .60
❑ 98 Nolan Ryan 10.00 3.00
❑ 99 Roy Halladay 2.00 .60
❑ 100 Jose Vidro 2.00 .60

2001 UD Reserve

	Nm-Mt	Ex-Mt
COMP.SET w/o SP's (180)	25.00	7.50
COMMON CARD (1-180)	.30	.09
COMMON (181-210)	4.00	1.20

❑ 1 Darin Erstad .30 .09
❑ 2 Tim Salmon .50 .15
❑ 3 Bengie Molina .30 .09
❑ 4 Troy Glaus .30 .09
❑ 5 Glenallen Hill .30 .09
❑ 6 Garret Anderson .30 .09
❑ 7 Jason Giambi .30 .09
❑ 8 Johnny Damon .50 .15
❑ 9 Eric Chavez .30 .09
❑ 10 Tim Hudson .30 .09
❑ 11 Miguel Tejada .30 .09
❑ 12 Barry Zito .50 .15
❑ 13 Jose Ortiz .30 .09
❑ 14 Tony Batista .30 .09
❑ 15 Carlos Delgado .30 .09
❑ 16 Shannon Stewart .30 .09
❑ 17 Raul Mondesi .30 .09
❑ 18 Ben Grieve .30 .09
❑ 19 Aubrey Huff .30 .09
❑ 20 Greg Vaughn .30 .09
❑ 21 Fred McGriff .50 .15
❑ 22 Gerald Williams .30 .09
❑ 23 Bartolo Colon .30 .09
❑ 24 Roberto Alomar .50 .15
❑ 25 Jim Thome .50 .15
❑ 26 Omar Vizquel .50 .15
❑ 27 Juan Gonzalez .30 .09
❑ 28 Ellis Burks .30 .09
❑ 29 Edgar Martinez .50 .15
❑ 30 Aaron Sele .30 .09
❑ 31 Jay Buhner .30 .09
❑ 32 Mike Cameron .30 .09
❑ 33 Kazuhiro Sasaki .30 .09
❑ 34 John Olerud .30 .09
❑ 35 Cal Ripken 2.50 .75
❑ 36 Brady Anderson .30 .09
❑ 37 Pat Hentgen .30 .09
❑ 38 Chris Richard .30 .09
❑ 39 Jerry Hairston Jr. .30 .09
❑ 40 Mike Bordick .30 .09
❑ 41 Ivan Rodriguez .50 .15
❑ 42 Rick Helling .30 .09
❑ 43 Rafael Palmeiro .50 .15
❑ 44 Alex Rodriguez 1.25 .35
❑ 45 Andres Galarraga .30 .09
❑ 46 Rusty Greer .30 .09
❑ 47 Ruben Mateo .30 .09
❑ 48 Ken Caminiti .30 .09
❑ 49 Nomar Garciaparra 1.25 .35
❑ 50 Pedro Martinez .50 .15
❑ 51 Manny Ramirez Sox .50 .15
❑ 52 Carl Everett .30 .09
❑ 53 Dante Bichette .30 .09
❑ 54 Hideo Nomo .75 .23
❑ 55 Mike Sweeney .30 .09
❑ 56 Carlos Beltran .30 .09
❑ 57 Jeff Suppan .30 .09
❑ 58 Jermaine Dye .30 .09
❑ 59 Mark Quinn .30 .09
❑ 60 Joe Randa .30 .09
❑ 61 Bobby Higginson .30 .09
❑ 62 Tony Clark .30 .09
❑ 63 Brian Moehler .30 .09
❑ 64 Dean Palmer .30 .09
❑ 65 Brandon Inge .30 .09
❑ 66 Damion Easley .30 .09
❑ 67 Brad Radke .30 .09
❑ 68 Corey Koskie .30 .09
❑ 69 Cristian Guzman .30 .09
❑ 70 Eric Milton .30 .09
❑ 71 Jacque Jones .30 .09
❑ 72 Matt Lawton .30 .09
❑ 73 Frank Thomas .75 .23
❑ 74 David Wells .30 .09
❑ 75 Magglio Ordonez .30 .09
❑ 76 Paul Konerko .30 .09
❑ 77 Sandy Alomar Jr. .30 .09
❑ 78 Ray Durham .30 .09
❑ 79 Roger Clemens 1.50 .45
❑ 80 Bernie Williams .50 .15
❑ 81 Derek Jeter 2.00 .60
❑ 82 David Justice .30 .09
❑ 83 Paul O'Neill .50 .15
❑ 84 Mike Mussina .50 .15
❑ 85 Jorge Posada .50 .15
❑ 86 Jeff Bagwell .50 .15
❑ 87 Richard Hidalgo .30 .09
❑ 88 Craig Biggio .50 .15
❑ 89 Scott Elarton .30 .09
❑ 90 Moises Alou .30 .09
❑ 91 Greg Maddux 1.25 .35
❑ 92 Rafael Furcal .30 .09
❑ 93 Andruw Jones .50 .15
❑ 94 Tom Glavine .50 .15
❑ 95 Chipper Jones .75 .23
❑ 96 Javy Lopez .30 .09
❑ 97 Richie Sexson .30 .09
❑ 98 Jeromy Burnitz .30 .09
❑ 99 Jeff D'Amico .30 .09
❑ 100 Jeffrey Hammonds .30 .09
❑ 101 Geoff Jenkins .30 .09
❑ 102 Ben Sheets .50 .15
❑ 103 Mark McGwire 2.00 .60
❑ 104 Rick Ankiel .30 .09
❑ 105 Darryl Kile .30 .09
❑ 106 Edgar Renteria .30 .09
❑ 107 Jim Edmonds .50 .15
❑ 108 J.D. Drew .30 .09
❑ 109 Sammy Sosa .75 .23
❑ 110 Corey Patterson .30 .09
❑ 111 Kerry Wood .30 .09
❑ 112 Todd Hundley .30 .09
❑ 113 Rondell White .30 .09
❑ 114 Matt Stairs .30 .09
❑ 115 Randy Johnson .75 .23
❑ 116 Mark Grace .50 .15
❑ 117 Steve Finley .30 .09
❑ 118 Luis Gonzalez .30 .09
❑ 119 Matt Williams .30 .09
❑ 120 Curt Schilling .30 .09
❑ 121 Gary Sheffield .30 .09
❑ 122 Kevin Brown .30 .09
❑ 123 Shawn Green .30 .09
❑ 124 Eric Karros .30 .09
❑ 125 Chan Ho Park .30 .09
❑ 126 Adrian Beltre .30 .09
❑ 127 Vladimir Guerrero .75 .23
❑ 128 Fernando Tatis .30 .09
❑ 129 Lee Stevens .30 .09
❑ 130 Jose Vidro .30 .09
❑ 131 Peter Bergeron .30 .09
❑ 132 Michael Barrett .30 .09
❑ 133 Jeff Kent .30 .09
❑ 134 Russ Ortiz .30 .09
❑ 135 Barry Bonds 2.00 .60
❑ 136 J.T. Snow .30 .09
❑ 137 Livan Hernandez .30 .09
❑ 138 Rich Aurilia .30 .09
❑ 139 Preston Wilson .30 .09
❑ 140 Mike Lowell .30 .09
❑ 141 Ryan Dempster .30 .09
❑ 142 Charles Johnson .30 .09
❑ 143 Matt Clement .30 .09
❑ 144 Luis Castillo .30 .09

Card	Nm-Mt	Ex-Mt
❑ 145 Mike Piazza UER Card lists him as a Dodger	1.25	.35
❑ 146 Al Leiter	.30	.09
❑ 147 Robin Ventura	.30	.09
❑ 148 Jay Payton	.30	.09
❑ 149 Todd Zeile	.30	.09
❑ 150 Edgardo Alfonzo	.30	.09
❑ 151 Tony Gwynn	1.00	.30
❑ 152 Ryan Klesko	.30	.09
❑ 153 Phil Nevin	.30	.09
❑ 154 Mark Kotsay	.30	.09
❑ 155 Trevor Hoffman	.30	.09
❑ 156 Damian Jackson	.30	.09
❑ 157 Scott Rolen	.50	.15
❑ 158 Mike Lieberthal	.30	.09
❑ 159 Bruce Chen	.30	.09
❑ 160 Bobby Abreu	.30	.09
❑ 161 Pat Burrell	.30	.09
❑ 162 Travis Lee	.30	.09
❑ 163 Jason Kendall	.30	.09
❑ 164 Derek Bell	.30	.09
❑ 165 Kris Benson	.30	.09
❑ 166 Kevin Young	.30	.09
❑ 167 Brian Giles	.30	.09
❑ 168 Pat Meares	.30	.09
❑ 169 Sean Casey	.50	.15
❑ 170 Pokey Reese	.30	.09
❑ 171 Pete Harnisch	.30	.09
❑ 172 Barry Larkin	.50	.15
❑ 173 Ken Griffey Jr.	1.25	.35
❑ 174 Dmitri Young	.30	.09
❑ 175 Mike Hampton	.30	.09
❑ 176 Todd Helton	.50	.15
❑ 177 Jeff Cirillo	.30	.09
❑ 178 Denny Neagle	.30	.09
❑ 179 Larry Walker	.30	.09
❑ 180 Todd Hollandsworth	.30	.09
❑ 181 Ichiro Suzuki SP RC	40.00	12.00
❑ 182 Wilson Betemit SP RC	5.00	1.50
❑ 183 A. Hernandez SP RC	4.00	1.20
❑ 184 Travis Hafner SP RC	8.00	2.40
❑ 185 Sean Douglass SP RC	4.00	1.20
❑ 186 Juan Diaz SP RC	4.00	1.20
❑ 187 H. Ramirez SP RC	5.00	1.50
❑ 188 M. Ensberg SP RC	6.00	1.80
❑ 189 B. Duckworth SP RC	4.00	1.20
❑ 190 Jack Wilson SP RC	5.00	1.50
❑ 191 Erick Almonte SP RC	4.00	1.20
❑ 192 R. Rodriguez SP RC	4.00	1.20
❑ 193 E. Guzman SP RC	4.00	1.20
❑ 194 Juan Uribe SP RC	5.00	1.50
❑ 195 Ryan Freel SP RC	5.00	1.50
❑ 196 C. Parker SP RC	4.00	1.20
❑ 197 J. Melian SP RC	4.00	1.20
❑ 198 Jose Mieses SP RC	4.00	1.20
❑ 199 Andres Torres SP RC	4.00	1.20
❑ 200 Jason Smith SP RC	4.00	1.20
❑ 201 J. Estrada SP RC	5.00	1.50
❑ 202 Cesar Crespo SP RC	4.00	1.20
❑ 203 C. Valderrama SP RC	4.00	1.20
❑ 204 Albert Pujols SP RC	80.00	24.00
❑ 205 Wilkin Ruan SP RC	4.00	1.20
❑ 206 Josh Fogg SP RC	4.00	1.20
❑ 207 Bert Snow SP RC	4.00	1.20
❑ 208 B. Lawrence SP RC	4.00	1.20
❑ 209 Esix Snead SP RC	4.00	1.20
❑ 210 T. Shinjo SP RC	5.00	1.50

2001 Ultimate Collection

	Nm-Mt	Ex-Mt
COMMON CARD (1-90)	4.00	1.20
COMMON CARD (91-100)	10.00	3.00
COMMON (101-110)	10.00	3.00
COMMON CARD (111-120)	15.00	4.50

Card	Nm-Mt	Ex-Mt
❑ 1 Troy Glaus	4.00	1.20
❑ 2 Darin Erstad	4.00	1.20
❑ 3 Jason Giambi	4.00	1.20
❑ 4 Barry Zito	4.00	1.20
❑ 5 Tim Hudson	4.00	1.20
❑ 6 Miguel Tejada	4.00	1.20
❑ 7 Carlos Delgado	4.00	1.20
❑ 8 Shannon Stewart	4.00	1.20
❑ 9 Greg Vaughn	4.00	1.20
❑ 10 Toby Hall	4.00	1.20
❑ 11 Roberto Alomar	4.00	1.20
❑ 12 Juan Gonzalez	4.00	1.20
❑ 13 Jim Thome	4.00	1.20
❑ 14 Edgar Martinez	4.00	1.20
❑ 15 Freddy Garcia	4.00	1.20
❑ 16 Bret Boone	4.00	1.20
❑ 17 Kazuhiro Sasaki	4.00	1.20
❑ 18 Cal Ripken	20.00	6.00
❑ 19 Tim Raines Jr.	4.00	1.20
❑ 20 Alex Rodriguez	10.00	3.00
❑ 21 Ivan Rodriguez	4.00	1.20
❑ 22 Rafael Palmeiro	4.00	1.20
❑ 23 Pedro Martinez	4.00	1.20
❑ 24 Nomar Garciaparra	10.00	3.00
❑ 25 Manny Ramirez Sox	4.00	1.20
❑ 26 Hideo Nomo	6.00	1.80
❑ 27 Mike Sweeney	4.00	1.20
❑ 28 Carlos Beltran	4.00	1.20
❑ 29 Tony Clark	4.00	1.20
❑ 30 Dean Palmer	4.00	1.20
❑ 31 Doug Mientkiewicz	4.00	1.20
❑ 32 Cristian Guzman	4.00	1.20
❑ 33 Corey Koskie	4.00	1.20
❑ 34 Frank Thomas	6.00	1.80
❑ 35 Maggio Ordonez	4.00	1.20
❑ 36 Jose Canseco	4.00	1.20
❑ 37 Roger Clemens	12.00	3.60
❑ 38 Derek Jeter	15.00	4.50
❑ 39 Bernie Williams	4.00	1.20
❑ 40 Mike Mussina	4.00	1.20
❑ 41 Tino Martinez	4.00	1.20
❑ 42 Jeff Bagwell	4.00	1.20
❑ 43 Lance Berkman	4.00	1.20
❑ 44 Roy Oswalt	4.00	1.20
❑ 45 Chipper Jones	6.00	1.80
❑ 46 Greg Maddux	10.00	3.00
❑ 47 Andruw Jones	4.00	1.20
❑ 48 Tom Glavine	4.00	1.20
❑ 49 Richie Sexson	4.00	1.20
❑ 50 Jeromy Burnitz	4.00	1.20
❑ 51 Ben Sheets	4.00	1.20
❑ 52 Mark McGwire	15.00	4.50
❑ 53 Matt Morris	4.00	1.20
❑ 54 Jim Edmonds	4.00	1.20
❑ 55 J.D. Drew	4.00	1.20
❑ 56 Sammy Sosa	6.00	1.80
❑ 57 Fred McGriff	4.00	1.20
❑ 58 Kerry Wood	4.00	1.20
❑ 59 Randy Johnson	6.00	1.80
❑ 60 Luis Gonzalez	4.00	1.20
❑ 61 Curt Schilling	4.00	1.20
❑ 62 Shawn Green	4.00	1.20
❑ 63 Kevin Brown	4.00	1.20
❑ 64 Gary Sheffield	4.00	1.20
❑ 65 Vladimir Guerrero	6.00	1.80
❑ 66 Barry Bonds	15.00	4.50
❑ 67 Jeff Kent	4.00	1.20
❑ 68 Rich Aurilia	4.00	1.20
❑ 69 Cliff Floyd	4.00	1.20
❑ 70 Charles Johnson	4.00	1.20
❑ 71 Josh Beckett	4.00	1.20
❑ 72 Mike Piazza	10.00	3.00
❑ 73 Edgardo Alfonzo	4.00	1.20
❑ 74 Robin Ventura	4.00	1.20
❑ 75 Tony Gwynn	8.00	2.40
❑ 76 Ryan Klesko	4.00	1.20
❑ 77 Phil Nevin	4.00	1.20
❑ 78 Scott Rolen	4.00	1.20
❑ 79 Bobby Abreu	4.00	1.20
❑ 80 Jimmy Rollins	4.00	1.20
❑ 81 Brian Giles	4.00	1.20
❑ 82 Jason Kendall	4.00	1.20
❑ 83 Aramis Ramirez	4.00	1.20
❑ 84 Ken Griffey Jr.	10.00	3.00
❑ 85 Adam Dunn	4.00	1.20
❑ 86 Sean Casey	4.00	1.20
❑ 87 Barry Larkin	4.00	1.20
❑ 88 Larry Walker	4.00	1.20
❑ 89 Mike Hampton	4.00	1.20
❑ 90 Todd Helton	4.00	1.20
❑ 91 Ken Harvey T1	10.00	3.00
❑ 92 Bill Ortega T1 RC	10.00	3.00
❑ 93 Juan Diaz T1 RC	10.00	3.00
❑ 94 Greg Miller T1 RC	10.00	3.00
❑ 95 Brandon Berger T1 RC	10.00	3.00
❑ 96 Brandon Lyon T1 RC	10.00	3.00
❑ 97 Jay Gibbons T1 RC	15.00	4.50
❑ 98 Rob Mackowiak T1 RC	15.00	4.50
❑ 99 Erick Almonte T1 RC	10.00	3.00
❑ 100 J.Middlebrook T1 RC	10.00	3.00
❑ 101 Johnny Estrada T2 RC	15.00	4.50
❑ 102 Juan Uribe T2 RC	15.00	4.50
❑ 103 Travis Hafner T2 RC	30.00	9.00
❑ 104 M.Ensberg T2 RC	25.00	7.50
❑ 105 Mike Rivera T2 RC	10.00	3.00
❑ 106 Josh Towers T2 RC	15.00	4.50
❑ 107 A.Hernandez T2 RC	10.00	3.00
❑ 108 Rafael Soriano T2 RC	10.00	3.00
❑ 109 Jackson Melian T2 RC	10.00	3.00
❑ 110 Wilkin Ruan T2 RC	10.00	3.00
❑ 111 Albert Pujols T3 RC	400.00	120.00
❑ 112 T.Shinjo T3 RC	25.00	7.50
❑ 113 B.Duckworth T3 RC	15.00	4.50
❑ 114 Juan Cruz T3 RC	15.00	4.50
❑ 115 D.Brazelton T3 RC	15.00	4.50
❑ 116 Mark Prior T3 AU RC	400.00	120.00
❑ 117 Mark Teixeira T3 AU RC	500.00	150.00
❑ 118 Wilson Betemit T3 RC	25.00	7.50
❑ 119 Bud Smith T3 RC	15.00	4.50
❑ 120 I.Suzuki T3 AU RC	1200.00	350.00

2002 Ultimate Collection

	Nm-Mt	Ex-Mt
COMMON CARD (1-60)	4.00	1.20
COMMON CARD (61-110)	10.00	3.00
61-110 PRINT RUN 550 SERIAL #'d SETS		.00
COMMON CARD (111-113)	25.00	7.50
COMMON CARD (114-120)	15.00	4.50

Card	Nm-Mt	Ex-Mt
❑ 1 Troy Glaus	4.00	1.20
❑ 2 Luis Gonzalez	4.00	1.20
❑ 3 Curt Schilling	4.00	1.20
❑ 4 Randy Johnson	6.00	1.80
❑ 5 Andruw Jones	4.00	1.20
❑ 6 Greg Maddux	10.00	3.00
❑ 7 Chipper Jones	6.00	1.80
❑ 8 Gary Sheffield	4.00	1.20
❑ 9 Cal Ripken	20.00	6.00
❑ 10 Manny Ramirez	4.00	1.20
❑ 11 Pedro Martinez	4.00	1.20
❑ 12 Nomar Garciaparra	10.00	3.00
❑ 13 Sammy Sosa	6.00	1.80
❑ 14 Kerry Wood	4.00	1.20
❑ 15 Mark Prior	6.00	1.80

❑ 16 Magglio Ordonez............ 4.00 1.20
❑ 17 Frank Thomas.................. 6.00 1.80
❑ 18 Adam Dunn...................... 4.00 1.20
❑ 19 Ken Griffey Jr. 10.00 3.00
❑ 20 Jim Thome 4.00 1.20
❑ 21 Larry Walker 4.00 1.20
❑ 22 Todd Helton 4.00 1.20
❑ 23 Nolan Ryan 15.00 4.50
❑ 24 Jeff Bagwell...................... 4.00 1.20
❑ 25 Roy Oswalt 4.00 1.20
❑ 26 Lance Berkman 4.00 1.20
❑ 27 Mike Sweeney.................. 4.00 1.20
❑ 28 Shawn Green.................... 4.00 1.20
❑ 29 Hideo Nomo 6.00 1.80
❑ 30 Torii Hunter....................... 4.00 1.20
❑ 31 Vladimir Guerrero 6.00 1.80
❑ 32 Tom Seaver....................... 4.00 1.20
❑ 33 Mike Piazza..................... 10.00 3.00
❑ 34 Roberto Alomar................. 4.00 1.20
❑ 35 Derek Jeter 15.00 4.50
❑ 36 Alfonso Soriano 4.00 1.20
❑ 37 Jason Giambi 4.00 1.20
❑ 38 Roger Clemens 12.00 3.60
❑ 39 Mike Mussina.................... 4.00 1.20
❑ 40 Bernie Williams................ 4.00 1.20
❑ 41 Joe DiMaggio 12.00 3.60
❑ 42 Mickey Mantle.............. 25.00 7.50
❑ 43 Miguel Tejada 4.00 1.20
❑ 44 Eric Chavez 4.00 1.20
❑ 45 Barry Zito 4.00 1.20
❑ 46 Pat Burrell......................... 4.00 1.20
❑ 47 Jason Kendall 4.00 1.20
❑ 48 Brian Giles 4.00 1.20
❑ 49 Barry Bonds 15.00 4.50
❑ 50 Ichiro Suzuki.................. 12.00 3.60
❑ 51 Stan Musial..................... 10.00 3.00
❑ 52 J.D. Drew 4.00 1.20
❑ 53 Scott Rolen 4.00 1.20
❑ 54 Albert Pujols.................. 12.00 3.60
❑ 55 Mark McGwire................ 15.00 4.50
❑ 56 Alex Rodriguez 10.00 3.00
❑ 57 Ivan Rodriguez 4.00 1.20
❑ 58 Juan Gonzalez.................. 4.00 1.20
❑ 59 Rafael Palmeiro................ 4.00 1.20
❑ 60 Carlos Delgado................. 4.00 1.20
❑ 61 Jose Valverde UR RC 10.00 3.00
❑ 62 Doug Devore UR RC 10.00 3.00
❑ 63 John Ennis UR RC.......... 10.00 3.00
❑ 64 Joey Dawley UR RC........ 10.00 3.00
❑ 65 Trey Hodges UR RC 10.00 3.00
❑ 66 Mike Mahoney UR............ 10.00 3.00
❑ 67 Aaron Cook UR RC 10.00 3.00
❑ 68 Rene Reyes UR RC 10.00 3.00
❑ 69 Mark Corey UR RC 10.00 3.00
❑ 70 Hansel Izquierdo UR RC 10.00 3.00
❑ 71 Brandon Puffer UR RC..... 10.00 3.00
❑ 72 Jeriome Robertson UR RC 10.00 3.00
❑ 73 Jose Diaz UR RC 10.00 3.00
❑ 74 David Ross UR RC 10.00 3.00
❑ 75 Jayson Durocher UR RC 10.00 3.00
❑ 76 Eric Good UR RC............ 10.00 3.00
❑ 77 Satoru Komiyama UR RC 10.00 3.00
❑ 78 Tyler Yates UR RC.......... 10.00 3.00
❑ 79 Eric Junge UR RC 10.00 3.00
❑ 80 Anderson Machado UR RC 10.00 3.00
❑ 81 Adrian Burnside UR RC.. 10.00 3.00
❑ 82 Ben Howard UR RC......... 10.00 3.00
❑ 83 Clay Condrey UR RC...... 10.00 3.00
❑ 84 Nelson Castro UR RC 10.00 3.00
❑ 85 So Taguchi UR RC 15.00 4.50
❑ 86 Mike Crudale UR RC....... 10.00 3.00
❑ 87 Scotty Layfield UR RC.... 10.00 3.00
❑ 88 Steve Bechler UR RC...... 10.00 3.00
❑ 89 Travis Driskill UR RC 10.00 3.00
❑ 90 Howie Clark UR RC......... 10.00 3.00
❑ 91 Josh Hancock UR RC 10.00 3.00
❑ 92 Jorge De La Rosa UR RC 10.00 3.00
❑ 93 Anastacio Martinez UR RC 10.00 3.00
❑ 94 Brian Tallet UR RC 10.00 3.00
❑ 95 Carl Sadler UR RC.......... 10.00 3.00
❑ 96 Cliff Lee UR RC.............. 15.00 4.50
❑ 97 Josh Bard UR RC 10.00 3.00
❑ 98 Wes Obermueller UR RC 10.00 3.00
❑ 99 Juan Brito UR RC 10.00 3.00
❑ 100 Aaron Guiel UR RC 10.00 3.00
❑ 101 Jeremy Hill UR RC 10.00 3.00
❑ 102 Kevin Frederick UR RC 10.00 3.00
❑ 103 Nate Field UR RC 10.00 3.00
❑ 104 Julio Mateo UR RC 10.00 3.00
❑ 105 Chris Snelling UR RC .. 15.00 4.50
❑ 106 Felix Escalona UR RC .. 10.00 3.00
❑ 107 Reynaldo Garcia UR RC 10.00 3.00
❑ 108 Mike Smith UR RC 10.00 3.00
❑ 109 Ken Huckaby UR RC 10.00 3.00
❑ 110 Kevin Cash UR RC 10.00 3.00
❑ 111 Kazuhisa Ishii UR AU RC 40.00 12.00
❑ 112 Fr. Sanchez UR AU RC 25.00 7.50
❑ 113 J.Simontacchi UR AU RC 25.00 7.50
❑ 114 Jorge Padilla UR AU RC 15.00 4.50
❑ 115 Kirk Saarloos UR AU RC 15.00 4.50
❑ 116 Ro. Rosario UR AU RC 15.00 4.50
❑ 117 Oliver Perez UR AU RC 50.00 15.00
❑ 118 Mi. Asencio UR AU RC 15.00 4.50
❑ 119 Fr. German UR AU RC.. 15.00 4.50
❑ 120 Jaime Cerda UR AU RC 15.00 4.50
❑ MM M.McGwire AU EXCH/100 .00 .00

2003 Ultimate Collection

MINT NRMT
COMMON CARD (1-84)............ 3.00 1.35
1-84 STATED ODDS TWO PER PACK .00
COMMON CARD (85-117)......... 5.00 2.20
COMMON CARD (118-140)........ 5.00 2.20
118-140 PRINT RUN 399 SERIAL #'d SETS .00
COMMON CARD (141-158)........ 6.00 2.70
COMMON CARD (159-168)....... 12.00 5.50
159-168 PRINT RUN 100 SERIAL #'d SETS .00
85-168 STATED ODDS ONE PER PACK .00
COMMON CARD (169-174)...... 15.00 6.75
169-174 AND ULT.SIG.OVERALL ODDS 1:4 .00
COMMON CARD (175-180)...... 15.00 6.75
175-180 AND BUYBACK OVERALL ODDS 1:8 .00
169-180 PRINT RUN 250 SERIAL #'d SETS .00
MATSUI PART LIVE/ PART EXCH.. .00
EXCHANGE DEADLINE 12/17/06 .. .00

❑ 1 Ichiro Suzuki................ 10.00 4.50
❑ 2 Ken Griffey Jr. 8.00 3.60
❑ 3 Sammy Sosa 5.00 2.20
❑ 4 Jason Giambi 3.00 1.35
❑ 5 Mike Piazza...................... 8.00 3.60
❑ 6 Derek Jeter 10.00 4.50
❑ 7 Randy Johnson 5.00 2.20
❑ 8 Barry Bonds 12.00 5.50
❑ 9 Carlos Delgado 3.00 1.35
❑ 10 Mark Prior...................... 5.00 2.20
❑ 11 Vladimir Guerrero 5.00 2.20
❑ 12 Alfonso Soriano 3.00 1.35
❑ 13 Jim Thome 5.00 2.20
❑ 14 Pedro Martinez 5.00 2.20
❑ 15 Nomar Garciaparra 8.00 3.60
❑ 16 Chipper Jones................ 5.00 2.20
❑ 17 Rocco Baldelli................. 3.00 1.35
❑ 18 Dontrelle Willis 5.00 2.20
❑ 19 Garret Anderson 3.00 1.35
❑ 20 Jeff Bagwell.................... 5.00 2.20
❑ 21 Jim Edmonds 5.00 2.20
❑ 22 Rickey Henderson 5.00 2.20
❑ 23 Torii Hunter..................... 3.00 1.35
❑ 24 Tom Glavine.................... 5.00 2.20
❑ 25 Hideo Nomo 5.00 2.20
❑ 26 Luis Gonzalez 3.00 1.35
❑ 27 Alex Rodriguez 8.00 3.60
❑ 28 Albert Pujols................. 10.00 4.50
❑ 29 Manny Ramirez 5.00 2.20
❑ 30 Rafael Palmeiro............... 5.00 2.20
❑ 31 Bernie Williams............... 5.00 2.20
❑ 32 Curt Schilling 3.00 1.35
❑ 33 Roger Clemens 10.00 4.50
❑ 34 Andruw Jones 5.00 2.20
❑ 35 J.D. Drew 3.00 1.35
❑ 36 Kerry Wood 3.00 1.35
❑ 37 Scott Rolen 5.00 2.20
❑ 38 Darin Erstad 3.00 1.35
❑ 39 Joe DiMaggio 8.00 3.60
❑ 40 Magglio Ordonez............. 3.00 1.35
❑ 41 Todd Helton 5.00 2.20
❑ 42 Barry Zito 3.00 1.35
❑ 43 Mickey Mantle.............. 15.00 6.75
❑ 44 Miguel Tejada 3.00 1.35
❑ 45 Troy Glaus....................... 3.00 1.35
❑ 46 Kazuhisa Ishii 3.00 1.35
❑ 47 Adam Dunn...................... 3.00 1.35
❑ 48 Ted Williams................. 10.00 4.50
❑ 49 Mike Mussina 5.00 2.20
❑ 50 Ivan Rodriguez 5.00 2.20
❑ 51 Jacque Jones 3.00 1.35
❑ 52 Stan Musial..................... 8.00 3.60
❑ 53 Mariano Rivera 5.00 2.20
❑ 54 Larry Walker 3.00 1.35
❑ 55 Aaron Boone 3.00 1.35
❑ 56 Hank Blalock................... 3.00 1.35
❑ 57 Rich Harden 5.00 2.20
❑ 58 Lance Berkman 3.00 1.35
❑ 59 Eric Chavez 3.00 1.35
❑ 60 Carlos Beltran 3.00 1.35
❑ 61 Roy Oswalt 3.00 1.35
❑ 62 Moises Alou 3.00 1.35
❑ 63 Nolan Ryan 12.00 5.50
❑ 64 Jeff Kent 3.00 1.35
❑ 65 Roberto Alomar................ 5.00 2.20
❑ 66 Runelvys Hernandez 3.00 1.35
❑ 67 Roy Halladay................... 3.00 1.35
❑ 68 Tim Hudson 3.00 1.35
❑ 69 Tom Seaver..................... 5.00 2.20
❑ 70 Edgardo Alfonzo 3.00 1.35
❑ 71 Andy Pettitte 5.00 2.20
❑ 72 Preston Wilson 3.00 1.35
❑ 73 Frank Thomas 5.00 2.20
❑ 74 Jerome Williams.............. 3.00 1.35
❑ 75 Shawn Green................... 3.00 1.35
❑ 76 David Wells...................... 3.00 1.35
❑ 77 John Smoltz 5.00 2.20
❑ 78 Jorge Posada 5.00 2.20
❑ 79 Marlon Byrd 3.00 1.35
❑ 80 Austin Kearns 3.00 1.35
❑ 81 Bret Boone 3.00 1.35
❑ 82 Rafael Furcal 3.00 1.35
❑ 83 Jay Gibbons 3.00 1.35
❑ 84 Shane Reynolds 3.00 1.35
❑ 85 Nate Bland UR T1 RC 5.00 2.20
❑ 86 Willie Eyre UR T1 RC 5.00 2.20
❑ 87 Jeremy Guthrie UR T1 ..... 5.00 2.20
❑ 88 Jeremy Wedel UR T1 RC .. 5.00 2.20
❑ 89 Jhonny Peralta UR T1 ..... 8.00 3.60
❑ 90 Luis Ayala UR T1 RC....... 5.00 2.20
❑ 91 Michael Hessman UR T1 RC 5.00 2.20
❑ 92 Michael Nakamura UR T1 RC 5.00 2.20
❑ 93 Nook Logan UR T1 RC 8.00 3.60
❑ 94 Rett Johnson UR T1 RC.... 5.00 2.20
❑ 95 Josh Hall UR T1 RC 5.00 2.20
❑ 96 Julio Manon UR T1 RC 5.00 2.20
❑ 97 Heath Bell UR T1 RC 5.00 2.20
❑ 98 Ian Ferguson UR T1 RC.... 5.00 2.20
❑ 99 Jason Gilfillan UR T1 RC.. 5.00 2.20
❑ 100 Jason Roach UR T1 RC .. 5.00 2.20
❑ 101 Jason Shiell UR T1 RC .. 5.00 2.20
❑ 102 Termel Sledge UR T1 RC 5.00 2.20
❑ 103 Phil Seibel UR T1 RC 5.00 2.20
❑ 104 Jeff Duncan UR T1 RC.... 5.00 2.20
❑ 105 Mike Neu UR T1 RC 5.00 2.20
❑ 106 Colin Porter UR T1 RC .. 5.00 2.20
❑ 107 David Matranga UR T1 RC 5.00 2.20
❑ 108 Aaron Looper UR T1 RC 5.00 2.20
❑ 109 Jeremy Bonderman UR T1 RC 15.00 6.75
❑ 110 Miguel Ojeda UR T1 RC 5.00 2.20
❑ 111 Chad Cordero UR T1 RC 10.00 4.50
❑ 112 Shane Bazzell UR T1 RC 5.00 2.20

❑ 113 Tim Olson UR T1 RC 5.00 2.20
❑ 114 Michel Hernandez UR T1 RC 5.00 2.20
❑ 115 Chien-Ming Wang UR T1 RC 25.00 11.00
❑ 116 Josh Stewart UR T1 RC 5.00 2.20
❑ 117 Clint Barmes UR T1 RC 8.00 3.60
❑ 118 Craig Brazell UR T2 RC 5.00 2.20
❑ 119 Josh Willingham UR T2 RC 8.00 3.60
❑ 120 Brent Hoard UR T2 RC 5.00 2.20
❑ 121 Francisco Rosario UR T2 RC 5.00 2.20
❑ 122 Rick Roberts UR T2 RC 5.00 2.20
❑ 123 Geoff Geary UR T2 RC 5.00 2.20
❑ 124 Edgar Gonzalez UR T2 RC 5.00 2.20
❑ 125 Kevin Correia UR T2 RC 5.00 2.20
❑ 126 Ryan Cameron UR T2 RC 5.00 2.20
❑ 127 Beau Kemp UR T2 RC 5.00 2.20
❑ 128 Tommy Phelps UR T2 5.00 2.20
❑ 129 Mark Malaska UR T2 RC 5.00 2.20
❑ 130 Kevin Ohme UR T2 RC 5.00 2.20
❑ 131 Humberto Quintero UR T2 RC 5.00 2.20
❑ 132 Aquilino Lopez UR T2 RC 5.00 2.20
❑ 133 Andrew Brown UR T2 RC 8.00 3.60
❑ 134 Wilfredo Ledezma UR T2 RC 5.00 2.20
❑ 135 Luis De Los Santos UR T2 5.00 2.20
❑ 136 Garrett Atkins UR T2 5.00 2.20
❑ 137 Fernando Cabrera UR T2 RC 5.00 2.20
❑ 138 D.J. Carrasco UR T2 RC 5.00 2.20
❑ 139 Alfredo Gonzalez UR T2 RC 5.00 2.20
❑ 140 Alex Prieto UR T2 RC 5.00 2.20
❑ 141 Matt Kata UR T3 RC 6.00 2.70
❑ 142 Chris Capuano UR T3 RC 6.00 2.70
❑ 143 Bobby Madritsch UR T3 RC 10.00 4.50
❑ 144 Greg Jones UR T3 RC 6.00 2.70
❑ 145 Pete Zoccolillo UR T3 RC 6.00 2.70
❑ 146 Chad Gaudin UR T3 RC 6.00 2.70
❑ 147 Rosman Garcia UR T3 RC 6.00 2.70
❑ 148 Gerald Laird UR T3 6.00 2.70
❑ 149 Danny Garcia UR T3 RC 6.00 2.70
❑ 150 Stephen Randolph UR T3 RC 6.00 2.70
❑ 151 Pete LaForest UR T3 RC 6.00 2.70
❑ 152 Brian Sweeney UR T3 RC 6.00 2.70
❑ 153 Aaron Miles UR T3 RC 10.00 4.50
❑ 154 Jorge DePaula UR T3 UER 6.00 2.70
Real name is Julio DePaula
❑ 155 Graham Koonce UR T3 RC 6.00 2.70
❑ 156 Tom Gregorio UR T3 RC 6.00 2.70
❑ 157 Javier A. Lopez UR T3 RC 6.00 2.70
❑ 158 Oscar Villarreal UR T3 RC 6.00 2.70
❑ 159 Prentice Redman UR T4 RC 12.00 5.50
❑ 160 Francisco Cruceta UR T4 RC 12.00 5.50
❑ 161 Guillermo Quiroz UR T4 RC 12.00 5.50
❑ 162 Jeremy Griffiths UR T4 RC 12.00 5.50
❑ 163 Lew Ford UR T4 RC 20.00 9.00
❑ 164 Rob Hammock UR T4 RC 12.00 5.50
❑ 165 Todd Wellemeyer UR T4 RC 12.00 5.50
❑ 166 Ryan Wagner UR T4 RC 12.00 5.50
❑ 167 Edwin Jackson UR T4 RC 20.00 9.00
❑ 168 Dan Haren UR T4 RC 20.00 9.00
❑ 169 Hideki Matsui AU RC 350.00 160.00
❑ 170 Jose Contreras AU RC 40.00 18.00
❑ 171 Delmon Young AU RC 300.00 135.00
❑ 172 Rickie Weeks AU RC 150.00 70.00
❑ 173 Brandon Webb AU RC 25.00 11.00
❑ 174 Bo Hart AU RC 15.00 6.75
❑ 175 Rocco Baldelli YS AU 25.00 11.00
❑ 176 Jose Reyes YS AU 25.00 11.00
❑ 177 Dontrelle Willis YS AU 50.00 22.00
❑ 178 Bobby Hill YS AU 15.00 6.75
❑ 179 Jae Weong Seo YS AU 25.00 11.00
❑ 180 Jesse Foppert YS AU 15.00 6.75

2004 Ultimate Collection

	Nm-Mt	Ex-Mt
COMMON CARD (1-42)	3.00	.90
COMMON CARD (43-126)	3.00	.90
1-126 STATED ODDS TWO PER PACK		.00
1-126 PRINT RUN 675 SERIAL #'d CARDS		.00
COMMON CARD (127-168)	5.00	1.50
127-209/222 STATED ODDS 3:4 PACKS		.00
127-168 PRINT RUN 525 SERIAL #'d SETS		.00
COMMON CARD (169-194)	6.00	1.80
169-194 PRINT RUN 299 SERIAL #'d SETS		.00
COMMON (195-209/222)	8.00	2.40
195-209/222 PRINT RUN 199 SER.#'d SETS		

210-221 STATED ODDS 1:10
210-221 PRINT RUN 75 SERIAL #'d SETS
EXCHANGE DEADLINE 12/28/07

❑ 1 Al Kaline 5.00 1.50
❑ 2 Billy Williams 3.00 .90
❑ 3 Bob Feller 3.00 .90
❑ 4 Bob Gibson 5.00 1.50
❑ 5 Bob Lemon 3.00 .90
❑ 6 Bobby Doerr 3.00 .90
❑ 7 Brooks Robinson 5.00 1.50
❑ 8 Cal Ripken 15.00 4.50
❑ 9 Catfish Hunter 5.00 1.50
❑ 10 Eddie Mathews 5.00 1.50
❑ 11 Enos Slaughter 3.00 .90
❑ 12 Ernie Banks 5.00 1.50
❑ 13 Fergie Jenkins 3.00 .90
❑ 14 Gaylord Perry 3.00 .90
❑ 15 Harmon Killebrew 5.00 1.50
❑ 16 Jim Bunning 3.00 .90
❑ 17 Joe DiMaggio 8.00 2.40
❑ 18 Joe Morgan 3.00 .90
❑ 19 Juan Marichal 3.00 .90
❑ 20 Lou Brock 5.00 1.50
❑ 21 Luis Aparicio 3.00 .90
❑ 22 Mickey Mantle 15.00 4.50
❑ 23 Mike Schmidt 10.00 3.00
❑ 24 Monte Irvin 3.00 .90
❑ 25 Nolan Ryan 12.00 3.60
❑ 26 Pee Wee Reese 5.00 1.50
❑ 27 Phil Niekro 3.00 .90
❑ 28 Phil Rizzuto 5.00 1.50
❑ 29 Ralph Kiner 5.00 1.50
❑ 30 Richie Ashburn 5.00 1.50
❑ 31 Robin Roberts 3.00 .90
❑ 32 Robin Yount 5.00 1.50
❑ 33 Rod Carew 5.00 1.50
❑ 34 Rollie Fingers 3.00 .90
❑ 35 Stan Musial 8.00 2.40
❑ 36 Ted Williams 10.00 3.00
❑ 37 Tom Seaver 5.00 1.50
❑ 38 Warren Spahn 5.00 1.50
❑ 39 Whitey Ford 5.00 1.50
❑ 40 Willie McCovey 5.00 1.50
❑ 41 Willie Stargell 5.00 1.50
❑ 42 Yogi Berra 5.00 1.50
❑ 43 Adrian Beltre 3.00 .90
❑ 44 Albert Pujols 10.00 3.00
❑ 45 Alex Rodriguez 8.00 2.40
❑ 46 Alfonso Soriano 3.00 .90
❑ 47 Andruw Jones 5.00 1.50
❑ 48 Andy Pettitte 5.00 1.50
❑ 49 Aubrey Huff 3.00 .90
❑ 50 Barry Larkin 5.00 1.50
❑ 51 Ben Sheets 3.00 .90
❑ 52 Bernie Williams 5.00 1.50
❑ 53 Bobby Abreu 3.00 .90
❑ 54 Brad Penny 3.00 .90
❑ 55 Bret Boone 3.00 .90
❑ 56 Brian Giles 3.00 .90
❑ 57 Carlos Beltran 3.00 .90
❑ 58 Carlos Delgado 3.00 .90
❑ 59 Carlos Guillen 3.00 .90
❑ 60 Carlos Lee 3.00 .90
❑ 61 Carlos Zambrano 3.00 .90
❑ 62 Chipper Jones 5.00 1.50
❑ 63 Craig Biggio 5.00 1.50
❑ 64 Craig Wilson 3.00 .90
❑ 65 Curt Schilling 5.00 1.50
❑ 66 David Ortiz 5.00 1.50
❑ 67 Derek Jeter 10.00 3.00
❑ 68 Eric Chavez 3.00 .90
❑ 69 Eric Gagne 3.00 .90
❑ 70 Frank Thomas 5.00 1.50
❑ 71 Garret Anderson 3.00 .90
❑ 72 Gary Sheffield 3.00 .90
❑ 73 Greg Maddux 8.00 2.40
❑ 74 Hank Blalock 3.00 .90
❑ 75 Hideki Matsui 10.00 3.00
❑ 76 Ichiro Suzuki 10.00 3.00
❑ 77 Ivan Rodriguez 5.00 1.50
❑ 78 J.D. Drew 3.00 .90
❑ 79 Jake Peavy 3.00 .90
❑ 80 Jason Schmidt 3.00 .90
❑ 81 Jeff Bagwell 5.00 1.50
❑ 82 Jeff Kent 3.00 .90
❑ 83 Jim Thome 5.00 1.50
❑ 84 Joe Mauer 3.00 .90
❑ 85 Johan Santana 5.00 1.50
❑ 86 Jose Reyes 3.00 .90
❑ 87 Jose Vidro 3.00 .90
❑ 88 Ken Griffey Jr. 8.00 2.40
❑ 89 Kerry Wood 3.00 .90
❑ 90 Larry Walker Cards 5.00 1.50
❑ 91 Luis Gonzalez 3.00 .90
❑ 92 Lyle Overbay 3.00 .90
❑ 93 Magglio Ordonez 3.00 .90
❑ 94 Manny Ramirez 5.00 1.50
❑ 95 Mark Mulder 3.00 .90
❑ 96 Mark Prior 5.00 1.50
❑ 97 Mark Teixeira 5.00 1.50
❑ 98 Melvin Mora 3.00 .90
❑ 99 Michael Young 3.00 .90
❑ 100 Miguel Cabrera 5.00 1.50
❑ 101 Miguel Tejada 3.00 .90
❑ 102 Mike Lowell 3.00 .90
❑ 103 Mike Piazza 8.00 2.40
❑ 104 Mike Sweeney 3.00 .90
❑ 105 Nomar Garciaparra 8.00 2.40
❑ 106 Oliver Perez 3.00 .90
❑ 107 Pedro Martinez 5.00 1.50
❑ 108 Preston Wilson 3.00 .90
❑ 109 Rafael Palmeiro 5.00 1.50
❑ 110 Randy Johnson 5.00 1.50
❑ 111 Roger Clemens 10.00 3.00
❑ 112 Roy Halladay 3.00 .90
❑ 113 Roy Oswalt 3.00 .90
❑ 114 Sammy Sosa 5.00 1.50
❑ 115 Scott Podsednik 3.00 .90
❑ 116 Scott Rolen 5.00 1.50
❑ 117 Shawn Green 3.00 .90
❑ 118 Tim Hudson 3.00 .90
❑ 119 Todd Helton 5.00 1.50
❑ 120 Tom Glavine 5.00 1.50
❑ 121 Torii Hunter 3.00 .90
❑ 122 Travis Hafner 3.00 .90
❑ 123 Troy Glaus 3.00 .90
❑ 124 Vernon Wells 3.00 .90
❑ 125 Victor Martinez 3.00 .90
❑ 126 Vladimir Guerrero 5.00 1.50
❑ 127 Aarom Baldiris UR T1 RC 8.00 2.40
❑ 128 Alfredo Simon UR T1 RC 5.00 1.50
❑ 129 Andres Blanco UR T1 RC 5.00 1.50
❑ 130 Jeff Bajenaru UR T1 RC 5.00 1.50
❑ 131 Bart Fortunato UR T1 RC 5.00 1.50
❑ 132 B.Medders UR T1 RC 5.00 1.50
❑ 133 Brian Dallimore UR T1 RC 5.00 1.50
❑ 134 Carlos Hines UR T1 RC 5.00 1.50
❑ 135 Carlos Vasquez UR T1 RC 8.00 2.40
❑ 136 Casey Daigle UR T1 RC 5.00 1.50
❑ 137 Chad Bentz UR T1 RC 5.00 1.50
❑ 138 Chris Aguila UR T1 RC 5.00 1.50
❑ 139 Chris Saenz UR T1 RC 5.00 1.50
❑ 140 Chris Shelton UR T1 RC 12.00 3.60
❑ 141 Colby Miller UR T1 RC 5.00 1.50
❑ 142 Dave Crouthers UR T1 RC 5.00 1.50
❑ 143 David Aardsma UR T1 RC 8.00 2.40
❑ 144 Dennis Sarfate UR T1 RC 5.00 1.50
❑ 145 Donnie Kelly UR T1 RC 5.00 1.50
❑ 146 Eddy Rodriguez UR T1 RC 8.00 2.40
❑ 147 Eduardo Villacis UR T1 RC 5.00 1.50
❑ 148 Edwardo Sierra UR T1 RC 8.00 2.40
❑ 149 Edwin Moreno UR T1 RC 8.00 2.40
❑ 150 Kyle Denney UR T1 RC 5.00 1.50
❑ 151 Evan Rust UR T1 RC 5.00 1.50

❑ 152 Fernando Nieve UR T1 RC 8.00 2.40
❑ 153 Frank Francisco UR T1 RC 5.00 1.50
❑ 154 Frank Gracesqui UR T1 RC 5.00 1.50
❑ 155 Freddy Guzman UR T1 RC 5.00 1.50
❑ 156 Greg Dobbs UR T1 RC .. 5.00 1.50
❑ 157 Hector Gimenez UR T1 RC 5.00 1.50
❑ 158 Jason Alfaro UR T1 RC .. 5.00 1.50
❑ 159 Jake Woods UR T1 RC .. 5.00 1.50
❑ 160 Andy Green UR T1 RC.... 5.00 1.50
❑ 161 Jason Bartlett UR T1 RC 8.00 2.40
❑ 162 Jason Frasor UR T1 RC .. 5.00 1.50
❑ 163 Jeff Bennett UR T1 RC.... 5.00 1.50
❑ 164 Jerome Gamble UR T1 RC 5.00 1.50
❑ 165 Jerry Gil UR T1 RC 5.00 1.50
❑ 166 Joe Hietpas UR T1 RC 5.00 1.50
❑ 167 Jorge Sequea UR T1 RC 5.00 1.50
❑ 168 Jorge Vasquez UR T1 RC 5.00 1.50
❑ 169 Josh Labandeira UR T2 RC 6.00 1.80
❑ 170 Justin Germano UR T2 RC 6.00 1.80
❑ 171 Justin Hampson UR T2 RC 6.00 1.80
❑ 172 Chris Young UR T2 RC 50.00 15.00
❑ 173 Justin Knoedler UR T2 RC 6.00 1.80
❑ 174 Justin Lehr UR T2 RC 6.00 1.80
❑ 175 Justin Leone UR T2 RC 10.00 3.00
❑ 176 Kaz Tadano UR T2 RC .. 10.00 3.00
❑ 177 Kevin Cave UR T2 RC 6.00 1.80
❑ 178 Linc Holdzkom UR T2 RC 6.00 1.80
❑ 179 Mike Rose UR T2 RC...... 6.00 1.80
❑ 180 Luis Gonzalez UR T2 RC 6.00 1.80
❑ 181 Mariano Gomez UR T2 RC 6.00 1.80
❑ 182 Rene Rivera UR T2 RC.... 6.00 1.80
❑ 183 Michael Wuertz UR T2 RC 10.00 3.00
❑ 184 Mike Gosling UR T2 RC 6.00 1.80
❑ 185 Mike Johnston UR T2 RC 6.00 1.80
❑ 186 Mike Rouse UR T2 RC..... 6.00 1.80
❑ 187 Nick Regilio UR T2 RC .. 6.00 1.80
❑ 188 Onil Joseph UR T2 RC .. 6.00 1.80
❑ 189 Orl Rodriguez UR T2 RC 6.00 1.80
❑ 190 Phil Stockman UR T2 RC 6.00 1.80
❑ 191 Renyel Pinto UR T2 RC 10.00 3.00
❑ 192 Roberto Novoa UR T2 RC 10.00 3.00
❑ 193 Roman Colon UR T2 RC 6.00 1.80
❑ 194 Ronald Belisario UR T2 RC 6.00 1.80
❑ 195 Ronny Cedeno UR T3 RC 12.00 3.60
❑ 196 Ryan Meaux UR T3 RC .. 8.00 2.40
❑ 197 Ryan Wing UR T3 RC 8.00 2.40
❑ 198 Scott Dohmann UR T3 RC 8.00 2.40
❑ 199 Joey Gathright UR T3 RC 12.00 3.60
❑ 200 Shawn Camp UR T3 RC 8.00 2.40
❑ 201 Shawn Hill UR T3 RC 8.00 2.40
❑ 202 Steve Andrade UR T3 RC 8.00 2.40
❑ 203 Tim Bausher UR T3 RC .. 8.00 2.40
❑ 204 Tim Bittner UR T3 RC 8.00 2.40
❑ 205 Brad Halsey UR T3 RC 12.00 3.60
❑ 206 William Bergolla UR T3 RC 8.00 2.40
❑ 207 Kameron Loe UR T3 RC 20.00 6.00
❑ 208 Jesse Crain UR T3 RC .. 12.00 3.60
❑ 209 Scott Kazmir UR T3 RC 25.00 7.50
❑ 210 Akinori Otsuka AU RC .. 50.00 15.00
❑ 211 Chris Oxspring AU RC 25.00 7.50
❑ 212 Ian Snell AU RC 40.00 12.00
❑ 213 John Gall AU RC 40.00 12.00
❑ 214 Jose Capellan AU RC .. 40.00 12.00
❑ 215 Yadier Molina AU RC .. 80.00 24.00
❑ 216 Merkin Valdez AU RC .. 40.00 12.00
❑ 217 R.Ramirez AU RC EXCH 25.00 7.50
❑ 218 Rusty Tucker AU RC 40.00 12.00
❑ 219 Scott Proctor AU RC 40.00 12.00
❑ 220 Sean Henn AU RC 25.00 7.50
❑ 221 Shingo Takatsu AU RC 50.00 15.00
❑ 222 Kazuo Matsui UR T3 RC 12.00 3.60

2005 Ultimate Signature

	Nm-Mt	Ex-Mt
COMMON CARD (1-50)	3.00	.90
COMMON CARD (51-100)	3.00	.90
1-100 PRINT RUN 825 SERIAL #'d SETS		.00
COMMON CARD (101-110)	15.00	4.50
MINOR STARS 101-110	25.00	7.50
SEMISTARS 101-110	40.00	12.00
UNLISTED STARS 101-110	40.00	12.00
101-110 AU PROSPECT ODDS 1:20		.00
101-110 PRINT RUN 225 SERIAL #'d SETS		.00

❑ 1 Al Kaline 5.00 1.50
❑ 2 Babe Ruth 10.00 3.00

❑ 3 Billy Williams .... 3.00 .90
❑ 4 Bob Feller 5.00 1.50
❑ 5 Bob Gibson 5.00 1.50
❑ 6 Brooks Robinson 5.00 1.50
❑ 7 Carlton Fisk 5.00 1.50
❑ 8 Cy Young 5.00 1.50
❑ 9 Dizzy Dean 5.00 1.50
❑ 10 Don Drysdale 5.00 1.50
❑ 11 Eddie Mathews 5.00 1.50
❑ 12 Enos Slaughter .... 3.00 .90
❑ 13 Ernie Banks 5.00 1.50
❑ 14 Fergie Jenkins .... 3.00 .90
❑ 15 Eddie Murray 5.00 1.50
❑ 16 Harmon Killebrew 5.00 1.50
❑ 17 Honus Wagner 5.00 1.50
❑ 18 Jackie Robinson 5.00 1.50
❑ 19 Jimmie Foxx 5.00 1.50
❑ 20 Joe DiMaggio 8.00 2.40
❑ 21 Joe Morgan .... 3.00 .90
❑ 22 Juan Marichal .... 3.00 .90
❑ 23 Larry Doby .... 3.00 .90
❑ 24 Jim Palmer .... 3.00 .90
❑ 25 Johnny Bench 5.00 1.50
❑ 26 Lou Brock 5.00 1.50
❑ 27 Lou Gehrig 8.00 2.40
❑ 28 Mel Ott 5.00 1.50
❑ 29 Mickey Cochrane .... 3.00 .90
❑ 30 Mickey Mantle 15.00 4.50
❑ 31 Mike Schmidt 10.00 3.00
❑ 32 Nolan Ryan 12.00 3.60
❑ 33 Pee Wee Reese 5.00 1.50
❑ 34 Phil Rizzuto 5.00 1.50
❑ 35 Ralph Kiner .... 3.00 .90
❑ 36 Robin Yount 5.00 1.50
❑ 37 Ozzie Smith 8.00 2.40
❑ 38 Roy Campanella 5.00 1.50
❑ 39 Satchel Paige 5.00 1.50
❑ 40 Stan Musial 8.00 2.40
❑ 41 Ted Williams 8.00 2.40
❑ 42 Thurman Munson 5.00 1.50
❑ 43 Tom Seaver 5.00 1.50
❑ 44 Ty Cobb 8.00 2.40
❑ 45 Walter Johnson 5.00 1.50
❑ 46 Warren Spahn 5.00 1.50
❑ 47 Whitey Ford 5.00 1.50
❑ 48 Willie McCovey 5.00 1.50
❑ 49 Willie Stargell 5.00 1.50
❑ 50 Yogi Berra 5.00 1.50
❑ 51 Adrian Beltre .... 3.00 .90
❑ 52 Albert Pujols 10.00 3.00
❑ 53 Alex Rodriguez 8.00 2.40
❑ 54 Alfonso Soriano .... 3.00 .90
❑ 55 Andruw Jones 5.00 1.50
❑ 56 B.J. Upton .... 3.00 .90
❑ 57 Ben Sheets .... 3.00 .90
❑ 58 Bret Boone .... 3.00 .90
❑ 59 Brian Giles .... 3.00 .90
❑ 60 Carlos Beltran .... 3.00 .90
❑ 61 Carlos Delgado .... 3.00 .90
❑ 62 Chipper Jones 5.00 1.50
❑ 63 Curt Schilling 5.00 1.50
❑ 64 David Ortiz 5.00 1.50
❑ 65 Derek Jeter 10.00 3.00
❑ 66 Eric Chavez .... 3.00 .90
❑ 67 Frank Thomas 5.00 1.50
❑ 68 Gary Sheffield .... 3.00 .90
❑ 69 Greg Maddux 8.00 2.40
❑ 70 Hank Blalock .... 3.00 .90
❑ 71 Hideki Matsui 10.00 3.00
❑ 72 Ichiro Suzuki 10.00 3.00
❑ 73 Ivan Rodriguez 5.00 1.50
❑ 74 Jason Schmidt .... 3.00 .90
❑ 75 Jeff Bagwell 5.00 1.50
❑ 76 Jim Thome 5.00 1.50
❑ 77 Johnny Damon 5.00 1.50
❑ 78 Jose Vidro .... 3.00 .90
❑ 79 Ken Griffey Jr. 8.00 2.40
❑ 80 Kerry Wood .... 3.00 .90
❑ 81 Manny Ramirez 5.00 1.50
❑ 82 Mark Prior 5.00 1.50
❑ 83 Mark Teixeira 5.00 1.50
❑ 84 Miguel Cabrera 5.00 1.50
❑ 85 Miguel Tejada .... 3.00 .90
❑ 86 Mike Mussina 5.00 1.50
❑ 87 Mike Piazza 5.00 1.50
❑ 88 Mike Sweeney .... 3.00 .90
❑ 89 Oliver Perez .... 3.00 .90
❑ 90 Pedro Martinez 5.00 1.50
❑ 91 Rafael Palmeiro 5.00 1.50
❑ 92 Randy Johnson 5.00 1.50
❑ 93 Roger Clemens 8.00 2.40
❑ 94 Sammy Sosa 5.00 1.50
❑ 95 Scott Rolen 5.00 1.50
❑ 96 Tim Hudson .... 3.00 .90
❑ 97 Todd Helton 5.00 1.50
❑ 98 Torii Hunter .... 3.00 .90
❑ 99 Victor Martinez .... 3.00 .90
❑ 100 Vladimir Guerrero 5.00 1.50
❑ 101 Adrian Gonzalez AU...... 15.00 4.50
❑ 102 Ambiorix Burgos AU RC 15.00 4.50
❑ 103 Ambiorix Concepcion AU RC 25.00 7.50
❑ 104 Dan Meyer AU 15.00 4.50
❑ 105 Ervin Santana AU 25.00 7.50
❑ 106 Gavin Floyd AU 15.00 4.50
❑ 107 Joe Blanton AU 15.00 4.50
❑ 108 Eric Crozier AU 15.00 4.50
❑ 109 Mark Teahen AU 15.00 4.50
❑ 110 Ryan Howard AU 40.00 12.00

1999 Ultimate Victory

	Nm-Mt	Ex-Mt
COMPLETE SET (180)	150.00	45.00
COMP.SET w/o SP's (120)	25.00	7.50
COMMON CARD (1-120)	.30	.09
COMMON SP (121-150)	2.00	.60
COMMON (151-180)	2.00	.60

❑ 1 Troy Glaus .... .50 .15
❑ 2 Tim Salmon .... .50 .15
❑ 3 Mo Vaughn .... .30 .09
❑ 4 Garret Anderson .... .30 .09
❑ 5 Darin Erstad .... .30 .09
❑ 6 Randy Johnson .... .75 .23
❑ 7 Matt Williams .... .30 .09
❑ 8 Travis Lee .... .30 .09
❑ 9 Jay Bell .... .30 .09
❑ 10 Steve Finley .... .30 .09
❑ 11 Luis Gonzalez .... .30 .09
❑ 12 Greg Maddux .... 1.25 .35
❑ 13 Chipper Jones .... .75 .23
❑ 14 Javy Lopez .... .30 .09
❑ 15 Tom Glavine .... .50 .15
❑ 16 John Smoltz .... .50 .15
❑ 17 Cal Ripken .... 2.50 .75
❑ 18 Charles Johnson .... .30 .09
❑ 19 Albert Belle .... .30 .09
❑ 20 Mike Mussina .... .50 .15

❑ 21 Pedro Martinez .50 .15
❑ 22 Nomar Garciaparra 1.25 .35
❑ 23 Jose Offerman .30 .09
❑ 24 Sammy Sosa .75 .23
❑ 25 Mark Grace .50 .15
❑ 26 Kerry Wood .30 .09
❑ 27 Frank Thomas .75 .23
❑ 28 Ray Durham .30 .09
❑ 29 Paul Konerko .30 .09
❑ 30 Pete Harnisch .30 .09
❑ 31 Greg Vaughn .30 .09
❑ 32 Sean Casey .50 .15
❑ 33 Manny Ramirez .50 .15
❑ 34 Jim Thome .50 .15
❑ 35 Sandy Alomar Jr. .30 .09
❑ 36 Roberto Alomar .50 .15
❑ 37 Travis Fryman .30 .09
❑ 38 Kenny Lofton .30 .09
❑ 39 Omar Vizquel .50 .15
❑ 40 Larry Walker .30 .09
❑ 41 Todd Helton .50 .15
❑ 42 Vinny Castilla .30 .09
❑ 43 Tony Clark .30 .09
❑ 44 Juan Encarnacion .30 .09
❑ 45 Dean Palmer .30 .09
❑ 46 Damion Easley .30 .09
❑ 47 Mark Kotsay .30 .09
❑ 48 Cliff Floyd .30 .09
❑ 49 Jeff Bagwell .50 .15
❑ 50 Ken Caminiti .30 .09
❑ 51 Craig Biggio .50 .15
❑ 52 Moises Alou .30 .09
❑ 53 Johnny Damon .50 .15
❑ 54 Larry Sutton .30 .09
❑ 55 Kevin Brown .50 .15
❑ 56 Adrian Beltre .30 .09
❑ 57 Raul Mondesi .30 .09
❑ 58 Gary Sheffield .30 .09
❑ 59 Jeromy Burnitz .30 .09
❑ 60 Sean Berry .30 .09
❑ 61 Jeff Cirillo .30 .09
❑ 62 Brad Radke .30 .09
❑ 63 Todd Walker .30 .09
❑ 64 Matt Lawton .30 .09
❑ 65 Vladimir Guerrero .75 .23
❑ 66 Rondell White .30 .09
❑ 67 Dustin Hermanson .30 .09
❑ 68 Mike Piazza 1.25 .35
❑ 69 Rickey Henderson .75 .23
❑ 70 Robin Ventura .30 .09
❑ 71 John Olerud .30 .09
❑ 72 Derek Jeter 2.00 .60
❑ 73 Roger Clemens 1.50 .45
❑ 74 Orlando Hernandez .30 .09
❑ 75 Paul O'Neill .50 .15
❑ 76 Bernie Williams .50 .15
❑ 77 Chuck Knoblauch .30 .09
❑ 78 Tino Martinez .50 .15
❑ 79 Jason Giambi .30 .09
❑ 80 Ben Grieve .30 .09
❑ 81 Matt Stairs .30 .09
❑ 82 Scott Rolen .50 .15
❑ 83 Ron Gant .30 .09
❑ 84 Bobby Abreu .30 .09
❑ 85 Curt Schilling .30 .09
❑ 86 Brian Giles .30 .09
❑ 87 Jason Kendall .30 .09
❑ 88 Kevin Young .30 .09
❑ 89 Mark McGwire 2.00 .60
❑ 90 Fernando Tatis .30 .09
❑ 91 Ray Lankford .30 .09
❑ 92 Eric Davis .30 .09
❑ 93 Tony Gwynn 1.00 .30
❑ 94 Reggie Sanders .30 .09
❑ 95 Wally Joyner .30 .09
❑ 96 Trevor Hoffman .30 .09
❑ 97 Robb Nen .30 .09
❑ 98 Barry Bonds 2.00 .60
❑ 99 Jeff Kent .30 .09
❑ 100 J.T. Snow .30 .09
❑ 101 Ellis Burks .30 .09
❑ 102 Ken Griffey Jr. 1.25 .35
❑ 103 Alex Rodriguez 1.25 .35
❑ 104 Jay Buhner .30 .09
❑ 105 Edgar Martinez .50 .15
❑ 106 David Bell .30 .09
❑ 107 Bobby Smith .30 .09
❑ 108 Wade Boggs .50 .15
❑ 109 Fred McGriff .50 .15
❑ 110 Rolando Arrojo .30 .09
❑ 111 Jose Canseco .50 .15
❑ 112 Ivan Rodriguez .50 .15
❑ 113 Juan Gonzalez .30 .09
❑ 114 Rafael Palmeiro .50 .15
❑ 115 Rusty Greer .30 .09
❑ 116 Todd Zeile .30 .09
❑ 117 Jose Cruz Jr. .30 .09
❑ 118 Carlos Delgado .30 .09
❑ 119 Shawn Green .30 .09
❑ 120 David Wells .30 .09
❑ 121 Eric Munson SP RC 5.00 1.50
❑ 122 Lance Berkman SP 3.00 .90
❑ 123 Ed Yarnall SP 2.00 .60
❑ 124 Jacque Jones SP 3.00 .90
❑ 125 K.Farnsworth SP RC 5.00 1.50
❑ 126 Ryan Rupe SP RC 2.00 .60
❑ 127 Jeff Weaver SP RC 5.00 1.50
❑ 128 Gabe Kapler SP 3.00 .90
❑ 129 Alex Gonzalez SP 2.00 .60
❑ 130 Randy Wolf SP 2.00 .60
❑ 131 Ben Davis SP 2.00 .60
❑ 132 Carlos Beltran SP 5.00 1.50
❑ 133 Jim Morris SP RC 5.00 1.50
❑ 134 J.Zimmerman SP RC 3.00 .90
❑ 135 Bruce Aven SP 2.00 .60
❑ 136 A.Soriano SP RC 40.00 12.00
❑ 137 Tim Hudson SP RC 20.00 6.00
❑ 138 Josh Beckett SP RC 40.00 12.00
❑ 139 Michael Barrett SP 2.00 .60
❑ 140 Eric Chavez SP 3.00 .90
❑ 141 Pat Burrell SP RC 15.00 4.50
❑ 142 Kris Benson SP 2.00 .60
❑ 143 J.D. Drew SP 3.00 .90
❑ 144 Matt Clement SP 3.00 .90
❑ 145 Rick Ankiel SP RC 5.00 1.50
❑ 146 Vernon Wells SP 3.00 .90
❑ 147 Ruben Mateo SP UER 2.00 .60
Card is misnumbered
❑ 148 Roy Halladay SP 3.00 .90
❑ 149 Joe McEwing SP RC 3.00 .90
❑ 150 Freddy Garcia SP RC 8.00 2.40
❑ 151 Mark McGwire MM 2.00 .60
❑ 152 Mark McGwire MM 2.00 .60
❑ 153 Mark McGwire MM 2.00 .60
❑ 154 Mark McGwire MM 2.00 .60
❑ 155 Mark McGwire MM 2.00 .60
❑ 156 Mark McGwire MM 2.00 .60
❑ 157 Mark McGwire MM 2.00 .60
❑ 158 Mark McGwire MM 2.00 .60
❑ 159 Mark McGwire MM 2.00 .60
❑ 160 Mark McGwire MM 2.00 .60
❑ 161 Mark McGwire MM 2.00 .60
❑ 162 Mark McGwire MM 2.00 .60
❑ 163 Mark McGwire MM 2.00 .60
❑ 164 Mark McGwire MM 2.00 .60
❑ 165 Mark McGwire MM 2.00 .60
❑ 166 Mark McGwire MM 2.00 .60
❑ 167 Mark McGwire MM 2.00 .60
❑ 168 Mark McGwire MM 2.00 .60
❑ 169 Mark McGwire MM 2.00 .60
❑ 170 Mark McGwire MM 2.00 .60
❑ 171 Mark McGwire MM 2.00 .60
❑ 172 Mark McGwire MM 2.00 .60
❑ 173 Mark McGwire MM 2.00 .60
❑ 174 Mark McGwire MM 2.00 .60
❑ 175 Mark McGwire MM 2.00 .60
❑ 176 Mark McGwire MM 2.00 .60
❑ 177 Mark McGwire MM 2.00 .60
❑ 178 Mark McGwire MM 2.00 .60
❑ 179 Mark McGwire MM 2.00 .60
❑ 180 Mark McGwire MM 2.00 .60

2000 Ultimate Victory

	Nm-Mt	Ex-Mt
COMP.SET w/o SP's (90)	25.00	7.50
COMMON CARD (1-90)	.30	.09

❑ 1 Mo Vaughn .30 .09
❑ 2 Darin Erstad .30 .09
❑ 3 Troy Glaus .30 .09
❑ 4 Adam Kennedy .30 .09

❑ 5 Jason Giambi .30 .09
❑ 6 Ben Grieve .30 .09
❑ 7 Terrence Long .30 .09
❑ 8 Tim Hudson .30 .09
❑ 9 David Wells .30 .09
❑ 10 Carlos Delgado .30 .09
❑ 11 Shannon Stewart .30 .09
❑ 12 Greg Vaughn .30 .09
❑ 13 Gerald Williams .30 .09
❑ 14 Manny Ramirez .50 .15
❑ 15 Roberto Alomar .50 .15
❑ 16 Jim Thome .50 .15
❑ 17 Edgar Martinez .50 .15
❑ 18 Alex Rodriguez 1.25 .35
❑ 19 Matt Riley .30 .09
❑ 20 Cal Ripken 2.50 .75
❑ 21 Mike Mussina .50 .15
❑ 22 Albert Belle .30 .09
❑ 23 Ivan Rodriguez .50 .15
❑ 24 Rafael Palmeiro .50 .15
❑ 25 Nomar Garciaparra 1.25 .35
❑ 26 Pedro Martinez .50 .15
❑ 27 Carl Everett .30 .09
❑ 28 Tomokazu Ohka RC .30 .09
❑ 29 Jermaine Dye .30 .09
❑ 30 Johnny Damon .50 .15
❑ 31 Dean Palmer .30 .09
❑ 32 Juan Gonzalez .30 .09
❑ 33 Eric Milton .30 .09
❑ 34 Matt Lawton .30 .09
❑ 35 Frank Thomas .75 .23
❑ 36 Paul Konerko .30 .09
❑ 37 Magglio Ordonez .30 .09
❑ 38 Jon Garland .30 .09
❑ 39 Derek Jeter 2.00 .60
❑ 40 Roger Clemens 1.50 .45
❑ 41 Bernie Williams .50 .15
❑ 42 Nick Johnson .30 .09
❑ 43 Julio Lugo .30 .09
❑ 44 Jeff Bagwell .50 .15
❑ 45 Richard Hidalgo .30 .09
❑ 46 Chipper Jones .75 .23
❑ 47 Greg Maddux 1.25 .35
❑ 48 Andruw Jones .50 .15
❑ 49 Andres Galarraga .30 .09
❑ 50 Rafael Furcal .30 .09
❑ 51 Jeromy Burnitz .30 .09
❑ 52 Geoff Jenkins .30 .09
❑ 53 Mark McGwire 2.00 .60
❑ 54 Jim Edmonds .30 .09
❑ 55 Rick Ankiel .30 .09
❑ 56 Sammy Sosa .75 .23
❑ 57 Julio Zuleta RC .30 .09
❑ 58 Kerry Wood .30 .09
❑ 59 Randy Johnson .75 .23
❑ 60 Matt Williams .30 .09
❑ 61 Steve Finley .30 .09
❑ 62 Gary Sheffield .30 .09
❑ 63 Kevin Brown .30 .09
❑ 64 Shawn Green .30 .09
❑ 65 Milton Bradley .30 .09
❑ 66 Vladimir Guerrero .75 .23
❑ 67 Jose Vidro .30 .09
❑ 68 Barry Bonds 2.00 .60
❑ 69 Jeff Kent .30 .09
❑ 70 Preston Wilson .30 .09
❑ 71 Mike Lowell .30 .09
❑ 72 Mike Piazza 1.25 .35

Card	Nm-Mt	Ex-Mt
❑ 73 Robin Ventura	.30	.09
❑ 74 Edgardo Alfonzo	.30	.09
❑ 75 Jay Payton	.30	.09
❑ 76 Tony Gwynn	1.00	.30
❑ 77 Adam Eaton	.30	.09
❑ 78 Phil Nevin	.30	.09
❑ 79 Scott Rolen	.50	.15
❑ 80 Bob Abreu	.30	.09
❑ 81 Pat Burrell	.30	.09
❑ 82 Brian Giles	.30	.09
❑ 83 Jason Kendall	.30	.09
❑ 84 Kris Benson	.30	.09
❑ 85 Gookie Dawkins	.30	.09
❑ 86 Ken Griffey Jr.	1.25	.35
❑ 87 Barry Larkin	.50	.15
❑ 88 Larry Walker	.30	.09
❑ 89 Todd Helton	.50	.15
❑ 90 Ben Petrick	.30	.09
❑ 91 Alex Cabrera/3500 RC	4.00	1.20
❑ 92 M.Wheatland/1000 RC	10.00	3.00
❑ 93 Joe Torres/1000 RC	10.00	3.00
❑ 94 Xavier Nady/1000 RC	15.00	4.50
❑ 95 Kenny Kelly/3500 RC	4.00	1.20
❑ 96 Matt Ginter/3500 RC	4.00	1.20
❑ 97 Ben Diggins/1000 RC	10.00	3.00
❑ 98 Danys Baez/3500 RC	4.00	1.20
❑ 99 Daylan Holt/2500 RC	5.00	1.50
❑ 100 K.Sasaki/3500 RC	5.00	1.50
❑ 101 D.Artman/2500 RC	5.00	1.50
❑ 102 Mike Tonis/1000 RC	10.00	3.00
❑ 103 Timo Perez/2500 RC	5.00	1.50
❑ 104 Barry Zito/2500 RC	10.00	3.00
❑ 105 Koyie Hill/2500 RC	5.00	1.50
❑ 106 B.Wilkerson/2500 RC	8.00	2.40
❑ 107 Juan Pierre/3500 RC	5.00	1.50
❑ 108 A.McNeal/3500 RC	4.00	1.20
❑ 109 J.Spurgeon/3500 RC	4.00	1.20
❑ 110 Sean Burnett/1000 RC	15.00	4.50
❑ 111 Luis Matos/3500 RC	4.00	1.20
❑ 112 Dave Krynzel/1000 RC	15.00	4.50
❑ 113 Scott Heard/1000 RC	10.00	3.00
❑ 114 Ben Sheets/2500 RC	10.00	3.00
❑ 115 D.Sardinha/1000 RC	10.00	3.00
❑ 116 D.Espinosa/1000 RC	10.00	3.00
❑ 117 Leo Estrella/3500 RC	4.00	1.20
❑ 118 K.Ainsworth/2500 RC	5.00	1.50
❑ 119 Jon Rauch/2500 RC	5.00	1.50
❑ 120 R.Franklin/2500 RC	5.00	1.50

1991 Ultra Update

	Nm-Mt	Ex-Mt
COMP.FACT.SET (120)	25.00	7.50
❑ 1 Dwight Evans	.75	.23
❑ 2 Chito Martinez	.25	.07
❑ 3 Bob Melvin	.25	.07
❑ 4 Mike Mussina RC	5.00	1.50
❑ 5 Jack Clark	.50	.15
❑ 6 Dana Kiecker	.25	.07
❑ 7 Steve Lyons	.25	.07
❑ 8 Gary Gaetti	.50	.15
❑ 9 Dave Gallagher	.25	.07
❑ 10 Dave Parker	.50	.15
❑ 11 Luis Polonia	.25	.07
❑ 12 Luis Sojo	.25	.07
❑ 13 Wilson Alvarez	.25	.07
❑ 14 Alex Fernandez	.25	.07
❑ 15 Craig Grebeck	.25	.07
❑ 16 Ron Karkovice	.25	.07
❑ 17 Warren Newson	.25	.07
❑ 18 Scott Radinsky	.25	.07
❑ 19 Glenallen Hill	.25	.07
❑ 20 Charles Nagy	.25	.07
❑ 21 Mark Whiten	.25	.07
❑ 22 Milt Cuyler	.25	.07
❑ 23 Paul Gibson	.25	.07
❑ 24 Mickey Tettleton	.25	.07
❑ 25 Todd Benzinger	.25	.07
❑ 26 Storm Davis	.25	.07
❑ 27 Kirk Gibson	.75	.23
❑ 28 Bill Pecota	.25	.07
❑ 29 Gary Thurman	.25	.07
❑ 30 Darryl Hamilton	.25	.07
❑ 31 Jaime Navarro	.25	.07
❑ 32 Willie Randolph	.50	.15
❑ 33 Bill Wegman	.25	.07
❑ 34 Randy Bush	.25	.07
❑ 35 Chili Davis	.50	.15
❑ 36 Scott Erickson	.25	.07
❑ 37 Chuck Knoblauch	.50	.15
❑ 38 Scott Leius	.25	.07
❑ 39 Jack Morris	.50	.15
❑ 40 John Habyan	.25	.07
❑ 41 Pat Kelly	.25	.07
❑ 42 Matt Nokes	.25	.07
❑ 43 Scott Sanderson	.25	.07
❑ 44 Bernie Williams	2.00	.60
❑ 45 Harold Baines	.50	.15
❑ 46 Brook Jacoby	.25	.07
❑ 47 Earnest Riles	.25	.07
❑ 48 Willie Wilson	.25	.07
❑ 49 Jay Buhner	.50	.15
❑ 50 Rich DeLucia	.25	.07
❑ 51 Mike Jackson	.25	.07
❑ 52 Bill Krueger	.25	.07
❑ 53 Bill Swift	.25	.07
❑ 54 Brian Downing	.25	.07
❑ 55 Juan Gonzalez	1.50	.45
❑ 56 Dean Palmer	.50	.15
❑ 57 Kevin Reimer	.25	.07
❑ 58 Ivan Rodriguez RC	8.00	2.40
❑ 59 Tom Candiotti	.25	.07
❑ 60 Juan Guzman RC	.50	.15
❑ 61 Bob MacDonald	.25	.07
❑ 62 Greg Myers	.25	.07
❑ 63 Ed Sprague	.25	.07
❑ 64 Devon White	.50	.15
❑ 65 Rafael Belliard	.25	.07
❑ 66 Juan Berenguer	.25	.07
❑ 67 Brian R. Hunter RC	.50	.15
❑ 68 Kent Mercker	.25	.07
❑ 69 Otis Nixon	.25	.07
❑ 70 Danny Jackson	.25	.07
❑ 71 Chuck McElroy	.25	.07
❑ 72 Gary Scott	.25	.07
❑ 73 Heathcliff Slocumb RC	.25	.07
❑ 74 Chico Walker	.25	.07
❑ 75 Rick Wilkins RC	.25	.07
❑ 76 Chris Hammond	.25	.07
❑ 77 Luis Quinones	.25	.07
❑ 78 Herm Winningham	.25	.07
❑ 79 Jeff Bagwell RC	8.00	2.40
❑ 80 Jim Corsi	.25	.07
❑ 81 Steve Finley	.50	.15
❑ 82 Luis Gonzalez RC	1.50	.45
❑ 83 Pete Harnisch	.25	.07
❑ 84 Darryl Kile	.50	.15
❑ 85 Brett Butler	.50	.15
❑ 86 Gary Carter	.50	.15
❑ 87 Tim Crews	.25	.07
❑ 88 Orel Hershiser	.50	.15
❑ 89 Bob Ojeda	.25	.07
❑ 90 Bret Barberie RC**	.25	.07
❑ 91 Barry Jones	.25	.07
❑ 92 Gilberto Reyes	.25	.07
❑ 93 Larry Walker	1.50	.45
❑ 94 Hubie Brooks	.25	.07
❑ 95 Tim Burke	.25	.07
❑ 96 Rick Cerone	.25	.07
❑ 97 Jeff Innis	.25	.07
❑ 98 Wally Backman	.25	.07
❑ 99 Tommy Greene	.25	.07
❑ 100 Ricky Jordan	.25	.07
❑ 101 Mitch Williams	.25	.07
❑ 102 John Smiley	.25	.07
❑ 103 Randy Tomlin RC	.25	.07
❑ 104 Gary Varsho	.25	.07
❑ 105 Cris Carpenter	.25	.07
❑ 106 Ken Hill	.25	.07
❑ 107 Felix Jose	.25	.07
❑ 108 Omar Olivares RC	.25	.07
❑ 109 Gerald Perry	.25	.07
❑ 110 Jerald Clark	.25	.07
❑ 111 Tony Fernandez	.25	.07
❑ 112 Darrin Jackson	.25	.07
❑ 113 Mike Maddux	.25	.07
❑ 114 Tim Teufel	.25	.07
❑ 115 Bud Black	.25	.07
❑ 116 Kelly Downs	.25	.07
❑ 117 Mike Felder	.25	.07
❑ 118 Willie McGee	.50	.15
❑ 119 Trevor Wilson	.25	.07
❑ 120 Checklist 1-120	.25	.07

1993 Ultra

	Nm-Mt	Ex-Mt
COMPLETE SET (650)	30.00	9.00
COMP. SERIES 1 (300)	15.00	4.50
COMP. SERIES 2 (350)	15.00	4.50
❑ 1 Steve Avery	.15	.04
❑ 2 Rafael Belliard	.15	.04
❑ 3 Damon Berryhill	.15	.04
❑ 4 Sid Bream	.15	.04
❑ 5 Ron Gant	.30	.09
❑ 6 Tom Glavine	.50	.15
❑ 7 Ryan Klesko	.30	.09
❑ 8 Mark Lemke	.15	.04
❑ 9 Javier Lopez	.50	.15
❑ 10 Greg Olson	.15	.04
❑ 11 Terry Pendleton	.30	.09
❑ 12 Deion Sanders	.50	.15
❑ 13 Mike Stanton	.15	.04
❑ 14 Paul Assenmacher	.15	.04
❑ 15 Steve Buechele	.15	.04
❑ 16 Frank Castillo	.15	.04
❑ 17 Shawon Dunston	.15	.04
❑ 18 Mark Grace	.50	.15
❑ 19 Derrick May	.15	.04
❑ 20 Chuck McElroy	.15	.04
❑ 21 Mike Morgan	.15	.04
❑ 22 Bob Scanlan	.15	.04
❑ 23 Dwight Smith	.15	.04
❑ 24 Sammy Sosa	.75	.23
❑ 25 Rick Wilkins	.15	.04
❑ 26 Tim Belcher	.15	.04
❑ 27 Jeff Branson	.15	.04
❑ 28 Bill Doran	.15	.04
❑ 29 Chris Hammond	.15	.04
❑ 30 Barry Larkin	.50	.15
❑ 31 Hal Morris	.15	.04
❑ 32 Joe Oliver	.15	.04
❑ 33 Jose Rijo	.15	.04
❑ 34 Bip Roberts	.15	.04
❑ 35 Chris Sabo	.15	.04
❑ 36 Reggie Sanders	.30	.09
❑ 37 Craig Biggio	.50	.15
❑ 38 Ken Caminiti	.30	.09
❑ 39 Steve Finley	.30	.09
❑ 40 Luis Gonzalez	.30	.09
❑ 41 Juan Guerrero	.15	.04
❑ 42 Pete Harnisch	.15	.04

❑ 43 Xavier Hernandez .15 .04
❑ 44 Doug Jones .15 .04
❑ 45 Al Osuna .15 .04
❑ 46 Eddie Taubensee .15 .04
❑ 47 Scooter Tucker .15 .04
❑ 48 Brian Williams .15 .04
❑ 49 Pedro Astacio .15 .04
❑ 50 Rafael Bournigal .15 .04
❑ 51 Brett Butler .30 .09
❑ 52 Tom Candiotti .15 .04
❑ 53 Eric Davis .30 .09
❑ 54 Lenny Harris .15 .04
❑ 55 Orel Hershiser .30 .09
❑ 56 Eric Karros .30 .09
❑ 57 Pedro Martinez 1.50 .45
❑ 58 Roger McDowell .15 .04
❑ 59 Jose Offerman .15 .04
❑ 60 Mike Piazza 3.00 .90
❑ 61 Moises Alou .30 .09
❑ 62 Kent Bottenfield .15 .04
❑ 63 Archi Cianfrocco .15 .04
❑ 64 Greg Colbrunn .15 .04
❑ 65 Wil Cordero .15 .04
❑ 66 Delino DeShields .15 .04
❑ 67 Darrin Fletcher .15 .04
❑ 68 Ken Hill .15 .04
❑ 69 Chris Nabholz .15 .04
❑ 70 Mel Rojas .15 .04
❑ 71 Larry Walker .30 .09
❑ 72 Sid Fernandez .15 .04
❑ 73 John Franco .30 .09
❑ 74 Dave Gallagher .15 .04
❑ 75 Todd Hundley .15 .04
❑ 76 Howard Johnson .15 .04
❑ 77 Jeff Kent .75 .23
❑ 78 Eddie Murray .75 .23
❑ 79 Bret Saberhagen .30 .09
❑ 80 Chico Walker .15 .04
❑ 81 Anthony Young .15 .04
❑ 82 Kyle Abbott .15 .04
❑ 83 Ruben Amaro .15 .04
❑ 84 Juan Bell .15 .04
❑ 85 Wes Chamberlain .15 .04
❑ 86 Darren Daulton .30 .09
❑ 87 Mariano Duncan .15 .04
❑ 88 Dave Hollins .15 .04
❑ 89 Ricky Jordan .15 .04
❑ 90 John Kruk .30 .09
❑ 91 Mickey Morandini .15 .04
❑ 92 Terry Mulholland .15 .04
❑ 93 Ben Rivera .15 .04
❑ 94 Mike Williams .15 .04
❑ 95 Stan Belinda .15 .04
❑ 96 Jay Bell .30 .09
❑ 97 Jeff King .15 .04
❑ 98 Mike LaValliere .15 .04
❑ 99 Lloyd McClendon .15 .04
❑ 100 Orlando Merced .15 .04
❑ 101 Zane Smith .15 .04
❑ 102 Randy Tomlin .15 .04
❑ 103 Andy Van Slyke .50 .15
❑ 104 Tim Wakefield .75 .23
❑ 105 John Wehner .15 .04
❑ 106 Bernard Gilkey .15 .04
❑ 107 Brian Jordan .30 .09
❑ 108 Ray Lankford .30 .09
❑ 109 Donovan Osborne .15 .04
❑ 110 Tom Pagnozzi .15 .04
❑ 111 Mike Perez .15 .04
❑ 112 Lee Smith .30 .09
❑ 113 Ozzie Smith 1.25 .35
❑ 114 Bob Tewksbury .15 .04
❑ 115 Todd Zeile .15 .04
❑ 116 Andy Benes .15 .04
❑ 117 Greg W. Harris .15 .04
❑ 118 Darrin Jackson .15 .04
❑ 119 Fred McGriff .50 .15
❑ 120 Rich Rodriguez .15 .04
❑ 121 Frank Seminara .15 .04
❑ 122 Gary Sheffield .30 .09
❑ 123 Craig Shipley .15 .04
❑ 124 Kurt Stillwell .15 .04
❑ 125 Dan Walters .15 .04
❑ 126 Rod Beck .15 .04
❑ 127 Mike Benjamin .15 .04
❑ 128 Jeff Brantley .15 .04
❑ 129 John Burkett .15 .04
❑ 130 Will Clark .50 .15
❑ 131 Royce Clayton .15 .04
❑ 132 Steve Hosey .15 .04
❑ 133 Mike Jackson .15 .04
❑ 134 Darren Lewis .15 .04
❑ 135 Kirt Manwaring .15 .04
❑ 136 Bill Swift .15 .04
❑ 137 Robby Thompson .15 .04
❑ 138 Brady Anderson .30 .09
❑ 139 Glenn Davis .15 .04
❑ 140 Leo Gomez .15 .04
❑ 141 Chito Martinez .15 .04
❑ 142 Ben McDonald .15 .04
❑ 143 Alan Mills .15 .04
❑ 144 Mike Mussina .50 .15
❑ 145 Gregg Olson .15 .04
❑ 146 David Segui .15 .04
❑ 147 Jeff Tackett .15 .04
❑ 148 Jack Clark .30 .09
❑ 149 Scott Cooper .15 .04
❑ 150 Danny Darwin .15 .04
❑ 151 John Dopson .15 .04
❑ 152 Mike Greenwell .15 .04
❑ 153 Tim Naehring .15 .04
❑ 154 Tony Pena .15 .04
❑ 155 Paul Quantrill .15 .04
❑ 156 Mo Vaughn .30 .09
❑ 157 Frank Viola .30 .09
❑ 158 Bob Zupcic .15 .04
❑ 159 Chad Curtis .15 .04
❑ 160 Gary DiSarcina .15 .04
❑ 161 Damion Easley .15 .04
❑ 162 Chuck Finley .30 .09
❑ 163 Tim Fortugno .15 .04
❑ 164 Rene Gonzales .15 .04
❑ 165 Joe Grahe .15 .04
❑ 166 Mark Langston .15 .04
❑ 167 John Orton .15 .04
❑ 168 Luis Polonia .15 .04
❑ 169 Julio Valera .15 .04
❑ 170 Wilson Alvarez .15 .04
❑ 171 George Bell .15 .04
❑ 172 Joey Cora .15 .04
❑ 173 Alex Fernandez .15 .04
❑ 174 Lance Johnson .15 .04
❑ 175 Ron Karkovice .15 .04
❑ 176 Jack McDowell .15 .04
❑ 177 Scott Radinsky .15 .04
❑ 178 Tim Raines .30 .09
❑ 179 Steve Sax .15 .04
❑ 180 Bobby Thigpen .15 .04
❑ 181 Frank Thomas .75 .23
❑ 182 Sandy Alomar Jr. .15 .04
❑ 183 Carlos Baerga .15 .04
❑ 184 Felix Fermin .15 .04
❑ 185 Thomas Howard .15 .04
❑ 186 Mark Lewis .15 .04
❑ 187 Derek Lilliquist .15 .04
❑ 188 Carlos Martinez .15 .04
❑ 189 Charles Nagy .15 .04
❑ 190 Scott Scudder .15 .04
❑ 191 Paul Sorrento .15 .04
❑ 192 Jim Thome .50 .15
❑ 193 Mark Whiten .15 .04
❑ 194 Milt Cuyler UER .15 .04
(Reversed negative on card front)
❑ 195 Rob Deer .15 .04
❑ 196 John Doherty .15 .04
❑ 197 Travis Fryman .30 .09
❑ 198 Dan Gladden .15 .04
❑ 199 Mike Henneman .15 .04
❑ 200 John Kiely .15 .04
❑ 201 Chad Kreuter .15 .04
❑ 202 Scott Livingstone .15 .04
❑ 203 Tony Phillips .15 .04
❑ 204 Alan Trammell .30 .09
❑ 205 Mike Boddicker .15 .04
❑ 206 George Brett 2.00 .60
❑ 207 Tom Gordon .15 .04
❑ 208 Mark Gubicza .15 .04
❑ 209 Gregg Jefferies .15 .04
❑ 210 Wally Joyner .30 .09
❑ 211 Kevin Koslofski .15 .04
❑ 212 Brent Mayne .15 .04
❑ 213 Brian McRae .15 .04
❑ 214 Kevin McReynolds .15 .04
❑ 215 Rusty Meacham .15 .04
❑ 216 Steve Shifflett .15 .04
❑ 217 Jim Austin .15 .04
❑ 218 Cal Eldred .15 .04
❑ 219 Darryl Hamilton .15 .04
❑ 220 Doug Henry .15 .04
❑ 221 John Jaha .15 .04
❑ 222 Dave Nilsson .15 .04
❑ 223 Jesse Orosco .15 .04
❑ 224 B.J. Surhoff .30 .09
❑ 225 Greg Vaughn .15 .04
❑ 226 Bill Wegman .15 .04
❑ 227 Robin Yount UER 1.25 .35
Born in Illinois, not in Virginia
❑ 228 Rick Aguilera .15 .04
❑ 229 J.T. Bruett .15 .04
❑ 230 Scott Erickson .15 .04
❑ 231 Kent Hrbek .30 .09
❑ 232 Terry Jorgensen .15 .04
❑ 233 Scott Leius .15 .04
❑ 234 Pat Mahomes .15 .04
❑ 235 Pedro Munoz .15 .04
❑ 236 Kirby Puckett .75 .23
❑ 237 Kevin Tapani .15 .04
❑ 238 Lenny Webster .15 .04
❑ 239 Carl Willis .15 .04
❑ 240 Mike Gallego .15 .04
❑ 241 John Habyan .15 .04
❑ 242 Pat Kelly .15 .04
❑ 243 Kevin Maas .15 .04
❑ 244 Don Mattingly 2.00 .60
❑ 245 Hensley Meulens .15 .04
❑ 246 Sam Militello .15 .04
❑ 247 Matt Nokes .15 .04
❑ 248 Melido Perez .15 .04
❑ 249 Andy Stankiewicz .15 .04
❑ 250 Randy Velarde .15 .04
❑ 251 Bob Wickman .15 .04
❑ 252 Bernie Williams .50 .15
❑ 253 Lance Blankenship .15 .04
❑ 254 Mike Bordick .15 .04
❑ 255 Jerry Browne .15 .04
❑ 256 Ron Darling .15 .04
❑ 257 Dennis Eckersley .30 .09
❑ 258 Rickey Henderson .75 .23
❑ 259 Vince Horsman .15 .04
❑ 260 Troy Neel .15 .04
❑ 261 Jeff Parrett .15 .04
❑ 262 Terry Steinbach .15 .04
❑ 263 Bob Welch .15 .04
❑ 264 Bobby Witt .15 .04
❑ 265 Rich Amaral .15 .04
❑ 266 Bret Boone .50 .15
❑ 267 Jay Buhner .30 .09
❑ 268 Dave Fleming .15 .04
❑ 269 Randy Johnson .75 .23
❑ 270 Edgar Martinez .50 .15
❑ 271 Mike Schooler .15 .04
❑ 272 Russ Swan .15 .04
❑ 273 Dave Valle .15 .04
❑ 274 Omar Vizquel .50 .15
❑ 275 Kerry Woodson .15 .04
❑ 276 Kevin Brown .30 .09
❑ 277 Julio Franco .30 .09
❑ 278 Jeff Frye .15 .04
❑ 279 Juan Gonzalez .30 .09
❑ 280 Jeff Huson .15 .04
❑ 281 Rafael Palmeiro .50 .15
❑ 282 Dean Palmer .30 .09
❑ 283 Roger Pavlik .15 .04
❑ 284 Ivan Rodriguez .50 .15
❑ 285 Kenny Rogers .30 .09
❑ 286 Derek Bell .15 .04
❑ 287 Pat Borders .15 .04
❑ 288 Joe Carter .30 .09
❑ 289 Bob MacDonald .15 .04
❑ 290 Jack Morris .30 .09
❑ 291 John Olerud .30 .09
❑ 292 Ed Sprague .15 .04
❑ 293 Todd Stottlemyre .15 .04
❑ 294 Mike Timlin .15 .04
❑ 295 Duane Ward .15 .04
❑ 296 David Wells .30 .09

❑ 297 Devon White .30 .09
❑ 298 Ray Lankford CL .15 .04
❑ 299 Bobby Witt CL .15 .04
❑ 300 Mike Piazza CL .75 .23
❑ 301 Steve Bedrosian .15 .04
❑ 302 Jeff Blauser .15 .04
❑ 303 Francisco Cabrera .15 .04
❑ 304 Marvin Freeman .15 .04
❑ 305 Brian Hunter .15 .04
❑ 306 David Justice .30 .09
❑ 307 Greg Maddux 1.25 .35
❑ 308 Greg McMichael RC .30 .09
❑ 309 Kent Mercker .15 .04
❑ 310 Otis Nixon .15 .04
❑ 311 Pete Smith .15 .04
❑ 312 John Smoltz .50 .15
❑ 313 Jose Guzman .15 .04
❑ 314 Mike Harkey .15 .04
❑ 315 Greg Hibbard .15 .04
❑ 316 Candy Maldonado .15 .04
❑ 317 Randy Myers .15 .04
❑ 318 Dan Plesac .15 .04
❑ 319 Rey Sanchez .15 .04
❑ 320 Ryne Sandberg 1.25 .35
❑ 321 Tommy Shields .15 .04
❑ 322 Jose Vizcaino .15 .04
❑ 323 Matt Walbeck RC .30 .09
❑ 324 Willie Wilson .15 .04
❑ 325 Tom Browning .15 .04
❑ 326 Tim Costo .15 .04
❑ 327 Rob Dibble .30 .09
❑ 328 Steve Foster .15 .04
❑ 329 Roberto Kelly .15 .04
❑ 330 Randy Milligan .15 .04
❑ 331 Kevin Mitchell .15 .04
❑ 332 Tim Pugh RC .30 .09
❑ 333 Jeff Reardon .30 .09
❑ 334 John Roper .15 .04
❑ 335 Juan Samuel .15 .04
❑ 336 John Smiley .15 .04
❑ 337 Dan Wilson .30 .09
❑ 338 Scott Aldred .15 .04
❑ 339 Andy Ashby .15 .04
❑ 340 Freddie Benavides .15 .04
❑ 341 Dante Bichette .30 .09
❑ 342 Willie Blair .15 .04
❑ 343 Daryl Boston .15 .04
❑ 344 Vinny Castilla .75 .23
❑ 345 Jerald Clark .15 .04
❑ 346 Alex Cole .15 .04
❑ 347 Andres Galarraga .30 .09
❑ 348 Joe Girardi .15 .04
❑ 349 Ryan Hawblitzel .15 .04
❑ 350 Charlie Hayes .15 .04
❑ 351 Butch Henry .15 .04
❑ 352 Darren Holmes .15 .04
❑ 353 Dale Murphy .50 .15
❑ 354 David Nied .15 .04
❑ 355 Jeff Parrett .15 .04
❑ 356 Steve Reed RC .30 .09
❑ 357 Bruce Ruffin .15 .04
❑ 358 Danny Sheaffer RC .30 .09
❑ 359 Bryn Smith .15 .04
❑ 360 Jim Tatum RC .30 .09
❑ 361 Eric Young .15 .04
❑ 362 Gerald Young .15 .04
❑ 363 Luis Aquino .15 .04
❑ 364 Alex Arias .15 .04
❑ 365 Jack Armstrong .15 .04
❑ 366 Bret Barberie .15 .04
❑ 367 Ryan Bowen .15 .04
❑ 368 Greg Briley .15 .04
❑ 369 Cris Carpenter .15 .04
❑ 370 Chuck Carr .15 .04
❑ 371 Jeff Conine .30 .09
❑ 372 Steve Decker .15 .04
❑ 373 Orestes Destrade .15 .04
❑ 374 Monty Fariss .15 .04
❑ 375 Junior Felix .15 .04
❑ 376 Chris Hammond .15 .04
❑ 377 Bryan Harvey .15 .04
❑ 378 Trevor Hoffman .75 .23
❑ 379 Charlie Hough .30 .09
❑ 380 Joe Klink .15 .04
❑ 381 Richie Lewis RC .30 .09
❑ 382 Dave Magadan .15 .04
❑ 383 Bob McClure .15 .04
❑ 384 Scott Pose RC .30 .09
❑ 385 Rich Renteria .15 .04
❑ 386 Benito Santiago .30 .09
❑ 387 Walt Weiss .15 .04
❑ 388 Nigel Wilson .15 .04
❑ 389 Eric Anthony .15 .04
❑ 390 Jeff Bagwell .50 .15
❑ 391 Andujar Cedeno .15 .04
❑ 392 Doug Drabek .15 .04
❑ 393 Darryl Kile .30 .09
❑ 394 Mark Portugal .15 .04
❑ 395 Karl Rhodes .15 .04
❑ 396 Scott Servais .15 .04
❑ 397 Greg Swindell .15 .04
❑ 398 Tom Goodwin .15 .04
❑ 399 Kevin Gross .15 .04
❑ 400 Carlos Hernandez .15 .04
❑ 401 Ramon Martinez .15 .04
❑ 402 Raul Mondesi .30 .09
❑ 403 Jody Reed .15 .04
❑ 404 Mike Sharperson .15 .04
❑ 405 Cory Snyder .15 .04
❑ 406 Darryl Strawberry .30 .09
❑ 407 Rick Trlicek .15 .04
❑ 408 Tim Wallach .15 .04
❑ 409 Todd Worrell .15 .04
❑ 410 Tavo Alvarez .15 .04
❑ 411 Sean Berry .15 .04
❑ 412 Frank Bolick .15 .04
❑ 413 Cliff Floyd .30 .09
❑ 414 Mike Gardiner .15 .04
❑ 415 Marquis Grissom .30 .09
❑ 416 Tim Laker RC .30 .09
❑ 417 Mike Lansing RC .50 .15
❑ 418 Dennis Martinez .30 .09
❑ 419 John Vander Wal .15 .04
❑ 420 John Wetteland .30 .09
❑ 421 Rondell White .30 .09
❑ 422 Bobby Bonilla .30 .09
❑ 423 Jeromy Burnitz .30 .09
❑ 424 Vince Coleman .15 .04
❑ 425 Mike Draper .15 .04
❑ 426 Tony Fernandez .15 .04
❑ 427 Dwight Gooden .30 .09
❑ 428 Jeff Innis .15 .04
❑ 429 Bobby Jones .30 .09
❑ 430 Mike Maddux .15 .04
❑ 431 Charlie O'Brien .15 .04
❑ 432 Joe Orsulak .15 .04
❑ 433 Pete Schourek .15 .04
❑ 434 Frank Tanana .15 .04
❑ 435 Ryan Thompson .15 .04
❑ 436 Kim Batiste .15 .04
❑ 437 Mark Davis .15 .04
❑ 438 Jose DeLeon .15 .04
❑ 439 Len Dykstra .30 .09
❑ 440 Jim Eisenreich .15 .04
❑ 441 Tommy Greene .15 .04
❑ 442 Pete Incaviglia .15 .04
❑ 443 Danny Jackson .15 .04
❑ 444 Todd Pratt RC .50 .15
❑ 445 Curt Schilling .30 .09
❑ 446 Milt Thompson .15 .04
❑ 447 David West .15 .04
❑ 448 Mitch Williams .15 .04
❑ 449 Steve Cooke .15 .04
❑ 450 Carlos Garcia .15 .04
❑ 451 Al Martin .15 .04
❑ 452 Blas Minor .15 .04
❑ 453 Dennis Moeller .15 .04
❑ 454 Denny Neagle .30 .09
❑ 455 Don Slaught .15 .04
❑ 456 Lonnie Smith .15 .04
❑ 457 Paul Wagner .15 .04
❑ 458 Bob Walk .15 .04
❑ 459 Kevin Young .30 .09
❑ 460 Rene Arocha RC .50 .15
❑ 461 Brian Barber .15 .04
❑ 462 Rheal Cormier .15 .04
❑ 463 Gregg Jefferies .15 .04
❑ 464 Joe Magrane .15 .04
❑ 465 Omar Olivares .15 .04
❑ 466 Geronimo Pena .15 .04
❑ 467 Allen Watson .15 .04
❑ 468 Mark Whiten .15 .04
❑ 469 Derek Bell .15 .04
❑ 470 Phil Clark .15 .04
❑ 471 Pat Gomez RC .30 .09
❑ 472 Tony Gwynn 1.00 .30
❑ 473 Jeremy Hernandez .15 .04
❑ 474 Bruce Hurst .15 .04
❑ 475 Phil Plantier .15 .04
❑ 476 Scott Sanders RC .30 .09
❑ 477 Tim Scott .15 .04
❑ 478 Darrell Sherman RC .30 .09
❑ 479 Guillermo Velasquez .15 .04
❑ 480 Tim Worrell RC .30 .09
❑ 481 Todd Benzinger .15 .04
❑ 482 Bud Black .15 .04
❑ 483 Barry Bonds 2.00 .60
❑ 484 Dave Burba .15 .04
❑ 485 Bryan Hickerson .15 .04
❑ 486 Dave Martinez .15 .04
❑ 487 Willie McGee .30 .09
❑ 488 Jeff Reed .15 .04
❑ 489 Kevin Rogers .15 .04
❑ 490 Matt Williams .30 .09
❑ 491 Trevor Wilson .15 .04
❑ 492 Harold Baines .30 .09
❑ 493 Mike Devereaux .15 .04
❑ 494 Todd Frohwirth .15 .04
❑ 495 Chris Hoiles .15 .04
❑ 496 Luis Mercedes .15 .04
❑ 497 Sherman Obando RC .30 .09
❑ 498 Brad Pennington .15 .04
❑ 499 Harold Reynolds .30 .09
❑ 500 Arthur Rhodes .15 .04
❑ 501 Cal Ripken 2.50 .75
❑ 502 Rick Sutcliffe .30 .09
❑ 503 Fernando Valenzuela .30 .09
❑ 504 Mark Williamson .15 .04
❑ 505 Scott Bankhead .15 .04
❑ 506 Greg Blosser .15 .04
❑ 507 Ivan Calderon .15 .04
❑ 508 Roger Clemens 1.50 .45
❑ 509 Andre Dawson .30 .09
❑ 510 Scott Fletcher .15 .04
❑ 511 Greg A. Harris .15 .04
❑ 512 Billy Hatcher .15 .04
❑ 513 Bob Melvin .15 .04
❑ 514 Carlos Quintana .15 .04
❑ 515 Luis Rivera .15 .04
❑ 516 Jeff Russell .15 .04
❑ 517 Ken Ryan RC .30 .09
❑ 518 Chili Davis .30 .09
❑ 519 Jim Edmonds RC 5.00 1.50
❑ 520 Gary Gaetti .30 .09
❑ 521 Torey Lovullo .15 .04
❑ 522 Troy Percival .50 .15
❑ 523 Tim Salmon .50 .15
❑ 524 Scott Sanderson .15 .04
❑ 525 J.T. Snow RC .75 .23
❑ 526 Jerome Walton .15 .04
❑ 527 Jason Bere .15 .04
❑ 528 Rod Bolton .15 .04
❑ 529 Ellis Burks .30 .09
❑ 530 Carlton Fisk .50 .15
❑ 531 Craig Grebeck .15 .04
❑ 532 Ozzie Guillen .30 .09
❑ 533 Roberto Hernandez .15 .04
❑ 534 Bo Jackson .75 .23
❑ 535 Kirk McCaskill .15 .04
❑ 536 Dave Stieb .15 .04
❑ 537 Robin Ventura .30 .09
❑ 538 Albert Belle .30 .09
❑ 539 Mike Bielecki .15 .04
❑ 540 Glenallen Hill .15 .04
❑ 541 Reggie Jefferson .15 .04
❑ 542 Kenny Lofton .30 .09
❑ 543 Jeff Mutis .15 .04
❑ 544 Junior Ortiz .15 .04
❑ 545 Manny Ramirez 1.25 .35
❑ 546 Jeff Treadway .15 .04
❑ 547 Kevin Wickander .15 .04
❑ 548 Cecil Fielder .30 .09
❑ 549 Kirk Gibson .50 .15
❑ 550 Greg Gohr .15 .04
❑ 551 David Haas .15 .04
❑ 552 Bill Krueger .15 .04
❑ 553 Mike Moore .15 .04
❑ 554 Mickey Tettleton .15 .04

❑ 555 Lou Whitaker .30 .09
❑ 556 Kevin Appier .30 .09
❑ 557 Billy Brewer .15 .04
❑ 558 David Cone .30 .09
❑ 559 Greg Gagne .15 .04
❑ 560 Mark Gardner .15 .04
❑ 561 Phil Hiatt .15 .04
❑ 562 Felix Jose .15 .04
❑ 563 Jose Lind .15 .04
❑ 564 Mike Macfarlane .15 .04
❑ 565 Keith Miller .15 .04
❑ 566 Jeff Montgomery .15 .04
❑ 567 Hipolito Pichardo .15 .04
❑ 568 Ricky Bones .15 .04
❑ 569 Tom Brunansky .15 .04
❑ 570 Joe Kmak .15 .04
❑ 571 Pat Listach .15 .04
❑ 572 Graeme Lloyd RC .50 .15
❑ 573 Carlos Maldonado .15 .04
❑ 574 Josias Manzanillo .15 .04
❑ 575 Matt Mieske .15 .04
❑ 576 Kevin Reimer .15 .04
❑ 577 Bill Spiers .15 .04
❑ 578 Dickie Thon .15 .04
❑ 579 Willie Banks .15 .04
❑ 580 Jim Deshaies .15 .04
❑ 581 Mark Guthrie .15 .04
❑ 582 Brian Harper .15 .04
❑ 583 Chuck Knoblauch .30 .09
❑ 584 Gene Larkin .15 .04
❑ 585 Shane Mack .15 .04
❑ 586 David McCarty .15 .04
❑ 587 Mike Pagliarulo .15 .04
❑ 588 Mike Trombley .15 .04
❑ 589 Dave Winfield .30 .09
❑ 590 Jim Abbott .50 .15
❑ 591 Wade Boggs .50 .15
❑ 592 Russ Davis RC .30 .09
❑ 593 Steve Farr .15 .04
❑ 594 Steve Howe .15 .04
❑ 595 Mike Humphreys .15 .04
❑ 596 Jimmy Key .30 .09
❑ 597 Jim Leyritz .15 .04
❑ 598 Bobby Munoz .15 .04
❑ 599 Paul O'Neill .50 .15
❑ 600 Spike Owen .15 .04
❑ 601 Mike Stanley .15 .04
❑ 602 Danny Tartabull .15 .04
❑ 603 Scott Brosius .30 .09
❑ 604 Storm Davis .15 .04
❑ 605 Eric Fox .15 .04
❑ 606 Rich Gossage .30 .09
❑ 607 Scott Hemond .15 .04
❑ 608 Dave Henderson .15 .04
❑ 609 Mark McGwire 2.00 .60
❑ 610 Mike Mohler RC .30 .09
❑ 611 Edwin Nunez .15 .04
❑ 612 Kevin Seitzer .15 .04
❑ 613 Ruben Sierra .15 .04
❑ 614 Chris Bosio .15 .04
❑ 615 Norm Charlton .15 .04
❑ 616 Jim Converse RC .30 .09
❑ 617 John Cummings RC .30 .09
❑ 618 Mike Felder .15 .04
❑ 619 Ken Griffey Jr. 1.25 .35
❑ 620 Mike Hampton .30 .09
❑ 621 Erik Hanson .15 .04
❑ 622 Bill Haselman .15 .04
❑ 623 Tino Martinez .50 .15
❑ 624 Lee Tinsley .15 .04
❑ 625 Fernando Vina RC .75 .23
❑ 626 David Wainhouse .15 .04
❑ 627 Jose Canseco .50 .15
❑ 628 Benji Gil .15 .04
❑ 629 Tom Henke .15 .04
❑ 630 David Hulse RC .30 .09
❑ 631 Manuel Lee .15 .04
❑ 632 Craig Lefferts .15 .04
❑ 633 Robb Nen .30 .09
❑ 634 Gary Redus .15 .04
❑ 635 Bill Ripken .15 .04
❑ 636 Nolan Ryan 3.00 .90
❑ 637 Dan Smith .15 .04
❑ 638 Matt Whiteside RC .30 .09
❑ 639 Roberto Alomar .50 .15
❑ 640 Juan Guzman .15 .04
❑ 641 Pat Hentgen .15 .04
❑ 642 Darrin Jackson .15 .04
❑ 643 Randy Knorr .15 .04
❑ 644 Domingo Martinez RC .30 .09
❑ 645 Paul Molitor .50 .15
❑ 646 Dick Schofield .15 .04
❑ 647 Dave Stewart .30 .09
❑ 648 Rey Sanchez CL .15 .04
❑ 649 Jeremy Hernandez CL .15 .04
❑ 650 Junior Ortiz CL .15 .04

1997 Ultra

	Nm-Mt	Ex-Mt
COMPLETE SET (553)	70.00	21.00
COMP.SERIES 1 (300)	30.00	9.00
COMP.SERIES 2 (253)	40.00	12.00
COMMON CARD (1-553)	.30	.09
COMMON RC	.40	.12

❑ 1 Roberto Alomar .50 .15
❑ 2 Brady Anderson .30 .09
❑ 3 Rocky Coppinger .30 .09
❑ 4 Jeffrey Hammonds .30 .09
❑ 5 Chris Hoiles .30 .09
❑ 6 Eddie Murray .75 .23
❑ 7 Mike Mussina .50 .15
❑ 8 Jimmy Myers .30 .09
❑ 9 Randy Myers .30 .09
❑ 10 Arthur Rhodes .30 .09
❑ 11 Cal Ripken 2.50 .75
❑ 12 Jose Canseco .50 .15
❑ 13 Roger Clemens 1.50 .45
❑ 14 Tom Gordon .30 .09
❑ 15 Jose Malave .30 .09
❑ 16 Tim Naehring .30 .09
❑ 17 Troy O'Leary .30 .09
❑ 18 Bill Selby .30 .09
❑ 19 Heathcliff Slocumb .30 .09
❑ 20 Mike Stanley .30 .09
❑ 21 Mo Vaughn .30 .09
❑ 22 Garret Anderson .30 .09
❑ 23 George Arias .30 .09
❑ 24 Chili Davis .30 .09
❑ 25 Jim Edmonds .30 .09
❑ 26 Darin Erstad .30 .09
❑ 27 Chuck Finley .30 .09
❑ 28 Todd Greene .30 .09
❑ 29 Troy Percival .30 .09
❑ 30 Tim Salmon .50 .15
❑ 31 Jeff Schmidt .30 .09
❑ 32 Randy Velarde .30 .09
❑ 33 Shad Williams .30 .09
❑ 34 Wilson Alvarez .30 .09
❑ 35 Harold Baines .30 .09
❑ 36 James Baldwin .30 .09
❑ 37 Mike Cameron .30 .09
❑ 38 Ray Durham .30 .09
❑ 39 Ozzie Guillen .30 .09
❑ 40 Roberto Hernandez .30 .09
❑ 41 Darren Lewis .30 .09
❑ 42 Jose Munoz .30 .09
❑ 43 Tony Phillips .30 .09
❑ 44 Frank Thomas .75 .23
❑ 45 Sandy Alomar Jr. .30 .09
❑ 46 Albert Belle .30 .09
❑ 47 Mark Carreon .30 .09
❑ 48 Julio Franco .30 .09
❑ 49 Orel Hershiser .30 .09
❑ 50 Kenny Lofton .30 .09
❑ 51 Jack McDowell .30 .09
❑ 52 Jose Mesa .30 .09
❑ 53 Charles Nagy .30 .09
❑ 54 Manny Ramirez .50 .15
❑ 55 Julian Tavarez .30 .09
❑ 56 Omar Vizquel .50 .15
❑ 57 Raul Casanova .30 .09
❑ 58 Tony Clark .30 .09
❑ 59 Travis Fryman .30 .09
❑ 60 Bob Higginson .30 .09
❑ 61 Melvin Nieves .30 .09
❑ 62 Curtis Pride .30 .09
❑ 63 Justin Thompson .30 .09
❑ 64 Alan Trammell .30 .09
❑ 65 Kevin Appier .30 .09
❑ 66 Johnny Damon .50 .15
❑ 67 Keith Lockhart .30 .09
❑ 68 Jeff Montgomery .30 .09
❑ 69 Jose Offerman .30 .09
❑ 70 Bip Roberts .30 .09
❑ 71 Jose Rosado .30 .09
❑ 72 Chris Stynes .30 .09
❑ 73 Mike Sweeney .30 .09
❑ 74 Jeff Cirillo .30 .09
❑ 75 Jeff D'Amico .30 .09
❑ 76 John Jaha .30 .09
❑ 77 Scott Karl .30 .09
❑ 78 Mike Matheny .30 .09
❑ 79 Ben McDonald .30 .09
❑ 80 Matt Mieske .30 .09
❑ 81 Marc Newfield .30 .09
❑ 82 Dave Nilsson .30 .09
❑ 83 Jose Valentin .30 .09
❑ 84 Fernando Vina .30 .09
❑ 85 Rick Aguilera .30 .09
❑ 86 Marty Cordova .30 .09
❑ 87 Chuck Knoblauch .30 .09
❑ 88 Matt Lawton .30 .09
❑ 89 Pat Meares .30 .09
❑ 90 Paul Molitor .50 .15
❑ 91 Greg Myers .30 .09
❑ 92 Dan Naulty .30 .09
❑ 93 Kirby Puckett .75 .23
❑ 94 Frank Rodriguez .30 .09
❑ 95 Wade Boggs .50 .15
❑ 96 Cecil Fielder .30 .09
❑ 97 Joe Girardi .30 .09
❑ 98 Dwight Gooden .30 .09
❑ 99 Derek Jeter 2.00 .60
❑ 100 Tino Martinez .50 .15
❑ 101 Ramiro Mendoza RC .30 .09
❑ 102 Andy Pettitte .50 .15
❑ 103 Mariano Rivera .50 .15
❑ 104 Ruben Rivera .30 .09
❑ 105 Kenny Rogers .30 .09
❑ 106 Darryl Strawberry .30 .09
❑ 107 Bernie Williams .50 .15
❑ 108 Tony Batista .30 .09
❑ 109 Geronimo Berroa .30 .09
❑ 110 Bobby Chouinard .30 .09
❑ 111 Brent Gates .30 .09
❑ 112 Jason Giambi .30 .09
❑ 113 Damon Mashore .30 .09
❑ 114 Mark McGwire 2.00 .60
❑ 115 Scott Spiezio .30 .09
❑ 116 John Wasdin .30 .09
❑ 117 Steve Wojciechowski .30 .09
❑ 118 Ernie Young .30 .09
❑ 119 Norm Charlton .30 .09
❑ 120 Joey Cora .30 .09
❑ 121 Ken Griffey Jr. 1.25 .35
❑ 122 Sterling Hitchcock .30 .09
❑ 123 Raul Ibanez .30 .09
❑ 124 Randy Johnson .75 .23
❑ 125 Edgar Martinez .50 .15
❑ 126 Alex Rodriguez 1.25 .35
❑ 127 Matt Wagner .30 .09
❑ 128 Bob Wells .30 .09
❑ 129 Dan Wilson .30 .09
❑ 130 Will Clark .50 .15
❑ 131 Kevin Elster .30 .09
❑ 132 Juan Gonzalez .30 .09
❑ 133 Rusty Greer .30 .09
❑ 134 Darryl Hamilton .30 .09
❑ 135 Mike Henneman .30 .09

❑	136	Ken Hill	.30	.09
❑	137	Mark McLemore	.30	.09
❑	138	Dean Palmer	.30	.09
❑	139	Roger Pavlik	.30	.09
❑	140	Ivan Rodriguez	.50	.15
❑	141	Joe Carter	.30	.09
❑	142	Carlos Delgado	.30	.09
❑	143	Alex Gonzalez	.30	.09
❑	144	Juan Guzman	.30	.09
❑	145	Pat Hentgen	.30	.09
❑	146	Marty Janzen	.30	.09
❑	147	Otis Nixon	.30	.09
❑	148	Charlie O'Brien	.30	.09
❑	149	John Olerud	.30	.09
❑	150	Robert Perez	.30	.09
❑	151	Jermaine Dye	.30	.09
❑	152	Tom Glavine	.50	.15
❑	153	Andruw Jones	.50	.15
❑	154	Chipper Jones	.75	.23
❑	155	Ryan Klesko	.30	.09
❑	156	Javier Lopez	.30	.09
❑	157	Greg Maddux	1.25	.35
❑	158	Fred McGriff	.50	.15
❑	159	Wonderful Monds	.30	.09
❑	160	John Smoltz	.50	.15
❑	161	Terrell Wade	.30	.09
❑	162	Mark Wohlers	.30	.09
❑	163	Brant Brown	.30	.09
❑	164	Mark Grace	.50	.15
❑	165	Tyler Houston	.30	.09
❑	166	Robin Jennings	.30	.09
❑	167	Jason Maxwell	.30	.09
❑	168	Ryne Sandberg	1.25	.35
❑	169	Sammy Sosa	.75	.23
❑	170	Amaury Telemaco	.30	.09
❑	171	Steve Trachsel	.30	.09
❑	172	Pedro Valdes RC	.30	.09
❑	173	Tim Belk	.30	.09
❑	174	Bret Boone	.30	.09
❑	175	Jeff Brantley	.30	.09
❑	176	Eric Davis	.30	.09
❑	177	Barry Larkin	.50	.15
❑	178	Chad Mottola	.30	.09
❑	179	Mark Portugal	.30	.09
❑	180	Reggie Sanders	.30	.09
❑	181	John Smiley	.30	.09
❑	182	Eddie Taubensee	.30	.09
❑	183	Dante Bichette	.30	.09
❑	184	Ellis Burks	.30	.09
❑	185	Andres Galarraga	.30	.09
❑	186	Curt Leskanic	.30	.09
❑	187	Quinton McCracken	.30	.09
❑	188	Jeff Reed	.30	.09
❑	189	Kevin Ritz	.30	.09
❑	190	Walt Weiss	.30	.09
❑	191	Jamey Wright	.30	.09
❑	192	Eric Young	.30	.09
❑	193	Kevin Brown	.30	.09
❑	194	Luis Castillo	.30	.09
❑	195	Jeff Conine	.30	.09
❑	196	Andre Dawson	.30	.09
❑	197	Charles Johnson	.30	.09
❑	198	Al Leiter	.30	.09
❑	199	Ralph Milliard	.30	.09
❑	200	Robb Nen	.30	.09
❑	201	Edgar Renteria	.30	.09
❑	202	Gary Sheffield	.30	.09
❑	203	Bob Abreu	.50	.15
❑	204	Jeff Bagwell	.50	.15
❑	205	Derek Bell	.30	.09
❑	206	Sean Berry	.30	.09
❑	207	Richard Hidalgo	.30	.09
❑	208	Todd Jones	.30	.09
❑	209	Darryl Kile	.30	.09
❑	210	Orlando Miller	.30	.09
❑	211	Shane Reynolds	.30	.09
❑	212	Billy Wagner	.30	.09
❑	213	Donne Wall	.30	.09
❑	214	Roger Cedeno	.30	.09
❑	215	Greg Gagne	.30	.09
❑	216	Karim Garcia	.30	.09
❑	217	Wilton Guerrero	.30	.09
❑	218	Todd Hollandsworth	.30	.09
❑	219	Ramon Martinez	.30	.09
❑	220	Raul Mondesi	.30	.09
❑	221	Hideo Nomo	.75	.23
❑	222	Chan Ho Park	.30	.09
❑	223	Mike Piazza	1.25	.35
❑	224	Ismael Valdes	.30	.09
❑	225	Moises Alou	.30	.09
❑	226	Derek Aucoin	.30	.09
❑	227	Yamil Benitez	.30	.09
❑	228	Jeff Fassero	.30	.09
❑	229	Darrin Fletcher	.30	.09
❑	230	Mark Grudzielanek	.30	.09
❑	231	Barry Manuel	.30	.09
❑	232	Pedro Martinez	.50	.15
❑	233	Henry Rodriguez	.30	.09
❑	234	Ugueth Urbina	.30	.09
❑	235	Rondell White	.30	.09
❑	236	Carlos Baerga	.30	.09
❑	237	John Franco	.30	.09
❑	238	Bernard Gilkey	.30	.09
❑	239	Todd Hundley	.30	.09
❑	240	Butch Huskey	.30	.09
❑	241	Jason Isringhausen	.30	.09
❑	242	Lance Johnson	.30	.09
❑	243	Bobby Jones	.30	.09
❑	244	Alex Ochoa	.30	.09
❑	245	Rey Ordonez	.30	.09
❑	246	Paul Wilson	.30	.09
❑	247	Ron Blazier	.30	.09
❑	248	David Doster	.30	.09
❑	249	Jim Eisenreich	.30	.09
❑	250	Mike Grace	.30	.09
❑	251	Mike Lieberthal	.30	.09
❑	252	Wendell Magee	.30	.09
❑	253	Mickey Morandini	.30	.09
❑	254	Ricky Otero	.30	.09
❑	255	Scott Rolen	.50	.15
❑	256	Curt Schilling	.30	.09
❑	257	Todd Zeile	.30	.09
❑	258	Jermaine Allensworth	.30	.09
❑	259	Trey Beamon	.30	.09
❑	260	Carlos Garcia	.30	.09
❑	261	Mark Johnson	.30	.09
❑	262	Jason Kendall	.30	.09
❑	263	Jeff King	.30	.09
❑	264	Al Martin	.30	.09
❑	265	Denny Neagle	.30	.09
❑	266	Matt Ruebel	.30	.09
❑	267	Marc Wilkins	.30	.09
❑	268	Alan Benes	.30	.09
❑	269	Dennis Eckersley	.30	.09
❑	270	Ron Gant	.30	.09
❑	271	Aaron Holbert	.30	.09
❑	272	Brian Jordan	.30	.09
❑	273	Ray Lankford	.30	.09
❑	274	John Mabry	.30	.09
❑	275	T.J. Mathews	.30	.09
❑	276	Ozzie Smith	1.25	.35
❑	277	Todd Stottlemyre	.30	.09
❑	278	Mark Sweeney	.30	.09
❑	279	Andy Ashby	.30	.09
❑	280	Steve Finley	.30	.09
❑	281	John Flaherty	.30	.09
❑	282	Chris Gomez	.30	.09
❑	283	Tony Gwynn	1.00	.30
❑	284	Joey Hamilton	.30	.09
❑	285	Rickey Henderson	.75	.23
❑	286	Trevor Hoffman	.30	.09
❑	287	Jason Thompson	.30	.09
❑	288	Fernando Valenzuela	.30	.09
❑	289	Greg Vaughn	.30	.09
❑	290	Barry Bonds	2.00	.60
❑	291	Jay Canizaro	.30	.09
❑	292	Jacob Cruz	.30	.09
❑	293	Shawon Dunston	.30	.09
❑	294	Shawn Estes	.30	.09
❑	295	Mark Gardner	.30	.09
❑	296	Marcus Jensen	.30	.09
❑	297	Bill Mueller RC	1.50	.45
❑	298	Chris Singleton	.30	.09
❑	299	Allen Watson	.30	.09
❑	300	Matt Williams	.30	.09
❑	301	Rod Beck	.30	.09
❑	302	Jay Bell	.30	.09
❑	303	Shawon Dunston	.30	.09
❑	304	Reggie Jefferson	.30	.09
❑	305	Darren Oliver	.30	.09
❑	306	Benito Santiago	.30	.09
❑	307	Gerald Williams	.30	.09
❑	308	Damon Buford	.30	.09
❑	309	Jeromy Burnitz	.30	.09
❑	310	Sterling Hitchcock	.30	.09
❑	311	Dave Hollins	.30	.09
❑	312	Mel Rojas	.30	.09
❑	313	Robin Ventura	.30	.09
❑	314	David Wells	.30	.09
❑	315	Cal Eldred	.30	.09
❑	316	Gary Gaetti	.30	.09
❑	317	John Hudek	.30	.09
❑	318	Brian Johnson	.30	.09
❑	319	Denny Neagle	.30	.09
❑	320	Larry Walker	.30	.09
❑	321	Russ Davis	.30	.09
❑	322	Delino DeShields	.30	.09
❑	323	Charlie Hayes	.30	.09
❑	324	Jermaine Dye	.30	.09
❑	325	John Ericks	.30	.09
❑	326	Jeff Fassero	.30	.09
❑	327	Nomar Garciaparra	1.25	.35
❑	328	Willie Greene	.30	.09
❑	329	Greg McMichael	.30	.09
❑	330	Damion Easley	.30	.09
❑	331	Ricky Bones	.30	.09
❑	332	John Burkett	.30	.09
❑	333	Royce Clayton	.30	.09
❑	334	Greg Colbrunn	.30	.09
❑	335	Tony Eusebio	.30	.09
❑	336	Gregg Jefferies	.30	.09
❑	337	Wally Joyner	.30	.09
❑	338	Jim Leyritz	.30	.09
❑	339	Paul O'Neill	.50	.15
❑	340	Bruce Ruffin	.30	.09
❑	341	Michael Tucker	.30	.09
❑	342	Andy Benes	.30	.09
❑	343	Craig Biggio	.50	.15
❑	344	Rex Hudler	.30	.09
❑	345	Brad Radke	.30	.09
❑	346	Deion Sanders	.50	.15
❑	347	Moises Alou	.30	.09
❑	348	Brad Ausmus	.30	.09
❑	349	Armando Benitez	.30	.09
❑	350	Mark Gubicza	.30	.09
❑	351	Terry Steinbach	.30	.09
❑	352	Mark Whiten	.30	.09
❑	353	Ricky Bottalico	.30	.09
❑	354	Brian Giles RC	1.50	.45
❑	355	Eric Karros	.30	.09
❑	356	Jimmy Key	.30	.09
❑	357	Carlos Perez	.30	.09
❑	358	Alex Fernandez	.30	.09
❑	359	J.T. Snow	.30	.09
❑	360	Bobby Bonilla	.30	.09
❑	361	Scott Brosius	.30	.09
❑	362	Greg Swindell	.30	.09
❑	363	Jose Vizcaino	.30	.09
❑	364	Matt Williams	.30	.09
❑	365	Darren Daulton	.30	.09
❑	366	Shane Andrews	.30	.09
❑	367	Jim Eisenreich	.30	.09
❑	368	Ariel Prieto	.30	.09
❑	369	Bob Tewksbury	.30	.09
❑	370	Mike Bordick	.30	.09
❑	371	Rheal Cormier	.30	.09
❑	372	Cliff Floyd	.30	.09
❑	373	David Justice	.30	.09
❑	374	John Wetteland	.30	.09
❑	375	Mike Blowers	.30	.09
❑	376	Jose Canseco	.50	.15
❑	377	Roger Clemens	1.50	.45
❑	378	Kevin Mitchell	.30	.09
❑	379	Todd Zeile	.30	.09
❑	380	Jim Thome	.50	.15
❑	381	Turk Wendell	.30	.09
❑	382	Rico Brogna	.30	.09
❑	383	Eric Davis	.30	.09
❑	384	Mike Lansing	.30	.09
❑	385	Devon White	.30	.09
❑	386	Marquis Grissom	.30	.09
❑	387	Todd Worrell	.30	.09
❑	388	Jeff Kent	.30	.09
❑	389	Mickey Tettleton	.30	.09
❑	390	Steve Avery	.30	.09
❑	391	David Cone	.30	.09
❑	392	Scott Cooper	.30	.09
❑	393	Lee Stevens	.30	.09

	Card	Nm-Mt	Ex-Mt
❑	394 Kevin Elster	.30	.09
❑	395 Tom Goodwin	.30	.09
❑	396 Shawn Green	.30	.09
❑	397 Pete Harnisch	.30	.09
❑	398 Eddie Murray	.75	.23
❑	399 Joe Randa	.30	.09
❑	400 Scott Sanders	.30	.09
❑	401 John Valentin	.30	.09
❑	402 Todd Jones	.30	.09
❑	403 Terry Adams	.30	.09
❑	404 Brian Hunter	.30	.09
❑	405 Pat Listach	.30	.09
❑	406 Kenny Lofton	.30	.09
❑	407 Hal Morris	.30	.09
❑	408 Ed Sprague	.30	.09
❑	409 Rich Becker	.30	.09
❑	410 Edgardo Alfonzo	.30	.09
❑	411 Albert Belle	.30	.09
❑	412 Jeff King	.30	.09
❑	413 Kirt Manwaring	.30	.09
❑	414 Jason Schmidt	.30	.09
❑	415 Allen Watson	.30	.09
❑	416 Lee Tinsley	.30	.09
❑	417 Brett Butler	.30	.09
❑	418 Carlos Garcia	.30	.09
❑	419 Mark Lemke	.30	.09
❑	420 Jaime Navarro	.30	.09
❑	421 David Segui	.30	.09
❑	422 Ruben Sierra	.30	.09
❑	423 B.J. Surhoff	.30	.09
❑	424 Julian Tavarez	.30	.09
❑	425 Billy Taylor	.30	.09
❑	426 Ken Caminiti	.30	.09
❑	427 Chuck Carr	.30	.09
❑	428 Benji Gil	.30	.09
❑	429 Terry Mulholland	.30	.09
❑	430 Mike Stanton	.30	.09
❑	431 Wil Cordero	.30	.09
❑	432 Chili Davis	.30	.09
❑	433 Mariano Duncan	.30	.09
❑	434 Orlando Merced	.30	.09
❑	435 Kent Mercker	.30	.09
❑	436 John Olerud	.30	.09
❑	437 Quilvio Veras	.30	.09
❑	438 Mike Fetters	.30	.09
❑	439 Glenallen Hill	.30	.09
❑	440 Bill Swift	.30	.09
❑	441 Tim Wakefield	.30	.09
❑	442 Pedro Astacio	.30	.09
❑	443 Vinny Castilla	.30	.09
❑	444 Doug Drabek	.30	.09
❑	445 Alan Embree	.30	.09
❑	446 Lee Smith	.30	.09
❑	447 Darryl Hamilton	.30	.09
❑	448 Brian McRae	.30	.09
❑	449 Mike Timlin	.30	.09
❑	450 Bob Wickman	.30	.09
❑	451 Jason Dickson	.30	.09
❑	452 Chad Curtis	.30	.09
❑	453 Mark Leiter	.30	.09
❑	454 Damon Berryhill	.30	.09
❑	455 Kevin Orie	.30	.09
❑	456 Dave Burba	.30	.09
❑	457 Chris Holt	.30	.09
❑	458 Ricky Ledee RC	.40	.12
❑	459 Mike Devereaux	.30	.09
❑	460 Pokey Reese	.30	.09
❑	461 Tim Raines	.30	.09
❑	462 Ryan Jones	.30	.09
❑	463 Shane Mack	.30	.09
❑	464 Darren Dreifort	.30	.09
❑	465 Mark Parent	.30	.09
❑	466 Mark Portugal	.30	.09
❑	467 Dante Powell	.30	.09
❑	468 Craig Grebeck	.30	.09
❑	469 Ron Villone	.30	.09
❑	470 Dmitri Young	.30	.09
❑	471 Shannon Stewart	.30	.09
❑	472 Rick Helling	.30	.09
❑	473 Bill Haselman	.30	.09
❑	474 Albie Lopez	.30	.09
❑	475 Glendon Rusch	.30	.09
❑	476 Derrick May	.30	.09
❑	477 Chad Ogea	.30	.09
❑	478 Kirk Rueter	.30	.09
❑	479 Chris Hammond	.30	.09
❑	480 Russ Johnson	.30	.09
❑	481 James Mouton	.30	.09
❑	482 Mike Macfarlane	.30	.09
❑	483 Scott Ruffcorn	.30	.09
❑	484 Jeff Frye	.30	.09
❑	485 Richie Sexson	.30	.09
❑	486 Emil Brown RC	.40	.12
❑	487 Desi Wilson	.30	.09
❑	488 Brent Gates	.30	.09
❑	489 Tony Graffanino	.30	.09
❑	490 Dan Miceli	.30	.09
❑	491 Orlando Cabrera RC	1.00	.30
❑	492 Tony Womack RC	.60	.18
❑	493 Jerome Walton	.30	.09
❑	494 Mark Thompson	.30	.09
❑	495 Jose Guillen	.30	.09
❑	496 Willie Blair	.30	.09
❑	497 T.J. Staton RC	.40	.12
❑	498 Scott Kamieniecki	.30	.09
❑	499 Vince Coleman	.30	.09
❑	500 Jeff Abbott	.30	.09
❑	501 Chris Widger	.30	.09
❑	502 Kevin Tapani	.30	.09
❑	503 Carlos Castillo RC	.40	.12
❑	504 Luis Gonzalez	.30	.09
❑	505 Tim Belcher	.30	.09
❑	506 Armando Reynoso	.30	.09
❑	507 Jamie Moyer	.30	.09
❑	508 Randall Simon RC	.40	.12
❑	509 Vladimir Guerrero	.75	.23
❑	510 Wady Almonte RC	.40	.12
❑	511 Dustin Hermanson	.30	.09
❑	512 Deivi Cruz RC	.40	.12
❑	513 Luis Alicea	.30	.09
❑	514 Felix Heredia RC	.40	.12
❑	515 Don Slaught	.30	.09
❑	516 S.Hasegawa RC	.60	.18
❑	517 Matt Walbeck	.30	.09
❑	518 David Arias-Ortiz RC	30.00	9.00
❑	519 Brady Raggio RC	.40	.12
❑	520 Rudy Pemberton	.30	.09
❑	521 Wayne Kirby	.30	.09
❑	522 Calvin Maduro	.30	.09
❑	523 Mark Lewis	.30	.09
❑	524 Mike Jackson	.30	.09
❑	525 Sid Fernandez	.30	.09
❑	526 Mike Bielecki	.30	.09
❑	527 Bubba Trammell RC	.40	.12
❑	528 Brent Brede RC	.40	.12
❑	529 Matt Morris	.30	.09
❑	530 Joe Borowski RC	.40	.12
❑	531 Orlando Miller	.30	.09
❑	532 Jim Bullinger	.30	.09
❑	533 Robert Person	.30	.09
❑	534 Doug Glanville	.30	.09
❑	535 Terry Pendleton	.30	.09
❑	536 Jorge Posada	.50	.15
❑	537 Marc Sagmoen RC	.40	.12
❑	538 Fernando Tatis RC	.40	.12
❑	539 Aaron Sele	.30	.09
❑	540 Brian Banks	.30	.09
❑	541 Derrek Lee	.50	.15
❑	542 John Wasdin	.30	.09
❑	543 Justin Towle RC	.40	.12
❑	544 Pat Cline	.30	.09
❑	545 Dave Magadan	.30	.09
❑	546 Jeff Blauser	.30	.09
❑	547 Phil Nevin	.30	.09
❑	548 Todd Walker	.30	.09
❑	549 Eli Marrero	.30	.09
❑	550 Bartolo Colon	.30	.09
❑	551 Jose Cruz Jr. RC	.60	.18
❑	552 Todd Dunwoody	.30	.09
❑	553 Hideki Irabu RC	.40	.12
❑	P11 Cal Ripken Promo Three Card Strip	2.00	.60

1998 Ultra

	Nm-Mt	Ex-Mt
COMPLETE SET (501)	160.00	47.50
COMP.SERIES 1 (250)	100.00	30.00
COMP.SERIES 2 (251)	60.00	18.00
COMP.SER.1 w/o SP's (210)	15.00	4.50
COMP.SER.2 w/o SP's (226)	15.00	4.50
COMMON (1-220/246-250)	.30	.09
COMMON (251-475/501)	.30	.09
COMMON SC (211-220)	2.00	.60
COMMON PROS (221-245)	3.00	.90
COMMON PZ (476-500)	1.00	.30

	Card	Nm-Mt	Ex-Mt
❑	1 Ken Griffey Jr.	1.25	.35
❑	2 Matt Morris	.30	.09
❑	3 Roger Clemens	1.50	.45
❑	4 Matt Williams	.30	.09
❑	5 Roberto Hernandez	.30	.09
❑	6 Rondell White	.30	.09
❑	7 Tim Salmon	.50	.15
❑	8 Brad Radke	.30	.09
❑	9 Brett Butler	.30	.09
❑	10 Carl Everett	.30	.09
❑	11 Chili Davis	.30	.09
❑	12 Chuck Finley	.30	.09
❑	13 Darryl Kile	.30	.09
❑	14 Deivi Cruz	.30	.09
❑	15 Gary Gaetti	.30	.09
❑	16 Matt Stairs	.30	.09
❑	17 Pat Meares	.30	.09
❑	18 Will Cunnane	.30	.09
❑	19 Steve Woodard	.30	.09
❑	20 Andy Ashby	.30	.09
❑	21 Bobby Higginson	.30	.09
❑	22 Brian Jordan	.30	.09
❑	23 Craig Biggio	.50	.15
❑	24 Jim Edmonds	.30	.09
❑	25 Ryan McGuire	.30	.09
❑	26 Scott Hatteberg	.30	.09
❑	27 Willie Greene	.30	.09
❑	28 Albert Belle	.30	.09
❑	29 Ellis Burks	.30	.09
❑	30 Hideo Nomo	.75	.23
❑	31 Jeff Bagwell	.50	.15
❑	32 Kevin Brown	.50	.15
❑	33 Nomar Garciaparra	1.25	.35
❑	34 Pedro Martinez	.50	.15
❑	35 Raul Mondesi	.30	.09
❑	36 Ricky Bottalico	.30	.09
❑	37 Shawn Estes	.30	.09
❑	38 Otis Nixon	.30	.09
❑	39 Terry Steinbach	.30	.09
❑	40 Tom Glavine	.50	.15
❑	41 Todd Dunwoody	.30	.09
❑	42 Deion Sanders	.50	.15
❑	43 Gary Sheffield	.30	.09
❑	44 Mike Lansing	.30	.09
❑	45 Mike Lieberthal	.30	.09
❑	46 Paul Sorrento	.30	.09
❑	47 Paul O'Neill	.50	.15
❑	48 Tom Goodwin	.30	.09
❑	49 Andruw Jones	.50	.15
❑	50 Barry Bonds	2.00	.60
❑	51 Bernie Williams	.50	.15
❑	52 Jeremi Gonzalez	.30	.09
❑	53 Mike Piazza	1.25	.35
❑	54 Russ Davis	.30	.09
❑	55 Vinny Castilla	.30	.09
❑	56 Rod Beck	.30	.09
❑	57 Andres Galarraga	.30	.09
❑	58 Ben McDonald	.30	.09
❑	59 Billy Wagner	.30	.09
❑	60 Charles Johnson	.30	.09
❑	61 Fred McGriff	.50	.15
❑	62 Dean Palmer	.30	.09
❑	63 Frank Thomas	.75	.23
❑	64 Ismael Valdes	.30	.09

❑ 65 Mark Bellhorn .30 .09
❑ 66 Jeff King .30 .09
❑ 67 John Wetteland .30 .09
❑ 68 Mark Grace .50 .15
❑ 69 Mark Kotsay .30 .09
❑ 70 Scott Rolen .50 .15
❑ 71 Todd Hundley .30 .09
❑ 72 Todd Worrell .30 .09
❑ 73 Wilson Alvarez .30 .09
❑ 74 Bobby Jones .30 .09
❑ 75 Jose Canseco .50 .15
❑ 76 Kevin Appier .30 .09
❑ 77 Neifi Perez .30 .09
❑ 78 Paul Molitor .50 .15
❑ 79 Quilvio Veras .30 .09
❑ 80 Randy Johnson .75 .23
❑ 81 Glendon Rusch .30 .09
❑ 82 Curt Schilling .30 .09
❑ 83 Alex Rodriguez 1.25 .35
❑ 84 Rey Ordonez .30 .09
❑ 85 Jeff Juden .30 .09
❑ 86 Mike Cameron .30 .09
❑ 87 Ryan Klesko .30 .09
❑ 88 Trevor Hoffman .30 .09
❑ 89 Chuck Knoblauch .30 .09
❑ 90 Larry Walker .30 .09
❑ 91 Mark McLemore .30 .09
❑ 92 B.J. Surhoff .30 .09
❑ 93 Darren Daulton .30 .09
❑ 94 Ray Durham .30 .09
❑ 95 Sammy Sosa .75 .23
❑ 96 Eric Young .30 .09
❑ 97 Gerald Williams .30 .09
❑ 98 Javy Lopez .30 .09
❑ 99 John Smiley .30 .09
❑ 100 Juan Gonzalez .30 .09
❑ 101 Shawn Green .30 .09
❑ 102 Charles Nagy .30 .09
❑ 103 David Justice .30 .09
❑ 104 Joey Hamilton .30 .09
❑ 105 Pat Hentgen .30 .09
❑ 106 Raul Casanova .30 .09
❑ 107 Tony Phillips .30 .09
❑ 108 Tony Gwynn 1.00 .30
❑ 109 Will Clark .50 .15
❑ 110 Jason Giambi .30 .09
❑ 111 Jay Bell .30 .09
❑ 112 Johnny Damon .50 .15
❑ 113 Alan Benes .30 .09
❑ 114 Jeff Suppan .30 .09
❑ 115 Kevin Polcovich .30 .09
❑ 116 Shigetoshi Hasegawa .30 .09
❑ 117 Steve Finley .30 .09
❑ 118 Tony Clark .30 .09
❑ 119 David Cone .30 .09
❑ 120 Jose Guillen .30 .09
❑ 121 Kevin Millwood RC .60 .18
❑ 122 Greg Maddux 1.25 .35
❑ 123 Dave Nilsson .30 .09
❑ 124 Hideki Irabu .30 .09
❑ 125 Jason Kendall .30 .09
❑ 126 Jim Thome .50 .15
❑ 127 Delino DeShields .30 .09
❑ 128 Edgar Renteria .30 .09
❑ 129 Edgardo Alfonzo .30 .09
❑ 130 J.T. Snow .30 .09
❑ 131 Jeff Abbott .30 .09
❑ 132 Jeffrey Hammonds .30 .09
❑ 133 Todd Greene .30 .09
❑ 134 Vladimir Guerrero .75 .23
❑ 135 Jay Buhner .30 .09
❑ 136 Jeff Cirillo .30 .09
❑ 137 Jeromy Burnitz .30 .09
❑ 138 Mickey Morandini .30 .09
❑ 139 Tino Martinez .50 .15
❑ 140 Jeff Shaw .30 .09
❑ 141 Rafael Palmeiro .50 .15
❑ 142 Bobby Bonilla .30 .09
❑ 143 Cal Ripken 2.50 .75
❑ 144 Chad Fox RC .30 .09
❑ 145 Dante Bichette .30 .09
❑ 146 Dennis Eckersley .30 .09
❑ 147 Mariano Rivera .50 .15
❑ 148 Mo Vaughn .30 .09
❑ 149 Reggie Sanders .30 .09
❑ 150 Derek Jeter 2.00 .60
❑ 151 Rusty Greer .30 .09
❑ 152 Brady Anderson .30 .09
❑ 153 Brett Tomko .30 .09
❑ 154 Jaime Navarro .30 .09
❑ 155 Kevin Orie .30 .09
❑ 156 Roberto Alomar .50 .15
❑ 157 Edgar Martinez .50 .15
❑ 158 John Olerud .30 .09
❑ 159 John Smoltz .50 .15
❑ 160 Ryne Sandberg 1.25 .35
❑ 161 Billy Taylor .30 .09
❑ 162 Chris Holt .30 .09
❑ 163 Damion Easley .30 .09
❑ 164 Darin Erstad .30 .09
❑ 165 Joe Carter .30 .09
❑ 166 Kelvim Escobar .30 .09
❑ 167 Ken Caminiti .30 .09
❑ 168 Pokey Reese .30 .09
❑ 169 Ray Lankford .30 .09
❑ 170 Livan Hernandez .30 .09
❑ 171 Steve Kline .30 .09
❑ 172 Tom Gordon .30 .09
❑ 173 Travis Fryman .30 .09
❑ 174 Al Martin .30 .09
❑ 175 Andy Pettitte .50 .15
❑ 176 Jeff Kent .30 .09
❑ 177 Jimmy Key .30 .09
❑ 178 Mark Grudzielanek .30 .09
❑ 179 Tony Saunders .30 .09
❑ 180 Barry Larkin .50 .15
❑ 181 Bubba Trammell .30 .09
❑ 182 Carlos Delgado .30 .09
❑ 183 Carlos Baerga .30 .09
❑ 184 Derek Bell .30 .09
❑ 185 Henry Rodriguez .30 .09
❑ 186 Jason Dickson .30 .09
❑ 187 Ron Gant .30 .09
❑ 188 Tony Womack .30 .09
❑ 189 Justin Thompson .30 .09
❑ 190 Fernando Tatis .30 .09
❑ 191 Mark Wohlers .30 .09
❑ 192 Takashi Kashiwada .30 .09
❑ 193 Garret Anderson .30 .09
❑ 194 Jose Cruz Jr. .30 .09
❑ 195 Ricardo Rincon .30 .09
❑ 196 Tim Naehring .30 .09
❑ 197 Moises Alou .30 .09
❑ 198 Eric Karros .30 .09
❑ 199 John Jaha .30 .09
❑ 200 Marty Cordova .30 .09
❑ 201 Ken Hill .30 .09
❑ 202 Chipper Jones .75 .23
❑ 203 Kenny Lofton .30 .09
❑ 204 Mike Mussina .50 .15
❑ 205 Manny Ramirez .50 .15
❑ 206 Todd Hollandsworth .30 .09
❑ 207 Cecil Fielder .30 .09
❑ 208 Mark McGwire 2.00 .60
❑ 209 Jim Leyritz .30 .09
❑ 210 Ivan Rodriguez .50 .15
❑ 211 Jeff Bagwell SC 2.00 .60
❑ 212 Barry Bonds SC 8.00 2.40
❑ 213 Roger Clemens SC 6.00 1.80
❑ 214 N.Garciaparra SC 5.00 1.50
❑ 215 Ken Griffey Jr. SC 5.00 1.50
❑ 216 Tony Gwynn SC 4.00 1.20
❑ 217 Randy Johnson SC 3.00 .90
❑ 218 Mark McGwire SC 8.00 2.40
❑ 219 Scott Rolen SC 2.00 .60
❑ 220 Frank Thomas SC 3.00 .90
❑ 221 Matt Perisho PROS 3.00 .90
❑ 222 Wes Helms PROS 3.00 .90
❑ 223 D.Dellucci PROS RC 3.00 .90
❑ 224 Todd Helton PROS 3.00 .90
❑ 225 Brian Rose PROS 3.00 .90
❑ 226 Aaron Boone PROS 3.00 .90
❑ 227 Keith Foulke PROS 3.00 .90
❑ 228 Homer Bush PROS 3.00 .90
❑ 229 S.Stewart PROS 3.00 .90
❑ 230 R.Hidalgo PROS 3.00 .90
❑ 231 Russ Johnson PROS 3.00 .90
❑ 232 H.Blanco PROS RC 3.00 .90
❑ 233 Paul Konerko PROS 3.00 .90
❑ 234 A.Williamson PROS 3.00 .90
❑ 235 S.Bowers PROS RC 3.00 .90
❑ 236 Jose Vidro PROS 3.00 .90
❑ 237 Derek Wallace PROS 3.00 .90
❑ 238 Ricky Ledee PROS SP 5.00 1.50
❑ 239 Ben Grieve PROS 3.00 .90
❑ 240 Lou Collier PROS 3.00 .90
❑ 241 Derrek Lee PROS 3.00 .90
❑ 242 Ruben Rivera PROS 3.00 .90
❑ 243 J.Velandia PROS SP 5.00 1.50
❑ 244 Andrew Vessel PROS 3.00 .90
❑ 245 Chris Carpenter PROS 3.00 .90
❑ 246 Ken Griffey Jr. CL .75 .23
❑ 247 Alex Rodriguez CL .75 .23
❑ 248 Diamond Ink CL .30 .09
❑ 249 Frank Thomas CL .50 .15
❑ 250 Cal Ripken CL 1.25 .35
❑ 251 Carlos Perez .30 .09
❑ 252 Larry Sutton .30 .09
❑ 253 Gary Sheffield .30 .09
❑ 254 Wally Joyner .30 .09
❑ 255 Todd Stottlemyre .30 .09
❑ 256 Nerio Rodriguez .30 .09
❑ 257 Charles Johnson .30 .09
❑ 258 Pedro Astacio .30 .09
❑ 259 Cal Eldred .30 .09
❑ 260 Chili Davis .30 .09
❑ 261 Freddy Garcia .30 .09
❑ 262 Bobby Witt .30 .09
❑ 263 Michael Coleman .30 .09
❑ 264 Mike Caruso .30 .09
❑ 265 Mike Lansing .30 .09
❑ 266 Dennis Reyes .30 .09
❑ 267 F.P. Santangelo .30 .09
❑ 268 Darryl Hamilton .30 .09
❑ 269 Mike Fetters .30 .09
❑ 270 Charlie Hayes .30 .09
❑ 271 Royce Clayton .30 .09
❑ 272 Doug Drabek .30 .09
❑ 273 James Baldwin .30 .09
❑ 274 Brian Hunter .30 .09
❑ 275 Chan Ho Park .30 .09
❑ 276 John Franco .30 .09
❑ 277 David Wells .30 .09
❑ 278 Eli Marrero .30 .09
❑ 279 Kerry Wood .50 .15
❑ 280 Donnie Sadler .30 .09
❑ 281 Scott Winchester RC .30 .09
❑ 282 Hal Morris .30 .09
❑ 283 Brad Fullmer .30 .09
❑ 284 Bernard Gilkey .30 .09
❑ 285 Ramiro Mendoza .30 .09
❑ 286 Kevin Brown .50 .15
❑ 287 David Segui .30 .09
❑ 288 Willie McGee .30 .09
❑ 289 Darren Oliver .30 .09
❑ 290 Antonio Alfonseca .30 .09
❑ 291 Eric Davis .30 .09
❑ 292 Mickey Morandini .30 .09
❑ 293 Frank Catalanotto RC .60 .18
❑ 294 Derrek Lee .50 .15
❑ 295 Todd Zeile .30 .09
❑ 296 Chuck Knoblauch .30 .09
❑ 297 Wilson Delgado .30 .09
❑ 298 Bobby Bonilla .30 .09
❑ 299 Orel Hershiser .30 .09
❑ 300 Ozzie Guillen .30 .09
❑ 301 Aaron Sele .30 .09
❑ 302 Joe Carter .30 .09
❑ 303 Darryl Kile .30 .09
❑ 304 Shane Reynolds .30 .09
❑ 305 Todd Dunn .30 .09
❑ 306 Bob Abreu .30 .09
❑ 307 Doug Strange .30 .09
❑ 308 Jose Canseco .50 .15
❑ 309 Lance Johnson .30 .09
❑ 310 Harold Baines .30 .09
❑ 311 Todd Pratt .30 .09
❑ 312 Greg Colbrunn .30 .09
❑ 313 Masato Yoshii RC .60 .18
❑ 314 Felix Heredia .30 .09
❑ 315 Dennis Martinez .30 .09
❑ 316 Geronimo Berroa .30 .09
❑ 317 Darren Lewis .30 .09
❑ 318 Bill Ripken .30 .09
❑ 319 Enrique Wilson .30 .09
❑ 320 Alex Ochoa .30 .09
❑ 321 Doug Glanville .30 .09
❑ 322 Mike Stanley .30 .09

	Card	Nm-Mt	Ex-Mt
❑	323 Gerald Williams	.30	.09
❑	324 Pedro Martinez	.50	.15
❑	325 Jaret Wright	.30	.09
❑	326 Terry Pendleton	.30	.09
❑	327 LaTroy Hawkins	.30	.09
❑	328 Emil Brown	.30	.09
❑	329 Walt Weiss	.30	.09
❑	330 Omar Vizquel	.50	.15
❑	331 Carl Everett	.30	.09
❑	332 Fernando Vina	.30	.09
❑	333 Mike Blowers	.30	.09
❑	334 Dwight Gooden	.30	.09
❑	335 Mark Lewis	.30	.09
❑	336 Jim Leyritz	.30	.09
❑	337 Kenny Lofton	.30	.09
❑	338 John Halama RC	.40	.12
❑	339 Jose Valentin	.30	.09
❑	340 Desi Relaford	.30	.09
❑	341 Dante Powell	.30	.09
❑	342 Ed Sprague	.30	.09
❑	343 Reggie Jefferson	.30	.09
❑	344 Mike Hampton	.30	.09
❑	345 Marquis Grissom	.30	.09
❑	346 Heathcliff Slocumb	.30	.09
❑	347 Francisco Cordova	.30	.09
❑	348 Ken Cloude	.30	.09
❑	349 Benito Santiago	.30	.09
❑	350 Denny Neagle	.30	.09
❑	351 Sean Casey	.50	.15
❑	352 Robb Nen	.30	.09
❑	353 Orlando Merced	.30	.09
❑	354 Adrian Brown	.30	.09
❑	355 Gregg Jefferies	.30	.09
❑	356 Otis Nixon	.30	.09
❑	357 Michael Tucker	.30	.09
❑	358 Eric Milton	.30	.09
❑	359 Travis Fryman	.30	.09
❑	360 Gary DiSarcina	.30	.09
❑	361 Mario Valdez	.30	.09
❑	362 Craig Counsell	.30	.09
❑	363 Jose Offerman	.30	.09
❑	364 Tony Fernandez	.30	.09
❑	365 Jason McDonald	.30	.09
❑	366 Sterling Hitchcock	.30	.09
❑	367 Donovan Osborne	.30	.09
❑	368 Troy Percival	.30	.09
❑	369 Henry Rodriguez	.30	.09
❑	370 Dmitri Young	.30	.09
❑	371 Jay Powell	.30	.09
❑	372 Jeff Conine	.30	.09
❑	373 Orlando Cabrera	.30	.09
❑	374 Butch Huskey	.30	.09
❑	375 Mike Lowell RC	1.00	.30
❑	376 Kevin Young	.30	.09
❑	377 Jamie Moyer	.30	.09
❑	378 Jeff D'Amico	.30	.09
❑	379 Scott Erickson	.30	.09
❑	380 Magglio Ordonez RC	2.00	.60
❑	381 Melvin Nieves	.30	.09
❑	382 Ramon Martinez	.30	.09
❑	383 A.J. Hinch	.30	.09
❑	384 Jeff Brantley	.30	.09
❑	385 Kevin Elster	.30	.09
❑	386 Allen Watson	.30	.09
❑	387 Moises Alou	.30	.09
❑	388 Jeff Blauser	.30	.09
❑	389 Pete Harnisch	.30	.09
❑	390 Shane Andrews	.30	.09
❑	391 Rico Brogna	.30	.09
❑	392 Stan Javier	.30	.09
❑	393 David Howard	.30	.09
❑	394 Darryl Strawberry	.30	.09
❑	395 Kent Mercker	.30	.09
❑	396 Juan Encarnacion	.30	.09
❑	397 Sandy Alomar Jr.	.30	.09
❑	398 Al Leiter	.30	.09
❑	399 Tony Graffanino	.30	.09
❑	400 Terry Adams	.30	.09
❑	401 Bruce Aven	.30	.09
❑	402 Derrick Gibson	.30	.09
❑	403 Jose Cabrera RC	.30	.09
❑	404 Rich Becker	.30	.09
❑	405 David Ortiz	.75	.23
❑	406 Brian McRae	.30	.09
❑	407 Bobby Estalella	.30	.09
❑	408 Bill Mueller	.30	.09
❑	409 Dennis Eckersley	.30	.09
❑	410 Sandy Martinez	.30	.09
❑	411 Jose Vizcaino	.30	.09
❑	412 Jermaine Allensworth	.30	.09
❑	413 Miguel Tejada	.75	.23
❑	414 Turner Ward	.30	.09
❑	415 Glenallen Hill	.30	.09
❑	416 Lee Stevens	.30	.09
❑	417 Cecil Fielder	.30	.09
❑	418 Ruben Sierra	.30	.09
❑	419 Jon Nunnally	.30	.09
❑	420 Rod Myers	.30	.09
❑	421 Dustin Hermanson	.30	.09
❑	422 James Mouton	.30	.09
❑	423 Dan Wilson	.30	.09
❑	424 Roberto Kelly	.30	.09
❑	425 Antonio Osuna	.30	.09
❑	426 Jacob Cruz	.30	.09
❑	427 Brent Mayne	.30	.09
❑	428 Matt Karchner	.30	.09
❑	429 Damian Jackson	.30	.09
❑	430 Roger Cedeno	.30	.09
❑	431 Rickey Henderson	.75	.23
❑	432 Joe Randa	.30	.09
❑	433 Greg Vaughn	.30	.09
❑	434 Andres Galarraga	.30	.09
❑	435 Rod Beck	.30	.09
❑	436 Curtis Goodwin	.30	.09
❑	437 Brad Ausmus	.30	.09
❑	438 Bob Hamelin	.30	.09
❑	439 Todd Walker	.30	.09
❑	440 Scott Brosius	.30	.09
❑	441 Len Dykstra	.30	.09
❑	442 Abraham Nunez	.30	.09
❑	443 Brian Johnson	.30	.09
❑	444 Randy Myers	.30	.09
❑	445 Bret Boone	.30	.09
❑	446 Oscar Henriquez	.30	.09
❑	447 Mike Sweeney	.30	.09
❑	448 Kenny Rogers	.30	.09
❑	449 Mark Langston	.30	.09
❑	450 Luis Gonzalez	.30	.09
❑	451 John Burkett	.30	.09
❑	452 Bip Roberts	.30	.09
❑	453 Travis Lee	.30	.09
❑	454 Felix Rodriguez	.30	.09
❑	455 Andy Benes	.30	.09
❑	456 Willie Blair	.30	.09
❑	457 Brian Anderson	.30	.09
❑	458 Jay Bell	.30	.09
❑	459 Matt Williams	.30	.09
❑	460 Devon White	.30	.09
❑	461 Karim Garcia	.30	.09
❑	462 Jorge Fabregas	.30	.09
❑	463 Wilson Alvarez	.30	.09
❑	464 Roberto Hernandez	.30	.09
❑	465 Tony Saunders	.30	.09
❑	466 Rolando Arrojo RC	.40	.12
❑	467 Wade Boggs	.75	.23
❑	468 Fred McGriff	.50	.15
❑	469 Paul Sorrento	.30	.09
❑	470 Kevin Stocker	.30	.09
❑	471 Bubba Trammell	.30	.09
❑	472 Quinton McCracken	.30	.09
❑	473 Ken Griffey Jr. CL	.75	.23
❑	474 Cal Ripken CL	1.25	.35
❑	475 Frank Thomas CL	.50	.15
❑	476 Ken Griffey Jr. PZ	4.00	1.20
❑	477 Cal Ripken PZ	8.00	2.40
❑	478 Frank Thomas PZ	2.50	.75
❑	479 Alex Rodriguez PZ	4.00	1.20
❑	480 Nomar Garciaparra PZ	4.00	1.20
❑	481 Derek Jeter PZ	6.00	1.80
❑	482 Andruw Jones PZ	1.50	.45
❑	483 Chipper Jones PZ	2.50	.75
❑	484 Greg Maddux PZ	4.00	1.20
❑	485 Mike Piazza PZ	4.00	1.20
❑	486 Juan Gonzalez PZ	1.00	.30
❑	487 Jose Cruz Jr. PZ	1.00	.30
❑	488 Jaret Wright PZ	1.00	.30
❑	489 Hideo Nomo PZ	2.50	.75
❑	490 Scott Rolen PZ	1.50	.45
❑	491 Tony Gwynn PZ	3.00	.90
❑	492 Roger Clemens PZ	5.00	1.50
❑	493 Darin Erstad PZ	1.00	.30
❑	494 Mark McGwire PZ	6.00	1.80
❑	495 Jeff Bagwell PZ	1.50	.45
❑	496 Mo Vaughn PZ	1.00	.30
❑	497 Albert Belle PZ	1.00	.30
❑	498 Kenny Lofton PZ	1.00	.30
❑	499 Ben Grieve PZ	1.00	.30
❑	500 Barry Bonds PZ	6.00	1.80
❑	501 Mike Piazza	1.25	.35
❑	S100 A.Rodriguez AU/750	120.00	36.00

2001 Ultra

	Nm-Mt	Ex-Mt
COMPLETE SET (275)	120.00	36.00
COMP.SET w/o SP's (250)	25.00	7.50
COMMON CARD (1-250)	.30	.09
COMMON (251-275)	3.00	.90
COMMON (276-280)	5.00	1.50

	Card	Nm-Mt	Ex-Mt
❑	1 Pedro Martinez	.50	.15
❑	2 Derek Jeter	2.00	.60
❑	3 Cal Ripken	2.50	.75
❑	4 Alex Rodriguez	1.25	.35
❑	5 Vladimir Guerrero	.75	.23
❑	6 Troy Glaus	.30	.09
❑	7 Sammy Sosa	.75	.23
❑	8 Mike Piazza	1.25	.35
❑	9 Tony Gwynn	1.00	.30
❑	10 Tim Hudson	.30	.09
❑	11 John Flaherty	.30	.09
❑	12 Jeff Cirillo	.30	.09
❑	13 Ellis Burks	.30	.09
❑	14 Carlos Lee	.30	.09
❑	15 Carlos Beltran	.30	.09
❑	16 Ruben Rivera	.30	.09
❑	17 Richard Hidalgo	.30	.09
❑	18 Omar Vizquel	.50	.15
❑	19 Michael Barrett	.30	.09
❑	20 Jose Canseco	.50	.15
❑	21 Jason Giambi	.30	.09
❑	22 Greg Maddux	1.25	.35
❑	23 Charles Johnson	.30	.09
❑	24 Sandy Alomar Jr.	.30	.09
❑	25 Rick Ankiel	.30	.09
❑	26 Richie Sexson	.30	.09
❑	27 Matt Williams	.30	.09
❑	28 Joe Girardi	.30	.09
❑	29 Jason Kendall	.30	.09
❑	30 Brad Fullmer	.30	.09
❑	31 Alex Gonzalez	.30	.09
❑	32 Rick Helling	.30	.09
❑	33 Mike Mussina	.50	.15
❑	34 Joe Randa	.30	.09
❑	35 J.T. Snow	.30	.09
❑	36 Edgardo Alfonzo	.30	.09
❑	37 Dante Bichette	.30	.09
❑	38 Brad Ausmus	.30	.09
❑	39 Bobby Abreu	.30	.09
❑	40 Warren Morris	.30	.09
❑	41 Tony Womack	.30	.09
❑	42 Russell Branyan	.30	.09
❑	43 Mike Lowell	.30	.09
❑	44 Mark Grace	.50	.15
❑	45 Jeromy Burnitz	.30	.09
❑	46 J.D. Drew	.30	.09
❑	47 David Justice	.30	.09
❑	48 Alex Gonzalez	.30	.09
❑	49 Tino Martinez	.50	.15
❑	50 Raul Mondesi	.30	.09
❑	51 Rafael Furcal	.30	.09
❑	52 Marquis Grissom	.30	.09

❑ 53 Kevin Young .30 .09
❑ 54 Jon Lieber .30 .09
❑ 55 Henry Rodriguez .30 .09
❑ 56 Dave Burba .30 .09
❑ 57 Shannon Stewart .30 .09
❑ 58 Preston Wilson .30 .09
❑ 59 Paul O'Neill .50 .15
❑ 60 Jimmy Haynes .30 .09
❑ 61 Darryl Kile .30 .09
❑ 62 Bret Boone .30 .09
❑ 63 Bartolo Colon .30 .09
❑ 64 Andres Galarraga .30 .09
❑ 65 Trot Nixon .30 .09
❑ 66 Steve Finley .30 .09
❑ 67 Shawn Green .30 .09
❑ 68 Robert Person .30 .09
❑ 69 Kenny Rogers .30 .09
❑ 70 Bobby Higginson .30 .09
❑ 71 Barry Larkin .50 .15
❑ 72 Al Martin .30 .09
❑ 73 Tom Glavine .50 .15
❑ 74 Rondell White .30 .09
❑ 75 Ray Lankford .30 .09
❑ 76 Moises Alou .30 .09
❑ 77 Matt Clement .30 .09
❑ 78 Geoff Jenkins .30 .09
❑ 79 David Wells .30 .09
❑ 80 Chuck Finley .30 .09
❑ 81 Andy Pettitte .50 .15
❑ 82 Travis Fryman .30 .09
❑ 83 Ron Coomer .30 .09
❑ 84 Mark McGwire 2.00 .60
❑ 85 Kerry Wood .30 .09
❑ 86 Jorge Posada .50 .15
❑ 87 Jeff Bagwell .50 .15
❑ 88 Andruw Jones .50 .15
❑ 89 Ryan Klesko .30 .09
❑ 90 Mariano Rivera .50 .15
❑ 91 Lance Berkman .30 .09
❑ 92 Kenny Lofton .30 .09
❑ 93 Jacque Jones .30 .09
❑ 94 Eric Young .30 .09
❑ 95 Edgar Renteria .30 .09
❑ 96 Chipper Jones .75 .23
❑ 97 Todd Helton .50 .15
❑ 98 Shawn Estes .30 .09
❑ 99 Mark Mulder .30 .09
❑ 100 Lee Stevens .30 .09
❑ 101 Jermaine Dye .30 .09
❑ 102 Greg Vaughn .30 .09
❑ 103 Chris Singleton .30 .09
❑ 104 Brady Anderson .30 .09
❑ 105 Terrence Long .30 .09
❑ 106 Quilvio Veras .30 .09
❑ 107 Magglio Ordonez .30 .09
❑ 108 Johnny Damon .50 .15
❑ 109 Jeffrey Hammonds .30 .09
❑ 110 Fred McGriff .50 .15
❑ 111 Carl Pavano .30 .09
❑ 112 Bobby Estalella .30 .09
❑ 113 Todd Hundley .30 .09
❑ 114 Scott Rolen .50 .15
❑ 115 Robin Ventura .30 .09
❑ 116 Pokey Reese .30 .09
❑ 117 Luis Gonzalez .30 .09
❑ 118 Jose Offerman .30 .09
❑ 119 Edgar Martinez .50 .15
❑ 120 Dean Palmer .30 .09
❑ 121 David Segui .30 .09
❑ 122 Troy O'Leary .30 .09
❑ 123 Tony Batista .30 .09
❑ 124 Todd Zeile .30 .09
❑ 125 Randy Johnson .75 .23
❑ 126 Luis Castillo .30 .09
❑ 127 Kris Benson .30 .09
❑ 128 John Olerud .30 .09
❑ 129 Eric Karros .30 .09
❑ 130 Eddie Taubensee .30 .09
❑ 131 Neifi Perez .30 .09
❑ 132 Matt Stairs .30 .09
❑ 133 Luis Alicea .30 .09
❑ 134 Jeff Kent .30 .09
❑ 135 Javier Vazquez .30 .09
❑ 136 Garret Anderson .30 .09
❑ 137 Frank Thomas .75 .23
❑ 138 Carlos Febles .30 .09
❑ 139 Albert Belle .30 .09
❑ 140 Tony Clark .30 .09
❑ 141 Pat Burrell .30 .09
❑ 142 Mike Sweeney .30 .09
❑ 143 Jay Buhner .30 .09
❑ 144 Gabe Kapler .30 .09
❑ 145 Derek Bell .30 .09
❑ 146 B.J. Surhoff .30 .09
❑ 147 Adam Kennedy .30 .09
❑ 148 Aaron Boone .30 .09
❑ 149 Todd Stottlemyre .30 .09
❑ 150 Roberto Alomar .50 .15
❑ 151 Orlando Hernandez .30 .09
❑ 152 Jason Varitek .75 .23
❑ 153 Gary Sheffield .30 .09
❑ 154 Cliff Floyd .30 .09
❑ 155 Chad Hermansen .30 .09
❑ 156 Carlos Delgado .30 .09
❑ 157 Aaron Sele .30 .09
❑ 158 Sean Casey .50 .15
❑ 159 Ruben Mateo .30 .09
❑ 160 Mike Bordick .30 .09
❑ 161 Mike Cameron .30 .09
❑ 162 Doug Glanville .30 .09
❑ 163 Damion Easley .30 .09
❑ 164 Carl Everett .30 .09
❑ 165 Bengie Molina .30 .09
❑ 166 Adrian Beltre .30 .09
❑ 167 Tom Goodwin .30 .09
❑ 168 Rickey Henderson .75 .23
❑ 169 Mo Vaughn .30 .09
❑ 170 Mike Lieberthal .30 .09
❑ 171 Ken Griffey Jr. 1.25 .35
❑ 172 Juan Gonzalez .30 .09
❑ 173 Ivan Rodriguez .50 .15
❑ 174 Al Leiter .30 .09
❑ 175 Vinny Castilla .30 .09
❑ 176 Peter Bergeron .30 .09
❑ 177 Pedro Astacio .30 .09
❑ 178 Paul Konerko .30 .09
❑ 179 Mitch Meluskey .30 .09
❑ 180 Kevin Millwood .30 .09
❑ 181 Ben Grieve .30 .09
❑ 182 Barry Bonds 2.00 .60
❑ 183 Rusty Greer .30 .09
❑ 184 Miguel Tejada .30 .09
❑ 185 Mark Quinn .30 .09
❑ 186 Larry Walker .30 .09
❑ 187 Jose Valentin .30 .09
❑ 188 Jose Vidro .30 .09
❑ 189 Delino DeShields .30 .09
❑ 190 Darin Erstad .30 .09
❑ 191 Bill Mueller .30 .09
❑ 192 Ray Durham .30 .09
❑ 193 Ken Caminiti .30 .09
❑ 194 Jim Thome .50 .15
❑ 195 Javy Lopez .30 .09
❑ 196 Fernando Vina .30 .09
❑ 197 Eric Chavez .30 .09
❑ 198 Eric Owens .30 .09
❑ 199 Brad Radke .30 .09
❑ 200 Travis Lee .30 .09
❑ 201 Tim Salmon .50 .15
❑ 202 Rafael Palmeiro .50 .15
❑ 203 Nomar Garciaparra 1.25 .35
❑ 204 Mike Hampton .30 .09
❑ 205 Kevin Brown .30 .09
❑ 206 Juan Encarnacion .30 .09
❑ 207 Danny Graves .30 .09
❑ 208 Carlos Guillen .30 .09
❑ 209 Phil Nevin .30 .09
❑ 210 Matt Lawton .30 .09
❑ 211 Manny Ramirez .50 .15
❑ 212 James Baldwin .30 .09
❑ 213 Fernando Tatis .30 .09
❑ 214 Craig Biggio .50 .15
❑ 215 Brian Jordan .30 .09
❑ 216 Bernie Williams .50 .15
❑ 217 Ryan Dempster .30 .09
❑ 218 Roger Clemens 1.50 .45
❑ 219 Jose Cruz Jr. .30 .09
❑ 220 John Valentin .30 .09
❑ 221 Dmitri Young .30 .09
❑ 222 Curt Schilling .30 .09
❑ 223 Jim Edmonds .50 .15
❑ 224 Chan Ho Park .30 .09
❑ 225 Brian Giles .30 .09
❑ 226 Jimmy Anderson .30 .09
Tike Redman
❑ 227 Adam Piatt .30 .09
Jose Ortiz
❑ 228 Kenny Kelly .30 .09
Aubrey Huff
❑ 229 Randy Choate .30 .09
Craig Dingman
❑ 230 Eric Cammack .30 .09
Grant Roberts
❑ 231 Yovanny Lara .30 .09
Andy Tracy
❑ 232 Wayne Franklin .30 .09
Scott Linebrink
❑ 233 Cameron Cairncross .30 .09
Chan Perry
❑ 234 J.C. Romero .30 .09
Matt LeCroy
❑ 235 Geraldo Guzman .30 .09
Jason Conti
❑ 236 Morgan Burkhart .30 .09
Paxton Crawford
❑ 237 Pasqual Coco .30 .09
Leo Estrella
❑ 238 John Parrish .30 .09
Fernando Lunar
❑ 239 Keith McDonald .30 .09
Justin Brunette
❑ 240 Carlos Casimiro .30 .09
Ivanon Coffie
❑ 241 Daniel Garibay .30 .09
Ruben Quevedo
❑ 242 Sang-Hoon Lee .30 .09
Tomo Ohka
❑ 243 Hector Ortiz .30 .09
Jeff D'Amico
❑ 244 Jeff Sparks .30 .09
Travis Harper
❑ 245 Jason Boyd .30 .09
David Coggin
❑ 246 Mark Buehrle .50 .15
Lorenzo Barcelo
❑ 247 Adam Melhuse .30 .09
Ben Petrick
❑ 248 Kane Davis .30 .09
Paul Rigdon
❑ 249 Mike Darr .30 .09
Kory DeHaan
❑ 250 Vicente Padilla 3.00 .90
Mark Brownson
❑ 251 Barry Zito PROS 5.00 1.50
❑ 252 Tim Drew PROS 3.00 .90
❑ 253 Luis Matos PROS 3.00 .90
❑ 254 Alex Cabrera PROS 3.00 .90
❑ 255 Jon Garland PROS 3.00 .90
❑ 256 Milton Bradley PROS 3.00 .90
❑ 257 Juan Pierre PROS 3.00 .90
❑ 258 Ismael Villegas PROS 3.00 .90
❑ 259 Eric Munson PROS 3.00 .90
❑ 260 T.De la Rosa PROS 3.00 .90
❑ 261 Chris Richard PROS 3.00 .90
❑ 262 Jason Tyner PROS 3.00 .90
❑ 263 B.J. Waszgis PROS 3.00 .90
❑ 264 Jason Marquis PROS 3.00 .90
❑ 265 Dusty Allen PROS 3.00 .90
❑ 266 C.Patterson PROS 3.00 .90
❑ 267 Eric Byrnes PROS 3.00 .90
❑ 268 Xavier Nady PROS 3.00 .90
❑ 269 G.Lombard PROS 3.00 .90
❑ 270 Timo Perez PROS 3.00 .90
❑ 271 G.Matthews Jr. PROS 3.00 .90
❑ 272 Chad Durbin PROS 3.00 .90
❑ 273 Tony Armas Jr. PROS 3.00 .90
❑ 274 F.Cordero PROS 3.00 .90
❑ 275 A.Soriano PROS 5.00 1.50
❑ 276 Junior Spivey RC 8.00 2.40
Juan Uribe RC
❑ 277 Albert Pujols RC 60.00 18.00
Bud Smith RC
❑ 278 Ichiro Suzuki RC 30.00 9.00
Tsuyoshi Shinjo RC
❑ 279 Drew Henson RC 8.00 2.40
Jackson Melian RC
❑ 280 Matt White RC 5.00 1.50
Adrian Hernandez RC

2003 Ultra

	Nm-Mt	Ex-Mt
COMP.LO SET (250)	100.00	30.00
COMP.LO SET w/o SP's (200)	25.00	7.50
COMMON CARD (201-220)	1.50	.45
COMMON CARD (221-250)	2.00	.60
COMMON CARD (251-265)	3.00	.90

No.	Player	Nm-Mt	Ex-Mt
❑ 1	Barry Bonds	2.00	.60
❑ 2	Derek Jeter	2.00	.60
❑ 3	Ichiro Suzuki	1.50	.45
❑ 4	Mike Lowell	.30	.09
❑ 5	Hideo Nomo	.75	.23
❑ 6	Javier Vazquez	.30	.09
❑ 7	Jeremy Giambi	.30	.09
❑ 8	Jamie Moyer	.30	.09
❑ 9	Rafael Palmeiro	.50	.15
❑ 10	Magglio Ordonez	.30	.09
❑ 11	Trot Nixon	.30	.09
❑ 12	Luis Castillo	.30	.09
❑ 13	Paul Byrd	.30	.09
❑ 14	Adam Kennedy	.30	.09
❑ 15	Trevor Hoffman	.30	.09
❑ 16	Matt Morris	.30	.09
❑ 17	Nomar Garciaparra	1.25	.35
❑ 18	Matt Lawton	.30	.09
❑ 19	Carlos Beltran	.30	.09
❑ 20	Jason Giambi	.30	.09
❑ 21	Brian Giles	.30	.09
❑ 22	Jim Edmonds	.50	.15
❑ 23	Garret Anderson	.30	.09
❑ 24	Tony Batista	.30	.09
❑ 25	Aaron Boone	.30	.09
❑ 26	Mike Hampton	.30	.09
❑ 27	Billy Wagner	.30	.09
❑ 28	Kazuhisa Ishii	.30	.09
❑ 29	Al Leiter	.30	.09
❑ 30	Pat Burrell	.30	.09
❑ 31	Jeff Kent	.30	.09
❑ 32	Randy Johnson	.75	.23
❑ 33	Ray Durham	.30	.09
❑ 34	Josh Beckett	.30	.09
❑ 35	Cristian Guzman	.30	.09
❑ 36	Roger Clemens	1.50	.45
❑ 37	Freddy Garcia	.30	.09
❑ 38	Roy Halladay	.30	.09
❑ 39	David Eckstein	.30	.09
❑ 40	Jerry Hairston	.30	.09
❑ 41	Barry Larkin	.50	.15
❑ 42	Larry Walker	.30	.09
❑ 43	Craig Biggio	.50	.15
❑ 44	Edgardo Alfonzo	.30	.09
❑ 45	Marlon Byrd	.30	.09
❑ 46	J.T. Snow	.30	.09
❑ 47	Juan Gonzalez	.30	.09
❑ 48	Ramon Ortiz	.30	.09
❑ 49	Jay Gibbons	.30	.09
❑ 50	Adam Dunn	.30	.09
❑ 51	Juan Pierre	.30	.09
❑ 52	Jeff Bagwell	.50	.15
❑ 53	Kevin Brown	.30	.09
❑ 54	Pedro Astacio	.30	.09
❑ 55	Mike Lieberthal	.30	.09
❑ 56	Johnny Damon	.50	.15
❑ 57	Tim Salmon	.50	.15
❑ 58	Mike Bordick	.30	.09
❑ 59	Ken Griffey Jr.	1.25	.35
❑ 60	Jason Jennings	.30	.09
❑ 61	Lance Berkman	.30	.09
❑ 62	Jeromy Burnitz	.30	.09
❑ 63	Jimmy Rollins	.30	.09
❑ 64	Tsuyoshi Shinjo	.30	.09
❑ 65	Alex Rodriguez	1.25	.35
❑ 66	Greg Maddux	1.25	.35
❑ 67	Mark Prior	.50	.15
❑ 68	Mike Maroth	.30	.09
❑ 69	Geoff Jenkins	.30	.09
❑ 70	Tony Armas Jr.	.30	.09
❑ 71	Jermaine Dye	.30	.09
❑ 72	Albert Pujols	1.50	.45
❑ 73	Shannon Stewart	.30	.09
❑ 74	Troy Glaus	.30	.09
❑ 75	Brook Fordyce	.30	.09
❑ 76	Juan Encarnacion	.30	.09
❑ 77	Todd Hollandsworth	.30	.09
❑ 78	Roy Oswalt	.30	.09
❑ 79	Paul Lo Duca	.30	.09
❑ 80	Mike Piazza	1.25	.35
❑ 81	Bobby Abreu	.30	.09
❑ 82	Sean Burroughs	.30	.09
❑ 83	Randy Winn	.30	.09
❑ 84	Curt Schilling	.30	.09
❑ 85	Chris Singleton	.30	.09
❑ 86	Sean Casey	.50	.15
❑ 87	Todd Zeile	.30	.09
❑ 88	Richard Hidalgo	.30	.09
❑ 89	Roberto Alomar	.50	.15
❑ 90	Tim Hudson	.30	.09
❑ 91	Ryan Klesko	.30	.09
❑ 92	Greg Vaughn	.30	.09
❑ 93	Tony Womack	.30	.09
❑ 94	Fred McGriff	.50	.15
❑ 95	Tom Glavine	.50	.15
❑ 96	Todd Walker	.30	.09
❑ 97	Travis Fryman	.30	.09
❑ 98	Shane Reynolds	.30	.09
❑ 99	Shawn Green	.30	.09
❑ 100	Mo Vaughn	.30	.09
❑ 101	Adam Piatt	.30	.09
❑ 102	Deivi Cruz	.30	.09
❑ 103	Steve Cox	.30	.09
❑ 104	Luis Gonzalez	.30	.09
❑ 105	Russell Branyan	.30	.09
❑ 106	Daryle Ward	.30	.09
❑ 107	Mariano Rivera	.50	.15
❑ 108	Phil Nevin	.30	.09
❑ 109	Ben Grieve	.30	.09
❑ 110	Moises Alou	.30	.09
❑ 111	Omar Vizquel	.50	.15
❑ 112	Joe Randa	.30	.09
❑ 113	Jorge Posada	.50	.15
❑ 114	Mark Kotsay	.30	.09
❑ 115	Ryan Rupe	.30	.09
❑ 116	Javy Lopez	.30	.09
❑ 117	Corey Patterson	.30	.09
❑ 118	Bobby Higginson	.30	.09
❑ 119	Jose Vidro	.30	.09
❑ 120	Barry Zito	.30	.09
❑ 121	Scott Rolen	.50	.15
❑ 122	Gary Sheffield	.30	.09
❑ 123	Kerry Wood	.30	.09
❑ 124	Brandon Inge	.30	.09
❑ 125	Jose Hernandez	.30	.09
❑ 126	Michael Barrett	.30	.09
❑ 127	Miguel Tejada	.30	.09
❑ 128	Edgar Renteria	.30	.09
❑ 129	Junior Spivey	.30	.09
❑ 130	Jose Valentin	.30	.09
❑ 131	Derrek Lee	.50	.15
❑ 132	A.J. Pierzynski	.30	.09
❑ 133	Mike Mussina	.50	.15
❑ 134	Bret Boone	.30	.09
❑ 135	Chan Ho Park	.30	.09
❑ 136	Steve Finley	.30	.09
❑ 137	Mark Buehrle	.30	.09
❑ 138	A.J. Burnett	.30	.09
❑ 139	Ben Sheets	.30	.09
❑ 140	David Ortiz	.50	.15
❑ 141	Nick Johnson	.30	.09
❑ 142	Randall Simon	.30	.09
❑ 143	Carlos Delgado	.30	.09
❑ 144	Darin Erstad	.30	.09
❑ 145	Shea Hillenbrand	.30	.09
❑ 146	Todd Helton	.50	.15
❑ 147	Preston Wilson	.30	.09
❑ 148	Eric Gagne	.30	.09
❑ 149	Vladimir Guerrero	.75	.23
❑ 150	Brandon Duckworth	.30	.09
❑ 151	Rich Aurilia	.30	.09
❑ 152	Ivan Rodriguez	.50	.15
❑ 153	Andruw Jones	.50	.15
❑ 154	Carlos Lee	.30	.09
❑ 155	Robert Fick	.30	.09
❑ 156	Jacque Jones	.30	.09
❑ 157	Bernie Williams	.50	.15
❑ 158	John Olerud	.30	.09
❑ 159	Eric Hinske	.30	.09
❑ 160	Matt Clement	.30	.09
❑ 161	Dmitri Young	.30	.09
❑ 162	Torii Hunter	.30	.09
❑ 163	Carlos Pena	.30	.09
❑ 164	Mike Cameron	.30	.09
❑ 165	Raul Mondesi	.30	.09
❑ 166	Pedro Martinez	.50	.15
❑ 167	Bob Wickman	.30	.09
❑ 168	Mike Sweeney	.30	.09
❑ 169	David Wells	.30	.09
❑ 170	Jason Kendall	.30	.09
❑ 171	Tino Martinez	.50	.15
❑ 172	Matt Williams	.30	.09
❑ 173	Frank Thomas	.75	.23
❑ 174	Cliff Floyd	.30	.09
❑ 175	Corey Koskie	.30	.09
❑ 176	Orlando Hernandez	.30	.09
❑ 177	Edgar Martinez	.50	.15
❑ 178	Richie Sexson	.30	.09
❑ 179	Manny Ramirez	.50	.15
❑ 180	Jim Thome	.50	.15
❑ 181	Andy Pettitte	.50	.15
❑ 182	Aramis Ramirez	.30	.09
❑ 183	J.D. Drew	.30	.09
❑ 184	Brian Jordan	.30	.09
❑ 185	Sammy Sosa	.75	.23
❑ 186	Jeff Weaver	.30	.09
❑ 187	Jeffrey Hammonds	.30	.09
❑ 188	Eric Milton	.30	.09
❑ 189	Eric Chavez	.30	.09
❑ 190	Kazuhiro Sasaki	.30	.09
❑ 191	Jose Cruz Jr.	.30	.09
❑ 192	Derek Lowe	.30	.09
❑ 193	C.C. Sabathia	.30	.09
❑ 194	Adrian Beltre	.30	.09
❑ 195	Alfonso Soriano	.30	.09
❑ 196	Jack Wilson	.30	.09
❑ 197	Fernando Vina	.30	.09
❑ 198	Chipper Jones	.75	.23
❑ 199	Paul Konerko	.30	.09
❑ 200	Rusty Greer	.30	.09
❑ 201	Jason Giambi AS	1.50	.45
❑ 202	Alfonso Soriano AS	1.50	.45
❑ 203	Shea Hillenbrand AS	1.50	.45
❑ 204	Alex Rodriguez AS	2.50	.75
❑ 205	Jorge Posada AS	1.50	.45
❑ 206	Ichiro Suzuki AS	3.00	.90
❑ 207	Manny Ramirez AS	1.50	.45
❑ 208	Torii Hunter AS	1.50	.45
❑ 209	Todd Helton AS	1.50	.45
❑ 210	Jose Vidro AS	1.50	.45
❑ 211	Scott Rolen AS	1.50	.45
❑ 212	Jimmy Rollins AS	1.50	.45
❑ 213	Mike Piazza AS	2.50	.75
❑ 214	Barry Bonds AS	4.00	1.20
❑ 215	Sammy Sosa AS	1.50	.45
❑ 216	Vladimir Guerrero AS	1.50	.45
❑ 217	Lance Berkman AS	1.50	.45
❑ 218	Derek Jeter AS	4.00	1.20
❑ 219	Nomar Garciaparra AS	2.50	.75
❑ 220	Luis Gonzalez AS	1.50	.45
❑ 221	Kazuhisa Ishii 02R	2.00	.60
❑ 222	Satoru Komiyama 02R	2.00	.60
❑ 223	So Taguchi 02R	2.00	.60
❑ 224	Jorge Padilla 02R	2.00	.60
❑ 225	Ben Howard 02R	2.00	.60
❑ 226	Jason Simontacchi 02R	2.00	.60
❑ 227	Barry Wesson 02R	2.00	.60
❑ 228	Howie Clark 02R	2.00	.60
❑ 229	Aaron Guiel 02R	2.00	.60
❑ 230	Oliver Perez 02R	2.00	.60
❑ 231	David Ross 02R	2.00	.60
❑ 232	Julius Matos 02R	2.00	.60

❑ 233 Chris Snelling 02R 2.00 .60
❑ 234 Rodrigo Lopez 02R 2.00 .60
❑ 235 Will Nieves 02R 2.00 .60
❑ 236 Joe Borchard 02R 2.00 .60
❑ 237 Aaron Cook 02R 2.00 .60
❑ 238 Anderson Machado 02R 2.00 .60
❑ 239 Corey Thurman 02R 2.00 .60
❑ 240 Tyler Yates 02R 2.00 .60
❑ 241 Coco Crisp 03R 2.00 .60
❑ 242 Andy Van Hekken 03R 2.00 .60
❑ 243 Jim Rushford 03R 2.00 .60
❑ 244 Jeriome Robertson 03R 2.00 .60
❑ 245 Shane Nance 03R 2.00 .60
❑ 246 Kevin Cash 03R 2.00 .60
❑ 247 Kirk Saarloos 03R 2.00 .60
❑ 248 Josh Bard 03R 2.00 .60
❑ 249 Dave Pember 03R RC 2.00 .60
❑ 250 Freddy Sanchez 03R 2.00 .60
❑ 251 Chien-Ming Wang PROS RC 8.00 2.40
❑ 252 Rickie Weeks PROS RC 8.00 2.40
❑ 253 Brandon Webb PROS RC 4.00 1.20
❑ 254 Hideki Matsui PROS RC 10.00 3.00
❑ 255 Michael Hessman PROS RC 3.00 .90
❑ 256 Ryan Wagner PROS RC 3.00 .90
❑ 257 Matt Kata PROS RC 3.00 .90
❑ 258 Edwin Jackson PROS RC 4.00 1.20
❑ 259 Jose Contreras PROS RC 4.00 1.20
❑ 260 Delmon Young PROS RC 10.00 3.00
❑ 261 Bo Hart PROS RC 3.00 .90
❑ 262 Jeff Duncan PROS RC 3.00 .90
❑ 263 Robby Hammock PROS RC 3.00 .90
❑ 264 Jeremy Bonderman PROS RC 8.00 2.40
❑ 265 Clint Barmes PROS RC 4.00 1.20

2004 Ultra

	MINT	NRMT
COMPLETE SERIES 1 (220)	60.00	27.00
COMP.SERIES 1 w/o SP's (200)	25.00	11.00
COMP.SERIES 2 w/o SP's (75)	25.00	11.00
COMP.SERIES 2 w/o L13 (162)	100.00	45.00
COMMON CARD (1-200)	.30	.14
COMMON CARD (201-220)	1.25	.55
201-220 APPROXIMATE ODDS 1:2 HOBBY		.00
201-220 RANDOM IN RETAIL PACKS		.00
COMMON CARD (296-382)	2.00	.90
296-382 ODDS TWO PER HOBBY/RETAIL		.00
COMMON CARD (383-395)	15.00	6.75
383-395 ODDS 1:28 HOBBY, 1:2000 RETAIL		.00
383-395 PRINT RUN 500 SERIAL #'d SETS		.00

❑ 1 Magglio Ordonez .30 .14
❑ 2 Bobby Abreu .30 .14
❑ 3 Eric Munson .30 .14
❑ 4 Eric Byrnes .30 .14
❑ 5 Bartolo Colon .30 .14
❑ 6 Juan Encarnacion .30 .14
❑ 7 Jody Gerut .30 .14
❑ 8 Eddie Guardado .30 .14
❑ 9 Shea Hillenbrand .30 .14
❑ 10 Andruw Jones .50 .23
❑ 11 Carlos Lee .30 .14
❑ 12 Pedro Martinez .50 .23
❑ 13 Barry Larkin .50 .23
❑ 14 Angel Berroa .30 .14
❑ 15 Edgar Martinez .50 .23
❑ 16 Sidney Ponson .30 .14
❑ 17 Mariano Rivera .50 .23
❑ 18 Richie Sexson .30 .14
❑ 19 Frank Thomas .75 .35
❑ 20 Jerome Williams .30 .14
❑ 21 Barry Zito .30 .14
❑ 22 Roberto Alomar .50 .23
❑ 23 Rocky Biddle .30 .14
❑ 24 Orlando Cabrera .30 .14
❑ 25 Placido Polanco .30 .14
❑ 26 Morgan Ensberg .30 .14
❑ 27 Jason Giambi .30 .14
❑ 28 Jim Thome .50 .23
❑ 29 Vladimir Guerrero .75 .35
❑ 30 Tim Hudson .30 .14
❑ 31 Jacque Jones .30 .14
❑ 32 Derrek Lee .50 .23
❑ 33 Rafael Palmeiro .50 .23
❑ 34 Mike Mussina .50 .23
❑ 35 Corey Patterson .30 .14
❑ 36 Mike Cameron .30 .14
❑ 37 Ivan Rodriguez .50 .23
❑ 38 Ben Sheets .30 .14
❑ 39 Woody Williams .30 .14
❑ 40 Ichiro Suzuki 1.50 .70
❑ 41 Moises Alou .30 .14
❑ 42 Craig Biggio .50 .23
❑ 43 Jorge Posada .50 .23
❑ 44 Craig Monroe .30 .14
❑ 45 Darin Erstad .30 .14
❑ 46 Jay Gibbons .30 .14
❑ 47 Aaron Guiel .30 .14
❑ 48 Travis Lee .30 .14
❑ 49 Jorge Julio .30 .14
❑ 50 Torii Hunter .30 .14
❑ 51 Luis Matos .30 .14
❑ 52 Brett Myers .30 .14
❑ 53 Sean Casey .50 .23
❑ 54 Mark Prior .50 .23
❑ 55 Alex Rodriguez 1.25 .55
❑ 56 Gary Sheffield .30 .14
❑ 57 Jason Varitek .75 .35
❑ 58 Dontrelle Willis .50 .23
❑ 59 Garret Anderson .30 .14
❑ 60 Casey Blake .30 .14
❑ 61 Jay Payton .30 .14
❑ 62 Carl Crawford .30 .14
❑ 63 Carl Everett .30 .14
❑ 64 Marcus Giles .30 .14
❑ 65 Jose Guillen .30 .14
❑ 66 Eric Karros .30 .14
❑ 67 Mike Lieberthal .30 .14
❑ 68 Hideki Matsui 1.50 .70
❑ 69 Xavier Nady .30 .14
❑ 70 Hank Blalock .30 .14
❑ 71 Albert Pujols 1.50 .70
❑ 72 Jose Cruz Jr. .30 .14
❑ 73 Randall Simon .30 .14
❑ 74 Javier Vazquez .30 .14
❑ 75 Preston Wilson .30 .14
❑ 76 Danys Baez .30 .14
❑ 77 Alex Cintron .30 .14
❑ 78 Jake Peavy .30 .14
❑ 79 Scott Rolen .50 .23
❑ 80 Robert Fick .30 .14
❑ 81 Brian Giles .30 .14
❑ 82 Roy Halladay .30 .14
❑ 83 Kazuhisa Ishii .30 .14
❑ 84 Austin Kearns .30 .14
❑ 85 Paul Lo Duca .30 .14
❑ 86 Darrell May .30 .14
❑ 87 Phil Nevin .30 .14
❑ 88 Carlos Pena .30 .14
❑ 89 Manny Ramirez .50 .23
❑ 90 C.C. Sabathia .30 .14
❑ 91 John Smoltz .50 .23
❑ 92 Jose Vidro .30 .14
❑ 93 Randy Wolf .30 .14
❑ 94 Jeff Bagwell .50 .23
❑ 95 Barry Bonds 2.00 .90
❑ 96 Frank Catalanotto .30 .14
❑ 97 Zach Day .30 .14
❑ 98 David Ortiz .75 .35
❑ 99 Troy Glaus .30 .14
❑ 100 Bo Hart .30 .14
❑ 101 Geoff Jenkins .30 .14
❑ 102 Jason Kendall .30 .14
❑ 103 Esteban Loaiza .30 .14
❑ 104 Doug Mientkiewicz .30 .14
❑ 105 Trot Nixon .30 .14
❑ 106 Troy Percival .30 .14
❑ 107 Aramis Ramirez .30 .14
❑ 108 Alex Sanchez .30 .14
❑ 109 Alfonso Soriano .30 .14
❑ 110 Omar Vizquel .50 .23
❑ 111 Kerry Wood .30 .14
❑ 112 Rocco Baldelli .30 .14
❑ 113 Bret Boone .30 .14
❑ 114 Shawn Chacon .30 .14
❑ 115 Carlos Delgado .30 .14
❑ 116 Shawn Green .30 .14
❑ 117 Tim Worrell .30 .14
❑ 118 Tom Glavine .50 .23
❑ 119 Shigetoshi Hasegawa .30 .14
❑ 120 Derek Jeter 1.50 .70
❑ 121 Jeff Kent .30 .14
❑ 122 Braden Looper .30 .14
❑ 123 Kevin Millwood .30 .14
❑ 124 Hideo Nomo .75 .35
❑ 125 Jason Phillips .30 .14
❑ 126 Tim Redding .30 .14
❑ 127 Reggie Sanders .30 .14
❑ 128 Sammy Sosa .75 .35
❑ 129 Billy Wagner .30 .14
❑ 130 Miguel Batista .30 .14
❑ 131 Milton Bradley .30 .14
❑ 132 Eric Chavez .30 .14
❑ 133 J.D. Drew .30 .14
❑ 134 Keith Foulke .30 .14
❑ 135 Luis Gonzalez .30 .14
❑ 136 LaTroy Hawkins .30 .14
❑ 137 Randy Johnson .75 .35
❑ 138 Byung-Hyun Kim .30 .14
❑ 139 Javy Lopez .30 .14
❑ 140 Melvin Mora .30 .14
❑ 141 Aubrey Huff .30 .14
❑ 142 Mike Piazza 1.25 .55
❑ 143 Mark Redman .30 .14
❑ 144 Kazuhiro Sasaki .30 .14
❑ 145 Shannon Stewart .30 .14
❑ 146 Larry Walker .30 .14
❑ 147 Dmitri Young .30 .14
❑ 148 Josh Beckett .30 .14
❑ 149 Jae Weong Seo .30 .14
❑ 150 Hee Seop Choi .30 .14
❑ 151 Adam Dunn .30 .14
❑ 152 Rafael Furcal .30 .14
❑ 153 Juan Gonzalez .30 .14
❑ 154 Todd Helton .50 .23
❑ 155 Carlos Zambrano .30 .14
❑ 156 Ryan Klesko .30 .14
❑ 157 Mike Lowell .30 .14
❑ 158 Jamie Moyer .30 .14
❑ 159 Russ Ortiz .30 .14
❑ 160 Juan Pierre .30 .14
❑ 161 Edgar Renteria .30 .14
❑ 162 Curt Schilling .30 .14
❑ 163 Mike Sweeney .30 .14
❑ 164 Brandon Webb .30 .14
❑ 165 Michael Young .30 .14
❑ 166 Carlos Beltran .30 .14
❑ 167 Sean Burroughs .30 .14
❑ 168 Luis Castillo .30 .14
❑ 169 David Eckstein .30 .14
❑ 170 Eric Gagne .30 .14
❑ 171 Chipper Jones .75 .35
❑ 172 Livan Hernandez .30 .14
❑ 173 Nick Johnson .30 .14
❑ 174 Corey Koskie .30 .14
❑ 175 Jason Schmidt .30 .14
❑ 176 Bill Mueller .30 .14
❑ 177 Steve Finley .30 .14
❑ 178 A.J. Pierzynski .30 .14
❑ 179 Rene Reyes .30 .14
❑ 180 Jason Johnson .30 .14
❑ 181 Mark Teixeira .50 .23
❑ 182 Kip Wells .30 .14
❑ 183 Mike MacDougal .30 .14
❑ 184 Lance Berkman .30 .14
❑ 185 Victor Zambrano .30 .14
❑ 186 Roger Clemens 1.50 .70
❑ 187 Jim Edmonds .50 .23
❑ 188 Nomar Garciaparra 1.25 .55
❑ 189 Ken Griffey Jr. 1.25 .55
❑ 190 Richard Hidalgo .30 .14

❑ 191 Cliff Floyd .30 .14
❑ 192 Greg Maddux 1.25 .55
❑ 193 Mark Mulder .30 .14
❑ 194 Roy Oswalt .30 .14
❑ 195 Marlon Byrd .30 .14
❑ 196 Jose Reyes .30 .14
❑ 197 Kevin Brown .30 .14
❑ 198 Miguel Tejada .30 .14
❑ 199 Vernon Wells .30 .14
❑ 200 Joel Pineiro .30 .14
❑ 201 Rickie Weeks AR 3.00 1.35
❑ 202 Chad Gaudin AR 1.25 .55
❑ 203 Ryan Wagner AR 1.25 .55
❑ 204 Chris Bootcheck AR 1.25 .55
❑ 205 Koyie Hill AR 1.25 .55
❑ 206 Jeff Duncan AR 1.25 .55
❑ 207 Rich Harden AR 2.00 .90
❑ 208 Edwin Jackson AR 1.25 .55
❑ 209 Robby Hammock AR 1.25 .55
❑ 210 Khalil Greene AR 3.00 1.35
❑ 211 Chien-Ming Wang AR 2.00 .90
❑ 212 Prentice Redman AR 1.25 .55
❑ 213 Todd Wellemeyer AR 1.25 .55
❑ 214 Clint Barmes AR 2.00 .90
❑ 215 Matt Kata AR 1.25 .55
❑ 216 Jon Leicester AR 1.25 .55
❑ 217 Jeremy Guthrie AR 1.25 .55
❑ 218 Chin-Hui Tsao AR 2.00 .90
❑ 219 Dan Haren AR 1.25 .55
❑ 220 Delmon Young AR 3.00 1.35
❑ 221 Vladimir Guerrero 1.25 .55
❑ 222 Andy Pettitte .75 .35
❑ 223 Gary Sheffield .50 .23
❑ 224 Javier Vazquez .50 .23
❑ 225 Alex Rodriguez 2.00 .90
❑ 226 Billy Wagner .50 .23
❑ 227 Miguel Tejada .50 .23
❑ 228 Greg Maddux 2.00 .90
❑ 229 Ivan Rodriguez .75 .35
❑ 230 Roger Clemens 2.50 1.10
❑ 231 Alfonso Soriano .50 .23
❑ 232 Miguel Cabrera .75 .35
❑ 233 Javy Lopez .50 .23
❑ 234 David Wells .50 .23
❑ 235 Eric Milton .50 .23
❑ 236 Armando Benitez .50 .23
❑ 237 Mike Cameron .50 .23
❑ 238 J.D. Drew .50 .23
❑ 239 Carlos Beltran .50 .23
❑ 240 Bartolo Colon .50 .23
❑ 241 Jose Guillen .50 .23
❑ 242 Kevin Brown .50 .23
❑ 243 Carlos Guillen .50 .23
❑ 244 Kenny Lofton .50 .23
❑ 245 Pokey Reese .50 .23
❑ 246 Rafael Palmeiro .75 .35
❑ 247 Nomar Garciaparra 2.00 .90
❑ 248 Hee Seop Choi .50 .23
❑ 249 Juan Uribe .50 .23
❑ 250 Nick Johnson .50 .23
❑ 251 Scott Podsednik .50 .23
❑ 252 Richie Sexson .50 .23
❑ 253 Keith Foulke Sox .50 .23
❑ 254 Jaret Wright .50 .23
❑ 255 Johnny Estrada .50 .23
❑ 256 Michael Barrett .50 .23
❑ 257 Bernie Williams .75 .35
❑ 258 Octavio Dotel .50 .23
❑ 259 Jeromy Burnitz .50 .23
❑ 260 Kevin Youkilis .50 .23
❑ 261 Derrek Lee .75 .35
❑ 262 Jack Wilson .50 .23
❑ 263 Craig Wilson .50 .23
❑ 264 Richard Hidalgo .50 .23
❑ 265 Royce Clayton .50 .23
❑ 266 Curt Schilling .75 .35
❑ 267 Joe Mauer .50 .23
❑ 268 Bobby Crosby .50 .23
❑ 269 Zack Greinke .50 .23
❑ 270 Victor Martinez .50 .23
❑ 271 Pedro Feliz .50 .23
❑ 272 Tony Batista .50 .23
❑ 273 Casey Kotchman .50 .23
❑ 274 Freddy Garcia .50 .23
❑ 275 Adam Everett .50 .23
❑ 276 Alexis Rios .50 .23
❑ 277 Lew Ford .50 .23
❑ 278 Adam LaRoche .50 .23
❑ 279 Lyle Overbay .50 .23
❑ 280 Juan Gonzalez .50 .23
❑ 281 A.J. Pierzynski .50 .23
❑ 282 Scott Hairston .50 .23
❑ 283 Danny Bautista .50 .23
❑ 284 Brad Penny .50 .23
❑ 285 Paul Konerko .50 .23
❑ 286 Matt Lawton .50 .23
❑ 287 Carl Pavano .50 .23
❑ 288 Pat Burrell .50 .23
❑ 289 Kenny Rogers .50 .23
❑ 290 Laynce Nix .50 .23
❑ 291 Johnny Damon .75 .35
❑ 292 Paul Wilson .50 .23
❑ 293 Vinny Castilla .50 .23
❑ 294 Aaron Miles .50 .23
❑ 295 Ken Harvey .50 .23
❑ 296 Onil Joseph RC 2.00 .90
❑ 297 Kazuhito Tadano RC 3.00 1.35
❑ 298 Jeff Bennett RC 2.00 .90
❑ 299 Chad Bentz RC 2.00 .90
❑ 300 Akinori Otsuka RC 2.00 .90
❑ 301 Jon Knott RC 2.00 .90
❑ 302 Ian Snell RC 3.00 1.35
❑ 303 Fernando Nieve RC 3.00 1.35
❑ 304 Mike Rouse RC 2.00 .90
❑ 305 Dennis Sarfate RC 2.00 .90
❑ 306 Josh Labandeira RC 2.00 .90
❑ 307 Chris Oxspring RC 2.00 .90
❑ 308 Alfredo Simon RC 2.00 .90
❑ 309 Rusty Tucker RC 3.00 1.35
❑ 310 Lincoln Holdzkom RC 2.00 .90
❑ 311 Justin Leone RC 3.00 1.35
❑ 312 Jorge Sequea RC 2.00 .90
❑ 313 Brian Dallimore RC 2.00 .90
❑ 314 Tim Bittner RC 2.00 .90
❑ 315 Ronny Cedeno RC 3.00 1.35
❑ 316 Justin Hampson RC 2.00 .90
❑ 317 Ryan Wing RC 2.00 .90
❑ 318 Mariano Gomez RC 2.00 .90
❑ 319 Carlos Vasquez RC 3.00 1.35
❑ 320 Casey Daigle RC 2.00 .90
❑ 321 Renyel Pinto RC 3.00 1.35
❑ 322 Chris Shelton RC 4.00 1.80
❑ 323 Mike Gosling RC 2.00 .90
❑ 324 Aarom Baldiris RC 3.00 1.35
❑ 325 Ramon Ramirez RC 2.00 .90
❑ 326 Roberto Novoa RC 3.00 1.35
❑ 327 Sean Henn RC 2.00 .90
❑ 328 Nick Regilio RC 2.00 .90
❑ 329 Dave Crouthers RC 2.00 .90
❑ 330 Greg Dobbs RC 2.00 .90
❑ 331 Angel Chavez RC 2.00 .90
❑ 332 Luis A. Gonzalez RC 2.00 .90
❑ 333 Justin Knoedler RC 2.00 .90
❑ 334 Jason Frasor RC 2.00 .90
❑ 335 Jerry Gil RC 2.00 .90
❑ 336 Carlos Hines RC 2.00 .90
❑ 337 Ivan Ochoa RC 2.00 .90
❑ 338 Jose Capellan RC 3.00 1.35
❑ 339 Hector Gimenez RC 2.00 .90
❑ 340 Shawn Hill RC 2.00 .90
❑ 341 Freddy Guzman RC 2.00 .90
❑ 342 Scott Proctor RC 3.00 1.35
❑ 343 Frank Francisco RC 2.00 .90
❑ 344 Brandon Medders RC 2.00 .90
❑ 345 Andy Green RC 2.00 .90
❑ 346 Eddy Rodriguez RC 3.00 1.35
❑ 347 Tim Hamulack RC 2.00 .90
❑ 348 Michael Wuertz RC 3.00 1.35
❑ 349 Arnie Munoz 2.00 .90
❑ 350 Enemencio Pacheco RC 2.00 .90
❑ 351 Dusty Bergman RC 2.00 .90
❑ 352 Charles Thomas RC 2.00 .90
❑ 353 William Bergolla RC 2.00 .90
❑ 354 Ramon Castro RC 2.00 .90
❑ 355 Justin Lehr RC 2.00 .90
❑ 356 Lino Urdaneta RC 2.00 .90
❑ 357 Donnie Kelly RC 2.00 .90
❑ 358 Kevin Cave RC 2.00 .90
❑ 359 Franklyn Gracesqui RC 2.00 .90
❑ 360 Chris Aguila RC 2.00 .90
❑ 361 Jorge Vasquez RC 2.00 .90
❑ 362 Andres Blanco RC 2.00 .90
❑ 363 Orlando Rodriguez RC 2.00 .90
❑ 364 Colby Miller RC 2.00 .90
❑ 365 Shawn Camp RC 2.00 .90
❑ 366 Jake Woods RC 2.00 .90
❑ 367 George Sherrill RC 2.00 .90
❑ 368 Justin Huisman RC 2.00 .90
❑ 369 Jimmy Serrano RC 2.00 .90
❑ 370 Mike Johnston RC 2.00 .90
❑ 371 Ryan Meaux RC 2.00 .90
❑ 372 Scott Dohmann RC 2.00 .90
❑ 373 Brad Halsey RC 3.00 1.35
❑ 374 Joey Gathright RC 4.00 1.80
❑ 375 Yadier Molina RC 5.00 2.20
❑ 376 Travis Blackley RC 2.00 .90
❑ 377 Steve Andrade RC 2.00 .90
❑ 378 Phil Stockman RC 2.00 .90
❑ 379 Roman Colon RC 2.00 .90
❑ 380 Jesse Crain RC 3.00 1.35
❑ 381 Edwardo Sierra RC 3.00 1.35
❑ 382 Justin Germano RC 2.00 .90
❑ 383 Kaz Matsui L13 RC 15.00 6.75
❑ 384 Shingo Takatsu L13 RC 15.00 6.75
❑ 385 John Gall L13 RC 15.00 6.75
❑ 386 Chris Saenz L13 RC 15.00 6.75
❑ 387 Merkin Valdez L13 RC 15.00 6.75
❑ 388 Jamie Brown L13 RC 15.00 6.75
❑ 389 Jason Bartlett L13 RC 15.00 6.75
❑ 390 David Aardsma L13 RC 15.00 6.75
❑ 391 Scott Kazmir L13 RC 30.00 13.50
❑ 392 David Wright L13 40.00 18.00
❑ 393 Dioner Navarro L13 RC 25.00 11.00
❑ 394 B.J. Upton L13 15.00 6.75
❑ 395 Gavin Floyd L13 15.00 6.75

2005 Ultra

	Nm-Mt	Ex-Mt
COMPLETE SET (220)	100.00	30.00
COMP.SET w/o SP's (200)	40.00	12.00
COMMON CARD (1-200)	.30	.09
COMMON CARD (201-220)	2.00	.60
201-220 ODDS 1:4 HOBBY, 1:5 RETAIL		.00

❑ 1 Andy Pettitte .50 .15
❑ 2 Jose Cruz Jr. .30 .09
❑ 3 Cliff Floyd .30 .09
❑ 4 Paul Konerko .30 .09
❑ 5 Joe Mauer .30 .09
❑ 6 Scott Spiezio .30 .09
❑ 7 Ben Sheets .30 .09
❑ 8 Kerry Wood .30 .09
❑ 9 Carl Pavano .30 .09
❑ 10 Matt Morris .30 .09
❑ 11 Kaz Matsui .30 .09
❑ 12 Ivan Rodriguez .50 .15
❑ 13 Victor Martinez .30 .09
❑ 14 Justin Morneau .30 .09
❑ 15 Adam Everett .30 .09
❑ 16 Carl Crawford .30 .09
❑ 17 David Ortiz .75 .23
❑ 18 Jason Giambi .30 .09
❑ 19 Derrek Lee .50 .15
❑ 20 Magglio Ordonez .30 .09
❑ 21 Bobby Abreu .30 .09
❑ 22 Milton Bradley .30 .09
❑ 23 Jeff Bagwell .50 .15
❑ 24 Jim Edmonds .50 .15
❑ 25 Garret Anderson .30 .09
❑ 26 Jacque Jones .30 .09

- ❑ 27 Ted Lilly .30 .09
- ❑ 28 Greg Maddux 1.25 .35
- ❑ 29 Jermaine Dye .30 .09
- ❑ 30 Bill Mueller .30 .09
- ❑ 31 Roy Oswalt .30 .09
- ❑ 32 Tony Womack .30 .09
- ❑ 33 Andruw Jones .50 .15
- ❑ 34 Tom Glavine .50 .15
- ❑ 35 Mariano Rivera .50 .15
- ❑ 36 Sean Casey .50 .15
- ❑ 37 Edgardo Alfonzo .30 .09
- ❑ 38 Brad Penny .30 .09
- ❑ 39 Johan Santana .50 .15
- ❑ 40 Mark Teixeira .50 .15
- ❑ 41 Manny Ramirez .50 .15
- ❑ 42 Gary Sheffield .30 .09
- ❑ 43 Matt Lawton .30 .09
- ❑ 44 Troy Percival .30 .09
- ❑ 45 Rocco Baldelli .30 .09
- ❑ 46 Doug Mientkiewicz .30 .09
- ❑ 47 Corey Patterson .30 .09
- ❑ 48 Austin Kearns .30 .09
- ❑ 49 Edgar Martinez .50 .15
- ❑ 50 Brad Radke .30 .09
- ❑ 51 Barry Larkin .50 .15
- ❑ 52 Chone Figgins .30 .09
- ❑ 53 Alexis Rios .30 .09
- ❑ 54 Alex Rodriguez 1.25 .35
- ❑ 55 Vinny Castilla .30 .09
- ❑ 56 Javier Vazquez .30 .09
- ❑ 57 Javy Lopez .30 .09
- ❑ 58 Mike Cameron .30 .09
- ❑ 59 Brian Giles .30 .09
- ❑ 60 Dontrelle Willis .30 .09
- ❑ 61 Rafael Furcal .30 .09
- ❑ 62 Trot Nixon .30 .09
- ❑ 63 Mark Mulder .30 .09
- ❑ 64 Josh Beckett .30 .09
- ❑ 65 J.D. Drew .30 .09
- ❑ 66 Brandon Webb .30 .09
- ❑ 67 Wade Miller .30 .09
- ❑ 68 Lyle Overbay .30 .09
- ❑ 69 Pedro Martinez .50 .15
- ❑ 70 Rich Harden .30 .09
- ❑ 71 Al Leiter .30 .09
- ❑ 72 Adam Eaton .30 .09
- ❑ 73 Mike Sweeney .30 .09
- ❑ 74 Steve Finley .30 .09
- ❑ 75 Kris Benson .30 .09
- ❑ 76 Jim Thome .50 .15
- ❑ 77 Juan Pierre .30 .09
- ❑ 78 Bartolo Colon .30 .09
- ❑ 79 Carlos Delgado .30 .09
- ❑ 80 Jack Wilson .30 .09
- ❑ 81 Ken Harvey .30 .09
- ❑ 82 Nomar Garciaparra .75 .23
- ❑ 83 Paul Lo Duca .30 .09
- ❑ 84 Cesar Izturis .30 .09
- ❑ 85 Adrian Beltre .30 .09
- ❑ 86 Brian Roberts .30 .09
- ❑ 87 David Eckstein .30 .09
- ❑ 88 Jimmy Rollins .30 .09
- ❑ 89 Roger Clemens 1.25 .35
- ❑ 90 Randy Johnson .75 .23
- ❑ 91 Orlando Hudson .30 .09
- ❑ 92 Tim Hudson .30 .09
- ❑ 93 Dmitri Young .30 .09
- ❑ 94 Chipper Jones .75 .23
- ❑ 95 John Smoltz .50 .15
- ❑ 96 Billy Wagner .30 .09
- ❑ 97 Hideo Nomo .75 .23
- ❑ 98 Sammy Sosa .75 .23
- ❑ 99 Darin Erstad .30 .09
- ❑ 100 Todd Helton .50 .15
- ❑ 101 Aubrey Huff .30 .09
- ❑ 102 Alfonso Soriano .30 .09
- ❑ 103 Jose Vidro .30 .09
- ❑ 104 Carlos Lee .30 .09
- ❑ 105 Corey Koskie .30 .09
- ❑ 106 Bret Boone .30 .09
- ❑ 107 Torii Hunter .30 .09
- ❑ 108 Aramis Ramirez .30 .09
- ❑ 109 Chase Utley .30 .09
- ❑ 110 Reggie Sanders .30 .09
- ❑ 111 Livan Hernandez .30 .09
- ❑ 112 Jeromy Burnitz .30 .09
- ❑ 113 Carlos Zambrano .30 .09
- ❑ 114 Hank Blalock .30 .09
- ❑ 115 Sidney Ponson .30 .09
- ❑ 116 Zack Greinke .30 .09
- ❑ 117 Trevor Hoffman .30 .09
- ❑ 118 Jeff Kent .30 .09
- ❑ 119 Richie Sexson .30 .09
- ❑ 120 Melvin Mora .30 .09
- ❑ 121 Eric Chavez .30 .09
- ❑ 122 Miguel Cabrera .50 .15
- ❑ 123 Ryan Freel .30 .09
- ❑ 124 Russ Ortiz .30 .09
- ❑ 125 Craig Wilson .30 .09
- ❑ 126 Craig Biggio .50 .15
- ❑ 127 Curt Schilling .50 .15
- ❑ 128 Kaz Ishii .30 .09
- ❑ 129 Marquis Grissom .30 .09
- ❑ 130 Bernie Williams .50 .15
- ❑ 131 Travis Hafner .30 .09
- ❑ 132 Hee Seop Choi .30 .09
- ❑ 133 Scott Rolen .50 .15
- ❑ 134 Tony Batista .30 .09
- ❑ 135 Frank Thomas .75 .23
- ❑ 136 Jason Varitek .75 .23
- ❑ 137 Ichiro Suzuki 1.50 .45
- ❑ 138 Junior Spivey .30 .09
- ❑ 139 Adam Dunn .30 .09
- ❑ 140 Jorge Posada .50 .15
- ❑ 141 Edgar Renteria .30 .09
- ❑ 142 Hideki Matsui 1.50 .45
- ❑ 143 Carlos Guillen .30 .09
- ❑ 144 Jody Gerut .30 .09
- ❑ 145 Wily Mo Pena .30 .09
- ❑ 146 Derek Jeter 1.50 .45
- ❑ 147 C.C. Sabathia .30 .09
- ❑ 148 Geoff Jenkins .30 .09
- ❑ 149 Albert Pujols 1.50 .45
- ❑ 150 Eric Munson .30 .09
- ❑ 151 Moises Alou .30 .09
- ❑ 152 Jerry Hairston .30 .09
- ❑ 153 Ray Durham .30 .09
- ❑ 154 Mike Piazza .75 .23
- ❑ 155 Omar Vizquel .30 .09
- ❑ 156 A.J. Pierzynski .30 .09
- ❑ 157 Michael Young .30 .09
- ❑ 158 Jason Bay .30 .09
- ❑ 159 Mark Loretta .30 .09
- ❑ 160 Shawn Green .30 .09
- ❑ 161 Luis Gonzalez .30 .09
- ❑ 162 Johnny Damon .50 .15
- ❑ 163 Eric Milton .30 .09
- ❑ 164 Mike Lowell .30 .09
- ❑ 165 Jose Guillen .30 .09
- ❑ 166 Eric Hinske .30 .09
- ❑ 167 Jason Kendall .30 .09
- ❑ 168 Carlos Beltran .30 .09
- ❑ 169 Johnny Estrada .30 .09
- ❑ 170 Scott Hatteberg .30 .09
- ❑ 171 Laynce Nix .30 .09
- ❑ 172 Eric Gagne .30 .09
- ❑ 173 Richard Hidalgo .30 .09
- ❑ 174 Bobby Crosby .30 .09
- ❑ 175 Woody Williams .30 .09
- ❑ 176 Justin Leone .30 .09
- ❑ 177 Orlando Cabrera .30 .09
- ❑ 178 Mark Prior .50 .15
- ❑ 179 Jorge Julio .30 .09
- ❑ 180 Jamie Moyer .30 .09
- ❑ 181 Jose Reyes .30 .09
- ❑ 182 Ken Griffey Jr. 1.25 .35
- ❑ 183 Mike Lieberthal .30 .09
- ❑ 184 Kenny Rogers .30 .09
- ❑ 185 Mike Mussina .50 .15
- ❑ 186 Preston Wilson .30 .09
- ❑ 187 Khalil Greene .50 .15
- ❑ 188 Angel Berroa .30 .09
- ❑ 189 Miguel Tejada .30 .09
- ❑ 190 Freddy Garcia .30 .09
- ❑ 191 Pat Burrell .30 .09
- ❑ 192 Luis Castillo .30 .09
- ❑ 193 Vladimir Guerrero .75 .23
- ❑ 194 Roy Halladay .30 .09
- ❑ 195 Barry Zito .30 .09
- ❑ 196 Lance Berkman .30 .09
- ❑ 197 Rafael Palmeiro .50 .15
- ❑ 198 Nate Robertson .30 .09
- ❑ 199 Jason Schmidt .30 .09
- ❑ 200 Scott Podsednik .30 .09
- ❑ 201 Casey Kotchman AR 3.00 .90
- ❑ 202 Scott Kazmir AR 5.00 1.50
- ❑ 203 Bucky Jacobsen AR 2.00 .60
- ❑ 204 Jeff Keppinger AR 2.00 .60
- ❑ 205 Dave Bush AR 2.00 .60
- ❑ 206 Gavin Floyd AR 2.00 .60
- ❑ 207 David Wright AR 8.00 2.40
- ❑ 208 B.J. Upton AR 5.00 1.50
- ❑ 209 David Aardsma AR 2.00 .60
- ❑ 210 Jason Bartlett AR 3.00 .90
- ❑ 211 Dioner Navarro AR 3.00 .90
- ❑ 212 Jason Kubel AR 2.00 .60
- ❑ 213 Ryan Howard AR 3.00 .90
- ❑ 214 Charles Thomas AR 2.00 .60
- ❑ 215 Freddy Guzman AR 2.00 .60
- ❑ 216 Brad Halsey AR 2.00 .60
- ❑ 217 Joey Gathright AR 3.00 .90
- ❑ 218 Jeff Francis AR 2.00 .60
- ❑ 219 Terry Tiffee AR 2.00 .60
- ❑ 220 Nick Swisher AR 3.00 .90

1989 Upper Deck

	Nm-Mt	Ex-Mt
COMPLETE SET (800)	80.00	32.00
COMP.FACT.SET (800)	100.00	40.00
COMP.HI FACT.SET (100)	10.00	4.00

- ❑ 1 Ken Griffey Jr. RC 50.00 20.00
- ❑ 2 Luis Medina RC .25 .10
- ❑ 3 Tony Chance RC .25 .10
- ❑ 4 Dave Otto .25 .10
- ❑ 5 S.Alomar Jr. RC UER 1.00 .40
  Born 6/16/66, should be 6/18/66
- ❑ 6 Rolando Roomes RC .25 .10
- ❑ 7 Dave West RC .25 .10
- ❑ 8 Cris Carpenter RC .25 .10
- ❑ 9 Gregg Jefferies .25 .10
- ❑ 10 Doug Dascenzo RC .25 .10
- ❑ 11 Ron Jones RC .25 .10
- ❑ 12 Luis DeLosSantos RC .25 .10
- ❑ 13 Gary Sheffield COR RC 5.00 2.00
- ❑ 13A G.Sheffield ERR RC 5.00 2.00
  SS upside down on card front
- ❑ 14 Mike Harkey RC .25 .10
- ❑ 15 Lance Blankenship RC .25 .10
- ❑ 16 William Brennan RC .25 .10
- ❑ 17 John Smoltz RC 5.00 2.00
- ❑ 18 Ramon Martinez RC .50 .20
- ❑ 19 Mark Lemke RC 1.00 .40
- ❑ 20 Juan Bell RC .25 .10
- ❑ 21 Rey Palacios RC .25 .10
- ❑ 22 Felix Jose RC .25 .10
- ❑ 23 Van Snider RC .25 .10
- ❑ 24 Dante Bichette RC 1.00 .40
- ❑ 25 Randy Johnson RC 15.00 6.00
- ❑ 26 Carlos Quintana RC .25 .10
- ❑ 27 Star Rookie CL .25 .10
- ❑ 28 Mike Schooler .25 .10
- ❑ 29 Randy St.Claire .25 .10
- ❑ 30 Jerald Clark RC .25 .10
- ❑ 31 Kevin Gross .25 .10
- ❑ 32 Dan Firova .25 .10
- ❑ 33 Jeff Calhoun .25 .10
- ❑ 34 Tommy Hinzo .25 .10

❑ 35 Ricky Jordan RC .50 .20
❑ 36 Larry Parrish .25 .10
❑ 37 Bret Saberhagen UER .40 .16
Hit total 931,
should be 1031
❑ 38 Mike Smithson .25 .10
❑ 39 Dave Dravecky .25 .10
❑ 40 Ed Romero .25 .10
❑ 41 Jeff Musselman .25 .10
❑ 42 Ed Hearn .25 .10
❑ 43 Rance Mulliniks .25 .10
❑ 44 Jim Eisenreich .25 .10
❑ 45 Sil Campusano .25 .10
❑ 46 Mike Krukow .25 .10
❑ 47 Paul Gibson .25 .10
❑ 48 Mike LaCoss .25 .10
❑ 49 Larry Herndon .25 .10
❑ 50 Scott Garrelts .25 .10
❑ 51 Dwayne Henry .25 .10
❑ 52 Jim Acker .25 .10
❑ 53 Steve Sax .25 .10
❑ 54 Pete O'Brien .25 .10
❑ 55 Paul Runge .25 .10
❑ 56 Rick Rhoden .25 .10
❑ 57 John Dopson .25 .10
❑ 58 Casey Candaele UER .25 .10
(No stats for Astros
for '88 season)
❑ 59 Dave Righetti .40 .16
❑ 60 Joe Hesketh .25 .10
❑ 61 Frank DiPino .25 .10
❑ 62 Tim Laudner .25 .10
❑ 63 Jamie Moyer .40 .16
❑ 64 Fred Toliver .25 .10
❑ 65 Mitch Webster .25 .10
❑ 66 John Tudor .40 .16
❑ 67 John Cangelosi .25 .10
❑ 68 Mike Devereaux .25 .10
❑ 69 Brian Fisher .25 .10
❑ 70 Mike Marshall .25 .10
❑ 71 Zane Smith .25 .10
❑ 72A Brian Holton ERR 1.00 .40
(Photo actually
Shawn Hillegas)
❑ 72B Brian Holton COR .40 .16
❑ 73 Jose Guzman .25 .10
❑ 74 Rick Mahler .25 .10
❑ 75 John Shelby .25 .10
❑ 76 Jim Deshaies .25 .10
❑ 77 Bobby Meacham .25 .10
❑ 78 Bryn Smith .25 .10
❑ 79 Joaquin Andujar .40 .16
❑ 80 Richard Dotson .25 .10
❑ 81 Charlie Lea .25 .10
❑ 82 Calvin Schiraldi .25 .10
❑ 83 Les Straker .25 .10
❑ 84 Les Lancaster .25 .10
❑ 85 Allan Anderson .25 .10
❑ 86 Junior Ortiz .25 .10
❑ 87 Jesse Orosco .25 .10
❑ 88 Felix Fermin .25 .10
❑ 89 Dave Anderson .25 .10
❑ 90 Rafael Belliard UER .25 .10
(Born '61, not '51)
❑ 91 Franklin Stubbs .25 .10
❑ 92 Cecil Espy .25 .10
❑ 93 Albert Hall .25 .10
❑ 94 Tim Leary .25 .10
❑ 95 Mitch Williams .25 .10
❑ 96 Tracy Jones .25 .10
❑ 97 Danny Darwin .25 .10
❑ 98 Gary Ward .25 .10
❑ 99 Neal Heaton .25 .10
❑ 100 Jim Pankovits .25 .10
❑ 101 Bill Doran .25 .10
❑ 102 Tim Wallach .25 .10
❑ 103 Joe Magrane .25 .10
❑ 104 Ozzie Virgil .25 .10
❑ 105 Alvin Davis .25 .10
❑ 106 Tom Brookens .25 .10
❑ 107 Shawon Dunston .25 .10
❑ 108 Tracy Woodson .25 .10
❑ 109 Nelson Liriano .25 .10
❑ 110 Devon White UER .40 .16
(Doubles total 46,
should be 56)

❑ 111 Steve Balboni .25 .10
❑ 112 Buddy Bell .40 .16
❑ 113 German Jimenez .25 .10
❑ 114 Ken Dayley .25 .10
❑ 115 Andres Galarraga .40 .16
❑ 116 Mike Scioscia .40 .16
❑ 117 Gary Pettis .25 .10
❑ 118 Ernie Whitt .25 .10
❑ 119 Bob Boone .40 .16
❑ 120 Ryne Sandberg 1.50 .60
❑ 121 Bruce Benedict .25 .10
❑ 122 Hubie Brooks .25 .10
❑ 123 Mike Moore .25 .10
❑ 124 Wallace Johnson .25 .10
❑ 125 Bob Horner .40 .16
❑ 126 Chili Davis .40 .16
❑ 127 Manny Trillo .25 .10
❑ 128 Chet Lemon .40 .16
❑ 129 John Cerutti .25 .10
❑ 130 Orel Hershiser .40 .16
❑ 131 Terry Pendleton .40 .16
❑ 132 Jeff Blauser .25 .10
❑ 133 Mike Fitzgerald .25 .10
❑ 134 Henry Cotto .25 .10
❑ 135 Gerald Young .25 .10
❑ 136 Luis Salazar .25 .10
❑ 137 Alejandro Pena .25 .10
❑ 138 Jack Howell .25 .10
❑ 139 Tony Fernandez .25 .10
❑ 140 Mark Grace 1.00 .40
❑ 141 Ken Caminiti .60 .24
❑ 142 Mike Jackson .25 .10
❑ 143 Larry McWilliams .25 .10
❑ 144 Andres Thomas .25 .10
❑ 145 Nolan Ryan 3X 4.00 1.60
❑ 146 Mike Davis .25 .10
❑ 147 DeWayne Buice .25 .10
❑ 148 Jody Davis .25 .10
❑ 149 Jesse Barfield .40 .16
❑ 150 Matt Nokes .25 .10
❑ 151 Jerry Reuss .25 .10
❑ 152 Rick Cerone .25 .10
❑ 153 Storm Davis .25 .10
❑ 154 Marvell Wynne .25 .10
❑ 155 Will Clark .60 .24
❑ 156 Luis Aguayo .25 .10
❑ 157 Willie Upshaw .25 .10
❑ 158 Randy Bush .25 .10
❑ 159 Ron Darling .40 .16
❑ 160 Kal Daniels .25 .10
❑ 161 Spike Owen .25 .10
❑ 162 Luis Polonia .25 .10
❑ 163 Kevin Mitchell UER .40 .16
('88/total HR's 18/52,
should be 19/53)
❑ 164 Dave Gallagher .25 .10
❑ 165 Benito Santiago .40 .16
❑ 166 Greg Gagne .25 .10
❑ 167 Ken Phelps .25 .10
❑ 168 Sid Fernandez .25 .10
❑ 169 Bo Diaz .25 .10
❑ 170 Cory Snyder .25 .10
❑ 171 Eric Show .25 .10
❑ 172 Robby Thompson .25 .10
❑ 173 Marty Barrett .25 .10
❑ 174 Dave Henderson .25 .10
❑ 175 Ozzie Guillen .40 .16
❑ 176 Barry Lyons .25 .10
❑ 177 Kelvin Torve .25 .10
❑ 178 Don Slaught .25 .10
❑ 179 Steve Lombardozzi .25 .10
❑ 180 Chris Sabo RC 1.00 .40
❑ 181 Jose Uribe .25 .10
❑ 182 Shane Mack .25 .10
❑ 183 Ron Karkovice .25 .10
❑ 184 Todd Benzinger .25 .10
❑ 185 Dave Stewart .40 .16
❑ 186 Julio Franco .40 .16
❑ 187 Ron Robinson .25 .10
❑ 188 Wally Backman .25 .10
❑ 189 Randy Velarde .25 .10
❑ 190 Joe Carter .40 .16
❑ 191 Bob Welch .40 .16
❑ 192 Kelly Paris .25 .10
❑ 193 Chris Brown .25 .10
❑ 194 Rick Reuschel .40 .16

❑ 195 Roger Clemens 2.00 .80
❑ 196 Dave Concepcion .40 .16
❑ 197 Al Newman .25 .10
❑ 198 Brook Jacoby .25 .10
❑ 199 Mookie Wilson .40 .16
❑ 200 Don Mattingly 2.50 1.00
❑ 201 Dick Schofield .25 .10
❑ 202 Mark Gubicza .25 .10
❑ 203 Gary Gaetti .40 .16
❑ 204 Dan Pasqua .25 .10
❑ 205 Andre Dawson .40 .16
❑ 206 Chris Speier .25 .10
❑ 207 Kent Tekulve .25 .10
❑ 208 Rod Scurry .25 .10
❑ 209 Scott Bailes .25 .10
❑ 210 R.Henderson UER 1.00 .40
Throws Right
❑ 211 Harold Baines .40 .16
❑ 212 Tony Armas .40 .16
❑ 213 Kent Hrbek .40 .16
❑ 214 Darrin Jackson .25 .10
❑ 215 George Brett 2.50 1.00
❑ 216 Rafael Santana .25 .10
❑ 217 Andy Allanson .25 .10
❑ 218 Brett Butler .40 .16
❑ 219 Steve Jeltz .25 .10
❑ 220 Jay Buhner .40 .16
❑ 221 Bo Jackson 1.00 .40
❑ 222 Angel Salazar .25 .10
❑ 223 Kirk McCaskill .25 .10
❑ 224 Steve Lyons .25 .10
❑ 225 Bert Blyleven .40 .16
❑ 226 Scott Bradley .25 .10
❑ 227 Bob Melvin .25 .10
❑ 228 Ron Kittle .25 .10
❑ 229 Phil Bradley .25 .10
❑ 230 Tommy John .40 .16
❑ 231 Greg Walker .25 .10
❑ 232 Juan Berenguer .25 .10
❑ 233 Pat Tabler .25 .10
❑ 234 Terry Clark .25 .10
❑ 235 Rafael Palmeiro 1.00 .40
❑ 236 Paul Zuvella .25 .10
❑ 237 Willie Randolph .40 .16
❑ 238 Bruce Fields .25 .10
❑ 239 Mike Aldrete .25 .10
❑ 240 Lance Parrish .40 .16
❑ 241 Greg Maddux 2.50 1.00
❑ 242 John Moses .25 .10
❑ 243 Melido Perez .25 .10
❑ 244 Willie Wilson .40 .16
❑ 245 Mark McLemore .25 .10
❑ 246 Von Hayes .25 .10
❑ 247 Matt Williams 1.00 .40
❑ 248 John Candelaria UER .25 .10
Listed as Yankee for
part of '87,
should be Mets
❑ 249 Harold Reynolds .40 .16
❑ 250 Greg Swindell .25 .10
❑ 251 Juan Agosto .25 .10
❑ 252 Mike Felder .25 .10
❑ 253 Vince Coleman .25 .10
❑ 254 Larry Sheets .25 .10
❑ 255 George Bell .40 .16
❑ 256 Terry Steinbach .40 .16
❑ 257 Jack Armstrong RC .50 .20
❑ 258 Dickie Thon .25 .10
❑ 259 Ray Knight .40 .16
❑ 260 Darryl Strawberry .40 .16
❑ 261 Doug Sisk .25 .10
❑ 262 Alex Trevino .25 .10
❑ 263 Jeffrey Leonard .25 .10
❑ 264 Tom Henke .25 .10
❑ 265 Ozzie Smith 1.50 .60
❑ 266 Dave Bergman .25 .10
❑ 267 Tony Phillips .25 .10
❑ 268 Mark Davis .25 .10
❑ 269 Kevin Elster .25 .10
❑ 270 Barry Larkin .60 .24
❑ 271 Manny Lee .25 .10
❑ 272 Tom Brunansky .25 .10
❑ 273 Craig Biggio RC 4.00 1.60
❑ 274 Jim Gantner .25 .10
❑ 275 Eddie Murray 1.00 .40
❑ 276 Jeff Reed .25 .10

❑	277	Tim Teufel	.25	.10
❑	278	Rick Honeycutt	.25	.10
❑	279	Guillermo Hernandez	.25	.10
❑	280	John Kruk	.40	.16
❑	281	Luis Alicea RC	.50	.20
❑	282	Jim Clancy	.25	.10
❑	283	Billy Ripken	.25	.10
❑	284	Craig Reynolds	.25	.10
❑	285	Robin Yount	1.50	.60
❑	286	Jimmy Jones	.25	.10
❑	287	Ron Oester	.25	.10
❑	288	Terry Leach	.25	.10
❑	289	Dennis Eckersley	.60	.24
❑	290	Alan Trammell	.40	.16
❑	291	Jimmy Key	.40	.16
❑	292	Chris Bosio	.25	.10
❑	293	Jose DeLeon	.25	.10
❑	294	Jim Traber	.25	.10
❑	295	Mike Scott	.40	.16
❑	296	Roger McDowell	.25	.10
❑	297	Garry Templeton	.40	.16
❑	298	Doyle Alexander	.25	.10
❑	299	Nick Esasky	.25	.10
❑	300	Mark McGwire UER (Doubles total 52, should be 51)	5.00	2.00
❑	301	Darryl Hamilton RC	.50	.20
❑	302	Dave Smith	.25	.10
❑	303	Rick Sutcliffe	.40	.16
❑	304	Dave Stapleton	.25	.10
❑	305	Alan Ashby	.25	.10
❑	306	Pedro Guerrero	.40	.16
❑	307	Ron Guidry	.40	.16
❑	308	Steve Farr	.25	.10
❑	309	Curt Ford	.25	.10
❑	310	Claudell Washington	.25	.10
❑	311	Tom Prince	.25	.10
❑	312	Chad Kreuter RC	.50	.20
❑	313	Ken Oberkfell	.25	.10
❑	314	Jerry Browne	.25	.10
❑	315	R.J. Reynolds	.25	.10
❑	316	Scott Bankhead	.25	.10
❑	317	Milt Thompson	.25	.10
❑	318	Mario Diaz	.25	.10
❑	319	Bruce Ruffin	.25	.10
❑	320	Dave Valle	.25	.10
❑	321A	Gary Varsho ERR (Back photo actually Mike Bielecki bunting)	2.00	.80
❑	321B	Gary Varsho COR (In road uniform)	.25	.10
❑	322	Paul Mirabella	.25	.10
❑	323	Chuck Jackson	.25	.10
❑	324	Drew Hall	.25	.10
❑	325	Don August	.25	.10
❑	326	Israel Sanchez	.25	.10
❑	327	Denny Walling	.25	.10
❑	328	Joel Skinner	.25	.10
❑	329	Danny Tartabull	.25	.10
❑	330	Tony Pena	.25	.10
❑	331	Jim Sundberg	.40	.16
❑	332	Jeff D. Robinson	.25	.10
❑	333	Oddibe McDowell	.25	.10
❑	334	Jose Lind	.25	.10
❑	335	Paul Kilgus	.25	.10
❑	336	Juan Samuel	.25	.10
❑	337	Mike Campbell	.25	.10
❑	338	Mike Maddux	.25	.10
❑	339	Darnell Coles	.25	.10
❑	340	Bob Dernier	.25	.10
❑	341	Rafael Ramirez	.25	.10
❑	342	Scott Sanderson	.25	.10
❑	343	B.J. Surhoff	.40	.16
❑	344	Billy Hatcher	.25	.10
❑	345	Pat Perry	.25	.10
❑	346	Jack Clark	.40	.16
❑	347	Gary Thurman	.25	.10
❑	348	Tim Jones	.25	.10
❑	349	Dave Winfield	.40	.16
❑	350	Frank White	.40	.16
❑	351	Dave Collins	.25	.10
❑	352	Jack Morris	.40	.16
❑	353	Eric Plunk	.25	.10
❑	354	Leon Durham	.25	.10
❑	355	Ivan DeJesus	.25	.10
❑	356	Brian Holman RC	.25	.10
❑	357A	Dale Murphy ERR (Front has reverse negative)	30.00	12.00
❑	357B	Dale Murphy COR	.60	.24
❑	358	Mark Portugal	.25	.10
❑	359	Andy McGaffigan	.25	.10
❑	360	Tom Glavine	1.00	.40
❑	361	Keith Moreland	.25	.10
❑	362	Todd Stottlemyre	.25	.10
❑	363	Dave Leiper	.25	.10
❑	364	Cecil Fielder	.40	.16
❑	365	Carmelo Martinez	.25	.10
❑	366	Dwight Evans	.60	.24
❑	367	Kevin McReynolds	.25	.10
❑	368	Rich Gedman	.25	.10
❑	369	Len Dykstra	.40	.16
❑	370	Jody Reed	.25	.10
❑	371	Jose Canseco UER (Strikeout total 391, should be 491)	1.00	.40
❑	372	Rob Murphy	.25	.10
❑	373	Mike Henneman	.25	.10
❑	374	Walt Weiss	.25	.10
❑	375	Rob Dibble RC	1.50	.60
❑	376	Kirby Puckett (Mark McGwire in background)	1.00	.40
❑	377	Dennis Martinez	.40	.16
❑	378	Ron Gant	.40	.16
❑	379	Brian Harper	.25	.10
❑	380	Nelson Santovenia	.25	.10
❑	381	Lloyd Moseby	.25	.10
❑	382	Lance McCullers	.25	.10
❑	383	Dave Stieb	.40	.16
❑	384	Tony Gwynn	1.25	.50
❑	385	Mike Flanagan	.25	.10
❑	386	Bob Ojeda	.25	.10
❑	387	Bruce Hurst	.25	.10
❑	388	Dave Magadan	.25	.10
❑	389	Wade Boggs	.60	.24
❑	390	Gary Carter	.40	.16
❑	391	Frank Tanana	.40	.16
❑	392	Curt Young	.25	.10
❑	393	Jeff Treadway	.25	.10
❑	394	Darrell Evans	.40	.16
❑	395	Glenn Hubbard	.25	.10
❑	396	Chuck Cary	.25	.10
❑	397	Frank Viola	.40	.16
❑	398	Jeff Parrett	.25	.10
❑	399	Terry Blocker	.25	.10
❑	400	Dan Gladden	.25	.10
❑	401	Louie Meadows	.25	.10
❑	402	Tim Raines	.40	.16
❑	403	Joey Meyer	.25	.10
❑	404	Larry Andersen	.25	.10
❑	405	Rex Hudler	.25	.10
❑	406	Mike Schmidt	2.00	.80
❑	407	John Franco	.40	.16
❑	408	Brady Anderson RC	1.00	.40
❑	409	Don Carman	.25	.10
❑	410	Eric Davis	.40	.16
❑	411	Bob Stanley	.25	.10
❑	412	Pete Smith	.25	.10
❑	413	Jim Rice	.40	.16
❑	414	Bruce Sutter	.40	.16
❑	415	Oil Can Boyd	.25	.10
❑	416	Ruben Sierra	.25	.10
❑	417	Mike LaValliere	.25	.10
❑	418	Steve Buechele	.25	.10
❑	419	Gary Redus	.25	.10
❑	420	Scott Fletcher	.25	.10
❑	421	Dale Sveum	.25	.10
❑	422	Bob Knepper	.25	.10
❑	423	Luis Rivera	.25	.10
❑	424	Ted Higuera	.25	.10
❑	425	Kevin Bass	.25	.10
❑	426	Ken Gerhart	.25	.10
❑	427	Shane Rawley	.25	.10
❑	428	Paul O'Neill	.60	.24
❑	429	Joe Orsulak	.25	.10
❑	430	Jackie Gutierrez	.25	.10
❑	431	Gerald Perry	.25	.10
❑	432	Mike Greenwell	.25	.10
❑	433	Jerry Royster	.25	.10
❑	434	Ellis Burks	.40	.16
❑	435	Ed Olwine	.25	.10
❑	436	Dave Rucker	.25	.10
❑	437	Charlie Hough	.40	.16
❑	438	Bob Walk	.25	.10
❑	439	Bob Brower	.25	.10
❑	440	Barry Bonds	5.00	2.00
❑	441	Tom Foley	.25	.10
❑	442	Rob Deer	.25	.10
❑	443	Glenn Davis	.25	.10
❑	444	Dave Martinez	.25	.10
❑	445	Bill Wegman	.25	.10
❑	446	Lloyd McClendon	.25	.10
❑	447	Dave Schmidt	.25	.10
❑	448	Darren Daulton	.40	.16
❑	449	Frank Williams	.25	.10
❑	450	Don Aase	.25	.10
❑	451	Lou Whitaker	.40	.16
❑	452	Rich Gossage	.40	.16
❑	453	Ed Whitson	.25	.10
❑	454	Jim Walewander	.25	.10
❑	455	Damon Berryhill	.25	.10
❑	456	Tim Burke	.25	.10
❑	457	Barry Jones	.25	.10
❑	458	Joel Youngblood	.25	.10
❑	459	Floyd Youmans	.25	.10
❑	460	Mark Salas	.25	.10
❑	461	Jeff Russell	.25	.10
❑	462	Darrell Miller	.25	.10
❑	463	Jeff Kunkel	.25	.10
❑	464	Sherman Corbett	.25	.10
❑	465	Curtis Wilkerson	.25	.10
❑	466	Bud Black	.25	.10
❑	467	Cal Ripken	3.00	1.20
❑	468	John Farrell	.25	.10
❑	469	Terry Kennedy	.25	.10
❑	470	Tom Candiotti	.25	.10
❑	471	Roberto Alomar	1.00	.40
❑	472	Jeff M. Robinson	.25	.10
❑	473	Vance Law	.25	.10
❑	474	Randy Ready UER (Strikeout total 136, should be 115)	.25	.10
❑	475	Walt Terrell	.25	.10
❑	476	Kelly Downs	.25	.10
❑	477	Johnny Paredes	.25	.10
❑	478	Shawn Hillegas	.25	.10
❑	479	Bob Brenly	.25	.10
❑	480	Otis Nixon	.25	.10
❑	481	Johnny Ray	.25	.10
❑	482	Geno Petralli	.25	.10
❑	483	Stu Cliburn	.25	.10
❑	484	Pete Incaviglia	.25	.10
❑	485	Brian Downing	.40	.16
❑	486	Jeff Stone	.25	.10
❑	487	Carmen Castillo	.25	.10
❑	488	Tom Niedenfuer	.25	.10
❑	489	Jay Bell	.40	.16
❑	490	Rick Schu	.25	.10
❑	491	Jeff Pico	.25	.10
❑	492	Mark Parent	.25	.10
❑	493	Eric King	.25	.10
❑	494	Al Nipper	.25	.10
❑	495	Andy Hawkins	.25	.10
❑	496	Daryl Boston	.25	.10
❑	497	Ernie Riles	.25	.10
❑	498	Pascual Perez	.25	.10
❑	499	Bill Long UER (Games started total 70, should be 44)	.25	.10
❑	500	Kirt Manwaring	.25	.10
❑	501	Chuck Crim	.25	.10
❑	502	Candy Maldonado	.25	.10
❑	503	Dennis Lamp	.25	.10
❑	504	Glenn Braggs	.25	.10
❑	505	Joe Price	.25	.10
❑	506	Ken Williams	.25	.10
❑	507	Bill Pecota	.25	.10
❑	508	Rey Quinones	.25	.10
❑	509	Jeff Bittiger	.25	.10
❑	510	Kevin Seitzer	.25	.10
❑	511	Steve Bedrosian	.25	.10
❑	512	Todd Worrell	.25	.10
❑	513	Chris James	.25	.10
❑	514	Jose Oquendo	.25	.10
❑	515	David Palmer	.25	.10
❑	516	John Smiley	.25	.10
❑	517	Dave Clark	.25	.10

❑ 518 Mike Dunne .25 .10
❑ 519 Ron Washington .25 .10
❑ 520 Bob Kipper .25 .10
❑ 521 Lee Smith .40 .16
❑ 522 Juan Castillo .25 .10
❑ 523 Don Robinson .25 .10
❑ 524 Kevin Romine .25 .10
❑ 525 Paul Molitor .60 .24
❑ 526 Mark Langston .25 .10
❑ 527 Donnie Hill .25 .10
❑ 528 Larry Owen .25 .10
❑ 529 Jerry Reed .25 .10
❑ 530 Jack McDowell .40 .16
❑ 531 Greg Mathews .25 .10
❑ 532 John Russell .25 .10
❑ 533 Dan Quisenberry .25 .10
❑ 534 Greg Gross .25 .10
❑ 535 Danny Cox .25 .10
❑ 536 Terry Francona .40 .16
❑ 537 Andy Van Slyke .60 .24
❑ 538 Mel Hall .25 .10
❑ 539 Jim Gott .25 .10
❑ 540 Doug Jones .25 .10
❑ 541 Craig Lefferts .25 .10
❑ 542 Mike Boddicker .25 .10
❑ 543 Greg Brock .25 .10
❑ 544 Atlee Hammaker .25 .10
❑ 545 Tom Bolton .25 .10
❑ 546 Mike Macfarlane RC .50 .20
❑ 547 Rich Renteria .25 .10
❑ 548 John Davis .25 .10
❑ 549 Floyd Bannister .25 .10
❑ 550 Mickey Brantley .25 .10
❑ 551 Duane Ward .25 .10
❑ 552 Dan Petry .25 .10
❑ 553 Mickey Tettleton UER .25 .10
(Walks total 175,
should be 136)
❑ 554 Rick Leach .25 .10
❑ 555 Mike Witt .25 .10
❑ 556 Sid Bream .25 .10
❑ 557 Bobby Witt .25 .10
❑ 558 Tommy Herr .25 .10
❑ 559 Randy Milligan .25 .10
❑ 560 Jose Cecena .25 .10
❑ 561 Mackey Sasser .25 .10
❑ 562 Carney Lansford .40 .16
❑ 563 Rick Aguilera .25 .10
❑ 564 Ron Hassey .25 .10
❑ 565 Dwight Gooden .40 .16
❑ 566 Paul Assenmacher .25 .10
❑ 567 Neil Allen .25 .10
❑ 568 Jim Morrison .25 .10
❑ 569 Mike Pagliarulo .25 .10
❑ 570 Ted Simmons .40 .16
❑ 571 Mark Thurmond .25 .10
❑ 572 Fred McGriff .60 .24
❑ 573 Wally Joyner .40 .16
❑ 574 Jose Bautista RC .25 .10
❑ 575 Kelly Gruber .25 .10
❑ 576 Cecilio Guante .25 .10
❑ 577 Mark Davidson .25 .10
❑ 578 Bobby Bonilla UER .40 .16
(Total steals 2 in '87,
should be 3)
❑ 579 Mike Stanley .25 .10
❑ 580 Gene Larkin .25 .10
❑ 581 Stan Javier .25 .10
❑ 582 Howard Johnson .40 .16
❑ 583A Mike Gallego ERR 1.00 .40
(Front reversed
negative)
❑ 583B Mike Gallego COR 1.00 .40
❑ 584 David Cone .40 .16
❑ 585 Doug Jennings .25 .10
❑ 586 Charles Hudson .25 .10
❑ 587 Dion James .25 .10
❑ 588 Al Leiter 1.00 .40
❑ 589 Charlie Puleo .25 .10
❑ 590 Roberto Kelly .25 .10
❑ 591 Thad Bosley .25 .10
❑ 592 Pete Stanicek .25 .10
❑ 593 Pat Borders RC .50 .20
❑ 594 Bryan Harvey RC .50 .20
❑ 595 Jeff Ballard .25 .10
❑ 596 Jeff Reardon .40 .16
❑ 597 Doug Drabek .25 .10
❑ 598 Edwin Correa .25 .10
❑ 599 Keith Atherton .25 .10
❑ 600 Dave LaPoint .25 .10
❑ 601 Don Baylor .40 .16
❑ 602 Tom Pagnozzi .25 .10
❑ 603 Tim Flannery .25 .10
❑ 604 Gene Walter .25 .10
❑ 605 Dave Parker .40 .16
❑ 606 Mike Diaz .25 .10
❑ 607 Chris Gwynn .25 .10
❑ 608 Odell Jones .25 .10
❑ 609 Carlton Fisk .60 .24
❑ 610 Jay Howell .25 .10
❑ 611 Tim Crews .25 .10
❑ 612 Keith Hernandez .40 .16
❑ 613 Willie Fraser .25 .10
❑ 614 Jim Eppard .25 .10
❑ 615 Jeff Hamilton .25 .10
❑ 616 Kurt Stillwell .25 .10
❑ 617 Tom Browning .25 .10
❑ 618 Jeff Montgomery .25 .10
❑ 619 Jose Rijo .40 .16
❑ 620 Jamie Quirk .25 .10
❑ 621 Willie McGee .40 .16
❑ 622 Mark Grant UER .25 .10
(Glove on wrong hand)
❑ 623 Bill Swift .25 .10
❑ 624 Orlando Mercado .25 .10
❑ 625 John Costello .25 .10
❑ 626 Jose Gonzalez .25 .10
❑ 627A Bill Schroeder ERR .60 .24
(Back photo actually
Ronn Reynolds buckling
shin guards)
❑ 627B Bill Schroeder COR .60 .24
❑ 628A Fred Manrique ERR .60 .24
(Back photo actually
Ozzie Guillen throwing)
❑ 628B Fred Manrique COR .25 .10
(Swinging bat on back)
❑ 629 Ricky Horton .25 .10
❑ 630 Dan Plesac .25 .10
❑ 631 Alfredo Griffin .25 .10
❑ 632 Chuck Finley .40 .16
❑ 633 Kirk Gibson .60 .24
❑ 634 Randy Myers .40 .16
❑ 635 Greg Minton .25 .10
❑ 636A Herm Winningham 1.00 .40
ERR (W1nningham
on back)
❑ 636B H.Winningham COR .25 .10
❑ 637 Charlie Leibrandt .25 .10
❑ 638 Tim Birtsas .25 .10
❑ 639 Bill Buckner .40 .16
❑ 640 Danny Jackson .25 .10
❑ 641 Greg Booker .25 .10
❑ 642 Jim Presley .25 .10
❑ 643 Gene Nelson .25 .10
❑ 644 Rod Booker .25 .10
❑ 645 Dennis Rasmussen .25 .10
❑ 646 Juan Nieves .25 .10
❑ 647 Bobby Thigpen .25 .10
❑ 648 Tim Belcher .25 .10
❑ 649 Mike Young .25 .10
❑ 650 Ivan Calderon .25 .10
❑ 651 Oswald Peraza .25 .10
❑ 652A Pat Sheridan ERR 15.00 6.00
(No position on front)
❑ 652B Pat Sheridan COR .25 .10
❑ 653 Mike Morgan .25 .10
❑ 654 Mike Heath .25 .10
❑ 655 Jay Tibbs .25 .10
❑ 656 Fernando Valenzuela .40 .16
❑ 657 Lee Mazzilli .40 .16
❑ 658 Frank Viola AL CY .25 .10
❑ 659A J.Canseco AL MVP .60 .24
Eagle logo in black
❑ 659B J.Canseco AL MVP .60 .24
Eagle logo in blue
❑ 660 Walt Weiss AL ROY .25 .10
❑ 661 Orel Hershiser NL CY .25 .10
❑ 662 Kirk Gibson NL MVP .40 .16
❑ 663 Chris Sabo NL ROY .40 .16
❑ 664 Dennis Eckersley .40 .16
ALCS MVP
❑ 665 Orel Hershiser .40 .16
NLCS MVP
❑ 666 Kirk Gibson WS 1.00 .40
❑ 667 O.Hershiser WS MVP .25 .10
❑ 668 Wally Joyner TC .25 .10
❑ 669 Nolan Ryan TC 1.25 .50
❑ 670 Jose Canseco TC .60 .24
❑ 671 Fred McGriff TC .40 .16
❑ 672 Dale Murphy TC .40 .16
❑ 673 Paul Molitor TC .40 .16
❑ 674 Ozzie Smith TC 1.00 .40
❑ 675 Ryne Sandberg TC 1.00 .40
❑ 676 Kirk Gibson TC .40 .16
❑ 677 Andres Galarraga TC .25 .10
❑ 678 Will Clark TC .40 .16
❑ 679 Cory Snyder TC .25 .10
❑ 680 Alvin Davis TC .25 .10
❑ 681 Darryl Strawberry TC .25 .10
❑ 682 Cal Ripken TC 1.00 .40
❑ 683 Tony Gwynn TC .60 .24
❑ 684 Mike Schmidt TC 1.00 .40
❑ 685 A.Van Slyke TC UER .40 .16
96 Junior Ortiz
❑ 686 Ruben Sierra TC .25 .10
❑ 687 Wade Boggs TC .40 .16
❑ 688 Eric Davis TC .25 .10
❑ 689 George Brett TC 1.00 .40
❑ 690 Alan Trammell TC .25 .10
❑ 691 Frank Viola TC .25 .10
❑ 692 Harold Baines TC .25 .10
❑ 693 Don Mattingly TC 1.00 .40
❑ 694 Checklist 1-100 .25 .10
❑ 695 Checklist 101-200 .25 .10
❑ 696 Checklist 201-300 .25 .10
❑ 697 Checklist 301-400 .25 .10
❑ 698 CL 401-500 UER .25 .10
467 Cal Ripkin Jr.
❑ 699 CL 501-600 UER .25 .10
543 Greg Booker
❑ 700 Checklist 601-700 .25 .10
❑ 701 Checklist 701-800 .25 .10
❑ 702 Jesse Barfield .40 .16
❑ 703 Walt Terrell .25 .10
❑ 704 Dickie Thon .25 .10
❑ 705 Al Leiter 1.00 .40
❑ 706 Dave LaPoint .25 .10
❑ 707 Charlie Hayes RC .50 .20
❑ 708 Andy Hawkins .25 .10
❑ 709 Mickey Hatcher .25 .10
❑ 710 Lance McCullers .25 .10
❑ 711 Ron Kittle .25 .10
❑ 712 Bert Blyleven .40 .16
❑ 713 Rick Dempsey .25 .10
❑ 714 Ken Williams .25 .10
❑ 715 Steve Rosenberg .25 .10
❑ 716 Joe Skalski .25 .10
❑ 717 Spike Owen .25 .10
❑ 718 Todd Burns .25 .10
❑ 719 Kevin Gross .25 .10
❑ 720 Tommy Herr .25 .10
❑ 721 Rob Ducey .25 .10
❑ 722 Gary Green .25 .10
❑ 723 Gregg Olson RC .50 .20
❑ 724 Greg W. Harris RC .25 .10
❑ 725 Craig Worthington .25 .10
❑ 726 Tom Howard RC .25 .10
❑ 727 Dale Mohorcic .25 .10
❑ 728 Rich Yett .25 .10
❑ 729 Mel Hall .25 .10
❑ 730 Floyd Youmans .25 .10
❑ 731 Lonnie Smith .25 .10
❑ 732 Wally Backman .25 .10
❑ 733 Trevor Wilson RC .25 .10
❑ 734 Jose Alvarez RC .25 .10
❑ 735 Bob Milacki .25 .10
❑ 736 Tom Gordon RC 1.00 .40
❑ 737 Wally Whitehurst RC .25 .10
❑ 738 Mike Aldrete .25 .10
❑ 739 Keith Miller .25 .10
❑ 740 Randy Milligan .25 .10
❑ 741 Jeff Parrett .25 .10
❑ 742 Steve Finley RC 2.00 .80
❑ 743 Junior Felix RC .25 .10
❑ 744 Pete Harnisch RC .50 .20
❑ 745 Bill Spiers RC .50 .20
❑ 746 Hensley Meulens RC .25 .10

❑ 747 Juan Bell RC .25 .10
❑ 748 Steve Sax .25 .10
❑ 749 Phil Bradley .25 .10
❑ 750 Rey Quinones .25 .10
❑ 751 Tommy Gregg .25 .10
❑ 752 Kevin Brown 1.00 .40
❑ 753 Derek Lilliquist RC .25 .10
❑ 754 Todd Zeile RC 1.00 .40
❑ 755 Jim Abbott RC 2.00 .80
Triple exposure
❑ 756 Ozzie Canseco .25 .10
❑ 757 Nick Esasky .25 .10
❑ 758 Mike Moore .25 .10
❑ 759 Rob Murphy .25 .10
❑ 760 Rick Mahler .25 .10
❑ 761 Fred Lynn .40 .16
❑ 762 Kevin Blankenship .25 .10
❑ 763 Eddie Murray 1.00 .40
❑ 764 Steve Searcy .25 .10
❑ 765 Jerome Walton RC .50 .20
❑ 766 Erik Hanson RC .50 .20
❑ 767 Bob Boone .40 .16
❑ 768 Edgar Martinez 1.00 .40
❑ 769 Jose DeJesus .25 .10
❑ 770 Greg Briley .25 .10
❑ 771 Steve Peters .25 .10
❑ 772 Rafael Palmeiro 1.00 .40
❑ 773 Jack Clark .40 .16
❑ 774 Nolan Ryan 4.00 1.60
(Throwing football)
❑ 775 Lance Parrish .40 .16
❑ 776 Joe Girardi RC 1.00 .40
❑ 777 Willie Randolph .40 .16
❑ 778 Mitch Williams .25 .10
❑ 779 Dennis Cook RC .50 .20
❑ 780 Dwight Smith RC .50 .20
❑ 781 Lenny Harris RC .50 .20
❑ 782 Torey Lovullo RC .25 .10
❑ 783 Norm Charlton RC .50 .20
❑ 784 Chris Brown .25 .10
❑ 785 Todd Benzinger .25 .10
❑ 786 Shane Rawley .25 .10
❑ 787 Omar Vizquel RC 3.00 1.20
❑ 788 LaVel Freeman .25 .10
❑ 789 Jeffrey Leonard .25 .10
❑ 790 Eddie Williams .25 .10
❑ 791 Jamie Moyer .40 .16
❑ 792 Bruce Hurst UER .25 .10
(Workd Series)
❑ 793 Julio Franco .40 .16
❑ 794 Claudell Washington .25 .10
❑ 795 Jody Davis .25 .10
❑ 796 Oddibe McDowell .25 .10
❑ 797 Paul Kilgus .25 .10
❑ 798 Tracy Jones .25 .10
❑ 799 Steve Wilson .25 .10
❑ 800 Pete O'Brien .25 .10

1990 Upper Deck

	Nm-Mt	Ex-Mt
COMPLETE SET (800)	25.00	7.50
COMP.FACT.SET (800)	25.00	7.50
COMPLETE LO SET (700)	25.00	7.50
COMPLETE HI SET (100)	5.00	1.50
COMP.HI FACT.SET (100)	4.00	1.20

❑ 1 Star Rookie Checklist .10 .03
❑ 2 Randy Nosek .10 .03
❑ 3 Tom Drees RC UER .10 .03
(11th line, hulred,
should be hurled
❑ 4 Curt Young .10 .03
❑ 5 Devon White TC .10 .03
❑ 6 Luis Salazar .10 .03
❑ 7 Von Hayes TC .10 .03
❑ 8 Jose Bautista .10 .03
❑ 9 Marquis Grissom RC .50 .15
❑ 10 Orel Hershiser TC .10 .03
❑ 11 Rick Aguilera .20 .06
❑ 12 Benito Santiago TC .10 .03
❑ 13 Deion Sanders .50 .15
❑ 14 Marvell Wynne .10 .03
❑ 15 Dave West .10 .03
❑ 16 Bobby Bonilla TC .10 .03
❑ 17 Sammy Sosa RC 4.00 1.20
❑ 18 Steve Sax TC .10 .03
❑ 19 Jack Howell .10 .03
❑ 20 Mike Schmidt Special 1.00 .30
UER (Suprising,
should be surprising)
❑ 21 Robin Ventura UER .50 .15
(Samta Maria)
❑ 22 Brian Meyer .10 .03
❑ 23 Blaine Beatty .10 .03
❑ 24 Ken Griffey Jr. TC .60 .18
❑ 25 Greg Vaughn UER .10 .03
(Association misspelled
as assiocation)
❑ 26 Xavier Hernandez RC .10 .03
❑ 27 Jason Grimsley RC .10 .03
❑ 28 Eric Anthony RC UER .10 .03
(Ashville, should
be Asheville)
❑ 29 Tim Raines TC UER .10 .03
(Wallach listed before Walker)
❑ 30 David Wells .20 .06
❑ 31 Hal Morris .10 .03
❑ 32 Bo Jackson TC .20 .06
❑ 33 Kelly Mann .10 .03
❑ 34 Nolan Ryan Special 1.00 .30
❑ 35 Scott Service UER .10 .03
(Born Cincinatti on
7/27/67, should be
Cincinnati 2/27)
❑ 36 Mark McGwire TC .60 .18
❑ 37 Tino Martinez 1.00 .30
❑ 38 Chili Davis .20 .06
❑ 39 Scott Sanderson .10 .03
❑ 40 Kevin Mitchell TC .10 .03
❑ 41 Lou Whitaker TC .10 .03
❑ 42 Scott Coolbaugh UER .10 .03
(Definately) RC
❑ 43 Jose Cano UER .10 .03
(Born 9/7/62, should
be 3/7/62)
❑ 44 Jose Vizcaino RC .25 .07
❑ 45 Bob Hamelin RC .25 .07
❑ 46 Jose Offerman RC UER .25 .07
(Posesses)
❑ 47 Kevin Blankenship .10 .03
❑ 48 Kirby Puckett TC .30 .09
❑ 49 Tommy Greene RC UER .10 .03
(Livest, should be
liveliest)
❑ 50 Will Clark Special .20 .06
UER (Perenial, should
be perennial)
❑ 51 Rob Nelson .10 .03
❑ 52 C.Hammond RC UER .10 .03
Chatanooga
❑ 53 Joe Carter TC .10 .03
❑ 54A B.McDonald RC ERR 2.00 .60
No Rookie designation
on card front
❑ 54B B.McDonald COR RC .25 .07
❑ 55 Andy Benes UER .20 .06
(Whichita)
❑ 56 John Olerud RC .75 .23
❑ 57 Roger Clemens TC .50 .15
❑ 58 Tony Armas .10 .03
❑ 59 George Canale .10 .03
❑ 60A Mickey Tettleton TC 2.00 .60
ERR (683 Jamie Weston)
❑ 60B Mickey Tettleton TC .10 .03
COR (683 Mickey Weston)
❑ 61 Mike Stanton RC .25 .07
❑ 62 Dwight Gooden TC .10 .03
❑ 63 Kent Mercker RC UER .25 .07
(Albuguerque)
❑ 64 Francisco Cabrera .10 .03
❑ 65 Steve Avery UER .10 .03
(Born NJ, should be MI,
Merker should be Mercker
❑ 66 Jose Canseco .30 .09
❑ 67 Matt Merullo .10 .03
❑ 68 Vince Coleman TC UER .10 .03
(Guererro)
❑ 69 Ron Karkovice .10 .03
❑ 70 Kevin Maas RC .25 .07
❑ 71 Dennis Cook UER .10 .03
(Shown with righty
glove on card back)
❑ 72 Juan Gonzalez RC UER 1.50 .45
(135 games for Tulsa
in '89, should be 133)
❑ 73 Andre Dawson TC .10 .03
❑ 74 Dean Palmer RC UER .25 .07
(Permanent misspelled
as perminant)
❑ 75 Bo Jackson Special .20 .06
UER (Monsterous,
should be monstrous)
❑ 76 Rob Richie .10 .03
❑ 77 Bobby Rose UER .10 .03
(Pickin, should
be pick in)
❑ 78 Brian DuBois UER .10 .03
(Commiting)
❑ 79 Ozzie Guillen TC .10 .03
❑ 80 Gene Nelson .10 .03
❑ 81 Bob McClure .10 .03
❑ 82 Julio Franco TC .10 .03
❑ 83 Greg Minton .10 .03
❑ 84 John Smoltz TC UER .30 .09
(Oddibe not Odibbe)
❑ 85 Willie Fraser .10 .03
❑ 86 Neal Heaton .10 .03
❑ 87 Kevin Tapani RC UER .25 .07
(24th line has excpet,
should be except)
❑ 88 Mike Scott TC .10 .03
❑ 89A Jim Gott ERR 2.00 .60
(Photo actually
Rick Reed)
❑ 89B Jim Gott COR .10 .03
❑ 90 Lance Johnson .10 .03
❑ 91 Robin Yount TC UER .50 .15
(Checklist on back has
178 Rob Deer and
176 Mike Felder)
❑ 92 Jeff Parrett .10 .03
❑ 93 Julio Machado UER .10 .03
(Valenzuelan, should
be Venezuelan)
❑ 94 Ron Jones .10 .03
❑ 95 George Bell TC .10 .03
❑ 96 Jerry Reuss .10 .03
❑ 97 Brian Fisher .10 .03
❑ 98 Kevin Ritz UER .10 .03
(Amercian)
❑ 99 Barry Larkin TC .20 .06
❑ 100 Checklist 1-100 .10 .03
❑ 101 Gerald Perry .10 .03
❑ 102 Kevin Appier .20 .06
❑ 103 Julio Franco .20 .06
❑ 104 Craig Biggio .50 .15
❑ 105 Bo Jackson UER .50 .15
('89 BA wrong,
should be .256)
❑ 106 Junior Felix .10 .03
❑ 107 Mike Harkey .10 .03
❑ 108 Fred McGriff .50 .15
❑ 109 Rick Sutcliffe .20 .06
❑ 110 Pete O'Brien .10 .03
❑ 111 Kelly Gruber .10 .03
❑ 112 Dwight Evans .30 .09
❑ 113 Pat Borders .10 .03
❑ 114 Dwight Gooden .20 .06
❑ 115 Kevin Batiste .10 .03
❑ 116 Eric Davis .20 .06

❑ 117 Kevin Mitchell UER .... .10 .03
(Career HR total 99,
should be 100)
❑ 118 Ron Oester .... .10 .03
❑ 119 Brett Butler .... .20 .06
❑ 120 Danny Jackson .... .10 .03
❑ 121 Tommy Gregg .... .10 .03
❑ 122 Ken Caminiti .... .20 .06
❑ 123 Kevin Brown .... .20 .06
❑ 124 George Brett UER .... 1.25 .35
(133 runs, should
be 1300)
❑ 125 Mike Scott .... .10 .03
❑ 126 Cory Snyder .... .10 .03
❑ 127 George Bell .... .10 .03
❑ 128 Mark Grace .... .30 .09
❑ 129 Devon White .... .20 .06
❑ 130 Tony Fernandez .... .10 .03
❑ 131 Don Aase .... .10 .03
❑ 132 Rance Mulliniks .... .10 .03
❑ 133 Marty Barrett .... .10 .03
❑ 134 Nelson Liriano .... .10 .03
❑ 135 Mark Carreon .... .10 .03
❑ 136 Candy Maldonado .... .10 .03
❑ 137 Tim Birtsas .... .10 .03
❑ 138 Tom Brookens .... .10 .03
❑ 139 John Franco .... .20 .06
❑ 140 Mike LaCoss .... .10 .03
❑ 141 Jeff Treadway .... .10 .03
❑ 142 Pat Tabler .... .10 .03
❑ 143 Darrell Evans .... .20 .06
❑ 144 Rafael Ramirez .... .10 .03
❑ 145 O.McDowell UER .... .10 .03
Misspelled Odibbe
❑ 146 Brian Downing .... .10 .03
❑ 147 Curt Wilkerson .... .10 .03
❑ 148 Ernie Whitt .... .10 .03
❑ 149 Bill Schroeder .... .10 .03
❑ 150 Domingo Ramos UER .... .10 .03
(Says throws right,
but shows him
throwing lefty)
❑ 151 Rick Honeycutt .... .10 .03
❑ 152 Don Slaught .... .10 .03
❑ 153 Mitch Webster .... .10 .03
❑ 154 Tony Phillips .... .10 .03
❑ 155 Paul Kilgus .... .10 .03
❑ 156 Ken Griffey Jr. UER .... 1.50 .45
(Simultaniously)
❑ 157 Gary Sheffield .... .50 .15
❑ 158 Wally Backman .... .10 .03
❑ 159 B.J. Surhoff .... .20 .06
❑ 160 Louie Meadows .... .10 .03
❑ 161 Paul O'Neill .... .30 .09
❑ 162 Jeff McKnight .... .10 .03
❑ 163 Alvaro Espinoza .... .10 .03
❑ 164 Scott Scudder .... .10 .03
❑ 165 Jeff Reed .... .10 .03
❑ 166 Gregg Jefferies .... .20 .06
❑ 167 Barry Larkin .... .30 .09
❑ 168 Gary Carter .... .20 .06
❑ 169 Robby Thompson .... .10 .03
❑ 170 Rolando Roomes .... .10 .03
❑ 171 Mark McGwire UER .... 1.25 .35
(Total games 427 and
hits 479, should be
467 and 427)
❑ 172 Steve Sax .... .10 .03
❑ 173 Mark Williamson .... .10 .03
❑ 174 Mitch Williams .... .10 .03
❑ 175 Brian Holton .... .10 .03
❑ 176 Rob Deer .... .10 .03
❑ 177 Tim Raines .... .20 .06
❑ 178 Mike Felder .... .10 .03
❑ 179 Harold Reynolds .... .20 .06
❑ 180 Terry Francona .... .20 .06
❑ 181 Chris Sabo .... .10 .03
❑ 182 Darryl Strawberry .... .20 .06
❑ 183 Willie Randolph .... .20 .06
❑ 184 Bill Ripken .... .10 .03
❑ 185 Mackey Sasser .... .10 .03
❑ 186 Todd Benzinger .... .10 .03
❑ 187 Kevin Elster UER .... .10 .03
(16 homers in 1989,
should be 10)
❑ 188 Jose Uribe .... .10 .03
❑ 189 Tom Browning .... .10 .03
❑ 190 Keith Miller .... .10 .03
❑ 191 Don Mattingly .... 1.25 .35
❑ 192 Dave Parker .... .20 .06
❑ 193 Roberto Kelly UER .... .10 .03
(96 RBI, should be 62)
❑ 194 Phil Bradley .... .10 .03
❑ 195 Ron Hassey .... .10 .03
❑ 196 Gerald Young .... .10 .03
❑ 197 Hubie Brooks .... .10 .03
❑ 198 Bill Doran .... .10 .03
❑ 199 Al Newman .... .10 .03
❑ 200 Checklist 101-200 .... .10 .03
❑ 201 Terry Puhl .... .10 .03
❑ 202 Frank DiPino .... .10 .03
❑ 203 Jim Clancy .... .10 .03
❑ 204 Bob Ojeda .... .10 .03
❑ 205 Alex Trevino .... .10 .03
❑ 206 Dave Henderson .... .10 .03
❑ 207 Henry Cotto .... .10 .03
❑ 208 Rafael Belliard UER .... .10 .03
(Born 1961, not 1951)
❑ 209 Stan Javier .... .10 .03
❑ 210 Jerry Reed .... .10 .03
❑ 211 Doug Dascenzo .... .10 .03
❑ 212 Andres Thomas .... .10 .03
❑ 213 Greg Maddux .... .75 .23
❑ 214 Mike Schooler .... .10 .03
❑ 215 Lonnie Smith .... .10 .03
❑ 216 Jose Rijo .... .10 .03
❑ 217 Greg Gagne .... .10 .03
❑ 218 Jim Gantner .... .10 .03
❑ 219 Allan Anderson .... .10 .03
❑ 220 Rick Mahler .... .10 .03
❑ 221 Jim Deshaies .... .10 .03
❑ 222 Keith Hernandez .... .20 .06
❑ 223 Vince Coleman .... .10 .03
❑ 224 David Cone .... .20 .06
❑ 225 Ozzie Smith .... .75 .23
❑ 226 Matt Nokes .... .10 .03
❑ 227 Barry Bonds .... 1.50 .45
❑ 228 Felix Jose .... .10 .03
❑ 229 Dennis Powell .... .10 .03
❑ 230 Mike Gallego .... .10 .03
❑ 231 Shawon Dunston UER .... .10 .03
('89 stats are
Andre Dawson's)
❑ 232 Ron Gant .... .20 .06
❑ 233 Omar Vizquel .... .50 .15
❑ 234 Derek Lilliquist .... .10 .03
❑ 235 Erik Hanson .... .10 .03
❑ 236 Kirby Puckett UER .... .50 .15
(824 games, should
be 924)
❑ 237 Bill Spiers .... .10 .03
❑ 238 Dan Gladden .... .10 .03
❑ 239 Bryan Clutterbuck .... .10 .03
❑ 240 John Moses .... .10 .03
❑ 241 Ron Darling .... .10 .03
❑ 242 Joe Magrane .... .10 .03
❑ 243 Dave Magadan .... .10 .03
❑ 244 Pedro Guerrero UER .... .10 .03
(Misspelled Guererro)
❑ 245 Glenn Davis .... .10 .03
❑ 246 Terry Steinbach .... .10 .03
❑ 247 Fred Lynn .... .10 .03
❑ 248 Gary Redus .... .10 .03
❑ 249 Ken Williams .... .10 .03
❑ 250 Sid Bream .... .10 .03
❑ 251 Bob Welch UER .... .10 .03
(2587 career strike-
outs, should be 1587)
❑ 252 Bill Buckner .... .10 .03
❑ 253 Carney Lansford .... .20 .06
❑ 254 Paul Molitor .... .30 .09
❑ 255 Jose DeJesus .... .10 .03
❑ 256 Orel Hershiser .... .20 .06
❑ 257 Tom Brunansky .... .10 .03
❑ 258 Mike Davis .... .10 .03
❑ 259 Jeff Ballard .... .10 .03
❑ 260 Scott Terry .... .10 .03
❑ 261 Sid Fernandez .... .10 .03
❑ 262 Mike Marshall .... .10 .03
❑ 263 Howard Johnson UER .... .10 .03
(192 SO, should be 592)
❑ 264 Kirk Gibson UER .... .30 .09
(659 runs, should
be 669)
❑ 265 Kevin McReynolds .... .10 .03
❑ 266 Cal Ripken .... 1.50 .45
❑ 267 Ozzie Guillen UER .... .20 .06
(Career triples 27,
should be 29)
❑ 268 Jim Traber .... .10 .03
❑ 269 Bobby Thigpen UER .... .10 .03
(31 saves in 1989,
should be 34)
❑ 270 Joe Orsulak .... .10 .03
❑ 271 Bob Boone .... .20 .06
❑ 272 Dave Stewart UER .... .20 .06
(Totals wrong due to
omission of '86 stats)
❑ 273 Tim Wallach .... .10 .03
❑ 274 Luis Aquino UER .... .10 .03
(Says throws lefty,
but shows him
throwing righty)
❑ 275 Mike Moore .... .10 .03
❑ 276 Tony Pena .... .10 .03
❑ 277 Eddie Murray UER .... .50 .15
(Several typos in
career total stats)
❑ 278 Milt Thompson .... .10 .03
❑ 279 Alejandro Pena .... .10 .03
❑ 280 Ken Dayley .... .10 .03
❑ 281 Carmelo Castillo .... .10 .03
❑ 282 Tom Henke .... .10 .03
❑ 283 Mickey Hatcher .... .10 .03
❑ 284 Roy Smith .... .10 .03
❑ 285 Manny Lee .... .10 .03
❑ 286 Dan Pasqua .... .10 .03
❑ 287 Larry Sheets .... .10 .03
❑ 288 Garry Templeton .... .10 .03
❑ 289 Eddie Williams .... .10 .03
❑ 290 Brady Anderson UER .... .20 .06
(Home: Silver Springs,
not Siver Springs)
❑ 291 Spike Owen .... .10 .03
❑ 292 Storm Davis .... .10 .03
❑ 293 Chris Bosio .... .10 .03
❑ 294 Jim Eisenreich .... .10 .03
❑ 295 Don August .... .10 .03
❑ 296 Jeff Hamilton .... .10 .03
❑ 297 Mickey Tettleton .... .10 .03
❑ 298 Mike Scioscia .... .10 .03
❑ 299 Kevin Hickey .... .10 .03
❑ 300 Checklist 201-300 .... .10 .03
❑ 301 Shawn Abner .... .10 .03
❑ 302 Kevin Bass .... .10 .03
❑ 303 Bip Roberts .... .10 .03
❑ 304 Joe Girardi .... .30 .09
❑ 305 Danny Darwin .... .10 .03
❑ 306 Mike Heath .... .10 .03
❑ 307 Mike Macfarlane .... .10 .03
❑ 308 Ed Whitson .... .10 .03
❑ 309 Tracy Jones .... .10 .03
❑ 310 Scott Fletcher .... .10 .03
❑ 311 Darnell Coles .... .10 .03
❑ 312 Mike Brumley .... .10 .03
❑ 313 Bill Swift .... .10 .03
❑ 314 Charlie Hough .... .20 .06
❑ 315 Jim Presley .... .10 .03
❑ 316 Luis Polonia .... .10 .03
❑ 317 Mike Morgan .... .10 .03
❑ 318 Lee Guetterman .... .10 .03
❑ 319 Jose Oquendo .... .10 .03
❑ 320 Wayne Tolleson .... .10 .03
❑ 321 Jody Reed .... .10 .03
❑ 322 Damon Berryhill .... .10 .03
❑ 323 Roger Clemens .... 1.00 .30
❑ 324 Ryne Sandberg .... .75 .23
❑ 325 Benito Santiago UER .... .20 .06
(Misspelled Santago
on card back)
❑ 326 Bret Saberhagen UER .... .20 .06
(1140 hits, should be
1240; 56 CG, should
be 52)
❑ 327 Lou Whitaker .... .20 .06
❑ 328 Dave Gallagher .... .10 .03
❑ 329 Mike Pagliarulo .... .10 .03
❑ 330 Doyle Alexander .... .10 .03

❑ 331 Jeffrey Leonard .10 .03
❑ 332 Torey Lovullo .10 .03
❑ 333 Pete Incaviglia .10 .03
❑ 334 Rickey Henderson .50 .15
❑ 335 Rafael Palmeiro .30 .09
❑ 336 Ken Hill .20 .06
❑ 337 Dave Winfield UER .20 .06
(1418 RBI, should be 1438)
❑ 338 Alfredo Griffin .10 .03
❑ 339 Andy Hawkins .10 .03
❑ 340 Ted Power .10 .03
❑ 341 Steve Wilson .10 .03
❑ 342 Jack Clark UER .20 .06
(916 BB, should be 1006; 1142 SO, should be 1130)
❑ 343 Ellis Burks .30 .09
❑ 344 Tony Gwynn UER .60 .18
(Doubles stats on card back are wrong)
❑ 345 Jerome Walton UER .10 .03
(Total At Bats 476, should be 475)
❑ 346 Roberto Alomar UER .30 .09
(61 doubles, should be 51)
❑ 347 Carlos Martinez UER .10 .03
(Born 8/11/64, should be 8/11/65)
❑ 348 Chet Lemon .10 .03
❑ 349 Willie Wilson .10 .03
❑ 350 Greg Walker .10 .03
❑ 351 Tom Bolton .10 .03
❑ 352 German Gonzalez .10 .03
❑ 353 Harold Baines .20 .06
❑ 354 Mike Greenwell .10 .03
❑ 355 Ruben Sierra .10 .03
❑ 356 Andres Galarraga .20 .06
❑ 357 Andre Dawson .20 .06
❑ 358 Jeff Brantley .10 .03
❑ 359 Mike Bielecki .10 .03
❑ 360 Ken Oberkfell .10 .03
❑ 361 Kurt Stillwell .10 .03
❑ 362 Brian Holman .10 .03
❑ 363 Kevin Seitzer UER .10 .03
(Career triples total does not add up)
❑ 364 Alvin Davis .10 .03
❑ 365 Tom Gordon .20 .06
❑ 366 Bobby Bonilla UER .20 .06
(Two steals in 1987, should be 3)
❑ 367 Carlton Fisk .30 .09
❑ 368 Steve Carter UER .10 .03
(Charlotesville)
❑ 369 Joel Skinner .10 .03
❑ 370 John Cangelosi .10 .03
❑ 371 Cecil Espy .10 .03
❑ 372 Gary Wayne .10 .03
❑ 373 Jim Rice .20 .06
❑ 374 Mike Dyer RC .10 .03
❑ 375 Joe Carter .20 .06
❑ 376 Dwight Smith .10 .03
❑ 377 John Wetteland .50 .15
❑ 378 Earnie Riles .10 .03
❑ 379 Otis Nixon .10 .03
❑ 380 Vance Law .10 .03
❑ 381 Dave Bergman .10 .03
❑ 382 Frank White .20 .06
❑ 383 Scott Bradley .10 .03
❑ 384 Israel Sanchez UER .10 .03
(Totals don't include '89 stats)
❑ 385 Gary Pettis .10 .03
❑ 386 Donn Pall .10 .03
❑ 387 John Smiley .10 .03
❑ 388 Tom Candiotti .10 .03
❑ 389 Junior Ortiz .10 .03
❑ 390 Steve Lyons .10 .03
❑ 391 Brian Harper .10 .03
❑ 392 Fred Manrique .10 .03
❑ 393 Lee Smith .20 .06
❑ 394 Jeff Kunkel .10 .03
❑ 395 Claudell Washington .10 .03
❑ 396 John Tudor .10 .03
❑ 397 Terry Kennedy UER .10 .03
(Career totals all wrong)
❑ 398 Lloyd McClendon .10 .03
❑ 399 Craig Lefferts .10 .03
❑ 400 Checklist 301-400 .10 .03
❑ 401 Keith Moreland .10 .03
❑ 402 Rich Gedman .10 .03
❑ 403 Jeff D. Robinson .10 .03
❑ 404 Randy Ready .10 .03
❑ 405 Rick Cerone .10 .03
❑ 406 Jeff Blauser .10 .03
❑ 407 Larry Andersen .10 .03
❑ 408 Joe Boever .10 .03
❑ 409 Felix Fermin .10 .03
❑ 410 Glenn Wilson .10 .03
❑ 411 Rex Hudler .10 .03
❑ 412 Mark Grant .10 .03
❑ 413 Dennis Martinez .20 .06
❑ 414 Darrin Jackson .10 .03
❑ 415 Mike Aldrete .10 .03
❑ 416 Roger McDowell .10 .03
❑ 417 Jeff Reardon .20 .06
❑ 418 Darren Daulton .20 .06
❑ 419 Tim Laudner .10 .03
❑ 420 Don Carman .10 .03
❑ 421 Lloyd Moseby .10 .03
❑ 422 Doug Drabek .10 .03
❑ 423 Lenny Harris UER .10 .03
(Walks 2 in '89, should be 20)
❑ 424 Jose Lind .10 .03
❑ 425 Dave Johnson (P) .10 .03
❑ 426 Jerry Browne .10 .03
❑ 427 Eric Yelding .10 .03
❑ 428 Brad Komminsk .10 .03
❑ 429 Jody Davis .10 .03
❑ 430 Mariano Duncan .10 .03
❑ 431 Mark Davis .10 .03
❑ 432 Nelson Santovenia .10 .03
❑ 433 Bruce Hurst .10 .03
❑ 434 Jeff Huson RC .10 .03
❑ 435 Chris James .10 .03
❑ 436 Mark Guthrie .10 .03
❑ 437 Charlie Hayes .10 .03
❑ 438 Shane Rawley .10 .03
❑ 439 Dickie Thon .10 .03
❑ 440 Juan Berenguer .10 .03
❑ 441 Kevin Romine .10 .03
❑ 442 Bill Landrum .10 .03
❑ 443 Todd Frohwirth .10 .03
❑ 444 Craig Worthington .10 .03
❑ 445 Fernando Valenzuela .20 .06
❑ 446 Joey Belle .50 .15
❑ 447 Ed Whited UER .10 .03
(Ashville, should be Asheville)
❑ 448 Dave Smith .10 .03
❑ 449 Dave Clark .10 .03
❑ 450 Juan Agosto .10 .03
❑ 451 Dave Valle .10 .03
❑ 452 Kent Hrbek .20 .06
❑ 453 Von Hayes .10 .03
❑ 454 Gary Gaetti .20 .06
❑ 455 Greg Briley .10 .03
❑ 456 Glenn Braggs .10 .03
❑ 457 Kirt Manwaring .10 .03
❑ 458 Mel Hall .10 .03
❑ 459 Brook Jacoby .10 .03
❑ 460 Pat Sheridan .10 .03
❑ 461 Rob Murphy .10 .03
❑ 462 Jimmy Key .20 .06
❑ 463 Nick Esasky .10 .03
❑ 464 Rob Ducey .10 .03
❑ 465 Carlos Quintana UER .10 .03
(Internatinoal)
❑ 466 Larry Walker RC 1.50 .45
❑ 467 Todd Worrell .10 .03
❑ 468 Kevin Gross .10 .03
❑ 469 Terry Pendleton .20 .06
❑ 470 Dave Martinez .10 .03
❑ 471 Gene Larkin .10 .03
❑ 472 Len Dykstra UER .20 .06
('89 and total runs understated by 10)
❑ 473 Barry Lyons .10 .03
❑ 474 Terry Mulholland .10 .03
❑ 475 Chip Hale .10 .03
❑ 476 Jesse Barfield .10 .03
❑ 477 Dan Plesac .10 .03
❑ 478A Scott Garrelts ERR 2.00 .60
(Photo actually Bill Bathe)
❑ 478B Scott Garrelts COR .10 .03
❑ 479 Dave Righetti .10 .03
❑ 480 Gus Polidor UER .10 .03
Wearing 14 on front, but 10 on back
❑ 481 Mookie Wilson .20 .06
❑ 482 Luis Rivera .10 .03
❑ 483 Mike Flanagan .10 .03
❑ 484 Dennis Boyd .10 .03
❑ 485 John Cerutti .10 .03
❑ 486 John Costello .10 .03
❑ 487 Pascual Perez .10 .03
❑ 488 Tommy Herr .10 .03
❑ 489 Tom Foley .10 .03
❑ 490 Curt Ford .10 .03
❑ 491 Steve Lake .10 .03
❑ 492 Tim Teufel .10 .03
❑ 493 Randy Bush .10 .03
❑ 494 Mike Jackson .10 .03
❑ 495 Steve Jeltz .10 .03
❑ 496 Paul Gibson .10 .03
❑ 497 Steve Balboni .10 .03
❑ 498 Bud Black .10 .03
❑ 499 Dale Sveum .10 .03
❑ 500 Checklist 401-500 .10 .03
❑ 501 Tim Jones .10 .03
❑ 502 Mark Portugal .10 .03
❑ 503 Ivan Calderon .10 .03
❑ 504 Rick Rhoden .10 .03
❑ 505 Willie McGee .20 .06
❑ 506 Kirk McCaskill .10 .03
❑ 507 Dave LaPoint .10 .03
❑ 508 Jay Howell .10 .03
❑ 509 Johnny Ray .10 .03
❑ 510 Dave Anderson .10 .03
❑ 511 Chuck Crim .10 .03
❑ 512 Joe Hesketh .10 .03
❑ 513 Dennis Eckersley .20 .06
❑ 514 Greg Brock .10 .03
❑ 515 Tim Burke .10 .03
❑ 516 Frank Tanana .10 .03
❑ 517 Jay Bell .20 .06
❑ 518 Guillermo Hernandez .10 .03
❑ 519 Randy Kramer UER .10 .03
(Codiroli misspelled as Codoroli)
❑ 520 Charles Hudson .10 .03
❑ 521 Jim Corsi .10 .03
Word "originally" is misspelled on back
❑ 522 Steve Rosenberg .10 .03
❑ 523 Cris Carpenter .10 .03
❑ 524 Matt Winters .10 .03
❑ 525 Melido Perez .10 .03
❑ 526 Chris Gwynn UER .10 .03
(Albeguergue)
❑ 527 Bert Blyleven UER .20 .06
(Games career total is wrong, should be 644)
❑ 528 Chuck Cary .10 .03
❑ 529 Daryl Boston .10 .03
❑ 530 Dale Mohorcic .10 .03
❑ 531 Geronimo Berroa .10 .03
❑ 532 Edgar Martinez .30 .09
❑ 533 Dale Murphy .30 .09
❑ 534 Jay Buhner .20 .06
❑ 535 John Smoltz UER .50 .15
(HEA Stadium)
❑ 536 Andy Van Slyke .30 .09
❑ 537 Mike Henneman .10 .03
❑ 538 Miguel Garcia .10 .03
❑ 539 Frank Williams .10 .03
❑ 540 R.J. Reynolds .10 .03
❑ 541 Shawn Hillegas .10 .03
❑ 542 Walt Weiss .10 .03
❑ 543 Greg Hibbard RC .10 .03
❑ 544 Nolan Ryan 2.00 .60
❑ 545 Todd Zeile .20 .06
❑ 546 Hensley Meulens .10 .03

❑ 547 Tim Belcher .10 .03
❑ 548 Mike Witt .10 .03
❑ 549 Greg Cadaret UER .10 .03
(Aquiring, should
be Acquiring)
❑ 550 Franklin Stubbs .10 .03
❑ 551 Tony Castillo .10 .03
❑ 552 Jeff M. Robinson .10 .03
❑ 553 Steve Olin RC .25 .07
❑ 554 Alan Trammell .20 .06
❑ 555 Wade Boggs 4X .30 .09
(Bo Jackson
in background)
❑ 556 Will Clark .30 .09
❑ 557 Jeff King .10 .03
❑ 558 Mike Fitzgerald .10 .03
❑ 559 Ken Howell .10 .03
❑ 560 Bob Kipper .10 .03
❑ 561 Scott Bankhead .10 .03
❑ 562A Jeff Innis ERR 2.00 .60
(Photo actually
David West)
❑ 562B Jeff Innis COR .10 .03
❑ 563 Randy Johnson 1.00 .30
❑ 564 Wally Whitehurst .10 .03
❑ 565 Gene Harris .10 .03
❑ 566 Norm Charlton .10 .03
❑ 567 Robin Yount UER .75 .23
(7602 career hits,
should be 2606)
In addition, the career doubles are
incorrect
❑ 568 Joe Oliver UER .10 .03
(Fl.orida)
❑ 569 Mark Parent .10 .03
❑ 570 John Farrell UER .10 .03
(Loss total added wrong)
❑ 571 Tom Glavine .30 .09
❑ 572 Rod Nichols .10 .03
❑ 573 Jack Morris .20 .06
❑ 574 Greg Swindell .10 .03
❑ 575 Steve Searcy .10 .03
❑ 576 Ricky Jordan .10 .03
❑ 577 Matt Williams .20 .06
❑ 578 Mike LaValliere .10 .03
❑ 579 Bryn Smith .10 .03
❑ 580 Bruce Ruffin .10 .03
❑ 581 Randy Myers .20 .06
❑ 582 Rick Wrona .10 .03
❑ 583 Juan Samuel .10 .03
❑ 584 Les Lancaster .10 .03
❑ 585 Jeff Musselman .10 .03
❑ 586 Rob Dibble .20 .06
❑ 587 Eric Show .10 .03
❑ 588 Jesse Orosco .10 .03
❑ 589 Herm Winningham .10 .03
❑ 590 Andy Allanson .10 .03
❑ 591 Dion James .10 .03
❑ 592 Carmelo Martinez .10 .03
❑ 593 Luis Quinones .10 .03
❑ 594 Dennis Rasmussen .10 .03
❑ 595 Rich Yett .10 .03
❑ 596 Bob Walk .10 .03
❑ 597A A.McGaffigan ERR 2.00 .60
Photo actually
Rich Thompson
❑ 597B A.McGaffigan COR .10 .03
❑ 598 Billy Hatcher .10 .03
❑ 599 Bob Knepper .10 .03
❑ 600 CL 501-600 UER .10 .03
599 Bob Kneppers
❑ 601 Joey Cora .20 .06
❑ 602 Steve Finley .20 .06
❑ 603 Kal Daniels UER .10 .03
(12 hits in '87, should
be 123; 335 runs,
should be 235)
❑ 604 Gregg Olson .20 .06
❑ 605 Dave Stieb .20 .06
❑ 606 Kenny Rogers .20 .06
(Shown catching
football)
❑ 607 Zane Smith .10 .03
❑ 608 Bob Geren UER .10 .03
(Origionally)
❑ 609 Chad Kreuter .10 .03
❑ 610 Mike Smithson .10 .03
❑ 611 Jeff Wetherby .10 .03
❑ 612 Gary Mielke .10 .03
❑ 613 Pete Smith .10 .03
❑ 614 Jack Daugherty UER .10 .03
(Born 7/30/60, should
be 7/3/60)
❑ 615 Lance McCullers .10 .03
❑ 616 Don Robinson .10 .03
❑ 617 Jose Guzman .10 .03
❑ 618 Steve Bedrosian .10 .03
❑ 619 Jamie Moyer .20 .06
❑ 620 Atlee Hammaker .10 .03
❑ 621 Rick Luecken UER .10 .03
(Innings pitched wrong)
❑ 622 Greg W. Harris .10 .03
❑ 623 Pete Harnisch .10 .03
❑ 624 Jerald Clark .10 .03
❑ 625 Jack McDowell UER .10 .03
(Career totals for Games
and GS don't include
1987 season)
❑ 626 Frank Viola .10 .03
❑ 627 Teddy Higuera .10 .03
❑ 628 Marty Pevey .10 .03
❑ 629 Bill Wegman .10 .03
❑ 630 Eric Plunk .10 .03
❑ 631 Drew Hall .10 .03
❑ 632 Doug Jones .10 .03
❑ 633 Geno Petralli UER .10 .03
(Sacremento)
❑ 634 Jose Alvarez .10 .03
❑ 635 Bob Milacki .10 .03
❑ 636 Bobby Witt .10 .03
❑ 637 Trevor Wilson .10 .03
❑ 638 Jeff Russell UER .10 .03
(Shutout stats wrong)
❑ 639 Mike Krukow .10 .03
❑ 640 Rick Leach .10 .03
❑ 641 Dave Schmidt .10 .03
❑ 642 Terry Leach .10 .03
❑ 643 Calvin Schiraldi .10 .03
❑ 644 Bob Melvin .10 .03
❑ 645 Jim Abbott .30 .09
❑ 646 Jaime Navarro .10 .03
❑ 647 Mark Langston UER .10 .03
(Several errors in
stats totals)
❑ 648 Juan Nieves .10 .03
❑ 649 Damaso Garcia .10 .03
❑ 650 Charlie O'Brien .10 .03
❑ 651 Eric King .10 .03
❑ 652 Mike Boddicker .10 .03
❑ 653 Duane Ward .10 .03
❑ 654 Bob Stanley .10 .03
❑ 655 Sandy Alomar Jr. .20 .06
❑ 656 Danny Tartabull UER .10 .03
(395 BB, should be 295)
❑ 657 Randy McCament .10 .03
❑ 658 Charlie Leibrandt .10 .03
❑ 659 Dan Quisenberry .10 .03
❑ 660 Paul Assenmacher .10 .03
❑ 661 Walt Terrell .10 .03
❑ 662 Tim Leary .10 .03
❑ 663 Randy Milligan .10 .03
❑ 664 Bo Diaz .10 .03
❑ 665 Mark Lemke UER .10 .03
(Richmond misspelled
as Richomond)
❑ 666 Jose Gonzalez .10 .03
❑ 667 Chuck Finley UER .20 .06
(Born 11/16/62, should
be 11/26/62)
❑ 668 John Kruk .20 .06
❑ 669 Dick Schofield .10 .03
❑ 670 Tim Crews .10 .03
❑ 671 John Dopson .10 .03
❑ 672 John Orton RC .10 .03
❑ 673 Eric Hetzel .10 .03
❑ 674 Lance Parrish .10 .03
❑ 675 Ramon Martinez .10 .03
❑ 676 Mark Gubicza .10 .03
❑ 677 Greg Litton .10 .03
❑ 678 Greg Mathews .10 .03
❑ 679 Dave Dravecky .20 .06
❑ 680 Steve Farr .10 .03
❑ 681 Mike Devereaux .10 .03
❑ 682 Ken Griffey Sr. .20 .06
❑ 683A Mickey Weston ERR 2.00 .60
(Listed as Jamie
on card)
❑ 683B Mickey Weston COR .10 .03
(Technically still an
error as birthdate is
listed as 3/26/81)
❑ 684 Jack Armstrong .10 .03
❑ 685 Steve Buechele .10 .03
❑ 686 Bryan Harvey .10 .03
❑ 687 Lance Blankenship .10 .03
❑ 688 Dante Bichette .20 .06
❑ 689 Todd Burns .10 .03
❑ 690 Dan Petry .10 .03
❑ 691 Kent Anderson .10 .03
❑ 692 Todd Stottlemyre .20 .06
❑ 693 Wally Joyner UER .20 .06
(Several stats errors)
❑ 694 Mike Rochford .10 .03
❑ 695 Floyd Bannister .10 .03
❑ 696 Rick Reuschel .10 .03
❑ 697 Jose DeLeon .10 .03
❑ 698 Jeff Montgomery .20 .06
❑ 699 Kelly Downs .10 .03
❑ 700A Checklist 601-700 2.00 .60
(683 Jamie Weston)
❑ 700B Checklist 601-700 .10 .03
(683 Mickey Weston)
❑ 701 Jim Gott .10 .03
❑ 702 Delino DeShields .50 .15
Marquis Grissom
Larry Walker
❑ 702A Mike Witt 10.00 3.00
Black rectangle covers much of back
❑ 703 Alejandro Pena .10 .03
❑ 704 Willie Randolph .20 .06
❑ 705 Tim Leary .10 .03
❑ 706 Chuck McElroy RC .10 .03
❑ 707 Gerald Perry .10 .03
❑ 708 Tom Brunansky .10 .03
❑ 709 John Franco .20 .06
❑ 710 Mark Davis .10 .03
❑ 711 David Justice RC .75 .23
❑ 712 Storm Davis .10 .03
❑ 713 Scott Ruskin .10 .03
❑ 714 Glenn Braggs .10 .03
❑ 715 Kevin Bearse .10 .03
❑ 716 Jose Nunez .10 .03
❑ 717 Tim Layana .10 .03
❑ 718 Greg Myers .10 .03
❑ 719 Pete O'Brien .10 .03
❑ 720 John Candelaria .10 .03
❑ 721 Craig Grebeck RC .10 .03
❑ 722 Shawn Boskie RC .10 .03
❑ 723 Jim Leyritz RC .25 .07
❑ 724 Bill Sampen .10 .03
❑ 725 Scott Radinsky RC .10 .03
❑ 726 Todd Hundley RC .25 .07
❑ 727 Scott Hemond RC .10 .03
❑ 728 Lenny Webster RC .10 .03
❑ 729 Jeff Reardon .20 .06
❑ 730 Mitch Webster .10 .03
❑ 731 Brian Bohanon RC .10 .03
❑ 732 Rick Parker .10 .03
❑ 733 Terry Shumpert .10 .03
❑ 734A Nolan Ryan 3.00 .90
6th No-Hitter
(No stripe on front)
❑ 734B Nolan Ryan 1.00 .30
6th No-Hitter
(stripe added on card
front for 300th win)
❑ 735 John Burkett .10 .03
❑ 736 Derrick May RC .10 .03
❑ 737 Carlos Baerga RC .25 .07
❑ 738 Greg Smith .10 .03
❑ 739 Scott Sanderson .10 .03
❑ 740 Joe Kraemer .10 .03
❑ 741 Hector Villanueva RC .10 .03
❑ 742 Mike Fetters RC .25 .07
❑ 743 Mark Gardner RC .10 .03
❑ 744 Matt Nokes .10 .03
❑ 745 Dave Winfield .20 .06
❑ 746 Delino DeShields RC .25 .07

❑ 747 Dann Howitt RC .10 .03
❑ 748 Tony Pena .10 .03
❑ 749 Oil Can Boyd .10 .03
❑ 750 Mike Benjamin .10 .03
❑ 751 Alex Cole RC .10 .03
❑ 752 Eric Gunderson .10 .03
❑ 753 Howard Farmer .10 .03
❑ 754 Joe Carter .20 .06
❑ 755 Ray Lankford RC .50 .15
❑ 756 Sandy Alomar Jr. .20 .06
❑ 757 Alex Sanchez .10 .03
❑ 758 Nick Esasky .10 .03
❑ 759 Stan Belinda RC .10 .03
❑ 760 Jim Presley .10 .03
❑ 761 Gary DiSarcina RC .25 .07
❑ 762 Wayne Edwards .10 .03
❑ 763 Pat Combs .10 .03
❑ 764 Mickey Pina .10 .03
❑ 765 Wilson Alvarez RC .25 .07
❑ 766 Dave Parker .20 .06
❑ 767 Mike Blowers RC .10 .03
❑ 768 Tony Phillips .10 .03
❑ 769 Pascual Perez .10 .03
❑ 770 Gary Pettis .10 .03
❑ 771 Fred Lynn .10 .03
❑ 772 Mel Rojas RC .10 .03
❑ 773 David Segui RC .50 .15
❑ 774 Gary Carter .20 .06
❑ 775 Rafael Valdez .10 .03
❑ 776 Glenallen Hill .10 .03
❑ 777 Keith Hernandez .20 .06
❑ 778 Billy Hatcher .10 .03
❑ 779 Marty Clary .10 .03
❑ 780 Candy Maldonado .10 .03
❑ 781 Mike Marshall .10 .03
❑ 782 Billy Joe Robidoux .10 .03
❑ 783 Mark Langston .10 .03
❑ 784 Paul Sorrento RC .25 .07
❑ 785 Dave Hollins RC .25 .07
❑ 786 Cecil Fielder .20 .06
❑ 787 Matt Young .10 .03
❑ 788 Jeff Huson .10 .03
❑ 789 Lloyd Moseby .10 .03
❑ 790 Ron Kittle .10 .03
❑ 791 Hubie Brooks .10 .03
❑ 792 Craig Lefferts .10 .03
❑ 793 Kevin Bass .10 .03
❑ 794 Bryn Smith .10 .03
❑ 795 Juan Samuel .10 .03
❑ 796 Sam Horn .10 .03
❑ 797 Randy Myers .20 .06
❑ 798 Chris James .10 .03
❑ 799 Bill Gullickson .10 .03
❑ 800 Checklist 701-800 .10 .03

1991 Upper Deck

	Nm-Mt	Ex-Mt
COMPLETE SET (800)	15.00	4.50
COMP.FACT.SET (800)	20.00	6.00
COMPLETE LO SET (700)	15.00	4.50
COMPLETE HI SET (100)	5.00	1.50

❑ 1 Star Rookie Checklist .05 .02
❑ 2 Phil Plantier RC .10 .03
❑ 3 D.J. Dozier .05 .02
❑ 4 Dave Hansen .05 .02
❑ 5 Maurice Vaughn .10 .03
❑ 6 Leo Gomez .05 .02
❑ 7 Scott Aldred .05 .02
❑ 8 Scott Chiamparino .05 .02
❑ 9 Lance Dickson RC .10 .03
❑ 10 Sean Berry RC .10 .03
❑ 11 Bernie Williams .25 .07
❑ 12 Brian Barnes UER .10 .03
(Photo either not him
or in wrong jersey)
❑ 13 Narciso Elvira .05 .02
❑ 14 Mike Gardiner .05 .02
❑ 15 Greg Colbrunn RC .25 .07
❑ 16 Bernard Gilkey .05 .02
❑ 17 Mark Lewis .05 .02
❑ 18 Mickey Morandini .05 .02
❑ 19 Charles Nagy .05 .02
❑ 20 Geronimo Pena .05 .02
❑ 21 Henry Rodriguez RC .25 .07
❑ 22 Scott Cooper .05 .02
❑ 23 Andujar Cedeno UER .05 .02
(Shown batting left,
back says right)
❑ 24 Eric Karros RC .50 .15
❑ 25 Steve Decker UER .05 .02
Lewis-Clark State
College, not Lewis
and Clark
❑ 26 Kevin Belcher .05 .02
❑ 27 Jeff Conine RC .50 .15
❑ 28 Dave Stewart TC .05 .02
❑ 29 Carlton Fisk TC .10 .03
❑ 30 Rafael Palmeiro TC .10 .03
❑ 31 Chuck Finley TC .05 .02
❑ 32 Harold Reynolds TC .05 .02
❑ 33 Bret Saberhagen TC .05 .02
❑ 34 Gary Gaetti TC .05 .02
❑ 35 Scott Leius .05 .02
❑ 36 Neal Heaton .05 .02
❑ 37 Terry Lee .05 .02
❑ 38 Gary Redus .05 .02
❑ 39 Barry Jones .05 .02
❑ 40 Chuck Knoblauch .10 .03
❑ 41 Larry Andersen .05 .02
❑ 42 Darryl Hamilton .05 .02
❑ 43 Mike Greenwell TC .05 .02
❑ 44 Kelly Gruber TC .05 .02
❑ 45 Jack Morris TC .05 .02
❑ 46 Sandy Alomar Jr. TC .05 .02
❑ 47 Gregg Olson TC .05 .02
❑ 48 Dave Parker TC .05 .02
❑ 49 Roberto Kelly TC .05 .02
❑ 50 Top Prospect Checklist .05 .02
❑ 51 Kyle Abbott .05 .02
❑ 52 Jeff Juden .05 .02
❑ 53 T.Van Poppel UER RC .25 .07
Born Arlington and
attended John Martin HS,
should say Hinsdale and
James Martin HS
❑ 54 Steve Karsay RC .25 .07
❑ 55 Chipper Jones RC 4.00 1.20
❑ 56 Chris Johnson RC UER .10 .03
(Called Tim on back)
❑ 57 John Ericks .05 .02
❑ 58 Gary Scott .05 .02
❑ 59 Kiki Jones .05 .02
❑ 60 Wil Cordero RC .10 .03
❑ 61 Royce Clayton .05 .02
❑ 62 Tim Costo RC .10 .03
❑ 63 Roger Salkeld .05 .02
❑ 64 Brook Fordyce RC .25 .07
❑ 65 Mike Mussina RC 1.50 .45
❑ 66 Dave Staton RC .10 .03
❑ 67 Mike Lieberthal RC .50 .15
❑ 68 Kurt Miller RC .05 .02
❑ 69 Dan Peltier RC .10 .03
❑ 70 Greg Blosser .05 .02
❑ 71 Reggie Sanders RC .75 .23
❑ 72 Brent Mayne .05 .02
❑ 73 Rico Brogna .05 .02
❑ 74 Willie Banks .05 .02
❑ 75 Len Brutcher .05 .02
❑ 76 Pat Kelly RC .10 .03
❑ 77 Chris Sabo TC .05 .02
❑ 78 Ramon Martinez TC .05 .02
❑ 79 Matt Williams TC .05 .02
❑ 80 Roberto Alomar TC .10 .03
❑ 81 Glenn Davis TC .05 .02
❑ 82 Ron Gant TC .05 .02
❑ 83 Cecil Fielder FEAT .05 .02
❑ 84 Orlando Merced RC .10 .03
❑ 85 Domingo Ramos .05 .02
❑ 86 Tom Bolton .05 .02
❑ 87 Andres Santana .05 .02
❑ 88 John Dopson .05 .02
❑ 89 Kenny Williams .05 .02
❑ 90 Marty Barrett .05 .02
❑ 91 Tom Pagnozzi .05 .02
❑ 92 Carmelo Martinez .05 .02
❑ 93 Bobby Thigpen SAVE .05 .02
❑ 94 Barry Bonds TC .50 .15
❑ 95 Gregg Jefferies TC .05 .02
❑ 96 Tim Wallach TC .05 .02
❑ 97 Len Dykstra TC .05 .02
❑ 98 Pedro Guerrero TC .05 .02
❑ 99 Mark Grace TC .10 .03
❑ 100 Checklist 1-100 .05 .02
❑ 101 Kevin Elster .05 .02
❑ 102 Tom Brookens .05 .02
❑ 103 Mackey Sasser .05 .02
❑ 104 Felix Fermin .05 .02
❑ 105 Kevin McReynolds .05 .02
❑ 106 Dave Stieb .05 .02
❑ 107 Jeffrey Leonard .05 .02
❑ 108 Dave Henderson .05 .02
❑ 109 Sid Bream .05 .02
❑ 110 Henry Cotto .05 .02
❑ 111 Shawon Dunston .05 .02
❑ 112 Mariano Duncan .05 .02
❑ 113 Joe Girardi .05 .02
❑ 114 Billy Hatcher .05 .02
❑ 115 Greg Maddux .40 .12
❑ 116 Jerry Browne .05 .02
❑ 117 Juan Samuel .05 .02
❑ 118 Steve Olin .05 .02
❑ 119 Alfredo Griffin .05 .02
❑ 120 Mitch Webster .05 .02
❑ 121 Joel Skinner .05 .02
❑ 122 Frank Viola .10 .03
❑ 123 Cory Snyder .05 .02
❑ 124 Howard Johnson .05 .02
❑ 125 Carlos Baerga .05 .02
❑ 126 Tony Fernandez .05 .02
❑ 127 Dave Stewart .10 .03
❑ 128 Jay Buhner .10 .03
❑ 129 Mike LaValliere .05 .02
❑ 130 Scott Bradley .05 .02
❑ 131 Tony Phillips .05 .02
❑ 132 Ryne Sandberg .40 .12
❑ 133 Paul O'Neill .15 .04
❑ 134 Mark Grace .15 .04
❑ 135 Chris Sabo .05 .02
❑ 136 Ramon Martinez .05 .02
❑ 137 Brook Jacoby .05 .02
❑ 138 Candy Maldonado .05 .02
❑ 139 Mike Scioscia .05 .02
❑ 140 Chris James .05 .02
❑ 141 Craig Worthington .05 .02
❑ 142 Manny Lee .05 .02
❑ 143 Tim Raines .10 .03
❑ 144 Sandy Alomar Jr. .05 .02
❑ 145 John Olerud .10 .03
❑ 146 Ozzie Canseco .10 .03
(With Jose)
❑ 147 Pat Borders .05 .02
❑ 148 Harold Reynolds .10 .03
❑ 149 Tom Henke .05 .02
❑ 150 R.J. Reynolds .05 .02
❑ 151 Mike Gallego .05 .02
❑ 152 Bobby Bonilla .10 .03
❑ 153 Terry Steinbach .05 .02
❑ 154 Barry Bonds 1.00 .30
❑ 155 Jose Canseco .15 .04
❑ 156 Gregg Jefferies .05 .02
❑ 157 Matt Williams .10 .03
❑ 158 Craig Biggio .15 .04
❑ 159 Daryl Boston .05 .02
❑ 160 Ricky Jordan .05 .02
❑ 161 Stan Belinda .05 .02
❑ 162 Ozzie Smith .40 .12
❑ 163 Tom Brunansky .05 .02
❑ 164 Todd Zeile .05 .02
❑ 165 Mike Greenwell .05 .02

❑ 166 Kal Daniels .05 .02
❑ 167 Kent Hrbek .10 .03
❑ 168 Franklin Stubbs .05 .02
❑ 169 Dick Schofield .05 .02
❑ 170 Junior Ortiz .05 .02
❑ 171 Hector Villanueva .05 .02
❑ 172 Dennis Eckersley .10 .03
❑ 173 Mitch Williams .05 .02
❑ 174 Mark McGwire .60 .18
❑ 175 F.Valenzuela 3X .10 .03
❑ 176 Gary Carter .10 .03
❑ 177 Dave Magadan .05 .02
❑ 178 Robby Thompson .05 .02
❑ 179 Bob Ojeda .05 .02
❑ 180 Ken Caminiti .10 .03
❑ 181 Don Slaught .05 .02
❑ 182 Luis Rivera .05 .02
❑ 183 Jay Bell .10 .03
❑ 184 Jody Reed .05 .02
❑ 185 Wally Backman .05 .02
❑ 186 Dave Martinez .05 .02
❑ 187 Luis Polonia .05 .02
❑ 188 Shane Mack .05 .02
❑ 189 Spike Owen .05 .02
❑ 190 Scott Bailes .05 .02
❑ 191 John Russell .05 .02
❑ 192 Walt Weiss .05 .02
❑ 193 Jose Oquendo .05 .02
❑ 194 Carney Lansford .10 .03
❑ 195 Jeff Huson .05 .02
❑ 196 Keith Miller .05 .02
❑ 197 Eric Yelding .05 .02
❑ 198 Ron Darling .05 .02
❑ 199 John Kruk .10 .03
❑ 200 Checklist 101-200 .05 .02
❑ 201 John Shelby .05 .02
❑ 202 Bob Geren .05 .02
❑ 203 Lance McCullers .05 .02
❑ 204 Alvaro Espinoza .05 .02
❑ 205 Mark Salas .05 .02
❑ 206 Mike Pagliarulo .05 .02
❑ 207 Jose Uribe .05 .02
❑ 208 Jim Deshaies .05 .02
❑ 209 Ron Karkovice .05 .02
❑ 210 Rafael Ramirez .05 .02
❑ 211 Donnie Hill .05 .02
❑ 212 Brian Harper .05 .02
❑ 213 Jack Howell .05 .02
❑ 214 Wes Gardner .05 .02
❑ 215 Tim Burke .05 .02
❑ 216 Doug Jones .05 .02
❑ 217 Hubie Brooks .05 .02
❑ 218 Tom Candiotti .05 .02
❑ 219 Gerald Perry .05 .02
❑ 220 Jose DeLeon .05 .02
❑ 221 Wally Whitehurst .05 .02
❑ 222 Alan Mills .05 .02
❑ 223 Alan Trammell .10 .03
❑ 224 Dwight Gooden .10 .03
❑ 225 Travis Fryman .10 .03
❑ 226 Joe Carter .10 .03
❑ 227 Julio Franco .10 .03
❑ 228 Craig Lefferts .05 .02
❑ 229 Gary Pettis .05 .02
❑ 230 Dennis Rasmussen .05 .02
❑ 231A Brian Downing ERR .05 .02
(No position on front)
❑ 231B Brian Downing COR .25 .07
(DH on front)
❑ 232 Carlos Quintana .05 .02
❑ 233 Gary Gaetti .10 .03
❑ 234 Mark Langston .05 .02
❑ 235 Tim Wallach .05 .02
❑ 236 Greg Swindell .05 .02
❑ 237 Eddie Murray .25 .07
❑ 238 Jeff Manto .05 .02
❑ 239 Lenny Harris .05 .02
❑ 240 Jesse Orosco .05 .02
❑ 241 Scott Lusader .05 .02
❑ 242 Sid Fernandez .05 .02
❑ 243 Jim Leyritz .05 .02
❑ 244 Cecil Fielder .10 .03
❑ 245 Darryl Strawberry .10 .03
❑ 246 Frank Thomas UER .25 .07
(Comiskey Park misspelled Comisky)

❑ 247 Kevin Mitchell .05 .02
❑ 248 Lance Johnson .05 .02
❑ 249 Rick Reuschel .05 .02
❑ 250 Mark Portugal .05 .02
❑ 251 Derek Lilliquist .05 .02
❑ 252 Brian Holman .05 .02
❑ 253 Rafael Valdez UER .05 .02
(Born 4/17/68, should be 12/17/67)
❑ 254 B.J. Surhoff .10 .03
❑ 255 Tony Gwynn .30 .09
❑ 256 Andy Van Slyke .15 .04
❑ 257 Todd Stottlemyre .05 .02
❑ 258 Jose Lind .05 .02
❑ 259 Greg Myers .05 .02
❑ 260 Jeff Ballard .05 .02
❑ 261 Bobby Thigpen .05 .02
❑ 262 Jimmy Kremers .05 .02
❑ 263 Robin Ventura .10 .03
❑ 264 John Smoltz .15 .04
❑ 265 Sammy Sosa .25 .07
❑ 266 Gary Sheffield .10 .03
❑ 267 Len Dykstra .10 .03
❑ 268 Bill Spiers .05 .02
❑ 269 Charlie Hayes .05 .02
❑ 270 Brett Butler .10 .03
❑ 271 Bip Roberts .05 .02
❑ 272 Rob Deer .05 .02
❑ 273 Fred Lynn .05 .02
❑ 274 Dave Parker .10 .03
❑ 275 Andy Benes .05 .02
❑ 276 Glenallen Hill .05 .02
❑ 277 Steve Howard .05 .02
❑ 278 Doug Drabek .05 .02
❑ 279 Joe Oliver .05 .02
❑ 280 Todd Benzinger .05 .02
❑ 281 Eric King .05 .02
❑ 282 Jim Presley .05 .02
❑ 283 Ken Patterson .05 .02
❑ 284 Jack Daugherty .05 .02
❑ 285 Ivan Calderon .05 .02
❑ 286 Edgar Diaz .05 .02
❑ 287 Kevin Bass .05 .02
❑ 288 Don Carman .05 .02
❑ 289 Greg Brock .05 .02
❑ 290 John Franco .10 .03
❑ 291 Joey Cora .05 .02
❑ 292 Bill Wegman .05 .02
❑ 293 Eric Show .05 .02
❑ 294 Scott Bankhead .05 .02
❑ 295 Garry Templeton .05 .02
❑ 296 Mickey Tettleton .05 .02
❑ 297 Luis Sojo .05 .02
❑ 298 Jose Rijo .05 .02
❑ 299 Dave Johnson .05 .02
❑ 300 Checklist 201-300 .05 .02
❑ 301 Mark Grant .05 .02
❑ 302 Pete Harnisch .05 .02
❑ 303 Greg Olson .05 .02
❑ 304 Anthony Telford .05 .02
❑ 305 Lonnie Smith .05 .02
❑ 306 Chris Hoiles .05 .02
❑ 307 Bryn Smith .05 .02
❑ 308 Mike Devereaux .05 .02
❑ 309A Milt Thompson ERR .25 .07
(Under yr information has print dot)
❑ 309B Milt Thompson COR .05 .02
(Under yr information says 86)
❑ 310 Bob Melvin .05 .02
❑ 311 Luis Salazar .05 .02
❑ 312 Ed Whitson .05 .02
❑ 313 Charlie Hough .10 .03
❑ 314 Dave Clark .05 .02
❑ 315 Eric Gunderson .05 .02
❑ 316 Dan Petry .05 .02
❑ 317 Dante Bichette UER .10 .03
(Assists misspelled as assissts)
❑ 318 Mike Heath .05 .02
❑ 319 Damon Berryhill .05 .02
❑ 320 Walt Terrell .05 .02
❑ 321 Scott Fletcher .05 .02
❑ 322 Dan Plesac .05 .02
❑ 323 Jack McDowell .05 .02

❑ 324 Paul Molitor .15 .04
❑ 325 Ozzie Guillen .10 .03
❑ 326 Gregg Olson .05 .02
❑ 327 Pedro Guerrero .10 .03
❑ 328 Bob Milacki .05 .02
❑ 329 John Tudor UER .05 .02
('90 Cardinals, should be '90 Dodgers)
❑ 330 Steve Finley UER .10 .03
(Born 3/12/65, should be 5/12)
❑ 331 Jack Clark .10 .03
❑ 332 Jerome Walton .05 .02
❑ 333 Andy Hawkins .05 .02
❑ 334 Derrick May .05 .02
❑ 335 Roberto Alomar .15 .04
❑ 336 Jack Morris .10 .03
❑ 337 Dave Winfield .10 .03
❑ 338 Steve Searcy .05 .02
❑ 339 Chili Davis .10 .03
❑ 340 Larry Sheets .05 .02
❑ 341 Ted Higuera .05 .02
❑ 342 David Segui .05 .02
❑ 343 Greg Cadaret .05 .02
❑ 344 Robin Yount .40 .12
❑ 345 Nolan Ryan 1.00 .30
❑ 346 Ray Lankford .10 .03
❑ 347 Cal Ripken .75 .23
❑ 348 Lee Smith .10 .03
❑ 349 Brady Anderson .10 .03
❑ 350 Frank DiPino .05 .02
❑ 351 Hal Morris .05 .02
❑ 352 Deion Sanders .15 .04
❑ 353 Barry Larkin .15 .04
❑ 354 Don Mattingly .60 .18
❑ 355 Eric Davis .10 .03
❑ 356 Jose Offerman .05 .02
❑ 357 Mel Rojas .05 .02
❑ 358 Rudy Seanez .05 .02
❑ 359 Oil Can Boyd .05 .02
❑ 360 Nelson Liriano .05 .02
❑ 361 Ron Gant .10 .03
❑ 362 Howard Farmer .05 .02
❑ 363 David Justice .10 .03
❑ 364 Delino DeShields .10 .03
❑ 365 Steve Avery .05 .02
❑ 366 David Cone .10 .03
❑ 367 Lou Whitaker .10 .03
❑ 368 Von Hayes .05 .02
❑ 369 Frank Tanana .05 .02
❑ 370 Tim Teufel .05 .02
❑ 371 Randy Myers .05 .02
❑ 372 Roberto Kelly .05 .02
❑ 373 Jack Armstrong .05 .02
❑ 374 Kelly Gruber .05 .02
❑ 375 Kevin Maas .05 .02
❑ 376 Randy Johnson .30 .09
❑ 377 David West .05 .02
❑ 378 Brent Knackert .05 .02
❑ 379 Rick Honeycutt .05 .02
❑ 380 Kevin Gross .05 .02
❑ 381 Tom Foley .05 .02
❑ 382 Jeff Blauser .05 .02
❑ 383 Scott Ruskin .05 .02
❑ 384 Andres Thomas .05 .02
❑ 385 Dennis Martinez .10 .03
❑ 386 Mike Henneman .05 .02
❑ 387 Felix Jose .05 .02
❑ 388 Alejandro Pena .05 .02
❑ 389 Chet Lemon .05 .02
❑ 390 Craig Wilson .05 .02
❑ 391 Chuck Crim .05 .02
❑ 392 Mel Hall .05 .02
❑ 393 Mark Knudson .05 .02
❑ 394 Norm Charlton .05 .02
❑ 395 Mike Felder .05 .02
❑ 396 Tim Layana .05 .02
❑ 397 Steve Frey .05 .02
❑ 398 Bill Doran .05 .02
❑ 399 Dion James .05 .02
❑ 400 Checklist 301-400 .05 .02
❑ 401 Ron Hassey .05 .02
❑ 402 Don Robinson .05 .02
❑ 403 Gene Nelson .05 .02
❑ 404 Terry Kennedy .05 .02
❑ 405 Todd Burns .05 .02

❑ 406 Roger McDowell .05 .02
❑ 407 Bob Kipper .05 .02
❑ 408 Darren Daulton .10 .03
❑ 409 Chuck Cary .05 .02
❑ 410 Bruce Ruffin .05 .02
❑ 411 Juan Berenguer .05 .02
❑ 412 Gary Ward .05 .02
❑ 413 Al Newman .05 .02
❑ 414 Danny Jackson .05 .02
❑ 415 Greg Gagne .05 .02
❑ 416 Tom Herr .05 .02
❑ 417 Jeff Parrett .05 .02
❑ 418 Jeff Reardon .10 .03
❑ 419 Mark Lemke .05 .02
❑ 420 Charlie O'Brien .05 .02
❑ 421 Willie Randolph .10 .03
❑ 422 Steve Bedrosian .05 .02
❑ 423 Mike Moore .05 .02
❑ 424 Jeff Brantley .05 .02
❑ 425 Bob Welch .05 .02
❑ 426 Terry Mulholland .05 .02
❑ 427 Willie Blair .05 .02
❑ 428 Darrin Fletcher .05 .02
❑ 429 Mike Witt .05 .02
❑ 430 Joe Boever .05 .02
❑ 431 Tom Gordon .05 .02
❑ 432 Pedro Munoz RC .10 .03
❑ 433 Kevin Seitzer .05 .02
❑ 434 Kevin Tapani .05 .02
❑ 435 Bret Saberhagen .10 .03
❑ 436 Ellis Burks .10 .03
❑ 437 Chuck Finley .10 .03
❑ 438 Mike Boddicker .05 .02
❑ 439 Francisco Cabrera .05 .02
❑ 440 Todd Hundley .05 .02
❑ 441 Kelly Downs .05 .02
❑ 442 Dann Howitt .05 .02
❑ 443 Scott Garrelts .05 .02
❑ 444 Rickey Henderson 3X .25 .07
❑ 445 Will Clark .15 .04
❑ 446 Ben McDonald .05 .02
❑ 447 Dale Murphy .15 .04
❑ 448 Dave Righetti .10 .03
❑ 449 Dickie Thon .05 .02
❑ 450 Ted Power .05 .02
❑ 451 Scott Coolbaugh .05 .02
❑ 452 Dwight Smith .05 .02
❑ 453 Pete Incaviglia .05 .02
❑ 454 Andre Dawson .10 .03
❑ 455 Ruben Sierra .05 .02
❑ 456 Andres Galarraga .10 .03
❑ 457 Alvin Davis .05 .02
❑ 458 Tony Castillo .05 .02
❑ 459 Pete O'Brien .05 .02
❑ 460 Charlie Leibrandt .05 .02
❑ 461 Vince Coleman .05 .02
❑ 462 Steve Sax .05 .02
❑ 463 Omar Olivares RC .10 .03
❑ 464 Oscar Azocar .05 .02
❑ 465 Joe Magrane .05 .02
❑ 466 Karl Rhodes .05 .02
❑ 467 Benito Santiago .10 .03
❑ 468 Joe Klink .05 .02
❑ 469 Sil Campusano .05 .02
❑ 470 Mark Parent .05 .02
❑ 471 Shawn Boskie UER .05 .02
(Depleted misspelled as depleated)
❑ 472 Kevin Brown .10 .03
❑ 473 Rick Sutcliffe .10 .03
❑ 474 Rafael Palmeiro .15 .04
❑ 475 Mike Harkey .05 .02
❑ 476 Jaime Navarro .05 .02
❑ 477 Marquis Grissom UER .10 .03
(DeShields misspelled as DeSheilds)
❑ 478 Marty Clary .05 .02
❑ 479 Greg Briley .05 .02
❑ 480 Tom Glavine .15 .04
❑ 481 Lee Guetterman .05 .02
❑ 482 Rex Hudler .05 .02
❑ 483 Dave LaPoint .05 .02
❑ 484 Terry Pendleton .10 .03
❑ 485 Jesse Barfield .05 .02
❑ 486 Jose DeJesus .05 .02
❑ 487 Paul Abbott RC .25 .07
❑ 488 Ken Howell .05 .02
❑ 489 Greg W. Harris .05 .02
❑ 490 Roy Smith .05 .02
❑ 491 Paul Assenmacher .05 .02
❑ 492 Geno Petralli .05 .02
❑ 493 Steve Wilson .05 .02
❑ 494 Kevin Reimer .05 .02
❑ 495 Bill Long .05 .02
❑ 496 Mike Jackson .05 .02
❑ 497 Oddibe McDowell .05 .02
❑ 498 Bill Swift .05 .02
❑ 499 Jeff Treadway .05 .02
❑ 500 Checklist 401-500 .05 .02
❑ 501 Gene Larkin .05 .02
❑ 502 Bob Boone .10 .03
❑ 503 Allan Anderson .05 .02
❑ 504 Luis Aquino .05 .02
❑ 505 Mark Guthrie .05 .02
❑ 506 Joe Orsulak .05 .02
❑ 507 Dana Kiecker .05 .02
❑ 508 Dave Gallagher .05 .02
❑ 509 Greg A. Harris .05 .02
❑ 510 Mark Williamson .05 .02
❑ 511 Casey Candaele .05 .02
❑ 512 Mookie Wilson .10 .03
❑ 513 Dave Smith .05 .02
❑ 514 Chuck Carr .05 .02
❑ 515 Glenn Wilson .05 .02
❑ 516 Mike Fitzgerald .05 .02
❑ 517 Devon White .10 .03
❑ 518 Dave Hollins .05 .02
❑ 519 Mark Eichhorn .05 .02
❑ 520 Otis Nixon .05 .02
❑ 521 Terry Shumpert .05 .02
❑ 522 Scott Erickson .05 .02
❑ 523 Danny Tartabull .05 .02
❑ 524 Orel Hershiser .10 .03
❑ 525 George Brett .60 .18
❑ 526 Greg Vaughn .05 .02
❑ 527 Tim Naehring .05 .02
❑ 528 Curt Schilling .25 .07
❑ 529 Chris Bosio .05 .02
❑ 530 Sam Horn .05 .02
❑ 531 Mike Scott .05 .02
❑ 532 George Bell .05 .02
❑ 533 Eric Anthony .05 .02
❑ 534 Julio Valera .05 .02
❑ 535 Glenn Davis .05 .02
❑ 536 Larry Walker UER .25 .07
(Should have comma after Expos in text)
❑ 537 Pat Combs .05 .02
❑ 538 Chris Nabholz .05 .02
❑ 539 Kirk McCaskill .05 .02
❑ 540 Randy Ready .05 .02
❑ 541 Mark Gubicza .05 .02
❑ 542 Rick Aguilera .10 .03
❑ 543 Brian McRae RC .25 .07
❑ 544 Kirby Puckett .25 .07
❑ 545 Bo Jackson .25 .07
❑ 546 Wade Boggs .15 .04
❑ 547 Tim McIntosh .05 .02
❑ 548 Randy Milligan .05 .02
❑ 549 Dwight Evans .15 .04
❑ 550 Billy Ripken .05 .02
❑ 551 Erik Hanson .05 .02
❑ 552 Lance Parrish .10 .03
❑ 553 Tino Martinez .25 .07
❑ 554 Jim Abbott .15 .04
❑ 555 Ken Griffey Jr. UER .50 .15
(Second most votes for 1991 All-Star Game)
❑ 556 Milt Cuyler .05 .02
❑ 557 Mark Leonard .05 .02
❑ 558 Jay Howell .05 .02
❑ 559 Lloyd Moseby .05 .02
❑ 560 Chris Gwynn .05 .02
❑ 561 Mark Whiten .05 .02
❑ 562 Harold Baines .10 .03
❑ 563 Junior Felix .05 .02
❑ 564 Darren Lewis .05 .02
❑ 565 Fred McGriff .15 .04
❑ 566 Kevin Appier .10 .03
❑ 567 Luis Gonzalez RC .75 .23
❑ 568 Frank White .10 .03
❑ 569 Juan Agosto .05 .02
❑ 570 Mike Macfarlane .05 .02
❑ 571 Bert Blyleven .10 .03
❑ 572 Ken Griffey Sr. .25 .07
Ken Griffey Jr.
❑ 573 Lee Stevens .05 .02
❑ 574 Edgar Martinez .15 .04
❑ 575 Wally Joyner .10 .03
❑ 576 Tim Belcher .05 .02
❑ 577 John Burkett .05 .02
❑ 578 Mike Morgan .05 .02
❑ 579 Paul Gibson .05 .02
❑ 580 Jose Vizcaino .05 .02
❑ 581 Duane Ward .05 .02
❑ 582 Scott Sanderson .05 .02
❑ 583 David Wells .10 .03
❑ 584 Willie McGee .10 .03
❑ 585 John Cerutti .05 .02
❑ 586 Danny Darwin .05 .02
❑ 587 Kurt Stillwell .05 .02
❑ 588 Rich Gedman .05 .02
❑ 589 Mark Davis .05 .02
❑ 590 Bill Gullickson .05 .02
❑ 591 Matt Young .05 .02
❑ 592 Bryan Harvey .05 .02
❑ 593 Omar Vizquel .15 .04
❑ 594 Scott Lewis RC .10 .03
❑ 595 Dave Valle .05 .02
❑ 596 Tim Crews .05 .02
❑ 597 Mike Bielecki .05 .02
❑ 598 Mike Sharperson .05 .02
❑ 599 Dave Bergman .05 .02
❑ 600 Checklist 501-600 .05 .02
❑ 601 Steve Lyons .05 .02
❑ 602 Bruce Hurst .05 .02
❑ 603 Donn Pall .05 .02
❑ 604 Jim Vatcher .05 .02
❑ 605 Dan Pasqua .05 .02
❑ 606 Kenny Rogers .10 .03
❑ 607 Jeff Schulz .05 .02
❑ 608 Brad Arnsberg .05 .02
❑ 609 Willie Wilson .05 .02
❑ 610 Jamie Moyer .10 .03
❑ 611 Ron Oester .05 .02
❑ 612 Dennis Cook .05 .02
❑ 613 Rick Mahler .05 .02
❑ 614 Bill Landrum .05 .02
❑ 615 Scott Scudder .05 .02
❑ 616 Tom Edens .05 .02
❑ 617 1917 Revisited .10 .03
(White Sox vintage uniforms)
❑ 618 Jim Gantner .05 .02
❑ 619 Darrel Akerfelds .05 .02
❑ 620 Ron Robinson .05 .02
❑ 621 Scott Radinsky .05 .02
❑ 622 Pete Smith .05 .02
❑ 623 Melido Perez .05 .02
❑ 624 Jerald Clark .05 .02
❑ 625 Carlos Martinez .05 .02
❑ 626 Wes Chamberlain RC .25 .07
❑ 627 Bobby Witt .05 .02
❑ 628 Ken Dayley .05 .02
❑ 629 John Barfield .05 .02
❑ 630 Bob Tewksbury .05 .02
❑ 631 Glenn Braggs .05 .02
❑ 632 Jim Neidlinger .05 .02
❑ 633 Tom Browning .05 .02
❑ 634 Kirk Gibson .15 .04
❑ 635 Rob Dibble .10 .03
❑ 636 Rickey Henderson SB .25 .07
Lou Brock
May 1, 1991 on front
❑ 636A R.Henderson SB .25 .07
Lou Brock
no date on card
❑ 637 Jeff Montgomery .05 .02
❑ 638 Mike Schooler .05 .02
❑ 639 Storm Davis .05 .02
❑ 640 Rich Rodriguez .05 .02
❑ 641 Phil Bradley .05 .02
❑ 642 Kent Mercker .05 .02
❑ 643 Carlton Fisk .15 .04
❑ 644 Mike Bell .05 .02
❑ 645 Alex Fernandez .05 .02
❑ 646 Juan Gonzalez .25 .07
❑ 647 Ken Hill .05 .02
❑ 648 Jeff Russell .05 .02

- ❑ 649 Chuck Malone .05 .02
- ❑ 650 Steve Buechele .05 .02
- ❑ 651 Mike Benjamin .05 .02
- ❑ 652 Tony Pena .05 .02
- ❑ 653 Trevor Wilson .05 .02
- ❑ 654 Alex Cole .05 .02
- ❑ 655 Roger Clemens .50 .15
- ❑ 656 Mark McGwire BASH .30 .09
- ❑ 657 Joe Grahe RC .10 .03
- ❑ 658 Jim Eisenreich .05 .02
- ❑ 659 Dan Gladden .05 .02
- ❑ 660 Steve Farr .05 .02
- ❑ 661 Bill Sampen .05 .02
- ❑ 662 Dave Rohde .05 .02
- ❑ 663 Mark Gardner .05 .02
- ❑ 664 Mike Simms .05 .02
- ❑ 665 Moises Alou .10 .03
- ❑ 666 Mickey Hatcher .05 .02
- ❑ 667 Jimmy Key .10 .03
- ❑ 668 John Wetteland .10 .03
- ❑ 669 John Smiley .05 .02
- ❑ 670 Jim Acker .05 .02
- ❑ 671 Pascual Perez .05 .02
- ❑ 672 Reggie Harris UER .05 .02
  (Opportunity misspelled
  as oppurtinty)
- ❑ 673 Matt Nokes .05 .02
- ❑ 674 Rafael Novoa .05 .02
- ❑ 675 Hensley Meulens .05 .02
- ❑ 676 Jeff M. Robinson .05 .02
- ❑ 677 Ground Breaking .10 .03
  (New Comiskey Park;
  Carlton Fisk and
  Robin Ventura)
- ❑ 678 Johnny Ray .05 .02
- ❑ 679 Greg Hibbard .05 .02
- ❑ 680 Paul Sorrento .05 .02
- ❑ 681 Mike Marshall .05 .02
- ❑ 682 Jim Clancy .05 .02
- ❑ 683 Rob Murphy .05 .02
- ❑ 684 Dave Schmidt .05 .02
- ❑ 685 Jeff Gray .05 .02
- ❑ 686 Mike Hartley .05 .02
- ❑ 687 Jeff King .05 .02
- ❑ 688 Stan Javier .05 .02
- ❑ 689 Bob Walk .05 .02
- ❑ 690 Jim Gott .05 .02
- ❑ 691 Mike LaCoss .05 .02
- ❑ 692 John Farrell .05 .02
- ❑ 693 Tim Leary .05 .02
- ❑ 694 Mike Walker .05 .02
- ❑ 695 Eric Plunk .05 .02
- ❑ 696 Mike Fetters .05 .02
- ❑ 697 Wayne Edwards .05 .02
- ❑ 698 Tim Drummond .05 .02
- ❑ 699 Willie Fraser .05 .02
- ❑ 700 Checklist 601-700 .05 .02
- ❑ 701 Mike Heath .05 .02
- ❑ 702 Luis Gonzalez 1.00 .30
  Karl Rhodes
  Jeff Bagwell
- ❑ 703 Jose Mesa .05 .02
- ❑ 704 Dave Smith .05 .02
- ❑ 705 Danny Darwin .05 .02
- ❑ 706 Rafael Belliard .05 .02
- ❑ 707 Rob Murphy .05 .02
- ❑ 708 Terry Pendleton .10 .03
- ❑ 709 Mike Pagliarulo .05 .02
- ❑ 710 Sid Bream .05 .02
- ❑ 711 Junior Felix .05 .02
- ❑ 712 Dante Bichette .10 .03
- ❑ 713 Kevin Gross .05 .02
- ❑ 714 Luis Sojo .05 .02
- ❑ 715 Bob Ojeda .05 .02
- ❑ 716 Julio Machado .05 .02
- ❑ 717 Steve Farr .05 .02
- ❑ 718 Franklin Stubbs .05 .02
- ❑ 719 Mike Boddicker .05 .02
- ❑ 720 Willie Randolph .10 .03
- ❑ 721 Willie McGee .10 .03
- ❑ 722 Chili Davis .10 .03
- ❑ 723 Danny Jackson .05 .02
- ❑ 724 Cory Snyder .05 .02
- ❑ 725 Andre Dawson .25 .07
  George Bell
  Ryne Sandberg
- ❑ 726 Rob Deer .05 .02
- ❑ 727 Rich DeLucia .05 .02
- ❑ 728 Mike Perez RC .10 .03
- ❑ 729 Mickey Tettleton .05 .02
- ❑ 730 Mike Blowers .05 .02
- ❑ 731 Gary Gaetti .10 .03
- ❑ 732 Brett Butler .10 .03
- ❑ 733 Dave Parker .10 .03
- ❑ 734 Eddie Zosky .05 .02
- ❑ 735 Jack Clark .10 .03
- ❑ 736 Jack Morris .10 .03
- ❑ 737 Kirk Gibson .15 .04
- ❑ 738 Steve Bedrosian .05 .02
- ❑ 739 Candy Maldonado .05 .02
- ❑ 740 Matt Young .05 .02
- ❑ 741 Rich Garces RC .10 .03
- ❑ 742 George Bell .05 .02
- ❑ 743 Deion Sanders .15 .04
- ❑ 744 Bo Jackson .25 .07
- ❑ 745 Luis Mercedes RC .10 .03
- ❑ 746 Reggie Jefferson UER .05 .02
  (Throwing left on card;
  back has throws right)
- ❑ 747 Pete Incaviglia .05 .02
- ❑ 748 Chris Hammond .05 .02
- ❑ 749 Mike Stanton .05 .02
- ❑ 750 Scott Sanderson .05 .02
- ❑ 751 Paul Faries .05 .02
- ❑ 752 Al Osuna RC .05 .02
- ❑ 753 Steve Chitren .05 .02
- ❑ 754 Tony Fernandez .05 .02
- ❑ 755 Jeff Bagwell RC UER 2.00 .60
  (Strikeout and walk
  totals reversed)
- ❑ 756 K.Dressendorfer RC .10 .03
- ❑ 757 Glenn Davis .05 .02
- ❑ 758 Gary Carter .10 .03
- ❑ 759 Zane Smith .05 .02
- ❑ 760 Vance Law .05 .02
- ❑ 761 Denis Boucher RC .10 .03
- ❑ 762 Turner Ward RC .10 .03
- ❑ 763 Roberto Alomar .15 .04
- ❑ 764 Albert Belle .10 .03
- ❑ 765 Joe Carter .10 .03
- ❑ 766 Pete Schourek RC .10 .03
- ❑ 767 H.Slocumb RC .10 .03
- ❑ 768 Vince Coleman .05 .02
- ❑ 769 Mitch Williams .05 .02
- ❑ 770 Brian Downing .05 .02
- ❑ 771 Dana Allison .05 .02
- ❑ 772 Pete Harnisch .05 .02
- ❑ 773 Tim Raines .10 .03
- ❑ 774 Darryl Kile .10 .03
- ❑ 775 Fred McGriff .15 .04
- ❑ 776 Dwight Evans .15 .04
- ❑ 777 Joe Slusarski .05 .02
- ❑ 778 Dave Righetti .10 .03
- ❑ 779 Jeff Hamilton .05 .02
- ❑ 780 Ernest Riles .05 .02
- ❑ 781 Ken Dayley .05 .02
- ❑ 782 Eric King .05 .02
- ❑ 783 Devon White .10 .03
- ❑ 784 Beau Allred .05 .02
- ❑ 785 Mike Timlin RC .50 .15
- ❑ 786 Ivan Calderon .05 .02
- ❑ 787 Hubie Brooks .05 .02
- ❑ 788 Juan Agosto .05 .02
- ❑ 789 Barry Jones .05 .02
- ❑ 790 Wally Backman .05 .02
- ❑ 791 Jim Presley .05 .02
- ❑ 792 Charlie Hough .10 .03
- ❑ 793 Larry Andersen .05 .02
- ❑ 794 Steve Finley .10 .03
- ❑ 795 Shawn Abner .05 .02
- ❑ 796 Jeff M. Robinson .05 .02
- ❑ 797 Joe Bitker .05 .02
- ❑ 798 Eric Show .05 .02
- ❑ 799 Bud Black .05 .02
- ❑ 800 Checklist 701-800 .05 .02
- ❑ HH1 H.Aaron Hologram 1.50 .45
- ❑ SP1 Michael Jordan SP 8.00 2.40
  (Shown batting in
  White Sox uniform)
- ❑ SP2 Rickey Henderson 2.00 .60
  Nolan Ryan
  May 1, 1991 Records

1991 Upper Deck Final Edition

	Nm-Mt	Ex-Mt
COMP.FACT.SET (100)	10.00	3.00

- ❑ 1F Ryan Klesko CL .25 .07
  Reggie Sanders
- ❑ 2F Pedro Martinez RC 8.00 2.40
- ❑ 3F Lance Dickson .05 .02
- ❑ 4F Royce Clayton .05 .02
- ❑ 5F Scott Bryant .05 .02
- ❑ 6F Dan Wilson RC .25 .07
- ❑ 7F Dmitri Young RC 1.00 .30
- ❑ 8F Ryan Klesko RC .75 .23
- ❑ 9F Tom Goodwin .05 .02
- ❑ 10F Rondell White RC .50 .15
- ❑ 11F Reggie Sanders .50 .15
- ❑ 12F Todd Van Poppel .05 .02
- ❑ 13F Arthur Rhodes RC .25 .07
- ❑ 14F Eddie Zosky .05 .02
- ❑ 15F Gerald Williams RC .25 .07
- ❑ 16F Robert Eenhoorn RC .10 .03
- ❑ 17F Jim Thome RC 2.00 .60
- ❑ 18F Marc Newfield RC .10 .03
- ❑ 19F Kerwin Moore RC .10 .03
- ❑ 20F Jeff McNeely RC .10 .03
- ❑ 21F Frankie Rodriguez RC .10 .03
- ❑ 22F Andy Mota .05 .02
- ❑ 23F Chris Haney RC .10 .03
- ❑ 24F Kenny Lofton RC .75 .23
- ❑ 25F Dave Nilsson RC .25 .07
- ❑ 26F Derek Bell .10 .03
- ❑ 27F Frank Castillo RC .25 .07
- ❑ 28F Candy Maldonado .05 .02
- ❑ 29F Chuck McElroy .05 .02
- ❑ 30F Chito Martinez .05 .02
- ❑ 31F Steve Howe .05 .02
- ❑ 32F Freddie Benavides .05 .02
- ❑ 33F Scott Kamieniecki RC .10 .03
- ❑ 34F Denny Neagle RC .25 .07
- ❑ 35F Mike Humphreys RC .10 .03
- ❑ 36F Mike Remlinger .05 .02
- ❑ 37F Scott Coolbaugh .05 .02
- ❑ 38F Darren Lewis .05 .02
- ❑ 39F Thomas Howard .05 .02
- ❑ 40F John Candelaria .05 .02
- ❑ 41F Todd Benzinger .05 .02
- ❑ 42F Wilson Alvarez .05 .02
- ❑ 43F Patrick Lennon RC .10 .03
- ❑ 44F Rusty Meacham RC .10 .03
- ❑ 45F Ryan Bowen RC .10 .03
- ❑ 46F Rick Wilkins RC .10 .03
- ❑ 47F Ed Sprague .05 .02
- ❑ 48F Bob Scanlan .05 .02
- ❑ 49F Tom Candiotti .05 .02
- ❑ 50F Dennis Martinez .10 .03
  (Perfecto)
- ❑ 51F Oil Can Boyd .05 .02
- ❑ 52F Glenallen Hill .05 .02
- ❑ 53F Scott Livingstone RC .10 .03
- ❑ 54F Brian R. Hunter RC .25 .07
- ❑ 55F Ivan Rodriguez RC 2.00 .60
- ❑ 56F Keith Mitchell RC .10 .03
- ❑ 57F Roger McDowell .05 .02
- ❑ 58F Otis Nixon .05 .02
- ❑ 59F Juan Bell .05 .02
- ❑ 60F Bill Krueger .05 .02

❑ 61F Chris Donnels .05 .02
❑ 62F Tommy Greene .05 .02
❑ 63F Doug Simons .05 .02
❑ 64F Andy Ashby RC .25 .07
❑ 65F Anthony Young RC .10 .03
❑ 66F Kevin Morton .05 .02
❑ 67F Bret Barberie RC** .10 .03
❑ 68F Scott Servais RC .25 .07
❑ 69F Ron Darling .05 .02
❑ 70F Tim Burke .05 .02
❑ 71F Vicente Palacios .05 .02
❑ 72F Gerald Alexander .05 .02
❑ 73F Reggie Jefferson .05 .02
❑ 74F Dean Palmer .10 .03
❑ 75F Mark Whiten .05 .02
❑ 76F Randy Tomlin RC .10 .03
❑ 77F Mark Wohlers RC .25 .07
❑ 78F Brook Jacoby .05 .02
❑ 79F Ken Griffey Jr. CL .40 .12
Ryne Sandberg
❑ 80F Jack Morris AS .05 .02
❑ 81F Sandy Alomar Jr. AS .05 .02
❑ 82F Cecil Fielder AS .05 .02
❑ 83F Roberto Alomar AS .10 .03
❑ 84F Wade Boggs AS .10 .03
❑ 85F Cal Ripken AS .40 .12
❑ 86F Rickey Henderson AS .15 .04
❑ 87F Ken Griffey Jr. AS .25 .07
❑ 88F Dave Henderson AS .05 .02
❑ 89F Danny Tartabull AS .05 .02
❑ 90F Tom Glavine AS .10 .03
❑ 91F Benito Santiago AS .05 .02
❑ 92F Will Clark AS .10 .03
❑ 93F Ryne Sandberg AS .25 .07
❑ 94F Chris Sabo AS .05 .02
❑ 95F Ozzie Smith AS .25 .07
❑ 96F Ivan Calderon AS .05 .02
❑ 97F Tony Gwynn AS .15 .04
❑ 98F Andre Dawson AS .05 .02
❑ 99F Bobby Bonilla AS .05 .02
❑ 100F Checklist 1-100 .05 .02

1992 Upper Deck

	Nm-Mt	Ex-Mt
COMPLETE SET (800)	25.00	7.50
COMPLETE LO SET (700)	20.00	6.00
COMPLETE HI SET (100)	5.00	1.50

❑ 1 Ryan Klesko CL .25 .07
Jim Thome
❑ 2 Royce Clayton SR .05 .02
❑ 3 Brian Jordan SR RC .40 .12
❑ 4 Dave Fleming SR .05 .02
❑ 5 Jim Thome SR .25 .07
❑ 6 Jeff Juden SR .05 .02
❑ 7 Roberto Hernandez SR .05 .02
❑ 8 Kyle Abbott SR .05 .02
❑ 9 Chris George SR .05 .02
❑ 10 Rob Maurer SR .05 .02
❑ 11 Donald Harris SR .05 .02
❑ 12 Ted Wood SR .05 .02
❑ 13 Patrick Lennon SR .05 .02
❑ 14 Willie Banks SR .05 .02
❑ 15 Roger Salkeld SR UER .05 .02
(Bill was his grand-
father, not his father)
❑ 16 Wil Cordero SR .05 .02
❑ 17 Arthur Rhodes SR .05 .02
❑ 18 Pedro Martinez SR 1.00 .30
❑ 19 Andy Ashby SR .05 .02
❑ 20 Tom Goodwin SR .05 .02
❑ 21 Braulio Castillo SR .05 .02
❑ 22 Todd Van Poppel SR .05 .02
❑ 23 Brian Williams SR RC .05 .02
❑ 24 Ryan Klesko SR .10 .03
❑ 25 Kenny Lofton SR .15 .04
❑ 26 Derek Bell SR .10 .03
❑ 27 Reggie Sanders SR .10 .03
❑ 28 Dave Winfield's 400th .05 .02
❑ 29 David Justice TC .05 .02
❑ 30 Rob Dibble TC .05 .02
❑ 31 Craig Biggio TC .10 .03
❑ 32 Eddie Murray TC .15 .04
❑ 33 Fred McGriff TC .10 .03
❑ 34 Willie McGee TC .05 .02
❑ 35 Shawon Dunston TC .05 .02
❑ 36 Delino DeShields TC .05 .02
❑ 37 Howard Johnson TC .05 .02
❑ 38 John Kruk TC .05 .02
❑ 39 Doug Drabek TC .05 .02
❑ 40 Todd Zeile TC .05 .02
❑ 41 Steve Avery .05 .02
Playoff Perfection
❑ 42 Jeremy Hernandez RC .05 .02
❑ 43 Doug Henry RC .10 .03
❑ 44 Chris Donnels .05 .02
❑ 45 Mo Sanford .05 .02
❑ 46 Scott Kamieniecki .05 .02
❑ 47 Mark Lemke .05 .02
❑ 48 Steve Farr .05 .02
❑ 49 Francisco Oliveras .05 .02
❑ 50 Ced Landrum .05 .02
❑ 51 Rondell White CL .10 .03
Mark Newfield
❑ 52 Eduardo Perez TP RC .25 .07
❑ 53 Tom Nevers TP .05 .02
❑ 54 David Zancanaro TP .05 .02
❑ 55 Shawn Green TP RC 1.50 .45
❑ 56 Mark Wohlers TP .05 .02
❑ 57 Dave Nilsson TP .05 .02
❑ 58 Dmitri Young TP .25 .07
❑ 59 Ryan Hawblitzel TP RC .10 .03
❑ 60 Raul Mondesi TP .10 .03
❑ 61 Rondell White TP .10 .03
❑ 62 Steve Hosey TP .05 .02
❑ 63 Manny Ramirez TP RC 4.00 1.20
❑ 64 Marc Newfield TP .05 .02
❑ 65 Jeromy Burnitz TP .10 .03
❑ 66 Mark Smith TP RC .10 .03
❑ 67 Joey Hamilton TP RC .25 .07
❑ 68 Tyler Green TP RC .10 .03
❑ 69 Jon Farrell TP RC .10 .03
❑ 70 Kurt Miller TP .05 .02
❑ 71 Jeff Plympton TP .05 .02
❑ 72 Dan Wilson TP .05 .02
❑ 73 Joe Vitiello TP RC .10 .03
❑ 74 Rico Brogna TP .05 .02
❑ 75 David McCarty TP RC .25 .07
❑ 76 Bob Wickman TP .25 .07
❑ 77 Carlos Rodriguez TP .05 .02
❑ 78 Jim Abbott .10 .03
Stay In School
❑ 79 Ramon Martinez .25 .07
Pedro Martinez
❑ 80 Kevin Mitchell .05 .02
Keith Mitchell
❑ 81 Sandy Alomar Jr. .10 .03
Roberto Alomar
❑ 82 Cal Ripken .50 .15
Billy Ripken
❑ 83 Tony Gwynn .15 .04
Chris Gwynn
❑ 84 Dwight Gooden .10 .03
Gary Sheffield
❑ 85 Ken Griffey Sr. .25 .07
Ken Griffey Jr.
Craig Griffey
❑ 86 Jim Abbott TC .10 .03
❑ 87 Frank Thomas TC .15 .04
❑ 88 Danny Tartabull TC .05 .02
❑ 89 Scott Erickson TC .05 .02
❑ 90 Rickey Henderson TC .15 .04
❑ 91 Edgar Martinez TC .10 .03
❑ 92 Nolan Ryan TC .50 .15
❑ 93 Ben McDonald TC .05 .02
❑ 94 Ellis Burks TC .05 .02
❑ 95 Greg Swindell TC .05 .02
❑ 96 Cecil Fielder TC .05 .02
❑ 97 Greg Vaughn TC .05 .02
❑ 98 Kevin Maas TC .05 .02
❑ 99 Dave Stieb TC .05 .02
❑ 100 Checklist 1-100 .05 .02
❑ 101 Joe Oliver .05 .02
❑ 102 Hector Villanueva .05 .02
❑ 103 Ed Whitson .05 .02
❑ 104 Danny Jackson .05 .02
❑ 105 Chris Hammond .05 .02
❑ 106 Ricky Jordan .05 .02
❑ 107 Kevin Bass .05 .02
❑ 108 Darrin Fletcher .05 .02
❑ 109 Junior Ortiz .05 .02
❑ 110 Tom Bolton .05 .02
❑ 111 Jeff King .05 .02
❑ 112 Dave Magadan .05 .02
❑ 113 Mike LaValliere .05 .02
❑ 114 Hubie Brooks .05 .02
❑ 115 Jay Bell .10 .03
❑ 116 David Wells .10 .03
❑ 117 Jim Leyritz .05 .02
❑ 118 Manuel Lee .05 .02
❑ 119 Alvaro Espinoza .05 .02
❑ 120 B.J. Surhoff .10 .03
❑ 121 Hal Morris .05 .02
❑ 122 Shawon Dawson .05 .02
❑ 123 Chris Sabo .05 .02
❑ 124 Andre Dawson .10 .03
❑ 125 Eric Davis .10 .03
❑ 126 Chili Davis .10 .03
❑ 127 Dale Murphy .15 .04
❑ 128 Kirk McCaskill .05 .02
❑ 129 Terry Mulholland .05 .02
❑ 130 Rick Aguilera .10 .03
❑ 131 Vince Coleman .05 .02
❑ 132 Andy Van Slyke .15 .04
❑ 133 Gregg Jefferies .05 .02
❑ 134 Barry Bonds 1.00 .30
❑ 135 Dwight Gooden .10 .03
❑ 136 Dave Stieb .05 .02
❑ 137 Albert Belle .10 .03
❑ 138 Teddy Higuera .05 .02
❑ 139 Jesse Barfield .05 .02
❑ 140 Pat Borders .05 .02
❑ 141 Bip Roberts .05 .02
❑ 142 Rob Dibble .10 .03
❑ 143 Mark Grace .15 .04
❑ 144 Barry Larkin .15 .04
❑ 145 Ryne Sandberg .40 .12
❑ 146 Scott Erickson .05 .02
❑ 147 Luis Polonia .05 .02
❑ 148 John Burkett .05 .02
❑ 149 Luis Sojo .05 .02
❑ 150 Dickie Thon .05 .02
❑ 151 Walt Weiss .05 .02
❑ 152 Mike Scioscia .05 .02
❑ 153 Mark McGwire .60 .18
❑ 154 Matt Williams .10 .03
❑ 155 Rickey Henderson .25 .07
❑ 156 Sandy Alomar Jr. .05 .02
❑ 157 Brian McRae .05 .02
❑ 158 Harold Baines .10 .03
❑ 159 Kevin Appier .10 .03
❑ 160 Felix Fermin .05 .02
❑ 161 Leo Gomez .05 .02
❑ 162 Craig Biggio .15 .04
❑ 163 Ben McDonald .05 .02
❑ 164 Randy Johnson .25 .07
❑ 165 Cal Ripken .75 .23
❑ 166 Frank Thomas .25 .07
❑ 167 Delino DeShields .05 .02
❑ 168 Greg Gagne .05 .02
❑ 169 Ron Karkovice .05 .02
❑ 170 Charlie Leibrandt .05 .02
❑ 171 Dave Righetti .10 .03
❑ 172 Dave Henderson .05 .02
❑ 173 Steve Decker .05 .02
❑ 174 Darryl Strawberry .10 .03
❑ 175 Will Clark .15 .04
❑ 176 Ruben Sierra .05 .02
❑ 177 Ozzie Smith .40 .12
❑ 178 Charles Nagy .05 .02

❑	179	Gary Pettis	.05	.02
❑	180	Kirk Gibson	.15	.04
❑	181	Randy Milligan	.05	.02
❑	182	Dave Valle	.05	.02
❑	183	Chris Hoiles	.05	.02
❑	184	Tony Phillips	.05	.02
❑	185	Brady Anderson	.10	.03
❑	186	Scott Fletcher	.05	.02
❑	187	Gene Larkin	.05	.02
❑	188	Lance Johnson	.05	.02
❑	189	Greg Olson	.05	.02
❑	190	Melido Perez	.05	.02
❑	191	Lenny Harris	.05	.02
❑	192	Terry Kennedy	.05	.02
❑	193	Mike Gallego	.05	.02
❑	194	Willie McGee	.10	.03
❑	195	Juan Samuel	.05	.02
❑	196	Jeff Huson (Shows Jose Canseco sliding into second)	.10	.03
❑	197	Alex Cole	.05	.02
❑	198	Ron Robinson	.05	.02
❑	199	Joel Skinner	.05	.02
❑	200	Checklist 101-200	.05	.02
❑	201	Kevin Reimer	.05	.02
❑	202	Stan Belinda	.05	.02
❑	203	Pat Tabler	.05	.02
❑	204	Jose Guzman	.05	.02
❑	205	Jose Lind	.05	.02
❑	206	Spike Owen	.05	.02
❑	207	Joe Orsulak	.05	.02
❑	208	Charlie Hayes	.05	.02
❑	209	Mike Devereaux	.05	.02
❑	210	Mike Fitzgerald	.05	.02
❑	211	Willie Randolph	.10	.03
❑	212	Rod Nichols	.05	.02
❑	213	Mike Boddicker	.05	.02
❑	214	Bill Spiers	.05	.02
❑	215	Steve Olin	.05	.02
❑	216	David Howard	.05	.02
❑	217	Gary Varsho	.05	.02
❑	218	Mike Harkey	.05	.02
❑	219	Luis Aquino	.05	.02
❑	220	Chuck McElroy	.05	.02
❑	221	Doug Drabek	.05	.02
❑	222	Dave Winfield	.10	.03
❑	223	Rafael Palmeiro	.15	.04
❑	224	Joe Carter	.10	.03
❑	225	Bobby Bonilla	.10	.03
❑	226	Ivan Calderon	.05	.02
❑	227	Gregg Olson	.05	.02
❑	228	Tim Wallach	.05	.02
❑	229	Terry Pendleton	.10	.03
❑	230	Gilberto Reyes	.05	.02
❑	231	Carlos Baerga	.05	.02
❑	232	Greg Vaughn	.05	.02
❑	233	Bret Saberhagen	.10	.03
❑	234	Gary Sheffield	.10	.03
❑	235	Mark Lewis	.05	.02
❑	236	George Bell	.05	.02
❑	237	Danny Tartabull	.05	.02
❑	238	Willie Wilson	.05	.02
❑	239	Doug Dascenzo	.05	.02
❑	240	Bill Pecota	.05	.02
❑	241	Julio Franco	.10	.03
❑	242	Ed Sprague	.05	.02
❑	243	Juan Gonzalez	.15	.04
❑	244	Chuck Finley	.10	.03
❑	245	Ivan Rodriguez	.25	.07
❑	246	Len Dykstra	.10	.03
❑	247	Deion Sanders	.15	.04
❑	248	Dwight Evans	.15	.04
❑	249	Larry Walker	.15	.04
❑	250	Billy Ripken	.05	.02
❑	251	Mickey Tettleton	.05	.02
❑	252	Tony Pena	.05	.02
❑	253	Benito Santiago	.10	.03
❑	254	Kirby Puckett	.25	.07
❑	255	Cecil Fielder	.10	.03
❑	256	Howard Johnson	.05	.02
❑	257	Andujar Cedeno	.05	.02
❑	258	Jose Rijo	.05	.02
❑	259	Al Osuna	.05	.02
❑	260	Todd Hundley	.05	.02
❑	261	Orel Hershiser	.10	.03
❑	262	Ray Lankford	.10	.03
❑	263	Robin Ventura	.10	.03
❑	264	Felix Jose	.05	.02
❑	265	Eddie Murray	.25	.07
❑	266	Kevin Mitchell	.05	.02
❑	267	Gary Carter	.10	.03
❑	268	Mike Benjamin	.05	.02
❑	269	Dick Schofield	.05	.02
❑	270	Jose Uribe	.05	.02
❑	271	Pete Incaviglia	.05	.02
❑	272	Tony Fernandez	.05	.02
❑	273	Alan Trammell	.10	.03
❑	274	Tony Gwynn	.30	.09
❑	275	Mike Greenwell	.05	.02
❑	276	Jeff Bagwell	.25	.07
❑	277	Frank Viola	.10	.03
❑	278	Randy Myers	.05	.02
❑	279	Ken Caminiti	.10	.03
❑	280	Bill Doran	.05	.02
❑	281	Dan Pasqua	.05	.02
❑	282	Alfredo Griffin	.05	.02
❑	283	Jose Oquendo	.05	.02
❑	284	Kal Daniels	.05	.02
❑	285	Bobby Thigpen	.05	.02
❑	286	Robby Thompson	.05	.02
❑	287	Mark Eichhorn	.05	.02
❑	288	Mike Felder	.05	.02
❑	289	Dave Gallagher	.05	.02
❑	290	Dave Anderson	.05	.02
❑	291	Mel Hall	.05	.02
❑	292	Jerald Clark	.05	.02
❑	293	Al Newman	.05	.02
❑	294	Rob Deer	.05	.02
❑	295	Matt Nokes	.05	.02
❑	296	Jack Armstrong	.05	.02
❑	297	Jim Deshaies	.05	.02
❑	298	Jeff Innis	.05	.02
❑	299	Jeff Reed	.05	.02
❑	300	Checklist 201-300	.05	.02
❑	301	Lonnie Smith	.05	.02
❑	302	Jimmy Key	.10	.03
❑	303	Junior Felix	.05	.02
❑	304	Mike Heath	.05	.02
❑	305	Mark Langston	.05	.02
❑	306	Greg W. Harris	.05	.02
❑	307	Brett Butler	.10	.03
❑	308	Luis Rivera	.05	.02
❑	309	Bruce Ruffin	.05	.02
❑	310	Paul Faries	.05	.02
❑	311	Terry Leach	.05	.02
❑	312	Scott Brosius RC	.40	.12
❑	313	Scott Leius	.05	.02
❑	314	Harold Reynolds	.10	.03
❑	315	Jack Morris	.10	.03
❑	316	David Segui	.05	.02
❑	317	Bill Gullickson	.05	.02
❑	318	Todd Frohwirth	.05	.02
❑	319	Mark Leiter	.05	.02
❑	320	Jeff M. Robinson	.05	.02
❑	321	Gary Gaetti	.10	.03
❑	322	John Smoltz	.15	.04
❑	323	Andy Benes	.05	.02
❑	324	Kelly Gruber	.05	.02
❑	325	Jim Abbott	.15	.04
❑	326	John Kruk	.10	.03
❑	327	Kevin Seitzer	.05	.02
❑	328	Darrin Jackson	.05	.02
❑	329	Kurt Stillwell	.05	.02
❑	330	Mike Maddux	.05	.02
❑	331	Dennis Eckersley	.10	.03
❑	332	Dan Gladden	.05	.02
❑	333	Jose Canseco	.15	.04
❑	334	Kent Hrbek	.10	.03
❑	335	Ken Griffey Sr.	.10	.03
❑	336	Greg Swindell	.05	.02
❑	337	Trevor Wilson	.05	.02
❑	338	Sam Horn	.05	.02
❑	339	Mike Henneman	.05	.02
❑	340	Jerry Browne	.05	.02
❑	341	Glenn Braggs	.05	.02
❑	342	Tom Glavine	.15	.04
❑	343	Wally Joyner	.10	.03
❑	344	Fred McGriff	.15	.04
❑	345	Ron Gant	.10	.03
❑	346	Ramon Martinez	.05	.02
❑	347	Wes Chamberlain	.05	.02
❑	348	Terry Shumpert	.05	.02
❑	349	Tim Teufel	.05	.02
❑	350	Wally Backman	.05	.02
❑	351	Joe Girardi	.05	.02
❑	352	Devon White	.10	.03
❑	353	Greg Maddux	.40	.12
❑	354	Ryan Bowen	.05	.02
❑	355	Roberto Alomar	.15	.04
❑	356	Don Mattingly	.60	.18
❑	357	Pedro Guerrero	.10	.03
❑	358	Steve Sax	.05	.02
❑	359	Joey Cora	.05	.02
❑	360	Jim Gantner	.05	.02
❑	361	Brian Barnes	.05	.02
❑	362	Kevin McReynolds	.05	.02
❑	363	Bret Barberie	.05	.02
❑	364	David Cone	.10	.03
❑	365	Dennis Martinez	.10	.03
❑	366	Brian Hunter	.05	.02
❑	367	Edgar Martinez	.15	.04
❑	368	Steve Finley	.10	.03
❑	369	Greg Briley	.05	.02
❑	370	Jeff Blauser	.05	.02
❑	371	Todd Stottlemyre	.05	.02
❑	372	Luis Gonzalez	.10	.03
❑	373	Rick Wilkins	.05	.02
❑	374	Darryl Kile	.10	.03
❑	375	John Olerud	.10	.03
❑	376	Lee Smith	.10	.03
❑	377	Kevin Maas	.05	.02
❑	378	Dante Bichette	.10	.03
❑	379	Tom Pagnozzi	.05	.02
❑	380	Mike Flanagan	.05	.02
❑	381	Charlie O'Brien	.05	.02
❑	382	Dave Martinez	.05	.02
❑	383	Keith Miller	.05	.02
❑	384	Scott Ruskin	.05	.02
❑	385	Kevin Elster	.05	.02
❑	386	Alvin Davis	.05	.02
❑	387	Casey Candaele	.05	.02
❑	388	Pete O'Brien	.05	.02
❑	389	Jeff Treadway	.05	.02
❑	390	Scott Bradley	.05	.02
❑	391	Mookie Wilson	.10	.03
❑	392	Jimmy Jones	.05	.02
❑	393	Candy Maldonado	.05	.02
❑	394	Eric Yelding	.05	.02
❑	395	Tom Henke	.05	.02
❑	396	Franklin Stubbs	.05	.02
❑	397	Milt Thompson	.05	.02
❑	398	Mark Carreon	.05	.02
❑	399	Randy Velarde	.05	.02
❑	400	Checklist 301-400	.05	.02
❑	401	Omar Vizquel	.15	.04
❑	402	Joe Boever	.05	.02
❑	403	Bill Krueger	.05	.02
❑	404	Jody Reed	.05	.02
❑	405	Mike Schooler	.05	.02
❑	406	Jason Grimsley	.05	.02
❑	407	Greg Myers	.05	.02
❑	408	Randy Ready	.05	.02
❑	409	Mike Timlin	.05	.02
❑	410	Mitch Williams	.05	.02
❑	411	Garry Templeton	.05	.02
❑	412	Greg Cadaret	.05	.02
❑	413	Donnie Hill	.05	.02
❑	414	Wally Whitehurst	.05	.02
❑	415	Scott Sanderson	.05	.02
❑	416	Thomas Howard	.05	.02
❑	417	Neal Heaton	.05	.02
❑	418	Charlie Hough	.10	.03
❑	419	Jack Howell	.05	.02
❑	420	Greg Hibbard	.05	.02
❑	421	Carlos Quintana	.05	.02
❑	422	Kim Batiste	.05	.02
❑	423	Paul Molitor	.15	.04
❑	424	Ken Griffey Jr.	.40	.12
❑	425	Phil Plantier	.05	.02
❑	426	Denny Neagle	.10	.03
❑	427	Von Hayes	.05	.02
❑	428	Shane Mack	.05	.02
❑	429	Darren Daulton	.10	.03
❑	430	Dwayne Henry	.05	.02
❑	431	Lance Parrish	.10	.03
❑	432	Mike Humphreys	.05	.02
❑	433	Tim Burke	.05	.02
❑	434	Bryan Harvey	.05	.02

❑ 435 Pat Kelly .05 .02
❑ 436 Ozzie Guillen .10 .03
❑ 437 Bruce Hurst .05 .02
❑ 438 Sammy Sosa .25 .07
❑ 439 Dennis Rasmussen .05 .02
❑ 440 Ken Patterson .05 .02
❑ 441 Jay Buhner .10 .03
❑ 442 Pat Combs .05 .02
❑ 443 Wade Boggs .15 .04
❑ 444 George Brett .60 .18
❑ 445 Mo Vaughn .10 .03
❑ 446 Chuck Knoblauch .10 .03
❑ 447 Tom Candiotti .05 .02
❑ 448 Mark Portugal .05 .02
❑ 449 Mickey Morandini .05 .02
❑ 450 Duane Ward .05 .02
❑ 451 Otis Nixon .05 .02
❑ 452 Bob Welch .05 .02
❑ 453 Rusty Meacham .05 .02
❑ 454 Keith Mitchell .05 .02
❑ 455 Marquis Grissom .10 .03
❑ 456 Robin Yount .40 .12
❑ 457 Harvey Pulliam .05 .02
❑ 458 Jose DeLeon .05 .02
❑ 459 Mark Gubicza .05 .02
❑ 460 Darryl Hamilton .05 .02
❑ 461 Tom Browning .05 .02
❑ 462 Monty Fariss .05 .02
❑ 463 Jerome Walton .05 .02
❑ 464 Paul O'Neill .15 .04
❑ 465 Dean Palmer .10 .03
❑ 466 Travis Fryman .10 .03
❑ 467 John Smiley .05 .02
❑ 468 Lloyd Moseby .05 .02
❑ 469 John Wehner .05 .02
❑ 470 Skeeter Barnes .05 .02
❑ 471 Steve Chitren .05 .02
❑ 472 Kent Mercker .05 .02
❑ 473 Terry Steinbach .05 .02
❑ 474 Andres Galarraga .10 .03
❑ 475 Steve Avery .05 .02
❑ 476 Tom Gordon .05 .02
❑ 477 Cal Eldred .05 .02
❑ 478 Omar Olivares .05 .02
❑ 479 Julio Machado .05 .02
❑ 480 Bob Milacki .05 .02
❑ 481 Les Lancaster .05 .02
❑ 482 John Candelaria .05 .02
❑ 483 Brian Downing .05 .02
❑ 484 Roger McDowell .05 .02
❑ 485 Scott Scudder .05 .02
❑ 486 Zane Smith .05 .02
❑ 487 John Cerutti .05 .02
❑ 488 Steve Buechele .05 .02
❑ 489 Paul Gibson .05 .02
❑ 490 Curtis Wilkerson .05 .02
❑ 491 Marvin Freeman .05 .02
❑ 492 Tom Foley .05 .02
❑ 493 Juan Berenguer .05 .02
❑ 494 Ernest Riles .05 .02
❑ 495 Sid Bream .05 .02
❑ 496 Chuck Crim .05 .02
❑ 497 Mike Macfarlane .05 .02
❑ 498 Dale Sveum .05 .02
❑ 499 Storm Davis .05 .02
❑ 500 Checklist 401-500 .05 .02
❑ 501 Jeff Reardon .10 .03
❑ 502 Shawn Abner .05 .02
❑ 503 Tony Fossas .05 .02
❑ 504 Cory Snyder .05 .02
❑ 505 Matt Young .05 .02
❑ 506 Allan Anderson .05 .02
❑ 507 Mark Lee .05 .02
❑ 508 Gene Nelson .05 .02
❑ 509 Mike Pagliarulo .05 .02
❑ 510 Rafael Belliard .05 .02
❑ 511 Jay Howell .05 .02
❑ 512 Bob Tewksbury .05 .02
❑ 513 Mike Morgan .05 .02
❑ 514 John Franco .10 .03
❑ 515 Kevin Gross .05 .02
❑ 516 Lou Whitaker .10 .03
❑ 517 Orlando Merced .05 .02
❑ 518 Todd Benzinger .05 .02
❑ 519 Gary Redus .05 .02
❑ 520 Walt Terrell .05 .02
❑ 521 Jack Clark .10 .03
❑ 522 Dave Parker .10 .03
❑ 523 Tim Naehring .05 .02
❑ 524 Mark Whiten .05 .02
❑ 525 Ellis Burks .10 .03
❑ 526 Frank Castillo .05 .02
❑ 527 Brian Harper .05 .02
❑ 528 Brook Jacoby .05 .02
❑ 529 Rick Sutcliffe .10 .03
❑ 530 Joe Klink .05 .02
❑ 531 Terry Bross .05 .02
❑ 532 Jose Offerman .05 .02
❑ 533 Todd Zeile .05 .02
❑ 534 Eric Karros .10 .03
❑ 535 Anthony Young .05 .02
❑ 536 Milt Cuyler .05 .02
❑ 537 Randy Tomlin .05 .02
❑ 538 Scott Livingstone .05 .02
❑ 539 Jim Eisenreich .05 .02
❑ 540 Don Slaught .05 .02
❑ 541 Scott Cooper .05 .02
❑ 542 Joe Grahe .05 .02
❑ 543 Tom Brunansky .05 .02
❑ 544 Eddie Zosky .05 .02
❑ 545 Roger Clemens .50 .15
❑ 546 David Justice .10 .03
❑ 547 Dave Stewart .10 .03
❑ 548 David West .05 .02
❑ 549 Dave Smith .05 .02
❑ 550 Dan Plesac .05 .02
❑ 551 Alex Fernandez .05 .02
❑ 552 Bernard Gilkey .05 .02
❑ 553 Jack McDowell .05 .02
❑ 554 Tino Martinez .15 .04
❑ 555 Bo Jackson .25 .07
❑ 556 Bernie Williams .15 .04
❑ 557 Mark Gardner .05 .02
❑ 558 Glenallen Hill .05 .02
❑ 559 Oil Can Boyd .05 .02
❑ 560 Chris James .05 .02
❑ 561 Scott Servais .05 .02
❑ 562 Rey Sanchez RC .25 .07
❑ 563 Paul McClellan .05 .02
❑ 564 Andy Mota .05 .02
❑ 565 Darren Lewis .05 .02
❑ 566 Jose Melendez .05 .02
❑ 567 Tommy Greene .05 .02
❑ 568 Rich Rodriguez .05 .02
❑ 569 Heathcliff Slocumb .05 .02
❑ 570 Joe Hesketh .05 .02
❑ 571 Carlton Fisk .15 .04
❑ 572 Erik Hanson .05 .02
❑ 573 Wilson Alvarez .05 .02
❑ 574 Rheal Cormier .05 .02
❑ 575 Tim Raines .10 .03
❑ 576 Bobby Witt .05 .02
❑ 577 Roberto Kelly .05 .02
❑ 578 Kevin Brown .10 .03
❑ 579 Chris Nabholz .05 .02
❑ 580 Jesse Orosco .05 .02
❑ 581 Jeff Brantley .05 .02
❑ 582 Rafael Ramirez .05 .02
❑ 583 Kelly Downs .05 .02
❑ 584 Mike Simms .05 .02
❑ 585 Mike Remlinger .05 .02
❑ 586 Dave Hollins .05 .02
❑ 587 Larry Andersen .05 .02
❑ 588 Mike Gardiner .05 .02
❑ 589 Craig Lefferts .05 .02
❑ 590 Paul Assenmacher .05 .02
❑ 591 Bryn Smith .05 .02
❑ 592 Donn Pall .05 .02
❑ 593 Mike Jackson .05 .02
❑ 594 Scott Radinsky .05 .02
❑ 595 Brian Holman .05 .02
❑ 596 Geronimo Pena .05 .02
❑ 597 Mike Jeffcoat .05 .02
❑ 598 Carlos Martinez .05 .02
❑ 599 Geno Petralli .05 .02
❑ 600 Checklist 501-600 .05 .02
❑ 601 Jerry Don Gleaton .05 .02
❑ 602 Adam Peterson .05 .02
❑ 603 Craig Grebeck .05 .02
❑ 604 Mark Guthrie .05 .02
❑ 605 Frank Tanana .05 .02
❑ 606 Hensley Meulens .05 .02
❑ 607 Mark Davis .05 .02
❑ 608 Eric Plunk .05 .02
❑ 609 Mark Williamson .05 .02
❑ 610 Lee Guetterman .05 .02
❑ 611 Bobby Rose .05 .02
❑ 612 Bill Wegman .05 .02
❑ 613 Mike Hartley .05 .02
❑ 614 Chris Beasley .05 .02
❑ 615 Chris Bosio .05 .02
❑ 616 Henry Cotto .05 .02
❑ 617 Chico Walker .05 .02
❑ 618 Russ Swan .05 .02
❑ 619 Bob Walk .05 .02
❑ 620 Bill Swift .05 .02
❑ 621 Warren Newson .05 .02
❑ 622 Steve Bedrosian .05 .02
❑ 623 Ricky Bones .05 .02
❑ 624 Kevin Tapani .05 .02
❑ 625 Juan Guzman .05 .02
❑ 626 Jeff Johnson .05 .02
❑ 627 Jeff Montgomery .05 .02
❑ 628 Ken Hill .05 .02
❑ 629 Gary Thurman .05 .02
❑ 630 Steve Howe .05 .02
❑ 631 Jose DeJesus .05 .02
❑ 632 Kirk Dressendorfer .05 .02
❑ 633 Jaime Navarro .05 .02
❑ 634 Lee Stevens .05 .02
❑ 635 Pete Harnisch .05 .02
❑ 636 Bill Landrum .05 .02
❑ 637 Rich DeLucia .05 .02
❑ 638 Luis Salazar .05 .02
❑ 639 Rob Murphy .05 .02
❑ 640 Jose Canseco CL .15 .04
Rickey Henderson
❑ 641 Roger Clemens DS .25 .07
❑ 642 Jim Abbott DS .10 .03
❑ 643 Travis Fryman DS .05 .02
❑ 644 Jesse Barfield DS .05 .02
❑ 645 Cal Ripken DS .40 .12
❑ 646 Wade Boggs DS .10 .03
❑ 647 Cecil Fielder DS .05 .02
❑ 648 Rickey Henderson DS .15 .04
❑ 649 Jose Canseco DS .10 .03
❑ 650 Ken Griffey Jr. DS .25 .07
❑ 651 Kenny Rogers .10 .03
❑ 652 Luis Mercedes .05 .02
❑ 653 Mike Stanton .05 .02
❑ 654 Glenn Davis .05 .02
❑ 655 Nolan Ryan 1.00 .30
❑ 656 Reggie Jefferson .05 .02
❑ 657 Javier Ortiz .05 .02
❑ 658 Greg A. Harris .05 .02
❑ 659 Mariano Duncan .05 .02
❑ 660 Jeff Shaw .05 .02
❑ 661 Mike Moore .05 .02
❑ 662 Chris Haney .05 .02
❑ 663 Joe Slusarski .05 .02
❑ 664 Wayne Housie .05 .02
❑ 665 Carlos Garcia .05 .02
❑ 666 Bob Ojeda .05 .02
❑ 667 Bryan Hickerson RC .10 .03
❑ 668 Tim Belcher .05 .02
❑ 669 Ron Darling .05 .02
❑ 670 Rex Hudler .05 .02
❑ 671 Sid Fernandez .05 .02
❑ 672 Chito Martinez .05 .02
❑ 673 Pete Schourek .05 .02
❑ 674 Armando Reynoso RC .25 .07
❑ 675 Mike Mussina .25 .07
❑ 676 Kevin Morton .05 .02
❑ 677 Norm Charlton .05 .02
❑ 678 Danny Darwin .05 .02
❑ 679 Eric King .05 .02
❑ 680 Ted Power .05 .02
❑ 681 Barry Jones .05 .02
❑ 682 Carney Lansford .10 .03
❑ 683 Mel Rojas .05 .02
❑ 684 Rick Honeycutt .05 .02
❑ 685 Jeff Fassero .05 .02
❑ 686 Cris Carpenter .05 .02
❑ 687 Tim Crews .05 .02
❑ 688 Scott Terry .05 .02
❑ 689 Chris Gwynn .05 .02
❑ 690 Gerald Perry .05 .02
❑ 691 John Barfield .05 .02

Card	Nm-Mt	Ex-Mt
❑ 692 Bob Melvin	.05	.02
❑ 693 Juan Agosto	.05	.02
❑ 694 Alejandro Pena	.05	.02
❑ 695 Jeff Russell	.05	.02
❑ 696 Carmelo Martinez	.05	.02
❑ 697 Bud Black	.05	.02
❑ 698 Dave Otto	.05	.02
❑ 699 Billy Hatcher	.05	.02
❑ 700 Checklist 601-700	.05	.02
❑ 701 Clemente Nunez RC	.05	.02
❑ 702 Mark Clark	.05	.02
Donovan Osborne		
Brian Jordan		
❑ 703 Mike Morgan	.05	.02
❑ 704 Keith Miller	.05	.02
❑ 705 Kurt Stillwell	.05	.02
❑ 706 Damon Berryhill	.05	.02
❑ 707 Von Hayes	.05	.02
❑ 708 Rick Sutcliffe	.10	.03
❑ 709 Hubie Brooks	.05	.02
❑ 710 Ryan Turner RC	.10	.03
❑ 711 Barry Bonds CL	.50	.15
Andy Van Slyke		
❑ 712 Jose Rijo DS	.05	.02
❑ 713 Tom Glavine DS	.10	.03
❑ 714 Shawon Dunston DS	.05	.02
❑ 715 Andy Van Slyke DS	.10	.03
❑ 716 Ozzie Smith DS	.25	.07
❑ 717 Tony Gwynn DS	.15	.04
❑ 718 Will Clark DS	.10	.03
❑ 719 Marquis Grissom DS	.05	.02
❑ 720 Howard Johnson DS	.05	.02
❑ 721 Barry Bonds DS	.50	.15
❑ 722 Kirk McCaskill	.05	.02
❑ 723 Sammy Sosa	.75	.23
❑ 724 George Bell	.05	.02
❑ 725 Gregg Jefferies	.05	.02
❑ 726 Gary DiSarcina	.05	.02
❑ 727 Mike Bordick	.05	.02
❑ 728 Eddie Murray 400 HR	.15	.04
❑ 729 Rene Gonzales	.05	.02
❑ 730 Mike Bielecki	.05	.02
❑ 731 Calvin Jones	.05	.02
❑ 732 Jack Morris	.10	.03
❑ 733 Frank Viola	.10	.03
❑ 734 Dave Winfield	.10	.03
❑ 735 Kevin Mitchell	.05	.02
❑ 736 Bill Swift	.05	.02
❑ 737 Dan Gladden	.05	.02
❑ 738 Mike Jackson	.05	.02
❑ 739 Mark Carreon	.05	.02
❑ 740 Kirt Manwaring	.05	.02
❑ 741 Randy Myers	.05	.02
❑ 742 Kevin McReynolds	.05	.02
❑ 743 Steve Sax	.05	.02
❑ 744 Wally Joyner	.10	.03
❑ 745 Gary Sheffield	.10	.03
❑ 746 Danny Tartabull	.05	.02
❑ 747 Julio Valera	.05	.02
❑ 748 Denny Neagle	.10	.03
❑ 749 Lance Blankenship	.05	.02
❑ 750 Mike Gallego	.05	.02
❑ 751 Bret Saberhagen	.10	.03
❑ 752 Ruben Amaro	.05	.02
❑ 753 Eddie Murray	.25	.07
❑ 754 Kyle Abbott	.05	.02
❑ 755 Bobby Bonilla	.10	.03
❑ 756 Eric Davis	.10	.03
❑ 757 Eddie Taubensee RC	.25	.07
❑ 758 Andres Galarraga	.10	.03
❑ 759 Pete Incaviglia	.05	.02
❑ 760 Tom Candiotti	.05	.02
❑ 761 Tim Belcher	.05	.02
❑ 762 Ricky Bones	.05	.02
❑ 763 Bip Roberts	.05	.02
❑ 764 Pedro Munoz	.05	.02
❑ 765 Greg Swindell	.05	.02
❑ 766 Kenny Lofton	.15	.04
❑ 767 Gary Carter	.10	.03
❑ 768 Charlie Hayes	.05	.02
❑ 769 Dickie Thon	.05	.02
❑ 770 D. Osborne DD CL	.05	.02
❑ 771 Bret Boone DD	.25	.07
❑ 772 A. Cianfrocco DD RC	.10	.03
❑ 773 Mark Clark DD RC	.10	.03
❑ 774 Chad Curtis DD RC	.25	.07
❑ 775 Pat Listach DD RC	.25	.07
❑ 776 Pat Mahomes DD RC	.25	.07
❑ 777 Donovan Osborne DD	.05	.02
❑ 778 John Patterson DD RC	.10	.03
❑ 779 Andy Stankiewicz DD	.05	.02
❑ 780 Turk Wendell DD RC	.25	.07
❑ 781 Bill Krueger	.05	.02
❑ 782 Rickey Henderson 1000	.15	.04
❑ 783 Kevin Seitzer	.05	.02
❑ 784 Dave Martinez	.05	.02
❑ 785 John Smiley	.05	.02
❑ 786 Matt Stairs RC	.25	.07
❑ 787 Scott Scudder	.05	.02
❑ 788 John Wetteland	.10	.03
❑ 789 Jack Armstrong	.05	.02
❑ 790 Ken Hill	.05	.02
❑ 791 Dick Schofield	.05	.02
❑ 792 Mariano Duncan	.05	.02
❑ 793 Bill Pecota	.05	.02
❑ 794 Mike Kelly RC	.10	.03
❑ 795 Willie Randolph	.10	.03
❑ 796 Butch Henry	.05	.02
❑ 797 Carlos Hernandez	.05	.02
❑ 798 Doug Jones	.05	.02
❑ 799 Melido Perez	.05	.02
❑ 800 Checklist 701-800	.05	.02
❑ HH2 T.Williams Hologram	2.00	.60
Top left corner says		
91 Upper Deck 92		
❑ SP3 Deion Sanders FB/BB	1.00	.30
❑ SP4 Tom Selleck	1.00	.30
Frank Thomas SP		
(Mr. Baseball)		

1993 Upper Deck

	Nm-Mt	Ex-Mt
COMPLETE SET (840)	40.00	12.00
COMP.FACT.SET (840)	50.00	15.00
COMP. SERIES 1 (420)	15.00	4.50
COMP. SERIES 2 (420)	25.00	7.50
❑ 1 Tim Salmon CL	.20	.06
❑ 2 Mike Piazza SR	3.00	.90
❑ 3 Rene Arocha SR RC	.50	.15
❑ 4 Willie Greene SR	.10	.03
❑ 5 Manny Alexander	.10	.03
❑ 6 Dan Wilson	.20	.06
❑ 7 Dan Smith	.10	.03
❑ 8 Kevin Rogers	.10	.03
❑ 9 Kurt Miller SR	.10	.03
❑ 10 Joe Vitko	.10	.03
❑ 11 Tim Costo	.10	.03
❑ 12 Alan Embree SR	.10	.03
❑ 13 Jim Tatum SR RC	.15	.04
❑ 14 Cris Colon	.10	.03
❑ 15 Steve Hosey	.10	.03
❑ 16 S. Hitchcock SR RC	.50	.15
❑ 17 Dave Mlicki	.10	.03
❑ 18 Jessie Hollins	.10	.03
❑ 19 Bobby Jones SR	.20	.06
❑ 20 Kurt Miller	.10	.03
❑ 21 Melvin Nieves SR	.10	.03
❑ 22 Billy Ashley SR	.10	.03
❑ 23 J.T. Snow SR RC	.75	.23
❑ 24 Chipper Jones SR	.50	.15
❑ 25 Tim Salmon SR	.30	.09
❑ 26 Tim Pugh SR RC	.15	.04
❑ 27 David Nied SR	.10	.03
❑ 28 Mike Trombley	.10	.03
❑ 29 Javier Lopez SR	.30	.09
❑ 30 Jim Abbott CH CL	.20	.06
❑ 31 Jim Abbott CH	.10	.03
❑ 32 Dale Murphy CH	.30	.09
❑ 33 Tony Pena CH	.10	.03
❑ 34 Kirby Puckett CH	.30	.09
❑ 35 Harold Reynolds CH	.10	.03
❑ 36 Cal Ripken CH	.75	.23
❑ 37 Nolan Ryan CH	1.00	.30
❑ 38 Ryne Sandberg CH	.50	.15
❑ 39 Dave Stewart CH	.10	.03
❑ 40 Dave Winfield CH	.10	.03
❑ 41 Joe Carter CL	.50	.15
Mark McGwire		
❑ 42 Joe Carter	.20	.06
Roberto Alomar		
❑ 43 Paul Molitor	.50	.15
Pat Listach		
Robin Yount		
❑ 44 Cal Ripken	.50	.15
Brady Anderson		
❑ 45 Albert Belle	.20	.06
Sandy Alomar Jr.		
Jim Thome		
Carlos Baerga		
Kenny Lofton		
❑ 46 Cecil Fielder	.10	.03
Mickey Tettleton		
❑ 47 Roberto Kelly	.60	.18
Don Mattingly		
❑ 48 Frank Viola	.50	.15
Roger Clemens		
❑ 49 Ruben Sierra	.50	.15
Mark McGwire		
❑ 50 Kent Hrbek	.30	.09
Kirby Puckett		
❑ 51 Robin Ventura	.30	.09
Frank Thomas		
❑ 52 Juan Gonzalez	.30	.09
Jose Canseco		
Ivan Rodriguez		
Rafael Palmeiro		
❑ 53 Mark Langston	.20	.06
Jim Abbott		
Chuck Finley		
❑ 54 Wally Joyner	.50	.15
Gregg Jefferies		
George Brett		
❑ 55 Kevin Mitchell	.50	.15
Ken Griffey Jr.		
Jay Buhner		
❑ 56 George Brett	1.25	.35
❑ 57 Scott Cooper	.10	.03
❑ 58 Mike Maddux	.10	.03
❑ 59 Rusty Meacham	.10	.03
❑ 60 Wil Cordero	.10	.03
❑ 61 Tim Teufel	.10	.03
❑ 62 Jeff Montgomery	.10	.03
❑ 63 Scott Livingstone	.10	.03
❑ 64 Doug Dascenzo	.10	.03
❑ 65 Bret Boone	.30	.09
❑ 66 Tim Wakefield	.50	.15
❑ 67 Curt Schilling	.20	.06
❑ 68 Frank Tanana	.10	.03
❑ 69 Len Dykstra	.20	.06
❑ 70 Derek Lilliquist	.10	.03
❑ 71 Anthony Young	.10	.03
❑ 72 Hipolito Pichardo	.10	.03
❑ 73 Rod Beck	.10	.03
❑ 74 Kent Hrbek	.20	.06
❑ 75 Tom Glavine	.30	.09
❑ 76 Kevin Brown	.20	.06
❑ 77 Chuck Finley	.20	.06
❑ 78 Bob Walk	.10	.03
❑ 79 Rheal Cormier UER	.10	.03
(Born in New Brunswick,		
not British Columbia)		
❑ 80 Rick Sutcliffe	.20	.06
❑ 81 Harold Baines	.20	.06
❑ 82 Lee Smith	.20	.06
❑ 83 Geno Petralli	.10	.03
❑ 84 Jose Oquendo	.10	.03
❑ 85 Mark Gubicza	.10	.03
❑ 86 Mickey Tettleton	.10	.03
❑ 87 Bobby Witt	.10	.03

❑ 88 Mark Lewis .10 .03
❑ 89 Kevin Appier .20 .06
❑ 90 Mike Stanton .10 .03
❑ 91 Rafael Belliard .10 .03
❑ 92 Kenny Rogers .20 .06
❑ 93 Randy Velarde .10 .03
❑ 94 Luis Sojo .10 .03
❑ 95 Mark Leiter .10 .03
❑ 96 Jody Reed .10 .03
❑ 97 Pete Harnisch .10 .03
❑ 98 Tom Candiotti .10 .03
❑ 99 Mark Portugal .10 .03
❑ 100 Dave Valle .10 .03
❑ 101 Shawon Dunston .10 .03
❑ 102 B.J. Surhoff .20 .06
❑ 103 Jay Bell .20 .06
❑ 104 Sid Bream .10 .03
❑ 105 Frank Thomas CL .30 .09
❑ 106 Mike Morgan .10 .03
❑ 107 Bill Doran .10 .03
❑ 108 Lance Blankenship .10 .03
❑ 109 Mark Lemke .10 .03
❑ 110 Brian Harper .10 .03
❑ 111 Brady Anderson .20 .06
❑ 112 Bip Roberts .10 .03
❑ 113 Mitch Williams .10 .03
❑ 114 Craig Biggio .30 .09
❑ 115 Eddie Murray .50 .15
❑ 116 Matt Nokes .10 .03
❑ 117 Lance Parrish .20 .06
❑ 118 Bill Swift .10 .03
❑ 119 Jeff Innis .10 .03
❑ 120 Mike LaValliere .10 .03
❑ 121 Hal Morris .10 .03
❑ 122 Walt Weiss .10 .03
❑ 123 Ivan Rodriguez .30 .09
❑ 124 Andy Van Slyke .30 .09
❑ 125 Roberto Alomar .30 .09
❑ 126 Robby Thompson .10 .03
❑ 127 Sammy Sosa .50 .15
❑ 128 Mark Langston .10 .03
❑ 129 Jerry Browne .10 .03
❑ 130 Chuck McElroy .10 .03
❑ 131 Frank Viola .20 .06
❑ 132 Leo Gomez .10 .03
❑ 133 Ramon Martinez .10 .03
❑ 134 Don Mattingly 1.25 .35
❑ 135 Roger Clemens 1.00 .30
❑ 136 Rickey Henderson .50 .15
❑ 137 Darren Daulton .20 .06
❑ 138 Ken Hill .10 .03
❑ 139 Ozzie Guillen .20 .06
❑ 140 Jerald Clark .10 .03
❑ 141 Dave Fleming .10 .03
❑ 142 Delino DeShields .10 .03
❑ 143 Matt Williams .20 .06
❑ 144 Larry Walker .20 .06
❑ 145 Ruben Sierra .10 .03
❑ 146 Ozzie Smith .75 .23
❑ 147 Chris Sabo .10 .03
❑ 148 Carlos Hernandez .10 .03
❑ 149 Pat Borders .10 .03
❑ 150 Orlando Merced .10 .03
❑ 151 Royce Clayton .10 .03
❑ 152 Kurt Stillwell .10 .03
❑ 153 Dave Hollins .10 .03
❑ 154 Mike Greenwell .10 .03
❑ 155 Nolan Ryan 2.00 .60
❑ 156 Felix Jose .10 .03
❑ 157 Junior Felix .10 .03
❑ 158 Derek Bell .10 .03
❑ 159 Steve Buechele .10 .03
❑ 160 John Burkett .10 .03
❑ 161 Pat Howell .10 .03
❑ 162 Milt Cuyler .10 .03
❑ 163 Terry Pendleton .20 .06
❑ 164 Jack Morris .20 .06
❑ 165 Tony Gwynn .60 .18
❑ 166 Deion Sanders .30 .09
❑ 167 Mike Devereaux .10 .03
❑ 168 Ron Darling .10 .03
❑ 169 Orel Hershiser .20 .06
❑ 170 Mike Jackson .10 .03
❑ 171 Doug Jones .10 .03
❑ 172 Dan Walters .10 .03
❑ 173 Darren Lewis .10 .03
❑ 174 Carlos Baerga .10 .03
❑ 175 Ryne Sandberg .75 .23
❑ 176 Gregg Jefferies .10 .03
❑ 177 John Jaha .10 .03
❑ 178 Luis Polonia .10 .03
❑ 179 Kirt Manwaring .10 .03
❑ 180 Mike Magnante .10 .03
❑ 181 Billy Ripken .10 .03
❑ 182 Mike Moore .10 .03
❑ 183 Eric Anthony .10 .03
❑ 184 Lenny Harris .10 .03
❑ 185 Tony Pena .10 .03
❑ 186 Mike Felder .10 .03
❑ 187 Greg Olson .10 .03
❑ 188 Rene Gonzales .10 .03
❑ 189 Mike Bordick .10 .03
❑ 190 Mel Rojas .10 .03
❑ 191 Todd Frohwirth .10 .03
❑ 192 Darryl Hamilton .10 .03
❑ 193 Mike Fetters .10 .03
❑ 194 Omar Olivares .10 .03
❑ 195 Tony Phillips .10 .03
❑ 196 Paul Sorrento .10 .03
❑ 197 Trevor Wilson .10 .03
❑ 198 Kevin Gross .10 .03
❑ 199 Ron Karkovice .10 .03
❑ 200 Brook Jacoby .10 .03
❑ 201 Mariano Duncan .10 .03
❑ 202 Dennis Cook .10 .03
❑ 203 Daryl Boston .10 .03
❑ 204 Mike Perez .10 .03
❑ 205 Manuel Lee .10 .03
❑ 206 Steve Olin .10 .03
❑ 207 Charlie Hough .20 .06
❑ 208 Scott Scudder .10 .03
❑ 209 Charlie O'Brien .10 .03
❑ 210 Barry Bonds CL .75 .23
❑ 211 Jose Vizcaino .10 .03
❑ 212 Scott Leius .10 .03
❑ 213 Kevin Mitchell .10 .03
❑ 214 Brian Barnes .10 .03
❑ 215 Pat Kelly .10 .03
❑ 216 Chris Hammond .10 .03
❑ 217 Rob Deer .10 .03
❑ 218 Cory Snyder .10 .03
❑ 219 Gary Carter .20 .06
❑ 220 Danny Darwin .10 .03
❑ 221 Tom Gordon .10 .03
❑ 222 Gary Sheffield .20 .06
❑ 223 Joe Carter .20 .06
❑ 224 Jay Buhner .20 .06
❑ 225 Jose Offerman .10 .03
❑ 226 Jose Rijo .10 .03
❑ 227 Mark Whiten .10 .03
❑ 228 Randy Milligan .10 .03
❑ 229 Bud Black .10 .03
❑ 230 Gary DiSarcina .10 .03
❑ 231 Steve Finley .20 .06
❑ 232 Dennis Martinez .20 .06
❑ 233 Mike Mussina .30 .09
❑ 234 Joe Oliver .10 .03
❑ 235 Chad Curtis .10 .03
❑ 236 Shane Mack .10 .03
❑ 237 Jaime Navarro .10 .03
❑ 238 Brian McRae .10 .03
❑ 239 Chili Davis .20 .06
❑ 240 Jeff King .10 .03
❑ 241 Dean Palmer .20 .06
❑ 242 Danny Tartabull .10 .03
❑ 243 Charles Nagy .10 .03
❑ 244 Ray Lankford .20 .06
❑ 245 Barry Larkin .30 .09
❑ 246 Steve Avery .10 .03
❑ 247 John Kruk .20 .06
❑ 248 Derrick May .10 .03
❑ 249 Stan Javier .10 .03
❑ 250 Roger McDowell .10 .03
❑ 251 Dan Gladden .10 .03
❑ 252 Wally Joyner .20 .06
❑ 253 Pat Listach .10 .03
❑ 254 Chuck Knoblauch .20 .06
❑ 255 Sandy Alomar Jr. .10 .03
❑ 256 Jeff Bagwell .30 .09
❑ 257 Andy Stankiewicz .10 .03
❑ 258 Darrin Jackson .10 .03
❑ 259 Brett Butler .20 .06
❑ 260 Joe Orsulak .10 .03
❑ 261 Andy Benes .10 .03
❑ 262 Kenny Lofton .20 .06
❑ 263 Robin Ventura .20 .06
❑ 264 Ron Gant .20 .06
❑ 265 Ellis Burks .20 .06
❑ 266 Juan Guzman .10 .03
❑ 267 Wes Chamberlain .10 .03
❑ 268 John Smiley .10 .03
❑ 269 Franklin Stubbs .10 .03
❑ 270 Tom Browning .10 .03
❑ 271 Dennis Eckersley .20 .06
❑ 272 Carlton Fisk .30 .09
❑ 273 Lou Whitaker .20 .06
❑ 274 Phil Plantier .10 .03
❑ 275 Bobby Bonilla .20 .06
❑ 276 Ben McDonald .10 .03
❑ 277 Bob Zupcic .10 .03
❑ 278 Terry Steinbach .10 .03
❑ 279 Terry Mulholland .10 .03
❑ 280 Lance Johnson .10 .03
❑ 281 Willie McGee .20 .06
❑ 282 Bret Saberhagen .20 .06
❑ 283 Randy Myers .10 .03
❑ 284 Randy Tomlin .10 .03
❑ 285 Mickey Morandini .10 .03
❑ 286 Brian Williams .10 .03
❑ 287 Tino Martinez .30 .09
❑ 288 Jose Melendez .10 .03
❑ 289 Jeff Huson .10 .03
❑ 290 Joe Grahe .10 .03
❑ 291 Mel Hall .10 .03
❑ 292 Otis Nixon .10 .03
❑ 293 Todd Hundley .10 .03
❑ 294 Casey Candaele .10 .03
❑ 295 Kevin Seitzer .10 .03
❑ 296 Eddie Taubensee .10 .03
❑ 297 Moises Alou .20 .06
❑ 298 Scott Radinsky .10 .03
❑ 299 Thomas Howard .10 .03
❑ 300 Kyle Abbott .10 .03
❑ 301 Omar Vizquel .30 .09
❑ 302 Keith Miller .10 .03
❑ 303 Rick Aguilera .10 .03
❑ 304 Bruce Hurst .10 .03
❑ 305 Ken Caminiti .20 .06
❑ 306 Mike Pagliarulo .10 .03
❑ 307 Frank Seminara .10 .03
❑ 308 Andre Dawson .20 .06
❑ 309 Jose Lind .10 .03
❑ 310 Joe Boever .10 .03
❑ 311 Jeff Parrett .10 .03
❑ 312 Alan Mills .10 .03
❑ 313 Kevin Tapani .10 .03
❑ 314 Darryl Kile .20 .06
❑ 315 Will Clark CL .20 .06
❑ 316 Mike Sharperson .10 .03
❑ 317 John Orton .10 .03
❑ 318 Bob Tewksbury .10 .03
❑ 319 Xavier Hernandez .10 .03
❑ 320 Paul Assenmacher .10 .03
❑ 321 John Franco .20 .06
❑ 322 Mike Timlin .10 .03
❑ 323 Jose Guzman .10 .03
❑ 324 Pedro Martinez 1.00 .30
❑ 325 Bill Spiers .10 .03
❑ 326 Melido Perez .10 .03
❑ 327 Mike Macfarlane .10 .03
❑ 328 Ricky Bones .10 .03
❑ 329 Scott Bankhead .10 .03
❑ 330 Rich Rodriguez .10 .03
❑ 331 Geronimo Pena .10 .03
❑ 332 Bernie Williams .30 .09
❑ 333 Paul Molitor .30 .09
❑ 334 Carlos Garcia .10 .03
❑ 335 David Cone .20 .06
❑ 336 Randy Johnson .50 .15
❑ 337 Pat Mahomes .10 .03
❑ 338 Erik Hanson .10 .03
❑ 339 Duane Ward .10 .03
❑ 340 Al Martin .10 .03
❑ 341 Pedro Munoz .10 .03
❑ 342 Greg Colbrunn .10 .03
❑ 343 Julio Valera .10 .03
❑ 344 John Olerud .20 .06
❑ 345 George Bell .10 .03

❑ 346 Devon White .20 .06
❑ 347 Donovan Osborne .10 .03
❑ 348 Mark Gardner .10 .03
❑ 349 Zane Smith .10 .03
❑ 350 Wilson Alvarez .10 .03
❑ 351 Kevin Koslofski .10 .03
❑ 352 Roberto Hernandez .10 .03
❑ 353 Glenn Davis .10 .03
❑ 354 Reggie Sanders .20 .06
❑ 355 Ken Griffey Jr. .75 .23
❑ 356 Marquis Grissom .20 .06
❑ 357 Jack McDowell .10 .03
❑ 358 Jimmy Key .20 .06
❑ 359 Stan Belinda .10 .03
❑ 360 Gerald Williams .10 .03
❑ 361 Sid Fernandez .10 .03
❑ 362 Alex Fernandez .10 .03
❑ 363 John Smoltz .30 .09
❑ 364 Travis Fryman .20 .06
❑ 365 Jose Canseco .30 .09
❑ 366 David Justice .20 .06
❑ 367 Pedro Astacio .10 .03
❑ 368 Tim Belcher .10 .03
❑ 369 Steve Sax .10 .03
❑ 370 Gary Gaetti .20 .06
❑ 371 Jeff Frye .10 .03
❑ 372 Bob Wickman .10 .03
❑ 373 Ryan Thompson .10 .03
❑ 374 David Hulse RC .15 .04
❑ 375 Cal Eldred .10 .03
❑ 376 Ryan Klesko .20 .06
❑ 377 Damion Easley .10 .03
❑ 378 John Kiely .10 .03
❑ 379 Jim Bullinger .10 .03
❑ 380 Brian Bohanon .10 .03
❑ 381 Rod Brewer .10 .03
❑ 382 Fernando Ramsey RC .15 .04
❑ 383 Sam Militello .10 .03
❑ 384 Arthur Rhodes .10 .03
❑ 385 Eric Karros .20 .06
❑ 386 Rico Brogna .10 .03
❑ 387 John Valentin .10 .03
❑ 388 Kerry Woodson .10 .03
❑ 389 Ben Rivera .10 .03
❑ 390 Matt Whiteside RC .15 .04
❑ 391 Henry Rodriguez .10 .03
❑ 392 John Wetteland .20 .06
❑ 393 Kent Mercker .10 .03
❑ 394 Bernard Gilkey .10 .03
❑ 395 Doug Henry .10 .03
❑ 396 Mo Vaughn .20 .06
❑ 397 Scott Erickson .10 .03
❑ 398 Bill Gullickson .10 .03
❑ 399 Mark Guthrie .10 .03
❑ 400 Dave Martinez .10 .03
❑ 401 Jeff Kent .50 .15
❑ 402 Chris Hoiles .10 .03
❑ 403 Mike Henneman .10 .03
❑ 404 Chris Nabholz .10 .03
❑ 405 Tom Pagnozzi .10 .03
❑ 406 Kelly Gruber .10 .03
❑ 407 Bob Welch .10 .03
❑ 408 Frank Castillo .10 .03
❑ 409 John Dopson .10 .03
❑ 410 Steve Farr .10 .03
❑ 411 Henry Cotto .10 .03
❑ 412 Bob Patterson .10 .03
❑ 413 Todd Stottlemyre .10 .03
❑ 414 Greg A. Harris .10 .03
❑ 415 Denny Neagle .20 .06
❑ 416 Bill Wegman .10 .03
❑ 417 Willie Wilson .10 .03
❑ 418 Terry Leach .10 .03
❑ 419 Willie Randolph .20 .06
❑ 420 Mark McGwire CL .30 .09
❑ 421 Calvin Murray CL .10 .03
❑ 422 Pete Janicki TP RC .15 .04
❑ 423 Todd Jones TP .20 .06
❑ 424 Mike Neill TP .10 .03
❑ 425 Carlos Delgado TP .50 .15
❑ 426 Jose Oliva TP .10 .03
❑ 427 Tyrone Hill TP .10 .03
❑ 428 Dmitri Young TP .30 .09
❑ 429 Derek Wallace TP RC .15 .04
❑ 430 Michael Moore TP RC .15 .04
❑ 431 Cliff Floyd TP .20 .06
❑ 432 Calvin Murray TP .10 .03
❑ 433 Manny Ramirez TP .75 .23
❑ 434 Marc Newfield TP .10 .03
❑ 435 Charles Johnson TP .20 .06
❑ 436 Butch Huskey TP .10 .03
❑ 437 Brad Pennington TP .10 .03
❑ 438 Ray McDavid TP RC .15 .04
❑ 439 Chad McConnell TP .10 .03
❑ 440 M.Cummings TP RC .15 .04
❑ 441 Benji Gil TP .10 .03
❑ 442 Frankie Rodriguez TP .10 .03
❑ 443 Chad Mottola TP RC .15 .04
❑ 444 John Burke TP RC .15 .04
❑ 445 Michael Tucker TP .20 .06
❑ 446 Rick Greene TP .10 .03
❑ 447 Rich Becker TP .10 .03
❑ 448 Mike Robertson TP .10 .03
❑ 449 Derek Jeter TP RC 10.00 3.00
❑ 450 Ivan Rodriguez CL .30 .09
David McCarty
❑ 451 Jim Abbott IN .20 .06
❑ 452 Jeff Bagwell IN .20 .06
❑ 453 Jason Bere IN .10 .03
❑ 454 Delino DeShields IN .10 .03
❑ 455 Travis Fryman IN .10 .03
❑ 456 Alex Gonzalez IN .10 .03
❑ 457 Phil Hiatt IN .10 .03
❑ 458 Dave Hollins IN .10 .03
❑ 459 Chipper Jones IN .30 .09
❑ 460 David Justice IN .10 .03
❑ 461 Ray Lankford IN .10 .03
❑ 462 David McCarty IN .10 .03
❑ 463 Mike Mussina IN .20 .06
❑ 464 Jose Offerman IN .10 .03
❑ 465 Dean Palmer IN .10 .03
❑ 466 Geronimo Pena IN .10 .03
❑ 467 Eduardo Perez IN .10 .03
❑ 468 Ivan Rodriguez IN .20 .06
❑ 469 Reggie Sanders IN .10 .03
❑ 470 Bernie Williams IN .20 .06
❑ 471 Barry Bonds CL .75 .23
Matt Williams
Will Clark
❑ 472 Greg Maddux .50 .15
Steve Avery
John Smoltz
Tom Glavine
❑ 473 Jose Rijo .20 .06
Rob Dibble
Roberto Kelly
Reggie Sanders
Barry Larkin
❑ 474 Gary Sheffield .20 .06
Phil Plantier
Tony Gwynn
Fred McGriff
❑ 475 Doug Drabek .20 .06
Craig Biggio
Jeff Bagwell
❑ 476 Will Clark .75 .23
Barry Bonds
Matt Williams
❑ 477 Eric Davis .20 .06
Darryl Strawberry
❑ 478 Dante Bichette .20 .06
David Nied
Andres Galarraga
❑ 479 Dave Magadan .10 .03
Orestes Destrade
Bret Barberie
Jeff Conine
❑ 480 Tim Wakefield .20 .06
Andy Van Slyke
Jay Bell
❑ 481 Marquis Grissom .30 .09
Delino DeShields
Dennis Martinez
Larry Walker
❑ 482 Geronimo Pena .50 .15
Ray Lankford
Ozzie Smith
Bernard Gilkey
❑ 483 Randy Myers .50 .15
Ryne Sandberg
Mark Grace
❑ 484 Eddie Murray .30 .09
Howard Johnson
Bobby Bonilla
❑ 485 John Kruk .10 .03
Dave Hollins
Darren Daulton
Len Dykstra
❑ 486 Barry Bonds AW .75 .23
❑ 487 Dennis Eckersley AW .20 .06
❑ 488 Greg Maddux AW .50 .15
❑ 489 Dennis Eckersley AW .20 .06
❑ 490 Eric Karros AW .10 .03
❑ 491 Pat Listach AW .10 .03
❑ 492 Gary Sheffield AW .10 .03
❑ 493 Mark McGwire AW .60 .18
❑ 494 Gary Sheffield AW .10 .03
❑ 495 Edgar Martinez AW .20 .06
❑ 496 Fred McGriff AW .20 .06
❑ 497 Juan Gonzalez AW .10 .03
❑ 498 Darren Daulton AW .10 .03
❑ 499 Cecil Fielder AW .10 .03
❑ 500 Brent Gates CL .10 .03
❑ 501 Tavo Alvarez DD .10 .03
❑ 502 Rod Bolton .10 .03
❑ 503 J.Cummings DD RC .15 .04
❑ 504 Brent Gates DD .10 .03
❑ 505 Tyler Green .10 .03
❑ 506 Jose Martinez DD RC .15 .04
❑ 507 Troy Percival .30 .09
❑ 508 Kevin Stocker DD .10 .03
❑ 509 Matt Walbeck DD RC .15 .04
❑ 510 Rondell White DD .20 .06
❑ 511 Billy Ripken .10 .03
❑ 512 Mike Moore .10 .03
❑ 513 Jose Lind .10 .03
❑ 514 Chito Martinez .10 .03
❑ 515 Jose Guzman .10 .03
❑ 516 Kim Batiste .10 .03
❑ 517 Jeff Tackett .10 .03
❑ 518 Charlie Hough .20 .06
❑ 519 Marvin Freeman .10 .03
❑ 520 Carlos Martinez .10 .03
❑ 521 Eric Young .10 .03
❑ 522 Pete Incaviglia .10 .03
❑ 523 Scott Fletcher .10 .03
❑ 524 Orestes Destrade .10 .03
❑ 525 Ken Griffey Jr. CL .50 .15
❑ 526 Ellis Burks .20 .06
❑ 527 Juan Samuel .10 .03
❑ 528 Dave Magadan .10 .03
❑ 529 Jeff Parrett .10 .03
❑ 530 Bill Krueger .10 .03
❑ 531 Frank Bolick .10 .03
❑ 532 Alan Trammell .20 .06
❑ 533 Walt Weiss .10 .03
❑ 534 David Cone .20 .06
❑ 535 Greg Maddux .75 .23
❑ 536 Kevin Young .20 .06
❑ 537 Dave Hansen .10 .03
❑ 538 Alex Cole .10 .03
❑ 539 Greg Hibbard .10 .03
❑ 540 Gene Larkin .10 .03
❑ 541 Jeff Reardon .20 .06
❑ 542 Felix Jose .10 .03
❑ 543 Jimmy Key .20 .06
❑ 544 Reggie Jefferson .10 .03
❑ 545 Gregg Jefferies .10 .03
❑ 546 Dave Stewart .20 .06
❑ 547 Tim Wallach .10 .03
❑ 548 Spike Owen .10 .03
❑ 549 Tommy Greene .10 .03
❑ 550 Fernando Valenzuela .20 .06
❑ 551 Rich Amaral .10 .03
❑ 552 Bret Barberie .10 .03
❑ 553 Edgar Martinez .30 .09
❑ 554 Jim Abbott .30 .09
❑ 555 Frank Thomas .50 .15
❑ 556 Wade Boggs .30 .09
❑ 557 Tom Henke .10 .03
❑ 558 Milt Thompson .10 .03
❑ 559 Lloyd McClendon .10 .03
❑ 560 Vinny Castilla .50 .15
❑ 561 Ricky Jordan .10 .03
❑ 562 Andujar Cedeno .10 .03
❑ 563 Greg Vaughn .10 .03
❑ 564 Cecil Fielder .20 .06
❑ 565 Kirby Puckett .50 .15

- ❑ 566 Mark McGwire 1.25 .35
- ❑ 567 Barry Bonds 1.50 .45
- ❑ 568 Jody Reed .10 .03
- ❑ 569 Todd Zeile .10 .03
- ❑ 570 Mark Carreon .10 .03
- ❑ 571 Joe Girardi .10 .03
- ❑ 572 Luis Gonzalez .20 .06
- ❑ 573 Mark Grace .30 .09
- ❑ 574 Rafael Palmeiro .30 .09
- ❑ 575 Darryl Strawberry .20 .06
- ❑ 576 Will Clark .30 .09
- ❑ 577 Fred McGriff .30 .09
- ❑ 578 Kevin Reimer .10 .03
- ❑ 579 Dave Righetti .20 .06
- ❑ 580 Juan Bell .10 .03
- ❑ 581 Jeff Brantley .10 .03
- ❑ 582 Brian Hunter .10 .03
- ❑ 583 Tim Naehring .10 .03
- ❑ 584 Glenallen Hill .10 .03
- ❑ 585 Cal Ripken 1.50 .45
- ❑ 586 Albert Belle .20 .06
- ❑ 587 Robin Yount .75 .23
- ❑ 588 Chris Bosio .10 .03
- ❑ 589 Pete Smith .10 .03
- ❑ 590 Chuck Carr .10 .03
- ❑ 591 Jeff Blauser .10 .03
- ❑ 592 Kevin McReynolds .10 .03
- ❑ 593 Andres Galarraga .20 .06
- ❑ 594 Kevin Maas .10 .03
- ❑ 595 Eric Davis .20 .06
- ❑ 596 Brian Jordan .20 .06
- ❑ 597 Tim Raines .20 .06
- ❑ 598 Rick Wilkins .10 .03
- ❑ 599 Steve Cooke .10 .03
- ❑ 600 Mike Gallego .10 .03
- ❑ 601 Mike Munoz .10 .03
- ❑ 602 Luis Rivera .10 .03
- ❑ 603 Junior Ortiz .10 .03
- ❑ 604 Brent Mayne .10 .03
- ❑ 605 Luis Alicea .10 .03
- ❑ 606 Damon Berryhill .10 .03
- ❑ 607 Dave Henderson .10 .03
- ❑ 608 Kirk McCaskill .10 .03
- ❑ 609 Jeff Fassero .10 .03
- ❑ 610 Mike Harkey .10 .03
- ❑ 611 Francisco Cabrera .10 .03
- ❑ 612 Rey Sanchez .10 .03
- ❑ 613 Scott Servais .10 .03
- ❑ 614 Darrin Fletcher .10 .03
- ❑ 615 Felix Fermin .10 .03
- ❑ 616 Kevin Seitzer .10 .03
- ❑ 617 Bob Scanlan .10 .03
- ❑ 618 Billy Hatcher .10 .03
- ❑ 619 John Vander Wal .10 .03
- ❑ 620 Joe Hesketh .10 .03
- ❑ 621 Hector Villanueva .10 .03
- ❑ 622 Randy Milligan .10 .03
- ❑ 623 Tony Tarasco RC .15 .04
- ❑ 624 Russ Swan .10 .03
- ❑ 625 Willie Wilson .10 .03
- ❑ 626 Frank Tanana .10 .03
- ❑ 627 Pete O'Brien .10 .03
- ❑ 628 Lenny Webster .10 .03
- ❑ 629 Mark Clark .10 .03
- ❑ 630 Roger Clemens CL .50 .15
- ❑ 631 Alex Arias .10 .03
- ❑ 632 Chris Gwynn .10 .03
- ❑ 633 Tom Bolton .10 .03
- ❑ 634 Greg Briley .10 .03
- ❑ 635 Kent Bottenfield .10 .03
- ❑ 636 Kelly Downs .10 .03
- ❑ 637 Manuel Lee .10 .03
- ❑ 638 Al Leiter .20 .06
- ❑ 639 Jeff Gardner .10 .03
- ❑ 640 Mike Gardiner .10 .03
- ❑ 641 Mark Gardner .10 .03
- ❑ 642 Jeff Branson .10 .03
- ❑ 643 Paul Wagner .10 .03
- ❑ 644 Sean Berry .10 .03
- ❑ 645 Phil Hiatt .10 .03
- ❑ 646 Kevin Mitchell .10 .03
- ❑ 647 Charlie Hayes .10 .03
- ❑ 648 Jim Deshaies .10 .03
- ❑ 649 Dan Pasqua .10 .03
- ❑ 650 Mike Maddux .10 .03
- ❑ 651 Domingo Martinez RC .15 .04
- ❑ 652 Greg McMichael RC .15 .04
- ❑ 653 Eric Wedge RC .50 .15
- ❑ 654 Mark Whiten .10 .03
- ❑ 655 Roberto Kelly .10 .03
- ❑ 656 Julio Franco .20 .06
- ❑ 657 Gene Harris .10 .03
- ❑ 658 Pete Schourek .10 .03
- ❑ 659 Mike Bielecki .10 .03
- ❑ 660 Ricky Gutierrez .10 .03
- ❑ 661 Chris Hammond .10 .03
- ❑ 662 Tim Scott .10 .03
- ❑ 663 Norm Charlton .10 .03
- ❑ 664 Doug Drabek .10 .03
- ❑ 665 Dwight Gooden .20 .06
- ❑ 666 Jim Gott .10 .03
- ❑ 667 Randy Myers .10 .03
- ❑ 668 Darren Holmes .10 .03
- ❑ 669 Tim Spehr .10 .03
- ❑ 670 Bruce Ruffin .10 .03
- ❑ 671 Bobby Thigpen .10 .03
- ❑ 672 Tony Fernandez .10 .03
- ❑ 673 Darrin Jackson .10 .03
- ❑ 674 Gregg Olson .10 .03
- ❑ 675 Rob Dibble .20 .06
- ❑ 676 Howard Johnson .10 .03
- ❑ 677 Mike Lansing RC .50 .15
- ❑ 678 Charlie Leibrandt .10 .03
- ❑ 679 Kevin Bass .10 .03
- ❑ 680 Hubie Brooks .10 .03
- ❑ 681 Scott Brosius .20 .06
- ❑ 682 Randy Knorr .10 .03
- ❑ 683 Dante Bichette .20 .06
- ❑ 684 Bryan Harvey .10 .03
- ❑ 685 Greg Gohr .10 .03
- ❑ 686 Willie Banks .10 .03
- ❑ 687 Robb Nen .20 .06
- ❑ 688 Mike Scioscia .10 .03
- ❑ 689 John Farrell .10 .03
- ❑ 690 John Candelaria .10 .03
- ❑ 691 Damon Buford .10 .03
- ❑ 692 Todd Worrell .10 .03
- ❑ 693 Pat Hentgen .10 .03
- ❑ 694 John Smiley .10 .03
- ❑ 695 Greg Swindell .10 .03
- ❑ 696 Derek Bell .10 .03
- ❑ 697 Terry Jorgensen .10 .03
- ❑ 698 Jimmy Jones .10 .03
- ❑ 699 David Wells .20 .06
- ❑ 700 Dave Martinez .10 .03
- ❑ 701 Steve Bedrosian .10 .03
- ❑ 702 Jeff Russell .10 .03
- ❑ 703 Joe Magrane .10 .03
- ❑ 704 Matt Mieske .10 .03
- ❑ 705 Paul Molitor .30 .09
- ❑ 706 Dale Murphy .30 .09
- ❑ 707 Steve Howe .10 .03
- ❑ 708 Greg Gagne .10 .03
- ❑ 709 Dave Eiland .10 .03
- ❑ 710 David West .10 .03
- ❑ 711 Luis Aquino .10 .03
- ❑ 712 Joe Orsulak .10 .03
- ❑ 713 Eric Plunk .10 .03
- ❑ 714 Mike Felder .10 .03
- ❑ 715 Joe Klink .10 .03
- ❑ 716 Lonnie Smith .10 .03
- ❑ 717 Monty Fariss .10 .03
- ❑ 718 Craig Lefferts .10 .03
- ❑ 719 John Habyan .10 .03
- ❑ 720 Willie Blair .10 .03
- ❑ 721 Darnell Coles .10 .03
- ❑ 722 Mark Williamson .10 .03
- ❑ 723 Bryn Smith .10 .03
- ❑ 724 Greg W. Harris .10 .03
- ❑ 725 Graeme Lloyd RC .50 .15
- ❑ 726 Cris Carpenter .10 .03
- ❑ 727 Chico Walker .10 .03
- ❑ 728 Tracy Woodson .10 .03
- ❑ 729 Jose Uribe .10 .03
- ❑ 730 Stan Javier .10 .03
- ❑ 731 Jay Howell .10 .03
- ❑ 732 Freddie Benavides .10 .03
- ❑ 733 Jeff Reboulet .10 .03
- ❑ 734 Scott Sanderson .10 .03
- ❑ 735 Ryne Sandberg CL .50 .15
- ❑ 736 Archi Cianfrocco .10 .03
- ❑ 737 Daryl Boston .10 .03
- ❑ 738 Craig Grebeck .10 .03
- ❑ 739 Doug Dascenzo .10 .03
- ❑ 740 Gerald Young .10 .03
- ❑ 741 Candy Maldonado .10 .03
- ❑ 742 Joey Cora .10 .03
- ❑ 743 Don Slaught .10 .03
- ❑ 744 Steve Decker .10 .03
- ❑ 745 Blas Minor .10 .03
- ❑ 746 Storm Davis .10 .03
- ❑ 747 Carlos Quintana .10 .03
- ❑ 748 Vince Coleman .10 .03
- ❑ 749 Todd Burns .10 .03
- ❑ 750 Steve Frey .10 .03
- ❑ 751 Ivan Calderon .10 .03
- ❑ 752 Steve Reed RC .15 .04
- ❑ 753 Danny Jackson .10 .03
- ❑ 754 Jeff Conine .20 .06
- ❑ 755 Juan Gonzalez .20 .06
- ❑ 756 Mike Kelly .10 .03
- ❑ 757 John Doherty .10 .03
- ❑ 758 Jack Armstrong .10 .03
- ❑ 759 John Wehner .10 .03
- ❑ 760 Scott Bankhead .10 .03
- ❑ 761 Jim Tatum .10 .03
- ❑ 762 Scott Pose RC .15 .04
- ❑ 763 Andy Ashby .10 .03
- ❑ 764 Ed Sprague .10 .03
- ❑ 765 Harold Baines .20 .06
- ❑ 766 Kirk Gibson .30 .09
- ❑ 767 Troy Neel .10 .03
- ❑ 768 Dick Schofield .10 .03
- ❑ 769 Dickie Thon .10 .03
- ❑ 770 Butch Henry .10 .03
- ❑ 771 Junior Felix .10 .03
- ❑ 772 Ken Ryan RC .15 .04
- ❑ 773 Trevor Hoffman .50 .15
- ❑ 774 Phil Plantier .10 .03
- ❑ 775 Bo Jackson .50 .15
- ❑ 776 Benito Santiago .20 .06
- ❑ 777 Andre Dawson .20 .06
- ❑ 778 Bryan Hickerson .10 .03
- ❑ 779 Dennis Moeller .10 .03
- ❑ 780 Ryan Bowen .10 .03
- ❑ 781 Eric Fox .10 .03
- ❑ 782 Joe Kmak .10 .03
- ❑ 783 Mike Hampton .20 .06
- ❑ 784 Darrell Sherman RC .15 .04
- ❑ 785 J.T. Snow .30 .09
- ❑ 786 Dave Winfield .20 .06
- ❑ 787 Jim Austin .10 .03
- ❑ 788 Craig Shipley .10 .03
- ❑ 789 Greg Myers .10 .03
- ❑ 790 Todd Benzinger .10 .03
- ❑ 791 Cory Snyder .10 .03
- ❑ 792 David Segui .10 .03
- ❑ 793 Armando Reynoso .10 .03
- ❑ 794 Chili Davis .20 .06
- ❑ 795 Dave Nilsson .10 .03
- ❑ 796 Paul O'Neill .30 .09
- ❑ 797 Jerald Clark .10 .03
- ❑ 798 Jose Mesa .10 .03
- ❑ 799 Brain Holman .10 .03
- ❑ 800 Jim Eisenreich .10 .03
- ❑ 801 Mark McLemore .10 .03
- ❑ 802 Luis Sojo .10 .03
- ❑ 803 Harold Reynolds .20 .06
- ❑ 804 Dan Plesac .10 .03
- ❑ 805 Dave Stieb .10 .03
- ❑ 806 Tom Brunansky .10 .03
- ❑ 807 Kelly Gruber .10 .03
- ❑ 808 Bob Ojeda .10 .03
- ❑ 809 Dave Burba .10 .03
- ❑ 810 Joe Boever .10 .03
- ❑ 811 Jeremy Hernandez .10 .03
- ❑ 812 Tim Salmon TC .20 .06
- ❑ 813 Jeff Bagwell TC .20 .06
- ❑ 814 Dennis Eckersley TC .20 .06
- ❑ 815 Roberto Alomar TC .20 .06
- ❑ 816 Steve Avery TC .10 .03
- ❑ 817 Pat Listach TC .10 .03
- ❑ 818 Gregg Jefferies TC .10 .03
- ❑ 819 Sammy Sosa TC .50 .15
- ❑ 820 Darryl Strawberry TC .10 .03
- ❑ 821 Dennis Martinez TC .10 .03
- ❑ 822 Robby Thompson TC .10 .03
- ❑ 823 Albert Belle TC .20 .06

❑ 824 Randy Johnson TC	.30	.09
❑ 825 Nigel Wilson TC	.10	.03
❑ 826 Bobby Bonilla TC	.10	.03
❑ 827 Glenn Davis TC	.10	.03
❑ 828 Gary Sheffield TC	.10	.03
❑ 829 Darren Daulton TC	.10	.03
❑ 830 Jay Bell TC	.10	.03
❑ 831 Juan Gonzalez TC	.10	.03
❑ 832 Andre Dawson TC	.10	.03
❑ 833 Hal Morris TC	.10	.03
❑ 834 David Nied TC	.10	.03
❑ 835 Felix Jose TC	.10	.03
❑ 836 Travis Fryman TC	.10	.03
❑ 837 Shane Mack TC	.10	.03
❑ 838 Robin Ventura TC	.10	.03
❑ 839 Danny Tartabull TC	.10	.03
❑ 840 Roberto Alomar CL	.20	.06
❑ SP5 George Brett	1.00	.30
Robin Yount		
❑ SP6 Nolan Ryan	2.00	.60

1994 Upper Deck

	Nm-Mt	Ex-Mt
COMPLETE SET (550)	50.00	15.00
COMP. SERIES 1 (280)	30.00	9.00
COMP. SERIES 2 (270)	20.00	6.00

❑ 1 Brian Anderson RC	.40	.12
❑ 2 Shane Andrews	.15	.04
❑ 3 James Baldwin	.15	.04
❑ 4 Rich Becker	.15	.04
❑ 5 Greg Blosser	.15	.04
❑ 6 Ricky Bottalico RC	.40	.12
❑ 7 Midre Cummings	.15	.04
❑ 8 Carlos Delgado	.50	.15
❑ 9 Steve Dreyer RC	.15	.04
❑ 10 Joey Eischen	.15	.04
❑ 11 Carl Everett	.30	.09
❑ 12 Cliff Floyd UER	.30	.09
(text indicates he throws left; should be right)		
❑ 13 Alex Gonzalez	.15	.04
❑ 14 Jeff Granger	.15	.04
❑ 15 Shawn Green	.75	.23
❑ 16 Brian L. Hunter	.15	.04
❑ 17 Butch Huskey	.15	.04
❑ 18 Mark Hutton	.15	.04
❑ 19 Michael Jordan RC	8.00	2.40
❑ 20 Steve Karsay	.15	.04
❑ 21 Jeff McNeely	.15	.04
❑ 22 Marc Newfield	.15	.04
❑ 23 Manny Ramirez	.75	.23
❑ 24 Alex Rodriguez RC	15.00	4.50
❑ 25 Scott Ruffcorn UER	.15	.04
(photo on back is Robert Ellis)		
❑ 26 Paul Spoljaric UER	.15	.04
(Expos logo on back)		
❑ 27 Salomon Torres	.15	.04
❑ 28 Steve Trachsel	.15	.04
❑ 29 Chris Turner	.15	.04
❑ 30 Gabe White	.15	.04
❑ 31 Randy Johnson FT	.50	.15
❑ 32 John Wetteland FT	.15	.04
❑ 33 Mike Piazza FT	.75	.23
❑ 34 Rafael Palmeiro FT	.30	.09
❑ 35 Roberto Alomar FT	.30	.09
❑ 36 Matt Williams FT	.15	.04
❑ 37 Travis Fryman FT	.15	.04
❑ 38 Barry Bonds FT	1.00	.30
❑ 39 Marquis Grissom FT	.15	.04
❑ 40 Albert Belle FT	.30	.09
❑ 41 Steve Avery FUT	.15	.04
❑ 42 Jason Bere FUT	.15	.04
❑ 43 Alex Fernandez FUT	.15	.04
❑ 44 Mike Mussina FUT	.30	.09
❑ 45 Aaron Sele FUT	.15	.04
❑ 46 Rod Beck FUT	.15	.04
❑ 47 Mike Piazza FUT	.75	.23
❑ 48 John Olerud FUT	.15	.04
❑ 49 Carlos Baerga FUT	.15	.04
❑ 50 Gary Sheffield FUT	.15	.04
❑ 51 Travis Fryman FUT	.15	.04
❑ 52 Juan Gonzalez FUT	.15	.04
❑ 53 Ken Griffey Jr. FUT	.75	.23
❑ 54 Tim Salmon FUT	.30	.09
❑ 55 Frank Thomas FUT	.50	.15
❑ 56 Tony Phillips	.15	.04
❑ 57 Julio Franco	.30	.09
❑ 58 Kevin Mitchell	.15	.04
❑ 59 Raul Mondesi	.30	.09
❑ 60 Rickey Henderson	.75	.23
❑ 61 Jay Buhner	.30	.09
❑ 62 Bill Swift	.15	.04
❑ 63 Brady Anderson	.30	.09
❑ 64 Ryan Klesko	.30	.09
❑ 65 Darren Daulton	.30	.09
❑ 66 Damion Easley	.15	.04
❑ 67 Mark McGwire	2.00	.60
❑ 68 John Roper	.15	.04
❑ 69 Dave Telgheder	.15	.04
❑ 70 David Nied	.15	.04
❑ 71 Mo Vaughn	.30	.09
❑ 72 Tyler Green	.15	.04
❑ 73 Dave Magadan	.15	.04
❑ 74 Chili Davis	.30	.09
❑ 75 Archi Cianfrocco	.15	.04
❑ 76 Joe Girardi	.15	.04
❑ 77 Chris Hoiles	.15	.04
❑ 78 Ryan Bowen	.15	.04
❑ 79 Greg Gagne	.15	.04
❑ 80 Aaron Sele	.15	.04
❑ 81 Dave Winfield	.30	.09
❑ 82 Chad Curtis	.15	.04
❑ 83 Andy Van Slyke	.50	.15
❑ 84 Kevin Stocker	.15	.04
❑ 85 Deion Sanders	.50	.15
❑ 86 Bernie Williams	.50	.15
❑ 87 John Smoltz	.50	.15
❑ 88 Ruben Santana	.15	.04
❑ 89 Dave Stewart	.30	.09
❑ 90 Don Mattingly	2.00	.60
❑ 91 Joe Carter	.30	.09
❑ 92 Ryne Sandberg	1.25	.35
❑ 93 Chris Gomez	.15	.04
❑ 94 Tino Martinez	.50	.15
❑ 95 Terry Pendleton	.30	.09
❑ 96 Andre Dawson	.30	.09
❑ 97 Wil Cordero	.15	.04
❑ 98 Kent Hrbek	.30	.09
❑ 99 John Olerud	.30	.09
❑ 100 Kirt Manwaring	.15	.04
❑ 101 Tim Bogar	.15	.04
❑ 102 Mike Mussina	.50	.15
❑ 103 Nigel Wilson	.15	.04
❑ 104 Ricky Gutierrez	.15	.04
❑ 105 Roberto Mejia	.15	.04
❑ 106 Tom Pagnozzi	.15	.04
❑ 107 Mike Macfarlane	.15	.04
❑ 108 Jose Bautista	.15	.04
❑ 109 Luis Ortiz	.15	.04
❑ 110 Brent Gates	.15	.04
❑ 111 Tim Salmon	.50	.15
❑ 112 Wade Boggs	.50	.15
❑ 113 Tripp Cromer	.15	.04
❑ 114 Denny Hocking	.15	.04
❑ 115 Carlos Baerga	.15	.04
❑ 116 J.R. Phillips	.15	.04
❑ 117 Bo Jackson	.75	.23
❑ 118 Lance Johnson	.15	.04
❑ 119 Bobby Jones	.15	.04
❑ 120 Bobby Witt	.15	.04
❑ 121 Ron Karkovice	.15	.04
❑ 122 Jose Vizcaino	.15	.04
❑ 123 Danny Darwin	.15	.04
❑ 124 Eduardo Perez	.15	.04
❑ 125 Brian Looney RC	.15	.04
❑ 126 Pat Hentgen	.15	.04
❑ 127 Frank Viola	.30	.09
❑ 128 Darren Holmes	.15	.04
❑ 129 Wally Whitehurst	.15	.04
❑ 130 Matt Walbeck	.15	.04
❑ 131 Albert Belle	.30	.09
❑ 132 Steve Cooke	.15	.04
❑ 133 Kevin Appier	.30	.09
❑ 134 Joe Oliver	.15	.04
❑ 135 Benji Gil	.15	.04
❑ 136 Steve Buechele	.15	.04
❑ 137 Devon White	.30	.09
❑ 138 S.Hitchcock UER	.15	.04
(two losses for career; should be four)		
❑ 139 Phil Leftwich RC	.15	.04
❑ 140 Jose Canseco	.50	.15
❑ 141 Rick Aguilera	.15	.04
❑ 142 Rod Beck	.15	.04
❑ 143 Jose Rijo	.15	.04
❑ 144 Tom Glavine	.50	.15
❑ 145 Phil Plantier	.15	.04
❑ 146 Jason Bere	.15	.04
❑ 147 Jamie Moyer	.30	.09
❑ 148 Wes Chamberlain	.15	.04
❑ 149 Glenallen Hill	.15	.04
❑ 150 Mark Whiten	.15	.04
❑ 151 Bret Barberie	.15	.04
❑ 152 Chuck Knoblauch	.30	.09
❑ 153 Trevor Hoffman	.50	.15
❑ 154 Rick Wilkins	.15	.04
❑ 155 Juan Gonzalez	.30	.09
❑ 156 Ozzie Guillen	.30	.09
❑ 157 Jim Eisenreich	.15	.04
❑ 158 Pedro Astacio	.15	.04
❑ 159 Joe Magrane	.15	.04
❑ 160 Ryan Thompson	.15	.04
❑ 161 Jose Lind	.15	.04
❑ 162 Jeff Conine	.30	.09
❑ 163 Todd Benzinger	.15	.04
❑ 164 Roger Salkeld	.15	.04
❑ 165 Gary DiSarcina	.15	.04
❑ 166 Kevin Gross	.15	.04
❑ 167 Charlie Hayes	.15	.04
❑ 168 Tim Costo	.15	.04
❑ 169 Wally Joyner	.30	.09
❑ 170 Johnny Ruffin	.15	.04
❑ 171 Kirk Rueter	.30	.09
❑ 172 Lenny Dykstra	.30	.09
❑ 173 Ken Hill	.15	.04
❑ 174 Mike Bordick	.15	.04
❑ 175 Billy Hall	.15	.04
❑ 176 Rob Butler	.15	.04
❑ 177 Jay Bell	.30	.09
❑ 178 Jeff Kent	.50	.15
❑ 179 David Wells	.30	.09
❑ 180 Dean Palmer	.30	.09
❑ 181 Mariano Duncan	.15	.04
❑ 182 Orlando Merced	.15	.04
❑ 183 Brett Butler	.30	.09
❑ 184 Milt Thompson	.15	.04
❑ 185 Chipper Jones	.75	.23
❑ 186 Paul O'Neill	.50	.15
❑ 187 Mike Greenwell	.15	.04
❑ 188 Harold Baines	.30	.09
❑ 189 Todd Stottlemyre	.15	.04
❑ 190 Jeromy Burnitz	.30	.09
❑ 191 Rene Arocha	.15	.04
❑ 192 Jeff Fassero	.15	.04
❑ 193 Robby Thompson	.15	.04
❑ 194 Greg W. Harris	.15	.04
❑ 195 Todd Van Poppel	.15	.04
❑ 196 Jose Guzman	.15	.04
❑ 197 Shane Mack	.15	.04
❑ 198 Carlos Garcia	.15	.04
❑ 199 Kevin Roberson	.15	.04
❑ 200 David McCarty	.15	.04
❑ 201 Alan Trammell	.30	.09
❑ 202 Chuck Carr	.15	.04
❑ 203 Tommy Greene	.15	.04
❑ 204 Wilson Alvarez	.15	.04
❑ 205 Dwight Gooden	.30	.09
❑ 206 Tony Tarasco	.15	.04

❑ 207 Darren Lewis .15 .04
❑ 208 Eric Karros .30 .09
❑ 209 Chris Hammond .15 .04
❑ 210 Jeffrey Hammonds .15 .04
❑ 211 Rich Amaral .15 .04
❑ 212 Danny Tartabull .15 .04
❑ 213 Jeff Russell .15 .04
❑ 214 Dave Staton .15 .04
❑ 215 Kenny Lofton .30 .09
❑ 216 Manuel Lee .15 .04
❑ 217 Brian Koelling .15 .04
❑ 218 Scott Lydy .15 .04
❑ 219 Tony Gwynn 1.00 .30
❑ 220 Cecil Fielder .30 .09
❑ 221 Royce Clayton .15 .04
❑ 222 Reggie Sanders .30 .09
❑ 223 Brian Jordan .30 .09
❑ 224 Ken Griffey Jr. 1.25 .35
❑ 225 Fred McGriff .50 .15
❑ 226 Felix Jose .15 .04
❑ 227 Brad Pennington .15 .04
❑ 228 Chris Bosio .15 .04
❑ 229 Mike Stanley .15 .04
❑ 230 Willie Greene .15 .04
❑ 231 Alex Fernandez .15 .04
❑ 232 Brad Ausmus .30 .09
❑ 233 Darrell Whitmore .15 .04
❑ 234 Marcus Moore .15 .04
❑ 235 Allen Watson .15 .04
❑ 236 Jose Offerman .15 .04
❑ 237 Rondell White .30 .09
❑ 238 Jeff King .15 .04
❑ 239 Luis Alicea .15 .04
❑ 240 Dan Wilson .15 .04
❑ 241 Ed Sprague .15 .04
❑ 242 Todd Hundley .15 .04
❑ 243 Al Martin .15 .04
❑ 244 Mike Lansing .15 .04
❑ 245 Ivan Rodriguez .50 .15
❑ 246 Dave Fleming .15 .04
❑ 247 John Doherty .15 .04
❑ 248 Mark McLemore .15 .04
❑ 249 Bob Hamelin .15 .04
❑ 250 Curtis Pride RC .40 .12
❑ 251 Zane Smith .15 .04
❑ 252 Eric Young .15 .04
❑ 253 Brian McRae .15 .04
❑ 254 Tim Raines .30 .09
❑ 255 Javier Lopez .30 .09
❑ 256 Melvin Nieves .15 .04
❑ 257 Randy Myers .15 .04
❑ 258 Willie McGee .30 .09
❑ 259 Jimmy Key UER .30 .09
(birthdate missing on back)
❑ 260 Tom Candiotti .15 .04
❑ 261 Eric Davis .30 .09
❑ 262 Craig Paquette .15 .04
❑ 263 Robin Ventura .30 .09
❑ 264 Pat Kelly .15 .04
❑ 265 Gregg Jefferies .15 .04
❑ 266 Cory Snyder .15 .04
❑ 267 David Justice HFA .15 .04
❑ 268 Sammy Sosa HFA .75 .23
❑ 269 Barry Larkin HFA .30 .09
❑ 270 Andres Galarraga HFA .15 .04
❑ 271 Gary Sheffield HFA .15 .04
❑ 272 Jeff Bagwell HFA .30 .09
❑ 273 Mike Piazza HFA .75 .23
❑ 274 Larry Walker HFA .15 .04
❑ 275 Bobby Bonilla HFA .15 .04
❑ 276 John Kruk HFA .15 .04
❑ 277 Jay Bell HFA .15 .04
❑ 278 Ozzie Smith HFA .75 .23
❑ 279 Tony Gwynn HFA .50 .15
❑ 280 Barry Bonds HFA 1.00 .30
❑ 281 Cal Ripken Jr. HFA 1.25 .35
❑ 282 Mo Vaughn HFA .15 .04
❑ 283 Tim Salmon HFA .30 .09
❑ 284 Frank Thomas HFA .50 .15
❑ 285 Albert Belle HFA .30 .09
❑ 286 Cecil Fielder HFA .15 .04
❑ 287 Wally Joyner HFA .15 .04
❑ 288 Greg Vaughn HFA .15 .04
❑ 289 Kirby Puckett HFA .50 .15
❑ 290 Don Mattingly HFA 1.00 .30
❑ 291 Terry Steinbach HFA .15 .04
❑ 292 Ken Griffey Jr. HFA .75 .23
❑ 293 Juan Gonzalez HFA .15 .04
❑ 294 Paul Molitor HFA .30 .09
❑ 295 Tavo Alvarez UDC .15 .04
❑ 296 Matt Brunson UDC .15 .04
❑ 297 Shawn Green UDC .30 .09
❑ 298 Alex Rodriguez UDC 5.00 1.50
❑ 299 S.Stewart UDC .75 .23
❑ 300 Frank Thomas .75 .23
❑ 301 Mickey Tettleton .15 .04
❑ 302 Pedro Munoz .15 .04
❑ 303 Jose Valentin .15 .04
❑ 304 Orestes Destrade .15 .04
❑ 305 Pat Listach .15 .04
❑ 306 Scott Brosius .30 .09
❑ 307 Kurt Miller .15 .04
❑ 308 Rob Dibble .30 .09
❑ 309 Mike Blowers .15 .04
❑ 310 Jim Abbott .50 .15
❑ 311 Mike Jackson .15 .04
❑ 312 Craig Biggio .50 .15
❑ 313 Kurt Abbott RC .40 .12
❑ 314 Chuck Finley .30 .09
❑ 315 Andres Galarraga .30 .09
❑ 316 Mike Moore .15 .04
❑ 317 Doug Strange .15 .04
❑ 318 Pedro Martinez .75 .23
❑ 319 Kevin McReynolds .15 .04
❑ 320 Greg Maddux 1.25 .35
❑ 321 Mike Henneman .15 .04
❑ 322 Scott Leius .15 .04
❑ 323 John Franco .30 .09
❑ 324 Jeff Blauser .15 .04
❑ 325 Kirby Puckett .75 .23
❑ 326 Darryl Hamilton .15 .04
❑ 327 John Smiley .15 .04
❑ 328 Derrick May .15 .04
❑ 329 Jose Vizcaino .15 .04
❑ 330 Randy Johnson .75 .23
❑ 331 Jack Morris .30 .09
❑ 332 Graeme Lloyd .15 .04
❑ 333 Dave Valle .15 .04
❑ 334 Greg Myers .15 .04
❑ 335 John Wetteland .30 .09
❑ 336 Jim Gott .15 .04
❑ 337 Tim Naehring .15 .04
❑ 338 Mike Kelly .15 .04
❑ 339 Jeff Montgomery .15 .04
❑ 340 Rafael Palmeiro .50 .15
❑ 341 Eddie Murray .75 .23
❑ 342 Xavier Hernandez .15 .04
❑ 343 Bobby Munoz .15 .04
❑ 344 Bobby Bonilla .30 .09
❑ 345 Travis Fryman .30 .09
❑ 346 Steve Finley .30 .09
❑ 347 Chris Sabo .15 .04
❑ 348 Armando Reynoso .15 .04
❑ 349 Ramon Martinez .15 .04
❑ 350 Will Clark .50 .15
❑ 351 Moises Alou .30 .09
❑ 352 Jim Thome .50 .15
❑ 353 Bob Tewksbury .15 .04
❑ 354 Andujar Cedeno .15 .04
❑ 355 Orel Hershiser .30 .09
❑ 356 Mike Devereaux .15 .04
❑ 357 Mike Perez .15 .04
❑ 358 Dennis Martinez .30 .09
❑ 359 Dave Nilsson .15 .04
❑ 360 Ozzie Smith 1.25 .35
❑ 361 Eric Anthony .15 .04
❑ 362 Scott Sanders .15 .04
❑ 363 Paul Sorrento .15 .04
❑ 364 Tim Belcher .15 .04
❑ 365 Dennis Eckersley .30 .09
❑ 366 Mel Rojas .15 .04
❑ 367 Tom Henke .15 .04
❑ 368 Randy Tomlin .15 .04
❑ 369 B.J. Surhoff .30 .09
❑ 370 Larry Walker .30 .09
❑ 371 Joey Cora .15 .04
❑ 372 Mike Harkey .15 .04
❑ 373 John Valentin .15 .04
❑ 374 Doug Jones .15 .04
❑ 375 David Justice .30 .09
❑ 376 Vince Coleman .15 .04
❑ 377 David Hulse .15 .04
❑ 378 Kevin Seitzer .15 .04
❑ 379 Pete Harnisch .15 .04
❑ 380 Ruben Sierra .15 .04
❑ 381 Mark Lewis .15 .04
❑ 382 Bip Roberts .15 .04
❑ 383 Paul Wagner .15 .04
❑ 384 Stan Javier .15 .04
❑ 385 Barry Larkin .50 .15
❑ 386 Mark Portugal .15 .04
❑ 387 Roberto Kelly .15 .04
❑ 388 Andy Benes .15 .04
❑ 389 Felix Fermin .15 .04
❑ 390 Marquis Grissom .30 .09
❑ 391 Troy Neel .15 .04
❑ 392 Chad Kreuter .15 .04
❑ 393 Gregg Olson .15 .04
❑ 394 Charles Nagy .15 .04
❑ 395 Jack McDowell .15 .04
❑ 396 Luis Gonzalez .30 .09
❑ 397 Benito Santiago .30 .09
❑ 398 Chris James .15 .04
❑ 399 Terry Mulholland .15 .04
❑ 400 Barry Bonds 2.00 .60
❑ 401 Joe Grahe .15 .04
❑ 402 Duane Ward .15 .04
❑ 403 John Burkett .15 .04
❑ 404 Scott Servais .15 .04
❑ 405 Bryan Harvey .15 .04
❑ 406 Bernard Gilkey .15 .04
❑ 407 Greg McMichael .15 .04
❑ 408 Tim Wallach .15 .04
❑ 409 Ken Caminiti .30 .09
❑ 410 John Kruk .30 .09
❑ 411 Darrin Jackson .15 .04
❑ 412 Mike Gallego .15 .04
❑ 413 David Cone .30 .09
❑ 414 Lou Whitaker .30 .09
❑ 415 Sandy Alomar Jr. .15 .04
❑ 416 Bill Wegman .15 .04
❑ 417 Pat Borders .15 .04
❑ 418 Roger Pavlik .15 .04
❑ 419 Pete Smith .15 .04
❑ 420 Steve Avery .15 .04
❑ 421 David Segui .15 .04
❑ 422 Rheal Cormier .15 .04
❑ 423 Harold Reynolds .30 .09
❑ 424 Edgar Martinez .50 .15
❑ 425 Cal Ripken Jr. 2.50 .75
❑ 426 Jaime Navarro .15 .04
❑ 427 Sean Berry .15 .04
❑ 428 Bret Saberhagen .30 .09
❑ 429 Bob Welch .15 .04
❑ 430 Juan Guzman .15 .04
❑ 431 Cal Eldred .15 .04
❑ 432 Dave Hollins .15 .04
❑ 433 Sid Fernandez .15 .04
❑ 434 Willie Banks .15 .04
❑ 435 Darryl Kile .30 .09
❑ 436 Henry Rodriguez .15 .04
❑ 437 Tony Fernandez .15 .04
❑ 438 Walt Weiss .15 .04
❑ 439 Kevin Tapani .15 .04
❑ 440 Mark Grace .50 .15
❑ 441 Brian Harper .15 .04
❑ 442 Kent Mercker .15 .04
❑ 443 Anthony Young .15 .04
❑ 444 Todd Zeile .15 .04
❑ 445 Greg Vaughn .15 .04
❑ 446 Ray Lankford .30 .09
❑ 447 Dave Weathers .15 .04
❑ 448 Bret Boone .30 .09
❑ 449 Charlie Hough .30 .09
❑ 450 Roger Clemens 1.50 .45
❑ 451 Mike Morgan .15 .04
❑ 452 Doug Drabek .15 .04
❑ 453 Danny Jackson .15 .04
❑ 454 Dante Bichette .30 .09
❑ 455 Roberto Alomar .50 .15
❑ 456 Ben McDonald .15 .04
❑ 457 Kenny Rogers .30 .09
❑ 458 Bill Gullickson .15 .04
❑ 459 Darrin Fletcher .15 .04
❑ 460 Curt Schilling .30 .09
❑ 461 Billy Hatcher .15 .04
❑ 462 Howard Johnson .15 .04
❑ 463 Mickey Morandini .15 .04

	No.	Player	Nm-Mt	Ex-Mt
❑	464	Frank Castillo	.15	.04
❑	465	Delino DeShields	.15	.04
❑	466	Gary Gaetti	.30	.09
❑	467	Steve Farr	.15	.04
❑	468	Roberto Hernandez	.15	.04
❑	469	Jack Armstrong	.15	.04
❑	470	Paul Molitor	.50	.15
❑	471	Melido Perez	.15	.04
❑	472	Greg Hibbard	.15	.04
❑	473	Jody Reed	.15	.04
❑	474	Tom Gordon	.15	.04
❑	475	Gary Sheffield	.30	.09
❑	476	John Jaha	.15	.04
❑	477	Shawon Dunston	.15	.04
❑	478	Reggie Jefferson	.15	.04
❑	479	Don Slaught	.15	.04
❑	480	Jeff Bagwell	.50	.15
❑	481	Tim Pugh	.15	.04
❑	482	Kevin Young	.15	.04
❑	483	Ellis Burks	.30	.09
❑	484	Greg Swindell	.15	.04
❑	485	Mark Langston	.15	.04
❑	486	Omar Vizquel	.50	.15
❑	487	Kevin Brown	.30	.09
❑	488	Terry Steinbach	.15	.04
❑	489	Mark Lemke	.15	.04
❑	490	Matt Williams	.30	.09
❑	491	Pete Incaviglia	.15	.04
❑	492	Karl Rhodes	.15	.04
❑	493	Shawn Green	.75	.23
❑	494	Hal Morris	.15	.04
❑	495	Derek Bell	.15	.04
❑	496	Luis Polonia	.15	.04
❑	497	Otis Nixon	.15	.04
❑	498	Ron Darling	.15	.04
❑	499	Mitch Williams	.15	.04
❑	500	Mike Piazza	1.50	.45
❑	501	Pat Meares	.15	.04
❑	502	Scott Cooper	.15	.04
❑	503	Scott Erickson	.15	.04
❑	504	Jeff Juden	.15	.04
❑	505	Lee Smith	.30	.09
❑	506	Bobby Ayala	.15	.04
❑	507	Dave Henderson	.15	.04
❑	508	Erik Hanson	.15	.04
❑	509	Bob Wickman	.15	.04
❑	510	Sammy Sosa	.75	.23
❑	511	Hector Carrasco	.15	.04
❑	512	Tim Davis	.15	.04
❑	513	Joey Hamilton	.15	.04
❑	514	Robert Eenhoorn	.15	.04
❑	515	Jorge Fabregas	.15	.04
❑	516	Tim Hyers RC	.15	.04
❑	517	John Hudek RC	.15	.04
❑	518	James Mouton	.15	.04
❑	519	Herbert Perry RC	.40	.12
❑	520	Chan Ho Park RC	.50	.15
❑	521	W.Va Landingham RC	.15	.04
❑	522	Paul Shuey	.15	.04
❑	523	Ryan Hancock RC	.15	.04
❑	524	Billy Wagner RC	1.50	.45
❑	525	Jason Giambi	.75	.23
❑	526	Jose Silva RC	.15	.04
❑	527	Terrell Wade RC	.15	.04
❑	528	Todd Dunn	.15	.04
❑	529	Alan Benes RC	.40	.12
❑	530	B.Kieschnick RC	.40	.12
❑	531	T.Hollandsworth	.15	.04
❑	532	Brad Fullmer RC	.50	.15
❑	533	S.Soderstrom RC	.15	.04
❑	534	Daron Kirkreit	.15	.04
❑	535	Arquimedez Pozo RC	.15	.04
❑	536	Charles Johnson	.30	.09
❑	537	Preston Wilson	.30	.09
❑	538	Alex Ochoa	.15	.04
❑	539	Derrek Lee RC	4.00	1.20
❑	540	Wayne Gomes RC	.15	.04
❑	541	J.Allensworth RC	.15	.04
❑	542	Mike Bell RC	.15	.04
❑	543	Trot Nixon RC	1.50	.45
❑	544	Pokey Reese	.15	.04
❑	545	Neifi Perez RC	.40	.12
❑	546	Johnny Damon	.75	.23
❑	547	Matt Brunson RC	.15	.04
❑	548	L.Hawkins RC	.50	.15
❑	549	Eddie Pearson RC	.15	.04
❑	550	Derek Jeter	2.50	.75
❑	A298	Alex Rodriguez AU	400.00	120.00
❑	P224	K.Griffey Jr. Promo	2.00	.60
❑	GM1	Ken Griffey Jr. AU Mickey Mantle AU/1000	1200.00	350.00
❑	KG1	K.Griffey Jr. AU/1000	250.00	75.00
❑	MM1	M.Mantle AU/1000	800.00	240.00

1995 Upper Deck

	Nm-Mt	Ex-Mt
COMP.MASTER SET (495)	110.00	33.00
COMPLETE SET (450)	50.00	15.00
COMP. SERIES 1 (225)	25.00	7.50
COMP. SERIES 2 (225)	25.00	7.50
COMMON CARD (1-450)	.15	.04
COMP.TRADE SET (45)	60.00	18.00
COMMON (451T-495T)	1.00	.30

	No.	Player	Nm-Mt	Ex-Mt
❑	1	Ruben Rivera	.15	.04
❑	2	Bill Pulsipher	.15	.04
❑	3	Ben Grieve	.30	.09
❑	4	Curtis Goodwin	.15	.04
❑	5	Damon Hollins	.15	.04
❑	6	Todd Greene	.15	.04
❑	7	Glenn Williams	.15	.04
❑	8	Bret Wagner	.15	.04
❑	9	Karim Garcia RC	.40	.12
❑	10	Nomar Garciaparra	2.00	.60
❑	11	Raul Casanova RC	.15	.04
❑	12	Matt Smith	.15	.04
❑	13	Paul Wilson	.15	.04
❑	14	Jason Isringhausen	.30	.09
❑	15	Reid Ryan	.30	.09
❑	16	Lee Smith	.30	.09
❑	17	Chili Davis	.30	.09
❑	18	Brian Anderson	.15	.04
❑	19	Gary DiSarcina	.15	.04
❑	20	Bo Jackson	.75	.23
❑	21	Chuck Finley	.30	.09
❑	22	Darryl Kile	.30	.09
❑	23	Shane Reynolds	.15	.04
❑	24	Tony Eusebio	.15	.04
❑	25	Craig Biggio	.50	.15
❑	26	Doug Drabek	.15	.04
❑	27	Brian L. Hunter	.15	.04
❑	28	James Mouton	.15	.04
❑	29	Geronimo Berroa	.15	.04
❑	30	Rickey Henderson	.75	.23
❑	31	Steve Karsay	.15	.04
❑	32	Steve Ontiveros	.15	.04
❑	33	Ernie Young	.15	.04
❑	34	Dennis Eckersley	.30	.09
❑	35	Mark McGwire	2.00	.60
❑	36	Dave Stewart	.30	.09
❑	37	Pat Hentgen	.15	.04
❑	38	Carlos Delgado	.30	.09
❑	39	Joe Carter	.30	.09
❑	40	Roberto Alomar	.50	.15
❑	41	John Olerud	.30	.09
❑	42	Devon White	.30	.09
❑	43	Roberto Kelly	.15	.04
❑	44	Jeff Blauser	.15	.04
❑	45	Fred McGriff	.50	.15
❑	46	Tom Glavine	.50	.15
❑	47	Mike Kelly	.15	.04
❑	48	Javier Lopez	.30	.09
❑	49	Greg Maddux	1.25	.35
❑	50	Matt Mieske	.15	.04
❑	51	Troy O'Leary	.15	.04
❑	52	Jeff Cirillo	.30	.09
❑	53	Cal Eldred	.15	.04
❑	54	Pat Listach	.15	.04
❑	55	Jose Valentin	.15	.04
❑	56	John Mabry	.30	.09
❑	57	Bob Tewksbury	.15	.04
❑	58	Brian Jordan	.30	.09
❑	59	Gregg Jefferies	.15	.04
❑	60	Ozzie Smith	1.25	.35
❑	61	Geronimo Pena	.15	.04
❑	62	Mark Whiten	.15	.04
❑	63	Rey Sanchez	.15	.04
❑	64	Willie Banks	.15	.04
❑	65	Mark Grace	.50	.15
❑	66	Randy Myers	.15	.04
❑	67	Steve Trachsel	.15	.04
❑	68	Derrick May	.15	.04
❑	69	Brett Butler	.30	.09
❑	70	Eric Karros	.30	.09
❑	71	Tim Wallach	.15	.04
❑	72	Delino DeShields	.15	.04
❑	73	Darren Dreifort	.15	.04
❑	74	Orel Hershiser	.30	.09
❑	75	Billy Ashley	.15	.04
❑	76	Sean Berry	.15	.04
❑	77	Ken Hill	.15	.04
❑	78	John Wetteland	.30	.09
❑	79	Moises Alou	.30	.09
❑	80	Cliff Floyd	.30	.09
❑	81	Marquis Grissom	.30	.09
❑	82	Larry Walker	.30	.09
❑	83	Rondell White	.30	.09
❑	84	W.VanLandingham	.15	.04
❑	85	Matt Williams	.30	.09
❑	86	Rod Beck	.15	.04
❑	87	Darren Lewis	.15	.04
❑	88	Robby Thompson	.15	.04
❑	89	Darryl Strawberry	.30	.09
❑	90	Kenny Lofton	.30	.09
❑	91	Charles Nagy	.15	.04
❑	92	Sandy Alomar Jr.	.15	.04
❑	93	Mark Clark	.15	.04
❑	94	Dennis Martinez	.30	.09
❑	95	Dave Winfield	.30	.09
❑	96	Jim Thome	.50	.15
❑	97	Manny Ramirez	.50	.15
❑	98	Goose Gossage	.30	.09
❑	99	Tino Martinez	.50	.15
❑	100	Ken Griffey Jr.	1.25	.35
❑	101	Greg Maddux ANA	.75	.23
❑	102	Randy Johnson ANA	.50	.15
❑	103	Barry Bonds ANA	1.00	.30
❑	104	Juan Gonzalez ANA	.15	.04
❑	105	Frank Thomas ANA	.50	.15
❑	106	Matt Williams ANA	.15	.04
❑	107	Paul Molitor ANA	.30	.09
❑	108	Fred McGriff ANA	.30	.09
❑	109	Carlos Baerga ANA	.15	.04
❑	110	Ken Griffey Jr. ANA	.75	.23
❑	111	Reggie Jefferson	.15	.04
❑	112	Randy Johnson	.75	.23
❑	113	Marc Newfield	.15	.04
❑	114	Robb Nen	.30	.09
❑	115	Jeff Conine	.30	.09
❑	116	Kurt Abbott	.15	.04
❑	117	Charlie Hough	.30	.09
❑	118	Dave Weathers	.15	.04
❑	119	Juan Castillo	.15	.04
❑	120	Bret Saberhagen	.30	.09
❑	121	Rico Brogna	.15	.04
❑	122	John Franco	.30	.09
❑	123	Todd Hundley	.15	.04
❑	124	Jason Jacome	.15	.04
❑	125	Bobby Jones	.15	.04
❑	126	Bret Barberie	.15	.04
❑	127	Ben McDonald	.15	.04
❑	128	Harold Baines	.30	.09
❑	129	Jeffrey Hammonds	.15	.04
❑	130	Mike Mussina	.50	.15
❑	131	Chris Hoiles	.15	.04
❑	132	Brady Anderson	.30	.09
❑	133	Eddie Williams	.15	.04
❑	134	Andy Benes	.15	.04
❑	135	Tony Gwynn	1.00	.30
❑	136	Bip Roberts	.15	.04

❑ 137 Joey Hamilton .15 .04
❑ 138 Luis Lopez .15 .04
❑ 139 Ray McDavid .15 .04
❑ 140 Lenny Dykstra .30 .09
❑ 141 Mariano Duncan .15 .04
❑ 142 Fernando Valenzuela .30 .09
❑ 143 Bobby Munoz .15 .04
❑ 144 Kevin Stocker .15 .04
❑ 145 John Kruk .30 .09
❑ 146 Jon Lieber .15 .04
❑ 147 Zane Smith .15 .04
❑ 148 Steve Cooke .15 .04
❑ 149 Andy Van Slyke .50 .15
❑ 150 Jay Bell .30 .09
❑ 151 Carlos Garcia .15 .04
❑ 152 John Dettmer .15 .04
❑ 153 Darren Oliver .15 .04
❑ 154 Dean Palmer .30 .09
❑ 155 Otis Nixon .15 .04
❑ 156 Rusty Greer .30 .09
❑ 157 Rick Helling .15 .04
❑ 158 Jose Canseco .50 .15
❑ 159 Roger Clemens 1.50 .45
❑ 160 Andre Dawson .30 .09
❑ 161 Mo Vaughn .30 .09
❑ 162 Aaron Sele .15 .04
❑ 163 John Valentin .15 .04
❑ 164 Brian R. Hunter .15 .04
❑ 165 Bret Boone .30 .09
❑ 166 Hector Carrasco .15 .04
❑ 167 Pete Schourek .15 .04
❑ 168 Willie Greene .15 .04
❑ 169 Kevin Mitchell .15 .04
❑ 170 Deion Sanders .50 .15
❑ 171 John Roper .15 .04
❑ 172 Charlie Hayes .15 .04
❑ 173 David Nied .15 .04
❑ 174 Ellis Burks .30 .09
❑ 175 Dante Bichette .30 .09
❑ 176 Marvin Freeman .15 .04
❑ 177 Eric Young .15 .04
❑ 178 David Cone .30 .09
❑ 179 Greg Gagne .15 .04
❑ 180 Bob Hamelin .15 .04
❑ 181 Wally Joyner .30 .09
❑ 182 Jeff Montgomery .15 .04
❑ 183 Jose Lind .15 .04
❑ 184 Chris Gomez .15 .04
❑ 185 Travis Fryman .30 .09
❑ 186 Kirk Gibson .50 .15
❑ 187 Mike Moore .15 .04
❑ 188 Lou Whitaker .30 .09
❑ 189 Sean Bergman .15 .04
❑ 190 Shane Mack .15 .04
❑ 191 Rick Aguilera .15 .04
❑ 192 Denny Hocking .15 .04
❑ 193 Chuck Knoblauch .30 .09
❑ 194 Kevin Tapani .15 .04
❑ 195 Kent Hrbek .30 .09
❑ 196 Ozzie Guillen .30 .09
❑ 197 Wilson Alvarez .15 .04
❑ 198 Tim Raines .30 .09
❑ 199 Scott Ruffcorn .15 .04
❑ 200 Michael Jordan 2.50 .75
❑ 201 Robin Ventura .30 .09
❑ 202 Jason Bere .15 .04
❑ 203 Darrin Jackson .15 .04
❑ 204 Russ Davis .15 .04
❑ 205 Jimmy Key .30 .09
❑ 206 Jack McDowell .15 .04
❑ 207 Jim Abbott .50 .15
❑ 208 Paul O'Neill .50 .15
❑ 209 Bernie Williams .50 .15
❑ 210 Don Mattingly 2.00 .60
❑ 211 Orlando Miller .15 .04
❑ 212 Alex Gonzalez .15 .04
❑ 213 Terrell Wade .15 .04
❑ 214 Jose Oliva .15 .04
❑ 215 Alex Rodriguez 2.00 .60
❑ 216 Garret Anderson .30 .09
❑ 217 Alan Benes .15 .04
❑ 218 Armando Benitez .30 .09
❑ 219 Dustin Hermanson .15 .04
❑ 220 Charles Johnson .30 .09
❑ 221 Julian Tavarez .15 .04
❑ 222 Jason Giambi .50 .15
❑ 223 LaTroy Hawkins .15 .04
❑ 224 Todd Hollandsworth .15 .04
❑ 225 Derek Jeter 2.00 .60
❑ 226 Hideo Nomo RC 2.50 .75
❑ 227 Tony Clark .15 .04
❑ 228 Roger Cedeno .15 .04
❑ 229 Scott Stahoviak .15 .04
❑ 230 Michael Tucker .15 .04
❑ 231 Joe Rosselli .15 .04
❑ 232 Antonio Osuna .15 .04
❑ 233 Bobby Higginson RC .75 .23
❑ 234 Mark Grudzielanek RC .75 .23
❑ 235 Ray Durham .30 .09
❑ 236 Frank Rodriguez .15 .04
❑ 237 Quilvio Veras .15 .04
❑ 238 Darren Bragg .15 .04
❑ 239 Ugueth Urbina .15 .04
❑ 240 Jason Bates .15 .04
❑ 241 David Bell .15 .04
❑ 242 Ron Villone .15 .04
❑ 243 Joe Randa .15 .04
❑ 244 Carlos Perez RC .40 .12
❑ 245 Brad Clontz .15 .04
❑ 246 Steve Rodriguez .15 .04
❑ 247 Joe Vitiello .15 .04
❑ 248 Ozzie Timmons .15 .04
❑ 249 Rudy Pemberton .15 .04
❑ 250 Marty Cordova .15 .04
❑ 251 Tony Graffanino .15 .04
❑ 252 Mark Johnson RC .40 .12
❑ 253 Tomas Perez RC .15 .04
❑ 254 Jimmy Hurst .15 .04
❑ 255 Edgardo Alfonzo .15 .04
❑ 256 Jose Malave .15 .04
❑ 257 Brad Radke RC .75 .23
❑ 258 Jon Nunnally .15 .04
❑ 259 Dilson Torres RC .15 .04
❑ 260 Esteban Loaiza .15 .04
❑ 261 Freddy Adrian Garcia RC .15 .04
❑ 262 Don Wengert .15 .04
❑ 263 Robert Person RC .40 .12
❑ 264 Tim Unroe RC .15 .04
❑ 265 Juan Acevedo RC .15 .04
❑ 266 Eduardo Perez .15 .04
❑ 267 Tony Phillips .15 .04
❑ 268 Jim Edmonds .50 .15
❑ 269 Jorge Fabregas .15 .04
❑ 270 Tim Salmon .50 .15
❑ 271 Mark Langston .15 .04
❑ 272 J.T. Snow .30 .09
❑ 273 Phil Plantier .15 .04
❑ 274 Derek Bell .15 .04
❑ 275 Jeff Bagwell .50 .15
❑ 276 Luis Gonzalez .30 .09
❑ 277 John Hudek .15 .04
❑ 278 Todd Stottlemyre .15 .04
❑ 279 Mark Acre .15 .04
❑ 280 Ruben Sierra .15 .04
❑ 281 Mike Bordick .15 .04
❑ 282 Ron Darling .15 .04
❑ 283 Brent Gates .15 .04
❑ 284 Todd Van Poppel .15 .04
❑ 285 Paul Molitor .50 .15
❑ 286 Ed Sprague .15 .04
❑ 287 Juan Guzman .15 .04
❑ 288 David Cone .30 .09
❑ 289 Shawn Green .30 .09
❑ 290 Marquis Grissom .30 .09
❑ 291 Kent Mercker .15 .04
❑ 292 Steve Avery .15 .04
❑ 293 Chipper Jones .75 .23
❑ 294 John Smoltz .50 .15
❑ 295 David Justice .30 .09
❑ 296 Ryan Klesko .30 .09
❑ 297 Joe Oliver .15 .04
❑ 298 Ricky Bones .15 .04
❑ 299 John Jaha .15 .04
❑ 300 Greg Vaughn .15 .04
❑ 301 Dave Nilsson .15 .04
❑ 302 Kevin Seitzer .15 .04
❑ 303 Bernard Gilkey .15 .04
❑ 304 Allen Battle .15 .04
❑ 305 Ray Lankford .30 .09
❑ 306 Tom Pagnozzi .15 .04
❑ 307 Allen Watson .15 .04
❑ 308 Danny Jackson .15 .04
❑ 309 Ken Hill .15 .04
❑ 310 Todd Zeile .15 .04
❑ 311 Kevin Roberson .15 .04
❑ 312 Steve Buechele .15 .04
❑ 313 Rick Wilkins .15 .04
❑ 314 Kevin Foster .15 .04
❑ 315 Sammy Sosa .75 .23
❑ 316 Howard Johnson .15 .04
❑ 317 Greg Hansell .15 .04
❑ 318 Pedro Astacio .15 .04
❑ 319 Rafael Bournigal .15 .04
❑ 320 Mike Piazza 1.25 .35
❑ 321 Ramon Martinez .15 .04
❑ 322 Raul Mondesi .30 .09
❑ 323 Ismael Valdes .15 .04
❑ 324 Wil Cordero .15 .04
❑ 325 Tony Tarasco .15 .04
❑ 326 Roberto Kelly .15 .04
❑ 327 Jeff Fassero .15 .04
❑ 328 Mike Lansing .15 .04
❑ 329 Pedro Martinez .50 .15
❑ 330 Kirk Rueter .15 .04
❑ 331 Glenallen Hill .15 .04
❑ 332 Kirt Manwaring .15 .04
❑ 333 Royce Clayton .15 .04
❑ 334 J.R. Phillips .15 .04
❑ 335 Barry Bonds 2.00 .60
❑ 336 Mark Portugal .15 .04
❑ 337 Terry Mulholland .15 .04
❑ 338 Omar Vizquel .50 .15
❑ 339 Carlos Baerga .15 .04
❑ 340 Albert Belle .30 .09
❑ 341 Eddie Murray .75 .23
❑ 342 Wayne Kirby .15 .04
❑ 343 Chad Ogea .15 .04
❑ 344 Tim Davis .15 .04
❑ 345 Jay Buhner .30 .09
❑ 346 Bobby Ayala .15 .04
❑ 347 Mike Blowers .15 .04
❑ 348 Dave Fleming .15 .04
❑ 349 Edgar Martinez .50 .15
❑ 350 Andre Dawson .30 .09
❑ 351 Darrell Whitmore .15 .04
❑ 352 Chuck Carr .15 .04
❑ 353 John Burkett .15 .04
❑ 354 Chris Hammond .15 .04
❑ 355 Gary Sheffield .30 .09
❑ 356 Pat Rapp .15 .04
❑ 357 Greg Colbrunn .15 .04
❑ 358 David Segui .15 .04
❑ 359 Jeff Kent .30 .09
❑ 360 Bobby Bonilla .30 .09
❑ 361 Pete Harnisch .15 .04
❑ 362 Ryan Thompson .15 .04
❑ 363 Jose Vizcaino .15 .04
❑ 364 Brett Butler .30 .09
❑ 365 Cal Ripken Jr. 2.50 .75
❑ 366 Rafael Palmeiro .50 .15
❑ 367 Leo Gomez .15 .04
❑ 368 Andy Van Slyke .50 .15
❑ 369 Arthur Rhodes .15 .04
❑ 370 Ken Caminiti .30 .09
❑ 371 Steve Finley .30 .09
❑ 372 Melvin Nieves .15 .04
❑ 373 Andujar Cedeno .15 .04
❑ 374 Trevor Hoffman .30 .09
❑ 375 Fernando Valenzuela .30 .09
❑ 376 Ricky Bottalico .15 .04
❑ 377 Dave Hollins .15 .04
❑ 378 Charlie Hayes .15 .04
❑ 379 Tommy Greene .15 .04
❑ 380 Darren Daulton .30 .09
❑ 381 Curt Schilling .30 .09
❑ 382 Midre Cummings .15 .04
❑ 383 Al Martin .15 .04
❑ 384 Jeff King .15 .04
❑ 385 Orlando Merced .15 .04
❑ 386 Denny Neagle .30 .09
❑ 387 Don Slaught .15 .04
❑ 388 Dave Clark .15 .04
❑ 389 Kevin Gross .15 .04
❑ 390 Will Clark .50 .15
❑ 391 Ivan Rodriguez .50 .15
❑ 392 Benji Gil .15 .04
❑ 393 Jeff Frye .15 .04
❑ 394 Kenny Rogers .30 .09

❑ 395	Juan Gonzalez	.30	.09
❑ 396	Mike Macfarlane	.15	.04
❑ 397	Lee Tinsley	.15	.04
❑ 398	Tim Naehring	.15	.04
❑ 399	Tim Vanegmond	.15	.04
❑ 400	Mike Greenwell	.15	.04
❑ 401	Ken Ryan	.15	.04
❑ 402	John Smiley	.15	.04
❑ 403	Tim Pugh	.15	.04
❑ 404	Reggie Sanders	.30	.09
❑ 405	Barry Larkin	.50	.15
❑ 406	Hal Morris	.15	.04
❑ 407	Jose Rijo	.15	.04
❑ 408	Lance Painter	.15	.04
❑ 409	Joe Girardi	.15	.04
❑ 410	Andres Galarraga	.30	.09
❑ 411	Mike Kingery	.15	.04
❑ 412	Roberto Mejia	.15	.04
❑ 413	Walt Weiss	.15	.04
❑ 414	Bill Swift	.15	.04
❑ 415	Larry Walker	.30	.09
❑ 416	Billy Brewer	.15	.04
❑ 417	Pat Borders	.15	.04
❑ 418	Tom Gordon	.15	.04
❑ 419	Kevin Appier	.30	.09
❑ 420	Gary Gaetti	.30	.09
❑ 421	Greg Gohr	.15	.04
❑ 422	Felipe Lira	.15	.04
❑ 423	John Doherty	.15	.04
❑ 424	Chad Curtis	.15	.04
❑ 425	Cecil Fielder	.30	.09
❑ 426	Alan Trammell	.30	.09
❑ 427	David McCarty	.15	.04
❑ 428	Scott Erickson	.15	.04
❑ 429	Pat Mahomes	.15	.04
❑ 430	Kirby Puckett	.75	.23
❑ 431	Dave Stevens	.15	.04
❑ 432	Pedro Munoz	.15	.04
❑ 433	Chris Sabo	.15	.04
❑ 434	Alex Fernandez	.15	.04
❑ 435	Frank Thomas	.75	.23
❑ 436	Roberto Hernandez	.15	.04
❑ 437	Lance Johnson	.15	.04
❑ 438	Jim Abbott	.50	.15
❑ 439	John Wetteland	.30	.09
❑ 440	Melido Perez	.15	.04
❑ 441	Tony Fernandez	.15	.04
❑ 442	Pat Kelly	.15	.04
❑ 443	Mike Stanley	.15	.04
❑ 444	Danny Tartabull	.15	.04
❑ 445	Wade Boggs	.50	.15
❑ 446	Robin Yount	1.25	.35
❑ 447	Ryne Sandberg	1.25	.35
❑ 448	Nolan Ryan	3.00	.90
❑ 449	George Brett	2.00	.60
❑ 450	Mike Schmidt	1.25	.35
❑ 451	Jim Abbott TRADE	2.00	.60
❑ 452	D.Tartabull TRADE	1.00	.30
❑ 453	Ariel Prieto TRADE	1.00	.30
❑ 454	Scott Cooper TRADE	1.00	.30
❑ 455	Tom Henke TRADE	1.00	.30
❑ 456	Todd Zeile TRADE	1.00	.30
❑ 457	Brian McRae TRADE	1.00	.30
❑ 458	Luis Gonzalez TRADE	1.50	.45
❑ 459	Jaime Navarro TRADE	1.00	.30
❑ 460	Todd Worrell TRADE	1.00	.30
❑ 461	Roberto Kelly TRADE	1.00	.30
❑ 462	Chad Fonville TRADE	1.00	.30
❑ 463	S.Andrews TRADE	1.00	.30
❑ 464	David Segui TRADE	1.00	.30
❑ 465	Deion Sanders TRADE	2.00	.60
❑ 466	Orel Hershiser TRADE	1.50	.45
❑ 467	Ken Hill TRADE	1.00	.30
❑ 468	Andy Benes TRADE	1.00	.30
❑ 469	T.Pendleton TRADE	1.50	.45
❑ 470	Bobby Bonilla TRADE	1.50	.45
❑ 471	Scott Erickson TRADE	1.00	.30
❑ 472	Kevin Brown TRADE	1.50	.45
❑ 473	G.Dishman TRADE	1.00	.30
❑ 474	Phil Plantier TRADE	1.00	.30
❑ 475	G.Jefferies TRADE	1.00	.30
❑ 476	Tyler Green TRADE	1.00	.30
❑ 477	H. Slocumb TRADE	1.00	.30
❑ 478	Mark Whiten TRADE	1.00	.30
❑ 479	M.Tettleton TRADE	1.00	.30
❑ 480	Tim Wakefield TRADE	1.50	.45
❑ 481	V. Eshelman TRADE	1.00	.30
❑ 482	Rick Aguilera TRADE	1.00	.30
❑ 483	Erik Hanson TRADE	1.00	.30
❑ 484	Willie McGee TRADE	1.50	.45
❑ 485	Troy O'Leary TRADE	1.00	.30
❑ 486	B.Santiago TRADE	1.50	.45
❑ 487	Darren Lewis TRADE	1.00	.30
❑ 488	Dave Burba TRADE	1.00	.30
❑ 489	Ron Gant TRADE	1.50	.45
❑ 490	B.Saberhagen TRADE	1.50	.45
❑ 491	Vinny Castilla TRADE	1.50	.45
❑ 492	F.Rodriguez TRADE	1.00	.30
❑ 493	Andy Pettitte TRADE	2.00	.60
❑ 494	Ruben Sierra TRADE	1.00	.30
❑ 495	David Cone TRADE	1.50	.45
❑ J159	R. Clemens Jumbo AU	100.00	30.00
❑ J215	A. Rodriguez Jumbo AU	120.00	36.00
❑ P100	K.Griffey Jr. Promo	2.00	.60

1999 Upper Deck

	Nm-Mt	Ex-Mt
COMPLETE SET (525)	100.00	30.00
COMP. SERIES 1 (255)	60.00	18.00
COMP. SERIES 2 (270)	40.00	12.00
COMMON (19-255/293-535)	.30	.09
COMMON SER.1 SR (1-18)	.50	.15
COMMON (266-292)	.50	.15

❑ 1	Troy Glaus SR	1.00	.30
❑ 2	Adrian Beltre SR	.60	.18
❑ 3	Matt Anderson SR	.50	.15
❑ 4	Eric Chavez SR	.60	.18
❑ 5	Jin Ho Cho SR	.50	.15
❑ 6	Robert Smith SR	.50	.15
❑ 7	George Lombard SR	.50	.15
❑ 8	Mike Kinkade SR	.50	.15
❑ 9	Seth Greisinger SR	.50	.15
❑ 10	J.D. Drew SR	.60	.18
❑ 11	Aramis Ramirez SR	.60	.18
❑ 12	Carlos Guillen SR	.60	.18
❑ 13	Justin Baughman SR	.50	.15
❑ 14	Jim Parque SR	.50	.15
❑ 15	Ryan Jackson SR	.50	.15
❑ 16	Ramon E.Martinez SR RC	.50	.15
❑ 17	Orlando Hernandez SR	.60	.18
❑ 18	Jeremy Giambi SR	.50	.15
❑ 19	Gary DiSarcina	.30	.09
❑ 20	Darin Erstad	.30	.09
❑ 21	Troy Glaus	.50	.15
❑ 22	Chuck Finley	.30	.09
❑ 23	Dave Hollins	.30	.09
❑ 24	Troy Percival	.30	.09
❑ 25	Tim Salmon	.50	.15
❑ 26	Brian Anderson	.30	.09
❑ 27	Jay Bell	.30	.09
❑ 28	Andy Benes	.30	.09
❑ 29	Brent Brede	.30	.09
❑ 30	David Dellucci	.30	.09
❑ 31	Karim Garcia	.30	.09
❑ 32	Travis Lee	.30	.09
❑ 33	Andres Galarraga	.30	.09
❑ 34	Ryan Klesko	.30	.09
❑ 35	Keith Lockhart	.30	.09
❑ 36	Kevin Millwood	.30	.09
❑ 37	Denny Neagle	.30	.09
❑ 38	John Smoltz	.50	.15
❑ 39	Michael Tucker	.30	.09
❑ 40	Walt Weiss	.30	.09
❑ 41	Dennis Martinez	.30	.09
❑ 42	Javy Lopez	.30	.09
❑ 43	Brady Anderson	.30	.09
❑ 44	Harold Baines	.30	.09
❑ 45	Mike Bordick	.30	.09
❑ 46	Roberto Alomar	.50	.15
❑ 47	Scott Erickson	.30	.09
❑ 48	Mike Mussina	.50	.15
❑ 49	Cal Ripken	2.50	.75
❑ 50	Darren Bragg	.30	.09
❑ 51	Dennis Eckersley	.30	.09
❑ 52	Nomar Garciaparra	1.25	.35
❑ 53	Scott Hatteberg	.30	.09
❑ 54	Troy O'Leary	.30	.09
❑ 55	Bret Saberhagen	.30	.09
❑ 56	John Valentin	.30	.09
❑ 57	Rod Beck	.30	.09
❑ 58	Jeff Blauser	.30	.09
❑ 59	Brant Brown	.30	.09
❑ 60	Mark Clark	.30	.09
❑ 61	Mark Grace	.50	.15
❑ 62	Kevin Tapani	.30	.09
❑ 63	Henry Rodriguez	.30	.09
❑ 64	Mike Cameron	.30	.09
❑ 65	Mike Caruso	.30	.09
❑ 66	Ray Durham	.30	.09
❑ 67	Jaime Navarro	.30	.09
❑ 68	Magglio Ordonez	.30	.09
❑ 69	Mike Sirotka	.30	.09
❑ 70	Sean Casey	.50	.15
❑ 71	Barry Larkin	.50	.15
❑ 72	Jon Nunnally	.30	.09
❑ 73	Paul Konerko	.30	.09
❑ 74	Chris Stynes	.30	.09
❑ 75	Brett Tomko	.30	.09
❑ 76	Dmitri Young	.30	.09
❑ 77	Sandy Alomar Jr.	.30	.09
❑ 78	Bartolo Colon	.30	.09
❑ 79	Travis Fryman	.30	.09
❑ 80	Brian Giles	.30	.09
❑ 81	David Justice	.30	.09
❑ 82	Omar Vizquel	.50	.15
❑ 83	Jaret Wright	.30	.09
❑ 84	Jim Thome	.50	.15
❑ 85	Charles Nagy	.30	.09
❑ 86	Pedro Astacio	.30	.09
❑ 87	Todd Helton	.50	.15
❑ 88	Darryl Kile	.30	.09
❑ 89	Mike Lansing	.30	.09
❑ 90	Neifi Perez	.30	.09
❑ 91	John Thomson	.30	.09
❑ 92	Larry Walker	.30	.09
❑ 93	Tony Clark	.30	.09
❑ 94	Deivi Cruz	.30	.09
❑ 95	Damion Easley	.30	.09
❑ 96	Brian L.Hunter	.30	.09
❑ 97	Todd Jones	.30	.09
❑ 98	Brian Moehler	.30	.09
❑ 99	Gabe Alvarez	.30	.09
❑ 100	Craig Counsell	.30	.09
❑ 101	Cliff Floyd	.30	.09
❑ 102	Livan Hernandez	.30	.09
❑ 103	Andy Larkin	.30	.09
❑ 104	Derrek Lee	.50	.15
❑ 105	Brian Meadows	.30	.09
❑ 106	Moises Alou	.30	.09
❑ 107	Sean Berry	.30	.09
❑ 108	Craig Biggio	.50	.15
❑ 109	Ricky Gutierrez	.30	.09
❑ 110	Mike Hampton	.30	.09
❑ 111	Jose Lima	.30	.09
❑ 112	Billy Wagner	.30	.09
❑ 113	Hal Morris	.30	.09
❑ 114	Johnny Damon	.50	.15
❑ 115	Jeff King	.30	.09
❑ 116	Jeff Montgomery	.30	.09
❑ 117	Glendon Rusch	.30	.09
❑ 118	Larry Sutton	.30	.09
❑ 119	Bobby Bonilla	.30	.09
❑ 120	Jim Eisenreich	.30	.09
❑ 121	Eric Karros	.30	.09
❑ 122	Matt Luke	.30	.09
❑ 123	Ramon Martinez	.30	.09
❑ 124	Gary Sheffield	.30	.09
❑ 125	Eric Young	.30	.09
❑ 126	Charles Johnson	.30	.09

❑ 127 Jeff Cirillo .30 .09
❑ 128 Marquis Grissom .30 .09
❑ 129 Jeromy Burnitz .30 .09
❑ 130 Bob Wickman .30 .09
❑ 131 Scott Karl .30 .09
❑ 132 Mark Loretta .30 .09
❑ 133 Fernando Vina .30 .09
❑ 134 Matt Lawton .30 .09
❑ 135 Pat Meares .30 .09
❑ 136 Eric Milton .30 .09
❑ 137 Paul Molitor .50 .15
❑ 138 David Ortiz .50 .15
❑ 139 Todd Walker .30 .09
❑ 140 Shane Andrews .30 .09
❑ 141 Brad Fullmer .30 .09
❑ 142 Vladimir Guerrero .75 .23
❑ 143 Dustin Hermanson .30 .09
❑ 144 Ryan McGuire .30 .09
❑ 145 Ugueth Urbina .30 .09
❑ 146 John Franco .30 .09
❑ 147 Butch Huskey .30 .09
❑ 148 Bobby Jones .30 .09
❑ 149 John Olerud .30 .09
❑ 150 Rey Ordonez .30 .09
❑ 151 Mike Piazza 1.25 .35
❑ 152 Hideo Nomo .75 .23
❑ 153 Masato Yoshii .30 .09
❑ 154 Derek Jeter 2.00 .60
❑ 155 Chuck Knoblauch .30 .09
❑ 156 Paul O'Neill .50 .15
❑ 157 Andy Pettitte .50 .15
❑ 158 Mariano Rivera .50 .15
❑ 159 Darryl Strawberry .30 .09
❑ 160 David Wells .30 .09
❑ 161 Jorge Posada .50 .15
❑ 162 Ramiro Mendoza .30 .09
❑ 163 Miguel Tejada .30 .09
❑ 164 Ryan Christenson .30 .09
❑ 165 Rickey Henderson .75 .23
❑ 166 A.J. Hinch .30 .09
❑ 167 Ben Grieve .30 .09
❑ 168 Kenny Rogers .30 .09
❑ 169 Matt Stairs .30 .09
❑ 170 Bob Abreu .30 .09
❑ 171 Rico Brogna .30 .09
❑ 172 Doug Glanville .30 .09
❑ 173 Mike Grace .30 .09
❑ 174 Desi Relaford .30 .09
❑ 175 Scott Rolen .50 .15
❑ 176 Jose Guillen .30 .09
❑ 177 Francisco Cordova .30 .09
❑ 178 Al Martin .30 .09
❑ 179 Jason Schmidt .30 .09
❑ 180 Turner Ward .30 .09
❑ 181 Kevin Young .30 .09
❑ 182 Mark McGwire 2.00 .60
❑ 183 Delino DeShields .30 .09
❑ 184 Eli Marrero .30 .09
❑ 185 Tom Lampkin .30 .09
❑ 186 Ray Lankford .30 .09
❑ 187 Willie McGee .30 .09
❑ 188 Matt Morris UER .30 .09
Career strikeout totals are wrong
❑ 189 Andy Ashby .30 .09
❑ 190 Kevin Brown .50 .15
❑ 191 Ken Caminiti .30 .09
❑ 192 Trevor Hoffman .30 .09
❑ 193 Wally Joyner .30 .09
❑ 194 Greg Vaughn .30 .09
❑ 195 Danny Darwin .30 .09
❑ 196 Shawn Estes .30 .09
❑ 197 Orel Hershiser .30 .09
❑ 198 Jeff Kent .30 .09
❑ 199 Bill Mueller .30 .09
❑ 200 Robb Nen .30 .09
❑ 201 J.T. Snow .30 .09
❑ 202 Ken Cloude .30 .09
❑ 203 Russ Davis .30 .09
❑ 204 Jeff Fassero .30 .09
❑ 205 Ken Griffey Jr. 1.25 .35
❑ 206 Shane Monahan .30 .09
❑ 207 David Segui .30 .09
❑ 208 Dan Wilson .30 .09
❑ 209 Wilson Alvarez .30 .09
❑ 210 Wade Boggs .50 .15
❑ 211 Miguel Cairo .30 .09
❑ 212 Bubba Trammell .30 .09
❑ 213 Quinton McCracken .30 .09
❑ 214 Paul Sorrento .30 .09
❑ 215 Kevin Stocker .30 .09
❑ 216 Will Clark .50 .15
❑ 217 Rusty Greer .30 .09
❑ 218 Rick Helling .30 .09
❑ 219 Mark McLemore .30 .09
❑ 220 Ivan Rodriguez .50 .15
❑ 221 John Wetteland .30 .09
❑ 222 Jose Canseco .50 .15
❑ 223 Roger Clemens 1.50 .45
❑ 224 Carlos Delgado .30 .09
❑ 225 Darrin Fletcher .30 .09
❑ 226 Alex Gonzalez .30 .09
❑ 227 Jose Cruz Jr. .30 .09
❑ 228 Shannon Stewart .30 .09
❑ 229 Rolando Arrojo FF .30 .09
❑ 230 Livan Hernandez FF .30 .09
❑ 231 Orlando Hernandez FF .30 .09
❑ 232 Raul Mondesi FF .30 .09
❑ 233 Moises Alou FF .30 .09
❑ 234 Pedro Martinez FF .50 .15
❑ 235 Sammy Sosa FF .50 .15
❑ 236 Vladimir Guerrero FF .75 .23
❑ 237 Bartolo Colon FF .30 .09
❑ 238 Miguel Tejada FF .30 .09
❑ 239 Ismael Valdes FF .30 .09
❑ 240 Mariano Rivera FF .50 .15
❑ 241 Jose Cruz Jr. FF .30 .09
❑ 242 Juan Gonzalez FF .30 .09
❑ 243 Ivan Rodriguez FF .50 .15
❑ 244 Sandy Alomar Jr. FF .30 .09
❑ 245 Roberto Alomar FF .50 .15
❑ 246 Magglio Ordonez FF .30 .09
❑ 247 Kerry Wood SH CL .30 .09
❑ 248 Mark McGwire SH CL 2.00 .60
❑ 249 David Wells SH CL .30 .09
❑ 250 Rolando Arrojo SH CL .30 .09
❑ 251 Ken Griffey Jr. SH CL 1.25 .35
❑ 252 T.Hoffman SH CL .30 .09
❑ 253 Travis Lee SH CL .30 .09
❑ 254 R.Alomar SH CL .30 .09
❑ 255 Sammy Sosa SH CL .50 .15
❑ 266 Pat Burrell SR RC 3.00 .90
❑ 267 S.Hillenbrand SR RC 1.50 .45
❑ 268 Robert Fick SR .50 .15
❑ 269 Roy Halladay SR .60 .18
❑ 270 Ruben Mateo SR .50 .15
❑ 271 Bruce Chen SR .50 .15
❑ 272 Angel Pena SR .50 .15
❑ 273 Michael Barrett SR .50 .15
❑ 274 Kevin Witt SR .50 .15
❑ 275 Damon Minor SR .50 .15
❑ 276 Ryan Minor SR .50 .15
❑ 277 A.J. Pierzynski SR .60 .18
❑ 278 A.J. Burnett SR RC 2.00 .60
❑ 279 Dermal Brown SR .50 .15
❑ 280 Joe Lawrence SR .50 .15
❑ 281 Derrick Gibson SR .50 .15
❑ 282 Carlos Febles SR .50 .15
❑ 283 Chris Haas SR .50 .15
❑ 284 Cesar King SR .50 .15
❑ 285 Calvin Pickering SR .50 .15
❑ 286 Mitch Meluskey SR .50 .15
❑ 287 Carlos Beltran SR 1.00 .30
❑ 288 Ron Belliard SR .50 .15
❑ 289 Jerry Hairston Jr. SR .50 .15
❑ 290 F.Seguignol SR .50 .15
❑ 291 Kris Benson SR .50 .15
❑ 292 C.Hutchinson SR RC .60 .18
❑ 293 Jarrod Washburn .30 .09
❑ 294 Jason Dickson .30 .09
❑ 295 Mo Vaughn .30 .09
❑ 296 Garret Anderson .30 .09
❑ 297 Jim Edmonds .30 .09
❑ 298 Ken Hill .30 .09
❑ 299 Shigetoshi Hasegawa .30 .09
❑ 300 Todd Stottlemyre .30 .09
❑ 301 Randy Johnson .75 .23
❑ 302 Omar Daal .30 .09
❑ 303 Steve Finley .30 .09
❑ 304 Matt Williams .30 .09
❑ 305 Danny Klassen .30 .09
❑ 306 Tony Batista .30 .09
❑ 307 Brian Jordan .30 .09
❑ 308 Greg Maddux 1.25 .35
❑ 309 Chipper Jones .75 .23
❑ 310 Bret Boone .30 .09
❑ 311 Ozzie Guillen .30 .09
❑ 312 John Rocker .30 .09
❑ 313 Tom Glavine .50 .15
❑ 314 Andruw Jones .50 .15
❑ 315 Albert Belle .30 .09
❑ 316 Charles Johnson .30 .09
❑ 317 Will Clark .50 .15
❑ 318 B.J. Surhoff .30 .09
❑ 319 Delino DeShields .30 .09
❑ 320 Heathcliff Slocumb .30 .09
❑ 321 Sidney Ponson .30 .09
❑ 322 Juan Guzman .30 .09
❑ 323 Reggie Jefferson .30 .09
❑ 324 Mark Portugal .30 .09
❑ 325 Tim Wakefield .30 .09
❑ 326 Jason Varitek .75 .23
❑ 327 Jose Offerman .30 .09
❑ 328 Pedro Martinez .50 .15
❑ 329 Trot Nixon .30 .09
❑ 330 Kerry Wood .30 .09
❑ 331 Sammy Sosa .75 .23
❑ 332 Glenallen Hill .30 .09
❑ 333 Gary Gaetti .30 .09
❑ 334 Mickey Morandini .30 .09
❑ 335 Benito Santiago .30 .09
❑ 336 Jeff Blauser .30 .09
❑ 337 Frank Thomas .75 .23
❑ 338 Paul Konerko .30 .09
❑ 339 Jaime Navarro .30 .09
❑ 340 Carlos Lee .30 .09
❑ 341 Brian Simmons .30 .09
❑ 342 Mark Johnson .30 .09
❑ 343 Jeff Abbott .30 .09
❑ 344 Steve Avery .30 .09
❑ 345 Mike Cameron .30 .09
❑ 346 Michael Tucker .30 .09
❑ 347 Greg Vaughn .30 .09
❑ 348 Hal Morris .30 .09
❑ 349 Pete Harnisch .30 .09
❑ 350 Denny Neagle .30 .09
❑ 351 Manny Ramirez .50 .15
❑ 352 Roberto Alomar .50 .15
❑ 353 Dwight Gooden .30 .09
❑ 354 Kenny Lofton .30 .09
❑ 355 Mike Jackson .30 .09
❑ 356 Charles Nagy .30 .09
❑ 357 Enrique Wilson .30 .09
❑ 358 Russ Branyan .30 .09
❑ 359 Richie Sexson .30 .09
❑ 360 Vinny Castilla .30 .09
❑ 361 Dante Bichette .30 .09
❑ 362 Kirt Manwaring .30 .09
❑ 363 Darryl Hamilton .30 .09
❑ 364 Jamey Wright .30 .09
❑ 365 Curtis Leskanic .30 .09
❑ 366 Jeff Reed .30 .09
❑ 367 Bobby Higginson .30 .09
❑ 368 Justin Thompson .30 .09
❑ 369 Brad Ausmus .30 .09
❑ 370 Dean Palmer .30 .09
❑ 371 Gabe Kapler .30 .09
❑ 372 Juan Encarnacion .30 .09
❑ 373 Karim Garcia .30 .09
❑ 374 Alex Gonzalez .30 .09
❑ 375 Braden Looper .30 .09
❑ 376 Preston Wilson .30 .09
❑ 377 Todd Dunwoody .30 .09
❑ 378 Alex Fernandez .30 .09
❑ 379 Mark Kotsay .30 .09
❑ 380 Matt Mantei .30 .09
❑ 381 Ken Caminiti .30 .09
❑ 382 Scott Elarton .30 .09
❑ 383 Jeff Bagwell .50 .15
❑ 384 Derek Bell .30 .09
❑ 385 Ricky Gutierrez .30 .09
❑ 386 Richard Hidalgo .30 .09
❑ 387 Shane Reynolds .30 .09
❑ 388 Carl Everett .30 .09
❑ 389 Scott Service .30 .09
❑ 390 Jeff Suppan .30 .09
❑ 391 Joe Randa .30 .09
❑ 392 Kevin Appier .30 .09
❑ 393 Shane Halter .30 .09

- ❑ 394 Chad Kreuter .30 .09
- ❑ 395 Mike Sweeney .30 .09
- ❑ 396 Kevin Brown .50 .15
- ❑ 397 Devon White .30 .09
- ❑ 398 Todd Hollandsworth .30 .09
- ❑ 399 Todd Hundley .30 .09
- ❑ 400 Chan Ho Park .30 .09
- ❑ 401 Mark Grudzielanek .30 .09
- ❑ 402 Raul Mondesi .30 .09
- ❑ 403 Ismael Valdes .30 .09
- ❑ 404 Rafael Roque RC .30 .09
- ❑ 405 Sean Berry .30 .09
- ❑ 406 Kevin Barker .30 .09
- ❑ 407 Dave Nilsson .30 .09
- ❑ 408 Geoff Jenkins .30 .09
- ❑ 409 Jim Abbott .50 .15
- ❑ 410 Bobby Hughes .30 .09
- ❑ 411 Corey Koskie .30 .09
- ❑ 412 Rick Aguilera .30 .09
- ❑ 413 LaTroy Hawkins .30 .09
- ❑ 414 Ron Coomer .30 .09
- ❑ 415 Denny Hocking .30 .09
- ❑ 416 Marty Cordova .30 .09
- ❑ 417 Terry Steinbach .30 .09
- ❑ 418 Rondell White .30 .09
- ❑ 419 Wilton Guerrero .30 .09
- ❑ 420 Shane Andrews .30 .09
- ❑ 421 Orlando Cabrera .30 .09
- ❑ 422 Carl Pavano .30 .09
- ❑ 423 Javier Vazquez .30 .09
- ❑ 424 Chris Widger .30 .09
- ❑ 425 Robin Ventura .30 .09
- ❑ 426 Rickey Henderson .75 .23
- ❑ 427 Al Leiter .30 .09
- ❑ 428 Bobby Jones .30 .09
- ❑ 429 Brian McRae .30 .09
- ❑ 430 Roger Cedeno .30 .09
- ❑ 431 Bobby Bonilla .30 .09
- ❑ 432 Edgardo Alfonzo .30 .09
- ❑ 433 Bernie Williams .50 .15
- ❑ 434 Ricky Ledee .30 .09
- ❑ 435 Chili Davis .30 .09
- ❑ 436 Tino Martinez .50 .15
- ❑ 437 Scott Brosius .30 .09
- ❑ 438 David Cone .30 .09
- ❑ 439 Joe Girardi .30 .09
- ❑ 440 Roger Clemens 1.50 .45
- ❑ 441 Chad Curtis .30 .09
- ❑ 442 Hideki Irabu .30 .09
- ❑ 443 Jason Giambi .30 .09
- ❑ 444 Scott Spiezio .30 .09
- ❑ 445 Tony Phillips .30 .09
- ❑ 446 Ramon Hernandez .30 .09
- ❑ 447 Mike Macfarlane .30 .09
- ❑ 448 Tom Candiotti .30 .09
- ❑ 449 Billy Taylor .30 .09
- ❑ 450 Bobby Estalella .30 .09
- ❑ 451 Curt Schilling .30 .09
- ❑ 452 Carlton Loewer .30 .09
- ❑ 453 Marlon Anderson .30 .09
- ❑ 454 Kevin Jordan .30 .09
- ❑ 455 Ron Gant .30 .09
- ❑ 456 Chad Ogea .30 .09
- ❑ 457 Abraham Nunez .30 .09
- ❑ 458 Jason Kendall .30 .09
- ❑ 459 Pat Meares .30 .09
- ❑ 460 Brant Brown .30 .09
- ❑ 461 Brian Giles .30 .09
- ❑ 462 Chad Hermansen .30 .09
- ❑ 463 Freddy Adrian Garcia .30 .09
- ❑ 464 Edgar Renteria .30 .09
- ❑ 465 Fernando Tatis .30 .09
- ❑ 466 Eric Davis .30 .09
- ❑ 467 Darren Bragg .30 .09
- ❑ 468 Donovan Osborne .30 .09
- ❑ 469 Manny Aybar .30 .09
- ❑ 470 Jose Jimenez .30 .09
- ❑ 471 Kent Mercker .30 .09
- ❑ 472 Reggie Sanders .30 .09
- ❑ 473 Ruben Rivera .30 .09
- ❑ 474 Tony Gwynn 1.00 .30
- ❑ 475 Jim Leyritz .30 .09
- ❑ 476 Chris Gomez .30 .09
- ❑ 477 Matt Clement .30 .09
- ❑ 478 Carlos Hernandez .30 .09
- ❑ 479 Sterling Hitchcock .30 .09
- ❑ 480 Ellis Burks .30 .09
- ❑ 481 Barry Bonds 2.00 .60
- ❑ 482 Marvin Benard .30 .09
- ❑ 483 Kirk Rueter .30 .09
- ❑ 484 F.P. Santangelo .30 .09
- ❑ 485 Stan Javier .30 .09
- ❑ 486 Jeff Kent .30 .09
- ❑ 487 Alex Rodriguez 1.25 .35
- ❑ 488 Tom Lampkin .30 .09
- ❑ 489 Jose Mesa .30 .09
- ❑ 490 Jay Buhner .30 .09
- ❑ 491 Edgar Martinez .50 .15
- ❑ 492 Butch Huskey .30 .09
- ❑ 493 John Mabry .30 .09
- ❑ 494 Jamie Moyer .30 .09
- ❑ 495 Roberto Hernandez .30 .09
- ❑ 496 Tony Saunders .30 .09
- ❑ 497 Fred McGriff .50 .15
- ❑ 498 Dave Martinez .30 .09
- ❑ 499 Jose Canseco .50 .15
- ❑ 500 Rolando Arrojo .30 .09
- ❑ 501 Esteban Yan .30 .09
- ❑ 502 Juan Gonzalez .30 .09
- ❑ 503 Rafael Palmeiro .50 .15
- ❑ 504 Aaron Sele .30 .09
- ❑ 505 Royce Clayton .30 .09
- ❑ 506 Todd Zeile .30 .09
- ❑ 507 Tom Goodwin .30 .09
- ❑ 508 Lee Stevens .30 .09
- ❑ 509 Esteban Loaiza .30 .09
- ❑ 510 Joey Hamilton .30 .09
- ❑ 511 Homer Bush .30 .09
- ❑ 512 Willie Greene .30 .09
- ❑ 513 Shawn Green .30 .09
- ❑ 514 David Wells .30 .09
- ❑ 515 Kelvim Escobar .30 .09
- ❑ 516 Tony Fernandez .30 .09
- ❑ 517 Pat Hentgen .30 .09
- ❑ 518 Mark McGwire AR 1.00 .30
- ❑ 519 Ken Griffey Jr. AR .75 .23
- ❑ 520 Sammy Sosa AR .50 .15
- ❑ 521 Juan Gonzalez AR .30 .09
- ❑ 522 J.D. Drew AR .30 .09
- ❑ 523 Chipper Jones AR .50 .15
- ❑ 524 Alex Rodriguez AR .75 .23
- ❑ 525 Mike Piazza AR .75 .23
- ❑ 526 N.Garciaparra AR .75 .23
- ❑ 527 Mark McGwire SH CL 1.00 .30
- ❑ 528 Sammy Sosa SH CL .50 .15
- ❑ 529 Scott Brosius SH CL .30 .09
- ❑ 530 Cal Ripken SH CL 1.25 .35
- ❑ 531 Barry Bonds SH CL 1.00 .30
- ❑ 532 Roger Clemens SH CL .75 .23
- ❑ 533 Ken Griffey Jr. SH CL .75 .23
- ❑ 534 Alex Rodriguez SH CL .75 .23
- ❑ 535 Curt Schilling SH CL .30 .09
- ❑ NNO Ken Griffey Jr. 1989 AU/100 800.00 240.00

2001 Upper Deck

	Nm-Mt	Ex-Mt
COMPLETE SET (450)	100.00	30.00
COMP. SERIES 1 (270)	40.00	12.00
COMP. SERIES 2 (180)	60.00	18.00
COMMON (46-270/300-450)	.30	.09
COMMON SR (1-45)	.50	.15

- ❑ 1 Jeff DaVanon SR .50 .15
- ❑ 2 Aubrey Huff SR .50 .15
- ❑ 3 Pasqual Coco SR .50 .15
- ❑ 4 Barry Zito SR .60 .18
- ❑ 5 Augie Ojeda SR .50 .15
- ❑ 6 Chris Richard SR .50 .15
- ❑ 7 Josh Phelps SR .50 .15
- ❑ 8 Kevin Nicholson SR .50 .15
- ❑ 9 Juan Guzman SR .50 .15
- ❑ 10 Brandon Kolb SR .50 .15
- ❑ 11 Johan Santana SR 5.00 1.50
- ❑ 12 Josh Kalinowski SR .50 .15
- ❑ 13 Tike Redman SR .50 .15
- ❑ 14 Ivanon Coffie SR .50 .15
- ❑ 15 Chad Durbin SR .50 .15
- ❑ 16 Derrick Turnbow SR .60 .18
- ❑ 17 Scott Downs SR .50 .15
- ❑ 18 Jason Grilli SR .50 .15
- ❑ 19 Mark Buehrle SR .60 .18
- ❑ 20 Paxton Crawford SR .50 .15
- ❑ 21 Bronson Arroyo SR 1.00 .30
- ❑ 22 Tomas De la Rosa SR .50 .15
- ❑ 23 Paul Rigdon SR .50 .15
- ❑ 24 Rob Ramsay SR .50 .15
- ❑ 25 Damian Rolls SR .50 .15
- ❑ 26 Jason Conti SR .50 .15
- ❑ 27 John Parrish SR .50 .15
- ❑ 28 Geraldo Guzman SR .50 .15
- ❑ 29 Tony Mota SR .50 .15
- ❑ 30 Luis Rivas SR .50 .15
- ❑ 31 Brian Tollberg SR .50 .15
- ❑ 32 Adam Bernero SR .50 .15
- ❑ 33 Michael Cuddyer SR .50 .15
- ❑ 34 Josue Espada SR .50 .15
- ❑ 35 Joe Lawrence SR .50 .15
- ❑ 36 Chad Moeller SR .50 .15
- ❑ 37 Nick Bierbrodt SR .50 .15
- ❑ 38 DeWayne Wise SR .50 .15
- ❑ 39 Javier Cardona SR .50 .15
- ❑ 40 Hiram Bocachica SR .50 .15
- ❑ 41 G.Chiaramonte SR .50 .15
- ❑ 42 Alex Cabrera SR .50 .15
- ❑ 43 Jimmy Rollins SR .50 .15
- ❑ 44 Pat Flury SR RC .50 .15
- ❑ 45 Leo Estrella SR .50 .15
- ❑ 46 Darin Erstad .30 .09
- ❑ 47 Seth Etherton .30 .09
- ❑ 48 Troy Glaus .30 .09
- ❑ 49 Brian Cooper .30 .09
- ❑ 50 Tim Salmon .50 .15
- ❑ 51 Adam Kennedy .30 .09
- ❑ 52 Bengie Molina .30 .09
- ❑ 53 Jason Giambi .30 .09
- ❑ 54 Miguel Tejada .30 .09
- ❑ 55 Tim Hudson .30 .09
- ❑ 56 Eric Chavez .30 .09
- ❑ 57 Terrence Long .30 .09
- ❑ 58 Jason Isringhausen .30 .09
- ❑ 59 Ramon Hernandez .30 .09
- ❑ 60 Raul Mondesi .30 .09
- ❑ 61 David Wells .30 .09
- ❑ 62 Shannon Stewart .30 .09
- ❑ 63 Tony Batista .30 .09
- ❑ 64 Brad Fullmer .30 .09
- ❑ 65 Chris Carpenter .30 .09
- ❑ 66 Homer Bush .30 .09
- ❑ 67 Gerald Williams .30 .09
- ❑ 68 Miguel Cairo .30 .09
- ❑ 69 Ryan Rupe .30 .09
- ❑ 70 Greg Vaughn .30 .09
- ❑ 71 John Flaherty .30 .09
- ❑ 72 Dan Wheeler .30 .09
- ❑ 73 Fred McGriff .50 .15
- ❑ 74 Roberto Alomar .50 .15
- ❑ 75 Bartolo Colon .30 .09
- ❑ 76 Kenny Lofton .30 .09
- ❑ 77 David Segui .30 .09
- ❑ 78 Omar Vizquel .50 .15
- ❑ 79 Russ Branyan .30 .09
- ❑ 80 Chuck Finley .30 .09
- ❑ 81 Manny Ramirez UER .50 .15
  Back photo is of David Segui
- ❑ 82 Alex Rodriguez 1.25 .35
- ❑ 83 John Halama .30 .09
- ❑ 84 Mike Cameron .30 .09
- ❑ 85 David Bell .30 .09
- ❑ 86 Jay Buhner .30 .09

❑ 87 Aaron Sele .30 .09
❑ 88 Rickey Henderson .75 .23
❑ 89 Brook Fordyce .30 .09
❑ 90 Cal Ripken 2.50 .75
❑ 91 Mike Mussina .50 .15
❑ 92 Delino DeShields .30 .09
❑ 93 Melvin Mora .30 .09
❑ 94 Sidney Ponson .30 .09
❑ 95 Brady Anderson .30 .09
❑ 96 Ivan Rodriguez .50 .15
❑ 97 Ricky Ledee .30 .09
❑ 98 Rick Helling .30 .09
❑ 99 Ruben Mateo .30 .09
❑ 100 Luis Alicea .30 .09
❑ 101 John Wetteland .30 .09
❑ 102 Mike Lamb .30 .09
❑ 103 Carl Everett .30 .09
❑ 104 Troy O'Leary .30 .09
❑ 105 Wilton Veras .30 .09
❑ 106 Pedro Martinez .50 .15
❑ 107 Rolando Arrojo .30 .09
❑ 108 Scott Hatteberg .30 .09
❑ 109 Jason Varitek .75 .23
❑ 110 Jose Offerman .30 .09
❑ 111 Carlos Beltran .30 .09
❑ 112 Johnny Damon .50 .15
❑ 113 Mark Quinn .30 .09
❑ 114 Rey Sanchez .30 .09
❑ 115 Mac Suzuki .30 .09
❑ 116 Jermaine Dye .30 .09
❑ 117 Chris Fussell .30 .09
❑ 118 Jeff Weaver .30 .09
❑ 119 Dean Palmer .30 .09
❑ 120 Robert Fick .30 .09
❑ 121 Brian Moehler .30 .09
❑ 122 Damion Easley .30 .09
❑ 123 Juan Encarnacion .30 .09
❑ 124 Tony Clark .30 .09
❑ 125 Cristian Guzman .30 .09
❑ 126 Matt LeCroy .30 .09
❑ 127 Eric Milton .30 .09
❑ 128 Jay Canizaro .30 .09
❑ 129 David Ortiz .50 .15
❑ 130 Brad Radke .30 .09
❑ 131 Jacque Jones .30 .09
❑ 132 Magglio Ordonez .30 .09
❑ 133 Carlos Lee .30 .09
❑ 134 Mike Sirotka .30 .09
❑ 135 Ray Durham .30 .09
❑ 136 Paul Konerko .30 .09
❑ 137 Charles Johnson .30 .09
❑ 138 James Baldwin .30 .09
❑ 139 Jeff Abbott .30 .09
❑ 140 Roger Clemens 1.50 .45
❑ 141 Derek Jeter 2.00 .60
❑ 142 David Justice .30 .09
❑ 143 Ramiro Mendoza .30 .09
❑ 144 Chuck Knoblauch .30 .09
❑ 145 Orlando Hernandez .30 .09
❑ 146 Alfonso Soriano .50 .15
❑ 147 Jeff Bagwell .50 .15
❑ 148 Julio Lugo .30 .09
❑ 149 Mitch Meluskey .30 .09
❑ 150 Jose Lima .30 .09
❑ 151 Richard Hidalgo .30 .09
❑ 152 Moises Alou .30 .09
❑ 153 Scott Elarton .30 .09
❑ 154 Andruw Jones .50 .15
❑ 155 Quilvio Veras .30 .09
❑ 156 Greg Maddux 1.25 .35
❑ 157 Brian Jordan .30 .09
❑ 158 Andres Galarraga .30 .09
❑ 159 Kevin Millwood .30 .09
❑ 160 Rafael Furcal .30 .09
❑ 161 Jeromy Burnitz .30 .09
❑ 162 Jimmy Haynes .30 .09
❑ 163 Mark Loretta .30 .09
❑ 164 Ron Belliard .30 .09
❑ 165 Richie Sexson .30 .09
❑ 166 Kevin Barker .30 .09
❑ 167 Jeff D'Amico .30 .09
❑ 168 Rick Ankiel .30 .09
❑ 169 Mark McGwire 2.00 .60
❑ 170 J.D. Drew .30 .09
❑ 171 Eli Marrero .30 .09
❑ 172 Darryl Kile .30 .09
❑ 173 Edgar Renteria .30 .09
❑ 174 Will Clark .50 .15
❑ 175 Eric Young .30 .09
❑ 176 Mark Grace .50 .15
❑ 177 Jon Lieber .30 .09
❑ 178 Damon Buford .30 .09
❑ 179 Kerry Wood .30 .09
❑ 180 Rondell White .30 .09
❑ 181 Joe Girardi .30 .09
❑ 182 Curt Schilling .30 .09
❑ 183 Randy Johnson .75 .23
❑ 184 Steve Finley .30 .09
❑ 185 Kelly Stinnett .30 .09
❑ 186 Jay Bell .30 .09
❑ 187 Matt Mantei .30 .09
❑ 188 Luis Gonzalez .30 .09
❑ 189 Shawn Green .30 .09
❑ 190 Todd Hundley .30 .09
❑ 191 Chan Ho Park .30 .09
❑ 192 Adrian Beltre .30 .09
❑ 193 Mark Grudzielanek .30 .09
❑ 194 Gary Sheffield .30 .09
❑ 195 Tom Goodwin .30 .09
❑ 196 Lee Stevens .30 .09
❑ 197 Javier Vazquez .30 .09
❑ 198 Milton Bradley .30 .09
❑ 199 Vladimir Guerrero .75 .23
❑ 200 Carl Pavano .30 .09
❑ 201 Orlando Cabrera .30 .09
❑ 202 Tony Armas Jr. .30 .09
❑ 203 Jeff Kent .30 .09
❑ 204 Calvin Murray .30 .09
❑ 205 Ellis Burks .30 .09
❑ 206 Barry Bonds 2.00 .60
❑ 207 Russ Ortiz .30 .09
❑ 208 Marvin Benard .30 .09
❑ 209 Joe Nathan .30 .09
❑ 210 Preston Wilson .30 .09
❑ 211 Cliff Floyd .30 .09
❑ 212 Mike Lowell .30 .09
❑ 213 Ryan Dempster .30 .09
❑ 214 Brad Penny .30 .09
❑ 215 Mike Redmond .30 .09
❑ 216 Luis Castillo .30 .09
❑ 217 Derek Bell .30 .09
❑ 218 Mike Hampton .30 .09
❑ 219 Todd Zeile .30 .09
❑ 220 Robin Ventura .30 .09
❑ 221 Mike Piazza 1.25 .35
❑ 222 Al Leiter .30 .09
❑ 223 Edgardo Alfonzo .30 .09
❑ 224 Mike Bordick .30 .09
❑ 225 Phil Nevin .30 .09
❑ 226 Ryan Klesko .30 .09
❑ 227 Adam Eaton .30 .09
❑ 228 Eric Owens .30 .09
❑ 229 Tony Gwynn 1.00 .30
❑ 230 Matt Clement .30 .09
❑ 231 Wiki Gonzalez .30 .09
❑ 232 Robert Person .30 .09
❑ 233 Doug Glanville .30 .09
❑ 234 Scott Rolen .50 .15
❑ 235 Mike Lieberthal .30 .09
❑ 236 Randy Wolf .30 .09
❑ 237 Bob Abreu .30 .09
❑ 238 Pat Burrell .30 .09
❑ 239 Bruce Chen .30 .09
❑ 240 Kevin Young .30 .09
❑ 241 Todd Ritchie .30 .09
❑ 242 Adrian Brown .30 .09
❑ 243 Chad Hermansen .30 .09
❑ 244 Warren Morris .30 .09
❑ 245 Kris Benson .30 .09
❑ 246 Jason Kendall .30 .09
❑ 247 Pokey Reese .30 .09
❑ 248 Rob Bell .30 .09
❑ 249 Ken Griffey Jr. 1.25 .35
❑ 250 Sean Casey .50 .15
❑ 251 Aaron Boone .30 .09
❑ 252 Pete Harnisch .30 .09
❑ 253 Barry Larkin .50 .15
❑ 254 Dmitri Young .30 .09
❑ 255 Todd Hollandsworth .30 .09
❑ 256 Pedro Astacio .30 .09
❑ 257 Todd Helton .50 .15
❑ 258 Terry Shumpert .30 .09
❑ 259 Neifi Perez .30 .09
❑ 260 Jeffrey Hammonds .30 .09
❑ 261 Ben Petrick .30 .09
❑ 262 Mark McGwire SH 1.00 .30
❑ 263 Derek Jeter SH 1.00 .30
❑ 264 Sammy Sosa SH .50 .15
❑ 265 Cal Ripken SH 1.25 .35
❑ 266 Pedro Martinez SH .50 .15
❑ 267 Barry Bonds SH 1.00 .30
❑ 268 Fred McGriff SH .30 .09
❑ 269 Randy Johnson SH .50 .15
❑ 270 Darin Erstad SH .30 .09
❑ 271 Ichiro Suzuki SR RC 15.00 4.50
❑ 272 W. Betemit SR RC .60 .18
❑ 273 Corey Patterson SR .50 .15
❑ 274 Sean Douglass SR RC .50 .15
❑ 275 Mike Penney SR RC .50 .15
❑ 276 Nate Teut SR RC .50 .15
❑ 277 R. Rodriguez SR RC .50 .15
❑ 278 B. Duckworth SR RC .50 .15
❑ 279 Rafael Soriano SR RC .50 .15
❑ 280 Juan Diaz SR RC .50 .15
❑ 281 H. Ramirez SR RC .60 .18
❑ 282 T. Shinjo SR RC .60 .18
❑ 283 Keith Ginter SR .50 .15
❑ 284 Esix Snead SR RC .50 .15
❑ 285 Erick Almonte SR RC .50 .15
❑ 286 Travis Hafner SR RC 4.00 1.20
❑ 287 Jason Smith SR RC .50 .15
❑ 288 J. Melian SR RC .50 .15
❑ 289 Tyler Walker SR RC .50 .15
❑ 290 Jason Standridge SR .50 .15
❑ 291 Juan Uribe SR RC .60 .18
❑ 292 A. Hernandez SR RC .50 .15
❑ 293 J. Michaels SR RC .50 .15
❑ 294 Jason Hart SR .50 .15
❑ 295 Albert Pujols SR RC 50.00 15.00
❑ 296 M. Ensberg SR RC 3.00 .90
❑ 297 Brandon Inge SR .50 .15
❑ 298 Jesus Colome SR .50 .15
❑ 299 K. Kessel SR RC UER .50 .15
L Missing from MLB experience
❑ 300 Timo Perez SR .50 .15
❑ 301 Mo Vaughn .30 .09
❑ 302 Ismael Valdes .30 .09
❑ 303 Glenallen Hill .30 .09
❑ 304 Garret Anderson .30 .09
❑ 305 Johnny Damon .50 .15
❑ 306 Jose Ortiz .30 .09
❑ 307 Mark Mulder .30 .09
❑ 308 Adam Piatt .30 .09
❑ 309 Gil Heredia .30 .09
❑ 310 Mike Sirotka .30 .09
❑ 311 Carlos Delgado .30 .09
❑ 312 Alex Gonzalez .30 .09
❑ 313 Jose Cruz Jr. .30 .09
❑ 314 Darrin Fletcher .30 .09
❑ 315 Ben Grieve .30 .09
❑ 316 Vinny Castilla .30 .09
❑ 317 Wilson Alvarez .30 .09
❑ 318 Brent Abernathy .30 .09
❑ 319 Ellis Burks .30 .09
❑ 320 Jim Thome .50 .15
❑ 321 Juan Gonzalez .30 .09
❑ 322 Ed Taubensee .30 .09
❑ 323 Travis Fryman .30 .09
❑ 324 John Olerud .30 .09
❑ 325 Edgar Martinez .50 .15
❑ 326 Freddy Garcia .30 .09
❑ 327 Bret Boone .50 .15
❑ 328 Kazuhiro Sasaki .30 .09
❑ 329 Albert Belle .30 .09
❑ 330 Mike Bordick .30 .09
❑ 331 David Segui .30 .09
❑ 332 Pat Hentgen .30 .09
❑ 333 Alex Rodriguez 1.25 .35
❑ 334 Andres Galarraga .30 .09
❑ 335 Gabe Kapler .30 .09
❑ 336 Ken Caminiti .30 .09
❑ 337 Rafael Palmeiro .50 .15
❑ 338 Manny Ramirez Sox .50 .15
❑ 339 David Cone .30 .09
❑ 340 Nomar Garciaparra 1.25 .35
❑ 341 Trot Nixon .30 .09
❑ 342 Derek Lowe .30 .09
❑ 343 Roberto Hernandez .30 .09

❑ 344 Mike Sweeney .30 .09
❑ 345 Carlos Febles .30 .09
❑ 346 Jeff Suppan .30 .09
❑ 347 Roger Cedeno .30 .09
❑ 348 Bobby Higginson .30 .09
❑ 349 Deivi Cruz .30 .09
❑ 350 Mitch Meluskey .30 .09
❑ 351 Matt Lawton .30 .09
❑ 352 Mark Redman .30 .09
❑ 353 Jay Canizaro .30 .09
❑ 354 Corey Koskie .30 .09
❑ 355 Matt Kinney .30 .09
❑ 356 Frank Thomas .75 .23
❑ 357 Sandy Alomar Jr. .30 .09
❑ 358 David Wells .30 .09
❑ 359 Jim Parque .30 .09
❑ 360 Chris Singleton .30 .09
❑ 361 Tino Martinez .50 .15
❑ 362 Paul O'Neill .50 .15
❑ 363 Mike Mussina .50 .15
❑ 364 Bernie Williams .50 .15
❑ 365 Andy Pettite .50 .15
❑ 366 Mariano Rivera .50 .15
❑ 367 Brad Ausmus .30 .09
❑ 368 Craig Biggio .50 .15
❑ 369 Lance Berkman .30 .09
❑ 370 Shane Reynolds .30 .09
❑ 371 Chipper Jones .75 .23
❑ 372 Tom Glavine .50 .15
❑ 373 B.J. Surhoff .30 .09
❑ 374 John Smoltz .50 .15
❑ 375 Rico Brogna .30 .09
❑ 376 Geoff Jenkins .30 .09
❑ 377 Jose Hernandez .30 .09
❑ 378 Tyler Houston .30 .09
❑ 379 Henry Blanco .30 .09
❑ 380 Jeffrey Hammonds .30 .09
❑ 381 Jim Edmonds .50 .15
❑ 382 Fernando Vina .30 .09
❑ 383 Andy Benes .30 .09
❑ 384 Ray Lankford .30 .09
❑ 385 Dustin Hermanson .30 .09
❑ 386 Todd Hundley .30 .09
❑ 387 Sammy Sosa .75 .23
❑ 388 Tom Gordon .30 .09
❑ 389 Bill Mueller .30 .09
❑ 390 Ron Coomer .30 .09
❑ 391 Matt Stairs .30 .09
❑ 392 Mark Grace .50 .15
❑ 393 Matt Williams .30 .09
❑ 394 Todd Stottlemyre .30 .09
❑ 395 Tony Womack .30 .09
❑ 396 Erubiel Durazo .30 .09
❑ 397 Reggie Sanders .30 .09
❑ 398 Andy Ashby .30 .09
❑ 399 Eric Karros .30 .09
❑ 400 Kevin Brown .30 .09
❑ 401 Darren Dreifort .30 .09
❑ 402 Fernando Tatis .30 .09
❑ 403 Jose Vidro .30 .09
❑ 404 Peter Bergeron .30 .09
❑ 405 Geoff Blum .30 .09
❑ 406 J.T. Snow .30 .09
❑ 407 Livan Hernandez .30 .09
❑ 408 Robb Nen .30 .09
❑ 409 Bobby Estalella .30 .09
❑ 410 Rich Aurilia .30 .09
❑ 411 Eric Davis .30 .09
❑ 412 Charles Johnson .30 .09
❑ 413 Alex Gonzalez .30 .09
❑ 414 A.J. Burnett .30 .09
❑ 415 Antonio Alfonseca .30 .09
❑ 416 Derrek Lee .50 .15
❑ 417 Jay Payton .30 .09
❑ 418 Kevin Appier .30 .09
❑ 419 Steve Trachsel .30 .09
❑ 420 Rey Ordonez .30 .09
❑ 421 Darryl Hamilton .30 .09
❑ 422 Ben Davis .30 .09
❑ 423 Damian Jackson .30 .09
❑ 424 Mark Kotsay .30 .09
❑ 425 Trevor Hoffman .30 .09
❑ 426 Travis Lee .30 .09
❑ 427 Omar Daal .30 .09
❑ 428 Paul Byrd .30 .09
❑ 429 Reggie Taylor .30 .09
❑ 430 Brian Giles .30 .09
❑ 431 Derek Bell .30 .09
❑ 432 Francisco Cordova .30 .09
❑ 433 Pat Meares .30 .09
❑ 434 Scott Williamson .30 .09
❑ 435 Jason LaRue .30 .09
❑ 436 Michael Tucker .30 .09
❑ 437 Wilton Guerrero .30 .09
❑ 438 Mike Hampton .30 .09
❑ 439 Ron Gant .30 .09
❑ 440 Jeff Cirillo .30 .09
❑ 441 Denny Neagle .30 .09
❑ 442 Larry Walker .30 .09
❑ 443 Juan Pierre .30 .09
❑ 444 Todd Walker .30 .09
❑ 445 Jason Giambi SH CL .30 .09
❑ 446 Jeff Kent SH CL .30 .09
❑ 447 Mariano Rivera SH CL .30 .09
❑ 448 Edgar Martinez SH CL .30 .09
❑ 449 Troy Glaus SH CL .30 .09
❑ 450 Alex Rodriguez SH CL .75 .23

2002 Upper Deck

	Nm-Mt	Ex-Mt
COMPLETE SET (745)	160.00	47.50
COMPLETE SERIES 1 (500)	110.00	33.00
COMPLETE SERIES 2 (245)	50.00	15.00
COMMON (51-500/546-745)	.30	.09
COMMON SR (1-50/501-545)	1.00	.30

❑ 1 Mark Prior SR 3.00 .90
❑ 2 Mark Teixeira SR 5.00 1.50
❑ 3 Brian Roberts SR 2.00 .60
❑ 4 Jason Romano SR 1.00 .30
❑ 5 Dennis Stark SR 1.00 .30
❑ 6 Oscar Salazar SR 1.00 .30
❑ 7 John Patterson SR 1.00 .30
❑ 8 Shane Loux SR 1.00 .30
❑ 9 Marcus Giles SR 1.00 .30
❑ 10 Juan Cruz SR 1.00 .30
❑ 11 Jorge Julio SR 1.00 .30
❑ 12 Adam Dunn SR 1.00 .30
❑ 13 Delvin James SR 1.00 .30
❑ 14 Jeremy Affeldt SR 1.00 .30
❑ 15 Tim Raines Jr. SR 1.00 .30
❑ 16 Luke Hudson SR 1.00 .30
❑ 17 Todd Sears SR 1.00 .30
❑ 18 George Perez SR 1.00 .30
❑ 19 Wilmy Caceres SR 1.00 .30
❑ 20 Abraham Nunez SR 1.00 .30
❑ 21 Mike Amrhein SR RC 1.00 .30
❑ 22 Carlos Hernandez SR 1.00 .30
❑ 23 Scott Hodges SR 1.00 .30
❑ 24 Brandon Knight SR 1.00 .30
❑ 25 Geoff Goetz SR 1.00 .30
❑ 26 Carlos Garcia SR 1.00 .30
❑ 27 Luis Pineda SR 1.00 .30
❑ 28 Chris Gissell SR 1.00 .30
❑ 29 Jae Weong Seo SR 1.00 .30
❑ 30 Paul Phillips SR 1.00 .30
❑ 31 Cory Aldridge SR 1.00 .30
❑ 32 Aaron Cook SR RC 1.00 .30
❑ 33 Rendy Espina SR RC 1.00 .30
❑ 34 Jason Phillips SR 1.00 .30
❑ 35 Carlos Silva SR 1.00 .30
❑ 36 Ryan Mills SR 1.00 .30
❑ 37 Pedro Santana SR 1.00 .30
❑ 38 John Grabow SR 1.00 .30
❑ 39 Cody Ransom SR 1.00 .30
❑ 40 Orlando Woodards SR 1.00 .30
❑ 41 Bud Smith SR 1.00 .30
❑ 42 Junior Guerrero SR 1.00 .30
❑ 43 David Brous SR 1.00 .30
❑ 44 Steve Green SR 1.00 .30
❑ 45 Brian Rogers SR 1.00 .30
❑ 46 Juan Figueroa SR RC 1.00 .30
❑ 47 Nick Punto SR 1.00 .30
❑ 48 Junior Herndon SR 1.00 .30
❑ 49 Justin Kaye SR 1.00 .30
❑ 50 Jason Karnuth SR 1.00 .30
❑ 51 Troy Glaus .30 .09
❑ 52 Bengie Molina .30 .09
❑ 53 Ramon Ortiz .30 .09
❑ 54 Adam Kennedy .30 .09
❑ 55 Jarrod Washburn .30 .09
❑ 56 Troy Percival .30 .09
❑ 57 David Eckstein .30 .09
❑ 58 Ben Weber .30 .09
❑ 59 Larry Barnes .30 .09
❑ 60 Ismael Valdes .30 .09
❑ 61 Benji Gil .30 .09
❑ 62 Scott Schoeneweis .30 .09
❑ 63 Pat Rapp .30 .09
❑ 64 Jason Giambi .30 .09
❑ 65 Mark Mulder .30 .09
❑ 66 Ron Gant .30 .09
❑ 67 Johnny Damon .50 .15
❑ 68 Adam Piatt .30 .09
❑ 69 Jermaine Dye .30 .09
❑ 70 Jason Hart .30 .09
❑ 71 Eric Chavez .30 .09
❑ 72 Jim Mecir .30 .09
❑ 73 Barry Zito .30 .09
❑ 74 Jason Isringhausen .30 .09
❑ 75 Jeremy Giambi .30 .09
❑ 76 Olmedo Saenz .30 .09
❑ 77 Terrence Long .30 .09
❑ 78 Ramon Hernandez .30 .09
❑ 79 Chris Carpenter .30 .09
❑ 80 Raul Mondesi .30 .09
❑ 81 Carlos Delgado .30 .09
❑ 82 Billy Koch .30 .09
❑ 83 Vernon Wells .30 .09
❑ 84 Darrin Fletcher .30 .09
❑ 85 Homer Bush .30 .09
❑ 86 Pasqual Coco .30 .09
❑ 87 Shannon Stewart .30 .09
❑ 88 Chris Woodward .30 .09
❑ 89 Joe Lawrence .30 .09
❑ 90 Esteban Loaiza .30 .09
❑ 91 Cesar Izturis .30 .09
❑ 92 Kelvim Escobar .30 .09
❑ 93 Greg Vaughn .30 .09
❑ 94 Brent Abernathy .30 .09
❑ 95 Tanyon Sturtze .30 .09
❑ 96 Steve Cox .30 .09
❑ 97 Aubrey Huff .30 .09
❑ 98 Jesus Colome .30 .09
❑ 99 Ben Grieve .30 .09
❑ 100 Esteban Yan .30 .09
❑ 101 Joe Kennedy .30 .09
❑ 102 Felix Martinez .30 .09
❑ 103 Nick Bierbrodt .30 .09
❑ 104 Damian Rolls .30 .09
❑ 105 Russ Johnson .30 .09
❑ 106 Toby Hall .30 .09
❑ 107 Roberto Alomar .50 .15
❑ 108 Bartolo Colon .30 .09
❑ 109 John Rocker .30 .09
❑ 110 Juan Gonzalez .30 .09
❑ 111 Einar Diaz .30 .09
❑ 112 Chuck Finley .30 .09
❑ 113 Kenny Lofton .30 .09
❑ 114 Danys Baez .30 .09
❑ 115 Travis Fryman .30 .09
❑ 116 C.C. Sabathia .30 .09
❑ 117 Paul Shuey .30 .09
❑ 118 Marty Cordova .30 .09
❑ 119 Ellis Burks .30 .09
❑ 120 Bob Wickman .30 .09
❑ 121 Edgar Martinez .50 .15
❑ 122 Freddy Garcia .30 .09
❑ 123 Ichiro Suzuki 1.50 .45
❑ 124 John Olerud .30 .09

❑ 125	Gil Meche	.30	.09
❑ 126	Dan Wilson	.30	.09
❑ 127	Aaron Sele	.30	.09
❑ 128	Kazuhiro Sasaki	.30	.09
❑ 129	Mark McLemore	.30	.09
❑ 130	Carlos Guillen	.30	.09
❑ 131	Al Martin	.30	.09
❑ 132	David Bell	.30	.09
❑ 133	Jay Buhner	.30	.09
❑ 134	Stan Javier	.30	.09
❑ 135	Tony Batista	.30	.09
❑ 136	Jason Johnson	.30	.09
❑ 137	Brook Fordyce	.30	.09
❑ 138	Mike Kinkade	.30	.09
❑ 139	Willis Roberts	.30	.09
❑ 140	David Segui	.30	.09
❑ 141	Josh Towers	.30	.09
❑ 142	Jeff Conine	.30	.09
❑ 143	Chris Richard	.30	.09
❑ 144	Pat Hentgen	.30	.09
❑ 145	Melvin Mora	.30	.09
❑ 146	Jerry Hairston Jr.	.30	.09
❑ 147	Calvin Maduro	.30	.09
❑ 148	Brady Anderson	.30	.09
❑ 149	Alex Rodriguez	1.25	.35
❑ 150	Kenny Rogers	.30	.09
❑ 151	Chad Curtis	.30	.09
❑ 152	Ricky Ledee	.30	.09
❑ 153	Rafael Palmeiro	.50	.15
❑ 154	Rob Bell	.30	.09
❑ 155	Rick Helling	.30	.09
❑ 156	Doug Davis	.30	.09
❑ 157	Mike Lamb	.30	.09
❑ 158	Gabe Kapler	.30	.09
❑ 159	Jeff Zimmerman	.30	.09
❑ 160	Bill Haselman	.30	.09
❑ 161	Tim Crabtree	.30	.09
❑ 162	Carlos Pena	.30	.09
❑ 163	Nomar Garciaparra	1.25	.35
❑ 164	Shea Hillenbrand	.30	.09
❑ 165	Hideo Nomo	.75	.23
❑ 166	Manny Ramirez	.50	.15
❑ 167	Jose Offerman	.30	.09
❑ 168	Scott Hatteberg	.30	.09
❑ 169	Trot Nixon	.30	.09
❑ 170	Darren Lewis	.30	.09
❑ 171	Derek Lowe	.30	.09
❑ 172	Troy O'Leary	.30	.09
❑ 173	Tim Wakefield	.30	.09
❑ 174	Chris Stynes	.30	.09
❑ 175	John Valentin	.30	.09
❑ 176	David Cone	.30	.09
❑ 177	Neifi Perez	.30	.09
❑ 178	Brent Mayne	.30	.09
❑ 179	Dan Reichert	.30	.09
❑ 180	A.J. Hinch	.30	.09
❑ 181	Chris George	.30	.09
❑ 182	Mike Sweeney	.30	.09
❑ 183	Jeff Suppan	.30	.09
❑ 184	Roberto Hernandez	.30	.09
❑ 185	Joe Randa	.30	.09
❑ 186	Paul Byrd	.30	.09
❑ 187	Luis Ordaz	.30	.09
❑ 188	Kris Wilson	.30	.09
❑ 189	Dee Brown	.30	.09
❑ 190	Tony Clark	.30	.09
❑ 191	Matt Anderson	.30	.09
❑ 192	Robert Fick	.30	.09
❑ 193	Juan Encarnacion	.30	.09
❑ 194	Dean Palmer	.30	.09
❑ 195	Victor Santos	.30	.09
❑ 196	Damion Easley	.30	.09
❑ 197	Jose Lima	.30	.09
❑ 198	Deivi Cruz	.30	.09
❑ 199	Roger Cedeno	.30	.09
❑ 200	Jose Macias	.30	.09
❑ 201	Jeff Weaver	.30	.09
❑ 202	Brandon Inge	.30	.09
❑ 203	Brian Moehler	.30	.09
❑ 204	Brad Radke	.30	.09
❑ 205	Doug Mientkiewicz	.30	.09
❑ 206	Cristian Guzman	.30	.09
❑ 207	Corey Koskie	.30	.09
❑ 208	LaTroy Hawkins	.30	.09
❑ 209	J.C. Romero	.30	.09
❑ 210	Chad Allen	.30	.09
❑ 211	Torii Hunter	.30	.09
❑ 212	Travis Miller	.30	.09
❑ 213	Joe Mays	.30	.09
❑ 214	Todd Jones	.30	.09
❑ 215	David Ortiz	.50	.15
❑ 216	Brian Buchanan	.30	.09
❑ 217	A.J. Pierzynski	.30	.09
❑ 218	Carlos Lee	.30	.09
❑ 219	Gary Glover	.30	.09
❑ 220	Jose Valentin	.30	.09
❑ 221	Aaron Rowand	.30	.09
❑ 222	Sandy Alomar Jr.	.30	.09
❑ 223	Herbert Perry	.30	.09
❑ 224	Jon Garland	.30	.09
❑ 225	Mark Buehrle	.30	.09
❑ 226	Chris Singleton	.30	.09
❑ 227	Kip Wells	.30	.09
❑ 228	Ray Durham	.30	.09
❑ 229	Joe Crede	.30	.09
❑ 230	Keith Foulke	.30	.09
❑ 231	Royce Clayton	.30	.09
❑ 232	Andy Pettitte	.50	.15
❑ 233	Derek Jeter	2.00	.60
❑ 234	Jorge Posada	.50	.15
❑ 235	Roger Clemens	1.50	.45
❑ 236	Paul O'Neill	.50	.15
❑ 237	Nick Johnson	.30	.09
❑ 238	Gerald Williams	.30	.09
❑ 239	Mariano Rivera	.50	.15
❑ 240	Alfonso Soriano	.30	.09
❑ 241	Ramiro Mendoza	.30	.09
❑ 242	Mike Mussina	.50	.15
❑ 243	Luis Sojo	.30	.09
❑ 244	Scott Brosius	.30	.09
❑ 245	David Justice	.30	.09
❑ 246	Wade Miller	.30	.09
❑ 247	Brad Ausmus	.30	.09
❑ 248	Jeff Bagwell	.50	.15
❑ 249	Daryle Ward	.30	.09
❑ 250	Shane Reynolds	.30	.09
❑ 251	Chris Truby	.30	.09
❑ 252	Billy Wagner	.30	.09
❑ 253	Craig Biggio	.50	.15
❑ 254	Moises Alou	.30	.09
❑ 255	Vinny Castilla	.30	.09
❑ 256	Tim Redding	.30	.09
❑ 257	Roy Oswalt	.30	.09
❑ 258	Julio Lugo	.30	.09
❑ 259	Chipper Jones	.75	.23
❑ 260	Greg Maddux	1.25	.35
❑ 261	Ken Caminiti	.30	.09
❑ 262	Kevin Millwood	.30	.09
❑ 263	Keith Lockhart	.30	.09
❑ 264	Rey Sanchez	.30	.09
❑ 265	Jason Marquis	.30	.09
❑ 266	Brian Jordan	.30	.09
❑ 267	Steve Karsay	.30	.09
❑ 268	Wes Helms	.30	.09
❑ 269	B.J. Surhoff	.30	.09
❑ 270	Wilson Betemit	.30	.09
❑ 271	John Smoltz	.50	.15
❑ 272	Rafael Furcal	.30	.09
❑ 273	Jeromy Burnitz	.30	.09
❑ 274	Jimmy Haynes	.30	.09
❑ 275	Mark Loretta	.30	.09
❑ 276	Jose Hernandez	.30	.09
❑ 277	Paul Rigdon	.30	.09
❑ 278	Alex Sanchez	.30	.09
❑ 279	Chad Fox	.30	.09
❑ 280	Devon White	.30	.09
❑ 281	Tyler Houston	.30	.09
❑ 282	Ronnie Belliard	.30	.09
❑ 283	Luis Lopez	.30	.09
❑ 284	Ben Sheets	.30	.09
❑ 285	Curtis Leskanic	.30	.09
❑ 286	Henry Blanco	.30	.09
❑ 287	Mark McGwire	2.00	.60
❑ 288	Edgar Renteria	.30	.09
❑ 289	Matt Morris	.30	.09
❑ 290	Gene Stechschulte	.30	.09
❑ 291	Dustin Hermanson	.30	.09
❑ 292	Eli Marrero	.30	.09
❑ 293	Albert Pujols	1.50	.45
❑ 294	Luis Saturria	.30	.09
❑ 295	Bobby Bonilla	.30	.09
❑ 296	Garrett Stephenson	.30	.09
❑ 297	Jim Edmonds	.50	.15
❑ 298	Rick Ankiel	.30	.09
❑ 299	Placido Polanco	.30	.09
❑ 300	Dave Veres	.30	.09
❑ 301	Sammy Sosa	.75	.23
❑ 302	Eric Young	.30	.09
❑ 303	Kerry Wood	.30	.09
❑ 304	Jon Lieber	.30	.09
❑ 305	Joe Girardi	.30	.09
❑ 306	Fred McGriff	.50	.15
❑ 307	Jeff Fassero	.30	.09
❑ 308	Julio Zuleta	.30	.09
❑ 309	Kevin Tapani	.30	.09
❑ 310	Rondell White	.30	.09
❑ 311	Julian Tavarez	.30	.09
❑ 312	Tom Gordon	.30	.09
❑ 313	Corey Patterson	.30	.09
❑ 314	Bill Mueller	.30	.09
❑ 315	Randy Johnson	.75	.23
❑ 316	Chad Moeller	.30	.09
❑ 317	Tony Womack	.30	.09
❑ 318	Erubiel Durazo	.30	.09
❑ 319	Luis Gonzalez	.30	.09
❑ 320	Brian Anderson	.30	.09
❑ 321	Reggie Sanders	.30	.09
❑ 322	Greg Colbrunn	.30	.09
❑ 323	Robert Ellis	.30	.09
❑ 324	Jack Cust	.30	.09
❑ 325	Bret Prinz	.30	.09
❑ 326	Steve Finley	.30	.09
❑ 327	Byung-Hyun Kim	.30	.09
❑ 328	Albie Lopez	.30	.09
❑ 329	Gary Sheffield	.30	.09
❑ 330	Mark Grudzielanek	.30	.09
❑ 331	Paul LoDuca	.30	.09
❑ 332	Tom Goodwin	.30	.09
❑ 333	Andy Ashby	.30	.09
❑ 334	Hiram Bocachica	.30	.09
❑ 335	Dave Hansen	.30	.09
❑ 336	Kevin Brown	.30	.09
❑ 337	Marquis Grissom	.30	.09
❑ 338	Terry Adams	.30	.09
❑ 339	Chan Ho Park	.30	.09
❑ 340	Adrian Beltre	.30	.09
❑ 341	Luke Prokopec	.30	.09
❑ 342	Jeff Shaw	.30	.09
❑ 343	Vladimir Guerrero	.75	.23
❑ 344	Orlando Cabrera	.30	.09
❑ 345	Tony Armas Jr.	.30	.09
❑ 346	Michael Barrett	.30	.09
❑ 347	Geoff Blum	.30	.09
❑ 348	Ryan Minor	.30	.09
❑ 349	Peter Bergeron	.30	.09
❑ 350	Graeme Lloyd	.30	.09
❑ 351	Jose Vidro	.30	.09
❑ 352	Javier Vazquez	.30	.09
❑ 353	Matt Blank	.30	.09
❑ 354	Masato Yoshii	.30	.09
❑ 355	Carl Pavano	.30	.09
❑ 356	Barry Bonds	2.00	.60
❑ 357	Shawon Dunston	.30	.09
❑ 358	Livan Hernandez	.30	.09
❑ 359	Felix Rodriguez	.30	.09
❑ 360	Pedro Feliz	.30	.09
❑ 361	Calvin Murray	.30	.09
❑ 362	Robb Nen	.30	.09
❑ 363	Marvin Benard	.30	.09
❑ 364	Russ Ortiz	.30	.09
❑ 365	Jason Schmidt	.30	.09
❑ 366	Rich Aurilia	.30	.09
❑ 367	John Vander Wal	.30	.09
❑ 368	Benito Santiago	.30	.09
❑ 369	Ryan Dempster	.30	.09
❑ 370	Charles Johnson	.30	.09
❑ 371	Alex Gonzalez	.30	.09
❑ 372	Luis Castillo	.30	.09
❑ 373	Mike Lowell	.30	.09
❑ 374	Antonio Alfonseca	.30	.09
❑ 375	A.J. Burnett	.30	.09
❑ 376	Brad Penny	.30	.09
❑ 377	Jason Grilli	.30	.09
❑ 378	Derrek Lee	.50	.15
❑ 379	Matt Clement	.30	.09
❑ 380	Eric Owens	.30	.09
❑ 381	Vladimir Nunez	.30	.09
❑ 382	Cliff Floyd	.30	.09

❑	383	Mike Piazza	1.25	.35
❑	384	Lenny Harris	.30	.09
❑	385	Glendon Rusch	.30	.09
❑	386	Todd Zeile	.30	.09
❑	387	Al Leiter	.30	.09
❑	388	Armando Benitez	.30	.09
❑	389	Alex Escobar	.30	.09
❑	390	Kevin Appier	.30	.09
❑	391	Matt Lawton	.30	.09
❑	392	Bruce Chen	.30	.09
❑	393	John Franco	.30	.09
❑	394	Tsuyoshi Shinjo	.30	.09
❑	395	Rey Ordonez	.30	.09
❑	396	Joe McEwing	.30	.09
❑	397	Ryan Klesko	.30	.09
❑	398	Brian Lawrence	.30	.09
❑	399	Kevin Walker	.30	.09
❑	400	Phil Nevin	.30	.09
❑	401	Bubba Trammell	.30	.09
❑	402	Wiki Gonzalez	.30	.09
❑	403	D'Angelo Jimenez	.30	.09
❑	404	Rickey Henderson	.75	.23
❑	405	Mike Darr	.30	.09
❑	406	Trevor Hoffman	.30	.09
❑	407	Damian Jackson	.30	.09
❑	408	Santiago Perez	.30	.09
❑	409	Cesar Crespo	.30	.09
❑	410	Robert Person	.30	.09
❑	411	Travis Lee	.30	.09
❑	412	Scott Rolen	.50	.15
❑	413	Turk Wendell	.30	.09
❑	414	Randy Wolf	.30	.09
❑	415	Kevin Jordan	.30	.09
❑	416	Jose Mesa	.30	.09
❑	417	Mike Lieberthal	.30	.09
❑	418	Bobby Abreu	.30	.09
❑	419	Tomas Perez	.30	.09
❑	420	Doug Glanville	.30	.09
❑	421	Reggie Taylor	.30	.09
❑	422	Jimmy Rollins	.30	.09
❑	423	Brian Giles	.30	.09
❑	424	Rob Mackowiak	.30	.09
❑	425	Bronson Arroyo	.30	.09
❑	426	Kevin Young	.30	.09
❑	427	Jack Wilson	.30	.09
❑	428	Adrian Brown	.30	.09
❑	429	Chad Hermansen	.30	.09
❑	430	Jimmy Anderson	.30	.09
❑	431	Aramis Ramirez	.30	.09
❑	432	Todd Ritchie	.30	.09
❑	433	Pat Meares	.30	.09
❑	434	Warren Morris	.30	.09
❑	435	Derek Bell	.30	.09
❑	436	Ken Griffey Jr.	1.25	.35
❑	437	Elmer Dessens	.30	.09
❑	438	Ruben Rivera	.30	.09
❑	439	Jason LaRue	.30	.09
❑	440	Sean Casey	.50	.15
❑	441	Pete Harnisch	.30	.09
❑	442	Danny Graves	.30	.09
❑	443	Aaron Boone	.30	.09
❑	444	Dmitri Young	.30	.09
❑	445	Brandon Larson	.30	.09
❑	446	Pokey Reese	.30	.09
❑	447	Todd Walker	.30	.09
❑	448	Juan Castro	.30	.09
❑	449	Todd Helton	.50	.15
❑	450	Ben Petrick	.30	.09
❑	451	Juan Pierre	.30	.09
❑	452	Jeff Cirillo	.30	.09
❑	453	Juan Uribe	.30	.09
❑	454	Brian Bohanon	.30	.09
❑	455	Terry Shumpert	.30	.09
❑	456	Mike Hampton	.30	.09
❑	457	Shawn Chacon	.30	.09
❑	458	Adam Melhuse	.30	.09
❑	459	Greg Norton	.30	.09
❑	460	Gabe White	.30	.09
❑	461	Ichiro Suzuki WS	.75	.23
❑	462	Carlos Delgado WS	.30	.09
❑	463	Manny Ramirez WS	.50	.15
❑	464	Miguel Tejada WS	.30	.09
❑	465	Tsuyoshi Shinjo WS	.30	.09
❑	466	Bernie Williams WS	.30	.09
❑	467	Juan Gonzalez WS	.30	.09
❑	468	Andruw Jones WS	.30	.09
❑	469	Ivan Rodriguez WS	.30	.09
❑	470	Larry Walker WS	.30	.09
❑	471	Hideo Nomo WS	.30	.09
❑	472	Albert Pujols WS	.75	.23
❑	473	Pedro Martinez WS	.50	.15
❑	474	Vladimir Guerrero WS	.50	.15
❑	475	Tony Batista WS	.30	.09
❑	476	Kazuhiro Sasaki WS	.30	.09
❑	477	Richard Hidalgo WS	.30	.09
❑	478	Carlos Lee WS	.30	.09
❑	479	Roberto Alomar WS	.30	.09
❑	480	Rafael Palmeiro WS	.30	.09
❑	481	Ken Griffey Jr. GG	.75	.23
❑	482	Ken Griffey Jr. GG	.75	.23
❑	483	Ken Griffey Jr. GG	.75	.23
❑	484	Ken Griffey Jr. GG	.75	.23
❑	485	Ken Griffey Jr. GG	.75	.23
❑	486	Ken Griffey Jr. GG	.75	.23
❑	487	Ken Griffey Jr. GG	.75	.23
❑	488	Ken Griffey Jr. GG	.75	.23
❑	489	Ken Griffey Jr. GG	.75	.23
❑	490	Ken Griffey Jr. GG	.75	.23
❑	491	Barry Bonds CL	1.00	.30
❑	492	Hideo Nomo CL	.30	.09
❑	493	Ichiro Suzuki CL	.75	.23
❑	494	Cal Ripken CL	1.25	.35
❑	495	Tony Gwynn CL	.50	.15
❑	496	Randy Johnson CL	.50	.15
❑	497	A.J. Burnett CL	.30	.09
❑	498	Rickey Henderson CL	.50	.15
❑	499	Albert Pujols CL	.75	.23
❑	500	Luis Gonzalez CL	.30	.09
❑	501	Brandon Puffer SR RC	1.00	.30
❑	502	Rodrigo Rosario SR RC	1.00	.30
❑	503	Tom Shearn SR RC	1.00	.30
❑	504	Reed Johnson SR RC	1.50	.45
❑	505	Chris Baker SR RC	1.00	.30
❑	506	John Ennis SR RC	1.00	.30
❑	507	Luis Martinez SR RC	1.00	.30
❑	508	So Taguchi SR RC	1.50	.45
❑	509	Scotty Layfield SR RC	1.00	.30
❑	510	Francis Beltran SR RC	1.00	.30
❑	511	Brandon Backe SR RC	1.50	.45
❑	512	Doug Devore SR RC	1.00	.30
❑	513	Jeremy Ward SR RC	1.00	.30
❑	514	Jose Valverde SR RC	1.00	.30
❑	515	P.J. Bevis SR RC	1.00	.30
❑	516	Victor Alvarez SR RC	1.00	.30
❑	517	Kazuhisa Ishii SR RC	1.50	.45
❑	518	Jorge Nunez SR RC	1.00	.30
❑	519	Eric Good SR RC	1.00	.30
❑	520	Ron Calloway SR RC	1.00	.30
❑	521	Val Pascucci SR	1.00	.30
❑	522	Nelson Castro SR RC	1.00	.30
❑	523	Deivis Santos SR	1.00	.30
❑	524	Luis Ugueto SR RC	1.00	.30
❑	525	Matt Thornton SR RC	1.00	.30
❑	526	Hansel Izquierdo SR RC	1.00	.30
❑	527	Tyler Yates SR RC	1.00	.30
❑	528	Mark Corey SR RC	1.00	.30
❑	529	Jaime Cerda SR RC	1.00	.30
❑	530	Satoru Komiyama SR RC	1.00	.30
❑	531	Steve Bechler SR RC	1.00	.30
❑	532	Ben Howard SR RC	1.00	.30
❑	533	An. Machado SR RC	1.00	.30
❑	534	Jorge Padilla SR RC	1.00	.30
❑	535	Eric Junge SR RC	1.00	.30
❑	536	Adrian Burnside SR RC	1.00	.30
❑	537	Mike Gonzalez SR RC	1.00	.30
❑	538	Josh Hancock SR RC	1.00	.30
❑	539	Colin Young SR RC	1.00	.30
❑	540	Rene Reyes SR RC	1.00	.30
❑	541	Cam Esslinger SR RC	1.00	.30
❑	542	Tim Kalita SR RC	1.00	.30
❑	543	Kevin Frederick SR RC	1.00	.30
❑	544	Kyle Kane SR RC	1.00	.30
❑	545	Edwin Almonte SR RC	1.00	.30
❑	546	Aaron Sele	.30	.09
❑	547	Garret Anderson	.30	.09
❑	548	Darin Erstad	.30	.09
❑	549	Brad Fullmer	.30	.09
❑	550	Kevin Appier	.30	.09
❑	551	Tim Salmon	.50	.15
❑	552	David Justice	.30	.09
❑	553	Billy Koch	.30	.09
❑	554	Scott Hatteberg	.30	.09
❑	555	Tim Hudson	.30	.09
❑	556	Miguel Tejada	.30	.09
❑	557	Carlos Pena	.30	.09
❑	558	Mike Sirotka	.30	.09
❑	559	Jose Cruz Jr.	.30	.09
❑	560	Josh Phelps	.30	.09
❑	561	Brandon Lyon	.30	.09
❑	562	Luke Prokopec	.30	.09
❑	563	Felipe Lopez	.30	.09
❑	564	Jason Standridge	.30	.09
❑	565	Chris Gomez	.30	.09
❑	566	John Flaherty	.30	.09
❑	567	Jason Tyner	.30	.09
❑	568	Bobby Smith	.30	.09
❑	569	Wilson Alvarez	.30	.09
❑	570	Matt Lawton	.30	.09
❑	571	Omar Vizquel	.50	.15
❑	572	Jim Thome	.50	.15
❑	573	Brady Anderson	.30	.09
❑	574	Alex Escobar	.30	.09
❑	575	Russell Branyan	.30	.09
❑	576	Bret Boone	.30	.09
❑	577	Ben Davis	.30	.09
❑	578	Mike Cameron	.30	.09
❑	579	Jamie Moyer	.30	.09
❑	580	Ruben Sierra	.30	.09
❑	581	Jeff Cirillo	.30	.09
❑	582	Marty Cordova	.30	.09
❑	583	Mike Bordick	.30	.09
❑	584	Brian Roberts	.30	.09
❑	585	Luis Matos	.30	.09
❑	586	Geronimo Gil	.30	.09
❑	587	Jay Gibbons	.30	.09
❑	588	Carl Everett	.30	.09
❑	589	Ivan Rodriguez	.50	.15
❑	590	Chan Ho Park	.30	.09
❑	591	Juan Gonzalez	.30	.09
❑	592	Hank Blalock	.50	.15
❑	593	Todd Van Poppel	.30	.09
❑	594	Pedro Martinez	.50	.15
❑	595	Jason Varitek	.75	.23
❑	596	Tony Clark	.30	.09
❑	597	Johnny Damon Sox	.50	.15
❑	598	Dustin Hermanson	.30	.09
❑	599	John Burkett	.30	.09
❑	600	Carlos Beltran	.30	.09
❑	601	Mark Quinn	.30	.09
❑	602	Chuck Knoblauch	.30	.09
❑	603	Michael Tucker	.30	.09
❑	604	Carlos Febles	.30	.09
❑	605	Jose Rosado	.30	.09
❑	606	Dmitri Young	.30	.09
❑	607	Bobby Higginson	.30	.09
❑	608	Craig Paquette	.30	.09
❑	609	Mitch Meluskey	.30	.09
❑	610	Wendell Magee	.30	.09
❑	611	Mike Rivera	.30	.09
❑	612	Jacque Jones	.30	.09
❑	613	Luis Rivas	.30	.09
❑	614	Eric Milton	.30	.09
❑	615	Eddie Guardado	.30	.09
❑	616	Matt LeCroy	.30	.09
❑	617	Mike Jackson	.30	.09
❑	618	Magglio Ordonez	.30	.09
❑	619	Frank Thomas	.75	.23
❑	620	Rocky Biddle	.30	.09
❑	621	Paul Konerko	.30	.09
❑	622	Todd Ritchie	.30	.09
❑	623	Jon Rauch	.30	.09
❑	624	John Vander Wal	.30	.09
❑	625	Rondell White	.30	.09
❑	626	Jason Giambi	.30	.09
❑	627	Robin Ventura	.30	.09
❑	628	David Wells	.30	.09
❑	629	Bernie Williams	.50	.15
❑	630	Lance Berkman	.30	.09
❑	631	Richard Hidalgo	.30	.09
❑	632	Greg Zaun	.30	.09
❑	633	Jose Vizcaino	.30	.09
❑	634	Octavio Dotel	.30	.09
❑	635	Morgan Ensberg	.30	.09
❑	636	Andruw Jones	.50	.15
❑	637	Tom Glavine	.50	.15
❑	638	Gary Sheffield	.30	.09
❑	639	Vinny Castilla	.30	.09
❑	640	Javy Lopez	.30	.09

❑ 641 Albie Lopez .30 .09
❑ 642 Geoff Jenkins .30 .09
❑ 643 Jeffrey Hammonds .30 .09
❑ 644 Alex Ochoa .30 .09
❑ 645 Richie Sexson .30 .09
❑ 646 Eric Young .30 .09
❑ 647 Glendon Rusch .30 .09
❑ 648 Tino Martinez .50 .15
❑ 649 Fernando Vina .30 .09
❑ 650 J.D. Drew .30 .09
❑ 651 Woody Williams .30 .09
❑ 652 Darryl Kile .30 .09
❑ 653 Jason Isringhausen .30 .09
❑ 654 Moises Alou .30 .09
❑ 655 Alex Gonzalez .30 .09
❑ 656 Delino DeShields .30 .09
❑ 657 Todd Hundley .30 .09
❑ 658 Chris Stynes .30 .09
❑ 659 Jason Bere .30 .09
❑ 660 Curt Schilling .30 .09
❑ 661 Craig Counsell .30 .09
❑ 662 Mark Grace .50 .15
❑ 663 Matt Williams .30 .09
❑ 664 Jay Bell .30 .09
❑ 665 Rick Helling .30 .09
❑ 666 Shawn Green .30 .09
❑ 667 Eric Karros .30 .09
❑ 668 Hideo Nomo .75 .23
❑ 669 Omar Daal .30 .09
❑ 670 Brian Jordan .30 .09
❑ 671 Cesar Izturis .30 .09
❑ 672 Fernando Tatis .30 .09
❑ 673 Lee Stevens .30 .09
❑ 674 Tomo Ohka .30 .09
❑ 675 Brian Schneider .30 .09
❑ 676 Brad Wilkerson .30 .09
❑ 677 Bruce Chen .30 .09
❑ 678 Tsuyoshi Shinjo .30 .09
❑ 679 Jeff Kent .30 .09
❑ 680 Kirk Rueter .30 .09
❑ 681 J.T. Snow .30 .09
❑ 682 David Bell .30 .09
❑ 683 Reggie Sanders .30 .09
❑ 684 Preston Wilson .30 .09
❑ 685 Vic Darensbourg .30 .09
❑ 686 Josh Beckett .30 .09
❑ 687 Pablo Ozuna .30 .09
❑ 688 Mike Redmond .30 .09
❑ 689 Scott Strickland .30 .09
❑ 690 Mo Vaughn .30 .09
❑ 691 Roberto Alomar .50 .15
❑ 692 Edgardo Alfonzo .30 .09
❑ 693 Shawn Estes .30 .09
❑ 694 Roger Cedeno .30 .09
❑ 695 Jeromy Burnitz .30 .09
❑ 696 Ray Lankford .30 .09
❑ 697 Mark Kotsay .30 .09
❑ 698 Kevin Jarvis .30 .09
❑ 699 Bobby Jones .30 .09
❑ 700 Sean Burroughs .30 .09
❑ 701 Ramon Vazquez .30 .09
❑ 702 Pat Burrell .30 .09
❑ 703 Marlon Byrd .30 .09
❑ 704 Brandon Duckworth .30 .09
❑ 705 Marlon Anderson .30 .09
❑ 706 Vicente Padilla .30 .09
❑ 707 Kip Wells .30 .09
❑ 708 Jason Kendall .30 .09
❑ 709 Pokey Reese .30 .09
❑ 710 Pat Meares .30 .09
❑ 711 Kris Benson .30 .09
❑ 712 Armando Rios .30 .09
❑ 713 Mike Williams .30 .09
❑ 714 Barry Larkin .50 .15
❑ 715 Adam Dunn .30 .09
❑ 716 Juan Encarnacion .30 .09
❑ 717 Scott Williamson .30 .09
❑ 718 Wilton Guerrero .30 .09
❑ 719 Chris Reitsma .30 .09
❑ 720 Larry Walker .30 .09
❑ 721 Denny Neagle .30 .09
❑ 722 Todd Zeile .30 .09
❑ 723 Jose Ortiz .30 .09
❑ 724 Jason Jennings .30 .09
❑ 725 Tony Eusebio .30 .09
❑ 726 Ichiro Suzuki YR .75 .23
❑ 727 Barry Bonds YR 1.00 .30
❑ 728 Randy Johnson YR .50 .15
❑ 729 Albert Pujols YR .75 .23
❑ 730 Roger Clemens YR .75 .23
❑ 731 Sammy Sosa YR .50 .15
❑ 732 Alex Rodriguez YR .75 .23
❑ 733 Chipper Jones YR .50 .15
❑ 734 Rickey Henderson YR .50 .15
❑ 735 Ichiro Suzuki YR .75 .23
❑ 736 Luis Gonzalez SH CL .30 .09
❑ 737 Derek Jeter SH CL 1.00 .30
❑ 738 Ichiro Suzuki SH CL .75 .23
❑ 739 Barry Bonds SH CL 1.00 .30
❑ 740 Curt Schilling SH CL .30 .09
❑ 741 Shawn Green SH CL .30 .09
❑ 742 Jason Giambi SH CL .30 .09
❑ 743 Roberto Alomar SH CL .30 .09
❑ 744 Larry Walker SH CL .30 .09
❑ 745 Mark McGwire SH CL 1.00 .30

2003 Upper Deck

	Nm-Mt	Ex-Mt
COMPLETE SERIES 1 (270)	50.00	15.00
COMPLETE SERIES 2 (270)	50.00	15.00
COMP.UPDATE SET (60)	20.00	6.00
COMMON (31-500/531-600)	.30	.09
COMMON (1-30/501-530)	1.00	.30
COMMON RC (541-600)	.50	.15

SR 1-30/501-530 ARE NOT SHORT PRINTS
CARD 19 DOES NOT EXIST
SCUTARO/NOMAR ARE BOTH CARD 96
541-600 ISSUED IN 04 UD1 HOBBY BOXES
UPDATE SET EXCH 1:240 '04 UD1 RETAIL
UPDATE SET EXCH.DEADLINE 11/10/06

❑ 1 John Lackey SR 1.00 .30
❑ 2 Alex Cintron SR 1.00 .30
❑ 3 Jose Leon SR 1.00 .30
❑ 4 Bobby Hill SR 1.00 .30
❑ 5 Brandon Larson SR 1.00 .30
❑ 6 Raul Gonzalez SR 1.00 .30
❑ 7 Ben Broussard SR 1.00 .30
❑ 8 Earl Snyder SR 1.00 .30
❑ 9 Ramon Santiago SR 1.00 .30
❑ 10 Jason Lane SR 1.00 .30
❑ 11 Keith Ginter SR 1.00 .30
❑ 12 Kirk Saarloos SR 1.00 .30
❑ 13 Juan Brito SR 1.00 .30
❑ 14 Runelvys Hernandez SR 1.00 .30
❑ 15 Shawn Sedlacek SR 1.00 .30
❑ 16 Jayson Durocher SR 1.00 .30
❑ 17 Kevin Frederick SR 1.00 .30
❑ 18 Zach Day SR 1.00 .30
❑ 19 Marcos Scutaro SR UER 1.00 .30
Card number 96 on back
❑ 20 Marcus Thames SR 1.00 .30
❑ 21 Esteban German SR 1.00 .30
❑ 22 Brett Myers SR 1.00 .30
❑ 23 Oliver Perez SR 1.00 .30
❑ 24 Dennis Tankersley SR 1.00 .30
❑ 25 Julius Matos SR 1.00 .30
❑ 26 Jake Peavy SR 1.00 .30
❑ 27 Eric Cyr SR 1.00 .30
❑ 28 Mike Crudale SR 1.00 .30
❑ 29 Josh Pearce SR 1.00 .30
❑ 30 Carl Crawford SR 1.00 .30
❑ 31 Tim Salmon .50 .15
❑ 32 Troy Glaus .30 .09
❑ 33 Adam Kennedy .30 .09
❑ 34 David Eckstein .30 .09
❑ 35 Ben Molina .30 .09
❑ 36 Jarrod Washburn .30 .09
❑ 37 Ramon Ortiz .30 .09
❑ 38 Eric Chavez .30 .09
❑ 39 Miguel Tejada .30 .09
❑ 40 Adam Piatt .30 .09
❑ 41 Jermaine Dye .30 .09
❑ 42 Olmedo Saenz .30 .09
❑ 43 Tim Hudson .30 .09
❑ 44 Barry Zito .30 .09
❑ 45 Billy Koch .30 .09
❑ 46 Shannon Stewart .30 .09
❑ 47 Kelvim Escobar .30 .09
❑ 48 Jose Cruz Jr. .30 .09
❑ 49 Vernon Wells .30 .09
❑ 50 Roy Halladay .30 .09
❑ 51 Esteban Loaiza .30 .09
❑ 52 Eric Hinske .30 .09
❑ 53 Steve Cox .30 .09
❑ 54 Brent Abernathy .30 .09
❑ 55 Ben Grieve .30 .09
❑ 56 Aubrey Huff .30 .09
❑ 57 Jared Sandberg .30 .09
❑ 58 Paul Wilson .30 .09
❑ 59 Tanyon Sturtze .30 .09
❑ 60 Jim Thome .50 .15
❑ 61 Omar Vizquel .50 .15
❑ 62 C.C. Sabathia .30 .09
❑ 63 Chris Magruder .30 .09
❑ 64 Ricky Gutierrez .30 .09
❑ 65 Einar Diaz .30 .09
❑ 66 Danys Baez .30 .09
❑ 67 Ichiro Suzuki 1.50 .45
❑ 68 Ruben Sierra .30 .09
❑ 69 Carlos Guillen .30 .09
❑ 70 Mark McLemore .30 .09
❑ 71 Dan Wilson .30 .09
❑ 72 Jamie Moyer .30 .09
❑ 73 Joel Pineiro .30 .09
❑ 74 Edgar Martinez .50 .15
❑ 75 Tony Batista .30 .09
❑ 76 Jay Gibbons .30 .09
❑ 77 Chris Singleton .30 .09
❑ 78 Melvin Mora .30 .09
❑ 79 Geronimo Gil .30 .09
❑ 80 Rodrigo Lopez .30 .09
❑ 81 Jorge Julio .30 .09
❑ 82 Rafael Palmeiro .50 .15
❑ 83 Juan Gonzalez .30 .09
❑ 84 Mike Young .50 .15
❑ 85 Hideki Irabu .30 .09
❑ 86 Chan Ho Park .30 .09
❑ 87 Kevin Mench .30 .09
❑ 88 Doug Davis .30 .09
❑ 89 Pedro Martinez .50 .15
❑ 90 Shea Hillenbrand .30 .09
❑ 91 Derek Lowe .30 .09
❑ 92 Jason Varitek .75 .23
❑ 93 Tony Clark .30 .09
❑ 94 John Burkett .30 .09
❑ 95 Frank Castillo .30 .09
❑ 96 Nomar Garciaparra 1.25 .35
❑ 97 Rickey Henderson .75 .23
❑ 98 Mike Sweeney .30 .09
❑ 99 Carlos Febles .30 .09
❑ 100 Mark Quinn .30 .09
❑ 101 Raul Ibanez .30 .09
❑ 102 A.J. Hinch .30 .09
❑ 103 Paul Byrd .30 .09
❑ 104 Chuck Knoblauch .30 .09
❑ 105 Dmitri Young .30 .09
❑ 106 Randall Simon .30 .09
❑ 107 Brandon Inge .30 .09
❑ 108 Damion Easley .30 .09
❑ 109 Carlos Pena .30 .09
❑ 110 George Lombard .30 .09
❑ 111 Juan Acevedo .30 .09
❑ 112 Torii Hunter .30 .09
❑ 113 Doug Mientkiewicz .30 .09
❑ 114 David Ortiz .50 .15
❑ 115 Eric Milton .30 .09
❑ 116 Eddie Guardado .30 .09
❑ 117 Cristian Guzman .30 .09
❑ 118 Corey Koskie .30 .09

❑	119	Magglio Ordonez	.30	.09
❑	120	Mark Buehrle	.30	.09
❑	121	Todd Ritchie	.30	.09
❑	122	Jose Valentin	.30	.09
❑	123	Paul Konerko	.30	.09
❑	124	Carlos Lee	.30	.09
❑	125	Jon Garland	.30	.09
❑	126	Jason Giambi	.30	.09
❑	127	Derek Jeter	2.00	.60
❑	128	Roger Clemens	1.50	.45
❑	129	Raul Mondesi	.30	.09
❑	130	Jorge Posada	.50	.15
❑	131	Rondell White	.30	.09
❑	132	Robin Ventura	.30	.09
❑	133	Mike Mussina	.50	.15
❑	134	Jeff Bagwell	.50	.15
❑	135	Craig Biggio	.50	.15
❑	136	Morgan Ensberg	.30	.09
❑	137	Richard Hidalgo	.30	.09
❑	138	Brad Ausmus	.30	.09
❑	139	Roy Oswalt	.30	.09
❑	140	Carlos Hernandez	.30	.09
❑	141	Shane Reynolds	.30	.09
❑	142	Gary Sheffield	.30	.09
❑	143	Andruw Jones	.50	.15
❑	144	Tom Glavine	.50	.15
❑	145	Rafael Furcal	.30	.09
❑	146	Javy Lopez	.30	.09
❑	147	Vinny Castilla	.30	.09
❑	148	Marcus Giles	.30	.09
❑	149	Kevin Millwood	.30	.09
❑	150	Jason Marquis	.30	.09
❑	151	Ruben Quevedo	.30	.09
❑	152	Ben Sheets	.30	.09
❑	153	Geoff Jenkins	.30	.09
❑	154	Jose Hernandez	.30	.09
❑	155	Glendon Rusch	.30	.09
❑	156	Jeffrey Hammonds	.30	.09
❑	157	Alex Sanchez	.30	.09
❑	158	Jim Edmonds	.50	.15
❑	159	Tino Martinez	.50	.15
❑	160	Albert Pujols	1.50	.45
❑	161	Eli Marrero	.30	.09
❑	162	Woody Williams	.30	.09
❑	163	Fernando Vina	.30	.09
❑	164	Jason Isringhausen	.30	.09
❑	165	Jason Simontacchi	.30	.09
❑	166	Kerry Robinson	.30	.09
❑	167	Sammy Sosa	.75	.23
❑	168	Juan Cruz	.30	.09
❑	169	Fred McGriff	.50	.15
❑	170	Antonio Alfonseca	.30	.09
❑	171	Jon Lieber	.30	.09
❑	172	Mark Prior	.50	.15
❑	173	Moises Alou	.30	.09
❑	174	Matt Clement	.30	.09
❑	175	Mark Bellhorn	.30	.09
❑	176	Randy Johnson	.75	.23
❑	177	Luis Gonzalez	.30	.09
❑	178	Tony Womack	.30	.09
❑	179	Mark Grace	.50	.15
❑	180	Junior Spivey	.30	.09
❑	181	Byung Hyun Kim	.30	.09
❑	182	Danny Bautista	.30	.09
❑	183	Brian Anderson	.30	.09
❑	184	Shawn Green	.30	.09
❑	185	Brian Jordan	.30	.09
❑	186	Eric Karros	.30	.09
❑	187	Andy Ashby	.30	.09
❑	188	Cesar Izturis	.30	.09
❑	189	Dave Roberts	.30	.09
❑	190	Eric Gagne	.30	.09
❑	191	Kazuhisa Ishii	.30	.09
❑	192	Adrian Beltre	.30	.09
❑	193	Vladimir Guerrero	.75	.23
❑	194	Tony Armas Jr.	.30	.09
❑	195	Bartolo Colon	.30	.09
❑	196	Troy O'Leary	.30	.09
❑	197	Tomo Ohka	.30	.09
❑	198	Brad Wilkerson	.30	.09
❑	199	Orlando Cabrera	.30	.09
❑	200	Barry Bonds	2.00	.60
❑	201	David Bell	.30	.09
❑	202	Tsuyoshi Shinjo	.30	.09
❑	203	Benito Santiago	.30	.09
❑	204	Livan Hernandez	.30	.09
❑	205	Jason Schmidt	.30	.09
❑	206	Kirk Rueter	.30	.09
❑	207	Ramon E. Martinez	.30	.09
❑	208	Mike Lowell	.30	.09
❑	209	Luis Castillo	.30	.09
❑	210	Derrek Lee	.50	.15
❑	211	Andy Fox	.30	.09
❑	212	Eric Owens	.30	.09
❑	213	Charles Johnson	.30	.09
❑	214	Brad Penny	.30	.09
❑	215	A.J. Burnett	.30	.09
❑	216	Edgardo Alfonzo	.30	.09
❑	217	Roberto Alomar	.50	.15
❑	218	Rey Ordonez	.30	.09
❑	219	Al Leiter	.30	.09
❑	220	Roger Cedeno	.30	.09
❑	221	Timo Perez	.30	.09
❑	222	Jeromy Burnitz	.30	.09
❑	223	Pedro Astacio	.30	.09
❑	224	Joe McEwing	.30	.09
❑	225	Ryan Klesko	.30	.09
❑	226	Ramon Vazquez	.30	.09
❑	227	Mark Kotsay	.30	.09
❑	228	Bubba Trammell	.30	.09
❑	229	Wiki Gonzalez	.30	.09
❑	230	Trevor Hoffman	.30	.09
❑	231	Ron Gant	.30	.09
❑	232	Bob Abreu	.30	.09
❑	233	Marlon Anderson	.30	.09
❑	234	Jeremy Giambi	.30	.09
❑	235	Jimmy Rollins	.30	.09
❑	236	Mike Lieberthal	.30	.09
❑	237	Vicente Padilla	.30	.09
❑	238	Randy Wolf	.30	.09
❑	239	Pokey Reese	.30	.09
❑	240	Brian Giles	.30	.09
❑	241	Jack Wilson	.30	.09
❑	242	Mike Williams	.30	.09
❑	243	Kip Wells	.30	.09
❑	244	Rob Mackowiak	.30	.09
❑	245	Craig Wilson	.30	.09
❑	246	Adam Dunn	.30	.09
❑	247	Sean Casey	.50	.15
❑	248	Todd Walker	.30	.09
❑	249	Corky Miller	.30	.09
❑	250	Ryan Dempster	.30	.09
❑	251	Reggie Taylor	.30	.09
❑	252	Aaron Boone	.30	.09
❑	253	Larry Walker	.30	.09
❑	254	Jose Ortiz	.30	.09
❑	255	Todd Zeile	.30	.09
❑	256	Bobby Estalella	.30	.09
❑	257	Juan Pierre	.30	.09
❑	258	Terry Shumpert	.30	.09
❑	259	Mike Hampton	.30	.09
❑	260	Denny Stark	.30	.09
❑	261	Shawn Green SH CL	.30	.09
❑	262	Derek Lowe SH CL	.30	.09
❑	263	Barry Bonds SH CL	1.00	.30
❑	264	Mike Cameron SH CL	.30	.09
❑	265	Luis Castillo SH CL	.30	.09
❑	266	Vladimir Guerrero SH CL	.50	.15
❑	267	Jason Giambi SH CL	.30	.09
❑	268	Eric Gagne SH CL	.30	.09
❑	269	Magglio Ordonez SH CL	.30	.09
❑	270	Jim Thome SH CL	.30	.09
❑	271	Garret Anderson	.30	.09
❑	272	Troy Percival	.30	.09
❑	273	Brad Fullmer	.30	.09
❑	274	Scott Spiezio	.30	.09
❑	275	Darin Erstad	.30	.09
❑	276	Francisco Rodriguez	.30	.09
❑	277	Kevin Appier	.30	.09
❑	278	Shawn Wooten	.30	.09
❑	279	Eric Owens	.30	.09
❑	280	Scott Hatteberg	.30	.09
❑	281	Terrence Long	.30	.09
❑	282	Mark Mulder	.30	.09
❑	283	Ramon Hernandez	.30	.09
❑	284	Ted Lilly	.30	.09
❑	285	Erubiel Durazo	.30	.09
❑	286	Mark Ellis	.30	.09
❑	287	Carlos Delgado	.30	.09
❑	288	Orlando Hudson	.30	.09
❑	289	Chris Woodward	.30	.09
❑	290	Mark Hendrickson	.30	.09
❑	291	Josh Phelps	.30	.09
❑	292	Ken Huckaby	.30	.09
❑	293	Justin Miller	.30	.09
❑	294	Travis Lee	.30	.09
❑	295	Jorge Sosa	.30	.09
❑	296	Joe Kennedy	.30	.09
❑	297	Carl Crawford	.30	.09
❑	298	Toby Hall	.30	.09
❑	299	Rey Ordonez	.30	.09
❑	300	Brandon Phillips	.30	.09
❑	301	Matt Lawton	.30	.09
❑	302	Ellis Burks	.30	.09
❑	303	Bill Selby	.30	.09
❑	304	Travis Hafner	.30	.09
❑	305	Milton Bradley	.30	.09
❑	306	Karim Garcia	.30	.09
❑	307	Cliff Lee	.30	.09
❑	308	Jeff Cirillo	.30	.09
❑	309	John Olerud	.30	.09
❑	310	Kazuhiro Sasaki	.30	.09
❑	311	Freddy Garcia	.30	.09
❑	312	Bret Boone	.30	.09
❑	313	Mike Cameron	.30	.09
❑	314	Ben Davis	.30	.09
❑	315	Randy Winn	.30	.09
❑	316	Gary Matthews Jr.	.30	.09
❑	317	Jeff Conine	.30	.09
❑	318	Sidney Ponson	.30	.09
❑	319	Jerry Hairston	.30	.09
❑	320	David Segui	.30	.09
❑	321	Scott Erickson	.30	.09
❑	322	Marty Cordova	.30	.09
❑	323	Hank Blalock	.30	.09
❑	324	Herbert Perry	.30	.09
❑	325	Alex Rodriguez	1.25	.35
❑	326	Carl Everett	.30	.09
❑	327	Einar Diaz	.30	.09
❑	328	Ugueth Urbina	.30	.09
❑	329	Mark Teixeira	.50	.15
❑	330	Manny Ramirez	.50	.15
❑	331	Johnny Damon	.50	.15
❑	332	Trot Nixon	.30	.09
❑	333	Tim Wakefield	.30	.09
❑	334	Casey Fossum	.30	.09
❑	335	Todd Walker	.30	.09
❑	336	Jeremy Giambi	.30	.09
❑	337	Bill Mueller	.30	.09
❑	338	Ramiro Mendoza	.30	.09
❑	339	Carlos Beltran	.30	.09
❑	340	Jason Grimsley	.30	.09
❑	341	Brent Mayne	.30	.09
❑	342	Angel Berroa	.30	.09
❑	343	Albie Lopez	.30	.09
❑	344	Michael Tucker	.30	.09
❑	345	Bobby Higginson	.30	.09
❑	346	Shane Halter	.30	.09
❑	347	Jeremy Bonderman RC	3.00	.90
❑	348	Eric Munson	.30	.09
❑	349	Andy Van Hekken	.30	.09
❑	350	Matt Anderson	.30	.09
❑	351	Jacque Jones	.30	.09
❑	352	A.J. Pierzynski	.30	.09
❑	353	Joe Mays	.30	.09
❑	354	Brad Radke	.30	.09
❑	355	Dustan Mohr	.30	.09
❑	356	Bobby Kielty	.30	.09
❑	357	Michael Cuddyer	.30	.09
❑	358	Luis Rivas	.30	.09
❑	359	Frank Thomas	.75	.23
❑	360	Joe Borchard	.30	.09
❑	361	D'Angelo Jimenez	.30	.09
❑	362	Bartolo Colon	.30	.09
❑	363	Joe Crede	.30	.09
❑	364	Miguel Olivo	.30	.09
❑	365	Billy Koch	.30	.09
❑	366	Bernie Williams	.50	.15
❑	367	Nick Johnson	.30	.09
❑	368	Andy Pettitte	.50	.15
❑	369	Mariano Rivera	.50	.15
❑	370	Alfonso Soriano	.30	.09
❑	371	David Wells	.30	.09
❑	372	Drew Henson	.30	.09
❑	373	Juan Rivera	.30	.09
❑	374	Steve Karsay	.30	.09
❑	375	Jeff Kent	.30	.09
❑	376	Lance Berkman	.30	.09

- ❑ 377 Octavio Dotel .30 .09
- ❑ 378 Julio Lugo .30 .09
- ❑ 379 Jason Lane .30 .09
- ❑ 380 Wade Miller .30 .09
- ❑ 381 Billy Wagner .30 .09
- ❑ 382 Brad Ausmus .30 .09
- ❑ 383 Mike Hampton .30 .09
- ❑ 384 Chipper Jones .75 .23
- ❑ 385 John Smoltz .50 .15
- ❑ 386 Greg Maddux 1.25 .35
- ❑ 387 Javy Lopez .30 .09
- ❑ 388 Robert Fick .30 .09
- ❑ 389 Mark DeRosa .30 .09
- ❑ 390 Russ Ortiz .30 .09
- ❑ 391 Julio Franco .30 .09
- ❑ 392 Richie Sexson .30 .09
- ❑ 393 Eric Young .30 .09
- ❑ 394 Robert Machado .30 .09
- ❑ 395 Mike DeJean .30 .09
- ❑ 396 Todd Ritchie .30 .09
- ❑ 397 Royce Clayton .30 .09
- ❑ 398 Nick Neugebauer .30 .09
- ❑ 399 J.D. Drew .30 .09
- ❑ 400 Edgar Renteria .30 .09
- ❑ 401 Scott Rolen .50 .15
- ❑ 402 Matt Morris .30 .09
- ❑ 403 Garrett Stephenson .30 .09
- ❑ 404 Eduardo Perez .30 .09
- ❑ 405 Mike Matheny .30 .09
- ❑ 406 Miguel Cairo .30 .09
- ❑ 407 Brett Tomko .30 .09
- ❑ 408 Bobby Hill .30 .09
- ❑ 409 Troy O'Leary .30 .09
- ❑ 410 Corey Patterson .30 .09
- ❑ 411 Kerry Wood .30 .09
- ❑ 412 Eric Karros .30 .09
- ❑ 413 Hee Seop Choi .30 .09
- ❑ 414 Alex Gonzalez .30 .09
- ❑ 415 Matt Clement .30 .09
- ❑ 416 Mark Grudzielanek .30 .09
- ❑ 417 Curt Schilling .30 .09
- ❑ 418 Steve Finley .30 .09
- ❑ 419 Craig Counsell .30 .09
- ❑ 420 Matt Williams .30 .09
- ❑ 421 Quinton McCracken .30 .09
- ❑ 422 Chad Moeller .30 .09
- ❑ 423 Lyle Overbay .30 .09
- ❑ 424 Miguel Batista .30 .09
- ❑ 425 Paul Lo Duca .30 .09
- ❑ 426 Kevin Brown .30 .09
- ❑ 427 Hideo Nomo .75 .23
- ❑ 428 Fred McGriff .50 .15
- ❑ 429 Joe Thurston .30 .09
- ❑ 430 Odalis Perez .30 .09
- ❑ 431 Darren Dreifort .30 .09
- ❑ 432 Todd Hundley .30 .09
- ❑ 433 Dave Roberts .30 .09
- ❑ 434 Jose Vidro .30 .09
- ❑ 435 Javier Vazquez .30 .09
- ❑ 436 Michael Barrett .30 .09
- ❑ 437 Fernando Tatis .30 .09
- ❑ 438 Peter Bergeron .30 .09
- ❑ 439 Endy Chavez .30 .09
- ❑ 440 Orlando Hernandez .30 .09
- ❑ 441 Marvin Benard .30 .09
- ❑ 442 Rich Aurilia .30 .09
- ❑ 443 Pedro Feliz .30 .09
- ❑ 444 Robb Nen .30 .09
- ❑ 445 Ray Durham .30 .09
- ❑ 446 Marquis Grissom .30 .09
- ❑ 447 Damian Moss .30 .09
- ❑ 448 Edgardo Alfonzo .30 .09
- ❑ 449 Juan Pierre .30 .09
- ❑ 450 Braden Looper .30 .09
- ❑ 451 Alex Gonzalez .30 .09
- ❑ 452 Justin Wayne .30 .09
- ❑ 453 Josh Beckett .30 .09
- ❑ 454 Juan Encarnacion .30 .09
- ❑ 455 Ivan Rodriguez .50 .15
- ❑ 456 Todd Hollandsworth .30 .09
- ❑ 457 Cliff Floyd .30 .09
- ❑ 458 Rey Sanchez .30 .09
- ❑ 459 Mike Piazza 1.25 .35
- ❑ 460 Mo Vaughn .30 .09
- ❑ 461 Armando Benitez .30 .09
- ❑ 462 Tsuyoshi Shinjo .30 .09
- ❑ 463 Tom Glavine .50 .15
- ❑ 464 David Cone .30 .09
- ❑ 465 Phil Nevin .30 .09
- ❑ 466 Sean Burroughs .30 .09
- ❑ 467 Jake Peavy .30 .09
- ❑ 468 Brian Lawrence .30 .09
- ❑ 469 Mark Loretta .30 .09
- ❑ 470 Dennis Tankersley .30 .09
- ❑ 471 Jesse Orosco .30 .09
- ❑ 472 Jim Thome .50 .15
- ❑ 473 Kevin Millwood .30 .09
- ❑ 474 David Bell .30 .09
- ❑ 475 Pat Burrell .30 .09
- ❑ 476 Brandon Duckworth .30 .09
- ❑ 477 Jose Mesa .30 .09
- ❑ 478 Marlon Byrd .30 .09
- ❑ 479 Reggie Sanders .30 .09
- ❑ 480 Jason Kendall .30 .09
- ❑ 481 Aramis Ramirez .30 .09
- ❑ 482 Kris Benson .30 .09
- ❑ 483 Matt Stairs .30 .09
- ❑ 484 Kevin Young .30 .09
- ❑ 485 Kenny Lofton .30 .09
- ❑ 486 Austin Kearns .30 .09
- ❑ 487 Barry Larkin .50 .15
- ❑ 488 Jason LaRue .30 .09
- ❑ 489 Ken Griffey Jr. 1.25 .35
- ❑ 490 Danny Graves .30 .09
- ❑ 491 Russell Branyan .30 .09
- ❑ 492 Reggie Taylor .30 .09
- ❑ 493 Jimmy Haynes .30 .09
- ❑ 494 Charles Johnson .30 .09
- ❑ 495 Todd Helton .50 .15
- ❑ 496 Juan Uribe .30 .09
- ❑ 497 Preston Wilson .30 .09
- ❑ 498 Chris Stynes .30 .09
- ❑ 499 Jason Jennings .30 .09
- ❑ 500 Jay Payton .30 .09
- ❑ 501 Hideki Matsui SR RC 5.00 1.50
- ❑ 502 Jose Contreras SR RC 1.50 .45
- ❑ 503 Brandon Webb SR RC 1.50 .45
- ❑ 504 Robby Hammock SR RC 1.00 .30
- ❑ 505 Matt Kata SR RC 1.00 .30
- ❑ 506 Tim Olson SR RC 1.00 .30
- ❑ 507 Michael Hessman SR RC 1.00 .30
- ❑ 508 Jon Leicester SR RC 1.00 .30
- ❑ 509 Todd Wellemeyer SR RC 1.00 .30
- ❑ 510 David Sanders SR RC 1.00 .30
- ❑ 511 Josh Stewart SR RC 1.00 .30
- ❑ 512 Luis Ayala SR RC 1.00 .30
- ❑ 513 Clint Barmes SR RC 2.00 .60
- ❑ 514 Josh Willingham SR RC 1.50 .45
- ❑ 515 Al. Machado SR RC 1.00 .30
- ❑ 516 Felix Sanchez SR RC 1.00 .30
- ❑ 517 Willie Eyre SR RC 1.00 .30
- ❑ 518 Brent Hoard SR RC 1.00 .30
- ❑ 519 Lew Ford SR RC 1.50 .45
- ❑ 520 Terrmel Sledge SR RC 1.00 .30
- ❑ 521 Jeremy Griffiths SR RC 1.00 .30
- ❑ 522 Phil Seibel SR RC 1.00 .30
- ❑ 523 Craig Brazell SR RC 1.00 .30
- ❑ 524 Prentice Redman SR RC 1.00 .30
- ❑ 525 Jeff Duncan SR RC 1.00 .30
- ❑ 526 Shane Bazzell SR RC 1.00 .30
- ❑ 527 Bernie Castro SR RC 1.00 .30
- ❑ 528 Rett Johnson SR RC 1.00 .30
- ❑ 529 Bobby Madritsch SR RC 1.50 .45
- ❑ 530 Rocco Baldelli SR 1.00 .30
- ❑ 531 Alex Rodriguez SH CL .75 .23
- ❑ 532 Eric Chavez SH CL .30 .09
- ❑ 533 Miguel Tejada SH CL .30 .09
- ❑ 534 Ichiro Suzuki SH CL .75 .23
- ❑ 535 Sammy Sosa SH CL .50 .15
- ❑ 536 Barry Zito SH CL .30 .09
- ❑ 537 Darin Erstad SH CL .30 .09
- ❑ 538 Alfonso Soriano SH CL .30 .09
- ❑ 539 Troy Glaus SH CL .30 .09
- ❑ 540 N.Garciaparra SH CL .75 .23
- ❑ 541 Bo Hart RC .50 .15
- ❑ 542 Dan Haren RC .75 .23
- ❑ 543 Ryan Wagner RC .50 .15
- ❑ 544 Rich Harden .50 .15
- ❑ 545 Dontrelle Willis .75 .23
- ❑ 546 Jerome Williams .30 .09
- ❑ 547 Bobby Crosby .50 .15
- ❑ 548 Greg Jones RC .50 .15
- ❑ 549 Todd Linden .30 .09
- ❑ 550 Byung-Hyun Kim .30 .09
- ❑ 551 Rickie Weeks RC 4.00 1.20
- ❑ 552 Jason Roach RC .50 .15
- ❑ 553 Oscar Villarreal RC .50 .15
- ❑ 554 Justin Duchscherer .30 .09
- ❑ 555 Chris Capuano RC .50 .15
- ❑ 556 Josh Hall RC .50 .15
- ❑ 557 Luis Matos .30 .09
- ❑ 558 Miguel Ojeda RC .50 .15
- ❑ 559 Kevin Ohme RC .50 .15
- ❑ 560 Julio Manon RC .50 .15
- ❑ 561 Kevin Correia RC .50 .15
- ❑ 562 Delmon Young RC 5.00 1.50
- ❑ 563 Aaron Boone .30 .09
- ❑ 564 Aaron Looper RC .50 .15
- ❑ 565 Mike Neu RC .50 .15
- ❑ 566 Aquilino Lopez RC .50 .15
- ❑ 567 Jhonny Peralta .50 .15
- ❑ 568 Duaner Sanchez .30 .09
- ❑ 569 Stephen Randolph RC .50 .15
- ❑ 570 Nate Bland RC .50 .15
- ❑ 571 Chin-Hui Tsao .30 .09
- ❑ 572 Michel Hernandez RC .50 .15
- ❑ 573 Rocco Baldelli .30 .09
- ❑ 574 Robb Quinlan .30 .09
- ❑ 575 Aaron Heilman .30 .09
- ❑ 576 Jae Weong Seo .30 .09
- ❑ 577 Joe Borowski .30 .09
- ❑ 578 Chris Bootcheck .30 .09
- ❑ 579 Michael Ryan RC .50 .15
- ❑ 580 Mark Malaska RC .50 .15
- ❑ 581 Jose Guillen .30 .09
- ❑ 582 Josh Towers .30 .09
- ❑ 583 Tom Gregorio RC .50 .15
- ❑ 584 Edwin Jackson RC .50 .15
- ❑ 585 Jason Anderson .30 .09
- ❑ 586 Jose Reyes .30 .09
- ❑ 587 Miguel Cabrera .75 .23
- ❑ 588 Nate Bump .30 .09
- ❑ 589 Jeromy Burnitz .30 .09
- ❑ 590 David Ross .30 .09
- ❑ 591 Chase Utley .75 .23
- ❑ 592 Brandon Webb .75 .23
- ❑ 593 Masao Kida .30 .09
- ❑ 594 Jimmy Journell .30 .09
- ❑ 595 Eric Young .30 .09
- ❑ 596 Tony Womack .30 .09
- ❑ 597 Amaury Telemaco .30 .09
- ❑ 598 Rickey Henderson .75 .23
- ❑ 599 Esteban Loaiza .30 .09
- ❑ 600 Sidney Ponson .30 .09
- ❑ NNO Update Set Exchange Card .00

2004 Upper Deck

	MINT	NRMT
COMPLETE SERIES 1 (270)	50.00	22.00
COMPLETE SERIES 2 (270)	50.00	22.00
COMP.UPDATE SET (50)	15.00	6.75
COMMON (31-480/541-565)	.30	.14
COMMON (1-30/481-540)	1.00	.45
COMMON CARD (566-590)	.50	.23
541-590 ONE SET PER '05 UD1 HOBBY BOX		.00
UPDATE SET EXCH 1:480 '05 UD1 RETAIL		.00
UPDATE SET EXCH.DEADLINE TBD	.00	

- ❑ 1 Dontrelle Willis SR 1.50 .70
- ❑ 2 Edgar Gonzalez SR 1.00 .45

❑ 3 Jose Reyes SR 1.00 .45
❑ 4 Jae Weong Seo SR 1.00 .45
❑ 5 Miguel Cabrera SR 1.50 .70
❑ 6 Jesse Foppert SR 1.00 .45
❑ 7 Mike Neu SR 1.00 .45
❑ 8 Michael Nakamura SR 1.00 .45
❑ 9 Luis Ayala SR 1.00 .45
❑ 10 Jared Sandberg SR 1.00 .45
❑ 11 Jhonny Peralta SR 1.00 .45
❑ 12 Wil Ledezma SR 1.00 .45
❑ 13 Jason Roach SR 1.00 .45
❑ 14 Kirk Saarloos SR 1.00 .45
❑ 15 Cliff Lee SR 1.00 .45
❑ 16 Bobby Hill SR 1.00 .45
❑ 17 Lyle Overbay SR 1.00 .45
❑ 18 Josh Hall SR 1.00 .45
❑ 19 Joe Thurston SR 1.00 .45
❑ 20 Matt Kata SR 1.00 .45
❑ 21 Jeremy Bonderman SR 1.00 .45
❑ 22 Julio Manon SR 1.00 .45
❑ 23 Rodrigo Rosario SR 1.00 .45
❑ 24 Robby Hammock SR 1.00 .45
❑ 25 David Sanders SR 1.00 .45
❑ 26 Miguel Ojeda SR 1.00 .45
❑ 27 Mark Teixeira SR 1.50 .70
❑ 28 Franklyn German SR 1.00 .45
❑ 29 Ken Harvey SR 1.00 .45
❑ 30 Xavier Nady SR 1.00 .45
❑ 31 Tim Salmon .50 .23
❑ 32 Troy Glaus .30 .14
❑ 33 Adam Kennedy .30 .14
❑ 34 David Eckstein .30 .14
❑ 35 Ben Molina .30 .14
❑ 36 Jarrod Washburn .30 .14
❑ 37 Ramon Ortiz .30 .14
❑ 38 Eric Chavez .30 .14
❑ 39 Miguel Tejada .30 .14
❑ 40 Chris Singleton .30 .14
❑ 41 Jermaine Dye .30 .14
❑ 42 John Halama .30 .14
❑ 43 Tim Hudson .30 .14
❑ 44 Barry Zito .30 .14
❑ 45 Ted Lilly .30 .14
❑ 46 Bobby Kielty .30 .14
❑ 47 Kelvim Escobar .30 .14
❑ 48 Josh Phelps .30 .14
❑ 49 Vernon Wells .30 .14
❑ 50 Roy Halladay .30 .14
❑ 51 Orlando Hudson .30 .14
❑ 52 Eric Hinske .30 .14
❑ 53 Brandon Backe .30 .14
❑ 54 Dewon Brazelton .30 .14
❑ 55 Ben Grieve .30 .14
❑ 56 Aubrey Huff .30 .14
❑ 57 Toby Hall .30 .14
❑ 58 Rocco Baldelli .30 .14
❑ 59 Al Martin .30 .14
❑ 60 Brandon Phillips .30 .14
❑ 61 Omar Vizquel .50 .23
❑ 62 C.C. Sabathia .30 .14
❑ 63 Milton Bradley .30 .14
❑ 64 Ricky Gutierrez .30 .14
❑ 65 Matt Lawton .30 .14
❑ 66 Danys Baez .30 .14
❑ 67 Ichiro Suzuki 1.50 .70
❑ 68 Randy Winn .30 .14
❑ 69 Carlos Guillen .30 .14
❑ 70 Mark McLemore .30 .14
❑ 71 Dan Wilson .30 .14
❑ 72 Jamie Moyer .30 .14
❑ 73 Joel Pineiro .30 .14
❑ 74 Edgar Martinez .50 .23
❑ 75 Tony Batista .30 .14
❑ 76 Jay Gibbons .30 .14
❑ 77 Jeff Conine .30 .14
❑ 78 Melvin Mora .30 .14
❑ 79 Geronimo Gil .30 .14
❑ 80 Rodrigo Lopez .30 .14
❑ 81 Jorge Julio .30 .14
❑ 82 Rafael Palmeiro .50 .23
❑ 83 Juan Gonzalez .30 .14
❑ 84 Mike Young .30 .14
❑ 85 Alex Rodriguez 1.25 .55
❑ 86 Einar Diaz .30 .14
❑ 87 Kevin Mench .30 .14
❑ 88 Hank Blalock .30 .14
❑ 89 Pedro Martinez .50 .23
❑ 90 Byung-Hyun Kim .30 .14
❑ 91 Derek Lowe .30 .14
❑ 92 Jason Varitek .75 .35
❑ 93 Manny Ramirez .50 .23
❑ 94 John Burkett .30 .14
❑ 95 Todd Walker .30 .14
❑ 96 Nomar Garciaparra 1.25 .55
❑ 97 Trot Nixon .30 .14
❑ 98 Mike Sweeney .30 .14
❑ 99 Carlos Febles .30 .14
❑ 100 Mike MacDougal .30 .14
❑ 101 Raul Ibanez .30 .14
❑ 102 Jason Grimsley .30 .14
❑ 103 Chris George .30 .14
❑ 104 Brent Mayne .30 .14
❑ 105 Dmitri Young .30 .14
❑ 106 Eric Munson .30 .14
❑ 107 A.J. Hinch .30 .14
❑ 108 Andres Torres .30 .14
❑ 109 Bobby Higginson .30 .14
❑ 110 Shane Halter .30 .14
❑ 111 Matt Walbeck .30 .14
❑ 112 Torii Hunter .30 .14
❑ 113 Doug Mientkiewicz .30 .14
❑ 114 Lew Ford .30 .14
❑ 115 Eric Milton .30 .14
❑ 116 Eddie Guardado .30 .14
❑ 117 Cristian Guzman .30 .14
❑ 118 Corey Koskie .30 .14
❑ 119 Magglio Ordonez .30 .14
❑ 120 Mark Buehrle .30 .14
❑ 121 Billy Koch .30 .14
❑ 122 Jose Valentin .30 .14
❑ 123 Paul Konerko .30 .14
❑ 124 Carlos Lee .30 .14
❑ 125 Jon Garland .30 .14
❑ 126 Jason Giambi .30 .14
❑ 127 Derek Jeter 1.50 .70
❑ 128 Roger Clemens 1.50 .70
❑ 129 Andy Pettitte .50 .23
❑ 130 Jorge Posada .50 .23
❑ 131 David Wells .30 .14
❑ 132 Hideki Matsui 1.50 .70
❑ 133 Mike Mussina .50 .23
❑ 134 Jeff Bagwell .50 .23
❑ 135 Craig Biggio .50 .23
❑ 136 Morgan Ensberg .30 .14
❑ 137 Richard Hidalgo .30 .14
❑ 138 Brad Ausmus .30 .14
❑ 139 Roy Oswalt .30 .14
❑ 140 Billy Wagner .30 .14
❑ 141 Octavio Dotel .30 .14
❑ 142 Gary Sheffield .30 .14
❑ 143 Andruw Jones .50 .23
❑ 144 John Smoltz .50 .23
❑ 145 Rafael Furcal .30 .14
❑ 146 Javy Lopez .30 .14
❑ 147 Shane Reynolds .30 .14
❑ 148 Horacio Ramirez .30 .14
❑ 149 Mike Hampton .30 .14
❑ 150 Jung Bong .30 .14
❑ 151 Ruben Quevedo .30 .14
❑ 152 Ben Sheets .30 .14
❑ 153 Geoff Jenkins .30 .14
❑ 154 Royce Clayton .30 .14
❑ 155 Glendon Rusch .30 .14
❑ 156 John Vander Wal .30 .14
❑ 157 Scott Podsednik .30 .14
❑ 158 Jim Edmonds .50 .23
❑ 159 Tino Martinez .50 .23
❑ 160 Albert Pujols 1.50 .70
❑ 161 Matt Morris .30 .14
❑ 162 Woody Williams .30 .14
❑ 163 Edgar Renteria .30 .14
❑ 164 Jason Isringhausen .30 .14
❑ 165 Jason Simontacchi .30 .14
❑ 166 Kerry Robinson .30 .14
❑ 167 Sammy Sosa .75 .35
❑ 168 Joe Borowski .30 .14
❑ 169 Tony Womack .30 .14
❑ 170 Antonio Alfonseca .30 .14
❑ 171 Corey Patterson .30 .14
❑ 172 Mark Prior .50 .23
❑ 173 Moises Alou .30 .14
❑ 174 Matt Clement .30 .14
❑ 175 Randall Simon .30 .14
❑ 176 Randy Johnson .75 .35
❑ 177 Luis Gonzalez .30 .14
❑ 178 Craig Counsell .30 .14
❑ 179 Miguel Batista .30 .14
❑ 180 Steve Finley .30 .14
❑ 181 Brandon Webb .30 .14
❑ 182 Danny Bautista .30 .14
❑ 183 Oscar Villarreal .30 .14
❑ 184 Shawn Green .30 .14
❑ 185 Brian Jordan .30 .14
❑ 186 Fred McGriff .50 .23
❑ 187 Andy Ashby .30 .14
❑ 188 Rickey Henderson .75 .35
❑ 189 Dave Roberts .30 .14
❑ 190 Eric Gagne .30 .14
❑ 191 Kazuhisa Ishii .30 .14
❑ 192 Adrian Beltre .30 .14
❑ 193 Vladimir Guerrero .75 .35
❑ 194 Livan Hernandez .30 .14
❑ 195 Ron Calloway .30 .14
❑ 196 Sun Woo Kim .30 .14
❑ 197 Wil Cordero .30 .14
❑ 198 Brad Wilkerson .30 .14
❑ 199 Orlando Cabrera .30 .14
❑ 200 Barry Bonds 2.00 .90
❑ 201 Ray Durham .30 .14
❑ 202 Andres Galarraga .30 .14
❑ 203 Benito Santiago .30 .14
❑ 204 Jose Cruz Jr. .30 .14
❑ 205 Jason Schmidt .30 .14
❑ 206 Kirk Rueter .30 .14
❑ 207 Felix Rodriguez .30 .14
❑ 208 Mike Lowell .30 .14
❑ 209 Luis Castillo .30 .14
❑ 210 Derrek Lee .50 .23
❑ 211 Andy Fox .30 .14
❑ 212 Tommy Phelps .30 .14
❑ 213 Todd Hollandsworth .30 .14
❑ 214 Brad Penny .30 .14
❑ 215 Juan Pierre .30 .14
❑ 216 Mike Piazza 1.25 .55
❑ 217 Jae Weong Seo .30 .14
❑ 218 Ty Wigginton .30 .14
❑ 219 Al Leiter .30 .14
❑ 220 Roger Cedeno .30 .14
❑ 221 Timo Perez .30 .14
❑ 222 Aaron Heilman .30 .14
❑ 223 Pedro Astacio .30 .14
❑ 224 Joe McEwing .30 .14
❑ 225 Ryan Klesko .30 .14
❑ 226 Brian Giles .30 .14
❑ 227 Mark Kotsay .30 .14
❑ 228 Brian Lawrence .30 .14
❑ 229 Rod Beck .30 .14
❑ 230 Trevor Hoffman .30 .14
❑ 231 Sean Burroughs .30 .14
❑ 232 Bob Abreu .30 .14
❑ 233 Jim Thome .50 .23
❑ 234 David Bell .30 .14
❑ 235 Jimmy Rollins .30 .14
❑ 236 Mike Lieberthal .30 .14
❑ 237 Vicente Padilla .30 .14
❑ 238 Randy Wolf .30 .14
❑ 239 Reggie Sanders .30 .14
❑ 240 Jason Kendall .30 .14
❑ 241 Jack Wilson .30 .14
❑ 242 Jose Hernandez .30 .14
❑ 243 Kip Wells .30 .14
❑ 244 Carlos Rivera .30 .14
❑ 245 Craig Wilson .30 .14
❑ 246 Adam Dunn .30 .14
❑ 247 Sean Casey .50 .23
❑ 248 Danny Graves .30 .14
❑ 249 Ryan Dempster .30 .14
❑ 250 Barry Larkin .50 .23
❑ 251 Reggie Taylor .30 .14
❑ 252 Wily Mo Pena .30 .14
❑ 253 Larry Walker .30 .14
❑ 254 Mark Sweeney .30 .14
❑ 255 Preston Wilson .30 .14
❑ 256 Jason Jennings .30 .14
❑ 257 Charles Johnson .30 .14
❑ 258 Jay Payton .30 .14
❑ 259 Chris Stynes .30 .14
❑ 260 Juan Uribe .30 .14

❑	261	Hideki Matsui SH CL	.75	.35
❑	262	Barry Bonds SH CL	1.00	.45
❑	263	Dontrelle Willis SH CL	.30	.14
❑	264	Kevin Millwood SH CL	.30	.14
❑	265	Billy Wagner SH CL	.30	.14
❑	266	Rocco Baldelli SH CL	.30	.14
❑	267	Roger Clemens SH CL	.75	.35
❑	268	Rafael Palmeiro SH CL	.30	.14
❑	269	Miguel Cabrera SH CL	.50	.23
❑	270	Jose Contreras SH CL	.30	.14
❑	271	Aaron Sele	.30	.14
❑	272	Bartolo Colon	.30	.14
❑	273	Darin Erstad	.30	.14
❑	274	Francisco Rodriguez	.30	.14
❑	275	Garret Anderson	.30	.14
❑	276	Jose Guillen	.30	.14
❑	277	Troy Percival	.30	.14
❑	278	Alex Cintron	.30	.14
❑	279	Casey Fossum	.30	.14
❑	280	Elmer Dessens	.30	.14
❑	281	Jose Valverde	.30	.14
❑	282	Matt Mantei	.30	.14
❑	283	Richie Sexson	.30	.14
❑	284	Roberto Alomar	.50	.23
❑	285	Shea Hillenbrand	.30	.14
❑	286	Chipper Jones	.75	.35
❑	287	Greg Maddux	1.25	.55
❑	288	J.D. Drew	.30	.14
❑	289	Marcus Giles	.30	.14
❑	290	Mike Hessman	.30	.14
❑	291	John Thomson	.30	.14
❑	292	Russ Ortiz	.30	.14
❑	293	Adam Loewen	.30	.14
❑	294	Jack Cust	.30	.14
❑	295	Jerry Hairston Jr.	.30	.14
❑	296	Kurt Ainsworth	.30	.14
❑	297	Luis Matos	.30	.14
❑	298	Marty Cordova	.30	.14
❑	299	Sidney Ponson	.30	.14
❑	300	Bill Mueller	.30	.14
❑	301	Curt Schilling	.30	.14
❑	302	David Ortiz	.75	.35
❑	303	Johnny Damon	.50	.23
❑	304	Keith Foulke Sox	.30	.14
❑	305	Pokey Reese	.30	.14
❑	306	Scott Williamson	.30	.14
❑	307	Tim Wakefield	.30	.14
❑	308	Alex S. Gonzalez	.30	.14
❑	309	Aramis Ramirez	.30	.14
❑	310	Carlos Zambrano	.30	.14
❑	311	Juan Cruz	.30	.14
❑	312	Kerry Wood	.30	.14
❑	313	Kyle Farnsworth	.30	.14
❑	314	Aaron Rowand	.30	.14
❑	315	Esteban Loaiza	.30	.14
❑	316	Frank Thomas	.75	.35
❑	317	Joe Borchard	.30	.14
❑	318	Joe Crede	.30	.14
❑	319	Miguel Olivo	.30	.14
❑	320	Willie Harris	.30	.14
❑	321	Aaron Harang	.30	.14
❑	322	Austin Kearns	.30	.14
❑	323	Brandon Claussen	.30	.14
❑	324	Brandon Larson	.30	.14
❑	325	Ryan Freel	.30	.14
❑	326	Ken Griffey Jr.	1.25	.55
❑	327	Ryan Wagner	.30	.14
❑	328	Alex Escobar	.30	.14
❑	329	Coco Crisp	.30	.14
❑	330	David Riske	.30	.14
❑	331	Jody Gerut	.30	.14
❑	332	Josh Bard	.30	.14
❑	333	Travis Hafner	.30	.14
❑	334	Chin-Hui Tsao	.30	.14
❑	335	Denny Stark	.30	.14
❑	336	Jeromy Burnitz	.30	.14
❑	337	Shawn Chacon	.30	.14
❑	338	Todd Helton	.50	.23
❑	339	Vinny Castilla	.30	.14
❑	340	Alex Sanchez	.30	.14
❑	341	Carlos Pena	.30	.14
❑	342	Fernando Vina	.30	.14
❑	343	Jason Johnson	.30	.14
❑	344	Matt Anderson	.30	.14
❑	345	Mike Maroth	.30	.14
❑	346	Rondell White	.30	.14
❑	347	A.J. Burnett	.30	.14
❑	348	Alex Gonzalez	.30	.14
❑	349	Armando Benitez	.30	.14
❑	350	Carl Pavano	.30	.14
❑	351	Hee Seop Choi	.30	.14
❑	352	Ivan Rodriguez	.50	.23
❑	353	Josh Beckett	.30	.14
❑	354	Josh Willingham	.30	.14
❑	355	Adam Everett	.30	.14
❑	356	Brandon Duckworth	.30	.14
❑	357	Jason Lane	.30	.14
❑	358	Jeff Kent	.30	.14
❑	359	Jeriome Robertson	.30	.14
❑	360	Lance Berkman	.30	.14
❑	361	Wade Miller	.30	.14
❑	362	Aaron Guiel	.30	.14
❑	363	Angel Berroa	.30	.14
❑	364	Carlos Beltran	.30	.14
❑	365	David DeJesus	.30	.14
❑	366	Desi Relaford	.30	.14
❑	367	Joe Randa	.30	.14
❑	368	Runelvys Hernandez	.30	.14
❑	369	Edwin Jackson	.30	.14
❑	370	Hideo Nomo	.75	.35
❑	371	Jeff Weaver	.30	.14
❑	372	Juan Encarnacion	.30	.14
❑	373	Odalis Perez	.30	.14
❑	374	Paul Lo Duca	.30	.14
❑	375	Robin Ventura	.30	.14
❑	376	Bill Hall	.30	.14
❑	377	Chad Moeller	.30	.14
❑	378	Chris Capuano	.30	.14
❑	379	Junior Spivey	.30	.14
❑	380	Rickie Weeks	.50	.23
❑	381	Wes Helms	.30	.14
❑	382	Brad Radke	.30	.14
❑	383	Jacque Jones	.30	.14
❑	384	Joe Mays	.30	.14
❑	385	Joe Nathan	.30	.14
❑	386	Johan Santana	.50	.23
❑	387	Nick Punto	.30	.14
❑	388	Shannon Stewart	.30	.14
❑	389	Carl Everett	.30	.14
❑	390	Claudio Vargas	.30	.14
❑	391	Jose Vidro	.30	.14
❑	392	Nick Johnson	.30	.14
❑	393	Rocky Biddle	.30	.14
❑	394	Tony Armas Jr.	.30	.14
❑	395	Braden Looper	.30	.14
❑	396	Cliff Floyd	.30	.14
❑	397	Jason Phillips	.30	.14
❑	398	Mike Cameron	.30	.14
❑	399	Tom Glavine	.50	.23
❑	400	Kenny Lofton	.30	.14
❑	401	Alfonso Soriano	.30	.14
❑	402	Bernie Williams	.50	.23
❑	403	Javier Vazquez	.30	.14
❑	404	Jon Lieber	.30	.14
❑	405	Jose Contreras	.30	.14
❑	406	Kevin Brown	.30	.14
❑	407	Mariano Rivera	.50	.23
❑	408	Arthur Rhodes	.30	.14
❑	409	Eric Byrnes	.30	.14
❑	410	Erubiel Durazo	.30	.14
❑	411	Graham Koonce	.30	.14
❑	412	Marco Scutaro	.30	.14
❑	413	Mark Mulder	.30	.14
❑	414	Mark Redman	.30	.14
❑	415	Rich Harden	.30	.14
❑	416	Brett Myers	.30	.14
❑	417	Chase Utley	.50	.23
❑	418	Kevin Millwood	.30	.14
❑	419	Marlon Byrd	.30	.14
❑	420	Pat Burrell	.30	.14
❑	421	Placido Polanco	.30	.14
❑	422	Tim Worrell	.30	.14
❑	423	Jason Bay	.30	.14
❑	424	Josh Fogg	.30	.14
❑	425	Kris Benson	.30	.14
❑	426	Mike Gonzalez	.30	.14
❑	427	Oliver Perez	.30	.14
❑	428	Tike Redman	.30	.14
❑	429	Adam Eaton	.30	.14
❑	430	Ismael Valdes	.30	.14
❑	431	Jake Peavy	.30	.14
❑	432	Khalil Greene	.75	.35
❑	433	Mark Loretta	.30	.14
❑	434	Phil Nevin	.30	.14
❑	435	Ramon Hernandez	.30	.14
❑	436	A.J. Pierzynski	.30	.14
❑	437	Edgardo Alfonzo	.30	.14
❑	438	J.T. Snow	.30	.14
❑	439	Jerome Williams	.30	.14
❑	440	Marquis Grissom	.30	.14
❑	441	Robb Nen	.30	.14
❑	442	Bret Boone	.30	.14
❑	443	Freddy Garcia	.30	.14
❑	444	Gil Meche	.30	.14
❑	445	John Olerud	.30	.14
❑	446	Rich Aurilia	.30	.14
❑	447	Shigetoshi Hasegawa	.30	.14
❑	448	Bo Hart	.30	.14
❑	449	Danny Haren	.30	.14
❑	450	Jason Marquis	.30	.14
❑	451	Marlon Anderson	.30	.14
❑	452	Scott Rolen	.50	.23
❑	453	So Taguchi	.30	.14
❑	454	Carl Crawford	.30	.14
❑	455	Delmon Young	.50	.23
❑	456	Geoff Blum	.30	.14
❑	457	Jesus Colome	.30	.14
❑	458	Jonny Gomes	.30	.14
❑	459	Lance Carter	.30	.14
❑	460	Robert Fick	.30	.14
❑	461	Chan Ho Park	.30	.14
❑	462	Francisco Cordero	.30	.14
❑	463	Jeff Nelson	.30	.14
❑	464	Jeff Zimmerman	.30	.14
❑	465	Kenny Rogers	.30	.14
❑	466	Aquilino Lopez	.30	.14
❑	467	Carlos Delgado	.30	.14
❑	468	Frank Catalanotto	.30	.14
❑	469	Reed Johnson	.30	.14
❑	470	Pat Hentgen	.30	.14
❑	471	Curt Schilling SH CL	.30	.14
❑	472	Gary Sheffield SH CL	.30	.14
❑	473	Javier Vazquez SH CL	.30	.14
❑	474	Kazuo Matsui SH CL	.50	.23
❑	475	Kevin Brown SH CL	.30	.14
❑	476	Rafael Palmeiro SH CL	.30	.14
❑	477	Richie Sexson SH CL	.30	.14
❑	478	Roger Clemens SH CL	.75	.35
❑	479	Vladimir Guerrero SH CL	.50	.23
❑	480	Alex Rodriguez SH CL	.75	.35
❑	481	Jake Woods SR RC	1.00	.45
❑	482	Tim Bittner SR RC	1.00	.45
❑	483	Brandon Medders SR RC	1.00	.45
❑	484	Casey Daigle SR RC	1.00	.45
❑	485	Jerry Gil SR RC	1.00	.45
❑	486	Mike Gosling SR RC	1.00	.45
❑	487	Jose Capellan SR RC	1.50	.70
❑	488	Onil Joseph SR RC	1.00	.45
❑	489	Roman Colon SR RC	1.00	.45
❑	490	Dave Crouthers SR RC	1.00	.45
❑	491	Eddy Rodriguez SR RC	1.50	.70
❑	492	Franklyn Gracesqui SR RC	1.00	.45
❑	493	Jamie Brown SR RC	1.00	.45
❑	494	Jerome Gamble SR RC	1.00	.45
❑	495	Tim Hamulack SR RC	1.00	.45
❑	496	Carlos Vasquez SR RC	1.50	.70
❑	497	Renyel Pinto SR RC	1.50	.70
❑	498	Ronny Cedeno SR RC	1.50	.70
❑	499	Enemencio Pacheco SR RC	1.00	.45
❑	500	Ryan Meaux SR RC	1.00	.45
❑	501	Ryan Wing SR RC	1.00	.45
❑	502	Shingo Takatsu SR RC	1.50	.70
❑	503	William Bergolla SR RC	1.00	.45
❑	504	Ivan Ochoa SR RC	1.00	.45
❑	505	Mariano Gomez SR RC	1.00	.45
❑	506	Justin Hampson SR RC	1.00	.45
❑	507	Justin Huisman SR RC	1.00	.45
❑	508	Scott Dohmann SR RC	1.00	.45
❑	509	Donnie Kelly SR RC	1.00	.45
❑	510	Chris Aguila SR RC	1.00	.45
❑	511	Lincoln Holdzkom SR RC	1.00	.45
❑	512	Freddy Guzman SR RC	1.00	.45
❑	513	Hector Gimenez SR RC	1.00	.45
❑	514	Jorge Vasquez SR RC	1.00	.45
❑	515	Jason Frasor SR RC	1.00	.45
❑	516	Chris Saenz SR RC	1.00	.45
❑	517	Dennis Sarfate SR RC	1.00	.45
❑	518	Colby Miller SR RC	1.00	.45

❑ 519 Jason Bartlett SR RC ...... 1.50 .70
❑ 520 Chad Bentz SR RC.......... 1.00 .45
❑ 521 Josh Labandeira SR RC.. 1.00 .45
❑ 522 Shawn Hill SR RC .... 1.00 .45
❑ 523 Kazuo Matsui SR RC ...... 1.50 .70
❑ 524 Carlos Hines SR RC ...... 1.00 .45
❑ 525 Mike Vento SR RC......... 1.50 .70
❑ 526 Scott Proctor SR RC ...... 1.50 .70
❑ 527 Sean Henn SR RC .... 1.00 .45
❑ 528 David Aardsma SR RC.... 1.50 .70
❑ 529 Ian Snell SR RC............. 2.00 .90
❑ 530 Mike Johnston SR RC .... 1.00 .45
❑ 531 Akinori Otsuka SR RC .... 1.00 .45
❑ 532 Rusty Tucker SR RC ...... 1.50 .70
❑ 533 Justin Knoedler SR RC .. 1.00 .45
❑ 534 Merkin Valdez SR RC .... 1.50 .70
❑ 535 Greg Dobbs SR RC .... 1.00 .45
❑ 536 Justin Leone SR RC ...... 1.50 .70
❑ 537 Shawn Camp SR RC ...... 1.00 .45
❑ 538 Edwin Moreno SR RC .... 1.00 .45
❑ 539 Angel Chavez SR RC...... 1.00 .45
❑ 540 Jesse Harper SR RC ...... 1.00 .45
❑ 541 Alex Rodriguez .... 1.25 .55
❑ 542 Roger Clemens .... 1.50 .70
❑ 543 Andy Pettitte .... .50 .23
❑ 544 Vladimir Guerrero .... .75 .35
❑ 545 David Wells.................... .30 .14
❑ 546 Derrek Lee...................... .50 .23
❑ 547 Carlos Beltran .... .30 .14
❑ 548 Orlando Cabrera Sox........ .30 .14
❑ 549 Paul Lo Duca.................. .30 .14
❑ 550 Dave Roberts.................. .30 .14
❑ 551 Guillermo Mota .... .30 .14
❑ 552 Steve Finley.................... .30 .14
❑ 553 Juan Encarnacion .... .30 .14
❑ 554 Larry Walker .... .30 .14
❑ 555 Ty Wigginton................... .30 .14
❑ 556 Doug Mientkiewicz .... .30 .14
❑ 557 Roberto Alomar .... .50 .23
❑ 558 B.J. Upton .... .50 .23
❑ 559 Brad Penny .... .30 .14
❑ 560 Hee Seop Choi .... .30 .14
❑ 561 David Wright 3.00 1.35
❑ 562 Nomar Garciaparra .... 1.25 .55
❑ 563 Felix Rodriguez .... .30 .14
❑ 564 Victor Zambrano .... .30 .14
❑ 565 Kris Benson..................... .30 .14
❑ 566 Aarom Baldiris SR RC ...... .50 .23
❑ 567 Joey Gathright SR RC .... 1.00 .45
❑ 568 Charles Thomas SR RC.... .50 .23
❑ 569 Brian Dallimore SR RC .... .50 .23
❑ 570 Chris Oxspring SR RC...... .50 .23
❑ 571 Chris Shelton SR RC...... 2.50 1.10
❑ 572 Dioner Navarro SR RC.... 1.50 .70
❑ 573 Edwardo Sierra SR RC...... .50 .23
❑ 574 Fernando Nieve SR RC .... .75 .35
❑ 575 Frank Francisco SR RC .... .50 .23
❑ 576 Jeff Bennett SR RC .... .50 .23
❑ 577 Justin Lehr SR RC............ .50 .23
❑ 578 John Gall SR RC .... .50 .23
❑ 579 Jorge Sequea SR RC .... .50 .23
❑ 580 Justin Germano SR RC .... .50 .23
❑ 581 Kazuhito Tadano SR RC .. .50 .23
❑ 582 Kevin Cave SR RC............ .50 .23
❑ 583 Jesse Crain SR RC .... .75 .35
❑ 584 Luis A. Gonzalez SR RC .. .50 .23
❑ 585 Michael Wuertz SR RC .... .50 .23
❑ 586 Orlando Rodriguez SR RC .50 .23
❑ 587 Phil Stockman SR RC ...... .50 .23
❑ 588 Ramon Ramirez SR RC .... .50 .23
❑ 589 Roberto Novoa SR RC...... .50 .23
❑ 590 Scott Kazmir SR RC........ 3.00 1.35
❑ NNO Update Set Exchange Card 10.00 4.50

2005 Upper Deck

	Nm-Mt	Ex-Mt
COMPLETE SERIES 1 (300)	50.00	15.00
COMMON CARD (1-500)..............	.30	.09
COMMON (211-250/426-450).....	1.00	.30
OVERALL PLATES SER.1 ODDS 1:1080 H		.00
PLATES PRINT RUN 1 #'d SET PER COLOR		.00
BLACK-CYAN-MAGENTA-YELLOW ISSUED		.00
NO PLATES PRICING DUE TO SCARCITY		.00

❑ 1 Casey Kotchman .... .30 .09

❑ 2 Chone Figgins..................... .30 .09
❑ 3 David Eckstein.................... .30 .09
❑ 4 Jarrod Washburn.................. .30 .09
❑ 5 Robb Quinlan .... .30 .09
❑ 6 Troy Glaus........................... .30 .09
❑ 7 Vladimir Guerrero .... .75 .23
❑ 8 Brandon Webb .... .30 .09
❑ 9 Danny Bautista .... .30 .09
❑ 10 Luis Gonzalez .... .30 .09
❑ 11 Matt Kata............................ .30 .09
❑ 12 Randy Johnson .... .75 .23
❑ 13 Robby Hammock................ .30 .09
❑ 14 Shea Hillenbrand................ .30 .09
❑ 15 Adam LaRoche .... .30 .09
❑ 16 Andruw Jones .... .50 .15
❑ 17 Horacio Ramirez .... .30 .09
❑ 18 John Smoltz .... .50 .15
❑ 19 Johnny Estrada .... .30 .09
❑ 20 Mike Hampton.................... .30 .09
❑ 21 Rafael Furcal .... .30 .09
❑ 22 Brian Roberts .... .30 .09
❑ 23 Javy Lopez .... .30 .09
❑ 24 Jay Gibbons .... .30 .09
❑ 25 Jorge Julio .... .30 .09
❑ 26 Melvin Mora .... .30 .09
❑ 27 Miguel Tejada .... .30 .09
❑ 28 Rafael Palmeiro .... .50 .15
❑ 29 Derek Lowe .... .30 .09
❑ 30 Jason Varitek...................... .75 .23
❑ 31 Kevin Youkilis...................... .30 .09
❑ 32 Manny Ramirez .... .50 .15
❑ 33 Curt Schilling .... .50 .15
❑ 34 Pedro Martinez .... .50 .15
❑ 35 Trot Nixon........................... .30 .09
❑ 36 Corey Patterson.................. .30 .09
❑ 37 Derrek Lee.......................... .50 .15
❑ 38 LaTroy Hawkins.................. .30 .09
❑ 39 Mark Prior........................... .50 .15
❑ 40 Matt Clement....................... .30 .09
❑ 41 Moises Alou .... .30 .09
❑ 42 Sammy Sosa .... .75 .23
❑ 43 Aaron Rowand.................... .30 .09
❑ 44 Carlos Lee.......................... .30 .09
❑ 45 Jose Valentin...................... .30 .09
❑ 46 Juan Uribe.......................... .30 .09
❑ 47 Magglio Ordonez................ .30 .09
❑ 48 Mark Buehrle...................... .30 .09
❑ 49 Paul Konerko...................... .30 .09
❑ 50 Adam Dunn .... .30 .09
❑ 51 Barry Larkin........................ .50 .15
❑ 52 D'Angelo Jimenez .... .30 .09
❑ 53 Danny Graves .... .30 .09
❑ 54 Paul Wilson........................ .30 .09
❑ 55 Sean Casey .... .50 .15
❑ 56 Wily Mo Pena .... .30 .09
❑ 57 Ben Broussard.................... .30 .09
❑ 58 C.C. Sabathia .... .30 .09
❑ 59 Casey Blake....................... .30 .09
❑ 60 Cliff Lee.............................. .30 .09
❑ 61 Matt Lawton .... .30 .09
❑ 62 Omar Vizquel...................... .30 .09
❑ 63 Victor Martinez .... .30 .09
❑ 64 Charles Johnson .... .30 .09
❑ 65 Joe Kennedy .... .30 .09
❑ 66 Jeromy Burnitz .... .30 .09
❑ 67 Matt Holliday...................... .30 .09
❑ 68 Preston Wilson .... .30 .09
❑ 69 Royce Clayton .... .30 .09
❑ 70 Shawn Estes .... .30 .09
❑ 71 Bobby Higginson .... .30 .09
❑ 72 Brandon Inge...................... .30 .09
❑ 73 Carlos Guillen .... .30 .09
❑ 74 Dmitri Young....................... .30 .09
❑ 75 Eric Munson .... .30 .09
❑ 76 Jeremy Bonderman .... .30 .09
❑ 77 Ugueth Urbina.................... .30 .09
❑ 78 Josh Beckett .... .30 .09
❑ 79 Dontrelle Willis .... .30 .09
❑ 80 Jeff Conine .... .30 .09
❑ 81 Juan Pierre .... .30 .09
❑ 82 Luis Castillo .... .30 .09
❑ 83 Miguel Cabrera .... .50 .15
❑ 84 Mike Lowell......................... .30 .09
❑ 85 Andy Pettitte .... .50 .15
❑ 86 Brad Lidge........................... .30 .09
❑ 87 Carlos Beltran .... .30 .09
❑ 88 Craig Biggio .... .50 .15
❑ 89 Jeff Bagwell......................... .50 .15
❑ 90 Roger Clemens .... 1.25 .35
❑ 91 Roy Oswalt .... .30 .09
❑ 92 Benito Santiago................... .30 .09
❑ 93 Jeremy Affeldt .... .30 .09
❑ 94 Juan Gonzalez.................... .30 .09
❑ 95 Ken Harvey .... .30 .09
❑ 96 Mike MacDougal.................. .30 .09
❑ 97 Mike Sweeney .... .30 .09
❑ 98 Zach Greinke....................... .30 .09
❑ 99 Adrian Beltre .... .30 .09
❑ 100 Alex Cora .... .30 .09
❑ 101 Cesar Izturis .... .30 .09
❑ 102 Eric Gagne......................... .30 .09
❑ 103 Kazuhisa Ishii .... .30 .09
❑ 104 Milton Bradley.................... .30 .09
❑ 105 Shawn Green..................... .30 .09
❑ 106 Danny Kolb .... .30 .09
❑ 107 Ben Sheets .... .30 .09
❑ 108 Brooks Kieschnick.............. .30 .09
❑ 109 Craig Counsell .... .30 .09
❑ 110 Geoff Jenkins .... .30 .09
❑ 111 Lyle Overbay .... .30 .09
❑ 112 Scott Podsednik .... .30 .09
❑ 113 Corey Koskie...................... .30 .09
❑ 114 Johan Santana................... .50 .15
❑ 115 Joe Mauer.......................... .30 .09
❑ 116 Justin Morneau .... .30 .09
❑ 117 Lew Ford............................ .30 .09
❑ 118 Matt LeCroy .... .30 .09
❑ 119 Torii Hunter........................ .30 .09
❑ 120 Brad Wilkerson .... .30 .09
❑ 121 Chad Cordero .... .30 .09
❑ 122 Livan Hernandez .... .30 .09
❑ 123 Jose Vidro.......................... .30 .09
❑ 124 Termel Sledge .... .30 .09
❑ 125 Tony Batista .... .30 .09
❑ 126 Zach Day............................ .30 .09
❑ 127 Al Leiter.............................. .30 .09
❑ 128 Jae Weong Seo .... .30 .09
❑ 129 Jose Reyes .... .30 .09
❑ 130 Kazuo Matsui .... .30 .09
❑ 131 Mike Piazza........................ .75 .23
❑ 132 Todd Zeile.......................... .30 .09
❑ 133 Cliff Floyd .... .30 .09
❑ 134 Alex Rodriguez .... 1.25 .35
❑ 135 Derek Jeter .... 1.50 .45
❑ 136 Gary Sheffield .... .30 .09
❑ 137 Hideki Matsui .... 1.50 .45
❑ 138 Jason Giambi .... .30 .09
❑ 139 Jorge Posada .... .50 .15
❑ 140 Mike Mussina .... .50 .15
❑ 141 Barry Zito .... .30 .09
❑ 142 Bobby Crosby .... .30 .09
❑ 143 Octavio Dotel...................... .30 .09
❑ 144 Eric Chavez .... .30 .09
❑ 145 Jermaine Dye .... .30 .09
❑ 146 Mark Kotsay .... .30 .09
❑ 147 Tim Hudson .... .30 .09
❑ 148 Billy Wagner .... .30 .09
❑ 149 Bobby Abreu .... .30 .09
❑ 150 David Bell .... .30 .09
❑ 151 Jim Thome .... .50 .15
❑ 152 Jimmy Rollins...................... .30 .09
❑ 153 Mike Lieberthal.................... .30 .09
❑ 154 Randy Wolf .... .30 .09
❑ 155 Craig Wilson........................ .30 .09

156	Daryle Ward	.30	.09
157	Jack Wilson	.30	.09
158	Jason Kendall	.30	.09
159	Kip Wells	.30	.09
160	Oliver Perez	.30	.09
161	Rob Mackowiak	.30	.09
162	Brian Giles	.30	.09
163	Brian Lawrence	.30	.09
164	David Wells	.30	.09
165	Jay Payton	.30	.09
166	Ryan Klesko	.30	.09
167	Sean Burroughs	.30	.09
168	Trevor Hoffman	.30	.09
169	Brett Tomko	.30	.09
170	J.T. Snow	.30	.09
171	Jason Schmidt	.30	.09
172	Kirk Rueter	.30	.09
173	A.J. Pierzynski	.30	.09
174	Pedro Feliz	.30	.09
175	Ray Durham	.30	.09
176	Eddie Guardado	.30	.09
177	Edgar Martinez	.50	.15
178	Ichiro Suzuki	1.50	.45
179	Jamie Moyer	.30	.09
180	Joel Pineiro	.30	.09
181	Randy Winn	.30	.09
182	Raul Ibanez	.30	.09
183	Albert Pujols	1.50	.45
184	Edgar Renteria	.30	.09
185	Jason Isringhausen	.30	.09
186	Jim Edmonds	.50	.15
187	Matt Morris	.30	.09
188	Reggie Sanders	.30	.09
189	Tony Womack	.30	.09
190	Aubrey Huff	.30	.09
191	Danys Baez	.30	.09
192	Carl Crawford	.30	.09
193	Jose Cruz Jr.	.30	.09
194	Rocco Baldelli	.30	.09
195	Tino Martinez	.50	.15
196	Dewon Brazelton	.30	.09
197	Alfonso Soriano	.30	.09
198	Brad Fullmer	.30	.09
199	Gerald Laird	.30	.09
200	Hank Blalock	.30	.09
201	Laynce Nix	.30	.09
202	Mark Teixeira	.50	.15
203	Michael Young	.30	.09
204	Alexis Rios	.30	.09
205	Eric Hinske	.30	.09
206	Miguel Batista	.30	.09
207	Orlando Hudson	.30	.09
208	Roy Halladay	.30	.09
209	Ted Lilly	.30	.09
210	Vernon Wells	.30	.09
211	Aarom Baldiris SR	1.00	.30
212	B.J. Upton SR	1.00	.30
213	Dallas McPherson SR	1.00	.30
214	Brian Dallimore SR	1.00	.30
215	Chris Oxspring SR	1.00	.30
216	Chris Shelton SR	1.00	.30
217	David Wright SR	2.00	.60
218	Edwardo Sierra SR	1.00	.30
219	Fernando Nieve SR	1.00	.30
220	Frank Francisco SR	1.00	.30
221	Jeff Bennett SR	1.00	.30
222	Justin Lehr SR	1.00	.30
223	John Gall SR	1.00	.30
224	Jorge Sequea SR	1.00	.30
225	Justin Germano SR	1.00	.30
226	Kazuhito Tadano SR	1.00	.30
227	Kevin Cave SR	1.00	.30
228	Joe Blanton SR	1.00	.30
229	Luis A. Gonzalez SR	1.00	.30
230	Michael Wuertz SR	1.00	.30
231	Mike Rouse SR	1.00	.30
232	Nick Regilio SR	1.00	.30
233	Orlando Rodriguez SR	1.00	.30
234	Phil Stockman SR	1.00	.30
235	Ramon Ramirez SR	1.00	.30
236	Roberto Novoa SR	1.00	.30
237	Dioner Navarro SR	1.00	.30
238	Tim Bausher SR	1.00	.30
239	Logan Kensing SR	1.00	.30
240	Andy Green SR	1.00	.30
241	Brad Halsey SR	1.00	.30
242	Charles Thomas SR	1.00	.30
243	George Sherrill SR	1.00	.30
244	Jesse Crain SR	1.00	.30
245	Jimmy Serrano SR	1.00	.30
246	Joe Horgan SR	1.00	.30
247	Chris Young SR	1.00	.30
248	Joey Gathright SR	1.00	.30
249	Gavin Floyd SR	1.00	.30
250	Ryan Howard SR	1.00	.30
251	Lance Cormier SR	1.00	.30
252	Matt Treanor SR	1.00	.30
253	Jeff Francis SR	1.00	.30
254	Nick Swisher SR	1.00	.30
255	Scott Atchison SR	1.00	.30
256	Travis Blackley SR	1.00	.30
257	Travis Smith SR	1.00	.30
258	Yadier Molina SR	1.00	.30
259	Jeff Keppinger SR	1.00	.30
260	Scott Kazmir SR	1.00	.30
261	Garret Anderson Vladimir Guerrero TL	.50	.15
262	Luis Gonzalez Randy Johnson TL	.50	.15
263	Andruw Jones Chipper Jones TL	.50	.15
264	Miguel Tejada Rafael Palmeiro TL	.30	.09
265	Curt Schilling Manny Ramirez TL	.50	.15
266	Mark Prior Sammy Sosa TL	.50	.15
267	Frank Thomas Magglio Ordonez TL	.50	.15
268	Barry Larkin Ken Griffey Jr. TL	.75	.23
269	C.C. Sabathia Victor Martinez TL	.30	.09
270	Jeromy Burnitz Todd Helton TL	.30	.09
271	Dmitri Young Ivan Rodriguez TL	.30	.09
272	Josh Beckett Miguel Cabrera TL	.30	.09
273	Jeff Bagwell Roger Clemens TL	.75	.23
274	Ken Harvey Mike Sweeney TL	.30	.09
275	Adrian Beltre Eric Gagne TL	.30	.09
276	Ben Sheets Geoff Jenkins TL	.30	.09
277	Joe Mauer Torii Hunter TL	.30	.09
278	Jose Vidro Livan Hernandez TL	.30	.09
279	Kazuo Matsui Mike Piazza TL	.50	.15
280	Alex Rodriguez Derek Jeter TL	1.50	.45
281	Eric Chavez Tim Hudson TL	.30	.09
282	Bobby Abreu Jim Thome TL	.30	.09
283	Craig Wilson Jason Kendall TL	.30	.09
284	Brian Giles Phil Nevin TL	.30	.09
285	A.J. Pierzynski Jason Schmidt TL	.30	.09
286	Bret Boone Ichiro Suzuki TL	.75	.23
287	Albert Pujols Scott Rolen TL	.75	.23
288	Aubrey Huff Tino Martinez TL	.30	.09
289	Hank Blalock Mark Teixeira TL	.30	.09
290	Carlos Delgado Roy Halladay TL	.30	.09
291	Vladimir Guerrero PR	.50	.15
292	Curt Schilling PR	.30	.09
293	Mark Prior PR	.50	.15
294	Josh Beckett PR	.30	.09
295	Roger Clemens PR	.75	.23
296	Derek Jeter PR	.75	.23
297	Eric Chavez PR	.30	.09
298	Jim Thome PR	.30	.09
299	Albert Pujols PR	.75	.23
300	Hank Blalock PR	.30	.09
301	Bartolo Colon	.30	.09
302	Darin Erstad	.30	.09
303	Garret Anderson	.30	.09
304	Orlando Cabrera	.30	.09
305	Steve Finley	.30	.09
306	Javier Vazquez	.30	.09
307	Russ Ortiz	.30	.09
308	Chipper Jones	.75	.23
309	Marcus Giles	.30	.09
310	Raul Mondesi	.30	.09
311	B.J. Ryan	.30	.09
312	Luis Matos	.30	.09
313	Sidney Ponson	.30	.09
314	Bill Mueller	.30	.09
315	David Ortiz	.75	.23
316	Johnny Damon	.50	.15
317	Keith Foulke	.30	.09
318	Mark Bellhorn	.50	.15
319	Wade Miller	.30	.09
320	Aramis Ramirez	.30	.09
321	Carlos Zambrano	.30	.09
322	Greg Maddux	1.25	.35
323	Kerry Wood	.30	.09
324	Nomar Garciaparra	.75	.23
325	Todd Walker	.30	.09
326	Frank Thomas	.75	.23
327	Freddy Garcia	.30	.09
328	Joe Crede	.30	.09
329	Jose Contreras	.30	.09
330	Orlando Hernandez	.30	.09
331	Shingo Takatsu	.30	.09
332	Austin Kearns	.30	.09
333	Eric Milton	.30	.09
334	Ken Griffey Jr.	1.25	.35
335	Aaron Boone	.30	.09
336	David Riske	.30	.09
337	Jake Westbrook	.30	.09
338	Kevin Millwood	.30	.09
339	Travis Hafner	.30	.09
340	Aaron Miles	.30	.09
341	Jeff Baker	.30	.09
342	Todd Helton	.50	.15
343	Garrett Atkins	.30	.09
344	Carlos Pena	.30	.09
345	Ivan Rodriguez	.50	.15
346	Rondell White	.30	.09
347	Troy Percival	.30	.09
348	A.J. Burnett	.30	.09
349	Carlos Delgado	.30	.09
350	Guillermo Mota	.30	.09
351	Paul Lo Duca	.30	.09
352	Jason Lane	.30	.09
353	Lance Berkman	.30	.09
354	Angel Berroa	.30	.09
355	David DeJesus	.30	.09
356	Ruben Gotay	.30	.09
357	Jose Lima	.30	.09
358	Brad Penny	.30	.09
359	J.D. Drew	.30	.09
360	Jayson Werth	.30	.09
361	Jeff Kent	.30	.09
362	Odalis Perez	.30	.09
363	Brady Clark	.30	.09
364	Junior Spivey	.30	.09
365	Rickie Weeks	.30	.09
366	Jacque Jones	.30	.09
367	Joe Nathan	.30	.09
368	Nick Punto	.30	.09
369	Shannon Stewart	.30	.09
370	Doug Mientkiewicz	.30	.09
371	Kris Benson	.30	.09
372	Tom Glavine	.50	.15
373	Victor Zambrano	.30	.09
374	Bernie Williams	.50	.15
375	Carl Pavano	.30	.09
376	Jaret Wright	.30	.09
377	Kevin Brown	.30	.09
378	Mariano Rivera	.50	.15
379	Danny Haren	.30	.09
380	Eric Byrnes	.30	.09
381	Erubiel Durazo	.30	.09
382	Rich Harden	.30	.09
383	Brett Myers	.30	.09

Card	Nm-Mt	Ex-Mt
❑ 384 Chase Utley	.30	.09
❑ 385 Marlon Byrd	.30	.09
❑ 386 Pat Burrell	.30	.09
❑ 387 Placido Polanco	.30	.09
❑ 388 Freddy Sanchez	.30	.09
❑ 389 Jason Bay	.30	.09
❑ 390 Josh Fogg	.30	.09
❑ 391 Adam Eaton	.30	.09
❑ 392 Jake Peavy	.30	.09
❑ 393 Khalil Greene	.50	.15
❑ 394 Mark Loretta	.30	.09
❑ 395 Phil Nevin	.30	.09
❑ 396 Ramon Hernandez	.30	.09
❑ 397 Woody Williams	.30	.09
❑ 398 Armando Benitez	.30	.09
❑ 399 Edgardo Alfonzo	.30	.09
❑ 400 Marquis Grissom	.30	.09
❑ 401 Mike Matheny	.30	.09
❑ 402 Richie Sexson	.30	.09
❑ 403 Bret Boone	.30	.09
❑ 404 Gil Meche	.30	.09
❑ 405 Chris Carpenter	.30	.09
❑ 406 Jeff Suppan	.30	.09
❑ 407 Larry Walker	.50	.15
❑ 408 Mark Grudzielanek	.30	.09
❑ 409 Mark Mulder	.30	.09
❑ 410 Scott Rolen	.50	.15
❑ 411 Josh Phelps	.30	.09
❑ 412 Jonny Gomes	.30	.09
❑ 413 Francisco Cordero	.30	.09
❑ 414 Kenny Rogers	.30	.09
❑ 415 Richard Hidalgo	.30	.09
❑ 416 Dave Bush	.30	.09
❑ 417 Frank Catalanotto	.30	.09
❑ 418 Gabe Gross	.30	.09
❑ 419 Guillermo Quiroz	.30	.09
❑ 420 Reed Johnson	.30	.09
❑ 421 Cristian Guzman	.30	.09
❑ 422 Esteban Loaiza	.30	.09
❑ 423 Jose Guillen	.30	.09
❑ 424 Nick Johnson	.30	.09
❑ 425 Vinny Castilla	.30	.09
❑ 426 Pete Orr SR RC	1.00	.30
❑ 427 Tadahito Iguchi SR RC	2.50	.75
❑ 428 Jeff Baker SR	1.00	.30
❑ 429 Marcos Carvajal SR RC	1.00	.30
❑ 430 Justin Verlander SR RC	2.50	.75
❑ 431 Luke Scott SR RC	1.50	.45
❑ 432 Willy Taveras SR	1.00	.30
❑ 433 Ambiorix Burgos SR RC	1.50	.45
❑ 434 Andy Sisco SR	1.00	.30
❑ 435 Denny Bautista SR	1.00	.30
❑ 436 Mark Teahen SR	1.00	.30
❑ 437 Ervin Santana SR	1.00	.30
❑ 438 Dennis Houlton SR RC	1.00	.30
❑ 439 Philip Humber SR RC	1.50	.45
❑ 440 Steve Schmoll SR RC	1.00	.30
❑ 441 J.J. Hardy SR	1.00	.30
❑ 442 Ambiorix Concepcion SR RC	1.50	.45
❑ 443 Dae-Sung Koo SR RC	1.00	.30
❑ 444 Andy Phillips SR	1.00	.30
❑ 445 Dan Meyer SR	1.00	.30
❑ 446 Huston Street SR	1.50	.45
❑ 447 Keiichi Yabu SR RC	1.00	.30
❑ 448 Jeff Niemann SR RC	1.50	.45
❑ 449 Jeremy Reed SR	1.00	.30
❑ 450 Tony Blanco SR	1.00	.30
❑ 451 Albert Pujols BG	.75	.23
❑ 452 Alex Rodriguez BG	.75	.23
❑ 453 Curt Schilling BG	.30	.09
❑ 454 Derek Jeter BG	.75	.23
❑ 455 Greg Maddux BG	.75	.23
❑ 456 Ichiro Suzuki BG	.75	.23
❑ 457 Ivan Rodriguez BG	.30	.09
❑ 458 Jeff Bagwell BG	.30	.09
❑ 459 Jim Thome BG	.30	.09
❑ 460 Ken Griffey Jr. BG	.75	.23
❑ 461 Manny Ramirez BG	.50	.15
❑ 462 Mike Mussina BG	.30	.09
❑ 463 Mike Piazza BG	.50	.15
❑ 464 Pedro Martinez BG	.30	.09
❑ 465 Rafael Palmeiro BG	.30	.09
❑ 466 Randy Johnson BG	.50	.15
❑ 467 Roger Clemens BG	.75	.23
❑ 468 Sammy Sosa BG	.50	.15
❑ 469 Todd Helton BG	.30	.09
❑ 470 Vladimir Guerrero BG	.50	.15
❑ 471 Vladimir Guerrero TC	.50	.15
❑ 472 Shawn Green TC	.30	.09
❑ 473 John Smoltz TC	.30	.09
❑ 474 Miguel Tejada TC	.30	.09
❑ 475 Curt Schilling TC	.30	.09
❑ 476 Mark Prior TC	.30	.09
❑ 477 Frank Thomas TC	.50	.15
❑ 478 Ken Griffey Jr. TC	.75	.23
❑ 479 C.C. Sabathia TC	.30	.09
❑ 480 Todd Helton TC	.30	.09
❑ 481 Ivan Rodriguez TC	.30	.09
❑ 482 Miguel Cabrera TC	.30	.09
❑ 483 Roger Clemens TC	.75	.23
❑ 484 Mike Sweeney TC	.30	.09
❑ 485 Eric Gagne TC	.30	.09
❑ 486 Ben Sheets TC	.30	.09
❑ 487 Johan Santana TC	.30	.09
❑ 488 Mike Piazza TC	.50	.15
❑ 489 Derek Jeter TC	.75	.23
❑ 490 Eric Chavez TC	.30	.09
❑ 491 Jim Thome TC	.30	.09
❑ 492 Craig Wilson TC	.30	.09
❑ 493 Jake Peavy TC	.30	.09
❑ 494 Jason Schmidt TC	.30	.09
❑ 495 Ichiro Suzuki TC	.75	.23
❑ 496 Albert Pujols TC	.75	.23
❑ 497 Carl Crawford TC	.30	.09
❑ 498 Mark Teixeira TC	.30	.09
❑ 499 Vernon Wells TC	.30	.09
❑ 500 Jose Vidro TC	.30	.09

2005 Upper Deck Baseball Heroes

	Nm-Mt	Ex-Mt
COMP.SET w/o SP's (100)	200.00	60.00
B.FELLER (1-5)	4.00	1.20
B.ROBINSON (6-10)	4.00	1.20
C.RIPKEN (11-15)	10.00	3.00
C.YASTRZEMSKI (16-20)	5.00	1.50
D.MATTINGLY (21-25)	8.00	2.40
T.SEAVER (26-30)	4.00	1.20
H.KILLEBREW (31-35)	5.00	1.50
J.PALMER (36-40)	4.00	1.20
M.SCHMIDT (41-45)	8.00	2.40
O.SMITH (46-50)	5.00	1.50
P.MOLITOR (51-55)	4.00	1.20
A.KALINE (56-60)	5.00	1.50
R.YOUNT (61-65)	5.00	1.50
R.SANDBERG (66-70)	8.00	2.40
S.MUSIAL (71-75)	5.00	1.50
S.CARLTON (76-80)	4.00	1.20
T.GWYNN (81-85)	5.00	1.50
W.BOGGS (86-90)	4.00	1.20
W.CLARK (91-95)	4.00	1.20
Y.BERRA (96-100)	5.00	1.50
B.RUTH (101-105)	10.00	3.00
R.MARIS (106-110)	10.00	3.00
D.DRYSDALE (111-115)	5.00	1.50
E.MATHEWS (116-120)	6.00	1.80
H.WAGNER (121-125)	6.00	1.80
J.ROBINSON (126-130)	8.00	2.40
J.FOXX (131-135)	5.00	1.50
J.DIMAGGIO (136-140)	8.00	2.40
J.MIZE (141-145)	5.00	1.50
L.GROVE (146-150)	5.00	1.50
L.GEHRIG (151-155)	8.00	2.40
M.OTT (156-160)	5.00	1.50
M.MANTLE (161-165)	20.00	6.00
R.CLEMENTE (166-170)	12.00	3.60
R.HORNSBY (171-175)	5.00	1.50
R.CAMPANELLA (176-180)	6.00	1.80
S.PAIGE (181-185)	6.00	1.80
T.WILLIAMS (186-190)	12.00	3.60
T.MUNSON (191-195)	6.00	1.80
T.COBB (196-200)	8.00	2.40

2005 Upper Deck Classics

	Nm-Mt	Ex-Mt
COMP.SET w/o SP's (100)	25.00	7.50
COMMON CARD (1-100)	.60	.18
COMMON CARD (101-130)	3.00	.90
101-130 STATED ODDS 1:4 H/R	.00	
❑ 1 Al Kaline	1.50	.45
❑ 2 Al Lopez	.60	.18
❑ 3 Allie Reynolds	.60	.18
❑ 4 Babe Herman	.60	.18
❑ 5 Bill Mazeroski	1.00	.30
❑ 6 Bill Russell	.60	.18
❑ 7 Billy Herman	.60	.18
❑ 8 Billy Williams	.60	.18
❑ 9 Bob Feller	1.00	.30
❑ 10 Bob Gibson	1.00	.30
❑ 11 Bob Lemon	.60	.18
❑ 12 Bobby Doerr	.60	.18
❑ 13 Boog Powell	.60	.18
❑ 14 Ken Hubbs	.60	.18
❑ 15 Brooks Robinson	1.00	.30
❑ 16 Buck Leonard	.60	.18
❑ 17 Cal Ripken	5.00	1.50
❑ 18 Carl Hubbell	.60	.18
❑ 19 Catfish Hunter	.60	.18
❑ 20 Johnny Hopp	.60	.18
❑ 21 Charlie Gehringer	.60	.18
❑ 22 Curt Flood	.60	.18
❑ 23 Jimmie Foxx	1.50	.45
❑ 24 Dave McNally	.60	.18
❑ 25 Davey Lopes	.60	.18
❑ 26 Don Drysdale	1.00	.30
❑ 27 Don Sutton	.60	.18
❑ 28 Earl Weaver	.60	.18
❑ 29 Early Wynn	.60	.18
❑ 30 Edd Roush	.60	.18
❑ 31 Eddie Mathews	1.50	.45
❑ 32 Enos Slaughter	.60	.18
❑ 33 Fergie Jenkins	.60	.18
❑ 34 Frank Howard	.60	.18
❑ 35 Leon Wagner	.60	.18
❑ 36 Frankie Crosetti	.60	.18
❑ 37 Gaylord Perry	.60	.18
❑ 38 George Bell	.60	.18
❑ 39 George Kell	.60	.18
❑ 40 Graig Nettles	.60	.18
❑ 41 Hal Newhouser	.60	.18
❑ 42 Harmon Killebrew	1.50	.45
❑ 43 Harvey Kuenn	.60	.18
❑ 44 Howard Johnson	.60	.18
❑ 45 Hoyt Wilhelm	.60	.18
❑ 46 Jack Clark	.60	.18
❑ 47 Jack Morris	.60	.18
❑ 48 Jim Bunning	.60	.18
❑ 49 Jim Palmer	.60	.18
❑ 50 Joe Adcock	.60	.18
❑ 51 Joe Carter	.60	.18

❑ 52 Casey Stengel 1.00 .30
❑ 53 Joe Morgan .60 .18
❑ 54 Joe Sewell .60 .18
❑ 55 Smokey Joe Wood .60 .18
❑ 56 Johnny Bench 1.50 .45
❑ 57 Johnny Mize .60 .18
❑ 58 Jose Canseco 1.00 .30
❑ 59 Juan Marichal .60 .18
❑ 60 Keith Hernandez .60 .18
❑ 61 Ken Griffey Sr. .60 .18
❑ 62 Kent Hrbek .60 .18
❑ 63 Kevin Mitchell .60 .18
❑ 64 Kirk Gibson .60 .18
❑ 65 Larry Doby .60 .18
❑ 66 Lou Boudreau .60 .18
❑ 67 Lou Brock 1.00 .30
❑ 68 Luis Aparicio .60 .18
❑ 69 Luke Appling .60 .18
❑ 70 Monte Irvin .60 .18
❑ 71 Nellie Fox 1.00 .30
❑ 72 Norm Cash .60 .18
❑ 73 Orlando Cepeda .60 .18
❑ 74 Pedro Guerrero .60 .18
❑ 75 Pee Wee Reese 1.00 .30
❑ 76 Phil Niekro .60 .18
❑ 77 Phil Rizzuto 1.00 .30
❑ 78 Ralph Kiner 1.00 .30
❑ 79 Ray Dandridge .60 .18
❑ 80 Red Schoendienst .60 .18
❑ 81 Richie Ashburn 1.00 .30
❑ 82 Rick Ferrell .60 .18
❑ 83 Robin Roberts .60 .18
❑ 84 Rollie Fingers .60 .18
❑ 85 Ron Cey .60 .18
❑ 86 Sparky Anderson .60 .18
❑ 87 Stan Coveleski .60 .18
❑ 88 Ted Kluszewski 1.00 .30
❑ 89 Ted Lyons .60 .18
❑ 90 Tom Seaver 1.00 .30
❑ 91 Tommie Agee .60 .18
❑ 92 Tommy Lasorda .60 .18
❑ 93 Tony Perez .60 .18
❑ 94 Vada Pinson .60 .18
❑ 95 Waite Hoyt .60 .18
❑ 96 Warren Spahn 1.00 .30
❑ 97 Willie McCovey 1.00 .30
❑ 98 Lyman Bostock .60 .18
❑ 99 Willie Stargell 1.00 .30
❑ 100 Yogi Berra 1.50 .45
❑ 101 Andre Dawson RSR 3.00 .90
❑ 102 Andy Van Slyke RSR 3.00 .90
❑ 103 Bret Saberhagen RSR 3.00 .90
❑ 104 Carl Yastrzemski RSR 8.00 2.40
❑ 105 Carlton Fisk RSR 5.00 1.50
❑ 106 Dale Murphy RSR 5.00 1.50
❑ 107 Darryl Strawberry RSR 3.00 .90
❑ 108 David Cone RSR 3.00 .90
❑ 109 Dennis Eckersley RSR 3.00 .90
❑ 110 Don Mattingly RSR 8.00 2.40
❑ 111 Dwight Gooden RSR 3.00 .90
❑ 112 Eddie Murray RSR 5.00 1.50
❑ 113 Eric Davis RSR 3.00 .90
❑ 114 Fred Lynn RSR 3.00 .90
❑ 115 George Brett RSR 8.00 2.40
❑ 116 Jim Rice RSR 3.00 .90
❑ 117 John Kruk RSR 5.00 1.50
❑ 118 Lenny Dykstra RSR 3.00 .90
❑ 119 Mickey Mantle RSR 15.00 4.50
❑ 120 Mike Schmidt RSR 8.00 2.40
❑ 121 Nolan Ryan RSR 10.00 3.00
❑ 122 Ozzie Smith RSR 8.00 2.40
❑ 123 Paul Molitor RSR 5.00 1.50
❑ 124 Robin Yount RSR 5.00 1.50
❑ 125 Ryne Sandberg RSR 8.00 2.40
❑ 126 Steve Carlton RSR 3.00 .90
❑ 127 Ted Williams RSR 8.00 2.40
❑ 128 Tony Gwynn RSR 8.00 2.40
❑ 129 Wade Boggs RSR 5.00 1.50
❑ 130 Will Clark RSR 5.00 1.50

2005 Upper Deck ESPN

	Nm-Mt	Ex-Mt
COMPLETE SET (90)	25.00	7.50
COMMON CARD (1-90)	.30	.09

❑ 1 Garret Anderson .30 .09

❑ 2 Troy Glaus .30 .09
❑ 3 Vladimir Guerrero .75 .23
❑ 4 Luis Gonzalez .30 .09
❑ 5 Randy Johnson .75 .23
❑ 6 Andruw Jones .50 .15
❑ 7 Chipper Jones .75 .23
❑ 8 J.D. Drew .30 .09
❑ 9 John Smoltz .50 .15
❑ 10 Miguel Tejada .30 .09
❑ 11 Rafael Palmeiro .50 .15
❑ 12 Curt Schilling .50 .15
❑ 13 David Ortiz .75 .23
❑ 14 Manny Ramirez .50 .15
❑ 15 Pedro Martinez .50 .15
❑ 16 Carlos Zambrano .30 .09
❑ 17 Greg Maddux 1.25 .35
❑ 18 Kerry Wood .30 .09
❑ 19 Mark Prior .50 .15
❑ 20 Nomar Garciaparra .75 .23
❑ 21 Sammy Sosa .75 .23
❑ 22 Carlos Lee .30 .09
❑ 23 Frank Thomas .75 .23
❑ 24 Magglio Ordonez .30 .09
❑ 25 Paul Konerko .30 .09
❑ 26 Adam Dunn .30 .09
❑ 27 Ken Griffey Jr. 1.25 .35
❑ 28 Travis Hafner .30 .09
❑ 29 Victor Martinez .30 .09
❑ 30 Todd Helton .50 .15
❑ 31 Ivan Rodriguez .50 .15
❑ 32 Carl Pavano .30 .09
❑ 33 Josh Beckett .30 .09
❑ 34 Miguel Cabrera .50 .15
❑ 35 Mike Lowell .30 .09
❑ 36 Carlos Beltran .30 .09
❑ 37 Craig Biggio .50 .15
❑ 38 Jeff Bagwell .50 .15
❑ 39 Lance Berkman .30 .09
❑ 40 Roger Clemens 1.25 .35
❑ 41 Roy Oswalt .30 .09
❑ 42 Mike Sweeney .30 .09
❑ 43 Adrian Beltre .30 .09
❑ 44 Brad Penny .30 .09
❑ 45 Eric Gagne .30 .09
❑ 46 Shawn Green .30 .09
❑ 47 Steve Finley .30 .09
❑ 48 Ben Sheets .30 .09
❑ 49 Scott Podsednik .30 .09
❑ 50 Joe Mauer .30 .09
❑ 51 Johan Santana .50 .15
❑ 52 Torii Hunter .30 .09
❑ 53 Jose Vidro .30 .09
❑ 54 Livan Hernandez .30 .09
❑ 55 Jose Reyes .30 .09
❑ 56 Mike Piazza .75 .23
❑ 57 Tom Glavine .50 .15
❑ 58 Alex Rodriguez 1.25 .35
❑ 59 Bernie Williams .50 .15
❑ 60 Derek Jeter 1.50 .45
❑ 61 Gary Sheffield .30 .09
❑ 62 Hideki Matsui 1.50 .45
❑ 63 Kevin Brown .30 .09
❑ 64 Mike Mussina .50 .15
❑ 65 Eric Chavez .30 .09
❑ 66 Mark Mulder .30 .09
❑ 67 Tim Hudson .30 .09
❑ 68 Bobby Abreu .30 .09
❑ 69 Jim Thome .50 .15
❑ 70 Craig Wilson .30 .09
❑ 71 Jason Kendall .30 .09
❑ 72 Oliver Perez .30 .09
❑ 73 Brian Giles .30 .09
❑ 74 Jake Peavy .30 .09
❑ 75 Jason Schmidt .30 .09
❑ 76 Bret Boone .30 .09
❑ 77 Ichiro Suzuki 1.50 .45
❑ 78 Albert Pujols 1.50 .45
❑ 79 Jim Edmonds .50 .15
❑ 80 Larry Walker .50 .15
❑ 81 Scott Rolen .50 .15
❑ 82 Aubrey Huff .30 .09
❑ 83 Carl Crawford .30 .09
❑ 84 Alfonso Soriano .30 .09
❑ 85 Hank Blalock .30 .09
❑ 86 Mark Teixeira .50 .15
❑ 87 Michael Young .30 .09
❑ 88 Carlos Delgado .30 .09
❑ 89 Roy Halladay .30 .09
❑ 90 Vernon Wells .30 .09

2004 Upper Deck Etchings

	Nm-Mt	Ex-Mt
COMP.SET w/o SP's (90)	25.00	7.50
COMMON CARD (1-90)	.50	.15
COMMON CARD (91-120)	4.00	1.20
91-120 STATED ODDS 1:6	.00	
91-120 PRINT RUN 2004 SERIAL #'d SETS		.00
COMMON AUTO (121-150)	8.00	2.40
121-150 OVERALL AU ODDS 1:4	.00	
121-150 PRINT RUN 700 SERIAL #'d SETS		.00

❑ 1 Albert Pujols 2.50 .75
❑ 2 Torii Hunter .50 .15
❑ 3 Jim Edmonds .75 .23
❑ 4 Alex Rodriguez 2.00 .60
❑ 5 Rafael Palmeiro .75 .23
❑ 6 Ken Griffey Jr. 2.00 .60
❑ 7 Adam Dunn .50 .15
❑ 8 Andruw Jones .75 .23
❑ 9 Carlos Lee .50 .15
❑ 10 Mike Piazza 2.00 .60
❑ 11 Jeff Bagwell .75 .23
❑ 12 Hideki Matsui 2.50 .75
❑ 13 Gary Sheffield .50 .15
❑ 14 Edgar Renteria .50 .15
❑ 15 Shawn Green .50 .15
❑ 16 Kerry Wood .50 .15
❑ 17 Ivan Rodriguez .75 .23
❑ 18 Josh Beckett .50 .15
❑ 19 Scott Rolen .75 .23
❑ 20 Brian Giles .50 .15
❑ 21 Derrek Lee .75 .23
❑ 22 Mike Lowell .50 .15
❑ 23 Mike Mussina .75 .23
❑ 24 Sammy Sosa 1.25 .35
❑ 25 Brandon Webb .50 .15
❑ 26 Jacque Jones .50 .15
❑ 27 Randy Johnson 1.25 .35
❑ 28 Luis Gonzalez .50 .15
❑ 29 Eric Chavez .50 .15
❑ 30 Carlos Delgado .50 .15
❑ 31 Phil Nevin .50 .15
❑ 32 Ichiro Suzuki 2.50 .75
❑ 33 Roy Oswalt .50 .15
❑ 34 Tim Hudson .50 .15
❑ 35 Juan Gonzalez .50 .15

❑ 36 Frank Thomas 1.25 .35
❑ 37 Mark Mulder .50 .15
❑ 38 Mark Teixeira .75 .23
❑ 39 Miguel Tejada .50 .15
❑ 40 Jeff Kent .50 .15
❑ 41 Andy Pettitte .75 .23
❑ 42 Barry Zito .50 .15
❑ 43 Roy Halladay .50 .15
❑ 44 Rocco Baldelli .50 .15
❑ 45 Derek Jeter 2.50 .75
❑ 46 Corey Patterson .50 .15
❑ 47 Javy Lopez .50 .15
❑ 48 A.J. Burnett .50 .15
❑ 49 Chipper Jones 1.25 .35
❑ 50 Curt Schilling .75 .23
❑ 51 Todd Helton .75 .23
❑ 52 Pedro Martinez .75 .23
❑ 53 Hideo Nomo 1.25 .35
❑ 54 Jose Reyes .50 .15
❑ 55 Vernon Wells .50 .15
❑ 56 Geoff Jenkins .50 .15
❑ 57 Troy Glaus .50 .15
❑ 58 Greg Maddux 2.00 .60
❑ 59 Jason Schmidt .50 .15
❑ 60 Preston Wilson .50 .15
❑ 61 Miguel Cabrera .75 .23
❑ 62 Hank Blalock .50 .15
❑ 63 Rafael Furcal .50 .15
❑ 64 Vladimir Guerrero 1.25 .35
❑ 65 Lance Berkman .50 .15
❑ 66 Javier Vazquez .50 .15
❑ 67 Bret Boone .50 .15
❑ 68 Mark Prior .75 .23
❑ 69 Maggilo Ordonez .50 .15
❑ 70 Dontrelle Willis .75 .23
❑ 71 Richie Sexson .50 .15
❑ 72 Alfonso Soriano .50 .15
❑ 73 Edwin Jackson .50 .15
❑ 74 Jose Vidro .50 .15
❑ 75 Jason Giambi .50 .15
❑ 76 Kevin Brown .50 .15
❑ 77 Orlando Cabrera .50 .15
❑ 78 Nomar Garciaparra 2.00 .60
❑ 79 Bobby Abreu .50 .15
❑ 80 Manny Ramirez .75 .23
❑ 81 J.D. Drew .50 .15
❑ 82 Roger Clemens 2.50 .75
❑ 83 Pat Burrell .50 .15
❑ 84 Ryan Klesko .50 .15
❑ 85 Garret Anderson .50 .15
❑ 86 Johan Santana .75 .23
❑ 87 Kevin Millwood .50 .15
❑ 88 Austin Kearns .50 .15
❑ 89 Jim Thome .75 .23
❑ 90 Carlos Beltran .50 .15
❑ 91 Kazuo Matsui FE RC 5.00 1.50
❑ 92 Jamie Brown FE RC 4.00 1.20
❑ 93 Brandon Medders FE RC 4.00 1.20
❑ 94 Carlos Vasquez FE RC 5.00 1.50
❑ 95 Chris Aguila FE RC 4.00 1.20
❑ 96 David Aardsma FE RC 5.00 1.50
❑ 97 Justin Leone FE RC 5.00 1.50
❑ 98 Mike Johnston FE RC 4.00 1.20
❑ 99 Tim Bittner FE RC 4.00 1.20
❑ 100 Mike Rouse FE RC 4.00 1.20
❑ 101 Dennis Sarfate FE RC 4.00 1.20
❑ 102 Jason Frasor FE RC 4.00 1.20
❑ 103 Jorge Vasquez FE RC 4.00 1.20
❑ 104 Mike Gosling FE RC 4.00 1.20
❑ 105 Jake Woods FE RC 4.00 1.20
❑ 106 Akinori Otsuka FE RC 4.00 1.20
❑ 107 Lincoln Holdzkom FE RC 4.00 1.20
❑ 108 Jesse Harper FE RC 4.00 1.20
❑ 109 Edwin Moreno FE RC 4.00 1.20
❑ 110 Shingo Takatsu FE RC 5.00 1.50
❑ 111 Ryan Meaux FE RC 4.00 1.20
❑ 112 Donnie Kelly FE RC 4.00 1.20
❑ 113 Jerome Gamble FE RC 4.00 1.20
❑ 114 Josh Labandeira FE RC 4.00 1.20
❑ 115 Ian Snell FE RC 5.00 1.50
❑ 116 Michael Wuertz FE RC 5.00 1.50
❑ 117 Greg Dobbs FE RC 4.00 1.20
❑ 118 Sean Henn FE RC 4.00 1.20
❑ 119 Dave Crouthers FE RC 4.00 1.20
❑ 120 Hector Gimenez FE RC 4.00 1.20
❑ 121 Renyel Pinto FE AU RC 10.00 3.00
❑ 122 Tim Hamulack FE AU RC 8.00 2.40
❑ 123 Chris Saenz FE AU RC 8.00 2.40
❑ 124 Carlos Hines FE AU RC 8.00 2.40
❑ 125 Justin Knoedler FE AU RC 8.00 2.40
❑ 126 Onil Joseph FE AU RC 8.00 2.40
❑ 127 Ryan Wing FE AU RC 8.00 2.40
❑ 128 Scott Proctor FE AU RC 10.00 3.00
❑ 129 Rusty Tucker FE AU RC 10.00 3.00
❑ 130 Fernando Nieve FE AU RC 10.00 3.00
❑ 131 Chad Bentz FE AU RC 8.00 2.40
❑ 132 Jerry Gil FE AU RC 8.00 2.40
❑ 133 Mariano Gomez FE AU RC 8.00 2.40
❑ 134 Justin Germano FE AU RC 8.00 2.40
❑ 135 Jason Bartlett FE AU RC 10.00 3.00
❑ 136 Ronald Belisario FE AU RC 8.00 2.40
❑ 137 E.Pacheco FE AU RC 8.00 2.40
❑ 138 Justin Hampson FE AU RC 8.00 2.40
❑ 139 Mike Vento FE AU RC 10.00 3.00
❑ 140 Merkin Valdez FE AU RC 10.00 3.00
❑ 141 Casey Daigle FE AU RC 8.00 2.40
❑ 142 Eddy Rodriguez FE AU RC 10.00 3.00
❑ 143 William Bergolla FE AU RC 8.00 2.40
❑ 144 Jose Capellan FE AU RC 10.00 3.00
❑ 145 Ronny Cedeno FE AU RC 10.00 3.00
❑ 146 F.Gracesqui FE AU RC 8.00 2.40
❑ 147 Roman Colon FE AU RC 8.00 2.40
❑ 148 Roberto Novoa FE AU RC 10.00 3.00
❑ 149 Ivan Ochoa FE AU RC 8.00 2.40
❑ 150 Shawn Hill FE AU RC 8.00 2.40

2001 Upper Deck Evolution

	Nm-Mt	Ex-Mt
COMP.SET w/o SP's (90)	15.00	4.50
COMMON CARD (1-90)	.30	.09
COMMON CARD (91-120)	4.00	1.20

❑ 1 Darin Erstad .30 .09
❑ 2 Troy Glaus .30 .09
❑ 3 Jason Giambi .30 .09
❑ 4 Tim Hudson .30 .09
❑ 5 Jermaine Dye .30 .09
❑ 6 Barry Zito .50 .15
❑ 7 Carlos Delgado .30 .09
❑ 8 Shannon Stewart .30 .09
❑ 9 Jose Cruz Jr. .30 .09
❑ 10 Greg Vaughn .30 .09
❑ 11 Juan Gonzalez .30 .09
❑ 12 Roberto Alomar .50 .15
❑ 13 Omar Vizquel .50 .15
❑ 14 Jim Thome .50 .15
❑ 15 Edgar Martinez .50 .15
❑ 16 John Olerud .30 .09
❑ 17 Kazuhiro Sasaki .30 .09
❑ 18 Cal Ripken 2.50 .75
❑ 19 Alex Rodriguez 1.25 .35
❑ 20 Ivan Rodriguez .50 .15
❑ 21 Rafael Palmeiro .50 .15
❑ 22 Pedro Martinez .50 .15
❑ 23 Nomar Garciaparra 1.25 .35
❑ 24 Manny Ramirez Sox .50 .15
❑ 25 Carl Everett .30 .09
❑ 26 Mark Quinn .30 .09
❑ 27 Mike Sweeney .30 .09
❑ 28 Neifi Perez .30 .09
❑ 29 Tony Clark .30 .09
❑ 30 Eric Milton .30 .09
❑ 31 Doug Mientkiewicz .30 .09
❑ 32 Corey Koskie .30 .09
❑ 33 Frank Thomas .75 .23
❑ 34 David Wells .30 .09
❑ 35 Magglio Ordonez .30 .09
❑ 36 Derek Jeter 2.00 .60
❑ 37 Mike Mussina .50 .15
❑ 38 Bernie Williams .50 .15
❑ 39 Roger Clemens 1.50 .45
❑ 40 David Justice .30 .09
❑ 41 Jeff Bagwell .50 .15
❑ 42 Richard Hidalgo .30 .09
❑ 43 Wade Miller .30 .09
❑ 44 Chipper Jones .75 .23
❑ 45 Greg Maddux 1.25 .35
❑ 46 Andruw Jones .50 .15
❑ 47 Rafael Furcal .30 .09
❑ 48 Geoff Jenkins .30 .09
❑ 49 Jeromy Burnitz .30 .09
❑ 50 Ben Sheets .50 .15
❑ 51 Richie Sexson .30 .09
❑ 52 Mark McGwire 2.00 .60
❑ 53 Jim Edmonds .50 .15
❑ 54 Darryl Kile .30 .09
❑ 55 J.D. Drew .30 .09
❑ 56 Sammy Sosa .75 .23
❑ 57 Kerry Wood .30 .09
❑ 58 Randy Johnson .75 .23
❑ 59 Luis Gonzalez .30 .09
❑ 60 Matt Williams .30 .09
❑ 61 Kevin Brown .30 .09
❑ 62 Gary Sheffield .30 .09
❑ 63 Shawn Green .30 .09
❑ 64 Chan Ho Park .30 .09
❑ 65 Vladimir Guerrero .75 .23
❑ 66 Jose Vidro .30 .09
❑ 67 Fernando Tatis .30 .09
❑ 68 Barry Bonds 2.00 .60
❑ 69 Jeff Kent .30 .09
❑ 70 Russ Ortiz .30 .09
❑ 71 Preston Wilson .30 .09
❑ 72 Ryan Dempster .30 .09
❑ 73 Charles Johnson .30 .09
❑ 74 Mike Piazza 1.25 .35
❑ 75 Edgardo Alfonzo .30 .09
❑ 76 Robin Ventura .30 .09
❑ 77 Jay Payton .30 .09
❑ 78 Tony Gwynn 1.00 .30
❑ 79 Phil Nevin .30 .09
❑ 80 Pat Burrell .30 .09
❑ 81 Scott Rolen .50 .15
❑ 82 Bob Abreu .30 .09
❑ 83 Brian Giles .30 .09
❑ 84 Jason Kendall .30 .09
❑ 85 Ken Griffey Jr. 1.25 .35
❑ 86 Barry Larkin .50 .15
❑ 87 Sean Casey .50 .15
❑ 88 Todd Helton .50 .15
❑ 89 Larry Walker .30 .09
❑ 90 Mike Hampton .30 .09
❑ 91 Ichiro Suzuki PROS RC 25.00 7.50
❑ 92 Albert Pujols PROS RC 50.00 15.00
❑ 93 W.Betemit PROS RC 5.00 1.50
❑ 94 Jay Gibbons PROS RC 5.00 1.50
❑ 95 Juan Uribe PROS RC 5.00 1.50
❑ 96 M. Ensberg PROS RC 6.00 1.80
❑ 97 C. Parker PROS RC 4.00 1.20
❑ 98 T. Shinjo PROS RC 5.00 1.50
❑ 99 Jack Wilson PROS RC 5.00 1.50
❑ 100 D. Mendez PROS RC 4.00 1.20
❑ 101 Ryan Freel PROS RC 5.00 1.50
❑ 102 Juan Diaz PROS RC 4.00 1.20
❑ 103 H. Ramirez PROS RC 5.00 1.50
❑ 104 R. Rodriguez PROS RC 4.00 1.20
❑ 105 E. Almonte PROS RC 4.00 1.20
❑ 106 J. Towers PROS RC 5.00 1.50
❑ 107 A.Hernandez PROS RC 4.00 1.20
❑ 108 B.Duckworth PROS RC 4.00 1.20
❑ 109 T. Hafner PROS RC 8.00 2.40
❑ 110 M. Vargas PROS RC 4.00 1.20
❑ 111 Kris Keller PROS RC 4.00 1.20
❑ 112 B. Lawrence PROS RC 4.00 1.20
❑ 113 Esix Snead PROS RC 4.00 1.20
❑ 114 Wilkin Ruan PROS RC 4.00 1.20
❑ 115 J. Mieses PROS RC 4.00 1.20
❑ 116 J. Estrada PROS RC 5.00 1.50
❑ 117 E. Guzman PROS RC 4.00 1.20

❑ 118 S. Douglass PROS RC 4.00 1.20
❑ 119 B. Sylvester PROS RC 4.00 1.20
❑ 120 Bret Prinz PROS RC 4.00 1.20

2003 Upper Deck Finite

	MINT	NRMT
COMMON CARD (1-100)	2.00	.90
COMMON CARD (101-150)	2.50	1.10
COMMON CARD (151-180)	4.00	1.80
COMMON CARD (181-200)	5.00	2.20
1-200 STATED ODDS TWO PER PACK		.00
COMMON CARD (201-300)	3.00	1.35
COMMON CARD (301-330)	5.00	2.20
301-330 PRINT RUN 599 SERIAL #'d SETS		.00
COMMON CARD (331-360)	10.00	4.50
331-360 PRINT RUN 299 SERIAL #'d SETS		.00
COMMON CARD (361-380)	15.00	6.75
361-380 PRINT RUN 150 SERIAL #'d SETS		.00
201-380/STARS 'N STRIPES ODDS 1:1		.00

❑ 1 Darin Erstad 2.00 .90
❑ 2 Garret Anderson 2.00 .90
❑ 3 Tim Salmon 2.50 1.10
❑ 4 Troy Glaus 2.00 .90
❑ 5 Luis Gonzalez 2.00 .90
❑ 6 Randy Johnson 2.50 1.10
❑ 7 Curt Schilling 2.00 .90
❑ 8 Andruw Jones 2.50 1.10
❑ 9 Gary Sheffield 2.00 .90
❑ 10 Rafael Furcal 2.00 .90
❑ 11 Greg Maddux 4.00 1.80
❑ 12 Chipper Jones 2.50 1.10
❑ 13 Tony Batista 2.00 .90
❑ 14 Jay Gibbons 2.00 .90
❑ 15 Johnny Damon 2.50 1.10
❑ 16 Derek Lowe 2.00 .90
❑ 17 Nomar Garciaparra 4.00 1.80
❑ 18 Pedro Martinez 2.50 1.10
❑ 19 Manny Ramirez 2.50 1.10
❑ 20 Mark Prior 2.50 1.10
❑ 21 Kerry Wood 2.00 .90
❑ 22 Corey Patterson 2.00 .90
❑ 23 Sammy Sosa 2.50 1.10
❑ 24 Moises Alou 2.00 .90
❑ 25 Maggilo Ordonez 2.00 .90
❑ 26 Frank Thomas 2.50 1.10
❑ 27 Paul Konerko 2.00 .90
❑ 28 Bartolo Colon 2.00 .90
❑ 29 Adam Dunn 2.00 .90
❑ 30 Austin Kearns 2.00 .90
❑ 31 Aaron Boone 2.00 .90
❑ 32 Ken Griffey Jr. 4.00 1.80
❑ 33 Omar Vizquel 2.50 1.10
❑ 34 C.C. Sabathia 2.00 .90
❑ 35 Brandon Phillips 2.00 .90
❑ 36 Larry Walker 2.00 .90
❑ 37 Preston Wilson 2.00 .90
❑ 38 Todd Helton 2.50 1.10
❑ 39 Eric Munson 2.00 .90
❑ 40 Ivan Rodriguez 2.50 1.10
❑ 41 Josh Beckett 2.00 .90
❑ 42 Roy Oswalt 2.00 .90
❑ 43 Craig Biggio 2.50 1.10
❑ 44 Jeff Bagwell 2.50 1.10
❑ 45 Dontrelle Willis 2.50 1.10
❑ 46 Carlos Beltran 2.00 .90
❑ 47 Brent Mayne 2.00 .90
❑ 48 Hideo Nomo 2.50 1.10
❑ 49 Rickey Henderson 2.50 1.10
❑ 50 Adrian Beltre 2.00 .90
❑ 51 Miguel Cabrera 2.50 1.10
❑ 52 Kazuhisa Ishii 2.00 .90
❑ 53 Richie Sexson 2.00 .90
❑ 54 Torii Hunter 2.00 .90
❑ 55 Jacque Jones 2.00 .90
❑ 56 A.J. Pierzynski 2.00 .90
❑ 57 Jose Vidro 2.00 .90
❑ 58 Vladimir Guerrero 2.50 1.10
❑ 59 Tom Glavine 2.50 1.10
❑ 60 Jose Reyes 2.00 .90
❑ 61 Mike Piazza 4.00 1.80
❑ 62 Jorge Posada 2.50 1.10
❑ 63 Mike Mussina 2.50 1.10
❑ 64 Robin Ventura 2.00 .90
❑ 65 Mariano Rivera 2.50 1.10
❑ 66 Roger Clemens 5.00 2.20
❑ 67 Jason Giambi 2.00 .90
❑ 68 Bernie Williams 2.50 1.10
❑ 69 Alfonso Soriano 2.00 .90
❑ 70 Derek Jeter 6.00 2.70
❑ 71 Miguel Tejada 2.00 .90
❑ 72 Eric Chavez 2.00 .90
❑ 73 Tim Hudson 2.00 .90
❑ 74 Barry Zito 2.00 .90
❑ 75 Pat Burrell 2.00 .90
❑ 76 Jim Thome 2.50 1.10
❑ 77 Bobby Abreu 2.00 .90
❑ 78 Brian Giles 2.00 .90
❑ 79 Reggie Sanders 2.00 .90
❑ 80 Ryan Klesko 2.00 .90
❑ 81 Edgardo Alfonzo 2.00 .90
❑ 82 Rich Aurilia 2.00 .90
❑ 83 Barry Bonds 6.00 2.70
❑ 84 Mike Cameron 2.00 .90
❑ 85 Kazuhiro Sasaki 2.00 .90
❑ 86 Bret Boone 2.00 .90
❑ 87 Ichiro Suzuki 5.00 2.20
❑ 88 J.D. Drew 2.00 .90
❑ 89 Jim Edmonds 2.50 1.10
❑ 90 Scott Rolen 2.50 1.10
❑ 91 Matt Morris 2.00 .90
❑ 92 Tino Martinez 2.50 1.10
❑ 93 Albert Pujols 5.00 2.20
❑ 94 Rocco Baldelli 2.00 .90
❑ 95 Hank Blalock 2.00 .90
❑ 96 Alex Rodriguez 4.00 1.80
❑ 97 Rafael Palmeiro 2.50 1.10
❑ 98 Eric Hinske 2.00 .90
❑ 99 Orlando Hudson 2.00 .90
❑ 100 Carlos Delgado 2.00 .90
❑ 101 Albert Pujols MF 6.00 2.70
❑ 102 Alex Rodriguez MF 5.00 2.20
❑ 103 Alfonso Soriano MF 2.50 1.10
❑ 104 Andruw Jones MF 3.00 1.35
❑ 105 Barry Zito MF 2.50 1.10
❑ 106 Bernie Williams MF 3.00 1.35
❑ 107 Carlos Delgado MF 2.50 1.10
❑ 108 Chipper Jones MF 3.00 1.35
❑ 109 Curt Schilling MF 2.50 1.10
❑ 110 Doug Mientkiewicz MF 2.50 1.10
❑ 111 Frank Thomas MF 3.00 1.35
❑ 112 Garret Anderson MF 2.50 1.10
❑ 113 Gary Sheffield MF 2.50 1.10
❑ 114 Greg Maddux MF 5.00 2.20
❑ 115 Hank Blalock MF 2.50 1.10
❑ 116 Hideki Matsui MF 6.00 2.70
❑ 117 Hideo Nomo MF 3.00 1.35
❑ 118 Ichiro Suzuki MF 6.00 2.70
❑ 119 Ivan Rodriguez MF 3.00 1.35
❑ 120 Jason Giambi MF 2.50 1.10
❑ 121 Jeff Bagwell MF 3.00 1.35
❑ 122 Jeff Kent MF 2.50 1.10
❑ 123 Jerome Williams MF 2.50 1.10
❑ 124 Jeromy Burnitz MF 2.50 1.10
❑ 125 Jim Thome MF 3.00 1.35
❑ 126 Jose Cruz Jr. MF 2.50 1.10
❑ 127 Ken Griffey Jr. MF 5.00 2.20
❑ 128 Kerry Wood MF 2.50 1.10
❑ 129 Lance Berkman MF 2.50 1.10
❑ 130 Luis Gonzalez MF 2.50 1.10
❑ 131 Manny Ramirez MF 3.00 1.35
❑ 132 Mark Prior MF 3.00 1.35
❑ 133 Miguel Cabrera MF 3.00 1.35
❑ 134 Miguel Tejada MF 2.50 1.10
❑ 135 Mike Piazza MF 5.00 2.20
❑ 136 Pat Burrell MF 2.50 1.10
❑ 137 Pedro Martinez MF 3.00 1.35
❑ 138 Rafael Furcal MF 2.50 1.10
❑ 139 Randy Johnson MF 3.00 1.35
❑ 140 Rich Harden MF 3.00 1.35
❑ 141 Rickey Henderson MF 3.00 1.35
❑ 142 Roberto Alomar MF 3.00 1.35
❑ 143 Roger Clemens MF 6.00 2.70
❑ 144 Sammy Sosa MF 3.00 1.35
❑ 145 Shawn Green MF 2.50 1.10
❑ 146 Todd Helton MF 3.00 1.35
❑ 147 Tom Glavine MF 3.00 1.35
❑ 148 Torii Hunter MF 2.50 1.10
❑ 149 Troy Glaus MF 2.50 1.10
❑ 150 Vladimir Guerrero MF 3.00 1.35
❑ 151 Adam Dunn PP 4.00 1.80
❑ 152 Albert Pujols PP 10.00 4.50
❑ 153 Alex Rodriguez PP 8.00 3.60
❑ 154 Alfonso Soriano PP 4.00 1.80
❑ 155 Andruw Jones PP 5.00 2.20
❑ 156 Barry Bonds PP 12.00 5.50
❑ 157 Carlos Delgado PP 4.00 1.80
❑ 158 Chipper Jones PP 5.00 2.20
❑ 159 Derek Jeter PP 12.00 5.50
❑ 160 Gary Sheffield PP 4.00 1.80
❑ 161 Hank Blalock PP 4.00 1.80
❑ 162 Hideki Matsui PP 10.00 4.50
❑ 163 Ichiro Suzuki PP 10.00 4.50
❑ 164 J.D. Drew PP 4.00 1.80
❑ 165 Jason Giambi PP 4.00 1.80
❑ 166 Jeff Bagwell PP 5.00 2.20
❑ 167 Jeff Kent PP 4.00 1.80
❑ 168 Jim Edmonds PP 5.00 2.20
❑ 169 Jim Thome PP 5.00 2.20
❑ 170 Ken Griffey Jr. PP 8.00 3.60
❑ 171 Luis Gonzalez PP 4.00 1.80
❑ 172 Magglio Ordonez PP 4.00 1.80
❑ 173 Manny Ramirez PP 5.00 2.20
❑ 174 Mike Lowell PP 4.00 1.80
❑ 175 Mike Piazza PP 8.00 3.60
❑ 176 Nomar Garciaparra PP 8.00 3.60
❑ 177 Rafael Palmeiro PP 5.00 2.20
❑ 178 Shawn Green PP 4.00 1.80
❑ 179 Troy Glaus PP 4.00 1.80
❑ 180 Vladimir Guerrero PP 5.00 2.20
❑ 181 Albert Pujols FC 12.00 5.50
❑ 182 Alex Rodriguez FC 10.00 4.50
❑ 183 Alfonso Soriano FC 5.00 2.20
❑ 184 Bernie Williams FC 6.00 2.70
❑ 185 Chipper Jones FC 6.00 2.70
❑ 186 Derek Jeter FC 15.00 6.75
❑ 187 Hideki Matsui FC 12.00 5.50
❑ 188 Ichiro Suzuki FC 12.00 5.50
❑ 189 Jim Thome FC 6.00 2.70
❑ 190 Joe DiMaggio FC 10.00 4.50
❑ 191 Ken Griffey Jr. FC 10.00 4.50
❑ 192 Mickey Mantle FC 20.00 9.00
❑ 193 Mike Piazza FC 10.00 4.50
❑ 194 Pedro Martinez FC 6.00 2.70
❑ 195 Randy Johnson FC 6.00 2.70
❑ 196 Roger Clemens FC 12.00 5.50
❑ 197 Sammy Sosa FC 6.00 2.70
❑ 198 Ted Williams FC 10.00 4.50
❑ 199 Troy Glaus FC 5.00 2.20
❑ 200 Vladimir Guerrero FC 6.00 2.70
❑ 201 Aaron Looper T1 RC 3.00 1.35
❑ 202 Alejandro Machado T1 RC 3.00 1.35
❑ 203 Alfredo Gonzalez T1 RC 3.00 1.35
❑ 204 Andrew Brown T1 RC 5.00 2.20
❑ 205 Anthony Ferrari T1 RC 3.00 1.35
❑ 206 Aquilino Lopez T1 RC 3.00 1.35
❑ 207 Beau Kemp T1 RC 3.00 1.35
❑ 208 Bernie Castro T1 RC 3.00 1.35
❑ 209 Bobby Madritsch T1 RC 5.00 2.20
❑ 210 Brandon Villafuerte T1 3.00 1.35
❑ 211 Brent Hoard T1 RC 3.00 1.35
❑ 212 Brian Stokes T1 RC 3.00 1.35
❑ 213 Carlos Mendez T1 RC 3.00 1.35
❑ 214 Chris Capuano T1 RC 3.00 1.35
❑ 215 Chris Waters T1 RC 3.00 1.35
❑ 216 Clint Barmes T1 RC 5.00 2.20
❑ 217 Colin Porter T1 RC 3.00 1.35
❑ 218 Cory Stewart T1 RC 3.00 1.35
❑ 219 Craig Brazell T1 RC 3.00 1.35
❑ 220 D.J. Carrasco T1 RC 3.00 1.35

❑ 221 Daniel Cabrera T1 RC 5.00 2.20
❑ 222 David Matranga T1 RC .. 3.00 1.35
❑ 223 David Sanders T1 RC 3.00 1.35
❑ 224 Diegomar Markwell T1 RC 3.00 1.35
❑ 225 Edgar Gonzalez T1 RC.... 3.00 1.35
❑ 226 Felix Sanchez T1 RC 3.00 1.35
❑ 227 Fernando Cabrera T1 RC 3.00 1.35
❑ 228 Francisco Cruceta T1 RC 3.00 1.35
❑ 229 Francisco Rosario T1 RC 3.00 1.35
❑ 230 Garrett Atkins T1 .... 3.00 1.35
❑ 231 Gerald Laird T1 .... 3.00 1.35
❑ 232 Guillermo Quiroz T1 RC 3.00 1.35
❑ 233 Heath Bell T1 RC............ 3.00 1.35
❑ 234 Delmon Young T1 RC .. 10.00 4.50
❑ 235 Jason Shiell T1 RC 3.00 1.35
❑ 236 Jeremy Bonderman T1 RC 8.00 3.60
❑ 237 Jeremy Griffiths T1 RC .. 3.00 1.35
❑ 238 Jeremy Guthrie T1.......... 3.00 1.35
❑ 239 Jeremy Wedel T1 RC...... 3.00 1.35
❑ 240 Carlos Rivera T1 .... 3.00 1.35
❑ 241 Joe Valentine T1 RC 3.00 1.35
❑ 242 Jon Leicester T1 RC 3.00 1.35
❑ 243 Jon Pridie T1 RC............ 3.00 1.35
❑ 244 Jorge Cordova T1 RC 3.00 1.35
❑ 245 Jose Castillo T1 .... 3.00 1.35
❑ 246 Josh Hall T1 RC 3.00 1.35
❑ 247 Josh Stewart T1 RC........ 3.00 1.35
❑ 248 Josh Willingham T1 RC 5.00 2.20
❑ 249 Julio Manon T1 RC........ 3.00 1.35
❑ 250 Kevin Correia T1 RC 3.00 1.35
❑ 251 Kevin Ohme T1 RC 3.00 1.35
❑ 252 Kevin Tolar T1 RC.......... 3.00 1.35
❑ 253 Luis De Los Santos T1 .. 3.00 1.35
❑ 254 Jermaine Clark T1.......... 3.00 1.35
❑ 255 Mark Malaska T1 RC...... 3.00 1.35
❑ 256 Juan Dominguez T1 ...... 3.00 1.35
❑ 257 Michael Hessman T1 RC 3.00 1.35
❑ 258 Michael Nakamura T1 RC 3.00 1.35
❑ 259 Miguel Ojeda T1 RC 3.00 1.35
❑ 260 Mike Gallo T1 RC 3.00 1.35
❑ 261 Edwin Jackson T1 RC 5.00 2.20
❑ 262 Mike Ryan T1 RC 3.00 1.35
❑ 263 Nate Bland T1 RC 3.00 1.35
❑ 264 Nate Robertson T1 RC..... 5.00 2.20
❑ 265 Nook Logan T1 RC 5.00 2.20
❑ 266 Phil Seibel T1 RC 3.00 1.35
❑ 267 Prentice Redman T1 RC 3.00 1.35
❑ 268 Rafael Betancourt T1 RC 5.00 2.20
❑ 269 Rett Johnson T1 RC 3.00 1.35
❑ 270 Richard Fischer T1 RC .. 3.00 1.35
❑ 271 Rick Roberts T1 RC........ 3.00 1.35
❑ 272 Roger Deago T1 RC........ 3.00 1.35
❑ 273 Ryan Cameron T1 RC 3.00 1.35
❑ 274 Shane Bazzell T1 RC 3.00 1.35
❑ 275 Erasmo Ramirez T1 .... 3.00 1.35
❑ 276 Termel Sledge T1 RC 3.00 1.35
❑ 277 Tim Olson T1 RC............ 3.00 1.35
❑ 278 Tommy Phelps T1 .... 3.00 1.35
❑ 279 Tommy Whiteman T1 .... 3.00 1.35
❑ 280 Willie Eyre T1 RC 3.00 1.35
❑ 281 Alex Prieto T1 RC 3.00 1.35
❑ 282 Michel Hernandez T1 RC 3.00 1.35
❑ 283 Greg Jones T1 RC.......... 3.00 1.35
❑ 284 Victor Martinez T1.......... 5.00 2.20
❑ 285 Tom Gregorio T1 RC...... 3.00 1.35
❑ 286 Marcus Thames T1 .... 3.00 1.35
❑ 287 Jorge DePaula T1 .... 3.00 1.35
❑ 288 Aaron Miles T1 RC 5.00 2.20
❑ 289 Reynaldo Garcia T1 .... 3.00 1.35
❑ 290 Brian Sweeney T1 RC 3.00 1.35
❑ 291 Pete LaForest T1 RC 3.00 1.35
❑ 292 Pete Zoccolillo T1 RC 3.00 1.35
❑ 293 Danny Garcia T1 RC 3.00 1.35
❑ 294 Jonny Gomes T1 .... 5.00 2.20
❑ 295 Rosman Garcia T1 RC.... 3.00 1.35
❑ 296 Mike Edwards T1............ 3.00 1.35
❑ 297 Marlon Byrd T1 .... 3.00 1.35
❑ 298 Khalil Greene T1 .... 8.00 3.60
❑ 299 Jose Valverde T1............ 3.00 1.35
❑ 300 Drew Henson T1 .... 3.00 1.35
❑ 301 Chris Bootcheck T2........ 5.00 2.20
❑ 302 Matt Belisle T2 .... 5.00 2.20
❑ 303 Kevin Gregg T2 .... 5.00 2.20
❑ 304 Bobby Jenks T2.............. 5.00 2.20
❑ 305 Jason Young T2 .... 5.00 2.20
❑ 306 Laynce Nix T2 .... 5.00 2.20
❑ 307 Robb Quinlan T2............ 5.00 2.20
❑ 308 Chase Utley T2 .... 8.00 3.60
❑ 309 Humberto Quintero T2 RC 5.00 2.20
❑ 310 Tim Raines Jr. T2 .... 5.00 2.20
❑ 311 Stephen Smitherman T2 5.00 2.20
❑ 312 Jason Anderson T2 .... 5.00 2.20
❑ 313 Joe Dawley T2................ 5.00 2.20
❑ 314 Chad Cordero T2 RC 10.00 4.50
❑ 315 Victor Alvarez T2............ 5.00 2.20
❑ 316 Jimmy Gobble T2 .... 5.00 2.20
❑ 317 Jared Fernandez T2........ 5.00 2.20
❑ 318 Eric Bruntlett T2 .... 5.00 2.20
❑ 319 Neal Cotts T2 .... 5.00 2.20
❑ 320 Ryan Madson T2............ 5.00 2.20
❑ 321 Rocco Baldelli T2 .... 5.00 2.20
❑ 322 Graham Koonce T2 RC .. 5.00 2.20
❑ 323 Bobby Crosby T2 .... 8.00 3.60
❑ 324 Mike Wood T2................ 5.00 2.20
❑ 325 Jesse Garcia T2.............. 5.00 2.20
❑ 326 Noah Lowry T2 .... 8.00 3.60
❑ 327 Edwin Almonte T2.......... 5.00 2.20
❑ 328 Justin Morneau T2 .... 5.00 2.20
❑ 329 Steve Colyer T2.............. 5.00 2.20
❑ 330 Vinnie Chulk T2 .... 5.00 2.20
❑ 331 Brian Schmack T3 RC .. 10.00 4.50
❑ 332 Stephen Randolph T3 RC 10.00 4.50
❑ 333 Pedro Feliciano T3 RC 10.00 4.50
❑ 334 Koyie Hill T3 .... 10.00 4.50
❑ 335 Geoff Geary T3 RC........ 10.00 4.50
❑ 336 Jon Switzer T3.............. 10.00 4.50
❑ 337 Xavier Nady T3 .... 10.00 4.50
❑ 338 Rich Harden T3 .... 15.00 6.75
❑ 339 Dontrelle Willis T3 ...... 15.00 6.75
❑ 340 Angel Berroa T3 .... 10.00 4.50
❑ 341 Jerome Williams T3 .... 10.00 4.50
❑ 342 Brandon Claussen T3 .. 10.00 4.50
❑ 343 Kurt Ainsworth T3........ 10.00 4.50
❑ 344 Horacio Ramirez T3...... 10.00 4.50
❑ 345 Hee Seop Choi T3........ 10.00 4.50
❑ 346 Billy Traber T3.............. 10.00 4.50
❑ 347 Brandon Phillips T3 .... 10.00 4.50
❑ 348 Jody Gerut T3 .... 10.00 4.50
❑ 349 Mark Teixeira T3.......... 15.00 6.75
❑ 350 Javier A. Lopez T3 RC .. 10.00 4.50
❑ 351 Miguel Cabrera T3 ...... 15.00 6.75
❑ 352 Brad Lidge T3 .... 10.00 4.50
❑ 353 Mike MacDougal T3 .... 10.00 4.50
❑ 354 Ken Harvey T3.............. 10.00 4.50
❑ 355 Chien-Ming Wang T3 RC 25.00 11.00
❑ 356 Aaron Heilman T3 .... 10.00 4.50
❑ 357 Jason Phillips T3 .... 10.00 4.50
❑ 358 Jason Bay T3................ 15.00 6.75
❑ 359 Arnie Munoz T3 RC...... 10.00 4.50
❑ 360 Ian Ferguson T3 RC 10.00 4.50
❑ 361 Ryan Wagner T4 RC 15.00 6.75
❑ 362 Rickie Weeks T4 RC 40.00 18.00
❑ 363 Chad Gaudin T4 RC 15.00 6.75
❑ 364 Jason Gilfillan T4 RC .. 15.00 6.75
❑ 365 Jason Roach T4 RC...... 15.00 6.75
❑ 366 Jhonny Peralta T4 .... 20.00 9.00
❑ 367 Mike Neu T4 RC 15.00 6.75
❑ 368 Jose Contreras T4 RC .. 25.00 11.00
❑ 369 Wilfredo Ledezma T4 RC 15.00 6.75
❑ 370 Lew Ford T4 RC 20.00 9.00
❑ 371 Luis Ayala T4 RC.......... 15.00 6.75
❑ 372 Bo Hart T4 RC.............. 15.00 6.75
❑ 373 Brandon Webb T4 RC .. 25.00 11.00
❑ 374 Dan Haren T4 RC 25.00 11.00
❑ 375 Hideki Matsui T4 RC 60.00 27.00
❑ 376 Jeff Duncan T4 RC 15.00 6.75
❑ 377 Matt Kata T4 RC 15.00 6.75
❑ 378 Oscar Villarreal T4 RC .. 15.00 6.75
❑ 379 Rob Hammock T4 RC .. 15.00 6.75
❑ 380 Todd Wellemeyer T4 RC 15.00 6.75

2003 Upper Deck Game Face

	Nm-Mt	Ex-Mt
COMP.SET w/o SP's (90)	25.00	7.50
COMMON CARD (1-120)	.50	.15
COMMON SP (1-120)	4.00	1.20
COMMON CARD (121-150)	4.00	1.20
COMMON CARD (151-171)	5.00	1.50
COMMON CARD (172-192)	5.00	1.50

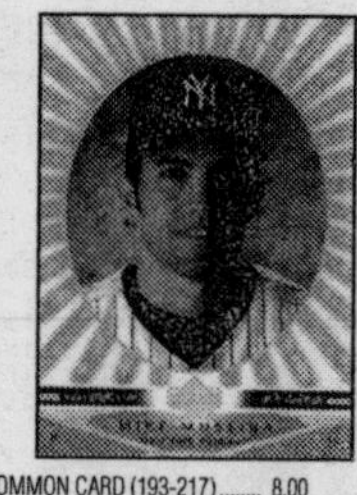

COMMON CARD (193-217)........ 8.00 2.40
193-217 RANDOM IN FINITE BONUS PACKS .00
193-217 PRINT RUN 299 SERIAL #'d SETS .00

❑ 1 Darin Erstad .... .50 .15
❑ 2 Garret Anderson .... .50 .15
❑ 3 Tim Salmon........................ .75 .23
❑ 4 Jarrod Washburn.................. .50 .15
❑ 5 Troy Glaus SP 4.00 1.20
❑ 6 Luis Gonzalez .... .50 .15
❑ 7 Junior Spivey .... .50 .15
❑ 8 Randy Johnson SP 5.00 1.50
❑ 9 Curt Schilling SP 4.00 1.20
❑ 10 Andruw Jones .... .75 .23
❑ 11 Gary Sheffield .... .50 .15
❑ 12 Rafael Furcal .... .50 .15
❑ 13 Greg Maddux SP.............. 8.00 2.40
❑ 14 Chipper Jones SP 5.00 1.50
❑ 15 Tony Batista .... .50 .15
❑ 16 Rodrigo Lopez.................. .50 .15
❑ 17 Jay Gibbons .... .50 .15
❑ 18 Shea Hillenbrand.............. .50 .15
❑ 19 Johnny Damon .... .75 .23
❑ 20 Derek Lowe .... .50 .15
❑ 21 Nomar Garciaparra .... 2.00 .60
❑ 22 Pedro Martinez SP 5.00 1.50
❑ 23 Manny Ramirez SP 5.00 1.50
❑ 24 Mark Prior.......................... .75 .23
❑ 25 Kerry Wood........................ .50 .15
❑ 26 Corey Patterson................ .50 .15
❑ 27 Sammy Sosa SP 5.00 1.50
❑ 28 Magglio Ordonez.............. .50 .15
❑ 29 Frank Thomas .... 1.25 .35
❑ 30 Paul Konerko.................... .50 .15
❑ 31 Adam Dunn........................ .50 .15
❑ 32 Austin Kearns .... .50 .15
❑ 33 Aaron Boone...................... .50 .15
❑ 34 Ken Griffey Jr. SP 8.00 2.40
❑ 35 Omar Vizquel.................... .75 .23
❑ 36 C.C. Sabathia .... .50 .15
❑ 37 Karim Garcia SP 4.00 1.20
❑ 38 Larry Walker...................... .50 .15
❑ 39 Preston Wilson .... .50 .15
❑ 40 Jay Payton.......................... .50 .15
❑ 41 Todd Helton SP................ 5.00 1.50
❑ 42 Carlos Pena........................ .50 .15
❑ 43 Eric Munson .... .50 .15
❑ 44 Mike Lowell........................ .50 .15
❑ 45 Josh Beckett .... .50 .15
❑ 46 A.J. Burnett .... .50 .15
❑ 47 Roy Oswalt .... .50 .15
❑ 48 Craig Biggio .... .75 .23
❑ 49 Jeff Bagwell SP 5.00 1.50
❑ 50 Lance Berkman SP 4.00 1.20
❑ 51 Mike Sweeney.................... .50 .15
❑ 52 Carlos Beltran.................... .50 .15
❑ 53 Hideo Nomo .... 1.25 .35
❑ 54 Odalis Perez .... .50 .15
❑ 55 Adrian Beltre...................... .50 .15
❑ 56 Shawn Green SP 4.00 1.20
❑ 57 Kazuhisa Ishii SP 4.00 1.20
❑ 58 Ben Sheets .... .50 .15
❑ 59 Richie Sexson .... .50 .15
❑ 60 Torii Hunter........................ .50 .15
❑ 61 Jacque Jones .... .50 .15
❑ 62 Eric Milton.......................... .50 .15
❑ 63 Corey Koskie...................... .50 .15
❑ 64 A.J. Pierzynski.................... .50 .15
❑ 65 Jose Vidro.......................... .50 .15

❑ 66 Bartolo Colon .50 .15
❑ 67 Vladimir Guerrero SP 5.00 1.50
❑ 68 Tom Glavine .75 .23
❑ 69 Mike Piazza SP 8.00 2.40
❑ 70 Roberto Alomar SP 5.00 1.50
❑ 71 Jorge Posada .75 .23
❑ 72 Mike Mussina .75 .23
❑ 73 Robin Ventura .50 .15
❑ 74 Raul Mondesi .50 .15
❑ 75 Roger Clemens SP UER 10.00 3.00
Card mistakenly numbered as 79
❑ 76 Jason Giambi SP 4.00 1.20
❑ 77 Bernie Williams SP 5.00 1.50
❑ 78 Alfonso Soriano SP 4.00 1.20
❑ 79 Derek Jeter SP 12.00 3.60
❑ 80 Miguel Tejada .50 .15
❑ 81 Eric Chavez .50 .15
❑ 82 Tim Hudson .50 .15
❑ 83 Barry Zito .50 .15
❑ 84 Mark Mulder .50 .15
❑ 85 Pat Burrell .50 .15
❑ 86 Jim Thome .75 .23
❑ 87 Bobby Abreu .50 .15
❑ 88 Brian Giles .50 .15
❑ 89 Jason Kendall .50 .15
❑ 90 Aramis Ramirez .50 .15
❑ 91 Ryan Klesko .50 .15
❑ 92 Phil Nevin .50 .15
❑ 93 Sean Burroughs .50 .15
❑ 94 J.T. Snow .50 .15
❑ 95 Rich Aurilia .50 .15
❑ 96 Benito Santiago .50 .15
❑ 97 Barry Bonds SP 12.00 3.60
❑ 98 Edgar Martinez .75 .23
❑ 99 John Olerud .50 .15
❑ 100 Bret Boone .50 .15
❑ 101 Ichiro Suzuki SP 10.00 3.00
❑ 102 J.D. Drew .50 .15
❑ 103 Jim Edmonds .75 .23
❑ 104 Scott Rolen .75 .23
❑ 105 Matt Morris .50 .15
❑ 106 Tino Martinez .75 .23
❑ 107 Albert Pujols SP 10.00 3.00
❑ 108 Aubrey Huff .50 .15
❑ 109 Carl Crawford .50 .15
❑ 110 Rafael Palmeiro .75 .23
❑ 111 Hank Blalock .50 .15
❑ 112 Alex Rodriguez SP 8.00 2.40
❑ 113 Kevin Mench SP 4.00 1.20
❑ 114 Juan Gonzalez SP 4.00 1.20
❑ 115 Shannon Stewart .50 .15
❑ 116 Vernon Wells .50 .15
❑ 117 Josh Phelps .50 .15
❑ 118 Eric Hinske .50 .15
❑ 119 Orlando Hudson .50 .15
❑ 120 Carlos Delgado SP 4.00 1.20
❑ 121 David Sanders FF RC 4.00 1.20
❑ 122 Rob Hammock FF RC 4.00 1.20
❑ 123 Rett Johnson FF RC 4.00 1.20
❑ 124 Mike Nicolas FF RC 4.00 1.20
❑ 125 Termel Sledge FF RC 4.00 1.20
❑ 126 Ryan Cameron FF RC 4.00 1.20
❑ 127 Prentice Redman FF RC 4.00 1.20
❑ 128 Clint Barmes FF RC 5.00 1.50
❑ 129 Brent Hoard FF RC 4.00 1.20
❑ 130 Willie Eyre FF RC 4.00 1.20
❑ 131 Phil Seibel FF RC 4.00 1.20
❑ 132 Chris Capuano FF RC 4.00 1.20
❑ 133 Bobby Madritsch FF RC 5.00 1.50
❑ 134 Shane Bazzell FF RC 4.00 1.20
❑ 135 Jeremy Griffiths FF RC 4.00 1.20
❑ 136 Jon Leicester FF RC 4.00 1.20
❑ 137 Brandon Webb FF RC 5.00 1.50
❑ 138 Todd Wellemeyer FF RC 4.00 1.20
❑ 139 Jose Contreras FF RC 5.00 1.50
❑ 140 Felix Sanchez FF RC 4.00 1.20
❑ 141 Arnie Munoz FF RC 4.00 1.20
❑ 142 Delvis Lantigua FF RC 4.00 1.20
❑ 143 Francisco Cruceta FF RC 4.00 1.20
❑ 144 Josh Willingham FF RC 5.00 1.50
❑ 145 Oscar Villarreal FF RC 4.00 1.20
❑ 146 Ian Ferguson FF RC 4.00 1.20
❑ 147 Pedro Liriano FF 4.00 1.20
❑ 148 Lew Ford FF RC 5.00 1.50
❑ 149 Jeff Duncan FF RC 4.00 1.20
❑ 150 Rich Fischer FF RC 4.00 1.20
❑ 151 Troy Glaus GF 5.00 1.50
❑ 152 Randy Johnson GF 8.00 2.40
❑ 153 Hideki Matsui GF RC 15.00 4.50
❑ 154 Chipper Jones GF 8.00 2.40
❑ 155 Nomar Garciaparra GF 15.00 4.50
❑ 156 Pedro Martinez GF 8.00 2.40
❑ 157 Ted Williams GF 20.00 6.00
❑ 158 Sammy Sosa GF 8.00 2.40
❑ 159 Ken Griffey Jr. GF 15.00 4.50
❑ 160 Vladimir Guerrero GF 8.00 2.40
❑ 161 Mike Piazza GF 12.00 3.60
❑ 162 Mickey Mantle GF 40.00 12.00
❑ 163 Alfonso Soriano GF 5.00 1.50
❑ 164 Derek Jeter GF 20.00 6.00
❑ 165 Roger Clemens GF 15.00 4.50
❑ 166 Jason Giambi GF 5.00 1.50
❑ 167 Barry Bonds GF 20.00 6.00
❑ 168 Ichiro Suzuki GF 15.00 4.50
❑ 169 Albert Pujols GF 15.00 4.50
❑ 170 Mark McGwire GF 20.00 6.00
❑ 171 Alex Rodriguez GF 12.00 3.60
❑ 172 Roy Oswalt 15.00 4.50
Ken Griffey Jr.
❑ 173 Barry Zito 5.00 1.50
Troy Glaus
❑ 174 Tim Hudson 15.00 4.50
Ichiro Suzuki
❑ 175 Mark Mulder 15.00 4.50
Alex Rodriguez
❑ 176 Tom Glavine 8.00 2.40
Vladimir Guerrero
❑ 177 Greg Maddux 15.00 4.50
Mike Piazza
❑ 178 Mark McGwire 30.00 9.00
Sammy Sosa
❑ 179 Mark Prior 8.00 2.40
Lance Berkman
❑ 180 Kerry Wood 15.00 4.50
Albert Pujols
❑ 181 Randy Johnson 8.00 2.40
Jeff Bagwell
❑ 182 Curt Schilling 20.00 6.00
Derek Jeter
❑ 183 Hideo Nomo 20.00 6.00
Barry Bonds
❑ 184 Kazuhisa Ishii 5.00 1.50
Todd Helton
❑ 185 Freddy Garcia 5.00 1.50
Eric Chavez
❑ 186 Al Leiter 8.00 2.40
Chipper Jones
❑ 187 Ted Williams 20.00 6.00
Nomar Garciaparra
❑ 188 Pedro Martinez 15.00 4.50
Hideki Matsui
❑ 189 Derek Lowe 8.00 2.40
Bernie Williams
❑ 190 Roger Clemens 20.00 6.00
Mike Piazza
❑ 191 Mike Mussina 8.00 2.40
Manny Ramirez
❑ 192 Mickey Mantle 30.00 9.00
Jason Giambi
❑ 193 Aaron Looper FF RC 8.00 2.40
❑ 194 Alex Prieto FF RC 8.00 2.40
❑ 195 Bo Hart FF RC 8.00 2.40
❑ 196 Chad Gaudin FF RC 8.00 2.40
❑ 197 Colin Porter FF RC 8.00 2.40
❑ 198 D.J. Carrasco FF RC 8.00 2.40
❑ 199 Dan Haren FF RC 10.00 3.00
❑ 200 Delmon Young FF RC 30.00 9.00
❑ 201 Dontrelle Willis FF 10.00 3.00
❑ 202 Jon Switzer FF 8.00 2.40
❑ 203 Edwin Jackson FF RC 10.00 3.00
❑ 204 Fernando Cabrera FF RC 8.00 2.40
❑ 205 Garrett Atkins FF 8.00 2.40
❑ 206 Jeremy Bonderman FF RC 15.00 4.50
❑ 207 Kevin Ohme FF RC 8.00 2.40
❑ 208 Khalil Greene FF 15.00 4.50
❑ 209 Luis Ayala FF RC 8.00 2.40
❑ 210 Matt Kata FF RC 8.00 2.40
❑ 211 Noah Lowry FF 10.00 3.00
❑ 212 Rich Harden FF 10.00 3.00
❑ 213 Rickie Weeks FF RC 25.00 7.50
❑ 214 Rosman Garcia FF RC 8.00 2.40
❑ 215 Ryan Wagner FF RC 8.00 2.40
❑ 216 Tom Gregorio FF RC 8.00 2.40
❑ 217 Wilfredo Ledezma FF RC 8.00 2.40
❑ NNO Ken Griffey Jr. Sample 5.00 1.50

2001 Upper Deck Gold Glove

	Nm-Mt	Ex-Mt
COMP.SET w/o SP'S (90)	15.00	4.50
COMMON CARD (1-90)	.60	.18
COMMON CARD (91-129)	5.00	1.50
COMMON (130-135)	10.00	3.00

❑ 1 Troy Glaus .60 .18
❑ 2 Darin Erstad .60 .18
❑ 3 Jason Giambi .60 .18
❑ 4 Tim Hudson .60 .18
❑ 5 Jermaine Dye .60 .18
❑ 6 Raul Mondesi .60 .18
❑ 7 Carlos Delgado .60 .18
❑ 8 Shannon Stewart .60 .18
❑ 9 Greg Vaughn .60 .18
❑ 10 Aubrey Huff .60 .18
❑ 11 Juan Gonzalez .60 .18
❑ 12 Roberto Alomar 1.00 .30
❑ 13 Omar Vizquel 1.00 .30
❑ 14 Jim Thome 1.00 .30
❑ 15 John Olerud .60 .18
❑ 16 Edgar Martinez 1.00 .30
❑ 17 Kazuhiro Sasaki .60 .18
❑ 18 Aaron Sele .60 .18
❑ 19 Cal Ripken 5.00 1.50
❑ 20 Chris Richard .60 .18
❑ 21 Ivan Rodriguez 1.00 .30
❑ 22 Rafael Palmeiro 1.00 .30
❑ 23 Alex Rodriguez 2.50 .75
❑ 24 Pedro Martinez 1.00 .30
❑ 25 Nomar Garciaparra 2.50 .75
❑ 26 Manny Ramirez Sox 1.00 .30
❑ 27 Neifi Perez .60 .18
❑ 28 Mike Sweeney .60 .18
❑ 29 Bobby Higginson .60 .18
❑ 30 Dean Palmer .60 .18
❑ 31 Tony Clark .60 .18
❑ 32 Doug Mientkiewicz .60 .18
❑ 33 Brad Radke .60 .18
❑ 34 Joe Mays .60 .18
❑ 35 Frank Thomas 1.50 .45
❑ 36 Magglio Ordonez .60 .18
❑ 37 Carlos Lee .60 .18
❑ 38 Bernie Williams 1.00 .30
❑ 39 Mike Mussina 1.00 .30
❑ 40 Derek Jeter 4.00 1.20
❑ 41 Roger Clemens 3.00 .90
❑ 42 Craig Biggio 1.00 .30
❑ 43 Jeff Bagwell 1.00 .30
❑ 44 Lance Berkman .60 .18
❑ 45 Andruw Jones 1.00 .30
❑ 46 Greg Maddux 2.50 .75
❑ 47 Chipper Jones 1.50 .45
❑ 48 Geoff Jenkins .60 .18
❑ 49 Ben Sheets 1.00 .30
❑ 50 Jeromy Burnitz .60 .18
❑ 51 Jim Edmonds 1.00 .30
❑ 52 Mark McGwire 4.00 1.20
❑ 53 Mike Matheny .60 .18
❑ 54 J.D. Drew .60 .18
❑ 55 Sammy Sosa 1.50 .45
❑ 56 Kerry Wood .60 .18

	Player	Nm-Mt	Ex-Mt
❑ 57	Fred McGriff	1.00	.30
❑ 58	Randy Johnson	1.50	.45
❑ 59	Steve Finley	.60	.18
❑ 60	Mark Grace	1.00	.30
❑ 61	Matt Williams	.60	.18
❑ 62	Luis Gonzalez	.60	.18
❑ 63	Shawn Green	.60	.18
❑ 64	Kevin Brown	.60	.18
❑ 65	Gary Sheffield	.60	.18
❑ 66	Vladimir Guerrero	1.50	.45
❑ 67	Tony Armas Jr.	.60	.18
❑ 68	Barry Bonds	4.00	1.20
❑ 69	J.T. Snow	.60	.18
❑ 70	Jeff Kent	.60	.18
❑ 71	Charles Johnson	.60	.18
❑ 72	Preston Wilson	.60	.18
❑ 73	Cliff Floyd	.60	.18
❑ 74	Robin Ventura	.60	.18
❑ 75	Mike Piazza	2.50	.75
❑ 76	Edgardo Alfonzo	.60	.18
❑ 77	Tony Gwynn	2.00	.60
❑ 78	Ryan Klesko	.60	.18
❑ 79	Scott Rolen	1.00	.30
❑ 80	Mike Lieberthal	.60	.18
❑ 81	Pat Burrell	.60	.18
❑ 82	Jason Kendall	.60	.18
❑ 83	Brian Giles	.60	.18
❑ 84	Ken Griffey Jr.	2.50	.75
❑ 85	Barry Larkin	1.00	.30
❑ 86	Pokey Reese	.60	.18
❑ 87	Larry Walker	.60	.18
❑ 88	Mike Hampton	.60	.18
❑ 89	Juan Pierre	.60	.18
❑ 90	Todd Helton	1.00	.30
❑ 91	Mike Penney GD RC	5.00	1.50
❑ 92	Wilkin Ruan GD RC	5.00	1.50
❑ 93	Greg Miller GD RC	5.00	1.50
❑ 94	Johnny Estrada GD RC	8.00	2.40
❑ 95	Tsuyoshi Shinjo GD RC	8.00	2.40
❑ 96	Josh Towers GD RC	8.00	2.40
❑ 97	H. Ramirez GD RC	8.00	2.40
❑ 98	Ryan Freel GD RC	8.00	2.40
❑ 99	M. Ensberg GD RC	8.00	2.40
❑ 100	A. Hernandez GD RC	5.00	1.50
❑ 101	Juan Uribe GD RC	8.00	2.40
❑ 102	Jose Mieses GD RC	5.00	1.50
❑ 103	Jack Wilson GD RC	8.00	2.40
❑ 104	Cesar Crespo GD RC	5.00	1.50
❑ 105	Bud Smith GD RC	5.00	1.50
❑ 106	Erick Almonte GD RC	5.00	1.50
❑ 107	E. Guzman GD RC	5.00	1.50
❑ 108	B. Duckworth GD RC	5.00	1.50
❑ 109	Juan Diaz GD RC	5.00	1.50
❑ 110	Kris Keller GD RC	5.00	1.50
❑ 111	J. Michaels GD RC	5.00	1.50
❑ 112	Bret Prinz GD RC	5.00	1.50
❑ 113	Henry Mateo GD RC	5.00	1.50
❑ 114	R. Rodriguez GD RC	5.00	1.50
❑ 115	Travis Hafner GD RC	10.00	3.00
❑ 116	Nate Teut GD RC	5.00	1.50
❑ 117	Alexis Gomez GD RC	5.00	1.50
❑ 118	Billy Sylvester GD RC	5.00	1.50
❑ 119	A. Pettyjohn GD RC	5.00	1.50
❑ 120	Josh Fogg GD RC	5.00	1.50
❑ 121	Juan Cruz GD RC	5.00	1.50
❑ 122	C. Valderrama GD RC	5.00	1.50
❑ 123	Jay Gibbons GD RC	8.00	2.40
❑ 124	D. Mendez GD RC	5.00	1.50
❑ 125	Bill Ortega GD RC	5.00	1.50
❑ 126	Sean Douglass GD RC	5.00	1.50
❑ 127	C. Parker GD RC	5.00	1.50
❑ 128	Grant Balfour GD RC	5.00	1.50
❑ 129	Joe Kennedy GD RC	8.00	2.40
❑ 130	Albert Pujols GD RC	120.00	36.00
❑ 131	W. Betemit GD RC	15.00	4.50
❑ 132	Mark Teixeira GD RC	40.00	12.00
❑ 133	Mark Prior GD RC	30.00	9.00
❑ 134	D. Brazelton GD RC	10.00	3.00
❑ 135	Ichiro Suzuki GD RC	50.00	15.00

2005 Upper Deck Hall of Fame

		Nm-Mt	Ex-Mt
	COMMON CARD (1-85)	4.00	1.20
	COMMON CARD (86-100)	4.00	1.20
	TWO BASIC AND/OR PARALLELS PER TIN		.00
	STATED PRINT RUN 550 SERIAL #'d SETS		.00
❑ 1	Al Kaline	6.00	1.80
❑ 2	Al Lopez	4.00	1.20
❑ 3	Bill Mazeroski	5.00	1.50
❑ 4	Billy Williams	4.00	1.20
❑ 5	Bob Feller	4.00	1.20
❑ 6	Bob Gibson	5.00	1.50
❑ 7	Bob Lemon	4.00	1.20
❑ 8	Bobby Doerr	4.00	1.20
❑ 9	Brooks Robinson	5.00	1.50
❑ 10	Buck Leonard	4.00	1.20
❑ 11	Carl Yastrzemski	8.00	2.40
❑ 12	Carlton Fisk	4.00	1.20
❑ 13	Casey Stengel	5.00	1.50
❑ 14	Catfish Hunter	4.00	1.20
❑ 15	Dave Winfield	4.00	1.20
❑ 16	Dennis Eckersley	4.00	1.20
❑ 17	Dizzy Dean	5.00	1.50
❑ 18	Don Drysdale	5.00	1.50
❑ 19	Don Sutton	4.00	1.20
❑ 20	Duke Snider	5.00	1.50
❑ 21	Early Wynn	4.00	1.20
❑ 22	Eddie Mathews	6.00	1.80
❑ 23	Eddie Murray	6.00	1.80
❑ 24	Enos Slaughter	4.00	1.20
❑ 25	Ernie Banks	6.00	1.80
❑ 26	Fergie Jenkins	4.00	1.20
❑ 27	Frank Robinson	4.00	1.20
❑ 28	Gary Carter	4.00	1.20
❑ 29	Gaylord Perry	4.00	1.20
❑ 30	George Brett	10.00	3.00
❑ 31	George Kell	4.00	1.20
❑ 32	George Sisler	4.00	1.20
❑ 33	Hal Newhouser	4.00	1.20
❑ 34	Harmon Killebrew	6.00	1.80
❑ 35	Hoyt Wilhelm	4.00	1.20
❑ 36	Jackie Robinson	6.00	1.80
❑ 37	Jim Bunning	4.00	1.20
❑ 38	Jim Palmer	4.00	1.20
❑ 39	Jimmie Foxx	5.00	1.50
❑ 40	Joe Morgan	4.00	1.20
❑ 41	Johnny Bench	6.00	1.80
❑ 42	Johnny Mize	4.00	1.20
❑ 43	Juan Marichal	4.00	1.20
❑ 44	Kirby Puckett	6.00	1.80
❑ 45	Larry Doby	4.00	1.20
❑ 46	Lefty Grove	4.00	1.20
❑ 47	Lou Boudreau	4.00	1.20
❑ 48	Lou Brock	5.00	1.50
❑ 49	Luis Aparicio	4.00	1.20
❑ 50	Mel Ott	5.00	1.50
❑ 51	Mickey Cochrane	4.00	1.20
❑ 52	Monte Irvin	4.00	1.20
❑ 53	Orlando Cepeda	4.00	1.20
❑ 54	Ozzie Smith	8.00	2.40
❑ 55	Paul Molitor	5.00	1.50
❑ 56	Pee Wee Reese	5.00	1.50
❑ 57	Phil Niekro	4.00	1.20
❑ 58	Phil Rizzuto	5.00	1.50
❑ 59	Pie Traynor	4.00	1.20
❑ 60	Ralph Kiner	4.00	1.20
❑ 61	Red Schoendienst	4.00	1.20
❑ 62	Richie Ashburn	5.00	1.50
❑ 63	Rick Ferrell	4.00	1.20
❑ 64	Robin Roberts	4.00	1.20
❑ 65	Robin Yount	6.00	1.80
❑ 66	Rod Carew	5.00	1.50
❑ 67	Rogers Hornsby	5.00	1.50
❑ 68	Rollie Fingers	4.00	1.20
❑ 69	Roy Campanella	5.00	1.50
❑ 70	Steve Carlton	4.00	1.20
❑ 71	Tony Perez	4.00	1.20
❑ 72	Warren Spahn	5.00	1.50
❑ 73	Whitey Ford	5.00	1.50
❑ 74	Willie McCovey	5.00	1.50
❑ 75	Willie Stargell	5.00	1.50
❑ 76	Yogi Berra	6.00	1.80
❑ 77	Babe Ruth	12.00	3.60
❑ 78	Honus Wagner	6.00	1.80
❑ 79	Lou Gehrig	8.00	2.40
❑ 80	Mickey Mantle	20.00	6.00
❑ 81	Ty Cobb	8.00	2.40
❑ 82	Ryne Sandberg	10.00	3.00
❑ 83	Satchel Paige	6.00	1.80
❑ 84	Wade Boggs	5.00	1.50
❑ 85	Reggie Jackson	5.00	1.50
❑ 86	Babe Ruth PC	12.00	3.60
❑ 87	Christy Mathewson PC	5.00	1.50
❑ 88	Cy Young PC	5.00	1.50
❑ 89	Honus Wagner PC	6.00	1.80
❑ 90	Joe DiMaggio PC	8.00	2.40
❑ 91	Lou Gehrig PC	8.00	2.40
❑ 92	Mickey Mantle PC	20.00	6.00
❑ 93	Mike Schmidt PC	10.00	3.00
❑ 94	Nolan Ryan PC	10.00	3.00
❑ 95	Satchel Paige PC	6.00	1.80
❑ 96	Stan Musial PC	8.00	2.40
❑ 97	Ted Williams PC	8.00	2.40
❑ 98	Tom Seaver PC	5.00	1.50
❑ 99	Ty Cobb PC	8.00	2.40
❑ 100	Walter Johnson PC	5.00	1.50

2001 Upper Deck MVP

		Nm-Mt	Ex-Mt
	COMPLETE SET (330)	40.00	12.00
❑ 1	Mo Vaughn	.20	.06
❑ 2	Troy Percival	.20	.06
❑ 3	Adam Kennedy	.20	.06
❑ 4	Darin Erstad	.20	.06
❑ 5	Tim Salmon	.30	.09
❑ 6	Bengie Molina	.20	.06
❑ 7	Troy Glaus	.20	.06
❑ 8	Garret Anderson	.20	.06
❑ 9	Ismael Valdes	.20	.06
❑ 10	Glenallen Hill	.20	.06
❑ 11	Tim Hudson	.20	.06
❑ 12	Eric Chavez	.20	.06
❑ 13	Johnny Damon	.30	.09
❑ 14	Barry Zito	.30	.09
❑ 15	Jason Giambi	.20	.06
❑ 16	Terrence Long	.20	.06
❑ 17	Jason Hart	.20	.06
❑ 18	Jose Ortiz	.20	.06
❑ 19	Miguel Tejada	.20	.06
❑ 20	Jason Isringhausen	.20	.06
❑ 21	Adam Piatt	.20	.06
❑ 22	Jeremy Giambi	.20	.06
❑ 23	Tony Batista	.20	.06
❑ 24	Darrin Fletcher	.20	.06
❑ 25	Mike Sirotka	.20	.06
❑ 26	Carlos Delgado	.20	.06
❑ 27	Billy Koch	.20	.06
❑ 28	Shannon Stewart	.20	.06

❑ 29 Raul Mondesi .20 .06
❑ 30 Brad Fullmer .20 .06
❑ 31 Jose Cruz Jr. .20 .06
❑ 32 Kelvim Escobar .20 .06
❑ 33 Greg Vaughn .20 .06
❑ 34 Aubrey Huff .20 .06
❑ 35 Albie Lopez .20 .06
❑ 36 Gerald Williams .20 .06
❑ 37 Ben Grieve .20 .06
❑ 38 John Flaherty .20 .06
❑ 39 Fred McGriff .30 .09
❑ 40 Ryan Rupe .20 .06
❑ 41 Travis Harper .20 .06
❑ 42 Steve Cox .20 .06
❑ 43 Roberto Alomar .30 .09
❑ 44 Jim Thome .30 .09
❑ 45 Russell Branyan .20 .06
❑ 46 Bartolo Colon .20 .06
❑ 47 Omar Vizquel .30 .09
❑ 48 Travis Fryman .20 .06
❑ 49 Kenny Lofton .20 .06
❑ 50 Chuck Finley .20 .06
❑ 51 Ellis Burks .20 .06
❑ 52 Eddie Taubensee .20 .06
❑ 53 Juan Gonzalez .20 .06
❑ 54 Edgar Martinez .30 .09
❑ 55 Aaron Sele .20 .06
❑ 56 John Olerud .20 .06
❑ 57 Jay Buhner .20 .06
❑ 58 Mike Cameron .20 .06
❑ 59 John Halama .20 .06
❑ 60 Ichiro Suzuki RC 10.00 3.00
❑ 61 David Bell .20 .06
❑ 62 Freddy Garcia .20 .06
❑ 63 Carlos Guillen .20 .06
❑ 64 Bret Boone .20 .06
❑ 65 Al Martin .20 .06
❑ 66 Cal Ripken 1.50 .45
❑ 67 Delino DeShields .20 .06
❑ 68 Chris Richard .20 .06
❑ 69 Sean Douglass RC .50 .15
❑ 70 Melvin Mora .20 .06
❑ 71 Luis Matos .20 .06
❑ 72 Sidney Ponson .20 .06
❑ 73 Mike Bordick .20 .06
❑ 74 Brady Anderson .20 .06
❑ 75 David Segui .20 .06
❑ 76 Jeff Conine .20 .06
❑ 77 Alex Rodriguez .75 .23
❑ 78 Gabe Kapler .20 .06
❑ 79 Ivan Rodriguez .30 .09
❑ 80 Rick Helling .20 .06
❑ 81 Kenny Rogers .20 .06
❑ 82 Andres Galarraga .20 .06
❑ 83 Rusty Greer .20 .06
❑ 84 Justin Thompson .20 .06
❑ 85 Ken Caminiti .20 .06
❑ 86 Rafael Palmeiro .30 .09
❑ 87 Ruben Mateo .20 .06
❑ 88 Travis Hafner RC 2.50 .75
❑ 89 Manny Ramirez Sox .30 .09
❑ 90 Pedro Martinez .30 .09
❑ 91 Carl Everett .20 .06
❑ 92 Dante Bichette .20 .06
❑ 93 Derek Lowe .20 .06
❑ 94 Jason Varitek .50 .15
❑ 95 Nomar Garciaparra .75 .23
❑ 96 David Cone .20 .06
❑ 97 Tomokazu Ohka .20 .06
❑ 98 Troy O'Leary .20 .06
❑ 99 Trot Nixon .20 .06
❑ 100 Jermaine Dye .20 .06
❑ 101 Joe Randa .20 .06
❑ 102 Jeff Suppan .20 .06
❑ 103 Roberto Hernandez .20 .06
❑ 104 Mike Sweeney .20 .06
❑ 105 Mac Suzuki .20 .06
❑ 106 Carlos Febles .20 .06
❑ 107 Jose Rosado .20 .06
❑ 108 Mark Quinn .20 .06
❑ 109 Carlos Beltran .20 .06
❑ 110 Dean Palmer .20 .06
❑ 111 Mitch Meluskey .20 .06
❑ 112 Bobby Higginson .20 .06
❑ 113 Brandon Inge .20 .06
❑ 114 Tony Clark .20 .06
❑ 115 Brian Moehler .20 .06
❑ 116 Juan Encarnacion .20 .06
❑ 117 Damion Easley .20 .06
❑ 118 Roger Cedeno .20 .06
❑ 119 Jeff Weaver .20 .06
❑ 120 Matt Lawton .20 .06
❑ 121 Jay Canizaro .20 .06
❑ 122 Eric Milton .20 .06
❑ 123 Corey Koskie .20 .06
❑ 124 Mark Redman .20 .06
❑ 125 Jacque Jones .20 .06
❑ 126 Brad Radke .20 .06
❑ 127 Cristian Guzman .20 .06
❑ 128 Joe Mays .20 .06
❑ 129 Denny Hocking .20 .06
❑ 130 Frank Thomas .50 .15
❑ 131 David Wells .20 .06
❑ 132 Ray Durham .20 .06
❑ 133 Paul Konerko .20 .06
❑ 134 Joe Crede .50 .15
❑ 135 Jim Parque .20 .06
❑ 136 Carlos Lee .20 .06
❑ 137 Magglio Ordonez .20 .06
❑ 138 Sandy Alomar Jr. .20 .06
❑ 139 Chris Singleton .20 .06
❑ 140 Jose Valentin .20 .06
❑ 141 Roger Clemens 1.00 .30
❑ 142 Derek Jeter 1.25 .35
❑ 143 Orlando Hernandez .20 .06
❑ 144 Tino Martinez .30 .09
❑ 145 Bernie Williams .30 .09
❑ 146 Jorge Posada .30 .09
❑ 147 Mariano Rivera .30 .09
❑ 148 David Justice .20 .06
❑ 149 Paul O'Neill .30 .09
❑ 150 Mike Mussina .30 .09
❑ 151 Christian Parker RC .50 .15
❑ 152 Andy Pettitte .30 .09
❑ 153 Alfonso Soriano .30 .09
❑ 154 Jeff Bagwell .30 .09
❑ 155 Morgan Ensberg RC 2.00 .60
❑ 156 Daryle Ward .20 .06
❑ 157 Craig Biggio .30 .09
❑ 158 Richard Hidalgo .20 .06
❑ 159 Shane Reynolds .20 .06
❑ 160 Scott Elarton .20 .06
❑ 161 Julio Lugo .20 .06
❑ 162 Moises Alou .20 .06
❑ 163 Lance Berkman .20 .06
❑ 164 Chipper Jones .50 .15
❑ 165 Greg Maddux .75 .23
❑ 166 Javy Lopez .20 .06
❑ 167 Andruw Jones .30 .09
❑ 168 Rafael Furcal .20 .06
❑ 169 Brian Jordan .20 .06
❑ 170 Wes Helms .20 .06
❑ 171 Tom Glavine .30 .09
❑ 172 B.J. Surhoff .20 .06
❑ 173 John Smoltz .30 .09
❑ 174 Quilvio Veras .20 .06
❑ 175 Rico Brogna .20 .06
❑ 176 Jeromy Burnitz .20 .06
❑ 177 Jeff D'Amico .20 .06
❑ 178 Geoff Jenkins .20 .06
❑ 179 Henry Blanco .20 .06
❑ 180 Mark Loretta .20 .06
❑ 181 Richie Sexson .20 .06
❑ 182 Jimmy Haynes .20 .06
❑ 183 Jeffrey Hammonds .20 .06
❑ 184 Ron Belliard .20 .06
❑ 185 Tyler Houston .20 .06
❑ 186 Mark McGwire 1.25 .35
❑ 187 Rick Ankiel .20 .06
❑ 188 Darryl Kile .20 .06
❑ 189 Jim Edmonds .30 .09
❑ 190 Mike Matheny .20 .06
❑ 191 Edgar Renteria .20 .06
❑ 192 Ray Lankford .20 .06
❑ 193 Garrett Stephenson .20 .06
❑ 194 J.D. Drew .20 .06
❑ 195 Fernando Vina .20 .06
❑ 196 Dustin Hermanson .20 .06
❑ 197 Sammy Sosa .50 .15
❑ 198 Corey Patterson .20 .06
❑ 199 Jon Lieber .20 .06
❑ 200 Kerry Wood .20 .06
❑ 201 Todd Hundley .20 .06
❑ 202 Kevin Tapani .20 .06
❑ 203 Rondell White .20 .06
❑ 204 Eric Young .20 .06
❑ 205 Matt Stairs .20 .06
❑ 206 Bill Mueller .20 .06
❑ 207 Randy Johnson .50 .15
❑ 208 Mark Grace .30 .09
❑ 209 Jay Bell .20 .06
❑ 210 Curt Schilling .20 .06
❑ 211 Erubiel Durazo .20 .06
❑ 212 Luis Gonzalez .20 .06
❑ 213 Steve Finley .20 .06
❑ 214 Matt Williams .20 .06
❑ 215 Reggie Sanders .20 .06
❑ 216 Tony Womack .20 .06
❑ 217 Gary Sheffield .20 .06
❑ 218 Kevin Brown .20 .06
❑ 219 Adrian Beltre .20 .06
❑ 220 Shawn Green .20 .06
❑ 221 Darren Dreifort .20 .06
❑ 222 Chan Ho Park .20 .06
❑ 223 Eric Karros .20 .06
❑ 224 Alex Cora .20 .06
❑ 225 Mark Grudzielanek .20 .06
❑ 226 Andy Ashby .20 .06
❑ 227 Vladimir Guerrero .50 .15
❑ 228 Tony Armas Jr. .20 .06
❑ 229 Fernando Tatis .20 .06
❑ 230 Jose Vidro .20 .06
❑ 231 Javier Vazquez .20 .06
❑ 232 Lee Stevens .20 .06
❑ 233 Milton Bradley .20 .06
❑ 234 Carl Pavano .20 .06
❑ 235 Peter Bergeron .20 .06
❑ 236 Wilton Guerrero .20 .06
❑ 237 Ugueth Urbina .20 .06
❑ 238 Barry Bonds 1.25 .35
❑ 239 Livan Hernandez .20 .06
❑ 240 Jeff Kent .20 .06
❑ 241 Pedro Feliz .20 .06
❑ 242 Bobby Estalella .20 .06
❑ 243 J.T. Snow .20 .06
❑ 244 Shawn Estes .20 .06
❑ 245 Robb Nen .20 .06
❑ 246 Rich Aurilia .20 .06
❑ 247 Russ Ortiz .20 .06
❑ 248 Preston Wilson .20 .06
❑ 249 Brad Penny .20 .06
❑ 250 Cliff Floyd .20 .06
❑ 251 A.J. Burnett .20 .06
❑ 252 Mike Lowell .20 .06
❑ 253 Luis Castillo .20 .06
❑ 254 Ryan Dempster .20 .06
❑ 255 Derrek Lee .30 .09
❑ 256 Charles Johnson .20 .06
❑ 257 Pablo Ozuna .20 .06
❑ 258 Antonio Alfonseca .20 .06
❑ 259 Mike Piazza .75 .23
❑ 260 Robin Ventura .20 .06
❑ 261 Al Leiter .20 .06
❑ 262 Timo Perez .20 .06
❑ 263 Edgardo Alfonzo .20 .06
❑ 264 Jay Payton .20 .06
❑ 265 Tsuyoshi Shinjo RC .50 .15
❑ 266 Todd Zeile .20 .06
❑ 267 Armando Benitez .20 .06
❑ 268 Glendon Rusch .20 .06
❑ 269 Rey Ordonez .20 .06
❑ 270 Kevin Appier .20 .06
❑ 271 Tony Gwynn .60 .18
❑ 272 Phil Nevin .20 .06
❑ 273 Mark Kotsay .20 .06
❑ 274 Ryan Klesko .20 .06
❑ 275 Adam Eaton .20 .06
❑ 276 Mike Darr .20 .06
❑ 277 Damian Jackson .20 .06
❑ 278 Woody Williams .20 .06
❑ 279 Chris Gomez .20 .06
❑ 280 Trevor Hoffman .20 .06
❑ 281 Xavier Nady .20 .06
❑ 282 Scott Rolen .30 .09
❑ 283 Bruce Chen .20 .06
❑ 284 Pat Burrell .20 .06
❑ 285 Mike Lieberthal .20 .06
❑ 286 B. Duckworth RC .50 .15

❑ 287 Travis Lee .20 .06
❑ 288 Bobby Abreu .20 .06
❑ 289 Jimmy Rollins .20 .06
❑ 290 Robert Person .20 .06
❑ 291 Randy Wolf .20 .06
❑ 292 Jason Kendall .20 .06
❑ 293 Derek Bell .20 .06
❑ 294 Brian Giles .20 .06
❑ 295 Kris Benson .20 .06
❑ 296 John VanderWal .20 .06
❑ 297 Todd Ritchie .20 .06
❑ 298 Warren Morris .20 .06
❑ 299 Kevin Young .20 .06
❑ 300 Francisco Cordova .20 .06
❑ 301 Aramis Ramirez .20 .06
❑ 302 Ken Griffey Jr. .75 .23
❑ 303 Pete Harnisch .20 .06
❑ 304 Aaron Boone .20 .06
❑ 305 Sean Casey .30 .09
❑ 306 Jackson Melian RC .50 .15
❑ 307 Rob Bell .20 .06
❑ 308 Barry Larkin .30 .09
❑ 309 Dmitri Young .20 .06
❑ 310 Danny Graves .20 .06
❑ 311 Pokey Reese .20 .06
❑ 312 Leo Estrella .20 .06
❑ 313 Todd Helton .30 .09
❑ 314 Mike Hampton .20 .06
❑ 315 Juan Pierre .20 .06
❑ 316 Brent Mayne .20 .06
❑ 317 Larry Walker .20 .06
❑ 318 Denny Neagle .20 .06
❑ 319 Jeff Cirillo .20 .06
❑ 320 Pedro Astacio .20 .06
❑ 321 Todd Hollandsworth .20 .06
❑ 322 Neifi Perez .20 .06
❑ 323 Ron Gant .20 .06
❑ 324 Todd Walker .20 .06
❑ 325 Alex Rodriguez CL .50 .15
❑ 326 Ken Griffey Jr. CL .50 .15
❑ 327 Mark McGwire CL .60 .18
❑ 328 Pedro Martinez CL .30 .09
❑ 329 Derek Jeter CL .60 .18
❑ 330 Mike Piazza CL .50 .15

2005 Upper Deck MVP

	Nm-Mt	Ex-Mt
COMPLETE SET (90)	25.00	7.50
COMMON CARD (1-90)	.25	.07

❑ 1 Adam Dunn .25 .07
❑ 2 Adrian Beltre .25 .07
❑ 3 Albert Pujols 1.00 .30
❑ 4 Alex Rodriguez .75 .23
❑ 5 Alfonso Soriano .25 .07
❑ 6 Andruw Jones .40 .12
❑ 7 Aubrey Huff .25 .07
❑ 8 Barry Zito .25 .07
❑ 9 Ben Sheets .25 .07
❑ 10 Bobby Abreu .25 .07
❑ 11 Bobby Crosby .25 .07
❑ 12 Bret Boone .25 .07
❑ 13 Brian Giles .25 .07
❑ 14 Carlos Beltran .25 .07
❑ 15 Carlos Delgado .25 .07
❑ 16 Carlos Lee .25 .07
❑ 17 Chipper Jones .50 .15
❑ 18 Craig Biggio .40 .12
❑ 19 Curt Schilling .40 .12
❑ 20 Dallas McPherson .25 .07
❑ 21 David Ortiz .50 .15
❑ 22 David Wright .75 .23
❑ 23 Derek Jeter 1.00 .30
❑ 24 Derek Lowe .25 .07
❑ 25 Eric Chavez .25 .07
❑ 26 Eric Gagne .25 .07
❑ 27 Frank Thomas .50 .15
❑ 28 Garret Anderson .25 .07
❑ 29 Gary Sheffield .25 .07
❑ 30 Greg Maddux .75 .23
❑ 31 Hank Blalock .25 .07
❑ 32 Hideki Matsui 1.00 .30
❑ 33 Ichiro Suzuki 1.00 .30
❑ 34 Ivan Rodriguez .40 .12
❑ 35 J.D. Drew .25 .07
❑ 36 Jake Peavy .25 .07
❑ 37 Jason Bay .25 .07
❑ 38 Jason Giambi .25 .07
❑ 39 Jason Schmidt .25 .07
❑ 40 Jeff Bagwell .40 .12
❑ 41 Jeff Kent .25 .07
❑ 42 Jim Edmonds .40 .12
❑ 43 Jim Thome .40 .12
❑ 44 Joe Mauer .25 .07
❑ 45 Johan Santana .40 .12
❑ 46 John Smoltz .40 .12
❑ 47 Johnny Damon .40 .12
❑ 48 Jorge Posada .40 .12
❑ 49 Jose Vidro .25 .07
❑ 50 Josh Beckett .25 .07
❑ 51 Kazuo Matsui .25 .07
❑ 52 Ken Griffey Jr. .75 .23
❑ 53 Kerry Wood .25 .07
❑ 54 Khalil Greene .40 .12
❑ 55 Lance Berkman .25 .07
❑ 56 Livan Hernandez .25 .07
❑ 57 Luis Gonzalez .25 .07
❑ 58 Magglio Ordonez .25 .07
❑ 59 Manny Ramirez .40 .12
❑ 60 Mark Mulder .25 .07
❑ 61 Mark Prior .40 .12
❑ 62 Mark Teixeira .40 .12
❑ 63 Miguel Cabrera .40 .12
❑ 64 Miguel Tejada .25 .07
❑ 65 Mike Mussina .40 .12
❑ 66 Mike Piazza .50 .15
❑ 67 Mike Sweeney .25 .07
❑ 68 Moises Alou .25 .07
❑ 69 Nomar Garciaparra .50 .15
❑ 70 Oliver Perez .25 .07
❑ 71 Paul Konerko .25 .07
❑ 72 Pedro Martinez .40 .12
❑ 73 Rafael Palmeiro .40 .12
❑ 74 Randy Johnson .50 .15
❑ 75 Richie Sexson .25 .07
❑ 76 Roger Clemens .75 .23
❑ 77 Roy Halladay .25 .07
❑ 78 Roy Oswalt .25 .07
❑ 79 Sammy Sosa .50 .15
❑ 80 Scott Rolen .40 .12
❑ 81 Shawn Green .25 .07
❑ 82 Steve Finley .25 .07
❑ 83 Tim Hudson .25 .07
❑ 84 Todd Helton .40 .12
❑ 85 Tom Glavine .40 .12
❑ 86 Torii Hunter .25 .07
❑ 87 Travis Hafner .25 .07
❑ 88 Troy Glaus .25 .07
❑ 89 Victor Martinez .25 .07
❑ 90 Vladimir Guerrero .50 .15

2001 Upper Deck Ovation

	Nm-Mt	Ex-Mt
COMP.SET w/o SP'S (60)	20.00	6.00
COMMON CARD (1-60)	.40	.12
COMMON WP (61-90)	5.00	1.50

❑ 1 Troy Glaus .40 .12
❑ 2 Darin Erstad .40 .12
❑ 3 Jason Giambi .40 .12
❑ 4 Tim Hudson .40 .12

❑ 5 Eric Chavez .40 .12
❑ 6 Carlos Delgado .40 .12
❑ 7 David Wells .40 .12
❑ 8 Greg Vaughn .40 .12
❑ 9 Omar Vizquel .60 .18
Travis Fryman is pictured on card front
UER
❑ 10 Jim Thome .60 .18
❑ 11 Roberto Alomar .60 .18
❑ 12 John Olerud .40 .12
❑ 13 Edgar Martinez .60 .18
❑ 14 Cal Ripken 3.00 .90
❑ 15 Alex Rodriguez 1.50 .45
❑ 16 Ivan Rodriguez .60 .18
❑ 17 Manny Ramirez Sox .60 .18
❑ 18 Nomar Garciaparra 1.50 .45
❑ 19 Pedro Martinez .60 .18
❑ 20 Jermaine Dye .40 .12
❑ 21 Juan Gonzalez .40 .12
❑ 22 Matt Lawton .40 .12
❑ 23 Frank Thomas 1.00 .30
❑ 24 Magglio Ordonez .40 .12
❑ 25 Bernie Williams .60 .18
❑ 26 Derek Jeter 2.50 .75
❑ 27 Roger Clemens 2.00 .60
❑ 28 Jeff Bagwell .60 .18
❑ 29 Richard Hidalgo .40 .12
❑ 30 Chipper Jones 1.00 .30
❑ 31 Greg Maddux 1.50 .45
❑ 32 Andruw Jones .60 .18
❑ 33 Jeromy Burnitz .40 .12
❑ 34 Mark McGwire 2.50 .75
❑ 35 Jim Edmonds .60 .18
❑ 36 Sammy Sosa 1.00 .30
❑ 37 Kerry Wood .40 .12
❑ 38 Randy Johnson 1.00 .30
❑ 39 Steve Finley .40 .12
❑ 40 Gary Sheffield .40 .12
❑ 41 Kevin Brown .40 .12
❑ 42 Shawn Green .40 .12
❑ 43 Vladimir Guerrero 1.00 .30
❑ 44 Jose Vidro .40 .12
❑ 45 Barry Bonds 2.50 .75
❑ 46 Jeff Kent .40 .12
❑ 47 Preston Wilson .40 .12
❑ 48 Luis Castillo .40 .12
❑ 49 Mike Piazza 1.50 .45
❑ 50 Edgardo Alfonzo .40 .12
❑ 51 Tony Gwynn 1.25 .35
❑ 52 Ryan Klesko .40 .12
❑ 53 Scott Rolen .60 .18
❑ 54 Bob Abreu .40 .12
❑ 55 Jason Kendall .40 .12
❑ 56 Brian Giles .40 .12
❑ 57 Ken Griffey Jr. 1.50 .45
❑ 58 Barry Larkin .60 .18
❑ 59 Todd Helton .60 .18
❑ 60 Mike Hampton .40 .12
❑ 61 Corey Patterson WP 5.00 1.50
❑ 62 Timo Perez WP 5.00 1.50
❑ 63 Toby Hall WP 5.00 1.50
❑ 64 Brandon Inge WP 5.00 1.50
❑ 65 Joe Crede WP 8.00 2.40
❑ 66 Xavier Nady WP 5.00 1.50
❑ 67 A. Pettyjohn WP RC 5.00 1.50
❑ 68 Keith Ginter WP 5.00 1.50
❑ 69 Brian Cole WP 5.00 1.50
❑ 70 Tyler Walker WP RC 5.00 1.50
❑ 71 Juan Uribe WP RC 5.00 1.50

Card	Nm-Mt	Ex-Mt
❑ 72 Alex Hernandez WP	5.00	1.50
❑ 73 Leo Estrella WP	5.00	1.50
❑ 74 Joey Nation WP	5.00	1.50
❑ 75 Aubrey Huff WP	5.00	1.50
❑ 76 Ichiro Suzuki WP RC	80.00	24.00
❑ 77 Jay Spurgeon WP	5.00	1.50
❑ 78 Sun Woo Kim WP	5.00	1.50
❑ 79 Pedro Feliz WP	5.00	1.50
❑ 80 Pablo Ozuna WP	5.00	1.50
❑ 81 Hiram Bocachica WP	5.00	1.50
❑ 82 Brad Wilkerson WP	5.00	1.50
❑ 83 Rocky Biddle WP	5.00	1.50
❑ 84 Aaron McNeal WP	5.00	1.50
❑ 85 Adam Bernero WP	5.00	1.50
❑ 86 Danys Baez WP	5.00	1.50
❑ 87 Dee Brown WP	5.00	1.50
❑ 88 Jimmy Rollins WP	5.00	1.50
❑ 89 Jason Hart WP	5.00	1.50
❑ 90 Ross Gload WP	5.00	1.50

2005 Upper Deck Pro Sigs

	Nm-Mt	Ex-Mt
COMPLETE SET (132)	50.00	15.00
COMMON CARD (1-90)	.30	.09
COMMON CARD (91-132)	.50	.15
❑ 1 Dallas McPherson	.30	.09
❑ 2 Garret Anderson	.30	.09
❑ 3 Steve Finley	.30	.09
❑ 4 Vladimir Guerrero	.75	.23
❑ 5 Luis Gonzalez	.30	.09
❑ 6 Shawn Green	.30	.09
❑ 7 Troy Glaus	.30	.09
❑ 8 Andruw Jones	.50	.15
❑ 9 Chipper Jones	.75	.23
❑ 10 John Smoltz	.50	.15
❑ 11 Tim Hudson	.30	.09
❑ 12 Miguel Tejada	.30	.09
❑ 13 Rafael Palmeiro	.50	.15
❑ 14 Sammy Sosa	.75	.23
❑ 15 Curt Schilling	.50	.15
❑ 16 David Ortiz	.75	.23
❑ 17 Johnny Damon	.50	.15
❑ 18 Manny Ramirez	.50	.15
❑ 19 Greg Maddux	1.25	.35
❑ 20 Kerry Wood	.30	.09
❑ 21 Mark Prior	.50	.15
❑ 22 Nomar Garciaparra	.75	.23
❑ 23 Frank Thomas	.75	.23
❑ 24 Paul Konerko	.30	.09
❑ 25 Adam Dunn	.30	.09
❑ 26 Ken Griffey Jr.	1.25	.35
❑ 27 Travis Hafner	.30	.09
❑ 28 Victor Martinez	.30	.09
❑ 29 Todd Helton	.50	.15
❑ 30 Ivan Rodriguez	.50	.15
❑ 31 Magglio Ordonez	.30	.09
❑ 32 Carlos Delgado	.30	.09
❑ 33 Josh Beckett	.30	.09
❑ 34 Miguel Cabrera	.50	.15
❑ 35 Craig Biggio	.50	.15
❑ 36 Jeff Bagwell	.50	.15
❑ 37 Lance Berkman	.30	.09
❑ 38 Roger Clemens	1.25	.35
❑ 39 Roy Oswalt	.30	.09
❑ 40 Mike Sweeney	.30	.09
❑ 41 Derek Lowe	.30	.09
❑ 42 Eric Gagne	.30	.09
❑ 43 J.D. Drew	.30	.09
❑ 44 Jeff Kent	.30	.09
❑ 45 Ben Sheets	.30	.09
❑ 46 Carlos Lee	.30	.09
❑ 47 Joe Mauer	.30	.09
❑ 48 Johan Santana	.50	.15
❑ 49 Torii Hunter	.30	.09
❑ 50 Carlos Beltran	.30	.09
❑ 51 David Wright	1.25	.35
❑ 52 Kazuo Matsui	.30	.09
❑ 53 Mike Piazza	.75	.23
❑ 54 Pedro Martinez	.50	.15
❑ 55 Tom Glavine	.50	.15
❑ 56 Alex Rodriguez	1.25	.35
❑ 57 Derek Jeter	1.50	.45
❑ 58 Gary Sheffield	.30	.09
❑ 59 Hideki Matsui	1.50	.45
❑ 60 Jason Giambi	.30	.09
❑ 61 Jorge Posada	.50	.15
❑ 62 Mike Mussina	.50	.15
❑ 63 Randy Johnson	.75	.23
❑ 64 Barry Zito	.30	.09
❑ 65 Bobby Crosby	.30	.09
❑ 66 Eric Chavez	.30	.09
❑ 67 Bobby Abreu	.30	.09
❑ 68 Jim Thome	.50	.15
❑ 69 Jason Bay	.30	.09
❑ 70 Oliver Perez	.30	.09
❑ 71 Brian Giles	.30	.09
❑ 72 Jake Peavy	.30	.09
❑ 73 Khalil Greene	.50	.15
❑ 74 Jason Schmidt	.30	.09
❑ 75 Moises Alou	.30	.09
❑ 76 Adrian Beltre	.30	.09
❑ 77 Bret Boone	.30	.09
❑ 78 Ichiro Suzuki	1.50	.45
❑ 79 Richie Sexson	.30	.09
❑ 80 Albert Pujols	1.50	.45
❑ 81 Jim Edmonds	.50	.15
❑ 82 Mark Mulder	.30	.09
❑ 83 Scott Rolen	.50	.15
❑ 84 Aubrey Huff	.30	.09
❑ 85 Alfonso Soriano	.30	.09
❑ 86 Hank Blalock	.30	.09
❑ 87 Mark Teixeira	.50	.15
❑ 88 Roy Halladay	.30	.09
❑ 89 Jose Vidro	.30	.09
❑ 90 Livan Hernandez	.30	.09
❑ 91 Tony Pena FC RC	.50	.15
❑ 92 Luis Hernandez FC RC	.50	.15
❑ 93 Pete Orr FC RC	.50	.15
❑ 94 Anibal Sanchez FC RC	4.00	1.20
❑ 95 Luis Mendoza FC RC	.50	.15
❑ 96 Stephen Drew FC RC	8.00	2.40
❑ 97 Russ Rohlicek FC RC	.50	.15
❑ 98 Casey Rogowski FC RC	.50	.15
❑ 99 Pedro Lopez FC RC	.50	.15
❑ 100 Tadahito Iguchi FC RC	3.00	.90
❑ 101 Daylan Childress FC RC	.50	.15
❑ 102 Juan Morillo FC RC	1.50	.45
❑ 103 Marcos Carvajal FC RC	.50	.15
❑ 104 Ubaldo Jimenez FC RC	.50	.15
❑ 105 Justin Verlander FC RC	2.50	.75
❑ 106 Chris Resop FC RC	.50	.15
❑ 107 Yorman Bazardo FC RC	.50	.15
❑ 108 Jared Gothreaux FC RC	.50	.15
❑ 109 Luke Scott FC RC	1.00	.30
❑ 110 Ambiorix Burgos FC RC	1.00	.30
❑ 111 Prince Fielder FC RC	5.00	1.50
❑ 112 Dennis Houlton FC RC	.50	.15
❑ 113 Franquelis Osoria FC RC	.50	.15
❑ 114 Norihiro Nakamura FC RC	3.00	.90
❑ 115 Oscar Robles FC RC	.50	.15
❑ 116 Steve Schmoll FC RC	.50	.15
❑ 117 Luis Pena FC RC	.50	.15
❑ 118 Dave Gassner FC RC	.50	.15
❑ 119 Ambiorix Concepcion FC RC	1.00	.30
❑ 120 Dae-Sung Koo FC RC	.50	.15
❑ 121 Matthew Lindstrom FC RC	.50	.15
❑ 122 Colter Bean FC RC	.50	.15
❑ 123 Keiichi Yabu FC RC	.50	.15
❑ 124 Philip Humber FC RC	2.00	.60
❑ 125 Wladimir Balentien FC RC	2.00	.60
❑ 126 Tony Giarratano FC RC	.50	.15
❑ 127 Shane Costa FC RC	.50	.15
❑ 128 Jeff Niemann FC RC	2.00	.60
❑ 129 Nick Masset FC RC	.50	.15
❑ 130 Ismael Ramirez FC RC	.50	.15
❑ 131 John Hattig FC RC	.50	.15
❑ 132 Brandon McCarthy FC RC	2.50	.75

2000 Upper Deck Pros and Prospects

	Nm-Mt	Ex-Mt
COMP.BASIC w/o SP's (90)	20.00	6.00
COMP.UPDATE w/o SP'S (30)	10.00	3.00
COMMON CARD (1-90)	.40	.12
COMMON PS (91-120)	5.00	1.50
COMMON PF (121-132)	4.00	1.20
COMMON PS (133-162)	5.00	1.50
COMMON (163-192)	.60	.18
❑ 1 Darin Erstad	.40	.12
❑ 2 Troy Glaus	.40	.12
❑ 3 Mo Vaughn	.40	.12
❑ 4 Jason Giambi	.40	.12
❑ 5 Tim Hudson	.40	.12
❑ 6 Ben Grieve	.40	.12
❑ 7 Eric Chavez	.40	.12
❑ 8 Shannon Stewart	.40	.12
❑ 9 Raul Mondesi	.40	.12
❑ 10 Carlos Delgado	.40	.12
❑ 11 Jose Canseco	.60	.18
❑ 12 Fred McGriff	.60	.18
❑ 13 Greg Vaughn	.40	.12
❑ 14 Manny Ramirez	.60	.18
❑ 15 Roberto Alomar	.60	.18
❑ 16 Jim Thome	.60	.18
❑ 17 Alex Rodriguez	1.50	.45
❑ 18 Freddy Garcia	.40	.12
❑ 19 John Olerud	.40	.12
❑ 20 Cal Ripken	3.00	.90
❑ 21 Albert Belle	.40	.12
❑ 22 Mike Mussina	.60	.18
❑ 23 Ivan Rodriguez	.60	.18
❑ 24 Rafael Palmeiro	.60	.18
❑ 25 Ruben Mateo	.40	.12
❑ 26 Gabe Kapler	.40	.12
❑ 27 Pedro Martinez	.60	.18
❑ 28 Nomar Garciaparra	1.50	.45
❑ 29 Carl Everett	.40	.12
❑ 30 Carlos Beltran	.40	.12
❑ 31 Jermaine Dye	.40	.12
❑ 32 Johnny Damon UER Picture on front is Joe Randa	.60	.18
❑ 33 Juan Gonzalez	.40	.12
❑ 34 Juan Encarnacion	.40	.12
❑ 35 Dean Palmer	.40	.12
❑ 36 Jacque Jones	.40	.12
❑ 37 Matt Lawton	.40	.12
❑ 38 Frank Thomas	1.00	.30
❑ 39 Paul Konerko	.40	.12
❑ 40 Magglio Ordonez	.40	.12
❑ 41 Derek Jeter	2.50	.75
❑ 42 Bernie Williams	.60	.18
❑ 43 Mariano Rivera	.60	.18
❑ 44 Roger Clemens	2.00	.60
❑ 45 Jeff Bagwell	.60	.18
❑ 46 Craig Biggio	.60	.18
❑ 47 Richard Hidalgo	.40	.12
❑ 48 Chipper Jones	1.00	.30
❑ 49 Andres Galarraga	.40	.12

❑ 50 Andruw Jones .60 .18
❑ 51 Greg Maddux 1.50 .45
❑ 52 Jeromy Burnitz .40 .12
❑ 53 Geoff Jenkins .40 .12
❑ 54 Mark McGwire 2.50 .75
❑ 55 Jim Edmonds .40 .12
❑ 56 Fernando Tatis .40 .12
❑ 57 J.D. Drew .40 .12
❑ 58 Sammy Sosa 1.00 .30
❑ 59 Kerry Wood .40 .12
❑ 60 Randy Johnson 1.00 .30
❑ 61 Matt Williams .40 .12
❑ 62 Erubiel Durazo .40 .12
❑ 63 Shawn Green .40 .12
❑ 64 Kevin Brown .40 .12
❑ 65 Gary Sheffield .40 .12
❑ 66 Adrian Beltre .40 .12
❑ 67 Vladimir Guerrero 1.00 .30
❑ 68 Jose Vidro .40 .12
❑ 69 Barry Bonds 2.50 .75
❑ 70 Jeff Kent .40 .12
❑ 71 Preston Wilson .40 .12
❑ 72 Ryan Dempster .40 .12
❑ 73 Mike Lowell .40 .12
❑ 74 Mike Piazza 1.50 .45
❑ 75 Robin Ventura .40 .12
❑ 76 Edgardo Alfonzo .40 .12
❑ 77 Derek Bell .40 .12
❑ 78 Tony Gwynn 1.25 .35
❑ 79 Matt Clement .40 .12
❑ 80 Scott Rolen .60 .18
❑ 81 Bobby Abreu .40 .12
❑ 82 Curt Schilling .40 .12
❑ 83 Brian Giles .40 .12
❑ 84 Jason Kendall .40 .12
❑ 85 Kris Benson .40 .12
❑ 86 Ken Griffey Jr. 1.50 .45
❑ 87 Sean Casey .60 .18
❑ 88 Pokey Reese .40 .12
❑ 89 Larry Walker .40 .12
❑ 90 Todd Helton .60 .18
❑ 91 Rick Ankiel PS 5.00 1.50
❑ 92 Milton Bradley PS 5.00 1.50
❑ 93 Vernon Wells PS 5.00 1.50
❑ 94 Rafael Furcal PS 5.00 1.50
❑ 95 Kazuhiro Sasaki PS RC 8.00 2.40
❑ 96 Joe Torres PS RC 5.00 1.50
❑ 97 Adam Kennedy PS 5.00 1.50
❑ 98 Adam Piatt PS 5.00 1.50
❑ 99 Matt Wheatland PS RC 5.00 1.50
❑ 100 Alex Cabrera PS RC 5.00 1.50
❑ 101 Barry Zito PS RC 12.00 3.60
❑ 102 Mike Lamb PS RC 8.00 2.40
❑ 103 Scott Heard PS RC 5.00 1.50
❑ 104 Danys Baez PS RC 5.00 1.50
❑ 105 Matt Riley PS 5.00 1.50
❑ 106 Mark Mulder PS 5.00 1.50
❑ 107 W.Rodriguez PS RC 5.00 1.50
❑ 108 Luis Matos PS RC 5.00 1.50
❑ 109 Alfonso Soriano PS 8.00 2.40
❑ 110 Pat Burrell PS 5.00 1.50
❑ 111 Mike Tonis PS RC 5.00 1.50
❑ 112 Aaron McNeal PS RC 5.00 1.50
❑ 113 Dave Krynzel PS RC 8.00 2.40
❑ 114 Josh Beckett PS 8.00 2.40
❑ 115 Sean Burnett PS RC 8.00 2.40
❑ 116 Eric Munson PS 5.00 1.50
❑ 117 Scott Downs PS RC 5.00 1.50
❑ 118 Brian Tollberg PS RC 5.00 1.50
❑ 119 Nick Johnson PS 5.00 1.50
❑ 120 Leo Estrella PS RC 5.00 1.50
❑ 121 Ken Griffey Jr. PF 10.00 3.00
❑ 122 Frank Thomas PF 6.00 1.80
❑ 123 Cal Ripken PF 20.00 6.00
❑ 124 Ivan Rodriguez PF 6.00 1.80
❑ 125 Derek Jeter PF 15.00 4.50
❑ 126 Mark McGwire PF 15.00 4.50
❑ 127 Pedro Martinez PF 6.00 1.80
❑ 128 Chipper Jones PF 6.00 1.80
❑ 129 Sammy Sosa PF 6.00 1.80
❑ 130 Alex Rodriguez PF 10.00 3.00
❑ 131 Vladimir Guerrero PF 6.00 1.80
❑ 132 Jeff Bagwell PF 6.00 1.80
❑ 133 Dane Artman PS RC 5.00 1.50
❑ 134 Juan Pierre PS RC 8.00 2.40
❑ 135 Jace Brewer PS RC 5.00 1.50
❑ 136 Sun Woo Kim PS RC 5.00 1.50
❑ 137 Jon Rauch PS RC 5.00 1.50
❑ 138 Juan Guzman PS RC 5.00 1.50
❑ 139 Daylan Holt PS RC 5.00 1.50
❑ 140 R.Washington PS RC 5.00 1.50
❑ 141 Ben Diggins PS RC 5.00 1.50
❑ 142 Mike Meyers PS RC 5.00 1.50
❑ 143 C.Wakeland PS RC 5.00 1.50
❑ 144 Cory Vance PS RC 5.00 1.50
❑ 145 Keith Ginter PS RC 5.00 1.50
❑ 146 Koyie Hill PS RC 5.00 1.50
❑ 147 Julio Zuleta PS RC 5.00 1.50
❑ 148 G.Guzman PS RC 5.00 1.50
❑ 149 Jay Spurgeon PS RC 5.00 1.50
❑ 150 Ross Gload PS RC 5.00 1.50
❑ 151 Ben Sheets PS RC 12.00 3.60
❑ 152 J.Kalinowski PS RC 5.00 1.50
❑ 153 Kurt Ainsworth PS RC 5.00 1.50
❑ 154 P.Crawford PS RC 5.00 1.50
❑ 155 Xavier Nady PS RC 8.00 2.40
❑ 156 B.Wilkerson PS RC 8.00 2.40
❑ 157 Kris Wilson PS RC 5.00 1.50
❑ 158 Paul Rigdon PS RC 5.00 1.50
❑ 159 R.Kohlmeier PS RC 5.00 1.50
❑ 160 Dane Sardinha PS RC 5.00 1.50
❑ 161 Javier Cardona PS RC 5.00 1.50
❑ 162 Brad Cresse PS RC 5.00 1.50
❑ 163 Ron Gant .60 .18
❑ 164 Mark Mulder .60 .18
❑ 165 David Wells .60 .18
❑ 166 Jason Tyner .60 .18
❑ 167 David Segui .60 .18
❑ 168 Al Martin .60 .18
❑ 169 Melvin Mora .60 .18
❑ 170 Ricky Ledee .60 .18
❑ 171 Rolando Arrojo .60 .18
❑ 172 Mike Sweeney .60 .18
❑ 173 Bobby Higginson .60 .18
❑ 174 Eric Milton .60 .18
❑ 175 Charles Johnson .60 .18
❑ 176 David Justice .60 .18
❑ 177 Moises Alou .60 .18
❑ 178 Andy Ashby .60 .18
❑ 179 Richie Sexson .60 .18
❑ 180 Will Clark 1.00 .30
❑ 181 Rondell White .60 .18
❑ 182 Curt Schilling .60 .18
❑ 183 Tom Goodwin .60 .18
❑ 184 Lee Stevens .60 .18
❑ 185 Ellis Burks .60 .18
❑ 186 Henry Rodriguez .60 .18
❑ 187 Mike Bordick .60 .18
❑ 188 Ryan Klesko .60 .18
❑ 189 Travis Lee .60 .18
❑ 190 Kevin Young .60 .18
❑ 191 Barry Larkin 1.00 .30
❑ 192 Jeff Cirillo .60 .18

2001 Upper Deck Pros and Prospects

	Nm-Mt	Ex-Mt
COMP.SET w/o SP's (90)	15.00	4.50
COMMON CARD (1-90)	.40	.12
COMMON CARD (91-135)	5.00	1.50
COMMON (136-141)	20.00	6.00

❑ 1 Troy Glaus .40 .12
❑ 2 Darin Erstad .40 .12
❑ 3 Tim Hudson .40 .12
❑ 4 Jason Giambi .40 .12
❑ 5 Jermaine Dye .40 .12
❑ 6 Barry Zito .60 .18
❑ 7 Carlos Delgado .40 .12
❑ 8 Shannon Stewart .40 .12
❑ 9 Raul Mondesi .40 .12
❑ 10 Greg Vaughn .40 .12
❑ 11 Ben Grieve .40 .12
❑ 12 Roberto Alomar .60 .18
❑ 13 Juan Gonzalez .40 .12
❑ 14 Jim Thome .60 .18
❑ 15 C.C. Sabathia .40 .12
❑ 16 Edgar Martinez .60 .18
❑ 17 Kazuhiro Sasaki .40 .12
❑ 18 Aaron Sele .40 .12
❑ 19 John Olerud .40 .12
❑ 20 Cal Ripken 3.00 .90
❑ 21 Rafael Palmeiro .60 .18
❑ 22 Ivan Rodriguez .60 .18
❑ 23 Alex Rodriguez 1.50 .45
❑ 24 Manny Ramirez Sox .60 .18
❑ 25 Pedro Martinez .60 .18
❑ 26 Carl Everett .40 .12
❑ 27 Nomar Garciaparra 1.50 .45
❑ 28 Neifi Perez .40 .12
❑ 29 Mike Sweeney .40 .12
❑ 30 Bobby Higginson .40 .12
❑ 31 Tony Clark .40 .12
❑ 32 Doug Mientkiewicz .40 .12
❑ 33 Cristian Guzman .40 .12
❑ 34 Brad Radke .40 .12
❑ 35 Magglio Ordonez .40 .12
❑ 36 Carlos Lee .40 .12
❑ 37 Frank Thomas 1.00 .30
❑ 38 Roger Clemens 2.00 .60
❑ 39 Bernie Williams .60 .18
❑ 40 Derek Jeter 2.50 .75
❑ 41 Tino Martinez .60 .18
❑ 42 Wade Miller .40 .12
❑ 43 Jeff Bagwell .60 .18
❑ 44 Lance Berkman .40 .12
❑ 45 Richard Hidalgo .40 .12
❑ 46 Greg Maddux 1.50 .45
❑ 47 Andruw Jones .60 .18
❑ 48 Chipper Jones 1.00 .30
❑ 49 Rafael Furcal .40 .12
❑ 50 Jeromy Burnitz .40 .12
❑ 51 Geoff Jenkins .40 .12
❑ 52 Ben Sheets .60 .18
❑ 53 Mark McGwire 2.50 .75
❑ 54 Jim Edmonds .60 .18
❑ 55 J.D. Drew .40 .12
❑ 56 Fred McGriff .60 .18
❑ 57 Sammy Sosa 1.00 .30
❑ 58 Kerry Wood .40 .12
❑ 59 Randy Johnson 1.00 .30
❑ 60 Luis Gonzalez .40 .12
❑ 61 Curt Schilling .40 .12
❑ 62 Kevin Brown .40 .12
❑ 63 Shawn Green .40 .12
❑ 64 Gary Sheffield .40 .12
❑ 65 Vladimir Guerrero 1.00 .30
❑ 66 Jose Vidro .40 .12
❑ 67 Barry Bonds 2.50 .75
❑ 68 Jeff Kent .40 .12
❑ 69 Rich Aurilia .40 .12
❑ 70 Preston Wilson .40 .12
❑ 71 Charles Johnson .40 .12
❑ 72 Cliff Floyd .40 .12
❑ 73 Mike Piazza 1.50 .45
❑ 74 Al Leiter .40 .12
❑ 75 Matt Lawton .40 .12
❑ 76 Tony Gwynn 1.25 .35
❑ 77 Ryan Klesko .40 .12
❑ 78 Phil Nevin .40 .12
❑ 79 Scott Rolen .60 .18
❑ 80 Pat Burrell .40 .12
❑ 81 Jimmy Rollins .40 .12
❑ 82 Jason Kendall .40 .12
❑ 83 Brian Giles .40 .12
❑ 84 Aramis Ramirez .40 .12
❑ 85 Ken Griffey Jr. 1.50 .45
❑ 86 Barry Larkin .60 .18
❑ 87 Sean Casey .60 .18
❑ 88 Larry Walker .40 .12

❑ 89 Todd Helton	.60	.18
❑ 90 Mike Hampton	.40	.12
❑ 91 Juan Cruz PS RC	5.00	1.50
❑ 92 Brian Lawrence PS RC	5.00	1.50
❑ 93 Brandon Lyon PS RC	5.00	1.50
❑ 94 A.Hernandez PS RC	5.00	1.50
❑ 95 Jose Mieses PS RC	5.00	1.50
❑ 96 Juan Uribe PS RC	8.00	2.40
❑ 97 M.Ensberg PS RC	8.00	2.40
❑ 98 Wilson Betemit PS RC	8.00	2.40
❑ 99 Ryan Freel PS RC	8.00	2.40
❑ 100 Jack Wilson PS RC	8.00	2.40
❑ 101 Cesar Crespo PS RC	5.00	1.50
❑ 102 Bret Prinz PS RC	5.00	1.50
❑ 103 H.Ramirez PS RC	8.00	2.40
❑ 104 E. Guzman PS RC	5.00	1.50
❑ 105 Josh Towers PS RC	8.00	2.40
❑ 106 B. Duckworth PS RC	5.00	1.50
❑ 107 Esix Snead PS RC	5.00	1.50
❑ 108 Billy Sylvester PS RC	5.00	1.50
❑ 109 Alexis Gomez PS RC	5.00	1.50
❑ 110 J. Estrada PS RC	8.00	2.40
❑ 111 Joe Kennedy PS RC	8.00	2.40
❑ 112 Travis Hafner PS RC	10.00	3.00
❑ 113 Martin Vargas PS RC	5.00	1.50
❑ 114 Jay Gibbons PS RC	8.00	2.40
❑ 115 Andres Torres PS RC	5.00	1.50
❑ 116 Sean Douglass PS RC	5.00	1.50
❑ 117 Juan Diaz PS RC	5.00	1.50
❑ 118 Greg Miller PS RC	5.00	1.50
❑ 119 C. Valderrama PS RC	5.00	1.50
❑ 120 Bill Ortega PS RC	5.00	1.50
❑ 121 Josh Fogg PS RC	5.00	1.50
❑ 122 Wilken Ruan PS RC	5.00	1.50
❑ 123 Kris Keller PS RC	5.00	1.50
❑ 124 Erick Almonte PS RC	5.00	1.50
❑ 125 R. Rodriguez PS RC	5.00	1.50
❑ 126 Grant Balfour PS RC	5.00	1.50
❑ 127 Nick Maness PS RC	5.00	1.50
❑ 128 Jeremy Owens PS RC	5.00	1.50
❑ 129 Doug Nickle PS RC	5.00	1.50
❑ 130 Bert Snow PS RC	5.00	1.50
❑ 131 Jason Smith PS RC	5.00	1.50
❑ 132 Henry Mateo PS RC	5.00	1.50
❑ 133 Mike Penney PS RC	5.00	1.50
❑ 134 Bud Smith PS RC	5.00	1.50
❑ 135 Junior Spivey PS RC	8.00	2.40
❑ 136 Ichiro Suzuki JSY RC	100.00	30.00
❑ 137 Albert Pujols JSY RC	200.00	60.00
❑ 138 Mark Teixeira JSY RC	120.00	36.00
❑ 139 D. Brazelton JSY RC	20.00	6.00
❑ 140 Mark Prior JSY RC	80.00	24.00
❑ 141 T. Shinjo JSY RC	20.00	6.00

2005 Upper Deck Pros and Prospects

	Nm-Mt	Ex-Mt
COMP.SET w/o SP's (100)	25.00	7.50
COMMON CARD (1-100)	.30	.09
COMMON CARD (101-150)	3.00	.90
COMMON CARD (151-175)	4.00	1.20
COMMON CARD (176-200)	5.00	1.50
❑ 1 Adam Dunn	.30	.09
❑ 2 Aramis Ramirez	.30	.09
❑ 3 Bobby Abreu	.30	.09
❑ 4 Mike Lowell	.30	.09
❑ 5 Josh Beckett	.30	.09
❑ 6 Derek Jeter	1.50	.45
❑ 7 Alex Rodriguez	1.25	.35
❑ 8 Andruw Jones	.50	.15
❑ 9 Brian Giles	.30	.09
❑ 10 Ivan Rodriguez	.50	.15
❑ 11 Aubrey Huff	.30	.09
❑ 12 Jake Peavy	.30	.09
❑ 13 Hank Blalock	.30	.09
❑ 14 Curt Schilling	.50	.15
❑ 15 Carlos Zambrano	.30	.09
❑ 16 Mike Mussina	.50	.15
❑ 17 Travis Hafner	.30	.09
❑ 18 Scott Rolen	.50	.15
❑ 19 Luis Gonzalez	.30	.09
❑ 20 Torii Hunter	.30	.09
❑ 21 Greg Maddux	1.25	.35
❑ 22 J.D. Drew	.30	.09
❑ 23 Kevin Brown	.30	.09
❑ 24 Carl Pavano	.30	.09
❑ 25 David Ortiz	.75	.23
❑ 26 Jose Reyes	.30	.09
❑ 27 Johan Santana	.50	.15
❑ 28 Todd Helton	.50	.15
❑ 29 Jason Kendall	.30	.09
❑ 30 Pedro Martinez	.50	.15
❑ 31 Chipper Jones	.75	.23
❑ 32 Ben Sheets	.30	.09
❑ 33 Garret Anderson	.30	.09
❑ 34 Carl Crawford	.30	.09
❑ 35 Jason Schmidt	.30	.09
❑ 36 Johnny Damon	.50	.15
❑ 37 Richie Sexson	.30	.09
❑ 38 Brad Penny	.30	.09
❑ 39 Carlos Delgado	.30	.09
❑ 40 Gary Sheffield	.30	.09
❑ 41 John Smoltz	.50	.15
❑ 42 Eric Chavez	.30	.09
❑ 43 Carlos Guillen	.30	.09
❑ 44 Jeff Kent	.30	.09
❑ 45 Miguel Tejada	.30	.09
❑ 46 Shawn Green	.30	.09
❑ 47 Vernon Wells	.30	.09
❑ 48 Albert Pujols	1.50	.45
❑ 49 Alfonso Soriano	.30	.09
❑ 50 Eric Gagne	.30	.09
❑ 51 Mark Prior	.50	.15
❑ 52 Rafael Furcal	.30	.09
❑ 53 Preston Wilson	.30	.09
❑ 54 Barry Larkin	.50	.15
❑ 55 Randy Johnson	.75	.23
❑ 56 Craig Wilson	.30	.09
❑ 57 Victor Martinez	.30	.09
❑ 58 Jim Thome	.50	.15
❑ 59 Paul Konerko	.30	.09
❑ 60 Jeff Bagwell	.50	.15
❑ 61 Lyle Overbay	.30	.09
❑ 62 Miguel Cabrera	.50	.15
❑ 63 Melvin Mora	.30	.09
❑ 64 Scott Podsednik	.30	.09
❑ 65 Mark Mulder	.30	.09
❑ 66 Mark Teixeira	.50	.15
❑ 67 Tom Glavine	.50	.15
❑ 68 Frank Thomas	.75	.23
❑ 69 Livan Hernandez	.30	.09
❑ 70 Kazuo Matsui	.30	.09
❑ 71 Jose Vidro	.30	.09
❑ 72 Ichiro Suzuki	1.50	.45
❑ 73 Roger Clemens	1.25	.35
❑ 74 Manny Ramirez	.50	.15
❑ 75 Michael Young	.30	.09
❑ 76 Rafael Palmeiro	.50	.15
❑ 77 Steve Finley	.30	.09
❑ 78 Andy Pettitte	.50	.15
❑ 79 Lance Berkman	.30	.09
❑ 80 Adrian Beltre	.30	.09
❑ 81 Carlos Lee	.30	.09
❑ 82 Bret Boone	.30	.09
❑ 83 Magglio Ordonez	.30	.09
❑ 84 Sammy Sosa	.75	.23
❑ 85 Tim Hudson	.30	.09
❑ 86 Vladimir Guerrero	.75	.23
❑ 87 Carlos Beltran	.30	.09
❑ 88 Kerry Wood	.30	.09
❑ 89 Jim Edmonds	.50	.15
❑ 90 Mike Sweeney	.30	.09
❑ 91 Nomar Garciaparra	.75	.23
❑ 92 Mike Piazza	.75	.23
❑ 93 Roy Halladay	.30	.09
❑ 94 Troy Glaus	.30	.09
❑ 95 Bernie Williams	.50	.15
❑ 96 Larry Walker	.50	.15
❑ 97 Craig Biggio	.50	.15
❑ 98 Roy Oswalt	.30	.09
❑ 99 Ken Griffey Jr.	1.25	.35
❑ 100 Hideki Matsui	1.50	.45
❑ 101 Bucky Jacobsen T1	3.00	.90
❑ 102 J.D. Closser T1	3.00	.90
❑ 103 Antonio Perez T1	3.00	.90
❑ 104 Chris Shelton T1	3.00	.90
❑ 105 David Aardsma T1	3.00	.90
❑ 106 Jake Woods T1	3.00	.90
❑ 107 Jung Bong T1	3.00	.90
❑ 108 Kazuhito Tadano T1	3.00	.90
❑ 109 John Van Benschoten T1	3.00	.90
❑ 110 Jesse Foppert T1	3.00	.90
❑ 111 Joe Borchard T1	3.00	.90
❑ 112 Brandon Phillips T1	3.00	.90
❑ 113 J.D. Durbin T1	3.00	.90
❑ 114 Brandon Claussen T1	3.00	.90
❑ 115 Robb Quinlan T1	3.00	.90
❑ 116 Aaron Harang T1	3.00	.90
❑ 117 Chris Burke T1	3.00	.90
❑ 118 Sergio Mitre T1	3.00	.90
❑ 119 David DeJesus T1	3.00	.90
❑ 120 Gustavo Chacin T1	3.00	.90
❑ 121 Xavier Nady T1	3.00	.90
❑ 122 Garrett Atkins T1	3.00	.90
❑ 123 Jimmy Gobble T1	3.00	.90
❑ 124 Yhency Brazoban T1	3.00	.90
❑ 125 David Kelton T1	3.00	.90
❑ 126 Dewon Brazelton T1	3.00	.90
❑ 127 Koyie Hill T1	3.00	.90
❑ 128 Roman Colon T1	3.00	.90
❑ 129 Daniel Cabrera T1	3.00	.90
❑ 130 Chris Bootcheck T1	3.00	.90
❑ 131 Brad Halsey T1	3.00	.90
❑ 132 Bobby Madritsch T1	3.00	.90
❑ 133 Grady Sizemore T1	3.00	.90
❑ 134 Akinori Otsuka T1	3.00	.90
❑ 135 Wilfredo Ledezma T1	3.00	.90
❑ 136 Russ Adams T1	3.00	.90
❑ 137 Joe Crede T1	3.00	.90
❑ 138 Chad Cordero T1	3.00	.90
❑ 139 Willie Harris T1	3.00	.90
❑ 140 Joey Gathright T1	3.00	.90
❑ 141 Logan Kensing T1	3.00	.90
❑ 142 Jon Leicester T1	3.00	.90
❑ 143 Freddy Guzman T1	3.00	.90
❑ 144 Jonny Gomes T1	3.00	.90
❑ 145 Jeff Bajenaru T1	3.00	.90
❑ 146 Andres Blanco T1	3.00	.90
❑ 147 Jhonny Peralta T1	3.00	.90
❑ 148 Jayson Werth T1	3.00	.90
❑ 149 Bill Hall T1	3.00	.90
❑ 150 Jason Davis T1	3.00	.90
❑ 151 Gabe Gross T2	4.00	1.20
❑ 152 Abe Alvarez T2	4.00	1.20
❑ 153 Josh Willingham T2	4.00	1.20
❑ 154 Merkin Valdez T2	4.00	1.20
❑ 155 Jeff Niemann T2 RC	5.00	1.50
❑ 156 Yadier Molina T2	4.00	1.20
❑ 157 Guillermo Quiroz T2	4.00	1.20
❑ 158 Ian Snell T2	4.00	1.20
❑ 159 Dan Meyer T2	4.00	1.20
❑ 160 Jason Lane T2	4.00	1.20
❑ 161 Adrian Gonzalez T2	4.00	1.20
❑ 162 Eddy Rodriguez T2	4.00	1.20
❑ 163 Jason DuBois T2	4.00	1.20
❑ 164 Juan Rincon T2	4.00	1.20
❑ 165 Ryan Wagner T2	4.00	1.20
❑ 166 Nick Swisher T2	4.00	1.20
❑ 167 Chad Tracy T2	4.00	1.20
❑ 168 Dioner Navarro T2	4.00	1.20
❑ 169 Gerald Laird T2	4.00	1.20
❑ 170 Alexis Rios T2	4.00	1.20
❑ 171 Aaron Rowand T2	4.00	1.20
❑ 172 Adam LaRoche T2	4.00	1.20
❑ 173 Kevin Youkilis T2	4.00	1.20
❑ 174 Philip Humber T2 RC	5.00	1.50
❑ 175 Chin-Hui Tsao T2	4.00	1.20
❑ 176 Jeff Francis T3	5.00	1.50
❑ 177 Chase Utley T3	5.00	1.50

❑ 178 Gavin Floyd T3	5.00	1.50
❑ 179 David Wright T3	10.00	3.00
❑ 180 B.J. Upton T3	5.00	1.50
❑ 181 Laynce Nix T3	5.00	1.50
❑ 182 Joe Mauer T3	5.00	1.50
❑ 183 Justin Morneau T3	5.00	1.50
❑ 184 Zack Greinke T3	5.00	1.50
❑ 185 Jose Capellan T3	5.00	1.50
❑ 186 Khalil Greene T3	8.00	2.40
❑ 187 Oliver Perez T3	5.00	1.50
❑ 188 Joe Blanton T3	5.00	1.50
❑ 189 Wily Mo Pena T3	5.00	1.50
❑ 190 Dallas McPherson T3	5.00	1.50
❑ 191 Edwin Jackson T3	5.00	1.50
❑ 192 Casey Kotchman T3	5.00	1.50
❑ 193 Jesse Crain T3	5.00	1.50
❑ 194 Ryan Howard T3	5.00	1.50
❑ 195 Bobby Crosby T3	5.00	1.50
❑ 196 Jason Bay T3	5.00	1.50
❑ 197 Rickie Weeks T3	5.00	1.50
❑ 198 Scott Proctor T3	5.00	1.50
❑ 199 Danny Haren T3	5.00	1.50
❑ 200 Scott Kazmir T3	5.00	1.50

2001 Upper Deck Prospect Premieres

	Nm-Mt	Ex-Mt
COMP.SET w/o SP's (90)	40.00	12.00
COMMON CARD (1-90)	.40	.12
COMMON AUTO (91-102)	15.00	4.50

Card	Nm-Mt	Ex-Mt
❑ 1 Jeff Mathis XRC	.50	.15
❑ 2 Jake Woods XRC	.40	.12
❑ 3 Dallas McPherson XRC	2.50	.75
❑ 4 Steven Shell XRC	.40	.12
❑ 5 Ryan Budde XRC	.40	.12
❑ 6 Kirk Saarloos XRC	.40	.12
❑ 7 Ryan Stegall XRC	.40	.12
❑ 8 Bobby Crosby XRC	3.00	.90
❑ 9 J.T. Stotts XRC	.40	.12
❑ 10 Neal Cotts XRC	.75	.23
❑ 11 J.Bonderman XRC	3.00	.90
❑ 12 Brandon League XRC	.40	.12
❑ 13 Tyrell Godwin XRC	.40	.12
❑ 14 Gabe Gross XRC	.50	.15
❑ 15 Chris Neylan XRC	.40	.12
❑ 16 Macay McBride XRC	.75	.23
❑ 17 Josh Burrus XRC	.40	.12
❑ 18 Adam Stern XRC	.40	.12
❑ 19 Richard Lewis XRC	.40	.12
❑ 20 Cole Barthel XRC	.40	.12
❑ 21 Mike Jones XRC	.50	.15
❑ 22 J.J. Hardy XRC	1.00	.30
❑ 23 Jon Steitz XRC	.40	.12
❑ 24 Brad Nelson XRC	.50	.15
❑ 25 Justin Pope XRC	.40	.12
❑ 26 Dan Haren XRC UER Blurb incorrectly lists him as a lefty	2.00	.60
❑ 27 Andy Sisco XRC	.50	.15
❑ 28 Ryan Theriot XRC	.40	.12
❑ 29 Ricky Nolasco XRC	.75	.23
❑ 30 Jon Switzer XRC	.40	.12
❑ 31 Justin Wechsler XRC	.40	.12
❑ 32 Mike Gosling XRC	.40	.12
❑ 33 Scott Hairston XRC	.50	.15
❑ 34 Brian Pilkington XRC	.40	.12
❑ 35 Kole Strayhorn XRC	.40	.12
❑ 36 David Taylor XRC	.40	.12
❑ 37 Donald Levinski XRC	.40	.12
❑ 38 Mike Hinckley XRC	.50	.15
❑ 39 Nick Long XRC	.40	.12
❑ 40 Brad Hennessey XRC	.50	.15
❑ 41 Noah Lowry XRC	3.00	.90
❑ 42 Josh Cram XRC	.40	.12
❑ 43 Jesse Foppert XRC	.50	.15
❑ 44 Julian Benavidez XRC	.40	.12
❑ 45 Dan Denham XRC	.40	.12
❑ 46 Travis Foley XRC	.40	.12
❑ 47 Mike Conroy XRC	.40	.12
❑ 48 Jake Dittler XRC	.50	.15
❑ 49 Rene Rivera XRC	.40	.12
❑ 50 John Cole XRC	.40	.12
❑ 51 Lazaro Abreu XRC	.40	.12
❑ 52 David Wright XRC	15.00	4.50
❑ 53 Aaron Heilman XRC	.40	.12
❑ 54 Len DiNardo XRC	.40	.12
❑ 55 Alhaji Turay XRC	.50	.15
❑ 56 Chris Smith XRC	.40	.12
❑ 57 Rommie Lewis XRC	.40	.12
❑ 58 Bryan Bass XRC	.40	.12
❑ 59 David Crouthers XRC	.40	.12
❑ 60 Josh Barfield XRC	1.25	.35
❑ 61 Jake Peavy XRC	4.00	1.20
❑ 62 Ryan Howard XRC	8.00	2.40
❑ 63 Gavin Floyd XRC	1.00	.30
❑ 64 Michael Floyd XRC	.40	.12
❑ 65 Stefan Bailie XRC	.40	.12
❑ 66 Jon DeVries XRC	.40	.12
❑ 67 Steve Kelly XRC	.40	.12
❑ 68 Alan Moye XRC	.40	.12
❑ 69 Justin Gillman XRC	.40	.12
❑ 70 Jayson Nix XRC	.40	.12
❑ 71 John Draper XRC	.40	.12
❑ 72 Kenny Baugh XRC	.40	.12
❑ 73 Michael Woods XRC	.40	.12
❑ 74 Preston Larrison XRC	.50	.15
❑ 75 Matt Coenen XRC	.40	.12
❑ 76 Scott Tyler XRC	.50	.15
❑ 77 Jose Morales XRC	.40	.12
❑ 78 Corwin Malone XRC	.40	.12
❑ 79 Dennis Ulacia XRC	.50	.15
❑ 80 Andy Gonzalez XRC	.40	.12
❑ 81 Kris Honel XRC	.40	.12
❑ 82 Wyatt Allen XRC	.40	.12
❑ 83 Ryan Wing XRC	.40	.12
❑ 84 Sean Henn XRC	.40	.12
❑ 85 John-Ford Griffin XRC	.40	.12
❑ 86 Bronson Sardinha XRC	.40	.12
❑ 87 Jon Skaggs XRC	.40	.12
❑ 88 Shelley Duncan XRC	.40	.12
❑ 89 Jason Arnold XRC	.40	.12
❑ 90 Aaron Rifkin XRC	.40	.12
❑ 91 Colt Griffin AU XRC	15.00	4.50
❑ 92 J.D. Martin AU XRC	15.00	4.50
❑ 93 Justin Wayne AU XRC	15.00	4.50
❑ 94 J.VanBenschoten AU XRC	15.00	4.50
❑ 95 Chris Burke AU XRC	40.00	12.00
❑ 96 C. Kotchman AU XRC	60.00	18.00
❑ 97 M. Garciaparra AU XRC	15.00	4.50
❑ 98 Jake Gautreau AU XRC	15.00	4.50
❑ 99 J. Williams AU XRC	25.00	7.50
❑ 100 Toe Nash AU XRC	15.00	4.50
❑ 101 Joe Borchard AU XRC	15.00	4.50
❑ 102 Mark Prior AU XRC	125.00	38.00

2002 Upper Deck Prospect Premieres

	Nm-Mt	Ex-Mt
COMP.SET w/o SP's (72)	25.00	7.50
COMMON CARD (1-60)	.40	.12
COMMON CARD (61-85)	5.00	1.50
COMMON CARD (86-97)	8.00	2.40
COMMON RIPKEN (98-99)	2.00	.60
COMMON MCGWIRE (100-105)	2.00	.60
COMMON DIMAGGIO (106-109)	1.50	.45
PENDER COR AVAIL.VIA MAIL EXCHANGE		.00

Card	Nm-Mt	Ex-Mt
❑ 1 Josh Rupe XRC	.40	.12
❑ 2 Blair Johnson XRC	.40	.12
❑ 3 Jason Pridie XRC	.40	.12
❑ 4 Tim Gilhooly XRC	.40	.12
❑ 5 Kennard Jones XRC	.40	.12
❑ 6 Darrell Rasner XRC	.40	.12
❑ 7 Adam Donachie XRC	.40	.12
❑ 8 Josh Murray XRC	.40	.12
❑ 9 Brian Dopirak XRC	1.25	.35
❑ 10 Jason Cooper XRC	.40	.12
❑ 11 Zach Hammes XRC	.40	.12
❑ 12 Jon Lester XRC	5.00	1.50
❑ 13 Kevin Jepsen XRC	.50	.15
❑ 14 Curtis Granderson XRC	1.25	.35
❑ 15 David Bush XRC	.50	.15
❑ 16 Joel Guzman	.75	.23
❑ 17A Matt Pender UER XRC Pictures Curtis Granderson	.75	.23
❑ 17B Matt Pender COR		
❑ 18 Derick Grigsby XRC	.40	.12
❑ 19 Jeremy Reed XRC	2.00	.60
❑ 20 Jonathan Broxton XRC	.75	.23
❑ 21 Jesse Crain XRC	.75	.23
❑ 22 Justin Jones XRC	.50	.15
❑ 23 Brian Slocum XRC	.40	.12
❑ 24 Brian McCann XRC	2.00	.60
❑ 25 Francisco Liriano XRC	4.00	1.20
❑ 26 Fred Lewis XRC	.40	.12
❑ 27 Steve Stanley XRC	.40	.12
❑ 28 Chris Snyder XRC	.50	.15
❑ 29 Dan Cevette XRC	.40	.12
❑ 30 Kiel Fisher XRC	.50	.15
❑ 31 Brandon Weeden XRC	.40	.12
❑ 32 Pat Osborn XRC	.40	.12
❑ 33 Taber Lee XRC	.40	.12
❑ 34 Dan Ortmeier XRC	.50	.15
❑ 35 Josh Johnson XRC	1.00	.30
❑ 36 Val Majewski XRC	.40	.12
❑ 37 Larry Broadway XRC	.40	.12
❑ 38 Joey Gomes XRC	.40	.12
❑ 39 Eric Thomas XRC	.40	.12
❑ 40 James Loney XRC	1.25	.35
❑ 41 Charlie Morton XRC	.40	.12
❑ 42 Mark McLemore XRC	.40	.12
❑ 43 Matt Craig XRC	.50	.15
❑ 44 Ryan Rodriguez XRC	.40	.12
❑ 45 Rich Hill XRC	1.00	.30
❑ 46 Bob Malek XRC	.40	.12
❑ 47 Justin Maureau XRC	.40	.12
❑ 48 Randy Braun XRC	.40	.12
❑ 49 Brian Grant XRC	.40	.12
❑ 50 Tyler Davidson XRC	.50	.15
❑ 51 Travis Hanson XRC	.40	.12
❑ 52 Kyle Boyer XRC	.40	.12
❑ 53 James Holcomb XRC	.40	.12
❑ 54 Ryan Williams XRC	.40	.12
❑ 55 Ben Crockett XRC	.40	.12
❑ 56 Adam Greenberg XRC	.75	.23
❑ 57 John Baker XRC	.40	.12
❑ 58 Matt Carson XRC	.40	.12
❑ 59 Jonathan George XRC	.40	.12
❑ 60 David Jensen XRC	.40	.12
❑ 61 Nick Swisher JSY XRC	15.00	4.50
❑ 62 Br.Clevlen JSY XRC UER Name mispelled as Cleven	8.00	2.40
❑ 63 Royce Ring JSY XRC	5.00	1.50
❑ 64 Mike Nixon JSY XRC	5.00	1.50
❑ 65 Ricky Barrett JSY XRC	5.00	1.50
❑ 66 Russ Adams JSY XRC	8.00	2.40
❑ 67 Joe Mauer JSY XRC	15.00	4.50
❑ 68 Jeff Francoeur JSY XRC	50.00	15.00
❑ 69 Joseph Blanton JSY XRC	8.00	2.40

❑ 70 Micah Schilling JSY XRC	5.00	1.50
❑ 71 John McCurdy JSY XRC	5.00	1.50
❑ 72 Sergio Santos JSY XRC	8.00	2.40
❑ 73 Josh Womack JSY XRC	5.00	1.50
❑ 74 Jared Doyle JSY XRC	5.00	1.50
❑ 75 Ben Fritz JSY XRC	5.00	1.50
❑ 76 Greg Miller JSY XRC	8.00	2.40
❑ 77 Luke Hagerty JSY XRC	5.00	1.50
❑ 78 Matt Whitney JSY XRC	5.00	1.50
❑ 79 Dan Meyer JSY XRC	8.00	2.40
❑ 80 Bill Murphy JSY XRC	5.00	1.50
❑ 81 Zach Segovia JSY XRC	5.00	1.50
❑ 82 St. Obenchain JSY XRC	5.00	1.50
❑ 83 Matt Clanton JSY XRC	5.00	1.50
❑ 84 Mark Teahen JSY XRC	8.00	2.40
❑ 85 Kyle Pawelczyk JSY XRC	5.00	1.50
❑ 86 Khalil Greene AU XRC	40.00	12.00
❑ 87 Joe Saunders AU XRC	10.00	3.00
❑ 88 Jeremy Hermida AU XRC	40.00	12.00
❑ 89 Drew Meyer AU XRC	8.00	2.40
❑ 90 Jeff Francis AU XRC	15.00	4.50
❑ 91 Scott Moore AU XRC	10.00	3.00
❑ 92 Prince Fielder AU XRC	80.00	24.00
❑ 93 Zack Greinke AU XRC	25.00	7.50
❑ 94 Chris Gruler AU XRC	8.00	2.40
❑ 95 Scott Kazmir AU XRC	60.00	18.00
❑ 96 B.J. Upton AU XRC	50.00	15.00
❑ 97 Clint Everts AU XRC	10.00	3.00
❑ 98 Cal Ripken TRIB	2.00	.60
❑ 99 Cal Ripken TRIB	2.00	.60
❑ 100 Mark McGwire TRIB	2.00	.60
❑ 101 Mark McGwire TRIB	2.00	.60
❑ 102 Mark McGwire TRIB	2.00	.60
❑ 103 Mark McGwire TRIB	2.00	.60
❑ 104 Mark McGwire TRIB	2.00	.60
❑ 105 Joe DiMaggio TRIB	1.50	.45
❑ 106 Joe DiMaggio TRIB	1.50	.45
❑ 107 Joe DiMaggio TRIB	1.50	.45
❑ 108 Joe DiMaggio TRIB	1.50	.45
❑ 109 Joe DiMaggio TRIB	1.50	.45

2003 Upper Deck Prospect Premieres

	MINT	NRMT
COMPLETE SET (90)	40.00	18.00
❑ 1 Bryan Opdyke XRC	.40	.18
❑ 2 Gabriel Sosa XRC	.40	.18
❑ 3 Tila Reynolds XRC	.40	.18
❑ 4 Aaron Hill XRC	.75	.35
❑ 5 Aaron Marsden XRC	.50	.23
❑ 6 Abe Alvarez XRC	.50	.23
❑ 7 Adam Jones XRC	.75	.35
❑ 8 Adam Miller XRC	1.50	.70
❑ 9 Andre Ethier XRC	1.50	.70
❑ 10 Anthony Gwynn XRC	.50	.23
❑ 11 Brad Snyder XRC	1.00	.45
❑ 12 Brad Sullivan XRC	.50	.23
❑ 13 Brian Anderson XRC	2.00	.90
❑ 14 Brian Buscher XRC	.40	.18
❑ 15 Brian Snyder XRC	.50	.23
❑ 16 Carlos Quentin XRC	2.50	1.10
❑ 17 Chad Billingsley XRC	2.50	1.10
❑ 18 Fraser Dizard XRC	.40	.18
❑ 19 Chris Durbin XRC	.40	.18
❑ 20 Chris Ray XRC	.75	.35
❑ 21 Conor Jackson XRC	3.00	1.35
❑ 22 Kory Casto XRC	.75	.35
❑ 23 Craig Whitaker XRC	.50	.23
❑ 24 Daniel Moore XRC	.40	.18
❑ 25 Daric Barton XRC	3.00	1.35
❑ 26 Darin Downs XRC	.50	.23
❑ 27 David Murphy XRC	1.00	.45
❑ 28 Dustin Majewski XRC	.50	.23
❑ 29 Edgardo Baez XRC	.50	.23
❑ 30 Jake Fox XRC	.40	.18
❑ 31 Jake Stevens XRC	.75	.35
❑ 32 Jamie D'Antona XRC	.75	.35
❑ 33 James Houser XRC	.50	.23
❑ 34 Jar. Saltalamacchia XRC	3.00	1.35
❑ 35 Jason Hirsh XRC	.75	.35
❑ 36 Javi Herrera XRC	.50	.23
❑ 37 Jeff Allison XRC	.40	.18
❑ 38 John Hudgins XRC	.40	.18
❑ 39 Jo Jo Reyes XRC	.50	.23
❑ 40 Justin James XRC	.40	.18
❑ 41 Kurt Isenberg XRC	.40	.18
❑ 42 Kyle Boyer XRC	.40	.18
❑ 43 Lastings Milledge XRC	3.00	1.35
❑ 44 Luis Atilano XRC	.40	.18
❑ 45 Matt Murton XRC	2.00	.90
❑ 46 Matt Moses XRC	1.25	.55
❑ 47 Matt Harrison XRC	.75	.35
❑ 48 Michael Bourn XRC	.75	.35
❑ 49 Miguel Vega XRC	.40	.18
❑ 50 Mitch Maier XRC	.75	.35
❑ 51 Omar Quintanilla XRC	.75	.35
❑ 52 Ryan Sweeney XRC	1.00	.45
❑ 53 Scott Baker XRC	1.50	.70
❑ 54 Sean Rodriguez XRC	.50	.23
❑ 55 Steve Lerud XRC	.50	.23
❑ 56 Thomas Pauly XRC	.40	.18
❑ 57 Tom Gorzelanny XRC	.50	.23
❑ 58 Tim Moss XRC	.40	.18
❑ 59 Robbie Wooley XRC	.50	.23
❑ 60 Trey Webb XRC	.40	.18
❑ 61 Wes Littleton XRC	.50	.23
❑ 62 Beau Vaughan XRC	.50	.23
❑ 63 Willy Jo Ronda XRC	.50	.23
❑ 64 Chris Lubanski XRC	1.00	.45
❑ 65 Ian Stewart XRC	8.00	3.60
❑ 66 John Danks XRC	1.50	.70
❑ 67 Kyle Sleeth XRC	.75	.35
❑ 68 Michael Aubrey XRC	.75	.35
❑ 69 Kevin Kouzmanoff XRC	.75	.35
❑ 70 Ryan Harvey XRC	2.00	.90
❑ 71 Tim Stauffer XRC	1.00	.45
❑ 72 Tony Richie XRC	.40	.18
❑ 73 Brandon Wood XRC	8.00	3.60
❑ 74 David Aardsma XRC	.50	.23
❑ 75 David Shinskie XRC	.40	.18
❑ 76 Dennis Dove XRC	.50	.23
❑ 77 Eric Sultemeier XRC	.40	.18
❑ 78 Jay Sborz XRC	.40	.18
❑ 79 Jimmy Barthmaier XRC	.40	.18
❑ 80 Josh Whitesell XRC	.40	.18
❑ 81 Josh Anderson XRC	.75	.35
❑ 82 Kenny Lewis XRC	.50	.23
❑ 83 Mateo Miramontes XRC	.40	.18
❑ 84 Nick Markakis XRC	2.00	.90
❑ 85 Paul Bacot XRC	.50	.23
❑ 86 Peter Stonard XRC	.40	.18
❑ 87 Reggie Willits XRC	.40	.18
❑ 88 Shane Costa XRC	.40	.18
❑ 89 Billy Sadler XRC	.40	.18
❑ 90 Delmon Young XRC	5.00	2.20

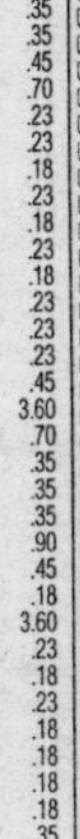
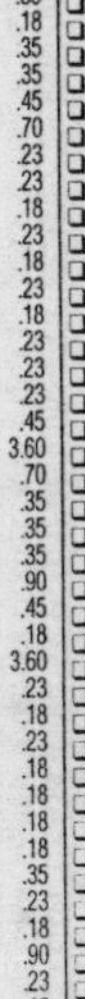

2005 Upper Deck Trilogy

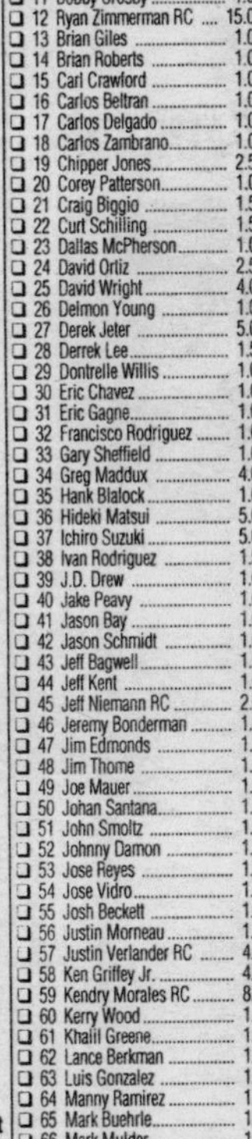

	Nm-Mt	Ex-Mt
COMPLETE SET (100)	50.00	15.00
COMMON CARD (1-100)	1.00	.30
❑ 1 A.J. Burnett	1.00	.30
❑ 2 Adam Dunn	1.00	.30
❑ 3 Adrian Beltre	1.00	.30
❑ 4 Albert Pujols	5.00	1.50
❑ 5 Alex Rodriguez	4.00	1.50
❑ 6 Alfonso Soriano	1.00	.30
❑ 7 Andruw Jones	1.50	.45
❑ 8 Aramis Ramirez	1.00	.30
❑ 9 Ben Sheets	1.00	.30
❑ 10 Bobby Abreu	1.00	.30
❑ 11 Bobby Crosby	1.00	.30
❑ 12 Ryan Zimmerman RC	15.00	4.50
❑ 13 Brian Giles	1.00	.30
❑ 14 Brian Roberts	1.00	.30
❑ 15 Carl Crawford	1.00	.30
❑ 16 Carlos Beltran	1.00	.30
❑ 17 Carlos Delgado	1.00	.30
❑ 18 Carlos Zambrano	1.00	.30
❑ 19 Chipper Jones	2.50	.75
❑ 20 Corey Patterson	1.00	.30
❑ 21 Craig Biggio	1.50	.45
❑ 22 Curt Schilling	1.50	.45
❑ 23 Dallas McPherson	1.00	.30
❑ 24 David Ortiz	2.50	.75
❑ 25 David Wright	4.00	1.20
❑ 26 Delmon Young	1.00	.30
❑ 27 Derek Jeter	5.00	1.50
❑ 28 Derrek Lee	1.50	.45
❑ 29 Dontrelle Willis	1.00	.30
❑ 30 Eric Chavez	1.00	.30
❑ 31 Eric Gagne	1.00	.30
❑ 32 Francisco Rodriguez	1.00	.30
❑ 33 Gary Sheffield	1.00	.30
❑ 34 Greg Maddux	4.00	1.20
❑ 35 Hank Blalock	1.00	.30
❑ 36 Hideki Matsui	5.00	1.50
❑ 37 Ichiro Suzuki	5.00	1.50
❑ 38 Ivan Rodriguez	1.50	.45
❑ 39 J.D. Drew	1.00	.30
❑ 40 Jake Peavy	1.00	.30
❑ 41 Jason Bay	1.00	.30
❑ 42 Jason Schmidt	1.00	.30
❑ 43 Jeff Bagwell	1.50	.45
❑ 44 Jeff Kent	1.00	.30
❑ 45 Jeff Niemann RC	2.50	.75
❑ 46 Jeremy Bonderman	1.00	.30
❑ 47 Jim Edmonds	1.50	.45
❑ 48 Jim Thome	1.50	.45
❑ 49 Joe Mauer	1.00	.30
❑ 50 Johan Santana	1.50	.45
❑ 51 John Smoltz	1.50	.45
❑ 52 Johnny Damon	1.50	.45
❑ 53 Jose Reyes	1.00	.30
❑ 54 Jose Vidro	1.00	.30
❑ 55 Josh Beckett	1.00	.30
❑ 56 Justin Morneau	1.00	.30
❑ 57 Justin Verlander RC	4.00	1.20
❑ 58 Ken Griffey Jr.	4.00	1.20
❑ 59 Kendry Morales RC	8.00	2.40
❑ 60 Kerry Wood	1.00	.30
❑ 61 Khalil Greene	1.50	.45
❑ 62 Lance Berkman	1.00	.30
❑ 63 Luis Gonzalez	1.00	.30
❑ 64 Manny Ramirez	1.50	.45
❑ 65 Mark Buehrle	1.00	.30
❑ 66 Mark Mulder	1.00	.30
❑ 67 Mark Prior	1.50	.45
❑ 68 Mark Teixeira	1.50	.45
❑ 69 Michael Young	1.00	.30
❑ 70 Miguel Cabrera	1.50	.45
❑ 71 Miguel Tejada	1.00	.30
❑ 72 Mike Mussina	1.50	.45
❑ 73 Mike Piazza	2.50	.75
❑ 74 Nomar Garciaparra	2.50	.75
❑ 75 Pat Burrell	1.00	.30
❑ 76 Paul Konerko	1.00	.30

❑ 77 Pedro Martinez 1.50 .45
❑ 78 Philip Humber RC 2.50 .75
❑ 79 Prince Fielder RC 10.00 3.00
❑ 80 Randy Johnson 2.50 .75
❑ 81 Richie Sexson 1.00 .30
❑ 82 Rickie Weeks 1.00 .30
❑ 83 Roger Clemens 4.00 1.20
❑ 84 Roy Halladay 1.00 .30
❑ 85 Roy Oswalt 1.00 .30
❑ 86 Sammy Sosa 2.50 .75
❑ 87 Scott Kazmir 1.00 .30
❑ 88 Scott Rolen 1.50 .45
❑ 89 Stephen Drew RC 10.00 3.00
❑ 90 Tadahito Iguchi RC 4.00 1.20
❑ 91 Tim Hudson 1.00 .30
❑ 92 Todd Helton 1.50 .45
❑ 93 Tom Glavine 1.50 .45
❑ 94 Torii Hunter 1.00 .30
❑ 95 Travis Hafner 1.00 .30
❑ 96 Troy Glaus 1.00 .30
❑ 97 Vernon Wells 1.00 .30
❑ 98 Victor Martinez 1.00 .30
❑ 99 Vladimir Guerrero 2.50 .75
❑ 100 Zack Greinke 1.00 .30

2001 Upper Deck Victory

	Nm-Mt	Ex-Mt
COMPLETE SET (660)	50.00	15.00

❑ 1 Troy Glaus .20 .06
❑ 2 Scott Spiezio .20 .06
❑ 3 Gary DiSarcina .20 .06
❑ 4 Darin Erstad .20 .06
❑ 5 Tim Salmon .30 .09
❑ 6 Troy Percival .20 .06
❑ 7 Ramon Ortiz .20 .06
❑ 8 Orlando Palmeiro .20 .06
❑ 9 Tim Belcher .20 .06
❑ 10 Mo Vaughn .20 .06
❑ 11 Bengie Molina .20 .06
❑ 12 Benji Gil .20 .06
❑ 13 Scott Schoeneweis .20 .06
❑ 14 Garret Anderson .20 .06
❑ 15 Matt Wise .20 .06
❑ 16 Adam Kennedy .20 .06
❑ 17 Jarrod Washburn .20 .06
❑ 18 Darin Erstad .20 .06
Troy Percival CL
❑ 19 Jason Giambi .20 .06
❑ 20 Tim Hudson .20 .06
❑ 21 Ramon Hernandez .20 .06
❑ 22 Eric Chavez .20 .06
❑ 23 Gil Heredia .20 .06
❑ 24 Jason Isringhausen .20 .06
❑ 25 Jeremy Giambi .20 .06
❑ 26 Miguel Tejada .20 .06
❑ 27 Barry Zito .30 .09
❑ 28 Terrence Long .20 .06
❑ 29 Ryan Christenson .20 .06
❑ 30 Mark Mulder .20 .06
❑ 31 Olmedo Saenz .20 .06
❑ 32 Adam Piatt .20 .06
❑ 33 Ben Grieve .20 .06
❑ 34 Omar Olivares .20 .06
❑ 35 John Jaha .20 .06
❑ 36 Jason Giambi .20 .06
Tim Hudson CL
❑ 37 Carlos Delgado .20 .06
❑ 38 Esteban Loaiza .20 .06
❑ 39 Brad Fullmer .20 .06
❑ 40 David Wells .20 .06
❑ 41 Chris Woodward .20 .06
❑ 42 Billy Koch .20 .06
❑ 43 Shannon Stewart .20 .06
❑ 44 Chris Carpenter .20 .06
❑ 45 Steve Parris .20 .06
❑ 46 Darrin Fletcher .20 .06
❑ 47 Joey Hamilton .20 .06
❑ 48 Jose Cruz Jr. .20 .06
❑ 49 Vernon Wells .20 .06
❑ 50 Raul Mondesi .20 .06
❑ 51 Kelvim Escobar .20 .06
❑ 52 Tony Batista .20 .06
❑ 53 Alex Gonzalez .20 .06
❑ 54 Carlos Delgado .20 .06
David Wells CL
❑ 55 Greg Vaughn .20 .06
❑ 56 Albie Lopez .20 .06
❑ 57 Randy Winn .20 .06
❑ 58 Ryan Rupe .20 .06
❑ 59 Steve Cox .20 .06
❑ 60 Vinny Castilla .20 .06
❑ 61 Jose Guillen .20 .06
❑ 62 Wilson Alvarez .20 .06
❑ 63 Bryan Rekar .20 .06
❑ 64 Gerald Williams .20 .06
❑ 65 Esteban Yan .20 .06
❑ 66 Felix Martinez .20 .06
❑ 67 Fred McGriff .30 .09
❑ 68 John Flaherty .20 .06
❑ 69 Jason Tyner .20 .06
❑ 70 Russ Johnson .20 .06
❑ 71 Roberto Hernandez .20 .06
❑ 72 Greg Vaughn .20 .06
Albie Lopez CL
❑ 73 Eddie Taubensee .20 .06
❑ 74 Bob Wickman .20 .06
❑ 75 Ellis Burks .20 .06
❑ 76 Kenny Lofton .20 .06
❑ 77 Einar Diaz .20 .06
❑ 78 Travis Fryman .20 .06
❑ 79 Omar Vizquel .30 .09
❑ 80 Jason Bere .20 .06
❑ 81 Bartolo Colon .20 .06
❑ 82 Jim Thome .30 .09
❑ 83 Roberto Alomar .30 .09
❑ 84 Chuck Finley .20 .06
❑ 85 Steve Woodard .20 .06
❑ 86 Russ Branyan .20 .06
❑ 87 Dave Burba .20 .06
❑ 88 Jaret Wright .20 .06
❑ 89 Jacob Cruz .20 .06
❑ 90 Steve Karsay .20 .06
❑ 91 Manny Ramirez .20 .06
Bartolo Colon CL
❑ 92 Raul Ibanez .20 .06
❑ 93 Freddy Garcia .20 .06
❑ 94 Edgar Martinez .30 .09
❑ 95 Jay Buhner .20 .06
❑ 96 Jamie Moyer .20 .06
❑ 97 John Olerud .20 .06
❑ 98 Aaron Sele .20 .06
❑ 99 Kazuhiro Sasaki .20 .06
❑ 100 Mike Cameron .20 .06
❑ 101 John Halama .20 .06
❑ 102 David Bell .20 .06
❑ 103 Gil Meche .20 .06
❑ 104 Carlos Guillen .20 .06
❑ 105 Mark McLemore .20 .06
❑ 106 Stan Javier .20 .06
❑ 107 Al Martin .20 .06
❑ 108 Dan Wilson .20 .06
❑ 109 Alex Rodriguez .50 .15
Kazuhiro Sasaki CL
❑ 110 Cal Ripken 1.50 .45
❑ 111 Delino DeShields .20 .06
❑ 112 Sidney Ponson .20 .06
❑ 113 Albert Belle .20 .06
❑ 114 Jose Mercedes .20 .06
❑ 115 Scott Erickson .20 .06
❑ 116 Jerry Hairston Jr. .20 .06
❑ 117 Brook Fordyce .20 .06
❑ 118 Luis Matos .20 .06
❑ 119 Eugene Kingsale .20 .06
❑ 120 Jeff Conine .20 .06
❑ 121 Chris Richard .20 .06
❑ 122 Fernando Lunar .20 .06
❑ 123 John Parrish .20 .06
❑ 124 Brady Anderson .20 .06
❑ 125 Ryan Kohlmeier .20 .06
❑ 126 Melvin Mora .20 .06
❑ 127 Albert Belle .20 .06
Jose Mercedes CL
❑ 128 Ivan Rodriguez .30 .09
❑ 129 Justin Thompson .20 .06
❑ 130 Kenny Rogers .20 .06
❑ 131 Rafael Palmeiro .30 .09
❑ 132 Rusty Greer .20 .06
❑ 133 Gabe Kapler .20 .06
❑ 134 John Wetteland .20 .06
❑ 135 Mike Lamb .20 .06
❑ 136 Doug Davis .20 .06
❑ 137 Ruben Mateo .20 .06
❑ 138 A. Rodriguez Rangers 1.50 .45
❑ 139 Chad Curtis .20 .06
❑ 140 Rick Helling .20 .06
❑ 141 Ryan Glynn .20 .06
❑ 142 Andres Galarraga .20 .06
❑ 143 Ricky Ledee .20 .06
❑ 144 Frank Catalanotto .20 .06
❑ 145 Rafael Palmeiro .20 .06
Rick Helling CL
❑ 146 Pedro Martinez .30 .09
❑ 147 Wilton Veras .20 .06
❑ 148 Manny Ramirez .30 .09
❑ 149 Rolando Arrojo .20 .06
❑ 150 Nomar Garciaparra .75 .23
❑ 151 Darren Lewis .20 .06
❑ 152 Troy O'Leary .20 .06
❑ 153 Tomokazu Ohka .20 .06
❑ 154 Carl Everett .20 .06
❑ 155 Jason Varitek .50 .15
❑ 156 Frank Castillo .20 .06
❑ 157 Pete Schourek .20 .06
❑ 158 Jose Offerman .20 .06
❑ 159 Derek Lowe .20 .06
❑ 160 John Valentin .20 .06
❑ 161 Dante Bichette .20 .06
❑ 162 Trot Nixon .20 .06
❑ 163 Nomar Garciaparra .50 .15
Pedro Martinez CL
❑ 164 Jermaine Dye .20 .06
❑ 165 Dave McCarty .20 .06
❑ 166 Jose Rosado .20 .06
❑ 167 Mike Sweeney .20 .06
❑ 168 Rey Sanchez .20 .06
❑ 169 Jeff Suppan .20 .06
❑ 170 Chad Durbin .20 .06
❑ 171 Carlos Beltran .20 .06
❑ 172 Brian Meadows .20 .06
❑ 173 Todd Dunwoody .20 .06
❑ 174 Johnny Damon .30 .09
❑ 175 Blake Stein .20 .06
❑ 176 Carlos Febles .20 .06
❑ 177 Joe Randa .20 .06
❑ 178 Mac Suzuki .20 .06
❑ 179 Mark Quinn .20 .06
❑ 180 Gregg Zaun .20 .06
❑ 181 Mike Sweeney .20 .06
Jeff Suppan
❑ 182 Juan Gonzalez .20 .06
❑ 183 Dean Palmer .20 .06
❑ 184 Wendell Magee .20 .06
❑ 185 Todd Jones .20 .06
❑ 186 Bobby Higginson .20 .06
❑ 187 Brian Moehler .20 .06
❑ 188 Juan Encarnacion .20 .06
❑ 189 Tony Clark .20 .06

❑ 190 Rich Becker .20 .06
❑ 191 Roger Cedeno .20 .06
❑ 192 Mitch Meluskey .20 .06
❑ 193 Shane Halter .20 .06
❑ 194 Jeff Weaver .20 .06
❑ 195 Deivi Cruz .20 .06
❑ 196 Damion Easley .20 .06
❑ 197 Robert Fick .20 .06
❑ 198 Matt Anderson .20 .06
❑ 199 Bobby Higginson .20 .06
Brian Moehler
❑ 200 Brad Radke .20 .06
❑ 201 Mark Redman .20 .06
❑ 202 Corey Koskie .20 .06
❑ 203 Matt Lawton .20 .06
❑ 204 Eric Milton .20 .06
❑ 205 Chad Moeller .20 .06
❑ 206 Jacque Jones .20 .06
❑ 207 Matt Kinney .20 .06
❑ 208 Jay Canizaro .20 .06
❑ 209 Torii Hunter .20 .06
❑ 210 Ron Coomer .20 .06
❑ 211 Chad Allen .20 .06
❑ 212 Denny Hocking .20 .06
❑ 213 Cristian Guzman .20 .06
❑ 214 LaTroy Hawkins .20 .06
❑ 215 Joe Mays .20 .06
❑ 216 David Ortiz .30 .09
❑ 217 Matt Lawton .20 .06
Eric Milton CL
❑ 218 Frank Thomas .50 .15
❑ 219 Jose Valentin .20 .06
❑ 220 Mike Sirotka .20 .06
❑ 221 Kip Wells .20 .06
❑ 222 Magglio Ordonez .20 .06
❑ 223 Herbert Perry .20 .06
❑ 224 James Baldwin .20 .06
❑ 225 Jon Garland .20 .06
❑ 226 Sandy Alomar Jr. .20 .06
❑ 227 Chris Singleton .20 .06
❑ 228 Keith Foulke .20 .06
❑ 229 Paul Konerko .20 .06
❑ 230 Jim Parque .20 .06
❑ 231 Greg Norton .20 .06
❑ 232 Carlos Lee .20 .06
❑ 233 Cal Eldred .20 .06
❑ 234 Ray Durham .20 .06
❑ 235 Jeff Abbott .20 .06
❑ 236 Frank Thomas .30 .09
Mike Sirotka CL
❑ 237 Derek Jeter 1.25 .35
❑ 238 Glenallen Hill .20 .06
❑ 239 Roger Clemens 1.00 .30
❑ 240 Bernie Williams .30 .09
❑ 241 David Justice .20 .06
❑ 242 Luis Sojo .20 .06
❑ 243 Orlando Hernandez .20 .06
❑ 244 Mike Mussina .30 .09
❑ 245 Jorge Posada .30 .09
❑ 246 Andy Pettitte .30 .09
❑ 247 Paul O'Neill .30 .09
❑ 248 Scott Brosius .20 .06
❑ 249 Alfonso Soriano .30 .09
❑ 250 Mariano Rivera .30 .09
❑ 251 Chuck Knoblauch .20 .06
❑ 252 Ramiro Mendoza .20 .06
❑ 253 Tino Martinez .30 .09
❑ 254 David Cone .20 .06
❑ 255 Derek Jeter .60 .18
Andy Pettite CL
❑ 256 Jeff Bagwell .30 .09
❑ 257 Lance Berkman .20 .06
❑ 258 Craig Biggio .30 .09
❑ 259 Scott Elarton .20 .06
❑ 260 Bill Spiers .20 .06
❑ 261 Moises Alou .20 .06
❑ 262 Billy Wagner .20 .06
❑ 263 Shane Reynolds .20 .06
❑ 264 Tony Eusebio .20 .06
❑ 265 Julio Lugo .20 .06
❑ 266 Jose Lima .20 .06
❑ 267 Octavio Dotel .20 .06
❑ 268 Brad Ausmus .20 .06
❑ 269 Daryle Ward .20 .06
❑ 270 Glen Barker .20 .06
❑ 271 Wade Miller .20 .06
❑ 272 Richard Hidalgo .20 .06
❑ 273 Chris Truby .20 .06
❑ 274 Jeff Bagwell .20 .06
Scott Elarton CL
❑ 275 Greg Maddux .75 .23
❑ 276 Chipper Jones .50 .15
❑ 277 Tom Glavine .30 .09
❑ 278 Brian Jordan .20 .06
❑ 279 Andruw Jones .30 .09
❑ 280 Kevin Millwood .20 .06
❑ 281 Rico Brogna .20 .06
❑ 282 George Lombard .20 .06
❑ 283 Reggie Sanders .20 .06
❑ 284 John Rocker .20 .06
❑ 285 Rafael Furcal .20 .06
❑ 286 John Smoltz .30 .09
❑ 287 Javy Lopez .20 .06
❑ 288 Walt Weiss .20 .06
❑ 289 Quilvio Veras .20 .06
❑ 290 Eddie Perez .20 .06
❑ 291 B.J. Surhoff .20 .06
❑ 292 Chipper Jones .30 .09
Tom Glavine CL
❑ 293 Jeromy Burnitz .20 .06
❑ 294 Charlie Hayes .20 .06
❑ 295 Jeff D'Amico .20 .06
❑ 296 Jose Hernandez .20 .06
❑ 297 Richie Sexson .20 .06
❑ 298 Tyler Houston .20 .06
❑ 299 Paul Rigdon .20 .06
❑ 300 Jamey Wright .20 .06
❑ 301 Mark Loretta .20 .06
❑ 302 Geoff Jenkins .20 .06
❑ 303 Luis Lopez .20 .06
❑ 304 John Snyder .20 .06
❑ 305 Henry Blanco .20 .06
❑ 306 Curtis Leskanic .20 .06
❑ 307 Ron Belliard .20 .06
❑ 308 Jimmy Haynes .20 .06
❑ 309 Marquis Grissom .20 .06
❑ 310 Geoff Jenkins .20 .06
Jeff D'Amico CL
❑ 311 Mark McGwire 1.25 .35
❑ 312 Rick Ankiel .20 .06
❑ 313 Dave Veres .20 .06
❑ 314 Carlos Hernandez .20 .06
❑ 315 Jim Edmonds .30 .09
❑ 316 Andy Benes .20 .06
❑ 317 Garrett Stephenson .20 .06
❑ 318 Ray Lankford .20 .06
❑ 319 Dustin Hermanson .20 .06
❑ 320 Steve Kline .20 .06
❑ 321 Mike Matheny .20 .06
❑ 322 Edgar Renteria .20 .06
❑ 323 J.D. Drew .20 .06
❑ 324 Craig Paquette .20 .06
❑ 325 Darryl Kile .20 .06
❑ 326 Fernando Vina .20 .06
❑ 327 Eric Davis .20 .06
❑ 328 Placido Polanco .20 .06
❑ 329 Jim Edmonds .20 .06
Darryl Kile CL
❑ 330 Sammy Sosa .50 .15
❑ 331 Rick Aguilera .20 .06
❑ 332 Willie Greene .20 .06
❑ 333 Kerry Wood .20 .06
❑ 334 Todd Hundley .20 .06
❑ 335 Rondell White .20 .06
❑ 336 Julio Zuleta .20 .06
❑ 337 Jon Lieber .20 .06
❑ 338 Joe Girardi .20 .06
❑ 339 Damon Buford .20 .06
❑ 340 Kevin Tapani .20 .06
❑ 341 Ricky Gutierrez .20 .06
❑ 342 Bill Mueller .20 .06
❑ 343 Ruben Quevedo .20 .06
❑ 344 Eric Young .20 .06
❑ 345 Gary Matthews Jr. .20 .06
❑ 346 Daniel Garibay .20 .06
❑ 347 Sammy Sosa .30 .09
Jon Lieber CL
❑ 348 Randy Johnson .50 .15
❑ 349 Matt Williams .20 .06
❑ 350 Kelly Stinnett .20 .06
❑ 351 Brian Anderson .20 .06
❑ 352 Steve Finley .20 .06
❑ 353 Curt Schilling .20 .06
❑ 354 Erubiel Durazo .20 .06
❑ 355 Todd Stottlemyre .20 .06
❑ 356 Mark Grace .30 .09
❑ 357 Luis Gonzalez .20 .06
❑ 358 Danny Bautista .20 .06
❑ 359 Matt Mantei .20 .06
❑ 360 Tony Womack .20 .06
❑ 361 Armando Reynoso .20 .06
❑ 362 Greg Colbrunn .20 .06
❑ 363 Jay Bell .20 .06
❑ 364 Byung-Hyun Kim .20 .06
❑ 365 Luis Gonzalez .30 .09
Randy Johnson CL
❑ 366 Gary Sheffield .20 .06
❑ 367 Eric Karros .20 .06
❑ 368 Jeff Shaw .20 .06
❑ 369 Jim Leyritz .20 .06
❑ 370 Kevin Brown .20 .06
❑ 371 Alex Cora .20 .06
❑ 372 Andy Ashby .20 .06
❑ 373 Eric Gagne .20 .06
❑ 374 Chan Ho Park .20 .06
❑ 375 Shawn Green .20 .06
❑ 376 Kevin Elster .20 .06
❑ 377 Mark Grudzielanek .20 .06
❑ 378 Darren Dreifort .20 .06
❑ 379 Dave Hansen .20 .06
❑ 380 Bruce Aven .20 .06
❑ 381 Adrian Beltre .20 .06
❑ 382 Tom Goodwin .20 .06
❑ 383 Gary Sheffield .20 .06
Chan Ho Park CL
❑ 384 Vladimir Guerrero .50 .15
❑ 385 Ugueth Urbina .20 .06
❑ 386 Michael Barrett .20 .06
❑ 387 Geoff Blum .20 .06
❑ 388 Fernando Tatis .20 .06
❑ 389 Carl Pavano .20 .06
❑ 390 Jose Vidro .20 .06
❑ 391 Orlando Cabrera .20 .06
❑ 392 Terry Jones .20 .06
❑ 393 Mike Thurman .20 .06
❑ 394 Lee Stevens .20 .06
❑ 395 Tony Armas Jr. .20 .06
❑ 396 Wilton Guerrero .20 .06
❑ 397 Peter Bergeron .20 .06
❑ 398 Milton Bradley .20 .06
❑ 399 Javier Vazquez .20 .06
❑ 400 Fernando Seguignol .20 .06
❑ 401 Vladimir Guerrero .30 .09
Dustin Hermanson CL
❑ 402 Barry Bonds 1.25 .35
❑ 403 Russ Ortiz .20 .06
❑ 404 Calvin Murray .20 .06
❑ 405 Armando Rios .20 .06
❑ 406 Livan Hernandez .20 .06
❑ 407 Jeff Kent .20 .06
❑ 408 Bobby Estalella .20 .06
❑ 409 Felipe Crespo .20 .06
❑ 410 Shawn Estes .20 .06
❑ 411 J.T. Snow .20 .06
❑ 412 Marvin Benard .20 .06
❑ 413 Joe Nathan .20 .06
❑ 414 Robb Nen .20 .06
❑ 415 Shawon Dunston .20 .06
❑ 416 Mark Gardner .20 .06
❑ 417 Kirk Rueter .20 .06
❑ 418 Rich Aurilia .20 .06
❑ 419 Doug Mirabelli .20 .06
❑ 420 Russ Davis .20 .06
❑ 421 Barry Bonds .75 .23
Livan Hernandez CL
❑ 422 Cliff Floyd .20 .06

❑ 423 Luis Castillo .20 .06
❑ 424 Antonio Alfonseca .20 .06
❑ 425 Preston Wilson .20 .06
❑ 426 Ryan Dempster .20 .06
❑ 427 Jesus Sanchez .20 .06
❑ 428 Derrek Lee .30 .09
❑ 429 Brad Penny .20 .06
❑ 430 Mark Kotsay .20 .06
❑ 431 Alex Fernandez .20 .06
❑ 432 Mike Lowell .20 .06
❑ 433 Chuck Smith .20 .06
❑ 434 Alex Gonzalez .20 .06
❑ 435 Dave Berg .20 .06
❑ 436 A.J. Burnett .20 .06
❑ 437 Charles Johnson .20 .06
❑ 438 Reid Cornelius .20 .06
❑ 439 Mike Redmond .20 .06
❑ 440 Preston Wilson .20 .06
Ryan Dempster CL
❑ 441 Mike Piazza .75 .23
❑ 442 Kevin Appier .20 .06
❑ 443 Jay Payton .20 .06
❑ 444 Steve Trachsel .20 .06
❑ 445 Al Leiter .20 .06
❑ 446 Joe McEwing .20 .06
❑ 447 Armando Benitez .20 .06
❑ 448 Edgardo Alfonzo .20 .06
❑ 449 Glendon Rusch .20 .06
❑ 450 Mike Bordick .20 .06
❑ 451 Lenny Harris .20 .06
❑ 452 Matt Franco .20 .06
❑ 453 Darryl Hamilton .20 .06
❑ 454 Bobby Jones .20 .06
❑ 455 Robin Ventura .20 .06
❑ 456 Todd Zeile .20 .06
❑ 457 John Franco .20 .06
❑ 458 Mike Piazza .50 .15
Al Leiter CL
❑ 459 Tony Gwynn .60 .18
❑ 460 John Mabry .20 .06
❑ 461 Trevor Hoffman .20 .06
❑ 462 Phil Nevin .20 .06
❑ 463 Ryan Klesko .20 .06
❑ 464 Wiki Gonzalez .20 .06
❑ 465 Matt Clement .20 .06
❑ 466 Alex Arias .20 .06
❑ 467 Woody Williams .20 .06
❑ 468 Ruben Rivera .20 .06
❑ 469 Sterling Hitchcock .20 .06
❑ 470 Ben Davis .20 .06
❑ 471 Bubba Trammell .20 .06
❑ 472 Jay Witasick .20 .06
❑ 473 Eric Owens .20 .06
❑ 474 Damian Jackson .20 .06
❑ 475 Adam Eaton .20 .06
❑ 476 Mike Darr .20 .06
❑ 477 Phil Nevin .20 .06
Trevor Hoffman CL
❑ 478 Scott Rolen .30 .09
❑ 479 Robert Person .20 .06
❑ 480 Mike Lieberthal .20 .06
❑ 481 Reggie Taylor .20 .06
❑ 482 Paul Byrd .20 .06
❑ 483 Bruce Chen .20 .06
❑ 484 Pat Burrell .20 .06
❑ 485 Kevin Jordan .20 .06
❑ 486 Bobby Abreu .20 .06
❑ 487 Randy Wolf .20 .06
❑ 488 Kevin Sefcik .20 .06
❑ 489 Brian Hunter .20 .06
❑ 490 Doug Glanville .20 .06
❑ 491 Kent Bottenfield .20 .06
❑ 492 Travis Lee .20 .06
❑ 493 Jeff Brantley .20 .06
❑ 494 Omar Daal .20 .06
❑ 495 Bobby Abreu .20 .06
Randy Wolf CL
❑ 496 Jason Kendall .20 .06
❑ 497 Adrian Brown .20 .06
❑ 498 Warren Morris .20 .06
❑ 499 Brian Giles .20 .06
❑ 500 Jimmy Anderson .20 .06
❑ 501 John VanderWal .20 .06
❑ 502 Mike Williams .20 .06
❑ 503 Aramis Ramirez .20 .06
❑ 504 Pat Meares .20 .06
❑ 505 Jason Schmidt .20 .06
❑ 506 Todd Ritchie .20 .06
❑ 507 Abraham Nunez .20 .06
❑ 508 Jose Silva .20 .06
❑ 509 Francisco Cordova .20 .06
❑ 510 Kevin Young .20 .06
❑ 511 Derek Bell .20 .06
❑ 512 Kris Benson .20 .06
❑ 513 Brian Giles .20 .06
Jose Silva CL
❑ 514 Ken Griffey Jr. .75 .23
❑ 515 Scott Williamson .20 .06
❑ 516 Dmitri Young .20 .06
❑ 517 Sean Casey .30 .09
❑ 518 Barry Larkin .30 .09
❑ 519 Juan Castro .20 .06
❑ 520 Danny Graves .20 .06
❑ 521 Aaron Boone .20 .06
❑ 522 Pokey Reese .20 .06
❑ 523 Elmer Dessens .20 .06
❑ 524 Michael Tucker .20 .06
❑ 525 Benito Santiago .20 .06
❑ 526 Pete Harnisch .20 .06
❑ 527 Alex Ochoa .20 .06
❑ 528 Gookie Dawkins .20 .06
❑ 529 Seth Etherton .20 .06
❑ 530 Rob Bell .20 .06
❑ 531 Ken Griffey Jr. .50 .15
Steve Parris CL
❑ 532 Todd Helton .30 .09
❑ 533 Jose Jimenez .20 .06
❑ 534 Todd Walker .20 .06
❑ 535 Ron Gant .20 .06
❑ 536 Neifi Perez .20 .06
❑ 537 Butch Huskey .20 .06
❑ 538 Pedro Astacio .20 .06
❑ 539 Juan Pierre .20 .06
❑ 540 Jeff Cirillo .20 .06
❑ 541 Ben Petrick .20 .06
❑ 542 Brian Bohanon .20 .06
❑ 543 Larry Walker .20 .06
❑ 544 Masato Yoshii .20 .06
❑ 545 Denny Neagle .20 .06
❑ 546 Brent Mayne .20 .06
❑ 547 Mike Hampton .20 .06
❑ 548 Todd Hollandsworth .20 .06
❑ 549 Brian Rose .20 .06
❑ 550 Todd Helton .20 .06
Pedro Astacio CL
❑ 551 Jason Hart .20 .06
❑ 552 Joe Crede .50 .15
❑ 553 Timo Perez .20 .06
❑ 554 Brady Clark .20 .06
❑ 555 Adam Pettyjohn RC .20 .06
❑ 556 Jason Grilli .20 .06
❑ 557 Paxton Crawford .20 .06
❑ 558 Jay Spurgeon .20 .06
❑ 559 Hector Ortiz .20 .06
❑ 560 Vernon Wells .20 .06
❑ 561 Aubrey Huff .20 .06
❑ 562 Xavier Nady .20 .06
❑ 563 Billy McMillon .20 .06
❑ 564 Ichiro Suzuki RC 5.00 1.50
❑ 565 Tomas De la Rosa .20 .06
❑ 566 Matt Ginter .20 .06
❑ 567 Sun Woo Kim .20 .06
❑ 568 Nick Johnson .20 .06
❑ 569 Pablo Ozuna .20 .06
❑ 570 Tike Redman .20 .06
❑ 571 Brian Cole .20 .06
❑ 572 Ross Gload .20 .06
❑ 573 Dee Brown .20 .06
❑ 574 Tony McKnight .20 .06
❑ 575 Allen Levrault .20 .06
❑ 576 Lesli Brea .20 .06
❑ 577 Adam Bernero .20 .06
❑ 578 Tom Davey .20 .06
❑ 579 Morgan Burkhart .20 .06
❑ 580 Britt Reames .20 .06
❑ 581 Dave Coggin .20 .06
❑ 582 Trey Moore .20 .06
❑ 583 Matt Kinney .20 .06
❑ 584 Pedro Feliz .20 .06
❑ 585 Brandon Inge .20 .06
❑ 586 Alex Hernandez .20 .06
❑ 587 Toby Hall .20 .06
❑ 588 Grant Roberts .20 .06
❑ 589 Brian Sikorski .20 .06
❑ 590 Aaron Myette .20 .06
❑ 591 Derek Jeter PM 1.25 .35
❑ 592 Ivan Rodriguez PM .20 .06
❑ 593 Alex Rodriguez PM .75 .23
❑ 594 Carlos Delgado PM .20 .06
❑ 595 Mark McGwire PM 1.25 .35
❑ 596 Troy Glaus PM .20 .06
❑ 597 Sammy Sosa PM .30 .09
❑ 598 Vladimir Guerrero PM .50 .15
❑ 599 Manny Ramirez PM .20 .06
❑ 600 Pedro Martinez PM .30 .09
❑ 601 Chipper Jones PM .30 .09
❑ 602 Jason Giambi PM .20 .06
❑ 603 Frank Thomas PM .30 .09
❑ 604 Ken Griffey Jr. PM .75 .23
❑ 605 Nomar Garciaparra PM .75 .23
❑ 606 Randy Johnson PM .30 .09
❑ 607 Mike Piazza PM .75 .23
❑ 608 Barry Bonds PM 1.25 .35
❑ 609 Todd Helton PM .20 .06
❑ 610 Jeff Bagwell PM .20 .06
❑ 611 Ken Griffey Jr. VB .75 .23
❑ 612 Carlos Delgado VB .20 .06
❑ 613 Jeff Bagwell VB .20 .06
❑ 614 Jason Giambi VB .20 .06
❑ 615 Cal Ripken VB 1.50 .45
❑ 616 Brian Giles VB .20 .06
❑ 617 Bernie Williams VB .20 .06
❑ 618 Greg Maddux VB .75 .23
❑ 619 Troy Glaus VB .20 .06
❑ 620 Greg Vaughn VB .20 .06
❑ 621 Sammy Sosa VB .30 .09
❑ 622 Pat Burrell VB .20 .06
❑ 623 Ivan Rodriguez VB .20 .06
❑ 624 Chipper Jones VB .30 .09
❑ 625 Barry Bonds VB 1.25 .35
❑ 626 Roger Clemens VB 1.00 .30
❑ 627 Jim Edmonds VB .20 .06
❑ 628 Nomar Garciaparra VB .75 .23
❑ 629 Frank Thomas VB .30 .09
❑ 630 Mike Piazza VB .75 .23
❑ 631 Randy Johnson VB .30 .09
❑ 632 Andruw Jones VB .20 .06
❑ 633 David Wells VB .20 .06
❑ 634 Manny Ramirez VB .20 .06
❑ 635 Preston Wilson VB .20 .06
❑ 636 Todd Helton VB .20 .06
❑ 637 Kerry Wood VB .20 .06
❑ 638 Albert Belle VB .20 .06
❑ 639 Juan Gonzalez VB .20 .06
❑ 640 Vladimir Guerrero VB .50 .15
❑ 641 Gary Sheffield VB .20 .06
❑ 642 Larry Walker VB .20 .06
❑ 643 Magglio Ordonez VB .20 .06
❑ 644 Jermaine Dye VB .20 .06
❑ 645 Scott Rolen VB .20 .06
❑ 646 Tony Gwynn VB .60 .18
❑ 647 Shawn Green VB .20 .06
❑ 648 Roberto Alomar VB .20 .06
❑ 649 Eric Milton VB .20 .06
❑ 650 Mark McGwire VB 1.25 .35
❑ 651 Tim Hudson VB .20 .06
❑ 652 Jose Canseco VB .20 .06
❑ 653 Tom Glavine VB .20 .06
❑ 654 Derek Jeter VB 1.25 .35
❑ 655 Alex Rodriguez VB .75 .23
❑ 656 Darin Erstad VB .20 .06
❑ 657 Jason Kendall VB .20 .06
❑ 658 Pedro Martinez VB .30 .09
❑ 659 Richie Sexson VB .20 .06
❑ 660 Rafael Palmeiro VB .20 .06

619 / Acknowledgments

Each year we refine the process of developing the most accurate and up-to-date information for this book. I believe this year's Price Guide is our best yet. Thanks again to all the contributors nationwide (listed below) as well as our staff here in Dallas.

Those who have worked closely with us on this and many other books have again proven themselves invaluable: Ed Allan, Frank and Vivian Barning, Levi Bleam and Jim Fleck (707 Sportscards), T. Scott Brandon, Peter Brennan, Ray Bright, Card Collectors Co., Dwight Chapin, Theo Chen, Barry Colla, Bill and Diane Dodge, Brett Domue, Dan Even, David Festberg, Fleer/SkyBox (Josh Perlman), Steve Freedman, Gervise Ford, Larry and Jeff Fritsch, Tony Galovich, Georgia Music and Sports (Dick DeCourcey), Dick Gilkeson, Steve Gold (AU Sports), Bill Goodwin (St. Louis Baseball Cards), Mike and Howard Gordon, George Grauer, Steve Green (STB Sports), John Greenwald, Bill Henderson, Jerry and Etta Hersh, Mike Hersh, Neil Hoppenworth, Hunt Auction, Mike Jaspersen, Jay and Mary Kasper (Jay's Emporium), Jerry Katz, Pete Kennedy, David Kohler (SportsCards Plus), Terry Knouse (Tik and Tik), Tom Leon, Lew Lipset (Four Base Hits), Mike Livingston (U-Trading Cards), Mark Macrae, Bill Madden, Bill Mastro, Dr.William McAvoy, Michael McDonald, Mid-Atlantic Sports Cards (Bill Bossert), Gary Mills, Ernie Montella, Brian Morris, Mike Mosier (Columbia City Collectibles Co.), B.A. Murry, Ralph Nozaki, Mike O'Brien, Oldies and Goodies (Nigel Spill), Oregon Trail Auctions, Pacific Trading Cards (Mike Cramer and Mike Monson), Playoff Trading Cards (Ben Ecklar, Steve Judd, and Tracy Hackler), Jack Pollard, Jeff Prillaman, Pat Quinn, Jerald Reichstein (Fabulous Cardboard), Tom Reid, Gavin Riley, Clifton Rouse, John Rumierz, Pat Blandford, Lonn Passon and Kevin Savage (Sports Gallery), Gary Sawatski and Jim Justus (The Wizards of Odd), Mike Schechter, Bill and Darlene Shafer, Barry Sloate, John E. Spalding, Phil Spector, Murvin Sterling, Ted Taylor, Lee Temanson, Topps (Marty Appel), Treat (Harold Anderson), Ed Twombly, Upper Deck (Justin Kanoya), Wayne Varner, Rob Veres, Bill Vizas, Waukesha Sportscards, Bill Wesslund (Portland Sports Card Co.), Kit Young, Rick Young, Ted Zanidakis, Robert Zanze (Z-Cards and Sports), Bill Zimpleman, and Dean Zindler. Finally we give a special acknowledgment to the late Dennis W. Eckes, "Mr. Sport Americana." The success of the Beckett Price Guides has always been the result of a team effort.

It is very difficult to be "accurate" — one can only do one's best. But this job is especially difficult since we're shooting at a moving target: Prices are fluctuating all the time. Having several full-time pricing experts has definitely proven to be better than just one, and I thank all of them for working together to provide you, our readers, with the most accurate prices possible.

Many people have provided price input, illustrative material, checklist verifications, errata, and/or background information. We should like to individually thank AbD Cards (Dale Wesolewski), Action Card Sales, Jerry Adamic, Johnny and Sandy Adams, Mehdi Ahlei, Alex's MVP Cards & Comics, Doug Allen, Will Allison, Dennis Anderson, Ed Anderson, Shane Anderson, Ellis Anmuth, Alan Applegate, Ric Apter, Clyde Archer, Randy Archer, Burl Armstrong, Neil Armstrong, Carlos Ayala, B and J Sportscards, Jeremy Bachman, Dave Bailey, Ball Four Cards (Frank and Steve Pemper), Bob Bartosz, Bubba Bennett, Carl Berg, Beulah Sports (Jeff Blatt), B.J. Sportscollectables, David Boedicker (The Wild Pitch Inc.), Louis Bollman, Tim Bond, Andrew Bosarge, Terry Boyd, Dan Brandenberry, Jeff Breitenfield, Scott Brockleman, John Broggi, Virgil Burns, Greg Bussineau, David Byer, California Card Co., Capital Cards, Danny Cariseo, Carl Carlson (C.T.S.), Jim Carr, Ira Cetron, Sandy Chan, Ric Chandgie, Ray Cherry, Bigg Wayne Christian, Josh Chidester, Michael and Abe Citron, Dr. Jeffrey Clair, Michael Cohen, Tom Cohoon (Cardboard Dreams), Gary Collett, Rick Cosmen (RC Card Co.), Lou Costanzo (Champion Sports), Mike Coyne, Tony Craig (T.C. Card Co.), Solomon Cramer, Kevin Crane, Taylor Crane, Chad Cripe, Scott Crump, Allen Custer, Dave Dame, Scott Dantio, Dee's Baseball Cards (Dee Robinson), Joe Delgrippo, Mike DeLuca, Ken Dinerman (California Cruizers), Rob DiSalvatore, Cliff Dolgins, Discount Dorothy, Richard Dolloff (Dolloff Coin Center), Joe Donato, Jerry Dong, Pat Dorsey, Double Play Baseball Cards, Joe Drelich, Richard Duglin (Baseball Cards-N-More), The Dugout, Ken Edick (Home Plate of Utah), Brad Englehardt, Doak Ewing, Terry Falkner, Mike and Chris Fanning, Linda Ferrigno and Mark Mezzardi, Jay Finglass, Bob Flitter, Fremont Fong, Paul Franzetti, Ron Frasier, Tom Freeman, Bob Frye, Bill Fusaro, Chris Gala, Richard Galasso, David Garza, David Gaumer, Georgetown Card Exchange, David Giove, Dick Goddard, Jeff Goldstein, Ron Gomez, Rich Gove, Jay and Jan Grinsby, Bob Grissett, Gerry Guenther, Neil Gubitz (What-A-Card), Hall's Nostalgia, Hershell Hanks, Gregg Hara, Todd Harrell, Robert Harrison, Steve Hart, Floyd Haynes (H and H Baseball Cards), Kevin Heffner, Joel Hellman, Hit and Run Cards (Jon, David, and Kirk Peterson), Vinny Ho, Johnny Hustle Card Co., John Inouye, Vern Isenberg, Dale Jackson, Marshall Jackson, Mike Jardina, Paul Jastrzembski, Jeff's Sports Cards, Donn Jennings Cards, George Johnson, Craig Jones, Chuck Juliana, Nick Kardoulias, Scott Kashner, Frank and Rose Katen, Kevin's Kards, Kingdom Collectibles, Inc., John Klassnik, Steve Kluback,Don Knutsen, Gregg Kohn,

Mike Kohlhas, Bob & Bryan Kornfield, Carl and Maryanne Laron, Howard Lau, Richard S. Lawrence, William Lawrence, Brent Lee, Morley Leeking, Irv Lerner, Larry and Sally Levine, Larry Loeschen (A and J Sportscards), Neil Lopez, Kendall Loyd (Orlando Sportscards South), Steve Lowe, Jim Macie, Peter Maltin, Paul Marchant, Brian Marcy, Scott Martinez, James S. Maxwell Jr., McDag Productions Inc., Bob McDonald, Steve McHenry, Tony McLaughlin, Mendal Mearkle, Carlos Medina, Ken Melanson, William Mendel, Blake Meyer (Lone Star Sportscards), Tim Meyer, Joe Michalowicz, Lee Milazzo, Cary S. Miller, George Miller, Wayne Miller, Dick Millerd, Frank Mineo, Mitchell's Baseball Cards, John Morales, William Munn, Mark Murphy, Robert Nappe, National Sportscard Exchange, Roger Neufeldt, Steve Novella, Bud Obermeyer, John O'Hara, Glenn Olson, Scott Olson, Ron Oser, Luther Owen, Earle Parrish, Clay Pasternack, Michael Perrotta, Tom Pfirrmann, Don Phlong, Loran Pulver, Bob Ragonese, Bryan Rappaport, Don and Tom Ras, Robert M. Ray, Phil Regli, Rob Resnick, Dave Reynolds, Carson Ritchey, Bill Rodman, Craig Roehrig, Mike Sablow, Terry Sack, Thomas Salem, Barry Sanders, Jon Sands, Tony Scarpa, John Schad, Dave Schau (Baseball Cards), Masa Shinohara, Eddie Silard, Mike Slepcevic, Sam Sliheet, Art Smith, Lynn and Todd Solt, Jerry Sorice, Don Spagnolo, Sports Card Fan-Attic, The Sport Hobbyist, Norm Stapleton, Bill Steinberg, Lisa Stellato (Never Enough Cards), Rob Stenzel, Jason Stern, Andy Stoltz, Rob Stenzel, Bill Stone, Ted Straka, Tim Strandberg (East Texas Sports Cards), Edward Strauss, Strike Three, Richard Strobino, Kevin Struss, Superior Sport Card, Dr. Richard Swales, George Tahinos, Brent Thorton, Ian Taylor, The The Thirdhand Shoppe, Brent Thornton, Paul Thornton, Jim and Sally Thurtell, Bud Tompkins (Minnesota Connection), Philip J. Tremont, Ralph Triplette, Umpire's Choice Inc., Eric Unglaub, Hoyt Vanderpool, Steven Wagman, T. Wall, Gary A. Walter, Joe and John Weisenburger (The Wise Guys), Brian and Mike Wentz (BMW Sportscards), Richard West, Mike Wheat, Richard Wiercinski, Don Williams (Robin's Nest of Dolls), Jeff Williams, John Williams, Kent and Louise Williams, Craig Williamson, Rich Wojtasick, John Wolf Jr., Jay Wolt (Cavalcade of Sports), Joe Yanello, Peter Yee, Tom Zocco, Mark Zubrensky, and Tim Zwick.

Every year we make active solicitations for expert input. We are particularly appreciative of help (however extensive or cursory) provided for this volume. We receive many inquiries, comments, and questions regarding material within this book. In fact, each and every one is read and digested. Time constraints, however, prevent us from personally replying. But keep sharing your knowledge. Your letters and input are part of the "big picture" of hobby information we can pass along to readers in our books and magazines. Even though we cannot respond to each letter, you are making significant contributions to the hobby through your interest and comments.

The effort to continually refine and improve this book also involves a growing number of people and types of expertise on our home team. Our company boasts a substantial Sports Data Publishing team, which strengthens our ability to provide comprehensive analysis of the marketplace. SDP capably handled numerous technical details and provided able assistance in the preparation of this edition.

Our baseball analysts played a major part in compiling this year's book, traveling thousands of miles during the past year to attend sports card shows and visit card shops around the United States and Canada. The Beckett baseball specialists are: Gabe Harro, Rich Klein, Dave Porter, and Grant Sandground (Senior Price Guide Editor). Their pricing analysis and careful proofreading were key contributions to the accuracy of this annual.

Grant Sandground's coordination and reconciling of prices as Beckett Baseball Card Monthly Price Guide Editor helped immeasurably. Rich Klein, as research analyst, contributed detailed pricing analysis and hours of proofing.

The effort was led by Dan Hitt, the Senior Manager of Sports Data Publishing. He was ably assisted by the rest of the Price Guide analysts: Clint Hall, Keith Hower, Tony Joseph, Beverly Mills, Bill Sutherland, Tim Trout, and Joe White.

The price gathering and analytical talents of this fine group of hobbyists have helped make our Beckett team stronger, while making this guide and its companion monthly Price Guide more widely recognized as the hobby's most reliable and relied upon sources of pricing information.

The Beckett Interactive Division played a critical role in technology. They spent countless hours programming, testing, and implementing it to simplify the handling of thousands of prices that must be checked and updated for each edition.

In the years since this guide debuted, Beckett Publications has grown beyond any rational expectation. A great many talented and hard working individuals have been instrumental in this growth and success. Our whole team is to be congratulated for what we together have accomplished.

The whole Beckett Publications team has my thanks for jobs well done. Thank you, everyone.